A DICTIONARY OF AMERICANISMS

A DICTIONARY OF AMERICANISMS

On Historical Principles

EDITED BY MITFORD M. MATHEWS

Dictionary Department · The University of Chicago Press

THE UNIVERSITY OF CHICAGO PRESS · CHICAGO · ILLINOIS

THE UNIVERSITY OF CHICAGO PRESS, CHICAGO 37
GEOFFREY CUMBERLEGE, OXFORD UNIVERSITY PRESS, London, E.C. 4, England
THE UNIVERSITY OF TORONTO PRESS, Toronto 5, Canada

Published 1951. Third Impression 1956. Composed and printed by THE UNIVERSITY OF CHICAGO PRESS, *Chicago, Illinois, U.S.A.*

PREFACE

AS USED in the title of this work, "Americanism" means a word or expression that originated in the United States. The term includes: outright coinages, as *appendicitis, hydrant, tularemia;* such words as *adobe, campus, gorilla,* which first became English in the United States; and terms such as *faculty, fraternity, refrigerator,* when used in senses first given them in American usage.

The purpose of this dictionary is to treat historically as many as possible of those words and meanings of words which have been added to the English language in the United States. The number of terms included might easily have been greater had it not been for the rigid exclusion of those for which, at the time of going to press, no printed evidence was on hand. The study of a people's language throws light upon every aspect of that people's culture. So far as American civilization is concerned, it is possible to focus attention on those terms with which the founders of the nation and those who came after them have felt impelled to augment their vocabulary. This dictionary is an index of the history and culture of the American people.

When work on this dictionary of Americanisms was begun in January, 1944, the groundwork for such an undertaking had already been laid. The *Oxford English Dictionary* (*OED*) with its *Supplement*, the *English Dialect Dictionary* (*EDD*) by Joseph Wright, and the *Dictionary of American English* (*DAE*) were all available, as well as special studies by W. A. Read, John F. McDermott, J. F. Bense, Francisco J. Santamaría, Harold Bentley, and other scholars. Had such works as these not been available, it would have been foolhardy to attempt the present dictionary.

The *DAE* in particular was most useful in the preparation of this work. The object of that dictionary was to cover a much larger field than that to which the present one is devoted, but, in achieving its other ends, the *DAE* greatly enlarged upon previous knowledge about those terms which first became English in this country. It was possible to utilize a large number of the illustrative quotations and definitions in that dictionary in the preparation of this one.

It has been necessary, however, to examine all the entries in the *DAE* in an effort to decide which of them deserved place in this dictionary. As a result of this examination, many of the terms marked in the *DAE* as Americanisms have been rejected, while others not so marked have here been placed in that category.

In trying to identify those words and word meanings which came first into the English language in the United States, one of the procedures followed has been to examine carefully the evidence in the *OED*—both the main work and its *Supplement*—and in the *EDD*. Along with the examination of these works, a serious effort has been made to evaluate whatever other evidence could be found. The mere fact that a term which has had some currency in America cannot be found elsewhere may under certain circumstances be an indication that it originated here, but it would not be wise, under all circumstances, to regard such a term as an American contribution. The fact has been kept in mind that many words must have eluded those who read for the *OED* and the *EDD*. These dictionaries, despite their completeness, are not to be regarded as having in them *all* the words that ever existed in the language. The dictionary dates of the first occurrences of terms have also been regarded with caution. So far as the great majority of the terms in the *OED* and *EDD* are concerned, their earliest use must go back much further than is shown.

The material found in the *OED* and *EDD* is often of a nature to puzzle a seeker after Americanisms. For example, the *OED* and its *Supplement* not infrequently use the label "U.S." in places where its significance is not clear. In the *OED*, "drummer" in one of its senses is defined as: "*fig.* One who solicits custom or orders; a commercial traveller; cf. DRUM, *v.* 5 and 6 b. U.S." The tag "U.S." in this definition is puzzling, for the first example, dated 1827, of the use of "drummer" in this sense is from Sir Walter Scott. No evidence of American use antedating the Scott passage has so far been found; and, until such evidence is forthcoming, this sense of "drummer" can hardly be regarded as having originated in the United States. Possibly all that Dr. Murray meant by his label in this case was that the word in this sense is used more in the United States than in England.

Anyone who examines carefully the *EDD* entries of terms that he suspects of being Americanisms may often come to the conclusion that a term originated in the United States, passed into one of the dialects of Great Britain, and subsequently showed up in Dr. Wright's monumental collection. In the *EDD*, *s.v.* "Stump," *v.*, the statement is made: "To stump Lancashire is to make speeches on politics or other subjects, in all the towns and centres of population in the county." The *EDD* evidence for this use appears to be meager and late; when it is compared with the evidence in this dictionary, the implication is unmistakable. The Lancashire phrase is a borrowing from American use.

The *EDD* records "sawyer" in the sense of "A fallen tree, floating down stream." A single example from an Irish source of 1848 is given. One who compares that evidence with what is supplied for the word in a somewhat related sense in this dictionary is likely to suspect that here again there is evidence of American influence on British dialect. The *EDD* records "Jim Crow" in the sense of a street actor, a "Billy Barlow," and the evidence supplied is of 1851 and from the London area. There is undoubtedly a connection between the American use of this expression and that shown in the *EDD*, but it is hardly possible at present to tell on which side of the ocean the term arose. A similar problem arises in connection with "bullfrog." The term was used by American speakers of English as early as 1698. But the *EDD* records "bullfrog" from north Devonshire in 1850, where it was used for an imaginary monster believed to live under the foundation stones of old houses. Possibly this term is centuries old in folk speech. It might have been brought to this country by some of the early colonists and applied to representatives of the genus *Rana*.

As may be seen from the foregoing, the task of identifying Americanisms has been essentially that of examining and weighing the evidence, both British and American, for thousands of terms and meanings of terms that have for one reason or another been suspected of having been coined in the United States or of having passed into the English of this country as independent borrowings. American borrowings from foreign languages are much more numerous and significant than has hitherto been suspected.

The student of American English has always to keep in mind the important fact that many people of many tongues took part in shaping the language of the United States. There are many linguistic phenomena in American English that cannot be intelligently explained within the limits of the English language.

In the *OED* the word "alcalde" is shown with four examples of its use. The two earliest, dated 1615 and 1666, are from British sources, the others from American works. The fact is, however, that neither in the British nor in the American examples is there any indication that "alcalde" became a part of the English language. The word was used by British and American writers with reference to Spain. There were no "alcaldes" in England; hence Dr. Murray, in entering the word in the *OED*, was entirely justified in indicating that it was without standing as an English word, having never become naturalized in the language.

An examination of the evidence for this same word given in the *DAE* reveals an entirely different situation. In the first place, the American evidence goes back only to 1803. From the evidence available, it is quite clear that the status of "alcalde" in American use has been entirely different from any that the term ever had in British use. The *DAE* supplies no fewer than thirteen examples of the use of the word from 1803 to 1925. So much had "alcalde" become a part of the American vocabulary that, in the days of the Gold Rush, western miners, in organizing local governments, provided for the election of alcaldes rather than mayors.

The fact that "alcalde" occurs in American use as late as it does, after the American frontier had been pushed as far west as the Mississippi River and beyond, suggests that, so far as its currency in this country is concerned, it is a new borrowing altogether. An examination of the amount and kind of American evidence available for the word confirms this view. Such British use as the term had once had in England clearly has no connection with, or bearing upon, its later use in America. The term would have made its appearance here just as it did, even if no British writer had ever made the least use of it.

The problem of how to deal with the thousands of plant and animal names used in the United States has been a difficult one. Many such names are old ones that have been brought over and applied, often quite loosely, to American objects. In this dictionary such old names have been included only in cases where American and British usage apply the same term to representatives of different genera. In working out this differentiation, it has often been necessary to secure the assistance of scholars well versed in the terminology of the various fields.

In presenting terms in this category, the earliest available evidence for them has been given. Since British scientists often supplied names for distinctively American plants and animals before Americans did, it sometimes happens that the earliest quotations given in this dictionary for such terms are from British sources. Animal and plant names that occur only locally have presented difficulty. Many such local expressions have been included, and, when possible, the area where they are known to prevail has been indicated.

Similar problems have come up with regard to other words which, so far as the present evidence shows, never enjoyed anything like widespread currency or appeared only sporadically. To include all such terms would, of course, be impossible, but a great many have been included. Undoubtedly, for many such terms further evidence will later be found which will show that they have or have had more currency than is indicated by the evidence so far collected.

ETYMOLOGIES

As a rule, in this dictionary only words such as "electrocute" and "hydrant" that originated in the United States and such as "campus" and "gorilla" that first became English here are provided with etymologies, and even in such cases no attempt has been made to do more than to point out as clearly as possible the immediate source from which the new terms passed into American use.

An effort has been made to be as specific as possible about terms from other languages. As is well known, the Spanish, French, Dutch, and German used in the United States is not always that of Europe. Consequently, the kind of Spanish, French, etc., involved in borrowed words has been carefully indicated in the etymologies. As in the case of "alcalde," many terms with some standing in British usage have come into American use quite independently. The expression "An Amer. borrowing" has been used in the etymologies of such terms as these. Also, the meaning of the term in the foreign language has been given, the better to enable the user of the dictionary to appreciate the background of the borrowed expression.

The many word combinations included in this dictionary are usually made up of terms that are old in the language, and in such cases it has not been regarded as worth while to belabor the obvious by giving any etymologies for them.

It would not have been wise, with the material on hand, to attempt to deal with the problem of hyphenation presented by many of the combinations given. The quotations showing the terms in use may or may not be helpful for those desirous of assistance in this direction. Furthermore, the plan followed in dealing with combinations made it somewhat inconvenient to point out all cases in which the first element is properly written with a capital. Usually, however, the nature of the combination and the quotations take sufficient care of this matter.

PRONUNCIATION

As a rule, pronunciation is given only for words regarded as having originated in this country or as having first become English here. Even for these words, only one pronunciation is usually cited, no attempt being made to represent American regional or British variants. Since the resources available to the project did not permit firsthand investigation of pronunciation, published works were relied upon wherever possible.

The problems encountered in indicating pronunciation have been many. A historical dictionary compiled from written evidence includes numerous words of rare and remote occurrence and many words that have been for a long time obsolete. Words from foreign languages—French, Spanish, American Spanish, Dutch, German, and American Indian tongues—which have become completely Anglicized present no exceptional difficulties, but many such words either are obsolete or have never come into general use. When words cannot be heard in actual use and when dictionaries have failed to record them, about all that can be done is to give conjectured pronunciations, based upon spelling (both standard and naïve), analogy, and the help rarely provided by the evidence brought together for the dictionary.

The pronunciations are given in the International Phonetic Association notation with the addition of ɜ and ɚ, well known through their use by Kenyon and Knott in their pronouncing dictionary, the magazine *American Speech*, and numerous other works. The symbols and their values are as follows:

VOWELS

[i] see si	[ɑ] ah ɑ	[ɜ] word wɜd	(in accented syllables)
[ɪ] city ˈsɪtɪ	[ɔ] raw rɔ	[ɚ] murder ˈmɜdɚ	(only in unaccented syllables)
[e] day de	[o] doze doz	[ə] above əˈbʌv	(only in unaccented syllables)
[ɛ] egg ɛg	[ʊ] pull pʊl	[ʌ] cut kʌt	
[æ] hat hæt	[u] moon mun		

DIPHTHONGS

[aɪ] five faɪv	[ɔɪ] joy dʒɔɪ
[aʊ] how haʊ	[ju] fuse fjuz

CONSONANTS

[p] pity ˈpɪtɪ	[s] song sɔŋ	[n] gnat næt
[b] bee bi	[z] zeal zil	[n̩] sudden ˈsʌdn̩
[t] tooth tuθ	[ʃ] shall ʃæl	[ŋ] sang sæŋ
[d] dash dæʃ	[ʒ] vision ˈvɪʒən	[l] lull lʌl
[k] king kɪŋ	[h] how haʊ	[l̩] saddle ˈsædl̩
[g] good gʊd	[tʃ] cheap tʃip	[w] watch wɑtʃ
[f] full fʊl	[dʒ] jaw dʒɔ	[hw] while hwaɪl
[v] voice vɔɪs	[m] men mɛn	[j] yet jɛt
[θ] theft θɛft	[m̩] keep 'em ˈkipm̩	[r] rate ret
[ð] then ðɛn		

The stress mark [ˈ] is used before a syllable having the principal accent. A corresponding mark below the line indicates that the syllable before which it stands has a weaker accentuation than that which receives the main stress. Secondary stress marks are regularly omitted in dissyllabic words unless each element of the term is recognizable as a word in its own right. Parentheses are used to indicate that the pronunciation of the word varies, being sometimes with and sometimes without the sound indicated by the inclosed symbol.

TYPOGRAPHICAL ARRANGEMENT

One of the problems inherent in historical lexicography is that of presenting material in an economical manner and at the same time in such a way that it can be readily found. The format employed in this work is the result of much study and experimentation.

In an effort to avoid the monotony that comes from too much uniformity in the appearance of the entries, those terms that are accompanied by only one or two quotations are usually given entirely in smaller (seven-point) type. In all other entries the entry words and the definitions are in larger (nine-point) type. Words that are old in the language and that are included in this dictionary because they have or have had a meaning or meanings that arose here are preceded by a star. Names such as "Franklin," in "Franklin rod," "Franklin stove," etc., and "Pickering," as in "Pickering frog," "Pickering's hyla," are preceded by a star, the assumption being that such names did not originate in this country.

Entry words, unless they require capitalization, are given with the initial letter in lower case. As a rule, no attempt has been made to give an exhaustive treatment of the variant spellings which some terms have had. To give such information in a useful fashion would require more material than has been available for this work.

The principal way in which the resources of the English vocabulary have been augmented in this country has been by forming new combinations. The number of such expressions that find a place in this dictionary is relatively large. At the outset it was realized that a method of dealing with terms of this kind would have to be found that would be clear and, at the same time, economical of space. The procedure followed has been to group under each entry word all the pertinent combinations into which it has entered, reserving for main entries only those combinations which merit more illustrative quotations than can well be given them in this group treatment. For example, under the entry * **fisher,** the combinations **fisher bean, fisher cat, fisher duck, fisher raccoon,** and **fisher weasel** are included, but mention is also made of the fact that * **fisherman** is to be looked for as a main entry.

It has often been possible to group combinations according to their nature into units that serve to bring together such terms as are in some way related. Such groupings, in addition to other advantages, make it possible to present a great many combinations in a way which avoids much of the stodginess in the appearance of the page which an undistributed arrangement would inevitably cause.

It will be observed that the quotations, numbered to correspond with the numbers of the definitions, have also been so grouped that those numbered 1, 5, 10, etc., begin new paragraphs. This arrangement enables the user of the dictionary to go with maximum ease from the definition of a particular term to the quotations that illustrate its use, and it has the further advantage of contributing to the appearance of the page. Entries such as * **black** and * **Indian** have tested severely the system followed. They are good examples of what it has been possible to achieve even with words whose adequate treatment was particularly troublesome.

No treatment of combinations is quite satisfactory which does not take into account those in which the given word appears as the second or last element in the combination. "Biscuit" is as much in combination in "beaten biscuit" as it is in "biscuit baker." Consequently, at the conclusion of those entries that justify it, a list is given of those expressions in which the given word occurs as the last element of a combination. Anyone who has ever used the large Dutch dictionary, *Woordenboek der Nederlandsche Taal*, has become acquainted with the advantages of an arrangement of this kind, and it was from that excellent work that this feature was borrowed. It should be noted also that many words have been given as entries merely for the purpose of pointing out the combinations into which they have entered. A good example of such an entry is * **bunting,** *n.*[1]

Obviously, no dictionary could possibly take account of all the combinations into which certain words have entered. In concluding the treatment of some words especially prolific in combinations, lists have been given, in italics, of combinations known to exist but regarded as belonging to types of a kind already adequately exhibited.

ILLUSTRATIONS

The decision to use pictures in this dictionary was reached after consultation with many friends and scholars. The more one has puzzled over the problems of defining and the more one has cudgeled one's brain in an effort to write definitions that need not be puzzled over, the more one is inclined to make thankful use of anything that assists in conveying information.

All the drawings were made especially for the dictionary by Mr. Irvin Studney. The sources from which Mr. Studney secured the models were varied. The editor and the artist diligently searched through all the museums in the Chicago area—the Natural History Museum, the Museum of Science and Industry, the collections of the Art Institute, and the Chicago Historical Society museum were all laid under contribution by the kind permission and generous help of those in charge. The dictionary staff, always on the alert for material for the drawings, made much use of such books as Knight's *Practical Dictionary of Mechanics*, Hodge's work on American Indians, George Catlin's well-illustrated volumes, old copies of Sears, Roebuck catalogues, and many others. They examined nineteenth-century travel books for the drawings with which these are sometimes embellished. Old volumes of the proceedings of agricultural societies were thumbed through, as well as old magazines, such as *Scribner's*, the *Century*, and *Outing*. The proceedings of antiquarian societies, particularly *Old-Time New England*, were carefully scanned. Modern books, such as Adams' well-known work on American history, heavily laden as it is with illustrations from a wide range of sources, and the beautifully written and illustrated work on American vehicles by Rittenhouse were fruitful sources of help.

ACKNOWLEDGMENTS

It is a pleasant duty to express my thanks to as many as possible of those who have in various ways assisted in the preparation of this dictionary.

Foremost among those to whom thanks are due is Rollin D. Hemens of the University of Chicago Press. Had it not been for his appreciation of the value of a work of this kind, the dictionary would never have been undertaken; without his continuous, enthusiastic support, the project would many times have languished.

Among those who have taken a continuing interest in the present work is Sir William Craigie, my friend and teacher for many years. Before I was able to devote my time exclusively to the study of Americanisms, I talked with him about the desirability of a dictionary devoted altogether to such terms, and the idea met with his warmest approval. At the outset of work on this dictionary, he turned over to me a considerable body of useful material.

One of the scholars whose counsel I early sought with regard to the scope and methodology of the dictionary was Dr. Kemp Malone. His enthusiasm for the undertaking encouraged me so much that I asked him if he would go over the galleys as they appeared, watching particularly for errors in the etymologies and definitions. He readily consented to take on this burden, which he has cheerfully borne, greatly to the enrichment of the dictionary and to the advantage of all who consult it.

Dr. James B. McMillan, of the University of Alabama, in addition to supplying much material, often of a kind sorely needed, kindly consented to look over the pronunciations in the dictionary. Fortunately, he was able to go over the entire work in the copy stage, and later, when the galleys were coming out, he continued his extremely helpful surveillance, watching not only the pronunciations but every other aspect of the work as well. The dictionary owes much to his fine discrimination and sound judgment.

Dr. Margaret Waterman during the two years she was a member of the dictionary staff did much preliminary editing, in addition to writing out the pronunciations for as much of the work as was available at the time. Dr. Barbara Garcia, of Mills College, Oakland, California, in addition to helping greatly with the pronunciation of many of the Spanish terms, gave invaluable assistance with the etymologies of Spanish words. Her interest in the work was so great that she consented to go over the galleys, watching particularly for the treatment given the hundreds of Spanish words with which it has been necessary to deal.

Dr. Lorenzo Turner, of Roosevelt College, has given freely of his time and scholarship in helping with the Africanisms included in the dictionary. His kindness in providing me with a manuscript of his book on Gullah long before the work was available in its present form places me still more under obligation to this fine scholar and gentleman.

Dr. Roland M. Harper, of the University of Alabama, has often given much needed help with information about plant names. Mr. W. L. McAtee, United States Fish and Wildlife Service, retired, has been most helpful, not only with bird names but also with material which he has come upon in his wide reading. Karl P. Schmidt, of the Chicago Natural History Museum, has gladly helped out with numerous snake names of a kind not easy to define. Dr. B. C. H. Harvey, of the Department of Anatomy of the University of Chicago, has never failed to respond helpfully to requests for assistance with medical terms. Other members of the University of Chicago faculty—Dr. Avery Craven, Dr. Daniel J. Boorstin, Dr. John M. Beal, Dr. Max Rheinstein, Dr. Gertrude E. Smith, Dr. Blanche B. Boyer, Dr. Jakob A. O. Larsen, Dr. William R. Keast—have placed me under obligations to them for their help on various terms.

One of those to whom I first turned when the production of the dictionary was being considered was H. L. Mencken. He was delighted that there was a possibility of a dictionary of this kind and pledged his heartiest co-operation. His promise of assistance was abundantly fulfilled. I have often had occasion to appeal to him concerning terms about which I needed enlightenment, and he has never failed to respond helpfully. In reply to a letter I wrote him about "Bible belt," he explained so neatly what he had meant by the term when he coined it that I made free use of his words in the definition which appears in the dictionary.

The unusual and extremely interesting nature of the undertaking may have contributed to the ready responses elicited by my many letters of inquiry. One of the most encouraging aspects of the work has been the readiness and competence shown by those to whom appeals for help have been directed. Limitation of space forbids a complete listing of those to whom my thanks are due. The following partial list indicates the scope of my indebtedness: C. G. Abbot, Secretary, Smithsonian Institution; L. R. Abrams, Natural History Museum, Stanford University, California; R. F. Adams, Dallas, Texas (see the list of works cited in the dictionary); Sidney J. Baker, Sydney, Australia; A. J. Barnouw, Columbia University; Steven T. Byington, Ballard Vale, Massachusetts; Elliott V. K. Dobbie, Columbia University; Isidore Dyen, Yale University; F. W. Gingrich, Albright College, Reading, Pennsylvania; Robert C. Gooch, Library of Congress, Washington, D.C.; W. Cabell Greet, Columbia University; Miles L. Hanley, University of Wisconsin; V. R. Hawthorne, Executive Vice-Chairman, Association of American Railroads, Chicago; Russell Leigh Jackson, Director, Essex Institute, Salem, Massachusetts; C. H. Johnson, Acting Chief, United States Department of the Interior, Bureau of Mines, Washington, D.C.; Lucille Kellar, McCormick Historical Association, Chicago; John S. Kenyon, Hiram College, Hiram, Ohio; Frederick H. Knight, Corning Glass Works, Corning, New York; W. S. Lacher, Association of American Railroads, Chicago; Thomas O. Mabbott, Hunter College, New York City; Alexander McQueen, Chicago; Winthrop A. McCarthy, Town Clerk, Town of Stoneham, Massachusetts; Helen McKearin, New York City; Mamie Meredith, University of Nebraska, Lincoln; J. Monaghan, State Historian, Illinois State Historical Library, Springfield; Lewis Pilcher, Association of American Railroads, Chicago; Louise Pound, University of Nebraska, Lincoln; Anne S. Pratt, Yale University Library; Robert L. Ramsay, University of Missouri; Allen Walker Read, Columbia University; William A. Read, Baton Rouge, Louisiana; Horace Reynolds, Cambridge, Massachusetts; Stephen T. Riley, Librarian, Massachusetts Historical Society, Boston; Jack D. Rittenhouse, Los Angeles, California; Frank H. H. Roberts, Jr., Smithsonian Institution, Washington, D.C.; Phillip C. Roettinger, Colt's Manufacturing Co., Hartford, Connecticut; Herbert H. Ross, State Natural History, Survey Division, Urbana, Illinois; I. Willis Russell, University, Alabama; M. W. Stirling, Director, Bureau of American Ethnology, Washington, D.C.; Dr. Catherine Sturtevant, Cornell University Press, Ithaca, New York; Sir St. Vincent Troubridge, London, England.

Unfortunately, a few of those who made substantial contributions to the work are now beyond the reach of these words of appreciation. Among these was Albert Matthews, of Boston, scholar and friend of scholars. It was my good fortune to be able to talk over with him plans for the projected dictionary. At the beginning of actual work, he, with his accustomed generosity, placed at my disposal his collectanea of Americana and was often good enough to give me help in working on particular words that presented difficulties.

Edward Wildeman, lover of literature and scholarship and for three years an ever ready helper, particularly on those terms having a Dutch background, gave assistance that could not have been obtained elsewhere. Born and brought up in Utrecht and a master not only of English but of other languages as well, he was one of the most gifted and inspiring friends and teachers I have ever met. Charles Exley, a devoted student of words and for many years a collector of evidence for the *OED*, placed at my disposal thousands of "slips" he had taken especially for this work. To him I am indebted for much new light on particular terms that had aroused his interest.

Among those to whom my obligations are especially heavy are the members of the small staff whose faithfulness and competence not only have hastened the appearance of the dictionary but have greatly enriched its contents as well. Patricia Martin Gibby, in addition to paying especial attention to the pronunciations, writing many of them herself, has served as the copy-editor for the work, in which capacity she examined and marked for the compositor the 126,600 "slips" of which the dictionary copy consisted. From the time work began in the composing room in October, 1948, until it ended in August, 1950, she saw to it that the compositor never ran out of copy. The care which she exercised in her work has, moreover, kept the cost of the alterations on the dictionary to a remarkably low figure. Her services in reading proof have been no less competent and valuable.

Charles J. Lovell, who joined the dictionary staff upon my invitation in November, 1946, has served since that time in the capacity of research and editorial assistant and has made an outstanding contribution to the work. In addition to the material which he brought with him, a veritable avalanche of some sixty pounds of "slips," including thousands of antedatings of the *DAE*, he has been able, along with his other duties, to supply the project with a surprisingly large amount of further material. Almost from the outset, he has been able to read the copy ahead of the copy-editor and to make many corrections in the definitions, besides augmenting the copy at spots where it was weakest. In addition to his other labors, he has prepared the bibliography of works cited in the dictionary.

During the researches he carried on before joining the dictionary staff, Mr. Lovell experienced helpful kindnesses at the hands of more friends and librarians than can here be enumerated. His obligations are particularly heavy to the following: Katherine E. Anderson, Library Association of Portland, Portland, Oregon; Carey Bliss, Henry E. Huntington Library and Art Gallery, San Marino, California; C. S. Brigham, American Antiquarian Society Library, Worcester, Massachusetts; Ethel M. Christoffers, University of Washington Library, Seattle, Washington; John Easley, *Daily Ardmoreite*, Ardmore, Oklahoma; Miss Mary Isabel Fry, Henry E. Huntington Library and Art Gallery, San Marino, California; Miss D. C. Gosling, Western History Department, Denver Public Library, Denver, Colorado; George P. Hammond, Bancroft Library, University of California, Berkeley; J. Henry Hefley, Ardmore, Oklahoma; L. Maria Kirkgaard, Fine Arts Department, Pasadena Public Library, Pasadena, California; Miss Caroline Wenzel, California State Library, Sacramento.

This dictionary, despite the care exercised in the preparation of it, cannot in the nature of things be free from error. If the work helps to stimulate increasingly competent study of the field to which it is devoted and if in its offerings and methodology it facilitates the efforts of those who will in time improve upon it, I shall be greatly pleased.

MITFORD M. MATHEWS

THE UNIVERSITY OF CHICAGO PRESS
September 1950

EXPLANATION OF SPECIAL LETTERING AND SYMBOLS

All entry words are given in boldface. When reference is made to them in the definitions or etymologies, they are in lightface if followed by *q.v.*

⁎ indicates that the word or expression before which it appears did not come first or independently into English in the United States. In the lists of combinations the star on the second element denotes that the combination is not of United States origin.

( ) are used in entry words sometimes to inclose a letter which may or may not be found in the spelling. In phrases parentheses are used about a word to indicate that it may or may not occur in the expression. Regularly, in the definitions of transitive verbs, parentheses are used for the direct object or to indicate the nature of the object.

[ ] regularly contain the etymologies. Brackets are also used to inclose matter supplied by the editor. Quotations are inclosed by brackets when they have some bearing upon, but do not contain, just the term being illustrated or when the quotation can hardly be cited as a legitimate or valid occurrence of the word in question.

† is used before spellings that are obsolete.

> is used for "whence," i.e., from which is derived.

< is used for "from, derived from."

+ is used for "and" in etymologies.

* is used before a hypothetical form.

The quotations are given in the form usual in historical dictionaries. Large capitals indicate volumes or other large divisions, small capitals parts or sections, and lower-case letters chapters or prefatory pages, e.g., III, II, xxi. When a subordinate sense marked **b** follows a sense which is not marked **a,** this signifies that the subordinate sense is regarded as being derived from the antecedent one.

LIST OF ABBREVIATIONS

a (before a date) = *ante*, before
a. = adjective
absol. = absolute, -ly
adv. = adverb
advt. = advertisement
Amer. = America(n)
Amer. Sp. = American Spanish
app. = apparently
attrib. = attributive, attributively
B. '48, etc. = J. R. Bartlett, *Americanisms* (1848, 1859, 1877)
B. and L. = Albert Barrère and C. G. Leland, *Dictionary of Slang* (1888–90)
Br. Wtb. = *Versuch eines Bremischniedersächsischen Wörterbuchs*
c (before a date) = *circa*, about
Camb. = Cambridge
Can. F. = Canadian French
cap. = capitalized
Cent. = *Century Dictionary* (1889–91)
cf. = confer, compare
collect. = collective, -ly
colloq. = colloquial -ly
combs. = combinations
DAB = *Dictionary of American Biography*
DAE = *Dictionary of American English*
dial. = dialect
dim. = diminutive
Doc. = Document, -ary
Du. = Dutch
Econ. = Economics
ed. = edition
EDD = *English Dialect Dictionary*
Educ. = Education, -al
ellipt. = elliptical
Eng. = English
esp. = especially
F. = French; J. S. Farmer, *Americanisms* (1889)
f. = from
F. and H. = J. S. Farmer and W. E. Henley, *Slang* . . . (1890–1904)
f(f). = following
fig. = figurative
fl. = *floruit*, flourished (followed by date)
freq. = frequently
G., Ger. = German
Geol. = Geology
Gk., Gr. = Greek
hist. = historical
i.e. = *id est*, that is
imper. = imperative
interj. = interjection
intr. = intransitive
irreg. = irregular, -ly
L. = Latin
LG = Low German
masc. = masculine
MF = Middle French (14th–16th cent.)
misc. = miscellaneous
n. = noun
N. Amer. = North America(n)
naut. = nautical
N. Eng. = New England
no. Eng. = northern England (English)
n.s. = new series
obs. = obsolete
OED = *Oxford English Dictionary*
OHG = Old High German
opp. = opposite
orig. = originally
p. = page
Pa. G. = Pennsylvania German
pass. = passive
Pg. = Portuguese
pl. = plural
Polit. = Political
poss. = possibly
prec. = preceding
prep. = preposition
prob. = probably
pron. = pronoun
pt. = part
quot(s) = quotation(s)
q.v., qq.v. = *quod vide*, which see
R. = Robert L. Ramsay, *Mark Twain Lexicon* (1938)
R., r. = river
Russ. = Russian
S. = Southern, South
sc. = *scilicet*, understand or supply
Ser. = Series
Sess. = Session
sing. = singular
specif. = specifically
Stand. = *Standard Dictionary* (Funk & Wagnalls, 1893–95)
Supp. = *Supplement*
S.W. = Southwest
Sp. = Spanish
s.v. = *sub verbum*, under the word
Th. = R. H. Thornton, *Glossary* (1912)
theat. = theatrical
Th. Supp. = R. H. Thornton, Supplement in *Dialect Notes*, Vol. VI
tr. = transitive, translation
transf. = transferred (sense)
usu. = usually
v. = verb
var. = variant
Ver. = Verwijs en Verdam, *Middelnederlandsch Woordenboek*
W. = West, Western, Webster
We. = Joseph A. Weingarten, *Supplementary Notes to the Dictionary of American English* (1948)
WNT = de Vries en te Winkel, *Woordenboek der Nederlandsche Taal*

A

∗**A,** *n.*

1. Abbreviation for Adultery (or Adulterer, Adulteress) formerly branded upon those convicted of this crime, or ordered worn by them as a badge. Now *hist.* Cf. **AD.**

The custom of branding criminals with the initial letter of their crimes is old (cf. *OED s.v.* F. III. **f.**), but evidence for such treatment of moral delinquents is available only from N. Eng. in early times. The law providing for the wearing of an A by those guilty of adultery remained in force in Mass. until 17 Feb., 1785. See Dow, *Every Day Life* 214. The offense referred to in the 1639 quot. below was adultery.

[**1639** *Plymouth Col. Rec.* I. 132 The Bench doth therefore censure the said Mary . . . to weare a badge vpon her left sleeue.] **1651** *Maine Province & Ct. Rec.* (1928) I. 164 Its ordered that mis Batcheller for her adultery shall . . . be branded with the letter A. **1850** HAWTHORNE *Scarlet Letter* 37 This rag of scarlet cloth . . . assumed the shape of a letter. It was the capital letter A. **1944** ADAMS *Album Amer. Hist.* I. 130 One harsh Puritan custom . . . compelled persons convicted of adultery to wear the letter 'A' sewed to their upper garments.

2. A brand used in early colonial times by the colonists of East Hampton, L.I., on stock owned by settlers there. *Obs.*

1665 in *Records E.-Hampton* I. 232 Mr Bond killed one red oxe 4 yeare ould cropt on both eares and marked with A uppon the horne. **1667** *Ib.* 262 Mr. Backer sould a horse . . . Brandmarked with ye letter A for East Hampton.

3. A mark denoting superior work done by a student in school.

The faculty minutes of Augustana College, Rock Island, Illinois, for June, 1877, refer to the adoption there of a marking system using the letters A, a, AB, ab, B. Augustana was founded by graduates of the Swedish universities of Upsala and Lund. In at least some of the elementary schools in Sweden letters were used as grade marks certainly as early as 1871, and the system adopted at Augustana apparently reflects earlier Swedish usage. The use of letters in this way at other institutions has not been investigated.

1877 [see note above]. **1897** FLANDRAU *Harvard Episodes* 57 'College life,' mutters the father of the man who got sixteen A's and brain fever. **1948** *Time* 12 Jan. 52/2 He pulled an A in Elizabethan literature, but he wasn't much of a student.

fig. **1946** *Chi. D. News* 22 July 8/7 A University of Wisconsin political scientist, who served one term in Congress and got A-plus on his report card as a New Dealer, is unopposed for the Democratic nomination.

A harrow

4. (See quot. 1879.)

1865 *Balt. Dly. Commercial* 4 Oct. 4/2 The refiners . . . now quote . . . Crushed, Powdered and Granulated, and Coffee Crushed at 19 1/4 cts for A White; 18 7/8 cts for Crushed A. **1879** WEBSTER *Supp.* 1539/1 A . . . In the United States the term is colloquially applied to other things [than ships] to imply superiority. **1925** MONROE & STRATTON *Good Buying* 46 She would know that for grade A the fruit must be sound and the color good, and she would know the size. **1943** OTTLEY *New World* 157 There is only one place in Harlem where meats of the finer cuts are sold, and few stores sell Grade A eggs.

5. a. A harrow, a harrow having the form of an A. **b. A tent,** a tent the sides of which slope evenly from the center-pole or the ridge-pole to the ground.

(a) **1867** *Iowa Agric. Soc. Rep.* (1868) 169 As soon as the corn appears in the row, drag with an A harrow. **1907** BAILEY *Cycl. Agric.* I. 394/2 Later a cross arm was attached and the implement was known as the 'A' harrow.

(b) **1863** GRAY *War Letters* 187 Beside them was a lot of negro laborers (not even soldiers) in brand new A tents. **1933** CHELEY *Camping Out* 432 An 'A' tent is almost as easy to pitch, especially if it is hung on a ridge rope tied between two trees.

For **A.B., A B C, AD, A.F. of L., A No. 1, A.P., A.P.A., AWOL,** see as main entries. Cf. also ∗**class 2.**

∗**Aaronic Priesthood.** Designating the order of lesser priests composed of deacon, teacher, and priest in the Mormon Church.

1838 FLAGG *Far West* II. 113 In the highest seat of the 'Aaronic priesthood' sit [*sic*] the venerable sire of the prophet. **1905** *Out West* Sep. 242 It is well understood in our Church that those holding the Aaronic Priesthood have authority to officiate only in outward ordinances. **1947** *This Week Mag.* 18 July 21/2 At least once a month, every family in a Mormon town can expect visits . . . from members of the 'Aaronic Priesthood'—deacons at 12, teachers at 14, priests at 17.

∗**A. B.** *Hist.* In combs: **A. B. conspirator, papers, plot,** (see quot. 1893).

1824 in *Ann. 18th Congress* 1 Sess. II. 2432 Notwithstanding all the canting about an 'A.B. plot,' . . . I assert . . . that it is known to your honorable body that neither of those committees extended their investigations into those statements. *Ib.* 2452 The charges . . . contain nothing but a reiteration of those made by the A.B. conspirators. **1854** BENTON *Thirty Years' View* I. xiv. 35/1 The A.B. papers . . . were a series of publications made in a Washington City paper, during the canvass, to defeat his [M. Crawford's] election. **1893** JAMESON *Dict. U.S. Hist.* (1931) 1 'A.B.' Plot, a plot to destroy Secretary of the Treasury Crawford's popularity and political power by accusing him, in 1824, of malfeasance in office. A series of letters appeared in a Washington newspaper signed 'A.B.,' reflecting upon Crawford's integrity, and demanding investigation. They were written by Ninian Edwards, who acknowledged their authorship. He failed to sustain his charges, so Crawford was exonerated.

∗**ab,** *n.* Usu. *pl.* One of the first two-letter combinations formerly found in elementary spelling books (see quot. 1899). — **1821** HOWISON *Sketches* 294 Yes, sir, only three years old, and knows his letters.—He was in the *abbs* and *ebbs* last week. **1899** GREEN *Va. Word-Book* 37 Ab, ab's and ba, ba's. The beginnings of spelling lessons; used to show that a person is in the very beginning of things, and has everything to learn. 'Why he is hardly in his *ab* and *ab's*, and *ba ba's* yet.' **1913** *American Mag.* Nov. 57/2 Louise-Marie, to do her credit, was a game little cluck-cluck when it come to a showdown and, more'n that, she'd learned her little a, b, abs, and, still more, she was a good woman.

abalone ˌæbəˈlonɪ, *n.* Also **abelone, avalone, avelone, avallonia, aulone,** etc. [Amer. Sp. *abulón* (f. Monterey Indian *aulun*) in same sense.] Any one of various mollusks or ear shells or sea ears of the genus *Haliotis* found on the coast of California. Cf. **bastard pearl.**

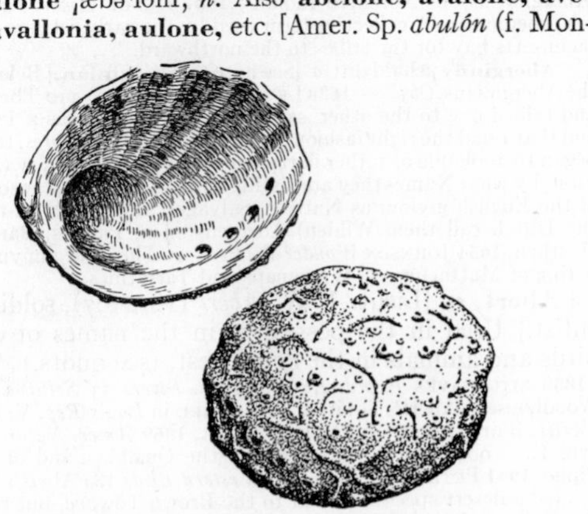

Shells of the abalone or bastard pearl

1850 B. TAYLOR *Eldorado* xvii. (1862) 174 The avelone, which is a univalve, found clinging to the sides of rocks, furnishes the finest mother-of-pearl. **1898** *Land of Sunshine* Mar. 181 The black abalone is more plentiful than the others, and the red abalone is the most beautiful of them all. **1947** *Newsweek* 20 Jan. 89/3 Between 20 and 30 . . . have jobs diving for abalone or harvesting agar at the ocean bottom.

attrib. **1882** *Harper's Mag.* Oct. 728 They [Chinamen in S. California] prepare the avallonia meat and avallonia shells for their home market. **1888** LINDLEY *Calif. of South* 304 Abalone shells are found on the rocks along all of these islands. **1897** *Land of Sunshine* Oct. 195 A Chinese abalone-hunter's cabin is buried to the eaves. **1947** *Denver Post* 2 Mar. 7/3 For several days we survived on an exclusive diet of abalone steaks.

***abate,** *v. tr.* To refrain from exacting (customs), to remit. *Obs.* — **1715** *Mass. H. Rep. Journals* I. 48 Praying that the Duty upon Eleven Negro Women and Children by him Imported, may be abated. **1718** *Ib.* II. 67 Praying that the Duty of Four Pounds on a Negro Boy he lately imported, may be abated. **1806** WEBSTER *Abate, v.*, to . . . remit as a tax (Con.).

abatied ˈæbətɪd, *a.* [f. ***abatis.**] *Mil.* Furnished with an abatis. *Obs.* — **1781** WASHINGTON *Diaries* II. 239 The Batteries . . . appeared to be well friezed, ditched and abbatied. *Ib.*, Fort N. 8 is also abatied and friezed at the top.

***A B C**

1. (See quot.) *Obs.*

1899 CHAMPLIN & BOSTWICK *Cycl. of Games s.v. A-B-C.* A game played by any number of persons with a pack of cards, on each of which are a letter of the alphabet and a picture. The pack is placed face upwards on the table, and each player in order names an object in the picture on the top card which begins with the letter on that card. Any one who cannot do so in less than one minute is out.

2. ABC table, some now indefinable gambling device. *Obs.*

1798 *N.C. Statutes* III. xix. 12 *And be it further enacted,* That any person whatsoever who shall suffer the game of Billiards, or any of the games played at the tables commonly called A B C, E O, or Faro Bank, or any other gaming table or bank of the same or like kind . . . shall . . . pay the sum of one hundred pounds. **1853** *Alta California* (S.F.) 1 May 2/2 There are a number of A.B.C. tables, but they are conducted in a different style, and probably the majority of them are perfectly fair.

Abe, see **Old Abe, Old Honest Abe, Uncle Abe.**

Aberginian ˌæbɚˈdʒɪnɪən, *n.* [See note.] (See quot. 1907.) *Obs.* or *hist.*

Hodge suggests that this word is a corruption of **Abnaki,** *q.v.*, or a misspelling of *aborigines.* In the first ed. (1623) of Cockeram's *The English Dictionarie,* the word *Aborigeni,* "people whose beginning is not knowne," occurs. In the 1626 and subsequent eds. the word is spelled Abergeni. Note the spelling *Aberieny* (i.e., *Aberjeny*) under **Aberginny,** *a.* below.

1634 WOOD *N. Eng. Prospect* II. i. 57 Our Indians that live to the North-ward of them be called Aberginians, who . . . are a cruell bloody people. **1764** HUTCHINSON *Hist. Mass.* I. 456 There was great enmity between the Tarrenteens and Aberginians, or Indians of Massachusets bay. **1832** WILLIAMSON *Maine* I. 459 The clans between the Pawkunawkutts and the Piscataqua . . . have been called the 'Abergineans,' or Northern Indians. **1907** HODGE *Amer. Indians.* I. 1/1 Abergenian. A collective term used by the early settlers on Massachusetts bay for the tribes to the northward.

Aberginny ˌæbɚˈdʒɪnɪ, *a.* [See note to **Aberginian.**] Belonging to the Aberginians. *Obs.* — **1628** LEVETT *Voyage* (1893) 110 They smiled and talked one to the other, saying the other man was a Iacknape, and that I had the right fashion of the *Aberieney Sagamores,* then they began to applaude or rather flatter me. **1643** WILLIAMS *Key* (1827) 19 First, by what Names they are distinguished. . . . First, those [names] of the English giving: as Natives, Salvages, Indians, Wild-men, (so the Dutch call them Wilden) Abergeny men, Pagans, Barbarians, Heathen. **1654** JOHNSON *Wonder-W. Prov.* 16 The Abarginnymen consisting of Mattachusets, Wippanaps and Tarratines.

***Abert,** *n.* [Lieut. J. W. *Abert* (1820–97), soldier, scientist.] Used in the possessive in the names of various birds and animals in the Southwest, (see quots.)

1853 SITGREAVES *Exped. Zuni & Colo. Rivers* 53 *Sciurus Abertii,* Woodhouse.—Abert's Squirrel. **1860** BAIRD in *Ives's Rep.* V. 6 *Pipilo abertis,* Baird, Abert's finch. Fort Yuma. **1869** *Amer. Naturalist* III. 476, I . . . obtained the first eggs of the Quail . . . and of Abert's Pipilo. **1941** PETERSON *Field Guide Western Birds* 184 Abert's Towhee . . . [is] a desert species, similar to the Brown Towhee, but browner, the entire under parts buffy-brown.

abisselfa ˌebaɪˈsɛlfə, *n.* [See note.] (See quot. 1848.) *Obs.*

Though this term has not been found in British use, the fuller expression, "A by itself, a" of which it is a contraction, occurs in Edward Moor's *Suffolk Words and Phrases* (1823), p. 119.

1835 LONGSTREET *Ga. Scenes* 76 In the good old days of fescues, abisselfas, and anpersants. **1848** BARTLETT 1 In the olden time, the first letter of the alphabet was denominated 'abisselfa' when it formed a syllable by itself, as in the word *able.* **1917** *D.N.* IV. 435.

abluvion æbˈluvɪən, *n.* [L. *abluvio, -onis* f. *abluere,* to wash away.] The action of washing away. *Obs.* — *a***1817** DWIGHT *Travels* II. 57 Several considerable lots have been washed away from the Hadley shore. . . . It cannot be wondered at, that this process of Alluvion, and abluvion, which has gone on ever since the deluge, . . . should produce even greater changes than these.

Abnaki æbˈnɑkɪ, *n.* [Algonquian *Wabunaki,* east land, morning land.] (See quot. 1907.)

[*a***1716** PERROT *Mémoire des Sauvages de l'Amérique* (1864) 70 Il n'y a que les Abenekis, et ceux qui demeurent les françois, par le conseil qu'on leur a donné.] **1721** *Mass. H. Rep. Jrnl.* III. 111 [A letter bearing] the Signature of the . . . Abnaquoise, and of . . . the Algonquins, the Hurons [etc.]. **1827** *Spirit of Seventy-Six* (Frankfort, Ky.) 8 Nov. 1/3 The Menominee and Wabanocky Indians squatting about in groups, (looking curious enough) on the left flank, a bit in advance of the line. **1907** HODGE *Amer. Indians* I. 2 Abnaki. . . . A name used by the English and French of the colonial period to designate an Algonquian confederacy centering in the present state of Maine, and by the Algonquian tribes to include all those of their own stock resident on the Atlantic seaboard, more particularly the 'Abnaki' in the N. and the Delawares in the S. **1947** COFFIN *Yankee Coast* 226 These Abenakis painted their faces the colors of death and their maple leaves in autumn when they went on the warpath and slew the Mohawks.

***aboard,** *adv.*

In British use *aboard* is used only nautically, but in Amer. English it has, as some other terms originally nautical, been extended to land use.

1. *All aboard,* the call of a conductor directing passengers to enter a train, streetcar, etc., that is about to start. Also transf.

1837 J. T. SMITH *Journal* 18 They describe a situation by the compass 'talk of the voyage' of being 'all aboard' &c this doubtless arises from *all* their ancestors having come hither over ocean & having in the voyage acquired nautical language. **1878** I. L. BIRD *Rocky Mts.* 148 'Head them [=cattle] off, boys!' our leader shouted; 'all aboard! hark away!' and . . . away we all went at a hand-gallop. **1902** MCFAUL *Ike Glidden* xxxi. 297 He and his bride boarded the train, and the conductor announced 'All aboard.' **1947** *Nat. Geog. Mag.* Feb. 157/2 (caption), All Aboard the Oxcarts.

2. On or into a train.

1856 M. J. HOLMES *L. Rivers* iv. 33 [She told] him that 'the trunks, box, feather bed, and all, were every one on 'em left!' 'No, they are not,' said John; 'I saw them aboard myself.' **1901** MERWIN & WEBSTER *Calumet K* xv. 297, I . . . jumped for the lever and hollered for him to get aboard. **1947** *Atlantic Mo.* Nov. 45/2 We're trying to . . . get us a special car on the eight-thirty. How about getting aboard?

b. On horseback. *Jocular.*

1884 SWEET & KNOX *Through Texas* v. 63 At one o'clock we were all aboard. **1946** *Outdoor Life* Oct. 7/1 You can hit the trail aboard a cayuse; hike or hunt . . . thrill to dude ranch life.

***aboard,** *prep.* On or into a train. — **1855** *Knickerb.* June 561, I . . . put myself 'a-board' the six-o'clock Train. **1901** MCCUTCHEON *Graustark* 26 You might have climbed aboard the train. **1948** *Popular Western* June 18/2 The brakeman, lantern swinging in the arcs of a high-ball signal, hopped aboard the rear platform.

abogado ˌɑboˈgɑdo, *n.* [Sp. in same sense.] In regions of former Spanish influence, a lawyer or advocate.

1803 *Ann. 8th Congress* 2 Sess. 1517 The fees of the Abogado, or person consulted by the judges on law points, are twelve and a half cents for every leaf of which the process consists. **1884** BRET HARTE *On Frontier* 199 Why did you send for the abogado Poindexter when my brother called? **1889** *Cent., Abogado* . . . [is thus] used in parts of the United States settled by Spaniards.

***abolition,** *n.* In combs. now obs. or hist.: (1) **abolition bill,** a bill in Congress favoring the abolition of slavery; (2) **colonist,** an early settler of Kansas friendly to the abolition of slavery; (3) **member,** a member of Congress favoring abolishing slavery; (4) **oil,** (see quot.); (5) **paper,** a newspaper advocating the abolishing of slavery, (6) **party,** a political party (1840–56) organized by those favoring the abolition of slavery in the District of Columbia and the Territories, suppression of the interstate slave trade, and general opposition to slavery to the full extent of constitutional power, cf. **Republican party;** (7) **society,** a society for promoting the abolition of slavery; (8) **soldiery,** northern or federal soldiers during the Civil War; (9) **state,** a state in which slavery was not tolerated; (10) **ticket,** a ticket put out by the Abolition party.

(1) **1862** S. Cox *In Congress* (1865) 239 Events, says Phillips, are grinding out the freedom of the negro; and these abolition bills are events. — (2) **1901** Duncan & Scott *Allen & Woodson Co.* (Kansas) 69 His sympathies were against the Abolition Colonists, and as he had the reputation of backing his opinion with his revolver, he was a terror to the 'Yankee Colonists.' — (3) **1852** Bristed *Upper Ten Th.* iii. 63 One of our Abolition members at Washington. — (4) **1881** C. M. Woodward *Hist. St. Louis Bridge* 247 The common remedy [for 'bends'] was the rubbing of the affected parts with oil or liniment of some kind. A certain 'Abolition Oil' gained great popularity.

(5) **1837** P. Hone *Diary* I. 278 An abolition paper was established . . . which, becoming obnoxious to the slave holders, was assailed. — (6) **1839** Marryat *Diary in Amer.* III. 58 For the stronger the abolition party may become, the more danger is there to be apprehended of a disastrous conflict between the States. **1890** Burney *J. G. Burney & His Times* 85 That was the last political effort of the abolition party in Maryland. — (7) **1790** Maclay *Deb. Senate* 169 Our President produced the petitions and memorials of the *Abolition* Society. — (8) **1866** Richardson *Secret Service* xv. 197 The people were greatly incensed at the 'Abolition Soldiery.' — (9) **1843** *Niles' Reg.* 13 May 175 That Great Britain would rather assist the country [=Texas] as an independent abolition state than purchase it. — (10) **1848** W. E. Burton *Waggeries* 65 It's rayther too far south for you to go the abolition ticket.

Also *abolition business, cause, chap, incendiarism, meeting, movement, priest, question, riot, speech, strength,* etc.

abolitional æbəˈlɪʃənl, *a.* [f. ∗*abolition.*] Pertaining to the abolition of Negro slavery in the U.S. *Obs.* — **1846** S. Smith *Theatrical Apprent.* ii. 30 Of course we could not encourage him in such abolitional ideas.

abolitionary æbəˈlɪʃənˌɛrɪ, *a.* [*abolition +-ary.*] Advocating the abolition of Negro slavery in the U.S. *Obs.* — **1859** J. Redpath *Roving Edi or* 118 If slavery had no other evils. the fact that it separates families, forever, . . . would make me an abolitionary insurrectionist.

abolitiondom æbəˈlɪʃəndəm, *n.* [∗*abolition +-dom.*] The realm or region of the abolitionists, hence the northern states. *Obs.* — **1857** *Lawrence* (Kansas) *Republican* 28 May 4 Brown the official . . . cursing . . . all abolitiondom for having stolen that precious four quires of paper. **1861** *N.Y. Times* 27 Dec., They [=people in Tenn.] cannot be sold to Abolitiondom. **1877** Bartlett 2.

abolitioner æbəˈlɪʃənɚ, *n.* [∗*abolition +-er.*] A believer in the abolition of Negro slavery. *Obs.* — **1855** *Herald of Freedom* 8 Sep. 2/4 Jist then, the man on my right whispered, 'that's an abolitioner.' **1865** *Madison* (Ind.) *Dly. Ev. Courier* 27 Sep. 4/1 They are 'afeerd the abolishiners will make the nigger their equal.'

abolitionize æbəˈlɪʃənˌaɪz, *v. tr.* To imbue with the principles of those favoring the abolition of slavery. Also transf. *Obs.*

1842 Joseph Sturge *Visit to U.S. 1841* 49 Appointing a sub-committee, to consist of one member for each block, square, section, sub-division, or neighborhood, whose duty it will be to endeavour to abolitionize his subdivision. **1854** C. Robinson *Kansas Conflict* (1892) 94 So it is with the colonizationist societies and their dupes they send to abolitionize Kansas. **1865** *Nat. Anti-Slavery Standard* (N.Y.) 23 Sep. 1/5 A great number of men of the Western army are being 'abolitionized.'

∗**aborigine,** *n.* As last term in **buck aborigine, white aborigine.**

abortionist əˈbɔrʃənɪst, *n.* [∗*abortion +-ist.*] One who practices the inducing of criminal abortions. — **1871** *N.Y. Herald* 16 Sep. 5/3 Hoping that your life and health may be spared to deal with abortionists as they deserve. **1885** Foster *Se-quo-yah* 199 Abortionists are imprisoned for not less than two or more than ten years. **1945** *Chi. Tribune* 16 Sep. (Book Sec.) 10/4 The most amazing criminal in the book is the midwife and abortionist.

∗**about,** *adv. about and about,* pretty much alike or the same. *Rare.* — **1867** *Congress. Globe* 8 Jan. 331/2 Men were created equal. That is, at the very outstart the cytoblast, the primal cell, . . . was about and about.

∗**above,** *prep.* **1.** *To go above* (one), in a spelling class, to spell a word another has missed and thus pass above him toward the head (*q.v.*) of the class. **2.** *above snakes,* quite high, *colloq., obs.* **3.** *above one's bend, huckleberry,* see the nouns.

(1) **1828** in *PMLA* LVI (June, 1941) 509 The pupil is generally allowed to spell at a word but once; if he errs, the one who is next in the class spells it if he can, and *'goes above him.'* **1881** Alcott *New Conn.* 132 If a word was misspelled, the next pupil who could spell it was allowed to take his place, or 'go above him,' as it was called. — (2) **1851** E. S. Wortley *Travels U.S.* xxiv. 154 Look at those two tall Kentuckians, with their tufted chins, somewhere about seven feet 'above snakes.'

abra ˈɑbrɑ, *n. S.W.* [Sp. in same sense.] A narrow pass or defile; a valley.

?**1892** in *D.N.* I. (1896) 243 abra: a narrow pass between mountains; in Texas, more specifically, a break in a *mesa* . . . or in a range of hills. **1912** Lumholtz *New Trails* 17 The intervening valleys, or *abras,* as the Mexicans call them, are rather flat. **1933** *Amer. Sp.* Oct. 9/1 The open spaces between very old, worn-down mountains, which have filled in with detritus, are called *abras.*

∗**Abraham,** see **Father Abraham.**

∗**absence,** *n. poet.* An absent form or face. *Obs.* — **1866** W. D. Howells *Venetian Life* 118 The balconies are full of the Absences of gay cavaliers and gentle dames. **1873** Higginson *Oldport Days* i. 14 What graceful Absences (to borrow a certain poet's phrase) are hunting those windows.

∗**absent,** *a.* In combs.: (1) **absent lot,** in the beginning of the New Haven colony, a lot left vacant by the non-arrival of a colonist expected to come later, *obs.;* (2) **treatment,** Christian Science treatment given at the request of one who is not present; (3) **voter,** an absentee voter, attrib. in context.

(1) [**1641** in Hoadly *Records New Haven* (1857) 61–62 Itt is ordered thatt all the voyde lotts in the towne shall be reserved for those for whom they were intended till the comeing of the first ships, and if then ye persons come nott for whom they are so reserved, the towne may dispose of them as they see cause.] **1643** *New Haven Col. Rec.* I. 95 The committee appointed to dispose of the absent lott mett. **1651** *New Haven Town Rec.* 74 [That] the land the Towne gave to Joseph Pecke out of the absent lotts, be disposed of. — (2) **1885** *Christian Science Jrnl.* III. 40 (caption), Absent Treatments. **1944** *Christian Science Sentinel* XLVI. 1713/1, I called for a Christian Science practitioner and asked her for absent treatment. — (3) **1936** *Dly. Oklahoman* (Okla. City) 4 Nov. 12/6 Welker Given, 83 years old, who conceived the idea of the absent voter ballot more than 40 years ago while editor of the Marshalltown Times-Republican, voted in person Tuesday.

∗**absentee,** *n.*

1. A loyalist who absented himself from his residence during the American Revolution. *Obs.*

1777 *Mass. Acts & Resolves* 9 April V. 630 The said agent . . . shall return an inventory . . . of such absentee's estate that has come to his hands, to the said judge of probate **1779** *N.H. Comm. Safety Rec.* 203 The farm . . . lately own'd by John Vance, an absentee. **1832** Williamson *Maine* II. 466 Copies of the confiscation or 'absentees act,' were transmitted [*c*1778] to every legislative assembly in the Union.

2. *attrib.* Denoting Indians living away from their former or customary abode.

1869 in Foreman *Last Trek* (1946) 176 A Resolution for the Relief of Settlers upon the Absentee Shawnee Lands in Kansas. **1946** *Ib.* 199 Steps were then taken to care for the more than three hundred 'Absentee Wyandots.'

3. Designating a qualified voter who, because of his circumstances, is permitted to vote by mail. Also **absentee vote, voting.**

1932 *N.Y. Times* 29 Oct. 17/2 (*heading*), Grandmother's 'Duty' to Child Wins Fight for Absentee Vote. *Ib.* 10 Oct. 2/3 Uniform laws governing absentee voting in the United States were urged today by John F. Costello. **1936** *Dly. Oklahoman* (Okla. City) 4 Nov. 12/6 Iowa was the first state to adopt the absentee voter idea. **1948** *Democrat* 23 Sep. 8/2 We found many, many irregularities in connection with the absentee voting.

b. Also **absentee ballot.**

1932 *Dly. Ardmoreite* (Ardmore, Okla.) 21 Oct. 3/4 It provides that only those who are absent from their homes on election day because of business which cannot be postponed are eligible to receive absentee ballots. **1944** *Steamboat* (Colo.) *Pilot* 9 Nov. 2/3 There are two types of absentee ballots in this state, those voted by the civilian people who are absent from their counties, and those voted by the military people.

∗**absenteeism,** *n.* (See quot.) — **1888** M. Lane *Pol. Catch-Words* 13 Sep. 15 *Absenteeism* . . . does duty in defining the position of congressmen, like the late Senator Nye, whose constituency is in one state and their residence in another.

absinthe ˈæbsɪnθ, *n.* [F. An Amer. borrowing. See McDermott, *s.v.*] The sage-brush or prairie sage, a species of artemisia. Also attrib. — **1841** P. J. De Smet *Letters* (1843) 108 It abounds in absynth, cactus, and all such plants and herbs as are chiefly found in arid lands. **1843** Frémont *Exped.* 56 *Absinthe bushes,* which grew in many thick patches. **1848** Parkman *Oregon Trail* x. 146 Multitudes of strange medicinal herbs, more especially the absanth, which covered every declivity.

∗**absolutely,** *adv.* Used colloquially as an emphatic affirmative. — **1892** Mark Twain *Amer. Cl.* xxiv 255 (R.), 'Do you mean to say that if he was all right and proper otherwise, you'd be indifferent about the early part of the business?' 'Absolutely.' **1927** *Collier's* 24 Dec. 36/3 'I do love a white Christmas, don't you?' 'Absolutely!' says Jack.

absorbent cotton. Raw cotton that has been freed of its natural fat or wax, thus rendering it suitable for medicinal dressings, etc. — **1889** *Cent.* **1923** *Outing* Feb. 198/2, I bought adhesive tape, peroxide, and absorbent cotton. **1947** *Hygeia* Oct. 767/2 The thermometer should be kept in a small tumbler, one-quarter filled with antiseptic solution, with a little absorbent cotton in the bottom of the glass.

absquatalize æbˈskwɑtl̩ˌaɪz, *v.* Also **absquatiate, absquattle.** [See next.] *tr.* and *intr.* Variants of next. *Slang. Obs.*

1839 *Ky. Observer* (Lexington) 31 Aug. 1/2 Yes, you low, vulgar, ill-born, illiterate scamp; I'll absquatalise you in an instant,'—and, raising his foot to effect his purpose, as luck would have it, a seam gave way. **1839** MARRYAT *Diary* II. 34 The editor of the *Philadelphia-Gazette* is wrong in calling *absquatiated* a Kentucky phrase. *Ib.*, By the way, there is a little corruption in the word as the *Gazette* uses it; *absqutalize* is the true reading. **1848** W. E. BURTON *Waggeries* 17 Let's licker one more round and then absquattle.

absquatulate æbˈskwɑtʃuˌlet, *v.* Also **absquatilate, absquotulate, -ilate,** etc. [Of fanciful classical formation as if based on **ab*+ **squat*, meaning the reverse of to squat (*q.v.*), i.e., to decamp, make off.] *intr.* To depart, go away, esp. in a clandestine, surreptitious or hurried manner, abscond, decamp. *Slang. Obs.*

1830 *Painesville* (Ohio) *Telegraph* 15 June 1/5 *Obsquatulate*—To mosey, to abscond. **1834** S. SMITH *A. Jackson* 36 By golly, if you absquotulate, you are ded before you can say Jack Robinson. **1861** J. LAMONT *Sea-horses* xi. 179 [An old bull-walrus] heard us, and lazily awaking, raised his head and prepared to absquatulate. **1890** *Buckskin Mose* i. 18 The vagabond had 'absquatulated' with the whole of the joint-stock funds.

b. Of things: To part, separate, fall away. Also **absquatulating,** *a.*

1842 *Spirit of Times* 29 June (Th.), When Mr. F. again called, the shingle had absquatulated from the shutter. **1846** DURIVAGE & BURNHAM *Stray Subjects* 70 Our boy is sick—has cut his stick—Absquatulating elf! **1858** *Salem* (Ill.) *Advocate* 17 Feb. 1/2 She might . . . give him a kiss. Ah, and a good one, too—not one of the touches that wouldn't make a dew drop absquatulate from a rose leaf.

absquatulation æbˌskwɑtʃuˈleʃən, *n.* [f. prec.] An instance of absquatulating, an absconding. *Slang. Obs.*

The first example is an allusion in "tall talk" to the old expression "Does your mother know you're out?"

1849 *Knickerb.* Nov. 407/1 I'l risk my pile that his mammy aint aprised of his absquatilation [*sic*]. **1862** *First Minnesota* (Berryville, Va.) 11 March 4/1 Our short residence in Berryville, and the sudden absquatulation of the local editor, is our apology for the meagre variety in the local column.

absquatulator æbˈskwɑtʃuˌletɚ, *n.* [f. **absquatulate.**] One who absquatulates. *Slang. Obs.* — **1842** *Spirit of Times* 20 June (Th.), [Sketch of] the career of a foreign absquatulator.

abstractionist æbˈstrækʃənɪst, *n.* One who is given to abstractions or ideals, an idealist (see quot. 1859). *Obs.* Cf. **Virginia abstractionist.**

1844 EMERSON *Ess.* II. viii, Nature . . . punishes abstractionists and will only forgive an induction which is rare and casual. **1859** GRATTAN *Civilized Amer.* I. 308 The Whig party . . . was formed of . . . Democrats like Henry Clay, old Federalists like Daniel Webster, Virginian theorists, nicknamed 'Abstractionists,' like John Tyler. **1865** *Atlantic Mo.* XV. 411 Though at first called an abstractionist and a fanatic by the looser thinkers of his own region, his inexorable argument . . . made itself felt at last.

***abut,** *v. tr.* To define (a piece of land) by stating the bounds. *Obs.* — **1651** *Dedham Rec.* 186 Eleazer Lusher is requested to refer those grants in the Record that ar entered unbutteled to those enteries that ar abutted to prevent questions & mistakes. **1663** *Groton Rec.* 10 Every man . . . shall bring a note of all his lands . . . bounded & abutted unto the Towne-Clark.

***abutment,** *n.* In *pl.*, bounds, limits. *Obs.* — **1665** *Hartford Land Distrib.* 405 All that land within these after abutments on the great River west. **1693** *Providence Rec.* IV. 244 A certaine tract of land & swampe . . . the bounds & abuttments whereof shall more amply appeare.

abuttalment əˈbʌtlmənt, *n.* [f. **abuttal* +*-ment.*] *pl.* Bounds of land. *Obs.* — **1700** *Dedham Rec.* V. 274 Any one of them with the Survaier Shall have power to . . . make return . . . of the qvantity bounds and abuttelments to be entered in the Booke of grants.

abutter əˈbʌtɚ, *n.* [f. **abut, v.*+*-er.*] An owner of contiguous property or land, an adjacent proprietor.

1673 *Boston Rec.* 82 Such of the present abuttrs. or borders on the said flatts as shall come in undertakes of the aforesaid wall or wharfe. **1807** *Boston Selectmen* 3 June 344 The abuttors . . . having regulated the side walk & paved the same with stone & brick. **1929** *Amer. City* Jan. 193/2 An abutter could not withdraw his name from a paving petition after it had been filed with the clerk.

***acacia,** *n.* The North American locust-tree, *Robinia pseudoacacia*, sometimes called false or bastard acacia. Also popularly applied to other species of this genus or to similar plants of other genera. Also attrib. Cf. **rose acacia.**

1640 PARKINSON *Theater of Plants* 1550 Robinus his false Acacia of America . . . I have given it a place with another *Virginia* like it, but not with the true ones as is most fit. **1763** in *Amer. Sp.* XX. (1945) 45 The *Acacia* (*Locust*) is the same in *Louisiana* as in *France*, much more common, and less streight. The natives . . . make their bows of it. **1785** MARSHALL *Amer. Grove* 53 *Gleditsia*. Triple-Thorned Acacia, or Honey Locust. **1880** G. W. CABLE *The Grandissimes* xxxvii. 287 Come . . . take right hold of the acacia-bush.

***academic,** *a.* and *n.*

1. *n.* An academic student. *Obs.*

1856 *S. Lit. Messenger* XXII. 248/1 If we compare these with our Masters of Arts, it seems in strong contrast with one out of every 43 (7 out of 304 Academics). **1894** *U. of Chi. Wkly.* 4 Oct. 4/1 One student, a member of the graduate school, . . . was heard one day soliciting an 'Academic' to set him right on the question of credits.

2. *a.* Pertaining or belonging to that department of a university or college which deals with classical, mathematical, and general literary studies, as distinguished from those that are technical or professional.

1856 *S. Lit. Messenger* XXII. 244/1 In the academic department of the university. **1892** *Nation* 22 Sep. 216/2 There is also a cross-line of cleavage between the sophomore and junior years of each of these colleges [of the University of Chicago]; the two lower years being termed the 'academic college' and the two higher years the 'university college.'

b. academic freedom, the freedom of a teacher to state the truth as he sees it without the fear of losing his position. Cf. *akademische Freiheit.*

1901 *World's Work* July 920/2 Every right-thinking man will stand firmly for academic freedom of thought. **1947** *Key Reporter* Autumn 5/3 Much is said about academic freedom, objective teaching of all science and all philosophies.

***academical,** *a.* =**academic,** *a.* (see quot. 1884). — **1813** *Yale Coll. Cat. Officers*, etc., Nov. 5 List of the Students in the academical Institution of Yale college. **1884** *Science* 425/4 The American use of 'academical' as applying to an undergraduate classical college, in distinction from a scientific or professional school.

***academy,** *n.* As the last term in **military, naval academy.**

Acadian əˈkedɪən, *n.* and *a.* [f. *Acadia.*]

See *Pub. Col. Soc. Mass.* XXIV. (1920–22), for a discussion of how this term came to be used for Nova Scotia.

1. *n.* A native or inhabitant of Acadia; one of the French settlers of Acadia, or of the descendants of these in Louisiana. Cf. **Cajan.**

1705 *Boston News-Letter* 14 May, At break of day . . . our harbour was beset with . . . some Accadians at Pessemequady and Port Royall, and Canadians. **1764** in *N.Y. Hist. Soc. Coll.* IX. 334 These Accadians were neither treated as Subjects in Rebellion nor as Prisoners of War. **1896** CLENDENIN *Fla. Parishes E. La.* 171 The Attakapas country is the home of the Acadians. **1931** READ *La. French* xviii, The Acadians of Louisiana are the descendants of the French who were formally expelled by the English from Acadie, or Nova Scotia, on Friday, September 5, 1755.

b. A French Louisianian of humble station.

1880 *Scribner's Mo.* Jan. 383/1 The term 'Acadian' . . . may frequently be heard applied to all the humbler classes of French origin throughout the state. **1947** *N. & Q.* Feb. 173/1 The Cajuns—southwest Louisiana Acadians of Norman and Breton ancestry—were seemingly very resourceful in this art.

2. *a.* In names of birds: **Acadian flycatcher, (night) owl,** (see quots.).

1839 AUDUBON *Synopsis Birds* 24 *Ulula Acadica*, . . . Acadian Night-Owl. . . . Saw-whet. **1874** COUES *Birds N.W.* 249 *Empidonax Acadicus*, . . . Acadian, or small Greencrested Flycatcher. *Ib.* 315 *Nyctale Acadica*, . . . Acadian or Saw-whet Owl. **1942** *U.S. Nat. Museum* Bul. 179, 194 The Acadian Flycatcher may be more active in the late summer than at any other season.

b. In the general sense, "of or belonging to Acadia," used in such expressions as *Acadian farmer, kin, land, race, settlement, wanderer*, etc.

3. Acadian French, (see quot.).

1939 LYLE SAXON *Fabulous New Orleans* 270–71 Then, of course, there was the Acadian French—or the Cajan French—which is the language spoken in the outlying districts of Louisiana.

Accidency ˈæksədənsɪ, *n.* [*f.* ∗*accident* +-*cy*.] A mock title, preceded by "His," applied to one succeeding to an office, esp. the presidency of the U.S., through the death of its holder.

1830 *Chautauque Phenix* (Westfield, N.Y.) 27 July 1/2 His Accidency is better, but his Accidency's malady, the palpitation of the heart, is not beyond danger. **1841** *Greene Co. Torchlight* (Xenia, O.) 16 Sep. 2/2 Mr. Tyler, 'his Accidency,' . . . has again interposed his 'reasons' between the welfare of his country and his 'conscientious scruples.' **1866** *Crumbs of Comfort* (Laporte, Penna.) 15 Oct. 2/2 The election returns, from Vermont and Maine, only prove to us, as the cheers for Gen. Grant during the Presidential tour did to his Accidency, that the People are with us.

∗**accidental,** *a.*

1. Used with reference to one who while serving as Vice-President of the U.S. becomes President through the death of that officer. Also **Accidental Johnson,** and (with reference to Millard Fillmore) **His Accidentalship.**

1856 *Town Talk* (S.F.) 29 July 2/3 'Mil Phil,' 'Jackson's Nephew,' 'His Accidentalship,' are already current coin. **1866** *Eastern Slope* (Washoe, Nev.) 6 Oct. 2/1 He fulfilled [these promises] to the entire satisfaction of his friends, by assuming the position rejected by Accidental Johnson, that of dictator. **1947** *Chi. Tribune* 19 Oct. 1. 24/6 In the future we should see to it that only men of Presidential stature are nominated to the Vice Presidency, thus avoiding 'accidental Presidents' of second or third rate ability.

2. accidental insurance, (see quot. 1865).

1865 *Boston Directory* 526/2 New York Accidental Insurance Company, . . . for insuring against accidents of all kinds. **1869** MARK TWAIN *Innocents Abroad* xxxvii. 401 (R.), He had what the accidental insurance people might call an extra-hazardous polish.

acclimation ˌæklɪˈmeʃən, *n.* [f. ∗*acclimate*, *v.*] The process of acclimating or of becoming accustomed to a different or less natural climate. Also attrib. — **1826** FLINT *Recoll.* 132 Emigrants generally suffer some kind of sickness, which is called 'seasoning,' implying that it is the summit of the gradual process of *acclimation.* **1873** MARK TWAIN & WARNER *Gilded Age* xvi. 154 Taking every morning before breakfast a dose of bitters . . . out of the acclimation jug.

acclimator ˈæklɪˌmetɚ, *n.* [f. ∗*acclimate*, *v.*] One who inures others to a new climate. *Rare.* — **1827** COOPER *Prairie* xxxi, He an acclimator! I will engage to get the brats acclimated to a fever-and-agy bottom in a week.

∗**accommodate,** *v. tr.* To provide or supply (a person) with (a loan of) money. "A commercial sense" (W. '28). — **1811** *Ann. 11th Congress* 3 Sess. 610 [Because] the Bank of the United States . . . has committed the fault of not accommodating everybody, it must now cease to accommodate anybody. **1880** BARNETT *Commercial Dict.* 10 Bills of exchange made . . . by a party . . . for the purpose of benefiting or accommodating some other party.

∗**accommodation,** *n.*

1. Land given a colonist by a colonial town. In full **accommodation of land.** *Obs.*

1636 *Essex Inst. Coll.* IV. 94/1 The town promised first acomodations vnto them. **1659** *Hempstead Town Rec.* I. 33 One halfe of my Accomodations of Land. **1684** *Maine Doc. Hist.* XXIV. 230 They will afford each of said Families equall accommodation of Lands with himself.

2. Financial aid, a loan.

1790 HAMILTON in *Ann. 1st Congress* II. 2058 The accommodations which they might derive in the way of their business, at a low rate. **1875** *Scribner's Mo.* Dec. 227/2 In general, every man who keeps an account at bank, and expects loans—'accommodations,'—is compelled by the law of custom to have a certain balance at all times standing to his credit.

3. Short for **accommodation stage, accommodation train.**

1829 A. ROYALL *Penna.* II. 9, I . . . intended to take the Accommodation in the morning. **1909** CALHOUN *Miss Minerva* 208 They went on the excursion and Sam Lamb is bringing them home on the accommodation. **1944** HOLTON *Yankees* 96 We would all arrive at the gate well before Willard had docked the Accommodation.

b. (See quots.)

1851 LOWELL *Letters* I. (1894) 212 She was built for a packet, has five accommodations. **1907** *St. Nicholas* May 669/1 When the miners go down into the mines, they get into a car called the accommodation.

4. *attrib.* Designating means of conveyance esp. suited in the times of their departure, stopping at all or nearly all stations, etc., to the convenience of travelers, as (1) **accommodation car,** (2) **coach,** (3) **stage,** (4) **train.**

These combs. are now obs. or hist., except **accommodation train** which in some localities is a mixed passenger and freight train (see quot. 1911).

(1) **1836** *Merchants' & Taylors' Guide* (Boston) 65 The price of the tickets is $2.00—accommodation cars $1.50. **1892** *Harper's Mag.* Feb. 426/1 What may be called accommodation cars [of an elevator] halt at the lower floors. — (2) **1830** *Collegian* 125 One of these vehicular conveniences that, by the association of contrast, are styled 'accommodation Coaches.' — (3) **1811** *Columbian Sentinel* (Boston) 25 Sep. 3/1. **1913** *Proc. Pa.-Ger. Soc.* XXII. 37 The other event was the arrival or departure of the accommodation stage. This, as its name implies, stopped at all points wherever a passenger beckoned to the driver. — (4) **1838** *Boston Almanac* 49 Depots on the Providence Rail Road. Accommodation Train. **1911** *Southern Reporter* LV. 595 A 'mixed or accomodation train' is a train equipped and having the appliances and facilities suited for the carriage of passengers as well as freight. **1946** *Amer. Sp.* Feb. 42 Dictionaries . . . seem confused over the relation between *local train, accommodation train,* and *mixed train.* The first two are synonyms, both being familiar colloquially but the shorter being preferred in official railroad documents; either of them means a mixed train which stops at every station, or at most of the stations.

b. Also **accommodation fare,** fare on an accommodation stage; **a. house,** a house for accommodating travelers; **a. line,** a line of accommodation stages. All *obs.*

1811 *Daily Advertiser* (Phila.) 11 July, From Philadelphia to New York. The Accommodation-fare through 3 dollars. — **1878** I. L. BIRD *Rocky Mts.* 165 Though the hosts kept 'an accommodation house for travellers,' they would take nothing for my entertainment! — **1832** MRS. TROLLOPE *Domestic Manners of the Americans* I. 284 As the accommodation line must not run on the sabbath. **1834** BAIRD *Valley Mississippi* 147 There are two lines daily called the Mail and Accommodation Lines.

5. Used with reference to financial arrangements: (1) **accommodation credit,** credit suited to one's needs; (2) **note,** "one drawn and offered for discount, for the purpose of borrowing its amount" (Web. '28); (3) **paper,** a negotiable paper made, indorsed, or accepted by a person to accommodate or favor another in the course of business.

(1) **1873** *Harper's Mag.* July 279/2 You will need no accommodation credits at two per cent. per month! — (2) **1797** *Ann. 5th Congress* I. 401 Accommodation notes . . . were often renewed. **1908** *Sat. Ev. Post* 26 Sep. 3/2 His law partner Captain Harvey, gave him an accommodation note for two hundred and fifty dollars. — (3) **1829** SHERWOOD *Gaz. Georgia* (ed. 2) 75 The Bank to collect the debts due the State, and debtors to be allowed to renew their notes, . . . as persons borrowing money on accommodation paper.

See also **bank accommodation, night accommodation.**

accommodational əˌkɑməˈdeʃənḷ, *a. local.* Offering accommodations; accommodative. *Rare.* — **1829** DUNGLISON in *Va. Lit. Museum* 102 A short time ago, we saw a tavern, recommended in a printed handbill as the most *accommodational* on the road.

∗**account,** *n.* *To hand in one's accounts,* to die. *Colloq.* — **1873** ALDRICH *Marj. Daw* 150 The hotel remains to-day pretty much the same as when Jonathan Bayley handed in his accounts in 1840.

As the last term in **charge, checking, government, no-, store account.**

∗**accounting,** *n.* and *a.* **1. accounting office,** an office in which accounts are kept. **2. accounting officer,** an officer who keeps or checks accounts. — (1) **1804** *Ann. 8th Congress* I. 266 The organization of the accounting offices of the Treasury, War, and Navy Department. — (2) **1802** *Ann. 7th Congress* App. 1304 That the accounting officers of the Treasury Department be . . . authorized . . . to make . . . allowances for clerk hire. **1841** TRUMBULL *Autobiog.* 96 In May, 1777, . . . my military accounts were audited and settled at Albany, by the proper accounting officer, John Carter.

∗**accredit,** *v. tr.* To attribute (a thing) *to* a person. — **1876** A. WILDER *R. P. Knight's Symb. Lang.* xxvii, To the fanatical hordes of Islam . . . is to be accredited the extinction of the Mystic Orgies of the East. **1900** *N. & Q.* 9th Ser. 22 Dec. 487/1 The introduction of the name [Columbia] as a poetic title for the United States is to be accredited to Dr. Timothy Dwight.

acculturation əˌkʌltʃəˈreʃən, *n.* [f. ∗*ac-* + ∗*culture* + ∗*-ation.*] The adoption or assimilation of an alien culture.

1880 J. W. POWELL *Study Ind. Lang.* (ed. 2) 46 The force of acculturation under the overwhelming presence of millions has wrought great changes. **1948** KERWIN *Civil-Military Relationships* 170 Cultural patterns are not inherited biologically but are transmitted from generation to generation by processes of education and what is properly called 'acculturation.'

b. Also **accultural,** *a.*, involving or produced by acculturation; **acculture,** cultural elements acquired by acculturation; **acculturize,** *v. tr.*, to affect the culture of (a people) by assimilation of foreign elements.

1897–8 J. W. POWELL *Bur. Amer. Ethnol. Rep.* I. xxi, When an invention is accepted and used by others it is accultural. — **1904** G. S. HALL *Adolescence* II. 726 There is little acculture [among American Indians]. — **1895** *Smithsonian Rep.* 44 The arts and industries of the partially acculturized Papago Indians.

accusive əˈkjusɪv, *a.* [f. ∗*accuse, v.*] Accusatory. *Rare.* — **1904** O. HENRY *Cabbages & Kings* 12 The comandante wrote in his secret memorandum book the accusive fact that Señor Goodwin had on that momentous date received a telegram **1906** —— *Four Million* ix. (1916) 95 Into this place Soapy took his accusive shoes and telltale trousers without challenge.

∗**ace,** *n.*

1. A point scored in baseball, a run. Now *hist.*

1845 in *Appleton's Ann. Cycl.* (1886) 77/2 The game [in baseball] to consist of twenty-one counts or aces. **1856** *Porter's Spirit of Times* 6 Dec. 229/2 *Yates—3d Base*—An excellent catcher; strikes well, and has been more successful in making aces in matches, than almost any other in this Club. **1947** R. SMITH *Baseball* 40 A turn at bat was a 'hand' and a run was an 'ace.'

2. ace-full, in poker, a hand consisting of three aces, together with one pair of a lesser denomination.

1849 *N.O. Picayune* 14 July 1/4 The game proceeded with the usual fluctuations for some length of time . . . when it happened that an 'ace-full,' was out against a 'king-full,' and Mr. Hancock . . . found himself loser $200. more. **1927** BURNS *Tombstone* 145 It makes a fellow feel like he was sitting behind an ace-full in a fat jackpot.

b. ace-high, quite high in favor or esteem, orig. a poker term used of a hand containing an ace, but not having a pair or better. *Colloq.*

[**1878** HART *Sazerac Lying Club* 154 A discussion on the Russo-Turkish war relieved the tedium of 'ace-high' and single pairs.] **1927** EUBANK *Horse & Buggy Days* 149 McWarg had an ace high showing. **1948** *Time* 12 Jan. 34/3 In one field, at least, the Russians were still ace-high with Americans last week.

c. ace in the hole, something particularly effective held in reserve. *Colloq.* Cf. **hole card.**

1922 *Collier's* 23 Sep. 24/1, I got a millionaire for an ace in the hole. **1948** *Chi. Tribune* 29 Feb. I. 14/1 (*heading*), Sumatra Held As Ace In Hole By Indonesians.

acequia əˈsekɪə, *n. S.W.* [Sp. in same sense.] An irrigation ditch. Cf. **irrigating acequia, sequia.**

1844 JAMES J. WEBB *Memoirs* 123 Following down the main Acequia for some distance towards the town, I was surprised to see beaver sign, so near a large town. **1891** Union Pac. R.R. *Utah* (ed. 4) 26 Ten years ago there were 10,000 miles of acequias, large and small, watering as many small farms in the valleys of Utah. **1941** FERGUSSON *Southwest* 278 They have saved . . . its acequias running clear mountain water, its trees, and a respect for its Spanish-speaking folk.

b. acequia madre, a main ditch.

1844 GREGG *Commerce of Prairies* I. 151 One *acequia madre* (mother ditch) suffices generally to convey water for the irrigation of an entire valley, or at least for all the fields of one town or settlement. **1887** *Overland Mo.* Aug. 159/2 The plough lands lay on a sort of natural terrace, and were all watered by numerous channels and runlets, which had their sources in the great *acequia madre*.

acid wood. The wood of various hardwood trees from which acetic acid, wood alcohol, and other chemicals are obtained by destructive distillation. — **1920** *U.S. Bulletin* 26 April 407 On privately owned land adjacent to this body of Government timber there is estimated to be approximately 200,000 cords of acid wood. **1941** ALLEY *Random Thoughts* 494, I saw a train with at least fifty cars, laden with pulp and acid wood.

Acoma ˈakəmə, *n.* [f. the native name meaning "people of the white rock."] *pl.* A tribe of Indians of the Keresan family occupying a pueblo of the same name in New Mexico. Also **Acoma Indian.**

1890 *Stock Grower* 26 July 6/2 For years the Acomas maintained a settlement twelve miles from the river. **1903** JAMES *Indian Basketry* 89 Among the Hopi, Zunis, Acomas and other pueblo Indians of Arizona and New Mexico . . . I have seen it thus used. **1912** SAUNDERS *Indian Terraced Houses* 20 We were greeted by Edward Hunt, a large, good-humoured Acoma Indian, who had picked up a Quakerish name, [and] a fair knowledge of English.

Hence **Acomanian,** a member of this tribe of Indians.

1934 MORRIS *Digging in Southwest* 75 The Acomanians are not much more pleased by tourists than they were by Spaniards.

∗**acorn,** *n.* In combs: (1) **acorn bread,** bread made of acorns; (2) **chestnut,** ?a white oak acorn; (3) **flour,** = next; (4) **meal,** meal of acorns; (5) **mush,** mush of acorn meal; (6) **oil,** the liquor obtained from crushed acorns; (7) **porridge,** porridge made of acorns; (8) **squash,** a squash somewhat resembling a huge acorn.

(1) **1847** *San Francisco* (Calif.) *Star* 24 July 2/2 On going into the village, these Indians manifested the most friendly feelings, offering acorn bread, and other food. **1882** J. HAWTHORNE in *Macm. Mag.* XLVI. 44 What I need now is a bellyful of venison and acorn-bread. — (2) **1797** IMLAY *Western Territory* (ed. 3) 268 There is another kind of chesnuts which are called the acorn chesnut, from its shape, and growing in a cup like the acorn. — (3) **1886** HUTCHINGS *Heart of Sierras* 425 The acorn flour needs to be relieved of its bitter tannin to prevent constipation. — (4) **1848** E. BRYANT *California* 345 Their breakfast . . . consisted of . . . a kettle of *atole* made of acorn-meal. (5) **1828** J. SMITH in M. S. Sullivan *Travels of Jedediah Smith* (1934) 58 These indians called themselves Machalunbrys . . . their principal living seems to be Acorn Mush. **1888** MUIR *Picturesque Calif.* 33 Raw or cooked, it is regarded as a fine luxury, and delicious dressing for other kinds of foods—acorn-mush, clover-salad, grass-seed-pudding, etc. — (6) **1709** LAWSON *Carolina* 178 As to the Indians foods, it is . . . fowl of all sorts . . . , acorns and acorn oil [etc.]. — (7) **1872** in *Overland Mo.* VIII. 426/1 In case of extreme suffering, it is probable that he [the Chareya-Indian fasting in mts.] takes a little acorn-porridge or *pinole* — (8) **1937** VERRILL *Foods Amer. Gave World* 84 There are the . . . scalloped squashes, vegetable marrows, Hubbard squashes and the little deeply-fluted diamond or acorn-squashes. **1948** *Spokesman-Review* (Spokane, Wash.) 23 Sep. 7/3 Spokane-grown endive and acorn squash are making their appearance on local markets this week.

b. *To come to the acorns,* to experience adversity. *Colloq. Obs.*

1835 BIRD *Hawks of Hawk-h.* I. xix. 256 You're no Johnny Raw, I see; but you'll come to the acorns yet!

∗**acre,** *n.* **1. acre foot,** the amount of water needed to cover an acre of land to the depth of one foot. **2. acre inch,** one twelfth of an acre foot. — (1) **1902** NEWELL *Irrigation* 83 The contents of reservoirs built for city water supply are usually stated in millions of gallons, while those for irrigation are almost always given in acre-feet. **1948** *Colo. Mag.* March 56 From 1941 to 1944 the annual average of all diversions from the Colorado to the South Platte . . . was roughly 15,000 acre-feet. — (2) **1909** WEBSTER. **1936** *Ariz. Agric. Exp. Sta. Bul.* 153, 489 Under cool coastal conditions, mature Washington navel orange trees used . . . 9.2 acre-inches of water.

See also **bee acre, Hollands acre.**

∗**act,** *n. To do the dude* (*hospitality, Melburn*) *act,* to act in a manner characteristic of a specified person or type. *Colloq.*

1887 *Harper's Mag.* May 990/2 He at once began . . . to abuse the Negro, accusing him of . . . doing the dude act in charcoal. **1904** W. H. SMITH *Promoters* iii. 72 They did the hospitality act up in great shape. **1907** M. C. HARRIS *Tents of Wickedness* 41 She thought she was going to do the Melburn act and ride roughshod over prejudices.

As the last term in **Algerine, alien, Alien and Sedition, Amnesty, baby, bounty, Desert Land, donation, Edmunds, Eight Section, Embargo, enabling, Exclusion, Fugitive Slave, gag, gold standard, homestead, land bounty, land grant, lumber, Missouri, non-importation, non-intercourse, Organic, reconstruction, sedition, Sherman, Sherman Anti-trust, Volstead, white face act.**

∗**act,** *v. intr. To act up,* to become unruly, to behave in an unusual or unbecoming manner. *Colloq.* — **1903** A. ADAMS *Log Cowboy* xviii. 115 The horse of some heeler . . . acted up one morning. **1929** F. E. MCCLINCHEY *Joe Pete* 182 They've lived here on this Island for years and this is the first time I've ever heard of their acting up.

∗**action,** *n.* As the last term in **back, double back, single action.**

actional ˈækʃənl, *a.* [f. ∗*action, v.*] *Law.* Actionable. *Obs.* — **1662** *R.I. Col. Rec.* I. 497 It shall be alowed on the actionall case aforesayd. **1664** *Ib.* II. 31 That two Courts of Triall in the yeare be held . . . for the triall of any actionall matter.

∗**actionist,** *n.* One who advocates or favors separate state action. *Rare.* — **1851** *Harper's Mag.* III. 557/2 A letter from Hon. J. L. Orr . . . , reflecting . . . upon the spirit manifested by the 'actionists' toward the 'co-operationists.'

actual settler, see **settler 1. b.**

∗**AD.,** *abbrev.* (See quots.) *Obs.* Cf. ∗**A,** *n.* **1.** — **1641** *Plymouth Col. Rec.* II. 28 The Court doth censure them as followeth: That they shall weare . . . two letters, viz., AD, for adulterers, daly, upon the outeside of their uppermost garment. **1658** *New Plymouth Laws* 113

Likewise to weare two capitall letters viz. AD. cut out in cloth and sowed on theire uper most Garments. **1895** *Proc. Amer. Antiq. Soc.* Apr. 110 A man and woman convicted of this offence were sentenced both to be severely whipped immediately, at the public post, and that they should wear (while they remained in the Government) two letters, viz., an 'AD,' for Adulterers, daily, upon the outside of their uppermost garment.

ad æd, *n.* Short for ∗*advertisement.* Often attrib. and in combs. Cf. **real estate ad, want ad.**

For some account of opposition that this term has encountered, see Mencken, *Supp.* I. 375.

1852 *Mountain Echo* (Downieville, Calif.) 14 Aug. 3/3 New Ads. **1889** *Portland* (Ore.) *Mercury* 22 June 3/3 Judging from the Register's 'ad' columns, it has come to stay. **1909** *Collier's* 22 May 15/2 So in a sense, the ad-man is a public entertainer. **1944** JOHNSON *As I Dare* 311 The class in writing became a sort of literary club, joined by a most satisfactory cross-section of the town's inhabitants: high-school teachers . . . the ad-writer from the one department store, . . . and others. **1948** *Time* 16 Feb. 74/3 Commercials for television are causing deep furrows in admen's brows.

∗**Adam,** *n.*

1. outward Adam, one's body. *Colloq. Obs.*

1836 CROCKETT *Adventures* 56, I had no sooner elongated my outward Adam, than they at it again, with renewed vigour. *Ib.* 91 Having the gentility of his outward Adam thus endorsed by his tailor . . . he managed to obtain an introduction to the planter's daughter.

2. In phrases and combs.: (1) ∗**Adam and Eve,** (see quot. 1897–8); (2) **Adam and Eve's thread and needle, = Adam's needle (and thread)**; (3) **Adam's cup,** (see quots.); (4) **Adam's leather,** the human skin, *rare;* (5) **Adam's needle (and thread),** (see quot. 1891).

(1) **1807** J. SCOTT *Descr. Md. and Del.* 25 Adam and Eve; this plant has two bulbous roots, joined together by a small filament, about two inches in length; when put into water, one of the roots swims, and the other sinks. **1897–8** *Bur. Amer. Ethnol. Rep.* I. 426 The putty-root (Adam-and-Eve, *Aplectrum hiemale*), which is of an oily, mucilaginous nature, is carried by the deer hunter, who, on shooting a deer puts a small piece of the chewed root into the wound, expecting as a necessary result to find the animal unusually fat when skinned. **1933** SMALL *Southeastern Flora* 388 Adam-and-Eve. Putty-root. — (2) **1831** *Boston Transcript* 5 June 2/1 Yucca filamentosa, or Adam and Eve's thread and needle. — (3) **1836** LINCOLN *Botany* 169 Side-saddle flower . . . is sometimes called Adam's cup, in reference also to the shape of the leaf. **1892** *Amer. Folk-Lore* V. 92 *Sarracenia purpurea*, Adam's cup. Dudley, Mass. — (4) **1835** BIRD *Hawks of Hawk-h.* II. i. 17 Never show an inch of Adam's leather to an Indian.

(5) **1765** J. BARTRAM *Diary* 15 July Ye other tree if we may so call it they call adams needle. **1891** *Cent. s.v. Yucca*, From their sharp-pointed leaves with threads hanging from their edges, *Y. filamentosa* and *Y. aloifolia* are known as Adam's needle and thread and as Eve's thread. **1938** DAMON *Grandma* 73 Just at the gate, each side, was a clump of yuccas, 'Adam's needle-and-thread,' and on the left against the house lilacs and twinberry and honeysuckle.

∗**adamantine,** *n.* and *a.* **1.** A candle made of hard wax, in full **adamantine candle.** *Obs.* **2.** (*cap.*) A member of the extreme faction of the Hardshells *q.v.* Also **Adamantine Hard.** *Obs.*

(1) **1845** *Ga. Messenger* (Augusta) 5 Sep. 2/2 (*Advt.*), Butter Crackers, Soda Biscuit, Adamantine Candles. **1882** *Rep. Indian Affairs* 342 Candles, adamantine: . . . 8,450 awarded. — (2) **1854** A. M. MURRAY *Lett. from U.S.* (1856) I. 197 Party terms . . . such as Adamantines, Hard-shells, Soft-shells, Loco-focos, Rick-burners, and Polly-wogs. It seems these names . . . have originated in casual expressions made use of by public speakers which have happened to hit the fancy of the hearers, so that they became cant terms. **1889** *Cent. s.v. Hard,* Of the more conservative of the two factions . . . the extreme members were called the Adamantine Hards.

Adamite 'ædəmaɪt, *n.* Also **Adamsite.** An adherent or supporter of John Adams, second President of the U.S. (1797–1801), or of his son, John Quincy Adams, sixth President (1825–29). *Obs.* Cf. next.

1799 WEEMS (*title*), The Philanthropist, or a Good Twenty-Five Cents Worth of Political Love Powder for Honest Adamites and Jeffersonians. **1825** in M. B. SMITH *Forty Yrs. Washington Soc.* (1906) 171 At Mr A's the other evening, there were Jacksonites and Adamites and Crawfordites all mingled harmoniously together. **1842** in *Amer. Sp.* XVIII. 119 'Think you I would have wasted a word on you, had I the slightest suspicion of your having hoisted the dirty colors of the Adamsites?'

∗**Adams,** *n.* Used attrib. in allusion to the political principles of John Quincy Adams (1767–1848), sixth President of the U.S. (1825–29).

1824 *Amer. Sentinel* (Georgetown, Ky.) 8 Oct. 2/4 It is thought that even should the Adams and Jackson men unite their strength, Mr. Clay will yet obtain the vote of that state. **1824** *Commentator* (Frankfort, Ky.) 27 Nov. 3/1 Any compromise, between the Adams and the Clay parties, would secure the latter a chance in the house of Representatives. **1858** T. S. WOODWARD *Reminiscences* (1939) 135, I could give you a long string of Jeffersonian Democrats who have descended from old Adams Federalists. **1935** ALEXANDER *Amer. Talleyrand* 219 The Adams and Jackson men might hate and distrust each other, but they held no bitterness for him.

b. Hence **Adamsism,** support or advocacy of John Quincy Adams. *Obs.*

1824 W. L. MARCY in Mackenzie *Van Buren* (1846) 199 The attack upon Mr. Mallory is by every body regarded as cruel and savage, . . . I hope this proceeding will cure him of his Adamsism. **1830** *Mechanics' Press* (Utica, N.Y.) 24 Apr. 191/3 We have nothing to do with the exploded notions of Jacksonism or Adamsism.

Adams press. (See quot.) *Obs.* — **1849** J. DIXON *Personal Narrative* 38 A great number of presses are at work; and one, called the 'Adams press,' from the name of the inventor, is remarkable. It was partly self-acting, an instrument of the nature of pincers, or rather a hand, taking hold of the paper as a roller revolved, and placing it so as to receive the designed impression.

adaptativeness ə'dæptəˌtɪvnɪs, *n.* [f. ∗*adaptative* + *-ness.*] Adaptiveness. *Rare.* — **1881** *Harper's Mag.* Apr. 645 He possessed plenty of that Yankee adaptativeness.

∗**adder,** *n.*[1] An adding machine. *Obs.* — [**1864** WEBSTER, Adder, one who, or that which, adds.] **1890** *N.Y. Herald* Jan. (*advt.*), The Adder is so called because really too simple to be styled a 'machine.' **1902** *Sears Cat.* (ed. 112) 168/3 Full instructions accompany each adder.

∗**adder,** *n.*[2]

1. ∗**adder's mouth,** an orchid of the genus *Malaxis.*

1840 DEWEY *Mass. Flowering Plants* 202 *Microstylis ophioglossoides.* Nutt. Adder-mouth [*sic*] . . . root bulbous; roots of trees; June. **1940** DEAM *Flora Indiana* 349 Malaxis unifolia Michx. Green Adder's Mouth.

2. ∗**adder's tongue,** the dogtooth violet, *Erythronium americanum.*

1821 *Mass. H. S. Coll.* 2 Ser. IX. 150 Plants, which are indigenous in the town of Middlebury, [Vermont, include] . . . *Erythronium lanceolatum*, (Pursh.) Adder's tongue. **1947** *Midland Naturalist* July 37 Yellow Adders-tongue [is] abundant in bottomland forest; rare in terrace and bluff forest.

As the last term in **blowing, checkered, deaf, flathead, puff, red, spreading, water adder.**

adding machine. A machine that performs arithmetical addition, and sometimes subtraction. — **1874** KNIGHT 12/2. **1911** HARRISON *Queed* viii. 102 He was as definite as an adding-machine, as practical as a cash register. **1947** *Denver Post* 2 Mar. 2C/5 But thou gavest me no adding machine, and the sum of the letters giveth the same answer on two sides of the post.

∗**addition,** *n.*

1. An added lot, plot, or extent of land, a piece *of* land added to existing holdings.

1636 *Springfield Rec.* I. 159 [A lot with] an adition . . . of as much marish as makes the whole twenty fouer acres. **1721** *Mass. H. Rep. Journals* III. 12 A Petition . . . praying for an addition of 3700 acres of land, to be added to their former grant.

b. An area near a city, town, or village, more recently laid out into lots, streets, etc., as an extension of the residential section.

1786 *Md. Journal* 6 Jan. (Th.), Found, in Howard's new Addition to Baltimore-Town, 127 panes of glass. **1923** R. HERRICK *Lilla* 24 The new Addition . . . was a new strip of prairie [near Chicago] which the Porter Realty Company was preparing to put on the market. **1947** *Steamboat* (Colo.) *Pilot* 9 Jan. 4/8 Sacrifice—Nine lots in Woolery addition $100.

2. A part added to a building. Cf. **frame addition.**

*c*1638 *Harvard Rec.* I. 172 For unloading the lumber prepard for the Addition: [£]3 10[*s*]. **1876** *Chico* (Calif.) *Enterprise* 23 June 3/3 Bryan & Cook have been awarded the contract to build the addition to the Court-house at Oroville. **1948** *Ariz. Republic* (Phoenix) 29 June 5/2 A $15,000 addition to the new juvenile detention home on West Apache street was approved yesterday by the county board of supervisors.

3. *Addition, division, and silence,* "a Philadelphia expression which, for a time, had a vogue as a catch phrase" (F.).

1867 W. H. KEMBLE *Lett. to T. J. Coffey* March (Cl.), Evans . . . has a claim of some magnitude that he wishes you to help him in. Put him through as you would me. He understands addition, division and silence.

∗**address,** *n.* As the last term in **inaugural, New Year's, post-office, self-, Tammany address.**

∗**address,** *v.tr.* To force (a judge) *out* (*of* office) by a petition to the executive. *Obs.* — **1822** *Missouri Intell.* 2 July 3/2 If any of the judges have corruptly discharged their duties, impeach them. If they are incompetent, address them out. **1874** R. H. COLLINS *Kentucky* I. 27 David Ballengall, an assistant judge . . . , [was] 'addressed' out of office, because a Scotchman unnaturalized.

addressee ədrɛsˈi, *n.* [f. ∗*address, v.*+*-ee.*] One to whom a letter, document, etc., is addressed.

[**1677** in E. D. NEILL *Virginia Carolorum* (1886) 374 Lieut Governor said he would lay £100 that the addressee would not be permitted to see the King, but would be sent to the Tower.] **1810** R. PETERS in *Life Jay* II. 332 Nothing must go with a pamphlet but the mere direction, under the pains and penalties of sousing the correspondent or addressee in all costs of enormous postage. **1947** *Dly. Oklahoman* (Okla. City) 5 Nov. 5/8 Many ballots were being returned, however, uncalled for by the addressees.

ade ed, *n.* [f. such expressions as lemon*ade*, orange*ade*.] A drink made of fruit juice and sweetened water. — **1895** *Amer. Folk-Lore* Jan.–Apr. 58 In the extraordinary use of these lemonades and other 'ades,' the Mexicans reveal the Moorish strain in their blood. **1945** MENCKEN *Supp.* I. 358 Drug stores and groceries sometimes announce lines of *ades*.

adelantado ædəlɑnˈtɑdo, *n. S.W.* [Sp. in same sense.] The governor of a province. — **1844** GREGG *Commerce of Prairies* 118 (Bentley), This adventurer . . . stipulates for some extraordinary provisions . . . with titles of Adelantado and the rank of Captain-general. **1885** *Wkly. N. Mex. Review* 22 Jan. 4/4 Juan de Onate, the first adelantado or governor, . . . writes with respect to the people [etc.]. **1932** C. C. LOVELL *Golden Isles Ga.* 5 In 1565, San Augustin was founded by Menendez de Avilés, adelantado and captain-general of Florida.

Adenostoma ædəˈnɑstəmə, *n.* [f. combining elements (f. Gk.) *adeno-* gland, +*-stoma* mouth, in allusion to the gland at the base of the calyx.] A genus of California shrubs of the rose family. Also (not *cap.*) a shrub of this genus. Cf. **chamiso.** — **1850** TORREY *Plantæ Fremontianæ* 11 The so-called glands in the throat of Adenostoma are only lobes of the free margin of the disk. **1869** MUIR *First Summer in Sierra* (1911) 18 The middle and background present fold beyond fold of finely modeled hills and ridges . . . all covered with a shaggy growth of chaparral, mostly adenostoma.

adios ɑdiˈos, *interj. S.W.* [Sp. *adiós*, in same sense.] Adieu, goodbye. Hence as *n.* a farewell. — **1837** *N.Y. Mirror* 23 Dec. 208/1 An overworked, spavined, broken-down set—but adios, Amigo. **1846–7** MAGOFFIN *Santa Fe Trail* (1926) 130 On receiving her pay she bowed most politely, shook hands with a kind *'adios.'* **1939** ROLLINS *Gone Haywire* 209 Adios, boys, an' may th' Lord have mercy on your souls.

Adirondack ˌædəˈrɑndæk, *n.* [f. Mohawk Indian term meaning "they eat trees" applied to a tribe of Canadian Indians.] *attrib.* Designating or with reference to things found in, or regarded as characteristic of, the Adirondack mountain region.

1870 *Rep. Comm. Agric.* 84 So far as they have been sufficiently tested, the Catawba, Iona, . . . and Adirondack [grapes] are the best. **1942** PEATTIE *Friendly Mts.* 235 To carry his duffle the hiker will need a pack, which may be an Adirondack pack basket. **1948** *Richmond* (Va.) *News Leader* 6 May 8/4 Sturdy Adirondack Chairs as shown, made of selected white pine ready to varnish or paint any color you choose.

Adirondacker ˌædəˈrɑndækɚ, *n.* A dweller in the region of the Adirondack Mountains. — **1920** *Outing* Dec. 115/1 That is how we Adirondackers entertain our friends.

adjourn əˈdʒɜn, *n.* [f. ∗*adjourn, v.*] (See quot.) *Obs.* — **1851** HALL *College Words* 3 At Bowdoin College, *adjourns* are the occasional holidays given when a Professor unexpectedly absents himself from recitation.

∗**adjourn,** *v. tr.* (See quot.) *Obs.* — **1856** HALL *College Words* (ed. 2) 4 At the University of Vermont, . . . the students *adjourn* a recitation, when they leave the recitation-room *en masse*, despite the Professor.

∗**adjunct,** *n.* A college or university teacher next in rank to a professor. In full **adjunct professor.** — **1826** *Cat. Univ. Cambridge* 6 John W. Webster, M.D., Adjunct Erving Professor of Chemistry. **1876** D. C. GILMAN *University Probl.* (1898) 29 Promoting them because of their merit to successive posts, as scholars, fellows, assistants, adjuncts, professors, and university professors. **1904** *N.Y. Tribune* 8 Nov. 5 A. D. F. Hamlin, now adjunct professor of architecture.

Adlumia ədˈlumɪə, *n.* [Named after Major John *Adlum*, an American gardener.] A genus of American plants of which the climbing fumitory is the only species. — **1847** WOOD *Botany* 158 Adlumia. . . . A. cirrhosa. . . . *Mountain Fringe.* A delicate climbing vine, native of rocky hills, Can. to N. Car. **1933** SMALL *Manual Southeastern Flora* 549 Adlumia fungosa. . . . Climbing-fumitory. Fairy-creeper. Mountain-fringe. Cliff-harlequin.

administrador ɑdˌmɪnɪstrɑˈdɔr, *n. La. & S.W.* [Sp. in same sense.] A manager or overseer; a steward. — **1803** *Ann. 8th Congress* 2 Sess. 1521 The administrador [in La.] is also subordinate to the Intendant, and . . . manages everything respecting the custom-house. **1895** REMINGTON *Pony Tracks* 66 The *administrador* . . . moves about in the discharge of his responsibilities, and they are universal; . . . from the negotiation for the sale of five thousand head of cattle to the 'busting' of a bronc which no one else can 'crawl.'

∗**administration,** *n.*

1. The President of the United States and his Cabinet.

1803 *Fredericktown* (Md.) *Herald* 30 Apr. 3/1 Much as the democrats may exult in the event, as brought about by the wisdom of the present administration; we still perceive a mystery in the business. **1884** BLAINE *20 Years of Congress* I. 498 The narrow escape of the Administration from total defeat . . . was demonstrated afresh by the roll-call of the House. **1948** *Chi. D. News* 22 May 6/1, I can well understand the Administration's determination to 'get tough' with Russia.

2. The term or terms during which a President holds office.

1796 WASHINGTON *Farewell Address* § 49 On reviewing the incidents of my administration, I am unconscious of intentional error. **1927** D. S. MUZZEY *History* 484 During Harrison's administration, . . . expenditures had mounted steadily. **1947** *Denver Post* 19 Jan. (*rotog.*) 4/4 The picture was taken during the Coolidge administration.

attrib. **1808** *Ann. 10th Congress* 2 Sess. 198 What he calls our own Administration paper [*sc.* the *National Intelligencer*]. **1870** *Congress. Globe* 21 Dec. 243/2, I am an administration man, and whatever you do will always find in me the most careful and candid consideration.

Also *administration bill, candidate, editor, measure, state,* etc.

See also **anti-administration, National Court Administration.**

administrationist ədˌmɪnɪˈstreʃənɪst, *n.* A supporter of a particular presidential administration. — **1899** *Boston Globe* 21 July 7/4 Gen. Alger has finally been forced by . . . certain administrationists at Washington to tender his resignation.

∗**admiration,** *n.* A word game designed to test the players' vocabularies. *Obs.* — **1828** *Yankee* Sep. 288/1 While the girls are at work [=quilting], they amuse themselves with . . . some sort of a play . . . ; one that we call admiration, is a very good one.

∗**admission,** *n.*

1. = **admittatur.** *Obs.*

1697 SEWALL *Diary* I. 456 Willard . . . went to Cambridge and was admitted and then went into the River, and was drowned with his admission in his pocket. **1734** *Harvard Coll. Rec.* I. 134 A true coppy of the College Laws . . . signed by the President, & major part of the tutors, shall be his admission into the College.

2. *admission to the bar*, the granting of authority to practice as a lawyer.

[**1766** ADAMS *Works* II. 197 A meeting of the bar at the Coffee House, for the admission of three young gentlemen.] **1881** *Mass. H.S. Proc.* XIX. 143 There seems to have been [in the eighteenth century] no regular time of study prescribed as requisite for admission to the bar. **1943** POWELL *Home Again* 12 The clerk told him that the Court was then engaged in other matters, but would take up admissions to the bar later in the day.

3. The formal admittance of a state *into* the Union.

1777 *Journals Cont. Congress* IX. 924/2 No other colony shall be admitted into the same [confederation of states] unless such admission be agreed to by nine states. **1876** *General Laws, Colo.* (1877) 84 The admission of the State of Colorado into the Union is now complete. **1948** JOHNSTON *Gold Rush* 33/1 At any rate, its appellation was changed in 1850 to Nevada, by which it continued to be known until the admission of the State of Nevada into the Union ten years later.

4. In combs: (1) **Admission Day,** in some western states a legal holiday commemorating the admission of the state into the Union, also attrib.; (2) **admission fee,** a fee for admittance.

(1) **1854** *Pioneer* (S.F.) Oct. 238 'Admission Day'—the day of days for California . . . has been appropriated as their anniversary by the Society of California Pioneers. **1946** *L.A. Times* 11 Sep. II. 12/3 The gambling ship Lux yesterday enjoyed a brisk Admission Day holiday business in the wake of heavy week-end patronage. — (2) **1842** *Knickerb.* Nov. 498 Certain persons under the title of 'Professors' being stationed at the gates to exact considerable admission fees. **1945** *Sat. Review* 6 Oct. 24/1 Admission fees, if any, . . . will be turned over to war sufferers.

∗**admit,** *v.*

1. *tr.* To receive (a state) *into* the Union, to invest with statehood.

1777 *Journals Cont. Congress* IX. 924/2 Canada acceding to this confederation . . . shall be admitted into and entitled to all the advantages of this Union. **1815** *Niles' Reg.* VIII. 67/2 Five new states have been admitted into the union. **1948** MENCKEN *Supp.* II. 147 At a later period, the State, which was admitted to the Union on December 28, 1846, received large accessions of population from the stream of European immigration.

2. *To admit to the bar*, etc., to give authority to practice law.

1768 in *Mass. H. S. Proc.* XIX. 149 We will not recommend any persons to be admitted to the Inferior Court, as attorneys, who have not studied with some barrister three years at least. **1835** HOFFMAN *Winter in West* I. 113 A graduate of Williams College had been recently admitted to the bar. **1931** ADAMS & ALMACK *Hist.* 384 In 1788, having gone over the mountains in the westward movement to Tennessee, he studied law and was admitted to the bar.

* **admittance,** *n.* **1.** A charge for admission. In full **admittance fee. 2.** Permission, leave. *Rare.* — **(1) 1798** H. M. BROOKS *Gleanings* 87 Admittance, for grown persons, one Quarter of a Dollar.—Children half price. **1838** *S. Lit. Messenger* IV. 61/1 Each auditor paid an admittance fee. **1867** *Ball Players' Chron.* 4 July 7/1 Each person was charged an admittance fee of twenty-five cents. — **(2) 1806** LEWIS & ORDWAY *Jrnls.* (1916) 355 Informed us that the most of our horses . . . were safe, but some . . . had been [made] use of by the admittance of the head chief.

admittatur ˌædmɪˈtetɚ, *n.* [f. the L. *admittatur*, "let him be admitted" used in the certificate.] A student's certificate of admission to college. *Obs.* or *hist.*

1683 SEWALL in *Mass. H. S. Coll.* 4 Ser. VIII. 516 What if I should print the Colledge-Laws? that so every student admitted may have a fair *Admittatur* to keep per him. . . . They are without both Laws and *Admittatur.* **1832** *N. Eng. Mag.* III. 238, I received my *admittatur* and returned home, to pass the vacation and procure the college uniform and other necessary equipments. **1923** W. C. LANE in *Pub. Col. Soc. Mass.* XXV. 245 Another copy [of the ms 1655 Laws of Harvard College] . . . followed by the 'Admittatur' of Jonathan Mitchell of the Class of 1687.

adobe əˈdobɪ, *n. S.W.* [Sp., a sun-dried brick of clay or mud.]

This word has been variously spelled **adaube, adobey, adobie,** etc. The attrib. uses are extremely numerous.

1. Sun-dried mud or clay, or a crude cement made of this. Also a brick or brick-like piece of such material used in building.

1759 trans. VENEGAS *Nat. Hist. Calif.* I. 77 Some, to please the fathers, have made themselves houses, if they may be called such, of adobe or unburnt bricks, covered with sedge; but few live in them. **1834** J. L. STEPHENS *Centr. Amer.* (1854) 224 The houses in Costa Rica are . . . built of adobes or undried bricks two feet long and one broad, made of clay mixed with straw to give adhesion. **1856** G. H. DERBY *Phoenixiana* xix. 133 We have . . . Indians employed . . . in mixing adobe for the type moulds. **1869** BROWNE *Adv. Apache Country* 118 The walls . . . are composed of a concrete of mud and gravel, very hard. . . . This concrete, or adobe, was cast in large blocks, several feet square. **1947** *Denver Post* 26 Jan. (*mag.*) 2/4 At Penasco, a town of 300, twenty-five miles south of Taos, the people brought their tools and built a clinic out of adobe.

transf. and *fig.* **1850** *Calif. Courier* (S.F.) 27 Sep. 2/4 Yesterday, the name of D. C. McCarty was announced as one of the nominees of the branch of Locofocos known as the 'Adobes.' **1851** *S. F. Picayune* 3 Oct. 2/4 The weary traveller who struggles up the hill, carries a comfortably large adobe on each foot. **1856** G. H. DERBY *Phoenixiana* viii. 83 Captain George P. Jambs, of the U.S. Artillery, a thorough-going *adobe*, as the Spaniard had it.

Also in allusion to the expression *to have a brick in one's hat, q.v. s.v.* **brick.**

1853 *Placer Times* (S.F.) 15 July 4/6 Another [hat] of the inverted 'lamp filler' pattern—vast in its proportions and capable of containing the biggest 'adobe' that ever respectable gentleman labored to transport to his 'fifth floor-back.'

b. An adobe house.

1821 DEWEES *Lett. from Texas* 21 The remainder of the buildings are adobes, except a few which are made of wood. **1879** *Chi. Tribune* 7 Feb. 9/6 Many of these adobes stand upon recent claims. **1948** *Popular Western* June 44/1 In the squat, thick-walled adobe, he lighted a reflector wall lamp above his battered flat-topped desk.

c. (See quot. 1889.)

1873 *Mining & Scientific Press* 21 Mar. The screenings and fine stuff is called 'tierras.' These 'tierras' are made into 'adobes' before being burnt. **1889** *Cent.* 80/1 Adobe. . . . In the quicksilver-mines of the Pacific coast, a brick made of the finer ores mixed with clay, for more convenient handling in the furnace.

2. Clay or soil suggestive of adobe. Also attrib.

1897 *Land of Sunshine* Sep. 187 There is no hardpan, alkali, or adobe to vex the tiller of the soil. **1925** BRYAN *Papago Country* 106 Orchard-like forests of mesquite are common on adobe flats. **1948** *Galveston* (Tex.) *News* 14 June 2/6 We have 17 different kinds of soil to work with, from blackland to adobe.

b. Esp. **adobe soil,** (see quot. 1891).

1858 *Hutchings' Mag.* Sep. 138/1 [Q.] What vegetables flourish best in the different Adobe soils? [A.] Big dornicks and scrubby cedars. **1891** *N. & Q.* VI. 216 Another use of the word adobe, not unknown in some parts of California, is that which makes it the name of a kind of clay. So distinguished a writer as Prof. E. W. Hilgard often speaks of *adobe* soils.

3. Often used in combs., as **adobe castle, ranch, ranch house, store.**

1839 T. J. FARNHAM *Great Western Prairies* 136 We spent the 2d and 3d most agreeably with Mr. Walker in his hospitable adobie castle. — **1881** ROMSPERT *Western Echo* 75, I will venture to say that there is not an Indian in the whole Cheyenne nation that could shoot me nearer the heart than did that school-marm in the little *adobe* ranche. — **1947** *Nat. Geog. Mag.* Feb. 137/2 Heading northeastward from the big adobe ranch house, we rode for an hour. — **1847** *Californian* (S.F.) 5 June 3/2 It is said that Mr. Parker at the Adobie store has plenty of it, and a great many other good things.

b. In the Southwest applied to Mexican things, as **adobe dollar,** the Mexican peso. *Colloq.* Cf. **dobe.**

1909 WEBSTER. **1936** McKENNA *Black Range* 271, I made big winnings—adobe silver dollars by the gallon.

Also *adobe brick, building, clay, corral, cottage, dust, dwelling, floor, house, hut, land, maker, palace, residence, stable, storehouse, structure, town, wall,* etc.

Adopting Act. (See quot. 1895.) *Obs.* — **1735** in BAIRD *Acts of Presbyterian Ch.* (1856) 6 Ordered, That each Presbytery have the whole Adopting Act inserted in their Presbytery book. **1895** THOMPSON *Hist. Presbyterian Churches* 26 The Adopting Act of 1729, by which its ministers and licentiates . . . were required to subscribe to the Westminster Confession and Catechisms.

* **adoption,** *n.* **1.** *traffic by adoption*, among the plains Indians traffic or barter on unusually friendly terms because of one party's having been adopted into the tribe of the other. **2. adoption dance,** a dance accompanying the ceremony of adoption among the Indians. Both *obs.* — **(1) 1804** LEWIS & CLARK *Journals* (1904) 221 They came to the nations in this quarter to trade or (make preasants) for horses the Method of this Kind of Trafick by adoption Shall be explained here after. — **(2) 1901** M. E. RYAN *Montana* ii. 38 The old squaw was sorely averse to the adoption dance for the white girl who lay on their blankets.

* **advance,** *n.*

1. An advance guard of troops. *Obs.*

1780 *Heath Papers* 96 The 1500 (the advance of the militia) will be supported by 1,500 more. **1826** COOPER *Mohicans* xiv., [The enemy] met us hard by, in our outward march to ambush his advance, and scattered us, like driven deer, through the defile to the shores of Horicon. **1866** F. KIRKLAND *Bk. Anecdotes* 309 The advance dashed around the camp, a group looking on in wonder.

2. (See quot. 1851.) *Obs.*

1848 N. AMES *Childe Harvard* 13 Even to save him from perdition He cannot get 'the advance,' forgets 'the review.' **1851** HALL *College Words* 6 The lesson which a student prepares for the first time is called *the advance*, in contradistinction to *the review.*

3. In combs.: (1) **advance agent,** an agent who goes before to make arrangements for a circus, theatrical company, etc.; (2) **bill,** (see quot.); (3) **corps,** an advance guard; (4) **guard,** a body of troops in front of the main army, also transf. [*OED* has one ex., 1677, of *advanced guard*, hence **advance guard** may be British, though not illustrated in *OED*].

(1) 1882 SWEET & KNOX *Texas Siftings* 38 Do you think I am the advance agent of a variety show? **1948** *Milwaukee Jrnl.* 18 July 2/2 While old Barnum worriedly looked on, he formed brigades of advance agents, brass bands and poster stickers. — **(2) 1889** *Cent. s.v.* Advance bill . . . [is] a draft on the owner or agent of a vessel, generally for one month's wages, given by the master to the sailors on their signing the articles of agreement. The practice was abolished . . . by act of Congress in 1884. — **(3) 1780** *Heath Papers* III. **33** An action . . . between the advance corps . . . and a body of the enemy. — **(4) 1758** *Essex Inst. Coll.* XVIII. 113 The Advance Guard . . . have cleared off the Trees and built Breastworks. *Ib.* XLV 343 They met an Indian within 1/4 of a Mile of the Advance-Guard. **1865** BOUDRYE *Fifth N.Y. Cavalry* 139 An advance guard was pushed to Allen's Mill. **1947** *Denver Post* 19 Jan. (*mag.*) 5/8 A group of Utes on the far side of the road were enabled to swing in behind the advance guard, and almost cut them off.

* **advanced,** *a.*

1. *Educ.* Beyond the elementary or introductory level of difficulty, attainment, rank, etc.

Provision for "admitting a scholar, who comes recommended from another College, into the same standing as he had there" was made at Harvard in 1767. See *Harvard Coll. Rec.* III. 348.
1790 *Laws of Harvard College* 7 No person shall be admitted to an advanced standing, unless, upon examination by the President, Professors and Tutors, he shall be found qualified. **1871** L. H. BAGG *At Yale* 689 Whether an 'advanced student' comes from a private tutor or from another college, or drops from a higher class at Yale, makes little difference. **1942** *Bul. Vanderbilt U.* 335 The student . . . has had educational experience beyond that of the secondary school and . . . wishes to be admitted to advanced standing.

b. advanced credit, academic credit allowed for work done elsewhere, as at another school.

1892 *Brigham Young Acad. Circular* 12 Requests for examination for advanced credit must be made to the faculty in writing, not later than one week after paying entrance fees. **1942** *U. of Mich. Gen. Reg.* Sec. 1, 67 All advanced credits are subject to revision after work in residence.

2. advanced female, a sarcastic designation formerly given a woman agitating for or favoring women's rights.

1871 *N.Y. Tribune* 2 Feb. (De Vere), The short-sightedness of the advanced female to the interest of her own cause. **1895** S. HALE *Letters* 288 She is a lion-hunter *enragée*, advanced female, views, everything.

***advent,** *n.* (*cap.*) Used attrib. in expressions denoting or pertaining to the Adventists, as **Advent Brethren, Christian, church.** Cf. **Second Advent.** — **1871** GEORGE EASTON *Travels in America* 37 It was not long, however, until I found that the 'Advent Brethren' were the parties at whom the speaker was throwing his darts. **1884** *Schaff's Relig. Encycl.* III. 2581/2 The most numerous branch [of Adventists] is the Advent Christians. . . . They have two or three weekly papers. **1922** CADY *Rhymes* (1926) 66 First, I want to know If there's an Advent church in Stowe.

Adventism ˈædvenˌtɪzəm, *n.* [See next.] The religious doctrine of the Adventists. Cf. **Second Adventism.** — **1874** WELLCOME *Hist. Second Advent Message* 592 Judaism is being taught: If brethren do not mean to teach it let them tell us so and not teach this under the cloak of Adventism. **1902** CLAPIN 7 The chief tenet of Adventism was a belief in the physical second advent of Jesus-Christ, which event Miller affirmed would take place on the 23rd of October 1844.

Adventist ˈædventɪst, *n.* [f. * *Advent*, second coming of Christ.] One of a religious denomination, comprising several branches, who believe in or look for the early second coming of Christ to reign personally on earth; a Millerite. More fully **Second Adventist.** Also **Age-to-come-Adventist.** Cf. **Seventh-day Adventist.**

1844 *Liberator* (Boston) 15 Nov. 184/4 Will you also inform me if you have been in any way 'embarrassed' by the 'inducements' of 'adventists'? **1881** *Amer. Cycl.* XIV. 745 Second Adventist, or Adventists . . . believe in the speedy second advent of Christ and the end of the world. **1884** *Schaff's Relig. Encycl.* III. 2581/2 The Age-to-come Adventists believe that the Jews are to be re-established in Jerusalem. . . . They are not numerous. **1945** *Christian Cent.* 7 Mar. 304/2 Thus Adventists were convinced that 'while there had been no mistake in regard to the time, there had been an error in interpreting the character of the event.'

***adventure,** *n.* (*cap.*) Used as a name for some localities occupied by early settlers in Maryland. *Obs.* See also **carpetbag adventure.** — **1700** *Md. Hist. Mag.* XX. 2921, (1644) Browns Adventure. *Ib.* 353, (1678) Goodmans Adventure. *Ib.* 365, (1695) Gilbert Adventure.

***advertising,** *a.* In combs.: (1) **advertising agency,** an agency or concern that, for a fee, handles all the details of writing and arranging for publication or broadcasting of publicity for a customer; (2) **agent,** a professional advertiser; (3) **blotter,** a blotter having on it an advertisement of the firm, business, etc., which provides it; (4) **car,** a railway car devoted to advertising a circus, theatrical troupe, etc.; (5) **curtain,** a stage curtain having advertisements painted upon it.

(1) **1850** *Hunt's Merch. Mag.* XXIII. 580 Mr. V. B. Palmer keeps what he terms the '*American Newspaper Advertising Agency*,' with offices established in New York, Boston, and Philadelphia. **1948** *Advertiser* April 9/3 The average advertising agency has a long life—much longer than many of the clients it deals with. — (2) **1832** MRS. TROLLOPE *Domestic Manners of Americans* I. 49 We went to the office of an advertising agent, who professed to keep a register of all such information, and described the dwelling we wanted. **1948** *Ponca City* (Okla.) *News* 1 July 1/7 He obtained a city license Wednesday as an advertising agent. — (3) **1931** *Durant* (Okla.) *Daily Democrat* 24 Dec. 6/3 (*advt.*) Advertising Blotters. — (4) **1896** *N.Y. Dramatic News* 4 April 21/1 What is unquestionably the finest and most perfect advertising car ever placed upon railway tracks, arrived in Jersey City. **1920** C. R. COOPER *Under Big Top* 4 So the departure of the 'bill car' or advertising car is a carefully thought out preconceived thing. — (5) **1863** *Chicago Post* 29 Sep., Last night the Varieties bloomed forth a set of magnificent new scenes and a beautiful advertising curtain.

aerodrome ˈɛrəˌdrom, *n.* [Gk. *aerodromos*, *a.* running through the air.] S. P. Langley's name for an early form of aeroplane. Also attrib. Now *hist.*

1891 S. P. LANGLEY *Exper. Aerodynamics* 49 An actual working aerodrome model with its motor. **1899** *N.Y. Journal* 25 June 28/1 The first machine actually to fly was successfully launched after ten months of persistent effort in 1897. It was christened the Aerodrome or "air-runner," and the name is still retained for the many improved machines that have been built since. **1948** *Chi. Tribune* 1 Feb. 1. 37/1 The Smithsonian institution several years ago withdrew its claims on behalf of Prof. Langley, whose 'aerodrome' failed in 1903 tests but was eventually flown in 1914.

***affairs** *n. pl.* As the last term in **Indian, prudential, Secretary of Foreign, Superintendent of Indian Affairs.**

affiant əˈfaɪənt, *n.* [F.] *Law.* One who makes an affidavit. — **1807** *Ann. 10th Congress* 1 Sess. I. 476 The affidavit of David Fisk, . . . that . . . a certain David Floyd . . . came to this affiant [etc.]. *Ib.* 477 This affiant asked what other object they had. **1878** *Congress. Rec.* 16 June (1879) 2041/1 Said deputy marshal denied affiant the right to make a bond . . . and carried affiant to the city of Montgomery.

***affiliate,** *v.*

1. *intr.* To associate, coöperate, be friendly, usu. *affiliate with.*

1843 T. WEED *Letters* (1866) 9 Our cabin passengers . . . are as diverse in characters and pursuit, as in birth and language. But we all affiliate and harmonize wonderfully. **1891** HARBEN *Almost Persuaded* 27 Our nearest neighbors live several miles away, and we don't affiliate with them much. **1947** *Rocky Mt. News* (Denver) 23 Feb. 28/1 The New York Yankees, when they affiliated with the local management, promised to give Denver a sound baseball man and a good baseball name as club manager.

2. To combine *with* something.

1877 RAYMOND *Mines & Mining* 98 Platinum . . . , though it does not amalgamate, . . . affiliates with the gold amalgam. **1887** *Century Mag.* July 431/2 Here they [*sc.* phenomena] affiliate with the whole mass of superstitions which accumulated in the early history of the human race.

***affiliation,** *n.* Relationship or association, as in politics or (more recently) church fellowship, etc.; freq. *pl.*, connections, relations.— **1852** *Congress. Globe* App. 15 Mar. 323/3 Certain merchants with whom he has affiliations in New Mexico. **1904** *Atlantic Mo.* March 293 The affiliation of local billboard interests into a national body, for the purpose of more successfully opposing adverse public action.

A.F. of L. Abbrev. for American Federation of Labor, *q.v.* Also **A.F.L.** Also attrib. — **1894** *Amer. Federationist* July 109/1 The Central Labor Union of E. St. Louis, Ill., passed a resolution requesting the unity and amalgamation of the A.F. of L. and K. of L. **1948** *Chi. Tribune* 10 May II. 3/3 The AFL union's statement is contained in its executive board's report.

***afoot,** *adv. Not to know whether one is afoot or horseback*, to be somewhat beside oneself. *Colloq.* — **1895** *Century Mag.* Aug. 570/1 Sam he had on a keg hat, all shiny silk, and a red necktie thet Car' Jane hed made him git, and he didn't know whether he was afoot or a-hossback. **1927** *Collier's* 22 Oct. 7/3 'Fay Daniels!' gasps the girl, which don't know if she's afoot or horseback—and neither did *I*.

afoul əˈfaʊl, *adv.* and *a.* [*a*, on +*foul.*] Entangled, fouled, in violent or hostile contact. Also jocose or humorous. — **1809** BARLOW *Columbiad* VII. 521 Above, with shrouds afoul and gunwales mann'd, Thick halberds clash. **1870** F. FERN *Ginger-Snaps* 10 The hostess . . . [may] set some maiden a-foul of the piano! **1892** *Harper's Mag.* Aug. 377/1 The ice crystals cannot grow out into the water very far without running afoul of other crystals.

***Africa,** *n.* **1.** Temper, anger. *Slang.* **2. Africa Negro,** a Negro born in Africa as distinguished from one born here. Both *obs.* — (1) **1838** *S. Lit. Messenger* IV. 162/1 Well, it sort o' raised his Africky [*sic*], at first. **1880** HARRIS *U. Remus* (1884) 231 Well, you des oughter see me get my Affikin up. **1928** BRADFORD *Ol' Man Adam* 199 So de people kept right on laughin' and passin' remarks about old Samson to finally old Samson got his Af'ican up. — (2) **1892** HARRIS *U. Remus & Friends* 36 He wuz one er deze yer Affiky niggers, en you know how dey is—bowlegged en bad tempered.

***African,** *a.* and *n.*

1. Of societies, congregations, or churches: Composed of or supported by Negroes. Cf. **Anglo-African.**

1798 (title), Laws of the Sons of the African Society, Instituted at Boston, Anno Domini, 1798. **1830** NEILSON *Recollections* 14 One of their congregations is styled 'African Presbyterian.' **1855** WELD *Va-*

cation Tour 294 At eleven I proceeded to the African Baptist Church. **1943** HOLT *Carver* 25 Sometimes she took George to the African Methodist Church which she attended.

2. (See quot. 1842.) In full **African Negro.** *Obs.*

1842 BUCKINGHAM *Slave States* II. 30 He is an African,* about forty five years of age. . . . *This means born in Africa, and recently imported from thence. **1892** HARRIS *U. Remus & Friends* 317 What I gwine to do in Affiky? I ain't no Affikin nigger.

3. a. African-American, an American of African origin. **b. African exodus,** an expression used with reference to a scheme by designing individuals to interest Negroes in leaving the U.S. Both *obs.*

(**a**) **1863** CONVERSE *Old Cremona Songster* 45 I'd buy up all de niggers—de niggers—de colored African-American citizens. — (**b**) **1874** *Int. Review* Sep. 594 Twenty years ago, the Cleveland Convention directed the African exodus to Central and South America, and the West Indies. **1892** HARRIS *U. Remus & Friends* 315 The Southern papers have not devoted much attention to the movement that is known as the "African exodus."

4. A Negro, in jesting allusion to "the Nigger in the woodpile."

1865 *Cairo* (Ill.) *Dly. Democrat* 4 Oct. 4/3 The house filled, the audience became anxious for a little gushing melody, but not a gush was heard, and it was soon evident that a 'free American of African "scent"' had become secreted in the woodpile. **1879** *Congress Rec.* 11 June 1931/1 There is a gigantic African here [i.e., in the Army Appropriation Bill]. . . . I want the African taken out of the bill. **1892** *Ib.* 19 Jan. 431/1 It is indeed difficult to know just how many Africans are hid away in this wood pile [*sc.* in the bill with reference to public printing].

5. African dominoes, golf, craps. *Slang.*

1920 *Collier's* 5 June 10/2, I got in that African golf tournament because I thought I could grab us enough doubloons to take us in to New York *right.* **1922** *Outing* Dec. 120/3 For one, to become proficient in African Dominoes has not been my lot, although the right arm has developed inches from exercise of rolling bones, while the left has increased in the same proportion from reaching for my pocket-book. **1948** MENCKEN *Supp.* II. 755/1 Golf . . . has also engendered *African golf,* crap-shooting.

Africanization ˌæfrɪkənɪˈzeʃən *n.* [f. next.] The action or fact of bringing under Negro supremacy; "the act of placing under negro domination" (B. '59). — **1856** S. CARTWRIGHT in *Life of Quitman* (1860) II. 230 The Clayton-Bulwer Treaty, the preposterous claims . . . , and the Africanization of tropical America. **1890** *Congress. Rec.* 23 Jan. 806/2, I said I was not in favor of the africanization of this continent or of any part of it.

Africanize ˈæfrɪkənˌaɪz, *v.* [f. *African.*]

1. *tr.* To bring under the supremacy of Negroes. *Obs.* "A cant term which has of late acquired very general and very melancholy currency" (De Vere).

1853 LD. CLARENDON in J. F. Rhodes *Hist. U.S.* II. 26 A violent and wholly unfounded article in the Washington *Union* charging them with an intrigue with Spain to 'Africanize' Cuba. **1868** *Sonoma Democrat* (Santa Rosa, Calif.) 11 Feb. 1/5 A resolution protesting against the slander which had been current that it was the idea of the colored people 'to Africanize the State,' was offered. **1884** *N. Amer. Rev.* Oct. 429 This is a white man's country, and a white man's government; and the white race will never allow a section of it to be Africanized.

2. To impart a Negro character to.

1865 *Cinci. Dly. Commercial* 4 July 1/2 The reply came from a thin vinegary-visaged woman, with a sharp nasal twang, a Yankee voice with Africanized accent. **1890** *Harper's Mag.* Jan. 224/1 Her recitals first developed in the white child . . . the power of fancy,—Africanizing it, perhaps, to a degree that after-education could not totally remove. **1930** WITTKE *Tambo & Bones* 143 In 1867, Kelly and Leon began 'Africanizing opera bouffe.'

Afro-American ˈæfroəˈmɛrəkən, *n.* and *a.* Designating or pertaining to an American Negro. — **1853** *Voice of the Fugitive* (Windsor, Ont.) 21 June 2/4 In our opinion, the true policy of the Afro-American race . . . is to emigrate to Canada, the West Indies, . . . where they can enjoy all the rights of freemen. **1890** *Advance* 23 Jan. 61/2 To encourage all State and local leagues . . . in obtaining for the Afro-American an equal chance. **1947** *N.Y. Herald-Tribune* 14 Dec. V. 6/7 New Orleans jazz is in the main line of development of Afro-American music.

after-ripening. A complex chemical change, often highly conducive to future germination and palatability, that takes place in fruits, seeds, etc., after harvesting. — **1867** *Soc. Iowa Agric. Rep.* (1868) 188 To make the wine: gather the fruit with the stems on. . . . Leave for three or four days in a cellar . . . thus causing after-ripening. **1872** *Vermont Bd. Agric. Rep.* 72 Shortly after, begins after-ripening, a chemical change, whereby the starch, abundant in the unripe or green fruit, is transformed into sugar.

***agate,** *n.*

1. A child's playing marble made originally of agate, but later of glass or clay. Cf. **aggie,** *n.*

1889 *Cent.* **1908** *D.N.* III. 285 agate, *n.* A marble made of glazed clay. Also called *jug.* The regular agate is called stone-glass. **1945** *Good Housekeeping* March 137/1 The revolutionary automatic machine that made this country supreme in the manufacture of marbles was brought out by the Akro Agate Company.

2. A size of type, approximately $5\frac{1}{2}$ point, between nonpareil and pearl.

1838 *Democratic Rev.* I. 61 Light faced Book and Job Printing Types . . . [including] Diamond, Pearl, . . . Agate. **1871** RINGWALT *Encycl. Printing* 24/2 Agate . . . is chiefly used in newspaper work, and . . . for pocket editions of the Bible and Prayer Books. **1948** *Chi. Tribune* 25 April IV. 6/2 In the agate statistics under the name of the players was the line: 'Home Run—Wagner.'

***age,** *n.* In poker the right possessed, under certain conditions, by the player to the left of the dealer of continuing in the game or dropping out, usu. *to have* (or *hold*) *the age.*

This poker term has app. given rise to the widespread colloq. expression *to have the edge* (*q.v.*) in the sense of to have the advantage.

1844 SHIELDS *S.S. Prentiss* (1883) 334 You can't expect me to take a hand in this game when he . . . has the age of me to boot. **1892** QUINN *Fools of Fortune* 216 The player entitled to bet first may withhold his wager until the others have bet round to him, which is called 'holding the age,' and this being considered an advantage, is very frequently done. **1907** MARK TWAIN in *N. Amer. Rev.* CIV. 569 How could I talk when he was talking? He 'held the age,' as the poker-clergy say.

b. The player having this right, the eldest hand.

1864 W. B. DICK *Amer. Hoyle* (1866) 176 Eldest Hand, or Age—The player immediately at the left of the dealer. **1887** KELLER *Draw Poker* 21 The ante must be placed on the table by the age before any cards are dealt.

As the last term in **coon's, dog's, dollar and cent, hog age.**

ageable ˈedʒəbl̩, *a. S.* Advanced in age. *Colloq.* — **1845** HOOPER *Taking Census* i. 153 Judy Tompkins, ageable woman, and four children. **1899** GREEN *Virginia Word-Bk.* 39 They are right ageable people. **1945** BOTKIN *My Burden* 84 My own daddy lived to be very ageable, but I don't know when he died.

***agency,** *n.*

1. The office of a government agent among the Indians, the headquarters of such an agent, or the area under his jurisdiction.

1707 *S. Car. Statutes at Large* (1837) II. 314, I will neither directly nor indirectly trade with any Indian . . . during the time of my agency. **1796** B. HAWKINS *Letters* 32, I do hereby authorize Stephen Hawkins . . . to pursue and apprehend the said offenders, wherever to be found within the agency South of the Ohio. **1824** *Statutes at Large* (1856) IV. 25 It shall be the duty of each Indian agent to reside and keep his agency within, or near the territory claimed by the tribe or tribes of Indians for which he may be agent. **1947** *Denver Post* 19 Jan. (*Mag.*) 7/3 An Indian courier was sent to the twenty remaining Utes, under Chief Douglas, at the agency.

2. In combs. of obvious meaning, as **agency cattle, clerk, doctor, farm, farmer, Indian, office.**

1866 *Rep. Indian Affairs* 90 A person to reside on the agency farm to attend to the cultivation of the crop. **1873** BEADLE *Undevel. West* 526 The party, consisting of Agent Miller, B. M. Thomas, Agency Farmer, . . . left Defiance. **1878** —— *Western Wilds* 252 Mr. Thomas V. Keams, Agency Clerk, was acting in place of Miller, deceased. **1891** *Boston* (Mass.) *Jrnl.* 1 Jan. 2/3 Does not our Government undertake to clothe and feed the agency Indians? **1907** WHITE *Ariz. Nights* 26, I was a kid then, about eighteen years old, and what I didn't know about Injins and Agency cattle wasn't a patch of alkali. **1945** *Reader's Digest* Aug. 51 Indians loll about agency offices waiting to ask permission on matters that a free farmer would decide in an instant. **1946** FOREMAN *Last Trek* 244 The Indian medicine man constantly fought the agency doctor.

Also *agency barn, building, house, storehouse,* etc.

As the last term in **advertising, blank, claim, commercial, crow, employment, forwarding, government, Indian, Navaho, news, Osage, real estate, route, sub agency.**

***agent,** *n.*

1. An officer in charge of an agency among the Indians.

1707 *S. Car. Statutes at Large* (1837) II. 311 For the further preventing abuses . . . Thomas Nairne . . . is . . . appointed the agent to reside among the Indians, subject to the Government of South Carolina. **1818** *Ann. 15th Congress* 1 Sess. 84 The expediency of requiring by law the nomination of agents to Indian tribes, to be submitted to the

Senate. **1890** *Harper's Mag.* April 734/2 The Indians had grown restless under the efforts of the agent to teach them farming and other industries of the whites.

2. A station agent or ticket agent.

1835 *Boston Mercantile Journal* 25 June, Tickets may be had at the Depot . . . Price $1. George M. Dexter, Agent. **1840** *N.Y. Mirror* 25 July 39/2 Nobody thinks nowadays of calling the conductor of a mud-cart on the rail-road, by any less dignified title than *an agent.* **1945** *Bent Co. Democrat* (Las Animas, Colo.) 27 July 1/4 Charles W. Hurd, local agent for the Santa Fe, told the Kiwanis . . . about his recent hike up Pike's Peak.

3. **=road agent.**

1876 *Calaveras Chronicle* (Mokelumne Hill, Calif.) 29 July 3/1 The driver finally succeeded in satisfying the 'agent' that no express box was carried by San Andreas. **1904** WHITE *Blazed Trail* 152 Nex' time I drives stage some of these yere agents massacrees me from behind a bush.

4. **agent of truancy,** in the state of New York, an officer who enforces attendance at school.

1877 *N.Y. City Bd. Education Rep.* 41 To carry out the provisions of the law relating to the inspection of . . . establishments where children are employed, it was found necessary to appoint an agent of truancy. **1884** *Encycl. Brit.* XVII. 461/2 The law [of compulsory education] is enforced in the city [of New York] by the city superintendent, who has twelve assistants known as 'agents of truancy.'

As the last term in **advance, advertising, baggage, bank, banking, Bible, blank, book, car, Cherokee, claim(s), colony, commercial, contracting, cotton, county, curbstone, depot, emigration, express, farm, freight, general passenger, government, Indian, land, lecture, lobby, navy, passenger, patent, pension, prohibition, purchasing, real estate, rent, revenue, road, route, school, sewing machine, special, special Indian, state, station, steamboat, sub, sub-Indian, ticket, train, transportation, traveling passenger, tree, truancy, under cover agent.**

aggie ˈægɪ, *n.* [f. agate *q.v.*] **=agate 1.** — *c***1918** *D.N.* V. 109 *ag, n.* An agate marble. Boy's usage [in Calif.]. *aggie*, n. See preceding. **1945** *Sat. Review* 4 Aug. 22 She pounced upon the 'aggies' and carried them off for her grandson.

Aggie ˈægɪ, *n.* [f. * *Agriculture*+*-ie.*]

1. A student at an agricultural college, usu. in the names of athletic teams representing such schools. *Colloq.*

1902 *Chi. Record-Herald* 28 Sep. 3/4 (*heading*), Swamp Michigan 'Aggies.' **1906** *K.C. Star* 30 Nov. 8/1 The 'Aggies' made both their touchdowns in the first half. **1947** *Rocky Mt. News* (Denver) 23 Feb. 31/3 The Aggies have been defeated only by Kansas State of the Big Six Conference this season.

2. An agricultural school or college.

1920 *Boston Ev. Transcript* 2 Oct. IV. 1/1 The man who thinks that the working farmer isn't interested in what Aggie does is mistaken. **1945** *Gunnison* (Colo.) *News-Champion* 22 Nov. 8/4 He will be at the home of his parents . . . until the beginning of the winter semester, when he will enroll at Colorado Aggies.

* **agrarian,** *n.* (See quots.) *Obs.*

1835 *Louisville Journal* 24 June 1/5 What are *his* claims to the support of the 'hurrah boys' and the 'agrarians'? **1841** BUCKINGHAM *America* I. 124 'Agrarians' is the name here given to people who meet to recommend the Government to keep the revenue in safe custody, in treasuries of their own, instead of intrusting it to speculating banks, at the risk of losing it all; though in other countries this term is usually, though erroneously, applied to those who are supposed to desire that the public lands and public wealth should be taken from the rich and divided among the poor. **1879** J. LALOR tr. *Von Holst's Const. Hist.* II. 397 'Agrarians' was the accursed name to be fastened on them [=the Equal Rights Party, 1835], and to make them an abomination in the eyes of all those who took any interest in law or social order.

agregado ˌɑgrəˈgɑdo, *n. S.W.* [Sp., a farmhand living on the farm of another.] (See quot.) *Obs.* — **1871** *Republican Review* (Albuquerque, N.Mex.) 14 Jan. 2/1 Then again there are others who are simply *agregados* or persons permitted by the consent of the rest to settle on the lands.

* **agricultural,** *a.*

1. Denoting institutions of learning in which agriculture is taught.

1819 SIMEON DEWITT (Title:) Considerations on the Necessity of Establishing an Agricultural College, and Having More of the Children of Wealthy Citizens Educated for the Profession of Farming. **1850** *N. Eng. Farmer* II. 42 Agricultural seminaries should be commenced on a moderate scale. **1857–58** *Ill. Agric. Soc. Trans.* III. 563 But the great want . . . is an Agricultural University. **1948** *Amer. Feed & Grain Dealer* April 6/2 Today the feed industry and the agricultural colleges are teaming together for added progress toward new goals in scientific feeding.

b. Esp. **agricultural and mechanical college.**

[**1852** *N.Y. Wkly. Tribune* 3 Jan. 3/6 Agriculture, with various branches of Manufacturing and the Mechanics Arts, shall be systematically prosecuted within the bounds of the College and its grounds. **1862** *Jrnl. of Senate* 5 May 444 Mr. Wade asked . . . leave to bring in a bill (S. 298) donating public lands to the several States and Territories which may provide colleges for the benefit of agriculture and the mechanic arts.] **1877** *Harper's Mag.* Apr. 724/2 Scientific [libraries] embrace the libraries of scientific schools, including agricultural and mechanical colleges and scientific societies. **1948** *Dly. Ardmoreite* (Ardmore, Okla.) 22 Jan. 1/7 R. T. Stuart, chairman of the board of regents for agricultural and mechanical colleges, declined to discuss the report.

2. In special combs.: (1) **agricultural ant,** any one of various stinging ants, as *Pogonomyrmex barbatus* of Texas, that clear away the verdure about their nests except one certain grass on whose seeds they feed; (2) **furnace,** (see quot.), *obs.;* (3) **scrip,** ?scrip sold to obtain money to be loaned for agricultural purposes; (4) **warehouse,** an establishment where agricultural tools and farm equipment are exhibited and sold, *obs.;* (5) **wheel,** see **wheel.**

(1) **1868** *Amer. Naturalist* II. 157 Such structures are remarkable . . . reminding us of the intelligence shown by the Agricultural Ant of Texas. — (2) **1850** *N. Eng. Farmer* II. 331 Agricultural furnace. This furnace is adapted to boiling vegetables, and cooking food generally for stock. — (3) **1870** MCCLUNG *Minnesota* 174 The $1.25 may be paid in cash, land warrants, or agricultural scrip, and may not really cost the purchaser over 90ct. or $1 per acre. — (4) **1848** C. L. FLEISCHMANN *Nordamerikanische Landwirth* 307 In den Agricultural Warehouses . . . findet man immer eine grosse Auswahl von den neuesten Maschinen und verbesserten Geräthen.

b. Also **agricultural agent, county, editor, newspaper, paper, periodical.**

1831 PECK *Guide* 300 Morgan County is destined to become one of the richest agricultural counties of the State. **1839** BUEL *Farmer's Companion* 281 The Agricultural periodicals of our country. **1843** *Quincy* (Ill.) *Whig* 11 Jan. 2/5 The 'Union Agriculturist' . . . was . . . an agricultural paper published at Chicago. **1847** *De Bow's Review* III. 4 How many agricultural newspapers are there in the country? **1848** *Ib.* VI. 160 We have not had time yet to pay our respects to this veteran agricultural editor. **1947** *Rocky Mt. News* (Denver) 23 Feb. 11/2 Hoar is Logan County agricultural agent.

agrippina ˌægrɪˈpinə *n.* [Origin unknown.] Some article of ship's furniture. *Obs.* — **1830** COOPER *Water Witch* II. ii. 39 Against the bulkhead of each state room stood an agrippina of mahogany. *Ib.* 40 The outer portion of the cabin . . . had its agrippina, its piles of cushions, its chairs.

aguardiente ɑˌgwɑrdɪˈɛntɪ, *n.* Also †**auquedent, aquadiente, aguadinte,** etc. [Sp. in same sense.] Any one of various distilled alcoholic drinks, esp. a strong or fiery one.

1818 *N.-Eng. Palladium* (Boston) 28 Sep. 3/2 Isaac McLellan & Co. . . . Have for sale . . . 100 pipes Spanish Rum or Auquedent, entitled to debenture. **1825** H. PAULDING *Journal of Cruise* (1831) 11 Our host indulged himself freely with the use of aquadiente. **1847** *N.O. Picayune* 12 Sep. 2/1 Many of the Mexicans were pretty well *corned,* [for] . . . *aguadinte* was plentiful. **1946** *Mazama* Dec. 31/2 However, before they left we gave each of them a good drink of Aguardiente which put them in good spirits.

* **ague,** *n.* In combs.: (1) **ague bark,** the wafer ash, *Ptelea trifoliata,* or its bark; (2) **grass, root,** the colicroot, *Aletris farinosa;* (3) **seed, =fever and ague seed,** *obs.;* (4) **weed,** (see quots.).

(1) **1889** *Cent.* 119/2 Ague-bark. . . . The bark of the wafer-ash, *Ptelea trifoliata.* **1931** CLUTE *Plants* 121 Among other plants reputed to be a cure for malaria were . . . the ague-bark or quinine tree (*Ptelea trifoliata*). — (2) **1687** CLAYTON *Virginia* 158 Some call it *Ague-grass,* other *Ague-root,* others Star-grass. **1876** HOBBS *Bot. Hand-Book* 2 Ague grass, Unicorn root, Aletris farinosa. — (3) **1869** in MCILWAINE *Poor-White* (1939) 136 The sallow, ashen or yellowish soil is full of ague seeds and unmeasured potentiality of yams and ugly spiders. — (4) **1889** *Cent.* 119/2 Ague-weed . . . 1. The common boneset of the United States, *Eupatorium perfoliatum.* 2. A species of gentian, *Gentiana quinqueflora.* **1907** LYONS *Plant Names* 189 *E. perfoliatum.* . . . Wild Sage, Ague-weed, Crosswort, Feverwort. . . . *G. quinquefolia* . . . Five flowered Gentian, Stiff Gentian, Ague-weed, Gall-weed, Blue Gentian.

As the last term in **buck, river, shaking, swamp, thump buck ague.**

* **ahead,** *adv.*

1. In an advanced or successful position or state.

1828 *Free Press* (Tarboro, N.C.) 14 Nov., In Virginia the Jackson Ticket is far a-head. **1878** *Ill. Dept. Agric. Trans.* XIV. 284 The Jersey was much ahead; had large cream globules which rise easy. **1948** *Dly. Ardmoreite* (Ardmore, Okla.) 30 May 8/3 J. M. Broughton, former governor, forged well ahead of W. B. Umstead, the incumbent, for the U.S. senatorial nomination in today's democratic primary.

b. In advance.

1900 DRANNAN *Plains & Mts.* 132 Johnnie West and I having enough meat ahead to last several days, we pulled out for Taos. **1947** *Redbook* Sep. 112/3 Henry's ahead of his time.

2. In colloq. phrases: (1) * *To go ahead,* to proceed forthwith, get on with the matter in hand, usu. as an imperative indicative of assent and approval, often with the force of "all right" [the association of this phrase with David Crockett may be based upon the incident, real or alleged, referred to in quot. 1833]; (2) * *to get ahead,* (*a*) to prosper, to succeed in accumulating money or property, (*b*) (see quot. 1877); (3) *to be ahead,* to have something on hand; (4) *to come out ahead,* to succeed, do well.

(1) 1831 *American* (Harrodsburg, Ky.) 25 Mar. 2/5 We say to our Clay friends, 'go ahead,' and . . . remember the Eleventh Commandment, 'every man mind his own business.' **1833** *Polit. Examiner* (Shelbyville, Ky.) 20 Apr. 4/1 A young gentleman . . . wrote to him requesting his permission that they might be married. The reply of the Colonel was in the following laconic style: Washington,—'Dear sir—I received your letter. Go ahead. David Crockett.' **1947** *Trail Riders Bul.* May 3/1 Jim Brewster was the first man whom they approached, and at once he said 'Go ahead! I'm for it.' — **(2)** (*a*) **1834** CARUTHERS *Kentuckian* I. 26 When the feller had got considerable ahead, the word came out that he was studyin to be a doctor. **1838** *Knickerb.* XII. 317 This, then, is the reason why Blueville never got ahead. (*b*) **1825** NEAL *Bro. Jonathan* I. 385, I was working, all the time, to get ahead of Edith. **1877** BARTLETT 775 Ahead. To 'get ahead of,' to outwit or outdo, by superior sagacity or activity.— **(3) 1882** BEADLE *Western Wilds* 615 My sheep had done well, and that was all I was ahead. **1904** W. H. SMITH *Promoters* i. 21 We can go on and finish our plant, and be ahead every dollar that they've blown in! — **(4) 1886** P. STAPLETON *Major's Christmas* 194 Your grandfather said you'd come out ahead, True, but this is so grand, so like the story.

ahsahta ɑ'sɑtə *n.* [Mandan Indian name.] The bighorn or Rocky Mountain sheep, *Ovis canadensis. Obs.* — **1805** LEWIS & CLARK *Journal* (1904) I. 239–40 The Mandan Indians call this Sheep Ar-Sar-ta. **1837** IRVING *Bonneville* I. 230 Numerous gangs of elk, large flocks of the ahsahta or bighorn.

a-huckleberring, see **huckleberrying.**

* **aid,** *n.* As the last term in **Indian, Kansas, ladies', Massachusetts, state, travelers' aid.**

Aid Society. An organization or society whose object it is to assist the indigent, needy, or helpless, esp. an organization of ladies which holds meetings or work-parties to promote charity and other church work. Also, ellipt., **Aid.**

1853 BRACE in *Dangerous Classes* (1872) 90 P.S.—I forgot to tell you the name we have chosen—'Children's Aid Society.' **1908** F. B. CALHOUN *Miss Minerva* 77 You can have so much fun when our mamas go to the Aid. **1948** *Dly. Ardmoreite* (Ardmore, Okla.) 20 Apr. 5/6 Women of the Advent Christian church met in the home of Mrs. C. A. Jensen, . . . recently, to form an aid.

aide ed, *n.* Short for "aide-de-camp."

1777 J. M. LINCOLN *Papers R. Lincoln* (1904) 11 They . . . fired on the flag, and killed our Ade. **1862** NORTON *Army Lett.* 91 Those in the rear of us received the order, but the aide sent to us was shot. **1948** *Time* 31 May 92/2 'We thought,' said Union Headquarters Aide Frank Haskell, 'that at the second Bull Run . . . we had heard heavy cannonading.'

b. aide-ship, an appointment as an aide-de-camp. *Rare.*

1862 JACKSON in M. A. Jackson *Life* 305, I will give him an aide-ship.

* **ail,** *n.* As the last term in **cripple, hoof, horn, horse ail.**

* **air,** *n.* In combs.: (1) * **air ball,** in baseball, a high fly or pop fly, *obs.;* (2) **brake,** a brake operated by compressed air, originally and chiefly used on railway trains, cf. *atmospheric brake;* (3) **conditioning,** the putting of air into a desired condition by washing, humidifying, etc., before admitting it into a room or building, also **air conditioned, air conditioner,** also attrib.; (4) **foundry,** a foundry provided with an air furnace or furnaces, *obs.;* (5) * **hole,** a hole in the ice covering streams or ponds, esp. one caused by the current or by springs; (6) **hose,** a hose used at garages for inflating tires; (7) **line,** see as a main entry; (8) **mail,** mail transported by airplane, also attrib.; (9) **plant,** (see quot. 1842); (10) **rifle,** a rifle-like gun shooting a dart or a single pellet; (11) **tight,** (*a*) a stove so constructed that the air can be almost entirely shut out, in full **airtight stove,** (*b*) (see quots.) *colloq.;* (12) **torpedo,** a torpedo driven by air or travelling through the air, *facetious;* (13) **town,** a town merely projected or "in the air," *humorous.*

Airtight stove

(1) 1867 *Chi. Times* 26 July 5/2 Williams hit an air ball which was sugared by Barnes at short stop. — **(2) 1871** *Rep. Comm. Patents* (1872) I. 253 Westinghouse, George, jr.. . . . Valve device for steam-power air-brake couplings July 4, 1871. **1947** *Reader's Digest* Sep. 135/2 Experts estimate that a train which travels 1500 feet after the air brakes are applied could be brought to a stop in 375 feet. — **(3) 1910** *Engineering Mag.* Aug. 697 Heating, ventilating and air-conditioning of factories. **1942** *Time* 7 Nov. 25/2 Promised in some [ads]: daily siestas, convenient trains, . . . home atmosphere, air-conditioned offices. **1945** *Boulder* (Colo.) *Dly. Camera* 27 Oct. 6/6 A short circuit in an electric motor of an air-conditioner caused a fire alarm this morning at 11:45. — **(4) 1814** *Pittsburgh Alman. 1815* 61 At Brownsville there is established an extensive air foundary, at which they cast all kinds of hollow work and machinery of every description. **1837** JENKINS *Ohio Gaz.* 370 Portsmouth . . . contained . . . one air foundery, with a cupola and brass foundery.

(5) 1829 HEAD *Forest Scenes* 47 And these air-holes, as they are called, are met with at times, no matter what the thickness of the ice may be. **1874** LONG *Wild-Fowl* 51 Great quantities of ducks are often killed in the air-holes about freezing-up time. **1933** CHELEY *Camping Out* 168 The trapper . . . sets his traps in the mud under the water of an air-hole near the beaver dam. — **(6) 1909** *Sat. Ev. Post.* 26 June 8/2 If she'd been my woman, about then and there I'd made a break to cure her of them there fancy notions with a good length of rubber air-hose. **1919** LEWIS *Free Air* 47 She noticed the sign on the air-hose of the garage—'Free Air.' — **(8) 1919** *Rep. Postmaster General* 13 The Post Office Department was successful in securing an appropriation by Congress of $100,000 for the fiscal year ending June 30, 1918, for an experimental air mail route. **1948** *Calif. Citrograph* April 273/3 The opening of this year's show was marked by a record transcontinental airmail flight that originated on the show grounds. — **(9) 1842** GRAY *Struct. Bot.* iii. § 1 (1880) 35 Epiphytes or Air-Plants have roots which are . . . unconnected with the ground. **1938** MATSCHAT *Suwannee River* 223 Tree orchids find a little food in the fallen leaves and dirt which collect around their roots, but most of their nourishment comes from the air; that is why so many people call them air plants.

(10) 1902 *Sears Cat.* (ed. 112) 298/2 Quackenbush Improved Nickel Plated Air Rifle . . . $4.35. **1948** *Chi. Tribune* 25 April IV. 6/1 No one is interested in hunting English sparrows with an air rifle. — **(11)** (*a*) **1841** *Greene Co. Torchlight* (Xenia, O.) 21 Oct. 4/2 The Air Tight Stove [is] known and warranted to be superior to every other in economy of time and expense. **1843** STEPHENS *High Life N.Y.* II.

xxxi. 227 Speakin' of stoves, Par, I got . . . what they call an air tight, and a little teenty tointy handful of wood keeps 'em warm as blazes a hull day and night tu. **1947** COFFIN *Yankee Coast* 162, I shall recall the wonder of seeing a boat grow beside an airtight-stove in the woodshed until the boat filled the woodshed full and stuck its nose right out into the snowy boughs of the apple orchard. (*b*) **1897** A. H. LEWIS *Wolfville* 330 What's air-tights? Which you Eastern shorthorns is shore ignorant. Air-tights is can peaches, can tomatters, an' sim'lar bluffs. **1923** *Outing* Mar. 263/1 One afternoon I decided the party had been on airtight (canned meat) long enough. — **(12) 1873** TWAIN & WARNER *The Gilded Age* 171 He was the inventor of the famous air-torpedo, which came very near destroying the Union armies in Missouri, and the city of St. Louis itself. — **(13) 1880** *Harper's Mag.* Oct. 729/1 The tent and 'dug out' can not long satisfy the men who see future Chicagoes in even the 'air towns' found at the termini of constructed track on the railroads.

b. In phrases: (1) *To put on airs*, to give oneself airs, also transf.; (2) *to give the air*, to dismiss, "fire," *slang;* (3) *to go up in the air*, see ∗**go,** *v.*

(1) **1832** *Congress Deb.* 30 Jan. 203, I am aware that, at times, States have attempted to put on airs, and set up their own against federal opinions. **1870** *Scribner's Mo.* I. 39 But the melodeon . . . behaved well. It put on no airs. — **(2) 1928** FOY & HARLOW *Clowning Thro' Life* 75 Finnegan got himself in bad with the great man, however, and was given the air before the engagement was over.

See also **fresh air, hot air.**

∗**airing,** *n.* A display, exposure to public notice. — **1873** MARK TWAIN *Speeches* (1923) 52 (R.), All the papers in America would have found out that I was a wife beater, and they would have given it a pretty general airing, too.

air line.

1. A straight or direct line. Also attrib.

1813 J. QUINCY in *Ann. 12th Congress* 2 Sess. 544 They will not rigidly observe any air-lines or water-lines in enforcing their necessary levies. **1863** DICEY *Six Months* II. 133 If you take any map of the West, and draw a straight, or what the Americans call an 'air-line,' from Racine to the nearest point of the Mississippi, you will have before you the exact course of the railroad in question. **1946** *Outdoor Life* Oct. 47/1 He had been driving over the Air Line Road, which bisects Washington County, and had seen the birds flying across the highway, easily visible in the bright moonlight.

fig. **1904** *N.Y. Tribune* 7 Nov. 2 The President . . . has marched straight up to his great fame by the air line, and not . . . by compromise with wrong.

2. A direct railroad route. In full **air-line railroad.** Also fig.

1853 *Congress. Globe* 18 Feb. 674/2 This 'air line' runs its whole length . . . through a country . . . eminently adapted for the construction . . . of a railroad. **1853** *Hunt's Merch. Mag.* XXVIII. 117 The South and East Hampton mines are located . . . on the canal, or air-line railroad. **1947** BEEBE *Mixed Train Dly.* 330 Its somewhat pretentious corporate title of Louisville, New Albany and Corydon dates from the time when it actually ran by trackage agreement over the Air Line rails of the Louisville, Evansville and St. Louis right to the Ohio River itself.

fig. **1888** *St. Louis Globe-Democrat* 24 Jan. (F.), An author must take the air-line or we will not travel.

b. The route covered by a system of transportation employing airplanes, a company maintaining such a route.

1921 *Outing* July 154 (*heading*), The Air Line to the Big Woods . . . Cutting Days to Hours in Getting Into the Land of Lakes and Wilderness. **1947** *Reader's Digest* April 31/1 The bill exempts from its scope the industries covered by the Railway Labor Act: railroads, air lines, interstate trucks and buses.

airophone ˈɛrə fon, *n.* [f. *airo-* (erron. for *aero-*) +*phone*.] (See quot.) *Obs.* — **1882–83** KNIGHT *Mech. Dict.* 671/1 A modification of the phonograph is called by Mr. Edison the *airophone*.

aisleman ˈaɪlˈmæn, *n.* One employed in a shop or store to have charge of an aisle. *Rare.* — **1906** *N.Y. Eve. Post* 8 Oct. 12 Simplify shopping by asking questions. . . . Ask the Aislemen and Elevator men.

ajo ˈɑho, *n. S.W.* [Sp., garlic.] Any plant of the genus *Allium*, common in the Southwest. Also widely misapplied to *Hesperocallis undulata*, the desert lily, a fragrant white lily of southern California and western Arizona desert regions. Also **ajo lily.**

1908 HORNADAY *Camp Fires on Desert* 77 The Ajo—which for convenience we may call the Ajo *Lily*, was found from Wall's Well to the Pinacate lava region. **1917** SAUNDERS *Western Wild Flowers* 4 The plant is reputed responsible for the name of the Ajo Mountains in Southwestern Arizona—*ajo*, the Spanish for garlic, being also the term locally applied to the Hesperocallis, which is very abundant in that vicinity. **1937** *Desert Mag.* Dec. 23/1 Dr. McDougal found two very interesting plants. One was Ajo lily. **1940** JAEGER *Desert Wild Flowers* 9 The Indians found the onion flavor agreeable, as did the early Spanish explorers, who called them *ajo*, garlic.

∗**à la.** In cookery phrases: (1) **chicken à la king,** said of a dish of chicken creamed with pimiento or green peppers; (2) **à la Maryland,** served with butter and cream sauce; (3) **à la Newburg,** served in a sauce the chief ingredients of which are cream, butter, flour, egg yolks, brandy and sherry.

(1) 1924 *Chi. Tribune* 5 Oct. 22/1 Chicken a la King is mentioned merely as an example of our exceptional food values. **1948** *Okla. Cotton Grower* 15 April 3/3 Fried noodles, chicken a la king and spring go hand in hand. — **(2) 1892** *Outing* Aug. 412/1 How they sailed into Mrs. Watt's chickens, *à la Maryland.* **1934** *Franklin School P.-T.A.* (Ardmore, Okla.) *Favorite Recipes* 12 Veal a la Maryland. — **(3) 1905** *Granville Centennial Cook Book* 11 Clams a la Newburg.

Alabama ˌæləˈbæmə, *n.* ["Alibamu (said to be from the Choctaw *alba ayamule*, 'I open or clear the thicket')" (Hodge I. 43).] The name of a Muskhogean tribe of Indians and later of a state named from them, used in combs.: (1) **Alabama bill,** a note issued by the Alabama State Bank (1823–46) or one of its four main branches, *obs.;* (2) **Guinea grass,** (see quot.); (3) **Indian,** an Indian of a Muskhogean tribe formerly living in what is now southern Alabama, *obs.;* (4) **screamer,** a ruffian or rowdy, *obs.*

(1) 1838 in BASSETT *South. Plant.* 112, I will forward the money to the publishers the first Ala. Bill I can get. — **(2) 1889** VASEY *Agric. Grasses* 36 *Sorghum halepense* (Johnson Grass; Mean's Grass) . . . has been called Egyptian Grass . . . [and] Alabama Guinea grass. — **(3)** [**1722** COXE *Desc. Carolana* 24 Below these on the same River, are the *Ullibalies*, or as some, the *Olibabalies* and according to the *French* the *Allibamous*.] **1770** MEASE *Narrative* 67 Set out at Day Break and soon after pass'd a Village of the Alibamous Indians on the West Side. **1808** JEFFERSON *Writings* III. 486, I lay before the legislature a letter . . . on the subject of a small tribe of Alabama Indians, on the western side of the Mississippi. — **(4) 1822** *Amer. Beacon* (Norfolk, Va.) 6 Sep. 4/1 (Th. Supp.), The bargemen . . . are divided into classes, such as Tuscaloosa Roarers, Alabama Screamers, Cahawba Scrougers, and the like gentle names.

b. Alabama claims, claims made by the United States upon Great Britain for losses sustained by the United States during the Civil War resulting from the construction of Confederate vessels, notably the privateer "Alabama," in British ports. Also **Alabama arbitrator, question.** Now *hist.*

1867 *Harper's Wkly.* 2 Feb. 67/1 The unsettled Alabama claims against England . . . will lead, we hope, to an international Congress to determine some general code of neutrality. **1886** A. JOHNSTON *Hist.* 376 The Alabama Arbitrators met at Geneva, in Switzerland, in 1872. **1889** FARMER 9 The political incident known as the 'Alabama Question.' **1948** KERWIN *Civil-Military Relationships* 39 We have often had the best of international horse-trading—from the Revolutionary debts owed to France, . . . down to our indemnity for the 'Alabama' claims.

Alabamian æləˈbæmɪən, *n.* Also **Alabaman.** A native or resident of the state of Alabama. Also as adj.

1832 *Deb. Congress.* 15 June 3570, I will not even discuss this great question of Southern wrongs as an Alabamian, but as a Southern man. **1842** in *Amer. Sp.* XVIII. 119 Your generosity is so truly Alabamian. **1948** MATHEWS *Southernisms* 51 Alabamians especially shoud be glad to know that.

b. An Indian living in what is now Alabama. *Rare.*

1851 HOWE *Hist. Coll. Great West* 269 Among the distinguished chiefs was the noted *Weatherford*, chief of the Alabamans, . . . leader in the capture and massacre of Fort Mimms.

alacran ˌæləˈkræn *n. S.W.* [Sp. *alacrán*, in same sense.] A scorpion. — [**1772** ULLOA *Noticias Americanas* 145 Es abundante en *Culebras* de la especies venenosa mas activas, como *Corales*, . . . en *Cientopies, Alacranes*, y de les demas clases comunes.] **1836** C. J. LATROBE *Travels in Mexico* 182 (Bentley) The alacran of Durango is the most venomous and hundreds of children are killed by them in that province. **1891** *D.N.* I. 243 *Alacran*, a scorpion. Different species of the genus *scorpio*, common in Texas and Mexico.

alameda ˌæləˈmedə, *n.* Chiefly *S.W.* [Sp. in same sense. An Amer. borrowing.] A public promenade or road with alamos or other trees on each side.

1831 PATTIE *Personal Narr.* 242 Upon the Alameda, a promenade north of the city. **1901** *Harper's Mag.* Dec. 72/2, I am about to take my ward out . . . to—er—taste the air in the Alameda. **1923** W.

SMITH *Little Tigress* 160 (Bentley) It was the memory of this that reminded me of him just a little while ago at the alameda.

alamo ˈælə,mo, *n.* [Sp. *álamo*, poplar.]

1. (*cap.*) Used with reference to the overwhelming and slaying of about 140 Texans and Americans at the Alamo, a Franciscan mission at San Antonio, Texas, in 1836. Now *hist.*

1836 *Niles' Reg.* 25 June 293/2 Colonel Sherman with his regiment, having commenced the action upon our left wing, the whole line, at the centre and on the right, advancing in double quick time, rung the war cry 'Remember the Alamo.' **1836** in *American War Songs* (1925) 59 And 'Alamo' hereafter be In bloodier fields, the battle cry. **1948** *Chi. Tribune* 2 May I. 22/2 Wake was not another Alamo, for, as has been said, 'Thermopylae had its messenger of defeat, The Alamo had none.'

2. *S.W.* A poplar. Also **alamo tree.**

1854 *H. Rep. Executive Doc. No. 91*, IV. (1856) 11 The alamos grow to a good large size and are quite abundant. **1893** DONALDSON *Moqui Pueblo Indians* 65 He repeated 'lena, lena' (firewood), but whether 'alamo' (cottonwood), or some other tree like the cedar or pine, I could not make out. **1910** *Century Mag.* March 767/1 Along its branches grow big alamo-trees. **1948** *D. Oklahoman* (Okla. City) 31 Oct. D. 8/5 The name came from a grove of cottonwoods (alamos) which once grew on the site.

* **alarm,** *n.* In combs.: (1) **alarm cord,** the cord of an alarm bell; (2) **duty,** the duty of being prepared to respond to an alarm, *obs.;* (3) **list,** a number of men required to perform military duty in an emergency, *obs.;* (4) **register,** on a streetcar a device used in registering the number of fares collected.

(1) 1872 EGGLESTON *End of World* v. 40 In behind the donjon chimney he pulled an alarm cord. — **(2) 1837** *S. Lit. Messenger* III. 644 There is a detachment of citizen soldiery . . . always on what is called alarm duty. — **(3)** *a***1752** W. DOUGLASS *Summary* II. 363 The alarum list, and the training militia [of Md.], are . . . under the same regulations as in the colonies already mentioned. **1835** *Biog. Isaac Hill* 6 Her father . . . commanded a company of alarmlist at the battle of Lexington. — **(4) 1895** WAIT *Car-Builder's Dict.* 8 The bell is intended to indicate or announce to the passengers that the conductor has recorded the fares collected. . . . The punching of the slip is now usually omitted, the device being then simply an *alarm register*, often made of large size and attached to the side of the car.

As the last term in **dinner, Indian, still, time alarm.**

Alaska əˈlæskə, *n.* [Eskimo *Alákshak, Aláyeksa*, the continental mainland of northwest America.]

1. An arctic (see also quot. 1921).

1902 *Sears Cat.* (ed. 112) 933/3 This is the only style of Alaska that will correctly fit a wide extension soled shoe. **1921** *Outing* Dec. 106/1 The Alaska type of snowshoe has the sides nearly parallel throughout its length, tapering quickly at the toe and heel.

2. In combs.: (1) **Alaska cedar,** =next; (2) **cypress,** (see quot.), also **Alaska ground cypress;** (3) **Day,** the anniversary, observed in Alaska as a holiday, of the day, Oct. 18, 1867, upon which Russia transferred the territory of Alaska to the U.S.; (4) **pine,** a hemlock, *Tsuga heterophylla*, found in northwestern North America; (5) **robin,** (see quot.); (6) **sable,** (see quot.).

(1) 1884 SARGENT *Rep. Forests* 7 The most valuable species of the northern Coast Forest [is] . . . the Alaska cedar (*Chamæcyparis* [*nootkatensis*]). **1947** *Alaska Life* Jan. 23/1 In many places red cedar and Alaska cedar are associated with them. — **(2) 1897** SUDWORTH *Arborescent Flora* 79 *Chamaecyparis nootkatensis* . . . Alaska Ground Cypress . . . Alaska Cypress. — **(3) 1932** *World Almanac* 70/2 Oct. 18—Alaska Day (in Alaska only). — **(4) 1897** SUDWORTH *Arborescent Flora* 45 *Tsuga mertensiana* . . . Alaska Pine [of] Northwestern lumbermen. — **(5) 1940** *Mt. Hood Guide* 18 The Western thrush or robin, a summer resident, differs only slightly from the varied thrush or Alaska robin, a shy resident seldom seen. — **(6) 1897** *Boston Transcript* 11 Sep. 24/3 Skunk skins are one of the biggest items in the fur market. They go under the attractive name of 'Alaska sable.'

b. Also **Alaska** (1) **current,** (2) **Indian,** (3) **salmon.**

(1) 1880 JACKSON *Alaska* 54 The former stream flowing northward has been named 'the Alaska Current,' and gives the great southern coast of Alaska a winter climate as mild as that of one third of the United States. — **(2) 1879** MUIR *John of Mts.* (1938) 275 A few good missionaries, a few good cannon with men behind them, and fair play, protection from whisky, is all the Alaska Indians require. **1947** *Christian Cent.* 8 Oct. 1205/1 The only hope the Alaska Indians have is that the Christian conscience of our country shall speak forcibly. — **(3) 1872** *Alaska Herald* 9 July 1/1 The great demand for Alaska salmon in California and the Eastern States has given the article a reputation which will develop the fisheries to a much greater extent than has yet been done. **1879** MUIR *John of Mts.* (1938) 260 The Alaska salmon are said to be inferior to those of the Columbia.

Alaskan əˈlæskən, *a.* and *n.* [f. prec.]

1. *a.* Of or pertaining to Alaska.

1870 W. H. DALL *Alaska* 286 The Rocky Mountain chain . . . passes to the west and south, combining with the coast ranges to form the Alaskan Range. **1901** *World's Work* June 816/2 Robert Moran, during the Alaskan rush, was left . . . with nearly three quarters of a million dollars worth of Yukon river steamers on his hands. **1947** *Alaska Life* Jan. 4/1 Interest in the new Alaskan industry has been mounting.

2. *n.* A native or inhabitant of Alaska.

1881 WILLARD *Life in Alaska* (1884) 16 It is the custom of the Alaskans to compel the murderer to stay beside the corpse until it is finally disposed of. **1947** *Democrat* 8 May 4/5 Hostesses, most of them native Alaskans, drive the soldiers.

b. English such as is used in Alaska.

1947 *This Week Mag.* 20 Sep. 4/2 They'll be Cheechakos—Alaskan for newcomers—for a few days, but plain Alaskans after that.

alaskaite əˈlæskə,aɪt, *n.* [So called from the Alaska mine in Colorado.] (See quot. 1927.) — **1889** [see **alaskite**]. **1927** *Amer. Mineralogist* Jan. 21 The alaskaite, which is an argentiferous variety of galeno-bismuthite, was found in the Saxon mine.

alaskite əˈlæskaɪt, *n.* [f. *Alaska.*] (See quots. 1889, 1918.)

The use of "alaskite" suggested in the first quot. has not prevailed, a different application having been made of the word.

1889 *Cent.* 128/3 alaskaite. . . . Better **alaskite*, . . . A sulphid of bismuth, lead, silver, and copper found at the Alaska mine in Colorado. **1915** *Nat. & Science on Pac. Coast* 68 The ore bodies are in intrusive alaskite porphyries of Mesozoic age. **1918** FAY *Gloss. Mining & Mineral Industry* 23/1 Alaskite. Any igneous rock consisting essentially of quartz and alkalic feldspar, without regard to texture.

Albanian ,ɔlˈbenɪən, *n.* [See next.] A native or inhabitant of Albany, N.Y.

1710 SHELDON *Deerfield* (1895) I. 375 You may adjust the Post as is proposed, . . . but the Albanians must not think to make a purse from us [Mass.], and to exact more than it would be done for by our people. **1863** BOOTH *N.Y.* 226 Terrified at the danger, the Albanians resolved to seek assistance from New York. **1933** *Am. Sp.* Oct. 78/1 One of my students, of obviously Anglo-Saxon ancestry, surprised me by saying that though he was born in Boston, his parents were both Albanians.

* **Albany,** *n.* [Named by the British in 1664 in honor of the Duke of York and Albany.] Name of the capital of New York State used in combs.: (1) **Albany ale,** an ale formerly made at Albany, *obs.;* (2) **beechdrops,** a purplish-brown parasitic plant, *Pterospora andromedea;* (3) **beef,** sturgeon meat, *obs.;* (4) **beer,** (see quot.), *obs.;* (5) **board,** (see quot.); (6) **pea,** a variety of field pea, *obs.;* (7) **plan,** (see quots.), now *hist.;* (8) **regency,** a coterie of Democratic politicians who met at Albany (1820–50) and exercised considerable influence in state and national politics, now *hist.;* (9) **slip,** (see quot.).

(1) 1821 DALTON *Travels* 74 Albany ale is almost as much famed in this country as London porter is throughout England. **1845** S. SMITH *Theatr. Apprent.* i. 21 My landlord hinted that I was in debt for . . . sundry pots of porter and Albany ale. — **(2) 1836** LINCOLN *Botany* App. 130 Albany beech-drops . . . is very tall, bearing a many-flowered raceme. **1847** WOOD *Botany* 380 Albany Beech-drops [are found] in various parts of N.Y. . . . First discovered by Dr. D. S. C. H. Smith, near Niagara Falls, 1816. **1915** ARMSTRONG *Western Wild Flowers* 360 It is also called Giant Bird's-nest and Albany Beech drops. — **(3) 1791** J. LONG *Voyages* 118 This fish [=sturgeon] is very common in Albany, and is sold at 1d. per lb. York currency. The flesh is called Albany beef. **1880** *Mag. of Am. Hist.* May 387 Of 'Albany Beef,' sturgeon, you can get enough for 12½ cts. to feed a family. — **(4) 1829** *Free Press* (Tarboro, N.C.) 23 Jan., Albany beer, best northern cider.

(5) 1904 *D.N.* II. 394 'The merchantable boards are three-fourths of an inch thick, from 10 to 15 feet long, and frequently deformed with knots; at New York they are called Albany boards.' Michaux, 1801, quoted by Fox, p. 15. — **(6) 1785** WASHINGTON *Diaries* II. 363 Sowed one Bushel and three Pecks of the Albany or field Pea. **1825** LORAIN *Pract. Husbandry* 513 The Albany and lady pea are lenient plants. — **(7) 1754** FRANKLIN *Writings* III. 235 The powers proposed by the Albany Plan of Union, to be vested in a grand council representative of the people, . . . are not so great as those the colonies of Rhode Island and Connecticut are entrusted with by their charters. **1891** ORDRONAUX *Const. Legislation* 83 This 'Albany plan,' as it has been called, contemplated establishing one general government over all the colonies, based upon the consent of the governed — (8) **1824** *Niles' Reg.* 25 Sep. 52/2, I observe the following as quoted from the *Mohawk Sentinel*, one of the few papers that thoroughly support the 'Albany regency.' **1832** J. Q. ADAMS *Mem.* VIII. 489 The proceedings of what are called the Albany Regency—the predominant party in the State of New York. — (9) **1909** *Cent. Supp.*, *Albany slip*, a clay dug from the shore of the Hudson river at Albany, New York used extensively . . . by American potters.

Albemarle pippin. (See quot. 1928.) — **1912** *Lit. Digest* 30 March 654/1 Our Va. Albemarle Pippins and Va. Winesap Apples have become famous on two continents. **1928** BAILEY *Cyclo. Horticulture* 322/2 The Yellow Newtown, rechristened Albemarle Pippin in the county of that name (under the impression it was a distinct sort) found its way from Virginia by railroad to the eastern seaboard cities.

Albert tie. A former fashion of bow or necktie. *Obs.* Cf. **Prince Albert.** — **1855** THOMPSON *Doesticks* xxxii. 289, I now discovered that he had stolen . . . an 'Albert tie' and a false collar from my neck.

* **Albright,** *n.* [Jacob *Albright* (1759–1808), a Methodist clergyman of Pennsylvania.] One of a religious denomination formerly also called **Albright's children, people,** or **brethren,** and now named the "Evangelical Association."

1815 STAPLETON *Evangelical Hist.* (1908) 8 This indenture . . . between Andrew Mowrer . . . [and the] trustees of the Evangelist Concretion and Albright's Children, or Albright's people, as they call themselves. **1847** HOWE *Ohio* 371 There are 15 churches, of which the . . . Albrights, Dunkers and African Baptists have each one. **1917** A. STAPLETON *Wonderful Story* 93 The first regular conference of 'The Albright Brethren,' as they were then called, was held . . . [in] Lebanon County, November 13–15, 1807.

***album,** *n.* As the last term in **bar, class, hair, album.**

albur ɑlˈbur, *n. S.W.* [Sp. in same sense.] A kind of card game. *Obs.* — **1851** *N.M. House Jrnl.* 31 All gambling at albur shall be prohibited.

alcabala ˌɑlkɑˈbɑlɑ, *n. S.W.* [Sp. in same sense.] A tax, esp. one on sales. *Obs.* — **1836** HOLLEY *Texas* xi. 213 All the produce of agriculture or industry of the new settlers, shall be free from excise duty, Alcabala, or other duties.

alcaide ælˈked, *n.* Also **alcade.** *S.W.* [Sp., governor of a fort or castle.] =**alcalde.** *Obs.*

1808 *Savannah Republican* 29 Sep. 3/3 A preacher . . . reports that the alcades or magistrates had called a meeting of the people [of Florida], and they were taking the oath of allegiance to Bonaparte. **1846** *Ore. Spectator* 26 Nov. 4/2 No less than seventy announcements of mines were made to the Alcado of San Jose within five months previous to June last. **1873** BEADLE *Undevel. West* 746 Edwin M. Bryant —first American Alcade of San Francisco.

alcalde ælˈkældɪ, *n. S.W.* [Sp. in same sense. An Amer. borrowing.] In regions of former Spanish influence, an administrative officer, as mayor, judge, or justice of the peace.

1803 *Ann. 8th Congress* 2 Sess. 1516 There are two Alcaldes [in Louisiana], whose jurisdiction, civil and criminal, extends through the city of New Orleans. **1892** DUVAL *Young Explorers* 17 We are carrying dispatches . . . from Gen'l Sam Houston to the Alcalde. **1948** JOHNSTON *Gold Rush* 5/2 The *alcaldes* themselves, whether elected or appointed, were usually honest and intelligent, anxious to deal out justice with an impartial hand, and well sustained alike by Mexican and American settlers.

attrib. **1885** C. H. SHINN *Mining Camps* 104 The various functions of government were performed without clashing, by this happily invented alcalde-system.

b. Hence **alcaldaism, alcaldeship.**

1848 *Calif. Star* (S.F.) 18 Mar. 2/2 His Alcaldeship, after favoring the parties with a 'hearing,' (though perspiring profusely meanwhile,) rises to the decision. **1857** *S.F. Call* 26 Mar. 1/2 Having shoulders strong and broad, he could make from twenty-five dollars to five ounces per day, and would not lose his time with Alcaldaism. **1885** C. H. SHINN *Mining Camps* 97 The most important alcaldeship in California . . . was that of San Francisco.

alchy ˈælkɪ, *n.* Colloquial or facetious reduction of **alcohol*, usu. with a prefixed term.

1844 *Akron Buzzard* 25 June 3/1 After strong devotional homage before the throne of old King Alchy, [he] is in the habit of manifesting his affection for his family by severely beating them. **1858** STONE *Put's Golden Songster* 15 'Old Alky' makes their bowels yearn, They stagger round and fall. **1948** *Chi. D. News* 15 March 14/1 The others used bread to make their Soviet alky.

b. Also **alchy-cooking, alchy gang.**

1931 ALLEN *Only Yesterday* 260 As the profits from beer and 'alky-cooking' (illicit distilling) rolled in, young Capone acquired more finesse. **1945** *Chi. D. News* 2 April 8/1 There was no 'singing widow' to help rub out the alky gangs at the inception of their careers.

alcoholist ˌælkəˈhɔlɪst, *n.* One who indulges in intoxicating liquor. — **1888** *Forum* Sep. 103 Of 250 chronic alcoholists nearly 90% had fatty degeneration of the liver. **1894** *Pop. Sci. Mo.* Nov. 99 Man may be a moderate alcoholist.

alcohol stove. A stove using alcohol as fuel. — **1879** BISHOP *4 Months in Sneak-box* 41 Alcohol stoves are small, and the fuel used too expensive. **1947** *Reader's Digest* Feb. 162/1 Today we tried to make soup on one of the alcohol stoves.

Alcorn Club. (See quot.), named from James L. Alcorn, Republican governor, and later senator, of Mississippi in Reconstruction times who openly sought the political support of Negroes. *Obs.* — **1904** FLEMING *Documents re Reconstruction* No. 3, 5 The dislike of the whites to the Union League was so great that the local bodies began to assume other names: . . . 'Alcorn Clubs' in Mississippi, 'National Guards' in Alabama, etc.

***alder,** *n.* As the last term in **black, box, candle, European, Oregon, seaside, speckled, spiked, swamp, tag, white, witch alder.**

alder swamp. A low, wet, marshy area where alder bushes are abundant.

1640 *Md. Hist. Mag.* VI. 67 Unto a swamp called Alder Swamp. **1775** *R.I. Hist. Soc.* VI. 14 [We] got into an alder swamp. **1849** CHAMBERLAIN *Indiana Gaz.* 11 White maple, tamarack and alder swamps; beautiful small lakes and iron ore . . . are scattered promiscuously together. **1947** *Midland Naturalist* July 9 These Alder swamps are ordinarily rapidly invaded by River Birch (*Betula nigra*) and occasionally by Black Willow (*Salix nigra*).

***alderwoman,** *n.* A woman who holds an aldermanic office. — **1884** *Chi. Tribune* 5 May 4/3 She cannot under the laws monopolize the holding of nice special offices like Mayoress, Alderwoman, Public Librarianess, or Superintendentess of Education. **1895** *N. Amer. Rev.* Sep. 267 When women shall have become, not only votresses, but . . . alderwomen.

ale cocktail. (See quot.) *Obs.* — **1838** UNCLE SAM in *Bentley's Misc.* IV. 47 The other passengers having all retired . . . to the bar-room, where ale-cocktail (ale with ginger and pepper in it) . . . and Monongahela (whisky-punch) were in great demand.

alegria æləˈgriə, *n. S.W.* [Sp. *alegria* in Amer. Sp. sense here shown.] The common pigweed. — **1844** GREGG *Commerce of Prairies* I. 218 The belles of the ranchos . . . have a disgusting habit of besmearing their faces with crimson juice of a plant called *alegria.* **1941** *Amer. Sp.* Oct. 185 Alegria (Spanish). Term used for herb or genus Amaranthus, common name pig weed. Leaves can be chewed or squeezed to produce bright red juice used as a cosmetic.

Aleut ˈælɪˌut, *n.* [Origin obscure. Poss. f. a native word *aliat*, island.] A member of an Eskimauan family living in the Aleutian Islands and on the north side of the Alaska peninsula. Usu. pl. with reference to the family.

1780 COXE *Discov. Between Asia & America* I. App. 263 The inhabitants of Unalashka . . . now begin to call themselves by the general name of Aleyut, given them by the Russians. **1890** *Independent* (N.Y.) 9 Oct. 1/2 The word *Aleut*, pronounced *al-lee-yoot*, is of uncertain origin. . . . The Aleuts themselves do not recognize the word, their own name for their tribe being Oonangan. **1947** *Alaska Life* Jan. 7/1 While in Afognak we talked with an old native Aleut who had spent his childhood in Katmai village.

Aleutian əˈluʃən, *n.* =prec. — **1806** LANGSDORFF *Voyages* (1817) 457 The sailors of the American States . . . carried their audacity so far, as to bring a number of Aleutians with them to catch sea-otters on the coast of California. **1870** *Alaska Times* (Sitka) 7 May 2/3 On last Monday afternoon war was declared between the Sitka Si-washes and the native Aleutians.

alewife ˈelˌwaɪf, *n.* Also **allize.** [See note.] A fish, *Pomolobus pseudoharengus*, found in great numbers along the Atlantic Coast, the branch herring. Cf. **spring herring** and see **inland alewife.**

The origin of this term is not clear. It has been suggested that it may be *ale* + *wife* (see quot. 1675), or an American Indian term. It is more likely an English dial. fish name. Cf. *EDD alley3*, also *allowes*, as a name for the allice-shad. The *Ling. Atlas of N. Eng.*, Map 233 lists *elwife*, *alewop*, and many variant pronunciations.

1633 *New Plymouth Laws* 32 That therefore the said herrings alewives or shadds comonly used in the setting of corne be appropriated. **1637** MORTON *New Canaan* 89 There is a fish, (by some called shadds, by some allizes,) that at the spring of the yeare passe up the rivers to spaune in the ponds. **1675** JOSSELYN *Two Voyages* 107 The alewife is like a herrin, but has a bigger bellie, therefore called an alewife. **1714** SEWALL *Diary* II. 436 Eat roste *Alewive* and very good Hasty Pudding. **1734** *Jrnls. Mass. Ho. Repr.* 50 A Bill entitled an Act to prevent the destruction of the fish commonly called alewives. **1838** *Mass. Zool. Survey Rep.* 42 The *Clupea vernalis*—alewife—is taken in immense quantities still, . . . although in several places . . . the various encroachments of man have sensibly diminished them. **1947** COFFIN *Yankee Coast* 297 Herring we have, . . . from the little brothers of seraphs that we call sardines and immortalize in olive oil in flat cans, up to the fat seraphs of alewives. (Pronounced L-Y's.)

attrib. **1634** WOOD *N. Eng. Prospect* I. x. 43 This town [of Salem] wants an alewife river, which is a great inconvenience; it hath two good harbours. **1755** *Cambridge Prop. Rec.* 352 To act and Do any matter or thing that they Shall Judge best with Respect to the alewive Fishery this year. **1945** *Nat. Geog. Mag.* Sep. 290 One of the oldest fisheries of Maine is probably alewife dipping.

b. Used of other fishes (see quots.).

1839 STORER *Mass. Fishes* 112 *Clupea fasciata* Le Sueur (fasciated Herring) is known under the name of alewive by the fishermen of Sandwich, and appears only in the spring. **1842** *Nat. Hist. N.Y., Zoology* IV. 258 The American Alewive. *Alosa tyrannus*. . . . In our waters, they appear with the Shad about the first of April, but are never sufficiently numerous to form a separate fishery. **1884** ROE *Nature's Story* 197 These half-grown fish [=shad] are taken in seines, and sold as herrings or 'alewives.'

* **Alexander,** *n.*

1. *pl.* The purple meadow parsnip, *Thaspium trifoliatum*, or its yellow variety, *T. t. aureum.*

1843 TORREY *Flora N.Y.* I. 272 *Thaspium atropurpureum*. . . . Purple Alexanders. **1942** PEATTIE *Friendly Mts.* 193 Flowers of the golden Alexanders now dot the meadows.

2. A variety of peach introduced in 1870 by O. A. Alexander, Mt. Pulaski, Illinois.

1890 *Stock Grower* 24 May 7/2 The Alexanders . . . are loaded with fruit [in the Mesilla Valley]. **1930** BAILEY *Cyclo. Horticulture* 2504/2 For shipping, Alexander, . . . Early Hale, . . . Elberta, and Salway are recognized as standards.

alfilaria æl͵fɪlə'riə, *n.* Also **alfileria, alfilerilla.** *W.* [Amer. Sp. *alfilerillo* in same sense.] The pin grass or pin clover, *Erodium cicutarium*, of the western plains.

1868 *Overland Mo.* Aug. 180/1 Burr clover, whose seed is enclosed in a prickly capsule, alfalfa, bunch grass and alfilarea represent the general pasture of the mountains. **1886** VAN DYKE *So. Calif.* 38 This is the bloom of the alfileria, and swiftly it spreads from the southern slopes, where it begins, and runs from meadow to hill-top. **1942** KEARNEY & PEEBLES *Flowering Plants Ariz.* 507 Both of the Arizona species are excellent forage plants but alfileria or 'fileree' (*E. cicutarium*) is especially important because of its great abundance.

alforja æl'fɔrhə, *n. S.W.* [Sp. in same sense.] A saddlebag. — **1847** RUXTON *Adv. Rocky Mts.* 77 To it flock venders of saddles, bridles, bits, spurs, whips, alforjas. **1922** P. A. ROLLINS *Cowboy* 155 All or a part of the parcels might have been stuffed into 'alforjas,' which were wide, leathern or canvas bags . . . hanging from the crosses on the saddle's top. **1946** *Trail Riders Bul.* May 11/1 At the drop of a hat, uke, fiddle, mouth organ or pleated piano come forth from his alforjas.

alfresco æl'frɛsko, *a. W.* [Sp. *al fresco*, in the open air.] Outdoors. Also as adv.

1853 PAXTON *Stray Yankee* (Bentley) This same camp was an extemporaneous affair, a kind of al fresco home, formed by setting up a few crotches to sustain a rude roof. **1857** *Spirit of Times* 21 Feb. 397/2 The governor would prefer playing Falstaff without stuffing, I guess, to taking his cigar *al fresco*, in front of his conservatory just now. **1890** *Outing* Oct. 53/1 We dined quite *al fresco*. **1948** *Time* 8 Mar. 21/1 This week, at an alfresco press conference, he refused comment about the Southern revolt.

algarroba ͵ælgə'robə, *n. W.* [Sp. in the Amer. Sp. senses shown here. An Amer. borrowing.] (See quots.)

1853 SITGREAVES *Exped. Zuni & Colo. Rivers* 39 There was to be seen occasionally a scattered willow (*Salix*,) mesquite (*Algarobia*,) . . . and a singular low shrub . . . covered with an adhesive varnish. **1898** RATTAN *West Coast Botany* 32 Honey Mesquit, or Algaroba (*Prosopis juliflora*) and Screw-pod Mesquit, or Tornilla, (*P. pubescens*), are small trees of Southern California. **1937** *Range Plant Handbook* B134 New Mexican locust, sometimes (though erroneously) called algaroba or, colloquially, agarroba, is a large, thorny shrub or small tree, varying from several feet up to 20 or 25 feet in height.

algeredo ͵ælgə'redə, *n. S.W.* [App., by confusion, f. **algerita.**] (See quots.) — **1937** PARKS *Valuable Plants Texas* 25 *Celtis pallida* [is] a bush-like shrub which is a honey plant and bears numerous berries in the fall which are collected for jellies and in many places sold under the name of algeredo. **1942** FRIEND *Plants for Rio Grande Valley* 53 *Celtis pallida*. Granjeno. . . . These fruits are used in making 'Algerado' jelly.

* **Algerine,** *n.* One who acts like an Algerine pirate, esp. (*pl.*) a local name of a faction in Rhode Island politics about 1842–50. Also **Algerineism.** *Obs.*

1841 FOOTE *Texas & Texans* 83 A transaction which doubtless will . . . call down retributive vengeance upon these American Algerines. **1843** *Providence Jrnl.* 7 Jan., Three times he waved it in the air; The cursed Algerines to scare. **1844** *Congress. Globe* 11 Mar. 360/1 The gentleman from Rhode Island had talked of 'ruffianism' in that State, and of 'Algerines'; but if the proposition he made to this House was not a specimen of 'Algerineism,' he apprehended it was not to be found in Rhode Island. **1885** *Congress. Rec.* 21 Jan. 912/1 Bitterly as the conflict was waged between the 'Dorrites' and the 'Algerines,' as the contending parties were called.

b. Algerine Act, (see quot. 1844).

1844 *No. Amer. Review* April 397 They also passed the 'Algerine Act,' making it a high offense, punishable by fine and imprisonment, for any persons to act as officers of illegal town meetings. **1859** KING *Life & Times T. W. Dorr* 68 The General Assembly had passed the act aforesaid, sometimes called the 'Algerine Act.'

algerita ͵ældʒə'ritə, *n. S.W.* Also **algireta, alderita.** [Amer. Sp., to designate the shrub here mentioned.] The berry of various shrubs of the genus *Mahonia* found in the Southwest. Also a shrub of this genus.

1890 *Geol. Survey Texas* 485 The most abundant berry is the algireta. . . . The berry resembles the cranberry of the North, in color, but is entirely different. **1904** WOOTON *Native Ornamental Plants N.M.* 26 *Berberis Fremontii* is a shrub which closely resembles the Algerita. **1942** CASTETTER & BELL *Pima & Papago Agric.* 26 Adjoining the desert are thickets of *jojoba* . . . (*Simmondsia californica*), with . . . *algerita* (*Berberis Fremontii*) and buckbrush in between.

attrib. **1936** MCKENNA *Black Range* 291 He told me he had lately gathered bushels of alderita berries to make wine.

Algic 'ældʒɪk, *a.* and *n.* (See quots.) *Obs.* — **1834** SCHOOLCRAFT in *Hist. & Scientific Sk. Mich.* 92 The . . . plan of a society of Inquiry respecting the Indians, was adopted . . . at Detroit in 1832, under the title of the Algic Society. **1839**——*Algic Researches* I. 12 The term Algic is introduced, in a generic sense, for all that family of tribes who, about A.D. 1600, were found spread out . . . along the Atlantic, . . . extending . . . west to the Mississippi. [The word is] derived from the words Alleghany and Atlantic.

algodon ɑlgo'don, *n.* [Sp. *algodón*, cotton or the cotton plant.] A cottonwood tree. *Rare.* — **1878** BEADLE *Western Wilds* 76 A little grove of algodones beyond the hacienda.

Algonkian æl'gɑŋkɪən, *a.* [f. **Algonquin.**] *Geol.* (See quot. 1918.) Also *absol.*

1897 *Md. Geol. Survey* I. 169 The supposed Algonkian rocks of the western division of the Piedmont Plateau are infolded with the Paleozoic deposits of Montgomery, Frederick, and Carroll counties. **1917** MOOREHEAD *Stone Ornaments Amer. Indian* 344 It resembles many of the graphitic schists of the Algonkian from the Black Hills or the Huronian period. **1918** FAY *Gloss. Mining & Mineral Industry* 24/2 Algonkian; Proterozoic. In the nomenclature of the United States Geological Survey, the second in order of age of the systems into which the stratified rocks of the earth's crust are divided; also the corresponding period of geological time. **1922** *Outing* June 100/3 In Glacier, all later deposits were washed away, leaving these Algonkian rocks upon the surface.

Algonquian æl'gɑŋkɪən, *a.* [f. **Algonquin,** 1st used by J. W. Powell (see 1st quot.).] Of or pertaining to the most widespread linguistic stock of American Indians whose territory is thought to have embraced, in general, much of the eastern half of the U.S., together with parts of Canada and portions of the West. Also as noun. Cf. next.

1885 POWELL in *Bur. Amer. Ethnol. Rep.* VII. 47 The area formerly occupied by the Algonquian family was more extensive than that of any other linguistic stock in North America. **1907** HODGE *Amer. Indians* I. 39/2 As a rule the relations of the French with the Algonquian tribes were friendly. **1946** *Nat. Geog. Mag.* Jan. 54/1 The Powhatan confederacy of Tidewater Virginia consisted of Algonquian-speaking tribes.

Algonquin æl'gɑŋkɪn, *n.* and *a.* [f. a native word of uncertain meaning.] Also **Algonquian.**

1. *n.* A member of an important widespread family of Indian tribes, formerly inhabiting various eastern and middle states and parts of Canada. Usu. pl. with reference to the family.

[**1603** CHAMPLAIN *Des Savvages* Bii, Les Algoumequins vne des trois nations sortirent de leurs cabanes; & se retirent à part dans vne place publique.] **1667** TRACY in Fernow *N.Y. Documents* (1853) III. 151 By our authority wee have hindred the Algonquins from making warre upon them [=the Dutch]. **1770** *Doc. Rel. Hist. N.Y.* VIII. 228 In the evening 16 Algonkins ettc. arrived. **1907** HODGE *Amer. Indians* I. 40 The central Algonquians are tall, averaging about 173 cm. **1948** *Sat. Ev. Post* 31 July 72/4 We went ashore there, hoping to get some pictures of the colorful Algonquins.

b. The language of these Indians.

1705 BEVERLEY *Virginia* III. 24 However they [Va. Indians] have a sort of general Language, like what Lahontan calls the Algonkine, which is understood by the Chief men of many Nations. **1869** PARKMAN *Discov. Gt. West* IV. 39 He spoke Algonquin fluently. **1948** *Sat. Ev. Post* 31 July 71/3 The Kapitachuan . . . means 'where the current stops' in Algonquin.

c. *a.* Designating or pertaining to this family of Indians or their language.

1705 HARRIS *Navigantium atque itinerantium* II. 909/2 Getting aboard as fast as we could, [we] made towards them, crying out in the *Iroquese* and *Algonquin* Languages. **1760** JEFFERYS *Hist. French Dominions* 47 The Christinax, a nation . . . speaking the Algonkin tongue. **1841** COOPER *Deerslayer* xv., Hurry, who had some knowledge of the Algonquin language. **1919** *Maine My State* 25 Canada, the original home of the great Algonkin family. **1945** *Reader's Digest* Aug. 76 My friend Alonzo, Algonquin trapper, . . . has spent 50 years in the forests of Quebec.

alguazil ælgwəˈzil, *n.* [Sp., an Amer. borrowing.] In regions of French or Sp. influence, a sheriff. *Obs.*

[**1671** OGILBY *America* 293 Every [New Mexican] Village was Govern'd by a *Casique*, whose Commands were published by the *Alguaziles*.] **1803** *Ann. 8th Congress* 2 Sess. 1520 This council distributes among its members several important offices, such as Alguazil Mayor or High Sheriff. **1858** *Texas Almanac* 162 The *Alguazil*, or Sheriff of the Colony, was appointed by the Supreme Judge.

***alibi,** *n.* An excuse. Also attrib. *Colloq.* — **1912** *Collier's* 20 April 15/2 'Getting your alibi ready?' asked Zeider. **1947** *Chi. D. News* 22 Jan. 14/4 [The] president of the . . . railroad is as good an executive as he is an alibi artist.

***alibi,** *v. intr.* To make an excuse. *Colloq.* — **1917** *Collier's* 13 Oct. 16/1, I ain't trying to alibi, it was a solid bone play. **1948** *Dly. Ardmoreite* (Ardmore, Okla.) 15 Jan. 1/1 Because some other towns of our comparable size are marked by their littered curbs and gutters doesn't alibi very effectively for our own situation.

Alice blue. [After *Alice* Roosevelt Longworth.] A color of a greenish-blue hue resembling Italian blue. Also attrib. — **1921** *Collier's* 19 Feb., Mood Change Carefree to Gay Record-Creation Causing Such Change Alice Blue Gown. **1936** *Sears Cat.* 397 [Colors:] Peach, Rose Pink, Maple Sugar, Alice Blue, White. **1946** T. JONES *Skinny Angel* 149 She sat straight-spined on the edge of her chair as she said this, a lovely figure in Alice blue.

***alien,** *n.*

1. (See quots.) *Obs.*

1882 *Nation* 19 Oct. 331/1 The State of Arkansas . . . certainly could not have supposed that capitalists at home and the aliens (as they were wont to call all Northern bondholders) had forgotten . . . the special acts of her Legislature. **1924** *Imperial Night-hawk* 4 June 3/3 More than ten thousand Klansmen and friends gathered to naturalize and to witness the naturalization of a class of one thousand aliens i.e. candidates for initiation into the K.K.K.

2. *Hist.* **Alien and Sedition Act, bill, law,** acts passed by Congress in 1798 against aliens, and sharply curtailing the freedom of the press to criticize the government.

1798 *Pittsburgh Gazette* 27 Oct. 1/4 The addressers complain of the 'odious Alien and Sedition Bills.' **1798** *Virginia Resolution* 21 Dec., The General Assembly doth particularly protest against the palpable and alarming infractions of the Constitution, in the two late cases of the 'Alien and Sedition Acts.' **1934** WINSTON *Robert E. Lee* 13 In the General Assembly of 1798 he endorsed the Alien and Sedition Laws, declaring them to be wise and constitutional.

alienism ˈeljən,ɪzəm, *n.* **1.** The state or condition of being an alien. *Rare.* **2.** The study and treatment of mental disease. — **(1) 1808** JOHNSON *Rep. Cases Supreme Ct., N.Y.* II. 381 The prisoner was convicted of murder. On his arraignment, he suggested his alienism, which was admitted. — **(2) 1881** *Nation* Dec. 433/1 As surgery is the very best department in medical science in this country (U.S.), alienism is the very worst.

aliso ɑˈliso, *n. W.* [Sp., used in Mexico for *Alnus mexicana*.] A shrub or tree of the genus *Alnus*, (see also quot. 1948). — **1908** INGERSOLL *Hist. Santa Monica Bay Cities, Calif.* xiii/1 Glossary . . . Aliso, Alder tree. **1948** *Pacific Discovery* July–Aug. 31/1 The name *El Aliso* is the Spanish-Californian for the sycamore or plane tree which is a conspicuous feature in the canyons and along the watercourses on the rancho.

***alkali,** *n.*

1. A region where the soil is heavily impregnated with alkali.

1870 MARK TWAIN *Sk., Petrified Man*, That awful five days journey through alkali, sagebrush, peril of body, and imminent starvation. **1902** WISTER *Virginian* ix. 101 Sunrise found the white stage lurching eternally on across the alkali. **1910** J. HART *Vigilante Girl* xxv. 351 The whitish stretches of alkali which lay like leprous patches on the desert's bosom.

b. An inhabitant of an alkali region. *Colloq.*

1904 WHITE *Mountains* 229 The cave . . . is inhabited by an old 'alkali' and half a dozen bear dogs. **1906** *McClure's Mag.* XXVI. 522 A man can do a heap with that much money. And yet an old 'alkali' is never happy anywhere else.

2. In combs.: (1) **alkali flat,** =**dry lake;** (2) **grass,** any one of various grasses found in alkaline regions; (3) **lake,** a lake in an alkaline region; (4) **spring,** a spring the water of which is alkaline; (5) **water,** water that is alkaline.

(1) 1871 DE VERE 177 The Alkali Flats are now crossed by the Pacific Railroad. **1947** *Time* 21 July 19/1 In 100 years the Mormons have won their war with wastes of sagebrush, sun-parched alkali flats and barren mountains. — **(2) 1870** PINE *Beyond the West* 376 Our horses recruited with a few blades of alkali grass about the spring. **1918** VISHER *So. Dakota* 90 On the somewhat alkaline soil of many 'blow-outs' and other undrained depressions, alkali grass replaces wheat grass. — **(3) 1848** CLAYTON *Latter-Day Saints' Emig. Guide* i, Emigrants have lost many of their teams in the neighborhood of the *Alkali lakes*, in consequence of not knowing the distance from any one of these lakes to good water. **1947** *Sat. Ev. Post* 8 Mar. 117/2 One night in 1914 he and his crew were sitting around the campfire at an alkali lake known as Stinkhole. — **(4) 1848** CLAYTON *Latter-Day Saints' Emig. Guide* (1928) 175 After this you have fifty miles to travel, which is dangerous to teams, on account of Alkali springs. — **(5) 1850** SAWYER *Way Sketches* (1926) 72 Last night about ten o'clock many of our animals were taken sick from drinking the alkali water. **1936** MCKENNA *Black Range* 61 Many of these openings were filled with alkali water unfit to use.

b. In other combs. of more obvious meaning or sufficiently explained in the quots.: (1) **alkali desert,** (2) **dust,** (3) **heath,** (4) **sink,** (5) **spot.**

(1) 1870 PINE *Beyond the West* 217 This road often led them . . . over alkali deserts. — **(2) 1868** BOWLES *Colorado* (1869) 28 The great mountain center of the Continent . . . cheers you through the rolling alkali dust of the Bitter Creek country. **1948** *Popular Western* June 25/2 They landed printed-side-up, puffing little spurts of alkali dust as they fell. — **(3) 1898** DAVY *Nat. Vegetation Alkali Lands* 65 At least two species, however, Salt-grass (*Distichlis spicata*) and Alkali-heath (*Frankenia grandiflora campestris*) may be called cosmopolitan. **1939** PICKWELL *Deserts* 17/1 One of the commonest [plants] on the mud flats of the Pacific Ocean is Alkali Heath, . . . which has the surface of its leaves covered with salt crystals. — **(4) 1886** *Boston Herald* 16 July, It is only an 'alkali sink'—a natural well, filled with a paste as yielding as water. — **(5) 1918** VISHER *So. Dakota* 27 Small gumbo areas, often popularly called 'alkali spots,' are found here and there even in the glaciated part of the state. **1948** *Dly. Ardmoreite* (Ardmore, Okla.) 30 Mar. 10/2 Long a primary problem to farmers is the appearance of alkali spots after a field has been in cultivation for years.

Also *alkali bed, bottom, cloud, land, marsh, plain, swamp, weed*, etc.

alkalied ˈælkə,laɪd, *a.* Impregnated with or affected by alkali.

1858 STONE *Put's Golden Songster* 53, I joined a train and travelled on . . . Until our grub was nearly gone, And I got alkalied. **1870** BEADLE *Utah* 444 It is only where small streams have run some distance across the plain that they are, in local phrase, 'alkalied.' **1929** A. J. DICKSON *Across Plains* 119 They made a business of buying alkalied or sore footed stock. **1942** LILLIARD *Desert Challenge* 140 A cure for alkalied cattle was a plug of tobacco between two slices of bacon.

***alkaline,** *a.* Used in the West to designate things and places impregnated with alkali, as **alkaline barren, bottom, flat, marsh, plain, seep, sink, slough, soil, valley, water.**

1850 SAWYER *Way Sketches* (1926) 109 Great care should be taken to avoid the alkaline waters found along the route and the animals should never be picketed out upon the low alkaline bottoms, if other grazing can be obtained. **1852** GUNNISON *Mormons* 16 On the south of the lake, and above the alkaline barrens, lie the more fertile valleys of the Jordan and Tuilla. **1862** HAYES *Pioneer Notes* (1929) 279 The exhalations, too, from this damp valley and from an alkaline soil must contribute to influence the atmosphere. **1869** BOWLES *New West* xiv. 277 These alkaline valleys of the Great Interior Basin. **1876** POWELL *Nevada* 211 Their waters . . . leave a thick deposit, which, glittering in large, white sheets over the hollows formerly occupied by the 'lakes,' procures for them, in their dry state, the name of '*alkaline flats*.' **1878** BEADLE *Western Wilds* 105 Salt lakes, alkaline 'sinks' and mud flats alone relieve the dreary monotony. **1886** VAN DYKE *So. Calif.* 125 The coyote is about the same as the coyote of the alkaline plains. **1929** CHALFANT *Death Valley* 123 More than half of the below-sea-level area of Death Valley is covered by a saline or alkaline marsh. **1940** JAEGER *Desert Wild Flowers* 9 Blue-eyed grass . . . is confined to alkaline seeps on the desert. **1946** THOMPSON *Am. Daughter* 163, I was willing to give all the beautiful flowers in St.

Paul for one ragged tumbleweed, all the beautiful lakes in Minnesota for one alkaline slough.

b. alkaline grass, (see quot.).

1889 VASEY *Agric. Grasses* 61 *Distichlis maritima* (Salt grass; Alkaline Grass) . . . is a perennial grass, growing . . . abundantly in alkaline soil throughout the arid districts of the Rocky Mountains.

* **all,** *a.* and *adv.*

1. In combs., chiefly *colloq.:* (1) **all aboard,** see **aboard;** (2) **-aged,** (see quot.); (3) **America(n),** see as a main entry; (4) **around,** good for all purposes or in all respects, also **all-aroundness;** (5) **a-setting,** in good condition, fine; (6) **-a-tanto,** completely, *rare;* (7) **day,** see as a main entry; (8) **face,** naked, *rare;* (9) **get out,** see **get out;** (10) * **in,** extremely weary, worn out; (11) **is,** (see quot. 1914, cf. *EDD all as is*); (12) **nature,** see **nature;** (13) * **of,** as much as, no less than, quite; (14) **outdoors,** see **outdoors;** (15) **overs,** the fidgets or creeps; (16) **rail,** entirely by rail; (17) **set,** see **set,** *a.;* (18) **star,** composed altogether of superior players or performers; (19) **wheat,** concerned only with wheat.

(2) **1905** *Forestry Bureau Bul.* 61 *s.v.* many-aged, A forest through all parts of which many different classes of trees tend to distribute themselves. When all age classes are thus distributed, the forest is all-aged. — (4) **1883** *Harper's Mag.* Aug. 453/1 It is not the best all-around boat. **1888** *Voice* (N.Y.) 6 Sep., Let all good people note the all-aroundness of our chieftain's character. **1920** *Harvey's Weekly* 5 June 4/1 Senator Knox in the best-equipped all-around internationalist.

(5) **1869** in MATHEWS *Beginnings* 155. They halt a few days, and allow the teams to graze undisturbed, which makes them 'all a-setting' again. **1898** HARRIS *Tales* 289 'All a-settin', ma'am!' said the Federal sharpshooter. 'Jest walk this way.' — (6) **1840** CROCKETT *Almanac* 10, I was rigged all-a-tanto. — (8) **1865** SALA *Diary* I. 335 It is true that when they have made you 'all face,' as the Indians say, the Virginian Rapparees will occasionally lend you a coat or a pair of pantaloons of their own, to cover your nakedness.

(10) **1902** A. D. MCFAUL *Ike Glidden* xxii. 201 The horse was holding steady up to his clip, but it could be easily seen that he was 'all in.' **1923** *Nation* 12 Dec. 687/1 If, after six hours' labor, one is 'all in' for the rest of the day, then his effective leisure is less. — (11) **1861** LOWELL *Biglow P.* II. p. lxxviii, All is, he couldn't love em. **1914** *D.N.* IV. 68 all is, conj. Considering every aspect of a matter. '*All is,* she's plumb wuthless.' — (13) **1829** SANDS *Writings* II. 57 They actually appointed a sub-committee, consisting of Miss Cross, who was all of six feet high. **1902** MARK TWAIN in *Harper's Mag.* Feb. 433 'About how far might it be to the scene of the explosion?' 'All of a mile!'

(15) **1884** J. C. HARRIS *Mingo* 127 She looks lonesome, an' she's got one er them kinder fur-away looks in her eyes that gives me the all-overs. **1942** RAWLINGS *C. Creek* 167, I came to Cross Creek with such a phobia against snakes that a picture of one in the dictionary gave me what Martha calls 'the all-overs.' — (16) **1876** *Outlook* (Santa Monica, Calif.) 19 July 3/3 An all-rail connection from Los Angeles to San Francisco now looks like a thing of the near future. **1879** *Lumberman's Gaz.* 3 Dec., This is probably the first all-rail shipment of lumber from the interior of Michigan to a far western State. — (18) **1889** *S.F. Bulletin* 13 July 1/6 Manager Harris' team is not now so much of an 'all star aggregation' now as it was when he first took hold of it. **1946** *Pueblo* (Colo.) *Chieftain* 1 July 6/1 Returned servicemen dominate the National league's all-star squad. — (19) **1884** *Rep. Comm. Agric.* 460 The districts where all-wheat farming is practiced.

b. allthorn, an exceedingly spiny shrub, *Koeberlinia spinosa,* of the southwestern desert region.

1908 HORNADAY *Camp Fires on Desert* 226 Of greater interest than they were the All-Thorn Bushes with large fleshy stems for the storage of water, and many thorns but no leaves. **1942** CASTETTER & BELL *Pima & Papago Agric.* 22 Commonly associated shrubs are lotebush (*Zizyphus lycoides*), skunkbush (*Rhus trilogata*), chamiso, (*Hymenoclea monogyra*), desert saltbush (*Atriplex polycarpa*) and allthorn (*Koeberlinia spinosa*).

2. Used with (1) **alligator,** (2) **horse,** (3) **man,** (4) **soul,** to designate a man or horse of superior strength, skill, tenacity, etc.

(1) **1814** *Analectic Mag.* IV. 63 The Mississippi navigator . . . affirmed himself to be 'all alligator but his head, which was of aquafortis.' — (2) **1860** HOLMES *Professor* vii. 197 It is a common saying of a jockey that he is 'all horse.' **1868** WOODRUFF *Trotting Horse* 50 At ten, you have probably got no horse at all worth mentioning: while mine is now 'all horse,' and in his true prime. — (3) **1895** REMINGTON *Pony Tracks* 77 If a man is to 'hold down' a big ranch in Northern Mexico he has got to be 'all man,' because it is 'a man's job.' — (4) **1831** ROYALL *Southern Tour* II. 44 He is not only all-soul, as the phrase is here [Camden, S.C.], but all heart.

3. Used with **createdly, gortiest, nation, possessed, wrath,** to denote something in the extreme or beyond the ordinary. *Colloq.*

1856 G. D. BREWERTON *War in Kansas* 317 So as I wor all-createdly riled, I jest up an' let 'em hev it. — **1845** J. J. HOOPER *Daddy Biggs' Scrape* 201, I throwed their guns in the roover, besides givin' 'em the all-gortiest scare they ever had. — **1847** *Knickerb.* XXX. 14 With the remark, that it was 'all-nation hot inside the clap-boards.' — **1833** S. SMITH *Life J. Downing* 209 [He] struck his fists together like all possessed. **1916** PORTER *David* 280 He danced and laughed and clapped his hands, . . . an' carried on like all possessed. — **1832** PAULDING *Westward Ho!* II. 182 He held back like all wrath, and wouldn't take any thing. **1857** *S. Lit. Messenger* XXV. 305/2 He will whale you like all wrath.

4. In colloq. phrases: (1) *To be all day with* (a person), to be all over or a hopeless case for one; (2) *all the way from,* the entire distance, within specified limits; (3) *all quiet on the Potomac,* (see quot. 1902,—the phrase is also ascribed to Gen. McClellan in B. Stevenson, *Home Bk. of Quots.,* 65:5); (4) *for all it is (they were) worth,* said with reference to action of a determined or persistent kind; (5) *all wool and a yard wide,* and variants, thoroughly all right, genuine.

(1) **1836** *Knickerb.* VIII. 205 Marlinspike now swore that it was all day with him; and . . . he might as well content himself. **1889** MUNROE *Golden Days* xiv. 153 If you hadn't toed the mark, good and square . . . , 'twould have been all day with me. — (2) **1838** DRAKE *Tales Queen City* 150 Upon the suggestion of a fierce little junior, all the way from Kentucky . . . a new plan . . . was adopted. **1878** BEADLE *Western Wilds* 493 The value of the booty taken has been estimated all the way from $150,000 to $300,000. **1905** *Atlantic Mo.* Nov. 580 The periodicals pay all the way from half a cent to fifteen cents a word. — (3) **1861** E. L. BEERS in *Harper's Wkly.* 30 Nov. 766/1 'All quiet along the Potomac,' they say, 'Except, now and then, a stray picket Is shot, as he walks on his beat to and fro, By a rifleman hid in the thicket.' **1902** CLAPIN *Americanisms* 14 All quiet on the Potomac. A phrase now become famous, and used in jest or ironically as indicative of a period of undisturbed rest, quiet enjoyment, or peaceful possession. It originated with Mr. Cameron, Secretary of War during the Rebellion, who made such a frequent use of it, in his war bulletins, that it became at last stereotyped on the nation's mind. — (4) **1874** MARK TWAIN *Sk., New & Old* 310 We shall fly our comet for all it is worth. **1897** THANET *Missionary Sheriff* 19 Paisley played his cough and his hollow cheeks for all they were worth.

(5) **1882** PECK *Sunshine* 85 You want to pick out (as the 'boss combination girl' of Rock Co.) a thoroughbred, that is, all wool, a yard wide. **1913** LONDON *Valley of Moon* 60 Now you're a live one, all wool, a yard long and a yard wide. **1946** *Chi. D. News* 2 Dec. 31/1 (Comics), A sweeter guy I never worked for. All wool and a yard wide.

As the last term in **carry, catch, cook, over, we-, you-all.**

all-America, *n.* A player, as in football or baseball, regarded as one of the best in the U.S. in his class. Also attrib. or as adj.

1904 *Independent* 27 Oct. 951/1 The selection of 'All-America' teams seems to have become a mania. **1944** *Reader's Digest* Feb. 56 He was persuaded to try football in his last year at Yale, and was chosen as an end on Walter Camp's first All-America eleven. **1947** *Denver Post* 2 Mar. 3E/7 Alex, a three-time all-America at guard, becomes a star in the pro ranks.

b. Also **all-American,** *a.* and *n.*

1888 *Outing* Nov. 166/2 The All-American team . . . is composed of men picked from the ranks of the representative ball teams of America. **1920** *Outing* Nov. 84/3 The little cripple, none other than Eddie Dillon, sometime All-American, caught the ball and ran with it through the entire opposing eleven for another touchdown. **1948** *Atlantic* March 24/1 You can't be an All-American on a losing team.

* **all day.** In combs.: (1) **all day horse,** one capable of working all day, *colloq.;* (2) **singing,** *S.,* a public gathering of persons to sing during a morning and afternoon session; (3) **sucker,** (see quot. 1901).

(1) *a***1870** CHIPMAN *Notes on Bartlett* 5 An all-day horse, etc. — *Ct.* — (2) **1933** JACKSON *White Spirituals* 68 We would have an all day singing and basket dinner but that has played out. **1948** *Carthaginian* (Carthage, Miss.) 19 Aug. 1/7 There will be an all-day singing in the Madison County courthouse next Sunday, August 22. — (3) **1901** *D.N.* II. 134 All-day sucker, n. A piece of candy on small stick to be disposed of by sucking for some time. **1945** *Barnum* (Colo.) *News* 20 July 1/8 Clothes were worn backwards and games and stunts were enjoyed with rules and events being run off in reverse. . . . The prizes, all day suckers, were eaten in the regular way.

Alleghania ˌæləˈgenɪə, *n.* [f. **Alleghany.**] (See quots.) *Obs.* or *hist.*

1839 W. IRVING in *Knickerb.* XIV. 161 We might still use the phrase, 'The United States,' substituting Appalachia, or Alleghania, (I should prefer the latter,) in place of America. **1847** *Daily Union* (Washington, D.C.) 18 Dec. 3/4 Columbia, which had become in some sort the poetic name for the United States, is not sufficiently specific; and Alleghania, which has been proposed, has, besides its unwelcome similarity with alligator, a character of newness without freshness. **1945** STEWART *Names on the Land* 173 Washington Irving proposed Appalachia or Alleghania. Much later the initials of United States of North America were combined to make Usona.

Alleghanian ˌæləˈgenɪən, *n.* and *a.* Also **Allegheni-an.** [See **Alleghany.**]

1. *n.* An inhabitant of the region of the Alleghany Mountains, or of Alleghania. *Obs.* Cf. **trans-Alleghanian.**

1820 (*Newspaper title*), Cumberland Alleghanian. **1839** *Knickerb.* Aug. 161 The title of Appalachian, or Alleghanian, would still announce us as Americans, but would specify us as citizens of the Great republic. ?**1847** HOFFMAN in Barnes *Hoffman* 281 A play to be called The First Alleghanian—or three years in the life of Washington [etc.].

2. *a.* Pertaining to the Alleghany Mountains. Cf. **trans-Alleghanian.**

1819 MEAD *Miss. Scenes* 27 The alleghanean summits rise, Amidst the clouds, and penetrate the skies. **1901** MOHR *Plant Life Ala.* 674 Butterfly Weed . . . [grows in the] Alleghenian, Carolinian, and Louisianian areas. **1942** WEYGANDT *Plenty of Penna.* 121 It is an unsung spectacle of our Alleghanian highlands, that far-spread blowing of shadbush on the mountain-sides this second Sunday of May.

Alleghany ˈæləˌgenɪ, *n.* Also **Allegheny.** [Amer. Indian of doubtful meaning.] The name of mountain ranges in the Appalachian system, and of a river in Pennsylvania, used in combs.: (1) **Alleghany alligator fish,** (see quot.), *obs.;* (2) **hellbender,** a salamander found in the Alleghany River; (3) **Hills,** the Alleghany Mountains; (4) **Indians,** (see quot. 1907); (5) **Mountains,** (see quot.); (6) **plum,** (see quot.); (7) **skiff,** (see quot. 1941); (8) **sloe,** (see quot.); (9) **vine,** the climbing fumitory, *Adlumia fungosa.*

(1) **1807** C. SCHULTZ *Travels* I. 123, I have been well assured that this river produces a fish which, from its resemblance to the alligator, is called the Alleghany alligator fish. — (2) **1842** *Nat. Hist. N.Y., Zoology* III. 89 The Allegany Hell-bender . . . feeds on worms, crayfish, fishes, and aquatic reptiles. — (3) **1818** J. BRISTED *Resources U.S.* 2 On the west by the Rocky Mountains; on the south by the Gulf of Mexico; on the east by the Alleghany Hills. — (4) **1738** *Va. Gazette* 23 June 4/1 An Express came here from *Orange* County . . . That some Indians had lately murder'd Eleven White Persons, . . . and that 'twas believ'd they were *Alleganey Indians.* **1907** HODGE *Indians* I. 45 *Alleghany Indians.* A geographical group, comprising Delawares and Shawnee, residing on Alleghany r. in the 18th century. —Rupp (1756), Northampton, etc., 106, 1845.

(5) **1812** MELISH *Travels* II. 430 By the general term, *Allegany mountains,* is meant the whole chain of mountains extending from the Mississippi Territory to the northern extremity of the union. — (6) **1892** APGAR *Trees Northern U.S.* 98 *Prunus Alleghaniensis,* Porter. (Alleghany Plum.) A low, straggling bush. . . . Mountains of Pennsylvania. — (7) **1884** *Harper's Mag.* June LXIX. 124 Of smaller vessels there were 'covered sleds,' 'ferry flats,' and 'Alleghany skiffs'; 'pirogues' made from two tree trunks, or 'dug-outs' consisting of one. **1941** BALDWIN *Keelboat Age* 42 The smaller bateaux were sometimes called skiffs, and this name was applied occasionally to the larger bateaux, usually with the prefix 'Allegheny' or 'Mackinaw,' which probably had little to do with the origin of the particular boat named. — (8) **1897** SUDWORTH *Arborescent Flora* 238 *Prunus alleghaniensis;* Porter: Alleghany Sloe. — (9) **1850** S. F. COOPER *Rural Hours* 169 Landed and gathered wild flowers . . . and Alleghany vine. *Ib.* 170 The Alleghany vine, with its pale pink clusters and very delicate foliage, is very common in some places. **1892** *Amer. Folk-Lore* V. 92 Allegheny vine [grows in] N. Ohio.

See also **trans-Alleghany.**

Alleghany ˈæləˌgenɪ, *v. tr.* (See quot.) *Obs.* — **1895** J. WINSOR *Mississippi Basin* 176 This 'trusting' process was so common hereabouts that, according to a memorial of some traders who had suffered by French blandishments interfering with the spring payments, it was termed 'Alleghanying' the poor Indians.

∗**Allen,** *n.* [Name of inventor.] Used, usu. in the possessive, in the name of an early type of revolver. *Obs.*

1850 JACKSON *Forty-Niner* (1920) 28 Donovan . . . jumped a claim, and when the rightful owner warned him off he drew an Allen's pepper box. **1864** *Ore. State Jrnl.* 23 April 1/5 The counsel for the prisoner insisted that an Allen's pepper-box was not a deadly weapon. **1906** in *Kansas Hist. Soc.* IX. 510, I got an Allen's revolver that night of Jim Stewart.

∗**alley,** *n.*

1. In some cities a road through the middle of a square or block giving access to the rear of buildings. Cf. **back alley.**

1729 *Baltimore Town Rec.* 10 The commissioners . . . shall cause the same Sixty Acres to be . . . divided into convenient Streets, Lanes, and Allies, as near as may be into Sixty equal lots. **1747** *Ib.* 22 To Survey the Same and lay it out into Lotts with convenient Streets and Alleys. **1809** *Ann. 10th Congress* 2 Sess. 1805 Whenever the proprietor . . . shall . . . subdivide such square or lot into convenient building lots . . . and alleys for their accommodation. **1948** *Democrat* 1 Jan. 4/2 Drivers now can park or back into alleys or up to loading platforms with much greater ease.

2. The space between the rows of a crop.

1833 SILLIMAN *Man. Sugar Cane* 17 There is great danger of disturbing the roots, which . . . extend far into the alleys. **1865** TURNER *Cotton* 133 The beds for cotton, corn, and potatoes, are all made in the same manner and distance apart, and reversed every other crop; that is, changed into the alleys of the proceding one; but no rotation of crops is practiced.

3. In combs.: (1) **alley cat,** a homeless cat that frequents alleys, also transf. in slang use; (2) **pin,** a ten-pin, *rare;* (3) **way,** (*a*) a narrow lane in a town, an alley, (*b*) a narrow passageway in a house.

(1) **1944** JOHNSON *As I Dare* 137 We would write an 'Elegy in a City Back Yard,' mourning the death of an alley cat. **1945** *Chi. D. News* 2 Aug. 10/7 I'm not trying to whitewash the alley-cats among the weekend war brides. **1948** *Chi. Tribune* 30 May IV. 6/3 First we learn of his friendship with an old alley cat. — (2) **1856** *Knickerb.* XLVII. 278 Occasionally the car is brought to a full stop, and the 'standees' are thrown against each other like alley-pins by a 'ten-strike.' — (3) (*a*) **1788** FRENEAU *Misc. Works* 223 The article stipulated expressly, that the alley-way should be sufficient for the passing and repassing of the plaintiff. **1850** C. MATHEWS *Moneypenny* 100 A very mean and low account of a writer who . . . lived in an alley-way. **1945** *Chi. D. News* 8 Dec. 5/2 She ran down her husband with her car, crushing him to death in an alleyway following an argument over a woman. (*b*) **1854** *Harper's Mag.* IX. 849/2, I was taken to the Auburn state-prison. And as I walked along the concealed alley-ways, . . . I bethought me of my theft of fruit. **1926** in *D.N.* V. 385 *Alley-way* (accent first syl.), n. A long hall in a house. 'Hang your coat in the alley-way.' Rare.

b. *To be up* (*down*) *one's alley,* to be entirely in the line of one's interests, wishes, capabilities, etc. Also allusively. *Slang.*

The first and last quots. below suggest that this term may have originated from baseball.

[**1912** *American Mag.* June 199/2 Alley—Imaginary lines between the right and center and right and left fielders down which hard hit balls go between the fielders, usually for home runs. 'Down the Alley' means a home run hit.] **1929** WITWER *Yes Man's Land* 253 Fun's fun, but box-fighting's your trick and anything else is out of your alley. **1944** *Vogue* 1 Oct. 108 Anything related to the making, designing, or repairing of hand-bags is right up Artkraft's alley. [**1947** *Redbook* July 29/1 First, like everybody else in the ball park, I keep at least one eye on the alley between the pitcher's mound and home plate.]

As the last term in **back, ball, broad, fore, gambling, lame duck, tin-pan, tom alley.**

∗**alligator,** *n.*

1. Used as a name or nickname for: **a.** A Mississippi keelboatman, rough-and-ready frontiersman, or Indian fighter, also attrib. *Slang. Obs.* **b.** A member of the Virginia House of Delegates. *Rare.* **c.** A hog of an inferior breed, a razor-back. *Obs.* **d.** *Mining.* (See quot. 1881), also attrib. *Obs.* **e.** (See quot.)

a. 1808 SCHULTZ *Travels* (1810) II. 145 One said, 'I am a man; I am a horse; I am a team. . . . The other replied, 'I am an alligator, half man, half horse; can whip any on the Mississippi, by G——d.' **1825** NEAL *Bro. Jonathan* II. 438 Somewhat o' the alligator tribe. *a***1861** T. WINTHROP *Canoe & Saddle* iii. 49 But the millions of Yankees—from codfish to alligators, . . . know little of these treasures of theirs.

b. *c***1870** BAGBY *Old Va. Gentleman* 290 This bell . . . called the truant 'Alligators' from their haunts in the barrooms and faro-banks when there was a close vote in the General Assembly.

c. 1841 *Cultivator* VIII. 152, I am anxious that he should soon get rid of his land-pikes and alligators at such prices as will enable him to buy a better breed. **1852** *Mich. Agric. Soc. Trans.* III. 332 Swine variously known as narragansetts, alligators, land sharks and flea breeders.

d. 1867 HOLLISTER *Mines of Colo.* 237 'The Hale Gold Mining Company' have here a new large alligator-cracker, Kingsley pulverizer (worthless,) and Keith shaking-table. **1881** RAYMOND *Glossary of Mining,* Alligator. . . . A rock-breaker operating by jaws.

c. **1900** *U.S. Nat. Museum Rep.* 269 [Chuckwallas] are common both along the canyon of the Lower Santa Clara and among the red sandstone cliffs near the village of St. George, and are called 'alligators' by the Mormons.

2. In the names of animals: (1) **alligator fish,** (*a*) an alligator gar, *obs.*, (*b*) (see quot. 1889); (2) **gar,** any one of various freshwater gars of the genus *Atractosteus;* (3) **snapper, terrapin, tortoise,** =next; (4) **turtle,** a snapping turtle, *Macrochelys temmincki*, found chiefly in southern streams.

(1) (*a*) **1772** ROMANS in Phillips *Notes* 124 There is also a fish Called the Gar Fish or Allegator Fish from the Shape of its head and teeth, by the french Called poisson arme, and not ill described by their Writers. (*b*) **1889** *Cent., Alligator fish*, an agonoid fish, *Podothecus acipenserinus*, . . . common from Puget Sound northward. — (2) **1821** in *Texas Hist. Quart.* VII. 300 Found another Karanqua encamp at which was . . . Alligator heads and the skins of Alligator Gars. **1944** *Reader's Digest* July 110 A huge alligator gar rips their nets to pieces, destroying the labor of weeks. — (3) **1884** GOODE *Nat. Hist. Aquat. Animals* 153, I have myself seen an 'Alligator Snapper,' of perhaps forty pounds weight. **1938** MATSCHAT *Suwannee River* 22 Alligator snappers, and cottonmouths inhabit the waters of the marsh. — **1835** SIMMS *Partisan* 317 Three enormous terrapins of that doubtful brood which the vulgar in the southern country describe as the alligator terrapin. **1934** *Nat. Geog. Mag.* LXV. 610 The turtle fauna . . . with aquatic preferences range in size from the musk turtle, with a carapace between three and four inches in length, to the mighty 75-pound alligator terrapin, with a head practically as large as a man's. — **1838** GOSSE *Letters* 98 The name of Snapping Turtle is given to one, but it is frequently called in books the Alligator Tortoise (*Chelydra serpentina*). — (4) **1798** DUNBAR *Life* 92 One of them is called the Alligator Turtle on account of his overgrown head and tail being covered with a species of scales resembling those which form the armour of the Crocodile. **1946** *Outdoor Life* Oct. 124/3 An old alligator turtle may weigh up to 140 lb. and have a shell close to 30 in. long.

b. In the names of shrubs and trees: (1) **alligator (bark) juniper,** an evergreen shrub, *Juniperus pachyphloea*, the bark of which has a checked, warty appearance, found in the Southwest; (2) **tree,** (see quots.).

(1) **1909** *Univ. Ariz. Agric. Exp. Sta. Timely Hints* No. 79, 5 The one-seeded juniper and the Utah juniper, both native to northern Arizona, grow at altitudes somewhat lower than the alligator bark juniper. **1925** BRYAN *Papago Country* 45 With these oaks are associated . . . the Mexican piñon . . . and the alligator juniper. **1947** *Primitive Man* Jan.–Apr. 9 'What kind of juniper? . . . Alligator bark juniper?' he asked. — (2) **1889** *Cent.* 148/3 Alligator-tree. . . . The sweet-gum tree, *Liquidambar Styraciflua*, of the southern United States. **1916** SETON *Woodcraft Man.* 288 Sweet Gum, Star-Leaved, or Red Gum, Bilsted, Alligator Tree, or Liquidambar (*Liquidambar Styraciflua*). A tall tree up to 150 feet high of low, moist woods, remarkable for the corky ridges on its bark, and the unsplitable nature of its weak, warping, perishable timber.

c. In miscellaneous combs.: (1) **alligator boat,** (*a*) a boat towed by an alligator or alligators, *humorous* and *obs.*, (*b*) a boat facetiously alleged to be used for dredging alligators out of the Mississippi River, a Mark Twainism; (2) **grip,** a handbag or valise made of alligator hide; (3) **gun,** a gun of large caliber suitable for shooting alligators; (4) **hole,** the nest or hibernating place of alligators; (5) **horse,** = **half horse half alligator,** *obs.;* (6) **swamp,** a swamp infested with alligators; (7) ***tooth,** (see quot.), *obs.*

(1) (*a*) **1844** *Spirit of Times* (Phila.) 10 Sep. (Th.), It takes a man . . . to ride one of these here alligator boats head on to a sawyer. (*b*) **1883** MARK TWAIN *Life Mississippi* xxiv. 230 He . . . observed that it was an 'alligator boat.' — (2) **1907** W. LILLIBRIDGE *Trail* 173 A dapper commercial salesman with an imitation alligator grip. — (3) **1856** PHILLIPS *Kansas* 285 Queer-looking, alligator guns these were, for we recaptured some of them when the war broke out. — (4) **1791** W. BARTRAM *Travels* (1793) 236 Our chief conducted me another way to show me a very curious place, called the Alligator Hole. **1842** BUCKINGHAM *Slave States* I. 155 In their retreats, or nests, called alligator-holes, as large a brood as a hundred are seen at a time. [**1944** BARBOUR *Eden* 189 The gator scoops out a hole of some considerable depth and in one side of this hole he forms his cave, a refuge where he may retire for rest by day or during cold weather.]

(5) **1826** S. WOODWORTH *Melodies* 221 We'll show him that Kentucky boys Are 'alligator horses.' **1850** *Quincy* (Ill.) *Whig* 9 Apr. 4/1 'Eh! hem, a horse, eh!' said the Judge. 'Yes, sir, an alligator horse.' — (6) [**1788** SCHÖPF *Reise* II. 154 Eine beruffene Gegend . . . ist der Dismal Swamp, auch great Dismal Swamp genannt, zum Unterschied des Alligator Dismal Swamp's [*sic*], welcher unweit von jenem in Nordkarolina zwischen Albermarle und Pemtikoe [*sic*]-Sound lieget.] **1842** in *Amer. Sp.* XVIII. 119 He would not have fought like a devil, with the Spaniards, to maintain an alligator swamp. **1907** COOK *Border & Buffalo* (1938) 40, I brought from cypress and alligator swamps of the South a case of malarial fever that tenaciously stayed in my system for four months. — (7) **1856** *Mich. Agric. Soc. Trans.* VII. 629 Alligator tooth, by S. B. Scranton. This tooth was one of a number designed to be used on marshes for tearing down the bogs and making them smooth.

Also *alligator bag, boot, cave, hide, hunt, leather, season, shooting, skin, steak, tail*, etc. For *alligator bed, pilot, reef, water,*—humorous nonce uses by Mark Twain, see Ramsay.

As the last term in **all, bull, cow, half, jumping, Mississippi, prairie alligator.**

alligatoring ˈæləˌgetərɪŋ, *n.* The cracking of paint, varnish, etc. caused by contraction. — **1911** *Engin. News* (N.Y.) 27 July 121 Many of the paints which lack any evidence of cracking, checking, or alligatoring.

alligatorism ˈæləˌgetərɪzəm, *n.* [See ***alligator 1. a.**] Roughness of character. *Obs.* — **1830** *Columbia Co. Register* (Bloomsburg, Penna.) 7 Sep. 1/4 Each party kept a half dozen bullies under pay—genuine specimens of Kentucky Alligatorism—to flog every poor fellow that would attempt to vote illegally.

allocochick ˈæləkəˌtʃɪk, *n.* [f. the native name.] (See quot. 1909.) Cf. **hiaqua.**

1851 in SCHOOLCRAFT *Indian Tribes* (1853) III. 142 This, under the name of the 'ali-qua-chick,' or Indian money, is more highly valued among them than any other article. **1872** *Overland Mo.* Apr. 329/2 This

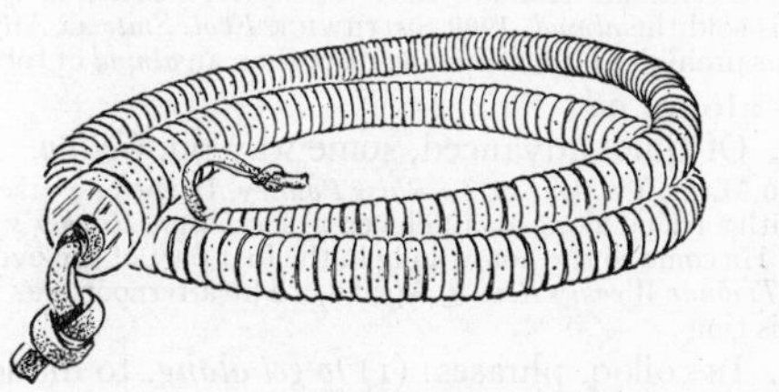

Allocochick, hiaqua, or shell money

shell money is called *álli-cochick*, not only on the Klamath, but from Crescent City to Eel River, though the tribes using it speak several different languages. **1909** *Cent. Supp.* 33/2 Allocochick. . . . The name of Indian shell-money used in northern California.

allotter əˈlatɚ, *n.* One of a group consisting of Gov. Winthrop and six others appointed at a general meeting in Boston, in Nov. 1634, to divide and dispose of all lands not already lotted out, to the inhabitants of the town according to the orders of the court. *Obs.* — **1635** *Boston Rec.* 5 That none shall sell their houses or allotments to any new comers, but with the consent and allowance of those that are appointed allotters. *Ib.* 7 Four of them shall, by the assignments of the Allotters, lay out their proportion of allotments for farmes att Rumley Marsh.

***allspice,** *n.* As the last term in **Carolina, Japan allspice.**

***alluvial,** *a.*

1. alluvial cone, fan, a fan-shaped deposit made by a stream at a place where its velocity is suddenly decreased.

1913 MEINZER & KETTON *Geol. Sulphur Springs Valley* 23 Instead of excavating for themselves definite stream valleys they build alluvial slopes, or fans, over which they spread. **1939** *Southwestern Lore* Sep. 29 Caves seen in this region were of two varieties, actual solution caves in sandstone and tunnels formed when talus slides or alluvial-cone material buries a gully. **1948** *Sierra Club Bul.* March 42 We find desert conditions and desert plants reaching the base of the eastern escarpment, advancing into the canyons along alluvial fans, and even mounting the rocky slopes.

2. alluvial way, (see quot.). *Obs.*

1824 TALBOT *Residence* II. 313 The road from Lewiston to Rochester is commonly called 'the Ridge Road,' or 'the Alluvial Way.'

alluviation əˌluvɪˈeʃən, *n.* [f. **alluviate v.*] The process of depositing alluvium. — **1847** C. LANMAN *Summer in Wild.* xxii. 132 They have been striped with various colors by mineral alluviations. **1877** GILBERT *Geol. Henry Mts.* 139 The same may be said of the changes by planation and alluviation. In each case . . . the watershed makes a leap.

***alluvion,** *n.* =**intervale.** *Obs.* — **1814** BRACKENRIDGE *Views La.* 158 The prairies or savannas, and alluvia, scarcely constitute the other two-fifths of the state. **1838** H. COLMAN *Mass. Agric. Rep.* (1839) 9 There are extended alluvions or intervales, which furnish a productive soil.

almighty dollar. The dollar thought of as "that great object of universal devotion" on the part of Americans.

1836 IRVING in *New Yorker* 12 Nov. 115 In a word, the almighty dollar, that great object of universal devotion throughout our land, seems to have no genuine devotees in these peculiar villages. **1857** *Phoenix* (Sacramento) 30 Aug. 4/3 In dreams they nod, and mutter 'God,' but mean the Almighty dollar. **1948** *Newsweek* 5 Jan. 56/1 Something had happened to his standard of value—the almighty dollar—which deeply disturbed him.

b. Alluded to in various expressions (see quots.).

1855 *Monterey* (Calif.) *Sentinel* 23 June 3/4 To-day is 'steamer day' every body is astir—the immortal dollar is jingling. **1866** *Beadle's Mo.* June 494/1 Even the Indian . . . is moved by the almighty dollar, or, rather, by the almighty half-dollar, for that is the only denomination of specie in which he will receive payments. **1884** *Las Vegas* (N.M.) *Gaz.* 6 Dec. 4/1 [The] street car driver made [him] walk up to the front of the car like a little man and deposit the almighty nickel in the box. **1947** *Time* 16 June 33/1 There is a limit to the sacrifices some Britons would make for the sake of the almighty greenback.

***almond,** *n.* As the last term in **laurel, Laurier, pine, soft-shelled almond.**

almond pine. (See quot.) *Obs.* — **1709** LAWSON *Carolina* 89 The small Almond-Pine . . . bears Kernels in the Apple, tasting much like an Almond. *Ib.* 98 The almond-pine serves for masts very well.

almud æl'mud, n. *S.W.* [Sp.] A dry measure of about a peck. *Obs.* — **1849** AUDUBON *Western Journal* (1906) 113 Beans are seventy-five cents an 'Almud.' **1864** *Weekly New Mexican* 4 Nov. 1/3 Corn is sold the *almud.* **1900** SMITHWICK *Evol. State* 42 Any one person was prohibited from planting more than an *almud* of tobacco seed.

***along,** *adv.*

1. Of time: advanced, some way on. *Colloq.*

*c***1870** MARK TWAIN *Sk., To Raise Poultry,* In the one case you start out with a friend along about eleven o'clock. **1886** *Harper's Mag.* Oct. 808/1 He come to the house 'long in the fust part of the evenin'. **1902** *N.Y. Tribune Weekly Rev.* 26 April 8/2 The afternoon was well along by this time.

2. In colloq. phrases: (1) *to get along,* to manage with at least some success, make a go of; (2) *to be along,* to arrive, come to a place; (3) *along back,* some time ago, recently; (4) *right along,* continuously, without interruption.

(1) **1830** S. SMITH *Lett. J. Downing* (1834) 34, I wish you'd write me . . . whether you think I could get along with the business [of Governorship]. **1896** J. C. HARRIS *Sister Jane* 5 She expressed supreme contempt for men who had no knack of getting along in the world. — (2) **1831** HOLLEY *Texas-Letters* (1833) 21 The captain . . . sent word that he would be along for us about sun-set. **1903** O. HENRY *Roads of Destiny* 107 'It'll be along,' said this queer Mr. Kearny; 'it'll be along on the beams of my bright but not very particular star.' — (3) **1851** N. KINGSLEY *Diary* 165 Worked as usual today, took-out 50 ounces and 4 dollars, which gains on our days along back. **1894** WILKINS *Pembroke* iii. 51, I've made up my mind that I've made a mistake along back. — (4) **1856** *Mich. Agric. Soc. Trans.* VII. 806 The result was, his corn grew right along, for it could not help it. **1906** *Springfield W. Republican* 25 Jan. 1 Public interest in the automobile is increasing right along.

***alphabet,** *n.* As the last term in **Cherokee, Deseret, Morse alphabet.**

***alpine,** *a.* In the names of plants and trees found in the Rocky Mountain region: (1) **alpine columbine,** a blue-flowered columbine, *Aquilegia coerulea,* the state flower of Colorado; (2) **fir,** a tall fir, *Abies lasiocarpa,* valued as a timber tree; (3) **hemlock,** a hemlock, *Tsuga mertensiana,* that yields valuable timber.

(1) **1922** *Outing* Apr. 295/3 The first part of her journey is over a grassy mountain meadow amid . . . the contrasting brilliant colors of the Alpine Columbine, Fringed Gentians, . . . Daisies and Buttercups. **1938** THOMPSON *High Trails* 86 In the alpine meadows we find . . . the alpine columbine and wild heliotrope. — (2) **1914** CLEMENTS *Rocky Mt. Flowers* 60 These [trees] are the Engelmann spruce, limber pine, Alpine fir, arctic willow, black birch, and quaking aspen. **1940** *Mt. Hood Guide* 12 The Alpine fir lifts tall and narrow amid the other evergreens near timberline. — (3) **1902** *Out West* Aug. 349 Inclosed by firs, . . . And alpine hemlocks 'gainst the mountain wall, A meadow lies, that holds my soul in thrall. **1940** *Mt. Hood Guide* 65 The Forest Service road passes through scattered reproduction of Alpine hemlock.

Also, in botanical books, *alpine azalea, enchanter's nightshade, hair grass, willow-herb,* etc.

also ran, *n. phr.* A nonentity. *Slang.* — **1904** *Cin. Enquirer* 6 Feb. 13/3 (*heading*), George B. Cox—He Heads The List Of Also Rans. **1945** *La Junta* (Colo.) *Tribune-Democrat* 3 March 2/4 Within a few hours some would be glorious in victory . . . some would be colorless 'also rans.'

***altar,** *n.* An inclosed area or platform immediately in front of the minister's stand or pulpit in an open-air religious service. Also attrib. *Obs.*

1820 FLINT *Letters* 236 The little inclosure, so often mentioned, is by the religious called *Altar,* and some scoffers are wicked enough to call it *Pen,* from its similarity to the structures in which hogs are confined. Its area was covered over with straw, in some parts more wetted than the litter of a stable. **1874** E. EGGLESTON *Circuit Rider* 204 [He] invited the penitents into the enclosed pen-like place called the *altar.* **1877** HABBERTON *Jericho Road* 127 In response to an exhortation, several persons had knelt at wooden benches inside the altar-rail. *Ib.* 128 There, on the altar-steps stood a man.

***alter,** *v. tr.* To castrate or spay. *Colloq.* — **1821** T. B. HAZARD *Nailer Tom's Diary* (1930) 555/2 Worner Knowles olterd my four Boar Piggs. **1852** *Florida Plant. Rec.* 62, I have sheared the sheep and altered the Lambs. **1948** *Dly. Racing Form* 29 June 2/2 One source of never ending amazement to a ranking Australian breeder was our failure to alter a larger percentage of male youngsters.

***alternate,** *n.* One chosen to act in place of a delegate at a political convention, etc., in case of the absence of the other.

1848 *N.Y. Wkly. Tribune* 26 Feb. 4/1 *Resolved,* That the Chair appoint a Committee . . . to report to this Convention thirty-six delegates to the National Convention; also an alternate to each delegate. **1888** BRYCE *Amer. Commonw.* II. lxix. 542 If the delegate is present to vote the alternate is silent; if from any cause the delegate is absent, the alternate steps into his shoes. **1948** *Chi. Tribune* 20 June 1. 1/1 More than 2,000 delegates and alternates . . . are in Philadelphia today for the 24th Republican national convention.

***alum,** *n.* In combs.: (1) **alum basket,** (see quot.), *obs.;* (2) **root,** any one of several North American plants of the genus *Heuchera,* having roots that are astringent; (3) **salt,** rock salt resembling alum; (4) **spring,** ?a spring whose waters are impregnated with salt; (5) **war,** a controversy over the healthfulness of baking powder, *obs.*

(1) **1883** MARK TWAIN *Life on Miss.* xxxviii. 404 Three 'alum' baskets of various colors—being skeleton-frame of wire, clothed-on with cubes of crystallized alum in the rock-candy style. — (2) **1813** MUHLENBERG *Cat. Plants* 29 American Heuchera (alum root) . . . Pens. fl. Maio. **1947** *Midland Naturalist* July 44 Alumroot [is] rare in bottomland forest and bluff forest. — (3) **1781** *Virginia State P.* I. 610 Small vessels with . . . a cargoe of Alum Salt . . . run up the Different Rivers & trade as friends. **1856** *Rep. Comm. Patents: Agric.* 311 A strong brine . . . made from good rock or alum salt. — (4) **1835** in *S. Lit. Messenger* IV. 517/1 The place selected is famous as the site of an alum spring of great power. — (5) **1904** *McClure's Mag.* April 593 Thus was begun the 'Alum War,' famous in chemistry, journalism, and legislation.

alumna ə'lʌmnə, *n. pl.* **-nae.** [L., fem. of *alumnus.*] A female pupil, esp. a graduate of a school or college.

1882 M. HARLAND *Eve's Daughters* 177 The statistics of the comparative death-rates of the Alumnæ and Alumni of Oberlin. **1910** *Vassar College Cat.* 3 The editors . . . have tried to obtain the information necessary for a complete record of the alumnae. **1946** *Chi. D. News* 20 May 13/7 She is an alumna of Wilson College in Chambersburg, Pa.

attrib. **1896** *Century Mag.* March 798/1 The average salary of the alumna teacher would be below rather than above $1000 a year. **1944** *Evanston Review* 2 Oct. 12/3 Members of the Northwestern chapter of Delta Omicron, music sorority, were guests of the North Shore Alumnae association.

***alumnus,** *n. pl.* **-ni.**

1. One who has been in attendance at, or graduated by, a particular university, college, or high school.

1696 SEWALL *Diary* I. 435 Lt. Govr. . . . promised his Interposition for them, as become such an Alumnus to such an Alma Mater. **1815** *Mass. H. S. Proc.* 2 Ser. V. 180 The oldest alumnus at Com[mencement] of whom I heard was Mr. Henry Hill (1756). **1855** *Harvard Mag.* I. 413 Speculations too abstruse for an Undergraduate to write or an Alumnus to understand. **1946** *Newsweek* 6 May 89/1 English High School in Boston . . . will mark the milestone on May 8 with a dinner for 2,500 alumni.

b. A former member, as of a baseball team. *Colloq.*

1948 *N.Y. Times* 9 May v. 5/2 Kirbe Higbee, another Dodger alumnus, came rushing to Lombardi's relief.

2. Used, esp. in the plural, in combs.; (1) **alumni day,** (see quots.); (2) **alumni professor,** a professor whose employment is made possible by gifts from the alumni; (3) **alumnus orator,** an orator or speaker selected from the alumni; (4) **alumni trustee,** (see quot.).

(1) **1906** *Springfield W. Republican* 28 June 10 Tuesday was alumni day at Yale, when hundreds of old graduates . . . gathered in alumni hall. **1942** *Bul. Vanderbilt U.* 38 The Alumni Association holds its annual meeting in Alumni Memorial Hall on the Saturday preceding Commencement. This day is termed Alumni Day on the University Calendar. — (2) **1890** S. W. NORTON in McLaughlin *Higher Educ. Mich.* (1891) 131 The faculty [of Hillsdale College] at present . . . consists of . . . Samuel Wilber Norton, acting alumni professor of rhetoric. — (3) **1843** HOPKINS in Hall *College Words* (1851) 8 Last year, for the first time, the voice of an Alumnus orator was heard at Harvard and at Yale. — (4) **1942** *Bul. Vanderbilt U.* 38 Every two years, each member of the Association in good standing may vote for the nomination of at least two alumni trustees on the Board of Trust of the University.

Also *Alumni Society, alumni banquet, dinner, meeting, song, weekly,* etc.

ama ˈɑmɑ, *n. S.W.* [Sp. in same sense.] The mistress of a house. *Rare.* — **1863** *Rio Abajo Press* 28 April 1 Señora Tules went to the ama's room to ask what time your honor's supper should be served.

amalgamationist əˌmælgəˈmeʃənɪst, *n.* One who favors amalgamation, or the union of the black and white races. Cf. **pan amalgamation.** — **1838** H. MARTINEAU *Western Travel* I. 229 You are an amalgamationist! cried she. I told her that the party term was new to me. . . . He had heard . . . that I was an amalgamationist. **1892** J. D. COX in *Atlantic Mo.* March 386/1 The charge that abolitionists were incendiaries and amalgamationists.

***amalgamator,** *n.* **1.** An amalgamationist. *Obs.* **2.** One who tends an amalgamating machine. Cf. **pan amalgamator.** — (1) **1865** *Atlantic Mo.* XV. 508 A lank Virginian . . . began pitching into me on the subject of 'Northern amalgamators.' — (2) **1882** *Rep. Precious Metals* 529 Mill: General foreman . . . Wood helpers, Amalgamators. **1936** DRURY *Editor on Comstock* 21 Their hundred helpers are catalogued in due order—superintendents, shift bosses, . . . battery-men, amalgamators, bulkheaders, fusemakers, wood passers, wire rope workers, giraffe-men, pilers, sluicers.

Amana Society. [f. *Amana*, a mountain mentioned in Song of Solomon iv. 8.] (See quot. 1909.) Cf. **Ebenezer Society.**

1885 *Outing* July 414/2 This is South Amana, one of the towns of the Amana Society. **1909** WEBSTER, Amana Society. . . . A religious and communistic society, consisting of several so-called *True Inspiration Congregations*, at Amana and elsewhere in Iowa county, Iowa. They came originally from Germany, and first settled near Buffalo, N.Y., from about 1842 to 1855. **1947** *Chi. Tribune* 8 June v. 12/5 Visitors to the seven cooperative villages of the Amana society, Amana, Iowa, are quick to note the air of tranquility that prevails over the colonies, said to be the only ones of their types in the United States.

b. Also **Amana colony, communist.**

1875 NORDHOFF *Communistic Societies U.S.* 37 The civil or temporal government of the Amana communists consists of thirteen trustees, chosen annually by the male members of the society. **1908** BAKER *Timber of Iowa* 19 The Amana colony, in Iowa County, has several large groves of white pine.

Amanite ˈæməˌnaɪt, *n.* [See **Amana Society.**] A member of an Amana organization. *Obs.* — **1901** *World's Work* Oct. 1257/2 Originally persecuted Pietists from Hesse, the Amanites to the number of 800 founded Ebenezer Community in New York in 1843.

amapola ˌɑmɑˈpolə, *n. S.W.* [Sp. in similar sense.] One of various wild poppies. — **1915** ARMSTRONG *Western Wild Flowers* 164 It is the State flower of California and has many poetic Spanish names, such as Torosa, Amapola, and Dormidera. **1920** RICE *Calif. Wild Flowers* 23 The sun-gold flower they 'Amapola' named. **1946** MCATEE *Local Names Plants* 10 *Argemone alba* Lestiboudis.—Amapola (Sp.) Southwest.

amargoso ˌɑməˈgoso, *n. S.W.* [Sp. in the Amer. Sp. sense shown here.] (See quot. 1889 in **b.**)

1885 HAVARD *Flora W. & S. Texas* 515 *Castela erecta* . . . the Amargoso of the Mexicans, . . . [is] common on the gravelly bluffs of the Lower Rio Grande. **1891** COULTER *Botany West. Texas* 55 The bark is intensely bitter and is much used in medicine by the Mexicans, who call it 'amargoso.' **1942** FRIEND *Plants for Rio Grande Valley* 53 Amargosa [is] a spiny native shrub that produces gray branches, small, dark green lanceolate leaves and small, four petal, red flowers.

b. Also **amargoso bark, bush.**

1878 *Proc. U.S. Nat. Museum* I. 122 This little bird was perched upon the topmost twig of an amargosa bush. **1889** *Cent.* 165/3 Amargoso-bark. . . . The bark of the goatbush, *Castela erecta*, a simarubaceous shrub of the Lower Rio Grande valley in Texas and of northern Mexico. It is intensely bitter, and is used by the Mexicans as an astringent, a tonic, and a febrifuge.

amazing əˈmezɪŋ, *adv.* [f. the adj.] Wonderfully; marvelously. *Colloq.* — **1805** in CRISWELL *Lewis & Clark* 8 In the afternoon their arose a storm of hard wind and rain and amazeing large hail. **1878** *Harper's Mag.* Sep. 574 Parson he reckoned he'd be amazin' forehanded this year.

***Amazon,** *n.* Designating a woman's bonnet of a type now undefinable and obs. — **1843** *Niles' Reg.* 6 May 160/1 Amazone bonnets . . . are altogether American, really beautiful and becoming.

***amber,** *n.*

1. amber-jack. a. A variety of yellow blende or blackjack. **b.** An amber-fish.

(a) **1888** *Harper's Mag.* June 48/1 Along the line of Spring River, lead, . . . galena, and zinc, as blende or black-jack and amber-jack, are abundant. (b) **1897** *Outing* Jan. 330/2 Not inferior to the kingfish for sport is the amber fish, or amberjack. *Ib.*, The amberjack . . . loves warm water, and . . . swarms in the neighborhood of Palm Beach. **1946** *Outdoors* May 51/1 Amberjack is a salt water fish of Florida and the tropics.

2. Amber Stream, (see quot.). *Obs.*

1841 CIST *Cincinnati* 66 This amber-colored loam imparts its tinge to the waters of the Ohio during its floods, and has given origin to the poetical name of the 'Amber Stream.'

***ambition,** *n.* (See 1st quots.) *Colloq.*

1826 *Va. Herald* 19 Aug. 1/4 Ambition, is used to express malice—an ambitious man means in common parlance a vindictive man. **1848** BARTLETT 9 In North Carolina this word is used instead of the word *grudge*, as, 'I had an ambition against that man.' I am credibly informed that it is even used in this manner by educated men. **1901** *Scribner's Mag.* April 395/1 His friends . . . kept urging him to revenge. A woman wanted them to stop. 'Hit jes' raises the ambition in him and don't do no good nohow.'

***ambitious,** *a.* (See quot. 1906.) — **1837** BIRD *Nick of Woods* I. 26 The fight had made him as ambitious as a wild-cat. **1906** *D. N.* III. 220 *ambitious, adj.* Mettlesome; full of animal spirits. [fr. N.W. Ark.]

***ambrosia,** *n.* **1.** Indian corn meal. *Obs.* **2.** (See quots.) Also **ambrosia beetle.**

(1) *c*1880 HAZARD *Jonny-Cake Papers* (1915) 61 Corn biscuit, or pound cake, another Indian meal luxury, used to be made with one pound of butter, one pound of sugar, ten eggs, and a pint of new milk, with enough ambrosia to mould it into thin cakes. — (2) **1896** *U.S. Dept. Agric. Year-bk.* 421 Their food consists not of wood, but of a substance to which the name ambrosia has been given, and which is a coating formed by a certain minute fungi and propagated on the walls of their galleries by the beetles. **1909** *Cent. Supp.* 39/1 Ambrosia-beetle. . . . Any one of a group of beetles of the family *Scolytidae*, which burrow in the wood of different trees, and in their burrows cultivate cergain fungi known as *ambrosia*. . . . Thirty species belonging to 6 genera in the United States are known to have this habit. **1948** BOYCE *Forest Pathology* 440 For the first three seasons of exposure most of the loss was occasioned by blue stain and ambrosia-beetle borings in the sapwood.

ambrotype ˈæmbrəˌtaɪp, *n.* [Gr. *ambro*tos, immortal, +*type*.] A type of photograph made by the collodion process. Also attrib.

1855 RICHARDS *V. Life* (1912) 62, I received a letter from my brother John in New Orleans, and his ambrotype. He has grown amazingly. **1858** *Spirit of Times* 20 Feb. 389/2 We rushed into friend Collogan's Ambrotype Saloon, in order that the sun might decide the question. **1904** WALLER *Wood-carver* 133, I wished I'd hed one er them new-fangled ambrotype boxes that the folks had up here. **1948** *Ore. Hist. Mag.* March 35 For three ambrotypes taken of Judge Olney he received one of those now out-of-date fifty dollar slugs.

ambrotypic ˌæmbrəˈtɪpɪk, *a.* [f. prec.] After the manner of an ambrotype. *Obs.* — **1861** *Ill. Agric. Soc.* IV. 264, I give a voice to a few thoughts ambrotypic of what the working-man is, and what he ought to be.

***ambulance,** *n.*

1. *W.* A passenger vehicle somewhat resembling a hospital ambulance. Now *hist.* Cf. **Dougherty wagon.**

1856 *N.Y. Herald* 9 Jan. 2/1 The vehicle, which, like most ambulances, or 'prairie wagons,' as they call them here, proved rather airy, was made comfortable by wrapping ourselves in buffalo robes and moccasins. **1899** T. HALL *Tales* 95 Once in a while she caught sight of a muffled figure in an ambulance that stopped for water for its thirsty mules. **1943** WOOD *W. Reed* 92 The road had turned out to be so rough that any progress faster than a walk threatened to shake both the ambulance (as the doherty wagon was also called) and its occupants apart.

2. ambulance chaser, (see quot. 1897). Also **ambulance chasing.**

1897 *Cong. Rec.* 24 July 2961/1 In New York City there is a style of lawyers known to the profession as 'ambulance chasers,' because they are on hand wherever there is a railway wreck, or a street-car collision, or a gasoline explosion with . . . their offers of professional service. **1937** *N.Y. Times* 1 Feb. 21/8 Part of the ambulance chasing and part of the disgraceful fake claims record is undoubtedly due to the fact that many companies make it a practice of settling the unfounded claim just to get rid of it. **1948** *Sat. Ev. Post* 8 May 129/2 He happened upon one of the ambulance-chasing types who started stirring up as much trouble as possible.

ambuscader ˌæmbəsˈkedɚ, *n.* [f. ∗*ambuscade, v.*] One who lies in ambush. *Obs.* — **1676** *Maine Doc. Hist.* VI. 152 There wilbe more danger of ambushcaders. **1775** ADAIR *Indians* 258 Perhaps, they are the most artful ambuscaders, and wolfish savages, in America.

∗**amen,** *n.* ∗**amen corner,** in some Protestant churches the corner immediately to the right of the pulpit formerly occupied by those who often expressed assent to the preacher's utterances. Also transf. and fig.

1860 *Harper's Mag.* Jan. 279/2 The Rev. Judson Noth, a local Methodist preacher, . . . was one of the best 'scotchers' that occupied the 'Amen Corner.' **1884** *Cong. Rec.* 24 April 3207/1 When commiserated upon the fact that he was compelled to go to what is commonly known here as the amen corner, [he] frankly said that any seat in the Senate was better than none. **1894** *Cong. Rec.* 24 Jan. 1502/2 One of those saintly Republican monopolists who sit in the 'Amen corner' of protected privilege. **1946** THOMPSON *Am. Daughter* 127 Ed Smith sat in the Amen corner and laughed softly to himself most of the service.

b. amen seat, a seat in the amen corner.

1876 HABBERTON *Jericho Road* xiv. 128 In an 'amen' seat sat an old half-breed.

amendatory əˈmɛndəˌtorɪ, *a.* [f. *amend, v.* possibly influenced by *emendatory.*] In the nature of an amendment. — **1790** MACLAY *Deb. Senate* 285 The message accompanying the proclamation calls for an amendatory law. **1803** *Ann. 7th Congress* 2 Sess. 603 Mr. Bayard . . . reported an amendatory bill; which was read twice. **1882** *National Bank Act* 77 That Congress may at any time amend, alter, or repeal this act and the acts of which this is amendatory.

∗**amendment,** *n.*

1. An additional piece of land, an addition. *Obs.*

1738 *Southampton Rec.* III. 125 The amendment . . . begins at the above sd. pine tree. *Ib.*, Two little hommocks . . . of segg at the S end of the amendment. *Ib.* 127 We proseded to lay out the Seder swamps for amendments to several of the poor lots.

2. An article added to the Constitution of the U.S. Cf. **mendment.**

1787 *Constitution* v., The Congress, whenever two thirds of both Houses shall deem it necessary, shall propose Amendments to this Constitution, or . . . shall call a Convention for proposing Amendments. **1834** *Advocate* (Shelbyville, Ky.) 4 Jan. 2/2 A resolution proposing an amendment to the Constitution of the United States, limiting the term of service of the President to a single term of six years, will probably pass the present Congress. **1943** OTTLEY *New World* 22 Ratification of the Thirteenth Amendment (1865), . . . gave friends of the Negro a sense of security.

As the last term in **constitutional, eighteenth, fifteenth, fourteenth, lame duck, prohibition, senate, slavery amendment.**

∗**America,** *n.*

1. The United States of America.

1781 WITHERSPOON *Druid P.* No. v., Some observations upon the present state of the English language in America. **1791** *Gazette U.S.* (Phila.) 16 Feb. 3/1 *America* is used very generally both by writers and public speakers, when they only intend the territory of the United States. . . . It may have first come into use as being much shorter to say *Americans*, than citizens of the United States: Some use Atlantic America for the United States—others United America—the last is the most proper. **1877** *Galaxy* XXIV. 379/1 Let us, however, for the sake of our examination, accept the limitation of the word 'America' to the United States of that name. **1945** *Wray* (Colo.) *Gazette* 22 Nov. 1/3 When he was 25, Mr. Peters came to America and made his home with a brother in Collinsville, Illinois.

b. Formerly used in the "Far West" for the eastern states or those east of the Mississippi.

1857 S. Oregon writer in *N.Y. Tribune* (Th.), [Some people here] are talking of going back to America. **1867** HOSMER *Trip to States by Way Yellowstone & Mo.* 10 We loafed around until three o'clock when most of the boats arrived and then we all set sail for America. **1931** WILLISON *Here They Dug Gold* 50 On every canvas top can still be read *Pikes Peak or Bust!* But to this has been added *Busted, by God!*—or some such sentiment as *Bound for America!*

2. A national hymn of the U.S. the words of which were written in 1832 by S. F. Smith.

1832 S. F. SMITH (title), *America.* **1907** *Washington Star* 30 Sep. 1 As he [the President] neared the school building the 1,700 children, grouped and dressed to represent the national flag, arose in a body and sang 'America.' **1948** *Time* 8 Mar. 21/1 The President . . . stopped to greet some 200 children who welcomed him by singing *America.*

3. America's cup, (see quot. 1851).

[**1851** *Living Age* 4 Oct. 42/2 The telegraphic despatch which appeared in *The Times* this morning stated the 'great fact' that the America had beaten the yachts which started against her on Friday for the Royal Yacht Club Cup of 100*l* value, in the most complete and triumphant manner.] **1885** *Sat. Review* 29 Aug. 289 Mr. Ashbury, after sailing the *Cambria* against the *Sappho* in English waters, . . . sailed against a fleet of American yachts for the *America*'s Cup. **1946** ADAMS *Album Amer. Hist.* III. 253 The *America*, which won 'America's Cup' in 1851, had served as a Confederate dispatch boat and had been captured during the War.

As the last term in **British, mid-, Miss, Russian, Sons of, South, Spanish, Young America.**

∗**American,** *n.*

1. A citizen of the United States, or the earlier British colonies included in these, not belonging to one of the aboriginal races.

?**1697** C. MATHER *Magnalia* (1855) I. 33 One poor feeble American, . . . capable of touching this work no otherwise than in a digression. **1782** J. H. ST. JOHN *Lett.* 53 The American is a new man, who acts upon new principles. **1887** DEPEW *Orations & Sp.* (1890) 85 The uprising which followed the guns of Sumter . . . expressed the value placed by Americans upon their institutions, their Constitution, and their liberty. **1947** *Reader's Digest* June 33/1 Coca-Cola, the world's best known commercial product, is older than nine out of ten Americans.

b. A member or supporter of the American party *q.v.*

1855 *Harper's Mag.* XI. 544/1 In North Carolina the Democrats are believed to have elected six of the eight Members of Congress, the Americans electing the other two. **1884** BARNES *Thurlow Weed* 224 An elaborate code of signals and passwords was adopted, and all operations of the 'Americans' were wrapped in profound secrecy. **1948** *Time* 12 Jan. 12/3 The Americans or 'Know-Nothings' . . . carried six states in 1854.

2. The English language as used in the United States. Cf. **American English, American language.**

[**1782** CHASTELLUX *Voyages dans l'Amérique* (1786) II. 202 Aussi évitoient-ils d'employer ces expressions: *vous parlez bien anglois, vous entendez bien l'anglois.* Je les ai entendus dire souvent: *vous parlez bien américain, l'américain n'est pas difficile à apprendre.*] **1799** DAVIS *Travels* (1803) 139 What think you of the style of *Johnson*, the Reviewer? It is not *English* that he writes, Sir, it is *American.* **1802** *Port Folio* 28 Aug. 266/2 [A Latin verse] which my schoolmaster has translated into American. **1947** *Prairie Schooner* Winter 390 Do you speak American?

Hence **Americanese.**

1929 *Chi. Tribune* 18 Jan. 12/4 It is dashed depressing, let me tell you, after one has crammed through an intensive course in Americanese, to listen to George Reedy, the journalist chap.

3. a. An American horse (see ∗**American,** *a.* **2. b**). *Obs.* **b.** =**American locomotive.**

(a) 1856 *Spirit of Times* 6 Dec. 228/1 There was 'Americans,' 'Black Hawks,' 'Hambletonians,' 'Bullocks,' 'Normans' and 'Rattlers'—all gathered to the show, and their owners claimed them all as trotters.— **(b) 1947** BEEBE *Mixed Train Dly.* 128 Ten-wheelers with diamond stacks, and Americans with huge wedge plows fixed to their pilot beams in winter, wheeled their tonnage down the Animas and over the Cumbres.

As the last term in **all-, Anglo, anti-, British, Early, Federal, Federo-, Franco-, German, Irish, little, Native, Orange, Pan-, Spanish, Young American.**

∗**American,** *a.*

1. Pertaining to the United States.

The lack of an adjective form corresponding to "United States" has inevitably given rise to this use which is now widespread.

1776 in *Dollar Newspaper* (Phila.) (1846) 16 Sep. 4/4 The colors of the American flag have a snake with thirteen rattles, the fourteenth budding, described in the attitude of going to strike, with the motto: '*Don't tread on me!*' **1804** J. ORDWAY in *Wis. Hist. Coll.* XXII. (1916) 138 Capt. Lewis & Capt. Clark . . . Gave the 3 Chiefs 3 niew meddals & 1 american flag Some knives & other Small articles. **1847** LANMAN *Summer in Wild.* xxii. 132 The American coast of Lake Superior extends to about twice the length of that which belongs to Canada. **1946** *Chi. D. News* 31 Aug. 5/7 American tourists are not the type to miss a trick.

b. Of or pertaining to the American party *q.v. Obs.*

1844 *Republican Sentinel* (Richmond, Va.) 13 Apr. 4/2 In the City of New York, James Harper, the American Republican candidate, is elected Mayor by about 3,000 over Coddington, Democrat. **1856** *Butte Record* (Bidwell, Calif.) 10 May 2/6 The American feeling was very strong in the central and eastern parts of that State, and to carry Pennsylvania, its aid must be secured to the Anti-Nebraskaites.

2. In the names of animals, birds, and fish native exclusively to the United States.

The expressions belonging here and under **3.** below are far too numerous for exhaustive treatment. For many more of a similar nature see other dictionaries and works of a special nature.

(1) **American alewife,** (see quot. and cf. **alewife**); (2) **antelope,** the pronghorn, *Antilocapra americana*, of the western plains, cf. **Missouri antelope;** (3) **carp, chameleon, cobra,** (see quots.); (4) **elk,** (*a*) the moose, (*b*) the wapiti; (5) **goldfinch,** any one of several small finches of the genus *Spinus;* (6) **nightingale,** (see quots.), *obs.;* (7) **ortolan,** the bobolink; (8) **partridge,** = **American quail;** (9) **pheasant,** the ruffed grouse; (10) **quail,** a quail of the genus *Colinus*, esp. *C. virginianus;* (11) **redstart,** a flycatching warbler, *Setophaga ruticilla*, of the eastern states; (12) **robin = robin.**

(1) **1867** De Voe *Market Ass't.* 249 Spring-herring or American alewive.—These fish are usually found much larger than the preceding, and have much of the form of a small shad; in fact, some fishermen call them *hickory shad.* — (2) **1868** *Amer. Naturalist* Dec. 537 American Antelope (*Antilocapra Americ*... [...]e] very abundant along the ...

tains. — (3) **1860**
netimes called the
at of *Pomotis vul-*
lizard . . . of the
erican chameleon,
Vorld. — **1894** in
laps I have found
own under several
nake,' and 'candy
wo pair of Ameri-
omans *Nat. Hist.*
e higher latitudes
to a state of do-
he American elk
nct animal from
American elk or
us: The Ameri-
Goldfinch . . . .
Gerrond *Poems*
hail the youth-
gale. [Author's
ue the honor of
e . . . of calling
Woods *Gold*
the American
homes we have
a . . . wonder-
, or American
esby *Carolina*
n half the size
fferson *Notes*
an partridge,
V. ix., Your
id 'American
inianus (Lin-
uail. — (**11**)
makes its ap-
l; and leaves
News 22 Sep.
n redstarts.'
o a different
iced several
ent, viz. the
n ours; and
of a good
h inferior

... 17 Mar. 2/3 Auction, . . . one American cow. **1875** *Cimarron News* 7 Aug. 4/4 What are cattle worth? . . . Texas cows, $12 to $16 per head; American cows, $25 to $50 per head. — [**1818** Fearon *Sks.* 155 He had committed the error of substituting an American horse, marked by the very long shaggy hair near the hoofs, by which they are distinguished.] **1846** E. Bryant *What I Saw in Cal.* (1849) 37 Such [Indians] as rode ponies were desirous of swapping them for the American horses of the emigrants. **1941** Fergusson *Southwest* 62 Mounts ranged from nimble Spanish ponies to big American horses.

Also in the names of animals and birds that are of genera occurring also in the Old World, as *American avocet, badger, barn owl, bear, bison, bittern, buffalo, bullfinch, buzzard, coot, crane, creeper, crossbill, crow, dipper, eagle, goshawk, hake, hare, magpie, merino* (*sheep*), *osprey, panther, pipit, ptarmigan, scoter, snipe, swan, thrush, widgeon, woodcock*, etc.

3. In the names of plants and trees native exclusively to the U.S.: (1) **American aloe,** a species of the agave,

...RATE ACCOUNTABILITY:
The Board of Directors

HAROLD M. WILLIAMS*

...rd with any pleasure to the possibility of federal ch...
...nilar measures designed to bring in their wake a...
...cted at the structure and governance of the corp...
...hasis should be on fostering private accountabil...
...e managers are held responsible for the results...
...n devising ways of intervening in the mechanism...
...ort to legislate a sort of federal "corporate morality."...
...can, over time, be such a thing as *corporate* mo...
...from that of the society of which it is a part, and th...
...I believe there is only a corporate environment that r...
...e individual behavior, morality, and ethics of th...
Government may have a role in creating an envir...
...ourages accountability. It should not, as a general...
...managerial decisions are reached or demand that a...
...n the conflicting groups affected by corporate action...
...the accelerating rush to federal corporate governan...
...fear this as the beginning of an effort which will...
...effort fails, that failure will, in turn, serve as the p...
...profound efforts to constrict the latitude of private d...
...ainful lesson may be that it is one thing for the...
...n discrete socially impacting issues, such as safety st...
...to deal directly with the process by which private ec...
...ntrolled.
...alternative to federal intervention—the developm...

esp. *Agave americana*, also **great American aloe;** (2) **ash,** the white ash, *Fraxinus americana;* (3) **aspen,** a variety of poplar, *Populus tremuloides;* (4) **banana,** (see quot.); (5) **beauty,** (*a*) a variety of apple, (*b*) a hybrid variety of cultivated rose with deep pink to crimson flowers; (6) **black thorn,** a pear haw, as *Crataegus tomentosa;* (7) **ceanothus,** see **ceanothus;** (8) **centaury,** either of two marsh plants of the genus *Sabbatia* found in the eastern states; (9) **columbo,** the American gentian, *Frasera carolinensis;* (10) **cowslip,** a plant of the genus *Dodecatheon*, as the shooting star, *D. meadia;* (11) **creeper,** the Virginia creeper; (12) **cypress,** the bald cypress, *Taxodium distichum*, of the southern states; (13) **dittany,** the small fragrant *Cunila origanoides;* (14) **hemp,** (see quot.); (15) **horse chestnut,** the common buckeye, *Aesculus glabra;* (16) **ivy, joy,** the woodbine or Virginia creeper; (17) **jute,** (see quots.); (18) **larch,** the tamarack or hackmatack; (19) **laurel,** the mountain laurel or calico bush, *Kalmia latifolia;* (20) **mezereon,** the leatherwood or moosewood, *Dirca palustris;* (21) **nettle tree,** a tree, as the hackberry, of the genus *Celtis*, having elm-like leaves; (22) **olive tree,** the devilwood, *Osmanthus americanus;* (23) **pride,** (see quot.), *obs.;* (24) **rosebay,** the great laurel or rhododendron; (25) **spikenard,** (see quot.); (26) **tea,** a variety of morning-glory, *obs.;* (27) **water cress,** a perennial herb, *Cardamine rotundifolia*, of the eastern states; (28) **wistaria,** a native woody climbing vine, *Wistaria* (syn. *Kraunhia*) *frutescens*, found along the edges of swamps from Virginia to Illinois and southward.

(1) **1731** Miller *Gard. Dict. s.v.* Aloe, A vulgar Error . . . relating to the large American Aloe, which is, that it never flowers until it is an hundred Years old. **1856** *Rep. Comm. Patents 1855: Agric.* 243 Dr. Henry Perine . . . introduced [into southern Fla.] . . . the 'Great American aloes,' or 'Century plant,' (*Agave americana*,) the fibre of which is manufactured into cordage. — (2) **1744** F. Moore *Voy. Georgia* 98 The trees in the grove are mostly bay, . . . hickory, American ash. — (3) **1785** Marshall *Amer. Grove* 107 American Aspen-tree. **1810** Michaux *Arbres* I. 39 American aspen (Tremble d'Amérique) . . . dans les états du milieu et du nord. — (4) **1902** Clara Morris *Life on Stage* 13 But never could I acquire a taste for the 'paw-paw,' that inane custard-like fruit, often called the American banana.

(5) (*a*) [**1827** *Cinci. Advertiser* 7 March 1/3 In the number [of wax figures] will be noticed some important personages, as our President J. Q. Adams, Commodore Porter, . . . Miss Patterson, better known as the American Beauty, (Jerome Buonaparte's wife) . . . and a number of other figures.] **1859** Elliott *Western Fruit Book* 122 American Beauty, [also called] Sterling Beauty. . . . Flesh, white, crisp, and juicy, with a sweet, rich, vinous flavor. (*b*) **1887** *Columbus* (O.) *Hort. Soc. Jrnl.* II. 43 The American Beauty is one of the finest introductions of late years, popular as a winter bloomer. **1946** *Sterling* (Colo.) *Advocate* 10 June 3/3 She carried a bouquet of American Beauty roses. — (6) **1817** *Detroit Gazette* I. 12 Sep. 2/3 The American black-thorn is the best for hedges—the crab-apple is a good substitute. — (8) **1831** J. Davies *Manual Mat. Med.* 116 American Centaury. This plant is pure bitter, justly held in estimation as a valuable tonic and febrifuge. **1836** Lincoln *Botany* App. 135 *Sabbatia angularis.* American centaury. — (9) *Ib.* 98 *Frasera verticillata.* American columbo. . . . Medicinal. [Grows in] swamps. **1941** R. S. Walker *Lookout* 49 This prominent floral bard is American Colombo, a giant among the members of the Gentian family to which it belongs.

(10) **1787** *Fam. Plants* I. 107 *Dodecatheon*, . . . American Cowslip. **1934** Webster. — (11) **1874** Mark Twain *Letters* (1917) I. xiii. 226 (R.) On the peak of the hill is an old arbor roofed with bark and covered with the vine you call the 'American creeper'—its green is almost bloodied with red. — (12) **1775** Romans *Nat. Hist. Florida* 25 American deciduous cypress. — (13) **1902** *Country Life* Aug. 159/3 In the latter part of the month will be found there the aromatic, fragrant stone-mint or American dittany. **1941** R. S. Walker *Lookout* 51 Stonemint, known by the makers of tea as American dittany, makes a thrifty growth. — (14) **1855** *Amer. Inst. N.Y. Trans.* 333 *Agave Americana.* . . . Admirable American Hemp.

(15) **1832** Browne *Sylva Amer.* 227 We have denominated it Ohio Buckeye, . . . and have prefixed the synonyme of American Horse Chestnut. — (16) **1785** Marshall *Amer. Grove* 59 *Hedera quinquefolia*, American Ivy, or Virginian Creeper. This hath a climing stem, attaching itself to any neighbouring support. — **1813** Muhlenberg *Cat. Plants* 26 American joy . . . , heart-leaved: Illini. Georg. Pens. — (17) **1863** *Rep. Comm. Agric.* 158 In the swamp . . . the surface is

beautiful in August with the yellow flowers of the *Hibiscus palustris*, or American 'Jute.' **1893** *Amer. Folk-Lore* VI. 139 *Abutilon avicennæ*, American jute. West Va. — **(18) 1785** MARSHALL *Amer. Grove* 104 *Pinus-Larix nigra*. Black American Larch-Tree. **1810** MICHAUX *Arbres* I. 31 American larch . . . Dénomination générale. **1892** APGAR *Trees Northern U.S.* 188 American Larch. . . . A tree of large size . . . growing wild in all the northern portion of our region. — **(19) 1785** MARSHALL *Amer. Grove* 71 *Kalmia*. Kalmia, or American Laurel. **1857** GRAY *Botany* 255 American Laurel . . . [grows on] rocky hills and damp soil, rather common from Maine to Ohio and Kentucky.

(20) 1784 CUTLER in *Mem. Academy* I. 421 American Mezerion. In hedges and woodland. . . . Blossoms greenish white. Berry pale red. — **(21) 1785** MARSHALL *Amer. Grove* 29 American Yellow-Fruited Nettle-tree. . . . The juice of the fruit is said to be astringent. — **(22) 1785** MARSHALL *Amer. Grove* 98 American Olive tree . . . grows naturally in Carolina and Florida, and is a beautiful ever-green tree. — **(23) 1784** CUTLER in *Mem. Academy* I. 484 *Lobelia*. . . . American Pride. Blossoms scarlet. Borders of brooks and rivers. — **(24) 1832** WILLIAMSON *Hist. Maine* I. 119 We begin with . . . the 'American Rose-bay.' . . . It is large, straggling, and quite irregular in its manner of growth.

(25) 1891 *Cent.* 5832/1 American spikenard, a much-branching herbaceous plant, *Aralia racemosa*, with a short thick rootstock. — **(26) 1784** CUTLER in *Mem. Academy* I. 417 *Ipomoea*. . . . American Tea. . . . By fences, and among bushes in loamy land. July. . . . The tea, when cured in this way, has an agreeable taste, and leaves a roughness on the tongue, somewhat resembling that of the bohea tea. — **(27) 1836** LINCOLN *Botany* App. 84 *Cardamine pennsylvanica*. American water-cress. — **(28) 1891** *Cent. s.v. Wistaria*, The American wistaria . . . is a native of swamp margins from Virginia to Illinois and southward. **1933** SMALL *Southeastern Flora* 699 American-wistaria. Banks of creeks and rivers, and swampy borders of woods, Coastal Plain and rarely adj. provinces, Fla. to Ala. and Va.

Also in the names of plants that are of genera occurring also in the Old World, as, *American beech, black poplar, cherry, chestnut, elm, hazelnut, hellebore, holly, hornbeam, lime, linden, linn, maple, mistletoe, mountain ash, pine, plane tree, poplar, primrose, raspberry, rhododendron, senna, sycamore, thorn, vetch, yew*, etc.

4. In miscellaneous combs., sometimes occasional and obs.: (1) **American bottom,** a name given a stretch of level ground in southwestern Illinois, extending along the east bank of the Mississippi from Alton to Chester; (2) **cheese,** cheddar cheese made in the U.S.; (3) **desert,** a vaguely defined area comprising a large part of the Great Plains, at one time regarded as a desert, now *hist.*, cf. **great American desert;** (4) **eagle,** a conventional representation of the bald eagle as a symbol of the U.S., cf. **eagle;** (5) **Empire,** the U.S.; (6) **English,** English such as is used in the U.S.; (7) **Federation of Labor,** an American federation of trade unions organized in 1886; (8) **language,** =**American English;** (9) **Legion,** an organization of men and women who served in the naval and military forces of the U.S. during the first and second World Wars; (10) **Middlewest,** the northern half, approximately, of the Mississippi River basin; (11) **plan,** a plan followed by some hotels of including the price of meals in the charge for rooms; (12) **Republic,** the U.S.; (13) **system,** the policy of high protective tariffs and encouragement of internal improvements; (14) **tongue,** =**American English;** (15) **way,** a way in conformity with U.S. customs and traditions, in full **American way of life.**

(1) 1807 SCHULTZ *Travels* II. 38 You next ride fifteen miles over one of the richest and most beautiful tracts I have ever seen. It is called the American Bottom, and is a prairie of such extent as to weary the eye in tracing its boundaries. **1860** HANCOCK *Five Years* 284 On the 'American bottom,' a tract extending for ninety miles along the Mississippi, the farms of the French settlers have produced great crops of corn every year. — **(2) 1804** *Guardian of Freedom* (Frankfort, Ky.) 10 Mar. 2/1 Cheese, American per lb. 18. **1911** *Ariz. Cook Book* 99 One-quarter teaspoon soda, one cup cream, one-half pound American cheese, [etc.]. **1948** *Dly. Ardmoreite* (Ardmore, Okla.) 22 April 8/2 One-half cup of grated American cheese may be added to a one-cup flour recipe for baking powder biscuits. — **(3) 1844** LEE & FROST *Oregon* xix. 207 These two ladies are the first white females who came to Oregon, and the first who adventured across the American desert. **1930** HENRY *Conquer. Plains* 256 As far as concerned the backbone of existence those earliest women in the American Desert had nearly always, in short, the requisite pith and gristle of the pioneer. — **(4) 1782** *Jrnls. Congress* (1823) IV. 39 The escutcheon on the breast of the American eagle displayed proper. **1944** HOLTON *Yankees* 261 It looked like dull-finished silver and had an American eagle engraved on it.

(5) 1783 R. PUTNAM in *Memoirs* 216 Such conditions of settlement, & purchess, for public securities, as Congress shall judge . . . of lasting consequence to the American Empire. — **(6) 1806** WEBSTER *Dict.* Pref. (ad fin.), In fifty years from this time, the American-English will be spoken by more people, than all the other dialects of the language. **1948** MENCKEN *Supp.* II. 11 Higginson rejected all of Hoar's evidence, and argued that American English showed very strong North Country influences. — **(7) 1894** *Amer. Federationist* March 14/2 The American Federation of Labor insists that the law shall be enforced in accordance with its plain reading, and in the spirit of its promoters. **1948** *Chi. D. News* 11 June 16/3 The American Federation of Labor supports him this year for the first time. — **(8) 1802** *Ann. 7th Congress* 1 Sess. 687 To express my idea still more clearly, and in American language. **1945** KENNY *West Va. Place Names* viii., My aims have been accuracy, the enrichment of the American language, the revelation of philological process and resource. — **(9)** [**1839** *Boston Wkly. Mag.* 1 June 310/2 The Irish and Germans belong to the American Legion, there being two in this city [New Orleans].] **1919** G. S. WHEAT *Story Amer. Legion* 8 At that dinner [Paris, 16 Feb. 1919] the American Legion was born. **1948** *Democrat* 30 Sep. 1/7 The Grove Hill Post of the American Legion had charge of the concessions.

(10) 1920 LEWIS *Main Street* 1 A rebellious girl is the spirit of that bewildered empire called the American Middlewest. — **(11)** [**1805** PARKINSON *Tour* 566 It is customary when you put your horse up and lodge in a tavern to pay a regular price, dine or not, for every meal, which is called boarding in the house, you occupying a bed: as to a room you cannot obtain one, it being general to have from two to twelve beds in each apartment.] **1879** *Appleton's Guide to U.S. & Canada* 1 The [N.Y.] hotels conducted on the regular or American plan. **1945** *Chi. D. News* 24 Dec. 6/7, I cannot, however, approve of what is called the 'American plan.' . . . When you know that regardless of what you eat, the price will be the same, you are almost certain to commit gluttony. — **(12) 1795** *Pittsburgh Gazette* 6 June 3/1 The Senate of the United States are to meet . . . to take into consideration the treaty made by Mr. Jay, on the part of the American Republic, with the court of Great-Britain. **1876** *Cinci. Enquirer* 14 June 4/4 This, if the truth, of the future prospects of the American Republic was melancholy. **1948** *Time* 12 April 112/3 At this point in its history the American Republic has arrived under the theory that the President of the United States possesses limitless authority publicly to misrepresent and secretly to control foreign policy. — **(13) 1824** H. CLAY in *Ann. 18th Congress* 1 Sess. II. 1978 That remedy consists in modifying our foreign policy, and in adopting a genuine American system. **1886** LOGAN *Great Conspiracy* 15 The institution of the now fully established American System of Protection. **1944** *Chi. D. News* 19 Feb. 1/1 And the American system has outproduced the world! — **(14) 1788** *American Mag.* April 347 A Number of Gentlemen in this city have formed themselves into a Society, by the name of the Philological Society, for the purpose of ascertaining and improving the *American Tongue*.

(15) 1885 *Century Mag.* April 953/2 To use an expression made popular, we believe, by General Hawley some years ago in regard to a very different question, dynamiting is '*not the American way!*' **1944** *Chi. D. News* 6 March 10/6 This is dangerous ground, as President Hutchins well knows, and it strikes at the very heart of what the business magazines like to call 'the American way of life.'

b. In similar combs. sufficiently explained in the quots., as (1) **American blight,** (2) **bowls,** (3) **China,** (4) **Knights,** (5) **locomotive,** (6) **Methodists,** (7) **oil,** (8) **party,** (9) **pestilence,** (10) **plague,** (11) **Protective Association,** (12) **refrigerator car,** (13) **Spaniard,** (14) **straight,** see **straight,** (15) **torpedo,** (16) **turtle,** (17) **water burner,** see **water burner.**

(1) 1851 BARRY *Fruit Garden* 366 The Woolly Aphis or American Blight . . . is a small insect, covered with a white woolly substance that conceals its body. They infest the apple tree in particular. — **(2) 1888–90** BARRERE-LELAND I. 26 The game was originally nine pins; but the Blue Laws of Connecticut having forbidden that game, the astute sons of the Puritans added a pin, and made the game ten pins, or as it is now called 'American bowls.' — **(3) 1881** *Harper's Mag.* Feb. 367/1 The 'ivory porcelain' of this pottery [at Trenton, N.J.] is . . . called variously semi-china, stone porcelain, and American china. — **(4) 1888** LANE *Pol. Catch-Words* 13 Sep. 15 *American Knights*, Knights of the Golden Circle.

(5) 1877 FORNEY *Catechism of the Locomotive* 430 The ten-wheeled locomotive . . . is similar in construction to an ordinary American locomotive, excepting that it has another pair of driving-wheels in front of the main driving-wheels. *Ib.* 429 Such locomotives have been called 'American' locomotives because they first originated in this country and are now more generally used here than anywhere else. **1909** FOWLER *Locomotive Dict.* 6 American Type Locomotive. . . . The prevailing type of locomotive several years ago. One having a four-wheel front truck and four-[*sic*] coupled driving wheels, but no trailing truck. — **(6) 1826** in PICKERING *Inquiries* 116 Only a few of the Wesleyan Methodists—the greater part being what are termed American Methodists, who have separated from the other, and are now subject to the American Conference. **1881** *Georgians* 149, I know nothing of the American Methodists. — **(7) 1904** *D.N.* II. 374 American oil, n. A commercial name for refined petroleum, about 1850. — **(8) 1835** *Louisville Public Advt.* 24 June, An 'American party' might have a good run. **1855** *Harper's Mag.* X. 829/1 The candidates presented by the 'Know Nothing' or 'American' party have to a great extent formed a centre around which all the elements of opposition to the Administration have gathered. **1946** ADAMS *Album Amer. Hist.* III. 48 The American, or Know-Nothing, Party nominated former President Millard Fillmore. — **(9) 1811** MEASE *Philadelphia* 37 Philadelphia has suffered severely by the American pestilence, commonly called yellow fever.

(10) 1830 J. F. WATSON *Philadelphia* 600 Noah Webster, speaking of this sickness, says, after the severe winter the city was severely visited with 'the American plague.' The same disease Doctor Bond has said was yellow fever, supposed to have been introduced by a load of sick people from Dublin. — **(11) 1883** *Chi. Tribune* 1 July 9/2 The American Protective Association, whichis fighting on secret orders, [has] 2 lodges. **1914** *Cyclo. Amer. Hist.* I. 51 The A.P.A., or American Protective Association, was organized in 1887, and was directed against the power of the Roman Catholics in the schools and other public institutions. It had its beginnings in the earlier Know Nothing party.—**(12) 1895** WAIT *Car-Builder's Dict.* 2 American refrigerator-car. One of the class of cars having the iceboxes at both ends of the car supplied from the roof. The drip-water passes off through troughs, and is utilized for cooling as it passes away. — **(13) 1827** *Spirit of Seventy-Six* (Frankfort, Ky.) 22 Mar. 1/4 There were two parties, one of them Americans and the other Spaniards and what are called American Spaniards. (The latter are white people who have been raised amongst the Spaniards by conduct.)

(15) 1823 J. THATCHER *Military Jrnl.* 146 The American Torpedo, and other . . . submarine machinery, invented by Mr. David Bushnell, for the purpose of destroying shipping while at anchor. — **(16) 1788** HUMPHREYS *Life Putnam* (1794) 114 A Machine . . . had been invented by Mr. David Bushnell, for submarine navigation. . . . To this Magazine (called the American Turtle) was attached a Magazine of Powder, which it was intended to be fastened under the bottom of a ship with a driving screw. **1946** S. H. HOLBROOK *Lost Men* 62 The *American Turtle* was conceived in the unusual mind of David Bushnell, a farmer boy of Saybrook, Connecticut, who had been graduated from Yale College in 1775.

Americaness əˌmɛrəˈkɑnɪs, *n.* A female American. *Obs.* — **1838** COOPER *Home as Found* I. vi. 93 Every true American and Americaness was expected to be at his or her post. **1879** *S.F. Argus* 22 Feb., One of these rascally responses threw the young Americaness into such fury that she was taken with a fit of hysterics. **1888–90** BARRERE-LELAND I. 36 Americanesses (American). This version of Americaine has begun to appear in Western newspapers.

Americanism əˈmɛrəkənˌɪzəm, *n.*

1. A word or expression originating in the U.S. (see also quot. 1781). Cf. **Yankeeism,** *n.* **2.**

1781 WITHERSPOON *Druid P.* No. 5, The first class I call Americanisms, by which I understand an use of phrases or terms, or a construction of sentences, even among persons of rank and education, different from the use of the same terms or phrases, or the construction of similar sentences, in Great Britain. **1855** *Georgetown* (Ky.) *Herald* 14 June, It is obviously a good old English word of classical usage, and no Americanism at all. **1947** R. K. LEAVITT *Noah's Ark* 32 There were Americanisms, solidly welded into our tongue by a century or more of usage.

2. "A love of America and preference of her interest" (W. '06).

1797 JEFFERSON *Let. to E. Rutledge* 24 June, The parties have in debate mutually charged each other . . . with being governed by an attachment to this or that of the belligerent nations, rather than the dictates of reason and pure Americanism. **1884** *Century Mag.* March 678/1 Those living Americans, whose Americanism did not begin within the last half century. **1948** *Chi. D. News* 1 May 6/3 Boston has refused to permit the use of its schools for contests on the kind of Americanism the D.A.R. advocates.

3. Adoption or display of American ideas, habits, etc. A peculiarity in manners, views, conduct, etc., thought to be typically American.

1835 N. P. WILLIS *Pencillings* (1942) 196 A bachelor friend of mine from New York is domesticated in the village with a German family. I was struck with the Americanism of their manners. **1893** *Nation* 2 Feb. 75/1 The spread of American influence and domination abroad, known as 'Americanism.' **1947** COFFIN *Yankee Coast* 143 The Maine man, the outsider notices at once, is a great one for gadgets, too. His Americanism breaks out all over him in that form.

b. Also applied to typically American things.

1856 *N.Y. Herald* 9 Jan. 2/1 Well, to locate the Gubernatorial apartment—it is some twenty feet square, has a door opening out upon (that Americanism) a 'piazza.' **1925** *Frontier* Mar. 20 On the opposite side of town one finds many Americanisms to blemish its vaunted Spanish antiquity—the state capitol of brick and stone, the federal building, the state penitentiary with its great walls and towers.

4. The principles of the American party *q.v.* *Obs.*

1855 *N.Y. Herald* 20 Nov. 8/4 (*heading*), Commodore Stockton on Americanism. **1856** *Western Citizen* (Paris, Ky.) 28 Mar. 3/2 Sectionalism, Negroism, and *Americanism* are, and must ever be, in utter oppugnation. **1856** *Ill. State Register* (Springfield) 1 May 2/6 In all the Western and New England states the republican party owes its strength in a very great degree to its alliance with Americanism.

As the last term in **little, Native, Virginia Americanism.**

Americanitis əˌmɛrəkənˈaɪtɪs, *n.* (See quot.) — **1896** *Nat. Geog. Mag.* Dec. 387 The east coast particularly affords relief from all forms of what is called 'americanitis,' or nerve exhaustion.

Americanization əˌmɛrəkənəˈzeʃən, *n.* "The act of rendering American, or of subjection to the laws and usages of the United States" (B. '59). — **1858** BROWNSON'S *Q. Rev.* April 190 All the Americanization I insist on is, that our Catholic population shall feel and believe that a man may be a true American, and a good Catholic. **1920** BOK *Americanization of E. Bok* 1 A family of four from the Netherlands who were to make an experiment of Americanization.

Americanize əˈmɛrəkənˌaɪz, *v.*

1. *tr.* To render American in character; to make similar to the people, customs, or institutions of the U.S. Also **Americanized,** *a.*, **Americanizing,** *n.*

1797 J. JAY *Corr. & P.* (1893) IV. 232, I wish to see our people more Americanized, if I may use that expression; until we feel and act as an independent nation, we shall always suffer from foreign intrigue. **1858** BROWNSON'S *Q Rev.* April 190 The Americanizing of the Catholic body does and will go on of itself. **1948** *Dallas Morn. News* 2 May 11.6/2 Common usage and Americanized spelling of the French words resulted in Ozarks.

2. *intr.* To become American in character.

1875 HOWELLS *Foregone Conclusion* 77 He was Americanizing in that good lady's hands as fast as she could transform him. **1905** *N.Y. Ev. Post* 19 Oct. 5, I fancy Asia will not Americanize very fast.

Americano əˈmɛrɪˈkɑno, *n. S.W.* [Sp. in same sense.] An American. — **1866** MELINE *Two Thousand Miles on Horseback* (1867) 189 With the advent of *los Americanos* came a changed state of things in the Church. **1923** W. SMITH *Little Tigress* 195 (Bentley) The blue-eyed, tawny-mustached *Americano* of fiction often as not turns out to be an affable cut-throat. **1948** *Neb. Hist.* March 45 These dilatory maneuverings of sixty hard-boiled, well armed *Americanos* had not gone unnoticed by Castro.

* **Americo-.** Combining form of America, as in **Americo-Indian, Mexican, Saxon.** *Obs.*

1844 GREGG *Commerce of Prairies* II. 235 All the Americo-Indian tribes have . . . preserved their traditions on this subject. **1847** *De Bow's Review* III. 440 Tariff for Americo-Mexican Ports. **1848** COOPER *Oak Openings* I. iv. 62 It was not so much Anglo-Saxon as Americo-Saxon, that was to be seen in the physical outlines and hues of this nearly self-destroyed being. **1878** CONKLIN *Picturesque Ariz.* 65 A conglomeration of individuals . . . embodied the characteristics of that class of people, so thoroughly identified with Americo-Mexican towns, who have nothing in view, have left nothing behind.

Amerind ˈæməˌrɪnd, *n.* [f. next.] (See quot. 1907.)

1897–8 POWELL *Rep. Bureau Amer. Ethnol.* I. xlviii, The brilliant work of Miss Alice Fletcher . . . on the tribal fraternities of the Amerinds. **1907** HODGE *Amer. Indians* I. 49 Amerind. A word composed of the first syllables of 'American Indian,' . . . used to designate the race of man inhabiting the New World before its occupancy by Europeans **1948** *Rotarian* Feb. 2/3 Rotarian Cosgrove is believed to be the only American Indian (Amerind) Rotarian.

Amerindian ˌæməˈrɪndiən, *a.* [*American*+*Indian.*] An American Indian. Also attrib. or as adj.

1897–8 *Ann. Rep. Bureau Amer. Ethnol.* II. 835 The four worlds of widespread Amerindian mythology. **1910** H. H. JOHNSTON *Negro in New World* vi, The Spaniards did not exterminate the Amerindian peoples of tropical America. **1947** EDMINSTER *Ruffed Grouse* 19 During Indian times the *papahcogh* was an important item in the economic life of the Amerindians of the Northeast.

amigo əˈmigo, *n. S.W.* [Sp. in same sense.] A friend. — **1837** *N.Y. Mirror* 23 Dec. 208/1 An overworked, spavined, broken-down set—but adios, Amigo. **1852** *S.F. Herald* 21 Dec. 2/2 Peligrine was an old *amigo* of Solomon Pico. **1947** *Mazama* Sep. 2/1 And, by the way amigo, if you have a car and can take one or more passengers, be sure to let Larry know.

Amish ˈæmɪʃ, *a.* and *n.* [See def. **1.**]

1. *n.* A body of strict Mennonites, so called after Jacob Amen, a Mennonite preacher of the seventeenth century.

1883 *Schaff's Relig. Encycl.* (1884) III. 2404/1 The Mennonites and the Amish baptize by pouring. **1947** *Time* 8 Dec. 12/3 Yoder repeatedly has shown himself out of harmony with the home-and peace-loving Amish.

2. *a.* Of or pertaining to this sect of Mennonites.

1844 RUPP *Relig. Denom.* 560 [Account of the] Omish or Amish Church. **1869** *Atlantic Mo.* Oct. 475/1 On a Sunday morning Amish wagons, covered with yellow oil-cloth, may be seen moving toward the house of that member whose turn it is to have the meeting. **1938** HARK *Hex Marks Spot* 18 Into many a neat and tidy barnyard my car has poked its nose; past many a spruce and spotless home with gates and blinds and shutters of vivid 'Amish blue.' **1948** *Dly. Ardmoreite* (Ardmore, Okla.) 23 Jan. 1/3 He was described by neighbors as a 'dictator of religious conduct' . . . in the northeastern Clinton township Amish church.

b. Amishman, a member of the Amish group.

1869 *Atlantic Mo.* Oct. 476/1 It was an Amish man, not well versed in the English language, from whom I bought poultry, and who sent me a bill for 'chighans.' **1925** *Ladies' Home Jrnl.* Apr. 18/1 Martin, who was an Amishman, had a thick, curling, silky beard. **1947** *Time* 17 Nov. 26/2 To the stubborn Amishmen, who frown upon court actions, God's law came before that of men.

See also **church Amish, hickory Amish, old order Amish.**

* **amnesty,** *n.* In hist. combs.: (1) **amnesty act,** an act by the Kansas legislature pardoning those who had participated in the struggle over slavery, 1854–58; (2) **oath,** (see quot. 1871); (3) **proclamation,** (see quot.).

(1) **1867** RICHARDSON *Beyond Mississippi* 148 The legislature [of Kansas in 1859] also passed an 'amnesty act' directing that all persons charged with crimes arising from political disturbances . . . should be set at liberty. — (2) **1865** ANDREW JOHNSON in *Docs. & Speeches in Am. Hist.* III. (1943) 6 The Secretary of State will establish rules and regulations for administering and recording the said amnesty oath. **1871** DE VERE 287 To secure the loyalty of conquered Southerners, a multitude of oaths were exacted of them . . . : the Amnesty Oath . . . secured pardon according to the terms of an amnesty granted by the President. — (3) **1865** *Ann. Cyclo. 1864* 778/1 The benefits of the amnesty proclamation issued by President Lincoln on December 8th, 1863, were sought by a large number of persons.

amole ə'mole, *n. S.W.* [Amer. Sp. (< Nahuatl) in the same or closely related senses.]

1. Any one of various plants parts of which are used as soap, a soap plant. Also attrib.

[**1780** CLAVIGERO *Storia della Messico* II. 228 La radice é quella dell' *Amolli*, pianta piccola, e comunissima in quel paese.] **1843** FRÉMONT *Exped.* 249 Near the river . . . are great quantities of *ammole,* (soap plant), the leaves of which are used in California for making . . . mats for saddle-cloths. **1885** HAVARD *Flora W. & S. Texas* 518 Lechuguilla is the most important of the soap or 'amole' plants of Southwestern Texas and Northern Mexico. **1903** JAMES *Indian Basketry* 33 A medicine basket containing amole root and water was placed in front of a circle made of sand and covered with pine boughs.

2. The root of a plant of this kind or the soap obtained from it.

1831 BEECHEY *Voyage* II. 43 They had also collected in great quantities a very useful root called in that country [California] *amoles.* **1940** JAEGER *Desert Wild Flowers* 13 The roots yield a soap, called *amole,* used especially in ceremonial hair-washing.

Amorpha ə'mɔrfə, *n.* [NL f. Gr. *amorphos,* shapeless.] A genus of leguminous shrubby plants having blue-violet flowers abnormally deficient in petals (whence the name); also (not *cap.*) a plant of this genus, false indigo.

1753 CHAMBERS *Cycl. Supp., Amorpha* . . . a genus of plants of the papilionaceous kind. **1843** FRÉMONT *Exped.* 14 Along our route the *amorpha* has been in very abundant but variable bloom. **1901** MOHR *Plant Life Ala.* 563 *Amorphaglabra.* Smooth Amorpha. . . . Flowers blue. May, June. Infrequent.

amovability ə,muvə'bɪlətɪ, *n.* Power to remove from office. *Rare.* — **1816** JEFFERSON *Writings* XV. 37 Let us retain amovability on the concurrence of the executive and legislative branches.

amphibiology æm,fɪbɪ'ɑlədʒɪ, *n.* [*amphibia* +-(*o*)*logy*] The science which treats of amphibious animals. *Obs.* — **1836** EATON *Man. Bot. N.A.* (ed. 7) 569 *Amphibiology,* the department of zoology, embracing animals which are capable of suspending respiration for a long time without injuring the action of the arterial system.

* **amphitheater,** *n.*

1. A large building in which circus acts as well as dramatic performances are given. *Obs.*

1858 *Chicago Dly. Press* 19 Feb., The play of the 'Fall of Delhi' is taking a most successful run at North's Amphitheater.

2. A room in a medical college or a hospital where operations are performed in the presence of students.

1797 MORSE *Amer. Gaz.* I., Philadelphia . . . (has) a medical theatre, a laboratory, an amphitheatre. **1851** CIST *Cincinnati* 112 Medical College of Ohio . . . contains large lecture rooms and an amphitheatre, together with apartments for the library. **1947** *Reader's Digest* Aug. 122 A dingy amphitheater where a few physicians gave occasional demonstrations.

3. (See quot. 1900.)

1900 *Am. Geog. Soc.* XXXII. 32 Amphitheater: A cove or angle of glacial origin near the summit of a high mountain and nearly surrounded by the highest summits. A small flat valley or gulch-like depression at the head of an alpine mountain drainage. Local in far West. **1947** *Sierra Club Bul.* May 32 The trail leads on and up through the great cirque or amphitheatre.

Amy Dardin. A widow of Mecklenburg County, Va., whose claim to be compensated for a horse came before Congress at intervals from 1796 to 1815. "Amy's case came to be a proverb for procrastination" (Th.). *Obs.*

1803 *Mass. Spy* 7 Dec. (Th.), This Amy Dardin is a Virginian, and has unremittingly applied to every Congress for nine years past for compensation. **1835** CROCKETT *Tour* 114 (Th.), [It would be] better than hanging on like Amy Dardin for fifty years; and then get pay for a horse pressed during the Revolution; and indeed this case of Amy Dardin shews much of the course of proceeding.

* **anaconda,** *n. fig.* At the outset of the Civil War, a name given in derision by the radical Union press of the North to a plan formulated by Gen. Scott for enveloping the South by a cordon of posts on the Mississippi and a sea blockade. Hence, the northern army. Also attrib. *Obs.* Cf. **Union anaconda.**

1861 NEWELL *Orpheus C. Kerr* I. 205 [McClellan's] great anaconda has gathered itself in a circle around the doomed rabbit of rebellion. **1862** *Yale Lit. Mag.* xxviii. 63 (Th.), How ridiculous was the '*anaconda* theory' of crushing the rebellion! **1863** O. J. VICTOR *Hist. Southern Rebellion* II. 471 [The army] was the *anaconda,* for so the people had christened it. **1879** *Southern Hist. Soc. P.* XI. 119 Our turn had come for a little squeeze in the folds of the traditional 'Anaconda,' that the New York Herald had so graphically depicted as encircling the South.

Anadarko ,ænə'dɑrko, *n. S.W.* [f. the native name.] "A tribe of the Caddo confederacy whose dialect was spoken by the Kadohadacho, Hainai, and Adai. . . . Their villages were scattered along Trinity and Brazos rs., Tex." (Hodge). — **1846** *Dollar Newspaper* (Phila.) 8 July 4/2 Represented in this delegation [are] the Camanches, . . . A-nah-dan-caes, Ionies, Caddoes, . . . and Delawares. **1856** PARKER *Unexplored Tex.* 213 At a council held here, the Jonies and Ah-nan-dah-kas were represented by Jose Maria.

anagreeta ,ænə'gritə, *n.* [Origin unknown.] (See quot.) *Obs.* — **1775** ROMANS *Florida* 122 Anagreeta is the corn gathered before maturity, and dried in an oven or the hot sun . . . , [making] a fine mixture in puddings especially with pease, but this is only practised in the provinces of New York and New Jersey.

* **Ananias,** *n.* Used, in allusion to the biblical Ananias (Acts v. 1–2), for a lie. Also **Ananias Club,** a club or group of liars. *Slang.*

"Ananias Club" attained wide popularity in connection with Theodore Roosevelt, but he did not coin the expression. See *N.Y. Times,* Nov. 25, 1923, Sec. 9, p. 16.

[**1878** *Gold Hill* (Nev.) *News* 15 March, It is a record of lies told in the Sazerac Lying Club, whose object, as its name implies, was lying.] **1888** *Kansas Hist. Coll.* IV. (1890) 273 An Ananias historian has tried to write a history that would make John Brown a demon, a thief and a murderer, and Lane a blackguard and a roustabout. **1896** J. F. B. LILLARD (*title*), Poker Stories as Told by Statesmen, Soldiers, . . . Members of the Ananias Club and the Talent. **1948** *Penna. Mag. Hist.* April 157, I have no wish for posthumous election to the Ananias Club.

ancheta æn'tʃetə, *n. S.W.* [Sp. in same sense.] A venture of merchandise sent to a distant region. *Obs.* — **1844** GREGG *Commerce of Prairies* 83 (Bentley), The Officer . . . was expecting an ancheta of goods.

* **anchor,** *n.*

1. anchor cattle, cattle used as the nucleus stock of a herd.

1890 *Stock Grower* 11 Jan. 11/2 All 'anchor' cattle belonging to this company are tally branded and all increase of 1884 is in the same brand.

2. anchor ice, ice which, under certain conditions, forms at the bottom of lakes and rivers (see quot. 1907).

1815 *Niles' Reg.* IX. 201/1 On the same day the anchor-ice began to run a little. **1907** *D.N.* III. 240 Anchor ice, *n. phr.* Detached ice (for the most part, *surface* ice) which floats down a river. 'A jam of *anchor ice* now fills the river for two miles.' **1948** *Chi. D. News* 30 Jan. 14/7 The intake pipes in the crib became blocked with anchor ice Thursday morning.

*ancient, *a.* In combs.: (1) **ancient diggings,** mining excavations thought to have been made by an ancient or prehistoric race, *obs.;* (2) **Ancient Dominion,** the colony and state of Virginia; (3) **metropolis,** (see quot.), *obs.;* (4) **Ancient Order Society,** a religious sect following certain teachings of Alexander Campbell (1788–1866), also **Ancient Gospel** with reference to the accepted teaching of this sect, *obs.*

(1) **1865** *Atlantic Mo.* XV. 308 This was the first instance where 'ancient diggings'—as they are familiarly called in the Lake Superior region—were ever recognized as such. — (2) **1699** *Va. State Papers* I. 63 A Generall Assembly of this his Majesties most ancient Colloney and Dominion of Virginia. **1705** MAKEMIE *Persuasive* (Dedication) To His Excellency Major Edward Nott, Her Majestys Governor of the Ancient Dominion of Virginia. **1850** FOOTE *Sk. Virginia* 393 The Smiths came to Virginia to commence log colleges in the 'Ancient Dominion.' — (3) **1859** *Ladies' Repository* XIX. 51/2 Chilicothe, Ohio, is the 'Ancient Metropolis,' from its being the former capital of the state. — (4) **1837** JENKINS *Ohio Gaz.* 130 Of this number . . . 725 are episcopal methodists; about 300 are supposed to belong to the ancient order society; 200 to the presbyterians. — **1843** H. CASWELL *Prophet of 19th Cent.* 11 This was denominated the 'Ancient Gospel,' and to these views all men were required to conform.

ancon,** *n.* A now extinct breed of sheep having short, crooked legs, and long bodies. Also attrib. Cf. **otter sheep.** *Obs.* — *a1811** SHATTUCK in *Phil. Trans.* CIII. 93 Its forelegs . . . appear like elbows, while the animal is walking. I have taken the liberty to call them *ancon,* from the Greek word. **1873** *Amer. Naturalist* VII. 742 Ancon or Otter Sheep . . . were raised till within a few years on the farm of Hon. William Hale of Barrington, N.H.

***and,** *conj.* (See quots.)

1867 MARK TWAIN *Sketches* 74 (R.), His last act was to go his pile on 'Kings-and' (calculatin' to fill, but which he didn't fill), when there was a 'flush' out agin' him. **1899** ——— *Man that Corrupted* 56 (R.), Yes, he saw my deuces-and with a straight flush, and by rights the pot is his. **1938** R. L. RAMSAY *Mark Twain Lexicon* 6/7 Neither 'kings-*and*' nor 'dueces-*and*' is explained in any dictionary, and neither combination seems to be any longer in use. Present day poker experts . . . are far from agreed in their interpretations. Compare the common American tennis expressions 'game-*and*' and 'thirty-*and*' for what the British call 'game-all' and 'thirty-all'; also the still more familiar Americanism 'ham-*and*' for a restaurant order of ham and eggs.

Andes grass. (See quot.) *Obs.* — **1835** P. SHIRREFF *Tour* 26, I saw [near Phila.] several fields of a newly introduced grass, called Andes grass, said to have been lately brought from the range of hills in South America bearing that name.

***anesthesia,** *n.* A state of insensibility to pain, entire or partial loss of sensation by means of ether, chloroform, cocaine, etc.

1846 HOLMES *Letter to W. T. G. Morton* 21 Nov., The state produced . . . should, I think, be called *anaesthesia.* This signifies insensibility. . . . The adjective will be *anaesthetic.* Thus we might say, the 'state of anaesthesia,' or the 'anaesthetic state.' **1876** BARTHOLOW *Materia Med.* (1879) 360 The term anaesthetic . . . means an agent capable of producing anaesthesia, or insensibility to pain. **1947** *U. of C. Mag.* Nov. 4/2 Anaesthesia by injection of sodium pentathol into a vein has become popular for short operations as it is safe and produces a minimum of discomfort and after effects.

anesthetic ˌænəsˈθɛtɪk, *a.* [Gk. *anaisthētos,* insensible.] Of the nature of, pertaining or belonging to, anesthesia; inducing anesthesia. — **1846** [see **anesthesia**]. **1866** *Nation* 20 June 812/1 The anaesthetic value of nitrous oxide. **1944** *Anesthesiology* V. Jan. 41 There are other criteria which serve as standards for comparing and evaluating local anesthetic agents.

***angel,** *n.*

1. A ten shilling bill of public credit issued in the Massachusetts Colony in 1713 under the direction of a committee of which S. Sewall was a member. In full **angel bill of credit.** *Obs.*

1713 SEWALL *Diary* II. 413, [I] gave him an Angel . . . to buy him and Madam Brattle a pair of gloves. **1717** *Ib.* III. 129 Give Mr. Little the Funeral Sermons . . . with an Angel Bill of Credit. **1724** *Ib.* 331 Mr. Barth. Green had an angel sent to him to insert it [=a notice] in his News-Letter of Feb. 13, which he did.

2. A financial backer, esp. a man of wealth who supports theatrical ventures or players. *Slang.*

Partridge includes this term, but does not ascribe it to the U.S.

1891 MAITLAND *Dict. Amer. Slang* 18 Angel. . . . One who possesses the means and inclination to 'stand treat.' **1900** GEORGE ADE *More Fables* 190 There was no more Capital coming from the Angels. **1948** *Newsweek* 18 Oct. 36/2 As a politician, she was an ardent Wallaceite, being both angel and office seeker.

3. In combs.: (1) ***angel cake,** a white cake of spongy texture the chief ingredients of which are flour, sugar, and egg whites, also attrib.; (2) **Angel City,** Los Angeles, in allusion to its name; (3) ***angel('s) food (cake),** =**angel cake,** also attrib.; (4) **angel sleeve,** an exceptionally wide, full sleeve hanging loose from the shoulder, also attrib.

(1) **1886** *Good Housekeeping* 10 July 127/2, I always use the pan sold as an 'angel cake pan.' **1944** HOLTON *Yankees* 175 Did you ever put better angel cake then hers into your mouth? — (2) **1874** J. VON KEITH *Westward* xiii, In no distant day You will see the Angel City Stretching twenty miles away. **1916** *Amer. City* Feb. 182/2 Los Angeles is the 'Angel City.' — (3) **1881** MRS. OWENS *Cook Bk.* 161 Angels' food. In other words, White Sponge Cake. **1920** LEWIS *Main Street* 88 Then they distributed . . . stuffed olives, potato salad, and angel's-food cake. **1948** *Chi. Tribune* 24 Feb. II. 6/1 It requires only seven eggs, and may be baked in your big angel food pan or in layers or loaves. — (4) **1862** in CHESNUT *Diary* 204 When she saw them coming in angel sleeves, displaying all their white arms and in their muslin, showing all their beautiful white shoulders and throats, she felt disposed to order them off the premises. **1939** *Vogue* 1 Feb., [She] expresses her house with an angel-sleeve tea-gown.

As the last term in **avenging, destroying, Mormon, swamp angel.**

Angeleno ˌændʒəˈlino, *n. local.* A native or inhabitant of Los Angeles. — **1888** LINDLEY *Calif. of South* 79 Governor Pico is still a resident of Los Angeles, and any Angeleño will cheefully point him out to the inquiring stranger. **1948** *L.A. Times* 10 May 1/6 Angelenos upheld summer traditions and went to the beach yesterday.

angelica tree. (See quot. 1931.)

1785 MARSHALL *Amer. Grove* 11 Virginian Angelica Tree . . . rises with a thick woody stem to the height of ten or twelve feet. **1892** APGAR *Trees Northern U.S.* 109 Angelica-tree . . . usually dies to the ground after flowering. **1931** CLUTE *Plants* 83 Another thorny species is the devil's walking-stick or devil's club (*Aralia spinosa*). Singularly enough, the same species is called angelica tree in some localities!

angeliferous ˌendʒəˈlɪfərəs, *n.* Angelic. *Slang.* — **1835** R. M. BIRD *Nick of Woods* I. 174 'Oh! you splendiferous creatur'! you anngeliferous anngel!' **1856** *Town Talk* (S.F.) 20 July 1/1, I didn't see . . . no nothin', 'cept one of the most splendifferous, angeliferous, . . . female critters I ever sot my two gooseberry eyes onto. **1888–90** BARRERE-LELAND I. 38 Angeliferous (American), a word signifying 'angelic,' and first used by Bird in his novel of 'Nick of the Woods,' in which roaring Ralph Stackpole frequently calls the heroine 'angeliferous Madam!'

***angle,** *v.* **1.** *intr.* To obtain an angle by which to find a hive of wild bees. Also **angling,** *n. Obs.* **2.** To move at an angle.

(1) **1848** COOPER *Oak Openings* I. i. 21, I must 'angle' for them chaps. . . . Many a man who can 'line' a bee, can do nothing at an 'angle.' *Ib.* II. iii. 36 Indians are not expert . . . on account of the 'angle-ing' part of the process, which much exceeds their skill in mathematics. — (2) **1860** in *Am. Sp.* XXII. 200/1 Thence angling across the country, we, on the second day, entered the Lane road. **1903** A. ADAMS *Log Cowboy* ix. 127 The old man started for him, angling across the street in disregard of sidewalks. *Ib.* xvii. 262 As we angled across it [i.e., the valley], the town seemed as dead as those that slept in the graveyard.

anglewing ˈæŋglˌwɪŋ, *n.* A butterfly belonging to a group characterized by having the outer edge of the forewings somewhat notched or angular. — **1901** *Everybody's Mag.* Apr. 390/2 When the warmer days approach, however, one may see a few mourning-cloak butterflies (*Vanessa*) or angle-wings (*Grapta*) flitting through the woods. **1948** *Sat. Ev. Post* 7 Aug. 5/1 With wings folded, an angle-wing resting on a tree trunk looks like a piece of rough bark.

***Anglican,** *n.* (See quot.) *Obs.* — **1836** EDWARD *Hist. Texas* 125 Thus the Creole party is divided into several factions. First, the Aristocratic. . . . They are also called Yorkinos and Anglicans, because under English influence, and leaning towards European connections.

***Anglicanism,** *n.* =next. *Obs.* — **1900** *Kansas Hist. Coll.* VI. 217 He resembled the best English pattern rather than our more acute American model. Of his unconscious Anglicanism, the most elaborate picture of Kansas that he ever drew in a sentence is an example.

***Anglicism,** *n.* Inclination towards England or English views. *Obs.* — **1810** JEFFERSON *Writings* XII. 373 The Anglicism of 1808, against which we are now struggling, . . . is a longing for a King, and an English King rather than any other.

Anglicizer ˈæŋglɪˌsaɪzɚ, *n.* One who assumes English manners or speech. *Obs.* — **1886** *American* XII. 181 A sense which our Anglicisers entirely ignore.

Anglify ˈæŋglɪˌfaɪ, *v.* [LL. *Angli,* the English +*-fy.*] *tr.* To Anglicize. Also **Anglified,** *a.*

1751 FRANKLIN *Wks.* (1840) II. 320 Why should Pennsylvania, founded by the English, become a colony of aliens, who will shortly be so numerous as to Germanize us instead of our Anglifying them?

1778 ADAMS *Fam. Lett.* (1876) 346, I can only say that we have many . . . difficulties . . . to give satisfaction to certain half-anglified Americans. **1890** H. C. BUNNER *Short Sixes* (1891) 217 They had two English servants and some other American 'help'; but they called the Americans by their last names, which anglified them to some extent.

∗ **Anglo,** *n.*

1. *S.W.* A person who is not of Spanish or Indian descent.

1941 FERGUSSON *Southwest* 70 Los ricos accepted the incoming Anglos as friends, as wives or husbands. **1948** *N.M. Quart. Rev.* Spring 67 Most non-Spanish city dwellers, the Anglos, so-called—Anglo-Saxon Anglos, Anglo-Serbian Anglos, Anglo-Greek Anglos, and Anglo-Celtic Anglos—are too busy.

2. Used as a combining form for "English" in noun and adjective combs. now chiefly obsolete: (1) **Anglo-African,** having a mixed character of English and African; (2) **-America,** those parts of the American continent under the influence of England [cf. **Anglo-American** as a main entry]; (3) **-centric,** having England as its center; (4) **-Confederate,** pertaining to the English and the Southern Confederacy during the Civil War; (5) **-federal,** pertaining to the Federalists who were accused of having leanings toward England, also **Anglo-federalism, -ist;** (6) **-Indian,** an American Indian under English influence, also as adj.; (7) **man,** an admirer or partisan of England; (8) **mania,** an excessive fondness for that which is English; (9) **-many,** =**anglomania;** (10) **phobia,** fear or dread of England; (11) **phobiac,** one having an intense dread or dislike of England, also as adj.; (12) **-Rebel,** pertaining to the forces of England and the Confederacy during the Civil War; (13) **-Yankee,** pertaining to New Englanders thought of as being under English influence.

(1) **1866** RICHARDSON *Secret Service* vi. 85 He speaks fluently, and with grammatical correctness but in the Anglo-African dialect. — (2) **1846** BROWNE *Trees Amer.* 1 Genus *Magnolia* . . . (grows in) Spain, Italy, Britain, and Anglo-America. *Ib.* 109 Horse-chesnut . . . (grows in) Britain and Anglo-America. — (3) **1886** *Ann. Rep. U.S. Treasury* p. ix., Which could but conceive an Anglo-centric monetary system. — (4) **1864** *National Almanac* (Phila.) 505/1 The Anglo-Confederate blockade-running steamer Chatham is captured.

(5) **1800** *Aurora* (Phila.) 8 Jan. (Th.), The nicknames Anglo-federal, Anglo-federalism, &c., were also current. **1817** FEARON *Sketches* (1818) 145 It is an unholy league between apostates . . . on the one part, and on the other the anglo-federalists, the monarchists. — (6) **1812** *Niles' Reg.* II. 6/2 We close this article by annexing the following Anglo-Indian account of the battle. **1845** DE SMET *Oregon Missions* (1847) 162 The worthy Bishop . . . has established his See on the Red River, a tributary of the Winnipeg, amidst the possessions of the Anglo-Indians. — (7) **1787** JEFFERSON *Writings* (1905) VI. 370 It will be of great consequence to France and England, to have America governed by a Galloman or Angloman. **1830** *Boston Transcript* 4 Sep. 2/2 The Anglomen, who have missed their union with England, . . . will never cease to bawl, on the breaking up of their sanctuary. — (8) **1787** JEFFERSON *Writings* VI. 145, I know your taste for the works of art gives you a little disposition to Anglomania. **1891** *Harper's Mag.* Aug. 372/2 If to swear by everything English, from togs to manners just because it is English, be Anglomania, the sooner we are rid of it the better. **1942** *Va. Q. Rev.* XVIII. 61 This set up an Anglomania in the South that still survives more or less. — (9) **1793** JEFFERSON *Writings* (1895) VI. 237 If the author of 'Plain truth' was now to be charged with that pamphlet, this put along side of his present Anglomany would decide the voice of the yeomanry of the country on the subject.

(10) **1793** JEFFERSON *Writings* VI. 250 We are going on here in the same spirit still. The Anglophobia has seized violently on three members of our council. **1944** *Chi. D. News* 7 Oct. 2/2 To the extent that this is mere Anglophobia it is unworthy. — (11) **1893** *N. Amer. Rev.* Aug. 170 The work of an anglo-phobiac who labors . . . to widen and prolong the schism. **1904** in BISHOP *Roosevelt & His Time* I. 348 If an Anglomaniac in social life goes into political life he usually becomes politically an Anglophobiac. — (12) **1863** *Boston Sun. Herald* 26 April 1/3 The Anglo-Rebel navy . . . was fitting out in England. — (13) **1846** EMORY *Military Reconn.* 96 They all spoke exultingly of having thrown off 'the detestable Anglo-Yankee yoke.'

Anglo-American 'æŋgloə'merəkən, *n.* and *a.*

1. An American of English descent.

[**1738** *Remarks on Trial of J. P. Zenger* i. 16 (Signature of letter:) I am yours, &c. Anglo-Americanus.] **1787** S. S. SMITH *Ess. Complexion* (1788) 194 The Anglo-Americans on the frontiers of the states, who acquire their sustenance principally by hunting. **1810** *Raleigh* (N.C.) *Register* 5 July 2/3 Those few who had been [to Oxford], had called themselves in the matriculation book, ANGLO *Americans.* **1948** *Seventeen* June 4/4 We had a Chinese boy cheerleader, a Mexican girl cheerleader, and three Anglo-Americans.

b. (See quot. 1786.) *Obs.*

1781–2 JEFFERSON *Notes Va.* (1787) 15 In case of war with our neighbours, the Anglo-Americans or the Indians, the route to New-York becomes a frontier through almost its whole length. **1786** — *Writings* V. 402 We can no longer be called Anglo-Americans. That appellation now describes only the inhabitants of Nova Scotia, Canada, &c.

2. *a.* Pertaining to both England and the U.S.

1809 F. CUMING *Western Tour* 219 At the conflux of the rivers Allegheny and Monongahela, the French . . . had the principal of a line line of posts . . . to prevent the spreading of Anglo-American colonization. **1880** CABLE *Grandissimes* liii. 402 It is not certain that they entered deeper . . . than a comparison of . . . Anglo-American and Franco-American conventionalities. **1948** *Sat. Ev. Post* 2 Oct. 51/1 One of the things that help exclude the Mexicans from a fuller part in Anglo-American doings is a residual Indian shyness that manifests itself in their clannishness.

b. *S.W.* Non-Spanish.

1943 DALE *Cow Country* 5 The fierce Comanches . . . were very warlike, raided in Mexico, and attacked the settlements of the Anglo-American settlers of Texas. **1947** *Denver Post* 19 Jan. (Mag.) 4/1 [He] will breed ten of the best Tee-la-wuket thoroughbred mares as a starter of what Venuti aspires to build up—an Anglo-American strain that will make history in this part of the country.

Anglo-Saxonize, *v. tr.* To imbue with English character or culture. *Rare.* — **1893** STRONG *New Era* iv. 80 This race is destined to dispossess many weaker ones, assimilate others, & mould the remainder, until . . . it has Anglo-Saxonized mankind.

Angola pea. (See quots.) — **1763** GRAINGER *Sugar-Cane* Bk. IV. 454 There let angola's bloomy bush supply, For many a year, with wholesome pulse their board. . . . [Note] *angola.* This is called pidgeon-pea, and grows on a sturdy shrub, that will last for years. . . . The botanic name is cytisus. **1856** *Rep. Comm. Patents: Agric.* 257 The celebrated 'Oregon pea' . . . has been cultivated . . . by my father about fifty years. He obtained the seed from the captain of a slaver, from the coast of Angola, a year or two after the cession of Louisiana; and it has been known and cultivated here ever since that period as the 'Angola pea.'

Anguilla seed. The seed of sea-island cotton. *Obs.* — **1828** COMMONS *Doc. Hist.* I. 268 The seed, as I have been informed by respectable gentlemen from the Bahamas, was in the first instance produced from a small island in the West Indies, celebrated for its Cotton, called Anguilla. It was therefore long after its introduction into this country called Anguilla seed.

anhinga æn'hɪŋgə, *n.* [f. Tupi (the lingua franca of the Amazon Valley) *anhinga.* The immediate source is not clear. Webster says Pg.; poss. Africans were the conveyors.] =**snake bird.** Also attrib.

1835 AUDUBON *Ornith. Biog.* III. 90 The hoarse cries of the Anhingas and the screams of the Herons. **1938** *Auk* Jan. 121 Here we found several American Egrets and Anhingas on nests. **c1945** HOPKINS *Okefenokee* 60, I found in 1933 thirty-one Anhinga nests in tall young cypress trees on one acre.

∗**animal,** *n. attrib.* Designating a *cooky* or *cracker* in the shape of an animal. See also **beef animal, calico animal.** — **1925** WITWER *Roughly Speaking* 52 The guests at Jonesy's party were as assorted as animal crackers, really. **1947** *Denver Post* 19 Jan. (Mag.) 7/1 She was to take a cake to a party. It fell, but she dressed it up with pink frosting and animal cookies.

∗**ankle,** *n.* **1. ankle express,** the feet. *Slang.* **2. ankle tie,** a low shoe or slipper fastened with ankle straps, laces, or ribbons. — (1) **1920** HUNTER *Trail Drivers Texas* I. 49, I took the 'ankle express' for my home. — (2) **1873** E. S. PHELPS *Trotty's Wedding* i, Her little ankle-ties swung tormentingly and carelessly to and fro against the wood-pile. **1943** HALE *Between Dark and Daylight* 162 There was a queer, tremulous feeling about being in your best dress, in your patent-leather ankle-ties; your legs felt long and cold in unaccustomed thin stockings.

Anna hummingbird. A hummingbird of a western species, *Calypte anna,* so named in 1829 by a French ornithologist in honor of Anna, Duchess of Rivoli. — **1898** *N.Y. Observer* 14 July 34/2 The Black-chinned Humming-bird and the Anna Humming-bird he mentions as common summer residents. **1948** *Pacific Discovery* Mar.–Apr. 14/2 Anna hummingbirds, with their flashing crimson gorgets, are with us all year round.

∗ **annex,** *n.*

1. An organization established at Harvard University in 1879 for giving women private collegiate instruction—the forerunner of Radcliffe College. Also transf. and attrib.

1880 *Harper's Mag.* Dec. 103 Of the success of the Annex in its first year there is only one opinion. **1884** *Century Mag.* Aug. 640/1 Well! he secured an Annex girl, And she beguiled a Yale professor. **1893** D. C. GILMAN *University Probl.* (1898) 304 The remarkable success which has attended what is called the Annex of Harvard University.

2. An addition or appendage. *Humorous.*

1887 *Harper's Mag.* Oct. 658/1 There arrived a dog, with a man annex, from the City of Brotherly Love. The way that dog went about . . . followed by his annex [etc.]. **1888** BILLINGS *Hardtack* 85 It would indeed have been a most admirable arrangement in many respects . . . could each man have been provided with an excellent Magee Range with copper-boiler annex.

*** annexation**, *n.* The adding of further territory to the U.S. See **Texas annexation.**

1820 CLAY *Speeches* (1860) I. p. xiv, The difference between those who may be disinclined to its annexation to our confederacy, and me, is, that their system begins where mine may . . . terminate. **1892** M. A. JACKSON *Gen. Jackson* 29 After the close of the Mexican war and the annexation of California. **1948** *Sat. Ev. Post* 10 July 68/4 He was sincerely opposed to the annexation of Texas, and brave enough to say so.

annexationist ænɛks'eʃənɪst, *n.* (See quot. 1888.) Also attrib. — **1845** *N.Y. Tribune* 31 Dec. 3/1 If the Annexationists really believe that the people of the U.S. will sanction their schemes, why do they not test them constitutionally? **1888** LANE *Pol. Catch-Words* 13 Sep. 15 *Annexationist*, one who advocates the annexation of outside territory to the United States. The word came prominently into use in the course of the discussions preceding the annexation of Texas.

Annie Oakley. [Annie Oakley (1860–1926) was a noted woman marksman who traveled for seventeen years with Buffalo Bill's Wild West Show. See *Amer. Sp.* for Feb. 1933, p. 76 ff.] (See quot. 1922.) — **1922** in *Amer. Sp.* VIII. 76/2 Miss Oakley explained that Ban Johnson is the man who invented the term 'Annie Oakley' for free passes. **1946** *Life* 17 June 108/2 A newspaper circulation man gave him two 'Annie Oakleys' to a boxing match.

anniversarian ˌænəvɚ'sɛrɪən, *n.* One who delivers an anniversary address. — **1898** *Official Congress. Directory* 31 William Henry Fleming . . . was chosen private anniversarian of the Phi Beta Kappa Society in 1873.

*** anniversary**, *n.* (1) (*cap.*) (*pl.*) The meetings in Anniversary Week. (2) **anniversary election sermon**, = **election sermon.** (3) **Anniversary Week**, the week during which religious societies and other organizations hold their annual meetings. All *obs.*

(1) **1856** *Harper's Mag.* July 269/1 The Anniversaries are long since over. **1857** *Harper's Mag.* May 842/2 A year ago we took occasion of the occurrence of the May Anniversaries to plead for a more just . . . remuneration of our ministers. — (2) **1704** *Boston News-Letter* 7 June 2/2 The anniversary Election Sermon was preached by the Rd. Mr. Jon. Russel. — (3) **1856** *Harper's Mag.* July 124/1 Imagine the thoughts of some well-educated but impoverished country minister as he looks upon our city during Anniversary Week. **1860** *Agric. Convention, Chicago* 3 The anniversary week . . . opened Tuesday, June 26th, with the annual meeting of the Illinois Natural History Society.

As the last term in **cracker, firemen's, national, Pilgrim anniversary.**

*** annual**, *a.* and *n.*

1. *n.* An examination held every year. Also attrib. or as adj. *Obs.*

1871 L. H. BAGG *At Yale* 277 On the morning of Presentation Day the Freshmen now assume their Annual hats. *Ib.* 278 The members of the committee . . . wear . . . tiny forks of gold, inscribed 'Annual.' . . . The last session of Freshman 'Annual' closes at noon of the Thursday before Commencement. *Ib.* 281 Each of the two factions also adopted its own style of Annual cap. **1895** W. S. TYLER *Amherst College* 175 In 1850–60, 'annuals' . . . [had] taken the place of the 'senior examination' on the whole course.

2. annual conference, in the Methodist Church a yearly assembly having jurisdiction over certain ecclesiastical matters and sending delegates to the general conference.

1832 WILLIAMSON *Maine* II. 697 There are seven Annual Conferences, composed only of those who are in full 'connexion,' that is, those who are in Elders' or Deacons' orders. **1936** *N.Y. Times* 8 Oct. 32/6 A formal demand was submitted today to officials of the Rock River annual conference of the Methodist Episcopal Church.

3. annual message, the message which the President of the U.S. delivers to Congress every year, or that of the governor to a state legislature.

1806 *Ann. 9th Congress* 2 Sess. 11 Annual Message. The following Message was received [by Congress] from the President of the United States. **1837** *Wisconsin H. Rep. Jrnl.* 440 Annual Message of Governor [= Henry Dodge]. **1945** *Newsweek* 15 Jan. 36/1 The President's comments on inter-Allied relationships, in his annual message to Congress, were intended to steady both American public opinion and the United Nations coalition.

*** annuity**, *n.* Used with reference to supplies and provisions annually given by the U.S. government to Indians, as (1) **annuity goods**, (2) **money**, (3) **salt.**

(1) **1868** *Indian Laws & Tr.* III. 716 The half-breeds of said tribe shall share equally . . . in the distribution of annuity goods. **1947** *Denver Post* 19 Jan. (Mag.) 5/5 The White river Utes, with little or no annuity goods for two years, would have starved if they had not killed wild game. — (2) **1849** *Pres. Mess. Congress* II. 1015 Besides this annuity-money, the band receives every year ten thousand dollars in goods. **1946** FOREMAN *Last Trek* 230 He could deposit the annuity money in a safe place. — (3) **1810** *Amer. Republic* (Frankfort, Ky.) 17 Aug. 1/5 About this time also, a boat which had been sent up the Wabash with the annuity salt for the Indians returned.

b. Also **annuity grounds, Indian, roll.** Cf. also **Indian annuity.**

1844 in *Amer. Sp.* XXII. 200/2 On the day following [I] visited the annuity-grounds, a few miles distant. [**1850** E. S. SEYMOUR *Sketches of Minnesota* 164 And the annuity-receiving Indians, will require for their consumption a large amount of agricultural products.] **1870** *Congress. Globe* 30 June 5010/2 When a tribe of annuity Indians take a frontier-man's cattle . . . , a deduction shall be made from the next annuity to be paid to those Indians. **1878** *Rep. Supt. Yellowstone Nat. Pk.* 9 The few Sheep-eaters, Bannocks, and Shoshones . . . now belong at their agencies with other annuity Indians. **1946** FOREMAN *Last Trek* 91 The annuity roll showed that these Indians numbered less than four hundred souls in 1836.

*** annunciator**, *n.* Also *** enunciator.** A signalling apparatus, or an indicator of some kind (see also quot. 1853).

1847 *Rep. Comm. Patents 1846* 101 Letters patent have also been granted for an improved enunciator, for use in hotels, etc. **1853** A. BUNN *Old Eng. & New Eng.* 39 There is an appendage to this office of a remarkable character called an 'Annunciator,' invented, we believe, by Jackson, of New York city, whereby all the bell-pulls of the house are brought within one focus. **1890** BIFF HALL *Turnover Club* 151 The effort of twirling the annunciator made him dizzy, but he found voice to call for the number he required. **1906** MARK TWAIN *Autobiog.* (1934) II. 78 (R.), The burglar-alarm let fly about two o'clock. I turned up the gas, looked at the annunciator, and turned off the alarm.

A No. 1, A number 1. First-class, superior, A 1, originally of ships (see quot. 1857). *Colloq.*

[**1835** in *Am. Sp.* XXII. 201/1 He is a splendid man, that; we class him No. 1, letter A.] **1857** BUTLER *Goodrich's Fifth School Reader* 55 Vessels are classified according to their age, strength, and other qualities. The best class is called A, and No. 1 implies that the Swiftsure stands at the head of the best class of vessels. **1886** MARK TWAIN *Speeches* (1923) 137 (R.), Tons of A No. 1, fourth-proof, hard-boiled, hide-bound grammar. **1947** *Sports Afield* Dec. 59/3 It's an A-No. 1 type of project for any club to sponsor.

***another**, *a.* **another sort**, differently. *Colloq.* — **1871** *Ill. Agric. Soc.* VIII. 229 His calves and his pigs would thrive another sort.

anquera æŋ'kɛra, *n. W.* [Amer. Sp. in same sense.] (See quot. 1944.) — **1881** FARROW *Mt. Scouting* 138 The Mexican or California saddle . . . [is] usually furnished with wool-lined bastas, llama-skin anqueras, sudaderos, tapaderos, and stirrup leathers handsomely cut-stamped. **1944** ADAMS *W. Words* 5/1 Anquera. . . . Americans use this term as meaning the broad leather sewn to the base of the cantle when there is no rear jockey, and extending beyond the cantle.

*** answer**, *n.* (See quots.) *Obs.*

1789 *Ann. 1st Congress* II. 32 The committee appointed to prepare an answer to the President's speech, delivered to the Senate and House of Representatives of the United States. **1816** PICKERING 32 *Answer* . . . is always used by us to signify the Reply of the Senate or House of Representatives to the Speech of the President (or of the Governor of a state) at the opening of a session of the Legislature. **1856** BENTON *30 Years* II. 32 The change from the address delivered in person, with its answer, to the message sent by the private secretary, and no answer, was introduced by Mr. Jefferson, and considered a reform.

*** ant**, *n.* In combs.: (1) *** ant catcher**, a rock wren, genus *Salpinctes*, of the arid desert regions of the western U.S.; (2) **country**, a region where ants are numerous, *rare;* (3) **killer**, the foot, *humorous;* (4) **rice**, (see quot. 1879).

(1) **1825** BONAPARTE *Ornithology* I. 9 The antcatchers are never found in settled districts, where their favorite insects are . . . less abundant. — (2) **1853** P. PAXTON *Yankee in Texas* 163 Texas, in fact, may be entomologically divided into . . . the ant country and the roach and flea country. — (3) *a***1846** *Quarter Race Kentucky* 85

'Bill Jones, quit a smashin that ar cat's tail!' 'Well let hir keep hir tail clar of my ant killers!' — (4) **1879** Lubbock *Sci. Lect.* iv. 109 A Texan ant . . . is also a harvesting species, storing up especially the grains of *Aristida oligantha*, the so-called 'ant rice.' **1885** H. C. McCook *Tenants Old Farm* 341 A sort of grass known as ant-rice, or needle grass.

As the last term in **agricultural, desert, occidental, velvet ant.**

***antagonize,** *v. tr.* "In England, antagonizing forces must be of the same kind, but in the political phraseology of the U.S. a person may antagonize (i.e., oppose) a measure" *OED.*

1882 *Boston Ev. Transcript* 4/3 Ex-Secretary Windom did not hesitate openly to antagonize ex-Secretary Sherman's Bill. **1904** L. O. Brastow *Repr. Mod. Preachers* 148 He antagonized theology and denied the rational possibility of it. **1932** *DAB* VIII. 226 This highly protectionist measure, antagonizing many voters as much as it pleased ardent protectionists like Hanna, led to a serious Republican setback.

ante 'æntɪ, *n.* Also **anti.** [App. f. **ante-*, before.] In card games as brag and poker, the preliminary stake or one put up in the course of the game. Also transf. Cf. **penny ante.**

1838 *Victims of Gambling* 86 The one next to the dealer [at brag] puts up into the pool . . . any sum he may choose, unless the amount has been . . . fixed by the company. This sum is called the ante. **1844** J. Cowell *Thirty Years* 94 The dealer makes the game, or value of the beginning bet, and called the anti. **1909** Wason *Happy Hawkins* 261, I had seen the ol' man sit in a game where steers was the ante an' car loads the limit. **1948** *Chi. D. News* 5 March 5/1, I . . . predicted that the $400 millions voted for the Truman Doctrine was but the initial ante in the international poker game.

b. A game involving an ante.

1835 *Essays on Var. Subjects* 7 Having several in company is also very convenient, when staying in the country, for a little *ante* in the evening, for which purpose a pack of cards is always put into the pocket with the powder flask.

c. ante-man, one who puts up an ante.

1887 Keller *Draw Poker* 68 If a number of players have gone in, it is best generally for the ante-man to make good and go in.

ante 'æntɪ, *v.* [f. the noun.] *tr.* and *intr.* To put up an ante in a game of chance. Often with *up.* Also transf. *Colloq.*

1845 Hooper *S. Sugg's Adv.* x. 129 'Yes!' . . . it's a game that all can win at! Ante up! ante up, boys—friends I mean—don't back out. **1854** in Thornton *Amer. Glossary* 971 Playin' at billiards an' monte Till they've nary red cent to ante. **1861** T. Polk in *N.Y. Tribune* 10 Aug., You have heard of the difficulty that *The Bulletin* has fallen into. I have had to 'ante up' there at the rate of $200. **1894** *Life* 4 Jan. 5 [Santa Claus:] Look here, my Christian friend! You want to ante up pretty liberally such a hard winter as this. **1948** *Dly. Ardmoreite* (Ardmore, Okla.) 13 Apr. 1/1, I had to ante up a buck.

b. To dispose of (money) in a card game, to push (one's way) into a place. *Rare.*

1845 Hooper *S. Sugg's Adv.* xii. 144 Exsept $500 dollers I anteed off amongst the boys of a night, I couldn't get off a sent. **1873** Mark Twain & Warner *Gilded Age* xiii. 124, I'd bet a hundred dollars he will ante his way right into the United States Senate when his territory comes in.

***ante-.** A prefix meaning "before" used in attrib. or adj. combinations: (1) **ante-bellum,** before the Civil War, 1861–65; (2) **revolutional, revolutionary,** prior to the American Revolution, 1775–83; (3) **-war, =ante-bellum.**

(1) **1867** *Fredericksburg* (Va.) *News* 2 Aug. 3/2 Attention, Ante Bellum Debtors to the News. **1947** Brown *Outdoors Unlimited* 77 Picture a composite, inside and out, of all the loveliest southern manors you've seen in the movies, and you're still only fairly close to Allourn, Hal's ante-bellum home. — (2) **1837** *S. Lit. Messenger* III. 464 These towns . . . still exist and are the only means we now have of becoming acquainted with the ante-revolutionary Frenchmen. **1839** Irving *Wolfert's Roost* (1855) 164 An old gentleman, whose dress was decidedly ante-revolutional. — (3) **1878** *N. Amer. Rev.* CXXVII. 123 To go back to Ante-war money, Ante-war wages, and ante-war prices, might be tolerable if, at the same time we could go back to ante-war freedom from debt and ante-war lightness of national taxation. **1880** *Bradstreet's* 19 May 5/4 The scaling down of the ante-war debt . . . will remain forever a stain.

***antelope,** *n.*

1. The pronghorn or prongbuck, *Antilocapra americana*, of the western plains area.

This animal differs so widely from the Old World creature of the same name that scientists have created for it a separate family of which it is the only representative.

1804 Lewis & Clark *Exped.* (1893) I. 120 Of all the animals we had seen the antelope seems to possess the most wonderful fleetness. **1867** Richardson *Beyond Mississippi* 165 The antelope gallops over the hills, with an elasticity surpassing the fleetest racehorse. **1947** *Steamboat* (Colo.) *Pilot* 30 Jan. 3/2 Approximately 500 antelope are wintering in the Browns Park area.

2. In combs.: (1) **antelope brush,** a branchy, silvery shrub common in the dry regions of the West; (2) **chipmunk, =antelope ground squirrel;** (3) **dance,** an Indian ceremonial dance; (4) **goat,** the Rocky Mountain goat, *Haplocerus montanus;* (5) **ground squirrel,** a ground squirrel found in the Southwest; (6) **jack rabbit,** a species of jack rabbit (see quot. 1925); (7) **range,** an area frequented by antelope; (8) **refuge,** a place set aside by the government for the protection of antelope;(9) **squirrel, =antelope ground squirrel;** (10) **surround,** a surround *q.v.* for killing antelope, *obs.*

(1) **1915** *Nat. & Science on Pac. Coast* 151 The most abundant species are the sagebrush, . . . antelope brush (*Purshia tridentata*), and in alkaline soil black greasewood. **1940** Jaeger *Desert Wild Flowers* 88 Antelope-brush . . . is considered to be the most important of Western browse species. — (2) **1915** *Nat. & Science on Pac. Coast* 111 Day-light-roaming rodents . . . include the striped antelope chipmunk which holds its short, flat, white-lined tail closely appressed to its back. — (3) **1942** Stegner *Mormon C.* 322 He lived among cowboys and Indians, danced the Antelope Dance with the Hopi, learned Navajo . . . and rode and fooled around with the Mormon kids. — (4) **1884** *Cent. Mag.* Dec. 193 Professor Spencer F. Baird . . . places this animal among the antelopes with the distinctive generic name of *Aplocerus montanus*. . . . As a popular name mountain antelope or antelope-goat might be suggested. **1888** Roosevelt in *Century Mag.* XXXVI. 202/2, [I] devoted my entire energies to the chase of but one animal, the white antelope-goat, at present the least known and rarest of all American game.

(5) **1939** Pickwell *Deserts* 3/1 For six weeks the Desert Antelope Ground Squirrel lived without a drop of water, yet it had water. **1940** Jaeger *Desert Wild Flowers* 3 The antelope ground squirrels, well aware of the nutritious qualities of the seeds, harvest them in quantity. — (6) **1909** Nelson *Rabbits of N.A.* 117 Antelope Jack Rabbit . . . is the handsomest . . . of the North American hares. **1925** Bryan *Papago Country* 50 The antelope jack rabbit (*Lepus alleni*) is one of the most interesting of the desert animals. — (7) **1846** Sage *Scenes Rocky Mts.* iv., We reached the antelope range, and saw four or five of these animals scouring the boundless expanse. — (8) **1943** Gabrielson *W. Refuges* 15 Steps were taken to establish . . . an antelope refuge in Nevada. — (9) **1908** Hornaday *Camp Fires on Desert* 66 During the day we saw . . . one coyote, two Harris's antelope squirrels, . . . one eagle, and eighteen ravens. — (10) **1845** Frémont *Exped.* 127 In the absence of the men, who were engaged in an antelope surround.

Also *antelope ham, meat, skin, steak.*

As the last term in **American, buck, forked-horned, goat, Missouri, mountain, prong horn(ed) antelope.**

Anthony rule. In the U.S. Senate an order of procedure for expediting the disposal of business devised by Henry B. Anthony, Senator from Rhode Island (1859–94). *Obs.*

1870 *Cong. Globe* 17 June 4541/3 The Chair will state the distinction between this and what was popularly known in the Senate as the 'Anthony rule,' under which the Calendar was gone over subject to objection. **1879** *Cong. Rec.* 5 Feb. 995/1 What is known as the Anthony rule can only be suspended on one day's notice given, or by unanimous consent. **1882** *Cong. Rec.* 3 Feb. 872/1 The great advantage we have . . . received from the . . . Anthony rule.

***anthracite,** *n.* In combs. designating things made by using anthracite coal or suitable for burning it, as **anthracite iron, nail, stove.**

1840 *Niles' Reg.* 20 June 256/1 Anthracite iron. Malleable iron has been made from pigs formed at the anthracite furnace at Roaring Creek, Pa. **1877** Raymond *Mines & Mining* 363 The development of the vast anthracite-iron industry, which has contributed so much to the prosperity of Pennsylvania.—**1840** *Niles' Reg.* 1 Aug. 352/1 Anthracite nails are made from the ore at the works of Messrs. Reeve & Whitaker, Phoenixville, Pa. in the short space of twenty-four hours. —**1853** Kane *Grinnell Exp.* ii. 21 Three anthracite stoves.

***anti,** *n.* Short for: (1) **antifederalist,** (2)**anti-Mason;** (3) **anti-Mormon.** All *obs.*

(1) **1788** *Columbian* July 414/1 After dinner it was agreed to raise the constitution that the anti's had burnt in the morning; a very respectable number went to the pine bush, and cutting down a pine tree, brought it to the fort, and raised it on the very spot where the anti's burnt the constitution. **1817** *N.Y. Herald* 2 April 1/2 Now the

democrats first called themselves antifederalists, and some, for shortness, antees, which means, that they were against those who wanted union and a national constitution. — (2) **1830** *Moral Envoy* (Fall River, Mass.) 9 June 2/6 This Most Worshipful and chivalrous Knight of the mallet and cable-tow . . . threatens to blow up the *Antis* 'sky high' with his 'damaged gunpowder.' **1831** *Vt. Statesman* (Castleton) 7 Dec. 2/5 They stayed at home and left the contest to be carried on between the Anties and the Jackson men. — (3) **1845** *Quincy* (Ill.) *Whig* 1 Nov. 2/2 A few more Mormon cabins had been burned in the county by the anties. *a***1850** FORD *Hist. Illinois* (1854) 419 But soon after the anties had arrived with their force near Nauvoo . . . Mr. Brayman came to Springfield. *Ib.* 417 This treaty was agreed to by Gen. Singleton . . . and others, on the side of the anties, and by Major Parker and some leading Mormons on the other side.

* **anti-.** A prefix denoting opposition or hostility, widely used in noun and attrib. or adj. combs.

The number of such combs. is extremely large. The more significant of them, as **anti-abolition, anti-American, anti-bank, anti-Democrat,** etc., are given as main entries. Those possessing at least some social or historic interest are dealt with here.

1. In relatively fixed but now often obs. combs.: (1) **anti-administration,** opposed to the President and his party; (2) **assumptionist,** one opposed to the assumption of state debts by the federal government; (3) **Clintonian,** one opposed to De Witt Clinton (1769–1825), candidate for the presidency in 1812, cf. **bucktail;** (4) **coolie,** opposed to the introduction of Chinese laborers into this country; (5) **fed,** abbrev. of **anti-federalist;** (6) **federalism,** the political principles of the anti-federalists; (7) **federalist,** one opposed to the Federalist party and to the adoption of the Constitution of 1787; (8) **imperialist,** an opponent of the policy of the U.S. of acquiring overseas territory; (9) **Lecompton,** designating a faction in the Democratic Party opposed to the proslavery constitution for Kansas drawn up at Lecompton, Oct.–Nov., 1857; (10) **liquor,** opposed to the liquor trade; (11) **mission, missionary,** used of a sect of Baptists opposed to missions and to missionary work; (12) **monopolist,** an opponent of monopolies; (13) **monopoly,** opposed to the power and influence of large corporations and their monopolies; (14) **nullification,** opposed to the doctrine that a state of the Union can nullify legislation of the federal government; (15) **nullifier,** one who opposes nullification, also with special reference to Andrew Jackson; (16) **polygamy,** opposed to polygamy, esp. with reference to the Mormons; (17) **relief party,** (see quot. 1887); (18) **secession,** opposed to the secession of the southern states from the Union; (19) **Southern,** opposed to the interests of the Southern States; (20) **suffragist,** one opposed to female suffrage; (21) **tariffite,** one opposed to tariffs, esp. to those of a protective nature, cf. **anti-tariff** below; (22) **Texas,** (*a*) opposed to the annexation of Texas, (*b*) also with reference to Texas fever quarantine laws; (23) **trust,** opposed to large monopolistic combinations in trade and industry.

(1) **1830** *Political Arena* (Fredericksburg, Va.) 10 Sep. 2/5 Administration and anti-administration, Nullification and Anti-Nullification, Whig & Enquirer, all unite in expressions of delight at the late events in France. **1945** *Daily Sentinel* (Grand Junction, Colo.) 26 Nov. 1/2 Anti-administration sentiment found another outlet in the lower house. — (2) **1841** *Cong. Globe* Jan. App. 153/1 The assumptionist and the anti-assumptionist . . . were united against the Democracy. **1883** MACMASTER *Hist.* I. 580 The Anti-assumptionists hoped to win through a bargain they had just completed with one of the Middle States. — (3) **1817** *Guardian of Liberty* (Cynthiana, Ky.) 7 June 3/2 The anti-Clintonians carried the election by a majority of 1900 votes. **1885** SCHOULER *Hist. U.S.* III. 227 Better success in constitutional reform was attained in New York, in spite of an incessant turmoil between Clintonians and the anti-Clintonians. — (4) **1869** BRACE *New West* xvi. 210 Employers found him too useful to permit him to be driven off by 'anti-coolie' vagabonds. **1888** *Cong. Rec.* App. 18 Aug. 439/2 The anti-cooly act became a law on the 9th of February, 1869.

(5) **1788** *Maryland Jrnl.* 3 June (Th.), The famous Dr. Spring asked a lady on which side she was, fed. or antifed. **1806** FESSENDEN *Democracy Unveiled* II. 83 Ye Tories, Demos, Antifeds, Of hollow hearts, and wooden heads. — (6) **1788** C. GORE in *Life & Corr. R. King* (1894) I. 348 One candidate . . . was abhorred for his antifederalism. **1840** HONE *Diary* II. 35, I was brought up after the manner of Virginian anti-Federalism. — (7) **1787** *Independent Gazetteer* (Phila.) 4 Oct., And I am the more inclined to espouse this opinion, because the author of 'Tar and Feathers' aims to destroy the distinction of *Whig* and *Tory*, and to establish one more odious, viz: *Federalists* and *Anti-Federalists*. **1948** *Chi. Tribune* 10 Oct. (Grafic Mag.) 5/5 Burr was an anti-Federalist. — (8) **1899** (*title*), The anti-Imperialist. Brookline, Mass. **1910** L. F. ABBOTT in *Outlook* 25 June 371 The extreme wing of the Liberal party, whom we should call Anti-Imperialists. — (9) **1859** *Tribune Almanac* 63/2 The candidates of the Anti-Lecompton or Broderick Democracy. **1886** LOGAN *Great Conspiracy* 94 Douglas, representing the Anti-Lecompton wing of Democracy, held that whether Slavery be right or wrong, [etc.].

(10) **1852** *N.Y. Wkly. Tribune* 14 Feb. 5/3 (*heading*), The Pending Anti-Liquor Law. **1910** C. HARRIS *Eve's Husband* 138, I have determined to run on the anti-liquor ticket. — (11) **1847** L. COLLINS *Kentucky* 112 To these add 7,085 anti-missionary Baptists, many of whom claim to be United Baptists. **1883** *Schaff's Relig. Encycl.* I. 212/1 Anti-Mission Baptists, with 40,000 members. **1910** *U.S. Census, Religious Bodies* (1919) II. 136 The antimission movement. — (12) **1850** *Corr. R. W. Griswold* (1898) 261, I was to be put in nomination by the anti-monopolists in the Legislature. **1888** LANE *Pol. Catch-Words* 13 Sep. 15 *Anti-Monopolists*, those who are opposed to the creation of corporations that have the control of any article of common use. — (13) **1881** *Nation* 10 March 160/2 The 'Anti-Monopoly League' meeting . . . has drawn out two or three excellent letters. **1886** *N. Amer. Review* July 87 The main purpose of the anti-monopoly movement is to resist public corruption and corporate aggression. — (14) **1830** [see **anti-administration**]. **1846** MANSFIELD *Winfield Scott* 234 The legislature of Georgia, also a strong anti-tariff state, passed anti-nullification resolutions, by strong majorities.

(15) **1830** *Mass. Spy* 27 Oct. (Th.), In Columbia [S.C.], the seat of Government, and the very focus of nullification, two Nullifiers, and two anti-Nullifiers are chosen to the Assembly. **1860** KENNEDY *Wirt* II. 346 All the loyal who enjoyed the favor or confidence of the great Anti-Nullifier. — (16) **1873** BEADLE *Undevel. West* 675 The Ninety-per-cent. Spring, which Gentiles call the Anti-polygamy Spring, is some two miles west of Hooper's. **1884** *Cent. Mag.* May 121/2 The passage of the Edmunds Anti-Polygamy Bill, disfranchising all persons living in polygamy. *Ib.* 122/1 It is entirely within the power of the Mormon women to turn any anti-polygamy bill into a farce, if they choose. — (17) **1824** *Commentator* (Frankfort, Ky.) 18 Dec. 3/3 It is as appropriate to the relief party as *court party* is to the anti-*relief party*. **1887** SCHURZ *Life Henry Clay* I. 203 The people of Kentucky . . . then sought 'relief' by legislative contrivances in favor of debtors, which caused a political division into the 'relief' and the 'anti-relief' parties. — (18) **1865** *Atlantic Mo.* XV. 745 The convention, when elected on the 4th of February preceding, was largely Anti-Secession. **1881** *Georgians* 77 They had both made anti-secession speeches in the beginning. — (19) **1842** *Southern Q. Rev.* II. 167 He was suspected of anti-Southern feelings. **1861** W. S. SPEER in *N.Y. Tribune* 8 Nov., I was stigmatized as an Abolitionist, or Black Republican, an anti-Southern man.

(20) **1886** HOWELLS in *Harper's Mag.* Dec. 64/2, I acknowledge that I made a speech . . . on behalf of the anti-suffragists. **1898** *Mo. So. Dakotan* I. 61 It has been said by some of our local anti-suffragists that the women of South Dakota have all they desire and with that ought to be content. — (21) **1833** *Niles' Reg.* XLIV. 1/1 Tariffites or anti-tariffites . . . have been so jostled that no party knows exactly where is its own present location. **1841** *Cong. Globe* Jan., App. 153/1 The high tariffite and the anti-tariffite . . . were united against the Democracy. — (22) (*a*) **1845** *Quincy* (Ill.) *Whig* 20 Dec. 2/4 The protective, anti-Texas, Oregon wing of the party will then rise in the ascendant. **1848** *N.Y. Wkly. Tribune* 1 April 5/3 A change of 2,600 votes in this State, or a saving of two-fifths of the anti-Texas votes thrown away on Birney, would have given us victory. (*b*) **1930** HOLDEN *Alkali Trails* 42 One naturally wonders what motive was behind so much quarantining and so many anti-Texas laws. — (23) **1890** *Cong. Rec.* 21 March 2465/2 Will the Senator inform me upon what ground the Missouri anti-trust bill was declared unconstitutional in his own State? **1948** *Atomic Scientists Bul.* May 135/2 We can rely on anti-trust remedies to control it.

2. In less frequent, now obs., combs.: (1) **anti-affirmant,** one opposed to the acceptance of an affirmation in place of an oath; (2) **amalgamist,** (see quot.); (3) **cholera,** (see quot.); (4) **effort Baptist,** a Baptist opposed to making any effort to further missionary work; (5) **embargo,** opposed to the embargo acts of the U.S. (1807 ff.), also **anti-embargoist;** (6) **filibusterism,** opposition to filibusterings, esp. such as those directed against various parts of Latin America; (7) **means Baptist,** (see quot.); (8) **Millerite,** one who opposed the views of the Millerites *q.v.;* (9) **populist,** opposed to the Populist party; (10) **protection,** opposed to the levying of a protective tariff; (11) **revolutionism,** opposition to the American Revolution, also **anti-revolutionist;** (12) **scalping,** opposed to the surreptitious securing and selling of railroad and other tickets; (13) **Snapper,** a New York State Cleveland Democrat who resented the calling of a snap state convention by D. B. Hill in 1892 to control, in Hill's favor, the election of delegates to the Chicago Democratic National Convention; (14) **state rights,** opposed to the doctrine of state rights; (15) **suffrage,** opposed to woman suffrage; (16) **tariff,** opposed to tariffs, esp. to those of a protective nature; (17) **Van Buren,** opposed to Martin Van Buren (1782–1862), eighth President of the U.S. (1837–41); (18) **Yazoo,** opposed to the land speculations known as "the Yazoo frauds."

(1) **1789** MACLAY *Deb. Senate* 89 Ran Ellsworth so hard, and the other anti-affirmants, on the anti-constitutionalism of the clause, that they at last consented to have a question taken. — (2) *c***1853** BENWELL *Travels* 58 Soon after he was mobbed in Maine-street by the young desperadoes I have referred to, who, from their determined opposition to intermixed marriages, were known in the place as 'anti-amalgamists.' — (3) **1833** E. T. COKE *Subaltern's Furlough* I. 146 Others . . . would only take 'anticholera,' as they termed brandy and port wine. — (4) **1867** W. H. DIXON *New America* II. 308 In a very short time this body was divided into Old School Baptists (called by their enemies Anti-effort Baptists), Sabbatarians, [etc.].

(5) **1808** *Ann. 10th Congress* 2 Sess. 607 The anti-embargo men of Massachusetts. *Ib.* 779 We anti-embargoists show that things would not have been thus, had our advice been taken. — (6) **1852** *N.Y. Wkly. Tribune* 24 Jan. 3/2 Our friend slipped over into fierce denunciation of Fillmore and anti-Filibusterism. — (7) **1872** EGGLESTON *Hoosier Schoolm.* xii. 102 They call themselves 'Anti-means Baptists' from their Antinomian tenets. — (8) **1842** *Boston Transcript* 4 Sep. 2/1 We now present it to our readers, with a hope that both the Millerites and Anti-Millerites will afford it a perusal. — (9) **1895** *Denver Times* 5 March 5/2 A citizens' caucus had been called . . . to place an anti-Populist ticket in the field for city offices in the near election.

(10) **1882** *Deb. Congress* 16 June 3636 The new race of statesmen in the anti-protection States regard the United States as . . . a quasi community not endowed with power to make the terms. — (11) **1789** MACLAY *Deb. Senate* 74 The old leaven of anti-revolutionism has leavened the whole lump; nor can we keep the Congress free from the influence of it. **1790** MACLAY *Deb. Senate* 300 We have thousands and tens of thousands of anti-revolutionists ready to blow the coals of contention. — (12) **1897** *Cong. Rec.* 19 Feb. 1989/1 A petition of sundry citizens of Massachusetts, praying for the passage of the anti-scalping railroad ticket bill. — (13) **1909** G. F. PARKER *G. Cleveland* 146 As if by magic, there sprang into being an organization known as the anti-Snappers. — (14) **1829** *Va. Herald* (Fredericksburg) 15 Apr. 3/1 Two of them, however, (Messrs Kercheval and Tuley) are anti state rights.

(15) **1886** HOWELLS in *Harper's Mag.* Dec. 66/2, I signed the anti-suffrage petition. — (16) **1820** *Niles' Reg.* XIX. 235 Report on the Anti-Tariff Petitions. — (17) **1834** *Beardstown* (Ill.) *Chronicle* 27 Dec. 3/1 We are informed that the anti-Van Buren men, voted for and elected Mr. Robinson, on the first ballot. — (18) **1796** *Aurora* (Phila.) 5 Dec. (Th.), [I was informed] that the Yazoo-men (as they are called in this place) were making every exertion to prevent General Jackson from being elected a Representative. . . . The people appeared to be of the anti-Yazoo party.

3. In recent combs.: (1) **anti-braintruster,** (2) **CIO,** (3) **freeze,** (4) **lynch(ing),** (5) **smoke law, ordinance,** (6) **vivisection.**

(1) **1935** *Gunnison* (Colo.) *News-Champion* 21 Nov. 4/4 What groups will be arrayed against the President? There will be the partisan Republicans, . . . the anti-brain trusters, the city press and the big magazines. — (2) **1946** *Longmont* (Colo.) *Times-Call* 10 June 2/2 They are saying they never agreed with Kenny, and are strongly anti-CIO. — (3) **1924** *Frontier* Nov. 20 It was so cold that the ten men who took care of Babe, Paul's big blue ox, had to make her drink anti-freeze solution of alcohol and glycerine. **1948** *Salt Lake Tribune* 17 Jan. 23/6 In late autumn and early winter antifreeze . . . was impossible to get most of the time. — (4) **1922** *Ardmore* (Okla.) *Dly. Press* 27 Jan. 1/7 The house declared itself in favor of the federal government exerting authority in an effort to stamp out lynching by passing the Dyer anti-lynching bill. **1948** *Dly. Ardmoreite* (Ardmore, Okla.) 30 Apr. 2/3 The convention endorsed fair employment practices, and anti-lynch and anti-poll tax measures.

(5) **1894** *Chi. D. News* 26 July 4/2 Anti-smoke ordinances have been passed and sustained in the courts. **1930** *N.Y. Times* 27 Apr. x. 5/3 New York's anti-smoke ordinance renders illegal the discharge of dense smoke from buildings. **1948** *Time* 26 April 66/3 They thought it was a petition for Palestine partition, or against the city anti-smoke law, or against war. — (6) **1899** *Land of Sunshine* Jan. 94 The New England Anti-Vivisection Society might probably win more converts to a good cause . . . by being a somewhat less numerous assortment of grandams. **1910** *Cosmopolitan* Oct. 806/1 Interest in the anti-vivisection movement is very much alive.

Also *Anti-Americanism, anglican, Benton democrat, caucus, Chinese, coercionist, constitutionalism, duelling, erosionist, frat, freemason, inoculator, Klan, Know Nothing, Ku Klux, Maine law, naturalization, Negro, Tammany, Texan.*

anti-abolition. Opposition to the abolition of slavery, usu. attrib. Also **anti-abolitionist.** — **1835** *S. Lit. Messenger* I. 772, I am both from conviction and expediency, a decided anti-abolitionist. **1842** BUCKINGHAM *Slave States* II. 76 Both are Anti-abolition papers. **1948** *N. Eng. Quart.* Sep. 327 By 1861, however, . . . the majority of the voters were no longer anti-abolitionists.

anti-American. Opposed to the interests of the U.S.

1773 in *Amer. Sp.* XX. (1945) 269 The Lieutenant-Governor by broaching afresh and supporting through the former assembly the anti-American doctrine of the parliament's right in all cases has given disgust to the public. **1838** in BUCKINGHAM *America* (1841) I. ix. 173 Now our young men are returned rogues and fops, with extravagant anti-American notions. **1947** *Chi. Tribune* 9 Nov. 1. 3/3 He has denied any anti-American sentiment.

b. Also as a noun to designate an opponent of the American party. *Obs.*

1855 *Louisville Times* 10 Aug. 2/1 If the anti-Americans are defeated to-day, they are extinguished as a party.

anti-bank. Opposed to the establishment or continuance of a U.S. bank. Also **anti-bankism, -bankite.** *Obs.*

1837 in MACKENZIE *Van Buren* (1846) 177 The final vote will not shew the full anti-bank strength. **1844** UNCLE SAM *Peculiarities* II. 46 I'm in for pulling an anti-bankite's nose. **1855** PRAY *Mem. J. G. Bennet* 358 Anti-bankism and anti-rentism . . . were prominent ones [*sc.* doctrines] upon which the leaders of this movement proposed to act. **1862** *N.Y. Tribune* 23 June, Had this Constitution been submitted whole, with all its anti-Bank, anti-Negro imperfections on its head, it would have stood a better chance.

Anti-Democrat. One opposed to the Democratic party. Also **anti-democratic.** — **1802** (*title*), The Republican; or, Anti-Democrat. **1837** *Democratic Review* Oct. 10 That extensive anti-democratic corruption of sentiment in some portions of our people. **1855** BRISTED in *Fraser's Mag.* LII. 521 Many of the Southern anti-Democrats in Jackson's and van Buren's time (under the name of *State-rights Whigs*) carried them [*sc.* doctrines] to greater lengths than the Democrats themselves.

anti-federal. Opposed to the granting of much power to the federal government, esp. with reference to a political party which opposed the adoption of the Constitution of 1787. Now *obs.* or *hist.*

1787 *Columbian* Aug. 612/2 The antifederal disposition of a great officer of New-York, it is said, has seriously alarmed the citizens of that State. **1801** A. HAMILTON *Works* (1886) VII. 187 Mr. Jefferson, Mr. Madison, and the great majority of the members . . . are now influential in the anti-federal party. **1882** COOPER *Amer. Pol.* I. 6 They were called Anti-Federals because they opposed a federal government and constitution and adhered to the rights of the States and those of local self-government.

anti-fogmatic. An alcoholic drink jocosely reputed to be valuable for counteracting the bad effects of fog. Also **anti-fogmatical.** Also transf. *Obs.*

1789 *Mass. Spy* 12 Nov. 4/2 Rum. Its great utility in preserving the planters from the effects of the damp and unwholesome air of the morning, has given it the medical name of an Antifogmatick. **1845** *Nauvoo Neighbor* 26 Feb. (Th.), We wish the present generation was a little more antifogmatical. *a***1877** *Baltimore Gazette* (B.), The typical Richmond man takes an 'eye-opener,' then . . . an 'anti-fog-matic,' then . . . his regular 'bitters.'

anti-Jackson. Opposed to Andrew Jackson and his political views. Also **anti-Jacksonian, anti-Jacksonite.** *Obs.* — **1827** *Central Watchtower* (Harrodsburg, Ky.) 29 Dec. 2/5 An attempt is now to be made, to organize an Anti-Jackson party in that state. **1830** *Maine Democrat* (Saco) 1 Sep. 1/1 Let him read . . . the written opinions of the Judges of the Supreme Court, a majority of whom they have claimed as anti-Jacksonian. **1842** in *Amer. Sp.* XVIII. 120 The majority are Creoles; consequently, Anti-Jacksonites.

anti-machine. Opposed to the domination of politics by political "machines." Also **anti-machinist.** — **1881** *Nation* 6 Jan. 1/2 In the contest for the Speakership of the Assembly, the Conklingite Machine [was] . . . represented by General Sharpe and the 'Anti-Machine' by Mr. Skinner. **1881** *Nation* 6 Jan. 1/2 The anti-Machinists tend to settle on Mr. Chauncey Depew. **1913** LA FOLLETTE *Autobiog.* 128, I had been elected as an anti-machine member.

anti-Mason. An opponent of Freemasonry. Also **anti-Masonic, anti-Masonry.**

1826 (*newspaper title*), Anti-Masonic Enquirer. **1827** BARNES *Mem. Th. Weed* (1884) 31 The subject of my communication was anti-masonry. **1828** BARNES *Life Th. Weed* (1884) I. 307 Under these multiplied difficulties the Anti-Masons incline to bestow their votes upon Mr. Southwick. **1879** H. O'REILLY (*title*), American Political-Antimasonry. **1948** *Time* 12 Jan. 12/3 Splinter parties were formed on such frenetic issues as a fanatical prejudice against Masons (the Anti-Masons).

anti-Mormon. One opposed to the Mormons or their religion. Also **anti-Mormonism.** — **1833** *Louisville D. Herald* 22 Nov. (*title*), The Mormons and the Anti-Mormons. **1845** *Quincy* (Ill.) *Whig* 4 Nov. 2/3 The noble stand, taken by the Whig, in favor of Anti-Mormonism, has made it a particular favorite in Hancock. **1881** ROMSPERT *Western Echo* 351 Soon anti-Mormons began to settle in the valleys east of the Sierra Nevada for the purposes of mining and stock-raising.

anti-Nebraska. Opposed to an act of 1854 by which the territory of Nebraska was organized free from slavery. Also **anti-Nebraskaism, anti-Nebraskaite.**

1854 *S.F. Chronicle* 21 Aug. 1/2 There is to be a convention of Anti-Nebraska men without distinction of party, tomorrow, at Worcester. **1855** *N.Y. Wkly. Tribune* 20 Jan. 4/2 Mr. Soulé returns in very ill humor, out of sorts with Know-Nothingism, Anti-Nebraskaism, and with the Administration. **1855** *N.Y. Herald* 10 Dec. 8/1 The caucus of the Anti-Nebraskaites, last night, effected nothing of importance. **1903** W. E. CURTIS *The True A. Lincoln* 146 With his usual candor, he had addressed letters to the Whigs and Anti-Nebraska men who had been elected to the Legislature, asking their support. **1948** *A. Lincoln Quart.* Mar. 27 Leading abolitionists were in charge, anti-Nebraska Democrats and Whigs refusing to be involved.

anting ˈæntɪŋ, *n.* [f. **ant, n.*] (See quot. 1948.)

1938 *Auk* Jan. 100 The phenomena involved in anting and the other actions of the birds here noted are both remarkable and obscure. **1948** *Dly. Ardmoreite* (Ardmore, Okla.) 26 April 4/6 'Bird anting' is an ornithological riddle. For reasons yet unknown, many species of birds have been observed in the peculiar ritual of grasping an ant in their beak, and rubbing it vigorously on their feathers. The performance has been given the name, 'bird anting.'

anti-prohibition. Opposition to prohibition, *q.v.* Also **anti-prohibitionist.**

1883 *Harper's Mag.* Oct. 804/1 Anti-Prohibition resolutions were passed. **1855** *N.Y. Herald* 6 Nov. 5/3 If anti-prohibitionists wish to know why it is necessary for them to defeat the fusion or republican ticket, we will refer them to the resolution adopted by the Prohibitionist State Convention. **1942** *Va. Q. Rev.* XVIII. 68 As for the Democratic party, Southerners have learned through the politically solid years to vote for it without liking everything it does or all of the people allowed in it—Tammany, the anti-Prohibitionists, the Catholics, and such.

anti-rent, *n. attrib.* Of or pertaining to the policy or practice of refusing to pay rent on the manorial lands of New York. Also **anti-renter, -rentism.** Now *hist.*

1844 *N.Y. Wkly. Tribune* 20 July 1/6 Anti-Rent Difficulties.—We understand . . . that the Sheriff of Rensselaer County . . . while attempting to serve a process upon some of the Manor tenants in Stephentown . . . met with forcible resistance. **1844** *St. Louis Reveille* 19 Dec. 1/6 We gave, last week, an attack made by the anti-renters of Scoharie county, upon Mr. Jacob Livingstone. **1845** COOPER *Chainbearer* xxii, Doctrines . . . published in journals devoted to anti-rentism in the State of New York. **1945** *Reader's Digest* Oct. 24/1 She wrote another one entitled 'Thirty-Six Feet of History,' dealing with the adventures of her little tract, under the feet of the Indians, the Dutch, the rebels of the Helderberg 'Anti-Rent Wars.'

anti-republican, *a.* and *n.*

1. *n.* A member of a group or party opposed to the Republicans of Jefferson's time. *Obs.*

1795 JEFFERSON *Writings* (1896) VII. 46 Hence the anti-Republicans appeared a considerable majority in both houses of Congress *Ib.* 47 The Anti-republicans consist of . . . tories [etc.].

2. *a.* Opposed or contrary to the rule of representatives elected by the people; aristocratic in sympathy or tendencies.

1790 MACLAY *Deb. Senate* 267 The practice [of dressing for levee day], however, considered as a feature of royalty, is certainly anti-republican. **1829** CHANNING *Works* (1884) 458/2 The taint of anti-Republican tendencies was fastened upon them [*sc.* the Federalists] by their opponents, and this reproach no party could survive. **1886** LOGAN *Great Conspiracy* 668 For the very purpose of nipping in the bud any anti-republican conspiracy likely to germinate from Slavery. **1947** *West. Penna. Hist. Mag.* March–June 57 Jefferson and Madison were determined that he should no longer be exposed to the contaminating influences of the Ernests, the Hulls, and other more or less anti-Republican elements of Detroit.

b. Opposed to the present Republican party.

1876 *Vallejo* (Calif.) *Chronicle* 5 Aug. 2/2 The Springfield *Republican* (anti-Republican) estimates that the Democrats can not possibly re-elect more than two or three. **1948** *Time* 5 July 13/2 Those, as Manhattan's stubbornly anti-Republican *Star* headlined them, were 'Noble Words, Proofs to Come.'

anti-saloon. Opposed to the liquor traffic. Also **Anti-Saloon League.** — **1888** *N. Amer. Rev.* Aug. 148 In the latter convention good men . . . wanted an anti-saloon plank put in the platform. **1892** (*title*), Documents . . . upon Law Enforcement. [Lowell, published by] The Anti-saloon League. **1948** *Time* 2 Feb. 15/2 At its annual meeting in Pittsburgh, the 52-year-old Anti-Saloon League of America changed its name to the Temperance League of America.

anti-slavery. In combs., now obs.: (1) **anti-slavery novel,** a novel designed to further opposition to slavery; (2) **party,** a group of those who opposed the extension of slavery to Kansas; (3) **ticket,** a list of candidates to be supported by those opposed to slavery; (4) **whig,** a whig who opposed slavery.

(1) **1865** *Atlantic Mo.* XV. 71 No anti-slavery novel has described a man of such marked ability. — (2) **1856** *Harper's Mag.* XII. 404/1 To such an extremity have the differences between the pro-slavery and anti-slavery parties been carried, that an actual appeal to arms was at one time considered most imminent. **1878** J. B. FREMONT in *Harper's Mag.* Jan. 275/2 In short, my pretty rooms were the headquarters of the antislavery party. — (3) **1820** *Niles' Reg.* XIX. 127 An attempt is making in Philadelphia to get up, what its projectors call, an 'anti-slavery' ticket, for electors of president and vice-president of the United States. — (4) **1856** HAMBLETON *Biog. H. A. Wise* 240 Buffington . . . and Morris [of Mass.] . . . are reliable anti-slavery whigs.

b. Also **anti-slavery convention, element, man, missionary.** *Obs.* or *hist.*

1839 *Ky. Observer* (Lexington) 14 Aug. 3/3 The National Anti-Slavery Convention, composing upwards of 400 delegates, . . . adjourned this afternoon, after a session of several days. **1842** *Southern Q. Review* I. 62 They are abolitionists,—at least anti-slavery men. **1867** J. N. EDWARDS *Shelby* 12 As early as May 10, 1860, the first meeting which ever assembled in a Slave State to consider the question of taking public position with the anti-slavery element of the North met in St. Louis and sent delegates to the Chicago Convention. **1946** FOREMAN *Last Trek* 170 The Reverend Gurley, an antislavery missionary among the Wyandots, was taken from his bed at midnight by 'the minions of slavery.'

c. anti-slaveryist, one opposed to slavery. *Obs.*

1862 WADSWORTH in *N.Y. Herald* 13 March, [Lincoln] had been teased and pressed by radical anti-slaveryists until he was compelled to offer a compromise.

anti-union. Opposed to the federal Union or to trade-unionism. Also **anti-unionist.** — **1800** JEFFERSON *Writings* (1896) VII. 447 However, as it has been made it shews who are the Anti-Unionists in principle. **1813** *Niles' Reg.* V. 3/2 They may expose the British anti-union demogagues. **1878** PINKERTON *Strikers* 206 The officers of the road secured a volunteer anti-union engineer and fireman to move the cars.

***Antwerp,** *n.* A variety of raspberry, usu. **red Antwerp.** — **1847** DARLINGTON *Weeds & Plants* 126 *Ida Rubus,* Antwerp Raspberry, Garden Raspberry . . . is much cultivated for its favorite fruit. **1851** CIST *Cincinnati* 296 Of these, the red Antwerp is the general favorite. **1884** ROE *Nature's Story* 258 Webb, carrying a little basket lined with grapevine leaves, gleaned the long row of Antwerp raspberries.

***anvil,** *n.*

1. An object resembling an anvil in use or shape.

1872 *Amer. Naturalist* April 228 Large stones [among N.J. prehistoric relics] that appear to have been utilized by the Redman, and are called 'anvils' for want of a more correct designation. **1874** LONG *Wild-Fowl* 35 From its construction, the anvil and ejector remaining in the shell, the extra tool for punching off caps needed with all other shells is dispensed with.

2. In combs.: (1) **anvil-block,** (cf. Du. *aanbeeldsblok*), the block of wood upon which an anvil rests; (2) **chorus,** the collective remarks of fault-finders or "knockers," *slang;* (3) **rock, -rock sandstone,** (see quots.).

(1) **1842** in BASSETT *South. Plant.* 162 Dear master I have Eleven children I have been faitheful over the anvill Block Evr cen 1811 and is still old Harry. **1870** BRYANT *Homer* II. XVIII. 219 He spake, and from his anvil-block arose. — (2) **1908** K. MCGAFFEY *Show-Girl* 29 If anyone starts the anvil chorus they get the skiddo. **1948** *Dly. Ardmoreite* (Ardmore, Okla.) 30 Sep. 14/4 A secret 'Azerbaijan democratic station' joined in the anvil chorus with two additional verbal attacks. — (3) **1862** DANA *Man. Geol.* 330 Above the twelfth [coal bed in Kentucky] there is the massive Sandstone . . . called the Anvil Rock, from the form of two masses of it in South-western Kentucky. **1869** *Amer. Naturalist* III. 44 The 'Anvil-rock Sandstones,' and the 'Mahoning Sandstone,' in the Kentucky section, are identical.

***anxious,** *a.*

1. *absol.* (See quot.) *Obs.*

1828 DEWEY *Letters* 8 Those who have not attained to this change, and yet are seeking for it, are usually denominated 'the anxious.' So that the whole community is divided into the three classes of the converts, the anxious, and the unconcerned.

2. In combs.: (1) **anxious bench,** in revival meetings, a seat near the front reserved for those who are concerned about their spiritual welfare, also *on the anxious bench,* uneasy, anxious; (2) **meeting,** (see quot.), *obs.;* (3) **mourner,** (see quot.), *obs.;* (4) **seat,** =**anxious bench,** also fig.

(1) **1832** MRS. TROLLOPE *Domestic Manners* I. III, As the poor creatures approached the rail, their sobs and groans became audible. They seated themselves in the 'anxious benches'; the hymn ceased, and two or three priests walked down from the tribune (etc.). **1839** H. CASWALL *America* 324 Women pray and exhort in public, persons under excitement are called forward to the '*anxious benches*' to make confession. **1906** *N.Y. Ev. Post* 23 Nov. 1 The entire diplomatic corps at Havana is . . . on the 'anxious bench.' — (2) **1859** BARTLETT, Anxious Meeting. A religious meeting consequent on a revival. — (3) **1871** DE VERE 234 Thus, persons who are peculiarly excited to a consciousness of their sinfulness, and the necessity of seeking salvation, are called *anxious mourners,* and are led by the ministers or deacons to the *anxious bench* or *seat,* a bench near the altar, there to receive aid and comfort. — (4) **1835** GRIFFITHS *Two Years* 181 At the close of the service those who felt anxious about their salvation, and wished to enjoy an interest in the prayers and counsels of God's people, were requested to come forward and occupy a seat which was vacated for them, called the *Anxious Seat.* **1846** CIST *Cin. Miscellany* II. 118/2 'It has pretty nigh starved me out'; and sure enough, he did look as if he had been on 'the anxious seat,' as he used to say, when things puzzled him. **1946** ANNE ROWE *Deadly Intent* 82 She had mailed a written confession to her Joe the night before and was now sitting on the anxious seat, waiting for his verdict.

***any,** *adv.* **any old,** any whatever. *Colloq.* — **1911** R. W. CHAMBERS *Common Law* ii. 63 'Would you like to have a chance to study?' . . 'Study? What?' 'Sculpture—any old thing!' **1948** *Chi. Tribune* 16 May (Comics) 6 I'll take on guys my size any old time.

***anybody,** *pron.* **anybody's game, race,** one in which the contestants are so evenly matched that any one of them may win. *Colloq.* — **1898** *Forum* Jan. 576 In Greater New York it was what is called 'anybody's race,' till close upon the day of election. **1930** *Randolph Enterprise* (Elkins, W.Va.) 23 Oct. 1/6 This will probably be a close game and anybodys game to the finish.

anything else. "A hyperbolical phrase, denoting a strong affirmation, which has recently sprung up and become quite common" (B. '59). — **a1859** *Newspaper* (B.), *Loco Foco.* Didn't Gen. Cass get mad at Hull's cowardice, and break his sword? *Whig.* He didn't do anything else. **1905** *D.N.* III. 2 'He didn't do *anything else,*' means he did just that.

***anywhere,** *adv.* *anywhere from . . . to,* anything between . . . and. *Colloq.* — **1897** *Outing* XXIV. 471/1 The tarpon will be anywhere from fifty to three hundred feet away when the boat is ready to follow him. **1909** O. HENRY *Options* 6, I'll guarantee an increase of anywhere from ten thousand to a hundred thousand a year.

A.P. 1. (See quot.) *Obs.* **2.** Abbrev. for **Associated Press.** Also attrib.

(1) **1817** M. BIRKBECK *Notes on a Journey* 71 The sections thus sold are marked immediately on the general plan, which is always open at the land office to public inspection, with the letters A.P. 'advance paid.' — (2) **1879** *Chi. Tribune* 4 March 5/4 Now, the A.P. may be a very wicked institution, but a 'Monopoly' it is not. **1948** *Time* 17 May 63/2 A.P. was not organized in its present pattern—a nonprofit cooperative—until 1892.

A.P.A. Abbrev. of "American Protective Association," a secret society founded in Iowa in 1887, to oppose unrestricted immigration and the influence of Roman Catholics in education and politics. Also attrib.

1893 *Chicago Record* 3 July 9/2 The American Protective association, or A.P.A., or Apes, as its members are called, have developed great strength in Ohio. **1893** J. P. ALTGOOD *Live Questions* (1899) 408 Do you think the A.P.A. sentiment is strongly diffused among Protestants? **1943** *Copper Camp* 56 The A.P.A., or American Protective Association, it is said, was an organization antagonistic to the Catholic Church.

Apache əˈpætʃɪ, *n.* [App. f. Amer. Sp. (<Zuni) *ápachu,* enemy.]

1. (See quot. 1907.) Also attrib. Cf. **prairie Apache.**

1745 *H. Moll's Atlas Minor* Plate 46, Apaches. **1808** PIKE *Exped.* App. III. 10 The Appaches are a nation of Indians who extend from the black mountains in New Mexico to the frontiers of Cogquilla, keeping the frontiers of three provinces in a continual state of alarm. **1907** HODGE *Amer. Indians* I. 63 Apache (probably from *ápachu,* 'enemy,' the Zuni name for the Navaho, who were designated 'Apaches de Nabaju' by the early Spaniards in New Mexico). A number of tribes forming the most southerly group of the Athapascan family. . . . They were first mentioned as Apaches by Oñate in 1598. **1947** *Desert* Feb. 8/3 Even after the death of the great Apache chief, . . . the Dragoon mountains was an Apache rendezvous.

2. Apache plume, a rosaceous shrub, *Fallucia paradoxa,* of the Southwest.

1889 *Cent.,* Apache-plume. . . . A low rosaceous shrub with long plumose carpels. **1940** JAEGER *Desert Wild Flowers* 89 Because of some fancied resemblance of the reddish, feathery-tailed seed clusters to the plumed war bonnets of the Apache Indians, the common name 'Apache-plume' was applied.

3. Apache state, (see quot. 1934).

1891 SWEETSER *King's Handbook U.S.* 54 It is also known as The Apache State, from the warrior tribe which for centuries fought the troops of Spain, Mexico, and the United States. **1934** SHANKLE *State Names* 99 The nickname, the *Apache State,* was applied to Arizona, doubtless, from the great numbers of Apache Indians originally inhabiting this territory.

aparejo ˌæpəˈreho, *n. S.W.* [Sp. in same sense.] A kind of packsaddle consisting chiefly of a square pad of stuffed leather or canvas. Cf. **arapajo.**

1844 J. GREGG *Commerce Prairies* I. 180 It is necessary too for the *aparejo* to be firmly bound on to prevent its slipping and chafing the mule's back. **1878** HART *Sazerac Lying Club* 51 We got a aparayho and put it on the burro. **1929** CHALFANT *Death Valley* 34 A pair of strong hickory shirts were sewed together at the tails, the necks were sewed up, and the combination put astride the ox, with a child in each, serving as what the Californians called '*aparejos.*'

Aparejo in place on a pack animal

b. aparejo grass, (see quots.).

1894 COULTER *Bot. West. Texas* 519 *S[porobolus] depauperatus.* . . . Aparejos grass. **1912** WOOTON & STANDLEY *Grasses N.M.* 69 Aparejo Grass (*Muhlenbergia utilis*) . . . receives its common name because it is used to stuff the pads (*aparejos*) used in certain parts of Mexico in lieu of pack saddles.

***apartment,** *n.*

1. a. One of the parts into which a railway passenger coach is divided. **b.** A set of rooms, among other sets in one building, designed for a single household, a suite, a flat.

(a) **1834** *Am. R.R. Jrnl.* III. 742/2 These coaches may have apartments to contain from 8 to 12 persons. — (b) **1876** *N.Y. Herald* 16 Aug. 2/2 To let . . . Nice apartments—from two to eight rooms. **1946** *Chi. D. News* 18 Nov. 17/7 Her fiance . . . has found an apartment for them on the Near North Side.

2. In combs.: (1) **apartment building,** an apartment house; (2) **hotel,** a hotel having housekeeping apartments for rent as well as supplying rooms and dining service for transient guests; (3) **house,** a building consisting of a number of separate housekeeping apartments.

(1) **1883** *Chi. Tribune* 4 May 9/3 To Rent. . . . Flat in elegant apartment building, 7 rooms. **1947** *Crim. Law & Criminology Jrnl.* Nov.–Dec. 330, I went into a room in an apartment building. — (2) **1902** EATON & UNDERHILL *Runaway Place* 238 The vast apartment hotels along the Park front. **1948** *Chi. Tribune* 25 April 49/6 A Modern apartment hotel, about 40 units, unfurnished, good location. — (3) **1876** *N.Y. Herald* 5 Oct. 2/3 A home . . . in the elegant new apartment-house. **1948** *L.A. Times* 4 May II. 1/5 The zoning . . . will allow construction of highly restricted apartment houses.

As the last term in **basement, brick, kitchenette, studio apartment.**

apee ˌeˈpi, *n.* (See quot.) *Obs.* — **1830** J. F. Watson *Philadelphia* 716 Philadelphia has long enjoyed the reputation of a peculiar cake called the apee. . . . Ann Page, still alive, . . . first made them, many years ago, under the common name of cakes. . . . On her cakes she impressed the letters A.P., the letters of her name.

apex, *n.* In mining, "the end or edge of a vein nearest the surface" (Raymond *Gloss.*, 1881). Hence **apex-right,** a mining right based upon the ownership of the apex of a vein. — **1898** *Engineering Mag.* XVI. 121/1 Besides, of such productive work No 'apex-right' or legal quirk Could thwart the rich requital.

apex, *v. Mining. intr.* Of a vein of mineral: To form an apex. — **1914** G. Atherton *Perch of Devil* I. xii. 79 'It dips towards the ranch.' . . . 'It's pretty close. That would be a kettle of fish—if it apexed on your land!' **1943** *Copper Camp* 43 Through his Rarus Mine, Heinze complacently moved into the Michael Davitt, an adjoining Amalgamated property, which he claimed 'apexed' on the Rarus.

apishamore əˈpɪʃəˌmɔr, *n.* (See quot. 1895.) — **1839** Townsend *Narr.* 145 We remained in camp, trading buffalo robes, apishemeaus, &c., of the Indians. **1851** W. Kelly *Across Rocky Mts.* (1852) 117 And our pack-saddles rigged, with cruppers, breechings, lash-ropes, and apichments. **1895** Gerard in *N.Y. Sun* 30 July, Apishamore, a saddle blanket made of buffalo calf skins, used on the great prairie; from Odjibway 'apishimon,' anything 'used for lying upon.'

Apollino ˌæpəˈlino, *n.* [f. *Apollo*, god of music + *-ino*, instrumental ending.] (See quots.) *Obs.* — **1819** *Plough Boy* I. 131/3 The Apollino combines the music of a Church Organ, a Grand Orchestra, a Martial Band, and a Harp. *Ib.* 147/1 The Apollino, a musical instrument invented by Mr. Job Plimpton, of this city. **1821** J. Howison *Recoll.* 322 The museum is also enriched with that astonishing piece of musical mechanism called the Apollino.

* **apostle,** *n.* One of a council of twelve men in the Mormon church functioning chiefly as an administrative body. Cf. **twelve Apostles.**

1842 in E. E. Folk *Mormon Monster* (1900) 52 My father's family received frequent visits from Apostles Brigham Young and Heber C. Kimball. **1906** *Congress. Rec.* Dec. 241/1 We protest that Apostle Reed Smoot ought not to be permitted to qualify . . . as a member of the United States Senate. **1947** Sessions *Cities of America* 37 Smoot was an apostle in the church, and the nation was still not convinced of the church's stand on plural marriage.

***apostleship,** *n.* The office of an apostle in the Mormon church. — *a*1861 Winthrop *J. Brent* xi. 121 My brethren in the Church of the Latter Day have their duties of stern apostleship.

Appalachee ˌæpəˈlætʃɪ, *n.* [Poss. f. Choctaw, meaning "people on the other side."] One of the principal native Indian tribes in Florida. Also attrib. — **1857** *Spirit of Times* 3 Oct. 65/2 There had been a fierce battle fought between the Yupaha tribes and the Appalaches. **1943** Peattie *Great Smokies* 18 DeSoto . . . left no memorial or trace, except the name Appalachian itself (from the Appalache tribe of Muskhogeans on the Gulf Coast), misapplied by him to the fair mountains he traversed so long ago.

Appalachia ˌæpəˈlætʃɪə, *n.* [See prec.]

1. The highland region in the southeastern portion of the U.S.

[**1705** Harris *Navigantium atque itinerantium* I. 806/1 *Soto* march'd toward *Apalache*, a very large and fruitful Province, as he was inform'd. *Ib.* 799/1 The *Indians* gave them to understand, by signs and words, that it came from a far distant Province call'd *Apalachen*.] **1913** *Outing* Feb. 551/1 Every stranger in Appalachia is quick to note the high percentage of defectives among the people. **1948** Mencken *Supp.* II. 16 Even the dialect of Appalachia, though it differs from General American, differs from it less than it differs from any regional variety.

2. (See quots.) Now *hist.*

1839 *Knickerb.* Aug. 161 We might still use the phrase, 'The United States,' substituting Appalachia, or Alleghania, (I should prefer the latter,) in place of America. **1947** *Amer. Sp.* Dec. 243 In 1839 . . . Washington Irving suggested . . . that *United States of America* be abandoned for *United States of Appalachia* or *Alleghania*, with *Appalachian*, or *Alleghanian* for a citizen thereof.

Appalachian ˌæpəˈlætʃɪən, *n.* and *a.* [f. **Appalachee.**]

1. Designating or pertaining to a range of mountains in the eastern U.S., or to the region where these occur.

[**1587** Hakluyt tr. Laudonnière *Notable Historie* 2v [The Indians] say that in the Mountaynes of Appalatacy there are mines of Copper, which I thinke to be golde. **1607** in Alvord & Bidgood *First Exploration Trans-Allegheny Region* (1912) 28 Mountaynes Apalatsi.] **1753** W. Douglass *Summary Brit. Setts.* II. 362 Col. *Spotswood* Lieut. Governor of *Virginia*, was the first who passed the *Apolacian Mountains*, or great *Blue-Hills*. **1906** V. A. Lewis *Rep. Dept. Archives & Hist., W.Va.* 31 West Virginia lies in part in three of these divisions—that is in the Potomac Area, the South Appalachian Area and the Ohio Valley Area. **1944** *Reader's Digest* Jan. (back cover), The . . . pulpwood must come primarily from . . . states in the . . . Appalachian and Great Lakes areas.

2. *pl.* The Indians formerly occupying the Appalachian region.

1888 Wallace *Land of Pueblos* 277 The Pimo Indians are not made of 'rose-red clay,' they are dark brown, differing in complexion from the Appalachians east of the Rocky mountains and the olive hues of the California tribes.

b. Designating a tribe of Muskhogean Indians formerly occupying part of northwest Florida.

1722 Coxe *Descr. Carolana* 22 Near it on both Sides towards the Sea-Coast, dwell divers Nations, . . . who are generally call'd by one name of Apalatchy Indians. **1797** Morse *Amer. Gaz., Apalachy* . . . is by some writers, applied to a town and harbour in Florida, 90 miles E. of Pensacola. . . . The tribes of the Apalachian Indians lie around it.

c. Appalachian bean, tea, (see quots.).

1763 tr. Lepage du Pratz *History Louisiana* (1758) II. 7 The *Apalachean* beans are so called because we received them from a nation of natives of that name. **1910** Shreve *Plant Life Md.* 485 Viburnum cassinoides L. Appalachian Tea [is] Rare in the Midland Zone, common in the Mountain Zone; in swamps and bogs.

d. Used with reference to the geology of the southeastern part of the U.S.

1878 Hinton *Handbook Ariz.* 54 A section thus arranged . . . presents a series of limestones, shales, sandstones, and conglomerates totally unlike that which has been established in the New York and Appalachian province. **1883** *The Virginias* (Staunton) Jan. 11/1 The Apalachian formations were studied by the brothers Rogers, forty years ago.

e. Used with reference to the language employed in this area.

1941 *Amer. Sp.* Oct. 180 *Ned* for bacon or salt pork, *set his hoss*, a gambling stake, are variously Appalachian.

appaloosa ˌɑpəˈlusə, *n.* [See note.]

The origin of this term is not clear. It may be a variant of *Opelousa*, a La. place name, formerly applied to a small band of Indians in that state. See W. A. Read, *La. Place-Names*, 44 ff., and quot. 1849 below. Adams in *W. Words* 5 says this breed of horses was developed by the Nez Percé Indians in the Palouse River country in Washington State, and *à Pelousé* became *appalousy, appaloosa*. Cf. Webster *s.v. palouser.*

1. A horse or breed of horses having characteristic color spots on the rump, a large amount of white in the eyes, and pink noses. Also attrib. Cf. **Palouse horse.**

1849 in *Amer. Sp.* XIX. 69 Nach diesen kommt das sogenannte Kreolen-pferdchen, auch Opelousas poney genannt, ein ausgezeichnetes Damenpferd. **1924** Davies *Skyline Trail* 49 They find death in a dramatic flare: Trying to ride the apaloochy mare. **1947** *Sooner Mag.* Nov. 30/2 The horseman discusses the various modern types—the Mustang, Quarter Horse, Appaloosa, Palomino, and the rest.

2. (See quot. 1909.)

1857 *Spirit of Times* 17 Jan. 319/3 He at length agreed to it, if we would say nothing about his 'catching the Apelousa.' **1909** *Cent. Supp.* 209/1 *Opelousas cat*, the long-jawed catfish, *Leptops olivaris*. **1948** *Dly. Ardmoreite* (Ardmore, Okla.) 23 April 7/1 Some of the larger, like Sand creek and Caney river, yield big blues and tackle-busting river cats, or Appaluchians.

***appeal,** *n.* As the last term in **court of appeal(s), sex appeal.**

appeal bond. A bond given by one who appeals a case to a higher court. — **1826** *Ill. Revised Laws* 404 The court shall render judgment against the party who removed the said case into the circuit court, and his security in the appeal bond, for all costs. **1877** *Ill. Revised Statutes* (1883) 841 Any informality or insufficiency of the appeal bond. **1948** *Time* 24 May 40/3 Another of the accused . . . is out on appeal bond under sentence of two years in prison.

appearance docket. (See quot.) — **1853** *Ohio Revised Statutes* (1860) II. 1034 On the appearance docket he [=clerk of the court of common pleas] shall enter all actions in the order in which they were brought, the date of the summons, . . . the time of filing the petition, and all subsequent pleadings.

***appellee,** *n.* The defendant in a case that is appealed. — **1771** *Mass. Col. Soc. Pub.* VI. 16 John Randal of Bristol . . . appellant vs. Thomas Bodkin of Boston . . . appellee, from the Judgment of an Inferior Court . . . when and where the appellee was Plt. (=plaintiff) and the appellant was Def. (=defendant). **1851** *Iowa Code* 27 The matter shall stand for hearing at that time if required by the appellee. **1949** *Amer. Gas Jrnl.* Jan. 39/2 Issues of actionable negligence on appellee's (gas company's) part were in failing to make a proper inspection when it undertook to do so, and in failing to . . . properly repair the pilot light found to be defective.

appendectomy ˌæpənˈdɛktəmɪ, *n.* [f. *append*ix + *-ectomy*.] An operation for the removal of the vermiform appendix. — **1903** *N.Y. Medical Jrnl.* 4 July 5/2 The methods of appendectomy can be divided into two classes, those with a stump and those without a stump. **1948** *This Week Mag.* 9 Oct. 29/2 Sixty per cent of all children's operations are tonsillectomies, and 20 per cent are appendectomies.

appendicitis əˌpɛndəˈsaɪtɪs, *n.* [f. *appendix* + *-itis.*] Inflammation of the vermiform appendix. — **1886** R. H. FITZ in *Amer. Jrnl. Med. Sci.* Oct. 323 As a circumscribed peritonitis is simply one event . . . in the history of inflammation of the appendix, it seems preferable to use the term appendicitis to express the primary condition. **1946** THOMPSON *Am. Daughter* 242 School hadn't been open a week when Kay had an attack of appendicitis.

* **apple,** *n.* In combs.

1. In the names of foods and drinks: (1) **apple brandy,** an alcoholic liquor made from apples; (2) **butter,** see as a main entry; (3) **cobbler,** (see quot. 1859); (4) **dowdy,** a deep-dish pie made of apples, cf. **pandowdy,** and see *Ling. Atlas* Map 292, also cf. **applecrowdy, dowler,** in *EDD* VI; (5) **duff,** a kind of apple pudding; (6) **frump,** =**apple slump;** (7) ***jack,** an alcoholic beverage made from apples; (8) ***john,** =**applejack;** (9) **leather,** (see quot.); (10) **pandowdy,** =**apple dowdy;** (11) **potpie,** =**apple slump;** (12) **sauce,** see as a main entry; (13) **slump,** (see quot. 1848); (14) **toddy,** a whisky or brandy punch flavored with roasted apples; (15) **waffle,** (see quot.); (16) **water,** juice from apples diluted with water; (17) **whisky,** liquor distilled from apples (see quot. 1929).

(1) *c***1780** *Md. Hist. Mag.* II. 256 [I] accepted 13 gals. of peach brandy in satisfaction of the damage. . . . He cheated me with apple brandy. **1929** *New Yorker* 25 May 22/1 [I remember] the apple brandy nipped at in the locker-room at the White Bear Yacht Club. — **(3) 1859** BARTLETT 90 Cobbler. . . . A sort of pie, baked in a pot lined with dough of great thickness, upon which the fruit is placed; according to the fruit, it is an apple or a peach *cobbler.* Western. **1948** *Chi. Tribune* 25 Jan. VI. 1/4 On the cupboard shelf a huge apple cobbler slowly cooled. — **(4) 1923** W. NUTTING *Massachusetts* 241 Did ever a dish of apple dowdy go to the spot like that? **1937** LUTES *Home G.* 147 If the Apple Dowdy went pretty well, you might try your hand at an Apple Frump.

(5) 1871 F. M. A. ROE *Army Lett.* 27 There were three long tables, fairly groaning with things upon them: . . . cakes, quantities of pickles, dried 'apple-duff,' and coffee. — **(6) 1937** [see **apple dowdy**]. — **(7) 1816** SCENE PAINTER *Emigrant's Guide* 30 A partial distillation is also made from apples . . . called Apple-Jack. **1947** *Hunting & Fishing* Feb. 25/1 A spot of apple-jack, fried country ham, baked potatoes, [etc.]. — **(8) 1856** *Spirit of Times* 6 Dec. 226/1 In the first place, get extremely 'how-came-you-so?' over night, no bad applejohn or worse rye-whiskey. **1872** DE VERE 415 Known even in the pretentious form of *Apple-John* in New England, it has the terrible name of *Jersey Lightning* farther south, and in Virginia rules supreme as *Apple-Brandy* although here a few peach-kernels are generally added to give it the flavor of peach-brandy. — **(9) 1877** BARTLETT 16 Apple-Leather. Apples parboiled and stirred into a paste of considerable consistency; then rolled out and dried in the sun. When dry, it is about as tough as leather, and comes away in sheets of the thickness of tanned cowhide,—whence its name.—Pennsylvania and Maryland.

(10) 1941 F. M. FARMER *Boston Cook Book* 545 Apple Pan Dowdy. Arrange 2 cups sliced apples in bottom of buttered baking dish. Sprinkle with 1/4 cup molasses or brown sugar. . . . Pour over Cottage Pudding batter and continue baking. **1947** BEROLZHEIMER *Regional Cookbook* 141 An excursion into one's childhood would hardly be complete without apple betty and apple pan-dowdy. — **(11) 1848** [see **apple slump**]. **1884** MRS. OWENS *Cook Book* 187. — **(13) 1831** *Finn's Comic Annual* 140 The pumpkin pies and apple slump . . . were smoking on the table. **1848** BARTLETT 311 A favorite dish in New England, called an *apple slump,* is made by placing raised bread or dough around the sides of an iron pot, which is then filled with apples and sweetened with molasses. Called in other parts of the country an *apple pot-pie.* **1947** BEROLZHEIMER *Regional Cookbook* 143 Rhode Island apple slump. — **(14) 1809** IRVING *Knickerb.* V. ii, The inhabitants . . . were prone to . . . get fuddled with . . . apple-toddy. **1904** GLASGOW *Deliverance* 155 Why, they use to say that you couldn't get to the Hall unless you swam your way through apple toddy.

(15) 1946 *Democrat* 21 Nov. 3/2 For supper some Sunday night, try apple waffles. Just add one and three-fourths cups grated or finely chopped apple to one standard waffle batter recipe. — **(16) 1832** L. M. CHILD *Frugal Housewife* 32 Apple water this [is] given as sustenance when the stomach is too weak to bear broth. — **(17) 1837** J. C. NEAL *Charcoal Sk.* (1838) 160 Pumpkins, cabbages, and apple whiskey is always good for a weakly constitution. **1929** *Amer. Sp.* IV. 387 The beverages known as *peach whiskey, apple whiskey* and *apricot whiskey* are really brandies, and are said to be made by distilling a mixture of dried fruit and water, but as a matter of fact they are probably synthetic.

2. In the names of plants: (1) **apple geranium,** a cultivated species of the common geranium; (2) **haw,** the May haw, *Crataegus aestivalis,* of the southern states; (3) **Peru,** (*a*) the jimson weed, *Datura stramonium,* (*b*) also **apple of Peru** in same sense (see also quots. 1847, 1901, 1941); (4) **pine,** the white pine, *Pinus strobus.*

(1) 1892 *Amer. Folk-Lore* V. 93 *Pelargonium* . . . apple geranium. Mansfield, O., and parts of Mass. — **(2) 1861** WOOD *Botany* 331 *Crataegus aestivalis* Torr. & Gr. Apple Haw. In the edges of ponds and rivers. S. Car. to Fla. and La. **1901** MOHR *Plant Life Ala.* 125 The smaller trees, of which the most conspicuous are planer tree, red maple, . . . and the apple haw. — **(3)** (*a*) **1784** CUTLER in *Mem. Academy* III. 419 Appleperu. . . . Common by the waysides. August. *a***1870** CHIPMAN *Notes on Bartlett* 219 Jamestown Weed. . . . Apple Peru,—at Salem, Mass. (*b*) **1705** BEVERLY *Virginia* II. 24 The James-Town Weed . . . resembles the thorny Apple of Peru. **1847** WOOD *Botany* 446 *Nicandra physaloides.* Apple of Peru. . . . Native of Peru, cultivated in fields. **1901** MOHR *Plant Life Ala.* 708 *Physalodes physalodes.* Apple of Peru. . . . Adventive and naturalized from southern Ontario to Pennsylvania, Ohio, and Missouri, and along the mountains to North Carolina. **1941** R. S. WALKER *Lookout* 52 In some of the oldest gardens on Lookout Mountain is still found a plant that for more than two centuries has followed the old settlers and filled an important niche in their economic lives. This is fly-poison plant, or the Apple-of-Peru. — **(4) 1832** BROWNE *Sylva Amer.* 242 This species . . . is known . . . in New Hampshire and Maine by the secondary denominations of Pumpkin Pine, Apple Pine.

b. *Within two rows of apple-trees,* within a fair distance. *Colloq.*

1869 CONKLING in *Cong. Globe* 2 March 1793/2 It does not come, if I may use the expression, within two rows of apple-trees of the point here at all.

3. In the names of insects, etc.: (1) **apple borer,** an insect, either *Saperda candida,* or *Chrysobothris femorata,* which infests apple trees, also **apple tree borer, apple twig borer;** (2) **bug,** (*a*) a species of water-beetle, (*b*) the plum weevil, *Conotrachelus nenuphar;* (3) **codling,** the codling moth; (4) **maggot,** a species of maggot which especially feeds on crab-apples and haws; (5) **smeller,** a species of water bettle, *Gyrinus natator;* (6) **worm,** a larva of the codling moth, *Carpocapsa pomonella,* also attrib.

(1) 1838 *Mass. Zool. Survey Rep.* 90 The most notoriously noxious insect of this genus is the *Saperda bivittata,* the parent of the apple-tree borer. **1856** A. FITCH *Noxious Insects* (3rd Rep. N.Y. Agric. Soc.) 330 Apple twig borer, *Nostrichus bicaudatus,* . . . has been common of late years in the orchards of Michigan and Illinois. **1858** *Ill. Agric. Soc. Trans.* III. 344 The most destructive of these, and the only one mentioned in fruit books, is that known as the apple borer. **1913** ESSIG *Injurious & Beneficial Insects Calif.* 235 The flat-headed apple-tree borer . . . is most destructive to young trees, the bases of which are often completely girdled. — **(2)** (*a*) **1832** KENNEDY *Swallow Barn* I. 129 The apple-bugs (as schoolboys call that glossy black insect which frequents the summer pools, and is distinguished for the perfume of the apple) danced in myriads over the surface of the still water. **1941** *Nature Mag.* March 138 A linguist innocent of entomological knowledge has assumed that the name apple bug means that the insect attacks apples. (*b*) **1889** FARMER 19/2 [The] Apple bug . . . deposits its eggs by puncturing the fruit, causing premature decay. — **(3) 1871** *Ill. Agric. Soc. Trans.* VIII. 158 Grapeberry moth, called also Grape-codling, for the reason that its destructive work in the vineyard is . . . similar to that of the Apple-codling in the orchard. — **(4) 1867** *Amer. Jrnl. Horticulture* Dec. II. 338 The apple maggot . . . breeds naturally in our wild haws and crabs, but . . . has been noticed to attack the cultivated apple. **1882** *Rep. Comm. Agric.* 195 The Apple Maggot (*Trypeta pomonella* Walsh.) . . . is becoming quite common in certain parts of New York and New England. *Ib.* 196 The Apple Maggot is much more apt to infest early apples than the winter varieties.

(5) *c***1830** GODMAN in *Waldie's Library* II. 85/1 Their distant relatives, called by the boys the water-witches and apple smellers, . . . [have] a delightful smell, exactly similar to that of the richest, mellowest apple. **1947** *Jrnl. N.Y. Entom. Soc.* Sep. 206 Apple smeller, N.J., Pa., Minn. — **(6) 1850** *New Eng. Farmer* II. 252 Tne others were bored by the common apple-worm. **1869** *Amer. Entomologist* Feb. 112/1 This moth is variously known as the Apple-worm Moth, or the Codling-worm Moth. **1882** *Rep. Comm. Agric.* 195 Without doubt the most important insect enemy of the apple is the codlin-moth or Apple-worm, as it is often called.

4. In miscellaneous combs.: (1) **apple bee,** a social gathering of neighbors to prepare and dry apples; (2) **bin,** a receptacle for apples; (3) **boy,** a boy who sells apples; (4) **chaff,** the refuse from an apple mill; (5) **cut, cutting,**

an apple bee; (6) **hole,** (see quot. 1876); (7) **parer,** an implement for paring apples; (8) **paring, =apple bee;** (9) **peeler,** an implement for peeling apples, jocosely, a knife; (10) **peeling, =apple bee;** (11) **pole,** a long pole used in gathering apples; (12) **roaster,** a receptacle in

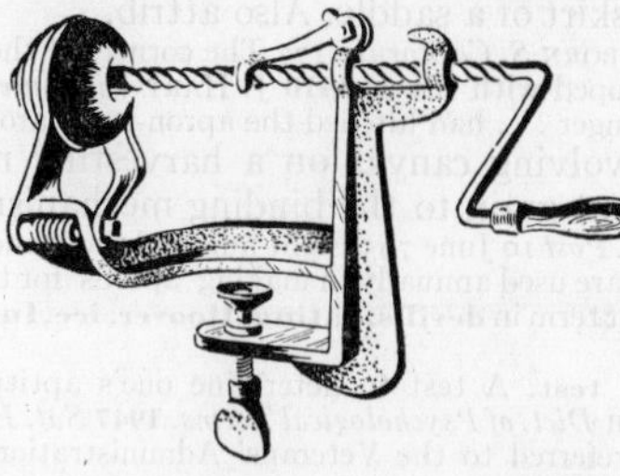

Apple parer of an early type

which apples are roasted; (13) **stand,** a stall or booth at which apples are sold.

(1) 1827 *Harvard Reg.* Nov. 273 Once Ebenezer Hodge invited me To help his Dolly at an apple bee. **1941** LEE *Stagecoach North* 27 At an apple bee enough greenings were parted and strung for drying to last the winter. — **(2) 1854** SHILLABER *Mrs. Partington* 16 What they suppose must have been a cellar, was in reality an apple-bin. **1904** DAY *Kin o' Ktaadn* 243 Warmth and peace within, And savory sniff from cellar door of spicy apple bin. — **(3) 1858** *N.Y. Tribune* 14 Jan., I got on the cars . . . after . . . flattening out an apple-boy and pop-corn vendor. — **(4) 1746** in *Amer. Sp.* XV. 226/1, 'I went out to the Cornfield and Sowed 2 Ld of apple Chaff.' **1752** HEMPSTEAD *Diary* 597 Wee carryed out some apple Chaff & plowd it in the S.W. cornner of his field.

(5) 1843 STEPHENS *High Life N.Y.* II. xxix. 172 Jest top them off with an apple cut or so. **1850** T. D. PRICE *MS Diary* 16 Sep., We had an apple cutting at D. E. Davis' home. **1894** R. E. ROBINSON *Danvis Folks* 118 'A apple cut? A parin'-bee? Good airth an' seas! you jest try it an' see.' — **(6) 1876** BURROUGHS *Winter Sunshine* VII. 154 Do you remember the apple hole in the garden? . . . In the fall we excavated a circular pit in the warm mellow earth, and covering the bottom with clean rye straw, emptied in basketful after basketful of hardy choice varieties. **1937** LUTES *Home Grown* 136 That unhappy day when the last apple in the bin, the last in the apple hole outside, was gone. — **(7) 1833** S. SMITH *Major Downing* 162 Peleg, who is all the while whitlin, and sawin, and makin clocks, and apple parers, and churns. **1876** INGRAM *Centennial Exp.* 328 The improved Turn-table apple parer is . . . arranged so as to loosen the apple on the fork after the paring is finished. — **(8)** [**1815** in *Morav. Hist. Soc. Trans.* Tr. IV. (1895) 131 A sociable apple-paring was started (about 75 miles north of Salem, N.C.), in which some neighbors joined, besides the numerous family.] **1819** NOAH *She would be a Soldier* I. i, I'm the boy for a race, for an apple-paring or quilting frolic—fight a cock . . . with any one. **1947** BEROLZHEIMER *Regional Cookbook* 54 Small gatherings such as quilting bees, cornhuskings, apple parings or barn-raisings were always an excuse for offering refreshment. — **(9) 1858** *Harper's Mag.* May 731/2 The president and some of his adherents whipped out their apple-peelers (pocket-knives), and threatening death to all who approached, heroically stood their ground. **1878** STOWE *Poganuc People* XXII. 244 A new patent apple-peeler and corer, warranted to take the skin from an apple with a quickness and completeness hitherto unimaginable.

(10) 1871 EGGLESTON *Hoosier Schoolm.* iv. 46 One night at a apple-peelin' I tuck a sheet . . . to splice out the table-cloth. — **(11) 1919** CADY *Rhymes of Vt.* (1923) 202, I s'pose they're using on the whole The same old sort of apple pole. — **(12) 1642** *Md. Archives* IV. 97 An apple-roster, & a meat-heater. **1717** *Mass. H. S. Coll.* 6 Ser. V. 365 One apple roaster, 2 brass skimmers. — **(13) 1834** *Sun* (N.Y.) 11 Mar. 2/2 Buying three cents worth of baked peanuts at an apple stand, . . . he reeled along as far as the Park. **1948** *Chi. Tribune* 23 May (Grafic Mag.) 2/3 It was 1932, when the only growing industries were apple stands and the WPA.

As the last term in **Astrachan, aunt's, bake-, Bicknell, bough, cedar, cheese, chunk, custard, Delicious, devil's, domine, fall, Gloucester white, ground, Hinchman, hog, honeysuckle, horse, huckleberry, ice, Indian, Jerusalem, May, Oregon crab, Osage, pine, pond, Porter, rope, Seven-Year, sheep, skunk, soap, Sodom, strawberry, swamp, thorn, white, wild, wild balsam apple.**

apple butter. A thick, usu. spiced, sauce of apples stewed to the desired consistency in cider or in their own juice.

*c*1774 CRÈVECOEUR *Sk. 18th-Cent. Amer.* (1925) 105 We often make apple-butter. **1819** NOAH *She would be a Soldier* I. i, Can she milk—knit garters—make apple butter and maple sugar—dance a reel after midnight? **1889** *Century Mag.* Jan. 409/2 Hot meats were surrounded by pickles, both sweet and sour; and over all predominated the conventional apple-butter. **1948** *Reader's Digest* March 104/2 A boy presented a bowl purporting to contain apple butter. It turned out to be mud.

attrib. **1851** CIST *Cincinnati* ii. 49 Apple-butter makers. **1856** *Harper's Mag.* Jan. 163/1 She looked mournfully around at each familiar object . . . the churn, the apple-butter pot, the venerable quilting frames. *Ib.*, She mounted the reversed apple-butter kettle. **1880** *Ib.* Aug. 354/2 There is church twice a month, sewing bees, and apple-butter stirrings.

***apple-sauce.**

1. A sauce made of stewed and sweetened apples. Also, *colloq.*, **apple sass.**

1776 in *R.I. Hist. Tracts* No. 13 (1881) 89 Our dinner, three chickens, baked in the oven, with apple sauce and Spanish potatoes. **1833** S. SMITH *Major Downing* 117 A load of apples and apple-sass, and a few sassages. **1897** W. E. BARTON *Hero in Homespun* 229 Jennie brought out . . . a high pie, . . . made of several layers of biscuit dough alternating with apple sauce. **1946** NEWTON *P. Bunyan* 55 Paul's belly pains were caused by eating too much apple sauce.

b. (See quot. 1929.) *Slang.*

1921 *Collier's* 1 Jan. 18/4 That's all apple sauce! **1929** *Cent. Mag.* Autumn 70 'Applesauce' means a camouflage of flattery, and is derived from the boarding-house trick of serving plenty of this cheap comestible when richer fare is scanty. **1948** *Chi. D. News* 4 March 10/7 That sentence doesn't mean a thing, my boy. It is just applesauce of the purest ray serene.

***appointee,** *n.* At Yale "one who receives an appointment at a college exhibition or commencement" (Hall). *Obs.* — **1847** J. MITCHELL *Scenes & Characters* 194 To the gratified appointee,—if his ambition for the honor has the intensity it has in some bosoms,—the day is the proudest he will ever see. **1852** BRISTED *Five Years Eng. Univ.* (ed. 2) 382, I suspect that a man in the first class of the 'Poll' has usually read mathematics to more profit than many of the 'appointees,' even of the 'oration men' at Yale.

appointive əˈpɔɪntɪv, *a.* [f. *appoint, v.*] Of a nature to be filled by appointment. — **1881** TOURGEE in *N. Amer. Rev.* CXXXII. 314 If the system is right why not apply it to every appointive place in the Government except the cabinet. **1913** LA FOLLETTE *Autobiog.* 115 We were then in the midst of the Wisconsin fight, and besides I did not desire an appointive office.

***appointment,** *n.*

1. (See quot. 1851 and cf. **appointee.**) *Obs.* See also **midnight appointment.**

1847 J. MITCHELL *Scenes & Characters* 69 The object of appointments is to incite to study, and promote good scholarship. **1851** HALL *College Words* 10 In many American colleges, students to whom are assigned a part in the exercises of an exhibition or commencement, are said to receive an *appointment.* Appointments are given as a reward for superiority in scholarship. **1871** L. H. BAGG *At Yale* 590 The honors' which are held out as an inducement for scholastic effort are chiefly in the form of appointments for Junior Exhibition and Commencement.

2. In combs.: (1) **appointment committee,** (see quot.); (2) **office,** an office in which appointments to positions or offices are made (see quot. 1843); (3) **appointments office,** (see quot.).

(1) 1897–8 *Harvard Univ. Cat.* 488 Appointment Committee. The Committee . . . recommends for positions of various kinds men who are studying or who have studied under this Faculty, whether or not holders of degrees. — **(2) 1843** *P.O. Laws & Reg.* II. 2 Appointment Office. To this office are assigned all questions which relate to the establishment and discontinuance of post offices . . . appointment and removal of deputy postmasters (etc.). **1880** LAMPHERE *U.S. Govt.* 52/1 The reception-room of the Appointment Office is always open to the public. — **(3) 1904–5** *Harvard Univ. Catalogue* p. xiii, The Appointments Office carries on the work hitherto in charge of the Appointment Committee, namely, that of procuring positions for undergraduates, graduates, and all past members of the University seeking employment.

appola əˈpɔlə, *n.* Also **apola.** [App. Can. Fr. f . . . Ind.] (See quots.)

1843 FRÉMONT *Exped.* 113 To-night the . . . *appolas* of fine venison, looked cheerf . . . **1850** GARRARD *Wah-To-Yah* (192 . . . meat were cooking *en appolas;* th . . . alternate fat and lean meat, makin . . . *Americanisms* 21 Apola. . . . An Ind . . . relations of the old French traders a . . . designating a certain variety of stew i . . .

March 6 *Appolas* [were] the sharpened sticks upon which meat was hung over the fire to cook.

* **appreciate,** *v.*

1. *tr.* To raise (currency, property, etc.) in value.

1778 J. Penn in *N.E. Hist. Reg.* XXX. 320, I expect Congress will in a few days agree on some plan for appreciating the currency. **1857** *Lawrence* (Kansas) *Republican* 4 June 4, I see . . . our farms teeming with abundant products, and greatly appreciated in value. ***a*1889** *Rural Register* (F.), These improvements will appreciate the farm immensely.

transf. **1864** *Cong. Globe* 8 June 2796/2 The terms of the letter certainly appreciate General Butler in my estimation.

2. *intr.* To rise in value.

1779 *Lett. to Franklin* 110, I trust our money will appreciate by just degrees. **1888** *Baltimore American* (F.), His Pennsylvania lands have not appreciated as he had hoped and when he left the Cabinet he was a poor man.

* **appreciation,** *n.* An increase in value or amount. — **1777** Adams *Wks.* (1854) IX. 470 An act is necessary for allowing a depreciation or an appreciation . . . upon specialties. **1869** *Cong. Globe* 27 Feb. 1669/1, I was glad to see our bonds appreciate in the market, and that the holders should get the benefit of that appreciation. **1896** *Boston Journal* 8 July 5/6 The act of 1873, demonetizing silver, . . . has resulted in the appreciation of gold.

* **approach,** *n.* **1.** Stealing up on an animal in hunting. **2.** Advances made to a person in an effort to influence improperly his actions. — (**1**) **1850** Garrard *Wah-To-Yah* i. 21 St. Vrain, dismounting took his rifle, and soon was on the 'approach.' — (**2**) **1893** *Congress. Rec.* 28 Sep. 1874/1 The idea that he [Samuel Hooper] was subject to approach is . . . ridiculous.

* **approach,** *v.*

1. *tr.* To steal up on (an animal or herd) in hunting. Also * **approaching,** *n.*

***c*1832** Catlin *Indians* I. 25 'Approaching'—(which is, all of us abreast, upon a slow walk, and in a straight line towards the herd, until they discover us and run). **1833** *Ib.* 219 We saw immense herds of buffaloes; and although we had no horses to run them, we successfully approached them on foot. **1850** Garrard *Wah-To-Yah* i. 13 Branson and I . . . 'approached' a band of bulls.

transf. **1847** Parkman in *Knickerb.* XXX. 129 'What do you mean to do?' 'I shall "approach,"' replied the Captain. 'You don't mean to "approach" with your pistols, do you?' **1872** Eggleston *Hoosier Schoolm.* iv. 49 He approached a word as Bull approached the raccoon.

2. To make overtures to (a person) in an effort to bribe or corrupt him.

1857 *Lawrence* (Kansas) *Republican* 30 July 2 An editor of this place had approached him, saying, they were about to start a Walker party in the Territory, and offering inducements to him to become an organ under it. **1893** *Cong. Rec.* Sep. 1874/1 Nearly every bit of everything that is said about public men being corrupted or approached is false.

approbamus ˌæprəˈbeməs, *n.* [L., "we approve."] A certificate of approbation given to a student. *Obs.* — **1774** Belknap in *Life* (1847) 71(Hall), [The Indian] appeared to be an ingenious, sensible, serious young man; and we gave him an *approbamus*, of which there is a copy on the next page.

* **approbate,** *v. tr.* To approve or sanction (a person) as qualified to preach. *Obs.* — **1779** E. Parkman *Diary* 113 He was graduated at Yale College, (and) approbated by the Association at New London. **1882** *Schaff's Relig. Encycl.* I. 720/2 In 1769 he [Nathanael Emmons] was approbated as a preacher.

* **apricot,** *n.* (See quots.) Also **apricot vine.** Cf. **maypop.** — **1867** Muir *Thousand-Mile Walk* (1916) 56 A species of passion flower is common, reaching back into Tennessee. It is here [Georgia] called 'apricot vine,' has a superb flower, and the most delicious fruit I have ever eaten. **1888** *Ark. Geol. Surv. Rep.* IV. 250 Passiflora incarnata, which is here called 'apricot,' is a straggling, careless vine with triple-lobed leaves. **1933** Small *Southeastern Flora* 896 May-pop. Apricot-vine. Dry roadsides, rocky slopes, and old fields, various provinces, Fla. to Tex., Mo., and Va.

April currant. (See quot.) *Obs.* — **1737** Brickell *N. Carolina* 89 April-Currans so call'd, from their being ripe in that month, grow on the banks of the rivers, or where clay has been thrown up; the fruit when ripe is red, and very soon gone.

* **apron,** *n.*

1. A device placed upon a ram to prevent his siring.

The early appearance of this use in this country renders questionable its having originated here, but no British evidence is at hand.

1651 in *Records E.-Hampton* I. 16 It is ordered yt all the rams that shall bee found amonge the goates without a apron the ptie that owneth the ram or rams shall be liable to pay 5s for every Defect herein and this order to stand in force till 5 weekes after myhillmus next ensueinge. **1862** *Rep. Comm. Patents: Agric.* 139 Ewes only being taken to him when in heat, such being selected from the flock, by the aid of a buck, with an apron called 'a teaser.'

2. A covering for the forward part of a canoe to prevent its shipping water and to keep out rain.

1805 *Lewis & Clark Jrnls.* (1904) III. ii. 166 Their canoes . . . verry light wide in the middle and tapers at each end, with aperns. **1880** *Harper's Mag.* Aug. 400/2 The outfit of every canoe should include a circular rubber cushion, and a rubber apron for covering the cockpit, to keep out the rain and seas.

3. The skirt of a saddle. Also attrib.

1893 K. Sanborn *S. California* 177 The corners of the aprons [on a saddle] are tipped with silver. **1910** J. Hart *Vigilante Girl* 137 The express messenger . . . had hitched the apron-strap around his leg.

4. A revolving canvas on a harvesting machine for conveying cut grain to the binding mechanism.

1899 *Sat. Ev. Post* 10 June 795 Eight hundred thousand yards of cotton duck . . . are used annually in making 'aprons' for the harvesters.

As the last term in **devil's, eating, Hoover, ice, Indian, leather apron.**

aptitude test. A test to determine one's aptitudes. — **1928** H. B. English *Dict. of Psychological Terms.* **1947** *Sat. Ev. Post* 8 Mar. 4/2 He was referred to the Veterans' Administration for aptitude tests.

aquardiente, variant of **aguardiente.**

arancel ɑranˈsel, *n. S.W.* [Sp. in same sense.] A fee, tariff or import duty. *Obs.* — **1836** Holley *Texas* xi. 214 In conformity with the last fee bill, Arancel, of notary public's of the ancient audience of Mexico. **1888** J. Webb *Adventures* 12 (MS), One third 'Aransel' or import duties on all goods sold in each state.

Arapaho əˈræpəˌho, *n.* [See note.]

This term is of uncertain derivation. It may be f. Pawnee *tirapihu, larapihu,* "trader." Santamaría equates *Arapaoes, Arrapahos* (no doubt the immediate source of the word in American English) with Sp. *desarrapados,* the ragged ones.

An Indian of an important warlike plains tribe of the Algonquian family, usu. pl. as a tribal name. Also attrib.

1812 J. C. Luttig *Jrnl. Exped. Upper Mo.* (1920) 101 Cadet Chevalier . . . was informed by the Arepaos, that 3 of them were Killed by the Blackfeet. **1851** Keller *Trip Across Plains* 15 This stream is so called, from a hunter and trapper of the same name, whose companions were killed, and his wife . . . carried away captive by the Arapahoes. **1907** Cook *Border & Buffalo* (1938) 135 The Cheyennes and Arapahoes hunt north of here. **1947** *Primitive Man* July 40 It is very similar in character to the present day Arapaho crow-dance.

b. The language of these Indians.

1866 *Beadle's Mo.* June 491/2 His entire ignorance of English was only equalled by my utter innocence of Arapahoe.

arapajo ˌærəˈpeho, *n. S.W.* Variant of **aparejo.** — **1854** Delano *Life on Plains* 334 We purchased 12 beautiful Peruvian mules, with necessary arapahoes (Mexican pack saddles). **1903** White *Forest* iii. 24 One hears strange, suggestive words and phrases—arapajo, capote, . . . and a dozen others coined into the tender of daily use.

* **arbor,** *n.* As the last term in **brush, bush, grape arbor.**

Arbor Day. A day in spring legally appointed for setting out trees.

Introduced by Nebraska in 1872, and now observed, usu. as a school or legal holiday, in most of the states. A day is similarly observed in Canada, Australia, and New Zealand.

1872 in Eggleston *Arbor Day* (1896) 14 Resolved, That Wednesday, the 10th day of April, 1872, be . . . consecrated for tree planting in the state of Nebraska, and the state board of agriculture hereby name it Arbor Day. **1903** *Nation* 29 Oct. 340 Miss Jarvis seems to think that on 'Arbor Day' every American is moved by an irresistible impulse to plant a tree. **1947** *Democrat* 16 Oct. 2/6 Ohio had its first Arbor Day in Cincinnati in 1882, when 20,000 school children paraded to parks to plant trees in honor of distinguished men.

* **arbutus,** *n.* = **trailing arbutus.** — **1846** Webb *Altowan* I. iv. 142 Dwarf arbutus . . . forms the principal ingredient of Indian fumigation. **1913** Eaton *Barn Doors & Byways* 255, I looked . . . toward the mountain, and the scent of arbutus came to me with almost physical distinctness. **1942** Weygandt *Plenty of Penna.* 267 We had come on another youngster with arbutus for sale less than a month earlier up near Clearfield.

* **arc,** *n.*

1. arc lamp, "a lamp in which the light is given out by an electric arc" (*Cent.*).

1883 H. Greer *Dict. Electricity* 183 Mr. Weston has devised several forms of automatic cut-outs for use in his arc lamps. **1901** Merwin & Webster *Calumet K* xvi. 307 She disappeared in the shadow of an arc lamp.

2. arc light, an electric light produced by an arcing current.

1885 Brockett *Our Country's Progress* 653/2 The arc light is no longer an experiment, either as regards its practicability or economy. *Ib.* 654/1 For small rooms, offices, and dwellings the arc light is utterly unsuited. **1946** ADAMS *Album Amer. Hist.* III. 309 The dynamo made by Charles F. Brush in 1876 began to bear fruit the following year when Brush announced the invention of an arc light—illumination brought about by an electric arc leaping from one carbon point to another.

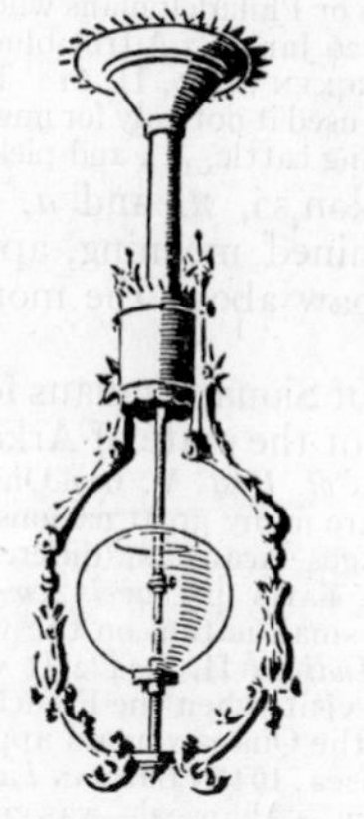

Arc light of an early type

***arch,** *n.*

1. An archway or arched-over opening used as a storage place at the base of a chimney in a dwelling house.

1786 PATTEN *Diary* 528 David began to build the wall of the Arch for our Chimney. **1845** *Lowell Offering* V. 256 We . . . descend into her cellar. . . . Here is a nice arch for potatoes and all other freeze-able commodities.

2. The fire chamber of a furnace for making maple sugar. Also attrib. Cf. **boiling arch, *evaporator.**

1867 *Harper's Wkly.* 4 May 286/2 The fluid thus extracted without further effort is then put in barrels, and drawn to 'the arch' or 'fire-place,' which is built of a few stones laid upon each other to hold the 'pans' or 'kettles,' where it is boiled down to a sirup. **1898** I. H. HARPER *S. B. Anthony* I. 7 Opening out of the kitchen was a room containing the cheese press, and the big arch kettle.

Archee ˈɑrˌtʃi, *n.* [Prob. fanciful coinage.] (See quot. 1882.) *Obs.* — **1876** *Amer. Cycl.* XVI. 795/2 [Brigham] Young was grand archee of the order of Danites, a secret organization within the [Mormon] church. **1882** MRS. WAITE *Adv. Far West* 250 Brigham Young and his two Counselors form the First Presidency, under the title of the Gods, or Grand Archees. . . . A few, also, of the Apostles, hold the rank of Grand Archees. . . . Next in importance, is a body of men called Archees. *Ib.* 251 The Archees have discretionary and independent power over the lives of all gentiles and 'apostates.'

Arch-stone State. The Keystone State, Pennsylvania. *Rare.* — **1840** *Congress. Globe* 25 Jan., App. 263 In this severance and sectioning, what would Pennsylvania, that 'arch-stone' State, say?

***arctic,** *n.* A warm, frequently fur-lined, waterproof overshoe, in full **arctic boot, overshoe,** usu. *pl.*

1867 *Territorial Enterprise* (Virginia, Nev.) 1 Mar. 1/1 The 'arctic' boots are taking the place of rubber overshoes . . . and are more

Pair of arctics

serviceable. **1890** *Harper's Mag.* June 69/2 To see Mr. Fox pacing the platform . . . with mittens and arctic overshoes. **1944** *Estes Park* (Colo.) *Trail* 25 Feb. 8/2 An . . . increase . . . in retail ceiling prices of . . . arctics, gaiters, and rubber boots . . . has been allowed.

***area,** *n.* As the last term in **cotton, experiment, wild, wilderness area.**

area of freedom. The U.S., a phrase used in connection with the annexation of Texas (see also quot. 1886). Both *obs.* — **1845** *Congress. Globe* 8 Jan., App. 79/1 Is our aid invoked to relieve her [*sc.* Texas] from a condition of servitude and extend 'the area of freedom'? Why, sir, in the same breath in which we are called upon to extend 'the area of freedom,' we are assured (etc.). **1886** ALTON *Among Law-Makers* 136 Mr. Dawes stood in front of the Clerk's desk . . . [in the space] . . . called the 'area of freedom.'

areaway ˈɛrɪəˌwe, *n.* A subsurface area about a building affording ready access to, and light and air in, cellars and basements, sometimes serving as a passage.

1899 BREEN *Thirty Years* 731 After the dust and mud became consolidated so as to absorb no more water, streams of surplus rain . . . made its way into area-ways. **1907** *Chicago Ev. Post* 4 May 3 The buiding is connected with the main hospital by a covered areaway. [**1909** *Cent. Supp.* 73/3 In cities it is becoming increasingly common to set buildings of all kinds in what seems a pit formed by areas on all the street-fronts.] **1947** *Chi. D. News* 20 Jan. 7/1 An unidentified man dragged her into an areaway near her home.

***Arethusa,** *n.* A genus of showy bog orchids, also (not *cap.*) a small swamp plant of this genus, *A. bulbosa,* having a handsome rose-like flower. Cf. **snakemouth.** — **1817–8** EATON *Botany* (1822) 180 *Arethusa bulbosa,* arethusa . . . flowers large, sweet-scented. . . . Damp. **1900** HIGGINSON *Outdoor Studies* 46 On peat-meadows . . . Arethusa (now called Pogonia) flowers profusely with a faint, delicious perfume. **1949** *Amer. Photography* Jan. 53/3 Somewhat resembling the rose pogonia and found growing in similar situations, is the arethusa.

argee ˈɑrˌdʒi, *n.* [Poss. a spelling out of r.g. =**rotgut** *q.v.*] Inferior liquor. In full **argee whisky.** *Obs.* — *a*1861 WINTHROP *J. Brent* ii. 22 Some like it . . . but taint like good old Argee to me. **1861** ——*Open Air* 147 What a hard lot we were all round, livin' on nothing but argee whiskey.

Argemone ɑrˈdʒɛmənə, *n.* [L. name of an herb.] (See quot. 1889.) — **1857** *Spirit of Times* 11 Apr. 90/3 To the above may be added . . . the Didiscus, the Argemone, and several others. **1889** *Cent.* 304/2 Argemone. . . . A small genus of plants, natural order *Papaveraceae.* The species are all ornamental, and natives of America, but are widely naturalized.

***Argonaut,** *n.* One who went to California to hunt gold soon after its discovery there in 1848. Also transf.

1848 in CUTLER *Greyhounds* (1930) 134 The ship will be commanded by a man of experience, and if the adventurers of the *Trescott* do not bring home their full share of the golden fleece, we have overestimated the qualities of the Argonautes. **1884** HILL *Colo. Pioneers* 18 A few of the Argonauts of '59, thinking 'a bird in the hand worth two in the bush,' took their helpmeets with them. **1948** JOHNSTON *Gold Rush* 28/1 How those argonauts who first beheld this contorted country must have labored to penetrate it with pack mules and ox-drawn wagons!

arid belt. (See quot. 1888.) — **1888** ROOSEVELT in *Cent. Mag.* Feb. 495/1 The great grazing lands of the West lie in what is known as the arid belt, which stretches from British America on the north to Mexico on the south, through the middle of the United States. **1894** *Cong. Rec.* 11 Aug. 8430/1 In this entire arid belt nature has provided in one way or another a sufficient amount of water, and all the necessary material for the construction of dams, basins, and reservoirs.

Arikara əˈrikərə, *n.* [See note.]

Ultimately f. the Skidi (a Caddoan tribe) word *ariki,* horn, referring to a former style of dressing the hair, +*ra,* pl. ending. *Aricaras,* also *Arrikaris, Ricaris,* occur in Santamaría, and the term may have come into Amer. use f. the Spanish.

"A tribe forming the northern group of the Caddoan linguistic family" (Hodge). Also attrib. Cf. **Ree, Ricaree.**

1811 in BRACKENRIDGE *Views of Louisiana* (1814) 242 Passed several old villages, said to be of the Arikara nation. **1814** *Ib.* 70 The only *fixed* or agricultural villages on the Missouri, are those of the Osage, Maha's, Poncas, Pani's, Arikara's, and Mandans . . . all on the S.W. side of the river. **1830** *St. Louis Beacon* 28 Oct., The Arickara Indians, who have been in an almost permanent state of hostility to the citizens of the United States, have lately committed new outrages. **1947** DEVOTO *Across Wide Missouri* 26 The Arikaras had finally got apprehensive of government retribution for years of murder and robbery.

***aristocracy,** *n.* As the last term in **Creole, Kansas, paper, planting, Tammany aristocracy.**

***aristocratic,** *a.* (See quots.) *Obs.* See also **anti-aristocratic.**

1846 COOPER *Redskins* x, Ravensnest was termed an 'aristocratic residence.' The word 'aristocratic,' I find since my return home, has got to be a term of expansive signification, its meaning depending on the particular habits and opinions of the person who happens to use it. **1859** BARTLETT 12 *Aristocratic,* strangely misapplied in those parts of the country where the population is not dense. The city, in the surrounding country towns, is deemed 'aristocratic.' The people in the villages consider the inhabitants of the towns 'aristocratic,' and so on. The term is . . . very common in small country newspapers and in political speeches in out of the way places.

Arizona ˌærəˈzonə, *n.* [f. Papago *Arizonac*, place of the few or little springs.]

1. Name of a southwestern state used attrib., chiefly in scientific works, in the names of birds and plants, as **Arizona cardinal, gnat-catcher, hooded oriole, quail, song sparrow, woodpecker.**

1869 *Amer. Naturalist* III. 474 The resident species not found westward of this valley were . . . the Arizona Song-sparrow (*Melospiza fallax*). **1880** *Cimarron News & Press* 30 Dec. 1/4 Three members of [the partridge] . . . family found here, the first of which is Gambell's partridge, or Arizona quail. **1881** *Amer. Naturalist* XV. 214 Later, in Arizona, I noticed . . . the Arizona or lead-colored gnat-catcher (*Polioptila plumbea*). **1891** *Cent. s.v. Woodpecker*, Arizona woodpecker, *Picus* (*Dendrocopus*) *arizonae*, [is] a bird lately discovered in Arizona. **1917** *Birds of Amer.* III. 64. **1940** JAEGER *Desert Wild Flowers* 6 From the copious loose threads hanging from the ends of the leaves, Arizona hooded and Scott orioles construct their unique, pendent nests. **1944** *Nat. Geog. Mag.* June 694/1 There were . . . western mockingbirds and Arizona cardinals; Bullock's orioles; [etc.].

Also *Arizona arbutus, bob-white, buckthorn, cork fir, crested flycatcher, cypress, gourd, jay, junco, longleaf pine, pine, screech owl, white pine, yellow pine*, etc.

2. a. Arizona fever, great desire to migrate to Arizona. *Obs.* **b. Arizona tenor,** (see quot.).

(a) **1873** BEADLE *Undevel. West* 669 All my friends who were 'footloose' had the 'Arizona fever.' — (b) **1945** *Everybody's Digest* Aug. 87 Among his own kind, the waddy calls a coughing tubercular an 'Arizona tenor.'

3. Arizona ruby, a garnet of a ruby color and of igneous origin found in the Southwest. Cf. **Navaho ruby.**

1893 DONALDSON *Moqui Pueblo Indians* 16 The Moqui Indians have quantities of garnets, Arizona rubies, and pieces of turquoise.

Arizonian ˌærəˈzonɪən, *a.* and *n.*

1. *n.* One who lives in Arizona. Also **Arizonan.**

1869 *Overland Mo.* June 495/1 So confident are the Arizonians of their agricultural future, that many merchants in Tucson and Wickenburg will advance seed and farming implements to an emigrant. **1947** *So. Sierran* Nov. 3/2 An Arizonan never climbs a mountain without first putting a horse under him.

2. *a.* Pertaining to Arizona.

*c*1857 WHITMAN *Amer. Primer* (1904) 35 Arizonian names have the sense of the ecstatic monk. **1869** *Overland Mo.* Jan. 19/2 The Chino valley is colossal for width; it is almost Arizonian.

***ark,** *n.*

1. A large, flat-bottomed boat, usu. employed as a house or freight boat on rivers in pre-steamboat days (see quot. 1819). Now *hist.*

It may be that Du. *aak*, and Ger. *arche*, used of flat-bottomed river boats, are in some way or degree contributory to this sense of **ark*.

1759 *Essex Inst. Coll.* XIX. 143 An ark that was built within about 12 Days was Launched into the Lake. **1819** HULME *Journal* 38 This ark, which would stow away eight persons, close packed, is a thing by no means pleasant to travel in, especially at night. It is strong at bottom, but may be compared to an orange-box, bowed over at top, and so badly made as to admit a boy's hand to steal the oranges: it is proof against the river, but not against the rain. **1823** JAMES *Exped.* I. 15 From Olean downward, the Alleghany and Ohio bear along with their current fleets of rude arks laden with cattle, horses, household furniture, [etc.]. **1942** WEYGANDT *Plenty of Penna.* 285 Coal has come from the anthracite fields by packhorse and by wagon, by arks on Lehigh and Delaware, by canal boat and train.

attrib. **1808** *Ann. 10th Cong.* 2 Sess. 52 Our dismantled, ark-roofed vessels . . . are indeed decaying in safety at our wharves. **1833** C. MINER in *Life* (1916) 62 The situation . . . rendered it necessary to obtain provisions, teams, miners, ark-builders, and other laborers. **1843** FRÉMONT *Exped.* 188 The emigrants . . . making ark-like rafts, on which they had embarked their families and household.

b. (See quots.)

1893 *Stand. Dict., Ark*, (Eastern United States) a moored scow covered by a house in which a business is done, as in oysters, etc. **1905** *Forestry Bureau Bul.* 61 *Ark*, see Wanigan . . . *Wanigan*, a houseboat used as sleeping quarters or as kitchen and dining room by river drivers. (N.W., L.S.)

2. A large freight wagon. *Obs.*

1838 *Knickerb.* XII. 191 They drove their long 'arks,' or market-wagons, filled with blaäing calves. **1891** S. M. WELCH *Recoll. 1830–40* 66 This tavern was so known by its patronage, the teamsters and freight handlers of the broad tire wheels; enormous arks of the so-called 'Pennsylvania wagons,' driven with four to ten horses.

As the last term in **Kentucky, land, lumber, Noah's, Pennsylvania ark.**

ark ɑrk, *v.* [A new formation from **ark,** *n.*] *tr.* To load (animals, etc.) on an ark or flat-boat. *Rare.* — **1845** *St. Louis Reveille* 4 Aug. (Th.), I stood by while all the animals were arked, each one more obstinate than the former.

Arkansan ɑrˈkænzən, *n.* Also **Arkansian.** One who lives in Arkansas. — **1844** *St. Louis Reveille* 29 Dec. 1/6 There is more gab in the newspapers on one Arkan*sian* who stabbeth than over ninety and nine New Yorkers or Philadelphians who do just the same thing. **1882** *Chi. Wkly. News* 26 Jan. 2/3 A true-blue Arkansan had the floor for a reply. **1948** MENCKEN *Supp.* II. 612 The legend was that the Arkansans of the time used it not only for murder, but also for fighting wild animals, butchering cattle, . . . and picking their teeth.

Arkansas ˈɑrkənˌsɔ, *n.* and *a.* Also **Arkansaw.** [f. name of undetermined meaning, applied by Illinois Indians to the Quapaw about the mouth of the Arkansas river.]

1. *pl.* A tribe of Siouan Indians formerly living in the northeastern part of the state of Arkansas.

1721 in *N.Y. Doc. Col. Hist.* V. 622 On the Mississippi, & the branches of it, there are many great nations, especially to the West, as the Missouris, Ozages, Acansias, (different from those of Acansa on the East). **1772** D. TAITT in *Travels Amer. Col.* 520 The Quarpas . . . or Arkansaws (a small nation on the west side of Mississippi). **1910** HODGE *Amer. Indians* II. 334/2 It was not until about 130 years after De Soto's visit, when the French began to venture down the Mississippi, that the Quapaw again appear in history, and then under the name Akansea. **1946** FOREMAN *Last Trek* 308 The name by which they were known—'Akansea'—was given to the stream, which afterward became the 'Arkansas.'

2. Short for **Arkansas stone.** *Obs.*

1869 G. A. ROGERS in *Eng. Mechanic* 22 Oct. 125 A sharp-edged Arkansas can be rubbed on the outside. *Ib.*, To sharpen them on the oilstone—slips of Turkey stone, Arkansas, or Washington being used with sweet oil.

3. Of or pertaining to the state of Arkansas.

1819 *Ann. 15th Congress* 2 Sess. I. 911 A petition of sundry inhabitants of the Arkansaw country, praying that a separate territorial government may be established for the said country. **1854** THORPE *Master's House* 233 'The laws be d——d,' said a fellow, in an Arkansas blanket coat, seizing hold of Toadvine's shoulder. **1901** DUNCAN & SCOTT *Allen & Woodson Co., Kansas* 35 The log cabin we lived in was built by an Arkansas man and, of course, had an Arkansas chimney to it, built with sticks above the fireplace, and daubed with mud; and, of course, it had to be repaired every fall.

4. In the names of birds and plants, as **Arkansas cabbage, finch, flycatcher, kingbird, siskin.**

1825 BONAPARTE *Ornithology* I. 18 The total length of the Arkansas Flycatcher is eight inches. The bill is similar to that of the Crested Flycatcher, but is more rounded above, and more abruptly inflected at tip, being of a blackish colour, as well as the feet. *Ib.* 54 The Arkansaw Siskin inhabits the country near the base of the Rocky mountains, south of the river Platte. **1836** EATON *Botany* (ed. 7) 549 *Streptanthus ovalifolius*, Arkansas Cabbage. . . . Grows in Arkansas. **1858** BAIRD *Birds Pacific R.R.* 422 *Chrysomitris Psaltria*, Bonap.; Arkansas-Finch . . . inhabits the southern Rocky mountains to the coast of California. **1870** *Amer. Naturalist* III. 477 McGillivray's Warbler . . ., Arkansas Kingbird (*Tyrannus verticalis*). **1945** *Mass. Audubon Soc. Bul.* Feb. 19 Arkansas Kingbirds and the Migrant Shrike—Western birds—are usually seen up from the shore in the fall.

Also *Arkansas coreopsis, goldfinch, greenback, soft pine*, etc.

5. In miscellaneous combs.: (1) **Arkansas Indians,** =**Arkansas 1.**; (2) **stone,** "a fine-grain whetstone found in Arkansas, and used to sharpen surgical and dental instruments" (*Cent.*); (3) **stool,** (see quot.), *obs.*; (4) **toothpick,** a bowie knife, or a knife resembling this; (5) **Traveler,** the name of a well-known tune and song; (6) **whetstone,** =**Arkansas stone.**

(1) **1770** PITTMAN *Present State* 40 The Arcansas or Quapas Indians live three leagues above the fort, on the side of the river. **1819** NUTTALL *Travels Ark.* (1821) 61 This evening we were visited by . . . a band of the Quapaws or Arkansa Indians. — (2) **1888** J. C. BRANNER *Geol. Survey* I. 49 Arkansas stone . . . produced . . . by the metamorphosis of chert. **1942** *Ark. Geol. Survey Bul.* VI. 67 The Arkansas stone is a very fine-grained, homogeneous rock with a waxy luster, is usually white, and is translucent on thin edges. — (3) **1858** *Spirit of Times* 13 Feb. 370/1 Seated on Arkansas stools (*i.e.* blocks sawed off the end of a log), by the fire, we had time to look around us. — (4) **1836** *Crockett Almanac* 1837 (Nashville) 46 [*Caption of woodcut*:] An Arkansaw Toothpick. **1948** *Sat. Ev. Post* 24 April 88/4 Arkansas itself was participating in the wildest kind of personal politics, replete with bombast, acrimony, pistols and 'Arkansas toothpicks.'

(5) **1856** BREWERTON *War in Kans.* 254 'Legs' is fiddling away . . . at that never-failing tune, 'The Arkansaw Traveller.' **1947** PAUL *Linden* 333 When we played 'The Arkansaw Traveller' or 'Turkey in the Straw,' the customers sometimes stamped the church until it threatened to

come down. — (6) **1878** *Harper's Mag.* Jan. 204 In commerce, under the name of the Arkansas whetstone or Ouachita oil-stone, [novaculite rock] has almost eclipsed its Turkish rival.

b. Also in derivatives (see quots.).

1885 *Outing* July 412/1 A dozen freckled Arkansawish faces are watching my movements with undisguised astonishment. **1910** BRONSON *Red-Blooded Heroes* 42 Arkansawyers don't count fer much nohow, do they? **1947** *Chi. Sun* (Bk. Week) 8 June 4/2 Most Arkansawyers . . . can find in this book a wealth of fresh information.

arkansite 'arkənˌsaɪt, *n.* (See quots.) — **1889** *Cent.* 311/1 Arkansite. . . . A variety of brookite from Magnet Cove, Arkansas. **1890** KUNZ *Gems & Precious Stones* 194 At Magnet Cove, Ark., brilliant crystals of the variety of this mineral known as arkansite are found in great profusion.

* **Arlington,** *n.* **1.** Designating a breed or variety of sheep developed on the Arlington estate of George Washington Parke Custis. **2. Arlington meal,** (see quot.). Both *obs.* — (1) **1809** LIVINGSTON *Sheep* (1810) 50 From these sheep I turn . . . to the Arlington long-woolled sheep. These . . . were derived from the stock of that distinguished farmer, soldier, statesman, and patriot, Washington. *Ib.* 59 The Arlington long-woolled breed. **1884** *Century Mag.* XXVII. 516/1 The Arlington sheep . . . seem to have been a valuable breed of long-wooled sheep, but are now unknown. — (2) **1879** MRS. WHITNEY *Just How* 41 Two heaping cups of 'Arlington meal,' or graham flour, in bread-bowl.

* **arm,** *n.*

1. arm band, a band worn around the arm, esp. by Indians, as an ornament.

1797 B. HAWKINS *Letters* 253 The goods he wants are . . . 3 pair arm bands, 3 pair wrist bands. **1846** M'KENNEY *Memoirs* I. 178, I opened a box . . . and took out a pair of silver arm-bands and a silver gorget.

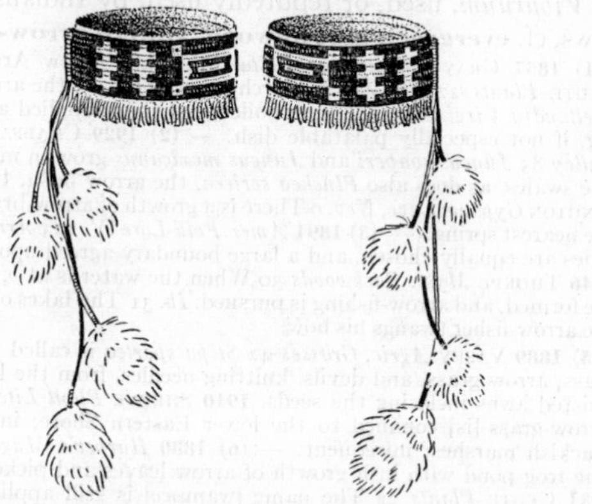

Arm bands of a type used by eastern Dakota Indians

1948 *Ill. State Arch. Soc. Bul.* April 28/2 They have two ornaments resembling large crab claws which were set with pearls, and 1,400 beads from necklaces and arm bands—some being perforated pearls.

2. arm-in-arm convention, (see quot.). *Obs.*

1892 BROWN & STRAUSS *Dict. Politics* (1907) 29 Arm-in-arm convention [was] a name given to a convention of Republicans that supported President Johnson's policy of reconstruction. Its name arose from the fact that the members from Massachusetts and from South Carolina entered the convention together at the head of the delegates.

See also **king's arm, long arm, strong arm.**

armist 'ɑrmɪst, *n.* (See quot.) *Rare.* — **1856** C. ROBINSON *Kansas Conflict* (1892) 397 One of them asked my husband, 'Are you a Northern armist,' He said, 'I am.' I understood the answer to mean that my husband was opposed to the Northern or free-soil party. I cannot say that I understood the question.

armoire ɑr'mwɑr, *n. S.* and *S.W.* [F., an Amer. borrowing.] A large cupboard or clothespress, often of expensive and ornate construction.

1834 BRACKENRIDGE *Recoll.* ii. 24 The furniture . . . was of the most common kind, consisting of an armoire, a rough table or two, and some coarse chairs. **1854** THORPE *Master's House* 118 The *armoire*, of massive proportions, is always composed of the richest of materials, and is very often inlaid with costly and different tinted woods, the panels are composed of costly mirrors that reach almost from the floor to the ceiling. **1936** ARTHUR *Old New Orleans* 63 The *armoire*, which is said to have been originated by him, is not an ordinary *armoire* of the wardrobe type, with two front doors opening into one large space within. The Seignouret *armoire* has, besides two front doors, a 'blind' door in the end, which opens into a separate space behind the large doors, forming, in this way, a sort of secret closet.

armonica ɑr'mɑnɪkə, *n.* [Ital., fem. of *armonico* harmonious.] The "musical glasses" invented by Franklin. Now *hist.* Cf. **harmonica.**

1762 FRANKLIN *Wks.* (1887) III. 204 In honor of your musical language, I have borrowed from it the name of this instrument, calling it the Armonica. **c1775** CARTER in Fithian *Journal* I. 59 *note*, An armonica, being the musical glasses without water, framed into a complete instrument. **1936** MORSE *Furniture* 305 Franklin invented an instrument for the musical glasses, which he called the Armonica, for which famous composers wrote music, and in which the glasses were arranged upon a rod which turned with a crank, while below was a trough of water which moistened the glasses as they dipped into it.

* **armor,** *n.* The steel plating or other protective covering of a warship, fortification, etc. Cf. **marine armor.** — **1855** W. M. GWIN (*title*), Report of the Committee on Naval Affairs, who were instructed to inquire into the expediency of using submarine armors in the United States navy. **1861** *Naval War Records* 1 Ser. IV. 222 This addition would nearly treble the strength of the armor and make it impervious to balls from Paixhans guns at . . . half a mile. **1948** *Sat. Ev. Post* 9 Oct. 31 She was sent against the Confederate batteries at Drewrys Bluff in the spring of 1862 to test her armor.

armor, *v. tr.* To furnish or cover (a warship) with armor-plating. — **1861** J. A. DAHLGREN in M. Dahlgren *Memoir* 249 So little having been determined with regard to the preferable mode of armoring ships. **1886** *Harper's Mag.* June 13/2 These vessels . . . will be armored with steel or compound armor.

* **armory,** *n.* A place where arms are manufactured. Cf. **government armory, state armory.**

1794 *Ann. 3rd Congress* 1428 There shall be established, at each of the aforesaid arsenals, a National Armory. **1883** MARK TWAIN *Life Miss.* lviii. 567 The Rock Island establishment is a national armory and arsenal. **1948** *Minneapolis Morn. Tribune* 28 Sep. 14/3 Production of M-1 rifles for the infantry and M-3 machine guns for jet planes is being stepped up at the Springfield, Mass., armory.

* **army,** *n.*

1. In miscellaneous combs.: (1) **army blue,** the blue uniform formerly worn by U.S. soldiers, or cloth for such a uniform, also as the name of a song; (2) **cloth,** "cloth from which soldiers' uniforms are made" (*Cent.*); (3) **correspondent,** one who is employed by a newspaper or other periodical to be with an army and contribute war news; (4) **duck,** (see quot. 1917); (5) **Register,** an annual publication by the War Department giving the names, relative standing, etc., of army officers; (6) **regulations,** the rules governing the conduct of soldiers, also as the title of a book of such rules.

(1) **1859** in E. A. DOLPH *Sound Off!* (1929) 570 We'll turn our eyes to brighter skies, And don the Army Blue. **1869** in *U.S. Army & Navy Jrnl.* 6 Nov. 179/1 On the frontier it is so common to see citizens dressed in the 'Army blue,' that it is difficult for a stranger to tell who is soldier and who is citizen. **1929** E. A. DOLPH *Sound Off!* 567 The time and circumstances of the song's origin . . . are unknown. It was in existence as early as 1846, for a poem of that year refers to the 'strains of "Army Blue."' — (2) **1877** *Rep. Indian Affairs* 5 We should have a uniform material, made of wool—like army-cloth—for Indian clothing. — (3) **1863** *Harper's Mag.* Oct. 627/1 From that day to this the 'army correspondent' has not ceased to be a concomitant of the army. **1886** POORE *Reminisc.* II. 126 With the war came the army correspondent. — (4) [**1780** T. JEFFERSON *Writings* (1893) II. 329 What is to be done for tents, I know not. I am assured that very little duck can be got in this country.] **1917** KEPHART *Camping* I. 32 *Army duck* is the best grade made, of selected cotton free from sizing, both warp and filling doubled and twisted, closely woven, and free from imperfections—if it comes up to army standard.

(5) **1815** (*title*), Army Register, Adjutant and Inspector General's Office, May 17, 1815. **1865** (*title*), Official Army Register of the Volunteer Force of the United States Army. — (6) **1820** *16th Cong.* 2 Sess., House Doc. 45 VI. 11 (*Note*), The articles marked . . . to be copied out of the *blue book* containing the present *army regulations.* **1847** *Gen. Regulations for Army* (*binder's title*), Army Regulations 1847. **1865** *Atlantic Mo.* XV. 626 They study the 'Army Regulations' to make sure that they concede no more.

b. In the names of insects: (1) **army cricket,** prob. the Mormon cricket, *q.v., obs.;* (2) **worm,** the larva of any one of various moths, as *Cirphis unipuncta*, that travel in great numbers and destroy grass and grain crops (see quot. 1888).

(1) **1860** A. D. H. SMITH ed. *Narrative S. Hancock* (1927) 22 Here we are much annoyed by the Army crickets, the whole surface of the ground being covered with these insects, about an inch and a half long. — (2) [**1743** THOMAS SMITH *Journals* (1821) 27 June 130 There are millions of worms, in armies, appearing and threatening to

cut off every green thing.] **1816** D. Thomas *Travels Western Country* (1819) 155 *A drowth,* the longest known in many years, which only ceased a few days ago,—and the *army worm,* which has ravaged the meadows,—prevent us from forming a proper judgment from our own observations. **1948** *Dly. Oklahoman* (Okla. City) 2 May 8/1 It also controls army worms, grasshoppers, and ants.

2. In the names of armies in operation during the Civil War, as (1) *Army of Northern Virginia,* (2) *Army of the Potomac,* (3) *Army of the Tennessee.*

(**1**) **1906** *McClure's Mag.* XXVI. 94 General William Henry Fitzhugh Lee, a son of General Robert E. Lee, Commander of the 'Army of Northern Virginia,' . . . was quite seriously wounded. **1948** *Time* 31 May 90/3 The Army of Northern Virginia hove in sight, 'wave after wave, billow after billow.' — (**2**) **1862** McClellan in *Own Story* 230 Even when in a subordinate position I always looked beyond the operations of the Army of the Potomac. **1945** *Ala. Hist. Quart.* Spring 121 In the Richmond sector, the Army of the Potomac had far more than met its match. — (**3**) **1866** Shanks *Recollections* 332 The Army of the Tennessee was composed of men from the West, and, as it existed under General Grant, was properly the representative army of the West.

As the last term in **continental, convention, Coxey's, Federal, gospel, grand, industrial, northern, patriot, provisional, rebel, secession, Union army.**

∗**Arnold,** *n.* [f. Benedict *Arnold* (1741–1801), Amer. Revolutionary traitor.] A traitor. — **1845** *St. Louis Reveille* 17 Apr. 2/4 *The 'Arnolds of the Press,'* is the very appropriate appellation given to the papers which are literally inviting the hostilities of Mexico against this country, since the . . . annexing of Texas. **1892** *People's Press* (S.F.) 27 Aug. 4/1 The truth is that Weaver is a paid Arnold; bought by British gold and promised Presidential patronage from Cleveland. **1948** *Chi. Sun-Times* 19 Feb. 42/2 For this he was denounced, back in Illinois, as a second Benedict Arnold.

arocoun, *n.* Variant of **raccoon.**

Aroostook War. [f. *Aroostook* River, Maine.] *Hist.* A controversy (1836–39) which threatened war between the U.S. and Gt. Britain over the northeastern bounds of the U.S. — **1895** *N. Eng. Mag.* Sep. 70/2 Houlton was the principal military station in the 'bloodless Aroostook war' over the boundary question. **1939** Chitwood *John Tyler* 308 These clashes (1838–39), sometimes called the 'Aroostook War,' might easily have led to international strife.

∗**around,** *n.* As the last term in **all, knock, run, turn, walk around.**

arpent ˈɑrpənt, *n.* [See note.]

Since this term occurs only in regions of former Fr. influence it is no doubt an Amer. borrowing from French. It is now *obs.*

1. An old French measure of land, varying greatly according to locality. Also attrib.

1800 Commons *Doc. Hist.* I. 253 The proprietor of several thousand arpents of land. **1808** *Ann. 10th Congress* 1. Sess. II. 2875 A tract of land bordering on the river Detroit, and not exceeding in depth forty arpens, French measure. **1852** Reynolds *Hist. Illinois* 48 The arpent lands of this common field extended . . . to the Mississippi. **1883** Cable in *Cent. Mag.* June 219 Truck-gardens covered the fertile arpents between and beyond.

2. (See quot. 1818.)

1751 J. Bartram *Observations* 92 The breadth of the island at its lower end is two thirds of an Arpent, or thereabouts. **1818** Darby *Emigrant's Guide* 6 The arpent is used also as a measure of length, being 180 feet, or 30 toises French, equal to 192 feet English or American feet, nearly. **1896** Clendenin *Fla. Parishes E. La.* 207 Before the State was divided into townships and sections, 'grants' were laid off with so many *arpents* frontage upon these bayous and so many *arpents* deep.

arrastre əˈræstrə, *n.* Also **arrastra.** [Sp. in Amer. Sp. sense here shown.] A crude contrivance, consisting essentially of a heavy stone dragged around on a circular stone bed, for pulverizing gold and silver ores. Cf. **drag mill, rastra.**

1836 Parker *Trip to West* 266 Upstream you catch the growl of the arrastra. **1909** Mark Twain *Is Shakespeare Dead?* vii. 74, I know all about . . . arastras and how to charge them with quicksilver and sulphate of copper. **1936** McKenna *Black Range* 31 All the different mining processes from arastra to cyanide were known to him.

attrib. **1943** *Copper Camp* 17 A small arastra smelter was built by Charles E. Savage to handle the silver ores from this mine.

arriero ɑrɪˈero, *n. S.W.* [Sp., an Amer. borrowing.] A muleteer. — **1838** *N.Y. Mirror* 6 Jan. 217/1 A train of soldiers, arrieros and attendants, composed the remainder of the group. **1897** Inman *Old Santa Fe Trail* 58 On the march the *arriero* is kept busy nearly all the time. **1941** *Amer. Sp.* Oct. 182 Arriero (Spanish). Mule driver.

arroba əˈrobə, *n. W.* [Sp., an Amer. borrowing.] A weight of 25 pounds.

1840 David Turnbull *Travels in West* 126 (Bentley), The agricultural produce is stated as follows: — Of white or clayed sugar 8,091,-837 arrobas of 25 pounds each. **1909** O. Henry *Options* 112 They wash the gold . . . and then they pack it in buckskin sacks of one arroba each. **1930** G. D. Lyman *John Marsh* 205 (Bentley), A cowhide repre-represented two dollars, and tallow fifty cents the arroba.

∗**arrow,** *n.* In combs.: (1) **arrow-arum,** an aquatic or marsh plant of the genus *Peltandra;* (2) **brush, bush,** =**arrowweed** (*b*); (3) **chase,** a children's tracking game in which arrow-shaped marks chalked on the pavement guide the pursuers; (4) **fisher,** one who takes fish with a bow and arrows, also **arrowfishing;** (5) ∗**grass,** (see quot. 1889 and cf. **seaside arrowgrass**); (6) **leaf,** any plant of the genus *Sagittaria;* (7) **-leaf** (or **leaved**) **tear-thumb,** *Polygonum sagittata,* so called from the hooked prickles on the angles of the stem and the petioles; (8) **-leaf** (or **leaved**) **violet,** (see quots.); (9) **reed,** prob. the giant reed, *Arundo donax,* also attrib.; (10) ∗**root,** see as a main entry; (11) **rush,** a rush with arrow-like stems or leaves, *rare;* (12) **shield,** a shield for protection against arrows, *rare;* (13) **stone,** an arrowhead, *rare;* (14) **tip,** an arrowhead; (15) **weed,** (*a*) a plant of the genus *Sagittaria,* some species of which have leaves shaped like arrowheads, (*b*) in the Southwest the arrowwood, *Pluchea sericea;* (16) **wood,** any one of various shrubs having straight tough shoots, as the sorrel tree and some species of *Viburnum,* used, or reputedly used, by Indians for arrows, cf. **evergreen arrow-wood, Indian arrow-wood.**

(**1**) **1857** Gray *Botany* 427 *Peltandra,* Raf., Arrow Arum. **1931** Clute *Plants* 22 The thick starchy rootstocks of the arrow-arum (*Peltandra Virginica*), . . . were boiled and thus supplied a nourishing, if not especially palatable dish. — (**2**) **1929** Chalfant *Death Valley* 85 *Juncus cooperi* and *Juncus mexicanus* grow in moist alkaline swales, as does also *Pluchea sericea,* the arrow bush. **1933** Harrington *Gypsum Cave, Nev.* 9 There is a growth of arrow-brush about the nearest spring. — (**3**) **1891** *Amer. Folk-Lore* IV. 223 *Arrow Chase.* Sides are equally chosen, and a large boundary agreed upon. — (**4**) **1846** Thorpe *Myst. Backwoods* 30 When the water is at *b,* the lakes are formed, and arrow-fishing is pursued. *Ib.* 31 The lakes over which the arrow-fisher twangs his bow.

(**5**) **1889** Vasey *Agric. Grasses* 42 *Stipa spartea* is called porcupine grass, arrow grass, and devils' knitting-needles, from the long, stiff, twisted awns inclosing the seeds. **1910** Shreve *Plant Life Md.* 395 Arrow-grass [is] confined to the lower Eastern Shore; in salt and brackish marshes; infrequent. — (**6**) **1880** *Harper's Mag.* June 70 The frog pond with lush growth of arrow leaves and pickerel weed. **1931** Clute *Plants* 22 The name [wampee] is still applied to the starchy tubers of the arrow-leaf (*Sagittaria latifolia*), though they are now more frequently known as duck potatoes, in reference to the wild duck's fondness for them. — (**7**) **1847** Darlington *Weeds & Plants* 282 Arrow-leaved Tear-thumb . . . [grows in] swampy meadows and thickets: New York to Florida. **1947** *Midland Naturalist* July 41 Arrow-leaf Tear-thumb [is] common (locally abundant) in marsh meadows and open shrub swamps. — (**8**) **1843** Torrey *Flora N.Y.* I. 71 *Viola sagittata.* Arrow-leaved Violet . . . [grows] in fields and on dry hill-sides. **1869** Fuller *Flower Gatherers* 110 That is the Arrow-leaf-violet, *Viola Sagittata.* **1947** *Midland Naturalist* July 51 Arrow-leaf Violet [is] common (locally abundant) in wet meadows. — (**9**) **1657** in *Amer. Sp.* XV. 151/2 Running west by North to Arrow reed swamp. **1666** *Ib.*, Beginning in a greate arrow read Swamp. **1933** Harrington *Gypsum Cave, Nev.* 9 Arrow reed or cane and other water-loving species, may be seen around Gypsum Spring.

(**11**) **1846** Emory *Military Reconn.* 11 The low grounds abound in . . . arrow rush. — (**12**) **1832** Catlin *Indians* I. 23 The Indian . . . mount[s] his snorting steed, with his bow and quiver slung, his arrow-shield upon his arm. — (**13**) **1843** *Amer. Pioneer* II. 196 Several Indian flint arrow-stones . . . were discovered by . . . Mr. Gridley. — (**14**) **1880** *Scribner's Mo.* April 884/1 They [=flintblocks] were doubtless split by the Indians from the oval nodules as materials for arrow-tips.

(**15**) (*a*) **1846** in Emory *Military Reconn.* 434 Some brackish pools, . . . bordered with the cat-tail (*typha latifolia*) and arrow weed, (*sagittaria sagittefolia*). **1886** S. W. Mitchell *R. Blake* 263 Those pools close by with purpled arrow-weed. (*b*) **1869** Browne *Adv. Apache Country* 51 Thickets of arrow-weed lined the way, and forests of cotton-wood loomed up ahead. **1947** *Rocky Mt. News* (Denver) 16 Feb. 22/4 It rolled more smoothly than the wood shavings, arrow-weed and corn silk that American boys have experimented with for generations. — (**16**) **1709** Lawson *Carolina* 100 Arrow-wood, growing on the Banks, is used, by the Indians, for Arrows and Gun-Sticks. **1892** Apgar *Trees Northern U.S.* 114 Arrow-wood . . . [is] a shrub or small tree, 5 to 15 ft. high, with ash-colored bark. **1942**

PEATTIE *Friendly Mts.* 202 On the left is a thick growth of spotted alder, arrowwood, highbush cranberry, and tamarack.

See also **broad arrow, medicine arrow, poison arrow.**

***arrowroot,** *n.* The coontie, *Zamia integrifolia*, or a starchy foodstuff prepared from the stem of this. Also **Florida arrowroot.**

1823 G. A. MCCALL *Lett. from Frontiers* (1868) 64 A half-worn sieve made of split cane, such as the Indian housewife used to bolt her flour, whether of corn or coonta-root, (a species of arrow-root). **1826** *Ib.* 157 The regions where the *coonta*, or arrow-root, the chief substitute for corn, or farinaceous food, is to be sought. **1860** CHAPMAN *Flora So. U.S.* 437 Coontie. . . . Low ground, South Florida. The stem abounds in starch, from which the Florida Arrowroot is obtained. **1899** M. GOING *Flowers* 295 But recently Mr. Herbert Webber has studied the whole process of fertilization in a subtropical gymnosperm, the coontie or arrow-root of southern Florida.

attrib. **1859** BARTLETT 98 An arrowroot preparation from the root of *Zamia integrifolia* by the Indians in Florida, where the plant is indigenous. **1876** M. F. HENDERSON *Cooking* 323 Arrowroot Jelly or Blanc-mange . . . may be flavored with lemon-juice if made with water. **1901** MOHR *Plant Life Ala.* 137 The tropical so-called sago palm (*Cycas revoluta*) and arrowroot palm (*Zamia integrifolia*) of southern Florida add to the number of decorative evergreen plants.

arroyo əˈrɔjo, *n. S.W.* [Sp.] A brook or creek, also a channel, gully, dry wash, stream bed, or valley.

[**1806** *Ann. 10th Congress* 1 Sess. I. 571 The country east of the Sabine to the Arroyo Hondo.] **1872** TICE *Across Plains* 49 There are many '*aroyas*,' that is beds of temporary streams with pools of water, which answer for stock purposes. **1947** *Nat. Geog. Mag.* Feb. 141/1 We finally came to a halt at a steep arroyo two miles from our destination.

b. arroyo seco, a dry arroyo or creek. Also as a proper name. Cf. **dry arroyo.**

1851 *Acad. Nat. Sci. Proc.* V. 215 Immediately on their arrival, they prepared their nests; one of these, built in the gravel bank of an *arroyo seco* or dry creek, I examined. **1948** *Chi. Tribune* 29 Feb. II. 3/8 At 10 o'clock Monday morning all hands are due to be in uniform at Brookside park in the Arroya Seco.

c. arroyo grape, a name applied in the western states to the riverside grape, *Vitis vulpina.*

1885 HAVARD *Flora W. & S. Texas* 511 Arroyo Grape . . . [is a] thrifty climber, the small but excellent berries maturing in October. **1891** COULTER *Botany West. Texas* 63 V. riparia Michx. (Riverside grape.) . . . Also known as 'arroyo grape.'

arse up ˈɑrsˌʌp, *n.* The white-breasted nuthatch, *Sitta carolinensis*. Cf. **tree mouse.** — *a***1870** CHIPMAN *Notes on Bartlett* 12 *Arse-up*. Small slate-colored woodpecker; so named from its facility and habit of running upward upon a tree's trunk while its head is lower than its tail. Local in Connecticut. **1945** MCATEE *Nomina Abitera* 42, I have a term variously spelled arce-up, arse-up, . . . the application of which to these upside-down birds is obvious.

art editor. The editor of a section dealing with art in a newspaper or periodical. — **1877** *Harper's Mag.* Dec. 53/2 The day editor puts news relating to art in the hands of the art editor. **1948** *Sat. Ev. Post* 24 April 6/3 That's what our art editor keeps telling us.

***artemisia,** *n.* (See quots.) *Colloq.* — **1846** SAGE *Scenes Rocky Mts.* xii, *Artemisie*, or rather *greasewood* of the mountaineers, became quite abundant, as did *absinthe*, or wild sage. **1889** R. T. COOKE *Steadfast* xxii. 236 A great bow-pot of early chrysanthemums, 'artemishys' Aunt Ruthy called them, filled the chimney.

***artery,** *n.*

1. A river, esp. the principal one in a river-system.

1805 JEFFERSON in *Life Wm. Dunbar* (1930) 177 We shall delineate with correctness the great arteries of this great country. **1850** G. HINES *Voyage* 329 This great artery of Oregon [=Columbia River] . . . receives the Cowilitz from the north. **1948** *Fargo* (N.D.) *Forum* 19 Sep. 22/2 The great rivers of the North American continent were then, and were for a long time, the chief arteries of transportation.

2. A road, railroad, or other artificial means of communication.

1850 GLISAN *Jrnl. Army Life* 27 When many of those great arteries of commerce—the railroads—shall have centered in this well-located city. **1947** *Chi. D. News* 31 Jan. 14/7 The trail long served as a great artery of travel.

***article,** *n.*

1. a. A Negro slave. **b.** In conveyancing (see quot.). Both *obs.*

(a) 1837 H. MARTINEAU *Society* II. 325 The creditors . . . answered that these young ladies [his 'quadroon' nieces] were a 'first-rate article,' too valued to be relinquished. **1869** TOURGEE *Toinette* v. (1881) 64 The recognition of 'the nigger' as a human being . . . instead of an article of merchandise. — **(b)** *a***1841** BUCKINGHAM *America* III. 103 The *article* was a device, of American origin, unknown in the English system of conveyancing; granting the possession, but not the fee of the land.

2. Articles of Confederation, a set of agreements providing for union among the original thirteen American states, framed in 1775, adopted by the Continental Congress in 1777, ratified by 1781, and in effect until 1789.

1775 *Journals Cont. Congress* II. 195 Articles of Confederation and perpetual Union, entred into . . . by the Delegates of the several Colonies. **1838** *Democratic Review* I. 226 The general dread of a return to the anarchy . . . of the old Articles of Confederation. **1948** *Antioch Review* Spring 10 As we have seen, even our old Articles of Confederation went this far!

As the last term in **annuity, cash, feature, money, school article.**

***artillery,** *n.*

1. Artillery election, the election of the officers in the Ancient and Honourable Artillery Company of Boston. Also **Artillery election sermon,** =next.

1673 *Mass. H.S. Coll.* 4 Ser. I. 19 Mr. Seaborn Cotton preacht ye Artillery Election [Sermon] at Boston. *c***1680** J. HULL *Diary* 202 So likewise did Mr. Higginson [preach a good sermon] upon the Artillery Election. **1865** *Nation* I. 674 'Evacuation Day' . . . has long since ceased to have any historical value for the great body of the People, much like the holiday called 'artillery election' in Boston. **1901** O. A. ROBERTS *Ancient & Hon. Artillery Co.* IV. 487 Rev. Phillips Brooks, D.D., of Boston, . . . delivered the Artillery Election sermon in 1872.

2. Artillery sermon, a sermon preached on the occasion of an Artillery election. *Obs.* See **state artillery.**

1644 *Mass. Bay Rec.* II. 71 The printer shall have leave to print the election sermon, . . . & the artillery sermon. **1701** SEWALL *Diary* II. 35 Mr. Pemberton preaches the artillery sermon, from Luke 3. 14.

***artist,** *n.* As the last term in **brand, bunko, chin-chin, comic, rawhide, sand, scenic, tonsorial artist.**

***as,** *prep.* In the role of.

1847 *Semi-Wkly. News* (Fredericksburg, Va.) 7 Oct. 1/4 His [*sc.* Forrest's] robust health and extraordinary *physique* give him great advantage where unusual muscular strength is necessary, as Damon, Matamor, the Gladiator, Brolla, &c. **1912** *Out West* June 359, I reproduce the accompanying sketch which gives the three principal characters, Miss Calhoun (Nellie) as *Rosalind*, Lady Archibald Campbell as *Orlando*, and Miss Schletter as *Celia*. **1947** *N.Y. Times Mag.* 12 Oct. 56/2 Above, Miss Anderson is seen with John Gielgud, the British actor-manager, as Jason.

***ascensionist,** *n.* A Millerite *q.v.* who expected to ascend to heaven at the end of the world in 1843. *Obs.* — **1869** MARK TWAIN *Innocents Abroad* xxxix. 416 (R.) The ascensionists came down from the mountain. **1884** *Harper's Mag.* May 980/2 Some years ago, in Georgia, that band of Christians known as Ascensionists were having a . . . revival.

Ascension robe. The garment donned by the Millerites *q.v.* on the day in 1843 when they expected the end of the world. *Obs.*

1843 *Nauvoo* (Ill.) *Neighbor* 7 June 3/5 Several Millerites in that city walked the streets and fields all day arrayed in their ascension robes. **1869** MARK TWAIN *Innocents Abroad* xxxix. 416 A multitude of people in America put on their ascension robes . . . and made ready to fly up into heaven. **1880** *Harper's Mag.* LX. 185/1 In New York, as Mrs. Child records, at a shop in the Bowery, muslin for ascension robes was offered. **1948** *Time* 22 Nov. 15/1 The Millerites, a religious sect, expected the world to end, and thousands of their members bought muslin Ascension Robes for the event.

***ash,** *n.*[1]

1. *Baseball.* A bat, freq. made of ash. *Colloq.*

1867 *Ball Players' Chron.* 24 Oct. 8/1 Doyle then shook the 'ash' by a liner to left field, upon which he made his second. **1886** CHADWICK *Art of Batting* 33 The ambition to excel in the home-run style of batting has been superseded by more scientific work in *handling the ash.* **1947** *This Week Mag.* 5 Oct. 4/2 Ted Williams, Boston's famed lambaster, stalked through the office . . . with a young Canadian tree, which, an Ontario pulp-and-paper man had assured him, would outwhack the American ash.

2. In combs.: (1) **ash breeze,** (see quot.); (2) **leaf maple, -leaved maple,** the box elder; (3) **maple,** the box elder; (4) **oak,** (see quot.); (5) ***pole,** a pole of ash, used as a political symbol by the followers of Henry Clay in allusion to his home, Ashland, near Lexington, Ky., *obs.;* (6) **rust,** (see quot.), *rare;* (7) **swale, swamp,** a swale or swamp in which ash is the prevailing growth.

(1) 1834 *Visit to Texas* xii, 105 We . . . took advantage of what is sometimes called the 'ash breeze': that is, our oars, and proceeded down the bay at a pretty good rate. — **(2) 1765** J. BARTRAM *Diary* 22 Sep., Below ye falls is very rich low land produceing . . . Ash hicory ash leaved maple. **1855–6** *Ill. Agric. Soc. Trans.* VI. 390 The

Box Elder of our river bottoms comes back to us under the name of . . . Ash Leaf maple. — (3) **1834** *S. Lit. Messenger* I. 98 On emerging from the wilderness, the customary variety of oak, ash maple, and hickory presents itself. **1861** *Ill. Agric. Soc. Trans.* IV. 449 The box elder or ash maple is decidedly and distinctly a maple. — (4) **1771** *N.H. Gazette* 30 Aug., Such persons as are desirous of contracting for white pine masts, yards and bowsprits, . . . lathwood, ash oak rafters, etc.

(5) **1844** *Louisville Pub. Advertiser* 17 Feb. 2/5 Mr. Clay dispatched his ash pole to Baltimore . . . [for] the grand national convention in the Monumental city. **1844** *Quincy* (Ill.) *Herald* 1 Nov. 2/1 The Old Coon himself, the daddy of all the little Coons will be tree'd on the Ash-Pole near a place they call Ashland. — (6) **1885** *Amer. Naturalist* XIX. 886 In Eastern Nebraska, . . . [there] has been . . . great abundance of the ash rust (*Æcidium fraxim*) upon the leaves . . . of the green ash. — (7) **1668** *Oyster Bay Rec.* I. 4 That . . . the Surveors are to lay out the Ash Swamp & so much upland to it, as yt shall see[m] convenyent. **1789** Morse *Amer. Geog.* 143 One species generally predominating in each soil, has originated the descriptive names of maple, ash, and cedar swamps. **1839** *Mich. Agric. Soc. Trans.* (1856) VII. 368 It follows mainly the course of two brooks . . . and embraces the intervening ash swales.

As the last term in **American, black, blue, brown, Carolina, European mountain, gray, green, hoop, jack-, live, Oregon, poison, prickly, red, stinking, swamp, Texas, wafer, water, western black, white, yellow ash.**

***ash,** *n.*[2] In combs.: (1) **ash barrel,** a barrel for ashes, also occas. **ashes barrel;** (2) ***cake,** a cake or pone of corn bread baked in ashes, cf. **corn ashcake;** (3) **can,** a large can for ashes; (4) ***cat,** a dirty or neglected child, also **ash-cat Sam,** *colloq.* or *slang;* (5) **gum,** (see quot. 1923), *colloq.;* (6) **hopper,** an ash-leach, also in phrase "to

One form of ash hopper

work one's own ash-hopper," to do one's own work, be independent, *colloq.;* (7) **house,** an outhouse for ashes and other refuse; (8) ***man,** a collector of, or dealer in, ashes; (9) **pone,** a pone of corn bread baked in an open fireplace in a container surrounded or covered by hot ashes; (10) **rake,** an implement for raking ashes; (11) **room,** a room for receiving ashes in a furnace, also attrib.; (12) **throat,** short for next; (13) **throated flycatcher,** a flycatcher, *Myiarchus cinerascens,* of the western U.S.; (14) **water,** water to which ashes have been added preparatory to boiling corn for hominy in it, *obs.*

(1) **1846** Corcoran *Pickings* 61 They were . . . knocking over the ashes barrels, shying stones at the lamps. **1947** Paul *Linden* 136 The Protestant deacons . . . did not fail to note . . . the empty bottles in the ash barrels, or thrown carelessly in piles. — (2) **1809** Ker *Travels* (1816) 111 The kind host regaled us with a good supper, or good for a wilderness country; it consisted of ash cake, venison, and bear's meat, besides coffee. **1946** *Chi. D. News* 29 Oct. 6/2, I worked in the fields, and had to eat fat meat and ash cakes in a chimney corner. — (3) **1910** *Collier's* 30 Apr. 34/2 Put 'em in the ash-can! **1948** *Chi. Tribune* 29 Feb. vii. 10/2 As those reviews persisted in giving Mr. Rodzinski credit for the orchestra's new brilliance, they must have landed in the Orchestra hall ashcan, for they certainly didn't appear on the program. — (4) **1869** Mark Twain *Innocents Abroad* xxv. 262 (R.) They [Italian women] sit in the alleys and nurse their cubs. They nurse one ash-cat at a time, and the others scratch their backs against the door-post and are happy. **1910** C. Harris *Eve's Husband* 120 He came home late at night looking like an ash-cat-Sam.

(5) **1851** Hooper *Widow Rugby's Husb.* 42 A dozen fowls clustered on the top of the ash-gum. **1923** *D.N.* V. 233 Ash-gum, n. A piece of a tree, generally of the trunk, hollowed out used to collect ashes for soap. A barrel thus employed is often so called. — (6) **1804** in *Mineral. Journal* I. 105 Cubic salts, . . . thrown upon the ash-hoppers, . . . are supposed to assist in precipitating the lime. **1843** Carlton *New Purchase* I. ix. 63 Mam, you'll have to work your own ash-hopper. **1948** *Chi. Tribune* 28 Mar. vii. 1/5 Soft soap was made at home by cooking lye water, drained from an ash hopper, with grease from cracklin's. — (7) **1807** Irving *Salmagundi* iv. 73 He once shook down the ash-house, by an artificial earthquake. **1922** Cady *Rhymes* (1926) 38 And say; I hid the dipper And water pail, the Fast Day night Our ashhouse got to smoking. — (8) **1836** *Franklin Repository* (Chambersburg, Pa.) 4 Oct. 1/3 Ever since these black stones [=coal] were brought to town, the wood-sawyers and pilers, and then soap-fat and hickory ashes-men, has been going down. **1947** *Harper's Mag.* Nov. 472/2 Some of us looked like ash-men, others more like Harlequin. — (9) **1816** A. Singleton *Lett. from S. & W.* (1824) 78 What slaves I have seen, have fared coarsely upon their hoe-cakes and ash-pone. **1946** Nixon *Va. Words.*

(10) **1861** *Atlantic Mo.* April 438/2 There he stands . . . leaning on his ash-rake. — (11) **1833** Silliman *Man. Sugar Cane* 50 It will be found advantageous, also, not to have the entrance for air united with the ash-room entrance. *Ib.* The ash-room need not be large, as it will be found best to remove its contents at short intervals, into an ash-house built of brick. — (12) **1903** *Atlantic Mo.* July 31 Up in the oaks the ashthroat chuckles. — (13) **1858** Baird *Birds Pacific R.R.* 179 Ash-throated Flycatcher. . . . The chin, throat, and fore part of the breast [are] ashy white. **1940** Jaeger *Desert Wild Flowers* 19 These [woodpecker holes] are later occupied by the ash-throated flycatcher. — (14) **1852** Mrs. Ellet *Pioneer Woman* 331 They had nothing but corn, which they boiled in ash-water with a little salt. [**1948** *Reader's Digest* Sep. 110/2 The wood ashes peeled off the skins from the swollen kernels of corn better than any lye had ever done.]

See also **hickory ashes, leached ashes.**

***ash,** *v. tr.* To treat (growing corn) with ashes as a preventive of damage by cutworms. *Obs.* — **1817** *Niles' Reg.* XII. 212/2 One hand may carefully ash three acres in a day, and . . . it will effectually destroy or drive away the cut worm.

ashery 'æʃərɪ, *n.* A place where potash is made, a potashery. — **1828** A. Sherburne *Mem.* (1831) viii. 185, I much wished to set up an ashery, as there was none very near me, and potash was in pretty good demand. **1884** L. F. Allen *New Farm Bk.* 62 Spent lye of the the asheries, is the liquid which remains after the combination of the lye and grease in manufacturing soap.

Ashlanders 'æʃləndəz, *n. pl.* A political club at Baltimore, Md., named "from Ashland Square, near which they lived" (B. '77), (see also quot. 1859). *Obs.* — **1859** Bartlett 13 *Ashlanders,* a club of Baltimore rowdies, so named probably from Henry Clay, of Ashland. **1888** Lane *Pol. Catch-Words* 13 Sep. 16 Ashlanders . . . took an active part in local politics; [their] . . . methods were like those of the Plug Uglies, etc.

***ashy,** *a.* Angry. *Colloq.* — **a1846** *Quarter Race Kentucky* 45 An the feller got rite ashy 'bout it, but I didn't mind him. **1903** *D.N.* II. 305 He argued awhile and then he began to get ashy. **1946** C. M. Woodard *Word-List from Va.* 4 ashy, *adj.* Ill-tempered, ill-humored. Pamlico. Common.

***aside,** *adv.*

1. Out of notice or consideration.

1860 Marsh *Eng. Lang.* 640 Leaving the question of competency aside. **1871** Grant White *Words & Uses* 21 But, pronouns . . . and 'auxiliary' verbs aside, it [Chaucer's English] is a mixture.

2. aside from. a. In addition to, besides. **b.** Except for. *Colloq.*

(a) **1818** Ticknor in *Life* I. 206 Indeed, aside from this, the mere show is more magnificent than can be seen at any other court in Europe. **1932** Beck *Wonderland* 29 These difficulties were aside from the seeming impossibility of the Congressional Committees to devise and enforce any accounting for public funds entrusted to paymasters to be disbursed for authorized purposes of the new government. — (b) **1861** *Md. Hist. Mag.* V. 303 Aside from the upheavals made by our engineer, . . . I don't think I have ever seen a more dreary region. **1906** *N.Y. Ev. Post.* 21 Aug. 1 The Department [of State] is without information . . . aside from press dispatches.

Asimina ə'sɪmənə, *n.* (See quots.)

In the Century and later dicts. this term is related to or derived from Can. Fr. *assiminier,* f. Illinois *rassimina,* papaw. If the "Osámener" in our 1588 quot. is, as it appears to be, the same word, this explanation of the source of term is obviously in error.

1588 Harriot *Briefe & True Report* Dv, There is a kind of berrie or acorne, of which there are fiue sorts that grow on seueral kinds of trees; the one is called Sagatémener, the second Osámener, the third Pummuckoner. **1889** *Cent.* 337/2 Asimina. . . . An anonaceous genus of shrubs of the Atlantic and Gulf States, including half a dozen species. Of these the most widely distributed is the common papaw, *A.*

triloba, which becomes a small tree and bears a large edible fruit. **1902** *Amer. Folk-Lore* 241 Asimina . . . the North American papaw (*Asimina triloba*). This word, which has probably come into English from the *assiminier* of Louisianian and Canadian French, is derived ultimately, perhaps, from the Illinois language. **1937** *Torreya* Sep.–Oct. 97 *Asimina triloba* Dunal.—Aciminier, assiminer, the fruit aciminie, assimine, Missouri (from an Algonquian term rassimina); acmine, jasmine, Louisiana.

asistencia ˌæsɪsˈtɛnsɪə, *n. W.* [Cf. Santamaría *s.v. asistencia pública* in same sense.] A charitable institution. — **1897** *Land of Sunshine* July 53 San Rafael Arcángel—the first Spanish settlement north of San Francisco, and with one exception the last Mission—was founded Dec. 18, 1817, as an *asistencia*. **1946** R. Peattie *Pac. Coast Ranges* 21 Of them all only the Asistencia de Pala, an appanage of San Luis, is still standing.

***asparagus**, *n.* **1. asparagus bean,** a tropical bean, *Vigna sesquipedalis*. **2. asparagus pea,** the Goa bean, *Psophocarpus tetragonolobus*, or its seed.

(1) **1856** Cozzens *Sparrowgr. Papers* vii. 85 The asparagus bean, a sort of long-winded esculent, inclined to be prolific in strings. — (2) **1859** A. Van Buren *Sojourn in South* 155 The Asparagus Pea, with a small round pod that grows from a foot to three in length, makes a choice dish at table.

***aspen**, *a.* **a. aspen-leaved birch,** see **birch. b. aspen poplar,** the asp or aspen.

(b) *a***1817** Dwight *Travels* I. 41 Varieties [of] poplar [are]: White, Aspen, Balsam or Black. **1875** *Amer. Naturalist* IX. 203 The prevalent timber growth [in Utah] was made up of interrupted groves of Aspen poplar. **1946** Stanwell-Fletcher *Driftwood Valley* 33 On drier, more open ridges, lodge pole pines and aspen poplars are the chief trees.

See also **American aspen, large-toothed aspen, trembling aspen.**

assapan ˌæsəˈpæn, *n.* (See quots.) Also **assapanic.**

1705 Harris *Navigantium atque itinerantium* I. 843/1 The *Assapanick* the *English* call a Flying-Squirrel, because by spreading their legs and extending their bodies to the full stretch, they will as it were fly along for 30 or 40 Yards together. **1902** *Amer. Folk-Lore* 241 *Assapan*. A name (almost solely a dictionary-term) for the flying-squirrel (*Sciuropterus volucella*). The form *assapanic* is also in the dictionaries. The word is derived from one of the south-eastern dialects. **1907** Hodge *Amer. Indians* I. 102/1 Assapan. A dictionary name for the flying squirrel (*Sciuropterus volucella*), spelt also *assaphan*, evidently cognate with Chippewa *ä'sipŭn*, Sauk and Fox *ä'sepäna*, 'raccoon.' (A. F. C. W. J.)

assassin collar. [Cf. G. *Vatermörder* in same sense.] A high stiff collar. *Rare.* — *a***1860** *Songs of Yale* 14 The Junior . . . ; Now he spouts hog-latin: Wears assassin collars, Turns up Jack for trump, sir.

***assay**, *n.* In combs.: (1) **assay master,** "an officer appointed, in the provincial period in Massachusetts, to test the quality of potash and pearlash intended for export, or the composition of the worms and still-heads used in distilling" (*Cent.*); (2) **office,** an office at which ores and metals are received to be assayed; (3) **stamp,** a stamp used by an assay office upon or with reference to materials assayed by it.

(1) *c***1790** *Mem. Academy* II. i. 165 Having had frequent applications from the manufacturers of pot ash, to examine that article, when condemned by the assay masters. **1796** *Boston Directory* 298 Town Officers [include] . . . Assay-Masters: Joshua Witherle, John Welles. — (2) **1851** *S.F. Herald* 1 Feb. 2/1 Arrangements for opening the United States Assay office in this city, are being rapidly completed. **1947** *Amer. Wkly.* 2 Nov. 21/1 He sent a sample of the blue alloy to a Sacramento assay office to see what it was. — (3) **1849** *Pacific News* (S.F.) 25 Aug. 3/2 We have the fullest confidence in Messrs. Moffat & Co., and consider their genuine Assay-Stamp equal to the United States or London Mints.

***assay**, *v. intr.* To contain, as shown by analysis, a certain proportion of (usu. precious) metal. Also fig.

1882 *Rep. Precious Metals* 305, 2-foot vein of carbonates, that assay as high as $100 to the ton. **1901** White *Westerners* xv. 112 He don't assay a cent a ton fo' sense! **1948** *Chi. Tribune* 26 April 1. 34/5 They located a vein of gold bearing sulphide ore assaying $96 a ton in nearby Maryland.

***assemble**, *v.tr.* To put together, to make up, from separate parts into a complete form. — **1852** *Harper's Mag.* V. 158/1 When the several parts are all finished, the operation of putting them together so as to make up the musket from them complete, is called 'assembling the musket.' **1894** *Harper's Mag.* July 256/2 The partly assembled gun remains in the pit for forty-eight hours to cool off.

assembling plant. A place where parts of machines are assembled into complete units. — **1926** *Time* 14 June 34/2 In 1924 he profited $25,000,000 by shipping parts to district assembling plants. **1930** Sherwood Anderson in *Nation* 28 May, The assembling plant assembles cars for a certain territory.

***assembly**, *n.* In combs.: (1) **assembly district,** an election district returning a member to the state legislature, as of New York; (2) **line,** in a manufacturing plant a grouping of machines and workmen so that a product passes from one operator or machine to another until it is completed, also attrib. and fig.; (3) **room,** (*a*) a room in which the parts of a machine are put together, (*b*) a room in which all the students of a school are from time to time assembled; (4) **ticket,** a political ticket for the election of an assemblyman.

(1) **1873** McElroy & McBride *Life Sk.* 149 Mr. Blackie represents the thirteenth Assembly district of New York in the present Legislature. **1929** Lynch *Epoch & Man* 211 It would have been playing with fate for Van Buren to seek election from either of its two Assembly Districts. — (2) **1930** *Fortune* Nov., What I have described is but the operation of several stations on unit No. 6, the general assembly line. **1943** Menefee *Assignment* 109 Actually the assembly-line method of putting bombers together has great possibilities. **1948** *Disabled Amer. Veterans' Semi-Mo.* 25 May 1/4 Next step in this assembly line procedure calls for the removal of the money and checks and ascertaining that the proper amount of money is attached. — (3) (*a*) **1897** *Outing* June 279/2 We have reached one corner of this assembly-room, and here are the workmen lacing the spokes into the hubs. (*b*) **1923** R. Herrick *Lilla* 75 It was the custom to send all pupils detained after school hours for failure in studies to the assembly room. — (4) **1830** *Williams's N.-Y. Ann. Reg.* 75n, This is the average vote given for the anti-masonic assembly tickets in New-York.

As the last term in **General, House of Indian, legislative, primary, state assembly.**

***assessment**, *n.*

1. *W.* A levy or call for money made upon stockholders by a board of directors for obtaining money for mining operations.

1857 *Hutchings Mag.* Sep. 98/1 Should it cost less or more—generally it is the latter—the proportion is diminished or increased by assessments, according to the number of shares. **1878** Hart *Sazerac Lying Club* 179 We now hold more corporate shares than we can pay assessments on. **1947** *Time* 27 Oct. 106/2 He sold most of his stock to avoid paying stock assessments, knowing that he could buy it back cheap when new ore was uncovered.

b. An expenditure on a mining claim of one hundred dollars annually so as to keep one's right to it in force.

1860 DeGroot *Washoe Mines* 23/1 Assessments begin with the breaking of the ground, returns only coming, in most cases, after months of expenditure and toil. **1936** McKenna *Black Range* 93 The law required a hundred dollars worth of work to be done as an annual assessment.

c. assessment work, work done on a mining claim to maintain a possessory title.

1877 Raymond *Mines & Mining* 193 Most holders having contented themselves with doing the 'assessment-work.' **1928** Breakenridge *Helldorado* 90 The two men finished the assessment work on the Broncho Mine.

2. A levy made upon, a payment required from, members of an organization, business concern, etc.

1882 Sala *Amer. Revisited* (1883) I. 186 His salary . . . is subject to considerable reductions by the 'assessments' made on the policeman by the committees of the political organisation. **1905** D. G. Phillips *Plum Tree* 131 My assessments upon the various members of my combine were sent, for several years, to me.

assignation house. A house of prostitution that caters to the well-to-do. Cf. **house of assignation.**

1854 Busch *Wanderungen* I. 107 'Nun aber könnte ich Sie in unsere *Assignationhouses* führen, wo diese jungferngoldnen Tugendspiel hinterm Rücken des Gemahls ihrem Liebhaber ihr Stelldichein geben, und Tomback, verdammtes Tomback würden Sie sagen, wie ich es thue.' **1882** Buel *Metropolitan Life Unveiled* 167 The assignation houses of Washington are sustained almost wholly by members of the two houses of Congress. **1943** Ottley *New World* 28 Don't come . . . bothering me with any more protests about assignation houses until you can bring concrete evidence of such houses.

***assignment**, *n.* A duty, task, position, etc. given to one to perform or fill. — **1848** Garlan in Church *Ulysses Grant* (1897) 45 Lieut. Grant can best serve his country in present emergencies under this assignment. **1897** *Scribner's Mag.* Aug. 232/2 The reporters . . . were waiting to be sent off on their first assignments before getting breakfast. **1910** Mulford *Hopalong Cassidy* xvii. 99 At first his assignment had pleased, but as hour after hour passed with growing weariness, he chafed more and more.

Assiniboin əˈsɪnəˌbɔɪn, *n.* [f. a native word of uncertain significance.] A large Siouan tribe first encountered by Europeans in the region between Lake Superior and Hudson Bay. Also attrib.

[**1681** in *N.Y. Doc. Col. Hist.* IX. 153 The first go to the original haunts of the Beaver, among the Indian tribes of the Assiniboüets.] **1794** *Mass. Hist. Soc. Coll.* 1 Ser. III. 24 The tribes of Indians which he passed through, were called the . . . Snake Indians, Ossnobians, Shiveyton tribe, . . . and several others. **1804** *Lewis & Clark Jrnls.* (1904) I. 221 The Assiliboille [Assiniboin], although numerous, and strong and robust men, are not brave; they are in great fear of the Sioux, whom they regard as braver. **1867** HOSMER *Trip to States by Way Yellowstone & Mo.* 36 These three tribes had joined themselves together for the purpose of defending themselves from the hostilities of the Sioux and Assinaboines. **1947** *Trail Riders Bul.* May 4/1 Less than a year had elapsed since the Assiniboine Indians made him a Chief in the tribe.

***assist,** *n. Baseball.* The act of a player who handles the ball in assisting to put an opposing player out, also the credit given by the scorer to a player so assisting. — **1877** *Constitution & By-laws Nat. League* 40 An assist should be given to each player who handles the ball in a run-out or other play of this kind. **1948** *Dly. Ardmoreite* (Ardmore, Okla.) 17 May 4/3 One morning newspaper . . . credited him with 22 putouts and an assist.

***assist,** *v. intr.* In baseball (see quot. 1872).

[**1867** *Ball Players' Chron.* 6 June 2/2 The next three strikers retired in one, two, three order, Shaw capturing the entire party, Hunniwell assisting him capitally twice and Ames once.] **1872** CHADWICK *Dime Base-ball Player* 27 A fielder assists when he throws a ball to the baseman on which the runner is put out, or in any way assists a fielder to put a player out. **1885** *Calif. Athlete* (S.F.) 19 Dec. 5/1 He assisted yesterday in 14 put outs.

***assistant,** *n.* In combs.: (1) **assistant marshal,** one who assists a census marshal; (2) **principal,** one who assists a school principal; (3) **professor,** in some colleges and universities a teacher ranking above an instructor and below an associate professor; (4) **Assistant Treasury,** a subtreasury or branch treasury of the U.S., *obs.*

(1) **1828** SHERBURNE *Mem.* (1831) x. 216 In addition to the census, government had directed that the assistant marshal should also take an account of the several manufacturing establishments in their several divisions. **1845** HOOPER *Taking Census* i. 149 The assistant marshals . . . were employed to take the last census. — (2) **1850** HALE *M. Percival in Amer.* 140 At first sight, however, the prospect of securing for Miss Percival the position of 'Assistant principal,' as, in the barbarous patois of the catalogue, it was called, did not seem very encouraging. — (3) **1851** CIST *Cincinnati* 304 In September . . . he received the appointment of assistant professor of mathematics. **1942** *Bul. Vanderbilt U.* 21 Assistant Professor of Clinical Surgery. — (4) **1865** *Washoe* (Nev.) *Times* 4 Nov. 2/4 The leading financial institution in the United States is the U.S. Assistant Treasury at New York.

See also **court of assistants, general assistant.**

associate, *n.* and *a.*

1. As an academic title or degree.

The signification varies in different institutions and departments.

1879 *Scribner's Mo.* Dec. 202/2 A number of young men . . . have been gathered about the university under the title of associates. **1891** D. C. GILMAN *Johns Hopkins Univ.* 63 The number of associates, readers, and assistants has been very large. **1904** E. G. DEXTER *Hist. Educ. U.S.* 293 With the completion of the two years' course, a certificate is granted giving the title of associate in the University.

2. ***Associate Justice,** one of the judges serving along with the Chief Justice as the Supreme Court of the U.S.

1789 *Acts of Congress,* Stat. 73 The supreme court of the United States shall consist of a chief justice and five associate justices. **1838** *Dem. Review* I. 146 But few of the Associate Justices of the Supreme Court, have been mere lawyers. **1914** *Cycl. Amer. Govt.* III. 248 *Supreme Court:* Chief Justice, $15,000; Associate Justices (8), $14,500.

3. Associate Reformed Church, a church resulting from a union in 1782 between the Reformed Presbyterians and various associate ministers and congregations.

1798 MASON (*title*), Letters on frequent communion . . . to the Members of the Associate-Reformed Church. **1824** R. H. BISHOP *Hist. Church Ky.* 172 He put himself under the care of the Kentucky Presbytery of the Associate Reformed Church. **1857** C. VAUX *Villas* 104 The Associate Reformed Church proposed to be erected in Newburgh.

b. In expressions relating to this church (see quots.).

1807 *Ann. 10th Congress* 1 Sess. I. 983 Mr. Findley presented a petition of the Associate Reformed or Presbyterian Congregation, in the city of Washington. **1811** MEASE *Philadelphia* 212 Sundry persons . . . made application to the associate synod in Edinburgh, for a supply of ministers. Two were accordingly sent, in 1754, and with ruling elders, constituted the 'Associate Presbytery of Pennsylvania.' **1837** PECK *Gaz. Illinois* (ed. 2) 74 There are also two or three societies of Associate Reformed Presbyterians, or Seceders.

c. Associate Reformed Methodists, a group of Methodists who agitated for lay representation in the General Conference, and in 1830 joined with others of similar views to form the Methodist Protestant Church in which lay representation in the Conference is equal to ministerial.

1830 *Free Press* (Tarboro, N.C.) 19 Mar., A Camp Meeting . . . held by the Associate Reformed Methodists.

4. associate professor, in colleges and universities a teacher ranking immediately below a professor.

1891 *U. of Chicago Official Bul. No. 1* 11 Lecturers and Teachers . . . shall be classified as follows. . . . (4) The associate professor. **1944** *Chi. D. News* 10 Jan. 10/6 Dr. Hellebrandt . . . is an associate professor in that excellent university.

Associated Press. An association of American newspapers for gathering and disseminating news. Cf. **A.P.**

1849 *N.O. Picayune* 9 May 2/2 The Associated press is next served, and their dispatches being voluminous, occupy the telegraph many hours. **1855** WELD *Vacation Tour* 380 The nine leading newspapers, under the designation of the New York Associated Press . . . combine to pay for daily telegraphic communications. **1948** *Dly. Ardmoreite* (Ardmore, Okla.) 25 April 11/1 The league's managers and sports writers picked the outcome of the race in a poll conducted by the Associated Press.

***association,** *n*

1. (See quot. 1848.) *Obs.*

1842 COMMONS *Doc. Hist.* (1910) VII. 185 The friends of Association in the City have founded a Society . . . to aid the propagation of the principles . . . of Association. . . . No responsibility is incurred by becoming a member of the Fourier Association. **1848** BARTLETT 14 Association. In civil affairs, this word is much used at the present day, to denote the principle of uniting the producing classes in societies, for the purpose of obtaining for themselves a larger share of the fruits of their labor. **1859** GRATTAN *Civilized Am.* II. 141 Among the principal converts to the belief in 'Association,' as the only true means of social happiness, was the Rev. George Ripley, a highly educated and talented man.

2. A group of pupils of an authorized teacher of Christian Science who meet annually.

1890 MARY B. EDDY *Misc. Writings* 137 My students can *now* organize their students into associations, form churches. **1945** L. C. BELL in *Christian Sci. Jrnl.* LXIII. 221/1 The association meets once a year, primarily to gain a further 'unfolding of Truth.'

As the last term in **alumni, Audubon, bar, baseball, claim, Equal Rights, Evangelical, Fair, fruit growers', general, Hunters', land, library, Lone Star, lyceum, Oklahoma Live Stock, parent teacher(s), press, squatter, state, State Teacher's, teachers', vigilance, William Poole association.**

associational əˌsosɪˈeʃənl, *a.* Pertaining to an association of clergymen or of churches. — **1815** DWIGHT *Remarks Inchiquin's Lett.* 56 In order to obtain a license, and afterwards to be admitted to ordination, they [=students in divinity] must in each case pass through the Associational or Presbyterial examination, mentioned above. **1899** *Boston Transcript* 1 Dec. 9/2 The Year Book . . . gathers associational reports covering the year preceding.

associationism əˌsosɪˈeʃənɪzəm, *n.* [Cf. **association 1.**] The doctrines of the Associationists. *Obs.* — *a***1840** N. EMMONS in Park *Memoirs* (1861) 163 Associationism leads to Consociationism; Consociationism leads to Presbyterianism.

Associationist əˌsosɪˈeʃənɪst, *n.* [Cf. **association 1.**] One advocating the doctrine of association as taught by the Fourierites. Also transf. *Obs.*

1844 COMMONS *Doc. Hist.* VII. 198 Resolved . . . that the Name which . . . we adopt for ourselves . . . is, The Associationists of the United States of America. We do not call ourselves Fourierists. **1845** JUDD *Margaret* II. i. 186 She . . . stepped with a kind of caution among these groups of dumb, . . . industrious Associationists [=ants]. **1846** *Knickerb.* XXVIII. 16 This is contemplated, I believe, in all the Phalansteries of Unitative Associationists.

Associatist əˈsosɪəˌtɪst, *n.* =**Associationist.** *Rare.* — **1848** *Howitt's Jrnl.* III. 109/2 The *Harbinger,* [is] the weekly organ of the American Associatists.

***associators,** *n. pl.* Used in Pennsylvania in the eighteenth century for the militia, the Quakers wishing to avoid a military name. Also **City Associators.** *Obs.*

1736 *Penna. Colonial Records* IV. 113 And, therefore, we think it proper that you call before you as many of the said Associators as possibly you can. **1788** FRANKLIN *Autobiog.* 362 Colonel Lawrence . . . and myself were sent [*c*1747] to New York by the associators, commission'd to borrow some cannon of Governor Clinton. **1877** *Pa. Mag. of Hist.* I. 194 Upon the commons near Centre Square he [George Washington] reviewed the City Associators, numbering about two thousand men.

assorter əˈsɔrtɚ, *n.* [f. the *v.*] One who assorts. — **1897** *Scribner's Mag.* Jan. 17/2 The assorter, who distributes the bundles [of goods] into lots to go to the different parts of the city.

***assumption,** *n.* The assuming of responsibility for the debts of the states by the federal government soon after its establishment. Also attrib. Now *hist.*

1789 GORE in *Life R. King* (1894) I. 362 Till the intention of Congress is known relative to the assumption of funds, the State cannot, with propriety, make any arrangement for the payment of their debts. **1797** *Ann. 4th Congress* 2 Sess. 1808 The endearing arguments . . . in favor of the assumption of the State debts. **1882** COOPER *Amer. Pol.* I. 8 Southern members . . . refused to vote for the Assumption Bill until the location of the capital in the District of Columbia had been agreed upon.

Hence **assumptionist.** Cf. **anti-assumptionist.**

1841 *Cong. Globe* Jan., App. 153/1 The distributionist, and the anti-distributionist—the assumptionist, and the anti-assumptionist . . . were united against the Democracy.

***aster,** *n.* As the last term in **frost, German, New England, Stokes's, wood aster.**

asthma weed. Indian tobacco, used as a remedy for asthma. *Colloq.* — **1819** *Western Rev.* I. 183 The *Lobelia inflata* or Asthma weed, a . . . plant with alternate hairy leaves, blue flowers, and swelled seed vessels. **1931** CLUTE *Plants* 123 Others are mildly tonic or possess some faint medicinal value, but have long ago been superseded by more powerful remedies. Familiar examples are asthma weed (*Lobelia inflata*), [etc.].

Astorian æsˈtorɪən, *n.* [*Astoria*, Oregon, fur-trading station founded in 1811 by J. J. Astor.] A fur-trader attached to Astoria. Now *hist.*

1837 IRVING *Bonneville* I. 24 The frightful hardships sustained by Wilson . . . and other intrepid Astorians, in their ill-fated expeditions across the mountains. **1850** G. HINES *Voyage* 372 The arrival of the ship Beaver . . . [with] supplies and reinforcements, encouraged the Astorians. **1943** DE VOTO *Yr. of Decis.* 413 He had lived in the mountains forever, his career going as far back as the Astorians.

***Astrachan,** *n.* An apple, introduced from Russia, of which there are two varieties, red and white. In full **Astrachan apple.** Cf. **red Astrachan.**

1852 *Horticulturist* VII. 437/2 Every householder who owns land . . . ought to have one tree of the Astrachan apple, both on account of its earliness, and its excellence for cooking. **1919** CADY *Rhymes of Vt.* (1923) 15 The apples wasn't doing well, There'd be no Astrakans to sell. **1943** DAMON *Sense of H.* 231 Before the Astrachans were all gone, the long-stemmed small Golden Sweets began to turn from pale green to pale yellow.

astral ˈæstrəl, *n.* (1) =next. *Obs.* (2) **astral lamp,** a lamp which has a ring-shaped reservoir for oil so placed that the descending light is not interrupted by it as in other lamps. (3) **astral oil,** (see quot. 1904).

(1) 1838 *Knickerb.* XII. 57 As she drew the flowers on the centre-table more under the light of the astral. **1865** *Atlantic Mo.* XV. 30 Mrs. Manlius . . . reappeared with an astral, which turned the somewhat gloomy aspect of affairs into cheerful light. — **(2)** *c***1830** *Encycl. Amer.* (1835) VII. 398/1 In the astral and sinumbral lamps . . . the oil is contained in a large horizontal ring, having a burner at the centre. **1856** M. J. HOLMES *Gable-Roofed House*, In Mr. Hubbell's parlor the astral lamp was lighted, and coals were heaped in the glowing grate. — **(3) 1883** *N.Y. World* in *Glasgow Weekly Herald* 9 June 8/3 An ordinary tin can very like that in which astral oil is sold. **1904** *D.N.* II. 375 Astral oil, *n.* A variety of refined petroleum, also called 150° *fire test.*

***asylum,** *n.* As the last term in **insane, juvenile, state asylum.**

***at,** *prep.*

1. In phrases designating parts of the country, as **at the East, North, South(ward). Colloq.*

"The very common expressions 'at the North,' 'at the West,' instead of 'in the North,' 'in the West,' offend an English ear" (B. '59). "This provincialism is not, however, promiscuously used, as, curiously enough, the better-known New-England States are generally spoken of as 'in the East'" (Clapin).

1636 *Mass. H. S. Coll.* 4 Ser. VI. 515 If Mr. Mayhew hath bought the provisions at the east. **1834** *Sun* (N.Y.) 25 Mar. 4/2 *Typographical Errors.*— . . . A man at the east offers for sale a large quantity of *fun powder* and several boxes of *pigs.* — **1910** G. C. EGGLESTON *Confederate War* I. 20 Slavery existed and was defended at the South while it was antagonized at the North. **1924** *Scribner's Mag.* May 560/2 Her words reminded me of an aged Southern mammy whose former charge, after spending ten years at the North, returned to her home in Virginia. — **1782** *Essex Inst. Coll.* XXXVIII. 55 My companey being at the sotherd the money was drawn for them for 3 months. **1885** EGGLESTON in *Century Mag.* April 880/2 The bright-blazing pitch-pine, called . . . 'lightwood' at the South.

2. *at auction*, by auction, for auctioning off.

1726 *Boston News-Letter* 3 March, Valuable books, many more than a thousand, to be sold at auction. **1852** STOWE *Uncle Tom* xxix, He and the lawyer think that the servants and furniture had better be put up at auction. **1932** GRAYSON *Leaders* 135 They got the land at $2 an acre and immediately offered it at auction realizing $17 per acre for it—not a bad day's work.

3. With, attended by.

1903 LORIMER *Old Gorgon Graham* 146 When husband and wife both love the same person, and that person is the wife, it's usually a life sentence at hard labor for the husband.

For *at that, at vendue*, see **that, vendue.**

atajo ɑˈtɑho, *n. S.W.* [Amer. Sp. spelling of Sp. *hatajo* in sense here shown.] A string or drove of pack mules. *Obs.* — **1844** GREGG *Commerce of Prairies* I. 181 It is apt to occasion much trouble to stop a heavily laden *atajo;* for, if allowed a moment's rest, the mules are inclined to lie down, when it is with much difficulty they can rise again with their loads. **1897** INMAN *Old Santa Fe Trail* 57 An old-time *atajo* or caravan of pack-mules generally numbered from fifty to two hundred.

atamasco ˌætəˈmæsko, *n.* [Virginian *attamusco*, stained with red.] A plant, *Zephyranthes atamasco*, having white or pinkish lily-like flowers, found in swampy regions from Virginia to Florida. In full **atamasco lily.**

[**1629** PARKINSON *Paradisus* 87 *Narcissus Virgineus*. The Virginia Daffodil. . . . The Indians in Virginia do call it Attamusco.] **1743** CATESBY *Carolina* I. App. 112 The Attamusco Lilly is a native of Virginia and Carolina, where in particular places the pastures are . . . thick sprinkled with them and martogons. **1901** MOHR *Plant Life Ala.* 123 On the shady borders of the hammock are found, flowering early in the spring, . . . the Atamasco lily . . . and hoary lupine. **1933** SMALL *Southeastern Flora* 320 Atamasco-lilies . . . are gathered about Easter time and sold especially in southern cities.

***Athenaeum,** *n.*

1. "An association of persons of literary or scientific tastes, for the purpose of mutual improvement" (W. '64).

1807 *Monthly Anthology* May 226 The Trustees with their associates are made a body corporate by the title of the Proprietors of the Boston Athenaeum. **1882** E. K. GODFREY *Nantucket* 13 The Athenaeum and other literary societies have from time to time given courses of lectures. **1948** *Dly. Ardmoreite* (Ardmore, Okla.) 25 April 13/6 (*heading*), Athenaeum to Discuss Health.

2. A reading room or library.

1818 FLINT *Letters* 112 The Atheneum, or reading-room [at Lexington, Ky.] is much frequented. **1883** MARK TWAIN *Life on Miss.* lvii., A great mass meeting was to be held on a certain day in the new Athenaeum [of Keokuk in 1861]. **1947** PERRY *Cities of America* 179 If you really want to read in the company of Brahmins, you take out a 'proprietorship' in Boston's famed Athenaeum, a society that bought George Washington's library.

***Athens,** *n.*

1. Used in nicknames of various American cities, esp. Boston, likened in culture to Athens, Greece.

1817 PAULDING *Lett. from South* II. 112 Along the banks of the Ohio, the Mississippi, . . . exists a race of men, . . . with as much learning, genuine politeness, and various intelligence, as those who inhabit the Athens of America. **1818** DARBY *Emigrant's Guide* 206 Education made rapid advances in some places, particularly Lexington, insomuch as to obtain for that town the title of the Athens of the western states. **1882** *Harper's Mag.* June 20/2, I have seen no women that equal the fair daughters of the monumental City. They make Baltimore the so-called Athens of America. **1947** *Time* 6 Jan. 61/1 Boston, which fancies itself the Athens of America, was crammed to its Beacon Street attics with scientists.

b. (See quot.) *Obs.*

1818 *W. Recorder* (Chillicothe, Ohio.) 25 Dec. 157/3 Why is New England deservedly called the Athens of America?

2. Athens marble, a variety of limestone quarried in Illinois.

1859 *New Amer. Cycl.* V. 67/1 The Athens marble, so called, is regarded as one of the finest building stones in the world. It is quarried only 20 m. from Chicago, directly on the banks of the canal. **1880** *Harper's Mag.* Oct. 717/1 Beautiful [Chicago] buildings of 'Athens marble'—nearly white—rose on all sides.

Atherton gag. [C. G. *Atherton* (1804–53), U.S. Rep. and Senator (1836–49).] A resolution introduced into Congress by Atherton in 1838, and in force until 1844, providing that all bills or petitions with reference to slavery should be tabled without debate. Cf. **gag.** *Obs.*

[**1840** J. Q. Adams *Memoirs* X. 273 Then came Atherton, of New Hampshire, the man of the mongrel gag.] **1865** Scofield in *Cong. Globe* 6 Jan. 144/3 [Slavery] demanded silence in this House and in the Senate, and we adopted the 'Atherton gag.' **1867** Sumner in *Cong. Globe* 5 July 493/2 The Senator from Maine [Mr. Fessenden] cannot have forgotten the Atherton gag.... If the Atherton gag was . . . odious . . . then [etc.].

athlete's foot. A form of ringworm often acquired by athletes in gymnasiums. — **1928** *Lit. Digest* 22 Dec. 16/1 Athlete's foot . . . is a popular name for ringworm of the foot, from which more than ten million persons in the United States are now suffering. **1948** *Woodlawn Booster* (Chi.) 12 May 4/1 You can get athlete's foot walking around barefoot.

athletic ground. A field or inclosed area where athletic contests, sports, etc., are held. — **1897** *N.Y. Journal* 5 Sep. 41/4 Captain Garrett Cochran will marshal a small army of gridiron warriors on the 'varsity athletic ground. **1899** Quinn *Pa. Stories* 37 There stood on the old Athletic Grounds a rickety structure which bore without reproach the name of 'grand stand.'

athleticize æθˈlɛtɪˌsaɪz, *v. tr.* To convert to the pursuit of athletics. *Obs.* — **1896** *Godey's Mag.* April 447/1 Are we to be so athleticized that we will disdain all fripperies. **1897** *Eclectic Mag.* Oct. 523 France, superficially, has become anglicized, athleticised.

* **-ativeness, -itiveness.** A suffix used to form abstract nouns denoting an indicated state of being, quality, etc. *Colloq.*

1831 *Boston Transcript* 13 July 3/1 (*heading*), 'Stay-at-homeativeness' [with reference to woman 88 years of age who never saw a road but three miles from her home]. **1839** *N.O. Picayune* 9 Mar. 2/1 A Phrenologist at the North finding a young lady he was examining possessed of the bump of *twenty-thousand-dollars-ativeness*, made overtures of marriage, which were accepted forthwith—the best bump he ever found. **1841** *N.O. Picayune* 17 Jan. 2/4 Tom Donahue . . . has the bump of come-it-over-green-ones-itiveness unusually largely developed. **1845** *St. Louis Reveille* 23 Apr. 2/2 The eccentric combination of cant, fanaticism, and worldly wide-a-wakeativeness, of which the Mormon papers are made up, renders them, in fact, journals of positive interest. **1879** Vivian *Wanderings Western Land* 112 A superintendent of detectives, noted for what is here termed his 'hang-to-itiveness,' was soon on the spot.

Atlantan ətˈlæntən, *n.* Also **Atlantian.** An inhabitant of Atlanta, Ga.

1889 *Chi. Tribune* 1 Aug. 3/6 The Atlantians, however, showed visible signs of dispirit at not being able to entertain the party today. **1946** *Life* 27 May 43/1 Fully grown men . . . got down on their knees on the ground before 100 white-sheeted and hooded Atlantans. **1948** *Highway Traveler* Aug.–Sep. 10/2 Atlantans, busy as they might be, will always take time out to show the stranger around.

* **Atlantic,** *a.*

1. Of, pertaining to, or situated on, the Atlantic Coast of the U.S., hence, eastern. Cf. **cisatlantic, South Atlantic, trans-Atlantic.**

1800 Weems *Washington* (1877) 163 Northern and southern—atlantic and western. **1803** *Ann. 8th Congress* 2 Sess. 1503 The peltry procured in the Illinois is the best sent to the Atlantic market. **1841** *S. Lit. Messenger* VIII. 551/1 It demands of our overgrown Atlantic towns, to throw open their advantages for the good of the distant country. **1900** Nelson *A B C Wall St.* 126 *Atlantic ports*, Boston, New York, Philadelphia and Baltimore—the leading export points.

2. In combs.: (1) **Atlantic flour,** flour produced or manufactured in the Atlantic states, *rare;* (2) **liner,** a liner that plies the Atlantic; (3) **plain,** =**Atlantic slope;** (4) **seaboard,** that part of the U.S. along the Atlantic Ocean; (5) **slope,** that part of the eastern U.S. that descends towards, and drains into, the Atlantic Ocean; (6) **states,** those states near or bordering upon the Atlantic Ocean; (7) **type locomotive,** (see quot. 1909).

(1) **1852** Reynolds *Hist. Illinois* 92 This mill manufactured great quantities of flour . . . which would compare well with the Atlantic flour. — (2) **1901** *Everybody's Mag.* Oct. 394/1 In other words, an Atlantic liner could be suspended from it in safety. — (3) **1854** W. Bromwell *Locomotive Sk.* 150 This zone . . . acquires a breadth of one hundred and fifty miles in the southern States. . . . This is called the Atlantic plain. — (4) **1851** Cist *Cincinnati* 312 Here are four trunk roads, each terminating . . . on the Atlantic seaboard. **1947** *Nat. Geog. Mag.* June 699/1 It is not an old settlement as Atlantic seaboard cities go.

(5) **1841** Lyell *Travels* I. 93 The region . . . sometimes called the 'Atlantic Slope,' corresponds nearly in average width with the low and flat plain. **1891** *Outing* Nov. 94/1 [Western cabins are] unlike the 'shanties' that one finds in the 'second-growth' forests of the Atlantic slope. — (6) **1789** *Ann. 1st Congress* I. 153 The policy of taxing the navigation of the Atlantic States for the purpose of encouraging their agriculture. **1871** De Vere 257 Another division, frequently found alluded to in books as well as in the daily press, . . . is that of Atlantic, Pacific, and Gulf States. — (7) **1899** *Railroad Gazette* 15 Dec. 863 But when trains of from six to nine cars are to be handled on fast schedules under ordinary conditions of grades such locomotives as the eight-wheel and Atlantic type become necessary. **1909** Fowler *Locomotive Dictionary* 9 Atlantic Type Locomotive. . . . A locomotive having a four-wheel front truck, four coupled driving wheels and a two-wheel trailing truck. Used for fast passenger service. **1945** Marshall *Santa Fe* 281 For the Santa Fe race east of La Junta the road used the 536, an Atlantic type ooOOo balanced compound.

atlatl ˈɑtlɑtl, *n.* [Nahuatl.] A throwing stick of any one of various types from sixteen to thirty inches long used by Indians and Eskimos.

1910 Hodge *Amer. Indians* II. 746/1 This implement, called also throwing board, dart sling, and atlatl, is an apparatus for hurling a

One form of atlatl, shown in detail and in use

lance, spear, or harpoon at birds and aquatic animals. **1934** Morris *Digging in Southwest* 44 The bow and arrow had not yet come into use, but instead game and enemies were reduced by long darts hurled with an *atlatl.*

* **atmosphere,** *n.* Environment, surroundings, tone, background, etc., that lends an impression of vividness or naturalness to a work of art. — **1886** *Harper's Mag.* Nov. 831/2 The constituent parts of literary society . . . are obliged to house themselves transiently in the most incongruous spots, with little, if any, 'atmosphere' about them. **1916** Bower *Phantom Herd* i. 1 Luck wanted several rehearsals of 'atmosphere' scenes before turning the camera on them. *Ib.* v. 66 There's a lot of atmosphere you couldn't get, anyway.

* **atmospheric,** *a.*

1. atmospheric brake, =**air brake.** *Obs.*

1869 *Harper's Wkly.* 21 Aug. 534/1 These are the atmospheric brakes —if one gives way there are three more to hold. **1879** Williams *Pacific Tourist* 233/1 How much better are iron rails than rugged rocks, and atmospheric brakes than treacherous cords!

2. atmospheric churn, (see quot. 1874). *Obs.*

1849 *Rep. Comm. Patents* (1850) 417 Most of these were styled atmospheric churns. **1857** *Trans. Mich. Agric. Soc.* VIII. 708 There was an atmospheric churn, a miniature steam-engine. **1874** Knight 176/2 Atmospheric churn. A churn in which atmospheric air is driven into the milk in order to agitate it, and also to obtain the specific effect of the air upon the milk in aggregation of the oleaginous globules.

atocha ɑˈtotʃə, *n.* [Sp. in same sense.] The esparto grass, *Stipa tenacissima.* Also attrib. — **1868** *Rep. Comm. Agric.* (1869) 262 There are two classes of this plant, the 'atocha,' properly so called, and the coarse or 'bastard' atocha. *Ib.*, The atocha grass, which is called esparto, is not cut like ordinary grass, but is pulled up from its socket. *Ib.* 264 It is at about this elevation [*sc.* 3,500 feet] where the snow usually commences, that the atocha plant ceases to grow.

atole əˈtolɪ, *n. S.W.* [Amer. Sp. (< Nahuatl) in same sense.] A kind of corn meal or gruel or porridge made of this. Also transf.

[1716 in *S.W. Hist. Quart.* XXXI. 56 They make large pots in which to keep water, make *atole*, and to preserve other things they need to carry.] **1790–95** PEYROUSE *Voyage* (1801) 89 A breakfast of barley meal awaits them at their return from the service. It is boiled in water; the Indians give this food the name of *atole*. **1844** GREGG *Commerce of Prairies* I. 153 A sort of thin mush, called *atole*, made of Indian meal, is another article of diet. **1881** *Amer. Naturalist* XV. 875 The scales [of sotol] . . . may be ground into atole. **1946** R. PEATTIE *Pac. Coast Ranges* 41 All partook of a morning meal of atole.

Atsina æt'sinə, *n.* [f. native name of uncertain meaning.] (See quot. 1907.)

1907 HODGE *Amer. Indians* I. 113/1 Atsina. . . . A detached branch of the Arapaho . . . , at one time associated with the Blackfeet, but now with the Assiniboin under Ft Belknap agency, Mont., where in 1904 they numbered 535, steadily decreasing. **1917** WILL & HYDE *Corn Among Indians* 45 The Atsinas, kinsmen of the Arapahoes, sometimes roved north of the Missouri and sometimes south of it. **1947** DEVOTO *Across Wide Missouri* 60 They were the Atsina or Gros Ventres of the Prairies, a tribe unrelated by blood or language to the three tribes of the Blackfeet but so closely associated with them that everybody called them Blackfeet.

attaboy 'ætəˌbɔɪ, *interj.* [Prob. f. *that's the boy!*] An exclamation of encouragement or admiration. *Slang.* — **1909** *American Mag.* May 40/2 Back of Chance's war cries, 'At-a-boy,' or 'Now ye're pitching,' may be hidden a whole command to his team. **1948** *Sat. Ev. Post.* 12 June 88/4 'At-a-boy,' I said, bringing my hand up in a casual salute.

Attacapa ɑ'tɑkɑpɑ, *n.* [f. a Choctaw term meaning cannibal.] "A tribe forming the Attacapan linguistic family, a remnant of which early in the 19th century occupied as its chief habitat the Middle or Prien lake in Calcasieu parish, La." (Hodge).

1896 CLENDENIN *Fla. Parishes E. La.* 181 Perhaps some of the aboriginal Attakapas tribes might, if consulted, still be able to bear testimony upon the subject. **1948** *Amer. Jrnl. Phys. Anthrop.* Mar. 65 The main Indian groups living in this region around the beginning of the historical period were the Atakapa, Karankawa, and Aranaman.

attendance money. ?Money paid for an attendant or servant. *Rare.* Cf. **sergeant attendant.** — **1733** *Harvard Rec.* II. 607 Mr. Goffe [is] to have the travelling Fees. 2s. for ten miles, & attendance money viz. 2s. per day.

attestant ə'testənt, *n.* [f. L. *attestans*, pr. part.] One who makes attestation, an attester. — **1680** *New Castle Court Rec.* 388 The attestant thereupon left the land.

* **attorney general.** The chief law-officer empowered to act for the U.S. Government in all cases that affect it.

"In the United States he is a member of the cabinet appointed by the President, has the general management of the departments of justice throughout the country, advises the President and departments on questions of law, and appears for the government in the Supreme Court and Court of Claims. The individual States of the Union also have their attorneys-general" (*Cent.*).

1789 *Ann. 1st. Congress* II. 2197 There shall also be appointed a meet person learned in the law to act as attorney-general for the United States. **1866** F. KIRKLAND *Bk. Anecdotes* 33 When the South Carolina 'ambassadors' came to Washington, Butler proposed to the Attorney-General to try them for treason. **1947** *Chi. D. News* 3 April 18/7 This makes the attorney general the interpreter and judge of the Bill of Rights.

b. A state official having corresponding duties with reference to a state.

1860 *Ohio Statutes* II. 1233 If payment thereof be not made in reasonable time . . . the comptroller shall file such claim with the attorney general. **1946** *Democrat* 3 Jan. 1/6 So far, the political dopesters have been giving the job to former attorney general Albert Carmichael.

c. (See quot.)

1903 *Nashville Banner* in *N.Y. Ev. Post* 14 Sep., It is a practice peculiar to Tennessee to dub all States' Attorneys Attorneys-General.

As the last term in **city, county, district, pension, prosecuting, sleeping, state's, title attorney.**

Auburn system. A system of prison management originating in the prison at Auburn, N.Y., about 1824, involving solitary confinement of the prisoners at night, shop work, and complete silence except at meals. *Obs.*

1833 E. T. COKE *Subaltern's Furlough* xxv, The Concord [N.H.] prison . . . was conducted partly on the Auburn system. **1842** BUCKINGHAM *E. & W. States* II. 306 The system of discipline pursued here, is that which is called the Auburn, or Silent System, in contradistinction to the Philadelphia, or Solitary System. **1869** HALL *Hist. Auburn* 352 The famous Auburn system then [1825] began to receive a careful trial.

* **auction,** *n.* In combs.: (1) **auction block,** a block or stand on which a slave stood when being sold by auction, now fig.; (2) **duty,** a duty or payment to public revenue levied on proceeds of sales by auction; (3) **pitch,** (see quot. 1890); (4) **sale,** a sale by auction; (5) **stand,** a stand at which slaves were sold, *obs.*, cf. **auction block;** (6) **store,** a store in which articles are sold by auction.

(1) 1860 ABBOTT *South & North* 198 In case of disobedience, to send them to the whipping-post, or the auction-block. **1889** MARK TWAIN *Conn. Yankee* xxxiv. 448 (R.) The auction-block came into my personal experience. **1948** *Chi. Tribune* 29 May 1. 11/7 The famous old steamer Meteor . . . will again be placed on the auction block. — **(2) 1827** DRAKE & MANSF. *Cincinnati* iv. 30 The General Assembly . . . gave for the permanent support of the establishment, half the Auction duties of the city. **1851** CIST *Cincinnati* 149 Others are supported out of a portion of the auction duties, collected in Cincinnati. — **(3) 1890** *Cent.* 4514/3 Auction-pitch, a game of pitch in which the player entitled to pitch the trump may sell the privilege to the highest bidder, adding the points bid to his score before play, or may reject all bids and himself lead the play, failure to make as many points as the highest bid reducing the pitcher's score correspondingly. **1946** MOREHEAD & MOTT-SMITH *Penguin Hoyle* 54 Auction Pitch is best for three to five players. — **(4) 1820** *Ann. 16th Congress* 1 Sess. I. 367 The evils arising from auction sales. **1948** *Dly. Ardmoreite* (Ardmore, Okla.) 9 May 1/4 (*heading*) Auction Sale Of Priceless Items Opens.

(5) 1846 L. M. CHILD *Fact & Fiction* 74 The gentle girl . . . was ruthlessly seized by a sheriff, and placed on the public auction-stand in Savannah. **1848** LOWELL *Biglow P.* 1. ix., How temptin' all on 'em would look upon an auction-stand! — **(6) 1785** *Pa. Packet* 24 Dec. 1/1 Northern-Liberty Auction Store, . . . At Ten o'clock . . . will begin the sale of . . . Merchandize. . . . Alex. Boyd, Auctioneer. **1878** COOKE *Happy Dodd* 150 Send 'em up to the auction store, and sell 'em.

See also **Negro auction, slave auction.**

* **audience,** *n.* The readers of a book or newspaper. Cf. **pay audience.**

1760 FRANKLIN *Wks.* (1887) III. 128, I assure you it often gives me pleasure to reflect how greatly the *audience* (if I may so term it) of a good English writer will, in another century or two, be increased by the increase of English people in our colonies. **1855** H. REED *Lect. Eng. Lit.* vii. (1878) 225 'Pilgrim's Progress' . . . has gained an audience as large as Christendom. **1883** G. HAMILTON in *N. Eng. Bygones* Pref. i, This book is published with no thought of an audience. **1949** *L. A. Times* 13 Feb. (Comics) 1 There may be neurotics in our audience!

audiphone 'ɔdɪˌfon, *n.* [L. *audire* to hear + *-phone*.] (See quots.) — **1880** *S.F. Globe* 16 May 2/5 The Audiphone enables the deaf to hear with ease through the teeth. **1882** AGNES CRANE in *Leisure H.* July 412 The audiphone, a fan-like instrument which materially alleviates certain phases of deafness.

* **audit,** *n.* A body of auditors of accounts. *Obs.* — **1657** *R.I. Court Rec.* 32 This Court have constituted . . . Mr. Benedict Arnold presid[en]t, Mr. Samuell Gorton, Mr. John Easton and John Sanford to be an awditt to heare accompts. **1691** *Boston Rec.* 206 One of the audit apoynted to adjust and settle the accompts of the selectmen.

* **auditor,** *n.* **1.** A money certificate. *Obs.* **2.** An official in Louisiana under Spanish rule (see quot.). [In this sense no doubt f. Sp.] *Obs.* Cf. **state auditor.** — **(1) 1790** *Steele Papers* I. 57 They were giving for Auditors 5s. paper, interest not counted, . . . and for Auditors after new coined, . . . ⅜ for principal and ¼ for Interest. — **(2) 1803** *Ann. 8th Congress* 2 Sess. 1521 The Auditor is the King's counsel, who is to furnish the Governor with legal advice in all cases of judicial proceedings, whether civil or military.

* **auditorium,** *n.* A building especially designed for the giving of lectures, concerts, etc. Also attrib.

1908 *Fra* Oct. xiv, Mr. Elbert Hubbard delivered a 'heart to heart' talk at the Windsor Auditorium. **1923** *Frontier* Nov. 17 It was in Los Angeles, and in an hour Chaliapin was to sing. A line waited in front of the auditorium box office. **1948** *Dly. Ardmoreite* (Ardmore, Okla.) 21 Mar. 1/2 The general admission tickets . . . are [for] the two top rows of the arena seats around the civic auditorium.

* **Audubon,** *n.* [J. J. *Audubon* (1785–1851), Amer. ornithologist.] Used in the possessive in the names of American animals, esp. birds: (1) **Audubon's bighorn,** a species of Rocky Mountain sheep, *Ovis cervina auduboni*, found in the Bad Lands of South Dakota; (2) **caracara,** a vulture-like hawk found chiefly in South and Central America but also in the southern states; (3) **oriole,** (see quot. 1917); (4) **shearwater,** (see quot. 1909); (5) **warbler,** the western yellow-rumped warbler, *Dendroica auduboni*, of the western U.S.; (6) **woodpecker,** the hairy woodpecker, *Dryobates villosus.*

(1) **1917** *Animals of Amer.* 48. **1942** *Nat. Pk. Service, Fading Trails* 50 To the east of the Rockies, Audubon's or Badlands bighorn inhabited the broken country of the Dakotas and part of Nebraska, Wyoming, and Montana. — (2) **1917** *Birds of Amer.* II. 92 The Caracaras are divided into three genera, *Polyborus, Milvago,* and *Ibycter,* of which the first-named comprises four species, including the Audubon Caracara. **1942** *Nat. Pk. Service, Fading Trails* 261 This [bird] is the Audubon's caracara, found in the United States only in Florida and the states bordering Mexico. — (3) **1858** Baird *Birds Pacific R.R.* 54 Audubon's oriole. . . . *Hab.* Valley of the Lower Rio Grande of Texas, southward. **1917** *Birds of Amer.* II. 253 Audubon's Oriole *Icterus melanocephalus auduboni* . . . is essentially a Mexican species, but its northern range brings it into Texas. **1941** Peterson *Western Birds* 165 Audubon's Oriole . . . [is] a *yellow* oriole with black head, wings, and tail. — (4) **1909** Webster 1938/1 The Manx shearwater . . . and the Audubon's shearwater (*P. lhermineiri*), common about the West Indies, Florida coasts, etc., are small species. **1938** *Auk* Jan. 119 An Audubon's Shearwater (*Puffinus lhermineiri lhermineiri*) was found dead on the beach at Chilmark, Martha's Vineyard, August 13, 1937. (5) **1837** Townsend in *Jrnl. Acad. Nat. Sci. Phila.* VII. 191 Audubon's Warbler . . . inhabits the forests of the Columbia river. **1948** *Pacific Discovery* Mar.–Apr. 17/1 The Audubon warbler's victory was short lived for the tree was usurped a moment later by five Oregon juncos. — (6) **1837** *Jrnl. Acad. Nat. Sci.* VII. 404 *Picus Auduboni.* Audubon's Woodpecker. . . . This species resembles the Hairy and Downy Woodpeckers in plumage, but is very distinct, and is intermediate in size between them. **1849** Audubon *Ornith. Biog.* V. 194 Audubon's Woodpecker . . . was presented to me by its discoverer [Dr. James Trudeau].

b. Audubon print, a reproduction of a drawing from Audubon's famous elephant folio work (1827–38) on the birds of America. Also **Audubon bird.**

1945 *New Yorker* 14 April 64 They are showing some rather nice trays—large oblongs . . . framing . . . colored Audubon prints of game birds. **1948** *Chi. Tribune* 10 Mar. II. 5/3 More formal is the artistic paper that shows Audubon birds in rectangular blocks on a white ground.

c. Also **Audubon Association, Law, Society.**

1886 *Forest & Stream* 11 Feb. 41/3 We propose the formation of an association for the protection of wild birds and their eggs, which shall be called the Audubon Society. **1921** *Outing* July 178/3 In most states this bill was known as the Audubon bill and in many places to-day is known as the Audubon Law. **1948** *Pacific Discovery* Mar.–Apr. 1/2 By virtue of other qualifications than an ornithological surname, Miss Crowe is Editor of the *Gull,* official journal of the Audubon Association of the Pacific.

* **auger,** *n.* As the last term in **pod, post, sand, screw, well auger.**

aulone, variant of **abalone.**

* **aunt,** *n.*

1. *N.Eng.* Designating a large winter apple of superior flavor. Also **Aunt Hannah.**

1817 W. Coxe *Fruit Trees* 134 Aunts Apple . . . is a beautiful and large apple. **1847** J. M. Ives *New Eng. Fruit* 47 *Aunt Hannah.*—A fine winter fruit, produced on the farm of Deacon Francis Peabody, of Middleton, Massachusetts. . . . We consider this to be one of the best eating winter apples of New England. **1859** Elliott *Western Fruit Book* 122 Aunt's Apple. Fruit, medium to large, . . . light yellow, streaked with red. *Ib.,* Aunt Hannah. From Massachusetts. . . . Flesh tender, crisp, sub-acid.

2. Aunt Jericho, (see quots.).

1894 *Amer. Folk-Lore* VII. 89 *Angelica,* sp., Aunt Jerichoes, N.E. **1931** Clute *Plants* 48 On the tongues of such folk, *Angelica* becomes Aunt Jericho.

* **auntie,** *n.*

1. *S.* An elderly or aged Negro woman.

1835 Ingraham *South-West* II. 241 Planters . . . always address them [*sc.* slaves] in a mild and pleasant manner—as 'Uncle,' or 'Aunty.' **1856** Murray *Letters from the U.S.* II. 159 This was an old nurse, an aunty, or mammy, as they are sometimes called (all ancient women of the darky kind here are addressed as aunties). **1947** Lumpkin *Southerner* 155 If I knew their names I at once forgot them, contenting myself with 'Sally' or 'Jim,' or if they were old, perhaps 'Uncle' or 'Auntie'—generic terms we were wont to use for Negroes whose names we did not know.

2. With punning allusion to "anti-." *Obs.*

1869 *Overland Mo.* Aug. 128/1 'Cousin Sal' . . . having been begotten by him [='Uncle Sam'] in the bonds of lawful wedlock with 'Aunty Extension.' **1899** *Review of Reviews* March p. xiv, In the States the Anti-Expansionists and Anti all other movements have been christened 'Aunties.'

Australian ballot. A type of ballot first used in South Australia and introduced into the U.S. about 1880, having upon it the names of all the candidates, so arranged that in voting secrecy is compulsory.

1888 *Nation* (N.Y.) 2 Aug. 91/2 By introducing the secret 'Australian ballot' in Congressional elections . . . the use of bribery in the choice of Congressmen might be discouraged to some extent. **1932** Lewinson *Race* 119 Where the election law permitted separate party 'tickets' instead of requiring a general Australian ballot, the Negro Republican was told that there were no Republican tickets available. **1944** *Chi. D. News* 25 July 8/2 Obviously electors with names beginning with 'A' had an advantage on an Australian ballot, with candidates arranged alphabetically.

attrib. **1898** *N.Y. Tribune* 7 Nov. 9/1 Last year there was an Australian ballot system, and that was advocated this year by many of the classes, and adopted again.

* **authors,** *n. pl.* A game played with sets of cards, each set dealing with an author.

1867 *Ball Players' Chron.* 27 June 5/4 For Two yearly subscriptions we will give: Bradley's Authors Improved. **1902** *Sears Cat.* (ed. 112) 1134/1 Authors. This popular game hardly needs any description. **1946** Morehead & Mott-Smith *Penguin Hoyle* 170 Authors is best for four or five players.

auto ˈɔto, *n.*

1. A colloquial shortening of **automobile.**

1899 *Boston Herald* 4 July 4/7 If we must Americanise and shorten the word, why not call them 'autos.' **1903** *Cin. Enquirer* 1 May 6/5 No matter how we get there . . . Foot or auto, 'coop' or bike. . . . We'll enjoy it all, you bet; When we all come down The Pike. **1948** *Pacific Discovery* Mar.–Apr. 27/1 There are many long stretches of road south of Ensenada passable for the modern, low-slung auto.

attrib. **1907** *Collier's* 20 Oct. 7/1 The auto-buggy is a distinctly new type of motor carriage. **1912** W. Irwin *Red Button* 197 A purple auto veil in my right hand. **1948** *Pacific Discovery* Mar.–Apr. 27/1 A regular auto ferry operates from Santa Rosalia to Guaymas.

2. Used as a prefix: (1) **auto-court,** (see quot. 1939); (2) **laundry,** a place where automobiles are washed; (3) **mat,** (see quot. 1909); (4) **plate,** "a curved stereotype which has been automatically cast, shaved, and beveled" (*Cent.*).

(1) **1939** *New Yorker* 14 Oct. 72 The usual phrase for cabin colonies in California is 'auto court.' **1948** *Coronet* June 22/2 In Los Angeles, a man buys property adjacent to a huge oil refinery and builds an auto court. — (2) **1919** *Polk St. Journal* (S.F.) 2 May 2/5 Auto Laundry De-Luxe. . . . Mr. Motorist, Something New. **1946** *Redbook* (Chicago) 98/1 Garfield Pk Auto Lndry Inc 14 Minute Car Washing. — (3) **1909** Webster Automat. . . . A café or restaurant in which orders are automatically delivered to customers who place coins or tokens in slots. *Cant.* **1948** *Time* 9 Feb. 50/3 Last week, she was in love with Manhattan—its Philharmonic, . . . its Automats, its Empire State Building. — (4) **1902** *Westm. Gaz.* 22 May 9/1 The Autoplate, a wonderful revolution in stereotyping. **1902** *Census Bul.* 28 June 51 (Cent. Supp.), A device known as the autoplate was invented in 1900 by means of which the time required for casting plates was . . . reduced.

b. Also with reference to various automotive vehicles, as **auto bus, cab, stage, truck, wagon.**

1899 *Boston Herald* 12 July 6/5 We should have the new words . . . autobus, [etc.]. **1915** *Nat. & Science on Pac. Coast* 155 The mesa and foothill flora may be examined to best advantage by taking the . . . daily San Jacinto auto-bus to 'the fill' on Box Springs Grade. — **1899** *Boston Herald* 12 July 6/5 We should have the new words . . . autocab. **1908** Phillips *Old Wives* 351 He took an auto cab, said 'Up the Riverside Drive' to the motorman, threw himself back in the corner and forgot his surroundings. — **1915** *Nat. & Science on Pac. Coast* 59 A daily auto stage meets the south bound Southern Pacific train. — **1899** *N.Y. Journal* 17 Jan. 5/2 The incorporation of the New York Auto-Truck Company. **1921** *Ohio State Jrnl.* (Columbus) 7 Apr. 5 Orm . . . is in the City Hospital . . . as a result of a 2,000-pound monument rolling off of an auto truck on him. — **1900** *Engineering Mag.* XIX. 733 This objection . . . does not hold good with the auto-waggon, which provides just that rapid and cheap form of independent direct transport for which so great a need exists at the present day. **1907** *Collier's* 20 Oct. 12/2 There were in the United States 120,000 pleasure cars of various models and 10,000 auto wagons.

autoist ˈɔto·ɪst, *n.* A motorist. *Colloq.* — **1903** *Sci. Amer.* 21 Feb. 134/1 Bills giving equal rights to autoists and the drivers of horses. **1944** *Chi. D. News* 19 Dec. 8/4 Have most of the police . . . looking out for irresponsible autoists who speed.

automatic ˌɔtəˈmætɪk, *n.* Short for automatic pistol or firearm.

1902 *Sears Cat.* (ed. 112) 305/2 Forehand Perfection Automatic, small frame, rebounding lock, positive stop on cylinder, and hammer blocked, same as in other Forehand Automatics. **1914** Gertrude Atherton *Perch of Devil* II. vii., I've even bought an automatic. I suppose I should call it a gun. **1947** *Hunting & Fishing* Feb. 11/1 Later in the season I was able to purchase a 'Remington' automatic which was the gun really wanted.

attrib. **1947** *Hunting & Fishing* Feb. 8/1, I have also heard dealers tell fellows that .32 Colt automatic cartridges wouldn't work in 7.65 mm guns of any kind.

automobile ˌɔtəˈmobɪl, ˈɔtəməˌbil *a.* and *n.* [F.]

1. *n.* A self-propelled vehicle, usu. of an internal combustion engine type, for use on roads and streets. Cf. **electric automobile.**

1895 in *Amer. Sp.* V. (1930) 273, I took part in the race of the automobiles from Paris to Bordeaux and back in carriage No. 16, the winner of the first prize. **1947** *Chi. D. News* 2 Jan. 6/1 The bodies . . . were found in Upp's automobile.

attrib. **1900** *Outing* Nov. 122 The influence of the Automobile Club of America. **1907** *Collier's* 20 Oct. 12/3 The Fifth Avenue stage . . . has just given way to a less picturesque but more powerful line of automobile buses. **1915** *Nat. & Science on Pac. Coast* 59 Oceanic Quicksilver Mine, near Cambria, can be reached by automobile stage from San Luis Obispo. **1923** Wyatt *Invis. Gods* IV. iii. 219 Dangling veils of the kind then [about 1903] known as 'automobile veils.' **1935** *Gunnison* (Colo.) *News-Champion* 21 Nov. 3/3 Until his election, he was an automobile dealer.

b. A waterproof mackintosh.

1903 *Sears Cat.* (ed. 113) 740/1 Ladies' and Misses' Iron Cloth Oxford Gray Covert Automobile. We are offering in this low priced automobile one of the strongest and best wearing cloths put on the market.

2. *a.* Self-propelling.

1883 H. Greer *Dict. Electricity* 48 There are half a dozen systems of electric traction . . . in use . . . 4. An auto-mobile car, with isolated rails. **1899** *Cent., Motorman,* . . . one whose business is to drive a motor-car, or automobile vehicle.

automobile ˈɔtəməˌbil, *v.* [f. the noun.] *intr.* To drive or travel in an automobile. Also **automobiling,** *n.*

1900 *N.Y. Journal* 11 Nov. 28/1 'Bubbling' . . . is the fashionable slang for automobling or locomobling or whatever you choose to call it. **1920** Lewis *Main Street* 70 The great trouble with this nation today is lack of spiritual faith—so few going to church, and people automobiling on Sunday. **1944** *Chi. D. News* 14 July 10/2 The growth of individual use of airplanes after the war will rival the growth of automobiling after World War I.

automobilize ɔtəˈmobɪˌlaɪz, *v. tr.* To habituate to the use of automobiles. *Obs.* — **1898** *Cosmopolitan* Sep. 480/1 It is scarcely an exaggeration to say that Paris is becoming 'automobilized.' **1902** *N.Y. Times* 26 March (*Cent. Supp.*).

***autumnal,** *a.* **1. autumnal herring,** the fall herring, *Pomolobus mediocris.* **2. autumnal warbler,** the blackpoll warbler, *Dendroica striata.* — (1) **1814** Mitchill *Fishes N.Y.* 451 Long-Island Herring. *Clupea mattowacca.* Called also the autumnal or fall herring. — (2) **1811** Wilson *Ornithology* III. 65 Autumnal Warbler: *Sylvia autumnalis:* This plain little species regularly visits Pennsylvania from the north in . . . October. **1917** *Birds of Amer.* III. 136.

auxiliary, *n.* (See quot. 1845.) *Obs.* — **1845** S. Smith *Theatr. Apprent.* i. 15 That useful, but much-despised class of individuals, indispensable in all theatres, called 'supers,' or more politely speaking 'auxiliaries.' **1854** E. Tompkins *Hist. Boston Theatre* (1908) 15 Wanted —Several respectable young men for Auxiliaries.

***avail,** *v. tr.* To give (a person) information about, or the benefit of, something. *Obs.* — **1781** Witherspoon *Druid P.* No. 7 The members of a popular government should be continually *availed* of the situation and condition of every part. **1843** Mrs. Trollope *Barnabys in Amer.* xviii. 119 'We should have got no invites, you may be avaled of that, I expect.'

***availability,** *n.* "That qualification in a candidate which implies or supposes a strong probability of his success, apart from substantial merit—a probability resulting from mere personal or accidental popularity" (B. '48).

1844 *Cong. Globe* 4 June 663/3 The *Eastern Argus* . . . describes the following as the traits of character which, in the estimation of the whigs, constitute the *ne plus ultra* of 'availability.' **1905** *N.Y. Ev. Post.* 13 Oct. 6 An illustration of the way in which what is called 'availability' is preferred to character and efficiency. **1948** *Chi. D. News* 6 Jan. 1/1 Gen. MacArthur's message congratulating Wisconsin upon her centennial celebration had no bearing on his political availability.

***available,** *a.* Having availability as a political candidate.

1837 *Baltimore Comm. Transcript* 20 June 2/2 (Th. Supp.), The New York papers are discussing whether the most talented, or the most available man, should be reëlected as candidate for the next presidency. **1888** Bryce *Amer. Commw.* II. lxx. II. 550 The man fittest to be adopted as candidate . . . is the man most likely to win, the man who, to use the technical term, is most 'available.' **1948** *Newsweek* 19 April 32/1 To call Vandenberg 'available' is not to question his sincerity in refusing to be a candidate.

***availableness,** *n.* =**availability.** *Obs.* — **1841** Emerson *Ess., Conserv.* 470 Conservatism . . . goes for availableness in its candidate, not for worth; and for expediency in its measures, and not for right.

* **avails,** *n. pl.* Commodities, property. *Rare.* — **1850** N. Kingsley *Diary* 99 She should not find profitable freight for Sacramento City, to take the avails of the company on board.

avalanche ˈævḷˌæntʃ, *n.* (See quots.) *Obs.* — **1859** Bartlett 15 *Avalanche,* a Texan corruption of the French *Ambulance.* A spring waggon. **1872** De Vere 580 *Avalanche,* a corruption of ambulance, was already before the late Civil War much used in Texas and the outlying territories. *Ib.,* Prince Polignac . . . showed very great excitement upon being informed by a [Southern] sergeant that the 'avalanche was just coming down the hill as fast as fury.'

avalanche lily. Any one of several large yellow erythroniums found near the snow line in the Northwest, esp. *Erythronium grandiflorum* or *E. montanum.*

1912 Wheeler *Selkirk Mts.* 74 Lily Glacier and Neve. . . . Some have thought that this so delicate appellation . . . for a river of 'thick-ribbed ice' came from the avalanche lilies . . . which follow the edges of the glaciers. **1946** R. Peattie *Pac. Coast Ranges* 72 Next in showiness, but surpassing in loveliness, are the avalanche lilies that burst from their bulbs at the very edge of the melting snow banks, and go dancing down to timber line.

avenging angel. (See quot. and cf. **Danite.**) *Obs.* — **1904** Steedman *Bucking the Sagebrush* 14, I saw here for the first time two real Danites, or 'avenging angels.' . . . They were the secret police of the Mormon Church. If any convert became weary of his surroundings or got disgusted and tried to leave the country, or if he bucked the authority of the Church, he disappeared from his 'sphere of influence.'

***avenue,** *n.*

1. A wide or principal street. Also a city thoroughfare, without particular regard to its character, often one merely running at right angles to others properly called "streets."

1780 J. Mason in *Boston Orations* (1785) 135 Till oppression stalked (in 1770) at noon-day through every avenue of your cities. **1830** Cooper *Water Witch* ii., The wide avenue in which Olaff Van Staats dwelt was but a few hundred yards in length. . . . This avenue . . . was then, as it is still, called the Broadway. **1948** *This Week Mag.* 3 Jan. 12/2, I started down Fifty-first Street towards Madison Avenue.

b. Often preceded by "the" with reference to a particular avenue. Cf. **Fifth Avenue.**

1852 *Knickerb.* XXXIX. 163 An old portrait which ornamented the back parlor in Wooster-street, and which hangs in the basement upon the Avenue. **1909** O. Henry *Options* 80 The Avenue was as quiet as a street of Pompeii.

2. In the phr. "the other end of the Avenue," with reference to the positions of the Capitol and the White House on Pennsylvania Ave., Washington, D.C.

1903 D. M. Dewitt *Impeachm. A. Johnson* 42 Thus far, it may be said, peace prevailed between the Capitol and 'the other end of the Avenue.' **1904** *N.Y. Ev. Post* 27 June 7 On the tariff question it seems almost certain that there will be a sharp difference of opinion between the White House group and the leaders at the other end of the avenue.

average book. At Harvard "a book in which the marks received by each student . . . are entered; also the deductions from his rank resulting from misconduct" (Hall '56). *Obs.* — **1848** W. F. Allen in Hall *Coll. Words* (1856) 15 In vain the Prex's grave rebuke, Deductions from the average book.

avitor ˈevɪtɚ, *n.* [App. f. **avi-* bird +*-tor* through association with *creator, orator,* etc.] (See quot.) *Obs.* — **1868** *Sonoma Democrat* (Santa Rosa, Calif.) 22 Feb. 4/6 Mr. Morrow, of Santa Rosa, is at work on his 'Avitor,' for navigating the air.

avocado ˌavəˈkado, *n.* [f. some Amer. Sp. form, as *abacado,* of *aguacate* (< Nahuatl). An Amer. borrowing.] The fruit of any one of various tropical trees of the genus *Persea,* an alligator pear. In full **avocado pear.**

1838 Texian *Mexico v. Texas* 10 In the orchards, the avigato pear, the citron and banana alternate with the apple, the plum and peach tree of Europe. **1902** *Fla. Hort. Soc. Proc.* XV. 64/2 The avocado pear . . . is to-day the most costly fruit on the American market. **1947** *Chr. Sci. Monitor* 1 Mar. III. 22/2 You'll find these giant avocados luscious and meaty.

attrib. **1947** *This Week Mag.* 8 March 16/3 *Avocado Sauce:* Peel medium-size avocado; cut in half and mash [etc.]. **1947** *Amer. Wkly.* 2 Nov. 36/3 Start the meal off with avocado cocktail, and for a surprise touch serve Mexican coffee. **1948** *Calif. Citrograph* April 261/3 A family orchard of avocado trees is maintained on the ranch.

***avoirdupois,** *n.* Personal weight. *Colloq.*

1858 *Spirit of Times* 13 Feb. 377/2 We directed the attention of our readers, a few weeks ago, to the increasing avoirdupois of the members of the new police. **1902** *Out West* Mar. 311 There is also more or less awareness . . . that Jordan and Wheeler differ in avoirdupois. **1928** *Collier's* 29 Dec. 28/4 My only idea, subscribers, was let's get this worry thing under way and take that poisonous avoirdupois off Jack before he weighed in for the champ.

Also **avoirdupoised,** *a.*

1922 *Outing* Jan. 165/2 If there be an idea that trails do not justify many words, listen to some avoirdupoised desk tender who tries to hike at 48 as he did at 18.

***awakening,** *n.* A spiritual revival. *Obs.* Cf. **great awakening.**

1736 EDWARDS *Faithful Narr.* (1737) 5 In these two years there were near twenty . . . converted; but there was nothing of any General Awakening. **1846** A. WILEY in *Indiana Mag. Hist.* XXIII. 428 He preached . . . until awakenings commenced, and the whole town . . . became religious. **1851** HOWE *Hist. Coll. Great West* 307 Excitements, or, in religious parlance, 'awakenings,' or 'revivals,' are common in all this region.

***away,** *adv.* In colloq. phrases: (1) *away back, from away back,* (*a*) far back in space or time, (*b*) said of a person or thing of great thoroughness or superiority in some respect; (2) *away below,* far below; (3) *away down, off,* (*a*) far down or off in an indicated direction, (*b*) *away down east,* far down in Maine or in some other district on the New England or Nova Scotia coast; (4) *away up,* far up, very high up; (5) *from away,* from a distance.

(1) (*a*) **1818** PALMER *Journal* 209 One of the passengers informed me, 'farms and settlements were thicker *a way back,* where the land was higher.' **1882** SWEET & KNOX *Texas Siftings* 45 Lawler . . . shot a deer, away back in 1840, on the spot where the capitol now stands. **1946** *Yankee* Sep. 4 The Allens, from away back, have been founts of wisdom. (*b*) **1884** *Chi. Tribune* 15 May 7/3 He was a State-rights Bourbon Democrat from away back. **1905** in *Kansas Hist. Soc.* IX. 68 Now, this Waters was full of jokes, and a fighter from away back.

(2) **1902** TOMPKINS *Hist. Rec. Rock Co., N.Y.* 348 A glass of hot gin would not be sufficient to keep the average man at church service with the mercury away below the freezing point.

(3) (*a*) *c*1849 PAIGE *Dow's Sermons* I. 16 Away down in the south . . . is a great country called California. **1871** CROFUTT *Tourist's Guide* 154 An Eastern lumberman, from 'away down in Maine,' . . . sank back in his seat and wept for joy. **1905** PHILLIPS *Social Secretary* 24 Even Tom don't seem natural any more, away off here in the East. (*b*) **1825** NEAL *Bro. Jonathan* III. 145 He-yankee, from 'away down east.' **1854** *Knickerb.* XLIII. 428, I am a miner, who wandered 'from away down-east.'

(4) **1818** PALMER *Journal* 130 Perhaps *away up* in Canada. **1834** DAVIS *Lett. J. Downing* 189 It's a present to me . . . from Starks & Co., away up in York State. **1904** *Minneapolis Times* 11 June 2 The rafters, away up high, were completely hidden under garlands of green.

(5) **1888** *Boston Journal* 6 Nov. 1/4 It is rumored that capitalists from away are making an effort to establish an industry in Rockland.

As the last term in **break, chuck, drive, run away.**

awful ˈɔfl, *adv.* [f. the *adj.*] Awfully. *Colloq.* — **1818** J. PALMER *Travels in U.S.* 131 (*note*), [It is] awful hot. **1861** NORTON *Army Lett.* 15 He was awful mad. **1921** PAINE *Comr. Rolling Ocean* iii. 39 A prairie town called Follansbee that looks awful good to me.

***awl,** *n.* As the last term in **moccasin, pegging, scratch awl.**

AWOL ˈewɔl, *n.* Also A.W.O.L. *Mil.* Abbreviation for "absent without leave."

1921 *Outing* June 137/1, I was surprised one day to find that unless I left the following morning to rejoin my regiment I would be an 'a-w-o-l.' **1944** in MENCKEN *Supp.* I. 410 [In the Confederate Army] unwarranted absences of short duration were often unpunished and in many other cases offenders received such trivial sentences as reprimand by a company officer, digging a stump, carrying a rail for an hour or two, wearing a placard inscribed with the letters AWOL. **1948** *Life* 15 March 130/2 After the furlough I went AWOL for a couple of weeks to keep working.

transf. **1946** *Chi. D. News* 7 Aug. 12/5 A 12-year-old musical prodigy in New York went A.W.O.L. **1947** *Chi. D. News* 31 Jan. 6/3 (*heading*), 4 Llamas Go A.W.O.L., Gambol in Jersey Fields.

***ax, axe,** *n.*

1. (See quot. 1883.) *Colloq.*

1883 DE VERE in *Encycl. Brit., Amer. Supp.* I. 200/1 The *axe,* or rather the guillotine, is made to represent the dismissal of Government officials upon the coming in of a new President or in case of some grave complication. **1928** *Hearst's International* Aug. 3/1 What assurance is yours that when the 'axe' falls, it will not hit you?

2. *An ax to grind,* a private or selfish end to gain, usu. *to have an ax to grind.*

The genesis of this expression is the well-known story of the foolish boy who was flattered by an affable stranger into turning a grindstone for him. This story was written by Charles Miner (alias Poor Robert) and first appeared in the *Luzerne* (Pa.) *Federalist* 7 Sep. 1810. After going the rounds of the newspapers the story was reprinted in a collection entitled *Essays from the Desk of Poor Robert the Scribe,* which many people confused with *Poor Richard's Almanac* with the result that the story is often erroneously ascribed to Franklin. See Charles F. and Elizabeth M. Richardson, *Charles Miner* (1916) 55 ff.

1810 C. MINER *Who'll turn the grindstone* in *Life* (1916) 56 When I see a merchant, over polite to his customers . . . thinks I, that man has an axe to grind. **1810** *Amer. Republic* (Frankfort, Ky.) 23 Nov. 4/3 Well, thinks I, no wonder the man is zealous in the cause, he evidently has an axe to grind. **1871** *N.Y. Tribune* 23 March 4/5 The number of axes which are taken to the various State Capitols, to be ground at the public expense, is perfectly enormous. **1947** *Chi. Sun* 20 Jan. 13/1 One can almost see the fine hand of somebody with an ax to grind.

3. In combs., usu. rare or obs.: (1) **ax blaze,** a blaze or mark on a tree made with an ax; (2) **cloth,** a cloth in which an ax is wrapped for safety; (3) **craft,** skillful use of an ax; (4) **factory,** a factory in which axes are made; (5) **gang,** the axmen in a timbering outfit; (6) **grinding,** (see quot. and cf. **2** above); (7) **hammer,** a stonecutter's ax, a hammer ax; (8) **hoe,** a form of hoe; (9) **man,** one who uses an ax in his work; (10) **mark,** a mark made by an ax; (11) **sling,** a sling for carrying an ax.

(1) 1903 WHITE *Forest* xviii. 261 The fresh axe-blazes the Indian had made. — **(2) 1853** FOWLER *Home for All* 190 Father . . . took his linen ax-cloth for a strainer. — **(3) 1843** CARLTON *New Purchase* I. xx. 188 During the day, this winter, I took lessons in axe-craft. — **(4) 1833** *Niles' Reg.* XLIV. 359/1 Ax Factories at New Haven. **1847** HOWE *Hist. Coll. Ohio* 348 The village contains . . . 1 woollen and 1 axe factory. *Ib.* 420 Garrettsville . . . has . . . 1 chair and 1 axe factory.

(5) 1901 WHITE *Westerners* xvi. 133 He must be pretty hot when his axe gang don't come any. — **(6) 1865** SALA *Diary* I. 421 'Axe-grinding' is a term borrowed from one of the most charming stories told by the great apologist of shrewd common-sense, Benjamin Franklin. — **(7) 1681** *New Castle Court Rec.* 476 Hee would beat him out with the ax hammer. — **(8) 1648** *Conn. Public Rec.* I. 492 An Inventory of the goods of Edward Chalkwell [includes] an axe howe, 6s. — **(9) 1671** *Essex Inst. Coll.* XX. 145 The time of meeting for ax men is to be by the Sun halfe an houre high. **1843** *Amer. Pioneer* II. 110 Colonel Brandt . . . finding him a superior axe-man and well acquainted with clearing new lands. **1948** *Hungry Horse News* (Columbia Falls, Mont.) 24 Sep. 1/3 Newest job developments at the Hungry Horse project this coming week will be hiring of about 30 axemen.

(10) 1832 *Louisville Directory* 107 Jacob Sodowsky . . . shewed a method of identifying the chops . . . made on the line and corner trees of old surveys, by cutting out the block containing the axe marks. **1845** SIMMS *Wigwam & Cabin* Ser. I. 79 A race [of frontiersmen] . . . who seldom make the real axe-marks of the wilderness. — **(11) 1812** *Niles' Reg.* II. 131/1 Axes, axe slings, muskets . . . have been bought.

As the last term in **belt, chopping, Collins, Indian, Kentucky, Mexican, narrow, settler's, squaw ax.**

axle grease. Grease made especially for use on the axles of wagons. — **1878** *Rep. Indian Affairs* 366 Class 10. Miscellaneous Articles. . . . Axle-grease—dozen boxes. **1948** *Hoosier Folklore* March 20 Put some axle grease on his face to grow whiskers.

ayuntamiento ɑˌjuntɑˈmjɛnto, *n. S.W.* [Sp. in same sense.] The magistracy or administrative body of a town or city under Spanish jurisdiction; a town council.

1831 DEWEES *Letters fr. Texas* xv. 140 If, after two years from the date of the concession, the colonists should not have cultivated his land . . . the respective Ayuntamientos can grant it to another. **1899** *Land of Sunshine* Apr. 241 The Ayuntamiento (town council) had appropriated $500 for the school. **1948** *True* May 126/2 Nacogdoches had no *ayuntamiento,* or city council, to ride herd on the *alcalde.*

***azalea,** *n.* As the last term in **flame, flame-colored, Lapland, scarlet, tree azalea.**

azotea ˌæzoˈteə, *n.* Orig. *S.W.* [Sp. in same sense.] The flat roof of a house or other building. — **1844** GREGG *Commerce of Prairies* I. 205 The roofs of the houses are all flat *azoteas* or terraces, being formed of a layer of earth two or three feet in thickness, and supported by stout joists or horizontal rafters. **1899** *Harper's Wkly.* 27 May 523/1 Above all is an *azotea* of such admirable proportions and commanding such a superb view [of New York] that it is in imminent danger of being called a 'Roof Garden.' *Ib.,* Flowers and shrubs will be used to decorate the *azotea.*

***azure,** *n.* (1) A bluefish. *Rare.* (2) **azure bluebird,** (see quot.). (3) **azure warbler,** the cerulean warbler, *Dendroica cerulea,* of the eastern U.S.

(1) 1720 *Broadside Verse* (1930) 161 Beside the Salmon. . . . Vast Shoals of Azures swim the Quinebauge. — **(2) 1917** *Birds of Amer.* III. 243/2 The Azure Bluebird (*Sialia sialis fulva*) wanders over the Mexican border into Arizona. — **(3) 1828** BONAPARTE *Ornithology* II. 28 The Female Azure Warbler is four and three-quarter inches long. **1946** HAUSMAN *Eastern Birds* 517 Cerulean Warbler *Dendroica cerulea.* . . . Other Names—Blue Warbler, Azure Warbler.

B

*B, *n.*

1. a. (See quot. and cf. **A, 1.** above.) **b.** (See quot.) Both *obs.*

(**a**) **1657** *Plymouth Col. Rec.* III. 112 Katheren Aines . . . for the blasphemos words that shee hath spoken, is centanced . . . to were a Roman B cutt out of ridd cloth and sowed to her vper garment on her right arme. (**b**) **1873** Aldrich *Marj. Daw.* etc. 122 Big Bethel and Bull Run and Ball's Bluff (the bloody B's, as we used to call them) hadn't taught us any better sense.

2. As a mark or grade given a student in school.

1877 [Provided for in June faculty minutes of Augustana College where B was equivalent to a grade of 60%–70%. See **A, 3.** note.] **1948** *Time* 1 Mar. 34/3 At school, where she always gets As or Bs, no one else is much impressed either.

b. As a grade for commodities.

1865 *Balt. Dly. Commercial* 4 Oct. 4/2 The refiners . . . now quote . . . 19 1/4 cts for A White; . . . 18 5/8 cts for B. **1886** *Harper's Mag.* June 93/1 'A' sugar is simply a term to designate the higher grades. . . . 'B' sugar is more brown. **1912** *American Mag.* Aug. 415/2 All milk sold in grades A and B must comply with high special requirements or else be pasteurized. **1945** *Newsweek* 4 June 31/3 About two days a week some Grades B and C beef to early or preferred customers.

ba, see **ab.**

babbitt ˈbæbɪt, n. [See 1st. quot. below.]

1. (See quot. 1874.) In full **babbitt metal.**

1874 Knight *Dict. Mechanics* 64/1 When the box is tinned it will take the Babbitt, but it must be pretty hot before the Babbitt is poured in. *Ib.* 205/1 Babbitt-metal. An alloy, consisting of 9 parts of tin and 1 of copper, used for journal-boxes; so called from its inventor, Isaac Babbitt, of Boston (patent, 1839). **1940** Eilmann *Medicolegal & Industrial Toxicology* 296 Metallic lead is used in . . . the making of . . . can seals, solder, babbitt, printers' type, etc.

2. (*cap.*) A derogatory term for a vulgar but smug, self-satisfied business man who readily conforms to the views and standards of his set, so called in allusion to the novel (and its hero) of this name by Sinclair Lewis.

1923 *Nation* 18 April 465/2 What is it I do find? A group of American business men! . . . A swarm of forward-lookers! A circle of Babbitts! **1947** *Atlantic Mo.* 76/1 Thousands of independent businessmen, or Babbitts, have been abolished and replaced with subordinate executives, or yes men, who, though smoother and more interchangeable, are unquestionably as a species a far lower form of animal life.

b. Hence **Babbittful, Babbittism, Babbittry.**

1923 *Nation* 17 Oct. 432/1 Busy, boasting, and Babbitt-ful, Kansas City holds a key position. **1938** Matschat *Suwannee River* 4 Near its junction with the Withlocoochee at Ellaville—marriage of Indian poetry to commercial Babbittry—the Alapaha pours into the brown tide. **1948** *New Leader* 24 April 9/1 There is a Babbittism of the Left spreading like an epidemic.

babiche baˈbiʃ, n. [See quot. 1907.] (See quots.)

1836 in *Life T. Simpson* (1845) x. 189 Babiche for snow-shoe lacing. **1894** *Outing* Nov. 127/1 The other article was . . . made from 'Babiche,' or narrow strips of reindeer skin woven into a fine mesh. **1907** Hodge *Amer. Indians* I. 123/1 Babiche. A thong of skin, particularly of eel skin. The word is derived through Canadian French, in which the term is old, occurring in Hennepin (1688), from one of the eastern dialects of Algonquian. **1948** *Sat. Ev. Post* 21 Aug. 72/4 No screws or nails are used at the joints, but *babiche* instead—rawhide thongs.

***baboon,** *n.* =**Illinois baboon.** *Obs.* — **1861** *Richmond* (Va.) *Examiner* 11 Dec. 2/4 To have come to reside in Charleston with an *exequatur* under the signature of the 'baboon' and that obtained after the war had actually begun, would have been, to say the least, a step of doubtful policy.

***baby,** *n.*

1. a. Some kind of article of convenience or equipment carried on a military expedition. *Rare.* **b.** A jocular or slang term of praise or approval applied to a person. Also used of a thing.

(**a**) **1710** Buckingham *Naval Exped.* 1 An ink-horn and tobacco stopper. . . . A baby. . . . A London Baby [listed among things taken on a military expedition]. — (**b**) **1911** H. S. Harrison *Queed* xiii. 167 Bad-eyed young men who congregate . . . to smirk at the working girls . . . 'Where you goin', baby?' **1932** *Blue Valley Farmer* (Okla. City) 11 Feb. 2/3 He may act somewhat queer, but that old baby knows his stuff. **1947** *Atlantic Mo.* Dec. 111/1 Yup, getting this baby out of the ground would come to a little expense.

2. In combs.: (1) **baby act,** the act of one who is immature or childishly weak, usu. *to plead* (or *play*) *the baby act;* (2) **beef,** a yearling calf 12 to 20 months old raised for beef; (3) **blue,** a pale shade of blue; (4) **blue-eyes,** one of several species of plants of the genus *Nemophila* (5) **bond,** (see quot. 1935); (6) **buggy,** a small carriage or perambulator for a baby; (7) ***bunting,** an infant's sleeping bag with an attached hood; (8) **carriage,** =**baby buggy;** (9) **coach,** =**baby buggy;** (10) **contest,** a con-

Baby carriage *c*1900

test in which babies are exhibited and a prize given to the one adjudged the prettiest, cf. **baby show;** (11) **hut,** (see quot. and cf. **booby, booby-hut, booby-hutch),** *obs.;* (12) **jumper,** a contrivance for supporting a baby in its early efforts to walk, cf. **baby walker;** (13) **kisser,** a politician who seeks to ingratiate himself with the voters by making much over babies, *colloq.;* (14) **parade,** a spectacle in connection with, and concluded by, a baby contest *q.v.;* (15) **show,** =**baby contest,** [such shows were app. originated by P. T. Barnum who went from city to city organizing them]; (16) **Baby State,** (see quot. 1934); (17) **talk,** talk for, or used to, a baby; (18) **tender,** a device for keeping a baby in safety; (19) **wagon,** =**baby carriage;** (20) **waist,** a type of short, full waist worn by women, also attrib.; (21) **walker,** a device for supporting a child learning to walk.

(**1**) **1868** *Putnam's Mag.* II. 570 'Don't plead the baby-act, Chinny!' **1904** Smith *Promoters* xv. 229 That's business honor, and anything else is the baby act. **1947** *Chi. Tribune* 28 June 8/6 In 1935, when the atrocious Wagner law went into effect, did employers and stockholders play the baby act and go on strike? — (**2**) **1890** *Stock Grower* 26 Apr. 5/3 Baby Beef. One of the marked changes in the method of cattle feeding is the increased number of yearling steers that are in the feed lots. **1946** *Reader's Digest* July 142/1 Cattlemen today are asking for steers that, instead of taking four to six years to mature, can be brought into the feed lot and finished off at 18 months to fetch a fancy price as 'baby beef.' — (**3**) **1889** Cable in *Century Mag.* Mar. 748/2 The small, square manuscript sewed at the back with worsted of the pale tint known as 'baby-blue.' **1947** *Time* 7 Apr. 26/1 Five bathrooms are done in various pastels—one in baby blue. — (**4**) **1887** *Overland Mo.* Aug. 152/1 Then, if we could have been there, we should have seen the . . . 'baby blue eyes' (nemophila). **1946** R. Peattie *Pac. Coast Ranges* 52 There it may be that baby blue-eyes cover the ground.

(5) **1935** *Lit. Digest* 9 Feb. 45/1 Next month the Government will enlarge its competition with savings-banks by beginning the sale of new 'baby bonds'—registered government bonds in denominations as small as $25 and as large as $10,000. **1945** *Greeley* (Colo.) *Tribune* 12 Feb. 1/2 The original government 'baby' savings bonds that went on sale 10 years ago are nearly grown-up now. — (6) **1890** *D.N.* I. 411. **1947** *N.Y. Times Mag.* 12 Oct. 26/3 A bunch of baby buggies are parked in front. — (7) **1926** *Mont. Ward Cat.* (ed. 104) 151 Mothers will find this little Baby Bunting exceptionally pretty. **1948** *Lisle* (Ill.) *Eagle* 21 Oct. 9/1 Infants Wear. Baby Buntings—White, Pink and Blue Detachable Hood $5.95. — (8) **1882** SWEET & KNOX *Texas Siftings* 48 There is a great deal of buggy riding but comparatively little pushing about of baby carriages. **1945** *Somerset News* 8 Feb. 2/2 Let us know by postcard if you have a second hand baby carriage for sale. — (9) **1903** *N.Y. Times* 1 Oct. 3 English baby coaches . . . The carriages are a distinctly English idea—they dub them 'Perambulators.' **1944** CARRINGTON *Safe Convoy* 171 The baby coach should be long enough that the passenger can stretch and grow.

Baby walker *c*1870

(10) **1921** *Ladies H. Jrnl.* June 84 Little Jayne Wheeler, [was] the . . . prize winner in a recent Chicago baby contest. — (11) **1772** A. G. WINSLOW *Diary* 60 If she had wanted much to have seen me, she might have sent either one of her chaises, her chariot, or her baby-hutt, one of which I see going by the door almost every day. *Ib.*, *Notes.* A baby hutt was a boobyhutch, a clumsy, ill-contrived covered carriage. — (12) **1852** EASTMAN *Aunt Phillis's Cabin* 52 And in the fifth corner was the baby-jumper, its fat and habitual occupant being at this time oblivious. **1872** *N.Y. Times* 24 April 8 (*advt.*), (Hoppe) Cradle, Baby-Jumper and Nursery Chair Combined. — (13) **1884** *Cin. Times-Star* 11 Sep. 4/6 As a baby-kisser, Ben Butler is not a success. **1928** *Collier's* 13 Oct. 8/4 The prizes in politics usually go to the back-slapper, the hand-shaker and the baby-kisser. — (14) **1913** *N.Y. Times* 6 July VII. 4/2 Titania's chief function, however, is to sit on review of the baby parade, a gorgeous spectacle that annually draws from 75,000 to 100,000 spectators to the Ocean Avenue concourse.

(15) **1855** *Golden Era* (S.F.) 8 Apr. 1/6 For one, as a Buckeye, I bid God speed the baby shows. **1948** *Chi. Tribune* 5 March II. 8/3 I'm surprised, because Morgan, a fine young man, never won a prize in a baby show. — (16) **1934** SHANKLE *State Names* 100 The *Baby State* refers to Arizona's being next to the last state to come into the Union. **1948** *Chi. Tribune* 21 Mar. VII. 18/1 James Minotto, former Chicago banker who has resided in Phoenix for many years . . . has become a political figure in the baby state. — (17) **1838** *Yale Lit. Mag.* III. 237 Parents and nurses are very unwise in attempting to simplify language by the use of what is termed 'baby talk.' **1947** *Dly. Oklahoman* (Okla. City) 11 Aug. 12/1 So-called baby talk is bad for children. — (18) **1845** *Knickerb.* XXV. 406 Some stove, button, baby-tender, or other of the most ingenious mysteries of inventive man. **1936** *Sears Cat.* 173 America's finest streamlined baby tender at all time low price! — (19) **1853** McCONNEL *Western Char.* 282 A steam-engine would have been clogged by the weight of a baby-wagon. **1903** A. ADAMS *Log Cowboy* xxii. 145 Well, at this church fair there was to be voted a prize of a nice baby wagon.

(20) **1897** TERHUNE *Old-field School* 19 The frock would have a full 'baby waist,' low in the neck and short-sleeved. **1902** MOORE *Songs & Stories* 26 This evening, in her baby-waist gown of white muslin, cut low-neck, and short sleeves . . . the girl was divine. — (21) **1856** *Mich. Agric. Soc. Trans.* VII. 81 Wm. Phelps . . . [exhibited] 1 baby walker. **1929** *Sears Cat.* 621 Low priced Baby Walker and Stroller.

As the last term in **blue-eyed, class, coon, cruller, cry, death, doll, Negro, rag, tar baby.**

***baccalaureate,** *n.* A sermon or other address delivered on the occasion when a class is receiving the baccalaureate degree. In full **baccalaureate address, discourse, sermon.**

1851 *Harper's Mag.* III. 560/2 At Rutgers College the Baccalaureate Address was delivered to a graduating class of 18 members. **1864** HOLMES *Soundings* 72 A baccalaureate sermon of President Hopkins. **1871** L. H. BAGG *At Yale* 666 A third or more of every class were always absent from the 'baccalaureate discourse' and graduation exercises. **1892** E. A. TANNER *Baccalaureate & Other Sermons* 6 All of the baccalaureates of the ten years of his presidency at Illinois College are published. **1945** *Gunnison* (Colo.) *Courier* 26 July 1/1 Because of college baccalaureate, Sunday morning, there will be no eleven o'clock service at the Church.

bach bætʃ, *n.* Abbreviation of "bachelor," an unmarried man. Usu. with *old. Colloq.*

1855 *Golden Era* (S.F.) 15 April 1/3 You will soon be . . . a 'dried up' old bach., and in fact, 'good for nix.' **1911** LINCOLN *Cap'n Warren's Wards* xvii. 278, I'm an old bach, you say, and ain't had no experience. **1947** *Chi. D. News* 14 May 18/4 No, I'm no old bach but a middle-aged father of two kids.

b. *To keep bach* (*hall*), =next.

1879 I. L. BIRD *Rocky Mts.* 157 A cabin where two brothers and a 'hired man' were 'keeping bach.' **1904** DAY *Kin o' Ktaadn* 76 Ye've kept bach hall since seventy-three!

bach bætʃ, *v.* Also **batch.** [f. **bach,** *n.*] *intr.* Of a man or men: To keep house without the aid of a woman. Also *to bach it*, =*to keep bach. Colloq.*

1870 *Repub. Dly. Jrnl.* (Lawrence, Kans.) 29 Jan. They 'bach.' **1888** *Century Mag.* Jan. 412/2 He had always 'bached it' (lived as a bachelor). **1948** *Chi. Tribune* 3 Apr. I. 16/3 He told how he was batching in a small apartment.

***bachelor,** *n.*

1. a. (See quots. and cf. **bank beaver.**) **b.** A local name for the crappie, *Pomoxis annularis.*

(a) **1870** PINE *Beyond West* 173 There are a certain few [beavers] . . . who have no family, make no dam, do no work, and never live in family lodges. . . . The trappers call them 'bachelors'! **1877** BARTLETT 809 As lonely as a catamount, and as dull as a bachelor beaver. — (b) **1877** *Smithsonian Misc. Coll.* XIII. 21 This fish is now, as in Rafinesque's time, abundant at the Falls of the Ohio, where it is now called 'Bachelor.' **1947** DALRYMPLE *Panfish* 84 Here, my friend, are the various names by which you would address that little gamester, the Crappie, depending on where you happened to be at the moment: Bachelor, Bachelor Perch, . . . Lamplighter, . . . White Perch.

2. In derivatives and combs.: (1) **bachelordom,** the state of being a bachelor, bachelors collectively; (2) **girl,** an unmarried girl who lives independently apart from her family or relations; (3) **-ism,** a trait or peculiarity of a bachelor, *obs.;* (4) **bachelors' ball,** in N.Y. *c*1827–50 an annual ball given by the bachelors of the city, *obs.;* (5) **bachelor's hall,** a bachelor's establishment, also transf., often *to keep bachelor's hall,* cf. **bach,** *v.;* (6) **bachelor('s) tax,** a tax upon bachelors.

(1) **1855** J. E. COOKE *Ellie* 198 Here I am, by no means averse to matrimony—tired of bachelordom in a word. **1932** *K.C. Star* 9 Jan. 10 Only Angelo C. Scott . . . remains alone in gloomy grandeur of bachelordom. — (2) **1899** *Tid-Bits* 8 Sep. 452/3 A latch-key—that prized possession and mark of identity of the American bachelor girl. **1944** JOHNSON *As I Dare* 97 We looked up a bachelor girl I knew, with leisure on her hands. — (3) **1808** W. IRVING *Salmag.* viii. (1860) 166 His character—fertile in . . . bachelorisms. **1860** J. KENNEDY *Swallow B.* 14 Chiding me roundly for certain waxing bachelorisms. — (4) **1827** *Cin. Advertiser* 7 March 2/2 (*heading*), Bachelors' Ball. **1896** HASWELL *New York* 407 On St. Valentine's Day was given at the Astor House the Bachelors' Ball, which had been long expected by our society and was long remembered for its brilliancy.

(5) **1731** G. WEBB (*title*), Batchelor's-Hall; a Poem. **1781** T. B. HAZARD *Nailer Tom's Diary* (1930) 26/1 Fixt the things in the house to keepe Bachelders Hall. **1870** PINE *Beyond the West* 173 Several of them [beavers] called bachelors are sometimes found in one abode, which the trappers denominate bachelor's hall. **1946** FORD *Honolulu Story* 13 The three of them and a boy named Ben Farrell were keeping what is sometimes called bachelor hall at Swede's aunt's place next door to mine. — (6) **1788** SCHÖPF *Reise* I. 192 Unter den verschiedenen Klassen von Taxen hat man in Pensylvanien auch eine eigene für Hagestolze (the Batchelor's Tax) angeleget. [**1821** *Olive Branch* (Danville, Ky.) 14 April 4/1 A bill has been introduced into the legislature of this state [N.Y.], laying a tax upon bachelors over the age of 28 years, for the support of Female Literature.] **1932** *Durant* (Okla.) *Dly. Democrat* 17 Dec. 3/3 Conner will propose a bachelor tax on all single men 30 years of age, increasing the tax progressively according to age.

b. *bachelor of science,* a degree conferred upon one who has completed a college course involving the study of prescribed scientific subjects. Usu. abbreviated **B.S.** or **S.B.**

1851 *Boston D. Advertiser* 17 July 2/1 The new degree of Bachelor in Science was conferred on the following gentlemen. **1940** *Harvard Gen. Cat.* 268 Candidates for the degree of A.B. or S.B. are required to show a reading knowledge of either French or German. **1948** *Democrat* 5 Aug. 1/7 Mr. Gray will receive the Bachelor of Science degree with a major in business administration.

See also **junior bachelor, senior bachelor.**

***back,** *a.* and *n.*

1. Denoting areas, geographical features, etc., in distant or frontier regions, as (1) **back country,** also attrib., (2) **county,** (3) **district,** (4) **farm,** (5) **(forest) plantation,** (6) **frontier,** (7) ***land,** [cf. Ger. *Hinterland*], (8) **mountains,** (9) **part,** (10) **prairie,** (11) **settlement,** (12) **swamp,** (13) **territory,** (14) **town,** (15) **trade,** (16) **wood(s),** see as a main entry.

(1) 1746 in WOODWARD *Ploughs* (1941) 332 In the back Country abt Paoqualin The Cattle feed is near over. **1787** in *Amer. Museum* (1789) II. *Chron.* 1/2 The back country people have killed three hundred Indians. **1948** *Sierra Club Bul.* Mar. 11 The back country would not be complete without wild animals. — **(2) 1755** FRANKLIN *Autobiog.* 397 The people of these back counties have lately complained to the Assembly that a sufficient currency was wanting. **1943** *Harper's Mag.* June 87 People who live in the back counties in this part of the country still have the old frontier tradition. — **(3) 1903** *N.Y. Ev. Post* 12 Sep., Rugs made by country women in the back districts. — **(4) 1904** WALLER *Wood-carver* 4 The driver . . . summons the dwellers on the 'back farms' to the rough box nailed to the guide-post. *Ib.* 96 Strangers . . . who have come to me on this 'back farm' in New England.

(5) 1700 *Virginia State P.* I. 70, I . . . have sent every way to search our ffrontears & back fforrist plantations. *Ib.* 71 Their ranging is . . . up to the uppermost inhabitants, soe down upon the back plantations. — **(6) 1755** CROGHAN *Journal* 82 An Indian from Ohio . . . says that the French will . . . lay all the back frontiers in ruins this winter. — **(7) 1681** PENN *Wks.* (1782) IV. 301 The back-lands being . . . richer, than those that lie by navigable rivers. **1795** JARDINE *Lett.* 21 You perceive the *Back Lands*, as they are called, recommend themselves by the cheapness of their purchase, and the great probability there is of their being, in the course of time, of considerable value. **1948** *Time* 3 May 33/2 He had already sent 600 leading Communists to the Chilean backlands, now had police rounding up small fry. — **(8) 1775** *R.I. Hist. Soc.* VI. 17 This place . . . is good land all to the back mountains. — **(9) 1698** G. THOMAS *West-N.J.* (1903) 79 Great Eggharbor River . . . runs by the back part of the Country into the Main Sea. **1856** GOODRICH *Recoll.* I. 96 Some years ago, a young New Englander found himself in the back parts of Pennsylvania, ashore as to the means of living.

(10) 1846 SAGE *Scenes Rocky Mts.* v, A dense band of buffalo cows made their appearance, from the back prairie. — **(11) 1758** in *Am. Sp.* XX. (1945) 269 They [the American Colonies] do not object to back settlement forts as they protect from Indians. **1759** FRANKLIN *Wks.* (1847) III. 420 These were to be followed . . . by a large number of Indians and French . . . in order to fall on the back settlements of Pennsylvania and Virginia. **1896** MARK TWAIN in *Harper's Mag.* Sep. 527/1 That was only a mud-turtle to a back-settlement lawyer. — **(12) 1772** J. HABERSHAM *Letters* 213 You cannot suffer so much here or there, as Planters in the back swamps. — **(13) 1817** PAULDING *Lett. from South* I. 82 Such [Atlantic States] as possess a back territory equal . . . in fertility . . . to the Western States. — **(14) 1778** in *Amer. Sp.* XX. (1945) 269 But for their clam-banks and fish, many would have perished if they had not removed into the back towns. **1883** *Harper's Mag.* April 705/2 The prospect of an illness in that back town . . . was not alluring.

(15) 1775 A. BURNABY *Travels* 27 These are two small towns lately built for the sake of the back trade. **1785** A. ELLICOTT in *Life & Lett.* 34 They expect in a short time to rival Hagers-town in the back trade.

b. Denoting those who live in such places or regions, as **back countryman** (also transf.), **farmer, inhabitant, member, people, settler.**

1796 *Gaz. U.S.* 19 Nov. (*advt.*) (Th.) A new Ballet Dance, called the Back Countryman, or the New Settlers. **1845** W. G. SIMMS *Wigwam & Cabin* 22 The boatman . . . knew by his dialect and dress that he was a back countryman. — **1770** *Md. Hist. Mag.* XII. 295 It is a Generall Complaint, not only here but among the Back farmers. — **1738** in KERCHEVAL *History* (1833) 61 First. I desire that you be very careful (being far and back inhabitants) to keep a friendly correspondence with the native Indians. **1789** *Ann. 1st Cong.* I. 169 The back inhabitants consumed five times as much as those on the sea-coast. — **1787** in *Speeches and Documents Amer. Hist.* I. 97 If the Western people get the power into their hands they will ruin the Atlantic interests. The Back members are always most averse to the best measures. **1791** WASHINGTON *Diaries* IV. 165 The Convention . . . made choice of a spot . . . lower than the back members . . . inclined to have it. — **1770** *Md. Hist. Mag.* XIII. 67, I shall write to the back people by Mr. Roberts. — **1754** in *Pub. Col. Soc* XI. 416 Accordingly we hear, that the Back Settlers in Virginia, are . . . terrify'd by the Murdering and Scalping of the Family last Winter. **1853** RAMSEY *Tennessee* 148 Charles Robertson had emigrated from that Province, and it may have been, was known to some of the disaffected back-settlers there.

c. In other expressions in which there is the idea of spatial relationship: (1) **back alley,** an alley in a disreputable section; (2) **Back Bay,** a district in Boston, Mass., reclaimed from the inner harbor and converted into a fashionable residential district, also attrib.; (3) **drop,** a curtain forming a barrier or background, also transf.; (4) **East,** the eastern states as contrasted with the Far West; (5) **fence,** a fence on the back or rear boundary of a lot, field, etc., also attrib.; (6) **field,** (*a*) in baseball, the outfield, (*b*) in football, the four players whose positions are back of the front line; (7) **fire,** a fire that is set to oppose another that is out of control, often fig., cf. next; (8) **firing,** the lighting of a fire to check an advancing one by depriving it of fuel; (9) **log,** a log, usu. of a large size, set at the back of a wood fire in a fireplace, also transf.; (10) **lot,** a lot on the back of a tract, also **back lotter;** (11) **porch,** a veranda at the back of a house; (12) **road,** a road, esp. an inferior one, leading or lying away from the main road; (13) **seat,** *fig.* a place of inferiority or insignificance, often *to take a back seat,* also **back seat driver,** one who from the back seat of an automobile insists on instructing the driver; (14) **states,** the New England states, *rare;* (15) ***stop,** (*a*) in baseball, a fence or other barrier behind the catcher to stop the ball if he fails to catch it, often the catcher himself, (*b*) a barrier to stop the shot or bullets in a shooting gallery; (16) **strap,** ?denoting boots or bootees having a strap at the back, also **back strappings,** *obs.*, cf. **2. b.** (11) below and see **back strap,** *v.;* (17) **stretch,** in a race course, the portion farthest from the main body of spectators, contrasted with home stretch *q.v.*, also fig.

(1) 1865 STOWE *House & Home P.* 38 We have been eating in a little dingy den, with a window looking out on a back-alley. **1947** *Denver Post* 2 March E. 3/1 Bring sports interest and training to every back alley in the land. — **(2) 1867** *Harper's Wkly.* 7 Sep. 563/4 New York has not, nor is she soon likely to have, an avenue like that which Boston is building across 'Back Bay,' and which has been called Commonwealth Avenue. **1948** *Good Housekeeping* Jan. 164/2 'Mr. Arthur, I'm Mavis Atterbury ' she said in a Midwestern version of a Back Bay accent. — **(3) 1913** *American Mag.* July 103/1 When the film is run off you see the back-drop right through him [*sc.* ghost] while he approaches Hamlet, and the two act in perfect unison. **1947** *So. Sierran* Oct. 3/1 Does any city have a more spectacular mountain back-drop? — **(4) 1876** *S.F. Dly. Examiner* 10 Oct. 1/3 O! you ought to see them administer justice back East. **1948** *So. Sierran* Mar. 3/1 The whole trip had the delightful aspects of a snow trip in winter 'up north' or 'back east.'

(5) 1912 MRS. WOODROW *Sally Salt* 24 She could really have believed that she could transform me from an eager back-fence prowler. **1946** *Sports Afield* Jan. 14/1 On a back fence, a magpie didn't even swear when a cat walked by. — **(6)** (*a*) **1911** *Collier's* 12 Aug. 21/2 From the home plate to the back field was a marked physical retrogression, ending in three strident but barely perceptible fielders. (*b*) **1923** *Outing* Mar. 287/1 Now look at the backfield, the terror of all elevens. **1948** *Dallas Morn. News* 2 May II. 1/7 They'll open with a good, seasoned first-string backfield. — **(7)** [**1784** *N.C. Morav. Rec.* (*tr.*) V. (1941) 2052 Below the mill fire broke out in the bush. . . . Toward evening the fire broke out again, so back-fires were lighted along the fences around the tavern land.] **1839** KIRKLAND *New Home* xxv. 204 The winds, though light, favored the destroyer, and the more experienced of the neighbors . . . declared there was nothing now but to make a 'back fire.' **1913** LA FOLLETTE *Autobiog.* 344 Thus starting a back fire on the Democratic legislators who were doubtful. **1948** *Range Riders Western* May 89/2 The fire set by the Indians raced toward the backfire and the two met and died down. — **(8) 1889** *Bellevue* (Ida.) *Press* 14 Sep. 3/2 The process known as 'back-firing' was resorted to, which resulted in saving the threatened buildings. **1946** *L.A. Times* 9 Sep. 1. 2/4 The blaze was stopped short of the Ridge Route by backfiring. — **(9) 1789** DUNLAP *Father* III. 1 It does my heart good to see him in the winter lay the shovel and tongs from the back-log to the hearth **1947** *Chi. D. News* 5 Feb. 14/1

This is hardly attributable to new-car productions, which still counts order back-logs into the millions.

(10) 1805 *Raleigh* (N.C.) *Register* 14 Jan., Back lots on the same square. **1850** Judd *R. Edney* xi. 158 There are the Gum-chewers,—all backlotters, and vulgar. **1911** *Collier's* 12 Aug. 21 The Real Baseball, Where Grit is Learned and Wits are Sharpened, is the Baseball of the Back Lots. — **(11) 1840** *S. Lit. Messenger* VI. 734/1 He was led by the hand into the back porch. **1903** *Harper's Mag.* July 176 He paced the back porch slowly. — **(12) 1788** Washington *Diaries* III. 444 Began a survey of the road leading from my Ferry to Cameron, and thence along the Back road by Mr. Lund Washington's. **1948** *Newsweek* 30 Aug. 77/1 Only after 'a storm of protest from all over the state . . .' was a new school built for the Negroes on a dirt back road. — **(13) 1859** *Harper's Mag.* June 54/2 This menagerie of . . . red skins, whom a score of indefatigable Coopers and Longfellows could never raise to merit a back seat in the heaven of romance. **a1863** *Southern Hist. Soc. P.* IX. 133, I tell you those able-bodied men who are sleeping in feather beds to-night . . . must be content to take back seats when we get home. **1927** *Collier's* 3 Dec. 10/1 You're just another one of them back-seat drivers. **1948** *Time* 9 Aug. 73/1 After the Democratic landslide of 1932 he retired to private law practice and a vociferous back seat in his party. — **(14) 1859** Hunter *Western Border Life* 21, I don't reckon she will though, for those folks from the back States are mighty green, they say.

(15) (*a*) **1889** *Cin. Commercial Gaz.* 17 March 7/1 The dash was for one hundred yards from the right field to the back-stop. **1901** *Denver Republican* 19 Aug. 6/3 The catcher is the crack back-stop of the Kearney, Neb., team. **1948** *Dly. Ardmoreite* (Ardmore, Okla.) 9 May 10/1 The lot had been graded and a well constructed backstop had been erected by carpenters. (*b*) **1946** *Sports Afield* Jan. 55/1 Put up two targets on the backstop for the second barrel practice, placing them at first on a horizontal line about 20 feet apart. — **(16) 1805** in *Amer. Ind. Soc.* III. 368 Back Strap Boots, fair tops, 4 Dols. 00 Cts. Back Strappings the top of do, 0. Dols. 75 Cts. . . . Back Strap Bootees, 3 Dols. 50 Cts. **1806** in Commons *Doc. Hist.* III. 63 For making fancy boots, the sum of five dollars; for making back strap boots, the sum of four dollars. — **(17) 1839** *N.O. Picayune* 2 Apr. 2/2 He went to work himself, soon passed the old black, made all sorts of a brush while rounding the last turn and commencing the back stretch. **1948** *Life* 21 June 32 (*caption*), Dewey, Taft and Stassen will get away fast, but watch out for Dark Horse Vandenberg on the backstretch.

2. In miscellaneous combs.

In some of these, "back" stems from the verbal and adverbial rather than from the adjectival use, but for convenience the expressions involved are included here.

(1) **back action,** backward or reversed action, also attrib., cf. **b.** (1) below; (2) **-bone Company,** "the New Orleans, Baton Rouge, and Vicksburg R. R. Co." (Th.), *obs.;* (3) **down,** an instance of backing down, tendency to back down; (4) **draw,** a drawback, disadvantage, *rare;* (5) **euchre,** see **euchre;** (6) **furrow,** a furrow plowed in the reverse direction; (7) **handed euchre,** see **euchre;** (8) **number,** *fig.*, a person or thing that is antiquated or out of date, also, *rare,* **back-numberish;** (9) **out,** an act or instance of backing out, withdrawing, or retreating, inclination or tendency to give way; (10) **pack,** a pack for the back, also attrib. and **back-packer, -packing;** (11) **slapper,** one given to slapping his friends familiarly on the back, a toady, flatterer, *colloq.;* (12) **slope,** type in which the letters slope backwards; (13) **tax,** taxes for past time, arrears of taxes, also **back tax collector,** cf. ***delinquent;** (14) **track,** (*a*) the track leading back to the starting point, also fig., (*b*) *to take the back track, to make back tracks,* to return, retreat, retrace one's steps, also fig.; (15) **tracker,** one who backtracks; (16) **trail,** =**back track,** also fig.

(1) 1845 *Knickerb.* XXV. 406 There lurks beneath it [the Yankee countenance] the knowledge of . . . some 'self-acting back-action sausage-stuffer.' **1873** Beadle *Undevel. West* 800 That sort of detraction has an awkward back-action about it. **1909** O. Henry *Options* 58 The sheep had to be driven up to the ranch, and . . . Mexicans would snip the fur off of them with back-action scissors. — **(2) 1884** *Cong. Rec.* June 5639/2 Here was the grant to the Backbone company; the five years' limit had about expired. *Ib.* 5645/2 The Backbone people were unable . . . to construct their road. *Ib.* 5695 The vote by which the Backbone Railroad land-grant bill had failed to pass. — **(3) 1862** Gray *War Letters* 35 The President's message . . . seems to me clearly a case of back down. **1894** Mark Twain *Pudd'nhead Wilson* xxi. 280 It's a clean back-down! he gives up without hitting a lick! — **(4) 1883** *Cent. Mag.* Oct. 815/2 There are great back-draws to the bee business, the irregularities of the flowers being chief.

(6) 1858 Flint *Milch Cows* 191 When arrived at the end of the piece, a back furrow is turned up to the potatoes, and a good ploughman will cover nearly all without difficulty. — **(8) 1882** Peck *Sunshine* 153 There is always some old back number of a girl who has no fellow. **1939** Brownell *Horse & Buggy Philos.* 199 They say there isn't a single [hitching] post on State Street and so why should we be back numberish and cluttered up with 'em. **1948** *Family Circle* June 13/3 He's the old man, a back number. — **(9) 1829** *Western Souvenir* 1830 314 There's no back out in none of my breed. **1888** *Boston W. Globe* 28 March (F.), Mr. Barber's back-out has not much surprised me.

(10) 1914 *Outing* June 312/1 By folding a blanket . . . it is convenient as a back-pack. **1916** Kephart *Camping & Woodcraft* I. 143 Back-packing is the cheapest possible way to spend one's vacation in the wilderness. **1921** *Outing* Mar. 254/1 How about that little back-pack tent you are going to have for your trip next summer or fall? **1946** *Trail & Timberline* June 88/1 The deplorable housing situation could never really affect a certain group of enthusiasts known as back-packers. — **(11) 1924** *Chi. Tribune* 1 Oct. 23/1 (*heading*), Here's a Comic Piece About a Back-Slapper. **1948** *Time* 10 May 22/1 No backslapper, he is well-liked but something of a lone wolf in the Senate cloakrooms. — **(12) 1835** H. C. Todd *Notes* 14 A [printing] type called backslope is much used in the city [N.Y.]. **1907** *Types of the De Vinne Press* 337 Backslope can be used properly in a list of names of persons or of places in narrow columns [etc.]. *Ib.*, These Backslopes are not totally acceptable with the Roman types that have stems of upright lines. — **(13) 1788** G. R. Minot *Insurrections in Mass.* 59 They completed an act providing for the payment of the back taxes in specifick articles. **1882** *Nation* 28 Dec. 544/3 The Grand Jury at Louisville, Kentucky, has found nine indictments against the Auditor, Back-Tax Collector, and Clerk of the Assessor's office of the city. **1948** *Chi. D. News* 13 July 20/2 Demands Stricter Law To Halt Back Taxes. — **(14)** (*a*) **1724** *Lancaster Rec.* 230 We lay still and kept scouts upon our back tracks to see if there would any pursue. **1839** *Maysville* (Ky.) *Eagle* 4 Dec. 3/2 Stocks are on the back track. **1929** Chalfant *Death Valley* 32 When on the back track they reached Elizabeth Lake with three horses, a mule, a sack of beans, . . . and some coarse flour. (*b*) **1837** *Cong. Globe* 13 Oct., App. 322/2 Does he mean to follow them as my young friend from Tennessee [=Crockett] felicitously expresses it, 'by taking the back tracks?' **1840** Hoffman *Greyslaer* II. x. 28 After giving up the chase, I made back-tracks up the river. **1864** Browne *A. Ward, His Book* 196 So we shall hate to whip the naughty South, but we must do it if you don't make back tracks at onct. **1903** White *Forest* xviii, Two days we lingered, then took the back track.

(15) 1946 *Nat. Geog. Mag.* Jan. 1/2 A small group of placer miners, many of them backtrackers from the California boom, had been gaining slender winnings in the gravel beds. — **(16) 1832** *Polit. Examiner* (Shelbyville, Ky.) 14 July 1/4 The whites . . . however soon discovered that they had taken the back trail, and renewed the pursuit. **1944** *Reader's Digest* Sep. 17/2 Immediately after it we hope to fare forth again on the back trail of the invasion of Folsom Man. **1948** *Range Riders Western* May 92/1 He sought higher ground to study his back trail.

b. In combs. the meanings of which are sufficiently explained in the quots.: (1) **back action,** cf. **2.** (1) above, (2) **campus,** (3) **fat,** (4) **lesson,** (5) **load(ing),** (6) **pay grab,** (7) **salary grab, grabber,** (8) **shad,** (9) **sight,** (10) **stamping,** (11) **strap,** cf. **1. c.** (16) above.

(1) 1870 *Terr. Enterprise* (Virginia, Nev.) 21 Apr. 3/1 Our teamsters use many words that are about the same as Greek to all but themselves, though some of them, such as back-action for a second wagon coupled behind the first, have come into general use. **1894** *S.F. Midwinter Appeal* 19 May 12/5 A back action passed through town two days ago with a load of cards and tangle-foot. — **(2) 1856** Hall *College Words* (ed. 2) 58 Back Campus, the privies [in College of New Jersey]. — **(3) 1867** De Voe *Market Ass't* 28 Animals in sound health, which have been fairly fed, will have a layer of fat between the skin and the flesh or muscles. This may be termed the outside or *back fat.* — **(4) 1827** *Harvard Reg.* Sep. 202 They have indulged in the luxury of 'sleeping over,'—a luxury, however, which is sadly diminished by the anticipated necessity of making up 'back-lessons.' **1851** Hall *College Words* 14 Back-lesson, a lesson which has not been learned or recited; a lesson which has been omitted.

(5) 1800 Tatham *Tobacco* 56 On their return, each one makes it his business to provide for his family, and for such neighbours as he can conveniently serve, by the conveyance of merchandize as part of their *back loads,* or returning freight. **1806** *Ann. 9th Cong.* 1 Sess. 619 If they were not to be certain of the back loading in returning, they would not take the gift of the flour on condition of hauling. **1842** *Amer. Pioneer* I. 70 Little did the first advocates of this system think, that . . . up river freight would be mere back loading. — **(6) 1890** [see **back salary grab**]. — **(7) 1873** *Newton* (Kansas) *Kansan* 26 June 2/1 If the people of the old Bay State don't lay this model back-salary grabber high and dry on the shelf, then we are mistaken. **1873**

Sat. Rev. Dec. 805/2 Congress . . . voted itself a few months ago an increase of pay, with retrospective effect—a proceeding known to American journalism as 'the back salary grab.' **1889** *Cent. s.v.* Grab, Back-pay grab, salary-grab, in U.S. hist., a retroactive congressional act of 1873 for the increase of the salaries of congressmen: an opprobrious name. — **(8) 1867** DE VOE *Market Ass't* 201 Those which are called *back shad* are sometimes improperly caught, after having spawned and are returning to the sea, when they are always poor, exhausted, and unfit to be eaten. **1868** B. LOSSING *Hudson* 145 They generally descend the river at the close of May, when they are called Back Shad. — **(9) 1867** MARSH in *N.Y. Nation* 9 May 373 A backsight is a sight or reading taken backwards; that is, in a direction opposite to that in which the levelling party is proceeding. **1947** *Mazama* Aug. 1/1 It was traveled by 'dead reckoning' with a granite crag for a foresight and a col in a ridge for a backsight, so the route is called 'gunsight.'

(10) 1887 *Postal Laws & Reg.* 232 Back stamping.—Every postmaster, upon receipt of the mail, will immediately place the postmark of his office upon the back of every letter therein received, showing the date and hour of the day when the letter was received. **1948** *Dly. Ardmoreite* (Ardmore, Okla.) 9 May 17/5 At the request of collectors desiring backstamps, covers mailed at New York will be backstamped at either Philadelphia or Washington. — **(11) 1904** WHITE *Mountains* 185 Next in order is the 'back strap' and tenderloin, which is always tender even when fresh. **1940** *Western Sportsman* Sep. 8/3 'Antelope saddle' was all that was considered edible—the so-called 'tenderloin,' or 'back strap'—which was sold in Denver and other western villages and hamlets for as low as 25 cents a 'saddle.'

c. In phrases: (1) *To be on one's back,* to be at the end of one's means or resources; (2) *to give one a back-cap,* (see quot. and cf. **backcap,** *v.*).

(1) 1840 DANA *Two Yrs.* xxviii. 312 He confessed the whole matter; acknowledged that he was on his back. **1904** *McClure's Mag.* Feb. 336/1 The employers of San Francisco are flat on their backs . . . ; when a labor leader makes a demand we give in without a word. — **(2) 1883** MARK TWAIN *Life on Miss.* lii. 514 (R.) Now I didn't fear no one giving me a back-cap (exposing his past life) and running me off the job.

3. In verbal combs., usu. colloq.: (1) **backcap,** (see quot. 1889); (2) **fire,** (see quots.); (3) **furrow,** (see quot. 1877); (4) **number,** to treat (someone) as a back number; (5) **set,** to restore (ridges of plowed land) to their original position by a later plowing, also **back-setting,** *n.;* (6) **stop,** to serve as a backstop or catcher in baseball; (7) **strap,** (*a*) to beat the back of (someone) with a strap, (*b*) to remove a back strip from pork; (8) **track,** to return along the same track, also fig.; (9) **trail,** to trace (someone) back to his starting point; (10) **up,** (*a*) = **back furrow,** *v.,* (*b*) to push (a vehicle) backwards, (*c*) of running water, to meet a barrier and become deeper, (*d*) to retreat or move backwards, also fig.; (11) **water,** *fig.* to retreat, withdraw.

(1) 1889 *Cent.,* Backcap . . . To depreciate or disparage. (U.S. slang). **1928** *Hearst's International* Aug. 34/2 Fine specimen you are—back-cappin' your own neighbors to town trash! — **(2) 1886** EBBUTT *Emigrant Life* 54 We all ran out immediately, and set to work to 'back fire' from the stables, and were only just in time to save the whole place from destruction, by burning a sufficiently wide piece of grass off, and thus stopping the rush of fire. **1912** DAWSON *Pioneer Tales* 291 Man learned to back-fire, and plow fire-guards, so but very few settlers lost their lives from prairie-fires. — **(3) 1855** *Ill. Agric. Soc. Trans.* I. 425 Plow first out from the row on both sides, then finish by *back-furrowing,* so as to leave the row a trifle higher than the surrounding surface. **1877** BARTLETT 24 Back-furrow, to plough so that the second and fourth ridge of earth made is laid against or on the first and third ridges; to turn the soil every other time reversely. — **(4) 1924** A. J. SMALL *Frozen Gold* vi. 140, I said, you lied when you told me Norvice was back numbered.

(5) 1880 FARRAR *Five Years Minn.* 243 It is common to cross-plough, or 'backset,' the same season. **1884** *Lisbon* (Dakota) *Star* 10 Oct., Farmers are now very busily engaged in plowing and backsetting and getting their land in readiness for crops next spring. **1894** *Congress. Globe* 31 July 8047/2 In some cases it will pay to 'break and back-set' the roadway to kill out the weeds. — **(6) 1918** *Amer. Mag.* April 39/1 He could back-stop and throw, and block runners and think. — (7) (*a*) **1807** IRVING, etc. *Salmagundi* x. 224 On his threatening to *backstrap* his adversary, the tailor was obliged to sheer off. (*b*) **1865–6** *Ill. Agric. Soc. Trans.* VI. 639 Mess Pork shall be packed from sides of well fatted hogs, cut into strips not exceeding six and a half (6½) inches wide . . . and not back strapped. — **(8) 1904** ELIZ. ROBINS *Magnetic North* II. 164 Now I'd advise you . . . to back-track home. **1947** *Time* 6 Oct. 25/2 During the week he had to back-track on three statements. — **(9) 1924** A. J. SMALL *Frozen Gold* i. 33 They back trailed him as far as Five Fingers and there the trail ended. **1945** MATHEWS *Talking* 24 Some have been more ingenious than others and have either back-trailed themselves or eventually worked out my trail.

(10) (*a*) **1785** PATTEN *Diary* 506 We backed up a piece of ground west of the Garden and planted it with yellow beans and I went to the falls. (*b*) **1834** *Visit to Texas* viii. 116 A small log building . . . in the rear of which a cart was backed up on the Prairie. **1883** *Harper's Mag.* Aug. 400 The wagons were backed up against the walls. (*c*) **1837** *Knickerb.* X. 409 They entered the Mississippi, and descended this river to the mouth of White river; and as this was backed up by the spring freshets, the voyagers turned their course up the stream. **1903** *N.Y. Times* 17 Sep., The wind, swelling the tide, caused the water to back up into the cellars. (*d*) **1864** MARK TWAIN *Sk., Killing Julius Caesar,* He then backed up against Pompey's statue, and squared himself to receive his assailants. **1906** O. HENRY *Four Million* 5 'Twill be convenient in the way of greeting when he backs up to dump off the good luck. — **(11) 1844** *N.O.Picayune* 18 March 33/2 Day before yesterday Boston waked up under a new coverlid of snow, dropped from the clouds overnight. This makes business back water. **1856** *Spirit of Times* 4 Oct. 70/2 Green was a large powerful man, but no grit, and Shortez offered to fight him for the money, but Green backed water. **1942** RICH *We Took to Woods* (1948) 263, I don't see why we can't rig it up. How many want to back water?

As the last term in **along, away, barnacle, bloody, blow, blue, break, brown, butter, calico, canvas, chair, chaw, cut, diamond, die, draw, eagle, eel, fall, fat, flash, foul, gray, green, hack, hairy, haul, hog, hold, horse, hump, kitchen, lazy, lead, leather, line, moss, mossy, olive, pull, put, razor, red, ridge, roach, rosin, russet, saddle, scrub quarter, set, shelf, skim, snap, snapper, soft, sparked, switch, talking, thorn, touch, trunk, turn, water, way, whale, white, yellowback.**

*__backed,__ *a.* As the last term in **canvas, moss, muslin, saddle, white backed.**

*__backer,__ *n.* As the last term in **bronze, green, way backer.**

backwood ˈbækˈwʊd, *n.* In combs. in the sense of "backwoods." Also, rarely, **backwoodishness.**

1792 BRACKENRIDGE *Adv. Capt. Farrago* xxv. 131 He thought it not amiss to make some inquiry, which by the by was rather an evidence of his backwood simplicity. **1836** *S. Lit. Messenger* II. 228/2 The oddities of a backwood reel are depicted with inimitable force. **1843** CARLTON *New Purchase* I. xviii. 152 Perhaps a novice, . . . in backwood life, may be pardoned for feeling a momentary sickness when [etc.]. **1855** OLIPHANT *Minnesota* 93 There was not a particle of backwoodishness about them.

backwoods ˈbækˈwʊdz, *n. pl.*

1. The woods lying back from the more settled areas; the uncleared forest to the west of the earlier settlements.

1709 LAWSON *Carolina* 139 He [pheasant] haunts the back Woods, and is seldom found near the Inhabitants. **1886** ALTON *Among Law-Makers* 145 The citizen from the backwoods of the West, and the citizen from the classic streets of Boston, may wander about the halls of Government with equal freedom and impunity. **1948** *Dly. Ardmoreite* (Ardmore, Okla.) 27 May 8/6 Instead of beating it for the backwoods, . . . people are reconciled to staying where they are.

attrib. **1784** J. SMYTH *Tour U.S.* I. i. 12 The American soldiery, chiefly then back-woods riflemen. **1880** *Amer. Punch* Feb. 22/1 The backwoods chaps are tickled almost to death to get five dollars a day. **1902** WHITE *Blazed Trail* viii. 58 Too big for a little backwoods farm. *Ib.* xvii. 133 Regular old backwoods mossback. **1948** *Life* 5 April 57/2 When the backwoods farmers of the Ozarks . . . find the night-blooming flowers they know that rain will come shortly.

2. In combs.: (1) **backwoodsman,** a man who lives in the backwoods, also, rarely, **backwoodsman-like;** (2) **backwoods woman,** a woman of the backwoods, *obs.*

(1) [**1710** *Miss. Prov. Arch., Frch. Dom.* (tr.) II. 57 Mr. De La Vente . . . is going to France and he will be able to represent to your Lordship the necessity that exists for having girls to draw in . . . the backwoodsmen.] **1774** DUNMORE *Correspondence* 24 Dec., Stired up the old inveteracy of those who are called the back-woods-men, who are Hunters like the Indians and equally ungovernable. **1848** PARKMAN in *Knickerb.* XXXI. 14 The impersonation of all that is wild and backwoodsmanlike. **1944** CLARK *Pills* 130 Southern backwoodsmen galloped home from their best girls' houses at Christmas firing pistols with wild abandon. — **(2) 1840** *Knickerb.* XV. 292 All the endless drudgery belonging to the life of a backwoods-woman. **1884** *Harper's Mag.* July 281/1 Mrs. Jackson—a plain, estimable backwoods-woman, . . . sat smoking her corn-cob pipe.

b. Also **backwoodsness,** the state of being from the backwoods, *rare;* **backwoodsy,** pertaining to, characteristic of, the backwoods, also, rarely, **backwoody.**

1832 WILLIAMSON *Maine* II. 645 He therefore spiked his guns, set fire to the Adams and the store-house, and retreated . . . through a back woody road, to Kennebeck. **1862** B. TAYLOR *At Home & Abroad*

2 Ser. II. 72 Wild and backwoodsy as the place appeared, it was to us the welcome herald of breakfast. **1867** *Harper's Mag.* Nov. 748/2 The peculiar *backwoodsness*, so to speak, of his costume and accoutrements. **1944** *Reader's Digest* Feb. 3 A young captain . . . had a session with a somewhat backwoodsy private who had been transferred to OSS because of an unusual linguistic background.

* **bacon,** *n.* In combs.: (1) **bacon beetle,** a beetle of the genus *Dermestes*, the larvae of which feed upon animal substance; (2) **box,** a box in which bacon is packed for transport; (3) **bug,** =**bacon beetle;** (4) **color, colored,** having the color of bacon skin, brownish; (5) **curer,** one engaged in the curing of bacon; (6) **fry,** (see quot.), *obs.;* (7) **ham,** app. a smoked ham, *rare.*

(1) **1832** WILLIAMSON *Hist. Maine* I. 171 *Dermestes Lardarius*, Bacon Beetle. **1889** *Cent. s.v. Dermestes*, One species, *D. lardarius*, is known by the name of bacon beetle. — (2) **1888** SHERIDAN *Memoirs* I. 27 About all that reached the post was what came in the shape of bacon boxes, and the boards from these were reserved for coffins in which to bury our dead. — (3) **1837** WILLIAMS *Florida* 68 The Insects of Florida are numerous. . . . Those most common, are . . . Bacon Bug. Dermestes. **1854** EMMONS *Agric. N.Y.* V. 60 The *Dermestes lardarius* commits its depredations in houses, usually in furs, meat, pork, bacon (whence it is sometimes called bacon bug). — (4) **1862** *N.Y. Tribune* 10 May, Maria is 18 years of age, very likely, has a very pleasant countenance, light bacon-colored skin. *Ib.*, Plato is about 19 years of age, and bacon color, squarely built.

(5) **1867–9** *Ill. Agric. Soc. Trans.* VII. 432, 4,118 hogs for bacon-curers and city consumption. — (6) *c*1746 in WOODWARD *Ploughs* (1941) 388 Bacon Fryes are made by slicing flitch bacon thin and fryed in Pancakes & are excellent eating. — (7) **1860** S. C. Cox *Recoll. Wabash Valley* 108 Took him back in the cellar and gave him an additional bacon ham.

b. Used with *collards, greens*, etc., in the names of dishes that are esp. popular in the South. *Colloq.*

1740 BYRD *Secret Diary* (1942) 82 Several gentlemen came . . . and dined and I ate bacon and greens. **1859** HUNTER *Western Border Life* 171 Who wants to trudge 'way over here for a bit of bacon and corn-bread? **1860** GREELEY *Overland Journey* 75 She gave us an excellent dinner of bacon and greens. **1877** BARTLETT 132 In the South . . . 'bacon and collards' are a universal dish.

c. In phrases: *bacon and rice aristocracy*, a nickname for those who had become wealthy through raising or dealing in these commodities, *obs.; to cook one's bacon*, to cook one's goose, *rare.*

1853 POYES *Peep into Past* 37 Thomas Smith bought his brother's lot, and remained [in Charleston, S.C.] to build up the 'bacon and rice aristocracy.' — **1868** H. WOODRUFF *Trotting Horse* xi. 120 The rating for six miles . . . 'had cooked his bacon'.

As the last term in **bear, belly, breakfast, hog and, Oregon, side, white bacon.**

bacon ˈbekən, *v. tr.* To convert into bacon. *Colloq.* — **1821** I. THOMAS *Diary* II. (1909) 76 Sent Legs of Pork to be baconed. **1829–30** DUNGLISON in *Va. Lit. Mus.* 102 In Virginia, we hear of a man intending to '*bacon* his pork.' **1917** *D.N.* IV. 407 bacon, v.t. To make bacon of. 'Reckon I'll haffter kill that hog and *bacon* it up.' [f. western N.C.].

Baconian beˈkonıən, *n.* =next. Also as adj. *Obs.* — **1676** in FORCE *Tracts* I. No. 9, 7 Sr. William . . . returns . . . in 5 shipps . . . in which was som 900 Baconians (for soe now they began to be called, for a marke of destinction). *Ib.* 9, Major Lawrence Smith, with 600 men, meeting with the like fate at coll. Pates Howse, in Gloster, a gainst Ingram, (the Baconian General).

Baconist ˈbekənıst, *n.* A follower of Nathaniel Bacon (*c*1642–1676) who opposed the arbitrary rule of representatives of the crown in the Jamestown colony. *Obs.* — **1837** BANCROFT *Hist.* (1854) II. xiv. 241 The party of 'Baconists' had obtained great influence in the public mind.

* **bad,** *a.*

1. Hostile, dangerous, murderous. *Colloq.*

1843 FRÉMONT *Exped.* 45 Our young men are bad, and, if they meet you, they . . . will fire upon you. **1920** MULFORD *J. Nelson* 7 A hard-drinking, two-gun man was 'bad.' **1927** SIRINGO *Riata* 155 The city marshall, Wilson, deputized him to arrest some 'bad niggers,' one of whom Wess killed.

2. In combs.: (1) **bad eye,** (see quot.), *slang, obs.;* (2) **folks,** a local name in the southern mountain country for Anabaptists, *obs.;* (3) **Bad Hearts,** (see quot. 1907); (4) **Indian,** an Indian who makes trouble for the whites; (5) **land,** see as a main entry; (6) **man,** a cattle thief, desperado, murderer of a type formerly found in the West; (7) **medicine,** a person or thing of a decidedly undesirable kind, *colloq.;* (8) **water,** *W.* =**alkali water.**

(1) **1875** MILLER *First Families* (1876) xv. 126 All of the following popular drinks, that is Old Bad Eye . . . were all made from the same decoction of bad rum, worse tobacco, and first-class cayenne pepper. — (2) **1804** MICHAUX *Voyage à l'Ouest* 160 Les personnes les plus instruites ne partagent pas l'opinion de la multitude sur état d'extase; c'est ce qui leur attire souvent la qualification de Bad folkes, mauvaises gens. — (3) **1852** MARCY *Explor. Red River* (1854) 3 We fell in with a party of Indians, of the nation of 'Kaskias,' or 'Bad Hearts.' **1907** HODGE *Amer. Indians* I. 701/2 Kiowa Apache. A small Athapascan tribe, associated with the Kiowa from the earliest traditional period and forming a component part of the Kiowa tribal circle. . . . They are possibly the Kaskaia. 'Bad Hearts,' of Long in 1820. — (4) **1846** J. W. WEBB *Altowan* I. vi. 178 [Gauchée is] a chochocoe chief, whose band have been considered bad Indians. **1885** *Weekly New Mex. Review* 21 May 1/5 Geronimo [the Apache] is the 'bad Indian' who caused so much trouble in Mexico a year ago. **1947** *Chi. Tribune* 8 June II. 5/7 Bad Indian who is proud of his ancestors is like turnip —best part of him underground.

(6) **1855** *Santa Barbara* (Calif.) *Gaz.* 28 June 1/4 At that precise moment the 'bad man' was floored by the weight of a walking stick that the quaker had been known to carry. **1948** *Dly. Ardmoreite* (Ardmore, Okla.) 4 May 4/3 The grandsons of the posses that chased the bad men out of town held conclave on how to welcome the good tourist. — (7) **1815** *Niles' Reg.* IX. 114/1 The former [Wyandotts] accuse the latter [Senecas] of administering *bad medicine.* **1947** *Beaver* June 11/1 Bad men, they said, the Mountain Men were, trading in to no post, keeping their country to themselves, bad medicine to strangers. — (8) **1865** *Washoe* (Nev.) *Times* 6 May 2/4 A lady of my acquaintance found her little son Jeff, bathing in a spring (of what they called 'bad water.')

b. In colloq. phrases: (1) *To be in a bad box*, "to be in a bad predicament" (B. '48); (2) *to put a bad mouth upon*, (see quot.), *rare;* (3) *to be in bad*, to be in disfavor *with* or *over.*

(1) **1818** WEEMS *Drunkard's Looking Glass* 5 You are now in a bad box; for if you take no notice of him at all, he is sure to turn mad. **1901** McCUTCHEON *Graustark* 288 By my soul, you are in a bad box, sir. — (2) **1835** SIMMS *The Partisan* 182 Maybe he would have a love charm . . . or he had an enemy and would have a bad mouth put upon him, shall make him shrivel up and die by inches, without any disease. — (3) **1923** R. HERRICK *Lilla* 103 He's in bad with the higher ups. **1931** *K. C. Star* 22 Oct., This column is in bad again . . . over a local.

Baden corn. A variety of corn said to have been developed by a Mr. Baden of Md. *Obs.*

1837 *Cultivator* March 9/1 The Dutton and Baden corn . . . are valued for the economy with which they convert food into solid grain. **1855** in SCHMIDT *Briefe* 106 Aus welchen durch sorgfältige Pflege eine Abart erzielt ist (Baden-corn genannt), worin sich die Fruchtbarkeit bis auf 6 und sogar 10 Aehren an einem halme steigert. **1856** *Mich. Agric. Soc. Trans.* VII. 528 Samples of Field Crops. . . . J. W. Armstrong, sample Baden corn.

badge pin. A fraternity pin. *Rare.* — **1871** L. H. BAGG *At Yale* 57 The badge pins worn by all the members constitute one of the most distinctive features of these societies.

* **badger,** *n.*

1. A thick-set animal, *Taxidea taxus*, about the size of a spaniel, found in central and western U.S. See also **Mexican badger, mountain badger.**

1654 JOHNSON *Wonder-w. Prov.* xxi. 173 A receptacle for . . . Foxes, Rockoones, Bag[er]s, Bevers, Otters, and all kind of wild creatures. **1781–2** JEFFERSON *Writings* II. 70 Kalm . . . tells us, that the lynx, badger, red fox, and flying squirrel, are the same in America as in Europe. **1903** AUSTIN *Land of Little Rain* 37, I have seen badgers drinking about the hour when the light takes on the yellow tinge it has from coming slantwise through the hills.

b. badger hole, a burrow made by a badger. Also transf. and attrib.

1823 W. KEATING *Narr.* 177 Many badger holes were observed. **1913** W. C. BARNES *Western Grazing Grounds* 150 They should be free from prairie dog and badger holes, for many a tottering little lamb has fallen into such a hole and perished. **1940** *Places to See in Wyo.* xx/2 Except for some badger-hole prospect diggings, the upper Teton country is virtually virgin mountain-forest. **1948** *Dly. Ardmoreite* (Ardmore, Okla.) 2 May 10/3 His cabin is known as 'badger hole,' and he has the neighbors he wants.

2. (*cap.*) A nickname for an inhabitant of the state of Wisconsin. Also **Badger State,** a nickname for Wisconsin.

1835 HOFFMAN *Winter in West* I. 176 There was . . . a keen-eyed, leather-belted 'badger' from the mines of Ouisconsin. **1850** E. S. SEYMOUR *Sks. Minnesota* 86 We have abundant reason to anticipate that Minnesota . . . will not lag far behind the Badger State. **1948** *Chi. Tribune* 25 Mar. I. 18/2 A survey of sentiment in 10 counties disclosed Badger citizens in rural and urban areas are increasingly concerned over the spread of communism.

Hence **Badgerite,** *n.*

1907 *No. Dak. Mag.* Dec. 45 It is in these counties that Wisconsin people find peculiar interest for there ex-Badgerites have settled in large numbers.

3. A decoy in a badger game *q.v.* Also **badger-worker.** *Slang.*

1858 *Spirit of Times* 27 Feb. 412/2 He was the 'badger' at Moll Hodge's famous 'panel' establishment, in West Broadway and was sent up for 4 years and 8 months. **1896** Francis *Frauds of Amer.* (1902) 175 A female badger and her lover may be poor and unable to rent a house. **1910** *N. Eng. Mag.* July 587/2 A woman who decoys men and then her accomplice (alleged husband) blackmails them is called a 'badger-worker.'

4. badger game, the blackmailing of a man by a woman who places him in a compromising situation. *Slang.*

1924 Henderson *Keys to Crookdom* 228, I know of one case where a man alone worked a variation of the badger game on women. **1941** Asbury *Gem of Prairie* 53 John Hill and his wife Mary . . . are said to have been the first persons in Chicago to work the badger game.

badland ˈbæd͵lænd, *n.*

1. *pl.* (*cap.*) A region in South Dakota and Nebraska where erosion has resulted in varied and fantastic land masses (see quot. 1882). Usu. **Bad Lands.**

1851 Owen *Geol. Surv. Wis.*, etc. (1852) 195 J. Evans . . . finally reached . . . the country of the 'Bad Lands' (*Mauvaise Terres*), lying high up on White River. **1882** *Cent. Mag.* XXIV. 510 The term Bad Lands does not apply to the quality of the soil. The Indian name was accurately rendered by the early French voyageurs as *Mauvaises Terres pour traverser*—bad lands to cross. The ground between the buttes is fertile, and the whole region is an excellent cattle-range, the rock formations affording the best possible winter protection. **1948** *Range Riders Western* May 44/1 He entered the intricate maze of the badlands.

b. *transf.* A slum section in Chicago. *Slang.*

1892 *Scribner's Mag.* July 8/1 'The Bad Lands' is a quarter more repellent because more pretentious than 'The Dive,' but being the abode of vice and crime rather than of poverty, it can properly be omitted here. **1947** *Chi. Tribune* 7 Dec. IV. 47/2, I remember a Christmas eve . . . when I toured the west side bad lands, tough saloons and brothels.

2. *attrib.* Designating formations, areas, etc., where erosion has been of a characteristic intricate and sculptural nature.

1876 Dodge *Black Hills* 17 All the country south is 'bad land' or tertiary formation, much cut by deep and abrupt ravines. **1899** *U.S. Geol. Surv., Water Supp. Paper* 19, 36 Among the first lands sold in small subdivisions was a tract of about 4,000 acres, located in the bad-land strip on the base of the hills about 6 miles north of Merced [Calif.]. **1927** James *Cow Country* 54 The country kept a-getting rougher and rougher as we rode, and pretty soon we begin to get in some bad-land breaks.

* **bag,** *n.*

1. A large bag packed with cotton ready for shipment. *Obs.*

1842 in Bassett *South. Plant.* 170, I have 26 bages pack and 20 or 30 thousand pickout not gin I had to have the gin work on which have through mea back in jining. **1849** *Ib.* 178 We have packed 112 Bags and hald them to the river.

2. A base in baseball, (see quot. 1857).

[**1857** *Spirit of Times* 28 Feb. 420/3 The first, second, and third bases shall be canvas bags, painted white, and filled with sand or saw-dust.] **1873** *Forest & Stream* 20 Nov. 231/1 In this inning, through error, the Princetons succeeded in getting the bags full, with no men out. **1948** *Chi. D. News* 3 Mar. 34/1 Our man on third could have stood on the bag and rolled home.

3. In combs.: (1) **bag holland,** Holland cloth used for bags, *obs.;* (2) **house,** in smelting, a house in which large filters in the form of huge cotton or woolen bags are used to recover particles from gas; (3) **-seed plant,** the bladdernut, *Staphylea trifolia;* (4) **worm,** one of the larvae of any one of several moths of the family Psychidae which construct and live in a bag of silk, leaves, etc.

(**1**) **1693** Sewall *Letter Book* I. 137 One piece Shepard's Holland or course Bag-Holland. **1741** *S.C. Gazette* 19–26 March, Just imported . . . and to be sold . . . bag hollands, brown hollands, table cloths. — (**2**) **1915** *Nat. & Science on Pac. Coast* 68 The Mammoth smelter, using a bag-house, may be seen to the west near Kennett. — (**3**) **1917** Bailey *Sand Dunes Indiana* 51 In the right foreground there may be observed a few specimens of the bag-seed plant, a small, hardy shrub which grows very rapidly in these seemingly impossible places. — (**4**) **1862** *Cong. Globe* 8 Jan. 232/1 On the avenue and in the parks you will find the evergreen trees . . . being destroyed by the bag-worm. . . . We have no bird that can tear or penetrate the tough cocoon or covering in which it lives. **1909** *Sat. Ev. Post* 12 June 25/3 The bag-worm which hangs its bags principally on the red cedar, . . . is destructive, but it is easily controlled. **1948** *Holland's* March 50/3 Bag worms . . . will practically devour the plants if not checked.

b. (1) *Somebody's cut the bag open,* a colloq. expression to explain the presence of a large number of birds, etc., at a particular place; (2) *in the bag,* assured, as if with reference to game already secured and in the game-bag, *slang.*

(**1**) **1874** J. W. Long *Amer. Wild-fowl* ix. 156, I reckon 'somebody's cut the bag open,' as the saying is out here, from the way they are coming. — (**2**) **1926** *Emporia Gazette* 24 Sep., After Gene landed with that terrific right the bout was in the bag. **1948** *Time* 8 March 18/3 The present leadership of the Democratic party will soon realize that the South is no longer in the bag.

As the last term in **base, bean, blanket, Boston, carpet, conjure, cotton, crocus, duffle, dust, emery, extension, factory, feed, feeding, fire, forage, gas, go-to-mill, grab, guano, hay, heart, hell, hunting, Indian, lucky, meal, medicine, merchant's, mill, overnight, piece, pill, sand, seed, shot, sleeping, smoking, splinter, tackling, tobacco, treasure, war, way bag.**

bagasse bəˈgæs, *n.* [F., an Amer. borrowing.] The refuse of sugar cane that has been crushed in sugar-making. Also attrib.

*c***1826** Stanley *Journal* 253 The canes are thrust . . . on one side by the machinery, crushed to atoms, and reduced to a perfectly dry mass. This, however, is by no means valueless, as it is in this shape, under the name of bagasse, a very fattening food for horses and cattle of all kinds. **1833** Silliman *Man. Sugar Cane* Two boys at bagasse (ground cane) carts. **1886** *Harper's Mag.* June 80/1 The juice flows from the crushers in one direction; the residual cane, now known as 'begass,' is carried off in another by an endless belt. **1947** *Atlantic Mo.* Oct. 55/2 Out of ordinary ground wood pulp, sugar cane, straw, and bagasse, they produced competitors as good and as profitable as Masonite.

b. (See quot.)

1944 *Newsweek* 26 June 80 Bagasse: A new industrial disease called bagasse was reported by Drs. W. A. Sodeman and R. L. Pullen of New Orleans, La. They observed it among sugarcane workers who handled bales of bagasse, the fibrous material left after sugar has been extracted from cane.

bagataway bəˈgætə͵we, *n.* [f. the Algonquian.] A form of Indian ball play from which lacrosse developed. *Obs.* Cf. **ball play, cross, lacrosse.**

1809 Henry *Travels* 77 *Baggatiway*, called by the Canadians, *le jeu de la cross*, is played with a bat and ball. **1833** *Polit. Examiner* (Shelbyville, Ky.) 9 Feb. 3/2 The Indians were in the habit of playing a game called Bag-gat-iway, which is played with a ball and bat, and decided by one of the party heaving the ball beyond the goal of their adversaries. **1851** Howe *Hist. Coll. Great West* 89 The *King's birth-day*, the 3rd of June, having arrived, a game of *baggatiway* was proposed by the Indians. **1947** *Parade* 22 June 2 Springing from an old Indian game known as baggataway, lacrosse had its start in Canada where it is by legislative action a national outdoor sport.

* **Bagdad,** *n.* [Name of the Oriental city.] Denoting a make of cigar. Also attrib. *Obs.* — **1834** Caruthers *Kentuckian* I. 11 Bring me a gin sling, . . . and half-a-dozen Bagdad segars. **1854** O. Optic *In Doors & Out* (1876) 200 Mrs. Washburn lit a Bagdad.

* **baggage,** *n.* In combs.: (1) **baggage agent,** a railroad employee who has supervision of the baggage of passengers; (2) **barrow,** (see quot.); (3) **blanket,** a blanket used in transporting baggage, *rare;* (4) **boat,** a boat for conveying baggage, *obs.;* (5) **car,** a railway car for transporting baggage; (6) **check,** a tag or label to be attached to a piece of baggage to indicate its destination; (7) **clerk,** =**baggage agent;** (8) **coach,** =**baggage car;** (9) **coupon,** =**baggage check,** *rare;* (10) **crate,** a crate or frame for protecting baggage in transit; (11) **express,** a company that takes charge of the baggage of passengers; (12) **expressman,** a man employed by a baggage express; (13) **house,** =**baggage car,** *obs.;* (14) **keeper,** =**baggage agent;** (15) **man,** a man having charge of passengers' baggage; (16) **master,** =prec.; (17) **mule, pony,** a mule or pony for transporting baggage; (18) **rack,** a rack for the accommodation of a passenger's baggage; (19)

room, a room, esp. aboard ship or at a railway station, for baggage; (20) **smasher,** one who handles baggage at a railroad station, dock, etc., also fig.; (21) **smashing,** (see first quot.); (22) **tag,** an identification tag or card for baggage; (23) **truck,** a truck for handling baggage at a railway station, etc.; (24) **van,** a van for handling baggage; (25) * **wagon,** = **baggage car.**

(1) **1858** W. P. SMITH *Railway Celebrations* 2 On almost all the trains will be found Baggage or Express Agents. **1884** CUMMINGS *Sk. Class 1862* 45 From this position he was promoted to the responsible place of General Baggage Agent. — (2) **1895** WAIT *Car-Builder's Dict.* 5 Baggage wagon-truck. . . . *A four-wheeled* vehicle with a frame or rack for carrying baggage. . . . A *two-wheeled* vehicle is a *baggage-barrow.* — (3) **1761** NILES *Indian Wars* II. 563, 60 Indians . . . were lying in wait for them, and drying their baggage-blankets in the sun. — (4) **1854** *Oregonian* (Portland) 10 June 2/3 We would advise them to apply to the commander of the Skookum Chuck for his boat, as a barge to be towed as a baggage-boat.

Baggage truck

(5) **1833** *Am. R.R. Jrnl.* II. 725/3 An agent is always stationed at the brake of the baggage car. **1948** *Chi. D. News* 17 Aug. 1/3 A mail car, a baggage car and a sleeper for train crew members also left the tracks. — (6) **1848** *Hunt's Merch. Mag.* XVIII. 334 (*caption*), Railroad Baggage checks. **1948** *Sat. Ev. Post* 25 Sep. 125 *One* ticket and *one* set of baggage checks takes you straight through to your overseas destination. — (7) **1870** W. F. RAE *Westward by Rail* 77 Frantic efforts are made to attract the attention of the baggage clerk, and to induce him to attach the necessary check to the trunk or portmanteau. — (8) **1878** PINKERTON *Strikers* 289 The inner track . . . was jammed full of engines, passenger and baggage coaches [etc.]. — (9) **1902** MARK TWAIN *Belated Russian Passport* (1928) 175 (R.), I couldn't get these tickets and baggage-coupons changed for St. Petersburg.

(10) **1839** *S. Lit. Messenger* V. 802/1 Our horses . . . were carried with the train in a large car partly filled with the baggage crates. **1863** GAIL HAMILTON *Gala-Days* 44, I suppose it [a trunk] would have kept on . . . had not Crene's dark eyes seen it tilting into a baggage-crate. — (11) **1859** *Harper's Mag.* Sep. 504/1 This accounts for the influx to the cars of the gentlemanly-looking men you . . . have taken at first for the agents of a baggage-express. — (12) **1872** T. W. TUCKER *Waifs* 114 Countless hosts of travellers . . . 'rise up and bless' the baggage expressman, as he . . . relieves them of the . . . care of their numerous trunks, valises, and hat-boxes. — (13) **1835** ABBOTT *N. Eng.* 194 The captain of the cars is arranging the passengers and securing the baggage in the baggage-house, an edifice on wheels. — (14) **1852** *Hunt's Merch. Mag.* XXVII. 75 A trunk and contents [were] placed in possession of the baggage-keeper.

(15) **1858** *N.Y. Tribune* 14 Jan. 2/3 [In] the baggage car . . . the baggage-man, who was not very polite, asked me what I wanted. **1944** *Harper's Mag.* June 12/1 One passenger, the engineer, the baggage-man, and two mail clerks on Passenger No. 122 were killed. — (16) **1845** *Hunt's Merch. Mag.* XIII. 581 The conductor . . . is also called baggage-master. **1926** *Amer. Mercury* Mar. 340/2 The baggage-master at the college transfer remembered re-checking his trunks. — (17) **1833** S. F. AUSTIN in *S.W. Hist. Quart.* II. 185 This same padre, when he left Nacogdoches for Bexar, lost a baggage mule, which a Tiger killed. **1840** *Knickerb.* XVI. 212 The cavalcade with its baggage-ponies . . . was getting into order for a march to the prairies. **1878** I.L. BIRD *Rocky Mts.* 30 The bundled up squaws riding astride on the baggage-ponies. — (18) **1889** *Harper's Mag.* Feb. 430/2 He found a member of Congress standing on the baggage rack. — (19) **1819** P. WAKEFIELD *Excursions in N.A.* 25 On deck there are numerous conveniences, such as baggage-rooms, smoking-rooms, &c. **1947** *Westerners' Brand Book* 43 River Station . . . consisted of a small waiting room for the passengers, the station agent's office and a baggage room.

(20) **1851** *S.F. True Standard* 6 Mar. 2/2 Baggage Smashers.—A disgraceful scene occurred on Long Wharf a day or two ago: a party of French emigrants having just arrived, the cartmen on the wharf seized their baggage and began packing it off in the most approved New York style. **1874** B. F. TAYLOR *World on Wheels* II. vi. 229 The word 'sagacity' is completely ruined for all human uses. It belongs to the baggage-smashers of the brute creation. **1947** *Westerners' Brand Book* 91 The box was banged, rolled, tossed and dropped in best baggage smasher style. — (21) **1883** *Ill. Revised Laws* 878 Baggage smashing. Any person employed by a railroad corporation in this state, who shall wilfully, carelessly or negligently break, injure, or destroy any baggage, shall be liable [etc.]. **1885** *Harper's Mag.* Aug. 418/2 His trunk . . . in a baggage-smashing mêlée . . . would, in the long run, come out victorious. — (22) **1879** STOCKTON *Rudder Grange* vii. 75, I went up-stairs and got a baggage tag. — (23) **1861** WINTHROP *Open Air* 228 The soldiers tramped forward and aft, danced on her decks, shot overboard a heavy baggage-truck. **1913** *Amer. Mag.* Sep. 41/1 Whoa—look out!! That's the fourth time that chap's tried to tag me with his automobile baggage truck. — (24) **1875** MARK TWAIN *Old Times on Mississippi* 190 (R.), Drays and baggage-vans were clattering hither and thither in a wild hurry.

(25) **1833** *Am. R.R. Jrnl.* II. 484/3 It has on several occasions taken a train of 8 carriages . . . with three baggage wagons.

b. *To get away with the baggage,* to escape detection in knavery. *Slang. Obs.*

1873 BEADLE *Undevel. West* xxxi. 672 How the swindlers 'got away with the baggage,' is it not all recorded?

As the last term in **blind, through baggage.**

***bagger,** *n.* As the last term in **carpet, four, sand, three, two bagger.**

baho, see **paho.**

baile 'baɪle, *n. S.W.* [Sp., a dance.] A dance or dance hall. Also attrib.

1844 GREGG *Commerce of Prairies* I. 243 The musical instruments used at the *bailes* and *fandangos* are usually the fiddle and *bandolin*, or *guitarra.* **1856** DAVIS *El Gringo* 264 The etiquette of the baile-room in New Mexico is quite accommodating, and there is no barrier against a person selecting whom he may desire for a partner. **1907** WHITE *Arizona Nights* x. 166 We . . . built a baile and saloon and houses out of adobe. **1946** *Ill. State Arch. Soc. Jrnl.* July 31/1 Street dancing in festival costumes . . . flourishes in the afternoon, with a baile, or indoor social dance, held that evening.

Also (diminutive) **bailecito.**

1853 *L.A. Star* 14 May 2/2 A nice bailecito came off at the house of Señor Celis last Tuesday evening, in which about twenty couples participated.

* **bailiwick,** *n. fig.* One's natural or proper place or sphere.

1843 *Knickerb.* XXI. 589 A friend and correspondent inside the southern division of Mason and Dixon's 'bailiwick' gives us the following. **1911** SAUNDERS *Col. Todhunter* ix. 119, I'm skeered to the marrow, . . . because I'm out o' my bailiwick. **1948** JOHNSTON *Gold Rush* 45/1 One of their number was chosen official representative to convince the man of God that he was *persona non grata* in their bailiwick.

***bailpiece,** *n. Law.* A warrant issued to a surety enabling him to arrest a person whom he has bailed. — *a*1821 C. BIDDLE *Autobiog.* i. 1 As he understood he was going off without settling the debt for which he was bound, my father took out a bail-piece. **1904** *Baltimore American* 24 Aug. 2 He was later released on bail . . . but was again arrested last night . . . on a bail piece, issued by . . . [the] clerk of the Criminal Court.

* **Baird,** *n.* [S.F. *Baird* (1823–87), Amer. naturalist Secy. Smithsonian Institution.] **1. Baird's sandpiper,** (see quot. 1891). **2. Baird wren,** = **Bewick's wren.**

(1) **1891** *Cent.* 5331/3 Baird's sandpiper, *Tringa* (*Actodromas*) *bairdi,* an abundant stint of both Americas, intermediate in size between the pectoral and the least sandpiper, and resembling both in coloration. *Coues,* 1861. **1946** HAUSMAN *Eastern Birds* 280 Baird's Sandpiper . . . is about 1 1/2 inches longer than the little Least Sandpiper, which it also resembles. — (2) **1940** JAEGER *Desert Wild Flowers* 19 These [woodpecker holes] are later occupied by the . . . Baird wren.

* **bait,** *n.* In combs.: (1) **bait mill,** a box in which knives mounted on a roller cut fish designed for bait into small pieces; (2) **stealer,** a local name for the cunner; (3) **stick,** a stick on which the bait of a trap is placed.

(1) **1846** *Knickerb.* XXVII. 513 Set the old bait-mill going. **1874** KNIGHT 212/1. — (2) **1884** GOODE *Fisheries* 273 At Salem they are called 'Nippers,' and occasionally here and elsewhere 'Bait-stealers.'— (3) **1834** A. PIKE *Sketches* 33 Lewis placed his trap still deeper under the water, and covered it with moss, placing no bait-stick.

As the last term in **bee, buffalo, clam, crazy, crow, eye, Hoosier, toll bait.**

***baiting,** *n.* The laying in of a supply of bait. See also **dollar baiting, still baiting.** — **1881** *Amer. Naturalist* XV. 369 Our vessel, a small one, made three 'baitings,' fishing each time about two weeks. *Ib.* 371 Twenty-five or thirty thousand are thus cared for at a 'baiting' and will keep in fit condition for use from two to three weeks.

bajada ba'hada, *n. S.W.* [Sp., a slope, a descent.] A descent, slope or downgrade. Also an alluvial fan.

1866 *Wkly. N. Mex.* 17 Nov. 2/3 The road from here to Algodones by way of the Bajada is being worked. **1931** M. AUSTIN *Starry Adventure* 105 (Bentley), There was a bajada just as you came out past the cienaga that dropped by way of zigzags. **1942** KEARNEY & PEEBLES *Flowering Plants Ariz.* 16 The bajadas are smooth, with gravelly surface, and are dominated by nearly pure stands of *Coleogyne ramosissima.* **1947** *Desert Mag.* Jan. 38/2 For those who like to camp out, I can suggest no more restful spot than the shrub-covered bajada at the base of the Koba.

∗**bake,** *n.*

1. A social gathering at which a meal, esp. of baked food, is partaken of by those present, a clambake, *q.v.*

1846 *Spirit of Times* (N.Y.) 6 June 174/3 In search of that five pound pickerel which he was bound to pull in every year, for the grand 'bake' at the village hotel. **1904** *Providence Jrnl.* 8 Aug. 8 The bake was prepared under the supervision of John Babbitt, and, with the 'fixings' which accompanied it, was pronounced excellent. **1948** *Nat. Geog. Mag.* Aug. 170/2 If Rhode Island had never produced anything but a bake like that . . . it would have been enough.

2. An act or the result of baking. *Rare.*

1851 *Knickerb.* XXXVIII. 187 Saint Peter [in stained glass] is a little cracked . . . ; but I've got a first-rate bake on Paul.

As the last term **hard, Missouri, potato, salmon, taffy bake.**

∗**bake,** *v.* In combs.: (1) **bake-apple,** the fruit of the cloudberry, *Rubus chamaemorus,* also **baked-apple;** (2) **beans,** baked beans; (3) **kettle,** a vessel for baking, ?a Dutch oven; (4) **oven,** [cf. Du. *bakoven*] =prec.; (5) **plate,** a bake pan, *rare;* (6) **shop,** a shop in which bread, pastry, etc., are baked or sold, also attrib.

(1) **1889** *Cent. s.v. baked-apple.* **1895** *Outing* XXVII. 18/1 The outlying islands furnish the curlew-berry and bake-apple in profusion. — (2) **1834** DAVIS *Lett. J. Downing* 26 Then we made the bake beans and salt pork fly. **1841** *N.O. Picayune* 2 Jan. 2/4 How to make . . . mince-pies, dumplins of all kinds, bake-beans, and so forth. — (3) **1836** TRAILL *Backwoods* 240 At first I was inclined to grumble and rebel against the expediency of bake-pans or bake-kettles. **1889** COOKE *Steadfast* i. 13 On one side of the fire stood a bake-kettle. **1938** DAMON *Grandma* 24 Cooking, what there was of it, was done in iron pots on a crane over the open fire, or in 'bake-kettles.' — (4) **1787** *Md. Gazette* 1 June 1/2 An excellent cellar, a large two-story Brick Kitchen and Bake-Oven. **1948** *L.A. Times* 2 May (Home Mag.) 22/2 There may be also a hot plate, a bake oven, a sink . . . and a large open fireplace to make chilly evenings comfortable.

(5) **1849** *One Man's Gold* (1930) 25 And baked in a pan of fat instead of in a bake plate. — (6) **1789** *Ky. Gazette* 25 April 1/4 Nicholas Wood . . . keeps a Bake Shop in Lexington, . . . Where may be had . . . several kinds of bread. **1908** PHILLIPS *Old Wives* 76 Suppose you saw a lot of loaves in a bakeshop window. **1945** *Boulder* (Colo.) *D. Camera* 29 Nov. 2/3 He is now stationed in the navy bake shop in Sasebo, Japan.

baked Alaska. A brick of ice cream inclosed within pieces of sponge cake, covered with meringue, and hurriedly baked in an oven until brown, before the center has time to melt.

[**1802** MITCHILL in *Harper's Mag.* (1879) Apr. 744/1 Among other things ice-creams were produced in the form of balls of the *frozen* material enclosed in covers of *warm pastry.*] **1909** FARMER *Boston Cook Book* 448 Baked Alaska. . . . Make meringue of eggs and sugar . . . , cover a board with white paper, lay on sponge cake, turn ice cream on cake . . . , cover with meringue, and spread smoothly. Place on oven grate and brown quickly in hot oven. **1948** *Time* 26 July 16/3 The party supped on roast beef and Baked Alaska.

∗**baker,** *n.*

1. A small tin oven for baking. See also **clam baker.**

1841 *Lowell Offering* I. 227 A peep into the baker told that the potatoes were cooked. **1897** *Outing* Feb. 489/1 The cooking utensils, consisting of three dripping pans, one patented baker and one large coffee-pot. **1940** *Western Sportsman* Sep. 34/2 This vest pocket size baker . . . weighs only a few ounces.

2. A tent having a fly which may be so raised that the heat of a campfire is reflected into the tent. In full **baker tent.**

1916 KEPHART *Camping & Woodcraft* II. 100 A fall of snow on the roof of an ordinary baker tent may cause trouble, unless an outside framework has been built and thatched with browse. **1922** *Outing* April 313/1 We tried a 7 by 12 tent something like the Baker. **1943** GEIST *Hiking* 34 [The] Baker tent . . . is a lean-to type of tent that weighs from 7 to 16 pounds.

∗**baking,** *n.*

1. baking powder, a white powder one of the elements of which is bicarbonate of soda used as a quick-acting leavening agent.

1853 *S.F. Whig* 28 July 3/6 (*advt.*), Judd's Baking Powders, extra superior. **1887** C. B. GEORGE *40 Yrs. on Rail* 81 Dr. Price, of whom I have just spoken, was the originator of the famous Price's baking powder. **1948** *Dly. Ardmoreite* (Ardmore, Okla.) 12 May 5/1 It takes face powder to catch 'em, but it takes baking powder to hold 'em!

attrib. **1900** *Harper's Mag.* Mar. 500 We cooked a loaf of baking-powder bread in a frying pan. **1944** *This Week Mag.* 7 Oct. 18 On the square is the way to cut baking-powder biscuits and cookies when time saving counts big.

2. baking soda, sodium bicarbonate.

1881 *Rep. Indian Affairs* 49 For weeks at a time, their storehouses were empty, with the exception of corn, baking soda, and soap. **1946** *This Week Mag.* 7 Sep. 27/1 Sift together flour, salt, baking powder and baking soda.

∗**balance,** *n.* The remainder, what is left. *Colloq.* See also **platform balance.**

1788 *Pa. Mag. Hist. & Biog.* (1894) XVIII. 62 Arose early and sent off the balance of our things. **1816** PICKERING 43, I spent a part of the evening at a friend's house, and the balance at home. **1946** *Mazama* Dec. 29/2 George told the Indians that if they would return and bring up the balance of the supplies that evening he would give them an extra half day's pay.

balao ba'lao, *n.* Also **ballaho.** [App. a var. of Amer. Sp. *balajú* in same sense.] The halfbeak, *Hemirhamphus brasiliensis.*

1867 DE VOE *Market Ass't* 199 There are likewise to be caught in the winter season, fish, by towing over this bank, if a person has suitable bait, such as the *ballaho,* which they have generally in the West Indies. **1896** JORDAN & EVERMANN *Fishes N. Amer.* 723 Hemirhamphus balao. . . . If a valid species, this must be the original *balao,* which is said to have the caudal bluish, and the common species will stand as *H. brasiliensis.* **1922** *Outing* Mar. 253/1 For sail and other large fish they use a sardine-sized, sword-nosed minnow called a ballyhoo. **1949** *Esquire* March 81 Bait—mullet, squid, balao [etc.].

∗**balcony,** *n.* (See quot.) *Obs.* See also **first balcony, second balcony.** — **1830** J. F. WATSON *Philadelphia* 177 The 'cushion head dress' was of gauze stiffened out in cylindrical form with white spiral wire. The border of the cap was called the balcony.

∗**bald,** *a.* and *n.*

1. A bare or treeless mountain top.

1838 *S. Lit. Messenger* IV. 231/2 At length, after considerable fatigue, we came to the top of the near Bald; from this we had an extensive and delightful prospect. **1877** *Field & Forest* III. 39 We come out upon 'The Bald,' as it is called, a mountain meadow extending over the crest of the mountain. **1943** PEATTIE *Great Smokies* 154 Aboriginally the Appalachian forests were vast in extent, clothing the mountains, except for the 'balds,' from top to bottom.

2. In combs.: (1) **bald brant,** the blue goose, *Chen caerulescens;* (2) **cypress,** a large tree of the genus *Taxodium* found in southern swamps; (3) **eagle,** the white-headed eagle, *Haliaeetus leucocephalus;* (4) **face, faced,** see as main entries; (5) **fall duck,** the American widgeon or baldpate, *Mareca americana;* (6) **head,** (*a*) a bald-headed eagle, (*b*) (see quot.); (7) **headed,** see as a main entry; (8) **head row, =bald-headed row;** (9) **hornet, =bald-faced hornet,** also transf.; (10) **pate, =bald face 1;** (11) **place,** a shallow pool in a salt marsh; (12) **prairie,** (see quots.); (13) **rush,** (see quot.).

(1) **1875** LONG *Wild-Fowl* 243 The younger [blue geese] . . . are further characteristically distinguished as bald brant or white-heads. — (2) **1709** LAWSON *Carolina* 96 Cypress is not an Ever-green with us, and is therefore call'd the Bald Cypress. **1916** SETON *Woodcraft Man.* 271 Bald Cypress. . . . A fine forest tree, up to 150 feet. . . . Sheds its leaves each fall so is 'bald' in winter. — (3) [**1634** WOOD *N. Eng. Prospect* (1865) 30 The Eagles of the Countrey be of two sorts, . . . the other is something bigger with a great white head, and white tayle: these bee commonly called Gripes.] **1688** J. CLAYTON in *Phil. Trans.* XVII. 989 The Second is the Bald Eagle, for the Body and part of the Neck being of a dark brown, the upper part of the Neck and Head is covered with a white sort of Down, whereby it looks very bald, whence it is so named. **1811** WILSON *Ornithology* IV. 89 [The] Bald Eagle . . . is the most beautiful of his tribe in this part of the world, and the adopted emblem of our country. **1948** *Democrat* 19 Aug. 6/4 The nest of the lordly American bald eagle in Lancaster county [Pa.] is vacant.

(5) **1835** J. MARTIN *Descr. Va.* 486 Very frequently there are found feeding among these fowl, the Bald Fall Duck; he has not the power of diving entirely under water in search of his food. — (6) (*a*) **1850** GARRARD *Wah-To-Yah* xii. 157 The magnificent bald-head unfolded his wings slowly. (*b*) **1945** *Mass. Audubon Soc. Bul.* March 41 Dr. Wallace has noted migratory movement over Baldhead, which is an exposed area atop the range several miles southwest of the Sanctuary. — (8) **1887** *Courier-Jrnl.* (Louisville) 16 Jan. 10/1 The arts and wiles of

the occupant of the bald-head row were of no avail, the proud Italian girl treating them with scorn. — **(9) 1859** TALIAFERRO *Fisher's R.* 194 It was as if you had assaulted a bald-hornet's nest. **1938** *Amer. Sp.* April 90 Lewis joined himself to a party of five men, including himself, headed by Tom Smith, the 'Bald Hornet,' for the purpose of trapping in the mountains north of Taos.

(10) 1808–14 WILSON *Ornithology* VIII. 86 On this account the Canvass backs and Widgeons, or as they are called round the bay, Bald pates, live in a state of perpetual contention. **1946** STANWELL-FLETCHER *Driftwood Valley* 177 The baldpates have white foreheads like bald old men, and white and gray sides. — **(11) 1813** WILSON *Ornithology* VII. 49 In the vicinity of these 'bald places,' as they are called by the country people [of N.J.], . . . among the thick tufts of grass. — **(12) 1846** *Freeman's Jrnl.* (N.Y.) 17 Oct. 120/2 [Sometimes Nature] will try her hand at a flower garden and throw in the midst of the groves a high rolling 'bald prairie' (so called from the absence of timber). **1901** MOHR *Plant Life Ala.* 104 The eminences of the lower swells of the plain with the strata of the limestone near the surface and destitute of arboreal growth are called bald prairies. — **(13) 1857** GRAY *Botany* 503 Bald-rush, . . . *Psilocarya scirpoides*, Torr., . . . [grows in] inundated places, Rhode Island and Plymouth, Massachusetts. July.

* **bald face,** *n.*

1. The white-crowned American widgeon, *Mareca americana.*

1709 LAWSON *Carolina* 151 The bald or white Faces are a good Fowl. **1768** WASHINGTON in Haworth *G. Washington* 255 Went a ducking between breakfast and dinner & killed 2 mallards & 5 bald faces.

2. Whisky fresh from the still without any aging. In full **bald face whisky.** *Colloq.* or *slang.*

1840 *Daily Pennant* 28 April (Th.) He called lustily for a horn of bald face and molasses. **1846** *S. Lit. Messenger* XII. 95/2 The loudest lungs were at a premium, and so was 'bald-face' whiskey. **1892** DUVAL *Young Explorers* 195 I'm not much on looks I know, but at any rate my breath don't smell of onions nor bald face whiskey.

3. bald-face bear, (see quot.), *rare;* **bald-face hornet,** =**bald-faced hornet; bald-face juice,** =**bald-face 2.** All *slang* and *obs.*

1876 *Fur Fin & Feather* Sep. 142 Green Martin tells of a bear rarely seen in the mountains which old hunters call the bald-face bear. — **1796** LATROBE *Journal* 104 The bald-face hornet. This dangerous fly is proverbially fierce. — **1844** *St. Louis Reveille* 20 June 2/3 Let us sing and dance, and drink old '*bald-face*' juice.

* **bald-faced,** *a.* In combs.: (1) **bald-faced hornet,** the white-faced hornet; (2) **shirt,** (see quots.), *colloq.* or *slang;* (3) **whisky,** =**bald face 2,** *slang, obs.*

(1) 1861 *Ill. Agric. Soc. Trans.* IV. 341 The nest of our bald-faced hornet is occasionally suspended in a house to kill off the houseflies. **1943** PEATTIE *Great Smokies* 287 Outlined against the sky, in a leafless maple, hangs a big oval nest of the bald-faced hornets. — **(2) 1889** FARMER Bald-faced shirt. The name by which a Western cowboy knows a white shirt. It is thought to come from the fact of Hereford cattle having white faces. [**1944** ADAMS *W. Words* 7/2 Baldfaced. A stiff-bosomed shirt, sometimes called boiled.] — **(3) 1836** *Wkly. Advertiser* (Russellville, Ky.) 21 Jan. 1/5 He has refused to keep any thing to drink but ball-[*sic*] faced whiskey. **1859** *Hutchings Mag.* Jan. 312/1 Give us some of your bald-faced whisky, fresh from the still-house—d'ye hear?

* **bald-headed,** *a.* In combs.: (1) **bald-headed eagle,** the bald eagle; (2) **mountain,** a bald mountain, *rare;* (3) **row,** (see quot. 1889 and cf. **bald head row**).

(1) 1836 M. A. HOLLEY *Texas* v. 100 The bald-headed eagle and the Mexican eagle . . . are among the birds of prey, and are very common. **1873** *Newton* (Kansas) *Kansan* 19 June 3/2 Let patriots everywhere . . . prepare to do the clean thing by Uncle Sam and his bald headed eagle.—**(2) 1854** HAMMOND *Hills, Lakes,* etc. 79 One day we came to an old baldheaded mountain. — **(3) 1889** FARMER 34 Bald-headed Row —The first row of stalls at theatres, especially those which make a feature of ballets. The term is a cynical allusion to the fact that these seats are generally occupied by men of mature age; the innuendo is obvious. **1943** ERNIE PYLE *Brave Men* 82 One night I went to a USO show given in a rest area and was put in the bald-headed row up front.

b. *To snatch (jerk) bald-headed,* to manhandle, "use up," treat with dispatch. *Colloq.*

1869 *Overland Mo.* Feb. 190/2 None but a wild and savage animal, of course, would 'snatch a gentleman bald-headed,' as the old man expressed it. **1909** MARK TWAIN *Is Shakespeare Dead?* i. 6 Can't you keep away from that greasy water? Pull her down! snatch her! snatch her baldheaded. **1945** *Jefferson Co. Republican* (Golden, Colo.) 28 Feb. 2/2 Just let me get hold of em, I'll jerk 'em bald-headed!

* **Baldwin,** *n.* A well-known winter apple of the northeastern U.S. developed from a seedling found about 1800 near Wilmington, Mass., by Col. Loammi Baldwin (1740–1807). Also a tree bearing such apples.

Authorities differ about the early history of this apple. The definition here is based on the account of Baldwin's life given in *DAB.*

1826 *Cat. Fruits* in *Garden Hort. Soc. London* 108 Apples. . . . Baldwin's. **1904** DAY *Kin o' Ktaadn* 21 There's bins full o' Baldwins an' Greenin's. **1944** *Life* 20 Nov. 82/1 The limbs of the Baldwins, Greenings and Snow apples are inclined to grow high into the air. **1948** *Chi. D.News* 27 May 2/2 The word 'apple' means just one thing in Connecticut: The Baldwin apple.

baldy ˈbɔldɪ, *n.*

1. A mountain top or peak covered with snow, usu. with reference to a particular peak. Also **Old Baldy.**

1863 *Rio Abajo Press* 28 Apr. 2/2 Within the perlieus [*sic*] of the Rio Chiquito and 'Old Baldy.' **1881** C. M. CHASE *Editor's Run* 59 Baldy is 12,000 feet above the sea, 5,000 feet above its eastern base. **1946** R. PEATTIE *Pac. Coast Ranges* 332 Upland and Claremont are on the alluvial fan or delta of San Antonio Creek, which pours out of Icehouse Canyon from the foot of Old Baldy.

2. Used as the name of a horse, and with reference to a bald-headed person. *Colloq.*

1894 *Outing* XXIV. 216/2 Well, I tried to wear it [=a whip] out on Baldy coming along. **1947** *Time* 15 Dec. 12/2 In Huntington, W.Va., bald Councilman R. J. Wilkinson Jr. pushed a measure to forbid barbers to charge baldies more than 25¢ for haircuts.

* **bale,** *n.*

1. A compact mass, now about 500 lbs., of ginned cotton securely wrapped and bound for shipping. Cf. **cotton bale.**

1803 *Ann. 8th Congress* 2 Sess. 1523, 20,000 bales of cotton, of three cwt. each, at twenty cents per pound. **1869** *Overland Mo.* July 10/1 The finished bales lie tumbled about, clean in gunny and blue hoops of iron. **1948** *Democrat* 23 Sep. 1/3 The . . . report . . . shows that 1098 bales of cotton had been ginned.

2. An amount of hay, usu. about 100 lbs., pressed and bound into a compact bundle. Cf. **hay bale.**

1834 *N.Y. City Ordinance* 15 April, All pressed hay, or hay in bales or bundles. **1874** KNIGHT 218/2 By these means the size of bale for a given weight of hay is materially reduced. **1948** *This Week Mag.* 10 July 14/3 Mabel was sent a bouquet of roses big as a bale of hay.

3. In combs.: (1) **bale boss,** of obscure origin and meaning, *obs.;* (2) **cloth,** cloth used for baling purposes; (3) **cotton,** cotton packed in bales, *obs.;* (4) **rope,** before the use of metal "ties," rope suitable for binding bales of cotton, cf. **baling rope.**

(1) 1832 *Louisville Pub. Adv.* 22 May, 100 lbs bale boss . . . for sale. — **(2) 1797** B. HAWKINS *Lett.* 346, 8 yds. bale cloth to Harry Dergin, at 12½c., $1.00. **1818** DARBY *Emigrant's Guide* 205 The demand for cordage and bale cloth must increase. **1922** *D.N.* V. 182 Bale cloth. Specially made heavy cloth, imported from Scotland for baling hops. — **(3) 1827** *Free Press* (Tarboro, N.C.) 22 Sep., Bale Cotton received and shipped to any merchant in Norfolk or elsewhere, for 12½ cents per bale. — **(4) 1821** *Missouri Intell.* 25 Dec. 3/3 (*advt.*), Bagging, Bale rope. **1874** R. H. COLLINS *Kentucky* I. 48 Tons [of hemp] were manufactured into bagging or bale rope in Mason county.

baler ˈbelɚ, *n.*

1. One who produces (so many) bales of cotton. *Colloq. Obs.*

1850 H. C. LEWIS *La. Swamp Doctor* 87 Every farmer in the South is a planter, from the 'thousand baler' to the rough, unshaved, unkempt squatter.

2. An apparatus or machine for baling hay, paper, etc. Also **baler-press.** Cf. **hay baler, paper baler.**

1888 *Voice* (N.Y.), Why are not balers as common as threshers? I believe it is owing to . . . manufacturers . . . not pushing the balers. **1932** W. KELLEY *Inchin' Along* 81 Seedless lint was stuffed into the baler-press and into its wrapper of burlap and metal ties. **1946** *Nat. Geog. Mag.* Jan. 31 One man drives the tractor down the windrow while the other two sit at the baler to tie the wires with which the hay is bound.

3. One engaged in baling.

1889 *Cent.* **1899** *Boston Globe* 22 Oct. 36/4 A baler and shipper of hay.

* **baling,** *n.*

1. The packing of ginned cotton into bales, the expense of this, or articles needed for it.

1836 BASSETT *Plantation Overseer* 100 The am[oun]t of the Sale of all the Cotton . . . is $3750 and the Bailing is to be taken out of that. **1854** *Harper's Mag.* VIII. 456/1 The baling of the cotton ends the labor of its production on the plantation.

2. In combs.: (1) **baling cloth,** coarse, heavy cloth for the outside covering of cotton bales, *obs.;* (2) **crew,** a group of men engaged in baling hay; (3) **linen,** baling cloth made of linen, *obs.;* (4) **press,** a press used in baling operations; (5) **rope,** rope formerly used for binding cotton bales; (6) **wire,** wire used in bailing, esp. in baling hay, cf. **hay wire.**

(1) **1809** F. Cuming *Western Tour* 165 There is [in Lexington, Ky.] one manufacturer of baling cloth for cotton wool, who employs thirty-eight hands. — (2) **1946** *Casper* (Wyo.) *Tribune-Herald* 26 Mar. 2/4 Food was dropped from a plane to 11 men in a hay bailing [*sic*] crew, marooned by snow. — (3) **1809** *Ann. 11th Congress* 1 Sess. II. 2171 There is manufactured, in Kentucky, a quantity of baling linen sufficient for the consumption of the greater part of the cotton country. — (4) **1815** *Niles' Reg.* IX. 187/1 They are considered much superior to all other baling presses. **1874** Knight 722/1 Double-acting baling-press . . . has two boxes in which the material is compressed.

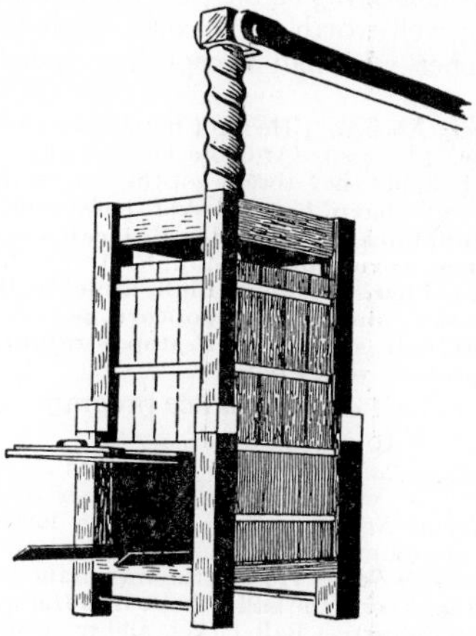

Baler (sense **2**)

(5) **1851** in J. S. Bassett *Plantation Overseer* 189, 1100 yards Coten bagginge; 1000 lbs baling rope. — (6) **1922** *Outing* June 110/2 The time was now come . . . to get out the pack saddles, panniers, rope and baling wire. **1946** Wilson *Fidelity* 181 Guide the clumsy old thing with a plowline or a piece of baling wire.

Balize bə'liz, *n.* [See note.] A small settlement on stilts or piling situated at Pass à la Outre, where lower Mississippi pilots were taken on and discharged.

Balize is Louisiana French for *balise*, beacon, and refers to the original tower erected by Iberville in 1700 at one of the passes of the Mississippi to guide vessels to the river's mouth. Others were afterwards erected and the place grew into a pilots' settlement. About the Civil War period the place fell into decay and has now vanished.

1821 *Olive Branch* (Danville, Ky.) 14 April 3/2 A pilot boat belonging to the Balize, having nine pilots on board, was blown off in the gale. **1882** Buel *Metropolitan Life Unveiled* 583 It is not difficult to account for the low depression and spongy character of the soil about New Orleans, after investigating the formations about the balise. **1942** Sinclair *Port of New Orleans* 267 Because the settlement was the first human thing seen in the Delta by inbound seafarers, vessels for New Orleans were commonly known as 'bound for Balize.'

* **balk,** *n. Baseball.* (See quot. 1887.) Also attrib. See also **claw balk.**

1845 in *Appleton's Ann. Cyclo.* (1886) X. 77/2 A runner can not be put out . . . when a balk is made by the pitcher. **1887** *Lippincott's Mag.* May 839 A *balk* is . . . any motion made by the pitcher to deliver the ball to the bat without delivering it, . . . *and any motion calculated to deceive a base-runner*, except the ball be accidentally dropped. **1913** *Amer. Mag.* Sep. 24/1 Out of the first nine men who reached first base, Kilroy caught seven by his balk motion, and turned their own game against the champions. **1948** *Dly. Ardmoreite* (Ardmore, Okla.) 14 May 8/6 They were disputing a balk called on Pauls Valley Pitcher Chuck Liska.

* **balk,** *v. intr.* Of a baseball pitcher: To make a balk *q.v.*

1857 *Spirit of Times* 26 Dec. 261/2 The pitcher is allowed to baulk as much as he pleases. **1867** *Ball Players' Chron.* 22 Aug. 2/1 In regard to the habit of baulking which Peters has, and must learn to get out of, we have to state that the movement of the foot—such as the lifting of the heel or toe—does not constitute a baulk unless the foot is *entirely* lifted from the ground. **1948** *Dly. Ardmoreite* (Ardmore, Okla.) 19 May 10/1 Willingham balked and Cooke scored with the tying run.

b. *tr.* To deliver (a ball) in a balking manner. *Obs.*

1867 *Ball Players' Chron.* 27 June 6/3 The rule does not state that called or balked balls are 'dead,' but only such balls as are *hit* or struck at. **1867** *Chi. Times* 26 July 5/2 Barker came home on a ball balked by Williams.

balker, *n.* A horse that balks. *Colloq.* — **1898** Westcott *D. Harum* 5 'When you get a balker to dispose of,' said David gravely, 'you can't alwus pick an' choose.'

balkiness 'bɔkɪˌnɛs, *n.* The quality of being balky. *Colloq.*— **1894** *Outing* July 349/1 The mules were the very embodiment of balkiness. **1909** Lincoln *Keziah Coffin* x. 143, I, bein' a Hammond, with some of the Hammond balkiness in me, I set my foot down as hard as his.

* **ball,** *n.*[1]

1. *Baseball.* (See quot. 1916.)

1867 *Ball Players' Chron.* 6 June 2/2 Jewell . . . had his base given him on three balls—the first of the game. **1916** Bancroft *Handbook* 78 Ball. A ball so pitched that it does not pass over the home plate between the height of the batter's knee and shoulder. If it does pass within these limits it is called a 'strike.' **1948** *Chi. Tribune* 1 Feb. II. 51 Is it a ball or a strike?

2. In combs.: (1) **ball alley,** a bowling alley, cf. **c.**(1) below; (2) **gun,** a gun for firing ball cartridges; (3) **patch,** a small piece of cloth or soft leather for inclosing the ball for a muzzle-loading rifle, *obs.;* (4) **roller,** one who participates in rolling a ball in a political parade, *obs.*, cf. *to keep the ball rolling;* (5) **rolling beetle,** a tumblebug; (6) **screw,** a screw attachable to the end of a ramrod for extracting a ball from a muzzle-loading gun, *obs.;* (7) **signal,** designating a railroad station where large balls used as signals are installed, cf. **highball;** (8) **stamp,** (see quot.), *obs.;* (9) **time,** (see quot.), *obs.;* (10) **toter,** a jocose term for a football player especially skilled in carrying the ball; (11) **willow,** (see quot.).

(1) **1831** *Ohio Revised Statutes* I. 448 Any keeper of a public house . . . who shall establish . . . any ball or ninepin alley. — (2) **1897** *Outing* March 567/1, I had changed my single rifle for a double-barreled ball gun. — (3) **1840** *Niles' Reg.* 4 April 74/1 [The] fatal shot . . . must have been near, as the ballpatch was sticking in her head. — (4) **1840** in *Sat. Review* (1941) 19 July 4 This gang of loafers and litterateurs . . . are said to number 1,000 braves, being the picked men of the old 'huge paws'—'butt enders'—'roarers,' and 'ball rollers.'

(5) **1850** S. F. Cooper *Rural Hours* 401 There is an insect very common in the lower parts of the State [of N.Y.], . . . : the ball-rolling beetle, so much resembling the sacred scarabæus of the Egyptians. — (6) **1846** Sage *Scenes Rocky Mts.* ii. 18 Beneath the right arm hangs a powder-horn transversely from his shoulder, behind which, upon the strap attached to it, are affixed his bullet-mould, ball-screw, wiper, awl, etc. — (7) **1864** *Mass. Statutes* lxv, The ball signal station, as it now stands. — (8) **1881** Raymond *Mining Gloss.*, Ball-Stamp, a stamp for crushing rock, operated directly by steam power. — (9) **1876** *Wide Awake* April 262/1 At the Naval Observatory in Washington [D.C., at noon] . . . a huge black ball, which is drawn up a few moments before, descends upon the dome of the Observatory; and hundreds all over the city stand, with watch in hand, to see it drop, to keep, as we say, 'ball time.'

(10) **1928** *Chi. Tribune* 13 Dec. 25/3 Where can you find a sweeter ball toter than Chuck Bennett? — (11) **1897** *Outing* XXIX. 538/1 A low swale filled with grass and a species of willow called locally [in north central states] 'ball' willow.

b. In combs. and derivatives of obvious meaning referring to baseball: (1) **ball club,** (2) **-dom,** (3) **field,** (4) * **game,** cf. **c.** (3) below, (5) **ground,** cf. **c.** (4) below, (6) **nine,** (7) **park,** (8) **player,** cf. **c.** (6) below, (9) **team,** (10) **tosser.**

(1) **1837** J. D. Whitney *Life & Lett.* 20, I can't see where the ball is coming soon enough to put the ball-club in its way. **1845–55** (*title*), Knickerbocker Ball Club. **1947** *Birmingham Age-Herald* 25 April 1/4 The two ball clubs ran up a total of 45 hits. — (2) **1867** *Ball Players' Chron.* 12 Sep. 2/2 His place has been filled by that fine young player, Sewell, who will doubtless make his mark in balldom soon. **1914** *Collier's* 17 Oct. 7/1 It is in this frame of mind that we come to our all-star selection from balldom's cast. — (3) **1867** *Ball Players' Chron.* 13 June 4/2 Let every true lover of the game come to its rescue from the attack made upon it by partizan and ignorant crowds, and let us train up assemblages to good behavior on ball-fields. **1948** *Sat. Ev. Post* 11 Sep. 28/1 The dog was always with him when he showed up at the ball field behind Stevenson's orchard. — (4) **1898** Susan Hale *Lett.* 335 These men were just like . . . Harvard men, after the ball game

has gone right for us. **1946** *Longmont* (Colo.) *Times-Call* 12 June 6/3 He lost his wallet containing $230 while watching a ball game.

(5) **1856** *Spirit of Times* 13 Dec. 245/1 The Club presented their President with an elegant silver Pitcher, with a view of the ball ground carved out upon it. **1917** Mathewson *Sec. Base Sloan* 218 A blue car buzzed past him bearing the legend 'Ball Grounds.' — **(6) 1889** *Gallup* (N.M.) *Gleaner* 18 Mar. 3/1 Where is Gallup's ball nine? — **(7) 1899** *Chicago News* 4 Aug. 6/1 Billy Phyle . . . went out to the ball park to see Burns this morning. **1948** *Sat. Ev. Post* 22 May 146/1 Come out to the ball park with me. — **(8) 1867** (*title*), The Ball Players' Chronicle. **1947** *Redbook* Oct. 100/2 Two of his uncles were bush-league ballplayers. — **(9) 1888** *Outing* July 353/2 Boston had begun to take municipal pride in its seemingly invincible ball-team. **1948** *Dly. Ardmoreite* (Ardmore, Okla.) 19 Apr. 6/5 Joe McCarthy may have a fine collection of players for the Red Sox but he hasn't got a ball team yet.

(10) 1867 *Ball Players' Chron.* 24 Oct. 7/1 The 'veteran ball-tosser' is a marked man, though he may be an indifferent player.

c. In expressions of obvious meaning with reference to Indian ball: (1) **ball alley,** cf. **2.** (1) above, (2) **court,** (3) ∗**game,** cf. **b.** (4) above, (4) **ground,** cf. **b.** (5) above, (5) **play,** (6) **player,** cf. **b.** (8) above, (7) **post,** (8) **stick.**

(1) **1802** Ellicott *Journal* 291 A convenient ball-alley was prepared. — (2) **1937** *Southwestern Lore* Sep. 29 Probably second in importance as an indication of Hohokam Culture is the presence of

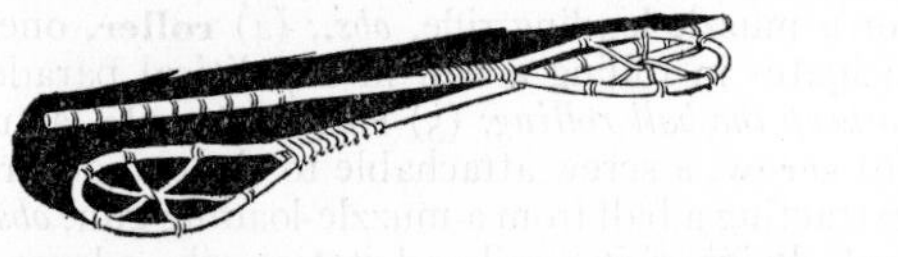

Ball sticks or crosse sticks such as Indians used

ball courts. — **(3) 1849** C. Lanman *Alleghany Mts.* xiii. 100 Since my arrival here the Indians have had one of their ball games. — **(4) 1772** D. Taitt in *Travels Amer. Col.* 546, [I] then went to a Ball ground . . . where the Eutchie and Geehaw people were playing Ball. **1894** *Outing* June 213/1 The ball ground is laid out on a piece of level prairie and is marked by two goal posts about one thousand feet apart.

(5) 1765 Timberlake *Mem.* 79, I was not a little pleased likewise with their ball-plays (in which they shew great dexterity) especially when the women played. *c*1836 Catlin *Indians* II. 124, I rode out . . . to the ball-play-ground of the Choctaws. **1899** Cushman *Hist. Indians* 149 While en route, they unexpectedly came upon a large company of Choctaws assembled for a ball play. — **(6) 1836** Catlin *Indians* II. 125 The most distinguished ball-player of the Choctaw nation represented in his ball-play dress, with his ball-sticks in his hands. **1894** *Outing* June 212 The ball players . . . dashed forward at full speed . . . brandishing their ball sticks. — **(7) 1899** Cushman *Hist. Indians* 185 Pieces of timber were firmly planted together in the ground; these were called amlbi (Ball posts). *Ib.* 230 He could throw a spell or charm . . . over the ball-post. — **(8) 1775** Adair *Amer. Indians* 400 The ball-sticks are about two feet long, the lower end somewhat resembling the palm of a hand, and . . . worked with deer-skin thongs. **1894** [see **ball player**].

3. In phrases: **a.** *ball and chain,* an iron ball and the chain for attaching it to a prisoner's legs to prevent escape. Also (*slang*) transf.

1835 Ingraham *South-West* II. 189 The threat of the Calaboose, or the 'ball and chain.' **1921** *Collier's* 25 June 24/3 He deliberately attempted to commit suicide by askin' me 'How's the ball and chain?' meanin' my wife. **1947** Baskins *Dr. Has Baby* 132 'Where's your ball and chain?' I demanded, as soon as she sat down. 'You mean my beloved daughter?' she laughed. 'In school.'

b. *To keep (set, start) the ball rolling,* to keep, etc., things going or moving in a suitable manner.

Partridge says this expression was established in British use by 1840. The *OED s.v.* "Ball" lists the phrase but gives no evidence of its use. Its currency in this country appears to have begun with the rolling of huge balls in political parades in the presidential campaign of 1840.

1840 *Log Cabin & Hard Cider Melodies* 58 Virginia will keep her ball rolling. **1850** W. Colton *Deck & Port* xiv. 390 That courageous organization . . . set the ball of Anglo-Saxon supremacy rolling in California. **1944** *Chi. D. News* 7 Feb. 1/6 The question now arises as to whether we have, or can acquire, sufficient power to start the ball rolling back in the other direction. **1948** *Sierra Club Bul.* March 66 Certainly no one was better prepared to take an active part in urging the Yosemite grant and to keep the ball rolling.

c. *To keep one's eye on the ball,* to be on the alert, to watch one's step. *Slang* from sports.

1907 in *Screen Book* (1937) 102 We were forever being told 'Keep your eye on the ball.'

d. *To hit the ball,* to work long and well, to go at a lively rate. *Slang.*

Prob. from baseball, but the practice of railroad men of calling the top of the rail "the ball" and of referring to fast trains as "hitting the ball" may account for the expression.

1939 *These Are Our Lives* 300 So, you see, it keeps a man hustling on his toes to make a go of it. You've sure got to hit the ball. **1943** in *Amer. Sp.* XIX. (1944) 35*n.* These grand trains . . . hit the ball at 50 miles an hour.

e. *To play ball with,* to get along with, coöperate with. *Slang.*

1930 Terrett *Only Saps Work* 149 The police of Buffalo are too dumb—it would be redundant, I suppose, to say 'and honest'—to play ball with the hold-up mobs. **1948** *Dly. Ardmoreite* (Ardmore, Okla.) 4 Apr. 1/1 The Americans and British are not playing ball the way the Russians anticipated.

f. *To have something on the ball,* to have special merit, or something well worth while, orig. with reference to a baseball pitcher who had exceptional speed or curves. *Slang.*

1912 *Collier's* 13 April 19/1 He's got nothing on the ball—nothing at all. **1948** *Dly. Ardmoreite* (Ardmore, Okla.) 23 Jan. 4 They've got nothin' on the ball, but they always got the boss on the pan.

As the last term in **barn, base, basket, basswood, bean, black, block, buck and, buckeye, butter, called, cap and, cedar, Chester, clay, coffee, corn, corner, dough, dropped, emery, fair, fish, fly, foul, golden, gum, hat, high, knuckle, line, molasses corn, pass, passed, pin, pitched, popcorn, potato, push, skew, sky, snow, soft, spit, spittle, stick, stop, straight, switch, tea, town, trade, unfair, volley ball.**

∗**ball,** *n.*[2] **1. ball card,** a dance program. **2. ball ticket,** an invitation to a ball.

(1) 1887 A. Daly *Railroad of Love* 65, I found an old ball-card of mine the other day, with his name written six times on it. **1897** Thanet *Missionary Sheriff* 60 Poor Jim Perley fought a duel with Captain Sayre over a misplaced dance on her ball-card. — **(2) 1835** Longstreet *Georgia Scenes* 130 For these assurances they look first to 'the face of the paper,' (the ball-ticket). **1860** *Harper's Mag.* Nov. 789/2 It was an ordination Ball Ticket, and read thus: 'Your company with lady is respectfully solicited at a ball [etc.].'

As the last term in **bachelor, calico, convention, creole, dollar, election, firemen's, forest, gumbo, homespun, inauguration, Jackson, king, silk, stag, union ball.**

∗**ball,** *v.*

1. ∗*To ball up,* (see quot.). *Obs.*

1856 Hall *College Words* (ed. 2) 19 *Ball up,* at Middlebury College, to fail at recitation or examination.

b. To bring into a state of entanglement, confusion, difficulty, etc. *Slang.*

1885 Mark Twain *Letters* (1917) II. xxv. 465 (R.), It will 'ball up' the binderies again. **1923** *Cent. Mag.* Mar. 753/2 His childhood had been tragically 'balled up' by circumstances which had branded him with such a passionate bitterness as I have seldom seen in a man. **1945** *Pueblo* (Colo.) *Chieftain* 18 June 5/5 The V. A. is hard pressed and, if you don't identify yourself thoroly, things are going to get balled up.

2. *To ball and chain,* to place a ball and chain on (a prisoner). *Rare.*

1867 *Harper's Wkly.* 5 Jan. 13/1 He was balled and chained at Macon, and forced to 'mark time' on the head of a barrel.

ballahou, see **ballyhoo.**

Ballard rifle. A once popular single-shot, breech-loading rifle of a type patented by C. H. Ballard in 1851. *Obs.* or *hist.*

1867 *Harper's Mag.* July 138/1 Each of the party had provided himself with a Ballard rifle. **1904** E. S. Farrow *Amer. Small Arms* 134 Ballard Rifle. This excellent American rifle is no longer made, being superseded by the Marlin. It is noted for its simple and effective breech mechanism. **1920** Sawyer *Our Rifles* 253 Ballard rifles, long ago obsolete, were perhaps the most popular single shot sporting rifles of black powder ammunition days.

∗**ballast,** *n.* **1. ballast fin,** a fin-shaped extension of a yacht keel to serve as ballast. **2. ballast stone,** one of the stones used to ballast a vessel. *Obs.*

(1) 1894 *Outing* (U.S.) XXIV. 194/2, I have not a word to say against the ballast-fin so far as racing is concerned. — **(2) 1761** S. Niles *Indian Wars* II. 490 The boat . . . with three Indians came under Captain Beale's stern; who, with small arms and ballast-stones, killed two of them. **1815** *Niles' Reg.* VIII. 140/1 Some of those which went to foreign ports were without cargoes; so that *ballast stones* were humorously 'quoted' in one of the papers . . . , as being in great demand at $150 per ton.

∗**baller,** *n.* =**baseballist.** *Obs.* See also **basket baller.** — **1867** *Ball Players' Chron.* 24 Oct. 7/1 Certain it is that two-thirds of the 'ballers' of to-day carry these marks about their persons.

ballist ˈbɔlɪst, *n.* =**baseballist.** *Obs.* — **1867** *Ball Players' Chron.* 17 Oct. 3/2 Young Rowe, next at the bat, being a young 'ballist,' of course, made a run. **1868** *N. Eng. Base Ballist* (Boston) 27 Aug., The title 'Ballist' is a verbal atrocity and bastard, and ought never to be uttered or printed.

∗**balloon,** *n.*

1. a. (See quot.) **b.** A fraudulent speculative venture. **c.** Short for **balloon frame.** All *obs.* See also **skin balloon.**

(**a**) **1787** *Independent Gazetteer* 24 Feb. 3/1 Continental certificates (or what some term balloons) . . . are those not adopted by any particular state. — (**b**) **1791** Hamilton *Works* (Lodge) VIII. 233 Raise it as high as possible by fictitious purchases, in order to take in the credulous. . . . Others are mounting the balloon as fast as possible. — (**c**) **1855** *Trans. Amer. Inst. N.Y.* 405, I start a balloon from the foundation and finish it to the roof.

2. In combs.: (1) **balloon building,** see **balloon frame,** *obs.;* (2) **car,** a type of horse-drawn streetcar, first built *c*1871, of an oval outline, the upper body turning freely on a stationary supporting truck, now *hist.;*

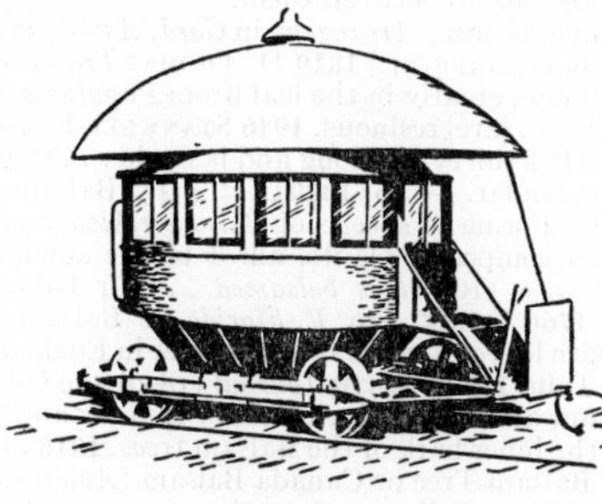

Balloon car

(3) **frame,** a frame for a building made of light materials easily and quickly nailed together, a house having such a frame, also **balloon-frame house, balloon framing,** *obs.;* (4) **hat,** an exceptionally large hat worn by women, *obs.;* (5) **house,** see **balloon frame** and cf. **balloon building,** *obs.;* (6) **sleeve,** a full sleeve drawn in at or near the wrist; (7) **vine,** the heartseed, *Cardiospermum halicacabum,* bearing large inflated pods.

(**1**) **1855** *N.Y. Wkly. Tribune* 27 Jan. 3/5 To erect a balloon-building requires about as much mechanical skill as it does to build a board fence. — (**2**) **1881** Marshall *Through Amer.* (1882) 265 The balloon car is a curious-looking device, reminding one more of a spread-out umbrella than a balloon, though either name would do for it. **1947** *Life* 24 Feb. 14/2 (*caption*), Balloon car of the '60s was the ancestor of the cable car. At the end of the line its horses pivoted its circular body while the wheels themselves remained stationary. — (**3**) **1853** J. W. Bond *Minnesota* 122 A little clump of shanties and balloon-frames in the neighborhood of the 'American house.' **1855** *Trans. Amer. Inst. N.Y.* 394 The balloon framing used in the Western States and California. **1873** Eggleston *Myst. Metrop.* xxxv. 302 When at last he saw the familiar balloon-frame houses. **1910** Burroughs *In Catskills* 58 Now that balloon frames are mainly used for houses, and lighter sawed timbers for barns, the old-fashioned raising is rarely witnessed. — (**4**) **1784** *Mass. Centinel* 3 July 1/1 Millenary . . . now ready for sale . . . consisting of . . . Ladies' Balloon-Hats. (**5**) **1855** *Trans. Amer. Inst. N.Y.* 399, I have seen balloon houses put up, and was very much surprised at the facility, quickness, and strength of them. — (**6**) **1837** *S. Lit. Messenger* III. 3 Women came to the spring for water in great balloon sleeves and prunelle shoes.— (**7**) **1836** Lincoln *Botany* App. 84 Balloon vine [Native of] East Indies. . . . Flowers white and green. **1901** Mohr *Plant Life Ala.*, Balloon Vine . . . [grows in] Louisianian area, South Carolina, Florida, and Texas, [etc.].

balloon, *v.tr.* (See quot. 1870.) Also **ballooning.** — **1854** H. H. Riley *Puddleford* 236 Mr. A. and B. are boating on the Mississippi, or 'ballooning' in some fancy speculation on the north shore of the Oregon. **1870** Medbery *Men & Myst. Wall St.* 134 *Ballooning,* to work up a stock far beyond its intrinsic worth, by favorable stories, fictitious sales, or other cognate means.

∗**ballot,** *n.* In combs.: (1) **ballot box stuffer,** one who puts spurious ballots into a ballot box; (2) **box stuffing,** "a new name for a new crime. This consists in the use of a box . . . so constructed with a false bottom and compartments as to permit the introduction of spurious ballots to any extent by the party having it in charge" (B. '59); (3) **stuffer,** =**ballot box stuffer;** (4) **stuffing,** =**ballot box stuffing.**

(**1**) **1856** *S.F. Bulletin* 3 Apr. 2/2 Does not every shoulder-striker, ballot-box stuffer and thief in the city, *know* he has a warm friend at court in the person of His Honor, James Van Ness. **1910** J. Hart *Vigilante Girl* xix. 264 He is said to be a notorious ballot-box stuffer. — (**2**) **1856** *Alta California* (S.F.) 24 May 2/2 This conclusion had been arrived at after reflecting upon the means used to elect the ticket, and the general disrepute of ballot-box stuffing of late. **1946** *Chi. D. News* 13 April 6/7 We shall lose, and no ballotbox stuffing or vote theft will help us. — (**3**) **1872** *Chi. Tribune* 11 Oct. 4/3 It is not Pennsylvania we have heard from, but merely an organized gang of ballot-stuffers. **1947** *True* Nov. 4/2 Send in your votes; we have an ex-ballot-stuffer on the staff. — (**4**) **1876** Nordhoff *Cotton States* 43/1 This small band of white men . . . have practiced all the basest arts of ballot-stuffing, false registration, and repeating, at election after election.

As the last term in **absentee, Australian, blanket, instructive, joint, Negro, sample, split, state, stuffed ballot.**

ballyhoo ˈbælɪˌhu, *n.* Also **ballahou.** [See note.]

This word has aroused considerable speculation. The senses here shown may all be of different words, since any relationship between them is not clear. Sense **I** is given by *Cent.* and Webster *s.v. ballahou, balahoo,* which they derive from Sp. *balahú,* schooner. In some edition or issue of *Cent.* subsequent to the 1st the Sp. word is suspected of being from Carib *balahua,* sea. See *Amer. Sp.* Dec. 1935, 289–91; Oct. 1945, 184–6.

1. (See quot. 1889.) Also **ballyhoo of blazes.**

1836 *Knickerb.* Aug. 203 Jack Marlinspike, who had been first dickey of an Indiaman, couldn't get a situation afore the mast of a Ballyhoo coasting-brig. **1847** in *Amer. Sp.* XX. (1945) 184 Be off wid ye, thin, darlints, and steer clear of the likes of this ballyhoo of blazes as long as ye live. **1889** *Cent.* 431/1 ballahou. . . . [Prob. of native origin.] 1. A fast-sailing two-masted vessel, rigged with high fore-and-aft sails, much used in the West Indies. The foremast rakes forward, the mainmast aft.—2. A term of derision applied to an ill-conditioned, slovenly ship.

2. ballyhoo bird, (see quot.). *Obs.*

1880 *Harper's Mag.* July 217/1 Another green South-Sider [i.e., a member of the South Side Club on Long Island] was sent in pursuit of birds as remarkable as anything in the mythology of the ancients: they were provided with four wings and two heads, and possessed the wonderful power of whistling through one bill while they sang through the other. Subsequent references to the 'ballyhoo bird' were never relished by the victim of the practical joke.

3. Noisy, sensational publicity, orig. used of the spiel of a barker at a sideshow, blarney, exaggerated praise. *Slang.*

1901 *World's Work* Aug. 1100/2 First there is the ballyhoo—any sort of a performance outside the show, from the coon songs of the pickaninnies in front of the Old Plantation, to the tinkling tamborines of the dancers on the stage of 'Around the World.' **1908** *Sat. Ev. Post* 21 Nov. 25/1 It is the practice of almost every statesman to prepare the country for his performance by beating the drum and blatting a few lines of ballyhoo. **1929** *Variety* 10 July 1/5 One of the greatest institutional ballyhoos for a commercial product conducted on showmanship lines is Catalina Island. **1948** *Sierra Club Bul.* March 84 Moving pictures of scenic travels and winter sports, and good music, would all be in keeping with the spirit of the place, while 'jazz' and 'ballyhoo' are not.

attrib. **1901** *Everybody's Mag.* Oct. 436/2 He got caught in the ebb of the Ballyhoo parade. **1948** *Sat. Ev. Post* 10 July 68/3 Even if the speaker is eventually able to finish, he will have depleted his ballyhoo reserves.

ballyhoo ˈbælɪˌhu, *v.* [f. the noun, sense **3.**] *tr.* and *intr.* To praise extravagantly, to indulge in ballyhoo. Also **ballyhooer,** *n.*, **ballyhooing,** *n.*

1901 *World's Work* Aug. 1100/2 Last of the professions on the Midway are those of the 'barker,' 'ballyhooer' and 'spieler' **1922** *Collier's* 4 March 7/1, I don't like to ballyhoo myself, Mickey, but here's a picture which will make you and Mr. D. Griffith bite your nails. **1924** *Amer. Mercury* Feb. 255/1 Unperturbed by the ballyhooing at other and more pretentious booths, Mrs. Watts continues to do business at the old stand. **1948** *Atlantic Mo.* March 24/1 They are ballyhooed, pushed, yelled, screamed, and in every way propagandized into the consciousness of the voters.

* **balm,** *n.* **1. balm geranium,** a plant not now identifiable. *Rare.* **2.** * **balm of Gilead,** see as a main entry. **3. balm of warrior's wound(s),** the St.-John's-wort.

(**1**) **1839** Mrs. Kirkland *New Home* xx. (1840) 146 A lady to whom I offered a cutting of my noble balm geranium . . . declined the gift. — (**3**) **1907** Lyons *Plant Names* 240 H[ypericum] perforatum . . . St. John, Herb John, Penny-John, Amber, Balm-of-warrior's-wound. **1931** Clute *Plants* 53 The inference is further borne out by its other common names of touch-and-heal and balm-of-warrior's wounds.

As the last term in **bee, horse, Indian, mountain, ox, snake oil balm.**

* **balm of Gilead.**

1. An American tree of the genus *Populus,* esp. the balsam poplar, *P. candicans.*

1784 Cutler in *Mem. Acad.* I. 491 *Populus,* . . . the Black Poplar, commonly called, in the northern states, the Balm of Gilead. **1844** Lee & Frost *Oregon* x. 116 It is a kind of rolling prairie . . . along its rivulets, fringed with the cottonwood or balm of Gilead. **1916** Seton *Woodcraft Man.* 273 Balsam Poplar, Balm of Gilead, or Tacamahac (*Populus balsamifera*).

attrib. **1832** L. M. Child *Frugal Housewife* 26 Balm-of-Gilead buds bottled up in N.E. rum, make the best cure in the world for fresh cuts and wounds. **1887** *Scribner's Mag.* Dec. 731/1 Just . . . pick me a handful o' balm o' Gilead buds. I want to put 'em in half a pint o' new rum.

2. The balsam fir, or the resin obtained from this. Also **balm of Gilead fir.**

1803 Lambert *Descr. Pinus* 48 Balm of Gilead Fir (*Pinus Balsamea.*) Habitat in Virginia, Canada. **1832** Browne *Sylva Amer.* 96 This resin [of the silver fir] is sold in Europe and the United States under the name of Balm of Gilead. **1902** Clapin 35 *Balsam Fir.* . . . The tree itself is also known as *Balm of Gilead,* in imitation of the Eastern terebinth.

b. Also **balm of Gilead (fir) tree.**

1785 Marshall *Amer. Grove* 102 *Pinus-Abies Balsamea.* Balm of Gilead Fir-Tree. **1945** MacDonald *Egg and I* 264 We parked the truck under a large Balm of Gilead tree near the restaurant. **1947** Paul *Linden* 104 The Balm of Gilead tree was twelve feet in diameter, with a spread of more than two hundred feet.

balmony ˈbælmənɪ, *n.* [Var. of **baldmoney.*] The turtlehead or snakehead, *Chelone glabra.* See also **salt balmony, turtle balmony.** — **1842** Mrs. Kirkland *Forest Life* I. 71 We stick to thoroughwort, —balmony,—soot tea,—'number six,'—and the like. **1857** Gray *Botany* 285 Turtle-head, snake-head, . . . *Chelone glabra.* . . . Called also shell-flower, balmony, etc.

baloney bəˈlonɪ, *n.* Also **boloney.** [Prob. f. *Bologna,* sausage.]

1. A contemptuous term for an unskilled prizefighter, a "palooka." *Slang.*

1920 *Collier's* 5 June 10/1 Kane Halliday, alias Kid Roberts, had won his first professional fight by knocking out a boloney with the *nom du ring* of Young Du Fresne. **1925** Witwer *Roughly Speaking* 103 D'ye see *now* what you could of did to that boloney? **1927** *Collier's* 12 Nov. 36/4 Cheez, what d'ye suppose I let a boloney like Burke cut me up for?

2. Bosh, stuff, nonsense. Also attrib. *Slang.*

1928 *Sat. Ev. Post* 28 Nov. 21 Gee, that's a long shot. Boloney! That's not the ball—it's the divot. **1935** *Amer. Sp.* Dec. 318/2 Alfred E. Smith's invention of the phrase 'the baloney dollar' to describe the managed currency of the present administration shows two departures in the use of a common type of slang. **1948** *Chi. D. News* 3 March 46/6 This law is the darndest hunk of baloney ever passed.

balsa ˈbɑlsə, *n.* [Sp. in same sense.] (See quots.) Also attrib.

[**1780** Clavigero *Storia della Messico* II. 168 Oltre alle barche si servivano per valicare i fuimi d'una macchina particolare, appellate *balsa* degli Spagnuoli dell' America.] **1806** Langsdorff *Voyages* (1817) 459 The Indians, are very seldom under the necessity of trusting themselves to the waves, and if such a necessity do occur, they make a sort of boat for the occasion of straw, reeds, and rushes, bound together so close as to be water-tight . . . these sort of boats are called by the Spaniards walza. **1907** Hodge *Amer. Indians* I. 920 The Mohave made no canoes, but when necessary had recourse to rafts, or balsas, made of bundles of reeds. **1948** *Reader's Digest* Jan. 105/1, I was able to float a balsa raft down to the Rio Negro.

b. (See quots.)

1910 *Cent. Mag.* March 765/1 The only hill we saw was in coming up out of the Cocoraqui *arroyo,* which proved to be no hill, but the wall of a *balsa,* or irrigation dam. **1942** Castetter & Bell *Pima & Papago Agric.* 169 At present, a method of irrigation from a *balsa* is employed in several places among the desert Papago. This *balsa* is a sort of embanked reservoir, supplied through a gate which allows water to enter from an arroyo.

* **balsam,** *n.* In combs.: (1) **balsam fir,** an American evergreen tree of the genus *Abies,* cf. **fir balsam;** (2) **hickory,** a species of hickory, *Carya ovalis;* (3) **of Gilead,** (see quots.), *obs.;* (4) **pine,** =**balsam fir;** (5) **poplar,** an American poplar, esp. the tacamahac; (6) **root,** (see quot.); (7) **spruce,** an American tree of the genus *Abies,* properly *A. lasiocarpa,* but also applied to *A. balsamea;* (8) **tree,** any one of various American trees, as the balsam fir or balsam poplar, from which balsam is obtained; (9) **weed,** (see quots.).

(**1**) **1805** J. Ordway in *Wis. Hist. Coll.* XXII. (1916) 274 Saw pitch pine and balsom fer which grow verry tall on the Spring runs and Sides of the mountains. **1947** *Time* 17 Nov. 46/2 In one spot the scrubby balsam firs had been cleared and a power shovel scooped deep into the earth. — (**2**) **1785** Marshall *Amer. Grove* 68 *Juglans alba odorata.* Balsam hickery. . . . The timber . . . is used for axle-trees of carriages, etc., mill coggs and rounds. **1815** Drake *Cincinnati* ii.80 Forest trees . . . of the Miami country . . . [include] Balsam hickory. — (**3**) **1810** Michaux *Arbres* I. 18 Sylvir fir, . . . Fir balsam, . . . [ou] Balsam of Gilead tree (Baumier de gilead). Dénominations également en usage. **1832** Browne *Sylva Amer.* 95 This species of spruce . . . is called Silver Fir, Fir Balsam, and Balsam of Gilead. — (**4**) **1805** Lewis & Clark *Journals* (1904) III. 279 We Continue to put up the Streight butifull balsam pine on our houses. **1878** I. L. Bird *Rocky Mts.* 15 Regal pines, straight as an arrow, with . . . firs and balsam pines filling up the spaces between them.

(**5**) [**1786** J. Abercrombie *Arrangem.* in *Gard. Assist.* 32/1 Tacamahacca, or great balsam poplar.] **1819** D. Thomas *Travels* 93 The true balsam poplar differs greatly in the leaf [from *Populus angulata*]; but the buds of both . . . [are] resinous. **1946** Stanwell-Fletcher *Driftwood Valley* 178 It's thirty feet long and is made . . . from the trunk of a huge balsam poplar. — (**6**) **1889** *Cent.* 434/3 Balsam-root. . . . A name given in California to species of *Balsamorrhiza,* a genus of low, coarse, perennial composite plants, allied to the sunflower. — (**7**) **1847** Wood *Botany* 516 *Abies balsamea.* . . . Fir balsam. Balsam spruce. — (**8**) **1766** Stork *Acc. E.-Florida* 46 Balsam-tree, of the same size and with leaves like the sycamore tree in England, yields the true balsam of Tolu. **1832** Wyeth *Journal* (1899) 159 On the highest point we had snow accompanied with heavy thunder and being out of meat fed upon the inner bark of the Balsam trees. **1916** Seton *Woodcraft Man.* 270 Balsam Tree or Canada Balsam (*Abies balsamea*). — (**9**) **1843** Torrey *Flora N.Y.* I. 25 *Impatiens fulva.* . . . Balsam-weed, Jewel-weed. . . . Common everywhere . . . possess[es] active medicinal properties. **1889** *Cent., Balsam-weed,* a name of the common everlastings . . . , *Gnaphalium decurrens* and *G. polycephalum,* . . . also called 'sweet balsam.'

As the last term in **black, Canada, Canadian, fir, hemlock, mountain, she, white balsam.**

balsamorrhiza ˌbɔlsəməˈraɪzə, *n.* [NL. f. Gr. *balsamon,* balsam +*-rhiza,* root.] (See quots.) — **1845** Wilkes *U.S. Explor. Exped.* IV. 434 The seed of the Balsamoriza (Oregon sunflower), is also used here, being pounded into a kind of meal, which they call mielito. **1919** Wilson *White Indian* 219 Balzamoriza. . . . A species of plant with showy yellow blossoms, and velvety leaves, belonging to the sunflower family. Commonly known as 'spring sunflower.'

* **Baltimore,** *n.* [Family title of the colonial proprietors of Maryland.]

1. Short for: **a. Baltimore oriole. b. Baltimore oyster.** Cf. **Baltimorean, b.**

(**a**) **1808** Wilson *Ornithology* I. 25 Orioles . . . with a few exceptions build pensile nests. Few of them, however, equal the Baltimore in the construction of these receptacles for their young. **1946** Hausman *Eastern Birds* 555 The bird is black and chestnut where the Baltimore is black and orange. — (**b**) **1844** *St. Louis Reveille* 16 Nov. 2/1, Clayton received yesterday, with the *other* eastern comforts, a fresh supply of the 'Baltimores.'

2. In combs.: (1) **Baltimore beauty,** (see quots.); (2) **belle,** (*a*) =**Baltimore beauty,** (*b*) a cultivated variety of the prairie rose having double pink flowers, in full **Baltimore belle rose;** (3) **bird,** =**Baltimore oriole;** (4) **clipper,** a fast sailing vessel of a type developed at Baltimore, now *hist.;* (5) **duck,** the canvas-back duck, *rare;* (6) **flyer,** =**Baltimore clipper,** *obs.;* (7) **hangnest,** =**Baltimore oriole;** (8) **iron,** app. a variety of iron produced at Baltimore, *rare;* (9) **oriole,** an American oriole, *Icterus galbula,* having colors, black and orange, like those of the coat of arms of Lord Baltimore; (10) **oyster,** an oyster from the vicinity of Baltimore, Md.; (11) **plan,** a plan proposed by the Baltimore clearing houses in 1894 to change the conditions under which bank notes were issued, *obs.;* (12) **platform,** a political platform adopted at Baltimore, as that adopted by the National Union party in a convention that met at Baltimore June 7, 1864, and nominated Lincoln and Johnson; (13) **proof,** (see quot.), *rare;* (14) **scarlet,** (see quot.); (15) **schooner,** a schooner built at Baltimore, *obs.;* (16) **stamp,** the make or form characteristic of a Baltimore product, *obs.;* (17) **vine,** (see quot.), *rare.*

(1) [**1828** BERNHARD *Reise* I. 259 Die Gesellschaften in *Baltimore* fand ich ungemein angenehm. . . . Die Damen, zum Theil sehr schön, pflegten zu singen, und sie sangen nich minder vortrefflich.] **1849** A. MACKAY *Western World* I. 105 Baltimore . . . is said to be full of pretty women, a 'Baltimore beauty' being a sort of proverbial expression. **1871** *Lippincott's Mag.* July 15/1 Being delicate, often fragile, spirituelle, sensitive, emotional, nervous, one might imagine for the Baltimore Beauty a fatality of early fading. — (2) (*a*) **1865** SALA *Diary* II. 350 'Lady,' indeed, is a term which the indignant

Baltimore clipper

loyalists refuse to apply to a Baltimore belle. 'Secesh woman' is good enough for her. (*b*) **1890** *Cent.* 5229/2 Here belong the prairie-rose, . . . the queen-of-the-prairies, Baltimore belle, etc., and the evergreen, Ayrshire, musk, many-flowered, and Banksian stocks. **1938** DAMON *Grandma* 88 A woman sitting in a barrel-stave hammock near a spouting fountain of Baltimore Belle roses. — (3) **1669** SHRIGLEY *Relation* 4 Fowle naturally to the Land are . . . Pidgions, Larks, Redbirds, the Baltenore [*sic*] bird, being black and yellow, blew Birds, mocking Birds, Woodpickers, and many sorts more. **1709** LAWSON *Carolina* 145 The Baltimore-Bird. . . . They are the Bigness of a Linnet, with yellow Wings, and beautiful in other Colours. **1917** *Birds of Amer.* II. 258. — (4) **1824** W. N. BLANE *Excursion* 33 At this port [Baltimore] are built those long sharp schooners, celebrated under the name of Baltimore Clippers. These vessels, which were once considered to sail faster than any in the world, are now surpassed by the New York pilot boats. **1946** *Sat. Ev. Post* 11 May 55/3 They built hundreds of the famous Baltimore clippers.

(5) **1835** in *Amer. Sp.* XVIII. 120 Baltimore Ducks. Eine Gattung Enten, die in der Chesapeak-Bay gefangen und erlegt werden. — (6) **1814** *Niles' Reg.* VI. 175/2 With many vessels of war lying in the Chesapeake Bay, 19 out of 20 of our 'Baltimore flyers' have passed safely! — (7) **1844** J. P. GIRAUD *Birds L.I.* 142 Baltimore Hangnest, or Oriole . . . is not very abundant on Long Island. **1853** SITGREAVES *Exped. Zuni & Colo. Rivers* 79 The Baltimore Hangnest [is] . . . common in the Indian territory. — (8) **1744** *Md. Hist. Mag.* XXI. 248, I hope . . . that altho it be not of the Baltimore Iron yet I may have the same Price for it. — (9) [**1771** JOHN R. FORSTER *Cat. Animals of N.A.* 10 Oriole Redwing, Oriolus Phoeniceus Baltimore, O. Baltimorus.] **1808** WILSON *Ornithology* I. 23 Baltimore Oriole . . . is generally known as the Baltimore bird. **1947** *Collier's* 29 Mar. 91/2 When you listen to the clear spring call of the Baltimore oriole, *here, here, look right here, here,* you hear a blackbird.

(10) **1887** *City of Balt., Half Century's Progress* 46 Baltimore oysters were already renowned, and probably will ever remain so. — (11) **1895** *Cong. Rec.* App. 8 Jan. 169/1 Those who venture to argue that the Baltimore plan is good, because the present system of national banking has proved so under the stress of thirty years' experience are even further astray. — (12) **1859** *Harper's Mag.* April 688/1 Aaron V. Brown, Postmaster-General . . . was chairman of the committee for constructing the 'Baltimore Platform.' **1866** *Cong. Globe* 5 May 2406/3, I desire to present here the Baltimore platform upon which Andrew Johnson was elected. — (13) **1850** BILL *Trip* 231 They have a distillery on the farm, where whiskey is produced from apples, the process of making which I witnessed; it is repeated until it is concentrated to 'Baltimore proof,' when it sells for 25 cents a gallon, but will pay at 20. — (14) **1862** *Rep. Comm. Patents: Agric.* 186 Baltimore Scarlet, . . . and Burr's New Pine are good early strawberries.

(15) **1818** PALMER *Journal* 27 Baltimore schooners are allowed to be the first in the world. — (16) **1815** *Niles' Reg.* VIII. 40/1 She appears to be a schooner of the 'Baltimore stamp.' — (17) **1867** W. H. DIXON *New America* II. 85 Next come a host of gardens, in which the Baltimore vine runs joyously up poles and along espaliers.

See also **bastard Baltimore.**

Baltimorean ˌbɔltəˈmorɪən, *n.* A resident of Baltimore, Md.

1816 U. BROWN in *Md. Hist. Mag.* X. 280 Baltimoreans, look; Land selling in the middle of the Alleghany Mountains. **1898** ATHERTON *Californians* 316 Rose went East and triumphantly captured a Baltimorean of distinguished lineage and depleted exchequer. **1947** *Time* 29 Dec. 31/2 Baltimoreans, observing their city's 150th anniversary, nominated their greatest citizen.

b. =**Baltimore oyster.** Cf. **Baltimore 1. b.** *Obs.*

1844 *St. Louis Reveille* 22 Nov. 2/1 He has, at the same time, received a magnificent shipment of the *Baltimoreans.*

* **bamboo,** *n.*

1. Short for next. Also **bamboo vine.**

1709 LAWSON *Carolina* 101 The small Bamboo is . . . a certain Vine, . . . growing in low Land. . . . Their Root is a round Ball, which the Indians boil . . . and eat them. **1853** P. PAXTON *Yankee in Texas* 22 [I aided] his rude attempts at road-making whenever a mass of bull-brier or bamboo-vines . . . called for action. **1934** *Nat. Geog. Mag.* LXV. 602 The 'hoorah bushes,' sweet gallberries, and other shrubs are interlaced with the thorny vines of 'bamboo' or smilax.

2. bamboo brier, *S.* an American climbing plant of the genus *Smilax.* See also **bay bamboo.**

1835 LONGSTREET *Ga. Scenes* 74 This came . . . over me, like a rake of bamboo briers. **1945** *Democrat* 4 Jan. 2/2 His progress was slowed up by a multitude of bamboo briers.

* **bamboozle,** *v.* **1.** *tr.* To hustle in various directions. **2.** (See quot.) Both *obs.* — (1) **1833** S. SMITH *Major Downing* 130 The President [was] . . . bamboozled about from four o'clock in the morning till midnight, . . . and then . . . jammed into Funnel Hall two hours. — (2) *a***1856** HALL *Coll. Words* 461 The various words and phrases . . . in use, at one time or another, to signify some stage of inebriation [include]: . . . shot in the neck, bamboozled, weak-jointed.

bamboula bʊmˈbulə, *n.* [f. Creole F. in sense shown here.] A primitive drum of bamboo, a dance performed to the beating of this. Also attrib. — **1883** *Cent. Mag.* Nov. 45/2 In New Orleans . . . a minute's walk . . . will bring you to Congo square . . . where the negro slaves once held their bamboulas. *Ib.,* Every Sunday afternoon the bamboula dancers were summoned to a wood-yard on Dumaine street. **1947** TALLANT *Voodoo in N.O.* 19 Here, while the white people gaped through the picket fence, they performed the Calinda and the Bamboula.

* **banana,** *n.*

1. The seed of a variety of cotton. In full **banana seed.** *Obs.*

1848 in TURNER *Cotton* (1865) 106 The Banana seeds are held at $100 per bushel, and no less than a peck can be sold by written agreement. **1849** *Rep. Comm. Patents: Agric.* (1850) 149 Cotton.—There have been some new varieties of seed introduced in this section, the banana and the sugar-loaf. **1850** in TURNER *Cotton* (1865) 110 The Banana seed of October, 1848, I saw. I culled a few seeds, and planted in 1849. I pronounced them identical with Hogan, and they were.

2. In combs.: (1) **banana belt,** a term used by railroad men in the Northwest to designate a region in the southern part of their territory where the temperature is relatively mild; (2) **boat,** a boat engaged in the banana trade; (3) **hole,** (see quot.); (4) **line,** the Atchison, Topeka and Santa Fe Railroad, in allusion to its handling of banana shipments from the west coast of Mexico into Santa Fe, *obs.;* (5) **split,** a dish served at soda fountains consisting essentially of a split banana and ice cream; (6) **steamer,** =**banana boat;** (7) **water lily,** a yellow water lily, *Nymphaea mexicana,* found in the southern states.

(1) **1898** *Cent. Mag.* Oct. 840/1 The glittering prospectuses that used to invite the world to come to the 'banana belt' of the Dakotas are not now . . . circulated by the millions. **1948** *Railroad Telegrapher* May 280/1 Tony Mancinni [is] all smiles these days, he's headed for the banana belt. — (2) **1916** W. A. DU PUY *Uncle Sam* 119 The skipper of the banana boat and Peterson, the smuggler, held a conference. **1948** *Chi. Tribune* 23 May (Grafic Mag.) 22/1 The big banana boat was due at 5. — (3) **1944** BARBOUR *Eden* 163 Scattered through al-

most all of these areas [in Fla.] are rocky sinks, usually not more than six or eight feet deep. . . . When the areas are burned off or cleared off these sinks usually become what are known as 'banana holes.' — (4) **1882** RADGES *Topeka Dir.* 124a, Along the route of the Great Banana Line, the Atchison, Topeka & Santa Fe Railroad.

(5) **1931** *Tulsa D. World* 15 Dec. 7/3 (*advt.*) Soda Fountain. . . . Banana Split 15¢. **1948** *Antioch Review* Spring 90 She had a maple walnut sundae and he had a banana split. — (6) **1894** *Harper's Wkly.* 21 Apr. 366/3 Unloading a banana steamer. — (7) **1926** *La. Dept. Conservation Rep. 1924–26* 144 Duckweeds, leafy pondweed and banana waterlily are most important.

As the last term in **American, Kansas, Mexican, Missouri banana.**

banco ˈbɑŋko, *n. Texas.* [Sp. in same sense.] A bank of sand or silt in a river. — **1888** *Cong. Rec.* 23 Sep. 8937/1 Sometimes the stream will suddenly cut a new channel, . . . and . . . a tract or 'banco' of a hundred acres will be found to be on the other side of the river. *Ib.*, Some bancos increase by deposit; some wear away till they are entirely swept off. **1941** FERGUSSON *Southwest* 64 The erratic habits of the Rio Grande and the Colorado which are always cutting *bancos* off one country and delivering them to the other, necessitate constant adjustments.

* **band,** *n.*

1. *W.* A herd or drove of animals.

1823 W. H. KEATING *Narr.* 395 The term *band*, as applied to a herd of buffalo, has almost become technical, being the only one in use in the west. **1868** *Overland Mo.* Nov. 443/2 The sheaves of grain were thrown on the ground, and a 'band' of 'mustangs' turned in to trample out the grain. **1946** *Outdoor Life* Oct. 37/1 The first year the road was cut through it was not uncommon to see moose, a few sheep, and sometimes bands of caribou.

2. A number of tobacco leaves or shingles tied up or packed together, a bundle.

1863 *Ill. Agric. Soc. Trans.* V. 668 The [tobacco] plants . . . are given to others, who strip off the remaining leaves, and tie them in bands of six or eight leaves. **1865–6** *Ib.* VI. 647 It is recommended that . . . bunches of shingles be packed in bands twenty (20) inches in length.

3. A light aluminum strip, bearing an appropriate address, used in tagging birds for studying their range, migrating habits, etc.

1914 *Country Life* July 36/2 These up-to-date bands are made in eight different sizes, some one of which is sure to fit the bird you wish to tag. **1948** *Auk* Jan. 88 It appears that credit belongs to our subject for the plan of establishing a central office for issuing bands and maintaining records.

4. In combs.: (1) * **bandbox,** see as a main entry; (2) **iron,** strap iron; (3) **man,** a bandsman, *rare;* (4) **mill,** a mill driven by a band or belt; (5) **playing,** ostentatious display, fanfare; (6) **saw,** a saw in the form of a narrow, flexible steel band which passes over and is driven by two large wheels, also **band-saw mill;** (7) **tail, -tailed pigeon,** a wild pigeon somewhat resembling the extinct passenger pigeon; (8) **wagon,** see as a main entry.

(2) **1866** *Internal Revenue Guide* 104 On band, hoop and sheet iron, . . . a tax of five dollars per ton. **1872** HUNTINGTON *Road-Master's Assistant* 28 It is a good plan to take hoop or band iron, 1 inch or 1½ inches wide. — (3) **1886** E. W. HOWE *Moonlight Boy* 76 Preparing music, and training an occasional band man who found time to come to him. — (4) **1823** JAMES *Exped.* I. 71 These corn mills are called band-mills. **1857** *Ill. Agric. Soc. Trans.* II. 314 Coeval with the band mill was the large wheel with cogs, drawn by horses.

(5) **1915** *Lit. Digest* (N.Y.) 21 Aug. 337/2 There has been no howl about impending calamity, no call to arms, no band-playing or trumpets blowing. — (6) **1864** WEBSTER *s.v. Saw.* **1874** KNIGHT 226/2 One advantage of the band-saw over the reciprocating saw. **1941** ALLEY *Random Thoughts* 489 The object for the establishment of this smaller plant being to manufacture furniture from the waste lumber left by the several great band sawmills then in operation. — (7) **1823** JAMES *Exped.* II. 10 This species . . . differs [from the ring-tailed pigeon] in the colour of the legs and bill. . . . It may be distinguished by the name of band-tailed pigeon. **1896** *Land of Sunshine* Dec. 18 The pigeon is called the Band-tail, from a dark band across the tail about the middle. **1946** *Mazama* Dec. 33/1 The band-tailed pigeon and the mountain beaver are two forms of wildlife that seem to prefer the west side.

b. *To beat the band,* (to do something) in a lively or excessive manner. *Colloq.*

1897 FLANDRAU *Harvard Episodes* 223, I was on the box-seat driving, you know,—lickety-split, to beat the band. **1911** SAUNDERS *Col. Todhunter* v. 64 I'm . . . primed for a campaign that'll . . . set 'em to whoopin' things up for you to beat the band. **1931** *K.C. Star* 28 Sep., Herman Levison . . . was at church Monday night praying to beat the band.

As the last term in **bird, breast, callithumpian, Canadian, citizen, crawfish, Danite, Destroying, Eastern, gin, head, minstrel, prairie, praying, river, rumba, saloon, shearing, sheet iron, Sioux, social, Spartan, sub, sweat, tail band.**

* **band,** *v.*

1. *tr.* (See quot. 1902.)

1878 B. F. TAYLOR *Between Gates* 266, I leave him to 'band' his sheep and herd his bees as he pleases. **1902** CLAPIN 36 In prairie parlance, *to band* means to form, to assemble cattle, sheep, into vast flocks.

2. To attach an identifying band to the leg of a bird in studying its range, habits, etc. Also * **banding,** *n.* Cf. **bird banding.**

1914 *Lit. Digest* 17 Jan. 102/2 Last year over 150 young American and snowy egrets were banded. **1937** *Bird Lore* Jan.–Feb. 84/2 After all, banding is only *one* of the methods of studying birds. **1948** *Nat. Hist.* Apr. 173/3 In a single season, 3000 ducks were banded.

bandannaed bænˈdænəd, *a.* Covered with a bandanna. *Colloq.* — **1831** Peck *Guide* 62 Negresses [in New Orleans] . . . carrying on their bandanaed heads . . . a whole table . . . covered with goodies.

bandanna turban. A bandanna fashioned into a turban-like headdress, formerly much worn by Negro women in the South. — **1869** ALDRICH *Bad Boy* ii. (1877) 16 Aunt Chloe . . . buried her face in the bright bandana turban. **1898** PAGE *Red Rock* 23 An old mammy in a white apron, with a tall bandanna turban around her head.

* **bandbox,** *n. To look as if one had just stepped out of a bandbox,* and variants, to look exceptionally tidy or dressed up. *Colloq.* See also **Saratoga bandbox.**

1825 WOODWORTH *Forest Rose* I. i, Why, he is a genteel, delightful looking fellow, neat as a starched tucker fresh from a banbox [*sic*]. **1833** *Knickerb.* I. 198 The old gentleman . . . popped into the room, looking as if he had stepped out of a bandbox. **1931** *K.C. Star* 28 July, My wife keeps me looking as though I had just stepped from a bandbox.

* **banded,** *a.* In combs.: (1) **banded drum,** the drumfish, *Pogonias cromis,* in its immature stage; (2) **gurnard,** an American gurnard, *Prionotus strigatus,* more commonly known as striped gurnard; (3) **leaf roller,** (see quot.), *rare;* (4) **rattlesnake,** the timber rattlesnake, a species common in the eastern and central states; (5) **woodpecker,** a woodpecker of the genus *Picoides.*

(1) **1842** *Nat. Hist. N.Y., Fauna* IV. 83 The Banded Drum, *Pogonias fasciatus*, . . . [has] four dusky bands over the body. — (2) **1842** *Nat. Hist. N.Y., Zoology* IV. 45 The banded gurnard is seldom eaten as food. — (3) **1877** *Vt. Bd. Agric. Rep.* IV. 146 One of the leaf-rollers is not uncommon, that called the Banded Leaf-roller. — (4) **1832** JAMES *Exped. Rocky Mts.* I. 267 *Crotalus horridus*, Banded rattlesnake. **1944** *Mass. Audubon Soc. Bul.* Dec. 262 The eight species of poisonous snakes found in the region under discussion are coral snake, copperhead, water moccasin, and five rattlers—massasauga, pigmy, diamond-back, banded, and canebrake rattlesnakes.

(5) **1844** *Nat. Hist. N.Y., Zoology* II. 191 The Banded Woodpecker, *Picus Hirsutus*, . . . is a rare northern species.

bandido bænˈdido, *n. S.W.* [Sp. in same sense.] A bandit or outlaw. — **1898** C. F. LUMMIS *Awakening of a Nation* 4 (Bentley), By every country road—even into the very heart of cities—the bandido robbed and murdered. **1928** DOBIE *Vaquero* 60 (Bentley), One issue . . . reported the following items from the lower country all pertaining to bandidos.

bandowzer bænˈdaʊzɚ, *n.* [Origin unknown.] A severe blow. *Slang. Obs.* — **1833** W. J. SNELLING *Exposé of Gaming* 26 We expected to see the man get a bounce on the nose, a dough bat, or a bandowzer.

band-wagon.

1. A large wagon, usu. ornamented and high, with a deck to seat bandsmen, as in a circus parade.

1855 BARNUM *Life* 205 At Vicksburg we sold all our land conveyances excepting four horses and the 'band wagon.' **1905** *N.Y. Ev. Post* 21 Oct. 1 Jerome's band wagon began to move over the town to-day. It bears on its sides announcements of these mass meetings on Monday night.

2. Used fig., esp. in the sense of a vehicle carrying political candidates, leaders, etc. forward to overwhelming victory at the polls. Also attrib.

1893 *Cong. Rec.* 25 Aug. 897/1 It is a lamentable fact that . . . our commercial enemy . . . should come along with a band wagon loaded with hobgoblins. **1906** in *N.Y. Ev. Post* 5 Sep. 4 Many of those Democrats . . . who rushed into the Bryan band-wagon . . . will now be seen crawling out over the tailboard. **1948** *Time* 22 March 22/2 In New Hampshire there was no real bandwagon enthusiasm for either.

b. Often in phrases with reference to joining a popular and apparently winning side or movement. *Colloq.*

1931 Reeve *Golden Age Crime* 58 The next serious outbreak was a three-cornered affair between the gangs of Joe Saltis (who had recently hopped on the Capone band-wagon) and 'Dingbat' O'Berta. **1948** *Time* 10 May 23/2 In the 1940 convention, Pennsylvania had made a celebrated boner by waiting too long to hop on the Willkie bandwagon.

***bandy,** *a.* **1. bandy porgy,** the spadefish of the eastern coast of the U.S. **2. bandy-shanked,** (see quot. 1908).

(1) 1883 Goode *Fishery Industries* 70 A station for the artificial propagation of . . . the Spanish mackerel . . . and the bandy porgy. — **(2) 1845** Hooper *Suggs* (1928) 81 'Go to h—l! you d—d old bandy-shanked red-skin!' shouted back Simon. **1908** *D.N.* III. 289 Bandy-shanked, *adj.* Having thin crooked shanks, bowlegged.

bang bæŋ, *n.* [The source in sense **1** is **beignet.** For sense **2** cf. **bang,** *v.*[2]] **1.** (See quot.) *Obs.* **2.** The front hair cut short and worn down over the forehead. Usu. *pl.*

(1) 1869 *Robert Kennicott's Journals* 200 For supper we had a rib of a large caribou roasted, and some 'bangs'—cakes made by frying a batter of flour, white-fish roe, and water in tallow. —**(2) 1880** Howells *Undisc. Country* viii. 113 When one lifted his hat . . . he showed his hair cut in front like a young lady's bang. **1883** *Harper's Mag.* Dec. 111/2 Miss Patty . . . [ran] her fingers over her 'bangs'—a very poor name for the lovely golden masses of wavy hair shading her brow and eyes. **1947** *Downtown Shop. News* (Chicago) 13 Feb. 2/3 Bangs are the most young-making hairstyle that has yet been found.

***bang,** *v.*[1] **1.** *To bang the bush,* see **bush. 2.** *To bang away,* to fire at, shoot. *Colloq.* — **(2) 1840** Dana *Two Years* xxxvi. 452 The watch on deck were banging away at the guns every few minutes. **1931** *K.C. Star* 29 Sep., If some men had been with the shepherds when the angels sang 'Glory to God in the Highest,' their first impulse would have been to grab a shotgun and bang away at the heavenly messengers.

***bang,** *v.*[2] *tr.* To cut (the hair) so as to form bangs. Also **banged,** *a.*

The relationship between this *v.* and **bang** *n.* **2** above is not clear. The *OED* derives the *v.* from the *n.*, Webster derives the *v.* from *bang, adv.*, and gives no source for the *n.* The evidence at present available for the *v.* is slightly earlier than for the *n.*

1878 B. F. Taylor *Between Gates* 171 A Digger Indian's papoose, with . . . hair cat-black and 'banged.' **1881** *Harper's Mag.* June 110/1 The old woman with the big bags under her eyes . . . a-askin' you to bang her hair, sir! **1941** in Clark *Elegant Eighties* xix, My hair was banged and fell in a thick mat over my brow.

***banged up.** *a.* Damaged by rough treatment. — **1886** *Harper's Mag.* June 107 Even the trig, irreproachable commercial drummer actually looks banged up and nothing of a man. **1886** E. L. Dorsey *Midshipman Bob* II. vii. 172 Then Young dragged himself on those banged up legs ever so far . . . to the Life-Saving Station.

***banger,** *n.* Formerly at Yale "a club like a cane or stick; a bludgeon" (Hall). Also attrib. See also **slam banger.**

1846 (*title*), The Yale Banger. **1853** *Yale Lit. Mag.* XIX. 2 (Th.), He is prone to sport a huge stick, suggestively called a 'Yale Banger.' **1871** L. H. Bagg *At Yale* 257 This challenge is accepted by the Sophomores and in the evening a 'banger rush' takes place. **1906** *Springfield W. Republican* 10 May 1 He has . . . rescued from some museum . . . his old 'banger' of student days.

***bangtail,** *n.* A horse, esp. a race horse. *Slang.* — **1921** *Collier's* 27 Aug. 20/2 If by some miracle the bangtail wins—beat it! That was Dopey's graft. **1947** *Sat. Ev. Post* 14 June 12/2 For centuries, bangtails have been drugged on occasion to make them run faster.

***bang-up,** *a.* and *n.*

1. *a.* (See quots.) *Obs.*

1825 Paulding *J. Bull in Amer.* x. 116 The driver being at length 'prime bang up,' that is to say, as drunk as a lord. **1854** O. Optic *In Doors & Out* (1876) 98 The other person, who to use his own classic expression, was 'bang up,' and wanted to borrow fifty dollars. *Ib.* 105, I am 'bang up.' I have got a note of four hundred to pay [etc.].

2. *n.* (See quot.) *Obs.*

1835 Abdy *Journal* III. 65 The road was hilly and bad; great part of it being what is vulgarly called 'corduroy,' or 'bang-up,' or 'railroad.' The term alludes to the planks or rails, which are placed transversely; so that the road presents the appearance of that sort of stuff which, in honor of some monarch, announces to the world that his majesty once deigned to have his inexpressibles made of it—(corde-du-roi).

banjo ˈbændʒo, *n.* Earlier **bangil, banjor, banger,** etc. [See note.]

Usu. explained as developing from a Negro mispronunciation of **bandore,* but this view is prob. in error. In *Amer. N. & Q.* July, 1946, 58, the view is given that the instrument and its name are both of African origin. The instrument became known to Europeans in the West Indies, and was early regarded as of African origin. The word undoubtedly passed into American use as a result of slavery.

1. A stringed musical instrument, usu. of five strings, having a neck like a guitar and a body like a tambourine, and played by plucking. See also **calabash banjo, Joey.**

1740 *Hist. Jamaica* 310 They have other Musical Instruments, as a *Bangil,* not much unlike our Lute in any thing but the Musick. **1774** Cresswell *Journal* 30 A great number of young people met together [in Va.] with a Fiddle and Banjo played by two Negroes, with plenty of Toddy. **1781–2** Jefferson *Notes Va.* (1787) 150 The instrument proper to them [*sc.* Negroes] is the Banjor, which they brought hither from Africa. **1841** E. R. Steele *Summer Journey* 210 The negro banjo . . . echoed from the lower deck. **1948** *New Yorker* 25 Sep. 23/2 The banjo, . . . out of vogue in the thirties, is now, like knickers, making an unexpected and vigorous comeback.

attrib. **1841** *N.O. Picayune* 1 Jan. 2/3 'Crichton the Admirable' . . . will be again performed to-night for the benefit of Mr. Sweeney, the unrivalled Banjo Player. **1947** *This Week Mag.* 16 Aug. 21/2 Last evening, Daddy, his nerves humming like banjo strings, crawled into his retreat.

2. a. banjo clock, a clock the shape of which suggests that of a banjo. **b. banjo drum,** (see quot.). *Obs.*

(a) 1932 *Old-Time N.Eng.* Jan. (cover) 4 Presentation Banjo Clock by Aaron Willard. **1945** Adams *Album of Amer. Hist.* II. 110 The 'Banjo Clock' was invented by Simon Willard or his brother, Aaron, in 1802.

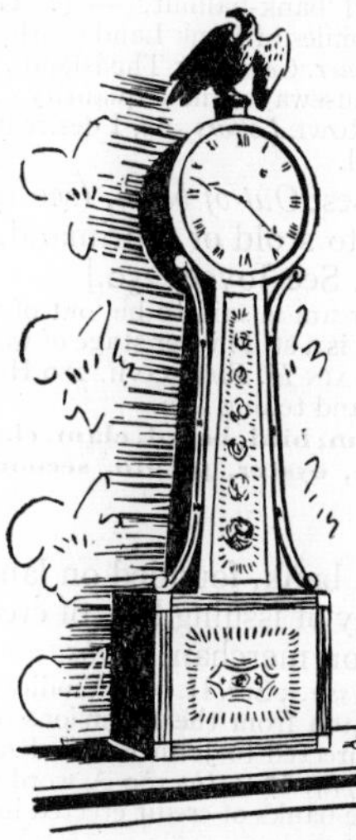

Banjo clock

— **(b)** *c***1824–38** G. Furman *Antiquities L.I.* 268 The music which usually accompanied this dance was the 'banjo drum,' formed of a hollow log, with a skin of parchment stretched over one end, the other being left open, on which they beat with a stick, making a rough, discordant sound.

banjorine ˌbændʒəˈrin, *n.* [f. **banjo.**] (See quot.) — **1907** *Sears Cat.* (ed. 117) 239/2 Banjorines are now used very extensively by all the best and up to date banjo clubs and orchestras. It is tuned one-fourth higher than the regular instrument, and takes the leading part, same as the flute or oboe in an orchestra.

***bank,** *n.*[1]

1. In lumbering, a place, usu. on the bank of a stream, where logs are piled awaiting further transportation.

1829 J. Mactaggart *Three Years* I. 241 The Shantymen . . . cut down the pine trees, . . . and afterwards draw the logs to what is termed the *bank,* with oxen. **1902** White *Blazed Trail* xiii. 91 An outline of the process after the logs have been piled on the banks.

b. *S.* A conical heap or pile of stored sweet potatoes covered with straw, earth, etc.

1837 Jacob D. Wheeler *Practical Treatise* 202 It appeared the slave was stealing potatoes from a bank near the defendant's house. **1856** Davis *Farm Bk.* 12 The Bank of cut potatoes was first used up but the cook failed to get all a few were left covered up in dirt.

c. *pl.* A colloq. shortening of "Newfoundland Banks."

1886 Bynner *Agnes Surriage* 48 Most of these loungers had been in younger days members of his congregation, who had graduated after their first trip 'to the Banks.'

2. In combs.: (1) **bank barn,** (see quot. 1942); (2) **beaver,** (see quots.); (3) **blasting,** *W.* ?the application of an explosive to a bank to facilitate mining operations; (4) **cellar,** ?a cellar which utilizes a bank or slope; (5) **diggings,** *W.* a place on a stream bank where gold is mined, cf. **diggings;** (6) **halibut,** (see quot.); (7) **land,** land along a bank, *rare;* (8) **meadow,** a meadow on the bank of a stream, *rare;* (9) **oil,** "menhaden oil" (*Cent.*).

(1) **1894** *Cong. Rec.* Jan. 1036/1 On my father's farm, when I was a boy, there stood a big bank-barn. **1942** Warnick *Dialect Garrett Co., Md.* 3 Bank-barn, n., barn built on the side of a hill with entrances to two floors from the ground. — (2) **1903** *Outing* Mar. 669/1 You find the bank beaver mostly on lakes, or large rivers, which they are unable to dam. **1943** Cahalane *Meeting the Mammals* 94 Occasionally, in swift rivers that would wash out the dam, or where the water level does not fluctuate and a dam is unnecessary, Castor lives in a bank den instead, and is called a 'bank beaver.' — (3) **1877** Raymond *Rep. Mines* 56 Bank-blasting is practiced. **1882** *Rep. Precious Metals* 627 The system of 'bank-blasting' generally in vogue. — (4) **1931** *Randolph Enterprise* (Elkins, W.Va.) 9 April 2/2 Charley Hart is putting a commodious bank cellar under his new house.

(5) **1852** *Mt. Echo* (Downieville, Calif.) 19 June 2/2 The Bank Diggins and sluicing claims at . . . ' bars in our vicinity are paying good wages. **1856** *Hutchings Mag.* Nov. 199/2 The 'bank' diggings pay regularly very good wages. — (6) **1883** Goode *Fish. Indust.* 51 These vessels salt down in their holds the Halibut which they obtain, and on their return it is smoked, producing smoked Halibut of the choicest kind—the so-called 'bank-halibut.' — (7) **1797** *Wilmington* (N.C.) *Gaz.* 8 June, Seven miles of Bank Land south of Cabbage-Inlet. — (8) **1789** Morse *Amer. Geog.* 295 The island . . . has four entrances over bridges and causeways, and a quantity of bank meadow adjoining. — (9) **1760** J. Rowe *Letters* 369, I desire it [=oil] may be of the pale sort or bank oyl.

b. In colloq. phrases: *Out of bank,* (see quot.), *to give (one) down the banks,* to scold or reprimand. [This use is said to be an Irishism. See Joyce, 250.]

1859 Bartlett 365 A stream is said to be 'out of ride' when it is past fording; 'out of bank,' is a still higher stage of water, i.e. over its banks. — **1884** Mark Twain *H. Finn* xxvii. 280 He give me down the banks for not coming and telling him.

As the last term in **berm, bird, board, clam, clay, coal, continental, cut, half, mine, oyster, potato, second, strawberry, thatch bank.**

* **bank,** *n.*[2]

1. *bank of credit,* a bank, founded on land as security and having a monopoly of issuing bills of credit, proposed in 1700 by some Boston merchants. *Obs.*

1714 in *Pub. Am. Econ. Assn.* 3 Ser. II. 90 A Vindication of the bank of credit projected in Boston from the aspersions of Paul Dudley, Esq., in a letter by him directed to John Burril, Esq., late speaker. . . . Printed in the year 1714. **1721** *Ib.* 100 A word of comfort to a melancholy country, or the banks of credit erected in the Massachusetts Bay.

2. In combs.: (1) **bank accommodation,** financial accommodation or help furnished by a bank; (2) **agent,** an agent or representative of a bank; (3) **capital,** the capital or aggregate of capital invested in banks; (4) **check,** an order issued on or by a bank to pay a designated amount, also attrib.; (5) **commissioner,** a commissioner charged with the supervision of banks; (6) **company,** a company organized to conduct banking operations; (7) **district,** the district served by a particular bank; (8) **draft,** a form of currency issued by the U.S. Bank and its branches and receivable in payment of public revenues, *obs.;* (9) **examiner,** (see quot. 1935); (10) **hours,** the hours when a bank is open for business; (11) **lock,** a lock used upon bank vaults; (12) **man,** (*a*) a man who favored the U.S. Bank in its contest with President Jackson, (*b*) =**bank robber,** *slang;* (13) **merger,** a merger (*q.v.*) affecting banks; (14) **messenger,** one who delivers messages, runs errands, etc. for a bank; (15) **monger,** a contemptuous term for an advocate of the first U.S. Bank, *obs.;* (16) **night,** the night upon which prizes are awarded in motion picture theaters, also transf.; (17) **note,** see as a main entry; (18) **party,** the political party or faction favoring the second U.S. Bank, also transf., *obs.;* (19) **president,** the chief officer of a bank; (20) **question,** the question or problem of providing a suitable banking system for the U.S.; (21) **rag,** a contemptuous designation for a bank note, *obs.;* (22) **robber,** one who robs a bank or banks; (23) **roll,** a roll of bank notes or bills; (24) **runner,** =**bank messenger;** (25) **snatcher,** =next, *slang, obs.;* (26) **sneak,** =**bank robber,** *slang;* (27) **tax,** a tax levied upon banks to provide a security fund for safeguarding depositors in banks that failed, also attrib., *obs.;* (28) **vault,** a room, usu. of steel, in which a bank keeps its funds; (29) **whig,** a whig who supported the second U.S. Bank, *obs.*

(1) **1811** *Ann. 11th Congress* 3 Sess. 612 By lessening or destroying bank accommodation, you transfer the credit from the city to the country. **1851** Cist *Cincinnati* 322 A deficiency, at Cincinnati, of bank capital and bank accommodations, . . . has induced many steamboat owners to build elsewhere. — (2) **1819** Mackenzie *Van Buren* (1846) 159 It is true that the Bank has not extended to speculators and bank agents that prompt accommodation which [etc.]. — (3) **1812** *Niles' Reg.* II. 77/1 The city of New-York already possesses a bank capital nearly double that of any other city in the Union. **1885** Brockett *Our Country's Progress* 605 [In] 1846 . . . the bank capital was at a low point. — (4) **1801** *Steele Papers* I. 225 Your letter enclosing a Bank check of $100 . . . has been duly received. **1876** Warner *Gold of Chickaree* 309 He opened a bank cheque book which lay there.

(5) **1829** in *Williams's N.Y. Ann. Reg.* (1830) 171 The income of such fund, after deducting the salaries of the bank commissioners, shall annually be paid, [etc.]. **1895** *Chi. Tribune* 6 April 1 The Bank Commissioner's report . . . says that . . . many investments are bad. — (6) **1805** *Ann. 8th Congress* 2 Sess. 1088 The bank company was again heard by counsel in favor of their exclusive monopoly. **1837** Peck *New Guide* 205 The general revenue . . . is collected . . . from insurance, bank and bridge companies, [etc.]. — (7) **1838** *Indiana H. Rep. Jrnl.* 174 The expediency of providing by law, for the distribution of the fund in the several branch banks . . . in the several counties of the bank districts. **1844** *Indiana Senate Jrnl.* 322 A bill repealing certain acts relative to the establishment of bank districts. — (8) **1834** *Deb. Congress* 20 March 1025 A certain description of paper . . . known by the appellation of 'bank drafts' . . . were made receivable in payment of the revenue. — (9) **1870** W. W. Fowler *Wall St.* 521 On the morning of the 24th, the bank examiners made their appearance for the purpose of investigating the books of the Tenth National Bank. **1935** Horwill *Amer. Usage* 120 A variety of examiner peculiar to Am. is the *bank examiner.* He is a public official, appointed to visit the banks and audit their accounts. **1948** *Dly. Ardmoreite* (Ardmore, Okla.) 21 July 6/7 You looked tougher than a bank examiner finding a $9 shortage when you turned the howitzers on those thugs yesterday.

(10) **1845** M. M. Noah *Gleanings* 51, I have seen a merchant . . . worn out with anxiety and fatigue, return to his house after bank hours, . . . finding no . . . cheerful voice to welcome him. — (11) **1849** *Rep. Comm. Patents* I. 48 Improvements in bank locks. — (12) (*a*) **1834** *Sun* (N.Y.) 21 Mar. 2/2 'Jackson is a *tyrant,*' . . . roars the bankman. **1923** Poage *Henry Clay & Whig Party* 25 Calhoun, of course, would see that no Bank man was chosen as Preston's successor. (*b*) **1901** Flynt *World of Graft* 78 Do you think Boston is as much of a bank-man's hang-out as it used to be? — (13) **1932** *Blue Valley Farmer* (Okla. City) 4 Feb. 8/1 Bank mergers in New York City alone have thrown more than 10,000 bank employes into idleness. **1943** *U.S. Investor* 25 Dec. 8/3 (*heading*), Cleveland Bank Merger. — (14) **1850** *Knickerb.* XXXV. 557 We knew a Wall-street bank-messenger . . . whose feet looked like two parcels of shag-bark walnuts. **1921** *Collier's* 26 March 25/1, I called upon the charmin' Dolores with a mysterious-lookin' and bulgin' black satchel in my hand, like the kind usually wore by bank messengers.

(15) **1814** Jefferson *Letter* Wks. XIV. 77, I was derided as a maniac by the tribe of bank-mongers. — (16) **1936** *Waco Sun. Tribune-Herald* 27 Dec. 2/6 Police Commissioner James P. Allman issued an order . . . to prohibit 'bank nights' and other drawings in all Chicago theatres. **1948** *Variety* 2 June 1/3 Radio's 'bank night' has snowballed into a giveaway orgy in which $7,000,000 radio cash is being pitched at listeners in a season's cycle. — (18) **1825** *Nat. Crisis* (Cin.) 8 Aug. 3/2 And Gentlemen I say, I am no Bank Party, I dont belong to the Bank. **1834** *State Advocate* (Vandalia, Ill.) 26 Nov. 2/5 The President of the Senate . . . finished his tirade . . . by . . . challenging him . . . to fight him, George Poindexter, the broken down Senator of Mississippi, and a distinguished leader of the Bank party. — (19) **1857** *Dly. Dispatch* (Richmond, Va.) 28 Sep. 1/5 The Bank Presidents have been in consultation this afternoon. **1902** A. D. McFaul *Ike Glidden* iii. 18 The bank president was fully satisfied.

(20) **1884** Blaine *20 Years of Cong.* I. 472 During the autumn of 1862 the bank question was subjected to a thorough discussion among the people. — (21) **1845** *N.Y. Comm. Adv.* 13 Dec. (B.), The Senator was shinning around, to get gold for the rascally bank-rags which he was obliged to take. — (22) **1799** *Aurora* (Phila.) 15 March (Th.), Groups of pickpockets, bank-robbers, and hen-pecked dotards. **1948** *America* 24 April 67/2 A New York bank robber seriously damaged a safe he cracked some years ago. — (23) **1887** *Courier-Journal* 23 Jan. 5/3 One night a well-dressed stranger went over and won the bank

roll. **1947** *Denver Post* 2 March A. 11/1 You won't get there unless you have . . . a bankroll the size of a section of the mint. — **(24) 1851** A. O. HALL *Manhattaner* 68 The jolly bank-runners carry their funds fearlessly under their arms, for the pickpockets are not to be found.

(25) 1890 R. WHEATLEY in *Harper's Mag.* Feb. 472/2 One of the most daring bank snatchers in the city effected two robberies in the course of a single day. — **(26) 1888** *Dly. Inter-Ocean* 16 Feb. (F.), Buffalo officers to-day picked out . . . Jones, the notorious bank sneak and burglar known professionally in every city of the United States. **1910** WILSON *Chicago Cess-Pool Infamy* 98 The bank sneak is simply a bank robber. — **(27) 1832** *Deb. Congress* 8 March 2073 The banks . . . [consented] to come in on the condition of being relieved from the payment of the bank tax. **1844** *Indiana Senate Jrnls.* 154 Two resolutions . . . one directing an enquiry in relation to the Bank tax fund. — **(28) 1842** *Knickerb.* XX. 340 No sooner has it [=money] . . . returned to the bank-vaults than it is again sent forth on another errand of iniquity. **1907** WHITE *Boniface to Bank Burglar* 408 It was a duplicate of the Yale lock on the outside door of the Corn Exchange Bank vault. — **(29) 1835** *Louisville Public Adv.* 26 June, The cognomen of Bank Whigs is to be doffed.

As the last term in **anti-, county, deposit, depositary, dime, district, Federal Reserve, free, gold, government, land, manufacture, member, monte, Mother, national, nickel, pet, real estate, reserve, rolling, safety fund, savings, shaving, specie-paying, state, United States, wildcat bank.**

***bank,** *v.*[1]

1. *tr.* To protect (a cellar, house, etc.), esp. against the cold, by piling earth against it, usu. with *up.*

1720 *Canton* (Mass.) *Rec.* 6 The same day there was ten Pounds granted . . . for to repaire the Roof of the meeting hovse and to bank the outside of the scils of said hovse. **1779** *Narrag. Hist. Reg.* I. 97 Banked up the cellar wall. **1845** KIRKLAND *Western Clearings* 103 The deacon . . . began thinking that the very next week he must bestir himself and get up a 'bee' to bank up his beloved meeting-house. **1948** *This Week Mag.* 10 July 9/3 We slept in canvas tents, banked around the sides with moss or larch branches to keep out the wind.

2. *S.* To store (sweet potatoes) in a bank. Cf. ***bank,** *n.*[1] **1. b.**

1851 *Fla. Plant. Rec.* 418, 2 [slaves] banking potatoes and so forth. **1855** DAVIS *Farm Bk.* 230 Finished Banking potatoes.

3. To stack or pile up (logs) on a river-bank or at a landing to await transportation. Also transf.

1856 *Mich. Agric. Soc. Trans.* VII. 828 There will be logs enough cut and 'banked' for 100,000,000 feet of lumber. We are informed that the amount now banked daily, will amount to 2,500,000 feet. **1895** KING *Fort Frayne* ii. 22 Double sacks of grain . . . were banked at the quartermaster's corral. *a***1904** S. E. WHITE *Blazed Trail* ii. 25 Richard Dorrell usually finished banking his season's cut a month earlier.

***bank,** *v.*[2] *intr.* To conduct the business of banking (or gambling) *on* or *upon* capital.

1831 *Deb. Congress* 2 Feb. 55 The name, the credit, and the revenues of the United States . . . constitute in themselves an immense capital to bank upon. **1838** *Democratic Rev.* I. 23 It being conceded that the banks must not hereafter, at any rate, bank upon the public money. **1853** *S. Lit. Messenger* XIX. 71/1 Simon found an opening on the thither side of a Faro table; and having disposed of the race mare for $300, banked on this capital.

b. Hence, to rely *on* or *upon* (a person or thing) with assurance. Also *to bank that. Colloq.*

1884 NYE *Baled Hay* 127 The man who ranks as a dignified snoozer and banks on winning wealth and a deathless name. **1903** A. ADAMS *Log Cowboy* vi. 39, I was banking plenty strong . . . that next year . . . I'd take her home with me. **1948** CHAPLIN *Wobbly* 299 The Centralia boys are banking on you.

bankable ˈbæŋkəbḷ, *a.* [f. *bank, n.* or *v.*] "Receivable at a bank, as bills; or discountable, as notes. (Of *recent origin.*)" (Web. 1828.)

1818 *Austin Papers* (1924) 329 The money must be *Bankable,* as none other will do. **1842** *Greene Co. Torchlight* (Xenia, O.) 20 Jan. 1/3 Their paper was not *bankable,* and it was looked upon with suspicion by the community. **1921** *Collier's* 19 Feb. 17/1 (*heading*), Good Will A Bankable Asset.

***banker,** *n.* **1.** An inhabitant of the North Carolina seacoast called the "banks." **2.** A person who fishes for cod on the banks.

(1) 1849 COOPER *Sea Lions* x., This term of 'Banker' applies to a scattering population of wreckers and fishermen, who dwell on the long, low, narrow beaches . . . from Cape Fear to near Cape Henry. **1871** DE VERE 334 The *bankers* of North Carolina . . . used to be wreckers of doubtful repute. They now combine the vocations of farming, fishing, and wrecking. — **(2) 1861** *Harper's Mag.* March 461/2 On the banks of Newfoundland . . . some of the old bankers predicted a gale, which, by ten o'clock, began to blow. **1880** *Ib.* Aug. 338/1 The establishment of a 'banker,' . . . whose occupation consisted in fishing in his schooner on the Grand Banks of Newfoundland.

As the last term in **high, land, monte, wildcat banker.**

***banking,** *n.*

1. Pulling earth with a hoe up on a list. *Obs.*

1865 *Nation* I. 683 Then he goes out again and pulls up the earth on the listing. That's *banking,* and he has so much a task for banking.

2. In combs. in which "banking" stems from various sources: (1) **banking agent,** an agent for a bank; (2) **board,** a board having supervision over the financial operations of a bank; (3) **game,** a gambling game; (4) **ground,** a place where logs are assembled for transportation.

(1) 1851 HALL *Manhattaner* 31 In one corner [is] the banking agent . . chatting familiarly with the jolly planter. — **(2) 1932** *Blue Valley Farmer* (Okla. City) 14 Jan. 6/7 What do the captains of finance, who had controlled the banking board since 1920, . . . care for a dry plank? — **(3) 1851** GREEN *Twelve Days* 191 We do hereby pledge ourselves, as gentlemen, to abstain from every species of gambling or banking games, or other games of chance. — **(4) 1880** *Lumberman's Gaz.* Jan. 728 The banking ground is about 125 feet above the bed of the river. **1929** F. E. MCCLINCHEY *Joe Pete* 167 The snow was deep and the logs should be hauled to the banking grounds on the shore, there to lie until a tug came in the spring.

See also **free banking, wheat banking.**

bankite ˈbæŋkˌaɪt, *n.* (See quot. 1838.) Also attrib. *Obs.* See also **anti-bankite.**

1832 *Deb. Congress* 14 March 2156 The distinguished bankite leader in the House had been elevated by the Governor to a place of the highest trust. **1838** UNCLE SAM in *Bentley's Misc.* IV. 584 There were only two bankites besides myself in the regiment. . . . Partisans of the United States bank, or 'Monster.' **1844** *Quincy* (Ill.) *Herald* 19 Apr. 2/2 We are just opening the campaign . . . and showing to the people the destructive policy of the bankite-high tariff-distribution politicians.

banklick bass. (See quots.) — **1909** *Cent. Supp.* 116/1 Banklick bass. Same as calico-bass. (Local, Indiana.) **1947** DALRYMPLE *Panfish,* Here, my friend, are the various names by which you would address that little gamester, the Crappie, depending on where you happened to be at the moment: . . . Banklick Bass, . . . Grass Bass, John Demon, . . . Perch, . . . White Perch.

***bank note.** In now obsolete combs.: (1) **bank note detector,** =**counterfeit detector;** (2) **reporter,** (see quots.); (3) **table,** a table showing the current value of bank notes.

(1) 1854 *Pa. Agric. Rep.* 421 Variegated soaps and bank note detectors. **1894** *Cong. Rec.* 5 June 5790/2 One of the old bank-note detectors which have been so often referred to. — **(2) 1855** WELD *Vacation Tour* 217 The wretched bank-notes of worthless paper commonly called *shin plasters,* are so frequently imitated that, unless the traveller is provided with a 'Bank-Note Reporter,' published monthly, and continually consults it, he is sure to be imposed upon. **1910** PRESCOTT *Early Day Railroading* 147 Printed bank note reporters failed to be a guide and were worthless and troubles multiplied daily. — **(3) 1834** *Deb. Congress* 23 Jan. 2523 Examine the bank note table which is almost daily furnished us in the public prints.

bankocracy bæŋˈkɑkrəsɪ, *n.* The domination of the U.S. Bank. *Obs.* — **1830** *Columbia & Greene Co. Envoy* (Hudson, N.Y.) 21 Sep. 2/4 Mr. Throop is the avowed friend of that monopolizing system—that Bankocracy—which is at war with all true republicanism.

***banner,** *n.*

1. A prize given for preëminence.

This sense developed from some such practice as is mentioned in quot. 1840 below. See also quot. 1840 *s.v.* **banner state.**

1840 *Log Cabin* (N.Y.) 5 Dec. 2/3 It is known that the Ladies of New Orleans early in the late contest offered a splendid Banner to the State which should give the largest relative majority for Harrison and Tyler in its popular vote for Presidential Electors. **1900** *Cent. Mag.* Feb. 636/1 Local authorities . . . united in the belief that . . . Ashtabula County might be accorded the banner.

2. Hence extensively used in combs. in the sense of foremost, leading, preëminent, etc. as (1) **banner city,** (2) **claim,** (3) **county,** (4) **crop,** (5) **day,** (6) **district,** (7) **parish,** (8) **salesman,** (9) **state,** (10) **town,** (11) **township,** (12) **veteran,** (13) **wheat.**

(1) 1844 *Louisville Democrat* 27 Nov. 2/1 This being the 'Banner City of the Banner State,' . . . we see no objection to her contributing as much light for our Democratic citizens as was burned to the whigs in 1840. **1882** *Cent. Mag.* Aug. 508 He is hired by the Chamber of Commerce . . . to ride upon the trains . . . and talk to emigrants about the advantages of settling near the Banner City. — **(2) 1901** WHITE *Westerners* xxiii. 212 The Great Snake . . . was admittedly the banner claim of the group. — **(3) 1840** *Niles' Reg.* 5 Dec. 210/2 The Banner County.—Designation is claimed by Worcester, Massachusetts, which gave Harrison the largest aggregate majority. **1887** *Courier-Journal* 13 Jan. 8/1 Trimble being the banner Democratic county of Kentucky, and being a citizen thereof . . . I desire to be heard through the columns of the Courier Journal. — **(4) 1886** *Harper's Mag.* July 237/2 She had the banner crop of tobacco in that county last year.

(5) 1911 S. E. WHITE *Bobby Orde* x. 128 On his banner day he brought down two fox-squirrels. **1941** *Reader's Digest* Oct. 89/2 One banner day last May the Knotts served 5910 dinners. — **(6) 1885** *Cent. Mag.* Nov. 28/1 The visitors . . . were mostly . . . miners on their way to the 'Banner district.' — **(7) 1909** *St. Stephen's Leaflet* (Portland, Ore.) May (Th.), It is clear that the Good Shepherd is the banner parish in its offering on Easter Day. — **(8) 1927** BENÉT *J. B.'s Body* 102 The directors [decide] with a sigh, to do without banner-salesmen. — **(9) 1840** *Niles' Reg.* 5 Dec. 210/1 The Whigs . . . proposed to designate whichever state should give the Harrison ticket the largest majority, as The Banner State. There has been considerable rivalry for the honor. **1887** GEORGE *40 Years on Rail* viii. 147 Obtaining the enormous land grant for Illinois, which makes her today the banner state of railroads. **1948** *Chi. Tribune* 17 Oct. I. 24/2 These were among the banner Republican states.

(10) 1882 E. K. GODFREY *Nantucket* 208 Nantucket during the Rebellion sent into the army two hundred and thirteen men, . . . gaining for herself the proud distinction of 'banner town' of this Commonwealth. **1892** *Vt. Bd. Agric. Rep.* XII. 128 Montgomery may be considered the banner town of the County for the manufacture of butter tubs. — **(11) 1883** *Harper's Mag.* Jan. 282/1 This constituency was solid for Bigler, and . . . this was the banner township of California. — **(12) 1843** *Knickerb.* XXII. 431 He who was for many years the banner-veteran of our worthies. — **(13) 1850** *N. Eng. Farmer* II. 360 A fine bunch of Kloss Blue Stem winter wheat or Banner wheat, as generally called in Maine.

b. banner stone, *archaeol.*, any one of variously-shaped polished stone objects with axial perforations and wing-like projections, prob. placed on a staff when in use.

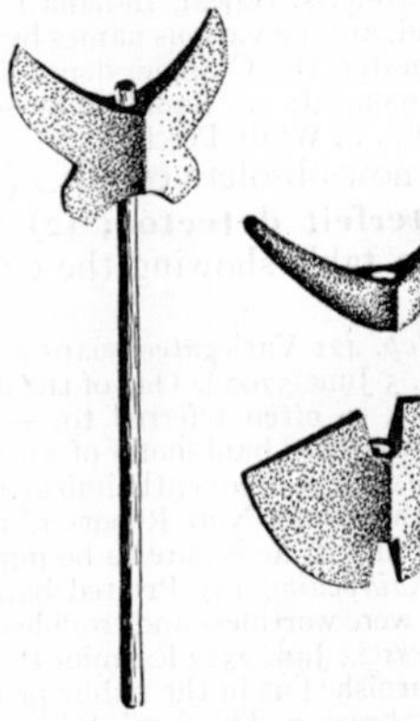

Banner stones

1881 *Smithsonian Rep.* 657 Some banner-stones of striped slate have been found in Camillus, and one on Skaneateles Lake [N.Y.]. **1948** *Ill. State Arch. Soc. Jrnl.* April 8/1 The six outstanding Bannerstones which constituted this group or cache were discovered individually over a period of years by different individuals who had worked that particular field.

As the last term in **Lone Star, palmetto, snow, Starry, Star-Spangled, State rights banner.**

***banner,** *v. tr.* (See quot.) *Rare.* — **1859** A. VAN BUREN *Sojourn in South* 19 We were 'bannered' away by the waving of handkerchiefs of friends on the other steamers and the levee.

bannerite 'bænəraɪt, *n.* (See quot.) — **1878** *Scribner's Mo.* XV. 636/2 My friend was a confirmed 'bannerite' as the printers term it—a careless, shiftless, strolling vagabond, here to-day and there to-morrow.

Bannock 'bænək, *n.* [f. *Panaítĭ*, their own tribal name. Note variant forms in the quots.] A Shoshonean Indian or (*pl.*) tribe of Indians formerly living chiefly in southern Idaho near their present reservation. Also attrib.

1834 in TOWNSEND *Narrative* 75 (Thwaites), The principal of these are Indians, of the Nez Percé, Banneck and Shoshone tribes. **1839** WISLIZENUS *Journey to Rocky Mts.* (1912) 158 Beyond them in Oregon, live the Crows, the Blackfeet, the Eutaws, the Snakes, the Nez Percés, the Flatheads, the Pannacks, etc. **1841** WILLIAMS *Tour to Ore.* (1921) 45 We passed the Ponock Indians. *Ib.* (1842) 77 Staid that night with a company of Ponark Indians, on a creek of Ham's fork of Green River. **1947** DE VOTO *Across Wide Missouri* 305 The Bannocks were detached Shoshones who lived in southern Idaho.

banquet lamp. An elaborate make of table lamp. *Obs.* — **1896** *N. Eng. Mag.* Nov. (*advt.*), Banquet lamps in Dresden, Onyx, Brass, Silver, and Wrought Iron. — **1903** WIGGIN *Rebecca* xiii. 139 The premiums . . . were three—a bookcase, a plush reclining chair, and a banquet lamp.

banquette 'bæŋkɛt, *n.* [For the source in **1**, see note; in **2.** app. an extension in meaning of English *banquette.*]

1. *La.* A raised sidewalk or footpath.

"As Standard-French *Banquette* is a diminutive formation from *banc*, 'bench,' the word *banquettes* was applied to benches which the Creoles of New Orleans placed on the sidewalks and occupied in the evenings. From this custom is said to have sprung the use of *banquette* in the sense of 'sidewalk.'" (Read)

1841 *N.O. Picayune* 28 Jan. 2/3 Bill Posey, the flower of loafers, was found stretched on the banquette on Tuesday night, like a turtle in a market cart. **1946** TALLANT *Voodoo in N.O.* 59 It was a low structure set behind a high fence, which almost, though not quite, concealed it from the *banquette*.

2. *Archaeol.* A shelf or bench-like platform along the wall of a cave.

1895 *Bureau Amer. Ethnol.* 17th Rep. II. (1898) 541 Broad lateral banquettes are prominent features in the most complicated caves, and there are many recesses and small closets or cists.

***Baptist,** *n.* Used with *Seceders, Reformers*, to designate particular sects of Baptists. *Obs.* — **1835** *S. Lit. Messenger* I. 259 The Baptist Seceders or followers of Alexander Campbell have 1 place of worship. **1837** PECK *Gaz. Illinois* 215 A charter has been obtained for a college, which is contemplated to be brought into operation by the Baptist Reformers.

As the last term in **feet washing, foot washing, forty gallon, Free, German, Hard-shell, Hard-shelled, iron-jacket, landmark, missionary, old, old school, old-sided, Potter, Primitive, regular, seed, Seventh-Day, Seventh-Day German, Six Principle, Snake, soft shell, United, water, whisky Baptist.**

baptized toast. (See quots.) *Obs.* — [**1818** PALMER *Journal* 241 One or two dishes are peculiar to New England, and always on the table, toast dipped in cream and *pumpkin pie.*] **1829** BOARDMAN *America & Americans* (1833) 105 The long tables exhibited . . . several favourite items peculiar to the American bill of fare, among which may be enumerated buckwheat cakes and baptized toast. . . . The baptized toast, which I at first mistook for spoiled toast, is the ordinary old-fashioned English buttered toast saturated with milk.

***bar,** *n.*[1]

1. A strip of solid color on a flag. *The Bars*, the flag of the southern Confederacy. Now *hist.* Cf. **Stars and Bars.**

1856 WHITTIER *Panorama*, Where'er our banner flaunts beneath the stars Its mimic splendors and its cloud-like bars. **1861** F. MOORE *Rebellion Rec.* I. 120/1 Down your Black-a-moor Stripes and Stars! We'll up, instead, the Confederate Bars! **1864** GRIGSBY *Smoked Yank* xxi. (1891) 185 On the bars there are thirteen stars.

2. The mouthpiece, when solid, of a bridle-bit.

1868 WOODRUFF *Trotting Horse* 391 A bar of moderate size, rather fine than thick, is what I have always preferred. **1898** P. L. FORD *Tattle-Tales* 35 He had had the reins buckled to the lower bar of the curb, so it must have been pretty bad for the grey.

3. (See quot.)

1872 *Harper's Mag.* Dec. 28/2 The deep valley widened, and the mountains, parting to right and left, made space for a small plateau or upland prairie—a *bar*, in [Colorado] mountain parlance.

4. The landside of a plow.

1876 *Ill. Dept. Agric. Trans.* XIII. 327 The French plow was destitute of iron, except a small piece . . . to cut the earth. . . . The bar, as it is called, was constructed of wood.

5. *W.* A straight horizontal line in a brand, also in the names of ranches.

1890 *Stock Grower* 29 March 6/4 Circle Bar Ranch. *Ib.* 15 March 6/3 The G-bar-outfit. **1911** *Outing* Mar. 736/1 With the beginning of Bonanza's espionage the Bar Cross cattle ceased to disappear. **1947** *Denver Post* 25 Feb. 26/7 Among the heavy losers are Lawrence Johnson, operator of the extensive Bar-A spread.

6. In combs.: (1) **bar album,** a guest register in a hotel or tavern, *obs.;* (2) **association,** an association of lawyers, judges, etc.; (3) **bass,** a rock bass; (4) **claim,** *W.* a claim for a piece of land upon which to begin bar-diggings; (5) **diggings,** *W.* (see quot. 1897); (6) **fish,** the calico bass (see also quot. 1888); (7) **fly,** a hanger-on at bars, a drunkard, *slang;* (8) **keep,** a bar-keeper; (9) **mine,** *W.* (see quot.); (10) **mining,** *W.* "the mining of river bars, usually between low and high waters, although the stream is sometimes deflected and the bar worked below water level" (Fay *Gloss. Mining Industry*); (11) **place,** a place in a fence where there are drawbars; (12) **post,** one of the posts supporting a set of drawbars; (13) **room,** a room or shop provided with a bar or counter at which liquors are sold, also attrib.; (14) **share,** a plowshare welded to the landside, also ellipt. for next; (15) **share plow,** a plow having a barshare; (16) **tender,** one who serves liquor at a bar.

(1) 1835 C. Colton *Four Years in Gt. Britain* (ed. 2) 94 In the United States, the moment a traveller arrives at an inn, before he can be assigned to his rooms, . . . the bar album is uniformly produced, and a pen put into his hand to record his name and residence! — **(2) 1838** *S. Lit. Messenger* IV. 581/2 There exist, at divers places in the southern country, certain combinations among the gentlemen of the bar, commonly styled Bar Associations. **1948** *Kankakee* (Ill.) *D. Jrnl.* 5 June 1/7 He has served on the official board of the bar association for a number of years. — **(3) 1798** Dunbar *Life* 88 In those lesser collections of waters generally fed by springs among many others are the Barbut . . . , the Sheep's head, Black trout, Bar or Rock, Bass, Perch, Sun-fish and a great variety of smaller fishes. — **(4) 1865** in *Frontier* VIII. (1928) 131 A bar claim (in Elk Creek district, Deer Lodge Co., Mont.) shall be fronting two hundred feet and shall extend from the first to the second rise of the rim rock. **1896** *Land of Sunshine* July 62 Some of the bar claims were quite rich—as high as $8 to the pan being obtained in some places.

(5) 1867 Hollister *Mines of Colo.* 60 Langley lighted upon some placer or bar-diggings in a gulch on South Boulder Creek. **1897** *U.S. Consular Rep.* Oct., 'Bar diggings' shall mean any part of a river over which the water extends when the water is in its flooded state and which is not covered at low water. — **(6) 1851** *De Bow's Review* XI. 56 *Bar Fish* [are found] in the spring time. **1888** Goode *Amer. Fishes* 33 The Yellow Bars . . . sometimes called Bar-fish in the South. **1947** Dalrymple *Panfish* 248, I could not seem to find anyone who knew the first thing about Barfish. — **(7) 1910** *Sat. Ev. Post* 16 July 5/2 Then, after having confessed to so much money, he hastened out, for he wud not be stung by bar-flies. **1920** *Collier's* 6 March 9/1 You know that I never at no time was no bar fly, bein' contented with a trifle beer . . . from time to time. **1944** *Military Surgeon* Aug. 127/1 The photographs of white and colored 'bar flies,' prostitutes, and vagrants who are arrested, are sent through the Provost Marshal to the Venereal Disease Control Officer. — **(8) 1846** *Spirit of Times* (N.Y.) 4 July 218/2 We embarked . . . in company with . . . a *barkeep* to mix the l——q——rs. **1947** *Steamboat* (Colo.) *Pilot* 16 Jan. 2/4 Tom, the head barkeep at the Jerome, never faltered once in several days of continuous operation. — **(9) 1867** Hollister *Mines of Colo.* 46 The Foot-hills furnished many gulch, placer, and bar-mines; that is surface deposits containing gold which could be got out by washing.

(10) 1871 Raymond *Mines* 199 It is not practical to carry on bar-mining in the Snake while the stream is high. — **(11) 1863** Mrs. Whitney *F. Gartney* xii, A little footpath that . . . stretched across the field, diagonally, to a bar-place and stile. *Ib.* xxviii, By and by, . . . she saw a chaise approaching. It was stopped at the corner, by the bar-place. — **(12) 1847** Webster. **1879** B. F. Taylor *Summer-Savory* xvii. 138 Awkward H's like a pair of leaning bar-posts with one bar. — **(13) 1797** Hiltzheimer *Diary* (1893) 28 July 245 Took a ride to the Upper Ferry to see Seider's contrivance for bringing water from a spring in his garden, through pipes into his bar-room. **1846** Durivage *Stray Subjects* 117 The bar-room loafers rose in affright. **1948** *New Yorker* 6 Nov. 65/1, I saw a justice of the Supreme Court of the United States drink one in a Washington barroom in 1886. — **(14) 1820** *Hillsborough* (N.C.) *Recorder* 12 July, When my corn is up, I run a barshear one round in each corn row. **1850** *Cultivator* VII. 369 The 'Empire' ploughs with wrought steel mould boards, made with bar shares and wrought iron standards . . . are superseding all other ploughs.

(15) 1785 Washington *Diaries* II. 438 Tools and Implemts: . . . Bar Shear Plows, 9s. **1876** *Ill. Dept. Agric. Trans.* XIII. 328 The bar-share and shovel plow have been succeeded by the Cary, the Diamond . . . and a wonderful number of other earth turners. **1944** Duncan *M. Graham* 115 Only a brief pageant was to be theirs, of oxcart and bar-share plow, spinning-wheel and gritter, well sweep and quilting bee, sulphur purgative and slippery-elm poultice. — **(16) 1836** *Franklin Repository* (Chambersburg, Pa.) 5 Apr. 3/3 My eldest son, my bar-tender, 18 years of age, has become a drunkard according to the course of trade. **1948** *New Yorker* 6 Nov. 64/2 Cocktails are now so numerous that no bartender, however talented, can remember how to make all of them, or even the half of them.

As the last term in **candy, county, crow, draw, finger, fish, gravel, hitching, mosquito, muck, refreshment, sand, sickle, slip, slipping, starting, throw, water bar.**

bar bɑr, *n.*[2] Also **bère, baire, bear.** [App. f. La. F. *baire,* a mosquito net. See Read, 3.] A mosquito bar or net. Also attrib.

1775 Romans *Concise Hist.* 189 Where musketoes are plenty, have a close covering, called in this country a *Bère,* made in form of a musketo net, to put up over your bed. **1797** F. Baily *Tour* 309 The bedrooms [in New Orleans] . . . are furnished with nothing but a hard-stuffed bed . . . covered with a clean, white sheet; and over the whole there is a large gauze net (called a *bear*), which is intended as a defence against the mosquitos. **1805** *Lewis & Clark Exped.* (1893) II. 417 *note,* I had left my bier, of course suffered considerably. **1847** Lanman *Summer in Wild* xxiv. 143 As to musketoes, had I not taken with me a quantity of bar netting . . . the creatures would have eaten me. **1894** Mark Twain *Those Twins* 415 Get their bed ready . . . and see that you drive all the mosquitoes out of their bar.

bar bɑr, *n.*[3] *S.W.* =**vara 1.** *Obs.* — **1836** Holley *Texas* xi. 208 Should his only occupation be raising of stock, he shall only receive a superficies of grazing land, equal to twenty-four million square bars.

bar bɑr, *v.* [App. f. **bar,** *n.*[1] **4.**] *S. tr.* To prepare young cotton plants for thinning and cleaning with the hoe by throwing the dirt away from the drill with a light turn-plow or sweep, usu. with *off.*

1835 Ingraham *South-West* II. 283 If there are many hoe-hands, there are several ploughs 'barring off,' as it is called. **1851** *Fla. Plant. Rec.* 367 Commenced baring cotton this Evening. **1948** *Democrat* 13 May 2/4 Do not waste the time barring cotton with a turn plow.

b. (See quot.)

1887 *Cent. Mag.* Nov. 111/1 In the stubble fields the first spring, work consists in 'barring off,' or moving the dirt away from the roots of the cane with plows and hoes.

barabara ˌbɑrəˈbɑrə, *n.* [Russian dial. *barabora* in same sense.] A hovel or hut, wholly or partially underground, such as Aleutian Islanders occupy.

1868 Whymper *Alaska* 162 We came to a small and very dilapidated shanty, not much better than an open camp, known by the Russians as 'Ivan's barabba.' **1880** Jackson *Alaska* 74 The centre of the town is occupied by the Russian church and the residence of the Greek priest, . . . and the eastern end is composed chiefly of the half-subterranean 'barabaras' of the Aleuts. **1903** *Amer. Folk-Lore* Jan.–Mar. 17 He preceded them, and cleared out of the barrabara all the straw and bedding. **1947** *Alaska Life* Jan. 33/3 Mr. Broderick states that this material lay beneath the floor of a baraba (half-underground house).

Baratarian ˌbɑrəˈtɑriən, *n.* [f. *Barataria,* name of a bay and island below N. Orleans. See Read, 188f.] A pirate of the Barataria Bay region on the coast of Louisiana. Also as adj. *Obs.*

1815 *Niles' Reg.* VII. 375/2 The privateering class, formerly yclept Baratarians, have produced a corps of skilful artillerists [at N.O.]. **1830** Marbois *Hist. La.* 383 The government . . . having no knowledge of the dispositions of the Baratarians, considered it to be its duty to reduce them by arms. **1882** Sala *Amer. Revisited* II. 41 And met with a most inglorious repulse at the hands of a slender force of American riflemen and Baratarian smugglers.

***barb,** *n.* **1.** (See quot.) **2. barbwire,** barbed wire, usu. in **barbwire fence.**

(1) 1888 Goode *Amer. Fishes* 123 The King-fish, . . . also known as . . . the 'Barb' about Barnegat. — **(2) 1880** *Cimarron News* 26 Feb. 1/7 The use of barb wire fence, which was almost unknown five years ago, has assumed great proportions. **1890** *Manti* (Utah) *Sentinel* 21 Nov. 4/1 We have three or four tons of barb wire which we are closing out at $4.80 per hundred pounds. **1947** *Hunting & Fishing* Feb. 11/1 The whole goose world seemed to break loose over on the Reservation, which was just across the barb wire fence.

Barbados distemper. One of the many terms formerly applied to yellow fever. *Obs.* — **1699** in J. F. Watson *Philadelphia* (1830) 599 This is quite the Barbadoes distemper—they void and vomit blood.

Barbary Coast. The tenderloin (*q.v.*) district of San Francisco. A nickname. — **1880** *Pacific Metropolis* (S.F.) 12 June 6/1 [On] the Barbary Coast . . . the patrolmen are above suspicion. **1947** Sessions *Cities of America* 75 The Barbary Coast, which in the old days was a huge attraction to out-of-town 'slummers,' is now something less than a reasonable facsimile of its former iniquitous glory.

***barbecue,** *n.* A social entertainment or political gathering, usu. outdoors, at which one or more large animals are barbecued and partaken of by those present. Also attrib.

1733 Lynde *Diary* (1880) 138 Fair and hot; Browne, Barbecue; hack overset. **1804** *Guardian of Freedom* (Frankfort, Ky.) 14 July 2/2 A number of gentlemen under the name of the Republican Society prepared a Barbecue for the celebration. **1946** *So. Sierran* Oct. 4/1 An outdoor barbecue was enjoyed by all at the barbecue pit.

b. The food at such a gathering or a device on which it is prepared.

1947 *Chi. Tribune* 15 June VII. 1/7 In the last spark of daylight he showed us the barbecue he had rigged for smoking fish. **1947** *Dly. Ardmoreite* (Ardmore, Okla.) 14 Nov. 10/5 The big party dined heartily on barbecue and all the fixings.

Also *barbecue dance, dinner, feast, supper,* etc.

∗ **barbed,** *a.*

1. barbed mesquite, = **mesquite grass.**

1877 Bartlett 788 *Barbed Mesquit,* a species of grass, from two to three feet in height, found in Western Texas. It is a favorite winter grass, and is much sought for by stock of all kinds.

2. barbed wire, a wire, or, usu., a twisted combination of two or three wires, having metal barbs or spurs securely attached at intervals of a few inches, much used in fencing. Also attrib. Cf. **barbwire.**

1881 Nye *Baled Hay* 126 The students at this school will wear barbed-wire masks while practicing. **1907** Lincoln *Old Home House*

Barbed wire on a wooden wire spool

103 We'll have to put up barbed wire to keep 'em off. **1947** *U. of C. Mag.* Nov. 17/1 The corner in which they stood was barred from the rest of the field by a barbed wire fence.

b. barbed-wire fence war, = **fence war.** *Obs.*

1884 *Nation* 24 Jan. 65/1 The 'barbed-wire fence war' which has broken out in Texas.

∗ **barber,** *n.*

1. *N. Eng.* A keen cold wind driving frozen snow crystals so violently as almost to cut one's face.

1833 M'Gregor *British Amer.* I. 133 The keen north-west wind, during winter, is often called the 'Barber' in America. **1892** H. F. Reddall *Fact and Fable* 57 Barber, The. A severe storm, accompanied by intense cold, peculiar to the Gulf of St. Lawrence. . . . The name is also applied to a phase of cold along the coasts of Nova Scotia and New England.

2. barber house, = next. *Rare.*

1889 Brayley *Boston Fire Dept.* 86 A fire at Gold's barber-house, in Southick's court, was put out by engine 6 during April.

3. barbershop, the shop of a barber.

One ex., 1579, of this term appears in *OED.* It was apparently formed anew in this country.

1832 Kennedy *Swallow Barn* I. Int. Ep. 8 A thorough-going violin . . . in an illuminated barber-shop, struggled in the contortions of a Virginia reel. **1947** *Duluth* (Minn.) *News-Tribune* 19 Jan. B. 4/7 More fish are 'caught' in a barber shop on an average winter afternoon than are taken in many lakes all summer.

b. barbershop quartet, a male quartet, orig. associated with barbershops, meeting occasionally to sing in close harmony.

1925 Witwer *Roughly Speaking* 302 Then there . . . [were] the barber shop quartette harmonizers and moonlight necking parties on the boat deck. **1948** *Dly. Ardmoreite* (Ardmore, Okla.) 2 May 12/3 Songs and music were provided by the barber shop quartet of Oklahoma City.

∗ **barberry,** *n.* As the last term in **Lewis barberry, sugar barberry.**

∗ **barefoot,** *a.* **1.** Of horses: unshod. **2.** Of a dance: performed with bare feet, *rare.* **3.** = **barefooted, 1.**

(1) 1805 Lewis & Clark *Journals* (1904) III. 15 Yet notwithstanding our horses traveled barefoot over them . . . fast . . . and did not detain us. **1927** Russell *Trails* 142 Barefoot ponies on well-grassed sod travel mighty silent, an' the savages ain't doin' no talkin' except with their hands. — **(2) 1852** Mrs. Ellet *Pioneer Women* 40 She would relate interesting anecdotes . . . of the 'barefoot and moccasin dance' and 'spice-wood tea-parties.' — **(3) 1866** Lowell *Biglow P.* II. p. lxii, 'I take my tea barfoot,' said a backwoodsman when asked if he would have cream and sugar. **1888** Whitman *November Boughs* 406 'Barefoot whiskey' is the Tennessee name for the undiluted stimulant.

∗ **barefooted,** *a.* **1.** Of drinks: uncontaminated, pure, unsweetened. *Colloq.* [Cf. Pa. G. *bârfiessich,* used of coffee without milk or sugar. See Lambert, 22.] **2. barefooted boys,** the ignorant, vicious frontiersmen and backwoodsmen in Illinois *c*1800. *Obs.* **3. barefooted democracy,** democracy of a pure, unadulterated kind, also (quot. 1870) with allusion to the hard times which prevailed 1836–39. *Obs.*

(1) *c***1845** W. I. Paulding *Madmen All* 194, I thought even a Yankee knew that 'stone fence barefooted' is the polite English for whiskey uncontaminated—pure, sir! **1878** Beadle *Western Wilds* 183 It was sod corn [= whisky] barefooted. — **(2) 1847** T. Ford *Hist. Illinois* 88 Since the butcher knife has been disused as an article of dress, the fashion has been, to call this class of people 'the bare-footed boys,' 'the flat-footed boys,' and 'the huge-pawed boys,' names with which they seem to be greatly tickled and pleased, and their influence is yet considerable in all elections. — **(3) 1870** *Cong. Globe* App. 9 June 528/1 In those days we were called the 'barefooted' Democracy, the 'great unwashed,' and other like significant names. **1888** Perrin *Ky. Pioneer Press* 32 It could be nothing else but an organ of the old Bourbon barefooted Democracy of the Jeffersonian type.

∗ **barelegged,** *a.* = **barefooted,** *a.* **1.** *Rare.* — **1704** S. Knight *Journal* 47 But the pumpkin and Indian mixt bred had such an aspect, and the bare-legg'd punch so awkerd or rather awfull a sound, that we left both.

∗ **bargain,** *n.* In combs.: (1) **bargain basement,** in some large stores, a basement in which lower-priced merchandise is sold, also attrib. and transf.; (2) **counter,** a counter in a store at which goods may be had at reduced prices, also fig.; (3) **day,** a day upon which goods are offered at reduced prices, also attrib.; (4) **room,** (see quot.); (5) **sale,** a sale of goods at reduced prices.

(1) 1925 *N.Y. Times* 22 Feb. II. 13/3 Another unprofitable department in the bargain basement is the grocery department. **1948** *Time* 24 May 44/3 When the 1948 season began, Connie Mack had his usual collection of bargain-basement ballplayers. — **(2) 1888** *Scribner's Mag.* Jan. 65/2 Ladies . . . in all the finery that the 'bargain counters' of Fourteenth Street could furnish. **1948** *Family Circle* June 14/1 Rushing to the nearest bargain counter to get a man before the supply is exhausted will likely result in a bad bargain. — **(3) 1893** *Standard* 164/1 B[argain] day [U.S.] a particular day on which a business house offers certain goods at reduced prices. **1909** O. Henry *Options* 118 It's a bargain-day rush. I've got one more line of goods to offer before I shut up shop. — **(4) 1880** Appel *Biog. Wanamaker* (1930) 104 Bargain Room: . . . a place where remainders of lots are sold at smaller prices.

(5) 1898 C. A. Bates *Clothing Bk.* No. 5211, Garments for which you pay the additional price at widely advertised 'bargain' sales. **1948** *Chi. Tribune* 21 Mar. I. 29 (*advt.*), Old Fashioned Bargain Sale.

b. *bargain and corruption,* = next.

1827 *Liberty Hall* (Cin.) 2 Aug. 2/1 It would have been fortunate for Gen. Jackson, had he contented himself with a simple statement of the person's name, who made to him a scandalous proposition of bargain and corruption, in respect to the late Presidential election. **1887** Schurz *Life Henry Clay.* I. 329 Eaton of Tennessee, whom Jackson selected as his Secretary of War, was the principal author of the 'bargain and corruption' story. **1935** Alexander *Amer. Talleyrand* 218 The cry of 'Bargain and Corruption' was a campaign slogan against him for thirty years to come.

c. *bargain and sale,* used with reference to an alleged "deal" in the presidential campaign of 1824 in which Henry Clay was accused of selling his influence to J. Q. Adams in return for the position of Secretary of State in Adam's cabinet.

1844 *Quincy* (Ill.) *Herald* 1 Nov. 2/1 A 'bargain and sale' after the Clay and Adams sort was entered into by the Whigs and Native Americans of the city and county of Philadelphia. **1937** Elliott *W. Scott* 241 He found objections to Mr. Clay, although he did not believe in the 'Bargain & Sale' charge which Jackson's supporters had raised after the election of 1824.

As the last term in **corrupt, gentleman's, political bargain.**

∗ **barge,** *n.* **1.** (See quot. 1864, and cf. **safety barge.**) *Obs.* **2.** *N. Eng.* A large omnibus or pleasure vehicle.

(1) 1864 Webster, Barge, a double-decked passenger and freight vessel, without sails or power, and towed by a steamboat. **1904** *Scribner's Mag.* May 561 During the heated days of August the towing of the big double-decked excursion barges became our chief occupation. — **(2) 1903** *Boston Herald* 19 Aug., The visitors were conveyed in barges to the crest of High Pole hill. **1907** *Springfield W. Republican* 21 Feb. 16 [A sleigh-ride] which required every four-horse barge in the north half of the county.

As the last term in **hay, hotel, safety, sand, Schenectady, schooner, steam barge.**

***bark,** *n.*[1]

1. a. Short for **bark canoe.** *Obs.* **b.** A small basket made of bark. *Rare.*

(a) 1791 BARTRAM *Travels* 305 My trusty and fortunate bark I presented to the old interpreter, Job Wiggens, often my travelling companion. **1826** COOPER *Mohicans* x, They now bore the light bark from the upper end of the rock, and placed it in the water. **1840** ——— *Pathfinder* v, The light bark shot across the intervening space. — **(b) 1853** J. S. BARRY *Sketch of Hanover* (Mass.) 37 Children . . . may be seen daily . . . [going berrying] with baskets, or tin kettles, or barks on their arms.

2. In combs.: (1) **barkborer,** a dark beetle of the genus *Dendroctonus;* (2) **eater,** the yellow-bellied sapsucker, *Sphyrapicus varius;* (3) **log,** a log with the bark on it, *rare;* (4) **louse,** any aphid that infests the bark of trees; (5) **mill,** a mill for grinding bark, esp. used by dyers and tanners; (6) **nutmeg,** a fake nutmeg made of bark, allegedly sold by Yankee peddlers, *rare;* (7) **peeling,** a place where the bark has been peeled from the trees; (8) **silk,** a silk-like fiber obtained from bark, *rare;* (9) **spudder,** a timberman who peels the bark from logs; (10) **stone,** a beaver stone or gland, allegedly so named from its secretion's resembling tanner's ooze in smell; (11) **wheel,** a wheel used in grinding bark.

(1) 1857–8 *Ill. Agric. Soc. Trans.* III. 345 Another species is that sometimes called the bark borer, from its feeding exclusively upon the cambium immediately beneath the bark. **1867** *Amer. Naturalist* I. 110 Cylindrical bark borers, . . . are little round black weevil like Beetles, often causing 'fire-blight' in pears, etc. — **(2) 1862** *Ill. Agric. Soc. Trans.* V. 731 The head of . . . the true bark-eater and Sap-Sucker. — **(3) 1674** *S.C. Hist. Soc. Coll.* V. 461 Wee our selfes carrying our trade upon barke logs swam over Aedistaw River. — **(4) 1841** HARRISON in Johnson *Farm Encycl.* (1868) 137/2 Early in the spring the bark lice are found apparently torpid, . . . sticking . . . closely to the bark. **1884** *Rep. Comm. Agric.* 352 The ordinary food-plant of this species of bark-louse is the soft or silver maple.

(5) 1749 ELIOT *Field-Husb.* ii. 30 Take your Clover Hay to a Tanners Bark-mill, where they use a stone Wheel, grind it. **1885** *Harper's Mag.* Jan. 276/1 Most tanners buy bark . . . and grind it in a bark mill, 'leaching' the bark to obtain the liquor. — **(6) 1837** *S. Lit. Messenger* III. 414 We of the south are mistaken in the character of these people, when we think of them only as peddlers in horn flints and bark nutmegs. — **(7) 1871** BURROUGHS *Wake-Robin* (1886) 85, I pass on through the old Bark-peeling, . . . now entering a perfect bower of . . . soft-maple. — **(8) 1813** *Niles' Reg.* V. Suppl. 176/1 He showed me a fishing net made of bark silk. — **(9) 1932** *DAB* VIII. 30 He was imposing, measuring six feet two inches; his strength had been gained as a 'bark spudder' and was considerable.

(10) 1799 J. SMITH *Acc. Captivity* 38, I asked, what was the use of the beaver's stones, or glands, to them;—as the she beaver has two pair, which is commonly called the oil stones, and the bark stones? **1890** *N. & Q.* V. 2 Aug. 162 *Barkstone.*—What is the origin of the term *barkstone,* a hunter's name for the castoreum of a beaver? — **(11) 1843** CARLTON *New Purchase* I. xviii. 149 A man who has already discovered two efficacious ways to make Christians—our bark-wheel, and now our boots!

b. Also in the sense "made of, or covered with, bark," as (1) **bark building,** (2) **cabin,** (3) **camp,** (4) **canoe,** (5) **coffin,** (6) **cradle,** (7) ***house,** (8) **hut,** (9) **lodge,** (10) **shanty,** (11) **tent,** (12) **wigwam.**

(1) 1881 *Harper's Mag.* May 869/2 Facing the lake . . . stand the bark buildings. — **(2) [1683** HENNEPIN in *Ill. Hist. Coll.* I. (1903) 67 We made a bark cabin . . . in order to say mass more conveniently.] **1738** BYRD in *N.C. Hist. Com. Pub.* XIX. (1929) 114 Within this Inclosure we found Bark Cabanes Sufficient to lodge all their people. **1843** CARLTON *New Purchase* I. ii. 10 Enthusiasm for bark cabins and forest life. — **(3) 1842** *Amer. Pioneer* I. 79 Here we found an old hunter in a bark camp, 'solitary and alone.' — **(4) [c1646** in *N.Y. Hist. Soc. Coll.* 2 Ser. III. 222 The enemy . . . awaited us, with all the advantage which a large number of picked men, fighting on land, can have over a smaller one of all kinds on the water in bark canoes.] **1725** *Lancaster Rec.* 232 We traveled down the river and found a bark cannow. **1947** *Canadian Alpine Jrnl.* June 145 The guide rushed on with his bark canoe.

(5) 1847 HOWE *Ohio* 56 The dead were wrapped in white hickory bark, . . . and buried in their bark coffins. — **(6) 1834** *Knickerb.* IV. 372 His mother swung Macoupin in his bark cradle. — **(7) 1669** *R.I. Col. Rec.* II. 272 Hee knew they were formerly his Indians, and had skill to bark cedar trees and to make bark houses. **1775** *Mass. Hist. Soc. Coll.* 2 Ser. II. 282 We found a good bark-house with one man in it. **1847** LANMAN *Summer in Wild.* xiv. 89 The grove-city . . . consisted of seventy-six bark houses like those I have described. — **(8) [1674** *S.C. Hist. Soc. Coll.* V. 457 The Indians being diligent in makeing two barke covered hutts, to shelter us from the injury of the weather.] **1881** *Rep. Indian Affairs* 40 Their descendants live, not in bark huts, or skin 'tipi,' but in comfortable log houses. — **(9) 1846** M'KENNEY *Memoirs* I. iii. 67 To exchange the polish of courts of Europe for a bark lodge on Drummond's Island. **1873** HOWELLS *Chance Acquaintance* 231 Mrs. Ellison . . . remained in the shadow of the bark-lodge.

(10) 1840 *Knickerb.* XVI. 163 Bob Mosely's house was a tolerably large bark shanty, with a clap-board roof. **1877** JOHNSON *Anderson Co., Kansas* 18 In the neighborhood above they built some bark shanties. — **(11) 1819** SCHOOLCRAFT *Journal* 28 We encamped in an Indian bark tent. — **(12) 1675** *Mass. Hist. Soc. Coll.* VI. 205 They have bark wigwams for shelter, and some mats. **1849** *Pres. Mess. Congress* II. 631, I built him a bark wigwam.

c. In colloq. phrases: (1) *To stick to (in) the bark,* to refrain from going deeply into a matter, to balk at; (2) *to take the bark off,* to give one a hiding; (3) *with the bark on,* plainly, in an unpolished natural state; (4) *to talk the bark off a tree,* to express one's feelings in very strong language; (5) *tighter than the bark on a tree,* extremely stingy.

(1) 1822 *Ann. 17th Congress* 1 Sess. I. 75 A technical judge . . . may conceive it his duty to stick to the bark of the case. **1848** A. CONKLING *Jurisdiction, Law and Practice* 8 But to give it so narrow a construction would be to 'stick in the bark.' **1904** *N.Y. Ev. Post* 27 July 6 He sticks in the bark about the mortal peril of promising 'independence'; but he does promise 'self-government.' — **(2) 1845** HOOPER *Simon Sugg's Adv.* i. 14 The old man's going to take the bark off both of us. — **(3) 1839** *Spirit of Times* 28 Dec. 511/3 (We.), I see Long has 'spoke the word with the bark on.' **1872** MARK TWAIN *Roughing It* xv. 124 That is the word with the bark on it. **1903** *N.Y. Sun* 28 Nov. 7 Your Westerner with the bark on is fond of . . . picturesque figures of speech. — **(4) 1891** *Outing* Nov. 137/1 The tracker will be led, perhaps, for mile after mile through just the sort of cover that tempts one to halt and 'talk the bark off a tree' now and then. — **(5) 1913** *Amer. Mag.* Nov. 46/2 If you wasn't tighter than the bark on a tree your wife wouldn't have to do her own washing. **1945** *Sat. Review* 27 Jan. 14/3 *Tighter'n the bark on a tree* and *harder'n climbin' a peeled saplin' heels uppard,* both have in them the good old backyonder flavor of frontier life.

As the last term in **ague, amargoso, bayberry, birch, butternut, canoe, clipper, elk, Georgia, hickory, Jesuit's, leather, nine, papaw, persimmon, Pilgrim, popple, red oak, scale-, scaly, seven, shell, slippery elm, tan, wahoo, wild cherry bark.**

***bark,** *n.*[2] In *pl.*, the barking exercise (*q.v.*). *Obs.* — **1807** R. M'NEMAR *Ky. Revival* 63 The quickest method to find releasement from the jerks and barks, was to engage in the voluntary dance.

***bark,** *v.*[1]

1. **To bark over,* to cover with bark.

1760 JENKS *Journal* 362, I spent most part of the day in my tent a overhawling orders & settling accounts, & seeing that my campanys tents well barked over the bottom, according to Brigadier General Ruggles order. **1847** in HOWE *Ohio* 151 The roof [of the hut] was barked over, strips being bent across from one eave over the ridge pole to the other and secured by poles on them.

2. (See quot. 1831.) Also ***barking,** *n.*

[1831 AUDUBON *Ornith. Biog.* I. 294 A common way of killing squirrels is . . . to strike with the ball the bark of the tree immediately beneath the squirrel; the concussion produced by which kills the animal instantly without mutilating it.] *Ib.* 293 [Kentuckians] will *bark* off squirrels one after another, until satisfied with the number procured. **1876** *Fur, Fin, & Feather* Sep. 167 Barking is an original method of killing squirrels pursued as a pastime . . . where these animals are numerous. **1944** FAST *F. Road* 254 Will Boone kept talking about his great-grandaddy, his great-grandaddy could bark a squirrel at a hundred yards.

3. To divest (oneself) of clothing. *Rare.*

1859 *S. Lit. Messenger* XXVIII. 143/2 Bill sed he'd dive doun and rise the pole. So he barks hisself, and in he goes.

***bark,** *v.*[2]

1. *To bark up the wrong tree,* said of a dog that mistakes the tree in which his quarry has taken refuge. Hence, *fig.*, to be mistaken and so fail in or misdirect one's efforts. *Colloq.*

1832 J. HALL *Legends of West* 46 You are barking up the wrong tree Johnson. **1833** *Sketches D. Crockett* 58, I told him . . . that he reminded me of the meanest thing on God's earth, an old coon dog, barking up the wrong tree. **1866** C. H. SMITH *Bill Arp* 73 If my coon dog does sometimes bark up the wrong tree, he don't mean any harm by it. **1948** *Chi. Tribune* 25 Jan. (Comics), The word is around that we're investigating. I want 'em thinkin' we're barkin' up the wrong tree.

2. To emit a short explosive sound. Now *slang.*

1853 F. W. THOMAS *J. Randolph* 129 The Shelby [a boat] was 'barking' after us like a bloodhound from the slip. *Ib.* 132 These boats bark so you can hardly hear yourself talk. **1907** WHITE *Arizona Nights* III xiii. 342 The Colt's forty-five barked once, and then again.

3. Of squirrels: To utter a bark-like sound.

1857 *Rep. Comm. Patents: Agric.* 61 But, though active at this time [in cold, rainy weather] and apparently engaged in play, they [fox-squirrels] do not now 'bark,' as on warm and pleasant days. **1917** *Animals of Amer.* 175 When alarmed, it lopes leisurely up to the base of a pine . . . barking and scolding at the intruder. **1949** *Sat. Ev. Post* 5 Feb. 68/4 A squirrel barked, staccato but muffled.

4. To advertise or solicit patronage for a cheap attraction or side show by noisily proclaiming its merits at the entrance. Also **barking,** *n. Slang.*

1908 MCGAFFEY *Show-Girl* 16 By gum, I'd take a job barking for a snake race. **1948** *Time* 19 July 90/2 [It] was another triumph for Liberty's brand of mass production plus carnival barking.

barken ˈbɑrkən, *a.* Made or consisting of bark. *Obs.*

1755 T. FORBES in Gist *Journals* (1893) 148 Easter Tuesday we embarked to the number of six or 700 in about 300 Batteaus or Canoes (not barken). **1835** R. M. BIRD *Hawks of Hawk H.* I. v. 61 Some tall and tawny hunter . . . may yet . . . urge his barken canoe over some cypress-fringed pool. **1890** *Harper's Mag.* Aug. 365 A sword-lunge of assailant thunder Slashed down thy barken mail.

barkentine ˈbɑrkəntin, *n.* [App. a variant of ∗*brigantine,* cf. *OED*'s one ex., 1555, of *bergantine,* from W. Indies area.] A vessel resembling a bark (see quot. 1867).

1693 *Pa. Col. Rec.* I. 379 Having sailed from Barbadoes in the barkenteen Ann. **1867** SMYTH *Sailors' Word-bk.* 79 *Barkantine* or *Barquantine,* a name applied on the great lakes of North America to a vessel square-rigged on the foremast, and fore-and-aft rigged on the main and mizen masts. . . . They are long in proportion to their other dimensions. **1903** *Boston Transcript* 6 Feb. 22/2 The first vessel ever built and rigged strictly a barkentine was the Leighton of 350 tons, built at Baltimore, Md. in 1852.

barkery ˈbɑrkərɪ, *n.* A building in which tanbark is stored or prepared. *Rare.* — **1843** CARLTON *New Purchase* I. xvi. 121 Such then was our barkery, our bark, and our bark grinder.

∗**barking,** *a.* In combs.: (1) **barking exercise,** a spasmodic nervous affection caused by excitement engendered at religious revivals, *obs.,* cf. **jerk,** *n.*²; (2) **pup,** a pistol, *rare;* (3) **squirrel,** a prairie dog; (4) **wolf,** a coyote.

(1) [**1807** R. M'NEMAR *Ky. Revival* 69 About the latter end of the year 1804, there were regular societies of these people, in the state of Ohio . . . praying, shouting, jerking, barking, or rolling.] **1834** *Biblical Repertory* VI. 350 A lady from Tennessee, who brought into a certain part of Virginia the barking exercise, immediately was imitated by certain of those affected with the jerks. **1922** KEPHART *So. Highlanders* 344 Thousands of men and women at the camp-meetings fell victims to 'the jerks,' 'barking exercises,' erotic vagaries, physical wreckage, or insanity. — (2) **1856** SIMMS *Charlemont* 443 He . . . amused himself by putting his two 'barking-pups' in order. — (3) **1811–4** BRACKENRIDGE *Journal* 239 In the course of my ramble, I happened on a village of barking squirrels, or prairie dogs, as they have been called. — (4) **1867** *Amer. Naturalist* I. 289 The Prairie or Barking Wolf (*Canis latrans* Say) is by far the most abundant carnivorous animal . . . in almost every part of the West.

∗**barley,** *n.* In combs. and derivatives: (1) **barley brand,** (see quot.); (2) **candy,** a brittle transparent mass made by heating and cooling cane sugar along with a decoction of barley, also attrib.; (3) **coffee,** a substitute for coffee, made of barley; (4) ∗**corn,** a particle, whit, *colloq.;* (5) **-earish,** ?denoting a soil in which the grains of sand somewhat resemble grains of barley, *rare;* (6) **stick,** a stick of barley candy.

(1) **1849** EMMONS *Agric. N.Y.* II. 131 Another diseased growth resembles the smut . . . and is called barley brand (*Uredo hardei*). — (2) **1844** EMERSON *Lect., Young American,* One man buys . . . a land title . . . and makes his posterity princes; . . . and the other buys barley candy. **1883** HALE in *Harper's Mag.* Jan. 277/1 In it were . . . barley-candy statuettes, jumping-jacks, and other . . . toys. — (3) [**1758** in FRIES *N.C. Morav. Rec.* I. (1922) 195 Our meals shall now be . . . for vesper barley-coffee, or sometimes brandy, or if the work is very hard a little beer.] **1820** *Plough Boy* I. 328/2 Barley Coffee.—A Western paper mentions that barley is much superior to rye and wheat as a substitute for green coffee. **1865** *Weekly New Mexican* 24 Mar. 1/4 After drinking a little barley coffee, we left Carizo Creek. — (4) **1803** *Ann. 8th Congress* 1 Sess. 611 This is but the saving of a barley-corn, and ought not to be regarded. **1882** STOCKTON in *Cent. Mag.* III. 83/2 This man, . . . every barleycorn a king, knew no tradition to which he owed . . . allegiance.

(5) **1702** SEWALL *Diary* II. 62 Our dear sister . . . is the first buryed in this new burying place, a barley-earish, pure sand. — (6) **1882** M. HARLAND *Eve's Daughters* 112 We had lollypops and barley-sticks, and clear lemon-bars.

barlow ˈbɑrlo, *n.* [f. the maker's name.] A pocket knife of a make so designated embracing single-bladed knives of various sizes. Also **barlow (pocket) knife, Russell Barlow knife.**

1819 *Mass. Spy* 29 Dec. (Th.), A barlow knife, bloody, and another knife, rusty, lay along side of him. **1873** HOLLAND *A. Bonnicastle* iii, Before her, on the table, were a Barlow pocket-knife, a boy's playing-ball [etc.]. **1884** SWEET & KNOX *Through Texas* xxxiv. 463 By the sale of a damaged barlow, . . . and a tailless kite, I became the possessor of twenty-five cents. **1944** WILSON *Passing Insts.* 59 A Russell Barlow knife can be used for all sorts of things. [**1946** ——— *Fidelity* 11 Boxes had to be whittled to their basic elements; Russell Barlow, whose knives we used for whittling, had he lived in earlier times, would have been made the patron saint of whittlers.]

b. Also **barlow penknife.**

1779 *N.J. Jrnl.* 12 Oct., To be sold by Stephenson and Canfield, In Morris Town, . . . Barlow penknives, knives and forks. **1830** J. F. WATSON *Philadelphia* 201 The buck-handled Barlow penknives [were] . . . a source of great gratification to the boys.

∗**barn,** *n.*

1. A hole in the ground lined and covered with bark and used by Indians to store their corn. Also attrib. *Obs.*

1634 WOOD *N. Eng. Prospect* II. xix. 95 Our hogges having found a way to unhinge their [*sc.* Indians'] barne doores, and robbe their garners. **1668** in *Rec. E. Hampton* I. 303 What old barns are there wch have no particular owner they shall shew them in convenient season, yt so they may be filled up.

2. A building in which horses, cattle, etc., as well as hay, corn, etc., are housed.

1770 FORSTER tr. *Kalm's Travels* I. 223 In the northern states of America, the farmers generally use barns for stabling their horses and cattle; so that among them, a barn is both a cornhouse or grange, and a stable. **1828** A. ROYALL *Black Book* II. 71 Every farmer has his small wooden barn, under which name they include stables. **1906** *Springfield W. Republican* 26 July 16 Thieves entered the barn . . . soon after midnight and stole a chestnut mare. **1948** *Democrat* 28 Oct. 3/3 Three years ago wind demolished a barn on a farm owned by the . . . estate

3. A carbarn.

1903 *N.Y. Tribune* 13 Sep., The signal to go ahead was given and the car shot into the barn. **1944** *Chi. D. News* 4 Aug. 6/4 But surface cars and busses were with a few exceptions still in the barns.

4. In combs.: (1) **barn ball,** a form of play in which a ball is thrown against the side of a barn or other building and caught on the rebound; (2) **boss,** one who is in charge of a barn; (3) **burner,** see as a main entry; (4) **burning,** pertaining to the Barnburner Democrats, *obs.;* (5) **cellar,** the lower story, beneath the ground level, of a barn; (6) **chamber,** a barn loft; (7) **dance,** a dance held in a barn, esp. a lively dance resembling a schottische; (8) ∗**door,** (*a*) (see quot. 1896), (*b*) (see quots. and cf. *WNT s.v. schuurdeur*), *colloq.;* (9) **dung,** dung obtained from a barn; (10) **grass,** short for **barnyard grass;** (11) **hill,** euphemism for "dunghill," *rare;* (12) **hold,** of or pertaining to a barn, *rare;* (13) **lot,** a piece of ground for or about a barn; (14) ∗**man,** a man in charge of horses in a barn; (15) **manure,** manure from a barn; (16) **preacher,** a preacher who conducts services in a barn; (17) **raising,** a social occasion for erecting the frame of a barn with the help of neighbors; (18) **ward,** toward the barn, *rare;* (19) **yard,** see as a main entry.

(1) **1841** *N.O. Picayune* 25 May 2/2 Who has not played 'barn ball' in his boyhood? **1947** R. SMITH *Baseball* 446 Boys and grown men . . . had played barn ball, two-hole cat, and round ball . . . since they were old enough to hold a stick. — (2) **1902** S. E. WHITE *Blazed Trail* xxix, So Shearer had picked out a barn-boss of his own. — (4) **1847** *Semi-Wkly. News* (Fredericksburg, Va.) 21 Oct. 2/2 If, then, the whole democratic party were Barnburning, the Hunkers would soon join the whigs. **1848** *N.Y. Wkly. Tribune* 5 Feb. 3/3 The spirit evinced is that of uncompromising hostility to the 'Barnburning' section. **1848** *Field Piece* (Chi.) 23 Aug. 2/1 The Barnburning papers are calling for the Establishment of 'Jeffersonian Leagues.'

(5) [1838 Colman *Mass. Agric. Rep.* 67 All the washings of the barn yard are received into the lower story or cellar.] **1842** T. Parker in Weiss *Life* I. 184 A bull . . . tied up in the corner of the barn cellar. — (6) **1838** Colman *Mass. Agric. Rep.* 16 The best method of curing it . . . is to . . . tie it in bundles; and set it upright in a barn chamber. **1871** Stowe *Sam Lawson* 28 That afternoon beheld Sam arranged at full length on a pile of top-tow in the barn-chamber. **1939** [see *L.A.* Map 102]. — (7) **1894** E. Scott *Dancing* 134 The Military Schottische or Barn Dance was known to and danced by the Americans long before it became generally popular over here. **1948** *Lisle* (Ill.) *Eagle* 21 Oct. 10/3 Everyone had a nice time at the barn dance Saturday night. — (8) (*a*) **1865** Mrs. Whitney *Gayworthys* xxvi. 256 Skirts were trodden on, and came out at the gathers; and there was more than one 'barn-door' rent. **1896** in *D.N.* I. 383 *Winklehawk*, triangular tear in cloth. (Cent. Dict. and Bartlett.) *Barndoor* is reported from Massachusetts in the same sense. (*b*) **1884** Cable *Dr. Sevier* xxxix. (1885) 297 His high waisted, barn-door trowsers. **1945** *Amer. Sp.* Oct. 231/1 A friend of a generation gone (1840–1916) told me about trousers, the front of which had an oblique row of buttonholes on each side, by means of which a large flap could be let down. This was the 'barn door,' giving origin to the name. **1947** *Ib.* Feb. 72 The term 'barn-door britches' was in common use in my home community in the southern part of Johnson County, Iowa, where the population is predominantly Pennsylvania Dutch in origin. — (9) **1802** *Mass. Hist. Soc. Coll.* 2 Ser. III. 3 The Indians use little barn dung; but about their hovels and stacks their land grows better

(10) **1894** Coulter *Bot. W. Texas* III. 502 Barn-grass, Cock's foot, . . . [is] apparently native to the Southern States. **1821** *Mass. Hist. Soc. Coll.* 2 Ser. IX. 153 Plants, which are indigenous in the township of Middlebury, [Vermont, include] . . . Dwarf groundnut. . . . Barn grass. — (11) **1843** Carlton *New Purchase* I. xvi. 121 And this after carrying barn-hill fowls a dozen at a time tied by the legs and dangling against his sides! — (12) **1801** R. B. Thomas *Farmer's Almanack 1802* 13–15 Feb. 2 Too much attention cannot be paid to barnhold economy, as cattle are made fat by clean stalls and full cribs. — (13) **1724** *N.H. Probate Rec.* II. 250, I give to my Daughters . . . the other half part of my afores[aid] Barn Lott in Salsbury. **1879** Tourgee *Fool's Errand* xxix. 179 You just . . . see that things is goin' right round the house and barn lot. **1947** *Dly. Oklahoman* (Okla. City) 28 Dec. 4/1 Sometimes the coyotes come right into the barn lot and kill calves and poultry. — (14) **1898** Westcott *D. Harum* 9, I ast the barn man if he knowed who they was.

(15) **1838** H. Colman *Mass. Agric. Rep.* (1839) 35 Drew on thirty loads short barn manure; principally the manure of sheep. — (16) [**1775** Fithian *Journal* II. 121 We held sermon in Mr. Fowley's barn. A rainy stormy day.] **1806** Fessenden *Democracy Unveiled* II. 173 We always possessed a violent antipathy to your bawling, itinerant, field and barn preachers. — (17) **1856** T. D. Price *MS Diary* 28 April, Went to D. D. Keller's barn raising. **1947** *Chi. Tribune* 1 July 19/3 Quite a crowd attended the barn raising Friday at the Talackson farm. — (18) **1884** Roe in *Harper's Mag.* July 247/2 The horses' heads were turned barnward.

b. *Between you and I and the barn*, confidentially. *Colloq.* Cf. *between you and me and the gatepost, s.v.* **gatepost.**

1854 O. Optic *In Doors & Out* (1876) 317 Between you and I and the barn, as we say out west, I am no friend of such folks as these over here.

As the last term in **bank, car, cattle, corn, cow, Dutch, farm, frame, horse, Indian, log, Shaker, sheep, stage, tobacco barn.**

barnacle-back ˈbɑrnəklˌbæk, *n.* A nickname for a sailor or marine. *Colloq.* — **1846** *Spirit of Times* 6 June 177/1 The monotony of this place has been relieved . . . by the drilling of 'Uncle Samuel's' 'web feet,' or 'barnacle backs' that came here from the squadron. **1890** *Cong. Rec.* 21 April 3637/1 This old 'barnacle back' was as surly a growler as ever went aloft.

Barnburner ˈbɑrnˌbɜnɚ, *n.* A member of a faction of the Democratic party in N.Y. State (*c*1840–50) so zealous for reforms that they would "burn the barn to get rid of the rats." Cf. **Hunker.**

1841 *Greene Co. Torchlight* (Xenia, O.) 19 Aug. 2/2 The meeting was attended by about 400 men and boys—such as Gov. Porter's brother has called 'barn-burners.' **1845** *Cong. Globe* 30 Dec. 117 The Whig party were no church-burners nor 'barn-burners' (a name which a certain portion of the Democratic party had delighted in taking to themselves). **1941** Buckmaster *Let My People Go* 159 The Democratic Convention had been forced to trample swiftly on its own rebels, the 'Barnburners.'

Hence **Barnburnerism,** *n. Obs.*

1848 *Field Piece* (Chi.) 9 Aug. 2/5 (*heading*), Barnburnerism in Cincinnati. **1848** *N.Y. Wkly. Tribune* 19 Aug. 1/2 Judge Nye of Madison Co. took the stand again and [spoke] . . . at some length on the origin and progress of Barnburnerism and the Free Soil movement.

Barnegat sneakboat. [*Barnegat* Bay, N.J.] A small decked boat used, concealed with weeds, brush, etc., in hunting wild fowl. Also **Barnegat sneakbox.**

1879 Bishop *4 Months in Sneak-box* vi, One of the smallest and most comfortable of boats—a purely American model, developed by the bay-men of the New Jersey coast of the United States, and recently introduced to the gunning fraternity as the Barnegat Sneak-Box. **1903** *Forest & Stream* 21 Feb. ix/4 For Sale: . . . one bushwhack boat with curtains; one Barnegat sneakboat, 15 ft. **1947** *Field & Stream* 102/3 Complete Plans for the Popular Barnegat Sneak Box.

* **barney,** *n.* (See quots.)

1851 Hall *College Words* 15 *Barney*. At Harvard College, about the year 1810, this word was used to designate a bad recitation. **1881** Raymond *Mining Gloss., Barney*, a small car attached to a rope and used to push cars up a slope or inclined plane. **1889** *Cent., Barney-pit*, in the anthracite mines of Pennsylvania, a pit at the bottom of a slope or plane into which the barney runs in order to allow the mine-car to run in over it to the foot of the plane.

* **barnstorm,** *v. Polit. intr.* To make a rapid tour, delivering campaign speeches and arousing political enthusiasm. Also **barnstorming,** *a.*

1896 *Congress. Rec.* 7 April 3661/1 The last I heard of him [*sc.* a cabinet official, he] was barnstorming down in Georgia in favor of a gold monometallism. **1944** *Chi. D. News* 27 Oct. 16/2 President Roosevelt indignantly denies that his New York and Chicago barnstorming trips violate his pledge not to campaign in the usual sense. **1947** *Time* 10 Mar. 21/1 Barnstorming Presidential Candidate Harold Stassen whirled through Belgium in one day.

* **Barnum,** *n.* [P. T. *Barnum* (1810–91), famous showman and "Prince of Humbugs."]

1. (See quot.) *Rare.* See also **Seven Mule Barnum.**

1856 Brewerton *War in Kans.* 17 In short he believed the whole affair to be a 'Barnum'—*alias* humbug, of the most unmitigated kind.

2. Hence in derivative expressions: **a. Barnumese, Barnumesque. b. Barnumism. c. Barnumize,** *v.* **d. Barnum-like.** *Colloq.* and chiefly *obs.*

(a) **1889** Farmer 40/1 From such circumstances we get words like *barnumese* and *telegraphese*, to signify exaggeration of style—what in slang parlance is known as the 'putting on of side.' **1929** *Variety* 29 May 31/1 He has circused and ballyhooed Whiteman's advent in Barnumesque manner. — (b) **1854** *Pioneer* (S.F.) July 59 Whether the offer was a piece of 'Barnumism' or not, it cannot be denied that it has been managed very clumsily. — (c) **1851** W. B. Hodgson in *Life* vi. (1883) 87 Barnumised and puffed as Napoleon has been, he is not popular. **1892** *Nation* 4 Aug. 88 Paris has the best advertised literature in the world, and confers a renown like that of a writer for syndicates here, only glorified and Barnumized. — (d) **1944** *Reader's Digest* Feb. 91 The crusader was not above using Barnumlike methods to advance her cause

* **barnyard,** *n.*

1. An inclosed area about a barn in which cattle, horses, etc., are kept, a farmyard. Also attrib.

1789 *Mass. Hist. Soc. Coll.* IV. 145 As this will always be a grazing country, the manure from the barn yard will be a fruitful source. **1867** T. Lackland *Homespun* III. 329 The city youth . . . supposed every farmer's barn-yard keeps at least one cow on purpose to give cream. **1948** *Chi. Tribune* 2 May VII. 1/1 On closer inspection, we could see it was only the farm wives shaking barnyard dirt from rag rugs.

b. *ellipt.* A barnyard fowl. *Rare.*

1868 *Putnam's Mag.* Feb. 241/1 An ale-house at Brooklyn, where the English mistress was superior in her choice of barnyards and their cooking.

c. Some indefinable game.

1939 Gilbert *Forty Yrs.* 58, I had charge of the boys' club, and we played Crokinole and Barnyard, a game . . . hard on the chairs.

2. In combs.: (1) **barnyard bell,** formerly on plantations, a bell rung as a signal or summons to slaves, *obs.*; (2) **fowl,** a domestic fowl; (3) **golf,** (see quots.); (4) **grass,** a coarse annual grass of the genus *Echinochloa*.

(1) **1856** Commons *Doc. Hist.* I. 118 The barn-yard bell will be rung by the watchman . . . half an hour before sunrise. — (2) **1843** *Knickerb.* XXI. 125 The chickens and tame barn-yard fowl were almost at his feet, scratching the soil. **1904** Stratton-Porter *Freckles* 32 I'll believe the birds of the Limberlost are tame as barnyard-fowl when I see it. — (3) **1930** *Dixon* (Ill.) *Ev. Telegraph* 24 Sep. 2/7 There were an even score of contestants who participated in the barn yard golf or horseshoe pitching contests. **1948** Mencken *Supp.* II. 755 Golf . . . has also engendered . . . *barnyard-golf*, horseshoe-pitching. — (4) **1843** Torrey *Flora N.Y.* II. 424 Barnyard Grass . . . [grows in] wet places, and about barnyards: common; the rough-sheathed variety along ditches near the salt water. **1922** Smiley *Weeds of Calif.* 12 In some cases at least, 'Billion Dollar Grass' has given rise,

after a year or two, to variants nearly indistinguishable from Barn-yard-grass.

Also *barnyard breed, cleaning, compost, goose, manure,* etc.

∗ **baron,** *n.*

1. A wealthy Carolinian in charge of a "barony" as provided for in John Locke's *Constitutions of Carolina. Rare.*

1776 J. ADAMS in *Familiar Lett.* 154 But the spirit of these Barons is coming down, and it must submit.

2. A commercial or financial magnate, one who dominates the trade in a specified commodity.

*c***1888** *Chicago Inter-Ocean* (F.), In all the 'steam rail baron's' reply to 'fair trade' . . . he calls upon the 'iron ore barons,' the 'coal and coke barons' and the 'labor barons' to aid him in meeting European competition. **1898** *Cent. Mag.* Oct. 838/2 The 'barons' certainly ought not to have been allowed to seize the watercourses. **1906** *N.Y. Ev. Post* 29 June 7 The ice 'barons' of this city have again raised the price of ice to the dealers. **1907** *Westm. Gaz.* 20 Dec. 9/4 The American beef barons, Armour's, Swift's, and Morris, are . . . the greatest captains of commerce in any market. **1948** JOHNSTON *Gold Rush* 1/2 John Augustus Sutter, pioneer Swiss land-baron and founder of Sutter's Fort, in 1847 had entered into a partnership.

As the last term in **iron ore, labor, lumber, meat, money, pig iron, rag, rum, silver, slave, water baron.**

barony, *n.* The domain over which a financial baron holds sway. — **1890** *Stock Grower* 1 Feb. 7/2 Texas is at a stage of progress now when there is more money in a small, well cultivated farm, with a few good cattle on it, than in the immense baronies held by cattlemen in the past. **1932** GRAYSON *Leaders* 477 He was to see John D. Rockefeller, the cold, stern, bloodless protagonist of acquisitive competition, collect into a mighty barony the wide-spread and disunited oil companies.

barouche bəˈruʃ, *v. intr.* To ride in a barouche. Also fig. *Obs.* — **1860** HOLMES *E. Venner* xxi, To think of seeing her barouching about Rockland behind a pair of long-tailed bays. **1881** HOWELLS *Modern Instance* xxvii. 334 I've been barouching round all over the moral vineyard with his friends.

∗**barque,** *n.* (See quot.) *Rare.* — **1735** *New Voyage to Georgia* 46 We concluded to tie some trees together, and make a barque, as the Indians call it, to ford over to the main.

barrack ˈbærək, *n.* [App. short for **hay-barrack** *q.v.* but cf. Pa. G. *bâre, bore,* a mow or haymow, in Lambert.] = **hay barrack.** Cf. **Dutch barn.** See also **log barrack, sick barrack.**

[**1697** in MUNSELL *Annals of Albany* (1852) III. 27 Desyred yt his Estate of Land, houses, Barns, Berghs, &c., should be apprized by

Barrack, hay barrack, or Dutch barn

indifferent good men.] **1756** in WOODWARD *Ploughs* (1941) 372, I have a Barrack 13 ft. Plant and —— ft. high it will hold but 12 Load when first halled in. **1854** *Harper's Mag.* IX. 849/2 We crept slyly around a 'barrack,' as it is called, of standing hay and by the pegs at a corner-post we climbed up to the top of the hay-mow. **1914** *Queens Univ. Dept. of Hist. Bul.* 12, 7 The earliest form of shelter for the crop was the 'barrack' or 'Dutch loft.'

barraclade ˈbærəˌkled, *n.* [App. f. Du. *baarkleed,* a bier-cloth, pall. See Bense 7.] (See quot.) *Obs.* — **1848** BARTLETT 24 Barraclade. (Dutch *barre kledeeren,* cloths undressed or without a nap.) A home-made woolen blanket without nap. This word is peculiar to New York city, and those parts of the State settled by the Dutch.

barrafou ˈbærəˌfu, *n.* [f. Bambara *balafo, barafo,* "to play the xylophone."] (See quot.) *Rare.* — **1775** HARROWER *Diary* 93 He also made a Niger come and play on an Instrument call'd a Barrafou. The body of it is an oblong box with the mouth up and stands on four sticks put in bottom, and cross the [top] is laid 11 lose sticks upon [which] he beats.

barracoon ˌbærəˈkun, *n.* [Sp. *barracón,* augmentative of *barraca* in Amer. Sp. sense shown here.] Slave quarters. Also transf. *Obs.*

1851 T. PARKER *Wks.* VII. 290 The chain . . . visible on the necks of the judges as they entered the Bastile of Boston—the Barracoon of Boston! **1868** *Overland Mo.* I. (Bentley), A barracoon is the place where those wretched captives are kept until opportunity serves to dispose of them. **1889** M. E. RIPLEY *From Flag to Flag* 172 (Bentley), The insurgent rebels . . . began to quiet down, gradually strolling to the veranda of their own barracoon. **1932** BENTLEY *Dict. of Sp. Terms* 99 *Barracon* is of chief interest because of the possibility that English 'coon' as applied to negroes was derived from it.

barranca bɑˈrɑŋkɑ, *n. S.W.* [Sp. in same sense.] A deep break or hole made by heavy rain, a ravine.

1836 C. J. LATROBE *Rambler in Mexico* 90 One of the gentlemen . . . was precipitated in the darkness into a profound barranca. **1856** REID *Desert Home* 15 There are vast caves piercing the sides of the mountains, and deep chasms opening into the plains—some of them so deep that you might fancy mountains had been scooped out to form them. They are called 'barrancas.' **1947** *Desert Mag.* Jan. 6/3 His ranch is cut with barrancas, spotted with sand dunes, and covered with salt flats and boulders.

∗ **barred,** *a.* **1.** Used locally in the names of fish. **2. barred owl,** the large swamp owl, *Strix varia,* barred with pale buff and deep brown feathers on its fore and upper parts. **3. Barred Rock,** a variety of Plymouth Rock chickens having grayish-white feathers evenly barred with bluish black, in full **Barred Plymouth Rock.**

(**1**) **1842** *Nat. Hist. N.Y., Zoology* IV. 218 The Barred Killifish, *Fundulus zebra,* . . . is found in the salt water creeks about New York. **1871** DE VERE 67 The *Mummachog* is hardly known beyond the waters around Long Island; the small carp-like fish is more generally called the Barred Killy. **1947** DALRYMPLE *Panfish* 273 The Barred Pickerel and the Little Pickerel (or Grass Pike) are both very small fish. — (**2**) **1811** WILSON *Ornithology* IV. 61 Barred Owl, *Strix nebulosa,* . . . is . . . frequently observed flying during day. **1945** *Mass. Audubon Soc. Bul.* March 58 The Barred Owl hooted for many minutes in the gathering dusk. — (**3**) **1890** *Harper's Wkly.* 8 Mar. 179/2 The late greatly revived interest in the barred Plymouth Rocks was helped along by $120 in specials offered. **1913** *Country Life* Mar. 16b Pittsfield Barred Rocks are bred for rapid development and heavy laying. **1947** *Science Illustr.* July 73/2 They [Conn. poultrymen] crossed an American chicken, the Dominique, with . . . a bright-eyed import from Asia, the Black Cochin. The new breed that resulted has become one of the most useful of all modern chickens, the familiar Barred Plymouth Rock. **1948** *Time* 22 March 1 The Barred Plymouth Rock is recognized by its distinctive plumage—light and dark gray bars.

∗ **barrel,** *n.*

1. A measure for corn (see quots.).

1641 *Md. Archives* 108 The Barrell to contein five of the said Bushell & no more or lesse. **1788** *Amer. Phil. Soc. Trans.* III. 226 A barrel is a measure of five bushels, much used in Virginia. **1837** COMMONS *Doc. Hist.* I. 221 Begun picking corn of plantation hands . . . their crop amounting to fifteen hundred barrels. **1903** *D.N.* II. 306 Barrel (of corn), n. A common way of measuring corn in the ear. One barrel of such corn is equivalent to a bushel of shelled corn.

b. (See quots.)

1818 PALMER *Journal* 22 A barrel of flour is 196 pounds. **1828** WEBSTER *s.v.,* In Connecticut, the barrel for liquors must contain 31½ gallons. . . . In New-York, a barrel of flour by statute must contain either 196 lb. or 228 lb. nett weight. The barrel of beef and pork in New-York and Connecticut, is 200 lbs. In general, the contents of barrels, as defined by state . . . must be from 28 to 31½ gallons. **1900** NELSON *A B C Wall St.* 128 The standard or commercial barrel of pork is reckoned at 200 pounds. . . . A barrel of flour contains 196 pounds.

2. A wastebasket. *Jocose* and *rare.*

1846 CORCORAN *Pickings* 38 The editor had not the good sense to appreciate [it], and therefore consigned it to the barrel.

3. A large sum (of money). *Colloq.*

1904 *McClure's Mag.* Feb. 379 [A place] good enough for old Jayes to make barrels of money in.

b. Esp. a slush fund provided by a political candidate or his henchmen. *Slang.*

"It is said to have originated in a dispatch to the St. Louis *Globe-Democrat* from Jefferson City about two weeks before the meeting of the Democratic Convention, in 1876, in St. Louis" (Lane *Pol. Catchwords* 16). "In this sense often written and pronounced *bar'l,* in humorous imitation of vulgar speech" (*Cent.*).

1876 *Harper's Wkly.* 19 Aug. 684/3 The 'barrel' is empty, the canvass ahead, And Still they are crying for more. **1876** *Solano Republican* (Suisun, Calif.) 24 Aug. 2/1 The great unwashed of Solano have resolved to make a brave struggle, whether they have to do it alone, or with the able assistance of Tilden's 'bar'l of money.' **1889** *Indianapolis D. Jrnl.* 23 Dec., The appearance of Mr. Bookwater, who owns a barrel as large as a hogshead, in the senatorial contest in Ohio . . . will happify the Democratic members of the Legislature. **1913** LA FOLLETTE *Autobiog.* 198 The nominations of the party will not be the result of 'compromise' or impulse, or evil design—'the barrel' and the machine.

4. In combs.: (1) **barrel bulk,** five cubic feet as a measure of capacity for freight; (2) **cactus,** any large cylindrical cactus of the genera *Echinocactus* or *Ferrocactus;* (3) **campaign, candidate,** (see quots.), *slang;* (4) **car,** (see quot.); (5) **chair,** an upholstered chair having a back shaped like a barrel; (6) **churn,** a barrel-shaped churn; (7) **copper,** (see quot. 1944 and cf. **barrel ore, barrel work**); (8) **fish,** the rudder fish, *Palinurichthys perciformis,* found off the N. Eng. coast; (9) **flour,** flour in barrels, i.e., "boughten" flour as contrasted with that made locally from home-grown wheat; (10) **gin,** a now obsolete type of cotton gin; (11) **house,** a low drinking place, often with a row of racked barrels along one side, also attrib.; (12) **jacket,** (see quot.), *obs.;* (13) **machine,** a barrel churn or similar device used in churning milk, *obs.;* (14) **ore,** copper ore in sizes suitable for shipping in barrels; (15) **plate,** an iron plate from which gun-barrels are made, also, in a machine-gun, a plate serving to hold the barrels in place; (16) **plow,** a form of grain drill devised by George Washington in which the seed was carried in a revolving barrel-like container and dropped through holes in this, *rare;* (17) **pork,** pork packed or intended for packing in barrels; (18) **seat,** a form of chair or seat cut out of a barrel; (19) **shirt,** =**barrel jacket,** *obs.;* (20) **shop,** =**barrel house,** *slang;* (21) **skirt,** a hoop skirt, *obs.;* (22) **spring,** (*a*) a cylindrical spring, (*b*) a spring of water provided with a barrel to serve as a catch-basin; (23) **stove,** a barrel-shaped stove; (24) **wheat,** (see quot.); (25) **work,** (see quot. 1881).

(1) 1853 *Harper's Mag.* VI. 581/2 Freights from Detroit to Lake Superior ports are usually $1 the barrel bulk—increased to $1 50 by the time of reaching the mines. — **(2) 1881** *Amer. Naturalist* XV. 984 Another species of the family is one commonly called the 'nigger-head' or 'barrel' cactus, a Mammalaria. **1948** *So. Sierran* May 5/2 We saw hundreds of barrel cacti crowned in yellow blossoms. — **(3) 1876** *Harper's Wkly.* 30 Sep. 804/1 The barrel campaign is a failure. **1884** *Boston Jrnl.* 1 Nov. 1 The Fifth District Barrel Campaign. *Ib.*, We are accustomed to 'barrel' campaigns here. Nobody supposes this district to be Democratic, but the Democrats depend upon carrying it with money. . . . But another 'barrel' candidate was discovered. **1889** *Cent. s.v.*, A *barrel* campaign is one in which money is lavishly employed to bribe voters. — **(4) 1895** WAIT *Car-Builder's Dict.* 6 Barrel-car. . . . A flat car, racked so as to carry many empty barrels. They are made long, and the racks are very high in order to make up a carload weight.

(5) 1887 I. ALDEN *Little Fishers* x, Those two barrel chairs were triumphs of art. **1947** *Downtown Shop. News* (Chi.) 10 Feb. 15 Curved back barrel chairs foster that new look in fine furniture. — **(6) 1864** *Rep. Comm. Patents* I. 364 A barrel churn of that class which have a large opening in the side to admit of the ready removal of the dasher. **1891** CHASE & CLOW *Industry* II. 105 The barrel-churn was made with beaters inside which flew round and round as the handle outside was turned. — **(7) 1895** *Standard Dict.* **1944** NUTE *Lk. Superior* 324 Copper was found in mass form and as 'barrel copper.' The latter occurred in small pieces that could be thrown into a barrel and thus easily transported. — **(8) 1885** KINGSLEY *Stand. Nat. Hist.* III. 191 They are most always found in the vicinity of floating barrels and spars, and sometimes inside of the barrels. Hence the fishermen call them barrel-fish, though the most usual name is rudder-fish. — **(9) 1877** *Vt. Bd. Agric. Rep.* IV. 75 At nearly every family where I boarded after that, the woman of the house . . . let me understand that I should not fare as well with them as at the other place, for they had no barrel flour.

(10) 1802 J. DRAYTON *S. Carolina* 133 Barrel gins are either worked by oxen or water; and may be said to be nothing more than foot gins, to which greater power is applied. — **(11) 1883** PECK *Bad Boy* 120 After I had put a few things in his brandy he concluded it was cheaper to buy it, and he is now patronizing a barrel house. **1888** *Missouri Republican* 11 Feb. (F.), The West-Side police are still arresting barrel-house loafers. **1948** CHAPLIN *Wobbly* 86 In dull times or in winter, seasonal workers made way for 'barrel-house stiffs' and human derelicts who constituted the backbone of the 'skid road's' population. — **(12) 1858** VIELÉ *Following Drum* 222 One delinquent was sentenced to wear a 'barrel jacket' every day. . . . It consisted of an old flour barrel with a hole cut for his head . . . and a pair of holes for his arms. — **(13) 1841** in *Wash. Hist. Quart.* XVI. 293 There were 70 milch cows at the dairy . . . (the churning is by a barrel machine—). — **(14) 1849** *Pres. Mess. Congress* II. 460 The barrel ore contains from 30 to 50 percent of copper.

(15) 1852 *Harper's Mag.* V. 147/2 The barrels are made from plates of iron, of suitable form and size, called scalps or barrel plates. **1888** *Cent. Mag.* Oct. 886/1 The breech-ends are firmly screwed into a disk or rear barrel-plate, which is fastened to the shaft. — **(16) 1786** WASHINGTON *Diaries* III. 38, I tried my drill or Barrel plow; which requiring some alteration in the harrow, obliged me to bring it to the Smiths shop. — **(17) 1851** CIST *Cincinnati* 228 The first floor . . . is used for cutting and packing barrel pork. — **(18) 1868** BEECHER *Norwood* 148 He plumped Barton into his own barrel seat. — **(19) 1865** *Nation* I. 367 If he didn't, they'd put a barrel-shirt on him.

(20) 1904 *N.Y. Tribune* 12 Oct. 1 A poisonous substitute for whiskey sold in the low 'barrel shops' along Tenth Avenue. — **(21) 1867** W. H. DIXON *New America* II. 33 Our women . . . eat pearl-ash for bread, they drink ice-water for wine; they wear tight stays, thin shoes, and barrel skirts. — **(22)** (*a*) **1773** *Boston Ev. Post* 4 Oct., A genteel curricle with patent barrel springs. (*b*) **1906** F. LYNDE *Quickening* 380 Then Farley was one of the three men who saw us up yonder at the barrel spring. — **(23) 1904** DAY *Kin o' Ktaadn* 47 Woodrow, tamping his pipe, retreats to the refuge of the 'Fabricator's Cabinet,' behind the barrel stove. — **(24) 1863** *Rep. Comm. Agric.* 90 The anecdote of the origin of the barrel wheat is well known. A farmer was in the habit of selecting his seed wheat by striking the sheaves across the head of an empty barrel; and as the largest, earliest matured, and the best grains shattered most easily, he thus selected them.

(25) 1849 *Pres. Mess. Congress* II. 468 The pieces which are raised to 30 per cent. of metal by beating off the rock are packed up in barrels, and this metal is called 'barrel-work.' **1881** RAYMOND *Mining Gloss., Barrel-work* (Lake Sup.), native copper occurring in pieces of a size to be sorted out by hand in sufficient purity for smelting without mechanical concentration.

As the last term in **ash-, cane, flour, grab, meal, meat, missionary, molasses, pork, pounding, rain, rain water, rice, tar, trash, turpentine, wash, water barrel.** For *cash on the barrel head* see **cash.**

* **barren,** *n.*

1. A tract of relatively open land, having little or no vegetation and usu. regarded by the earliest pioneers as lacking in fertility. Often *pl.*

1651 in *Amer. Sp.* XV. 153/1 To a Nother quarter tree on the barrons. **1697** *N. Eng. Hist. & Gen. Reg.* XXX. 65 As to the Soyle [of S.C.] . . . whether here and ther some rich Spot, and the Barrens are farr the greater in Quantitie. **1824** *Amer. Sentinel* (Georgetown, Ky.) 10 Sep. 2/5 Some of this Land is well improved, and that that is not, is easy to improve, being fine rich Barren. **1946** R. PEATTIE *Pac. Coast Ranges* 362 Ridge faces and summits are scarred by numerous 'balds' or 'barrens.'

b. A particular area of this kind usu. preceded by a designating term.

1723 *Weekly Mercury* 4 July 4/1 An Orchard lying at the Eastern End of the Loadstones Barren. **1784** FILSON *Kentucke* 20 Below a creek . . . on this river, . . . a great territory begins, called Green River Barrens. **1796** IMLAY *Western Territory* (ed. 3) 523 The Cumberland barrens, so called, where the land, though without timber, is frequently very good. **1844** HOWE *Ohio* (1847) 163 A small tract, called 'the barrens,' so termed from the land being divested of undergrowth and tall timber; it is covered with a grass well adapted to pasturage. **1949** *Sat. Ev. Post* 12 Mar. 17/2 Don't confuse the Pines with the Jersey Barrens, a like district sixty miles to the southwest, across a belt of rich farm lands.

2. In combs.: (1) **barren hickory,** a variety of hickory often found on barrens; (2) **oak,** any one of various oaks, as the blackjack and bear oak, growing in barrens; (3) **plum,** a wild plum, as *Prunus americana, obs.;* (4) **scrub oak,** the turkey oak, *Quercus catesbaei,* of the southern states; (5) **strawberry,** (see quot. 1891); (6) **white oak,** (see quots.), *obs.*

(1) 1882 WORTHEN *Econ. Geol. Ill.* II. 105 The post-oak . . . prevails . . . together with black oak, some white oak, black jack, barren hickory. — **(2) 1797** PRIEST *Travels* 12 Water and barren oak are small and bushy, and only used for firing. **1901** MOHR *Plant Life Ala.* 96 The turkey or barren oak and the blue jack . . . are frequent companions of the long-leaf pine. — **(3) 1792** IMLAY *Western Territory* 210 Barren, or red plumb. — **(4) 1810** MICHAUX *Arbres* I.24

Barrens scrub oak. **1897** SUDWORTH *Arborescent Flora* 170 Turkey oak. . . . Common names [include] . . . Barren Scrub Oak (Tenn.). (5) **1891** *Cent., Waldsteinia,* The barren strawberry . . . [is] widely diffused through northern and mountainous parts of the Eastern and Central States. — (6) **1785** MARSHALL *Amer. Grove* 120 *Quercus alba minor,* Barren White Oak, . . . grows generally upon poor, barren, or waste land. **1847** DARLINGTON *Weeds & Plants* 308 Barrens White Oak. . . . Rough Oak. . . . This tree seems to be confined to barren hills, and exposed ridges.

b. Barren Land, in ironic use, Canada. *Rare.*

1812 *Beauties of Brother Bull-us* 82 Jonathan . . . forthwith dispatched his chief bailiff, Benjamin Brave, into the Barren Lands of John Bull, with orders to annex them to Jonathan's farm.

As the last term in **cedar, hickory, ice, mountain, oak, pine, pitch pine, sand, sandy barren.**

barreny ˈbærənɪ, *a.* Of the nature of barrens. — **1834** AUDUBON *Ornith. Biog.* II. 492 A certain tract of Barreny country in the latter state [Maine]. **1882** WORTHEN *Econ. Geol. Ill.* II. 161 Rocks . . . may be found by digging to a small depth nearly all over the barreny hills.

barring plow. A plow used in "barring off" cotton. *Rare.* — **1865** TURNER *Cotton* 44 As soon as a stand makes its appearance, the barring-plough should be run round.

barronet ˈbærəˌnɛt, *n.* A kind of carriage, possibly a confusion of "barouche." *Rare.* — **1829** M. BAYARD SMITH *Forty Yrs. Washington Soc.* (1906) 292 By ten o'clock the Avenue was crowded into carriages of every description, from the splendid Barronet and coach, down to waggons and carts.

***barrow,** *n.* As the last term in **baggage barrow, wheelbarrow,**

* **Bartlett,** *n.* A pear of an early variety introduced into this country from England and distributed by Enoch Bartlett of Dorchester, Mass. In full **Bartlett pear,** used of the fruit and the tree.

1831 *Boston Transcript* 19 Sep. 2/2 Mr. Enoch Bartlett of Roxbury, [contributed] the Bartlett pear and specimens for names. **1867–8** *Ill. Agric. Soc. Trans.* VII. 506 Trees affected with this disease have been grafted with Bartlett and other pears. **1882** HOWELLS *Modern Instance* xxiii, I wonder the old Bartlett pear didn't burst into a palm-tree over your heads. **1947** *Reader's Digest* April 80/2 Collins now is getting from 1000 to 1500 boxes of Bartlett and Bosc pears per acre.

* **Bartram,** *n.* [Wm. *Bartram* (1739–1823), Amer. naturalist.] In combs., usu. in the possessive: (1) **Bartram('s) oak,** an oak, *Quercus heterophylla,* found in the eastern states; (2) **Bartram's sandpiper,** the upland plover, *Bartramia longicauda,* of the eastern states, also **Bartramian sandpiper;** (3) **Bartram's tattler,** =prec.

(1) **1810** MICHAUX *Arbres* I. 24 Bartram's Oak . . . , sur la rivière Schuylkill. **1868** *Exp. U.S. Comm. Agric.* (1869) 202 Bartram oak. . . . This unique plant forms one of the most beautiful as well as the most interesting of all the oaks. **1901** MOHR *Plant Life Ala.* 473 Bartram Oak . . . [is] sparsely diffused and local from Staten Island to Delaware, North Carolina, northern Alabama, and northeastern Texas. — (2) **1813** WILSON *Ornithology* VII. 63 Bartram's Sandpiper . . . being as far as I can discover a new species, . . . I have honored it with the name of my very worthy friend, near whose Botanic Gardens . . . I first found it. **1942** *Nat. Pk. Service, Fading Trails* 259 The increase of the upland plover (commonly known as the Bartramian sandpiper) in Oregon would be a biological miracle. — (3) **1839** PEABODY *Mass. Birds* 370 Bartram's Tattler . . . is considered a great luxury. **1844** *Nat. Hist. N.Y., Zoology* II. 247 The Grey Plover. . . . In the books it is described under the names of Bartram's Tatler and Sandpiper.

barvel ˈbɑrvḷ, *n.* [Prob. a variant of **barbel.*] App. a variety of sucker. *Colloq.* — **1832** *N.H. Hist. Soc. Coll.* III. 85 The Barvil are taken in the spring of the year . . . with the spear. **1900** *Boston Transcript* 10 March 26/3, I think that the word barvel as applied to a fish, must be a localism rather peculiar to the region about Lake Winipiseogee. I remember that one day, more than fifty years ago, Horace Langley . . . brought into Concord a large number of barvels which had been taken from the lake at Alton, N.H.

bascule pan. *La.* [F. *bascule,* a seesaw.] A form of tilt-pan used in sugar making. — **1833** SILLIMAN *Man. Sugar Cane* 38 Bascule pan of a circular form and moveable on its axis. *Ib.* 100 This is so elevated, that the syrup flows, readily, into the evaporating vessels—which are the (now well known,) bascule pans, called also, tilt or seesaw pans.

* **base,** *n.*

1. The name of a ball game somewhat resembling baseball. Also transf.

1841 *N.O. Picayune* 25 May 2/2 Who has not played 'barn ball' in his boyhood, 'base' in his youth, and 'wicket' in his manhood? **1856** *Spirit of Times* 27 Dec. 277/1 Base is also a favorite game upon the green in front of village school-houses in the country throughout New England. **1866** C. H. SMITH *Bill Arp* 129 Sherman was playin base around about Atlanta.

2. In general combs.: (1) **baseboard,** a board at the base of something, as the washboard of a room, hall, etc., a board at the bottom of a fence; (2) **burner,** a stove in which the fuel is fed automatically from a container according as the lower stratum is consumed, hence **base-burning,** *a.;* (3) * **line,** in government surveys of public land, an east and west line serving as the base upon which township lines are later run, parallel with it, also fig., cf. **b.** (3) below.

(1) **1853** FOWLER *Home for All* 159 After mop or base-boards are nailed on, and before lathing, fill in between these boards . . . with stone or mortar. **1925** BRYAN *Memoirs* 17 Our yard was enclosed in the old-fashioned paling fence with a baseboard about a foot high. — (2) **1874** KNIGHT 242/1 The principle of the base-burner is also found in the furnace [etc.]. **1874** KNIGHT 242/1 *Base-burning Furnace,* a furnace or stove in which the fuel . . . is fed to the fire as the lower stratum burns. *Ib.* 242/2 Base-burning Stove. **1948** *Chi. Tribune* 18 Mar. IV. 1/2 It's going the way of the base burners and bed warmers. — (3) **1817** *Niles' Reg.* XII. 97/1 A standard line . . . is run due north and south, through the tract, . . . which line is crossed at right angles by another standard line, running due east and west, which is called the *base-line.* **1883** SMITH *Geol. Survey Ala.* 450 The narrow trough of Roup's Valley . . . is well defined as far south as the base line between the two surveys. **1944** *Chi. D. News* 30 Oct. 6/2 After victory we must move forward from a base line set many years since 1933.

b. With reference to the bases in baseball (*q.v.* as a main entry): (1) **base bag,** a bag of sand or sawdust used to mark first, second, or third base; (2) **hit,** a hit which enables the batter to reach first base; (3) * **line,** the line from one base to another, cf. **2.** (3) above; (4) **man,** a player stationed at a base, cf. **first, second, third baseman;** (5) * **plate,** (see quot., and cf. **home plate**); (6) **player,** a baseman; (7) **playing,** fielding at first, second, or third base; (8) **post,** formerly a post to which the basebag was attached, *obs.;* (9) **runner,** a player making the circuit of the bases; (10) **running,** running from one base to another; (11) **stealer,** a player who steals a base; (12) **steal(ing),** reaching a base without the aid of a hit or of an error, also attrib.

(1) **1864** *Wilkes' Spirit of Times* 10 Dec. 229/1 The player shall not be declared out if he maintains his position with any part of his person on the place where the base-bag belongs. **1948** *Time* 3 May 43/1 Williams angrily kicked the first base bag. — (2) **1875** *Chi. Tribune* 26 Oct. 2/7 The Philadelphians made twenty base hits to their opponents' six, and earned six runs. **1948** *Chi. Tribune* 8 May II. 3/4 O'Neill said there was nothing wrong with Wakefield that a couple of base hits wouldn't correct. — (3) **1867** *Ball Players' Chron.* 4 July 5/1, Foul balls are those striking the ground or a player back of the base lines. **1948** *Chi. D. News* 3 Mar. 34/1 But he was down the baseline, had to run back to tag and left too soon. — (4) **1857** *Spirit of Times* 28 Nov. 196/1 Logan, as third base, is excellent, and probably the best baseman on the club. **1912** *Amer. Mag.* Sep. 463/2 He . . . made a desperate, diving slide around and under the baseman only to be called out.

(5) **1889** *Cent.* 464/2 Base-plate. . . . In *base-ball* one of the plates formerly often used to mark the bases; hence, by extension, one of the bases. — (6) **1867** *Ball Players' Chron.* 6 June 3/3 Smith [is] . . . eminently a base player. **1896** CHADWICK *Spalding's Base B. Guide* 79 The fault lies with the catcher's inability to throw well to base, or to the base-player who fails to properly accept chances to put the runners out. — (7) **1868** CHADWICK *Base Ball* 34 We now come to base playing, and we propose to show that each position has its peculiar points of play. **1891** *Triangle* Feb. 3 The special training should include . . . under base-playing: . . . avoiding the runner in playing base. — (8) **1867** *Ball Players' Chron.* 25 July 2/2 The bases, instead of being canvass bags strapped to base posts, were nailed down tight, a plan that allows too many risks of sprained ankles. — (9) *Ib.* 6 June 2/1 The play was of no account, the struck ball being a called one, and consequently dead, both as regards the striker and base runner. **1948** *Dly. Ardmoreite* (Ardmore, Okla.) 7 April 10/2 Some believe he may develop into one of the fleetest base runners in the game.

(10) **1867** *Ball Players' Chron.* 6 June 4/2 The rule known as section 10 was checked off as adopted, and one of a similar tenor, *but prohibiting base running on called balls* was checked as lost. **1912** *Amer. Mag.* July 302/2 Remember that, in base running, the more the situation seems to call for an effort to steal the less chance to steal is given. — (11) **1896** CHADWICK *Spalding's Base B. Guide* 88 We have made up a record of the most successful base-stealers of the twelve League

clubs who have a record of total stolen bases for at least three seasons. **1948** *Dly. Ardmoreite* (Ardmore, Okla.) 27 May 5/2 The catcher threw to second base trying to catch a base stealer. — **(12) 1886** *Chi. Tribune* 14 May 3/3 The fifth inning was characterized by a cheeky bit of base-stealing by Dalrymple. **1889** *S.F. Bulletin* 29 July 1/7 The home nine up to last Thursday had to their credit 200 base steals. **1947** *Redbook* July 72/3 The catcher, of course, is important in the base-stealing act.

c. In phrases having reference to baseball (see quots.). Often *colloq.*

1867 *Ball Players' Chron.* 6 June 3/4 Only four were rewarded with runs, Walters, after taking his base on 3 balls, being sent home by Sweezy's hit. **1868** CHADWICK *Base Ball* 38 *Bases on Errors.*—When a base is made by a muffed or dropped ball, or by an overthrow, the batsman is not entitled to the credit of a base on a hit. **1888** MARK TWAIN *Meisterschaft* 463 (R.) It's about the gaudiest thing in the book, if you boom it right along and don't get left on a base. **1948** *Dly. Ardmoreite* (Ardmore, Okla.) 26 May 6/4 There are more men caught off base at cocktail parties than ball games.

d. *To change one's base,* to retreat or decamp. *Colloq.*

Gen. McClellan's euphemistic reference (see quot. 1862) to his defeat in the Peninsula campaign against Richmond, from April to August, 1862 provoked the satirical use of this phrase.

1862 MCCLELLAN in *Own Story* (1887) 485 Never did such a change of base, involving a retrograde movement, and under incessant attacks . . . partake so little of disorder. **1863** *Rio Abajo Press* 28 July 4/3 Judge Baird's defeat . . . caused him to change his 'base' to California. **1919** DUNN *Indiana* II. 996 The medical profession had resolved on a change of base.

e. *To be off* (one's) *base,* out of one's right mind, off one's rocker. *Colloq.*

1882 PECK *Sunshine* 42 The Boston lady held up her hands in holy horror, and was going to explain . . . how she was off her base. **1907** M. C. HARRIS *Tents of Wickedness* III. iii. 251 Mrs. Butterbeans was so off her base about it, it was ludicrous. **1947** *Time* 20 Oct. 11/1 Your Latin American department was off base in its comparison of the Portillo Hotel in Chile with our famous Sun Valley.

As the last term in **earned, first, home, king's, second, stolen, sub, third, work base.**

***baseball,** *n.*

1. A well-known game now played according to official rules, on a "diamond" ninety feet square, by teams of nine players each.

The first mention so far found of "baseball" is in *A Little Pretty Book* brought out in London in 1744. (See *The Month At Goodspeed's,* Jan. 1943, 89–90.) Hence neither the term nor the game originated in this country, but the game has been so modified and modernized here as to justify regarding the present meaning of "baseball" as distinctively American.

1850 *Knickerb.* XXXV. 84 As we . . . never indulged in a game of chance . . . save the 'bass-ball' . . . and 'barn-ball' of our boyhood. **1857** *Spirit of Times* 24 Oct. 117/2 Base Ball . . . has, no doubt, been played in this country for at least one century. **1869** *Nation* 26 Aug. 168/2 He would indeed be an unfaithful chronicler who should attempt to question the hoary antiquity of 'Two-Old-Cat,' or the parental relation in which it stands to base-ball. **1945** *This Week Mag.* 1 Sep. 4/3 He pointed to a stocky kid playing baseball in the middle of the street.

b. The ball used in this game.

1863 GAIL HAMILTON *Gala-Days* 50 You may . . . hurl the base-ball, follow the plough, . . . and yet you may be a hero. **1947** *Nat. Geog. Mag.* July 96/2 A hundred other products of the two cities range from baseballs to baby food.

2. In derivatives and combs.: (1) **baseball association,** an association comprising a number of baseball teams or clubs; (2) **club,** (*a*) a club of baseball players and officials, (*b*) a baseball bat; (3) **column,** a column in a newspaper devoted to baseball news or comment; (4) **diamond,** the square, ninety feet on a side, making up the infield of a baseball field; (5) **-dom,** all those interested in baseball; (6) **baseballer,** see as a main entry; (7) **fever,** enthusiasm for baseball; (8) **ground,** an area where baseball is played; (9) **baseballism,** (*a*) the practice or pursuit of baseball, (*b*) an expression used in baseball; (10) **baseballist, = baseballer a;** (11) **league,** an association of baseball clubs; (12) **nine,** the nine players composing a baseball team; (13) **park,** an area, usu. inclosed and provided with a grandstand, where baseball is regularly played; (14) **team,** a group, at present nine, of players composing a "side" in baseball.

(1) 1888 *Battle Creek* (Mich.) *Jrnl.* 12 Dec., The managers of the Western Base Ball Association convened . . . Saturday morning. — (2) (*a*) **1855** (*title*), Atlantic Base Ball Club, Jamaica, N.Y. **1913** *Amer. Mag.* Sep. 23/2 The Orioles, carefully studied, never were a great baseball club—on paper, although probably the greatest that ever played on the field. (*b*) **1884** NYE *Baled Hay* 207 Should the immediate lime continue to remain deliberate, lay the water down on a stone and pound it with a base ball club. **1891** S. M. WELCH *Recoll.* 1830–40 173 They were hideous devices . . . seeming to have been formed by dipping various sizes of bent base ball clubs in melted gum. — **(3) 1867** *Brooklyn Union* 10 June Mr. C. has for some time been in charge of the familiar base ball column of the *Union.* — **(4) 1944** *Nat. Geog. Mag.* Jan. 79 There are baseball diamonds set in jungle glades to the specifications of Abner Double-day. **1948** *Pacific Discovery* Mar–Apr. 18/2 Flocks of Brewer blackbirds pass overhead on their way to forage on the baseball diamond.

(5) 1867 *Ball Players' Chron.* 22 Aug. 2/4 All base balldom were gathered together on the Union grounds. **1928** *Dly. Ardmoreite* (Ardmore, Okla.) 29 March 8/5 (*heading*), Spitball Pitchers Are Fast Fading From Baseballdom. — **(7) 1867** *Norwich* (Conn.) *Bulletin* 24 July, Whenever a club chances to become expert, the locality in which it abides has base ball fever. — **(8) 1867** *Ball Players' Chron.* 27 June 6/3 Both clubs appeared on the field in neat uniforms, that of the Dartmouth players being more tasteful and better adapted for its use than is often seen on a base ball ground. — **(9)** (*a*) **1870** *Northern Vindicator* 14 May, We disserted briefly upon the present popular 'ism' of the day, viz.: base ballism. (*b*) **1898** *Boston Sun. Globe* 15 May 36/4 There are two kinds of salesmen, the 'pikers,' who grind away all the time, and the men who bunch their hits, to use a baseballism.

(10) 1867 *Harper's Wkly.* 30 Nov. 758/1 Not having the fear of 'baseballists' before his eyes, . . . [he] suggested to the various clubs that if they needed physical exercise they had better turn their attention to sawing wood for the poor. **1896** *Ohio Chronicle* (Columbus) 5 Dec., The brilliant record our own Pickaway boy . . . has made for himself as a crack base and footballist. — **(11) 1887** *Lippincott's Mag.* Aug. 312 The parties to this were the four base-ball leagues then in existence. **1930** WILLIAMSON *Amer. Hotel* 293 The Broadway Central has been the scene of several noteworthy episodes. It was there that the National Baseball League was organized in 1876. — **(12) 1871** L. H. BAGG *At Yale* 49 *University* . . . [signifies] the picked base-ball nine. **1948** *Chi. Tribune* 5 March II. 18/2 He was the third best boxer in school and the first string pitcher on the baseball nine. — **(13) 1868** *N.E. Baseballist* 22 Oct. 45/1 The matches . . . at the base ball park . . . were decidedly the most interesting of the series. **1948** *Chi. Sun-Times* 2 June 83/2 A published report stated that the Braves 'will become owners of their own baseball park.' — **(14) 1888** *Outing* XII. 117/1 The first regular professional baseball team ever established . . . went into practical operation in 1868. **1947** *Chi. D. News* 10 April 1/8 Aboard the plane were members of a soldier baseball team.

Also *baseball bat, contest, czar, fan, follower, game, ground, magnate, match, pennant race, player, practice, stadium,* etc.

baseball ˈbesˌbɔl, *v. intr.* To play at baseball. Also with *it.* Also **baseballing,** *n.*

1867 *Ball Players' Chron.* 12 Dec. 4/3 Possibly we may be walking and base-balling ourselves into a better reputation. **1871** *Northern Vindicator* (Estherville, Iowa) 22 March, The Blizzards [Club] are beginning to base-ball-it again this spring. **1896** *Ohio Chron.* (Columbus) 5 Dec., Even if he proposes to follow baseballing.

baseballer ˈbesˌbɔlə, *n.* **a.** One who plays or supports baseball. **b. base bawler,** (see quot. 1867). *Slang. Obs.*

(a) 1867 *Ball Players' Chron.* 24 Oct. 7/1 Could the experiences of his chequered career be vividly portrayed, . . . there would be fewer base-ballers. **1948** *Chi. Maroon* 7 May 19/4 Chicago's baseballers outscored their three weekend opponents 19 to 14. — **(b) 1867** *Chi. Times* 29 July 4/3 Base-bawlers—the men who, having lost some money in the late match, are asserting that they have been swindled. **1869** *Terr. Enterprise* (Virginia, Nev.) 14 Oct. 3/2 There is getting to be a great number of 'base bawlers' in this city.

***basement,** *n.*

1. basement apartment. An apartment in a basement.

1863 C. C. HOPLEY *Life in South* I. 4 Vast hotels rise bodily to admit a new foundation and a new suite of 'basement' apartments. **1948** *Chi. Tribune* 26 June I. 10/7 An advertisement in a neighborhood paper last week read, '2 1/2 Rm. Unfurn. Basement Apt., call Anonymous 0000.'

2. basement house. A house in which the rooms for receiving company are one story above the ground level, having an entrance at the basement level.

1852 BRISTED *Upper Ten Th.* ii. 43 Even in a double house, or a house and a half, or a basement house, three different styles which would all admit of cloaking-rooms on the lower floor, no one ever thinks of having them there. **1886** *Cent. Mag.* Feb. 549/1 We have since built basement-houses in not inconsiderable numbers, but they have never been really popular in New York.

See also **bargain basement, English basement.**

baser ˈbesɚ, *n.* In baseball, a hit that enables the batter to reach a base. *Obs.* Cf. **base hit,** and see **three baser, two baser.** — **1879** *Chi. Tribune* 16 May 5/2 Peters knocked the sphere for a baser, sending in Anson. **1889** *Cin. Commercial Gaz.* 17 March 7/1 Three [runs] in the fifth, by McPhee's single, Corkhill's home runner to right field fence, West's infield baser, a passed ball and an excusable error by Creamer.

Bashaba bɑˈʃebə, *n.* [Native word.] The titular name of a chief or king among the Abnaki Indians in Maine. Now *hist.*

1605 Rosier in *Mass. Hist. Soc. Coll.* 3 Ser. VIII. 142 [The Indians] often would . . . sign unto us, that their Bashebes (that is their king) had great plenty of furs. *a***1704** Hubbard *Hist. N. Eng.* vii. 30 In the . . . places more eastward, they called the chief rulers . . . bashabeas. **1795** J. Sullivan *Hist. Maine* 88 Tribes . . . had above these [chiefs,] higher officers called Bashabas. **1937** Coffin *Kennebec* 204 The 'bashaba,' the chief bottle washer of the tribe, had the honor of giving the sea monster the iron.

***bashaw,** *n.* A local name for the mud cat. — **1888** Goode *Amer. Fishes* 378 'The Mud Cat' 'Yellow Cat,' 'Soujon' or 'Bashaw' is found in all the large rivers of the West and South. **1923** *Public Opinion* 12 Oct. 357/3 A good-sized fish, itself Carnivorous, called a basha. **1938** Schrenkeisen *Fresh-Water Fishes* 164.

***basil,** *n.* Any one of various kinds of mountain mint. See also **scarlet basil.**

1791 Muhlenberg *Index Florae* 172 *Clinopodium vulgare,* Basil-weed. **1836** Lincoln *Botany* App. 130 *Pycnanthemum . . . incanum,* ('wild basil, mountain mint . . .) leaves oblong-ovate . . . flowers in compound heads. **1901** Mohr *Plant Life Ala.* 699 *Koellia albescens* (Torr. & Gr.) . . . Whitish Basil. [Grows in] Louisianian area. Florida to Texas and Arkansas.

***basin,** *n.* **1.** (*cap.*) Short for **Great Basin. 2. Basin State,** a nickname for Utah.

(1) **1902** Wister *Virginian* xxv. 282 The Judge has friends goin' to arrive from New Yawk for a trip across the Basin. **1930** Henry *Conquer. Plains* 255 Hence I propose a tribute to the noble women of our transcendent Basin. — (2) **1852** Stansbury *Gt. Salt Lake* 140 The sustenance of a population so numerous as will ere long be congregated within the limits of the 'Basin State.'

As the last term in **catch, grand, Great, steamboat basin.**

***basis,** *n.* As the last term in **compound, federal, mixed, paper, specie, white basis.**

***basket,** *n.*

1. One of the goals in basketball, originally a fruit basket or box, now a metal ring 18 in. in diameter from which a net of white cord, open at the bottom, is suspended.

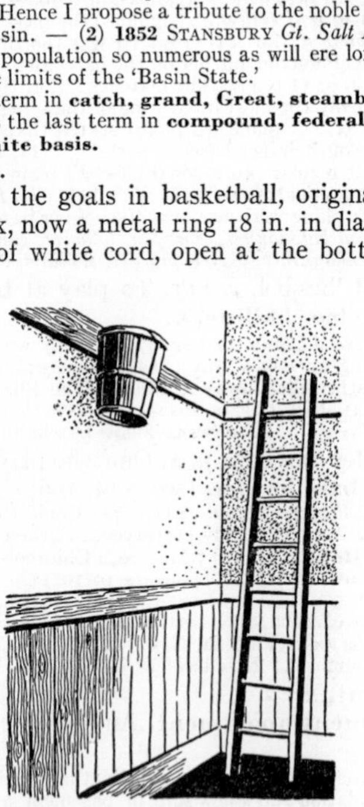

Basket of the kind originally used in basketball

1892 J. Naismith in *Triangle* Jan. 145 The baskets [are] hung up, one at each end on the railing. The goals are a couple of baskets or boxes about fifteen inches in diameter across the opening, and about fifteen inches deep. **1945** *Chi. D. News* 8 Aug. 22/2 He had an uncanny knack of hitting the basket with a right-handed hook shot.

b. A score or point in basketball.

1907 Smith *Basket Ball Guide* 31 He . . . always succeeded in outscoring his opponent at least to the extent of two baskets to one. **1948** *Dly. Ardmoreite* (Ardmore, Okla.) 21 Mar. 15/2 They broke through the Lions' loosening defenses for five straight baskets.

2. In combs. designating meals carried in baskets or gatherings at which meals so brought are partaken of, as (1) **basket dinner,** (2) **lunch,** (3) **meeting,** (4) **party,** (5) **picnic,** (6) **social,** (7) **supper.**

(1) **1892** *Ill. Kentuckian* (Lexington) Dec. 88/3 This is a noted place for picnics where pies and cake and basket dinners prevail. **1904** *Charlotte D. Observer* 21 Aug. 8 After the speech a basket dinner will be enjoyed by the picnickers. **1946** *Nat. Speleological Soc. Bul.* July 53/1 One of the caves was formed to provide a large room where basket dinners could be served. — (2) **1905** *Springfield W. Republican* 11 Aug. 14 At noon a bountiful basket lunch was served under the trees in the park. — (3) **1859** Bartlett 24 *Basket-meeting,* in the West, a sort of picnic, generally with some religious 'exercises.' **1892** *N. & Q.* VIII. 309 'Basket meetings' are not confined to the Southern negroes. On the contrary they are more common among the white people. Neither are they always religious. Quite frequently they are political, sometimes educational. When purely social they are called picnics. — (4) **1868** *Cong. Globe* 6 Feb. 1008/3 In the southern part of Illinois . . . they have what they call basket parties where every man carries his own refreshments.

(5) **1882** in Foreman *Last Trek* (1946) 198 This year witnessed a good, old-fashioned basket picnic. **1910** *Collier's* 14 May 29/2 These Farmers' Days are usually basket-picnics, and the people come by train, trolley, team, and even automobiles. — (6) **1895** *Denver Times* 5 Mar. 5/4 The Prohibitionists will give a basket social (cake only) at the Women's Exchange. — (7) **1944** *Chi. D. News* 16 June 25/5 Have sack or basket or box suppers that are plain but delicious. **1948** *Tishomingo* (Okla.) *Capital-Democrat* 17 June 5/6 In addition to hearing the inspiring Indian singers, we will have a basket supper at six-thirty.

3. In miscellaneous combs.: (1) **basketball,** see as a main entry; (2) **baller,** one who plays basketball; (3) **clause,** a clause of a general or comprehensive character; (4) **dance,** (of obscure meaning), *obs.;* (5) **darning,** darning in which the threads cross and interlace somewhat like the twigs in basketwork; (6) **Basket Maker,** one of the earliest inhabitants of the Southwest, prior to the use there of pottery, also designating the period (A.D. *c*100–500) when these Indians lived, or the culture which they possessed; (7) **oak,** thin strips of oak for making baskets, cf. **b.** (4) below; (8) **rack,** (see quot.); (9) **stuff,** material, as thin strips of white oak, for making baskets; (10) **timber,** timber which supplies basket stuff; (11) **wood,** =**basket stuff.**

(2) **1922** *Dly. Ardmoreite* (Ardmore, Okla.) 5 Jan. 2/1 A double-header will be staged in the Junior High gymnasium . . . when both the boys and girls teams of the Ardmore High School basketballers play. **1948** *Ib.* 15 April 7/4 Jimmy Littlejohn . . . won considerable fame as an East Texas State basketballer. — (3) **1883** *Cong. Rec.* 13 Feb. 2580/1 This basket clause seems to be a sort of prophetic fine-comb with which to search all the possibilities of the future. **1897** *Ib.* 26 March 367/2 Mr. Bailey:—If we strike . . . [an item] from the dutiable list we transfer it to the 'basket clause' at 25 per cent . . . Mr. Dingley:—There is no 'basket clause' to the free list. — (4) **1886** Poore *Reminisc.* I. 74 The '*minuet de la cour*' and stately 'quadrille,' varied by the 'basket dance,' and, on exceptional occasions, the exhilarating 'cheat,' formed the staple for saltatorial performance.

(5) **1884** *Harper's Mag.* Aug. 346/2 The darned threads are carried across either the woof or warp . . . and are not crossed by a returning thread, as in ordinary basket darning. — (6) **1904** Burdick *Mystic Mid-Region* 92 The basket-makers of that time had all the skill that is known to their descendants to-day. **1938** *Southwestern Lore* June 5 We now place the beginning of the Basket Maker II period as about the opening of the Christian Era and its end about 400 A.D., with the Basket Maker III period lasting up to 700 A.D. **1948** *Atlantic Mo.* Jan. 61/1 In this red-walled wash . . . the archeologist Prudden first clearly isolated the Basket Maker culture as separate from and earlier than the Pueblo. — (7) **1856** *Fla. Plant. Rec.* 506, 1 hand giting out basket oake today. — (8) **1895** Wait *Car-Builder's Dict.* 93 Parcel-net (English). American equivalent, *basket-rack.* In a carriage, a netting placed transversely above the seats for the purpose of carrying light baggage, parcels, etc. — (9) [**1824** *N.H. Hist. Soc. Coll.* I. 251 A few ash trees . . . were stripped of bark and limbs, and split literally into basket-stuff.] **1877** *Vermont Bd. Agric. Rep.* IV. 91 The chairs were bottomed with elm bark, . . . or of split ash called basket stuff.

(10) **1845** *Cultivator* II. 303 What are they going to do when the supply of basket timber is exhausted? **1929** F. E. McClinchey *Joe Pete* 69 When April came—the month when came the first chance to get basket timber if the season were an advanced one—she was glad that Charlotte was there. — (11) **1855** Davis *Farm Bk.* 205 Got basket wood & began to make baskets.

b. In the names of or with reference to plants and animals: (1) **basket elm, =cedar elm;** (2) **fish,** a sand-star found on the N. Eng. coast; (3) **horse,** (of obscure meaning), *obs.;* (4) **oak,** the cow oak, cf. **3.** (7) above; (5) **plant,** a plant suitable for growing in a basket (see quot.); (6) **worm,** (see quot. 1889).

(1) **1851** *De Bow's Review* XI. 46 *Basket Elm and Water Elm.* — (2) **1671** WINTHROP in *Phil. Trans.* VI. 2223 Until a fitter English name be found for it, why may it not be called . . . a Basket-Fish, or a Net Fish, or a Purs-net Fish? **1881** E. INGERSOLL *Oyster Industry* 241 Basket-Fish, *Astrophyton Agassizii*, a kind of many armed star-fish. — (3) **1847** FIELD *Drama in Pokerville*, etc. 188 A long, lumbering wagon, canvas-topped, &c., a 'basket-horse' snuffing the breeze out of the after end. — (4) **1876** DODGE *Black Hills* 103 The oak is a white oak, of sometimes a straight fiber, like the basket oak of the Eastern States. **1899** SUDWORTH *Arborescent Flora* 158 *Quercus michauxii*, Cow Oak. . . . Common names [include] Basket Oak (Ala., Miss., La., Tex., Ark.). *Ib.* 159 *Quercus breviloba*, Durand Oak. . . . Common names [include] . . . Basket Oak (Ala., La., Tex.).

(5) **1862** *Ill. Agric. Soc. Trans.* V. 796 The *stanhopen sigrina* (or basket plant) is exceedingly rare and fragrant. — (6) **1862** T. HARRIS *Insects Injur. Veg.* 415 In Philadelphia and the vicinity . . . trees are often very much injured by the insects inhabiting them. These are there popularly called drop-worms and basket-worms. **1889** *Cent.* 420/3 Bag-worm. . . . The larva of a lepidopterous insect, *Thyridopteryx ephemeraeformis* (Harris), common throughout the more northern part of the United States. The larva is called bag-worm because it spins a silken bag for its protection, and moves with it hanging downward; it has also received the names *basket-worm, drop-worm*, etc.

As the last term in **alum, birchbark, chip, corn, cotton, feed, fish, Indian, key, May, oriole, papoose, Saratoga, scrap, shuck, splinter, split, steamer, stocking, trash, wash basket.**

basketball ˈbæskɪtˌbɔl, *n.* [The name and the sport were brought into use in 1891 by James Naismith at the Y.M.C.A. College at Springfield, Mass.] A game, usu. played indoors and chiefly in winter, in which the players, commonly five on a side, try to toss a large inflated ball through an elevated basket or goal.

1892 NAISMITH in *Triangle* Jan. 144 Basket Ball [*article heading*]. We present to our readers a new game of ball. . . . It fills the same place in the gymnasium that foot ball does in the athletic field. Any number of men may play at it, and each one get plenty of exercise. **1893** *Physical Education* April 21 Basket Ball as an In-door Game for Winter Amusement and Exercise. **1947** *Chr. Sci. Monitor* 16 Jan. 6/1 Basketball remains the only major sport of purely American origin, and the sport which, year in and year out, attracts more spectators than any other.

attrib. **1913** *Outing* Feb. 639/1 The Princeton basket ball team defeated the New York University five. **1921** HALL *Yosemite Nat. Park* 280 Basket-ball or similar shoes with heavy rubber soles are good for smooth rock surfaces. **1948** *P. C. C. Chronicle* (Pasadena, Calif.) 31 Mar. 2/1 Handball courts, top basketball courts, and other physical improvements have been recently made.

b. The ball used in this game.

1902 *Sears Cat.* (ed. 112) 325/2 Victor Official Basket Ball, made of the best English grain leather 30 1/2 to 30 inches circumference, the best basket ball made. **1948** *Athletic Jrnl.* April 3/1 We have done 'miracles' in taking old basketballs, footballs . . . and punching bags and returning them beautifully reconditioned.

basketeer ˌbæskəˈtɪr, *n.* A basketball player. — **1922** *Ardmore* (Okla.) *D. Press* 1 Jan. 1/6 The Wilson Knights of Pythias basketeers defeated the Loco High School five Friday night. **1948** *Salt Lake Tribune* 17 Jan. 20/8 The University of Utah basketeers . . . will play their first home conference game Saturday night.

***bass,** *n.* **1. bass plug,** a cylindrical casting bait used for bass. **2. bass rock,** *N. Car.* ?the rockfish or striped bass. *Rare.*

(1) **1923** *Outing* Apr. 13/1 We even tried flies . . . and several home-made (fearfully and wonderfully made) bass plugs. **1947** DALRYMPLE *Panfish* 212 Now and again a big Rock Bass will smash a large Bass plug with as much vigor as the Old Boy himself. — (2) **1784** J. SMYTH *Tour U.S.* I. xi. 89 Amazing numbers of those fishes, here called Bass-Rocks . . . [come] up to the falls at the same time to spawn.

As the last term in **bar, black, brass, brassy, buck, bull, calico, channel, dotted, grass, green, hog, lake, large mouth(ed) (black), minny, moss, mud, mungo, Oswego, Otsego, red, river, rock, sea, shad, silver, slough, spotted-tail, state, strawberry, striped, sunfish, tiger, white, yellow bass.**

basswood ˈbæsˌwʊd, *n.*

1. A tree of the genus *Tilia*, in full **basswood tree,** or the wood of this. See also **white basswood.**

1670 *Rowley Rec.* 210 The Northwest Angle is a basswood tree. **1728** *Boston Rec.* 222 We are of opinion that no popler, chestnut, pine, hemlock [*sic*], sassifax, black ash, basswood, or ceder shall be corded up. **1841** COOPER *Deerslayer* ii. 9 Deerslayer pointed out . . . the trunk of a huge linden, or bass-wood. **1946** *Sports Afield* Nov. 92/2 An occasional old basswood or sugar maple provided good den trees.

2. Attrib. in sense "made or consisting of basswood," as (1) **basswood ball,** (2) **log,** (3) **paddle,** (4) **paper,** (5) **plank,** (6) **spout,** (7) **trough,** (8) **whistle.**

(1) **1895** *Outing* XXVI. 474/1 There is no better light cavalry exercise than an hour in the saddle chasing the bounding basswood ball. — (2) **1843** *Yale Lit. Mag.* VIII. 361 The half of a basswood log with the bark peeled off . . . was placed under his head, in lieu of a pillow. **1892** *Vermont Agric. Rep.* XII. 155 The farmer of fifty years ago . . . tapping his trees with an axe and catching the sap in troughs dug from bass wood logs. — (3) **1845** JUDD *Margaret* I. ii. 7 Her brother . . . was at work with a piece of glass, smoothing a snow-white bass-wood paddle. — (4) **1857** *Knickerb.* XLIX. 109 We have received, through a friend, four different kinds of Basswood Paper.

(5) **1855** THOMPSON *Doesticks* 220 Magnificent forest scene— . . . a mossy bank . . . made of canvass, stretched over a basswood plank, and painted mud color. — (6) **1851** *Knickerb.* XXXVII. 377 The country-bred traveller . . . smells the bass-wood 'spouts,' . . . and inhales the odor of the red-cedar buckets. — (7) **1849** *Ib.* XXXIII. 279 The bass-wood troughs or sweet-smelling cedar buckets. — (8) **1879** B. F. TAYLOR *Summer-Savory* xi. 99 It looked like a basswood whistle, but it was bliss.

b. Used jocosely in the names of articles of trade allegedly made of basswood and dispensed by Yankee peddlers, as **basswood button, ham, pumpkin seed.**

1824 *Microscope* (Albany, N.Y.) 27 March 4/1 (Th.), All the heroes of wooden nutmegs, horn gun-flint, and bass-wood button memory. **1830** *Newark* (N.J.) *Monitor* 7 Sep. 2/5 Freemasonry is as gross an imposture on the public as the *wooden nutmegs*, or *horn flints*, or the *beach hams*, or *leathern clocks*, or *basswood pumpkin seeds*. **1850** *Cong. Globe* 30 April 861/3, I want to see how many wooden nutmegs, horn flints, and basswood hams have been made and sent to the South since the last census. [**1856** *Western Citizen* (Paris, Ky.) 20 June 1/4 The cucumber seeds of those days were not all 'basswood.']

transf. **basswood Mormon,** an imitation Mormon. *Rare.*

*a***1859** B. YOUNG *Sermons* (B.), You Gentiles and hickory and basswood Mormons can write it down, if you please; but write it as I speak it.

c. basswood township, a township where basswood is abundant, a backwoods or frontier township. *Rare.*

1882 *Cong. Rec.* 2 Feb. 832/1 Every man who has ever practiced before a justice of the peace in a hog case in a bass-wood township would know.

bassy ˈbæsɪ, *a.* Frequented by bass. *Rare.* — **1897** *Outing* June 222/2 An opening in a mat of weeds, a shadowed nook . . . where a tree overhangs the water, into which insects may drop—these are very 'bassy' spots.

***bastard,** *n.* and *a.*

1. *n.* (See quot.)

1889 *Cent.* 470/2 bastard. . . . A local name of Kemp's gulf-turtle, *Thalassochelys* (*Colpochelys*) *kempi*, of the Gulf of Mexico.

2. *a.* In combs.: (1) **bastard Baltimore,** the orchard oriole, *Icterus spurius*, of eastern North America, smaller than the Baltimore oriole; (2) **halibut,** a large flounder of the Pacific Coast; (3) **hornsnake,** the hornsnake, *Farancia abacura*, of the southern states, or a snake similar to this; (4) **marsh,** app. an inferior kind of meadow ground, *rare;* (5) **pearl,** the abalone, *rare;* (6) **pennyroyal,** a plant of the genus *Trichostema* having irregular blue flowers; (7) **pine,** any one of various pines (see quots.); (8) **rattlesnake,** the ground rattler or massasauga; (9) **trout,** a weakfish found on the southern coasts of the U.S.

(1) *c***1728** CATESBY *Carolina* I. 49 *Icterus minor.* The Bastard Baltimore. Weighs thirteen pennyweight. **1808** WILSON *Ornithology* I. 23 Buffon, and Latham, have both described the male of the bastard Baltimore (*Oriolus spurius*), as the female Baltimore. — (2) **1907** JORDAN *Fishes* (1925) 702 In the bastard halibuts, *Paralichthys*, the eyes and color are on the left side. — (3) **1888** CABLE *Bonaventure* 291 The maimed form and black and red markings of a 'bastard hornsnake.' — (4) **1684** *Essex Inst. Coll.* XXII. 2 Also I give him . . . two acres of bastard and salt marsh or ruff meadow.

(5) **1805** *Lewis and Clark Journals* (1904) III. i. 10 The most sacred of all the orniments of this nation is the sea shells of various Sizes and Shapes and colours, of the bassterd perl kind, which they inform us they get from the Indians to the South. — (6) **1859** BARTLETT 37 Blue curls. (*Trichostema dichotomum.*) From the shape and color of its

flowers. A common plant resembling pennyroyal, and hence called bastard pennyroyal. — (7) **1785** MARSHALL *Amer. Grove* 100 *Pinus echinata.* Three leaved prickly-coned Bastard Pine. This grows naturally in Virginia. **1884** SARGENT *Rep. Forests* 202 *Pinus Cubensis.* . . . Bastard Pine. Meadow Pine. — (8) **1791** BARTRAM *Travels* 274 The bastard rattle snake, by some called ground rattle snake, is a dangerous little creature. — (9) **1888** GOODE *Amer. Fishes* 120 The Silver Squeteague, *Cynoscion nothum,* called at Charleston the 'Bastard Trout.' The 'White Trout' . . . is caught with hook and line.

b. In similar combs sufficiently explained in the quots.: (1) **bastard canoe,** (2) **china root,** (3) **dowitcher,** (4) **hickory,** (5) **limestone,** (6) **locust,** (7) **margaret,** (8) **oak,** (9) **pecan,** (10) **sandstone,** (11) **snapper,** (12) **Spanish,** (13) **yellowlegs.**

(1) **1944** NUTE *Lk. Superior* 114 There was also the intermediate size, the North canoe, and still a third size, called the bastard canoe, which was larger than the Indian, but not so large as a North canoe. — (2) **1737** BRICKELL *N. Carolina* 22 Tisinaw, or Bastard China-Root, these grow in great Clusters, together, and have a stalk like a Brier, whereon grow small Black-Berries, the Indians boil these Roots and eat them, and sometimes make them into Bread. — (3) **1889** *Cent.* 1749/2 Bastard dowitcher or dowitch, the stilt-sandpiper, *Micropalama himantopus.* — (4) **1948** *Sci. Amer.* Sep. 41/1 Occasionally a tree has clear, not shaggy, bark, and is called by lumbermen 'Bastard Hickory.'

(5) **1882** WORTHEN *Econ. Geol. Ill.* II. 81, I observed . . . a layer of hard, firmly cemented, calcareous sandstone. . . . It is generally called bastard limestone in this vicinity. — (6) **1851** *S. Lit. Messenger* XVII. 374/2, I am convinced that it is the Mezquite; which is not known to exist in our prairies; their frequenters have no name for it that I have heard except perhaps 'bastard locust.' — (7) **1903** J. A. HENSHALL *Bass,* etc. 330 The Sailor's Choice (*Hæmulon parra*). This grunt is sometimes called bastard margaret by the Key West fisherman. — (8) **1901** MOHR *Plant Life Ala.* 470 *Quercus brevilobata,* Texan White Oak, Pin Oak, Bastard Oak, . . . [is] of some value for its timber. — (9) **1818** DARBY *Emigrant's Guide* 80 (*note*), *Juglans aquatica,* Water hickory, . . . This tree bears, in Louisiana, the name of bastard paccan.

(10) **1882** WORTHEN *Econ. Geol. Ill.* II. 160 A hard calcareous sand rock, or, in the language of the people, a bastard sandstone. — (11) **1888** GOODE *Amer. Fishes* 78 The Mangrove Snapper . . . of Charleston, called at Pensacola the 'Bastard Snapper.' *Ib.* 84 The Bream, or 'Bastard Snapper,' *Sparus aculeatus.* — (12) **1709** LAWSON *Carolina* 92 Bastard-Spanish is an Oak betwixt the Spanish and Red-Oak. — (13) **1909** WEBSTER 190/3 *B[astard] yellowlegs,* the stilt sandpiper. *Mass. & Long Island.* **1917** *Birds of Amer.* I. 231/1 The similarity of the two species is acknowledged by the popular name, 'Bastard Yellow-legs,' which the sportsmen of Long Island have given to the Stilt Sandpiper.

bastos ˈbɑstos, *n. S.W.* [pl. of Sp. *basto* in Amer. Sp. sense shown here.] A leather lining of a saddle. Also the skirt of a saddle.

1881 FARROW *Mt. Scouting* 138 The Mexican or California saddle . . . [is] usually furnished with wool-lined bastas. **1907** *Outing* Nov. 139/2 Even then I] could not avoid a sharp prod that would have ripped him up had not my leather *bastos* intervened. **1946** *Trail Riders Bul.* May 11/1 They're as much a part of a cowpoke's equipment as the *bastas* and *mochila* of his saddle.

∗**bat,** *n.*[1] The bull-bat, *Chordeiles virginianus.*

1709 LAWSON *Carolina* 144 East-Indian Bats or Musqueto Hawks, are the Bigness of a Cuckoo, and much of the same Colour. **1808–14** WILSON *Ornithology* V. 65 Night-Hawk. . . . This bird in Virginia and some of the southern districts, is called a bat. **1899** GREEN *Va. Word Book* 52 *Bat,* the night hawk.

b. bat-tick, a small spider-like insect parasitic on bats.

1852 T. HARRIS *Insects New Eng.* 501 A remarkable group of insects, which seems to connect the flies with the true ticks and spiders. Such are sheep-ticks and bat-ticks. **1868** *Amer. Naturalist* II. 198 The Bee-louse of Europe . . . [is] allied to . . . the wingless Bat-tick (*Nycteribia*).

As the last term in **brown, bull, Carolina, East India, New York, red, squirrel, Virginia bat.**

∗**bat,** *n.*[2]

1. = **cotton bat.**

1847 in THOMPSON *M. Jones* (1872) 194 Becky was cardin away as hard as she could, makin bats of cotton for a quiltin they was gwine to have, and lookin as mischievous as she could be. **1867** G. W. HARRIS *Sut Lovingood* 128 Hit wud rain aigs, an' bats ove cottin.

2. bat boy, in baseball a boy selected or employed to look after bats during a game.

1925 *Boston Ev. Transcript* 16 Nov. 11. **1946** *Chi. D. News* 30 Dec. 1/1 How would you like to be batboy for the Chicago White Sox?

3. In colloq. expressions stemming from baseball: (1) *at (the) bat,* said of a side whose turn it is to bat, also fig; (2) *hot from (off) the bat,* promptly; (3) *step to the bat,* go ahead, take your turn; (4) *right off the bat,* at once; (5) *to come (go) to bat for,* to come or go to the assistance of (someone or something).

(1) **1875** *Chi. Tribune* 18 Aug. 5/6 The fine play of the home nine for seven innings, . . . both in the field and at the bat. **1884** NYE *Baled Hay* 52 Common decency ought to govern conversation without its being necessary to hire an umpire to announce who is at bat and who is on deck. — (2) **1888** MARK TWAIN *Meisterschaft* 459 (R.), Whoever may ask us a Meisterschaft question shall get a Meisterschaft answer —and hot from the bat! **1910** W. M. RAINE *B. O'Connor* 65 Turn loose your yarn at me hot off the bat. — (3) **1889** MARK TWAIN *Connecticut Yankee* vii. 88 (R.), Step to the bat, it's your innings. — (4) **1916** EATON *Idyl of Twin Fires* 210 It would have been hard to name so many correctly right off the bat. **1948** *Dly. Oklahoman* (Okla. City) 5 June 6/3 Why don't you come to some reasonable conclusions right off the bat?

(5) [**1868** *Iowa State Reporter* (Des Moines) 21 Oct. 2/4 The penny was flipped to see who should go first to the bat, and the juniors won it.] **1928** J. P. MCEVOY *Show Girl* 194 The daughter of old man Brewster who owns the Evening Tab, my meal ticket, came to bat when my show was ready to close. **1946** *Newsweek* 15 July 30/1 Patterson, . . . visited the Batavia plant and went to bat for him.

As the last term in **baseball, dough, fungo bat.**

bat bæt, *n.*[3] [App. < *batter* in same sense; cf. *on the batter,* on a spree, in *EDD s.v. batter, sb.*[2] 3.] A spree, usu. *on (upon) a bat. Slang.*

1848 DURIVAGE & BURNHAM *Stray Subjects* 102 Zenas had been on 'a bat' during the night previous. **1894** *S.F. Midwinter Appeal* 19 May 15/1 He hasn't taken a bath or shave since he started in on his big bat. **1945** SERVICE *Ploughman* 342 Once in a while he would go on a bat that lasted for days.

∗**bat,** *v. tr.* In baseball, to hit safely balls served by (a pitcher). Often in the passive.

1867 *Ball Players' Chron.* 20 June 3/4 He was batted freely all over the field in a style that must have considerably astonished him. **1887** *Courier-Journal* (Louisville) 4 June 2/7 The Cleveland nine . . . batted Lynch freely and beat the Mets. **1944** *Sat. Ev. Post* 12 Aug. 91/1 Believe it or not, he was never once relieved. He was never batted from the hill.

batamote ˌbɑtɑˈmot, *n.* Also **guatamote.** *S.W.* [See note.]

The Amer. Sp. *batamote* (ultimate origin obscure), used in Mexico for the *Baccharis glutinosa,* gave rise among English speakers to "guatamote," which in turn, by a misapprehension of its 1st element (since the plant grows in wet places), led on to **water wally.**

One of several species of *Baccharis* growing in moist places in the Southwest. Also attrib.

1886 VAN DYKE *So. Calif.* 17 It meanders through meadows green with perennial grass, then amid jungles of wild-rose, sweet-brier, and guatemote. **1927** MEINZER *Plants in Relation Ground Water* 31 The batamote bush (*Baccharis glutinosa*) is regarded by G. E. P. Smith as an indicator of ground water. **1938** GOODDING *Native & Exotic Plants* 131 *Baccharis glutinosa,* Batamote or Seep Willow . . . is one of the best erosion control plants in the Gila water shed.

batch, see **bach,** *v.*

batea bɑˈteə, *n. S.W.* [Sp. in same sense.] A large shallow bowl or pan, often used for washing gold ore.

1759 VENEGAS (tr.) *Nat. Hist. Calif.* I. 81 The manner of negociating their marriages . . . was to present the bride by way of earnest with a batea or jug . . . made of mezcale thread. **1844** GREGG *Commerce of Prairies* I. 169 A round wooden bowl called *batea,* about eighteen inches in diameter, is the washing vessel. **1898** *Engineering Mag.* XVI. 51 Wooden bateas about eighteen inches in diameter (probably used to carry the ore out of the mine). **1946** MCWILLIAMS *So. Calif. Country* 56 The panning system was based upon the use of a wooden bowl, or *batea,* with which they were long familiar.

bateau bæˈto, *n.* Also **battoe, batteau.** [App. borrowed first from the French in Canada, and later from those in La. See McDermott, 20.] A light, high-nosed, flat-bottomed boat, tapering toward the ends, for use chiefly on rivers.

1711 *Boston News-Letter* 23–30 July 2/1 All our Battoes are finished, and several of them gone to Albany last week with several Indians. **1717** *N.J. Archives* IV. 318, I pressed all the carpenters in the place . . . for the dispatch of these batteaux. **1847** LANMAN *Summer in Wilderness* 171 At present they are navigable about half their length for small steamboats and bateaux. **1947** *Sports Afield* Dec. 21/1 They'll jump in with us and sink this bateau.

attrib. **1756** *Doc. Hist. N.Y. State* (1849) I. 477 Upwards of 500 Battoe Men were sent different Ways into the Woods. **1837** JENKINS *Ohio Gaz.* 397 A bateaux navigation upon this line of communication, has been . . . had with only four miles portage. **1932** W. KELLEY *Inchin' Along* 4 He looped his bateau chain over a cypress knee which grew out of the water's edge.

b. (See quots.)

1916 SURREY *Commerce of La.* 64 'Bateau' had a still more general use. As a name it could be applied to any sort of small boat whether propelled by sails or oars, or by both sails and oars. Moreover, the term was used quite as often in reference to boats on the river as to those on the open sea. **1947** *Amer. Dial. Soc. Pub.* No. 8, 34 Bateau: In southern Virginia this is not a small boat but a flat-bottomed freight boat.

bateau bæˈto, *v.* Also **battoe.** [f. the noun.]

1. *intr.* To proceed by bateau. Also **bateauing,** *n.*

1759 R. PUTNAM *Journal* (1886) 84 This day a detachment . . . marched up the Mohawk River in order to Battoe up that River. **1760** *Essex Inst. Coll.* XX. 199 To-day there was a draught out of our company for battowing from fort Miller to fort Edward. **1905** in *Amer. Sp.* XV. (1940) 326 We batteauxed up the St. Croix River with the goods and traveled on foot the barrens alongside.

2. *tr.* To convey by bateau. *Obs.*

1764 F. B. HOUGH *Siege of Detroit* (1860) 280, I cannot discharge the Teamster & Waggoner . . . , being obliged to employ them at . . . Battoeing Provisions to Port Erie, making Hay, &c. **1773** WALDEN *Narrative of Travels* 10 The army went forward to Detroit, and left about sixty men to batoe provisions up from the Great Falls.

* **bath,** *n.* In combs.: (1) **bath bonnet,** (see quot. 1830), prob. so called in allusion to Bath, England, *obs.*, cf. **bathing hat;** (2) * **house,** a cabin or building in which open-air bathers change clothes; (3) **robe,** a loose, full length robe such as is worn to and from a bath; (4) **towel,** a large towel, esp. suitable for use in all-over bathing; (5) **tub,** a tub for bathing, esp. the large bathroom fixture so called; (6) **tub gin,** during prohibition days, a jocular term for homemade gin.

(1) **1751** in SINGLETON *Social N.Y.* 213 Hats, Bath Bonnets, Hoods, and Pullareens for Ladies. **1830** WATSON *Philadelphia* 176, I have seen what was called a bath-bonnet, made of black satin, and so constructed to lay in folds that it could be set upon like a chapeau bras. — (2) **1884** SWEET & KNOX *Through Texas* 30 Although the beach was dotted with numerous bath-houses, few persons were disporting themselves in the brine. **1886** C. D. WARNER *Their Pilgrimage* xi, All down the shore were pavilions and bath-houses. — (3) **1902** *Sears Cat.* (ed. 112) 846/2 Fine Terry Cloth Bath Robe with Hood, in fancy fast color design. **1947** *Sat. Ev. Post* 17 May 116/2 She put on her bathrobe and went downstairs. — (4) **1935** *Montgomery Ward Cat.* 123 318/5 Our heaviest, firmest and largest Turkish Bath Towel. **1945** *Chi. D. News* 31 Aug. 16/2 The WPB has authorized unlimited production of bath towels.

(5) **1870** MARK TWAIN *Sk., Ghost Story*, I . . . was sorry that he was gone . . . and sorrier still that he had carried off my red blanket and my bath-tub. **1896** *D.N.* I. 434 *Mad* (for *angry*), *wrathy*, *bath-tub* (for *bath*), . . . though many of them are excellent and idiomatic, are, I believe, peculiar to America, or nearly so. **1948** *Calif. Citrograph* May 326/3 Do you avoid leaving small children alone in the bath tub? — (6) **1932** *Variety* 8 Oct. 1/4 The liquid served in most of the spots is called punch. Principle ingredient is bathtub gin and this 'punch' lives up to its name. **1947** *Acad. Polit. Science Proc.* May 90 It is a seasoned generation . . . that learned to handle its alcohol the hard way, with bath tub gin and hip flasks and speak-easies.

As the last term in **bird, cradle, plunge, shower bath.**

bathinette ˌbæθəˈnet, *n.* A small bath, supported on a stand, and provided with conveniences needed in bathing a baby. Also attrib. — **1936** *Sears Cat.* (Ed. 173) 173 Genuine Bathinette. . . . Pull hand grip, white duck dressing table comes over Dupont rubber coated fabric tub. Safety strap. Towel rack, enameled hardwood stand. Rustproof metal parts. Rubber hose, shut-off. **1947** *Chi. Sun* 14 Oct. 10/4 Back on the bathinette table I patted her dry, again making sure to get into the creases of loose skin.

* **bathing,** *n.* In combs.: (1) **bathing beauty,** a beautiful girl who, in a bathing suit, frequents bathing beaches, esp. one who enters beauty contests, cf. **bathing girl;** (2) **box,** (see quot.); (3) **girl,** = **bathing beauty,** also attrib.; (4) **hat,** (see quot.), *obs.;* (5) **pavilion,** a light, often ornamented building erected at a bathing beach for the comfort and convenience of bathers; (6) **suit,** a garment, now much abbreviated, designed to be worn while swimming.

(1) **1922** *Ardmore* (Okla.) *D. Press* 1 June 5/2 Somebody started the rumor that the famous Sennett bathing beauties were to be eliminated from all future comedies. **1945** *Greeley* (Colo.) *D. Tribune* 11 July 2/1 America to Brazilians, the speaker said, is the skyscrapers of New York, . . . the stars of Hollywood, and the bathing beauties of Miami beach. — (2) **1883** *Harper's Mag.* Feb. 336/2 'Bathing-boxes' (as the seaside cottages are called) perched about on the . . . hill-sides. — (3) **1921** *N Y. Times* 9 Sep. 15/1 'Miss Washington' scored again by being acclaimed the most beautiful bathing girl in the bathing girl contest. — (4) **1851** WORTLEY *Travels* 44 She looks particularly pretty in the *bathing* hat, a large Swiss-looking straw hat which she sometimes wears also out walking.

(5) **1880** *Scribner's Mo.* July 356/2 The Manhattan Beach bathing-pavilion is five hundred feet long. — (6) **1881** MARSHALL *Through Amer.* (1882) 398 There had appeared in the *Salt Lake Daily Tribune*, in the morning, the following announcement: 'Bathing Suits to order in six hours.' **1946** WILSON *Fidelity* 113 In those days bathing suits had not yet arrived.

* **battalion,** *n.* **1.** *local.* A muster day. **2.** A group of fire companies. Also attrib. See also **Mormon battalion, shirt battalion.**

(1) **1882** GIBBONS *Penna. Dutch* 424 The battalion (Pennsylvania Dutch, *Badolya?*) is an annual day of joy and festivity, in Berks County. — (2) **1884** JOSEPH HATTON *Henry Irving's Impressions of America* II. 227 The captain of the [fire] company that arrives first on the ground takes command of all the companies that arrive after his, until the chief of a battalion arrives. **1948** *Sat. Ev. Post* 21 Aug. 107/1 He checks all alarms in neighboring battalion areas against a card index.

batteau, see **bateau.**

* **batten,** *n. Logging.* (See quot.) — **1879** VIVIAN *Wanderings in Western Land* 54 In the saw mills the logs are cut up into . . . planks three inches thick, and seven, nine, and eleven inches in width; if less than seven inches they are called 'battens.'

* **batter,** *n.* In combs.: (1) **batter bread,** (see quots.); (2) **cake,** a griddlecake, (see also **corn, Indian, rice battercake**); (3) **pot,** a pot in which batter is set to rise. See also **buckwheat batter, Indian batter.**

(1) **1897** TERHUNE *Old-field School* 87 Batter-bread is a mixture of Indian meal, milk and eggs, beaten light and baked in a mould. When hot and fresh, it is puffy and delicious. In cooling, it becomes heavy and sticky. **1901** *D.N.* II. 136 *Batter-bread*, a preparation like hominy, eaten with butter. **1906** *Ib.* III. 125 Batter-bread, *n.* 1. Soft corn bread containing lard or butter, and served with a spoon. 2. Thick griddle-cakes, made of flour and meal. — (2) **1835** LONGSTREET *Ga. Scenes* 36 Waffles were handed to Ned, and he took one; batter-cakes were handed, and he took one. **1943** POWELL *Home Again* 200 Once upon a time there was a little boy who was very fond of battercakes. — (3) **1851** *Knickerb.* XXXVIII. 392 The civilizing encroachments of the batter-pot, that most persuasive of missionaries. *Ib.* 394 That old red earthen batter-pot! We see it now, as of yore it sat upon the kitchen hearth, capped with a pie-plate.

* **battery,** *n.*[1] [Sense **1.** shows an extension of the proper name as used in N.Y. City. Sense **2.** is an Amer. borrowing from F. See Read, 70, *s.v. Sirop de batterie.*]

1. (*cap.*) (See quot. 1848.)

1787 TYLER *Contrast* I. i, But to . . . walk on the Battery, N.Y., give me the luxurious, jaunty, flowing, bell-hoop. *Ib.*, I was dangling o'er the battery with Billy Dimple. **1848** COOPER *Oak Openings* I. xi 160 Our language . . has changed . . . public promenades on the water into 'batteries.' **1869** *Overland Mo.* July 12/1 Sitting on the low drab-colored sea-walls of the Battery, I watched the sun make pleasant summer around the head of Sumter. **1948** *Chi. Tribune* 4 Apr. (Grafic Mag.) 20/3 He became discouraged and went down to the Battery, where he sat on a dock and looked out to sea.

2. Chiefly *La.* The last of a series, usu. five, of kettles in which sugar-cane juice is treated in sugar making, and from which it goes, as a thick sirup, into the cooling kettle. *Obs.* Cf. **flambeau, prop,** *n.*[2]

1833 SILLIMAN *Man. Sugar Cane* 33 The names apropriated to the different kettles are as follows: the largest is called the *grande*, . . . and the last the *battery*. **1888** CABLE *Bonaventure* 14 She was as sweet as the last dip of cane-juice from the boiling battery.

b. (See quot.)

1886 *Harper's Mag.* June 80/2 These processes, in the old-fashioned plantation sugar-houses, are effected by what is known as a 'battery' of open pans or 'taches.'

3. "A sort of boat used for duck-shooting in the Chesapeake, in which the shooter lies below the surface of the water" (B. '59). Also attrib.

*a***1841** W. HAWES *Sporting Scenes* I. 198 A machine or battery, is a wooden box of the necessary dimensions to let a man lie down upon his back, just tightly fitting enough to let him rise again. **1875** *Fur, Fin & Feather* 122 The battery gunner . . . has a great advantage over the fowler who shoots from the shore. **1947** BROWN *Outdoors Un-*

limited 49 I've tumbled velour-headed canvasbacks from Currituck batteries and taken like toll at shore blinds along Potomac broadwaters.

4. A series of stamps, or the box in which they are operated, used in dressing ore. Also attrib. Cf. **quartz battery.**

1853 *Harper's Mag.* VI. 578/2 There being openings in this opposite each cover or battery of stamps, the stone comes through, as fast as it is removed and shoveled into the covers. **1871** RAYMOND *3rd Rep. Mines* 340 The battery box is . . . cast in one piece with the mortar-bed. **1936** DRURY *Editor on Comstock* 21 Their hundred helpers are catalogued in due order—superintendents, . . . battery-men, . . . fuse-makers, wood passers, . . . pilers, sluicers.

5. *Baseball.* The pitcher and catcher, orig. used of the pitcher alone. Also attrib.

1867 *Ball Players' Chron.* 6 June 2/2 He soon resumed his position, once more facing the battery of Lovett. **1886** CHADWICK *Art of Pitching* 8 The 'battery' of a club's team, that is the pitcher and catcher. **1948** *Capital-Democrat* (Tishomingo, Okla.) 3 June 7/2 Bobby Cox, experienced battery mate for Smith, . . . is due to get the catching assignment, regardless of who starts on the mound.

6. A revolver. *Obs.*

1871 HARTE *Works* (1910) XII. 139 A man would pull out his battery For anything—maybe the price of whisky. **1906** MARK TWAIN *Horse's Tale* 327, 16/2 (R.), There's no telling how much he does weigh when he is out on the war-path and has his batteries belted on.

As the last term in **boat, home, water battery.**

* **batting,** *n.*

1. Cotton, wool, or other fibrous material, prepared in matted sheets, frequently used for making quilts or coverlets. See **cotton batting.**

1829 *Oneida Republican* (Rome, N.Y.) 30 Dec., N. Draper . . . will be enabled to keep constantly on hand and for sale . . . Ticking, Wicking, Batting, Threads and Cotton Yarn. **1888** *Cent. Mag.* Sep. 767/2 Carding-combs of a rough pattern were constructed for the purpose of converting the raw cotton into batting. **1936** *Sears Cat.* (ed. 173) 457/2 Ranch Rose batting makes warmer, plumper, more beautiful quilts!

2. In combs. relating to baseball: (1) **batting average,** the ratio of times at bat to the number of base hits obtained, also fig.; (2) **cage,** see **cage;** (3) **list,** a list of names of players showing the order in which they bat; (4) **order,** (see quot. 1916 and cf. prec.); (5) **practice,** practice in batting; (6) **score,** the score or batting average made at bat by a player; (7) **side,** the side at bat.

(1) **1867** *Ball Players' Chron.* 12 Dec. 5/3 The best players are those making the best batting and fielding averages. **1931** REEVE *Golden Age Crime* 169 The tabloids all fattened up their batting averages on it. **1944** *Railway Age* 16 Dec. 45 The commission evidently has not been sufficiently impressed with the batting average of the bureaucrats' revenue forecasts. — (3) **1917** MATHEWSON *Sec. Base Sloan* xiii. 173 Toonalta started the seventh with the head of her batting list up. — (4) **1883** *Chi. Tribune* 3 July 6/5 The manager of the Bisons would do well to change the batting order of his men. **1916** BANCROFT *Handbook* 78 Batting order. The order in which the players of a team go to the bat. The batting order is arranged by the captain of a team, and given to the Umpire before the game begins. The score keeper calls the players to the bat in the order of this list, from which there may be no departure. **1948** *Time* 10 May 62/3 He is also clean-up man in the batting order.

(5) **1910** *Amer. Mag.* April 785/1 Wagner showed up at the grounds with a five-cent bat he had purchased from a small boy and started batting practice. **1947** *Harper's Mag.* June 557/1 He'd keep us for hours while we should have been out at batting practice, and talk on and on. — (6) **1867** CHADWICK *Base Ball Player's Bk.* 30 A regular scorer . . . should be competent to record the fielding as well as batting score of the game. — (7) **1868** CHADWICK *Base Ball* 41 An innings, in base ball, is played when three men on the batting side have been put out.

* **battle,** *n.* [The term "battle" used in (5) and (6) is app. from obs. * *battle, v.*, to grow fat, thrive. The terms are included in this list for convenience.]

1. In combs.: (1) **Battle-born State,** (see quots.); (2) **correspondent,** = **war correspondent;** (3) **fish,** *local* (see quot.); (4) **flag,** a distinctive flag carried by troops in battles, also transf.; (5) **hammed,** ?thick- or fat-hammed, *rare;* (6) **kneed,** ?thick-kneed, *rare;* (7) **pin,** a pin showing the battle or battles in which a soldier has served; (8) **ship,** a line-of-battle ship, also **battleship gray,** a gray-bluish color often used for battleships.

(1) **1891** SWEETSER *King's Handbook U.S.* 533 The popular names of Nevada are the Silver State, from its chief product; . . . and the Battle-Born State, commemorating its admission to the Union during the Civil War. **1948** MENCKEN *Supp.* II. 636 Nevada . . . prefers to be called the *Battle-born* State, to recall the fact that it was admitted to the Union on October 31, 1864, while the Civil War was raging. — (2) **1862** *S.F. Herald & Mirror* 4 July 1/6 The battle correspondent says that the cannonading and musketry were terrific. — (3) **1878** *Harper's Mag.* Jan. 203/1 In the creek [Hot Springs, Ark.] there are many species of fish, one of which, from its scales of red, white, and blue, is dubbed the 'battle-fish.' — (4) **1862** MCCLELLAN in *Own Story* 614 My tent is filled quite to overflowing with trophies in the way of captured secesh battle-flags. **1892** MARK TWAIN *Amer. Claimant* xv. 161 Now, old fellow, take in your battle-flag out of the wet. **1900** *Dly. Ardmoreite* (Ardmore, Okla.) 28 Aug. 1/5 Twelve heralds in costume blowing French horns, announced the coming of fifty tattered battle flags, carried by New Yorkers during the war.

(5) **1727** *N. Eng. Wkly. Journal* 11 Sep., Ran-away from his Master . . . a young Negro Man-Servant, about 20 Years of Age, a stout Fellow, speaks pretty good English, has thick Lips, battle-ham'd, and goes something waddling. — (6) **1743** *N.J. Archives* 1 Ser. XII. 181 They were stolen by one David Howell, . . . ruddy Complexion, light Hair, and battel-knee'd [*sic*]. — (7) **1863** NORTON *Army Lett.* 188, I have another name to put on my battle pin (when I get it), that of 'Rappahannock Station, November 8th.' — (8) **1794** HUMPHREYS *Industry* 20 Give me the music, where the dock equips, With batt'ries black and strong, the battle-ships. **1898** *Boston Herald* 1 June 12/4 In her day she was a battleship, but she . . . would be little more than sport for a modern ironclad. **1942** RAWLINGS *C. Creek* 9 The walls were painted a battleship gray. **1946** *Sat. Ev. Post* 11 May 26/2 Long lines of buildings painted a battleship gray covered hundreds of acres.

2. In phrases: (1) *Battle Hymn of the Republic,* the title, said to have been suggested by Jas. T. Fields, editor of the *Atlantic Monthly,* of a now well-known patriotic poem and song first drafted in Nov. 1861 by Julia Ward Howe; (2) *Battle in the Clouds,* the battle of Lookout Mountain, near Chattanooga, Tenn., during the Civil War; (3) *Battle of the Kegs,* the title of a humorous poem by Francis Hopkinson on the theme of an unsuccessful attempt by the Americans in Jan., 1778, to destroy British shipping at Philadelphia by floating combustibles, also used with reference to the episode itself.

(1) **1862** *Atlantic Mo.* Feb. 145 (*title*), Battle Hymn of the Republic. **1948** *Chi. Tribune* 23 June 1. 4/5 The orchestra, perched high under the vaulted roof in the rear of the auditorium, played 'Battle Hymn of the Republic.' — (2) **1867** LATHAM *Black and White* 69 Mrs. F. told me that at Chattanooga where General Hooker's 'Battle in the Clouds' was fought she stood on a hill from which the whole battle-field was visible, and on the slope at her feet were the assembled graves of 7,000 men. — (3) **1778** in *Amer. Museum* I. 56/1 Not a chip, stick, or drift log, passed by, without experiencing the vigour of the British arms. . . . In short, Monday the 5th . . . day of January, 1778, will be ever memorable in history, for the renowned *battle of the kegs.* **1833** WATSON *Hist. Tales Phila.* 297 Among the amusing and facetious incidents of the war . . . was that of the celebrated occurrence of 'the Battle of the Kegs' at Philadelphia.

As the last term in **buffalo, grasshopper, gun, junk battle.**

batture bəˈtjur, *n.S.*[F.] "That part of the inner shore of a stream which has been thrown up by the action of the current, and which, at certain seasons of the year, may be covered as a whole or in part by the water" (Read). Also attrib.

[**1713** JOUTEL *Journal* 8 A l'égard de l'autre Canal, le même sieur Joutel croit qu'il est plus au Sudoüest & vers des batures qu'ils trouvèrent le 6 Janvier 1685.] **1784** HUTCHINS *La. & West Fla.* 66 Behind it, there is a large bay called L'ance de la Grand Bature, 8 miles East of Pascagoula bluff. **1841** *N.O. Picayune* 17 Mar. 2/2 There is the Batture case, to which the Second Municipality is a party. **1941** DORSEY *Master of Miss.* 125 Livingston, *Duc de la Batture!* By what right did he order a free citizen brought before him?

baum bɔm, *v.* [Cf. * *balm.*] (See quot.) *Obs.* — **1851** HALL *College Words* 16 *Baum.*, at Hamilton College, to fawn upon; to flatter; to court the favor of anyone.

Baumont root. (See quot. and cf. **bowman's root.**) —**1789** *Amer. Philos. Soc.* III. p. xviii, *Spiraea trifoliata.* . . . Indian physic, Baumont-root, is an effectual and safe emetic.

* **bawl,** *v.* *To bawl out,* to reprimand severely. *Slang.* — **1907** REX BEACH *Barrier* xvii. (1908) 270 If you'll go back on your word like this you'll 'bawl me out' before the priest. **1937** SUTHERLAND *Professional Thief* 39 She started to argue with him while in a store in regard to what articles they were supposed to be stealing, so, after bawling her out, he announced himself as quitting.

bay, *n.[1]

1. (*cap.*) The Colony of Massachusetts Bay. *Obs.*

1636 *Maine Doc. Hist.* III. 79 No one place in the world comes neere itt; I meane in the Baye, where there is such a holly [=holy] walking. **1660** *New Haven Col. Rec.* II. 374 The maintaining children at the Schooles or colledg in the Bay. **1680** *Conn. Prob. Rec.* 586, I give . . . what mony I have comeing to me in the bay.

2. A tract of prairie or open land partially surrounded by a forest. Cf. **bay prairie.**

1820 GILLELAND *Ohio & Miss. Pilot* 205 Several long lines of prairie, which are called *Bays*, extend from the main Opelousas prairie. **1850** W. COLTON *Three Years Calif.* 370 Still, in some of its [=San Joaquin valley's] bays, the evidences of fertility exist. **1907** *D.N.* III. 209 *Bay*, a piece of land partly surrounded by woods. (N.E. Ark.)

3. (*cap.*) San Francisco, situated on the bay of that name. Also attrib. Cf. **Bay City.**

1869 *Overland Mo.* July 64/2 The impromptu treasurer . . . is to send the money to the afflicted widow and unprotected orphans down at 'the Bay.' **1910** J. HART *Vigilante Girl* xxi. 294 The miners up there look with much suspicion on the arrival of any lawyer from 'down at the Bay,' as they say. **1948** *Sierra Club Bul.* Feb. 4/1 An excellent grove of San Mateo county redwoods, about to feel the ax, is badly needed for recreational purposes, owing to its proximity to the Bay Area population.

4. (See quot.)

1910 *S.C. Hist. Mag.* XI. 44 From the description of the lots in this deed [dated 1744] it appears that one street, fronting on the river, was known as the 'Bay.' This word 'bay' . . . seems very generally to have been applied in Lower South Carolina at that period in towns on rivers or water courses, to the streets which fronted directly on the water.

5. In combs.: (1) **bay bird,** (see quot. 1889); (2) **Bay City,** San Francisco, a nickname, cf. **3.** above; (3) **craft,** a vessel built to navigate a bay; (4) **prairie,** (see quot. and cf. **2.** above); (5) **salmon,** a salmon found in bays, *rare;* (6) **shiner,** (see quot.); (7) **shooting,** shooting or hunting along a bay, *obs.;* (8) **shore,** the shore of a bay; (9) **side,** (see quot. 1899); (10) **snipe,** "a bay-bird, or bay-birds collectively" (*Cent. s.v. snipe*); (11) **State,** see as a main entry; (12) **stater,** a native or inhabitant of Massachusetts; (13) **vessel,** a bay craft.

(1) **1889** *Cent., Bay-birds*, a collective name of numerous small wading birds or shore-birds, chiefly of the snipe and plover families, which frequent the muddy shores of the bays and estuaries along the Atlantic coast of the United States. **1895** ELLIOT *N.A. Shore-Birds* 52 On the Atlantic seaboard, . . . this species [the Dowitcher] is one of the most common and well known of the 'Bay-birds.' — (2) **1855** *Golden Era* (S.F.) 4 Mar. 1/6 On the evening of the second day he arrived at the Bay City. **1933** *Variety* 21 Mar. 51/5 Now comes the Bay City's opportunity to get back at the City of Angels, which it has started to do with a great amount of energy. — (3) **1725** in *N. Eng. Quarterly* (1929) II. 660 We met a Ship which they took and Burnt them sending away what Prisoners they thought fit in a Bay Craft. **1835** INGRAHAM *South-West* II. 150 The Gulf, 'accessible,' says Flint, 'by small vessels and bay-craft.' — (4) **1831** HOLLEY *Texas* (1833) vi. 58 This island constituted what is now called the Bay Prairie; a large, rich, and very beautiful prairie, lying between the timbered lands of Caney, and those of Colorado.

(5) **1857** *Harper's Mag.* Nov. 817/1 The bay salmon is larger than the cod in the bays of California. — (6) **1842** *Nat. Hist. N.Y., Zoology* IV. 211 The Bay Shiner. *Leuciscus chrysopterus*. . . . This beautiful species is caught in the harbor of New York, and is popularly called Bay Shiner, or simply Shiner. — (7) **1852** FLEISCHMANN *Wegweiser* 245 Die Wasserjagd (*Bay shooting*), an den Küsten mit Segel—oder Ruderbooten oder auf andere Weise getrieben, umfasst Tatlers, See-Enten, Rallen u.s.w. — (8) **1732** in *Amer. Sp.* XV. 154/2 Beginning at a pine Standing on Batt's Bay . . . then North West Twenty Six Degrees Thirty Six pole to Chesapeak Bay Side then South West . . . along the Bay Shore. **1850** FOOTE *Sk. Virginia* 357 The neighborhood must have been between the Blue Ridge and the Bay Shore. — (9) **1642** in *Amer. Sp.* XV. 154/2 The land beginning from the land of Edmund Scarburgh on the one Side and goeing in breadth on the Bayeside Northwest to the land of Thomas Hunt. **1849** F. DOUGLASS *Life* 53 In August, 1832, my master attended a Methodist camp-meeting held in the Bay-side. **1899** GREEN *Va. Word-Book* 52 *Bay-side*, the Chesapeake Bay side of Accomack and Northampton counties.

(10) **1856** *Spirit of Times* 6 Sep. 9/1 Bay Snipe shooting is at its acme, and can be enjoyed everywhere on Long Island. **1875** *Fur, Fin, & Feather* 121 It is also a capital place for bay-snipe shooting in summer. — (12) **1845** *St. Louis Reveille* 14 May 2/4 The inhabitants of . . . Massachusets [are called] Bay Staters. **1888** WHITMAN *November Boughs* 70 The soldiers . . . from . . . Massachusetts [were called] Bay Staters. — (13) **1789** *Md. Journal* 2 Jan. (Th.), I will exchange a small Bay Vessel for a large one, and give the difference.

b. In combs. now obs. or hist. with reference to the Colony of Massachusetts Bay, as (1) **bay colony,** (2) **council,** (3) **government,** (4) **leader,** (5) **line,** (6) **man,** see as a main entry, (7) **old tenor,** (cf. **old tenor**), (8) **shilling,** (9) **soldier.**

(1) **1777** *Hist. Pelham* (1898) 130 In the name of the People & Stats of the Bay Colony. **1931** DAVIS *We Are Alaskans* 12 After your ancestor had been a Bay Colony man for thirty years, was he an American—or an Algonquian Indian? — (2) **1675** in *Conn. Public Rec.* II. 367 The Councill prepared . . . a covert to a letter from the Bay Councill. — (3) **1665** *Mass. Bay Rec.* IV. II. 249 The king's commissioners summoned the people . . . and possessed them of their inevitable ruine in case they continued vnder the Bay gouernment. **1680** *N.H. Hist. Soc. Coll.* VIII. 53 As for the Bay government, we have lived under the plague of the Bay government long enough. — (4) **1946** *Reader's Digest* Dec. 68/2 Conferences between the Bay leaders and the Indian chiefs were commonly held in his house.

(5) **1725** *Providence* (R.I.) *Rec.* XIII .24 The highway from Town to the Bay Line. — (7) **1770** PATTEN *Diary* 250, I had . . . a Dozen of fish hook from Meins for which I paid him 1-18-2 Bay old Tenor. — (8) **1704** S. KNIGHT *Journal*, 42 *Mony* is pieces of Eight, Ryalls,or Boston or Bay shillings. — (9) **1675** *Wyllys Papers* 223 The Indians . . . have slain & wounded nigh thirty men; most of them bay souldiers.

c. *A little over the bay,* somewhat intoxicated. *Slang.*

1833 GREENE *D. Duckworth* II. 176 He was seldom downright drunk; but was often—a little over the bay. **1896** *D.N.* I. 398 'He was a little over the bay.' [Current in] Minn., N.Y.

bay, *n.[2]

1. Any one of various trees and shrubs somewhat resembling the European bay.

1587 HAKLUYT tr. Laudonnière *Notable Historie* 2[r] There is great store of Ceders, Cypresses, Bayes, Palme trees, Hollies, and wilde Vines. **1634** WOOD *N. Eng. Prospect* I. v. 133 In the woods, without eyther the art or the helpe of man, . . . [grow] mirtle, . . . bayes, &c. **1853** SIMMS *Sword & Distaff* 151 A clump of bays, or dwarf-laurel. **1928** R. M. HARPER *Economic Botany Ala.* 25 Right here in Alabama we have two short-leaf pines, two cypresses, several red oaks and water oaks, three or four bays, two tytys, [etc.].

2. *S.E.* A low, marshy area where bay trees are abundant.

1795 ASBURY *Journal* II. 285 This country [*sc.* S. Carolina] abounds with bays, swamps, and drains. **1802** J. DRAYTON *S. Carolina* 7 They are called *bays*, from the quantities of bay trees which grow therein. And which are so tall and closely connected with each other, as to throw a continual shade over the lands below. Hence their soil is naturally sour and spungy. **1855** SIMMS *Forayers* 354 The bay was the abiding place only of the reptile and the wild cat.

b. *Florida.* (See quots.).

1884 *Harper's Mag.* March 601/1 Swamp and 'bay' (the word applied in Florida to slough and water-grass meadows) amplify the area. **1938** MATSCHAT *Suwannee River* 30 In the weird, hobgoblin world of the bays there is perpetual twilight. These bays are flooded forests of close-growing cypresses mixed with a few other trees. They stretch away from the prairies and runs into unexplored depths of shadow and mystery.

3. In combs.: (1) **bayberry,** see as a main entry; (2) **bush,** the sweet gale, *Myrica gale;* (3) **gall,** *S.E.* and *S.* (*a*) a low tract of boggy or spongy land overgrown with the sweet bay and other shrubs, (*b*) (see quot.); (4) **land,** =**bay 2. b;** (5) **laurel,** an American laurel, as the magnolia; (6) **leaf bamboo,** (see quot.); (7) **nut,** the fruit of the California laurel; (8) **rum,** a perfume obtained originally from bayberry leaves; (9) **swamp,** a swamp in which bay grows abundantly; (10) **tree,** (see quot.); (11) **tulip tree,** ?the bull bay, *Magnolia grandiflora, rare;* (12) **wax,** =**bayberry wax;** (13) **willow,** (see quot.).

(2) **1688** *Huntington Rec.* I. 517 The east bounds is a hamake of bay bushes and a rocke. **1845** SIMMS *Cabin & Wigwam* I. 19 He heard something like a sudden breeze that rustled through the bay bushes at his feet. **1913** EATON *Barn Doors & Byways* 170 The shores of the ponds are broken by small promontories crowned with oak, bay bushes, and huckleberries. — (3) (*a*) **1775** ROMANS *Florida* 15, I shall treat of them by the names of pine land, hammock land, savannahs, swamps, marshes, and bay, or cypress galls. **1839** *S. Lit. Messenger* V. 375/2 On the left was a large bay-gall . . . thickly beset with catbriers and undergrowth. **1905** *Bureau of Forestry* Bul. No. 64, 14 Partially inundated depressions, locally known as 'bay galls,' . . . serve as

the natural drainage channels of the flat longleaf pine land. . . . The bay galls . . . receive their name from the sweet bay . . . the characteristic tree of such situations. (*b*) **1897** SUDWORTH *Arborescent Flora* 201 Red bay [is called] . . . Bay Galls (Tenn.). — (**4**) **1886** I. D. HARDY *Oranges and Alligators* 48 We talk glibly of pine-land and bay-land, of high and low hammock, and 'flat-woods.'

(**5**) **1836** HOLLEY *Texas* 88 Among the underwood are found the bay laurel—the poet's own tree. **1877** BARTLETT 33 Bay . . . [or] Bay laurel . . . is of the same family as the *Magnolia grandiflora*, which it resembles except in size. — (**6**) **1901** MOHR *Plant Life Ala.* 446 *Smilax laurifolia*, . . . Bay-leaf Bamboo. . . . Flowers in May. — (**7**) **1902** CHESNUT *Plants Used by Indians* 297 Some of the native food stuffs, such as the bay nut and the numerous liliaceous bulbs, might be introduced into our markets or at least into our home gardens for human consumption. — (**8**) **1840** *Knickerb.* XVI. 34 Perfumed 'as to our locks' with the bay-rum or fragrant cologne. **1902** HARBEN *A. Daniel* 99 When the barber finished he soaked my face in bay-rum. — (**9**) **1741** W. STEPHENS *Proc. Georgia* II. 237 The Land in these Parts, setting aside the Pine-Barren, and some Bay-swamps or the like, with proper Cultivation, will yield a reasonable Increase. **1832** BROWNE *Sylva Amer.* 164 These spots are entirely covered with the loblolly bay, and are called Bay Swamps. **1947** *Sports Afield* Dec. 20/2 These woods, dotted with bay and gum swamps, provide the choice deer and turkey hunting in the state.

(**10**) **1911** RICHTER *Honey Plants of Calif.* 990 *Umbellularia californica* . . . California Laurel. Bay Tree. Pepper Wood. Spice Tree. — (**11**) **1709** LAWSON *Carolina* 95 The Bay-Tulip-Tree is a fine evergreen which grows frequently here. — (**12**) **1721** *N. Eng. Courant* 2–9 Oct. 2/2 We the Subscribers . . . [will] give our Attendance to assist any Person . . . that will come with . . . Eggs, Bees-Wax, Bay-Wax, or, in short, any Commodity that may be brought. — (**13**) **1892** APGAR *Trees Northern U.S.* 164 *Salix lucida*, Mühl. Shining or American Bay Willow. . . . New Jersey, north and westward.

b. Also **bay flower, sprout, thicket, tree.**

1851 *Polly Peablossom* 21 Polly was dressed in white, and wore a bay-flower with its green leaves in her hair. — **1932** W. KELLEY *Inchin' Along* 2 And around the house . . . were clumps of sassafras bushes, stunted bay sprouts, and patches of swamp sedge. — **1845** SIMMS *Wigwam & Cabin* I. 18 He proceeded to traverse the margin of the bay until he came to . . . the high-road. The youth . . . soon found himself on the opposite side of the bay thicket. — **1843** *Amer. Pioneer* II. 447 The boughs of the fragrant bay tree . . . imparted to the lard a rich flavor. **1944** *Sat. Ev. Post* 9 Sep. 13/1 The bay tree or shrub abounds in them.

As the last term in **bull, California, cow, cypress, great, holly, loblolly, red, swamp, tan, white bay.**

∗**bay,** *n.*[3] (See quots.) — **1888** BILLINGS *Hardtack* 385 The distance between the centres of two boats [of a pontoon bridge] in position is called a *bay*. **1895** WAIT *Car-Builder's Dict.* 7/1 Bay-window parlor-car. . . . A common style of parlor-car construction, designed to give more variety to the interior and improve the line of vision of the passenger.

∗**bay,** *a.* In combs.: (1) **bay breast,** short for next; (2) **breasted warbler,** a handsome warbler, *Dendroica castanea;* (3) **ibis,** a glossy ibis; (4) **lynx,** (see quot. 1890); (5) ∗**steer,** used in the colloq. or slang phrase, *to kick like a bay steer*, to protest violently; (6) **winged,** having bay-colored wings, (see quots.).

(**1**) **1892** TORREY *Foot-Path Way* 190 A hurried search showed . . . one yellow redpoll, and one clearly marked bay-breast. **1942** WHITE *One Man's Meat* 286 Remember not to confuse the issue with 'adults in spring' or with the Bay-breast at *any* season. — (**2**) **1810** WILSON *Ornithology* II. 97 Bay-Breasted Warbler. *Sylvia Castanea*. . . . This very rare species passes the Pennsylvania about the beginning of May, and soon disappears. **1948** PEATTIE *Berkshires* 103 Black-poll and bay-breasted warblers, for instance, so distinct in the spring, are of nearly identical appearance in the fall. — (**3**) **1833** BONAPARTE *Ornithology* IV. 36 The Bay or Glossy Ibis is twenty-six inches in length. **1874** COUES *Birds N.W.* 513 Two species of Ibis, the Wood and Bay, are known to occur . . . near the Missouri region. — (**4**) **1784** PENNANT *Arctic Zoology* I. 51 Bay Lynx. . . . This species is found in the internal parts of the province of New York. **1890** *Cent. s.v. Lynx*, the common wildcat of North America is the bay lynx, . . . which runs into several varieties.

(**5**) **1931** *K.C. Times* 28 Sep., The next morning he came down town kicking like a bay steer. — (**6**) **1811** WILSON *Ornithology* IV. 51 Bay-winged Bunting: *Emberiza graminea* . . . delights in frequenting grass and clover fields. **1889** *Cent., s.v.,* Bay-winged longspur, . . . *Rhynchophanes maccowni*, a common fringilline bird of the western prairies. *Ib.*, Bay-winged summer-finch, *Peucæa carpalis* of Arizona. **1946** HAUSMAN *Eastern Birds* 600 Eastern Vesper Sparrow . . . Bay-winged Bunting, Ground Bird, Grass Finch, Grass Sparrow.

∗**bayberry,** *n.*

1. The fruit of the wax myrtle or the shrub which produces this. Also attrib.

1690 in *Pub. Col. Soc.* XIV. 152 One thing I would annexe of a rare sort of Candle found out last y. 1689 wch is made of a gumous matter gathered by boiling of ye berries of a little bush or shrub wch they here call bay berries but I take it to be a sort of myrtle but ye leaves are deciduous in sharp winters. **1709** LAWSON *Carolina* 89 The Bay-Berries yield a Wax, which besides its Use in Chirurgery, makes Candles that, in burning, give a fragrant Smell. **1792** BELKNAP *Hist. N.H.* III. 123 The bayberry . . . the leaves of which yield an agreeable perfume, and the fruit a delicate green wax, which is made into candles. **1947** *Nat. Geog. Mag.* Sep. 325/2 Song sparrows sing in the bayberry bushes.

2. In special combs.: (1) **bayberry bark,** (see quot.); (2) **candle,** a candle made of bayberry wax; (3) **day,** (see quot.), *obs.;* (4) **dip,** a dip candle made of bayberry wax; (5) **meadow,** a meadow in which bayberry shrubs are the natural growth; (6) **tallow,** the wax obtained from the bayberry; (7) **wax,** =prec.

(**1**) **1901** MOHR *Plant Life Ala.* 464 *Myrica caroliniensis*. . . . Bayberry . . . Candleberry. . . . The bark of the root, as 'bayberry bark,' is used medicinally. — (**2**) **1739** *Harvard Rec.* II. 689 [Voted] That Mr. Treasurer Hutchinson be empower'd to send to Mr. Mico, Merchant in London, a box of thirty or fourty weight of Bay-berry Candles. **1912** *Country Life* Dec. 130 Bayberry candles and dips are being revived to-day for holiday and other special use on account of their peculiar fragrance. **1947** COFFIN *Yankee Coast* 226 They slept on balsam and lighted their nights with whale-oil and bayberry candles. — (**3**) **1911** *Boston Ev. Transcript* 27 May II. 3/7 In the annals of those [colonial] days, Sept. 15 was 'Bayberry Day,' when . . . old and young, sallied forth with pail and basket, each eager to secure his share in this gift of nature. — (**4**) **1903** *Boston Herald* 19 Aug., The bayberry dips are made by boiling bayberries down to a thick wax and dipping cords into the mixture. **1912** *Country Life* Dec. 130 Bayberry dips and candles went out with the invention of new methods of lights and the wholesale manufacture of tallow and wax candles.

(**5**) **1687** *Manchester Town Rec.* 32 Near Vincsons baiberry medow . . . where the meeting house timber was cut. — (**6**) **1720** *Mass. H. Repr. Journals* II. 333 The enhabitants of this province shall have liberty . . . to pay the several sums . . . in . . . oyl, whalebone, bayberry wax or tallow [etc.]. **1891** *N. & Q.* VI. 210, I have often heard old people tell about the former use of 'bayberry tallow,' or wax, for candle-making. — (**7**) **1695** W. WINTHROP in *Winthrop P.* IV. 509, I shall send . . . a cake of the bayberry wax, about 23 lb, which is som I had by me since last year. **1891** [see **bayberry tallow**].

Also *bayberry marsh, root, shrub,* etc.

bayeta baˈjetə, *n. S.W.* [Sp., baize.] (See quots.) Also attrib.

1852 in DONALDSON *Moqui Pueblo Indians* (1893) 25 This evening we bought enough corn for the mules at $5 per faneja (2.5 bushels), paying in bayjeta, or red cloth. **1902** *Everybody's Mag.* Jan. 33/2 The loomsticks he either borrowed or copied from the Pueblos, and then by ravelling a very hard-twist Spanish cloth, known as 'vayeta,' he rewove it and made the 'Serape Navaho' of the old traders and explorers. **1936** REICHARD *Navajo Shepherd & Weaver* 23 Bayeta yarn thus respun is fine and even in twist.

b. bayeta blanket, (see quots.).

1902 *Everybody's Mag.* Jan. 37/1 Some of the old vayeta blankets have a very dark blue design. **1912** *Out West* Feb. 114/1 The most highly prized of Navajo blankets are known as bayeta blankets.

bayman ˈbemən, *n.*[1]

1. A man who resides on or close to a bay; esp. (*cap*) a native or resident of the colony of Massachusetts Bay.

1641 *Plymouth Col. Rec.* II. 23 That clause . . . which concerned the boundes from Narragansetts Bay to . . . Pockanockett, in regard the Bay men would haue had Sicquncke from us. **1788** W. GORDON *History* (1789) I. 193 Scurrilous publications . . . were craftily calculated . . . , and suited the too levelling disposition of the Bay-men. **1827** *Spirit of Seventy-Six* (Frankfort, Ky.) 29 Mar. 4/2 He was a Bayman, that captain. **1944** JOHNSON *As I Dare* 220 His odd costume was probably what a bayman thought it best to wear on Easter Sunday.

b. (See quot.)

1930 *Old-Time N. Eng.* April 192 In October, 1851, there occurred a memorable storm in the Gulf of St. Lawrence. Large numbers of Yankee fishing vessels, 'Baymen,' so called, were engaged there at the time and so many of these craft either foundered or were driven ashore when attempting to beat out of the Bay that the storm took the name 'The American Breeze.'

2. One engaged in cutting baywood in the Bay of Honduras. *Obs.*

1715 *Boston News-Letter* 10 Oct. 2/2 [They] report that 250 of the Bay-Men . . . were designed to Campeche, to burn the Shipping there. *a*1821 C. BIDDLE *Autobiog.* i. 17 The baymen at this time would frequently sell their wood to two or three different captains.

bayman ˈbemən, *n.*[2] (See quot. 1900.) — [**1888** Churchward *Blackbirding* 25, I stole a beautiful knife from the sick bayman's locker.] **1889** *Cent., Bayman,* . . . a sick-bay attendant; a nurse for sick or wounded men on a vessel of war. **1900** Webster *Supp. s.v.,* Bayman, . . . in the United States navy, . . . [is] a sick-bay nurse; now officially designated as *hospital apprentice.*

bayo ˈbɑjo, *n. W.* [Prob. f. Amer. Sp. Cf. Santamaría, "Bayo, ya, adj. En Méjico, dícese del color amerillo claro de cierta especie de frijol nativo."] App. an edible but not highly esteemed bean native to the Southwest. Now *hist.*

1855 [see **California bayos**]. **1875** Phillips *Letters from Calif.* (1877) 92 Then, and finally, came a sort of purple-colored bean, called 'bayo,' and the desert [*sic*], in the shape of a pie. **1947** Lovell in *Amer. Sp.* April 90/1 Considering the poor repute in which they were held, they [beans] may well have been *Bayos* . . . ; for this name has been found in many contemporary advertisements of foodstuffs.

* **bayonet,** *n.* In combs.: (1) **bayonet fish,** ?a cutlass fish, *rare;* (2) **palmetto,** the common dwarf palmetto, *Sabal minor;* (3) **rush,** a plant of the genus *Juncus.*

(1) **1888** Goode *Amer. Fishes* 390 The sword-fish and the bayonet-fish destroy many, rushing through the schools and striking right and left with their powerful swords. — (2) **1829** Hall *Travels* III. 173 It is called on the spot, the bayonet palmetto, from each division of its broad leaf being in the form of that weapon. **1856** Fergusson *America* 143 The dwarf palmetto grows abundantly on St John's Island. It is called the Spanish bayonet, or bayonet palmetto. — (3) **1840** Dewey *Mass. Flowering Plants* 203 *Juncus militaris.* Big. Bayonet Rush . . . flowers at the summit in a panicle.

As the last term in **Spanish bayonet, trowel bayonet.**

bayou ˈbaɪu, *n. S.* Also formerly **bayoue, bayoe, bayeau, bayau,** etc. [Amer. F. from Choctaw *bayuk,* river, creek. See *The Nation,* 59 (1894), 15 Nov. 361, and Read, *La. Pl.-Names,* p. xii.]

1. A sluggish stream or body of water, often connecting larger waters or emptying into adjacent streams. See also **blind, dry, pine bayou.**

Various applications of this term are shown in some of the quots.

[**1699** in Read *La. Pl.-Names* p. xii, A cinq lieues plus loin, en tournant tousjours à la gauche sur le lac, on trouve une eau dormante, que les Sauvages appellent Bayouque.] **1766** H. Gordon in *Travels Amer. Col.* 484 We left New Orleans . . . and lay that night at the Bayouc. **1792** *Amer. Philos. Soc.* III. 217 A place called the Bio-Piere. **1841** W. Kennedy *Texas* I. 25 The word *bayou* . . . is rather loosely applied in the topography of Texas and the West. In strictness, I believe it means a deep inlet, which affords a channel for the water in time of flood, and remains dry, or nearly so, at other seasons. **1914** R. S. Tarr *Physiography* 150 Some abandoned [river] courses along the lower Mississippi are called *bayous.* **1947** *Sat. Ev. Post* 17 May 19/1 At first there had been some land along the bayou.

2. bayou blue, an alcoholic drink, *slang, obs.* Also **bayou cabin, road, State, steamboating, version.**

1870 Nowland *Indianapolis* 36 He thought (especially if he had taken a little 'bayou blue') he would weigh several ton. — **1888** Cable *Bonaventure* 106 Sitting and pondering one evening in the little bayou cabin. — **1850** H. C. Lewis *La. Swamp Doctor* 161, I saw the dust up the bayou road shaken up by a half-naked negro. — **1867** *Trubner's Amer. Lit. Rec.* Aug. 41/1 Maine is popularly known as The Lumber or Pine-Tree State; . . . Mississippi as the Bayou State. **1886** *Chi. Wkly. News* 29 Apr. 4/3 Mississippi is the Bayou state, and its people are Tadpoles, both for obvious reasons. — **1946** *Reader's Digest* May 95/1 Bayou steamboating was steamboating at its worst. — **1886** *Harper's Mag.* Aug. 483/1 The following bayou version of one of the negro folk-lore stories is translated by a lady.

3. Bayou Salade, the name given, poss. by early French trappers, to South Park, Colo. Also attrib.

A. Matthews, in *Mass. Col. Soc. Pub.* VIII. (1904) 392, explains this expression as coming from Sp. *Valle Salado,* South Park having long been noted for its salt springs.

1848 Allen *Ten Yrs. in Ore.* 381 [The Arapahoes] in summer hunt the buffalo in the New Park, or 'Bull Pen,' in the 'Old Park,' on Grand river, and in 'Bayou Salade,' on the south fork of the Platte. **1948** *Chi. Tribune* 29 Feb. IV. 6/4 The novel reaches a peak in both interest and writing during the years Johnny spends with the Ute Indians in the Bayou Salade region of the Rockies.

Bay State.

1. (See quot. 1886.) Cf. **Old Bay State.**

1789 in *Mass. Hist. Soc. Proc.* 1 Ser. XI. (1869) 14 The style of building varies somewhat from that of the Bay State, as they (people at Wethersfield, Conn.) term Massachusetts. **1886** *Chi. Wkly. News* 29 Apr. 4/3 Massachusetts is the Bay state because it was originally the colony of Massachusetts Bay and its people are Bay-Staters. **1948** *Democrat* 24 June 6/3 Bay State Asked to Void Anti-Rhode Islander Law.

b. (See quot.) *Obs.* Cf. **Bay State Shawl.**

1877 Bartlett 575 A tall man well bundled up in a Scotch plaid, or 'Bay State.'

2. Attrib. in **Bay State dialect, name, shawl.**

*c***1848** Lowell *Look on who will* ii, 'Tis but but my Bay-State dialect,—our fathers spoke the same! — **1919** Cady *Rhymes of Vt.* (1923) 109, I'd like to see this meeting choose A good old Bay State name. — **1856** Hannah Ropes *Kansas* 62 The 'Bay State shawls' are fastened up and turned into tapestry against the walls, back of the lounges. **1858** Holmes *Autocrat* i. 21 When I fling a Bay-State shawl over my shoulders.

bazoo bəˈzu, *n.* [Prob. f. Du. *bazuin,* trumpet.] (See quots.) *Slang.*

1877 Bartlett 49 *Blowin' his bazoo,* gasconade; braggadocio. Tennessee. **1884** Nye *Baled Hay* 237 People . . . listen to the silvery tinkle of his bazoo. **1888** Whitman *November Boughs* 407 Among the far-west newspapers, have been, or are, . . . *The Bazoo,* of Missouri. **1902** Harben *A. Daniel* 81 You are jest my sort of a Christian—better'n me, a sight, fer you don't shoot off yore bazoo on one side or t'other. **1948** *Sat. Ev. Post* 24 April 173/2 Shut yer big bazoo!

bazooka bəˈzukə, *n.* [App. f. **bazoo.**] (See quots.) Also **bazookist.**

1935 *Newsweek* 14 Dec. 29/1 (*caption*), A Local Bazookist Makes Good in Some Big Cities. *Ib.* 29/2 Burns peps up his lengthy yarns with periodic outbursts on his own invention, the bazooka, a trombone-like instrument confected of two gaspipes and a whisky funnel. **1943** *Pop. Sci. Mo.* Dec. 69 By developing the bazooka, our Army Ordnance Department modernized an old and almost forgotten weapon—the artillery rocket. . . . Resemblance to comedian Bob Burns's famous 'bazooka' inspired the modern launcher's name. **1948** *Chi. Tribune* 2 May 1. 45/2 The army . . . will be in the market for improved guns, [and] rocket launchers like the bazooka.

* **BB,** *n.*

1. BB gun, an air rifle that shoots BB shot.

1932 *Kansas City Times* 2 April 28 They put bird baths and bird boxes in their yards to attract the birds and then equip their small sons with B. B. guns. **1945** Wallace *Barington* 13 His favorite pastime with the high-powered Benjamin BB-gun was shooting the buttons off Lee Graham's coat.

2. BB shot, a size of shot intermediate between B and BBB, measuring .18 of an inch in diameter.

[**1874** Long *Wild-Fowl* 240 B or BB may with propriety be used in large or very close shooting guns.] **1891** *Scribner's Mag.* X. 460 A Canada goose . . . had been struck with one 'BB' shot, which had penetrated the left ventricle. **1947** *Chi. D. News* 21 July 12/1 The University of Chicago law library had an adventure with a trespassing bird, which was finally abated by a BB shot.

* **beach,** *n.*

1. *N. Jersey.* A low sand island or part of an island lying along or parallel to the coast.

1743 *N.J. Archives* VI. 155 A certain beach or island of sand lying next and adjoining to the main sea. **1855** *Knickerb.* XLVI. 221 The coast line of New-Jersey consists of a continuous chain of long narrow islands, known as 'beaches.' **1893** *Jerseyisms* in *D.N.* I. 328 'Young' or 'little beach' is new-made beach containing younger timber; 'old beach,' parallel ridges crowned by old timber.

2. In combs.: (1) **beach bird,** any one of various birds that frequent beaches; (2) **clam,** a surf clam, esp. *Mactra solidissima;* (3) **flea,** any one of various small leaping crustaceans of the family Orchestiidae found on seacoasts; (4) **front,** a strip or tract of land that fronts on a beach, also attrib.; (5) **grape,** ?the riverside grape, *Vitis vulpina, rare;* (6) **grass,** a coarse grass, *Ammophila arenaria,* found on beaches and often planted in dune reclamation, also attrib.; (7) **heather,** (see quot. 1931); (8) **hill,** a hill or dune on a beach; (9) **ivy,** = **beach grass,** *rare;* (10) **land,** land on or near a beach; (11) **lantern,** a lantern for use on a beach; (12) **lot,** a lot on a water front; (13) **pajamas,** pajamas for women suitable for wearing over bathing suits at a beach; (14) **pea,** a wild pea, *Lathyrus maritimus,* found on beaches; (15) **plum,** a shrub, *Prunus maritima,* also attrib.; (16) **wagon,** "a light open wagon with two or more seats" (W. '79).

(1) **1800** Bentley *Diary* II. 348 Dined . . . upon a Pie of beach birds. **1893** *Outing* May 94/1 Curlew, willet, plover and other beach birds swarm upon the flats in the spring, summer and fall months. —

(2) **1791** *Huntington Rec.* III. 170 That no Beach Clams on the south side of the Islands . . . be catched by any Person whatsoever to sell to Boatmen. **1889** *Cent. s.v.* — (3) **1843** *Nat. Hist. N.Y., Zoology* VI. 35 These small crustaceans are well known under the name of Sand-flea, or Beachflea. **1890** *Cent.* 4140/3 *Orchestiidæ.* . . . The species are inhabitants of the littoral region, and some are known as 'beach-fleas.' — (4) **1921** *N.Y. Times* 9 Sep. 15/1 It is calculated that $100,000 was spent by the great beach front hotels, business places and visitors in decorating the chairs, which were solid masses of blossoms. **1931** *Atlantic City News* 7 Aug. 4/2 The beachfront here . . . and large tracts of land in the most fertile parts of New Jersey . . . are all part of the Steelman heritage.

(5) **1819** SCHOOLCRAFT *Mo. Lead Mines* 29 The poplar . . . and beach grape . . . are only found to flourish on the rich alluvial lands composing the banks of rivers. — (6) **1681** *East-Hampton Rec.* II. 102 Thomas Bee doth . . . maintaine a sofisient three raile fence one the beach . . . down so low as any Beach grass groues. **1782** CRÈVECOEUR *Lett.* 128 Those declining grounds which lead to the sea-shores abound with beach grass, a light fodder when cut and cured, but very good when fed green. **1947** *Atlantic Mo.* Sep. 35/2 We made headquarters on a small beach-grass rise opposite Fish Hog Eddy. — (7) **1907** LYONS *Plant Names* 237 H[udsonia] tomentosa Nutt. Canada and northeastern U.S. Woolly Hudsonia, False Heather, Beach Heather. **1931** CLUTE *Plants* 69 The heather is rare or missing with us, but a little heather-like plant of sandy regions is a good substitute as the beach heather (*Hudsonia tomentosa*). — (8) **1815** *Mass. H.S. Coll.* 2 Ser. III. 173 Shifting cove on the Manomet shore, where there are beach hills, is the outlet for Beaver-dam brook. — (9) **1802** *Mass. H.S. Coll.* VIII. 145 Beach grass, the beach pea, beach ivy, . . . grow here luxuriantly.

(10) **1658** *East-Hampton Rec.* I. 148 A certayne tract of beach land with all the rest of the grass that joynes to it not seperated from it by water. **1753** *Brookhaven Rec.* 167 Several tracts or persels of . . . Swomp land, beach land, . . . situate within the township. — (11) **1878** *Harper's Mag.* Feb. 331/2 Each patrolman will carry a beach lantern, also a red coston hand-light. — (12) **1847** E. BRYANT *California* (1848) 438 All the ungranted tract of ground on the east front of the town of San Francisco, . . . known as the water and beach lots. **1910** J. HARTE *Vigilante Girl* 208 They say Burke has made a large fortune out of his beach and water lots. — (13) **1931** *K.C. Star* 3 Sep., The thing we like about beach pajamas . . . is that the wide legs are almost as handy as a skirt in lifting hot kettles. — (14) **1802** [see **beach ivy**]. *a***1862** THOREAU *Cape Cod* vii, Here and there were tracts of Beach-grass mingled with the Sea-side Golden-rod and Beach-pea, which reminded us still more forcibly of the ocean. **1939** *Nat. Geog. Mag.* 249/1 The beach pea (*L. maritimus*) of eastern lake shores or sea beaches is . . . similar in size and coloring to this ornate sweet pea farther west.

(15) **1784** CUTLER in *Mem. Amer. Acad. Arts & Sci.* (1785) I. 449 The Beach, or Sea-Side Plumb. **1892** B. TORREY *Footpath-Way* 78 The beach-plum crop was a failure. **1946** *Sat. Ev. Post* 3 Aug. 70/1 We plunged into the woods and descended toward the marsh, . . . keeping in the concealment of the trees, and later, as we descended, of the sumacs and bayberries and beach plums. — (16) **1869** ALCOTT *Little Women* II. 35, I shall hire a beach-wagon. **1948** *Chi. Tribune* 9 May II. 10/4 Use of the parking facilities is restricted to automobiles, beach wagons, and motorcycles.

As the last term in **old field beach, Palm Beach, sand beach.**

* **bead,** *n.*

1. The front sight of a rifle.

1831 AUDUBON *Ornith. Biog.* I. 294 He raised his piece gradually, until the *bead* . . . of the barrel was brought to a line with the spot which he intended to hit. **1853** SIMMS *Sword & Distaff* 483 Each with the bead of his rifle prepared to tell upon an enemy's button. **1936** *Sears Cat.* (ed. 173) 817 Gold Bead. . . . Standard Ivory Bead.

b. *To draw a bead on,* to take aim upon with a rifle. Also transf. Also *to have a bead on.*

1833 CATLIN *Indians* I. 77, I made several attempts to get near enough to 'draw a bead' upon one of them. **1846** *Spirit of Times* (N.Y.) 18 April 91/2 The percussion cap on their gun exploded without igniting the powder in the barrel, while they had a 'bead' on the game in question. **1853** *S. Lit. Messenger* XIX. 221/1 As Chuck levelled the pipe and drew a bead on them [*sc.* a crowd], and as it [*sc.* water] shot into the faces of the crowd—vip, vip, vip, they fell back. **1948** *Dly. Ardmoreite* (Ardmore, Okla.) 10 May 2/1 He draws a bead on squirrels and other game by sound alone and rarely misses.

2. In combs.: (1) **bead-line,** a line of aim; (2) **ruby,** a small two-leaved herb, *Maianthemum canadense,* having red bead-like berries; (3) **snake,** the small poisonous harlequin snake, *Micrurus fulvius,* of the southern U.S.

(1) **1866** F. KIRKLAND *Bk. Anecdotes* 319 He had his rifle on the bead-line ready. — (2) **1850** S. F. COOPER *Rural Hours* 105 Violets . . . grow there, with . . . bead-ruby, squaw-vine, partridge-plant, [etc.]. **1894** *Amer. Folk-Lore* VII. 102. — (3) **1736** CATESBY *Carolina* II. 60 The Bead Snake. . . . They have nothing of a Viper, either in Form or Quality, but are very inoffensive. **1808** T. ASHE *Travels* xxviii. 243 The conversation as usual, turned on the serpent tribe, and we called the following at least to our recollection . . . brown snake, little bead snake.

* **beaded,** *a.* Adorned with Indian beads or shells, as **beaded moccasin, shot-pouch, wampum.**

1809 F. CUMING *Western Tour* 269 A pair of very handsome beaded mockesons. **1829** COOPER *Wish-Ton-Wish* xxvi, Belts of richly-beaded wampum. **1838** *S. Lit. Messenger* IV. 224/1 This warrior was a young man . . . with . . . a beautiful beaded shot-pouch over his shoulder. **1948** *Norman* (Okla.) *Transcript* 1 July 3/2 Other Oklahoma souvenirs will include . . . miniature beaded moccasins made by Indian children of Anadarko.

* **beagle,** *n.* (*cap.*) A nickname for an inhabitant of Virginia. — **1845** *St. Louis Reveille* 14 May 2/4 The inhabitants of . . . Virginia [are called] Beagles. **1886** *Chi. Wkly. News* 29 Apr. 4/3 Virginia is the Old Dominion or the Mother of Presidents, but its people are Beagles.

* **beam,** *n.* As the last term in **brake, eave(s), finger, fore, log, pole, walking beam.**

beamster ˈbimstɚ, *n.* A man who prepares hides at a beam. — **1865** *Harper's Mag.* Oct. 678/1 A neighbor of his . . . is a morocco dresser—or a 'beamster.' **1885** *Ib.* Jan. 274/2 The beamsters, bending to their task, look as if they had taken in a large week's washing.

* **bean,** *n.*

1. A poker chip. Cf. **bean poker.**

1903 *Cin. Enquirer* 2 May 12/1, I recall the night you mention when we were pinched and there were several fellows who didn't turn up when we reopened to cash in their beans.

2. The head. *Slang.* Cf. **bean ball,** and **bean,** *v.*

1911 LEWIS *Apaches N.Y.* 20 Beat it, before I bump me black-jack off your bean! **1921** R. D. PAINE *Comr. Rolling Ocean* x. 168 If these Dutchmen get nasty, bang their blighted beans together.

3. In combs.: (1) **beanbag,** a small bag filled with beans used in children's games, also attrib.; (2) **ball,** (see quot. 1912); (3) **beetle,** the Mexican bean beetle; (4) **blow,** the flower of the bean plant, *obs.;* (5) **club,** a group of political boodlers, *obs.* [from *bean,* money in slang use], cf. **beanite;** (6) **Bean Eater,** a Bostonian, a nickname; (7) **hole,** a hole in the ground suitably lined with stone or brick for use in baking beans; (8) **patch, plot,** a patch or plot in which beans are grown; (9) **poker,** poker in which beans serve as chips, *obs.;* (10) **pole,** (*a*) a pole upon which bean vines climb, (*b*) a tall, thin person, [cf. Du. *boonstaak* in these senses]; (11) **porridge,** porridge made from bean meal [cf. Du. *boonpotage*]; (12) **pot,** a pot in which beans are cooked; (13) * **shell,** *transf.* a light flimsy vessel, *rare;* (14) **shooter,** a kind of small blowgun, a slingshot or catapult; (15) **tree,** (see quot. 1907); (16) **vine,** the vine of the bean plant; (17) **weevil,** any one of various small weevils injurious to beans.

(1) **1887** *Courier-Journal* 23 Jan. 6/4 The evening was spent in the games of 'Jackstraws,' bean-bag and cards. **1892** *Canebrake Herald* 15 April 3/2 The 'Christian Workers' will give a 'Bean Bag' party at the Parsonage, Saturday 15th. **1947** R. SMITH *Baseball* 28 There was an even older game, as refined as bean-bag, but called base or goal ball. — (2) **1912** *Amer. Mag.* June 199/2 Bean ball—A fast ball pitched at or near the head of a player who is standing too close to the plate with intent to drive him back. **1948** DIMAGGIO *Baseball for Everyone* 121 We'll go into no signs for dusters or bean-balls here. — (3) **1931** *Randolph Enterprise* (Elkins, W.Va.) 22 Oct. 1/5 The bean beetles almost totally destroyed the bean crop around here. — (4) **1854** PAIGE *Dow's Sermons* IV. 73 (Th.), As gently as a breeze ever scupped a bean-blow.

(5) **1875** *Chi. Tribune* 1 Sep. 4/3 These persons can well afford to . . . join hands in the bean-club in the common cause of plunder. — (6) **1881** *Detroit Free Press* 22 Sep. 6/2 An equal number of fielding errors by the bean eaters allowed the visitors to pocket four runs. **1948** *Chi. Tribune* 23 May II. 6/2 The second baseman of the Boston Bean-eaters . . . never was noted for his long ball hitting. — (7) **1923** *Outing* March 252/2 A bean hole can be made by digging a hole some larger than the largest kettle and a foot deeper. — (8) **1850** *Knickerb.* XXXV. 23, I know that rank corn is now grown on the bean-patch below. **1775** ADAIR *Indians* 232 Their young married people . . . had . . . broke down and polluted many of the honest neighbours bean-plots. — (9) **1866** *Eastern Slope* (Washoe, Nev.) 14 July 3/2 The crazy man looked around upon a bar-room full of men drinking red-eye and playing bean poker. **1878** HART *Sazerac Lying Club* 150 They were talking politics and playing bean poker—twenty beans for a quarter.

(10) (*a*) **1821** *Mass. Hist. Soc. Coll.* 2 Ser. IX. 143 This [sprout] when it rises sufficiently high, should be tied to a strong stake or pole, similar to a bean pole. **1860** *Harper's Mag.* Apr. 581/2 A tall, gaunt specimen of humanity. . . . His costume was as singular as his figure, and

hung upon him 'like a shirt upon a bean-pole.' (*b*) **1837** HALIBURTON *Clockmaker* I. Ser. xxix, Mr. Jehiel, a bean pole of a lawyer, was at the bottom or it. **1881** STODDARD *E. Hardery* 62 Not till she's married, and goodness knows when that'll be, the great, stuck-up beanpole. — (**11**) **1828** *Yankee* March 83/3 A sandy complexioned boy . . .eating bean-porridge with a pewter spoon. **1878** B. F. TAYLOR *Between Gates* 286 Two days more would . . . ripen bean-porridge to the fine perfection of 'nine days old.' — (**12**) **1846** *Quarter Race Ky.* 85 Jim Smith, hand over that spoon, an quit a lickin it like 'sank in a bean-pot.' **1904** O. HENRY *Heart of West* 88 He's got pots of money—bean-pots full of it. — (**13**) **1777** *Md. Journal* 25 Feb. (Th.), The Continental bean-shells, mann'd with Yankies, and armed with innocent pop-guns. — (**14**) **1889** *Cent.* 488/3 *Bean-shooter*, a toy for shooting beans, shot, or other small missiles; a pea-shooter. **1890** *Cong. Rec.* 4 March 1920/1, I have not excused this rudeness or shooting with a bean-shooter. **1948** *Sat. Ev. Post* 29 May 4/4 We boys in the Midwest 50 years ago called it a beanshooter.

(**15**) **1842** in *Amer. Sp.* XVIII. 120 Still, we are surrounded by . . . a colossal vegetation of cotton, live oak, bean and cypress trees. **1907** HODGE *Amer. Indians* I. 213 The two species native in the United States are the common catalpa, bean-tree, Indian bean, or candle-tree (*Catalpa catalpa*); and the western catalpa. — (**16**) **1828** WEBSTER *s.v. Vine*, Thus we speak of the hop vine [and] the bean vine. **1912** MRS. WOODROW *Sally Salt* 181 The bean vines, twining in luxuriant wreaths and festoons over their tall poles. — (**17**) **1870** PACKARD in *Mass. Agric. Rep.* I. 370, I sent specimens of the bean weevil . . . to Dr. G. A. Horn, of Philadelphia, who pronounces it to be . . . a native species (*B. varicornis* of Leconte). **1928** BAILEY *Cyclo. Horticulture* 460/2 A somewhat serious pest, however, which attacks the seeds both in the pod and dry, after being shelled, is the bean-weevil.

4. In colloq. phrases, meaning a small or the least amount as (1) *to know* (*not to know*) *beans*, (2) *not to care* (*say*) *beans*. Cf. *hill of beans*, *s.v.* **hill.**

(**1**) **1833** GREENE *D. Duckworth* II. 66 He don't know beans. **1888** *Chicago Herald* (F.), One has to know beans to be successful in the latest Washington novelty for entertainment at luncheons. **1948** *Range Riders Western* May 83/2 Captain Willard didn't know beans about fighting Apaches. — (**2**) **1857** *Knickerb.* XLIX. 138, I don't care beans for the rail-road, not a single old red-eyed bean, not a string bean. **1868** W. BAKER *New Timothy* (1870) 122 He'll never say 'beans' again!

b. *To spill the beans*, to divulge something secret, to say or do something indiscreet. *Slang.*

1919 T. K. HOLMES *Man fr. Tall Timber* xxviii. 355 'Mother certainly has spilled the beans!' thought Stafford in vast amusement. **1948** *N.Y. Times* 23 May v. 2/6 Leo spills the beans in needless style.

c. In miscellaneous expressions (see quots.).

1842 UNCLE SAM *Peculiarities* I. 98, I . . . was at the battle of New Orleans, when we gave the British beans. **1860** HOLLAND *Miss Gilbert* xxvi. 454, I felt meaner than beans about it. **1878** R. T. COOKE *Happy Dodd* 73 They don't think no small beans o' themselves.

As the last term in **Appalachian, asparagus, Boston baked, buffalo, bunch, bush, bushed, butter, Carolina, castor, castor-oil, coffee, coral, cornfield, cranberry, early comfort, English, fisher, Gloucester, green, ground, high, hominy, honey, Indian, jack, jelly, jumping, Magotty bay, mesquite, Mexican, Mohawk, mole, navy, pearl, pinto, prairie, refugee, Saba, sacred, screw, shell, short, shuck, smoking, snap, squeak, steady, string, tepary, valentine, velvet, wax, wild bean.**

bean bin, *v.* [f. **bean,** *n.* **2.**] *tr.* To strike or hit (someone) on the head. *Slang.* — **1910** *Amer. Mag.* 398/2 He is in extreme danger of being 'beaned,' which, in baseball, means hit in the head. **1948** *Dly. Ardmoreite* (Ardmore, Okla.) 22 April 6/4 He was beaned in an exhibition game at Topeka, Kan., April 14.

beanery ˈbinərɪ, *n.* A cheap restaurant where beans are often served. *Slang.* — **1894** *S.F. Midwinter Appeal* 10 Feb. 4/1 Papa Peakers gave a baked bean blowout to . . . the Press Men at his beanery. **1947** *Chi. Herald-American* 31 Aug. 1/7 Jake was slinging hash in a beanery on Cermak road near Wabash Ave.

beanite ˈbinaɪt, *n.* A member of a bean club. *Rare.* — **1875** *Chi. Tribune* 1 Sep. 4/3 Boss Tweed held about the same relationship to the Americans which the Head-Centre of the beanites holds to the Union.

* **bear,** *n.* Chiefly *attrib.*

1. *ellipt.* Bear's meat.

The fact that the European bear had become extinct in Britain by the eleventh century (see *Ency. Brit.*), strengthens the supposition that this sense, and the combs. given below, and no doubt many more, originated in this country.

1733 BYRD *Journey to Eden* (1901) 310 For those Stomachs . . . there was plenty of fat Bear, we having kill'd two in this day's March. **1750** WALKER *Journal* 23 April, Then Ambrose Powell . . . and I departed, leaving the others to provide and salt some Bear.

2. In miscellaneous combs.: (1) **Bear and Star,** in allusion to the Bear Flag Republic in California in 1846, *obs.*, cf. **Bear Flag, bear man, Bear Revolution;** (2) **blanket,** a bearskin used as a blanket, *rare;* (3) **cat,** a person who is superior in energy, strength, etc., *slang;* (4) **dance,** an invocative dance engaged in by Indians on the eve of a bear hunt; (5) **Flag,** see as a main entry; (6) **ground,** a region where bears are found; (7) **gun,** a gun suitable for killing bears; (8) **hunt,** a hunt after a bear or bears; (9) **hunter,** one who hunts bears; (10) **hunting,** the hunting of bears; (11) **man,** one of those interested in setting up the Bear Flag Republic in California in 1846, *obs.;* (12) **mouse,** (see quot. 1889); (13) * **paw,** (see quots.), also **bear's paw,** cf. **b.** (9) below; (14) **Bear Revolution,** the revolt of the Americans in California in 1846 against the Mexican authorities, *obs.;* (15) **rough,** a thicket such as bears frequent; (16) **'s handkerchief,** the caul of a bear, *obs.;* (17) **sign,** a track, or other indication of its presence left by a bear, cf. **c.** (6) below; (18) **skin,** see as a main entry; (19) **song,** ?a song sung by bear hunters, *rare;* (20) **Bear State,** (see quots.); (21) **story,** a story, often exaggerated, about bears, bear hunting, etc., also transf.; (22) **trail,** a trail made by a bear or bears, cf. **beat,** *n.* **1. b;** (23) **trap,** a trap for catching bears, also transf.; (24) **tree,** a hollow tree in which a bear or bears hibernate; (25) **wallow,** a shallow depression, usu. filled with water, attributed to the wallowing of bears, also attrib.

(**1**) **1849** *Bankers' Mag.* (May) III. 656 The corps of volunteers . . . raised the flag of the 'Bear and Star.' The number of grizzly bears in the country and the single star of the Texan flag, probably suggested the device of their own banner. — (**2**) **1850** H. C. LEWIS *La. Swamp Doctor* 168 The quantity of bear-blankets in the neighbouring cabins. — (**3**) **1916** *Amer. Mag.* April 77/1 The director said he had 'discovered' a bearcat, and engaged Alec at once. **1948** *Sat. Ev. Post* 8 May 40/2 I'm a bear cat on the Dodg'-Em. You know, the little cars at the amusement parks. — (**4**) **1820** in NUTE *Lake Superior* (1944) 75 They have . . . the Bear Dance & the Buffalo Dance, descriptive of their respective achievements in the chase. **1938** *Southwestern Lore* Sep. 32 He performed a leading part in the famous Bear Dance of the Utes.

(**6**) **1797** B. HAWKINS *Lett.* 70 This was our beloved bear ground, and reserved as such as long as it was of value for bear. **1923** J. H. COOK *On Old Frontier* 137 When we reached the place where I knew there was good bear ground, I instructed the men to move, in line with me. — (**7**) **1888** LINDLEY *Calif. of South* 189 A heavy shot from Lang's bear-gun sent an ounce-and-a-half bullet into Bruin's breast. **1929** *Randolph Enterprise* (Elkins W.Va.) 28 Nov. 1/1 We hope Mr. Piercy will be waiting for him with a good bear gun. — (**8**) **1803** *Lit. Mag.* (Phila.) Oct. 64 A grand bear hunt is proposed on the third Wednesday in October. **1948** *Minneapolis Star* 17 Sep. 1/3 He went on his first bear hunt at nine and shot a black bear in southeastern Alaska. — (**9**) **1765** ROGERS *Acc. N. Amer.* 259 An alliance with a noted bear-hunter, who has killed several in one day, is . . . eagerly sought after. **1922** *Outing* Oct. 22/1 He had had a successful season guiding Eastern 'dudes' who thought they were bear hunters.

(**10**) **1705** BEVERLEY *Virginia* IV. 65 Some few years agoe, I was a Bear-Hunting in the Woods above the Inhabitants. **1709** LAWSON *Carolina* 117 Bear-hunting is a great Sport in America, both with the English and Indians. **1948** *Outdoor Life* June 31/1, I did *not* go bear hunting. — (**11**) *c*1847 in IDE *California* 117 Early on the 5th of July Capt. Fremont requested the 'bear men,' as the 'Independents' were designated, to assemble 'without arms.' **1849** *Bankers' Mag.* III.656 These [insurgents] were styled the Bear Men. — (**12**) **1857** *Rep. Comm. Patents: Agric.* 84 Where several species [of meadow-mice] are found in one locality, they are commonly considered by farmers as one animal, known under various names, as 'Short-tailed Field Rats or Mice,' 'Bear Mice,' 'Bull-headed Mice,' 'Ground Mice,' 'Bog Mice,' &c. **1889** *Cent.* 492/2 bear-mouse. . . . A book-name of a marmot or a woodchuck, translating the generic name *Arctomys*. — (**13**) **1784–1812** D. THOMPSON *Narrative* (1916) 556 Having made for ourselves Bears Paws, which are rough made snow shoes round at each end. **1921** *Outing* Dec. 105/3 In climbing a mountain where it is known that snowshoes will be needed for only an hour or two during the day, the bear-paws can be strapped on the back or carried in a knapsack where they will not be an incumbrance. **1947** *Harper's Mag.* July 82/1 He wore ordinary snowshoes for fairly level country but bearpaws for rough and hilly terrain. — (**14**) **1846** BRYANT *California* (1848) 333 Among the passengers . . . were Mr. Ide, who acted so conspicuous a part in what is called the 'Bear Revolution,' and Messrs. Nash and Grigsby. **1849** *Bankers' Mag.* III. 656 The movement of the American settlers under Mr. Ide . . . was called the 'Bear revolution.'

(15) 1837 *Knickerb.* X. 413 Here security was made doubly sure by the bear-rough that sheltered them. — (16) *a*1846 *Quarter Race Kentucky* 144 He opened the 'bear's handkerchief,' or caul, and wrapped it round the whole [skewer of fat and liver], and thus roasted it before the fire. — (17) 1839 *S. Lit. Messenger* V. 377/1 To be sure I did see a powerful sight of bear signs. 1946 R. PEATTIE *Pac. Coast Ranges* 84 You may note 'bear sign' from the Gualala River to the Siskiyous and beyond. — (19) 1850 H. C. LEWIS *La. Swamp Doctor* 167 The preparations being completed [for amputation], Mik refused to have his arms bound, and commenced singing a bear song; and throughout the whole operation, ... he never uttered a groan, or missed a single stave.

(20) 1848 BARTLETT 392, I once asked a Western man if Arkansas abounded in bears, that it should be designated as the 'Bear State. 1944 *This Week Mag.* 23 Dec. 5/3 Arkansas, often known as the 'Bear State,' can boast a mere 30 black bears while California has 17,020. — (21) 1856 *Spirit of Times* 25 Oct. 129/1 Whether the forty-bear-in-a-day story ... was founded on fact, or was merely a *bear-story*, we are unable to decide. 1871 *Atlantic Mo.* Nov. 564/2 A company of hunters ... went on in their old eternal way of making bear-stories out of whole cloth. 1948 *N.Y. Folklore Quart.* Spring 82 Two bear stories also come from Collins. — (22) 1858 IVES *Colo. River* (1861) 111 A fresh bear trail crossing the slope was a good sign that the almost despaired of element was not far distant. — (23) 1825 NEAL *Bro. Jonathan* I. 108 What are ye arter there, squattin' so; jess like a cub in a bear trap? 1835 BIRD *Hawks of Hawk-hill* I. 269 Look you, boy, you are in a bear-trap, and the log will soon be on your back. 1841 *Week in Wall St.* 81 Bear-traps ... signifies ... [brokers who] have sold stock which they have not got, and trust to circumstances to be able to supply it. 1947 *Chi. D. News* 22 Oct. 47/2 (*comics*), Good gosh! Not satisfied to git caught in almost a bear trap, he has to pick up a mouse trap too! — (24) 1808 F. CUMING *Western Tour* 423 About five miles from our hut I found a bear tree. 1860 *Harper's Mag.* March 447/2 Visits are made to neighboring camps, bear-trees routed of their tenants, and traps inspected.

(25) 1766 in *Amer. Sp.* XV. 155/1 Thence ... to two White Oaks Saplings by the Bear Wallow Drains. 1872 W. J. FLAGG *Good Investment* i. 46/2 Sometimes he will meet with one of those almost mysterious shallow basins of water called 'bear-wallows.' 1947 *Harper's Mag.* July 84/1 He might be following a hardwood ridge of beech and maple, or working in the bear-wallow sort of land that often lies atop a mountain.

b. In the names of plants: (1) ∗**bearberry,** (*a*) the cranberry, *Vaccinium oxycoccus, obs.*, (*b*) =**bear huckleberry,** (*c*) the cascara buckthorn, *Rhamnus purshiana*, of the Pacific Coast; (2) **clover,** a rosaceous evergreen bush, *Chamaebatia foliolosa*, common to the California mountains; (3) **grass,** *S.* and *W.* any one of various species of yucca and similar plants, also attrib.; (4) **huckleberry,** the common huckleberry, *Gaylussacia baccata*, of the eastern states; (5) **mat,** =**bear clover;** (6) **oak,** a low evergreen oak, *Quercus pumila*, forming dense thickets in the southeastern states; (7) **root,** (see quot.), *rare;* (8) **'s bush,** =**inkberry;** (9) **'s paw,** (see quot.), cf. **2.** (13) above; (10) **weed,** the yerba santa, *Eriodictyon californicum;* (11) **wood,** =**bearberry** (*c*), see also **Oregon bearwood.**

(1) (*a*) 1672 JOSSELYN *N. Eng. Rarities* 65 Cran Berry, or Bear Berry, because Bears use much to feed upon them, is a small trayling plant that grows in Salt Marshes. (*b*) 1883 [see **bear huckleberry**]. (*c*) 1884 SARGENT *Rep. Forests* 41 *Rhamnus Purshiana*. ... Bearberry. Bear Wood. Shittim Wood. 1893 *Amer. Folk-Lore* VI. 139 *Rhamnus Californica*, wild coffee; bearberry. — (2) 1897 PARSONS *Wild Flowers Calif.* 92 Along the line of the railroad in Placer County it is often called 'bear-clover,' perhaps in accordance with our felicitous custom of giving names, because it bears not the least resemblance to clover, and the bear will have nothing to do with it. 1944 *Sat. Ev. Post* 12 Aug. 25/1 Watkins ... used to specialize in exotic honeys—manzanita, wild lilac, cedar, honey dew, creeping sage, bear clover—'honeys that taste like the mountains smell in spring.' — (3) 1750 WALKER *Journal* 12 April, On the Banks is some Bear-Grass. 1802 *Farmer's Library* (Louisville) 1 Apr. 3/4 The following articles of produce will be received in payment, viz. Wheat delivered at any of the Merchant Mills on Goose-Creek or Bear Grass Hemp, Country Linen or Sugar at the market price. 1946 R. PEATTIE *Pac. Coast Ranges* 72 In these meadows the most conspicuous plant is likely to be the bear grass, whose great white heads of bloom are a favorite subject with western mountain photographers. — (4) 1883 HALE *Woods & Timbers N.C.* 140 Bear Huckleberry. Bearberry. (*Gaylussacia ursina*, Gray.) ... The berry is purplish or dark red, insipid and dry, ripening in July and August.

(5) 1915 ARMSTRONG *Western Wild Flowers* 222 The smell and foliage attract attention and the shrub has many names, such as Bear-mat and Kittikit. — (6) 1810 MICHAUX *Arbres* I. 24 Bear oak (Chêne d'ours), connu sous ce nom dans les Etats de New-Jersey et de New-York. 1814 PURSH *Flora Amer.* II. 631 *Quercus Banisteri*. ... This shrub ... is known by the name of bear oak, black scrub oak, and dwarf red oak. 1935 *Ecological Monog.* Jan. 67 In addition, there were open brushy places in certain regions, composed largely of bear oak. — (7) 1751 ELIOT *Field-Husb.* iii. 66 Take the Roots of Swamp Hellebore, sometimes called Skunk Cabbage, Tickle Weed, Bear Root. — (8) 1787 CUTLER in *Life*, etc. I. 201 Brought home Bear's-bush and two species of Sumach. — (9) 1824 SINGLETON *Letters* 63 Here [in Va.] are ... the prickly pear or bear's paw.

(10) 1887 BURROUGHS in *Cent. Mag.* July 325 The stem [is] two feet high, very leafy, and coarser than bear-weed. — (11) 1869 *Amer. Naturalist* III. 407 Oregon Bearwood (*Frangula Purshiana*). This species of Buckthorn occurs on both slopes of the Coeur d'Alene Mountains. 1897 PARSONS *Wild Flowers Calif.* 68 In Oregon it is known as 'chittemwood' and 'bitter bark,' and also as 'wahoo' and 'bear-wood.'

c. Designating foods, usu. parts of a bear prepared as food or used in cooking, as (1) **bear bacon,** (also **bear's bacon**), (2) **chowder,** (3) **fat,** (also **bear's fat**), (4) **ham,** (5) **meat,** (also **bear's meat**), (6) **sign,** cf. **2.** (17) above, (7) **'s oil,** (8) **steak.**

(1) [1737 BRICKELL *N. Carolina* 111 The Bacon made thereof is extraordinary good. ... I have seen very good Hams ... made of these Bear's-flesh.] 1818 SCHOOLCRAFT *Journal* 45 We have homony ... and bear's bacon for dinner. 1909 T. W. ENGLISH in *Pioneer Days* 246 It was bear bacon and it was real good. — (2) 1847 LANMAN *Summer in Wilderness* xiv. 88 When the bear chowder was done, it was equally distributed among the assembled crowd. — (3) 1709 LAWSON *Carolina* 207 A roasted or barbakued Turkey, eaten with Bears Fat, is held a good dish. 1852 WATSON *Nights in Block-house* 135 Then bear-meat, looking very much like pork; bear-fat in separate dishes; a few squirrels ... filled up the rest of the table. — (4) 1766 W. STORK *Acc. East-Florida* 50 It is reckoned very good food, especially the bear hams, &c. 1850 H. C. LEWIS *La. Swamp Doctor* 165 From the joists depended bear-hams and tongues innumerable.

(5) 1772 D. TAITT in *Travels Amer. Col.* 513 One of the head men intertained us at his house with some bears meat for breakfast. 1787 in RAMSEY *Tennessee* (1853) 504 Good bear meat, without bones, eight dollars per hundred wt. 1890 RYAN *Told in Hills* 96 Jimmy brought out ... some bits of salt meat—evidently bear meat. — (6) 1903 A. ADAMS *Log Cowboy* xviii. 279 She asked me to make the bear sign — doughnuts, she called them—and I did. — (7) 1674 in ALVORD & BIDGOOD *Trans-Allegheny Region* 213 Aboundance of corne [was brought] ... with fish, flesh and beares oyle. 1750 WALKER *Journal* 20 June, My riding Horse was bit by a Snake this day, and having no Bear's Oil I rub'd the place with a piece of fat meat, which had the desired effect. 1888 EGGLESTON in *Cent. Mag.* July 341/2 His hair was well kept in place by bear's oil. — (8) 1788 J. MAY *Journal & Lett.* 59 Had an elegant dinner. Amongst the variety was ... boiled fish, bear-steak, roast venison, etc. 1883 ZEIGLER & GROSSCUP *Alleghanies* 48 The hounds may be 20 miles away, and the drivers and standers [may be] toasting bear steaks in their cabins.

3. In colloq. phrases: (1) *as cross as a bear*, and variants, quite angry or cross; (2) *to skin the bear at once*, to proceed to essentials, to get down to brass tacks; (3) *bring on your bears*, a challenge of defiance, an invitation to an adversary to do his worst.

(1) 1826 *Va. Herald* (Fredericksburg) 13 Sep. 2/1 All hands except one, were as cross as bears. 1837 BIRD *Nick of Woods* I. 89 Major Smalleye war as mad as a beaten b'ar. 1859 G. A. JACKSON *Diary* 522 Phil has been as cross as a bear all day. — (2) 1844 *N.O. Picayune* 16 Sep. 241/4 But now, to skin the *bar* at once, can you give me and five other gentlemen employment? — (3) 1886 *Chi. Tribune* 13 Sep. 4/3 Bring On Your Bears. What with offensive Ministers and erratic Consuls, ... burden after burden of trouble has been laid upon Secretary Bayard's shoulders. *Ib.*, He can request England or Canada ... to bring on their bears.

As the last term in **bald faced, black, cinnamon, hog, Mexican, Missouri, mule, naked, over, range, ranging, Rocky Mountain, skunk, slough, white, yellow bear.**

∗**bear,** *v.* ∗*To bear off*, (see quot.). — 1869 *Overland Mo.* Aug. 126 Another rides in, selects a stray brand, and 'cuts it out,' by chasing it out with his horse. At other times they 'bear off' a single animal, by riding between it and the herd, when in motion.

∗**beard,** *n.* As the last term in **crown, gray, lion's, old man's, silver, Spanish beard.**

beardtongue ˈbɪrdˌtʌŋ, *n.* An herb of the genus *Penstemon.*

1821 *Mass. Hist. Soc. Coll.* 2 Ser. IX. 153 *Pentstemon pubescens*, Beard tongue. 1847 WOOD *Botany* 400 Beard-tongue ... [grows on] river banks, bluffs, hills, and barrens, Western N.Y. to Ohio, Iowa and Illinois. 1940 JAEGER *Desert Wild Flowers* 235 This tall (2–5 ft.), extraordinarily sweet-scented beard-tongue comes to perfection in mid-May.

∗**bearer,** *n.* As the last term in **chain, eave(s), signal, sword bearer.**

Bear Flag. A white flag having a grizzly bear as its device raised in June, 1846, by a small group of American insurgents in California, who, in defiance of the Spanish authorities, proclaimed "The California Republic." Now used as the California state flag.

[**1848** *Calif. Claims* (Senate Rep. 23 Feb.) 27 A settler . . . had hoisted a flag—a grizzly bear upon a white field—as the insignia of the new State.] *Ib.* 50 The most valuable portion of the beautiful valley . . . and the wealthy missions of the country would have been ceded and granted away, but for the opportune hoisting of the bear flag. **1880** IDE *California* 47 The said 'Bear Flag'—made of plain cotton cloth, and ornamented with the red flannel of a shirt from the back of one of the men, and christened by the words 'California Republic,' in red-paint letters on both sides—was raised upon the standard where had floated on the breezes the Mexican flag aforetime. It was on the 14th of June, '46. **1946** R. PEATTIE *Pac. Coast Ranges* 82 Not even a hint of an echo of his growl comes down the winds, flutter-

Bear Flag of the California Republic

ing proudly the Bear Flag which, as California's official State flag, floats beside the national colors. **1948** *Chi. Tribune* 25 April I. 24/3 They marched on the local presidio and on June 14, 1846, raised the famous Bear Flag.

attrib. **1856** *Wide West* (S.F.) 1 Oct. 2/1 The bear which forms a portion of the present escutcheon of the State of California, was introduced as a memento of the Bear Flag movement, by the Constitutional Committee. **1880** in IDE *California* 127 During these twenty days there was no obstruction, by a conflicting party, to the exercise by the Bear Flag Government, of its entire functions and prerogatives of National Independence. **1943** DEVOTO *Year of Decision* 461 They were afraid of such half or wholly irregular military forces as the Bear Flag stalwarts and the California Battalion.

***bearing,** *n.* As the last term in **gold, oil, roller bearing.**

bearing tree. In land surveying, a tree, suitably marked, serving to indicate the position of a "corner," a witness tree *q.v.*

1817 *Niles' Reg.* XII. 98/2 At each corner the courses are taken to two trees, in opposite directions as nearly as may be, and their distance from the post measured. These trees are called 'bearing trees,' and are blazed on the side next the post. **1878** *Harper's Mag.* Jan. 210/2 A 'bearing' tree has been blocked to get at a 'blaze' made in the spring of '38. **1948** *Time* 8 March 87 [Painting by Glenn Grohe:] 'Cruisers at Bearing Tree.'

***bearskin,** *n.* **1.** A coarse woolen cloth for overcoats. **2. bearskin moccasin,** a moccasin made of bearskin. *Obs.* See also **doe bearskin.**

(1) **1762** H. M. BROOKS *Gleanings* 37 Broad cloths, German serges, bearskins, beaver coating, half-thick, red shagg, bays. **1805** PARKINSON *Tour* 381 A top-coat for a boy twelve years old, of the cloth called bear-skin, eight dollars. — (2) **1775** ADAIR *Indians* 390 The victors . . . put on their feet a pair of bear-skin maccaseenes.

***beat,** *n.*

1. =**yard,** *n.* **2.** See also **buffalo, deer, horse, moose beat.**

1834 AUDUBON *Ornith. Biog.* II. 433 When we went to look for the other [moose], . . . we found that he had . . . gone to the 'beat,' about a mile and a half distant.

b. (See quot.)

1857 *Harper's Mag.* Nov. 819/1 The bear goes to and from his den or cover . . . by certain paths, called 'beats.' A bear will use the same beat for years, going by night on one beat, and in the day taking another, more circuitous.

2. A person or thing that excels or surpasses. *Colloq.*

1833 S. SMITH *Major Downing* 129, I never see the beat of it. **1847** *Knickerb.* XXIX. 62, I suppose this Teeples ha'n't got his beat in old Potter. **1902** L. RICHARDS *Mrs. Tree* 70 'There! you hear her!' murmured Direxia. 'Oh, she is the beat of all!'

3. Chiefly *S.* An election precinct. Also attrib. Cf. **Captain's beat.**

1842 *Vermont Militia Act.* 11., Every commanding officer may enroll as musicians in his company, at least two and not more than five persons residing in his beat. **1860** CLAIBORNE *Saml. Dale* x. 166 Governor Holmes appointed me . . . commissioner to take the census and organize beats or precincts. **1870** HOWE *Presby. Church in S.C.* I. 584 Shortly after commencing his schooling, a draft was ordered in the Beat company in which he resided. **1944** *Democrat* 6 April 3 List of Qualified Electors [in] . . . Beat No. 1 . . . Beat No. 2. [etc.].

4. =**deadbeat.** *Slang.*

1865 *Canteen Songster* (1868) 26 Before 'this cruel war' broke out, he was what's termed 'a beat.' **1901** J. RIIS *Making of an American* 139 When the grocer on my corner complained that he was being ruined by 'beats' who did not pay their bills . . . I started in at once to make those beats pay up. **1948** *Chi. Tribune* 4 Apr. (*comics*) 7 Well, you can't get money out of a turnip!! You're no turnip—you're a beat!

b. (See quot.) *Obs.*

1871 L. H. BAGG *At Yale* 138 In sophomore year, Beta Xi men are are called 'Dead Beats,' or simply 'Beats,' by those of Theta Psi.

5. In journalism, the securing and publishing of a piece of news before one's competitors, the news item itself.

1873 *Harper's Mag.* July 231/1 One of these 'enterprising' individuals secured his first 'beat' by riding in from the first Bull Run defeat on a horse not his own, and taking news of the disaster to Philadelphia by rail, before an injunction was laid on the transmission of the truth. **1948** *Time* 5 April 68/1 Shorty . . . fumbled a chance for a beat on a gangster slaying.

b. *To get a beat on (one),* to get the advantage of. *Slang.*

1889 FARMER 46 As used by thieves and their associates, *to get a beat on one* . . . also implies that the point has been scored by underhand, secret, or unlawful means.

As the last term in **king, live, panhandle, road beat.**

***beat,** *a.*

1. Overcome by astonishment, taken aback. *Colloq.*

1835 LONGSTREET *Ga. Scene* 212 Well, the law me, I'm clear beat! **1881** A. HAYES *New Colorado* ii. 25 When the feller . . . got the light on the [railroad] pass, . . . he was the wust beat feller you ever see.

b. beat out, exhausted, worn out by fatigue, out of patience. *Colloq.*

1746 in G. SHELDON *Hist. Deerfield* I. 548, I . . . ordered him to put on faster. He told me his horse was about beat out. **1891** RYAN *Pagan* ix. 123 'I'm beat out,' he acknowledged; 'and I ain't a going to keep up this sort of canter the whole trip.' **1943** PEATTIE *Great Smokies* 128 The North Carolina woman . . . 'got so plumb beat out with the no-account ways of her fam-il-ee, that she just tuk to the bed and stayed thar, year in and year out.'

2. a. beat biscuit, =**beaten biscuit. b. beat meat,** (see quot.). *Obs.*

(a) 1881 *Georgians* 123 This is regular old-fashioned hoe-cake; and here I see part of a pone; and this is beat-biscuit, I'm sure. **1923** WATTS *Luther Nichols* 306 A delicacy known all over the South as beat biscuit. — **(b) 1784–1812** D. THOMPSON *Narrative* (1916) 434 Pemican . . . is made of the lean and fleshy parts of the Bison dried, smoked and pounded fine; in this state it is called Beat Meat.

***beat,** *v.*

1. *tr.* To cheat, defraud, often with *out.* Cf. *to beat one's way.*

1851 *Oquawka* (Ill.) *Spectator* 5 Feb. 1/7 He then went to Cincinnati where he *beat* another man out of $12. **1889** *Western Herald* (S.F.) 26 July 1/4 What did you put the man off for? Was he trying to beat a ride? **1944** KAHN *Cable Car Days* 82 One never attempted to 'beat' the conductor out of his fare.

2. To arrive before (another). Also absol.

1869 *Overland Mo.* July 65/2 'The Pacific beat by two minutes thirty-one and two-fifths seconds,' interposes an outsider, with a double-tinned imitation gold watch, and an itching for fame as an exact statistician. **1948** *Chi. Tribune* 30 May I. 7/1 Chief Harry Tracy of the Calais department takes command if his men beat the St. Stephen boys to a St. Stephen alarm.

3. In colloq. and slang phrases: (1) *To beat all,* and variants, to surpass or excel decisively; (2) *it beats my time,* it surpasses my comprehension; (3) *to beat one's way,* to travel without paying one's way; (4) **to beat out,* to get the start of, defeat, surpass, often of a baseball player who reaches a base before the arrival there of the ball; (5) *to beat one to it,* to anticipate, forestall (one) in doing something; (6) **to beat up,* to thrash soundly; (7) *to beat it,* to go away, clear out.

(1) **1831** *Boston Transcript* 10 May 1/1 By forty! . . . if this dont beat all the milintary [*sic*] movements I ever heerd of! **1873** *Harper's*

Mag. XLVI. 680 'Don't that beat the deuce?' says Grey. **1948** *Chi. Tribune* 1 Feb. VII. 1/4 Don't it beat all how folks plunge into things, when they've already got more money than it'd take to burn a wet mule! — **(2) 1869** MARK TWAIN *Innocents Abroad* lvii. 616 Well, you take it along—but I swear it beats my time, though. **1898** PAGE *Red Rock* 224 It clean beats my time. I don't know what's got into her. — **(3) 1878** RUEDE *Sod-House Days* 230 Herman Glicker is out here again. He 'beat' his way to Chicago, where he got a ticket for the balance of the way. **1945** *Reader's Digest* Jan. 46/1 He beat his way to Cambridge. — **(4) 1893** *Outing* May 155/2 The act of starting consisted in beating out the pistol. It was a footless sprinter then who could not steal a fifth of a second on the start. **1905** N. DAVIS *Northerner* 227 Jiminy! . . . This beats out all creation! **1912** *Amer. Mag.* July 302/1 Ty Cobb informed me that during the entire season he did not bunt with the idea of beating out the ball, except in one case. **1948** *Dly. Ardmoreite* (Ardmore, Okla.) 30 May 10/3 It was not until the sixth when Stephens beat out a slow roller through the pitcher box that the Raiders got another safety.

(5) 1904 *McClure's Mag.* March 556/2 'They simply beat us to it,' complained Barrett, as we rode south. **1923** WATTS *Luther Nichols* 198 If the sheriff don't beat me to it. — **(6)** *a***1906** O. HENRY *Trimmed Lamp* 159, I wouldn't have a man . . . that didn't beat me up at least once a week. — **(7) 1908** A. RUHL *Other Americans* ii. 10 He'll be beatin' it for Paris pretty soon where the rest of 'em all went. **1947** *Savings News* Nov. 12/2 Dull party, isnt it? . . . Let's beat it.

beatemest ˈbitəməst, *a.* Also **beatomest.** [f. Eng. dial. *beatem* (i.e., beat them) "the conqueror, one who excels all others"—*EDD.*] Best, finest, greatest. *Colloq. Obs.* Cf. **beatenest,** *a.* — **1831** *Boston Transcript* 9 Aug. 2/3 He . . . sees old Susap . . . stan' there with his gun pyntin' right into the door—beatemest feller with a gun ever you seed. **1851** JUDD *Margaret* (ed. 2) III. 245 Take it by and large fifty head a season, and she is the beatomest.

beaten biscuit. *S.* A hard biscuit made of dough consisting of flour, shortening, and water, lightened by thorough beating and frequent folding.

1876 M. F. HENDERSON *Practical Cooking* 69 Little machines . . . for the purpose of making beaten biscuit. **1908** LORIMER *J. Spurlock* 207 There was a chicken gumbo soup, and then cold boiled Virginia ham, and hot fried chicken, . . . beaten biscuits. **1948** *Chi. D. News* 23 Feb. 12/7 The famous beaten biscuit deserved just what it got—a beating.

beatenest ˈbitnəst, *a.* [Whimsical superlative of the participle *beating* (or *beaten*).] One who or that which "beats" or surpasses everyone else or everything. *Colloq.* Cf. **beatemest,** *a.*

1860 *Harper's Mag.* 135 A countryman . . . attracted by the white slab . . . exclaimed, 'Well, if this ain't the beatenest town I ever saw!' **1908** K. D. WIGGIN *Rebecca* xix. 209 Ain't she the beatin'est creetur that ever was born int' the world! **1947** *Atlantic Mo.* June 58/2 He was the beatinest and the eatinest durn man I ever seed.

* **beater,** *n.*

1. One of the vats used in making indigo. *Obs.*

1784 J. SMYTH *Tour U.S.* II. 60 They judge that the fermentation has attained its due pitch . . . ; this directs the managers to open a cock, and let off the water into another vat which is called the *beater*. **1835** INGRAHAM *South-West* I. 273 The liquor is at length drawn off into another vat, called the beater.

2. One who excels others. *Colloq.*

1845 JUDD *Margaret* II. v. 283 Take it by and large, fifty head a season, and she is the beater of all. **1886** *Harper's Mag.* Nov. 835/1 Well, for getting sunthin outer northing, she's a beater!

3. beater press, (see quot. 1874).

1865 *Chi. Tribune* 10 April 1 A No. 1 Beater Hay Press. **1874** KNIGHT 259 Beater-press. For baling. One in which the bale is made by beating it into smaller bulk; or, which is more usual, in which the bale is packed by beating, and finally solidified by direct and maintained pressure.

As the last term in **bush, egg, gold, hominy, world beater.**

beateree ˌbitəˈri, *n.* That which surpasses. *Colloq. Obs.* — **1861** R. T. COOKE in *Atlantic Mo.* Aug. 159/2 That was the beateree of all the weddin'-towers I ever heerd tell on. **1878** R. T. COOKE *Happy Dodd* x. 99 Mis' Potter sent that, and it is the beateree for bread, but 'tain't rye.

beatermost ˈbitɚˌmost, *a.* [Whimsical superlative of *beater,* one who excels.] =**beatenest.** *Colloq. Obs.* — **1843** STEPHENS *High Life N.Y.* II. xix. 28 Now if this don't beat all, aint I the beatermost feller for losing things? **1845** MRS. KIRKLAND *Western Clearings* 98 The Maineman . . . will declare [his cow] to be the 'beatermost critter under the canopy.'

* **beating,** *n.* The drumming of the ruffed grouse. — **1752** Lett. of Mr. Brooke of Md. in EDWARDS *Gleanings Nat Hist.* (1758) I. 82 The beating of the Pheasant, as we term it, is a noise chiefly made in the spring of the year.

beaut bjut, *n.* [Short for *beauty.*] A person or thing exceptionally handsome or splendid, often ironical. *Colloq.*

1866 F. KIRKLAND *Bk. Anecdotes* 178 Hopeful is not a beauty, and he knows it; and though some of the rustic wits call him 'Beaut,' he is well aware that they intend it for irony. **1903** C. L. BURNHAM *Jewel* 18 'Ain't she a beaut!' exclaimed Zeke as he led out the mare. **1948** *Dly. Ardmoreite* (Ardmore, Okla.) 15 April 6/2 I'm glad I don't drink any more because this is a cue to go on a beaut.

beautician bjuˈtɪʃən, *n.* One in charge of, or employed as an operative in, a beauty parlor. *Cant.* — **1926** *Amer. Mercury* Feb. 162/2 Arkansas, Connecticut, Illinois, Louisiana, Missouri, New Mexico, Oregon, Utah and Wisconsin are already in the fold with state licenses for beauticians. **1947** *Denver Post* 5 March 1/8 The former state service tax . . . provided for a flat 2 per cent tax on . . . the services of physicians, dentists, . . . beauticians, . . . etc.

* **beauty,** *n.* In combs.: (1) **beautyberry,** a plant of the genus *Callicarpa,* of the verbena family; (2) **contest,** a competition in which girls or women compete for a prize to be given the most beautiful, also transf.; (3) **culture,** used attrib. to designate a beauty parlor; (4) **doctor,** one who cares for the beauty of his clients; (5) **parlor,** a shop or establishment in which the business of caring for and beautifying the hair, hands, and complexions of the patrons is carried on; (6) **queen,** a beautiful girl or woman, esp. one adjudged a winner in a beauty contest, also attrib.; (7) **shop,** =**beauty parlor;** (8) **show,** an occasion upon which girls or women participate in a beauty contest.

(1) 1923 *Standardized Plant Names* 61/1 Hort. var. of Callicarpa: White Beautyberry (*C. americana alba*). **1942** VAN DERSAL *Ornamental Amer. Shrubs* 260 In its native habitat beautyberry grows in rich woodlands, old fields, woods edges, or sometimes in very poor eroded soil. — **(2) 1903** *Cin. Enquirer* 23 May 11/4 They hired seven girls, whom they picked up in the street, to sit in short skirts and pose as candidates in a 'beauty contest.' **1947** *Time* 3 Feb. 21/3 In a beauty contest I am paired with the Senator from Ohio. — **(3) 1927** *Sat. Ev. Post* 23 Apr. 73/1 Many of the other large beauty-culture concerns recruit their assistants from graduates of beauty schools, of which there are several hundred throughout the country. — **(4) 1909** O. HENRY *Roads of Destiny* 74 Looking handsome. Oh, what a mistake! It's the larynx that the beauty doctors ought to work on. **1912** *Ladies' Home Jrnl.* Nov. 14/2 The 'treatments' of the 'beauty doctors' were given in their own establishments—'Institutes' and 'Colleges' they prefer to call them.

(5) 1908 *Harper's Wkly.* 24 Oct. 22/1 Scene:—The 'beauty parlors' of a large department store. There are a number of booths divided off by wooden partitions. **1948** *Family Circle* June 84/3 She consulted her purse, adopted a rashly extravagant attitude, and started phoning beauty parlors. — **(6)** [**1865** *Harper's Wkly.* 7 Oct. 637/1 Three tilts or courses in succession is the general number tried, the knight who takes three rings oftenest has the honor of choosing the Queen of Love and Beauty. **1909** *Amer. Review of Reviews* Sep. 362/1 From these six by a further plebiscite the 'Queen of Beauty' was to be chosen.] **1922** *N.Y. Times* 5 Sep. 19/6 The winning beauty will be heralded as America's 'Beauty Queen.' **1939** BROWNELL *Horse & Buggy Days* 153 Since the 'Beauty Queen' craze started, we've had one for spring and summer, for tulips and hollyhocks. — **(7) 1901** *Current Lit.* Apr. 446/1 (*title*), The Oldest Beauty-Shop. **1939** *Industrial Market Data Handbook U.S.* 164 Beauty shop equipment. — **(8) 1924** *Lit. Digest* 31 May 35/1 The Atlantic City beauty shows have for their object the exploitation of loveliness of face and form—mostly form.

As the last term in **American, Baltimore, bathing, highland, meadow, Ohio, pine barren, Rutland, spring beauty.**

* **beaver,** *n.*

1. A beaver skin. *Obs.*

1602 BRERETON *Relation* 9 So the rest of the day we spent in trading with them [Indians] for Furres, which are Beauers, . . . black Foxes, Conie skinnes, . . . and other beasts skinnes to us unknowen. **1692** *Md. Hist. Mag.* XIII. 211 They presented him with a beaver in expectation of having some corn. **1721** *Mass. H. Repr. Jrnls.* III. 111 Thou didst . . . promise to remit those four men, by giving thee two hundred Beavers.

b. (See quot.) *Rare.*

1848 RUXTON *Far West* (1924) iii. 99 'Ho, boys! hyar's a deck, and hyar's the beaver' (rattling the coin).

c. An amount equivalent in value to a beaver pelt.

1902 WHITE *Conjuror's House* iii. 26 He too reported of the trade—so many 'beaver' of tobacco, of powder, of lead, of pork.

2. A person. *Colloq.*

1850 GARRARD *Wah-To-Yah* xix. 216 Why, the old beaver says as how he was in hell once. **1866** SHANKS *Recollections* 47 The soldiers called each other 'gophers' and 'beavers;' and 'gopher-holes' were more common in the armies' track than were camp-fires. *Ib.* 345 The rebels used to call our men, when working on forts, rifle-pits, etc., 'beavers in blue.'

3. In combs.: (1) **beaver blanket,** a blanket of beaver skins, *obs.;* (2) **Beaverboard,** a trade-mark for a kind of fiberboard; (3) **buffalo,** (see quot.), *rare;* (4) **coat,** (*a*) a coat made of beaver skins, *obs.*, (*b*) (see quot.); (5) **coin,** used collectively for the coins, of California gold, issued in 1849 by the Oregon Exchange Co., *obs.;* (6) **Beaver Hunters,** the Tsattine ("dwellers among the beavers") Indians; (7) **Beaver Indians,** =prec.; (8) **maker,** a maker of beaver hats, *rare;* (9) **pay,** payment in beaver, or at the value of it, *obs.;* (10) **plew,** a beaver skin, *obs.;* (11) **price,** (see quot. and cf. **beaver pay**), *obs.;* (12) **robe,** a robe of beaver skins (see also quot. 1918); (13) * **tail,** the tail of a beaver used as food, cf. **b.** (3) below; (14) **trade,** beaver as an article of trade, trade in beaver skins; (15) **trading,** trading for beaver skins.

(1) 1752 W. TRENT *Journal* 96 The Twightwees made the following speech, with a beaver blanket, with a green painted spot in the middle. **1778** CARVER *Travels* 24 He prayed '. . . that I might lie down, by night, on a beaver blanket.' — **(2) 1909** *Sat. Ev. Post* 20 Feb. 35/1 [Advt. Beaver Mfg. Co., Buffalo, N.Y.:] Beaver Board . . . Takes Place of Both Lath and Plaster. **1948** *Baby Post* Spring 6/3 Paste the tracing on the . . . beaverboard. — **(3) 1892** *Scribner's Mag.* Sep. 277/1 The 'beaver buffalo' . . . has been vaguely described to me by northern Indians as small and having a very curly coat. — **(4)** (*a*)**1628** LEVETT *Voyage into N. Eng.* (1893) 110 They brought me a Beauer Coate, and two Otter skines. **1748** WEISER *Journal* 36 The Delawares made a Speech to me & presented a Beaver Coat & a String of Wampum. (*b*) **1908** VISSCHER *Pony Express* 92 All the Indians liked 'Beaver Coat,' as they called Gen. Miles.

(5) 1866 *Beadle's Mo.* Aug. 184/2 A few specimens of the early money, the 'Beaver Coin,' are still in existence. — **(6) 1845** DE SMET *Oregon Missions* (1847) 16 Within the limits . . . are found the Black-Feet, Crees, . . . Beaver Hunters, Flat-side Dogs, Slaves, and Deer-Skins. — **(7) 1791** *Mass. Hist. Soc. Coll.* 1 Ser. III. 24 The tribes of Indians . . . were called the . . . Great Belly Indians, Beaver Indians [etc.]. — **(8) 1652** *Suffolk Deeds* I. 235 Theodore Atkinson of Boston, . . . beauer maker. [Elsewhere called 'hatter' and 'felt-maker.'] — **(9) 1662** *Jamaica* (L.I.) *Rec.* I. 14 [They] are to pay twentie three pounds in bever pay that is to say wheat at sixe shillings & indian corn at three shillings sixe pence the bushell. **1685** *N.J. Archives* 1 Ser. I. 504 The disbursement off four pounds a peice in bever pay.

(10) 1850 GARRARD *Wah-To-Yah* xix. 220 The rocks on the sides was pecked as smooth as a beaver plew rubbed with the grain. — **(11) 1662** *Hempstead Town Rec.* I. 127, I William Smith do prise the halfe of the mill at ffourty pounds sterling, to be paid in beaver or cattell at beaver prise. — **(12)** [**1678** MARQUETTE in *La. Hist. Coll.* IV. (1852) 37 The third scene consists of a speech delivered by the holder of the calumet . . . and as a reward, he who presides at the dance presents him with a beautiful beaver robe, or something else.] **1791** J. LONG *Voyages* 136 The father covers them with a beaver robe. **1892** *Scribner's Mag.* Sep. 277/2 The rare and valuable 'silk' or 'beaver' robe owes its name to its dark color and its peculiar sheen or gloss. **1918** W. E. CONNELLEY *Hist. Kansas* I. 290 Of the qualities of [buffalo] hides, one of the rarest was the 'Beaver-robe,' a soft fur resembling the animal it was named for. — **(13)** [**1656** VAN DER DONCK in *N.Y. Hist. Soc. Coll.* 2 Ser. I. (1841) 225 Beaver tails excel all other flesh taken on land and in the water.] **1805–9** HENRY *Camp. Quebec* 23 They returned two fresh beaver tails, which when boiled, renewed ideas, imbibed with the May butter of our own country. **1904** in *Kansas Hist. Soc.* IX. 41 Their meals were not always regular, but always hearty, consisting of such delicious morsels as beaver-tail soup (the trapper's dish par excellence), roast wild turkey, . . . or buffalo meat. — **(14) 1632** *Mass. H.S. Coll.* 2 Ser. VIII. 231 Received for beaver trade at 12*d* per lb of Mr. Turner of Sagus . . . £1. 6. 6. **1687** *Doc. Hist. N.Y. State* (1849) I. 173 Finding such contest between the Government of Canada & this about the Beaver trade.

(15) *Ib.* 259 Major McGregory . . . went with 60 of the young men of Albany, and some of the Albany Indians a Beaver trading.

b. In the names of plants: (1) **beaver poison,** the water hemlock, *Cicuta maculata;* (2) **root,** the yellow pond lily, *Nuphar advenum;* (3) * **tail,** (see quot. 1940), cf. **3.** (13) above; (4) **tree,** a species of magnolia [cf. Du. *beverboom* in same sense]; (5) **wood,** a beaver tree or a hackberry, also attrib.

(1) 1857 GRAY *Botany* 157 Spotted cowbane. Musquash-root. Beaver-poison. . . . The root is a deadly poison. — **(2) 1832** WILLIAMSON *Maine* I. 126 Of the Lily tribe, we have several species . . . such as the yellow water-lily, or dog-lily, or beaver-root. — **(3) 1940** JAEGER *Desert Wild Flowers* 159 Beavertail Cactus. *Opuntia basilaris.* **1948** *Nat. Hist.* April 18 Beavertail in Bloom: a gay little plant that entices you with its massed blossoms of bright lavender-red but punishes the hand that touches it with hundreds of tiny prickers. — **(4) 1753** KALM *N. Amerika* II. 324 *Magnolia*, . . . Beaver-Tree. **1856** REID *Desert Home* 195 It was the *magnolia glauca*, . . . generally known among hunters and trappers as the 'beaver tree.' It is so named by them, because the beaver is fonder of its roots than of any other food; so fond of it, indeed, that it is often used as a bait to the traps by which these animals are caught. **1911** RICHTER *Honey Plants of Calif.* 990 *Magnolia glauca* L. Sweet Swamp, or White Bay Beaver Tree.

(5) 1810 MICHAUX *Arbres* I. 33 Small magnolia. . . . Swamp sassafras, . . . Sweet Bay, . . . ou Beaver wood, nom tombé en désuétude, autrefois dans le New Jersey. **1859** BARTLETT 27 Beaver-tree . . . is called also Beaver-wood, and sometimes Castor-wood, probably from the preference shown by the beavers for the bark as food, or for the wood as useful in their structures. **1948** *Sat. Ev. Post* 25 Sep. 154/3 One may remember the clean, bright blaze of a beaverwood fire, and green tents against the darkness, and the laughter and good companionship of the trail.

c. Designating structures, etc., made or caused by beavers, or places or regions frequented by them, as (1) **beaver canal,** (2) **country,** (3) **creek,** (4) **cutting,** (5) **dam,** (6) **den,** (7) **house,** (8) **lands,** (9) **lodge,** (10) **meadow,** (11) **path,** (12) **pond,** (13) **sign,** (14) **slide,** (15) **stream,** (16) **town,** (17) **works.**

(1) 1868 *Amer. Naturalist* May 157 Is there not some evidence of a progress in knowledge to be found in the beaver-canal and the beaver-slide? **1939** HAMILTON *American Mammals* 218 The long and often elaborate beaver canals are constructed for the purpose of furnishing a suitable and accessible highway over which the beaver may transport food to the pond and storage quarters. — **(2) 1761** NILES *Indian Wars* II. 541 [The fort] stands in the midst of the extensive territories of the Six Nations, and commands their beaver country entirely. **1907** *Ladies' Home Jrnl.* July 18/2 The three days more the Boy and Jabe remained in the beaver country. — **(3) 1850** DRAKE *Treatise* 221 The river no longer passes over its banks, but throwing its backwater up the estuaries of its tributary streams, and into the beaver-creeks, spreads over the rear of the bottoms. — **(4) 1792** CARTWRIGHT *Labrador Jrnl.* 373 Beaver-cuttings, A furrier's term for those trees or sticks which have been cut down by beavers. It is also used for the stumps which are left. **1889** *Harper's Mag.* Jan. 234/2 Not unless severed roots and other marks of beaver-cutting are found is this conclusive. **1923** *Lit. Digest* 24 Nov. 63/1 For days not a fresh track or beaver cutting had I found.

(5) 1638 in *Amer. Sp.* XV. 155/1 Upon the branches of a swamp runing North west up into the woods from the head of the said Vlyes Creeke out of a Bever dam. **1829** HEAD *Forest Scenes* 305 He told me of a beaver dam, as it is called, in the neighbourhood: a work erected by the animals for the purpose of rearing their young, and where they live in considerable numbers. **1944** *Life* 23 Oct. 73 The waters from snow-fed mountain springs are held back briefly by a beavers' dam. — **(6) 1804** LEWIS & CLARK *Journals* (1904) I. i. 104 [We] camped on the L.S. above a Beaver Den. — **(7) 1748** H. ELLIS *Hudson's Bay* 160 The Situation of these Beaver-Houses is always by the Side of a Lake or Pool. **1809** A. HENRY *Travels* 29 In passing one of them, we saw many beaver-houses and dams. **1946** *Outdoors* June 48/2, I guessed that the trouble had been that the trout were out in the deepest water in front of the beaver house. — **(8) 1873** BEADLE *Undevel. West* 764 In the lower portions of the valley the road traverses what are called 'Beaver Lands,' said to be the choicest of all the lands in Oregon. — **(9) 1805** ORDWAY in *Journals* 257 [We] saw abundance of beaver lodges. **1925** HEMING *Living Forest* 133 'Do you see that dome-shaped mound of earth an' barkless sticks showin' above the bushes over there?' and the old hunter pointed. 'That's a beaver lodge.'

(10) 1644 *New Haven Col. Rec.* I. 126 A proposition . . . thatt they may have the Bever meadowes granted to them. **1809** KENDALL *Travels* III. 176 The dams being in the end abandoned by the beaver, and broken through by the water, large tracts of meadow-land are formed, which, from their origin, are described as beaver-meadows. **1904** *Outing* Apr. 77/2 Here and there was a beaver meadow with a dam, perhaps, and a *cabane* or two. — **(11)** [**1655** DE VRIES in *N.Y. Hist. Soc. Coll.* 2 Ser. III. 128 In consequence of there being no sun, I had . . . taken the beaver's path. **1661** *Doc. Col. Hist. New-York* II. 460 To powder, 6 lbs., to salute the ship *Arent* in sailing past the fort going to the Beaver-path.] **1889** *Harper's Mag.* Jan. 238/2 The jaws of the trap are so placed that their length coincides with the direction of the beaver path. — **(12) 1640** *New Haven Col. Rec.* I. 27 The cow pasture shall begin on the hither side of the Beever ponds. **1765** CROGHAN *Journal* 18 Our course was through a thick woody country, crossing a great many swamps, morasses, and beaver ponds. **1948** *Pacific Discovery* Jan–Feb. 14/2 Canada geese nest on the Snake River bars and at beaver ponds. — **(13) 1822** J. FOWLER *Journal* 126 The ice begins to thaw and all [are] makeing for the Bever Sign. **1900**

DRANNAN *Plains & Mts.* 49 From Arkansas river . . . carefully examining every stream we came to for beaver signs. — **(14) 1868** [see **beaver canal**].

(15) 1837 IRVING *Bonneville* I. xxi. 210 [The exploration] would be attended with great profit, from the numerous beaver streams with which the lake must be fringed. **1916** THOBURN *Hist. Oklahoma* II. 27 They ascended the courses of the rivers and of the tributary beaver streams. — **(16) 1877** STANLEY *Rambles in Wonderland* 146 Desolation . . . will in a few years pervade the now densely-inhabited 'beaver-towns' amid these remote mountains and valleys. — **(17) 1889** *Harper's Mag.* Jan. 230/1 These burrows, of which there are several in every 'beaver-works,' as the trappers call the range of land and water occupied by a colony of beavers, open into the water.

d. In other combs. of obvious meaning, or sufficiently explained in the quots.: (1) **beaver eater,** (2) **field mouse,** (3) **hunt,** (4) **hunter,** (5) **hunting,** (6) **medicine,** (7) **shot,** (8) **trap,** (9) **trapper,** (10) **trapping.**

(1) 1771 PENNANT *Synopsis* 197 Wolverene . . . in America is called the Beaver-Eater, watching those animals as they come out of their houses, and . . . devours them. **1804–5** LEWIS & CLARK *Journals* (1904) VI. i. 107 Carkajous, wolverine or Beaver Eaters . . . or Links. — **(2) 1842** *Nat. Hist. N.Y., Zoology* I. 86–88 The Beaver Field-Mouse. *Arvicola hirsutus* . . . the popular name of Beaver Rat or Beaver Mouse, is derived from the abundance and fineness of its fur. — **(3) 1848** PARKMAN in *Knickerb.* XXXI. 194 He and three or four of his companions were out on a beaver hunt. — **(4) 1687** *Doc. Hist. N.Y. State* (1849) I. 258 The French King . . . has built a Fort . . . where all our Traders & Beaver Hunters must pass. **1847** RUXTON *Adv. Rocky Mts.* (1848) 234 The beaver-hunter has set his traps in every creek and stream.

(5) [1656 VAN DER DONCK in *N.Y. Hist. Soc. Coll.* 2 Ser. I. (1841) 209 For beaver hunting the Indians go in large parties, and remain out from one to two months.] **1701** in J. W. LYDEKKER *Faithful Mohawks* (1938) 191 Came and settled there twenty years agoe disturbed our beaver hunting against which nation wee have warred ever since. **1774** *Doc. Hist. N.Y. State* (1849) I. 742 The Five Nations . . . Beaver hunting country being bounded to the West by that Lake [=Lake Huron]. — **(6) 1877** J. S. CAMPION *On Frontier* 157 The 'beaver medicine,' for so the bait is called, requires extraordinary care in its preparation. — **(7) 1725** *N. Eng. Courant* 17–24 May 1/2 He . . . slightly wounded Capt. Lovewell and one of his Men with Beaver Shot. — **(8) 1709** LAWSON *Carolina* 48 The old King . . . went to look after his Bever-Traps, there being abundance of those amphibious Animals in this River. **1946** STANWELL-FLETCHER *Driftwood Valley* 112 Twigs and strips of dogwood bark are used by the Indians as a scent for beaver traps. — **(9) 1819** SCHOOLCRAFT *Journal* 63 It is by a skilful preparation of [sweet-scented herbs and spicy barks] that beaver-trappers are enabled to take such quantities of them [beavers]. **1856** J. B. JONES *Western Scenes* 70 An old beaver trapper and deer hunter took it into his head that [etc.].

(10) 1823 E. JAMES *Exped.* I. 162 He remained . . . a considerable time after his nation had departed down the river to their beaver trapping.

4. In colloq. phrases: (1) *To work like a beaver*, to work very hard or industriously; (2) *as mad as a beaver*, very angry; (3) *as busy, industrious, as a beaver*, quite busy; (4) *not to be up to beaver*, not sufficiently cunning to outwit a beaver; (5) *to be a gone beaver*, to be hopelessly lost, cf. **gone,** *a.*

(1) 1741 in BROOKS *Days of Spinning-Wheel* (1886) 31 To be sold . . . the very best negro woman in this town, who . . . will work like a beaver. **1948** *Chi. Tribune* 27 Mar. I. 5/2 She's really been working like a little beaver. — **(2) 1809** *Mass. Spy* 5 July (Th.), He is naturally as mad as a beaver, and will scold like a termagant. — **(3) 1817** PAULDING *Lett. from South* I. 68 This competitor, was heavy and cunning, but as industrious as a beaver. **1879** in *Cong. Rec.* 28 April (1881) 419/1 Another member of my society was as busy as a beaver circulating statements. — **(4) 1837** IRVING *Bonneville* II. i. 16 The trapper now gives up the contest of ingenuity, and shouldering his traps, marches off, admitting that he is not yet 'up to beaver.' **1948** *Nebr. Hist.* March 6 The phrase, *up to beaver*, [was] used of a person who was wise enough to catch even the most cautious beaver.

(5) 1848 RUXTON *Far West* ii. 86 From that moment he was 'gone beaver'; 'he felt queer,' he said. **1857** *Harper's Mag.* Oct. 645/2 We are 'gone beaver,' sure—the whole of us!

As the last term in **bank, court, ground, made, mountain, musk, prickly, ram, spring, stovepipe beaver.**

beaverette ˌbivəˈret, *n.* A material, as rabbit fur, resembling beaver fur; a hat made of this, in full **beaverette hat.** *Obs.* — **1718** *Md. Hist. Mag.* XVIII. 202 One new Beaveret, cost prime 1£ Ster[ling]. **1770** *Mass. Gazette* 15 Jan. 4/2 Castor & Beverett Hatts. **1820** *Boston D. Advertiser* 19 May 2/6 (*advt.*), Beaveretts.

beavering ˈbivərɪŋ, *n.* The hunting of beavers. *Rare.* — **1841** COOPER *Deerslayer* ii, I do a little beavering myself, as occasion offers.

beccasse beˈkɑs, *n.* [F. *bécasse*, woodcock, *bécassine*, snipe. See Read, 5.] (See quot.) — **1841** *S. Lit. Messenger* VII. 77/1 Innumerable species of the snipe are . . . met with, from the little Bobtail of the sandbar, up to the Beccasse of the plain.

bec-croche ˈbɛkˈkrɔʃ, *n. La.* [F. "crooked bill."] (See quot. 1931.) — **1827** G. A. MCCALL *Lett. from Frontiers* 178, I saw a large flock of the white ibis or, as it is called here, Becroche, settle down at the water's edge near by. **1931** READ *La. French* 7 The *bec-croche*, for which the technical name is 'white ibis' (*Guara alba* L.), inhabits the swampy regions of lower Louisiana.

*** bed,** *n.*

1. (See quot.)

1913 BARNES *Western Grazing Grounds* 368 There are an endless number of hitches used by western men, as the squaw, the stirrup, the bed and the basco; all are good and for their purposes quite as satisfactory in every way as the diamond.

2. In combs.: (1) * **bed-bug,** in the colloq. phrase, *as crazy as a bed-bug*, completely crazy; (2) **bunt,** [f. Du. *beddebont*, cf. Dijkstra *s.v. Bont*], a colored linen or cotton material used for bed covers, *obs.;* (3) **cap,** ?a night cap, *rare;* (4) **clothing,** bed-clothes; (5) **ground,** a place where cattle sleep at night, also transf.; (6) **log,** a log forming the foundation of a structure; (7) **pan,** [f. Du. *bedpanne*, cf. *WNT s.v. beddepan* 2], a sanitary vessel for use in bed by the sick; (8) * **piece,** (see quot. and cf. **bed,** *v.* **1.,** and **bedding timber**); (9) **quilting,** a social gathering for making quilts, *rare;* (10) **rock,** see as a main entry; (11) **roll,** bedding that may be rolled into a bundle convenient for carrying; (12) **sack,** ?a stout cover or case for bedding, a bed-tick [cf. Du. *beddezak* in this sense]; (13) **shoe,** a bedroom slipper, *rare;* (14) **spread,** [perhaps after Du. *beddesprei*, L. G. *bedsprêd*], a coverlet or counterpane; (15) **wagon,** *W.* a wagon providing sleeping accommodations, also attrib.; (16) **warmer,** a pad, electrically warmed, for use in bed.

(1) 1832 S. SMITH *Major Downing* 104 Nabby run about from house to house like a crazy bed-bug. **1904** *Buffalo Commercial* 2 Aug. 6 On the subject of the relations of organized capital and organized labor it [N.Y. *Sun*] is as crazy as a bed-bug. — **(2) 1761** *Newport* (R.I.) *Mercury* 3 Nov. 4/2 To be sold by Naphtael Hart, . . . Flanders Bed-tick, Bed Bunt, . . . superfine and middling Camblets. **1770** *Md. Hist. Mag.* III. 146 We will not hereafter . . . import . . . Cotton and Linen Stuff, Bed-Bunts, and Bed-Ticken of all sorts. **1787** *Md. Gazette* 1 June 3/3 Callicoes and Printed Linens; Bed-Ticking and Bed Bunts; . . . Bar-Iron and Steel; Iron Castings. — **(3) 1820** *Missouri Intell.* 18 April 4/1 A general Assortment of Merchandise, . . . Bed Caps, . . . Buttons, coat, pantaloon & Vest. — **(4) 1852** STOWE *Uncle Tom* xxxii, A tattered blanket . . . formed his only bed-clothing. **1876** HABBERTON *Jericho Road* 16 The Parson . . . awoke, and accused Slim of appropriating his bed-clothing.

(5) 1874 MCCOY *Cattle* 99 When all is still, and the herd well over its scare, they are returned to their bed-ground, or held where stopped until daylight. **1903** A. ADAMS *Log Cowboy* ii. 18 He could use the poorest judgement in selecting a bed ground for our blankets. **1942** DALE *Cow Country* 53 Toward sundown the herd was moved out away from the stream to a stretch of level land which would furnish a suitable 'bed ground.' — **(6) 1883** *Amer. Naturalist* Nov. 1197 Five beavers came out from holes in the bank. . . . The[ir] first effort was to get back to its place the bed log. — **(7) 1678** *New Castle Court Rec.* 361 Twoo Earthen bed Pans. **1756** *Lett. to Washington* I. 168 Half a dozen Bed-panns for the Hospital. **1947** *Collier's* 31 May 26/2 They make you wait an hour for a bedpan. — **(8) 1851** J. S. SPRINGER *Forest Life* 94 Before felling the Pine, small trees are cut for bed-pieces, the Pine-tree falling across them transversely. **1858** *Harper's Wkly.* 25 Sep. 618/2 Others fell smaller trees for 'bed-pieces,' to prevent the pine from sinking into the snow. — **(9) 1819** *Mass. Spy* 12 May (Th.) They were to assist at a bed-quilting he intended to have at his raising.

(11) 1916 KEPHART *Camping & Woodcraft* II. 136 A bed roll made with flaps and sides and ends is best for this purpose. **1947** *Steamboat* (Colo.) *Pilot* 13 Feb. 2/8 Some of them had trouble carrying their bedrolls and took a few spills in the snow. — **(12) 1661** *Essex Probate Rec.* I. 323 A bead sacke . . . a cheste. **1811** *Niles' Reg.* I. 45/2 In this valuable class of cotton goods are included . . . bed sacks. **1888** BILLINGS *Hardtack* 304 Each ambulance was required to carry . . . the following articles:—Three bed-sacks, . . . one leather bucket. — **(13) 1912** W. IRWIN *Red Button* 17 Professor Noll . . . slipped into ulster and bed-shoes and rushed across the street to rouse the house physician. — **(14)** *c***1845** *Big Bear Ark.* 30, I made a bed-spread of his skin, and the way it used to cover my bar mattress . . . would have delighted you. **1948** *Good Housekeeping* Jan. 26/3 Some manufacturers make washable draperies to match their bedspreads.

(15) **1869** in *Colo. Mag.* 1948 March 71 He, upon seeing my condition, very kindly asked me to rest in his bed wagon. **1909** *Sat. Ev. Post* 2 Jan. 8/2 I've got to shoe that lil' ol' bedwagon mule. **1948** *Southwest Review* Winter 29 When they picked him up he was 'flat as a wet leaf and headed for a week in the bed-wagon.' — (16) **1931** *K.C. Star* 2 Sep., We have one German machine gun, one electric bed warmer and a set of Balzac's works.

As the last term in **bunker, button, canyon, cot, cotton, double deck, deer, feather, hog, husk, Indian, kermis, lettuce, mortar, muck, pink, plant, rail, red, rice, road, seed, shuck, single, sleigh, spool, thatch, tobacco, twin bed.**

* **bed,** *v.*

1. *tr.* (See quots.)

1792 Belknap *Hist. N.H.* III. 103 When a mast tree is to be felled, . . . the workmen have a contrivance which they call *bedding* the tree. . . . They cut down a number of smaller trees. . . . and place them so that the falling tree may lodge on their branches. **1905** *Forestry Bureau Bul. 61* Bed a tree, to level up a path in which a tree is to fall, so that it may not be shattered.

2. To plow (ground, esp. for cotton) in beds or broad ridges preparatory to planting, also with *up*.

1830 W. Edwards *MS Diary* 13 April (N.C.H.C.), Bedding low grounds. **1858** *Texas Almanac 1859* 81 The ploughs . . . should be started to bed up the ground. **1947** Lumpkin *Southerner* 24 In March the first corn could go in, and what plows could be spared from corn could be used for bedding cotton land.

3. To place (sweet potatoes) in a specially prepared bed for sprouting.

1854 Davis *Farm Bk.* 19 Bedded it & planted it in spanish & yam Potatoes—then bedded about 35 or 40 bushels of Potatoes for slips. **1858** *Texas Almanac 1859* 82 If he has bedded his sweet potatoes early, . . . the ground should be sufficiently moist . . . he will have slips to set for early use.

4. *W.* (See quot. 1888.)

1888 Roosevelt in *Cent. Mag.* April 862/2 The first guards have to bed the cattle down, . . . it simply consists in hemming them into as small a space as possible, and then riding round them until they lie down and fall asleep. **1903** A. Adams *Log Cowboy* ii. 18 Flood and all the herd men turned out to bed down the cattle for our first night. **1945** Mathews *Talking* 168 They . . . kept stopping to look back toward the sunny side of the canyon directly under me where they had been bedded down.

b. *intr.* Also transf.

1903 A. Adams *Log of Cowboy* viii. 110 Not a hoof would bed down. **1912** Bower *Flying U* 7 Throw out your war-bag and make yourself to home, Mig-u-ell; some of the boys'll show you where to bed down. **1931** Dobie *Coronado* 128 Cattle in a brush country often bed down in open roads.

5. (See quots.)

1881 E. Ingersoll *Oyster Industry* 241 *Bedding*, transplanting oysters of any size to beds prepared for them, from which they are to be removed before the frosts of the ensuing winter. *Ib.*, Bedding-down [oysters].

* **bedding,** *a.* **1. bedding ground,** = **bed ground. 2. bedding roll,** = **bed roll. 3. bedding timbers,** (see quot.).

(1) **1884** Aldridge *Life on Ranch* 51 Our herd now amounted to some six hundred head, and it was a pretty sight of an evening to see them streaming in from various quarters towards the bedding ground. **1920** Hunter *Trail Drivers Texas* 215 It looked like a 'round-up' when turning them off of the bedding ground. — (2) **1926** Cooper *Oklahoma* 97 They were Pawnee Bill, Mort and Honest John, their bedding rolls fastened tightly behind saddles, vicious appearing rifle butts protruding from their scabbards. — (3) **1853** Strickland *Twenty-seven Yrs.* II. 280 A gang of men cut down the trees, taking care to throw small trees, called bedding timbers, across the path the tree will fall, for the purpose of keeping it from freezing to the ground or endangering the edge of the workmen's axes against stones or earth.

bedrock ˈbɛdˌrɑk, *n.*

1. *Mining.* The solid rock underlying detrital beds or strata. Also attrib.

1850 N. Kingsley *Diary* 154 We go down but we are in for seeing the bed rock all along the bottom. **1871** Raymond *Mines* 69 The running of a bed-rock tunnel to drain . . . these diggings. **1899** *Mo. So. Dakotan* I. 173 We decided to build a China pump to be run by water power and try to reach bed rock from the bottom of this ditch with it. **1947** *This Week Mag.* 4 Jan. 12/2 When he reached bedrock . . . his first day's operations with the new flume and riffles netted him one hundred ounces of nuggets and dust.

2. *fig.* The bottom, lowest extremity, the fundamental or essential part. Also attrib. *Colloq.*

1873 Miller *Amongst Modocs* vi. 71 But I have thought it all out, clean down to the bed-rock. **1897** *Land of Sunshine* Oct. 224 Los Alamitos town lots . . . can today be secured at bed-rock prices. **1948** *Family Circle* June 13/1 Okay, let's get down to bedrock on this problem.

b. A thing exceptionally fine. *Colloq.*

1902 Wister *Virginian* xxvii. 346 That play is bed-rock, ma'am! Have you got something like that?

c. Often in phrases.

1869 S. Bowles *Our New West* v. 99 We came down to 'bed-rock,' as the miners say, i.e. an extra flannel shirt and a pocket-comb. **1887** *Lippincott's Mag.* Jan. 195 Whether a man be hell-bent or heaven-bent, somewhar in his tracks thar will be found the prints of a woman's feet. That's it, isn't it? And your poet has brought the matter down to bed-rock. **1945** *Chi. D. News* 24 March 4/2 The number now available is down to bedrock and even grandpap had to go back to the pits to make up that number.

* **bee,** *n.*[1]

1. Short for **beeline.** *Rare.*

1850 H. C. Lewis *La. Swamp Doctor* 93 I'd take a 'bee' for home, an' come to this slew, an' then have to head it.

2. In combs.: (1) **bee acre,** an opening in the woods where there are flowers frequented by bees, *rare;* (2) **bait,** honey used to attract wild bees; (3) **box,** a box used by a bee hunter for catching bees; (4) **culture,** the keeping of bees; (5) **gum,** see as a main entry; (6) * **hive,** (*a*) a kind of fireworks, *obs.*, (*b*) **Beehive State,** Utah, a nickname alluding to the device on the state shield, cf. **Deseret;** (7) **hiving,** = **bee culture;** (8) **hunt,** a hunt for wild bees to get their honey; (9) **hunting,** searching for bee-trees and wild honey; (10) **line,** the direct course taken by a bee returning to its hive, hence a direct or straight line, also attrib. and fig.; (11) **paddle,** *local,* a light paddle of convenient length used by boys in fighting bumble-bees, yellow jackets, etc.; (12) **pasture,** a region where flowers frequented by bees abound; (13) **ranch,** an establishment with its houses, etc., where bee-culture is carried on, also **bee-ranching;** (14) **range,** = **bee pasture;** (15) **stand,** a hive of bees; (16) **suck,** a wet, marshy area frequented by bees, *obs.;* (17) **sweetening,** (see quots.); (18) **tree,** a hollow tree in which wild bees have a nest; (19) **treeing,** locating bee-trees by observing the flight of wild bees.

(1) **1882** *Cent. Mag.* June 226/2 Around the lofty redwood walls of these little bee-acres there is usually a fringe of chestnut-oak. — (2) **1900** Smithwick *Evolution of State* 292, I had occasion to speak of 'bee bait.' . . . When we went out in search of a 'bee tree' we took along a vessel containing honey; this we placed . . . to attract the attention of any bee. — (3) **1869** *Harper's Mag.* March 573/1 Once, on the approach of the [bee-]hunting season, he went out, as usual, armed with bee-box and honey-bottle, and soon had a worker caught. — (4) **1856** *Rep. Comm. Patents: Agric.* 121 My profits from bee culture seldom fail from the loss of colonies in winter. **1948** *Dly. Ardmoreite* (Ardmore, Okla.) 16 May, Styles will show motion pictures on bee culture following his lecture.

(6) (*a*) **1766** *R.I. Col. Rec.* VI. 494 In the evening, one hundred and eight sky-rockets, with a bee-hive, containing one hundred and six serpents, was [*sic*] played off before the court house. (*b*) **1934** Shankle *State Names* 149 The Bee Hive State commemorates the fact that the coat of arms of Utah depict 'a conical beehive, with a swarm of bees round it, emblematic of the industry of the people.' **1947** *Denver Post* 25 Feb 17/7 Most of the ninety skiers who will test their skill at the national slalom and downhill on Utah slopes this weekend had arrived in the Beehive state Tuesday. — (7) **1868** *Rep. Comm. Agric.* (1869) 275 To make bee-hiving successful, it is necessary to have strong swarms early in spring. — (8) **1837** Irving *Bonneville* I. ii. 37 In the autumn, when the harvest is over, these frontier settlers . . . prepare for a bee hunt. **1884** Roe *Nature's Story* 347 Nutting expeditions will soon be in order, and we have a bee-hunt on the programme. — (9) **1824** W. N. Blane *Excursion U.S.* 239 It is a favourite amusement, at a particular season of the year, to go bee-hunting; and great quantities of honey are then collected. **1940** *Life* 14 Oct. 59 Bee hunting is best in late summer because then the bees are cramming their hives.

(10) **1830** *Mass. Spy* 24 Nov. (Th.), The squirrel took a bee line, and reached the ground six feet ahead. **1853** Thomas *J. Randolph* 122 You'll have a bee line drawed upon you some of these days, in consequence of that tongue of yours. **1862** Lowell *Biglow P.* II. ii. 52 Concord Bridge, thet Davis . . . Found was the bee-line track to heaven an' fame. **1948** *Chi. D. News* 9 Feb. 14/7, I covered the trail last year by . . . ducking out the back way and making a beeline for Mexico. — (11) **1931** *K.C. Times* 4 July, The child who has never been spanked with a bee paddle has missed something worth while in this life. —

(12) **1882** *Cent. Mag.* June 226/2 The bee-pastures of the coast-ranges last longer and are far more varied than those of the great plain. **1948** *Dly. Ardmoreite* (Ardmore, Okla.) 1 Aug. 8/2 One of the most successful plans inaugurated thus far has been demonstrated in contests for gardens, pasture establishment, bee pastures, upland crops and bottomland crops. — (**13**) **1878** B. F. TAYLOR *Between Gates* 266 To call a place where bees are harbored and robbed, a ranch, is about as bad as to name the grazing range of lowing herds a cattle academy. . . . If bees are either cattle, sheep or horses, then there is such a thing as a bee ranch. **1884** *State Republican* (Colo. Springs, Colo.) 4 Oct. 1/2 California is the greatest bee-ranching or honey-making region in the world. **1906** *Out West* Apr. 353 A number of bee-ranches are maintained in the cañons east of Orange. **1946** MCWILLIAMS *S. Calif. Country* 114 Introduced about 1858, bee-ranching had become a type of bonanza farming by 1870. — (**14**) **1845** JUDD *Margaret* III. i. 402 In the garden is a large bee-range.

(**15**) **1882** *Harper's Mag.* Nov. 968/1 He ran right over a bee stand . . . and was stung in thirty places. — (**16**) **1823** in *Amer. Sp.* XV. 155/2 At a white oak on the north side of a hill near a small run and thirty poles West of a Bee Suck in a run. — (**17**) **1888–90** BARRERE-LELAND I. 102 Bee-sweetening (American), honey, more jargon than slang. **1893** LELAND *Memoirs* 294 There was no sugar at his supper-table, but he had three substitutes for it—'tree-sweetnin', bee-sweetnin', and sorghum'—that is, maple sugar, honey, and the molasses made from Chinese maize. — (**18**) **1782** CRÈVECOEUR *Letters* 37 If we find anywhere in the woods (no matter on whose land) what is called a bee-tree, we must mark it. **1838** GOSSE *Letters* 178 And the urchin, having carefully marked the spot, comes home with the triumphant intelligence that he has found a 'Bee-tree.' **1948** *Reader's Digest* Dec. 148/2 'Course we ain't found the bee tree yet,' Jerry said. — (**19**) **1913** *Outing* Apr. 120/1 Bee-treeing as we practiced it was too unsure and hit-or-miss in its general working out to attract the encyclopedic type of outdoor expert.

b. In the names of birds, insects, etc.: (1) * **bee bird,** the bee martin *q.v.* [quot. 1946 may refer to a hummingbird in allusion to its smallness]; (2) **catcher,** a robber fly; (3) * **eater,** = **bee martin;** (4) **fly,** any one of various flies making up the family Bombyliidae; (5) **martin,** the kingbird, *Tyrannus tyrannus,* also attrib.; (6) **miller,** the bee moth or its larva; (7) **moth,** a moth, *Galleria mellonella* (see quot. 1889).

(1) **1862** *Ill. Agric. Soc. Trans.* V. (1865) 734 The Bee bird will eat bees, and working bees even, when he cannot get drones. **1883** *Cent. Mag.* Oct. 816/2 The bee . . . is an irresistible treat to the bee-bird. **1946** RICHTER *Fields* 255, I seed a bee bird last summer. It's no bigger'n a snake doctor. — (**2**) **1838** GOSSE *Letters* 211, I have since observed this powerful and predaceous fly carrying insects heavier than itself, on several occasions, and so well are its instincts recognised, that it has obtained the common name of the 'Bee-catcher.' — (**3**) **1811** R. SUTCLIFF *Travels* (1815) xiv. 272 His bee-hives [in Penna.] having been considerably annoyed by a bird, called the bee-eater, he . . . shot one of them. — (**4**) **1852** T. HARRIS *Insects New Eng.* 484 The bee-flies . . . often hover . . . over the early flowers. **1881** *Amer. Naturalist* XV. 143 The 'parasitism' of these bee-flies upon locust-eggs.

(**5**) **1805** LEWIS in *Journals* (1904) II. 141 The bee martin or Kingbird is common to this country; tho' there are no bees . . . , nor have we met with a honey bee since we passed the entrance of the Osage River. **1851** *Polly Peablossom* 121 Had she a d——d tall thing like a bee-martin pole stuck up forard? **1946** HAUSMAN *Eastern Birds* 397 Eastern Kingbird . . . Bee Bird, Bee Martin, Field Martin, Tyrant Flycatcher. — (**6**) **1823** *Amer. Farmer* 2 May 45/2 To Destroy The Bee Miller. This troublesome insect is making great ravages among the bees in this vicinity. — (**7**) **1829** *Mass. Spy* 27 May (Th.), Instinct teaches the bee-moth to secrete herself, during the day, in the corners of the hive. **1889** *Cent., s.v. Galeria,* The bee-moth [is] a great pest in apiculture, the destructive larvae of which feed on wax.

c. In the names of plants: (1) **bee balm,** an aromatic plant of the genus *Monarda* or *Melissa,* cf. **monarda, Oswego tea;** (2) * **flower,** the common aster, *Aster novae-angliae,* of the eastern states; (3) **harvest,** the oxeye daisy; (4) **weed,** the heartleaf aster, *Aster cordifolius,* also the poison milkweed, *Asclepias galioides.*

(1) **1847** DARLINGTON *Weeds & Plants* 232 *Monarda didyma,* . . . Oswego Tea, Bee Balm. . . . New England West and South. July–August. A very showy plant, . . . very common in gardens. **1948** *Household* June 71/1 Others to divide later will be plantain lily, hardy phlox, bell-flower, bee-balm, coral bells, and coreopsis. — (**2**) **1840** DEWEY *Mass. Flowering Plants* 135 The most beautiful of our species [of asters], . . . called by the people, bee-flower, because it is in September so sought for by the honey-bee. — (**3**) *a***1847** HOWE *Ohio* 358 The white-weed or bee-harvest, as it is called, so profusely spread over our bottom and wood lands, was not then seen among us. — (**4**) **1907** LYONS *Plant Names* 59 A[ster] cordifolius. L. Blue Wood-aster, Bee-weed, Tongue. **1931** CLUTE *Plants* 95 The bee-weed (*Aster cordifolius*), and the bee balms (*Monarda didyma* and *Melissa officinalis*), derive their names from the fact that bees favor them. **1937** *Range Plant Handbook* W29 Horsetail milkweed, also known . . . locally as beeweed, a poisonous perennial herb, ranks among those plants most deadly to range livestock, especially sheep.

d. *As busy as a bee in a tar-barrel,* exceptionally busy. *Colloq.*

1859 L. WILMER *Press Gang* 199 He established a Democratic paper, and . . . made himself 'as busy as a bee in a tar-barrel.' **1889** COOKE *Steadfast* 197, I've been busier'n a bee in a tar-barrel ever sence the folks come home.

bee bi, *n.*[2] [See note.]

1. A meeting of neighbors and friends for performing some task in common for the assistance of one of their number, a social gathering for this or a similar purpose.

Usu., but prob. erroneously, regarded as the same word as the prec. George Casper Homans, *English Villagers . . .* (1942) 265 ff. traces the bee as a social institution back to the Yorkshire *bêan days,* and regards *bee* as derived from 13c. *bêan, bene.* Cf. *boon* sb.[2] and its variants in *EDD.* Du. *bee* (<*bede* <*bededienst*) is another possible source. See *Archief voor Nederlandsche Taalkunde* I. (1847) 246, *s.v. bede, beë.* For sense **2** below cf. *Br. Wtb. s.v. bede, beë.*

1769 *Boston Gazette* 16 Oct. 1/3 Last Thursday about Twenty young Ladies met at the House of Mr. Nehemian Liscome, here [Taunton, Mass.], on purpose for a Spinning Match: (or what is call'd in the Country a Bee). **1816** in KITTREDGE *Old Farmer* (1904) 169 Husking is now a business for us all. If you make what some call a *Bee,* it will be necessary to keep an eye on the boys, or you may have to husk over again the whole heap. **1890** E. B. CUSTER *Following Guidon* 257 If one of us was plunged into difficulties . . . the rest came in for a 'bee,' and made light work about the sewing-machine. **1945** SERVICE *Ploughman* 154 Best of all was the threshing. We joined in to form a bee.

2. A combined presentation of gifts to a minister by members of his congregation. *Obs.*

1823 I. HOLMES *Account* 358 For the clergy, in country places, once or twice a year, they have what they denominate a 'bee,' or 'hive.' . . . The members of his congregation . . . repair to the minister's dwelling, each person taking something, either an article of clothing or victuals. **1852** MRS. DUNCAN *America* 160 With such people it is much easier to give gifts to their pastor, than to insure him a regular money income. From this circumstance has arisen the plan of having what has got the name of 'A Bee,' once a year.

As the last term in **apple, building, candy, checker, chopping, drawing, hanging, house cleaning, husking, kissing, knitting, logging, lynching, paring, picking, political, raising, rattlesnake, sewing, shingle, shooting, shouting, shucking, spelling, spinning, squirrel, stone, tailor, whipping, wood bee.**

* **beech,** *n. attrib.* Designating areas, regions, etc., where beeches abound, as (1) **beech bottom,** (2) **flat,** (3) **ground,** (4) **knob,** (5) **land,** (6) **ridge,** (7) **swamp.** See **beechdrops, beech seal** as main entries.

(1) **1770** WASHINGTON *Diaries* I. 442 Beach Bottoms are excepted against, on acct. of the difficulty of clearing them. **1841** *Amer. Pioneer* I. 39 The tree is sixty-five feet high; it stands on a flat beech bottom, with many other trees of the same kind near it. — (**2**) **1847** *Ind. Hist. Soc. Pub.* III. 440 The knobs and beech flats of some poorer sections of the State. — (**3**) *a***1817** DWIGHT *Travels* IV. 60 The beech and maple grounds were too wet to be burned. — (**4**) **1779** W. FLEMING in *Travels Amer. Col.* 623 We fell on a Creek that emptied into Chaplains Fork of Salt River over bad beach knobs.

(**5**) **1789** MORSE *Amer. Geog.* 143 One species generally predominating in each soil, has originated the descriptive names of birch, beach, and chesnut lands. **1808** F. CUMING *Western Tour* 416 Some plats of beech land, that appears to be second rate, as it frequently produces spice-wood. — (**6**) **1789** MORSE *Amer. Geog.* 197 The interior parts are interspersed with beech ridges. **1805** PARKINSON *Tour* 113 There are likewise a great many swamps in the beech-ridge, which occasioned me very often to lie wet. — (**7**) [**1781** ZEISBERGER *Diary* I. (1885) 45 The bush (near Detroit) is either beech-swamp or ash, linden, elm, and other trees, such as grow in wet places.] **1805** ASBURY *Journal* III. 201 [In Ohio] we had a beach-swamp [*sic*], mud up to the hubs, stumps as high as the wagon-body, logs, trees. **1843** CARLTON *New Purchase* II. xliv. 95 The cream-coloured mud in beech swamps, the black mud and water in bayous.

As the last term in **blue, buck, European, red, water, white beech.**

beechdrops ˈbitʃˌdrɑps, *n.* A plant, *Epiphegus virginiana,* found as a parasite on the roots of beech trees. See also **Albany, Carolina, false beechdrops.**

1815 DRAKE *Cincinnati* ii. 86 Plants useful in medicine [include] . . . Beech-drops, the root. **1836** LINCOLN *Botany* App. 96 Beech-drops, cancer root. . . . The whole plant is yellowish-white. **1947** *Midland*

Naturalist July 58 Beech-drops [is] common (locally abundant) under Beech in terrace forest and bluff forest.

beecher ˈbitʃɚ, *n.* (See quot.) *Obs.* — **1868** *Putnam's Mag.* June 709/2 Its low-down class is by no means so degraded as . . . the 'beechers,' and other wild paupers of North Carolina.

Beecher's Bible. A Sharps' rifle. Now *hist.*

1856 *Western Citizen* (Paris, Ky.) 2 May 2/3 The great notoriety which the Rev. Beecher has given himself in furnishing Sharpe's rifle to Kansas emigrants, has given these weapons the name of Beecher's Bibles. **1879** *Cong. Rec.* 5 April 262/2 You marched an armed body of men into my town before ever a 'Beecher's bible' was sent to Kan. . . . Then, thank God, Beecher did send his 'bibles.' **1946** Adams *Album Amer. Hist.* III. 44 Soon the eastern supporters of the Emigrant Aid Company began shipping in Sharps rifles, dubbed 'Beecher's Bibles,' due to the fact that Henry Ward Beecher . . . helped to raise funds for their purchase.

Beecher's Bible or Sharps' rifle *c*1855

beech seal. In Vermont during the trouble over conflicting land grants *c*1775, a beech rod or a sound flogging with this. *Obs.* or *hist.*

1832 *Green Mt. Repository* (Burlington, Vt.) Aug. 171 The punishment most frequently inflicted was the application of the 'beech seal' to the naked back and banishment from the grants. **1856** *Cong. Globe* App. 30 April 552 The Vermonters . . . caught one of the [N.Y.] officers and tied him to a tree, and laid upon him what they called a 'beech-seal,' which grows in the woods in the shape of what boys call switches. **1893** J. Auld *Picturesque Burlington* 17 The 'land grabbers' . . . were often admonished and sometimes punished by whippings—'the beech-seal.' **1942** Peattie *Friendly Mts.* 66 Sheriffs were seized and beaten up—or, as Ethan more elegantly put it, 'severely chastised with twigs of the wilderness' and given the 'beech seal.'

beech seal, *v. Vermont. tr.* To whip soundly with a beech rod. Also **beech sealer.** *Obs.* — **1840** Thompson *Green Mt. Boys* I. v. 54 Why, he was the one that so handsomely beech-sealed one of the York authorities down Bennington way, last year. *Ib.* xiii. 145 Boys, you may as well be getting a brace of genteel beech-sealers; for I feel very confident of a decision in my favor.

* **beef,** *n.* and *a.* In combs.

1. Designating animals or groups of animals designed for beef, as (1) **beef animal,** (2) **cattle,** (3) **cow,** (4) **creature,** (5) **herd,** (6) **ox.**

(1) 1837 Colman *Mass. Agric. Rep.* 73 They agree to pay 32 cents for the offal of every beef animal there slaughtered. **1947** *Denver Post* 2 Feb. A. 8/3 Send a division of troops in to slaughter every beef animal in the country. — **(2) 1758** in *Amer. Antiq. Soc. Proc.* New Ser. XLI. 130 This day the Waggons set off from Pearises and about five Hundred Beef Cattle are to set off tomorrow. **1811** *Niles' Reg.* I. 101/2 We can . . . discontinue . . . some of our cotton and beef cattle farming. **1943** *Gunnison* (Colo.) *News-Champion* 23 Sep. 4/2 The men are now busy gathering beef cattle from high ranges. — **(3) 1783** Patten *Diary* 471, I got word of our Beaf Cow (who has been mising a fortnight) by Mr Benjn Stevens of Goffestown who came to tell me of her. **1902** McFaul *Ike Glidden* ix. 71 To inquire . . . if he cared to buy a beef cow that he was fatting. — **(4) 1782** *N.H. Comm. Safety Rec.* 299 Authorized Col. Badger to dispose of one beef creature towards his own Expenses. **1858** *Harper's Mag.* May 854/2 Here [central Mass.] in the country, when one of the neighbors kills a 'beef creature,' he is expected to send a piece to each one of the families near by.

(5) 1927 James *Cow Country* 204 Dude took in his beef herd. **1942** Dale *Cow Country* 118 The fat, mature animals ready for market [are] thrown into the 'beef herd.' — **(6) 1834** S. Smith *Major Downing* 124 Quick as ever you see a beef ox knocked down with an ax.

b. Denoting persons having to do with such cattle, as (1) **beef buyer,** (2) **contractor,** (3) **curer,** (4) **driver,** (5) **packer.**

(1) 1912 Raine *Brand Blotters* 244 I've had a talk with that beef buyer from Kansas City. — **(2) 1849** in *Calif. Hist. Soc. Quart.* XVIII. (1939) 119 Last night the Beef Contractor lost all his Cattle. . . . I much fear the Indians stole them. **1915** Young *Hard Knocks* 127 Leaving the agency on the twenty-fifth, my duty was to ride forty-five miles to the beef contractor's range. — **(3) 1851** Cist *Cincinnati* 228 There are as many as thirty-three pork and beef packers and ham and beef curers on a large scale. — **(4) 1834** in *N. Mex. Hist. Rev.* II. (1927) 297 The Ajt. Com., of Subsistence, will cause one of the Beef drivers to watch the Beeves at night.

(5) **1796** *Boston Directory* 271 Nutt, Isaac, beef packer. **1904** *N.Y. Tribune* 17 July 8 Now even many rural districts are as dependent on the beef packer, the vegetable canner . . . as the veriest cockney.

2. In miscellaneous combs.: (1) **beef biscuit,** *local,* a kind of biscuit made of beef and bread; (2) **chuck,** the part of the side of a dressed beef which includes the first three ribs, nearly all of the neck, and the parts around the shoulder blade; (3) **contract,** a contract to supply beef; (4) **dodger,** =**beef biscuit;** (5) **Beef-Head,** a nickname for a Texan, *obs.;* (6) **issue,** an issue of cattle made by the government to reservation Indians, also attrib.; (7) **packing,** the packing of beef for preservation and sale; (8) **raising,** the raising of cattle for beef; (9) **stall,** a stall where beef is sold; (10) **-steak-house,** an eating house supplying beefsteaks; (11) **steak plant,** (see quot.); (12) **store,** a store in which beef is sold; (13) **tax,** a tax payable in beef, *obs.;* (14) **ticket,** a ticket issued to an Indian authorizing him to draw beef from a government contractor, *obs.;* (15) **treaty,** a treaty by the terms of which the federal government obligated itself to provide Indians with beef, *obs.;* (16) **worm,** ?the larva of a meat fly.

(1) 1856 Goodrich *G. Go-Ahead* 191 A sort of meat-bread, like the beef-biscuit made in Texas. — **(2) 1886** Howells in *Century Mag.* April 861/1 'Refrigerator in the next room,' the mate lectured on. 'Best beef-chucks in the market.' — **(3)** *c***1867** Mark Twain *Sk., Great Beef Contract,* He had nothing to do with beef contracts for General Sherman **1942** Dale *Cow Country* 160 The first beef contracts had been made at a time when the Indians could eke out their beef ration very considerably by hunting buffalo. — **(4) 1853** in Bartlett (1859) 28 It is a small party . . . and goes unincumbered with superfluities . . . pinole, pemmican, and beef-dodgers for their principal support.

(5) 1872 *Harper's Mag.* Jan. 318/1 Texas, Beef-Heads; Vermont, Green Mountain Boys **1886** *Chi. W. News* 29 Apr. 4/3 Texas is the Lone-Star state, . . . its people are Beef-Heads for some unknown reason. — **(6) 1895** R. H. Davis in *Cong. Rec.* 15 Jan. 1005/2 A beef issue is not a pretty thing to watch. **1911** Quick *Yellowstone N.* xii. 299 The 'O.M.' Mr. Elkins . . . casually landed a juicy contract with Uncle Sam f'r supplyin' beef-issue cattle over on the Rosebud. **1942** Dale *Cow Country* 160 The beef issue was not increased in quantity and the Indians were often hungry and in consequence restive and ripe for trouble. — **(7) 1851** Cist *Cincinnati* 229 Their avowed business is pork and beef packing on commission, for the home and foreign markets. — **(8) 1892** *Vt. Agric. Rep.* XII. 144 When beef raising was remunerative, here the Shorthorn Cattle grew to perfection.— **(9) 1812** *Boston Selectmen* 29 July 69 The Clerk of the Market is directed to lease the vacant beef stalls in Ann street. **1813** *Ib.* 10 Nov. 103 Remonstrance was received . . . relative to beef stalls . . in Union Street.

(10) 1764 in E. Singleton *Social N.Y.* 366 Wm. Adams opens . . . upon the New Dock, a Beef Steak House. **1860** Mordecai *Virginia* iv. 58 The Globe Tavern . . . closed its career, a few years ago, as an 'oyster and beef-steak house, with other refreshments.' — **(11) 1907** Lyons *Plant Names* 342 P[edicularis] canadensis. . . . Wood Betony, Lousewort, High Heal-all, Beefsteak plant. — **(12) 1796** *Boston Directory* 295 Windship, Jonathan, beef store, Nathan Spear's wharf. — **(13) 1781** *Va. State P.* I. 530 Convinced of the impossibility of collecting the Beef Tax, in this County, I have agreed to accept of the People, the same quantity of Pork. **1782** *Mass. Acts & Resolves* 7 May (1890) 983 Where execution hath been levied . . . on any town Treasurer. . . . for either of the two first beef-taxes. — **(14) 1842** E. A. Hitchcock *Journal* (1930) 79 Thompson came to an understanding with the contractors agent, that they should be paid three cents per pound for all the beef tickets they could purchase.

(15) 1852 *Western American* (S.F.) 1 Mar. 2/1 The Indians have been spoiled by beef treaties, &c., &c., so much that they are at this time more troublesome than perhaps at any other period since the organization of the country. — **(16) 1872** Morrell *Flowers & Fruits* 381 A fly . . . about double the size of a house-fly, infests certain localities among the brush, and deposits a worm on the human flesh every opportunity; that is known as the 'beef worm,' and it immediately bores into the flesh.

As the last term in **Albany, baby, blue, buffalo, Congress, elk, prairie, wild beef.**

* **beef,** *v.*

1. *tr.* To put more muscle into, to drive harder. *Slang.*

1860 *Yale Lit. Mag.* XXVI. 83 (Th.), The first boat in is the winner of the race, so round they turn, and 'beef her' for the home stretch. **1948** *Time* 12 April 35/1 The Russians were worried by recent public reports that the U.S. was about to beef up its espionage service.

2. To kill (a beef animal) for food.

1869 *Harper's Mag.* Jan. 159/1 Then, as he expressed it, they [*sc.* the buffalo] were to be beefed and sent East or put into cattle-cars, and killed after they had arrived in the Eastern cities. **1919** CADY *Rhymes of Vt.* (1923) 43 Well; I shan't call it no disgrace To beef that critter on the place.

3. *intr.* To complain, usu. in a fussy, disagreeable manner. Also **beefing,** *n. Slang.*

1889 *The Road* (Denver) 28 Dec. 4/3 He will be coming down town again soon on crutches, 'beefing' about cancer of the stomach. **1944** *Chi. D. News* 19 Dec. 8/3, I hear a lot of beefing. **1948** *Time* 17 May 78/3, I guess they're entitled to beef if they want to.

beefery ˈbifərɪ, *n.* A packing plant for beef. *Rare.* — **1890** *Stock Grower* 12 Apr. 3/1 How does it come that no one else started a Pacific beefery?

bee gum.

1. A hollow gum tree or log which houses a swarm of bees or from which beehives are made. Also **bee gum tree.**

Bee gum or honey gum of an early type

1817 WEEMS *Letters* III. 215 To be run . . . round & round the circumference of a Bee-Gum like a Dog in chase of his tail, is enough to try the patience of ten Jobs. **1852** REGAN *Emigrant's Guide* 85 Thar I . . . tore up Sam. Kirkham's Grammar, and hid it in a bee gum. **1888** C. D. WARNER *On Horseback* 92 Big Tom was always on the alert to discover and mark a bee-gum. **1926** ROBERTS *Time of Man* 130 Erastus found a bee-gum tree and robbed the wild bees of their fruit.

2. A beehive, orig. one made of a section of a hollow gum tree.

[**1818** PALMER *Journal* 126 The environs of the house are often ornamented with a peach or apple orchard, a small garden, patch of tobacco, cotton or indigo, and bee-hives (made of hollow pieces of logs, or square boxes).] **1846** *Quincy* (Ill.) *Whig* 28 Feb. 2/5 Is it not a delightful picture for a high-souled democrat to contemplate, to see a Mormon, with a stolen pig under one arm, a stolen sheep under the other, and a bee-gum strapped on his back, pointed to, by the whigs, as a member of our party? **1913** M. W. MORLEY *Carolina Mts.* 180 Neither are there 'hives' in the mountains, only 'bee-gums,' which the bees fill with 'right smart of honey.' **1939** HARRIS *Purslane* 10 Dele rolled rags into smokers for the bee gums.

b. (See quot. 1904.) *Colloq.*

1880 HARRIS *U. Remus* (1884) 230 One er deze yer slick-lookin' niggers, wid a bee-gum hat an' a brass watch ez big ez de head uv a beer bar'l, come 'long an' bresh up agin me—so. **1904** *D.N.* II. 416 Bee-gum hat, n. Silk hat.

***beer,** *n.* In combs.: (1) **beer cellar,** [cf. G. *bierkeller*, Du. *-kelder*], a beer shop in a cellar or basement; (2) **fountain,** a beer pump, a counter at which beer is dispensed; (3) **garden,** [cf. G. *biergarten*], an open-air spot furnished with tables and chairs where beer is retailed; (4) **hall,** [G. *bierhalle*], a beer shop; (5) **jerker,** one who draws beer, *slang;* (6) **mill,** a beer shop; (7) **saloon,** a saloon at which beer is sold; (8) **sleigh,** a sleigh for hauling beer in barrels, cf. **beer wagon;** (9) **spruce,** a variety of spruce fir; (10) **store,** a store where beer is sold; (11) **wagon,** a wagon for hauling beer in barrels, see **lager beer wagon.**

(1) **1732** *S.C. Gazette* 28/2 At the Beer Cellar, over against Mr. Elliot's Bridge on the Bay. **1947** *Atlantic Mo.* Sep. 6 6/1 Whitman may seem, when we view the fifties in retrospect, to have dominated the writers that foregathered at Pfaff's beer-cellar under Broadway. — (2) **1849** *Rep. Comm. Patents* (1850) 243 Improvement in Portable Beer Fountains. **1873** BAILEY *Life in Danbury* 279 It is no unusual thing to see five boys file up to a Peruvian beer fountain. — (3) **1870** *Scribner's Mo.* I. 115/2 When the war broke out . . . photographs of Bismarck were speedily for sale in all the great German beer-gardens on the Bowery. **1948** *Sat. Ev. Post* 23 Oct. 18/1 Its forty-one square miles were largely farm lands, wilderness and parks; with numerous beer gardens, it was highly favored for picnics. — (4) **1882** *Black Hills Pioneer* (Deadwood, Dak. Terr.) 1 Jan. 18/6 (*advt.*), Go to the export beer hall . . . where you can get your beer for five cents a glass! **1928** FOY & HARLOW *Clowning Thro' Life* 60 The only hope for young aspirants like Finnegan and myself lay in what were later called 'honky tonks'—the 'beer halls' or 'wine rooms.'

(5) **1873** *Newton Kansan* 15 May 2/1 You will have the beer jerker at a disadvantage. **1936** ASBURY *French Quarter* 320 Plenty to eat and drink, served at little tables by waiter girls, popularly known as 'beer-jerkers,' who sometimes doubled as singers and dancers. — (6) **1879** MARK TWAIN *Letters* (1917) I. xix. 367 (R.), We went to a beer mill to meet some twenty Chicago journalists. — (7) **1861** NORTON *Army Lett.* 15 Night before last a row broke out in a beer saloon near the depot. **1891** *Cent. Mag.* April 932 Beer saloons, cheap grocery stores, . . . marked the increasing poverty . . . of the population. — (8) **1886** M. D. WOODWARD in *Checkered Yrs.* (1937) 120 Sullivan's beer sleigh went by today. — (9) **1787** SARGENT in *Mem. Academy* II. I. 158 Spruce Pine grows on cliffs near heads of waters, and is of the same qualities with the northern Beer Spruce; it is from one to three feet diameter.

(10) **1825** J. PICKERING *Inquiries Emigrant* (1831) 31 Almost all the roads leading to a town in America are full of houses on their sides, called 'taverns,' or 'liquor,' 'beer and cake,' or 'grocery,' stores. — (11) **1861** NEWELL *Orpheus C. Kerr* I. 290 The brigade is formed in the shape of a clam-shell, with the right resting on a beer wagon. **1947** *Chi. Tribune* 1 Nov. 19/6 Do You Remember 'Way Back When . . . the teams of heavy draft horses pulled the rumbling beer wagons.

As the last term in **birch, bock, buck, cane, corn, double, eager, maple, near, peach, persimmon, root, 'simmon beer.**

***beet,** *n.* In combs.: (1) **beet bird,** the American goldfinch, *Spinus tristis;* (2) **greens,** the leaves and stems of garden beets boiled for food; (3) **lifter, loader,** agricultural machines for pulling up and loading sugar beets.

(1) **1931** *Randolph Enterprise* (Elkins, W.Va.) 24 Sep. 5/4 We used to wonder why old folks of early days called the wild canary the 'beet bird' until this summer they eat our beet tops. — (2) **1938** DAMON

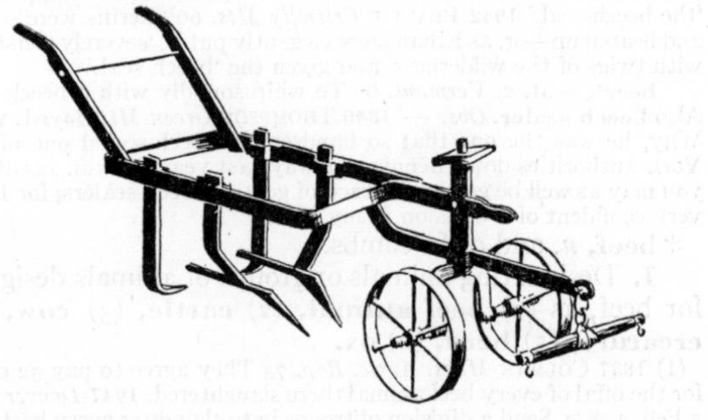

Early form of beet lifter

Grandma 277, I found in the buttery a platter of cold beet greens. — (3) [**1918** MOORHOUSE *Growing Beets in Utah & Idaho* 33 The 1-row lifter was used uniformly in these three districts.] **1945** *Hardin* (Mont). *Tribune-Herald* 15 Feb. 7/4 Machinery—1 2-row John Deere beet lifter. *Ib.* 8/2 For Sale: . . . ballbearing beet loader.

As the last term in **blood, mineral, sugar beet.**

***beetle,** *n.* In combs.: (1) **beetle bug,** (see quot.), *rare;* (2) ***head,** the black-breasted plover, *Squatarola squatarola;* (3) **headed plover,** =prec.; (4) **wood,** (see quot.).

In (2), (3) and (4) **beetle* alludes to a hammer.

(1) **1824** DODDRIDGE *Notes* 85 The beetle bug, or curculio, an insect unknown to the country, at its first settlement . . . perforates the green fruit, for the deposition of its egg. — (2) **1829** TICKNOR in *Life* I. 386 Mr. Webster has been out shooting all day, and brought home a fine quantity of beetle-heads, curlews, and other things. **1946** HAUSMAN *Eastern Birds* 258 The young, lighter in color, are known to the hunters as Beetleheads or Bottleheads. — (3) **1839** PEABODY *Mass. Birds* 361 The beetle-headed plovers . . . toward the last of September . . . collect in great flocks, preparatory to their migration. — (4) **1916** SETON *Woodcraft Man.* 279 Ironwood, Hard-hack, Leverwood, Beetle-wood, or Hop Hornbeam (*Ostyra Virginiana*). A small tree; 20 to 30, rarely 50, feet high; named for its hardness and its hop-

like fruit. Bark furrowed . . . One of the strongest, heaviest, and hardest of timbers.

As the last term in **apple, bacon, bean, Black Hills, buffalo, Colorado, cucumber, fire, four spot, grape, grapevine, larder, Mexican, pear blight, pine-tree, potato, saw-tooth grain, snapping, snout, squash, striped cucumber, sweet potato, three lined potato, tobacco, tumble beetle.**

***beggar,** *n.*

1. Used colloq. with ***lice, tick, weed,** as names for the prickly awns of various species of plants, esp. of the genus *Desmodium,* which cling to clothing. Also such a plant itself. Cf. **2.** below and see **daisy beggartick.**

1859 BARTLETT 27 A species of *Desmodium* whose pods break at the joints . . . is sometimes called Beggar-Lice. **1941** *Nature Mag.* March 136 Most of us have had experience with the three-cornered burs so unesthetically called beggar-lice. — **1836** LINCOLN *Botany* App. 76 *Bidens cernua,* . . . water beggar ticks. . . . Ponds and ditches. **1947** *Midland Naturalist* July 63 Common Beggar-ticks [were] abundant in south end and along west shore of Lake Redington in 1946. — **1889** VASEY *Agric. Grasses* 94 *Desmodium.* . . . There are about forty species native in the United States. . . . These are often called beggar-tick, beggar-lice, beggar weed, or tick-weed.

2. Used in the possessive in combs.: (1) **beggar's dance,** (see quot. 1788 and cf. **begging dance**), *obs.;* (2) **lice, tick,** (see **beggar lice, tick**).

(1) **1788** W. BIGGS *Captivity* 31 They took me with them to dance what is called the 'Beggar's Dance.' It is a practice for the Indians every spring, when they come in from their hunting ground, to go to the trading towns and dance for presents. **1901** *Everybody's Mag.* Feb. 149/1 Nor did he dream that his daughters would one day watch under the light of a Northern sun . . . the antics of crafty Pau-Puk-Keewis in the 'Beggar's Dance.' — (2) **1847** DARLINGTON *Weeds & Plants* 245 Beggar's Lice . . . [grows in] fence-rows and borders of thickets: Northern and Middle States. **1893** *Amer. Folk-Lore* VI. 140 *Desmodium Canadense,* beggar's lice. Concord, Mass. — **1869** FULLER *Flower Gatherers* 273 The lower flowers had gone to seed, and first attracted our attention by their prickly capsules, which clung to us like beggar's ticks. **1897** TERHUNE *Old Field* I. 8 'Beggars' ticks' and 'Spanish needles,' sticking to his clothes, told of a tramp through marsh and field.

3. beggars' presses, (see quot.). *Colloq.*

1870 EGGLESTON *Queer Stories* iv. 28 She had put it [a dress] away carelessly and it was all in 'beggars' presses.'

As the last term in **cider, office beggar.**

***begging,** *n.* **1. begging dance,** =**beggar's dance. 2. begging party,** (see quot. and cf. prec.). Both *obs.*

(1) **1820** *Western Rev.* III. 161 The begging dance is performed by young men and boys, who dress like warriors and go about through the village singing war songs and dancing. **1942** CASTETTER & BELL *Pima & Papago Agric.* 46 When the Papago became very hungry they would journey to the Gila and present for the Pima a 'Begging Dance.' — (2) **1831** *Illinois M. Mag.* 459 In the spring of '14 a calumet party of about twenty Grand Pawnees paid them [=Ponca Indians] a visit in their village. . . . These are generally called by whites *begging parties,* but . . . I would ascribe to them less degrading motives: for though custom decrees that presents be made on such occasions, all alike give and receive. The visitors were . . . feasted on fat dogs, and then they danced.

***begin,** *v.*

1. *intr.* With preceding negative and infinitive following: To make not the least approach (*to* be or do something), to have not the slightest pretension to.

1833 *Niles' Reg.* XLIV. 348/1 The one in Bleecker street . . . cost ten thousand dollars, and that does not begin to be as expensive as this. **1868** *Putnam's Mag.* June 672/2 These girls . . . didn't begin to be as strong as Marthy. **1907** HOWELLS *Through Eye of Needle* 43 Often there's a . . . dinner that you couldn't begin to get for the same price anywhere else.

2. *ellipt.* To compare at all (*with* something). *Colloq.*

1862 NORTON *Army Lett.* 47 There is no other man whom I would be so much pleased to have taken as . . . Floyd. Jeff Davis wouldn't begin. **1897** MARK TWAIN *Following Equator* xxxviii. 347 Indeed, our working-women cannot begin with her as a road-decoration.

beginning tree. A tree from which descriptions of land are reckoned. *Obs.* — **1769** *Md. Hist. Mag.* XII. 284 The former [plot] . . . calls for the beginning tree of Concord at the end of the second course. *Ib.* 285 The beginning tree of Concord should be fixed at C.

***begonia,** *n.* As the last term in **coral begonia, pond lily begonia.**

behaving party. (See quot.) *Obs.* — **1829** T. FLINT *George Mason* 148 They had been at what . . . [in New Orleans] are very significantly termed 'behaving parties.' In these, . . . the persons present are supposed to be on their good behaviour.

beheader bɪˈhɛdɚ, *n.* (See quot.) — **1765** R. ROGERS *Acc. N. America* 21 One of them [*sc.* fishermen], who is called the Beheader, opens the fish with a two-edged knife, and cuts off his head.

***behind,** *n.* A baseball catcher. Also as adv. *Obs.*

1856 *Porter's Spirit of Times* 4 Oct. 86/1 The Eagle Club now made a very judicious change by placing Mr. Gelston behind. **1857** *Spirit of Times* 3 Jan. 293/1 The first nine of the Gotham Club are:—Burns, behind; T. G. Van Cott, pitcher; [etc.]. [**1947** R. SMITH *Baseball* 27 There was a player [in town ball], called 'behind,' who stood behind each striker and received the underhand toss of the bowler.]

behindments bɪˈhaɪndmənts, *n. pl.* Payments in arrear. *Obs.* — **1758** *Essex Inst. Coll.* XXI. 159 Henry William, Mr. Frances Pool, . . . [to] be a Committe to make up with the treasurer consarning the be-hindments of the Parish taxes for years past. **1877** BARTLETT 37 *Behindments,* arrearages.

beignet ˈbɛɲe, *n.* [F., a fritter.] (See quots.) *Obs.* — **1835** IRVING *Tour Prairies* xxxiii. 306 We . . . supped heartily upon stewed buffalo meat, roasted venison, beignets, or fritters of flour fried in bear's lard. **1941** MCDERMOTT *Glossary* 22 Beigne, n.m. A fried cake, a kind of doughnut. . . . Sometimes written *beigné, beignet,* and, by Americans, *bang.*

belduque belˈduke, *n. S.W.* [Amer. Sp. in same sense.] (See quot. c1892.)

1838 TEXIAN *Mexico v. Texas* 218 Away went the quarteroon, armed with a large knife, or *beldúque,* to dig up the roots. **c1892** *D.N.* I. 188 Beldúque (or Spanish *verdugo*) a sheath knife, smaller than the *machete* . . . and larger than the *cuchillo.* The forms used in Texas and Mexico are *verduque, berduque, belduque.* **1894** *Scribner's Mag.* May 606/2 The smuggler . . . quickly drew his terrible 'belduque,' and slashing right and left he made his escape.

belefelde ˈbiləˌfeld, *n.* [f. *Bielefeld,* Westphalia, famed for its linens.] A kind of linen. *Obs.* — **1833** *Niles' Reg.* XLIV. 269/1 Linens to be admitted at an ad valorem duty . . . [include] Bretagnes: belefeldes: bodenwerders.

***Belgian,** *a.* Denoting a block of granite or other hard stone used for paving, or a pavement made of such blocks. Also absol.

1855 *N.Y. Herald* 26 Dec. 6/4 In addition, the small cobble stone is used to some extent, and the small square stone, or Belgian pavement —as it is here called—in many of the chief thoroughfares. **1864** A. DALY in *Life* (1917) 62 As full of rocks . . . as Broadway when Russ or Belgian is being laid. **1896** HASWELL *New York* 273 It was about this year [1832–3] that the first block, or Belgian, pavement was laid in a street of this city or country. **1904** *Brooklyn D. Eagle* 5 June, It ought also to be possible to leave well-defined routes of belgian blocks over which heavy loads may be drawn to every part of the city.

belittle bɪˈlɪtl, *v.*

1. *tr.* To make small, reduce in size.

1781–2 JEFFERSON *Notes on Va.* (1788) 69 So far the Count de Buffon has carried this new theory of the tendency of nature to belittle her productions on this side the Atlantic. **1816** PICKERING 48 To *Belittle* . . . is sometimes heard here in conversation; but in writing, it is, I believe, peculiar to that gentleman [=Jefferson]. **1910** *Bookman* May 290/2 The pictures seldom fail to put 'Mutt' in the same class with his name, proving his belittled compatriot, 'Jeff,' to be the cleverer man.

2. To disparage, speak of slightingly.

1797 *Independent Chron.* 30 March, [He] is . . . an honorable man, . . . let the writers . . . endeavour to belittle him as much as they please. **1844** *Republican Sentinel* (Richmond, Va.) 8 June 3/1 The Whigs may attempt to 'belittle' our candidates—that is a favorite game with them. **1948** *America* 24 April 44/2 The Communist smear technique . . . has been used to belittle certain supporters of the strike.

3. To cause to appear small.

1850 S. COOPER *Rural Hours* I. 127 The hills . . . [do not] belittle the sheet of water. **1883** H. GEORGE *Social Problems* (1884) 20 We have already corporations whose revenues and pay-rolls belittle those of the greatest States. **1947** *Chi. Sun* 2 June 11/1 Long Line Bra styled to belittle generous proportions.

belittler bɪˈlɪtlɚ, *n.* One who belittles. — **1901** *Out West* Dec. 474 Why do not these sly belittlers come out and launch a popular movement to change the name 'United States' to 'McKinleya?' **1947** *Time* 14 Apr. 59/3 Some belittlers, exaggerating Dressen's importance, think the Dodgers won't be the same without him.

belittling bɪˈlɪtlɪŋ, *a.* Reducing in size, disparaging discrediting. Also as a *n.*

1796 MORSE *Amer. Univ. Geog.* I. 230 The Abbe Raynal, in a former edition of his works, supposed this belittling tendency or influence had its effect on the race of whites transplanted from Europe. **1843** *Knickerb.* XXI. 411 A condition even more inevitably belittling . . . than any mechanical employment. **1948** *Time* 17 May 80/3 Eddie used to cry over the belittling he got.

* **bell,** *n.*

1. *pl.* The rattles of a rattlesnake. *Obs.*

1781 S. PETERS *Hist. Conn.* 261 Before they bite, they [*sc.* rattle-snakes] rattle their bells three or four times. **1846** in *Tall Tales of S.W.* (1930) 318 [The Irishman] would have given long odds in favor of a Stock Creek gouging, rather than face an 18 inch moccasin with 'bells on his tail,' as he termed rattles.

2. ?A Spanish real. *Obs.*

c1788 in *Ann. 11th Congress* 2363 Hire of Jesse twenty-five days, at six bells.

3. A small pouch of hairy skin that hangs from the neck of a moose (misapplied in quot. 1895).

1895 *Outing* Dec. 218/2 He [a caribou] had a fine bell—*i.e.*, long, hanging white hair under the throat. **1908** *Sat. Ev. Post* 10 Oct. 12/2 His 'bell'—as the long, shaggy appendage that hangs from the neck of a bull moose, a little below the throat, is called—was of unusual development, and the coarse hair adorning it peculiarly glossy. **1947** CAHALANE *Mammals No. Amer.* 44 Hanging about six inches below his throat is the bell or ropelike flap of skin covered with long hair.

4. In combs.: (1) **bellboy,** (*a*) a boy who rings a bell, (*b*) a boy or man who answers a bell, as in a hotel; (2) **button,** an ornamental button, usu. of copper or brass, shaped like a sleigh bell, formerly used by Indians as a bead, also **bell-buttoned;** (3) **captain,** one who has the supervision of a group of bellboys; (4) **cart,** a cart announced by the ringing of a bell, *rare;* (5) **cord,** a cord which being pulled rings a bell or sounds a signal, also attrib.; (6) **crown,** a bell-shaped crown on a hat, a hat having such a crown, in full **bell crown hat,** *obs.;* (7) **crowned,** of a hat, having a crown shaped like a bell, *obs.;* (8) **factory,** a factory where bells are made, *rare;* (9) **hop, hopper,** a hotel bellboy, *slang,* cf. **coon bell-hop;** (10) **puller,** a bellpull, *rare;* (11) **punch,** (see quot. 1895); (12) **strap,** a strap by which a bell is rung on a street car; (13) **time,** the time, announced by the ringing of a bell, for resuming or stopping work.

(1) (*a*) **1838** E. FLAGG *Far West* I. 22 The hated clang of the bell-boy was . . . heard resounding far and wide . . . throughout the cabins. **1851** MELVILLE *Moby Dick* xxxix, Eight bells there! d'ye hear, bell-boy! (*b*) **1861** BERKELY *Sportsman* 366 'What are you, then, young fellow?' 'I'm bell-boy.' **1944** *Reader's Digest* March 109 A bellboy of some 70 summers stood on the threshold. **1947** *Democrat* 15 May 7/5 Old Lady (to bell boy)—I tell you I won't live in this room. — (2) **1775** ADAIR *Indians* 7 The beaus . . . choose bell-buttons, to give a greater sound. **1839** *S. Lit. Messenger* V. 329/1, I had on, for the first time, a pair of new blue breeches . . . adorned with bell-buttons. *Ib.*, I just began to move in, glittering (that is the bell-buttons) like the morning star. **1871** O. E. WOOD *West Point Scrap Book* III., The bell-buttoned brevity of the cadet's coat-tail. **1917** R. C. RICHARDSON *West Point* 97 The present list includes . . . a single-breasted coat of blue gray cloth, with three rows of gilt bell buttons in front. — (3) **1944** *Reader's Digest* March 108 The coruscating bell captain commands an army of bell-boys. — (4) **1766** BUCKINGHAM *Newspaper Lit.* I. 35 The Bell Cart will go through Boston before the end of the next month, to collect Rags for the Paper-Mill at Milton.

(5) **1843** *Knickerb.* XXI. 332 The man . . . look'd for a bell-rope to summon the host [of the inn] for writing materials; but he found no bell-cord to pull. **1940** *Quiz* 152 What do the various bell-cord signals mean? — (6) **1843** STEPHENS *High Life N.Y.* 149 With that, I took off old bell-crown with one hand. **c1870** BAGBY *Old Va. Gentleman* 27 The typical Yankee, in bell-crown hat, swallow-tail coat. **1879** B. F. TAYLOR *Summer-Savory* vi. 51 The roomy bell-crowns, that flared like an old-time wooden churn bottom side up. — (7) **1821** DODDRIDGE *Backwoodsman & Dandy*, Betsy . . . said it was a thing called a Dandy, . . . with your bell crowned hat. **1865** MARK TWAIN in *Sk. Sixties* (1926) xiv. 203 Pictures . . . of men with swallow-tailed coats and bell-crowned hats. **1947** DOWNEY *Lusty Forefathers* 235 Back from the ever-advancing frontier to St. Louis flowed beaver pelts by the hundred thousand, bought at a thousand dollars a pack, and shipped so that dandies of the eastern cities . . . might have fine bell-crowned beaver hats to doff proudly to the ladies. — (8) **1841** *Niles' Reg.* 24 July 336/2 The Huntsville Democrat reports the destruction by fire, of the bell factory in Madison county, Ala. — (9) **1900** GEORGE ADE *More Fables* 5 When he got back to his Room the Bell-Hopper came around and asked him if he cared to Sit in a Quiet Game. **1919** CADY *Rhymes of Vt.* (1923) 99 The traveler saw no bellhops hop. **1947** *Chi. D. Times* 30 Jan. 3/3 Another bellhop helped an elderly lady from Newark.

(10) **1843** *Amer. Pioneer* II. 91 He rapped with his knuckles, for knockers and bell-pullers were unknown. — (11) **1877** BARTLETT 253 *Gong-Punch,* an instrument used by conductors [etc.] . . . ; a bell-punch. **1895** WAIT *Car-Builder's Dict.* 8 Bell-punch. An instrument for punching a hole on a recording slip of paper or tickets, so as to register the fares collected by a conductor. The instrument has a bell attached which is rung every time a fare is recorded by punching the paper or ticket. **1922** CADY *Rhymes* (1926) 52 Sim Jacobs bossed a Boston car, Until the bell-punch stung his star. — (12) **1888** WHITMAN *November Boughs* 406 [The conductor's] characteristic duty is to constantly pull or snatch the bell-strap, to stop or go on. — (13) **1845** *Lowell Offering* V. 98 Just look at the clock and you will find that it is but five minutes to 'bell time.'

b. In names of plants and animals: (1) **bellflower,** the bellefleur apple, or the tree bearing this, also attrib., cf. **yellow bellflower;** (2) **frog,** a frog, *Hyla cinerea,* having a voice of a bell-like sound, also known as **cow bellfrog;** (3) **pear,** a pear or variety of pear shaped somewhat like a bell, a tree bearing such a pear, *obs.;* (4) **squash,** a squash, as the acorn squash, shaped somewhat like a bell; (5) * **wort,** any one of various plants of the genus *Uvularia.*

(1) **1817** W. COXE *Fruit Trees* 120 *Bell-Flower,* a remarkably large, beautiful and excellent apple, both for the dessert and for cooking. **1857** WARDER *Pomology* 712 Bellflower Pippin . . . [is cultivated] in Ind. **1937** LUTES *Home Grown* 141 Bellflower, Gillyflower—ah, the old Black Gillyflower, an apple that may be, for all I know, entirely extinct. — (2) [**1688** in FORCE *Tracts* III. No. 12, 38 Another small sort of Frog, . . . makes a Noise like Pack-horse Bells all the Spring long.] **1791** BARTRAM *Travels* 277 The bell frog, so called because their voice is fancied to be exactly like the sound of a loud cow bell. **1942** A. A. & A. H. WRIGHT *Handbook of Frogs* 136 Bell Frog . . . Cow-bell Frog. . . . The voice is loud and at a distance sounds like a cow-bell. The individual call is quonk, quonk, [etc.]. — (3) **1786** WASHINGTON *Diaries* III. 24 In the No. Et. square of this garden . . . 7 Row, 3 Bell Pears East. **1899** VANDERBILT *Flatbush* 278 The 'bell pear,' named from its shape, was a rich juicy pear, and bore very abundantly. — (4) **1843** STEPHENS *High Life N.Y.* II. xxi. 52 A great smashing bunch of posies as big as a bell-squash choked in at the neck.

(5) **1784** CUTLER in *Mem. Academy* I. 434 *Uvularia,* . . . Bellwort, Sweet-smelling Solomon's Seal, Jacob's Ladder. **1947** *Midland Naturalist* July 37 Little Bellwort . . . [is] common in bottomland forest; rare in seepage swamps and terrace forest.

c. Designating a person or animal serving as a leader or guide, as (1) **bell cow,** (2) **leader,** (3) **mare,** (4) **mule.**

(1) **1860** in A. D. H. SMITH (ed.) *Narr. Sam. Hancock* (1927) 3 The Indians finding it impossible to get near this 'bell cow' endeavoured to kill her. **1896** G. ADE *Artie* xi. 103 If you can't travel with the bell-cows, why stick to the gang? **1904** T. WATSON *Bethany* 20, I hear the 'toll, tolang, toll, tolang,' of the bell-cows down in the meadow by the creek. — (2) **1932** *Randolph Enterprise* (Elkins, W.Va.) 28 Jan. 1/2 A delegation of about ten members from the Parsons Temple was present, headed by the old bell-leader from that section. — (3) **1844** GREGG *Commerce of Prairies* I. 183 The mules at night . . . are all turned loose without tether or hopple, with the . . . bell-mare, to prevent them from straying abroad. **1936** MCKENNA *Black Range* 21 My little Mexican mules sometimes stole away from the bell mare to call on me, knowing their visit meant salt, a chunk of bread, or a lump of sugar. — (4) **1876** MILLER *First Families* iii. 23 She had ridden the bell mule of the pack-train. **1922** *Outing* Dec. 124/3 Our guide, starting old Mose, the Bell-mule, with a few picturesque epithets and a cut of his whip, led our party around the corner.

d. (1) *To ring the bell,* to score a success, take the prize,—from hitting the bull's eye and so ringing a bell in target shooting, *colloq.;* (2) *to be there with bells on,* to be present in fine fettle (see first quot.), *colloq.*

(1) **1928** *Publishers' Weekly* 26 May 2094 This book liberally illustrated, with a great jacket, rings the bell. **1947** *Time* 14 Apr. 38/3 A local correspondent in Rangoon last week rang the bell with the following summary of the situation. — (2) **1946** *Newsweek* 15 April 51 'There with bells on' originated among Conestoga freighters proud of the bronze harness-bells that advertised safe arrival in a town. But, if the wagon bogged down, it brought the driver the humiliation of having to hand over his bells to the team that towed his wagon out. **1946** NEWTON *P. Bunyan* 63 We'll be there with bells on and lard in our hair.

As the last term in **barnyard, bird, car, chestnut, dinner, dumb, electric, engine, fog, gong, Liberty, plantation, recording, satin, shore, silver, sleigh, thimble, Virginia, war, winter bell.**

* **Bell,** *n.* [J. G. *Bell* (1812–89), a taxidermist who accompanied Audubon up the Missouri R. in 1843.] Used in the possessive in the names of American birds as **Bell's greenlet, sparrow, vireo,** (see quots.).

1844 AUDUBON *Birds of Amer.* VII. 333 Bell's Vireo or Greenlet, *Vireo Bellii,* . . . is usually found in the bottom lands along the shores of the Upper Missouri river. **1874** COUES *Birds N.W.* 101 Bell's

Vireo . . . [is] abundant in Kansas. **1917** *Birds of Amer.* III. 49 On the alkali plains of the Southwest, where only yuccas, sagebrush, and cacti grow, is the home-land of Bell's Sparrow and its variants.

***belle,** *n.* As the last term in **Baltimore belle, college belle.**

belled snake. A rattlesnake. *Rare.* — **1781** S. PETERS *Hist. Conn.* 260 The belled or rattle snakes are large.

bellefleur ˌbɛlˈflɜ, *n.* [F.] A variety of winter apple producing large sweet fruit of a yellow color. Cf. **bellflower.** — **1856** *Rep. Comm. Patents: Agric.* 292 Winter apples [include] . . . Ortley, or White Belle-fleur. **1864** *Ohio Agric. Rep.* XVIII. App. 49 The Belle-fleur apple grafted upon the Sweet Bough was less acid than usual.

***bellied,** *a.* As the last term in **blue-bellied, red-bellied, shad-bellied.**

***belling,** *n.* A charivari. *Colloq.*

1862 G. W. WILDER *MS Diary* 18 July, E. thought we would probably get a belling. **1878** *Dly. State Jrnl.* (Lincoln, Neb.) 1 Jan. 1/3 A number of uninvited guests gave the couple a belling. **1948** MENCKEN *Supp.* II. 208 A noisy serenade to a bridal couple is called both a *callathumpian* and a *belling.*

bellota bəˈlotə, *n.* [Sp., acorn.] An oak, or its acorn, found in the Southwest.

1910 THORNBER *Grazing Ranges Ariz.* 272 Of the various oaks, scrub oak, bellota, *Quercus arizonica* and *Q. turbanella* may be noted as examples of brouse species. **1925** BRYAN *Papago Country* 381 The acorns, under the name bellota, are eaten by the Indians. **1948** *Desert* Feb. 8/2 The Bellota extends east through southern New Mexico into Texas.

***bellows,** *n.*

1. (See quot.) *Colloq.*

1888–90 BARRERE-LELAND I. 104 Bellows, bellowses (American), the heaves in a horse. 'And when old Tom Jefferson sent for me to go to Washington, I was still here with fifteen children and as good a hoss as any man ever sid, only she was blind and had the bellusses.' —Uncle Steve's Stump Speech.

2. In combs.: (1) ***bellows fish,** (see quot. 1889); (2) **top,** a chaise with a collapsible top or the top itself, (see also quot. 1873); (3) **trousers,** (see quot.), *obs.*

(1) **1807** *Mass. H.S. Coll.* 2 Ser. III. 55 The puff fish, or swell fish, or bellows fish, is a cartilaginous fish. It is seven inches long; and . . . its proportions are those of a sculpion nearly. **1889** *Cent.* 516/3 *Bellows fish,* . . . a local name in Rhode Island of the angler, *Lophius piscatorius.* — (2) **1815** *Columbian Centinel* 28 June 3/3 (*advt.*), 4 new bellows top chaises. **1873** J. PARKER *Centenn. Address* (B.), When egg was beaten in it [flip], it was called bellows-top; partly, perhaps, from its superior quality and partly from the greater quantity of white froth that swelled to the top of it. **1890** *Harper's Mag.* Oct. 718/1 Willis . . . drove a square-topped gig, being that two-wheeled vehicle known as a Boston 'chaise,' but with a square instead of a bellows top. — (3) **1861** *Vanity Fair* 26 Jan. 45/1 The original pair [of trousers was] . . . plaited prominently over the hips and gathered in with a drawing-string round the ankles. They were called bellows trowsers in those days, from their form.

***belly,** *n.*

1. In miscellaneous combs.: (1) **belly bacon,** [cf. Du. *buikspek*] bacon from the belly of a hog, *rare;* (2) **bender,** (see quot. and cf. **tiddledies**); (3) **cutter,** (see quot.); (4) **flump,** (see quot.); (5) **guts,** (see quots.); (6) **shot,** (see quot.).

(1) *a*1775 J. BOUCHER *Glossary* 50 At dinner, let me that best buckskin dish, Broth . . . and belly bacon see. — (2) **1877** BARTLETT 38 Belly-Bender. Floating pieces of ice, or weak ice, which bend under one, as he passes from one cake to another. Boys take great pleasure in this precarious amusement. — (3) **1871** DE VERE 441 *Belly-guts* is the unaesthetic name given in Pennsylvania to molasses candy, and, in New England, by a corruption of belly-cutter, to low sleds on which boys slide downhill in winter, lying flat on their bellies. — (4) **1859** GRATTAN *Civilized Amer.* II. 314 The great fun of the boys is 'coasting' down hill on the frozen snow, lying flat on little square boxes called 'belly-flumps.'

(5) **1849** WM. DUANE *Let. to Bartlett* (MS.) 22 Jan., *Belly Guts,* a Pennsylvania word, now becoming obsolete, being supplanted by the more elegant, though perhaps not quite correct, name of molasses candy. **1870** *Nation* (N.Y.) July 56/2 The molasses candy which had been 'worked' till it became white went by another name. . . . 'Belly-guts' was the name it bore. **1871** [see **belly cutter**]. — (6) **1688** in FORCE *Tracts* III. No. 12, 26 After that sweet Food they are not so prompt to brouze on the Trees, and the coarse Grass which the Country affords; so that thus their Guts shrink up, and they become Belly-shot as they call it.

2. Used in children's language in numerous expressions, (nouns, verbs, adverbs), referring to diving awkwardly so that the belly strikes flat against the water, and with reference to coasting on a sled on one's belly or to casting oneself on the sled belly-down, after a short run to obtain speed, as **belly bump, bumper, bumping, bung, flop, flounder, flumps, gut, whopper.**

1845 JUDD *Margaret* 173, 'I shall take it knee-bump, next time.' . . . 'Try bellygut, you'll like that better,' said another. **1855** WILLIS *Convalescent* 75 The only attitude he patronizes on his sled('belly-flumps') is slightly apoplectic. **1860** *Marysville* (Calif.) *Appeal* 30 Mar. 4/1 None of your belly-flounders! This lying down on a sled [is] not the thing. **1868** *Harper's Mag.* Feb. 355/2 Running at full speed [with the sled], he tumbled 'belly-bung' upon it. **1868** G. C. CHANNING *Recoll. Newport* 33 The boy who happened to make the 'belly-bumper' movement, as it was termed, was ejected from the circle. **1888** *Chi. Inter-Ocean* (F.), Barney had his sled out yesterday, belly-bumping on a little patch of ice and snow. **1904** WALLER *Wood-carver* 63 There is a fine coast for good two thirds of the way down the Pent Road; . . . she tells me she always slides 'bellybump.' **1943** M. FLAVIN *Journey in Dark* 18 The only way to coast was belly-whopper, and you had the whole sled to yourself. **1947** *Denver Post* 5 March 1/2 Taking no chance of missing the fun of sliding on the snow, Tommy . . . took what he feared might be one of his last 'belly-flops.'

The number of these expressions is very large. See Bartlett '77, p. 39, *Dial. Notes* I. (index *s.vv. belly-bump, belly-bumper*), and *Linguistic Atlas,* map 576.

As the last term in **big, blue, checker, copper, red, salmon, saw, shad, speckled, squash, toad, yellow belly.**

bellyache ˈbɛlɪˌek, *v. intr.* (See quot. 1889.) Also **bellyacher, bellyaching.**

1889 FARMER 50 Bellyache, to.—A coined word, meaning 'to grumble without good cause.' Employés *bellyache* at being overworked, or when they fancy themselves underfed. A vulgarism. **1929** DOBIE *Vaquero* 104 If in the midst of such gruelling and desperate work there was plenty of 'belly-aching,' there was plenty of cheer. **1930** HENRY *Conquer. Plains* 221 These voluble doubters were commonly called old croakers, backbiters, 'bellyachers.' **1947** BROWN *Outdoors Unlimited* 237 Halfway home, with the tide racing against us, Jack began bellyachin' about Harry-the-Horse's heft, his tackle store and why didn't he do his share of rowin' instead of sitting a-stern there like a stuffed hop toad.

bellyache root. Any one of various plants (see quots.) thought to be useful in cases of bellyache. *Colloq.*

1762 CLAYTON *Flora Virginica* 43 Angelica lucida canadensis fortasse, vulgo Belly-ach-root. **1789** *Amer. Philos. Soc.* III. p. xviii, Cholick is removed, by the oil of the Spicewood-berries: the flatulent and hysteric kind, eminently so by Angelica *lucida* . . . , called therefore *belly-ach root.* **1931** CLUTE *Plants* 124 Others are mildly tonic or possess some faint medicinal value. . . . Familiar examples are . . . belly-ache root (*Solidago bicolor*).

Belshnickle ˈbɛlʃˌnɪkl, *n.* Chiefly *Pa.* [G. (Palatinate and Saar) dial. *Pelznickel,* f. *pelz,* fur, *Nickel,* Nicholas.] Santa Claus, Christmas.

1823 JAMES *Long's Exped.* I. 188 This dance is called *La Gineolet,* and may have had its origin in the same cause that produced our Belshnickles, who make their appearance on Christmas-eve. **1830** WATSON *Philadelphia* 242 The 'Belsh Nichel' and St. Nicholas has been a time of Christmas amusement from time immemorial among us. **1869** *Atlantic Mo.* Oct. 485/2 Pelznickel is the bearded Nicholas, who punishes bad ones; whereas Krisskringle is the Christkindlein, who rewards good children. **1936** MENCKEN *Amer. Lang.* 159 Santa Claus, in such areas, is usually *Belsnickel,* as indeed he was among the Germans of Baltimore when I was a boy [*c*1890].

attrib. **1940** WRIGHT *Pioneer Life* 90 Among the Germans the Beltznickel Man, a member of the community disguised in a panther skin with trailing tail, black bearskin cap, and mask, romped with the children and filled their stockings with apples and nuts.

***belt,** *n.*

1. An Indian belt made of wampum, usu. *belt of wampum,* a girdle from one to five inches broad, used among Indians for ornamental and ceremonial purposes.

1663 *Md. Archives* 472 A vast Expence of 70 Belts of Peake. **1778** CARVER *Travels* 362 These belts are made of shells found on the coasts of New England and Virginia, which are sawed out into beads of an oblong form, about a quarter of an inch long, and round like other beads. Being strung on leather strings, and several of them sewed neatly together with fine sinewy threads, they then compose what is termed a Belt of Wampum. **1891** S. M. WELCH *Recoll. 1830–40* 121 A young Indian, a brave or chief, would improve upon this dress by wearing belts of wampum.

b. (See quots.) Now *hist.*

1797 *State P.* (1819) II. 403, I have it from indubitable authority, that a large belt [by which he meant a speech] from the Spaniards is now travelling through the different nations. **1948** *Indiana Mag. Hist.* Sep. 245 When delivered at treaties, each so-called belt, some more than six feet in length, served as an official 'statement' or 'word.'

2. Short for **time belt.**

1942 *Nat. Geog. Mag.* May 590 The closest station to the west is on Yukon time; we use Pacific time, though we're in the Yukon belt.

3. In combs.: (1) **belt line,** see as a main entry; (2) **plate,** the plate or buckle of a waist-belt; (3) **railroad,** =**belt line 1;** (4) **saw,** =**band saw.**

(2) **1866** F. KIRKLAND *Bk. Anecdotes* 212 His cap box had slipped from his belt plate. **1884** *Cent. Mag.* Oct. 809/1 Some men were . . . constantly polishing buttons and belt-plates. — (3) **1880** *Bradstreet's* 14 Jan. 2/1 The Standard Oil Company . . . has just purchased ground on our Belt Railroad. **1948** *Chi. D. News* 28 April 20/1 Installation of four diesel locomotives by the Indiana Harbor Belt railroad . . . should make Chicago's southern skies a bit clearer. — (4) **1819** *Niles' Reg.* XVI. 93/2 The editor . . . was invited a few days since, to see the newly invented Belt or Strap saw, in operation. **1874** KNIGHT 273/2.

b. Designating tools or weapons carried at the belt, as (1) **belt ax,** (2) **knife,** (3) **pistol.**

(1) **1859** G. A. JACKSON *Diary* 521, [I] marked the big fir tree with belt axe and knife. *Ib.*, I had broken his back with belt axe. **1947** *Boys' Life* Oct. 22/2, I have seen a lot of belt axes just like it. — (2) **1840** C. F. HOFFMAN *Greyslaer* I. 234 The hand of the Mohawk clutched the belt-knife . . . half drawn from its sheath. **1859** *Harper's Mag.* Aug. 425/1 The Judge . . . whipped out his belt-knife and made at the aggressor. — (3) **1775** ADAIR *Indians* 326 In the middle of the river, I was forced to throw away one of my belt-pistols. **1848** F. BRYANT *California* 466 A revolving belt pistol may be found useful.

c. *To hold the belt,* (see quot. 1889). Also fig.

1889 *Cent.* 519/2 *To hold the belt,* to hold the championship in pugilism or some other athletic exercise. **1906** MARK TWAIN *Autobiog.* (1924) ii. (R.), He easily held the belt for honesty in that country.

As the last term in **banana, black, Bible, carrying, chain, corn, cotton, fever, forest, fruit, gold, grain, grape, Great, Indian, iron, limestone, lynching, money, oil, orange, peace, peag, prairie, redwood, road, shelter, speech, sugar, thermal, thimble, timber, time, tobacco, wampum, war, wheat belt.**

* **belt,** *v.* **1.** *tr.* To girdle a tree in order to kill it. **2.** To swallow, put under one's belt. *Slang. Obs.*

(1) **1812** MARSHALL *Kentucky* These improvements . . . consisted principally, in cutting the under brush, and belting the larger trees. **1880** BURNETT *Old Pioneer* 14 The large trees were belted around with the axe. — (2) **a1846** *Quarter Race Ky.* 82 He can belt six shillins worth of corn-juice at still-house rates and travel.

belted kingfisher. An American kingfisher, *Megaceryle alcyon,* having a band or stripe across the chest.

1811 WILSON *Ornithology* III. 59 [The] Belted Kingsfisher, *Alcedo Alcyon*, . . . is a general inhabitant of the banks and shores of all our fresh water rivers from Hudson's bay to Mexico. **1885** M. THOMPSON *By Ways & Bird Notes* 82 A belted kingfisher, that most beautiful of all our birds of the streams, suddenly appeared. **1929** W. HEYLIGER *Builder of Dam* 1 A belted kingfisher, crying shrilly as it flew, suddenly poised in flight and dropped with a thud and a splash into the waters below.

* **belter,** *n.* As the last term in **corn, rain belter.**

belting 'bɛltɪŋ, *n.* The girdling of a tree. — **1829** *Va. Lit. Museum* 16 Dec. 418 *Belting* in Virginia—the same as *girdling.* **1855** *S. Lit. Messenger* XXI. 662/2 Killing the larger forest trees without removal, but the process of belting, or girdling.

belt line.

1. A railroad that goes wholly or partially around a city. Also attrib. and transf.

1894 *Cent. Mag.* Dec. 290 De Belt Line stables ain't no Hoffman House, but dey're Vanderbilts 'longside o' Kansas. **1903** *N.Y. Times* 24 Oct. 2 George B. McClellan and Edward M. Grout were scheduled for a belt line tour of speechmaking last night. **1935** HORWILL 27 The term *belt line* is applied in Am. to a tram-line which takes a circular route. It is also used fig.

2. A highway.

1922 *Dly. Ardmoreite* (Ardmore, Okla.) 6 Jan. 6/5 A belt line of gravel highway is now under construction around the city of Ardmore. **1948** *Chi. Tribune* 15 Apr. III. 1/3 The Illinois highway department decided to by-pass the community with a belt line for route 150 coming from the east.

ben bɛn, *v.* [Origin and precise meaning obscure.] *tr.* App. to repair (a mill) in some manner. *Obs.* — **1669** *Huntington* (L.I.) *Rec.* I. 31 The defendant . . . did git a work-man in the spring to ben the mill. *Ib.*, He did . . . send to Henery Lininton . . . to come to ben the mill. *Ib.*, The defendant is bound to git Goodman Webb to ben the mill if posable.

* **bench,** *n.*

1. A level, somewhat narrow plain bordering upon an upland region or mountains.

1803 LEWIS in *Journals of L. & Ordway* 34 What is called the third bottom is more properly the high benches of the large range of hills. **1917** KEPHART *Camping* I. 217 In cold weather seek . . . a 'bench' (natural terrace backed by a cliff) on the leeward side of a hill. **1946** *Mazama* Dec. 13/1 On July 19 we established a high camp on a bench at timberline east of and below Snowpatch.

2. A level tract between a river or lake and neighboring mountains.

1811 *Ann. 12th Cong.* 1 Sess. 2116 Towards the left flank this bench of high land widened considerably. **1858** GOVE *Letters* 340 These are called benches; they . . . are plainly visible, exactly level, and are the ancient shores of the Great Salt Lake. **1912** WHEELER *Selkirk Mts.* 125 Any knowing reliable pony will carry you over the 'benches' to the high margin of Columbia Lake. **1944** *Nat. Geog. Mag.* June 658 (Pl. II.) In the foreground, where the 'bench' breaks away to the Boise River Valley floor, are the Howard Platt Gardens, outside the Union Pacific station.

3. In combs.: (1) **bench bottom,** ground forming a bench by a river; (2) **judging,** judging at a bench show *q.v.;* (3) **land,** land that forms a bench; (4) **legged,** (see quot. 1902), *colloq.;* (5) **show,** an exhibition of dogs or other animals; (6) **wagon,** a wagon having bench-like seats for the occupants; (7) **warmer,** one who sits idly on a bench, as a player not used in a game (see also quot. 1925), *slang.*

(1) **1867** *Iowa Agric. Soc. Rep.* (1868) 160 On the second or bench-bottoms on the Missouri . . . are our best wheat lands. — (2) **1897** *Outing* May 125/1 Feet and legs are therefore the prime points in bench-judging and score the highest. — (3) **1857** CHANDLESS *Visit Salt Lake* II. x. 326 The coast is walled by steep mountain ridges; . . . sometimes with bench-land fifty or hundred feet above the water-level intervening. **1931** *Randolph Enterprise* (Elkins, W.Va.) 23 April 3/4 The other half is second bench land and is a very desirable property. — (4) **1866** C. H. SMITH *Bill Arp* 159 Dodds says before he'd pull a trigger for Thad Stevens he'd have his soul transmigrated to a bench-leg'd fice, and bark at his daddy's mules 2,000 years. **1902** *D.N.* II. 226 Bench-legged, adj. With legs set wide apart, as in a *'bench-legged* fiste.'

(5) **1874** *Forest & Stream* 29 Oct. 182/1 The first regular bench show of dogs we have ever held in this country in connection with agricultural fairs took place at Mineola, Long Island, on the 7th of October. **1948** *Dly. Ardmoreite* (Ardmore, Okla.) 16 May 12/3 Southern Oklahoma Fox and Wolf Hunters association will open a two-day meet and bench show on the Robert Mitchell farm. — (6) **1885** HOWELLS *Silas Lapham* (1891) I. 88 Lapham arrived . . . in his four-seated bench-wagon. — (7) **1912** *Sat. Ev. Post* 3 Aug. 48/4 A certain rich man . . . offered a manager ten thousand dollars . . . if the manager would carry his son along with the regular team as a combination of mascot and benchwarmer. **1925** *D.N.* V. 438 bench-warmer, *n.* A weary hobo whose home is a park bench. **1932** *K.C. Times* 17 Feb. 18 And that is a good thought for a bench warmer at that.

As the last term in **anxious, deacon, log, mourners', shoe, Supreme, wash bench.**

* **bench,** *v.* **a.** *tr.* To raise to the bench, appoint as a judge. *Rare.* **b.** In baseball, football, etc., to take a player out of a game or prevent his taking part in it. *Slang.*

(a) **1846** M'KENNEY *Memoirs* I. ii. 54 What are you going to do with Mr. M'Lean? . . . 'D—n him, we'll bench him.' — (b) **1917** MATHEWSON *Sec. Base Sloan* xvi. 224 Some of you stuffed sausages will be benched mighty quick if you don't wake up. **1947** *Harper's Mag.* June 560/2, I should have benched him long ago, he got only nineteen hits all season.

* **benching,** *n.* A continuous bench-like seat along a wall or the side of a room. — **1866** HOWELLS *Venet. Life* xx. 335 The benching that passes round the shop. **1886** *Cent. Mag.* April 860/1 A large, square room, with benching against the wall for them to sit on.

bench warrant, *v. tr.* To issue a bench warrant for (a person). *Rare.* — **1862** *Trial C.M. Jefferds* 145 The District Attorney has not bench-warranted me yet.

* **bend,** *n.*[1] **1.** *Above* (one's) *bend,* beyond one's abilities. **2.** =**bender 1.** *Slang.*

(1) **1835** CROCKETT *Tour Down East* 44, I shall not attempt to describe the curiosities here [at Peale's Museum]; it is above my bend. **1888–90** BARRERE-LELAND I. 6 It would be *above my bend* to attempt telling you all we saw among the Redskins.—J. F. Cooper: The Oak Openings. — (2) **1887** F. FRANCIS, JR. *Saddle & Moccasin* 84 They do say as he was 'customed to go on a scoop'—on a bend, occasionally, as it were.

As the last term in **big bend, cypress bend.**

bend bɛnd, *n.*[2] [f. **Grecian bend.** See *The Nation,* 13 Feb. 1908, p. 146.] =**caisson disease.** Usu. *pl.*

1894 *Westm. Gaz.* 16 Oct. 3/2 The pressure . . . is quite enough to give the men a dose of the 'bend' [*sic*] as it is called. **1908** *Nation*

30 Jan. 101/1 All your New York papers call this ailment 'the bends.' The more usual term is 'caisson disease.' **1948** *Chi. Tribune* 15 Feb. (*Comics*) 6 I'm shootin' for the surface without decompression! I'll git th' bends!

Ben Davis. A red and yellow American winter apple valued more for its keeping than for its eating qualities. — **1863** *Horticulturist* Aug. 262/1 Of Apples, we may mention . . . Gravenstein, Ben Davis, Rambo. **1945** *Hardin* (Mont.) *Tribune-Herald* 15 Feb. 4/3 Uncle Ben Davis—$1–89 bu.

Ben Day. 1. In photoengraving, a pattern effect produced on a zinc etching by a process developed by Benjamin Day (1838–1916), a N.Y. printer. **2. Ben Day process,** (see quot. 1949).

(1) **1927** Paul D. Hugon *Morrow's Word Finder s.v. Cut.* A Ben Day, shaded printing surface on a line cut. — (2) **1912** F. Weitenkampf *Amer. Graphic Art* 217 The 'Ben Day' process of quick mechanical production of tints by 'rapid shading mediums' has also been a time-saver. **1949** *Manual of Style* 245 Ben Day Process—An engraving process for producing a variety of shaded tints by the use of gelatin films, particularly in connection with line (zinc) etchings.

Hence **Ben Dayed,** *a.*, produced by the Ben Day process.

1931 *Retailing* 7 Nov. The Ben Dayed design, in conjunction with the panels, gives the ad the perfect illusion of greater depth than it actually has.

* **bender,** *n.* **1.** A drinking frolic, or spree. Also transf. *Slang.* See also **hell bender. 2.** A facetious euphemism for "leg." *Rare.*

(1) **1846** Corcoran *Pickings* 62, I was on a almighty big bender last night . . . and the way we *did* walk into the highly concentrated hard cider. **1857** *Knickerb.* XLIX. 43 It was . . . a regular Thanksgiving made perfect—a bender of friendship preserved in the syrup of pleasant recollections. **1947** *This Week Mag.* 17 May 4/2, I pulled the shade down over that terrific last bender. — (2) **1849** Longfellow *Kavanagh* xii, Young ladies are not allowed to cross their benders in school.

bene ˈbinə, *n.* [L., well.] "A word sometimes attached to a written college exercise, by the instructor, as a mark of approbation" (Hall). *Obs.* — **1837** *Harvardiana* III. 402 When I look back upon my college life, And think that I one starveling *bene* got. **1840** Dana *Two Years* xi. 89, I . . . heard the 'well done' of the mate . . . with as much satisfaction as I ever felt at Cambridge on seeing a '*bene*' at the foot of a Latin exercise.

beneficial society. A society whose members are entitled to certain benefits in return for their payments to its funds. *Obs.* — **1811** Mease *Picture of Phila.* 278 The following Benefit Societies also exist in Philadelphia. American Beneficial Society, 105 members, . . . Union Beneficial Society, [etc.]. **1865** *Atlantic Mo.* XV. 317 Varick had in better days become a member of a beneficial society which allowed forty dollars to a widow for the funeral expenses of her husband.

beneficiate bɛnəˈfɪʃɪˌet, *v. W.* [Sp. *beneficiar*, in same sense.] *tr.* To reduce (ores). Also **beneficiation,** *n.*

1871 Raymond *Trans. Amer. Mining Eng.* I. 91 This paper will treat of such works only as beneficiate ores directly in the mining districts. **1877** *8th Rep. Mines* 317 Mr. Keck has completed his beneficiating works. *Ib.*, This ore is now . . . subjected to the rest of the beneficiating process. **1881** Raymond *Mining Gloss. s.v. beneficiation.* **1883** W. Bishop *Old Mexico* 238 His ancient beneficiating hacienda of Regla. **1949** *Sat. Ev. Post* 16 Apr. 155/1 If techniques for handling the leaner ore improve just enough, great beneficiating plants and increased pay rolls may appear in the iron ranges for which Duluth is supplier, outlet and shopping center.

* **benefit,** *n.*

1. *To take the benefit,* to take advantage of bankruptcy laws. *Obs.*

1823 I. Holmes *Account* 215 To shew the extreme facility of obtaining the benefit of the Insolvent Act, an attorney . . . informed me, that a person applied to him to assist him 'in taking the benefit,' as it is termed, of the act. **1846** Cooper *Redskins* xii, I took 'the benefit,' as it is called, myself.

2. benefit bridge (party), luncheon, a bridge party or luncheon the proceeds of which are donated to some cause.

1931 *K.C. Star* 11 Nov., One woman went home from the benefit bridge party last night just before the scores were tallied. **1932** *Durant* (Okla.) *D. Democrat* 27 Oct. 5/5 Mrs. J. T. May will be hostess for the Garden club benefit bridge. **1947** *Chi. D. News* 13 Sep. 11/3 Arden Shore-ites are hereby abolishing benefit luncheons in favor of the cocktail hour.

benevolence circle. A society for benevolent purposes. *Rare.* — **1872** *Harper's Mag.* March 637/1 The wife . . . after a time joined a ladies' 'benevolence circle,' of which she was elected secretary.

* **benevolent,** *n.* (See quot. 1908, and cf. Washington Benevolent Society.) *Obs.* — **1813** *Northern Centinel* (Burlington, Vt.) 3 Dec., But, the bold benevolents of Vermont have lately smuggled from the enemy a Governor of the true British stamp. **1908** *Amer. Antiq. Soc. Proc.* XIX. n.s. 26 By 'benevolents' are meant members of the Washington Benevolent Societies, then [i.e., during the war of 1812] common.

* **benevolent,** *a.* In the names of, or with reference to, charitable organizations.

[**1792** Brissot *Reise* 179 Ferner gehört hieher [in Philadelphia] *the benevolent institution*, dessen Zweck es ist, armen kriessenden Weibern in ihren eignen Wohnungen bei der Entbindung helfen zu lassen.] **1811** Mease *Philadelphia* 277 Columbian Benevolent Society [was] instituted 1804. All well known, healthy citizens of Pennsylvania are eligible. *Ib.* 287 St. Patrick's Benevolent Society [was] incorporated 1804. **1895** *N.Y. Dramatic News* 23 Nov. 14/3 Two boxes in the Pleasure Palace have been donated the fairs given by the Ladies' Benevolent Sewing Society. **1911** *Okla. Session Laws* 3 Legisl. 34 Benevolent institutions which own, maintain and operate cemeteries under the laws of the state shall be permitted to retain ten per centum of the gross proceeds of all lots sold by such institutions.

Bengal grass. The foxtail millet, *Setaria italica.* — **1847** Wood *Botany* 607 Bengal Grass . . . [grows] in fields, not often cultivated. **1890** *Cent. s.v. Grass,* Bengal grass . . . [is] now very extensively cultivated as a forage-plant.

benitoite bəˈnitoˌaɪt, *n.* [See def.] A titanosilicate found in San Benito County, California, greenish-blue in color, and used as a gem. — **1915** *Nat. & Science on Pac. Coast* 55 The gem mineral benitoite . . . is the only mineral representative of a particular class of crystal symmetry.

* **benjamin,** *n.*

1. *local.* A plant of the genus *Trillium*, esp. the common red or purple species *T. erectum.*

1887 *Harper's Mag.* July 303/1 In the woods the painted trilliums—the 'Benjamins' of the country folk—were unfolding their delicate pink and white flowers. **1891** *Amer. Folk-Lore* IV. 149 My father used to gather the early plants [*T. erectum,*] in Gilsum, N.H. for greens, and called them Benjamins.

2. benjamin bush, the spicebush, *Benzoin aestivale.*

[**1765** J. Bartram *Diary* 24 July, The trees common in this rich neck of land is as follows . . . tupelo, water tupelo. shrubs fartle berry stewartia benjamin Cephalanthus halesia.] **1857** Gray *Botany* 379 Benjamin-bush . . . [grows in] damp woods; rather common. **1893** Dana *Wild flowers* 114 Spice-bush. Benjamin-Bush. Fever-bush.

3. benjamin tree. =prec.

1640 Parkinson *Theatr. Bot.* 1572 The fruite of this Benjamin-tree, or of the browne American Balsame before set down. **1741** Miller *Gardener's Dict.* (ed. 2) I., *Benzoin*, the Benjamin-tree. . . . This Tree was brought from Virginia into England, some Years since. **1837** Darlington *Flora Cestrica* 253 Spice-wood. Wild All-spice. Fever bush. Benjamin tree.

benne ˈbɛnə, *n.* Also **bene, bhené** [*bene,* native name of the plant among the Mendi of Sierra Leone, West Africa]. The sesame, *Sesamum indicum.* Also attrib.

1769 in *Amer. Philos. Soc.* I. 309, I send you [from Savannah, Ga.] a small keg of Bene or Bene Seed, which you will please to present to your Society for their inspection. **1818** Darby *Emigrant's Guide* 185 That species of sesamum, called oriental bhené. *Ib.*, The bhené is certainly one of the most productive vegetables that ever was cultivated by man. It is known in Louisiana, but much neglected. **1824** *Amer. Farmer* 9 Jan. 331/3 The Bene mucilage is useful in all cases where other mild and mucilaginous remedies are proper to be recommended. **1867** De Voe *Market Ass't* 358 Bene plant. This plant is much used in the South for culinary purposes. **1946** Hibben *Cookery* 316 Charleston Benné Wafers . . . 1 cup light brown sugar . . . ½ cup parched benné seeds.

* **bent,** *n.* "One section of the frame of a building, which is put together on the ground or foundation and then raised by holding the feet of the posts, and elevating the upper portion. A bent consists of posts united by the beams which pass transversely across the building" (Knight).

1815 *Niles' Reg.* IX. 200/2 The floats were placed at proper distances, with their ends to the shore, and on each of them were raised two bents or frames. *Ib.*, This made sixteen bents, on which the grand and enormous structure was raised. **1842** Mrs. Kirkland *Forest Life* I. xvii. 136 An immense bent was about to be raised, . . . and as many men as could find hands-breadths on its edge were applying their united energies to the task. **1853** Strickland *Twenty-seven Yrs.* I. 51 When ready, the building is put together in what is called bents, each bent consisting of two posts, one on each side of the building, connected together by a strong beam running across the building. **1910**

Burroughs *In Catskills* 57 Slowly the great timbers go up; louder grows the word of command, till the bent is up.

***bent,** *a.* Tipsy. *Slang. Obs.* —**1833** Greene *Dod. Duckworth* II. 176 He was seldom downright drunk; but was often . . . confoundedly bent.

Bentonian ˌbenˈtonɪən, *a.* [Thomas Hart *Benton* (1782–1858), Amer. political figure.] **1. Bentonian delegation,** a delegation made up of the political followers of T. H. Benton. **2. Bentonian shiner,** =**mint-drop.** Both *obs.*

(1) **1852** *N.Y. Wkly. Tribune* 28 Feb. 4/3 The Bentonian delegation from Missouri will doubtless be favorable to his nomination. — (2) **1834** *State Advocate* (Vandalia, Ill.) 19 Nov. 3/3 For our own part, did we feel a disposition to hoard, it should be the real Bentonian shiners, and no such stuff as Banks are made of.

Bentonite bentənaɪt, *n.*[1] [See prec.] A political follower of T. H. Benton. *Obs.* — **1855** *N.Y. Wkly. Tribune* 6 Jan. 7/4 The Legislature of Missouri, either now in session or shortly to assemble, is composed of 40 Bentonites, 60 Whigs and 60 Atchison Loco-Focos.

bentonite ˈbentənaɪt, *n.*[2] [f. Fort *Benton*, Montana.] A soft clay containing chiefly silica, alumina, and water.

1909 *Cent. Supp.* 128/3 bentonite. . . . A variety of clay occurring extensively in the Fort Benton strata of the Cretaceous of Wyoming. **1942** *Ark. Geol. Survey Bul.* VI. 57 Bentonite is used principally as a fuller's earth to decolorize oils, waxes and fats. **1948** *Desert* Feb. 26/3 Bentonite, a clay used in oil filtering, . . . is being mined three miles south of Kersarge, Inyo county.

***benzine,** *n.* Inferior whisky. Hence **benzinery,** a low drinking joint. *Slang.*

1877 Burdette *Rise & Fall of Mustache* 160 Clustering all around the young poet's head, . . . were . . . 'Mountain Dew,' 'Benzine,' . . . and several other spirits. **1884** Sweet & Knox *Through Texas* 624 The fellow had been sent, for a flask of mescal, to the Mustang Spring—the name of the benzinery probably. **1902** *N.Y. Sun* Nov. 23 If a student has 'hit the benzine can' too hard on the night before he is apt to be anxious to get 'on to the water wagon.'

***bergamot,** *n.* =**wild bergamot.** — **1822** J. Woods *English Prairie* 218 The prairie-roses, balm, here called bergamot, and sassafraswood, are exceptions, and have all powerful scents.

bergschrund ˈbɜgˌʃrʌnd, *n.* [G. *Bergschrunde*, mountain crevice.] A crevasse in a mountain glacier. — **1888** Muir *Picturesque Calif.* 5 At the head of the glacier where the *neve* joins the mountain it is traversed by a huge yawning *bergschrund.* **1947** *Can. Alpine Jrnl.* 33 It looked particularly steep in parts and there were several bergschrunds we could not be certain of.

***Berkshire,** *n.* The name of an English county used attrib. with reference to articles brought from there. *Obs.* — **1788** Washington *Diaries* III. 311 The next land to this a bushel of Berkshire Beans from Mr. Peachy was sown. *c*1797 Latrobe *Journal* 61 The Berkshire iron plow he held next in estimation.

berm bɜm, *n.* [f. G. *Berme* (Du. *berm*) a path or strip of ground along a dike.] The bank of a canal opposite the towing path. Also the side or shoulder of a road. Orig. **berm-bank.**

1854 in *N. & Q.* 1 Ser. IX. 12/2 The bank of a canal opposite to the towing-path is called the birm-bank. **1883** *Williamsport* (Pa.) *Gaz.* 30 March (Th.), The horse plunged over the berm bank into the bed of the canal. **1943** Powell *Home Again* 54 It tilted the car into the air and pitched the passengers off on to the berm of a cut through which the train was passing.

b. (See quot.)

1947 *Nat. Geog. Mag.* Sep. 326/1, I listened to Coast Guardsmen expounding . . . how to climb a steep bank and cross the soft berm, or crest.

***Bermuda,** *n.*

1. Used attrib. or absol. to designate onions, potatoes, etc., coming, or regarded as coming, originally from the Bermuda Islands. Cf. **moody,** *n.*

1736 Mortimer in *Phil. Trans.* XXXIX. 258 The Author enumerates five Kinds: the common *Potato*, the *Bermudas*, the *Brimstone*, the *Carrot*, and *Claret Potatoes.* **1854** *Penna. Agric. Rep.* 206 Robert Wallace, for a lot of Bermuda potatoes. **1883** Hale *Woods & Timbers N.C.* 143 Bermuda or French Mulberry (*Callicarpa Americana*) [is] quite common in light soils and dry, open woods. **1943** *Copper Camp* 248 The buckets were sure to [contain] . . . a button or two of garlic, and perhaps a whole Bermuda onion.

2. Bermuda (grass), a lawn and pasture grass, *Cynodon dactylon*, common in the warmer parts of the U.S.

1808 in Dunbar *Life* 199 The *Bermuda grass* is . . . the same with Cumberland grass, the famous East Indian grass Agrostis linearis, it has been known and described by the name of Panicum dactylon in Linnaei work, but dont agree well with the character of Panicum. **1822** *Agric. Papers* (Raleigh, N.C.) (1825) 55 Mr. Elliott . . . when speaking of the *Digitaria Dactylon*, or *Bermuda Grass*, remarks, 'We have two varieties of this plant, one coarser, growing in damp soils, native—the other, said to be imported—a tender, delicate Grass, growing over and binding the most loose and arid soils in our country.' **1945** Wallace *Barington* 91 The earthy fragrance of bermuda and the delicate scent of clover filled the yard.

berrendo beˈrendo, *n. S.W.* [Sp. in Amer. Sp. sense shown here.] The pronghorn. — **1847** Coulter *Adventures* I. 133 This peculiar specimen of the goat kind our guide termed 'berendos,' and are known, all through California, by the same name. **1906** *Out West* May 422 Her eyes were brown also, and big like those of the little antelope that was always playing about the courtyard. Very like, these two were, Theresa and the *berendo*, and both stepped lightly.

***berry,** *n.*

1. In various slang uses, as: **a.** An easy mark. **b.** (See quot.) **c.** (See quot.)

(a) 1887 *Courier-Journal* 27 May 2/4 Harkins started to pitch, . . . for the Brooklyns, but he proved to be a berry for the local sluggers. **1902** Clapin 49 Berry. In college slang, anything easy or soft; a good thing. Also used adjectively in sense of good-looking. — **(b) 1929** *Chi. Tribune* 11 Oct. 14/3 The [dope-] peddler takes his stock to a point on the street or possibly a pool hall. . . . A package of drug wrapped in paper is called a 'deck,' a 'check' or a 'bundle.' If it is in a capsule it is called a 'berry,' a 'bean' or a 'cap.' — **(c) 1929** *Amer. Sp.* IV. 358 'Dollar,' of course, is well represented. It is a *bean, berry, bone, buck,* [etc.].

2. In combs.: (1) **berry boat,** a boat carrying berries to market; (2) **field,** a field where berries grow; (3) **house,** (see quot.), *rare;* (4) **lot,** a berry patch, *rare;* (5) **money,** money earned by picking berries; (6) **moth,** the moth of the cranberry worm, the larvae of which are injurious to cranberries; (7) **party,** a party for picking berries; (8) **pasture,** a pasture in which wild berries are plentiful; (9) **patch,** a place where wild berries grow; (10) **pemmican,** (see quots. and cf. **pemmican**); (11) **spoon,** a spoon used in serving or eating berries; (12) **wagon,** a wagon in which berries are hauled.

Berry wagon

(1) 1880 *Scribner's Mo.* Mar. 762/1 The village of Highland, opposite Poughkeepsie, runs a berry boat [*sc.* for raspberries] daily to New York. — **(2) 1861** *Harper's Mag.* Aug. 363/2 Granny Woodban . . . living in the berry fields all summer, and wandering off no one knew where in winter. **1879** *Harper's Mag.* June 68/2 They are a merry, jolly, happy-go-lucky tribe, . . . finding food in the berry fields. — **(3) 1879** *Harper's Mag.* June 69/2 In the berry-house where the packing of boxes is done, a huge pile of empty crates reaches nearly to the roof. — **(4) 1845** Cooper *Chainbearer* xxiii, I went a berryin' this forenoon, and up ag'in the berry lot . . . I saw a young woman.

(5) **1886** P. Stapleton *Major's Christmas* 168 The things she bought us one Christmas with the berry-money she arnt herself. — **(6) 1884** *Rep. Comm. Agric.* 395 Where the water was taken off [the bogs] early, the berry-moth was found in some numbers. — **(7) 1860** *Harper's Mag.* Nov. 789/1 Aunt Tabby . . . inquired what she could give me to make me . . . not mind the berry party. — **(8) 1880** Howells *Undiscovered Country* 204 The women went, five or six in a wagon, . . . to the berry pasture a mile or two away. **1893** B. Torrey *Footpath Way* 176 The thrasher is silent in the berry pasture. — **(9) 1896** Wilkins *Madelon* 344 She resolved that she would go away . . . to another berry patch that she knew of.

(10) 1944 *Military Surgeon* Aug. 90/2 The other kind was berry pemmican, flavored with dried fruit, usually choke cherries or saskatoon berries. **1947** DeVoto *Across Wide Missouri* 164 The luxury article was 'berry pemmican,' into which pulverized dried fruits of any available kind had been mixed, most often wild cherries with their stones. — **(11) 1875** Stowe *We & Our Neighbors* 474 Of course the reader knows that there were the usual amount of berry-spoons, and pie-knives, and crumb-scrapers. **1936** *Sears Cat.* (ed. 173) 740

Sugar Spoon, Gravy Ladle, Berry Spoon. — (12) **1879** *Harper's Mag.* June 69/2 The loaded [crates are] . . . placed in a large berry wagon.

As the last term in **bay, bear, beauty, box, brown, buck, buffalo, bull, bunch, button, candle, cap, cedar, chaparral, checker, chick, chicken, China, Chinese, choke, Christmas, coffee, coral, cow, cracker, dangle, deer, dog, farkle, finger, fox, gall, gin, ground, gum, hack, hog, ink, June, liver, locust, logan, moose, nanny, one, partridge, pigeon, poison, poke, rabbit, raccoon, razz, red, salal, salmon, scoot, service, shad, sheep, sheepteats, snow, sour, spice, squaw, straw, sugar, swamp, swamp red, tallow, tea, thimble, twin, winter, wintergreen, wolf berry.**

berrying ˈbɛrɪ·ɪŋ, *n.* The gathering of berries. Also attrib. or as adj. See also **buffalo berrying, huckleberrying.**

1845 Cooper *Chainbearer* xxi, It's berryin' time now. I'll run and get a basket. *c***1853** Miss Sedgwick in *Life & Lett.* (1871) 44, I went with herds of school-girls nutting, and berrying, and bathing by moonlight. **1868** *Amer. Naturalist* May 133 A man who had been out berrying stated that he suddenly came across a Rattlesnake with her young. **1880** *Harper's Mag.* March 546/1 With no companions but another woman, who had 'gone berrying.' **1890** Marah E. Ryan *Told in Hills* v. 58 A berrying crowd from the Kootenai tribe.

***berth,** *n.*

1. A place to sleep in a sleeping car.

1838 *Am. R.R. Jour.* VII. 328 If you travel in the night you go to rest in a pleasant berth. **1885** *Harper's Mag.* Apr. 698/2 The traveller . . . goes to sleep in his Pullman berth.

2. (See quot. and cf. **logging berth, lumber berth.**)

*a***1862** Thoreau *Maine Woods* 234 The chopper . . . speaks of a 'berth' of timber, a good place for him to get into, just as a worm might.

3. a. berth deck, the deck where the sailors' hammocks are swung, or upon which the berths are situated, also transf. and attrib. **b. berth saloon,** ?a saloon on the berth deck of a vessel.

(a) 1814 *Niles' Reg.* VI. 36/1 Captain Lambert and Mr. Waldo were the only wounded persons not removed to the *birth* [*sic*] *deck*, on this occasion. **1830** Cooper *Water Witch* III. i. 21 What is the opinion of the berth-deck concerning this strange brigantine? **1886** *Cent. Mag.* April 908/2 From the berth-deck ports we had a fair look at her. — **(b) 1897** Mark Twain *Following Equator* iii. 57 The young diver descended . . . and entered the berth-saloon of the boat.

beshow bəˈʃo, *n.* [Indian *bishowk*, in the Makah dialect of the Wakashan stock.] The candle-fish, *Anoplopoma fimbria*, found along the west coast of North America. — [**1884** Goode *Fisheries U.S.* I. 268 Black Candle-fish . . . in the Straits of Fuca . . . is called by the Indians 'Beshow.'] **1888** ——— *Amer. Fishes* 271 The Beshow . . . is generally known in Puget Sound by the name of 'Horse mackerel.'

***best,** *a.* In combs.: (1) **best bet,** the best one, the one most likely to succeed, *slang;* (2) **girl,** (see quot. 1889), *colloq.;* (3) **looker,** a very good-looking person, *colloq.;* (4) ***man,** (see quot.), *colloq.;* (5) **seller,** a thing, esp. a book, which sells better than anything else in its class, also attrib.; (6) **selling,** *a.* that is a best seller.

(1) 1908 O. Henry *Gentle Grafter* (1920) 18 I carried only one best bet just then, and that was Resurrection Bitters. **1932** *Durant* (Okla.) *D. Democrat* 2 Feb. 2/3 Out of 45 actresses who were considered as the 'best bets,' he ranks Sylvia Sidney as outstanding. — **(2) 1889** Barrere & Leland 109 Best girl (American), the preferred one; a sweetheart. **1944** *Sat. Review* 8 July 16/2 The black-eye susans that in spring adorned the campus did not arouse in him any desire to pluck a bouquet for his best girl. — **(3) 1911** R. W. Chambers *Common Law* i. 10 There's always something wrong with the best lookers. — **(4) 1835** Longstreet *Ga. Scenes* 53 Two men . . . were admitted on all hands to be the very *best men* in the county . . . which, in the Georgia vocaculary, means they could flog any other two men in the county.

(5) 1905 *Out West* Sep. 363 To be able to discuss the Six Best Sellers has become as much an article of faith as any in the Longer Catechism. **1912** *Ib.* Feb. 143/1 The fiction reading public is divided into two classes: those who are set on being supplied from the 'six best seller' stand and those who are avid for Arnold Bennett. **1948** *Christian Cent.* 7 Jan. 18/1 The earliest best seller, for instance, was the Rev. Michael Wigglesworth's religious tract, Day of Doom. — **(6) 1895** *Bookman* July 429/2 The best selling new book is Mr. Stockton's *Adventures of Captain Horn.* **1948** *Rotarian* April 12/2 The novel . . . no doubt stands second to the *Bible* as the world's all-time best selling book.

b. For *best licks, best . . . in the shop*, see the nouns.

***bet,** *v.* Used in various colloq. expressions of an emphatic nature, as: (1) *bet your* (*sweet*) *life,* (2) *bet your boots,* see **boot,** *n.* **2. c.** (3), (3) *you bet, you bet you,* (4) *I bet you.*

(1) 1852 *S.F. Sun. Dispatch* 18 Jan. 1/5 He's around when there's money in the pipe—bet your life on t-h-a-t. **1865** *Carson* (Nev.) *Appeal* 17 Oct. 2/3 You bet your sweet life we fellows stand by Clagett. **1923** Cobb *Kansas* 61 Am I my Brother's Keeper? You bet your sweet life I am! — **(3) 1857** *Phoenix* (Sacramento) 22 Nov. 2/2, I saw all the 'boys,' and distributed to them the papers and 'you bet,' they were in great demand. **1917** Sinclair *King Coal* 116 'You bet you!' **1939** Brownell *Horse & Buggy Days* 125 'You bet I did,' said Jack as he straightened his shoulders. — **(4) 1945** *Craig* (Colo.) *Empire-Courier* 25 July 2/4 You'll all agree to that, I betcha!

***Bethel,** *n.* A place where religious services are held for seamen. Also **Bethel flag, ship, union.**

1823 *Amer. Baptist Mag.* IV. 178/2 New-Orleans Bethel Union, in the establishment of which the friends of seamen have great cause of rejoicing. *Ib.* 179 Having received from the New York Bethel Union . . . a Bethel Flag. **1862** *Harper's Mag.* Aug. 310/1 There, Sir, is the Bethel ship, one of many. **1944** Mencken in *New Yorker* 30 Dec. 20/3 'Are You Ready for the Judgment Day?' [was] the prime favorite of the period in all the sailors' bethels, helping-up missions.

Bethlemite, *n.* (See quot.) *Obs.* — **1816** Scene Painter *Emigrant's Guide* 37 A sect denominated Bethlemites, from the name of a parish or township called Bethlem, which they exclusively inhabit, a few miles from Philadelphia, follow the example of the primitive Christians, by throwing their property into one common stock.

betrustment bɪˈtrʌstmənt, *n.* [f. *betrust, v.* +*-ment.*] (See quot. 1806.) *Obs.*

1702 C. Mather *Magnalia* v. ii. (1852) 255 To make over church-betrustments 'unto faithful men.' **1806** Webster *Compend. Dict.* 29 Betrustment, *n.* act of entrusting, thing entrusted. **1836** Matthews *Lectures on Eloquence* 130 We sometimes . . . hear *missionate, variate, betrustment,* and *bestowment.* in conversation or prayer. But none of these I presume can be said to have the stamp of good use among us.

***betsy,** *n.*

1. (*cap.*) A popular colloquial name for a favorite gun. Also **old Betsy.**

1856 *Spirit of Age* (Sacramento) 4 Nov. 3/1 Jest let them raise that check agin me, and if I don't shoot why old Betsy won't blizzard. **1869** *New No. West* (Deer Lodge, Mont.) 20 Aug. 2/7 Mr. Fredericks proceeded immediately on the horse, loaded 'Betsey,' (his shot gun). **1946** *Outdoors* June 82/2 I'll just bet you old Betsy here against that machine-gun of yours that I can get off 25 shots faster'n you can!

2. betsy bug, a pinch bug, but often used facetiously without specific reference to any particular bug, esp. in the phrase *as crazy as a betsy bug.* Also **bess bug, bess beetle, betty bug.** *Colloq.*

1910 C. Harris *Eve's Husband* 234 A young congressman has to . . . encourage them [his constituents] to ask for little things like sample betty-bugs to eat other bugs, garden seed [etc.]. . . . The Government furnishes the betty-bugs. **1910** W. S. Blatchley *Coleoptera* 908 This well-known species, commonly known as the 'horn' or 'bess-beetle,' occurs abundantly throughout the state [Indiana]. **1934** Vines *Green Thicket World* 193 He had made her as crazy as a bess bug. **1944** *Harper's Mag.* March 373/2 He always lived over the crick from us. Crazy as a betsey bug most of the time.

***better,** *adv.*

1. Used in ellipt. expressions, as *I, you, he,* etc., *better,* the *had* being omitted. *Colloq.*

1831 S. Smith *Major Downing* 65 My clothes had got so shabby, I thought I better hire out a few days and get slicked up a little. **1888** *Vt. Agric. Rep.* X. 14 If a man has a cheese factory he better keep it. **1916** Bower *Phantom Herd* i. 7 What you better do is this.

2. *You'd better believe,* you may be sure, without doubt. *Colloq.*

1856 *Yale Lit. Mag.* XXI. 171 (Th.), If I catch your daughter from home, You'd better believe, I'll live in the clover. **1872** Holmes *Poet* x. 331 My old gentleman means to be Mayor . . . before he goes off the handle, you'd better b'lieve.

***bettering house.** Formerly a benevolent institution in Philadelphia primarily for the poor and sick but serving also as a workhouse and place of detention for those of loose habits. Now *hist.*

1767 in J. C. Parsons *Diary of Jacob Hiltzheimer* (1893) 12 Called in my sleigh for Mrs. Reynell, took her to see the Bettering House, and then left her at Edward Penington's. **1774** J. Adams *Diary* 17 Sep. II. (1850) 380 Visited the Bettering House, a large building, very clean, neat, and convenient for the poor. **1877** *Pa. Mag. Hist.* I. 8 The Bettering or Alms House stood on the south side of Spruce Street between 10th and 11th Streets. **1917** Lippincott *Early Philadelphia* 312 These quiet people knew well of the Bettering House. [**1939**

Padelford *Colonial Panorama* 18 The Alms House, opened in Oct. 1767, was located on the block bounded by Spruce, Pine, Tenth, and Eleventh Streets.]

***betterment,** *n.* An improvement on real property. Usu. *pl.*

"This term was first used, as I have understood, in the State of Vermont; but it has for a long time been common in the State of New Hampshire: And it has been getting into use in some parts of Massachusetts, since the passing of the late law, similar to the Betterment Acts (as they are called) of the states abovementioned" (Pickering). **1785** *Vt. State P.* (1823) 490 An Act to secure Daniel Marsh, in the possession of a certain farm, until he shall have opportunity of recovering his betterments. **1809** Kendall *Travels* III. 160 These men . . . demand either to be left owners of the soil or paid for their betterments, that is, for what they have done towards clearing the ground. **1900** Dix *Deacon Bradbury* 162 The small amount . . . melted away under his hands in absolutely required replenishments and betterments.

attrib. **1854** Kent *Commentaries* (ed. 8) 393 The statute law in Massachusetts, New Hampshire and Vermont is called the 'Betterment Law.' **1890** J. Rae in *Contemporary Rev.* May 644 The betterment tax . . . has been known in America for two hundred years.

***bettor,** *n.* One who holds the stakes of those betting on an Indian ball game. *Rare.* — **1894** *Outing* XXIV. 214/2 When two countries are playing, local feeling runs high, and one of the features of the day is the 'bettor' or go-between. He is mounted on a pony . . . , and carries anything and everything that is betted. He ties the articles together; thus you will see a pair of boots traded for a shawl, or several small articles for a coat, and if the owner of the coat wins he takes everything that is tied to it.

***Betty,** *n.*

1. (See quot. and cf. **apple, brown, sweet betty.**)

1918 *Ladies' Home Jrnl.* July 25/1 Use rhubarb to make a 'Betty,' now or next winter, with bread crumbs, butter substitute, lemon peel and raisins.

2. Betty lamp, (see quots.). Also attrib. Cf. **brown Betty** (*b*).

1898 Earle *Customs Old N. Eng.* 125 Betty lamps were the earliest form. They were a shallow receptacle, usually of pewter, iron, or brass, circular or oval in shape, and occasionally triangular, and about two or three inches in diameter, with a projecting nose an inch or two

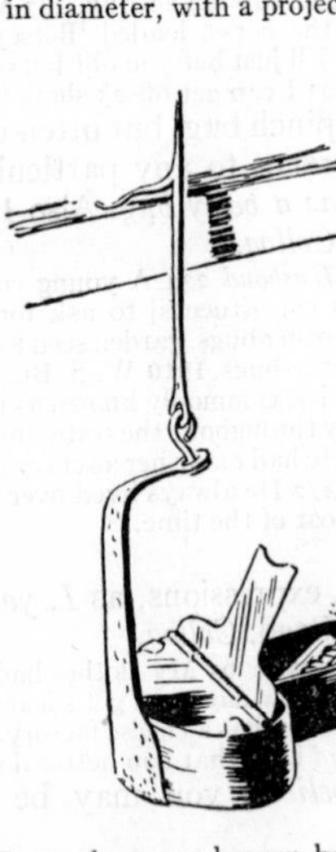

Betty lamp or brown betty (*b*)

long. When in use they were filled with tallow or grease, and a wick or piece of twisted rag was placed so that the lighted end could hang on the nose. **1935** *Col. of Conn.* 15 Betty lamps: These were much like the early Roman lamps. . . . They were small, shallow receptacles, 2 or 3 inches in diameter . . . [and] about an inch in depth . . . , rectangular, oval, round, or triangular . . . with a . . . nose or spout an inch or 2 long. . . . Each lamp had a hook and a chain to hang on a nail on the wall. . . . They were filled with tallow, grease, and oil. . . . [A] piece of . . . rag wick hung out at the nose when it was lighted. . . . They were usually made of pewter. **1942** Weygandt *Plenty of Pa.* 221 A slant top desk in cherry and curly maple, . . . has on its top two painted birds, a Betty lamp stand of wood with two iron lamps hanging from it, and a pewter communion goblet and tankard.

As the last term in **black, calico, dumb betty.**

between-lands. Lands lying between those on a lower and higher level. *Colloq.* — *c***1900** R. L. Hale *Log of Forty-Niner* 86 These higher, or between lands, as they are called, are unhealthy.

Bewick('s) wren. [Thomas *Bewick* (1753–1828), an English artist, wood engraver, and naturalist.] The long-tailed house wren, *Thyromanes bewicki*, common in the southern part of the U.S.

1831 Audubon *Ornith. Biog.* I. 96 Bewick's Wren, *Troglodytes Bewickii*. . . . In shape, colour and movements, it nearly resembles the Great Carolina Wren, and forms a kind of link between that bird and the House Wren. **1898** Torrey *Atlantic Mo.* April 457/1 The singer was at home for the season: . . . a Bewick's wren, as I had guessed. **1948** *Pacific Discovery* Mar.–Apr. 15/1 Like the chickadees, the Bewick wrens find the dark foramina of the whale skulls desirable places for nesting.

***bias,** *v. tr.* To cut bias. — **1883** *Cent. Mag.* XXVI. 960/1 You may baste, you may bias the Gore if you will.

***Bible,** *n.* Also ***bible.**

1. Among whalers, a large piece of blubber minced for the trying pot by being sliced transversely.

1884 *U.S. Nat. Mus. Bul.* XXVII. 292 These slices are called bibles or books; they are not detached at the base of the piece, but are held together as are the leaves of a book.

2. In combs.: (1) **Bible agent,** a seller of Bibles; (2) **Belt,** a term coined about 1925 by H. L. Mencken to designate those parts of the country in which the literal accuracy of the Bible is credited and clergymen who preach it have public influence; (3) **class,** a class of those studying the Bible; (4) **communism,** =**Oneida communism;** (5) **communist,** a member of the Oneida Community *q.v.*; (6) **leaf,** (see quot.).

(1) **1847** Briggs *Tom Pepper* I. 16, I turned a bible agent out of the schooner the day before we left. — (2) **1926** *Amer. Mercury* Feb. 141/2 The *Baptist Record*, of Jackson, Miss., [is] in the heart of the Bible and Lynching Belt. **1948** *Sat. Ev. Post* 5 June 20/3 Founded in a single day by 10,000 lusty pioneers, Oklahoma City is now the sedate capital of the Bible Belt. — (3) **1824** *Baptist Mag.* IV. 371, I intimated my intention to establish . . . Bible classes for the study of the sacred oracles. **1948** *Good Housekeeping* Jan. 108/3 Every time I'd get it in my mind, Mr. Creech, I'd see you in the Bible Class a-tellin' the story of Cain and Abel. — (4) **1867** Dixon *New America* I. x, I have received from Father Noyes, the Founder of Bible Communism, a criticism—addressed, in the place, to his own people—of my account of the Bible Family at Oneida. **1870** J. H. Noyes *Hist. Amer. Socialisms* 638 They invented the term *Free Love* to designate the social state of the Kingdom of Heaven as defined in *Bible Communism*.

(5) **1867** Dixon *New America* I. xii, Mr. Noyes explains that my account of the Bible Communists must be taken as my own, not as his, and not as sanctioned by him. **1869** J. H. Noyes *Hist. Amer. Socialisms* 631 Bible Communists are not held responsible for the proceedings of those who meddle with the sexual question. — (6) **1931** Clute *Plants* 60 More appealing names are . . . bible-leaf (*Chrysanthemum balsamita*) for that fragrant-leaved plant whose leaves were often carried to church.

As the last term in **college, freshman's, Gold, golden, Indian, Jefferson, kiss-the-, school Bible.**

Bicknell ˈbɪknel, *n.* [App. from a proper name or names.] **a.** Short for "Bicknell's Detector" *q.v.*, *s.v.* ***detector. b. Bicknell apple,** (see quot.). Both *obs.* — (a) **1852** Regan *Emigrant's Guide* 88 You'll show me the Bicknell then. I guess I can manage it myself. — (b) **1816** *Mass. H.S. Coll.* 2 Ser. VII. 116 The 'Bicknell apple,' so termed, is here cultivated. It yields a great proportion of juice, but as to quality is rather watery.

bicycler ˈbaɪˌsɪklɚ, *n.* [f. ******bicycle, v.*] One who rides a bicycle. — **1879** *Lippincott's Mag.* Nov. 626/1 Two bicyclers rode one hundred miles in the suburbs of Boston in twelve hours. **1913** Eaton *Barn Doors & Byways* 32, I used to notice that a road the bicycler cursed by day, picking his path, seemed smooth enough as he bowled along in the dark.

***bid,** *n.* **1.** A request for (one's) services. *Rare.* **2.** An invitation to a student to join a fraternity or sorority. Also a student who has received such a bid. **3.** An invitation of any kind. See also **straw bid.**

(1) **1855** J. E. Cooke *Ellie* 67 Mrs. Brown had more 'bids' for her work, at the moment, than she could supply. — (2) **1887** *Lippincott's Mag.* July 100 Our new man has a 'bid,' and . . . must be initiated into the mysteries of a 'dyke.' **1913** *Ladies' Home Jrnl.* Nov. 19/2 The 'Betas' were to entertain their 'bids' that evening. — (3) **1893** *Kansas U. Q.* Jan. 136 A bid to the wedding. **1948** *Time* 24 May 23/2 New York newspapers blazoned the story that Russia had accepted a U.S. bid to talk about their differences.

*bid, v.

1. bid to, *pp.*, invited to. *Rare.*

1729 J. COMER *Diary* (1923) 81 A child's funeral bid to. *Ib.* 98 This morning Gideon Wanton's child's funeral bid to.

2. *To bid off*, to dispose of, or obtain by bidding, at auction.

1780 *N.H. Comm. Safety* 235 Provided the heirs of Joseph Simmes . . . should bid off at Vendue any of said Estate laying in the town of Middle-town. **1833** *Niles' Reg.* XLIV. 347/1 The school master is often 'bid off' or 'put up at auction,' as are our paupers—and the *lowest* bidder in the district takes him. **1855** *Harper's Mag.* X. 853/1 At an auction in the country a fiddle was put up for sale. It was 'bid off' by a green-looking Yankee. **1907** C. C. ANDREWS *Recoll.* 276 It was bid-off by the lumber-men themselves, who formed a combination to prevent it from falling into the hands of other purchasers.

3. *To bid in*, to buy at auction.

1857 *Quinland* I. 130 If any can pay, well and good. Farms are to be bid in at not more than half of their estimated value, and as much under as possible. **1917** J. F. DALY *Life A. Daly* 345 The costly books . . . were bid in at the sale of 1878.

bidar ˈbaɪdɑr, *n. Alaska.* [Russian *baidara*, adaptation of *paithak, paithaalik*, in the Kanaigmiut dial. used of a three-paddle boat.] A large skin-covered boat used by the Aleuts.

1802 SAUER *Geog. & Astron. Exped.* 171 The customs of these savages are nearly allied to those of Oonalashkas [*sic*]. They have the same kind of implements, darts, and boats, or baidars, but much worse made; nor are they so active upon the water. **1868** WHYMPER *Alaska* 137 Their 'baidarres,' similar to the 'oomiak' of the Greenlander, vary in size from those intended for three or four persons to others capable of holding fifteen or twenty persons. **1880** JACKSON *Alaska* 336 Launching their walrus-skin boats (baidars), they boldly cross to and fro from Siberia.

bidarka baɪˈdɑrkə, *n. Alaska.* [Russian *baidarka*, dim. of *baidara*. Cf. **bidar.**] A small portable completely decked boat, resembling a kayak but usually having hatchways for two or three rowers.

1868 WHYMPER *Alaska* 137 Their 'baidarkes' are similar to the Greenland 'kyack,' but are more commonly constructed with three holes than with one. **1899** MUIR *John of Mts.* (1938) 401 Two men in a canoe were badly beaten by two men in a three-hatch bidarka. **1942** JAMES *First Explor. Russian Amer.* 44 The baidark was a light skin canoe with a covering of skin which fitted tightly to the skin tunic, worn by the native, so as to be waterproof.

***biennial,** *n.* (See quot. 1853.)

1853 *Songs of Yale* 4 The 'Biennial' is an Examination occurring twice during the course,—at the close of the Sophomore and of the Senior years,—in all the studies pursued during the two years previous. It was established in 1850. **1871** L. H. BAGG *At Yale* 277 As the 'Biennial' was superseded by the 'Annual' examinations, so the 'Biennial caps' gave way to 'Annual caps,' and the 'Biennial Jubilee' found a successor in the 'Annual Dinner.' **1876** W. S. TYLER *Amherst Coll.* 237 Amherst had already led the way in dispensing with biennials and senior examinations in the whole curriculum.

biennialist ˌbaɪˈenɪəlɪst, *n.* One who favors biennial rather than annual sessions of a legislative body. *Rare.* — **1894** *Columbus* (O.) *Dispatch* 7 March, The Lieutenant Governor, an intensely partisan biennialist, told him he need not answer any questions.

biff bɪf, *n.* [App. imitative.] A blow. Also transf. and as interjection. *Colloq.*

1847 ROBB *Squatter Life* 137, I hit him, *biff*, alongside his smeller. **1904** F. LYNDE *Grafters* xxviii, 368 But Hawk's next biff was more to the purpose. **1947** *Sat. Ev. Post* 15 March 146/3 Giving her a good biff on the nose . . . might . . . create the erroneous idea that he was a bully.

bifocal ˌbaɪˈfokḷ, *a.* Having two foci, used of spectacles the lenses of which give assistance for both near and distant vision. Also as noun. Cf. **double spectacles, Franklin spectacles.**

1894 GOULD *Dict. Med.* 205/1 Bifocal lens. **1895** *Pop. Science Mo.* Aug. 470 Ordinary bifocal glasses. **1948** *Hygeia* Jan. 38/1, 1888 or 1889 are the dates of the Morck patents on cement bifocals and 'perfection'. bifocals. . . . The invention of the Kryptok, or fused bifocal, is accredited to an American by the name of Borsch in 1899 and a short time after this the solid or one piece bifocals were invented by another American, Connor.

***big,** *a.*

1. In Indian talk or with reference to Indian usage, as **big canoe, chief, dog** (cf. **5.** (3) below), **hearts, lodge, medicine, river** (cf. **5. c.** (6) below), **speak, talk, village, waters.**

1813 *Niles' Reg.* V. 78/2 The Indians . . . [were] determined to see which of the *big canoes* had the command of the lake. **1846** MELVILLE *Typee* 31 When the inhabitants of some sequestered island first descry the 'big canoe' of the European rolling through the blue waters toward their shores. — *a***1861** T. WINTHROP *Canoe & Saddle* X. 199 'You big chief, got plenty thing.' — **1899** H. B. CUSHMAN *Hist. Indians* 256 Some whipped their own dogs during an eclipse because a '*Big Dog*' was eating the sun or moon, and believed the '*Big Dog*' might be induced to postpone his meal by the howls of their whipped curs. — **1837** IRVING *Bonneville* II. vii. 81 The old chief . . . did all that he could to glorify the Big Hearts of the East. — **1848** RUXTON in *Blackw. Mag.* LXIV. 440 A trader from the 'big lodge' (the fort) has been in his village. — **1848** RUXTON *Far West* (1849) 128 The valley [contains] . . . many thermal . . . springs . . . considered, moreover, to be the 'biggest kind' of 'medicine' to be found in the mountains. **1911** WRIGHT *Winning Barbara Worth* 132 Word had gone out that the Seer, beloved by all the tribe, and his lieutenant, almost equally beloved, were making 'big medicine' in The King's Basin Desert. — **1827** COOPER *Prairie* II. i. 7 The runners, from the people on the Big-river, Hard Heart. — **1804** *Fredericktown* (Md.) *Herald* 18 Feb. 2/2 Upon hearing a 'big speak' as our Indians phraze it, from one of Bonaparte's aids-du-camp, His Royal Highness withdrew his troops. — **1837** IRVING *Bonneville* I. xxii. 216 The military were stationed at some little distance from the scene of the 'big talk'; . . . the general and the chiefs were smoking pipes and making speeches. **1863** *Sacramento Union* 30 Oct. 3/3, I was introduced to Captain Tom who said, 'By-and-by big talk.' — **1848** RUXTON in *Blackw. Mag.* LXIII. 726 Their 'big village' has wintered there for many successive years. — **1899** H. B. CUSHMAN *Hist. Indians* 66 They also had a tradition that their fore-fathers came from a country beyond the '*Big Waters*' far to the northwest.

See also **Big Feather, Big Knife.**

2. Used colloquially in the sense of great, excellent, important.

1845 HOOPER *Taking Census* ii. 167 Throw a mealbag . . . over your head, twell my little 'squire gits sorter usen to the big ugly! **1889** FARMER 53 What in England would be called fine old whiskey and brandy would, in America, be designated 'big whiskey.' **1914** H. JAMES *Ivory Tower* II. i. 77 What was before him at the least was a 'big' experience. **1932** *Durant* (Okla.) *D. Democrat* 12 Nov. 4/2 Come to town and tell your neighbor to come, for there'll be big doings for all.

3. In the names of plants: (1) **big buckeye,** the sweet or yellow buckeye, *Aesculus octandra*, often cultivated; (2) **bud,** designating the mockernut hickory; (3) **cone(d),** see as a main entry; (4) **cottonwood,** the necklace poplar, *Populus balsamifera;* (5) **laurel,** (*a*) a magnolia, *Magnolia grandiflora*, of the southern states, (*b*) the rhododendron of the eastern U.S.; (6) **leaf maple,** the Oregon maple, *Acer macrophyllum*, of the Pacific Coast; (7) **root,** a cucurbitaceous plant of California, *Echinocystis fabacea*, having an enormous tuberous root; (8) **shellbark,** a species of hickory, *Carya lacinosa*, common in the eastern states; (9) **tree,** the sequoia tree of the Sierra Nevada, also attrib.

(1) **1832** BROWNE *Sylva* 226 Large Buckeye . . . is here [in the Southern states] called Big Buckeye, to distinguish it from the *Paria rubra.* — (2) **1916** SETON *Woodcraft Man.* 276 Mockernut, White Heart, or Big-bud Hickory (*Hicoria alba*), A tall forest tree, up to 100 feet. Wood much like that of Shagbark, but not quite so heavy. . . . Its bark is smooth and furrowed like that of the Pignut. — (4) **1901** MOHR *Plant Life Ala.* 465 *Populus deltoides*, Carolina Poplar, Big Cottonwood, . . . [is] a timber tree.

(5) (*a*) **1810** MICHAUX *Arbres* I. 32 The large magnolia, . . . [or] Big laurel. **1883** HALE *Woods & Timbers N.C.* 110 *Magnolia grandiflora*. . . . Farther south it is often called Big Laurel. (*b*) **1853** STROTHER *Blackwater Chron.* vii. 89 This dale is girt round . . . by a broad belt of the *Rhododendron*—commonly called the big laurel out here. **1931** *Randolph Enterprise* (Elkins, W.Va.) 12 March 1/2 The shrubbery should not be cut down along the banks, but more planted, 'Big Laurel,' rose-bushes, [etc.]. — (6) **1905** *Calif. Acad. Sci. Occasional Papers* IX. 66 Big-leaf Maple . . . grows along water courses in the Coast Ranges and Sierra Nevada from the northern to the southern boundaries of the state. **1940** *Mt. Hood Guide* 70 The Salmon River Trail parallels Salmon River through a deep canyon shaded by forests of Douglas fir, . . . big leaf maple, alder and western yew. — (7) **1897** PARSONS *Wild Flowers Calif.* 26 Seeing its rather delicate ivy-like habit above ground, one would never dream that it came from a root as large as a man's body, buried deep in the earth. From this root, it has received two of its common names, 'big-root' and 'man-in-the-ground.' **1942** KEARNEY & PEEBLES *Flowering Plants Ariz.* 864 Marah. Bigroot, Wild-cucumber. — (8) **1884** SARGENT *Rep. Forests* 133 *Carya sulcata*, . . . Big Shellbark. *Ib.* 175 *Populus monilifera*, . . . Big Cottonwood. — (9) **1853** *Placer Times* (S.F.) 27 June 2/2 The Big Tree at the World's Fair. **1886** HUTCHINGS *Heart of Sierras* 274

The sugar and yellow pine, fir and big tree wood, were converted into doors, blinds, sashes, etc. **1948** *Pacific Discovery* Mar.–Apr. 1/1 Not all Big Trees are grizzled patriarchs of 2,000 years or more, nor are they necessarily a doomed race.

4. In the names of fishes and other animals: (1) **big drum,** the common drumfish, *Pogonias cromis,* of the Atlantic Coast; (2) **-eared deer,** =?**mule deer;** (3) **-eyed scad,** the goggler, *Trachurops crumenophthalmus,* found along the Atlantic Coast; (4) **head,** see as a main entry; (5) **horn,** the Rocky Mountain sheep, *Ovis canadensis,* in full **bighorn sheep,** cf. **5. b.** (6) below; (6) **mouth,** =**warmouth.**

(1) 1842 *Nat. Hist. N.Y., Zoology* IV. 80 The Big Drum, *Pogonias chromis,* . . . is a large and deep fish. — **(2) 1839** WEBBER *Old Hicks* 89 Hicks says it is most abundant along the foot of the Rocky Mountains, and that the hunters call it the 'big-eared deer,' and sometimes the 'black throat,' from a black mark along the dew-laps. It is much heavier and darker than the common deer; the ears rounder, and a third larger in proportion. — **(3) 1885** J. S. KINGSLEY *Riverside Nat. Hist.* III. 187 The big-eyed scad, also more generally known as the goggler, and goggle-eyed Jack—the *Trachurops crumenophthalmus* of naturalists. **1903** T. H. BEAN *Fishes N.Y.* 427 The big-eyed scad *Trachurops crumenophthalmus* is taken in the fall in Gravesend bay.

(5) 1784–1812 D. THOMPSON *Narrative* (1916) 557 Four sheep, an animal peculiar to these mountains, and by the Americans named Big Horn. **1838** PARKER *Tour* 194, I am not able . . . to describe the Rocky Mountain, or big-horn sheep, as I did not have the opportunity to see it. **1946** *Wyo. Wild Life* May 30/2 Protective coloration of Big Horns is the perfect camouflage. — **(6) 1820** [see **big head 2.**]. **1888** GOODE *Amer. Fishes* 67 *Chocnobryttus antistius,* a species also called 'Warmouth,' 'Big-mouth,' . . . abounds in the tributaries of the Upper Mississippi.

b. In more occasional names of this kind (see quots.)

1814 MITCHILL *Fishes N.Y.* 40 Big Porgee of New-York, *Labrus versicolor.* **1818** *Jrnl. Science* I. 79 The big-eye herring (*Clupea megalops*) begin to be seen at the fish-market. **1844** *Nat. Hist. N.Y., Zoology* II. 285 The Great Diver, or Big Loon, may be regarded as a perpetual resident in this State. **1874** COUES *Birds N.W.* 573 *Fuligula Marila,* . . . Greater Scaup Duck; Big Black-head. **1944** *Reader's Digest* Sep. 52/1 He's . . . an expert on the best way to catch bigmouth bass.

5. In miscellaneous combs.: (1) **big board,** the New York Stock Exchange or a quotation board for securities listed on this, *colloq.;* (2) **business,** large mercantile transactions, organizations, etc., often derogatorily; (3) ***dog,** a person of great or fancied importance, frequently with additions (see quots.), *slang,* cf. **1.** above; (4) **game,** an important athletic contest between traditional rivals; (5) **gate,** a large gate, one sufficiently wide for a wagon to be driven through; (6) **greasy cut,** a cut in card playing, *slang, obs.;* (7) **hand,** (see quot. 1909), *colloq.;* (8) **head,** see as a main entry; (9) **horned,** having big horns, cf. **big horn;** (10) ***house,** (*a*) a manor, esp. on a plantation, the master's house, (*b*) a penitentiary, *slang;* (11) **idea,** an exceptionally fine idea, aim, purpose, *colloq.;* (12) **jaw,** =**big head 1.,** also an animal affected with this or a similar disease, also attrib.; (13) **league,** either of the two major rival baseball leagues or clubs in the U.S., also transf. and attrib.; (14) **leaguer,** a player on a big league baseball team, also transf.; (15) **meeting,** (see quot. 1942); (16) **mitt,** (see quots.), *slang;* (17) **money,** a large amount of money, as profits, salary, etc.; (18) ***pond,** the Atlantic Ocean, *humorous;* (19) **shot,** a "big bug," *slang;* (20) **stick,** *fig.* strength or power sufficient to obtain, by force if need be, what one wants, also transf., hence, *rare,* **big sticker** [this term was introduced by Theodore Roosevelt in a speech advocating a large navy]; (21) **thing,** a promising scheme, a fine chance to make money, *slang;* (22) **time,** (*a*) (see quot. 1942), (*b*) major league baseball, also transf. and attrib.; (23) **top,** the main tent of a circus, also transf.

(1) 1934 WEBSTER. **1948** *Time* 14 June 88/2 In some respects, the Dow-Jones averages—which record the rise and fall of 65 (out of 1,398) stocks on the Big Board—did not show the true strength of the baby bull market. — **(2) 1905** *McClure's Mag.* 49 The stench of the vice graft did not repel, it attracted big business. **1947** *Acad. Polit. Science Proc.* May 25 There is no public chorus to sing 'Big Business, we love you.' — **(3) 1833** J. S. JONES *Green Mt. Boy* I. iii, For the rale genuine grammar larnin' I am a six-horse team and a big dog under the wagon. **1845** J. J. HOOPER *Simon Sugg's Adv.* x. 126 The reverend gentleman . . . was the 'big dog of the tanyard.' **1847** FIELD *Drama in Pokerville* 35 At any rate, he belonged to 'one of the first families in Virginia,' . . . and [was], altogether, the 'big dog' at Pokerville. **1859** BARTLETT 31 In some parts of the country the principal man of a place or in an undertaking is called the 'big dog with a brass collar,' as opposed to the little cuss not thought worthy of a collar. — **(4) 1923** *L.A. D. News* 23 Nov. 19/2 The Stanford rooting section was originally designed to hold 1900 students at the big game. **1948** *Reader's Digest* Feb. 31/1 That year we had all gone up to San Francisco from Los Angeles to see the Big Game—Stanford versus California.

(5) *c***1866** BAGBY *Old Va. Gentleman* 51 The traveller enters this domain [of grassland] through a rickety 'big-gate.' **1904** TOM WATSON *Bethany* (1920) 13 You might have seen this aged slave making his regular tour from the Big Gate to Germany Creek. — **(6)** *a***1846** *Quarter Race Ky.* 92 He gin 'em [*sc.* the cards] the Sunflower 'shuffle,' and I the Big Greasy 'cut,' and pushed 'em back. **1855** OLIPHANT *Minnesota* 134 There was the game of Seven-up, . . . involving the mysteries of the 'Sunflower-shuffle' and the 'big greasy cut.' — **(7) 1909** *Sat. Ev. Post* 5 June 17/2 A big hand . . . Much applause. **1948** *Prairie Club Bul.* June 14 Three lusty cheers and a big hand for Charles, Our Star Square Dance Host! — **(9) 1805** LEWIS in *Orig. Journals* (1904) II. 92 We have met with great abundance of the argalia or bighorned animals. **1822** J. FOWLER *Journal* 114 We find nothing to kill exsept two of the Big Horned Sheep, one of which Robert Fowler shot but cold not git it.

(10) (*a*) **1823** COOPER *Pioneers* xli, Yes! the big house has rung with merriment this month past! **1854** DAVIS *Farm Bk.* 122 Wright working at the big house. **1947** LUMPKIN *Southerner* 7 The plantation 'big house' . . . was situated on a rise of ground above the road leading to the county seat of Lexington. (*b*) **1916** *Lit. Digest* 19 Aug. 424/3 Then comes . . . the final curtain of the piece, when the malefactor is sent away to the 'big house.' **1948** *Chi. D. News* 10 May 14/4 Austin, who was converted to religion in the big house, planned to begin at once his studies for the priesthood. — **(11) 1923** C. J. DUTTON *Shadow on Glass* 240 'What's the big idea of sitting in the dark?' he asked in a gruff tone. **1948** *Chi. Tribune* 20 June (Comics) 13 In that case I will take my big ideas elsewhere. — **(12) 1867** *Iowa Agric. Soc. Rep.* (1868) 130, I have not lost but two of the bovine species . . . ; one in 1861 had big head or jaw. **1890** *Stock Grower* (Las Vegas, N.M.) 10 May 3/1 We still advise ranchmen to shoot down what few big jaws may be found on the range. **1936** BARNARD *Rider* 111 He killed big jaw steers. — **(13) 1899** *Chi. D. News* 10 May 6/1 They are telling a story on one of Chicago's crack players new in the big league. **1943** *Sat. Ev. Post* 1 May 11/3 It was what the circus, a big-league baseball game, Tommy Harmon, Joe Louis, Jimmy Doolittle and a ride in an airplane, all combined, would be to the average boy of fifteen. **1947** *Time* 14 Apr. 66/3 They announced a prize book contest baited with enough cash to make big-league authors sit up & take notice. — **(14) 1910** *Amer. Mag.* May 6/1 College players stop eight out of nine grounders and big leaguers stop 15 out of 16 or thereabout. **1946** *Chi. D. News* 31 Aug. 6/6 Let's train our men to be big leaguers if they are to compete, as our representatives, in the big leagues!

(15) [**1805** in FRIES *N.C. Morav. Rec.* VI. (1943) 2814 There was a Methodist *big meeting* in the neighborhood.] **1857** *Mag. of Travel* April 230 A peculiar feature of the country is the Methodist camp meetings, usually called 'big meetins,' to which the whole country flock indiscriminately. **1942** WARNICK *Dialect Garrett Co., Md.* 4 Big-meeting, n., protracted or revival meeting. — **(16) 1903** *Dly. Chron.* 6 May 7/2 The St. Louis scandal is constantly referred to as a 'big mit.' *Ib.* 27 May 7/2 A 'big mit,' . . . is a big boodle game, a graft. **1940** MAURER *Big Con* 242 Each large fair or exposition brings a revival of these short-con games . . . : the tear-up, the big-mitt, the big joint, . . . three-card monte. — **(17) 1876** *Dly. Stock Report* (S.F.) 9 Oct. 1/2 We are getting our heads accustomed to larger works, better machinery, and the putting in of 'big money' by consolidating capital. **1947** *Harper's Mag.* Oct. 352/2 'Big money,' represented by the slicks, the book clubs, and especially Hollywood, 'is the ruination of many a promising writer.' — **(18) 1840** HALIBURTON *Clockmaker* III. xviii, He is . . . the best live one that ever cut dirt this side of the big pond. **1902** *Outing* June 345/1 Irish and Gordon setters of late years have hardly sustained their reputation on either side of the big pond.— **(19) 1929** *Cin. Enquirer* 5 Oct. 10/3 The McMillans, Englishes, Boleys and Bishops are to be heard from, and one of them is just as likely to win the series as one of the 'big shots.' **1948** *Chi. D. News* 9 Jan. 14/1 There is no proof that 'big shots' of labor have . . . power to divert votes from Wallace.

(20) 1900 ROOSEVELT in Pringle *Roosevelt* (1931) 214, I have always been fond of the West African proverb: 'Speak softly and carry a big stick; you will go far.' **1905** *Springfield W. Republican* 9 June 1 A big-sticker after Mr. Roosevelt's own heart. **1947** *Harper's Mag.* Nov. 459/2 A technique based on a judicious combination of the soft wood and the big stick, it has already begun to make revolutionary changes in employment policies. — **(21) 1862** *Campfire Songster* 48 There's a big thing coming, boys, 'A big thing on ice'; There's a big thing coming, boys, Wait a little longer. **1884** NYE *Baled Hay* 65 If it could be so arranged . . . it would be a big thing for humanity. — **(22)** *(a)* **1863** Norton *Army Lett.* 183 The brigade was flying round, getting into line, drums beating and a big time generally. *Ib.* 190 We had big times that night for fires. **1942** Warnick *Dialect Garrett Co., Md.* 4 Big time, n. phr., lots of fun, also used ironically as 'They had a big time at Smiths when he came home drunk.' *(b)* **1921** *Collier's* 25 June 3/3 Like as not I will have to go back pitchin' baseball in some bush league on the account I am too old for the Big Time. **1928** Foy & Harlow *Clowning Thro' Life* 75 Such plays as Brutus, Virginius, etc., . . . were considered big time stuff half a century ago. **1947** *Sooner Mag.* Nov. 18/1 O.U. is a 'big-time' university with three campuses at Norman, including two large Navy bases and the medical school and hospitals campus at Oklahoma City. — **(23)** **1896** *N.Y. Dramatic News* 29 Aug. 6/1 If times were not so hard the large 'big top' would not have held the people. **1946** *U. of C. Mag.* Dec. 9/2 The fact is that he was not really a good showman under the academic big-top. **1948** *Dly. Ardmoreite* (Ardmore, Okla.) 12 May 5/2, I stood with a circus official one night watching the workmen take down the 'big top' and smaller tents.

For **big figure, hominy, lick, noon, pay, stiff, strike,** see the nouns.

b. In more occasional or rare combs., chiefly obs.: (1) **big bore,** a rifle of large caliber; (2) **buggery,** conceit, arrogance; (3) **bugocracy,** "big bugs" collectively; (4) **dust,** a sham or fraud, *slang;* (5) **fish,** a "big bug," *slang;* (6) **horn,** (see quot. and cf. **4.** (5) above); (7) **Ike,** a person of great importance, esp. in his own estimation, *colloq.;* (8) **noise,** a "big bug," *slang;* (9) **show,** a big league baseball club, *slang;* (10) **smoke, squeeze,** a "big bug," *slang;* (11) **swimming,** (see quot.); (12) **water,** the Mississippi River, from the significance, "big river," of its name; (13) **wheel,** (see quot.).

(1) **1843** Carlton *New Purchase* II. xxxvi. 31, I had a powerful big bore to fix for a feller going out West. — **(2)** **1843** Carlton *New Purchase* I. xxv. 235 Mistaken opinions in the neighbours about 'Mr. Carlton's bigbuggery and stuckupness.' — **(3)** **1865** *Three Yrs. Among Working Classes in U.S.* 14 Republican 'big bugocracy' sports its jewels, silks and drapery. — **(4)** **1844** M. C. Field in Sol. Smith *Theatr. Apprent.* 207 'Well, you're a big dust of a doorkeeper!' said the rowdy as he went in.

(5) **1836** Howard *Stewart* 139 He is a big fish—anything he says will be believed. — **(6)** **1859** Bartlett 31 The 'big horn,' for the last trumpet, is almost profane. — **(7)** **1902** Harben *Abner Daniel* 72 He's a big Ike in some church in Atlanta. — **(8)** **1927** Vachell *Dew of the Sea* 268 You're the big noise; you own this castle. — **(9)** **1912** C. Mathewson *Pitching* i. 1. During his first two years in the big show. . . . [he] looked like a cripple at the plate.

(10) **1936** Barnard *Rider* 133 He had charge of all the roundups and arranged dates upon which to hold them, and was considered a big smoke. **1912** London *Smoke Bellew* 13 He's the editor and proprietor and all-round big squeeze of *The Billow.* — **(11)** **1923** J. H. Cook *On Old Frontier* 55 This first year that I was on the trail, every river from the Red River to the Arkansas was 'big swimming,' as the boys termed it. — **(12)** **1896** Mark Twain *Tom Sawyer, Detective* iii. 351 (R.), The boat was slipping along, swift and steady, through the big water in the smoky moonlight. — **(13)** **1853** Strickland *Twenty-seven Yrs.* II. 292 The Grecian lady spun with a distaff, and had never known the superior aid of the modern spinningwheel, much less the great-wheel, or big-wheel, as our American neighbours call the Irish importation.

c. In proper names and in nicknames: (1) **Big Belly,** an Indian of an Algonquian stock or tribe now settled in Montana, usu. pl., with reference to the tribe, cf. **Gros Ventre;** (2) **bend,** see as a main entry; (3) **Devils,** the Watopachnato, a division of the Assiniboin Indians, *obs.;* (4) **Dipper,** see **dipper;** (5) **Ditch,** see as a main entry; (6) **Drink,** *(a)* the Mississippi River, *obs.*, *(b)* the Atlantic Ocean, *rare;* (7) **Fan,** (see quots. and cf. **Danite, *fan,** *v.* **2.**), *obs.;* (8) **Father,** see ***father 2,** quot. 1867; (9) **Four,** a combination of four important things, persons, etc., esp. the Cleveland, Cincinnati, Chicago, and St. Louis Railroad; (10) **General,** *local* (see quot.); (11) **Hungry,** a nickname for the poor country region around Tuskegee, Ala., site of Tuskegee Institute; (12) **Knife,** a designation formerly used by Indians for an American, esp. a Virginian, as contrasted with an Englishman, also transf., cf. **great knife, long knife** [see A. Matthews in *The Nation* 14 March 1901, pp. 213–4]; (13) **Muddy,** the Missouri River, from the notion, prob. erroneous, that this translates the Indian name; (14) **Pasture,** (see quot.); (15) **Timber,** (see quot. 1848); (16) **Woods,** (see quot.).

(1) **1805** A. Henry *Journal* 338 They are much more agricultural than their neighbors, the Big Bellies, raising an immense quantity of corn, beans, squashes, tobacco. **1812** J. C. Luttig *Jrnl. Exped. Upper Mo.* (1920) 68 They reported that a Skulking Big belly entered the Village at dark yesterday and Killed 1 Ree. **1841** De Smet *Letters* (1843) 52 A country still more exposed to the incursions of the Black Feet, the Assiniboins, the Big Bellies, the Arikaras, the Scioux. — **(3)** **1814** Biddle *Lewis & Clark Exped.* I. 61 Yanktons of the (North or) Plains, or Big Devils, who rove on the heads of the Sioux, Jacques, and Bed rivers; the most numerous of all the tribes numbering about 500 men.

(6) *(a)* **1844** *N.O. Picayune* 24 Mar. 2/2 There never would have been any Atlantic ocean if it hadn't been for the Mississippi, nor never will be after we've turned the waters of that big drink into the Mammoth Cave! **1867** W. H. Dixon *New America* I. 59 The states lying east of the Mississippi [are divided from] the states and territories lying west of the Big Drink. *(b)* **1884** *Illustr. Lond. News* 1 Nov. 410/1 Many of the Transatlantics will doubtless take a journey across what they call the 'big drink' to hear her. — **(7)** **1843** Henry Caswall *Prophet 19th Cent.* 154 They amounted to about three hundred, and, at first, took the name of the 'Big Fan' in reference to their purpose of separating the dissenters from the 'church' like chaff from grain. **1852** Gunnison *Mormons* 109 The chief persons organized a secret society, with signs and 'Key-words,' called the Big Fan, and afterwards known as the Danites. — **(9)** **1886** *Outing* Nov. 156/1 The trial races . . . proved beyond a doubt that the *Mayflower* was the queen of the 'big four.' **1890** Wheeler & Cardwill *W. A. W.* p. vi, Big 4 Route. . . . Best Modern Day Coaches on all Trains. **1948** *Dly. Ardmoreite* (Ardmore, Okla.) 2 May 2/1 All the 'big four' meat packers took steps today to speed up meat production, despite the 48-day-old strike.

(10) **1848** J. Mitchell *Nantucketisms* 40 *Big General,* The largest bill of a fishing vessel. — **(11)** **1943** Holt *Carver* 105 This little corner of his kingdom, stretching as far as the main line of the railroad, was known deservedly as Big Hungry. — **(12)** **1750** Gist *Journals* 36 Upon his understanding I came from Virginia, he called Me the Big Knife. **1779** *Va. State P.* I. 316 The Grand Kite and his Nation living at Port St. Vincent told Mr. Hamilton that he and his people was Big Knives and would not give their hands anymore to the English. **1817** J. Bradbury *Travels* 95 The Americans are called 'the Big Knives' by the Indians of the Missouri. [**1899** H. B. Cushman *Hist. Indians* 439 The big knives (referring to the swords of the officers) are coming on us and we will all be killed.] — **(13)** **1825** in S. F. Cooper *Rural Hours* (1850) 481 Ye plains where sweet Big-Muddy rolls along, And Teapot, one day to be found in song. **1948** *Newsweek* 30 Aug. 21/3 We're going clear to the Missouri River and smash this stuff back across the Big Muddy. — **(14)** **1873** Beadle *Undevel. West* xxii. 436 Our route this afternoon and to-night is through the 'Big Pasture' of America. It extends from latitude 52°, in British America, to Texas, and has an average width of 250 miles.

(15) **1821** J. Fowler *Journal* 16 The Indeans advise us to cross the Arkensaw at the big timber. **1848** Ruxton *Adventures* 277 Our next camping-place was the 'Big Timber,' a large grove of cotton-woods on the left bank of the [Arkansas] river, and a favorite wintering-place of the Cheyennes. — **(16)** **1870** McClung *Minnesota* 14 The Big Woods is a belt of hard timber, 100 miles long by about 40 wide, extending south-westerly from Crow Wing to Rice and Blue Earth counties, interspersed with numerous prairies, lakes and natural meadows, and embracing the richest arable land in the Northwest.

d. For *to cut a big swath,* see **cut,** *v.*, for *biggest toad in the puddle,* see **toad.**

bigamize ˈbɪgəˌmaɪz, *v. intr.* To commit bigamy. *Rare.* — *a*1861 T. Winthrop *F. Brent* vi. 61 When he came back the pretty girl had bigamized.

*** big bend.**

1. A region adjacent to, or embraced by, a large bend in a river, esp. (*cap.*) such a region in northern Oregon and southern Washington near the Columbia River.

1817 *N.Y. Herald* 12 July 1/3 We fell in with an Indian trail, which we followed a circuitous route, bearing for the big bend of St. Mary's [in Fla.]. **1855** *N.Y. Herald* 29 Nov. 2/4 The depredations thus far committed have been all between what is called Big Bend on Rogue river and the ferry at the crossing of the Oregon trail leading to Jacksonville. **1947** *Can. Alpine Jrnl.* June 138 They . . . soon reached the shore of the lower lake opposite Jasper House, having been ten days travelling from Boat Encampment on the Big Bend.

attrib. **1889** *Union Pac. R.R. Ore. & Wash.* 122 To the west, is the Washington Central—and stretching out in the same direction the Seattle, Lake Shore and Eastern, both penetrating the Big Bend country.

2. A region in southwestern Texas. Also attrib.

1931 DOBIE *Coronado* 158 The great bow thus made, its string the Southern Pacific Railroad and its arc the Rio Grande, is known as the Big Bend country of Texas. 1947 *Sierra Club* (So. Calif. Chap.) *Sched.* 125, 16 Enjoy this newest of our National Parks, located in the 'Big Bend' of the Rio Grande along the Mexican Border.

3. Big Bend State, (see quot. 1948).

1886 *Chi. W. News* 29 Apr. 4/3 Tennessee is the Big Bend state, from the circular course of its main river, but its people are Cotton-Manies. 1948 MENCKEN *Supp.* II. 639 At various times Tennessee has also been known as the *Big Bend State*, the *Hog and Hominy State* and the *Lion's Den.*

big-cone(d). In the names of western trees: (1) **big-coned fir,** = **big-cone spruce;** (2) **pine,** the Coulter pine of California, the cones of which sometimes reach a length of fourteen inches and weigh six pounds; (3) **spruce,** a tree, *Pseudotsuga macrocarpa*, resembling the Douglas spruce, also **big-cone hemlock spruce.**

(1) 1851 in SCHOOLCRAFT *Indian Tribes* (1853) III. 104 One of the big-coned firs was noticed. — (2) 1906 *Out West* Mar. 181 (*caption*), The big-cone pine (*Pinus Coulteri*). 1923 SAUNDERS *So. Sierras Calif.* 31 Because of its monster cones, the mountain folk generally speak of the tree as the big-cone pine, but I like to think of it as Coulter pine—the name the botanists record it by (*Pinus coulteri*), in honor of its discoverer, Dr. Thomas Coulter. — (3) 1906 *Out West* Mar. 175 The cone of the Big-cone Hemlock Spruce of the San Bernardino Mountains is five to seven inches long. 1908 SUDWORTH *Forest Trees Pac. Slope* 104 Bigcone spruce, which is a little-known tree, is distinct in appearance and conspicuous among its usually lower growing associates. 1948 *So. Sierran* Apr. 1/3 At Sturtevant's Camp in Santa Anita Canyon stands a Big Cone Spruce 185 feet high and 18 feet in circumference.

Big Ditch.

1. The Erie Canal. Also attrib.

1825 in *Amer. Sp.* (1946) XXI. 305/1 The project (for what was called by its friends 'the great Canal,' and by its opponents the 'big ditch,') met with considerable, and very able opposition. 1835 H. C. TODD *Notes* 64 The Erie canal . . . was at first attempted to be laughed down, under the cognomen of 'The Big, and Clinton's Ditch.' 1872 *Harper's Mag.* May 841/1 Tammany used the 'big ditch' scheme as one of the most effective weapons against him [*sc.* Clinton].

b. Also other canals (see quots.).

1880 *Cimarron News & Press* 19 Aug. 3/3 The head of water in the Big Ditch is pretty fair and so are the clean ups. 1928 *Collier's* 25 Aug. 15/4 Many's the day . . . before I'll forget that voyage . . . , Panama City, the Big Ditch with its marvelous locks; . . . Balboa, Colon, Havana. 1948 *Sat. Ev. Post* 9 Oct. 15/1 Our vaunted Big Ditch is vulnerable to planes, submarines—and saboteurs.

c. The Atlantic Ocean. *Rare.*

1909 WASON *Happy Hawkins* 11, I'm the biggest fool this side o' the big ditch.

2. *W.* The main ditch in an irrigation system. Cf. **acequia madre.**

1894 *Irrigation Age* April 165/1 The survey for the big ditch on the North river, near Julesburg, is being pushed rapidly forward.

bighead ˈbɪgˌhed, *n.*

1. A disease, as osteoporosis, of horses and cattle causing an enlargement of the head.

1805 *Lancaster* (Pa.) *Intelligencer* 3 Dec. (*advt.*), [A brown steer had] what they call the Big Head. 1887 *Courier-Journal* 16 Jan. 16/6 A veterinary authority tells us that 'the "big-head" of the Mississippi valley is the manifestation of a general fault in nutrition.'

2. Any one of various fish having large heads.

1820 RAFINESQUE *Ichth. Ohiensis* 49 Vulgar names, Chub, Bigmouth, and Big-head. It has really the largest head and mouth of this tribe. 1842 *Nat. Hist. N.Y., Zoology* IV. 204 Chub, Big-head, *Leuciscus cephalus.* 1889 *Cent.* 549/3 *Bighead*, a local name of a California species of sculpin, *Scorpoenichthys marmoratus*, a fish of the family *Cottidae.* Also called *cabezon.*

3. Conceit, egotism. *Colloq.*

[1846 *Warsaw* (Ill.) *Signal* 6 Feb. 3/1 A certain Jack-mormon of Hancock county, we won't call him big head, (but the Saints used to) is in the habit of shaving the hair off his forehead, in order to give it an intellectual appearance.] 1850 H. C. LEWIS *La. Swamp Doctor* 157 Pride, that busy devil that . . . lets human nature die of the big-head before common sense can bleed freely. 1902 LORRIMER *Lett. Merchant* 226 A boss with a case of big-head will fill an office full of sore heads.

b. Hence **bigheadism,** *rare.*

1856 CARTWRIGHT *Autobiog.* xxviii. 431 It was surely begotten in the regions, or sprang from the soil of 'Bigheadism.'

bike baɪk, *n.* A bicycle. *Colloq.* — 1882 *Wheelman* I. 189 Much I should like To know why you . . . take such a header From off of your 'bike.' 1947 *Denver Post* 23 Feb. A. 5/2 Denver's bike riding population is growing with the rest of the city.

bike baɪk, *v. intr.* To ride on a bicycle. Hence **biker, biking,** *n. Colloq.*

1883 *Wheelman* I. 336 It seemed as if Nature had rallied all her forces for one grand attack on us three poor, miserable 'bikers.' *Ib.*, We very modestly declined, informing them that 'biking' and drinking are inconsistent. 1895 *N.Y. Dramatic News* 6 July 7/2 Frank Weston and his wife . . . are to be seen 'biking' it nearly every evening. 1947 *Trail & Timberline* Feb. 20/1 Another time we biked around.

∗**Bilboa,** *n.* A variety of potato. *Obs.* — 1830 J. F. WATSON *Philadelphia* 718 Probably about 65 years ago, they then first introduced a larger kind, more like the present in use, which were called, in New England, the Bilboa. . . . In Pennsylvania the same kind of potatoes were called Spanish potatoes.

∗**biled,** see **boiled.**

biler, see **boiler.**

∗**bilge,** *v. intr.* To fail in one's studies at the U.S. Naval Academy and be forced to resign. *Slang.* — 1917 MORGAN *Recollections* 215, I discovered that he was an old classmate of mine at Annapolis who had 'bilged.'

∗**bilious,** *n.* **1.** (See quot. 1870.) **2.** ∗**bilious fever,** yellow fever. Both *obs.*

(1) 1819 THOMAS *Travels* 213 The prevailing diseases of this country are *bilious*, which sometimes terminate in malignant typhus. 1870 *Nation* 28 July 57/1 To be 'overing the bilious' is to be getting well of the bilious fever. — (2) 1802 DRAYTON *S. Carolina* 27 The *typhus icterodes*, or putrid bilious or yellow fever, is however particularly local to Charleston. 1831 PECK *Guide* 230 The bilious fever put on its most malignant type.

∗**bill,** *n.*[1]

1. A dramatic entertainment or performance, esp. in vaudeville.

1855 W. B. WOOD *Recoll. Stage* 155 Warren had prepared, as he conceived, a strong bill on the return from New York of Jefferson and myself. 1896 *N.Y. Dramatic News* 4 April 14/2 Vernona Jarbeau fairly led Keith's bill.

2. An order for lumber cut to specified dimensions, or the lumber so cut. Also **bill stuff.**

1864 in EASTERBY *S.C. Rice Plant.* (1945) 312 Do you Remember a conversation betwen me and you in refferance to Sawing a bil of lumber for Mr Buchanan. 1881 *Chi. Times* 16 April, Last fall our mill shut down with contracts for bill stuff still on their order books. 1910 *Country Life* 15 Dec. 189/2 From the plan you can see just what wood you need, and its dimensions—in other words, your 'bill of lumber.'

3. In combs.: (1) **billboard,** a bulletin board, often a large flat-surfaced structure put up in a conspicuous place for advertising purposes; (2) ∗**book,** a billfold, a pocketbook; (3) **clerk,** a clerk who makes out bills; (4) **fold(er),** a form of pocketbook for carrying bills; (5) **puffing,** "puffing" by advertising in playbills, *rare;* (6) **stuff,** (see **2.** above).

(1) 1851 W. K. NORTHALL *Curtain* 15 With excusable vanity, the bill-boards of the Park . . . still continued to style the Park 'The Theatre.' 1948 *This Week Mag.* 9 Oct. 22/2 Stay away from empty lots and don't walk near billboards. — (2) 1905 *N.Y. Times* 3 Feb. 3 In a billbook in an inside pocket were many checks for various sums on Plainfield banks. — (3) 1909 O. HENRY *Options* (1916) 77 Young New Yorkers who might be millionaires or bill clerks. — (4) *Ib.* 35 When he drew out his bill-folder to pay the cabman you couldn't help seeing hundreds and thousands of dollars in it. 1947 *Democrat* 16 Oct. 7/3, I must have dropped it when I opened my billfold.

(5) 1855 W. B. WOOD *Recoll. Stage* 451 Newspaper and bill puffing and lying, and every other possible sort of vaunting, swaggering, and imposition.

b. In phrases: (1) ∗*bill of credit,* a form of paper money issued by the colonies and later by Congress and some of the states, now *hist.;* (2) ∗*Bill of Rights,* the first ten amendments to the Constitution of the U.S., also transf.; (3) *bill of liberty,* an indenture of chattel slavery signed by a slave upon being taken to Texas, *obs.;* (4) *to fill the bill,* to come up to expectations or requirements, *colloq.*

(1) 1695 SEWALL *Diary* I. 399 Voted . . . an additional Impost for a fund of 4000. Bills of Credit. 1704 *Boston News-Letter* 31 July 2/1 A Proclamation. Whereas it's manifest, That some evil minded Persons . . . have attempted to Counterfeit the Twenty Shilling Bill of Credit on this Province. 1840 *Niles' Reg.* 28 March 63/2 Does not this bill authorise the issue of 'bills of credit,' to circulate and be used as money by the government and the people? 1948 *Chi. Tribune* 14 Nov. (Grafic Mag.) 4/2 One week after Bunker Hill the issuance of 2,000,000 dollars' worth of bills of credit was sanctioned. — (2) 1798 MANNING *Key of Liberty* 11 In the Bill of Rights it declares all men

to be free & equel. **1874** B. F. TAYLOR *World on Wheels* 49 Though the herder is quiet, civil, self-reliant, yet he is a peripatetic Bill of Rights. **1948** *Kankakee* (Ill.) *D. Jrnl.* 5 June 12/3 The first ten amendments to the Constitution of the United States, called the Bill of Rights, are clear. — **(3) 1844** in *Amer. Sp.* XVIII. 120 There are hundreds, and hundreds of thousands, who have drawn similar bills of liberty. — **(4) 1860** *Ill. Agric. Soc. Trans.* IV. 471 Shaker's Seedling [strawberry] Dr. W. hopes well from because of its great vigor, but doubts if it fills the bill. **1945** *Mass. Audubon Soc. Bul.* Feb. 8 When good shrub cover is at a distance from the house and no tree is handy from which to hang a feeder, one upon a post will fill the bill.

As the last term in **abolition, advance, Alabama, Angel, Australian, board, boarding, butter, butter boat, cinch, Civil Rights, colony, corporation, Crown Point, doctor, dollar, embargo, enabling, enrolled, exchequer, fee, five cent, five dollar (bank), force, fractional, fugitive slave, gag, homestead, horse, house, Indian appropriation, irrigation, Jim Crow, Kansas, Nebraska, Kentucky, lame duck, land, land bank, land grant, land relief, loan office, lumber, Old Charter, omnibus, pension, pop gun, pork, pork barrel, portledge, post, province, public, rate, revenue, ripper, sale, Sherman Anti-trust, sight, silver, soup house, store, ten-dollar, time, treasury, under, wait, wash, way, Wild, wildcat bill.**

* **bill,** *n.*[2] In combs.: (1) **billbug,** any one of various weevils with long snouts, injurious to grass and cereal crops; (2) **fish,** any one of various fishes, as the garfish, having long narrow bodies and pike-like snouts; (3) **hold,** a hold on one's nose, *humorous, rare;* (4) **scale,** (see quot.).

(1) 1861 *Harper's Mag.* Aug. 319/1 The next . . . belongs to the family of *Rhyncophorus*, or 'Weevils.' . . . It is familiarly called at the South and West, 'Bill-bug,' 'Corn-borer,' and 'Cane-piercer.' **1909** *Cent. Supp.* 133/3 The genus *Sphenophorus* [includes] . . . Blue-grass bill-bug . . . Calloused bill-bug . . . Clay-colored bill-bug . . . Sculptured corn bill-bug . . . Tenacious bill-bug. — **(2)** [**1782** P. H. BRUCE *Memoirs* xii. 424 The sea hereabouts [Bahamas, etc.] abounds with fish unknown to us in Europe, . . . bill-fish, hound-fish, etc.]. **1793** *Mass. H.S. Coll.* III. 119 We also have the bill-fish in great plenty in the month of October. **1884** GOODE *Amer. Fishes* I. 458 'Bill-fish' . . . is also applied by our fishermen to the slender species [of silver garfishes] of the sword-fish family. — **(3) 1833** *Ky. Gazette* 18 May, It would have been well to let the Old Chief take a *bill-hold* upon him. — **(4) 1889** *Cent., s. v.* Bill-scale: The hard scale or nib on the tip of the beak of a chick, aiding it to peck the shell in order to make its escape from the egg.

As the last term in **hen, hook, ivory, moon, over, ring, saw, shovel, sickle, white bill.**

* **bill,** *v.*

1. *To bill out,* to allocate or assign in or by a bill. *Obs.*

1735 *N.H. Hist. Soc. Coll.* II. 76 [A committee was] appointed to bill out this money according to the proprietors' directions.

2. To consign (freight) by rail to a destination.

1867 *Vt. Rep.* XL. 326 The Station agent . . . billed the plaintiff's goods through to Charlestown, Mass. **1922** TITUS *Timber* 165 Thursday afternoon John was in Pancake, billing out another shipment of his lumber.

3. To divorce (a wife). *Rare.*

1885 H. H. JACKSON *Zeph* ii. 42 He's a blamed fool he don't bill her.

* **billiard,** *n. attrib.* In combs., as (1) **billiard hall,** a room or hall in which billiards is played; (2) **parlor,** a room or establishment where billiards is played; (3) **saloon,** =prec.

(1) 1873 *Winfield* (Kansas) *Courier* 18 Jan. 3/2 The lower room [of the gallery building] will soon be occupied . . . as a saloon and billiard hall. **1882** *Wheelman* I. 103 The smoky and spirituous atmosphere of the card-room or billiard-hall. — **(2) 1906** MARK TWAIN *Speeches* (1910) 269 One day a stranger came to town and opened a billiard-parlor. — **(3) 1840** *N.Y. Mercury* 6 Sep. 3/5 (*advt.*), Billiard Saloon.—187 Broadway, directly opposite John Street. **1875** MARK TWAIN *Old Times on Miss.* xvii. (1876) 144 Bogart's billiard-saloon was a great resort for pilots in those days.

billiardist ˈbɪljədɪst, *n.* One who plays billiards.

1865 *Phila. Sun. Mercury* 15 Oct. 6/3 Nelms, the great billiardist, covered himself with glory. **1898** *N.Y. Journal* 29 Aug. 8/3 Two wonderful little billiardists. **1948** FUNK *Hog on Ice* 109 The real story of the phrase, according to Charles C. Peterson, the noted billiardist, is that it originated in 1919 in a billiard room on John Street, New York.

* **billiards,** *n.* As the last term in **horse, Presbyterian billiards.**

* **billion,** *n.* A thousand million.

The Amer. usage here follows the French, cf. F. *billion.* In the English and German method of numeration, a billion is a million million, or 1,000,000,000,000.

1834 DAVIES *School Arithmetic* 13, 6,245,289,421 [reads] 6 Billions, 245 millions, 289 thousand, 421. **1904** E. B. HOLT, tr. Munsterberg *Americans* 91 The total sum of appropriations in one session of Congress amounted to over $1,000,000,000, in America called a billion. **1948** *Cong. Rec.* 705/2 Mr. Speaker, I should like to strike the word 'billion' out of the English language. . . . I prefer the actual statement of a thousand millions.

billionaire ˌbɪljənˈɛr, *n.* One whose wealth amounts to a billion dollars or more. Also attrib.

1860 HOLMES *E. Venner* vii, One would like to give a party now and then, if one could be a billionnaire. **1923** *Nation* 25 July 78 Can you contend with a billionaire industrialist? **1947** *Sat. Ev. Post* 8 March 80/3 'Uncle Andy' . . . was a billionaire.

* **billy,** *n.* A policeman's club. See also **hillbilly, old billy.**

1856 *Santa Barbara* (Calif.) *Gaz.* 14 Feb. 2/5 He was knocked down by a blow from a 'billy.' **1903** *N.Y. Times* 11 Sep., Eight men set upon a policeman this morning and after taking his revolver and billy away from him kicked and beat him. **1948** CHAPLIN *Wobbly* 169 The plain-clothesmen charged with upraised 'billies,' smashing right and left through the crowd.

bilsted ˈbɪlstəd, *n.* Also **boilsted, billsted.** [Origin obscure. The suggestion in quot. 1890 seems improbable.] (See quots. 1832, 1890, 1916.)

[**1694** *Annals of Albany* (1850) II. 135 One hundred and fity lood of good oak, ippere, bill, stell or dry pine and ashy.] **1765** R. ROGERS *Acc. N. America* 138 This soil [in N. & S.C.] is a blackish sand, producing . . . ash, laurel, boilsted, &c. **1832** J. F. WATSON *Hist. Tales N.Y.* 164 The general furniture [about 1780] was made of 'billstead,' another name for maple. **1890** *N. & Q.* V. 14 June 79 *Bilsted.*—In some parts of this country the sweet-gum tree (otherwise called copalm, Vol. iv, p. 34; bilster, bilsterd, or liquid-amber) is known as the bilsted. Prof. Meehan derives this word from the Dutch *bijlsteel,* bill-handle, or axe-handle. But I do not see how *bijlsteel* could become *bilsted* except through a misprint. A still more formidable objection is this: there is probably no kind of wood less fitted for axe-handle material than this same bilsted. **1916** SETON *Woodcraft Man.* 288 Sweet Gum, Star-Leaved, or Red Gum, Bilsted, Alligator Tree, or Liquidambar (*Liquidambar Styraciflua*). A tall tree up to 150 feet high of low, moist woods, remarkable for the corky ridges on its bark, and the unsplitable nature of its weak, warping, perishable timber.

bimbo ˈbɪmbo, *n.* [Origin obscure. For sense **1.** cf. * *bumbo* in similar sense. Sense **2.** may be of a different word.] **1.** (See quots.) *Obs.* **2.** An inconsequential person. *Colloq.*

(1) 1837 *Baltimore Commerc. Transcript* 5 Sep. 2/3 (Th.), *Bimbo* is a rascally compound of brandy and sugar, flavored with lemon peal [*sic*]. An invention of the devil to make drunkards. **1853** G. H. DERBY *Phoenixiana* (1856) xxviii. 173 My morning glass of bimbo (a temperance drink, composed of 'three parts of root beer and two of water-gruel, thickened with a little soft squash, and strained through a cane-bottomed chair'). — **(2) 1919** *Amer. Mag.* Nov. 69/1 Nothing but the most heroic measures will save the poor bimbo. **1928** *Chi. Tribune* 7 Oct. (Comics) 2 I'll show these bimboes how to tackle. **1948** *L.A. Times* 8 Aug. II. 5/5 Lots of people who would treat a bimbo, a Ford or a pup kindly treat their comedones very roughly indeed.

* **bin,** *n.* As the last term in **apple, feed, toll bin.**

bind baɪnd, *v.* [Erroneously for * *bound, v.*] *intr.* To have the boundary, to border *on* a place. *Obs.*

1677 *N.Y. State Col. Hist.* XII. 574 From thence southwest binding vpon a little Creeke one hundred & Eighty five pertches to a marked white oake. **1746** *N.H. Probate Rec.* III. 454 His single share . . . runs North . . . then binding on said way by the water side. **1808** *Mass. Spy* 11 May (Th.), [New York] binds on Lake Erie to Niagara, on the whole extent of Lake Ontario, [etc.] . . . Vermont binds on lakes which communicate with Canada. **1899** GREEN *Va. Word-Book* 59 Land binding on the north side of the inlet.

* **binder,** *n.* A machine that cuts and binds grain into bundles.

1857 *Ill. Agric. Soc. Trans.* II. 120 A self raker, and even a binder, may be just as simple in its structure as some *hand raker,* considering what it does. **1948** *Life* 23 Aug. 103 On every farm . . . reapers and binders churned the crop, shockers in straw hats followed behind to set up the bundles into rows of shocks.

b. binder twine, =**binding twine.**

1946 *Reader's Digest* Jan. 141/2 They flew it with five balls of binder twine. **1946** WILSON *Fidelity* 183 In fact, the cracker that came on the whip was usually replaced, when it wore out, with a piece of binder twine.

As the last term in **cinch, high, self-, twine, wire binder.**

bindery ˈbaɪndərɪ, *n.* [Cf. Du. *binderij.*] A place where books are bound. See also **book bindery.**

1810 I. THOMAS *Printing* I. 402 At Worcester Mass., he also . . . set up a bindery. **1888** PERRIN *Ky. Pioneer Press* 25 In 1808 he sold his bindery. **1946** *Chi. D. News* 29 Aug. 8/6 (*heading*), Bindery Union Agrees To NLRB Election.

∗**binding,** *n.* As the last term in **self-binding, twine binding.**

binding twine. A coarse, loosely twisted twine for use in binders. — **1890** *Cong. Rec.* Aug. 9260/1 The observations of . . . [Senator Davis] in respect to binding-twine are very important to the people of La. **1948** *Sat. Ev. Post* 24 April 102/3 McAlester made binding twine for the farmers.

bindle ˈbɪndl̩, *n.* [App. var. of ∗*bundle.*]

1. (See quot.)

1916 *Lit. Digest* 19 Aug. 425/1 A package is a 'bindle,' derived from 'bundle.'

2. bindle man, roll, stiff, (see quots.). *Slang.*

1900 FLYNT *Itinerant Policeman* 167 Among the 'Bindle Men,' 'Mush Fakers,' and 'Turnpikers' of the middle West, the East, and Canada, there exists a crude system of marking 'good' houses. **1925** *Forum* Aug. 232 Carrying his 'bindle roll' or roll of blankets on his back, he is prepared to make his home wherever night finds him. *Ib.* 235 *Bindle stiff*—a western hobo, who carries his blankets in a roll or bindle. **1946** R. PEATTIE *Pac. Coast Ranges* 233 The bindle stiff who got gay with the boss was a lucky boy if he lived with the wish to fight another day.

Bing cherry. A dark, sweet cherry introduced by S. Lewelling of Milwaukie, Oregon, in 1875. — **1925** BAILEY *Cyclo. Hort.* I. 741/1 Black Tartarian, Lewelling and Bing are the mainstay for black cherries. **1948** *L.A. Times* 2 May (Home Mag.) 32/3 If canned bing cherries are used, thicken juice with a little cornstarch.

bingle ˈbɪŋgl̩, *n.* [Origin obscure.] In baseball, a safe hit. *Slang.* — **1902** *Sporting Life* 6 Sep. 4 He is not a good ground coverer, loses bingle after bingle near second base and is a light hitter. **1948** *Dly. Oklahoman* (Okla. City) 13/6 Lombardi limited the Indians to one bingle in the five shutout innings.

bingo ˈbɪŋgo, *n.* [In **1.** of obscure origin; in **2.** imitative.]

1. A game resembling lotto.

1936 *Time* 21 Dec. 26/2 In many a U.S. Catholic diocese during the past few years the simple gambling game of bingo (or beano, or keno) has served as a principal money-raiser. **1948** *Chi. D. News* 1 March 1/7 Their parents played bingo to help pay for a community fire truck.

2. An exclamation indicative of a sudden sharp impact. *Colloq.*

1937 *Amer. Sp.* Oct. 244/1 Anyone who has taken part in outdoor sports, either as a player or spectator, has heard the exclamation 'bingo.' **1948** *Sat. Ev. Post* 7 Aug. 22/2 That was bingo, right there.

binnacle ˈbɪnəˌkl̩, *n.* Also **binacle, binocle.** *local.* [App. f. Du. *binnen,* within, inner +*kil,* channel.] A side channel of a river, a millrace.

1860 in *D.N.* II. 132 Along the shore of said river at low water mark to a point at the mouth of the binacle, then up along the western side of said binacle at low water mark. **1881** J. BURROUGHS *Pepacton* i. (1895) 19 There was a whirlpool, a rock eddy, and a binocle within a mile. **1902** CLAPIN, *Binnacle,* in parts of New York, the flume of a mill stream, a mill race.

∗**biograph,** *n.* A trade-mark for an early form of motion picture machine. Also attrib. Cf. **mutoscope.**

1896 *Chi. Tribune* 20 Dec. 39/7 The American Biograph . . . producing views of natural scenes with most perfect detail. **1901** *Everybody's Mag.* Aug. 227/1 On the night of October 26, 1896, the first biograph pictures were shown to the American public. **1904** *St. Louis Globe-Democrat* 3 July 9/5.

∗**biography,** *n.* As the last term in **campaign, congressional biography.**

∗**birch,** *n.* and *a.*

1. Used with qualifying terms to designate American varieties of birch, as **aspen-leaved, brown (bark) birch,** (see quots.).

1785 H. MARSHALL *Amer. Grove* 19. **1916** SETON *Woodcraft Man.* 278 Gray Birch or Aspen-leaved Birch (*Betula populifolia*). A small tree found on dry and poor soil; rarely 50 feet high. . . . It has a black triangular scar at each armpit. — **1903** AUSTIN *Land of Little Rain* 132 The willow and brown birch, . . . have come back to the streamside. *Ib.* 221 The brown-bark western birch [is] characteristic of lower stream tangles.

b. running birch, (see quot.).

1931 CLUTE *Plants* 69 The running birch (*Chiogenes hispida*) is a heathwort, but its aromatic leaves make it a birch on the popular tongue.

See also **bog, broom, canoe, cherry, European white, gray, old field, paper, pin, poplar, poplar-leaved, poverty, red, river, scrub, silver, sugar, sweet, water, white, yellow birch.**

2. A canoe made of birchbark. Cf. **birch-builder.**

1858 THOREAU in *Atlantic Mo.* June 4/2 The lake to-day was rougher than I found the ocean, either going or returning, and Joe remarked that it would swamp his birch. **1895** *Outing* Oct. 47/1 The precious birch was secured to its sled, and anxiously watched by all hands.

3. In combs.: (1) ∗**birchbark,** see as a main entry; (2) **beer,** a beverage of slight alcoholic content obtained from the birch, also a carbonated soft drink flavored to resemble this; (3) **bucket,** a bucket made of birchbark; (4) **builder,** a maker of birchbark canoes; (5) **canoe,** a canoe made of birchbark; (6) **horn, =moose call;** (7) **land,** land upon which birch is the prevailing growth; (8) **partridge,** (see quot. 1917); (9) **stump,** the stump of

Birchbark canoe

a birch tree; (10) **swamp,** a swamp in which birch is the prevailing growth.

(2) **1883** *Wheelman* I. 392 We reached Bushkill at 12:30 P.M., stopping—for birch beer—at odd places. **1929** *Amer. Sp.* IV. 387, I have heard also of . . . *birch beer* and *dandelion beer,* but have been unable to find out anything very definite about these beverages. **1948** PEATTIE *Berkshires* 65 Birch beer, made by fermenting the sap, is perhaps better known. — (3) **1866** *Rep. Indian Affairs* 293 The mococks (birch buckets) hold from sixty to eighty pounds of sugar. — (4) **a1861** T. WINTHROP *Life in Open Air* (1863) 49 These aborigines are the birch-builders.

(5) **a1649** WINTHROP *Hist.* II. 85 They went up Saco river in birch canoes. **1726** S. PENHALLOW *Indian Wars* (1824) 68 From thence they came to Chamblee, and brought with them three birch canoes. **1916** C. A. EASTMAN *From Deep Woods* 178, I set out with an Ojibway guide in his birch canoe. — (6) **1858** THOREAU *Maine Woods* 101 While Joe was preparing his birch-horn . . . we collected fuel. — (7) **1789** MORSE *Amer. Geog.* 143 One species generally predominating in each soil, has originated the descriptive names of . . . birch, beach and chesnut lands. — (8) **1917** *Birds of Amer.* II. 15/1 But it is called Spruce Partridge in common parlance to distinguish it from the Birch Partridge (Ruffed Grouse), and ornithologists have adopted the popular misnomer, well knowing it to be incorrect. **1947** BUMP *Ruffed Grouse* 4 Throughout the Northeast, where birches were a favorite food, it is commonly known as the 'birch partridge.' — (9) **1684** *Manchester Rec.* 15 From s[ai]d tree cros the Neck . . . to a burtch stump. And from s[ai]d burtch stump to a pine stump. **1760** *N.H. Probate Rec.* III. 375 Thence northeasterly about seventy Rods to a Birch Stump with Stones.

(10) **1660** *Warwick* (R.I.) *Rec.* 326 Bounded . . . on the Southeast towards the burch Swamp. **1740** *N.H. Probate Rec.* II. 240 Fifteen acres of land laying above the Birch Swamp so called.

birch bɜtʃ, *v. intr. To birch it,* to journey in a birchbark canoe. *Rare.* — **1861** WINTHROP *Open Air* 50 He had birched it down to Lake Chestuncook in bygone summers.

∗**birchbark,** *n.*

1. A canoe made of birchbark, in full **birchbark canoe.**

1805 LEWIS in *Ann. 9th Cong.* 2 Sess. 1070 Principally birch bark canoes. **1868** WHYMPER *Alaska* 212 Birch-barks are so easily navigated that I should adopt them exclusively if travelling in that country again. **1945** SERVICE *Ploughman* 419, I became the possessor of the finest birch-bark canoe in the North.

2. Attrib. in the sense "made of or covered with birchbark," as **birchbark basket, box, cradle, dish, hut, lodge, package, tube, wigwam.**

1803 in *Wis. State H.S. Coll.* XX. 417, I bought of a woman a Big birch bark basket Full of rice, that I paid a 2½ pt blanket for. — **a1800** *Spirit Farmers' Museum* (1801) 244 Mother Draper rides, With panniers. . . . Laden with birch bark boxes, berries tart, [etc.]. — **1846** L. M. CHILD *Fact & Fiction* 168 Her mother used to sing to her, when she swung from the boughs in her queer little birch-bark cradle. — **1925** HEMING *Living Forest* 131 This he did by heating stones and then placing them in a birchbark dish containing water. — **1880** *Harper's Mag.* July 181/2 She and Sarah were soon sound asleep in their birchbark hut. — **1907** C. C. ANDREWS *Recollections* 121 A caravan of Red Lake Indians . . . were encamped round in tents or birch bark lodges. — **1903** WHITE *Forest* x. 128 This birch-bark package contains maple sugar. — **1925** HEMING *Living Forest* 127 How to prevent our bowstrings from breaking placing them in a birch-bark tube along with wet moss to keep them moist. — **1829** BASIL HALL *Travels* I. (Edinburgh ed.) 266 Some of the party [of Indians] were encamped under the brushwood, in birch-bark wigwams, or huts.

b. Also (1) **birchbark mocock,** (see **mocock**); (2) **rogan,** a bowl-like receptacle made of birchbark.

(1) **1903** WHITE *Forest* iii. 26 In a loft a birchbark mokok . . . dispenses a faint perfume. — (2) **1925** HEMING *Living Forest* 132 After using our birchbark rogans to fill the canoe half full of water.

* **birchen,** *a.*

1. Having a growth of birch trees. *Obs.*

1657 *Warwick* (R.I.) *Rec.* 297 A 6 acre Lott, on the south side bounded with his own Birchin ffeeld. **1673** *Springfield Rec.* II. 245 Jeremy Horton hath graunted unto him twenty acres of land in the birchen playn above Skeepmuck.

2. birchen bark, The bark of a birch tree.

1643 WILLIAMS *Key* 61 Burching barke, and Chesnut barke which they dresse finely, and make a Summer-covering for their houses. **1826** COOPER *Mohicans* xx, You showed knowledge in the shaping of birchen bark, Uncas, when you chose this from among the Huron canoes. **1870** LOWELL *Study Windows* 304 How would birchen bark, as an educational tonic, have fallen in repute!

3. Made from birchbark or birch wood.

1634 WOOD *N. Eng. Prospect* II. xvi. 90 In the night time they [*sc.* Indians] betake them to their Burtchen Cannows . . . [to catch] the Sturgeon. **1865** PARKMAN *Pioneers of France* 300 Indefatigable canoe-men, in their birchen vessels, light as egg-shells.

bircher, *n.* One who operates a birchbark canoe. *Rare.* — **1861** WINTHROP *Open Air* 51 Cancut, though for this summer boatman or bircher, had other strings to his bow.

* **bird,** *n.*

1. A fellow, guy. *Slang.*

1842 *Spirit of Times* 12 Feb. (Th.), Chippendale slept in the watch-house. . . . Chippendale is certainly a bird. **1924** *S.F. Herald* 3 May 17/3 I've been reading this bird Homer—It's Greek to me. **1946** *Sports Afield* June 25/2 This bird, or some syndicate he represented, had a heavy bet on Black Diamond to win.

b. (See quot.)

1887 A. JENKS in *Lippincott's Mag.* Aug. 291 There are men in every college, of whom Yale has its full number, denominated in student slang as 'birds.' The 'birds' are firm believers in the old Epicurean theory that everything in life is subservient to pleasure.

2. A person or thing of excellence, often *perfect bird. Slang.*

1849 *N.O. Picayune* 3 June 2/4 *Mr. E. P. S.* was the next witness called, a perfect 'bird' in his way, and who can't be beat. **1856** *Knickerb.* April XLVII. 429 A sleigh, drawn by a 'perfect bird' of a three-mile bay mare. **1911** H. QUICK *Yellowstone N.* ix. 230 He's got a disguise that's a bird.

3. A gold coin having an eagle stamped on it. *Obs.* Cf. **eagle.**

1853 SIMMS *Sword & Distaff* 496, I won't trust you . . . ontel the money's put down here, the yellow birds, all a-flying about me. **1857** *Quinland* II. xiv. II. 76 Bill dropped on his knees before her, and put in her white soft hand the 'bird' he had received from Morley.

4. In combs.: (1) **bird band,** a light identification band placed on a bird's leg in studying its range, habits, etc., also **bird bander, banding;** (2) **bank,** (see quot.); (3) **bath,** a shallow receptacle set up in a yard or garden for birds to bathe in; (4) **box,** a box put up for birds to nest in; (5) * **cage,** (see quot. 1938); (6) **charge,** a charge of small shot for shooting birds; (7) **day,** in some states, a day set aside for school children to study birds and their protection; (8) **dog,** a dog trained to hunt birds; (9) **egging frolic,** an excursion for wild-birds' eggs, *rare,* cf. **d.** below; (10) **gun,** a smooth-bore gun for shooting birds; (11) **hawk,** a pigeon hawk, *rare;* (12) **hound,** = **bird dog;** (13) **house,** a small house-like structure for birds to nest in; (14) **-line view,** a bird's eye view, *rare;* (15) **market,** a market where birds are bought and sold; (16) **peep,** dawn, *rare;* (17) **people,** (see quot.); (18) **point,** = **bird stone;** (19) **refuge,** a bird sanctuary; (20) **'s-eye (limestone),** (see quot. 1890); (21) **'s-eye marble,** = prec.; (22) **stone,** (see quot. 1907); (23) **store,** a store where birds are bought and sold; (24) **thrashing,** killing birds at night by thrashing the bushes, thickets, etc., where they roost, also as verb; (25) **woman,** (*a*) (*cap.*) the Shoshoni woman who accompanied Lewis and Clark to the Rocky Mountains and served as a guide, (*b*) a woman who is a lover of birds.

(1) **1914** *Country Life* July 36/2 One of the first questions asked of the bird-bander, is 'How do you get hold of the bird in order to band it?' **1914** *Lit. Digest* 17 Jan. 103/1 He is pursuing several interesting local problems in bird-banding. **1939** *Nat. Geog. Mag.* March 368 My companion placed bird bands around their legs and released them one by one to join their friends in the treetop. — (2) **1835** AUDUBON *Ornith. Biog.* II. 242 They flew directly towards their place of rest [in Cole's Island, S.C.], called the 'Bird Banks.'—(3) **1912** *Collier's* 27 April 34/2 Martin houses and food houses and bird baths like those in this village, are now to be found in every one of the New England States. **1948** *Richmond* (Va.) *News Leader* 6 May 8/2 We carry replacement pots for all bird baths in stock. — (4) **1934** in *Nat. Geog. Mag.* LXV. 578 The homes are located . . . in bird boxes, which are filled with dead leaves and other rubbish.

(5) **1938** ASBURY *Sucker's Progress* 52 It [chuck-a-luck] in recent years has often been called Bird Cage. **1947** BEEBE *Mixed Train Dly.* 291 Then you pass through the roulette room and then the bird cage and hazard room and then you come to the big gaming apartment. — (6) **1876** *Fur, Fin, & Feather* Sep. 135 The doctor soon drew a bird charge from his gun. — (7) **1897** *Land of Sunshine* Dec. 33 The efforts made by our late Secretary of Agriculture, Mr. Morton, toward the adoption of a 'Bird Day' in our public schools, are to be supplemented by the women's clubs. **1901** *World's Work* May 776/1 On May 4th of last year Wisconsin celebrated Arbor and Bird Day. — (8) **1889** *Cent.* **1946** *Democrat* 22 Aug. 2/1 Bill Brooks, of The Brewton Standard, has bought a bird dog. — (9) **1860** *Harper's Mag.* Nov. 753/1 We had choice of a cruise on the Sound for scup fishing, or a bird-egging frolic to Muskegeet.

(10) **1853** SIMMS *Sword & Distaff* 115 This Frenchman . . . owned . . . a miserable little single-barrel bird-gun, small in bore, but something taller than its owner. **1904** GLASGOW *Deliverance* 193 Christopher . . . had waited with his bird-gun in the bushes to shoot Fletcher when he came in sight. — (11) [**1772** FORSTER in *Phil. Trans.* LXII. 382 This species [Pigeon Hawk] is called a small-bird hawk at Hudson's Bay.] **1832** WILLIAMSON *Maine* I. 141 The Whetsaw . . . frequents logging camps; and is thought to be the same as the Bird-hawk, though as to this naturalists differ. — (12) **1913** *Outing* Mar. 767/1 Oliver Blatchford came in second behind a team of Missouri bird hounds. — (13) **1870** F. FERN *Ginger-Snaps* 54, I look at that elaborate little bird-house for sparrows. **1947** EDMINSTER *Fish Ponds* 16 The tree swallows nesting in the birdhouse. — (14) **1803** *Mass. Spy* 8 June (Th.), The bright bird-line view of American glory being thus intercepted.

(15) **1831** AUDUBON *Ornith. Biog.* I. 110 The first brood is frequently brought to the bird-market in New Orleans as early as the middle of April. — (16) **1859** STOWE *Minister's Wooing* xxx, It was jest arter bird-peep. I kinder allers wakes myself den. — (17) **1907** HODGE *Amer. Indians* I. 367 *Crows.* (trans., through French *gens des corbeaux,* of their own name, *Absároke,* crow, sparrowhawk, or bird people). A Siouan tribe forming part of the Hidatsa group, their separation from the Hidatsa having taken place, as Matthews (1894) believed, within the last 200 years. Hayden, following their tradition, placed it about 1776. — (18) **1923** *Arrow Points* 5 Jan. 18 Nearly every one of us enhanced our collection of aboriginal objects by the addition of 'Bird Points' from this ever yielding source. **1948** *Ill State Arch. Soc. Jrnl.* April 40/1 My own finds at the site have consisted of . . . drills and birdpoints. — (19) **1912** *Outing* Dec. 382/1 Marsh Island, on the Louisiana Gulf coast, has been turned into a bird refuge. **1946** *Mazama* Dec. 34/1 The Malheur bird refuge south of Burns has more different kinds of migratory birds visit its sanctuary than any other refuge in the United States.

(20) **1843** *Nat. Hist. N.Y., Geology* III. 38 At Fort-Plain . . . the change from Birdseye to Trenton limestone is perfectly abrupt. *Ib.,* The surface of the upper layers of birdseye, at its point of connection with the superior rock. **1890** *Cent.* 3457/2 Bird's-eye limestone, a part of the Black River limestone, one of the subgroups into which the Lower Silurian has been divided by the New York geologists; so called because it has crystalline points scattered through it which have a fancied resemblance to the eyes of birds. **1894** *State Geol. N.Y. Rep.* 422 Here there is a three-foot bed of dense, dark limestone which has the characteristic white weathering, etc., of Birdseye limestone. — (21) **1857** DANA *Mineralogy* (1872) 365 The bird's-eye marble of Western New York is a compact limestone, with crystalline points scattered through it. **1893** *Stand.* 1079/3 Marble is variously distinguished by special names: (1) from its structural features or resemblances; as, bird's-eye marble, black-and-gold m., [etc.]. — (22) **1881**

ABBOTT *Primitive Industry* 365 The curious carved 'bird stones,' common to our Atlantic coast states, are, as a class, even of greater interest. **1907** HODGE *Amer. Indians* I. 148/1 Bird-stones. A name given to a class of prehistoric stone objects of undetermined purpose, usually resembling or remotely suggesting the form of a bird. **1917** MOORHEAD *Stone Ornaments Amer. Indian* 83 The bird-stones with projections on either side, which by some are called ears, and by others eyes, are quite frequently found in the eastern United States and Canada. — **(23) 1870** *Amer. Naturalist* March IV. 58 There is an albino rat at a bird-store in town. — **(24)** [**1838** GOSSE *Letters* 296 Three or four lads proceeded to some thickets soon after night.... The torch being elevated at some little distance from a thick bush, the lad with the staff began to thresh the bush.] **1886** *Cent. Mag.* Feb. 586/1 The boys were off in the thickets bird-thrashing. **1934** VINES *Green Thicket World* 150 The little group got up a bird thrashing.

(25) (*a*) **1805** LEWIS & CLARK *Orig. Journals* 20 May II. 52 This stream we called Sah-ca-ger-we-ah (Sancagahewa) [*sic*] or bird woman's River, after our interpreter the Snake woman. **1948** *Pac. Northwest Quart.* April 167 Bakeless identifies the aged Indian woman who died on the Shoshone reservation in 1884 as the Bird Woman, but the evidence is not conclusive. (*b*) **1932** *Randolph Enterprise* (Elkins, W. Va.) 5 Feb. 1/1 Jean Stratton Porter's 'Girl of the Limberlost' and 'Freckles' made famous the bird-woman of northern Indiana.... Greenbriar County, W. Va., has been the home of a more real and more interesting bird-woman than ever lived on the pages of any story-book.

b. In the names of plants: (1) **bird bell,** the rattlesnake root, *Prenanthes altissima;* (2) **cherry,** the pin cherry; (3) **eye maple, =bird's-eye (maple),** *obs.;* (4) **foot clover,** bird's-foot clover, *obs.;* (5) **foot violet, =bird's-foot violet;** (6) **grass,** a forage grass, *Poa trivialis,* introduced into the U.S. from Europe, also attrib.; (7) * **'s beak,** any one of various California flowers of the genus *Cordylanthus,* so named from their beak-shaped flowers, also **bird beak;** (8) * **seed,** (see quot.); (9) **'s-eye (maple),** a kind of wood obtained from the sugar maple in which the grain has wavy markings suggestive of a bird's eye; (10) **'s-foot violet,** a common violet of the eastern U.S., having large pansy-like pale blue or purple flowers; (11) **'s nest,** the Indian pipe, *Monotropa uniflora;* (12) **'s nest pine,** (see quot.); (13) **wood,** (see quot.).

(1) 1850 S. F. COOPER *Rural Hours* 283 Another flower, common in our woods just now, is the Bird-bell, the Nabalus of botanists. **1894** *Amer. Folk-Lore* VII. 92 *Prenanthes altissima,* ... bird-bell. N.Y. — **(2) 1931** CLUTE *Plants* 93 Other species besides the cornels that are often called dog-woods are the bird cherry (*Prunus Pennsylvanica*), [etc.]. — **(3) 1807** J. MEASE *Geol. Account of U.S.* (1807) 259 A species of maple abounds in Nova Scotia, and, no doubt, farther south, called bird-eye maple ... very beautiful. **1832** J. F. WATSON *Hist. Tales N.Y.* (1832) 202 Every touch of it (painting of church pulpit) is true of the character of the bird-eye maple, and having the finest possible polish. — **(4) 1814** J. TAYLOR *Arator* 155 The wheat ... has been free from what is called the bird foot clover. **1818** *Ib.* 67 The bird-foot clover, as it is called, is one of considerable promise.

(5) 1840 DEWEY *Mass. Flowering Plants* 78 Bird-foot Violet ... blossoms in May, grows in woods and dry soils; flowers large and blue. **1947** *Midland Naturalist* July 51 Birdfoot Violet [is] rare in sandy margins of pine-oak forest. — **(6) 1785** WASHINGTON *Diaries* II. 361 Sowed 5 Rows and a small piece of the bird grass seed. **1797** I. THOMAS *N. Eng. Farmer* 33 Bird Grass, *Poa avaria, spicalis subbifloris.* Usually known in this country by the name Fowl Meadow Grass. **1890** *Cent.* 4575/3 *P*[*oa*] *trivialis* [is cultivated] as 'bird grass.' — **(7) 1917** SAUNDERS *Western Flower Guide* 192 Bird-beak (*Cordylanthes filifolius*). **1923** —— *So. Sierras Calif.* 139 If you press the sides of the flower together between your finger and thumb, the slender beak opens like the bill of a hungry bird, and it is the most natural thing in the world to call the flower 'bird-beak,' the sensible popular name by which it goes. **1925** JEPSON *Flowering Plants Calif.* 945 Cordylanthus Nutt. Bird's Beak. **1940** JAEGER *Desert Wild Flowers* 244 The name 'bird's-beak' has reference to the flower, which resembles the broad beak of a young bird. — **(8) 1931** CLUTE *Plants* 91 The list of plants named for animals supposed to feed on them is a long one ... bee-balm (*Monarda didyma*), and bird-seed (*Lepidium Virginicum*). — **(9) 1820** HIBERNICUS *Letters* (1822) June 75 Curled maple ... sometimes is shaped into a formation singularly elegant, called *birdseye,* from its appearance. **1820** *Niles' Reg.* XVIII. 152/1 The case ... is of that kind of wood called bird's eye maple. **1948** BOYCE *Forest Pathology* 283 Black walnut and black cherry burls are highly valued for furniture, the figure being somewhat similar to that of bird's-eye maple.

(10) 1839 *Columbian Reg.* (New Haven, Conn.) 19 Feb. 4/5 The pedate violet ... is sometimes called, bird's foot, or parsley violet. **1948** *Sat. Ev. Post* 14 Aug. 27/2 Beyond was the spring where the great velvet bird's-foot violet and yellow lady's-slipper grew. — **(11) 1784** CUTLER in *Mem. Academy* I. 442 Birdsnest. Blossoms yellow. About Great Ossapy pond, in ... New-Hampshire. **1847** WOOD *Botany* 380 Bird's nest ... [is] a small, succulent plant, ... common in woods, near the base of trees, on whose roots it is said to be parasitic. **1889** *Cent.* 561/3 Bird's nest ... [is] a parasitic ericaceous plant ... the leafless stalks of which resemble a nest of sticks. — **(12) 1788** SCHÖPF *Reise* II. 275 Die *Birds-nest Pine,* Vogelnest-Kiefer.—Man hat ihr diesen Namen gegeben, weil längst dem ganzen Stamm eine Menge kleine und kurze buschichte Sprossen durch die Rinde hervorbrechen, welche ihr ein besonderes, und auf den ersten Anblick unterschiedendes Ansehen geben [Charleston, S.C.]. — **(13) 1935** ROLLINS *Discovery Ore. Trail* 225 According to Lilian Linder Fitzpatrick, the name Birdwood is either a parallelism or literal translation of *Zintka-chan wakpala,* the Dakota indians' title for this same stream, each so given because the birdwood or indigo shrub, *Amorpha fruticosa,* was common along its banks.

c. (1) *bird of freedom,* the bald eagle, emblematic of the U.S., also *our country's bird, bird of our country, bird of America;* (2) * *bird of Paradise,* (see quot.); (3) *bird of Washington,* the bald eagle in its immature stage.

(1) 1846 LOWELL *Biglow P.* I. ii, Our country's bird alookin' on an' singin' out hosanner. *Ib.*, I'm safe enlisted for the war, Yourn, Birdofredom Sawin. **1847** *Ib.* iv, Ef the bird of our country could ketch him, she'd skin him. **1848** PARKMAN in *Knickerb.* XXXII. 514 Tête Rouge declaring that he would kill the bird of America, borrowed Delorier's gun and set out on his unpatriotic mission. **1906** *Harper's Mag.* Mar. 638 The short story is peculiarly an American institution, and we are as proud of it as we are of the 'Bird of Freedom.' — **(2) 1858** BAIRD *Birds Pacific R.R.* 169 *Milvulus forficatus,* Scissor-tail, Swallow-tailed Flycatcher, ... [is the] 'Bird of Paradise' of the Texans. — **(3) 1831** AUDUBON *Ornith. Biog.* I. 58 This new species of Eagle, 'The Bird of Washington,' ... is indisputably the noblest bird of its genus that has yet been discovered in the United States. *Ib.* 60–61. **1917** *Birds of Amer.* II. 81 These large immature birds deceived Audubon who thought they were a distinct species and named them 'Birds of Washington.'

d. *Go on with your birds'-egging,* etc., (see quots.). *Colloq.*

1854 S. SMITH *Down East* 32 So now go on with your birds'-egging, and make your Christmas as fast as you please. **1896** *D.N.* I. 412 'That's none of my bird's-egging,' that's none of my affair. 'Go on with your bird's-egging,' go on with your story.

As the last term in **Baltimore, bay, beach, bee, black, blue, brant, brown, buffalo, bush, calumet, cardinal, carpenter, carrion, cat, cattle, cedar, chaparral, cherry, chimney, chip, chipping, corn, cow, cowpen, crown, doe, dough, dumb, dun, eastern blue, eastern snow, egg, fat, fire, fire hang, flat, flutter, fool, French black, French mocking, frost, goose, grass, gray, ground, gull, hair, hang-, hanging, heart, hemp, hominy, hum, humming, indigo, Jersey, king, Lapland snow, lazy, letter, maize, May, meadow, meat, medicine, mock, mocking, moon, mountain blue, mountain mocking, mouse, mule, myrtle, national, officer, Oregon snow, oven, pasture, pea, Peabody, plow, prairie, rail, rain, red, reed, rice, rock, runner, salad, sand, sandy mocking, sewing, shad, skunk, snake, snow, spider, spring, spruce, state, stone, sugar, summer yellow, surf, sweetpotato, Sydney, teacher, thistle, thunder, tweezer, venison, vesper, Wakon, war, wheat, whistling, white, yawker, yellow bird.**

***birdie,** *n.* In golf, a score of one stroke less than par on a hole. — **1922** *N.Y. Times* 1 July 11/2 He won the 17th with a birdie 2, his iron leaving him an eight foot putt. **1948** *Dly. Ardmoreite* (Ardmore, Okla.) 30 April 10/1 He sank another birdie on the 16th.

birding grass, =bird grass. *Rare.* — **1787** WASHINGTON *Diaries* III. 198, I sowed ... 19 rows of the Birding-grass sent me by Mr. Sprigg of Annapolis.

* **birl,** *v. tr.* Among lumberjacks in the North Woods, to revolve a log in the water while standing on it. Also **birler,** *n.,* **birling,** *a.* Cf. **log birling.**

*a*1904 S. E. WHITE *Blazed Trail* i. 4 'Birling match,' he explained briefly. *Ib.* 7 They commenced to birl the log from left to right. *Ib.* 10 Dorrell still trod the quarter-deck as champion birler for the year. **1948** *Chi. Tribune* 23 June III. 4/3 The sport of birling started in lumber camps.

birthroot 'bɜθ,rut, *n.* The purple trillium, *Trillium erectum,* of the eastern states, so called from supposed usefulness in parturition. — **1822** *Jrnl. Science* IV. 62 Plants collected by Professor B. Douglass ... around the great Lakes ... [include] Birth root: Black Rock, May 3d. **1933** SMALL *Southeastern Flora* 305 Trillium ... Wake-robins. Birth-roots.

*biscuit, *n.*

1. A small, soft cake of wheat bread, made of rolled dough raised in the baking by baking powder, or soda, and cooked quickly.

"The name, in England, is given to a composition of flour, eggs, and sugar. With us the name is given to a composition of flour and butter, made and baked in private families. But the compositions under this denomination are very various" (W. 1828).

1818 PALMER *Journal* 125 Our living consisted almost invariably of coffee, [and] hot short cakes, called biscuits. **1908** PHILLIPS *Old Wives* 158 A plate of hot biscuits, three eggs, and two chops. **1947** *Harper's Mag.* July 81/1 He would . . . mix up a batch of biscuits . . . and in no time produce an excellent meal.

2. In combs.: (1) **biscuit baker,** a reflector oven or baker; (2) **block,** a block upon which dough for beaten biscuits is rolled or beaten; (3) **potato,** (see quot.), *rare;* (4) **punch,** a circular implement for cutting biscuits out of rolled dough; (5) **root,** (see quot. 1889 and cf. **camass**); (6) **shooter,** a cook or waitress, *slang.*

(1) **1829** *Va. Herald* (Fredericksburg) 11 Feb. 1/3 (*advt.*), Pots, Skillets, Biscuit Bakers, Griddles, . . . of all sizes. — (2) **1895** CRADDOCK *Myst. Witch-Face Mt.* 219 Mrs. Blakely. . . had observed him at the gate, while she stood at the biscuit-block in the shedroom. **1947** BEROLZHEIMER *Regional Cookbook* 217 Many homemakers still have wooden blocks called 'biscuit blocks' used to beat the dough [for beaten biscuits]. — (3) **1838** COLMAN *Mass. Agric. Rep.* 33 The Biscuit potato, [is] a round potato with brown rough skin, mealy and productive. — (4) **1889** MARK TWAIN *Conn. Yankee* ii. 38 [There are] men . . . in scale armor whose scales are represented by round holes—so that the man's coat looks as if it had been done with a biscuit-punch.

(5) **1837** IRVING *Bonneville* II. ix. 99 The cowish, also, or biscuit root, about the size of a walnut, . . . they reduce to a very palatable flour. **1889** *Cent.*, biscuit root. A name given to several kinds of wild esculent roots which are extensively used for food by the Indians of the Columbia river region, especially to species of *Camassia* and *Peucedanum.* **1947** DEVOTO *Across Wide Missouri* 432 Some of these were very important sources of food, notably the camas, . . . the biscuitroot, . . . and many species of lilies. — (6) **1893** *Harper's Mag.* Dec. 57/2 His helpmeet in her night-gown and the biscuit-shooter each seized a broom. **1927** *Collier's* 12 Nov. 11/1 The former biscuit shooter's photo begin hitting the rotogravures and fan magazines regularly.

As the last term in **beat, beaten, beef, corn, corner, cream, graham, hot, Maryland (beaten), meat, New York, pilot, president's, rat, saleratus, salt, soda, water biscuit.**

*bishop, *n.*

1. A lady's bustle. *Obs.*

1787 *Newport Herald* 11 Oct. 1/4 Tear off that load of horsehair foolishly called a *bishop,* from thy back. **1875** G. P. BURNHAM *Three Years* 219 Indeed, in the early days, when the 'bishop' or 'bustle,' . . . first came into vogue, Mrs. Roberts sported a tremendous ornament of this description.

2. In combs., sometimes in the possessive: (1) **bishop pine,** a California pine, *Pinus muricata,* having a spreading, flattened crown, and small prickly cones that remain on the tree for many years, also **bishop's pine;** (2) ***bishop's cap,** a plant of the genus *Mitella,* bearing pods suggestive of a bishop's miter; (3) **bishop sleeve,** a wide sleeve resembling that of an Anglican bishop's robe, worn by women; (4) **weed,** (see quots.), also ***bishop's weed.**

(1) **1890** *Cent.* 4495/3. **1948** *Pacific Discovery* Jan.–Feb. 2 (*caption*), Bishop pines, Mendocino County, California. — (2) **1839** LONGFELLOW *Voices of Night* Prelude viii, When . . . Bishop-caps have golden rings. **1869** FULLER *Flower Gatherers* 45 The flowers of the 'Bishop's Cap' are small and white, and grow usually upon wet rocks. **1900** HIGGINSON *Outdoor Studies* 37 One may still find, usually close together, the Hobble-bush and the Painted Trillium, the Mitella, or Bishop's Cap, and the snowy Tiarella. — (3) **1846** CORCORAN *Pickings* 56 Instead of making the sleeves tight they are the old fashioned *bishop* sleeves; and instead of putting in the Elssler buttons, she has substituted hooks and eyes. *a***1906** O. HENRY *Trimmed Lamp* 198 They . . . found their tastes in art, chicory salad and bishop sleeves so congenial that the joint studio resulted. — (4) **1833** EATON *Botany* (ed. 6) 127 *Discopleura capillacea,* bishop weed. **1889** *Cent.* 564/3 Bishop's weed . . . [is] a name given . . . in the United States to a somewhat similar umbelliferous plant, *Discopleura capillacea.*

***bishoped,** *a.* Furnished with a bishop or bustle. *Rare.* — **1807** IRVING *Salmagundi* ii. 40 When our ladies in stays, and in bodice well laced, when bishop'd, and cushion'd, and hoop'd to the chin.

Bishopites ˈbɪʃəpˌaɪts, *n. pl.* A minor Mormon sect. *Obs.* — **1851** *Ore. Statesman* 23 Dec. 1/5 The Bishopites, new lights, established at Kirtland, Lake county, Ohio.

bisnaga bɪsˈnagə, *n. S.W.* [See note.] A globular or cylindrical, strongly ribbed, spiny cactus, *Echinocactus visnaga,* also any one of various thorny barrel cacti of the genus *Ferocactus.*

Early Spanish explorers brought to this country their word *biznaga* used of a European plant of the carrot family the rays of the umbel of which become tough and hard and are sometimes used as toothpicks. In this country the explorers found a cactus having spines or thorns that were likewise suitable for use as toothpicks. This point of similarity may have suggested to the Spaniards the applicability of *biznaga* to the new plant.

This application may have been helped along or entirely inspired by the fact that the name, *huitz-nahuac,* which the Aztecs used for this cactus was not very distant in sound from the Spanish *biznaga.* Santamaría derives the word in its American application directly from the Aztec, and he may be entirely justified in doing so.

[**1789** CLAVIGERO *Storia della Calif.* I. 50 La Visnaga spinosa è un' altra specie di pianta carnosa, striata, sfogliata, è spinosa.] **1845** FRÉMONT *Exped.* 264 Fuentes pointed out one [cactus] called by the Spaniards bisnada [*sic*], which has a juicy pulp, slightly acid, and is eaten by the traveler to allay thirst. **1906** JAMES *Colo. Desert* 223 The Mexicans call it 'bisnaga,' and they and the Indians often use its water storage when traveling across the desert. **1940** JAEGER *Desert Wild Flowers* 168 The bisnaga, at first globular in form, eventually becomes cylindrical and may grow to a height of 5 or 6 ft.

*bison, *n.* Attrib. in the sense "of or pertaining to the American bison" with **bull, path, robe, skin, tallow, trace, wool.** See also **half bison, wood(land) bison.**

1827 COOPER *Prairie* xix, A few enormous bison-bulls were first observed. — **1821** NUTTALL *Trav. Arkansa* 162 We . . . kept up along the banks of the Kiamesha, by a bison path. — **1823** JAMES *Exped.* I. 114 Large wooden bowls, which were placed on bison robes or mats. — *Ib.* 113 Bison-skins supply them with a comfortable bedding. — **1821** NUTTALL *Journal* 237 At this time nearly the whole town, men and women, were engaged in their summer hunt, collecting bison tallow and meat. — *Ib.* 212 We proceeded along a blind bison trace. — **1838** AUDUBON *Ornith. Biog.* IV. 487 The nest itself was made of small twigs . . . , lined with stripes of bark and bison wool.

*bit, *n.*

1. *Bit of eight,* a piece of eight, a Spanish dollar. *Rare.*

1676 TOMPSON *Poet. Works* 50 Twas ere a Barge had made so rich a fraight As chocholatte, dustgold, and bitts of eight.

2. A small Spanish silver coin (the real) or a substitute for this, and latterly a nominal coin or amount, having the value of 12½ cents.

Orig. *bit* was app. (as in sense 1) a rendering of the Spanish *pieca,* but its general use was probably assisted by the fact that the "bit" was sometimes the result of dividing a coin of greater value. The second group of quots. shows how the value of the coin so called has varied.

(1) **1683** *Md. Hist. Mag.* I. 101 [In this one the grantee was put in possession by the delivery of a silver coin] called in Spanish a Bit fixed on the Seal of these presents. **1705** *Provincial Press Mass.* I. 192 Prohibiting the importation of any clipt money of Bitts . . . into this colony. **1821** in ARTHUR *Old New Orleans* 116 The price of Fresh Flour being this day $10 a bbl. according to the tariff the bakers must give during the ensuing week 31 ounces of bread for a bit. **1942** LILLARD *Desert Challenge* 218 Most drinks were priced at one bit—twelve and a half cents.

attrib. **1865** *Gold Hill* (Nev.) *News* 11 May 2/3 Sacks . . . even condescends to drink bit gin at a fourth class dead-fall, and on tick. **1897** LEONARD *Gold Fields Klondike* 28 In ordinary placer mining a claim is considered quite good when it yields from ten to fifteen cents to the pan: 'bit dirt' as they say in California. **1926** *Collier's* 30 Oct. 19/4 O'Brien, in a towering rage, swore he would some day 'sell bit whisky over the counter of the Bank of California.'

(2) **1824** SINGLETON *Letters* 127 A *bit* [in New Orleans] is the Pennsylvanian eleven-pence, the New York *shilling,* and the New England *nine-pence.* **1840** *Boston Transcript* 11 Feb. 2/2 Ten cent pieces are forced upon you for bits, and bits are taken from you for only ten cents. **1885** *Knowledge* 28 Aug. 172 *Bit.* I must admit great ignorance as to the real meaning of this word. In the South, a 'bit' is generally half-a-quarter; *i.e.* 12½¢., equal in value to our English sixpence; but I have known a quarter and a dime (25¢ and 10¢ respectively) called a 'bit.' I believe, however, a bit usually means 12½¢. **1941** FLORENCE L. DORSEY *Master of Mississippi* 29 Mexican silver dollars, worth about fifty cents each, cut into four 'bits' with a chisel.

b. Usu. preceded by even multiples, as (1) **two,** see **two bits,** (2) **four,** (3) **six,** but also (rarely) (4) **three bits.**

(2) **1836** Edward *Hist. Texas* 162 The party who does not conform with the determination, shall pay four bits for cost. **1945** Botkin *My Burden* 30 Old Bab Russ charge me four bits for that hand, and I have to give four bits more for a pint of whiskey. — **(3) 1840** *Jamestown* (N.Y.) *Jrnl.* 12 Aug. 3/4 If he grumbles we'll give him six bits. **1948** *Galveston* (Tex.) *News* 14 June 4/1 What's it like to be an American in a nation where six bits make you a millionaire? — **(4) 1859** A. Van Buren *Sojourn in South* 36 My second trunk was brought, the charge asked, and answered, 'Three bits.'

c. (1) **half-bit,** a nominal or cut coin having half the value of a bit; (2) **long bit,** (see quot. 1877); (3) **short bit,** a dime.

(1) [1723 *Smithtown Rec.* 80 Shuball Marchant, Pounder, . . . doth oblige himself to have but half a bit for turning of the key.] **1775** *Pa. Ev. Post.* (Phila.) 30 Dec. 601/2 The half bit loaf of bread to weigh fourteen ounces, and all other loaves in proportion. **1860** Mordecai *Virginia* 277 A quarter of a dollar would be radiated and subdivided into six parts, or a pistareen into five parts, each one of which called a 'half bit,' passed for three-pence. — **(2) 1857** *S.F. Call* 8 Jan. 1/1 *Dissolved,* Dat from and after dis date . . . we will receive nuffin but long bits for brackin of boots. **1877** W. Wright *Big Bonanza* 354 The smallest coin in use is the bit, ten-cent piece,—sometimes spoken of as a 'short bit,' as not being twelve and one-half cents, the 'long bit.' — **(3)** *c***1854** Paige *Dow's Sermons* IV. 219 (Th.), The will, that cuts off an expectant heir with a 'short bit.' **1936** McKenna *Black Range* 196 Gus was rather stingy, so he hied him to the brewery where a schooner of beer could be had for a short bit.

d. bit house, *W.* a saloon where drinks, cigars, etc., are sold for a bit. *Obs.*

[1839 *Ill. Temperance Herald* (Alton) Feb. 3/1 It is a bit a drink at the *genteel* drunkeries.] **1856** *Spirit of Age* (Sacramento) 1 Sep. 2/2 At long intervals they have a few shillings in their pockets, most of which they spend for poor whisky at 'bit houses.' **1880** Edmund Leathes *An Actor Abroad* 283 All drinks are one price, from a glass of beer to a champagne cocktail; in a 'one bit house' they charge 'one bit.'

As the last term in **devil's, double, elevenpenny, fip(p)enny, five penny, frog, lever, long, Louisiana, Mexican, over, ring, short, Spanish, ten penny bit.**

bit bɪt, *v.* To "tap" (a tree) with a bit or auger. *Rare.* — **1857** *Lawrence* (Kansas) *Republican* 11 June 4 Of course, he hadn't any auger to bit or tap the trees.

***bitch,** *n.* (See quot. 1927.) Cf. **slut* in same sense in *OED* from 1609. — **1904** E. Robins *Magn. North* I. 233 'I'll light a piece of fat pine,' shouted the Boy. . . . 'Where's your bitch?' said Dillon. **1927** Russell *Trails* 159 In the long winter nights their light was coal oil lamps or candles—sometimes they were forced to use a 'bitch,' which was a tin cup filled with bacon grease and a twisted rag wick.

***bite,** *n.* As the last term in **devil's, hog, short, snake bite.**

***bite,** *v.*

1. *tr.* To bother, exercise, worry. *Slang.*

1909 *Sat. Ev. Post* 27 March 7/3 Say! what's biting you? **1911** H. S. Harrison *Queed* vii. 84 Liberties—what's bitin' ye, man?

2. In colloq. and slang phrases: (1) *To bite off,* to conclude speaking, to "shut up"; (2) *to bite off more than one can chew,* to undertake something beyond one's powers.

(1) **1843** Stephens *High Life N.Y.* II. xxi. 48, I had to bite off short, for a chap come aboard the sloop with Captin Doolittle. **1911** Vance *Cynthia* 172 'Ah, bite that off!' Rhode interrupted impatiently. — **(2) 1877** Beadle *Western Wilds* ii. 42 Men, you've bit off more'n you can chaw. **1948** *Dly. Ardmoreite* (Ardmore, Okla.) 4 May 4/1 Some people go hungry for fear of biting off more than they can chew.

***biter,** *n.* As the last term in **ear biter, pie biter.**

***bitter,** *a.* In combs.: (1) **bitter brush,** (see quot. 1925); (2) **buttons,** (see quots.); (3) **cottonwood,** a species of cottonwood, *Populus angustifolia,* found chiefly west of the Rocky Mountains; (4) **ender,** one who fights or holds out to the very last in some cause, *colloq.;* (5) **head,** a local name for the calico bass; (6) **hickory,** a hickory, *Carya cordiformis,* of the eastern states having a bitter nut; (7) **land,** sour land or soil; (8) **nut,** a hickory, esp. the bitter hickory, bearing a bitter nut, in full **bitter-nut hickory;** (9) **orange,** an orange having an acid, slightly bitter, pulp; (10) **pecan,** =**water hickory;** (11) **root,** tobacco-root, *Lewisia rediviva,* or the bigroot, *Echinocystis fabacea,* also attrib.; (12) **rot,** a destructive fungus disease that attacks apples, grapes, etc.; (13) ***sweet,** the climbing shrub, *Celastrus scandens,* also called false bittersweet; (14) **weed,** any one of various American plants, as ragweed and sneezeweed, etc., having a bitter principle.

(1) **1925** Jepson *Flowering Plants of Calif.* 504 *P[urshia] tridentata* DC. Antelope Brush. . . . Also called Bitter-Brush, Greasewood . . . and Buckbrush. **1937** *Range Plant Handbook* B115 Bitterbrush is one of the most widely distributed of all western shrubs, ranging from Montana to New Mexico, California, and British Columbia. — **(2) 1909** *Cent. Supp.* 138/2 Bitter-buttons . . . The tansy, *Tanacetum vulgare.* **1944** *Chi. D. News* 2 Aug. 12/8 'Tansy. Otherwise known as Bitter Buttons,' John was saying, . . . as he inspected a yellow flower which we had spent a lifetime ignoring. — **(3) 1844** Gregg *Commerce of Prairies* I. 159–60 Another [cottonwood] . . . found on the mountain streams of New Mexico . . . has been called willow-leaf or bitter cottonwood, and has been reckoned by some a species of cinchona. — **(4) 1850** *Cong. Globe* 12 March, App. 303 The disunionist looks forward to a southern confederacy; the bitter-ender to the triumph of his party. **1948** *Time* 26 Jan. 15/3 Except for half a dozen bitter-enders, most were willing to accept the Marshall Plan in principle.

(5) 1888 Goode *Amer. Fishes* 69 The names 'Bitter Head' and 'Lamplighter' are also ascribed to it. **1947** Dalrymple *Panfish* 84 Here, my friend, are the various names by which you would address that little gamester, the Crappie, depending on where you happened to be at the moment: Bachelor, . . . Banklick Bass, . . . Bitterhead, . . . Lake Bass. — **(6) 1813** Muhlenberg *Cat. Plants* 88 *Juglans sulcata, amara:* bitter hickory, white, [grows in] Pens. — **(7) 1837** Williams *Florida* 89 The third kind of swamps are those spongy tracts, where the waters continually ooze through the soil, and finally collect in streams and pass off. These are properly termed galls, sometimes sour, sometimes bitter land . — **(8) 1810** Michaux *Arbres* I. 19 Bitter nut hickory . . . , seul nom en usage dans N.Y. **1814** Pursh *Flora Amer.* II. 638 *Juglans amara.* . . . This is known by the name of Bitter Nut, White or Swamp Hickory. **1947** *Midland Naturalist* July 39 Bitternut [is] occasional in bottomland forest and wood margins. — **(9) 1827** *Liberty Hall* (Cin.) 4 Oct. 1/6 The orange (sweet, sour and bitter) grows wild in the county. **1901** Mohr *Plant Life Ala.* 96 In sheltered situations, the sweet and bitter orange and loquat . . . are cultivated.

(10) 1884 Sargent *Rep. Forests* 136 *Carya aquatica.* . . . Water Hickory. Swamp Hickory. Bitter Pecan. — **(11) 1835** Parker *Exploring Tour* (1838) 204 To these may be added the racine amère, or bitter root, which grows on dry ground, fusiform, and though not pleasant to the taste, yet it is very conducive to health. **1885** *Cent. Mag.* Jan. 447 It was too late to find the exquisite camellia-like flower of the bitter-root, which in May stars the ground. **1945** Macdonald *Egg & I* 20 The bitterroot daisies, the Montana State flower, had little foliage and no stems and lay flat and pink and exquisite on the brown hard earth. — **(12) 1861** *Ill. Agric. Soc. Trans.* IV. 115 The bitter rot makes its appearance as a brown spot on the side of the apple. *Ib.* 117. **1890** *Cent.* 5235/3 The bitter rot [of the grape is caused] by *Greeneria fuliginea.* — **(13) 1813** Muhlenberg *Cat. Plants* 25 Climbing Stafftree or bittersweet. **1901** Mohr *Plant Life Ala.* 605 Waxwork. False Bitter-sweet. . . . The bark is used as a domestic medicine. **1943** Damon *Sense of H.* 57 A bittersweet vine twines above the front door. — **(14) 1819** Thomas *Travels* 222 *Ambrosia artimisifolia* hog or bitter weed. **1944** *Democrat* 18 May 3/5 Bitterweed, a serious pasture pest which causes unpalatable milk, can be controlled by proper management of the pasture.

bittered sling. A cocktail. *Obs.* — **1806** *Balance* (Hudson, N.Y.) 13 May 146 (Th.), Cocktail is a stimulating liquor, composed of spirits of any kind, sugar, water, and bitters—it is vulgarly called bittered sling, and is supposed to be an excellent electioneering potion.

***bitters,** *n. pl.* **1.** =**gall bitters, prairie bitters.** *Obs.* **2.** *To get one's bitters, fig.* to meet one's deserts or fate. *Colloq.*

(1) **1846** Sage *Scenes Rocky Mts.* xvi. 132 A kind of beverage very common among mountaineers, . . . 'bitters' . . . is prepared by the following simple process, viz: with one pint of water mix one-fourth gill of buffalo-gall, and you will then have before you a wholesome and exhilarating drink. — **(2) 1812** *Md. Hist. Reg.* IX. 70 You might get your bitters in Baltimore Town. *a***1846** *Quarter Race Ky.* 194 The seal soon got his bitters, and the captin cut a big hunk off the tail end.

As the last term in **fig, gall, plantation, prairie, Swedish, wahoo bitters.**

biz bɪz, *n.* Short for **business. Slang.*

1862 Browne *A. Ward His Book* 222, I must forth to my Biz. **1892** *Slater* (Mo.) *Index* 11 Aug. 3/3 Constable Bridges was down to Blue Lick Spring Tuesday on official biz. **1948** *Pac. Northwest Quart.* April 109 After warning the mayor to 'go slow' and 'let the Chinese biz alone,' it told him of a cache of dynamite . . . ready to be utilized at any time.

***blab,** *n. W.* (See quot. 1884.)

1884 Aldridge *Life on Ranch* 183 A 'blab' is a piece of thin board, six inches by four inches, which has a piece cut out of the middle of one of the longer sides, so shaped that you can just force it on to the membrane that divides the nostrils of a calf. When put on it hangs down over the mouth of an animal so that it cannot suck, but is able to graze without difficulty. **1922** ROLLINS *Cowboy* 193 The calf and his mater had to be chased so far apart as to permit the cowboy to rope and throw the calf, attach the blab, and remount his horse.

Hence **blabbing,** *n.*

1884 ALDRIDGE *Life on Ranch* 183 When you start out on a blabbing expedition you place several blabs in your pocket and ride along until you see a big calf whose dam looks as if she would be the better for being relieved of the support of her progeny. **1922** ROLLINS *Cowboy* 193 Blabbing was not always easy of accomplishment.

blab school. A school in which the pupils study aloud and recite in concert. *Obs.* — **1890** in *Congress. Rec.* 10 Feb. 1165/1 It is a school at study and all studying at the top of their voices. Such a din! This is a 'blab' school. *Ib.*, Of these mountain children in our mission schools . . . I never talked with one who had not been accustomed to the blab school, except the younger ones.

* **black,** *a.*

1. In the names of trees and shrubs: (1) **black alder,** (*a*) an American species of holly, *Ilex verticillata*, (*b*) (see quot.); (2) **American larch,** the tamarack, *Larix laricina;* (3) **balsam,** a white fir, *Abies concolor;* (4) * **berry,** see as a main entry; (5) **birch (tree),** any one of various birches, esp. the cherry birch, *Betula lenta*, or *B. fontinalis;* (6) **brush,** any one of several shrubs, esp. *Coleogyne ramosissima*, having spiny twigs, found in arid regions in the Southwest (in quot. 1856 prob. an error for **black-rush**); (7) * **cap,** used of, or designating, the black raspberry, *q.v.;* (8) **gum** (*a*) the tupelo, *Nyssa sylvatica*, (*b*) **black gum toothbrush,** a small black gum twig a few inches long, one end of which is chewed until it is suitable for use as a brush for the teeth, or, often, to dip snuff; (9) **jack,** see as a main entry; (10) **larch,** the tamarack or hackmatack, *Larix laricina;* (11) **locust,** the honey locust (see also quot. 1901); (12) **moosebush,** the hobblebush, *Viburnum alnifolium;* (13) **oak,** any one of various American oaks, as the blackjack, quercitron, etc., having dark bark and foliage, also attrib.; (14) **sage,** any one of various plants native to California and the Southwest, as *Salvia mellifera*, *Trichostema lanatum;* (15) **scrub oak,** = **bear oak;** (16) **walnut,** an American tree of the genus *Juglans*, esp. *J. nigra*, the wood or fruit of this, also attrib.; (17) **willow,** (*a*) any one of various American willows, esp. *Salix nigra*, having dark bark, (*b*) the Californian mule fat; (18) **wood,** = **black tree,** also attrib., cf. **4. e.** (11) below.

(1) (*a*) **1805** LEWIS in *L. & Clark Exped.* (1904) III. 261 The large black alder. **1942** PEATTIE *Friendly Mts.* 206 At the border of the bog among the tall cinnamon ferns grows the black alder or winterberry. (*b*) **1889** *Cent.* 134/1 In the eastern United States the common species are the smooth alder, *A. serrulata*, and the speckled alder, *A. incana*. Both are also known as black alder. — **(2) 1785** MARSHALL *Amer. Grove* 104 Black American Larch-Tree. This is also a variety differing in having dark coloured cones. — **(3) 1883** ZEIGLER & GROSSCUP *Alleghanies* 57 Every grove is composed of both black and white balsams, and no single tree is widely separated from its opposite sex. **1888** S. D. WARNER *On Horseback* 50 The black balsam [of Car. or Va.] is neither a cheerful nor a picturesque tree.

(5) 1675 JOSSELYN *Two Voyages* 69 The Birch-tree is of two kinds, ordinary Birch, and black Birch. **1721** *Braintree Rec.* 152 From thence we run to a black burch Tree by the side of a swamp. **1904** WALLER *Woodcarver* 85 I've often wondered what became of it. It was a black birch, wasn't it? — **(6) 1856** *Spirit of Times* (N.Y.) 8 Nov. 161/1 The next day we worked . . . until our poor pointers were . . . cut up by the bog-grass and sharp *black brush.* **1937** *Range Plant Handbook* B63 Blackbrush flowers in April and May. **1940** CASSADY & GLENDENING *Revegetating Semidesert Range Lands* 2 Brushy areas on the mesas . . . [are] dominated by such shrubs as creosotebush, honey mesquite, tarbush or 'blackbrush,' . . . and various other thorny shrubs. — **(7)** [**1656** VAN DER DONCK in *N.Y. Hist. Soc. Coll.* 2 Ser. I. (1841) 152 Strawberries in abundance all over the country . . . ; blueberries, raspberries, black-caps, &c.] **1847** DARLINGTON *Weeds & Plants* 127 *Rubus occidentalis.* . . . Wild or Black Raspberry. Thimbleberry. Black Caps. **1940** SMITH *Puyallup-Nisqually* 248 Blackcaps might be mixed with the blackberries and dried and formed into cakes with them. — **(8)** (*a*) **1709** LAWSON *Carolina* 95 Of the Black Gum there grows, with us, two sorts. . . . The one bears a black well-tasted Berry. . . . The Bears crop these trees for the Berries, which they mightily covet. **1785** WASHINGTON *Diaries* II. 346 Planted all the . . . Blackgums in my Serpentine Walks. *c***1945** HOPKINS *Okefenokee* 50 This fire killed forty to fifty million feet of Swamp black gum. (*b*) **1930** VINES *River Goes with Heaven* 234 Verda wanted a black gum toothbrush. **1944** CLARK *Pills* 149 Filling their lower lips, or rolling frazzled ends of black-gum toothbrushes in ounce tin boxes, females consumed huge quantities of tobacco in its vilest form.

(10) [**1785** MARSHALL *Amer. Grove* 104 Black American Larch-Tree. This is also a variety differing in having dark coloured cones.] **1884** SARGENT *Rep. Forests* 215 *Larix Americana.* . . . Larch. Black Larch. Tamarack. Hackmatack. — **(11) 1787** W. SARGENT in *Mem. Acad.* II. I. 157 The Black Locust . . . grows from six inches to two feet and a half diameter. **1901** MOHR *Plant Life Ala.* 77 On its flanks [Lookout Mt.] the black locust (*Robina pseudacacia*) is found, one of the few localities in Alabama where it can be considered to be indigenous. **1945** *Prairie Farmer* 22 Dec. 4/1 Honey locusts are harmless but the common or black locust tree is responsible for many cases of animal poisoning. — **(12)** *a***1817** DWIGHT *Travels* II. 418 Here, also, I first observed the black-moose bush; a pretty shrub with a rich pulpy leaf, and a tuft of brilliant white flower at the end of every branch. — **(13) 1634** WOOD *N. Eng. Prospect* I. v. 16 Of Oakes there be three kindes, the red Oake, white, and black. **1703** *Conn. Col. Rec.* IV. 422 To a black oak tree by a ledge of rock on the side of a hill. **1947** *Midland Naturalist* July 40 Black Oak [is] common in upland oak forest; occasional in terrace forest. — **(14) 1876** BOURKE *Journal* 12 March, Across the Southern boundary of Montana, in a region well grassed with gramma and the 'black sage,' a plant almost as nutritious as oats. **1946** R. PEATTIE *Pac. Coast Ranges* 53 White sage, black sage, and purple sage all yield fine honeys.

(15) 1810 MICHAUX *Arbres* I. 24 Bear' Oak, . . . Black Scrub Oak. **1892** APGAR *Trees Northern U.S.* 157 Bear or Black Scrub-oak. . . . Sandy barrens and rocky hills. New England to Ohio, and south. — **(16) 1612** R. JOHNSON *New Life of Va.* B3r They cut downe wood for wanscot, blacke walnut tree, Spruce, Cedar & Deale. **1624** *Va. House of Burgesses* 28 [We] weare . . . wholly imployed in cuttinge downe of masts, cedar, black wallnutt, clapboarde. **1737** BRICKELL *N. Carolina* 69 The Indians gather great Quantities of these Nuts, and the Black Wall-nuts (being ripe in Autumn). **1948** *Pacific Discovery* Mar.–Apr. 15/2 The purple finches brought their three offspring to the black walnut tree on four consecutive mornings last spring. — **(17)** (*a*) **1802** ELLICOTT *Journal* 284 Black-willow . . . [is] not in great abundance, and becomes more scarce as you descend the river. **1947** *Midland Naturalist* July 38 Black Willow [is] occasional (locally common) in river swamps. (*b*) **1894** *Amer. Folk-Lore* VII. 91 *Baccharis viminea*, . . . black willow; Santa Barbara Co., Cal. — **(18) 1775** ROMANS *Florida* App. 27 There are some mangrove and blackwood bushes on them. *Ib.* 80 The chief growth on the keys are mangrove and blackwood bushes. **1897** SUDWORTH *Arborescent Flora* 334 Blackwood. . . . Common names [include] Blackwood (Fla.), Blacktree (Fla.).

b. In similar names sufficiently defined in the quots.: (1) **black ash,** (2) **cypress,** (3) **elder,** (4) **haw,** (5) **hickory,** (6) **huckleberry,** (7) **maple,** (8) **persimmon,** (9) **pine,** (10) **raspberry,** (11) * **seed (cotton),** (12) **slash pine,** (13) **snaps,** (14) **spruce,** (15) **sugar maple,** (16) * **thorn,** (17) **tree,** (18) **whortleberry.**

(1) 1673 *Essex Hist. Coll.* VI. 178/2 From thence . . . to a forked black ash. **1737** J. HEMPSTEAD *Diary* 316, I cut a black ash ladder pole. **1916** SETON *Woodcraft Man.* 295 Black Ash, Hoop Ash, or Water Ash (*Fraxinus nigra*) A tall forest tree of swampy places; 70, 80, or rarely 100 feet high. — **(2) 1810** MICHAUX *Arbres* I. 30 *Cypress*, . . . *Bald Cypress*, . . . [ou] *Black* et *White Cypress.* **1901** MOHR *Plant Life Ala.* 325 *Taxodium distichum.* . . . Black Cypress. . . . Most valuable timber tree, the largest of Atlantic North America. — **(3) 1807** GASS *Journal* 136 There are black elder, and bore-tree, pitch and spruce pine, all growing together on these mountains. *a***1862** THOREAU *Maine Woods* 310 The prevailing shrubs and small trees along the shore were: . . . *Sambucus Canadensis* (black elder), rose, . . . [etc.]. — **(4) 1709** LAWSON *Carolina* 107 A slender Tree . . . bears the black Haw, which People eat, and the Birds covet also. **1785** WASHINGTON *Diaries* II. 346 Planted . . . all the black haws, all the large berried thorns. **1948** *Household* March 50/4 Black haw . . . is not a Crataegus but a Viburnum—*V. prunifolium.*

(5) 1787 W. SARGENT in *Mem. Acad.* II. I. 157 Black Hickory [of the Ohio valley], with a small thin shell nut. **1897** SUDWORTH *Arborescent Flora* 114 *Hicoria alba*, Mockernut (Hickory), . . . is also called Black Hickory (Tex., Miss., La., Mo.). — **(6) 1847** DARLINGTON *Weeds & Plants* 209 *Gaylussacia resinosa* is the plant which furnishes the larger share of the 'black huckleberries' of the northern markets. **1947** *Midland Naturalist* July 53 Black Huckleberry [is] abundant in pine-oak forest and upland oak forest. — **(7)** *a***1817** DWIGHT *Travels* I. 40 The Hard Maple, sometimes called the Black, is extensively called the Sugar Maple. **1947** *Amer. Sp.* April 152/1 Black maple (*saccharum nigrum*). One of the two varieties of maples from which sirup is made. — **(8) 1846** GREGG *Diary & Letters* (1941) I. 239 Among other wild fruits of this vicinity, [is] that called by Mexicans chapote and generally by Americans, black persimmon. **1897** SUDWORTH *Arborescent Flora* 321 *Diospyros texana*, Mexican Persimmon.

. . . Common names [include] . . . Black Persimmon (Tex.), Chapote (Tex.). — **(9) 1681** *N.H. Probate Rec.* I. 47 From that 48 Pole S.W. to a black Pine Stump on the West. **1809** KENDALL *Travels* III. 146 The black pine or pitch pine (pinus taeda) grows in sands, has a very long leaf, and a bark in very large scales. **1854** GLISAN *Jrnl. Army Life* 152 In Arkansas—the birch, honey-locust, cyprus, black and white pine.

(10) 1781–2 JEFFERSON *Notes Va.* (1787) 37 Native plants [of Va. include] Black raspberries. **1901** MOHR *Plant Life Ala.* 541 Black Raspberry . . . [was] frequently transplanted by the settlers to their gardens. — **(11) 1796** B. HAWKINS *Letters* 30, I advised him . . . as from his information the black seed cotton will not do here, to plant only the green seed. **1810** LAMBERT *Travels* III. 69 In the lower country, the *black seed* produces from 100 to 300 lbs. of clean cotton, per acre. In the middle and upper country, *green seed* does the like. **1882** *Cent. Mag.* Feb. 573/1 The long staple or black seed cotton of the Sea Island variety. — **(12) 1897** SUDWORTH *Arborescent Flora* 26 *Pinus tæda,* Loblolly Pine. . . . Common names [include] . . . Longshucks (Md., Va.), Black Slash Pine (S.C.), Franckincense Pine (lit.). — **(13) 1894** *Amer. Folk-Lore* VII. 93 *Gaylusaccia resinosa* . . . black snaps, Wells, Me. **1931** CLUTE *Plants* 42 One might be puzzled to know why one species of huckleberry (*Gaylussacia baccata*) is called crackers, cracker berry, and black-snaps, until in eating the fruit he finds the seeds cracking between his teeth. — **(14) 1765** R. ROGERS *Acc. N. America* 48 You will find beach, hemlock, and some white pines; higher up [in N.H.] the growth is chiefly black spruce. **1803** LAMBERT *Descr. Genus Pinus* 41 Black Spruce Fir, *P. nigra,* grows wild only in New England, Canada, Nova Scotia. **1947** *Atlantic Mo.* Sep. 116/1 The black spruce suffered severely from the blight of the 1920's.

(15) 1817 RAFINESQUE tr. C. C. Robin *Florula Ludoviciana* 158 *Acer nigrum.* . . . Rare, called black sugar maple. **1832** BROWNE *Sylva* 104 Black Sugar Maple *Acer nigrum* . . . [is so called,] probably, on account of the dark color of its leaves in comparison with those of the sugar maple. **1892** APGAR *Trees Northern U.S.* 86 Black Sugar-maple. . . . Found with the other Sugar-maple, and quite variable. — **(16)** (*a*) **1737** BRICKELL *N. Carolina* 79 The Black Thorn, or Sloe Tree grows plentifully in several parts of this Province, . . . but is quite different from our Sloe Tree in Ireland. **1901** MOHR *Plant Life Ala.* 99 *Crataegus molle* (black thorn) . . . [is] rarely found north of the Central Pine belt. (*b*) **1833** EATON *Botany* 1, *A. farnesiana,* black thorn . . . New Orleans. **1845** LINCOLN *Botany* App. 69/1 *Acacia farnesiana,* (black thorn). . . . Flowers fragrant; legumes fusiform. *S.* — **(17) 1884** SARGENT *Rep. Forests* 117 *Avicennia nitida.* . . . Black Mangrove. Black Tree. Black Wood. **1897** SUDWORTH *Arborescent Flora* 334 Blackwood. . . . Common names [include] Blackwood (Fla.), Blacktree (Fla.). — **(18) 1784** CUTLER in *Mem. Acad.* I. 438 The Black Whortleberry. **1847** WOOD *Botany* 368 *Vaccinium resinosum,* Black Whortleberry or Huckleberry. . . . Berries black, globose, sweet and eatable, ripe in Augut.

c. In the names of herbaceous plants: (1) **black bindweed,** the ivy bindweed, *Bilderdykia convoluvulus,* introduced from Europe; (2) **calabash,** (see quot.); (3) **cohosh,** the bugbane, *Cimicifuga racemosa,* or a preparation made from this; (4) ***eye,** the black-eyed cowpea, *Vigna sinensis,* usu. **black-eyed pea;** (5) ***eyed Susan,** any one of various plants, as the yellow daisy, *Rudbeckia hirta,* having flowers with a black or dark center; (6) **flower,** =**bunch flower;** (7) **grass,** a species of rush, *Juncus gerardi,* that grows in salt marshes and is valued as hay; (8) **moss,** the Spanish moss of the southern states, "so called from the black fiber that remains after the outer covering of the stem is removed" (*Cent.*); (9) **oat grass,** an oat grass, *Stipa avenacea,* common in the eastern and southern states; (10) ***pea,** =**black-eyed pea;** (11) **root,** any one of various American plants, as Culver's root, colicroot, etc., having black rootstocks often used in medicine; (12) **rush,** one or other species of *Juncus,* cf. **black grass;** (13) **sampson,** *S.* the purple coneflower, the roots of which were formerly thought to have powerful medicinal virtues; (14) **snakeroot,** any one of several American plants, as bugbane, having real or alleged medicinal value.

(1) 1843 TORREY *Flora N.Y.* II. 146 Black Bindweed . . . [grows in] cultivated grounds and sandy fields; very common. **1901** MOHR *Plant Life Ala.* 486 Black Bind Weed . . . [grows] in waste places. . . . June to August; frequent. Annual. — **(2) 1897** SUDWORTH *Arborescent Flora* 336 *Crescentia ovata,* Burmann. Black Calabash Tree. — **(3) 1830** *Huntingdon* (Penna.) *Courier* 15 Sep. 4/5 American Remedies Wanted . . . Rattle Weed or Black Cahash. **1851** CIST *Cincinnati* 211 Jacob S. Merrel, Steam Drug mills, prepares . . . concentrated extracts of vegetable medical articles . . . such as . . . macrotin or black cohosh, leptandrin or black-root extracts. **1948** *Chi. D. News* 26 Feb. 16/3 But the real tonic . . . was made of a root called 'black cohoosh.' — **(4) 1738** BYRD *Dividing Line* 74 Each Cell (of N.C. pine cone) contains a Seed of the Size and Figure of a black-ey'd Pea, which, Shedding in November, is very good Mast for Hogs, and fatens them in a Short time. **1788** WASHINGTON *Diaries* III. 357 Finished planting of Pease here yesterday . . . two . . . were of the large and early blackeye. **1948** *Capital-Democrat* (Tishomingo, Okla.) 17 June 7/2, I also want to plant some black-eyed peas.

(5) 1891 *Cent. s.v. Thunbergia,* The hardy annual *T. alata,* known locally by the name *black-eyed Susan* from its buff, orange, or white flowers with a purplish-black center. **1947** *Midland Naturalist* July 62 Black-eyed Susan [is] occasional in fallow fields and abandoned fields; rare in pine fields. — **(6) 1817** S. BROWN *Western Gaz.* 322 Mr. Granger enumerates the following species [found in New Connecticut], viz: . . . Seneca snake root, black flower, white hellebore, [etc.]. — **(7) 1788** SCHÖPF *Reise* I. 12 Nur eine Art davon, nemlich *Juncus bulbosus* L. wird unter dem Namen schwarzes Gras (Black-grass), als die dem Vieh angenehmste und erspriesslichste Weide, auf solchen Wiesen am liebsten gesehen, aber nur sehr selten angesäet. **1871** DE VERE 408 Salt-Hay, a very important product of salt-marshes, is of two principal sorts, called *salt-grass* and *black-grass.* — **(8) 1774–6** JANET SCHAW *Jrnl. of Lady of Quality* (1923) 152 The trees that keep clear from this black moss (as it is called) are crowned with the Mistletoe. **1894** COULTER *Bot. W. Texas* III. 426 Common Long-moss. Black moss. . . . Hanging on trees, forming long tufts; southern Texas. — **(9) 1843** TORREY *Flora N.Y.* II. 433 Black Oat-grass . . . [is found in] Dry sandy or rocky woods, not uncommon in the valley of the Hudson. **1941** R. S. WALKER *Lookout* 49 Black oat grass, thrives in the open woodlands on the mountain.

(10) 1855 DAVIS *Farm Bk.* 183 We thrashed 24 Bushels black peas. — **(11) 1709** BYRD *Secret Diary* (1941) 4 Feb. 13, I sent him some blackroot . . . for the gripes. **1843** T. TALBOT *Journals* 45 We traded some Kooyah or Black root . . . a black, sticky, suspicious looking compound, of very disagreeable odor. . . . It is a very palatable and soon a favorite mess. **1891** *Cent. s.v. Veronica,* A few [species] are of medicinal repute, especially *V. Virginica,* known as black-root and *Culver's-root* or *Culver's-physic* . . . occurring in Canada, the eastern and central United States [etc.]. — **(12) 1840** DEWEY *Mass. Flowering Plants* 204 *Juncus bulbosus,* Black Rush, . . . [grows] about salt marshes, and 'makes good hay.' **1901** MOHR *Plant Life Ala.* 50 Paludial plants confined to the salt marshes of the seashore . . . [include] black rush (*Juncus roemerianus*). — **(13) 1857** GRAY *Botany* 214 Purple coneflower. . . . Root thick, black, very pungent to the taste, used in popular medicine under the name of Black Sampson. **1901** MOHR *Plant Life Ala.* 799 Black Sampson, . . . Open woods and prairies. — **(14) 1698** G. THOMAS *Penna. & N.J.* 19 There grows also in great plenty the Black Snake-Root, (fam'd for its sometimes preserving, but often curing the Plague, being infused only in Wine, Brandy or Rumm.) **1840** DEWEY *Mass. Flowering Plants* 21 Cohosh. Black snakeroot. . . . Strong medicinal purposes. **1941** R. WALKER *Lookout* 48 Among the wild plants once employed as antidotes for the bites of poisonous reptiles, are rattlesnake master, blacksnake root, rattlesnake-weed, Samson snakeroot, or scurfy.

2. In the names of birds: (1) **black and white creeping warbler,** (see quots.); (2) **-bellied,** designating various American birds (see quots.); (3) **-billed cuckoo,** a common North American cuckoo, *Coccyzus erythropthalmus,* so called to distinguish it from the yellow-billed cuckoo; (4) ***-bird,** see as a main entry; (5) **brant,** a species of dark-colored brant found on the Pacific Coast (see also quot. 1872); (6) **breast,** (*a*) (see quot.), (*b*) the black-bellied plover, *Squatarola squatarola,* in full **black breast plover;** (7) **breasted,** (see quots.); (8) **capped,** (*a*) designating various American birds (see quots.), (*b*) esp. the common chickadee; (9) **-chinned hummingbird,** a species of hummingbird, *Archilochus alexandri;* (10) **-crowned night heron,** an American variety of night heron; (11) ***duck,** any one of several American ducks, as the dusky duck, *Anas rubripes tristis,* having dark plumage, also transf.; (12) **hawk,** the American rough-legged hawk, cf. **3. c.** (8) and **4. c.** (7) below; (13) ***head,** a scaup duck, cf. **4. d.** (4) below; (14) **-headed grosbeak,** a grosbeak, *Hedymeles melanocephala,* found in the western U.S. and Mexico; (15) **poll,** a species of warbler, *Dendroica striata,* the males of which when in full plumage have the top of the head black, in full **black-poll warbler;** (16) **skimmer,** a long-winged marine bird, *Rhynchops nigra,* common on the southern coast of the U.S.; (17) **-throated blue warbler,** the blue flycatcher, *Dendroica caerulescens,* of the eastern states; (18) **-throated bunting,** =**dickcissel;** (19) **-throated gray warbler,** a warbler, *Dendroica nigrescens,* of the western states; (20) **warrior,** a large black hawk, *Buteo borealis barlani,* of the southern states; (21) **woodcock,** =**pileated woodpecker.**

(1) **1874** COUES *Birds N.W.* 45 *Mniotilta Varia,* . . . Black-and-white Creeping Warbler. **1946** HAUSMAN *Eastern Birds* 497 Black and White Warbler *Mniotilta varia*—Other Names—Black and White Creeping Warbler, Creeping Warbler, . . . Whitepoll Warbler. — (2) **1813** WILSON *Ornithology* VII. 41 Black-bellied Plover, *Charardrius apricarius;* . . . called by many gunners along the coast the Black-bellied Kildeer. *Ib.* IX. 79 Black-bellied Darter, or Snake-bird: *Plotus melanogaster.* **1874** COUES *Birds N.W.* 122 *Plectrophanes Ornatus,* Chestnut-collared Bunting; Black-bellied Longspur. *Ib.* 489 *Tringa Alpina* var. Americana, . . . Black-bellied or Red-breasted Sandpiper. **1948** *Chi. Tribune* 29 Sep. 1. 1/4 Small flocks of golden and black bellied plover dotted the shores of Wolf lake and Lake Calumet. — (3) **1908** KNIGHT *Birds Maine* 267 The Black-billed Cuckoo is found throughout the State and may be expected to arrive in spring as early even as May 18. **1945** *Nat. Geog. Mag.* June 733 This Black-billed Cuckoo built her nest in a currant bush, and the first of the eggs has just hatched a youngster that only a mother could love.

(5) **1858** BAIRD *Birds Pacific R.R.* 767 *Bernicla Nigricans,* Black Brant. . . . [Inhabits] Pacific coast of North America. Very rare on the Atlantic coast. **1872** *Amer. Naturalist* July 401 Two other interesting birds found here are the double-crested cormorant and the white pelican, the former bearing the singular local name of 'black brant!' **1946** R. PEATTIE *Pac. Coast Ranges* 99 Wild geese and black brant are also fairly numerous. — (6) (*a*) **1844** *Nat. Hist. N.Y., Zoology* II. 240 This species [of sandpiper, *Tringa cinclus*] is common on the coast of New-York, which it reaches in April, and is then called Black-breast. (*b*) **1856** *Spirit of Times* (N.Y.) 6 Sep. 9/2 Great sport is also to be had at Curlew, black-breasts, [and] red-breasted snipe. **1882** GODFREY *Nantucket* 157 In May spring black-breast plover are at times numerous. — (7) **1844** *Nat. Hist. N.Y., Zoology* II. 240 The Black-Breasted Sandpiper. *Tringa cinclus* . . . returns to us in the autumn, . . . and is then called Winter Snipe. **1871** LEWIS *Poultry Book* 57 Black-Breasted Red is another breed of game that has its hosts of admirers. — (8) (*a*) **1808** WILSON *Ornithology* I. 134 The Black-Capt Titmouse, *Parus Altricapillus,* . . . is one of our resident birds, active, noisy and restless. **1878** *Proc. U.S. Nat. Museum* I. 407 *Myiodioctes pusillus,* (var.) pileolata.-Californian Black-capped Green Warbler. **1948** *Prairie Club Bul.* Sep. 18 Among birds identified were the pine siskin, the black-capped sparrow, the pine grosbeak, and of course jays. (*b*) **1874** COUES *Birds N.W.* 20 *Parus Atricapillus,* . . . Black-capped Chickadee. **1946** HAUSMAN *Eastern Birds* 428 Carolina Chickadee [is] . . . similar to the Black-capped Chickadee but smaller by about an inch. — (9) **1858** BAIRD *Birds Pacific R.R.* 133 *Trochilus Alexandria,* Black chinned Humming Bird. **1940** JAEGER *Desert Wild Flowers* 245 Black-chinned hummingbirds probe the blossoms both for insects and nectar.

(10) **1844** [see ∗**quawk**]. **1939** LINCOLN *Migration* 101 Black-crowned Night Herons, particularly those individuals that nest in the central part of the breeding range, likewise drift to the northward. — (11) **1637** MORTON *New Canaan* II. iv, Ducks there are of three kindes, pide Ducks, gray Ducks, and black Ducks in great abundance. **1767** HUTCHINSON *Hist. Mass.* (1795) II. iii. 267 From this or a like action, probably took rise a common expression among English soldiers and sometimes English hunters, who, when they have killed an Indian, make their boast of having killed a black duck. **1946** HAUSMAN *Eastern Birds* 167 American Scoter [has] . . . some twenty-five or thirty local names, among which are: Black Scoter, Black Sea Duck, Black Coot, Black Duck, . . . Gray Coot, Smutty Coot. — (12) **1812** WILSON *Ornithology* VI. 82 The Black Hawk, *Talco niger,* . . . is . . . found most frequently along the marshy shores of our large rivers. . . . The Black Hawk . . . is a native of North America alone. **1869** *Amer. Naturalist* III. 228 The Black-hawk, by some supposed to be only a darker race of this species [=Rough-legged Buzzard], and once occasionally to be met with, is now unknown [in New England]. — (13) **1781–2** JEFFERSON *Notes Va.* (1787) 77 Black head. **1945** *Md. Conservationist* 17/1 The field glasses disclosed that they were black heads, or blue bills. — (14) **1889** *Cent.* 2632/3. **1939** LINCOLN *Migration* 84 Examples are the Pine Warbler, Rock Wren, Field Sparrow, Loggerhead Shrike and Black-headed Grosbeak.

(15) **1785** PENNANT *Arctic Zoology* II. 401 Black-poll Warbler . . . . Inhabits during summer, Newfoundland and New York. **1811** WILSON *Ornithology* IV. 40 Black-poll Warbler, *Sylvia striata,* . . . has considerable affinity to the Flycatchers in its habits. **1946** *Chi. D. News* 8 March 8/2 Black-poll warblers fly some 35 miles a day when they leave South America. — (16) **1813** WILSON *Ornithology* VII. 85 Black Skimmer, or Sheerwater: *Rhynchops nigra;* . . . is a truly singular fowl. **1946** HAUSMAN *Eastern Birds* 332 Black Skimmer *Rynchops nigra nigra* . . . skims and flies with vigor and grace just above the surface, its long lower mandible cleaving the water like a knife. — (17) **1808** WILSON *Ornithology* II. 115 Black-Throated Blue Warbler, *Sylvia Canadensis.* **1946** HAUSMAN *Eastern Birds* 513 Cairns's Warbler *Dendroica caerulescens cairnsi* [is] similar to the Black-throated Blue Warbler but with back more or less spotted with black. — (18) [**1785** PENNANT *Arctic Zoology* II. 363 Black-throated bunting . . . inhabits New York.] **1917** *Birds of Amer.* III. 75 The bird has been called the Black-throated Bunting and also the Little Meadowlark. — (19) **1858** BAIRD *Birds Pacific R.R.* 270 *Dendroica Nigrescens,* Baird. Black-throated Gray Warbler. *Hab.*—Pacific Coast, United States; Fort Thorn, New Mexico. **1917** *Birds of Amer.* III. 141 When the wise men gave names to the different birds, the Black-throated Gray Warbler got its name from the male, for he only has the black throat.

(20) **1831** AUDUBON *Ornith. Biog.* I. 441 The Black Warrior has been seen to pounce on a fowl, kill it almost instantly, and . . . conceal it. *Ib.* 442. **1874** COUES *Birds N.W.* 352 Harlan's Buzzard; Black Warrior. . . . I regard the claims of this species to validity as not yet established. — (21) **1811** WILSON *Ornithology* IV. 27 In Pennsylvania and the northern states he is called the Black Woodcock; in the southern states, the Log-cock. **1858** BAIRD *Birds Pacific R.R.* 107 Black Wood Cock; Log Cock. *Hab.*—North America from Atlantic to Pacific.

b. In less frequent bird names: (1) **black-billed magpie,** an American magpie found in the Rocky Mountain region, and so called to distinguish it from the yellow-billed magpie; (2) **-crested titmouse** (see quot.); (3) **flusterer,** the surf scoter, *Oidemia perspicillata* [quot. 1743 prob. quotes, inaccurately, the 1709 reference]; (4) ∗**heart,** =**black breast** (*b*); (5) **partridge,** the spruce partridge or grouse, *Canachites canadensis;* (6) **shouldered hawk,** ?the white-tailed hawk, *rare;* (7) **snipe,** (see quot.); (8) **snowbird,** the junco, *Junco hyemalis,* of northeastern America.

(1) **1869** *Amer. Naturalist* April 80 Black-billed Magpie (*Pica Hudsonica*) . . . continued common throughout the route westward [from the Bad Lands]. — (2) **1934** *Nat. Geog. Mag.* LXV. 578 The black-crested titmouse (*Baeolophus atricristatus atricristatus*) is found from the Rio Grande Valley in Texas south into eastern Mexico. — (3) **1709** LAWSON *Carolina* 149 Black Flusterers; some call these Old Wives. They are as black as Ink. The Cocks have white Faces. **1743** CATESBY *Carolina* App. p. xxxvii, The Coast of Virginia and Carolina in Winter [is visited by] . . . Black Duck, Black Flutterers, Whistlers. — (4) **1893** *Outing* June 224/1 A storm of 'black-hearts' drove down on us, flying but a few feet above the water.

(5) **1778** CARVER *Travels* 471 There are three sorts of partridges here, the brown, the red, and the black, the first of which are most esteemed. — (6) **1858** BAIRD *Birds Pacific R.R.* 37 The Black-shouldered Hawk . . . [has] lesser wing coverts glossy black, which forms a large oblong patch from the shoulder. — (7) **1872** *Amer. Naturalist* VI. 400 The glossy ibis (called 'black snipe!') is now a common summer bird. — (8) **1869** *Amer. Naturalist* VII. 634 The Black Snowbird breeds on the Graylock Range.

3. In the names of fishes: (1) **black-banded sunfish,** a small sunfish, *Mesogonistius chaetodon,* marked with vertical black bars; (2) **bass,** a fish of the genus *Micropterus* (see also quots. 1855, 1889), also attrib.; (3) **buffalo,** a buffalo fish, *Ictiobus urus;* (4) **drum,** the common drumfish, *Pogonias cromis,* found along the Atlantic Coast; (5) **eared pondfish,** a sunfish, *Lepomis auritus,* found in the eastern and southern states; (6) **ears,** a sunfish, *Xenotis megalotis,* found in the central and southern states; (7) **-eye sunfish,** a greenish sunfish, *Apomotis cyanellus,* found in the Great Lakes region; (8) **fin,** a Great Lakes cisco, *Leucichthys nigripinnis;* (9) **fish,** see as a main entry; (10) **grunts,** the black perch, *Lobotes surinamensis;* (11) **nurse,** a shark of inactive habits of the family Scymnidae; (12) **perch,** any one of numerous perch-like American fishes as the black sea bass, the tripletail, etc.; (13) **trout,** any one of various trout or trout-like fish having a very dark skin.

(1) **1934** *Nat. Geog. Mag.* LXV. 605 With it are found . . . the pygmy sunfish; [and] the black-banded sunfish, formerly known no farther south than North Carolina. — (2) **1815** *Trans. Lit. & Phil. Soc. N.Y.* I. 146 Basse; is a Dutch word, signifying perch. Black, or Oswego, basse, a fine fish, like our black fish. **1855** BAIRD in *Smithsonian Rep.* 323 Black Bass, Sea-Bass, *Centropristes nigricans.* . . . The black fish, as an article of food, may be reckoned among the best of the fishes of the coast. **1889** *Cent.* 571 Black-bass, a local name, along portions of the Pacific coast of the United-States, of a scorpaenoid fish, *Sebastichthys melanops,* or black rock-fish. **1947** *Sports Afield* Feb. 26/1 Ranch Branch, a tributary to the San Saba River, is a paradise for the black

bass fisherman in wet seasons. — (3) **1842** *Nat. Hist. N.Y., Zoology* IV. 203 *Catostomus elongatus*. The Missouri Sucker, Black Horse and Black Buffalo. — (4) **1709** LAWSON *Carolina* 156 Black Drums are . . . shap'd like a fat pig; they are . . . not so common with us as to the Northward. **1884** GOODE *Aquat. Animals* 367 The adult is known as the 'Black Drum,' the young as the 'Striped Drum.'

(5) **1818** MITCHILL in *Amer. Monthly Mag.* II. 247 Black eared Pond-Fish, *Labrus appendix*. **1842** *Nat. Hist. N.Y., Zoology* IV. 32 The Black-Eared Pondfish. *Pomotis appendix*. . . . Its broad appendix distinguishes it. — (6) **1820** RAFINESQUE in *Western Rev.* II. 49 Big-ear Sunfish, *Icthelis megalotis*, . . . a fine species, called Red-belly, Black-ears, Black-tail Sunfish, &c. It lives in the Kentucky, Licking, and Sandy rivers, &c. — (7) **1819** *Western Rev.* I. 376 Blackeye Sunfish, *Icthelis melanops*. Vulgar names, blue-fish, black-eyes, sun-fish, blue-bass, &c. — (8) **1875** *Amer. Naturalist* IX. 135 This Indiana Argyrosomus appears to be quite distinct from the species found in Lake Michigan; *i.e.*, the shallow-water 'herring' . . . and 'black fin' (*A. nigripennis* Gill).

(10) **1814** MITCHILL *Fishes N.Y.* 419 Some of the fishermen call him . . . black grunts. — (11) **1883** *Harper's Mag.* Jan. 186/2 One of the most interesting luminous fishes is a shark . . . that resembles the black nurse, or scymnus, that I have often caught on the Florida coast. — (12) **1706** in *Amer. Hist. Rev.* XII. (1907) 335 There are . . . Pearch of severall sorts. the white Bellied Pearch, the Red Bellied Pearch the Black Pearch and the Yellow Bellied Pearch. **1780** W. FLEMING *Travels Amer. Col.* 646 The Inhabitants of this place [in Ky.] catched numbers of fish yesterday and today all Cat fish except a black perch such as in Roanoke. **1883** *Cent. Mag.* July 376/2, I have heard them [=black bass] called black perch, yellow perch, and jumping perch up the Rockcastle & Cumberland rivers. — (13) **1849** LANMAN *Alleghany Mts.* ix. 65 On inquiring of a homespun angler what fish the river did produce, he replied: 'Salmon, black-trout, red horse, hog-fish suckers and cat-fish.' **1883** *Cent. Mag.* July 376/2, I have heard them [=black bass] called . . . white and black trout in Tennessee. **1891** *Cent.* 6503 *Black trout*, the Lake Tahoe trout; specified as *Salmo henshawi*.

b. In other fish names sufficiently defined in the quots.: (1) **black back,** (2) **candlefish,** (3) **catfish,** (4) **grouper,** (5) **Harry,** (6) * **horse,** (7) **salmon,** (8) **sea bass,** (9) * **smith,** see as a main entry, (10) **snapper,** (11) **sucker, suckrel.**

(1) **1815** *Mass. H.S. Coll.* 2 Ser. IV. 294 The second [kind of alewife], less in size, and usually called 'black backs,' equally true to instinct, as invariably seek the Agawaam. — (2) **1884** GOODE *Fisheries U.S.* I. 268 Black Candlefish (*Anoplopoma fimbria*). This species is known in Puget Sound by the name of 'Horse-mackerel.' At San Francisco it is usually called 'Candle-fish.' — (3) **1805** T. M. HARRIS *State of Ohio* 116 The *Black Cat-Fish* are caught weighing from six to one hundred and ten pounds. **1842** *Nat. Hist. N.Y., Zoology* IV. 185 The Black Catfish, *Pimelodus atrarius*, . . . occurs commonly in Wappingers creek. — (4) **1878** *Proc. U.S. Nat. Museum* I. 182 The Black Grouper (*Epinephelius nigritus*) of the Southern Coast.

(5) **1814** MITCHILL *Fishes N.Y.* 416 Black harry, hannahills, and blue-fish, are some of the names by which he [*sc.* sea bass] is known. **1842** *Nat. Hist. N.Y., Zoology* IV. 25 The Black Sea Bass, *Centropristes nigricans*, . . . [is] sometimes called Blue-Fish, Black Harry. **1888** GOODE *Amer. Fishes* 39 In the Middle States the Sea Bass is called . . . 'Black Harry.' — (6) **1842** *Nat. Hist. N.Y., Zoology* IV. 203 *Catostomus elongatus*. The Missouri Sucker, Black Horse and Black Buffalo. — (7) **1832** WILLIAMSON *Maine* I. 160 There are three varieties; the *black* Salmon, which is smallest; the *hawkbill* . . . ; and the *smoothnosed*. **1856** *Spirit of Times* (N.Y.) 20 Dec. 253/1 We have two kinds of this fish [the pike-perch, in the Ohio River]; one is called the white, the other the black salmon. **1890** *Cent.*, 5315/1 Black salmon, a local name of the great lake-trout, *Salvelinus* (*Cristivomer*) *namaycush*. — (8) **1842** *Nat. Hist. N.Y., Zoology* IV. 24 The Black Sea Bass. *Centropristis nigricans* . . . is one of the most savory and delicate of the fishes which appear in our markets from May to July.

(10) **1775** ROMANS *Nat. Hist. Fla.* App. 52 The fish caught here . . . are such as . . . red, grey and black snappers, dog-snappers, mutton-fish. **1888** GOODE *Amer. Fishes* 79 The Gray Snapper, *Lutjanus caxis*, . . . is called the 'Gray Snapper' in South Florida, and the 'Black Snapper' at Pensacola. **1891** *Cent.* 5727/2 Black snapper, a local name of a form of the cod, *Gadus morrhua*, living near the shore. — (11) **1839** STORER *Mass. Fishes* 86 *Cyprinus nigricans*. . . . The Black Sucker. . . . Color of the back, black; sides reddish yellow. **1820** RAFINESQUE in *Western Rev.* II. 355 Black Suckrel. *Cycleptus nigrescens*. . . . A rare fish, whose flesh is very much esteemed. It is also found in the Missouri, whence it is sometimes called the Missouri Sucker. Length two feet. **1870** *Amer. Naturalist* IV. 386 Mud-loving species . . . common to the Delaware and its tributaries . . . [include] Black Sucker.

c. In the names of, or with reference to, various other animals: (1) * **black and tan,** see as a main entry; (2) **bear,** the common American bear, *Ursus americanus;* (3) **cat,** =**fisher 1;** (4) * **cattle,** (*a*) buffalo, *rare*, (*b*) slaves, *slang*, *obs.;* (5) **elk,** (see quot.), *obs.;* (6) **footed ferret,** an American weasel, *Mustela nigripes*, found in western states; (7) **fox,** a red fox, *Vulpes fulva*, of a color phase in which its fur is black; (8) **Black Hawk (horse),** =**Morgan horse,** cf. **2.** (12) and **4. c.** (7); (9) **moose,** a color-variety of the moose, *Alces americanus;* (10) **racer,** a fleet sub-species, *Coluber constrictor constrictor*, of the blacksnake; (11) **rattlesnake,** =**massasauga;** (12) **runner,** =**black racer;** (13) **skunk,** a skunk having only a small bit or strip of white, the fur of which is regarded in the fur trade as the choicest; (14) **snake,** see as a main entry; (15) **squirrel,** a color-variety of the common gray squirrel or fox squirrel; (16) * **tail,** * **tailed,** see as main entries; (17) **water snake,** ?a blacksnake, *obs.*

(2) **1805** LEWIS in *Ann. 9th Cong.* 2 Sess. 1041 Skins of the small deer, black bear, some beaver. **1945** *Outdoor Life* Oct. 76/2 Naturalists declare the Arizona black bear is omnivorous and normally content to feed on herbs, seeds, roots, insects, rodents, carrion, and honey. — (3) **1791** *Mass. Laws* (1801) I. 509 No person . . . shall hereafter, in either of the months of June, July, August or September, . . . kill, any Otter, Beaver, . . . Black-Cat, [etc.]. **1882** *Cent. Mag.* March 719/2 The black cat is the most successful cub slayer. — (4) (*a*) **1812** STUART *Narratives* 191 The sides are 3 feet high and the whole covered with Buffalo skins, so we have now a tolerable shelter and eighteen Black Cattle. (*b*) **1819** FAUX *Mem. Days* 59 Their black cattle (alias slaves) do not breed freely. **1823** in MATHEWS *Memoirs* III. 387 'I guess you have considerable hogs and niggers?'—'Yes, we have plenty of them black cattle.'

(5) **1842** *Nat. Hist. N.Y., Zoology* I. 116 The Moose . . . is known with us under the various names of Flat-Horned Elk, Black Elk [etc.]. — (6) **1885** *Amer. Naturalist* Sep. 922 The long lost black-footed ferret, or prairie dog-hunter, of Western Kansas, whose rediscovery was recorded a few years since by Dr. Coues. **1917** *Mammals of Amer.* 126 The Black-footed Ferret is a true Weasel, but differs from the other members enough to be placed in a group by itself. — (7) **1602** BRERETON *Virginia* 13 We saw . . . Luzernes, Black Foxes [etc.]. **1826** GODMAN *Nat. Hist.* I. 276 The black fox is found throughout the northern parts of America, . . . where it is considered among the richest and most valuable of furs. **1925** HEMING *Living Forest* 99 The fur o' the so-called black fox is a very dark slaty blue, an' both th' inner an' outer hair is of that color. — (8) **1856** *Spirit of Times* 27 Sep. 55/3 There was a big show of horses; the Black Hawks were in their glory. . . . A yearling Black Hawk changed hands at $900 and over. **1872** *Vt. Board Agric. Rep.* I. 208 The close built, sound, swelled muscled Black Hawk or Morgan horses. — (9) **1724** KIDDER *Exped. Lovewell* (1865) 16 [We] . . . killed a Black Moose that day. **1858** THOREAU *Maine Woods* 141 He had the horns of what he called 'the black moose that goes in low lands.' . . . The 'red moose' was another kind.

(10) **1819** THOMAS *Travels* 163 Some garter snakes are found; and I learn that the water snake and black racer will complete the list. **1908** *D.N.* III. 291 *Black-runner*, a black snake noted for fleetness. Also called *black racer*, or simply *racer*. — (11) **1778** CARVER *Travels* 4 The Rattle Snake. There appears to be two species of this reptile; one of which is commonly termed the Black, and the other the Yellow. — (12) **1788** SCHÖPF *Reise* II. 214 Eine Schlange, der schwarze Läufer (Black Runner) genannt, wurde vor einiger Zeit getödet, und 12 Fuss lang gefunden. **1908** [see **black racer**]. — (13) **1947** *Hunting & Fishing* Feb. 13/2 To my surprise, one morning I had two nice black skunk and one ten pound turkey hen in one No. 2 Victor Trap.

(15) [**1602** BRERETON *Virginia* 16 Squirrels, which to the Northward are blacke, and accounted very rich furres.] **1682** ASH *Carolina* 22 There are . . . the flying Squirrel, . . . the Red, the Grey, the Fox and Black Squirrels. **1945** MATHEWS *Talking* 156 The black squirrel is seldom seen. He is the black phase of the gray squirrel. — (17) **1791** J. LONG *Voyages* 160 The black water snake is used by the Indians when they go to war.

d. In the names of insects: (1) **black bug,** (*a*) the larva of a pine sawyer, (*b*) ?the chinch bug, *rare* in both senses; (2) * **fly,** (see quot. 1889); (3) **Black Hills beetle,** (see quot. 1909), also **black hill beetle;** (4) **wasp,** =?**dirt-dauber;** (5) **weevil,** a name used in the South for the rice weevil, *Sitophilus oryzae;* (6) **widow,** any one of various spiders of the genus *Latrodectus*, esp. the female, *L. mactans*, so called from its color and its habit of devouring its mate; (7) **worm,** any one of various black grubs that attack plants and trees.

(1) (*a*) **1859** G. W. PERRY *Turpentine Farming* 103 Black Bug.—This insect is found as small as a hair up to its full-grown state, which

is about the size of a common straw, and a quarter of an inch long. It will cut through the thickest kind of bark to the skin at any size, and commences to do so at the appearance of warm weather. (*b*) **1861** *Ill. Agric. Soc. Trans.* IV. 316 When the black bug is plenty, you may expect the grub in three years. — **(2) 1776** in *Md. Hist. Mag.* XXVII. 258 Bit very much with black flies, face in lumps. **1889** *Cent.* 2294/1 Black fly, any one of the species of the genus *Simulium*, some of which are extraordinarily abundant in the northern woods of America, and cause great suffering by their bites. **1946** *Outdoors* June 23/2 There is no place under God's heavens where the black flies are so numerous and so enthusiastic, and so hungry, as round-about a beaver bog. — **(3) 1905** *U.S.D.A. Bureau of Entom. Bul. 56* (*title*), The Black Hills Beetle, with further notes on its distribution, life history, and methods of control. **1909** Hopkins *Scolytid Beetles of N.A. Forests* 90 The Black Hills beetle . . . [attacks] living and sometimes injured and felled, yellow pine, lodgepole pine, limber pine, Mexican white pine, white spruce, and Engelmann spruce from the Black Hills, South Dakota, to Southern Arizona, and westward into Utah, and is very destructive. **1945** *Boulder* (Colo.) *D. Camera* 12 Nov. 5/6 The campaign during the past year against the black hill beetle [was] carried out by the forest service. — **(4) 1789** Morse *Amer. Geog.* 62 Insects found in America . . . [include the] Black wasp. **1902** Harben *A. Daniel* 52 'You look fer the world like a dirt-dauber.' This comparison to a kind of black wasp came from Pole Baker.

(5) 1849 *Rep. Comm. Patents: Agric.* (1850) 153 These are the *Calandra oryzae*, the true rice weevil; distinguished from his European cousin by the two reddish spots on each wing-cover, and known among us [in Mississippi] as the 'black weevil.' — **(6) 1922** *Science* 19 May 539/2 In regard to the 'Black Widow,' *Lactrodectus mactans* he quotes Dr. McCook as of the opinion that the bite of this spider is 'in most instances of small consequence.' **1948** *Democrat* 22 April 4/3 [She] crawled back into bed with a black widow spider after having been bitten one time. — **(7) 1773** in N. Webster *Hist. Epid. and Pest. Dis.* I. (1799) 259 In 1770, cotemporary with the clouds of flies in India and a most fatal pestilence among men and cattle in Europe, appeared in America a black worm . . . which devoured the grass and corn. . . . They all moved nearly in one direction. **1861** *Ill. Agric. Soc. Trans.* V. 476 The army worm . . . has probably existed there [=New England] for a century, . . . being known by the popular name of 'black worm.'

4. In miscellaneous combs.: (1) **black betty,** a liquor or whisky bottle, *obs.*, cf. **Black Betts,** in **f.** (1) below; (2) **boy,** one of those Pennsylvania backwoodsmen who on occasion from 1763 to 1769 served under James Smith in defending their frontier, esp. Conococheague Valley, against Indian depredations, and who in 1765 attacked and burned a pack train carrying trading goods, including arms and ammunition, to the Indians, *obs.*, cf. **c.** (2) below; (3) **cockade,** (see quot. 1914); (4) **Black Dan,** Daniel Webster, a nickname; (5) **-eyed Susan,** (see quots.), *obs.*, cf. **1. c.** (5); (6) **Black Friday,** a day upon which an exceptional calamity occurs, esp. in the U.S. Sep. 24, 1869, and Sep. 19, 1873, days upon which financial panics began; (7) **gold,** oil, also transf.; (8) * **Black Hand,** a secret society of Italians in the U.S. chiefly concerned in blackmail; (9) **Black Hander,** member of a Black Hand Society; (10) * **Black Horse Cavalry,** (*a*) a company of cavalry organized in Jefferson County, Va., just before the Civil War, which played a prominent role in that struggle (see also quot. 1866), *obs.*, (*b*) a legislative coterie that practices a form of blackmail by threatening to enact laws against corporations unless paid not to do so; (11) **Black Maria,** a closed vehicle in which prisoners are conveyed to and from prison; (12) **money,** a term formerly used in Maryland in distinguishing the red money, *q.v.*, of that state from that printed in black, *obs.;* (13) **ore,** a variety of iron ore, *rare;* (14) **pony,** ?variant of "dark horse," *obs.;* (15) **ride,** a performance of black riding, *obs.;* (16) **Black Rider,** one of a band of mounted banditti represented as having operated during the Revolutionary War, *rare;* (17) **riding,** (see quot.), *obs.;* (18) **roller,** designating a dust cloud or dust storm, *colloq.;* (19) **salter,** one who makes black salts, *obs.;* (20) **salts,** crude potash, *obs.;* (21) * **sand,** sand that is dark in color because of its ferrous content, often associated with gold; (22) **smithery,** (*a*) a smithy, (*b*) the work of a blacksmith or that done in a blacksmith's shop; (23) **Blackspots,** the Molly Maguires, *obs.*, cf. **b.** (11) below; (24) **tariff,** a term used by the Democrats for the high protective tariff passed by the Whigs in 1842, *obs.;* (25) * **top,** designating an improved road finished off with material that leaves its surface black.

(1) 1821 Doddridge *Backwoodsman & Dandy*, He that got first to the bride's house, got black betty. *Ib.*, The company stopt and every boy and girl, old and young, . . . must kiss black betty; that is to take a good slug of dram. **1880** in Greve *Cent. Hist. of Cincinnati* (1904) I. 463 They didn't forget to pass the 'old black betty,' filled with good old peach brandy, among the old pioneers. — **(2) 1769** *Pa. Gazette* 2 Nov., There appeared an extract of a letter from Bedford . . . relative to James Smith, as being apprehended on suspicion of being a black boy. *Ib.*, James Smith . . . is stiled the principal ring leader of the black boys. **1831** A. S. Withers *Chron. Border Warfare* 79 A company of riflemen, called the Black boys (from the fact of their painting themselves red and black, after the Indian fashion,) . . . contributed to preserve the Conococheague valley, during the years 1763 and 1764. — **(3) 1798** Hiltzheimer *Diary* (1893) 10 May 255 Last evening there was some disturbance in the streets, occasioned by men of the Black Cockade and those of White Cockade, and some arrests were made. **1856** *Western Citizen* (Paris, Ky.) 18 July 1/5 He was an old federalist, wore the black cockade, [and] defended the alien and sedition laws. **1914** McLaughlin & Hart *Cyclo. Amer. Govt.* I. 133 Black Cockade. The badge of the Federalist party, assumed during the X Y Z agitation with France in 1798, as an expression of disapproval of the French tricolor cockade worn frequently by the Republicans, and as a patriotic reminder of the American Revolution when the black cockade was worn as a symbol of patriotism. — **(4) 1844** *Republican Sentinel* (Richmond, Va.) 4 Oct. 2/4 Mr. Clay has changed places with Black Dan, and is annoyed to death in endeavoring to reach the proper position on the Texas question.

(5) 1869 in Mathews *Beginnings* 153 Among names of revolvers I remember the following: Meat in the Pot, . . . Black-eyed Susan. **1945** *Everybody's Digest* Aug. 89 For his gun he has various names: 'blue lightnin',' 'black-eyed susan,' 'equalizer,' 'smoke iron,' 'six' and 'Colt.' — **(6) 1873** Lawrence *Silverland* 17 The audacity of our 'bulls' and 'bears' pales before the ordinary operations of Wall Street —not taking into account such crises as the Black Friday, or the recent conflict over Erie's. **1911** Hovey *Morgan* 53 Black Friday and the Gold Corner were synonymous with his name. **1948** *Time* 14 June 89/1 There was . . . Jay Gould, . . . whose attempt to corner gold brought on the 'Black Friday' of 1869 and disrupted the nation's whole credit structure. — **(7) 1924** Witwer *Roughly Speaking* (1925) 27 Gold—black gold—this farm is a hotbed of *oil!* **1948** *So. Bend* (Ind.) *Tribune* 3 Apr. 5/1 The 'Black Gold' of the farm belt—grunting hogs—is beginning to tarnish. **1948** *Dly. Ardmoreite* (Ardmore, Okla.) 1 Aug. 9/1 His company instructed him to return here and file a claim on the land where he drilled the 'makeshift' well that poured forth the black gold. — **(8) 1904** *N.Y. Tribune* 31 July 2 For months the black hand society has been forcing Italians to contribute to its treasury with threats of death. **1931** Reeve *Golden Age Crime* 43 The labor unions, some of them, have been as contributory as the Camorra, the Mafia and the Black Hand. — **(9) 1923** L. J. Vance *Baroque* viii. 49 The Wop detective that used to play horse with the Black Handers.

(10) (*a*) **1862** in S. Cox *In Cong.* (1865) 221 A cry was raised that the Black Horse, a formidable body of the rebel cavalry . . . were charging upon us. **1866** *39th Cong.* 2 Sess. 6 Sen. Ex. Doc. 55 Bands of men styling themselves 'Regulators,' 'Jay-Hawkers,' and 'Black-horse cavalry,' have infested different parts of the State [Ga.], committing the most fiendish and diabolical outrages on the freedmen. (*b*) **1893** *Congress. Rec.* Dec. 453 Speaking for New Jersey, I know something of the black-horse cavalry force and the way they do their work at Trenton sometimes. I know . . . the way the black horse does business around Legislatures. **1914** *Cyclo. Amer. Govt.* I. 133 Black Horse Cavalry. A derogatory appellation given to a coterie of Republican members in the New York legislature charged with selling legislative privileges and extorting money from corporations by the introduction of blackmailing legislation. — **(11) 1847** *Boston Ev. Traveller* 25 Sep. 2/3 A new Black Maria . . . a new wagon for the conveyance of prisoners to and from the courts of justice. **1948** Chaplin *Wobbly* 45 Once or twice the 'Black Maria' clattered up, and the shamefaced kids were dragged off to the precinct lockup. — **(12) 1782** *Md. Journal* 31 Dec. (Th.), The House is against taking either black or red Money in Payment for taxes. **1787** *Ib.* 28 Sep., (*advt.*) (Th.), Cash given for black and Continental State Money. — **(13) 1804** *Mass. H.S. Coll.* IX. 255 Black ore [is] found in deep water on a muddy bottom in cakes of a dirty black colour, and of an earthy appearance. **1845** *Hunt's Merch. Mag.* XIII. 172 It was estimated, that this argentiferous ore, locally termed 'the black ore,' produced on an average from $87.50 to $100 per ton. — **(14) 1833** *Niles' Reg.* XLIV. 345/2 Another black poney—The new brig John Gilpin, built at Baltimore, left that port in June, 1832. **1834** C. A. Davis *Lett. J. Downing* 137, I wish you'd git a black pony goin this season, like the folks did last year, who print a paper down-cellar under yourn.

(15) **1857** *Letter* in E. L. Green *Hist. Univ. S.C.* 243 Friday night we had a beautiful sight—a black-ride in the Campus. There were four or five riders half masked with their faces blacked. . . . It was a splendid sight to see them galloping up and down the Campus, waving their flambeaux. *Ib.*, This morning some four or five were called up before the faculty . . . to answer as to the part they took in the blackride. — **(16) 1841** SIMMS *Kinsmen* v. (1882) 51 The Black Riders of Congaree . . . were dressed in complete black—each carried . . . all the usual equipments of the well-mounted dragoon. *Ib.* 65 The chief of the Black Riders. — **(17) 1851** HALL *College Words* 20 At the College of South Carolina, it has until within a few years been customary for the students, disguised and painted black, to ride across the college-yard at midnight, on horseback, with vociferations and the sound of horns. *Black riding* is recognized by the laws of the College as a very high offence. — **(18) 1936** *Dly. Oklahoman* (Okla. City) 17 Mar. 5/1 He disappeared just before a 'black roller' dust cloud made midnight of mid-day Sunday. — **(19) 1880** E. KIRKE *Garfield* 6 The boy overcame her scruples, and thus our future President became prime-minister to a black-salter. **1882** THAYER *From Log Cabin* 150 The manufacturer of the article [i.e., black salts] was called a 'black salter.'

(20) 1864 T. L. NICHOLS *Amer. Life* II. 213 The process . . . of boiling the lye into black salts, was commonplace. **1924** MCCONNELL *Frontier Law* 6 The lye thus obtained [i.e., by leaching wood ashes] was boiled down in large iron kettles until it became what was called by pioneers 'black salts,' now known as concentrated lye. — **(21) 1844** GREGG *Commerce of Prairies* I. 170 In this manner they continue till nothing remains in the bottom of the *batea* but a little heavy black sand mixed with a few grains of gold. **1936** MCKENNA *Black Range* 5 Before long I could pan the black sand and even count the colors to the pan. — **(22)** *(a)* **a1855** KELLEY *Humors* 303 Of course the town—of some four houses, six 'groceries,' a *store* and blacksmithery—was aroused, indignant! *(b)* **1889** *Advance* (Chicago) 21 March 229 Carpentry, blacksmithery, and carriage making are also chief industries for the Indian on the plain. — **(23) 1888** M. LANE *Pol. Catch-Words* 18 Oct. 15 They were known in one locality as 'Blackspots,' and in another as 'Buckshots,' and committed all sorts of murders, and outrages. — **(24) 1846** *Cong. Globe* Jan. 92 Let this state of things about the 'black tariff.' *Ib.* App. 1 July 1043/1, I might compromise a little rather than see the country longer consigned to the tender mercies of the black tariff of 1842.

(25) 1931 *Amer. City* Oct. 112/1 This was done by adding a black border for the letters and other characters, which for black top pavements are yellow. **1948** *Chi. Tribune* 7 March 1. 2/3 He promised . . . a black-top road running by every rural mail box.

For **black bottom, *jack, *smith, *snake** see as main entries.

b. Used of or in allusion to Negroes: (1) **Black and Brown,** =**Black Republican,** cf. **black and tan 2;** (2) **belt,** *(a)* a southern region, esp. in Alabama and Mississippi, characterized by rich black prairie soil, and by a preponderantly Negro population, *(b)* any region of dense Negro population; (3) **code,** a legal code applying to the colored population, esp. to that of a southern state before emancipation; (4) **county,** a southern county in which the Negro population predominates; (5) ***face,** *(a)* a Negro, *obs.*, *(b)* an actor made up to play a Negro role or a theatrical entertainment given by such actors, usu. attrib.; (6) **flesh,** =**black stock,** *obs.;* (7) **law,** a law that discriminates against Negroes; (8) **liner,** during Reconstruction in the South, one who in drawing the color line gave preference to Negroes, *obs.;* (9) **mammy,** *S.* a colored nurse, *colloq.;* (10) **Black Republican,** see as a main entry; (11) ***spot,** the area in the U.S. over which slavery was formerly prevalent, *rare,* cf. **4.** (23) above; (12) **state,** a southern state in which the colored population is numerous, *obs.;* (13) **stock,** Negro slaves, *obs.;* (14) **university,** a school for the underprivileged, esp. Negroes, *rare.*

(1) 1860 *Olympia* (Wash.) *Pioneer* 9 Mar. 1/5 (*headline*), Co-operation of the Black and 'Brown' Republicans. — **(2)** *(a)* **1875** *Cong. Rec.* 8 Jan. 342/1 During this last campaign . . . I made a number of speeches in Georgia. I spoke in what is known as the 'Black Belt.' **1910** *Sat. Ev. Post* 29 Oct. 25/2 Summed up, they have bought the most mortgages in the following regions: Iowa, western Ohio, . . . [and] that part of Texas known as the 'Black Belt,' which is bounded by Paris on the east, Wichita Falls on the west, Oklahoma on the north and Austin on the south. **1945** *Democrat* 23 Aug. 2/3 calves gain two pounds per day on central Alabama pastures, according to the figures of the Black Belt experiment station. *(b)* **1943** OTTLEY *New World* 63 Negroes mostly sought their entertainment at house-rent parties, a distinctly Harlem innovation that became the vogue in other Black Belts of the country. **1948** *Chi. D. News* 7 May 6/3 A slow expansion of Negro families into white communities adjoining the overcrowded 'Black Belt' is expected. — **(3) 1840** *N.O. Picayune* 30 July 2/1 A black man . . . has been arrested and . . . [will] be tried before Judge Preval, under the Black Code. **1947** LUMPKIN *Southerner* 65 South Carolina, with its usual forthrightness of action, had its so-called 'Black Code' written and ready for operation by Christmas of 'sixty-five. — **(4) 1888** *Cong. Rec.* 26 Sep. 8947/1 Justices of the peace in the black counties . . converted their offices into engines of oppression to both races.

(5) *(a)* **1704** S. KNIGHT *Journal* 40 Order the master to pay 40s to black face. **1899** CUSHMAN *Hist. Indians* 312 Do they not even now kick and strike us as they do their black-faces? *(b)* [**1869** DUMONT *Benedict's Cong. Songster* 9 Lew made his first bow before the public at the Metropolitan Theatre in a black face.] **1901** *Cosmopolitan* Sep. 637/2 The old-time brand of performance in black face has not undergone improvement, for its sphere of usefulness has been superseded by the variety-hall. **1947** *Redbook* Sep. 12 When two young men walked into an Arkansas radio station prepared to do a blackface act, they found the preceding acts had all been blackface, so they made a quick switch to homespun mountain folk. — **(6) 1827** COOPER *Prairie* viii, The newspapers of Kentuck have called you a dealer in black flesh a hundred times, but little did they reckon that you drove the trade into white families. — **(7) 1848** *N.Y. Wkly. Tribune* 12 Feb. 5/3 Bills to repeal the atrocious Black Laws of Ohio have been defeated in the House by votes of 42 to 23 and 40 to 25. **1852** T. HUGHES in J. Ludlow *Hist. U.S.* 342 The Topeka constitution . . . contained one article . . . which must not be passed over. I mean that commonly known as the 'black law,' by which coloured people were excluded from the territory. **1943** OTTLEY *New World* 23 In the South, there was the emergence of the Ku Klux Klan, the enactment of Black Laws which sharply restrict the Negro even to this day. — **(8) 1875** *44th Congress* 2 Sess. 45 Sen. Misc. Doc. 583 Warren County . . . made a clean sweep of the county officers for the black-liners, and to-day scores of their ignorant dupes lie buried in the ditches. — **9) 1886** B. P. POORE *Reminisc.* I. 538 He loved his 'old black mammy,' and she loved him. **1904** F. LYNDE *Grafters* vi. 81 Old Chloe . . . was my black mammy.

(11) 1851 A. LAWRENCE *Diary & Corr.* 307 We have allowed the 'black spot' to be too far spread over our land; it should have been restrained more than thirty years ago. — **(12) 1814** *Niles' Reg.* VI. 189/1 In 1792 the exports of the 'black' state of South Carolina were equal to the exports of . . . Massachusetts and New Hampshire. **1902** *Everybody's Mag.* Apr. 394/2, I recalled . . . the low level of public life in all the 'black' States. — **(13) 1861** VICTOR *Southern Rebellion* I. 234 The oldest families in the State . . . derived their chief revenue from their annual sales of 'black stock.' — **(14) 1870** MACRAE *Americans* I. 241 Then come its chartered colleges at Berea (Kentucky), Nashville (Tennessee), and Atlanta (Georgia). 'Black Universities' they are sometimes called, though at Berea College nearly 100 of the students are white.

See also **black and tan 3, black bottom 1.**

c. Used of or in allusion to Indians or those having to do with them, chiefly obs.: (1) **Blackarms,** a name formerly used for Cheyenne Indians, app. through an error in interpreting their tribal sign in the sign language; (2) ***boy,** (see quots.), cf. **4.** (2); (3) **dance,** =**powwow 2;** (4) **drink,** a decoction of the leaves of the yaupon, *Ilex vomitoria,* formerly used by the Indians of the southern states as a ceremonial drink and as a medicine; (5) **Blackfoot,** see as a main entry; (6) ***Black Gown,** a Jesuit missionary among the western Indians, *obs.;* (7) **Black Hawk War,** a war waged by the U.S. Government against the Sac and Fox Indians in Illinois and southern Wisconsin in 1831–32, cf. **2.** (12), **3. c.** (8); (8) **medicine,** (see quot.); (9) **Blackmouth dance,** (see quot.), *obs.;* (10) **Black Robe,** (see quots. and cf. **Black Gown**); (11) **seed,** (see quot.), *rare,* cf. **1. b.** (11); (12) **-wood dance,** see **Blackmouth dance.**

(1) 1813 *Niles' Reg.* IV. 265/1 He had been considerably to the south and east among the nations called Blackarms and Arapahays. — **(2) 1635** *Relat. Md.* v. 34 The Children live with their Parents; the Boyes untill they come to the full growth of men; then they are put into the number of Bow-men, and are called Black-boyes. **1749** ROBERT GOADBY *Life Bampfylde Moore Carew* 93 They [*sc.* the American Indians] have servants whom they call black boys. — **(3) 1778** CARVER *Travels* 270 The nations to the westward of the Mississippi, and on the borders of Lake Superior, still continue to make use of the Powwow or Black Dance. — **(4) 1772** D. TAITT in *Travels Amer. Col.* 503, I went this Morning to the Hot house and Stayed there about two hours smoking and drinking black drink. **1946** *Nat. Geog. Mag.* Jan. 59/1 In practically all important ceremonies held in the Southeast, the use of the black drink was an essential feature.

(6) **1804** tr. VOLNEY *Climate & Soil U.S.* 409 This is as difficult to the *black gowns* as to ourselves. **1880** CABLE *Grandissimes* 25 The year 1682 saw a humble 'black gown' dragging and splashing his way . . . through the swamps of Louisiana, . . . backed by French carbines and Mohican tomahawks. — **(7) 1838** *Chi. Democrat* 21 Nov. 1/2 At the commencement of the Black Hawk war, there were but seventeen families. **1948** *Ill. State Arch. Soc. Jrnl.* April 43/2 Historic figures had to do with the park area at the time of the Black Hawk war. — **(8) 1868** H. A. BOLLER *Among the Indians* 27 The Council concluded with a feast, consisting of 'black medicine' (coffee) and hard bread. — **(9) 1899** CUSHMAN *Hist. Indians* 499 The Chickasaws had two dances sacred to women alone and in which they only participated—one was called . . . Blackwood Dance; the other, . . . Blackmouth Dance.

(10) 1811 tr. HUMBOLDT *Political Essay* I. 116 The Canadian savages call themselves Metoktheniakes, born of the sun, without allowing themselves to be persuaded of the contrary by the *black robes*, a name which they give to the missionaries. **1846** *Freeman's Mag.* (N.Y.) 14 Mar. 294/1 The Winnebago Indian Chief . . . [reported] that the nation wished their brother of the Black Robe (meaning a Catholic Priest) to reside in the nation. **1947** *Nat. Geog. Mag.* July 67/2 The first of the 'Black Robes' died martyrs' deaths under torture and tomahawk. — **(11) 1809** IRVING *Knickerb. Hist. of N.Y.* I. v. 48 They [Indians] were a perverse, illiterate, dumb, beardless, bare-bottomed *black-seed*.

d. Designating or with reference to diseases in plants and animals: (1) ***black ball,** smut in wheat, *obs.;* (2) ***canker,** the disease melanosis; (3) **foot,** (see quot.); (4) ***head,** a fatal infectious disease of turkeys, peacocks, etc., cf. **2.** (13); (5) ***hearted,** (see quots.); (6) **knot,** (see quot. 1889); (7) **leg,** scurvy, *obs.;* (8) **rot,** (*a*) any one of various diseases of plants that cause black discoloration and decay, (*b*) a disease affecting poultry; (9) **rust,** the wheat rust, or a disease resembling this; (10) **smallpox,** a fatal form of smallpox marked by cutaneous hemorrhages; (11) **tongue,** an affection of the tongue, in human beings or cattle, symptomatic of various diseases, also the disease itself; (12) **tooth,** (see quot. 1909); (13) **wart,** =**black knot.**

(1) 1856 *Rep. Comm. Patents: Agric.* 186 The spores of parasitical fungi . . . may still be present in sufficient quantities to produce 'black-ball,' or 'smut,' in the succeeding crop. — **(2) 1909** WEBSTER. **1942** STEGNER *Mormon C.* 60 They left graves behind them, hundreds of graves, because the black canker had gone through their camps like a scythe. — **(3) 1820** *Plough Boy* I. 320 A correspondent has sent us the following receipt for curing a disease now prevalent among horses, called the black foot. — **(4) 1901–2** *Dept. Agric. Experiment Station Rec.* XIII. 287. **1945** *Nat. Geog. Mag.* May 542 'We have found by experiment,' said the professor who was showing me around, 'that blackhead, the worst disease that menaces turkeys, is eliminated if the young birds are kept clear of their own droppings.'

(5) 1872 *Vt. Bd. Agric. Rep.* I. 94 The lower branches are suffered to grow until of such size that a dry, dead knot is left when they are cut off, which sometimes kills the center of the tree, making it 'black-hearted.' **1874** *Ib.* II. 290 He expressed the opinion that all the trees that split from frost are black hearted, and that a tree not black hearted will not split from frost. — **(6)** [**1845** DOWNING *Fruits Amer.* 270 The knots is a disease attacking bark and wood . . . [with] the appearance of large, irregular black lumps, with a hard, cracked, uneven surface, quite dry within.] **1889** *Cent.* 573/1 Black-knot. . . . A species of pyrenomycetous fungus, *Sphoeria morbosa*, which attacks plum-trees and some varieties of cherry, forming large, black, knot-like masses upon the branches. — **(7) 1847** RUXTON *Adv. Rocky Mts.* (1848) 279 (fn.), [Scurvy is] Called 'Black Leg' in Missouri. — **(8)** (*a*) **1849** *Rep. Comm. Patents: Agric.* (1850) 438 In the southern part of the State winter apples are very liable to the black-rot, spots, [etc.]. **1893** *Rep. Secretary Agric.* 249 Experiments in the Treatment of Black Rot of the Grape. (*b*) **1871** LEWIS *Poultry Book* 97 Black Rot.—The symptoms of this disease are blackening of the comb, resembling mortification [etc.]. — **(9) 1790** S. DEANE *New-Eng. Farmer* 20/1 The pods are liable to be hurt by a black rust, if they are exposed much to the sun. **1847** *Rep. Comm. Patents* (1848) 108 If followed by wet weather the black rust or smut is produced or, if by dry weather the red rust.

(10) 1881 *Harper's Mag.* Jan. 196 Presently one of the assistants cried out that the sleepers had 'the black small-pox.' — **(11) 1834** *Amer. R.R. Jrnl.* III. 120/3 A disease in horses and cattle [is] called the *Black Tongue* or *Burnt Tongue*. **1919** DUNN *Indiana* II. 804 In 1842–3 epidemic erysipelas prevailed in a number of counties in southern Indiana, and was known by a number of popular names, as 'black tongue,' 'sore throat,' 'swelled head,' etc. **1932** *Durant* (Okla.) *D. Democrat* 2 Dec. 1/5 Black-tongue, a fatal disease common to deer of that section, is prevalent at this time. — **(12) 1877** *Vt. Dairym. Assoc. Rep.* VIII. 107 Black tooth is a popular disease of swine. **1909** *Cent. Supp.* 140/2 black-tooth. . . . A condition of hogs in which the teeth are black from accumulation of tartar. The condition produces no ill effect upon the health of the animal, and is not, as is commonly supposed, a disease. — **(13) 1861** *Ill. Agric. Soc. Trans.* IV. 454 The Black Cherry . . . is sometimes affected by the black wart. **1867** *Amer. Naturalist* April 112 The members then discussed the origin of the *Black Wart* on the Plum Tree. The disease was regarded as being due to a constitutional decline of the tree, during which the bark loosens and cracks open.

e. Designating soils, areas having distinctive types of soil, or vegetation of a particular kind: (1) **black alkali,** see as a main entry; (2) **growth,** (see quots.), also **black soft growth;** (3) **land,** land of a dark color, also attrib.; (4) **muck,** (see quot. 1855); (5) **pocosin,** ?a pocosin in which black growth *q.v.* abounds, *obs.*, cf. **black slash, swamp, timber, wood;** (6) **prairie,** a prairie the soil of which is black; (7) **slash,** ?a wet marshy area where black growth *q.v.* abounds, *obs.;* (8) **swamp,** =**black pocosin,** *obs.*, cf. **black growth, slash, timber, wood;** (9) **timber,** =**black growth;** (10) **wax,** *local*, a black soil which becomes sticky and wax-like when wet, also attrib., also **black waxy;** (11) **wood,** =**black growth.**

(2) 1814 *Mass. H.S. Coll.* 2 Ser. III. 121 The wood is chiefly black growth, viz. hemlock and spruce; but there is some rock maple and beach. **1834** AUDUBON *Ornith. Biog.* II. 398 This took place in what hereabouts [in Maine] is called the 'black soft growth' land, that is the spruce, pine, and all other firs. *a*1862 THOREAU *Maine Woods* 307 The fir has the darkest foliage, and, together with the spruce, makes a very dense 'black growth.' **1942** RICH *We Took to Woods* (1948) 212, I was in the middle of a black-growth swamp that I hadn't ever known existed. — **(3) 1860** *Charleston* (S.C.) *Mercury* 27 Nov. 4/2, I hear from the 'black-land' counties that nearly every man is for Secession. **1910** *Sat. Ev. Post* 8 Oct. 10/3 John Simmons lived on a black-land farm in central Missouri. **1948** *Galveston* (Tex.) *News* 14 June 2/5 We have 17 different kinds of soil to work with, from black-land to adobe. — **(4) 1849** CHAMBERLAIN *Indiana Gazetteer* 283 The soil being a mixture of clay, marl, and black muck. **1855** *Trans. Amer. Inst. N.Y.* 343 The Newark meadows . . . are formed of black, carbonaceous soil, usually known as black muck.

(5) 1696 in *Amer. Sp.* XV. 156/2 Ye Black poquoson near by ye Beaver Dam of the head of Indian Creek. . . . A mark't Gum . . . Standing in ye Black poquoson. — **(6) 1893** LERCH *Hills of La.* 88 The gray clays . . . pass into fossiliferous yellow marls, capped here and there with thin ledges of white limestone and giving rise to the peculiar physiographic feature previously noted—'the black prairies' of North Louisiana. **1896** CLENDENIN *Fla. Parishes E. La.* 206 The 'black prairies' of St. Landry and the Attakapas country owe their color to the fact that the silt covering is sufficiently attenuated to place the calcareous substratum within easy reach of the plow even in ordinary cultivation. — **(7) 1849** *N. Eng. Farmer* 235 A large portion of the land in Indiana, as well as some other of the Western States, is technically called 'flat woods,' 'wet lands,' 'black slashes,' &c. — **(8) 1687** in *Amer. Sp.* XV. 156/2 To a Water Oake Standing by ye side of ye black Swamp. — **(9) 1943** DAMON *Sense of H.* 85 The colors of New Hampshire are . . . the green of pines, the darker green of firs—'black timber,' they call it.

(10) 1895 *Stand. Dict* 2042/1 Black wax. . . . A tenacious black mud found in Texas. **1927** *My Okla.* April 24/1 The crop may be grown on about any type of soil except the 'black-waxy' and extremely heavy clays. **1939** LANGE & TAYLOR *American Exodus* 85 Beyond the Black Wax Prairie of Texas gently undulating grass lands invited the farmer to move west. **1948** *Scientific Mo.* April 327 The eastern half of the county, in the Black Prairie Division, is a treeless, level to gently rolling prairie, with rich black sticky soils locally known as 'black-waxy.' — **(11) 1812** F. A. MICHAUX *Arbres de l'Amérique* II. 220 On désigne ces terreins sous le nom de *Black wood lands*, terreins à essence noire. **1859** HILLHOUSE tr. *Michaux's Sylva* I. 154 The first class comprises the resinous trees, such as Pines and Spruces, and covers the low grounds and bottoms of the valleys; these forests are called Black-wood lands.

f. Designating foods and drinks: (1) **Black Betts,** alcoholic liquor, *obs.*, cf. **black betty,** in **4.** (1) above; (2) **cake,** a cake of a dark appearance from having been made with molasses, fruits, etc.; (3) **fat,** (see quot.), *obs.;* (4) **jack,** see as a main entry; (5) **strap,** (*a*) a mixture of rum and molasses used as a liquor, *obs.*, (*b*) a by-product obtained in manufacturing sugar, in full **blackstrap molasses.**

(1) 1845 L. CRAWFORD *Hist. White Mts.* 45 There I was loaded . . . with a plenty of what some call 'Black Betts,' or 'O be joyful,' as it was the fashion in those days, to make use of this kind of stuff.— **(2) 1885** *La Cuisine Creole* 144 Rich Wedding Cake, or Black Cake. **1898** *Epworth League Cook Book* 21 Black Cake. — **(3) 1897** *Brad-*

street's 24 Dec. 8/1 It has been for years the custom of certain tobacco manufacturers to pack in hogsheads and bales, for foreign trade, a brand of leaf tobacco known as 'blackfat.'

(5) (*a*) **1817** J. M. SCOTT *Blue Lights* 130 It was afterwards observed by an English sailor, that instead of making switchel of the molasses, the Yankees had converted it into blackstrap. **1944** DUNCAN *M. Graham* 37 He thought court-week games bully, loved to watch them, and came home to teach them to the children; but then there were those ticklers of whiskey and those 'flips of blackstrap' against which the preacher railed. (*b*) **1917** ROLPH *Something About Sugar* 82 The liquor, from which the crystals formed in repeated boilings have been removed as made, at length becomes so charged with impurities that further crystallization is impossible and this residue, or final waste, is known as blackstrap molasses. **1946** NEWTON *P. Bunyan* 55 Sam stewed the dried apples in black-strap molasses. **1948** *Chi. D. News* 26 Feb. 16/3 The most common, of course, was sulphur and molasses —the blackstrap kind.

g. *into the black*, used of business operations that are making money in contrast with those *in the red*, *q.v.* *Colloq.*

1935 *Amer. Mercury* July 357/2 This time she appeared at the Italian Village, and within two weeks she had pulled it out of the red ink and into the black. **1948** *Time* 2 Feb. 76/3 The World Bank, which had lost money since it opened two years ago, finally climbed into the black.

black alkali. *W.* An area where the soil has been blackened by the decomposition of its organic matter by alkali.

1894 *Irrigation Age* March 117/1 The soda generally makes what is called 'black alkali' and the potash what is called 'white alkali.' **1898** *U.S. Geol. Surv.* Water Supp. Paper 18, 79 Spots of black alkali now mar its bed and sides, which before were a light sand, apparently free from any excess of alkaline salts.

attrib. **1931** DAYTON *Western Brouse Plants* 34 The species is especially characteristic of black alkali sites. **1933** BROWN & EVANS *Diseases Peas* 73 Destructive action of this type in black alkali soils attributed to the presence of sodium carbonate is probably due to sodium hydroxide.

black and tan.

1. A dog, esp. a foxhound, of a black color spotted with tan. Also **black tan.** Usu. attrib.

1856 *Spirit of Times* 1 Nov. 140/2 Dan brought home two of the finest *black tans* you ever laid your eyes on. **1857** *Ib.* 15 Aug. 376/1 We can furnish you with a brace of black and tan fox-hounds for about $60. **1884** *Harper's Mag.* Aug. 464/1 A jealous little black-and-tan stood by. **1947** *Democrat* 18 Sep. 8/2 Lost—Large black and tan hound dog . . . Tan spots over each eye.

2. (*cap.*) Of or pertaining to a faction of the Republican party in the South favoring proportional representation in the party for whites and Negroes. Cf. **lily white.**

1868 *Sonoma Democrat* (Santa Rosa, Calif.) 7 Mar. 5/2 Our friends of the black and tan stripe, will hold their primaries on Saturday, March 21st. **1890** *Why the Solid South?* 328 [Such] men . . . were shining exceptions to the rule of ignorance and depravity which pervaded what became memorable as the Black and Tan Convention. **1914** MCLAUGHLIN & HART *Cyclo. Amer. Govt.* I. 133 The national Republican party is almost bound by tradition to support the Black and Tan faction, and give it the federal patronage.

3. A mulatto. Usu. designating cabarets, clubs, etc., frequented by blacks and whites.

1879 HAVERLEY *Colored Minstrels* 36 Black and tan—meersham, No happier mokes can be found within this land. **1891** RYAN *Pagan of Alleghanies* 26 'Well, this ain't no duck quackin', Mister Hubbard,' said the black-and-tan, pushing a droopy, wide hat to the back of his head. **1925** W. C. RECKLESS *Nat. Hist. Vice Areas in Chicago* 273 The so-called Black and Tan cabarets. **1945** *Reader's Digest* June 110/1 Harlem is ablaze with black-and-tan bars, one-room cafés and cellar dance dives.

4. A kind of buffalo robe (see quot.).

1918 W. E. CONNELLEY *Hist. Kansas.* I. 290 The 'Black-and-tan' was also rare. In it, the nose, flank, and inside of the forelegs were black-and-tan—the rest of the hide jet black.

∗ **blackberry,** *n.*

1. blackberry cobbler, a cobbler the chief ingredient of which is blackberries.

1936 KROLL *Share-cropper* 106 Maw then would bake a huge blackberry cobbler. **1945** *Chi. Tribune* 3 June VII. 1/3, I have fresh blackberry cobbler and things like that.

2. blackberry winter, (see quots.).

1905 JOHNSON *Highways* 162 Then, later, when the blackberries are in blossom, we have another cold spell what we call the blackberry winter. **1920** THOMAS *Ky. Super.* 189 Cool weather in May is called blackberry winter. **1933** *Amer. Sp.* Feb. 80 In addition to *blackberry winter, dogwood winter,* and *snowball winter* mentioned in preceding issues of *American Speech*, Oklahoma has *whippoor-will storms.*

As the last term in **bush, high, low, low bush, running, sand, swamp, thimble blackberry.**

∗ **blackbird,** *n.* One or other of various birds belonging to the family Icteridae, esp. the crow-blackbird or grackle, *Quiscalus purpureus*, or the marsh blackbird.

1602 BRERETON *Discovery of N. Virginia* 12 We saw in the country . . . Doves, Sea-pies, Black-birds with carnation wings. **1709** LAWSON *Carolina* 139 Black-Birds. Of these we have two sorts, which are the worst Vermine in America. **1880** *Harper's Mag.* June 69/1 The noisy blackbirds hold high carnival in the top of the old pine-trees. **1945** MATHEWS *Talking* 35 The meadowlarks sing, and the blackbirds flock to the blackjacks to bow and ruffle their feathers.

As the last term in **Brewer's, cow, crow, French, marsh, red-shouldered, red-winged, rusty, rusty-winged, skunk, swamp, white-winged, yellow-headed blackbird.**

black bottom.

1. In a town a relatively low-lying section inhabited by Negroes.

1915 *Lit. Digest* 4 Sep. 500/2 Uncle Mose aspired to the elective office of justice of the peace in the 'black bottom' part of town.

2. A form of Negro clog dance involving prominent movements of the hips.

1926 *New Yorker* 9 Oct. 18/2 [The Black Bottom] . . . was constructed to simulate the movements of a cow mired in black bottom river mud. **1926** *N.Y. Times* 19 Dec. VII. 4/6 It occurred to the producer that if you could dance before the beat you would have a new rhythm. . . . The result is the Black Bottom. **1947** *Chi. Herald-Amer.* (Home Mag.) 11 Jan. 7/3 After the Charleston, it was the Black Bottom, then Truckin', and Peckin'—then the Big Apple and the Lambeth Walk.

Blackburnian ˌblækˈbɜnɪən, *n.* [After Mrs. Hugh *Blackburn*, an Englishwoman.] An orange-throated warbler, *Dendroica fusca*, of eastern N.A. In full **Blackburnian warbler.**

1783 LATHAM *Gen. Syn. Birds* II. II. 861. **1811** WILSON *Ornithology* III. 64 Blackburnian Warbler, *Sylvia Blackburniae*. . . . This is another scarce species in Pennsylvania, making its appearance here about the beginning of May; and again in September on its return. . . . Inhabits also the state of New York, from whence it was first sent to Europe. **1844** *Nat. Hist. N.Y., Zoology* II. 93 The Blackburnian Warbler . . . was first discovered by an English collector named Ashton Blackburn. **1947** *Harper's Mag.* May 480/1 There is no more socially defensible joy than that of following with a field glass the orange flittings of a Blackburnian in the treetops.

blackfish ˈblækˌfɪʃ, *n.*

1. Any one of various small-toothed whales of the genus *Globicephala*. See also **New York blackfish, Virginia blackfish.**

1688 SEWALL *Diary* I. 239 [We saw] Birds, and a number of Fishes called Bottle-noses. Some say they are Cow-fish, or Blackfish. **1809** KENDALL *Travels* II. 149 A small species of whale, here called *black-fish*. **1904** *Sci. Amer. Supp.* 3 Sep. 23969/1 In addition to the blackfish secured by the spermwhalers, large numbers have been captured on the shore of Cape Cod, where they are attracted by squids on which they feed.

2. =**tautog.**

1765 R. ROGERS *Acc. N. America* 68 In the sea adjacent to this island [*sc.* L.I.] are sea-bass and black-fish in great plenty. **1842** *Nat. Hist. N.Y., Zoology* IV. 176 The Common Black-fish, or Tautog, . . . is a well known and savory fish, affording equal pleasure to the angler and the epicure. **1947** *Hunting & Fishing* Feb. 32/2 Blackfish (Tautog): from May to November you will find them on their runs in the salty waters, and it is said that around 'apple blossom' time is one of the best early runs.

3. (See quots.)

1855 BAIRD in *Smithsonian Rep.* 323 Black Bass, Sea-Bass, *Centropristes nigricans*. . . . The black fish, as an article of food, may be reckoned among the best of the fishes of the coast. **1888** GOODE *Amer. Fishes* 39 The Sea Bass is also known south of Cape Hatteras as the 'Blackfish.'

∗ **Blackfoot,** *n.* [A translation of the tribal name, *Siksika*, believed to refer to their moccasins.]

1. An Algonquian Indian of the Siksika tribe.

1834 in *Overland to Pacific* IV. (1934) 192 The Blackfoot is a sworn and determined enemy to all white men. **1890** RYAN *Told in Hills* 187 Genesee bought her of a beast of a Blackfoot.

attrib. **1805** LEWIS & CLARK *Orig. Journals* (1904) II. 98 The Minetares or black foot Indians . . . inhabit the country watered by the Suskashawan. **1836** IRVING *Astoria* I. XV. 246 Colter . . . [had] some knowledge of the Blackfoot language. **1917** EATON *Green Trails* 49

He was a trapper for the Hudson Bay Company, married a Blackfoot squaw, and spent most of his long life in this region.

2. An important confederacy of Algonquian Indians of the northern plains, embracing the Siksika, Blood, and Piegan tribes. Usu. attrib.

1794 *Mass. Hist. Soc. Coll.* 1 ser. III. 24 The tribes of Indians which he passed through, were called the Maskeyo tribe, . . . Beaver Indians, Blood Indians, the Blackfeet tribe, . . . and several others. **1812** STUART *Narratives* 161 On the headwaters of the Missouri . . . many of their people, were killed by the Blackfeet. **1832** *St. Louis Republican* 16 Oct., One of our friendly Indians, who spoke the Blackfeet language, . . . held a conversation with them during the engagement. **1945** *Reader's Digest* Aug. 50 For the Blackfeet tribe in Montana, $95,252 was spent for land, although the tribe has leased out 747,068 acres of its vast holdings.

* **blackjack,** *n.*

1. Any one of various oaks, esp. *Quercus marilandica,* having dark bark. In full **blackjack oak.** Also the wood of such an oak. Cf. **fork-leaf.**

1765 J. BARTRAM *Diary* 31 July Ye oaks black which is reconed ye best fire wood they have they call them black Jacks seldom grow above A foot diameter very scruby & of good use for timber for boats. **1782** JEFFERSON *Virginia* (1787) 62 Black jack oak. *Quercus aquatica.* **1879** TOURGEE *Fool's Errand* xv. 75 The wide fireplace, in which the dry hickory and black-jack was blazing brightly. **1946** *Reader's Digest* Feb. 93/1 He started off through the Texas blackjack oaks.

fig. **1835** KENNEDY *Horse Shoe Robinson* II. xvii. 142 Stop your bawling, you stunted black-jack!

attrib. **1775** ROMANS *Florida* 156 *Silk Grass* grows on the most barren sand hills of Florida (called black Jack ridges). **1802** B. HAWKINS *Letters* 426 One peck of blackjack ashes to a hide. *a***1909** O. HENRY *Roads of Destiny* x. 165 A little town five miles off the railroad down in the black-jack country of Arkansas. **1947** *Harper's Mag.* July 47/2 Elmer moved over a few steps and squatted, leaning against a black-jack sapling.

b. fork-leaf blackjack, and variants, =**turkey oak.**

1842 in TURNER *Cotton* (1865) 58 It is a high ridge-land, readily recognized, and its quality distinctly understood, in our southern country, under the name of *forked-leaf, black-jack, pine-barren,* a deep, porous, sandy, superstratum, lying under a tolerable good clay, at a distance of two to three feet below the surface. **1894** *Amer. Folk-Lore* VII. 99 *Quercus Catesbaei,* . . . forked-leaved blackjack. S.C. **1901** MOHR *Plant Life Ala.* 471 Forked-leaf Black Jack, . . . Small tree. Abundant in sandy pine barrens.

2. (See quot. 1877.)

1863 E. KIRKE *Southern Friends* ix. 112 A mug of 'black jack' helps him amazingly. **1877** BARTLETT 45 *Black-Jack,* . . . rum sweetened with molasses. New England. **1880** *Scribner's Mo.* June 293/1 A father whose sole object in life was to vie with his neighbors in the consumption of 'black jack' and corn whisky.

3. A small leather-covered club having a weighted head and a pliant shaft. Also fig. and attrib.

1895 *Denver Times* 5 March 8/5 During the scuffle, Miss Alderfer . . . saw the 'black jack' up his sleeve, . . . and as a result, swore out the concealed weapons charge. **1947** *Dly. Oklahoman* (Okla. City) 21 Sep. 5-D/1 Behind it all is the Indian claim that the palefaces used blackjack methods—sometimes with the military poised behind the chief doing the signing.

4. =**Vingt-et-un,** a card game. Also attrib.

1931 *K.C. Star* 28 Dec. 16 The governor knows his politics and is too poor a black jack player to mingle with gobs, anyway. **1946** R. PEATTIE *Pac. Coast Ranges* 205 Other loggers played blackjack for pastime. **1947** *Criminal Justice* May 21/2 The gambling room . . . operated a hand book, with loud speaker service, black jack tables and crap tables.

blackjack ˈblæk͵dʒæk, *v.* [f. **blackjack** *n.* **3.**] *tr.* To strike (a person) with a blackjack. — **1905** *N.Y. Ev. Post* 2 Sep., 'I got a partner there' [in the penitentiary], Red said, . . . 'blackjacked a man.' **1948** *Chi. Maroon* 3 Dec. 1/5 University students . . . were the victims of black-jacking and slugging while serving as canvassers and poll watchers in the First ward on election day.

Black Republican. A contemptuous nickname used in the South for a Republican friendly to the cause of Negro emancipation. Also transf. and attrib. Now *hist.*

[**1833** in *S. Atlantic Quart.* Jan. 15 When I have sufficiently disgusted myself with contemplating the *white* Negroes, I shall perhaps . . . examine the black republicans, and then compare them.] **1855** *N.Y. Herald* 20 Nov. 2/3 The black republicans here now bow their heads in deep despair. **1856** *N.Y. Herald* 5 Jan. 8/3 The black republican party, embracing the abolitionists, the free soilers and the Seward whigs, will be in the field with Seward as a candidate. **1948** *Pacific Spectator* Summer 259 It had existed that way for eighty years and . . . could continue indefinitely so to exist if only Lincoln and his black Republicans would recognize the sacred right of each State to decide the question for itself.

Hence **Black Republicanism,** *obs.*

1855 *N.Y. Herald* 19 Nov. 8/2, I can only say that I will—*a la mode* Jackson—fervently affectively rule black 'republicanism'; I will rule them!

* **blacksmith,** *n.*

1. a. (See quot. 1887.) **b.** (See quot.)

(**a**) **1878** RUEDE *Sod-House Days* 234 We had a regular 'blacksmith' at work in the office, and he beat Keever out of a week's board, and Mrs. Korb ditto, and today he lit out after taking an old pepperbox revolver belonging to somebody else. **1887** *N.Y. Ev. Post* 20 Jan., Shiftless newspaper reporter or journalist [is called] a blacksmith. — (**b**) **1888** GOODE *Amer. Fishes* 300 Another somewhat noteworthy species is known in California, on account of its dusky colors, as the 'Blacksmith,' *Chromis punctipinnis.*

2. blacksmith shop, a blacksmith's shop.

1791 FRENEAU *Poems* (1795) 421 Unless the [stage] driver . . . Has made some business for the black-smith-shop. **1889** *Harper's Mag.* Aug. 390/1 Perhaps he had better ride over to the blacksmith shop. **1948** JOHNSTON *Gold Rush* 53/1 John Carr, whose blacksmith shop was a going concern at the time, wrote as follows.

black snake.

1. Any one of various snakes, as *Coluber constrictor,* having very dark skins.

1634 WOOD *N. Eng. Prospect* I. xi. 46 A great long blacke snake, two yards in length, which will glide through the woods very swiftly. **1898** *Smithsonian Rep.* 794 The *Zamenis constrictor* is the 'black snake' of the East and the 'blue' and 'green racer' of the West. **1945** MATHEWS *Talking* 150 The blacksnakes, having no young rabbits to prey on, are a greater menace to the birds.

2. An abolitionist. Also attrib. *Obs.*

Introduced as a retort to "Copperhead," the adj. apparently being suggested by "Black Republican."

1863 *Crisis* 18 March 63 'Copperhead' Victory in Sullivan! 'Black Snakes' Cleaned out. *Ib.* April 77 The Abolition Blacksnakes are now using every effort to obtain subscribers to a new *ism. Ib.,* The Blacksnake editors appear to be urging their followers up to 'blood letting' among us. *Ib.* 6 May 119 The Black Republicans . . . are now very industriously applying the term 'Copperheads' to the Democrats. . . . Now, the representative of the Republicans, opposite to the Copperhead, is the Blacksnake.

3. A long tapering whip made of plaited leather thongs. In full **blacksnake whip.**

1863 J. FISK *Exped. Rocky Mts.* 5 A 'black snake' . . . brought him on his legs. **1889** *Ellensburgh* (Wash.) *Capital* 28 Nov. 2/2 One constable recently laid the blacksnake on a quintette of hobos who refused to work. **1948** CHAPLIN *Wobbly* 211 There they were tied to trees and beaten with blacksnake whips.

blacksnake ˈblæk͵snek, *v.* [**black snake,** *n.* **3.**] *tr.* To lash with a blacksnake whip. — **1870** MARK TWAIN *Sk., History Repeats Itself,* I lay I'll blacksnake you within an inch of your life! **1901** *Kansas H.S. Coll.* VII. 49 One wagon boss blacksnaked him.

* **blacktail,** *n.*

1. A (or the) black-tailed deer.

1846 ABERT *Exam. N.M.* 23 Of the latter there are two varieties, the common deer, and the black tail. **1903** AUSTIN *Land of Little Rain* 196 When such a storm portends the weather-wise black-tail will go down across the valley. **1947** *Sports Afield* Feb. 29/2 The little Sitka black-tails furnish food for the wolf packs.

2. In combs.: (1) **blacktail buck,** a male black-tailed deer; (2) **deer,** =**black-tailed deer;** (3) **fox,** the common red fox in one of its color phases; (4) **rabbit,** =**black-tailed rabbit.**

(**1**) **1828** in *Ashley-Smith Explor.* (1918) 259 Several of us went hunting, and I killed a fine black tail buck, that was fat. **1886** *Outing* Oct. 45/2 Next morning we . . . had two large black-tail bucks and a doe lying before our little tent. — (**2**) **1826** J. GODMAN *Nat. Hist.* II. 304 The Black-tail Deer, *Cervus Macrolis.* — (**3**) **1819** *Western Rev.* I. 235 The black-tail fox is of mixed grizzled color on the back. — (**4**) **1859** in *S.W. Hist.* Ser. XI. (1942) 315 We have seen two black tail rabbits—some of the boys thought they were young antelope. . . . Their ears are about eight inches long.

* **black-tailed,** *a.* In combs.: (1) **black-tailed deer,** (*a*) the mule deer, or a deer, *Odocoileus columbianus,* of the Northwest intermediate between this and the Virginia deer, (*b*) a Hidatsa band or secret order; (2) **hare,** (see quot. 1859); (3) **(jack)rabbit,** =prec.; (4) **roebuck,** =**blacktail buck,** *rare.*

(**1**) (*a*) **1806** LEWIS in *L. & Clark Exped.* (1904) IV. 87 The black tailed fallow deer. **1946** *Mazama* Dec. 33/1 The blacktailed deer is a separate species. (*b*) **1907** HODGE *Indians* I. 153 *Black-tailed Deers*. A Hidatsa band or secret order.—Culbertson in Smithson. Rep. 1850, 143, 1851. — (**2**) **1827** J. S. SMITH in *Ashley-Smith Explor.* (1918) 187 From this lake (Utah Lake) I found no more signs of buffalo; there are a few antelope and mountain sheep, and an abundance of black tailed hares. **1859** BARTLETT 218 Jackass Rabbit (*Lepus callotis*) . . . is known also by the names of Mule Rabbit, Texan Hare, and Black-tailed Hare. — (**3**) **1846** EMORY *Military Reconn.* 15 The only animals seen were one black-tailed rabbit and an antelope. **1946** R. PEATTIE *Pac. Coast Ranges* 92 Long-legged and long-eared, the black-tailed jack rabbits are hares renowned for their burst of speed on the getaway and in flight, exceeding the celerity of coyotes, even. — (**4**) **1841** DE SMET *Letters & Sketches* (1843) 54 The black-tailed roebuck, so richly dressed in its brown coat, frequently excited our admiration, by its elegant shape, and abrupt, animated movements, in which it appears scarcely to touch the earth with its feet.

bladderbush ˈblædɚˌbʊʃ, *n.* The bladdersage, *Salazaria mexicana*, a plant of southwestern desert regions notable for its curiously inflated fruiting calyxes. — **1915** ARMSTRONG *Western Wild Flowers* 448 Bladder-bush [is] a very curious spiny desert shrub, about three feet high, varying a great deal in general appearance in different situations.

blade,** ***n.

1. *pl. S.* The leaves of Indian corn used as fodder.

1688 JOHN CLAYTON in *Phil. Trans.* XVII. 986, I advised her likewise to save, and carefully gather her Indian Corn-tops, and blades, and all her straw, and whatever could be made Fodder. **1724** JONES *Present State* 40 *Indian Corn* is the best Food for *Cattle* . . . and the Blades and Tops are excellent *Fodder*, when well cured. **1828** *Webster*, blade, *n.* . . . A leaf. In this sense much used in the Southern States of N. America, for the leaves of maize, which are used as fodder. **1899** GREEN *Va. Word-book* 60 Blades, *n. pl.* The leaves of corn pulled and dried for fodder.

2. In combs.: (1) **blade fodder,** fodder consisting of the cured blades of corn tied into bundles; (2) **house,** (see quot.).

(**1**) **1823** COMMONS *Doc. Hist.* I. 256 For example, the tops are not cut from the corn. The blade fodder only is pulled, and that not always. **1905** JOHNSON *Highways* 321 In a few days the 'blade fodder' was ready for storage. — (**2**) **1865** *Nation* I. 333 Later in the day they could be seen coming up out of the fields, carrying on their heads great stacks of the dried fodder, which is at once stowed away in blade-houses. These are small buildings with walls of logs, between which are left wide apertures for the admission of air, as the fodder is apt to grow musty.

As the last term in **corn, fodder, scalp, winding blade.**

blade bled, *v.* [f. **blade,** *n.*] *tr.* To strip (corn) of its leaves. *Rare.* — **1791** IMLAY *Western Territory* (1797) 477 August . . . he sows his turnips, tops his Indian corn, and blades it for the cattle.

blah blɑ, *n.* [Imitative.] Nonsense, bunk. *Slang.* — **1921** *Collier's* 15 Jan. 10/3 Then a special announcer began a long debate with himself which was mostly blah blah. **1948** *Southwestern Rev.* Summer 302/1, I never heard such a hum of strong b's in my life: 'Balderdash, bathos, bushwah, buncombe, bombast, and blah!'

Blaineism ˈblenɪzəm, *n.* The political philosophy of James G. Blaine (1830–93), a senator from Maine and frequent presidential candidate. Also **Blaineite,** a political follower of James G. Blaine. *Obs.* — **1884** *Cin. Times-Star* 11 Sep. 4/3 They can only speak for that monstrosity of political falsehood and impudence which calls itself Republicanism, but which is but Blaineism. **1880** *Dly. Inter-Ocean* (Chi.) 3 June 5/1 He is stopping among the Blaineites at the Sherman House.

blamenation ˈblemˈneʃən, *n.* and *adv.* [App. f. *blame, v.* after *damnation*. Cf. *Blamnatschon* in Berghaus and *Blast-nation* in *EDD s.v. Blast. v.* II. 2.] Used as an expletive or mild oath. *Colloq.* — **1837** J. C. NEAL *Charcoal Sk.* (1838) 106 Don't stand . . . all day a blockin' up the gangvay, or I'll drive right over you—blamenation if I don't! **1863** E. KIRKE *Southern Friends* iv. 63 But, blamenation, ye ar!

Bland dollar. The standard silver dollar of 412½ grains coined in accordance with the Bland-Allison Silver Act of 1878. *Obs.*

From 1873–78 there had been no coining of standard silver dollars, the trade dollar (1873–87) *q.v.* having been coined during this time. By 1878 there had arisen a need for the standard silver dollar.

[**1876** *Chi. Tribune* 3 Aug. 5/1 The morning hour was occupied with useless filibustering upon the Bland Silver bill.] **1879** *Congress. Rec.* 15 May 1369/2 Notwithstanding this sad fate of the Bland silver dollar, it is now seriously proposed to repeat that folly on a much larger scale. **1896** *Cong. Rec.* 15 May 4935/2, I simply call the attention of the Senate to the fact that the so-called Bland dollar was never a full legal tender.

blank,** ***n.

1. *Baseball.* A zero score. Also **blank score.**

1867 *Ball Players' Chron.* 6 June 2/2 Sharp fielding should have disposed of the Harvards for a blank. **1867** *Ib.* 2/3 The finest fly catch of the match by Shaw on a foul ball, caused the Lowells to retire for a blank score. **1948** *Dly. Ardmoreite* (Ardmore, Okla.) 25 June 6/4 Grove held Iola to a pair of hits and a blank on runs.

2. In combs.: (1) **blank agency,** (see quots.); (2) **agent,** a postal official having charge of the issue of blank forms; (3) **book,** a book of clean writing paper in which to make entries, keep accounts, etc., also attrib.; (4) **work,** the printing of blank forms.

(**1**) **1868** *Statutes at Large* 27 July XV. 196 The Postmaster-General . . . is hereby, authorized . . . to establish a blank agency for the Post-Office Department . . . ; and all other blank agencies are hereby abolished. **1880** LAMPHERE *U.S. Govt.* 240/1 The Blank Agency, to which is assigned the duty of supplying the post-offices entitled thereto with blanks. — (**2**) **1854** *Statutes at Large* 22 April X. 276 That the stamp and blank agent for the Post Office Department receive the same salary as clerks of the second class. — (**3**) **1712** C. MATHER *Diary* II. 199, I would scarce lett a day pass me, without obliging my son, Increase, to transcribe . . . into a blank book, some instructive passage. **1831** *Boston Directory* 18 (*advt.*), Blank book manufacturers. **1886** S. W. MITCHELL *R. Blake* ii. 14 He spent a few minutes more over the details of daily duty set out in a little blank-book. — (**4**) **1873** *Winfield* (Kan.) *Courier* 11 Jan. 1/7 The Courier Job Office . . . [is] prepared to do all kinds of job work, Blank work, Circulars, Posters, etc., at reduced rates.

blank,** ***v. tr. To retire (a team) without a score.

1870 *N.Y. Herald* 2 July 5/4 By good hitting St. John made four runs in the second inning, again blanked the Mutuals and then scored two. **1887** *Courier-Journal* 26 May 2/6 In the eighth and ninth innings both teams were blanked. **1948** *Dly. Ardmoreite* (Ardmore, Okla.) 4 Apr. 12/6 The Boston Red Sox blanked the Cincinnati Reds 5–0.

blanket,** ***n.

1. (See quot.) *Rare.*

1851 GREEN *Twelve Days* 165, I have money enough to singe a cane-brake. Yes, sir, enough of Uncle Sam's thousand dollar blankets (meaning one thousand dollar notes) to make a carpet for a steam-boat!

2. *Mining.* A heavy coarse cloth, usu. of wool with a long nap, used to catch particles of gold or other minerals. Also attrib.

1857 *Hutchings Mag.* Oct. 151/1 The blankets are allowed to remain upon the tables from ten to thirty minutes, according to the quality of the rock beng crushed. **1882** C. KING *Rep. Precious Metals* 606 The blanket washings can be passed through a simple machine.

3. Attrib. in the sense of "covering," "inclusive." Cf. **blanket ballot** in **4.**

1886 *Sec. Treasury Rep.* I. p. xli, Suitable annual appropriations . . . require no blanket clause to justify or cover them. **1889** *Cent.*, Blanket-mortgage, a mortgage intended to cover an aggregation of property, or secure or provide for indebtedness previously existing in various forms. **1932** BECK *Wonderland* 166 Section 251, Revised Statutes, gives almost blanket authority to the Secretary of the Treasury.

4. In combs.: (1) **blanket bag,** a bag for blankets, a sleeping bag; (2) **ballot,** a large ballot upon which the names of all the candidates of all political parties appear; (3) **brave,** =**blanket Indian;** (4) **deposit,** (see quot.), *obs.;* (5) **fish,** a devilfish, *Manta birostris*, found along the coast of the Gulf of Mexico; (6) **flower,** (see quots.); (7) **grass,** (see quot.); (8) **Indian,** an Indian of a low cultural level who uses a blanket as a garment instead of adopting the dress of white men, a semi-civilized Indian supplied with blankets and food by the government; (9) **man,** (see quot.); (10) **primary,** a primary in which blanket ballots are used; (11) **roll,** a blanket made up into a roll, a soldier's field equipment made up thus, and worn on one shoulder; (12) **sheet,** a newspaper consisting of one large sheet folded once, in full **blanket sheet newspaper;** (13) **stiff,** *W.* (see quots.), *slang;* (14) **tribe,** an Indian tribe among whom blankets serve as garments, a primitive or uncivilized tribe; (15) **waisted,** (see quot.), *obs.;* (16) **washer,** (*a*) an apparatus for washing blankets, (*b*) one who washes gold by means of a coarse blanket, *obs.*, cf. **blanket 2.**

(**1**) **1724** *N.-Eng. Courant* 5 Oct. 2/2 My Wife . . . made Preparation (by making sundry Blanket Baggs) to transport away what Goods she could. **1885** *Outing* Oct. 77/2, I crept into my blanket-bag, and slept . . . soundly. — (**2**) **1900** *Cong. Rec.* 14 Feb. 1801/1 When we had the blanket ballot, if he wanted to vote the Republican ticket, his Republican judge scratched out the Democratic name by drawing a line through it, the People's Party, the Prohibition ticket, and so on, and left the Republican column unmarked. **1914** McLaughlin & Hart *Cycl. Amer. Govt.* I. 101 Nine out of ten of the states have provided for an official 'blanket ballot.' — **(3) 1891** Ryan *Told in Hills* 166 You should hear her talking Chinook to a blanket brave. — **(4) 1889** *Cent.* 577/3 Blanket-deposit.... The name given in some parts of the Cordilleran mining region, especially in Colorado and Utah, to deposits of ore occurring in a form having some of the characters of those elsewhere designated as flat sheets, bedded veins, beds, or flat masses.

(5) 1870 *Amer. Naturalist* IV. 597 Large numbers of 'blanket fish' (a species of *Thymallus*) were to be seen ascending the small rivers. — **(6) 1909** *Cent. Supp.* 141/1 Blanket-flower.... A plant of the genus *Gaillardia*. **1915** Armstrong *Western Wild Flowers* 555 Blanket flower. *Gaillardia pinnatafida.* — **(7) 1889** Vasey *Agric. Grasses* 23 *Paspalum platycaule* ... forms such a thick turf that it is called here [*sc.* n. Fla.] 'blanket grass.' — **(8) 1859** Bartlett 35 *Blanket-Indian*, a wild Indian, whose principal article of dress is the blanket. **1873** Roe *Army Lett.* 95 It shows in detail the everyday dress of the genuine blanket Indians. **1946** Foreman *Last Trek* 219 Some were blanket Indians who still followed the chase. — **(9) 1872** Powers *Afoot & Alone* 309 One of the notable phenomena of California is the multitude of its tramps, the so-called 'blanket-men.'

(10) 1948 *Pac. Northwest Q.* Jan. 33 Twelve years ago the state of Washington adopted a new type of direct primary law—the blanket primary. — **(11) 1891** *Harper's Mag.* June 8/1 His bridle hand is raised by the blanket roll or carbine. **1908** *Sat. Ev. Post* 7 Nov. 11/1 He found an empty bunk which suited him, [and] threw down his heavy blanket-roll. **1927** Burns *Tombstone* 294 Saddle the ponies and slip the blanket rolls and the grub and the old camp kit on the pack mule. — **(12) 1839** *Boston W. Mag.* 2 Feb. 175 [The] Baltimore Athenæum ... is a *blanket sheet*, very well executed, and always filled with interesting matter. **1870** Maverick *Raymond & N.Y. Press* 36 The heavy, old-fashioned, 'blanket sheet' newspaper. **1901** Churchill *Crisis* 342 Black headlines, and grim lists three columns long,—three columns of a blanket sheet! — **(13) 1900** Flynt *Itinerant Policeman* 167 Among the 'Blanket Stiffs' in the far West ... there exists a crude system of marking 'good' houses. **1917** Sinclair *King Coal* 50 He was what is called a 'blanket-stiff,' wandering from mine to harvest-field and from harvest-field to lumber-camp. **1945** Service *Ploughman* 191, I hardly think they would have wanted to know a blanket-stiff, idly dreaming, while his few dollars melted away. **1948** Chaplin *Wobbly* 91 The 'blanket-stiff' now packs his bed Along their trails of yesteryear. — **(14) 1866** *Rep. Indian Affairs* 173 There is ... great ignorance concerning the location of the prairie or blanket tribes.

(15) 1877 Bartlett 776 *Blanket-waisted.* Cattle distinguished by a broad band of white hair completely encircling the body. — **(16)** *(a)* **1876** Ingram *Centennial Exp.* 345 A blanket-washer, a mangle, a frame for stretching and dyeing lace curtains, etc. *(b)* **1876** Raymond *8th Rep. Mines* 330 For 24 hours.... Wages of two blanket-washers were $4.

b. Designating various articles, usu. of clothing, made of blankets or blanketing material, as **blanket cap, capeau, capot, coat** (also transf.), **overcoat, shawl, tent.** Chiefly *obs.*

1842 *American Pioneer* I. 427 My friend ... took out a sort of blanket cap, and put it on my head. — **1821** Nuttall *Travels Arkansa* 79 The dresses of the men consist of blanket capeaus, buckskin pantaloons, and mockasins. — **1807** Pike *Exped.* III. App. 62 Presented to the commandant-general in a blanket cappot. — **1775** *Penna. Ev. Post* 31 Oct. 497/1 Our people had taken from the regulars some blanket coats, stockings and shoes, four hogsheads of rum and some wine. **1837** Bird *Nick of Woods* I. 58, I'm for any man that insults me! log-leg or leather-breeches, green-shirt, or blanket-coat. **1948** *Trail Riders Bul.* June 8/1 We suggest you bring along a good heavy sweater, blanket coat, leather windbreaker or something equally snug to wrap yourself in at the evening singsong. — **1822** Quitman in *Life & Corr.* 72 Straw hats and no neck-cloths in summer, and in winter coarse shoes and blanket overcoats. **1889** Cable in *Cent. Mag.* Jan. 364/1 The younger was muffling himself in an old blanket-overcoat such as we give to plantation negroes. — **1837** *S. Lit. Messenger* III. 660 The blanket shawls with their varied coloring looked pretty and comfortable. **1898** Westcott *D. Harum* 165 Hullo, John! what you got there? ... Slips, blanket-shawl, petticut, stockin's. — **1823** E. James *Exped.* II. 109 The wind blew so violently that our blanket-tent could afford us no protection. **1865** Kellogg *Rebel Prisons* 143 A man ... was quietly sleeping in his little blanket tent.

5. In colloq. phrases: *To wear the blanket,* (see quot.) *obs.; to stretch the blanket,* to exaggerate; *to split the blanket,* (see quot.).

1859 Bartlett Blanket. A term used distinctively for the clothing of an Indian. To say of one's father or mother that they 'wore the blanket,' implies that they were but half civilized Indians. Western. — **1892** Harris *U. Remus & Friends* 123 When he git ter talkin' he'll stretch his blanket-spite er de worl.' — **1903** *D.N.* II. 331 split the blanket, *v. phr. i.* Parted (man and wife). 'They *split the blanket* after living together ten years.' (Facetious.)

As the last term in **baggage, bayeta, bear, beaver, California, Dutch, gum, mackinaw, Mexican, Navaho, Negro, Northwest (Company), painter, pinning, point, rose, rubber, saddle, sluice, squaw, tear blanket.**

***blanket,** *v.* **1.** *tr.* To include under one head or category, to take inclusively. **2.** To suppress, put in the shade. *Colloq.* in both uses.

(1) 1892 *N.Y. Law Journal* in *Law Times* XCIII. 413/1 A bona fide immigrant ... blanketed the aforesaid quarter-section with his own claim, and the court held that the blanketer ... was *potior in jure.* **1913** La Follette *Autobiog.* 365 The employees then holding office were not blanketed into the service. — **(2) 1903** *N.Y. Sun* 6 Nov. 6 In this way the Republican campaign was blanketed. **1908** *Springfield W. Republican* 17 Dec. 4 It so happened that Mr. Taft was completely blanketed by the San Francisco earthquake.

blast wall. (See quots.) — **1852** *Harper's Mag.* April 643/1 A great black slanting structure ... [forms] a 'blast-wall.' *Ib.* 644/2 A structure of black timber ... set up in the shape of an acute angle. This is a 'blast-wall,' intended to offer some resistance to a rush of air in case of an explosion [at the powder-mill].

***blaze,** *n.*[1] **1.** A metal shield on a fireman's cap. **2.** A blazed trail or road, in full **blaze road.** Both *obs.* Cf. **ax blaze.**

(1) 1764 *Boston Selectmen* 121 Such person ... shall ... at every Fire wear a black leather jocky cap with a pewter blaze in the front of it. — **(2) 1817** Fordham *Narrative* 100 Blaze roads are merely lines, marked through the forests by slices of bark, like a *blaze*, being chopped off the trees. **1853** P. Paxton *Yankee in Texas* 100 He will see them pouring in ... by every possible road, ... wagon roads, main roads, 'cow trails,' and 'blazes.'

***blaze,** *n.*[2] **1.** Continuous or sustained firing. *Obs.* **2.** (See quots.)

(1) 1777 *Md. Journal* 2 Sep. (Th.), [They] kept up such a blaze upon the enemy, that they were forced to retreat. — **(2) 1866** *Wilkes' Spirit of Times* 24 March 60/2 A, B and C are playing poker, blases [*sic*] to count. **1887** Keller *Draw Poker* 9 *Blaze*, a hand consisting of five court cards. **1891** Quinn *Fools of Fortune* 218 *Blaze.*—This hand consists of five court cards, and, when it is played, beats two pairs.

***blazed,** *a.* Denoting a path or way the trees along which have been blazed.

1788 Schöpf *Reise* I. 367 Diese Methode wurde anfänglich aus Furcht, sich in den Waldungen zu verlieren, eingeführt. Man nennt diese so bezeichneten Wege blazed Paths. **1819** J. Flint *Lett. from Amer.* 154 Not neglecting to carry with him a pocket-compass, to enable him to follow the blazed lines marked out by the surveyor. **1853** P. Paxton *Yankee in Texas* 122, I went up country a bit, struck 'Trammel's Trace'—nothing but a blazed road then. **1932** *Old-Time N. Eng.* Jan. 136/1 My grandfather ... came on foot to this country from a town near Boston following a blazed trail. **1938** Matschat *Suwannee River* 37 John Bartram ... traveled with his son William ... following the waterways and blazed Indian trails.

blazer 'blezɚ, *n.*[1] One who blazes trees. *Obs.* — **1775** Romans *Florida* 195 These same two men serve as chain-bearers, and two as blazers. **1833** Galt *Autobiography* II. 122 After them a band of blazers, or men to mark the trees in the line.

***blazer,** *n.*[2]

1. *fig.* A person or thing of a surpassing or pre-eminent kind. *Slang. Obs.*

1845 Mrs. Kirkland *Western Clearings* 127 T'other gal is likely enough, but the mother's a blazer!

2. (See quot. 1889.)

1889 *Cent., Blazer,* ... a dish under which there is a receptacle for coals to keep it hot. **1900** R. Grant *Unleavened Bread* 111 Pauline's oyster suppers, cooked in her grandmother's blazer, were still a stimulus to high thinking.

3. *W.* An error, or lie. Also *to run a blazer,* to endeavor to deceive. *Slang.*

1906 *Springfield W. Republican* 19 April 1 The Kaiser's telegram to Count Goluchowski recalls some of his blazers in the past. **1907** White *Arizona Nights* 11 It was just a cold, raw blazer. **1910** Bronson *Remin. Ranchman* 115 The disfigurement was so placed that it seemed evident the rustlers planned to run a blazer on us by undertaking to cut them on the spring round-up under cover of a gun bluff.

***blazes,** *n. pl.* As the last term in **blue blazes, hell's blazes.**

blazing iron. (See quot.) *Rare.* — **1778** Anburey *Travels* II. 218 To meet a New Englander riding in the woods with his blazing iron (the term they give to a musket or gun) you might mistake him for the knight of the Woeful Countenance.

***blazing star.**

1. Any one of various American plants having flower clusters suggestive of a star.

1789 *Amer. Philos. Soc.* III. p. xx, The root of *Aletris farinosa* is taken in powder, or bruised and steeped in liquor: this root is called star-root, blazing star, devil's bit; and greatly esteemed . . . for many qualities. **1830** *Huntingdon* (Penna.) *Courier* 15 Sep. 4/5 American Remedies Wanted . . . Angelica, Wild, Devil's Bit or Blazing Star, (*Helonias Dioica.*) **1947** *Desert Mag.* May 28/3 Until the middle of June visitors will find . . . mimulus, chia, blazing star, . . . and ground cherry in the Valley of Fire and other rocky areas.

2. (See quot. 1889.)

1889 *Cent.* 582/2 blazing-star. . . . A stampede of pack-mules or other animals from a central point. (Western U.S. slang.) **1901** *Munsey's Mag.* XXV. 403/2 The herd . . . burst like a bombshell into that most disastrous of all plains mishaps—a 'blazing star.' The solid herd streamed suddenly in all directions, scattered in knots and bunches, and twos and threes, and vanished into the storm and darkness.

***bleach,** *n.* (See quot. 1902.) — **1849** Willis *Rural Lett.* xii. 112 The breachy ox has run over the 'bleach and lavender' of a seven days' wear and washing. **1902** Clapin 56 Bleach. A family washing hung out to dry.

bleach, *v. intr.* (See quot. 1851.) *Obs.* — **1836** *Harvardiana* III. 123 'Tis sweet Commencement parts to reach, But, oh! 'tis doubly sweet to *Bleach.* **1851** Hall *College Words* 20 At Harvard College, he was formerly said to *bleach* who preferred to be *spiritually* rather that *bodily* present at morning prayers.

***bleacher,** *n.* **1.** A vessel used in processing almonds for the market. *Rare.* **2.** *pl.* The low-priced, sometimes roofless, seats for spectators at outdoor events, esp. baseball and football games, also attrib. (in the sing.); those who occupy these seats. Cf. **bleaching boards.**

(1) **1883** *Cent. Mag.* Oct. 812/2 The nuts are then poured into bleachers—boxes with perforated bottoms. — (2) **1889** *Chi. Tribune* 18 May 6/1 The grand stand and bleachers were well filled with something over 2,000 spectators. **1889** *Sporting Life* (Phila.) 10 July 3/6 There is one thing in which Gloucester 'beats' the world, and that is in the 'bleacher.' There that irrepressible blooms unregenerate and develops his lungs to their full fog-horn capacity. **1917** Mathewson *Sec. Base Sloan* xviii. 238 More than half of the bleacher seats were empty. **1948** *Chi. Tribune* 20 Apr. 1. 20/4 They didn't whoop it up like the crowd in the grandstand and bleachers.

bleacherite ˈblitʃəˌraɪt, *n.* [f. **bleacher 2.**] (See quot. 1909.)

1896 *Chi. Tribune* 3 July 9/3 The money for it is being subscribed by the bleacherites. **1909** *Cent. Supp.* 142/1 bleacherite. . . . One who must be content to stand or occupy a bench in the open air while witnessing a base-ball or other game. (Slang, U.S.) **1947** *Time* 16 June 71/2 It was like the old days—when bleacherites chanted a song called *Joltin' Joe Di Maggio.*

bleaching boards. The bleacher seats or bleachers in a ball park. Cf. **bleacher 2.** — **1888** *Cosmopolitan* Oct. 445 [Illustration of] B.B. Audience—The Bleaching Boards. **1947** R. Smith *Baseball* 98 There were ladies in the audience, too, and a heavy sprinkling of kids, both in the grandstand and on the bleaching boards, the uncovered benches which are now called the bleachers.

***bleat,** *n.* = **deer bleat.** — **1832** Irving *Tour of Prairies* (1835) 211 A stratagem some times used in deer hunting . . . consists in imitating, with a small instrument called a bleat, the cry of the fawn, so as to lure the doe within reach of the rifle. **1859** Taliaferro *Fisher's R.* 92, I made me a blate, went out to the laurel and ivy thicket whar I'd killed the doe, blated, and the fawn answered me.

***bleat,** *v. tr.* and *intr.* To decoy and so kill deer by imitative bleating, also with *up. Obs.* — **1806** Lewis in *L. & Clark Exped.* (1904) V. 156 The does now having their fawns the hunters can bleat them up and in that manner kill them with more facility and ease. **1832** Irving *Tour on Prairies* (1835) 212, I never could bring myself to bleating deer. **1859** [see **bleat,** *n.*].

***bleed,** *v. tr.* To draw sap, gum, etc., from (a tree) by wounding it. Cf. ***milk,** *v.* — **1856** *Spirit of Times* (N.Y.) 22 Nov. 198/2 Bleeding Trees to make them bear, consists in cutting the bark up and down the tree, from the limbs to the ground, about the 1st of May. **1895** *Yearbook Dept. Agric.* 1894 45 The pineries of the Southern States which are being 'bled' for turpentine.

***bleeding,** *a.* **1.** ***bleeding heart,** *S.*, the burning bush or wahoo. **2. bleeding Kansas,** Kansas during the period (1854–60) of violence and bloodshed over slavery. Now *hist.*

(1) **1897** Sudworth *Arborescent Flora* 281 *Evonymus atropurpureus,* . . . Bleeding Heart (N.C.). — (2) **1856** *Cleveland Plain-Dealer* 7 Nov., The ladies, dear creatures, who 'part their hair in the middle,' just like Fremont, were on their kerchy-benders, too, sighing and sobbing for 'bleeding Kansas.' **1948** Mencken *Supp.* II. 152 In the great days of Bleeding Kansas the inmates of the State prided themselves upon the alleged fact that what they called the *Kansas language* was simpler, franker and more vivid than that of the decadent East.

blenker ˈblɛŋkɚ, *v. tr.* (See quot). *Obs.* — **1862** *Yankee Volunteer's Songster* 71 His knapsack with chickens was swelling; He'd 'Blenker'd' those dainties, and thought it no wrong. . . . (Note. 'Blenkered,' . . . a term quite common, just now, in the army for anything stolen, which came into use soon after General Blenker's division passed down the Shenandoah Valley.)

blickey ˈblɪkɪ, *n. local.* [Du. *blikje,* a small tin or container such as is used for canned goods.] (See quots.)

1859 Bartlett 36 *Blickey,* . . . in New York, a tin pail. **1899** Vanderbilt *Flatbush* 56 The tin dipper that hung at the well curb was a 'blikke,' from the Dutch word 'blik,' for tin. **1948** Mencken *Supp.* II. 181 He found a number of Dutch loans, also surviving in New York, *e.g., blickey,* a small bucket.

***blights,** *n. pl.* (See quot.) *Obs.* — **1828** Webster *s.v.,* In America, I have often heard a cutaneous eruption of the human skin called by the name of *blights.*

As the last term in **American, frozen sap, pear, twig blight.**

***blind,** *a.* and *n.*

1. A place of concealment used by hunters, an ambush. See also **brush blind, log blind.**

1818 *Niles' Reg.* XV. 64/2 Col. Boon rode to a deer lick, seated himself within a blind raised to conceal him from the game. **1873** *Forest & Stream* 4 Sep. 52/1 Red cedar . . . is invaluable to the sportsman for the making of 'blinds.' **1938** Matschat *Suwannee River* 145 Obadiah had a duckblind here.

2. In poker, a compulsory stake put up by the elder hand or age before the deal, and thus without seeing the cards. (See also quot. 1946.)

1850 Bohn *Handbook Games* 383 Should a party see fit to call the blind, [he] must put twice the number in the pool, with the privilege of running over the blind. **1894** *Cong. Rec.* 4 May 4408/2 When the fourth [school] boy . . . handed in his composition, it read, 'Put up your blind. It is my deal.' **1946** Morehead & Mott-Smith *Penguin Hoyle* 132 The first bet, which will be called the 'blind' here, is often called the ante.

3. *Baseball.* (See quots.)

1867 *Ball Players' Chron.* 20 June 1/3 A blank score at Albany, N.Y., is called 'a blind.' *Ib.* 12 Sep. 2/1 After the Excelsiors gave their opponents a 'blind' in the first innings, the tables turned.

4. = **blind baggage.**

1893 *Chi. Record* 14 July 11/3 In hobo language 'beating the blinds' means to steal a ride on the mail car next to the engine. **1948** *Sat. Ev. Post* 31 July 89/1 If there were any hobos on the blind, they would step off into my arms.

5. In combs.: (1) **blind baggage,** a railroad car without any end doors or with no door at the end placed toward the front of the train or next to the locomotive, in full **blind baggage car;** (2) **bridle,** a bridle fitted with blinds or blinkers; (3) **crossing,** a railroad crossing that is obscured; (4) **door,** a door made of slats, as a window blind; (5) **fast,** a device for closing or fastening a window blind; (6) ***fish,** any one of various fish of the family Amblyopsidae found in Mammoth Cave; (7) **hand,** ?in poker a player who bets before examining his hand, cf. **blind poker;** (8) **lead, lode,** in mining a lead or lode that does not crop out above the surface; (9) **pig,** a place where liquor is sold illegally, *slang,* cf. **blind tiger, fifteen gallon law, striped pig;** (10) **pigger,** one who operates a blind pig, *slang;* (11) **pool,** an amount of stock, or other resources, placed at the disposal of a manager, who alone knows how it is to be managed, cf. **c.** (5); (12) **staggers,** the staggers, a disease which affects the brain and spinal cord of horses, hogs, etc., causing them to have a staggering gait; (13) **tiger,** = **blind pig;** (14) **tooth,** a wolf tooth in horses, alleged to be a cause of blindness.

(1) **1893** *Dly. Ardmoreite* (Ardmore, Okla.) 8 Nov. 1/4 They didn't even have an opportunity to fire a tramp off the blind baggage. **1901** *Scribner's Mag.* April 429/1 The train's got a blind baggage-car on. . . . That's a car that ain't got no door in the end that's next the engine. **1945** Marshall *Santa Fe* 320 Thousands of hoboes rode free, clinging to the rods, huddling in the 'blind baggage' and on the roofs of cars. — (2) **1833** J. Hall *Harpe's Head* 30 Some rode with blind-bridles. **1944** Clark *Pills* 142 For the first six months of that year he bought . . . fifty-six plugs of tobacco, . . . a blind bridle, . . . and a bottle of Hoyt's cologne. — (3) **1861** *Remin. Life Locomotive Engineer*

124, I heard his whistle sound at a 'blind crossing' about a mile distant. — **(4) 1881** *Cent. Mag.* Nov. 131/1 One of those deceptive New England cottages . . . with its front hall, now cooled by the light sea-breeze drifting through the blind-door.

(5) 1846 *Knickerb.* Sep. 279 A. Fuller . . . has fitted up a [machine] shop at his house . . . where he will attend to the manufacture of Blind Fasts. — **(6) 1843** *Journal of Sci. & Arts* XLV. 94 Description of a 'Blind Fish,' from a cave in Kentucky. **1897** HOVEY & CALL *Mammoth Cave* 100 Soon after the rivers were discovered, . . . the earliest specimens of crayfish and blind-fish were also found. — **(7) 1882** *Poker* 88 For some reasons players never give the blind hand credit for a good or even an average hand. — **(8) 1872** MARK TWAIN *Roughing It* xl. 218 It's a blind lead, for a million!—hanging wall—foot wall—clay casings—everything complete! — **1880** *Cimarron News* 1 July 2/2 A blind lode cut within the first 20 feet assayed 98½ oz. of silver. — **(9)** [**1870** MACRAE *Americans* II. 315 In desperate cases it has to betake itself to the exhibition of Greenland pigs and other curious animals, charging 25 cents for a sight of the pig and throwing in a gin cocktail gratuitously.] **1887** *Minn. Gen. Statutes Supp.* (1888) 248 Whoever shall attempt to evade or violate any of the laws of this state . . . by means of the artifice or contrivance known as the 'Blind Pig' . . . shall . . . be punished. **1945** *Chi. D. News* 5 Feb. 8/2 Such a sleuth was 'Pussyfoot' Johnson. Because he was, perhaps, the most notable figure associated in the public mind with . . . 'blind pigs,' 'speakeasies' and—above all—'pussyfooters,' he should merit at least a footnote in the dictionaries of the future, if not in the histories.

(10) 1894 *Voice* (N.Y.) 6 Dec. 1/5 Headed by one of the blind-piggers who was under arrest, Rev. McNamara was severely beaten. **1917** D. PICKETT *Cyclo. of Temperance* 55 The blind pigger in wet territory can procure his liquor shipments without exciting suspicion. — **(11) 1882** *Nation* 31 Aug. 168/1 He denies the charge that he managed the 'blind pool' dishonorably, and declares that although made up on paper, it never went into effect. — **(12) 1784** in *N.J. Hist. Soc. Proc.* LIX. 169 Here (Princeton) we discovered that my horse had a distemper called the blind staggers. **1946** WILSON *Fidelity* 49 Father kept his instruments and used them on horses and mules afflicted with 'blind staggers.' — **(13) 1857** *Spirit of Times* 23 May 182/1, I sees a kinder pigeon-hole cut in the side of a house, and over the hole, in big writin', 'Blind Tiger, ten cents a sight.' . . . Says I to the feller inside, 'here's your ten cents, walk out your wild-cat.' Stranger, instead of showin' me a wild varmint without eyes, I'll be dod-busted if he didn't shove out a glass of whiskey. You see, that 'blind tiger' was an arrangement to evade the law, which won't let 'em sell licker there, except by the gallon. **1941** DANIELS *Tar Heels* 9 An old Negress let us watch her put the corks in blind tiger liquor bottles. — **(14) 1843** *Cultivator* Dec. 198/1 One [horse] had gone entirely blind before I was apprised of the cause, and the other two I relieved by immediately extracting the *blind teeth.* **1856** *Spirit of Times* 13 Dec. 243/2 In no work on the diseases of horses, so far as we know, is what are called 'blind teeth,' noticed.

b. In expressions of obvious meaning or sufficiently defined in the quots.: (1) **blind chisel** (or **blind-slat chisel**), (2) **date,** (3) **eel,** (4) **ink,** (5) **mess,** (6) **poker,** (7) **robin,** (8) **snake,** (9) **snipe.**

(1) 1851 CIST *Cincinnati* 258 Brand, stamp, and blind chisel makers. **1874** KNIGHT 298 Blind-slat Chisel. A hollow chisel, specially adapted for cutting the mortises in a common blind-stile for the reception of the ends of the slats. — **(2) 1925** *Lit. Digest* 14 March 65/1 No, got a blind date on to-night. **1929** *Amer. Sp.* IV. 420 A blind date — A date with someone whom the datee does not know but which is arranged by a third person. **1947** *Chi. Tribune* 14 June 18/8 In describing your blind date, I would say she has a wonderful personality. — **(3) 1865** *Atlantic Mo.* Jan. 96/1 A new hook had been put on mine [*sc.* fishing line], as on the last excursion the old one had caught in what the boys call a 'blind eel,' that is, a sunken log. **1877** BARTLETT 47 When a fisherman brings up a piece of sea-weed on his hook, he is said to have caught a blind eel. — **(4) 1884** KNIGHT *Dict. Mech. Supp.* Blind Ink. Invented by Edison. An ink which . . . swells up into relief on the paper.

(5) 1828 A. SHERBURNE *Mem.* (1831) iv. 86 The messes in rotation, send one of their number into the cook room every day. The mess which sends the man, is called the blind mess [because the lots of meat were indicated by a blindfolded man]. — **(6) 1871** SCHELE DE VERE *Americanisms* 328 Poker, when played by betting before looking at one's hand, is called *Blind Poker.* — **(7) 1889** RILEY *Pipes o' Pan* 32 A reputed banquet whose menu's range confined itself to herrings, or 'blind robins,' dried beef, and cheese. **1926** *Amer. Sp.* I. 616 One day the owner of the stall . . . said to me when I had asked for smoked herring, 'We call them blind-robins,' and I have since learned to use the term. — **(8)** *Ib.*, First come those in which blind is used in its ordinary sense of 'destitute of sight, or so supposed to be.' Such are *blind-beetle, blind-fish, . . . blind-snake, blind-worm.* — **(9)** *a***1841** W. HAWES *Sporting Scenes* I. 179 Sportsmen, generally, among themselves, talk of killing a 'cock'; but if they meet an old woman in the woods . . . they ask her if she has seen any 'blind snipes.' **1844** *Nat. Hist. N.Y., Zoology* II. 258 The American Woodcock, *Rusticola minor,* . . . in some parts of the State . . . is known under the name of Blind Snipe; but for what reason I have not been able to discover. **1890** *Cent.* 5731/3 *Blind snipe,* the stilt-sandpiper, *Micropalama himantopus.*

c. Designating depressions, bodies of water, etc., having little or no inlet or outlet, as (1) **blind bayou,** (2) **gully,** (3) **lake,** (4) **pocosin,** (5) **pool,** cf. **5.** (11).

(1) 1842 *Knickerb.* XX. 309 He had had some experience in 'blind' bayous. — **(2) 1903** AUSTIN *Land of Little Rain* 183 Here and there in the hill country one comes upon blind gullies fronted by high stony barriers. — **(3) 1903** *Ib.* 207 It is always a favorite local tradition that one or another of the blind lakes is bottomless. — **(4) 1770** WASHINGTON *Diaries* I. 365, [I] found a fox at the head of the blind Pocoson.

(5) 1903 AUSTIN *Land of Little Rain* 207 The stream . . . sometimes breaks out of a hillside as a spring where the ear can trace it under the rubble of loose stones to the neighborhood of some blind pool.

***blind,** *v.* **a.** *tr.* (See quots.) **b.** In draw poker, to make use of blinds. Cf. ***blind,** *a.* and *n.* **2.** Also to give an opponent a blind (sense **3.**).

(a) 1859 BARTLETT 36 *To blind a trail,* to conceal a person's footprints, or to give them the appearance of going in a different direction; figuratively, to deceive a person by putting him on the wrong track. **1862** *Rep. Comm. Patents: Agric.* 513 The eyes on these canes (except the two on the top) should be rubbed off, or, as it is technically called, 'blinded,' so as to concentrate the strength into the two. — **(b) 1870** *Boise* (Ida.) *Statesman* 30 Sep. 1/6 They blinded, straddled, straddled back, drew, bet, raised, went better, and so on, until they got $3,000 in the pot. **1871** *Cin. Commercial* 8 Sep. 5/4 The Chicagos were again blinded, Simmons being the last out by an expert catch of a hot liner by Schafer.

***blinder,** *n.* **a.** A window shutter. **b.** In baseball, a blank score. Cf. ***blind,** *n.* and *a.* **3.** Both *obs.*

(a) 1790 BENTLEY *Diary* I. 187 Whether blinders upon the outside of windows are not more troublesome than within? — **(b) 1867** *Ball Players' Chron.* 24 Oct. 3/1 On the second innings, the Mutuals received a blinder. **1868** *N.E. Baseballist* 29 Oct. 51/1 Pratt went out on a foul fly by Bush—First blinder.

As the last term in **board blinder.**

***blink,** *n.* [The origin of the term in sense **1.** is unknown. It may be a different word from that in **2.**] **1.** (See quots.) **2.** *on the blink,* in a bad way, out of order. *Slang.*

(1) 1856 GOODE *Fisheries* (1884) 298 The mackerel . . . are not sold by weight, but are culled, and are denominated as follows: Large ones, second size, tinkers, and blinks. **1888** ATWOOD in Goode *Fishes* 174 Fish of this size are sometimes called 'Spikes.' . . . The next year I think they are the 'Blinks,' being one year old. — **(2) 1904** O. HENRY *Cabbages & Kings* iii. 51 This café looks on the blink, but I guess it can set out something wet. **1948** *Reader's Digest* Sep. 82/1 If the radio goes on the blink it is foolish to worry about the tubes or transformer.

***blister,** *n.* **1.** (See quot.) **2.** *blister and curl,* (see quot.). *Rare.* **3. blister pine,** (see quot). See also **pine rust blister.**

(1) 1881 E. INGERSOLL *Oyster Industry* 241 *Blister,* A young oyster, not larger than a quarter dollar. . . . (Barnegut to Cape May.) — **(2) 1864** *Ohio Agric. Rep.* XVIII. 460 For some years, in this country, the disease which produces the 'Blister and Curl' in the peach leaf, and decay in the peach fruit, has . . . produced extensive ravages. — **(3) 1894** *Amer. Folk-Lore* VII. 99 *Abies balsamea,* . . . blister pine, balm of Gilead fir, West Va.

blisterer ˈblɪstərɚ, *n.* [f. dial. **blister, v.,* to punish, cf. *D.N.* III. 127.] A severe disciplinarian. *Rare.* — **1883** EGGLESTON *Hoosier School-Boy* xxiii. 157 Bob Halliday said 'the young master was a blisterer.'

blizz blɪz, *n.* [Cf. next **1.c.**] A violent rainstorm. *Rare.* — **1770** L. CARTER *Diary* 31 May (*William & Mary Coll. Q. Hist. Mag.* XIII. 51), At last a mighty blizz of rain.

blizzard ˈblɪzɚd, *n.* [See note.]

This term has evoked much discussion. See A. W. Read in *Amer. Sp.* III. 191–217, V. 232–35. The *Cent.* (1913 ed., and poss. earlier) regards the word as a dial. var. of *blizzer,* and as having passed from Eng. prov. use into Amer. Eng. At present neither the word nor its now most prevailing sense, shown in **1. c.** below, can be conclusively shown to have originated in this country. See note to **1. c.** below.

1. Something extreme or exceptional of its kind, regarded as sudden, severe, startling, violent, overwhelming, superior, as (*a*) a sharp blow, (*b*) a squelching retort, (*c*) *pl.* as the name of a baseball club, (*d*) a drink of liquor. All *obs.*

(*a*) **1829** *Va. Lit. Mus.* 16 Dec. 418 **Blizzard.* 'A violent blow—' perhaps from *Blitz,* [*Germ.*] lightning. *Kentucky.* **1881** *Nation* 14 April 260 In 1836 I first heard the word 'blizzard' among the young men at Illinois College, Jacksonville. If one struck a ball a severe blow in playing town-ball it would be said 'That's a blizzard.' **1891** *N.Y. Tribune* 19 July 14/5 It was not till within the last thirty years . . . that it was ever heard in the Eastern States, and in the Western a blizzard meant a knock-down blow from an argument, and not a knock-down blow from a snow-blast.

(*b*) **1835** CROCKETT *Tour down East* 16 During dinner the parson . . . called on me for a toast. Not knowing whether he intended to . . . have some fun at my expense, I concluded to go ahead, and give him and his likes a blizzard.

(*c*) **1871** *Northern Vindicator* (Estherville, Iowa) 22 March, The Blizzards are beginning to base-ball it again this spring.

(*d*) **1881** *Nation* 31 March 220 There has been an extensive use of the word in Pennsylvania for many years, as witness the following: (1) A drink of any intoxicant, generally applied to whiskey. . . . 'Let's take a blizzard.'

b. A shot or volley of shots. *Obs.*

1834 CROCKETT *Life* 152, I saw two more bucks, very large fellows, too. I took a blizzard at one of them and up he tumbled. **1846** *Spirit of Times* 6 June 117/3 We turned one of our 18 pounders to bear on the mass and gave them a 'blizzard' to help them along. **1892** DUVAL *Young Explorers* 103, I wish Mass Seth only let me gib 'em one blizzard, I bet I make 'em yelp toder side dere mouth.

c. A violent storm of fine driving snow accompanied by intense cold. Also fig. Hence **blizz,** *v., colloq.*

The first two quots. given below suggest that blizzard in this sense may have originated in Eng., as the *Cent.* (1913 ed.) sets forth in some detail. The original of the diary supplying quots. 1859, 1861, is app. lost. The editor of it for the *Kans. Hist. Quart.* says "some of the entries apparently were expanded somewhat at a later date." Whether these examples of blizzard occur in these possibly expanded portions it is not possible to say.

(1) [**1881** in *Am. Sp.* III. (1928) 195 A sudden or unexpected storm. This use was in existence as early as 1836 in this part of the state [Perry Co., Pa.] Charcoal-burners, watching their pits, would fear a blizzard. **1888** *N. & Q.* 7 Ser. V. 17 March 217 The word *blizzard* is well known through the Midlands, and its cognates are fairly numerous. I have known the word and its kin fully thirty years. Country folk use the word to denote blazing, blasting, blinding, dazzling, or stifling. One who has had to face a severe storm of snow, hail, rain, dust, or wind, would say on reaching shelter that he has 'faced a blizzer,' or that the storm was 'a regular blizzard.']

(2) **1859** L. B. WOLF *Diary* in *Kans. Hist. Quart.* I. (1932) 205 Zounds, boys; we've got it this morning . . . a blizzard had come upon us about midnight . . . shot 7 horses that were so chilled could not get up. **1861** *Ib.* 210 The officers' and company headquarters are occupied, with the four corral stables completed. And well it is so as we get a terrible blizzard. **1870** *Northern Vindicator* (Estherville, Iowa) 23 April, Campbell has had too much experience with northwestern 'blizards' [*sic*] to be caught in such a trap. *Ib.* 30 April, The unfortunate victim of the March 'blizzard' . . . is rapidly improving. **1881** ROMSPERT *Western Echo* 119 At daylight we were in the midst of a *blizzard*. This is a *heavy gale* in which sharp ice, as fine as salt, falls so thickly that you can not see two feet ahead; and it is not safe to leave camp twenty steps without a rope around the waist. **1910** *Sat. Ev. Post* 23 July 39/2 A train every thirty minutes over our rails will do more toward keeping them usable than a rotary [snowplow] going over them after a night's inaction. So, when she begins to blizz, we just fall back on our roundhouses, that's all. *Ib.* 24 Sep. 74/3 To guard 'gainst the blow of the business blizzard when an able leader dies, The Equitable Life Assurance Society now issues a Corporate Policy. **1948** *L.A. Times* 19 Nov. 1/4 The storm in the central part of the country was almost a true blizzard, lacking only the severe drop in temperature to be called a blizzard.

2. In combs.: (1) **blizzard blown,** blown or swept by a blizzard, *rare;* (2) **shoot,** an occasion of shooting ducks in a blizzard of snow, *rare;* (3) **signal-light,** (see quot.); (4) **State,** South Dakota, a nickname.

(1) **1898** *Mo. So. Dakotan* I. 129 In the winter time, [he] alternated the farm chores with tramping to the blizzard blown prairie school house. — (2) **1897** *Outing* March 536/2 In my younger days I participated in several of these blizzard shoots, one of which I will relate. — (3) **1895** WAIT *Car-Builder's Dict.* 11 Blizzard. A fierce storm with high wind. Hence the trade name *blizzard signal-light,* . . . to designate one of extra quality, with careful provisions to prevent extinction by wind. — (4) **1907** *Boston Transcript* 9 Nov. **1948** MENCKEN *Supp.* II. 638 In its early days it was known variously as the *Blizzard State*, the *Artesian State*, . . . and the *Land of Plenty.*

b. Also **black, ground, western blizzard,** (see quots.). Cf. **dust blizzard.**

1936 *Durant* (Okla.) *Dly. Democrat* 16 March 1/4 Steve Benson stumbled into a farmhouse alive today after spending the night lost in one of the worst 'black blizzard' dust storms ever to strike this area. **1947** *Reader's Digest* Oct. 78/1 Black blizzards roared across the Plains. — **1939** ABBOTT-SMITH *We Pointed* 212 What they call ground blizzards in this country Montana, where you couldn't see twenty feet ahead of you because the wind was blowing the loose snow, and yet overhead the sky would be shining. — **1857** in J. K. WINKLER *J. P. Morgan* (1931) 62 The terrible panic of 1857, 'The Western Blizzard,' this panic was ironically called.

blizzardly ˈblɪzədlɪ, *a.* Like a blizzard. *Obs.* — **1883** *Letter* in *Advance* (Chi.) 1 March, The rain changed to driving snow, with very blizzardly tendencies, the mercury dropped forty-three degrees. **1885** *Milnor* (Dakota) *Teller* 2 Jan. 3/2 A trifle blizzardly this week.

blizzardous ˈblɪzədəs, *a.* Marked by blizzards. *Rare.* — **1883** *Dansville* (Ohio) *Advertiser*, I'm hazardous and blizzardous. . . I'm bad and my name is March.

blizzardy ˈblɪzədɪ, *a.* =**blizzardly.** — **1888** *S.F. News Letter* (F.), I should like to have seen the Colonel's face when he got that very cold, blizzardy letter. **1946** *Chi. D. News* 5 March 8/4 [It] would ruin the disposition of the throngs . . . especially on blizzardy nights.

bloat blot, *n.*

1. A pompous, conceited, contemptible person, (see also quot. 1889). *Slang.* Cf. **whisky bloat.**

1860 in *Am. Sp.* XXII. 299, I considered such an old bloat not worth minding. *a***1861** WINTHROP *Open Air* 147 When I think . . . what a mean bloat I was, going to the stub-tail dogs with my hat over my eyes. **1889** FARMER 64 Bloat (Cant), a drowned body; also a drunkard.

2. A condition produced in cattle, horses, etc., characterized by pronounced distention of the stomach.

1881 *Cimarron News* 3 March 2/2 There is danger of bloat if cattle are turned on [alfalfa]. **1890** *Stock Grower & Farmer* 18 Jan. 4/4 The only objection which southwestern stockmen have raised against alfalfa as a forage plant is its tendency to cause bloat.

***bloater,** *n.* A large, fat mackerel suitable for curing by salting and smoking. — **1857** *Harper's Mag.* Sep. 539/2 They are hauling in mackerel, genuine bloaters, as fast as they can. *Ib.* 540/1 The captain shouted, 'Here they are, boys!' and with the word landed a real bloater.

***blob,** *n.* A miller's thumb or similar small fish. — **1881** *Amer. Naturalist* Nov. 879 These [s. Tenn. fishes] were the common blob, *Potamocottus meridionali* , and sucker, *Catostomus teres.* **1888** GOODE *Amer. Fishes* 320 *Uranidea* and allied genera, known in some localities by the English name of 'Miller s Thumb,' also called 'Bull-heads,' 'Goblins,' 'Blobs,' and 'Muffle-jaws

***bloc,** *n.* As the last term in **farm bloc, silver bloc.**

***block,** *n.* [Sense **1.** shows the influence of Du. *blok.* See *WNT s.v. blok,* 14, 15.]

1. A connected or compact mass of houses or other buildings, in later use esp. one mainly or wholly occupying the space bounded by four streets. Also *block of buildings*, or *houses.*

1796 *Aurora* (Phila.) 13 Dec. (Th.), The whole block of buildings included between that slip, Front Street, and the Fly Market. **1801** CUTLER in *Life* II. 50 The buildings [in Washington] are brick, and erected in what are called large blocks, that is, from two to five or six houses joined together, and appear like one long building. **1833** ALEXANDER *Transatlantic Sk.* II. 121, I was tempted to stay in Louisville by an offer of an introduction to certain young ladies with blocks of houses, (a block is half a dozen or a dozen contiguous dwellings built on the same plan). **1881** *Harper's Mag.* April 712/2 In the case of Milwaukee . . . solid blocks of houses flush with the sidewalk are very few.

b. One of the square or rectangular areas in which American towns and cities are commonly laid out, often as an indication of distance. In early use occas. *block of lots.*

1815 DRAKE *Cincinnati* vi. 202 The principal wall or embankment, encloses an entire block of lots and some fractions. **1855** BRISTED in *Cambridge Ess.* 63 We were only two blocks from the steamboat. **1947** *Denver Hotel Greeters Guide* 31 Jan. 11/1 Numbering of houses in the business district commences at Broadway and Colfax . . . and 100 numbers are used for each block.

c. (See quots.)

[**1829** J. MACTAGGART *Three Years* II. 283 In some of the new townships in the western part of [Upper Canada], . . . that seventh part of the land . . . was laid out in blocks . . . containing from 2000 to 10,000 acres.] **1887** *Cent. Mag.* Nov. 115/1 A sugar plantation is divided by main ditches and roads into sections known in some parishes . . . as 'blocks.' **1902** MCFAUL *Ike Glidden* vii. 45 Ansel explained that he owned the east half of the two-thousand-acre block, and the deacon owned the west half. **1925** BRYAN *Memoirs* 34 Our farm contained five hundred twenty acres in one block.

2. A blockhouse. *Obs.*

1829 COOPER *Wish-ton-Wish* vii. 108 He . . . will take but little [rest] . . . until his head be safely housed within some such building as yon block. **1840** —— *Pathfinder* xxiv, He next examined the door of the block, to ascertain its security. **1852** WATSON *Nights in Block-*

house 27 D'ye see, arter Vansan and I left the block, we paddled up the stream.

b. A large single building of any kind.

1849 in ADAMS *Pioneer Hist.* (1923) 149 A little old 'corner grocer' building occupied the corner where Pratt & Millsapugh's block now stands. **1923** ADAMS *Pioneer Hist.* 64 Elected register of deeds in 1866, he built a three-story block in Mason, and purchased and improved 640 acres of land south of the city. **1945** *Springfield* (Mass.) *Union* 13 March 3/1 Negotiations were completed today between trustees . . . and the purchasers of the Botsford and Warner blocks on Main Street. **1947** *Westerners' Brand Book* 43 This block was probably better known to you as the Good Will Block, and at that time belonged to Arcadia de Baker.

3. A number of vessels used in salt-making. *Obs.* (Cf. *WNT s.v. blok* 17.)

1850 JOHNSTON *Notes* I. 189 The third method is by boiling the water in deep iron pots, or kettles, as they are called, of which forty, built up in two parallel rows, form what is called a block.

4. The stand on which a slave stood when being sold at auction. Also fig. *Obs.*

1853 *Chambers' Jrnl.* Oct. 39 Boy mounts the block, . . . the auctioneer kindly lends him a hand. **1866** BRYANT *Death of Slavery* 79 There shall the grim block remain At which the slave was sold. **1875** *Chi. Tribune* 22 July 2/5 The gold is not cried orally from 'the block' by our auction-treasurer.

5. (See quots.)

1896 CHADWICK *Spalding's Base B. Guide* 173 A Block is a batted or thrown ball that is touched, stopped or handled by any person not engaged in the game. **1948** *Athletic Jrnl.* Jan. 17/1 A block is the impeding of the progress of an opponent who has not the ball.

6. In combs.: (1) **block ball,** (see quot.); (2) **captain,** one who has supervision over certain matters of public concern in a city block (cf. Du. *blokmeester*); (3) **coal,** splint coal; (4) **committee,** (see quot.); (5) **fort,** a fort of logs, *rare;* (6) * **house,** (*a*) a house built of squared logs (see quots.), *obs.*, (*b*) a house built of a child's toy blocks; (7) **pavement,** pavement consisting of squared blocks of stone; (8) **play,** (see quot. 1931); (9) **step,** a stump of a convenient height with steps cut in one side by which to mount or dismount from a horse; (10) **truck,** a solid wooden wheel, *rare;* (11) **up,** a temporary blockage, *rare.*

(1) **1891** N. CRANE *Baseball* 79 *Block ball,* a batted or thrown ball handled by an outsider. — (2) **1943** *Chi. D. News* 30 Oct. 6/7 It is the block captains and parents, . . . and all the other run-of-the-mill ordinary citizens that this conference is trying to reach. — (3) **1871** *Amer. Naturalist* V. 177 On this excursion [to Terre Haute] a visit will be made to the celebrated Block-coal field (iron smelting coal) and Blast furnaces, of Clay County. *Ib.* 554 Block coal has a laminated structure and is composed of alternate thin layers of vitreous, dull black coal, and fibrous, mineral charcoal. **1874** R. H. COLLINS *Kentucky* I. 210 The Peach Orchard coal, the cannel coal, and the block coal (now best known at Ashland and used in the raw state for smelting iron ore), are among the finest in the world. — (4) **1839** T. BROTHERS *U.S.* 134 The politicians, or office-hunters, form their 'block committees,' the duty of each of which committees is to organise and drill all the whigs, or democrats, as the case may be, that live in a certain number of houses adjoining each other, which they are pleased to call 'blocks.'

(5) **1798** I. ALLEN *Hist. Vermont* 47 He, with a number of men, repaired to New Haven falls, and built a block fort. — (6) (*a*) **1821** Z. HAWLEY *Jrnl. of Tour* (1822) 52 A block-house in Ohio differs from a log one in this particular: in the former the logs are hewn square, so that they are smooth within and without, and the latter are hewn only within, having the bark on the outside. **1826** J. BRADFORD *Ky. Notes* 74 *Blockhouse,* a strong log house the second story of which overjuts or protrudes beyond the first 18 inches or more all round. **1857** *Mich. Agric. Soc. Trans.* VIII. 398 The house that Mr. Campau built is yet standing; it is what is called a block-house, *i.e.*, a house built of logs that have been hewed square before being laid up. (*b*) **1919** CUNNINGHAM *Chronicle* 247 We had planned a big cake and a lot of block houses for him to build. — (7) **1896** HASWELL *New York* 273 It was about this year [1832] that the first block, or Belgian, pavement was laid in a street of this city or country. — (8) **1931** *Chi. Tribune* 18 Jan. II. 4/1 What is a block play in basketball? The term, frequently used since general adoption of a man-to-man defense, indicates that a defensive player has been deliberately prevented from guarding his opponent by another opponent. In collegiate and high school basketball this is legal. **1935** *Lit. Digest* 9 Feb. 40/1 The referee declared that the play 'was a deliberate block,' that 'it is regretted that Kentucky is taught illegal block plays.' — (9) **1916** MASSEY *Reminisc.* 31 At almost every home and at the churches there were block steps for the ladies to mount from.

(10) **1860** *Harper's Mag.* Jan. 282/2 In Kentucky . . . there is a region so rocky and rough that the people do most of their hauling on . . . a frame mounted on wide block trucks sawed from a log. — (11) **1855** *N.Y. Wkly. Tribune* 10 March 5/2 They reported that there was still a block-up at Oak Ridge, and advised us to sit down quietly until to-morrow.

b. In phrases. (1) *On the block,* (of cattle) slaughtered and dressed, opposed to "on the hoof"; (2) *to go on the block,* to be put up for auction, cf. **4.** above; (3) *block of five,* see * **five.**

(1) **1864** *Weekly New Mexican* 17 June 2/4 Proposals . . . for furnishing United States troops . . . with Fresh Beef on the Hoof and on the Block. — (2) **1929** R. B. VANCE *Human Factors in Cotton Culture* 65 Planters failed and plantations went on the block.

As the last term in **anvil, auction, biscuit, brick, building, business, city, head, hominy, lick, sale, salt, school, silver block.**

* **block,** *v.* **1.** *To block one's game,* to thwart one's plans. **2.** *To block off,* to head off, stop.

(1) **1844** KENDALL *Santa Fe Exped.* II. 260 Soon after [he] ordered his own men to leave the gambling cot of the leper, and by this means 'blocked the game.' **1884** *Boston Journal* 20 Dec. 2/2 Their little game was blocked. — (2) **1893** POST *Harvard Stories* 86 The two opposing crowds . . . swept across the diamond, 'blocking off' the owners of the two dogs. **1899** QUINN *Pa. Stories* 190, I tried to fix up two or three things with Miss Fitzgerald and she blocked me off each time, very nicely, it is true, but still she blocked me off.

* **blockade,** *n.*

1. =**blockade whisky.**

1867 SCOTT *Partisan Life* 195 The truth is, the parson had taken about half a pint of 'blockade,' and did not care the snap of a finger for the reproachful looks of all the black eyes in Christendom. **1913** M. W. MORLEY *Carolina Mts.* 66 For corn . . . supplies as well that important beverage, variously known as 'blockade,' 'brush whiskey,' and in the outer world, 'corn-whiskey.'

2. A block or stoppage of transport or traffic, esp. on a railroad, by snow or some accident. Also attrib.

1856 *N.Y. Herald* 8 Jan. 1/4 The railroads are being slowly relieved from the blockade of snow, but serious detention of trains still exists. **1890** *Boston Transcript* 29 Jan. 1/4 It now seems probable that the great blockade in the Sierras will soon be over. **1904** *N.Y. Times* 5 May 3 After it had become known that the system was paralyzed, 'blockade signs' were hung out at all the stations. **1947** *R.R. Telegrapher* May 279/1 Much credit and appreciation is due the many Brothers who stayed with the job for many long hours . . . ; thereby assisting in getting the blockade cleared up.

3. A barrier on a river. *Rare.*

1871 *N.C. Game Laws* in *Fur, Fin, & Feather* (1872) 153 It shall not be lawful for any person to draw a seine . . . between the blockade near Hill's Point . . . and the falls at Wm. S. Battles' factory.

4. In combs.: (1) **blockade cotton,** during the Civil War, cotton barred from foreign markets by the federal blockade, *obs.;* (2) **liquor,** =**blockade whisky;** (3) **run,** denoting something brought in through a blockade; (4) **runner,** a vessel that tries to evade a blockade, a captain or crew member of such a vessel; (5) **running,** the action of getting or attempting to get through a blockade; (6) **still,** an illegal still that produces blockade liquor; (7) **tobacco,** (see **blockader,** quot. 1886); (8) **whisky,** illicit whisky.

(1) **1865** *Chi. Tribune* 10 April 1 It may fairly be inferred . . . that the patriotic citizens making these donations . . . had the choice of . . . taking blockade cotton at government prices. — (2) **1922** KEPHART *So. Highlanders* 126 Here an illicit distiller is called a blockader, his business is blockading, and the product is blockade liquor. — (3) **1865** *Atlantic Mo.* XV. 508/2, I should like to see the negroes whom I knew most thoroughly intrusted with blockade-run rifles. — (4) **1863** *Rep. Secy. of Navy* p. v, Not a single blockade-runner has succeeded in reaching the city [of Charleston] for months. **1889** *Cent. Mag.* Feb. 601/1 She was built for a blockade-runner, I suppose you know. **1944** *Newsweek* 24 Apr. 14/1 The Germans . . . have redoubled their efforts to sneak through blockade runners from Japan.

(5) **1864** *Nautical Almanac* 505/1 The Anglo-Confederate blockade-running steamer Chatham is captured by the United States gunboat Huron. **1947** *Newsweek* 17 Feb. 20/3 Gibbs, finishing a novel for spring publication, and Williams, working on the history of blockade running. — (6) **1909** *Sat. Ev. Post* 10 April 9/3 Those puzzling, intangible lines of communication . . . serve the mountain in lieu of telegraph and telephone, . . . often forestalling the swiftest raid on blockade stills. **1913** KEPHART *So. Highlanders* 133 At the little blockade still a slower process is used, for malt is hard to get. — (8) **1883** ZEIGLER & GROSSCUP *Alleghanies* 52 Like blockade whisky, a bah

outer thet black bore allus goes to the spot. **1922** KEPHART *So. Highlanders* 138 Blockade whiskey, until recently, sold to the consumer at from $2.50 to $3.00 the gallon.

b. *To run the blockade,* to escape capture by eluding or outdistancing a blockading force.

1861 *Harper's Mag.* Sep. 547/1 The 'Sumter' . . . succeeded in running the blockade of the mouth of the Mississippi. **1883** *Cent. Mag.* Nov. 142/1 Colonel Thorburn . . . afterward became engaged in running the blockade, bringing supplies into the Confederate States.

As the last term in **constructive, cotton, paper, snow blockade.**

* **blockade,** *v. tr.* To block by snow or ice. Also transf.

1816 *Niles' Reg.* X. 216/2 In consequence of the vast body of ice with which it [the harbor] is yet *blockaded,* they were unable to get in. **1872** *Vt. Bd. Agric. Rep.* I. 24 An exceedingly severe snow storm having completely blockaded many of the roads, many were prevented from attending the meetings. **1909** A. C. RICE *Mr. Opp* 289 You've carried this through, but I'll blockade you. I am going to tell the truth to the whole community.

* **blockader,** *n. S.* An illicit distiller of whisky (see also quot. 1886). Cf. **blockade liquor, still, whisky.**

1883 ZEIGLER & GROSSCUP *Alleghanies* 141 In the wilderness, we would be taken for revenue officers and, as such, shot on sight by blockaders. **1886** *Boston Beacon* 2 Jan., The dealers in illicit tobacco, who flourished principally in North Carolina, were called *blockaders,* and the illicit untaxed tobacco *blockade tobacco.* **1943** *Nat. Geog. Mag.* Dec. 762 The preacher converted the 'king' of the 'blockaders' (moonshiners) and built a tiny log schoolhouse.

* **blockading,** *n.* The making of liquor without a license, moonshining.

1883 ZEIGLER & GROSSCUP *Alleghanies* 141 Blockading, or 'moonshining' as it is sometimes called, . . . is not as prevalent in these mountains as is generally supposed. **1921** *Outing* July 190/3 'Blockading' has become so profitable that there are ten men engaged in it now to what there were a short time ago. **1943** *Nat. Geog. Mag.* Dec. 766/1 Naturally Henderson in this 'blockading' (moonshining) . . . had made many enemies.

Blocker loop. *W.* (See quots.) — **1929** DOBIE *Vaquero* 263 No doubt many people who speak of the 'Blocker loop' nowadays never heard of John Blocker, although all the real cattle people in Texas know who John Blocker was. **1944** ADAMS *W. Words* 13 *Blocker loop* An extra-large loop, taking its name from John Blocker, a well-known roper of Texas, who originated and used this loop.

* **blocking,** *n.* **1.** The set of blocks used in shipbuilding. **2. blocking-man,** (see quot.). Both *obs.*

(1) **1706** SEWALL *Diary* II. 156 A great ship, . . . building at Salem, runs off her blocking in the night. **1883** *Harper's Mag.* May 937/2 The blocking is knocked away. — (2) **1835** in HOFFMAN *Winter in West* II. 117 The hogs are . . . first weighed by the weigher, then passed to the 'blocking-men,' who placed them on the several blocks . . . when they are received by the 'cutters.'

blondine blɑnˈdin, *a.* and *n.* [f. * *blond, a.*] **1.** *n.* A preparation for making the hair blond. **2.** *a.* Artificially blond. Also **blondined.**

(1) **1909** F. CALHOUN *Miss Minerva* 73 Jimmy . . . returned with a big bottle of a powerful 'blondine' in one hand. — (2) **1920** LEWIS *Main Street* 312 'You know this new dressmaker, Mrs. Swiftwaite?—swell dame with blondine hair? **1931** *K.C. Star* 5 Aug., Did you notice . . . the hula dancer . . . —the blondined Hawaiian?

* **blood,** *n.*

1. (See quots.) *Slang. Obs.*

1851 HALL *College Words* 178 At Washington College, Penn., students of a religious character are called *lap-ears* or *donkeys.* The opposite Class are known by the common name of *bloods.* **1851** HALL *College Words* 20 *Blood.* At some of the Western colleges, this word signifies excellent; as a *blood* recitation. A student who recites well is said to *make a blood.*

2. (*cap.*) =**Blood Indian.** Also attrib.

1832 CATLIN *Indians* I. 52 The Blackfeet proper are divided into four bands or families, as follow:—the 'Blood' band, of 450 lodges; and the 'Small Robes.' **1855** in *Mont. Hist. Soc. Contrib.* X. (1940) 45 He was unable to find the Principal Camp of the Bloods but about 8 miles from the Fort overtook a small party of them. **1892** *Amer. Anthropologist* April 156 The Blackfoot name for the Blood tribe is Kainah. The term Blood was probably given them by the Hudson Bay people on account of their custom of painting their faces with a red streak extending from ear to ear. **1947** DEVOTO *Across Wide Missouri* 90 When he sighted some Bloods and his men began to shoot, they too flew a white flag.

3. In special combs.: (1) **Blood Atoner,** a Mormon who holds that certain sins can be atoned for only by shedding of the sinner's blood, *obs.;* (2) **beet,** the common red beet; (3) **Indian,** an Indian of the Kainah group, a division of the Blackfeet; (4) * **root,** the red puccoon or its root, also a medicinal preparation made from this; (5) **Blood Tubs,** a gang of roughs once active in Baltimore, *obs.;* (6) **turnip,** a turnip-shaped variety of the blood beet; (7) * **wort,** any one of various American plants, as the red puccoon, red root, etc., also the rattlesnake weed.

(1) **1900** *Congress. Rec.* 24 Jan. 1131/1 The 'Blood Atoners' silenced in death the voice of apostacy. *Ib.,* Mr. Eldredge was a Danite. Mr. Eldredge was a Blood Atoner. — (2) **1829** *Free Press* (Tarboro, N.C.) 20 Feb., Blood Beets. **1941** LEE *Stagecoach North* 29 Grandmother took as much pride in the display of marrow fat peas, parsnips, blood beets, and limas as she did in her china roses. — (3) **1794** in *Mass. H.S. Coll.* 1 Ser. III. 24 The tribes of Indians which he passed through [between Montreal and the Lake of the Woods], were called . . . Blood Indians, the Blackfeet tribe, . . . and several others. **1863** *Amer. Philos. Soc. Trans.* XII. 249 The Blood Indians range through the district along Maria, Teton, and Belly Rivers. — (4) **1722** DUDLEY in *Phil. Trans.* XXXII. 295 Remedies for the Sting of a Rattlesnake; among others, . . . is a Root they call Blood-root. **1832** WILLIAMSON *Maine* I. 120 The *Blood-root* is an acrid narcotic; and a large dose of it occasions nausea, heart-burn, and faintness. **1948** *Life* 5 April 57/1 Spring comes to the Ozarks in March, a few weeks after the white bloodroot shoots through dead leaves on barely thawed ground.

(5) **1856** *Butte Record* (Oroville, Calif.) 29 Nov. 3/7 The 'Blood Tubs' . . . went to Philadelphia on election day . . . to fight off and whip the democracy from the polls. **1888** M. LANE in *America* 20 Sep. 15 Blood tubs . . . got the name by dipping the head of an obnoxious German in a tub of blood and then chasing him along the streets. At one time these gangs of roughs, like the Ashlanders and Plug Uglies, practically controlled the ward politics of Baltimore. — (6) **1857–8** *Ill. Agric. Soc. Trans.* III. 503 The early blood turnip is a standard sort [of beet], turnip shaped, blood red, very tender and good for early use and late keeping. — (7) **1705** BEVERLEY *Virginia* IV. 56 Others degenerate, and will not continue above a year or two at the most; such are July-Flowers, . . . Clary, and Bloodwort. **1833** EATON *Botany* (ed. 6) 174 Vein-leaf hawkweed, bloodwort. . . . *S.* **1889** *Cent.* 594 Bloodwort, the leaves of which are veined with red.

b. In phrases: (1) * *blood and thunder,* and variants, "the term generally applied to works dealing with the exploits of desperadoes, cutthroats, and other criminals" (F.); (2) * *blood-and-wounds, S.* a species of bullfrog, so called from its cry, also **bloodnoun.**

(1) **1852** *Lantern* (N.Y.) II. 67/2 Most, however, of these 'blood, thunder, and whiskey articles,' are written by raw lads, who were originally caught by Barnum's agent in the Bogs of Slievegammon. **1882** STEELE *Frontier Army* (1883) 3 There is an interesting phase of American life that hitherto had its chief chronicler in the dime novel and its most frequent interpreter in the blood-and-terror drama. **1947** *Denver Post* 23 Feb. A. 7/1 The 'thriller' scribblers of the 1870's turned out miles of blood-and-thunder copy. — (2) **1872** FLAGG *Good Investment* XX. 901/1 Monstrous frogs, named 'blood-an-'ounds', from the sounds they utter, called in loud, deep bass for 'blood and wounds.' **1909** *Cent. Supp.* 145/2 *Bloodnoun,* a local name of the bullfrog, *Rana catesbiana.* (Southern U.S.).

As the last term in **full, half, hot, mixed, Morgan, pure, warm blood.**

* **blooded,** *a.* Of horses or other animals: Of good blood, of a pure or superior breed or stock. See also **fine, full, mixed, pure blooded.**

1778 *Md. Journal* 20 Jan., (*advt.*) (Th.), Several blooded mares and fillies will also be sold. **1784** *Ib.* 2 Nov., (*advt.*) (Th.), A natural trotter but not free spirited, though part blooded. **1898** PAGE *Red Rock* 43 Jacquelin, on a blooded colt, was trying to keep . . . in line with him. **1948** *Democrat* 1 April 1/3 Blooded Calves Bring Fancy Price Tuesday.

b. Used jocularly of persons.

1804 *Mass. Spy* 11 Jan. (Th.), When one of our blooded young fellows separates from the crowd, he only, &c. **1899** CHESNUTT *Wife of His Youth* 292 'Pears ter me Ben gettin' mighty blooded, . . . drivin' a hoss an' buggy.

bloodee ˌblʌdˈi, *n.* (See quot.) *Obs.* — **1797** *Farmer's W. Museum* (Walpole, N.H.) 21 Aug. (Hall), Seniors about to take degrees Not by their wits, but by *bloodees. Ib.* (*footnote*), A kind of cudgel . . . borne . . . by the bloods of a certain college in New England, 2 feet 5 inches in length, . . . with a huge piece of lead at one end.

* **Bloodgood,** *n.* [f. proper names.] **1.** A variety of pear. **2. Bloodgood pie,** (see quot.). Both *obs.*

(1) **1847** IVES *N. Eng. Fruit* 58 *Bloodgood.* This pear was first brought into notice by the late James Bloodgood, of Flushing, Long Island. **1867–8** *Ill. Agric. Soc. Trans.* VII. 523, I got four dollars per box for Bloodgoods last year. — (2) **1896** HASWELL *New York* 168 Frequently parties, suffering from the neglect by the accumulation of filth in

the streets [c1825], would pile it up in a great mass and then label it 'Corporation Pudding,' and, in later years, 'Bloodgood Pies,' etc.; Bloodgood being the head of the department.

* **bloody,** *a.*

1. Filled with, or the scene of, strife and danger (attributed to Indian speech). *Obs.* Cf. **Bloody Ground, land.**

1751 C. GIST *Journals* 51 Their Father . . . said the Road was clear, but He understood it was made foul and bloody, and by them. **1777** *Va. State P.* I. 286 [The Indians] also observing it was a bloody Country, and if he went to it they would not hold him by the hand any longer. **1802** J. DRAYTON *S. Carolina* 14 The path over this mountain, has been crooked and straight, bloody and clean; (according to the Indian talks).

2. (See quot.) *Slang. Obs.*

1819 A. PEIRCE *Rebelliad* 44 Arriving at Lord Bibo's study, They thought they'd be a little bloody . . . [*footnote*] Formerly a College term for daring, rowdy, impudent. *Ib.* 76.

3. In combs.: (1) **bloody back,** a contemptuous nickname for a British soldier, *obs.*, cf. **red coat;** (2) **bill,** an act passed by Congress in 1833 providing for the enforcement of the tariff laws in South Carolina, *obs.*, cf. **force bill;** (3) **bub,** (see quot.), *obs.;* (4) **cardinal,** the cardinal flower, *Lobelia cardinalis, rare;* (5) **chasm,** the estrangement between North and South caused by the Civil War; (6) **code,** =**black code,** *obs.;* (7) **Bloody Ground,** = **Dark and Bloody Ground,** *obs.;* (8) **land,** used of Kansas, cf. **bleeding Kansas;** (9) ***nose,** (see quot.); (10) **season,** (see quot.), *rare;* (11) ***shirt,** any means used to stir up sectional hostility between the North and South since the Civil War, often *to wave the bloody shirt,* also attrib., hence **bloody shirter.**

(1) 1770 *Mass. Gaz. Extraordinary* 21 June 2/2 The Mob still increased, and were outrageous . . . calling out 'Come, you Rascals, you bloody Backs, you Lobster Scoundrels; fire if you dare.' **1781** PETERS *Hist. Conn.* (1829) 292 That the lead of it [=George III's statue] should be run into bullets, for the destruction of the English bloody-backs. — **(2) 1833** *Niles' Reg.* XLIV. 36/1 The law 'further to provide for the collection of duties on imports,' is called 'the bloody bill,' by all the nullifiers, and some yet talk about letting blood, because of its passage! *Ib.* 384/1 May those who voted for the bloody bill to coerce South Carolina, a free and sovereign state, into shameful submission, never go down to their graves in peace. — **(3) 1882** *Alta California* (S.F.) 25 July 1/1 'Bloody Bub' literature is the latest name for dime novels. — **(4) 1851** D. G. MITCHELL *Dream Life* 199 The bloody cardinal of the swamp-lands.

(5) 1876 *Congress. Rec.* 14 June 3791/1 This measure is one of conciliation. It reunites; it fills up the 'bloody chasm.' **1916** *Amer. Mag.* May 20/1 The Kentucky Confederates and the Kentucky Unionists embraced across the Bloody Chasm. **1924** *Amer. Mercury* April 390/1 Greeley had spent his life abusing the Southern slaveholders and the absurdity and hollowness of their supporting him could hardly be veiled by any pretext of shaking hands across the bloody chasm. — **(6) 1855** *S. Lit. Messenger* XXI. 2 At the time in question no Southern State was as much noted for subserviency to the Bloody Code as Mississippi. — **(7) 1777** *Va. State P.* I. 283 The Dragging Canoe told them it was the bloody Ground, and would be dark, and difficult to settle it. **1836** IRVING *Astoria* I. xviii. 301 Edward Robinson . . . had been one of the first settlers of Kentucky, and engaged in many of the conflicts of the Indians on 'The Bloody Ground.' **1840** *Knickerb.* XVI. 161 He . . . had signalized himself in the hard conflicts with the Indians, which gained Kentucky the appellation of 'the Bloody Ground.' — **(8) 1855** *Herald of Freedom* 18 Aug. 2/4 The bloody land [*sc.* Kansas]. — **(9) 1931** CLUTE *Plants* 44 Occasionally a bit of sly humor has dictated the names as . . . the red trillium (*T. erectum*) is bloody nose.

(10) 1846 LEVINGE *Echoes* II. 60 They expected what they termed a 'bloody season.' The ball-room is the arena chosen for catching their enemies, when with 'an Arkansas toothpick' or a 'bowie knife' they pay off old scores. — **(11) 1875** J. S. REYNOLDS *Reconstruction S.C.* (1905) 304 A diligent attempt is now being made to hide with the 'bloody shirt' the appalling wrongs committed by the Republican party. **1877** J. M. BEARD *K.K.K. Sketches* 156 These men . . . went forth to lay their knives at the throats of a sufficient number of innocents to afford a text for bloody-shirt invectives. **1880** *Chi. Tribune* 25 Jan. 4/2 It turns out, then, that the 'bloody-shirters' have lost a Senator in Wisconsin and the advocates of 'civil rule' have gained one. **1948** KERWIN *Civil-Military Relationships* 31 The G.A.R. waved the Bloody Shirt in many a political campaign, advising its boys in blue to 'vote as you shot.'

blooey ˈbluˑɪ, *a.* [Imitative.] Awry, askew, usu. *to go blooey. Slang.* — **1929** *Collier's* 5 Jan. 40/4 But in 1920 I weakened. As a result, my bank roll went blooie. **1932** *K.C. Star* 2 Feb. 20 We note that the caviar market has gone 'blooie.'

bloomer ˈblumɚ, *n.* [After Mrs. Amelia *Bloomer* (1818–94), an early advocate of the costume.]

1. Orig. a complete costume or suit for women, consisting of a short skirt worn over pantalets gathered at the ankles, and usu. with a loose coat and broad-brimmed hat, latterly used of loose trousers gathered at the knees, and now often a woman's knee-length undergarment. Regularly *pl.* and orig. *cap.*

1851 *Worcester Spy* in *Boston Transcript* 29 May 2/4 The first 'Bloomer' made its appearance in our city yesterday. **1851** *Harper's Mag.* Sep. 576/2 The ladies seem determined to reduce the volume of their dresses. This is manifested . . . at home by the general favor in which the 'bloomers' are held. **1895** *N.Y. Dramatic News* 12 Oct. 3/3 Beneath this costume may be worn bloomers or any style of nether garment your fancy or the weather may suggest. **1920** LEWIS *Main Street* 2 The hulking young women . . . with calves bulging in heavy-ribbed woolen stockings beneath decorous blue serge bloomers, thuddingly galloped across the floor of the 'gym.' **1946** THOMPSON *Am. Daughter* 40 My lingerie consisted solely of black sateen bloomers.

attrib. **1851** *Boston Transcript* 26 May 2/3 The daughter of Dr. Hanson, of this city, appeared in the Bloomer suit at a convention in South Reading last week. *Ib.* 31 May 2/4 Quite a large number of young ladies in that city [=Lowell] have made arrangements to attend church tomorrow in the Bloomer costume.

2. A woman wearing a bloomer costume. *Obs.*

1851 in *Pioneer* (S.F.) (1854) Nov. 277, I knew a 'strong-minded Bloomer,' at home, of some talent, and who was possessed, in a certain sense, of an excellent education. **1856** *Spirit of Times* (N.Y.) 22 Nov. 190/3 His mind was made up as quickly as a Bloomer makes up her mind to get married, when she can. **1860** HOLMES *Professor* vii. 195 I don't like the Bloomers any too well,—in fact, I never saw but one, and she . . . had a mob of boys after her. **1865** *Wilkes' Spirit of Times* 5 Aug. 363/3, I go in for woman's rights, and shall attend the next convention of *bloomers.*

3. A hat such as was often worn with a bloomer costume. In full **bloomer hat.** *Obs.*

1859 A. HOPE in *Amer. Agriculturist* XVIII. 183 She . . . did wear an immense bloomer hat streaming with blue ribbons. **1883** *Life Mrs. Prentiss* vi. 177 A small shawl and my bloomer on.

4. =**bloomer car.** *Obs.*

1904 *Providence Jrnl.* 1 Aug. 3 The car was one of the new eight-wheel bloomers.

5. In special combs.: (1) **bloomer car,** a type of streetcar formerly used in Providence, R.I., and perhaps elsewhere, having such a high running board, which served as a step, along the side that ladies in boarding it were compelled to lift their skirts sufficiently high to expose their bloomers, *obs.;* (2) **fence,** (see quot.), *obs.;* (3) **meeting,** a meeting attended by bloomers, *rare;* (4) **pantalets,** pantalets forming part of a bloomer costume, *obs.;* (5) **stern,** a type of stern for sailing boats, *rare.*

(1) 1904 *Providence Journal* 1 Aug. 3 Attempting to board a moving Crescent Park bloomer car caused James Cooper to lose both feet and may cost him his life. — **(2) 1862** in *Ill. State Agric. Soc. Trans.* V. (1861–64) 692 At present many men in opening new farms are compelled to make 'Shanghai' or 'Bloomer' fences (two-boarded fences). — **(3) 1865** SALA *Diary* I. 397 There is a Spiritualist Convention next door; there is a Bloomer meeting over the way. — **(4)** *a***1855** KELLEY *Humors* 167 Maria Evangeline Roxana Matilda was to be fitted out in Polka boots, gipsey bonnet, and Bloomer pantalettes.

(5) 1897 *Outing* April 9/1 Tartar was generally recognized to have won her races without benefit from the 'bloomer stern,' which had excited so much adverse criticism earlier in the year.

Also *bloomer clad, girl, vagary.*

bloomered ˈblumɚd, *a.* Characterized by wearing bloomers. *Rare.* — **1895** S. T. KIDDER in *Advance* (Chi.) 6 June 1287 The 'new woman,' . . . though not necessarily of the bloomered type, is marching . . . to victory in Wisconsin.

bloomerism ˈbluməˌrɪzəm, *n.* [f. **bloomer.**] The practice or advocacy of wearing the bloomer costume. *Obs.*

1851 (*title*), 'Bloomerism,' or The New Female Costume of 1851. **1860** HANCOCK *Five Years* 54 The Tribune . . . assisting to give a sickly vitality to the doctrines of Bloomerism, Freeloveism, and woman's rights. **1865** SALA *Diary* II. 14 Is Bloomerism on the wane, or gaining ground?

Bloomerite ˈbluməˌraɪt, *n.* =**bloomer 2.** *Obs.* — **1851** in *Annals of Iowa* 3 Ser. V. 58 The Bloomerites will carry the day. **1852**

Ore. Statesman 27 Jan. 1/4 The Bloomerites made their appearance last week on the Boulevard de la Madelaine.

blooper ˈblupɚ, *n. Baseball.* [Imitative.]

1. (See quot. 1937.) Hence **blooping,** *a.*

1937 *N.Y. Times* 8 Oct. 29/6 A 'blooper' is a soggy fly to an unoccupied spot behind the backs of the infielders and under the nose of some disgruntled outfielder. **1948** *Dly. Ardmoreite* (Ardmore, Okla.) 28 April 8/3 Hughes forced Smith at third on an infield blooper, which narrowly missed being caught, to score two runs. **1948** *N.Y. Times* 23 May v. 2/4 Lupien reached second on the error and a blooping single by Ralph Hodgin let Baker score.

2. A kind of pitched ball (see quot. 1946). Also attrib.

1946 *Time* 22 July 48/2 Rip called it an ephus ball after an old crap-shooting phrase, *ephus—iphus—ophus;* sportwriters called it a blooper. Whatever its name, it was lobbed up to the plate . . . with lots of backspin. **1948** *Chi. Tribune* 27 June II. 4/8 His homer on one of Rip Sewell's famous blooper pitches was the only one ever knocked against the Pittsburgh veteran's specialty.

* **blossom,** *n.*

1. a. A variety of quartz thought to indicate the presence of lead. **b.** (See quot. 1881.)

(a) **1819** SCHOOLCRAFT *Mo. Lead Mines* 71 This variety of quartz . . . has acquired the popular name of blossom of lead, or mineral blossom. *Ib.* 91 In searching for ore, the soil, the slope of the hills, spar, blossom, trees, etc. are taken as guides. **1883** BEADLE *Western Wilds* xxxiv. 560 We are certainly near the outcrop from which the 'blossom' was broken. **1936** MCKENNA *Black Range* 287 After the great finds of Lake Valley, those croppin's being mostly manganese of iron, all prospectors were lookin' for that kind of blossom. — (b) **1871** *Colo. Gazetteer* 158 The first object of the prospector is to find the 'blossom'; the next, where it comes from. **1881** RAYMOND *Mining Glossary, Blossom,* the oxidized or decomposed outcrop of a vein or coal-bed, more frequently the latter.

2. In combs.: (1) **blossom hemp,** (see quot. 1862); (2) **rock,** a variety of rock believed to indicate the presence of a mineral.

(1) **1766** WASHINGTON *Diaries* I. 228 Began to pull Hemp at the Mill and at Muddy hole—too late for the blossom Hemp by three Weeks or a Month. **1862** *Rep. Comm. Patents: Agric.* 114 The male [hemp] is called the blossom-hemp, and the female the seed-hemp. When the blossom-hemp has shed its pollen, it dies. — (2) **1871** *Colo. Gazetteer* 156 The 'blossom rock' (quartz stained with metallic oxides), which indicates the proximity of mineral deposits, differs but little in gold and silver lodes.

As the last term in **bosom, bubby, gold, May, mineral, orange, shad blossom.**

* **blotter,** *n.* **1.** A book, as in a police station, in which events are recorded as they occur. See also **advertising blotter. 2.** *W.* =**brand blotter.**

(1) **1887** *Harper's Mag.* Mar. 500/2 Every item of police duty, and of civil or criminal occurrence, is inscribed on the 'blotter.' **1906** *Atlantic Mo.* Feb. 264 It was necessary . . . to examine the day-book or blotter in the chief clerk's office [at the Patent Office]. **1946** *Chi. D. News* 20 July 1/4 Strange doings were recorded on today's police blotter here. — (2) **1920** MULFORD *J. Nelson* xii. 126 There ain't no sense in totin' it by th' glass to a crowd of blotters. They'll hold more liquor than a gopher hole.

* **blow,** *n.*

1. (See quot. 1851.) *Slang. Obs.*

1827 *Harvard Reg.* Aug. 172 My fellow-students had been engaged at a 'blow' till the stage horn had summoned them to depart. **1851** HALL *College Words* 21 Blow. A merry frolic with drinking; a spree.

2. Scenting distance.

1851 WM. KELLY *Across Rocky Mts.* 94, I did not fire until they [antelope] came almost within 'blow' of me, and then shot two.

3. A short rest. *Colloq.*

1855 *Knickerb.* Aug. 146, I determined that the horses should now have a good 'blow,' let what would happen. **1948** *Sat. Ev. Post* 11 Sep. 19/3 He stopped to give the horses a blow.

3. *What's the blow?* What's the matter? *Rare.*

1852 STOWE *Uncle Tom* viii, What's the blow now?

As the last term in **horn, peach, sand, shad blow.**

* **blow,** *v.*

1. *intr.* Of firearms: Upon being discharged to blow up or undergo a blowing out, usu. along the line of weld in the barrel. *Obs.*

1774 in *Champlain Soc. Pub.* XXI. 125, 15 Gallons of the Brandy ware Expended before they ariv'd, and 2 of the guns Blown—but all the other goods came Safe. **1779** *Ib.* 258, I think the trading Guns must be very slightly proved as one that I bought of Your Honors made by Wilson being loaded to four Inches including powder, shot & wading the third time it was fired blowed into two pieces about 15 Inches from the britch. **1835** LONGSTREET *Ga. Scenes* 224 'Gentlemen,' said he, as he came to the mark, 'I don't say that I'll win beef; but if my piece don't blow, I'll eat the paper; or be mighty apt to do it.

2. *tr.* To send (a ball), make (a hole), through a person.

1790 FANNING *Narrative* 7 They threatened blowing a ball through me every instant, if I did not surrender. **1860** CLAIBORNE *Sam Dale* iv. 73 Fall back, or I will blow you through. **1891** ROBERTS *Adrift in Amer.* 153 If you talk to me like that, I'll blow a hole through you that a rat could crawl through.

3. *intr.* To emit or discharge.

1805 DUNBAR *Life* 317 It happens not rarely as I am informed that the mountains blow as it is termed that is the Earth opens & a quantity of earthy & mineral matter is thrown up with considerable force. **1886** WINCHELL *Walks & Talks* 143 Personal information from Mr. Neff . . . assures me that these wells continue to 'blow.'

4. (See quot.)

1868 *Amer. Naturalist* Oct. 467 Another sound is a kind of snort,—a forcible emission of air from the nostrils. . . . At the season when the doe is rearing her young, . . . she will stand and 'blow.' The bucks also blow, but less frequently.

5. The verb or verb stem in combs.: (1) * **blowback,** a backward draught or air current; (2) **bladder,** (see quot.); (3) **down,** a tree that has been blown down, or an area where trees or other vegetation have been blown down; (4) **gun,** (see quots.); (5) **hard,** a blustering braggart, also attrib., *slang;* (6) **leaf,** (see quot.); (7) * **out,**

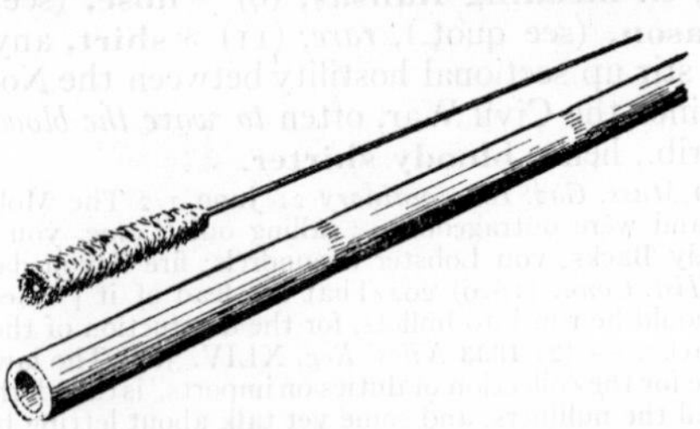

Portion of an Indian blowgun and dart

(*a*) an irregular surface outcropping of a lode, (*b*) a hollow made by the wind in sandy or light soil, (*c*) **blowout grass,** any one of various grasses found in such a blowout; (8) **snake,** the blowing adder, snake, or viper, *qq.v.;* (9) **torch,** a blow lamp or blast torch, also fig.; (10) * **up,** (*a*) a business failure, a bankruptcy, (*b*) a tank or vat used in sugar refining.

(1) **1883** FULTON *Sam Hobart* 224 The flames originated from the '*blow back*' on the engine, forcing the flames out of the furnace when the door was opened. — (2) **1877** BARTLETT 776 'A blow-bladder figure for it,' a price inflated beyond all reason. — (3) **1895** *Outing* Aug. 448/2 After that, a line of blazes wanders erratically back and forth up the side of the mountain, dodging 'blow-downs' and ledges. **1946** *Time* 30 Dec. 2/2 We could have got our limit many times over. Hurricane blow-down full of them. **1946** *Democrat* 26 Dec. 1/1 These cankers . . . weaken the tree structurally, causing a large number of blow-downs. — (4) **1810** WILSON *Prose* I. 213, I first observed the Indian boys with their blow-guns. **1907** HODGE *Amer. Indians* I. 155 *Blowgun.* A dart-shooting weapon, consisting of a long tube of cane or wood from which little darts are discharged by blowing with the mouth. The darts are slender splints or weed stems, pointed at one end and wrapped at the butt with cotton, thistle down, or other soft material. This implement was common in the more southerly parts of the United States, the habitat of the fishing cane of which it was made.

(5) **1855** *Oregon Wkly. Times* 21 July (Th.), The Oregonian of last week has a blowhard article on the subject. **1867** *Weekly New Mexican* 13 Apr. 2/1 The blow-hard at the handle of the Gazette's bellows . . . puts forth the following. **1948** *Sat. Ev. Post* 11 Sep. 152/3 You're a blowhard. A great big loudmouthed blowhard. — (6) **1891** *Amer. Folk-Lore* IV. 148 *Sedum telephium* . . . in New Hampshire I have found it called Blow-leaf, also Aaron's Rod. — (7) (*a*) **1873** BEADLE *Undevel. West* 333 All the strange terms in mining parlance: 'true lodes, . . . blow-outs.' **a1904** WHITE *Blazed Trail Stories* xii. 233 The doubtful spot on the *Jim Crow* was not a blow-out, but a 'horse.' (*b*) **1892** SMITH & POUND *Bot. Survey Nebraska* II. 8 If a spot on a dry hill becomes bare, the loose sand is blown away, a small hollow is

made, the surrounding grass dies from drought.... Such blow outs were seen 100 meters in diameter and 15 ... meters deep. **1943** *Jrnl. Wildlife Management* Jan. Pl. 2 Old 'blow-out' in sand dunes partly stabilized by vegetation since grazing was eliminated. (*c*) **1897** POUND & CLEMENTS *Phytogeography of Nebraska* 248 The blow out grasses ... bind the sand together with their roots. **1935** HITCHCOCK *Manual of Grasses* 173 Redfieldia flexuosa.... Blowout Grass.... A sandbinding grass. — (**8**) **1850** E. S. SEYMOUR *Sketches of Minn.* 132 There is a snake called the blow-snake, whose breath is said to be poisonous. This snake is probably rare, as I could not find any person who had ever seen one. **1899** *Animal & Plant Lore* 86 The breath of a 'blow snake' ... is 'sure death' to the one who breathes it. Illinois. **1934** WEBSTER. — (**9**) **1909** *Cent. Supp.* 146/1 Blow-torch.... An apparatus for applying heat to a small area. **1935** *Amer. Mercury* Aug. 487/2 It would take all the picks and blowtorches in the world to make a sizable dent in that Gargantuan chunk of ice.

(**10**) (*a*) **1820** *Petersburg* (Va.) *Republican* 18 July 3/1 Another Blow-up.... A view of the affairs of the bank has just concluded, and ... the ... deficiency is ascertained. **1895** *N.Y. Dramatic News* 7 Dec. 18/1 The People's theatre and everybody connected with it are still head-over-ears in trouble and the grand blow-up may be expected at any time. (*b*) **1833** SILLIMAN *Man. Sugar Cane* 77 The vats, or blow-ups, as they are called, containing the sugar, ... are heated by steam tubes passing through them. **1886** *Harper's Mag.* June 82/2 These 'mixers' or 'blow-ups' are really great stew-pans set in the ground.

6. In colloq. and slang phrases: (1) *blow high, blow low,* come what may; (2) *∗to blow in,* to appear unexpectedly, to drop in; (3) *∗to blow* (money, etc.) (*in*), to spend money or resources recklessly, to squander; (4) *∗to blow off,* to cease an activity, cf. **dog;** (5) *to blow oneself* (or another), to treat, regale; (6) *to blow the lid off,* to expose a state of affairs, *slang;* (7) *∗to blow up,* (*a*) to become furiously angry, to go to pieces, muff one's part, (*b*) to summon (dogs) by blowing a horn.

(**1**) **1774** FITHIAN *Journal* I. 235 Ben is in a wonderful Fluster lest he shall have no company tomorrow at the Dance—But blow high, blow low, he need not be afraid; Virginians are of genuine blood—They will dance or die! **1921** PAINE *Comr. Rolling Ocean* x. 171 Here were three musketeers ... who were blithely resolved to stand by each other through thick and thin, blow high, blow low.

(**2**) **1895** REMINGTON *Pony Tracks* 104 We were all very busy when William 'blew in' with a great sputtering. **1948** *News-Dispatch* (Michigan City, Ind.) 3 Apr. 11 He never fails to check in at the post office the first thing when he blows into a new town!

(**3**) [**1887** F. FRANCIS *Saddle & Moccasin* 144 'Sam went off on a bend,' 'To blow in?' Jake laughed assent.] **1889** *Cent. Mag.* March 784/1 His story was that the brother sold out his share and 'blew it all in' in about a week. **1946** *Sat. Ev. Post* 3 Aug. 26/3 Most kids had only about a dime of pocket money to last them all week, and they thought twice about blowing it all at one time.

(**4**) **1845** HOOPER *Suggs* (1928) 37 When we blowed off, I judge he had the wust of it; he looked like he had any how.

(**5**) **1896** *D.N.* I. 412 'To *blow* oneself,' to spend money freely. **1948** *Woman's Day* March 9/1 The Long Island Railroad recently blew itself to some new upholstery and fresh paint.

(**6**) **1928** *Daily Tel.* 1 May 9/5 He 'blew the lid' off a notorious national condition of affairs.

(**7**) (*a*) **1871** MARK TWAIN *Letters* (1917) I. x. 189 Redpath tells me to blow up. Here goes! **1944** *Chi. D. News* 14 Dec. 22/1 You must learn to carry insults, anxieties, anger, fear and grief without blowing up. **1944** *Reader's Digest* April 122 Barrymore 'blew up' in his lines at almost the same place in the scene as before. (*b*) **1891** SLOAN *Fogy Days* 175 As the hour approached, I mounted my Bucephalus, and blew up the dogs, they were all keen, in for the hunt, and in finest trim.

∗blower, *n.*

1. A blow snake.

[**1745** in BEAUCHAMP *Moravian Jrnls. Rel. to Cen. N.Y.* (1916) 15 A little farther lay a snake (a blower) as thick as the arm, in the middle of the path. **1764** in FRIES *Records of the Moravians in N.C.* II. 581 (*Blässer*) is a black or slate-colored snake. If one goes too near to it the snake raises itself and puffs itself out until it is quite thick. It is said to blow out poison, and therefore be worse than a Rattlesnake, but I have not heard of any harm being done, and think that this is probably not true.] **1857** E. BEADLE *To Nebraska in '57* (1923) 47 We found a snake called here a blower. this one was as much as five feet long. they are spoted like a milk snake and perfectly harmless. [**1871** DE VERE 87 But *Blauser,* from the Dutch *blazer,* is still the name of the Deaf Adder.]

2. (See quot.)

1842 *Nat. Hist. N.Y., Zoology* IV. 327 The Common Puffer. *Tetradon turgidus*.... This curious fish receives its popular names of Puffer and Blower from its being enabled to inflate itself when taken from the water.

3. A contrivance for producing a strong current of air.

1858 SIMMONS *Dict. Trade,* Blower, ... a fan used on board American river steam-boats, to increase the current of air. **1931** *K.C. Star* 3 Dec. 32 One of the men called the beauty parlor and asked the operator if she had 'her blower on.'

As the last term in **fan, horn, pea, putty blower.**

∗blowing, *a.* In combs.: (1) **blowing adder, =blowing snake;** (2) **cave, cavern,** one through which a strong current of air passes; (3) **fly,** a blowfly, *obs.;* (4) **horn,** a cow horn suitably prepared for being blown; (5) **sand,** sand or sandhills shifted by the winds; (6) **snake,** a hognose snake; (7) **spring, =blowing cave;** (8) **viper, =blowing snake,** also attrib.

(**1**) **1882** *Amer. Naturalist* XVI. 566 Of all strange habits in snakes, none equals that observed in the blowing adder (*Heterodon simus*). **1901** *Everybody's Mag.* April 384/1 We may sometimes find a milk snake, garter snake, or blowing adder (hognosed snake) sunning himself upon a rock. — (**2**) **1781–2** JEFFERSON *Notes Va.* (1788) 22 There is another blowing cave in the Cumberland mountain. **1805** CLARK in *Lewis & C. Exped.* (1904) II. 176 A nois ... as might be caused by running water in some of the caverns ..., on the principal of the blowing caverns. **1843** *Nat. Hist. N.Y., Geology* I. 107 If the outlet of the cave be left open, it will form a blowing cave. **1944** *Speleological Soc. Bul.* July 50/1 These smaller caves are three or four hundred feet east of Blowing Cave, and are about twenty feet above the Three Sisters. — (**3**) **1805** LEWIS in *L. & Clark Exped.* (1904) II. 51 This stream we named Blowing Fly Creek, from the immence quantities of these insects found in this neighbourhood. **1823** JAMES *Exped.* I. 108 The blowing flies swarmed in inconceivable numbers, attacking ... the provision of the party. — (**4**) **1836** C. GILMAN *Recollections* (1838) xxx. 209 The usual dress of a hunter is composed of a cap, a frock coat, ... boots, spurs, and blowing-horn. **1933** T. WILLIAMSON *Woods Colt* 74 What was that noise? It sounded like a horn, a blowin'-horn.

(**5**) **1839** BUEL *Farmer's Comp.* 89 We have used the blue clay upon blowing sands. **1861** in *Maine Bd. Agric. Rep.* X. (1865) 149 The most striking geological characteristic on the road from Winthrop to the Androscoggin River, are the sand hills, or 'blowing sands' of Wayne and South Livermore. — (**6**) **1688** J. CLAYTON *Acc. Va.* in *Phil. Trans.* XVIII. 134 The Blowing-Snake [is] an absolute species of a Viper, but larger than any I have seen in Europe. **1806** CLARK in *Lewis & C. Exped.* (1905) VI. 224 [We] saw a blowing snake. — (**7**) **1825** KEATING *Exped. St. Peter's River* I. 23 In this vicinity there is a blowing spring, which is situated in an excavation on the side of a hill. — (**8**) **1869** *Amer. Naturalist* III. 555 A female snake, *Heterodon platyrhinus,* commonly known in this locality [Lancaster, Pa.] as the 'Blower,' or 'Blowing Viper,' was killed in Martic Township. **1941** STUART *Men of Mts.* 164 Never saw nothin' but a blowin viper snake and a couple of crows.

blown blon, *n.* (See quot.) — **1890** *Stock Grower & Farmer* 22 Feb. 6/2 Acute Tympanitis or Hoven in Cattle. This peculiar affection is known by a variety of terms, hoven, hoose, blown, dew blown, grass sickness, fog-sickness, etc.

∗blue, *n.*

1. A blueberry.

1587 HAKLUYT tr. Laudonnière *Notable Historie* 2r There are Raspisses, and a little bearie which we call among us Blues, which are very good to eate. **1709** LAWSON *Carolina* 104 The Hurts, Huckle-Berries, or Blues of this Country, are four sorts, which we are well acquainted withal. **1944** HOLTON *Yankees* 177 One day a dark-skinned Cape Verde Portuguese came to her door with a bucket of fine ripe blues.

2. A blue heron or a bluefish.

1838 in AUDUBON *Ornith. Biog.* IV. 604 We brought home with us forty-six of the large White Herons, and three of the great Blues. **1897** *Outing* Sep. 546/1 The blues are here! ... an' they're bitin' like savages. **1947** BROWN *Outdoors Unlimited* 288, I haven't caught a blue for two seasons. They're temperamental fish.

3. A student (at Dartmouth or Yale) of a strict or serious character. *Slang. Obs.* Cf. **blue-skin 4.**

1842 *Dartmouth* IV. 117 The students here are divided into two parties, ... the *Rowes* and the *Blues.* The Rowes are very liberal in their notions; the *Blues* more strict. **1850** *Yale Lit. Mag.* XV. 81, I wouldn't carry a novel into chapel to read, ... because some of the blues might see you.

4. The ashy gray winter coat of deer.

1843 OLIVER *Eight Months* 135 The American deer ... is in summer of a pale red, and in winter of a dunnish brown, or, as the hunter terms it, *blue.* **1877** CATON *Antelope & Deer of Am.* (1881) 149 There is a bluish shade observed on the Common Deer, which is so prevalent as to have given the winter coat the general appellation ... of the *blue,* among frontiersmen and hunters, who say the deer is in the *red* or the *blue,* as it may be in the summer or the winter coat. **1947** CAHALANE *Mammals N. Amer.* 28 Because of the much larger diameter and greater length of the winter hairs, they form a coat sometimes two inches thick. It is gray, and the deer is said by hunters to be 'in the blue.'

5. The blue uniform formerly worn by U.S. soldiers. Also transf.

1848 *West Point Graduating Class Song*, But with right stout hearts we'll play our parts, When we change the Grey for the Blue. **1895** C. KING *Fort Frayne* xx. 290 Farrar was . . . just about the happiest fellow that wore the army blue. **1907** *Collier's* 9 Nov. 9/2 The Blue and the Gray have organized together, in Missouri, the 'United Veterans of the Civil War.' **1946** HOLBROOK *Lost Men* 223 With the Blue and the Gray dead safely buried, . . . it was probably inevitable that Americans should go into a period of the grossest materialism.

6. A blue chip or counter used in poker.

1890 BIFF HALL *Turnover Club* 206 When turned to faro, You sometimes caused 'a stack of blues' to win. **1920** MULFORD *J. Nelson* xxi. 228 'Two pairs . . . Well I'll see it an' add a blue.' **1928** *Sat. Ev. Post* 15 Dec. 35/1 White chips were ordinarily worth $1, red chips $5, blues $10, yellows $100.

7. (See quot.)

1920 C. R. COOPER *Under Big Top* 200 He knows the vagaries of the human mind as represented in the reserved seats as apart from that of the 'blues' or general admission seats.

*** blue**, *a.*

1. a. Intoxicated, drunk. [Cf. G. *blau* in same sense.] **b.** (See quot.) Both *slang* and *obs.*

(a) 1818 WEEMS *Drunkard's Looking Glass* 4 The patient goes by a variety of nicknames . . . such as boozy—groggy—blue—damp. **1851** *Polly Peablossom* 105 The blue tickets he sold out to some upper-country flatboatmen who were pretty *blue*. — **(b) 1851** HALL *College Words* 21 'Our real delvers, midnight students,' says a correspondent from Williams College, 'are called *blue*.'

2. In the names of trees and shrubs: (1) * **blue ash,** an American ash, esp. *Fraxinus quadrangulata*, having bluish-green foliage, also attrib.; (2) **beech,** (see quot. 1916); (3) **berry,** see as a main entry; (4) **dangles,** = **blue huckleberry;** (5) **dogwood,** a species of dogwood producing blue berries; (6) **huckleberry,** the dangleberry; (7) **jack,** a species of small oak, *Quercus cinerea* or *brevifolia*, growing in the southern states, also attrib.; (8) **lilac,** =**blue myrtle;** (9) **locust,** =**black locust;** (10) **myrtle,** (see quots.); (11) **oak,** any one of several American oaks (see quots. 1869, 1884); (12) **palmetto,** the needle palm, *Rhapidophyllum hystrix*, or dwarf palmetto, *Sabal minor;* (13) **pearmain,** a large winter apple or apple tree, the bloom of which is bluish in color, also attrib.; (14) **poplar,** (see quot.); (15) **spruce,** (see quots.); (16) **tangles,** the dangleberry, cf. **blue huckleberry;** (17) **whortleberry,** a species of blueberry; (18) **wood,** a small shrub or tree, *Condalia obovata*, of the Southwest.

(1) 1783 W. FLEMING in *Travels Amer. Col.* 667 Blue Ash a species of the White Ash and called so from the bark tinging water of that colour, grows to be a large tree. **1847** in DRAKE *Pioneer Life Ky.* ii. 34 We charged upon the beautiful blue-ash and buckeye groves. **1897** SUDWORTH *Arborescent Flora* 330. — **(2) 1821** *Mass. H.S. Coll.* 2 Ser. IX. 148 Plants, which are indigenous in the township of Middlebury, [Vermont, include] *Carpinus americana*, Blue beech. **1916** SETON *Woodcraft Man.* 280 Blue Beech, Water Beech, or American Hornbeam (*Carpinus caroliniana*) A small tree, 10 to 25, rarely 40, feet high; bark smooth. Wood hard, close-grained, very strong; much like Ironwood. — **(4) 1861** WOOD *Botany* 481 *Gaylussacia frondosa*. . . Blue Dangles. Grows in open woods, N. Eng. to Fla. and La.

(5) 1897 SUDWORTH *Arborescent Flora* 309 *Cornus alternifolia*, Blue Dogwood. — **(6) 1883** HALE *Woods & Timbers N.C.* 139 Blue Huckleberry (*Gaylussacia frondosa*). . . . The berries are dark blue, large and sweet. — **(7) 1860** *So. Cultivator* XVIII. 384 As the traveller journeys westward [in Texas] he passes through what are called 'blue-jack' lands, the soil being very loose and the growth stunted and gnarled. **1901** MOHR *Plant Life Ala.* 91 The upland willow oak or blue jack, common in the lower Coast Pine belt, in this isolated pine forest reaches its most northern station — **(8) 1899** *Land of Sunshine* Apr. 265 As far as the eye could reach the blue lilac had spread a mantle of the tenderest azure upon the hillsides. — **(9) 1897** SUDWORTH *Arborescent Flora* 262 *Robinia . . . glaucescens*, Blue Locust.

(10) 1884 SARGENT *Rep. Forests* 41 *Ceanothus thyrsiflorus*, . . . Blue Myrtle. **1889** *Cent.* 874/2 The blue myrtle of California, *Ceanothus thyrsiflorus*, becomes a small tree. — **(11) 1817** S. BROWN *Western Gaz.* 25 Sugar maple, blue and white oak, black locust. **1869** MUIR *First Summer* (1911) 10 The trees, mostly the blue oak, (*Quercus Douglasii*), are about thirty to forty feet high, with pale blue-green leaves and white bark. **1884** SARGENT *Rep. Forests* 143 *Quercus Douglasii*. . . . Mountain White Oak. Blue Oak. **1921** HALL *Yosemite Nat. Park* 127 The Upper Sonoran Zone has been entered and may always be recognized by the presence of digger pines, buckeyes, blue oaks, and interior live oaks. — **(12) 1861** WOOD *Botany* 667 *Chamærops*. Blue Palmetto. **1901** MOHR *Plant Life Ala.* 96 The appearance of the dwarf or blue palmetto (*Sabal adansonii*) . . . indicates that the subtropical region of the State has been entered. — **(13) 1804** S. DEANE *Diary* (1849) 5 Oct. 385 Got in blue pearmains, eight and a half bushels. **1876** BURROUGHS *Winter Sunshine* 165 Late in November he found a blue-pearmain tree growing within the edge of a swamp. **1943** DAMON *Sense of H.* 235 The very best keeper of all was the Blue Pearmain—called blue from the bluish bloom all over it like that on Concord grapes, and Pearmain from Parma—a most ancient variety, and described back in 1577 in Gerarde's *Herbal*. — **(14) 1897** SUDWORTH *Arborescent Flora* 198 Tulip Tree; . . . Blue Poplar.

(15) 1884 SARGENT *Rep. Forests* 205 *Picea pungens*. . . . White Spruce. Blue Spruce. **1897** SUDWORTH *Arborescent Flora* 34 *Picea mariana*, Black Spruce. . . . Common names [include] . . . Blue Spruce (Wis.). — **(16) 1814** PURSH *Flora Amer.* I. 286 *Vaccinium lanceolatum*. . . . About three feet high; . . . berries large, blue, globular, eatable; called by the country people Blue-tangles. **1857** GRAY *Botany* 247 Blue Tangle, Dangleberry, . . . grows in low copses, coast of New England to Kentucky, and southward. — **(17) 1763** tr. LEPAGE DU PRATZ *Louisiana* II. 18 The blue *whortle berry* is a shrub somewhat taller than our largest gooseberry bushes, which are left to grow as they please. **1821** *Mass. H.S. Coll.* 2 Ser. IX. 157 *Vaccinium frondosum*, Blue whortleberry. — **(18) 1884** SARGENT *Rep. Forests* 4 *Condalia obovata*, . . . Blue Wood, Log Wood, Purple Haw. **1897** SUDWORTH *Arborescent Flora* 297 *Condalia obovata* . . . Bluewood . . . Common Names Bluewood (Tex.).

b. In the names of herbaceous plants: (1) * **bluebonnet,** =**blue lupine;** (2) **cohosh,** see **cohosh;** (3) **cotton,** (see quot.); (4) **curls,** (*a*) =**bastard pennyroyal,** (*b*) the selfheal, *Prunella vulgaris;* (5) **devil,** see as a main entry; (6) **flag,** a species of iris, esp. *Iris versicolor*, having blue flowers; (7) **flint,** designating a variety of flint corn; (8) **grass,** see as a main entry; (9) **hearts,** (see quot. 1901); (10) **joint (grass),** a tall bluish-stemmed grass, *Calamagrostis canadensis*, also a grass of the western states, *Agropyron smithi;* (11) **lettuce,** (see quots.); (12) **lupine,** a species of lupine, esp. *Lupinus perennis*, having blue flowers; (13) **nose,** see as a main entry; (14) **potato,** =**bluenose 2;** (15) **sage,** (see quot.); (16) **spike,** (see quot.); (17) **squash,** (see quot.), *rare;* (18) **stem,** see as a main entry.

(1) 1928 *Nat. Geog. Mag.* June 681 Chosen by the Legislature as the State flower, the bluebonnet rules a region more limited than do most State flowers. **1948** *Dly. Ardmoreite* (Ardmore, Okla.) 22 April 7/1 The Texas legislature named the bluebonnet as the state flower March 7, 1901. — **(3) 1844** in TURNER *Cotton* (1865) 173 There has been no remedy applied for Blue Cotton. . . . By this term we mean such cotton as comes up and grows very luxuriantly, without any fruit, reaching at times the height of eight or ten feet, having large leaves, with crimped edges, and of a deep lead color. . . . At other times, . . . the plant, after growing several feet, and bearing well, sheds all its fruit and becomes *blue*. — **(4)** (*a*) **1817** EATON *Botany* (1822) 490 *Trichostema dichotoma*, blue curls. **1931** VANSELL *Nectar & Pollen Plants* 14 Blue Curls . . . produces as much as 100 pounds to the colony in some years at certain locations. (*b*) **1847** WOOD *Botany* 424 Self-heal. Blue curls a very common plant, in meadows and low grounds. **1894** *Amer. Folk-Lore* VII. 96 *Brunella vulgaris*, . . . blue curls; somewhat general.

(6) 1784 CUTLER in *Mem. Academy* I. 406 *Iris*, . . . Blue-Flag. . . . A decoction of the fresh roots is a powerful cathartic. **1947** DALRYMPLE *Panfish* 9 Here mint and arrowhead, blue flag and watercress grow in abundance. — **(7) 1897** INMAN *Old Santa Fe Trail* 148 Aside from the bread,—usually only *tortillas*, made of the blue-flint corn of the country,—and coffee . . . the meals were excellent. — **(9) 1817** EATON *Botany* (1822) 213 *B. americana*, blue hearts. **1843** TORREY *Flora N.Y.* II. 39 Blue Hearts . . . [grows in] moist meadows. **1901** MOHR *Plant Life Ala.* 728 *Buchnera americana*. . . . Blue-hearts. [Grows in] dry open woods. . . . Flowers violet, May to July.

(10) 1832 *N.H. Hist. Soc. Coll.* III. 205 Hay of good quality is cut upon the upland; . . . in the intervals and meadows . . . bluejoint and several other kinds of grasses. **1855** *Mich. Agric. Soc. Trans.* VI. 149 The plants on the uplands are columbo . . . and two kinds of bluejoint grass. **1935** H. L. DAVIS *Honey in the Horn* 21 They went behind a stand of tall blue-joint grass. — **(11) 1890** *Cent.* 3422 *Blue lettuce*, a plant of the section *Mulgedium* of the genus *Lactuca*, with blue flowers. (U.S.) **1937** STEMEN & MYERS *Okla. Flora* 529 Lactuca pulchella . . . Large-flowered Blue Lettuce. — **(12) 1852** STANSBURY *Gt. Salt Lake* 27 A blue lupine and a white mallow were also gathered. **1948** *Dly. Ardmoreite* (Ardmore, Okla.) 4 May 6/1 The blue lupine grows wild in this section. — **(14) 1814** T. B. HAZARD

Nailer Tom's Diary (1930) 434/1 Carried Elish R Potter Six bushels of Blew Pottatoes. **1846** W. R. Brown in *Minn. Farmers' Diaries* (1939) 75 Harrison went ove(r) to Haskels & got 30 bushels of Blue Potatoes.

(15) 1901 Mohr *Plant Life Ala.* 15 There he [W. Bartram] also found the blue sage, *Salvia azurea*, 'with its spikes of flowers of celestial blue.' — **(16) 1784** Cutler in *Mem. Academy* I. 433 *Pontederia*.... Pickerelweed. Blue Spike. Blossoms blue. Common on the borders of ponds and rivers. July. — **(17) 1814** Bentley *Diary* IV. 280 This squash is commonly known by the name of the Blue Squash . . . and is also called the African Squash.

3. In the names of birds: (1) **blue crane,** the great blue heron, *Ardea herodias*, also **great blue crane;** (2) **crow,** =**piñon jay;** (3) **-darter,** (see quot. 1917); (4) **-fronted jay,** (see quot. 1917 and cf. **Steller's jay**); (5) **goose,** the blue-winged goose, *Chen caerulescens;* (6) **gray,** used to designate various birds (see quots.); (7) **grosbeak,** a grosbeak, *Guiraca caerulea*, found in the eastern and central states, or a subspecies found in the Southwest; (8) **grouse,** the dusky grouse, *Dendragapus obscurus*, of the Rocky Mountain region; (9) **hawk,** = **marsh hawk;** (10) **headed,** denoting certain species or varieties of birds (see quots.); (11) **heron,** the little blue heron, *Florida caerulea;* (12) * **kite,** =**Mississippi kite;** (13) **linnet,** the indigo bird, *Passerina cyanea*, or the lazuli finch, *P. amoena;* (14) **Blue Peter,** (see quots.); (15) **quail,** the scaled quail, *Callipepla squamata*, of the Southwest; (16) **robin,** the bluebird, *Sialia sialis;* (17) **scoggin,** a local name for the little blue heron, cf. **blue heron;** (18) **tail(ed) hawk,** =**blue darter;** (19) **warbler,** a species of warbler with blue plumage, also **black-throated blue warbler;** (20) **water hen,** ?a coot, *rare;* (21) **yellow-back(ed) warbler,** =**parula warbler,** also called **blue yellowback.**

(1) 1781–2 Jefferson *Notes Va.* (1788) 74 *Ardea caerulea*, . . . Blue heron [or] Crane. **1946** Hausman *Eastern Birds* 100 Great Blue Heron *Ardea herodias herodias*.... Other Names—Blue Crane, Crane, Red-shouldered Heron. — **(2) 1874** Coues *Birds N.W.* 209 *Gymnokitta Cyanocephala*, . . . Blue Crow; Cassin's Jay; Maximilian's Jay. **1917** *Birds of Amer.* II. 234. — **(3) 1892** Harris *U. Remus & Friends* 5 Dey er done broke in ter ketchin' chickens—de goshawk, de swamp hawk en de bluedarter. **1917** *Birds of Amer.* II. 68 *Goshawk Astur atricapillus atricapillus*.... Other Names.—American Goshawk; Blue Hen Hawk; Blue Darter. **1947** *Democrat* 22 May 4/3 There are only three species of hawks—the sharp-shinned, the blue darter, and the goshawk—which prey largely on poultry. — **(4) 1917** *Birds of Amer.* II. 220 These are known as the Blue-fronted Jay or Sierra Nevada Jay (*Cyanocitta stelleri frontalis*). **1941** Lofberg *Sierra Outpost* 209, I could recognize the scolding of the blue-fronted jay, the sharp 'quickers' of the flickers, the whistle of a mountain quail.

(5) 1874 Coues *Birds N.W.* 553. **1947** *Wildlife Management Jrnl.* Jan. 50/1 The blue goose, the snow goose, and the muskrat are conspicuous. — **(6) 1810** Wilson *Ornithology* II. 164 [The] Small Blue Grey Flycatcher, *Muscicapa Caerulea*, . . . is a very dexterous Flycatcher. **1844** *Nat. Hist. N.Y., Zoology* II. 92 The Blue-Grey Warbler, *Sylvicola caerulea*, . . . reaches Louisiana from Mexico in the spring. **1874** Coues *Birds N.W.* 17 *Polioptila Caerulea*, . . . Blue-gray Gnat-catcher. — **(7) c1729** Catesby *Carolina* I. 39 The blue Grossbeak.... I have not seen any of these Birds in any parts of America but Carolina. **1882** *Cent. Mag.* Jan. 359/2 Of these birds, all except the . . . blue grosbeak are familiar summer songsters throughout the Middle and Eastern States. **1944** *Nat. Geog. Mag.* June 696/1 Near Stockton Jack Arnold showed us a colony of blue grosbeaks. — **(8) 1860** in Coues *Birds N.W.* 395 This bird, called generally in Oregon the Blue Grouse, and also known as the Pine Grouse, Dusky Grouse, &c. **1948** *Pacific Discovery* Jan.–Feb. 14/2 Ruffed grouse, blue grouse . . . bald eagles, meadows of wild geraniums, . . . these are the Teton country. — **(9) 1917** *Birds of Amer.* II. 64. **1936** *Dly. Oklahoman* (Okla. City) 5 Nov. 11/6 Herman Glenz's cheese-baited rat trap to catch corn-stealing rats caught instead a bluehawk Wednesday.

(10) 1858 Baird *Birds Pacific R.R.* 340 *Vireo solitarius*, Blue-headed Flycatcher. *Ib.* 608 *Starnoenas cyanocephala*, Blue-headed Pigeon. **1892** Torrey *Foot-path Way* 244 Solitary (or blue-headed) Vireo. **1917** *Birds of Amer.* II. 39 Passenger Pigeon.... [Also called] Blue-headed Pigeon. **1944** *Mass. Audubon Soc. Bul.* Dec. 261 October 24, Phoebe, Blue-headed Vireo, Nashville Warbler (latest ever). — **(11) c1730** Catesby *Carolina* I. 76 *Ardea cœrulea*. The blue Heron.... These Birds are not numerous in Carolina, and are rarely seen but in the Spring of the Year. **1857** Thoreau *Maine Woods* (1894) 316 He found the blue heron's nest in the hard-wood trees. **1947** *Chr. Sci. Monitor* 15 Jan. 8/1 In our valley, we feel that winter has arrived when we see the blue heron. — **(12) 1873** *Amer. Naturalist* VII. 202 Soaring gracefully above them with a similar flight were smaller numbers of the 'blue kite' (*Ictinia Mississippiensis*). **1917** *Birds of Amer.* II. 62.— **(13) c1730** Catesby *Carolina* I. 45 The blue Linnet . . . is rather less than a Gold-finch.... The whole Bird appears, at a little Distance, of an intire blue Colour. **1869** *Amer. Naturalist* III. 77 Blue Linnet (*Cyanospiza amœna*). I saw this bird on the eastern slope of the Rocky Mountains. — **(14) 1709** Lawson *Carolina* 151 Blue-Peters, The same as you call Water-Hens in England, are here very numerous, and not regarded for eating. **1917** *Birds of Amer.* I. 214 Coot. *Fulica americana*.... Other names.—American Coot; . . . Flusterer; Blue Peter.

(15) 1846 Emory *Military Reconn.* 62 We saw here also, in great numbers, the blue quail. **1851** in Schoolcraft *Indian Tribes* (1853) III. 103 We saw during the day great numbers of the blue or crested quail. **1930** McLean *Quail of Calif.* 20. — **(16) 1844** *Nat. Hist. N.Y., Zoology* II. 65 The Blue-bird, or Blue Robin as it is called in the western counties, . . . is hailed with us as the first harbinger of spring. **1884** Roe *Nature's Story* 95 He resembles your English redbreast closely both in appearance and habits, and our New England forefathers called him the 'blue robin.' — **(17) 1938** Matschat *Suwannee River* 56 Blue scoggins, or herons, were late-nesting in the bushes five or six feet above the water. — **(18) 1859** Taliaferro *Fisher's R.* 117 'Gius had his eye on her like a blue-tailed hawk watchin' a chicken. **1867** G. W. Harris *Sut Lovingood* 250 Yere's the blue-tail hawk, an' he's a-flyin low. — **(19) 1810** Wilson *Ornithology* II. 115 Black-Throated Blue Warbler, *Sylvia Canadensis*. **1858** Baird *Birds Pacific R.R.* 280 *Dendroica Cærulea*, Blue Warbler. *Hab.*—Eastern United States to the Missouri river. **1892** Torrey *Foot-Path Way* 191, I came upon . . . three goodly throngs, including . . . black-throated blue warblers, [and] pine warblers.

(20) 1851 *De Bow's Review* XI. 55 *Blue Water Hen*, or *Indian Hen* . . . sits still over the water. — **(21) 1811** Wilson *Ornithology* IV. 17 Blue Yellow-back Warbler: *Sylvia pusilla* . . . is remarkable for frequenting the tops of the tallest trees, where it feeds on . . . small winged insects. **1868** *Amer. Naturalist* II. 177 The Blue Yellow-backed Warbler (*Parula americana*) is one of the smallest, as well as one of the most beautiful of all [warblers]. **1917** *Birds of Amer.* III. 123/1 The Parula Warbler has been called the Blue Yellowback.

See also as main entries **blue back, bluebird, blue hen,** ***blue jay,** ***blue stocking, blue wing.**

b. In the names of fishes, crabs, etc.: (1) **blue back,** see as a main entry; (2) **bream,** (see quot.); (3) **cat(fish),** a catfish, *Ictalurus furcatus*, of the Mississippi Valley; (4) **claw,** (see quot.); (5) **cod,** (see quot.); (6) **crab,** an edible swimming crab of a blue color belonging to the genus *Callinectes*, esp. *C. sapidus* or *C. hastatus*, found on the Atlantic and Gulf coasts; (7) **fin,** "a local name in the United States of the lake-herring or whitefish of Lake Michigan, *Coregonus nigripinnis*" (*Cent.*); (8) **fish,** any one of various fishes, as the salt water fish, *Pomatomus saltatrix*, the California weakfish, greenfish, etc., of a bluish color, also attrib.; (9) **gill,** a sunfish, *Helioperca incisor*, found chiefly in the Mississippi Valley; (10) **herring,** a fresh water clupeoid fish, *Pomolobus chrysochloris*, found chiefly in the Mississippi Valley; (11) **perch,** a local name for the cunner; (12) **point (oyster),** a small oyster of superior flavor, obtained from a bed near Blue Point, L.I., or any oyster similar to this; (13) **pointer,** =prec.; (14) **racer (snake),** a bluish subspecies of the common black snake; (15) **tail(ed) lizard,** a harmless lizard or skink, *Eumeces fasciatus*, the under surface of the tail of which is blue; (16) **tailed skink,** =prec.; (17) **-tail fly,** a fabled fly represented in minstrel songs *c*1850 as particularly active and troublesome.

(2) 1888 Goode *Amer. Fishes* 67 The Blue Sun-fish, *Lepomis pallidus*, is also known as the 'Blue Bream.' — **(3) 1832** N. J. Wyeth *Journal* (1899) 20 Aug. 211 Caught just at dusk last night plenty of Blue Catfish. **1835** Martin *Descr. Va.* 347 The mud and blue cat . . . are very much celebrated among travellers for their fine flavor and astonishing size. **1947** Dalrymple *Panfish* 291 The Blue Cat, *Ictalurus furcatus*, which ranges down the Mississippi Valley and throughout the Gulf States, grows very large, some specimens weighing one hundred and fifty pounds. — **(4) 1807** *Mass. H.S. Coll.* 2 Ser. III. 58 There is the large crab, called here [Duke's Co., Mass.] the blue claw. **(5) 1907** Hodge *Indians* I. 371 *Cultus-cod*. A name of the blue, or buffalo, cod (*Ophiodon elongatus*), an important food fish of the Pacific coast from Santa Barbara to Alaska. — **(6) 1883** Rathbun in *U.S. Mus. Bul.* 27 109 The most valuable of these are the Blue Crab (*Callinectes hastatus*), Lady Crab [etc.]. — **(7) 1884** Goode *Fisheries U.S.* I. 541 The 'Blue-fin' or 'Black-fin' . . . has . . . been taken only in the deeper waters of Lake Michigan. **1944** NUTE *Lake Superior* 185 Fishing continued until about 1915 but the bluefins became rarer and rarer and practically disappeared. . . . This fish and the bluefin are not recorded prior to 1893 — **(8)** *c***1622** PORY *Plymouth & N. Eng.* (1918) 39 As concerning the blew fish, in delicacie it excelleth all kinde of fish that ever I tasted. **1714** J. HEMPSTEAD *Diary* 38 Wm Pendal . . . fell out of a small Boat in the horserace catching blue-fish. **1948** *N.Y. Times* 23 May v. 5/7 As the bluefish schools move northward they will hit in toward the beach at several points. — **(9) 1881** *Forest & Stream* 11 Aug. 31/3 (*heading*), The Blue Gills—1881. **1948** *Gary* (Ind.) *Post-Tribune* 1 July 24/1 A bluegill under average conditions will reach legal length of six inches during its fourth summer of life.

(10) 1814 MITCHILL *Fishes N.Y.* 457 Blue Herring. . . . The skin is free from spots and stripes; and is a bluish colour — **(11) 1839** STORER *Mass. Fishes* 78 *Crenilabrus burgall.* . . . The Conner. Blue Perch. Chogset . . . is an excellent fish for the table. **1895** GERARD in *N.Y. Sun* 30 July, Chogset, an eastern Algonquian name for the blue perch or burgall.— **(12) 1789** in *Mass.Hist.Soc.Proc.* 1 Ser. XI (1869) 24 Judge Hobart . . . treated us with Blue Point oysters from the shell. **1868** ROSE *Great Country* 25 [Oysters] are called by many names; 'saddle rocks,' 'blue points,' and 'Shrewsburys,' being the most popular. **1947** *Sat. Ev. Post* 15 Mar. 40/3, I think I'll drop by the market a little later in the evening and pick up a dozen blue points. — **(13) 1828** PAULDING *New Mirror* 68 Reynard was fishing for oysters with his tail, he had the good luck to put the end of it into the jaws of a fine *Blue Pointer* that lay gaping with his mouth wide open. **1853** *Harper's Mag.* VII. 275/2, I am told that, . . . when a demijohn of brandy had been burst, a large blue pointer was found lying in a little pool of liquor, just drunk enough to be careless of consequences. — **(14) 1886** EBBUTT *Emigrant Life in Kansas* 66 The 'blue-racer' snake . . . is a quick traveller; in fact, it is no sooner seen than gone, like a flash of greased lightning with the brake off. **1947** *Reader's Digest* Oct. 143/2 A blue racer came looping through the grass at me.

(15) 1738 CATESBY *Carolina* II. 67 *Lacertus cauda cærulea.* The Blue-Tail Lizard. . . . They are seen often on the ground, and frequent hollow trees. . . . They are found in Virginia and Carolina. **1839** STORER *Mass. Reptiles* 219 *Scincus fasciatus.* Lin. The Blue-tailed Lizard. — **(16) 1842** *Nat. Hist. N.Y., Zoology* III. 29 Blue-tailed Skink. . . . This harmless little animal miscalled the Blue-tailed Lizard and Striped Lizard, is not uncommon in the southern counties of the State. **1934** *Nat. Geog. Mag.* LXV. 609 The blue-tailed skink, or red-headed scorpion, is common, especially in old logs in hammocks and cypress bays. — **(17) 1849** HOWE *Glee Book* 165 De 'skeeters bites ye through your close, De gallinipper sweeten high, But wusser yet de blue tail fly. **1880** NYE *B. Nye & Boomerang* 92 Nurse them and read the Scriptures to them and drive away the blue-tail fly and other domestic insects. [**1945** *Chr. Sci. Monitor* 25 Apr. 8/1 The blue-tailed fly . . . is an old minstrel song which tells how the blue-fly bit the pony and the pony threw Old Massa, with disastrous consequences.]

4. In miscellaneous combs.: (1) **blue blazes,** an expression denoting anything excessive or in the extreme, *slang;* (2) **chip,** one of the blue counters used in poker, also transf.; (3) **cockade,** a cockade formerly used as a symbol of secession, *obs.;* (4) **dog,** (see quot. 1875 and cf. **blue pup**), *obs.;* (5) **fishing,** fishing for bluefish; (6) **marsh,** ?a marsh with blue-colored soil, *obs.;* (7) **mass,** (see quot. 1889); (8) **mixed,** =**cadet cloth;** (9) **norther,** see **norther;** (10) * **pill,** a bullet, *slang*, cf. **c.** (8) below; (11) **pup,** (see quots.), *obs.;* (12) **streak,** *fig.* anything depicted as resembling a flash of lightning in speed, quickness, vividness, etc., *colloq.;* (13) **stripe,** (see quot. and cf. **blue-bellied, belly**); (14) **whistler,** (*a*) a buckshot of the largest size, (*b*) =**blue norther;** (15) **Blue William,** (see quot.), *obs.*

(1) 1818 WEEMS *Drunkard's Looking Glass* 49 Ye steep down gulphs of liquid fire! Ye blue blazes of damnation! **1934** VINES *Green Thicket World* 149 It was as cold as blue blazes. — **(2)** *a***1904** S. E. WHITE *Blazed Trail* viii. 146, I reckon I don't stack up very high in th' blue chips. **1948** *Time* 2 Feb. 71/3 Even such a blue chip as U.S. Steel went begging at $73½. — **(3) 1860** *Charleston* (S.C.) *Mercury* 6 Nov. 3/2 They wore the blue cockade, we understand, and warmly endorsed the noble Southern sentiments uttered by the distinguished orator. *Ib.* 20 Dec. 2/4 This emblem of secession has become very prevalent with our New Orleans ladies, who wear the blue cockade on bonnets in the street, and at home in their hair. — **(4) 1875** *Chi. Tribune* 24 Aug. 6/1 'Blue Dog' was a State issue for canal extension. **1893** *Cong. Rec.* 25 Aug. 936/2 Then we had the Michigan wild-cat money; then we had throughout Indiana, Illinois, and Ohio what is known as blue-dog and yellow-pup.

(5) 1860 *Harper's Mag.* July 194/2 Spent three or four weeks at Muskeogue every summer for the sake of the bluefishing. **1935** LINCOLN *Cape Cod Yesterdays* 127 Bluefishing is *fun;* any sane person will agree to that. — **(6) 1747** in *Am. Sp.* XV. 156/2 To a Pine in the blew Marsh Meadow. **1764** *Ib.*, To a Pine near where the mouth of blue marsh Branch makes into Rackoon swamp. — **(7) 1855** DAVIS *Farm Bk.* 154 Johnson & Rance sick—Influenza—treatment adopted. Blue mass—castor oil & then the pleurisy root tea both are doing well now. **1889** *Cent.* 600/2 blue-mass . . . A drug made by rubbing up metallic mercury with confection of roses until all the globules disappear. Of this blue-pills are made. **1945** BOTKIN *My Burden* 86 First off they'd give some castor oil, and if that didn't cure, they'd give blue mass. — **(8) 1845** HOOPER *Suggs* (1928) 128 His coat was 'blue mixed,' with a very acute terminus, and it seems to have a particular affection for the hump of his shoulders, for it touched no other part of his person. **1887** *Postal Laws* 266 For Winter Wear . . . a single-breasted sack coat of 'cadet gray,' or, technically, 'blue-mixed cadet cloth.'

(10) 1834 J. DOWNING *Andrew Jackson* 111 They saw no hopes from fitin, they wern't fond of blue pills, and . . . were preparin tu take care of *number one*. **1861** *Missouri let.* in *N.Y. Tribune* 10 Nov., Between blue pills, halters and the penitentiary, we shall soon work of[f] the element of rascaldom. — **(11) 1848** BARTLETT 272 In Michigan, they apply the term 'blue pup money' to bank notes having a blue stamp on their backs. **1875** *Chi. Tribune* 24 Aug. 6/1 'Blue Pup' was a shinplaster currency issued by canal contractors, and redeemable in 'Blue Dog.' — **(12) 1830** *Kentuckian* 14 May, A gentleman . . . has only to get into a Sunday Mail Coach . . . to pass Mr. Rowan with such rapidity as not even to leave a 'blue streak' behind him. **1914** ATHERTON *Perch of Devil* i. 24 You must be considerable in earnest to talk a blue streak! **1947** *This Week Mag.* 11 Oct. 7/1 He began talking a blue streak. — **(13) 1878** BEADLE *Western Wilds* 443 There will, perhaps, be the Yankee type: the people north and east of Pennsylvania, . . . with that traditional 'blue stripe on the belly.' — **(14)** (*a*) **1843** in BLAIR *Amer. Humor* (1937) 300, I determined to go this time for the 'antlered monarch,' by loading one barrel with fifteen 'blue whistlers,' reserving the other for small game. **1894** *Outing* Mar. 439/1 Didn't they all watch me count the blue-whistlers for my gun? (*b*) **1929** DOBIE *Vaquero* 278 We were on the plains country, and no one who has not experienced a blue whistler on the open prairies of West Texas really knows what a cold north wind is like. **1932** in *Amer. Sp.* VIII. (1933) 80 The blue whistler that come up Friday night sure came from the north pole Saturday and Sunday.

(15) 1869 *Overland Mo.* III. 128, $100 bills were there [in Texas] called 'Williams,' and $50 bills 'Blue Williams.'

Also see as main entries **blue book, b. coat, b. hen, b. law b. light,** ***b. Monday, b. nose, b. skin,** ***b. sky.**

b. Designating kinds of earth, soil, etc.: (1) **blue clay,** a clay of a bluish color, also fig. and attrib.; (2) **dirt,** =**blue gravel;** (3) **gravel,** (see quots.); (4) **lead,** (see quots. and cf. **blue dirt, gravel**); (5) **limestone,** a variety of limestone of a bluish color; (6) **marl,** (see quots.); (7) **mud,** (see quot. 1882), also *as clear as blue mud*, quite obscure, *colloq.;* (8) **slate,** (see quot.), *rare;* (9) **stone,** a bluish argillaceous sandstone, used as a building material and for flagstones, also attrib.; (10) **stuff,** (see quot. 1877).

(1) 1778 CARVER *Travels* 101 This country likewise abounds with a milk white clay, . . . and also with a blue clay that serves the Indians for paint. **1879** *Scribner's Mo.* Dec. 242/2 Then I excavated great deep holes, but came to a blue clay that held water like rubber. **1906** MARK TWAIN *Autobiog.* (1924) I. 293 (R.), Any person who is familiar with me knows how to get at the jewel of any fact of mine and dig it out of its blue-clay matrix. — **(2) 1853** *Mt. Echo* (Downieville, Calif.) 11 June 2/3 The ground is a Quartz gravel, and so far has turned out to be 'blue dirt and bed rock pitching.' **1856** *Hutchings Mag.* July 13/2 This claim looked as favorable as could be, and paid as well as it did last year, in *that* the blue dirt seemed to be running out. — **(3) 1873** LAWRENCE *Silverland* 181 It is, of course, proportionately more valuable—averaging, as we were informed, about eight dollars per ton; whereas about twenty cents in the blue gravel . . . seems a fair average. **1874** RAYMOND *6th Rep. Mines* 15 The term 'blue-gravel' has come into general use among hydraulic miners, to distinguish . . . the lower and richer portions which have often, but not always, a peculiar bluish color. **1882** *Rep. on Prec. Metals U.S.* 623 The blue gravel . . . is the bluish, grayish, or greenish colored gravel nearest to the bed rock. — **(4) 1855** *Pioneer* (S.F.) Oct. 218 Others were sinking shafts, which are intended to pierce the 'blue lead,' as it is called—a hard bluish gravel, where it is supposed a river once ran, and where the gold is 'lying about loose,' waiting to be gathered up. **1880** G. INGHAM *Digging Gold* ii. 46 The class of deposits known as the ancient river channels or the 'blue-lead' of California . . . are gold-bearing gravels found deep beneath the surface.

(5) *a***1817** DWIGHT *Travels* II. 480 The rock over which the Hudson descends at this place, is a vast mass of blue limestone, horizontally stratified. **1883** *Harper's Mag.* Oct. 719/1 The Kentucky blue-limestone too is a quarry for the turnpike-roads. — **(6) 1883** SMITH *Geol. Survey Ala.* 269 The unchanged rock [=rotten limestone] . . . is frequently spoken of as the blue-marl rock. *Ib.* 488 These subsoils frequently have limy concretions and are underlaid with a blue marl (Rotten Limestone) at ten to twelve feet depth. — **(7) 1839** *N.O. Picayune* 10 Feb. 2/3 The natur' of the case is as clear as blue mud. **1882** WORTHEN *Econ. Geol. Illinois* I. 521 Below these beds of clay and gravel, a deposit is often met with in this county [=Jackson], . . . consisting of a dark blue or black mud, containing branches of trees. *Ib.* II. 4 Below these beds we find at some localities the same 'blue mud.' — **(8) 1805** DUNBAR *Life* 305 But the blue slate as it is called is only bluish shistus, hard tho' brittle & not at all proper for the roofing of houses. — **(9) 1709** LAWSON *Carolina* 50 This [river] is call'd Heighwaree, and affords as good blue Stone for Mill-Stones, as that from Cologn. **1851** A. CARY *Clovernook* 106 A little puddle of water had thawed from his boots and soiled the bluestone hearth. **1944** *New Yorker* 7 Oct. 22/1 One of these was the mining of bluestone, a hard, slatelike rock.

(10) 1876 RAYMOND *8th Rep. Mines* 19 The celebrated 'blue stuff' . . . vexed and bewildered Comstock and his companions, when working below the great Washoe lode. **1877** WM. WRIGHT *Big Bonanza* 52 They, however, did not know that the 'blue stuff' (sulphuret of silver), which they had dug into, was of any value.

c. Used of or with reference to persons or groups of persons: (1) **blue-bellied,** a contemptuous term used in the South, esp. with *Yankee,* to designate a northerner, particularly one from New England, *slang;* (2) * **belly,** (*a*) a Yankee, esp. a New Englander, (*b*) a southern nickname for a northern or federal soldier during the Civil War, any U.S. soldier, *slang;* (3) **bottle,** a person of no consequence, *rare;* (4) **dyer,** one who dyes fabrics blue; (5) **fisher,** a boat engaged in catching bluefish; (6) * **lodge,** a secret society formed by Missourians in 1854 to extend slavery into Kansas and other territory of the U.S., *obs.;* (7) **Bluemouths,** app. a tribe of Indians west of the Choctaws, about whom little is known, *obs.;* (8) * **pill,** a druggist, *slang, rare,* cf. **4.** (10) above; (9) **ribbon jury,** a jury whose members are selected on the basis of intelligence and income rather than at random, also **blue ribbon panel.**

(1) 1852 *S. Lit. Messenger* XVIII. 681/1 I'd disgrace the party—and am no better than a dratted, blue-bellied, federal whig! **1865** *Gold Hill* (Nev.) *News* 8 May, To-day the mackerel-eating, blue-bellied, psalm-singing, Abolitionist is far ahead of the high-toned, card-playing, horse-racing, nigger-producing, need hanging chivalry of the South, in the eyes of the civilized world. **1948** *Realty & Bldg.* 15 May 11/2 We fell upon the blue-bellied horde and beat them into dastardly flight. — **(2)** (*a*) **1827** J. PICKERING *Inquiries Emigrant* (1831) 92 The inhabitants are chiefly Americans. . . . In short 'blue bellies' of all sorts and condition, equal to any of the frontier towns on both sides of the 'lines.' **1857** T. GLADSTONE *Englishman in Kansas* 43 No highfalutin' airs here, you know. Keep that for them Blue-bellies down East. **1945** *Everybody's Digest* Aug. 87 The Southern cowman refers to a Yankee as a 'blue belly.' (*b*) **1863** *S. F. Call* 18 Oct. 4/1 A Provost Marshal's pass . . . must be presented to a pair of drunken blue-bellies, who are stationed at each church door. **1905** REX BEACH *Pardners* ii. 54 Well! them bodies has got to be hid, or we'll have the tribe [of Indians] and the blue-bellies from the fort a scouring the hills. — **(3) 1840** W. G. SIMMS *Border Beagles* II. 101 Why here, you blue-bottle, here in Cane Castle, hard by, within a Choctaw's mile. — **(4) 1788** *Kentucky Gazette* 15 March 1/3 The subscriber . . . has set up the blue diers business . . . and will take in Hemp, Flax and Cotton thread to dye. **1809** F. CUMING *Western Tour* 164 There is one excellent umbrella manufactory. . . . Three blue-dyers. Five hatters [etc.].

(5) 1898 *Boston Transcript* 9 April 9/6 Bluefisher, (as the boats engaged in catching this class of fish are officially known). — **(6) 1855** *Herald of Freedom* 1 April 4 In the slave States, . . . what is called the 'Blue Lodge' . . . is now lending every energy, to make Kansas a slave State. **1887** *Cent. Mag.* April 870/1 The conspirators had already spent some months in organizing their 'Blue Lodges.' — **(7) 1740** *Ga. Col. Rec.* IV. 663 The Eastern and Southern Parts of it [*sc.* Georgia, are] inhabited by the Creek Indians; . . . the Western by the Chactaws, the Blewmouths, and other Indian Nations, to South Sea. [**1870** in HODGE *Amer. Indians* I. 155/1 According to the French Indians [Choctaw] there is a large city where a blue-lipped people live, of whom they have often heard it said that if any one tries to kill them he becomes insane.] — **(8) 1861** NEWELL *Orpheus C. Kerr* I. 316 'See here, old blue-pills,' says one of the firemen pleasantly, 'if you don't let us in, your own crib will go to blazes in ten minutes.' — **(9) 1937** *N.Y. Times Index* 1178/1 Irwin's lawyer protests exclusion of women from blue-ribbon panel in murder case. **1948** *Southwestern Rev.* Winter 3/2 In the South . . . there are no Blue Ribbon juries and there has never been a legal lynching of the kind that makes 'Massachusetts justice' a synonym for judicial murder.

See also as main entries **bluebird, b. coat, b. devil, b. light, b. nose, b. skin, b. stocking.**

d. Used with reference to foods and drinks: (1) **blue beef,** very poor, lean beef; (2) **dumpling,** a food formerly used by the Gulf Coast Indians (see quot.), *obs.;* (3) **head,** app. cheap whisky, or a barrel of this, the head being painted blue, *obs.,* cf. **redhead;** (4) * **John,** (see quots.), [cf. Du. *blauwjan* in local use for milk to which water has been added].

(1) 1876 *Dalles* (Ore.) *Tribune* 22 Jan. 3/2 One of our exchanges in the Valley complains that the butchers down there are now dealing out 'blue beef' to their customers. **1916** MASSEY *Reminisc.* 192 Our rations consisted of 'blue' beef and cornbread made out of musty meal. — **(2) 1910** HODGE *Amer. Indians* II. 613 Water is kept on the *sofki* for hours at a time, and, finally, after the mixture has become very thick, it is removed and allowed to cool. A half-dozen 'blue dumplings' (a very palatable cornmeal preparation) are almost a necessary accompaniment of a mug of *sofki.* — **(3) 1856** *Herald of Freedom* (Lawrence, Kans.) 5 Apr. 1/6 A man can only make one dollar on a barrel of flour, but he can ticket a ten on each 'blue head.' **1856** *Spirit of Times* (N.Y.) 6 Sep. 7/1, I thought I would ask you if you wouldn't swallow a 'slug' of Carthage blue-head. — **(4) 1869** *Overland Mo.* III. 129 North Carolinians call skim milk 'blue John.' **1891** *N. & Q.* VIII. 62 Blue-john is a thin blue milk that has been skimmed, that is, 'sour sweet-milk.' **1944** *D.N.* Nov. 6 *Blue-John,* less often *blue-Johnny:* n. Milk, skimmed (hence blue) and slightly sour.

5. In phrases: (1) *blue and white,* (see quot.), *obs.;* (2) *to make a blue fist of,* to make a dismal failure of, *colloq.* or *slang;* (3) *as clear as blue mud,* see **blue mud.**

(1) 1830 NEILSON *Recollections* 320 A detatchment of country militia who were called to town [Charleston, S.C.] during the Negro disturbance, made a somewhat grotesque appearance, being dressed with trowsers and frocks made of common drugget, (or blue and white as it is called). — **(2) 1834** CARUTHERS *Kentuckian* I. 25 A chap would make a blue fist of takin a dead aim through double sights, with the butt end of a psalm in his guzzle.

As the last term in **army, baby, bayou, cotton, dark, federal, Jersey, long-tailed, Pennsylvania, sky blue.**

* **blueback,** *n.*

1. Any one of various fishes, birds, etc., so called from their color.

1812 BENTLEY *Diary* IV. 125 Mrs. Osgood . . . had taken great numbers of the Herrings called Bluebacks at the mills this season. **1843** *Nat. Hist. N.Y., Zoology* V. 24 There is a variety of the Lobster, termed Blue-backs, on account of their dark bluish color. They are derived from the coast about Cape Cod, have comparatively thin shells, and are highly prized by epicures. **1883** *Cent. Mag.* Sep. 684/1 The blue-back's nest was scarcely a foot from the ground. **1945** *Md. Conservationist* 8/1 There are five species of Pacific salmon: . . the sockeye, also known as blue-back and red salmon. **1948** *Scientific Mo.* April 283/2 It is often assumed that the blueback salmon spawn rather generally throughout the upper Columbia Basin.

2. One of the notes or bills issued by the Southern Confederacy. *Obs.*

1869 in MATHEWS *Beginnings* 156 The Rebels had their 'bluebacks' for money; but in Texas, . . . they made slow progress. **1871** DE VERE 47 During the Civil War, . . . the original Blue Backs of the Confederacy (so-called in opposition to *Green Backs* of the Union) soon became known as Shucks.

3. Used attrib. or as adj. to designate a well-known elementary spelling book written by Noah Webster and first published in 1783. Also **blue-backed.**

1858 *Harper's Mag.* May 724/1 The scholars sat on rough-hewn benches conning their well-thumbed primers, or blue-backed spelling books. **1916** MASSEY *Reminisc.* 47 From a Webster's blue-back spelling book my father taught me the alphabet. **1947** LUMPKIN *Southerner* 160 Instead of the 'Blue Back' speller, we studied spelling from the dictionary.

* **bluebell,** *n.* As the last term in **Ohio bluebell, Virginia bluebell.**

* **blueberry,** *n.*

1. The sweet, edible fruit of any one of various species of *Vaccinium,* or the plant producing this.

1709 LAWSON *Carolina* 104 The first sort is the same Blue or Bilberry, that grows plentifully in the North of England, and in other Places. **1842** *Lowell Offering* II. 131 We want to spread currants and blueberries on the table to be dried. **1937** VERRILL *Foods Amer. Gave World* 135 By far the greater number of the blueberries and huckleberries that are marketed are the wild berries.

b. blueberrying, gathering blueberries.

1861 *Harper's Mag.* Jan. 188/1 Several acres . . . had long been put to no other use than that of a general 'blue-berrying' region. **1948**

PEATTIE *Berkshires* 67 To me blueberrying doesn't really start until the high-bush are ready.

2. Attrib. with **bush, cake, flat, folks, pie, swamp.**

1787 CUTLER in *Life* I. 278 Under the trees and on the sides of the hill, are many blueberry, whortleberry, and bilberry bushes. **1828** *Western Mo. Rev.* Sep. 206 Unenclosed and naked pastures, looking for all the world, like New-England blueberry swamps, spread almost from the foot [of the House of Congress]. **1853** *Farmington* (Me.) *Chronicle* 14 July 3/1 George Bass . . . intends keeping Beer by the bottle . . . for the accommodation of blueberry folks, at the foot of the mountain. **1895** *Outing* Dec. 217/1 We put in the next day hunting over the blue-berry flat after bear. **1943** MENEFEE *Assignment* 296 But the average soldier is still, as one writer put it, 'fighting for blue-berry pie.' **1948** *Reader's Digest* Sep. 111/2 Her blueberry cakes would make the heart sing.

As the last term in **Canada, low, mountain, swamp blueberry.**

***bluebird,** *n.*

1. Any one of various small American songbirds of the genus *Sialia*, of a predominantly blue color.

1688 JOHN CLAYTON in *Phil. Trans.* XVII. 996 They have a Bird they call a Blew-bird, of a curious azure colour about the bigness of a Chafinch. **1844** *Nat. Hist. N.Y., Zoology* II. 65 The Bluebird, or Blue Robin as it is called in the western counties, . . . is hailed with us as the first harbinger of spring. **1945** PEARSON *Country Flavor* 17 The bluebirds carol from the apple trees in the back yard.

2. A Union soldier during the Civil War. *Obs.*

1861 NEWELL *Orpheus C. Kerr* I. 199, I reached the side of the Commander of the Accomac. . . . 'How are you, my blue-bird; and what do you think of this brilliant assemblage?' **1867** CRAWFORD *Mosby* 129 John Munson and Walter Whaley brought in two bluebirds, one walking and the other riding, The one riding was a guard and bearer of despatches to General Gregg's headquarters.

As the last term in **azure, eastern, mountain, western, Wilson's bluebird.**

***blue book.**

1. The "Biennial Register" of information about the U.S. Government, or an authoritative report issued by a department of the government.

1836 BENTON in *Deb. Congress* June 1719 An array of names more numerous . . . than was to be found in the 'Blue Book,' with the Army and Navy Register inclusive. **1886** POORE *Reminisc.* I. 108 Mr. Force, while printing the *Biennial Register*, better known as the Blue Book from the color of its binding, began to collect manuscripts. **1912** F. J. HASKIN *Amer. Govt.* 323 A graphic illustration of the growth of the civil service of the United States is afforded by a contrast of the Government Blue Books published in 1816 and 1905. The one published in 1816 is not much larger than a child's 'reader,' and had but 176 pages. The one for 1905 had 4,219 pages. **1929** *Lit. Digest* 12 Oct. 6/2 He told of . . . making use of an official Navy Department 'blue book' of statistics in passing naval information on to the correspondents.

b. A similar register published by a state.

1879 (*title*), The Blue Book of the State of Wisconsin for 1879. **1915** (*title*), The Nebraska Blue Book and Historical Register.

2. (Meaning obscure.) *Obs.*

1837 *Globe* (Washington, D.C.) 10 April, Yesterday was a hard day in State street, *two* per cent. a month was paid on post notes and blue books having six months to run.

3. A directory of a business or a professional class (see also quot. 1940).

1868 *Harper's Mag.* July 241/2 'Lloyds List' finds more than one parallel in another department of commerce in America, in the circulars or 'Blue books' of the various commercial agencies in which the standing, pecuniary condition, and moral character of merchants throughout the country are given. **1895** (*title*), Blue Book: Official Directory of the Practicing Dental Profession of Chicago, Ill. **1940** RIESENBERG *Golden G.* 309 The *Worker* urged the men to revolt against their 'company union,' the Longshoremen's Association of San Francisco, called the 'Blue Book.'

4. A directory of persons of social prominence.

1846 in *Amer. Sp.* (1948) Feb. 43/2 Well—they are poor and stylish looking, and the Yankee knows nothing of the blue-book. **1882** HOWELLS *Modern Instance* xxi, I suppose you wont refuse to come because I don't ask the whole Blue Book to meet them. **1943** *Copper Camp* 24 As early as 1901, a *Blue Book*, a tiny social register with about two thousand names, was published.

5. A booklet of blank paper used in some colleges for writing examinations.

1893 POST *Harvard Stories* 240 Jack . . . walked up to the desk at the end of the [examination] room, and put his blue book on the pile of others. **1943** BAKER *Trio* (1946) 135 We might have stayed here the rest of our lives, making lectures, having the mob to tea, correcting blue-books.

***blue coat,** *n.*

1. A U.S. soldier, used esp. during the Civil War. Cf. *boys in blue s.v.* ***boy.**

1833 CATLIN *Indians* I. 240 The United States and British governments . . . paid them [*sc.* Indians] . . . for every 'scalp' of a 'red' or a 'blue coat' they could bring in! **1864** CATE *Two Soldiers* 46 During the day I remained about the premises, though in constant anticipation of seeing the blue-coats coming. **1945** MARSHALL *Santa Fe* 9 Then the Texans came rampaging west and whipped the bluecoats in the Glorietas.

2. A policeman. *Colloq.*

1875 *Chi. Tribune* 29 Aug. 5/4 Occasionally one of the blue coats would attempt to put back the crowd, but they would not be put back. **1947** *Denver Post* 23 Feb. A. 7/1 While the bluecoats lately have had only 'God's Little Acre' to cover, the risque scribblers of the pioneer era were turning out miles of blood-and-thunder copy.

3. A bluish color-stage in the coats of deer at a certain season. *Rare.* Cf. **blue,** *n.* **4.**

1870 *Amer. Naturalist* May 1908 The spike-horn was shot just as deer were attaining the 'blue coat.'

***blue devil,** *n.*

1. As a plant name (see quots.).

1837 DARLINGTON *Flora Cestrica* 119 Blue weed. . . . Blue Devils. **1894** *Amer. Folk-Lore* VII. 91 *Aster cordifolius.* . . . Blue Devil, stick-weed, bee-weed, Fall Aster; West Va. **1931** CLUTE *Plants* 111 The little blue-flowered *Echium vulgare* is known as viper's grass, viper's bugloss, adder's meat . . . but it is . . . more commonly known, to the farmer at least, as blue devils.

2. One of the fence cutters in the so-called "fence war" in Texas in the early 1880's when the open ranges were fenced. *Obs.*

1884 *Nation* 24 Jan. 65/1 The fence-cutters, or 'blue devils,' as they are called, represent the primitive Texas of the ante-bellum period *Ib.* 65/2 It is evident that the blue devils . . . are endeavoring to give the fence war the air of a struggle between poverty and banded wealth.

blue devil, *v. tr.* To make despondent. *Rare.* — **1836** in *So. Hist. Jrnl.* (1935) I. 364 To be hemmed up in a strange place without . . . anything to interest you, expecting every minute to get off and every minute disappointed, is enough to Blue Devil one.

***blue-eyed,** *a.*

1. (See quot.) *Slang. Obs.*

a1856 *Burlington Sentinel* in Hall *Coll. Words* (ed. 2) 461 Words and phrases which have been in use . . . to signify some stage of inebriation [include] . . . fogmatic, blue-eyed, a passenger in the Cape-Ann stage.

2. In combs.: (1) **blue-eyed babies,** a local name for **Quaker-ladies;** (2) **grass,** one or other species of iridaceous grass-like plants of the genus *Sisyrinchium* having small blue flowers; (3) **Mary,** a delicate annual, *Collinsia verna*, of the eastern states; (4) **yellow warbler,** the golden warbler, *Dendroica aestiva*.

(1) **1892** *Amer. Folk-Lore* V. 97 *Houstonia cærulea*, blue-eyed babies. Springfield, Mass. — (2) **1784** CUTLER in *Mem. Academy* I. 48 *Sisyrinchium.* . . . Blue-Eyed Grass. Blossoms blue. In grass lands. . . . It makes very pretty edging for borders in gardens. **1939** *Nat. Geog. Mag.* Aug. 219/2 Marsh marigolds . . . and blue-eyed grass enlivened meadows. — (3) **1894** *Amer. Folk-Lore* VII. 96 *Collinsia verna*, . . . blue-eyed Marys. Anderson, Ind. **1945** *Sat. Review* 5 May 12/3 The author has an artist's eye and ear for . . . the 'blue-eyed Mary' that closes at night and opens with the sun. — (4) **1810** WILSON *Ornithology* II. 111 Blue-Eyed Yellow Warbler, *Sylvia Citrinella* . . . This is a very common summer species. . . . It arrives in Pennsylvania about the beginning of May. **1917** *Birds of Amer.* III. 126.

***bluegrass,** *n.*

1. Any one of various American grasses of the genus *Poa*, some of which, as the Kentucky bluegrass, *P. pratensis*, are highly valued for pasturage and hay.

1751 ELIOT *Field-Husb.* iii. 61 The Land that you would improve this way, must be intirely free from Blue Grass, called by some Dutch Grass, or Wire Grass. **1835** HOFFMAN *Winter in West* II. 130 This was the grazing portion of the farm, and the hardy blue grass, even thus early, afforded a rich sward beneath the boughs. **1898** *Cong. Rec.* March 2417/2 The blue grass of Kentucky, which when more grazed is always better.

b. With a distinguishing term.

1864 *Ohio Agric. Rep.* XVIII. 461 Under and near the peach trees were noticed the leaves of the Ohio Blue Grass (*Poa pratense*). **1889** *Cent. s.v.*, The red-topped blue-grass of Montana and westward is *Poa tenuifolia*.

2. The region of the bluegrass, esp. with reference to Kentucky.

1871 DE VERE 407 Both the region where it grows naturally, and the settlers there, are known as Blue Grass simply, and hence the State of Kentucky is often thus designated. **1897** BRODHEAD *Bound in Shallows* 17 Even her I don't see much of; she's mostly visiting her kin in the blue grass. **1946** *Sat. Review* 8 June 65/1 He is honest enough to admit that *all* of Kentucky did not have the lush fertility of the section now known as the Bluegrass.

Hence **Bluegrassdom,** the bluegrass region. *Rare.* — **1887** *Courier-Journal* 19 Feb. 6/7 The first time people in Bluegrassdom were ever assessed for anything like what they are worth.

3. *ellipt.* as *adj.* Belonging to or coming from the bluegrass country.

1889 *Harper's Mag.* Aug. 459/2 Bud rode into the yard on Mollie. . . . 'Blue-grass all over, I wonder how he came by her.' **1913** STRATTON-PORTER *Laddie* x. 274 There's a strain of Arab in the father, . . . and the mother is bluegrass.

4. Bluegrass State, Kentucky.

1886 *Chi. W. News* 29 Apr. 4/3 Kentucky's desperate Indian wars gave it the name of the Dark and Bloody Ground; it is also called the Blue Grass state. **1947** *Dly. Racing Form* (Chi.) 6 Nov. 36/3 He never raced in his native Blue Grass State.

b. bluegrass country, a region, chiefly in Kentucky, noted for its bluegrass.

1883 *Harper's Mag.* Oct. 715/1 The blue-grass country is reached by traversing central Virginia and Kentucky. **1947** *Newsweek* 22 Dec. 22/3 He was born in Kentucky—in the bluegrass country—and he likes it there.

5. Attrib. with **hay, horseman, Kentuckian, pasture, region.** Also *bluegrass county, farm, land, man, seed,* etc.

1772 *Penna. Gazette* 16 April 4/3 Timothy and blue grass hay to be sold. **1823** DEWEES *Lett. from Texas* 35 The musquit grass grows very thick and about three feet high, and looks very much like a blue grass pasture. **1863** DICEY *Six Months* II. 64 In any of the country towns of what is called the Blue Grass region of Kentucky, you require the sight of the railroad running along the streets to show you that you are not in an English county town. **1944** *Chi. D. News* 4 Aug. 24/4 The new records were enough to convince Blue Grass horsemen they have a good thing in the Lexington market. **1946** *Newsweek* 26 Aug. 72/3 His successor . . . is a blue-grass Kentuckian.

As the last term in **Canada, Colorado, English, Kentucky, Pennsylvania, Texas bluegrass.**

blue hen.

1. blue hen's chickens, (see quots.).

The reason for the association of this term with Delaware and its citizens is not clear. The explanation in quot. 1840 is often given.

1840 *Niles' Reg.* 9 May 154/3 In the revolutionary war, . . . Captain Caldwell had a company recruited from Kent and Sussex [Counties, Del.], called by the rest 'Caldwell's game cocks,' and the regiment after a time in Carolina was nicknamed from this 'the blue hen's chickens' and the 'blue chickens.' . . . But after they had been distinguished in the south the name of the *Blue Hen* was applied to the state. **1844** *Ib.* May 183 The Blue Hen's Chickens, was the name of a club from Kent county, having with them a significant banner, representing a chicken coop. **1856** *Louisville Courier* 8 Nov. 3/1 Delaware, small but mighty in its influence, well represents the character and reputation of the Blue Hen's Chicken. **1864** *Cong. Globe* June 2968/2, I remember the early history of the 'Blue-Hen's Chickens,' . . . The record is as proud as that of the early 'Jersey Blues.' **1946** MCWILLIAMS *S. Calif. Country* 172 People from Delaware are 'the Blue Hen's chickens.'

b. (See quots. 1927, 1948.) *Colloq.*

1830 A. ROYALL *Lett. from Ala.* 69 [Andrew Jackson said] he was 'one of the blue hen's chickens.' **1927** *D.N.* V. 473 *blue hen's chicken,* . . . A formidable fighter. 'You-uns git Hank rousted up now, an' he shore is one o' th' ol' *blue hen's chickens.*' [Reported from Ozarks.] **1948** MENCKEN *Supp.* II. 232 [In Salem, Virginia] *Blue hen's chickens,* usually applied to natives of Delaware, is used to designate the local gentry.

2. Blue Hen (State), Delaware, a nickname.

1840 *Niles' Reg.* 9 May 154/3 The whigs of the revolution never ceased to boast of the Blue Hen and her chickens. **1897** *Cong. Rec.* App. 23 March 68, I am thankful to the gentleman from the 'Blue Hen State' for his suggestion. **1905** *Nation* 31 Aug. LXXXI. 177/2 Their political conditions . . . could not be compared with those which were smelling to Heaven in the Old Blue Hen State.

3. blue hen hawk, the blue darter, *Astur atricapillus.*

1884 ROE *Nat. Ser. Story* iv, The American goshawk is the dreaded blue hen hawk of New England. **1917** *Birds of Amer.* II. 68 American Goshawk; Blue Hen Hawk; Blue Darter; Partridge Hawk; Dove Hawk; Chicken Hawk.

blue jay. Any one of various North American jays, esp. the common jay, *Cyanocitta cristata.* See also **mountain blue jay.**

1709 *Bristol Rec.* in *Narrag. Hist. Reg.* III. 211 The same order shall extend to the killing of blew Jawes [*sic*]. **1808–14** WILSON *Ornithology* I. 12 The Blue Jay is an almost universal inhabitant of the woods, frequenting the thickest settlements, as well as the deepest recesses. **1944** DUNCAN *M. Graham* 17 Faintly hearing the blue jays that called and scolded near the cabin, Mary stirred and woke.

b. blue-jay camp meeting, a group of chattering jays. *Colloq.*

1907 LINCOLN *Old Home House* 12 Everybody was togged up till Jonadab and me, in our new cutaways, felt like a couple of moulting blackbirds at a blue-jay camp-meeting.

blue law(s).

1. The severe puritanical regulations alleged to have been in force at New Haven, Conn., and its neighborhood, in the seventeenth and eighteenth centuries.

The term was first used by the Rev. Samuel A. Peters (see 1st quot. below), an ardent loyalist, who fled this country in 1774. The "laws" were in large part splenetic fabrications. See *N. & Q.* 4th S. VII. (1871) 191 ff.

1781 PETERS *Hist. Conn.* 43 Even the rigid fanatics of Boston, and the mad zealots of Hertford, . . . christened them the *Blue Laws. Ib.* 69 They . . . were very properly termed Blue Laws; i.e. bloody Laws; for they were all sanctified with . . . whippings, cutting off the ears, burning the tongue, and death. **1829** L. DOW *Omnifarious Laws Exempl.* 13 One of the blue laws of Conn. was, neither to give meat, drink, or lodging to a Quaker, or to tell him the road. **1871** BARNUM *Struggles & Triumphs* 53 The following scene makes a chapter in the history of Connecticut, as the State was when 'blue laws' were something more than a dead letter. **1944** JOHNSON *As I Dare* 42 The 'blue laws,' a term which nine-tenths of my friends think of only in association with New England, were in part imaginary.

b. Blue Law State, Connecticut.

1839 BRIGGS *H. Franco* II. xviii. 180 'But, you were not a member of the Hartford Convention?' exclaimed Mr. Bloodbutton. . . . 'Never was in the Bluelaw State in my life, Sir.' **1854** *Cong. Globe* 6 July 1618/1, I know that Connecticut, in the olden time, was libeled by a Tory renegade . . . as the Blue Law State.

2. Any laws regarded as excessively rigorous, esp. those seeking to regulate conduct in matters of individual conscience, sometimes in the singular.

1815 *Niles' Reg.* VIII. 363/1 This is a notable instance of the efficacy of *blue laws.* **1895** *N.Y. Dramatic News* 7 Dec. 2/2 The arrest was made under an old blue law, which provides for the punishment of those who commit adultery. **1948** *Dly. Ardmoreite* (Ardmore, Okla.) 7 April 1/2 The Ardmore junior chamber of commerce [is] concerned about the recent invoking of the old blue laws of 1910.

* **blue light.** (Also *cap.*) A New England Federalist who opposed the War of 1812. Usu. *pl. Obs.*

"The expression originated in 1813 from the claim of Commodore Decatur that blue light signals set to warn the British had prevented him on several dark nights from getting to sea from the port of New London with his two frigates."—McLaughlin & Hart I. 136/2.

[**1813** DECATUR *Lett.* in *Niles' Reg.* (1814) V. 302 In the course of the evening [of 12 Dec.] two blue lights were burnt on both the points at the harbor's mouth as signals to the enemy, and there is not a doubt, but that they have, by signals and otherwise, instantaneous information of our movements.] **1814** *Niles' Reg.* VI. 2/1 Such is the universal sentiment of our invincible and invaluable seamen. They hate 'blue-lights' and traitors. **1815** *Ib.* VIII. 140/2 Many of our best and most patriotic citizens are emigrants from New England; and even a very 'blue light' loses that factious, grumbling and suspicious spirit that distinguished him at home. **1847** *Cong. Globe* 20 Jan., App. 252/1 Where, tell me where, have you buried the sins of these 'old blue lights' of New Hampshire? [**1848** *Field Piece* (Chi.) 2 Aug. 3/5 No doubt they will tell us next that the blue lights, said to have been exhibited for the benefit of the British in the last war, was also an evidence of patriotism.]

attrib. **1818** H. B. FEARON *Sketches of A.* The mode of doing this is said to have been by the throwing up blue lights; a circumstance which has given rise to the party appellation of 'blue light men'—a term of reproach used by the democrats against the federalists. **1844** *Cong. Globe* App. 6 March 399/2 J. C. Wright [was] . . . as rank a blue-light federal whig as ever justified the Hartford convention. **1848** *Ib.* 2 March 418/2 The late war with Great Britain was unpopular with the blue-light Federalists. **a1859** *N.Y. Herald* (B.), Horace Greeley, and a train of real blue light Clayites from your State, have arrived this morning.

b. (See quots.) *Obs.*

1856 GOODRICH *Recollections* I. 484 *Blue Lights,* meaning treason on the part of Connecticut federalism during the war [of 1812], is a standard word in the flash dictionary of low democracy. **1856** HALL (ed. 2) 30 At the University of Vermont this term is used, writes a correspondent, to designate 'a boy who sneaks about college, and reports to the Faculty the short-comings of his fellow students.'

***blue Monday.**

1. A Monday that is depressing or trying, esp. by reason of reaction from undue indulgence the preceding day.

This expression as used in this country may stem from G. *der blaue Montag,* Du. *blauwe maandag,* in the sense of a holiday.

1840 *Boston Transcript* 2 Mar. 2/2 This was blue Monday in the House. **1923** SAUNDERS *So. Sierras Calif.* 97 One Blue Monday in Los Angeles . . . he thought to relieve a fit of despondency by looking over his old book of records. **1946** *Chi. D. News* 28 Feb. 8/7 Every day is Blue Monday at the Navy.

2. A day spent in jollification.

1862 *Yankee Volunteer's Songster* 51 Uncle Sam, the son of *Johnny Bull,* the boss, On Blue-Monday took a spree, sirs. **1885** *Harper's Mag.* 873/1 The workman getting sober after his usual 'blue Monday.'

3. (See quot. 1870.)

1870 F. FERN *Ginger-Snaps* 67 'Blue Monday!' By this name clergymen designate the day; . . . the worn-out clergyman takes Monday for a day of rest, for truly the Sabbath is none. . . . But Blue Monday does not belong exclusively to clergymen. **1898** M. DELAND *Old Chester Tales* 136 Dr. Lavendar never had 'blue Mondays'—perhaps because he preached old sermons.

***bluenose,** *n.* (Also *cap.*)

1. A nickname for a New Englander or a Canadian. Also attrib.

[**1830** *Northern Watchman* (Troy, N.Y.) 30 Nov. (Th.), A real 'blue-nose,' fresh from the land of steady habits.] **1839** *N.O. Picayune* 12 Mar. 2/3 The blue noses *may* be visited shortly by a few more 'Yankee Doctors.' **1864** *Sacramento Union* 14 Jan. 3/2 It is believed there are from twelve to twenty gangs of 'Blue-nose' blockade runners. **1883** F. INGERSOLL in *Harper's Mag.* Jan. 206/2 The Americans employed are very often graduates of the Maine Woods, or 'Blue-noses' from Lower Canada. **1948** *Range Riders Western* May 108/2 I'll say what I got to say standin' up, you danged blue-nose Yankee!

b. One who is excessively puritanical or inquisitive.

1929 *Variety* 3 April 11/4 That this picture may aggravate blue nose censors is not beyond the bounds of possibility. **1945** *Chi. D. News* 2 Aug. 10/7 It seems to me that our bluenoses are doing a grave injury to the men serving overseas, who have got the impression that married women are running wild. **1948** *Laff* Apr. 16/2 Boston, city of Puritans and blue noses, home of the Apleys and the Cabots and the Lodges, . . . has its own burlesque theatre!

2. A variety of potato.

*c***1840** HALIBURTON *Sam Slick* (B.), 'Blue Noses' . . . is the name of a potatoe . . . which they [=Nova Scotians] produce in great perfection. **1872** *Vt. Bd. Agric. Rep.* I. 232 He . . . sighs for a potato that will yield as much and cook as well as the old Blue Noses used to do forty years ago.

3. A variety of clam. *Rare.*

1883 *Leisure Hour* 252/1 The coarsest is the mud-clam, or blue nose, which is dug out of the mud with tongs.

***blue-nosed,** *a.*

1. Used as a disparaging or contemptuous term.

1809 IRVING *Knickerb.* III. ii, As a mouse eats his way into a comfortable lodgment in a goodly, blue-nosed, skim'd milk, New-England cheese. **1866** C. H. SMITH *Bill Arp* 87 General Johnston was retreating and the blue-nosed yankees were to pollute our sacred soil the next morning. **1948** *Atlantic Mo.* March 25/1 Apart from . . . hypercritical bluenosed censorship, . . . the motion picture is bad because 90 per cent of its source material is tripe.

2. blue-nosed potato = bluenose 2.

1833 J. S. JONES *Green Mt. Boy* I. ii, We can raise more . . . blue-nosed potatoes than we can harvest, a darned sight. **1841** *Knickerb.* XVII. 49 A face whose combined features strikingly resembled a half-peck of blue-nosed potatoes.

blues bluz, *n. pl.* [Short for **blue devils.*]

1. Depression of spirits, despondency, melancholy, usu. with *the.*

1807 IRVING *Salmagundi* xv, [He] concluded his harangue with a sigh, and I saw he was still under the influence of a whole legion of the blues. **1873** HAYCRAFT *Elizabethtown, Ky.* 148 One evening in winter he was walking out to relieve ennui and a heavy spirit, warmly clad, but as miserable as he could be—that is, completely in the *blues.* **1945** *Chi. D. News* 17 May 23/2 (*heading*), The Old Medicine Man Still Cures the Blues.

2. A type of mournful, haunting Negro folk song adapted and often burlesqued for use in music halls, vaudeville shows, etc. Also attrib.

1917 *Lit. Digest* 25 Aug. 29/2 Jazz crept slowly up the Mississippi from resort to resort until it landed in South Chicago at Freiburg's, whither it had been preceded by the various stanzas of 'Must I Hesitate?' 'The Blues,' 'Franky and Johnny,' and other classics of the levee underworld. **1921** *Outward Bound* May 58/2 These 'labour songs,' . . . like the 'blues' of to-day, were rather humorous. **1948** *Time* 1 Mar. 34/2 The words were written specially for her, to an old blues tune.

b. blues singer, one accustomed to sing such songs.

1931 *K.C. Star* 23 Oct., Twin girls, age 4, rendered a program as blues singers at a dime store in Emporia the other day. **1947** *Chi. Sun* 14 Oct. 43/4, I got her a job understudying the blues singer in the show I'm handling.

blue-skin. (Also *cap.*)

1. An ardent supporter of the American Revolution. *Obs.*

1782 *Loyal Verses* (1860) 100 Tho' the Colour's unlike both Christian and Jew Skin, Yet it greatly resembles a true Rebel Blue-Skin. **1783** in FRENEAU *Poems* II. 157 Let him stand where he is—don't push him down hill, And he'll turn a true *Blue-Skin,* or just what you will.

2. A term of depreciation for a person of strict morals, a Presbyterian. *Obs.*

1787 TYLER *Contrast* II. ii, It is no shame, my dear Blueskin, for a man to amuse himself with a little gallantry. **1848** BARTLETT 39 *Blue-skins,* a nickname applied to the Presbyterians, from their alleged grave deportment. **1855** BARNUM *Life* 50 There the congregation would sit and shiver, and their faces would look so blue, that it is no wonder 'the world's people' sometimes called them 'blue skins.'

3. A Negro. *Obs.*

1821 COOPER *Spy* vii, You seem very careful of that beautiful person of yours, Mr. Blueskin. **1847** ROBB *Squatter Life* 111 'What, Missus dar, *too!*' shouted the nigger, . . . and off the cussed blueskin started fur the house.

4. = blue, *n.* **3.** (see also quot. 1871). *Obs.*

1823 *Crayon* (Yale) 22, I . . . issued from my cell, To see if we could over-hear, Or make some blue-skin tell. **1856** HALL (ed. 2) 31 *Blue-skin* . . . was formerly in use at some American colleges, with the meaning now given to the word *Blue.* **1871** G. R. CUTTING *Student Life at Amherst College* 132 During the years from 1821 to 1826. . . . It was the practice to hang in effigy those students who, by special attention to the Faculty, had gained the obnoxious name of 'Blue-skins.'

5. *W.* (See quots.) *Obs.*

1863 J. L. FISK *Exped. Rocky Mts.* 31, I went to the tabernacle and heard Bishop Woolley incite his flock to sneer at the 'blue skins,' (meaning our soldiers stationed there). **1866** F. KIRKLAND *Bk. Anecdotes* 302 Darn the blueskins, any how; who's scared of the blue-bellies? (That is, Eastern men.)

***blue-sky,** *n.*

1. (See quot. 1948.) Also as adj.

1906 WOOLRIDGE *Grafters of Amer.* 48 They were what I would term 'blue sky and hot air' securities. **1948** MENCKEN *Supp.* II. 149 Carruth . . . suggested that *blue-sky,* to indicate a bad investment, might be from the German *blauer dunst.*

2. blue-sky law, a law to protect the public from purchasing stocks and bonds that are unsound or that do not meet certain standards.

1912 *N.Y. Ev. Post* 13 Jan. (Fin. Supp.), The 'Blue Sky' law of Kansas prohibits the sale . . . of stock or bonds of any company chartered outside the State. **1921** *Springfield W. Republican* 3 Mar. 1 The origin of 'blue sky law'—legislation providing for State regulation of the sale of corporate securities—is middle western. **1946** *Reader's Digest* Sep. 20/1 'You're operating illegally,' he said. 'Either you are selling stock in violation of the blue-sky law or you are asking charity.'

bluestem 'blu͵stɛm, *n.*

1. A variety of wheat, in full **bluestem wheat.** *Obs.*

1853 *Mich. Agric. Soc. Trans.* (1854) 72, 2 bushels blue stem wheat. **1856** *Rep. Comm. Patents: Agric.* 194 In 1853, I obtained from Baltimore 2 bushels of 'White Blue-stem' wheat. **1861–2** *Ill. Agric. Soc. Trans.* V. 209 Mr. C. sows the Blue Stem and the May or Alabama, in about equal quantities.

2. Either of two valuable forage grasses, *Andropogon furcatus,* or *Agropyron smithi,* of the western U.S. In full **bluestem grass.** Cf. **gumbo grass.**

1879 H. KING in *Scribner's Mo.* Nov. 138 A belt of the tall, thick blue-stem. **1927** SIRINGO *Riata* 53 If the fire was down in the arroyo, where the blue-stem grass grows tall, it was allowed to burn its way onto a level flat covered with buffalo grass. **1945** MATHEWS *Talking* 4 Their absorption with the practical working-out of the maze of field-mice trails and the grazing of the rank bluestem.

3. bluestem goldenrod, (see quots.), also **blue-stemmed goldenrod.**

1817–8 EATON *Botany* (1822) 467 *Solidago caesia*, blue-stem golden-rod. **1846** WOOD *Botany* 329 *Solidago caesia*, Blue-stemmed Golden-rod.... Flowers of a deep, rich yellow. **1901** MOHR *Plant Life Ala.* 772 Blue-stem Golden-rod . . . [grows in] open damp woods; . . . flowers, July, August. *Ib.*, *Solidago caesia paniculata*, Southern Blue-stem Golden-rod.

***bluestocking,** *n.*

1. A professing Christian. Also attrib. *Obs.*

1829 A. ROYALL *Pennsylvania* I. 152 The sole and all-weighing cause of my partiality for the Germans, is their aversion to the gray coats, or, as they are called in Pennsylvania, *blue stockings.* **1868** *Harper's Mag.* Jan. 267/1 A Presbyterian minister of the genuine old 'blue stocking' school.

2. (See quot. 1844.)

1844 *Nat. Hist. N.Y., Zoology* II. 267 The American Avoset, or Blue-stocking as it is called in New Jersey, is a scarce bird on the shores of this State. **1892** *Outing* Sep. 457/1 A lonely blue-stocking, the first of its kind I had seen in many a year, stood motionless by a bed of rock-weed.

***bluet,** *n.*

1. A small plant, *Houstonia caerulea*, with "delicate little flowers, light blue, pale lilac, or nearly white" (Gray).

1821 BARTON *Flora* I. 119 Fairy-flax. Bluett. Innocence. Venus' Pride. **1887** BURROUGHS in *Cent. Mag.* July 333 We have one flower which grows in vast multitudes, yet which is exquisitely delicate and beautiful in and of itself, I mean the houstonia, or bluets. **1948** *Life* 5 April 57/2 In March . . . the low field flowers like the bluets begin to bud.

2. A similar plant of the genus *Oldenlandia* (syn. *Hedyotis*).

1843 TORREY *Flora N.Y.* I. 315 *Hedyotis caerulea*.... Common Bluets. Dwarf Risk. *Ib.* 316 *Hedyotis longifolia*.... Long-leaved Bluets [etc.].

3. The farkleberry.

In this sense f. Amer. Fr. *beluet, bluet,* huckleberry. See McDermott.

[*a*1716 PERROT *Mémoire des Sauvages de l'Amérique* (1864) 52 On y ramasse cependant des bluets dans les mois d' août et de septembre.] **1897** SUDWORTH *Arborescent Flora* 312 *Vaccinium arboreum*.... Tree Huckleberry.... Bluet (La.).

bluewing, *n.*

1. A North American teal, *Querquedula discors.* In full **bluewing(ed) teal.**

1709 LAWSON *Carolina* 148 The Blue-Wings are less than a Duck, but fine Meat. These are the first Fowls that appear to us in the Fall of the Leaf. *c*1731 CATESBY *Carolina* I. 99 *Querquidula americana fusca*, the Blue-wing Teal, . . . in August . . . come in great plenty to Carolina. **1945** MATHEWS *Talking* 153 The first bluewinged teal stop on the ponds and the private pools.

2. bluewing shoveler, a shoveler duck, *Spatula clypeata*, or *S. rhynchotis.*

*c*1731 CATESBY *Carolina* I. 96 *Anas Americanus luto rostro*, the Blue wing Shoveler.... The upper part of the wing is covered with pale blue feathers.

bluff blʌf, *n.*[1] [See note.] A steep river bank or shore, or the top of such a bank.

This noun use is poss. f. the adj., or short for **bluff land.** See **c.** below. All the early examples refer to South Carolina and Georgia, and many of them relate to Savannah.

1687 in *S.C. Hist. & Gen. Mag.* (July, 1929) 26 April 131 . . . We landed on a Bluffe where some shads were.... At night with the Ebb we came to a Bluffe. *Ib.* 30, 132. This morning . . . we came . . . to ane old Indian plantation on a Bluffe. **1737** JOHN WESLEY *Journal* I. (1910) 402 Savannah stands on a flat *bluff* (so they term any high-land hanging over a creek or river), which rises forty-five feet perpendicular from the river. **1801** *Hist. Review* II. 307 The river forms a half moon, with banks on the south-side 40 feet high, having on the top a flat which sailors call a *bluff.* **1881** *Rep. Indian Affairs* 37 The bottom lands here are about one and one-fourth of a mile wide, the land rising with a gentle slope from the river to the bluffs in the rear. **1948** *So. Sierran* May 1/1 Before us were limestone cliffs, red sandstone walls, spectacular views of the gorge with its fantastic crags and bluffs.

attrib. **1765** J. BARTRAM *Diary* 24 July, Water ouseth thro ye strata of sand shels or gravel so that they cant dig very deep except it is in bluf banks near ye river. **1850** DRAKE *Treatise* 168 This is another bluff-town on the same right-hand bank of the river, fifty miles higher up, and one hundred and eighty-seven from the mouth of the Missouri. **1861–4** *Ill. Agric. Soc. Trans.* V. 628 The term loess is applied to a deposit which . . . has been sometimes called the 'bluff' deposit. **1886** *Outing* May 131/1 One of my foremen shot a mountain ram on a ragged bluff-crest but half a mile away.

b. Bluff City, (see quots.).

1859 *Harper's Mag.* March 591/2 The Shelby Agricultural Society's fair grounds, a mile and a half from this, the 'Bluff City' [= Memphis]. **1871** DE VERE 663 Hannibal, in Missouri, is known as the *Bluff City*, being built on high bluffs overhanging the river.

c. bluff land(s), land that rises steeply, high land.

1666 *S.C. Hist. Soc. Coll.* V. 62 The North East side is a bluffe land, rounding from the River. **1685** *Let.* in *S.C. Hist. & Gen. Mag.* April (1929) We settled ourselves altogether in a verie convenient place for a town . . . a high bloffe land excellently weel [*sic*] watered. **1884** *Encycl. Brit.* XVII. 309/2 These so-called 'bluff-lands,' [are] composed of loess materials.

As the last term in **burnt, cedar, clam, clay, clay rock, limestone, pine, prairie, river, rock, salt, sand, sandstone, shell, sulphur, wash bluff.**

bluff blʌf, *n.*[2] [See note.]

Bense regards the word as of LG. origin, and cites LG. *bluffen, blüffen,* to frighten by menacing conduct, and Middle Du. *bluffen* for *buffen* (mod. Du. *boffen*), to make a trick at cards.

1. The game of poker.

1838 BURTON *Comic Songster* 10 Those who play at pharo bank, At poko, brag, or loo, or bluff, Must all be sure to lose enough. **1845** *St. Louis Reveille* 2 May 1/6 The reader who does not understand the game of 'bluff,' or 'poker,' as it is most generally called, may as well leave off here. **1885** *Cent. Mag.* Aug. 639/1 Sutler's pasteboard checks were very useful in playing the game of 'bluff.' **1939** WELLMAN *Trampling Herd* 256 Even then, for another thirty years, it remained a simple game called 'bluff' as often as poker.

fig. **1859** *Harper's Mag.* Oct. 713/2 Hazlit felt abashed at the formidable appearance of the culprit, but determined to *play bluff.* **1866** *Harvard Mem. Biographies* I. 400 It is a very magnificent game of Bluff that we are playing. **1878** *Pt. Townsend* (Wash.) *Wkly. Argus* 22 Mar., 'Too thin, old man,' said the deputy, 'the game of bluff won't win.'

2. An instance of, or the practice of, bluffing in poker. Also transf.

For *to call one's bluff, throw the bluff,* see the verbs.

1859 *No. Californian* (Union) 27 Apr. 1/4 'My call,' rejoined Bob; 'show your hand,' at the same time planking down two dollars and a half to make good the bluff. **1882** *Cent. Mag.* XXIV. 864 The games played are faro and 'stud poker,' the latter being the favorite. It is a game in which 'bluff' goes farther than luck or skill. **1945** *Birmingham Age-Herald* 5 Nov. 9/4 He . . . said it would be a complete impossibility, a bluff, one couldn't do it.

b. Also **bluff game.**

1845 HOOPER *Suggs* (1928) 91 'No' said Simon, still indulging in his favourite style of metaphor; 'the bluff game aint played here! **1906** RIDLEY *Battles* 489 At Athens, after Campbell surrendered the fort of 1,800 men to Forrest (bluff game), a Dutchman commanding a block-house filled full of negro soldiers refused to surrender.

3. A stake in a card game. *Rare.*

1870 NOWLAND *Indianapolis* 163 While playing he kept his money in his mouth, it held just twenty dollars in silver; his usual 'bluff' was a mouthful, which he emptied from his mouth on to the table.

4. A bluffer. *Colloq.* or *slang.*

*a*1904 WHITE *Blazed Trail* ii. 27 'You're a bluff!' he said insultingly. **1910** *Fra* April 23/1 Oh, yes, I'm a bit of a bluff it's true; What sort of a bluff are you?

bluff blʌf, *v.*[1] [f. **bluff,** *n.*[1]] *tr.* To raise in the form of a bluff. *Rare.* — **1809** BARLOW *Columbiad* I. 643 Where dread Niagara bluffs high his brow.

bluff blʌf, *v.*[2] [App. of LG. origin. See note on **bluff,** *n.*[2]]

1. *tr.* To impress, intimidate, frighten (one) by pretense, swagger, mere show, etc., also with *off.*

1839 *N.O. Picayune* 17 Mar. 2/4 It was currently reported that the race was postponed; it however proved otherwise, and as many (not very few) whom no rain, mud or doubt could bluff off, went to see such sport as might chance. **1887** *Cent. Mag.* March 974 He would propose such a sort of fight as would bluff off Shields. **1944** *Chi. D. News* 14 Dec. 3/7 With five guns frozen up and inoperative, the gunners successfully bluffed the Germans.

b. Esp. in poker to deceive an opponent as to the strength of one's hand by betting heavily upon it, speaking, gesticulating, etc., to scare *off* an opponent by such means. Also fig.

1845 *St. Louis Reveille* 2 May 1/6 Therefore, inasmuch as I believe you are only trying to bluff me off, I go two hundred. **1885** *N.Y. Wkly.*

Sun 13 May 2/7 One evening . . . he went his whole heart, soul, and pocket on three aces and was bluffed by his opponent with a pair of trays. **1890** RYAN *Told in Hills* 224, I think it's playing it pretty low down on Providence to bluff him on an empty hand.

2. *intr.* To act so as to bluff, or seek to impress someone.

1854 *Cong. Globe* 3 May 1070 We both know how that game of brag is played. I thought I would bluff back on him. **1893** POST *Harvard Stories* 237 Write only on those questions that you can answer. . . . Don't try to bluff on the questions that you don't know. **1948** *L.A. Times* 2 May (Home Mag.) 2/3 A dog which has been 'bluffed' into running by the neighbor's dog, then suddenly turns and thrashes the 'bully,' is an inspiration to his young master.

bluffer ˈblʌfɚ, *n.* [f. **bluff,** *v.*²] One who bluffs, at poker or otherwise.

1850 GARRARD *Wah-To-Yah* ix. 122 Others . . . gasconaded and looked fierce enough to stare a mad 'bluffer' out of countenance. **1889** *Sporting Life* (Phila.) 5 June 7/3 He is beyond doubt the greatest living manager of ball players, and likewise the greatest bluffer and boaster in the business. **1946** *Sci. News Letter* 23 March 188/1 The *puff adder,* a common snake in America, is one of the world's biggest bluffers.

bluffing ˈblʌfɪŋ, *n.* [f. **bluff** *v.*²] The action of using bluff, *q.v.* Also attrib.

*c***1850** *Southern Sketches* 137 (B. '59), Jim . . . tried the bluffing system; but Joe said he . . . would put up with no more insults from his bullying neighbor. **1882** *Nation* 12 Oct. 301/1 The other method, which might be called the bluffing method, . . . has been frequently applied to civil-service reform. **1887** KELLER *Draw Poker* 6 It must be remembered that in poker 'bluffing' or betting on nothing, is not only permissible, but is one of the most seductive features of the game. **1948** *Redbook* March 23/1 Andy was a blustering, bluffing, not too straitlaced fellow.

***bluffy,** *a.* Resembling bluffs, steep. — **1851** *Knickerb.* XXXVII. 182 The shores have a bluffy appearance, and the river has scooped out hollows all along the banks. **1882** *Cent. Mag.* Sep. 707 The Penobscot winds around the bluffy headlands.

***bluing,** *n.* (See quot. 1864.) Also attrib.

1842 MRS. KIRKLAND in *Knickerb.* XX. 419 The harvest-moon . . . is like 'the yelk of an egg that's been froze, and then dropt into a great tub o' bluin'-water.' **1864** WEBSTER, Bluing. . . . Something to give a bluish tint, as indigo used by washerwomen. **1881** *Harper's Mag.* Dec. 73/2 In color the melon is of a deep indigo blue, rotund in form —indeed, facetiously suggesting a small bluing-bag. **1913** STRATTON-PORTER *Laddie* i, The bluing settled in the rinse water and stained her white clothes. **1948** *Chi. D. News* 7 May 1/2 Do Mayor Kennelly use bluing to get his hair white?

blummie ˈblʌmɪ, *n. local.* [Dim. of Du. *bloem,* flower.] (See quots.)

[**1848** BARTLETT Blumachies. (Dutch.) This Dutch word for flowers is still preserved in the New York markets.] **1881** *Harper's Mag.* March 526/1 [The Pinkster king] and his followers were covered with Pinkster *blummies,* the wild azalia or swamp-apple. **1936** MENCKEN *Amer. Lang.* 109 In isolated communities in the Catskills there is still a considerable admixture [of Dutch] in the common speech, e.g. *clove* (ravine), *killfish, pinxter* (a variety of azalea), *speck* (fat), *fly* (swamp), *blummie* (flower) [etc.].

blunderbuss boots. ?Wide-topped boots. *Rare.* — **1873** *Newton* (Kansas) *Kansan* 31 July 3/3 Geo. Hagerty [was] in hunting trim with his cow hide blunderbuss boots on.

***blunt,** *a.* Of cartridges: Blank. *Obs.* — **1799** *Aurora* (Phila.) 9 July 2/5 The Militia Legion will form on its parade . . . , provided as heretofore with blunt cartridge. **1800** *Ib.* 30 April.

blurb blɜb, *n.* [See note.] A brief and highly commendatory notice or advertisement, esp. of a book. Also attrib.

Said to have been originated in 1907 by Gelett Burgess in a comic book jacket embellished with a drawing of a pulchritudinous young lady whom he facetiously dubbed Miss Blinda Blurb. See Mencken, *Supp.* I. 329.

1923 *Nation* 1 Aug. 121/2 The publishers . . . clapped on a jacket containing a blurb. **1924** *Spectator* 27 Sep. 426 The note of vanity is ominously accentuated by the publisher's blurb on the dust-cover, as silly and vulgar as the present writer has ever seen. **1947** *Sat. Review* 18 Oct. 10/2, I suppose it is too much to expect that the publisher should have shown its faith in the work to the extent of making its blurb-writer read it. **1948** *Good Housekeeping* Jan. 9/1 Blurbs insult their intelligence and they want no part of them.

blutwurst ˈblʌtˌwɜst, *n.* [G.] A form of sausage containing so much blood that it is almost black in color. — **1856** *Spirit of Age* (Sacramento, Calif.) 27 Mar. 3/1 'What is the German Diet?' 'Sourkrout, pretzels, plutworst, and lager beer.' **1911** *Cosmopolitan* Feb. 314/1 See that I have blutwurst, brattwurst, and mettwurst every day for breakfast.

B'nai B'rith bəˈne·bəˈrɪθ, *n.* [Heb., "sons of the covenant."] A Jewish fraternity founded in New York City in 1843 and now widely extended.

1879 *Chi. Tribune* 14 May 6/1 (*heading*), B'nai B'rith. **1883** *Chi. Tribune* 1 July 9/2 The Jewish benevolent order of B'nai B'rith has ten lodges. **1909** *Cent. Supp.* 147/3 B'nai B'rith. . . . [Heb., 'children of the covenant' (i.e., circumcision).] An independent Jewish order. **1948** *Dly. Ardmoreite* (Ardmore, Okla.) 23 April 10/1 He helped to organize the B'nai B'rith fraternal group here.

bo bo, *n.* [Prob. short for **bozo, hobo.**] A hobo, also as a mere term of familiar address meaning man, fellow, buddy. *Slang.*

1893 *Chi. Record* 14 July 11/3 An' den w'en ye meets one uv yer own kind ye feels like old pals, 'cause he calls ye 'Ho' an' ye calls him 'Bo.' See? **1903** *Cin. Enquirer* 2 May 12/2 Said I to myself, ''Bo, I really fear that there is quite some mussiness impending.' **1912** *Sat. Ev. Post* 27 July 33/2 Say, bo, shove us a plank or a ladder, will you? **1945** MARSHALL *Santa Fe* 285 The 'boes shifted uneasily and looked at Doc with new respect.

***board,** *n.*

1. Short for "blackboard."

1842 in THOMPSON *M. Jones* (1872) 37 'Go to the board,' said the master—and maybe she didn't shine when she walked up to a grate black board, what stood in the corner, and tuck hold of a piece of chalk not half so white as her pretty little hand itself. **1862** G. C. STRONG *Cadet Life West Point* 185 A number of cadets, say three, four, or five, are successively sent to the board. Each . . . turning to the blackboard writes his name at the top and begins his work.

2. *S.* A piece of board suitably fashioned (see quot.) to use in leveling off a planted ridge.

1852 in TURNER *Cotton* (1865) 14 These I would cover with a board, made of some hard wood, an inch or an inch and a-half thick, about eight inches broad, and thirty inches long, beveled on the lower edge so as to make it sharp, slightly notched in the middle so as to straddle a row, with a hole bored in the centre one inch from the upper edge.

3. In gambling, the bank.

1848 JUDSON *Mysteries of N.Y.* 20 (We.) Make your bets, gentlemen; the board is open. **1893** K. SANDBORN *S. Calif.* 103 The owner was implored to sit down and gamble himself, hoping in this way to win more money and get back the board.

4. A stock exchange. Also attrib. Cf. **big board, board book, room,** *Board of Brokers.*

1837 *Hennepin* (Ill.) *Jrnl.* 26 Oct. 1/4 The sales of specie to-day, at the Board, were $1,700 in American gold, at 5 1/2 premium. **1853** *Hunt's Merch. Mag.* XXVIII. 488 Sales at the Board for the year 1852 have more than doubled. **1905** *Dly. Chron.* 28 April 4/4 None of the 'board members'—as the Stock Exchange men are called—ever appears on the kerb. . . . While fortunes are made and lost on the kerb, it does not seem so serious a business as 'on the board.'

b. A listing of stocks, with prices, sales, etc., at a particular time (see quot. 1909).

1852 *N.Y. Wkly. Tribune* 7 Feb. 8/4 Between the Boards, 64 1/2 was bid for 2,000 shares, but it left off the Second Board at 64 5/8. **1855** *N.Y. Herald* 14 Nov. 3/5 At the first board Illinois Central bonds advanced one per cent. **1865** *Balt. D. Commercial* 4 Oct. 4/1 At the second board it advanced 1/8 to 3/8, selling from 144 1/8 to 144 3/8 regular. **1909** WEBSTER 820/3 *First board,* . . . New York Stock Exchange. The printed list of the sales from 10 A.M. to 12 M.

5. (See quots.) Cf. **board card, log, pine, timber, tree.**

1853 P. PAXTON *Yankee in Texas* 65 This same camp was . . . formed by setting up a few crotches to sustain a rude roof of undressed shingles, . . . there known as 'boards.' **1859** BARTLETT 40 In the South-west, boards are strips of wood from two to four feet in length riven from blocks, and differing only in size from shingles. All sawed stuff, which at the North is called *boards,* is here called *plank.* **1889** *Cent.* 604 To riven pieces of this kind, not more than 3 feet long, used for roofing, the name *board* is exclusively applied in the southern United States.

6. * *on board,* in or into a boat or train. Also, jocosely, atop or astride a horse. Cf. **aboard.**

1860 MRS. S. COWELL *Diary* 168 At Island Point . . . the custom house officer . . . came 'on board' as the Yankees say. **1884** SWEET & KNOX *Through Texas* i. 21, I at once decided . . . to take a trip through the comparatively unknown wilds of Texas on board of a Mexican mustang. **1904** *N.Y. Times* 11 May 3 Half a dozen . . . guards and three private detectives were on board the train when it left Boston.

7. *Printing.* (See quot.)

1893 M. PHILIPS *Making of a Newspaper* 103 The 'copy-cutter' cut the despatch into two parts . . . , and then laid them upon 'the board,' a sort of counter where the compositors came to be supplied with copy.

8. Attrib. in the sense "made of boards" with (1) **bank,** (2) **chimney,** (3) **fence,** (4) **fencing,** (5) **floor,** (6) **house,** (7) **pavilion,** (8) **shack,** (9) **shanty,** (10) **sidewalk,** (11) **walk.**

(1) 1902 CLAPIN 62 Board-bank. On the coast of New Jersey, a floor of boards placed on the bed of a creek near the shore, on which oysters are laid to fatten. — **(2) 1769** PATTEN *Diary* 225 John finished a board Chimney in our outside Cellar and I got some Walnut bark the back side of james Littles field. — **(3) 1718** *Boston Selectmen* 48 They . . . shall . . . maintain a substanciall board fence . . . from the Barn to three rods distant southerly from the dwelling house. **1856** BREWERTON *War in Kans.* 105 Upon reaching the board fence which enclosed a sort of flower-garden, just in front of the Superintendent's dwelling, we rode up to a tying-post. **1948** *Country Gentleman* May 175/2 He had cut the fence rows from the board fence around the shack, barn and garden. — **(4) 1871** *Ill. Agric. Soc. Trans.* VIII. 232 By means of hedging and movable board fencing, keep up a great deal of pasturage.

(5) 1836 *Knickerb.* VIII. 150 The trail from St. Augustine to this great bend, about thirty miles, is almost as level as a board floor. **1882** *Cent. Mag.* March 793/2 In preparing cellars or basements, it is often desirable to have board-floors. — **(6) 1883** *Rep. Indian Affairs* 19 The Indians are all living in board houses, with fire-places and chimneys. — **(7) 1923** R. HERRICK *Lilla* 37 He had induced some credulous capitalist to erect a big shambling board 'Pavilion' above the lake, with a restaurant and a dance hall attached. — **(8) 1912** MRS. WOODROW *Sally Salt* 148 Hidden deep in the woods was a board shack roughly put together. **1940** BABER & WALKER *Longest Rope* 36 Most of the buildings were board shacks, scattered along the banks of Clear Creek. — **(9) 1849** T. T. JOHNSON *Sights Gold Region* xiv. 139 In an old board shantee and cook shop, . . . we obtained . . . a piece of beef and cup of tea. **1910** J. HART *Vigilante Girl* xxiv. 330 Along the single street he walked, lined with its rough board shanties.

(10) 1883 MARK TWAIN *Life on Miss.* xxx. 295 The board sidewalks on the ground level were loose and ruinous. **1946** *Reader's Digest* March 139/2 Pretty soon the stores began . . . and no front yards at all, only board sidewalks shaded by wooden awnings. — **(11) 1872** F. M. A. ROE *Army Letters* 53 We reached a narrow board walk that was supposed to run along by her side fence. **1948** *Airlines* Mar. 3/1 It is probably best known for its 8-mile long Boardwalk, beaches and special beauty shows crowning 'Miss America' every year.

9. In special combs.: (1) **board bill,** an amount charged for board; (2) **blinder,** a board secured in place on a cow's head so as to prevent vision in a straight-ahead direction; (3) **book,** a book in which a broker records daily sales at the Exchange; (4) **cart,** a cart having the body made of boards; (5) **foot,** the volume of wood in a piece of timber 12 in. × 12 in. × 1 in. used as a unit in measuring lumber; (6) **log,** a log from which boards may be obtained; (7) **merchant,** a merchant who buys and sells boards, *rare;* (8) ***nail,** in phrases (see quots.), *colloq.;* (9) **pine,** the white pine of the eastern states; (10) **room,** the room in which a board regularly meets, esp. the main room or hall of a stock exchange building; (11) **round,** = **boarding round,** *rare;* (12) **timber,** timber, esp. pine, suitable for making boards; (13) **tree,** (*a*) a tree, usu. a pine, suitable for making boards, (*b*) a shrubby plant, *Euonymus obovatus;* (14) **yard,** a place where boards and other lumber are kept for sale, a lumber yard, also attrib.

(1) 1833 E. T. COKE *Subaltern's Furlough* ii, He has gone away without paying his tailor's bill, or his board bill. **1931** *Randolph Enterprise* (Elkins, W. Va.) 17 Sep. 5/4 Ralph Kesling charged with not paying a board bill. — **(2) 1812** *Boston Gazette* 9 July 3/4 (*advt.*), The other [cow], when she went away, had on a board blinder. — **(3) 1872** TALMAGE *Abom. Mod. Society* 112 The inevitable board-book that the operator carries in his hand may be as pure as the clothing merchant's ledger. [*c***1887** E. V. SMITH *Plain Truths* 13 The Board met at 11 A.M. and adjourned at 12. Each broker carried a small book in which the prices current and transactions of the day were recorded.] — **(4) 1867** *Atlantic Mo.* April 406/1 Father made a small board cart, into which he threw the chickens, the little pigs, and the young children.

(5) 1896 *Vt. Agric. Rep.* XV. 83 About 24 cubic feet per acre is added . . . annually—this means about 150 board feet. **1948** *Democrat* 23 Sep. 1/2 Sawmills in this county cut 66,963,000 board feet of pine . . . last year. — **(6) 1647** *Springfield Rec.* I. 190 No man shall hence forth transport out of the town to other places, any buildinge tymber, board loggs, or sawn boardes or planks. **1832** WILLIAMSON *Maine* II. 25 The General Court [in 1693] thought it expedient to encourage him, by permitting him to take board-logs from the public lands. — **(7) 1790** *Penna. Packet* 24 Aug. 3/4 The Partnership of M'Culloh and Peterson, board merchants, is this day disolved by mutual consent. — **(8) 1833** S. SMITH *Major Downing* 193 Two of the Senators . . . looked cross enough for a week to bite a board nail off. **1854** ——— *Way Down East* 62 Then father would look gritty enough to bite a board-nail off. — **(9) 1672** JOSSELYN *N. Eng. Rarities* 61 Board Pine, is a very large Tree two or three Fadom about. . . . It yields a very soveraign Turpentine for the Curing of desperate Wounds. **1675** ——— *Two Voyages* 64 The Pine-Tree challengeth the next place, and that sort which is called Board-pine is the principal.

(10) 1883 *Harper's Mag.* May 816/1 The board-room within is amphitheatre-shaped, and a bronze railing protects the circle of seats. **1900** S. A. NELSON *A B C Wall St.* 13 Most of the building, however, is an immense board room or hall. **1945** *Chi. D. News* 19 Oct. 20/4 These boys holding soft jobs and big pay in the boardrooms don't care about your children. — **(11) 1849** in ADAMS *Pioneer Hist.* (1923) 151 Numerous hired pedagogues whaled the rising generations of Mason six months of the year, at a salary of from $16 to $25 per month, and 'board 'round.' — **(12) 1705** BEVERLEY *Virginia* II. (1705) 9 The Wood grows at every Man's Door so fast, that after it has been cut down, it will in Seven Years time, grow up again from Seed, to substantial Fire-Wood; and in Eighteen or Twenty Years 'twill come to be very good Board-Timber. **1856** *Florida Plant. Rec.* 458, 2 [men] sawing bord timber.

(13) (*a*) **1878** GUILD *Old Times* 117 The first was interrogated very closely as to the cutting of some rail-timber and its value; the second, as to the cutting of five board trees. **1946** STUART *Plum Grove Hills* 228 Got so anymore there isn't enough good timber for a board tree. (*b*) **1945** KENNY *West Va. Place Names* 12 Today one rarely hears mention of the Cameron or board tree, yet West Virginia's maps contain two Board Tree Branch'es, a Board Tree Gap, and the village, Board Tree. — **(14) 1790** *Penna. Packet* 24 Aug. 3/4 The board-yard business is now carried on by John M'Culloh, at Mr. Thomas Morris's wharf. **1811** MEASE *Philadelphia* p. xii, An open space near the Delaware, in the southern part of the city, . . . has been rented for a board yard!! **1850** H. C. WATSON *Camp-Fires Revol.* 86 Jack White and I were peeping from behind a pile of logs in the old board-yard.

b. In the names of (official) bodies or groups: (1) *Board of Brokers,* (see quot.); (2) *of Education,* a group in a county, city, or state, charged with the direction and supervision of public schools within its jurisdiction; (3) *of Equalization,* =next; (4) *of Equalizers,* a board for equalizing state taxes; (5) *of Internal Improvements,* a board having charge of directing the internal improvements in a state; (6) *of Regents,* a governing board of a university; (7) *of Registrars,* in some states, a board for registering those entitled to vote; (8) *of Supervisors,* a board in a county, city, etc., charged with certain supervisory duties over matters relating to the public welfare; (9) * *of trade,* a chamber of commerce (see also quot. 1948); (10) *of Trustees,* a board for administering the affairs of a university.

(1) *c***1887** E. V. SMITH *Plain Truths* 13 The Board of Brokers, as it was called before it claimed to be entitled the New York Stock Exchange, commenced business with eighteen members, and met in a room over what was known as Jauncey's Stables, in Wall Street. — **(2) 1872** BRACE *Dangerous Classes N.Y.* 360 Four different classes of officers . . . namely, School-Visitors, the Board of Education, [etc.]. **1946** *Chi. D. News* 24 May 16/1 James B. McCahey has been re-elected president of the Board of Education for the 14th year. — **(3) 1837** PECK *New Guide* 207 Members and Clerks of the Board of Equalization. **1945** *Nashville Tennesseean* 19 Oct. 22/7 The state board of equalization will meet this morning to pass on several assessment appeal cases. — **(4) 1851** *Mich. Gen. Statutes* (1882) I. 167 The board of equalizers shall hear any evidence which may be laid before them.

(5) 1827 *Mass. Resolves 1824–8* 479 The Governor of the Commonwealth . . . is authorized to appoint . . . a Board of Internal Improvements, whose duty it shall be to attend to the examination of such routes for Canals and Railways, as the Legislature may . . . direct. — **(6) 1911** *Okla. Session Laws* 3 Legisl. 121 The Board of Regents of the State University . . . shall have the following additional power and duties. **1948** *Duncan* (Okla.) *D. Banner* 1 July 10/1 There would be nine members on the board of regents. — **(7) 1943** *Democrat* 1 July 1/2 The Clarke County Board of Registrars will meet in Grove Hill on Monday. — **(8) 1821** *Const. of State of N.Y.* Art. IV. VII., The board of supervisors in every county in this state, shall, at such times as the legislature may direct, meet together. **1947** *Pasadena* (Calif.) *Star-News* 9 Sep. 16/5 The suggestion will be considered tomorrow by the Board of Supervisors. — **(9) 1871** *Harper's Mag.* Aug. 415/2 Copies of the telegrams of 'probabilities' are also instantly sent to all boards of trade, chambers of commerce, merchants' exchanges, scientific societies, etc. **1886** *Harper's Mag.* July 207/2 No black-board in the elegant hall of the Chicago Board of Trade is so eagerly watched as that which, every five minutes, records the prices current in New York. **1901** *World's Work* Aug. 1068/2

Some manufacturers may consider that exhibiting at the many exhibitions and fairs . . . is poor advertising, but the boards of trade of leading California cities do not think so. **1948** *Chi. Tribune* 21 Mar. 1. 2/2 The Chicago Board of Trade, world's largest grain exchange, will be 100 years old April 3.

(10) 1807 *Ann. 10th Congress* 1 Sess. I. 1206 Mr. Newton, . . . to whom was referred . . . the petition of the Board of Trustees of the University of Vincennes, . . . made a report thereon. **1948** *Calif. Acad. Sci. Ann. Rep.* 4 Our Board of Trustees is now prepared to proceed actively with work looking to actual construction.

As the last term in **banking, base, beaver, bill, bleaching, bosom, box, bread, breast, buck, bulletin, call, canvassing, card, center, chair, checker, child, cooling, county, crap, dirt, double, dropping, finger, flap, foot, grave, guide, hand, health, index, jiggling, johnny, johnnycake, jolly, land, lazy, lighthouse, loading, mile, open, ouija, outside, papoose, parole, police, press, punch, returning, ridge, running, sand, school district, sea, seat, second, sign, spring, state, stock, summer, sweat, table, tally, teeter, treasury, wagon, walking, wash, washing board.**

* **board,** *v.*

1. *To board out*, to secure meals away from one's room or home, or outside of a college dormitory.

1655 *Harvard Coll. Rec.* III. 331 Noe student shall board or lye out of the Colledge without just Cause allowed by the President. **1734** *Harvard Rec.* I. 140 No Undergraduate shall lodge or board out of the College. **1818** DUNCAN *Travels* I. 146 'Boarding out,' as it is called, is now much less necessary, in consequence of the erection of two new buildings, with increased accommodation for lecture rooms and sleeping apartments. **1871** EGGLESTON *Hoosier Schoolm.* ix. 81 Ralph would not find it very pleasant 'boarding out' all the time he was entitled to spend at Pete Jones's.

b. To recover a debt by boarding with the debtor.

1829 *Detroit Gaz.* XII. 5 Mar. 4/2 Weighed, and found I had lost six pounds the past week . . . had a talk with Mr. B——, and concluded I had boarded out his share. **1864** TROWBRIDGE *Cudjo's Cave* ix. 83 It would be equally impossible for him ever to board it out.

2. *To board round* or *around:* **a.** *intr.* (See quot. 1828.) **b.** *tr.* To furnish (a teacher) with meals and lodging in different homes in turn.

a. 1828 *Ladies' Mag.* (Boston) I. 215 The Village Schoolmistress . . . I boarded *round*, as they termed it, that is, I boarded with every family in proportion to the number of scholars they sent. **1871** *Harper's Mag.* XLIII. 915/2 This was quite a luxury for the pedagogue of that district, who had heretofore been accustomed to 'board around.' **1923** ADAMS *Pioneer Hist.* 241 Not until well along in the '80's was the old system of having the teacher 'board 'round,' sampling all the viands in the district, as well as all the beds, done away with.

b. 1833 *Niles' Reg.* XLIV. 347/1 Our schoolmasters are . . . 'boarded round,' so as to save the drawing the pay of the schoolmaster's board from the school fund. **1876** JOSH BILLINGS *Wks.* 325 (F.), The school-committee . . . board him around the neighborhood.

3. *tr.* To go on or into a vehicle.

1848 BURNS *Notes* 108 About 10 in the forenoon we reached Warren, and then *boarded*, to use a Yankeeism, the stage for Cleveland. **1909** *Public Ledger* (Phila.) 24 June 7/1 The two men boarded a car on 20th street. **1947** *Atlantic Mo.* Nov. 46/1 Tommy Burton always boarded the eight-thirty at Stamford.

* **boarder,** *n.* An unprofitable dairy cow. — **1936** BARNARD *Rider* 226 He may not have the oratorical ability of Henry Johnston, but he possesses the information that enables him to determine a money-making dairy cow from a 'boarder.' **1938** NIXON *Forty Acres* 75 Other cooperative activities might include local breeding associations, for instance, to displace . . . those milch cows which are expensive boarders.

As the last term in **center, cow, day, self, star boarder.**

* **boarding,** *n.* and *a.* In combs.: (1) **boarding bill,** a board bill, *rare;* (2) **car,** a railroad car where those at work on a line of road can secure meals and sometimes sleeping accommodations; (3) **cottage,** a cottage at a resort where meals are served; (4) **hall,** a residence for students in which meals are served; (5) * **house,** (see quots.), *rare;* (6) **house runner,** one who solicits patronage for a boarding house; (7) **place,** a house, hotel, etc., where people board; (8) **round,** of a schoolteacher, the practice of having meals and room at different homes in turn; (9) * **school,** (see quot.), *slang;* (10) **shanty,** a shanty in which people board; (11) **stable,** a stable where horses are boarded; (12) **table,** a home in which meals are supplied to boarders.

(1) 1857 *Quinland* II. 159, I have finished with Dr. Spooney, my boarding bill is paid, a few dollars are left in my pocket. — **(2) 1867** *Com. & Fin. Chron.* 8 June 726 The equipment of the road consists of 132 broad and 18 narrow-gauge locomotives; and . . . 4 boarding and 8 wrecking cars. **1900** *Engineering Mag.* XIX. 794/1 Double deck boarding cars built by and in use on the St. Paul & Duluth R.R. — **(3) 1878** *Harper's Mag.* Feb. 336/1 The hotels, saloons, restaurants, and boarding cottages [of Atlantic City] . . . are innumerable. — **(4) 1868** *Mich. Agric. Rep.* VII. 17 Bill of boarding hall, $79.49. **1882** *Dakota Mission Conf. of M.E. Ch.* 3 Sess. 19 Two college boarding halls—one for ladies and one for gentlemen—are carried on.

(5) 1853 A. BUNN *Old Eng. & New Eng.* 64 Instead of the familiar sign of 'horses taken in to bait and stand at livery,' you may read stuck up, 'boarding-house for horses,' as if they were a set of human beings. **1859** MATSELL *Vocabulum* 13 Boarding-house. City prison; the Tombs. — **(6) 1840** DANA *Two Years* xxxvi. 459 The decks were filled with people; custom-house officers . . . and boarding-house runners. **1947** FISCHER *Focs'le Days* 80 The tough-looking individuals aboard were boarding-house runners from the dives along South and Cherry Streets. — **(7) 1854** M. CUMMINS *Lamplighter* xx. 170, [I] represented to her that I wanted a boarding-place for the winter. **1911** H. S. HARRISON *Queed* iii. 28 She runs this boarding-place, and people of various kinds come to her. — **(8) 1845** *S. Lit. Messenger* XI. 755/1, I was formally appointed 'schoolmaster' of the 'Octagon Schoolhouse,' upon the half a dollar per month and 'boarding round' basis. **1946** WILSON *Fidelity* 150 Though 'boarding round' had gone out of style at Fidelity, it was still customary for the teacher to spend a night at as many homes as possible. — **(9) 1859** MATSELL *Vocabulum* 13 Boarding-school. Penitentiary.

(10) 1848 MASON in E. Bryant *California* 457 A store was erected, and several boarding shanties in operation. — **(11) 1903** *N.Y. Tribune* 20 Sep. (*advt.*), Boarders wanted at Rochville Boarding Stable. **1905** *N.Y. Ev. Post* 27 Sep. 5 Many horses were suffocated . . . when fire destroyed the two-story boarding stable. — **(12) 1886** JAMES *Bostonians* 28 She had gone out to her supper; she got her supper at a boarding-table about two blocks off.

boasting dance. A dance by Indians. *Rare.* — **1833** CATLIN *Indians* I. 126 Dancing . . . may be seen in a variety of forms: such as the buffalo dance, the boasting dance, the begging dance, [etc.].

* **boat,** *n.* In combs.: (1) **boat battery,** a vessel, heavily armed and armored, designed for bombarding purposes, *obs.;* (2) **book,** a book for keeping accounts and other records on board a river boat, *obs.;* (3) **canal,** an artificial navigable waterway for boats, *obs.;* (4) **corn,** corn brought south by boat, *rare;* (5) **hand,** a laborer employed aboard a boat; (6) **horn,** (*a*) a horn for blowing used by boatmen in signaling, (*b*) (see quot.), *obs.;* (7) **landing,** a place on the bank of a river where boats stop to discharge or take on freight, passengers, etc.; (8) **ride,** a sail or row in a boat; (9) **shooting,** shooting ducks, etc., from a boat; (10) **sleigh,** (see quot. and cf. **steamboat 1. c.**); (11) **stone,** (see quot. 1907); (12) **store,** (*a*) *pl.* equipment, supplies, etc., needed aboard a boat, *obs.*, (*b*) (see quot.); (13) **tail,** =next; (14) **tailed grackle,** a large grackle, *Cassidix mexicanus major*, found in the southern states, having a tail a transverse section of which is V-shaped; (15) **water,** water navigable by boats, *rare;* (16) **yard,** a place where boats are built.

(1) 1864 PENNIMAN. *Tanner-Boy.* 178 The commanding officer . . . was authorized to turn him over to the captain of some boat-battery or transport. — **(2) 1831** *Louisville Public Advt.* 1 July, Boat Books —Ledgers, journals, freight, passage books. — **(3) 1813** *Ann. 13th Congress* 1 Sess. I. 49 The supply of water drawn from Elk river, by a feeder six miles in length, (already completed, which is itself a boat canal), . . . is calculated to fill . . . one hundred and forty-four locks. **1841** PARK *Pantology* 450 Ship Canals are usually 20 feet deep; sloop canals, 8 or 10 feet; and boat canals, from 3 to 6 feet deep. — **(4) 1849** *Rep. Comm. Patents: Agric.* (1850) 164 Every planter [of Miss.] . . . may secure a supply, at least six weeks before his main crop will ripen, by planting a few acres of *boat corn*, that is, corn . . . of a more northern climate, most commonly of Ohio or Kentucky.

(5) 1821 *Ann. 17th Cong.* 1 Sess. I. 46 This admiralty jurisdiction had done much to ruin those who were engaged in . . . [steamboat] navigation, by making the boat-hands unfaithful. **1880** *Harper's Mag.* Dec. 53 This simile is borne out by the action of the double stream of . . . colored boat hands. — **(6)** (*a*) **1835** CROCKETT *Tour* 87 One fellow tried to sing, that was not half up to a Mississippi boat-horn. **1946** RICHTER *Fields* 280 Oh, that was the liveliest sound in these woods, the music of a boat horn on the water. (*b*) **1838** C. MATHEWS *Motley Bk.* (1840) 149 A boat-horn . . . consists of the horn of an ox attached to the extremity of a wooden handle, and is used in our sloops and other river craft to wet the sails. — **(7) 1826** FLINT *Recoll.* 13 The first thing that strikes a stranger . . . arrived at the boat-landing [in

Pittsburgh], is the . . . spectacle of the varieties of water-craft. **1946** FOREMAN *Last Trek* 97 While waiting to be embarked on steamboats, they were located for the night near a boat-landing. — **(8) 1838** *N.Y. Mirror* 2 June 387/1 His nonsense will furnish us variety during our monotonous boat-ride. **1947** *Mazama* Dec. 56/1 Then for variety, a thrilling boatride up the 52-mile length of this loveliest of lakes. — **(9) 1874** LONG *Wild-Fowl* 21 In boat-shooting, . . . he uses *two* muzzle-loaders.

(10) 1937 MITCHELL *Horse and Buggy Age* 84 It was possible to charter one of those enormous boat sleighs drawn by six or eight horses and capable of accommodating anywhere from a score to half a hundred persons. — **(11) 1907** HODGE *Amer. Indians* I. 157/1 Boat-stones. Prehistoric objects of polished stone having somewhat the shape of a canoe, the use of which is unknown. **1917** MOOREHEAD *Stone Ornaments Amer. Indian* 76 The ruder boat-stones occur occasionally in the extreme South and throughout the Delaware-Hudson region, and New England. — **(12)** *(a)* **1835** A. PARKER *Trip to Texas* 12 They are all ornamented with grog-shops, containing, among other miscellaneous matter, an abundant supply of 'boat-stores.' **1841** CIST *Cincinnati* 42 Dealers in boat-stores, iron, [etc.]. *(b)* **1881** J. MCCABE *New York* 364 In the neighborhood of Christopher street are the 'boat stores,' curious looking floating edifices devoted mainly to the sale of oysters and fish. — **(13) 1857** *Rep. Comm. Patents: Agric.* 129 They [the red-winged starlings] move more gracefully and quickly than either the purple-grackle or the 'boat-tail' of the Southern States. **1934** *Nat. Geog. Mag.* LXVI. 126 The boat-tails . . . may often be seen wading clear up to their breasts in the shallows. — **(14) 1839** AUDUBON *Ornith. Biog.* V. 480 Boat-Tailed Grakle. *Quiscalus Major. Ib.*, The name of Boat-tailed Grakle has been of late given to our Common Crow Blackbird, *Quiscalus versicolor.* **1934** *Nat. Geog. Mag.* LXVI. 126 The Boat-Tailed Grackle (*Cassidix mexicanus major*).

(15) 1804 *Mass. H.S. Coll.* 2 Ser. VIII. 112 We left our canoes at the head of boat-waters, in a small clear stream of spring water. — **(16) 1805** R. H. COLLINS *Kentucky* (1874) I. 408 There are also . . . a coal yard and boat yard; and, it is said, several saltpetre caves. **1897** *Outing* XXX. 5/2 Before there was a sign of activity about any of the boatyards, a rumor was afloat . . . that six contracts had been let for first-class sloops.

b. *To lash boats,* (see quot.). *Obs.*

1834 C. D. ARFVEDSON *United States* II. 116 The boatmen travel about from boat to boat, make inquiries and acquaintances, agree to 'lash boats,' as it is called, and form alliances, to yield mutual assistance to each other on the way to New Orleans.

As the last term in **baggage, banana, berry, box, buffalo, bull, Chebacco, chip, cotton, day, down, Durham, Erie, family, fire, folding, freight, French, gun, Hampton, hay, horse, hunting, India rubber, jebacco, joe, John, keel, Kentuck, Kentucky, light, line, lumber, mackinaw, Mohawk, Monroe, morning, Moses, Moses-built, mud, New Orleans, news, ninety-day, Ohio, opposition, Orleans, oyster, packet, paddling, pass, pole, pound, pull, rawhide, religious, road, saloon, sand, Schenectady, scout, scow, scraping, sedge, shanty, show, sink, snag, sneak, steam, steam ferry, steam tow, sternwheel, stone, store, sucker, sugar, surface, team, tobacco, tobacco chebacco, torpedo, tow, trading, transfer, tule, twin, up, weed, whale, wharf, wheelbarrow, whitehall boat.**

***boat,** *v. intr.* To engage in the business of conveying by boat. *Rare.* — **1885** *Graceville* (Minn.) *Transcript* 3 June 2/1 Scores of men who have grown up on the canal are disposing of their boats at a sacrifice, and will boat no longer.

boatable ˈbotəbl̩, *a.* Navigable by boat.

1683 PENN *Descr. Pa. Wks.* (1782) IV. 315 The Schuylkill being an hundred miles boatable above the Jules. **1804** *Fredericktown* (Md.) *Herald* 4 Feb. 4/2 The Potomack is already boatable, without risque, below the mouth of the river Monocasy. **1888** *Harper's Mag.* Sep. 510/1 Occasionally a caribou is killed . . . while seeking the grass growing in some boatable stream. **1941** BALDWIN *Keelboat Age* 39 When Thomas Hart Benton and Governor William Clark of the Missouri Territory undertook to estimate the extent of the 'boatable waters' of the Mississippi Valley they arrived at a grand total of fifty thousand miles.

***boater,** *n.* As the last term in **shanty boater, steam boater.**

***boating,** *n.* As the last term in **keel boating, pole boating.**

***boatman,** *n.* As the last term in **keel boatman, Ohio boatman, shanty boatman.**

* **bob,** *n.*[1]

1. *On the bob,* as one is bobbing about, on the go. *Colloq.*

1834 CARUTHERS *Kentuckian* I. 21 You see he always took 'em on the bob, jist as you would shoot a diving bird. **1864** O. W. NORTON *Army Letters* 240 The status of the poor quartermaster may be graphically described as 'on the bob' from morning till night.

2. An attachment to the tail of a kite, serving to ballast it. Also fig.

1844 *Knickerb.* XXIV. 260 Once in a while a bob gets reinforced, just as the kite has nearly reached the ground. **1867** HOLMES *Guardian Angel* 198 Cut off the bobs of your kite . . . and see if it doesn't pitch, and stagger, and come down head-foremost.

3. A bobsled. Also attrib. Sometimes **bobs.**

1856 M. Y. JACKSON in *Minn. Farmers' Diaries* (1939) 145 Went to Kinnik-kinnik yesterday with the bobs. Had to stay over night & return to day with part of a load of lumber. **1888** *Troy D. Times* 31 Jan. (F.), The bob race will be held in the evening. **1945** PEARSON *Country Flavor* 109 A one-horse bob with its four tall, sturdy oak stakes is a good vehicle to handle.

4. *pl.* (See quot. *c*1873.)

1857 *Knickerb.* XLIX. 67 The 'stage' consisted of a rickety pair of bobs—an open box, of course—two miserably gaunt horses, and a Dutchman. *c***1873** DE VERE *MS Notes* 186 *Bobs*, short, stout sleds, 2 of which are gen[erally] placed under 1 sleighbox or wagon box and

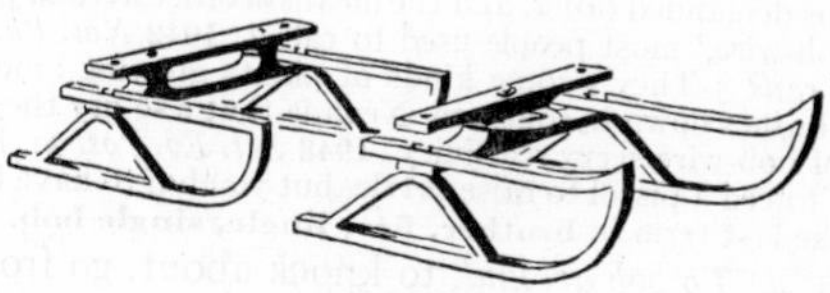

Pair of bobs

called a pair of bobs. **1898** *Mo. S. Dakotan* I. 134 Lucky the bobs are on the wagon, they don't make such a blamed racket as wheels. **1948** RITTENHOUSE *Vehicles* 53 In winter, any farm or commercial vehicle could be converted into a bobsled by simply attaching the body to 'bobs' such as these.

5. (See quot.)

1888–90 BARRERE-LELAND I. 230 Bob, to catch a bob (American), a boy's expression for getting on behind and taking a ride gratis; getting a lift.

bob bɑb, *n.*[2] Short for: **a. bobwhite. b. bobolink.**

(a) 1883 *Cent. Mag.* Aug. 483/2 The European partridge . . . weighs twice as much as Bob White, but he has not Bob's sturdy, rapid . . . flight. **1902** E. SANDYS & VAN DYKE *Upland Game Birds* 9 Then brave, brown Bob . . . enters Love's fateful lists. — **(b) 1912** *Outing* Oct. 228/2 Numbers of gay bobolinks drifted over, and sang as they traveled. Like the Lapland longspur, Bob does not believe in keeping his music till he reaches his summer home. **1923** MCATEE *Local Names Migratory Game Birds* 75 Bobolink (originally a New York and New England name, now in rather general use, not among gunners, however; sometimes nicked to Bob or Robert).

bob bɑb, *interj.* An intensive particle. *Colloq.*

1856 *Iroquois Republican* (Middleport, Ill.) 29 May 1/5 He can't get me with his big words, nosiree bob. **1859** *No. Californian* (Union) 22 June 1/5 A witness before Judge H—— of Missippi [*sic*], in answer to a question, replied 'Yes, siree, Bob!' **1909** *D.N.* III. 362 No, siree, Bob! **1947** *Amer. Wkly.* 2 Nov. 21/2 No sirree, Bob! Not me, boys.

* **bob-.** In combs.: (1) **bobcat,** the bay lynx or a wildcat; (2) **coat,** a bobtailed coat, *rare;* (3) **crackery,** gimcrackery, *rare;* (4) **Bob Ruly,** (see quot.), *obs.;* (5) **sawyer,** = **sawyer,** *obs.;* (6) **sled,** see as a main entry; (7) **sleigh,** a bobsled; (8) **sleighing,** riding for pleasure with a group in a bobsleigh; (9) **squirt,** a worthless young fellow, a whippersnapper, *colloq.;* (10) **tail,** see as a main entry; (11) **veal,** veal of a newly born or unborn calf; (12) **white,** see as a main entry; (13) **wire,** a colloquial variant of "barbwire."

(1) 1888 ROOSEVELT in *Cent. Mag.* March 656 We also keep hens, which, in spite of the damaging inroads of hawks, bob-cats, and foxes, supply us with eggs. **1946** R. PEATTIE *Pac. Coast Ranges* 120 If ever all the coyotes and lions and bobcats were gone, I wouldn't want to live in these hills. — **(2) 1835** LONGFELLOW *Outre-Mer* I. 64 The procession was led by a long orang-outang of a man, in a straw hat and white dimity bob-coat. — **(3) 1837** *Harvardiana* III. 238, I was dispatched . . . for a load of pumpkins and such other bob-crackeries. — **(4) 1848** COOPER *Oak Openings* I. 14 (*fn.*), This unfortunate name [Bois Brûlé], which it may be necessary to tell a portion of our readers means 'Burnt Wood,' seems condemned to all sorts of abuses among the linguists of the west. Among other pronunciations is that of 'Bob Ruly.'

(5) 1879 BISHOP *4 Months in Sneak-box* 65 This trap for careless sailors is a tree, with its roots held in the river's bottom, and its broken top bobbing up and down with the undulations of the current. Boatmen give it the euphonious title of 'bob sawyer' because of the bobbing and sawing motions imparted to it by the pulsations of the water. — **(7) 1853** STRICKLAND *Twenty-Seven Yrs.* II. 283 A large-sized mast, after being loaded on a bob sleigh, requires from twelve to sixteen span of horses or oxen to draw it. **1941** SETON *Trail of Artist-Naturalist* 38 Out in the yard stood the light bobsleighs with their wagon box on them. — (8) **1913** *Outing* Jan. 492/1 Balls, concerts and dances go hand in hand with ice skating, bob sleighing, bandy and skiing. **1948** *Sat. Review* 19 June 34/3 Polo and bob-sleighing apart, one can pursue pretty nearly every kind of sport. — (9) **1891** WILKINS *N. Eng. Nun* 26 S'pose they should turn you out in your old age an' call in some young bob squirt, how'd you feel? **1905** ——— *Debtor* 469 But you look as if you could do more and better work in an hour than that young bob-squirt.

(11) **1855** in DE VOE *Market Ass't* (1867) 421 He saw nine quarters of plated veal hanging up in a meat-shop in Grandstreet, which, if the whole nine quarters were tried out, after taking away the pork-fat, which the kidneys were placed with, enough fat could not be got out to grease a jackknife. Butchers call this *bob-veal*. **1945** WEBSTER *Town Meeting Country* 232 Deacon Osgood! How in hell be ye, Deacon? Sellin' much bob veal these days? — (13) **1929** DOBIE *Vaquero* 116 Chaos demanded order, and the means of order were to be barbed wire—'bob-wire,' most people used to call it. **1942** *Nat. Pk. Service, Fading Trails* 5 They's some kinds of plants growing amongst the creosote bushes down in southern Nevada that's so dry they'd make a piece of bob-wire seem real juicy. **1948** *Sat. Ev. Post* 31 July 54/2 You don't need a pistol to raise cattle, but you haf to have bob-wire.

As the last term in **brother, fire, jingle, single bob.**

* **bob,** *v.*[1] *To bob around*, to knock about, go from place to place. *Colloq.*

The popularity, and poss. the origin, of this expression may have been occasioned by a popular song "Bobbing Around," sung by Stephen C. Massett, a minstrel, in California mining camps during the fifties.

1855 *N.Y. Herald* 10 Dec. 4/2 All this time the loose Whigs of the South, and the twelfth section Know Nothings, have been 'bobbing around,' as if singly for the purpose of enforcing upon the Seward alliance the largest possible vote necessary to secure a majority. **1857** *Harper's Mag.* March 443/2 You may take me if you can catch me while I'm bobbin' around, but I can't stop for you. **1869** BROWNE *Adv. Apache Country* 182 She had prospected awhile in Australia, and bobbed around Frisco for the last few years. **1871** DE VERE 585 'Bobbing around' is . . . a favorite expression in the United States.

bob bɑb, *v.*[2] [f. *bob, n.*, a horse's tail docked short.] *tr.* To cut short or dock (a horse's tail, etc.).

1822 J. FOWLER *Journal* 112 We this day seen six wild Horses, tho two of them must have been in Hands, as their tails ware bobed short. **1889** *Cent.* 606/2 *Bob*, . . . to cut short; dock: often with off: as, to *bob* or *bob off* a horse's tail. **1894** *Cong. Globe* App. 11 Jan. 43/1 The [Republican] party . . . have adopted every English 'fad,' from a gold standard down to 'bobbing' their horses' tails.

bob bɑb, *v*3.[f. **bob,** *n.*[1] **3.**] *intr.* To ride or coast on a bobsled. — **1880** *Wisconsin Rep.* 254 For injuries suffered . . . by collision with persons 'bobbing' or 'coasting' on such street, the city is not liable. **1893** *Outing* Mar. 125/1 Grown men and women took to 'bobbing' because they liked the sensation of school-boyishness and girlishness it recalled.

bobbing ˈbɑbɪŋ, *n.* [f. **bob,** *n.*[1] **3.**] Riding on bobsleds or bobsleighs. Attrib. in contexts.

1888 *Troy D. Times* 31 Jan. (F.), All the village bobbing clubs will participate in the carnival at Albany tomorrow. . . . There are seventy-eight entries for the bobbing parade. **1888** *Harper's Mag.* May 973/1 Ruby and Ned displeased their mother by joining a 'bobbing' party on a neighbouring 'hill' street. **1893** *Outing* Mar. 125/2 The 'bobbing' party is always a gay one.

bobble ˈbɑbl̩, *n.* [f. *bobble, v.*] A mistake, a failure. *Colloq.*

1908 *St. Louis Globe-Democrat* 2 July 4/1 Wallace, Williams and Ferris starred in the fielding line for the Browns, Wallace accepting eight chances without a bobble. **1920** *Cosmopolitan* Aug. 101/1 The Committee on Arrangements had made it impossible for the Dinner to be a Bobble. **1948** *Galveston* (Tex.) *News* 14 June 7/2 Vidor got off to a shaky start, committing six bobbles.

bobolink ˈbɑbəˌlɪŋk, *n.* Also **bob-o-lincoln, bob-link,** etc. [f. its call.] The skunk blackbird, *Dolichonyx oryzivorus*, an American songbird found chiefly in the eastern and central states. Also transf. Cf. **prairie bobolink.**

1774 J. ADAMS *Works* II. 401 Young Ned Rutledge is a perfect Bob-o-Lincoln,—a swallow, a sparrow, a peacock. *a***1801** FESSENDEN *Orig. Poems* (1806) 146 In strains as sad as you can think on, In unison with bob-o-link horn. **1826** FLINT *Recollections* 243, I saw early in the spring a flock of those merry and chattering birds, that we call bob-a-link, or French black-bird. **1903** *Mich. Ornith. Club Bul.* March 11 In some sections the Bobolink is known only as the Skunk-head Blackbird, while the Towhee or Chewink is called Bobolink. **1947** *Sports Afield* Dec. 26/3 A bobolink poured out its tiny jugful of rhythmic melody.

b. The call-note of this bird.

1839 *Boston Transcript* 8 June 2/4 The songster then varied his note, 'Boblink—Boblink!' **1855** BRYANT *Robert of Lincoln* i, Robert of Lincoln is telling his name: Bob-o'-link, bob-o'-link, Spink, spank, spink.

bobolition ˌbɑbəˈlɪʃən, *n.* An alleged Negro variant of "abolition." Also attrib. *Obs.*

1818 (*title*), Bobolition of Slavery!!! Grand selebrashum by de Africum Shocietee!!! **1839** GAUND *Aristocracy* II. 137 For G——d's sake! cried the old gentleman; let us not have *bobolition*. **1861** F. MOORE *Rebellion Record* I. III. 126/2 Wake up, I tell yer! Git up, Jefferson! Bobolishion's comin'—Bob-o-lish-i-on. **1862** *Vanity Fair* 29 March (front cover), Gineral McClellan don't go strong 'nuff for Bobolition. **1898** EARLE *Customs Old N. Eng.* 226 The 14th of July was observed by Boston negroes for many years to commemorate the introduction of measures to abolish the slave trade. It was derisively called Bobalition Day, and the orderly convention of black men was greeted with a fusillade of rotten fruit and eggs and much jesting abuse.

Hence **bobolitionist,** *n.* — **1887** *Cent. Mag.* Apr. 845 Is dese yer bobolitionists got horns en huffs?

bobsled ˈbɑbˌslɛd, *n.*

1. A sled mounted on "bobs" (see **bob,** *n.*[1] **4.**) often used in hauling timber, etc. Also attrib.

1839 in *Amer. Sp.* (1948) Feb. 44/1 Then there would be wear and tear of bob-sled, teamster's wages, and your dead pull springs—the horses' knees. **1848** BARTLETT 40 *Bob-sled*, a sled prepared for the transportation of large timber from the forest to a river or public road. *Maine*. **1931** *K C. Times* 26 Dec. 14 Bob-sled parties were quite the thing. **1948** RITTENHOUSE *Vehicles* 53 In winter, any farm or commercial vehicle could be converted into a bobsled by simply attaching the body to 'bobs' such as these.

2. A sled for coasting made of two pairs of runners connected by a long board.

1890 *D.N.* I. 72 *Bob-sled*, a 'double-runner' (only of a boy's sled). **1891** *Amer. Folk-Lore* IV. 160 The 'double-runner' of New England becomes, however, on Long Island, a 'bob-sled,' or even a 'bob.' **1904** *N.Y. Ev. Post* 21 Jan. 11 Three boys are in the Englewood Hospital as the result of a collision between two bob sleds.

bobsled ˈbɑbˌslɛd, *v. intr.* To ride or coast on a bobsled. — **1883** PECK *Bad Boy* 154 You have got to be darn careful when you have the mumps, and not go out bob-sledding. **1945** MACDONALD *Egg & I* 18, I remember icicles . . . and bobsledding at night with Daddy.

* **bobtail,** *n.*

1. =**bobtail coat.** Also one who wears such a coat. *Obs.*

1824 *Free Press* (Halifax, N.C.) 17 Sep., Bobtails and hunting shirts! you are a set of d——d ignorant fellows. **1850** C. MATHEWS *Moneypenny* 61 The checker-board hat was changed to a fall beaver; . . . but the bob-tail and barber-pole were on duty in strong force. **1880** *Harper's Mag.* Feb. 358/1 Braddock's troops nicknamed the Virginia rangers, in derision at the scanty coats which Dinwiddie had given them, 'Bobtails.'

2. The spotted sandpiper or teeter-tail, *Actitis macularia.*

1841 *S. Lit. Messenger* VII. 77/1 Innumerable species of the snipe are every where to be met with, from the little Bobtail of the Sandbar, up to the Beccasse of the plain.

3. =**bob,** *n.*[1] **2.**

1844 *Knickerb.* XXIV. 251 'Brother Jonathan' made a long 'bobtail' [for the kite].

4. Short for **bobtail car.**

1875 *Chi. Tribune* 16 Oct. 11/3 Witness . . . [had] been conductor on a two-horse car since last May; . . . [and not] conductor on a 'bobtail.'

5. In colloq. or slang combs.: (1) **bobtail car,** (see quots.); (2) **coat,** a short coat; (3) **cuss,** a term of mild disparagement for a short person; (4) **discharge,** a dishonorable discharge; (5) **flush,** =**bobtailed flush,** also fig.; (6) **representation,** (see quot.); (7) **streetcar,** (see quot.); (8) **train,** a train not having its full complement of coaches, *rare.*

(1) **1875** *Chi. Tribune* 8 Sep. 8/2 The bobtail cars ought to be taken off the streets right away, or conductors put on them. **1889** FARMER 71 Bobtail Car.—The popular name for a small tram-car horsed by a single animal, and on which the only official is a driver. **1948** *Nebr. Hist.* March 17 The bob-tail car had a ten foot car body, with five windows on a side, a driver's platform in front and a step but no platform in the rear. — (2) **1832** KENNEDY *Swallow Barn* II. 5 A shad-bellied blue bobtail coat . . . was well adapted to show the breadth of his brawny chest. **1880** MARK TWAIN *Tramp Abroad* xxxv. 400 They gave my bobtail coat to somebody else, and sent me an ulster suitable for a giraffe. — (3) **1856** *Spirit of Times* (N.Y.) 25 Oct. 130/2 He was a leetle yaller bob-tail cuss, but he could run. — (4)

1886 *Outing* Dec. 227/2 Upon the expiration of his first enlistment, he was given what is called a *bobtail* discharge, a discharge without character.

(5) **1875** *Cin. Enquirer* 2 July 2/3 The gentlemen have shown their hand a little too soon, and, in our opinion, can not 'bluff' to any success on their 'bob-tail flush.' **1894** Chopin *Bayou Folk* 2 Mr. Wallace Offdean hurried to the bank in order to replenish his portemonnaie which had been materially lightened at the club through the medium of unpropitious jack-pots and bobtail flushes. **1948** *Houston* (Tex.) *Post* 14 June 10/1 At Yalta and Teheran old Joe took Roosevelt's aces with a bobtail flush, paving the way for the troubles and tribulations of the cold war. — (6) **1880** *Cong. Rec.* 6 May 3078/2 The Territories have only a part of what is called here 'bobtail' representation, a power to speak but not to vote. — (7) **1895** Wait *Car-Builder's Dict.* 11 Bob-tail street-car. A term used to designate a street-car with a platform in front only and a small step behind. Such cars are usually drawn by one horse only. — (8) **1873** *Newton Kansan* 5 June 3/3 The 'bob-tail' train to Hutchinson is taken off entirely.

* **bobtailed,** *a.* In colloq. uses.

1. Denoting vehicles curtailed in some respect.

1875 *Chi. Tribune* 16 Oct. 11/3 The witness professed ignorance in regard to public feeling being against 'bobtailed' cars. **1881** Marshall *Through Amer.* (1882) 29 A bobtailed stage or car is one without a conductor or man to collect the fares, there being a box inside with a slit in the top, into which the passenger is trusted to drop the exact amount of the fare. **1901** White *Westerners* i. 4 He owned . . . a light, two-wheeled wagon of the bob-tailed type. **1906** *Out West* May 438 [With] modern transit . . . Los Angeles, for instance, could be forty miles square and still 'nearer together' than the little island of New York was with its bob-tailed horse cars of ten years ago.

2. Denoting a coat shorter than usual.

1843 Stephens *High Life N.Y.* II. 203, I got on my figgered vest and my little bob-tailed coat. **1856** Snodgrass [Mark Twain] in *Keokuk Sat. Post* 1 Nov. 9 Then some soldiers with bobtailed tin coats on (high water coats we used to call 'em in Keokuk) come in.

3. bobtailed flush, (see quot. 1944).

1873 *Winfield* (Kansas) *Courier* 15 Feb. 1/5 For a little man Senator Allen could play a pretty large game. The clerical part of the House was also well up in all the mysteries of a 'pair' or a 'bobtailed flush.' **1922** McNeal *When Kans. Was Young* 265 The western man . . . declared that a bob-tailed flush was just as good as the real thing if you only had the nerve to bet it high enough, and at the same time look as if you really held the cards. **1944** *N. & Q.* Sep. 85/1 Bobtailed Straight Or Flush: a three-card (and therefore worthless) straight or flush in a five-card poker hand; a term hitherto confined to the South but apparently in general use at present in the Army.

bobwhite ˈbɑbˈhwaɪt, *n.* [Imitative.]

1. The call or note of the quail or partridge.

1812 Wilson *Ornithol.* VI. 25 The quail . . . will sometimes sit, repeating, at short intervals, 'Bob White,' for half an hour at a time. **1884** Aldridge *Life on Ranch* 195 The cheerful 'Bob White' of the quails can be heard any day during the breeding season without going out of doors. **1917** Eaton *Green Trails* 112 He could sit down in a field by the edge of the woods, motion me to silence, and then whistle 'Bob White' till sometimes a whole flock of quail would be gathered on the ground about us.

2. A quail of the genus *Colinus*, esp. *C. virginianus*. Cf. also **masked bobwhite.**

1837 *N.Y. Mirror* 18 Nov. 164/3 Only thou, dear Bob White . . . will remain. **1886** Van Dyke *So. Calif.* 77 Bob White is one of nature's noblemen. **1945** *N. Eng. Homestead* 13 Oct. 6/4 The bob-white is a special friend as well as a popular game bird and will readily take advantage of bushy fence rows.

Also as a plural. — **1948** *Sierra Club Bul.* Mar. 16 Working with bobwhite, he was able to demonstrate that the number of birds present in the spring is determined by the suitability of the winter range.

b. Also **bobwhite quail.**

1920 *Outing* Oct. 15/1 No birds in the United States . . . lie as well to the dog as bob-white quail. **1948** *Durant* (Okla.) *Dly. Democrat* 4 July 2/2 Artificial propagation of bob white quail at the state game farm may mean more this year than ever before.

c. (See quot.)

1894 *Outing* xxiv. 227/1 Bass flies of proved merit include the bob white, grizzly queen, grizzly king.

boca ˈbokə, *n.* [Sp. in same sense.] The mouth of a river, gorge, etc. Also in proper names.

1832 *Boston Transcript* 4 May 2/2 On Saturday last, the crowd of bathers was immense, amounting we might say to thousands, who occupied the banks of the river from the Boca to the Recoleta. **1896** *Land of Sunshine* June 16 At the right the gorge narrows to the *Bocas*, grim and practically impassable, by which it enters the Rio Grande's chasm. **1947** *Field & Stream* June 21/2 Useppa Island is only twenty minutes by boat from both Boca Grande and Captiva passes.

bock bɑk, *n.* [G. *bockbier.*] A dark, extra strong variety of beer, brewed in December and January and drunk in spring. In full **bock beer.**

1856 *Ill. State Reg.* 26 June 4/3 There is a Bavarian lager beer which is called 'bock'—in English buck or goat—and is so called because of its great strength making its consumers prance and tumble about like these animals. [**1869** *New No. West* (Deer Lodge, Mont.) 13 Aug. 3/1 His 'buck' beer is the delight of Teutonic bibulists.] **1897** F. Norris *Stories & Sk.* (1931) 65 An open car had appeared on the crosstown cable line and Bock beer was on draught at the 'Wein Stube,' and Polk Street knew that Spring was at hand. **1932** *K.C. Times* 5 March 26 That causes the Mail to recall that it is almost the season of the year when bock beer signs appeared.

bockey ˈbɑkɪ, *n.* [Du. *bakje*, cup, bowl.] (See quots.) *Obs.* — **1848** Bartlett 41 *Bockey*, a bowl, or vessel made from a gourd. A term probably derived from the Dutch, as it is peculiar to the city of New York and its vicinity. **1880** *Harper's Mag.* May 826/1 There was an abundance of flip and toddy in *bockjes*, or wooden bowls.

bodega boˈdigə, *n.* [Sp. in same sense. An Amer. borrowing.] A wineshop or liquor store.

1849 *N.O. Picayune* 10 May 4/1, I found the *bodega* and poor old Bocanega; the proprietor of the same. **1855** *N.Y. Herald* 14 Nov. 3/4 The police . . . traced Sanchez to a *bodega* (grocery) where he had been in the habit of going to drink. **1910** *Sat. Ev. Post* 8 Oct. 4/3 In one bodega there was quite a crowd.

bodewash ˈbodˌwɑʃ, *n. W.* (See quots.) *Obs.* Cf. **bois de vache.** — **1871** De Vere 110 *Bodewash* . . . [is] the *Buffalo Chips* of the Western hunter and trader. **1877** Bartlett 56 *Bodewash.* (Fr. *bois de vache.*) Dried cow-dung, used for fuel on the treeless plains of the Far West.

bodily exercise, =**exercise,** *n.* **2.** *Obs.*

1824 R. H. Bishop *Hist. Church Ky.* 353 The first bodily exercise, which appeared in our worshipping assemblies, was *falling*. **1834** *Biblical Repertory* VI. 338 Here was the commencement of disorder and confusion. The sermon had scarcely commenced, when some one or more would become the subject of *bodily exercise*. This was commonly called the *falling exercise;* or, as it was often said, such and such an one was *'struck down.'* **1850** Gallaher *Western Sketch-Book* 32 The Falling Down. This was one of the forms of that *bodily exercise*, as it was then called, which accompanied this remarkable work. **1944** Duncan *M. Graham* 22 From the child's earliest months until he was three years old, the hotly belabored question of 'bodily exercises' at camp meetings took the center of the Brush Creek stage.

bodock ˈbodɑk, *n. S.W.* Also **bowdark, bodarc, bodok,** etc. [f. F. *bois d'arc.*] =**bois d'arc.** Cf. **bowwood, brasswood, osage orange.**

1844 Gregg *Commerce of Prairies* II. 199 In many of the rich bottoms from the Canadian to Red River . . . is found the celebrated *bois d'arc* . . . usually corrupted in pronunciation to *bowdark*. **1871** De Vere 110 The Osage Orange . . . was called *bois d'arc* by French settlers; the unfamiliar name became in the hands of English hunters *Bowdark*. **1933** *Amer. Sp.* Feb. 48 Bodark, n. The Osage orange or *bois d'arc*, a tree which is very common in the prairie country north and west of the Ozark hills.

* **body,** *n.*

1. An area *of* land or timber.

[**1635** in *Amer. Sp.* XV. 156/2 The body of the land lyeth South East into the woods.] **1700** *Providence Rec.* IV. 199 A heape of stones neere a small rock . . . is the Norwesterne Cornner of the said Body of land. **1857** *Lawrence* (Kansas) *Republican* 4 June 3 It is beautifully situated . . . near a heavy body of timber. **1899** Green *Va. Word-Book* 63 He has a good *body* of land on the river.

2. The walls of a log cabin. *Rare.*

1844 Lee & Frost *Oregon* xxii. 275 Mr. Smith . . . had laid up the body of a log cabin, about fifteen feet square, and was living in it without floor or roof.

3. In combs.: (1) **body meeting,** (see quot.), *obs.;* (2) **pew,** (see quot. 1877).

(1) **1823** Tudor *Otis* 418 [At Boston in 1773] a body-meeting was an assembly after public notification, at which any citizens might attend, and at which many of the principal inhabitants of the neighbouring towns attended. . . . These body meetings were in fact, only an orderly, well regulated mob. — (2) **1823** *Baptist Mag.* IV. 145 Elder A—— requested those who were willing to own themselves concerned for their souls, to seat themselves in the body pews. **1877** Bartlett 608 Slip, . . . in New England, a long seat or narrow pew in a church with or without doors, in contradistinction to the old-fashioned 'square' or 'body pew.' **1891** M. W. Freeman *N. Eng. Nun* 108 In one of the foremost body-pews sat John Arnold.

b. *body and breeches*, wholly, entirely. *Slang.*

1878 *Cong. Rec.* 12 April 2492/1 The yankee notions produced by Newark every year will buy out, body and breeches, any thoroughly Democratic State in the Union. **1901** W. A. White in *McClure's Mag.*

Dec. 151/2 Platt . . . got nearly to the door; then turned back, and surrendered, body and breeches.

As the last term in **dog, home, pick up, wagon body.**

* **bog,** *n.* In combs.: (1) **bog birch,** *local,* the Indian cherry or yellow wood, *Rhamnus caroliniana;* (2) **hoe,** a hoe used in cutting up and removing hummocks in bog meadows; (3) **lime,** an impure earthy form of calcium carbonate deposited in lakes and ponds, chiefly through the agency of aquatic plants; (4) **meadow,** meadow that is exceptionally wet, marshy, or swampy; (5) **mouse,** (see quot.); (6) **onion,** any one of various plants, as the royal fern, jack-in-the-pulpit, etc., somewhat resembling an onion, also the root of such a plant; (7) **plow,** a kind of plow used in removing bogs or grass hummocks from land; (8) **potato,** a species of wild potato found in swampy places, *obs.;* (9) **rider, riding,** *W.* (see quots.); (10) **sucker,** (see quot.); (11) **torch,** (see quot. 1909); (12) **willow,** (see quots.).

(1) **1897** SUDWORTH *Arborescent Flora* 298 *Rhamnus Caroliniana.* . . . Common names [are] . . . Stinkwood (La.), Bog Birch (Minn.). — (2) **1854** THOREAU *Walden* 221 My host . . . worked 'bogging' for a neighboring farmer, turning up a meadow with a spade or bog hoe. **1874** *Vt. Bd. Agric. Rep.* II. 551 Then with axes, potato hooks, and bog hoes, the turf was all peeled off. — (3) **1840** in *Mich. Agric. Soc. Trans.* (1853) 298 This condition is that which is very commonly designated as '*bog-lime.*' **1856** *Ib.* VII. 367 It is . . . scarcely known to our farmers that marl, or bog lime, may be used with . . . profit. — (4) **1748** ELIOT *Field-Husb.* i. 4 The Bog Meadow [will be] the next in Charge, because the Bogs must be cut up with a Bog Plough or with the Hoe. **1843** *Nat. Hist. N.Y., Geology* I. 371 The argillite portion of the county of Orange embraces an unusual number . . . of swamps, or, as they are called, bog meadows. **1860** *Harper's Mag.* April 583/2 They turned short to the left in the direction of the road, and in a few moments found themselves in an open space of bog meadow.

(5) **1857** *Rep. Comm. Patents: Agric.* 84 Where several species [of meadow-mice] are found in one locality, they are commonly considered by farmers as one animal, known under various names, as . . . 'Ground Mice,' 'Bog Mice,' &c. — (6) **1832** WILLIAMSON *Maine* I. 120 The Brake, of which there are several varieties, the root of which is sometimes called the 'bog-onion,' . . . is good for sprains. **1880** ROLLINS *N. Eng. Bygones* 32 Bog onions curled their brown coils against the rocks. **1892** *Amer. Folk-Lore* V. 104 *Arisæma triphyllum,* bog onion. — (7) **1748** [see **bog meadow**]. — (8) **1800** B. HAWKINS *Sk. Creek Country* 21 In the old beaver ponds, in thick boggy places, they have the bog potatoe. — (9) **1913** W. C. BARNES *Western Grazing Grounds* 122 Generally in the Southwest the cattle began to 'bog down' in March, and bog-riding was necessary until the cows began to gain strength, which was in May. **1920** HUNTER *Trail Drivers Texas* I. 299 A 'bog rider' is the cowboy who 'tails' up the poor cows which get stuck in the mud.

(10) **1897** *Ann. Rep. Comm. of Fisheries* 322 *Philohela minor* Gmelin. American woodcock. Popular synonyms: Bog-sucker; mud snipe; blind snipe. — (11) **1909** *Cent. Supp.* Bog-torches. . . . The golden-club, *Orontium aquaticum:* so called from the shape and color of its flower-stalk and flowers. **1934** *Nat. Geog. Mag.* LXV. 599 The swamp boatman amuses himself by pushing the dark-green blades of the bog torch beneath the water and watching them emerge to justify their local name of 'never-wets.' — (12) **1833** EATON *Botany* (ed. 6) 319 *S[alix] discolor,* bog willow, red-root willow. **1892** APGAR *Trees Northern U.S.* 166 Glaucous or Bog Willow . . . [is] a very variable species, common in low meadows and on river banks.

As the last term in **caribou bog, cranberry bog.**

* **bog,** *v. tr.* and *intr.* To clear (land) of bogs, or grass tussocks, to remove hummocks from a bog meadow. *Obs.* — **1680** *Springfield Rec.* I. 430 Denton is to . . . occupy & improve the whole said medow, provided he do bog & clean the said medow. **1854** THOREAU *Walden* 221 My host . . . worked 'bogging' for a neighboring farmer, turning up a meadow with a spade or bog hoe.

bogan ˈbogən, *n.* (See quot.) Cf. **logan,** *n.* — **1903** *Amer. Folk-Lore* Apr.–June 128 A word much used by guides and others who go into the New Brunswick woods is bogan—a still creek or bay branching from a stream—exactly the same thing the Indians call a pokologan and I think the former is a corruption of the latter word.

bogue bog, *n. S.* [Amer. F., f. Choctaw *bok, bouk,* creek, stream, shortened f. *báyuk.* See **bayou.** For the use of this word in place names, Bogalusa, Bogue Chitto, Bogue Falaya, see Read p. 157.] **1.** (See quots.) *Obs.* **2.** A nickname for an inhabitant of western Florida. *Obs.*

(1) **1826** FLINT *Recoll.* 317 The rivers that run through these level and swampy pine forests, are called, in the Indian language, 'Bogue,' with some attribute denoting the character of the stream. **1923** *Arrow Points* 5 Jan. 4 Many of the streams in the Choctaw country carry the affix 'Bogue,' in designating their present name. **1931** W. A. READ *La.-French* 157. — (2) **1826** FLINT *Recollections* 319 They are a wild race, with but little order or morals among them; they are generally denominated 'Bogues,' and call themselves 'rosin heels.'

bogue bog, *v.* [Of obscure origin. Cf. **brogue,** *v.*] *intr.* To go around, walk about, take part *in. Colloq.*

1775 G. W. RAUCK *Boonesborough* 179 [We] were four days boguing in the woods seeking the way. **1867** LOWELL *Biglow P.* II. p. lvii, I don't git much done 'thout I *bogue* right in along 'th my men. **1870** DUVAL *Big-Foot Wallace* 132 The first thing he knows he will have his 'hair lifted,' 'boging' about alone, with nothing but that 'pop-gun' of his to fight with. **1889** *Cent.* 611/2 *To bogue in,* to 'sail in'; take a hand; engage in a work. (Local, New England.) **1944** *D.N.* Nov. 40 *bogue around:* vb. To wander around aimlessly, restlessly, and nervously. Albermarle Co., Va. Reported.

bogus ˈbogəs, *n.*[1] [See note.]

The origin of this term is obscure. In the *OED s.v.* it is said that its use with reference to an apparatus for coining false money was inspired by the mysterious-looking nature of one of these objects found in the hands of a gang of coiners at Painesville, Ohio, in May, 1827. A bystander called the thing a "bogus" and this name was adopted in the *Painesville Telegraph.* The word may thus be connected with *EDD tantrabobus, tantarabobus,* a name for the devil or a bogie. Charles P. G. Scott in *Trans. Amer. Phil. Ass'n.* XLII. (1911), 157–74, derives **bogus** from *barghest* (see *EDD*), a ghost, goblin, bogie.

1. An apparatus for making counterfeit money. Also **bogus press, bogus machine.** *Obs.*

1827 *Painesville* (Ohio) *Telegraph* 6 July He never procured the casting of a Bogus at one of our furnaces. *Ib.* 2 Nov., The eight or ten boguses which have been for some time in operation. **1844** *Spirit of Times* 12 Oct. (Th.), A bogus press for making counterfeit money was dug up near Lyme, Huron County, Pa., on Monday last. **1850** *Frontier Guardian* 23 Jan. (Th.), We employed that same Bill Hickman to ferret out a bogus press and a gang of counterfeiters. . . . A part of the bogus machine has been found here in Mulholland's possession.

2. Counterfeit money made on a bogus. Also fig. *Obs.*

1839 MRS. KIRKLAND *New Home* xxxii. (1840) 227 The boxes of the 'real stuff' . . . contained a heavy charge of broken glass and tenpenny nails, covered above and below with half-dollars, principally 'bogus.' **1842** *Life in West* 297 They had attempted to pass bogus (base coin). **1848** W. E. BURTON *Waggeries* 90 No luggage, nor no nothing, but a roll of bogus. **1853** B. YOUNG *Journal Discourses* I. 270 (Th.), [The Magicians of Egypt] produced a very good bogus, but it was not quite the true coin. **1875** G. P. BURNHAM *Three Years* p. iv, *Bogus,* counterfeit bank notes, or false coins of any kind.

attrib. **1841** *S. Lit. Messenger* VII. 54/1, I am a minter, A bogus moulder, from about Sandusky. **1844** *Nauvoo Neighbor* 12 June (Th.), To bolster up the interests of blacklegs and bogus-makers. **1850** *Frontier Guardian* 23 Jan. (Th.), James M. Mulholland was one of the principal actors in the bogus business. **1943** MORGAN *Humboldt* 209 At the time of the Mormon migration . . . he had made himself useful along the Missouri River bottoms, breaking up a gang of bogus-makers.

b. Any counterfeit article.

1857 *Knickerb.* XLIX. 278 Don't run your bogus [*sc.* cigars] on me this time. **1944** *Chi. D. News* 13 Nov. 1/2 The broadcast . . . was officially described in London as 'obviously an enemy propaganda story' and 'a complete bogus.'

c. *Journalism.* (See quot. 1886.) Also attrib.

1886 MARK TWAIN *Speeches* (1910) 184 (R.), Well, we did have one or two kinds of 'bogus.' . . . To make up for short matter we would 'turn over ads'—turn over whole pages and duplicate it. The other 'bogus' was deep philosophical stuff, which we judged nobody ever read; so we kept a galley of it standing, and kept on slapping the same old batches of it in every now and then. **1948** *Time* 3 May 65/1 The New York publishers wanted to kill the costly 'bogus rule' that the I.T.U. had been writing into contracts for more than 40 years.

bogus ˈbogəs, *n.*[2] Short for **calibogus.** *Obs.*

1848 BARTLETT 40 *Bogus,* a liquor made of rum and molasses. **1871** DE VERE 444 *Bogus,* the name of a beverage . . . is occasionally heard in the Eastern States, especially among fishermen. **1898** EARLE *Customs Old N. Eng.* 179 'Calibogus,' or 'bogus,' was cold rum and beer unsweetened.

bogus ˈbogəs, *a.* [f. **bogus,** *n.*[1]] Spurious, counterfeit, fraudulent.

1838 in HUNT *Hist. Mormon War* (1844) 206 During the free career of Oliver Cowdery and David Whitmer's bogus-money business, information got abroad into the world that they were engaged in it. **1857** *Lawrence* (Kansas) *Republican* 11 June 2 They ask us to *humble* to those bogus laws. **1880** MARK TWAIN *Letters* (1917) I. xx. 377 The small bogus king has a . . . cussed time of it on the throne. **1948** *Chi. D. News* 8 Sep. 1/7 She was sentenced to a year in the County Jail . . . for cashing bogus checks.

bogusly ˈbogəslɪ, *adv.* In a fraudulent manner. *Rare.* — **1862** *N.Y. Herald* 2 May, When this post office came under the rebel government, and the oath was sent to us, we filed it bogously [*sic*], and sent it to Richmond without swearing to it.

***bohea tea.** A local name for the carrion flower. — **1833** Eaton *Botany* (ed. 6) 343 *Smilax herbacea*, bohea tea. **1839** in *Mich. Agric. Soc. Trans.* VII. 419.

***Bohemian,** *n.* A newspaper reporter. Also attrib. *Obs.*

1861 Browne *Four Years in Secessia* (1865) 14 The nineteenth-century Bohemians narrate the acts of others; make their name and fame without themselves gaining any glory. **1864** *Gold Hill* (Nev.) *News* 25 Jan. 2/3 Notwithstanding his antipathy for 'Bohemians,' I shall be present on the occasion, and take down his message phonographically and send it to you. **1872** *Las Cruces* (N.M.) *Borderer* 3 July 2/1 This specimen of newspaper Bohemian made the trip in the interest of a Cincinnati paper. **1884** Hill *Colo. Pioneers* 186 A few years later, following up my Bohemian life, as reporter for a newspaper, I drifted.

***Bohn,** *n.* (See quot. 1856.) *Slang. Obs.* — **1855** *Songs of Yale* (1860) 40 'Twas plenty of skin with a good deal of Bohn. **1856** Hall *College Words* (ed. 2) 32 *Bohn*, a translation; a pony. The volumes of Bohn's Classical Library are in such general use among undergraduates in American colleges, that *Bohn* has come to be a common name for a translation.

bohunk ˈbohʌŋk, *n.* [*Bo*hemian + *Hun*garian.] Originally an unskilled laborer from the region of the former Austria-Hungary or Bohemia, now any low-class, rough looking fellow, esp. one from southern or southeastern Europe. Also attrib. *Slang.* Cf. **Hunk,** *n.*[2]

1903 *Cin. Enquirer* 9 May 13/1 Bohunk—A Bohemian; a foreigner. **1910** *Butte* (Mont.) *Ev. News* 24 July 1 The bohunk miner is a low grade foreigner who buys his job from the foreman and pays him for keeping it. **1927** Eubank *Horse & Buggy Days* 75 The steers went over the hill at about the same rate of speed a Bohunk dishwasher turns the corner in dodging the police. **1946** Thompson *Am. Daughter* 112 Knudt called them flat-headed Polacks or square-headed bohunks.

***boil,** *n.* A turbulent swirl or eddy in a river, usu. with reference to the Mississippi. Cf. **boiling pot.**

1805 Clark in *Lewis & C. Exped.* (1904) III. 151 In those narrows the water was agitated in a most shocking manner, boils, swells, & whorlpools [*sic*]. **1826** T. Flint *Recoll.* 87 The Mississippi . . . is full of singular boils, where the water rises with a strong circular motion. **1875** Mark Twain *Old Times* iii. (1876) 59 Those tumbling 'boils' show a dissolving bar and a changing channel there. **1948** *Dly. Oklahoman* (Okla. City) 4 June 8/1 The water churned through in boils, and seeped up on the inner side.

***boiled,** *a.* Also ***biled** (humorous or illit.) In combs.: (1) **boiled cake,** (see quot.), *obs.;* (2) **cider,** cider that has been brought to a boil to preserve it, also attrib.; (3) **corn,** (see quot.), *colloq.;* (4) **crow,** see **crow;** (5) **dinner,** a dinner consisting chiefly of meat, usu. corned beef, and vegetables boiled together, cf. **New England boiled dinner;** (6) **dish,** =**boiled dinner,** also **boil dish,** *colloq.;* (7) **goods,** =**boiled shirt,** *obs.;* (8) **owl,** see **owl;** (9) **pie crust,** (see quot.), *rare;* (10) **rag,** =next; (11) **shirt,** orig. a shirt boiled in washing contrasted with one merely doused in cold water, later a starched shirt, esp. a white one with a stiff bosom; (12) **shirted,** *a.* clad in a boiled shirt, *rare.*

(1) 1895 *D.N.* I. 387 Doughnut . . . was biled-cakes if in twisted form . . . on Cape Cod, and generally in Eastern Mass. — **(2) 1705** *Lancaster Rec.* 153 They drank a barell of boyled Cyder & a barell of Strong bear. **1832** *Louisville Public Advt.* 13 March, 25 bbls. boiled cider, for sale. **1948** *Amer. Sp.* Feb. 49 Boiled cider is boiled . . . to get rid of whatever alcoholic content it has, and to bring its non-alcoholic contents to such concentration as shall tend to prevent the formation of any alcohol in it. — **(3) 1836** *Quarter Race Ky.* (1846) 14 Colonel, let us have some of your byled corn [=whisky]—pour me out a buck load.

(5) 1805 *Pocumtuc Housewife* (1906) 9 Directions for a Boiled Dinner may seem unnecessary. **1886** Poore *Reminisc.* I. 384 She could . . . prepare the old-fashioned New Hampshire 'boiled dinner.' **1944** Holton *Yankees* 245 'I'm going to have a boiled dinner.' And a boiled dinner she had, regardless of protest. — **(6) 1895** A. Brown *Meadow-Grass* 269 Do you remember how you used to come over an' eat cold b'iled dish for supper? **1907** *D.N.* III. 182 Boil-dish, n. New England boiled dinner. — **(7) 1892** *Outing* Feb. 361/1 The sombrero and flannel shirt he scorned and sported a derby and 'biled' goods instead. — **(9) 1844** Featherstonhaugh *Excursion* 50 But it turned out they had no bread even of Indian corn, and in its place the landlady placed before us a filthy-looking mess of what she called *boiled pie-crust.* **(10) 1861** Artemus Ward in *Vanity Fair* 23 Feb. 95/1 The Shakers axed me to go to their meetin, as they was to hav services that mornin, so I put on a clean biled rag and went. **1886** *Outing* May 167/1 For the first time since leaving port I wore 'boiled rags' as the mate calls them. — **(11) 1851** A. T. Jackson *Forty-niner* (1920) 113 He had shaved his beard off, except his mustache, and was dressed up in a 'biled shirt.' **1872** Mark Twain *Roughing It* lvii. 416 The miners [of Calif.] . . . had a particular and malignant animosity toward what they called a 'biled shirt.' **1948** *Time* 17 May 73/1 Socialites in boiled shirts or mink coats and plainer citizens in their Sunday best swarmed in to take over every one of the 3,300 seats. — **(12) 1869** *New No. West* (Deer Lodge, Mont.) 23 July 2/5 There [are] now confined in the county jail . . . a Frenchman who went 'daft' on quartz, and a 'boiled shirted' gent, who put a 'head' on his girl.

***boiler,** *n.* In combs.: (1) **boiler deck,** (see quot. 1830), [Ramsay points out that this was not the lower deck, as in *OED*, but "part of the upper deck, and *above* the main deck"]; (2) **plate,** stereotyped matter supplied to small publishers, esp. editors of country newspapers, also attrib.; (3) **yard,** a place where boilers for steam engines are made, *rare.*

(1) 1830 *Steamboat Disasters* (1846) 127 The boiler-deck,—being that part of the upper deck situated immediately over the boilers. **1875** Mark Twain *Old Times* ii. (1876) 32 The boiler deck (*i.e.* the second story of the boat, so to speak) was as spacious as a church. **1894** Eggleston in *Harper's Mag.* Feb. 467/1 Mr. Scudder and myself stood on the boiler-deck of the boat in conversation. — **(2) 1893** *Cong. Rec.* 18 Aug. 465/1 The country weeklies have been sent tons of 'boiler plates,' accompanied by . . . wily letters asking the editors to use the matter as news. **1905** D. G. Phillips *Plum Tree* 190 He attended to the subsidizing of news agencies that supplied thousands of country papers with boiler-plate matter to fill their inside pages. **1948** *Dly. Ardmoreite* (Ardmore, Okla.) 9 July 10/2 Forty-eight years ago small town dailies received shipments of boiler plate news services. — **(3) 1851** C. Cist *Cincinnati* 174 There are ten boiler yards, employing ninety-seven hands.

b. *To burst one's boiler*, etc., *fig.* to break down seriously, to come, or bring, to grief. *Slang.*

[**1824** in *Franklin* (Greenfield, Mass.) *Herald* 2 March (giving 'a short essay, repeating this phrase at the end of every paragraph' Thornton.)] **c1845** W. I. Paulding *Madmen All* 189 May my boiler be eternally busted, if there isn't that are young lady. **1856** *Sacramento Union* 24 Mar. 4/1 My dynder kept a risin' higher and higher, till I thought my biler would bust, unless I let out steam. **1916** *Amer. Mag.* Sep. 21/2, I am going to pack that bag of samples to Pine Valley in time for next week's stage if I bust a boiler!

As the last term in **coffee, double, farina, ribbed, sap, sorghum, tar, wash boiler.**

***boiling,** *n.* and *a.* In combs. now chiefly obs.: (1) **boiling arch,** a type of furnace arch upon which the kettles or evaporators used in making maple sugar rest; (2) **frolic,** a bee or frolic for making apple butter; (3) **place,** the place where maple sap is boiled in making sugar; (4) **pot,** a place in a river where the water is violently agitated, a whirlpool, cf. **boil,** *n.;* (5) ***spring,** a spring of cool water that rises quietly from some depth.

(1) 1874 *Vt. Bd. Agric. Rep.* II. 728 Boiling arches should be of good depth, not filled up at back end. — **(2) 1857** D. H. Strother *Virginia* 202 Whether you saw her carrying eggs to market . . . or helping to stir apple-butter at a boiling frolic. — **(3) 1844** *Knickerb.* XXIII. 444 And now we are at the 'boiling place' . . . The cauldron . . . is filled with the fresh sap two or three times a day. **1876** Burroughs *Winter Sunshine* v. 123 The 'boiling-place,' with its delightful camp-features, is just beyond the first line [of maple trees]. — **(4) 1790** Washington *Diaries* IV. 78 A place called the Suck, or boiling pot, where the river runs through the Cumberland Mountains. **1837** Bird *Nick of Woods* I. 225 Thar's a boiling-pot above and a boiling-pot below.

(5) 1664 in *Amer. Sp.* XV. 157/1 Running along the same into the Boyling Spring Swamp. **1946** *Nat. Speleological Soc. Bul.* July 5/2 An unexplored cave and a large 'boiling spring' occur on the Henkel estate near Quicksburg.

As the last term in **corn boiling, sap boiling.**

Boisbrûlé ˌbwɑbruˈle, *n.* [See note.]

Usu. explained as simply F. =burnt wood, with allusion to the complexion of these Indians. Poss. the name orig. had reference to the fact that they were a woods-dwelling people, rather than plains Indians. Cf. **Brulé,** and note in Hodge such designations as Wood Assiniboines, Woods Bloods, Woods Chippewas, Wood Crees, Woods Indians. See also **forest Indian.**

A Canadian half-breed Indian, esp. one of French and Indian extraction, or the tribe of such an Indian. Also attrib.

1805 LEWIS in *Ann. 9th Congress* 2 Sess. 1047 The Tetons Bois brûlè killed and took about 60 of them last summer. **1851** HOWE *Hist. Coll. Great West* 156 There has arisen around the trading-posts large numbers of half-breeds. Of these the males . . . are nicknamed *Bois Brule, i.e.* Burnt Wood, from their dark complexion. **1871** EGGLESTON *Duffels* (1893) iv. 380 Most of the drivers were of the pure Bois Brules stock. **1881** *Amer. Naturalist* XV. 123 Buffalo make good tractable work cattle when caught young, and the *Bois Brules* frequently use them as such.

bois d'arc. [F., "bow-wood."] The Osage orange, the wood of which was used by the Indians for making bows. Also attrib. Cf. **bodock.**

1805 in *Ann. 9th Congress* 2 Sess. 1138 At this place Mr. Dunbar obtained one or two slips of the '*bois d'arc,*' (bow wood, or yellow wood,) from the Missouri. **1842** E. A. HITCHCOCK *Journal* (1930) 74 His party . . . used bows and arrows for killing buffalo—bow made of the bois d'arc wood. **1885** M. THOMPSON *By-Ways* 158 The cat-bird . . . is . . . the musical deity of our blackberry jungles and *bois d'arc* hedges. **1947** *Dly. Oklahoman* (Okla. City) 28 Dec. 4/1 More men will carry hickory or bois d'arc clubs and hoe handles than will use shotguns.

bois de diable. = **vine maple** (*a*). — **1823** D. DOUGLAS *Journal* (1914) 108 This Acer forms part of the underwood in the pine forests. . . . It is called by the voyageurs Bois de Diable from the obstruction it gives them in passing through the woods. **1942** VAN DERSAL *Ornamental Amer. Shrubs* 194 The coiling, writhing stems . . . explain why early voyageurs called the plant *bois-de-diable* when they tried to penetrate characteristic thickets of this species.

bois de vache. *W.* [F.] Buffalo chips.

1843 FRÉMONT *Exped.* 22 Our fires were partially made of the *bois de vache*, . . . a very good substitute for wood, burning like turf. **1850** GARRARD *Wah-To-Yah* i. 11 [We used] *bois de vache* (buffalo chips) for want of better fuel. *Ib.* i. 19 We made a small bois de vache fire. **1897** *Land of Sunshine* July 49 Then she builds an out-door fire of *bois de vache*, sets up her circle of vessels about the slow, pungent blaze, and toasts them till they are done.

Bokhara clover. [*Bokhara*, Asia.] The sweet clover, *Melilotus alba*, widely dispersed throughout North America.

1868 GRAY *Field Botany* 101 *M. alba*, White Melilot, Bokhara or Tree Clover, . . . has been cult[ivated] for green fodder. **1884** *Rep. Comm. Agric.* 125 Bokhara clover . . . has recently been considerably cultivated [in some parts of the South] and apparently with satisfactory results. **1911** RICHTER *Honey Plants of Calif.* 999 Sweet (White Bokhara and Stone) Clover . . . [is] much esteemed by beekeepers wherever grown, and may be found from Siskiyou to San Diego County.

* **bold,** *a.* and *adv.* **1.** Of water: Having a strong current, flowing in an abundant, free manner. *Colloq.* **2. bold hives,** (see quot.). *Obs.*

(1) **1805** CLARK in *Lewis & C. Exped.* (1904) I. 298 The little Missouri . . . is 134 yards wide at it's Mouth and sets in with a bould current. *Ib.* 362 A beautiful bold running stream. **1821** J. FOWLER *Journal* 28 A streem of bold running water one hundred and fifty feet wide. **1895** *D.N.* I. 370 *Bold:* freely, plentifully. 'The spring don't flow as bold as it did.' — (2) **1824** J. DODDRIDGE *Notes* 148 The croup, or what was then [*c*1775] called the 'Bold hives' was a common disease among the children, many of whom died of it.

* **Bolingbroke,** *n.* (See quot.) *Obs.* — **1823** *N. Eng. Farmer* II. 85 Our city has been much amused with a low tripod-kind of a hat, made of fine beaver, and worn by our Bang-ups. Some call them the *Touch* others the *Gape and Stare*, the real name is the Bolingbroke.

* **Bolivar,** *n.* [Simon *Bolivar* (1783–1830), a Venezuelan patriot.]

1. Designating articles of clothing (see quots.). *Obs.*

1826 *Va. Herald* (Fredericksburg) 6 Sep. 3/4 Mrs. Kelley, Has just received an elegant lot of Ladies' Bolivar and Leghorn Flats. **1848** BARTLETT 393 *Bolivar Hat*, a Leghorn bonnet, with a broad brim, worn a few years since. **1857** *Spirit of Times* 26 Sep. 55/2 Contrast it with the 'poke bonnet' of 1820; the broad brim black fur 'Bolivar' of 1825. **1886** B. P. POORE *Reminisc.* I. 75 Those gentlemen [at Washington, D.C., *c*1827] who dressed fashionably wore 'Bolivar' frock-coats of some gay-colored cloth.

2. A local term formerly in use for a large round gingercake. *Obs.*

1860 HARTE in *Golden Era* (S.F.) 4 Nov., [In my pocket was] a peculiar kind of cake—resembling in shape the almanac cuts of the sun —called a Bolivar. **1869** *Harper's Mag.* Oct. 753/1 With that penny he bought a 'bolivar'—as the huge molasses-cake was called in those days [1854]. **1889** MELLICK *Story Old Farm* 607 Nance and the children were placed on chairs in front, and behind was . . . a corn-basket full of large round ginger cakes—they called them bolivars.

* **boll,** *n.*

1. The seed vessel of the cotton plant. Cf. **cotton boll.**

1776 CARTER in *W. & M. Coll. Quar.* XX. 174 To give it (cotton) its natural growth it must be planted in May . . . ; and if later the same cotton may be got by having it up as soon as the boles are full, then you can't make good seed. **1862** in *Ill. Agric. Soc. Trans.* V. (1865) 509 The late planted [cotton] will only produce a small return of bolls. **1948** *Democrat* 5 Aug. 1/2 He recently counted 112 well matured bolls on one stalk.

2. In combs.: (1) **boll rot,** (see quot.); (2) **weevil,** a weevil, *Anthonomus grandis*, which destroys cotton squares and young bolls by depositing its eggs in them, also attrib.; (3) **weevil democrat,** (see quot.), *rare;* (4) **worm,** the larva of the moth *Heliothis armigera*, which feeds upon immature cotton bolls, also called **corn-ear worm, corn worm,** also attrib.

(1) **1889** *Cent.* Boll-rot. . . . A disease to which the boll of the cotton-plant is liable, manifesting itself at first by a slight discoloration resembling a spot of grease, and culminating in the rupture of the boll and the discharge of a putrid mass. — (2) [**1895** *Insect Life* March 295 Report on the Mexican Cotton-Boll Weevil in Texas, . . . by C. H. Tyler Townsend, . . . [dated] December 20, 1894.] **1904** W. D. HUNTER *Mexican Cotton Boll Weevil* 10 Up to the present time (January, 1904) the boll weevil has been found outside of the State of Texas in only three instances. **1948** *Ada* (Okla.) *Ev. News* 4 July 11/3 In all of these fields the boll weevil count is lower than at any time last year. — (3) **1906** *Springfield W. Republican* 19 July 16 The 'boll-weevil democrats' is the term of opprobrium which a southern paper applies to democrats who favor Hearst. — (4) **1847** *Rep. Comm. Patents* (1848) 171 In view then of . . . the destruction caused by the boll worm . . . the receipts will show another short crop. **1856** *Rep. Comm. Patents: Agric.* 67 Mocking-birds and bee-martins catch and destroy the boll-worm moth. **1948** *Democrat* 30 Sep. 2/6 Pink bollworm is the most destructive pest of cotton. The worm damages both the boll and the seeds, resulting in loss of cotton yield and reducing the oil content of the seeds.

***bolled,** *a.* Of cotton: furnished with bolls. *Colloq.* — **1854** *Fla. Plant. Rec.* 90 All so the cotton crop is good and it seames to be groing finly at present and is bold well.

bolly ˈbɒlɪ, *n. S.* [Dim. of **boll.*] *pl.* Cotton bolls which have not opened or not fully opened so that the cotton can be picked out easily, and which, hence, are harvested whole. — **1929** R. B. VANCE *Human Factors in Cotton Culture* 132 Frost bitten bolls harvested whole are called 'bollies.' **1931** *Blue Valley Farmer* (Okla. City) 10 Sep. 2/1 The cotton farmer who realized from three to four dollars a bale out of the cotton that he had kept his children out of school to pick, is grateful for a better price for the few bolies he has left.

* **bologna,** *a.* Designating or referring to bulls suitable for converting into beef of an inferior quality. Cf. * *Bologna sausage.*

1899 *Chi. D. News* 7 June 11/5 Choice fat light bulls went at stronger prices but the heavy bologna stock was dragging at the bottom. **1904** *Cin. Enquirer* 2 Feb. 8/1 Bulls—Good bologna grades active and 10 @ 15c higher; fat bulls unchanged and slow. **1947** *Chi. Tribune* 14 June 18/3 Cattle Pr[i]m[e] steers . . . $28.00 — 30.00 . . . Bulls, bologna, com-choice $15.50 @ 18.00.

boloney, see **baloney.**

Bolongaro ˌbolɒŋˈgero, *n.* [Origin unknown.] "A kind of snuff made of various grades of leaves and stalks of tobacco" (*Cent.*). — **1833** *Knickerb.* II. 57 A villainous snuff-box rolled from my pocket, and scattered . . . a thousand pinches of Bolongaro, full in the face of Miss Tabby.

bolsa ˈbolsə, *n.* [Sp. in same sense.] A purse. — [**1829** *El Español* (New Orleans) 6 Apr. 4/2 Contentate con la bolsa, Tolsa.] **1852** *Calif. Express* (Marysville) 25 Aug. 2/2 On some, *fortune*, the *jade*, is lavishing her kindness more bountifully by filling their *bolsa's* with *the Ora* in an incredibly short space of time.

bolson bolˈson, *n. S.W.* [Sp. *bolsón*, in Amer. Sp. sense here shown.] A low area or basin completely surrounded by higher ground or mountains. Also attrib.

1838 TEXIAN *Mexico v. Texas* 9 A desert known, in the maps [of Mexico], under the name of 'Bolson of Mapimi.' **1847** RUXTON *Adv. Mexico* xiii. 96 The sun was fast sinking behind the ragged crest of the 'Bolson,' tinging the serrated ridge . . . with a golden flood of light. **1904** *Amer. Geologist* Sep. 164 The bolson plains may be considered as sections of an upraised peneplain surface in its earliest infancy. **1906** BRAY *Vegetation of Texas* 95 The extreme desert aspects of bolson vegetation and its meagerness are due more to the presence of alkali in the soil than to actual lack of rainfall.

*__bolt,__ *n.*[1] An earmark for animals. *Obs.* — **1732** *Edgecombe Co. Marks & Brands* 15 Aug. (N.C.H.C.), A Bolt in the left & the right ear cut off.

*__bolt,__ *n.*[2] **1.** A refusal to support a candidate, policy, etc., proposed by one's political party. **2.** (See quot.) *Slang. Obs.*

(1) **1858** *N.Y. Tribune* 8 Jan. 2/3 (Th.), It is known that there would have been some such a bolt from the nominations, had the nominations been made. *Ib.* 1 April 3/3 (Th.), The Lecomptonists and the 'anti-Lecompton' Democracy of Lecompton went off on this bolt, doing it secretly. **1903** A. H. LEWIS *Boss* 116 You can say that we . . . are goin' to make a bolt for better government. — (2) **1851** HALL *College Words* 22 *Bolt*, an omission of a recitation or lecture.

*__bolt,__ *v.*

1. *tr.* To split (trees, timber, etc.) into bolts.

1685 in TEMPLE & SHELDON *Hist. Northfield, Mass.* 99 It is ordered . . . that if any person or persons whatsoever shall fall timber on the Commons, after three months its to be crossted or cut off; and after 3 months more to be cleft out or bolted or squared. **1776** DUNBAR *Life* 28 Monday the 15th sent Mr. Simpson with the Negro Boys to begin stave making, bolting all day to teach the Boys. **1917** *D.N.* IV. 376 Bolt, v.t. To cleave (wood) into bolts.

2. To avoid (an issue) by not voting.

1813 *Portsmouth* (N.H.) *Oracle* 20 Nov. 2/3 (Th.), Others, ashamed to make further opposition, but without sufficient courage to do their duty, bolted the question. **1814** *N.Y. Herald* 13 April 3/4 When a member wishes to 'bolt,' he 'totes' himself out of the house before the ayes and noes are called.

3. *intr.* To break away from a political party or its representative; to go over to the opposition party.

1833 *Louisville Herald* 17 Oct., Does the Doctor apprehend that the editor is about to 'bolt'? **1875** *Scribner's Mo.* Nov. 124/2 Voters, even though they have little to do with forming platforms and nominating men, can bolt. **1944** *Chi. D. News* 6 April 1 (*headline*), Question—Will Willkie Bolt?

b. To draw back from an agreement.

1840 *Ill. State Reg.* (Springfield) 8 Jan. 2/1 Mr. Lincoln, a Whig representative of Sangamo, . . . who was *pledged* to sustain the system of internal improvements, . . . has *bolted*, . . . and has left the system to shift for itself. **1849** T. T. JOHNSON *Sights Gold Region* ii. 16 Surprised at our facile compliance with their original demand, they determined at once to bolt from their contract.

4. *tr.* To break away from, desert, turn against (a party, program, or candidate).

1847 *Cong. Globe* 4 Feb. 322/2, I had never bolted a regular nomination of the Democratic party, from President to constable. **1880** *Dly. Inter Ocean* (Chi.) 1 June 2/4, I do not see how any of them can vote to break the unit rule and bolt their instructions. **1901** W. A. WHITE in *McClure's Mag.* Dec. 149 If he bolts the caucus, a new man often appears from his district the next session. **1948** *Newsweek* 8 March 88/3 But half the voters it got to the polls bolted the candidate.

*__bolter,__ *n.* **1.** One who converts timber into bolts. **2.** One who "bolts" in politics.

(1) **1776** DUNBAR *Life* 37 The bolters being chiefly employed in falling Timber. — (2) [**1812** *Salem Gaz.* 10 July 4/1 (Th.), D. Tompkins would . . . send home the bolters by new prorogation.] **1848** *Albany Argus* 8 Jan. 1/3 The bolters from the democratic party, have abandoned their proposed convention. **1948** *Dly. Ardmoreite* (Ardmore, Okla.) 30 Mar. 3/4 'I'm not a bolter,' the chairman of the California democratic committee told newsmen.

*__bolting,__ *n.* and *a.* Desertion of party, making a "bolt".

1845 BENNETT in Mackenzie *Van Buren* (1846) 236, I stuck to the movement, and left the *Courier and Enquirer* on account of this bolting. **1867** *Cong. Globe* 16 Feb. 1445/2 This bolting convention of Radicals at Cleveland was condemned . . . by the great mass of the Union Party. **1900** *Dly. Ardmoreite* (Ardmore, Okla.) 14 June 4/5 Not exceeding two hundred delegates went with the bolting crowd. **1948** *Newsweek* 27 Sep. 19/1 Rival Truman delegations from the bolting counties . . . had been waiting outside around loudspeakers and a chuck-wagon.

bombo ˈbɑmbo, *n.* [?var. of **boomer,** *n.* **a.**] (See quots.) — *a***1877** *Westover Papers* 28 (B. '77) When the people [of North Carolina] entertain their friends, they fail not to set before them a capacious bowl of *Bombo*, so called from the animal of that name. **1877** BARTLETT 57 Bombo. An animal of North Carolina, said to resemble the hedgehog, and by some called a Badger.

*__bomb-proof,__ *n.* In the South, during the Civil War, one who occupied a place of safety. Also a place so occupied. *Obs.*

1869 *Overland Mo.* III. 128 In the cis-Mississippi States [such Southerners] . . . were generally dubbed 'bomb-proofs.' **1876** *Southern Hist. Soc. P.* II. 229 While the war lasted, it was the delight of some of the stoutly built fellows to go home for a few days, and kick and cuff and tongue-lash the able-bodied bomb-proofs. **1891** *Scribner's Mag.* X. 367 Mrs. Wagoner's husband had been in a bomb-proof during the war.

b. Also attrib. or as adj.

1867 *Harper's Wkly.* 6 Apr. 211/1 The 'bomb-proof' editors will probably continue to repeat the heroics of the war. **1895** *Cong. Rec.* 11 Jan. 887/2 He asked to be relieved from a bombproof situation under the Government in order to join his regiment. **1927** BENÉT *J. B.'s Body* 155 Muddy Washington . . . [is] full of . . . 'Bombproof' officers, veterans back on leave.

bonanza bəˈnænzə, *n.* [See note.]

From Sp. (prosperity, success) app. in Amer. Sp. senses shown in **1.** and **3.**, though the *Diccionario de la Real Academia Española* records *bonanza* in sense **3.** without ascribing it to Amer. Sp.

1. *In bonanza*, of a mine: Producing very profitable ore.

1844 GREGG *Commerce of Prairies* I. 170 The Placer was in its greatest *bonanza*—yielding very large profits to those engaged in the business. **1888** J. J. WEBB *Adventures* 50 The products of the gold mines . . . did not amount to more than $200,000 dollars a year when in bonanza, and very seldom to anything near that amount.

2. In mining, the accidental discovery of a rich vein or pocket, good luck. Also transf.

1844 GREGG *Commerce of Prairies* I. 173 The progress of the foreign adventurer is always liable to be arrested by the jealousy of the government, upon the first flattering *bonanza*, as the cited instances abundantly demonstrate. **1881** RAYMOND *Mining Glossary*, *Bonanza*, in miners' phrase, good luck. **1886** *Stamp Collector* (Chi.) July 11 At one small bookshop . . . I ran across what some would consider a bonanza.

3. An especially rich vein or pocket of ore. Also transf.

1864 MOWRY *Ariz. & Sonora* 131 Their successors no sooner struck a *bonanza* than . . . they commenced to enjoy life in pretty much the same manner. **1880** *Custer* (Dakota Terr.) *Chronicle* 31 Jan. 1/8 This mine situated about seven miles west from town is fast proving itself a bonanza. **1948** *Colo. Mag.* March 88 Loading a stamp mill on to a wagon at St. Joseph, Smith and Chaffee started for the new bonanza.

4. Used attrib. of persons who have become rich through mining operations or to properties yielding rich returns or conducted on a large scale, as **bonanza family, king, mine, mine owner, property, state, stock.**

1898 ATHERTON *Californians* 61 A 'Bonanza' family, whose huge fortune, made out of the Nevada mines, had recently lifted it from obscurity to social fame. — **1876** *Boston Post* 5 May (B.), The Bonanza king was bitterly indignant at the means employed to depreciate his mines. **1947** *Time* 27 Oct. 106/2 Mackay hated the title of 'Bonanza King.' — **1876** DE GROOT in Powell *Nevada* 73 The 'Bonanza Mines' of the Comstock occupy a section of that lode situate near the northerly extremity of what has thus far proved to be the more fertile portion thereof. — **1884** *Cent. Mag.* Sep. 796 The railroad king, . . . the bonanza mine owner, the Texas rancher, and the Pennsylvania iron prince. — **1902** LONDON *Daughter of Snows* 66 A Bonanzo property, or a block of Bonanzo properties, does not entitle you to a pound more than the oldest penniless 'sour-dough.' — **1893** WAGNER *More About Names* 35 Montana is The Bonanza State, in allusion to its many Bonanza mines, the word *Bonanza* being Spanish for prosperity. **1948** MENCKEN *Supp.* II. 635 Montana, in its earlier days, was the *Bonanza State.* — **1876** *Boston Post* 5 May (B.), The recent decline in Bonanza stocks in the San Francisco market. **1883** MRS. FOOTE *Led-Horse Claim* i. 9 The ark of the mining interest . . . had drifted about unsteadily after the break in bonanza stocks in the summer of 1877.

Hence, transf., **bonanzist.** *Rare.* — **1879** *Chi. Tribune* 8 Feb. 5/2 The market must be stiffened or values will go down to such a figure that the average price will not allow the great bonanzist to come out with what was originally put in the deal.

b. Esp. **bonanza farm, farmer, farming.**

1878 CONKLIN *Picturesque Ariz.* 32 One can get an extended . . . and at least a flattering idea of a bonanza farm of Southern California. **1904** *Minneapolis Times* 8 July 4 The 'bonanza' farm, not many years ago a subject of much boasting in the west, is a thing of the past, and from now on intensified instead of expansive farming will prevail. **1943** HOWARD *Montana* 175 As a matter of fact, up to this time the famous 'bonanza' farms in Montana were primarily livestock operations. — **1882** *Uncle Rufus & Ma* 46 The large 'bonanza' farmers in Cass County have been successful. **1937** M. D. WOODWARD *Checkered Years* 10 One bonanza farmer alone had, at one time, 600,000 bushels of No. 1 hard in the elevators which he was holding for better prices. — **1909** *Sat. Ev. Post* 30 Jan. 30/2 What bonanza-farming is in any way equal to that? **1945** GRAY *Pine, Stream & Prairie* 17 The soil is rich and deep; great dramas of bonanza farming have been enacted on it.

*__Bonaparte,__ *n.* [f. C.L.J.L. *Bonaparte* (1803–57), Amer. ornithologist.] **1.** Used in the possessive in names of birds, as **Bonaparte's flycatcher, sandpiper,** (see quots.). **2. Bonaparte's gull,** one of the smaller North American gulls, *Larus philadelphia*, often found in flocks in plowed fields and swamps.

(1) **1858** BAIRD *Birds Pacific R.R.* 295 *Myiodioctes Bonapartii.* . . . Bonaparte's Flycatcher. **1873** *Forest & Stream* 4 Sep. 59/3 The 'Ring Necks' . . . are found upon sandy beaches . . . with the Semi-palmate and Bonaparte's Sand-pipers. **1874** COUES *Birds N.W.* 487 *Tringa Fuscicollis.* . . . Bonaparte's Sandpiper. — (2) **1839** PEABODY *Mass. Birds* 379 Bonaparte's Gull, *Larus Bonapartii*, is seen occasionally, early in autumn, on the coast of this State. **1946** *Nat. Geog. Mag.* Sep. 338/1 Bonaparte's gull frequently 'dive-bombed' the author from behind, though it rarely struck with its bill.

***bond,** *n.* As the last term in **cotton, division, drawn, government, land grant sinking fund, Liberty, Mississippi, registered, school, state, straw bond.**

* **bond,** *v.*

1. *tr.* To issue bonds upon (property), to finance in this way. Also absol.

1812 *Ann. 12th Congress* 2 Sess. 1273 We have only bonded for three thousand seven hundred and fifty dollars. **1880** G. INGHAM *Digging Gold* xvii. 386 Gold parties . . . who bought [the Dakota lode] . . . , when approached in regard to selling it, would not offer to bond it for less than one hundred thousand dollars. **1883** *Harper's Mag.* Nov. 939/1 Conservative investors . . . said the [Northern Pacific] road . . . was too heavily bonded.

2. To bind (one) by a legal bond, to put under bond.

1896 *N. Amer. Rev.* CLXIII. 711 The [Western] settlers . . . were so willing to bond themselves. **1948** *Insurance Index* 15 April 12/3 In the various governmental departments all employees who handle money are bonded.

* **bone,** *n.*

1. The tougher or more fibrous part of a plant.

1843 OLIVER *Eight Months* 93 Besides, when it was mown late, there was some *bone* in it, and it took some eating. **1913** O. A. ROTHERT *Hist. Muhlenberg Co. (Ky.)* 114 The harvesting began by pulling the [flax] plant out by the roots. It went through a number of processes before the fibre was finally separated from the 'bone.'

2. *pl.* The performer in a Negro minstrel company, usu. an end man, who uses bones. Usu. *cap.*

1849 *Placer Times* (S.F.) 7 March 3/7 Brudder bones will again appear in his new Dances, Burlesques, Tragedies, &c. **1857** *S.F. Call* 1 Feb. 2/2 The witticisms of Bones and his friend of the Tamborine, were delivered in fine style. **1927** BENÉT *J. B.'s Body* 285 The minstrels have raised their prices, but every night Bones and Tambo play to a crowded house. **1930** WITTKE *Tambo & Bones* 140 Originally, all endmen were addressed as 'Mistah Tambo' and 'Mistah Bones,' names derived from the instruments with which they added to the hilarity and din of the show.

b. Attrib. with **convention, end, performer, player.**

1846 *Spirit of Times* 25 April 100/1 He is brother to the *bone* performer belonging to the troupe of Ethiopian Serenaders. **1867** *N.Y. World* 14 Dec. 2/1 The Virginia Bones and Banjo Convention is in its first stage [at Richmond, Va.]. **1880** E. JAMES *Negro Minstrel's Guide* 6 Much . . . depends on the drolleries and antics of the Tambo and Bone ends to insure a good time for the spectators. *Ib.*, 2 Bone-player on the extreme right; Triangle-player next to Bones' end.

3. =**boner.** Also attrib. *Slang.*

1916 *Amer. Mag.* Aug. 9/2 Shrapnel, seeing he's made a bone, switches systems sudden. **1917** *Collier's* 13 Oct. 16/1 It was a solid bone play.

4. In special combs.: (1) ***bone-dry,** absolutely without intoxicating drink; (2) **fish,** any one of various marine fishes, as the ladyfish, *Bodianus rufus*, right whale, etc.; (3) **gathering,** (see quot.), *obs.;* (4) **head,** (*a*) a blockhead, also attrib., (*b*) =**boner,** *rare, slang* in both uses; (5) **headed,** stupid, *slang;* (6) **hunter,** *W.* one who hunts for animal bones, esp. those of the buffalo, to sell them to fertilizer plants, cf. **bone pilgrim;** (7) **meal,** bones ground for use as fertilizer, or to feed farm stock; (8) **mill,** a place where bones are ground into meal; (9) ***picker,** (see quots.); (10) **pilgrim,** (see quot. and cf. **bone hunter**); (11) **pit,** (see quot.); (12) ***set,** see as a main entry; (13) **shark,** (see quot. 1889); (14) **yard,** see as a main entry.

(1) **1932** *K.C. Times* 27 April 22 Both towns were bone dry. — (2) **1734** *Phil. Trans.* XXXVIII. 317 *Mormyrus, ex cinereo nigricans*, the Bone-Fish. **1809** E. A. KENDALL *Travels* II. 204 The species of whale taken was . . . that which is technically called the bone-fish, or fish valued for the article called in commerce whale-bone. **1897** *Outing* XXIX. 331/1 The bone-fish somewhat resembles a whiting in shape, with the mouth of a sucker and no teeth. — (3) **1775** ADAIR *Indians* 180 Those who lose their people at war, . . . are so observant of this kindred duty, as to appropriate some time to collect the bones of their relations; which they call *bone gathering*. — (4) (*a*) **1912** BOWER *Flying U.* 27 Us boneheads don't appreciate him, is all that ails us. **1921** *Ladies' H. Jrnl.* Apr. 40/3, I guess I've pulled a bone-head play. **1947** *Dly. Oklahoman* (Okla. City) 28 Dec. 6/4 The boss is mad at this buyer for making such bonehead buys. (*b*) **1931** *K.C. Times* 24 July, He pulled one of the biggest boneheads one night this week.

(5) **1903** *Smart Set* IX. 96 You talk like a bone-headed fool. **1929** A. J. DICKSON *Across Plains* 143 If some boneheaded mule displayed characteristic traits, the muleskinner was very expert with his long lash. — (6) **1927** RUSSELL *Trails* 41 'Tain't long ago the country was covered with these relics, but since the bone hunters cleaned up you seldom see one. Down on the Missouri I've seen bunches of skeletons, runnin' from ten to sixty. — (7) **1850** *N. Eng. Farmer* II. 44 On Mr. Preston's farm, . . . they began to use bone-meal. **1948** *Amer. Feed & Grain Dealer* April 6/1 Some of the colleges . . . would recommend only the simple mixtures of oil meal, cottonseed, a little bone meal and salt to be fed. — (8) **1874** *Dept. Agric. Rep. 1873* 285 On a small stream running through the farm a bone-mill has been built. **1884** SWEET & KNOX *Through Texas* 634 The animal must be a superannuated plug, . . . fit only for the bone-mill. — (9) **1809** CUMING *Western Tour* 261 Some priest or privileged person [among the Indians], who was called the bone picker, was always sent for to the nation to come and cleanse the bones from the flesh [of a corpse] . . . that the bones might be carried home and interred in the general cemetery. **1948** MATHEWS *Southernisms* 62 Decomposition had so far advanced as to make it possible for old men known as bone-pickers to . . . scrape away the flesh from the bones.

(10) **1884** ALDRIDGE *Life on Ranch* 169 The bone-pilgrim used to be quite an institution in Western Kansas, gathering up the remnants of defunct bisons and hauling them to the railway, to be sent east for manufacturing into artificial manure. — (11) **1871** DE VERE 25 In the State of New York and in Canada there are, besides, many places found, where the Indians buried their dead, and these are known as *bonepits*. — (13) **1802** *Mass. H.S. Coll.* VIII. 199 There is a large shark in the harbour, named the bone-shark, and similar in shape to the man-eating shark, but harmless. **1889** *Cent.* 621/3 *Bone-shark*, a common name along the New England coast of . . . the basking shark.

b. *To feel it* (etc.) *in one's bones*, to feel certain about, to have an intuition of, something. Also of the thing, *to be in one's bones. Colloq.*

1844 in BARNES *Mem. Thurlow Weed* (1884) 123 It was in my bones all summer. **1857** *Lawrence* (Kan.) *Republican* 11 June 4 They feel in their bones, that, as American citizens, they have a right to it [political power]. **1947** *Sat. Ev. Post* 8 Mar. 148/3 We have a feeling in our bones that this plan for the revival of Europe will not do so badly with American public opinion.

As the last term in **break, buffalo, chicken, crazy, feather, herring, horse, jaw, pull, pulling, side, soup, spinal, whale bone.**

* **bone,** *v.*

1. *intr.* To work hard; to apply oneself closely or strenuously. Freq. with *in, into, down. Colloq.* or *slang.*

1841 GREELEY in *Corr. R. W. Griswold* (1898) 53 Webb wants to be Postmaster. . . . He has been round boring every big-bug in the State to bone for him. *a***1861** WINTHROP *Open Air* 148 We was about sick of putty-heads and sneaks that . . . didn't dare to make us stand round and bone in. *a***1870** CHIPMAN *Notes on Bartlett* 42 *Bone*, to apply one's self closely. 'To bone into it.' **1883** *Cent. Mag.* June 273, 'I suppose you'll keep up your reading along with your law?' 'No, . . . I'm going to bone right down to it.'

2. *tr.* and *intr.* To study hard, to prepare (a subject), or get well acquainted with it by close study. *Colloq.* or *slang.*

Clapin, 64, implies that this sense is derived from **Bohn,** *q.v.* No evidence, other than that in Clapin, has been found for *Bohn, v.*

1862 G. C. STRONG *Cadet Life West Point* 198 Not unfrequently I took the liberty to suggest to him that if he did not leave poetry, and 'bone math' ' more than he was doing, we should be deprived ere long of his excellent society. **1926** DE KRUIF *Microbe Hunters* 26 But in every spare moment he boned away at mathematics. **1948** *Chi. D. News* 23 Oct. 6/2 Children are boning up in preparation for the Spelling Bees.

Hence * **boning,** *n.*

1859 in O. E. WOOD *West Point Scrap Book* (1871 ed.) 88 Much study, too, you must admit, when starting out afresh, Although you call it 'boning,' is quite weary to the flesh. **1886** E. L. DORSEY *Midshipman Bob* 72 Mr. Dugald . . . said a few weeks' more 'boning' would brace me up to the mark. (That's what they call studying here.)

*boner, *n.* A stupid or ridiculous blunder, often *to pull a boner*. *Slang.*

1912 *Amer. Mag.* June 200/1 Boner—a stupid play; a blunder in the science of the game. **1913** *Ib.* Sep. 94/3 Got his signals mixed and pulled a boner. **1948** *Hygeia* Feb. 99 When a 'boner' bares a hidden thought it may be embarrassing, but it is by no means always tragic.

***Bones,** *n. pl.* The common name of "Skull and Bones," the oldest senior society at Yale University, founded in 1832. Also attrib.

1871 L. H. BAGG *At Yale* 145 Popularly the society is known as 'Bones,' and its members as 'Bones men.' *Ib.* 148 A half-dozen extra men are chosen in Bones, in addition to the regular fifteen. **1895** *Bachelor Arts Mo.* June 192 The would-be host circulates . . . , tapping the elect on the shoulder and speaking a word beneath his breath, as they select Bones men at Yale. **1912** JOHNSON *Stover at Yale* 204 Who do you think will be first tapped for Bones?

As the last term in **dry bones, faggot bones, side bones.**

***boneset,** *n.*

1. Any one of various North American herbs of the genus *Eupatorium*, esp. *E. perfoliatum*, formerly much used in medicine.

[**1764** in FRIES *N.C. Morav. Rec.* II. 565 *Boneset* is so called because the Indians use it as splints in binding a broken arm or leg. The plant looks much like Willow, and has white on stem and leaves. It grows in large patches, but is not often found.] **1817-8** EATON *Botany* (1822) 278 Boneset, thoroughwort. **1880** W. H. GIBSON in *Harper's Mag.* June 80 Out in the swamp meadow the tall clumps of boneset show their dull white crests. **1948** *Hoosier Folklore* March 5 Gather boneset, which grows in wild swamps, when in bloom in the fall and hang up to dry.

b. *ellipt.* Boneset leaves or tea.

*c***1850** WHITCHER *Bedott P.* xiii. 136, I send you herewith a paper o' boneset. **1876** M. F. HENDERSON *Cooking* 327 Pour one and one-half pints of boiling water on a ten-cent package of boneset. **1890** *Harper's Mag.* April 713/2 Dosin' with ginger tea, an' boneset an' sage an' saffron.

2. Designating a *lozenge* or *tea* prepared from boneset.

1831 *Boston Transcript* 26 Nov. 3/1 A discerning public will reward him, as does the writer, for the benefit he has received from the Boneset Lozenges, in an irritable cough. **1839** BRIGGS *H. Franco* II. 153 'Dear soul,' said the good woman, 'let me warm your bed, and give you some boneset tea.' [**1931** CLUTE *Plants* 121 A cup of bitter tea, brewed from the boneset, even if it did not cure, was calculated to make the patient forget all else for a time at least.]

bone yard. A storage place for bones. Also, *slang*, a cemetery. Also fig.

1862 *Rep. Comm. Patents: Agric.* 127 After that, to commence a liberal supply of grain, will doubtless hasten many of them to the bone-yard. **1872** MARK TWAIN *Roughing It* xlvii. 334 When some roughs jumped the Catholic bone-yard and started in to stake out town-lots in it he went for 'em! **1903** A. H. LEWIS *Boss* 205 Along comes a scientist an' tells him it's all off an' nothin' for it but the boneyard! **1948** *Sat. Ev. Post* 2 Oct. 20/3 Dozens of times the powerful Republican press has buried him in the political boneyard.

b. (See quot.)

1903 W. J. LONG *Beasts of Field* 70, I have met men . . . who speak of 'bone yards' which they have discovered—places where they can go at any time and be sure of finding a good set of caribou antlers. And they say that the caribou go there to die.

c. *jocular.* "In the game of dominoes, the pieces reserved to draw from" (*Cent.*).

***bonito,** *n.* A local name for the sergeant fish, *Rachycentron canadus*. Cf. **striped bonito.** — **1884** GOODE *Fisheries U.S.* I. 444 The cobia or crab-eater—*Elacate canada*. This fish, known in the Chesapeake Bay as the 'Bonito' and 'Coal-fish,' and as the 'Sergeant-fish' in Southern and Eastern Florida, . . . is considered one of the most important food-fishes of Maryland and Virginia.

bonito bə'nito, *a. S.W.* [Sp. in same sense.] Pretty, nice. — *c***1892** *D.N.* I. 188 Bonito: pretty, nice. It supersedes in Spanish America *lindo*, and is of frequent occurrence in Western Texas. **1941** FERGUSSON *Southwest* 16 This is the damnedest country you ever saw. You dig for wood, climb for water, spell hickory with a j, and call a pretty girl a bone-eater. The Spanish **j** is pronounced h, and *bonita* means 'pretty' in the feminine sense.

***bonnet,** *n.*

1. The spatterdock, *Nuphar advenum*, a yellow water lily.

1836 *Knickerb.* VIII. 283 The banks of the river [near Rolls Town, Fla.] generally are . . . lined with 'bonnets,' as they are called there. **1934** *Nat. Geog. Mag.* LXV. 598 The golden, globular flowers of yellow pond-lilies, or 'bonnets,' glow in a setting of huge green leaves.

2. In combs.: (1) **bonnet curtain,** (see quot. 1852), *obs.*; (2) **grass,** a species of bent grass or redtop, *Agrostis stolonifera*; (3) **head,** (see quots.), also **bonnet-headed shark;** (4) **leaf,** the American lotus, *Nelumbo lutea*; (5) **paper,** ?paper used in making bonnets, *obs.*; (6) **pasteboard,** ?pasteboard used in bonnets, *obs.*; (7) **squash,** ?the common vegetable sponge, *Luffa cylindrica*; (8) **wire,** wire used in the framework of bonnets and hats; (9) **worm,** the larva of a leaf-beetle of the genus *Donacia* found on water lilies.

(1) **1845** MRS. KIRKLAND *Western Clearings* 19, I was 'a-goin' to want that 'ere flowery white bunnet-curting' of mine. **1852** REGAN *Emigrant's Guide* 139 Green veils or 'bonnet curtings,' as they are called predominated with the young ladies. [**1889** *Cent. Mag.* Dec. 260/2 When our grandmothers had curtains to their bonnets.]— (2) **1836** EATON *Botany* (ed. 7) 147 *Agrostis alba*, white top, bonnet grass. **1889** *Cent.* 623/1. — (3) **1878** *Proc. U.S. Nat. Museum* I. 387 *Reniceps Tiburo*,—Shovel-headed Shark, Bonnet-head. Abundant [near Beaufort Harbor, N.C.]. **1890** *Cent.* 5552/2 Bonnet-headed shark [is] a hammer-headed shark of the genus *Reniceps*. — (4) **1822** W. H. SIMMONS *Notices of E. Fla.* 29 (Th.S.), The bonnet leaf, a species of lotus, abounds in the dead water formed by the meeting currents.

(5) **1786** *Middlesex Gazette* 13 Nov., To be sold or exchanged for clean cotton or Linen Rags, by the printers hereof. . . . Bonnet paper and Bonnet Linings. **1803** *Ib.* 10 Jan., Writing—Printing—Sheathing —Bonnet, and Press Paper, upon as good terms as can be had in New York or Boston. — (6) **1780** *N.J. Archives* 2 Ser. IV. 316 Parchment and Bonnet Pasteboard, to be sold at the Printing-Office. — (7) **1892** HARRIS *Plantation* 124 The girls made their hats of rye and wheat straw, and some very pretty bonnets were made of the fibrous substance that grows in the vegetable known as the bonnet squash. — (8) **1862** *Harper's Mag.* Jan. 224/1 The apparatus used consisted of two coils of wire . . . somewhat like ordinary bonnet-wire. — (9) **1888** GOODE *Amer. Fishes* 58 In Florida . . . [black bass] feed on a grub called the 'bonnet-worm.'

As the last term in **bath, blue, Boston, cape, convention, Lafayette, log cabin, Methodist, muskmelon, Navarino, scoop, scoop shovel, secession, Shaker, shovel, slab, slat, splinter, wagon, war bonnet.**

Bonnie Blue Flag. Prob. the secession flag of South Carolina, consisting of a blue field with at first a single star for that state. Also as the title of a song popular in the South during the secession period.

1861 H. MACARTHY *Song, The Bonnie Blue Flag* i, Hurrah for the Bonnie Blue Flag that bears a Single Star! **1865** SALA *Diary* I. 260 The young lady who wore the Union flag in her bosom begins to hum the 'Bonnie Blue Flag.' **1889** FARMER 75 *Bonny Blue Flag*, the Blue Flag, the standard of the Confederates, was thus affectionately named. Round it gathered the whole sentiment and earnestness of the Southern cause. **1947** *Atlantic Mo.* Aug. 70/2 Some East Texans, in particular, still have vague romantic feelings about the Bonny Blue Flag.

bony 'bonɪ, *n.* [f. the adj.] (See quot.) Cf. **bony coal.** — **1874** RAYMOND *6th Rep. Mines* 39 The coal . . . is interstratified with sandrock and shale. In some of the mines the roof consists of a mixture of the two, called by the men 'bony.' *Ib.* 41 The Black Diamond vein has for roof and floor shale, slate, and 'bony.'

***bony,** *a.* In combs.: (1) **bony coal,** coal containing a considerable amount of slate, shale; (2) **fish,** a local name for various fishes, esp. the menhaden; (3) **gar,** (see quot. and cf. next); (4) **pike,** (see quot. 1889).

(1) **1857** *Harper's Mag.* Sep. 463/1 Much of the slate and 'bony coal' that occurs in the vein is separated . . . and thrown around the slope [in Pa.]. — (2) **1814** MITCHILL *Fishes N.Y.* 453 Bony-fish, Hard-heads, or Marsbankers . . . [are] about fourteen inches long. **1892** *Outing* Apr. 54/1 Giving my line a little jerk I reeled in a couple of 'bony fish,' the captain called them. **1939** *L.A.* Map 233. — (3) **1821** NUTTALL *Travels Arkansa* 177 The boney gar (*Esox osseus*), and the large grey cat-fish, are also sufficiently common. — (4) **1842** *Nat. Hist. N.Y., Zoology* IV. 272 The Buffalo Bony Pike, *Lepisosteus bison*, . . . was obtained at Buffalo, Lake Erie, where it is called the Bony Pike, Alligator and Alligator Gar. **1889** *Cent.* 2459 *Garpike*, any fish of the family *Lepidosteidae*; a gar. Also called *bony pike*.

boob bub, *n.* [f. **booby*.] A simpleton, dunce. *Slang.*

1909 *Sat. Ev. Post* 27 March 7/3, I had to tell her the boob had gone for the day. **1919** *Amer. Mag.* April 40/3 If this boss of yours is such a boob, what must *you* be? **1948** *Lawton* (Okla.) *Constitution* 2 July 2/3 Amiable, conscientious, learned Mr. Morris has more knowledge than the ignorant boobs he represents in congress.

***booby,** *n. N. Eng.* (See quot. 1889.) Also **booby hack.**

1888 *Boston Globe* (F.), A party . . . coming down the steep grade . . . on a double ripper, . . . collided with Crowley's booby hack. **1889**

Cent. 623/3 *Booby*, . . . a hack on runners; a sleigh kept for hire. **1896** Haswell *New York* 34 Carts and wheeled vehicles were replaced by sleds and sleighs, even to carriage- and hack-bodies being set upon runners, as is still the case in Boston, for example, when they were termed booby hacks.

booby-hut, *n.* [Alteration of next.] "A carriage body put upon sleigh runners. New England" (B. '59).

1795 *Columbian Centinel* 24 Jan. 3/4 Two second hand Booby-Huts. **1835** in Mathews *Memoirs* IV. 325, I induced him on Wednesday to accompany Mrs. Eliot and myself in a 'Booby Hut,' (for so a *covered* sleigh is called). **1867** *Atlantic Mo.* March 306/1 Miss Dudley, in her Siberian sables, sprang lightly from the *booby-hut*, and caught me in her arms. **1929** *Old Time N. Eng.* April 158/2 A Coach House of Colonial design has been recently constructed, in which has been placed the Hancock Coach, or 'Booby-Hut.' This vehicle belonged to John Hancock.

***booby-hutch,** *n.* [In former British use, a small or clumsy carriage.] =prec. *Obs.* Cf. **close sleigh.** — **1766** *Boston Gazette* 29 Dec. (Th.), A very neat Booby-hutch to be sold cheap for Cash. **1767** *Mass. Gazette* 12 Feb. 4/2 A close Sleigh, or Booby-Hutch, to go with either one or two horses, . . . to be sold.

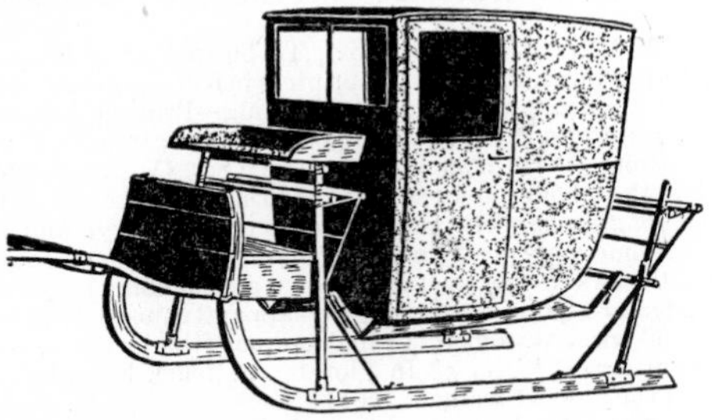

Booby hutch *c*1775

booby prize. A prize given to the one who has the lowest score in a game, contest, etc. Also transf. and fig.

1893 Dana *Wild Flowers* 170 It seems as though the flowers of the witch-hazel were fairly entitled to the 'booby-prize' of the vegetable world. **1932** *K.C. Star* 1 Feb. 18 The Pulitzer committee gives an annual award for the best news story of the year, but offers no booby prize for the worst. **1948** *Southern Wkly.* 3 July 18/1 In spite of all the recent booby-prize nominations, no one has thought to accuse Henry of being the worst third-party candidate the country has ever seen.

boodle ˈbudḷ, *n.* [See note.]

In senses **1.** and **2.** f. Du. as the result of two separate borrowings. See *WNT s.v. boedel* 1 and 5 (*De heele, gansche, boel*), and cf. Bense *s.v.*

1. Property, goods, effects. *Obs.*

1699 Mansell *Ann. Albany* (1852) III. 53 Elisabeth . . . hath ye Boedel of Jan Verbeek, deceased, in hands.

2. *The whole boodle*, the whole lot, number, or amount. *Slang.* See **kit and caboodle.** Cf. **caboodle, kerboodle.**

1833 J. Neal *Down-Easters* I. 61, I know a feller 'twould whip the whool [*sic*] boodle of 'em an' give 'em six. **1858** Holmes *Autocrat* v. 139 He would like to have the whole boodle of them (I remonstrated against this word, but the Professor said it was a diabolish good word, and he would have no other) . . . shipwrecked on a remote island. **1891** S. Fish *Holiday Stories* (1900) 158 A few diamonds, and a lot of jewelry; in fact . . . the whole boodle that we have been searching for so long.

3. Counterfeit money, money used in graft, money in general. *Slang.*

1858 *Harper's Weekly* 3 April 222/1 'Boodle' is a flash term used by counterfeiters. *Ib.* 222/2 The leaders [of the band] were the manufacturers and bankers of the 'boodle.' **1884** *Amer. Hist. Mag.* XII. 566/2 *Boodle*, a slang word adapted to political usage from the *argot* of counterfeiters. Originally it meant the main portion of the counterfeit money, and by an easy translation has come to mean a large roll of bills such as political managers are supposed to divide among their retainers. **1942** Warnick *Dialect Garrett Co., Md.* 4 Boodle, n., ordinary money, with no implication of graft. **1948** *Houston* (Tex.) *Post* 14 June 6/5 It was boodle when a gas company or a streetcar company or a paving company bribed a city council to pass a swindling franchise or contract.

attrib. **1887** *Nation* 14 April 307/3 New York is better known all over the . . . world for boodle Aldermen and municipal rings than for anything else. **1891** Scott *Amer. Lawyers* 398 His services were most valuable in what have become known as the 'Boodle Cases' in the City of New York. **1904** Steffens in *McClure's Mag.* April 591/1 'Driftwood' was boodle bills for business men, and some of it was blackmail, but it was all irregular.

b. The use of bribery. *Slang.*

1904 W. H. Smith *Promoters* iii. 72 The game of boodle isn't near as easy to play as it used to be.

boodle budḷ, *v.* [f. the noun.] *tr.* and *intr.* To bribe. *Slang.* — **1904** W. H. Smith *Promoters* iv. 86 If you're going to boodle you've got to do it on a party basis.

boodleism ˈbudḷˌɪzəm, *n.* [Cf. **boodle,** *n.* **3.**] The practice of political bribery and corruption. *Slang.* — **1889** *Metropolitan* (Hyde Park, Ill.) 5 Nov. 4/3 An Insidious Scheme in the Direction of Boodleism. **1904** *Minneapolis Times* 6 July 6 He has been making war on boodleism for political effect.

boodleistic ˌbudḷˈɪstɪk, *a.* [f. **boodle,** *n.* **3.**] Characterized by boodleism. *Slang. Rare.* — **1898** *Cong. Rec.* 28 April 4385/1 The barking of this mangy Wall street boodleistic cur . . . reminds me of a lonely coyote baying the moon.

boodleize ˈbudḷˌaɪz, *v.* [f. **boodle,** *n.* **3.**] *tr.* To corrupt, bribe, or influence illegally or improperly. *Slang.* — **1886** *Cong. Rec.* 21 July 7730/1 We seven men have been boodleized, and there are no seven men in the State of Ohio, unless they were boodleized, who would agree to any such proposition. **1895** A. O. Myers *Bosses & Boodle* 290 Mr. Brice took Mr. Payne's thoroughly boodleized seat in 1891.

boodler ˈbudlɚ, *n.* [f. **boodle,** *n.* **3.** and **b.**] **1.** One who practices or takes part in political bribery and corruption. Also attrib. **2.** One who tries to obtain money by dishonest means. *Slang* in both uses.

(1) 1887 *Chi. Tribune* 3 May 6/7 When the boodlers met in the lower corridor explanations were made and 'Buck' McCarthy was sent back to act as watch-dog. **1887** *Courier-Journal* 6 May 4/8 Chicago Boodler Trials. **1896** *Chi. Times-Herald* 14 July 10/6 He is elected by republican votes, only to rescue the schemes of democratic boodlers from the fires of investigation. **1904** Steffens in *McClure's Mag.* April 588/2 If he had confined his chase to that unprotected bird, the petty boodler, all might have been well. — **(2) 1888** J. J. Webb *Memoirs* 147 We were fortunate enough not to be drawn into any compromise . . . and left the next morning in high spirits, and the boodlers mortified.

boodlerism ˈbudlɚˌɪzəm, *n.* [f. prec.] The practice of bribery or corruption in politics. Also **boodlery.** *Slang.* — **1887** *Advance* (Chicago) 30 June 408 'Boodlerism' in the management of our city and county and State affairs. *Ib.*, Let her not plead great conscience . . . but grant open licence to boodlery.

boodling ˈbudlɪŋ, *n.* [f. **boodle,** *n.* **3.**] The use of fraud and corruption in politics. *Slang.* — **1890** *School Board* Feb., Something akin to 'boodling' has been unearthed in the public educational system of New York city. **1903** *N.Y. Ev. Post* 31 Aug., We fancy that the people of Missouri will conclude to diminish boodling rather by taking from than adding to the powers of the dominant machine.

* **book,** *n.*

1. In various rare or obs. senses: **a.** A pack of folded hides. **b.** *Ellipt.* Book-muslin. **c.** An accumulation of the sticks, pebbles, etc., left on a trail by passing Indians for the information of their friends.

(a) 1840 Dana *Two Years* xxix. 329 A large 'book' was made of from twenty-five to fifty hides, doubled at the backs, and put into one another, like the leaves of a book. — **(b) 1875** *Chi. Tribune* 26 July 1/1 We are offering splendid Bargains in . . . Lawns, Swisses, Books, Nainsooks, etc. — **(c) 1917** Abbott *Recollections* 189 Upon reaching the summit of this mountain we came to an Indian 'book' which must have been hundreds of years old, for it was now thirty feet in diameter and nearly five feet high in the center.

2. In combs.: (1) **book agent,** a person who sells books, usu. by going from house to house; (2) **bindery,** [cf. Du. *boekbinderij*] (*a*) a place where books are bound, (*b*) the product of the book binder's art, *rare;* (3) **count,** *W.* a count or estimation of the number of cattle on a ranch made from an examination of the ranch records; (4) **factor,** a book agent, *rare;* (5) **farmer,** (see quot. 1852); (6) **farming,** farming in accordance with information obtained from books; (7) **house,** a book-publishing house or concern; (8) ***keeper,** at Harvard College, a student appointed to record the names of those students not returning to their rooms by a specified hour in the evening, *obs.;* (9) **peddler,** one who travels about selling books; (10) **social,** (see quot.), *rare;* (11) **stand,** a place or station occupied by a vendor of books, magazines, etc.; (12) **store,** a store or shop where books are sold, cf. **gift bookstore, village bookstore.**

(1) 1830 *Williams's N.-Y. Ann. Reg.* 1830 299 John Emory and Beverly Waugh, Book Agents, New-York. **1946** T. Jones *Skinny*

Angel 135 He returned with slightly over two hundred dollars, having fallen into the hands of some of the book agents who swarmed to the Institutes for the easy pickings. — **(2)** (*a*) **1815** *Niles' Reg.* VIII. 141/2 There are [in Pittsburgh] . . . 5 printing offices; 4 book binderies. **1885** *Harper's Mag.* Feb. 370/1 Flavilla . . . served an apprenticeship at the book-bindery. (*b*) **1887** *Courier-Journal* 2 May 5/2 It is a sad thing that some of the most beautiful book-bindery and some of the finest rhetoric have been brought to make sin attractive. — **(3)1926** Branch *Cowboy* 109 But in the fervor of speculation, book counts were the basis of transactions, and were accepted as security by the banks. **1942** Dale *Cow Country* 108 They soon discovered that book count in selling cattle was a thing of the past. — **(4)1797** Weems *Letters* II. 86, I . . . think you have borne much harder upon me than upon the rest of your Book Factors.

(5) 1841 *Spirit of Times* 30 Oct. 417/1 (We.), This, however, is like all the other assertions of the Book farmers. **1852** Regan *Emigrant's Guide* 254 But he was what we call in this country, a 'Book Farmer,' that is, one who farms on scientific principles—reads books on the subject, and makes experiments. **1865** Gail Hamilton *Skirmishes* ix. 133 We want them to be practical farmers, book-farmers and gentlemen-farmers in one. — **(6) 1823** R. B. Thomas *Farmer's Almanack 1824* 18–24 Dec./2 Be not stubborn and unreasonable in your prejudices against what is called *book-farming* . . . .Farmers may acquire much useful knowledge by reading. **1930** Holden *Alkali Trails* 244 The average farmer had a profound contempt for scientific farming, 'book farming' as he called it. — **(7) 1867** *Atlantic Mo.* March 343/2 Such books, too, as the people of Chicago and the Northwest are buying! Already three large book-houses are competing to supply the demand of this great market. — **(8) 1830** *Collegian* 225, I strode over the bridge, with a rapidity which grew with . . . my anxiety to reach my goal ere . . . the book-keeper's light should disappear from his window. **1851** Hall *College Words* 136 The College Freshman . . . was commonly called the bookkeeper. The duties of this office are now performed by one of the Proctors. — **(9) 1844** *Lowell Offering* IV. 146 Some book-pedlers, shoe-pedlers, essence-pedlers, and candy boys came in. **1889** *Cent. Mag.* April 847/1 First seen in the neighborhood of Alexandria [Va.] as a book-peddler for a Philadelphia firm.

(10) 1892 *Courier-Journal* 1 Oct. 12/4 The Women's Auxiliary will give a 'book social' Friday evening, October 7. . . . Admission, a well-bound book or twenty-five cents. — **(11) 1875** A. Daly *Big Bonanza* (1884) 20 Stocks? Shares? Short? Why, sir, that's what I hear continually at my book-stand down near the Exchange. — **(12) 1763** *Boston Ev. Post* 3/3. **1810** *Edinburgh Rev.* XVII. 121 Their booksellers' shops passing under the name of book-stores. **1947** *Chi. Sun* (Bk. Week) 7 Sep. 7/3 North shore readers gained another bookstore this week.

As the last term in **average, bill, blank, blue, board, boat, brand, campaign, class, comic, complaint, conduct, cook, cooking, cotton, Democratic Campaign Text, entry, estray, grade, hand, horse, jargon, loan office, mileage, offering, pass, plantation, plantation account, pocket, rule, score, source, stock, store, stub, stub ballot, style, ticket, trip book.**

booky ˌbʊkɪ, *a.* Fond of books, bookish. *Colloq.* — **1832** Paulding *Westward Ho* I. 194 You're one of the booky fellers that think of one thing while they are talking about another. **1898** Atherton *Californians* 28 It became known that she was 'booky,'—a social crime in San Francisco.

***boom,** *n.*[1]

1. A barrier of connected floating timbers placed across a stream or around an area of water to retain floating logs. Cf. **catch boom, log boom, mill boom, pocket boom, side boom.**

1676 Sewall *Diary* I. 23 Squaw and Sonne taken at Salmon Falls Mill, being seen as they went over the Boom. **1789** *Mass. Acts* (1894) V. 94 The laying a boom across the River Androscoggin . . . for the purpose of stopping and securing logs and other lumber. **1839** *Louisville Journal* 26 June 2/3 The flood . . . has carried away the Yankee booms on the Aroostook and Fish River, and most of the British and Yankee booms on the St. Johns. **1947** *Sat. Ev. Post* 8 Mar. 53/2 Logs or men wouldn't halt until they reached the mill boom in Stillwater, two hundred miles of white water away.

2. In combs.: (1) **boom company,** a company that collects logs in booms; (2) **gatherer,** one who collects logs in booms; (3) **head,** (see quot.); (4) **house,** a house in which those who work at a boom live; (5) **log,** =**boom stick;** (6) **master,** one in charge of a boom; (7) **stick,** one of the logs fastened together in making a boom to hold floating logs.

(1) 1862 *Harper's Mag.* June 28/1 There are organizations entitled 'Boom Companies' who have the means provided . . . to interrupt the passage of the logs. — **(2) 1850** Judd *R. Edney* xviii. 220 This flood was both springtime and harvest for log-drivers, boom-gatherers, and lumber-men generally. — **(3) 1848** Thoreau *Maine Woods* 42 The logs . . . are thus towed altogether . . . across the lake, . . . by a windlass or boom-head such as we sometimes saw standing on an island or head-land. — **(4) 1892** *Harper's Mag.* Dec. 84 [She] must 'a' ben hidin' up in the boom-house. **1897** E. W. Brodhead *Bound in Shallows* 10, I thought you might recall the little black-eyed, brown-legged girl who used to play around the boom-house.

(5) 1945 *Reader's Digest* Aug. 86 He and Dad are looking for boom logs and they won't let me in a canoe till I can swim. — **(6) 1851** Springer *Forest Life* 175 It is the duty of the boom-master . . . to raft the logs of each individual in parcels by themselves. — **(7)1850** Judd *R. Edney* xvi. 207 They found Chuk in trouble; his guys had parted, and his boom-sticks were broken. **1897** E. W. Brodhead *Bound in Shallows* 10 She could walk the boom-sticks like a cat, and ride on the log cars in a most amazing fashion.

boom bum, *n.*[2] [f. **boom,** *v.*[2]]

1. *W.* In gold mining, a rush of water from a reservoir to wash out gold deposits. Also **boom-flume.**

1874 Raymond *6th Rep. Mines* 302 The use of a boom permits the working of ground that could by no other means be made to pay. **1876** ——— *8th Rep. Mines* 318 A force of thirty-five men was set at work . . . building boom-flumes and reservoirs.

b. (See quot. 1890.)

1890 *N. & Q.* IV. 8 March 227 All persons at all familiar with the every-day speech of any large part of the Southern and South-western States are familiar with the fact that a boom in a river is the same as a freshet or spate. **1948** *Galveston* (Tex.) *News* 14 June 4/6 The Rio Grande, for the first time in two years, was on a regular boom yesterday, reaching a 12-foot rise by morning.

2. A sudden increase in business activity; a rapid rise in prices; a sudden, and occas. artificial, inflation of real-estate values.

1879 *Lumberman's Gaz.* 19 Dec., There has not been the 'boom' upon lumber experienced in many other articles of merchandise. **1894** Robley *Bourbon Co., Kansas* 9 Rogers thought he was in the midst of a 'boom,' and he asked them $1,000 an acre. **1947** *Chi. D. News* 4 Feb. 10/1 Then the boom lasted for two years after Armistice Day.

b. Attrib. with **city, magic, maker, time, town, year.**

1904 *Public Ledger* (Phila.) 14 June 8 No 'boom city' of the West can boast such a record of amazing and substantial growth. — **1886** *Leslie's Mo.* March 306/1 Cities . . . whose inhabitants had yet to be gathered in from the four corners of the earth by boom magic. — **1895** *Cent. Mag.* Aug. 638/2 The troop of boom makers has actively given its perennial leisure to extravagant schemes of town-platting. — **1896** *N. Amer. Rev.* CLXIII. 711 The West is harvesting the fruitage of the seed sown in the boom time of seven . . . years ago. **1943** *Reader's Digest* Oct. 98 (*title*), Boomtime for Bootleggers. **1948** *Appraisal Jrnl.* April 172/2 It seemed to be reasonable, temporarily, under boom time conditions. — **1900** Smithwick *Evol. of State* 19 Colonel De Witt was as enthusiastic as the real estate dealer in a boom town nowadays. **1947** *Steamboat* (Colo.) *Pilot* 16 Jan. 1/4 The Jerome was built in 1889, when Aspen was one of the boom towns of the West. — **1944** *Harper's Mag.* March 364/2 After the war and during the boom years Reynolds busied himself making a living in Asheville.

Also **boom and bust,** a period of great prosperity followed by a severe depression.

1947 *Harper's Mag.* June 527/1 On the basis of the experience after World War I, we can write out today an almost sure-fire prescription for another cycle of Boom and Bust about 1955. **1948** *Time* 22 March 85/1 This is the stuff out of which booms and busts are made.

3. Enthusiastic support of, or admiration for, a particular person; esp. great or rapidly increasing sentiment in favor of a political candidate. Also attrib.

1879 *Chi. Tribune* 15 May 11/5 The more the Democrats in Congress back down, the worse it is for the Grant boom. **1880** *Nation* XXXI. 285/1 Forward the boom brigade; 'Vote for Grant,' Conkling said. **1948** *Time* 10 May 21/1 The boom for Justice William O. Douglas had collapsed.

As the last term in **cotton, diamond, immigration, Kansas, oil, Oklahoma, paper, presidential, real estate, soap, store, trade, war, wildcat boom.**

boom bum, *v.*[1] [f. **boom,** *n.*[1]] *tr.* **1.** To impound (logs) in a boom. **2.** To equip (a river, lake, etc.) with a boom for stopping floating timber.

(1) 1850 Judd *R. Edney* xxviii. 312 It was arranged that the elder Edney should furnish the logs, Chuk boom them, and Richard saw them. **1879** Vivian *Wanderings in Western Land* 81 About nine miles above Newcastle we passed a large lumber station, called 'Parker's,' where quantities of timber are 'boomed' (that is, collected between 'booms' previous to its being divided off into rafts or 'joints'). **1948** *Green Bay* (Wis.) *Press-Gazette* 13 July 1/3 Suspected 'log rustlers' liberated 3,000,000 board feet of boomed logs and set them swinging in the tide towards the United States. — **(2) 1879** *Lumberman's Gaz.*

1 Oct., Numerous lakes communicating with the main Slough have been boomed.

***boom,** *v.*²

1. *intr.* **a.** Of a river: To rush strongly. Also of logs carried down by a river. **b.** To move with speed or vigor. Also fig.

(a) 1852 *Knickerb.* XL. 154 The Licking added her tribute very modestly to the total, which, not now estopped . . . by the 'gorge' on the bar, went booming by. **1879** *Lumberman's Gaz.* 19 Dec., The three drives . . . are all this side of Big Rapids, and with plenty of water come booming along at a most lively rate. **1944** DUNCAN *M. Graham* 131 Steamboats could come to New Salem only when the Sangamon was booming with snow-water, a few days in the spring. — **(b) 1873** MARK TWAIN & WARNER *Gilded Age* xvii. 60 Mr. Jeff Thompson was the most popular engineer who could be found for his work. . . . In his own language he 'just went booming.' **1904** W. H. SMITH *Promoters* xi. 175 His spirits boomed to the top notch.

2. *intr.* To display sudden activity or briskness; to rise rapidly into notice or prosperity.

1873 MARK TWAIN & WARNER *Gilded Age* xxvii. 244 There's 200,000 coming, and that will set things booming again. **1928** FOY & HARLOW *Clowning Thro' Life* 103 Big strikes of silver had occurred at Leadville, the place was beginning to boom, and had as yet no railroad. **1948** JOHNSTON *Gold Rush* 46/2 They will tell of the days when 'she was booming and wide open' and when the deserted bars and benches swarmed with men who plied picks and gold pans.

3. *intr.* To show enthusiasm *for* a candidate, etc.

1879 *Indianapolis Journal* 23 April, The rest [of the stalwarts] are in varying degrees positive, if not all 'booming' for U. S. Grant. **1889** FARMER 78/1 The whole State is booming for Smith.

4. *tr.* To bring prominently into public notice; to support or promote in this way; to cause a "boom" in.

1882 E. V. SMALLEY in *Cent. Mag.* Aug. 506/1 To 'boom' a town in Dakota is an art requiring a little money, a good deal of printer's ink, and no end of push and cheek. **1909** H. N. CASSON *Life McCormick* 190 Then the sudden scarcity of laborers created a panic among the farmers, and boomed the sale of all manner of farm machinery. **1948** *Chi. Tribune* 6 July II. 1/3 He invited other Democrats to abide in his mountain wonderland, and boom it.

boomage ˈbumɪdʒ, *n.* Toll for the use of a boom in which saw logs are collected. — **1818** *Mass. Laws* (1822) VIII. 51 A toll or boomage . . . is hereby granted . . . for the benefit of the said proprietors . . . according to the rates following. **1864** C. L. FLINT *Eighty Years* 74 The boom is owned by an individual, who derives a large profit from the boomage, which is 35 cents per thousand on all logs coming into it.

boomer ˈbumɚ, *n.*¹ [f. **boom, v.*]

1. = **mountain boomer.**

1878 C. COALE in *Ann. S.W. Va.* (1929) 1544 The formidable animal proved to be a boomer, a species of mountain squirrel. **1943** R. CHASE *Jack Tales* 201 Boomer: small red mountain squirrel. **1948** *Sat. Ev. Post* 31 July 35/1 He pulled the squirrel from his pocket. . . . Well, I'll just clean this here old boomer for you and be gittin' along.

2. (See quot. 1889.)

1884 KINGSLEY *Stand. Nat. Hist.* V. 121 The 'Showt'l' or 'Sewellel' of the aborigines . . . [is] known to more prosaic hunters and trappers as the 'Boomer.' **1889** *Cent.* 626/3 *Boomer*, . . . a name of the showt'l or mountain beaver, *Haplodon rufus* or *Aplodontia leporina.* **1943** CAHALANE *Meeting the Mammals* 98 Although he usually shuns human traffic, a 'boomer' once made his home near the head of the trail to Crater Lake, where hundreds of people passed every day.

boomer ˈbumɚ, *n.*² [f. **boom,** *v.*² **4.**]

1. One who "booms" a town, enterprise, person, etc.; an enthusiastic supporter or advocate.

1880 *Ill. State Jrnl.* (Springfield) 27 May 4/1 The Illinois Republican Convention took care that the 'unit rule' should not be broken, as the Blaine boomers threaten to do in Pennsylvania and New York. **1882** *Cent. Mag.* XXIV. 508 Bismarck has a 'boomer.' He is hired by the Chamber of Commerce, at a good salary, to ride upon the trains east of Fargo and talk to emigrants about the advantages of settling near the Banner City. **1908** *St. Louis Globe-Democrat* 4 July 2/4 One of the Ridgely 'boomers' said to me: 'Why not Mr. Ridgely?' **1943** *Reader's Digest* Oct. 6/1 The normal American is a natural boomer and booster. **1946** MCWILLIAMS *So. Calif. Country* 115 Boosters and boomers came with the tourists, convinced that the completion of the Southern Pacific line to Southern California would transform the region.

2. An unusual or phenomenal success.

In the sense of something notable, impressive, Baker reports this from Australia in 1860.

1887 *Courier-Journal* 30 Jan. 8/4 This sale will be a boomer for the very finest soft or stiff hat goes for $1.98. **1889** *Idaho City* (Ida.) *World* 3 Sep. 1/2 If the Custer mill starts again this fall . . . old Custer with her numerous mines of high grade ore will be a 'boomer.'

3. *W.* A participant in a rush for unsettled lands; a settler or "squatter" on a ranch; a nester or homesteader.

1884 *Chi. Tribune* 13 May 5/4 The boomers report a large number of people—fully 1,000—now in the Indian Territory. **1930** FERBER *Cimarron* 11 It was known he had been one of the early Boomers who followed the banner of David Payne in the first wild dash of that adventurer into Indian Territory. **1941** *Nat. Geog. Mag.* March 269/2 Again and again as 'boomers,' 'sooners,' and squatters, whites invaded the country.

b. "A migratory workman" (Web. '34). Also attrib.

1926 *Amer. Mercury* Jan. 64/2 The footloose *boomer* looks down on the *homeguard* with the condescending scorn of a globe-trotter for the . . . yokel, and the *homeguard* considers the *boomer* a tramp. **1945** MARSHALL *Santa Fe* 89 Town boosters were called 'boomers' in those days, although later the word, especially among railroaders, came to have the meaning of transient worker, as against the 'home guard.' **1947** *Harper's Mag.* Jan. 67/2 Then, restless, he became a boomer machinist.

As the last term in **land, Oklahoma, town boomer.**

booming ˈbumɪŋ, *n.*¹ [f. **boom,** *n.*¹] The formation of a boom, the impounding of logs in a boom. Also attrib. Cf. **log booming.**

1798 *Boston Rec.* 45 That . . . the said Corporation be allowed the Privilege of securing by booming their logs on such parts of the beach at the foot of the Common . . . as the Selectmen . . . may appoint. **1850** JUDD *R. Edney* xxviii. 312 Bill Stonners' Point was the best booming privilege on the River. **1879** *Mich. Gen. Statutes* (1882) I. 550 Each log running or booming company doing business on any waters on which the logs or timber are floated or run. **1944** BINNS *Timber Beast* 70 The ox teams had dragged the best of the timber over that road, to be dumped in the booming ground in the cove.

***booming,** *n.*² [Cf. **boom,** *n.*² **2.** and *v.*² **4.**]

1. The fact of flourishing by a boom; the creation of a boom or the attempt to make one. Also attrib.

1873 *Newton Kansan* 3 July 1/6 'Booming' is the name of an operation with which probably our readers are not generally familiar. **1880** *Harper's Mag.* Feb. 383 This little town [Rosita, Colo.] was founded in 1872, and led a quiet existence, with occasional episodes of what is here called 'booming.' **1888** *Chicago Herald* (F.), Ben Butterworth, of Ohio, one of the mainstays of John Sherman's booming squad.

2. *W.* A method of using impounded water in placer mining (see first quot.).

1874 RAYMOND *6th Rep. Mines* 299 The practice of booming has permitted the successful working of poorer ground than has been before worked in the county. [*Note.*] A rude form of hydraulic mining, in which a torrent of water, obtained by the accumulation of smaller supplies, is suffered to escape from the reservoir at intervals. *Ib.* 302 Booming may be considered as the best labor-saving invention introduced into the country of late years.

***booming,** *n.*³ = **drumming,** *n.* **2.** Also **booming ground.**

1864 *Wilkes' Spirit of Times* 26 Nov. 195/1 As the sharp-tailed grouse celebrates his wooing with a dance and a fight, and the ruffed grouse by drumming, so the blue grouse, in honor of his mate, makes an extraordinary noise called by hunters 'booming.' **1941** LEHMANN *Atwater's Prairie Chicken* 13 Key areas during the courtship season are the booming grounds where males assemble each morning from daybreak until 8 A.M. and each afternoon from 5:30 P.M. until dark and give their courtship display. **1945** SCHWARTZ *Ecology of Prairie Chicken* 57 The fall booming-ground display is similar to that of the spring but booming is not so loud or resonant and the activities do not lead to mating.

***booming,** *a.*

1. Of a river: Rushing strongly. Cf. ***boom,** *v.*² **1.**

1831 AUDUBON *Ornith. Biog.* I. 155 To give you some idea of a *Booming Flood* of these gigantic streams, it is necessary to state the causes which give rise to it. **1868** *Putnam's Mag.* I. 596/1 The chutes, the landslides, the booming torrents [of the Miss. R.] . . . —all these supply . . . themes of conversation.

2. (See quot. 1889.)

1867 *Harper's Wkly.* 12 Jan. 29/2 On 'panic' or 'booming' days the excitement is proportionately increased. **1889** *Cent.* 627/1 Booming. . . . Active; lively; advancing; buoyant: as, a *booming* market. **1948** *Sat. Ev. Post* 7 Aug. 10/2, I came across a picture taken while that Colorado town was a booming silver camp.

3. Splendid, grand. Also as intensive adv.

1884 MARK TWAIN *H. Finn* xvii. 151 We can just have booming times—they don't have no school now. *Ib.* xxiv. 242 They was booming mad, and gave us a cussing.

boomlet ˈbumlɪt, *n.* [Cf. **boom,** *n.*² **2.**] An attempted boom, one that does not attain expected proportions.

1887 *Saginaw Ev. Jrnl.* 7 Dec., The boomlet of W. R. Burt for governor grows about an inch a day. **1907** *Collier's* IX. 28 He [Gov.

Hughes] was introduced by Chanler who has a Presidential boomlet of his own, and was hailed as our next President. **1947** *Time* 16 June 27/2 The old gold camp of Fairbanks in the interior also enjoys a boomlet.

Boomopolis ˌbumˈɑplɪs, *n.* [Cf. **boom,** *n.*² **2.**] A jesting name for a boom town. *Rare.* — **1890** J. K. Bangs in *Harper's Mag.* Dec. 160/1 A Boomopolis Wedding. *Ib.*, The undisputed belle of Boomopolis . . . that Eden of sand and corner lots.

boomster ˈbumstɚ, *n.* [Cf. **boom,** *v.*² **4.**] One who works up a boom. *Obs.* — **1879** *Nation* 9 Oct. 236 The trickery and usurpation . . . of the leading boomster. **1887** *Courier-Journal* 8 Jan. 4/4 Henry Watterson goes for the Southern boom in his usual style. . . . A few of his favorite epithets . . . for the progressive men of the South are: . . . 'Boomsters,' 'Ringsters,' [etc.].

boonder ˈbundɚ, *n.* [Du. *boender.*] A brush used in scrubbing.

1791 Freneau *Poems* (1795) 423 Fate early had pronounc'd this building's doom, Ne'er to be vex'd with boonder, brush, or broom. **1859** Bartlett. **1933** Cheley *Camping Out* 97, I am including a photograph of a 'boonder' made this way by Frank Stoll, also several withes made by him from hickory switches, as well as hickory bark rope.

boondoggle ˈbunˌdɑgl̩, *v.* [Origin unknown.] *intr.* To engage in trifling, inconsequential, or piddling work. Also as a noun and in derivatives, as **boondoggler, boondoggling.** *Slang.*

1935 *Chi. Tribune* 4 Oct., To the cowboy it meant the making of saddle trappings out of odds and ends of leather, and they boondoggled when there was nothing else to do on the ranch. **1942** *Ib.* 20 April 8/3 No good American wants to see our form of government or our system of economy overturned by boondogglers or social experimenters. **1947** *Ib.* 8 June 1. 22/2 The cost of this boondoggle has been estimated at perhaps 50 million dollars. **1947** *Steamboat* (Colo.) *Pilot* 2 Jan. 1/4 Nor do I believe in worldwide boondoggling or free and easy loans from our treasury to support decadent empires.

booshway ˈbuʃwe, *n.* [?Var. of **bourgeois,** *q.v.*] (See quot.) *Obs.* — **1871** Pine *Beyond West* (ed. 2) 276 After a camp [of fur traders] is organized, and is on the march, a military discipline is observed; a leader is chosen, known as a 'Booshway,' whose business is to take the supervision—look after the condition of the whole camp.

boost bust, *n.* [f. the verb.] A push or shove that assists one to rise; commendation, praise. *Colloq.*

1825 Neal *Bro. Jonathan* II. 101 What say you, mayor?—shall I give him a boost?—or no? **1889** *Kansas Times & Star* 25 Nov., The Star prints a half-column boost of the new Young Women's Christian Association home here, signed 'An Inmate of the Home.' **1945** *Estes Park* (Colo.) *Trail* 9 Nov. 2/2 Good old Estes will look good to us and don't think I don't give Estes a boost every time I can.

b. A ride along one's way, a lift. *Colloq.*

1891 Garland *Main-travelled Roads* (1922) 73 'Want a boost?' 'Well, yes. Are you down with a team?' 'Yep. 'Bout goin' home. Climb right in.'

boost bust, *v.* [Origin unknown.] *tr.* To raise or lift, to hoist, push, shove up. Also fig.

1815 Humphreys *Yankey* 103 *Boost*, raise up, lift up, exalt. **1833** S. Smith *Major Downing* 139 You . . . give me a lift into public life, and you've been a boosting me along ever since. **1847** Field *Drama in Pokerville* 117 [He clambered] back into the box, . . . the sanctimonious manager assisting to 'boost him' with the most friendly solicitude. **1855** *N.Y. Herald* 20 Nov. 2/3 They discovered that his martyrdom would not 'boost' them into power in the Keystone State.

b. *To boost* (*up*), to cheer, encourage, praise.

1887 F. Francis *Saddle & Moccasin* 121 You think that I'm trying to boost the place up because it belongs to us. **1887** N. Perry *Flock of Girls* 239 She did talk about herself when she cried herself down, and we were always boosting her up to make her feel better. **1948** *Chi. Tribune* 20 Apr. 1. 9/2 One of southern California's biggest industries is 'boosting' the opportunities and virtues of the region.

c. To raise in amount or price.

1907 *Phila. Inquirer* 28 Nov. (Th.), Little disposition to boost the cost of this or that musty, dog-eared volume was apparent. **1945** *Dly. Sentinel* (Grand Junction, Colo.) 25 Nov. 13/5 To increase minimum class room expenditures and boost teachers' salaries—Two conflicting sets of proposals offered in house and a third in senate.

booster ˈbustɚ, *n.* [f. **boost,** *v.*]

1. One who or that which supports or promotes the interests of a person, cause, etc. Cf. **land booster.**

1890 *Stock Grower* 1 Feb. 3/2 The Rio Grande Inflammation and Preliminary Dividend company, of which Col. Partial Smyth is chief booster, seems to be worried. **1910** *Sparks* (Nev.) *Forum* 15 Feb. 1/5 We are very likely to go back on the best booster for our town that we have and incidentally lose half our trade. **1948** *Capital-Democrat* (Tishomingo, Okla.) 24 June 3/4 Tishomingo has won two more boosters as a favorite spot for spending a vacation.

Hence **boosterism,** *n.* — **1939** in McWilliams *So. Calif. Country* (1946) 225 At bottom it was garish, a bit crude, lacking in pure form and subtlety, devoid of finesse, largely boosterism run amuck. **1948** *Dly. Ardmoreite* (Ardmore, Okla.) 8 April 12/2 'Boosterism' will be out when a new Maryland Department of Information begins to warm up the typewriters this year.

b. A capper or decoy as for gamblers (see also quot. 1910). *Slang.*

1906 Woolridge *Grafters of Amer.* 241 The booster meets the victim and conducts him to a saloon or byway and there the operator is found shaking three dice. **1910** *N. Eng. Mag.* July 587/2 A shoplifter is called a 'booster' or 'hoister' or 'hyster,' and an exceptionally smart one a 'swell booster.' **1947** *Amer. Sp.* XXII. 164 The *boosters* come in to keep the game going.

2. (See quot. 1896.) Also attrib.

1896 S. P. Thompson *Dynamo-Electric Mach.* (ed. 5) 726 Motor-dynamos are employed . . . to compensate the drop in voltage on long mains by inserting into the main at a distant point a series motor. . . . American electricians term it a 'booster.' **1945** *Reader's Digest* April 97/2 Under orders from London, certain agents had become conversant with the operations of the 74 booster stations in France's long-distance telephone system. Now, equipped with German passes, they went to the booster stations and blew them up.

3. a. booster club, a club composed of boosters. **b. booster engine,** an engine that boosts or assists another over heavy grades.

(a) 1922 S. Lewis *Babbitt* i. § 4. 19 He stuck in his lapel the Boosters' Club button. **1947** *Chi. Sun* 30 May 17/1 Delegations from the booster clubs . . . feel the question turning uneasily around in their subconscious minds. — **(b) 1945** *Greeley* (Colo.) *Tribune* 12 Feb. 1/3 Several piled up behind the freight's lead locomotive and others near the booster engine at the rear

***boot,** *n.*

1. (See quots.)

1828 Webster, Boot. . . . Also, an apron or leathern cover for a gig or chair, to defend persons from rain and mud. This latter application is local and improper. **1911** Lincoln *Cap'n Warren* 9 The 'boot' was a rubber curtain buttoned across the front of the buggy, extending from the dashboard to just below the level of the driver's eyes.

2. In combs.: (1) **boot and shoe-store,** a store where boots and shoes are sold; (2) **black,** one who blacks and polishes shoes; (3) **blacking,** polishing boots and shoes with blacking, also attrib.; (4) **crimp,** (see quot. 1874); (5) **crimper,** a person or device that crimps boot leather; (6) **graveyard,** *W.* (see quot. and cf. next); (7) **Hill,** *W.* designating a cemetery or graveyard for those who died with their boots on, *jocular;* (8) **hook,** (see quot. 1874); (9) ***jack,** (*a*) a dolt, blockhead, *rare,* (*b*) (see quot.); (10) **jack signal,** on railroads the Gravit signal or right-angle semaphore; (11) **leg,** see as a main entry; (12) **legger,** (*a*) one who sells alcoholic liquor clandestinely and illegally, (*b*) one who deals illicitly in anything, also with a specifying term, *slang;* (13) **lick,** =next, cf. **bootlick,** *v.;* (14) **licker,** one who curries favor with another, a toady, orig. college slang; (15) **licking,** toadying, also as adj., *slang;* (16) **pack,** (see quot. 1926 and cf. **pack**).

(1) 1789 *Boston Directory* 174 Baxter John and Com. boot and shoe-store, No. 14, State-street. — **(2) 1817** *Essex Inst. Coll.* VIII. 246 At the house where we stopped they had a boot-black and barber. **1945** *Sat. Review* 31 March 7/3 To his bewilderment, he found himself suddenly limited to the economic role of a bootblack or janitor. — **(3) 1866** Gregg *Life in Army* 139 Here are . . . candy shops, pea nut stands, cake wagons, and boot-blacking establishments. **1870** O. Logan *Before Footlights* 173 Men have the whole field of labor before them, from Wall street speculation down—or up—to boot-blacking. **1923** Watts *Luther Nichols* 68 There were . . . saloons, barber-shops and boot-blacking 'parlors' on the first floors. — **(4) 1847** Webster. **1849** *Rep. Comm. Patents* (1850) 212 Improvement in Boot Crimps. **1874** Knight 335/2 *Boot-crimp,* a tool or a machine for giving the shape to the pieces of leather designed for boot uppers.

(5) 1830 *U.S. Patents* 19 Feb. **1841** *Boston Almanac* 53 Boot Crimpers. Ross, Jacob, Wilson lane [etc.]. — **(6) 1881** Romspert *Western Echo* 210 There is at this place [Dodge City] a yard called the *Boot Grave-yard,* a place well known to all western men, and called thus from the fact that thirty-eight men have been buried there with their boots on. — **(7) 1901** *Everybody's Mag.* June 582/2 Occasionally his six-shooter brought order and a new grave or two in Boot Hill cemetery. **1930** Ferber *Cimarron* 160 The body, unclaimed, was interred in Boot Hill, with only the prowling jackals to mourn him, their own kin. **1948** *So. Sierran* May 2/3 The rest of us took Wednesday for an auto trip . . . through Tombstone of the one and only Boothill Cemetery. — (8) **1851** *Polly Peablossom* 188 The first article that presented itself was a pair of boot-hooks. **1874** KNIGHT 336/1 *Boot-hook*, a device for drawing on boots and shoes, consisting essentially of a stout wire bent into a hooked form and provided with a handle. — (9) (*a*) **1842** *Dartmouth* IV. 116 A stupid fellow, a dolt, a boot-jack, an ignoramus, is called here a *gonus*. (*b*) **1890** T. M. COOLEY *Railways Amer.* 222 At all places where two rails cross or approach each other . . . dangerous boot-jacks are formed by the rail-heads.

(10) **1898** *Engineering Mag.* XVI. 161/2 The 'Bootjack' Signals of the Lake Shore and Michigan Southern Ry. — (12) (*a*) **1889** SANGER *Rep.* in Thoburn *Hist. Oklahoma* I. 223 Gamblers, liquor dealers (or as they are called here 'boot-leggers'), lot-jumpers. **1948** *Dly. Ardmoreite* (Ardmore, Okla.) 17 May 1/4 The illegal moonshine had probably been dumped by a fleeting bootlegger. (*b*) **1946** *Sports Afield* June 120 Duck bootleggers also were fined, as were hunters who illegally killed or possessed woodcocks, waterfowl, doves . . . and robins. **1946** *Chi. D. News* 27 Aug. 12/3 One of these bootleggers [in lumber] who had taken on a few drinks too many . . . confided to a friend of mine that he had made one of these round trips. — (13) **1849** *Yale Banger* 6 Nov. 6 The rites of Wooden Spoon we next recite, When Boot-lick hypocrites upraised their might. **1899** GREEN *Va. Word-Book* 64 *Bootlick*, a person who tries to gain favour by mean behavior. — (14) **1848** *Yale Banger* 23 Oct., Three or four boot-lickers rise. **1924** B. J. HENDRICK *W. H. Page* I. 19 The recipient is either a humbug or a bootlicker.

(15) **1849** *Gallinipper* Dec., The 'Wooden Spoon' exhibition passed off without any such hub-hub, except where the pieces were of such a character as to offend the delicacy and modesty of some of those crouching, fawning, boot-licking hypocrites. **1851** HALL *College Words* 24 Some [students are] . . . very apt to linger after recitation to get a clearer knowledge of some passage. They are *Bootlicks*, and that is known as *Bootlicking*. **1894** *Current Hist.* IV. 472 Working his way by scheming and bootlicking into the good graces of . . . a young idiot of a lord. — (16) **1893** *Scribner's Mag.* June 715 Logger's Footgear. . . . Old-fashioned boot-pack. Modern rubber-soled boot-pack. **1926** RICKABY *Ballads* 233 *Boot-pack.* A heavy and roomy foot-wear, usually of rubber, somewhat higher than a shoe buckled or laced. Its roominess allowed the wearing of several pairs of thick woolen socks. This was worn mainly in the winter or cutting period, giving way to the calked shoe or boot on the drive.

b. *In the boot*, of wheat: In the stage of developing the inflorescence.

1858 *Texas Almanac 1859* 70 A severe frost fell in Northern Texas on the 5th of April, 1857, when the wheat was in the boot.

c. In colloq. phrases: (1) *To go it boots*, to act quickly or vigorously; (2) *to move* (*start*) *one's boots*, to set off, depart; (3) *to bet your boots*, to be quite sure about; (4) *big in one's boots*, proud, conceited; (5) *to beat out of one's boots*, to beat decisively; (6) *to go down in one's boots*, to be scared.

(1) **1843** *Quincy* (Ill.) *Herald* 24 Feb. 4/1 He is then prepared to stem the torrent of mud which clothes our streets . . . and yell out with unusual self-importance, 'go it boots.' **1872** *Borderer* (Las Cruces, N.M.) 5 June 1/2 Then go it 'progress,' go it 'boots.' — (2) **1851** *Alta California* (S.F.) 29 July, It needed not this display to assure the spectators that they were bent on 'moving their boots.' **1886** *Leslie's Mo.* May 614/2 Now start your boots, and go home. — (3) **1856** *Spirit of Times* (N.Y.) 6 Sep. 3/3 You may bet your old boots on that. **1878** HART *Sazerac Lying Club* 51 You better bet your boots, boys, I wasn't slow in takin' aim. **1909** *Sat. Ev. Post* 10 April 9/3 Monk grinned and exclaimed: 'You bet your boots!' — (4) **1879** TOURGEE *Fool's Errand* 84 They are gittin so big in ther boots they cant rest.

(5) **1890** *Adrian* (Mich.) *Times* 6 March, 'Gov. Luce,' he said, '. . . can beat Barnes out of his boots.' — (6) **1901** WHITE *Claim Jumpers* viii. 113 'You hits hard, sonny,' said he, 'and you don't go down in your boots a little bit.'

As the last term in **blunderbuss, carriage, Congress, cowhide, gum, hip, Indian, logging, Oregon, rubber, shoe, store, Suwarrow, wrapping boot.**

bootee buˈti, *n.* [* *boot* + * *-ee.*] A half-boot or high shoe.

1799 *Aurora* (Phila.) 15 Nov. (Th.), For sale, 180 pairs of bootees. **1819** *Ky. Herald* (Louisville) 30 June 1/5 (*advt.*), Just received . . . Children's leather and morocco Bootees and Shoes. **1854** *Pioneer* (S.F.) Jan. 57 In came Sally with her bootees on,—A hundred years ago! **1929** A. ELLIS *Life* 279 She got a pencil and drew three designs on her booty.

b. A baby's boot or shoe of knitted wool.

1929 *Sears Cat.* Fall 76 These bootees make a warm and cozy place to tuck little feet. **1945** *This Week Mag.* 3 March 5/3 On all his missions he carried a pair of knitted baby bootees.

* **bootleg,** *n.* Illicit or bootlegged liquor. Also attrib. *Slang.*

*a***1889** *Omaha Herald* (B. & L.), There is as much whisky consumed in Iowa now . . . on the boot-leg plan. **1920** *Collier's* 6 March 9/1 They call it bootleg licker . . . because it's prob'ly made outa castaway boots. **1947** *Harper's Mag.* Nov. 445/1 He was going to . . . buy a pint of bootleg rotgut, and get drunk.

b. Used attrib. to denote anything that is inferior or illegal. Also **bootleg days,** the period (1920–33) when federal prohibition was in force.

1895 CHAMBLISS *Diary* 324 The menu at the meal stations along through Texas and Arizona consists of whit-leather steak, overdue eggs, bad-smelling butter, corn dodgers, and 'boot-leg' coffee. **1941** *Harper's Mag.* Oct. 541/2 Massachusetts hams recently engaged a bootleg station in lengthy conversations so that Federal monitoring stations had plenty of time to ply their direction finders and apprehend the operator. **1946** *Newsweek* 7 Jan. 56/2 As a prohibition agent in Chicago in bootleg days Eliot Ness got to know a lot about safes.

bootleg ˈbutˌlɛg, *v.* [f. the noun.] *tr.* Orig. to carry liquor about concealed on one's person, as in a bootleg, for disposing of it illegally. Hence to sell or deal in liquor or anything else illegally or surreptitiously.

1906 in *D.N.* III. 127 William Castell, charged with bootlegging whiskey, was tried before Mayor Eason this morning. **1929** *Variety* 10 Apr. 1/2 There is almost as big a market for bootleg disk records as there is for bootlegged books. **1948** *Chi. Tribune* 28 Nov. 41/5 The sale of liquor is banned here on the Sabbath, and that's when the bootlegger bootlegs.

b. Also **bootlegging,** *n.* Also attrib.

1903 *Cinci. Enquirer* 3 Jan. 1/3 (*caption*), In the Pulpit Was a Minister When Arrested For 'Boot-Legging.' **1946** *Chi. D. News* 24 May 16/1 The black market is becoming as big as prohibition bootlegging ever was. **1948** *Capital-Democrat* (Tishomingo, Okla.) 10 June 11/4 There is not a bootlegging joint or gambling house in Johnston county.

bootlick ˈbutˌlɪk, *v. tr.* and *intr.* To curry favor with (a person), to be a toady. *Slang.*

1845 HOOPER *Suggs* v. 58 A young man . . . was inclined to bootlick anybody suspected of having money. **1885** *Milnor* (Dakota) *Teller* 1 May 2/3 They must drink, truckle, and bootlick to keep their greatness uppermost. **1915** *N.Y. Tribune* 24 March 5/3 It . . . accused 'The Spectator's' staff of grafting and bootlicking their advertisers.

* **booze,** *n.* In slang combs.: (1) **booze fight,** a fight occasioned by strong drink; (2) **fighter,** a heavy drinker; (3) **hound,** =prec.; (4) **joint,** a low dive where whisky is sold.

(1) **1922** H. L. FOSTER *Adv. Trop. Tramp* ix. 127 Riotous booze-fights . . . were less in evidence. — (2) **1903** *Cinci. Enquirer* 9 May 13/1 Booze fighter—One who drinks whisky to excess. **1926** *Chi. Drovers' Jrnl.* 24 Apr. 4/1 The Illinois Steel company's safety council suggests the following for married booze fighters. — (3) **1948** *Dly. Ardmoreite* (Ardmore, Okla.) 29 Apr. 14/1 What chance has the poor boozehound who imbibes too freely and gets stiff as a board? — (4) **1896** G. ADE *Artie* xii. 110 He's . . . dug up the long green and he's puttin it out at the booze joints. **1931** *K.C. Times* 18 July, Officers have raided booze joints in Bates County.

borasca bəˈrɑskə, *n. W.* [Sp. *borrasca* in Amer. Sp. sense here shown.] In a mine, the lack of rich ore. Also transf.

1864 MOWRY *Ariz. & Sonora* 130 When a *borasca* made its appearance, as it will in every mine once in a while, they . . . found themselves . . . without the requisite funds to enable them to pierce through the poor ores and dead rock in order to strike rich ores again. **1896** SHINN *Story of Mine* 156 Here's wishin', . . . that you may hev as many days in bonanza as you hed in borrasca. **1913** GOODWIN *As I Remember Them* 127 There were times when the obstacles in the way would have broken the heart of any other man, for sometimes it looked as though the whole lode was going into perpetual borasca. **1947** BEEBE *Mixed Train Dly.* 208 The V. & T.'s ups and downs, its perilous descents into borrasca and its climbs to dizzy heights of bonanza have been almost continuous.

borax lake. *W.* A lake the water of which has a high concentration of borates from which borax is often prepared commercially by evaporation. Also, loosely, a salt lake or alkali lake. — **1876** *Calaveras Chronicle* (Mokelumne Hill, Calif.) 29 July 2/3, I found Columbus to be a sleepy little town of five hundred inhabitants, situated on a dry borax lake. **1947** *Mazama* Dec. 39/1 Someone supplied the information that the borax lake was inhabited by a species of fish peculiar to that body of water.

bordage ˈbɔrdɪdʒ, *n.* [Can. F.] (See quots.) — **1807** HERIOT *Travels* 267 The ice on the rivers in Canada, acquires a thickness of two feet and upwards, and is capable of supporting any degree of weight. That on the borders of the Saint Lawrence, called the *bordage* sometimes exceeds six feet. **1821** HOWISON *Sketches* (1822) 219 The severity of the weather had frozen the Detroit river . . . but a thaw soon coming on, destroyed the ice so completely, that no part of it remained except a narrow strip along the shore, such as the Canadians call a *bordage*.

border, n. attrib.* Living on or constituting a border, as **border Indians, Missouri, prairie, ranchman, tribe. See also, as main entries, **Border Ruffian, B. Ruffianism, B. State,** and cf. **Indian border.**

1837 IRVING *Bonneville* II. 106 He had . . . betaken himself to the society of the border Indians. — **1857** *Lawrence* (Kans.) *Republican* 11 June 2 Already the pro-slavery papers of Border Missouri raise a shout of expected triumph. — **1846** SAGE *Scenes Rocky Mts.* i, I shall never forget the pleasing sensations produced by my first visit to the border-prairies. — **1916** EASTMAN *From Deep Woods* 127 The border ranchmen called me in now and then. — **1849** PARKMAN *Oregon Trail* 19, I was . . . already familiar with many of the border tribes.

b. Border Eagle (State), (see quots.).

1846 *Warrock's Alman.* (Richmond) 22 *Flash Names*. . . . Mississippi, Border Beagles [*sic*]. **1893** L. WAGNER *More About Names* 30 Mississippi also bears the name of The Border Eagle State, from the American eagle which appears on her arms.

c. Border Patrol, a customs or immigration agent on the Mexican or Canadian border, or the service to which such an agent belongs.

1928 *Collier's* 27 Oct. 81/3 'You know damned well who I am,' said the customs man. 'Border patrol.' **1947** *So. Sierran* Jan. 4/2 Bill Sherrill of the Border Patrol gave us some interesting and humorous comments on his experiences.

d. border tier, designating counties or a railroad on the border of a state.

1861 *Charleston* (S.C.) *Mercury* 26 Feb. 3/1. **1869** *Repub. D. Jrnl.* (Lawrence, Kans.) 25 July, Letter from Border Tier Counties. **1873** BEADLE *Undevel. West* 203 [The] Gulf Railroad runs . . . in a few places within five miles of the Missouri line, and is popularly known here as the 'border tier road.'

Border Ruffian. (Also not *cap.*)

1. A member of the pro-slavery party in Missouri who in 1854–58 often crossed the border into Kansas to vote illegally and to intimidate the opponents of slavery. Now *hist.*

1855 *Free State* (Lawrence, Kans.) 24 Sep. 2/3 It is from their papers at Lawrence that the Press in the States have taken so many accounts of 'Kansas outrages,' and 'Border Ruffians.' **1881** J. W. BUEL *Border Outlaws* 12 The border counties of Missouri and Kansas suffered terribly from the incursions of 'Jayhawkers' and 'Border Ruffians,' afterward guerrillas, as the opposing factions were called. **1948** *Ohio State Arch. & Hist. Quart.* Jan. 5 He warned that the people of the North had no more right to interfere in Kansas than did the 'Border Ruffians' of Missouri.

b. (See quots.)

1856 *Spirit of Times* 29 Nov. 204/3 Mr. Brown and myself have averaged nearly a dozen bass a day, and twice that number of horse-mackerel (our blue-fish), which, on account of their rapacious qualities, are here [R.I.] called 'border-ruffians.' **1857** J. TAYLOR in *Jrnl. Discourses* V. 116 A great majority of the people of the West, on the borders, may be emphatically termed 'Border ruffians.' The Eastern people call them by that name. **1948** *Sat. Review* 22 May 18/3 The old man is one of those [Florida] frontier land-and-slave-stealers whose band of cutthroats and border ruffians murder poor white settlers as well as ruin the broken Indian tribes around them.

2. Attrib. (or as adj.) with **candidate, decision, incursion, nest,** in allusion to Kansas and the troubles there over slavery.

1855 *Free State* (Lawrence, Kans.) 24 Sep. 2/1 Gen. J. W. Whitfield is Atchinson's border ruffian candidate. **1858** *N.Y. Tribune* 12 July 6/5 (*headline*), Jack Henderson discharged. A Border-Ruffian Decision. **1860** GREELEY *Overland Journey* 18 Atchinson, Kansas was long a Border-Ruffian nest. **1867** A. D. RICHARDSON *Beyond Miss.* 28, I asked if there was any doubt about the border ruffian incursions.

b. Border Ruffian State, Kansas. *Obs.*

1856 *Western Citizen* (Paris, Ky.) 24 Apr. 3/3 Abolition organs throughout the north, are sending up jubilant shouts over the Abolition triumph in what they call the 'Border Ruffian State.' **1856** *Spirit of Times* (N.Y.) 27 Dec. 269/3, I wonder if there is any chance for an outsider of the Border Ruffian State to come in.

border-ruffianism, *n.* The acts of violence that characterized the border strife in Kansas and Missouri over slavery. Now *hist.*

1856 *Herald of Freedom* (Lawrence, Kans.) 6 Dec. 1/7, I was a constant reader of your paper till Border Ruffianism interrupted it. **1871** EGGLESTON *Hoosier School.* vi. 71 It is out of these materials [desperadoes and thieves] that border ruffianism has grown. **1905** VALENTINE *H. Sandwith* 162 The *Tribune* was eagerly scanned by pious Republicans for latest exaggerations of Border ruffianism.

Border State. Also **border state.**

1. One of the United States situated on the border between the North and the South.

1842 JOSEPH STURGE *Visit to U.S.* 166 Many planters, with their slaves, have emigrated thither [to Texas] to escape their creditors from the border States. **1866** GREGG *Life in Army* xxv. 212 Thousands of the time-serving trimmers of the border states . . . should be disqualified. **1948** *Chi. D. News* 20 Feb. 1/3 Southern Democrats in Congress, except for a few from the border states, stayed away from the dinner.

b. 1. border free state, a state on the northern side of the border between the North and the South. **2. border slave state,** a state on the southern side of this border. Both *obs.*

(1) **1863** DICEY *Six Months* II. 34 My road lay through Western Virginia, whence the Confederates had just retreated, through Ohio, the great Border Free State. — (2) **1860** *Cong. Globe* 19 Dec. 139/3 Virginia, Maryland, Kentucky, and Missouri . . . constitute the first tier of the border slave States. **1863** DICEY *Six Months* I. 283 Kentucky . . . [is] the staunchest of the Border Slave States.

2. Attrib. with **accent, convention, Democrat, man, manners, mind, policy, proposition.**

1861 *Chi. Tribune* 26 May 1/6 Affairs in Louisville. . . . The Border State Convention meets at Frankfort on Monday. **1862** KETTELL *Hist. Rebellion* I. 73 Neither the Crittendon resolutions, nor the border state propositions were, however, destined to pass Congress. **1863** G. HAMILTON *Gala-Days* 92 For these Border State men . . . I have a profound contempt. **1875** *Chi. Tribune* 8 Dec. 1/5 'Here we are again!' . . . Deacon Pogram, with his band of Border-State Democrats. **1884** BLAINE *20 Years of Congress* I. 467 If the border-state policy of Mr. Lincoln . . . had not required [etc.]. **1886** LOGAN *Great Conspiracy* 555 In both Houses of Congress . . . they had been striving . . . to poison the loyal Northern and Border-State mind. **1888** A. C. GUNTER *Mr. Potter* viii, Miss Potter still keeps her Border-State accent and her Border-State manners.

bore bor, *n.* [f. **bore, v.*] A hoax, trick, deception. *Slang. Obs.* — **1800** *Aurora* (Phila.) 3 July (Th.), A Federal bore [concerning the reported death of Jefferson]. **1811** *Mass. Spy* 1 May (Th.), Tis thus that Hymen cracks his joke, A hoax, a quiz, a bore.

***bore,** *v.* **1. bore-well,** a bored well. Cf. ***bored.** *Rare.* **2. bore-worm,** a caterpillar or borer that attacks the cotton plant.

(1) **1873** *Winfield* (Kans.) *Courier* 18 Jan. 2/2 At Bunker Hill . . . they have a bore-well two hundred and seventy feet deep. — (2) **1840** *N.O. Picayune* 10 Sep. 2/1 Not more than half an average crop of cotton will be made this year. The caterpillar and cut or bore worm have done irreparable mischief. **1856** *Rep. Comm. Patents: Agric.* 86 This [dropping off of young cotton-buds] has been attributed to the agency of the young larvæ of the 'bore-worm.'

***bored,** *a.* Of a well: Made by drilling or boring as distinguished from digging. Cf. **dug well,** and see **bore-well.** — **1883** SMITH *Geol. Survey Ala.* 444 Drinking water in this region is obtained from bored or artesian wells. **1922** T. A. MCNEAL *When Kansas was Young* 205 A fair-haired child who was so unfortunate as to fall into a bored well out in western Kansas.

***borer,** *n.* **1.** (See quot. 1836.) *Slang. Obs.* **2.** A lobbyist. *Rare.*

(1) **1836** *Public Ledger* (Phila.) 23 Aug. (Th.), [In Philadelphia drummers] are called borers, probably from some resemblance in qualities to a worm that infests fruit trees. **1856** *Knickerb.* Oct. 407 Felicien B. blessed the drummers and borers of New York. — (2) **1854** *Cong. Globe* App. 20 May 893/2, I should like to say a few words about these 'legislative borers.'

As the last term in **apple, apple tree, apple twig, bark, corn, cornstalk, gold, grape, grapevine, hickory, locust, maple, peach, peach tree, pine, poplar, poplar tree, shot, shot hole, square, squash, stalk, tap, water, yucca borer.**

***boring,** *n.* Trying to influence members of a legislature for private ends. *Rare.* — **1841** in COMBE *Notes* I. 322 Great impediments are thrown in the way of the fulfilment of imperative duties by the monstrous increase of boring and lobbying on behalf of the interests of corporate associations.

***borough,** *n.*

1. In Connecticut, Pennsylvania, and a few other states, a form of municipal corporation corresponding approximately to incorporated towns and villages in other states.

1718 *Pa. Col. Rec.* III. 58 The sd town might be erected into a Borough by a Charter of Incorporacon. **1828** WEBSTER *s.v.*, In Connecticut, this word, *borough*, is used for a town or a part of a town, or a village, incorporated with certain privileges, distinct from those of other towns and of cities; as the *Borough* of Bridgeport. **1919** MENCKEN *Amer. Lang.* 355 This is now [spelled] . . . Allegheny for the Pittsburgh borough and the Pennsylvania county.

2. One of the five major administrative subdivisions of New York City.

1897 N. M. BUTLER in *Independent* 11 March 306/1 The Charter provides . . . that the Borough of Brooklyn may have a professionally conducted school system. **1948** *Chi. Tribune* 18 Mar. III. 4/5 The jubilee commemorates the 50th anniversary of the consolidation of the boroughs of Manhattan, Brooklyn, Bronx, Queens and Staten Island into New York City.

borracho bəˈratʃo, *n. S.W.* [Sp. in same sense.] A drunkard. — **1836** LATROBE *Rambler in Mexico* 70 (Bentley), When you have said that he was a borrachio you have recorded all the positive evil in his character. **1932** BENTLEY *Dict. Sp. Terms* 102 In the sense of a drunkard one hears it along the border in such expessions as 'I was disturbed during the night by two *borrachos*.'

bos bɔs, *n.* [Origin unknown.] (See quot.) *Obs.* — **1851** HALL *College Words* 25 At the University of Virginia, the desserts which the students . . . are allowed twice per week, are respectively called the senior and junior *bos*.

bosal boˈsæl, *n.* Also **bozal.** *S.W.* [Sp. *bozal*, in Amer. Sp. sense here shown.] A halter fitting tightly about a horse's nose.

1844 GREGG *Commerce of Prairies* 184 (Bentley), The head of the animal is turned towards his subduer, who seldom fails to throw a bozal around the nose. **1853** P. PAXTON *Yankee in Texas* 117 A fish spear is to him [the Texan] a *groin;* . . . a halter, a *bosaal;* a whip, a *quirt;* a house, no house, but a *log-pen.* **1917** MORGAN *Recollections* 9 He was then quickly blindfolded and a bridle without a bit, but with a tight-fitting halter to keep him from biting,—it was called a 'bosal'—and prevented the animal from opening his jaws,—was fitted to him. **1948** ROLLINSON *Wyo. Cattle Trails* 87 The men were mostly from Oregon, and all rode with the 'Macarty' (*mecate*) attached to the hackamore noseband or bozal, with the free end tucked into or through their cartridge or money belts.

bosman ˈbɔsmən, *n.* [Can. F., f. French *bosseman*, a naval officer ranking just below a quartermaster.] (See quots. and cf. **bowsman.**) *Obs.*

[**1807** C. C. ROBIN *Voyages* II. 212 Les rameurs sont distribués également de chaque côté; à l'arrière est le patron qui gouverne, et en avant un homme, nommé *bosman*, une perche à la main, sonde les lieux où l'on craint de toucher.] **1876** HALE *P. Nolan's Friends* i, A man in the bow called the bosman, who generally wielded a sort of boathook, watched the course. **1904** in *Kansas Hist. Soc.* IX. 272 The captain of the boat, called the 'patron,' did the steering, and his assistant, called the 'bosseman,' stood on the bow, pole in hand, and gave directions to the men at the cordelle.

* **bosom,** *n.*

1. A false shirt front, a dickey.

1863 *Horticulturist* Dec. 4 Shirt and Bosom makers. **1905** *N.Y. Ev. Post* 26 May 12 Men's Unlaundered Shirts. . . . Three-ply linen bosoms reinforced back and front. **1945** BOTKIN *My Burden* 51 Please don't let my gal see under my coat, 'cause I got on a bosom and no shirt.

2. In combs.: (1) **bosom blossom,** the flower of the strawberry shrub, *colloq.*, cf. **bubby flower;** (2) **board,** a board upon which the bosoms of shirts, waists, etc., may be ironed; (3) **bottle,** (see quot. 1904), *obs.;* (4) **piece,** =**bosom,** *rare;* (5) **pin,** a breastpin.

(1) *c***1845** W. T. PORTER *Big Bear Ark.* 103, I used to save bosim blossoms for him, which some people call sweet sentid shrubs. — (2) **1869** E. PUTNAM *Receipt Bk.* 319 For the washroom, have . . . an ironing blanket and sheet; a dress-board and bosom-board well covered. *a***1918** G. STUART *On Frontier* I. 256, I have been called upon to make a 'bosom board'; . . . and she has starched front, neck, and wristbands of our shirts. — (3) **1714** *Essex Inst. Coll.* XLIII. 52, 2 diamond cut Bottles 24/, . . . 7 Bosome ditto 7/. **1904** MCCLELLAN *Dress* 383 Bosom-bottle.—A small flat glass bottle, sometimes covered with silk to match the gown, concealed in the stomacher of the dress to hold water for flowers, so generally worn by ladies in the last half of the eighteenth century. — (4) **1850** JUDD *R. Edney* xi. 154 Richard fairly struck his high colors to the persuasions of his sister, and ran up instead a white collar and bosom-piece.

(5) **1855** BARNUM *Life* 123 What a fool I was to give you that finger-ring and bosom-pin. **1889** CUSTER *Tenting on Plains* 213 This cambric finery, ornamented with three old-fashioned bosom-pins.

As the last term in **hog, palpitating, shirt, sow bosom.**

bosque ˈbɔske, *n. S.W.* [Sp. in same sense.] A wood or forest, a clump or grove of trees. Also attrib.

1771 MEASE *Narrative* 79 Upon some of the Eminences are Bosquets or Clumps of Pine Trees which seem to have been left expressly both as Shade for Cattle and the Adornment of the Country. **1834** PIKE *Prose Sketches* 44 The Bosque Redondo is about one hundred and twenty miles from San Miguel. **1902** GARCIA *Shade Trees* 17 It is native in our valleys, and many places have dense 'bosques' or forests of it. **1948** *Popular Western* June 33/1 At the bosque of cottonwoods . . . one of the riders halted in the shade.

boss bɔs, *n.*[1] [Du. *baas*, master.]

1. An employer, foreman, master.

[*a***1649** WINTHROP *Hist.* I. 166 Here arrived a small Norsey bark . . . with one Gardiner, an expert engineer or work base [=Du. *werkbaas*], and provisons.] **1653** HAZARD *Hist. Collections* II. 236 From our place of residence at the Basses house in the Manhatoes. **1806** IRVING *Life & Lett.* (1862) I. 96, I had completely forgotten the errand, . . . so I had to return, make an awkward apology to *boss*, and look like a nincompoop. **1884** MARK TWAIN *H. Finn* vi, He said he would show who was Huck Finn's boss. **1944** *This Week Mag.* 18 March 16/1 Fishing Boss Ickes gives you some tips on seafood prospects.

b. Also transf. and as a term of address.

1839 C. F. BRIGGS *H. Franco* I. 31 'Why don't you get in boss?' said one of the men on the dock. **1850** *N.Y. Herald* 24 May (B.), Rothschild is the real Pope and boss of all Europe. **1891** THANET *Otto the Knight* 328 That's my chile! Take him 'way, boss!

2. A professional politician in charge of, or involved in, a political machine. *Slang.* Cf. **bossdom, bossism, boss-ship.**

1861 *Carrolton* (Ill.) *Gazette* 2 March 2/2 Abe . . . was sent for by 'boss' Seward. **1899** BREEN *Thirty Years* 31 It was while the Tweed Ring was in the height of its power that the term Boss was applied to the man who had control of the dominant political organization of the city. **1946** *Chi. D. News* 5 March 8/2 Those voters, not virtually disfranchised by the bosses, should exercise their franchise with discrimination.

attrib. **1880** *Bradstreet's* 22 Dec. 4/4 [It] is now called the 'boss' system. **1882** COOPER *Amer. Pol.* I. 261 The complaint of 'Boss Rule' in these States—by which is meant the control of certain leaders—still obtains to some extent. Wayne MacVeagh was the author of this very telling political epithet, and he used it with rare force in his street speeches at Chicago when opposing the nomination of Grant. **1906** in *Kansas Hist. Soc.* IX. 419 There were no 'boss busters' then.

3. Often used attributively or as an adj. to denote a person or thing of superior kind, rank, etc.

1836 in COMMONS *Doc. Hist.* IV. 287, I am a boss shoemaker. **1848** *N.Y. Wkly. Tribune* 24 June 5/4 He then presented to the meeting Hon. *Stephen A. Douglas*, U.S. Senator from Illinois, and one of the particular cronies and eulogists of Lewis Cass, the Boss Dough-face of the country. **1858** *Harper's Wkly.* 25 Sep. 618/1 The 'boss swamper' lays out the line. **1876** *Union* (Champaign, Ill.) 7 Sep. 3/4 This is not the only big farm in this vicinity, but is the 'boss farm' of a dozen or more running 600 to several thousand acres. **1948** *Reader's Digest* March 64/2 By that time Merle Brown, our neighborhood boss carpenter, had some plans drawn up.

As the last term in **barn, camp, cellar, city, cow, ditch, ex-, fire, gang, grog, head, herd, jigger, labor, logging, machine, party, pit, political, range, Republican, river, section, shanty, shift, straw, sub, trail, vice, wagon, walking, ward, weigh, whipping, woods, yard boss.**

* **boss,** *n.*[2] **1.** (See quots.) *Obs.* **2.** A word used in calling or soothing a cow. *Colloq.*

(1) **1846** SAGE *Scenes Rocky Mts.* iii, 'Come, boss!—Poor boss!—bossy, bossy!' addressing the buffalo, which commenced advancing. **1848** BARTLETT 44 *Boss* (Lat. *bos*), among the hunters of the prairies, a name for the buffalo. — (2) **1874** *Vt. Bd. Agric. Rep.* II. 706 So-o-boss! There, you've kicked it over—All that milk, now, I declare! **1901** HEMPL in *Nation* 18 April 314/2 The call 'Co' boss is familiar to most of the inhabitants of our Northern States and Canada.

boss bɔs, *v.* [f. **boss,** *n.*[1]] *tr.* To manage, control, be in authority over. Also *to boss it.*

1856 M. THOMPSON *Plu-ri-bus-tah* 222 He 'bossed' a splendid 'ked'n'-try.' **1856** *Nat. Intelligencer* 3 Nov. (B.), The little fellow that sits up in the pulpit and kinder bosses it over the crowd gin us a talk. **1887** L. M. ALCOTT *Under Lilacs* 110 Nobody is going to boss me but Miss Celia. **1948** *Chi. D. News* 6 Jan. 10/7 Farrell . . . has bossed the entertainment in the lounge for five years.

bossdom ˈbɔsdəm, *n.* The position or influence of a political boss; the control of politics by bosses. — **1888** BRYCE *Amer. Commonwealth* II. lxiii. 462 The extinction of the Boss himself and of bossdom. **1894** *Citizen* (Albion, Mich.) 293 It is not healthy for a party, if the few are allowed to do all and say all. That way Rings and Bossdom lie.

bossible ˈbɔsəbl, *a.* Capable of being bossed. *Rare.* — **1926** D. COLVIN *Prohibition in U.S.* 563 The liquor vote was the largest . . . bossible and corruptible vote which existed.

bossism ˈbɔsɪzəm, *n.* The system of political control by bosses.

1881 *Scribner's Mo.* Aug. 626/1 The event shows, also, that the days of 'bossism' are closing. **1903** *Nation* 30 April 358/3 There is even edification for votes, for would-be office-holders and others in the exposition of Bossism and corruption which Mr. Fowler makes. **1948** *Green Bay* (Wis.) *Press-Gazette* 12 July 2/7 He said Democrats 'must make a crusading fight against bossism.'

bosslet ˈbɔslɪt, *n.* A subordinate or minor political boss. — **1903** *Nation* 23 April LXXVI. 325/3 Serviceable to the old boss as he had been, and to the bosslet Quigg, he counted confidently upon their machine. **1947** *Atlantic Mo.* July 24/1 The Republican bosslet of that County is Mr. Flynn's stooge.

bossloper ˈbɔsˌlopɚ, *n.* [App. f. Du. *boschlöper*, lit. "woods runner" but in *WNT* as "highwayman, robber."] One who traverses the forest, a frontiersman, trapper, trader, etc. Cf. **bushloper.** *Obs.*

1687 *Doc. Hist. N.Y. State* (1849) I. 254 The Governour of Canida sent for all the Bosslopers that were at Ottowawa. **1690** *N.Y. Hist. Soc. Coll.* II. 175 Four hundred men were gone from Quebek under command of Mons. Pirneusse, and Monsieur Courtimanche, being all Bosse-lopers Inhabitants and Indians. **1691** *Mass. Bay Currency Tracts* 26 Had they not gone with the Fleet to Canada, a thousand Boss-Lopers had been upon our Country Towns and laid them waste. **1893** *Harper's Mag.* Dec. 215 Incomparable as is the modern Boston 'drummer,' he is but the evolution of the Dutch *bos-loper*, or wood-ranger, who scoured the forests for trade.

boss-ship ˈbɔsʃɪp, *n.* The rule of a political boss.

1882 *Nation* 2 Nov. 371/3 The gross and wholesale prostitution of the service . . . to enable Mahone to build up a new and repudiating boss-ship in Virginia. **1894** *Voice* (N.Y.) 6 Sep., It was thought to be an auspicious time to shake off the 'bossship' exercised by Mr. Platt for many years. **1904** *N.Y. Ev. Post* 16 Dec. 6 [To] make the time ripe for a party to revolt against a hideous boss-ship.

bossy ˈbɔsɪ, *a.* [f. **boss,** *n.*[1]] Inclined to boss, to manage, or dictate. Hence **bossiness.**

1882 *Harper's Mag.* Dec. 108/1 There was a lady manager who was dreadfully bossy. **1945** Webster *Town Meeting Country* 166 None of them could be tied down to a wife who was bound to be bossy. **1948** *Dly. Oklahoman* (Okla. City) 5 June 1/2 They love her for her bossiness.

* **Boston,** *n.* [*Boston,* Mass.]

1. A Chinook term for a native or citizen of the U.S. Often attrib.

1844 Lee & Frost *Oregon* 148 He boasted that the 'Bostons,' as he termed us, 'should never make him good.' **1880** Jackson *Alaska* 137 These Indians have patriotic ideas, are proud to call themselves 'Boston Siwashes' (United States Indians), and glory in the possession of a 'star-spangled banner.' **1946** R. Peattie *Pac. Coast Ranges* 190 The long-lived Indians out on the coast could have heard from their grand-parents of the coming of the 'King George men,' the English, and the 'Bostons,' the American traders.

Also **Boston man.**

1868 Whymper *Alaska* 25 'Boston man,' or 'Boston' simply, stands for an American; the first vessels bearing the stars and stripes, hailed from that port. **1909** *Nation* 29 July 104/1 Almost to this day a 'Boston man' among the Indians [Pacific Coast] is the more intelligent equivalent for American. **1924** *Smithsonian Misc. Coll.* 76 No. 10, 120 The . . . white visitors were 'Boston men' concerning whom it was said 'they dug large deep holes and buried a great many bottles to prove they discovered Neah Bay.'

b. Boston papers, pre-emption papers secured by an Indian in the Northwest.

1879 *No. Pacific Coast* (Tacoma, Wash.) 15 Dec. 7/2 The Indians in this neighborhood, a majority of them, are securing their 'Boston papers,' and locating on the most desirable portions.

2. Learned talk, **Bostonese.** *Rare.*

1861 *Harper's Mag.* May 726/1 In short—to use the phrase of an envious and gibing New Yorker—'we talked Bosting' enough in an hour to have lasted reasonable people a month.

3. A kind of waltz (see quot. 1913). Also **Boston dip.**

1879 *Amer. Punch* Oct. 116/1 The Hardshell Baptists will not dance even the Boston Dip Waltzes. **1911** Harrison *Queed* 108 She could make even 'the Boston' look graceful. **1913** E. Scott *All About the Boston* 24 The term 'Boston' is applied to the kind of movement that in its best and most graceful form would be far more consistently described as Rectilineal or Diagonal waltzing. **1948** *Time* 19 April 22/1 He liked to play charades in the White House and dance the Boston with Martha Bowers.

4. =**Boston terrier.**

1948 *Chi. Tribune* 4 Apr. (Grafic Mag.) 20/4 The Boston originated from a cross between the English bulldog and the white English terrier.

5. In special combs.: (1) **Boston bag,** a form of handbag kept closed by having a handle on each side of the top opening; (2) **culture,** superior culture such as is thought of as prevailing in Boston; (3) **fern,** (see quot. 1909); (4) **money,** money passing current in Boston, *obs.;* (5) **news,** out-of-date or stale news, *obs.;* (6) **notion,** any small article of trade, as a bead, bowl, clock, etc., formerly sold by Yankee peddlers, also transf., *obs.,* cf. **notion;** (7) **pine,** a variety of strawberry, *obs.;* (8) **Resolves,** resolves drawn up in Boston, as those of 1767 looking to the restoration of puritanical simplicity through the non-importation of any luxuries, *obs.;* (9) **rocker,** a modified Windsor chair, usu. having a curved

Boston rocker

wooden seat, spindle back, and flat headrail, also attrib.; (10) **Tea Party,** the gathering of some Boston Citizens, Dec. 16, 1773, to enforce the non-importation resolves of the colony by going on board three recently arrived ships and throwing overboard the tea which they carried; (11) **terrier,** (see quot. 1909); (12) **type,** an embossed alphabet for the blind originated by Doctor S. G. Howe of the Massachusetts Asylum for the Blind about 1830; (13) **white,** a variety of potato, *obs.*

(1) 1922 *Mont. Ward Cat.* (ed. 97) 316 New Type Boston Bag with Lock and Catches. **1936** *Sears Cat.* (ed. 172) 1024/2 Boston bags. — **(2) 1881** R. H. Stoddard *Homes* 155 To be a missionary of Boston culture, rather than the apostle of political or theological revolution, must have pleased the anxious thought of this medical Brahmin. — **(3) 1909** *Cent. Supp.* 466/3 Boston fern, a luxuriant cultivated form (*Nephrolepis exalta* var. *Bostoniensis*) of the common sword-fern. **1920** *Outing* Dec. 135/1 No home was considered complete unless it contained, on a pedestal in the window next to the Boston fern, a brimming bowl wherein were more or less happily domiciled a quintette of glittering gold fish. — **(4) 1679** *East-Hampton Rec.* II. 87 In consideration of the sume of five pounds in boston monney to mee in hand paid. **1833** *Niles' Reg.* XLIV. 316/2 A piece of british cotton shirting, bought . . . in the autumn of 1813, at eighty-five cents per yard, cash, (Boston money or specie).

(5) 1846 *Spirit of Times* 16 May 138/2 Preserving the freshness, novelty, and interest of the subject, which by age . . . may be deprived of its interest, and rank among 'Boston news' to you. — **(6) 1832** *Boston Transcript* 24 Aug. 2/2 We sincerely wish that some of these 'Boston notions' would find their way into other places. **1889** Farmer 80/1 *Boston Notions,* . . . is a well-known expression and dates back many years. It was used during the last century, and even at that time had become proverbial. — **(7) 1852** *Horticulturist* 352 Boston Pine has done nobly this season. **1862** *Rep. Comm. Patents: Agric.* 186 For medium season: Brighton Pine, Boston Pine [etc.]. — **(8) 1774** *Hist. Manuscripts Com.* 14th Rep. App. X. (1895) 234 Boston Resolves adopted by the Congress which also advises non-importation. — **(9) 1856** Robinson *Kansas* 215 A large Boston rocker, with mahogany squab-seat chairs and cricket, made up the removable furniture. **1948** *Chi. Tribune* 12 Mar. II. 3/2, I am a Boston rocker man myself, though I'll not quarrel with those whose contours fit better into other styles.

(10) 1834 G. A. Kirtland (*title*), Retrospect of the Boston Tea Party. **1947** *Reader's Digest* March 26/2 In Boston, young men and women dressed as Indians tossed inflation-priced merchandise into the harbor, in a humorous imitation of the Boston Tea Party. — **(11) 1894** *Outing* Mar. 465/1 After much discussion the name of Boston Terrier was finally selected because all other names indicating the origin of the dog were more or less in conflict with those of older breeds. **1909** *Cent. Supp.* 1332/3 *Boston terrier,* a breed of dogs supposed to be a cross between the English bulldog and terrier. It originated in Boston, Massachusetts. **1943** LYON *So to Bedlam* 196 Judy, the Boston terrier, lifted her head from her cushion on the davenport. — **(12) 1892** *Scribner's Mag.* Sep. 30/2 The books were generally in Boston type, but text-books were nowhere used in the classes, while the Braille system, although known to a few—chiefly teachers—was not recognized in the course of study of any school. — **(13) 1856** *Rep. Comm. Patents: Agric.* 221 The 'Boston Whites' are . . . early, good flavored, and yield well.

b. In the names of, or with reference to, foods: (1) **Boston baked beans,** navy beans baked slowly with pork and flavored with molasses, also attrib.; (2) **brown bread,** brown steamed bread made usu. of rye and corn meal or wheat flour, molasses, soda, and milk or water; (3) **butt,** (see quot.); (4) **butter roll,** a form of roll once popular in Boston; (5) **cracker,** a rather large, round, porous, semi-sweet cracker; (6) **cream cake,** prob. Boston cream pie, a form of two-layer cake put together with whipped cream, cream filling, etc.; (7) **shoulder,** (see quot.); (8) **strawberry,** (see quot.), *slang.*

(1) 1853 WEBSTER *Improved Housewife* 147 Boston Baked Beans. **1904** *Omaha Bee* 16 Aug. 4 The maker of Boston baked bean pots is dead, but the fame of the Boston baked bean is perpetual. **1947** *Chi. Tribune* 21 Dec. I. 39/3 Miss Fannie's recipe for Boston baked beans. — **(2) 1856** *Rep. Comm. Patents: Agric.* 163 The 'Boston Brown Bread' contains two parts of corn to one of rye-meal, by measurement. **1947** BEROLZHEIMER *Regional Cookbook* 101 Boston brown bread was a traditional accompaniment [of baked beans]. — **(3) 1903** *Sears Cat.* (ed. 113) 18/1 Boston heavy Butts, made from top of shoulder after cutting California hams, and consists of about two thirds lean and one-third fat. — **(4) 1853** *S.F. Whig* 28 July 1/4 (*advt.*), Boston Butter Rolls, Graham Bread.

(5) 1818 FEARON *Sketches of Amer.* 44 In the evening . . . the table is filled with cheese, biscuits (called Boston crackers,) molasses, and slices of raw dried beef. **1944** HOLTON *Yankees* 239 People used to think chowder should be poured into a tureen lined with Boston crackers. — **(6) 1855** *N.Y. Herald* 24 Dec. 1/6 Confectioneries. Boston cream cakes. Almond macaronies. Ladies' fingers. **1865** *Republican Banner* (Nashville, Tenn.) 5 Nov. 1/2 Pastry . . . Vanilla Macaroons. Boston Cream Cake. — **(7) 1910** L. D. HALL *Market Classes of Meat, Picnics or Calas* (formerly termed California hams) are cut 2-½ ribs wide. . . . They are sold almost entirely as sweet-pickled, smoked and boiled meats. The lighter averages (4 to 8 pounds) are sometimes termed Boston Shoulders. . . . But Chicago and other western packers now trim them like Calas and designate both as Picnic. — **(8) 1884** in *Amer. Sp.* XX. (1945) Feb. 71/1 'Give me a plate of beans,' he said to the waiter. 'One plate of Boston strawberries,' yelled that functionary.

c. In other combs., often occasional and obs., in the sense "of or pertaining to Boston, Massachusetts," as (1) **Boston bonnet,** (2) **boy,** (3) **Brahmin,** (4) **chaise,** (5) **china,** (6) **chip,** (7) **cloak, coat,** (8) **coffee,** (9) **cottons,** (10) **dollar,** (11) **dray,** (12) **fashion,** (13) **kettle,** (14) **manner,** (15) **particular,** (16) **philosophy,** (17) **scorn,** (18) **shilling,** (cf. **bay shilling**), (19) **snap,** (20) **style,** (21) **truck,** (22) **window glass.**

(1) 1868 MRS. WHITNEY *P. Strong* 124 People who go [to Boston] every day or two keep 'Boston bonnets' of a meaner sort. — **(2) 1859** GRATTAN *Civilized Amer.* II. 318 A 'Boston boy' is a melancholy picture of prematurity. It might be almost said that every man is born middle-aged in that and every other great city of the Union. — **(3) 1940** *Life* 16 Dec. 69 Congressman Tinkham, a Boston Brahmin, looks like a Russian commissar, but loathes Communism, wears whiskers because it is the manly thing to do. **1947** *Time* 29 Dec. 66/3 Parkman was born a Boston Brahmin. — **(4) 1890** *Harper's Mag.* Oct. 718/1 That two-wheeled vehicle known as a Boston 'chaise.'

(5) 1846 C. MATHEWS *Writings* II. 309 (Th.), She had a cargo of notions, consisting of Boston china (Hingham wooden ware), onions, apples, coffins in nests, cheese, potatoes, &c. — **(6) 1813** *Ann. 12th Congress* 2 Sess. 1118 Shingles, called *Boston chips,* not more than 12 inches in length. — **(7) 1836** T. POWER *Impressions* I. 190 Each [was] carrying a small valise, a carpet-bag, [and] a long Boston coat or cloak. — **(8) 1830** N. AMES *Mariner's Sk.* 132 She [=a boat] was supplied with . . . a keg of molasses, another of 'Boston particular,' 'lacking six days of being a week old' and a quantity of Boston coffee, videlicet rye. — **(9) 1814** *Louisville* (Ky.) *Correspondent* 24 Apr. 4/1 (*advt.*), 10 cases of Boston Cottons, each case containing about 60 pieces, and well assorted.

(10) 1902 *Out West* July 30 Where the tradition was to toss at least 'four bits' to a beggar, it was revolutionary to see the new-comer carefully hand him a 'Boston dollar.' [Note:] Cowboy satire for a copper. — **(11) 1862** E. KIRK *Among Pines* 166 The vehicle . . . was mounted on wheels that had probably served their time on a Boston dray. — **(12) 1850** G. HINES *Voyage* 167 Their dresses were an imitation of the Boston fashions. — **(13) 1697** *Conn. Probate Rec.* I. 551 To my daughter Hannah my warming pan and my Boston Kettle. — **(14) 1788** FRANKLIN *Lett. to Lathrop* 31 May, The Boston manner, turn of phrase, and even tone of voice, and accent in pronunciation, all please, and seem to refresh and revive me.

(15) 1830 [see **Boston coffee**]. — **(16) 1886** *Harper's Mag.* Nov. 946/1 What is the Boston philosophy? Why, it is not to care about anything you do care about. — **(17) 1901** CHURCHILL *Crisis* 151 Graven on his face was what is called the 'Boston scorn.' — **(18) 1704** S. KNIGHT *Journal* 42 Mony is pieces of Eight, Ryalls, or Boston or Bay shillings (as they [=people of Conn.] call them). — **(19) 1937** MITCHELL *Horse & Buggy Age* 68 The snappers on the cheap whips were not made separately, but were all of a piece with the plaiting, an attenuated extension of the lash. They were known as Boston snaps, while the others—the loose snappers—were called Philadelphia snaps.

(20) 1834 in *Monthly Mag.* XLII. (1834) III. 161 To do a thing 'in Boston style' is proverbial throughout the country, as signifying a thing done with superior promptness and execution. — **(21) 1860** E. EVERETT *Mt. Vernon Papers* iii. 24 The Boston truck is constructed of two parallel shafts, hewn from the best of oak. — **(22) 1923** *Old-Time N. Eng.* Jan. 135 A works for making crown window glass was established in Boston in 1787, but led a precarious existence until 1803 when an experienced workman from abroad arrived and took charge, and twenty years later 'Boston Window Glass' was a quality of glass known everywhere in the New England States.

Bostoner ˈbɔstənɚ, *n.* An inhabitant of Boston.

1671 OGILBY *America* 164 The . . . *Bostoners* were from the beginning the most Potent and Predominant of all the rest of the Colonies. **1676** *N.H. Doc. and Rec.* I. 326 All ways have been tried and methods used to obtain justice from the Bostoners, but all have proved ineffectual. **1758** *Micmakis & Maricheets* 65 On condition of the Bostoners returning to Petitpas. **1915** *Amer. Mag.* Oct. 47/3 He was too much a Bostoner himself not to understand how Miss Susan, and possibly her niece, would regard his exploits at Coronado.

Bostonese ˌbɔstənˈiz, *n.* **1.** (See quots. 1809, *c*1818), also inhabitants of Boston. **2.** (See quot. 1889.) Also attrib.

(1) [**1809** GRAY *Letters* 367 *Les sacra* [*sic*] *Bostonois,* is the usual epithet [in Canada] for all Americans, from whatever part of the country they may come.] **c1818** HADFIELD *Diary* 61 He asserted he had tomahawked and scalped 50 Bostonese, a name they [*sc.* Indians in Canada] give generally to the Americans of the states. **1888** *N.Y. Herald* 29 July 7/6 There were a number of people present, principally Bostonese. **1925** *N.Y. Times* 8 Sep. 24/3 The real culprit was Squire Sam Jones, who in the second inning surrendered four runs to the Bostonese. — **(2) 1876** *Cinci. Enquirer* 17 June 3/2 His reply was not negro at all, it was purest Bostonese. **1889** FARMER 79/2 Bostonese . . . is a method of speech or manners supposed to be specially affected by the residents of that city. **1914** BRININSTOOL *Trail Dust* 246 I'm tryin' to tame my rough manner To fit with her Bostonese style. **1948** MENCKEN *Supp.* II. 179 The educated speech of the State . . . , though 'not as harsh as the Middle Western' variety, is 'untainted by Bostonese.'

∗ **Bostonian,** *n.* and *a.*

1. *n.* A native or inhabitant of Boston.

1682 J.W. *Lett. from N.-Eng.* 7 In short, Sir, these *Bostonians* enrich themselves by the ruine of Strangers. **1897** FLANDRAU *Harvard Episodes* 18 When I say 'a Bostonian,' . . . I mean of course a Bostonian that one knows. **1947** *N. & Q.* Oct. 109/2 A clipper captain tried unsuccessfully to enlist Bostonians in 1787.

2. *pl.* A designation formerly used, esp. by foreigners and Indians, for Americans in general.

1785 GROSE *Classical Dict. Vulgar Tongue,* Gouge, to squeeze out a man's eye with the thumb, a cruel practice used by the Bostonians in America. **1799** *Mass. H.S. Coll.* VI. 150 In the years 1775 and 1776, the French, . . . called all the inhabitants belonging to the then thirteen revolted colonies, by the general name of *Bostonians.* **1820** W. TUDOR *Lett. E. States* 307 Americans were then, in France, often called *Bostonians,* the term by which they are designated in Canada to this day.

3. *a.* Pertaining to Boston, Mass.

1698 C. MATHER (*title*), The Bostonian Ebenezer. Some Historical Remarks on the state of Boston. **1778** BILLINGS *Singing Master's Assistant* 34 Forbid it Lord God that those who have sucked Bostonian Breasts should thirst for American Blood. **1881** *Harper's Mag.* April 648/2 She uttered 'culture' with the sibilant Bostonian twang. **1948** *N.E. Quart. Rev.* June 151 He subscribes to the Bostonian conviction that Harvard is the best of all universities.

Bostonianism bɔsˈtonɪənˌɪzəm, *n.* [f. prec.] Features or traits characteristic of Boston. — **1845** W. I. PAULDING *Noble Exile* 107 When we get abroad in Europe, we are ready enough to copy: not but that we do mingle a little Bostonianism in every style we assume. **1881** *Harper's Mag.* April 712/2 A third [house or shop-front in Milwaukee] adopts a peculiar bit of Bostonianism.

Bostonism ˈbɔstən͵ɪzəm, *n.* = prec. Also an expression regarded as typical of Boston. — **1881** *Harper's Mag.* Feb. 381/2 There is such a thing as New York Bostonism. **1944** JOHNSON *As I Dare* 276 Well, I can add that to my collection of Bostonisms.

Bostonite ˈbɔstən͵aɪt, *n.* An inhabitant or native of Boston (see also quot. 1884).

1775 *First Book Amer. Chronicles* 1 Tidings came to the great city . . . how the men of Boston, even the Bostonites, had arose, a great multitude, and destroyed the tea. **1848** *Knickerb.* XXXI. 175 Part of his cargo was living pork for the Bostonites. **1884** *Boston Journal* 12 Sep., Wuston is the Iroquois name for Boston, and Wustonaka or Bostonites represents to these Indians the whole American people, since Boston was in the early days the rallying place of Americans.

Bostonized ˈbɔstən͵aɪzd, *a.* Rendered like Boston, Mass. or its inhabitants.

1679 *N.C. Col. Rec.* I. 245 The rest of His Majesty's people so trading must become Bostoniz'd or relinquish dealing. **1825** *Boston Mo. Mag.* I. 145 In plain language, my outward man was not quite *Bostonized*. **1882** *Boston Ev. Transcript* 18 Jan. 2 To show how the villages of the Massachusetts sea coast were being 'Bostonized.'

bota ˈbota, *n. S.W.* [Sp. in same sense.] A kind of ample boot, often ornamented, used by cowboys and ranchers.

1834 A. PIKE *Prose Sks. and Poems* 138 Everything is new, striking, and quaint: the men with their pantalones of cloth, gaily ornamented with lace, . . . the botas of striped and embroidered leather; the zarape or blanket of striped red and white. **1896** *Land of Sunshine* Aug. 109 Clad in short jacket and slashed trousers of velvet, . . . soft leather *botas* embroidered in fancy patterns, . . . the California vaquero . . . was a sight to rejoice the eye. **1901** *Out West* June 481 She . . . looked up . . . at the pretty red-stained *botas* studded with silver buttons.

* **botanic,** *a.* (See quot. 1877.) *Obs.*

1835 *Stimpson's Boston Directory* 17 (*advt.*), Mass. Botanic Infirmary, or Thomsonian Hospital—for the reception of the sick and the lame. **c1844** TOWNES *Hist. Marion* 29 The town of Marion, at this time numbers, among it's inhabitants: . . . 3 Botanic or Steam Doctors. **1877** BARTLETT Thomsonian System. A peculiar treatment of diseases, so named from its inventor, Samuel Thomson, a native of Alstead, New Hampshire. . . . The medicines are . . . compounds of Cayenne pepper, lobelia, &c. His followers have discarded much that he adopted, and are now known as Eclectic or Botanic physicians.

***botanical,** *a.* (See prec.) *Obs.* — **1836** M. A. HOLLEY *Texas* v. 89 Where every man, in time of sickness, becomes a 'botanical quack and steam doctor.' **1849** CHAMBERLAIN *Indiana Gazetteer* 374 There are . . . five botanical and 12 other physicians.

* **bottle,** *n.* In combs.: (1) **bottle cap,** a small piece of metal suitably shaped for closing and sealing a bottle; (2) **capper,** a device for putting caps on bottles; (3) **gentian,** (see quot. 1909); (4) **grass,** (see quots.); (5) **head,** *local* (see quot.); (6) * **neck,** *fig.* a place, condition, situation, etc., by which progress, production, etc., is handicapped, also **bottle-necked,** *a.;* (7) **night,** (see quot.), *obs.;* (8) * **nose,** a river fish, as the long-nosed sucker, *Catostomus catostomus,* having a bottle-shaped nose; (9) **opener,** a utensil for removing caps from bottles, cf. **can opener;** (10) **proof,** immune from intoxication, *slang, obs.;* (11) * **stopper,** (see quot.).

(1) **1928** *Collier's* 1 Sep. 9/2 The bottle caps and cappers are for people who put up ketchup. **1948** *Chi. Tribune* 16 May VII. 1/7 'If I crash,' he would say, 'please put bottle caps on my grave!' — (2) **1928** *Collier's* 1 Sep. 47/1 The great Woolworth chain . . . has a special department for corks, bottle cappers, tubing, crown caps, etc. **1931** *K.C. Times* 15 Sep., The lad who makes a better bottle capper is the genius who walks under the shekel shower. — (3) **1909** *Cent. Supp.* 518/3 Bottle gentian, the closed gentian, *Gentiana Andrewsii.* **1917** BAILEY *Sand Dunes Indiana* 156 Purple asters, goldenrod, daisies, bottle and fringed gentians once grew in plenty near-by. — (4) **1840** DEWEY *Mass. Flowering Plants* 244 *Setaria.* Bottle Grass. . . . Four species of the grass, *viridis, glauca, Italica, verticillata, P. de B.* are pretty common. . . . *S. veridis,* is found in the vicinity of Boston. **1863** *Ill. Agric. Soc. Trans.* V. (1865) 867 *Setaria viridis,* Green Fox-tail or Bottle-grass, is from the South of Europe.

(5) **1877** BARTLETT, Bottle-Head. . . . The black-bellied plover, also called 'beetle-head' and 'green head.' — (6) **1923** *Nation* 24 Oct. 461/2 The situation is that we have a congestion of law-enforcement traffic and movement. . . . The 'bottleneck' yards, which cannot be widened except by new enormous expenditures of public money, are jammed and clogged. **1947** *Rocky Mt. News* (Denver) 23 Feb. 18/2 The present condition at that point is crude, disgraceful and a traffic bottle-neck on the most heavily traveled vehicular artery through town. **1948** W. MILLER *Fatal Step* 186 It could be entered only through a sloping bottle-necked drive. — (7) **1907** *Springfield W. Republican* 13 June 12 On bottle night, which usually is celebrated on the night of the last examination, everything breakable, from a spring water bottle to a cut glass pitcher, is hurled from the dormitory windows of the freshmen, and when dawn breaks the streets and sidewalks are covered inches deep with broken crockery and glass. — (8) [**1756** KALM *Resa* II. 159 Kl. 1. efter middagen kom en stor svärm af det fiskslag, som kallas Bottle-noses, tumlade i vatnet från S.W. til NO. de voro faseligen stora, väl af 6 alnars längd.] **1805** LEWIS *L. & Clark Exped.* (1904) II. 304 The fish of this part of the river are trout and a species of scale fish of a white colour and a remarkable small long mouth which one of our men inform us are the same with the species called in the Eastern states *bottlenose.* — (9) **1931** *K.C. Times* 17 Dec. 20 There were a few keys and a corkscrew and bottle-opener in the bunch.

(10) **1838** KENNEDY *Rob of the Bowl* I. 43 Dauntrees was bottle-proof. — (11) **1875** *Amer. Naturalist* IX. 143 The singular fistulous-stemmed species *Eriogonum inflatum* . . . from the peculiar bulging appearance of its main stalk and upper branches . . . has received the fanciful popular name of 'bottle stoppers.'

b. *Grind the bottle,* a game played by young people in pioneer times. *Obs.*

1782 DALRYMPLE *Journal* (1871) 36 We have diverted ourselves playing *grind the bottle.* **1833** CROCKETT *Sketches* 49 Plays which had been fashionable when their grandmothers were girls, such as . . . Grind the Bottle . . . were called up and wearied out.

As the last term in **blue, bosom, chunk, pill bottle.**

bottling works. A place where beverages are bottled. — **1881** *L.A. Times* 28 Dec., The men ran through the rear building and escaped in the darkness back of the Vizina bottling works. **1883** *Cent. Mag.* Oct. 957/1 The beer-sellers have been openly retailing their wares without license under the sign of 'Bottling Works.'

* **bottom,** *n.*

1. Level land, usu. fertile and cultivable, on the margin of rivers and creeks.

[**1634** *Boston Rec.* IV. 9 The hedgey ground that lies in the bottom betwixt his house and the water.] **1750** GIST *Journals* 34 The Land from Shannopin's Town is good along the River, but the Bottoms [are] not broad. **1788** in IMLAY *Western Territory* (1797) 595 The intervals or what the people of this country call bottoms, are from one half to three quarters of a mile wide. **1885** M. THOMPSON *By Ways & Bird Notes* 162 Along the Wabash river, in the broad, wooded 'bottoms,' I have heard it [=Wilson thrush] singing long after sunset. **1945** MCATEE *Pheasant* 39 The birds show a strong tendency to drift toward stream bottoms.

2. first, second, third bottom, the first and succeeding levels or plains along the shore of some rivers.

1788 in IMLAY *Western Territory* (1797) 595 Next to these are what is called second bottoms, which are elevated plains, and gentle risings of the richest uplands, and as free from stone as the low or first bottom. **1803** LEWIS in *Journals of L. & Ordway* 34 What is called the third bottom is more properly the high benches of the large range of hills. **1893** LERCH *Hills of La.* 107 The second bottoms of the smaller streams and creeks . . . seem to be of more recent origin and not to be cotemporaneous with the formation of these immense valleys. **1948** *Durant* (Okla.) *Dly. Democrat* 4 July 5/4 The first bottom is the red tide lands, the second bottom is the mixed land and the third bench is the sandy lands.

3. The bulbous roots of such plants as turnips, onions, etc. *Colloq.*

1833 GREENE *Dod. Duckworth* I. 25 Another of their notions was that turnips, onions, and all manner of bulbous roots, would be utterly destitute of bottoms, if not sown in the old of the moon.

4. A vat used in salt-making. *Obs.*

1833 *Niles' Reg.* XLIV. 395/1 The vat, or bottom, as it is generally called, was constructed 100 feet in length and 10 in width and all on the same level.

5. *pl.* "The impure metallic copper . . . which separates from the matt, and is found below it" (Raymond).

1876 RAYMOND *8th Rep. Mines* 393 Four tons of white metal, from the Ziervogel treatment, give 600 pounds of bottoms.

6. In combs.: (1) **bottom claim,** (see quot. and cf. **claim**); (2) **dollar,** the last dollar which one possesses, often in the phrase *to bet one's bottom dollar, colloq.;* (3) **ground,** =next; (4) **land,** level, low-lying land along a stream; (5) **log,** the log first laid down in making a log fence, *obs.;* (6) **lot,** a lot in an area of bottom land; (7) **plain,** a plain consisting of a river bottom; (8) **prairie,** a low-lying prairie, one not much elevated above neighboring streams; (9) **rail,** *fig.* in the expression *bottom rail* *on top*, denoting a reversal in circumstances, used esp. in the South after the Civil War in allusion to the changed relations between former slaves and those who had owned them, *colloq.;* (10) **rock,** the lowest stratum of rock, also fig.; (11) **sand,** true grit or courage, *slang;* (12) **side upwards,** topsy-turvy, *colloq.;* (13) **timber,** timber growing in a bottom.

(1) **1877** RUEDE *Sod-House Days* 12 An upland claim lies on top of a divide, and it is hard to find water sometimes. A bottom claim is one along a creek or river. — (2) **1857** *S.F.Call* 24 Jan. 4/1 Sometimes, however, luck will run against him, and, to use his own expressive phraseology, he 'slips up for his bottom dollar.' **1868** *Terr. Enterprise* (Virginia, Nev.) 18 June 3/1 You bet your bottom dollar and go your boots blind. **1948** *Chi. Tribune* 22 Feb. II. 1/8 You can bet your bottom dollar they'll start firing with everything they have tomorrow night at 7 o'clock. — (3) **1637** MORTON *New Canaan* II. ii, If any man be desirous to finde out in what part of the Country the best Cedars are, he must get into the bottom grounds. **1823** JAMES *Exped.* I. 80 Above this both shores [of the Mo. R.] are low bottom grounds. **1843** *Amer. Pioneer* II. 253 They concluded to leave the bottom grounds. — (4) **1728** *Boston News-Letter* 23–30 May 2/2 To be Sold Fifty Acres of Extraordinary good Meadows and Meadow Bottom Land. **1948** *Life* 23 Aug. 101 Raised just as good crops as the rich bottom lands.

(5) **1770** PATTEN *Diary* 241 We hauled some bottom logs for fence alongside the road on this side holms bridge. — (6) **1818** MELISH *Trav. U.S.* 485 To the south along the creek are handsome rich bottom lots. — (7) **1804** CLARK in *Lewis & C. Exped.* (1904) I. 49 Next to the river is an ellegent bottom Plain which extends several miles in length. — (8) **1804** J. ORDWAY in *Wis. Hist. Coll.* XXII. (1916) 95 Opposite this Island on the South Side is a beautiful Bottom Prarie . . . about 2000 acres of Land covered with wild rye and wild potatoes. **1946** FOREMAN *Last Trek* 70 The difficulty in crossing wet bottom prairies, Brish said, could scarcely be imagined. — (9) **1879** TOURGEE *Fool's Errand* xi. 50 It is . . . reported that he has been sent down here . . . to assist in overturning our institutions, and putting the bottom rail on top. **1898** PAGE *Red Rock* 321 Yes, the bottom rail is on top, and we mean to keep it so till the fence rots down. **1944** CLARK *Pills* 188 Some southerners regarded public education and civil rights as insidious devices for putting the bottom rail on top.

(10) **1864** DANA *Geology* (1874) 45 The whole thickness above the unfossiliferous bottom-rocks is about 100,000 feet. **1887** C. B. GEORGE *40 Years on Rail* 93 About the time I had reached bottom rock in my financial troubles, . . . I met A. B. Pullman. — (11) **1882** BAILLIE-GROHMAN *Camps in Rockies* 17 It takes moments of danger to discover a man's true grit—the 'bottom sand,' as a plainsman would say. — (12) **1858** GOVE *Letters* 362 But, alas for Mormon hopes, we entered the hotel to find it 'bottom side upwards,' as country folks say. — (13) **1837** PECK *Gaz. Illinois* 125 The bottom timber consists of oaks. **1874** LONG *Wild-Fowl* 150 How much better walking it is in this bottom-timber than in the woods of New England.

As the last term in **American, beech, bench, black, branch, broad, cane, cedar, chestnut, cistern, corn, creek, dry, fever and ague, free, grease (wood), hickory, Mingo, Mississippi, Missouri, oyster, prairie, river, rock, rush, salt, sand, sandy, second, shuck, sleigh, split, swamp, third, timber, tule, valley, walnut, willow, wooden bottom.**

***bottom,** *v. tr. Mining.* To underlie. — **1876** RAYMOND *8th Rep. Mines* 56 The company is extending and straightening the bed-rock tunnel, so that it . . . will 'bottom' all the land on this end of the claim.

***bottomed,** *n.* As the last term in **broad bottomed, hickory bottomed, hide bottomed.**

bot worm. A grub or larva of the bot fly. — **1799** *N.Y.State Soc. Arts* I. 391, I think it out of doubt . . . that the egg on the horse's hair produces the botworm. **1877** *Vt. Dairym. Assoc. Rep.* VIII. 105 Grub-in-the-head is a bot-worm, . . . cousin to the bots in horses.

boudin buˈdæn, *n. W.* [F., sausage, blood-pudding.] A kind of sausage prepared by stuffing forcemeat made of selected tidbits of a buffalo into the large intestine of the animal, and cooked by boiling and frying. *Obs.*

App. in imitation of an Indian practice. See quot. 1877.

1805 in THWAITES *Lewis and Clark* II. 15 We saved the necessary materials for making what our wrighthand cook Charbono calls the *boudin* (*poudingue*) *blanc*, and immediately set him about preparing them for supper. **1852** STANSBURY *Gt. Salt Lake* 35 Today the hunters killed their first buffalo . . . and a busy scene ensued of roasting, boiling, and making boudin, which is a sort of sausage boiled and eaten hot. [**1877** MATTHEWS *Ethnog. Hidatsa* 23/4 Sometimes they [Mandan Indians and their allies] chopped the fresh meat fine, put in it a piece of bowel, and thus made a sort of sausage, which was usually boiled.] **1948** *Neb. Hist.* March 6 *Boudins* [were] a trapper delicacy made from buffalo intestines and containing the chyme.

***boudoir,** *n.* **1. boudoir car,** (see quot. 1939). Now *hist.* **2. boudoir theater,** a small, elegantly furnished theater. *Rare.*

(1) **1887** C. B. GEORGE *40 Yrs. on Rail* 248 Smoking, buffet, drawing-room, boudoir, dining and sleeping cars have all been added to meet the needs and tastes of this enterprising age. **1893** M. PHILIPS *Making of a Newspaper* 179 The train . . . had one of the Mann boudoir cars; I engaged a section [and] adjusted the table. **1939** CLARK *Railroads & Rivers* 140 One rival of Pullman was the so called 'boudoir car,' a development in which beds were placed in rooms across the beam of the car as well as fore and aft. *Ib.*, The boudoir cars failed to attract sufficient patronage and eventually vanished. —(2) **1856** *Spirit of Times* (N.Y.) 22 Nov. 200/1 This beautiful boudoir theatre has been placed by him under my guardianship.

***bough,** *n.* **1. bough apple,** a variety of apple. **2.** ***bough house,** a temporary structure made of boughs, serving as a blind in wild-fowl shooting or as a camp.

(1) **1899** VANDERBILT *Flatbush* 279 'Bough apples' began to ripen in harvest-time, and they were followed by a regular succession of ripening varieties until, latest of all, the russets were gathered. — (2) **1811** WILSON *Ornithology* III. 111 Their destroyers construct for themselves lurking holes made of pine branches, called *bough-houses*. . . . Hither they repair with their fowling-pieces . . . and wait the appearance of the birds. **1894** *Outing* July 281/1 Down in the bough house the campers reclined in attitudes comfortable if not always picturesque.

As the last term in **sour bough, sweet bough.**

***bough,** *v. To bough down,* (see quot.). — **1861** WINTHROP *Open Air* 89 Iglesias and I stripped off armfuls of boughs and twigs from the spruces to 'bough down' our camp. 'Boughing down' is shingling the floor elaborately with evergreen foliage.

***boulevard,** *n.* A broad, well-made street, avenue, or main road. Also attrib.

"Now sometimes extended to . . . a street which is of especial width, is given a park-like appearance by reserving spaces at the sides or center for shade-trees, flowers, seats, and the like, and is not used for heavy teaming" (*Cent.*).

1875 *Scribner's Mo.* Sep. 541/2 The boulevard which started from Lincoln Park, connects the Central and Douglas Parks. **1912** *Out West* April 271/1 Alhambra is centrally located in a fine boulevard system. **1948** *Okla. City Times* 14 June 8/6 Forty new convertibles were lined up on the ramp to take the president and his party . . . up Wilshire boulevard to the Ambassador hotel for a luncheon meeting.

b. boulevard stop, a place at which traffic stops before crossing a boulevard.

1934 *Amer. Sp.* April 114/2 On the way to business, school, or entertainments those who drive have to make allowances for . . . boulevard stops and traffic lights. **1948** *Sat. Ev. Post* 31 July 16/3 Go up to the first boulevard stop, turn to the left, go up the hill for four blocks.

bounce baʊns, *n.*[1] [Cf. **cherry-bounce*.] A kind of cordial, usu. flavored with the juice of certain fruits.

1800 *Mass. H.S. Coll.* VII. 247 The usual drink of the fishermen [of Shoals Islands], at that period [*c*1730——], was liquor which they called *bounce*, composed of two thirds spruce beer and one third wine. **1835** BIRD *Hawks of Hawk H.* II. 171 Here I've mixed you a brandy cock-tail, and you've spilled the bounce into it. **1888** HARGIS *Graded Cook Book* 474 [In making] blackberry bounce, . . . to two quarts of juice put about three-fourths of a pound of sugar.

bounce baʊns, *n.*[2] [Poss. f. **bounce,** *v.*, but cf. Du. *de bons geven, krijgen*, etc., in *WNT s.v. Bons* (II) 1, *b.*] An abrupt, summary dismissal, discharge, rejection, usu. **grand bounce,** *q.v. Slang.* — **1910** O. HENRY *Rolling Stones* 122 'Had you ever thought,' I asks, . . . 'of giving her the bounce yourself?' **1944** *Chi. Sun* 20 May 15/1 He was given the bounce by Umpire John Conlan.

***bounce,** *v.*

1. a. *tr.* To cause (deer) to start from cover. *Colloq.* **b.** *bounce out*, to set off or set out smartly. *Rare.*

(a) **1840** *Crockett Almanac* 11 The rest of the time he spent in . . . bouncing deer. **1858** *Harper's Mag.* Oct. 615/2 It is a common thing for still-hunters, when a deer is suddenly 'bounced up,' . . . to bleat, imitating the noise of the fawn. — (b) **1859** G. A. JACKSON *Diary* 523 No town for us. We will bounce out for the head of Vasquez in the early spring.

2. *tr.* To discharge or dismiss summarily, as an employee from his position, a member from a church. Also to cast off or reject (a suitor). *Slang.*

This use is app. an extension of dial. "bounce" in the sense of "to eject forcibly." See *EDD s.v. Bounce*, *v.* II. 2.

1876 *Cong. Rec.* 10 Aug. 5403/1 Where are the soldiers of the Union army . . . ? Nearly all gone, a clean sweep; to use a phrase that I never heard before, although I am told it is common in some sections of the country, they are 'bounced.' **1893** THANET *Stories Western Town* 213 You don't suppose it would be any use to offer Esther a cool hundred thousand to promise to bounce this young fellow? **1948** *Time* 16 Feb. 25/3 Wallace had to bounce him and 20 other AAA employees because too many people complained that the group was trying to change the world too fast.

3. To "jump" (a claim). *Rare.*

1889 K. MUNROE *Golden Days* 69 We've got to . . . stake out the others [*sc.* claims] so the Injuns can't bounce 'em.

4. *tr.* (See quot. *s.v.* **bouncer, b.**)

***bouncer,** *n.* A man employed in a hotel, theater, saloon, etc., to eject undesirables, or otherwise maintain order. *Slang.*

1865 *Nat. Police Gaz.* (N.Y.) 29 Apr. 4/2 Old Moyamensing is almost as famous for its lawless gangs of boys and young men as it was in the days of the 'killers' and 'bouncers.' **1894** *Life* 17 May 321/2 Have you ever been a prize fighter or a bouncer in a saloon? **1945** STEINBECK *Cannery Row* 53 'The bouncer fixed her up,' said Mack. **1948** *Sat. Ev. Post* 4 Dec. 18/2 He and his staff of eight bouncers can handle 4000 customers with no trouble at all.

b. (See quot.)

1927 *New Republic* 26 Jan. 277/2 'Bouncer,' for instance, may be either (1) a rubber check, returned by the bank as no good, or (2) the person who passes (bounces) the rubber check.

c. A railroad caboose.

1947 BEEBE *Mixed Train Dly.* 324 About the only uniform and universal attributes of short-line bouncers are the round wheels, automatic couplers, air brakes and a variable degree of availability to human occupancy.

***bound,** *n.* As the last term in **corner, east, eastern, north, south, tip, up, water, west bound.**

***bound,** *v. tr.* To name the boundaries of (a country or state) as a school exercise in studying geography.

1847 WEBSTER, Bound, v.t. . . . To mention the boundaries of a country; as, to bound France. **1877** *Harper's Mag.* March 558 Lessons literally went in at one ear and out of the other; if she bounded Pennsylvania correctly to-day . . . she was as likely to put Texas on the east and Georgia on the north of it tomorrow. **1946** WILSON *Fidelity* 140 We bounded all the states and countries, named capes and rivers and bays and lakes.

***bound,** *a.* Of a boy or girl: Articled to service.

1843 *Amer. Pioneer* II. 140 Our family consisted of my father, mother, and three children, . . . and a bound boy of fourteen. **1871** EGGLESTON *Hoosier Schoolm.* iv. 51 Ralph recognized Hannah, the bound girl at old Jack Means's. **1896** S. O. JEWETT *Country of Pointed Firs* 157 A scatter-witted little bound girl came running to the meetin'-house door.

b. (See quot.)

1846 *Cong. Globe* 6 Feb. 322/3 He has to stand by, as we say in the West, 'like a bound boy at a husking.'

***boundary,** *n.* An area, tract, or extent of land. *Colloq.*

1881 in *Amer. Sp.* XV. 158/1 In the Clinch Mountain are large boundaries of chestnut, chestnut oak, with hickory, etc. **1933** *Ib.*, He increased his acreage from time to time by purchasing adjoining lands until he owned a large boundary. **1941** ALLEY *Random Thoughts* 482 They bought a considerable boundary of timber lands.

As the last term in **Indian, Oregon, out, section boundary.**

***bounded,** *a.* Of a tree: Selected or distinguished as a boundary mark. *Local* and *obs.*

1674 *Md. Hist. Mag.* I. 9 Beginning at the northernmost bounded tree of the land . . . and running north . . . to a bounded oak by a small branch. **1685** *Col. Rec. Penn.* I. 128 Such as Cutt or fall Marked or bounded trees. **1786** *Md. Hist. Mag.* XIX. 262 If he had cut it down he could have been hung, as it was a bounded tree.

bounder ˈbaʊndɚ, *n.* **1.** A device causing objects to rebound. *Rare.* **2.** In baseball, a batted ball which bounds over the ground.

(1) 1858 *Rep. Comm. Patents* (1859) I. 364, I claim the inclined plane and bounder . . . for bounding cranberries, to separate the good from the bad. — **(2) 1868** CHADWICK *Base Ball* 37 The short-stop, too, has to field more ground balls and short bounders than any other fielder. **1914** *Chi. Tribune* 6 Aug. 15/1 Mel got rid of Baker on an easy bounder.

bound game. In the early days of baseball a game in which the balls were caught with the bare hands on the first bounce. *Obs.* Cf. **fly game.** — **1864** *Wilkes' Spirit of Times* 17 Dec. 244/3 The following argument asserting the superiority of the fly-game over the bound-game we clip from a local contemporary.

bound house. A house erected to mark the bounds, actual or intended, of a colony. *Obs.*

1660 in SHURTLEFF *Log Cabin* (1939) 81 At there first coming over they sett up a house and named it the bound House as finding it three miles from Meromack, the North bound of there Patent. **1676** *N.H. Doc. & Rec.* I. 325 They thought fit at length to declare themselves mistaken in what they had done in the year 1631, when they erected bound-houses. **1784** in SHURTLEFF *Log Cabin* (1939) 82 An house was built, and commonly called the Bound-house; though it was intended as a mark of possession rather than of limits.

***bounty,** *n.*

1. A premium or reward given to encourage the slaying of wild animals or Indians. Also attrib.

1726 PENHALLOW *Indian Wars* 106 Capt. Lovewell [and 30 men] . . . came on . . . two Indians, one of which they killed and . . . for which they received the promised bounty of one hundred pounds a scalp. **1873** *Newton Kansan* 20 Feb. 4/1 The bounty of 15 cents on gopher scalps is said to have cost Nebraska $25,000 in two years. **1901** DUNCAN & SCOTT *Allen & Woodson Co., Kansas* 15 They [the county board] . . . offered a bounty of twenty-five cents for wolf scalps. **1947** *Sports Afield* Feb. 24/1 Both of these states have had long experience in bounty control of wild vermin.

2. In special combs., chiefly obs. or hist.: (1) **bounty act,** a legislative enactment providing for the payment of a bounty; (2) **broker,** one who traded in the enlistment of soldiers during the Civil War; (3) **fund,** during the Civil War a fund provided for paying bounties to those enlisting in the army; (4) **grant,** a payment in land made to one as compensation for military service; (5) **jumper,** one who enlists as a soldier, obtains the bounty paid to recruits, and then deserts; (6) **jumping,** the practice of enlisting to obtain the bounty and then deserting, also attrib. or as adj.; (7) **land,** land given as bounty for military service, also attrib.; (8) **lot,** a lot consisting of bounty land; (9) **reward,** a bounty given as a reward; (10) **tract,** (see quot.).

(1) 1726 PENHALLOW *Indian Wars* 99 The frontiers being thus alarmed, two companies of volunteers went from New-Hampshire on the bounty act, one hundred pounds a scalp. — **(2) 1864** SALA in *Daily Telegraph* (Lond.) 9 Aug., A bounty-broker is simply a crimp, or what the recruiting sergeants in Charles-street, Westminster, call a 'bringer.' **1891** SCOTT *Amer. Lawyers* 193 Upon the establishment of the provost marshal department by act of Congress, certain persons engaged in the recruiting service entered into a conspiracy with 'bounty-brokers' to defraud the Government. — **(3) 1863** F. MOORE *Rebellion Rec.* V. I. 48 A large amount of money was subscribed to the bounty fund. — **(4) 1837** BIRD *Nick of Woods* I. 47 The bounty-grants earned by himself in virtue of military service rendered in the army of his native State.

(5) 1864 WHITMAN *November Boughs* (1888) 80 There are many hundreds of 'bounty jumpers,' and . . . eighty thousand deserters! **1941** ASBURY *Gem of Prairie* 66 Bounty-jumpers, thugs and rowdies who enlisted for the pay, deserted as soon as they had collected their bounty. — **(6) 1865** P. V. NASBY *Struggles* 169 Vallandigum and Voorhees hev gone into the law; I shel embark into bounty-jumpin. **1867** GOSS *Soldier's Story* 157 Thus ended the lesson of retribution that . . . broke up a gang of bounty-jumping desperadoes. **1914** MCLAUGHLIN & HART *Cyclo.* I. 169/1 Gangs were organized by substitute brokers to repeat the 'bounty jumping' in different localities. — **(7) 1779** *Ky. Petitions* 49 This would entitle every man to draw a free lott in Town, and also entitle him to his Bounty Land. **1836** *Niles' Reg.* 24 Sep. 62/1 [Appropriation] for messenger in the bounty land bureau, [$]400. **1889** *Cent.* 642/3 *Bounty Land Act*, a United States statute of 1850 (9 Stat., 520), granting lands to those engaged in the military service, or to their widows or minor children. **1944** DUNCAN *M. Graham* xxvii, He had bounty land of thousands of acres. — **(8) 1820** *Missouri Intell.* 27 May 2/3 The Lands in the Military Tract . . . could not be distributed to soldiers, being . . . too small or too large for bounty lots. **1832** WILLIAMSON *Maine* II. 543, 80 settlers, who were entitled to the bounty-lots of government. — **(9) 1761** S. NILES *Indian Wars* II. 354 A fresh company . . . soon found the Indian Ashley had shot, and scalped him; for which he received a hundred-pound bounty reward, according to the order of the Assembly.

(10) 1831 PECK *Guide* 319 The Military Bounty Tract . . . was set aside by Congress and patented for soldiers who served in the last war.

As the last term in **fishing, military, Negro, scalp bounty.**

bounty ˈbaʊntɪ, *v.* [f. the noun.] *tr.* To assist, encourage, or reward with a bounty. *Obs.* — **1788** JEFFERSON *Writings* VII. 210 The eighty-five ships, . . . bountied, as the English are, will require a sacrifice of twelve hundred and eighty-five thousand two hundred livres a year. **1863** NORTON *Army Lett.* 180 The government may get considerable money to bounty volunteers, but they will be too late.

***bouquet,** *n. To throw bouquets,* to pay compliments. *Colloq.* — **1904** *Journalist* 28 May 89 We do not wish to say 'I told you so,' or to 'throw any bouquets' in our own direction. **1905** A. ADAMS *Outlet* 230 Quince . . . threw bouquets at me regarding my ability always to find water.

* **Bourbon,** *n.* Also * **bourbon.**

1. *attrib.* Denoting varieties of sugar-cane and cotton, possibly introduced from the Isle of Bourbon. *Obs.*

1814 *Niles' Reg.* VI. 200/1 Thirteen years ago some Bourbon canes were given to Mr. Couper, of St. Simons, by a gentleman who had emigrated from one of the Bahama Islands. **1818** J. PALMER *Travels U.S.* 443 Cotton, Bourbon and other foreign varieties. **1853** *Harper's Mag.* VII. 749/1 The Bourbon cane is of a dark purplish color. **1856** *Rep. Comm. Patents: Agric.* 227 In the earlier experiments, the Bourbon cotton was mainly relied upon.

2. Used in allusion to the New Court party *q.v.* in Kentucky. *Obs.* Cf. **4.** below.

1827 *Spirit of Seventy-Six* (Frankfort, Ky.) 4 Jan. 3/3 What '*Bourbons*' ever existed in Kentucky? What '*Bourbons*' are restored?

3. A kind of whisky, originally made in Bourbon County, Ky. Also attrib. Cf. **Old Bourbon.**

1851 *Knickerb.* XXXVII. 280 A somewhat freedrinker in Kentucky . . . purchased a hogshead of the 'Bourbon whiskey' of that region. **1856** G. H. DERBY *Phoenixiana* xxxii. 195 We had an opportunity of ascertaining whether there was any Bourbon among us. **1867** W. H. DIXON *New America* II. 96 These people say they want no Cherokee medicines, no plantation bitters, no Bourbon cocktails. **1947** BEEBE *Mixed Train Dly.* 89 Would you gentlemen care for the refreshment of a little bourbon whisky?

4. A conservative in politics, used esp. of southern Democrats of old-fashioned "before-the-war" political views. Cf. **Southern bourbon.**

In allusion to the Bourbon royal family of France, of whom it was said on their return to power after Napoleon's downfall that they had "learned nothing and forgotten nothing."

1866 *Harper's Mag.* Sep. 536/1 To the query 'Have we a Bourbon among us?' I would say a great many of them. **1884** NYE *Baled Hay* 140 Colonel Thomas . . . Dayton entered the democratic headquarters, . . . the stamping ground of the bourbons. **1947** *Christian Cent.* 8 Oct. 1204/1 Even the most reactionary bourbons of the south have not proposed that the lands of our colored citizens should be seized and turned over to more progressive citizens.

b. Attrib. with **ally, candidate, democrat, family, organ, regime, white.**

1859 *Olympia* (W.T.) *Pioneer & Democrat* 15 April (Th.), The 'Bourbon' family have attempted to rule this territory from the earliest hour of its creation. **1875** *Cong. Rec.* 2 March 2111/1 Baxter's success depended upon the influence of his Bourbon allies. **1881** *Ib.* 7 Feb. 1305/2, I am not sufficiently acquainted with history to know why a man should dislike to be called a 'Bourbon' democrat. **1883** *Cent. Mag.* July 398/1 A man's opinions on . . . the Bourbon regime in the South, were no test of his fitness to collect taxes. **1884** *Boston Journal* 20 Sep., That chief of Bourbon organs, the Charleston (S.C.) News. *Ib.* 23 Sep., Major J. W. McDaniel of Virginia, the Bourbon candidate for Governor three years ago. **1944** FAST *F. Road* 49 He had no love for Bourbon whites, whom he hated instinctively.

Bourbonish ˈbʊrbənɪʃ, *a.* Having the character of Bourbon democracy. *Rare.* — **1906** *Springfield W. Republican* 22 Nov. 8 On this matter that section is to-day more exclusive and bourbonish and reactionary than it was 30 years ago.

Bourbonism ˈbʊrbənˌɪzəm, *n.* Conservatism in politics.

1876 *Arcola* (Ill.) *Record* 26 Feb. 4/2 The ancient Courthouse Bourbons . . . helped to start the *Review* in this county, for the purpose of building up Bourbonism and breaking down the Independent Reform movement. **1904** *Buffalo Commercial* 22 Nov. 8 The young and liberal men in the South are encouraged to throw off the yoke of Bourbonism. **1944** *Christian Cent.* 12 July 823/1 The Democratic convention will reveal quite as much bourbonism on the part of its powerful southern state and northern city machines as did the Republicans in their cheers for 'free enterprise.'

Bourbonite, *n.* One who prefers Bourbon whisky to gin. Cf. **Bourbon,** *n.* **3.** *Colloq.* — **1865** *Wilkes' Spirit of Times* 26 Aug. 402/1 And those who don't participate in the juice of the juniper are Bourbon-ites.

Bourbonized ˈbʊrbənˌaɪzd, *a.* Affected by Bourbonism. — **1906** *N.Y. Ev. Post* 7 May 6 This difficulty in bringing 'Bourbonized' Republicans around to a successful advocacy of the old Democratic doctrines.

bourgeois ˈbʊrʒwa, *n.* [F., an American borrowing.] "In the fur trade of the West and North, a partner in a company who was in charge of a trading post or expedition" (McDermott).

[**1791** J. LONG *Voyages* 75 The Canadians . . . encounter these difficulties [forcing canoes through shallow water] with uncommon chearfulness, though they sometimes exclaim, 'c'est la misère, mon bourgeois.'] **1837** *N.Y. Mirror* 8 July 11/1 Our brigade consisted of two canoes, manned by seventeen Canadians, voyageurs: John Reed, an Irishman, and myself, an American 'commiss,' and Donald McKenzie, bourgeois, or proprietor, who had charge of the whole. **1855** ROSS *Fur Hunters* I. 5 Clerks have charge of posts, bourgeois of districts, and the ambition of the clerk is naturally to become a bourgeois. **1912** WHEELER *Selkirk Mts.* 13 The camp-fire, flickering among the dark shadows of the pines, has lighted up the bronzed and strikingly characteristic features of bourgeois, voyageur and redskin. **1948** *Pac. Northwest Quart.* April 53 The previous year he had become a *bourgeois* or partner in the company.

b. (See quots.) *Obs.*

1836 T. B. THORPE *Life on Lakes* I. 179 Next, a frame, or rather a stout lattice-work, is laid on in the centre, where the '*Bourgois*,' as the Canadians call the passengers, are to sit. **1857** *Spirit of Times* 5 Dec. 209/1 A standing position in a bark canoe is not to be thought of for a *bourgeois*—as travellers are called by the boatmen.

boute baʊt, *n.* [Du. *bocht*, or G. *bucht*. Cf. *OED s.v.* **bought*.] A bend in the course of a river. *Rare.* — **1675** *Penna. Archives* I. 34 Two Necks or points of land, lying and being in this River of Delaware and on the east-side thereof over ag[ains]t the Boute above Verdick-teige-hooke.

* **bow,** *n.*

1. *pl.* The rims or framing of a pair of spectacles.

1711 *Essex Inst. Coll.* IV. 187/1 To Madam Rebekah Brown, I give my spectacles with gold bows. **1847** LONGFELLOW *Evangeline* I. iii. 4 Glasses with horn bows Sat astride on his nose. **1861** STOWE *Pearl Orr's Isl.* I. 65 Mrs. Kittredge glared through the horn bows of her glasses. **1890** *Harper's Mag.* Oct. 720/1 A pair of ancient silver-rimmed spectacles from which the bows were lost. **1905** *Sears Cat.* (ed. 115) 431/1 This method of making the bows renders them very flexible and somewhat larger than the regulation style, making it impossible for them to cut into the flesh back of the ears.

2. A bent strip of wood serving as an arch to support the canvas or tilt of a covered wagon.

1856 WHIPPLE *Explor. Ry. Route* I. 10 As our wagons were packed to the bows, . . . we offered to purchase his wagon and horses. **1877** F. M. A. ROE *Army Lett.* 161 The high top will be of canvas drawn over 'bows,' in true emigrant fashion. **1929** A. J. DICKSON *Across Plains* 138 The whole was surmounted by a canvas cover supported by bows which widened outward if the box was flaring.

3. In combs.: (1) **bow-key,** a bowpin for an oxbow; (2) **stick,** ?a bowstave, *rare;* (3) **timber,** wood for making oxbows; (4) **whip,** (see quot.), *rare;* (5) **wood,** (see quot. 1916 and cf. **bodock, brasswood**).

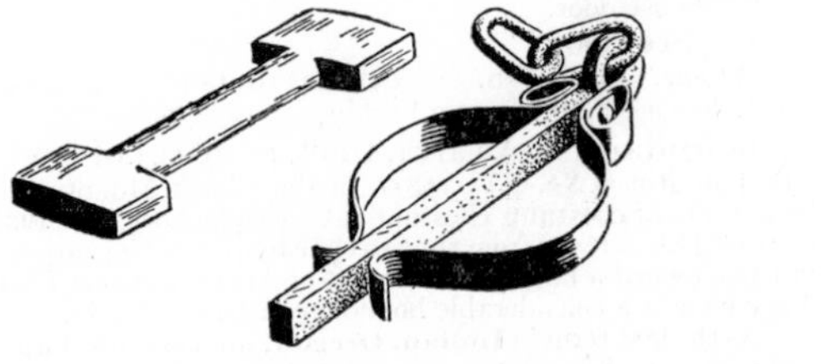

Bow-keys of different types

(**1**) **1857** J. YOUNG in *Journal Discourses* VI. 230 You that have on such a yoke had better pull out the bow-keys. **1921** H. QUICK *Vandemark's Folly* 304, I would be gosh-blasted if I wouldn't, by Golding's Bow-key! [*Footn.*], 'By Golding's bow-key' was a very solemn objurgation. . . . It harks back to the time when every man who had oxen named them Buck and Golding, and the bow-key held the yoke on. — (**2**) **1729** *Essex Inst. Coll.* XLII. 132 The storm . . . obliged them to clear & heave what was in her over board as Apples, Bow Sticks, &c. — (**3**) **1846** SAGE *Scenes Rocky Mts.* iii, We . . . encamped at Big Vermilion for the purpose of procuring a quantity of hickory for gun-sticks and bow-timber. — (**4**) **1890** *Harper's Mag.* Oct. 718/1 His whip was the fashionable 'bow-whip' of the period, common enough now, to be sure, with a long lash, tapering down to a fine silk 'snapper' on the end.

(**5**) **1806** *Ann. 9th Congress* 2 Sess. 1138 One or two slips of the bois d'arc, bow wood, or yellow wood, from the Missouri. **1842** BUCKINGHAM *Slave States* I. 476 The first of these is the bow-wood, so called because its branches were used by the native Indians for making their bows. **1916** SETON *Woodcraft Man.* 287 Osage Orange, (Bois D'arc) Bodarc, or Bow-Wood (*Toxylon pomiferum*). A small tree, rarely 60 feet high. Originally from the middle Mississippi Valley, now widely introduced as a hedge tree. Famous for supplying the best bows in America east of the Rockies.

As the last term in **choke, cornstalk, flat, ox, rain, wagon bow.**

bowdark, see **bodock.**

*__bowed,__ *a.* **1.** Of spectacles: Having "bows" or rims of a specified kind. **2.** (See quots.) *Obs.*

(1) **1840** *Knickerb.* XVI. 296 In addition to this, he had a pair of large bowed spectacles, resting upon the tip of his ruby nose. **1870** W. W. FOWLER *Ten Years in Wall Street* 303 A corpulent gentleman, who wore gold-bowed spectacles. — (2) **1841** *Hunt's Merch. Mag.* March 212 [Georgia upland cotton] was long called Bowed, because it was originally cleared from its seeds by the blows of a bowstring. *Ib.* 217 The species of cotton long known as the bowed Georgia, derives its name from the mode of cleaning it. **1848** *Banker's Mag.* III. 78 The *upland cotton,* or that grown in the interior, is known by the name of *short staple* or *bowed cotton.*

As the last term in **horn bowed, steel bowed.**

*__bowel,__ *n.* (See quots.) *Slang. Obs.* — *c***1844** R. H. COLLYER *Amer. Life* 7 Almost every house or room has in one corner a bar where the various evil spirits of rum, gin and brandy, and various fancy mixtures called, 'Toenails, Bowel Ploughers, Corn Cobs, Eye Snappers,' are retailed. **1856** HALL *College Words* (ed. 2) 37 At Harvard College, a student in common parlance will express his destitution or poverty by saying, 'I have not a bowel.' The use of the word with this signification has arisen, probably, from a jocular reference to a quaint Scriptural expression.

bower ˈbaʊɚ, *n.* [G. *bauer,* peasant, knave in cards.] One of the two highest cards in some card games, esp. euchre. The *right bower* is the higher of the two, being the knave of the trump suit; the *left bower* is the knave of the suit having the same color as the trump suit.

1830 *Cin. Chronicle* 2 Jan. 1/2 As I was sauntering by a house in Broad Way, I heard the words, 'bowers,' 'hearts,' 'trumps,' &c. **1839** *Spirit of Times* 24 Aug. 294/2 (We.), The *right* and *left bower* in the game of *Euchre.* **1898** WESTCOTT *D. Harum* 36 We have played . . . fifteen hundred games, in which he had held both bowers and the ace of trumps . . . fourteen hundred times. **1946** MOREHEAD & MOTT-SMITH *Penguin Hoyle* 29 The second-highest is the jack of the trump suit, called the *right bower.*

b. *fig.* In various applications.

1850 H. C. LEWIS *La. Swamp Doctor* 125 'What is calomel?' 'A drug, sir, that may be called the right bower of quackery.' **1884** *Milnor* (Dakota) *Teller* 8 Aug., Little Maud S. . . . once again reigns as the queen of the turf and holds a right bower over the King. **1929** DOBIE *Vaquero* 60 Cortina's 'right bower' was Alberto Garza, popularly known as 'Caballo Blanco.' **1947** *Time* 29 Dec. 14/2 As Ed's successor, the convention picked shaggy-browed Allan Kline, 52, of Iowa, who has long been Ed's right bower.

c. *To christen the bower,* to indulge in strong punch or drink. *Obs.*

*c***1861** in *Pub. Col. Soc.* XXVII. 79 July 25. Nine of the Class of 1823 at Harvard receive public admonitions for pursuing the ancient ceremony of 'christening the bower.'

bowery ˈbaʊərɪ, *n.* [Du. *bouwerij,* farm.]

1. A farm or country estate in the early Dutch settlements in New York. Now *obs.* or *hist.*

1650 in SHURTLEFF *Log Cabin* (1939) 113 The report in question, by Secretary Cornelis van Tienhoven, is dated March 4, 1650, and called 'Information relative to taking up land in New Netherland, in the form of Colonies or private bouwries.' **1675** *N.Y. State Col. Hist.* XIII. 490 The boweryes or farmes of Schanechtade are to pay . . . four Bushells of winter wheate per Annum as a quitt Rent. **1885** *Harper's Mag.* May 841/2 The farm called the Domine's Bouwery . . . was granted by Governor Van Twiller to Roeloff Jansen and his wife in 1636. **1944** ADAMS *Album Amer. Hist.* I. 143 A few blocks from Fort Amsterdam one came to the farms or 'boweries' of the Dutch squires.

b. The farm or country seat of Governor Stuyvesant of New York, afterwards a resort of pleasure parties from the city. *Obs.*

1679 in WOLLEY *Journal* (1902) 13 We left the village called the *Bouwerij,* lying on the right hand, and went through the woods to New Harlem, a tolerably large village situated on the south side of the island. **1704** S. KNIGHT *Journal* 55 Their Diversions in the Winter is riding Sleys about three or four Miles out of Town, where they have Houses of entertainment at a place called the Bowery. **1890** *Cent. Mag.* Nov. 46 Their adoration took the form of steady pilgrimages to Mynheer Van Witt's mansion, 'Bovenkirk,' just beyond Governor Stuyvesant's 'Bowery.'

c. (*cap.*) A well-known street or region in New York City, located on or near the site of the Governor's farm, noted for cheap theaters, beer halls, etc.

1787 CUTLER in *Life & Corr.* I. 305, I . . . left the city by way of the Bowery. *c***1844** COLLYER *Lights & Shadows Am. Life* 7 You may leave the brilliant walks of fashion, beauty and lustre of Broadway, or the crowd and bustle of business in Chatham street, and the Bowery. **1948** *Dly. Ardmoreite* (Ardmore, Okla.) 18 Apr. 22/3 So far it has been seen here chiefly in poor men's clubs along the bowery and third avenue.

attrib. **1852** BRISTED *Upper Ten Th.* 29 Its occupants are of not-to-be-mistaken Bowery cut—veritable 'b'hoys.' **1859** *Harper's Mag.* April 616/2 As they drove by, one of them, with a most remarkable 'Bowery twang,' sang out. **1891** *Ib.* Dec. 41/1 The shining bodies of men, bare naked, and frescoed like a Bowery bar-room, were not lacking. **1947** *Chi. Tribune* 1 Nov. 8/1 He was arrested in a Bowery flophouse where a bed for the night costs 50 cents.

2. In special combs.: (1) **Bowery boy,** a rough or rowdy of a type characteristic of the Bowery about 1835–45, in the pl. a gang of such roughs, now *hist.;* (2) **bum,** a

Bowery boy *c*1840

bum who frequents the Bowery; (3) **girl,** (see quot. 1882), *obs.*

(1) **1840** *N.O. Picayune* 28 Aug. 2/1 The Bowery boys of New York have, in our opinion, eclipsed the nice young men of Baltimore. **1860** HANCOCK *Five Years* 46 The term 'Bowery Boy,' or to give the customary pronunciation, 'Bowery B'hoy,' is understood as implying the personification of vulgarity of manner, showiness of costume, facilty in the use of slang, and mental imbecility generally, in their highest development. **1941** A. TRAIN *Story Everyday Things* 291 A fight broke out in New York between the partisans of Edwin Forrest and William Charles Macrady, . . . which was delightedly joined in by . . . members of such well-known gangs as the 'Bowery Boys' and the 'Dead Rabbits.' — (2) **1943** MENEFEE *Assignment* 27 Even the Bowery Bum of legend is being rehabilitated. **1946** *Reader's Digest* Dec. 16/1 Wondering why he should be competing with the Bowery bums for alms, I said, 'Don't you think you would do better some place like Park Avenue?' — (3) **1856** *Spirit of Times* 1 Nov. 149/1 Star-flower of the blooming Bower-y girls, Come hither, the spoonies are gone. **1861** HORTON RHYS *Theatrical Trip* 29 To say nothing of the Bowery bo-hoys and ga-hals. **1882** MCCABE *New York* 642 The original 'Bowery Girl' must have been made of a rib of the original 'Bowery Boy,' so exactly was she his counterpart. There was this difference, however, between them. While he affected a severely simple style of dress, she loved to deck herself out in all the glories of dry-goods and millinery.

Bowery-boy-ish, *a.* Of or pertaining to a Bowery boy. *Rare.* — **1852** *Knickerb.* Aug. 187 There was something very 'Bowery-boy'-ish in a question asked by one 'soap-lock' of another.

Boweryish ˈbaʊərɪ·ɪʃ, *a.* Suggestive of the Bowery in N.Y. *Rare.* — **1846** POE *Literati, L. G. Clark,* Its best friends are forced to admit [this Editor's Table] is a little Boweryish.

Boweryism ˈbaʊərɪˌɪzəm, *n.* Conduct characteristic of a Bowery boy. Also **Bowery-boyism.** *Obs.* — **1852** *Lantern* (N.Y.) I. 135/1 His valor and Bowery B'hoyism is, however, too strong; and it thus mildly escapes. **1896** HASWELL *New York* 355 They were mostly men of regular occupations and industry, the Boweryism being only their form of amusement in leisure hours.

bowfin ˈboˌfɪn, *n.* A freshwater ganoid fish, *Amia calva,* found chiefly in the Mississippi Valley.

1845 STORER *Synopsis Fishes N.A.* 213 Called the 'Bowfin,' at Lake Champlain. **1897** *Outing* Aug. 437 This fish, the bowfin . . . , was always termed 'dogfish,' and he was an ugly-looking fellow. His greenish-yellow, snaky-looking body was not pleasant to contemplate, and there was an ugly expression about his big mouth. **1947** DALRYMPLE *Panfish* 27 If you want a *real* battle, find a spot where Bowfins (Dogfish) abound.

bowie ˈbu·ɪ, *n.* (Also *cap.*)

1. Short for next.

1842 *Spirit of Times* 29 Jan. 566/2 (We.), I hung my bowie to my side. **1880** *Sat. Review* 18 Sep. 369/2 Every now and then Mr. Mercer goes for the citizens with a bowie. **1901** *Munsey's Mag.* XXIV. 450/2 The term 'bowie' came to mean almost any kind of a knife carried in a sheath. The real bowie is from nine to ten inches long, with one edge.

2. bowie knife, a heavy sheath knife, having a strong single-edged blade from nine to fifteen inches long, originally made by frontier blacksmiths from old files, horse-rasps, etc., and differing much in size and pattern.

The first such knife is said to have been made by Rezin Bowie (see *Amer. Sp.* Feb. 1937, 77 ff.), but the name is usu. associated with his more illustrious brother, Col. James Bowie, one of the heroes of the Alamo.

1836 *Niles' Reg.* 4 June 234 With two large Bowie-knives (an instrument about twelve inches in length, and an inch and a half wide, with two edges tapering to a sharp point). **1894** *Life* 12 July 32/1 A big, burly fellow, bristling with revolvers and bowie knives, stepped in the door. **1945** *Chi. D. News* 17 Jan. 10/6 Wait until a portly lady is paying her fare. Then, when her back is turned, thrust your Bowie knife deep into her derriere—this is known the army as 'the softening-up process.'

attrib. **1837** in COMMONS *Doc. Hist.* II. 299 The introduction of their lawless customs among us, in the shape of gamblers and bowie knife assassins. **1857** T. H. GLADSTONE *Englishman in Kansas* 252 And that day, the 29th of November, 1854, the slaveholding interest, from which there is no appeal, achieved the first of its great bowie-knife victories, and witnessed the establishment of rifle-rule in Kansas. **1877** BERRY in Morris *Pub. Service Alaska* (1879) 24 British Columbia tolerates no cutting and shooting, and it soon tames our pistol and bowie-knife gentry.

b. Also **bowie-knifing,** fighting with bowie knives. *Obs.*

1844 *St. Louis Reveille* 29 Dec. 1/6 Many, especially far east, . . . hear nothing of these people, except their bowie-knifing and rifle-shooting.

3. Bowie whiskers, (see quot.). *Rare.*

1837 *Commercial Trans.* (Balt.) 16 Nov. 2/1 (Th.), *The Philadelphia Ledger* insinuates that those who wear these appendages encircling the face are no better than they should be. He says *Bowie whiskers* are the signs of Bowie knives.

* **bowl,** *n.*

1. (See quot. 1907.) Also attrib. Now *hist.*

1778 CARVER *Travels* 365 The game of the Bowl or Platter . . . is played between two persons only. Each person has six or eight little bones . . . two of the sides of which are coloured black, and the others

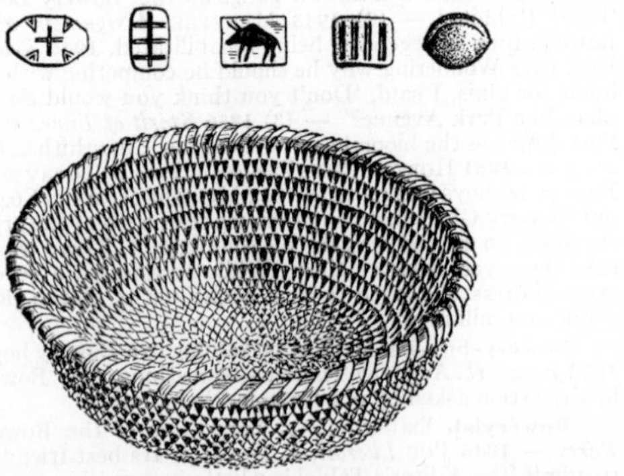

Objects used in the bowl game as played by Cheyenne Indians

white. These they throw up into the air, from whence they fall into a bowl or platter placed underneath. **1855** LONGFELLOW *Hiawatha* XVI. vii, Then from out his pouch of wolf-skin Forth he drew . . . All the game of Bowl and Counters. **1907** HODGE *Amer. Indians* II. 484/2 *Bowl game.*—A kind of dice game widely played by women among the Algonquian, Iroquois, Sioux, and other northern tribes. The dice consist of bone disks, or of peach or plum stones, which are tossed in a wooden bowl or a basket.

2. A bowl-shaped amphitheater where athletic events are held., usu. in the names of particular places of this kind.

1923 *Pasadena* (Calif.) *Star-News* 1 Jan. 1 Cheered to the echo, . . . a crowd of about 50,000 people in the great Rose Bowl, Pasadena's new Stadium in the Arroyo Seco. **1940** *Mt. Hood Guide* 110 An enlarged area . . . was also put into use in the space lying between the Ski Bowl and the Ski Jump. **1944** *Chi. D. News* 10 Jan. 11/7 Two men rapped on the door of the Sports Bowl . . . and told the janitor . . . they had come to repair the lights. **1946** *Trail & Timberline* Apr. 53/1 The Arizona Snow Bowl, one of the most popular ski areas in the Southwest, is located on the slope of San Francisco Peaks. **1947** *Chi. Sun* 18 Nov. 30/2 Undefeated Compton (Calif.) Junior College is receiving top consideration for a spot in the Papoose Bowl against an Oklahoma team.

transf. **1947** *Steamboat* (Colo.) *Pilot* 9 Jan. 1/5 Nestling in a snug valley entirely surrounded by mountains, Steamboat calls itself the 'Snow Bowl of the Rockies.'

As the last term in **bread, bubble, corncob, dust, Indian, knot, set, slop, wash bowl.**

bowldered ˈboldərd, *a.* Paved with cobblestones. *Rare.* — **1873** J. H. BEADLE *Undevel. West* xxxi. 682 There is not a foot of regular turnpike, a rod of bowldered street, or a mile of navigable canal in the entire Territory.

bowling saloon. A building equipped with bowling alleys where patrons may engage in bowling. — **1846** *Dollar Newspaper* (Phila.) 1 July 2/3 Elder Knapp . . . addressed a large congregation on the immoral tendencies of 'theatres and bowling saloons.' **1889** BRAYLEY *Boston Fire Dept.* 211 The same day fire originated in a wooden building used for bowling-alleys, and known as the 'Neptune Bowling Saloon.'

Bowlist ˈbolɪst, *n.* [Origin unknown.] A member of a former New England religious sect. — **1781** PETERS *Hist. Conn.* 280 The Bowlists, Separatists and Davisonians, are peculiar to the Colony. The first allow neither singing nor prayer.

bowman ˈbaʊmən, *n.* [?f. *bâtman*, batman, with *bât* pronounced as in French.] (See quot.) *Obs.* — **a1859** *Sk. Virginia* (B.), Each captain and lieutenant [in Va.] was entitled, and I believe is so now, to select from the rank of his company a soldier to wait on him, to carry messages, to cater for him, and to cook for him; and the soldier thus selected was called *bowman.*

bowman's root. [Cf. the earlier **baumont root.**] Any one of various common plants as Culver's root, flowering spurge, Indian physic, etc. Also **bowman root.**

1815 DRAKE *Cincinnati* ii. 87 [In the] forest of the Miami country [grows] *Euphorbia colorata*, Bowman's root. **1824** DODDRIDGE *Notes* 148 Indian physick, or bowman root, a species of epicacuanha [*sic*] was frequently used for a vomit. **1901** MOHR *Plant Life Ala.* 539 *Porteranthus trifoliatus.* . . . Bowman's Root. *Spiraea trifoliata.* . . . *Gillenia trifoliata.* . . . Alleghenian and Carolinian area; . . . rare west of the Alleghanies. **1931** CLUTE *Plants* 126 Some plants have been so regularly used by certain individual medical practitioners as to have become indissolubly connected with their names. This is the case with . . . Bowman's root (*Gillenia trifoliata*).

bowsman ˈbaʊzmən, *n.* [An alteration of F. *bosseman*, bosman, misapprehended as "bow's-man."] = **bosman.**

1804 LEWIS in *L. & Clark Exped.* (1904) I. 34 The one not engaged at the oar [of the batteau] will attend as the Bows-man. **1846** M'KENNEY *Memoirs* I. 97, I ordered the bowsman to stick a pole down in the river. **1902** WHITE *Conjuror's House* ii. 16 New leggings, of holiday pattern, were intermittently visible on the bowsmen and steersmen.

* **box,** *n.*

1. A cavity made in the trunk of a tree, usu. a maple tree or pine, for collecting sap or turpentine. Also attrib.

1720 P. DUDLEY in *Phil. Trans.* XXXI. 27 You box the Tree, as we call it, i.e. make a hole with an Axe, or chizzel, into the side of the Tree, within a Foot of the Ground; the Box you make may hold about a Pint. **1775** ROMANS *Nat. Hist. Florida* 150 A hole is cut in the tree on the side most exposed to the solar rays. . . . This hole is called a box, and the turpentine is dipped out of it. **1896** *Pop. Science Mo.* Feb. 478 The French turpentine workman does not cut a big, deep, broad box into the tree [as our southern workman does]. **1938** DANIELS *Southerner* 316 But Dr. Herty in those days was already teaching the South to use the less destructive cups in place of the old box system in collecting the crude turpentine from the scarred pine trees.

b. *To hack boxes,* (see quot.).

1859 G. W. PERRY *Turpentine Farming* 77 When chipping is commenced on the faces, it is called 'hacking boxes.'

2. (See quots.) *Obs.*

1809 KENDALL *Travels* III. 218 Rafts, composed of boards and other lumber, are called *boxes.* **1836** T. POWER *Impressions* II. 145 A mail conveyance bearing a name so novel excited my curiosity; so, . . . I walked down to the starting-place, where, ready-harnessed and loaded, stood literally the *Box,* made of rough fir plank, eight feet long by three feet wide, with sides two feet deep: it was fixed firmly on an ordinary coach-axle. **1881** MARSHALL *Through Amer.* (1882) 192 Mormons are great bathers, and have erected fifty or sixty 'boxes' or dressing-sheds on the shore, at a place called Lake Point.

3. A receptacle or pigeon-hole in a post office in which a subscriber's mail is placed. Cf. **box letter, box rent.**

1833 *Trial E. K. Avery* 43 E. K. Avery had a private box at my office. **1865** *Erie* (Penna.) *Wkly. Gazette* 5 Oct. 3/1 A very necessary addition to the number of boxes at the post office is being made. **1948** *Lawton* (Okla.) *Constitution* 4 July 1/4 Regular deliveries will be suspended with the exception of special delivery and mail in boxes at the post office.

4. (See quots.) Cf. **battery,** *n.*[1] **3.**

1859 BARTLETT 24 Battery. A sort of boat used for duck-shooting in the Chesapeake, in which the shooter lies below the surface of the water. It is also called, among other local names, a Surface-boat, Coffin-boat, Sink, or Box. **1874** LONG *Wild-Fowl* 52 Perhaps the very best blind . . . is the sunken box . . . a deep box of pine. *Ib.* 253 The box in which the shooter lies should be of pine.

5. The body of a sleigh or wagon. Cf. **box pung, sledge, sleigh, wagon; sleigh box, wagon box.**

Du. *bak*, bowl, trough, in some of its uses corresponds to Eng. "body." Cf. *WNT s.v. bak* (I) 5 *a*, where *bak* is given as "dat deel van eene kar waarin de vracht geladen wordt." One of the exs. given here has ref. to a sleigh, "De bak der sleê was laag bij den grond, . . . fraai beschilderd en verguld."

[*c*1774 CRÈVECOEUR *Sketches of 18th Cent. Amer.* (1925) 146 The pleasure-sleigh is accommodated with a box handsomely painted, and seats which can easily carry six persons.] **1869** J. R. BROWNE *Adv. Apache Country* 193 One of the escort picked up a few sticks of wood . . . and threw them in the box of the forage-wagon. **1899** *Mo. So. Dakotan* I. 175 The box is in the slough and the hind axle hangs on the demolished harvester. **1936** *Sears Cat.* (ed. 173) 943 Steel Wagon Box Rods. . . . For narrow box.

6. The station occupied by various players in baseball, now usu. applied to that of the batter.

1881 *Detroit Free Press* 26 Sep. 1/5 Weidman . . . will have to go into the box for the remaining four games. **1909** *Collier's* 15 May 14/1 The pitcher was now contained in a box six feet square. **1916** BANCROFT *Handbook* 78 Box. The places where the pitcher and batter stand. They are level with the surface of the ground, and in official games consist, for the pitcher, of a plate of whitewashed rubber; and for the batsman, of an enclosure merely outlined on the ground. **1948** *Alva* (Okla.) *Review-Courier* 2 July 2/6 Both of these boys are tough babies in the batter's box.

b. *To knock out of the box,* to hit so successfully the balls delivered by the pitcher as to cause him to be retired from his position.

1886 *Chi. Tribune* 6 May 8/2 Twitchell was knocked out of the box, and in the seventh inning Richardson took his place. **1887** *Outing* May 100/1 A glass of mercury instead of a glass of something else should be held responsible for a pitcher getting 'knocked out of the box.' **1948** *Time* 10 May 61/3 Feller was knocked out of the box and Cleveland lost its first game of the season, 10–3.

7. *transf.* A voting precinct.

1946 *Democrat* 9 May 1/7 A number of boxes failed to send in the returns to the Democrat office. **1948** *Ib.* 3 June 1/7 State returns from a large percentage of the boxes showed Folsom trailing in seventh place.

8. In combs. in which the first element is from various sources but brought together here for convenience of reference: (1) **box board,** a board suitable for making boxes; (2) **calf,** a trade-mark name for calfskin tanned with chrome salts and rolled in such a way as to leave square markings on the grain; (3) **length,** *W.* (see quot.), *obs.;* (4) **letter,** a letter intended to be placed in a private box at the post office; (5) **party,** =**box supper;** (6) **rent,** rent paid for a post-office box, also attrib.; (7) **rustler,** (see quot.), *obs.;* (8) **score,** in baseball a complete record of a game, giving in tabular form the scores, names, and positions of the players, errors, hits, etc., also transf.; (9) **settle,** (see quot. 1877), *obs.;* (10) **sheet,** ?a sheet upon which are written the names of guests in a theater box; (11) **social,** =**box supper;** (12) **stair, staircase,** a stair or staircase in which the outer ends of the treads are inclosed in the supporting strings; (13) **stew,** (see quot.); (14) **stuffing,** stuffing of ballot boxes; (15) **supper,** (see quot. 1942).

(1) **1853** FOWLER *Home for All* 34 [When] you . . . are ready for your walls, procure common pine box boards, . . . and cut them off to the length required for your wall. **1905** *Bureau of Forestry Bul.* No. 63, 15 The lumber is usually of a low grade, but it is always in demand at good prices for match blocks, pail staves, and box boards. — (2) **1904** P. N. HASLUCK *Leather Working* 15 Box Calf. The grain side is the face of this leather. It is somewhat like firm ooze calf, only black. **1933** *OED Supp.* 111/1 Box-calf. . . . Named about 1890 by Edward L. White, of White Bros. & Co., Mass., U.S.A., after Joseph *Box*, boot-maker, of London. (The picture of a calf in a box was adopted as an advertising device.) — (3) **1897** LEONARD *Gold Fields Klondike* 38 The principal part of his $130,000 came from thirty 'box-lengths' of dirt. A 'box length' is fifteen feet long and twelve feet wide. — (4) **1832** *U.S. Postal Reg.* 43 Box-letters. **1843** *P.O. Laws & Reg.* II. 17 All letters placed in a post office, to be delivered from it to the persons addressed [are] called 'Box letters.' *Ib.* 28 Drop and box letters are not to be advertised.

(5) **1939** HARRIS *Purslane* 257 The teacher suggested a box party to raise a little money for baseballs and bats. — (6) **1841** *Congress. Globe* App. 20 Feb. 343/2 This House was constrained . . . to adopt my proposition to cure the abuse growing out of box-rents. **1887** *Postal Laws* 18 The Division of Salaries and Allowances . . . prepares orders for regulation of box-rents rates. **1948** *Dly. Ardmoreite* (Ardmore, Okla.) 6 July 5/6 Box rents are due and many old-time holders have not paid their rent. — (7) **1939** ABBOTT-SMITH *We Pointed* 95 In that kind of theaters they used to have curtained boxes running all around inside, and box rustlers was what they called the girls that worked them. — (8) **1913** *Outlook* 19 April 856/1 A box-score is a pretty intricate thing to be sent by telegraph and copied on a type-writer. **1944** *Sat. Review* 6 May 20/1 Grizzled baseball enthusiasts are going slightly nuts trying to keep track of major-league box scores in the budding and unprecedented campaign of 1944. **1948** *Galveston* (Tex.) *News* 14 June 4/2 He is expected to call the roll on what he has asked of congress and what he has received, giving his listeners a sort of box score. — (9) **1860** HOLMES *E. Venner* v, A man slept in a box-settle at night, to wake up early passengers. **1877** BARTLETT, Box-Settle. A settle whose seat is the cover of a box (*i.e.* a bunk). *O. W. Holmes.*

(10) **1837** in W. R. ALGER *Life of Edwin Forrest* (1877) I. 324 And her box-sheet already shows a fine display of fashionable names. — (11) **1929** *Randolph Enterprise* (Elkins, W. Va.) 14 Nov. 5/4 Old time Fiddling, Banjo, Songs, Pie and Box Social. **1946** *Grizzly Growl* (Yampa, Colo.) 20 Dec. 3/2 There is to be an old-time box social and dance at Toponas Saturday night. — (12) **1902** STURGIS *Dict. Arch.*, *Box Stair*, one made with two closed strings, so that it has a boxlike form of construction. **1907** M. H. NORRIS *The Veil* i. 5 Returning to the hall he opened the door of a box stair-case, ascending unconsciously on tiptoe a broad flight of shallow stairs to an immense attic. — (13) **1891** *Cent.* 5940/2 Box-stew, an oyster-stew made of box-oysters—that is, of large select oysters. — (14) **1944** CLARK *Pills* 68 A generous amount of box stuffing went on, and the Coleman ledger showed a goodly quantity of liquor sold that day.

(15) **1942** WARNICK *Dialect Garrett Co., Md.* 4 Box-supper, n., an event for raising church or other funds by auctioning box lunches donated by the women of the community. **1947** *Dly. Oklahoman* (Okla. City) 28 Dec. 5/1 An 'old-fashioned box supper' was recently given by the Rose unit at Guymon.

b. In the names of vehicles, structures, etc., consisting of, or having features suggesting, a box, as (1) **boxboat,** (2) **canyon,** (3) **car,** (see as a main entry), (4) **cart,**

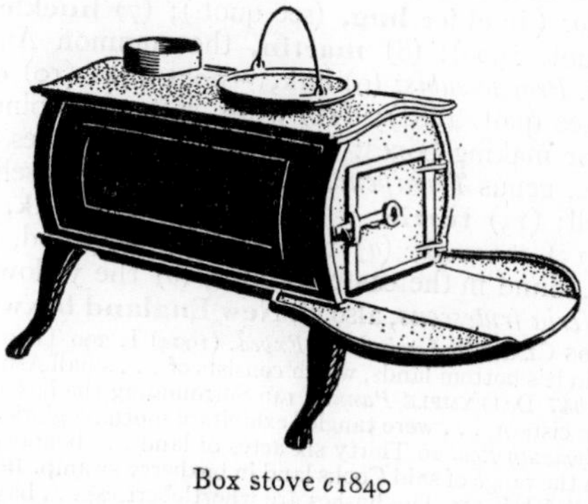

Box stove *c*1840

(5) **cornsheller,** (6) **freight car,** (7) **gulch,** (8) **house,** (9) **pung,** (10) **sledge, sleigh,** (11) **stall,** (12) **stock car,** (13) **stove,** (14) **trap,** (15) **trunk,** (16) **tubing,** (17) **wagon.**

(1) **1873** in ADAMS *Pioneer Hist.* (1923) 25 Cooley went to Eaton Rapids, made a box boat and moved down the river. — (2) **1873** BOURKE *Journal* 21 March, We descended into a box cañon and made camp. **1947** *Canadian Alpine Jrnl.* June 91 We were unable to follow this route (with a packhorse) beyond a box çanyon. — (4)

1890 *Harper's Mag.* March 569/2 Jim . . . returned with the box-cart and horse.

(**5**) **1865** Turner *Cotton* 135 These simple machines are 3½ feet high, 2 feet long, and 1 wide, with an iron fly-wheel like that of a 'box corn-sheller,' upon each side. — (**6**) **1850** *Hunt's Merch. Mag.* XXII. 105 The company have . . . three four wheel luggage cars, 105 eight wheel box freight cars, 113 eight wheel platform cars. **1903** E. Johnson *Ry. Transportation* 141 In the military and fourth classes the coaches are but little better than box freightcars. — (**7**) **1927** Russell *Trails* 192 He thinks he's safe, but after ridin' up it a way, discovers it's a box gulch, with walls straight up from 600 to 1,000 feet. — (**8**) **1881** *Rep. Indian Affairs* 83 The school was . . . conducted in . . . the house formerly used by the agent, and some box-houses constructed for the purpose. **1936** Barnard *Rider* 161 Douthitt had built a house on the west side of the claim, and Sniderwine built a box house on the east side. — (**9**) **1864** *Wilkes' Spirit of Times* 10 Dec. 225/2 Our conveyance, though not at all showy, was well adapted for the purpose, . . . it being a small box pung.

(**10**) **1855** *Knickerb.* Feb. 168 The widow and he were often seen riding side by side, on fine moon-light evenings, in Mr. Lean's large box-sleigh. **1884** Roe *Nature's Story* 11 After seeing that her trunks were safely bestowed in a large box-sledge, . . . he drove rapidly homewards. **1891** A. M. Earle *Sabbath* 103 The horses were saddled or were harnessed and hitched into the great box-sleighs or 'pungs.' — (**11**) **1885** *Harper's Mag.* May 949/2 His choicest colt . . . had been fed from his birth in a box stall. **1939** *L.A.* Map 109. — (**12**) **1868** *Com. & Fin. Chron.* VI. 521/1 [*s.v.* paymaster car.] These cars are described as follows . . . paymaster 2 . . . box stock 47, rack stock 36. **1895** Wait *Car-Builder's Dict.* 68 Horse-car. A box-car fitted up especially for carrying horses, but leaving certain slatted openings, etc. They are then classed under the general name of *box-stock car.* — (**13**) **1820** *Columbian Centinel* 1 Jan. 3/3 Oblong and oval Box Stoves. **1945** *Chi. Tribune* 18 Nov. vii. 1/5 Low unpainted benches stood in three rows with a woodburning box stove in the middle. — (**14**) **1785** T. B. Hazard *Nailer Tom's Diary* (1930) 78/2 Made door for Box Trap for Biger Babcock Jun(io)r. **1884** Roe *Nature's Story* 41 Webb helped him make two box-traps, and the boy concealed them in the copse where the rabbit-tracks were thickest. **1948** *Nat. History* Apr. 187/1 Box traps, similar to fish or lobster traps but not baited, can be made of quarter-inch mesh hardware cloth.

(**15**) **1783** in *Mass. H.S. Collections* I. 178 What will be the charge of land transportation of a box trunk? — (**16**) **1874** *Vt. Bd. Agric. Rep.* II. 520 Mr. Andrews used a box-tubing, twelve inches square, to the roof to ventilate his barns. — (**17**) **1846** Bushnell *Work & Play* (1864) 246 If you will make up your mind to . . . live on the coarsest fare, to ride in a box wagon or cart . . . you will see how it is. **1880** *Bradstreet's* 7 July 6/1 The heads of the grain are . . . shot into a great box wagon.

c. In the names of, or with reference to, plants and animals: (1) **box alder,** =**box elder;** (2) **berry,** the American wintergreen, *Gaultheria procumbens,* or the partridge berry, *Mitchella repens,* also attrib.; (3) **coot,** the surf scoter, *Melanitta perspicillata;* (4) **crab,** one or other species of crab of the genus *Calappa* resembling a box when at rest; (5) **elder,** the ash-leaved maple, *Acer negundo;* (6) **elder bug,** (see quot.); (7) **huckleberry,** (see quot. 1909); (8) **martin,** the common American martin, *Progne subis;* (9) **oak,** =**post oak;** (10) **oyster,** *local* (see quot. 1881); (11) **pine,** soft white pine often used for making boxes; (12) **tortoise,** a species of land tortoise, genus *Terrapene,* capable of closing itself up in its shell; (13) **turtle,** =prec.; (14) **white oak,** =**box oak;** (15) ***wood,** (*a*) the flowering dogwood, *Cornus florida,* found in the eastern states, (*b*) the yellow wood, *Schaefferia frutescens,* also cf. **New England boxwood.**

(**1**) **1805** Clark in *Lewis & C. Exped.* (1904) I. 299 There is some timber in it's bottom lands, which consists of . . . small Ash and box alder. **1947** Dalrymple *Panfish* 146 Surrounding the box alder behind the cistern, . . . were tangled exhibits of morning-glories. — (**2**) **1706** *Plymouth Rec.* 26 Thirty six acres of land . . . bounded from a stake in the range of said Cooks land in boxberry swamp. **1802** *Mass. H.S. Coll.* VIII. 197 The bushes are whortleberries, . . . bay-berries, and box-berries. **1881** McLean *Cape Cod Folks* 243 We had boxberry bread, boxberry stews and pies, and one day, I caught a glimpse of Grandma . . . frying boxberry griddle-cakes. — (**3**) **1844** *Nat. Hist. N.Y., Zoology* II. 335 The Box Coot, Spectacle Duck, . . . is very common on the coast of New-York during the winter. **1917** *Birds of Amer.* I. 151. — (**4**) **1889** *Cent.* 759/1 *C. depressa* and *C. granulata* are among the species known as *box-crabs.*

(**5**) **1787** Sargent in *Mem. Academy* II. i. 158 Box Elder, from six inches to two feet, and a very crooked tree. **1948** *Chi. Sun-Times* 20 Apr. 32/2 The box elder leafs almost as early. — (**6**) **1892** V. Kellogg *Kansas Insects* 99 Box-elder bug (*Leptocoris trivittatus*). . . . In winter the bugs frequent houses, and many appear in sunny places on warm days. — (**7**) **1909** *Cent. Supp.* 602/1 Box-huckleberry, *Gaylussacia brachycera,* a low stiff huckleberry, with somewhat the habit and foliage of box. It is found in dry woods from Pennsylvania to Virginia. **1942** Weygandt *Plenty of Penna.* 131 How many of you have visited the oldest living thing in Pennsylvania, the patch of box huckleberry in Perry County near New Bloomfield? — (**8**) *a***1857** *R.I. Rev. Stat.* lxxxiii § 2 Any person who shall take, kill or destroy any swallow or box martin, between the first day of May and the first day of October, shall forfeit for every such bird two dollars. — (**9**) **1785** Washington *Diaries* II. 360 These [acorns] grew on a tree resembling the box Oak. **1810** [see **box white oak**].

(**10**) **1881** E. Ingersoll *Oyster Industry* 242 *Box Oyster,* an oyster from seven to ten years old, of round, handsome shape, not less than three inches wide and five inches long. (Connecticut and New York) . . . The name is due to the fact that many years ago it was customary to ship oysters of this grade to New York in boxes instead of the ordinary barrel. **1886** *Good Housekeeping* 30 Oct. 324/1 Box oysters are $2, and extra sizes are $3 a hundred. — (**11**) **1944** Clark *Pills* 48 The country store was the only place in the South where a man could find a piece of soft northern box pine on which to use his razor-sharp barlow knife. — (**12**) **1839** Storer *Mass. Reptiles* 214 From the circumstance of the sternum being divided into two portions, . . . enabling the animal when disturbed, to encase itself entirely within its shell, the species is generally known under the name of 'box tortoise.' **1945** McAtee *Nomina Abitera* 22 The box tortoises draw attention . . . by the knocking together of their hard shells. — (**13**) **1804** *Cabinet of Nat. History* (N.Y.) 14 A small N. A. Box Turtle. Testudo terrestris Amer. Sept. **1918** Visher *So. Dakota* 104 The turtles of the state are aquatic (except a box turtle in the sandhills of Bennett County). — (**14**) **1810** Michaux *Arbres* I. 22 Post oak, . . . Iron Oak, . . . Box oak (chêne buis), [ou] Box White-Oak . . . dans l'Etat de Maryland. **1832** Browne *Sylva* 275 In Maryland and a great part of Virginia where it abounds, . . . it is called Box White Oak, and sometimes Iron Oak and Post Oak. **1892** Apgar *Trees Northern U.S.* 153 *Quercus stellata,* . . . Post-Oak, Rough or Box White Oak, . . . [is] a medium-sized tree, 40 to 50 ft. high, with very hard, durable wood.

(**15**) (*a*) **1832** Browne *Sylva* 141 In the United States at large, it is known by the name of Dogwood, and in Connecticut it is also called Box Wood. **1884** Sargent *Rep. Forests* 91 *Cornus florida,* . . . Flower-Dogwood, Box Wood. (*b*) **1884** Sargent *Rep. Forests* 39 *Schaefferia frutescens,* . . . Yellow wood, Box wood. **1890** *Cent.* 5386/3 *S. frutescens,* a small tree of southern Florida and the neighboring islands, produces a valuable wood which from its color and hardness is known by the names of *yellow-wood* and *boxwood.*

As the last term in **bacon, bad, ballot, band, bathing, bee, birchbark, bird, buggy, butter, call, cheese, chuck, contribution, cracker, crank, dealing, devil's snuff, driving, drop, dry goods, fare, feed, flume, foot, full, garbage, goods, grab, grape, gumbo, honey, hot, ice, Jeff Davis, jury, kittereen, lint, lock, lumber, mail, martin, monkey, moon, mosquito, musical, musical sardine, Pandora's, parterre, patch, patrol, pepper, piece, pig, pitcher's, pool, post-office, press, rattle, riffle, riffler, ripple, salt, sand, seed, shad, shad-hatching, shoe-shine, sink, sleigh, sluice, snake, sneak, snuff, soap, spring, store, sweat, talking, telephone, treasure, tree, turpentine, wagon box.**

***box,** *v.*

1. *tr.* To cut a "box" in the trunk of a pine or maple tree for obtaining its turpentine or sap.

1700 *Springfield Rec.* II. 357 No Stranger . . . shal box any trees or Improve the sam for Turpintine. **1737** Brickell *N. Carolina* 265 Negroes cut large Cavities on each side of the Pitch-Pine Tree (which they term Boxing the Tree) wherein the Turpentine runs. **1944** Barbour *Eden* 79 This, of course, is not the case where the trees have been 'boxed' for turpentine.

2. To provide with planking to prevent caving.

1816 *Boston Selectmen* 18 April 179 The ground having been boxed last fall and the well sunk to the depth of about 30 feet. **1821** *Ib.* 7 Sep. 216 After consideration . . . of the probable cost of digging and boxing a cellar under the building [etc.].

3. To place (incoming mail) in the post-office boxes of patrons.

1945 *Greeley* (Colo.) *D. Tribune* 17 Aug. 10/7 Incoming mail at the post office was boxed and outgoing mail distributed but no home deliveries were made Thursday.

boxcar ˈbɑks,kɑr, *n.*

1. A railroad car for carrying freight, resembling a huge box.

1856 *Mich. Agric. Soc. Trans.* VII. 334 There are on the road . . . 11 four-wheeled box cars. **1884** *Las Vegas* (N.M.) *Optic* 20 Mar. 3/2 San Antonio's pioneer station agent . . . first had his office, three years ago, in a box car. **1948** *Chi. D. News* 20 Feb. 1/4 The . . . home was a tinder-box structure constructed of two boxcars.

transf. **1946** *Reader's Digest* March 17/2 Prescott had flown them, and believed them to be steady, reliable aerial boxcars.

2. a. boxcar building, a building shaped like a boxcar. **b. boxcar figures,** large numbers, as those common on the sides of boxcars. **c. boxcar letter,** a very large letter.

(a) 1921 *Rural Organization* 133 Eight million . . . children attend one- and two-teacher rural schools, scattered over the continent in 210,000 box-car buildings. — **(b) 1948** *L.A. Times* 14 Jan. I. 2/6 (*heading*), Those Boxcar Figures [of the Marshall Plan] Just Confuse Them. — **(c) 1912** *Sat. Ev. Post* 3 Aug. 50/4 An enterprising tailor once put a notice in box-car letters on the Polo Grounds fence, offering a fifteen dollar suit for every home run made by a member of the local team. **1945** *Salida D. Mail* (Salida, Colo.) 22 Jan. 1/5 Box Car letters did not really originate with this writer. An illiterate boy said it back in the long ago, but the Mail was the first to put it into print.

***boxed,** *a.* (See quot. 1939 and cf. **box house.**) — **1939** in *U. of Ala. Studies in Educ.* I. 133 Most of the remaining houses were of a structure known as 'boxed,' which consisted of a single boarded wall of rough lumber with narrow strips nailed over the cracks. **1946** WILSON *Fidelity* 3 The log houses that were built in the earliest pioneer times were still numerous, but some had given way to boxed or frame structures.

***boxing,** *n.*

1. The practice or method of making boxes in the trunks of trees to collect turpentine or sap.

1703 *First Cent. Hist. Springfield* (1899) II. 75 It is voted . . . that what ever Cart way . . . shal be stoped or incumered by reason of any Persons boxing of Pine trees, the Improvers of sd Trees shal remove such Nusances, wthin a weeks warning. **1708** *Springfield Rec.* II. 376 It was voted to restraine the boxing of Turpentine Trees within the inmost Comons. **1880** *Vt. Agric. Rep.* VI. 112 An aged maple tree may be found with the scars made by an axe in tapping by the method then known as 'boxing.'

2. *boxing of a table,* (see quot. 1891).

1888 *2nd Ann. Rep. Interstate Com. Commission* 271 (*Cent. s.v. Table*), The use of miscellaneous in the boxing of this table requires a word of explanation. **1891** *Cent.* 6148/2 Boxing of a table, the words, figures, or signs on one or both sides and over the columns of a mathematical, statistical, or similar table, intended to indicate or explain the nature of its contents. Also called *argument of a table.*

***boy,** *n.*

1. A lounger, loafer, political follower or hanger-on. *Colloq.*

Often "b'hoy" in allusion to Irish pronunciation.

1832 *Polit. Examiner* (Shelbyville, Ky.) 9 June 3/1 The Jackson boys are too smart to be beaten if they have the choice of their competitors. **1885** *Mag. Amer. Hist.* Jan. 98/1 *Boys.*—This word is often used nowadays to designate the political hangers-on of a candidate or party. **1906** *N.Y. Ev. Post* 1 March 8 Machine politicians . . . always want some one who will be kind to 'the boys.'

2. a. *boys in blue,* northern or federal soldiers in the Civil War. Now *hist.* **b.** *Boy Orator of the Platte,* (see quot.).

(a) 1866 *Cong. Globe* 27 Jan. 460/1 The brave 'boys in blue' fought manfully, and through their efforts, thank God, the Union has been preserved. **1948** *Chi. D. News* 1 June 5/1 Plan to Bury One of Last 'Boys in Blue.' — **(b) 1896** *Cin. Enquirer* 10 July 9/7 The demonstration that followed Russell from the platform was submerged beneath the storm of cheers that greeted the appearance on the stage of W. J. Bryan, the 'Boy Orator of the Platte,' whose star as a Presidential possibility had for twenty-four hours burned brightly on the convention horizon.

3. boy friend, a girl's sweetheart or steady companion. *Colloq.*

1925 WITWER *Roughly Speaking* 259 She had no heavy boy friend and craved none. **1947** *Mazama* Aug. 2/2 Bring your supper, the husband, the girl friend or boy friend.

As the last term in **apple, bell, black, Boston, Bowery, bully, bus, butcher, canal, chore, college, copy, corner, cow, cracker, dough, draw, drummer, elevator, fair-haired, field, gal, Granite, Green Mountain, hall, hat, herd, high, hopper, hurrah, Kentuck, log cabin, low, mail, mountain, page, plain, plate, play, press, rah-rah, red, Rocky Mountain, roller, sand-hill, shanty, shirt tail, shoe-shine, short, small, store, tow, train, wagon, water, whisky, white, whoop, yellow boy.**

Cf. also **huge-pawed, Liberty, Paxton, Swill boys.**

boysenberry ˈbɔɪzn̩ˌberɪ, *n.* A berry developed by Rudolph Boysen of California by experiments involving the blackberry, raspberry, and loganberry. Also attrib.

1941 *Reader's Digest* Oct. 89/1 Boysenberry pies baked by Mrs. Knott sold for 50 cents apiece. **1945** *Greeley* (Colo.) *D. Tribune* 15 Mar. 10/7 Eldorado [blackberry] is plenty hardy, but Boysenberries, both thorny and thornless must be covered thru the winter. **1948** *Household* June 52/2 Boysenberries and loganberries are here.

bozal, see **bosal.**

bozo ˈbozo, *n.* [Origin obscure. Cf. Sp. *bozal, a.,* inexperienced, stupid, foolish, and see quot. 1939 below.] A fellow, guy. *Slang.*

1921 *Collier's* 11 June 5/1 Joe is the bozo which I write all them letters to from France. **1939** *Amer. Sp.* April 97 The origin of this slang equivalent of *fellow, guy,* so far entirely unknown, might well be sought in the Caribbean, namely in the so-called *Papiamento* of Dutch-owned Curacao. . . . In this language . . . the second person singular of the personal pronoun is *bo =you* . . . ; the second person plural is *boso =you people*. . . . *Boso,* used at the beginning of many sentences in daily conversation, may well have been mistaken by outsiders for an indefinite term of address. **1947** *Denver Post* 15 Feb. 16/2 When partner plays bridge at the lowest degree, refrain from an impulse to shout it. Consider how lucky the bozo must be when knowing so little about it.

brace bres, *n.*[1] [F. *brasse,* an Amer. borrowing.] A measure of length, 1.62 meters. *Obs.* — **1805** CLARK in *Lewis & C. Exped.* (1904) I. 269 He . . . had received . . . from M. Chaboillez . . . the following articles 3 Brace of Cloth 1 Brace of Scarlet a par Corduroy overalls.

***brace,** *n.*[2]

1. *To take a brace,* to pull oneself together, as for a fresh start, to mend one's ways, etc. *Colloq.*

1884 *Cent. Mag.* Nov. 154 Vane 'takes a Brace.' He goes to America in the steerage, . . . sternly lives in down-town lodgings [etc.]. **1910** RAINE *B. O'Connor* 40 You want to take a brace and act like a man.

2. A "bracer." *Colloq.*

1890 RYAN *Told in Hills* 183 They needed that swallow of brandy as a brace against the cold wind of the hills. **1897** THANET *Missionary Sheriff* 123 He passed the tumbler to Harned, who shook his head 'Don't need a brace?'

3. In combs.: (1) **brace box,** in faro a dealing box designed to facilitate cheating; (2) **faro,** a form of faro in which the cards are secretly marked, after being dealt, by the casekeeper, attrib. in context; (3) **gambler,** a gambler who participates in cheating by brace games; (4) **game,** a card game, esp. faro, in which there is concerted cheating, also fig.; (5) **shot,** in artillery fire, a bracket.

(1) 1908 G. H. LORIMER *J. Spurlock* vi. 116 Life's not even a gamble in this age of commercialism, fo' Fo'tune deals from a brace box.— **(2) 1891** QUINN *Fools of Fortune* 45 My pursuits included the use of marked cards, . . . and 'bunko steering' for 'brace' faro banks. — **(3) 1891** ROMAINE *Gambling* 228 Then it is that fraud and theft are triumphant: that 'brace' gamblers . . . and their conscienceless harpies pray [*sic*] in secret upon the unwary. — **(4) 1875** *Chi. Tribune* 25 Aug. 8/1 The brace game flourishes for no other purpose than to cheat the gambling fraternity. **1908** WHITE *Riverman* vi. 58, I tell you, you can't win! . . . It's a brace game pure and simple. **1938** ASBURY *Sucker's Prog.* 317 As a matter of fact, there were hundreds of brace games throughout the town, and even in the largest establishments . . . skullduggery on the part of the artists and croupiers was common.

(5) 1915 R. H. DAVIS *With the Allies* 134 To find the range the artillery sends what in the American army are called brace shots.

***brace,** *v.*[1]

1. *intr. To brace up,* to pull oneself together for an effort, to take a drink or "bracer" for this purpose, to become more encouraging.

1809 *Ann. 10th Cong.* 2 Sess. 1148 We have been home, and bracing up; we have had plenty of good wine. **1816** U. BROWN *Journal* II. 44 He minutely examines the same & began to Brace up in the following Manner. **1887** *Courier-Journal* 1 May 10/2 Come out and take a hummer with me and brace up. **1930** HENRY *Conquer. Plains* 218 But the outlook for the next summer's profits, in the excluding pursuit of money-making, tended always to 'brace up.'

2. *tr.* To press or plant firmly, to render firm by pressure. Also *intr.* for *refl.*

*a***1846** *Quarter Race Ky.* etc. 97 Braced back in my phaeton, . . . I touches her [=the mare] up On an elegant 'raw.' **1857** M. J. HOLMES *Meadow-Brook* xxviii, Bolt upright upon the box, with his brawny feet firmly braced against the dash-board so as to give him more power, sat Bill. **1885** MARK TWAIN in *Cent. Mag.* Dec. 196/2 It would sit down and brace back, and no one could budge it.

3. (See quot. 1889.) Also, to charge extortionately. *Slang.*

1889 FARMER, *brace*, To (Cant.), to get credit by swagger.—To brace it through, to succeed by dint of sheer impudence. **1923** WATTS *Luther Nichols* 269, I haven't quite the cheek to brace you for board and lodging both.

b. To assume a defiant attitude toward. *Slang*.

1922 ZANE GREY *To Last Man* vii. 165 He must have been crazy or drunk—to pop up there—an' brace us that way.

4. (See quot. and cf. **brace box, faro, game.)**

1931 WILLISON *Here They Dug Gold* 217 Although not easily done, faro is sometimes 'braced.' Tiny holes are punched in the cards so that the dealer may see what is coming and to the bank's advantage pull two cards instead of one, giving the wink to the case-keeper to arrange his part of the swindle.

bracket shoes. Snowshoes. *Rare*. — **1648** *Good News from N. Eng.* in *Mass. H.S. Coll.* 4 Ser. I. 203 The tripping Deer . . . burst through frozen snow, Hunters pursue with bracket shooes.

Braddockian bræˈdɑkɪən, *n.* An imitator of Gen. Edward Braddock (1695–1755), who scorned "bush warfare." *Rare*. — **1842** in *Amer. Sp.* XVIII. 121 They don't . . . know anything at bush warfare—they are *Braddockians*.

* **brag,** *a.* Fine, excellent, first-rate.

[**1818** in W. B. WOOD *Personal Recollections* (1855) 231 Five Celebrated Wyandott Chiefs. . . . Green Corn, or National Dance Buffaloe Dance, or Dance of Plenty. Brag Dance, and War Speech.] **1838** *Jeffersonian* 5 May 96 The Moselle was a new *brag* boat and had recently made several exceedingly quick trips. **1848** D. P. THOMPSON *L. Amsden* 14, I took the syrup from the kettle . . . and filled up anew [with sap], thinking I would boil down a few pounds as nice as I could for brag-sugar. **1904** HARBEN *Georgians* 291 Our brag murderer . . . recently laid low one of our most popular citizens.

* **brag,** *v. tr.* To stake in the game of brag. *Obs.*

1835 *Vade Mecum* (Phila.) 23 May 4/4 After any player has *bragged*, the rest must either *go it*, . . . or *bolt*. **1845** *St. Louis Reveille* 2 May 1/6, I commenced the game by bragging a dollar. **c1845** *Big Bear Ark.* 110 Once in awhile . . . they would venture a bet of five or ten dollars, but they were always compelled to back out by the tremendous bragging of the Captain *or* pilot.

* **bragger,** *n.* (See quots. 1838, 1909.)

1807 IRVING *Salmagundi* 502 Presently one of them . . . exclaimed triumphantly, 'Two bullets and a bragger!' and swept all the money into his pocket. **1838** *Victims of Gambling* 89 Every nine-spot and every knave is called a bragger. All the other cards rank as at whist. The effect of a bragger is to assimilate all other cards; thus, an ace and two braggers, one bragger and two aces, is the same as three aces, and so on. **1909** *Cent. Supp.* 159/3 Bragger. . . . In the game of brag, the ace, the nine of diamonds, the jack of clubs. The holder of any of these cards can call it anything he pleases. **1938** ASBURY *Sucker's Prog.* 21 In American Brag there were eight 'braggers'—the jacks and nines of each suit.

* **Brahmin,** *a.* and *n.*

1. *a.* Of New Englanders: Exclusive with respect to culture and society. Cf. **Boston Brahmin.**

1860 HOLMES in *Atlantic Mo.* Jan. 93 He comes of the *Brahmin caste of New England*. This is the harmless, inoffensive, untitled aristocracy to which I have referred. **1903** TRENT *Hist. Amer. Lit.* 112 The fact . . . bears testimony to the growing tolerance of New England, but it does not prove that the Brahmin clergy had by any means been driven from the field. **1947** *Amer. Wkly.* 2 Nov. 4/1 He took delight, too, in shocking his Brahmin relatives, who belong to one of the oldest and richest families in Massachusetts.

2. *n.* A New Englander belonging to the aristocratic, conservative class.

1881 R. H. STODDARD *Homes* 155 To be a missionary of Boston culture, rather than the apostle of political or theological revolution, must have pleased the anxious thought of this medical Brahmin. **1900** HOWELLS *Literary Friends* 278 This light and joyous creature could not but be a Pariah among our Brahmins, and I . . . never met him in any of the great Cambridge houses. **1947** *Atlantic Mo.* Nov. 160/2 The Brahmins do not think of themselves as Brahmins: the word is as antique as the wooden cod hanging in the State House.

3. A species of cattle, orig. imported from India. Now **Brahma.**

1893 G. W. CURTIS *Horses* 210 Dr. James Bolton Davis, of Charleston, S.C., . . . imported [in 1849] the first pair of Brahmins ever brought to the United States. *Ib.*, The name 'Brahmin,' however, is . . . firmly fixed among those who have bred or known them in the Southern States. **1948** *Galveston* (Tex.) *News* 14 June 2/5 Brahmas and Herefords have been cross-bred before.

***Brahminical,** *a.* =**Brahmin,** *a.* — **1900** HOWELLS *Literary Friends* 272 He was ancestrally of the Swiss 'Brahminical caste,' as so many of his friends in Cambridge were of the Brahminical caste of New England.

* **braid,** *n.* A string of corn, onions, etc., tied together. Cf. **candy braid.**

1857 HAMMOND *Northern Scenes* 149 The stories contained in that work hang together so like a string of onions, or a braid of seed corn. **1871** *Ill. Agric. Soc. Trans.* VIII. 177 Onions, in our climate, . . . are best kept thinly spread, or in braids, in a dry place. **1917** WILL & HYDE *Corn Among Indians* 127 There was a standard size for these braids, the length being from knee down around the foot and up to the knee again. One of these braids was the standard measure for corn on the ear.

braided rug. A home-made rug made of long strips of cloth braided and sewed together.

1884 WILKINS in *Harper's Mag.* July 307/2 She wants some braided rugs. **1943** DAMON *Sense of H.* 202 On the braided rug in front of the stove Tiger, with his tail curled around his toes, purrs loudly. [**1948** *L.A. Times* 2 May (Home Mag.) 5/3 Braid rugs cover the floor.]

brail brel, *n.* [F. *brelle*, in similar sense.] (See quots. 1881, 1905.)

1879 *Lumberman's Gaz.* 1 Oct., This part of the Slough is wide and deep, and is used for coupling up the strings into brails and rafts. **1881** T. B. WALKER *Letter* 4 June, A brail of logs is a crib of loose logs surrounded by a boom of longer ones whose ends are fastened together. . . . Three or four brails are put side by side and fastened together to form a raft and towed by steam tugs. **1905** *Forestry Bureau Bul.* 61 *Brail*, a section of a log raft, six of which make an average tow.

* **brain,** *n.*

1. *To take brains*, to absorb the boiled brains of the deer (or other animal) used in dressing the skin. *Rare*.

1868 *Amer. Naturalist* Oct. 474 The [deer-]skin . . . should be stretched and broken still more, while drying, that it may 'take brains' more readily.

2. In combs.: (1) **brain-dressed,** of skins, dressed or tanned by a process in which brains are used; (2) * **fag,** mental exhaustion; (3) **storm,** (see quot. 1894), also in popular use any transitory state of mental confusion; (4) **tanned,** =**brain-dressed;** (5) **trust,** a derisive term for an administrative group, usu. political, selected on the basis of intellectual qualifications rather than on political records, orig. **brains trust;** (6) **truster,** a member of, or one suitable for membership in, a brain trust.

(1) **1887** *Harper's Mag.* June 61/2 These [deerskin leggings] were prepared of brain-dressed skins that perfectly turned the rain and dew. — (2) **1851** DUNGLISON *Med. Lex.* 596 A hypochondriacal condition . . . termed by some *cerebropathy;* by others, *brain-fag.* **1884** W. JAMES in *Mind* IX. 17 In states of extreme brain-fag the horizon is narrowed almost to the passing word. — (3) **1894** G. M. GOULD *Illustr. Dict. Med., Brain-storm*, a succession of sudden and severe phenomena, due to some cerebral disturbance. **1948** *Sat. Ev. Post* 3 July 79/1 Nobody paid much attention, however, and for forty years Crichton-Browne's brainstorm was forgotten. — (4) **1880** *Harper's Mag.* Dec. 159 The picturesque hunting shirt, with the brain-tanned moccasin and belt . . . were as sure to put in their appearance . . . as the hunter himself.

(5) **1933** *Newsweek* 2 Sep. 4/1 The President's Brain Trust, a little band of intellectuals, sat at the center of action as similar bands have done in revolutions of the past. **1939** *Amer. Sp.* Dec. 246 (*fn.*), The term *brains trust*, about which you inquire, was originally used by James Kieran during the campaign of 1932. He used the plural, *brains*. However, Ernest Lindley states in one of his books that because of frequent repetition by newspapermen during that period, the term appeared more often as *brain trust*. **1948** *Time* 31 May 51/1 The Dodger brain trust traded away two of Brooklyn's favorite heroes: Dixie Walker and Eddie Stanky. — (6) **1943** DE VOTO *Yr. of Decis.* 10 Shortly after he was inaugurated, he explained his objectives to George Bancroft, the scholar, historian, and man of letters who had been a Democratic Brain-Truster since Jackson's time. **1948** *Time* 12 Jan. 14/1 One by one, Franklin Roosevelt's brain-trusters of the early New Deal had vanished from Harry Truman's Administration.

***brain,** *v. tr.* To treat (skins) with brains in the process of tanning. — **1868** *Amer. Naturalist* Oct. 474 There are three principal operations: graining, braining, and smoking. *Ib.*, It is known when the skin is brained in this manner.

braireau, see **brarow,** *n.*

***brake,** *n.*[1] Short for **canebrake.** *Rare*. — **1852** REYNOLDS *Hist. Illinois* 195 The cane grew so thick and strong that man, or beast, could scarcely penetrate it. These were called brakes.

* **brake,** *n.*[2] In combs.: (1) **brake beam,** (see quot. 1874); (2) **man,** (*a*) one who operated the brakes on an old-fashioned fire engine, *obs.*, (*b*) a railroad employee whose duty formerly was to operate the brakes on a train, but now, except on freight trains not provided with air brakes, chiefly engaged in assisting the conductor, cf. **freight brakeman, railroad brakeman;** (3) **shoe,**

(see quot. 1874); (4) **wheel,** a hand-operated wheel by which a brake is controlled.

(1) 1874 KNIGHT 357 *Brake-beam,* . . . the transverse beam connecting the shoes of opposite wheels. A brake bar. **1898** HAMBLEN *Gen'l Manager's Story* 29 Oh, came in on a break beam, did you? — **(2)** *(a)* **1831** *Boston Transcript* 23 Apr. 2/2, I hope that each and every 'break-man' and 'hose-man' will do all that lies in his power to achieve this coming 17th celebration. *(b)* **1833** *Am. R.R. Jour.* II. 738/1 Two brakemen $450 00. **1948** *Calif. Citrograph* May 277/3 The law continues in force and the extra brakemen still are riding the trains. — **(3) 1874** KNIGHT 357 *Brake-shoe,* that part of a brake which is brought in contact with the object whose motion is to be restrained. **1910** J. HART *Vigilante Girl* 147 As the brake-shoes left the wheel-tires, the heavy coach lurched forward. **1934** LOMAX *Amer. Ballads* 26 When she hove in sight far up the track, She was working steam, with her brake-shoes slack. — **(4) 1872** HUNTINGTON *Road-Master's Ass't* 114 Brakemen, instead of taking the most comfortable vacant seat they can find, sit astride the brake-wheel. **1891** C. ROBERTS *Adrift Amer.* 78 The very devil of mischief . . . put it into Mr. Hiram's head to pick up the oil can and pour a stream of oil on the brake-wheel.

As the last term in **air, atmospheric, cane, cedar, cliff, cypress, hog, laurel, reed brake.**

***brake,** *v.* **1.** *intr.* To serve as brakeman on a train. **2.** Of a train: To slow *up* under the application of the brakes. *Rare.*

(1) 1879 *Scribner's Mo.* Oct. 925/1 You see I know this road pretty well. I've been braking here on a through freight for something more'n a year now. **1892** GUNTER *Miss Dividends* 263, I'm braking on the Burlington again, and we're bound for Chicago. — **(2) 1891** E. S. ELLIS *Check No. 2134* 86 The conductor discovered the strange blunder the moment the cars began braking up.

brakie ˈbrekɪ, *n.* =**brakeman,** *(b). Colloq.* — **1887** M. ROBERTS *Western Avernus* 238 The brakie came down a step and made a kick at him. **1927** RUSSELL *Trails* 149 Lookin' over the tombstone, sizin' me up, is the toughest lookin' brakie I ever see.

***bran,** *n.* In combs.: (1) **bran-dance,** (see quots.), *obs.* [The method alluded to of preparing a surface for dancing is not unknown now]; (2) **duster,** a machine for separating flour and bran after the bolting process, also attrib.; (3) **rising,** a leavening agent prepared of bran, *obs.*

(1) 1833 *Sketches of Crockett* 148 This is the famous bran-dance of the west, and derives its name from the fact that the ground is generally sprinkled with the husk of Indian meal. **1851** *Arkansas Doctor* 52 (Th.), There I stood, looking kin to a fool at a bran-dance. [**1883** S. BONNER *Dialect Tales* 155 We found the dancers in a rustic arbor, roofed with green boughs intertwined with hickory withes. Floor there was none save the smooth earth covered three inches deep with wheat-bran. Slightly dampened, it was pleasant to dance on; but Heaven preserve them when they danced it dry! **1942** RAWSON *N.H. Borns a Town* 246 Any old rough board could be made slippery and danceable by sowing cornmeal across it.] — **(2) 1849** *Rep. Comm. Patents* 374 No. 6952.—Improvement in Bran Dusters. . . . Robt. M. Dempsey. **1884** *Rep. Comm. Agric.* 99 The bran-duster flour is a dirty, lumpy by-product. — **(3) 1836** TRAILL *Backwoods* 241 There are several other sorts of rising similar to the salt-rising. . . . 'Bran-rising,' . . . is made with bran instead of flour, and is preferred by many persons to either of the former kinds.

***branch,** *n.*[1]

1. Chiefly *S.* A small stream, a brook or run.

[**1624** in *Amer. Sp.* XV. 158/2 Here doth the river divide it selfe into 3 or 4 convenient branches. **1642** *Md. Hist.* V. 171 A Line drawn . . . unto a branch of St. George's Creek called Weston's branch.] **1663** *N.C. Col. Rec.* I. 20 That Parcell of land lying and being on the same Neck, Beginning at a small creek or Branch. **1750** T. WALKER *Jrnl. Explor.* (1888) 57 We could not get our Horses till almost Night, when we went down the Branch. **1838** GOSSE *Letters* 109 A brook is a 'branch.' When I came first, I was inquiring for a neighbour's house, and was directed to pursue a certain path through the woods, till I crossed the *branch.* **1946** *Atlanta Jrnl. Mag.* 3 March 9/3 A stream too small to be a river or creek is a branch.

b. Attrib. with **bottom, creek, head, herring, land, side, swamp, water.**

1880 *New Virginians* I. 82 The land being what is called branch-bottom, i.e. alluvial in character. — **1938** MATSCHAT *Suwannee River* 141 Swamp fowkses sing a little rhyme about that branch crick runnin' back of the island. — **1670** in *Amer. Sp.* XV. 159/1 Beginning at a Corner white oak by a Slash or branch hed. **1948** *Time* 15 March 30/2 He traveled to the 'crossroads, the branch-heads and the brush arbors' with a hillbilly band. — **1884** GOODE *Fisheries* I. 580 *C[lupea] vernalis* is known along the Potomac River as the 'Branch' Herring. **1943** CARSON *Food From Sea* 16 These are the true alewives (*Pomolobus pseudoharengus*), called also 'branch herrings.' — **1870** *Rep. Comm. Agric.* 270 The soil was 'branch land' (creek bottom), black mud or muck swamp, five feet deep, containing a mixture of sand. — **1640** in *Amer. Sp.* XV. 159/1 Beginning at a marked pine standing on a point by the maine branch side. — **1832** BROWNE *Sylva* 195 Red Bay . . . is profusely multiplied in the branch swamps. **1883** HALE *Woods N.C.* 132 Loblolly Bay [is] . . . confined, I think, to the branch-swamps and bays within 100 miles of the coast. — **1850** *Quincy* (Ill.) *Whig* 7 May 4/2 Come in and we'll take a sip of branch-water, and I'll norate it to you. **1859** BARTLETT 47 '*Branch*-water' is distinguished from '*well*-water.' **1943** PEATTIE *Great Smokies* 117 If it is branch water they drink, it must come from some stream running in laurel and rock.

2. A chapter of a Greek-letter fraternity. In full **branch chapter.** *Obs.*

1779 in *Cat. of Harvard Chap. of ΦBK* (1912) 90 Petition of Mr Parmelie for a Charter Party to institute a Branch of this Society at Cambridge in Massachusetts, granted. **1835** *Cat. of Conn. Alpha of ΦBK* 3 The branches of the Society at the present time, are six in number. **1871** L. H. BAGG *At Yale* 55 Sigma Eps at Yale, calling itself the 'Kappa' chapter, established a branch 'Alpha' chapter at Amherst.

3. In special combs.: (1) **branch church,** in the Christian Science Church, a local congregation, a branch of the Mother Church; (2) **grass,** (see quot.); (3) **road,** a road or railroad which is a minor division of a larger system; (4) **store,** a store that is a part or branch of a larger institution.

(1) 1895 EDDY *Church Manual* 27 Branch churches shall not take the title of *The* First Church of Christ, Scientist. **1948** *Chr. Sci. Jrnl.* 66 (Jan.) 43, I studied our Lesson-Sermon . . . daily and joined the branch church in that city. — **(2) 1837** COLMAN *Rep. Agric. Mass.* (1838) 18 Branch Grass, a short reedy grass, resembling much the fox grass . . . branches much and from this circumstance derives its name. — **(3) 1831** *Cong. Deb.* I March 830 The right of Congress to pass laws hereafter for the opening of branch roads [etc.]. **1902** HARBEN *A. Daniel* 137 Wanting to know if there were not many branch roads that did not own their rolling stock. — **(4) 1842** E. A. HITCHCOCK *Journal* 109, I find Chapman is here in charge of Hill's branch store. *a***1918** G. STUART *On Frontier* I. 216 Warden and Higgins concluded to start a branch store in our village and leave a portion of their goods here.

As the last term in **cane, dry, green, head, logging, mesquite, prairie, spring, swamp branch.**

branch bræntʃ, *n.*[2] [If quot. 1910 is correct, no doubt from F. *branche.*] (See quot. 1910.) *Obs.* — **1822** MORSE *Rep. Indian Affairs* I. 55 A half point blanket is sold for four skins. . . . Five branches, or two hundred and fifty grains of wampum, one skin. . . . Forty branches of white beads, one skin. **1910** HODGE *Amer. Indians* II. 907/1 The first variety was made originally by stringing the wampum beads on small strands of skin or sinew, and later on a strong thread or on several threads twisted together; these strings of shell beads were called 'branches' by French writers generally, probably including the bunches or sheaves.

***brand,** *n.*

1. *W.* A bovine animal of a particular brand, usu. collect. with reference to a herd of such cattle.

1881 ROMSPERT *Western Echo* 186 It is seldom they kill their own brands; but when there is no mavorick, they slide a ball into another man's calf. **1885** *Rep. Indian Affairs* 166 They have many small brands of cattle. **1903** A. ADAMS *Log Cowboy* 90, I must have inspection papers before I can move a brand out of the county in which it is bred.

2. In combs., usu. of western provenience: (1) **brand artist,** (see quot. 1944); (2) **blotter,** a cattle thief who blots out or otherwise obscures the legitimate brands on cattle, also **brand blotting;** (3) **book,** a book in which brands used on stock are recorded (see also quot. 1944); (4) **burner,** =**brand blotter,** also **brand burning;** (5) **owner,** the owner of a particular brand of cattle; (6) **reader,** one skilled in distinguishing the brand on cattle.

(1) 1934 *Denver Post* 4 Aug. 10/4 Another tradition credits him [Samuel Maverick] with being a 'brand artist' of little scruple. **1944** ADAMS *W. Words* 17/1 Brand artist. A rustler, one expert at changing brands. — **(2) 1910** W. M. RAINE *B. O'Connor* 107 Move, you red-haided son of a brand blotter, and I'll pump holes in you! **1926** BRANCH *Cowboy* 117 The simple process of roping and branding an unmarked cow, a 'maverick,' was soon supplemented by a complicated technique of brand-blotting and branding, thievery on an audacious, organized basis. **1930** RAINE & BARNES *Cattle* 147 They fought brand blotters and homesteaders no less than they did wolves and blizzards. — **(3) 1665** *Conn. Public Rec.* II. 28 They shal enter such saile within 10 daies in the said brand booke, with the artificial and natural marks, coulor and age of such horses. **1944** ADAMS *W. Words* 17/1 Brand book. An official record of brands of a cattle association.

1948 *Ore. Hist. Mag.* March 17 There have been, and perhaps there still are, brand books in circulation. — **(4) 1926** BRANCH *Cowboy* 118 Brand-burning was the altering of brands so that owners, if they found their stolen cattle, had no proof by which they could identify them. **1929** DOBIE *Vaquero* 122, I had recognized some of the men as brand burners.

(5) 1931 *Frontier* Nov. 33/2 They're branded. . . . Brand owners get a right to claim them when they're advertised. — **(6) 1888** ROOSEVELT in *Cent. Mag.* April 860 A man must have natural gifts, as well as great experience, before he becomes a good brand-reader and is able to really 'clean up a herd.'

As the last term in **barley, burnt, cattle, cross, dust, lightwood, picked, ranch, road, running, sale, slough, vent brand.**

***brand,** *v. tr.* To place a mark of ownership upon (horses and cattle) by means of a hot iron or brand.

1644–5 *Conn. Rec.* I. 118 The owners of any Catle within thes Plantations shall earemarke or brand all their Cattle and swyne that are above halfe a yeare old (except horsses). **1765** WASHINGTON *Diaries* I. 216 In all 24 head [of cattle] branded on the Buttock GW. **1902** WISTER *Virginian* 54 We emerged from a narrow cañon suddenly upon . . . some cow-boys branding calves by a fire in a corral.

***branded,** *a.* Of certain fishes: Having spots suggestive of brand marks, esp. **branded drum,** (see quot. 1890).

1814 MITCHILL *Fishes N.Y.* 411 Beardless Drum. *Sciaena imberbis.* . . . Upon the upper part of the tail, on each side, is a black spot, . . . resembling the brand of a hot iron upon wood; whence he has been called the *branded* drum. **1842** *Nat. Hist. N.Y., Zoology* IV. 75 The Branded Corvina. *Corvina ocellata.* . . . This beautiful fish, which appears but occasionally on our coast, is more common at the south. **1890** *Cent.* 1782/1 The branded drum or beardless drum, *Sciœna ocellata,* [is] the redfish of south Atlantic and Gulf States.

***brander,** *n.* One who brands horses and cattle. Cf. **calf brander, cross brander.** — **1681** *Conn. Rec.* III. 79 It shall be done by the publique officer appoynted to brand horses, . . . and the sayd brander shall record all such horss kind as he markes or brands. **1920** HUNTER *Trail Drivers Texas* I. 297 The flanker and assistants . . . call out 'hot iron' or 'sharp knife,' the brander responding, 'Right here with the goods.'

***branding,** *n.*

1. The action of placing brands upon horses and cattle, an occasion of this.

1740 W. STEPHENS *Proc. Georgia* 513 They were not of his branding. **1841** *S. Lit. Messenger* VII. 77/2 Our stranger friend was on his way to the branding. **1948** *Ore. Hist. Mag.* March 17 Recently an interest in one aspect of the management of range stock in the Oregon Country—that of branding—has unfolded itself.

2. Used attrib. with **camp, chute, corral, crew, fire, pen, season,** with reference to branding operations on cattle ranches in the West.

1904 O. HENRY *Heart of West* 16 A portable furnace, such as are seen in branding-camps. — **1882** *Lippincott's Mag.* May 429/2 Several small fenced enclosures, or corrals, and a branding-chute are soon completed, and the ranch may be considered established. **1920** HUNTER *Trail Drivers Texas* I. 297 A branding chute where an arrangement for holding the cattle while they are being branded is called a 'squeezer.' — **1937** COOLIDGE *Texas Cowboys* 88 The bawling cows and calves were thrown into the strong branding corral. — **1907** WHITE *Arizona Nights* 146 Three branding crews were told to brand the calves we had collected. — **1907** *Outing* Dec. 325/1 The horse turned and began methodically, without undue haste, to walk toward the branding fire. **1914** BRININSTOOL *Trail Dust* 41 Where your branding-fires gleamed are seas of grain. — **1866** in *Annals of Iowa* 3 Ser. XIV. 250 Recd 241 cattle & finished Branding Pen. **1927** EUBANK *Horse & Buggy Days* 47 During the season he worked in the branding pens and the foreman observed that he was not only an expert cowboy, but took an interest in the affairs of the ranch. — **1884** ALDRIDGE *Life on Ranch* 159 When the branding season comes and we are fussing, . . . Then a cow-boy's lot is not a happy one. **1929** DOBIE *Vaquero* 24 The cow people of the lower country came to speak of the 'skinning season' as naturally as they spoke of the 'branding season.' A settler short on a corn crop could count on a 'hide crop.'

As the last term in **chute, open, road, sleeper branding.**

***Brandon,** *n.* A note of a wildcat bank at Brandon, Miss.; the bank itself. Also attrib. *Obs.*

1839 *N.O. Picayune* 6 Feb. 2/1 The gentleman handed over his wallet, but it was 'no go' with the freebooter, who exclaimed, '*No you don't stranger. I scorn Brandon!*' **1839** *Ky. Observer* (Lexington) 25 May 3/1 The sheriff's office is full of Brandon paper. **1840** *Boston Transcript* 29 Jan. 1/1, I have actually failed oftener than all the banks put together, including all the Wild Cat institutions and the Brandon.

***brandy,** *n.* In combs.: (1) **brandy cocktail,** (see quots.) (2) **galaxy,** ?brandy and milk, *rare;* (3) **sling,** sling in which brandy is used; (4) **smash,** (see quot. 1909); (5) **smasher,** =prec., *obs.;* (6) **sour,** a drink composed of brandy, lime or lemon juice, bitters, and water; (7) **toddy,** brandy mixed with hot water and sweetened.

(1) 1845 DURELL *New Orleans* 25 A brandy-toddy is made by adding together in a little water, a little sugar, and a great deal of brandy—mix well and drink. A brandy-cocktail is composed of the same ingredients, with the addition of a shade of Stoughton's bitters. **1936** ARTHUR *Old New Orleans* 29 The original cocktail was a mixture of sugar, cognac, and aromatic bitters . . . and was known to those who first sampled the apothecary's mixture as a 'brandy cocktail.' — **(2) 1845** *P. Parley's Ann.* VI. 176 Will was especially fond of mint julip, and brandy galaxy. — **(3) 1810** M. V. H. DWIGHT *Journey* 49 He . . . invited us into the house & call'd for some brandy sling. **1851** W. K. NORTHALL *Curtain* 219 With trembling lips [he] called for a brandy sling. — **(4) 1850** THAXTER *Poem before Iadma* 7 Or didst thou at the Pemberton absorb a brandy-smash? **1909** *Cent. Supp.* 161/1 *Brandy-smash,* a drink made by mixing brandy with crushed ice and putting a few sprigs of mint in the glass. **1927** *Amer. Mercury* Jan. 28/1 Little Phil Sheridan . . . was fond of brandy smashes.

(5) 1846 *Knickerb.* XXVII. 59 Another banner shall be stationed opposite the hotels and coffee-houses, . . . 'Beware of Cock-Tails and Brandy Smashers!' **1848** *N.Y. Wkly. Tribune* 27 May 5/4 Think of a mass meeting in every bar-room in the city of Baltimore—and the perfect din of brandy 'smashers' keeping up a shrill treble over the deep bass of the base party watch-words with which partisans appeal to their followers! — **(6) 1861** NEWELL *Orpheus C. Kerr* I. 212 [The South Carolina gentleman] . . . clears a mighty track of everything that bears the shape of whiskey-skin, gin-and-sugar, brandy-sour [etc.]. — **(7) 1840** *N.O. Picayune* 23 Aug. 2 He was suffering . . . for a stiff brandy toddy. **1891** SLOAN *Fogy Days* 195 We'd bet he's got but little brain, Yes, we'd bet a brandy toddy.

As the last term in **apple, burnt, cider, papaw, peach, pug brandy.**

Brandywine cowslip. *local.* (See quot.) — **1937** LINCOLN *Wilmington Del.* 147 In the spring the children went a-Maying on the meadows which then extended from Orange to West streets and between Second and Third. They gathered the wild honey-suckle, the blood-root, May-apple and violet, as well as the now almost extinct Brandywine cow-slip (*Mertensia Virginica*).

branle ˈbrænlə, *n.* [F., a pendulum-like motion.] (See quot.) *Obs.* — **1894** CHOPIN *Bayou Folk* 197 So away they [the family] all went. All but Bibine, who was left swinging in his branle. . . . This branle consisted of a strong circular piece of cloth, securely but slackly fastened to a large, stout hoop suspended by three light cords to a hook in a rafter of the gallery.

***brant,** *n.* As the last term in **bald, black, fish, goose, sea, speckled, white brant.**

brant bird. A name applied locally to several birds, esp. the ruddy turnstone. — **1844** *Nat. Hist. N.Y., Zoology* II. 216 The Turnstone . . . is known among our gunners . . . under the names of Brant-bird, Heart-bird, Horsefoot Snipe, and Beach-bird. **1917** *Birds of Amer.* I. 268.

brarow ˈbrɛro, *n. W.* Variously spelled, see quots. [F. *blaireau,* badger.] The American badger, *Taxidea taxus.* Also attrib. *Obs.* Cf. **prarow.**

1804 WHITEHOUSE in *Lewis & Clark Exped.* (1905) VII. 67 Capt. Clark killed a Deer and a brarow. **1814** LEWIS & CLARK *Exped.* (1893) 64 One of our men brought in yesterday an animal called by the Pawnees chocartoosh, and by the French blaireau, or badger. **1860** *Charleston* (S.C.) *Mercury* 6 Nov. 3/2 This fur is called 'Blaireau Fur,' or 'Ocean Bay Sable.'

brasada brəˈsædə, *n. S.W.* [?Sp. *brazada,* armful of firewood.] Brush country, a region covered with thickets. — **1929** DOBIE *Vaquero* 204 (Bentley), The Brasada is still a *brasada,* the openings in it fewer and smaller. *Ib.* 229 In short, the Brasada was a strategic point for stealing and smuggling. **1939** WELLMAN *Trampling Herd* 107 Between the Rio Grande and the Nueces was the Brasada, composed of the worst jungle in the entire cow country of America.

brashly ˈbræʃlɪ, *adv.* Hastily, rashly. — **1865** MARK TWAIN *Sketches* (1926) 179, I mixed into this business a little too brashly—so to speak—and without due reflection. **1884** *Mexican Lett.* in *Boston* (*Mass.*) *Jrnl.* Aug., This department of business that started off so brashly has played out.

brash oak. *local.* The post oak. — **1897** SUDWORTH *Arborescent Flora* 154 *Quercus minor.* . . . Common names [include] . . . Box Oak (Md.), Brash Oak (Md.).

brasil brəˈsil, *n. S.W.* [Sp. in Amer. Sp. sense shown here.] (See quots.) — **1891** COULTER *Botany W. Tex.* 58 *C*[*ondalia*] *obovata.* . . . Known as 'brasil' and 'logwood,' and one of the common 'chaparral' plants of western Texas, forming dense impenetrable thickets. **1942** *Bul. Texas Agric. Exper. Station* March 24 *Condalia obovata.* Brasil, Brazil Wood. This native evergreen tree or tall shrub is sometimes called 'Bright Green Ebony.'

* **brass,** *n.*

1. A collective term for high-ranking army and navy officers in allusion to the gold braid on their uniforms. Also attrib. *Slang.*

1899 *Boston Herald* 26 July 4/8 It was not a big brass general that came; But a man in khaki kit. **1947** *Chi. Times* 28 June 16/5 When I visited Annapolis I found out those plebes are really taught to respect brass.

2. In combs.: (1) **brass ankle,** a mulatto, also transf., *colloq.;* (2) **brass-bass,** (see quot. 1889), also **brassy-bass;** (3) **button brigade,** (see quot.), *obs.;* (4) **eye,** the American goldeneye duck; (5) **eyed whistler,** =prec.; (6) **knuckles,** a protective metal device for the knuckles

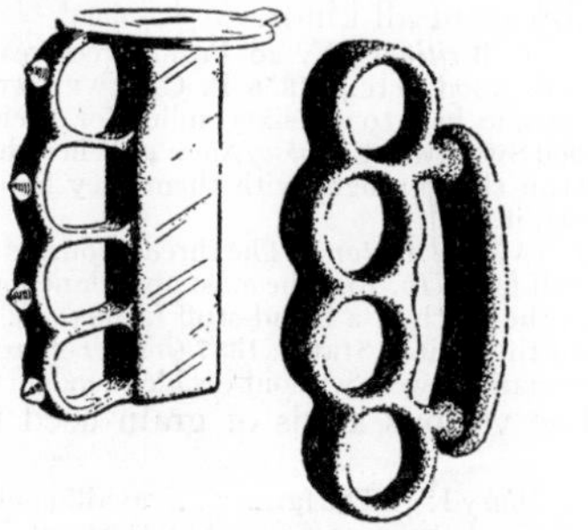

Brass knuckles, brass knucks, iron knuckles, knuckle dusters, knuckles, or knucks

of the closed fist, used in fights by roughs, thugs, etc., also **brass knucks;** (7) **monkey,** used fig. in phrases (see quots.); (8) **toe(s),** (see quots.); (9) **toed,** wearing boots capped with brass; (10) **wood,** =**bowwood,** also attrib., cf. **bodock.**

(1) **1940** *Amer. Sp.* XV. 446/2 Brass Ankle. Mulatto. 'The hotel cook is a brass ankle.' **1947** *S. Folklore Quart.* Sep. 190 Barty, the 'brass ankle' of Po' Buckra, says, 'If you can't git a horse, ride a cow.' — (2) **1884** GOODE *Fisheries U.S.* I. 424 The Brassy Bass of the Lower Mississippi Valley, *Roccus interruptus.* **1889** *Cent.* 664/1 *Brass-bass,* a percoideus fish, *Morone interrupta:* so called from its bright brassy color, tinged with blue on the back. . . . It attains the size of the common white perch, and inhabits fresh waters of the Mississippi valley. — (3) **1887** *Courier-Journal* 3 May 1/2 The Army and Navy people ruled in Washington society as well as in Congress. . . . Many wealthy civilians were anxious to get into the giddy whirl, but they were barred out by the brass-button brigade.— (4) **1844** *Nat. Hist. N.Y., Zoology* II. 330 *Fuligula clangula,* the Brass-eye, Whistler or Great-head, . . . is another northern species.

(5) **1839** PEABODY *Mass. Birds* 393 The Golden Eye . . . [has also] the name of Brass-eyed Whistler. — (6) **1855** *Chicago Times* 13 March 3/1 That new implement in modern *Mohawkism*—brass knuckles. **1922** F. A. SONDLEY *Asheville and Buncombe Co.* 200 Good old-fashioned fighting without rocks, knifes, pistols or 'brass knucks' was one of the most common and popular amusements of those days. **1947** *Dly. Oklahoman* (Okla. City) 30 Dec. 12/3 A rummaging detective found a pair of brass knuckles. — (7) **1870** DUVAL *Big-Foot Wallace* 148 It is hot enough to scald the throat out of a brass monkey. **1879** *Cin. Commercial* 2 Feb. 6/4 The wrath of the New York *Sun,* over the way those sacred cipher telegrams were handled, . . . would singe the hair on a brass monkey. **1929** J. PARKER *Old Army* 120 It was 'cold enough to freeze the tail off a brass monkey.' — (8) **1908–9** *D.N.* III. 293 *Brass-toes,* n. Brass-toed boots worn by children. Also called *copper-toes.* **1944** CLARK *Pills* 211 Despite its poor quality and general unsuitability the famous old 'brass toe' was an object of sentiment which older generations of southerners recall with affection.— (9) **1884** CRADDOCK *Where Battle Was Fought* 111 She could see his hilarious, brass-toed hosts kicking his brothers.

(10) **1830** *Newark* (N.J.) *Monitor* 7 Sep. 2/5 Freemasonry is as gross an imposture on the public as the *wooden nutmegs,* or *horn flints,* . . . or *brasswood pumpkin seeds.* **1844** *Cong. Globe* App. 31 May 500/1 On the Arkansas and Red rivers, an extremely valuable wood, . . . called the bois d'arc, or brass wood, grows in great quantities.

b. *To get down to brass tacks, nails,* to get down to fundamentals. *Colloq.*

1903 *N.Y. Sun* 28 Nov. 3 This bold sister was the first . . . to get down to brass tacks in a discussion of the scandal. **1911** H. QUICK *Yellowstone N.* xi. 288 When you come down to brass nails. **1948** *Life* 29 March 127/1 After the exchange of a few pleasantries we immediately got down to brass tacks.

* **brave,** *n.*

1. An Indian warrior. Cf. **blanket brave, Sioux brave.**

1819 SCHOOLCRAFT *Mo. Lead Mines* 176 Their warriors are called braves, to which honour no one can arrive, without having previously plundered or stolen from the enemy. **1902** TOMPKINS *Hist. Rec. Rockland Co. N.Y.* 35 The crew replied with bullets, hitting three braves and repulsing the rest. **1948** *True* May 130/2 The full-grown braves carried seven-foot bows a white man could not bend.

2. A member of the Tammany Society. Cf. **Tammany brave.**

1856 *N.Y. Herald* 9 Jan. 1/3 Among the attractions of the evening was a committee room where the 'braves' indulged in fire water, which was served up in the shape of nice brandy punches. **1907** BROWN & STRAUSS *Dict. Amer. Politics* 390 Its organization [i.e., of Tammany Society] was supposed in a general way to imitate Indian customs, . . . the members being called braves, its meeting place the wigwam, etc. **1935** ALEXANDER *Amer. Talleyrand* 379 By a prodigious effort the Braves had won him the City with 982 votes to spare.

brazen bullhead. (See quot. 1814.) — **1814** MITCHILL *Fishes N.Y.* 380 Brazen Bullhead. *Cottus aeneus.* With brass-coloured complexion, thorny head, and rusty blotches over the sides. **1839** STORER *Mass. Fishes* 20 The brazen Bullhead . . . is very voracious, catching at almost any kind of bait offered to it, and distending itself immensely with food.

Brazil tobacco. (See quot. 1788.) *Obs.*

1774 in *Pub. Champlain Soc.* XXI. 97 We ware in all 5 cannoes and tho deep laden we had but about 180 lbs Brazil Tobaco. [**1788** SCHÖPF *Reise* I. 540 Die Maryländischen und Virginischen Tobackpflanzer unterscheiden vielerley Abarten von Toback, nach dessen Wachsthum: als Long-green, Thick-joint, Brazil, Shoestring u.s.w.] **1791** in *Pub. Champlain Soc.* XXI. 495, I got a few articles as supplies from Mr Ross such as 6 Womens & 2 Mens Knives, 4 Awls, 2 Steels, ½ lb of Common beads, 2 fathems of Brazile Tobacco.

brea ˈbreə, *n. W.* [Sp. in same sense.] (See quots.) Also attrib.

1855 *Santa Barbara* (Calif.) *Gaz.* 1 Nov. 2/4 Such was the intense heat that the *brea* or pitch with which its flat roof was covered, became liquid and ran through on to the billiard tables. **1896** *Land of Sunshine* June 7 There is . . . the large, placque-shaped basket on which the Indians gamble with dice made of walnut shells, halved, filled with brea (tar) into which wampum is pressed. **1912** *Harper's Wkly.* 18 Dec. 11/2 It is interesting to note the presence in the same asphalt bed of the great American lion along with the sabre-tooth tiger, the two representing the highest environs of the Brea pool.

* **bread,** *n.*

1. *S.* Corn bread.

[**1643** WILLIAMS *Key* (1866) 121 The Indians bruise them [*sc.* strawberries] in a morter and mixe them with meale and make Strawberry bread.] **1705** BEVERLEY *Virginia* III. 14 They make their Bread of the Indian Corn, Wild Oats, or the Seed of the Sunflower. **1903** *D.N.* II. 307 bread, *n.* Corn-bread. **1942** RAWLINGS *C. Creek* 208 If I asked a neighbor for some bread in an emergency, I should receive a pan of cornbread.

2. (See quot.) *Obs.*

1824 J. DODDRIDGE *Notes* 101 The lean venison and the breast of the wild turkies, we were taught to call bread. The flesh of the bear was denominated meat.

b. *pl.* (See quots.)

1835 LONGSTREET *Ga. Scenes* 36 He ate his meat and *breads* in the usual way, but he drank liquids in all ways. **1863** C. C. HOPLEY *Life in South* II. 237 'Breads,' as all the variety of corn cakes, waffles, hot rolls, and hominy are called.

3. In combs.: (1) **bread board,** a board on which dough is kneaded; (2) **bowl,** a bowl in which the ingredients for bread are mixed; (3) **colony,** a colony furnishing breadstuffs, *rare;* (4) ***corn,** Indian corn particularly suitable for bread; (5) ***fruit,** wheat, *rare;* (6) **grain,** wheat, corn, etc., used for making bread; (7) **line,** a line of poor people waiting to receive bread or other food given as charity, also transf.; (8) **meal,** corn meal; (9) **pudding,** a pudding consisting of stale bread crumbs, suitably moistened with milk, sweetened, and seasoned; (10) **root,** =**prairie turnip,** cf. **Indian breadroot, Missouri breadroot;** (11) **stuff,** see as a main entry; (12) **ticket,** a ticket entitling the possessor to bread; (13) **toaster,** a fork or other device used in toasting bread; (14) **tray,** a large shallow wooden receptacle in which dough is kneaded; (15) **trough,** a kneading trough; (16) **weigher,** an official who supervises the weighing of bread offered for sale; (17) **wheat,** wheat used for making bread.

(1) **1869** E. PUTNAM *Receipt Bk.* 4 Mix . . . the dough; roll it, on a bread-board, about an inch thick. **1945** *Chi. Tribune* 13 May VII. 1/7 A mass of soft fluffy dough was put out on the breadboard. — (2) **1819** PEIRCE *Rebelliad* 15 The bread-bowls fly at woful rate. **1896** WILKINS *Madelon* 14 She passed him with the bread-bowl on her hip and her soft arm curved around it. — (3) **1769** *Amer. Philos. Soc.* I. 190 All the foregoing sorts [of vines] will do very well for the three bread colonies, viz. New-York, New-Jersey, Pennsylvania. — (4) **1668** *East-Hampton Rec.* I. 288 Whosoever shall grind Malte at the mill shall after[wards] . . . clear the mill with at least halfe apeck of bread corne. **1775** ADAIR *Indians* 407 The third [kind of corn grown by the Indians] is the largest, of a very white and soft grain, termed 'bread-corn.' **1899** GREEN *Va. Word-Book* 67 Bread-corn, *n.* The white, and best corn, was always used for grinding into meal for bread.

(5) **1853** *S.F. Whig* 28 July 2/3 This vast extent of bread-fruit spreads often, on either hand, for miles—and the sight of rich winrows, sheaves, and knolls of life-preserving cereal, fails not with the level soil, but crowns the rolling lands and hillsides. — (6) **1793** JEFFERSON *Writings* III. 263 Bread-stuff, that is to say, bread-grains, meals, and bread. **1814** J. TAYLOR *Arator* 175 Their food [i.e., of horned cattle] for half the year consists of the coarse offal of bread grain. — (7) **1900** *Lippincott's Mag.* LXV. 12 That's the bread line. They get a cup of coffee and a loaf of bread every night at twelve o'clock. **1946** *Chi. D. News* 17 June 10/2 Up to now the dread word 'breadline' has always had a twin—'unemployment.' **1948** *Reader's Digest* May 149/2 But I was there pretty regularly when the bread line formed. — (8) **1931** *Randolph Enterprise* (Elkins, W. Va.) 5 Feb. 3/2 T. Newland and father are grinding some fine bread meal Saturday of each week for any one bringing in corn. — (9) **1810** *New System Domestic Cookery* 132 Boiled Bread Pudding. **1948** *Calif. Citrograph* May 327/2 (*heading*), Dried Fruit Bread Pudding.

(10) **1829** EATON *Botany* (ed. 5) 349 *Psoralea esculenta*, bread root. . . . The root affords a staple article of diet to the western Indians. **1947** DE VOTO *Across Wide Missouri* 432 Some of these were very important sources of food, notably the camas, . . . the breadroot or prairie turnip, . . . and many species of lilies. — (12) **1855** *Chicago Times* 21 March 3/1 To await trial for entering a bakeshop and stealing therefrom bread tickets to the value of $16. — (13) **1783** T. B. HAZARD *Nailer Tom's Diary* (1930) 44/1, I made a Bread Toaster and Finisht agridiron for Robert Hazard. **1851** HALL *Manhattaner* 18 Furnished rooms and cafés elbow each other wistfully; and bachelor bread-toasters, coffee-boilers, and the like, are soon picked up from the neighboring shops. — (14) [**1854** TROWBRIDGE *M. Merrivale* 6 They [the rays of sunset] fell upon the gray plates and the worn Japan of the old bread-tray.] **1865** *Harper's Mag.* April 665/1 You men can make bread-trays,—there's plenty of fine cypress on the plantation. **1898** PAGE *Red Rock* 182 She was busy with a bread-tray.

(15) **1638** *Md. Proc. Council* 76, I have seised . . . a bread troughe [and] . . . a reaping hooke. **1783** E. PARKMAN *Diary* 299 A Meal Seive /6. Bread Trough /8. — (16) **1725** *N.-Eng. Courant* 7 Aug. 1/1 Bread very often wants near a quarter Part of its due Weight, notwithstanding the extraordinary Diligence of the Bread-weighers, who daily seize great quantities of it. — (17) **1814** J. TAYLOR *Arator* 153 The best bread and seed wheat, is invariably that gotten out and cleaned within a day or two after it is cut.

b. In phrases: (1) **bread-and-butter*, (see quots.), *colloq.;* (2) *bread and butter brigade*, a contemptuous term for politicians desirous of securing for Congress all the patronage possible, *obs.;* (3) *bread and butter letter*, a letter of thanks to one's host for hospitality; (4) *bread and butter man*, a member of the bread and butter brigade, *obs.;* (5) *bread and cheese apple*, (see quot.), *obs.*

(1) **1892** *Amer. Folk-Lore* V. 104 Smilax rotundifolia, biscuit-leaves; bread-and-butter . . . Allston, Mass. . . . The young leaves eaten by children. **1931** CLUTE *Plants* 133 Failure to observe this requirement has been the chief fault of the toad-flax (*Linaria vulgaris*). . . . It flaunts its banners in a thousand fields where it is known as . . . bread-and-butter. — (2) **1866** *Cong. Globe* 19 Dec. 206/3 There are gentlemen here, who in the last political contest went over the country saying that a certain party was a 'bread and butter brigade.' **1884** *Chi. Tribune* 3 June 4/4 The bone and muscle of his strength in the convention consist of the Bread-and-Butter Brigade, delegates from the hopeless Democratic States of the South. — (3) **1901** HOWELLS *Pair of Patient Lovers* 82 His prompt bread-and-butter letter. **1942** RAWLINGS *C. Creek* 207 There came to me in the mail a copy of the *Boston Cook Book*, even ahead of the conventional bread and butter letter. — (4) **1867** *Cong. Globe* 12 April 835/3 [They] were removed by Andrew Johnson to make place for unreliable, irresponsible Copperheads in most cases, or bread and butter men, who are worse. — (5) **1817** W. COXE *Fruit Trees* 116 [The] Rambo, or Romanite . . . is much cultivated in Delaware. . . . It is in some parts of the country, called the Bread and Cheese apple.

As the last term in **acorn, batter, Boston brown, brown, corn, crackling, devil's, diet, egg, fatty, flat, good, Graham, gritted, hominy, hornet's nest, Indian, Indian corn, johnny, large, light, nutmeg, peach, persimmon, pilot, plum, pone, pumpkin, root, saleratus, salt, spoon, strawberry bread.**

bread brɛd, *v. tr.* To supply with bread.

1797 *Steele Papers* I. 152, I cannot return you corn again this fall as what I have . . . will Scarcely Bread the Negroes and feed the Work Horses. **1885** *Rep. Indian Affairs* 148 These Indians raised sufficient amount of wheat last year to bread them until the present crop is gathered. **1946** *Atlanta Jrnl. Mag.* 3 March 9/2 Farmers usually make enough corn to bread them.

breadstuff ˈbrɛdˌstʌf, *n.*

1. Cereals, flour, meal, etc., out of which bread is made; also bread of all kinds.

1793 JEFFERSON *Writings* IX. 20 France receives favorably our bread stuff, rice, wood, [etc.]. **1856** P. CARTWRIGHT *Autobiog.* 254 Some of the people had to go sixty miles for their grinding and bread-stuff. **1900** SMITHWICK *Evol. of State* 15 When the colonists used up the breadstuff they brought with them they had to do without until they raised it.

attrib. **1814** J. TAYLOR *Arator* 92 The three resources . . . common to every bread stuff farm. *Ib.* 102 The most abundant source of artificial manure within the reach of a bread-stuff farmer. *Ib.* 170 The bread stuff country of the United States. **1887** *Courier-Journal* 11 Jan. 4/1 The breadstuff markets were without decided tendencies.

2. *pl.* The various kinds of grain used for this purpose.

1831 P. HONE *Diary* I. 31 The farmer . . . availing himself of the increased price of bread-stuffs, occasioned by the brisk foreign demand. **1838** BELL *Men & Things* 163 Two things I saw on this road then new to me, Indian corn and buck wheat—the giant and the dwarf of 'bread-stuffs,' as the Americans call edible grain. **1904** *N.Y. Times* 13 May 11 For April the decrease in our exports of bread-stuffs was $11,319,993. The foreigners can get wheat cheaper elsewhere.

***break,** *n.*[1]

1. *pl. W.* A succession of sharp interruptions of the terrain, broken country.

1820 GILLELAND *Ohio & Miss. Pilot* 171 Some of the breaks rise in deep circular glens called coves, each of which has a gap at one side for the stream to pass out. **1854** MARCY *Expl. Red River* 5 Manuel . . . pointed out to him breaks or bluffs upon a stream to the south of the Canadian. **1918** VISHER *So. Dakota* 117 In each of these areas badlands or 'breaks' afforded protection from winter storms, permanent streams supplied water, and pasturage was available.

2. A break-down, collapse, failure.

1827 J. RANDOLPH in *Life* (1851) II. 289, I am of opinion that (as we say in Virginia) we have made 'a great break.' In fact the administration have succeeded in no one measure. **1931** ADAMS & ALMACK *Hist.* 511 President Buchanan, always a conciliator, tried to find ways to make another compromise that would prevent the break.

3. A rush or dash from a place, an attempt to escape.

1833 *Sketches of Crockett* 82 Just before I got there, the old bear made a break and got loose. **1888** ROOSEVELT in *Cent. Mag.* May 49 Our three men . . . understood perfectly that the slightest attempt at a break would result in their being shot down. **1948** *Dly. Ardmoreite* (Ardmore, Okla.) 29 June 7/3 They will be handcuffed and chained with the chain running between their legs to trip them if they attempt a break.

b. A dash *for* a place.

1845 J. J. HOOPER *Simon Sugg's Adv.* xii. 143, I maid a brake on a bee line for Urwinton. **1899** A. H. QUINN *Penn. Stories* 50 Field, in the meantime, had made a break for third and reached it safely.

c. An attempt or try *at* something.

1886 P. STAPLETON *Major's Christmas* 27 Maybe now a cornerser [=connoisseur] . . . would give you more, but I'll make a break at it as best I know how.

4. An agitated or disturbed area on the surface of water, as that made by the rising of a fish, or by the ripple from a snag.

1852 *Mich. Agric. Soc. Trans.* III. 231 They will make a break in the water near the shore with their tail. **1894** MARK TWAIN *P. Wilson* xvi, She passed many a snag whose 'break' could have told her a thing to break her heart. **1900** F. NORRIS *Blix* 144 The two watching from the boat . . . saw that most inspiriting of sights—the 'break' of a salmon-trout.

5. A sudden interruption in gait or speed on the part of a horse, esp. of a race horse. Cf. ***break,** *v.* **4.**

1839 *Spirit of Times* 13 July 222/3 (We.), It was as bad a break as we ever saw. **1902** McFAUL *Ike Glidden* 200 When rounding into the home stretch his horse broke, and suddenly went to a wild swerving break that carried him to the complete outside of the track. **1948** *L.A. Times* 2 May 1. 21/2 Farcry made bad break entering back-stretch, was far back thereafter.

6. (See quot. 1859.)

1859 BARTLETT 48 *Break*, a regular sale of tobacco at the 'breaking' or opening of the hogsheads. Local in Virginia. **1865** *Louisville D. Democrat* 30 Oct. 3/6 The breaks to-day amounted to 127 hhds, with rejection of bids on 20 hhds. **1943** *Jrnl. of Business* July 149/1 However, to avoid visiting these auctions or 'breaks' in the different warehouses, which involved time and wading through muddy streets, the commercial merchants came to sell in their offices from samples.

7. = **gallows stalk.** *Rare.*

1862 *Ill. Agric. Soc. Trans.* (1865) V. 160, I selected the gallows stalks, or breaks of my shocks [of sorghum].

8. A sudden decline in the prices of stocks and commodities on an exchange. Cf. * **break,** *v.* **5.**

1870 MEDBERY *Men of Wall St.* 203 It is partly for want of courage to endure an occasional 'break' in stocks, . . . that . . . the outsiders . . . meet with misfortune. **1900** S. A. NELSON *A B C Wall St.* 130 The attack of a bear crowd or the actual inability of the holders will produce a decline, which is called 'a break.' **1948** *Gainesville* (Tex.) *D. Register* 3 July 1/7 The break in corn had some influence on other grains, but they did not fall as much as the yellow cereal.

9. An awkward social blunder, a mistake, error. Often a *bad break. Slang.*

1884 NYE *Baled Hay* 200 Possibly science may be wrong. We have known science to make bad little breaks. **1898** HAMBLEN *Genl. Manager's Story* 136 He kept this kind of thing [i.e., an examination] up for a good hour. . . . On the whole, I didn't make any very bad breaks. **1908** *St. Louis Globe-Democrat* 1 July 11/1 But for what seemed a bad break on the part of Umpire Billy Evans, in the eighth inning, the Browns might have tied the score. **1930** *Randolph Enterprise* (Elkins, W. Va.) 20 Nov. 4/1 The Republicans [have been] licked out of their boots over this and a lot more such breaks.

10. A critical or decisive point or moment.

1888 BRYCE *Amer. Commonwealth* II. 568 One balloting follows another till what is called 'the break' comes. . . . The break, when it comes, comes with fierce intensity. **1909** *Amer. Mag.* June 107/1 Among the players, who do not study psychology, the crucial moment is known as 'the break.' **1923** *N.Y. Times* 7 Oct. 1. ii. 1/4 The two teams, in my opinion, are evenly matched, and the breaks of the game, plus good pitching, will decide the series.

11. *Baseball.* The swerve of a pitched curve ball at or near the plate. Cf. * **break,** *v.* **11.**

1905 *Chi. D. News* 31 July 4/3 He seems to possess everything necessary for a pitcher, having fine speed, a curve ball which has a very quick break to it and a good change of pace. **1912** *Collier's* 20 April 14/2 Walsh could . . . control its 'break,' knowing with certainty whether its sudden swerve would be to right, to left, or straight down.

12. A chance, luck, fortune, often with a qualifying term, as *even break, good break,* etc. *Slang.*

1911 H. QUICK *Yellowstone N.* v. 126 It's allus an even break whether they'll stan' and freeze in their tracks, or chase after some bunch of . . . natives. **1922** *Collier's* 29 April 4/3 Then comes the first of a world's series of bad breaks which just missed turning [them] . . . into a set of raging maniacs. **1926** J. BLACK *You Can't Win* xxi. 331 After gathering every scrap of information available, I was sure I could 'take' the spot if I got a fair break on the luck. **1948** *Dly. Ardmoreite* (Ardmore, Okla.) 2 May 13/5 By a series of good breaks, he possessed the required elements to result in his being presented with one 1948 model Ford car Saturday afternoon.

As the last term in **fire break, ice break, wind break.**

break brek, *n.*[2] [App. f. **brake*, *v.*, to dress hemp.] (See quot. 1907.) — **1796** *Mass. Mercury* 29 April (*Cent.*), Best St. Petersburg clean Hemp of the break of the year 1796. **1907** *Dly. Chronicle* 7 March 6/6 A 'break' of hemp, which in America means the quantity sold in a year.

* **break,** *v.*

1. *intr.* (See quot.) *Rare.*

1809 F. CUMING *Western Tour* 135 A fine dog, led by a string to prevent his breaking (or hunting the game beyond the reach of their rifles).

2. To run, make a rush, dash *for* or *to* a place.

1834 CROCKETT *Life* xiv. 96 When my lead dog found him [*sc.* a bear] and raised his yell, all the rest [of the dogs] broke to him. **1835** LONGSTREET *Ga. Scenes* 125 The way she [a horse] now broke for Springfield 'is nothing to nobody.' **1902** LORIMER *Lett. Merchant* xvi. 237 Just as the crowd yelled and broke for the house, two patrol wagons full of policemen got there. **1907** WHITE *Arizona Nights* v. 98 The cattle would attempt to 'break' past the end and up the valley.

For *to break for high* or *tall timber* see **timber.**

3. *tr.* To soften (hard water).

1837 E. L. WILLSON *Journey* (1929) 22 June, We have to break all the water to wash with for we can not catch any rain water. **1853** *Harper's Mag.* VI. 582/2 The water of Lake Superior . . . being . . . entirely unfit for the laundry without a previous 'breaking,' by soda or other means.

4. *intr.* Of a horse, esp. in racing: To change gait, to lose a level stride. Also transf. Cf. * **break,** *n.*[1] **5.**

1839 *Spirit of Times* 13 July 222/3 (We.) While Awful was ahead, and his backers were counting the spoils in advance, he broke! **1865** *Louisville D. Democrat* 30 Oct. 2/3 On the back stretch Dorsey broke, while Dimmock went ahead and opened a considerable gap on him. **1902** LORIMER *Lett. Merchant* 60 Never start off at a gait that you can't improve on, but move along strong and well in hand to the quarter. . . . Take it calm enough up to the half not to break. **1948** *L.A. Times* 2 May 1. 21/2 Norris Hanover was far back after breaking at start.

b. *fig.* To break away from a party and vote contrary to its leadership.

1904 *N.Y. Ev. Post* 17 May 1 Kane County deserted Yates. . . . Will County broke also, and gave twenty-six votes for Lowden. **1908** *Springfield W. Republican* 8 Oct. 2 The word 'break' applied to political campaigners has the same meaning [as in horse racing]. **1948** *Time* 5 July 17/3 Connecticut was ready to break for Dewey.

5. Of prices of commodities, stocks, etc.: To fall suddenly or sharply. Cf. * **break,** *n.*[1] **8.**

1870 W. W. FOWLER *Ten Yrs. in Wall St.* 435 Gold had broken to 87, and then, on the news of the repulse at Fayetteville, North Carolina, ran up to 194. **1902** LORIMER *Lett. Merchant* 23 He is the chap that's buying wheat at ninety-seven cents the day before the market breaks. **1948** *Time* 7 June 34/1 Gold shares broke wide open on the stock exchange, tumbled more than $300 million.

6. *tr.* (See quot.) *Obs.*

1871 DE VERE *Break*, to, is in Virginia, and other tobacco-raising States, applied to the opening of the hogsheads, as they are sent from the plantations, previous to a public sale.

7. *intr.* To break up or disperse, usu. of a religious meeting.

1881 H. W. PIERSON *In the Brush* 177 The benediction was then pronounced, and, in their vernacular, the 'meeting broke.' **1939** HARRIS *Purslane* 86 De meetin' breaks tomorrow, and Mariah's bound to see Duck come th'ugh.

8. Of fish: To leap out or partially out of the water.

1885 *Outing* Oct. 75/2 Just then a trout broke under the olders [*sic*]. **1885** *Harper's Mag.* Jan. 216/1 Once I tried to fool them with sham colored feathers; but no, sir, they [*sc.* the fish] never broke. **1948** *Dly. Ardmoreite* (Ardmore, Okla.) 28 July 16/5 As everyone was watching the water around his line a six pound channel catfish broke.

9. *tr.* (See quot.)

1889 *Cent.* 669/1 *To break a gun*, to open it by the action.

10. *Lumbering.* (See quot.)

1893 *Scribner's Mag.* June 710/2 This is active work and requires . . . care in so placing the logs that they will 'break' or roll in easily when the ice goes out.

11. *Baseball. intr.* Of a pitched curve ball: To swerve or curve at or near the plate. Cf. * **break,** *n.*[1] **11.**

1899 *Chi. D. News* 8 May 6/1 Katoll is spoken of as the possessor of a sizzling curve that comes up with a phenomenal burst of speed and breaks lightning fast. **1909** *Collier's* 15 May 29/2 A fast, breaking outshoot . . . goes naturally to first and right. **1948** *Durant* (Okla.) *D. Democrat* 2 July 4/3 Both pitchers handcuffed the opposition for five full innings, Leader with a sharp breaking curve and Marshall with a fireball.

12. With adverbs: (1) * *break away*, of the weather, to clear up, fair off; (2) * *break down*, (*a*) to dance or perform (a dance) in a violent or stamping manner, (*b*) to break (a horse), *rare;* (3) *break even*, to gain and lose equally; (4) * *break in*, to wear (shoes or boots) until comfortably adjusted to the feet, also transf.; (5) *break out*, (*a*) to free a way or road from snow, (*b*) (see quots.), (*c*) in lumbering, to trip the key logs in a rollway and allow the logs to roll into a stream; (6) * *break up*, of a race horse, to "break" (see **4.** above), also transf. to upset or make (a person) nervous, *slang.*

(1) **1758** *Essex Inst. Coll.* XVIII. 98 Cloudy cool Morning wind West Northerly breaks away about Noon. **1816** U. BROWN *Journal* II. 221 This morning rains very much, about ten o'Clock breaks away. — (2) (*a*) **1838** *Lexington Observer & Rep.* 8 Aug., He got to 'breaking down' so hard toward the end of his dance, that the head [of the barrel] went in. **1873** MARK TWAIN & WARNER *Gilded Age* xvi, The twang of a banjo became audible as they drew nearer, and they saw a couple of negroes, from some neighboring plantation, 'breaking

down' a juba. (*b*) *c***1835** CATLIN *Indians* II. 59 This 'breaking down' or taming, however, is not without the most desperate trial on the part of the horse. — **(3) 1938** ASBURY *Sucker's Prog.* 15 Break even—A system of betting by which each card was played to win and lose an even number of times. **1944** CLARK *Pills* 135 Where cash resources were limited, one- and two-pound orders were common, but customers who wound up the crop year by breaking even with a little clear money were satisfied with nothing short of a hoop of cheese. — **(4) 1846** *Spirit of Times* (N.Y.) 25 April 99/2 A pair of his new boots require no 'breaking in.' **1884** NYE *Baled Hay* 119, I had . . . been breaking in a pair of new boots that day. **1948** *Chi. Tribune* 21 Mar. (Comics) 12, I got a new pair of brass knuckles that need breaking in.

(5) (*a*) **1780** PATTEN *Diary* 410 We broke out to our wood and I shoveled snow about the door. **1831** C. C. BALDWIN *Diary* (1901) 3 Feb. 92 The people are busy in breaking out roads which have been blocked up with snow. **1947** *Pub. Amer. Dial. Soc.* No. 8, 5 break out: To break a road through deep snow by means of a team and an empty sled so that the sap will not be overturned when hauling it to the sugar house. (*b*) *a***1870** CHIPMAN *Notes on Bartlett* 49 *To break out in a new spot*, to do some new thing; to do something else.—Ct. [= Connecticut]. **1878** I. L. BIRD *Rocky Mts.* 215 Even their [*sc.* Indians'] 'reservations' do not escape seizure practically; for if gold 'breaks out' on them they are 'rushed.' (*c*) **1901** *Munsey's Mag.* XXV. 393/1 Bold men with peevies 'break out' the rollways; the logs rattle down. — **(6) 1844** *N.O. Picayune* 19 Feb. 4/3 There was . . . one match that was first rate—competitors, a Yankee horse, attached to wheels, and a Canadian pony, to runners. The wheels conquered, after a short, but spirited contest—the pony 'breaking up.' **1860** HOLMES *Professor* i. 12 This episode broke me up, as the jockeys say. **1902** L. BELL *Hope Loring* 240 What language you use! . . . If you knew how it breaks me up when you use slang!

b. In various contextual and phrasal uses: (1) *To break corn*, to remove ears of corn from the stalks in harvesting; (2) *to break the pope's (man's) neck*, a game played indoors in which a plate is spun preparatory to other activities on the part of the players, cf. *spin the plate*, *s.v.* **plate;** (3) *to break ground (camp) (corral)*, to leave a camp, etc., and move elsewhere; (4) *to break one's nose*, to administer a rebuff or setback; (5) *to break the slate*, see **slate;** (6) *to break the golden harp*, (see quot.); (7) *to break brush*, to live in the backwoods and become accustomed to riding through rough, brushy country (see quot. 1941); (8) *to break yard*, of moose, to leave a moose-yard; (9) ∗ *to break into*, to get into some occupation, activity, status, etc., to succeed in having a contribution published in (a magazine); (10) *to break stalks*, to break down or chop up corn or cotton stalks in beginning a new crop.

(1) [**1701** WOLLEY *Journal* (1902) 43 Their Harvest is in *October*, their Corn grows like clusters of Grapes, which they pluck or break off with their hands. **1776** DUNBAR *Life* 32 The Other negroes employed in hoeing and breaking down corn. *Ib.* 33, 4 Negroes cutting stave timber. . . . Employed all day all hands in breaking down Corn.] **1864** in EASTERBY *S.C. Rice Plant.* (1945) 313, I have finished Picking Peas & commencd Breakeing the Corn but have to stop on account of Rain. [**1948** *Democrat* 24 June 8/3 Farmers should notice especially the highly fertilized hybrid corn from now to breaking season.] — **(2) 1773** P. V. FITHIAN *Journal* I. 65 Mr. Lee, by the voice of the Company, was chosen Pope, . . . and the rest of the company were appointed Friars, in the Play call'd 'break the Pope's neck.' *c***1830** FURMAN in *N.Y. Hist. Soc. Bul.* (Jan., 1939) 6 'To break the man's neck,' chairs were placed around the room for all the company save one; one person stood in the centre of the room, with a plate in his hand; the whole company forming a circle round him,[etc.]. **1890** *N. & Q.* VI. 53 There used to be a game played by young persons of either sex in New England called 'Break the Pope's Neck.' . . . It was an in-door game, played of a winter's evening in country places, and I think a pewter plate was twirled in a certain way at one stage of the game. — **(3) 1827** BERNARD *Retrospections of Amer.* 179 Such was the squatter's illustration of the instability of things, he being known sometimes to 'break ground' as it was termed, three or four times, before the advancing flood of population. **1929** DICKSON *Across Plains* 108 Everyone was now growing impatient of further delay, and it was decided to break corral. **1946** *So. Sierran* Sep. 2/3 Early next morning we broke camp. — **(4) 1864** NORTON *Army Letters* 217 The new major 'has broken the doctor's nose' and given him to understand that his duties are to attend to the sick.

(6) 1874 *Southern Mag.* XIV. 378 What do you mean by that—breaking the golden harp? My lor! don't you know, Miss Jennie? He meant ef I done a murder I couldn't never have nothin' to play on in hebben. — **(7) 1881** H. W. PIERSON *In the Brush* 6 Father A—— . . . is an old Brush-Breaker. . . . He has broken a right smart chance of brush. **1941** *Reader's Digest* Oct. 155 Just to show what my failure consisted of, I may say that 'breaking brush,' as we called it, is a specialized kind of cowpuncher horsemanship. New Mexico cowboys hooted derisively at cowboys from the Texas plains who hesitated to ride full tilt at a clump of trees whose branches interlaced to form a veritable hedge. — **(8) 1887** *Harper's Mag.* Feb. 459/1 They 'break yard,' as it is called, and falling in one behind the other, start down the mountain in close column. — **(9) 1899** *Chi. D. News* 10 May 6/1 Nichols will be anxious to break into the game pretty soon. **1907** *Collier's* 5 Oct. 11/2 After reading newspapers and periodicals for a quarter of a century, Mr. F. C. Wheeler . . . decided recently for the first time in his life to break into print. **1926** *Scribner's Mag.* Aug. 230/1 We are compelled to read of ambitious writers who 'break into' the leading magazines. **1928** *Dly. Ardmoreite* (Ardmore, Okla.) 25 March 12/2 He is the best outfield prospect I have seen since 'Shoeless Joe' Jackson broke into the American league.

(10) 1931 *K.C. Star* 20 Oct., The Chicago teachers who have had no pay since farmers began breaking stalks last spring, begin to want money.

∗**break-** The verb stem in combs.: (1) **breakback,** (see quot. 1859), *obs.;* (2) **bone (fever)** = **dengue,** cf. **Russian breakbone fever;** (3) **down,** see as a main entry; (4) ∗ **up,** (*a*) the Civil War, *colloq.*, *obs.*, (*b*) *W.* the time in the late 1870's when, because of drought, thievery, sheep raising, etc., cattle were remarkably scarce in the cattle country of southwest Texas.

(1) 1856 GOODRICH *Recoll.* I. 78 The house itself was a low edifice . . . ; the rear being what was called a *breakback*, that is, sloping down to a height of ten feet; this low part furnishing a shelter for garden tools, and various household instruments. **1859** BARTLETT 48 *Breakback*, a term applied to a peculiar roof, common in the country, where the rear portion is extended beyond the line of the opposite side, and at a different angle. — **(2) 1862** *N.Y. Tribune* 16 May, The warm weather is adding . . . another fever, to which the natives [of the southwestern states] give the name (said to be very graphic) of Breakbone, in which every bone in the body feels as if it were broken. **1948** *Reader's Digest* May 32/2 He was among the first 16 to be exposed to the virus of dengue fever, the 'breakbone fever' which was causing more casualties among our troops in the Pacific than the enemy. — **(4)** (*a*) **1869** J. R. BROWNE *Adv. Apache Country* 133 It [*sc.* Tucson] became during the few years preceding the 'break-up' quite a place of resort for traders, speculators [etc.]. **1884** SWEET & KNOX *Through Texas* 74 Before the civil war, or, as a Texan would say, ''fore the break-up,' [etc.]. (*b*) **1929** DOBIE *Vaquero* 227 It is true that the Break-up did not mark sharply the end of the old order, for more than a decade was to pass before the trails were fenced.

∗**break-down,** *n.*

1. A noisy, rollicking dance of rustic origin. Also attrib. and transf. Cf. **Ethiopian, Negro, Old Virginia, Virginia breakdown.**

1819 QUITMAN in *Life & Corr.* I. 42 Lay at Point Pleasant, where Whiting and I visited a Virginia 'break-down.' **1844** *N.O. Picayune* 18 Mar. 33/2 Old Hickory's birthday is to be celebrated at Faneuil Hall by a *fête* similar to the Clay Club's, to be styled the 'Jackson Jubilee'—another political breakdown. **1849** KENT in *Calif. Hist. Soc. Quart.* XX. 41 One of our men had a violin . . . and once in a while we could get up a sort of break down dance. **1944** WILSON *Passing Inst.* 53 My first knowledge of breakdowns was gained from hearing the boys play on such occasions.

2. *local.* A cedar tree which in falling from natural causes breaks above the roots instead of uprooting.

1857 *Geology of Cape May N.J.* 77 He can tell whether it was a *windfall* or a *breakdown;* that is, whether it was blown down or broken off. **1893** *D.N.* I. 336 break down and windfall are terms describing conditions in which cedar logs are found beneath the surface. The log is chipped and its condition indicated by the odor of the chip.

∗**breaker,** *n.*

1. One engaged in breaking hemp. *Obs.*

1720 *Mass. Bay Currency Tracts* 389 Two breakers for 1 day 6 *s.* . . . Four swinglers for 1 day 12 *s.*

2. A kind of plow used in breaking land.

1857 *Lawrence* (Kansas) *Republican* 28 May 3 A large assortment of Breakers of all sizes, especially of my extra Two-Horse Moldboard Breakers. **1876** *Rice Co. Gazette* (Sterling, Kans.) 20 Jan., All styles of breakers and stirring plows will be kept in stock and at lowest prices.

3. One who plows or breaks up land.

1859 *Letter* in *Kans. Hist. Quart.* VIII. 308 The Breakers are running two plows in our pasture cutting broad furrows 70 rods long.

4. A horse that in racing breaks from the prescribed gait.

1868 H. WOODRUFF *Trotting Horse* 201 Although a trotter of remarkably fine speed and power, he was such a bad breaker, . . . that at first he was beaten by horses much inferior to himself.

5. =**coal breaker.**

1901 *Cosmopolitan* Sep. 629/1 First, the boy of eight or ten is sent to the breaker to pick the slate and other impurities from the coal which has been brought up from the mine. **1948** *Chi. D. News* 18 June 1/7 He veered way from a huge anthracite breaker towering 265 feet into the air.

As the last term in **brush, circuit, clod, coal, fence, fog, gall, head, horse, ice, jaw, Negro, prairie, rock, stone, wind breaker.**

Breaker (sense **2**), prairie breaker, or clipper plow

***breakfast,** *n.* In combs.: (1) **breakfast bacon,** bacon especially prepared for use at breakfast; (2) **cap,** a small fancy cap worn by women at breakfast time; (3) **cereal,** a cereal specially prepared for serving at breakfast; (4) **food,** food, such as specially prepared cereals, served at breakfast; (5) **horn,** a horn blown as a summons to breakfast; (6) **house,** a house on a stage road where passengers may obtain breakfast; (7) **nook,** a nook or recess in a house or apartment provided with tables, chairs, etc., where breakfast may conveniently be served; (8) **station,** a place on a stage route where breakfast is obtained; (9) **tea,** a kind of tea used at breakfast, cf. **English breakfast tea.**

(1) **1884** Shepherd *Prairie Exp.* 220 A slightly better quality is sold in smaller joints, wrapped in yellow water-proof cloth, and styled breakfast bacon. **1942** Rawlings *C. Creek* 213 We call it white bacon to distinguish it from breakfast bacon, or side meat. — (2) **1863** G. Hamilton *Gala-Days* 28 What had I to do with breakfast-caps? . . . If I had wanted breakfast-caps, shouldn't I have asked for breakfast-caps? **1873** C. D. Warner *Backlog Studies* 71 The Mistress, in a pretty little breakfast-cap, is moving about the room with a feather-duster. — (3) **1902** *Amer. Federationist* Sep. 602 Gluten Grits and Barley Crystals, Perfect Breakfast and Dessert Health Cereals. **1945** *Reader's Digest* Aug. 32 He cites the instance in which two fires within a week wiped out enough stored grain to provide a year's supply of Breakfast cereal for an army of 600,000 men. — (4) **1898** *Ladies' Home Jrnl.* Feb. 28/1 (*advt.*), Ralston Health Club Breakfast Food. **1948** *Reader's Digest* Feb. 68/2 There, in 1893, a prepared breakfast food was sold publicly for the first time.

(5) **1845** Noah *Gleanings* 78 We returned to the house, warned by the shrill echo of the breakfast horn. **1884** Mark Twain *H. Finn* 361 He broke off there, because we heard the breakfast-horn blowing. — (6) **1867** Latham *Black & White* 118 At the 'breakfast house' on the line, a sort of farm house, two stations beyond Wilmington, the good-wife was willing to board and lodge us both for ten dollars . . . a-week. — (7) **1931** *K.C. Times* 9 Oct., They are at home snacking on a rickety but modern breakfast table, in a cute little room called the breakfast nook. **1945** *Chi. D. News* 1 Sep. 15/2 They got him thru to Canada six times, but they never got him thru a breakfast nook! — (8) **1872** Mark Twain *Roughing It* xii. 97 Just beyond the breakfast-station we overtook a Mormon emigrant train of thirty-three wagons. **1891** *Scribner's Mag.* X. 216 Gerard talked with him until they reached the breakfast station. — (9) **1865** Stowe *House & Home P.* 262 Breakfast-tea must be boiled!

b. *hell-bent for breakfast,* see **hell-bent.**

***breakfast,** *v. tr.* To supply with breakfast. — **1793** T. Jefferson *Writings* IV. 83 They will breakfast you. **1885** M. Pattison *Mem.* 50, I was breakfasted by Copleston. **1928** *Wisconsin Alumni Mag.* Dec. 86 The Wisconsin Alumni Association . . . breakfasted the football team.

***breaking,** *n.*

1. Land newly broken up by the plow.

1860 Greeley *Overland Journey* 10 Despite the hard times, Illinois is growing. There are new blocks in her cities, . . . new breakings on this or that edge of almost every prairie. **1883** *Pamphlet Jamestown* (Dakota) *Board of Tr.*, He earned enough besides, with what he had raised on his breaking, to keep himself.

2. In combs.: (1) **breaking exercises,** (see quot.); (2) **plow,** =**breaker 2;** (3) **team,** a team for drawing a breaking plow.

(1) **1881** H. W. Pierson *In the Brush* 253 These 'breaking' or parting exercises have afforded me the opportunity of hearing the grandest . . . African melodies to which I have ever listened. — (2) **1853** *Knickerb.* XLII. 593 The great 'breaking-plough,' with its dozen yoke of cattle, in the first place, goes tearing and groaning through the roots and grubs that lie twisted under it. **1948** *Sat. Ev. Post* 4 Dec. 35/1 His father turned away to yoke the oxen, hitch on the breaking plow and go into the meadow. — (3) **1839** J. Plumbe *Sk. Iowa* 40 This route would also answer well for persons . . . wishing to purchase their breaking-team, plow, &c. at the West. **1896** *Cong. Rec.* 5 May 4843/2, I do not brag of my voice. I came honestly by it driving breaking teams.

As the last term in **brush breaking, candy breaking, prairie breaking.**

***breaking-up,** *n.* **1.** =**break-up** (*a*). *Colloq.* **2.** Used attrib. to designate tools, etc., used in breaking land, as **breaking-up hoe, plow, team.**

(1) **1945** Botkin *My Burden* 86 Most the niggers I know, who had their marriage put in the book, did it after the breaking-up. — (2) **1773** Patten *Diary* 307, I went to the meadow to help the boys toward night and I Cut my left legg with the breaking up hoe. — **1781** *Ib.* 438 David and our 4 oxen and breaking up plow helped James Walker break up. **1830** *Cortland Observer* (Homer, N.Y.) 2 July 1/3 They also make . . . a large assortment of ploughs, heavy and light, . . . from the large breaking-up or greensward ploughs, to the small light corn ploughs, . . . and side hill ploughs. **1942** Cannon *Mountain* 100, I see MacLaughlin down t' the smithy gettin' some irons f'r his breakin'-up plow. — **1764** *N.H. Hist. Soc. Coll.* IX. 168, [I] mustered my breaking up team. **1868** Greeley *Autobiog.* 36 A breaking-up team, in my early boyhood, was made up of four yoke of oxen and a horse, where an acre per day was seldom ploughed.

***breast,** *n.*

1. (See quot.) *Rare.*

1868 S. E. Todd *Amer. Wheat Culturist* 24 In some sections of the country, a spikelet is better understood if it is spoken of as a *breast of wheat.*

2. In combs.: (1) **breast band,** a leather band or strap passing across a draft animal's breast; (2) **board,** on a steamboat "a board placed at the breast-beam—the beam where the quarter-deck or forecastle breaks" (R.); (3) **complaint,** consumption, tuberculosis, *colloq.;* (4) ***pin,** a brooch; (5) ***plate,** a metal plate or disk worn as an ornament on the breast, esp. by Indians; (6) **weed,** (see quot. 1889); (7) ***work,** (*a*) a breast-high partition, *rare,* (*b*) the breast of a fireplace, cf. **log-breastwork.**

(1) **1837** Irving *Capt. Bonneville* (1849) 135 Breast-band, saddle and crupper, are lavishly embroidered. **1912** London *Smoke Bellew* 160 The dogs sprang into the breast-bands, and the sled jerked abruptly ahead. — (2) **1883** Mark Twain *Life on Mississippi* xxiv. 264 (R.), Every detail of the pilot-house was familiar to me, with one exception—a large-mouthed tube under the breast-board. — (3) [**1835** in Bassett *South. Plant.* 44 Your Boy Hardy is not able to go he has had a breast complaint about five months, has a very violent cough.] **1837** Sherwood *Gaz. Georgia* (ed. 3) 82 Dyspepsy carries off some; consumption, or breast complaint, as it is termed, affects some persons. **1838** in Bassett *South. Plant.* 115, I had good atten(tion) paid to her I call in and other phisian to Loosa she died with the breast complaint. — (4) **1835** N. P. Willis *Pencillings* (1942) 515 No shirt, but a very smart black glass breast-pin, holding together the stringy ends of his cravat. **1942** Warnick *Dialect Garrett Co., Md.* 4 Breast-pin, n., brooch.

(5) **1765** Timberlake *Memoirs* 50 They [*sc.* Cherokees] that can afford it wear a collar of wampum, a silver breast-plate, and bracelets on their arms and wrists. **1807** *Ann. 10th Congress* 1 Sess. I. 458 He made me a present of a silver breastplate. *Ib.* 639 Mr. Owens . . . presented me with a very handsome breastplate. — (6) **1829** Eaton *Botany* (ed. 5) 509 Lizard's tail, breastweed. . . . Rare in New York east of Cayuga Lake—abundant west of it. **1889** *Cent.* 672 Breast-weed [is] a name given to the lizard's-tail of the United States . . . from its use as a remedy in mammary inflammation. — (7) (*a*) **1747** *Md. Hist. Reg.* IX. 52 [The Vestrymen] ordered that a Breast-Work be erected in the Chapel of this Parish. (*b*) **1806** *Mass. Spy* 23 July (Th.), On the breastwork over the fire-place was the distinct impression of a bloody hand. **1824** *N.H. Hist. Soc. Coll.* I. 249 At the same instant the breast work and chimney gave way.

As the last term in **bay, black, broken, muddy, red breast.**

breasting,** *n.* A method of hunting deer in which the hunters ride abreast and shoot from horseback. — *a1889** G. B. Grinnell *Gun & Rod* 152 (*Cent.*), Breasting is employed where the deer make their home in very high grass, such as is to be found on some of the prairies in the South-west.

Breckite ˈbrɛkaɪt, *n.* A political follower of John C. Breckenridge (1821–75), Vice-President of the U.S. (1857–61). *Obs.* — **1860** *Charleston* (S.C.) *Mercury* 24 Nov. 4/2, I am a Breckite; but since the reception of the news of Lincoln's election, not only the friends of Breckenridge, but of Bell and Douglas here, are with you in secession, heart and hand.

***bred,** *n.* As the last term in **eastern bred, full bred, pure bred.**

***breech,** *n. attrib.* Designating a (1) **cloth,** (2) **clout,** (3) **piece,** a cloth worn as a loin cloth, usu. by Indians.

(1) **1793** B. Lincoln in *Mass. H.S. Coll.* 3 Ser. V. 152 They all have Indian stockings, made of woollen cloth; the males a breech cloth and the females a woollen petticoat. **1890** *Harper's Mag.* April 730 Stripped to their breech-cloths, . . . the Indian scouts . . . surrounded and guarded the sullen renegade guide. **1946** *Nat. Geog. Mag.* Jan. 15 Once Paiutes wore only breechcloths in summer and buckskin suits

Breechclout, flap, or gee of a type used by the Dakota Indians

with rabbitskin blankets in winter. — (2) **1757** Putnam *Memoirs* (1903) 12 Nothing to cover us from the Natts & Musketoes but a Shirt and Breech-Clout. **1889** *Cent. Mag.* April 908/2 Lieutenant Jim only needed breech-clout and long hair in order to draw rations at the agency. **1946** *This Week Mag.* 17 Aug. 5/2 Tuxedos and ties replace breachclouts and moccasins. — (3) **1846** Cooper *Redskins* xx, Habitually he wore his Indian vestments; the leggings, moccasins, breech-piece, blanket or calico shirt, according to the season.

***breeches,** *n. pl.* As the last term in **copperas, crocus, Dutchman's, foot, Indian, leather, little boys' breeches.**

breeches flower. =**Dutchman's breeches.** — **1814** Pursh *Flora Amer.* II. 462 *Corydalis Cucullaria.* . . . This singularly constructed flower is known among the inhabitants by the name of Breeches-flower or Yellow-breeches. **1893** *Amer. Folk-Lore* VI. 137 *Dicentra cucullaria,* Little boy's breeches. Central Iowa. Breeches flower. N.Y.

***breeching,** *n.* A breechcloth *q.v. Rare.* — **1842** *Amer. Pioneer* I. 47 On going to bed the men [*sc.* Indians] pull off all but their breeching, and the women all but their shrouds.

***breed,** *n.* A person of mixed racial descent, esp. one of Indian and white blood. Also transf. and attrib. Cf. **half breed.**

1889 Mark Twain *Connecticut Yankee* xxiii. 288 (R.), All the different breeds of rockets. **1892** *Harper's Mag.* Feb. 387/2 One-quarter of the number of 'breeds' could read and write. **1892** *Outing* Jan. 287/1 With him dwelt a tall, wiry 'Breed' hunter, called Dave, or 'Injun Dave,' according to taste. **1947** *Reader's Digest* June 143/2 It was Lola, the 'breed wife of one of the trappers.

As the last term in **buffalo, Gore, half, Holderness, mixed, Morgan, otter breed.**

***breeder,** *n.* As the last term in **flea breeder, grade breeder, slave breeder.**

***breeding,** *n.* **1.** *W.* Designating a **ranch** or **range** where cattle are bred. **2.** *S.* **breeding woman,** a slave woman who bears children. *Obs.*

(1) **1890** *Stock Grower* 1 Feb. 11/2 Breeding range, on the Pecos River, New Mexico. **1923** Evarts *Tumbleweeds* 87 In a breeding-ranch country the herd would have been worked on the spot. — (2) **1851** *De Bow's Review* X. 326 A breeding woman gets too heavy to go to the field. **1856** Olmsted *Slave States* 55 A breeding woman is worth from one-sixth to one-fourth more than one that does not breed.

As the last term in **fox breeding, line breeding, slave breeding.**

***breeze,** *n.* As the last term in **ash breeze, horn breeze.** For *a breeze of luck* see ***luck.**

***breeze,** *v. intr.* To move or proceed briskly. *Colloq.* — **1907** *Chi. Ev. Post* 4 May 9 He breezed through the Louvre at such a pace that he broke all the rapid sightseeing records. **1948** *Dly. Ardmoreite* (Ardmore, Okla.) 3 May 6/3 Charley Deal . . . had set the Indians down with two hits and apparently was breezing along to victory with a six run working margin.

breezeway ˈbrizˌwe, *n.* (See quots.) Also attrib. Cf. **dogtrot.**

1931 K. N. Burt *Man's Own Country* 39 A small log building attached to the end of his own ranch-house by means of what is known to the Far West as a breeze-way. This construction is a floored and roofed-over passage, open at the sides. It is used for the protection of buckets of water, washtubs, firewood, stray tools, fishing-tackle, guns, skiis, and occasionally for a clothesline. **1944** *D.N.* Nov. 8 *dog-trot,* also called *breeze-way:* n. A wide, floored passageway running between two halves of a house, built, except for a common roof and floor level as two separate structures. **1948** *Household* March 14/1 The breezeway porch is an extension of the main roof.

brer brə, *n.* Also **br'er.** *proclitic.* An illiterate Negro pronunciation of "brother." *Colloq.*

1880 Harris *U. Remus* (1884) 51 Brer Rabbit kep' on gainin', en bimeby he dart in a brier-patch. **1890** *Harper's Mag.* Feb. 440/1 If you read what this author says about Brer Albucasis. **1948** *Range Riders Western* May 84/1 Ole Br'er Jack Rabbit don't like Apaches anymore'n what we do.

***Brethren,** *n. pl.* A German-American religious sect, also known as German Baptists and Dunkers. Also attrib.

1822 *Ann. 17th Congress* 1 Sess. I. 230 The Brethren (for by that name they began to be known,) established themselves in a village [50 miles west of Hartford, Conn.]. **1844** Rupp *Relig. Denominations* 697 The Brethren Church is . . . comparatively small, owing to the fact, that until within twenty years, its religious exercises have all been conducted in the German language. **1884** *Schaff's Relig. Encycl.* III. 2401/2 The name originally adopted by themselves [i.e., the Dunkers], and . . . now generally used, is simply 'The Brethren'; but they frequently use the term 'German Baptists,' even in their official documents.

b. *Brethren in Christ,* (see quot. and cf. **River Brethren**).

1938 Hark *Hex Marks Spot* 101 The River Brethren . . . are also called Brethren in Christ.

As the last term in **Advent, red, River, Southern, United Brethren.**

***brevet,** *n.* **1. brevet Democrat,** a derisive term for a Democrat who had served as an officer in the Confederate Army. **2. brevet-hell,** (see quot.). **3.** *children by brevet,* "suppositious or illegitimate children. A popular jest during and after the Civil War" (R.). All *obs.*

(1) **1884** *Boston Jrnl.* 18 Sep., The brevet Democrats catch the spirit of pro-slavery Bourbonism naturally. — (2) **1871** De Vere 284 The 'boys,' with a witty turn of the military significance of the word, were in the habit of terming a battle a brevet-hell. — (3) **1883** Mark Twain *Life on Mississippi* i. 27 (R.), Lax court morals and the absurd chivalry business were in full feather . . . religion was the passion of the ladies, and the classifying their offspring into children of full rank and children by brevet their pastime.

***Brewer,** *n.* [T. M. *Brewer* (1814–80), Amer. ornithologist.] **1. Brewer's blackbird,** a handsome blackbird found chiefly in western North America. **2. Brewer's sparrow,** the field sparrow, *Spizella pusilla.*

(1) **1858** Baird *Birds Pacific R.R.* 552. **1946** Stanwell-Fletcher *Driftwood Valley* 172 There has been a pair of Brewer's blackbirds, also new to us, but easy to identify. — (2) **1858** Baird *Birds Pacific R.R.* 475 *Spizella Breweri,* . . . Brewer's Sparrow. **1945** *Auk* July 392 Brewer's Sparrows occur in some numbers in spring and fall through the Transition Zone.

***Brewster,** *n.*

1. A hat of a make so designated. *Obs.*

1840 Kennedy *Quodlibet* 110 William was smoothing the nap of his glossy black Brewster, with a brush as soft as silk.

2. *attrib.* (1) Designating vehicles in some way associated with one J. B. Brewster, *obs.;* (2) **Brewster chair,** (see quot. 1937), [so named after Wm. Brewster (1566–1644), the Elder of the Pilgrim church, who is said to have owned such a chair].

(1) **1884** *N.Y. Herald* 27 Oct. 1/2 J. B. Brewster sidebar top buggy, Sleigh, sets of . . . Harness. *Ib.,* Two Brewster Carriages, sets of Harness, Blankets, Robes. — (2) **1924** Nutting *Furniture Pilgrim Cent.* 294 It used to be presumed that the Brewster and Carver chairs of Plymouth were brought over in the Mayflower. **1937** Langdon *Everyday Things* 32 From Plymouth Colony mostly there has come a type of chair, or two similar types of chair which are indeed instinct with dignity and a certain formality but not so repellent in their magnificence. These are the Carver Chair and the Brewster Chair. . . . The main difference between the two types is that the Carver Chair is much the simpler, having for example only 3 spindles, in the

back, while the Brewster Chair has many,—8 in the back, 12 on each side, above and below the seat, and 4 more in front, below the seat.

Brewsterite ˈbrustəˌraɪt, *n.* A follower of James C. Brewster, a dissenting Mormon, who with others formed a new church in 1849. *Obs.* — **1851** *Ore. Statesman* 23 Dec. 1/5 The Brewsterites, new lights, from Ill., now settled at Socorro, New Mexico. **1870** BEADLE *Utah* 124 Most of the other aspirants took off various sects, known in the Brighamite church as . . . 'Brewsterites,' 'Cutlerites,' 'Gatherers,' etc.

Brewster chair, 17th century

***brick,** *n.*

1. A brick house.

1845 *Cincinnati Misc.* 11 The tearing down of Frames to make way for Bricks, and the great excess of new bricks over new frame buildings, will increase the disparity between the two. **1895** SULLIVAN *Tenement Tales* 45 On a certain corner in a West Side tenement neighborhood stands a cheaply constructed five-story brick. **1948** *N.Y. Post* 2 May 36/1 (*advt.*), 3-family brick, detached, oil, stall showers, finished basement, double garages.

2. In combs.: (1) **brick apartment,** an apartment house of brick construction; (2) **block,** a large house or building unit made of brick, cf. **block, *n.* 2. b;** (3) **pond,** a pond in connection with a brickyard; (4) **stove,** a stove made of bricks or tiles, *rare;* (5) **top,** a shock-head of red hair, also **brick-topped,** *a., colloq.;* (6) ***wall,** designating a snake, *rare;* (7) **wood,** firewood for a brick kiln, *rare;* (8) **yard,** a place where bricks are made, a brickfield, also in nonce use **brickyardy,** *a.*

(1) **1944** *Chi. Tribune* 1 March 25/3, 2 Story Brick Apt. . . . $12,600. — (2) **1899** *Caddo* (Okla.) *Herald* 5 May 3/2 The new brick block on Buffalo street belonging to W. J. Moon is going up fast. — (3) [**1731** see **brickyard.**] **1811** *Mass. Spy* 9 Jan. 3/3 Two boys . . . were drowned in a brick pond in the vicinity of the city [=Philadelphia]. **1850** *Wilmington* (N.C.) *Commercial* 5 Sep. 2/3 (Th. Supp.), Water brought from the neighbouring brick-ponds [at Philadelphia] in buckets. — (4) **1810** in *Essex Antiq.* I. (1897) 185 The Subscriber last winter invented a *brick stove* for the purpose of warming dwelling-houses, churches, compting rooms, &c.

(5) **1856** M. THOMPSON *Elephant Club* 163 A head of hair which the youth of America are accustomed to designate as a 'brick-top.' **1912** *D.N.* III. 572 Brick-topped, *adj.* Red-headed. — (6) **1851** *De Bow's Review* XI. 54 *Thunder* and *Lightning* or *Brick Wall Snake*—Small, harmless. — (7) **1788** WASHINGTON *Diaries* III. 295 The Negro Men were employed in cutting Rail stuff and Brick Wood. — (8) **1731** *Essex Inst. Coll.* XLII. 229 The water here . . . is as thick of mudd & Clay as in the Pond of a Brick yard. **1871** *Rep. Indian Affairs* (1872) 531, I have had a brick-yard made, and a kiln of one hundred thousand is ready to burn. **1897** MARK TWAIN *Following the Equator* xlix. 460 (R.), A plain, perfectly flat, dust-colored, and brickyardy, stretching limitlessly away in the dim gray light.

b. In slang and colloq. phrases: (1) *like a thousand of brick*, and variants, most violently or vigorously; (2) *to feel like bricks*, to feel wretched or miserable, *rare;* (3) *to have a brick in one's hat*, and variants, (*to be*) *tight as a brick*, to be intoxicated or tipsy.

(1) **1836** HILL *Yankee Stories* 32 (We.), If I don't be into him with a thousand of brick. **1841** *N.O. Picayune* 16 Mar. 2/2 After they had . . . rounded the first turn pretty much in a heap like a thousand of brick, Marshal led off and sustained this position for the first half mile. **1896** H. FREDERIC *Damnation of T. Ware* 158 You've got to be mighty particular in such matters, you know, or you'll have the trustees down on you like a 'thousand of bricks.' **1945** *This Week Mag.* 21 April 15/2 Well, I found the cache all right and Joe fell like a ton of bricks. — (2) **1846** *Spirit of Times* (N.Y.) 11 July 232/1, I have been hard at work all day—I feel like bricks—had no supper. — (3) **1846** DURIVAGE *Stray Subjects* 61 A 'shocking bad 'un' was his hat, and matted was his hair. He wore a 'brick' within that hat. **1847** *Knickerb.* XXIX. 569 A youth who came home one night, prepared 'to build,' having 'a brick in his hat.' **1894** MARK TWAIN *Those Twins* (Intro.), Her half had never drunk a drop in his life, and, although tight as a brick three days in the week, was wholly innocent of blame.

As the last term in **face, front, gold, Kansas, mud, Nebraska, Philadelphia, red, silver, wine brick.**

brickbat ˈbrɪkˌbæt, *v. tr.* To hurl brickbats at (a house, person, etc.). Also fig.

1833 *Ev. & Morning Star* (Kirtland, Ohio) July 114/1 About the middle of July last, yea, in fact previous, they commenced brickbatting our houses again. **1866** in EASTERBY *S.C. Rice Plant.* (1945) 222 It is common to brick bat white people in the street at night. **1947** *Time* 27 Jan. 43/1 Perennially brickbatted Sculptor Epstein got another lump on the head.

***bricky,** *a.* Intoxicated, having "a brick in one's hat." *Slang.* — **1852** *S.F. Picayune* 14 Apr. 2/4 Peter Smith was taken up for being a bit 'bricky.'

***bridal,** *n.* In combs.: (1) ***bridal chamber,** (see quots.), *obs.;* (2) **rose,** (see quot. 1861); (3) **suite,** a hotel suite fitted up in an especially attractive or luxurious manner; (4) **tour,** a journey taken for pleasure by a newly married couple.

(1) **1853** A. BUNN *Old Eng. & New Eng.* 51 A room, called a bridal-chamber (originally introduced, we understood, in the huge steamboats of the various rivers,) has been fitted up in the most luxurious and fascinating manner at the aforesaid 'St. Nicholas.' **1860** HANCOCK *Five Years* 189 This is the fitting up, in hotels and steamboats, of what are called 'bridal chambers'; apartments furnished and decorated in a style of the most profuse and extravagant luxury. **1871** DE VERE 356 It is the same unfortunate tendency which makes him adorn his magnificent steamers with that outrage on decency, *Bridal Chambers.* — (2) **1832** HALE *Flora* 139. **1861** WOOD *Botany* 240 Bridal rose. . . . A delicate house plant, with snow white double flowers. Native of Mauritius. **1899** *Animal & Plant Lore* 107 When the 'bridal rose' blossoms, there will follow a death in the family. Massachusetts. — (3) **1938** ASBURY *Sucker's Prog.* 265 The bridal suite was called 'Paradise,' while drunken guests were assigned to a meagerly furnished chamber known as 'Hell.' — (4) *a***1855** WITCHER *Widow Bedott* 185 (We.), Bridal tewer. **1856** M. J. HOLMES *Homestead on H.*, Gilberts v, The next morning Mr. and Mrs. Sherwood departed on their bridal tour. **1880** MARK TWAIN *Tramp Abroad* xxxv. 388 She was newly married, and was on her bridal tour.

***bride,** *n.*

1. bride perch, (see quots.).

1819 RAFINESQUE in *Western Rev.* I. 375 Calliurus. Painted Tail. Callicure. . . . Vulgar names, painted-tail or bride-perch. **1820** *Ib.* II. 54 Ohio Red-eye, *Aplocentrus calliops*, . . . lives in the lower parts of the Ohio, in Green river, &c. Vulgar names Red-eyes, Bride perch, Batchelor's pearch, Green bass, &c. **1947** DALRYMPLE *Panfish* 84 Here, my friend, are the various names by which you would address that little gamester, the Crappie, depending on where you happened to be at the moment: . . . Bride Perch, . . . Grass Bass, . . . Rockfish.

2. *bride's room, =bridal chamber. *Obs.*

1855 BESTE *Wabash* I. 148, I found on board the steamer, two or three separate rooms on deck with full sized beds in them; . . . They called them Bride's rooms.

As the last term in **picture bride.**

***bridge,** *n.*

1. (See quots. and cf. **corduroy bridge.**) *Obs.*

1839 MRS. KIRKLAND *New Home* (1840) ii. 19 The 'beautiful bridge,' a newly-laid causeway of large round logs. *Ib.* vii. 40 A marsh which we were crossing by the usual bridge of poles, or *corduroy* as it is here termed.

2. In combs.: (1) **bridge cases,** instances of the bends or caisson disease observed during the building of the St. Louis bridge across the Mississippi River about 1875, *obs.;* (2) **company,** a company engaged in building bridges; (3) **jumper,** one who makes sensational leaps from bridges or other high places, *obs.;* (4) **lamp,** a light, movable floor lamp, usu. with an adjustable arm, and esp. suitable for use at or near a bridge table; (5) **perch,** a local name for the crappie; (6) **pewee,** the phoebe bird,

Sayornis phoebe; (7) **spectacles,** (see quot. 1830); (8) **tender,** one who has charge of a drawbridge.

(1) **1881** C. M. Woodward *Hist. St. Louis Bridge* 258 The 'Bridge cases' excited great interest and discussion in medical and scientific circles. — (2) **1817** *Niles' Reg.* XII. 142/1 Among the laws passed were 24 for incorporating turnpike and bridge companies. **1837** Peck *New Guide* 205 The general revenue is obtained from moderate taxes . . . collected from insurance, bank and bridge companies [etc.]. — (3) **1887** *Courier-Journal* 19 Feb. 4/5 Lawrence Donovan, the Brooklyn bridge-jumper, leaped into the Schuylkill river. — (4) **1929** *Sears Cat.* Spring 771 (*caption*), Neat Bridge Lamp. **1945** Maxwell *Folded Leaf* 19 Mrs. Latham reached up and turned on the bridge lamp at her elbow.

(5) **1888** Goode *Amer. Fishes* 71 *Pomoxys annularis* . . . has other names of local application as 'Tin Mouth,' 'Bridge Perch.' **1947** Dalrymple *Panfish* 84 [Synonyms:] Bridge Perch, Calico, . . . Sand Perch, Shad. — (6) **1867** *Amer. Naturalist* I. 54 Ornithological Calendar for March—Meadow Larks, Bridge Pewees or Phoebes, [arrive]. **1917** *Birds of Amer.* II. 199 The bird . . . builds occasionally . . . on a beam under a bridge. From the last mentioned site the bird is often called the 'Bridge Pewee,' though the true Pewees are of a different species. — (7) **1830** J. F. Watson *Philadelphia* 180 In her early years the only spectacles she ever saw were called 'bridge spectacles,' without any side supporters, and held on the nose solely by nipping the bridge of the nose. **1845** Judd *Margaret* I. xiv. 103 She provided him with a pair of broad horn-bowed bridge spectacles. — (8) **1853** A. Bunn *Old Eng. & New Eng.* 149 The draw was opened by the bridge-tender for the passage of the steam-boat. **1887** *Cent. Mag.* Aug. 495/1 The bridge-tender, called in for consultation, thought the *Cowles* 'a little mite' longer than that laker.

As the last term in **benefit, chip, corduroy, county, covered, dry, farm, ferry, floating, grapevine, ground, hanging, ice, Indian, Kissing, log, low, natural, pole, raccoon, raft, slab, slough, trail bridge.**

∗**bridge,** *v.* **a.** *tr.* (See quot.) *Obs.* **b.** To tide over, carry through. *Colloq.* **c.** *intr.* To arch the recumbent body.

(a) **1809** E. A. Kendall *Travels* I. 235 In the lowlands are some marshy tracts; but, here, a sufficient, though not very agreeable road, is formed by causeys of logs; or, in the language of the country, it is *bridged*. — (b) **1931** *Randolph Enterprise* (Elkins, W. Va.) 19 March 3/3 We wish to thank Mr. C. L. Armentrout as he has let several have a load of hay to bridge them over till grass comes. — (c) **1913** Mulford *Coming of Cassidy* i. 21 The under man . . . bridged so suddenly as to throw the hunter off him. *Ib.* iii. 58 Trying in vain to bridge on his head and heels.

∗**bridle,** *n.* In combs.: (1) **bridle leather,** leather suitable for making bridles; (2) **pin,** a pin or peg in a bridle rack to facilitate hitching; (3) **post,** a hitching post; (4) **rack,** a hitching bar; (5) **track,** a bridle path; (6) **wisdom,** the quality of being **bridle-wise** (*b*); (7) **wise,** (*a*) *adv.* the long way, (*b*) *adj.* (see quot. 1889), also transf.

(1) **1760** in Chalkley *Scotch-Irish Settlement Va.* III. 63, 19 hides tanned leather, 16 sides soal leather, 11 sides bridle leather. **1874** Long *Wild-Fowl* 163 A narrow strip of bridle-leather about two feet in length. — (2) **1824** Singleton *Letters* 90 There is commonly in the front yard a horse-rack, with bridle pins over head for a dozen of steeds. — (3) **1866** Whittier *Snowbound* line 60 The bridle-post an old man sat With loose-flung coat and high cocked hat. — (4) **1832** Kennedy *Swallow Barn* I. 21 A bridle-rack stands on the outer side of the gate.

(5) **1837** W. Jenkins *Ohio Gaz.* 321 The country was yet a wilderness, with no other ingress than by Indian trails, and bridle tracks opened by themselves. **1885** *Cent. Mag.* Oct. 917 Wheelways ample, smooth, clean, a springy bridle-track adjoining the road [etc.] . . . — these are the essential physical features of a grand promenade. — (6) **1895** *Outing* XXVI. 477/1 Not that in the heat of play one relies upon this bridle-wisdom [of a polo-pony]. — (7) (*a*) **1830** *Ky. Reporter* 17 Feb., You had better cut it bridlewise. **1867** De Voe *Market Ass't* 71 'Shall I cut this loin of mutton saddle-wise?' 'No,' said his friend. 'Cut it bridle-wise, for then we may have a chance to get a *bit* in our mouths.' (*b*) **1840** *N.O. Picayune* 6 Oct. 2 Phrases in use among the 'natives' [of Ill.]: . . . The horse was not fit for a lady to ride; he was not *bridle wise*. **1889** *Cent.*, *Bridle-wise*, trained to obey the bridle. Applied to a horse which is guided by pressure of the bridle against his neck instead of by pulling on the bit. **1898** H. S. Canfield *Maid of Frontier* 100 Just like a woman. You can't never make 'em bridle-wise.

As the last term in **blind bridle, grapevine bridle.**

bridled tern. A species of tern, *Sterna anaethetus melanoptera*, found in the southern part of the U.S. — **1869** *Amer. Naturalist* III. 340 When Dr. Gambel found out that it was different from both these species, he bestowed upon it the title of the Bridled Tern (*S. frenata*). **1891** *Cent.* 5937/2 Some middle-sized terns with dark upper parts, widely distributed in tropical and warm temperate regions, are the subgenus *Haliplana*, as the common sooty and bridled terns.

brieflet ˈbriflɪt, *n.* A brief news item. — **1882** *Boston Transcript* 18 Jan. 1/3 (*heading*), Brieflets. **1890** *Register* (Whitewater, Wis.) 12 June, (*heading*), Wisconsin Brieflets. Interesting Items Gathered from various Sources.

∗**brier,** *n.* Also **briar.** In combs.: (1) **brier hook,** a kind of reaping hook for cutting briers, also transf.; (2) **patch,** a piece of ground overgrown with briers; (3) **scythe,** a scythe for cutting briers.

(1) **1819** *Plough Boy* I. 130 The common red pea . . . should be cut with a small briar-hook. **1843** Carlton *New Purchase* II. xxxvii. 42 With a genuine far-east barber's flourish, [I] touched the vile old briar-hook to my cheek. — (2) **1838** B. Drake *Queen City Tales* 124 (We.), This new inroad upon his favorite brier-patch. **1948** *Richmond* (Va.) *News Leader* 6 May 17/2 Sammy Jay found Peter Rabbit dozing under his favorite bramble bush in the dear Old Brier Patch. — (3) **1813** Warder *Hedges & Evergreens* 181 The best method of cutting the tops off is to use a mowing-machine or briar-scythe. **1876** *Ill. Dept. Agric. Trans.* XIII. 301 The weeds are kept down with the hoe or briar scythe.

As the last term in **bamboo, bull, cat, China, green, horse, Indian, Mohawk, sand, saw, sensitive brier.**

brig brɪg, *n.* [Origin unknown.] A place for the confinement of prisoners, orig. on board a vessel; a nautical or military prison. See also **clipper brig.**

1852 *Knickerb.* XXXIX. 404 In less than a minute I was in the 'brig,' in double irons. *Ib.*, They call the place where prisoners are confined, 'the brig.' **1921** R. D. Paine *Comr. Rolling Ocean* 62 The master-at-arms stowed them for safe-keeping in a small building with barred windows which he called the brig. **1948** Chaplin *Wobbly* 272 The comparatively minor offense of being A.W.O.L. on account of a woman . . . called for a night in the brig.

∗**brigade,** *n.* [In **2.** f. F.]

1. A train of wagons or railroad cars. Now *hist.*

1780 *Md. Hist. Reg.* IX. 242 This is to inform your Excellency that we have sent of to Brigades of waggons loaded with flour. **1830** *Baltimore Amer.* 24 May, A brigade of cars will run three times a day each way from Baltimore to Ellicott's Mills—Damage 25 cents. **1887** George *40 Years on Rail* 31 Freight cars in the early days were called 'burthen cars' and trains were known as 'brigades.' **1944** *Reader's Digest* August 106 So Susan joined the other passengers outside, staring curiously at the train, which consisted of a locomotive and a 'brigade' of six cars.

2. (See quots.) Now *hist.*

1793 in Gates *Fur Traders* 68 Mr Frobisher wishing to keep Faignan for the last or June Brigade, say Canoes, gave the Brigade in charge to Francois Huneau. . . . A Brigade of canoes in the Grand River is generally four. **1860** *Harper's Mag.* Oct. 587/2 The hunter . . . never goes alone. He and his friends and neighbors make up a brigade—large or small, it is called a brigade. **1944** Nute *Lake Superior* 43 In May an expedition would set out from Montreal—several canoes organized into a 'brigade.'

As the last term in **brass button, dinner pail, European, Stone-wall brigade.**

∗**brigade,** *v.* **1.** *tr.* To group (wagons) into a brigade. *Obs.* **2.** To command in a military brigade. *Rare.* — (1) **1781** *Cal. Virginia St. P.* I. 594 You will therefore lose no time in sending them [=Public Wagons] to the Army, properly brigaded, with good Conductors and drivers. — (2) **1864** Nichols *Amer. Life* II. 156, I'll be d——d if I will be brigaded by a man who kept a —— in Washington, and killed his best customer.

∗**brigadier,** *n.* (*cap.*) =**Southern Brigadier.** *Obs.* Cf. **Confederate, rebel brigadier.** — **1879** *Chi. Tribune* 29 Jan. 4/1 In the House the Brigadiers who wore the gray are spoiling for a chance to get the floor for an extended onslaught on Gen. Bragg, of Wisconsin. **1880** *Chi. Inter-Ocean* 4 May, We doubt very much whether the class known as 'Brigadiers' of the South are any more patriotic or loyal than they were four years ago.

∗**Brigham,** *n. attrib.* Designating a plant of the genus *Ephedra*, widely distributed in the West, so called in allusion to Brigham Young (1801–77), well-known Mormon leader. — **1915** Wooton & Standley *Flora N. Mex.* 38 The shrubs are variously known as 'popotillo,' 'cañatillo,' 'Mormon tea,' and 'Brigham Young weed,' as also by several other names. **1931** Dayton *Western Browse Plants* 12 All the species are known also as Mormon-tea, canatillo, Brigham tea. **1945** McAtee *Nomina Abitera* 7 Such medication and popular opinion as to those in need of it are indicated in the vernacular names: Brigham's tea, . . . Brigham Young weed, . . . clapweed, . . . teamster's tea.

Brighamite ˈbrɪgəmˌaɪt, *n.* A follower or adherent of the Mormon leader Brigham Young. Also attrib. *Obs.*

1854 Simms *Southward Ho!* 181 He was driving . . . with one of his wives—and, to do him justice, we must assure the reader that, unlike our modern Brighamites, he had but one at a time. **1878** Beadle *Western Wilds* 342 The cannon and long-range rifles of the Brighamite militia completely raked the interior of the camp. **1890** *Cong. Rec.* 2 April 2933/1 The Mormons are divided into two classes, known as Josephites and Brighamites. . . . It is the . . . Brighamites alone who believe in bigamy and in polygamy.

* **bright,** *a.* and *adv.*

1. Denoting tobacco of a light shade or color. Cf. **kitefoot tobacco.**

1765 in *Amer. Hist. Rev.* XXVII. 71 Saw some of the bright coloured tobaco which sels So Dear in foreign markets. it is of a light yelow Coulour. . . . the Inhabitants call it bright tobacco. **1822** *Missouri Intell.* 17 Dec. 1/3 None but the brightest tobacco is now worth marketing. **1941** Daniels *Tar Heels* 106 The Slade brothers, Eli and Elisha, accidentally produced bright leaf tobacco in 1852.

2. Used with reference to the complexion of mulattoes.

1831 *Georgian* (Savannah) 5 April 3/3 For sale, a bright Mulatto Man. **1888** C. D. Warner *On Horseback* 116 Mary, the 'bright' woman (this is the universal designation of the light mulatto), was a pleasing but bold yellow girl. **1911** Harrison *Queed* 211 Now a young bright-skin negro wishes to marry Laura.

3. bright-work, metal fixtures on a ship that are kept bright by polishing.

1841 *S. Lit. Messenger* VII. 769/2 It was a part of my duty, when I had to watch, to superintend the cleaning of the 'bright work.' **1911** Vance *Cynthia* 123 [The dining-saloon] was also dingy . . . , the lustre of its brightwork dulled, its white paint tarnished.

4. *bright and early,* very early in the morning. *Colloq.*

1837 Irving *Bonneville* II. ii. 17 Captain Bonneville and his three companions set out, bright and early, to rejoin the main party. **1917** McCutcheon *Green Fancy* 50 All three promised to be up bright and early in the morning to speed him on his way.

brilliantine ˈbrɪljənˌtin, *n.* [F. *brillantine.*]

1. A superior kind of glossy dress fabric made of mohair and cotton.

1873 Mrs. Whitney *Other Girls* iii. 15 Nobody really looked down to see that the underskirt was the identical black brilliantine that had done service all the spring. **1908** *Sears Cat.* (ed. 118) 898 White mohair brilliantine, natural finished fabric. **1948** *American Fabrics* No. V. 143/1 Brilliantine: Cloth in which a birdseye pattern is woven into the material on the Jacquard loom.

2. (See quot. 1905.)

1884 *Harper's Mag.* Oct. 706/1 The same devotion to starch and brilliantine. **1905** *Sears Cat.* (ed. 115) 391 Brilliantine, an imported French hair oil for making the hair soft and glossy. **1948** *Miss America* June 18/1 His usually shaggy mop of hair was slicked against his scalp with brilliantine.

* **brim,** *n.* The long-eared sunfish, *Xenotis megalotis,* found in the central and southern parts of the U.S.

1795 Scott *U.S. Gazeteer* Hv, [The rivers of Georgia] are stored with a great variety of fish, as rock, mullet . . . catfish, white, brim, and sturgeon. **1887** *Harper's Mag.* July 270/1 If they could slip away . . . there would be a diminished number of 'brim' and 'goggle-eye,' in the ditch. **1947** Dalrymple *Panfish* 4, I recalled the South Carolina gentleman . . . who suddenly and haughtily withdrew from the conversation, because I had called his 'Brim' a Sunfish.

* **brimstone,** *n.*

1. = **glass snake.** *Rare.*

1709 Lawson *Carolina* 134 The Brimstone is so call'd, I believe, because it is almost of a Brimstone Colour.

2. In allusive and slang uses (see quots.). *Obs.*

1823 in Mrs. Mathews *Memoirs of Charles Mathews* (1839) III. 39 By the by, they call the nigger meetings 'Black Brimstone Churches.' **1832** Paulding *Westward Ho!* I. 121 Hold your tongue, you beauty, or you shall smell brimstone through a nail hole. **1843** Uncle Sam *Peculiarities* I. 161 I'm all brimstone, and drive the roughest rocking-horse in any three of these United States. **1856** P. Cartwright *Autobiog.* 202, [I] shook my brimstone wallet over him [=I threatened him with hell] till he was sick and tired of it. **1886** Glazier *Amer. Cities* 55 It [i.e., Park Street Church, Boston, Mass.] used to be known as 'brimstone corner.'

brimstone ˈbrɪmˌston, *v.* [f. the noun.] *tr.* To smoke or kill (bees) with brimstone. — **1868** *Rep. Comm. Agric.* (1869) 275 The yield is principally derived from hives that are 'brimstoned' in the fall, or from old combs that are unfit for use. **1880** *Harper's Mag.* Oct. 777/1 This fearless being, however, knew only one way to 'take up the honey,' viz., to brimstone the bees, killing every one.

* **brindle,** *n.* **1.** (See quot.) *Rare.* **2. Brindle-tail,** used attrib. with **party,** etc., to designate a faction of the Republican party in Arkansas about 1871.

(1) **1834** Pike *Sketches* 27, I tumbled old brindle [his gun] to the ground . . . my fingers were so froze. — (2) **1871** *Cong. Globe* 7 Jan. 350/1 The 'Brindle-tail party,' as it is called, . . . opposed Governor Clayton's usurpations of power. *Ib.*, The Lieutenant-Governor . . . still remains in the Republican party, but belongs to the 'Brindle-tail' wing of that party. **1872** *Ib.* 9 Feb. 935/2 In the township of Ashley, more than in any other . . . did the 'Brindle-tail' mob hold high carnival.

* **bring,** *v.*

1. *tr.* To produce (curd, butter) from milk.

1855 *Mich. Agric. Soc. Trans.* VI. 183 The milk for cheese is made into curd . . . by adding sufficient rennet to 'bring' it in about fifteen minutes. **1881** Rittenhouse *Maud* 8, I got up and churned awhile (Corinne had almost brought the butter before I began) and then worked it.

2. In phrases: (1) * *To bring round,* to occupy, to while away; (2) * *to bring to,* (see quot. 1814); (3) * *to bring in,* (*a*) of a batter in baseball, to enable, with a hit, a runner or runners to score, also *to bring home,* (*b*) to get an oil well into active production.

(1) 1847 Field *Drama in Pokerville* 73 Juleps, milk punches, and ten-pins . . . brought round the evening. — **(2) 1814** in *Amer. Sp.* XXII. 273 To *bring* to a piece of land—to bring it into a state of cultivation, or rather perhaps into a state fit for cultivation. **1837** Colman *Mass. Agric. Rep.* (1838) 77 One of these gentlemen . . . has found this sort of land, after it was thus 'brought to,' extremely favorable to the growth of rye. — **(3)** (*a*) **1865** *Wilkes' Spirit of Times* 19 Aug. 387/3 The Captain himself, got excited, and attempted to put a man out running from first to second base, when a man was on the third, and the result was an overthrow which brought two men home. **1867** *Ball Players' Chron.* 11 July 2/2 The Eckfords began play with fine batting, Swandell sending a fair ball clean over the house at right field, on which he made a home run and brought two men in. **1875** *Chi. Tribune* 16 Sep. 8/4 Warren made the best hit of the day, clean over centerfielder's head for two bases bringing in Waterman and Golden. **1900** *Chi. Times-Herald* 10 May 4/1 Smith brought in two more runs in the same inning by a good clean hit. (*b*) **1944** *Christian Science Mon.* 25 April (Editorial), Oil has been discovered—in fact, a gusher has been brought in—on the Lewis farm.

For *to bring on your bears, to bring down the persimmon,* see the nouns.

brinjer ˈbrɪndʒɚ, *n.* Also **bringer.** *S.* [Prob. related to n. England dial. * *bringe, v.,* to rush forward violently.] A name for a dog; also as a nonsense refrain. Also in colloq. expressions, as *like bringer,* furiously; *to give one bringer,* to give one a beating.

1851 *Polly Peablossom* 52 He 'gin pickin' up rocks an' slingin' um at the dogs like bringer! **1880** Harris *Uncle Remus* (1883) 190 Nuthin' neber 'sturbs his mine, Twel he hear ole Bringer bark. **1892** ——— *U. Remus & Friends* 60 High, my lady! Brinjer, ho. **1908** *D.N.* III. 315 *Give one bringer, v. phr.* To give one severe punishment, make it hot for one.

bristlecone pine. (See quot. 1912.) Cf. **hickory pine** (*b*).

1894 Coville *Death Valley Exped.* 221 In none of the other mountains east of the Sierra Nevada . . . did the bristle-cone pine occur. **1912** Wooton & Standley *Grasses N.M.* 13 The commonest trees are the Bristle-cone Pine (*Pinus aristata*), . . . the Quaking Aspen (*Populus tremuloides*), and one or two willows of the Transition Zone. **1949** *Pacific Discovery* Jan.–Feb. 29/1 Thus we find . . . 'hickory pine' for 'bristle-cone' pine, and 'silver pine' for western white pine.

* **bristly,** *a.* Used in the specific names of plants, etc., bearing bristles, as **bristly crowfoot, currant, dory, foxtail, locust, raspberry, sarsaparilla.**

1814 Mitchill *Fishes N.Y.* 384 Bristly Dory, *Zeus setapinnis,* . . . [is] taken in the bay of New-York. **1833** Eaton *Botany* (ed. 6) 310 *Rubus setosus,* bristly raspberry. **1840** Dewey *Mass. Flowering Plants* 27 *Ranunculus Pennsylvanicus,* Bristly Crowfoot, flowers in August in woods and meadows. *a***1862** Thoreau *Maine Woods* 315 *Aralia hispida* (bristly sarsaparilla). **1878** Killebrew *Tennessee Grasses* 218 *Setaria Verticillata,* Bristly Foxtails . . . is one of the foxtail grasses, some of which are very good grazing when young. **1883** Hale *Woods & Timbers N C.* 139 Bristly currant (*R. resinosum*). . . . It is covered in every part, not excepting the fruit, with resinous glandular hairs, by which it may be recognized. **1892** Apgar *Trees Northern U.S.* 94 *Robinia hispida* (Bristly Locust, Rose-Acacia), with bristly leaf-stalks and branchlets.

* **Britannias,** *n. pl.* ?Trousers of Britannia linen. *Rare.* — **1798** B. Hawkins *Letters* 352 One pair of Britannias . . . $3.50.

Briticism ˈbrɪtəˌsɪzəm, *n.* Also **Britishism.** A word or expression characteristic of, or peculiar to, Great Britain.

1868 R. G. White in *Galaxy* March 335 This use of the word is a widespread Briticism. **1883** *Boston Journal* 17 Sep., The smaller of the two [books] is a well arranged handbook of Briticisms, Americanisms, Colloquial Phrases, &c. **1894** *Harper's Mag.* Jan. 315/1 Doubtless he could use 'Britishisms' if he chose. *Ib.* 315/2 Nor should we advise an American statesman to attempt a 'Britishism.' **1949** *Amer. Coll. Dict.* xxx/1 Words like *blizzard, jingoism, O.K.*, or *teetotaler* are well known either as Americanisms or Briticisms in origin.

* **British,** *a.*

1. Of American Indians: Acting as allies of Great Britain. *Obs.*

1835 Hoffman *Winter in West* I. 277 Behind these the British Indians lay concealed. **1852** J. Reynolds *Hist. Illinois* 9 It was a band of these natives, called the 'British,' or 'Black Hawk Band,' that caused so much trouble and expense to the United States.

2. In special combs.: (1) **British America,** that part of North America formerly occupied by British settlers or claimed by Great Britain, Canada; (2) **American,** a Britisher, also as adj.; (3) **cousin,** a Britisher; (4) * **gold,** funds allegedly given by the English to influence American elections; (5) * **lady,** a local name for the red-winged blackbird; (6) * **merchant,** (see quot.), *obs.;* (7) **oil,** (see quot. 1837), *obs.;* (8) * **tory,** (see quot.), *obs.;* (9) **Whig Trap,** a derisive term for the log cabin used as a political symbol in the presidential campaign of 1840, *obs.*

(1) 1764 Otis *Rights* (1766) 77 The ministry [of Gt. Britain] . . . may rely on it, that British America will never prove undutiful, till driven to it. **1784** Smyth *Tour* II. 34 The houses here [in Florida] have a very singular appearance within, being floored with a kind of reddish stucco, . . . no where else to be met with in British America. **1869** Bowles *Our New West* 23 From British America on the north to Mexico on the south is from one thousand to twelve hundred miles. **1907** Lyons *Plant Names* 189 E. purpureum L . . . British America, south to Florida and Utah. — **(2) 1764** J. Otis *Rights* 80 The services and sufferings of the British American colonies. **1765** J. Habersham *Letters* 45 We are speaking of the indefeasible Birth Right of a Brittish American Subject. **1784** Smyth *Tour* I. 346 The Indians indeed do not appear to entertain any dislike to the British or French . . . nor have the real British or French any particular aversion to them, as the British Americans have. — **(3) 1910** in *Pub. Col. Soc.* XIII. 120 An amusing episode that occurred on the last day of the session (March 29) is recorded for the benefit of those Americans who think that our British cousins are lacking in a sense of humor. — **(4) 1780** *Va. Gazette* 2 Dec. 2/3 Say, was it thirst for *British gold;* Could tempt to deed, this son of earth, At once so *base* and *bold*. **1844** *Sucker* (Pittsfield, Ill.) 19 July 4/3 It is probable that the Locofoco editor has been paid in British Gold for the publication of his tracts. **1884** *Colo. Springs Gazette* 7 Oct. 1/2 (*headline*), British Gold for Cleveland.

(5) 1920 Thomas *Ky. Super.* 28 If you kill the 'British lady' (the red-winged blackbird), you will marry the next man you meet. . . . Mountains. — **(6) 1860** S. Mordecai *Virginia* II. 33 The term 'British merchants' is here used *not* in its general acceptation, but as it was formerly applied in Virginia to those who had establishments here and who in fact had the monopoly of trade in the Southern States. — **(7) 1787** *Kentucky Gazette* 15 Dec. 2/3 Robert Barr . . . has lately received a general assortment of Grocery and Dye Stuffs with the following medicines, viz. Glauber salts, . . . British oil, [etc.]. **1837** Irving *Bonneville* I. xxiii. 223 The bituminous oil, called petrolium or naphtha, . . . forms a principal ingredient in the potent medicine called British Oil. — **(8) 1813** *Salem* (Mass.) *Gaz.* 12 Mar. 2/4 To pronounce him a friend to Great-Britain; or, in their language of vulgar abuse, a *British Tory*. — **(9) 1840** *N.O. Picayune* 4 Oct. 2/2 The Log Cabin, set upon triggers and called by the New York Era 'the British Whig Trap,' has been improved upon in this city.

Britisher ˈbrɪtɪʃɚ, *n.* A native of Great Britain, a person of British origin.

The question of the place of origin of this term has been debated without decisive results. According to the evidence at present available it is of American origin.

1829 Marryat *F. Mildmay* xx, [American mate speaking:] 'Are we going to be bullied by these . . . Britishers?' **1863** Russell *Diary* II. 97 Why even the Northern chaps get angry with a Britisher, as they call us, if he attempts to say a word against those cursed niggers. **1947** *Denver Post* 28 Feb. 10/4 They must be forever on the qui vive not to do anything that will offend the critical Britishers back home.

Britishite ˈbrɪtɪʃaɪt, *n.* = **Britisher.** *Rare.* — **1788** *Independent Chronicle* 20 Mar. 3/3 He [S. Adams] is the man . . . whom the Britishites excluded from all hopes of pardon.

* **brittle,** *a.* **1. brittlebush,** any one of various plants of the genus *Encelia* found in desert regions in the Southwest and in Mexico. **2. brittlewood,** a local name for the Indian cherry.

(1) 1908 Hornaday *Camp Fires on Desert* 182 The White Brittle-Bush, as seen standing alone on bare black lava, is truly a thing of beauty. **1948** *Time* 26 Jan. 44/3 The brittlebush . . . always grows alone in a patch of ground bare of potential competitors. — **(2) 1897** Sudworth *Arborescent Flora* 298 *Rhamnus caroliniana*, . . . Indian Cherry. . . . Common Names [include] . . . Brittlewood.

broad brɔd, *n.* Also **'broad.** [f. *abroad, adv.*, mistaken for "a broad," *n.*] A going abroad or away, a journey or trip. *Colloq.*

1823 Cooper *Pioneers* xv, I heer'n say that the Judge was gone a great 'broad, and that he meant to bring his darter hum. **1841** *S. Lit. Messenger* VII. 40/1 You must give up your broad to-day, Corally, for I want to have rails right away to fix the fences. **1921** C. Greer-Petrie *Angeline at Seelbach* 25, I was sorry the Jedge was in sich a swivvit to git back to Louisville, bekase I didn't half git my broad out.

* **broad,** *a.* and *adv.* In combs.: (1) **broad aisle,** see as a main entry; (2) **alley,** = **broad aisle,** *obs.;* (3) * **arrow,** a badge or symbol, allegedly, of the Yamassee Indians, *obs.;* (4) * **bottom,** a member of the Anti-federalist party, *obs.;* (5) * **bottomed,** *a.* anti-federalist, *obs.;* (6) * **cast,** *a.* of machines, adapted for sowing grain broadcast; (7) * **cloth,** a derisive term for a man dressed in a superior manner, *rare,* cf. **swamp broadcloth;** (8) **constructionist,** = **loose constructionist,** cf. **strict constructionist;** (9) * **gauge,** *fig.* on a large or liberal scale, also as adj., large-minded, cf. **narrow gauge;** (10) **gauger,** one who professes to hold broad or liberal views, as in religion and politics; (11) **hoe,** (see quot. 1899); (12) **horn,** see as a main entry; (13) **road,** a main road, a big road; (14) **seal,** see as a main entry; (15) * **side,** the part of an animal, esp. a hog, that lies between the ham and the shoulder, a side of bacon; (16) **tread,** *a.* of carts, etc., having wheels with a wide bearing surface; (17) **Broadway,** see as a main entry.

(2) 1731 *Suffield Doc. Hist.* 250 It being put to the Town whether ye Broad alley in ye meeting House should be fil'd up, it pass'd in ye Negative. **1806** *Intelligencer* (Lancaster, Pa.) 21 Oct. (Th.), Mr. Deming was sitting in the Pew east of the broad alley. — **(3) 1835** Simms *Yemassee* I. 97 Does Sanutee speak for the Yemassee—and where are the other chiefs of the broad-arrow? — **(4) 1816** *Mass. Spy* 10 Jan. (Th.), The Broad Bottoms are increasing in strength. The Federalists rest on their oars.

(5) 1819 *Ib.* 13 Jan. (Th.), Many broad-bottomed measures have been enacted. — **(6) 1856** *Mich. Agric. Soc. Trans.* VII. 56 C. B. Seymour, Scio, [exhibited a] broadcast sower. **1905** E. W. Pringle *Rice Planter* 162, I bought a Cahoon broad-cast seeder, and have tried to make Willing . . . understand the directions. — **(7) 1835** Longstreet *Ga. Scenes* (1840) 211 I'll be dod darned if Broadcloth don't give some of you the dry gripes. — **(8) 1882** Cooper *Amer. Pol.* I. 7 The Federalists became 'Broad Constructionists,' because they interpreted the constitution in a way calculated to broaden the power of the national government. — **(9) 1858** Brannan in *Tall Tales of S.W.* (1930) 255 [The 'hard-shell' religion is] not like the Methodists, what specks to get to heaven by hollerin' hell-fire, nor like the Univarsalists, that get on the broad gage and goes the hull hog-ah! **1887** George *40 Years on Rail* 234 Out West everthing is done on the broad-gauge plan. **1889** *Harper's Mag.* May 989/1 Those who have . . . known English men and women of the broad-guage variety.

(10) *c***1873** De Vere *MS Notes* 242 *Broad Gauge* church in [the] West = Universalist or no church. A Broad Gauger may be an infidel, atheist, etc. **1914** *Cyclo. Amer. Govt.* III. 78/1 In the Pittsburgh Convention of 1896 were two factions, the 'narrow gaugers,' opposed to the free silver principle, and the 'broadgaugers.' — **(11) 1672** *Oyster Bay Rec.* I. 69 A broade hooe. **1754** *S.C. Gazette* 1 Jan. 2/2 Just imported . . . a large assortment of . . . broad hoes. **1899** Green *Va. Word-book* 70 Broad-hoe, *n.* A hoe with a blade a foot wide, and long handle for weeding corn. — **(13) 1871** Stowe *Pink & White Tyranny* 292 The bustle and animation . . . on the turnpike, spoken of familiarly as the 'broad road', will be somewhat increased.

(15) 1831 Peck *Guide* 172 Their method is to salt it [= pork] sufficiently to prepare it for smoking, and then to make bacon of hams, shoulders, and midlings or broadsides. **1846** Melville *Typee* I. viii. 69 A rapidity and loudness of utterance that almost led me to suspect he had been slyly devouring the broadside of an ox in some of the adjoining thickets. **1853** *Harper's Mag.* VII. 276/2 The old Doctor quietly obeyed directions and layer after layer of fat 'broadside' was hoisted out to him. — **(16) 1866** W. Reid *After the War* 471 Great 'broad-tread' carts, with a stout mule hitched in the shafts and a pair of lighter ones in front, are used to haul the cane to the mill. **1875** *Chi. Tribune* 11 Sep. 3/6 The cars . . . are new and of 'broad tread.'

b. In the names of, or with reference to, plants and animals: (1) **broadbill,** see **creek broadbill;** (2) * **leaf,**

see **Maryland broadleaf;** (3) **leaf(ed) maple,** "a fine species, *Acer macrophyllum*, of California and Oregon, the wood of which is largely used locally for furniture, etc." (*Cent. s.v. maple*); (4) **leafed tobacco,** (see quot.); (5) **leaved laurel,** mountain laurel, *Kalmia latifolia;* (6) **leaved maple, =broad-leafed maple;** (7) **tailed humming bird,** a species of humming bird found in the western U.S.; (8) **wing,** =next; (9) **winged buzzard,** a common though locally distributed hawk, *Buteo platypterus;* (10) **winged hawk,** =prec.

(3) **1890** *Cent.* 3622/2. **1948** *Mazama* June 2/2 Bob Platt, as an ex Mazama President, planted as a memorial tree a broad leaf maple.— (4) **1891** *Cent.* 6362/3 *Broad-leafed* tobacco, the Maryland tobacco.

(5) **1823** James *Exped.* I. 10 The deep umbrageous hue of hemlock spruce . . . is exchanged for the livelier verdure of the broad-leaved laurel. — (6) **1869** Muir *First Summer in Sierra* (1911) 33 It has a fine, deep, clear little lake with mossy banks embowered with broad-leaved maples. **1902** *Out West* Sep. 350 There, where those broad-leaved maple branches bed, Are cool, brown shadows. — (7) **1858** Baird *Birds Pacific R.R.* 135 *Selasphorus Platycercus*, . . . Broad-tailed Humming Bird. **1881** *Harper's Mag.* June 27/1 Doctor Coues describes a similar antic practiced by the broad-tailed humming bird . . . of the Rocky Mountains. — (8) **1945** *Mass. Audubon Soc. Bul.* March 39 There are some pairs of nesting Red-shoulders, Sharp-shins or Broad-wings. — (9) **1844** *Nat. Hist. N.Y., Zoology* II. 11 The Broad-winged Buzzard, *Buteo Pennsylvanicus*, . . . is a rare species in our State. . . . In Virginia and Maryland, it is more common. **1874** Coues *Birds N.W.* 360 Broad-winged Buzzard.

(10) **1812** Wilson *Ornithology* VI. 92 [This] Broad-Winged Hawk, *Falco Pennsylvanicus*, . . . was perched on the dead limb of a high tree. **1895** *Dept. Agric. Yearbook 1894* 222 The broad-winged hawk . . . feeds largely on insects, small mammals, snakes, toads, and frogs.

broad aisle. The main aisle or passageway in a church.

1806 *Repertory* (Boston) 16 June (Th.), For sale, a Pew in the broad Isle of the Chapel Church. **1889** *Harper's Mag.* Dec. 147/1 When I see her parade up the broad aisle, I want to stick out my tongue at her. **1945** *Chi. Tribune* 16 Sep. VII. 1/5 Wide handmade benches were set in two rows, leaving a broad aisle, and on a raised platform were the piano, high pulpit and benches for a choir.

Also *attrib.* and *transf.*

1850 Judd *R. Edney* ix. 141 Then there was Mrs. Tunny, . . . who owned a broad-aisle pew in Dr. Broadwell's Church. **1866** Lowell *Biglow P.* II. xi. 244 No white man sets in airth's broad aisle Thet I ain't willin' t' own ez brother.

broadhorn ˈbrɔdˌhɔrn, *n.* [See quots. 1936, 1941.]

1. A kind of flatboat formerly used on American rivers, esp. the Mississippi and the Ohio. Now *hist.* Cf. **Kentucky broadhorn, Mississippi broadhorn.**

1819 Dewees *Lett. from Texas* 11 The vessels upon this river consist in part of barges and keel boats; but mostly of upper country flat boats, (generally called broad-horns). **1852** Casey *Two Yrs.* 113 The flat boat or 'broad horn' may be called a feature of the river; it is met with at every bend, and consists of a square boat some 150 feet long, and 25 broad, manned by from four to eight or ten men, laden with various cargoes, and floated down by the current. **1936** Asbury *French Quarter* 77 The flatboat, . . . was simply an oblong ark with a curved roof to shed the rain, and sometimes a curved bow, with a great oar or sweep projecting from either side whence the name 'broadhorn.' [**1941** Baldwin *Keelboat Age* 48 Two or more sweeps, or broadhorns, similarly pivoted on the sides, were used to keep the boat in the current.]

b. A somewhat similar boat but designed for carrying coal. Also attrib. in transf. sense.

1851 *Knickerb.* XXXVII. 182 The river is dark as night; but we see, every now and then, 'broad-horns' and coal-flats, with a twinkling light. **1867** Devens *Pictorial Bk.* 169 His Burnside hat surmounted with a feeble plagiarism of the 'Prince's feather,' his feet encased snugly in a pair of 'broadhorn' coal boots. **1883** *Encyclo. Amer.* I. 440/2 When the coal mines in the vicinity of Pittsburgh began to ship coal to Southern markets, the 'broad-horn,' or 'coal-boat,' was invented.

c. broadhorn dialect, language thought of as typical of Kentuckians and keelboatmen. *Obs.*

1833 *Polit. Examiner* (Shelbyville, Ky.) 20 Apr. 1/3 Mr. Paulding . . . made a hunter and companion of Daniel Boone not only loquacious, but 'running over' with the most exaggerated superlatives in the 'broad horn' dialect.

2. The bighorn or Rocky Mountain sheep. *Obs.*

1847 *Knickerb.* XXX. 141 He had wandered some distance up the mountain in search of wild sheep, or 'broad-horns.'

3. =**longhorn.**

1872 *Kans. Mag.* Jan. 92/1 You can't go foolin' 'round and keep Five hundred steers all right; Jest try them broad-horns once yourself Some ugly stormy night. **1900** Garland *Eagle's Heart* 164 Reynolds and Mose rode out toward the slowly 'milling' herd, a hungry, hot, and restless mob of broadhorns, which required careful treatment.

* **broad seal.** Also *cap.*

1. Used allusively with reference to the Broad-seal war. *Obs.*

1839 *N.Y. Semi-Wkly. Express* 11 Dec. 1/5 Mr. Duncan began a speech about corsets . . . enumerations and contested seats, broad seals and narrow ones, which when half made was interrupted. **1840** *Niles' Reg.* 9 May 153/3 They [i.e., a political delegation from New Jersey] brought with them a number of beautiful banners. In front was carried the arms of the state, beneath which was inscribed the appropriate motto 'The Next Impression of Her Broad Seal Will Be Respected.' **1843** *Quincy* (Ill.) *Herald* 8 Dec. 21/1 Then follows little New Jersey, and with her Democratic broom makes a clean sweep of every Coon from the State. Even Pennington's 'Broad Seal' could not save them.

2. Broad-seal war, (see quot. 1889). *Obs.*

1877 Raum *New Jersey* II. 399 The Whigs refused to vote; but the question was decided by the rest of the House in favor of the Democratic claimants. . . . This was called Governor Pennington's 'broad seal war.' **1889** *Cent.* 689/3 Broad-seal war, in *U.S. hist.*, a contest in the House of Representatives, in December, 1839, as to the admission or exclusion of five Whig members from New Jersey, who had certificates of election under the broad seal of the State, but whose seats were contested by Democratic claimants.

Broadway ˈbrɔdˌwe, *n.* [See quot. 1673.]

1. Used, often grandiloquently, for a street likened to Broadway in N.Y. City.

[**1673** in *Coll. N.Y. Hist. Soc.* XLVI. (1913) 8 A Certaine house & Lott of ground, scituate Lying and being wthin this City, to ye west of the street Commonly Called the heere Street or bredewegh.] **1835** *Vade Mecum* (Phila.) 14 Feb. 3/3 The future Broadways and Pall Malls were marked upon the trees. **1884** *Cent. Mag.* March 678/2 No sooner is the 'Interocean City' of some farthest Western frontier of civilization out of the log-cabin period, than it has at once a Broadway, a Fifth Avenue, and an Academy of Music.

2. Often used attrib. in such expressions as **Broadway beau, buck, cabaret, exquisite, idea, idler, nostalgia, squad, swell,** etc.

1835 N. P. Willis *Pencillings* (1942) 399 The driver was dressed like a Broadway idler. **1844** in *Amer. Sp.* XVIII. 121 You could not have distinguished them from the first Broadway bucks and beaux. **1849** A. Mackay *Western World* I. 67 It is impossible to meet with a more finished coxcomb than a Broadway exquisite, or a 'Broadway swell,' which is the designation attached to him on the spot. **1881** *Harper's Mag.* April 712/2 Another suggests some Broadway idea. **1891** Lovett *U.S. Pictures* 34 The 'Broadway Squad'—that is, the stalwart policemen whose duty it is to pilot pedestrians across. **1904** *N.Y. Ev. Post* 9 May 7 Mr. Townsend of Chemulpo, an American who has lived out here twenty years without any Broadway nostalgia. **1913** *Nation* XCVI. 352/3 No one who has spent an hour at a Broadway cabaret can doubt that we are splendidly casting off the shackles of academicism.

b. Also in derivatives, as **Broadwayese, -ite.** *Colloq.*

1918 *Amer. Mag.* Jan. 65/1 The loophound of Chicago differs visibly from the Broadwayite of Manhattan and the boulevardier of Paris. **1947** *Sat. Ev. Post* 8 Mar. 28/1 Although he is fluent in four languages, his working vocabulary runs heavily to Broadwayese with drugstore-cowboy trimmings. **1948** *Time* 16 Aug. 70/3 Most show-wise Broadwayites agreed with the directors that the Met couldn't safely raise the price of its orchestra seats above the present $7.50.

Brodiaea ˌbrodɪˈiə, *n.* [Named for J. J. *Brodie*, a Scotchman.] (See quot. 1909.) Cf. **covena.**

1909 *Cent. Supp.* 166/3 Brodiaea. . . . An untenable name for *Hookera*, a genus of plants of the family *Liliaceae*. . . . A plant of the genus *Hookera*. The brodiaeas are bulbous plants of the Pacific coast, some of great beauty and gathered wild or cultivated for ornament. From the habit of some species has arisen the name *California hyacinth.* **1915** *Nat. & Science on Pac. Coast* 149 Another lilaceous group, the Brodiaeas, which grow from edible corms and bear umbels of usually bluish flowers, inhabit clay soils. **1947** *Desert Mag.* May 28/3 Visitors in May and June will find a good display of blue brodiaea.

***brogan,** *n. local.* (See quot.) See **ice brogan.** — **1881** E. Ingersoll *Oyster Industry* 242 *Brogan*, a kind of large boat used by the oystermen of the Chesapeake.

broglio ˈbroglɪo, *n.* [Origin unknown.] A kind of cloth. *Obs.* — **1759** in H. M. Brooks *Gleanings* 33 Cross-bar'd stuffs, rich brunets, broglios, stript & plain camblets & cambleteens. **1762** *Newport Mercury* 7 Sep. 3/2 To be sold by Gideon, . . . figur'd . . . broglio's, light and cloth colour'd belladine.

brogue brog, *v.* [App. related to ∗*brogue*, *n.* a stout, coarse shoe. Cf. **bogue.**] *intr.* To go about on foot in a leisurely, aimless manner, to bogue. *Colloq.*

The initial *p* in the 1856 quot. may be an error for *b*, or poss. an *i* has dropped out after it, "piroguein" being meant. The meaning given in the 1883 quot. is not that shown in the other quots. and may be an error, or humorous.

1856 *Knickerb.* XLVIII. 433 (Th.), Nex mornin' airly I goes down to the mash [marsh], an' while proguein round I got a shot at some black ducks. **1883** ZEIGLER & GROSSCUP *Alleghanies* 51 'I've brogued it through every briar patch an' laurel thicket' . . . 'What do you mean by "brogued it"?' . . . 'Crawled, thet's what hit means.' **1917** *D.N.* IV. 409 Brogue, *v.i.* To go afoot. 'Where are you a-goin?'—'Jes' "*broguin*" about.'

∗**broiler,** *n.*

1. A utensil for broiling meat.

[**1828** WEBSTER, *Broiler*, that which dresses by broiling.] **1846** WORCESTER, *Broiler*, . . . a gridiron. **1902** *Harper's Mag.* May 966 Phil . . . shot away from her and into the kitchen to turn the wire broiler. **1948** *Dly. Ardmoreite* (Ardmore, Okla.) 23 Jan. 3/3 Creamed flaked fish

Broilers of different types

spooned into individual baking shells and sprinkled with cheese before going under the broiler is a good dish to serve for Sunday night supper.
fig. **1890** BIFF HALL *Turnover Club* 193 The Agent and the Purveyor had a new scheme on the broiler.

2. (See quot.)

1909 *Cent. Supp.* 166/3 broiler. . . . In *railroading*, a parlor car fitted with a grill kitchen or a kitchen in which broiling of chops, etc., can be done without the more elaborate cooking of a dining-car; a grill-room car.

∗**broken,** *a.* In combs.: (1) **Broken Arrows,** (see quot. 1907); (2) **bone fever,** =**breakbone fever,** *obs.;* (3) **breast,** abscess of the mammary gland; (4) **days,** see as a main entry; (5) **dose,** (see quot. 1903); (6) **field,** in American football, a field upon which the players are widely scattered, as after a kick, usu. attrib., also transf.; (7) **marsh,** ?a marsh having in it elevations or "islands" of firm ground; (8) **stove lid,** the name of a quilt pattern, prob. *facetious, obs.*

(1) **1848** RUXTON in *Blackwood Mag.* LXIV. 141 The Indians . . . were mostly of the Sioux nation, including the tribes of Burnt-woods. . . . Broken Arrows, all of which belong to the great Sioux nation. **1907** HODGE *Amer. Indians* I. 166 Broken Arrows. A hunting band of Sioux found on the Platte by Sage . . . ; possibly the Cazazhita. — (2) **1872** *Newton Kansan* 22 Aug. 4/2 Dengue fever—what is known in South Carolina and Georgia as 'Broken Bone' fever—is still on the increase in Calcutta and the neighborhood. **1880** *Bradstreet's* 1 Sep. 3/1 Nearly one-half the city [Charleston] is down with the broken-bone fever. — (3) **1877** *Vt. Dairymen's Assoc. Rep.* VIII. 105 In the human subject this is known as 'broken breast.'

(5) **1806** LEWIS in *L. & Clark Exped.* (1905) IV. 73 We gave him broken dozes of diluted nitre. **1903** *D.N.* II. 307 Broken dose or doste, *n.* A little at a time. 'I always give quinine in *broken doses.*' — (6) **1899** *Offic. Football Guide* 39 He is one of the strongest men carrying a ball through a broken field. **1923** *Outing* Jan. 149/1 Kaw of Cornell offered a combination of power and elusiveness in broken field running. **1945** *Nation* CLX. II. 17 March 315/1, I also thought it . . . satisfying and encouraging in its broken-field run through the problems of cost. **1948** *Redbook* April 103/1 Every ticket-holder on Franklin Field knew he had seen the greatest broken-field runner of all time! — (7) **1657** in *Amer. Sp.* XV. 160/2 Runing Northerly With a narrow Slippet in Hummocks & broken Marshes. **1872** *Ib.*, The rest of the country was low, broken marshes. — (8) **1898** HARRIS *Tales* 317 'That is what they call the broken stove lid,' explained Jack, seeing the big Irishman's apparent interest in the quilt pattern.

broken days. Among the southeastern Indians, the time intervening before an event, usu. a ceremony, symbolized by a bundle of sticks one of which was to be broken each day. *Obs.*

1775 ADAIR *Indians* 318 Seventeen were the broken days, according to the Indian phrase, when the Choktah engaged to return with the French scalps. *Ib.* 329, I . . . arrived in the Choktah country before the expiration of the broken days, or time we had appointed. **1798** B. HAWKINS *Letters* 318 The chiefs request the agent . . . that when he sends a written notice to them, he will send the broken days to the head man. *Ib.*, When the broken days are out they are to commence their journey of banishment. **1842** E. A. HITCHCOCK *Journal* 132 On the fourth meeting they give out the 'broken days' for the Busk.

∗**broker,** *n.* Short for **bounty broker.** *Obs.* — **1865** SALA *Diary* II. 371 Let them visit a few offices 'down town,' tenanted by the crimps—here politely termed brokers.

As the last term in **bounty, cattle, curb, curbstone, flour, government, note, play, real estate, street, substitute, ticket, vote, Wall Street, wildcat broker.**

∗**brokerage,** *n.* As the last term in **cotton brokerage, substitute brokerage.**

∗**bromide,** *n.*

1. A dull, tiresome person, in allusion to medicinal bromides as sedatives. *Slang.*

1906 G. BURGESS (*title*), Are you a Bromide? **1909** *Sat. Ev. Post* 13 March 20/3 We'll say that the sucker is about an average-minded man—what they're calling a 'bromide' nowadays. **1936** *Publisher's Wkly.* 24 Oct. 1705/1 The first printing of that useful word was on the dust-jacket of Gelett Burgess' 'Are You a Bromide?'

2. A commonplace saying, trite remark, conventionalism. Also **bromidic, bromidity.**

1920 *Outing* June 160/3 Even at the risk of being somewhat bromidic I am forced to remark that in the expansive West distances between places are very great. **1926** *Publisher's Wkly.* 20 Feb. 563 The old bromide that poetry never sells is once again proved to be wrong. **1948** *Time* 31 May 20/3 In a letter to Peace-in-our-Timer Henry Wallace he administered the familiar bromide: [etc.]. **1948** *Sat. Ev. Post* 26 June 71/1 (*heading*), It isn't the heat, it's the bromidity.

bronc braŋk, *n.* Also **bronch, bronk.** *W., S.W.* Short for **bronco.** Also as adj. *Colloq.*

1893 ROOSEVELT *Wilderness Hunter* 418, I saddled up the bronc' and lit out for home. **1910** MULFORD *Hopalong Cassidy* 138 That ain't a bad cayuse you got there. . . . Is it very bronc? **1948** *Range Riders Western* May 30/2 Two tired broncs stamped their hoofs restlessly at the tie-rail.

b. bronc peeler, rider, twister, =**bronco buster.**

1914 BRININSTOOL *Trail Dust* 114 He used to brag he was the boss Bronc-peeler at this ridin' game. **1923** EVARTS *Tumbleweeds* 93 The surplus bronc peelers . . . have been drifting up there. — **1938** G. BALCH *Tiger Roan* 56 An expert bronc-rider himself. . . . Sleed had been smart enough to see that there was more money to be made. — **1916** H. TITUS *I Conquered* 92 You'd have made a fine bronc twister. **1948** *Southwestern Rev.* Winter 27/1 A bronc twister maybe ain't strong on brains, . . . but he ain't short on guts.

Also **bronc-busting, riding.**

1927 JAMES *Cow Country* 152 The money they won at them events at steer roping, bull dogging, and bronk-riding kept 'em up respectable and all. **1945** *Greeley* (Colo.) *Tribune* 18 Jan. 1/8 Bronc-busting Jack Wade . . . topped a twisting chestnut critter.

bronco ˈbraŋko, *n.* and *a.* Also **broncho.** Chiefly *W.* and *S.W.* [Sp., rough, unruly.]

1. *n.* A small, wiry, half-wild horse of the western plains, probably descended from horses that escaped from early Spanish explorers and settlers. Cf. **outlaw bronco.**

?**1850** *Life in Rocky Mts.* 41 (Bentley), A buggy drawn by light broncos. **1868** BOWLES *Colorado* (1869) 57 If a well-broken Indian pony or a 'broncho' (a California half-breed horse) can be got, either is probably better than a mule. **1944** *Nat. Geog. Mag.* June 656/1 But the greatest fun is the rodeo—a real Wild West spectacle in which hard-working ranch cowboys ride unbroken broncos and steers fresh from the ranges.

b. (See quots.)

1877 McDANIELD and TAYLOR *Coming Empire* 374 These mules are from Mexico and are called broncos. **1893** *Outing* Apr. 75/1 Many a bold buck looked as though he would have swapped his whole herd of ponies and thrown in a few squaws and papooses in exchange for my trim, steel broncho [a bicycle] from the far East.

2. *a.* Unruly, rough, crude. *Colloq.*

1866 *Weekly New Mexican* 21 July 1/4 Then the Territory did not keep fast horses and other things, and go to bronco bailes and play whiskey poker. **1910** *Cent. Mag.* March 763/2 Away to the north . . . were the Bacatete Mountains, the stronghold for ages of the wild or bronco Yaquis. **1947** *Westerners' Brand Book* 75 He always felt that a man who made a false step wasn't necessarily all bad or 'broncho' as he expressed it.

3. In special colloq. combs.: (1) **bronco buster,** one who breaks broncos to the saddle; (2) **busting,** the breaking of broncos to the saddle; (3) **tag,** (see quot.).

(1) **1888** ROOSEVELT in *Cent. Mag.* Feb. 507/1 The flash riders, or horse-breakers, always called 'bronco busters,' can perform really marvelous feats. **1943** *Nat. Geog. Mag.* May 618/1 Veteran buckaroos whoop with delight when a bronco-buster gets 'piled.' — (2) **1891** *Harper's Mag.* July 208/1 Bronco busting is a distinct art. **1947** *Trail Riders Bul.* Feb. 20/2 That's how I come tuh give up bronco bustin' an' foun' me a healthier climate. — (3) **1943** *Nat. Geog. Mag.* Dec. 767 Among the most popular games of mountain young people is 'bronco tag.' The girl who has her hands on her partner's waist must keep him between herself and her competitor or lose him.

Also *bronco breaker, horse, mare, mule, pony, riding, twister, type,* etc.

Bronx braŋks, *n.* [A part of N.Y. City, so named after Jonas Bronck, an early landholder.]

1. A kind of alcoholic drink. Also attrib.

1909 *Sat. Ev. Post* 10 April 37/2 The first-night death-watch, ... in its sophistication could recognize a block away a Bronx, Martini or Manhattan cocktail by its color. **1921** *Collier's* 24 Sep. 4/1 How d'ye mix a Bronx cocktail? **1931** F. L. ALLEN *Only Yesterday* 11 He finds there a group of men downing Bronxes and Scotch highballs.

2. Bronx cheer, a sound of contempt made by vibrating the tongue between the lips.

1929 *Collier's* 23 Feb. 10/4 Maxim give him a Bronx cheer. **1948** *Sat. Ev. Post* 22 May 145/3 There were quite a few Bronx cheers when my name was announced over the public address system.

***bronze,** *n.* or *a.* **1. bronze backer,** a local name for the small-mouthed black bass. **2. Bronze John,** (see quot.). *Slang. Obs.* — (1) **1888** GOODE *Amer. Fishes* 56 'Bronze-backer' is one of its pet names among the anglers. — (2) **1869** *Overland Mo.* Aug. 130/1 'Bronze John' is pretty well known [in the South] for yellow fever.

bronzed grackle. A western variety of the purple grackle. — **1895** *Dept. Agric. Yearbook 1894* 233 The common purple grackle ... and its two subspecies, the bronzed grackle (*Quiscalus q. æneus*) and the Florida grackle. **1945** *Nat. Geog. Mag.* June 739 Reflections on a Corn-fed Bronzed Grackle Gleam in Splendor.

***brooder,** *n.* A heated contrivance, often box-like in form, used in raising chickens hatched in an incubator. Also attrib.

Brooder for incubator chicks

1880 H. TOMLINSON *Artificial Incubation* 32 [Chickens] may ... be transferred to an artificial mother, or *brooder* as the Yankees call it. **1935** *Weatherford* (Okla.) *News* 4 April 8/7 Simplex brooder stove in good condition and a lot of other baby chick equipment. **1945** *La Junta* (Colo.) *Tribune-Democrat* 12 June 2/1 Turkeys, we are told are actually too dumb to come in out of the rain and that is why they are kept carefully in heated brooder houses during this kind of weather. **1948** *Okla. Cotton Grower* 15 Jan. 3/5 Build a new brooder house or repair the old one.

brood frame. One of the frames in a patent bee hive. — **1861** *Ill. Agric. Soc. Trans.* IV. 82 Cut E is the brood frame. Little *g* represents the upper one full of comb.

***brook,** *n.* In combs.: (1) **brook drive,** (see quot.); (2) **driving,** floating logs down a brook in time of high water; (3) **Brook Farm,** (see quot. 1893), also attrib.; (4) **fish,** a fish frequenting brooks (see quot. 1889); (5) **fishing,** fishing in a brook; (6) **trout,** the speckled trout, *Salvelinus fontinalis;* (7) **trouting,** fishing for brook trout.

(1) **1851** SPRINGER *Forest Life* 164 Brook-drives are ... usually distinct parcels of logs belonging to an individual or company. — (2) **1851** SPRINGER *Forest Life* 156 In brook-driving it is necessary to begin early, in order to get the logs in to the ... current of the main river while the freshet is yet up. — (3) **1847** *N.Y. Wkly. Tribune* 13 Nov. 7/1 You have all, doubtless, heard of the Brook Farm Association. **1893** JAMESON *Dict. U.S. Hist.* (1931) 63 *Brook Farm,* a communistic industrial and literary establishment founded in Massachusetts, in 1841, by George Ripley and other persons of socialistic tendencies. The establishment failed in 1846. **1947** *Harper's Mag.* July 1/2 This dream had obsessed the American people since Brook Farm and Robert Owen's New Lanarck. — (4) **1846** *Knickerb.* XXVIII. 177 In that stream ... lurk scores of the aristocracy of brook-fish, which are to dangle upon our lines tomorrow. **1889** *Cent.* 695/1 *Brook-fish,* a fish of the family *Cyprinodontidae* and genus *Fundulus:* same as *killifish* and *mummychog.* (Local U.S.)

(5) **1857** D. H. STROTHER *Virginia* 17, I have a rod here, ... the very thing for brook-fishing, for whipping the smaller streams. **1857** S. H. HAMMOND *Northern Scenes* 112 Let him rig for brook-fishing and take to that stream. — (6) **1836** DUNLAP *Mem. Water Drinker* I. 57, I am not one of your brook trout to be played back and forth with a hair line. **1948** *Ga. Review* Spring 74 The brook trout has moved into the headwaters where the streams are small and cold. — (7) **1855** *Knickerb.* XLVI. 308 In brook-trouting it is always better to pass on, and not seek to get all the fish out of any one hole.

As the last term in **pine brook, spring brook.**

Brooklynite ˈbrʊklənˌaɪt, *n.* An inhabitant of Brooklyn, N.Y.

1835 W. L. GARRISON in *Life* II. 67 Mr. and Mrs. May sat at my right hand, propounding many questions about the Brooklynites. **1881** *Harper's Mag.* May 817/1 With the exception of a few Brooklynites ... the place [=Coney Island] has been abandoned to cardsharpers and the roughest class from New York. **1943** MENEFEE *Assignment* 23 Brooklyn houses are studded with service stars, and Brooklynites, like Texans, are continually popping up in the war news.

***broom,** *n.* In special combs.: (1) **broom birch,** (see quots.); (2) **brush,** (*a*) a shrubby American species of St. John's wort, (*b*) (see quot.); (3) **clover,** wild indigo or yellow broom, *Baptisia tinctoria;* (4) **corn,** a variety of common sorghum the panicles of which are used for making brooms, brushes, etc., also attrib.; (5) **crowberry,** a shrub, *Corema conradi,* resembling the common crowberry; (6) **grass,** one or other species of the genus *Andropogon* of perennial grasses, esp. broom sedge; (7) **hickory,** pignut hickory, *Carya glabra,* formerly used for making brooms; (8) **pine,** the long leaf or Georgia pine, *Pinus palustris;* (9) **sedge,** a species of coarse grass of the genus *Andropogon,* broom grass, also attrib. with **grass;** (10) **straw,** broom sedge or a single stalk of this, also attrib. in fig. use; (11) **tail,** a western range pony having a short bushy tail, *colloq.;* (12) ***weed,** a yellow-flowered shrub-like plant, *Gutierrezia texana,* found on the prairies of the Southwest.

(1) **1810** MICHAUX *Arbres* I. 26 *Red birch,* ... dans New York et Penn. *Broom birch,* nom secondaire. **1813** H. MUHLENBERG *Cat. Plants* 88 Broom birch [or] poplar-leaved birch (*Betula populifolia*). — (2) (*a*) **1888** *N.Y. World* (F.), The Shakers ... were the first to make brooms of broom brush, and, in fact, originated the entire broom business. **1893** *Amer. Folk-Lore* VI. 138 *Hypericum proliferum,* broom brush, West Va. (*b*) **1889** *Cent.* 695/1 *Broom-brush,* a whisk-broom or clothes-brush made from broom-corn. — (3) **1790** S. DEANE *N.-Eng. Farmer* 25/2 Broom clover and mustard are said to afford bees an excellent pasture. — (4) **1781–2** JEFFERSON *Notes Va.* (1788) 40 Our farms produce wheat, rye, barley, oats, buck wheat, broom corn, and Indian corn. **1821** W. COBBETT *Amer. Gardener* iv. Par. 201 Upon these (small poles) lay, corn-stalks, broom-corn stalks, or twigs or brush of trees. **1947** *Nat. Geog. Mag.* July 105/1 Large quantities of broomcorn were once grown in the Mohawk and Schoharie Valleys.

(5) **1857** GRAY *Botany* 393 *Corema,* Broom-Crowberry. ... Much-branched little shrubs. **1892** B. TORREY *Foot-Path Way* 80 Equally new to me ... were the broom crowberry and the greener kind of poverty grass. — (6) *a*1686 in ALVORD & BIDGOOD *Trans-Allegheny Region* (1912) 189 'Old fields' is a common expression for land that has been cultivated by the Indians and left fallow, which are generally overrun with what they call broom grass. **1793** *N.Y. State Soc. Arts* I. 181 Broom grass, two species, (*bromi*). **1901** MOHR *Plant Life Ala.* 336 Broom-Grass. ... Over the State, on poor sandy soil. Common everywhere. — (7) **1813** H. MUHLENBERG *Cat. Plants* 88 Heart hickory, or Broom hickory. **1897** SUDWORTH *Arborescent Flora* 115 *Hicoria glabra,* Pignut (Hickory). ... Common names [include] ... Broom Hickory (Mo.). — (8) **1791** BARTRAM *Travels* 58 The trees were tall, and generally of the species called Broom-pine. **1832** BROWNE *Sylva* 229 This invaluable tree ... is called Long-leaved Pine ... and Broom Pine. — (9) **1819** AGRICOLA *Ess. Agriculture* 26 Worn-out fields, which have ... grown up in broom sedge, may be highly improved by ... ploughing them deep. **1859** G. W. PERRY *Turpentine Farming* 9 Every kind of turf should be turned over, such as ... wire grass, savanna grass and broom-sage grass. **1947** LUMPKIN *Southerner* 154 Here and there would be a shack set down in a field of plowed land or broom sage.

(10) **1785** WASHINGTON *Diaries* II. 365 Had the Roots, shrubs (which had been grubbed) and tussics of broom Straw ... raked of[f]

and burnt. **1845** J. J. HOOPER *S. Sugg's Adv.* iii. 38 In two hours more he wont be able to step over the butt cut of a broom straw. **1855** *S. Lit. Messenger* XXI. 222 A sham society, with 'broom straw' aristocracy, whose wealth, refinement, and education the schoolmaster estimated as a mathematically minus quality. **1939** HARRIS *Purslane* 233 He helped Letha wring a supply of broom straw. — **(11) 1913** W. C. BARNES *Western Grazing Grounds* 119 Hair ropes ('mecates') spun from the very choicest mane hair taken from some bunch of 'broom tails' (mares) which the boys rounded up on an afternoon and spent hours in throwing in order to obtain the hair. **1940** BABER & WALKER *Longest Rope* 32 Broomtails were killed off by the thousands then. — **(12) 1908** *Sat. Ev. Post* 21 Nov. 9/3 Once he paused, in a patch of broomweed, to send his doleful cry to the stars. **1945** MATHEWS *Talking* 163, I have crawled through the broomweeds and the dead bluestem for a quarter of a mile.

As the last term in **brush, corn, hemlock, horse, sage, Scotch, splinter, split, stick, straw, twig broom.**

***broom,** *v. tr.* To fray or splinter at the end. Also **broomed,** *a.*

1796 J. DABNEY *Address* 25 Stir the liquor with a broomed stick, until it shall be found to ferment. **1923** COOPER *Pilot* I. xvii. 228, I would rather drop my anchor on a bottom that won't broom a keel. **1872** HUNTINGTON *Road-Master's Assistant* 95 When a rail gets badly broomed at the ends, it is taken to a shop and repaired by welding on a piece of bar-iron to level it up to its former shape.

***brother,** *n.*

1. Friend, in Indian usage or with reference to Indians. Also **red brother.**

1684 I. MATHER *Providences* (1856) ii. 39 When the Indian was set free, he came to me, . . . and said I was his brother. **1779** in *Pub. Col. Soc.* XIII. 263 We are sure our good Brothers the Delawares will always be so. **1848** COOPER *Oak Openings* I. 121 'Has my brother lost a warrior?' was the calm reply. **1939** BROWNELL *Horse & Buggy Philos.* 46 Our red brothers (as soon as we took their land we started to call them brothers) were getting along pretty well until we appeared in the offing.

2. A fellow member of a college fraternity.

1779 in SHEPARDSON *Phi Beta Kappa* (1915) 12 Brother: It is an uncommon pleasure which I feel in being able to address you by this tender appellation. *Ib.*, You are to become the brother of unalienable Brothers. **1899** A. H. QUINN *Penna. Stories* 74 He was a member of Kappa Phi, and . . . he had a right to anything his brothers could give him. **1944** *Delta of Sigma Nu* Oct. 6/2 Grant lives in Kansas City himself, so he was quite at home—with familiar faces, old friends, and lifelong Brothers.

3. In combs.: (1) **brother Bob,** the name of a party game; (2) ***brother-in-law,** (see quot. 1888), *slang;* (3) ***Brother Jonathan,** see as a main entry; (4) **Brother Jonathanism,** exaggerated Americanism, *obs.;* (5) **Brothers of Light,** the Penitentes or Penitent Brothers, a Spanish religious sect in the Southwest that practices severe bodily chastisement and other severe rites.

(1) 1843 in THOMPSON *M. Jones* (1872) 101 Spose we play brother Bob—lets play brother Bob. — **(2) 1888** *Boston* (Mass.) *Jrnl.* 31 Oct. 2/4 The street car conductors at Los Angeles have been 'knocking down' from $100 to 200 a day, and several have been arrested. They used an instrument called a 'brother-in-law.' **1944** KAHN *Cable Car Days* 68 The accused conductor, when brought before his employer, confessed that he was the originator of this ingenious mechanism, called a 'brother-in-law,' and demonstrated how it worked. — **(4) 1886** RICHARDSON *Amer. Lit.* (1891) II. 295 American literature, between 1775 and 1825, veered swiftly to and fro between humble subservience to European . . . leadership, and a self-conscious indignant 'Brother-Jonathanism.'

(5) 1929 FORREST *Missions Old Southwest* I. 199 The brotherhood of each morada is governed by ten officers, known as Los Hermanos de Luz, or the Brothers of Light. **1941** FERGUSSON *Southwest* 344 Alice Corbin Henderson has written of them (Penitentes) under the name they prefer: Brothers of Light.

***brotherhood,** *n.* As the last term in **Fenian Brotherhood, Lincoln Brotherhood, White Brotherhood.**

***Brother Jonathan.** A nickname orig. applied in derision by the British and loyalists to an American patriot, latterly a personification of the U.S. or one of its citizens.

This term, with reference to American patriots, appears to have been first used by British soldiers, see quot. 1776 below. There is no evidence that the expression grew out of allusions to Gov. Jonathan Trumbull of Conn. See A. Matthews in *Pub. Col. Soc. Mass.* VII. (1901), 94–125, and XXXII. (1937) 374–386. Also cf. ***Jonathan.**

1776 EZRA STILES in *Pub. Col. Soc. Mass.* VII. (1901) 125, I saw several Gentlemen who came out of Boston last Evening. . . . They [i.e., the British] left Bunker Hill last Ldsday Morning 17th at Eight o'Clock, leaving Images of Hay dressed like Sentries standing, with a Label on the Breast of one, inscribed 'Welcome Brother Jonathan.' **1802** J. T. CALLENDER *Lett. to Hamilton* ii. 20, I am not . . . very much alarmed at the . . . furious thunderbolts of brother Jonathan. **1871** *Overland Mo.* March 273/1 Since that day, a great many people have found 'Brother Jonathan' a very helpful relative in time of need. **1903** *N. & Q.* 9 Ser. XI. 115/1 But it would probably be too ambiguous to call 'Jehu-car' the vehicle which Brother Jonathan designates a 'runabout.'

Brotherly-love vireo or **greenlet** =**Philadelphia vireo.** Cf. **City of Brotherly Love.** — **1874** COUES *Birds N.W.* 97, 233. **1917** *Birds of Amer.* III. 104 The popular name 'Brotherly-love Vireo' is, of course, in reference to the use of the name Philadelphia. . . . The bird was discovered by Cassin [*c*1851], near Philadelphia, who named it in honor of that city.

Brotherton ˈbrʌðɚtən, *n.* [Cf. next.] (See quots.) — **1856** *N.Y. Herald* 5 Jan. 2/5 The Brothertons reside on Lake Winnebago, adjacent to the Stockbridges. **1907** HODGE *Amer. Indians* I. 166 Brotherton. The name of two distinct bands, each formed of remnants of various Algonquian tribes. The best-known band was composed of individuals of the Mahican, Wappinger, Mohegan, Pequot, Narraganset, etc., of Connecticut and Rhode Island.

Brothertown Indians. (See quots.) *Obs.*

1795 in *Mass. Hist. Soc. Col.* 1 Ser. IV. 68 The Brothertown Indians are the scanty remnant of the Moheakaunuck Indians, called formerly the *seven tribes on the sea coast.* They lived in Farmington, Stonington, Mohegan, and some other towns in the state of Connecticut, and Narragansett, in the state of Rhode-Island. ***c*1824–38** G. FURMAN *Antiquities of L.I.* 45 A considerable number of the Montauk Indians appear to have emigrated in 1783, together with some other fragments of the great Mohegan nation, of which they formed a part, into the western part of this State [N.Y.] under the direction of the Rev. Samson Occom, where they all together merged into one tribe and became known as the *Brothertown Indians.*

brotus ˈbrɔtəs, *n.* [Cf. British dial. *brot(t)*, scraps, fragments, a small quantity.] (See quot.) *Obs.* — **1877** BARTLETT 69 *Brotus* means the superfluity of a helping,—the running over of a measure which has been 'heaped up and shaken down.' It is the extra and gratuitous surplusage which the vendor of peanuts gives her customer for his patronage. In New Orleans, the Creole word (in Gumbo French) which exactly represents *brotus* is lagniappe (lan-yap).

***brown,** *n.* In the names of birds: (1) **brown-back,** the red-breasted snipe or dowitcher in summer plumage (see also quot. 1889); (2) ***bird,** the upland plover, also a local name of the towhee; (3) **capped chickadee,** (see quot.); (4) **capped rosy finch,** a rosy finch, *Leucosticte australis,* found in the Southwest; (5) **crane,** the sandhill crane; (6) **creeper,** a small creeper, *Certhia familiaris americana,* found chiefly in the eastern half of the U.S.; (7) **curlew,** (see quot. 1805); (8) **eagle,** (*a*) the bald eagle, (*b*) the golden eagle; (9) **flycatcher,** (see quot. 1730); (10) **hawk,** (*a*) the sharp-shinned hawk, (*b*) Swainson's hawk, found chiefly in the western states; (11) **lark,** the American pipit, *Anthus rubescens;* (12) **oriole,** (see quot.); (13) **pelican,** a dark brown pelican, *Pelecanus occidentalis,* found chiefly along the Gulf Coast of the southern states; (14) **thrasher,** the common thrasher or sandy mocking bird, *Toxostoma rufus,* also transf.; (15) **thrush,** =prec.; (16) **titlark,** =**brown lark.**

(1) 1844 *Nat. Hist. N.Y., Zoology* II. 255 The Dowitchee, Red-breasted Snipe, Quail Snipe, or Brown-back, arrives on the coast of New-York towards the latter part of April. **1889** *Cent.* 697/3 *Brown-back,* . . . a name of the great marbled godwit, *Limosa fedoa.* — **(2) 1882** GODFREY *Nantucket* 157 Large numbers of the upland gray-back, otherwise known as the brown-bird, made their appearance here on the marshes. **1939** *Nat. Geog. Mag.* March 353 Most people know it, but not everyone calls it 'towhee.' Many speak of it as 'brown bird' and others call it 'bush bird.' — **(3) 1916** SETON *Woodcraft Man.* 318 *Chickadee* (*Penthestes atricapillus*) . . . it is well known in the winter woods of eastern America up to the Canadian region where the brown-capped or Hudson Chickadee takes its place. — **(4) 1917** *Birds of Amer.* III. 11/2 The Brown-capped Rosy Finch . . . breeds above the timber-line on the high mountains of Colorado. **1945** *Auk* July 390 The Brown-capped Rosy Finch nests in the cliffs above timberline.

(5) 1805 LEWIS in *L. & Clark Exped.* (1904) II. 255 Saw several of the large brown or sandhill Crain today with their young. **1890** *Cent.* 5330/3 *Grus canadensis* . . . properly applies only to the northern brown or sand-hill crane, somewhat smaller and otherwise different from the southern brown or sand-hill crane, *Grus mexicanus* or *G. pra-*

tensis. — **(6) 1808** WILSON *Ornithology* I. 122 The Brown Creeper is an extremely active and restless little bird. **1934** *Nat. Geog. Mag.* LXV. 581 The brown creeper spends its days in climbing actively with long claws and bracing tail up the rough bark of trees. — **(7) 1731** CATESBY *Carolina* I. 83 *Numenius fuscus.* The Brown Curlew. . . . They . . . come annually about the middle of September, and frequent the watery Savannas in numerous flights, continuing about six weeks, and then retire. **1805** LEWIS in *L. & Clark Exped.* (1904) II. 119 Brown curloos, a small species of curloo or plover of a brown colour about the size of a common snipe and not unlike it. — **(8)** *(a)* **1815** *Mass. H.S. Coll.* 2 Ser. IV. 274 It is probably the brown, or 'fisher eagle,' we have noticed in the winter season. *(b)* **1844** *Nat. Hist. N.Y., Zoology* II. 5 The Brown or Bald Eagle . . . is found in every part of the United States, feeding upon fish, wild fowl and small quadrupeds. **1917** *Birds of Amer.* II. 82. — **(9)** *c***1730** CATESBY *Carolina* I. 54 *Muscicapa fusca.* The little brown Fly-catcher. . . . All the upper part of the body [is] of a dark ash-colour. . . . These breed in Carolina, and retire Southward in Winter. **1832** WILLIAMSON *Maine* I. 143 The brown Fly-catcher . . . caught them [=flies] and cleared them all out of the chamber in one day.

(10) *(a)* **1828** BONAPARTE *Synopsis* 434 The American Brown Hawk, *Falco fuscus.* **1839** PEABODY *Mass. Birds* 266 The American Brown, or Slate Colored Hawk, *Falco fuscus* . . . is said to abound in the thinly settled parts of the southern states, where it often makes great havoc among the domestic poultry. *(b)* [**1874** COUES *Birds N.W.* 357, I took no specimens [of Swainson's buzzard] in the melanistic state of plumage in which the bird has been described as another supposed species (*B[uteo] insignatus*).] **1881** *Amer. Naturalist* XV. 209 The brown hawk (*Buteo insignatus*) is not . . . [seen often] owing to its frequenting quiet secluded places. — **(11) 1812** WILSON *Ornithology* V. 89 Brown Lark: *Alauda rufa* . . . flies in loose scattered flocks; is strongly attached to flat, newly-ploughed fields. **1874** COUES *Birds N.W.* 231 Brown Lark, [is] abundant; migratory; breeds in great numbers above timber-line. — **(12) 1917** *Birds of Amer.* II. 256 Orchard Oriole . . . [Also called] Brown Oriole; Basket Bird. — **(13) 1828** BONAPARTE *Synopsis* 401 The Brown Pelican . . . [is] common in southern states, where it breeds. **1870** *Amer. Naturalist* IV. 58 The Brown Pelican I have not known to occur previously so far north [i.e., Mass.]. — **(14) 1810** WILSON *Ornithology* II. 83 The Ferruginous Thrush, *Turdus Rufus*, . . . is the Brown Thrush, or Thrasher of the middle and eastern states. **1948** *Chi. Tribune* 20 Apr. II. 4/3 We hadn't hiked more than 200 feet when we saw the first brown thrasher on the farm this spring.

(15) 1805 LEWIS in *L. & Clark Exped.* (1904) VI. 190 18th [April] . . . the brown thrush or mocking bird has appeared. **1885** M. THOMPSON *Byways & Bird Notes* 156 The brown-thrush, next to the mocking-bird, [is] the most famous singer of our woods. — **(16) 1831** AUDUBON *Ornith. Biog.* I. 49 The Brown Titlark, *Anthus Spinoletta*, . . . is met with in every portion of the United States which I have visited. **1844** *Nat. Hist. N.Y., Zoology* II. 76 The Little Brown Titlark winters in Louisiana, and as far south as Brazil.

b. In miscellaneous combs.: (1) **brown ash,** the American ash, *Fraxinus pennsylvanica,* or hoop ash, *F. nigra;* (2) **bat,** (see quots.); (3) **berry,** (see quot. 1806), *obs.;* (4) **Bet,** a brown jug, *colloq.;* (5) **Betty,** *(a)* a pudding of fruit, usu. apples, and bread crumbs, *(b)* (not *cap.*) =**betty lamp;** (6) ***bread,** *(a)* (see quot. 1889), *(b)* also attrib.; (7) **cat, catfish,** (see quot.); (8) **corn,** an early-maturing variety of Indian corn, *obs.;* (9) **-eyed Susan,** a name for various plants having bright flowers with dark centers, as the black-eyed Susan *q.v.;* (10) **house,** = **brownstone front;** (11) **meal,** (see quot.), *obs.;* (12) **Brown Mule,** the trade-mark of a popular brand of chewing tobacco (see also quot. 1918); (13) ***people,** mulattoes, *obs.;* (14) ***snake,** any one of various small harmless American snakes of a brown color, as the *Storeria dekayi,* and related species; (15) **snapper,** (see quot.); (16) ***stone,** see as a main entry.

(1) 1832 BROWNE *Sylva* 157 In . . . the provinces of New Brunswick and Nova Scotia the White Ash and the Black Ash, which is sometimes called Water Ash and Brown Ash, are the most abundant in the forests. **1874** *Vt. Bd. Agric. Rep.* II. 529 In Whiting part of this swamp produces brown ash, birch, soft maple and elm. — **(2) 1842** *Nat. Hist. N.Y., Zoology* I. 8 The Little Brown Bat, *Vespertilio subulatus. Ib.* 9 The Little Brown Bat appears to be subject to great variations in size and color. **1867** *Amer. Naturalist* I. 284 The well-known little Brown Bat (*V. subulatus* Say) is generally and abundantly distributed throughout the territory [of Arizona.] — **(3) 1785** WASHINGTON *Diaries* II. 342 Planted eight young Pair Trees . . . in the following places . . . 3 Brown Berries in the west square in the Second plat. **1806** CLARK in *Lewis & C. Exped.* (1905) IV. 13 The Vineing or low brown berry, a light brown berry rather larger and much the Shape of a black haw. — **(4) 1807** J. R. SHAW *Life* (1930) 150 By tipping me a little out of brown Bet, which contained some double fortified stimulous [etc.].

(5) *(a)* **1864** *Yale Lit. Mag.* XXIX. 187 Tea, coffee, pies and 'brown Betty' must next be sacrificed. **1936** LUTES *Country Kitchen* 41 A light dessert followed—an apple dumpling, perhaps, brown Betty, or a custard. *(b)* **1898** EARLE *Customs Old N. Eng.* 125 These lamps were sometimes called 'brown-bettys,' or 'kials,' or 'cruiseys.' — **(6)** *(a)* **1831** *Boston Transcript* 7 Mar. 2/1 'It is not their hilly country nor their fine climate, but their sweet *brown bread,*' to which the rosy cheeks of New England's lads and lasses are to be attributed. **1889** FARMER 90 Brown Bread.—Unlike English brown or bran-bread, the component parts of the American comestible of this name are two-thirds maize meal and one-third rye meal; formerly confined to New England and now, in consequence, known in other parts of the Union as Boston-Bread. **1941** *L.A.* Map 287. *(b)* **1831** *Boston Transcript* 7 Oct. 2/1 It is . . . quite another . . . sort of a thing to be roused from sound sleep at 3 o'clock in the morning, and transported twenty mile, in a driving rain storm to a *dejeuner* of rye coffee and brown bread toast. **1916** EATON *Idyl of Twin Fires* 25, I haven't eaten brown bread Joes since I was a boy. — **(7) 1820** RAFINESQUE in *Western Rev.* II. 359 *Silurus nebulosus* . . . is a large fish, from two to four feet long, and commonly called Yellow cat, Mud cat, and Brown cat, but these names are common to other species. **1842** *Nat. Hist. N.Y., Zoology* IV. 184 The Brown Catfish, *Pimelodus pullus,* . . . is very common in Lake Pleasant, Lake Janet, and many other lakes in the northern districts of the State. — **(8) 1848** C. L. FLEISCHMANN *Nordamerikanische Landwirth* 113 Canada Corn, oder Eight Rowed Yellow Small Corn. . . . Eine veredelte Abart davon, zwölfzeilig, fuhrt den Namen Browne Corne. **1849** *Rep. Comm. Patents: Agric.* (1850) 87 The common eight-rowed, mixed with a kind called the Brown corn, does the best. **1856** *Ib.* xi, The Improved King Philip or Brown Corn . . . was extensively disseminated in all the States north of New Jersey, and throughout the mountainous districts of Pennsylvania, Maryland, and Virginia. — **(9) 1907** LYONS *Plant Names* 404 R[udbeckia] hirta L. Western prairies, nat. in eastern U.S. Black-eyed-Susan, Brown-eyed Susan, Yellow Daisy. **1948** *Dly. Ardmoreite* (Ardmore, Okla.) 11 July 21/4 Dixie and I enjoyed . . . the brown-eyed Susans especially.

(10) 1845 S. JUDD *Margaret* II. viii. 324 The Deacon's . . . was a small, one story brown house. **1861** MRS. STOWE *Pearl Orr's Island* I. ii. 10 Down near the end of Orr's Island . . . stands a brown house. — **(11) 1839** MARRYAT *Diary* II. 35 In the West, when you stop at an inn, they say—'What will you have? Brown Meal and common doings, or white wheat and chicken fixings';—that is, 'Will you have pork and brown bread, or white bread and fried chicken?' — **(12) 1918** *D.N.* 18 *Brown's mule,* any chewing tobacco. **1944** CLARK *Pills* 148 At an early date R. J. Reynolds entered the country-store field with his great rural favorite, Brown Mule, packed in caddies. — **(13) 1836** C. GILMAN *Recoll.* (1838) 270 *n.*, I have known *brown people,* as they are termed, feel too great a contempt for a black leader to become a class-leader. — **(14) 1832** WILLIAMSON *Maine* I. 170 Eight species of Serpents have been seen among us: viz. . . . the little brown Snake, [etc.]. **1868** *Amer. Naturalist* II. 136 On opening a large Black-snake . . . a full-sized Brown-snake (*Tropidonotus occipito-maculatus*) was found in its stomach. **1890** *Cent.* 5724/3 Brown snake, *Haldea striatula* of the southern United States.

(15) 1884 GOODE *Nat. Hist. Aquat. Anim.* 410 The Red Grouper . . north of Florida . . . is called the 'Brown Snapper,' or 'Red-bellied Snapper.'

As the last term in **high brown, John Brown, prairie-dog brown.**

***brownie,** *n.* A kind of chocolate cooky. — **1909** FARMER *Boston Cook Book* 495 [Recipe:] Brownies. **1948** *Household* March 46/2 A moderately slow oven (325°F.) is used for brownies.

***Browning,** *n.* A firearm designed by J. M. Browning (1855–1926), an American inventor. Usu. attrib.

1905 *Dly. Chron.* 9 Feb. 5/2 Hohental fired all the seven chambers of a Browning revolver at Herr Johnsson. **1918** *Collier's* 30 March 17/2 The Browning light machine rifle has yet to show a slight malfunction in action. **1935** *Amer. Mercury* June 207/2 For low-flying pursuit planes and scouts on groundstrafing missions there is the 50-caliber Browning, automatically aimed and loaded. **1948** *Chi. Tribune* 11 April (Grafic Mag.) 8/1 It is now generally known that the Browning 'fifty' was the greatest gun ever carried by a warplane in World War II.

***brownstone,** *n.*

1. A reddish-brown sandstone extensively used as a building material.

[**1836** *Knickerb.* VIII. 390 His poor remains may be found in one corner of a doctor's garden—a brown stone at his head and foot.] **1851** J. H. ROSS *In New York* 207 The stone on which the man was at work was a brown, or what is frequently called red stone. **1871** *N.Y. Tribune* 19 Jan. (De Vere), The brown stone, now so fashionable, is perhaps the most perishable of all materials used in New York house-building. **1894** O. HENRY *Cabbages & Kings* 244 The

Casa Morena . . . was a building of brown stone, luxurious as a palace in its interior.

b. A building made of stone of this kind.

1948 *Time* 8 March 25/1 Nightclubs in sorry brownstones crowd each other like bums in a breadline.

c. brownstone front, a house having a front made of brownstone, in full **brownstone-front house, brownstone-front residence.**

1858 *Spirit of Times* 13 Feb. 377/2 The intended little bijou, which is to be conferred upon the General by these good people, is . . . a solid substantial brown-stone front house and lot. **1866** J. E. COOKE *Surry* 361, I think it would be better than to have a 'brown-stone front' on Fifth or any other avenue. **1909** O. HENRY *Options* 22 The (so-called) Vallambrosa Apartment House . . . is composed of two old-fashioned, brownstone-front residences welded into one. **1946** ADAMS *Album Amer. Hist.* 360 In New York the well-to-do lived in brownstone front houses such as that shown *left*.

2. *attrib.* Designating or pertaining to the well-to-do.

1865 G. HAMILTON *New Atmosphere* 32 The brown-stone friends are shocked and scandalized, which is probably the best thing that could happen to them. **1873** *Winfield* (Kansas) *Courier* 15 Feb. 1/4 There has been some poker in the Manhattan Club, but the brownstone members of that institution have pretty generally attempted to keep it a secret. **1888** BRYCE *Amer. Commonwealth* II. III. lxii. 443 *n.*, The so-called 'brownstone districts' in New York City have, I believe, good [political] Machines. **1909** *N.Y. Sun* 3 Nov. 6 The 'brownstone vote,' as it is called, is cast as completely as is the vote of the most crowded tenement house districts.

***browse,** *n.* (See quot.) — **1879** VIVIAN *Wanderings in Western Land* 54 These logs are hauled over the surface of the hard snow to the 'browse,' which is the bank overhanging the stream down which the timber is to be 'driven' or floated when the ice breaks up in the spring. . . . When the spring comes and the ice breaks up, . . . the 'browses' are let go.

***browse,** *v. intr.* (See quot.) *Rare.* — **1888–90** BARRERE-LELAND I. 185 Browse, to browse, In the United States, to eat here and there, now and then, an expression of Abraham Lincoln's.

browsing line. The level to which cattle browse the foliage of trees. — **1857** OLMSTED *Jour. through Texas* 64 The browsing line under the dense mass of trees was almost as clean cut as that of Busby Park.

bruised,** *a.* (See quot.) *Slang. Obs.* — *a1856** *Burlington Sentinel* in Hall *Coll. Words* (ed. 2) 461 We give a list of a few of the various words and phrases which have been in use . . . to signify some stage of inebriation: . . . Boosy, bruised, screwed [etc.].

* **bruiser,** *n.*

1. (See quot. 1889.) *Slang.*

1830 *Painesville* (Ohio) *Telegraph* 15 June 1/3 He is a fellow of pretty good outward show, but a real *bruiser*, and has also some brains. **1889** FARMER Bruisers.—A generic name in large cities for a rowdy or bully. Sometimes, however, the term has been limited in its application to a particular band of ruffians. This was the case once in Baltimore. **1948** CHAPLIN *Wobbly* 195 Bruisers didn't like to fool around with Frank.

2. (See quots.)

1879 P. L. ISAAC *Notes on Shipping* 65 The old-fashioned bluff-bowed craft, sometimes called 'bruisers.' **1881** E. INGERSOLL *Oyster Industry* 242 *Bruiser*, a short paddle used for beating sponges in process of cleaning. (Florida).

brujo 'bruho, *n. W.* Also **bruja.** [Sp. in same sense.] A sorcerer or witch. — **1922** HERGESHEIMER *Bright Shawl* 156 He caught this negro hysteria, he became a brujos. **1941** FERGUSSON *Southwest* 254 Crescenciana used to tell me that any old hag we met with her blouse stuck full of pins was a bruja. . . . Brujas may cause illness, crop failure, loss of love, and general bad luck.

brulé 'bruˌle, *n.* Also **brule.** [F.]

1. (See quots.)

1793 in GATES *Fur Traders* 77 We could see . . . a large clearing apparently made by fire and which the Canadians would call a Grand-Brulé. **1849** M'LEAN *Notes* I. 122 Our guide, discontented with the short allowance, gave no assistance, till coming to an extensive 'brulé,' he was completely *at fault*, as no marks of any kind could be discovered. **1922** KEPHART *So. Highlanders* 99 It was above the Fire-scald, a brulé or burnt-over space on the southern side of the ridge between Briar Knob and Laurel Top.

attrib. **1925** HEMING *Living Forest* 89 'What's a brule country?' I asked. 'A forest of burnt timber.'

2. (*cap.*) Short for **Boisbrûlé.**

1831 in FRIEDERICI (1947). **1847** PARKMAN in *Knickerb.* XXX. 290 The *Brulé*, and other western bands of the *Dahcotahs*, are thorough savages. **1898** KING *Warrior Gap* 28 The great war-chief of the Brulés —Sintogaliska—Spotted Tail, the white man's friend, gave solemn warning not to trust the Ogallallas. **1948** *Scientific Mo.* July 46/1 Mostly French or *Brûlés* (half-breeds), these swarthy men were truly the heroes of the canoe.

attrib. **1908** VISSCHER *Pony Expr.* 96 Many names were parleyed over, and at last the general commanding was informed that the Brules Sioux would listen to and believe in the Great Father's 'First Good Man' that had been sent to them as agent after the War of 1876.

brulot 'brulo, *n.* [F. *brûlot*, in the Amer. F. sense shown here.] A gnat or midge, prob. a buffalo gnat *q.v.*

1705 HARRIS *Navigantium atque itinerantium* II. 926/2 The Brulots are a sort of Hand Worms, which cleave so hard to the Skin, that their prickling occasions the same pain as though it were a spark of Fire. **1758** LE PAGE DU PRATZ *Histoire de la Louisiane* II. 149 Il n'en est pas de même des Brûlots: ceux ci, quoiqu'ils ne soient pas plus gros que la pointe d'une épingle, sont insupportables aux gens de travail dans la campagne. **1841** DE SMET *Letters* (1843) 115 Another species of insects, called brulots, are found by myriads in the desert, and are not less troublesome than the musquito. **1857** *Spirit of Times* 5 Dec. 210/1 The voyageurs say, that nothing but a wet blanket will keep off these *brulons*. **1941** MCDERMOTT *Glossary* 35 Probably the *brûlot* and the buffalo gnat . . . are the same insect. In the Minnesota Country the word is used for midges.

brummer 'brumɚ, *n. Pa.* (See quot. 1924.) — **1898** *Lebanon* (Pa.) *News* 20 Jan. in *Cong. Rec.* Feb. 1506/1 Our people can again hear the sweet familiar sounds of the 'brummer,' which to many is more agreeable music than any of the Wagner compositions. **1924** LAMBERT *Dict. Pa.-Ger.* 33 Brummer . . . , m. steam factory whistle. G Brummer.

* **Brunonian. 1.** *n.* A student or alumnus of Brown University, Providence, R.I. **2.** *a.* Pertaining to Brown University.

(1) **1829** (*title*), The Brunonian. Edited by the Students of Brown University. **1889** *Cent.* 699/2. **1900** *Brown Alumni Mo.* I. 6/1 (*caption*), Brunonians far and near. — (2) **1909** *Memories of Brown* 8 The editors . . . have desired to . . . create in the contemporary mind a fuller consciousness of the continuity of Brunonian tradition and aspiration. **1917** *Brown Alumni Mo.* XVII. 259/1 To the consternation of the Brunonian rooters, Umpire Lanigan called it a ball.

Brunswick stew. (See quot. 1899.)

1856 DAVIS *Farm Bk.* 56 Our dinner consisted of the following Bill of Fare. . . . Soup Gumbo Brunswick Stew. **1899** GREEN *Va. Word-Bk.* 71 Brunswick Stew, *n.* A stew made of squirrel or chicken meat, lima beans and green corn cooked together and seasoned with pepper and salt. **1947** BEROLZHEIMER *Regional Cookbook* 200 Brunswick Stew [was] originated by one of the race of 'born cooks' . . . Dr. Haskins' 'Uncle Jimmy' of Brunswick County, Virginia. . . . The original stew was made of squirrel with no vegetables, but onions.

* **brush,** *n.*

1. A region where small trees, shrubs, chaparral, etc., abound; the backwoods.

Baker finds this in Australian use as early as 1799. See *Amer. Sp.* Dec. 1943, 254. This sense therefore may be old in British use.

?**1775** in *Amer. Sp.* XV. 161/2 Carr hunted over in Kentucky beyond the Cumberland montaine to the right of Cumberland gap in a

Brush fence

place called the brush. **1791** *Ib.*, To a white Oak & red Oak near a hollow in the Edge of Brush. **1881** PIERSON *In the Brush* 9, I was once present at an ecclesiastical meeting in the Brush. *Ib.*, My experiences in the Brush. [**1929** DOBIE *Vaquero* 201 The worst brush in the United States . . . is . . . McMullen, Webb, Duval, Live Oak, and other counties between the Nueces River and the Rio Grande.]

2. A brush harrow or drag.

1943 DAMON *Sense of H.* 122 After the plowing is over, Samuel . . . can go about his next business of making a 'brush.'

3. *attrib.* Designating structures, usu. temporary, made of brush, as (1) **brush arbor,** (2) **blind,** (3) **cabin,** (4) **camp,** (5) **chute,** (6) **dam,** (7) **drag,** (8) **fence,** (9) **heap,** (10) **house,** (11) **hut,** (12) **lodge,** (13) **net,** (14)

pile, (15) **shade,** (16) **shanty,** (17) **shed,** (18) **stable,** (19) **tent.**

(1) **1851** Woods *Gold Diggings* 62 W. is now putting up a brush arbor, to guard us more effectually against the heat of the sun. **1948** *Democrat* (Negro Supp. 1) April 3/3 This organization built a brush arbor to serve for a church. — (2) **1895** *Outing* XXVII. 231/2 Daybreak . . . found us ensconced in a brush blind on the spot where the flock had been scattered. — (3) **1825** Neal *Bro. Jonathan* III. 404 After many weeks of incredible hardship, he slept in a brush cabin. where he found part of a mocassin. — (4) **1776** *Essex Inst. Coll.* LIII. 89 Marched to Lake Champlain, 10 miles. . . . Staid in a brush camp. **1897** *Outing* XXX. 190/2 The outfit from Maine, log-cabin, brush-camps, guides and all, was busy at the old stand.

(5) **1903** A. Adams *Log Cowboy* 16 When we reached the brush chute, all hands started them on a run for the water. — (6) **1854** Marcy *Expl. Red River* 34 It occurred to me that the plan of erecting our brush dams must have been originally suggested from witnessing those of the beavers. — (7) **1801** *Mass. Spy* 21 Oct. (Th.), They had met at Franklin with a view of fishing the Miami with what is called a brush drag. **1857** *Spirit of Times* 7 Mar. 6/1 They cut them [grapevines] away, and interweaving them with the thick branches of the buckeye and paw-paw, soon constructed what they called a 'brush drag'; and commenced on the upper part of some deep pool of water, they stretched it across from shore to shore. — (8) **1729** Hempstead *Diary* 212, I made 42 Rod Brush fence from the Hill of Rocks at the old orch[ar]d towards the new. **1880** *Scribner's Mo.* Feb. 504/1 A lawful brush fence must be a rod wide, with no specification as to its height. **1948** *Neb. Hist.* June 97 Once a field had been cleared the branches were trimmed from the tree trunks with an axe and used to construct a 'brush fence' about the clearing. — (9) **1809** Irving *Knickerb.* v. ii. 28 He was a perfect brush-heap in a blaze, snapping and crackling for a time, and then ending in smoke. **1945** McAtee *Pheasant* 106 The birds roosting on the ground were in brush heaps and brier patches.

(10) **1862** Norton *Army Lett.* 64 When we came back we burned all the log barracks and brush houses at the forts. **1883** *Rep. Indian Affairs* 21 While these Indians live entirely in tents, tepes, and brush houses, . . . they are fast adopting the customs of whites in manner of dress. — (11) **1889** *Cent. Mag.* April 908/2 We were never out of sight of the brush huts of the Indians. **1893** K. Sanborn *S. California* 140 They had substantial brush huts, supported by pillars. —(12) **1805** Lewis in *L. & Clark Exped.* (1905) III. 6 At the distance of five miles he arrived at some brush lodges of the Shoshones. — (13) **1807** Gass *Journal* 29 What [fish] we caught were taken with trails or brush nets. — (14) **1865** Whittier *Snow-Bound* l. 59 A smooth white mound the brush-pile showed. **1945** Botkin *My Burden* 247 When we got cold we'd crawl in a brushpile and hug up close together to keep warm.

(15) **1850** L. Sawyer *Way Sketches* 94 These enterprising traders had just arrived and set up a brush shade for a house. – (16) **1857** Hammond *Northern Scenes* 111 Our boatman built for our accommodation, a brush shanty in the place of our tents. — (17) **1877** W. Wright *Big Bonanza* 65 Some . . . did their cooking in the open air under a brush-shed. — (18) **1835** *S. Lit. Messenger* I. 581 The pony . . . moves homeward . . . leaping every obstacle in his way to his brush stable. — (19) **1862** *Harper's Mag.* June 16/1 In the yard . . . were several chapadens or brush-tents in which whisky, gin, aguardiente and other refreshments . . . were for sale. **1873** Beadle *Undevel. West* 654 John D. Lee has pre-empted the pool, and has his wife Rachel living there in a sort of brush tent. **1879** C. F. McGlashan *Donner Party* (1947) 117 The rest of us went to work and built a brush tent in which to keep our provisions.

b. In the sense "overgrown with brush," as (1) **brush country,** (2) **land,** (3) **lot,** (4) **patch,** (5) **plain.**

(1) **1923** J. H. Cook *On Old Frontier* 33 The buffalo never ranged in the 'brush country.' **1946** *This Week Mag.* 12 Jan. 5/1 They began to make their way through the brush country. — (2) **1853** *Mich. Agric. Soc. Trans.* 631 The fields . . . look more like what is commonly called brush land than they do like a white man's improvements. **1947** Bump *Ruffed Grouse* 234 Brushlands, be they overgrown pastures or slashings, seldom contain adequate amounts of species furnishing winter shelter for grouse. — (3) **1943** Damon *Sense of H.* 122, I remember the years when this field we plow was a 'brush lot.' **1947** Edminster *Ruffed Grouse* 43 The grouse were to be found along wood-land edges, in brush lots and even out along hedge-rows. — (4) **1867** J. N. Edwards *Shelby* 206 Furloughed militia darted out from every haystack and brush patch to have one good shout for Lincoln.

(5) **1661** *Manchester Town Rec.* 15 Where the way now is that gose to . . . and through the brushee plain. **1856** *Spirit of Times* (N.Y.) 18 Oct. 113/1 Rabbit . . . can only now be found . . . where there are extensive brush-plains.

4. In special combs.: (1) **brush ape,** a term of contempt for a backwoodsman or mountaineer, *rare;* (2) **breaker,** one who lives in the brush or backwoods; (3) **breaking,** *W.* the breaking off of brush by riding boldly through it, cf. prec.; (4) **broom,** (*a*) *S.* a large broom made of shrubs, as young dogwoods, used chiefly for sweeping yards, (*b*) (see quot.); (5) **burner,** one who burns brush, esp. in clearing land for cultivation, also **brush burning;** (6) **ends,** the tips or points of brush-wood; (7) **fire,** a fire in brush or fed by brush, also transf.; (8) **hand,** *W.* a cowboy accustomed to work in a brush country; (9) **hat,** a kind of fur hat made from Russian hare skins which were brushed for hours at a time in preparing them, *obs.;* (10) **horse,** *W.* a cow pony used to a brush country; (11) **meeting,** a meeting held in the brush or backwoods; (12) **plow,** (see quot.); (13) **popper,** *W.* a cowboy accustomed to handling cattle in a brush country, also **brush popping,** *a.;* (14) **rabbit,** a small rabbit, *Sylvilagus bachmani,* found on the Pacific Coast; (15) **road,** a country or backwoods road; (16) **whisky,** whisky made illicitly in the brush or backwoods; (17) **wolf,** a coyote.

(1) **1933** T. Williamson *Woods Colt* 69, I want to git out of here before a bunch of these *brush apes* swarm down out of the woods an' take him away from me. — (2) **1881** H. W. Pierson *In the Brush* 6 Father A—— . . . is an old Brush-Breaker. . . . He has broken a right smart chance of brush. — (3) **1941** *Reader's Digest* Oct. 155 'Brush breaking' derives its name from the peculiar brittleness of the timber in the high dry altitude of the Southwest. One can ride at full speed into a piñon tree and the chances are that the momentum will smack off even good-sized branches. — (4) (*a*) **1864** Cate *Two Soldiers* 30, I had every man to turn out with his brush broom to clean the battery for inspection. **1898** Harris *Tales* 179 Don't you tell mistiss dat I been free, kaze she'll take a bresh-broom an' run me off'n de place when I go back home. (*b*) **1910** *D.N.* III. 438 Brush-broom, *n.* A whisk-broom made from broom-corn.

(5) **1859** A. Cary *Country Life* 7 The half-holiday was less welcome than as if it had brought a log-rolling, brush-burning, or stone quarrying with it. **1890** *Juliaetta* (Idaho) *Gem* 9 Aug. 1/1 Have you noticed how queer the creek bottom looks since the brush burners have tackled it? — (6) **1868** *Rep. Comm. Agric.* 256 In single-line hedge the saplings are so wound between as to press against the stakes, the tips or brush ends being all turned to the beveled or slanting side. **1889** *Harper's Mag.* Jan. 230/2 The brush ends inclined towards the bottom of the stream. — (7) [**1777** *N.C. Morav. Rec.* III. (1926) 1145 The hard wind brought the brush-fire toward Peter Rose's fence so rapidly that he was obliged to call several Brethren to help put it out.] **1850** Garrard *Wah-To-Yah* xviii. 213 The spiral smoke, turning gray in the twilight, rose from the brushfire through Louys' exertions. **1947** *Chi. D. News* 15 May 1/3 The family outcast is stirring up a brush fire of liberal resentment against the Truman administration. — (8) **1929** Dobie *Vaquero* 205 A brush hand can work on the prairie as well as any prairie-trained cowboy. — (9) **1865** *Three Yrs. in the U.S.* 183 The business of this latter firm may be looked upon as of an exceptional character, being wholly confined to the manufacture of 'brush hats.' This class of goods is only known to the trade in Great Britain by name.

(10) **1929** Dobie *Vaquero* 206 Like the brush hand, the brush horse is a distinct type. — (11) **1890** *Cong. Rec.* 9 May 4376/2, I remember in 1887 attending a great prohibition meeting that was held over in Virginia, called a brush meeting. — (12) **1889** *Cent.* 700/2 brush-plow. . . . A strong plow used for breaking up rough land covered with brush and small trees. — (13) **1929** Dobie *Vaquero* 86 Walton knew that I was a brush popper and that I hankered for ranger service; so he gave me the chance. **1947** *Chi. D. News* 14 Jan. 29/2 He's an' old brush-poppin' hoss, Wes. — (14) **1907** White *Arizona Nights* 10 And me squatting behind that ore dump about as formidable as a brush rabbit. **1912** *Out West* March 161/2 One of the greatest difficulties with which the forester met in his replanting scheme was the destruction of young trees by the brush rabbits.

(15) **1878** Beadle *Western Wilds* 36 Didn't you come sneakin' along brush-road from Nauvoo t'other day, then? — (16) **1885** Craddock *Prophet* 22 The brush whiskey [was] warming his heart. **1913** M. W. Morley *Carolina Mts.* 66 That important beverage, variously known as . . . 'blockade,' 'brush whiskey,' and in the outer world, 'corn whiskey,' which is extracted from the grain and surreptitiously distributed. — (17) **1923** *Frontier* March 11 Presently a brush wolf yapped. **1946** Stanwell-Fletcher *Driftwood Valley* 24 A little 'brush wolf,' or coyote, stared at us from a high bank, and vanished.

As the last term in **antelope, arrow, bitter, black, break, broom, buck, bugle, cane, chemise, deer, Flora's paint, gin, hazel, mesquite, paint, painter's, pea, quail, rabbit, sage, scarlet painter's, Shaker, snuff, tooth, under brush.**

*__brush,__ *v.*[1] **1.** *tr.* To mend, repair (a fence, road) with brush. **2.** To provide (peas) with brush to climb on. — (1) **1730** Hempstead *Diary* 219 Jno. Larkins workt cutting of fenceing Stuff & brushing fence. **1905** *Forestry Bureau Bul.* 61 *s.v.*, *To brush a road,* to cover with brush the mud-holes and swampy places in a logging road,to make it solid. (N[orthern] F[orest]). — (2) **1889** *Cent.* 700/1 To brush peas.

∗ **brush,** *v.*[2]

1. *tr.* To force, bring on. Also to drive (a horse) smartly or briskly.

1755 *Conn. Gazette* 29 Nov. (De Vere), As tending to beget ill will, and brushing a disunion in the several governments in America. **1868** WOODRUFF *Trotting Horse* 70 Eight or ten days prior to the race . . . brush him half a mile. **1904** *N.Y. Times* 28 Nov. 5 The drivers . . . spent a couple of hours before dusk brushing their fast steppers on the upper stretch.

2. a. *brush in,* to plant small grain or seed by covering it lightly, as with a light brush. **b.** ∗ *brush off,* to smarten, tidy up by brushing. **c.** ∗ *brush over,* to cultivate rapidly or superficially. *Colloq.*

(a) 1912 DAWSON *Pioneer Tales* 270 Wheat, rye, and oats were sown broadcast and brushed in with log-spiked harrows or bushy tree-tops dragged across the fields. — **(b) 1882** G. A. SALA *America Revisited* I. 270 The Transatlantic Brush Fiend does not brush you 'down.' He brushes you 'off.' **1944** *Dict. Amer. Eng.* 2473/2 Whisk broom. A small broom used for brushing off clothes. — **(c) 1788** WASHINGTON *Diaries* III. 416 The other hands [were] brushing over the Potatoes in the Corn.

3. To nose out, trail (a deer); to hunt out, reconnoiter (woods).

1827 COOPER *Prairie* x, I have at this moment a dog brushing a deer, not far from this. **1829** ——— *Wish-Ton-Wish* xxviii, There was a party sent to brush the woods on the trail of Indians. **1855** SIMMS *Forayers* 207 Whether knocked up or not, we must brush that wood before dark.

∗ **brushed,** *a.* **1.** Overgrown with brush. **2.** Bewildered, confused, as if lost in the brush. *Rare.*

(1) 1666 *Duxbury Rec.* 16 A certain parcel of land . . . marked with divers trees, until you come to a low brushed swamp. **1888** *Cent. Mag.* Jan. 453/1 A cañon, liberally wooded or 'brushed' with wild plums. — **(2) 1881** H. W. PIERSON *In the Brush* 7 Didn't you think the Bishop got badly *brushed* in the first part of his sermon? . . . It's a comfort to a beginner to know that an old preacher sometimes gets brushed.

Bryanism ˈbraɪənˌɪzəm, *n.* The political philosophy of Wm. J. Bryan (1860–1925).

1896 *Chi. Tribune* 20 Aug. 6/2 The Democrats of New York have repudiated . . . Bryanism in an overwhelming outburst of enthusiasm for honest money. **1900** *Boston Transcript* 15 May 3/3 James Belford . . . who was converted to Bryanism in 1896, has come out for the Republican party again. **1908** *St. Louis Globe-Democrat* 2 July 6/1 Some rather crude attempts are being made . . . to show that the Bryan ticket of 1908 will not mean Bryanism at all, but something which will be harmless to the country.

Bryanite ˈbraɪənˌaɪt, *n.* A political follower of Wm. J. Bryan (1860–1925). — **1908** *St. Louis Globe-Democrat* 6 July 4/1 None but Bryanites are to be on guard at Denver. **1947** *Newsweek* 8 Sep. 24/1 The Bryanites promised. This week, on Labor Day, the statue was dedicated.

bub bʌb, *n.* [Perhaps f. dial. ∗ *bubby,* see *EDD s.v.* **booby,** but cf. ex. 1889 below.] Brother, little fellow, boy. *Colloq.* See also **bloody bub.**

[1837 *Knickerb.* X. 521 Have you at present any of the *chastised idiot-brother*. . . . What I want is what *you* call *whipped syllabub*.] **1839** BRIGGS *H. Franco* II. 189 'Speak louder, Bub,' said one of the vice presidents, encouragingly. **1889** BARRERE-LELAND I. 187 Bub, bubby (American), a term very commonly applied to a little boy. It came from Pennsylvania, where it was derived from the German bube, which is commonly abbreviated to bub.**1948** *Chi. Star* 24 April 3/4 Hey bub—can I get a squint at yer uppers?

∗ **bubble,** *n.* As the last term in **Mississippi bubble, oil bubble, Washoe bubble.**

bubble bowl. A small-mouthed bowl, usu. of clear glass, into which, when half-filled with water, short-stemmed flowers are put and allowed to float. — **1936** *Durant* (Okla.) *D. Democrat* 28 March 4/1 Small bubble bowls filled with pansies and other cut flowers were used as decorations.

∗ **bubbler,** *n.*

1. The fresh-water drumfish, *Aplodinatus grunniens,* found in the Great Lakes and Mississippi Valley.

1819 *Western Rev.* I. 372 Grunting Bubbler, *Amblodon grunniens.* . . . The vulgar names of this fish are white perch, . . . bubbler, and muscle-eater. **1832** FLINT *Miss. Valley* I. 79 Bubbler *amblodon,* Buffalo perch. Found in all the waters of the Ohio. . . . It is a fine fish for the table. **1871** DE VERE 383 The Bubbler . . . when drawn from the waters of the Ohio, . . . makes an extraordinary bubbling noise, as if protesting against such treatment.

2. A drinking fountain consisting of a small nozzle from which water bubbles up.

[1911 *Survey* 22 April 146/2 The Board of Public Improvements has ordered that bubbling fountains must take the place of the drinking cup.] **1926** *Sanitary and Heating Eng.* July 582 Every Test, Century *Bubblers* are Sanitary and Attractive. **1944** C. LAWRENCE *Narrowing Wind* 137 She left the washroom and went to the bubbler, which she let run a long time before drinking from it.

bubbling ˈbʌblɪŋ, *n.* [f. "automobubble," jocular term for an automobile. See L.A. Map 185.] (See quot.) *Obs.* — **1900** *N.Y. Journal* 11 Nov. 28/1 Perhaps the most popular fad of the week was 'bubbling.' This you know is the fashionable slang for automobiling or locomobling or whatever you choose to call it.

∗ **bubby,** *n.* In combs., as **bubby blossom, bush, flower, shrub,** as names for the strawberry shrub or one of its fragrant dark-red flowers (see quots. 1791 and 1945). Cf. **sweet bubby.**

1791 ANBUREY *Travels* II. 352 A shrub peculiar to this province [Va.] . . . bears a small flower, which the inhabitants term the bubby flower; . . . the name . . . arises from a custom that the women have of putting this flower down their bosoms, . . . till it has lost all its grateful perfume. **1883** HARRIS *Nights* (1911) 70 Ole Brer Rabbit, he mouter had some bubby-blossoms wrop up in his hankcher. **1893** *Amer. Folk-Lore* VI. 141 *Calycanthus glaucus,* bubby-bush. Banner Elk, N.C. **1945** MCATEE *Nomina Abitera* 12 Strawberry Shrubs (Calycanthus spp.)—These are familiar garden shrubs, the globular flowers of which probably inspire the common names of bubby, bubby-blossoms, bubby-bush, bubby-shrub.

buccarebou bʌkˈkærəbu, *n.* =**caribou.** *Obs.* — **1795** J. SULLIVAN *Hist. of Maine* 11 There was an animal called by the natives the *buc-carebou,* which was peculiar to the District. **1796** MORSE *Amer. Geog.* I. 388 An animal called by the natives, buccarebou, of a size between the moose and the deer, was formerly found in this country [Maine].

Buchanier ˌbjukəˈnɪr, *n.* Also **Buchananer.** [f. Jas. *Buchanan* (1791–1869), 15th Pres. of the U.S.] A term used by Buchanan's political opponents for his followers or supporters, in punning allusion to "buccaneer." Also attrib. *Obs.*

1856 *Iroquois Republican* (Middleport, Ill.) 17 July 2/6 He claimed that he had never changed his creed and that he was now a Buecaneer Democrat. **1856** *Western Citizen* (Paris, Ky.) 1 Aug. 3/3 The dirtiest trick of the Buchananers is the statement that Herbert, who killed the Irish waiter at Washington, is a Know Nothing. **1860** *Press & Tribune* (Chi.) 23 Feb. 1/1 Henry L. Lane and O. P. Morton are a pair of nags that will distance any team that the Douglasites or Buchaneers may put on the track.

∗ **buck,** *n.*[1]

1. A deerskin, as a standard of value among Indians. *Obs.*

1748 C. WEISER *Journal* 41 He has been robbed of the value of 300 Bucks, & you [Indians] all know by whom. *Ib.,* Every cask of Whiskey shall be sold to you [Indians] for 5 Bucks in your town. **1789** in CIST *Cincinnati* 215 Another Indian . . . was forced to pay two bucks more. **1834** *Mass. H.S. Coll.* 3 Ser. VI. 147 If they [the Indians] took him away so that he should lose him, he would make them pay him a thousand bucks.

2. A male sheep. [So. G. *bock,* Du. *bok.*]

1812 *Niles' Reg.* II. 240/1 The product [of wool] was as follows: a Buck (*Judas*) 12 lbs. 4 oz. **1881** HAYES *New Colorado* 60 His 'bucks' (say about three to each hundred ewes) will generally be Merinos. **1948** *Dly. Ardmoreite* (Ardmore, Okla.) 25 June 2/2 Bulk good and choice native spring lambs 29.00; bucks out at 28.00.

3. Ellipt. for (1) **buckskin,** referring to the skin of a buck and to a Virginian, *obs.,* (2) **buckshot,** (3) **buck private.**

(1) 1787 M. CUTLER in *Life* (1888) I. 250 In the stage were General Armstrong and Colonel Franks . . . Both of them high Bucks, and affected, as I conceived, to hold the New England States in contempt. **1845** J. W. NORRIS *Chi. Directory* 119 Retail Dealers in . . . Buffalo Robes, Buffalo Overshoes, Buck Mitts. — **(2) 1845** SIMMS *Wigwam & Cabin* II. 107 On using big buck, he numbered two sevens for a load; the small buck, three. **1895** *Outing* Dec. 214/2, I vainly searched for a charge of buck. — **(3) 1922** *Ardmore* (Okla.) *D. Press* 14 Jan. 1/5 The former leather-necks, gobs, bucks, shavetails, etc., had finally taken their places

4. A counter used in poker. Cf. **6.** (2) below.

1878 HART *Sazerac Lying Club* 33 The boys was playin' poker at four bits ante and shove the buck. **1891** *Hoffmann's Cyclo. Card & Table Games* 203 Straight Poker. . . . To avoid dispute as to whose turn it may be, a pocket-knife, known as the 'buck,' is passed round, resting with the player whose turn it is to 'chip' for the remainder. **1938**

ASBURY *Sucker's Prog.* 27 The buck could be any object, but was usually a knife, and most Western men in those days carried knives with buck horn handles, hence the name.

5. In combs.: (1) **buck aborigine,** =**buck Indian;** (2) **ague,** nervous excitement felt by a hunter at the sight of game, orig. deer, also transf., cf. ***thump,** *n.;* (3) **and ball,** (see quot. 1889); (4) **and wing,** a kind of tap dance, poss. of Negro origin, orig. and usu. attrib.; (5) **bathing,** (see quot.), *slang;* (6) **beer,** =**bock beer,** *obs.;* (7) **dance, dancer, dancing,** (see **buck and wing**); (8) **eye, -eyed,** see as main entries; (9) **fever,** =**buck ague;** (10) **handled,** having a handle made of buckhorn; (11) **horn,** see as a main entry; (12) **Indian,** a male Indian; (13) **load,** a load or charge used in shooting a buck, also transf.; (14) **nigger,** a male Negro; (15) **nun,** (see quot. 1944), *slang;* (16) **private,** a common soldier below the rank of private first class; (17) **rake,** an exceptionally large rake for raking hay; (18) **scrape,** a place where the ground has been scraped by deer; (19) **scraper,** a single-handed road scraper having steel runners for elevating the load, a fresno scraper; (20) **shot,** see as a main entry; (21) **snatcher,** a river boat used in piratical undertakings, *obs.;* (22) ***tail,** see as a main entry; (23) **warrior,** a male Indian warrior, *obs.*

(1) 1879 MIGHELS *Sagebrush Leaves* 167 The buck aborigine takes more solid comfort than the female of his tribe. — **(2) 1844** GREGG *Commerce of Prairies* II. 24, I have often heard backwoodsmen speak of the 'buck ague,' but commend me to the 'buffalo fever' of the Prairies for novelty and amusement. **1945** *Democrat* 19 April 1/1 Willie Tucker . . . found that turkey hunting and buck ague don't go together. — **(3)** [**1776** MACKENZIE *Diary* I. 138 The Rebels had thier pieces loaded with a ball and 3 Buckshot each. **1867** DEVENS *Pictorial Bk.* 463 Buck, Ball & Co., take charge of all baggage.] **1889** *Cent.* 704/3 buck-and-ball. . . . A cartridge for smooth-bore firearms containing a spherical bullet and three buck-shot: now little used. — **(4) 1895** *N.Y. Dramatic News* 23 Nov. 13/4 Burt Jordon, an exceedingly agile buck and wing dancer, was a hit at Keith's last week. **1902** LORIMER *Lett. Merchant* 177 Get something that won't keep people guessing whether you follow the horses or do buck and wing dancing for a living. **1945** MATHEWS *Talking* 45 He would get up from his chair, wave his great black hat, and do a buck-and-wing on the pine flooring, giving a Comanche yell as he finished.

(5) 1931 *Atlantic City News* 7 Aug. 4/3 Devotees of 'buck bathing' who dance in the nude in and out of the surf are also unwelcome in Brigantine. — **(6) 1859** BARTLETT 51 *Buck beer.* (German, *bock bier.*) The strongest kind of German beer. . . . It is, of course, intoxicating. **1880** NYE *B. Nye & Boomerang* 37 He looked like the man who first discovered and introduced Buck beer into the country. — **(7) 1840** *Spirit of Times* 2 May 103/2 (We.), The extra clearing in turn for the finishing buck dance. **1896** *N.Y. Dramatic News* 29 Aug. 8/3 Conwell and O'Day, buck dancers, made a gigantic hit at Ferris Wheel park. **1897** G. ADE *Pink Marsh* 73, I use' to know cullud boy in Tuhkish bath place 'at got job on' e stage doin' buck-dancin'. **1925** J. BLACK *You Can't Win* iv. (1926) 39 The young negroes began singing and buck dancing. — **(9) 1841** *S. Lit. Messenger* VII. 224/2 If you see a deer . . . you'll be sure to git the buck fever. **1946** *Fur, Fish, & Game* July 4/2 In cases of the sort fishermen are often afflicted with a species of 'buck fever.'

(10) 1840 *S. Lit. Messenger* VI. 507/1 [He] was a tall strapping fellow, with a mouth always standing half-open, like an old case of buck-handled knives. **1911** *Cosmopolitan* March 504/2 Where's my buck-handled knife? — **(12) 1840** HOFFMAN *Greyslaer* II. 54 There they lay on the grass, six big buck Injuns, likely fellows all. **1936** BARNARD *Rider* 61 We cowpunchers had no use for the boomers. They came into our country, plowed up good grass, and started to nesting and working like the devil. Even the buck Indians did not work! — **(13) 1836** *Quarter Race Ky.* (1846) 14 Colonel, let us have some of your *byled* corn—pour me out a buck load—there—never mind about the water. **1891** SLOAN *Fogy Days* 16 Bang, bang, our double-barrel went, And two buck loads at him we sent. — **(14) 1835** *Vade Mecum* (Phila.) 17 Jan. 3/6 A buck nigger is worth the slack of two or three hundred dollars. **1844** *N.O. Picayune* 19 Feb. 1/4 Among the rest, a big buck nigger got at it, and mesmerised all the darkies in the settlement. **1941** DANIELS *Tar Heels* 49 Sometimes in summer there is almost a pulse in it like a buck nigger panting.

(15) 1907 WHITE *Arizona Nights* III. iii. 286, I might as well go be a buck nun and be done with it. **1944** ADAMS *W. Words* 22 Buck-nun. A recluse, a man who lives alone. — **(16) 1926** *Collier's* 29 May 6/4 Some of the novels was all the rage when Julius Cæsar was a buck private, what I mean! **1947** *Chi. Sun* 26 Dec. 36/3 A little buck private on the plane casually explained that the stop was to let him off. — **(17) 1908** *U.S. Dept. Agric. Farmer's Bul.* 339 24 This is then in proper shape for loading on to the hayrack with a hay loader or for handling with sweep rakes, buck rakes, or 'go-devils.' **1948** *Dly. Ardmoreite* (Ardmore, Okla.) 3 May 7/8 For Sale—Grain binder; IHC tractor, mower, tractor buck rake, sulky rake. — **(18) 1885** *Outing* Oct. 68/1 We had walked about a quarter of a mile when we found a fresh buck-scrape. — **(19) 1890** *Stock Grower* 31 May 6/1 Level off with buck scraper all knolls. **1911** FORBES *Irrigation & Agric. Practice* 65 The buck scraper is one of the most effective tools known for moving dirt by horse-power.

(21) 1830 *Western Mo. Review* III. 356 For night and secret work Plug had a fleet of Bucksnatchers with chosen crews, to row up and down the river. — **(23) 1876** *Cong. Rec.* June 3505/1 These buck warriors smell the warpath.

b. In the names of, or with reference to, plants and animals: (1) **buck antelope,** a male pronghorn; (2) **bass,** a species of black bass; (3) **berry,** a berry eaten by deer, as a southern huckleberry, *Gaylussacia ursina,* or the fruit of *Polycodium stamineum,* of the eastern states, cf. **seedy buckberry;** (4) **brush,** any one of various shrubby plants upon which deer browse; (5) **bush,** a species of *Symphoricarpos,* also a buckbrush; (6) **elk,** a male elk; (7) **fly,** (see quot.); (8) **lamb,** a male lamb, cf. G. *bocklamm;* (9) **moth,** (see quot.); (10) **mouse,** (see quot.); (11) **root,** *Psoralea canescens,* a blue-flowered herb of the pea family, known also as scurvy pea, wild alfalfa, cf. **Indian turnip, prairie potato;** (12) **wood,** (see quot. 1810).

(1) 1812 STUART *Narratives* 160 Our living has been and is of the meanest kind being poor Bull meat or Buck Antelope, both too bad to be eat except in cases of starvation. — **(2) 1883** *Cent. Mag.* July 376/2 Other names have been conferred on account of their pugnacity or voracity, as, tiger, bull, sow, and buck bass. **1888** *Wildwood's Mag.* (Chicago) June 64 In the north and west both species are known as 'bass,' with the addition of various adjectives expressive of gameness, coloration, or habitat, as . . . 'buck-bass'; black, green, or yellow-bass. — **(3) 1824** J. DODDRIDGE *Notes* 86 An indifferent kind of fruit, called buckberries, used to grow on small shrubs. . . . This fruit has nearly vanished from the settled parts of the country. **1920** STEPHENS *Life at Laurel Town* 14 Such substitutes as nature . . . is able to plant in Kansas—sumach and buckberry [etc.]. — **(4) 1874** LONG *Wild-Fowl* 179 He may find good shooting, . . . when the buck-brush is so close that the boat cannot be easily pushed through it. **1948** *Democrat* 24 June 6/2 The animal . . . is an asset to a farmer since it helps clear buck brush.

(5) 1918 VISHER *So. Dakota* 93 The buck-bush, is a transition stage between grassland and woodland, and the sage brush between grassland and desert. — **(6) 1750** T. WALKER *Journal* 26 May 64 Our Dogs roused a large Buck Elk. **1839** Z. LEONARD *Adventures* (1904) 62 I have killed two big Buck Elk. — **(7) 1859** BARTLETT 52 *Buck fly.* an insect which torments the deer at certain seasons. — **(8) 1852** *Mich. Agric. Soc. Trans.* III. 25 Best pen of 5 buck lambs. — **(9) 1889** *Cent.* buck-moth. . . . A name given to a delicate crape-winged moth, *Hemileuca maia* (Drury), of the family *Bombycidae:* so called, it is said, on account of its flying late in the fall, when the deer run.

(10) 1857 *Rep. Comm. Patents: Agric.* 90 The white-footed wood-mouse is known under the names of 'Deer Mouse,' 'Buck Mouse,' 'White-footed Field Mouse.' — **(11) 1765** J. BARTRAM *Diary* 24 July, Rode to observe A lovely species of onobrichis with large aromatick root & very regular branched stalk 3 foot high people calls it here buck root & say it is very good for inward pains. — **(12) 1787** M. CUTLER in *Life,* etc. II. 397 The prevailing growth of timber and the more useful trees are maple or sugar-tree, . . . butternut, . . . buckwood. **1810** MORSE *Amer. Gazetteer s.v. Ohio,* Hickory, cherry, buckwood or horse chesnut, [etc.].

6. In colloq. phrases: (1) *as hearty as a buck,* quite hale and hearty; (2) *to pass the buck,* originally in poker to ante and pass or hand on the buck to the next player in token of one's desire not to deal, latterly to shift responsibility to another, also in allusive contexts.

(1) 1835 CROCKETT *Tour* 8 So, so middlin'. I'm hearty as a buck, but can't jump jest so high. — **(2) 1865** *Weekly New Mexican* 14 July 1/3 They draw at the commissary, and at poker after they have passed the 'buck.' **1912** W. IRWIN *Red Button* 341 The Big Commissioner will get roasted by the papers and hand it to the Deputy Comish, and the Deputy will pass the buck down to me, and I'll have to report how it happened. **1947** *Sat. Ev. Post* 8 Mar. 148/3 It puts the buck squarely up to the newspaper publishers, who are, after all, the men who print the leakage. **1948** *Dly. Ardmoreite* (Ardmore, Okla.) 29 Apr. 14/6 So far, this has turned into something of a buck-passing game.

As the last term in **blacktail, prong, spike, spiked, swamp buck.**

buck bʌk, *n.*[2] [App. f. Du. *beuk*, or G. *buche.*] A species of beech. In full **buck beech.** *Obs.* Cf. **buckwheat.**

1709 Lawson *Carolina* 94 Beech. . . . Another sort call'd Buck-Beech is here found. **1790** Maclay *Deb. Senate* 182 It [i.e., Northumberland County, Pa.] is covered with an immense forest of timber. Maple; sugar tree; buck; beech; oak of all kinds. **1835** *Survey of Property* Nov., *Pettigrew P.* (N.C. Univ.), To a maple & 2 buck beaches corner Trees.

buck bʌk, *n.*[3]

1. Short for **sawbuck.** [Cf. Berghaus *bukk* =*sage-bukk*].

1817 J. K. Paulding *Letters from South* I. 189 He first carried wild pigeons about to sell; but this business not answering, he bought himself a buck and saw, and became a redoubtable sawyer. **1848** Bartlett 393 *Buck*, a frame or stand of peculiar construction on which wood is sawn for fuel. In New England it is called a *saw-horse.* **1867** *Ball Players' Chron.* 14 Nov. 5/1 The next [would] stumble and almost fall, in his endeavors to keep out of the way of a huge stick which an assistant would tumble into the buck.

2. bucksaw, (see quot. 1874).

1856 in *Amer. Sp.* XII. 115 Or cutting out three or four ribs with a buck-saw or a broad-axe. **1874** Knight 398/1 Buck-saw, . . . a frame-saw with one extended bar to form a handle, and adapted to a nearly vertical motion, in cross-cutting wood held by a saw-buck. **1946** *Reader's Digest* Jan. 139/2, I made my bucksaw out of black walnut.

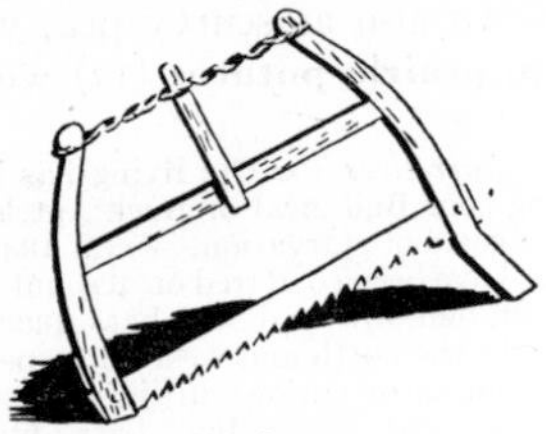

Bucksaw

buck bʌk, *n.*[4] [f. **buck,** *v.*[2]]

1. The act of bucking, the power to buck.

*a*1877 *Texas corr.* in *Chi. Tribune* (B.), The *buck* consists of the mustang's springing forward with quick, short, plunging leaps, and coming down stiff-legged [etc.]. **1890** L. C. D'Oyle *Notches* 34 In two months from now the worst 'buckers' amongst them will not have a 'buck' left in them. **1891** *Harper's Mag.* July 206/2 After a series of bucks, more or less severe, during which his spurs go time and again into the pony's flanks [etc.].

2. In football, an instance of charging into an opponent's line. Cf. ***buck,** *v.*[2] **3. c.**

1902 *Out West* Feb. 234 (*caption*), A Buck Through the Center. **1910** *Chi. Tribune* 15 Nov. III. 1 A straight buck and forward pass.

***buck,** *n.*[5]

1. (See quot. and cf. quot. 1839 in **2.**) *Obs.*

1881 *Harper's Mag.* April 786/2 The 'buck' is a more modern word to describe the long plank attached to runners—a device which was developed from the old custom of holding the small single sleds together in a train.

2. buckboard, orig. a plank laid upon the bare bolsters of a wagon, later a light four-wheeled vehicle having

Buckboard of a once popular type

a single seat placed on an elastic platform connecting the two axles. See also **mail buckboard, springboard b.**

1839 Hoffman *Wild Scenes* i. 10 [Did you] ever see a teamster riding upon a buckboard? a stout, springy plank, laid upon the bare bolsters of a wagon? **1869** Tourgee *Toinette* iv. (1881) 45 The kind-hearted old slave woman folded her sooty arms about the shivering, splattered figure on the 'buck-board.' **1948** *Dly. Oklahoman* (Okla. City) 16 May E. 2/1 Prairie schooners and buckboards have been replaced by airplanes, automobiles, fine trains, tractors and motor coaches.

b. Attrib. with **buggy, ride, road, wagon.**

1871 *Republican D. Journal* (Kansas) 25 Aug., Dr. Wilder was indulging yesterday in a new buckboard buggy. **1885** *Outing* Oct. 74/2 At 2.20 exchanged my seat in a . . . railway carriage, for a place beside Frank Johnson, in a long buck-board wagon. **1890** C. King *Sunset Pass* 9 Officers . . . had to . . . take a four or five days' 'buckboard' ride across the dusty deserts of Colorado. **1944** Johnson *As I Dare* 28 Folks want to know why I don't fix up this buckboard road.

buck bʌk, *n.*[6] [See note.] A dollar. *Slang.*

The origin of this term is not clear. It has been suspected of being a development from ***buck,** *n.*[1] **1.** above.

1856 *Dem. State Jrnl.* (Sacramento) 3 July 3/2 Bernard, assault and battery upon Wm. Croft, mulcted in the sum of twenty bucks. **1896** G. Ade *Artie* 106 Jimmy can afford to buy wine at four bucks a throw when he's only gettin' three a week out o' the job. **1946** *New Yorker* 28 Dec. 50/2 Every soldier in our small headquarters squadron was taxed about five bucks.

buck bʌk, *v.*[1] [Origin obscure.]

1. *tr.* To lose or bet away (money) in gambling, esp. at faro.

1851 *Alta Californian* 8 July, The money Percy took to the El Dorado [San Francisco saloon], where he duly bucked it off against a faro bank. **1851** Mrs. Clappe *Lett. from Calif.* 121 Little John was then at the Humboldt betting, or, to speak technically, 'bucking' away large sums at monte.

b. *To buck the tiger*, (see quot. 1938). *Slang.*

1859 *Police Gazette* 12 Mar. 4/4 A third amused the company by informing them as to the luck he had had that day 'bucking the tiger.' **1873** *Las Cruces* (N.M.) *Borderer* 22 Mar. 1/3 A young man in Santa Fe found an old deacon he knew 'bucking the tiger' in a gambling hell. **1938** Asbury *Sucker's Prog.* 15 *Bucking the tiger*—Playing Faro.

2. *intr.* To play monte, faro, etc. Usu. with *at* or *against*. Also fig.

1849 *N.O. Picayune* 18 May 1/6 Several were in their seats, and I left them 'bucking' away, desiring only once more to 'get even,' and then they 'would quit.' **1863** *Rio Abajo Press* 12 May 1 Do you expect me to believe a Saint would buck at monte? **1871** Bret Harte *Luck of Roaring Camp*, etc. 95 Why don't you say you want to buck agin' Faro? **1898** Canfield *Maid of Frontier* 109 The man who bucks against that kind of game is a fool.

Also *tr.*

1948 *Sat. Ev. Post* 10 July 74/3 Professional gamblers will not buck a new game until they have carefully studied the layout and have assured themselves that it is on the level.

buck bʌk, *v.*[2] [Origin obscure. See note.]

It is not entirely clear that all the meanings given here belong to this verb. In sense **1.** the word occurs earlier (1848), in Australia, and the first example (1859), in *OED* refers to that country. G. *bocken* may be the source of the word in both Australian and American use. Positive evidence for this is lacking, however, as is evidence of borrowing between Australia and U.S. See note *s.v.* **bucker,** *n.*[1]

1. *intr.* Of horses and sometimes of other animals: To make a sudden leap upwards and come down with the hind legs in the air, the forelegs stiff, and the head held low, in an effort to cast off a rider or load. Also transf.

1869 *Overland Mo* III. 127 A mustang is generally any thing in the world but 'religious,' for he will both 'sull,' (have the sulks) and 'buck.' **1929** Dickson *Across Plains* 118 While the animals reared back, twisted, bucked and bowled simultaneously. **1948** *Denison* (Tex.) *Herald* 1 July 9/2 The old adage of what goes up must come down still held when the broncs and the bulls started to buck.

b. To object to, be recalcitrant, make a fuss about. Also *tr. Colloq.* Cf. **2.**

1851 A. T. Jackson *Forty-Niner* 89 Anderson has been asked to deliver the oration and although he bucked at first he finally accepted. **1898** *Boston Journal* 10 July 10/1 Even when uniformed men of this generation mutiny, or buck, in a body, they very rarely make their point stick. **1948** *Lawton* (Okla.) *Constitution* 2 July 2/3 As the possessor of superior wisdom, he bucks the bi-partisan foreign policy, embodied in the European Aid Program.

c. *To buck up*, of a horse: To "break," refuse to perform in a race.

1902 McFaul *Ike Glidden* 169 All I know is, they say he bucked up on that race they started him in.

d. *tr.* To shake, jar, cast off by bucking. Also transf.

1871 *Atlantic Mo.* Nov. 570 [The colt] had 'nearly bucked her to pieces.' **1889** *Cent. Mag.* Jan. 338/2 A person who had just been 'bucked' violently from the back of a descendant of the Barbs. **1948** *Time* 10 May 24/2 His own Republican state legislature had bucked off every reform proposal like an unbroken pony with a burr under the saddle.

2. *intr.* To exert oneself, usu. *at, against*, or *through* something, to drive hard against. *Colloq.* Cf. **1. b.**

1857 *S.F. Call* 21 May 3/1 A great many gamblers left. They think it hardly worth while to 'buck' against the present law prohibiting the pursuit of their 'science.' **1865** *Cairo* (Ill.) *D. Democrat* 4 Oct. 4/2 We earnestly advise him, however, not to let those who desire to curry favor with him, to persuade him into an attempt at 'bucking' against the president. **1921** PAINE *Comr. Rolling Ocean* 106 A good many of the boys seem to look up to you as a sort of leader since we bucked through that big gale of wind.

b. *To buck up to*, to "shine up to" a girl, to seek to make a good impression upon. *Colloq.*

1832 *Polit. Examiner* (Shelbyville, Ky.) 8 Dec. 4/1, I seed her at church one day fixed up kinder pretty snug; so . . . darn my seelskin pumps if I dont buck up to her next Fust day. **1868** PAULDING *Book of Vagaries* 265 Single gentlemen . . . should beware how they 'buck up' to widows.

c. *To buck into*, to begin boldly the study of, to run into (a person).

1856 PH. BROOKS in Allan's *Life* I. (1900) 151, I am beginning to buck into Hebrew. **1904** G. STRATTON-PORTER *Freckles* 100 If you was to buck into Mr. McLean in your prisint state, without me there to explain matters the chance is he'd cut the liver out of you.

d. *To buck for*, to strive earnestly for.

1881 in HAYES *Guiteau* 73, I was bucking very strong for the job. **1948** *Time* 10 May 23/1 Favorite Son Martin had run a poor third behind Harold Stassen (whose backers had bucked hard for him) and Tom Dewey.

e. To spring *over* (an obstacle).

1886 ROOSEVELT in *Cent. Mag.* July 338/1 The horse generally has to be brought to a canter . . . , and then bucks over the obstacle by sheer strength.

3. *tr.* To drive or smash into (snow or ice), to clear a way through it.

1883 *Colo. Springs Republic* 31 Dec. 2/2 Trainmaster Downey has been bucking snow . . . since Saturday night, and has not succeeded in getting through with his four engines yet. **1902** McKEE *Land of Nome* 145 The *Jeannie*, a steam-whaler, specially fitted to 'buck' the ice, was the only vessel known to have discharged its passengers and freight at Nome. **1947** *Time* 3 Feb. 68/1 In winter months they buck four to ten foot snow drifts.

b. *fig.* To try to overcome or get the better of (anything). *Colloq.*

1902 LORIMER *Lett. Merchant* 32 Jim's father had a lot of money till he started out to buck the universe and corner wheat. **1913** LA FOLLETTE *Autobiog.* 75 If he thinks he can buck a railroad company with 5,000 miles of line, he'll find out his mistake. **1948** *Time* 12 April 26/1 If they bucked the machine, they were liable to personal harm.

c. *To buck center*, in football, to charge into the center of the opponent's line.

1904 O. HENRY *Cabbages & Kings* (1916) 95, 'I'm going to buck centre,' says Henry, in his football idioms. **1911** P. H. DAVIES *Football* 122 Emrich takes the ball and bucks the Army's centre for a touchdown.

4. To thrust or force (one) *in*.

1897 FLANDRAU *Harvard Episodes* 158 He wanted Sears Wolcott on the Signet [club]. . . . His best motives for wishing to 'buck' Sears in were hardly formulated in his own mind.

buck bʌk, *v.*³ [Poss. the same word as *EDD buck v.*³ 7. "to beat, overcome."]

1. *tr.* To punish a person by tying the wrists together, passing the arms over the bent knees, and inserting a stick over the arms and beneath the knees, also **buck and gag.**

1848 *Protestant Monitor* (Alton, Ill.) 24 May 3/1 A man is not considered a soldier until he . . . has been bucked and gagged once or twice. **1851** *Sacramento Transcript* 26 Mar., Jackson was sentenced to be bucked, receive forty-five lashes, and have his head shaved. **1903** STILES *Four Years* 231 Calloway had him bucked and gagged and sequestered his pay to reimburse the woman.

2. To bend, to bend and hold (a person) across a log, preparatory to flogging.

1879 TOURGEE *Fool's Errand* 80 They might have bucked 'em across a log. . . . It's a powerful handy way to larrup a man. **1883** *American* VI. 237 (*Cent.*), To *buck*, meaning to bend, is a common word in the South.

b. (See quot. 1946.)

1939 HARRIS *Purslane* 202 Most of the children scampered away, intent on exploring the woods, hunting sweet gum, wading in the water, and bucking the boys that needed it. **1946** WOODARD *Word-List* 7 Buck: *vb.* To tame a tough or mommock a small boy by seizing his arms and legs and banging his fundament against the fundament of another boy or against a tree or wall. It takes two 'initiators' to do the bucking. Pamlico. Common among boys.

buck bʌk, *v.*⁴ [f. **buck,** *n.*³] *tr.* To saw wood with a buck or bucksaw (see quot. 1905).

1870 *Phila. Press* 8 Jan., [The] Pennsylvanian does not saw wood; he 'bucks' it. **1905** *Forestry Bureau Bul. 61 s.v., Buck*, to saw felled trees into logs (Pacific Coast Forest). **1939** BROWNELL *Horse & Buggy Philos.* 208 In the spring father would hire a man to 'buck it up' and then it was our job to pile it up in the woodhouse.

Buck and Breck. (See quot. 1914.) *Obs.* or *hist.*

1856 *Spirit of Age* (Sacramento) 21 Sep. 4/2, I . . . expected any minute to hear No. 5's boys come down with three times three and a 'tiger' for 'Buck and Breck.' **1902** *Bookman* Oct. 117/2 When November's ides arrive, To greet the Colonel's sight, Straight from the Democrat hive, *Two* B's will on him light—Buck and Breck. **1914** *Cyclo. Amer. Govt.* I. 179 Buck and Breck. The nickname of James Buchanan . . . and John C. Breckenridge . . . President and Vice-President 1857–1861, current during the campaign of 1856, Buchanan was also nicknamed 'Old Public Functionary.'

buckaroo ˈbʌkəˌru, *n.* Also **buckhara, bukkarer, buccaroo,** etc. *S.W.* [Sp. *vaquero*, cowboy.] =**vaquero.** Also attrib.

1827 DEWEES *Lett. from Texas* x. 66 These [rancheros] are surrounded by . . . peons and bakharas, or herdsmen. **1889** *Oregonian* (Portland) 7 Oct. 6/3 Our feats were as nothing to what we saw at 'Buckaroo' camp some distance from 'The Cove.' **1924** DAVIES *Skyline Trail* 15 The buckaroo . . . takes his fall, but, after all, bends the broncho's will to his own. **1948** *Popular Western* June 28/1 Local buckaroos competed with world champion riders and ropers.

bucker ˈbʌkɚ, *n.*¹ [f. **buck,** *v.*²] **1.** A horse that bucks. **2.** *transf.* An individual who rebels, grumbles, nurses a grievance, etc.

Baker reports this word, in the sense of a horse that bucks, from Australia in 1853. See note to **buck,** *v.*²

(1) **1881** ROMSPERT *Western Echo* 205 To see a big tender-foot back a bucker is about as funny a thing as I ever witnessed. **1948** *Southwestern Rev.* Winter 27/2 He is not ashamed of being 'grassed' by a good bucker. — (2) **1887** *Scribner's Mag.* II. 508 So I heard, last year, a politician speak of a bolter of the Republican ticket as a 'bucker.' **1898** *Boston Journal* 10 July 10/1 Yet the army is never without its buckers.

bucker ˈbʌkɚ, *n.*² [f. **buck,** *v.*¹] One who "bucks" at faro. — **1898** BRET HARTE *Stories in Light* 91 The unfortunate 'bucker' was cleared out not only of his gains, but of his original investment. **1900** SMITHWICK *Evolution of State* 75 One of the buckers was in my shop one day and . . . was struck with an idea.

bucker ˈbʌkɚ, *n.*³ [f. **buck,** *v.*⁴] *Lumbering.* One who saws felled trees into saw logs. — **1900** *Treasurer's Bur. Statistics* Nov. 1116 A logging crew consists of 1 foreman . . . 2 swampers, 2 buckers, 3 hook tenders. **1946** R. PEATTIE *Pac. Coast Ranges* 222 As the tree falls, buckers are ready to cut it into forty-foot logs.

***bucket,** *n.* [In **1.** and in **bucket letter** f. "Ned Bucket." See **bucket letter.**]

1. Short for **bucket letter.** *Obs.*

1843 in THOMPSON *M. Jones* (1872) 153 'Maybe it's a bucket,' ses the postmaster; 'you better open it and see, and if it is you won't have to pay no postage.'

2. In combs.: (1) **bucket letter,** originally one of the letters written anonymously to Pres. J. Q. Adams by David Holt of Ga. under the pseudonym of Edward Bucket, later any anonymous letter, *obs.;* (2) ***maker,** a nickname for an inhabitant of Hingham, Mass., *obs.;* (3) **plank,** a plank forming a part of the bucket of a water wheel; (4) **shop,** see as a main entry.

(1) **1843** in THOMPSON *M. Jones* (1872) But I could tell by the feelin it wasn't no bucket letter. **1865** A. H. STEPHENS *Diary* (1910) 380 Dave Holt [*c*1830] was author of the letters signed 'Ned Bucket,' and published all over the country. . . . Anonymous letters came to be called 'Bucket letters.' — (2) **1840** DANA *Two Years* xxiii. 229 He was born in Hingham, and of course was called 'Bucketmaker.' *Ib.* xxxvi. 453 One of our boys was the son of a bucket-maker. — (3) **1901** CHURCHILL *Crisis* 322 The bells clanged and the bucket-planks churned, and the great New Orleans packet crept slowly to the Barbara's side.

As the last term in **birch, candy, clamshell, dinner, dope, Hingham, sap, shake, Shaker bucket.**

bucket shop.

1. (See quots.)

1875 STOWE *We & Our Neighbors* 380 The lowest, the most dreadful of all, was what they called the bucket shops. There the vilest of liquors are mixed in buckets and sold to wretched, crazed people. **1881** *N.Y. Ev. Post.* Oct. (Th.), A 'bucket-shop' in New York is a low 'gin-mill,' or 'distillery,' where small quantities of spirits are dispensed in pitchers and pails (buckets). When the shops for dealing in one-share or five-share lots of stocks were opened, these dispensaries of smaller lots than could be got from regular dealers were at once named 'bucket-shops.'

2. *Finance.* An office or place posing as a legitimate stock exchange, but being in reality a gambling establishment, and therefore illegal, where bets are accepted in the form of orders or options on the current prices of securities and commodities.

1880 *Bradstreet's* 1 Dec. 1/4 The failure of the 'Produce Exchanges,' or bucket shops . . . caused little excitement. **1881** [see sense **1**]. **1887** *Ev. Jrnl.* (Atlanta) 30 June 1/2 'About nine-tenths bucket shop and one-tenth bank' would have been a fair description of the business carried on by Crumb & Baslington. **1948** *Time* 5 July 70/2 Fusaro . . . was convicted of grand larceny and operating a bucket shop.

b. Hence **bucket shopper.**

1924 Henderson *Key to Crookdom* 254 Bookmakers are closely allied to the bucket shopper in their method of operation.

c. Also attrib.

1906 Woolridge *Grafters of Amer.* 91 There is no form of gambling more disastrous to the player than 'bucketshop' gambling. **1922** *Ardmore* (Okla.) *D. Press* 14 May 7 I'm surprised that a man of your seeming intelligence would deal with a bucket shop broker! **1947** *Time* 6 Jan. 82/3 As Curb traders grew richer . . . they . . . got rid of 'bucket-shop' brokers, and became a respectable proving ground for new securities.

* **buckeye,** *n.*

1. One or other species of horse chestnut native to the U.S., esp. the Ohio buckeye, *Aesculus glabra.* Also a tree of such a species. Cf. * **buck's eye.**

"The tree was so called on account of the resemblance which its dark-brown nut bears to a buck's eye, when the shell first cracks and exposes it to sight" (Clapin).

1763 in R. T. Durrett *Louisville* (1893) 132 Beginning at a hoop-ashe and buckeye, the lower corner of Major Edward Ward's land [etc.]. **1784** J. Filson *Kentucke* 23 Here also is the buck-eye, an exceeding soft wood, bearing a remarkable black fruit. **1842** Buckingham *Slave States* II. 296 The tree called the buck-eye . . . was here first seen by us, growing to a height of about thirty feet, and having a fine foliage. **1901** Mohr *Plant Life Ala.* 92 The delicate white-flowered spikes of the small-flowered buckeye (*Aesculus parviflora*). **1921** Deam *Trees Indiana* 253 In our area the buckeye is the very first tree to put out its leaves.

b. Attrib. with **ball, grove, leaf stem borer, log, nut, poison, tree.**

1838 Drake *Tales & Sk.* 179 Our sons . . . assembling in the 'muster field,' divide themselves into armies, and pelt each other with Buck-eye balls. — **1847** in Drake *Pioneer Life Ky.* 34 We charged upon the beautiful blue-ash and buckeye groves. — **1882** *Amer. Naturalist* XVI. 913 The Buckeye Leaf Stem Borer. . . . We gave a short abstract of Mr. E. W. Claypole's paper on the above insect. — **1897** Brodhead *Bound in Shallows* 142 'Bout like a buckeye log that'll rot at one end while it sprouts at the other. — **1785** Washington *Diaries* II. 360 Sowed . . . the following things: . . . Six buck eye nuts. — **1867** *Iowa Agric. Soc. Rep.* 129 Cattle have few diseases in this locality except the 'buck eye' poison. *Ib.* 129 When they run out in the bottom timber they often eat the buck eye balls and are badly poisoned. — **1804** *Md. Hist. Mag.* IV. 15 Sugar trees of enormous size . . . blue ash, oak, buckeye trees . . . all very large. **1945** Tryon *Poor Man* 10 He stood on the brick sidewalk a moment, as if to enjoy the . . . buckeye trees' shade.

c. Buckeye State, a nickname of Ohio, from the buckeye trees native there.

1837 *Russellville* (Ky.) *Advertiser* 27 Oct. 3/1 (*heading*), The way they use up an 'Ex-Governor in the Buck Eye State. **1948** *Chi. Sun-Times* 20 Apr. 32/2 At the last Republican convention, buckeyes were used as a campaign emblem by Bricker of the Buckeye State.

2. The nut or fruit of the buckeye, often carried as a charm or for luck.

1797 in *Filson Club Hist. Quart.* II. (1928) 166 The natural fruit is . . . black walnut, Chestnut . . . & Buck eye, this last resembles the Chestnut, but is as large as a hickory nut of the largest Size. **1877** *Field & Forest* Sep. 39 The nut of the Buckeye is frequently carried in the pocket, as a prevention against piles. **1892** *Amer. Folk-Lore* V. 20 In Talladega, Alabama, the negroes believe if one carries buckeyes in the pocket he will have no chills through the year. **1948** *Chi. Tribune* 28 Mar. VII. 1/3 You carried a buckeye to ward off rheumatism.

attrib. **1910** O. Henry *Strictly Business* 36, I'd be . . . better satisfied if the citizens . . . run more to velveteen vests and buckeye watch charms.

b. buckeye-bean, the fruit of the buckeye.

1867 *Harper's Wkly.* 7 Dec. 773/3 It [smuggled liquor] is nearly all *very bad*, owing to the quantity of buck-eye bean used in its preparation, to give it what is called a *bead.*

3. A nickname for a backwoodsman (see first quots.), later applied especially to Ohioans.

1823 James *Exped.* I. 20 In allusion to this circumstance, the indigenous backwoodsman is sometimes called buck-eye, in distinction from the numerous emigrants who are introducing themselves from the eastern states. **1842** Buckingham *Slave States* II. 296 It [the buck-eye] is so abundant in the neighbouring State of Kentucky . . . that the Kentuckians are often called 'buck-eyes.' **1895** A. O. Myers *Bosses & Boodle* 64 It has been claimed that this device [a buckeye tree] on this seal [i.e., of Gov. St. Clair] gave the appellation of 'Buck-eyes' to Ohio and her people. **1948** *Chi. D. News* 10 May 23/3 The men who run against the Buckeye know him for a driving runner, who has terrific acceleration.

b. *attrib.* Of or pertaining to Ohio. Cf. **1. c.** above.

1834 *Western Mo. Mag.* 145 Our own Buckeye population. **1842** *Amer. Pioneer* I. 436 His son of that name was my school-mate at a buckeye log cabin school-house. **1893** *Columbus* (O.) *Dispatch* 6 Sep., The Buckeye place-seekers can now and then be seen peering down upon the occupant of the Vice President's chair.

Hence **Buckeyeism,** *obs.*

1846 Cist *Cin. Miscellany* II. 97/2 I might claim to be a greater Buckeye than most of you who were born in the city, for my Buck-eyeism belongs to the country, a better soil for rearing Buckeyes than the town.

4. A person or thing of an inferior or cheap kind (see quots.). Also attrib.

1846 Cist *Cin. Miscellany* II. 97/1 The buckeye . . . could not be used in building, nor for fences, nor even for fuel. As a tree it consequently stood very low in the estimation of early settlers, and by a figure of speech very forcible to them, it was applied to lawyers and doctors whose capacity and attainment were of a low grade. **1906** *Atlantic Mo.* Nov. 640 The serious painters whose work is found in exhibitions, and the despised 'buckeye' painter who paints for department stores and cheap picture shops. **1947** *New Yorker* 15 Feb. 59 A buckeye is a small shop in which cigars are made by hand in a back room and sold across the counter out front. . . . There are just a few buckeyes left in New York, but as recently as thirty years ago there was one on almost every block downtown.

5. (See quots.) *Obs.*

*c*1844 Townes *Hist. Marion* 7 The medical springs . . . have such remarkable properties that their full benefit cannot be realized, unless commingled with nearly the proportion of four to one of distilled liquid, known and called by the pet name of Buck-eye, which is supposed to be [because] of frequent use of the waters is apt to put the eyes in that condition or color. **1865** *Nashville Dly. Union* 25 Nov. 4/1 Potatoes . . . 110 brls buckeyes and 100 sacks flukes at 35c.

6. (See quots. and cf. * **bugeye.**)

1885 C. P. Kunhardt *Small Yachts* 234 (*Cent.*), The buckeyes . . . are an exaggeration of the dugout canoe. **1889** *Cent.* 705/2 buckeye. . . . A flat-bottomed centerboard schooner of small size (3 to 15 tons), decked over, and with a cabin aft, used in oyster-fishing in Chesapeake Bay. **1923** *Outing* Jan. 187/1 The craft he suggests is one of 'those Chesapeake Bay buckeyes.'

As the last term in **big, California, common, large, Mexican, mountain, Ohio, purple, red, small, small flowering, spiked, stinking, sweet, tall, yellow buckeye.**

***buckeyed,** *a.* Poisoned from eating of the buckeye. — **1867** *Iowa Agric. Soc. Rep.* 129 From half a pound to one pound of lard put down the animal's throat when 'buckeyed' is a pretty safe antidote for the poison.

* **buckhorn,** *n.*

1. = **staghorn sumac.** Cf. * **buck's horn.**

1629 Parkinson *Paradisus* 611 *Rhus Virginiana.* The Virginia Sumach, or Buckes horne tree of Virginia. **1712** Petiver in *Phil Trans.* XXVII. 424 Virginia Sumach . . . the first branches are very soft and velvety, like the horns of a young deer, for which reason it is called Buckhorn by the country people.

2. A rifle sight having somewhat the shape of a pair of deer horns, the sighter looking through the curved antlers. In full **buckhorn sight.**

1877 R. I. Dodge *Hunting Grounds Gt. West* vii. 105 The very best sight, and the one almost universally in use by sportsmen and professional hunters on the plains, is the plain 'buckhorn.' *Ib.*, Sportsmen who use the 'buckhorn' must learn to sight 'on the barrel.' **1901** White *Westerners* xi. 78 Innumerable times he had viewed the doctor, Prue, and the scout through the buck-horn sights of his long rifle.

3. buckhorn cactus, an arborescent cactus, *Opuntia versicolor,* having cylindrical joints.

1897 *Land of Sunshine* Mar. 138 The most familiar cacti of the Southwest in a state of nature are the huge and ghostly zahuaro; the buckhorn cactus, . . . whose stems make the familiar 'lattice-work canes'; [and] the prickly pear. **1948** *Desert Mag.* July 8/3 On the mountainside nearby were mountain lilac in blossom, . . . agave and buckhorn cactus.

bucking ˈbʌkɪŋ, *n.*[1] and *a.* [f. **buck** *v.*[2]]

1. *n.* The action on the part of a horse of trying to throw its rider. Also attrib. and transf.

1869 McClure *Rocky Mts.* 302 The native horses become singularly skilled in 'bucking,' and there are few riders who can keep the saddle or make them yield to the lines. **1902** Wister *Virginian* 291 Stooping to investigate the bucking-strap on his saddle—a superfluous performance, for Pedro never bucked. **1907** White *Arizona Nights* viii. 151 Naturally Mr. Calf entered his objections, which took the form of . . . the most comical bucking. **1927** James *Cow Country* 61 Doggone queer . . . how a man that's had so much teaching in horsemanship, as they call it, can fall off a horse the way he's done, without that horse even bucking.

2. *a.* Of a horse: Accustomed to buck.

1877 W. Wright *Big Bonanza* 87 He was killed . . . by being thrown from a 'bucking' mustang. **1901** White *Claim Jumpers* v. 74 The curley-haired young man who had lent him the bucking horse. **1948** *Gainesville* (Tex.) *D. Register* 3 July 1/1 Livestock, including bucking horses and a large herd of Brahma cattle, were said to be in excellent condition.

bucking ˈbʌkɪŋ, *n.*[2] [f. **buck** *v.*[3]] **1.** (See quot. 1864.) Also **bucking-down. 2. bucking paddle,** a paddle used upon one undergoing bucking. *Obs.*

(1) **1864** Pittenger *Daring & Suffering* 228 The guards came up, and seizing Pierce, . . . and tying his hands before his knees, with a stick inserted across under his knees and over his arms, in the way that soldiers call 'bucking,' they left him there all night. **1921** R. M. Jones *Later Period of Quakerism* II. 744 The bucking-down was resorted to for two hours. — (2) **1861** H. Jacobs *Life Slave Girl* 98 Others were tied hand and feet, and tortured with a bucking paddle.

bucking ˈbʌkɪŋ, *n.*[3] [f. **buck,** *v.*[2]] (See quot.) — **1882** *Harper's Mag.* Dec. 3/2 Presently the swiftest water is reached, the race of the rapid. Now commences what Western steamboat men call 'bucking'; the wheel flies round fast enough, and there is a great kicking up of water behind, and a tremendous exhaust of steam.

bucking ˈbʌkɪŋ, *n.*[4] [Origin unknown.] (See quot.) *Rare.* — **1888** *Troy D. Times* 8 Feb. (F.), There is, as far as I know, but one thing in which they [poor whites] believe, and that is what is termed further South voudouism, or, as they term it here, bucking.

***buckle,** *n. To make buckle and tongue meet, fig.* to get along, to manage successfully. *Colloq.* — **1859** *Fisher's River* 249 All they cared for was 'to make buckle and tongue meet' by raising stock, a few bales of cotton, and a little corn for bread. **1888** *Harper's Mag.* Apr. 703/1 Beginning without money, he had as much as he could do to make 'buckle and tongue meet,' as the phrase goes.

***buckle,** *v. To buckle down to,* to set to work seriously or steadily at (something). — **1865** *Atlantic Mo.* XV. 301 If he would only buckle down to serious study. **1889** Custer *Tenting on Plains* 145, I was constantly mystified . . . how our officers . . . could, as they expressed it, 'buckle-down' to the dull, exhausting days of a monotonous march.

***buckler,** *n.* A local name for a crab at the stage when the shell yields to the pressure of the fingers. — **1879** *St. Nicholas* Nov. Letter-Box Dept., I don't know what a crab is usually called at first, whether a soft or hard crab. We say he is a 'Buckler.' **1884** Goode *Nat. Hist. Aquat. Anim.* 776 The terms 'Soft Crab,' 'Paper-shell,' and 'Buckler' denote the different stages of consistency of the shell.

buckra ˈbʌkrə, *n.* Also **buccara, boccra,** etc. [Efik *(m)bakara,* white man.]

1. A white man, master, boss. Also transf. See also **poor buckra, white buckra.**

1736 in *S.C. Gazette* 23 April (1737) 2 A Negro who had been Evidence against the former, seeing his master (Maj. Nuegent) come home, went to him and told him, *Bockorau* go to sleep too soon. **1787** B. Franklin in *Amer. Museum* II. 212/2 They are pleased with the observation of a negro, and frequently mention it, that Boccarorra (meaning the white man) make de black man workee, make de horse workee, make de ox workee, make ebery ting workee; only de hog. **1886** *Amer. Philol. Assoc.* XVII. 45 *Buck-ra* (for boss or master in South Carolina). **1892** Harris *On the Plantation* 75 Miss Chicken Hawk she coyspon' wid Mr. Eagle, which he was de big buckra er all de birds. **1948** *Reader's Digest* March 93/1 Now repeat the exact words to the *Bahkra.*

2. Attrib. with **gentleman, God, man, overseer, people, woman.**

*c*1775 Janet Schaw *Journal Lady of Quality* 108 Every Negro infant can tell you, that he owes this happiness to the good Buckara God, that he be no hard Master, but loves a good black man as well as a Buccara man. **1831** *Naval Songster* 180 Great way off at sea, when at home I've been-ee, Buckra man fetch me from de coast of Guinea. **1838** Gilman *Recollections* 127 Miss Neely, one buckra woman want for track up all de clean floor. **1845** *Knickerb.* XXVI. 332 So thought Mr. Thomas Rice, a 'buckra gemman' of great imitative powers. **1872** W. J. Flagg *Good Investment* 549/2 No mo' . . . dan . . . de buckra people 'bout yere kin be like Miss Bella. **1891** Sloan *Fogy Days* 41 Didn't love poor bucra overseer, Your terror was the patter-roll. **1945** Botkin *My Burden* 169 You never see classy buckra man a-paterolling.

b. buckra yam, (see quot.).

1871 De Vere 151 Negroes thus speak of buckra yam, with the understanding, however, that it is not only white, but peculiarly good also.

***buckram,** *n.* **1.** *In buckram,* (see quot.). **2.** (*cap.*) *fig.* One inclined to favor metallic rather than paper currency. *Obs.* — (1) *c*1830 Godman in *Waldie's Select Library* II. 87/3 Twelve hours later the shell is sufficiently stiffened to require some slight force to bend it, and the crab is said to be in *buckram.* — (2) **1855** Hambleton *H. A. Wise* 448 Some Softs who are 'Buckrams,' tending to Hards.

bucksa ˈbʌksə, *n.* ?A feminine form of **buckra.** *Rare.* — **1830** *Somerset* (Pa.) *Whig* 18 Aug. 1/5 Dat black mus have strong stummack, to marry a bucksa, and desert de *fair sex* ob his own colour.

***buck's-eye,** *n.* =**buckeye 1.** *Obs.*

1762 Clayton *Flora Virginica* 57 Dear's Eye, & Buck's Eyes. **1781–2** Jefferson *Notes Va.* (1788) 38, I will sketch out those [plants which would principally attract notice . . . : Red flowering maple, *Acer rubrum;* Horse-chestnut, or Buck's-eye, *Æsculus pavia.* **1836** Latrobe *Rambler* II. 8 The buck's eye, a shrub with bright green leaves and red flower-buds, and the red-berry, covered with peach-coloured blossoms, were seen every where.

***buck's-horn,** *n.* (See quots.)

1629 Parkinson *Paradisus* 611 *Rhus Virginiana.* The Virginia Sumach, or Buckes horne tree of Virginia. **1821** *Mass. H.S. Coll.* 2 Ser. IX. 153 *Onoclea struthiopteris.* Buck's horn brake. **1890** *Cent.* 3552/2 *Lycopodium clavatum* . . . has also been called stag's horn, buck's horn, fox's claws, foxtail, etc.

buckshot ˈbʌkˌʃɑt, *n.* [f. **buck,* a male deer +*shot.*]

1. A large lead shot having a diameter of .24 in. to .36 in., used for large game, esp. deer.

1775 *Gaines Mercury* 14 Aug. (B.), The reason that so many more of the King's troops were wounded than killed in the late action [of Breed's Hill] in New England . . . is that the Americans use a small shot, called buck-shot, which is much smaller than the soldiers' bullets. **1852** Moodie *Roughing It* 94 Jacob, you have no chance; there is but one charge of buck-shot in the house. **1948** *This Week Mag.* 10 July 17/3 He completely convinced another hunter who promptly winged him with buckshot.

2. *pl.* (*cap.*) =**Molly Maguire.** Cf. **Blackspots.** *Obs.*

1877 J. D. McCabe *Hist. Great Riots* 463 The members of this organization were popularly termed 'Buckshots.' They gave considerable trouble to the authorities. **1888** M. Lane in *America* 18 Oct. 15 They were known in one locality as 'Blackspots,' and in another as 'Buckshots,' and committed all sorts of murders, and outrages.

3. In combs.: (1) **buckshot sinker,** a sinker for a fishing line made of a buckshot; (2) **Buckshot War,** an election disturbance in Harrisburg, Pa., in 1838, in which the troops called out were ordered to use buckshot cartridges.

(1) **1889** Mellick *Story Old Farm* 5 Again we are boys, with cork dobbers, buckshot sinkers and hickory poles, angling in the pond. — (2) **1842** *Cong. Globe* June 609/1 Mr. B. believed that was the phrase used in Pennsylvania, in time of the buckshot war. **1875** *Cong. Rec.* March 38/1 This buckshot war was a ridiculous affair from beginning to end.

b. Designating *land* or *soil* of a quite porous, often clayey, nature that cracks and becomes crumbly in dry weather with the formation of small lumps or nodules somewhat resembling buckshot.

1871 R. Somers *Southern States since War* 144 The soil is a dry deep red loam—what is called, in the language of the country, 'a buckshot soil.' **1896** Clendenin *Fla. Parishes E. La.* 206 Along the coulees and bayous are certain black or grayish black, waxy lands known as 'buckshot' lands. **1938** Daniels *Southerner* 9 A little man . . . may . . . fail to make even a living trying to grow cotton out of buckshot land.

buckshot ˈbʌkˌʃɑt, *v. tr.* To shoot with buckshot. *Rare.* — **1887** *Courier-Journal* 8 May 4/7 He was buck-shotted to death on Friday afternoon at his home near Kerrville.

***buckskin,** *n.*

1. A nickname for a backwoodsman, esp. a Virginian or Southerner. Usu. *cap.*

1744 Hamilton *Itin.* 150, I told him that the most dangerous wild beasts in these woods were shaped exactly like men, and they went by the name of Buckskins, or Bucks, tho' they were not Bucks either, but something as it were, betwixt a man and a beast. 1776 in Jas. Thacher *Military Jrnl.* 72 We too frequently hear the burlesque epithet of Yankee from one party, and that of Buckskin, by way of retort, from the other. 1835 H. C. Todd *Notes* 8 *Buckskin* is the nickname for Southerns and Westerns. 1944 Adams *Album Amer. Hist.* I. 215 There was a distinct social cleavage between Tidewater and Piedmont, between landed gentry and 'buckskins.'

b. *attrib.* Virginian or native American.

1776 J. Leacock *Fall Brit. Tyranny* III. vi, His jetty black hair, such as Buckskin saints wear. 1800 J. Boucher *Gloss.* p. 1, At dinner, let me that best buck-skin dish, Broth made of bacon, cream, and eke cat-fish, with toss 'em boys, and belly bacon see. 1809 Weems *Marion* (1833) 233 To be treated thus by buckskin girls, the rebel daughters of convict parents, was more than the British officers could put up with. 1845 Green *Texian Exped.* 281 One of our buckskin Republicans, . . . threw the larieta over the head of the young Jesus.

c. buckskin man, one of a group of outlaw Indians formerly making trouble on the Round Valley Reservation. *Obs.*

1866 *Rep. Indian Affairs* 97 The haunts of the notorious 'buckskin men,' or kidnappers, in the small valleys or on the mountains would be under our control.

2. A horse the color of buckskin. Usu. attrib.

1874 *Vt. Bd. Agric. Rep.* II. 402 The buckskin McClellan was a regular hollow or sway back. 1914 Brininstool *Trail Dust* 115 He drawed a little buckskin mare. 1946 R. Peattie *Pac. Coast Ranges* 126 When deer season comes, nor Jersey cow or buckskin horse is safe in the hills, and the only thing that cheers me is that hunters frequently shoot each other.

b. The color of buckskin. Also **buckskin color.**

1880 Nye *B. Nye & Boomerang* 105 The palfrey was a delicate buckskin color. 1902 McFaul *Ike Glidden* 23 Only thing he has against him's his color; says he can't bear buck-skin.

3. A buffalo robe of a buckskin color.

1918 W. E. Connelley *Hist. Kansas* I. 290 The rarest skin of them all was the 'Buckskin,' a freak of nature. It was a dirty white in color, and because of its rarity, rather than its beauty, sold for two hundred dollars.

* **bucktail,** *n.*

1. (*cap.*) A member of the Tammany Society in N.Y. City (*c*1817–25), later a political opponent of Gov. De Witt Clinton. Now *hist.*

1818 J. M. Duncan *Travels U.S.* II. 247 Tammany Hall is one of the public hotels, and noted for the public meetings of the democratic party, or Bucktails, as they are called. [*Note.* From their wearing the tail of a buck in their hats at an annual festivity.] 1833 Greene *Fibbleton's Travels* 158 The Bucktails, in point of power and numerical strength, doubtless hold first rank. 1872 *Harper's Mag.* April 695/1 The 'Bucktails' (so called from a conspicuous feature in Tammany's Indian uniform). 1935 Alexander *Amer. Talleyrand* 203 He had 17 trusty Bucktails in the State Senate, a majority that could block anything the House or Governor proposed.

b. Attrib. with **council, flag, legislature, paper, party.** All *obs.*

1846 Mackenzie *Life Van Buren* 167 The Bucktail Council very unpopular. — 1838 in Mackenzie *Life Van Buren* 198 You may remember when in 1817 we ran up the Bucktail flag we had but eighteen men with us in the Legislature. — 1846 *Ib.* 188 In Feb. 1823, the bucktail legislature reappointed . . . Marcy as Comptroller. — 1821 Quitman in *Life & Corr.* I. 57 We take the American, the most violent of the Bucktail papers. — 1822 Gall *Auswanderung* II. 25 Nur die Parthei von Hirschschwanze (*the bucktail party*) frech genug seyn könne, dem Augenschein zum Trotz, das erstaunende Werk noch länger als unausführbar darzustellen. 1827 *Cin. Advertiser* 26 Sep. 2/2 The Bucktail party are daily rallying to the Hero. 1843 J. D. Hammond *Polit. Hist. N.Y.* I. 450 Hence the party opposed to the administration of Mr. Clinton were . . . called the 'Bucktail Party.'

2. *pl.* A regiment of Pa. troops in the Civil War. Also **Bucktail Rifles.** *Obs.*

1862 Moore *Rebellion Rec.* V. 394 Colonel Kane of the Pennsylvania Bucktail Rifles reported himself to you with a battalion of his men. 1863 Victor *Hist. Southern Rebellion* II. 470/2 The Kentuckians first showed themselves, when the fiery Bucktails advanced upon them. 1876 *Southern H.S. Papers* I. 436 We awaited with beating hearts, the sure and steady approach of the 'Pennsylvania Bucktails.' 1910 *Sat. Ev. Post* 30 July 26/2 Did you hear those dirty Bucktail veterans back there poking fun at us?

3. An artificial fly made of hairs of a deer's tail.

1920 *Outing* June 175 (*advt.*), Fuzzy Buck-Tail No. 1034RR Hook No. 2. 1947 *Field & Stream* June 10/2, I tried a spinner, with a black bucktail, made several casts, but didn't do any good.

* **buckthorn,** *n.* As the last term in **Carolina, Jamaica, southern buckthorn.**

* **buckwheat,** *n.*

1. Short for **buckwheat cake.**

1830 *Collegian* 41 For tea, [take] six muffins, a dozen buck-wheats, and 6 cups of shells. 1900 E. A. Dix *Deacon Bradbury* 224 'Mandy came in with another plate of hot buckwheats.

2. (*cap.*) A rustic Pennsylvanian, so called from the use he made of buckwheat in barter trade. *Obs.*

1866 *Beadle's Mo.* March 248/2 The most novel and sometimes very funny experiences are with the aborigines, or, as they are called, the 'Buckwheats.'

3. Meal, flour, or batter made from buckwheat.

1881 W. O. Stoddard *E. Hardery* 63 A sack of flour and some cornmeal and some buckwheat and a load of shorts. 1904 Glasgow *Deliverance* 225 On the table was the bowl of buckwheat which Cynthia had been preparing.

4. Short for **buckwheat coal.**

1925 *Wall St. Jrnl.* 12 Jan. 13/5 Steam sizes have improved a little, so that certain of the large companies have stopped dumping No. 1 buckwheat. 1928 *Sat. Ev. Post* 10 March 147/1 Spencer Heaters are specially constructed to burn this low-cost No. 1 Buckwheat.

5. *W.* Any one of various plants of the genus *Eriogonum.* Also **buckwheat butterfly,** (see quot. 1940).

1940 Jaeger *Desert Wild Flowers* 31 If one at all closely examines the old red stems of this and other buckwheats, one is certain to note the broad-ringed scars where the feeding larvae of the buckwheat butterfly (*Apodemia deserti*) have girdled them. 1946 R. Peattie *Pac. Coast Ranges* 105 Dryness intensifies the smell of sage and buckwheat and greasewood. 1948 *Sierra Club Bul.* March 45 *Oxytropis Parryi* was a depressed dwarf scarcely to be distinguished on the tundra-like flat among the low condensed buckwheats, drabas, phloxes, and daisies with which it grew.

6. In special combs.: (1) **buckwheat character,** a buckwheat note or shaped note *qq.v., obs.;* (2) **coal,** (see quots.); (3) **itch,** (see quot.); (4) **-nose, -nosed,** (see quots.); (5) **notes,** see as a main entry; (6) **pine,** ?the white pine, so called from the appearance of its cone; (7) **pot,** a pot in which buckwheat or buckwheat batter is prepared; (8) **tree,** the ironwood, *Cliftonia monophylla*, of the southern states; (9) **worm,** a species of cutworm that attacks buckwheat, as well as corn, cabbage, etc.

(1) 1883 Howe *Country Town* (1926) 17 He had a collection of religious songs preserved in a leather-bound book, the notes being written in buckwheat characters on blue paper. — (2) 1881 Raymond *Mining Gloss. s.v. Coal,* Buckwheat-coal . . . is the smallest size, and usually included in the dirt or culm. 1889 *Cent.* 707/1 *Buckwheat coal,* in the anthracite region of Pennsylvania, the smallest size of coal sent to market. It is sufficiently small to pass through a half-inch mesh. — (3) 1909 *D.N.* III. 409 Buckwheat itch, *n. phr.* A skin eruption supposed to be caused by eating buckwheat. (In Me.) — (4) 1842 *Nat. Hist. N.Y., Zoology* III. 52 The Hog-nosed Snake, *Heterodon platyrhinos.* . . . This well known species. . . is also called Deaf Adder, Spreading Adder, Hog-nose and Buckwheat-nose. 1848 Bartlett 34 The other popular names [of the hog-nosed snake] in New York are Deaf-adder and Buckwheat-nosed.

(6) 1873 *Atlas of Michigan* Pref. 20 Upon a somewhat similar soil is found the 'Buckwheat' and 'grove' pine. — (7) 1851 *Knickerb.* XXXVIII. 393 Enter into an alliance with the kitchen, keep your eye upon the over-night buckwheat pot. — (8) 1813 Muhlenberg *Cat. Plants* 45 Buckwheat tree. *Mylocarium.* 1938 Matschat *Suwannee River* 262 Other flowers were mint, forming a sea of blue flowers . . . and the titi, or buckwheat tree. — (9) 1854 Emmons *Agric. N.Y.* V. 261 (Index) Buckwheat worms, 243. *Ib.* 243 *Agrotidae* . . . they are called cut-worms. . . . The attacks of these larvae extend to many of our most useful cultivated plants, corn, cabbages, wheat, buckwheat, grasses, together with cultivated flowers.

b. Used with (1) **bannock,** (2) **batter,** (also transf.), (3) **cake,** [cf. Du. *boekweitkoek*], (4) **flour,** (5) **meal,** (6) **pancake,** in the sense "made of buckwheat or of buckwheat meal or flour."

(1) 1909 *D.N.* III. 409 Buckwheat bannocks, *n. phr.* Thick fritters made of buckwheat (in Me.). — (2) 1878 Stowe *Poganuc People* 108 She hurried down into the kitchen to find Nabby stirring up her buckwheat batter. 1919 Cady *Rhymes of Vt.* (1923) 151 And then, By George! I know what's up—It's time for buckwheat batter. — (3) [1748 P. Kalm *Travels No. Amer.* I. (1937) 184 Buckwheat cakes . . . are common at Philadelphia and in other English colonies, especially in winter.] 1774 J. Adams *Diary* 21 Sep. II. (1850) 381 Mrs. Yard entertained us with muffins, buckwheat cakes, and common toast. 1893 *Harper's Mag.* Dec. 218 As for the popular American winter breakfast luxury, the buckwheat cake, it was introduced from Central Asia

by the Hollanders, acclimated, cultivated, named 'beech-mast' (*boekweit*), and in the form associated with heat, sweets, aroma, and good cheer is a Dutch invention. **1939** BROWNELL *Horse & Buggy Philos.* 82 Remember how you used to love buckwheat cakes and sausages.— (4) **1805** PARKINSON *Tour* 223 A farmer's waggon in America, when she comes into market, is something like a pedlar's pack: it consists of . . . buckwheat-flour, rye-flour, chopped straw, &c.
(5) **1768** FRANKLIN *Writings* V. 96, I have received also the Indian and buckwheat meal, that they brought from you. **1804** J. ROBERTS *Penn. Farmer* 62 Potatoes boiled and mixed with a small quantity of Indian, pea, bean or buckwheat meal, is a good fattener for them. — (6) **1856** M. THOMPSON *Plu-ri-bus-tah* 28 To his lips he raised the buckwheat Pancakes, dripping with molasses.

As the last term in **false buckwheat, wild buckwheat.**

buckwheat notes. In music, notes having the heads of various shapes somewhat suggestive of buckwheat kernels. Cf. **shaped notes.**

Such notes were used in Albany, N.Y. as early as *c*1800. See G. P. Jackson, "Buckwheat Notes," in *The Musical Quarterly* XIX. (1933), 393–400.

1853 GOULD *Church Music* 55 After making two attempts without success, he [Andrew Law] desisted; and others profited by the form of the characters, which were afterwards by way of reproach, called, by some, buckwheat notes. *Ib.* 140 Still, however, we have reason to believe that *buckwheat* notes are not all eaten up, but are to this time preserved and used in many places in the great west. **1895** HOWELLS *Recollections* 143 The books were printed in what they called patent notes, or, in ridicule, *buckwheat* notes. Instead of having the note-heads round, they were made of different shapes, the seven notes of the scale being made up by repeating three of the notes. **1933** *Amer. Sp.* Feb. 52 Shape Notes, n. The peculiar notation which the Ozark singing-teachers still use rather than the ordinary *round* or *sol* notes. Sometimes called *buckwheat notes.*

bud bʌd, *n.*[1] [App. short for **buddy,** brother.] Brother, also in extended use.

1851 *Polly Peablossom* 19 'An't you joking, bud?' asked Polly of her boy brother. **1889** *Harper's Mag.* Aug. 450/1 He said that his name was 'Bud' Lightwood. . . . 'It's brother,' he said, . . . '"bud" and "sis" you know.' **1948** *Chi. Tribune* 9 May (Comics) 4 Go right ahead, Bud. Where'd you get it?

***bud,** *n.*[2]

1. A girl just entering society.

1880 R. GRANT *Confessions of Frivolous Girl* 39 'This is your first party, I believe, Miss Palmer?' 'Yes, I am what is called a "bud".' **1947** *Chi. D. News* 14 Nov. 29 (*heading*), Lunch on Day Before to Put Buds In Swing for Big Party.

2. budworm, any one of various worms or larvae that attack the buds of plants.

[**1803** *Mass. Spy* 29 June (Th.), The means of destroying the canker and bug worms.] **1849** *Rep. Comm. Patents: Agric.* (1850) 459 With the bud-worm you must be more particular, as you are apt to destroy the bud of the plant in killing it. **1945** *Boulder* (Colo.) *D. Camera* 12 Nov. 5/6 The budworm appears to be attacking the Douglas fir more than any other tree in this region.

3. *To give the bud,* (see quot.). *Slang.*

1891 THANET *Otto the Knight* 237 But what fur did he kill the feller? Why cudn't he of given him the bud an' taken the money back? *Ib. n.*, 'To give the bud' or 'give the hickory' in Arkansas for to thrash.

As the last term in **big, peach, red, rose, rum, tory, twist bud.**

***bud,** *v. intr.* Of birds, etc.: To eat buds. *Colloq.* — **1888** *Forest & Stream* XXVIII. 131 Last night I saw a number of grouse budding upon a neighboring apple tree. **1892** DUVAL *Young Explorers* 123 He was up thar buddin', fur at this time of the year they lives mostly on the buds and twigs of some sorts of trees.

buddy ˈbʌdɪ, *n.* [Origin obscure. See *Amer. Sp.* IV. 389. Possibly a variant of *butty* (see *EDD*), early associated with *bubby* and *brother.*] Brother, bud, comrade, assistant.

1850 PREMIUM *Eight Yrs. Brit. Guiana* 218 Buddy (brother) how you can fink me sha' talk so to you? **1852** WHITMORE *Diary* 25 Dec., Wrote to my folks and took a Christmas dinner with my buddy. **1921** *Frontier* Feb. 29 He was Fred's 'buddy' on the steel gang, and he was also not naturalized. **1948** *Dly. Ardmoreite* (Ardmore, Okla.) 21 April 6/4 They were buddies in school.

b. Buddy poppy, a replica of a Flanders poppy sold by veterans on Poppy Day.

1935 *Amer. Mercury* July 381/2 Does it reveal a nationwide campaign to protect the Federal credit and condemn Buddy poppies? **1947** *Railroad Telegrapher* May 267/2 Wear a V.F.W. 'Buddy' Poppy Memorial Day.

***budge,** *n.* **1.** (See quot. 1824.) Also *pl. Colloq.* **2.** Intoxicating liquor. *Slang.*

(1) **1824** JEFFERSON in *Private Corr. D. Webster* (1857) I. 373 Madame Neckar . . . was not very pleasant in conversation, for she was subject to what in Virginia we call the 'Budge,' that is, she was very nervous and fidgety. **1904** GLASGOW *Deliverance* 102 Having unfortunately crossed her knees in the parlor after supper, she suffered untold tortures from 'budges' for three mortal hours rather than be seen to do anything so indelicate as to uncross them. — (2) **1906** in *Kansas Hist. Soc.* IX. 536 Loaded with budge, a certain individual once cleaned out a house, and was out in the street with a rock in each hand when Tom arrived. . . . The individual has never drank a drop since.

***budget,** *n.* **1.** (See quot.) **2. budget-husband,** a bundle of clothes representing an Indian widow's deceased husband. Also **budgeted husband.** All *rare.* See also **fuss budget, war budget.**

(1) **1833** FLINT *D. Boone* 143 When an attack is to be made . . . each man takes out his budget, or *totem,* and attaches it to that part of his body which has been indicated by tradition from his ancestors. — (2) *Ib.* 141 Her budgetted husband is permitted, when drams are passing, to be considered as a living one. . . . [The Indian widow] is allowed to cheer her depressed spirits with a double dram, that of her budget husband and her own.

buff bʌf, *n.* Short for **buffalo.** *Rare.* — **1884** *Bismarck Tribune* Aug., The ball struck the unsuspecting animal in the thigh, inflicting a slight wound. But the old 'buff' took the fling as an insult.

***buffalo,** *n.*

1. The North American bison, *Bison bison.* Also in collective use or as *pl.*

[**1544** DE SOTO in *La. Hist. Coll.* II. (1850) 106 The Indians informed us there was a province eleven days off, where they killed buffaloes.] **1635** *Relat. Maryland* iii. 23 In the upper parts of the countrey there are Bufeloes, Elkes, Lions, Beares, Wolves, and Deare there are in great Store. **1709** LAWSON *Carolina* 115 The Buffelo is a wild Beast of America, which has a Bunch on his Back. **1895** C. KING *Fort Frayne* 260 A deep cleft in the foothills through which the buffalo in bygone days had made their way. **1947** *Denver Post* 2 Mar. c. 3/4 It thrilled me no end to read of those intrepid archers risking their lives against those ferocious bucket-fed buffalo.

b. Ellipt. for "buffalo meat."

1743 CATESBY *Carolina* App. p. xiii, Our Indians being loaded with skins, and barbacued buffalo. **1894** ROBLEY *Bourbon Co., Kansas* 38 And then again they had nothing to eat but jerked buffalo and Pawnee macarroni.

c. The representation of a buffalo on the "buffalo nickel."

1920 LEWIS *Main Street* 309 But at home he pinches a nickel till the buffalo drips blood.

2. Any one of various large fish of the sucker family, also **sucker-mouth buffalo.** Cf. **black buffalo.**

1788 J. MAY *Jrnl. & Lett.* 32 The [Ohio] river abounds in fish, such as cat, perch, pike, buffalo, sturgeon, etc. **1886** *Nat. Museum Proc.* VIII. 13 *Ictiobus bubalus,* Rafinesque. Sucker-mouth Buffalo. **1944** *Reader's Digest* July 108 The buffalo leaves the muddy water of the Mississippi to be sold in the delicatessen stores of New York's East Side as sturgeon.

3. A hornless cow or creature of the cow kind. Also attrib. *Obs.* Cf. **buffalo cow** (*b*).

1804 *Fredericktown* (Md.) *Herald* 11 Feb. 4/2 Two Stray Heifers came to the Subscriber's plantation . . . one of them a buffaloe, marked with a crop off both ears and slit in the left. **1819** *Amer. Farmer* I. 315 The buffaloe breed of cattle, or those without horns, will not answer well for working. **1858** C. FLINT *Milch Cows* 78 Hornless cattle . . . have been crossed with the common stock . . . to produce hornless grades. . . . These are not unfrequently known under the name of buffalo cattle.

4. Short for **buffalo grass, robe.**

1829 *Yankee* (Boston) July 29 Every creature about me [was] chilled through and through, muff, tippet, and all—bricks, buffaloes and stones to the contrary nevertheless. **1880** HAYES *New Colorado* 37 The ranchero well knows the tufts of buffalo and gramma growth, . . . and remembers that it grows afresh twice a year. **1922** CADY *Rhymes* (1926) 32 One buffalo, I'd have you know, With red and scolloped trimmin, Was all you needed, 'less it snowed, Or 'less you took the wimmen.

5. Used as a nickname: (1) (see quot.), *obs.;* (2) a North Carolinian who favored the Union cause during the Civil War, *obs.;* (3) (see quot.).

(1) **1842** F. BYRDSALL *History of Loco-Foco* 178 Hence the Equal Rights party became divided within itself; the majority for union called the opposing minority Rumps, and the latter called the majority Buffaloes. — (2) **1865** KELLOGG *Rebel Prisons* 243 The rebels were very bitter against these 'buffaloes,' as they called them for many of them had been on their side, and left it for the service of the

Union. **1867** W. L. Goss *Soldier's Story* 61 The Buffaloes, as the North Carolina companies were called, escaped in some cases by swimming the river. — **(3) 1890** *N. & Q.* IV. 1 Feb. 166 The 'poor whites' of North Carolina are nicknamed Buffaloes.

6. In miscellaneous combs.: (1) **buffalo beef,** meat of the buffalo, *obs.;* (2) **boat,** a boat made by stretching buffalo hides over a frame, *obs.;* (3) **bone,** the bone of a buffalo, often *pl.* as an object of traffic; (4) **calfskin,** the skin of a buffalo calf; (5) **chip,** a piece of dried buffalo dung; (6) **coat,** a coat made of buffalo skins; (7) **crossing,** a place on a stream where buffalo herds cross, *obs.;* (8) **dance,** a ritualistic, invocatory dance practiced by plains Indians in their ceremonial preparations for a buffalo hunt, *obs.;* (9) **eaters,** (see quots.), *obs.;* (10) **fever,** =**buck ague,** *obs.;* (11) **ford,** =**buffalo crossing;** (12) **Buffalo Gals,** the title of a formerly popular song; (13) **ground,** a region where buffalo abound, *obs.;* (14) **gun,** a rifle of large caliber for shooting buffalo; (15) **horn,** (*a*) the horn of a buffalo, (*b*) (see quot.); (16) **hump,** meat from the hump of a buffalo; (17) **plain,** a plain frequented by buffalo; (18) **Buffalo platform,** an anti-slavery political platform adopted in Buffalo, N.Y., Aug. 9, 1848, at the organization of the Free-Soil party, *obs.;* (19) **road,** a road, path, or trail made by buffalo herds, *obs.;* (20) **robe,** see as a main entry; (21) **rug,** a buffalo robe, *obs.;* (22) **sod,** sod from a buffalo range preferred for building sod houses, *obs.;* (23) **soldier,** (see quots.); (24) **trace,** a way or road made by the passage of buffalo; (25) **trail,** =**buffalo road;** (26) **tug,** a thong of buffalo hide; (27) **wallow,** (see quot. 1834), now *hist.*

(1) [**1722** *Miss. Prov. Arch.* Fr. Dom. II. (1929) 272 Prices.... Buffalo beef at eight sous a pound.] **a1738** Byrd *Secret History* (1929) 289 Our People were so well pleas'd with Buffalo-Beef, that the Grid-Iron was upon the Fire all Night. **1852** Kelly *Across Rocky Mts.* 91 We ... shot a good many [prairie dogs], several of the party preferring them even to buffalo beef. — **(2) 1844** Gregg *Commerce of Prairies* I. 65 On some occasions caravans have been obliged to construct what is called a buffalo boat, which is done by stretching the hides of these animals over a frame of poles, or, what is still more common, over an empty wagon-body. **1880** Hayes *New Colo. & Santa Fe Trail* 138 Across swamps, quagmires, and even rivers, the teams were driven, men being sent ahead to make temporary bridges ... and sometimes to fabricate 'buffalo boats.' — **(3) 1833** Catlin *Indians* I. 116 'Marrow-fat' is collected by the Indians from the buffalo bones which they break to pieces, yielding a prodigious quantity of marrow, which is boiled out and put into buffalo bladders. **1938** Asbury *Sucker's Prog.* 341 The largest and farthest west, and also the worst, was Dodge City, the principal shipping point of the trail herds from Texas; and, in later years, when the town had fallen on evil days, headquarters of an extensive traffic in buffalo bones, which were hauled in from the prairie and shipped by the hundreds of carloads to Eastern factories to be converted into fertilizer. — **(4) 1847** Ruxton *Adv. Rocky Mts.* (1848) 253 The wolf ... was soon tugging away at an apishamore or saddle-cloth of buffalo calfskin which lay on the ground. **1868** in Custer *Following Guidon* (1890) 15, I am to have a vest made from a dressed buffalo calf-skin, with the hair on.

(5) 1840 *N.O. Picayune* 11. Oct. 2 We raised an extensive cloud of smoke from burning 'buffalo chips' to keep off the musquitos. **1947** De Voto *Across Wide Missouri* 36 Captain Stewart ... was now cooking over buffalo chips. — **(6) 1845** J. W. Norris *Chi. Directory* 119 Retail Dealers in Hats, Caps, Muffs, Boas, Buffalo Coats, Buffalo Robes. **1943** *Copper Camp* 125 They braved the cold wrapped in many layers of clothing over which was frequently worn a shaggy, buffalo coat, cinched tight at the middle with an enormous brass-studded leather belt. — **(7) 1775** Cresswell *Journal* 80 Proceeded a little way up the River to a great Buffalo crossing. **1856** Whipple *Explor. Ry. Route* I. 24 Here, deep-furrowed trails show a regular buffalo crossing. — **(8) 1805** Clark in *Lewis & C. Exped.* (1904) I. 245 A Buffalo Dance (or Medeson) for 3 nights passed in the 1st. Village, a curious Custom the old men arrange themselves in a circle & after Smoke a pipe which is handed them by a young man Dress[ed] up for the purpose. All this is to cause the buffalow to Come near So that they may Kill them. **1945** Mathews *Talking* 51 They might possibly have a ceremony more like the Osage buffalo dance. — **(9) 1847** *H.R. Doc.* 76, 6 The Co-che-ta-cah, or 'Buffalo Eaters.' They have something upwards of three hundred lodges, and number about two thousand souls, and are located principally upon the headwaters of the Brazos. **1852** Marcy *Explor. Red River* (1854) 102 The Northern and Middle Comanches subsist almost entirely upon the flesh of the buffalo; they are known among the other Indians as 'buffalo-eaters.'

(10) 1844 Gregg *Commerce of Prairies* II. 24, I have often heard back woodsmen speak of the 'buck ague,' but commend me to the 'buffalo fever' of the Prairies for novelty and amusement. **1862** *Harper's Mag.* Sep. 452/1, I took the 'buffalo fever' at once in its severest form, had my gun ready in the twinkling of an eye, and ... sallied forth. — **(11) 1779** in *Amer. Sp.* XV. 161/2 Crossing the creek to a buckeye, hickory, and Walnut, near the creek; by a Buffaloe ford. **1837** Bird *Nick of Woods* II. 84 Crossing the river at the buffalo-ford above ... they made their way through the forest. — **(12) 1848** Ruxton *Adventures* 273 He was a musician, and of course could play the fiddle; Lucy Neal, Old Dan Tucker, and Buffalo Gals, were heard at all hours of the day and night. **1932** *Frontier* March 217/2 The band boys got up steam on free bourbon and played *Buffalo Gals* and *Marchin' Through Georgia* and *Maggie.* — **(13) 1824** in *Ore. Hist. Quart.* XIV. 375 The enemies proved to be six friendly Nez Perces separated from their camp on the buffalo ground and in snow shoes made way to us across the mountains. **1946** Foreman *Last Trek* 243 Six privates of the Fourth Cavalry, left the reservation on November 1, 1877, for the buffalo ground near Camp Supply. — **(14) 1907** Mulford *Bar-20* 21 Cowan, closing the door and taking a .60-caliber buffalo gun from under the bar, went out also and slammed the rear door forcibly. **1947** *Denver Post* 2 Mar. (Mag.) 3/3 They were armed with a few old trade guns and bows and arrows; we all had muzzle-loading muskets, mine an old Sharp's buffalo gun.

(15) (*a*) [**1683** in *Ill. Hist. Coll.* I. (1903) 71 We found ... a number of buffalo horns.] **1838** *N.O. Picayune* 3/5 Shell, Buffalo-horn, Brazilian and Ivory Combs of every description. **1939** Brownell *Horse & Buggy Philos.* 166 The ground was plentifully spattered with buffalo horns as the settlers had not yet come to gather them and send them to the folks back home. (*b*) **1887** *Scribner's Mag.* II. 507 The latter fixes his attention on the saw-like, serrated crowns, or summits, which are ... typical ... of true mountainous form. There are plenty of such features in the Rocky Mountains, and natives call them 'buffalo-horns.' — **(16) 1827** *Western Mo. Rev.* I. 281 It affords him a delightful theme to recount to his listening companions ... feasting on the smoking buffalo hump, on a winter evening. **1927** Siringo *Riata* 48 Being out of meat, and seeing a band grazing at the head of a gulch, about a mile distant, I concluded to get some buffalo humps. — **(17) 1781–2** Jefferson *Notes Va.* (1788) 8 The Kaskaskia is 100 yards wide at its entrance into the Missisipi [*sic*] and preserves that breadth to the Buffalo plains, 70 miles above. **1918** Connelley *Kansas* 248 Two Delawares and their wives were encamped on the buffalo-plains and engaged in hunting. — **(18) 1850** *Cong. Globe* App. 19 Feb. 160 Mr. Webster ... congratulates them [=northern Whig Party] that the Buffalo platform, though having some rotten planks ... [gives] a secure place to stand upon. **1864** *Ib.* App. 27 Feb. 49/2 Was he an unwilling advocate of emancipation who first unfurled that banner in Missouri on the Buffalo platform in 1848? — **(19) 1750** T. Walker *Journal* 55 We went up Naked Creek to the head and had a plain Buffaloe Road most of the way. **1850** *Cong. Globe* Dec. 57 The wild animals ... are the first engineers to lay out a road in a new country; the Indians follow them, and hence a buffalo road becomes a war-path.

(21) 1805 in *Ann. 9th Congress* 2 Sess. 1082 The surplusage [of vegetables, etc.] they exchange with the Hietans for buffalo rugs, horses and mules. **1844** Gregg *Commerce of Prairies* II. 213 The annual 'export' of *buffalo rugs* from the Prairies and bordering 'buffalo range,' is about a hundred thousand. — **(22) 1877** H. Ruede in *Sod-House Days* (1937) 28 Sod for building ... regulation thickness is $2\frac{1}{2}$ inches, buffalo sod preferred on account of its superior toughness. **1943** Holt *Carver* 49 With a plow they cut the buffalo sod four inches thick and twelve inches wide. — **(23) 1872** F. M. A. Roe *Army Lett.* 65 The officers say the negroes make good soldiers and fight like fiends. ... The Indians call them 'buffalo soldiers,' because their woolly heads are so much like the matted cushion that is between the horns of the buffalo. **1946** Woodard *Word-List* 7 Buffalo soldier: *n.* A Southerner who, near the end of the Civil War, fought for, or sympathized with, the North in order to curry favor with the probable winner. Pamlico, 1900–. Occasional. **1948** *Range Riders Western* May 95/2 There were other Long Knives coming, a small body of Buffalo Soldiers—Negro troopers—on their way to join the Long Knives at the corral. — **(24) 1823** *S.D. Hist. Coll.* I. 190 We had to pursue the intricate windings of a buffalo trace, among rocks, trees, etc. **1886** Z. F. Smith *Kentucky* 22 The hardy explorers took one of these roads, or buffalo traces, as they are called and known even yet.

(25) c1834 Catlin *Indians* II. 18 We will take that buffalo trail, where the traveling herds have slashed down the high grass. **1948** *Southwestern Rev.* Summer 235, I was attempting to cross the creek in a buffalo trail. — **(26) 1832** J. A. McClung *Sks. Western Advent.* 165 [The Indian] ... pinioned his arms until the buffalo tug was buried in the flesh. **1852** Mrs. Ellet *Pioneer Woman* 57 They omitted the precaution of binding him closely one night, merely tying the buffalo tug around his wrists, and fastening it to their bodies. — **(27) 1834** A. Pike *Sketches* 18 Traveled all day, and encamped again in the prairie, at a hole where buffalo had been rolling, called by hunters a buffalo wallow, and containing water. **1948** *Sat. Ev. Post* 25 Sep. 105/2 He gathered up his dead and buried them in a buffalo wallow.

b. In less frequent combs., often rare or obs.: (1) **buffalo bait,** the baiting or badgering of a buffalo; (2) **battle,** a fight or engagement with buffalo; (3) **beat,** (see quot.); (4) **berrying,** the gathering of buffalo berries; (5) **cider,** (see quot. and cf. **buffalo gall**); (6) **fuel,** buffalo chips; (7) **gall,** = **buffalo cider;** (8) **landing-place,** the place on the bank of a stream where buffalo land in crossing; (9) **pistol,** a pistol of large caliber for shooting buffalo; (10) **pond,** ?a pond frequented by buffalo, cf. **buffalo wallow;** (11) **pound,** a park (see **park,** *n.* **1.**) where buffalo congregate during the winter; (12) **ranger,** a buffalo that has wandered from the herd; (13) **run,** (see quot.); (14) **running,** hunting buffalo on horseback; (15) **slayer,** a name for a particular buffalo gun; (16) **stamp,** (see quots.); (17) **stove,** ?a stove of a type made in Buffalo, N.Y.; (18) **wagon,** ?an exceptionally large wagon; (19) **whooper,** (see quot.); (20) **wood,** buffalo chips.

(1) 1837 IRVING *Bonneville* II. xii. 126 Several admirable horsemen and bold hunters, who amused themselves with a grotesque kind of buffalo bait. — **(2) 1847** D. COYNER *Lost Trappers* 32 Their horses too were . . . well trained in all those dexterous movements to be practised in a buffalo battle. — **(3) 1805** T. M. HARRIS *State of Ohio* 179 There are found open cleared spots on the summit of hills, called 'Buffalo beats,' because supposed to be occasioned by the resort of those animals thither in fly time. — **(4) 1887** I. R. *Lady's Ranche Life Mont.* 20 Two afternoons we spent in buffalo-berrying and shooting combined.

(5) 1872 DE VERE 367 *Buffalo-Cider* is the ludicrous name given to the liquid in the stomach of a buffalo, which the thirsty hunter drinks, when he has killed his game at a great distance from water. — **(6) 1848** ROBINSON *Santa Fe Exped.* 13 The men scattered themselves about to pick up . . . buffalo-fuel. — **(7) 1846** SAGE *Scenes Rocky Mts.* xvi, With one pint of water mix one-fourth gill of buffalo-gall, and you will then have before you a wholesome . . . drink.— **(8) 1837** IRVING *Bonneville* II. xvi. 165 It was the lot of the voyagers, one night, to encamp at one of these buffalo landing-places, and exactly on the trail. — **(9) 1847** PARKMAN in *Knickerb.* XXIX. 509 He . . . jerked a huge buffalo-pistol from his holster, and set out at full speed after her.

(10) 1782 in *Amer. Sp.* XV. 162/1 To an Elm Standing on Souths line at the edge of a small Buffaloe pond. — **(11) 1775** in *Pub. Champlain Soc.* XXI. 159 Messrs Francis, Patterson & Homes are by the best authority the most Comodiously Situated for that artical, being within a few days Journies of the Buffalow Pounds where many old Men and some lazey Young Fellow resort the whole winter and never trouble themselves about any kind of Furrs Except a few wolves which are very Plenty in that Part. — **(12) 1859** A. JACKSON *MS Diary* 10 Kit caught a buffalo ranger. — **(13) 1867** DIXON *New America* I. 31 They must keep the buffalo-runs of Kansas and Colorado (as the white men have begun to call the plains—on paper) free from intrusion of mail and train. — **(14) 1849** PARKMAN in *Knickerb.* XXXIII. 8 The hunter came trotting back to the party, disgusted with buffalo-running.

(15) 1852 *S. Lit. Messenger* XVIII. 315/2, I now draw my old Harper's Ferry 'buffalo slayer,' and select a barren cow . . . and deliver my fire. — **(16) 1873** BEADLE *Undevel. West* 205 'Buffalo stamps,' are tracts of hard blue soil. **1878** ——— *Western Wilds* 131 The rock lies . . . but a few inches below the surface, which is largely dotted with 'buffalo stamps.' These are said to have been caused by buffaloes crowding together, stamping and licking the ground, led thereto by a saline element in the soil. — **(17) 1835** TODD *Notes* 6 In houses of the second order, firing is usually economised in the parlor by a Buffalo stove, having a flat top, with indentures for receiving stew pans or boilers, so that the character of cook may be enacted by the mistress. — **(18) 1853** *Mich. Agric. Soc. Trans.* (1854) 53 Chas. Hager, Detroit, [exhibited] 1 buffalo wagon. — **(19) 1915** YOUNG *Hard Knocks* 53 It was necessary to keep the cattle on the range; we also kept two additional men whose duty it was to keep the buffalo off the range; they were called 'buffalo whoopers.'

(20) 1855 STONE *Put's Calif. Songster* 16 It's fun to cook with buffalo wood.

c. In the names of, or with reference to, animals: (1) **buffalo beetle,** the carpet beetle or bug, *Anthrenus scrophulariae,* which damages woolen goods, esp. carpets; (2) **bird,** the cow blackbird, *Molothrus ater* (see also quot. 1876); (3) **bony pike,** (see quot.); (4) **bug,** = **buffalo beetle;** (5) **bull,** a male buffalo, also attrib.; (6) **calf,** the young of the buffalo; (7) **carp,** (see quot.); (8) **cod,** (see quot. 1907); (9) **cow,** (*a*) a female buffalo, also attrib., (*b*) a domestic cow having no horns, cf. **3.** above; (10) **dog,** a dog used in hunting buffalo; (11) **fish,** (see quot. 1889); (12) **fly,** = **buffalo gnat;** (13) **gnat,** any one of various small insects of the genus *Simulium,* esp. common in the lower Mississippi Valley, cf. **buffalo fly;** (14) **head,** = **bull neck;** (15) **horse,** a horse trained for hunting buffalo; (16) **moth,** the moth of the buffalo beetle; (17) **pecker,** ?a buffalo bird, *rare;* (18) **perch,** (see quots.), *obs.;* (19) **runner,** = **buffalo horse;** (20) **wolf,** the gray wolf, *Canis occidentalis.*

(1) 1892 V. KELLOGG *Kansas Insects* 109 Buffalo beetle. . . . Small, dark-colored, hairy creatures, infesting carpets. — **(2) 1876** DODGE *Black Hills* 124 Found in the Hills proper . . . [is the] Buffalo-bird—a large species of jay. **1912** *Animals of Amer.* 43 It is interesting to note that . . . the Buffalo had one little companion and friend—the cowbird or Buffalo bird. 'Sometimes the cowbirds walk sedately behind their grazing monster; sometimes they flit over, snapping at flies; often they sit along the ridgepole of his spine.' **1934** *Nat. Geog. Mag.* LXVI. 118 In early accounts of prairie life they [cowbirds] were known as 'buffalo birds' for the same reason. — **(3) 1842** *Nat. Hist. N.Y., Zoology* IV. 271 The Buffalo Bony Pike, *Lepisosteus bison,* . . . occurs in many of the small lakes of the Western district, and has been taken at Ogdensburgh three feet long. — **(4) 1889** *Cent.* 239/3 A larger species . . . is known as the carpet-beetle and buffalo-bug, and is very destructive to carpets and other woolen fabrics.

(5) 1774 D. JONES *Journal* (1865) 27 Mr. Owens killed . . . a stately buffalo bull. **1780** W. FLEMING in *Travels Amer. Col.* 641, I had lived for a constancy on poor dried Buffalo bull beef cured in the smoak. **1947** *Denver Post* 15 Feb. 9/5 Exception to the smooth running of the hunt was the first buffalo bull which ran the gantlet of archers without incurring a scratch. — **(6) 1775** ADAIR *Indians* 421 [Indians] change the regimen in nurturing their young females; these they lay on the skins of fawns or buffalo calves, because they are shy and timorous. **1890** CUSTER *Following Guidon* 183 The ranchmen devised a plan to capture buffalo calves. — **(7) 1820** RAFINESQUE in *Western Review* II. 299 Buffalo Carp Sucker, *Catostomus anisopturus,* . . . is found in the lower part of the Ohio, and is called Buffalo carp, Buffalo perch, Buffalo sucker [etc.]. — **(8) 1890** *Cent.* 4124 *O. elongatus,* a Californian species, attains a length of 5 feet and . . . is known by various names, as . . . green-cod, buffalo-cod, and codfish. **1907** HODGE *Amer. Indians* I. 371 *Cultus-cod.* A name of the blue, or buffalo, cod (*Ophiodon elongatus*), an important food fish of the Pacific coast from Santa Barbara to Alaska. — **(9)** (*a*) **1775** *Jrnl. Nicholas Cresswell* (1925) 84 This morning Killed a Buffalo Cow crossing the River. **1853** BOND *Minnesota* 302 Our tents were pitched, horses staked, supper cooked of buffalo cow-steaks. **1947** *Boulder* (Colo.) *D. Camera* 15 Feb. 2/1 The bowmen missed the first animal and killed a buffalo cow by mistake. (*b*) **1850** *N. Eng. Farmer* II. 52 The buffalo, or hornless cows, spoken of in Statement No. 1, . . . are there considered as natives. **1902** CLAPIN 80 Buffalo-cow, a common expression, among colored people of Virginia, for a cow without horns, because its head somewhat resembles that of the female buffalo, whose horns are very short.

(10) 1867 in E. B. CUSTER *Tenting on Plains* (1889) 575 One of them accidentally shot his horse, and also a large buffalo-dog. — **(11)** [**1768** ZEISBERGER & ZENSEMAN *Diary* (1912) 29 May, Another variety of fish . . . is the so-called Buffalo-fish, named thus because of the cattle-like lowing attributed to them.] **1774** D. JONES *Journal* (1865) 111 There is another kind of fish called buffaloe fish, many of which are larger than our sheepshead. **1889** *Cent.* 709/2 buffalo fish. . . . The popular name of fishes of the family *Catostomidae,* or suckers, and genus *Ictiobus* or *Bubalichthys.* They are among the largest of the suckers, somewhat resemble carp, and abound in the lakes and rivers of the United States. **1946** *Democrat* 27 June 2/1 A colored fisherman of this county caught a buffalo fish with no mouth. — **(12) 1846** LYELL *Second Visit* (1849) II. 89 There were swarms of buffalo flies to torment his horses, and sand flies to sting him and his family. **1889** *Secy. of Agric. Rep.* 346 [The Horn Fly] . . . has also been called the 'Texas Fly,' the 'Buffalo Fly,' and the 'Buffalo Gnat.' — **(13) 1822** J. WOODS *English Prairie* 278 As the first part of it [= summer] was so dry, we had no buffalo gnats, and but few prairie flies or musquetoes. **1933** CHELEY *Camping Out* 423 Black-fly, Buffalo Gnat, or Turkey Gnat. — **(14) 1791** BARTRAM *Travels* (1940) 243 *A*[*nas*] *bucephala;* the bull neck and buffaloe head.

(15) 1827 *Phila. Gazette* 27 Sep., On this trip I lost 1 horse by accident, and the last spring 2 by the Utaws, who killed 3 for the purpose of eating them 1 of which was a favorite buffalo horse. **1927** SIRINGO *Riata* 46 Here I saw my first expert lancing of buffalo, by Apache Indians on swift buffalo horses. — **(16) 1892** V. KELLOGG *Kansas Insects* 109 Small, dark-colored, hairy creatures, infesting carpets . . . known to housekeepers as 'fish moths,' 'buffalo moths,' etc. — **(17) 1806** LEWIS in *L. & Clark Exped.* (1905) V. 201 Killed a buffaloe pecker a beautifull bird. — **(18) 1832** FLINT *Miss. Valley* I. 79 Bubbler *amblodon,* Buffalo perch. Found in all the waters of the Ohio. . . . It is a fine fish for the table. **1845** KIRTLAND in *Boston Jrnl. Nat. Hist.* V. 266 Buffalo Sucker. Brown Buffalo. . . . The young is nearly elliptical in outline, and is often sold in the market as a distinct species, under the name of *Buffalo Perch.* — **(19) 1848** in *Blackw. Mag.* LXIII. 717 He had his horse, a regular buffalo-runner, picketed round the fire quite handy **1860** *Harper's Mag.* Oct. 586/2 Since 1850 the Sioux have stolen from the people of St. Jo more than four hundred horses, many of them buffalo-runners.

(20) 1846 SAGE *Scenes Rocky Mts.* vi, Of these [=wolves] there are five distinct classifications, viz: The big white, or buffalo wolf; the shaggy brown; the black; the gray, or prairie wolf; and the cayeute, (wa-chunka-monet,) or medicine-wolf of the Indians. **1947** *True* Nov. 90/1 They could be found . . . everywhere that the buffalo wolf roamed.

d. In the names of plants: (1) **buffalo bean,** any one of various leguminous plants of the genus *Astragalus* or closely related genera; (2) **berry,** the edible fruit of a western shrub of the genus *Shepherdia*, or the shrub itself, also attrib.; (3) **bur,** the sandbur, *Solanum rostratum;* (4) **bush,** the bush bearing the buffalo berry; (5) **clover,** a species of clover found chiefly in the western states, also the Texas blue bonnet, *Lupinus texensis;* (6) **currant,** a currant, *Ribes odoratum*, of the western states, valued as an ornament and for its black fruit; (7) **flower,** the bluebonnet; (8) **grass,** a perennial low-growing grass, *Buchloë dactyloides*, common on the former buffalo ranges of the West, also a species of grama grass, also attrib.; (9) **grease bush,** ?=**buffalo berry,** *rare;* (10) **nut,** the rabbitwood, *Pyrularia pubera*, or the water chestnut; (11) **pea,** =**buffalo bean;** (12) **plum,** =**buffalo bean;** (13) **tree,** (see quot.).

(1) 1906 RYDBERG *Flora of Colo.* 202 Geoprumnon . . . Buffalo Beans, Ground Plums. **1918** VISHER *So. Dakota* 81 The Legume family . . . includes some of the more abundant plants of these plains, notably . . . buffalo-bean, loco, lupine, and wild alfalfas. — **(2) 1805** *Mass. Spy* 17 July (Th.), Scions of a newly discovered berry, called the buffaloe berry. **1887** I. R. *Lady's Ranche Life Mont.* 67 A haunch of venison with buffalo-berry jelly. **1941** MCCOWAN *Naturalist* 214 Some of these Buffalo Berry shrubs have orange-coloured berries, others have fruit that when ripe is a brilliant crimson. — **(3) 1894** *Amer. Folk-Lore* VII. 95. **1931** CLUTE *Plants* 98 The buffalo-bur (*Solanum rostratum*), comes rightly by its name. It doubtless perfected its trick of catching hold of all sorts of animals by practicing on the buffalo. — **(4) 1833** CATLIN *Indians* I. 72 The buffalo bushes, which are peculiar to these northern regions, lined the banks of the river and defiles in the bluffs, sometimes for miles together. **1860** GREELEY *Overland Journey* 271 Half a dozen specimens of a large, worthless shrub, known as buffalo-bush or bull-berry, . . . comprise the entire timber of this delectable stream.

(5) [1764 *N.C. Morav. Rec.* II. (1925) 565 Buffalo Clover is a particularly large clover, of which these animals, that is the Buffaloes, are very fond.] **1767** *N. Car. Col. Rec.* VII. 1007 Buffalow Clover was extremely thick here it is a species of grass much like the red clover not much coveted by any cattle but the Buffalow. **1931** DOBIE *Coronado* 108 Yet the hills could hardly be so lush with buffalo-clover—as we used to call the blue bonnet—and red bunch grass, so soft and lovely, as they are in the eyes of memory. — **(6) 1863** GRAY *Botany* p. lii, Buffalo . . . Currant . . . is planted for its bright-yellow spicy-scented flowers, . . . berries blackish, useless. **1931** CLUTE *Plants* 98 It is not at all likely that the buffalo ate the . . . buffalo currant (*Ribes aureum*). — **(7) 1946** *Mag. of South* April 33/1 Other names include Buffalo flower, because the early settlers believed that the buffalo grazed on this member of the Clover family. — **(8) 1784** FILSON *Kentucke* 24 Where no cane grows there is abundance of wild-rye, clover, and buffalo-grass, . . . affording excellent food for cattle. **1888** *Harper's Mag.* July 244/2 The buffalo-grass sod which has covered these plains for centuries. **1948** *Reader's Digest* Nov. 133 We lived five miles southwest of him on the hard-soil buffalo-grass plains. — **(9) 1806** CLARK in *Lewis & C. Exped.* (1904) V. 302 The bottoms on the Stard. Side low and extencive and covered with timber such as . . . Grapevines together with the red berry or Buffalow Grees bushes.

(10) 1857 GRAY *Botany* 382 Buffalo-nut . . . [is] a low straggling shrub, with small greenish flowers. . . . [It grows on] rich wooded banks, mountains of Penn. and southward throughout and near the Alleghanies. **1931** CLUTE *Plants* 99 The buffalo nut (*Trapa natans*), however, is an inhabitant of watery places and has nothing to do with the buffalo, except that the hard black two-horned fruit has considerable resemblance to the head of the animal. — **(11) 1907** LYONS *Plant Names* 59 A[stragalus] crassicarpus Nutt. . . . Ground Plum, Buffalo Apple, Buffalo Bean, Buffalo Pea. *Fleshy legumes* edible. **1913** CATHER *My Antonia* 145 The buffalo-peas were blooming in pink and purple masses along the roadside. — **(12) 1939** *Nat. Geog. Mag.* Aug. 219/1 Buffalo plums like purple shadows lingered past their season.— **(13) 1883** HALE *Woods & Timbers N.C.* 154 Oil-Nut, Buffalo Tree, (*Pyrularia oleifera*, Gray) [is] a bush 3 to 6 feet high, abundant through our mountain range, and reaching north to the mountains of Pennsylvania.

e. Designating a fabric of a large square-checked pattern or a garment made of such a fabric.

1907 *Sears Cat.* (ed. 117) 969/2 Buffalo California Flannel Overshirts $1.95. **1947** *Dly. Ardmoreite* (Ardmore, Okla.) 25 Nov. 10 All-Wool Buffalo Plaid $9.98.

Also *buffalo blanket, chase, country, hair, hunting, meat, overcoat, range, region, sign, tallow, wool, wrapper*, etc.

As the last term in **black, bull, cow, half-breed, king, medicine, mongrel, mountain, prairie, razor, white buffalo.**

buffalo ˈbʌflˌo, *v.* [f. the noun.] **1.** *absol.* To hunt or kill buffalo, *rare.* **2.** *tr.* To intimidate or overawe. *Slang.*

(1) 1848 RUXTON in *Blackw. Mag.* LXIV. 23 Passing the Wa-ka-rasha . . . they met a band of Osages going 'to buffalo.' — **(2) 1903** *Cin. Enquirer* 9 May 13/1 Buffaloed—Bluffed. **1948** *Range Riders Western* May 58/1 That had me buffaloed for a while.

Buffalonian ˌbʌfəˈlonɪən, *n.* and *a.* **1.** *n.* An inhabitant of Buffalo, N.Y. **2.** *a.* Of or pertaining to Buffalo, N.Y.

(1) 1836 *Knickerb.* VIII. 352 A magnificent thoroughfare, Old Main, as the Buffalonians call it, stretched for miles before my eye. **1948** *Dly. Ardmoreite* (Ardmore, Okla.) 6 May 8/2 Nat Harris, a fellow Buffalonian, [is] now owner of Broadway's huge club, The Harem. — **(2) 1893** M. PHILIPS *Making of a Newspaper* 81 Its difficulties were imposed by the Buffalonian *mauvaise honte* of Mr. Cleveland.

buffalo robe. The skin of a buffalo dressed with the hair on for use as a covering, carriage robe, etc.

[1681 MARQUETTE AND JOLIET in *La. Hist. Coll.* II. 291 To reward him (Indian who holds the calumet), the chief presents him with a buffalo robe.] *c***1723** *Ib.* III. (1851) 73 Two of the chiefs took him

Buffalo robe of a type used by the Arapaho Indians

(M. de la Harpe) to a spot and seated him on a buffalo robe. **1804** CLARK in *Lewis & C. Exped.* (1904) I. 130 The [Sioux] Squars wore Peticoats & a white Buffalow roabe. **1833** J. E. ALEXANDER *Transatlantic Sketches* II. 316, I found the inhabitants driving about in sleighs at a great rate, seated on red-edged 'buffalo robes.' **1948** JOHNSTON *Gold Rush* 40/2 Miles Goodyear died, and was buried in a rocker with a buffalo robe as a shroud.

attrib. **1841** in *Minn. Hist. Bul.* IV. (1922) 428 On our faces we had *Buffalo robe masks*, and yet got our noses ears and cheeks frozen.

b. (See quots.)

1776 A. HENRY *Travels* 265 We were obliged to wrap ourselves continually in beaver blankets, or at least in ox-skins, which the traders call buffalo-robes. **1817** J. BRADBURY *Travels* 130 He wished for more time to fix the price of dried buffaloe skins, (usually called buffaloe robes). **1852** REGAN *Emigrant's Guide* 43 A buffalo robe* hung upon a peg near the door. . . . *The dried hide with the hair on.

* **buffet,** *n.* **1. buffet car,** (see quot. 1895), also **buffet smoking car. 2. buffet kitchen,** the kitchen of a buffet car. **3. buffet sleeper,** =**buffet car.**

(1) 1887 GEORGE *40 Yrs. on Rail* 248 Buffet, . . . dining and sleeping cars have all been added to meet the needs and tastes of this enterprising age. **1895** WAIT *Car-Builder's Dict.* 21 Buffet-car. A term (meaning, literally, *sideboard-car*) applied to a style of sleeping-car or parlor-car which has an ornamental buffet where light lunches can be prepared for the passengers. *Buffet-smoking cars* are also built in the same general style of finish. **1916** *Amer. Mag.* Aug. 8/3 The Pullman conductor got fresh and said we was driving everyone out of the buffet car. — **(2) 1895** *Cent. Mag.* June 273/1 Her own order for breakfast was confined to a cup of coffee, which the porter was preparing in the buffet-kitchen. — **(3) 1887** *Ev. Jrnl.* (Atlanta) 30 June 1/8 Double daily service of elegantly appointed coaches and buffet sleepers.

bufflehead ˈbʌflˌhɛd, *n.* [See quot. 1917.] A small, well-known fresh-water duck, *Charitonetta albeola.*

1858 BAIRD *Birds Pacific R.R.* 798 The name buffle head is a corruption of buffalo head, under which name it is mentioned by Bartram, in 1791. **1917** *Birds of Amer.* I. 140/1 It was named Buffle-head (or Buffalo-head) because of its large fluffy head, which looks particularly big when its feathers are erected. **1948** *Field & Stream* June 128/3 A diver, the buffle-head seldom flies high, but breezes busily across the water.

buffle-headed duck. Also **buffelheaded, †buffel's head duck, bufflehead,** =prec.

1731 CATESBY *Carolina* I. 95 *Anas minor purpureo capite.* The Buffel's Head Duck.... These Bird's frequent fresh waters, and appear in Carolina only in Winter. **1813** WILSON *Ornithology* VIII. 51 The Buffel-headed Duck, or rather as it has originally been, the Buffaloe-headed Duck, ... is fourteen inches long, and twenty-three inches in extent. **1946** STANWELL-FLETCHER *Driftwood Valley* 179 Two pairs of little bufflehead ducks arrived last week.

buffler ˈbʌflɚ, *n.* Variant of buffalo. *Colloq. Obs.* — **1848** RUXTON *Far West* i. 30 A clever man was Bill Bent as I ever know'd trade a robe or throw a bufler in his tracks. **1886** *Outing* June 323/2, I want ter show this 'ere young man where I got that big stand on buffler last fall.

∗**Buffum,** *n.* A variety of pear introduced by D. Buffum in 1828.

1853 FOWLER *Home for All* 145 The Buffum, very prolific, and almost equal to Vergalue. **1863** *Rep. Comm. Agric.* 182 The Buffum is a native of Rhode Island, a remarkably erect and vigorous grower, with reddish brown, short-jointed wood. **1863** *Horticulturist* Aug. 262/1 Of Pears, [we mention] Bartlett, ... Sheldon, Seckel, Buffam, Beurré Diel.

∗**bug,** *n.* [In sense **1.** possibly f. ∗*bug, a.*, pompous, big.]

1. An individual obsessed by some idea or enthusiasm, also an obsession, mania. *Slang.*

For various colloq. or dial. uses see *D.N.*

1841 *Cong. Globe* June 133 Mr. Alford of Georgia warned the 'tariff bugs' of the South that ... he would read them out of church. *a***1909** O. HENRY *Roads of Destiny* xiii. 208 He's got bugs. Sitting on ice and calling his best friends pseudonyms. **1947** *Denver Post* 2 Feb. A. 11/2 Basketball bugs believe Colorado never had a prep team like the Windsor Wizards.

b. A device used by a sharper to cheat at cards. *Slang.*

1889 *Thompson St. Poker Club* 69 The Rev. Mr. Smith unloaded himself from Mr. Williams' abdomen, arose, crossed the room, and possessed himself of the extra cards pinned to the table. '*Dis* whadjer call de *bug?*' he asked. **1891** QUINN *Fools of Fortune* 234 As soon as the party receives, in the regular course, a card, or perhaps a pair of the same denomination as the one which he has secreted in the 'bug,' he puts his hand over the edge of the table, under which he puts his thumb, he then deftly raises the card which he has concealed, at the same time taking an inferior card from his hand and placing the latter in the 'bug.'

c. A defect or fault. *Slang.*

1934 WEBSTER. **1945** *Pueblo* (Colo.) *Star-Journal* 17 June 11. 1 Distribution Bug Blamed for Nation's Meat Shortage.

2. In combs.: (1) **bug catcher,** a jocose term for a student of bugs and insects, an entomologist; (2) **eater,** see as a main entry; (3) ∗**eye,** (see quot. 1881 and cf. ∗**buckeye 6.**); (4) **eyed,** *a.* having bulging eyes; (5) **fish, head,** *local* (see quots.); (6) **horned,** *a.* having bug horns, *obs.;* (7) **horns,** horns curving inward, *obs.;* (8) **house,** see as a main entry; (9) ∗**hunter,** =**bug catcher;** (10) **juice,** bad or inferior liquor, *slang;* (11) **lamp, lantern,** a lamp or lantern giving only a feeble light; (12) **light,** a small harbor or channel light that flashes intermittently, suggesting a **lightning bug,** also transf.; (13) **masher,** the foot, *jocular;* (14) **poison,** =**bug juice,** *slang;* (15) **shad,** see **bug fish;** (16) **sharp,** =**bug catcher, bug hunter, bugologist,** *slang.*

(1) 1843 in *Miss. Val. Hist. Rev.* VI. 108 We had doctors, Lawyers, botanists, Bugg Ketchers, Hunters and men of nearly all professions. — **(3) 1881** E. INGERSOLL *Oyster Industry* 242 *Bugeye*, a flat-bottomed, center-board schooner of three to fifteen tons, built of heavy timbers, without a frame. A bugeye is always decked over and has a cabin aft. **1947** *Amer. Dial. Soc. Pub.* No. 8, 35 The boat used in the Chesapeake Bay is called bug-eye, but it is not a small boat. — **(4) 1934** WEBSTER. **1948** *Desert* Feb. 40/3 The patrons will be bug-eyed.

(5) 1857 *Harper's Mag.* March 442/1 Other varieties [of refuse fish] are sometimes taken, and among them the bug-fish.... Its characteristic peculiarity is only discovered on opening the mouth, in which it carries a sort of parasitical bug. **1888** GOODE *Amer. Fishes* 386 Virginia gives us 'Bug-fish,' 'Bug-head' and 'Bug-shad,' referring to the parasitic crustacean found in the mouths of all Southern Menhaden. **1941** *Nature Mag.* March x. 138 In Virginia, bug-fish is the word; it refers to parasitic crustaceans (not bugs, i.e. insects) that are often found in the mouth of the menhaden. — **(6) 1823** *Somerset* (Me.) *Jrnl.* 28 Nov. 1/1 (Th.), Come into the enclosure of the subscriber ... a Red Cow, with a white face, and bug horned. — **(7) 1766** *Mass. Gazette* 23 Oct. 4/3 Strayed away from the Owner in Boston, ... a small dark brown Cow, with bug Horns. **1821** *Mass. Spy* 22 Aug., Strayed, a pair of three-year-old Steers,—one of brown colour, with bug horns. — **(9) 1898** *Mo. So. Dakotan* I. 75 When the bug hunter was killed on the Little Cheyenne Captain Miner was acting field officer of the day.

(10) 1869 *New No. West* (Deer Lodge, Mont.) 22 Oct. 1/5 Citizens glad to see us—freedom of the city—'bug juice,' *ad lib.* **1940** WILSON *Wabash* 228 Abe had no taste for the blue ruin, the bug juice, or the moral suasion that was consumed in those days in great quantities. — **(11)** *c***1849** PAIGE *Dow's Sermons* I. 75 You may wander outside in the darkness of ignorance—guided by the bug-lamps of instinct. **1924** R. CUMMINS *Sky-High Corral* 104 He produced a candle and a can from his pack and made a 'bug' lantern by cutting a hole in the side of the can and poking the candle through it. — **(12) 1882** GODFREY *Nantucket* 217 The Cliff lights, sometimes called 'Bug lights,' ... are situated on the beach northwest of Nantucket Harbor. **1899** SUSAN HALE *Letters* 341 My room is called the 'Buglight' because it is a little house all by itself set upon four legs over a sort of piazza where we read and sew. **1945** *Chi. D. News* 28 Sep.6/5 He became keeper of a bug-light in Boston Harbor and sometime after that buried the money. — **(13) 1871** *Harper's Mag.* XLIII. 640/2 He is best known as 'Barefooted Jake.' However, it is not with Jake's 'bug-mashers' that we have to do. — **(14) 1888** *Texas Siftings* 7 July (F.), Nearly every character introduced by Charles Dickens into his numerous novels, was addicted to drinking ... ; each and every individual took his bug-poison with surprising regularity and eminent satisfaction.

(16) 1877 *Field & Forest* III. 94 One [*Amblychila cylindriformis*] ... was viewed with emotions too deep for words by jostling crowds of bug-sharps.

3. In figurative colloq. phrases: (1) *To put a bug on* (a person), to hoax (see quot. 1900); (2) *to smell a bug,* to become suspicious, to "smell a rat"; (3) *to go to the bugs,* to go to the mischief; (4) *the bug under the chip,* the ulterior or hidden motive or cause, also in allusive context; (5) *to beat the bugs,* to beat the dickens; (6) *to put a bug in one's ear,* (see quot.).

(1) 1848 W. T. THOMPSON *Major Jones's Sk. Trav.* 126 (Th.), This may be a bug what they put on me, but one thing I do know [etc.]. **1900** *D.N.* II. 16 With customary inconsistency, however, *to put a bug on* a person is to score a point in repartee. — **(2) 1853** P. PAXTON *Yankee in Texas* 96, I smell a bug. Dave and that ar stranger's only playin' possum. — **(3) 1856** J. D. WHITNEY *Life & Lett.* 160 Shall I let the survey go to the bugs and return home immediately? — **(4) 1885** *Cong. Rec.* Jan. 998/1, I know as well what the bug is under this chip as I know that the resolution is pending here. **1909** O. HENRY *Options* 9 How about this write-up of the Atlanta, New Orleans, Nashville, and Savannah breweries? ... What's the chip over the bug? **1946** *Newsweek* 15 July 36/3 To those uneasy over the alliance he gave his word that there are 'no such bugs under the chips.'

(5) 1891 E. S. ELLIS *Check No. 2134* 261 'That beats the bugs!' exclaimed the operator. — **(6) 1905** *D.N.* III. 72 Bug in one's ear, *n. phr.* Hint. 'I want to put a *bug in your ear.*' Common.

As the last term in **apple, bacon, bed, beetle, betsey, bill, black, box elder, buffalo, cabbage, calico, cherry, China, chinch, Colorado, cow, Croton, cucumber, daddy, daw, dollar, doodle, dor, electric light, elm tree, false, fire, flea, gall, gold, great, hammer, Hessian, horn, horned, June, Juney, kissing, lightning, money, Negro, pea, peach, pill, pinch, pinching, plant, potato, red, rose, sand, saw, scale, scorpion, shore, silver, snap, snap-jack, snapping, soldier, spit, spittle, squash, steamboat, stick, stink, strawberry, striped, tariff, thunder, tumble, water, wheel bug.**

bug bʌg, *v.*[1] [See note.]

In the *OED* and in Webster senses **1.** and **2.** are regarded as being from different sources. They are prob. both from ∗*bug, n.* the insect.

1. *tr.* To clear (trees or plants) of insects.

1869 *Champaign Co.* (Ill.) *Gazette* 26 May 2/1 If every tree in the township was 'bugged' daily, ... the destruction of this little pest would be certain. **1877** *Vt. Bd. Agric. Rep.* IV. 113 For several years this 'bugging the potatoes,' as it was frequently termed, was the only effectual mode of combatting these insects that was known. **1917** *D.N.* IV. 409 Jim's out buggin' taters.

2. *intr.* Of the eyes: To stick out, protrude. *Colloq.*

1877 MARK TWAIN in *Atlantic Mo.* XL. 446 His dead-lights were bugged out like tompions; and his mouth stood ... wide open. **1947** *This Week Mag.* 12 April 22/3 He talks and listens for a minute and his eyes bug out.

bug bʌg, *v.*[2] [App. f. ∗*bug, n.*, a trick or hoax, as in *to put a bug on, to smell a bug* (see ∗**bug,** *n.* **1. b.** and **3.**)] **1.** *tr.* To deceive or hoax. **2.** *bugged up to kill,* dressed to kill. Both *colloq.* — **(1) 1843** in TURNER *Cotton* (1865) 62 You will first observe the bloom, and the description given, and you will agree with me at once, that Mr. Sears has been bugged by an okra flower. — **(2) 1898** WISTER *Lin McLean* 3 'Bugged up to kill!' exclaimed one, perceiving Lin's careful dress.

bug-eater.

1. An insignificant or trifling fellow. *Obs.*

a1859 *Southern Sketches* 99 (B.), Congo is a scrougher; he's up a gum, and no bug-eater, I tell you. **1878** *Field & Forest* Jan. 132/2 Our old teamster informed us that in Rocky Mountain parlance, a worthless fellow is called a 'bug eater.' **1891** SLOAN *Fogy Days* 134, I was going to get even with them before I left, to show them I wasn't the kind of a bug-eater they took me for.

2. (*cap.*) A nickname for a Nebraskan.

1872 *Harper's Mag.* Jan. 318/1 Below will be found a careful compilation of the various nicknames given to the States and people of this republic. . . . Nebraska, Bug-Eaters. **1889** *N. & Q.* III. 15 June 83 bug eater. . . . I imagine this name as applied to the people of Nebraska comes from the fact that at a time when that State was overrun by locusts (or 'hoppers'), the proposal was made to turn the insects to good account by making them an article of food, after the manner of the Arabs. Several entomologists and journalists actually got up a dinner at which the locusts were served up in various styles.

***buggy,** *n.*

1. A light four-wheeled vehicle, drawn usu. by one horse, and having a collapsible top. See also **Concord buggy.**

The first example may refer to an English-type buggy having two wheels.

[**1807** IRVING *Salmagundi* viii. 174 An honest cit packs up . . . in a buggy . . . and rattles away on Sunday.] **1843** *Knickerb.* XXI. 49 He has recently become sole proprietor of . . . a nondescript four-wheeled vehicle, dignified with the name of 'buggy.' **1861** BERKELY *Sportsman* 158 A very pretty girl of about 14 or 15 was once permitted to drive me out in what her father called his buggy, but which carriage had four wheels, and was a sort of curricle drawn by a pair of horses. **1948** RITTENHOUSE *Vehicles* 3 The buggy was a truly distinctive American type of vehicle, popular because of its lightness and economy.

b. A doll carriage or baby buggy.

1929 *Nebraska Alumnus* June 166 There are also a doll bed and dresser and buggy with several dolls and their wardrobes. **1944** *Chi. D. News* 4 Oct. 4/2 Iris fell from the buggy when she stood up. **1947** *Jrnl. Crim. Law & Criminology* Nov.–Dec. 313 At 7 months, while unattended, he fell from his buggy to a cement basement areaway 12 feet below and injured his head.

2. (See quots.)

1875 *Chi. Tribune* 11 Sep. 4/2 The yard men load little iron carts,—called 'buggies' . . . .—, with the due proportions of ordinary pig and charcoal iron. **1883** *Harper's Mag.* LXVI. 939/2 The men who do this work [=on the Brooklyn Bridge cables] go out for the purpose on the strand in a 'buggy' so called, which is a board slat slung by ropes from the axis of a grooved wheel fitting and travelling on the strand as bound together.

3. The caboose of a freight train.

1899 *Boston Globe* 18 March 12/2 During the first eight weeks of this year 31,271 freight cars passed through Concord, N.H. Estimating the total length of these cars, with the engines and buggies, we find [etc.]. **1904** *Ib.* 28 Feb. 40/6 The caboose, or as it is better known, the buggy, is . . . a peculiar little car, and is the home of the crew while on the rail. It has four bunks, two at either end; while in the center is a compartment of about a dozen feet square. In one corner is a stove, in another a sink, while in the center is a stairway, leading up the monitor.

4. In combs.: (1) **buggy box,** the box or body of a buggy; (2) **collar,** a collar for a buggy animal; (3) **cultivator,** (see quot.); (4) **cushion,** the cushioned seat of a buggy; (5) **harness,** harness suitable for a buggy animal; (6) **horse,** a horse that pulls a buggy; (7) **lines,** the lines or reins used in driving a buggy animal; (8) **mare, nag,** a mare or nag that pulls a buggy; (9) **plow,** a riding plow; (10) **ride,** a ride in a buggy; (11) **robe,** =**lap robe;** (12) **seat,** a seat of a buggy or buggy plow; (13) **shed,** a shed for housing a buggy; (14) **sleigh,** ?a buggy provided with runners like a sleigh, *obs.;* (15) **wagon,** a light four-wheeled wagon; (16) **whip,** a long switch-like whip for use in a buggy, also attrib.

(1) **1860** *S. Cultivator* XVIII. 127 What do you think of the 'stimulated industry' which can start from Ohio with a buggy-box full of Ohio grafts, and *graft its way* clear through to Alabama. — (2) **1853** *Mich. Agric. Soc. Trans.* V. 53 Farm Implements [exhibited include] . . . 1 fine buggy collar. — (3) **1874** KNIGHT 400/1 Buggy-cultivator, . . . one having wheels and a seat so that the person may ride. — (4) **a1841** W. HAWES *Sporting Scenes* II. 81 The light of the lantern . . . now disclosing a hat . . . , now an umbrella, and now a buggy-cushion. **1906** in *Kansas Hist. Soc.* IX. 178 In this, with buffalo skins for beds and buggy cushions for pillows, they slept comfortably and securely.

(5) **1840** *Boston Directory* 11 Coach, Gig, & Buggy Harnesses. **1944** CLARK *Pills* 51 It was of wax on saddles, horse collars and buggy harness. — (6) **1858** GLISAN *Jrnl. Army Life* 398, I succeeded in purchasing a splendid saddle and buggy horse, known all over the Territory. **1911** HARRISON *Queed* 174 In the grove stood carriages; buggy horses reined to the tall trees. — (7) **1944** CLARK *Pills* 269 The most common practice was to use buggy lines with buckles stripped off so that when the casket came to rest at the bottom the straps could be pulled out from one side. — (8) **1870** MACRAE *Americans* I. 283 Those who have horses to dispose of ride up and down . . . shouting, 'Here's your fine saddle-horse!' . . . 'Here's your buggy-nag!' **1934** VINES *Green Thicket World* 52 Winnie had often heard him cluck to Morgan and a little red buggy mare. — (9) **1870** MACRAE *Americans* II. 180 Yes, that's what we call a buggy-plough. It makes ploughing pleasanter. A woman or a boy could plough with it just as well as that man. **1876** *Cong. Rec.* 17 June 4656/1 We are developing our wheat interest . . . by the addition of . . . the turning plow, the gang plows, . . . the buggy plow, and so on.

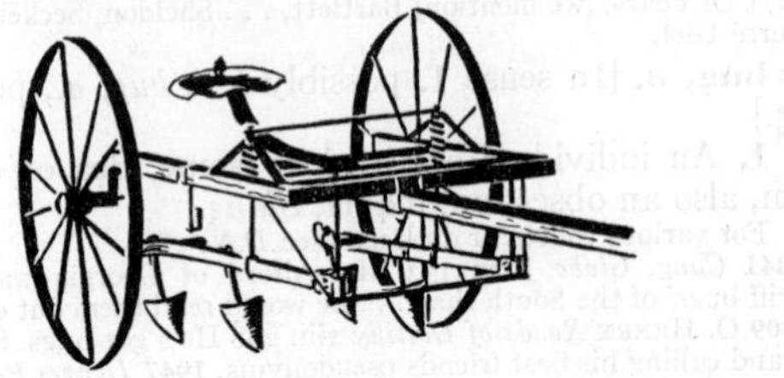

Buggy cultivator or riding cultivator

(10) **1863** *Ill. Agric. Soc. Trans.* (1865) V. 255 The one on the gang plow would have a fine buggy ride. **1944** KAHN *Cable Car Days* 107 A good part of the livery stable's income was derived from the Sunday buggy rides through Golden Gate Park. — (11) **1939** HARRIS *Purslane* 100 He tucked the buggy robe around her feet and slipped it over her lap. **1943** DAMON *Sense of H.* 80 He had on what I took to be a brown buffalo buggy robe. — (12) **1863** *Ill. Agric. Soc. Trans.* V. (1865) 255 The old plow jogger will be mounted on his buggy seat. **1884** HOWELLS *Silas Lapham* i. 23 Lapham, gathering up the hitching-weight, slid it under the buggy-seat and mounted. — (13) **1944** CLARK *Pills* 294 Soon buggy sheds were used to house automobiles, and buggies, harness and carriage fixtures disappeared from the market. — (14) **1842** HALE *If, Yes and Perhaps* (1868) 84 The dear girl . . . agreed to go to Mrs. Pollexfen's ball that evening, ready to leave it with me in my buggy sleigh.

(15) **1841** L. B. SWAN *Journal* (1904) 38 Left Huron in a buggy wagon for Norwalk (Ohio), 12 miles over a bad road. **1856** BREWERTON *War in Kans.* 305 John Smith says he's expectin' a buggy-wagon, along with some other notions, which his folks are a sendin' out from New York State. — (16) **1839** *Amer. Comic* (We.), She'll sometimes grip The buggy whip. **1873** *Winfield* (Kansas) *Courier* 10 July 3/2 Buggy whips, cattle whips and riding whips at Old Log Store. **1948** *Sat. Ev. Post* 26 June 47/1 The surviving whalers voyaged to the Arctic and Antarctic to bring back the whalebone still demanded by the buggy-whip makers and corset manufacturers.

As the last term in **baby, buckboard, covered, doll, double, horse-and-, hug-me-tight, no top, pembina, pie, shifting-top, side-bar, single, spider-wheeled, spring, swamp, top, two horse buggy.**

buggy ˈbʌgɪ, *v.tr.* To convey (a person) in a buggy. Also *intr.* — **1869** *New No. West* (Deer Lodge, Mont.) 17 Sep. 3/1 J. B. Hubell . . . buggied into town on Thursday evening from Helena. **1872** *Newton Kansan* 5 Sep. 3/2 Our whilom friend . . . buggied Mrs. S. over to Augusta.

bughouse ˈbʌgˌhaʊs, *n.* and *a.*

1. *n.* A lunatic asylum. *Slang.*

1904 O. HENRY *Heart of West* 226, 'I thought he was in the bughouse,' said the passenger who was nobody in particular. **1943** DAMON *Sense of H.* 163 Thet thar man yer've jest hired 's a lunatic, or was, last I knew. Was in the bughaouse a long spell, anyhaow.

b. Bughouse Square, a place, usu. in a park, to which those resort, often for prolonged discussions, who are regarded as not quite compos mentis. *Colloq.*

1923 *Jrnl. Amer. Inst. Crim. Law & Criminology* Aug. 302 Washington Square or 'Bughouse' Square, Grant Park and the docks are also favorite rendezvous for the homeless men. **1948** CHAPLIN *Wobbly* 71 We made the acquaintance of the rough-and-ready free-lance orators at 'Bughouse Square' near Newberry Library on the Near North Side.

2. *a.* Insane, crazy. *Slang.*

1895 *Cent. Mag.* L. 291/2 How's that for bein' bug-house, eh? **1913** *Industrial Worker* (Spokane) 14 Aug. 4/2 Whom the gods would destroy they first make bughouse!

b. *To go bughouse*, to go crazy. *Slang.*

1909 *Sat. Ev. Post* 15 May 39/2 All the inhabitants of this country have gone synchronously bughouse, batty and dopy on the same subject. **1947** PAUL *Linden* 396 Before the first day was up, I had to get a job, washing dishes at one of the hotels, to keep from going bughouse.

***bugle,** *n.*

1. The nose or head. *Slang.*

1865 MARK TWAIN in Paine *Biography* I. 275 (R.), Tore his coat, clutched his throat, And split him in the bugle. **1918** *D.N.* V. 111 *bugle*, n. Head. From the noise made with the head. [At U. of Calif.]

2. In combs.: (1) **bugle brush,** ?a species of chaparral, *rare;* (2) **cranberry,** a cranberry of an oblong or bugle-like shape; (3) **weed,** (see quot. 1890).

(1) **1885** L. W. SPRING *Kansas* 259 Not a building of any sort existed on the proposed site of it; nothing was there except 'prairie grass, bugle-brush, and weeds.' — (2) **1874** *Dept. Agric. Rep. 1873* 445 The American cranberry is divided by growers and writers into three different varieties, viz., the Bell cranberry . . . ; the Bugle cranberry, which somewhat resembles a bugle-head . . . ; the Cherry cranberry. — (3) **1817–8** EATON *Botany* (1822) 345 *Lycopus virginicus*, bugle weed . . . var. *quercifolius*. . . . Damp. **1890** *Cent.* 3552/2 *L. Virginicus* is a common American species [of mint] with some medicinal properties, called *bugleweed*.

bugologist ˌbʌgˈɑlədʒɪst, *n.* An entomologist. *Jocular.*

1881 *Nat. Republican* 24 Feb. 2/4 Mr. Riley, the eminent bugologist, has had an interview with General Garfield on the subject of agriculture. **1901** G. S. HALL *Confess. Psychol.* 110 The 'Bugologist' . . . has long been the stalking horse or awful example of . . . narrowness. **1910** *Sat. Ev. Post* 2 July 49/2 Government bugologists camped on his trail and studied his habits until they got so they could read his mind.

bugology ˌbʌgˈɑlədʒɪ, *n.* Entomology. *Jocular.* — **1843** CARLTON *New Purchase* II. 171 Chemistry, botany, anatomy, conchology, bugology. **1898** *Cong. Rec.* App. 22 April 455/2 Those of you who are acquainted with bugology know there is rather a disreputable bug that looks one way and rolls the other.

***build,** *v.*

1. *tr.* Used somewhat jocosely in a quite general sense (see quots.).

1845 J. F. COOPER *Satanstoe* (B.), In this manner it was thought we should . . . sooner 'build up a settlement,' as the phrase goes. In America, the reader should know, everything is 'built.' The priest 'builds up' a flock; the speculator, a fortune; the lawyer a reputation; and the landlord a settlement. **1877** BARTLETT 76 *To build clothes:* tailors use this expression for making clothes. 'Guess we can build you a neat pant off these goods, sir.' **1907** *Collier's* 5 Oct. 21/3 Mother's at the kitchen stove Building lemon pie. **1930** FERBER *Cimarron* 232 They built angel-food cakes whose basis was the whites of thirteen eggs, and their husbands, at breakfast, said, 'What makes these scrambled eggs so yellow?'

2. To make, construct (a railroad).

1873 *Republic* I. 54 In the last forty years 61,480 miles of railroad have been built. **1929** *Times* 23 Dec. 27/3 Before a railroad may build a new line, it must make application.

3. *Cards.* (See quot. 1901.) Also transf.

1901 *Munsey's Mag.* XXIV. 871/2 To build down . . . is to place a card upon one of the next higher denominations. To build up . . . is to do just the opposite—that is, to place an eight on a seven. **1903** A. ADAMS *Log Cowboy* vi. 76, I built right up to him.

***builder,** *n.* As the last term in **ark, birch, car, ground, house, mound builder.**

builder's paper. =**building paper.** — **1917** MATHEWSON *Sec. Base Sloan* vii. 88 Red builder's paper superseded the boards across the window frames.

***building,** *n.* In combs.: (1) **building bee,** a bee for erecting a house; (2) **block,** a small wooden block for children's use in building; (3) **lot,** a plot of land laid out as a building site; (4) **paper,** heavy paper used for warmth or to deaden sound in the walls and roofs of buildings; (5) **rock,** stone suitable for use as building material; (6) **spot,** a site suitable for a building.

(1) **1848** RUXTON *Far West* (1849) 257 A buildin' bee or a raisin' bee is when they want to set up the frame or the logs of a house or barn. **1948** *Popular Western* June 72/2 You cain't wind up a buildin' bee witout a doin's uh some sort, an' count me in on it. — (2) **1846** *Boston Herald* 14 Oct. 3/1 Jewsharps, Games, Building Blocks, Harmonicas. **1857** *Miners' Own Book* iii, Wheel Barrows, Race and Grace Hoops, Building Blocks. — (3) **1701** *Conn. Col. Rec.* IV. 357 On the west side of old Jacksons lotts (vizt,) pasture, building lott, and long lott. **1948** *So. Bend* (Ind.) *Tribune* 3 Apr. 10/5 A beautiful building lot awaits you in Wooded Estates Second Addition. — (4) **1873** *Newton Kansan* 20 Feb. 3/4 Building paper, the best substitute for plastering, for sale by Lehman & Co. **1947** *Democrat* 14 Aug. 6/1 If floors and walls are not tight, cover them with building paper.

(5) **1800** B. HAWKINS *Sk. Creek Country* 28 The hill sides fronting the river, exhibit this building rock. **1849** CHAMBERLAIN *Indiana Gazetteer* 191 Iron ore, marble, excellent building rock and hydraulic cement are found in abundance. — (6) **1802** *Mass. H.S. Coll.* VIII. 201 So many houses and works have been erected, . . . that building spots now sell at a high price. **1872** *Ill. Dept. Agric. Trans.* 174 In the west part of the city . . . are the finest building spots in the world.

As the last term in **apartment, balloon, bark, commissary, county, elevator, frame, log, mound, office, saloon, seven, six, state building.**

build-up, *n. fig.* The aggregate of interest in or enthusiasm for a person or thing. *Slang.* — **1927** *Collier's* 3 Dec. 10/4 That's the old build-up for the Patsys. **1948** *Dly. Ardmoreite* (Ardmore, Okla.) 12 May 12/3 After all that buildup—it got the country into a kind of crisis mood—they had to call off the strike.

***built,** *p.p. To be built that way*, to be so constituted or disposed. *Colloq.*

[**1868** *Mo. Republican* 25 Jan. (F.), 'Why didn't you roll down?' 'I wasn't built that way.'] **1889** FARMER 100/1 The expression is even extended to individuals, to be built being used with the meaning of formed. 'I was not built that way'; and hence in a still more idiomatic sense to express unwillingness to adopt a specified course or carry out any inconvenient plan. **1942** WARNICK *Dialect Garrett Co., Md.* 4 Built, v., adapted to. 'I'm not built that way.'

As the last term in **log built, scow built.**

***bulge,** *n.*

1. Advantage, upper hand, superiority over something or somebody, usu. *to have*, (or *get*) *the bulge on. Colloq.*

1841 *Spirit of Times* 18 Dec. 498/3 (We.), Kate got the bulge on her at the start. **1860** *Richmond Enquirer* 30 Nov. 4/5 (Th.), It is in this respect [*sc.* of field products] that the South has 'the bulge' on the North. **1891** SLOAN *Fogy Days* 110 All these latter sins, are called passions, and they go in and come out of a fellow's bosom as they please, when they get the bulge on him. **1947** *N.Y. Times* 12 Oct. v. 1/8 Yale enjoyed a 10–0 bulge that did not begin to tell the story of its domination of the contest.

2. *fig.* An increase in prices. *Colloq.*

1890 BIFF HALL *Turnover Club* 208 There is quite a bulge on June cocktails, and I fear a corner. **1908** G. H. LORIMER *J. Spurlock* xi. 272 The city house which the Bonsalls had occupied just before the big bulge in Southern Pacific landed them on top.

***bulge,** *v.* **1.** *intr.* To rush, dash. *Colloq.* **2.** *tr.* To force at high speed. *Rare.*

(1) **1834** CROCKETT *Narr. Life* 96 My dogs . . . bulged in, and in an instant the bear followed them out. *Ib.* 105 As soon as we struck, I bulged for my hatchway. **1884** MARK TWAIN *H. Finn* 372 Whilst we was a-standing there in the dimmish light here comes a couple of the hounds bulging in from under Jim's bed. — (2) **1868** WOODRUFF *Trotting Horse* xxiii. 207 Brooks and Harry Jones bulged them [*sc.* the horses] in the lead at such a rate that I was forced to let them take the pole on the turn.

bulger ˈbʌldʒɚ, *n.* [f. ***bulge,** *v.*] (See quot. 1871.) *Colloq.* — **1835** CROCKETT *Tour* 37 We . . . soon came in sight of the great city of New York, and a bulger of a place it is. **1871** DE VERE 587 *Bulger* . . . in the United States generally designates anything very large. 'That's a *bulger* of a story.'

***bulk,** *n.*

1. A pile of tobacco made up to undergo sweating.

1678 *New Castle Court Rec.* 253 Tobacco which was struck & lay in balke. **1784** SMYTH *Tour* II. 136 The hands or bundles thus tied up are also laid in what is called a bulk, and covered with the refuse tobacco or straw, to preserve their moisture. **1880** TOURGEE *Bricks* 359 The spicy odor of the 'bulks' of tobacco, which was stored there. **1902** *Farmers' Bul. No. 60* (Dept. Agric.) 14 Before the sweat is completed the bulk is pulled down and built up eight or ten times.

2. *attrib.* Of commodities, etc.: Kept, sold, dealt with, in bulk or large quantities. See also **barrel bulk,** and ***bulkhead.**

1693 *Virginia State P.* I. 48 An answer to a former message of yours relating to the Act for Ports & Bulke Tubacco. **1847** *Rep. Comm. Patents* (1848) 527 Bulk pork is that which is intended for immediate use or smoking. **1888** *Voice* (N.Y.) June, I have noticed that wherever baled hay is used it supersedes the use of bulk hay rapidly.

***bulk,** *v. tr.* To put (tobacco) in bulks for curing, to store wheat in a heap.

1849 *Rep. Comm. Patents: Agric.* (1850) 322 To 'bulk' tobacco requires judgment and neatness. **1884** *Rep. Comm. Agric.* 350 The bulking of early-threshed wheat without separating the chaff. **1902** *Farmer's Bul. No. 60* (Dept. Agric.) 17 The leaves [of White Burley tobacco] . . . are tied into hands and bulked down for a short time, after which they are 'prized' into hogsheads.

*__bulker__, *n.* One who places tobacco, etc., in bulk. — **1863** *Ill. Agric. Soc. Trans.* V. (1865) 668 This is done by lapping the bundles over each course similar to shingling a roof, the bulker having his knees upon the bulk.

*__bulkhead__, *n.*

1. (See quots.)

1848 *Calif. Courier* (S.F.) 10 June 4/1 Look yonder, what a wonder! Jones' 'bulk-head,' yclept pier, Half hid under piles of 'plunder.' **1896** HASWELL *New York* 7 What are termed docks here are piers and bulkheads, constituting a wharf.

2. (See quot. 1907.)

1854 THOREAU *Walden* iv. 132 Some trader among the Green Mountains, . . . stands over his bulk-head and thinks of the last arrivals on the coast. **1907** *D.N.* III. 182 Bulkhead, *n.* Outside cellar-entrance with nearly horizontal doors under which is the upright door leading directly into the cellar. 'The barrel rolled down into the *bulkhead* against the cellar-door.' **1947** *Harper's Mag.* May 472/2 He went out and sat on the bulkhead in the backyard, safe from interruption.

3. (See quot. 1881.) Also transf.

1881 RAYMOND *Mining Gloss.*, *Bulkhead*, 1. A tight partition or stopping in a mine for protection against water, fire, gas. 2. The end of a flume, whence water is carried in iron pipes to hydraulic workings. **1934** LYMAN *Saga of Comstock Lode* 119 A promoter was organizing a company to build a 'bulkhead' around Virginia to keep out the Washoe zephyr. **1948** *Railway Conductor* June 177/1 He noticed that the pressure of the Columbia river was cracking railroad track bulkheads.

4. (See quot.)

1890 WEBSTER, bulkhead. . . . A boxlike structure rising above a floor, roof, etc., as for a cover for an elevator or stairway.

*__bulkheaded__, *a.* Of a water front: Provided with bulkheads or piers. Cf. *__bulkhead 1.__ — **1896** HASWELL *New York* 17 The North River above Barclay Street was not fully bulkheaded, and on it but eight piers existed.

bulk window. ?A bow window. Also **bulk-windowed,** *a. Rare.* — **1846** H. N. MOORE *Fitzgerald and Hopkins* 144 He [a runaway horse] lost all sense of propriety and danger, and blindly dashed himself right through an apothecary's bulk window. *Ib.* 51 The neighbor kept a bulk-windowed and mahogany countered shop for the sale of cigars.

*__bull__, *n.*[1]

1. A male buffalo.

[**1723** DIRON D'ARTAGUIETTE in *Travels Amer. Col.* 84 Both sides of the river (were) lined with bulls and cows.] **1825** in *Mo. Hist. Rev.* VI. 5 Saw this day (June 9, 1824) at least five thousand buffaloe, chiefly bulls. **1897** INMAN *Old Santa Fe Trail* 217 The young bulls were on duty as sentinels on the edge of the main herd watching the vedettes. **1947** *Denver Post* 15 Feb. 9/5 One final arrow loosed by an excited archer missed the fleeing bull and lodged in the chest cavity of one of the cows in the herd.

b. (See quot.) *Obs.*

1841 DE SMET *Letters* (1843) 120 To preserve the [buffalo] meat it is cut in slices, thin enough to be dried in the sun; sometimes a kind of hash is made of it, and this is mixed with the marrow taken from the largest bones. This kind of mixture is called Bull or Cheese, and is generally served up and eaten raw.

c. The male of the moose or elk.

1857 *Spirit of Times* 31 Jan. 353/2 A few hours' run suffices to overtake the moose . . . one old bull having three or four calves, with their cows, and two year old bulls and heifers under his charge. **1882** BAILLIE-GROHMAN *Camps in Rockies* 112 Wapiti are called elk out West; and the stag is spoken of as a 'bull.' **1941** SETON *Trail of Artist-Naturalist* 359 Sure enough, there was the big bull [i.e., elk] with horns and nose up high, seeking for me as I sought for him.

2. A bulldog.

1848 *Knickerb.* XVIII. 119 He was . . . a 'reg'lar thorough-bred bull.' **1901** WHITE *Westerners* xxii. 207 Your bull wouldn't be ace high. Look at the teeth on him!

3. A Britisher, a citizen of John Bull's realm. *Rare.*

1845 *Quincy* (Ill.) *Whig* 11 Dec. 1/5 'Is that the tune the old cow died of?' said an Englishman, nettled at the industry with which a New Englander whistled 'Yankee Doodle.' 'No, beef,' replied Jonathan, 'that are's the tune old *Bull* died of!' **1858** *N.Y. Tribune* 18 Mar. 2/2 So the aristocratic Senator [Hammond, of S. Car.] is half Yankee, half Bull.

4. (See quot. and cf. **bullgine.**)

1889 FARMER 101 *Bull*, . . . a locomotive.

5. A policeman. *Slang.*

1900 J. FLYNT *Tramping* 385 'Bull' (policeman) [comes] from the plunging, bullying attitude of these officers when dealing with rowdies. **1948** CHAPLIN *Wobbly* 88 Between the 'hi-jacks,' railroad 'shacks' and 'bulls' who bullied us, . . . we were everlastingly out of luck.

6. Foolish talk, stuff, claptrap. *Slang.* Cf. **bull session.**

1924 *Chi. Tribune* 1 Oct. 25/8 Applesauce is used, of course, in its aspect of this Autumn's equivalent of what we have known in other Autumns as the Bull, the Glad Hand, the Old Oil, and Il Bushwa. **1939** *Amer. Sp.* April 97, I have in mind the journalistic and more generally used *bull* in the sense of *bunk*, in such idioms as *shoot, throw the bull, hold a bull-session.*

7. In the names of, or with reference to, animals: (1) **bull alligator,** a large male alligator; (2) **bass,** (see quot.); (3) **bat,** a nighthawk, *Chordeiles minor*, also transf.; (4) **buffalo,** a male buffalo; (5) ***dog,** any one of various small horseflies of the genus *Chrysops* or related genera, in full **bulldog fly;** (6) **-eyed mackerel,** =**chub mackerel, fall mackerel;** (7) ***frog,** any one of various large frogs, esp. of the genus *Rana*, also attrib. and transf.; (8) **-gator,** =**bull alligator,** *colloq.;* (9) **head,** see as a main entry; (10) **moose,** see as a main entry; (11) ***neck,** a local name for any one of various ducks, as the canvasback, ruddy duck, and the ring-necked duck; (12) **nose,** (see quot. and cf. **8.** (7) below); (13) **plover,** the black-bellied plover, *Squatarola squatarola;* (14) **pout,** =***bullhead 1;** (15) **snake,** =**gopher snake.**

(1) **1935** *Today's Literature* 430/2 The bull alligator Roars from the swamp. — (2) **1888** *Wildwood's Mag.* (Chicago) June 64 Both species are known as 'bass,' with the addition of various adjectives expressive of gameness, coloration, or habitat, as 'tiger-bass,' 'bull-bass' [etc.]. — (3) **1838** GOSSE *Letters* 62 The common people here [i.e., near Selma, Ala.] generally call these birds by the name of bull-bats. **1859** BARTLETT 55 *Bull-bat*, night-hawk; whippoorwill. A gang of blackguard boys in Washington City have adopted this very appropriate name. **1945** MATHEWS *Talking* 103 The nighthawks [are] called bullbats because of the sound made by the air passing along the edges of their tremendous mouths. — (4) **1733** BYRD *Land of Eden* (1928) 299 In coming back to the camp we discovered a solitary bull buffalo, which boldly stood his ground. **1898** *K.C. Star* 18 Dec. 1/2 A huge bull buffalo . . . was driven into the cattle pens at the packing house.

(5) **1792** in *Pub. Champlain Soc.* XXI. 488 A kind of fly about the size of a bee and not much unlike them in colour but flat and resemble the gad fly of England in this country called bull dogs are the most numerous and troublesome I ever knew and their bite is as sudden as the sting of a bee. **1848** BALLANTYNE *Hudson Bay* (1890) 176 It was the height of summer, . . . the whole room was filled with mosquitoes and bull-dog flies. **1946** *Sky Line Trail* Nov. 6/1 Others . . . endure the impertinence of bull-dog flies and mosquitoes cheerfully and wade through icy water for the sheer joy of being actually and literally on the top of the world. — (6) **1814** MITCHILL *Fishes N.Y.* 422 Thimble eyed, bull eyed, or chub mackerel, *Scomber grex*, . . . comes occasionally in prodigious numbers to the coast of New-York, in autumn. **1842** *Nat. Hist. N.Y.*, *Zoology* IV. 102. — (7) **1698** G. THOMAS *Penna. & N.J.* 16 There are among other various sorts of Frogs, the Bull-Frog, which makes a roaring noise, hardly to be distinguished from that well known of the Beast, from whom it takes its Name. **1818** PALMER *Journal* 12 For the first time, I saw and *heard* a bull frog, they are something larger than the largest frog in England, and bellow as loud as a bull! **1947** PERRY *Cities of America* 118 The spent, bullfrog voice of Wendell Willkie called out for 'production, production, production!' — (8) **1938** MATSCHAT *Suwannee River* 61 From the bay a bull gator roared challenge and another answered.

(11) **1709** LAWSON *Carolina* 150 Bull-Necks. These are a whitish fowl, about the bigness of a Brant; they come to us after Christmas, in very great flocks, in all our Rivers. **1743** CATESBY *Carolina* App. p. xxxvii, The following American Sea-Fowl also frequent the Coast of Virginia and Carolina in Winter, and are called . . . Whistlers, Bull-neck, [etc.]. **1857** *Spirit of Times* 14 Feb. 380/3 They consist of all the varieties of duck species known in our latitude, such as canvas backs, . . . sprigtails, bullnecks, baldfaces, (or widgeons), shovelers, &c. — (12) **1881** E. INGERSOLL *Oyster Industry* 242 *Bull Nose*, an old, overgrown, heavy quahaug, unfit for food (Cape May). — (13) **1844** *Nat. Hist. N.Y.*, *Zoology* II. 215 The large Whistling Plover, or Bull and Beetle-head Plover as it is called in its autumnal dress, appears with us from the south in May. — (14) **1823** COOPER *Pioneer* xxiii, 'Away with you, you varmint!' said Billy Kirby, plucking a bull-pout from the rushes. **1897** ROBINSON *Uncle Lisha* 91 Two hours later he appeared, . . . bringing a number of dressed bull pouts.

(15) **1784** FILSON *Kentucke* 27 Serpents are not numerous, and are such as are to be found in other parts of the continent, except the bull, the horned and the mockason snakes. **1873** BEADLE *Undevel. West* 231,

I killed one of the species known as 'bull snake,' which was five feet three inches long. **1948** *Nat. History* Apr. 185/1 The U.S. Fish and Wildlife Service found it necessary to devise means of controlling bull snakes in a wildlife refuge where these serpents destroyed more than 40 per cent of the duck nests.

8. In the names of, or with reference to, plants: (1) **bull bay,** the big laurel, *Magnolia grandiflora;* (2) **berry,** = **buffalo berry;** (3) **brier,** either of two species of *Smilax, S. pseudo-china* and *S. hispida;* (4) ∗**face,** a variety of tobacco, *obs.;* (5) **grape,** (see quots.); (6) **nettle,** the spurge nettle, (see quot. 1894); (7) **nose,** (see quot. and cf. **7.** (12) above); (8) **nut,** (see quot.); (9) **pine,** any one of several varieties of pine, esp. the yellow pine, *Pinus ponderosa,* of the western states; (10) **rattle,** (see quot. 1923); (11) **sap, sapling,** (see quot. 1902).

(1) 1883 Smith *Geol. Survey Ala.* 292. **1884** Sargent *Rep. Forests* 19. — **(2) 1839** Farnham *Travels West. Pariries* (1841) 121 There is in this valley, and in some other parts of the mountains, a fruit called bullberry. **1946** Thompson *Amer. Daughter* 190, I . . . went bullberry-picking down in the sharp ravines. — **(3) 1853** P. Paxton *Yankee in Texas* 22, [I aided] his rude attempts at road-making whenever a mass of bull-brier or bamboo-vines . . . called for action. **1859** Bartlett 55 *Bull Briar,* a large briar in the alluvial bottoms of the South-west, the root of which contains a farinaceous substance from which the Indians make bread. — **(4) 1800** Boucher *Glossary* p. l, In twist-bud, thick-joint, bull-face, leather-coat, I'd toil all day.

(5) 1847 Darlington *Weeds & Plants* 84 Vulpine or Foxy Vitis, Fox-Grape, of the Southern States; also called 'Muscadine,' and 'Bullet- or Bull-Grape.' **1893** *Amer. Folk-Lore* VI. 139 *Vitis vulpina,* bull grape. Ala. — **(6) 1876** *Cong. Rec.* 18 May 3166/2 [He] beat down the wild-brier and bull-nettle, . . . felled the forest, and hewed out his humble home. **1894** *Amer. Folk-Lore* VII. 95 *Solanum Carolinense,* . . . bull-nettle, Perrysville, Ind. — **(7) 1857–8** *Ill. Agric. Soc. Trans.* III. 508 The squash, the bull nose, the sweet mountain and sweet Spanish are [good varieties of peppers] for pickling.— **(8) 1859** Bartlett 55 *Bull-nut,* a large kind of hickory-nut. **1884** Sargent *Rep. Forests* 134 *Carya tomentosa.* . . . Mocker Nut. Black Hickory. Bull Nut. — **(9) 1884** Sargent *Rep. Forests* 193 *Pinus Jeffreyi,* . . . Bull pine, Black Pine. **1947** Chalfant *Gold, Guns, & Ghost Towns* 10, I stumbled onto a small so-called 'bull pine.'

(10) 1907 Lyons *Plant Names* 282 L[ychnis] alba . . . Bull-rattle, Cow-rattle, Snake-flower. **1923** W. N. Clute *Amer. Plant Names* 63 Bladder Campion.—Cow-paps, cow-bell, bull-rattle, . . . maiden's tears. — **(11) 1851** Springer *Forest Life* 41 That variety called sapling Pine, bull sapling, &c., usually grows on high, hard-wood land. **1902** White *Blazed Trail* vii. 59 In a moment Thorpe found himself waist deep in the pitchy aromatic top of an old bull-sap.

9. In miscellaneous combs.: (1) **bull boat,** a boat of buffalo or elk hides stretched over a light wooden framework, now *hist.,* cf. **buffalo boat, rawhide boat;** (2) **butter,** (see quots.); (3) **chip,** = **buffalo chip;** (4) **-dog edition,** an early edition of a newspaper brought out for sending to distant points; (5) **dogging,** (see quot. 1907); (6) **fiddle,** a bass viol; (7) **-gine,** a locomotive or steam engine, *colloq.;* (8) ∗**hide,** *attrib.* designating objects made of the hide of a domestic bull or of a buffalo; (9) **meat,** buffalo meat or meat of a domestic bull; (10) **nigger,** = **buck nigger,** *obs.;* (11) **outfit,** *W.* a wagon train drawn by oxen, now *hist.;* (12) **pen,** see as a main entry; (13) **rake,** (see quot. 1913); (14) **session,** an occasion

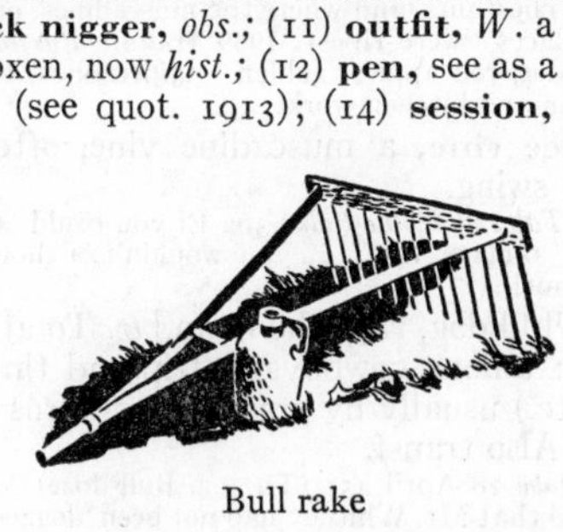

Bull rake

when there is much informal talk, *slang,* cf. ∗**bull,** *n.* **6;** (15) **strong,** of a fence, strong enough to hold back a bull, usu. in phrases; (16) **tailing,** *W.* the action by mounted cowboys of chasing bulls, seizing them by the tail, and throwing them; (17) **team,** a team of oxen; (18) **-tongue plow,** a simple form of plow, so called from its shape; (19) **train,** a wagon train drawn by oxen, now *hist.;* (20) **wagon,** a wagon drawn by oxen; (21) **whacker,** see as a main entry; (22) **whacking,** the occupation of a **bull whacker;** (23) **wheel,** see as a main entry; (24) **whip,** a whip for driving oxen, cf. **bull whack.**

(1) 1832 N. Wyeth *Journal* 160 We are now employed in making bull boats. **1859** Marcy *Prairie Traveler* 83 Two men can easily build a bull-boat of three hides in two days which will carry ten men with perfect safety. **1947** DeVoto *Across Wide Missouri* 51 At rivers that could not be forded he had to take off the wheels and make bull-boats of the wagon boxes, sheathing them in hides so that they could be ferried across. — **(2) 1886** *Chi. Tribune* 13 May 3/2 If they personally prefer bull and boar butter to the genuine dairy article, no one can have any objection to their eating it. **1948** *Time* 10 May 20/2 Farm-area Congressmen had long sneered at margarine as 'bull butter,' had taxed it, regulated and abused it for more than half a century. — **(3) 1866** in *Neb. Hist. Mag.* XIII. (1932) 152 Our first call after corralling . . . is for fuel for cooking, and shouted in stentorian tones—'bull chips,' 'bull chips' . . . the manure of oxen or buffalo. **1870** Beadle *Utah* 221 We took to the plains and gathered the fuel known to plainsmen as 'bull-chips,' which made a very hot fire. — **(4) 1926** *Amer. Mercury* Oct. 188 Bull-dog editions, dated as of the next day and put on the street as soon as the afternoon papers' sale slowed down helped to swell the circulation. **1948** *Ga. Review* Spring 58, I would rather play fan-tan at the Chinaman's when the 'bull-dog' edition has been put to bed.

(5) 1842 *Cong. Globe* 4 May 478/1, I made the reply about bull-dogging for the gentleman from Virginia. **1907** White *Arizona Nights* 151 One of the men . . . reached well over the animal's back to get a slack of the loose hide next the belly, lifted strongly, and tripped. This is called 'bull-dogging.' **1948** *Dly. Ardmoreite* (Ardmore, Okla.) 26 May 10 From the turgid cattle trail days of the Old West come the cowboy skills—bull-dogging, roping, bronco riding—which excite breathless crowds today at the rodeo. — **(6) 1882** G. A. Sala *Amer. Revisited* II. 160 The form of which reminded one of the case of a 'bull-fiddle'—which is Americanese for a viol violoncello. **1946** Newton *P. Bunyan* 180 He no longer practiced evenings on the saxophone and the big bull fiddle. — **(7) 1846** Durivage *Stray Subjects* 38 [He made] himself agreeable to his officers by jumping Jim Crow, playing on the bones, and imitating the 'bull-gine.' **1939** Rollins *Gone Haywire* 21 His bullgine was new an' shiny, an' there it was with tomater ketchup all over th' boiler an' th' cab. — **(8) 1762** in Woodward *Ploughs* (1941) 378 In the Fall when you kill your Cattle, Recollect whether you want Bull hide Traces as they are usually called, Well Ropes or Leading Lines. **1842** *S. Lit. Messenger* VIII 465/1 The Indians instantly scattered to avoid a shot from the corporal, one of them dropping his bull-hide shield. **1846** W. G. D. Stewart *Altowan* I. vi. 164 Two men . . . had just landed from a small boat composed of raw bull-hide. — **(9) 1812** Stuart *Narratives* 160 Our living has been and is of the meanest kind being poor Bull meat or Buck Antelope, both too bad to be eat except in cases of starvation. **1947** *Prairie Schooner* Winter 452 Pressure cookers have been so perfected that housewives would never be dismayed at the prospect of serving bull meat.

(10) 1828 *Yankee* May 175/1 [The traveler in the South] sees one solitary man—a great bull nigger, coming toward him. **1840** Haliburton *Clockmaker* 3 Ser. 46 If there was a thing on airth that Ahab hated like pyson, I do believe it was a great bull-nigger. — **(11) 1888** Buffalo Bill *Wild West* 432 The wagon-master, in the language of the plains, was called the 'bull-wagon boss' . . . and the whole train was denominated a 'bull-outfit.' **1939** Abbott-Smith *We Pointed* 101 Zeke Newman had sold his bull outfit and was quitting the country. — **(13) 1895** *D.N.* I. 396 bull rake: very heavy hand rake. N.Y.c. **1913** *D.N.* IV. 55 bull-rake, n. A large drag-rake, drawn by hand. 'You can rake twice as fast with a *bull-rake* as you can with one o' them little things.' [Cape Cod.] **1944** *Greeley* (Colo.) *D. Tribune* 30 Sep. 2/7 [For sale] Bull rake, 2 row go-dig, McD feed grinder. — **(14) 1939** [see ∗**bull** *n.* **6.**]. **1948** *Time* 22 March 71/2 That starts a family bull-session about sex, to make the audience realize that sex can be casually and decently discussed.

(15) 1859 *Harper's Mag.* Oct. 712/2 A Buncombe fence, Sir, is a fence that is bull strong, horse high, and pig tight! **1943** Crow *Amer. Customer* 179 This appeared to solve the problem, though the farmers had to wait four years before the fence would be 'pig tight, horse high and bull strong.' [**1948** *Dly. Ardmoreite* (Ardmore, Okla.) 4 July 9/4 She gave the reins to her father and hopped off the horse and scaled the bull tight fence like a squirrel.] — **(16) 1848** Ruxton *Adventures* 92 We arrived at the rancho of La Punta in the afternoon, in time to witness the truly national sport of the *coléa de toros*—in English, bull-tailing. **1929** Dobie *Vaquero* 19 Bull-tailing . . . was practiced by the first Mexican vaqueros of Texas, and long after the Civil War it was a popular sport among the Mexicans of Southwest Texas. — **(17) 1855** *Golden Era* (S.F.) 1 Apr. 4/2 The music of your voice . . . shall be used in the humbler occupation of swaying a bull-team. **1948** *Popular Western* June 64/1 He hadn't seen any logging operations for a long time, not since he'd hauled by bull team the logs that formed his squat shack and barn and chicken house. — (18) **1831** MARY A. HOLLEY *Texas* (1833) 139 Many farmers use the coulter and bull-tongue ploughs. **1948** *Range Riders Western* May 45/1 The farmer . . . walked away behind a bull-tongue plow. — (19) **1877** J. S. CAMPION *On Frontier* 99 A Kansas City 'bull-train,' lately come in, had passed an encampment of over six hundred tents. **1929** DICKSON *Across Plains* 173 The streets were lined with bull-trains and pack animals.

(20) **1888** BUFFALO BILL *Wild West* 432 The wagon-master, in the language of the plains, was called the 'bull-wagon boss.' **1896** *Harper's Mag.* XCIV. 62/2, I was standing in the bull-wagon road. — (22) **1870** J. WHITE *Sks. from Amer.* 259 The profession of 'bull-whacking' has, in ante-railway days, been one of the foremost in the West. **1880** NYE *B. Nye & Boomerang* 34 The closing ten years of the regular course might be profitably used in learning a practical knowledge of . . . bull whacking, etc. — (24) **1852** *S. Lit. Messenger* XVIII. 749/2 If an overseer . . . omitted . . . laying down at once his bull-whip for the yard-stick. **1948** *Time* 7 June 24/1 Earl Long picked up Brother Huey's bull-whip and laid it manfully across the backs of his submissive legislators.

b. In less frequent combs., often rare and usu. obs.: (1) **bull bass,** the bass supplied by a bull fiddle; (2) **curl,** ?the curl of hair in the crown of the head; (3) **dance,** =**buffalo dance;** (4) **-dog Indian,** a pure-blooded Indian; (5) **fever,** =**buck fever;** (6) ***hole,** (see quot.); (7) **ledge,** *W.* a non-mineralized quartz vein, cf. **bull quartz;** (8) **punching,** working as a bullpuncher; (9) **push log raising,** ?the raising of a log house by the use of oxen; (10) **quartz,** =**bull ledge;** (11) **ranch,** *W.* a place where the bulls of a herd of cattle are wintered; (12) **rock,** (see quot.); (13) **schooner,** =**prairie schooner;** (14) **tonguing,** plowing with a bull tongue plow; (15) **whack,** (see quot.); (16) **yard,** an inclosure for cattle.

(1) **1867** G. W. HARRIS *Sut Lovingood* 22 From the tribil down ter the bull base ove a fiddil. — (2) *Ib.* 188 He loaned the passun a mos' tremenjus contashun, rite in the bull curl. — (3) **1833** CATLIN *Indians* I. 165 On the first day, this 'bull-dance' is given once to each of the cardinal points. — (4) **1870** O. LOGAN *Before Footlights* 286 There are lots of 'big Injuns' in Milwaukee. There is the unapproachable or Bull-dog Indian, who wears the aboriginal dress.

(5) **1839** TOWNSEND *Narrative* 168 Just then I was attacked with the 'bull fever' so dreadfully, that for several minutes I could not shoot. — (6) **1887** *Harper's Mag.* Feb. 350/1 These little ponds are called 'bull-holes.' The traveller is told that they are started in this watery soil by the pawing of bulls. — (7) **1897** *Land of Sunshine* Mar. 170 What are styled in the vernacular of the miner 'bull ledges' of quartz, are found traversing the district in all directions. — (8) **1887** M. ROBERTS *Western Avernus* ii. 20, I found this bull-punching a very wearisome and dangerous business. — (9) **1923** ADAMS *Pioneer Hist.* 320 There were many scenes, incidents and accidents I might recall, and will mention a few: pike pole barn raisings with hair raising incidents and accidents; bull push log raising with many happenings.

(10) **1897** *Land of Sunshine* Mar. 170 Great dykes of porphyry, mica schist and 'bull quartz' are here in evidence, running from north to south. — (11) **1939** ABBOTT-SMITH *We Pointed* 227 North of the DHS bullranch . . . we run out of flour. — (12) **1920** THOMAS *Ky. Super.* 263 A 'bullrock,' also called a 'jackrock' (a small round rock), in the ashes keeps hawks away from chickens. — (13) **1947** *Steamboat* (Colo.) *Pilot* 2 Jan. 7/3 The officers hunted around and dug up an old bull schooner. — (14) **1861** *Ill. Agric. Soc. Trans.* IV. 248 Whether hoeing the small corn or rolling or bull-tonguing or hilling up.

(15) **1885** *Mag. Amer. Hist.* XIII. 98 In Texas and western Louisiana the 'bull-whack' is a terrible whip with a long and very heavy lash and a short handle. It is used by drovers to intimidate refractory animals. — (16) **1868** *Mich. Agric. Rep.* VII. 99 The manure in this experiment was all taken from the 'bull yard.'

c. In slang and colloq. expressions designating those having to do with oxen and other cattle: (1) **bull cook,** in a logging camp, one who feeds and attends to the oxen; (2) **dogger,** *W.* a cowboy who throws and holds calves for branding, cf. **bulldog,** *v.;* (3) **driver,** a man engaged in driving cattle; (4) **puncher,** a cowboy or ox driver; (5) **pusher,** an ox driver; (6) **skinner,** =prec.; (7) **whacker,** see as a main entry.

(1) **1921** *Outing* Nov. 94/3 There was a sentimental 'bull cook' who between and after meals wrote poetry on a typewriter. **1948** *Popular Western* June 60/2 I've done most every kind uh work, from bull-cook to river drivin' with the Canadian-French an' I've met a lot uh men. — (2) **1907** *Outing* Dec. 325/1 The two 'bull-doggers' immediately pounced upon the victim. **1946** *Fort Collins Coloradoan* 16 June 2/3 Director of the rodeo is L. U. (Shorty) Creed, world champion bulldogger. — (3) **1863** *Gold Hill* (Nev.) *News* 13 Dec. 3/1 Away went the bull-drivers up the hill. **1891** GARLAND *Main-travelled Roads* (1922) 136, I know what manners are, if I am a bull-driver. — (4) **1874** *Chambers's Jrnl.* 543/2 Commissariat beeves, guarded by the commissariat 'bull-punchers.' **1893** *Scribner's Mag.* June 711/2 A young 'bull-puncher' in a Wisconsin logging camp became in middle life Congressman, then United States Senator.

(5) **1879** *Chi. Tribune* 14 May 7/4 But a few years ago, every hog-driver and 'bull-pusher' was armed with an implement of torture that would make the old Roman inquisitors ashamed of themselves. — (6) **1932** W. KELLEY *Inchin' Along* 212 'Ba-a-ack, Ball,' commanded the bull skinners. **1948** *Chr. Sci. Monitor* 22 April 14/6 The swashbuckling cat-skinners, descendants of the bull-skinners and mule-skinners of yesterday, ride their roaring caterpillar tractors, full of the daredevil swagger of mounted men.

d. Used in the possessive in combs.: (1) **bull's eye,** a thick, round, bulging watch with a relatively small face, in full **bull's-eye watch;** (2) **foot,** (see quot.); (3) **milk,** an alcoholic drink, *obs.*

(1) **1833** NEAL *Down-Easters* I. 78 Lugging out a heavy silver watch, . . . a genuine bull's-eye with a huge copper logging-chain, [etc.]. **1866** *Eastern Slope* (Washoe, Nev.) 20 Oct. 1/2 He stood [there], every now and then consulting an enormous bull's eye watch. **1892** DUVAL *Young Explorers* 217 As soon as Uncle Seth had finished his yarn, he slowly extracted his big bullseye silver watch from his fob. — (2) **1872** HUNTINGTON *Road-Master's Assistant* 76 There are a good many kinds of claw-bars, some of which work well; . . . and probably the old style of 'bull's-foot' claw is as good as any. — (3) **1858** *Salem* (Ill.) *Advocate* 17 Feb. 1/2 No gunticklers [*sic*], and necktwisters, and brandy smashes and bullsmilk and tongue-scrapers.

e. In colloquial phrases (see quots.).

1830 *Village Record* (Westchester, N.Y.) 23 June 2/3 You never heard nothing like it but uncle bens bull, when he gets tearing mad in fly time. **1836** CROCKETT *Adv.* 90 He belonged to that numerous class, that it is perfectly safe to trust (as far as a tailor can sling a bull by the tail). **1851** *Oquawka* (Ill.) *Spectator* 11 June 4/3 In the afternoon brother-in-law come up to me, madder than a short-tailed bull in hornet time. **1868** ROSE *Great Country* 124 Out of office they are miserable, wretched, God-forsaken—as uncomfortable as that famous stump-tailed bull in fly time. **1913** *Industrial Worker* (Spokane) 12 June 4/1 The 'bull of the woods,' Oscar Enloc, was in Bellingham most of the day hunting a new crew. **1946** R. PEATTIE *Pac. Coast Ranges* 233 The bullwacker yielded precedence only to the big boss of all the works, the 'bull of the woods' as he was called on the Saginaw.

As the last term in **buffalo, dumb, harness, poor, spike bull.**

***bull,** *n.*[2] An absurd error or mistake. — **1855** P. PAXTON *Capt. Priest* 226, I had committed a bull myself, by intruding where I evidently was *de trop.* **1911** HARRISON *Queed* 392 He had never once made a bull in 'Mr. Queed's copy' since the day of the famous fleas.

***bull,** *v.*[1] *intr.* To push ahead boldly. *Slang.* — **1884** MARK TWAIN *H. Finn* 144 Up-stream boats . . . bull right up the channel against the whole river. *Ib.* 276 It injured the frauds some; but the old fool he bulled right along, spite of all the duke could say or do.

bull bʊl, *v.*[2] [f. ***bull** *n.*[2]] *intr.* (See quot.) *Obs.* — **1851** HALL *College Words* 25 *Bull,* at Dartmouth College, to recite badly.

***bullace,** *n.* In the southern states the fruit of the muscadine, *Vitis rotundifolia.* In full **bullace grape.**

1862 *Rep. Comm. Patents: Agric.* 479 The Muscadine, Bullace, or Scuppernong grape, (*Vitis rotundifolia* of Michaux.). **1892** HARRIS *Plantation* 71 He knew where the wild strawberries grew, and the chincapins and chestnuts, and where the muscadines, or, as he called them, the 'bullaces,' were ripest. **1939** HARRIS *Purslane* 84 White fields, ripe fodder, red apples, golden scuppernongs, black bullaces defined the farm and kitchen work.

b. bullace vine, a muscadine vine, often used by children as a swing.

1898 HARRIS *Tales of Home Folks* 362 Ef you could 'a' seed 'em a-swingin' in the bullace vine, . . . you wouldn't 'a thought Loorany was bothered much.

bulldog ˈbʊlˌdɔg, *v.* [f. the noun.] *tr.* To attack like a bulldog, spec. among cowboys to trip and throw (a running steer, etc.) usually by grasping its horns and twisting its neck. Also transf.

1842 *Cong. Globe* 28 April 457 (Th. *s.v.* Bull-doze) Mr. Stanly of N. Carolina said that Mr. Whitney had not been 'dogged' to the door of the Committee-room, but, when inside, he had been 'bull-dogged' with a vengeance. **1907** *Outing* Dec. 329/1 'No more necked calves,' they announced, 'catch 'em by the hind legs, or bull-dog 'em yourself.' **1941** *Nat. Geog. Mag.* March 300/1 He's too old now to bulldog a steer or bust a bronco.

bulldose ˈbʊlˌdos, *n.* [See note.] A severe beating. *To come the bulldose on,* to administer a severe beating to. *Obs.*

The origin of this term, and of the corresponding verb, is not clear. It app. consists of *bull*+*dose*, a dose suitable for a bull. There is no evidence to confirm Bartlett's (1877) statement that it originally had reference to the flogging of Negroes in La., nor is it clear which came first, the noun or the verb. Cf. note to **bulldozer.**

1877 BARTLETT 77 Give him a bulldose meant give him a flogging,—a 'cowhiding.' **1881** *Harper's Mag.* Feb. 479/2 The old man secured the subsidy [for voting], remarking, 'Ef you is comin' de bulldose on dis ole niggah, he weakens.'

bulldoze ˈbʊlˌdoz, *v.* [See note to the noun above.]

1. *tr.* To intimidate by violence or threats, often for political purposes. Also **bulldozed,** *a. Colloq.*

1876 *N.Y. Tribune* 23 Dec. 6/4 If the State of Connecticut . . . had any apprehensions lest . . . their representatives . . . might be 'intimidated,' or 'bulldozed,' or 'terrorized,' [etc.]. **1877** *N.Y. Herald* 7 March 6/2 If he [Pres. Hayes] yields he will be only a nominal President; will not be even a peer of the party leaders, but only their bulldozed vassal. **1883** DE VERE in *Ency. Br. Supp.* I. 200/2 To bulldoze is a later political term, originating in the South, and denoting the intimidation of voters. **1944** *Chi. D. News* 15 May 10/2 'The customer was tough and determined, but I bulldozed him out of buying,' says today's supersalesman.

2. To use a bulldozer (sense 3.), to bulldog a steer.

1944 *Reader's Digest* August 125 Men were coming out of the sea continually and starting to work—digging, hammering, bulldozing, . . . shooting and being shot at. **1944** LANKS *Alaska* 2 There are the usual contests of wild calf roping, broncho busting, steer bulldozing, and wild cow milking.

bulldozer ˈbʊlˌdozɚ, *n.*

1. One who practices bulldozing or intimidation.

"The term 'Bulldozers,' which is so variously printed in the New Orleans despatches, is the name applied to an organization of armed white men, whose ostensible business it is to keep the Negroes from stealing the cotton crop. On election day, however, the 'Bulldozers' go gunning for Negroes who manifest a disposition to vote the Republican ticket" (*N.Y. Tribune* cited in B. '77).

1876 in *Cong. Rec.* 9 Jan. (1877) 500/1 A band of bull-dozers came into Saint Francisville, and by their yelling and hallooing . . . put the entire inhabitants in a mortal terror. **1892** *Courier-Journal* 1 Oct. 6/3 The people of Louisville . . . will never surrender their rights to Johnny Davenport's proposed gang of ballot-box stuffers and bulldozers.

2. (See quots.) *Obs.*

1881 *Sat. Review* 9 July 40/2 A Californian bull-doser is a pistol which carries a bullet heavy enough to destroy human life with certainty. **1889** *Cent.* 715 *Bull-dozer,* a revolver.

3. A powerful machine of a caterpillar tractor type having in front an adjustable steel blade or scraper, used for clearing and leveling ground, making terraces, etc.

1930 *Water Works & Sewerage* June 262/3 The bulldozer is built for heavy duty. **1948** *Capital-Democrat* (Tishomingo, Okla.) 3 June 1/4 A bulldozer will be put to work as soon as the ground hardens.

bulldozing ˈbʊlˌdozɪŋ, *n.* Intimidating, overawing with threats, etc. Also as adj.

1876 *N.Y. Tribune* Dec. (B.), There was a bad case of 'bulldozing' in Cincinnati on Monday night. . . . Mr. C. was in the chair, . . . and declared . . . that he was not to be intimidated. **1900** *Engineering Mag.* XIX. 761/1 The cursing, bulldozing foreman . . . creates so much confusion about casting time that one-third of the work is likely to be lost. **1948** *Tenn. Hist. Quart.* March 20 He accused the General . . . among other things, of bulldozing and corruption in the Senate election of 1823.

* **bullet,** *n.*

1. (See quot. 1889.)

1807 IRVING *Salmagundi* 501 Presently one of them exclaimed triumphantly, 'Two bullets and a bragger!' and swept all the money into his pocket. **1878** HART *Sazerac Lying Club* 151 'Here's four bullets,' said Brown, as he reached for the pot. **1889** BARRERE & LELAND, *Bullets* (cards) in American brag are aces. . . . The highest hand in the game is three white (or real) aces, the next highest is 'two bullets and a bragger.'

2. A guessing game resembling thimblerig adopted by American frontiersmen from Indians. Now *hist.*

1879 in STEWART CULIN *Games N. Amer. Indians* (1907) 343 Subsequently the whites modified the game slightly by placing caps on the table, and the game became changed to bullet. . . . On the early statutes stands a law making gambling at bullet a finable offense. **1907** *Ib.*, Dr. Walter J. Hoffman described the moccasin or bullet game, as follows.

3. A nugget of gold. *Obs.*

1889 MUNROE *Golden Days* 112 In the clay he was . . . likely to strike 'bullets,' lumps . . . or pockets of pure gold.

4. In combs.: (1) **bullet-bush,** (see quot.), *obs.;* (2) **button,** [cf. Du. *kogelknoop*] a bullet-shaped button, also **bullet-buttoned,** *a.;* (3) **grape,** =**bull grape;** (4) **hawk,** any one of various American hawks as the pigeon hawk, *Falco columbarius;* (5) * **head,** *fig.* an obstinate person, also **bullet headedness;** (6) **ladle,** a ladle in which lead for making bullets for muzzle-loading rifles is melted; (7) **patch,** (*a*) a small piece of cloth, leather, etc., in which bullets for muzzle-loading rifles are wrapped in loading (see quot. 1871), (*b*) (see quot.); (8) **vote,** a vote cast for one candidate where several are to be voted for, *colloq.*

(1) *c***1730** CATESBY *Carolina* I. 75 The Bullet-Bush. . . . The height is usually five feet. . . . The berries hang to the smaller branches by footstalks not half an inch long, and are globular, somewhat larger than a Black Cherry. — **(2) 1816** in *Centennial West Point* I. 511 *Vest,* gray cloth for winter, single breasted, yellow gilt bullet buttons, and trimmed with black silk lace. **1843** *Knickerb.* XXI. 49 He often . . . flourishes in a bullet-buttoned coat in which he once marched in the country's service. **1859** *West Point Life* 3 When you doze in bed . . . [you] Dream of bullet buttons. — **(3) 1829** EATON *Botany* (ed. 5) 447 *Vitis rotundifolia,* bullet grape, . . . berries large. **1847** DARLINGTON *Weeds & Plants* 84 Vulpine or Foxy Vitis, Fox-Grape, of the Southern States; also called 'Muscadine,' and 'Bullet- or Bull-Grape.' — **(4) 1844** *Nat. Hist. N.Y., Zoology* II. 15 The Pigeon Hawk, *Falco Columbarius,* . . . has been termed the Bullet Hawk, in allusion to its swiftness. **1917** *Birds of Amer.* II. 89.

(5) 1846 LOWELL *Biglow P.* ix, He aint No more 'n a tough old bullethead. *a***1849** POE *Marginalia* lxxiv, The disgusting sternness, captiousness, and bulletheadedness of her husband. — **(6) 1891** SLOAN *Fogy Days* 94 After supper we . . . secured an old bullet ladel for melting the metal, then repaired to a deep hollow not far away, built a fire and started the factory. — **(7)** (*a*) **1824** DODDRIDGE *Notes* 289 They went on with their work of carrying water and cutting bullet patches for the men. **1871** *Pat. Off. Rep.* II. 240/1 *Bullet-Patch.*—Alfred C. Hobbs, Bridgeport, Conn. *Claim.*—A patch for bullets composed of paper-pulp applied to the bullet. (*b*) **1933** *Amer. Sp.* Feb. 50 A man whose trousers fit very tightly over the seat is said to be *makin' bullet patches.* I have heard this expression many times. — **(8) 1897** *Boston Ev. Rec.* 23 Dec. 1/7 In . . . Dixon's ward, between 500 and 600 voters cast 'bullet' votes. These were ballots on which the only name crossed for alderman was that of Dixon.

As the last term in **trade bullet, wolf bullet.**

***bulletin,** *v. tr.* To display on a bulletin board. — **1871** *Scribner's Mo.* I. 412 It was bulletined at noon . . . in the Merchants' Exchange at Chicago. **1884** *Reading* (Pa.) *Herald* 3 April, Mr. L—— has made arrangements to have all . . . championship games bulletined at the Casino during the season.

bulletin board. A board on which bulletins, notices, etc., are posted.

1831 *Boston Transcript* 5 July 2/4 From the City Hall Bulletin Board. **1904** F. LYNDE *Grafters* 14 Train Number Three . . . was late . . . ; and pending the chalking-up of its arriving time on the bulletin board, the two men sat on an empty baggage truck and smoked. **1949** *Lisle* (Ill.) *Eagle* 10 March 5/1 With the new scroll placed on the bulletin board all may see who made the honor roll this time.

* **bullhead,** *n.*

1. Any one of various American fresh-water fish of the genus *Ameiurus* and allied genera. See also **brazen bullhead.**

1674 JOSSELYN *Acc. 2 Voyages N.E.* 113 Blew-fish, Bull-head, Burfish. **1758** J. WILLIAMS *Hist. Captivity* 18 There seven of us supped on the Fish, called Bull-head or Pout, and did not eat it up, the Fish was so very large. **1886** *Leslie's Mo.* June 742/2 It is now a penal offence to place bull-heads, perch or pickerel in waters where they do not exist. **1947** *Sports Afield* Feb. 21/2 Our lake is full of bullheads, and Mr. Cornelius, have you ever fished for bullheads in the moonlight?

2. The golden plover.

1838 AUDUBON *Ornith. Biog.* IV. 281 In the Eastern States, as well as in Kentucky, it is called the Bull-head. **1856** *Spirit of Times* 27 Sep. 51/3 'Been?' said I, 'been after bull-heads, a very large flock, but they are as wild as hawks.' **1917** *Birds of Amer.* I. 257.

3. Attrib. with **eel, lily, plover, snipe, whiting.**

1842 *Nat. Hist. N.Y., Zoology* IV. 313 The Bull Head Eel, *Anguilla macrocephala,* . . . inhabits Saratoga lake. Mr. Lesueur states that it is a good table fish. **1856** *Spirit of Times* (N.Y.) 27 Sep. 51/3 Hunting bullhead plover in a swamp. **1878** *U.S. Nat'l Museum Proc.* I. 440 *Ægialitis montana,* Mountain Plover, . . . [which is] known here [in Calif.] as the 'Bull-head Snipe,' usually arrives at Stockton and Marysville in November. **1889** *Cent.* 716/2 Bull-head whiting, a sciænoid fish, *Menticirrus alburnus;* the southern king-fish. [Florida.]

1891 *Amer. Folk-Lore* IV. 147 [In New Hampshire] *Nuphar advena* was Bullhead Lily.

b. bullhead luck, (see quot.). *Rare.*

1879 *Scribner's Mo.* Oct. 834/2 By exercising skill and judgment, or 'bull-head luck,' as an old veteran of the pass calls it, a little execution may be done.

***bullheaded,** *a.* **1. bullheaded mouse,** (see quot.). **2. bullheaded plover,** =**bullhead 2.** — (1) **1857** *Rep. Comm. Patents: Agric.* 84 Where several species [of meadow-mice] are found in one locality, they are commonly considered by farmers as one animal, known under various names, as . . . 'Bear Mice,' 'Bullheaded Mice,' 'Ground Mice,' 'Bog Mice,' &c. — (2) **1835** Audubon *Ornith. Biog.* III. 623 The account which Wilson gives of this species refers in part to the 'Bull-headed Plover,' *Charadrius helveticus.*

Bullion State. (See quot. 1859.) — **1848** *N.Y. Herald* 13 June (B.), In my own State, the Bullion State, they did not succeed in depreciating our majority. **1859** Bartlett 55 *Bullion State,* the State of Missouri; so called in consequence of the exertions made by its Senator, Mr. Benton, in favor of a gold and silver currency.

bull moose.

1. A male moose.

1839 Hoffman *Wild Scenes* 58 The Indians . . . celebrate the death of a bull-moose, when they are so fortunate as to kill one, with all the songs of triumph that they would raise over a conquered warrior. **1917** *Mammals of Amer.* 24 This Cow was lured to within fifteen feet of the camera by the operator, who grunted like a Bull Moose. **1948** *Ariz. Republic* (Phoenix) 28 Feb. 1/1 A nonchalant bull moose played tag with a passenger train for more than five hours near here today.

2. (*cap.*) A nickname applied to Theodore Roosevelt and his supporters during the political campaign of 1912. Also attrib.

1912 *Lit. Digest* XLV. 769/1 The Wisconsin Senator . . . went on to say that the treatment of this disease [growth of trusts] 'is no job for a Bull Moose,' nor for 'an amiable, easy-going man.' **1948** *Galveston* (Tex.) *News* 14 June 4/5 It was the split in the Republican ranks over Roosevelt and his Bull Moose ticket which caused Capper to lose his first try for governor of Kansas.

Hence **Bull Mooser.**

1912 *Harper's Wkly.* 5 Oct. 7/2 Perhaps, as appears, the Bull-Moosers have got it fixed so nobody can vote for Taft in California. **1948** *Time* 21 June 20/3 He remains a Bull Mooser to this day.

***Bullock,** *n.* [f. Wm. *Bullock* (*fl.* 1827) British naturalist.] Used in the possessive in combs.: (1) **Bullock's oriole,** a western oriole, *Icterus bullocki,* of striking black and orange coloration; (2) **troupial,** =prec.

(1) **1858** Baird *Birds Pacific R.R.* 549 Bullock's Oriole. . . . *Hab.*—High Central Plains to the Pacific; rare on upper Missouri; south into Mexico. **1946** R. Peattie *Pac. Coast Ranges* 97 The Bullock's oriole, closely akin to the celebrated Baltimore and showing the relationship in the male's bright orange-and-black attire. — (2) **1839** Audubon *Ornith. Biog.* V. 9 Bullock's Troopial, *Icterus Bullockii,* . . . resembles the Common Baltimore Bird, which it supersedes from the first great bifurcation of the Platte, to the shores of the Columbia. **1881** *Amer. Naturalist* XV. 216 The hooded troupial . . . and the Bullock's troupial . . . are the most common around Tucson.

Bullock's pippin. A variety of apple. — **1817** W. Coxe *Fruit Trees* 125 Bullocks Pippin, or Sheep Nose, . . . is one of the finest apples in New-Jersey. . . . It is sometimes called the Long Tom; it derives one of its names from the family of Bullock. **1867** Warder *Pomology* 714 Bullock's Pippin, synonym of American Golden Russet.

bull pen.

1. An inclosure of logs or other heavy materials for bulls. *Obs.*

1848 Robinson *Santa Fe Exped.* 60 The bull pen also attracts the notice of every traveller. **1879** *Cong. Rec.* 27 May 1626/1 You give him [a government official] authority about the cow-yards and the bull-pens of the country.

b. Orig. such an inclosure serving as a temporary prison, in later use a jail of any kind. *Slang.*

1809 Weems *Marion* (1833) 225 The tories were all handcuffed two and two, and confined together under a centinel, in what was called a bull-pen, made of pine trees, cut down so judgmatically, as to form by their fall, a pen or enclosure. **1843** *Times & Seasons* (Nauvoo, Ill.) 1 July 253/4 All the witnesses, even forty at a time, have been taken by force of arms, and thrust into the '*bullpen*' in order to prevent them from giving their testimony. **1920** *Nation* 31 Jan. 137/1 From 130 to 140 men were herded into the police 'bull-pen,' a room built to hold petty offenders for not more than three or four hours. **1947** *Chi. D. News* 16 Dec. 1/1 He swallowed poison Monday in the bull pen in Federal Court.

c. In the Rocky Mountains, an elevated level area surrounded by lofty mountains. Cf. **park.**

1820 in *Pub. Col. Soc. Mass.* VIII. (1906) 391 It has its source in numerous small streams, which descend from the hills surrounding a circumscribed valley within the mountains, called the Bull-pen. . . . The diameter of the circumscribed valley, called the Bull-pen, is one day's travel, about twenty miles. **1872** Tice *Across Plains* 183 The Indian name for these parks signified 'cow-lodge,' or 'bull-pen' on account of the immense herds of buffalo with which they abounded.

d. In baseball, a place outside the playing limits where pitchers are exercised for possible use during the progress of a game.

1924 *Chi. Tribune* 5 Oct. II. 1/1 Four fellows stepped up and knocked the cover off the ball while only one retired, and Blake was rushed from the battlefield and Rip Wheeler summoned from the bullpen. **1948** *N.Y. Times* 2 May 55 McQuinn propelled a homer into the Sox bull-pen in right field.

e. The waiting room in an employment office.

1944 *Chi. D. News* 10 Feb. 10/3 After waiting two hours in the 'bull pen' outside the employment office, I was finally escorted into the inner sanctum.

2. A boys' ball game involving an area called the "bull-pen" outlined by players on corners who throw at those in the "pen."

1857 *Spirit of Times* 19 Dec. 241/1 About twenty boys and girls were assembled, . . . some of both sexes conning their lessons, and some playing—the boys at bull-pen, the girls at jumping the rope. **1871** Eggleston *Hoosier Schoolm.* iv. 48 He could not throw well enough to make his mark in that famous western game of bull-pen. **1944** Duncan *M. Graham* 99 Sometimes he joined the boys at 'bull pen'—not very often but often enough to win their homage.

bullwhack ˈbʊlˌhwæk, *v.* [f. the noun.] *tr.* To drive (an ox-team) with a whip. *Colloq.* — **1896** McClure *Rocky Mts.* 102 You will often find some graduate of Yale 'bull-whacking' his own team from the river to his mines, looking as if he had seldom seen soap and water. **1906** *D.N.* III. 129 'What's Jim doin'?' 'O, he's a bull-whackin'.'

bullwhacker ˈbʊlˌhwækɚ, *n.*

1. The driver of a bull team or bull train.

1858 *Valley Tan* (Salt Lake City) 17 Dec. 2/2 This valley . . . will set an example that will make the blush of shame mantle upon the cheek of the bull-whacker. **1946** R. Peattie *Pac. Coast Ranges* 251 When bullwhackers or teamsters heard the bright warning of bells they halted at the first passing place.

attrib. **1873** *Winfield* (Kansas) *Courier* 7 Aug. 4/1 Cotemporary with that, was what might be called 'bull-whacker' literature, detailing the immense traffic of the plains. **1875** *Chi. Tribune* 6 Nov. 8/7 The bull-whacker element in the Texas Constitutional Convention . . . thus far has defeated every proposition for the establishment of the free-school system.

2. =**bullwhack,** *n.* Also attrib. with **whip.**

1889 Custer *Tenting on Plains* 229 There is no sound like the snap of the lash of a 'bull-whacker.' **1898** Wister *Lin McLean* 271 Limber Jim called for another drink, and, with his cigar between his teeth, cracked his long bull-whacker whip. **1902** Clapin 83 *Bull-whacker,* a heavy whip used in the South-West, for driving cattle.

bull wheel. The main driving wheel in a system of machinery.

1830 *Cortland Observer* (Homer, N.Y.) 2 July 1/3 All kinds of machinery, mill cranks and gudgeons of all sizes, . . . bull wheels. **1873** in Adams *Pioneer Hist.* (1923) 19 The first grist mill was started by Mr. Danforth, who got a pair of mill stones—about twenty inches in diameter—set them in the corner of his saw mill and propelled them by the bull-wheel of the mill.

b. A drum upon which a rope is wound for hoisting purposes.

1874 Raymond *6th Rep. Mines* 415 By means of a bull-wheel, rope, car, and rail-road, the slimes were delivered . . . directly to the pans.

c. In oil well drilling (see quots.).

1883 *Cent. Mag.* July 329/2 Attached to the derrick is also a big windlass; called the 'bull-wheel', which hoists the drilling apparatus out of the [oil] well. **1900** *Everybody's Mag.* July 78/1 The engine operated a 'bull wheel,' which is a big wooden reel, on which is wound thousands of feet of rope.

d. *pl.* =**logging wheels.**

1946 Newton *P. Bunyan* 129 With a pair of bull-wheels and the right kind of a chain Babe could walk off with the biggest log that ever grew in the northwoods.

***bully,** *n.*

1. A class leader at Yale, or the office of leader. *Obs.*

1843 E. P. Belden *Sk. Yale College* 171 The 'Bully' was still acknowledged as class leader. He marshalled all processions, was moderator of all meetings, and performed the various duties of a chief. **1871** L. H. Bagg *At Yale* 501 Each class . . . chose as leader their largest and most muscular man, to whom they gave the name of 'Bully.' **1948** *Chi. Tribune* 20 June I. 22/3 The students found it necessary to organize for defense and elect a chief who was called the class bully and carried a club as his badge of office.

2. In combs. now obs.: (1) **bully boy,** in old field schools on occasions of barring out the teacher, the leader of the pupils; (2) **club,** the club or stick intrusted to a class leader at Yale as a symbol of his office as bully; (3) **-ship,** the office held by a student bully at Yale, the profession or status of bully.

(1) **1878** GUILD *Old Times* 332 The following is a graphic description of one of these episodes by a man who was a 'bully boy' on that occasion. — (2) **1843** E. P. BELDEN *Sk. Yale College* 171 The *Bully Club* was every year, with procession and set form, bestowed upon the newly acknowledged leader. **1895** *Bachelor Arts Mo.* May 3 The original Bully Club—a stout oaken stick two inches in diameter—was taken from a sailor by a powerful student in 1801, and, until 1841, was handed down from class to class as an emblem of supremacy. — (3) **1871** L. H. BAGG *At Yale* 501 As the collisions with the 'townies' grew less frequent, . . . the 'bullyships' came to be looked upon in the light of honors. **1908** MARK TWAIN *Autobiog.* (1924) II. 124 (R.), Brooks apologized and retired from his bullyship.

* **bully,** *a.* Fine, capital, first-rate, apparently first used of boats.

1844 *Scribblings & Sk.* 181 (Th.), A two days' race with bully-boats combines every sort of pleasing excitement. It were well to inform you that a bully-boat means a boat that beats everything on those [Mississippi] waters. *c***1898** CHRISTIAN *Days* 42 [He] exclaimed as she walked off, 'Look, boys, aint she bully?' **1929** H. L. GATES *Lipstick* 122 Others thought it a bully play.

b. Used as an exclamation and as an adv.

1860 *S.F. Gaz.* 28 Nov. 1/1 Hays galloped his bull around the track again, and won the money. Bully for the bull! **1861** *Yankee Doodle Songster* 15 Bully, O Bully, O bully good song, Bully for all, Bully for all. **1899** VAN DYKE *Fisherman's Luck* 201 'Bully for us . . . we got him!'

bullyism ˈbʊlɪˌɪzəm, *n.*

1. The system of bullies at Yale. *Obs.*

1843 E. P. BELDEN *Sk. Yale College* 170 *Bullyism* had its origin, like everything else that is venerated, far back in antiquity. **1871** L.H. BAGG *At Yale* 501 It was from this feud [between townspeople and students] that the custom of 'Bullyism' arose.

2. Conduct characteristic of a bully. *Obs.*

1845 POE in *Broadway Journal* 29 March, The Outises who practise this species of bullyism are, as a matter of course, anonymous. **1860** ABBOTT *South & North* 264 They will raise a howl, which will split the public ear, about the violation of the privileges of debate, Southern bullyism, etc. **1886** *All Year Round* 27 Feb. 35 The spirit of 'bullyism' . . . peculiarly prevalent in the Northern States.

bum bʌm, *n.* [App. (esp. in sense **2.**) f. earlier **bummer.**]

1. A drunken spree or debauch. Also *on a bum. Slang.*

1871 L. H. BAGG *At Yale* 153 Aside from the annual convention on Commencement night, there are two other 'bums' held during the year . . . which bring many graduates from out of town. **1879** *Caddo* (Indian Terr.) *Free Press* 23 May 7/2 Mrs. M. E. Hawkins and Mrs. G. A. Gaillie, went to Denison Wednesday—as the boys say—on a 'bum.' **1885** CUSTER *Boots & Saddles* xx. 193, I intend to celebrate their return by going on a tremendous 'bum.'

2. A loafer, tramp, idler, vagrant. *Slang.*

[**1862** *Union Canteen Songster* 33 Lather and shave 'em, frizzle 'em bum.] **1864** *Gold Hill* (Nev.) *News* 15 Apr. 5/1 The policemen say that even their old, regular and reliable 'bums' appear to have reformed, and they have absolutely nothing to do. **1947** FISHER *Focs'le Days* 76 [The sailors] would always desert the ship the first port reached, to be replaced by bums and drunks.

b. bum's rush, a forceful ejection of one not entitled to be present. *Slang.*

1941 *Yankee* Dec. 4/3 We'll give him an able demonstration of what we used to call in the old days the 'bum's Rush.' **1948** *Dly. Oklahoman* (Okla. City) 7 June 1/6 Ritchie. . . declared Nebraska and Iowa Democrats 'were given the bum's rush' during the president's Omaha visit.

3. *On the bum,* **a.** in a disordered or bad condition, **b.** tramping about as a vagrant or bum.

(**a**) **1896** G. ADE *Artie* 28, I sized it up that the house was on the bum and she didn't want me to see it. **1945** *Ledger-News* (Antonito, Colo.) 19 July 1/2 Wednesday the regular carrier, Paul Strawn's car went on the bum, and had to be taken to Alamosa for repair. — (**b**) **1895** *Cent. Mag.* Oct. 941/2 Plans are made also for going 'on the bum' the moment they are free. **1948** CHAPLIN *Wobbly* 88 Most of the stiffs were working for a winter stake without which they would be 'on the bum' all winter.

bum bʌm, *a.* [f. **bum,** *n.*] Of poor or inferior quality, bad. *Slang.*

1859 in *Pacif. N.W. Quart.* XXXI. 292 Bum River Ferry, Slight showers on first watch from 8 until 1 A.M. **1903** *Cin. Enquirer* 10 May IV. 3/1 You've got the bummest lot of birds I've ever listened to. **1948** *Dly. Ardmoreite* (Ardmore, Okla.) 25 May 6/4 She tried to perk coffee and, to her, it seemed bum.

b. bum ball, in baseball a bunt *q.v. Obs.*

1870 *N.Y. Herald* 7 July 10/1 McAtee hit a 'bum' ball towards Wolters, which rolled along so slowly that the striker secured base ere it was fielded.

c. bum steer, false information or advice. *Slang.*

[**1903** *Cin. Enquirer* 9 May 13/1 Bum ox —— wrongly directed.] **1924** HENDERSON *Key to Crookdom* 399 Bum steer, poor advice. **1932** *K.C. Times* 8 March 16 Official Washington has given us so many 'bum steers' about no depression and prosperity just around the corner. **1948** *Chi. Tribune* 31 Oct. (Comics) 2 Fred wouldn't 'a' given me a bum steer.

bum bʌm, *v. Slang.* [Cf. *bummeln* in Berghaus.]

1. *intr.* To loaf around, idle about, act as a bum.

1863 *Boston Herald* 2 Aug. 2/5 They are just fit to stay in this city, vegetate in the back slums, read the News and Express, bum round rum-shops [etc.]. **1876** *Wheatland* (Calif.) *Free Press* 4 March 2/2 The Professor is readier with his stock of puzzling questions to 'flunk' the student, who spent his time 'bumming' the night before, depending on luck for his next day's success. **1946** THOMPSON *Amer. Daughter* 72 Bummed in here broke, got a job working right here in this very shop.

2. *tr.* To obtain (a ride, food, money, etc.) by surreptitious means or by begging.

1863 *Unionville* (Nev.) *Humboldt Register* 4 July 2/1 He offered to pay, and didn't undertake to bum a puff out. **1896** *Pop. Science Jrnl.* L. 25 Several of the 'lads' had been 'pulled' at the Rapids for 'bumming the freights.' **1948** *So. Bend* (Ind.) *Tribune* 3 Apr. 6/8 On the basis of the full payment an aged man would have to . . . bum or steal his clothes and would still starve.

* **bumblebee,** *n.* Used in jocose or slang combs. as **bumblebee cotton, dust, whisky,** (see quots.).

1943 HOLT *Carver* 158 They need not keep on producing two-bolls-to-a-stalk, bumblebee cotton—a bumblebee had hardly to lift his wings to reach the big pink blossoms. **1946** *N. & Q.* Oct. 104/1 Bumblebee Cotton: cotton so stunted by drought that bumblebees can sit on the ground and suck nectar from the blossoms. — **1940** *Amer. Sp.* XV. 83 The parent was 'only using a little *bumble-bee dust.*' The procedure, he finally informed me, was the dabbing of a bit of snuff under the upper lip. Snuff is often spoken of simply as *dust.* — **1867** G. W. HARRIS *Sut Lovingood* 33, I tuck me a four finger dost ove bumblebee whiskey.

bum-booing ˈbʌmˌbuɪŋ, *n.* [Imitative.] The drumming of grouse. *Obs.* — **1843** OLIVER *Eight Months* 145 The males . . . strut about with erect tail, . . . uttering a peculiar sound, called by the natives *bum-booing.*

bum-foozle, see **dumbfoozle.**

bummer ˈbʌmɚ, *n.* [Origin obscure, cf. G. *bummler.*]

1. An idler, loafer, sponger. Also attrib. *Slang.*

1855 *Oregonian* (Portland) 27 Jan. 1/4 Come, clear out, you trunken loafer! Ve don't vant no *bummers* here! **1856** *Spirit of Age* (Sacramento) 11 Dec. 4/2 There are duplicate Jerry Sullivans in this city; the one, a decent and orderly looking man; the other, a seedy example of the 'Bummer' family. **1890** N. P. LANGFORD *Vigilante Days* I. 202 For years he has been a 'bummer' among men of his class. He has lived off his friends.

Hence **Bummerdom,** *obs.*

1858 *Varieties* (S.F.) 22 May 8/2 If this be so, there will be war in the camp of Bummerdom.

2. During the Civil War, a soldier who deserted the ranks and plundered promiscuously; loosely a member of a raiding force. See also **Sherman's bummers.**

1861 *Md. Hist. Mag.* V. 324 We have a fair sprinkling of bummers, but instead of demoralizing their betters by their presence, they are only laughed at. **1866** *Beadle's Mo.* May 398/2 We are decided in our opinion that the 'Bummer Brigade,' as conducted, was neither a credit to the service nor an organization permissible by any known laws of war. **1946** ADAMS *Album Amer. Hist.* III. 182 Straggling soldiers, known as 'bummers,' looted and burned without restraint.

b. (See quot. 1870.) *Obs.*

1869 BROWNE *Adv. Apache Country* 292 The newly-discovered silver regions, which were then making a prodigious stir among the bummers, bankers, and other men of enterprising genius on Montgomery Street. **1870** MEDBERY *Men Wall St.* 144 There are numerous workers in this rich mine, some with far less capital than assurance. These latter form an outlying fringe, to which the slang of the street has given the expressive term, borrowed from the army, of 'bummers.'

c. (See quot. 1888.) *Obs.*

1872 *Chi. Tribune* 24 Dec. 2/3 Without general acquaintance here [*sc.* Washington] and utterly unknown as a Congressional bummer. **1888** *America* 20 Sep. 16 *Bummer.* The name is now applied to party hangers on, who are of no value, but expect to be taken care of for doubtful services in the past. **1898** *Forum* Dec. 414 Ward heelers and slum 'bummers' were conspicuous factors in the Presidential campaign of 1876.

As the last term in **Congressional, party, ward, Yankee bummer.**

bummerish ˈbʌmerɪʃ, *a.* Characteristic of a bummer or loafer. *Rare.* — **1872** C. King *Sierra Nevada* 36 Indians, . . . lying off with that peculiar bummerish ease, associated with natural mock dignity.

bummerism ˈbʌmɚˌɪzəm, *n.* The habits or ways of bummers *Obs.* — **1858** *Varieties* (S.F.) 22 May 8/3 There is bummerism in politics—in fact, it is the heart core. **1898** *Forum* Dec. 426 We are so far beyond the age of low 'bummerism' in Federal office that we can afford to hesitate and ask questions.

bummery ˈbʌmərɪ, *n.* =prec. *Rare.* — **1894** *Advance* (Chicago) 3 May 277/4 Petitions in Boots & Bummery. To some these straggling adventurers [=Coxey's followers and their imitators] have been a sort of . . . abnormal lesson in bummerism and vagabondage.

bumming ˈbʌmɪŋ, *n.* Carousing, loafing, begging, acting like a bum. *Slang.*

1857 *S.F. Call* 9 Jan. 1/2 The 'Bumming and Gassing Company' were out in full strength, the novelty of labor being a new experience in their existence. **1860** *Yale Lit. Mag.* XXV. 398 (Th.), Another great shame connected with our social life is that of spreeing or 'bumming.' **1891** C. Roberts *Adrift Amer.* 66 The idea of begging, or 'bumming,' as it is popularly called out there, went strongly against my stomach.

bummy ˈbʌmɪ, *n.* Bumming, living off the country. *Obs.* — **1865** in *Jrnl. South. Hist.* IX. (1943) 252 Ordered to forage again off from the country. It was sad to see the system of *Bummy* commence again.

∗**bump,** *n.* As the last term in **belly bump, goose bump, turkey bump.**

∗**bump,** *v.* *To bump off,* to kill. *Slang.*

1910 W. M. Raine *B. O'Connor* 117 I've got several good reasons why I don't aim to get bumped off just yet. **1920** *Collier's* 6 March 9/1 A good drunk would prob'ly bump you off. **1948** *Omaha World-Herald* (Mag.) 20 June 18/3 How long will it be until John bumps you off?

∗**bumper,** *n.*

1. A contrivance for reducing the impact of bumps, collisions, etc., often a buffer at the ends of railroad cars and automobiles.

1839 *Franklin Inst. Jrnl.* XXIV. 156 The bumpers or elastic cushions are to be attached . . . to the front and rear drawbar. **1890** *Salida* (Colo.) *Mail* 3 Jan. 1/7 We came in on the bumpers last night and he got a fall under the wheels down in the yards. **1948** *New Yorker* 25 Sep. 23/1 The pilot [has] a view of the thirty feet of road immediately ahead of his front bumper.

2. a. A form of rocker used in gold mining. **b.** A contrivance for administering a jar or bump. Both *obs.* See also **belly bumper.**

(a) 1860 *Harper's Mag.* April 609/2 Our machine, which resembled the 'bumper,' or Virginia rocker, consisted of a wooden trough, . . . so hung as to be rocked to and fro by hand. — **(b) 1871** *Ill. Agric. Soc. Trans.* VIII. 247 He uses the wheelbarrow curculio bumper, his own invention.

bumwood ˈbʌmˌwʊd, *n.* [Origin obscure. Cf. **burnwood.**] The coral sumac, *Metopium linnaei.* — **1884** Sargent *Rep. Forests* 54 *Rhus Metopium* . . . Poison Wood. Coral Sumach. Mountain Manchineel. Bum Wood. **1897** Sudworth *Arborescent Flora* 274 *Rhus metopium.* Poisonwood. . . . Common names [include]. . . . Bumwood, Hog Plum, Doctor Gum.

bun bʌn, *n.* [Origin obscure. Cf. *EDD bung,* intoxicated, *bungie,* tipsy.] *To have (get) a bun on,* to be drunk. *Slang.*

1915 *Amer. Mag.* Sep. 93/1, I suppose . . . that we ought to get a slight bun on—but I have to work to-morrow. **1922** *Collier's* 7 Oct. 26/2 You got a bun on downstairs and I couldn't do nothin' with you. **1931** Reeve *Golden Age Crime* 92 Didn't he come into the city room with an occasional bun on to receive his assignments the same as the rest?

∗**bunch,** *n.*

1. A clump of trees.

1683 *Topsfield Rec.* 49 A bunch of mapels at ye brooke. **1742** *N.H. Probate Rec.* III. 101 The pine . . . is the Bounds . . . at said Mote River by the Bunch of Burches. **1917** Kephart *Camping* II. 64 They would merely mark the easiest route for a prospective road from the river to some 'bunch' of timber.

2. A compact bundle of 1,000 sawed shingles. *Rare.* Cf. ∗**bundle,** *n.* **2.**

1872 *Harper's Mag.* Nov. 950/1 The good people . . . contracted with him to have him deliver them a certain number of sermons at the price of a bunch (1000) of shingles for a sermon.

3. In combs.: (1) **bunch bean,** a bean, as the kidney bean, of a non-running variety; (2) ∗**berry,** the dwarf cornel, *Cornus canadensis,* or its fruit, also attrib.; (3) **cherry,** (see quot.); (4) **cotton,** handfuls of cotton taken from bales, *rare;* (5) **flower,** any one of various herbs of the genus *Melanthium,* esp. *M. virginicum* of the eastern and southeastern states; (6) **grass,** any one of various grasses, chiefly western, that grow in bunches or tufts, also attrib.; (7) **oysters,** (see quot.); (8) **pink,** the sweet william, *Dianthus barbatus;* (9) **plum,** =**bunch-berry.**

(1) 1787 Washington *Diaries* III. 212 At Muddy hole . . . ordered . . . the 9th square allotted for experiments (to be previously dunged as the others had been) in order to receive the bunch Nomeny bean, the common hominy bean. **1805** Parkinson *Tour* 341 What are termed Indian peas, are a sort of kidney-bean; the bunch-bean is the same, and produces abundantly. **1948** *Dly. Ardmoreite* (Ardmore, Okla.) 2 May 13/3 Carrots, bunch beans, pole beans, okra and cucumbers are numbered among his thriving garden plants. — **(2) 1845** Judd *Margaret* I. xiv. 106 She came to the shadows of the woods . . . where she got boxberry flowers and fruit, bunch-berry and star-of-Bethlehem flowers. **1946** Stanwell-Fletcher *Driftwood Valley* 23 We trod . . . over beds of deep moss, lit by scarlet bunchberry, beneath great dark spruces. — **(3) 1825** Wm. Cobbett *Woodlands* 185 American Wild Black Cherry. . . . The Americans call it the *Bunch-cherry,* because its fruit hangs in long bunches, somewhat like grapes. — **(4) 1865** *World* (N.Y.) 18 Feb. 1/2 They were all loaded with leather to barter for bunch cotton. **1872** *Harper's Mag.* Oct. 677/2 Stealing 'bunch cotton' from bales, . . . is guarded against.

(5) 1817–8 Eaton *Botany* (1822) 350 *Melanthium racemosum* bunch flower. **1845** Lincoln *Botany* App. 127/1 *Melanthium hybridum,* bunch-flower. [Also in later botanies.] — **(6) 1837** Irving *Bonneville* I. xii. 129 Their horses . . . [grazed] upon the upland bunch grass, which grew in great abundance, and, though dry, retained its nutritious properties. **1948** *Popular Western* June 26/1 Back on the bunchgrass flats, Grant checked to reassure himself that the rented saddles were not carrying booted carbines. — **(7) 1881** E. Ingersoll *Oyster Industry* 242 *Bunch Oysters,* those growing in clusters (South). — **(8) 1857** Gray *Botany* 54 Sweet William or Bunch Pink. **1877** *Vt. Bd. Agric. Rep.* IV. 99 The quantity of . . . bunch pinks and candy-tufts coming from self-sown seeds is quite startling. — **(9) 1840** *S. Lit. Messenger* VI. 518/2 There were the fringed polygula, the butter-cup, wild geranium, bunch-plum, ivy-berry. **1892** *Amer. Folk-Lore* V. 97 *Cornus Canadensis,* bunch plums; pudding-berry, N.H.

∗**bunch,** *v.*

1. *tr.* To collect or herd (cattle, horses, etc.) into a compact group.

1869 McClure *Rocky Mountains* 99 The horses not captured by the Indians have been 'bunched' at either end of the hostile country, and I doubt whether there will be regular coaches. **1907** White *Arizona Nights* 108 It was somewhere near noon by the time we had bunched and held the herd. **1930** *Denver Post* 22 June II. 9/3 When I sent the riders out, I told them we would bunch the cattle at the crossing on Troublesome [Creek].

b. In baseball, to secure (hits) in close succession. Also transf.

1883 *Chi. Tribune* 3 July 6/5 Detroit played a wretched muffing game today and failed to bunch hits. **1898** *Boston Globe* 15 May 36/4 There are two kinds of salesmen, the 'pikers,' who grind away all the time, and the men who bunch their hits, to use a baseballism. **1948** *Dly. Ardmoreite* (Ardmore, Okla.) 15 April 7 1 The Indians bunched hits in the second, fifth and eighth innings to build up a seven run margin.

2. *intr.* To collect in a close group or mass. Also with *up.*

1873 Beadle *Undevel. West* 60 Buffalo grass and gama grass take its place, and there show a tendency to bunch together, leaving large portions of the surface bare. **1916** Bower *Phantom Herd* 11 In certain parts cattle still were wild enough to bunch up at sight of a man afoot. **1948** *Democrat* 3 June 1/3 This worm usually waits until corn bunches for tasseling or begins to silk before they attack.

bunco, see **bunko.**

buncocrat ˈbʌŋkoˌkræt, *n.* =next. — **1944** *Chi. D. News* 17 July 8/4 It is further hoped that never again, again, again, will any more buncocrats ever sit in the White House.

buncoer ˈbʌŋkoɚ, *n.* Also **buncoist.** [f. bunko, *n.* and *v.*] A swindler. — **1894** *Columbus* (O.) *Dispatch* 28 May, A noted buncoist, who attempted to turn a trick on Farmer Abel Comstock, of Wood county,

1932 *K.C. Times* 22 March 16 An interesting race for first place as official buncoer this year is between Hon. Graham McNamee and Hon. Walter Winchell.

Buncombe ˈbʌŋkəm, *n.* and *a.* Also **buncombe, bunkum,** etc. [See note.]

1. In the phrase "to talk to (or for) Buncombe," or variants of this (see quot. 1828).

This use is alleged to have originated in a speech in Congress by Felix Walker who served in Congress from 1817 to 1823, representing a district in N.C. which included Buncombe Co. Over the protests of his colleagues, in the 16th Congress (1819–21) he once persisted in going through with a tiresome speech, later explaining his persistence by saying that the people of his district expected him to do so, and that come what might he was bound "to make a speech for Buncombe."

The two contradictory meanings of the term, especially where the adj. is involved (cf. senses **1.** and **2.** with **3.** below), are difficult to reconcile with the evidence now at hand. One possibility is pointed out in the note under **3.** below.

1828 *Niles' Reg.* XXXV. 66/2 'Talking to Bunkum!' This is an old and common saying at Washington, when a member of congress is making one of those hum-drum and unlistened to 'long talks' which have lately become so fashionable. . . . This is cantly called 'talking to Bunkum': an 'honorable gentleman,' long ago, having said that he was not speaking to the house, but to the people of a certain county in his district, which, in local phrase, he called 'Bunkum.' **1841** *N.O. Picayune* 26 Mar. 2/2 There is a deal of 'speaking for Buncombe,' or as some would call it, 'for grandeur,' in our legislative assemblies nowadays. **1862** *Mass. Hist. Soc. Proc.* V. 370 He made no speeches for *Buncombe*, and seldom addressed the House at much length.

2. Stuff, nonsense, humbug, often with reference to legislative action designed merely to satisfy or impose upon public opinion. *Colloq.*

1847 J. S. Robb *Squatter Life* 17 To sum it up, it is a little of government—a great deal of 'bunkum,' sprinkled with a high seasoning of political juggling. **1894** Mark Twain *P. Wilson* xvii, He said that he believed that the reward offered for the lost knife was humbug and buncombe. **1944** *Chi. D. News* 14 Dec. 10/1 Isn't it about time for Chicago and Illinois to have done with quibbles and buncombe about 'American sovereignty over Lake Michigan' and go to bat for our real interests?

b. Attrib. or as adj. with a derogatory or contemptuous signification, as **Buncombe adviser, day, drama, legislation, oratory, order, proclamation, speech, style.**

1845 *Ill. State Register* (Springfield) 28 Feb. 2/7 He read some *Buncombe* orders from Brown's history of Illinois, which is a good offset to his Buncombe speeches. **1845** *St. Louis Reveille* 8 Feb. 2/3 All that has been done . . . is fully embodied in the reports of some very good 'Bunkum' speeches. **1846** *Quincy* (Ill.) *Whig* 5 Feb. 2/5 In the opinion of my Buncombe advisor, the tall gentleman in the long boots, (No. 11) from Illinois, we are not afraid. **1858** *Spirit of Times* 9 Jan. 304/2 She deserves a bumper, if only for the courage and abnegation she has displayed in playing, at the behest of the management, a worthless and most ungracious *rôle* in a 'bunkum' drama. **1860** Olmsted *Back Country* 467 The South sends more 'orators' to Washington than the North, and the nuisance of Washington is 'bunkum' oratory. **1862** *N.Y. Tribune* 11 Feb., The rebel Brigadier-General, H. H. Sibley, was within 30 miles of Fort Craig . . . and had issued a bunkum proclamation. **1867** *Harper's Wkly.* 2 Feb. 67/1 Buncomb legislation is not admirable, but Congress seems peculiarly liable to it when treating our foreign affairs. **1880** G. A. Pierce *Zachariah* 196 It was Saturday, a day known in House parlance as 'buncombe day,' when members who desire to get their speeches before their constituents, are permitted to repeat them on the floor, and have them taken down by the official reporters and printed in the official 'Record.' **1887** *Nation* 27 Oct. 333/2 Oratory, other than of the bunkum or maudlin style, has long been rare.

3. A thing of superior excellence, esp. in the name of, or with reference to, a boat. *Slang. Obs.* Cf. **Bunkumite,** *n.*

This use may stem from Canadian F. *le buncum sa* (F. *il est bon comme ça*) it is good as it is. Cf. quot. 1849 under **b.** below.

1836 *Knickerb.* VII. 19 'Ain't she [=a boat] the raal bunkum?' exclaimed Hal. **1857** *Harper's Mag.* Feb. 348/1 When the packet-ship *Bunkum* was announced as 'below,' there was a great stir at the Astor House.

b. Fine, excellent, first-rate. *Colloq.*

1834 Tremaine in *Military & Naval Mag. U.S.* III. 24 My companions caused to be put up in parcels, a quantity of candy and cakes; 'for,' said Santin, '. . . these will be *bunkum* about taps.' **1849** *Knickerb.* Nov. 407/1 Ye see, the Yankees say a thing's 'bunkum' when it's good enuff as it is; the Canada Frenchers say '*Bunq cum sa.*' **1880** *Harper's Mag.* XLI. 615/1, I had heard the word 'bunkum' often used by bumpkins, but always with reference to something of an edible character, as an apple being 'bunkum,' or a piece of cake or pie.

buncombe ˈbʌŋkəm, *v. intr.* To talk buncombe. *Rare.* — **1855** *Herald of Freedom* (Kansas) 8 Sep. 2/4 (Th.), Now, when we want anything done we jist come together and do it right up, . . . and when it's done 'tis done, without buncomin' and gassin' on't two or three days.

bund bund, *n.* [G.] A band, group, society for a particular purpose. — **1867** *Harper's Wkly.* 28 Sep. 620 (*caption*), Festival of the German Singing Bund of North America at Indianapolis—the Sangerfest Hall. **1948** *Chelsea* (Mass.) *Record* 30 Nov. 4/5 Former National Commander of American Legion, Daniel J. Doherty, assails Bund, all 'Isms' at Brotherhood dinner of Congregation Emmanuel.

* **bundle,** *n.*

1. A number of corn blades for use as forage bound into a compact bunch.

1755 in *Pub. Col. Soc.* XII. 92 By 500 bundles of Fodder of Jacobs. **1881** Pierson *In the Brush* 67 'Fodder' in these regions [i.e., the Southwest] has a limited signification, and is applied only to the leaves which are stripped from the corn-stalks, tied in small bundles, and generally stacked for preservation. **1948** *Chi. Tribune* 4 Jan. I. 14/8 Other items sold included . . . several hundred bundles of corn fodder.

b. Used also of tobacco leaves and wheat.

1784 Smyth *Tour* II. 136 Every night the negroes are sent to the tobacco house to strip, that is to pull off the leaves from the stalk, and tie them up in hands or bundles. **1827** *Albany Gazette* 25 Sep. 2/3 The agent has provided a few bundles of wheat in the sheaf, for the purpose of operation, and solicits the public patronage. **1910** *D.N.* III. 438 bundle, *n.* Sheaf. 'I'm going to pitch *bundles* when they draw wheat tomorrow.' **1947** *Tobacco* 25 Dec. 28/1 All tobacco was given a preliminary rough classification by bundle as soon as it was brought to the warehouse from the curing barns in the country.

2. bundle shingles, shingles put up in compact bundles each containing, at present, enough shingles to cover 250 sq. ft. Cf. * **bunch,** *n.* **2.** See also **shingle bundle.**

1819 *Amer. Farmer* I. 142 North-Carolina, bundle Shingles, the run and average quality, retail, $16.

bungo ˈbʌŋgo, *n.* [See note.]

This term is f. Amer. Sp. *bongo* in our sense **1.** The source of the Spanish term is prob. African. See W. A. Read in *Language* 1948 (April–June) 253.

1. A kind of boat, a dugout, used esp. in California and the Southwest.

1763 W. Roberts *Acct. of First Discovery & Nat. Hist. Fla.* Map opp. p. 11 A Bungo. **1842** *Diplom. Corr. Texas* (1911) III. 954, I have made a voyage to the Islands of Cozumel for which purpose I had occasion to charter a Bungo, and . . . the captain (owner) of the Bungo remarked, that he with several other Bungos went from Sisal to the Alacranes. **1852** A. J. Stone *Corr.* (Huntington Lib.) 1 June 1 We started up the river in a bungo. It was a large log dug out, and thirteen of us passengers and five natives to row embarked with our baggage. **1934** *Calif. Hist. Soc. Quart.* Mar. 4 Our party finally succeeded in engaging two 'bungoes' manned by two black men each.

2. (See quots.) *Obs.*

1849 T. T. Johnson *Sights Gold Region* 18 Our party of four took possession of a light little canoe or dug-out, provided, as in all cases, with a bungo, or species or roof made of the branches and leaves of the palmetto. **1889** K. Munroe *Golden Days* 16 In the stern . . . was a palm-thatched bungo, or shelter from the weather.

Bungtown ˈbʌŋˌtaʊn, *n.* [Of obscure origin. Poss. in some way related to *bung*, a pickpocket.] A counterfeit coin, usu. attrib. with **cent, copper, money,** (see quot. 1890).

1787 *Newport Mercury* 13 Aug. 3/2 By a Correspondent of good Intelligence we are informed—that all Coppers by law in New-York, except Bungtowns, are fixed at 160 for a Dollar. **1835** H. C. Todd *Notes* 83 Brantford [in Canada] is the focus of coiners: spurious half dollars and base currency, are called, at Hamilton [Canada], *Bungtown* money, in which place a band of regular burglars from the old country have been just broken up. **1853** *Weekly Oregonian* 13 Aug. (Th.), What is the currency of the U.S.? Coppers, bogus Bungtown cents, . . . pistareens, and shinplasters. **1879** *Chi. Tribune* 11 March 4/3 The mania for old coins . . . advanced the prices of old bungtown coppers so far beyond the value of the coins of the realm as to make the dollar of the fathers ashamed of its insignificance. **1890** *N. & Q.* VI. 76 *Bungtown Coppers*. . . . Among numismatists this term is often used to designate any battered or otherwise mutilated old coins, which on account of their poor condition have practically no value.

* **bunk,** *n.*[1] (See quots. 1848, 1907.)

1770 Patten *Diary* 238 My brors boys helpt me more than half the day to Draw logs we took 3 to the mill and I hewed a bunk and a Slat for my brors loging Sled it snowed about an inch today. **1848** Bart-

Lett 55 *Bunk*, a piece of wood placed on a lumberman's sled to enable it to sustain the end of heavy pieces of timber.—*Maine.* **1902** White *Blazed Trail* 72 They were tremendous affairs, these sleighs, with runners six feet apart, and bunks nine feet in width for the reception of logs. The bunks were so connected by two loosely-coupled rods that, when emptied, they could be swung parallel with the road, so reducing the width of the sleigh. **1907** *D.N.* III. 241 bunk, n. 1. A piece of timber placed across a lumberman's sled to support the ends of logs. 2. A lumberman's sled thus arranged. Linneus, Aroostook Co. [Me.].

* **bunk,** *n.*^{2} In combs.: (1) **bunk car,** in railroading, a car in which workmen sleep; (2) **house,** a (temporary) structure in which miners, cowboys, lumbermen, etc., sleep; (3) **mate,** one who shares a bunk; (4) **room,** a room containing bunks.

(1) **1896** P. L. Ford *P. Stirling* xl, By the light one of the superintendents found the bunk-cars gone. **1918** Sandburg *Cornhuskers* 80 Then they go to the bunk cars and eat mulligan and prune sauce. — (2) **1876** Raymond *8th Rep. Mines* 332 Bunk-house [of the Little Annie Mill cost] . . . [$]228.00. **1946** Newton *P. Bunyan* 163 Down crashed a thousand boots on the bunkhouse floor. — (3) **1877** Habberton *Jericho Road* 16 Folding his blanket double and piling it over his bunk-mate, . . . the Parson stretched himself in his bunk with no covering whatever. **1902** London *Daughter of Snows* 233 Yes, strange sort of a chap. Wouldn't hanker to be bunk-mates with him. — (4) **1848** Baker *Glance at N.Y.* 24 (We.), De way de boys laid out of de old bunk-room was sinful. **1924** Mulford *Rustlers' Valley* vi, The cook was busy in the bunkroom.

bunk bʌŋk, *n.*^{3} [f. **Buncombe** (sense **2**).] Nonsense, tommyrot, also **bunco, bunkalorum.** *Slang.*

1900 George Ade *More Fables in Slang* 15 But the Business Manager was a Lightning Calculator, and he surmised that the Bunk was about to be Handed to him. **1912** London *Smoke Bellew* 287 But when it comes to fi-nance we're sure the fattest suckers that ever fell for the get-rich-quick bunco. **1940** Riesenberg *Golden G.* 305 It's a lot of bunkalorum. **1948** *Chi. D. News* 4 March 10/7 The politician feels he is justified in handing out bunk to fool the people.

bunk bʌŋk, *v.* [?f. **buncombe.**] *tr.* To fool or deceive. *Slang.*

1877 Bartlett 84 To bunk. . . . Among lumbermen, to pile wood deceitfully so as to increase the apparent quantity in the survey. **1915** *Amer. Mag.* Aug. 28/3 He wasn't exactly wild, but he wasn't given' 'em no good balls to hit and he couldn't bunk 'em into swingin' at bad ones. **1948** *Chi. Tribune* 9 May 1. 24/7 The Great I Am, old Again and Again and Again himself, couldn't possibly have done a better job of bunking the American people than this fellow Stassen.

bunker ˈbʌŋkɚ, *n.* Short for **mossbunker.** See also **Joe Bunker.**

1842 *Nat. Hist. N.Y., Zoology* IV. 260 The Mossbonker, *Alosa menhaden.* . . . At the east end of the island, they are called Skippangs or Bunkers. **1888** Goode *Amer. Fishes* 386 New Jersey uses the New York name with its local variations, such as 'Bunker' and 'Marshbunker.' **1898** *N.Y. Journal* 26 July 14/7 Thousands of bunkers, otherwise known as 'Long Island herring,' floated lifeless on the surface of the water.

bunker bed. ?A bunk. *Rare.* — **1796** B. Hawkins *Letters* 44, I saw a few bunker beds and the cannon, the only remains of the French establishment.

Bunker Hill price. An excessively high price, in allusion to the heavy loss of men by the British at Bunker Hill. *Rare.* — **1776** T. Paine *Common Sense* (1928) 25 'Tis as great a folly to pay a Bunker-hill price for law as for land.

bunkie ˈbʌŋkɪ, *n.* = **bunk mate.** *Colloq.*

1858 Viele *Following the Drum* 218, I rewarded [his affection for the dog] by giving him Jack for his 'bunkie'! **1907** Mulford *Bar-20* 27 Why didn't he say suthin' about it? Anyhow, Jimmy was my bunkie. **1948** *Southwestern Rev.* Winter 29/2 The next morning Bud's 'bunkie' sat watching him shave.

bunko ˈbʌŋko, *n.* [App. f. Sp. *banca*, a game of chance at cards.]

1. A cheat or swindler. *Slang.*

1884 *Las Vegas* (N.M.) *Gazette* 7 Dec. 4/1 The tramps, thugs, and bunkos must go.

2. A party game played with dice (see quot. 1938). Also attrib.

1921 *Outing* June 132/2 (*advt.*), 'Joker' Tops. . . . Have them at home for Bunko Parties, etc. **1938** Asbury *Sucker's Prog.* 57 Eight-Dice Cloth . . . was introduced into San Francisco by a crooked gambler who made various changes in the method of play and christened it Banco. After a few years this was corrupted into Bunco, sometimes spelled Bunko and in time Bunco came to be a general term applied to all swindling and confidence games. **1948** *News-Dispatch* (Michigan City, Ind.) 3 Apr. 6/5 Bunco was played.

3. In special combs.: (1) **bunko artist,** an adept in cheating operations; (2) **game,** a gambling or swindling game, also transf.; (3) **joint,** (see quot.); (4) **man,** a swindler or cheat; (5) **sharp,** = prec.; (6) **show,** a show or exhibition designed for swindling; (7) **skin,** (see quot.); (8) **steerer,** (see quot. 1875); (9) **steering,** the activity of a bunko steerer; (10) **thief,** a swindler or cheat.

(1) **1946** *Newsweek* 18 March 34/1 The bunco artists start literally from the skin out, trading on the clothing shortage and the soldier's natural desire to get into civvies. **1948** *Time* 12 April 22/2 He swept up shoals of bootleggers, con men, grifters, oil stock swindlers, bunco artists. — (2) **1875** *Chi. Tribune* 8 Dec. 12/3 This marriage was merely a 'confidence' or 'bunko' game on both sides,—purely a Mormon affair. **1902** Pidgin *Quincy A.S.* 121 Well, Strout ought to know what a good bunco game is. — (3) **1889** *Cent.* 721/3 bunko-joint. . . . A house or rendezvous to which strangers are allured, and in which they are victimized by bunko-men. — (4) **1883** *Putnam Co. Jrnl.* (Palatka, Fla.) 28 Jan. 3/1 Bunko men are with us. Give them a wide street. **1938** Asbury *Sucker's Prog.* 57 In time Bunco came to be a general term applied to all swindling and confidence games, while the sharpers who practiced them were called Bunco men.

(5) **1894** C. H. Hoyt *Texas Steer* (1925) III. 39 You're a . . . bunco sharp. — (6) **1884** Cable *Dr. Sevier* (1885) 205 The tenpin alleys, the chop-houses, the bunko shows, and shooting-galleries. — (7) **1938** Asbury *Sucker's Prog.* 57 The game [Banco] was in full growth in New York during the 1870's and the early 1880's, when scores of Banco Skins, as the police called the games were scattered throughout the city. — (8) **1875** *Chi. Tribune* 1 Oct. 4/3 A 'bunko-steerer' seems to be a subordinate confidence-man who . . . conducts them [= countrymen] into a back room of some large building where they are 'confidenced' of what money they may have about them. **1945** Service *Ploughman* 377 This burg's full of bunco steerers. — (9) **1875** *Chi. Tribune* 30 Sep. 4/2 The criminal classes . . . proceeded to introduce the business of 'bunko-steering.' **1892** *Daily News* 1 Jan. 7/3 Obtaining a sum of money . . . in Albany, New York, by what at first appeared to be a variation of the confidence trick, locally known as 'bunco-steering.'

(10) **1872** *Chi. Tribune* 18 Oct. 8/4 A quintet of bunco thieves were tried by jury. . . . Such verdicts are powerless to inspire gamblers with the proper respect for the law.

bunko ˈbʌŋko, *v.* [Cf. **bunko,** *n.*] *tr.* To swindle by a bunko game or other form of deception. *Slang.*

1875 *Chi. Tribune* 6 July 8/1 The fugitive is the same person who bunkoed a stranger out of $75 recently. **1894** C. H. Hoyt *Texas Steer* (1925) II. 21 I'd been here six hours, and they'd buncoed me out of more than a hundred dollars. **1919** Dunn *Indiana* II. 658 Hines felt that they had been 'bunkoed' in some way, and says, 'When the count was taken of the number of Sons of Liberty on whom we could rely, it seemed worse than folly to attempt to use them.'

Bunkumite ˈbʌŋkəmˌaɪt, *n.* [Cf. **Buncombe 3.**] One who is smug, self-satisfied, pleased with the status quo. *Obs.* — **1849** *Knickerb.* Nov. 407/1 They're so sot up in thar own noshuns and consarns, that the naybors all calls 'em 'Bunkumites.' **1861** *Oregon Argus* 16 Feb., A poor, shoeless, shirtless, and hatless Bunkumite.

bunny hug. A couple dance done to syncopated music. Hence **bunny hugger.**

1914 *Art* 290 It is not in the souls of bunny-huggers that the new ferment is potent; they will not dance and sing the world out of its lethargy. **1934** Webster. **1947** *Chi. Herald-Amer.* 11 Jan. (Sat. Home Mag.) 7/2 Along with this music appeared the 'animal' dances—the Bunny Hug, the Grizzly Bear, the Chicken Scratch, the Turkey Trot, the Lame Duck, and the Fish Walk.

* **bunt,** *n.* In baseball, a mere blocking of a pitched ball with the bat. Cf. **bum ball.**

1889 *Chi. Tribune* 8 Aug. 6/1 Connor got around on bases on balls given himself and Richardson, Ward's bunt toward third, . . . and a wild pitch. **1914** *Chi. Tribune* 6 Aug. 15/1 Bush dropped a bunt six feet in front of the plate. **1946** *Longmont* (Colo.) *Times-Call* 6 June 7/2 Iverson beat out a bunt and scored on Red Dexter's triple.

* **bunt,** *v.* **1.** *tr.* In baseball, to stop (the ball) with the bat without swinging the latter. **2.** (See quot.)

(1) **1889** *Reach's Base Ball Guide* 144 Bunted Ball. **1912** Mathewson *Pitching* 23 Doyle bunted and was safe, filling the bases. **1947** *Redbook* July 29/2, I like to see the smart hitters take close pitches, bunt unexpectedly when they catch the infield playing deep, or bluff a bunt and swing around for a full cut at the ball as the infield is drawn in. — (2) **1892** *Amer. Folk-Lore* V. 146 When a boy throws himself upon a sled . . . he *bunts*, or *bumps*, or *plumps*, etc., upon it, according to the manner of speech in his locality. (Maine.)

bunter bʌntɚ, *n.*

1. a. (See quot.) **b.** A heavy obstruction built at the end of a railroad track to prevent cars from running off.

(a) **1884** KNIGHT *Supp.* 147/1 Bunter. The bumper or buffer of a railway car. The bar on the front end of the car, which strikes against a similar bar on an adjacent car in coupling. — **(b) 1898** *Boston Herald* 12 Aug. 4/7 A number of passenger cars were shunted into the trainshed . . . and, for some reason . . . the bunter received a terrific blow that splintered a part of the woodwork and severely wrenched two of the coaches.

2. One who bunts in baseball.

1912 *Amer. Mag.* June 200/2 The play is extremely dangerous to bad bunters, as a double play is almost certain if they hit a fly into the air. **1948** *Athletic Jrnl.* April 28/3 Good bunters as a rule develop a good eye in looking over each pitch.

***bunting,** *n.*[1] As the last term in **chestnut-collared, clay-colored, cow, cowpen, Indigo, lark, lazuli, lazuli painted, Leconte's, Henslow's, McCown, painted, rice, savanna, silk, towhee, Townsend, varied bunting.**

***bunting,** *n.*[2] =**baby bunting.**

1922 *Mont. Ward Cat.* (ed. 97) 93 This attractive Bunting is just the thing to keep baby warm and comfortable. **1935** *Ib.* (ed. 123) 128 Chinchilla Bunting. Warm—because it's Beacon Cotton Chinchilla—white cotton flannel lining. **1948** *Baby Post* Spring 20/2 Baby will be nice and cozy buttoned into this toast-warm outdoor bunting with an attached hood.

Buntlinism 'bʌntlɪn,ɪzəm, *n.* [f. "Ned *Buntline,*" pen name of Edward Z. C. Judson (1823–86), one of the chief organizers of the Know-Nothing party.] The rowdy, jingoistic, nativistic political and social doctrines of "Ned Buntline" and his group. *Rare.* — **1855** *Olympia* (W.T.) *Pioneer* 6 July (Th.), In these days of Buntlinism, it is a common thing to hear men boast that some fellow has 'seen Sam,' or is 'Right on the Goose.'

***bur,** *n.*

1. =**pine bur.**

1859 G. W. PERRY *Turpentine Farming* 24 We shall find that where pines are situated so that they are not exposed, and are perfectly sound, they will drop their burs clear and regular every year. **1905** *Bureau of Forestry Bul.* No. 63, 6 The seed of the white pine is borne in a cone, sometimes called a 'bur.'

2. In combs.: (1) **bur clover,** a prickly-podded plant of the genus *Medicago;* (2) **fish,** any one of various spiny globefish; (3) **marigold,** beggar ticks, a species of *Bidens* with conspicuous yellow flowers; (4) **oak,** the overcup or mossy-cup oak, *Quercus macrocarpa,* found chiefly in the central U.S., also attrib.; (5) **seed,** (see quot. 1909); (6) **tomato,** (see quot.), also called **buffalo bur.**

(1) 1868 *Overland Mo.* Aug. 180/1 Burr clover, whose seed is enclosed in a prickly capsule, alfalfa, bunch grass and alfilarea represent the general pasture of the mountains. **1901** MOHR *Plant Life Ala.* 135 Vetch . . . , cowpeas, and bur clover . . . will yield crops for soiling in the earliest days of spring. *Ib.* 560 *Medicago arabica,* . . . Spotted Bur Clover. — **(2) 1674** JOSSELYN *Acc. Voy. New-Eng.* 113 Blew-fish, Bull-head, Bur-fish. **1884** GOODE *Fisheries U.S.* I. 170 The Porcupine Fishes—*Diodontidæ.* . . . The best known is the Swell Fish of New England. *Chilomycterus geometricus.* These fishes are commonly known by such names as 'Burr Fish,' 'Ball Fish,' 'Swell Fish', and 'Toad Fish.' — **(3) 1817–18** EATON *Botany* (1822) 205 *Bidens frondosa,* burr-marygold. **1939** *Nat. Geog. Mag.* Aug. 220/2 Conspicuous among these are . . . the closely related bur marigolds or tickseeds. — **(4) 1815** DRAKE *Cincinnati* 82 The most valuable timber trees are the . . . white, black, low-land chesnut and bur oaks. **1835** HOFFMAN *Winter in West* I. 154, I struck a burr-oak opening. **1947** *Better Homes & Gardens* Feb. 23/2 Bur oak wears snow as an adolescent boy might wear his sister's sweater, with elbows and wrists much in evidence.
(5) 1847 WOOD *Botany* 435 *Echinospermum Lappula.* . . . Burr-seed, an erect herb, in dry soils, roadsides, N. States to Arc. Am. **1909** *Cent. Sup.* 178/1 Burseed, a species of stickseed, *Lappula Lappula,* introduced into the United States from Europe. — **(6) 1918** VISHER *So. Dakota* 90 The bur-tomato (*Solanum rostratum*) is another annual which is sometimes conspicuous in similar situations.

***Burbank,** *n.* Used attrib. or in the possessive with reference to varieties of plants developed by Luther Burbank (1849–1926), American naturalist.

1894 *N.Y. at World's Columb. Expos.* 279/1 Potatoes. American Giant, Beauty of Hebron, Belle, Blush, Burbank's Seedling. **1901** *World's Work* Sep. 1210/2 Perhaps the three most useful things that he has yet introduced are the Wickson and Burbank plums and the Shasta daisy. **1906** *Out West* Apr. 340 Strawberries, . . . Burbank berries, and all the berry tribe, flourish well in the warm, sandy soils. **1908** *Sat. Ev. Post* 29 Aug. 9/1 The Burbank potato . . . has yielded probably the largest aggregate of additional wealth of any of the new things created by the American school of plant breeders. **1948** *News-Palladium* (Benton Harbor, Mich.) 14 Aug. 7/1 Burbank plums in half-bushel baskets ranged from $1.00 to $1.40.

Hence **Burbankian,** *a.*

1930 FERBER *Cimarron* 287 In the sitting room was a lamp with a leaded glass shade in the shape of a strange and bloated flower—a Burbankian monstrosity, half water lily, half petunia.

***burden,** *n.* **1. burden car,** a freight car. *Obs.* **2. burden grass,** redtop, an important pasture grass, *Agrostis stolonifera major. Obs.*

(1) 1834 *Am. R.R. Jour.* III. 742/2 Steel springs are still being placed upon the burthen cars. **1909** CARTER *When Railroads Were New* 52 (*ill.,*) Type of 'burden' or freight car used on the Baltimore and Ohio in 1832. — **(2) 1749** FRANKLIN *Writings* II. 386, I threw in the following seed . . . a peck of Burden grass . . . and two Pints of Red Clover per acre.

Burden car or freight car *c*1835

***burdensome,** *a.* Of vessels: Capable of carrying a good burden. *Obs.*

1763 *Boston Ev. Post* 9 May (Th.), A very good and burthensome Schooner for sale. **1817** *Cape-Fear Recorder* 5 April, The good substantial and burthensome brig Hibernia, of 145 tons' burthen. **1834** M. SCOTT *Cruise Midge* xviii, 'Pull under the stern of that large ship' . . . 'A fine burdensome craft that, sir.' **1835** HOFFMAN *Winter in West* II. 68 The burthensome steamboats from New-Orleans reach here at the lowest stage of the river.

***bureau,** *n.*

1. An article of furniture for holding clothing, usu. surmounted by an adjustable mirror; a chest of drawers. Also attrib.

In the first example the name may be used in the original sense of a writing-desk with drawers.

1751 *Boston Ev. Post* 29 July, Fashionable furniture, consisting of mahogany, India & stone tables, buroes [etc.]. **1819** *St. Louis Enquirer* 15 Sep. (Th.), Look in the bureaus and trunks of modern men of fashion, and see the number of coats, waistcoats, pantaloons, hats, and boots. **1853** B. F. TAYLOR *Jan. & June* (1871) 100 At our house, bureau-drawers tumbled out their treasures of flannels and linens. **1948** *Antioch Review* Spring 88 Ella still looked young in the light of the pink-shaded lamp on her bureau.

Bureau trunk or dresser trunk *c*1871

b. (See quot.) *Obs.*

1888 J. D. BILLINGS *Hardtack* 319 Their course could have been followed by the well stuffed knapsacks—or 'bureaus,' as some of the old vets called them—that sprinkled the roadside.

c. bureau trunk, a trunk which can be arranged somewhat as a bureau. Cf. **dresser trunk.**

[**1892** B. BUTTERWORTH *Growth of Industrial Art* 151 Trunks. . . . U.S. Patent Bureau—A.D. 1871.] **1907** *Sears Cat.* (ed. 117) 991/2 Strongest, most convenient bureau trunk made.

2. A subdivision in an executive department of the U.S. Government. Also attrib.

1831 *Deb. Congress* 26 Feb. 318 [The growing cost of government] is easily accounted for by the increased expense in every department—by establishing new bureaus—by erecting new offices. **1846** M'KENNEY *Memoirs* I. 24 To dismiss from office in those days without cause . . . —and especially the dismissal of a bureau officer or clerk . . . would have been deemed an outrage. **1880** E. KIRKE *Garfield* 43 What can a bureau do with the whole weight of congressional influence pressing for the appointment of men because they are our friends?

b. Used in the official name of such a subdivision. (For **Bureau of Labor** see **Labor Bureau.**)

1850 *N. Eng. Farmer* II. 30 The establishment of a 'Bureau of Agriculture,' at Washington, is a subject that has received considerable attention for the year past. **1870** *Comm. Educ. Rep.* 5 [The] Bureau of Education, . . . established as an independent Department, . . . was afterward reduced to an office in the Interior Department, where now the law styles it a Bureau. **1944** *U.S. Govt. Manual* 69 The Bureau of Areas coordinates the development of area programs. **1945** *Farmington* (N.M.) *T. Hustler* 16 Feb. 1/1 The Bureau of Reclamation thru its own engineers openly declared that there is not sufficient water in the San Juan River to water all the potential lands in this county.

As the last term in **commissary, currency, dressing, employment, farm, Freedmen's, Hydrographic, Indian, labor, Negro, news, pension, Weather bureau.**

∗ **burg,** *n.* Also **burgh.** A town, village, city. *Colloq.* See also **mining burg.**

1845 SOL. SMITH *Theatrical Apprent.* 151 It so happened that the stranger who had played poker with us, also disembarked at the same burgh. **1889** *Gallup* (N.M.) *Gleaner* 27 Mar. 3/2 Judge Brinker paid this burg a short visit last week. **1948** *Hungry Horse News* (Columbia Falls, Mont.) 24 Sep. 8/1 The law cracked down on our burg the other evening, and several arrests were made.

burgaloo, see **vergaloo.**

∗ **burgess,** *n.*

1. Formerly a member of a colonial legislative body. *Obs.* Cf. **House of Burgesses.**

1619 *Va. Ho. of Burgesses* 3 Every man [should] . . . pay into the hands . . . of the burgess one pound of the best tobacco . . . to be distributed to the speaker. *c***1680** *Mass. H.S. Coll.* 2 Ser. I. 35, He returns home, and while here submits himselfe to be chosen burgess of the County. **1800** JEFFERSON *Notes* 115 They on the 24th of July 1621, by charter under their common seal, declared that from thenceforward there should be two supreme councils in Virginia, the one to be called the council of state . . . the other to be called the general assembly to be convened by the governor once yearly or oftener, which was to consist of the council of state, and two burgesses out of every town, hundred, or plantation, to be respectively chosen by the inhabitants.

2. A representative on a local governing body (see quot. 1889).

*a***1821** C. BIDDLE *Autobiog.* 194 Being Chief Burgess of the borough, I attended, and rode near the prisoner, who marched with great firmness. **1889** *Cent.* 725/2 In Connecticut boroughs the *board of burgesses* corresponds to the township board or board of trustees in some other States, or to the common council of a city. The chief executive officer of a Pennsylvanian borough is called the *chief burgess*.

burgher ˈbɜgɚ, *n.* [Du. *burger.*] One of the early Dutch inhabitants of New York. *Obs.*

1677 *N.Y. State Col. Hist.* XII. 576 The Court have ordered that the Burgers in generall bee called together. **1809** IRVING *Knickerb.* VII. ix, The ancient burghers contended who should have the privilege of bearing the pall. **1830** COOPER *Water Witch* III. 69 Day had dawned on the industrious burghers of Manhattan.

b. Attrib. with **excise, packt.** *Obs.*

1688 *Annals of Albany* (1850) II. 104 The mayor . . . having taken into consideration ye burger or small pakt which hath been paid by ye inhabitants of this towne time out of mind, towards ye defraying of publike charge thereof, which said packt or excise is continued by his excellency ye govr for ye space of two years. *Ib.* 105 By ye ancient custome of this citty hes been liable to pay ye sd burger packt. **1691** *Ib.* 116 The assistants propose yt order to taken concerning ye burger excise in the time of the revolution, that it may be collected for the cittyes use.

burglarize ˈbɜglǝˌraɪz, *v. tr.* and *intr.* To steal, break into (a house) and rob, to practice burglary. Also **burglarizing,** *n.*

1871 *Southern Mag.* April (De Vere), The Yankeeisms donated, collided, and burglarized, have been badly used up by an English magazine writer. **1871** DE VERE 655 In like manner the burglar's occupation has been designated as burglarizing. **1947** *Jrnl. Crim. Law & Criminology* Nov.–Dec. 319, I tried to resist the urge to get outside and burglarize.

∗ **burgoo,** *n.* (See quots.) Also attrib.

1853 MCCONNEL *Western Char.* 363 Around a burgou pot, or along the trenches of an impromptu barbecue, he shone in meridian splendor. . . . *Note.* A kind of soup, made by boiling all sorts of game with corn, onions, tomatoes, and a variety of other vegetables. When skilfully concocted and properly seasoned, not at all unsavory. So called from a soup made by seamen. **1885** *Mag. Amer. Hist.* Jan. 98/2 *Burgoo.*—A Southern and Southwestern term akin to barbecue. . . . The feast, however, was furnished by hunters and fishermen—everything, fish, flesh, and fowl, being compounded into a vast stew. **1944** *Chi. D. News* 4 May 21 Burgoo Stew . . . is such an old and ancient dish in Kentucky that no two people tell the same story of its origin and no two people will give you the same recipe.

Burgoynade ˌbɜgɔɪnˈed, *n.* A military reverse, in allusion to the capture of General John Burgoyne at Saratoga, N.Y., during the Revolution. *Obs.*

1779 *S.C. Gazette* 3 March, Col. Campbell's expedition from Savannah to Augusta . . . has proved as unfortunate as Major Gardner's to Port Royal; to escape a Burgoynade he has made a very sudden and precipitate retreat down the country. **1780** in *Mag. Amer. Hist.* V. 379 Our affairs to the Southward look blue. So they did when you took the command before the Burgoynade. **1814** *Col. Centinel* 24 Sep. 1/3 News of another *Burgoynade*, or a retreat from the peninsula between Lakes Ontario and Erie, may therefore be daily looked for.

Burgoyne ˈbɜgɔɪn, *v.* [f. the name of Gen. John *Burgoyne*, captured at Saratoga in 1777.] *tr.* To capture, take prisoner. *Obs.*

1777 *N.J. Archives* 2 Ser. I. 531 Our army by this time, 'tis hoped have come up with them, and will either have him burgoyned or driven off. **1787** *New Haven Gaz.* 8 March 22/3 (Th. Supp.), Help us to burgoyn Lincoln and his army. **1816** *Niles' Reg. Supp.* IX. 85/1 Macomb would have *Burgoyn'd* John, your governor Prevo', But ah! he was too nimble, oh Johnny Bull, my Joe.

∗ **burial,** *n.* In combs.: (1) **burial case,** a form of coffin, often of metal; (2) **casket,** = prec.; (3) **lot,** a private lot in a cemetery; (4) **permit,** a certificate issued by the proper authorities granting permission to bury.

(1) **1851** CIST *Cincinnati* 191 Foundery castings.—This . . . is carried on in every possible variety, in which iron can be cast from a butt hinge to a burial case. **1941** in MENCKEN *Supp.* I. (1945) 570 Caskets, Coffins, Burial-Cases, and Other Morticians' Goods. — (2) **1866** *Rep. Comm. Patents* I. 676 Removing from the side of a coffin or burial casket . . . so much of its front side as is required to sufficiently expose the person of the corpse. **1892** *Harper's Mag.* March 506/2 A dog-cariole of the best pattern—a little suggestive of a burial casket, to be sure. — (3) **1833** *Knickerb.* II. 259 The whole of this extensive area is laid off in burial lots, which were offered by the original proprietors for sale. **1915** *Kansas Stat.* 2270 [Cemetery corporations are] hereby empowered to acquire and hold lands for cemetery purposes . . . and to divide said lands into burial lots. — (4) **1888** *St. Louis Globe-Democrat* (R.), Yesterday's Burial Permits. **1924** A. L. H. STREET *Amer. Funeral Law* 208 The local registrar . . . shall take up the transit and removal permit and issue a burial permit.

burion ˈbjurɪǝn, *n.* [Amer. Sp. *burrión*, sparrow, "corrupción vulgar de gorrión"—Santamaría.] = **house finch.** — **1858** BAIRD *Birds Pacific R.R.* 415. **1889** *Cent.* 832/1 The burion or house-finch of the southwestern United States is *Carpodacus frontalis.*

∗ **Burley,** *n.* [App. f. proper name.] A variety of tobacco grown esp. in Kentucky, often **white Burley.** See also **Kentucky burley.**

1881 in B. W. ARNOLD *Tobacco Ind.* (1897) 35 The White Burley produced in the West has now thoroughly substituted our dark grades. **1909** *Cent. Supp.* 177/1 *Burley*, a well known American variety of tobacco, having two subvarieties, red and white. **1945** *Chi. D. News* 8 Jan. 6/2 From here it looks as if the typical Victory garden in '45 will have to include five rows of Kentucky burley, five of Carolina types, two of latikia and one of perique.

∗ **Burlington,** *n.* [*Burlington*, N.J.] *attrib.* Of or pertaining to Burlington. *Obs.*

[**1771** TAYLOR *Voyage* 164 This town [Burlington, capital of West N.J.] is vastly in fame for producing the best fed pork in America.] **1777** CRESSWELL *Journal* 264 The Jerseys . . . are famous for Hams, which go under the name of Burlington Hams and are esteemed the best in the world. **1817** W. COXE *Fruit Trees* 129 Jersey, or Rhode-Island Greening. Sometimes called the Burlington Greening. **1817** *Ib.* 126 Newton Spitzemberg. This apple is in some parts of this State called the English, or Burlington Spitzemberg: it was brought from Newton on Long-Island. **1818** *Amer. Mo. Mag.* II. 428/2 Table Apples [include] . . . 16. Burlington Greening, October and November. **1867** DE VOE *Market Ass't.* 227 The Burlington herring have also had quite a reputation for the table.

***burn,** *n.*

1. An instance of burning the vegetation, debris, etc., on land in clearing it for cultivation, esp. *a good burn. Colloq.*

1792 J. BELKNAP *Hist. of New Hampshire* III. 132 Much depends on getting what is called a *good burn,* to prepare the ground for planting. **1874** *Vt. Bd. Agric. Rep.* II. 455 This land is not very difficult to clear, although a good burn is rare. **1942** CANNON *Mountain* 97 If he was to get a good burn, he'd have room enough ready by the end of June, probably, to get a fair crop of corn—if the weather was right.

2. A place where the trees, grass, etc., have been burned.

1839 HOLMES *Explor. Aroostook River* 69 Very little ploughing is as yet done, as most of the crops are raised on a 'burn.' **1920** HUNTER *Trail Drivers Texas* I. 274 We escaped by fleeing in a part of the plain which had been burned before, called 'a burn' by people of that section. **1947** *Trail & Timberline* May 82/1 The U.S. Forest Service will have 10,000 three-year-old lodgepole pines waiting for us at the old Mammoth Burn a mile and a half southwest of Tolland.

As the last term in **house burn, powder burn.**

***burn,** *v.*

1. *tr.* **a.** To roast (coffee). *Rare.* **b.** In gold mining to sink (a hole) with the help of fires to thaw the frozen ground. *Obs.* Cf. ***burning, 2.**

(a) **1842** *Lowell Offering* II. 137 'What! going to burn coffee now? We shan't have breakfast today.' — (b) **1912** LONDON *Smoke Bellew* 150 Gilchrist, who has the next claim below, has got six hundred dollars in a single pan of bedrock. He's burned one hole down.

2. In colloq. phrases: (1) *To burn powder,* to use or expend ammunition, to fire shots; (2) *to burn off,* to prepare (land) for cultivation by burning the brush, etc. (see quot. 1926); (3) *to burn the prairie, earth,* or *wind,* to go at full speed; (4) *to have (money, time,* etc.) *to burn,* to have abundance of.

(1) **1775** *Md. Hist. Mag.* V. 159 Atkinson said he intended to burn powder that day. **1785** in *Amer. Museum* V. 578/1 The principal officers . . . were employed in preparing and ordering an expensive entertainment, for spectators and officers, while the soldiers were left to burn powder to no purpose.

(2) **1852** MOODIE *Roughing It* 90 Moodie and Jacob had chopped eight acres during the winter, but these had to be burnt off and logged-up before we could put in a crop of wheat for the ensuing fall. **1926** *D.N.* V. 386 *burn off, or up,* v. phr. Clear away, applied to fog, 'The fog will burn up before noon.' Common. [In Me.]

(3) **1881** ROMSPERT *Western Echo* 164 Of course, the first day the mustangs will burn the prairie. **1891** THANET *Otto the Knight* 219 An' we all ayfter 'm, hollerin' with all the power. . . . Didn't he burn the wind, though! **1903** ADAMS *Log Cowboy* 23, I was half a mile in the lead, burning the earth like a canned dog. **1946** WILSON *Fidelity* 180 When something went fast in the older days, we said it 'burned the wind.'

(4) **1897** *Cong. Rec.* 27 March 400/1 Mr. Simpson of Kansas. You have plenty of time. Mr. Payne. No; I have not got time 'to burn.' **1904** *Courier-Journal* 2 July 5 She has . . . already had literary experience to burn. **1911** QUICK *Yellowstone N.* 240 The gall of my swearing against these big men that had money to burn. **1945** *N. Eng. Homestead* 22 Sep. 18/2 Because we live on a farm we have land to burn. Only we do not burn it.

b. burned piece, a piece of ground cleared for cultivation by burning. *Rare.*

1860 *Harper's Mag.* Feb. 290/2 Here was a fellow who had come . . . twenty miles to see the circus. He had left his 'burned-piece' just in the nick of time.

***burner,** *n.* As the last term in **Barn, base, brand, brush, church, foot, hay, prairie, rose gas, tar, water burner.**

***burning,** *a.* and *n.*

1. An area cleared of underbrush, debris, etc., by burning.

1830 J. F. WATSON *Philadelphia* 53 The 'clearings' and the 'burnings' of the 'brushwood' and 'undergrowth,' had begun to mark, in rude lines, the originals of the present paved and stately streets. **1902** WHITE *Blazed Trail* x. 77 Down in the swamp the covey of partridges were beginning to hope that in a few days more they might discover a bare spot in the burnings.

2. In gold mining, an instance of working or digging frozen ground by first thawing it with a fire.

1897 LEONARD *Gold Fields Klondike* 23 Drifting was carried on by the usual winter process of 'burning.' **1899** *Harper's Wkly.* 8 April 344/1 The lay-men struck it the first hole, and out of thirty burnings took out $40,000. *Ib.* 344/2 The first hole to be put down by burning is credited to Shookum Jim. **1949** *Boston Globe* 15 May (Fiction Mag.) 2/4, I got to thinkin' about all the hard work there is shovellin', an' pannin', an' sluicin', an' choppin' wood, an' burnin' in, an' crankin' a windlass.

3. In combs.: (1) **burning bush,** see as a main entry; (2) **fluid,** see as a main entry; (3) **fly,** =**punkie;** (4) **ground,** a place where Indians executed victims by burning, *obs.;* (5) **spring,** a spring whose waters are so impregnated with inflammable gas that they appear to burn when the gas is ignited.

(3) **1791** BARTRAM *Travels* (1792) 383 The sting of this is intolerable, no less acute than a prick from a red-hot needle, or a spark of fire on the skin; these are called the burning flies. — (4) **1847** in HOWE *Hist. Coll. Ohio* 404 The burning-ground, in the suburbs of Grenadier Squawtown, represented in the map, was also situated on an elevated spot. . . . The burning-ground at Old Chillicothe was somewhat similar, being in full view of the burning-ground at Squawtown. — (5) **1819** SCHOOLCRAFT *Mo. Lead Mines* 216 A phenomenon . . . under the name of a *burning spring,* exists on one of the principal forks of Licking River, Kentucky. **1855** BESTE *Wabash* I. 118 In this neighbourhood, is one of those natural phenomena, so frequent in America, called the Burning spring; gas bubbles up through the water of a small stream, or through the snow that covers it in the winter; and, when a light has been applied, burns steadily down to the snow or the water's edge.

As the last term in **barn, brush, counter, fall, house burning.**

burning bush. The spindle tree, *Euonymus americanus,* or *E. atropurpureus,* having bright red capsules.

1785 MARSHALL *Amer. Grove* 45 Ever-green Spindle Tree. From their [=its fruit's] red appearance [it] obtained the name of the Burning Bush. **1838** GOOSE *Letters* 237 The plant is called the Burning Bush (*Euonymus angustifolius*). **1939** *These Are Our Lives* 137 A neighbor give us them three burning bushes the past spring

b. (See quot.)

1893 M. A. OWEN *Old Rabbit* 71 He hid himself in a thicket of plums and burning bush (bittersweet).

burning fluid. (See quots. 1932.) Also **burning fluid lamp.** Now *hist.*

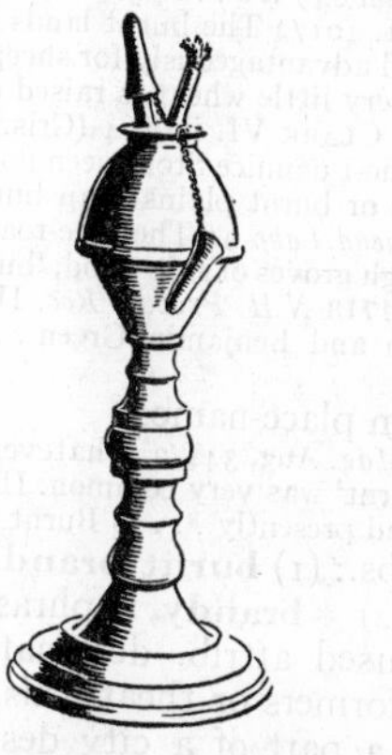

Burning fluid lamp *c*1840, forerunner of the kerosene lamp

1855 *Mass. Acts & Resolves* 903 Establishments for the manufacture of camphene or burning fluid. **1887** *Courier-Journal* 16 Jan. 14/2 We used 'burning fluid' and camphine lamps in those days. **1932** *Old-Time N. Eng.* Oct. 61/2 'Camphene' (burning fluid) lamps had a bad reputation for explosiveness, particularly if a little ether was a part of the mixture. *Ib.* 62/2 Burning Fluids may be an American invention, as Isaiah Jennings of New York, in 1836, received a patent for 'a lamp used for burning compounds of alcohol and spirits of turpentine or other analogous mixtures.'

***Burnside,** *n.* Also **burnside.** [Gen. A. E. *Burnside* (1824–81).]

1. *pl.* (See quot. 1909.)

1881 RITTENHOUSE *Maud* 36 The two Lydston gentlemen came home on the same car with us. . . . The older one has *lovely* burnsides. **1909** *Cent. Supp.* 177/3 *Burnsides,* . . . a style of beard such as that affected by General Burnside (1824–81), consisting of a mustache, whiskers, and a clean-shaven chin. **1945** *Reader's Digest* April 34 By 1890 beards and burnsides (sideburns are the same thing, only there isn't so much to them) were distinctly obsolete.

attrib. **1875** *Cin. Enquirer* 6 July 2/1 His whisker was of the Burnside type, consisting of mustache and 'mutton-chop,' the chin being perfectly clean. **1917** EATON *Green Trails* 197 He had ample Burnside whiskers which gave him a most benevolent expression.

2. A type of breech-loading carbine invented by A. E. Burnside, in full **Burnside carbine.** *Obs.*

1899 WYETH *Forrest* 174 The five-shooters of the Second Michigan, and the rapidity with which the Burnside carbine could be loaded, poured . . . a constant and deadly volley into their ranks. **1901** MONTGOMERY *Reminiscences* 68 They were armed with Burnsides, a better gun than mine.

3. *attrib.* Designating or pertaining to a hat of a style worn by Gen. Burnside. *Obs.*

1866 F. KIRKLAND *Bk. Anecdotes* 169 A stalwart descendant of the Nubian race, . . . his Burnside hat surmounted with a feeble plagiarism of the 'Prince's feather.' **1866** SHANKS *Recollections* 56 The hat which he generally wears is of the same order of faded 'regulation,' with the crown invariably puffed out instead of being pushed in, in

Burnsides or sideburns

the 'Burnside style.' **1881** VAWTER *Prison Life* 33 But my neat, soft felt hat of the Burnside pattern, was lifted off my head by a long-haired fellow, who gave me in exchange his C.S. regulation tile.

* **burnt,** *a.*

1. Denoting a place or area over which fire has swept, as **burnt bluff, land, plain, slash, swamp.**

1807 GASS *Journal* 249 We . . . proceeded on to the burnt bluffs. — **1811** *Niles' Reg.* I. 101/2 The burnt lands of many neighbourhoods could be employed advantageously for sheep walks. **1864** *Rep. Agric. Soc. Maine* 25 Very little wheat is raised except on burnt land. — **1804–6** LEWIS & CLARK VI. ii. 164 (Cris.), The Tract of Country which furnishes the Pummice Stone seen floating down the Missouri, is rather burning or burnt plains than burning mountain. — **1882** HUBBARD *Moosehead Lake* 94 The tote-road . . . is as a whole quite good, lying through groves of soft-wood, 'burnt-slash,' and over hard-wood ridges. — **1718** *N.H. Probate Rec.* II. 5, I give and bequeath to my sons John and Benjamin Green . . . my land in the burnt swamp.

b. (*cap.*) In place-names.

1880 *Harper's Mag.* Aug. 344/2 Whatever had happened to justify it, the prefix 'burnt' was very common. He came now . . . to Burnt Thoroughfare, and presently . . . to Burnt Cove.

2. In combs.: (1) **burnt brand,** *W.* a changed or defaced brand; (2) * **brandy,** in phrase (see quots.), *colloq.*; (3) * **cork,** used attrib. designating or pertaining to blackface performers or theatricals, also **burnt-corker;** (4) **district,** a part of a city destroyed by a fire; (5) **Burnt Thighs,** the Brûlé Indians, also attrib.; (6) **tongue,** =**black tongue;** (7) **wheat coffee,** a coffee substitute made of roasted wheat; (8) **wood,** see **Bois-brûlé,** *obs.*

(1) **1890** *Stock Grower* 5 July 5/4 The Nolan and Fisher Live Stock association is doing some good work in ferreting out burnt brands. — (2) **1836** CROCKETT *Adventures* 18 It must be done soon, or even burnt brandy wouldn't save me. **1894** SEARIGHT *Old Pike* 150 It was often lighted by a taper and burnt, under the influence of a popular tradition that 'if burnt brandy couldn't save a man' in need of physical tension, his case was hopeless. — (3) **1863** *Chicago Post* 27 Sep., This favorite troupe of burnt cork performers . . . commence the fall season in Metropolitan Hall, Monday evening. **1880** E. JAMES *Negro Minstrel's Guide* 10 A pair of legs such as Nelse Seymour had and Cool Burgess has are great attractions in a burnt-cork artist. **1890** BIFF HALL *Turnover Club* 124 To cast aside the air of unseemly hilarity which had characterized the recent visit of the burnt-corkers. **1895** *N.Y. Dramatic News* 20 July 5/3 In the vaudeville there are no more amusing . . . features than those introduced by . . . versatile burnt cork comedians. — (4) **1839** *Spirit of Times* 138/3 (We.), The Exchange is most finished . . . and is situated in what they call the burnt district. **1904** T. WELLS *Life Dr. Wilson* vii. 3 What the Americans call, in Western phrase, 'a burnt district.'

(5) **1846** SAGE *Rocky Mt. Life* (1859) 130 While there a dog-soldier of the Burnt-thighs received the offer of six horses from an Oglalla brave for his only daughter. **1937** DOUGLAS *Amer. Bk. of Days* 397 In addition to these contests members of the Burnt Thigh tribe of the Sioux Indians participate in the celebration [of Frontier Day in Wyoming] with native dances and the like. — (6) **1820** *Plough Boy* I. 255 The disease called the Burnt Tongue has lately made its appearance among the cattle in Baltimore county, Md. **1834** [see **black tongue**]. — (7) **1940** RIESENBERG *Golden G.* 44 Before he had visited many of the ships, burnt-wheat coffee, frijoles, and *gistado* had lost their taste. — (8) **1827** COOPER *Prairie* iv. 'Am I a fool not to know a burnt-wood Teton?' demanded the trapper. *Ib.* vii, You think to escape the craft and hatred of the burnt-wood Indians. **1848** RUXTON in *Blackw. Mag.* LXIV. 141 The Indians . . . were mostly of the Sioux nation, including the tribes of Burnt-woods, Yanka-taus, Pian-Kashas, Assinaboins, Oglallahs, Broken Arrows, all of which belong to the great Sioux nation.

burnwood ˈbɜnˌwʊd, *n.* [Origin obscure.] (See quots.) — **1889** *Cent.* 4588/1 poisonwood, a small poisonous tree, *Rhus Metopium,* of the West Indies and southern Florida . . . [which is] also called *burn wood.* **1897** SUDWORTH *Arborescent Flora* 277 *Cyrilla racemiflora,* Ironwood. . . . Common names [include] . . . He Huckleberry (N.C., S.C.), Burnwood (N.C.), Burnwood Bark (S.C.).

* **burr,** *n.* [f. various sources, placed together here for convenience.]

1. Flour ground by burr millstones. *Rare.*

1773 WASHINGTON *Writings* (1931) III. 109, I have now a vessell waiting . . . to take in flour. . . . Perhaps there may be about 200 barr'ls of super fine burr; 50 of midling do.

2. In combs.: (1) **burr-flower,** any one of various species of waterleaf; (2) **burr potato,** (see quots.), *obs.*

(1) **1817–8** EATON *Botany* (1822) 311 *Hydrophyllum virginicum,* burr-flower. . . . The flowers have the appearance of a burr several weeks before they expand. **1839** in *Mich. Agric. Soc. Trans.* VII. 409 *Hydrophyllum canadense,* Rough burr-flower. — (2) **1839** COLEMAN *Mass. Agric. Rep.* 88 The first seven rows were planted with the Burr or flesh-coloured potatoes. **1849** EMMONS *Agric. N.Y.* II. 41 Flesh-color or Burr Potato. . . . It will be observed that this potato contains less starch than many others in common use.

Burrier's oak. =**Bartram('s) oak.** *Obs.*

1813 H. MUHLENBERG *Cat. Plants* 87 *Quercus heterophylla,* (Burrier's oak) various-leav'd oak. **1817–8** EATON *Botany* (1822) 418 Burrier's oak. . . . Pursh says there is but one individual of this species known in the world, which is now growing on the Bartram plantation near Philadelphia. **1897** SUDWORTH *Arborescent Flora* 178 Bartram oak . . . common names [include] . . . Burriers Oak (Lit.).

Burrism ˈbɜˌɪzəm, *n.* The political views of Aaron Burr. *Obs.* — **1806** *Ann. 9th Congress* 1 Sess. 13 March 775, I will take gentlemen on another principle — on the principle of Burrism, as it is called. *Ib.* 776 Are we for administering the Government on principles of Burrism? **1808** *Ann. 10th Congress* 1 Sess. I. 1321 Mr. G[ardenier] was no advocate of Burrism; nor was he one of those opposed to General Wilkinson for putting down Burrism.

Burrite ˈbɜˌaɪt, *n.* A political adherent of Aaron Burr (1756–1836). *Obs.*

1802 *Balance* (Hudson, N.Y.) 10 Aug. 250 (Th.), Burrites! Clintonians! Democrats! hear me for my family. **1841** FOOTE *Texas & Texans* I. 148 Blennerhasset's Journal . . . asserts . . . that they were both *Burrites.* **1883** *Cent. Mag.* Apr. 859/1 There is a fourth description of men, commonly called *Burrites.*

burro ˈbɜo, *n. S.W.* [Sp. in sense 1. An Amer. borrowing.]

1. A donkey. Also attrib.

1844 GREGG *Commerce of Prairies* I. 187 The chief riding animal of the peasant is the *burro,* upon which saddle, bridle, or halter, is seldom used. **1929** A. ELLIS *Life* 21 Two other prospectors followed them two days later with their burros and prospecting outfit. **1948** *Pacific Discovery* Mar.–Apr. 26/2 Burro trips into the mountains for hunting and collecting of specimens are inexpensive.

2. In special combs.: (1) **burro bush,** (see quot. and cf. **burroweed**); (2) **deer,** (see quot. 1917); (3) **school,** (see quot.); (4) **weed,** *W.* loosely applied to various plants on the range, considered palatable to burros (see quots.).

(1) **1940** JAEGER *Desert Wild Flowers* 279 Burro bush is our second most widespread and dominant xeric plant, . . . erroneously it is generally called burro *weed.* **1946** *Sierra Club Bul.* Dec. 18 Even burro bushes look dead and cacti shrivel. — (2) **1895** REMINGTON *Pony Tracks* 130 After hunting down the valley for a few days for 'burro deer' and wild turkey, we found that the tobacco was promptly giving out. **1917** *Mammals of Amer.* 15 Burro Deer, or Desert Mule Deer. *Odocoileus hemionus eremicus* (Mearns.) Very pale, large, with heavy horns. Western Desert Tract of the United States. **1943** CAHALANE *Meeting the Mammals* 18 The Canadian hunters call him also 'muley deer,' the Utah prospectors 'burro deer,' and the Mexican rancheros 'venado burro.' — (3) **1885** *Weekly New Mexican* (Santa Fe) 9 Apr. 4/6 Marsh & Co. have opened a burro school at the Las

Vegas hot springs, and will furnish tourists with burro transportation when they want to fool away an idle day in mountain climbing. — (4) **1913** WOOTON *Trees & Shrubs N.M.* 64 Burro Weed (*Allenrolfea occidentalis*) is a very peculiar, almost leafless alkali-loving shrub with cylindrical jointed green succulent branches. **1929** CHALFANT *Death Valley* 80 *Franseria dumosa*—Burro weed, sand bur. **1947** *Desert* Feb. 17/1 *C*[*uscuta*]. *denticulata* favors creosote bush, burro-weed, etc.

As the last term in **muskrat burro, pack burro.**

* **burrowing,** *a.* In combs.: (1) **burrowing owl,** a prairie owl, *Speotyto cunicularia hypuogaea,* found chiefly in the western states, often living in burrows of prairie dogs; (2) **squirrel,** any one of various western ground squirrels of the genus *Citellus;* (3) **wasp,** any one of various wasps, as the digger wasp, that build their nests in burrows and provision them.

(1) **1820** E. JAMES *Exped. Rocky Mts.* III. (1823) 285 Mr. Peale killed a burrowing owl. **1948** *Pacific Discovery* Mar.–Apr. 18/2 Much of the present park area was rolling sand dunes, dotted, no doubt, with clumps of lupine and inhabited by burrowing owls. — (2) **1805** LEWIS in *L. & Clark Exped.* (1904) II. 301 In the course of the day they passed some villages of burrowing squirrels. **1868** *Amer. Naturalist* II. 532 The 'burrowing squirrel' of Lewis and Clarke . . . was undoubtedly . . . founded on at least two distinct animals. — (3) **1884** *Rep. Comm. Agric.* 400 Among the few insects that destroy the worms in this State, several species of burrowing wasps are quite conspicuous.

bursom ˈbɜsəm, *n.* [Origin unknown.] (See quot.) — **1853** *Harper's Mag.* VI. 580/2 At each stage of the process [=the extraction of copper] there is a quantity of refuse matter, or poor-stuff, which is wheeled off in barrows to the *bursom,* or waste pile. This is also the term for a similar deposit of poor-stuff from the mine.

***burst,** *n.* As the last term in **cloud burst, sand burst, sun burst.**

***burster,** *n.* See ***buster,** *n.*

* **bursting,** *n.* **1.** Bankruptcy. Also **bursting up.** *Obs.* **2. bursting heart,** the burning bush, *Euonymus atropurpureus.*

(1) **1834** CLAY *Cong. Deb.* 27 Feb. 747 You must lend us $300,000, to prevent a general bursting. **1846** in *Amer. Sp.* XXIII. (1948) Feb. 44/1 This is to be extended into a 'Daily Prandial Gazette,' and furnished to each guest with the soup, containing the arrivals of the day at the hotel, the range of the thermometer, the prospect of rain, 'burstings-up' in Wall street. — (2) **1866** *Land We Love* (Charlotte, N.C.) May 80 Bursting Heart. . . . The bright crimson berries of this plant, open their embossed covering into four leaves, and display within the smooth scarlet seeds, which gives it the name of bursting heart. **1883** HALE *Woods & Timbers N.C.* 165 Strawberry Bush . . . [is] a shrub 2 to 5 feet high, found in all the Districts, and known by the names of Burning Bush, Fish-wood, and Bursting Heart.

burthenage ˈbɜðənɪdʒ, *n.* An impost levied on transported goods. *Rare.* — **1725** G. CHICKEN in *Travels Amer. Col.* 128 The Traders are obliged to pay double burthenage for every Pack.

***burthened,** *a.* Having a capacity of, capable of carrying (so much cargo). *Obs.* — **1704** *Boston News-Letter* 22 May 2/2 Arrived here this Day the Sloop Mary, . . . from New-York, burthen'd about 40 Tuns. **1723** *Weekly Mercury* 19 Sep. 2/2 The ship Globe, . . . burthened about 150 tons. **1761** *Essex Inst. Coll.* XLVIII. 94 A Snow burthened about one hundred and seventy Tons.

burthener ˈbɜðənɚ, *n.* One who carries a burden, a burden-bearer. *Obs.* — **1725** G. CHICKEN in *Travels Amer. Col.* 105 This Opportunity happening by two Burtheners who are going to Mr. Hasford's Cowpen, I thought it would be proper to acquaint your Honour of my Arrival. *Ib.* 128, I am Sorry to hear that its so hard for our Traders to get Burtheners among you.

***burthensome,** see **burdensome.**

***bury,** *v.* **1.** *tr. To bury the hatchet, tomahawk,* see these nouns. **2.** *intr.* Of a vessel: To dip or submerge the bows. — (2) **1886** *Outing* Nov. IX. 117/1 It was asserted that she [*sc.* keel schooner] was too fine forward, . . . that she would bury in driving hard.

* **burying,** *n.* In combs.: (1) **burying cloth,** a cloth for covering the coffin at a funeral, *obs.;* (2) **lot,** =**burial lot;** (3) * **place,** a storage place or cache for baggage, canoes, etc., *obs.;* (4) **yard,** a cemetery, graveyard.

(1) **1729** *Manchester Rec.* 176 It was voted that the present Select men shall provide a Desant buring [*sic*] Cloth at the Charge of ye town. **1777** *Smithtown Rec.* 49, I also bequeath to the town of Setauket a burying cloth to be purchased for them by my executors. — (2) **1848** *Hunt's Merch. Mag.* XIX. 569 This burying lot . . . has been neglected for many years. **1882** *Harper's Mag.* Dec. 129/2 One golden bright afternoon, quite a crowd was assembled around the little burying-lot in the orchard. — (3) **1807** GASS *Journal* 101 We finished the burying place, so that we will be ready to start as soon as Capt. Clarke returns. **1808** F. CUMING *Western Tour* 415 When we came to the falls of Sandusky, we buried our birch bark canoes . . . at a large burying place for that purpose. — (4) **1664** *Conn. Hist. Soc. Coll.* VI. 144 He is at no time to sufer hoogs to com in to the s[ai]d bering yard nor to foder catel in it. **1770** in *N.H. Hist. Soc. Coll.* IV. 127 The burying yard should be cleared, and fenced with a good and sufficient board fence. **1846** *Hunt's Merch. Mag.* XIV. 243 In the burying yard of Plattsburgh there is a group of little grave-stones.

bus boy, girl. A boy or girl who clears away the dishes in an eating place.

The *OED* shows *omnibus* in this use from 1888. The expressions here given may not be American in origin.

1913 *Industrial Worker* (Spokane) 12 June 4/2 They are cooks, bus boys, dishwashers. **1945** *New Yorker* 6 Jan. 16 During a particularly hazardous lunch hour, a bus girl in an automat was heard to say to a teammate, 'I'm gettin' outta this job the end of the week.' **1948** *Atlantic Mo.* Jan. 105/1 I'm a bus boy at the Hotel Hibiscus.

As the last term in **auto, hotel, school, trolley bus.**

* **bush,** *n.* [In sense **1.** app. directly f. Du. *bosch, busch.*]

1. The wilderness or uncleared forest, often with *the.*

[**1657** *Doc. Rel. to Col. Hist. New-York* (tr.) XII. 168 The Commander again told me to leave and that the land was his . . . ; I therefore called on Hudde to survey for me a piece of land, situate there (Southriver, New-Netherland) in the bush.] **1779** S. LOVELL *Jrnl. Penobscot Exped.* (1881) 102 The Gentlemen took to the Bush and escaped being made prisoners. **1827** BEAUFOY *Tour* 79, I there [*sc.* N.Y.] had an opportunity of seeing the wilderness or 'bush,' untouched by man, and in all its solemn magnificence. **1890** RYAN *Told in Hills* 191 From their tones one would gather the impression that all the splendors of a metropolis were as nothing when compared with the luxuries of 'shack' life in the 'bush.' **1948** *Canadian Alpine Jrnl.* June 39 He followed the Kwadacha River, and was forced in the end to make a cross country journey through the bush.

b. In *pl.* in the same sense.

[**1677** W. HUBBARD *Indians in New-England* I. 37 Captain Beers . . . with Thirty six men . . . before they came very near to the Town . . . were set upon by many hundreds of the Indians out of the Bushes by a Swamp-side. **1743** C. WEISER in *Penna. Col. Rec.* IV. 661, I, with Shikellimo, visited Canassatego, desired him to meet Us in the Bushes to have a private Discourse. . . . We met a little way distant from the Town.] **1879** TOURGEE *Fool's Errand* 130 That refuge of free thought at the South, the woods (or 'the bushes,' as the scraggly growth is more generally termed).

2. A grove of sugar maple trees where sugar-making is carried on.

[**1782** ZEISBERGER *Diary* I. (1885) 76 (tr.), The whites were for the most part making sugar in the bush.] **1823** COOPER *Pioneer* II. i. 12 The underwood had been entirely removed from this grove, or bush, as, in conjunction with the simple arrangements for boiling, it was called. **1919** CUNNINGHAM *Chronicle* 281 It was good sap: sweeter than that of the trees growing in the thick of the bush.

3. *pl.* In baseball, the minor leagues. Cf. **bush league.**

1910 *Amer. Mag.* July 91/2 The scouts returned from the deepest part of the 'bushes' proclaiming that the crop was poor. **1948** *Dly. Ardmoreite* (Ardmore, Okla.) 28 April 9/8 Some smart baseball men deep in the bushes aren't too happy about 1948 prospects.

Bush arbor or brush arbor

4. In miscellaneous combs.: (1) **bush arbor,** a temporary shelter or shade made of boughs, bushes, etc., usu. for holding a bush meeting, also attrib.; (2) **fighter,** one who engages in bush fighting, *obs.;* (3) **fighting,** fighting from behind trees, rocks, etc., also transf. and attrib.;

(4) **hook,** a heavy scythe-like hook or bill for clearing away underbrush; (5) **league,** in baseball, a minor league including semiprofessional teams, also transf.; (6) **leaguer,** a baseball player who plays in a bush league, also transf.; (7) **loper,** see as a main entry; (8) **meeting,** a religious meeting held in a forest or grove; (9) **pasture,** a pasture composed of uncleared woodland, *obs.;* (10) * **ranger,** see as a main entry; (11) **whack,** (*a*) a tool for cutting bushes or shrubs, (*b*) making one's way through timber where there is no trail by brushing aside the bushes, etc.

(1) **1848** E. BRYANT *California* 457 The hill-sides were thickly strewn with canvas tents and bush arbors. **1904** HARBEN *Georgians* 3 He raised a regular bedlam at the bush-arbor meetin' below town. **1943** OTTLEY *New World* 95 Daddy Grace . . . was considered a 'bush arbor' preacher until he crashed the urban circuit! — (2) **1760** WESLEY *Jrnl.* 22 Nov. (1827) III. 27 If it should happen, that any one of these silly bush-fighters steps out into the plain. **1840** HOFFMAN *Greyslaer* I. 116 If it means an old bushfighter, there's no man in all Tryon county . . . , but must knock under to old Balt in expayrience. — (3) **1758** *Essex Inst. Coll.* XVIII. 101, I improved this Day Chiefly in the exercise of Bush Fiting. *Ib.* 187 The Rangers exercise in Scout Marches and Bush fighting. **1783** STOKES *View* 141 They [i.e., the Crackers] are equally skilled in the arts of bush fighting, and discovering the enemy by their tracks. **1860** HOLMES *Professor* ii. 45 A barren interchange of courtesies, or a bush-fighting argument. — (4) **1813** T. B. HAZARD *Nailer Tom's Diary* (1930) 339/1 Thomas Champlin . . . took his bush hook and paid for it Cotten yearn. **1884** ROE *Nature's Story* 3 The angular fields, . . . marked by trees and shrubs that, in their earlier life, ran the gauntlet of the bush-hook.

(5) **1909** *Collier's* 15 May 15 Rockford is in the bush leagues. **1944** *Reader's Digest* Oct. 55/1 They have left the political bush leagues and are now in the majors. **1948** *Chi. Tribune* 25 Mar. I. 22/3 In 2,000,000 years—a split second in infinity—Mount Baldy, a bush league mountain in San Bernardino county, would be as high as Mount Whitney. — (6) **1907** SMITH *Basket Ball Guide* 19 Serious cause for complaint and concern has lately arisen from the conduct of a certain set of worthies styling themselves 'the Bush Leaguers.' **1945** *Chi. D. News* 27 June 12/3 You may think Sherlock Holmes was pretty good, but he is just a bush leaguer compared to the modern detective. — (8) **1863** *Young Parson* 175 She jined the last camp-meetin' I had, or rather last *bush*-meetin'. **1942** WARNICK *Dialect Garrett Co., Md.* 4 Bush-meeting, n., religious services held in a grove. — (9) *a***1817** DWIGHT *Travels* II. 460 The proprietor is always ready to sell: for he loves this irregular . . . life, and hates the sober industry . . . by which his bush pasture is changed into a farm. **1844** *Knickerb.* XXIV. 300 It was a little Dutch cow, she was in our bush-pasture, and it was a very dry summer.

(11) (*a*) **1865** *Atlantic Mo.* XV. 521 It is so far escaping from the axe and the bushwhack as to have opened communication with the forest and mountain beyond by straggling lines of Cedar, Laurel, and Blackberry. (*b*) **1946** *Sierra Club Bul.* Dec. 121 The descent by the cable and long bushwhack back to camp may be avoided by an enjoyable 800-foot rappel starting somewhat to the north of the climbing route.

b. In less frequent combs., often rare or obs.: (1) **bush beater,** [cf. Du. *boschklopper*, a highwayman], = **bushwhacker 1;** (2) **country,** unsettled country; (3) **fence,** (see quot. and cf. **brush fence**); (4) **field,** (see quot.); (5) **fight,** a fight from behind trees, rocks, etc., in the forest; (6) **fire,** the shots of bushfighters; (7) **firing,** exchange of shots by bushfighters; (8) **hammer,** [app. f. G. *bosshammer*], a hammer with a serrated face for dressing stone; (9) **house,** a brush shelter or ambush; (10) **hut,** a hut made of bushes or boughs; (11) **knife,** = **bush hook;** (12) **light,** (see quot.); (13) **lot,** a lot or area of uncleared land; (14) **pond,** a pond in the bush or among bushes; (15) **shanty,** a shanty of bushes or boughs; (16) **tea,** a tea made of some variety of bush or plant; (17) **tent,** a temporary shelter made of bushes or boughs, cf. **brush tent.**

(1) **1809** IRVING *Knickerb.* VI. iv, Such was the legion of sturdy bush-beaters that poured in at the grand gate of New-Amsterdam. — (2) **1855** SIMMS *Forayers* 544 Who would have thought of any fellow being such a bloody booby as to bring a bathing-tub and chamber crockery into a pond and bush country? — (3) **1790** S. DEANE *N. Eng. Farmer* (1790) 92/1 Bush fences are sometimes made by piling bushes, or small trees with the limbs on them; finished with cross stakes and riders. — (4) **1857** HAMMOND *Northern Scenes* 147 On my father's farm was a bush field, a place that had been chopped and burned over, and then left to grow up with bushes.

(5) **1758** S. THOMPSON *Diary* (1896) 8 Ye general had given leave for four or five hundred Rangers to go out and hold a bush fight for 1/4 of an hour. — (6) **1761** S. NILES *Indian Wars* II. 435 The enemy . . . were beaten back by the bush-fire of Lieutenant Stark and his party. — (7) **1779** *N.J. Archives* 2 Ser. III. 578 A constant bush-firing then commenced, in which capt. Tyler . . . was killed, and several privates wounded. — (8) **1885** *Harper's Mag.* Mar. 558/1 They took the bush hammer out . . . that the ladies might see the varieties with five, six, eight or ten edges, which gave the granite the slightly lined or ridged appearance. — (9) **1834** C. A. DAVIS *Lett. J. Downing* 367 Saratogue, for politicians, is jist like the bush-houses for killing pigeons.

(10) **1775** S. THAYER *Journal* (1867) 12 Our troops . . . had not the satisfaction or conveniency to build ourselves . . . a Bush hut to pass the tedious night in. — (11) **1851** *Florida Plant. Rec.* 439 Rec'd 6 scooter Ploughs, three axes and one Bush knife . . . and eight turn

Bush tent, brush tent, or Indian tent

ploughs. — (12) **1836** C. GILMAN *Recoll.* (1838) xi. 82 A bush-light was flaming near Jacque's habitation. [*Note.*] A fire of light wood kindled on a small mound of earth. — (13) **1694** *Conn. Prob. Rec.* 497 Orchards, Gardens and Yards, and a pasture, Plow Land and Bush Lott. — (14) **1897** *Outing* XXX. 434/1 The crawfish . . . were very abundant in the shallow water at the river-banks, in the creeks, and in certain bush-ponds.

(15) **1857** HAMMOND *Northern Scenes* 169 Crop crept close alongside of me, in our bush-shanty. — (16) **1768** *Holyoke Diaries* 30 Began to take Bush Tea. [**1777** *N.C. Morav. Rec.* III. (1926) 1193 The Council was consulted about the Lovefeasts, for coffee, tea and sugar have become very expensive; it is suggested that bush-tea and barley-coffee be used.] — (17) **1758** L. LYON in *Mil. Jrnls.* (1855) 16 We Lodged in Bush tents and very wet it was.

c. In the names of plants: (1) **bush bean,** a dwarf bean, as *Phaseolus vulgaris;* (2) **blackberry,** a species of blackberry, *Rubus trivialis,* found in the southern states; (3) **clover,** any one of various plants, usu. of an upright habit, of the genus *Lespedeza;* (4) **cranberry,** = **cranberry tree;** (5) **honeysuckle,** any one of various shrubs of the genus *Diervilla*, esp. *D. lonicera,* having yellow flowers; (6) * **poppy,** (see quot. 1869); (7) **squash,** the summer squash, so called from its short vine.

(1) **1821** *Plough Boy* II. 358/3 An opinion prevails here (Columbus, Ohio) that our soil is *too rich,* for the profitable culture of the *bush bean,* (called, I believe, at the eastward, the *fisher bean*). **1887** *Harper's Mag.* Jan. 307/2 Those who need much instruction in regard to bush-beans should remain in the city. — (2) **1899** VANDERBILT *Flatbush* 293 These running blackberries were known as dewberries, and were much larger and sweeter than the 'bush blackberry,' as, for distinction, those were called. — (3) **1817–8** EATON *Botany* (1822) 335 *Lespedeza sessiliflora,* bush clover. . . . Var. *reticulata.* **1939** *Nat. Geog. Mag.* Aug. 222/1 The ubiquitous pea family is represented by a number of tick trefoils and bush clovers, but of greater interest are the trailers, the groundnut with its brown-purple clusters and sweet tubers. — (4) **1835** PARKER *Exploring Tour* (1838) 203 The pambina is a bush cranberry. **1843** TORREY *Flora N.Y.* I. 307 *Viburnum opulus,* . . . Bush Cranberry or High Cranberry. . . . The acid fruit is sometimes used as a substitute for cranberries.

(5) **1817–8** EATON *Botany* (1822) 266 *Diervilla canadensis,* bush honeysuckle. . . . Variable in size, 1 foot to 6. **1944** HOLTON *Yankees* 84 The perfume of bush honeysuckle and sweet pepper from the swamps on the landward side of the road. — (6) **1869** MUIR *First Summer in Sierra* (1911) 51 A marked plant is the bush poppy (*Dendromecon rigidum*), found on the hot hillsides near camp, and the only woody member of the order I have yet met in all my walks. **1942** VAN DERSAL *Ornamental Amer. Shrubs* 240 Found also in southern California,

and often rated as one of the ten best native shrubs of that state, is the bushpoppy. — (7) **1897** R. M. Stuart *Simpkinsville* 146 Reckon I'll plant bush-squash myself after this.

d. In the names of or with reference to animals: (1) **bush bird,** (see quot.); (2) **rat,** a species of wood rat; (3) **sheep,** (see quot.); (4) **sparrow,** the song sparrow or the field sparrow; (5) **tit(mouse),** (see quot. 1889).

(1) **1939** *Nat. Geog. Mag.* March 353 Most people know it, but not everyone calls it 'towhee.' Many speak of it as 'brown bird' and others call it 'bush bird.' — (2) **1867** *Amer. Naturalist* I. 399 The Bush Rat. (*Neotoma Mexicana*) is abundant throughout the Territory [Ariz.], and forms no small item in the economy of the Indians. — (3) **1867–8** *Ill. Agric. Soc. Trans.* VII. 457 Sheep shipped in for sale because they 'didn't flourish' on prairie grass. These 'bush sheep,' as they are called, have been in abundant supply. — (4) **1858** *Atlantic Mo.* Oct. 594/2 In several localities these two species [the song sparrow and vesper bird] are distinguished by the names of Bush-Sparrow and Ground-Sparrow, from their supposed different habits of placing their nests, one on a bush and the other on the ground. **1869** Burroughs in *Galaxy* Aug. 139/2 A favourite sparrow of my own . . . is the wood, or bush-sparrow, usually called *spizella pusilla.*

(5) **1881** *Amer. Naturalist* XV. 213 At Colton, Cal., I first found the nest of that diminutive little bird, the least bush titmouse (*Psaltriparus minimus*). **1889** *Cent.* 732/2 bush-tit. . . . An American oscine passerine bird, of the genus *Psaltriparus* and family *Paridae.* There are several species in the western United States and Mexico. **1948** *Pacific Discovery* Mar.–Apr. 15/2 The bush-tits constructed their gray, pouch-shaped nest in a bride tree (*Hoheria*) just outside the window.

5. In colloq. phrases meaning to surpass, excel, take first place, as (1) *To take the rag off the bush,* [cf. *EDD, to take the rag off the edge* in similar sense], (2) *to bang the bush,* (3) *to drag the bush up.*

(1) **1810** *Norfolk Gazette* 19 Sep. 2/3 (Th. Supp.), This 'takes the rag off the bush' so completely, that we suppose we shall hear no more . . . about the Chesapeake business. **1833** *Advocate* (Shelbyville, Ky.) 14 Sep. 3/5 Well, stranger, you can take the rag off the bush about the leetle cleanest I ever heard tell. **1871** De Vere 197 The fact that the improvised target is not unfrequently a rag hung on a bush, has suggested to Professor S. S. Haldeman the thought that the familiar phrase: 'That takes the rag off the bush,' may have likewise originated from the use of the rifle in the hands of the Western hunter. — (2) **1835–7** Haliburton *Clockmaker* 1 Ser. 52 That's a cap sheef that bangs the bush. **1848** W. E. Burton *Waggeries* 70 It happifies me to say that we bang the bush! — (3) **1845** J. J. Hooper *Simon Sugg's Adv.* xii. 142 That uther picture . . . kums nigher draggin the bush up by the roots an a most enny thing I ever seed.

As the last term in **amargoso, arrow, bayberry, bear's, bird-in-the, brittle, bubby, buck, buffalo, bullet, burning, burro, butter, button, calico, candy, deer, desert, elbow, fetter, fever, gall, goat, greased, greasewood, high, hobble, huckleberry, hurrah, indigo, jack, leatherwood, liberty, locust, maple, May, medicine, medlar, mesquite, moose, Osage orange, palmetto, papaw, partridge, pepper, persimmon, pineapple, pigeon berry, poke, pond, pucker, rabbit, sage, sap, sassafras, service-berry, shad, shot, skunk, snowball, sour berry, spice, squaw, stag, stagger, strawberry, sugar, tallow, tar, tie, toothache, wine bush.**

* **bush,** *v.* **1.** *To bush out,* to clear out or make (a road) through bush country. **2.** *To bush up,* (see quot. 1926). *Colloq.*

(1) **1851** Springer *Forest Life* 91 A road was bushed out to the spot where the poor creature lay. **1882** Hubbard *Moosehead Lake* 114 His guides 'bushed out' the old tote-roads where there were any, and cut new roads where none had before existed. — (2) **1926** *D.N.* V. 398 bush up, v. phr. To hide in the shrubbery. Tom he went an' *bushed up* down back o' th' church house. **1933** T. Williamson *Woods Colt* 178 'You tell your paw I'm goin' to bush up for a while,' he says.

bushed buʃt, *a.*

1. Tired, worn out. *Colloq.*

1870 *Nation* July 57/1 To be 'bushed' was to be tired [in Penna.]. **1885** M. D. Woodward in *Checkered Yrs.* (1937) 67 Walter owned, for once in his life, that he was nearly bushed. (That expression will not apply on our Dakota farm where there is not a bush on the whole two sections.) **1948** *Dly. Ardmoreite* (Ardmore, Okla.) 13 Apr. /44 Whew! I'm bushed!

2. Confused, bewildered, frightened by being in the woods.

1920 *Outing* Nov. 77/1 Soundless and wonderful he floated . . . through the unspeakable tangle that would have pulled you or me up in half-a-dozen yards, hopelessly 'bushed.' **1946** Stanwell-Fletcher *Driftwood Valley* 1 8 If I hadn't gone crazy 'bushed,' I knew that something alive was there, close to me, in the deep snowy woods.

bushel ˈbuʃl, *n.* [Origin obscure, cf. **bushel,** *v.*] **1.** (See quot.) **2. bushelman,** = **busheler. 3. bushelwoman,** (see quot.).

(1) **1889** *Cent.* 731/2 bush. . . . A tailor's thimble. Also called bushel. — (2) **1864** Webster 177/3. **1909** O. Henry *Options* 109 You would say he had been brought up a bushelman in Essex Street. **1948** *Chi. Tribune* 25 April 62/2 Help Wanted . . . Bushelman Experienced and Presser on Men's Clothing. — (3) **1889** *Cent.* 732/1 bushelwoman. . . . A woman who assists a tailor in repairing garments.

bushel ˈbuʃl, *v.* [?f. G. *bosseln,* to work carefully at a petty job.] *tr.* To repair or renovate garments (see quot. 1893). Also **busheling,** *a.*

1877 Bartlett 777 *To bushel,* . . . to repair garments. **1890** *Boston Transcript* 9 Sep., Returning from the country, you will find last winter's woollens . . . needing to be pressed, cleaned and repaired. Our Busheling Department employs twenty men who do nothing but attend to this class of work. **1893** in *Cong. Rec.* (1894) 8327/1 To allow [this building] to be 'busheled up' or repaired by a private purchaser would be to court inevitable disaster.

bushel-bean. (See quot.) *Obs.* — **1709** Lawson *Carolina* 76 Of the Pulse-kind, we have many sorts. The first is the Bushel-Bean, which is a spontaneous Product. They are so called, because they bring a Bushel of Beans for one that is planted. . . . The Bean is white and mottled, with a purple Figure on each side it, like an Ear.

busheler ˈbuʃlər, *n.* [f. **bushel,** *v.*] (See quots.)

1860 Worcester 184/2 *Busheller,* one who repairs garments for tailors. (Local, U.S.) *Dr. Gilman.* **1877** Bartlett 777 *Busheler, Bushelman,* . . . a tailor's assistant, whose business it is to repair garments.

b. (See quot.)

1948 *Sat. Ev. Post* 24 Jan. 44/3 Buckers and fallers . . . are known in the woods as bushelers.

busher ˈbuʃər, *n.* (See quot. 1912.) — **1912** *Amer. Mag.* June 200/2 Busher—A Major league term of scorn applied to players from the smaller leagues. **1948** *Life* 5 April 21/1 During the past several weeks these raw bushers . . . have been subjected to microscopic scrutiny for major-league aptitude.

bush hammer, *v. tr.* To dress (stone) with a bush hammer. — **1884** Knight *Dict. Mech. Supp. s.v.,* Roughpointing, tooth-axing, bush-hammering. *Ib.,* Sandstone is seldom bush-hammered, as the stunning makes it scale.

bushloper ˈbuʃˌlopər, *n.* = **bossloper.** Also transf. Now *hist.*

1694 in Munsell *Ann. Albany* II. 128 [That] there may be a company of buss Loopers raised to scour the cost for schulking partyes of the enemy. **1752** *Importance of Friendship* 17 By this means a number of *Bush-lopers,* as the Dutch call them, and the French, who are indefatigable in this point, *Coureurs de bois,* are created; a set of men, who from their acquaintance with the woods and Indians are very useful. **1893** Eggleston *Duffels* Pref. iii, The outfit of this young 'bushloper' . . . consisted mainly of a sort of cloth suited to Indian wants. **1926** Doudore *Prairie* 102 The most valuable single early record of the 'bush-lopers' in the lake country is Cadwallader Colden's *History of the Five Indian Nations.*

* **bushranger,** *n.* A frontiersman or borderer. Also * **bushranging,** *n.*

[**1758** *N.C. Morav. Rec.* I. (1922) 195 Outside of ordinary meal-times the following Brethern need butter: the night-watchman, the herdsmen, the Bush-Ranger sometimes, the threshers, and sometimes the carpenters.] **1830** H. H. Porter *Bethrothed of Wyoming* 171 Joseph's small party of bush-rangers, as they were called, were stationed in a valley about a mile distant. **1885** L. W. Spring *Kansas* 287 Quantrill, who led the raid, once lived in Lawrence—a dullish, sullen, uninteresting knave, giving no promise of unusual bushranging genius. **1947** *True* Nov. 107/1 Six canvas sacks, the remains left by the bushrangers, came by packhorse into Fairplay.

bushwhack ˈbuʃˌhwæk, *v.*

1. *intr.* To orate or harangue with vigorous gesticulations suggestive of a man chopping bushes. *Obs.*

1836 Crockett *Exploits* 17 So I mounted the stump that had been cut down for the occasion and began to bushwhack in the most approved style.

2. *intr.* and *tr.* (See quot. 1936.) Cf. **bushwhacking,** *n.* **1.**

1834 R. Baird *Valley Mississippi* vii. 60 Instead of spending many months in warping a barge, or 'cordelling' and 'poling,' and 'bushwhacking' a keelboat from New Orleans to Pittsburg . . . a steam boat now makes the voyage in fifteen or twenty days. **1861** Winthrop *Open Air* 84 Bushwhacking thus for a league, we circumvented the peril, and came upon the river flowing fair and free. **1936** Asbury *French Quarter* 76 In high water some were bushwhacked up the river—that is, the boat was kept close to shore, and the crew moved it along by pulling on the bushes which grew on the bank.

3. *tr.* To attack, fire upon (an enemy or game) in the manner of bushwhackers.

1866 C. H. SMITH *Bill Arp* 116 The truth is, that Confederate cavalry can fight 'em, and dog 'em, and dodge 'em, and bushwhack 'em, and bedevil 'em for a thousand years. **1874** LONG *Wild-Fowl* 133, I . . . jumped into a paddle-boat, paddled ashore, and proceeded to 'bushwhack' them [*sc.* ducks]. **1918** MULFORD *Bar-20* 193 Here he is over this end of th' trail an' givin' you a fine chance to sneak up an' bushwhack him.

4. *intr.* To dwell in, to prowl or search among, the bushes or forest. *Colloq.*

1868 *Putnam's Mag.* I. 22 An old Dutch Continental, Bushwhacked up there a spell. **1881** BUEL *Border Outlaws* 192 The three survivors bushwhacked about for some time, two of them eventually escaping. **1888** CRADDOCK *Broomsedge Cove* 428, I b'lieve we sarched every squar' mile fur ten mile, a-bushwhackin' fur 'em. **1889** MARK TWAIN *Conn. Yankee* xxv. 324 He knew something about . . . bushwhacking around for ogres.

bushwhacker ˈbʊʃˌhwækɚ, *n.*

1. A dweller in the backwoods, a frontiersman.

1809 IRVING *Knickerb.* II. 107 They were gallant bush-whackers and hunters of raccoons by moon-light. **1885** *Harper's Mag.* Sep. 519/2 The General was a natural bushwhacker, in the sense of having an intuitive knowledge of country.

b. One who bushwhacks a boat up a stream. Cf. **bushwhack,** *v.* **2.**

1942 HEREFORD *Old Man River* 99 Folks called those early boatmen bushwhackers, but they were a different breed than the outlaw bushwhackers you hear about.

2. A bill or hook for cutting bushes. Also fig.

*c***1849** PAIGE *Dow's Sermons* I. (B.), I know not the victim soon destined to fall before the keen-edged bushwhacker of Time, or I would point him out. **1870** EMERSON *Soc. & Sol.* 81 He is a graduate of the plough, and the stub-hoe, and the bushwhacker.

3. One who lurks in woods or thickets and carries on guerrilla warfare or engages in plundering. See also **rebel bushwhacker.**

This sense apparently originated during the Civil War.

1861 *N.Y. Herald* 21 Nov. 4/2 Nineteen bushwhackers arrived at Cincinnati . . . as prisoners. **1906** RIDLEY *Battles* 486 Champ Ferguson's company of Confederate Bushwhackers could place a ball at any given point. **1948** *Range Riders Western* May 109/1 Dusty Trail opened up with his .45–70 on the fast-shooting bushwhacker on the north bank.

b. *transf.* (See quots.)

1862 *Lawrence* (Kans.) *Republican* 11 Sep. 4/1 That faction of Democracy who sympathise with the rebels are known in Ohio as 'Vallandinghamers,' . . . in Missouri as 'butter-nuts,' in Kansas as 'jayhawkers,' in Kentucky as 'bushwhackers.' **1885** *Mag. Amer. Hist.* Jan. 99/1 *Bushwhacker*, in politics, as in war, simply a 'free-lance.' **1944** *Chi. D. News* 10 Jan. 6/1 [The] prewar isolationist and bushwhacker against the administration, was all set today to make an issue of the affair.

bushwhackerism ˈbʊʃˌhwækɚˌɪzəm, *n.* The principles and practices of bushwhackers. *Rare.* — **1883** *American* VI. 356 The 'border ruffianism' and the 'bushwhackerism' which disgraced Missouri.

bushwhacking ˈbʊʃˌhwækɪŋ, *n.*

1. Pulling a boat against the current by grasping bushes along the bank. *Obs.*

1826 T. FLINT *Recoll.* 86 We began to pull the boat up the stream, by a process, which in the technics of the boatmen [of the Miss. R.], is called bush-whacking. **1833** HAWKS *Hist. Western States* (1844) 30 When the waters are high, and the boat can run along under bushes on the river-bank, pulling up by the bushes, this is called 'bush-whacking.' **1941** DORSEY *Master of Miss.* 23 By this ancient device of 'bushwhacking,' the craft moved laboriously ahead.

b. Making one's way through unbroken forest by pushing aside bushes, etc. Cf. **bushwhack,** *n.* (*b*).

1945 *Sky Line Trail* June 5/1 A small amount of bushwhacking allows the visitor to make his way to camp over Odaray Plateau. **1948** *Sierra Club Bul.* March 122 About an hour of talus hopping and bush-whacking is necessary to reach the gulley at the base of the East Arrowhead Chimney where the route begins.

2. Carrying on guerrilla warfare, marauding. Also transf.

1841 *Cong. Globe* 8 Jan. 91 He again thanked the Senator—they should now have a fair contest, and no 'bush whacking.' **1845** *Ib.* App. 3 Feb. 152/1 All he asked for was a clear field and a fair fight—no *bushwhacking*, if he might be indulged in an expressive word, well understood in the border wars of the West; no masked batteries. **1862** *N.Y. Herald* 29 June (B.), We would be glad to meet any number of the Confederates in a fair fight; but this infernal bushwhacking shall not be practised on the men of my command. **1891** CRADDOCK in *Harper's Mag.* Feb. 368/1 He had been a brave soldier, although the flavor of bushwhacking clung to his war record.

bushwhacking ˈbʊʃˌhwækɪŋ, *a.* Practicing guerrilla warfare. Also transf.

1813 *Mass. Spy* 27 Jan. (Th.), These bush-whacking Yankees won't do. **1866** F. KIRKLAND *Bk. Anecdotes* 179 It was only a skirmish, a bushwhacking fight for the possession of a swamp. **1911** *Springfield W. Republican* 24 Aug. 8 It has been altogether a confusing, disturbing, bushwhacking session—a playing for party position and issues in a political war to come. **1947** *True* Nov. 106/2 [He] increased to $2,500 the reward offered by the Territory for the bushwhacking murder merchants, dead or alive.

bushy ˈbʊʃɪ, *n.* Prob. a guessing game involving forfeits, better known as "jack-in-the-bush." *Obs.* — **1873** L. S. PHELPS *Trotty's Wedding Tour* 23 She let him beat at 'Bushy' all the time.

* **bushy,** *a.* In the names of plants (see quots.).

1784 CUTLER in *Mem. Academy* I. 481 Bushy aster. Florets in . . . the center yellow. By fences. September. **1843** TORREY *Flora N.Y.* II. 46 *Gerardia Pedicularia*, . . . Bushy Gerardia, . . . [is] rather common throughout the State. *Ib.* 144 *Amaranthus Græcizans*, . . . Bushy Amaranth . . . [grows in] cultivated grounds, waste grounds, and road-sides; common. **1932** W. KELLEY *Inchin' Along* 6 From behind a clump of the bushy dogfennel came the giggle of a girl.

* **business,** *n.* In combs.: (1) **business block,** (*a*) a large building in which a business is carried on, (*b*) a city block occupied by business houses; (2) * **card,** (see quot. 1889); (3) **college,** a school where only commercial subjects are taught; (4) **doctor,** (see quot. 1909); (5) **end,** the effective or active part, the commercial aspect; (6) **girl,** = **business woman;** (7) **lot,** in a city a piece of land suitable for erecting business houses; (8) **notice,** = **business card;** (9) **office,** the office where the financial transactions and bookkeeping for a firm or institution are carried on; (10) **school,** = **business college;** (11) **store,** a general store; (12) **street,** a street along which business houses are located; (13) **suit,** a suit such as a business man usu. wears; (14) **woman,** a woman engaged or employed in business; (15) **world,** that portion of society concerned with business interests.

(1) (*a*) **1871** *Colo. Gazeteer* 375 Many of the residences and business blocks are large, well constructed, neatly painted, and tastefully ornamented. **1899** *Mo. So. Dakotan* I. 184 That year he erected the fine business block in Watertown which bears his name. (*b*) **1948** *Kankakee* (Ill.) *D. Jrnl.* 5 June 1/1 Fire swept sections of two Duluth business blocks today. — **(2) 1868** *Commercial and Financial Chronicle* VI. 333/2 The business card of Messrs. Gray, Prince & Co. . . . is published on the first page of this paper. **1889** *Cent.* 732/3 Business card . . . an advertisement in a public print, giving a tradesman's name and address, with particulars as to the nature of his business. — **(3) 1865** *Indianapolis D. Jrnl.* 14 Sep. 2/4 Hoosiers . . . are here as students in Bryant's Business College, which is conducted by Mr. T. J. Bryant. **1946** THOMPSON *Amer. Daughter* 148, I wanted to attend the local business college, but there was no money. — **(4) 1908** *Accountant* 8 Aug. 157/2 The method of so-called 'business doctors.' **1909** *Modern Business* Jan. 606/1 In America . . . there exists a body of men who are known as 'Business Doctors,' men who are called in to give advice upon the proper conduct of business.

(5) 1878 M. L. HOLBROOK *Hygiene of Brain & Nerves* 56 The business end of a carpet-tack. **1901** CHURCHILL *Crisis* 113 Just now they callate I'm about good enough to manage the business end of an affair like this here. **1933** HARRINGTON *Gypsum Cave, Nev.* 140 We have no perfect digging-sticks from Gypsum Cave, our specimens consisting merely of the 'business ends' of the implements, and one handle-end. — **(6) 1944** *Chi. Tribune* 17 Sep. v. 3/1 (*advt.*), Business girl will share modern 4 room apartment with same: reasonable. — **(7) 1871** *Colo. Gazeteer* 129 The town site was subdivided into 520 business lots, 25×190 feet. **1900** *Dly. Ardmoreite* (Ardmore, Okla.) 27 Aug. 4/3 These new rules provide that all business lots shall be 25×150 feet. — **(8) 1854** BUSCH *Wanderungen* I. 95 Da steht unter den *Business Notices* eines andern Blattes folgendes ergötzliche Beispiel. — **(9) 1849** *De Bow's Review* VII. 400 The accommodations for passengers and the business offices of the company [have been] materially improved. **1893** M. PHILIPS *Making of a Newspaper* 18 In this partial survey of the process and cost of making a 'mammoth newspaper,' no account has been taken of the business office, the mailing room, the foundry, and the press-room.

(10) 1916 *Nat. Educ. Assn. Addresses & Proc. 1915* 325 (*heading*), The Service of Business Schools at the Close of the Great War. **1948** *Chi. Maroon* 7 May 10/1 The curricula in many Business Schools consisted mainly of a series of more or less unrelated courses. — **(11) 1922** *Hotel Mo.* XXX. 57/2 Around the lobby is the writing room, the ladies' lounge, cafe, lunch room, cigar stand, and business stores. — (12) **1881** *Harper's Mag.* April 711/1 Its [i.e., Milwaukee's] broad, Nicholson-paved business streets are bounded for block after block with warehouses and offices. — (13) **1870** *Harper's Bazaar* 5 Nov. 707 High-crowned beaver hats are, however, used more than any other, with business suits as well as with those for more dressy occasions. **1948** J. L. LINKLATER *Bishop's Cap* 19 He was wearing a navy blue pin stripe business suit, but Daisy didn't think he was a business man. — (14) **1844** *S. Lit. Messenger* X. 486/1 Mrs. Jemima Jowers . . . had the universal reputation of being a 'business woman.' **1944** *Chi. Tribune* 17 Sep. v. 3/1 (*advt.*), Large, light room, with or without board; business woman preferred.

(15) **1837** *S. Lit. Messenger* III. 391 An extra-ordinary convulsion in the business-world prostrated his hopes.

As the last term in **big, bogus, cahoot, cotton, cow, dollar store, dry-goods, express, firing, forwarding, funny, land office, leg, lumber, lumbering, mail order, monkey, monkey-doodle, morning, Negro, oil, peanut, pork, running, saloon, spoils, through, turpentine business.**

busk bʌsk, *n.* [Creek *pûskita*, a fast.] An annual feast of first fruits held by the Creek Indians when green corn was ripe enough to eat.

1759 *Newport Mercury* 18 Sep. 3/1 A very fortunate Accident revealed a dangerous Conspiracy . . . to break out a War with the English, to begin it by a general Massacre of our Traders, at their great Busk or Greene-Corn-Dance, on the 24th Instant. **1842** E. A. HITCHCOCK *Journal* 116 The fire at the Round House is kept alive throughout the Busk. **1946** *Nat. Geog. Mag.* Jan. 59/1 A typical ceremony was the busk, or green corn, ceremony of the Creeks, a New Year's celebration.

***bust,** *n.*

1. A failure, a bankruptcy. *Colloq.*

1842 *Knickerb.* XX. 99 'A mistake!' exclaimed the other; 'not a bit of it! It's a reg'lar built bu'st!' **1931** *K.C. Times* 18 June, We have about came[*sic*] to the conclusion that politics as a means of providing sustenance is a complete 'bust.' **1947** *Chr. Sci. Monitor* 24 Jan. 1/1 We had an agricultural 'boom and bust' after the other World War.

2. A drinking bout or spree, esp. *on a bust.* Also fig. *Colloq.*

EDD records *burst*, "an outburst of drinking."

1843 *Ky. Yeoman* (Frankfort) 2 Jan. 4/3 I'll pay—d——n the expense, I say, when a fellow is on a bust. **1867** A. DALY *Legend of 'Norwood'* 35 The darned old thing [a clock] goes on a regular bust when it strikes. **1944** *Chi. D. News* 21 Oct. 4/1 You don't exactly figure that a display of gold sequins and flesh-colored foundations at a Hollywood bust is exactly a contribution toward winning the war.

***bust,** *v.* Also **burst.**

1. *intr.* To fail financially, become bankrupt. *Colloq.*

1833 W. J. SNELLING *Exposé of Gaming* 10 Two persons who had bursted were sitting vis a vis by the fire-place. **1868** ROSE *Great Country* 198, I shall do business with that man again, for though he busted he means honourable, I'm sure. **1904** O. HENRY *Cabbages & Kings* (1916) 146 'Twas the project of a private corporation, but it busted, and then the government took it up.

2. (See quots.)

1851 HALL *College Words* 33 *Burst*, to fail in reciting; to make a bad recitation. This word is used in some of the Southern colleges. **1900** *D.N.* II. 25 Bust, v.i. To fail in recitation or examination.

3. To go on "busts," to dissipate.

1866 C. H. SMITH *Bill Arp* 118 Ike was at home on a busting furlow. **1869** *N.O. Picayune* 14 Feb. (De Vere), I had to go with them, frolicking, . . . excursioning, and busting generally.

4. *W. tr.* To break or render (a horse) tractable.

1891 *Harper's Mag.* July 210/1 Two rides will usually bust a bronco so that the average cow-puncher can use him. **1941** *Nat. Geog. Mag.* March 300/1 He's too old now to bulldog a steer or bust a bronco.

b. (See quot.)

1929 DOBIE *Vaquero* 8, [I] tossed a half hitch over a post so that when she hit the end of the rope I held it without giving a foot and 'busted' her flat.

5. In colloq. phrases: (1) *To burst a cap*, (see quot.); (2) *to burst a bank*, to break the bank in gambling.

(1) **1846** *Spirit of Times* 18 April 91/2 You often hear this or that acquaintance speak of the misfortune of having '*bursted a cap*' at a five buck or other valuable game, meaning thereby, that the percussion cap on their gun exploded without igniting the powder in the barrel. — (2) **1850** RYAN *Adv. Calif.* II. 209 An experienced player from New Orleans . . . not only regained his former losses, but . . . bursted the bank.

***bustard,** *n.* The Canada goose, *Branta canadensis.*

[**1583** EDWARD HAIES *Narr. Exped. Sir H. Gylberte* (1903) 136 Foule both of water and land in great plentie and diuersitie. All kind of green foule: Others as bigge as Bustards, yet not the same. A great white foule called of some a Gaunt.] **1759** (tr.). VENEGAS *Nat. Hist. Calif.* I. 39 About the harbour of Monte-Rey are bustards . . . and other birds. **1804** in GATES *Fur Traders* 234 We saw Bustards to day for the first time. **1896** A. NEWTON *Dict. of Birds*, The distribution of the Bustards is confined to the Old World—the bird so-called in the Fur-Countries of North America, and thus giving its name to a lake, river, and cape, being the Canada Goose, *Bernicla canadensis.*

***busted,** *a.* Ruined, destitute, esp. financially. *Slang.*

1837 *Knickerb.* X. 170 I've hear'n tell since that he was a busted man. **1881** MARSHALL *Through Amer.* (1882) 114 When, however, a break-down occurred, a very different motto would be painted on the waggon-sheet, revealing the deplorable condition of the party, and this was, 'Busted, by thunder!' **1946** *Sat. Ev. Post* 11 May 55/2 When the war was over, Baltimore's good customer, the South, was busted.

***buster,** *n.* Also **burster.**

1. A spree or drinking frolic, esp. *on a buster.* Also one who goes on such a spree. *Slang. Obs.*

1831 *Boston Transcript* 26 Apr. 2/2 Now he is fairly initiated into the various grades of dissipation, and is looked upon as a 'Regular Burster.' **1848** BARTLETT 57 They were on a buster, and were taken up by the police. **1850** W. COLTON *3 Years Calif.* 290 You had some trouble with me in Monterey; I was on a burster.

2. (See quots.)

1879 *St. Nicholas Mag.* Nov., He [=young crab] still keeps on eating and gets bigger still, and then cracks a little, and is called a 'Crack-buster.' He still grows till he is called a 'Buster,' and then sheds. **1943** PENN *Ecology* XXIV. 11 As the crawfish [*Cambarus clarkii* Girard] grows beyond the limits of its hardened exoskeleton, a white 'waist' appears between the cephalothorax and the abdomen (this stage is termed the 'buster').

3. =**bronco buster.**

1891 *Harper's Mag.* July 208/1 The bronco buster . . . cannot stick it out very long, for the business is sure to end by busting the buster. **1914** BRININSTOOL *Trail Dust* 136 Who as a 'buster' was the boss? Could tame the wildest outlaw hawss? **1948** *Southwestern Rev.* Winter 26/2 As one buster told me, 'Ridin' the rough string ain't like attendin' a knittin' bee.'

As the last term in **bronco, middle, ridge, sod, trust, turkey buster.**

busthead ˈbʌstˌhɛd, *n.* Whisky of an inferior quality. Also attrib. *Slang.*

1857 *S.F. Call* 27 Feb. 4/1 A big strapping six-footer, full of 'bust head' and Dutch courage, . . . slapped his fists together, swearing he was 'spiling for a fight.' **1881** *Uniontown Press* 26 March 3/2 The merchants can supply you with anything from a pocket saw mill to bust-head liquor. **1935** *Amer. Mercury* May 106/1 The hunter . . . now spent most of his time on his back, and consoling himsef for the poorness of his shooting with a jug of what he himself had named 'busthead.'

bustic ˈbʌstɪk, *n.* [Origin unknown.] A tree found in Florida and the West Indies having heavy, hard, dark-brown wood. — **1884** SARGENT *Rep. Forests* 101 *Dipholis salicifolia*. . . . Bustic. Cassada.

***busting,** *n.* The breaking-in or taming of horses. Also attrib. See also **bronco busting, trust busting.** — **1891** *Harper's Mag.* July 208/2 The whole secret of 'busting' . . . lies in completely exhausting the bronco at the first lesson. **1913** MULFORD *Coming of Cassidy* 15 But the rider had learned his art in . . . the 'busting' corrals.

***busting,** *a.* Immense, splendid. *Colloq.* — **1851** *Polly Peablossom* 151, I soon see thar was gwine to be the bustinest fight that ever was. **1859** *S. Lit. Messenger* XXVIII. 143/1 Turkey, thar's the biggest, bustinest pike in that hole you uvver seed.

bustler ˈbʌslɚ, *n.* A bustle. *Rare.* [The article from which our quot. comes appears to be the only authority for the statement that the word originated in the visit to London in 1783 of the German duchess of "Bustledorfe."] — **1787** *Amer. Museum* II. 483 Wool, which might cover the legs of hundreds, is diverted from that use, and manufactured into odious *bustlers*.

***bust-up,** *n.* A plight, dilemma, bank failure. *Colloq.* — **1846** *Knickerb.* XXVIII. 313 This is the houdaciousest bust-up I ever seed, any how! **1902** HARBEN *Abner Daniel* 205, I wanted to talk to you about Alan an that bank bu'st-up. *Ib.* 213 Fincher's his best friend sence his bu'st-up, an' they are mighty thick.

***busy,** *a.* *To get busy*, to go into action, become active. *Colloq.* — **1904** *Courier-Journal* 27 Sep. 3 It was necessary to call upon the sergeant-at-arms. . . . When that functionary got busy there came near being a riot. **1906** O. HENRY *Four Million* 121 'Ikey,' said he, . . . 'get busy with your ear. It's drugs for me if you've got the line I need.'

***butcher,** *n.*

1. (See quots.)

1867 HOLMES *Guardian Angel* 297 These are the manuscript poems that we receive, and the one sitting at the table is commonly spoken of among us as The Butcher. **1902** CLAPIN 88 *Butcher*, in newspaper jargon, a term applied to the copy-reader, who uses mercilessly the blue-pencil in cutting short reporters' stories.

2. A vendor of candy, fruit, etc., esp. a boy who sells a variety of such articles on a train. In full **butcher boy.**

1883 Peck *Bad Boy* 54 They never prayed in circus, 'cept the lemonade butchers. **1926** Branch *Cowboy* 8 So Charlie Siringo wrote a book for butcher-boys to sell in smoking-cars. **1945** Marshall *Santa Fe* 110 The butchers sold cheap, dirty books, bad candy and cheap cigars.

3. (See quot.)

1889 Barrere-Leland I. 253 Butcher, clam butcher (American), a man who opens clams.

As the last term in **candy, clam, news, shop, train, wood butcher.**

butcher knife. A large knife now used chiefly as a kitchen utensil.

[**1714** *Boston News-Letter* 1–8 March 2/2 To be sold by public vendue . . . fans, butchers knives [etc.].] **1822** *Mass. Spy* 25 Dec. (Th.), Her foot slipt, and she fell upon a large butcher-knife which she had in her hand. **1866** Goss *Soldier's Story* 125 We had a pocket compass, which was intrusted to me, a small quantity of salt, and a butcher-knife, such as was issued to Massachusetts soldiers at Readville. **1948** Johnston *Gold Rush* 11/2 Butcher knives which miners used to dig gold from crevices [were] thirty dollars each.

b. *attrib.* Used of the vicious, illiterate, butcher-knife-wearing element in the early population of Illinois. *Obs.*

1847 T. Ford *Hist. Illinois* 88 These 'butcher knive boys,' as they were called, made a kind of balance of power party. *Ib.*, Most of the elections in early times were made under 'butcher knife influence.'

Butlerize ˈbʌtləˌraɪz, *v.* [f. Gen. B. F. *Butler* (1818–93) who while commandant of New Orleans after its capture in the Civil War was accused by the Southerners of stealing and looting.] *tr.* To steal, appropriate. *Obs.* — **1870** Macrae *Americans* I. 157 Several times in the south-west I heard people speak of having things 'Butlerized.' 'Now, don't you Butlerize all that pie,' said one little urchin to his sister, who was helping herself rather liberally.

* **butt,** *n.*

1. The base of a wing, where it joins the body of a bird. *Colloq.*

1806 Lewis in *L. & Clark Exped.* (1905) IV. 28 A third stripe . . . passes from the sides of the neck just above the butts of the wings across the croop in the form of a gorget.

2. A short piece, a butt end. *Rare.*

1888 Billings *Hardtack* 89 Even those troops having nearly three years to serve would exclaim, . . . 'It's only two years and a but.'

3. butt cut, the first portion of a tree cut off above the stump. Also transf. Cf. **jump butt.**

1830 *Northern Watchman* (Troy, N.Y.) 19 Oct. (Th.), [He] weighs little short of 450 lbs. and is familiarly known as the But-cut. **1840** *N.Y. American* 24 Nov. 3/2 The overshadowing sycamore . . . was a scraggy affair whose butt-cut would hardly make a back-log for an Illinois cabin. **1948** *Country Gentleman* May 177/1, I rived enough boards to kiver it from the butt-cuts.

4. * **butt end,** the part of a tree trunk or sapling immediately above the ground. Also fig.

1642 T. Lechford *Plain Dealing* 51 They [*sc.* Indians] cut downe a tree with axes and hatchets, . . . & bring in the butt-end into the wigwam, upon the hearth, and so burne it by degrees. **1760** Winthrop in *Phil. Trans.* LII. 10 A great tree, 2½ feet in diameter at the butt-end. **1846** Cist *Cin. Miscellany* II. 18/1 The freight from New Orleans, which is the butt end of the expense, is only 18 cents per cwt. **1889** *Harper's Mag.* Jan. 230/2 The largest poles are perhaps as thick as a man's wrist, the butt ends sticking up in the air.

b. Butt-End Coon-Hunters, (see quot. 1844). *Obs.* or *hist.*

1844 *N.Y. Wkly. Tribune* 5 Oct. 4/2 There exists in the City an association of whole-hog Loco-Focos who rejoice in the cognomen of the 'Butt-End Coon-Hunters.' **1935** Styron *Cast-Iron Man* 266 Similar political groups—the Butt-end Coon Hunters and the Subterraneans, the latter composed of New York City radicals led by Mike Walsh—also made their appearance.

c. Butt-Enders, (see quots.). *Obs.* or *hist.*

1840 *Boston Transcript* 4 Jan. 2/2 A riot was raised at New York, on New Year's Day, by a body of young men, called Butt-Enders, belonging to the noisy and turbulent portion of the Fire Department. **1840** *Nat. Intelligencer* 7 April 1/2 Already the Locofocos have got out their banners and procession, and 'the Butt-enders' and 'Point-enders' are marching at night through our streets, led by the so-called 'O.K.' club, which is just now a cant phrase in Tammany. **1938** Asbury *Sucker's Prog.* 370 They consisted of members of the 36th Engine, known as the Original Hounds, reinforced by a gang of Buttenders and Short Boys.

5. butt log, a log from the butt end of a tree.

1779 Patten *Diary* 396 John and I with both our Teams together hauled 2 butt logs that I Cut to Orrs mill. **1851** Springer *Forest Life* 41 The butt log was so large that the stream did not float it in the spring, and when the drive was taken down we were obliged to leave it behind. **1902** White *Blazed Trail* ii. 12 The teamster clamped the bite of his tongs to the end of the largest, or butt, log.

* **butt,** *v.*

1. *tr.* (See quot. 1850.)

1774 Patten *Diary* 331, I cut of 9 Rail cuts and butted 8 at the west end of Wm Barnetts land. **1850** Judd *R. Edney* 41 Richard took an axe and very neatly proceeded to 'butt' a log; that is, to cut the end of it square off. **1926** Rickaby *Ballads* 63 They will measure, top, and butt you. Into saw-logs they will cut you.

2. (See quot. 1840.) *Colloq.*

1840 Thompson *Green Mt. Boys* II. 364 Her oldest son, having at length been enabled to butt his mother, to use a chopper's phrase, that is to get off his cut first, in a trial of skill on the same log, she concluded to betake herself to household duties. **1884** E. Ingersoll *Country Cousins* i, I had an uncle . . . who was a famous chopper. . . . When he was past seventy, he had a man working for him . . . and my uncle offered to butt him.

3. *butt in,* to intrude. *Slang.*

1901 *Denver Republican* 19 Aug. 1/7 (*headline*), Ecuador 'Butting In.' **1939** Brownell *Horse & Buggy Philos.* 237 He had the pernicious habit indulged in by some merchants today of 'butting in' when we were waiting on a customer. **1947** *Harper's Mag.* Dec. 498/1 A eight-year-old young 'un ain't got no call to be buttin' into grown folks's business.

Hence **butter-in, butt-in, butt-iner,** one who intrudes. *Slang.* Cf. **buttinsky.**

1907 *Collier's* 30 Nov. 20/2 Collier's is . . . a butter-in of the first water. **1910** O. Henry *Rolling Stones* (1915) 194 Any of the Flat bush or Hackensack Meadow kind of butt-iners. **1911** J. C. Lincoln *Cap'n Warren's Wards* viii. 124 If I had my way the old butt-in should understand exactly that I think of him.

butte bjut, *n. W.* (See quot. 1843.)

[**1659** *Rec. Providence, R.I.* III. 76 Also six acres of Land lieing upon the small fresh streame which runneth into the Coave which is Called Bailies Coave, neere unto the two litle hills called Bailyes Buttes.] **1805** Clark in *Lewis & C. Exped.* (1904) II. 61, I walked out after dinner and assended a but [*sic*] a few miles [off] to view the country. **1843** Frémont *Exped.* 161 The French word *butte* . . . is naturalized in the region of the Rocky mountains; and, even if desirable to render it in English, I know of no word which would be its precise equivalent. It is applied to the detached hills & ridges which rise abruptly, and reach too high to be called hills or ridges, and not high enough to be called mountains. **1914** Brininstool *Trail Dust* 7 The black buttes loom up yonder, grim and spectral-like and strange. **1942** Stegner *Mormon C.* 39 The country spreads away in broad, colored plains broken by buttes and mesas and split by canyons and washes.

transf. **1936** Richter *Sea of Grass* 4, I can see his huge parlor, . . . piled to the pine rafters with white sacks of flour . . . and wooden buttes of . . . dried fruits and canned tomatoes.

As the last term in **mud, sand, sandstone, soda, tepee butte.**

* **butter,** *n.*[1] In combs.: (1) **butterball,** a small ball or individual serving of butter, cf. **b** (2); (2) **bean,** a variety of lima bean, also attrib.; (3) **bush,** = **buttonbush;** (4) * **cake,** (see quot.); (5) **corn,** a candy shaped and colored to resemble a slightly enlarged grain of corn; (6) **cow,** a cow valued for her butter-producing qualities; (7) **factory,** a place where butter is made in large quantities; (8) **family,** a breed of cows especially valued as butter producers; (9) * **fly,** * **milk, nut,** see as main entries; (10) **pear,** the avocado; (11) **print,** the Indian mallow; (12) **sauce,** a sauce the main ingredient of which is butter; (13) **squash,** a variety of squash; (14) **worker,** see as a main entry.

(1) **1911** J. C. Lincoln *Cap'n Warren's Wards* xi. 184 Mrs. Dickens wishes another butter-ball. **1937** *Dly. Oklahoman* (Okla. City) 24 Jan. C-11/2 Has the vogue for 'butter balls' gone out? — (2) **1821** Wm. Cobbett *Amer. Gardener* iv. Par. 197 The *Lima*-bean . . . is sometimes called the *butter*-bean. *c***1866** Bagby *Old Va. Gentleman* 45 The frost lies heavy on the palings, and tips with silver the tops of the butter-bean poles. **1948** *Democrat* 22 July 1/7 The chief products being canned are corn, tomatoes, soup mixtures, peas, butterbeans and snapbeans. — (3) **1843** Torrey *Flora N.Y.* I. 313 *Cephalanthus occidentalis*. . . . Butter-bush, or Pond-Dogwood. . . . Borders of ponds and rivers, and in swamps. **1861** *N.Y. Tribune* 24 July, [The] butter-bush . . . grows in swamps, and low, wet, marshy grounds. — (4) **1906** *N.Y. Ev. Post* 14 July 1 The 'butter-cake,' a fearful and wonderful hat with a tall crown and a brim an inch wide.

(5) **1945** *Reader's Digest* Dec. 103/1 There was butter-corn, or 'chicken feed,' a favorite confection. — (6) **1877** *Vt. Bd. Agric. Rep.* IV. 46 We . . . believe that the Jersey as a butter-cow has the ad-

vantage of at least the average life time of man. **1896** *Ib.* XV. 29 She is a specially bred butter cow. — **(7) 1868** *Mich. Agric. Rep.* VII. 228 The system of 'butter-factories,' [was] first organized in Orange county, N.Y. **1888** *Vt. Bd. Agric. Rep.* X. 14 If a man has a cheese factory he better keep it, but other things being equal a butter factory is better. — **(8) 1888** *Ib.* 16 The dairyman should raise his own stock, using the best males from the best butter families.

(10) 1909 *Cent. Supp.* 23/2 The alligator-pear. The tree yields a reddish-brown, soft, and very brittle wood. Also known as the *butter-pear* and *vegetable marrow.* [**1942** WEYGANDT *Plenty of Penna.* 106, I saw the ruby crown . . . in the butter-pear tree on our lawn, or in the dwarf Bartlett, or in the Sheldon.] — **(11) 1872** *Ill. Dept. Agric. Trans. 1871* p. ix, The Indian Mallow (*Abutilon Avicennae*) is variously known as 'stamp weed,' 'velvet leaf,' 'butter print,' 'Mormon weed,' etc. **1899** *Animal & Plant Lore* 120 *Abutilon Avicennae* is called 'butter-print,' 'pie-print,' and 'pie-marker,' because its pods are used to stamp butter or pie crust. Ohio, Illinois, Iowa, and Missouri. — **(12) 1896** J. C. HARRIS *Sister Jane* 61 She was sweet as butter sauce. — **(13) 1849** EMMONS *Agric. N.Y.* II. 296 The Butter squash was less sweet than the Vegetable Marrow.

b. In the names of birds: (1) **butter back,** a small North American duck, *Charitonetta albeola;* (2) **ball,** = prec., cf. (1) above; (3) **bill,** the American scoter duck, *Oidemia americana;* (4) **boat-bill(ed coot),** the surf scoter, *Melanitta perspicillata;* (5) **box,** = **butter back;** (6) **duck,** (see quot.); (7) **munk,** (see quot.).

(1) 1796 MORSE *Amer. Geog.* I. 213 Little Black and White Duck, called Butter Back, *Anas minor picta.* — **(2) 1813** WILSON *Ornithology* VIII. 51 Buffel-headed Duck. . . . This pretty little species, usually known by the name of the Butter-box, or Butter-ball, is common to the sea shores, rivers and lakes of the United States. **1948** *Sat. Ev. Post* 2 Oct. 1 The identifying feature of the Buffle-head or Butter-ball, is an oversized head that seems almost too big for his body. — **(3) 1844** *Nat. Hist. N.Y., Zoology* II. 329 *Fuligula albeola.* This little duck is known under the various popular names of . . . Butter-bill [etc.]. *Ib.* 336 *Fuligula Americana.* This duck, which is known . . . farther east by the name of Butter-bill, is described in the books under the name of American Scoter Duck. — **(4) 1838** AUDUBON *Ornith. Biog.* IV. 163 In the States of Maine and Massachusetts, this species is best known by the name of 'Butter-boat-billed Coot.' **1844** *Nat. Hist. N.Y., Zoology* II. 335 *Fuligula Perspicillata,* . . . Black Sea Duck or Butter-boat-bill, is very common on the coast of New-York during the winter.

(5) 1806 CLARK in *Lewis & C. Exped.* (1905) IV. 150, I take this to be the same species of duck common to the Ohio, as also the atlantic coast, and sometimes called the butterbox. **1917** *Birds of Amer.* I. 140. — **(6) 1857** J. G. SWAN *Northwest Coast* 357 The Colonel saw a 'butter-duck' in a shallow creek. . . . These ducks are the black surf-duck. — **(7) 1889** *Cent.* 738/1 buttermunk. . . . [A variant of *butterbump.*] A local New England name of the night-heron, *Nyctiardea grisea naevia.*

c. In phrasal expressions: (1) **butter-and-egg man,** a wealthy, extravagant man who spends money lavishly on theatrical ventures, chorus girls, night clubs, etc., *slang;* (2) **butter-and-egg money,** (see quot.). [*EDD* records "butter money" in a similar sense.]

(1) 1925 WITWER *Roughly Speaking* 229 J. Overland Cunningham and Hudson Chalmers. . . . A couple of big butter and egg men from Verona, New Jersey. **1948** *Antioch Review* Spring 105 There is also the 'butter-and-egg man' who startles the foreign lecturer with blunt questions. — **(2) 1942** WARNICK *Dialect Garrett Co., Md.* 4 Butter and egg money, n. phr., money derived from the sale of butter and eggs, a portion or all of which was the wife's share of returns for produce sold.

As the last term in **apple, bull, Californian, commissary, drawn, egg, factory, fall, Goshen, grass, June, lemon, lump, milled, peach, peanut, pieplant, prairie, pumpkin, ranch, school, September, soul, squatter, tomato butter.**

***butter,** *n.*² **1.** One who butts a log. *Obs.* **2.** (See quot.) — **(1) 1850** JUDD *R. Edney* 98 He teazed a butter with it, making as if he would thrust it under his axe. — **(2) 1874** KNIGHT 414/1 *Butter,* . . . a machine for sawing off the ends of boards.

***butterfly,** *n.* In combs.: (1) **butterfly cape,** a cape or scarf suggestive in its shape of a butterfly's wing; (2) **lily,** = **Mariposa lily;** (3) **milkweed,** = **butterfly weed;** (4) **pea,** any one of various wild peas of the genus *Clitoria,* or a related plant, *Centrosema virginianum;* (5) **root,** = **butterfly weed;** (6) **shawl,** a shawl of a shape suggestive of a butterfly's wing; (7) **tree,** (see quot. 1932); (8) **tulip,** = **Mariposa lily;** (9) **weed,** a milkweed, *Asclepias tuberosa,* having brilliant orange blossoms; (10) **wort,** = prec.

(1) 1893 *Chi. Tribune* 23 April 29/5 Fine Cloth Butterfly Capes—butterfly silk lined—ribbon and embroidery trimmed, at $8. *Ib.,* 25 April 4/6 The maiden spends her money for a butterfly cape. — **(2) 1902** CHESNUT *Plants Used by Indians* 323 Calochortus venustus . . . [is] the commonest species of the Mariposa or butterfly lilies which grow, often in great tracts, on open hillsides throughout the region. — **(3) 1899** *Animal & Plant Lore* 118 *Asclepias tuberosa,* the butterfly milkweed, is called 'chigger flower,' from the belief that insects known as chiggers harbor in it. Southwestern, Missouri. **1939** *Nat. Geog. Mag.* Aug. 220/2 Striking contrast is provided by some of the most brilliant flowers of the prairie, notably . . . the purple cone-flower, the butterfly milkweed, . . . and the prickly pears. — **(4) 1857** GRAY *Botany* 106 *Clitoria,* Butterfly Pea. . . . *Centrosema,* Spurred Butterfly Pea. **1941** R. S. WALKER *Lookout* 58 Butterfly-pea is one of the many kinds of beautiful members of the legume family growing on the mountain.

(5) 1789 *Philos. Soc. Trans.* III. xviii, The best among pleuretic remedies must be the *pleuresy-root.* . . . Another asclepias bears high value in Maryland; called also *butterfly root.* **1888** *Cent. Mag.* XXXVI. 768/1 'A brilliant yellow' may be obtained by pouring boiling water upon other component parts of 'sassafras, swamp bay, and butterfly root.' — **(6) 1852** *Southern Ladies Book* I. 47 The grounds were crowded with fashion, gay bonnets, butterfly shawls, etc. — **(7) 1881** *Amer. Naturalist* XV. 572, I have been to Monterey, and was fortunate enough to see the 'butterfly tree,' or trees, as there are three of them. These trees are the Monterey pine. **1932** CLARK *Butterflies Dist. Columbia* 121 The milkweed butterfly is especially remarkable . . . for its habit of swarming in incredible numbers on the twigs and branches of trees and bushes. In some places the trees frequented by these insects in the swarming season have come to be known as 'butterfly trees.' — **(8) 1886** HUTCHINGS *Heart of Sierras* 294 Our course . . . is . . . around oak knolls, intermixed with flowering shrubs and flowers; among which is the charming Mariposa, or 'Butterfly Tulip.' **1947** *Nat. Geog. Mag.* July 60/1 And the Mariposas or Butterfly-Tulips (*Calochortus*); except for a few forms, they mostly spurn permanent sanctuary with humans. — **(9) 1816** D. THOMAS *Travels Western Country* (1819) 222 *Asclepias decumbens* butterfly weed. **1927** CATHER *Death Comes* 167 Evening primroses, the fireweed, and butterfly weed grew to a tropical size.

(10) 1830 *Huntingdon* (Penna.) *Courier* 15 Sep. 4/5 Harvest Root or Butterfly Wort, (Asclepias Tuberosa.).

As the last term in **buckwheat, hop, milkweed, semicolon butterfly.**

butterick ˈbʌtərɪk, *n.* [f. Ebenezer *Butterick* (1826–1903), Amer. inventor of standardized clothes patterns.] A dressmaker's pattern. *Obs.* — [**1901** J. L. FORD in *Munsey's Mag.* July 534 What is technically known as the 'butterick,' a picture of two or more persons in conversational attire [*sic*], and usually amid the most luxurious surroundings.] *a***1910** O. HENRY *Rolling Stones* (1917) 178 A buttonless flannel dressing sacque whose lines had been cut by no tape or butterick known to mortal women.

***buttermilk,** *n.* In combs.: (1) **buttermilk land,** wet, marshy land, *colloq.;* (2) **ranger,** a nickname given a cavalryman by southern infantrymen during the Civil War, *obs.* [cf. *EDD buttermilk-man,* "an opprobrious term for a trooper of the Cheshire Yeomanry"]; (3) **sand,** (see quot.).

(1) 1843 R. CARLTON *New Purchase* IX. 58 They had been sufficiently fortunate as to get a taste of 'buttermilk land,' . . . and to learn the nature of 'mash land'—'rooty and snaggy land.' — **(2) 1870** MACRAE *Americans* I. 261 When, on the advance of the enemy's infantry, the cavalry were ordered to the rear, the troops generally greeted them with shouts of,—'Here come the buttermilk rangers; there's goin' to be a fight, sartin, when they're clearin' out o' the road.' **1898** HARRIS *Tales* 343 The hit was as palpable as it was daring, for the men of this command were known far and wide as the Buttermilk Rangers. — **(3) 1904** *D.N.* II. 377 buttermilk sand, *n.* The driller's name for a sandstone found about 914 feet down in Westmoreland Co., Pa. Cf. Carll, *Seventh Report,* 1890, p. 219.

butternut ˈbʌtəˌnʌt, *n.*

1. The white walnut, *Juglans cinerea,* or its fruit.

1741 COLLINSON in *Mem. Bartram* (1849) 148 The butter-nut . . . with the Medlar and Sagamore's head. **1753** CHAMBERS *Cyclo. Supp. s.v., Butter-nut,* a fruit in New England, whose kernel yields a great quantity of sweet oil. **1832** BROWNE *Sylva Amer.* 174 The black walnut and butternut, when young, resemble each other in their foliage, and in the rapidity of their growth. **1944** HOLTON *Yankees* 137 His emotional life was as secretive as a butternut.

attrib. **1936** LUTES *Country Kitchen* 59 There, however, was the required ingredient for our hickory-nut cake, walnut cake, and for butternut candy. **1948** *Chi. Tribune* 15 Feb. (Comics) 14, I made you some butternut cookies.

b. The wood, bark, or hull of the tree or nut.

1781 J. THATCHER *Military Jrnl.* 309 A single dose of jalap and calomel, or of the extract of butternut, *juglans cinerea,* is in general administered previous to the appearance of the symptoms. **1843** T. TALBOT *Journals* 29 The following are external applications: . . . Star root, Rattlesnake plantain, Butternut, Daphne Mezereum, or Spurge Olive. **1886** *Leslie's Mo.* XXI. 388/2 One of the finest boats on the Hudson is built of butternut. **1902** S. G. FISHER *Amer. Revol.* 261 Many regiments, [in the Revolutionary War] stained their hunting-shirts with butternut, which was used for a similar purpose by the Confederates of the Civil War.

c. butternut bark, the bark of the butternut used in medicine and in dyeing.

[**1776** *Burlington Almanac.* (N.J.) Cr, Take bark of the butter-nut-tree, put a layer in the bottom of a brass kettle, then a layer of wool, and so alternately till you have it full, or as much as you intend to die [*sic*].] **1838** *Harvardiana* IV. 374, I had . . . the best butternut bark. **1877** *Vt. Bd. Agric. Rep.* IV. 92 The wool was colored with butternut bark.

2. The color obtained by using the bark, roots, etc., of the butternut tree as a dye. Also the cloth or garments so colored.

1810 *Mass. Spy* 21 Feb. (Th.), Two pair home-made pantaloons, the one dark-colored, the other light butternut. **1867** E. KIRKE *On Border* 150, I must add that this angel wore seedy butternuts, chewed tobacco. **1947** CHALFANT *Gold, Guns, & Ghost Towns* 12 Two gentlemen in butternuts were running a rocker in a manner that indicated they would much prefer to hunt coons.

b. *attrib.* Designating kinds of cloth dyed a brownish color with dye obtained from the butternut, as **butternut flannel, homespun, jean(s), linsey, woolsey.**

1883 *Harper's Mag.* Sep. 626/2 A big young fellow in butternut flannel appeared. — **1863** E. KIRKE *Southern Friends* viii. 106 He was dressed in a suit of 'butternut homespun.' **1879** TOURGEE *Fool's Errand* 139 He was clad now in 'butter-nut-gray' homespun. — **1867** E. KIRKE *On Border* 310 He was dressed in the common butternut jean of the district. **1912** CRUMPTON *Two Boys* 110 They were all dressed in butternut jeans. — **1848** DRAKE in *Pioneer Life Ky.* 74 My equipments were a substantial suit of butternut-linsey, a wool hat. — **1881** PIERSON *In the Brush* 117 Her arms were colored to above her elbows, where she had had them in the dye tub, preparing the 'butternut-woolsey' for the family use.

Also *butternut breeches, cloth, clothes, clothing, coat, color, colored, dyed, garment, hue, suit, trousers,* etc.

3. A Confederate soldier in the Civil War. Now *hist.*

1862 *N.Y. Tribune* 28 May 3/1 Capital shots are many of these 'Butternuts'—long, lank, loose-jointed Mississippians and Texans though they are. **1875** G. P. BURNHAM *Three Years* 28 'Who ar yer? Whar yer from?' asked the butternut, rudely. **1948** *Reader's Digest* Jan. 67/2 When the backwoods boys fought beside Robert E. Lee in their homespuns dyed with butternut, they were known as 'Butternuts,' and that tree became a synonym for tattered valor.

b. =**copperhead.** Also attrib. *Obs.*

See A. Matthews "The Origin of Butternut and Copperhead" in *Pub. Col. Soc. Mass.* XX. (1918) 205–37.

1862 *Independent* 27 March 1/6 The butternut gentry, . . . availing themselves of Government passes over railroads, have flocked to the Northern watering-place [=Chicago]. **1862** *Lawrence* (Kans.) *Republican* 11 Sep. 4/1 That faction of Democracy who sympathise with the rebels are known in Ohio as 'Vallandinghamers,' . . . in Missouri as 'butter-nuts,' in Kansas as 'jayhawkers,' in Kentucky as 'bushwhackers.' **1885** *Amer. Hist. Mag.* Jan. 99/1 *Butternuts.*— Equivalent at the North to 'copperheads.'

4. (*cap.*) A nickname for a Missourian. Also attrib.

1881 *Kansas Hist. Colls.* II. 187 A knowledge of this claim made by Mr. Thayer spread like wildfire through western Missouri. It fired the 'butternut' heart amazingly. . . . They offered a thousand dollars reward for Eli Thayer's head. **1895** *Ib.* (1896) V. 131 Kansas City . . . [is] 'a city,' as a Butternut told me, 'of 371 souls, and about a dozen Indians.'

b. Butternut State, Missouri. A nickname.

1863 *Rocky Mt. News* (Denver) 19 March (Th.), We expect ere long to stand on the banks of the 'Big Muddy,' and meet the hominy-fed lasses of the Butternut State.

As the last term in **Georgia, Mississippi Butternut.**

butterworker 'bʌtɚˌwɝkɚ, *n.* An implement for kneading and pressing butter in salting it and freeing it from buttermilk.

Though included in the *DAE* as an Americanism, this term occurs in the *OED* but without quots. Its status as an Americanism is doubtful.

1853 *Rep. Comm. Patents* (1854) 247 Improvement in Butter Workers. **1872** *Vt. Bd. Agric. Rep.* I. 152 Work [it] again in butter-worker, using a large sponge and a cloth to absorb all moisture that remains in the butter. **1882** *Maine Bd. Agric. Rep.* XXVI. 153 A good butter worker of some kind should be provided, and also a thermometer, if one expects to make a uniform article.

butting pole. A pole against which the lower ends of the clapboards forming the roof of a log cabin rested. Now *hist.*

1791 in JILLSON *Dark & Bl. Ground* (1930) 109 The eave bearers [of a log cabin] are the end logs which project over to receve the butting poles, against which the lower tier of clapboards rest in forming the roof. **1843** *Amer. Pioneer* II. 445 The knees are pieces of heart timber placed above the butting poles, successively, to prevent the weight poles from rolling off. **1940** WRIGHT *Pioneer Life* 46 Two end logs projected a foot or eighteen inches beyond the wall to receive the butting poles, as they were called, against which the ends of the first row of clapboards was supported.

Butterworker of a type popular *c*1875

buttinsky ˌbʌˈtɪnskɪ, *n.* Also **butterinsky.** (See quot. 1903 and cf. **butt in,** *v.*) *Slang.*

1903 *Cin. Enquirer* 9 May 13/2 Piker— . . . a cheap grafter; a noser; a butterinsky. **1912** RAINE *Brand Blotters* 156 'You're making a heap of formality out of this, Mr. Buttinsky,' sneered the cowpuncher. **1931** *K.C. Star* 21 Nov. 12 We saw Bill's arms around both of the girls making each girl think the other was a mean little buttinsky.

* **button,** *n.*

1. Short for **button tree** (*a*). *Obs.*

1746 *Boston Records* (1887) XVII. 135 They . . . Plant . . . an Elm and a Button at the same Distance from each other with the Trees already Planted on the Neck. **1773** in T. HUTCHINS *Topo. Descr. Virginia* (1778) 59 The timber is generally Birch, Button, and Paccan.

2. The hard, bonelike terminal segment at the end of the rattles of a rattlesnake.

1822 in *South. Hist. Jrnl.* VII. (1941) 385 Killed a rattle snake this afternoon (24 Apr) 3 feet 6 inches long, with four rattles and a button. **1845** SIMMS *Wigwam & Cabin* I Ser. 83 A little way behind him lay a dead rattlesnake, one of the largest I ever did see, counting twenty-one rattles besides the button. **1948** *Nat. Hist.* Apr. 187/2 Other snakes vibrate their tails, but only the rattlesnakes have rattles (at birth a bell-shaped 'button').

3. A pin having a circular front, usu. of celluloid, on which there is some sort of political propaganda.

[**1884** *N.Y. Times & Express* June, An engraver . . . made a couple of dozen such buttons for a leading actress.] **1900** *Daily News* 5 Nov. 7/1 Another feature of an American Presidential campaign is the lavish display of political 'buttons.' 3000000 buttons have been sent out from the Republican headquarters. **1948** *Chi. D. News* 24 June 16/7 The pretty girls passing out buttons, the general circus atmosphere—all this seems ill-matched with the solemnity of the decision to be taken.

3. In combs.: (1) **button ball,** (see quot. 1916); (2) **bed,** (see quot.); (3) **berry,** =**salmonberry,** cf. **swamp buttonberry;** (4) **bush,** the pond dogwood, *Cephalanthus occidentalis;* (5) * **flower,** =prec.; (6) **-nose mole,** (see quot.); (7) **pear,** ?a variety of small pear, *obs.;* (8) **(rattle)snakeroot,** one or other species of eryngo, esp. *Eryngium aquaticum* of the southern states, or a plant of the genus *Liatris;* (9) **stick,** ?a button-hook, *obs.;* (10) **tree,** (*a*) (see quot. 1859), (*b*) =**buttonbush;** (11) **wood,** see as a main entry.

(**1**) **1821** *Mass. Hist. Soc. Coll.* 2 Ser. IX. 153 [Trees indigenous at Middlebury, Vt.] Button-ball tree. **1916** SETON *Woodcraft Man.* 288 Sycamore, Plane Tree, Buttonball, or Buttonwood (*Platanus occidentalis*). One of the largest of our trees; up to 140 feet high; commonly hollow. . . . Famous for shedding its bark as well as its leaves. — (**2**) **1932** *Montgomery Advt.* 11 Sep., The typical Alabama spool-bed, or as some call it, the button-bed, made of maple is the product of the shop right here at home. — (**3**) **1876** DODGE *Black Hills* 84

[There is] a curious raspberry which grows on a stalk between two broad leaves. It is sometimes called button-berry. — **(4) 1754** ELIOT *Field-Husb.* v. 124 There was not the same Success attending the cutting these Button Bushes as the other Sorts. **1870** *Amer. Naturalist* IV. 216 The Button-bush . . . is odd, with its buttons of white flowers, and worthy of cultivation. **1947** *Midland Naturalist* July 59 Buttonbush [is] occasional (locally common) in shrub swamps.

(5) 1819 THOMAS *Travels* 222, I noticed the following vegetables growing indigenously, near the Wabash, between Vincennes and Fort Harrison. . . . *Cephalanthus occidentalis* button flower. — **(6) 1842** *Nat. Hist. N.Y., Zoology* I. 14 The Star-nose is abundant throughout New-York, where it is occasionally called the Button-nose Mole. — **(7) 1687** SEWALL *Diary* I. 173 Grafted the Button-pear tree stock. **1713** *Charlestown Land Rec.* 211 From the corner of Deericks & Eades Land to the butten pare trees is 23 foot. **1759** *Newport Mercury* 8 May 1/1 Plough it in, and harrow it . . . with a Thorn-bush Harrow, or a Harrow made of Plum Tree, or Button-pear Tree. — **(8) 1775** ADAIR *Indians* 156 A thick whip, . . . composed of plaited silk grass, and the fibres of the button snake-root stalks. *Ib.* 160 This purifying physic, is warm water highly imbittered with button-rattlesnake-root, which as hath been before observed, they apply only to religious purposes. **1800** HAWKINS *Sk. Creek Country* 79 Every new moon, he drinks for four days the posson, (button snakeroot), an emetic. **1941** R. S. WALKER *Lookout* 48 Among the wild plants once employed as antidotes for the bites of poisonous reptiles are . . . Samson snakeroot, . . . Virginia snakeroot, button snakeroot, and rattlesnake-root. — **(9) 1890** GOSS *Recollections* 6 There were in it a pair of trousers, . . . a button-stick, chalk, razor and strop.

(10) *(a)* **1751** WM. A. DOUGLASS *Summary* II. 213 The button tree, or plantanus occidentalis, is of a fine parabolick form fit for avenues, but its verdure is of short continuance, and the tree is not long lived. **1859** BARTLETT 61 Buttonwood or button tree (*Platanus occidentalis*) [is] the popular name in New England, of the sycamore tree; so called from the balls it bears, the receptacle of the seed. . . . Sometimes called Button-ball tree. *(b)* **1785** MARSHALL *Amer. Grove* 30 *Cephalanthus occidentalis.* Button tree. This shrub grows pretty common by creek sides and ponds. **1815** DRAKE *Cincinnati* 76 The botanical resources of this . . . Forest of the Miami country [include] . . . *Cephalanthus occidentalis*, Button tree.

As the last term in **basswood, bell, bitter, bullet, campaign, collar, death-head, dog, Georgia, mescal, palmetto, peyote, push, sleeve button.**

* **button,** *v.* **1.** *button down on,* settle down to, fix upon. **2.** *tr.* "To buttonhole" (a person). Both *colloq.* and *rare.* — **(1) 1857** *Knickerb.* XLIX. 277 Why the d——l don't you button down *on one thing;* take up some line, spread yourself on it, and go your die? — **(2) 1862–3** HALE *If, Yes & Perhaps* (1868) 8 But, if the reader wishes to lengthen out this story, he may button the next silver-gray friend he meets.

* **Buttoners,** *n. pl.* (See quot. and cf. **Hook and Eye, Hooker.**) — **1880** *Harper's Mag.* May 810/1 The stricter Mennonites . . . were called 'Hookers,' in distinction from the more lax brethren, who were called 'Buttoners.'

buttonhole twist. A kind of stout thread for making button-holes. — **1868** *Rep. U.S. Comm. Agric.* (1869) 289 Button-hole twist is the same, with a tighter twist.

buttonwood ˈbʌtn̩ˌwud, *n.*

1. A plane tree or species of tree, esp. *Platanus occidentalis*, and *P. orientalis.* Also attrib.

1674 *Cambridge Rec.* 1 A button wood tree to make two beams of. **1674** *Cal. State P., Amer. & West Indies* VII. 581 [In Maine] grow . . . alder, shumack, willow, button wood, poplar [etc.]. **1778** CARVER *Travels* 499 The Button Wood is a tree of the largest size, . . . covered with small hard burs which spring from the branches, that appear not unlike buttons. **1833** NEAL *Down-Easters* I. 81 Dont care how close a feller is—closer an' button-wood bark, all the better for me. **1948** *Hoosier Folklore* March 7 Take the twigs of buttonwood, . . . and boil them in a brass kettle so that the liquor is strong.

2. =**buttonbush.**

1802 DRAYTON *S. Carolina* 62 Button wood. (*Cephalanthus Occidentalis.*) Grows in watery places: blossoms in June. A wash of the decoction of this plant, is said to be good for the palsey. **1813** MUHLENBERG *Cat. Plants* 15 Globe-flower shrub, (button wood, or pond dog-wood).

3. buttonwood caterpillar, (see quot.). *Rare.*

1854 EMMONS *Agric. N.Y.* V. (Index), 261 Buttonwood Caterpillar. *Ib.* 234 *Dryocampa imperialis* . . . its caterpillar feeds upon the button-wood . . . oak, and sweetgum.

As the last term in **large buttonwood, pond buttonwood.**

buy baı, *n.* [Recorded in *EDD* VI. *s.v.*, from Ireland. Possibly borrowed in U.S. from Irish.] A bargain, purchase. *Colloq.*

1882 *Cent. Mag.* Aug. 540 Do you not think that 'Denver' has a future? . . . I think myself it is a first-rate buy. **1911** QUICK *Yellowstone N.* 191, I believe it's a good buy! **1948** *Savings News* Jan. 15/3 Homemakers often pass up unusually good buys in medium and small eggs by the mistaken notion that they are not of as good a quality as the larger eggs.

* **buyer,** *n.* **buyer thirty, three,** ellipt. for "a buyer's option good for thirty (or three) days." Cf. **seller.** Also attrib.

1864 *Wilkes' Spirit of Times* 17 Dec. 250/3 By dint of bidding for gold largely, at 'buyer three,' they had shoved the market up again to retrieve their losses by turning Bulls. **1867** *Harper's Wkly.* 23 Feb. 114/3 'Puts' and 'calls' fly thick and fast, and 'seller 3,' 'buyer 30,' 'regular,' 'flat,' and the whole vocabulary of brokers' terms are bandied about from mouth to mouth in rapid succession. **1879** *Chi. Tribune* 5 Feb. 5/2 The Baron is a capitalist who does the carrying over for members or outsiders who desire to engage in the 'buyer 3,' or 'buyer 5,' or 'buyer 30' business.

As the last term in **beef, cattle, cotton, hair, hide, vote buyer.**

* **buzz,** *n.*

1. Short for next. *Colloq. Obs.*

1821 *Mass. Spy* 26 Sep. (Th.), A circular buz, of thin, soft sheet iron, six inches in diameter. **1830** S. SMITH *Major Downing* 27, I met a man . . . that said they've got them are wheels going now like a buz.

2. buzz saw, a circular saw. Also fig. and attrib.

1858 *Varieties* (S.F.) 17 July 3/1 'Any taste for music?' 'Strong. Buzz and buck saws in the day time, and wolf howling and cat fighting nights.' **1895** WILLIAMS *Princeton Stories* 69 All summer long she sat on the sand without a veil and was nice to two little boys in clean duck trousers and buzz-saw hats which blew off sometimes. **1948** *Parents' Mag.* March 92/3 Some were bookworms who lost themselves in a library to escape the buzz-saws of life.

b. (See quots.)

1921 *Outing* Mar. 247/2 There are several styles of spur in use in the West, the O.K. or 'petmaker' and the 'buzz saw' being the worst. Both have large rowels with small, sharp points, and few riders use them to-day. **1939** ROLLINS *Gone Haywire* 38 The favorite shapes among the punchers were the cartwheels (spokes radiating from an axle), . . . buzz saw (points fewer, longer and sharper than the sunburst), and the star.

* **buzz,** *v. Baseball. tr.* ?To catch a ball and so put out (a runner). *Obs.* — **1867** *Ball Players' Chron.* 22 Aug. 8/2 By a wild pitch he reached his second, and by a passed ball his third, and but for being 'buzzed' by Pike would have got home.

* **buzzard,** *n.*

1. The California vulture or condor, *Gymnogyps californianus. Obs.*

1805 CLARK in *Lewis & C. Exped.* (1905) III. 174 Those Buzzards are much larger than any other of ther Spece or the largest Eagle white under part of their wings. **1807** GASS *Journal* 168 They killed a remarkably large buzzard, of a species different from any I had seen. It was 9 feet across the wings, and 3 feet 10 inches from the bill to the tail.

2. =**turkey buzzard.**

1824 DODDRIDGE *Notes* 69 The buzzards, or vultures . . . were very numerous here in former times. **1903** AUSTIN *Land of Little Rain* 47 The buzzards sit on the fences and low hummocks. **1948** *Chi. Tribune* 9 May I. 27/4 Air lines have recorded crashes with buzzards, condors, and swans weighing up to 38 pounds.

b. (See quots.)

1845 *St. Louis Reveille* 14 May 2/4 The inhabitants of . . . Georgia [are called] Buzzards. **1913** RUOFF *Dict. Facts* 372 Names given to the inhabitants of the different States by popular use: . . . Georgia, buzzards.

3. (See quot.)

1871 in DE VERE 588 *Buzzard* is the half-facetious half-contemptuous term applied in several mechanical professions to a badly-spoiled piece of work. 'Said the venerable Mr. G. to one of his jours: Sir, I pronounce that job an unmitigated *buzzard.*'

4. (Harris') buzzard, (see quot. 1922).

*a***1888** in J. PHELAN *Hist. Tenn.* 381 It's all over; there is Harris's infernal buzzard in the mail. **1922** MCCORMAC *Biog. Polk* 141 Harris had a spread-eagle woodcut prepared. . . . As its appearance in the *Union* was always accompanied by news of Democratic victory, the Whigs expressed their contempt by calling it 'Harris's buzzard.' *Ib.*, 150 On August 1 [1839] Polk was elected by a majority of three thousand votes, and Harris got out his 'buzzard' to adorn the front page of the *Union.*

5. In combs.: (1) **buzzard dollar,** the standard dollar, having on it the figure of an eagle derisively called a buzzard, as distinguished from the trade dollar, *obs.;* (2) **lope,** (see quot.); (3) **plow,** ?a plow with a single handle and single shovel, *obs.*, cf. **buzzard sweep, wing;** (4) **roost,** *(a)* a place where buzzards roost (see also quot.

1906), (*b*) the name of a quilt pattern; (5) **sweep, wing,** *S.* an extremely large sweep or plow shovel, cf. **turkey wing plow.**

(1) **1878** *Nation* 19 Sep. 170/2 The 'buzzard dollar' [is] the designation applied by indignant holders of the trade-dollar to the now standard dollar. **a1890** *Chi. Tribune* (B. & L.), The waiters . . . will take anything you give them, from a nickel up to a buzzard dollar, and look happy. — (2) **1890** *Standard Dict.* 24 Apr., Buzzard Lope—'the latest social institution of America . . . a dance taught to a Georgian negro by the turkey buzzard.' — (3) **1848** *De Bow's Review* VI. 150 It is more like the scooter or buzzard plow. — (4) (*a*) **1889** MARK TWAIN *Connecticut Yankee* iv. 53 After suffocating body and mind . . . in that intolerable old buzzard-roost. **1906** *D.N.* III. 129 buzzard-roost, *n.* A dilapidated building. **1945** BOTKIN *My Burden* 56 You can go to a buzzard roost and see for yourself. (*b*) **1938** MATSCHAT *Suwannee River* 121 The names were enchanting: Wild Goose Chase, . . . Buzzard's Roost, Star of the East, Log Cabin.

(5) **1854** *Florida Plant. Rec.* 575, 16 Buzzard Sweeps, old patern. **1944** CLARK *Pills* 282 By colloquial designations the various strange shapes were known to the trade as . . . buzzard wings, scrapers and subsoilers.

As the last term in **broad-winged, ferruginous, red-shouldered, red-tailed, star, turkey, vulture buzzard.**

buzz saw, *v. tr.* To cut with a buzz saw, also fig. *Rare.* — **1883** M. D. LANDON *Wit & Humor* 118, I was buzz-sawed, sure.

B.V.D. The trade-mark of an undergarment for men. Also **beeveedees.**

1908 *Sat. Ev. Post* 4 July 1 All B.V.D. Garments are made of thoroughly tested woven materials selected for their *cooling* and *wearing* qualities. **1915** in *Sooner Mag.* (1947) Nov. 14/1 The 'frosh' started a 'back to nature' movement but compromised on 'beeveedees.' **1947** COFFIN *Yankee Coast* 71 He rushed out on the parade grounds in his B.V.D.'s.

*** by,** *prep., adv., a.*

1. *adv. S.* At, in, or into another's house when passing, as *go by, come by, call by, stop by. Colloq.*

1918 in *Amer. Sp.* XXII. 283 'Will you *go by* and dine with me.' When I mentioned this singular expression to some gentlemen afterwards, I was told it was often used. **1863** C. C. HOPLEY *Life in South* I. 58 The Southerners . . . deem it a thing impossible that a friend should pass the house and not come in; so that 'come by' implies 'take *our* road home, and of course come in.' **a1906** O. HENRY *Trimmed Lamp,* etc. 220 Granger . . . would call by for Mary Adrian. **1928** F. N. HART *Bellamy Trail* v. 172 They were going to stop by for her.

b. *prep.* At or into (another's house on passing it).

1896 *D.N.* I. 385 'Come by my house and stay all night' =not pass by, but stop at the house. **1923** *Ib.* V. 244 *Stop by,* to visit 'Stop by my house.'

2. * *by and large,* on the whole, in general.

1767 in *S. Lit. Messenger* XXVII. 183/2 [He] hath made prize of the President's daughter, Miss Betsey, a charming frigate, that will do honour to our country, if you take her by and large, as the sailors say. **1845** C. MATHEWS *Writings* II. 150 (Th.), He had been speaking for four hours, ostensibly on the Panama mission, but actually travelled over everything by and large. **1948** *Nat. Hist.* Apr. 188/1 By and large, the worries of summer residents concerning snakes are far out of proportion to the dangers that potentially exist.

3. In combs.: (1) **by letter,** a letter to be delivered by the way, *rare;* (2) **line,** the name of an author appearing beneath the title of an article, also **by-liner;** (3) **settlement,** an out-of-the-way or back settlement, *rare;* (4) **trail,** a bypath, *rare.*

(1) **1792** *Ann. 2nd Congress* 62 The deputy postmasters . . . shall . . . answer to him, for all by or way letters, and shall specify the same . . . in the post bill. — (2) **1928** *Sat. Ev. Post* 12 May 36/2 The too generous use of what we call by-lines on the sporting pages should have made the fans a little skeptical long ago, but it hasn't. *Ib.,* The term 'by-line' means the signature of the writer. **1946** *New Yorker* 16 Nov. 66/2 Seven crews . . . travelled fourteen thousand miles throughout the state, according to Jack Turcott, the *News* byliner who furnished the continuity. **1948** *Time* 3 May 66/3 The foundations of good coverage are laid in the staff of district reporters, who never get bylines or much notice, but who have lots of friends among the police. — (3) **1780** R. PUTNAM in *Memoirs* 153 He saw no foot, but heard of small partys being out and plundering some bye settlements. — (4) **1873** MILLER *Amongst Modocs* iii. 53, I remember . . . that I always took some by-trail, if possible.

bye bai, *n.* [Origin obscure.] The goal used in the Indian game of ball. *Rare.* — **c1836** CATLIN *Indians* I. 124 We . . . witnessed the ceremony of . . . erecting the 'byes' or goals which were to guide the play. Each party had their goal made with two upright posts, about 25 feet high and six feet apart, set firm in the ground, with a pole across at the top.

*** Byfield,** *n.* [?f. personal name.] A breed of hogs. *Obs.*

1838 COLMAN *Mass. Rep. Agric.* 74 A cross with some of our small boned breed, such as the Byfield or the China. **1851** CIST *Cincinnati* 279 The hogs raised for this market, are generally a cross of Irish Grazier, Byfield, Berkshire, [etc.]. **1864** *Me. Rep. Agric.* 28 Mr. Haines gave an account of the old Newbury White breed. They were introduced . . . under the name of 'Byfield.' . . . They had small ears, short legs, and long bodies.

C

*C, n.

1. A hundred dollars, esp. a bill of that denomination. Also **C note.** Cf. **century note.** *Colloq.*

1839 *Spirit of Times* 13 April 66/3 (We.), I had no idea of betting more than an 'L,' or a 'C.' **1845** Sol. Smith *Theatr. Apprent.* 149 So there's my hundred—and as my pocket-book's out, and my hand's in, there's another C. **1946** *Science Digest* Aug. 23/2 Barney Baruch likes to start out each day with a goodly supply of crisp C-notes.

b. C speck, a hundred-dollar bill. *Rare.*

*a***1846** *Quarter Race Ky.* 117 Sol. Lauflin matched his bay four year old colt . . . to run a quarter, in the lane near this place, for a C speck.

2. (See quot.) *Rare.*

1848 N. Ames *Childe Harvard* 33 These last six stanzas, I suppose, may seem Rather out of place, and should be marked with 'C'; That is, 'want of connection' in 'the theme.'

3. Used to denote the grade or quality of a commodity.

1865 *Balt. D. Commercial* 4 Oct. 4/2 The refiners . . . now quote . . . 18 5/8 cts for B, and 18 1/4 cts for C extra. **1912** *Amer. Mag.* Aug. 415/2 Lederle laid down the law that all milk sold in the city should be classified into three grades: (A)—suitable for infants and children. (B)—suitable for adults. (C)—suitable for cooking and manufacturing purposes. **1945** *Newsweek* 4 June 31/3 About two days a week some Grades B and C beef to early or preferred customers.

b. Used as a grade or mark in school. See also **high C.**

1889 *Harvard Faculty Rec.* in M. L. Smallwood *Exams. & Grading Systems* 59 Any member of the graduating class who has attained Grade C or a higher grade in eighteen courses . . . will be recommended for a degree. **1948** *Dly. Ardmoreite* (Ardmore, Okla.) 31 Mar. 14/4 On her last report card she received 4 A's and 4 B's and only one C.

ca- kə. Also **co-, ka-.** [Perhaps imitative. Stone suggests it may be from G. *ge-*. Cf. **ker-.**] Widely used colloquially as an emphatic or intensive prefix. Cf. **caboodle, chewallop, cowallop.**

The 1758 exs. may be the result of misreading a *w* poorly written in the MS.

1758 *Essex Inst. Coll.* XLV. 343 They came within a mile & 1/2 of this Stockade, where lay in Ambush near 50 of the Enemy, who cahoop'd. *Ib.*, The Indian sprung out of the Road towards the Enemy, and cahoop'd likewise. **1832** *Polit. Examiner* (Shelbyville, Ky.) 8 Dec. 4/1 By gum, if I dident sit plump cowallish right down on Deby's aunt's cat. **1843** Stephens *High Life N.Y.* II. 63 It was lucky the [theater-] curtain went down ca-smash as it did. *Ib.* 67 It [*sc.* a bouquet] fell ca-swash right down to Miss Elssler's feet. *c***1845** *Big Bear Ark.* 124 Chunkey lathered away, and *ca chunk!* he went into the creek. **1924** *D.N.* V. 264 *Ca-blam* (sound of blow) *ca-blub.*

*cab, n. The covered compartment of a locomotive that houses the engineer and fireman. Also attrib.

1859 Worcester 187/1 *Cab.* . . . A small structure on a locomotive engine serving as a shelter to the engineer. **1901** Merwin & Webster *Calumet K* 94 The fireman [was] leaning far out of the cab window, closely scanning the track for signs of an obstruction. **1947** *Chr. Sci. Monitor* 1 Mar. III. 23/2 The cab of a railroad engine is no feather bed. *transf.* **1887** C. B. George *40 Years on Rail* 31 The brakes of all cars were on top, and the brake-man sat in that elevated position in a little cab.

b. Hence **cabless,** *a.* Of a locomotive engine: Not furnished with a cab. *Rare.*

1887 C. B. George *40 Years on Rail* 24 We had a small cabless engine, weighing about five tons.

As the last term in **auto, electric, engine, locomotive cab.**

caba ˈkæbə, *n.* [F. *cabas*, basket.] "A flat basket . . . for figs, &c.; hence, a lady's flat work-basket or reticule" (W. '64). — **1877** Ruede *Sod-House Days* 27 At N's we stopped at the pump, which furnished the liquor and the caba furnished the solids for the meal. **1898** Deland *Old Chester Tales* 317 So Lucy came, with . . . her little caba full of worsted work.

cabalgada ˌkabəlˈgadə, *n. S.W.* [Sp. in same sense.] A cavalcade. *Obs.* — **1849** Audubon *Western Journal* (1906) 95 Those intending to run off the 'cabalgada' of a travelling party, take a strong horse.

caballada ˌkabəlˈjadə, *n. S.W.* [Sp. in similar sense.] A herd of horses or mules, often the supply of mounts kept by a ranching outfit.

This term is illustrated with unusual fulness here to show the number and complexities of its variants.

1821 S. F. Austin in *Texas Hist. Quart.* VII. 288 Found that Erasmo had captured a Caviard of mules & horses which some traders were taking in from the Comanches. **1836** Dewees *Lett. from Texas* 208 Several persons . . . went round calling themselves press-masters, and by this means soon obtained a fine cavalyard of horses. **1844** Gregg *Commerce of Prairies* I. 27 The savages mounted those they had already secured, . . . and drove off the entire *caballada.* **1874** McCoy *Cattle* 11 We will here say for the benefit of our northern readers that the term 'ranch' is used in the Southwest instead of 'farm,' . . . the horse used a 'cow horse,' and the herd of horses a 'cavvie yard.' **1901** in *Kansas Hist. Coll.* (1902) VII. 52, I was driving a cavayado. . . . The Mexicans always drove their cavayado in front of their trains. **1941** Fergusson *Southwest* 32 Unskilled boys wrangled the horse herd, called the 'caviya' from the Spanish caballada. **1942** Dale *Cow Country* 47 The band of horses was variously known as the *remuda,* 'saddle band,' or the *caballado,* sometimes corrupted into 'cavvy yard,' 'cavalry yard,' or 'cavvy.'

caballerango kaˌbaljəˈræŋgo, *n. S.W.* [Amer. Sp. in same sense.] (See quot. 1902.) Cf. **horse wrangler, wrangler.** — **1902** *Out West* June 619 Among the first American cowboys—who were of course Spanish—the man who took care of the riding horses was known as the *Caballerango.* **1925** Will James *Drifting Cowboy* 80 (Bentley), The cavy-wrango had brought the horses in, and they were all there to pick from one another day's riding.

caballero ˌkabəlˈjero, *n. S.W.* [Sp. in same sense.] A horseman, gentleman, lady's escort.

1837 Irving *Astoria* iii. 85 (*headline*), A Californian caballero. **1892** Duval *Young Explorers* 69 Gayly dressed 'caballeros' were prancing along the streets on their gaudily caparisoned steeds. **1948** *P.C.C. Chronicle* (Pasadena, Calif.) 7 May 2/1 Gay caballeros and beautiful senoritas danced under the warm California sun.

caballo kəˈbaljo, *n. S.W.* [Sp. in sense **1.** Amer. Sp. in sense **2.**]

1. A horse.

[**1685** Joutel *Journal* (1719) 118 They [Indians] spoke some words of broken *Spanish,* as . . . *Cohavillo* instead of *Cavallo,* a Horse.] **1845** T. J. Green *Texian Exped.* 205 How, then, . . . do you catch your cavallos and chickens? **1907** White *Arizona Nights* 23 Get your cavallos and follow me. *Ib.* 261 That cavallo of his is a heap sight better than the Shorty horse. **1945** Marshall *Santa Fe* 4 Then the creature split and here was a man and something he called a *caballo,* which was not a part of the man but a separate animal.

2. A lively dance of one or more groups of four couples.

1910 J. Hart *Vigilante Girl* 226 Some of them set dances in which many joined, others for single couples, such as the bamba, the borrego, and the caballo.

cabana kəˈbanə, *n.* Orig. *S.W.* [Sp. *cabaña*, hut, cabin.] A cabin, also a small bathhouse, usu. of canvas, on a beach. — **1890** *Outing* July 232 He lives in a little *cabane* on a rough hillside. **1898** *Land of Sunshine* Jan. 61 Though not lacking a certain picturesqueness, what the *cabana* means, and what it stands for, is a large thing. **1948** *Airlines* Mar. 3/1 Gay, colorful Cabanas and big umbrellas line the beaches.

cabaret ˌkæbəˈre, *n. S.W.* [F., an Amer. borrowing.] A small liquor shop. *Obs.* Cf. **Broadway cabaret.** — **1835** J. H. Ingraham *South-West* I. 92 Ten, out of seventeen successive shops, or *cabarets,* upon the shelves of which I could discover nothing but myriads of claret or Madeira bottles. **1851** Hall *Manhattaner* 102 Picayune dram-houses (better known among Crescent citizens as cabarets) smoke each other (tobaccowise) at every few steps.

*cabbage. In combs.: (1) **cabbage bug,** = **harlequin cabbage bug;** (2) **cigar,** (see **cabbage leaf**); (3) **hammock,** a hammock overgrown with cabbage palms, *rare;* (4) **land,** land covered with cabbage palm, *rare;* (5) ***leaf,** an inferior cigar, suggestive of one made of cabbage leaves, in full **cabbage leaf cigar,** *colloq.;* (6) **palmetto,** a palm, *Sabal palmetto,* also attrib.; (7) **pea,** (see quot.), *obs.;* (8) **pear,** a species of *Opuntia* found in the southwest, *rare;* (9) **plusia,** a moth the larva of which feeds on cabbage; (10) **radish,** (see quot.), *rare;* (11) **turnip,** a species of turnip now unidentifiable, *obs.;* (12) **yard,** ?a cabbage garden, *obs.*

(1) **1889** *Cent.* 746/3 [The] cabbage-bug . . . has spread from Guatemala to Mexico, and thence into the United States, and is destructive to cabbages. — **(2) 1870** in MARK TWAIN *The Judge's 'Spirited Woman'* (1875) 272 Smoking one of those cabbage cigars the San Francisco people used to think were good enough for us in those times. — **(3) 1837** J. L. WILLIAMS *Florida* 142 Occasionally cabbage hammocks of considerable extent, rise in the midst of these glades. — **(4) 1837** WILLIAMS *Terr. of Florida* 54 The St. Johns rises . . . in the extensive grass meadows . . . separated from the waters that run south into the Everglades, by a very crooked rise of cabbage land.

(5) **1851** HALL *Manhattaner* 158 The fog . . . was heavy enough to give the cows a bronchitis, and as disagreeable to breathe as the smoke of a cabbage-leaf regalia cigar. **1912** NICHOLSON *Hoosier Chron.* 62 Try one of those cigars. . . . If they're cabbage leaf it isn't my fault. — **(6) 1802** J. DRAYTON *S. Carolina* 66 Cabbage palmetto. (*Corypha palmetto.*) Grows on the sea islands, and on lands adjacent to salt water rivers, a few miles from the sea. **1947** *Wildlife Management Jrnl.* Jan. 25/1 The birds traveled through a thick forest undergrowth of yaupon (*Ilex vomitoria*) and cabbage palmetto (*Sabal palmetto*). — **(7) 1859** A. VAN BUREN *Sojourn in South* 155 The Cabbage Pea, with its large broad pod, makes a fine soup. — **(8) 1827** in DALE *Ashley-Smith Explor.* (1918) 188, I here found a kind of plant of the prickly pear kind, which I called the cabbage pear, the largest of which grows about two feet and a half high and 1½ feet in diameter . . . nearly of the substance of a turnip . . . its form . . . similar to that of an egg, being smaller at the ground and top than in the middle. — **(9) 1890** *Cent.* 4571/2 *P. brassicae* of the United States is one of the worst enemies of the cabbage. . . . [It is] known as the *cabbage-plusia.* **1892** V. KELLOGG *Kansas Insects* 61 Cabbage plusia (*Plusia brassicae*). . . . The caterpillars have but five pairs of legs instead of eight pairs, as is the case with the Imported Cabbage-worms.

(10) **1806** in *Ann. 9th Congress* 2 Sess. 1127 This cabbage must be considered as indigenous to this sequestered quarter, and may be denominated as the cabbage radish of the Washita. — **(11) 1773** FRANKLIN *Corr. Wks.* (1840) VIII. 32 Herewith I send you a few seeds of what is called the cabbage turnip. — **(12) 1742** HEMPSTEAD *Diary* 394, I was at home fenceing in a Cabage yard. **1778** *Essex Inst. Coll.* LII. 13 Another shot I saw tearing up the ground . . . & burying itself in a cabbage yard.

b. In colloq. phrases (see quots.). *Obs.*

1828 A. ROYALL *Black Book* II. 243 It is flint to cabbage emphatically. **1902** CLAPIN 90, *I don't boil my cabbage twice,* a very common expression in the country towns of Pennsylvania, and signifying that the person uttering it does not intend to repeat an observation. Allusion to the cabbage which when boiled a second time, is not always palatable.

As the last term in **Arkansas, goss, palmetto, skunk, skunk's, squaw, swamp, wild cabbage.**

cabestro kəˈbestro, *n.* Also **cabresta, cabresto, caberos.** *S.W.* [Sp., halter; Amer. Sp., hair rope.] A hair rope, esp. one used as a halter or lariat. Cf. **cabras.**

1846 *Knickerb.* XXVII. 251 He felt himself violently seized from behind, his arms pinioned, his mouth filled with the end of a hair cabresta. **1902** CLAPIN 90 The *cabestro* is also employed for fastening animals to stakes or pegs driven into the ground. **1936** RIDINGS *Chisholm Trail* 371 Many of them carried a *cabestros* or hair-rope, and at night time, when they lay down on their blankets on the prairie, would lay the hair-rope on the ground, entirely encircling their beds.

cabeza kaˈbesə, *n. S.W.* [Sp. in same sense.] Head. — **1858** *Phoenix* (Sacramento) 31 Jan. 4/1 But the world . . . shall yet feel the potency of this *cabeza* and this right arm. **1877** WM. WRIGHT *Big Bonanza* 374 He's got more instink, that dog has . . . right in that ugly old cabeza of his, nor can be found in the heds of a whole plaza full of eddicated town dogs.

cabezon ˌkæbəˈzɑn, *n.* [Sp. *cabezón,* bighead, aug. of *cabeza.*] (See quot.) — **1889** *Cent.* 549/2 bighead. . . . A local name of a Californian species of sculpin, *Scorpaenichthys marmoratus,* a fish of the family *Cottidae.* Also called *cabezon.*

cabildo kaˈbildo, *n. S.W.* [Sp. in same senses.] The chapter house of a cathedral church, or the chapter itself. Usu. *cap.*

1880 CABLE *Grandissimes* (1883) 320 He saw his clerks . . . standing idle and shabby in the arcade of the Cabildo and on the banquette of Maspero's. **1924** in HEARNE *Amer. Miscellany* lxviii, I wish to thank those who did this service for me . . . at the Cabildo, in New Orleans. **1948** *N.O. Times-Picayune* (Mag.) 24 Oct. 7/3 Tidewater red cypress lasts forever when used in buildings, such as many of New Orleans historic old landmarks, the Cabildo, the Presbytere and St. Louis Cathedral.

* **cabin,** *n.*

1. Formerly at Harvard, a closet or cubicle assigned a student as a study. *Obs.*

*c***1644** in *Pub. Col. Soc.* XV. 9 Let to George Stirk 1644 wthout charging him wth ye Cabin. *c***1673** *Ib.* 12 The right to a Cabin in ye great chamber. *c***1890** *Ib.* lxxiii, In the chambers were 'cabins' or closets which were specifically assigned. Sometimes the cabin assigned to a student was not situated in the chamber where he lodged.

2. In a Creek Indian council house a bench-like structure used as a seat and as a bed. *Obs.*

1772 TAITT in *Travels Amer. Col.* 503 The Square [at Tuckabatchi on the Tallapoosa river] is formed by four houses about forty feet in Length and ten wide. Open in front and devided into three different Cabins each. **1791** BARTRAM *Travels* 368 All around the inside of the building, betwixt the second range of pillars and the wall, is a range of cabins or sophas. *Ib.* 451 The aged chiefs and warriors are seated on their cabbins or sophas.

3. In combs.: (1) **cabin car,** (see quot. 1895); (2) **fever,** an alleged ailment that confines one to his cabin, *rare;* (3) **guard,** on a river steamer the lateral extension of the deck outside the ladies' cabin; (4) **mate,** one who shares with another a cabin on a boat; (5) **raising,** a gathering of neighbors to erect a log cabin, *obs.;* (6) **roof,** a form of house roof similar to that used on cabins, *obs.;* (7) **ship,** a passenger ship providing accommodations for cabin passengers only; (8) **song,** a song such as those who live in cabins, esp. Negroes, sing.

(1) **1879** *Scribner's Mo.* Nov. 23/2 This road has also cabin cars, with stove, bunks, etc. which it will switch off at any station. **1895** WAIT *Car-Builder's Dict.* 22 Caboose cars are either *four-wheel* or *eight-wheel,* and both are in general use; four-wheeled cabooses are sometimes termed *cabin-cars.* — **(2) 1924** SHEPHARD *P. Bunyan* 135 But that year they got the spring-fever or the cabin-fever or somethin', and got lazy and laid down on their jobs. — **(3) 1875** MARK TWAIN *Old Times on Miss.* 569 It has been up on the ladies' cabin-guard two days. — **(4) 1870** MARK TWAIN *Sketches* (1875) 312 Will the new candidate explain . . . the little circumstance of his cabin-mates . . . losing small valuables from time to time?

(5) **1845** *Ind. Mag. Hist.* 11 Between log-rollings and cabin-raisings, we were together several days in each week. — **(6) 1822** *Missionary Herald* XVIII. 81 A large dwelling house, . . . covered by a cabin roof 90 feet by 40. **1847** in H. HOWE *Ohio* 198 It [*sc.* a new jail] was a rough log building; two stories high, with a cabin roof. — **(7) 1928** *Sat. Ev. Post* 4 Feb. 89/4 The same fine accommodations . . . will be maintained on the *George Washington,* now the largest American Cabin-ship. — **(8) 1893** *Voodoo Tales* 58 Cabin songs, she frankly added, were a great deal nicer than hymns.

As the last term in **bark, bayou, brush, camp, claim, double, double-penned, ghost, half-faced, hunting, improvement, Indian, log, lottery, musquash, Negro, palmetto, pine pole, pole, shake, sugar, trunk, war cabin.**

cabineer ˌkæbɪˈnɪr, *n.* One who lives in a cabin. *Rare.* — **1776** Z. F. SMITH *Kentucky* (1886) 75 Not one has arrived except a few cabineers down the Ohio.

* **cabinet,** *n.*

1. (*cap.*) The advisory council of the President of the U.S. composed of the heads of the executive departments.

1800 J. MCHENRY in Gibbs *Memoirs Admin. Washington & Adams* (1846) II. 347 We have had, for some time past, a disjointed Cabinet. **1813** *Ann. 12th Congress* 2 Sess. 562 For these twelve years past the whole affairs of this country have been managed . . . under the influence of a Cabinet little less than despotic. **1890** C. MARTYN *W. Phillips* 325 He urged Lincoln to dismiss Seward from the Cabinet as a hopeless obstructive. **1948** *Chi. D. News* 6 Nov. 6/4 Mr. Wallace . . . had previously been honored with a position in his Cabinet.

attrib. **1830** *Deb. Congress* 15 March 256/2 From the first organization of the Government, the Heads of Departments have been . . . a cabinet council. **1855** *S. Lit. Messenger* XXI. 14 His popularity . . . was fatally shaken by his acceptance of a cabinet office under John Quincy Adams. **1948** *Time* 21 June 22/2 It has been suggested that I am anxious to be a Cabinet member in the next Administration.

b. A similar body in other republics having governments modeled on that of the U.S., or in church governments.

1836 *Diplom. Corr. Texas* (1908) I. 74 Will you please, in conjunction with the Cabinet, take this matter into consideration. **1885** *Methodist Review* LXVII. 15 Nothing that he [Bishop Simpson] did was done more satisfactorily than his work in what has come to be known as the *cabinet.* **1886** LOGAN *Great Conspiracy* 196 The *immediate* 'shedding of blood' . . . was . . . the subject of excited agitation in the Confederate Cabinet at this time.

c. (See quot.)

1889 *Cent.* 747/3 The term *cabinet* is also sometimes applied to the executive council of a governor or of a mayor.

2. In special combs.: (1) **cabinet cherry,** the wild black or rum cherry, *Padus serotina;* (2) **factory,** a factory in which cabinet work is done; (3) **furniture,** furniture made by cabinet makers, also attrib.; (4) * **maker,** one who assists or seeks to assist in forming the President's Cabinet; (5) * **minister,** a member of the President's Cabinet; (6) **secretary,** =prec.; (7) **shop,** a cabinet-maker's shop; (8) **work,** cabinet ware.

(1) 1817–8 EATON *Botany* (1822) 411 *Prunus virginiana,* wild cherry, rum cherry, cabinet cherry. . . . In dense forests it grows to a very great height. . . . The bark is an excellent tonic. — **(2) 1832** WILLIAMSON *Maine* II. 609 Here is a cabinet factory worked by water power, where ten or twelve men are employed, who make 'annually from 8 to 10,000 chairs.' — **(3) 1815** *Niles' Reg.* IX. 36/1 The principle manufactures in wood are the following:—sideboards, secretaries, bureaus, and other articles of cabinet furniture. **1827** DRAKE & MANSF. *Cincinnati* 59 Our Steam Engines, Castings, Cabinet Furniture, Chairs, Hats, etc. etc. are sent to Kentucky, Alabama, Louisiana. *Ib.,* 64 Thirteen Cabinet Furniture Shops. — **(4) 1884** *Boston Journal* 22 Nov. 2/4 The New York Sun says that 'the Cabinet-makers, the office seekers, and the schemers who abound in Washington are busy in laying-out plans for the future.' **1944** *Chi. D. News* 22 Nov. 6/7 The congressional cabinet-makers told me he was doing his best to keep senatorial chairs from collapsing.

(5) 1806 *Ann. 9th Congress* 1 Sess. 561 My answer was, (and from a Cabinet Minister too,) 'There is no longer any Cabinet.' **1873** MARK TWAIN & WARNER *Gilded Age* xxxii. 290 The first reception took place at a Cabinet Minister's—or rather, a Cabinet Secretary's—mansion. — **(6) 1873** [see **cabinet minister**]. — **(7) 1817** S. BROWN *Western Gaz.* 93 There are [in Lexington, Ky.] five cabinet shops. **1877** JOHNSON *Anderson Co., Kansas* 65 Burns has built several buildings in the town, [and] opened the first cabinet shop. **1948** *Red Book* (Chi.) March 279/4 (*advt.*), Quality Cabinet Shop. — **(8) 1732** *S.C. Gazette* 104/2 [There] will continue to be sold all sorts of Cabinet Work. **1834** PECK *Gaz. Illinois* 24 The black walnut is much used for building materials and cabinet work. **1908** GRIFFITH *Essential Woodworking* 105 The most elementary of cabinet work necessitates groove cutting, [etc.].

As the last term in **kitchen, Martha Washington sewing, rebel, spoils cabinet.**

cabinette ˌkæbɪ'net, *n.* A small cabin. *Rare.* — **1879** *Scribner's Mo.* Oct. 822/2 Can I ever forget that low-cowled cabinette . . . up on the hill-side?

* **cable,** *n.*

1. Short for **cablegram.** Also attrib.

1876 *Outlook* (Santa Monica, Calif.) 19 July 4/2 To-day we have cable letters from Paris, London, Rome, Berlin, Vienna, Athens and other cities. **1910** *Bookman* June 403/1 The cables to the American journals were filled with the news. **1948** *Chi. D. News* 14 Oct. 59/2 Then this cable from pop was really an S.O.S.

b. Short for **cable car.** *Obs.*

1892 S. HALE *Letters* 269 There are cables, and electrics. . . . I mounted a cable, took a transfer [etc.].

2. In derivatives and combs.: (1) **cable car,** a form of streetcar drawn by a cable operated by a stationary engine, cf. **cable grip** [Edgar M. Kahn in *Cable Car Days* (1940), 27 ff., says such cars were invented by Andrew S. Hallidie, a Scotchman, in San Francisco, about 1873]; (2) **celebration,** a celebration on the completion of the Atlantic cable to Europe in 1858; (3) **-gram,** a message sent by means of a submarine telegraphic cable [In Web. '79 called "Colloq. and low"]; (4) **grip,** a device on a cable car for gripping and releasing the moving cable beneath the car, now *hist.;* (5) **railroad, railway,** a street or other railway on which the cars are drawn by a cable, also attrib., *obs.;* (6) **road,** =prec.; (7) **walk,** a narrow footway to the top of a tower of a suspension bridge, cf. * *catwalk.*

(1) [**1873** *S.F. D. Ev. Bulletin* 1 Aug., At five o'clock this morning the first car on the Clay Street Railroad was sent down the hill and back again by means of the wire rope.] **1887** J. B. SMITH *Cable Traction* 42 The excellent control of the cable car is . . . admirably demonstrated upon this line. **1945** *Sat. Review* 26 May 6/3 Wilder Foote, assistant to Secretary Stettinius, said that a journey on the cable cars was well worth the trip to San Francisco. — **(2) 1858** *Harper's Wkly.* 11 Sep. 585 (*caption*), Atlantic Cable Celebration—Presentation to Cyrus W. Field in the Crystal Palace. **1896** HASWELL *New York* 517 The 'Cable Celebration' in New York will be long remembered; the city was illuminated, *Te Deum* was sung in Trinity Church, a banquet was given to Cyrus W. Field, whose energy had accomplished the great work. — **(3) 1868** *Daily News* (London) 26 Sep., The new word *cablegram* is used by a New York contemporary to characterise a telegraphic despatch. **1883** *Harper's Mag.* March 605/2 My suspense was . . . relieved by a telegram, or cablegram as some say. **1948** *Spokesman-Review* (Spokane, Wash.) 23 Sep. 16, I sent a cablegram to your Cousin Bedelia. — **(4)** [**1944** KAHN *Cable Car Days* 108 James W. Harris, with cable-car grips.] **1947** *Life* 24 Feb. 16 Cable grip fits into the slot between the tracks. With it the gripman inside the car can grasp or release the cable, which moves at a constant 9.5 mph.

(5) 1889 *N.J. Laws* 332 Every cable railroad company . . . and every corporation owning, using or operating any cable, electric or horse railroad [etc.]. **1946** MCWILLIAMS *So. Calif. Country* 148 He also designed a plan by which he could operate a swinging cable railway from the hotels on Mt. Lowe across a vast gorge to the proposed hotel. — **(6) 1882** *Ideographic* (S.F.) 25 July 2/3 The cable- or 'grip' road, as

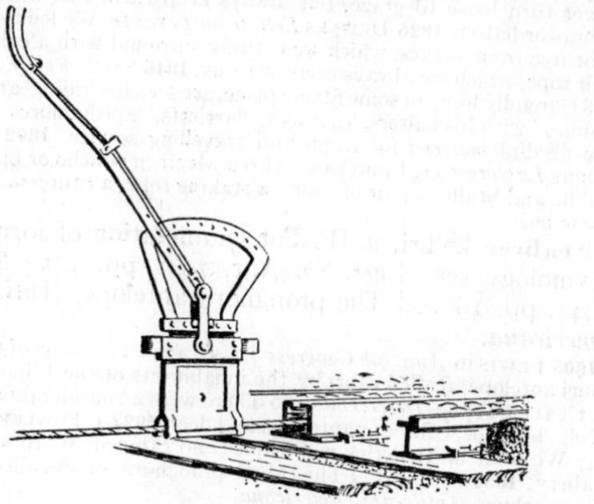

One form of cable grip

they term it in Cincinnati, seems to have made an unenviable reputation in that city, having caused the death of several persons during its short existence. **1891** *Harper's Mag.* Dec. 162/1 It was along a street traversed by a cable road. — **(7) 1929** *Literary Digest* 11 May 36/2 Climbing the cable walk of the Brooklyn Bridge to the top of one of its towers . . . is one of the routine jobs which is guaranteed to make photographers slightly nervous.

caboodle kə'budḷ, *n.* Also **capoodle,** etc. [App. from **ca-**+**boodle.**] The (entire) lot, number, crowd, usu. *the whole caboodle. Colloq.* Cf. **boodle 2, kerboodle.**

*a***1848** *Ohio State Jrnl.* (B.), The whole caboodle will act upon the recommendation of the Ohio Sun. **1884** L. W. BALDWIN *Yankee School Teacher in Va.* 27, I wish the hull keboodle on ye a Merry Christmas. **1946** *Yankee* Aug. 11 The citizens of Long Island claimed the whole 'caboodle' as salvage.

* **caboose,** *n.* [For sense **1.** cf. LG. *kabuse,* a wretched dwelling.]

1. A hut or poor dwelling. *Obs.*

1839 *Cong. Globe* App. 15 Feb. 343/1 We have a postmaster in our own little village . . . and in his little caboose of a post office I have found electioneering interferences. **1874** *Opelika Times* (Ala.) 30 Sep., [Such] a colored man . . . should be preferred as tenant of our houses, cabooses on the farm, drayman upon the streets.

b. =**calaboose.** *Slang.*

1865 *Republican Banner* (Nashville, Tenn.) 12 Oct. 3/2 The 'caboose' is neatly packed with 'pickled' offenders of municipal law. **1939** *These Are Our Lives* 346 It's going to be kept clean as long as I'm there if they put me in the caboose for cruelty to roaches and water bugs.

2. =**caboose car.** Cf. **double caboose.**

1861 *Remin. Life Locomotive Engineer* 90, I never prepared myself for another midnight ride in the 'Caboose' of a freight train by telling horrid stories before I started. **1947** *Chi. D. News* 17 Jan. 4/2 A freight car and caboose were destroyed by fire.

attrib. and *transf.* **1870** *R.R. Gazette* 30 Apr. 100/3 He remembers . . . the caboose brakeman. **1903** *N.Y. Ev. Post* 25 Aug., The rest of the crew . . . saw from the caboose windows the bodies . . . lying along the tracks. **1894** *Life* 11 Oct. 238/1 Every town has . . . scores of men with the caboose of their trousers worn smooth as glass. **1944** MENCKEN in *New Yorker* 30 Dec. 19/2 Larry and the other comedians began paddling the girls' cabooses with slapsticks.

3. (See quots.) *Obs.*

1920 HUNTER *Trail Drivers Texas* I. 213 Under a camp wagon is usually suspended an old cowhide called the 'caboose,' and in that we throw stray pieces of wood, etc. **1939** WELLMAN *Trampling Herd* 113 Below the wagon was slung a peculiar device known as a 'cooney' or 'caboose.'

4. In special combs.: (1) **caboose car,** (see quot. 1895); (2) **stove,** (see quot.).

(1) **1862** *Ashcroft's Railway Directory* 76 No. of Caboose Cars [on Central Railroad of New-Jersey], 6. **1895** WAIT *Car-Builder's Dict.* 22 Caboose-car. . . . A car attached to the rear of all freight trains, for the accommodation of the conductor and trainmen, and for carrying the various stores, tools, etc., required on freight trains. — (2) *Ib.*, Caboose-stoves. . . . A stove for heating a caboose-car and by which trainmen may warm their lunch, and even do some cooking if necessary.

cabras kə'bras, *n.* Also **caboras,** etc. Variants of **cabestro.**

1805 SIBLEY in *Ann. 9th Congress* 2 Sess. 1082 Their horses they never turn loose to graze, but always keep them tied with a long cabras or halter. **1826** DEWEES *Lett. from Texas* 61 We look us out a spot free from snakes, which we entirely surround with a caboras or hair rope, which we always carry with us. **1846** SAGE *Rocky Mt. Life* 348 Carefully hung in some fitting place, are seen his 'riding' and 'pack saddles,' with his halters, 'cavraces,' 'larrietts,' 'apishamores,' and all the needful *materiel* for camp and travelling service. **1892** DUVAL *Young Explorers* 11, I purchased also a Mexican poncho or blanket, a saddle and bridle, a pair of spurs, a staking rope, a cabressa made of horse hair.

cabree kə'bri, *n.* [F. For enumeration of forms and etymology see *Amer. Sp.* Apr. 1941, pp. 125–26; Feb. 1944, pp. 19–20.] The pronghorn antelope, *Antilocapra americana.*

1805 LEWIS in *Ann. 9th Congress* 2 Sess. 1046 The skins of the Missouri antelope, (called cabri by the inhabitants of the Illinois). **1812** J. CUTLER *Topog. Descr. Ohio* 166 There were a considerable number of elk, buffaloe, cabree or antelope, and deer. **1822** J. FOWLER *Journal* 147 We went up the crick eight miles and camped. Ward killed one Cabery. **1889** *Cent.* 245/2 The cabril, pronghorn, or so-called American antelope, *Antilocapra americana.*

cabrón kə'bron, *n. S.W.* [Sp., a cuckold.] (See quot. 1932.) — **1931** AUSTIN *Starry Adventure* 310 (Bentley), As if in reference to her you would admit even the impulse to pound the guts out of that filthy *cabron.* **1932** BENTLEY *Sp. Terms* 110 Cabron. . . . Masculine augmentative of *cabra,* goat. Although the term literally means 'a big goat' and therefore often not taken seriously by Americans who use it, *cabron* is, in the mind of the Mexican, as strong as English 'fool' or even 'damn fool.'

cache kæʃ, *n.* [F.] A secret place of deposit, often a hole in the ground, used by explorers, trappers, etc.; the goods, provisions, etc., stored in such a place. Cf. ***deposit 1.**

1805 LEWIS & CLARK *Exped.* (1904) VII. 99 We put in the carsh or hole . . . the bellowses. **1888** ROOSEVELT in *Cent. Mag.* XXXVI. 42/2 The plunderers of our cache were a pair of cougars. **1948** *Sierra Club Bul.* Mar. 6 There was only enough food at the cache to give four men 45-pound packs.

transf. and *attrib.* **1929** W. HEYLIGER *Builder of Dam* 14 I'm down in a cache of small rocks. **1947** *Steamboat* (Colo.) *Pilot* 16 Jan. 3/3 He was suffocated in a cache-cellar used by a sheep company to store supplies.

b. The pebble or other small object used by Indians in the game of hand *q.v. Obs.*

1837 IRVING *Bonneville* II. xviii. 185 In the present game, the object hidden, or the *cache* as it is called by the trappers, is a small splint of wood, or other diminutive article, that may be concealed in the closed hand.

c. *To make (a) cache,* to cache. *Obs.*

1843 FRÉMONT *Exped.* 22 As this was to be a point in our homeward journey, I made a *cache* (a term used in all this country for what is hidden in the ground) of a barrel of pork. **1846** SAGE *Scenes Rocky Mts.* (1859) 196 A company of traders . . . made câche of one hundred and sixty packs of robes, which they were compelled to leave. **1856** EMERSON *Eng. Traits* 120 The wolf . . . makes a cache of his prey.

As the last term in **grub, log, salmon, seed cache.**

cache kæʃ, *v.* [F. *cacher,* to hide.]

1. *tr.* To hide or place in a cache. Also **cached,** *a.*

1805 *Lewis & Clark Exped.* (1904) VII. 139 In the evening after dark we carried our baggage we concluded to carsh to the place of cashing. **1901** WHITE *Westerners* 47 Lone Wolf's band took up quarters within striking distance of the cached schooners. **1948** *Canadian Alpine Jrnl.* June 12 We decided to cache our packs and begin our return to the cabin.

2. *intr.* or *refl.* To hide oneself.

1827 *Michigan Herald* (Detroit) 29 Sep., The women and children were all cached, that is, hidden in holes dug in the ground. **1857** *Spirit of Times* 14 Mar. 18/2 This child smells trouble a-comin'; so let's *cache* at once, for it ain't safe, no how. **1897** INMAN *Old Santa Fe Trail* 43 If he is out hunting and desires to secrete himself from approaching game, he will say, 'I am going to *cache* behind that rock.'

cachimilla katʃə'miljə, *n.* Also **cachinilla, cachanilla.** *S.W.* [Amer. Sp. in same sense.] (See quots.)

1909 *Cent. Supp.* 183/3 cachimilla. . . . A west American composite shrub, *Pluchea sericea,* called *arrow-wood* by travelers because it is used by the Indian in making arrows. It ranges from western Texas to California and northern Mexico. Also called *arrow-weed.* **1913** WOOTON *Trees & Shrubs N.M.* 146 Arrow Wood or Cachinilla (*Berthellotia borrealis*) is a common shrub, forming large patches in the valleys of the southern part of the State. **1931** DAYTON *Western Browse Plants* 164 Arrowweed [is] . . . also known by the vernacular names arrowbush, arrowwood, cachanilla, cachimilla, and osikakamuk.

cacique kə'sik, *n.* [Sp. in same sense. An Amer. borrowing.] Among the Indians in the Southwest, a chief, ruler, petty king.

1838 TEXIAN *Mexico v. Texas* 82 A man in a hideous mask . . . rules the dance, and not infrequently applies the lash to the caciques and the grandees. **1878** *Mesilla Valley* (N.M.) *Independent* 16 Mar. 1/2 The meal having been disposed of, the Cacique produced a huge gourd of native wine. **1942** CASTETTER & BELL *Pima & Papago Agric.* 229 It is customary among the Pueblos for the people of a village to prepare, plant, hoe, irrigate and harvest the cacique's field.

Hence **caciqueship.**

1882 *Atlantic Mo.* Oct. 551/2 The head chief combines with his political office the caciqueship, or that which in Zuni is distinctly religious, . . . a kind of high-priesthood.

b. (See quot.)

1871 DE VERE 71 The West India term *Cacique* . . . is often most absurdly applied . . . to mayors of New Mexican towns, and any somewhat pompous and self-sufficient man is apt to be nicknamed the Cacique of his town.

cacomistle 'kækə,mɪsl, *n.* Also **cacomixl.** *S.W.* [Amer. Sp. *cacomixtle* (< Nahuatl) in same sense.] (See quot. 1889.) Cf. **tree civet.**

[**1869** FLOWER *Proc. Zool. Society* i, Acomistle or Bassa. vis, an American animal of the racoon family.] **1889** *Cent.* 469/2 *B[assaris] astuta* is the type-species, inhabiting the southwestern United States and Mexico, where it is called *mountain-cat* and *cacomixl.* It is a pretty and intelligent creature, about as large as a cat, resembling the racoon in some respects, but slenderer, and with a long furry tail marked with black and white rings, as in the common lemur. **1939** SNEDIGAR *Small Native Mammals* 48 A very close relative of the raccoon . . . the cacomixtle has drifted north to us from its native Mexican home. **1947** CAHALANE *Mammals No. Amer.* 166 Modern Mexicans frequently have used the Aztec title: *cacomixtle,* although in Baja California *babisuri* is preferred.

***cactus,** *n.* In combs.: (1) **cactus candy,** candy made by boiling the pulp of certain cacti with sugar; (2) **forest,** an extensive growth of arborescent cacti; (3) **mouse,** a white-footed mouse, *Peromyscus eremicus,* found in the Southwest; (4) **rat,** =prec.; (5) **woodpecker,** =**Gila woodpecker;** (6) **wren,** any one of various large wrens found in the Southwest.

(1) [**1858** VIELE *Following Drum* 186 Then came the dessert, dulcies of candied cactus and melons.] **1895** *Amer. Folk-Lore* Jan.–Apr. 51 This is the best kind of cactus candy. **1925** BRYAN *Papago Country* 47 The pulp of bisnaga is not bitter like that of sahuaro and is used in making the cactus candy, a famous Arizona product. — (2) **1910** *Cent. Mag.* March 763/1 A moment's walk . . . took me to the heart of the giant cactus forest. **1921** *Outing* May 68/2 These sites are . . . in the cactus forest on the Gold Roads route, six or eight miles southwest of Kingman, Arizona, and at Newberry Springs in the Mohave desert. — (3) **1939** *Mammalogy Jrnl.* 14 Nov. 443 On the plain, cactus-mouse burrows were grouped around the base of the mesquite. **1946** HALL *Mammals Nev.* 510 The cactus mouse . . . is a species of the Lower Sonoran Life-zone. — (4) **1904** BURDICK *Mystic Mid-Region* 63 A common creature in the portions of the desert with cacti is the cactus rat.

(5) **1914** *U.S. Nat. Museum Bul.* No. 50, 254 *Dryobates scalaris cactophilus* Oberholser. Cactus Woodpecker. **1940** JAEGER *Desert Wild Flowers* 22 The dried stems of this agave are used as nesting sites by the cactus woodpecker. — (6) **1869** *Amer. Naturalist* III. 183 The Rock Wren and Cactus Wren . . . chirrup loudly from the tiled roof or dense thickets. **1948** *Desert* Feb. 28/1 The cactus wrens were friendly and curious.

As the last term in **barrel, buckhorn, candle, cane, Christmas, elk-horn, fish hook, giant, globe, grizzly bear, hedgehog, ice cream, jumping, king, monumental, old man, organ, pear, pillar, rainbow, saguaro giant, snake, strawberry, tree, tuna, yucca cactus.**

Caddo 'kado, *n.* ["Contracted from *Kä' dohädä' cho,* real Caddo" (Hodge).] A member of a tribe of Indians formerly living in Louisiana, Arkansas, and eastern Texas. Also attrib. *Obs.*

1805 DUNBAR *Life* 319 The Cadaux Nation is 50 leagues above the raft. **1807** in *S.W. Hist. Quart.* XLV. 295, I think by dividing of it (23 barrels of flour) among the Caddos it would have a good Effect. **1844** *Cong. Globe* 377/1 [The House agreed to pay] expenses attending the holding a treaty with the Caddoes and other wandering tribes. **1947** *Dly. Ardmoreite* (Ardmore, Okla.) 14 Aug. 12/3 Both are wearing traditional Caddo dress with intricate, well-designed beadwork.

Hence **Caddoan,** *a.*

1905 DORSEY *Traditions of Caddo* 5 The Caddos, numbering 530 in 1903, are of the Caddoan stock, and since 1859 have lived in southern Oklahoma between the Washita and Canadian rivers. **1946** *Nat. Geog. Mag.* Jan. 53/2 The Caddoan stock was found in northeastern Texas, southern Oklahoma, southwestern Arkansas, and western Louisiana.

* **cadet,** *n.*

1. A man who is kept by a prostitute; one who procures for brothels young women whom he first seduces. Also attrib. *Slang.*

1911 *Crim. Law & Criminology Jrnl.* Jan. 835 Twenty-eight topics are here treated, examples of which are the tenement house law, the disorderly house law, the cadet system, [etc.]. **1941** H. ASBURY *Underworld of Chicago* 265 In some cases they [prostitutes] were accompanied by their cadets who were continually on the lurk for fresh victims.

2. In combs.: (1) **cadet cloth,** (see quot. 1948); (2) **gray,** =prec., also transf.

(1) **1879** F. ROE *Army Lett.* 221 A tight chamois skin waist underneath my cadet-cloth habit and a broad fur collar completes a riding costume. **1948** *Amer. Fabrics* No. V. 145/2 Cadet Cloth: The standard blue, gray, or indigo and white mixture, made of woolen yarn, as decreed by the United States Miliary Academy at West Point, New York. — (2) **1865** in E. A. DOLPH *Sound Off!* (1929) 567 In a month or two We'll bid farewell to 'Cadet Gray,' And don the 'Army Blue.' **1887** *Postal Laws* 266 For Winter Wear . . . a single-breasted sack coat of 'cadet gray,' or, technically, 'blue-mixed cadet cloth.' **1894** CABLE *J. March* xvii, All Rosemonters were required to sit together at Sunday morning service, in a solid mass of cadet gray.

b. *Cadet of temperance,* (see quot.). *Obs.*

1906 MARK TWAIN *Autobiog.* (1924) II. 99 In Hannibal, when I was about fifteen, I was for a short time a Cadet of Temperance, an organization which probably covered the whole United States during as much as a year. It consisted in a pledge to refrain, during membership, from the use of tobacco.

'Cadian 'kedɪən, *n.* Short for **Acadian.** *Colloq.* Cf. **Cajan.** — **1880** CABLE *Grandissimes* 220 Agricola Fusilier . . . was loth to resell him with the rest to some unappreciative 'Cadians. **1894** CHOPIN *Bayou Folk* 59 The little 'Cadians had already disappeared like rabbits. *Ib.* 194 Madame Laballière . . . knew a respectable family of 'Cadians living some miles below.

***Caesar,** *n.* Used colloquially in exclamations, esp. *great Caesar's ghost!* — **1865** *Memphis D. Argus* 19 Nov. 3/2 (*heading*), Great Caesar! **1868** MARK TWAIN in C. Clemens *My Father* (1931) 15 Great Caesar's ghost. **1947** *Chi. Tribune* 25 May (Comics) 4 Great Caesar's ghost! Who's takin' who to the prom?

* **café,** *n.* **1.** A barroom. **2. café car,** (see quot. 1895).

(1) **1893** *Standard.* **1910** *Boston Ev. Transcript* 17 Nov. 1/6 The word 'cafe' is hereafter to be substituted for the name [*sc.* saloon] heretofore commonly employed in connection with places devoted to the purveying of alcoholic liquid refreshments. — (2) **1895** WAIT *Car-Builder's Dict.* 22 Cafe-car. . . . A buffet-dining car, in which only a light lunch is served. It differs from a *dining-car* in that the food is not cooked or prepared on the car. **1897** *Boston Herald* 11 Aug. 8/3 Instead of dining cars, the Illinois Central has placed on all its western lines cafe cars, in which meals are served a la carte.

cafeteria kæfə'tɪrɪə, *n.* [Amer. Sp. *cafetería,* retail coffee store.] A restaurant or café where the patrons serve themselves from a long counter, taking their trays to nearby tables to eat (see also quot. 1916).

1839 J. L. STEPHENS *Travel in Russian & Turkish Empires* I. 157 Every third shop, almost, being a cafteria [*sic*] where a parcel of huge turbanded fellows were at their daily labours of smoking pipes and drinking coffee. **1853** in *Amer. Sp.* II. (1927) 488 It is rather a place for drinking than for eating; and in this respect, the name has little of the meaning current in parts of Mexico where a *cafeteria* is a small restaurant serving ordinary alcoholic drinks and plain meals. **1916** NEWMARK *60 Yrs. S. Calif.* 133 Then [*c*1853] came the *cafeteria,* but the term was used with a different significance from that now in vogue. It was rather a place for drinking than eating. **1946** *Ala. School Journal* March 16/3 How do you manage your cafeteria? *attrib.* and *transf.* **1912** *Out West* Feb. 135/1 Instead of breakfast with the landlady, lunch at a cafeteria and dinner at a little cafe, there was just breakfast now and a carefully selected cafeteria dinner. **1925** *Frontier* May 14 The girl . . . energetically began dabbing at her face with a powder-puff while she half crouched, and squinted into the slit of looking glass of a penny chewing-gum cafeteria. **1948** *Hygeia* Jan. 19/2 The mice also like to congregate around the incinerators. They were veritable rodent cafeterias.

b. Designating or with reference to a court in which traffic offenders are allowed to pay certain standard fines, rather than being compelled to appear for formal court trial.

1947 *Chi. Tribune* 17 March 20/1 The total was double what the violators would have paid in 'Cafeteria' court, where no hearings are held. *Ib.* 11 Dec. 18/3 He would cooperate with the proposal that cafeteria branches of Municipal court be established under the stands of Soldiers' field for the payment of traffic fines by motorists.

* **cage,** *n.*

1. *Baseball.* An inclosed or wired-in place or area for practice, esp. a movable screen used in batting practice. Also **batting cage.**

1893 W. CAMP *College Sports* 194 Some of the best equipped of these gymnasiums have long, low alleys, completely bounded by two walls and a wire netting, in which throwing and batting can be practiced. These are known as 'cages.' **1902** *Harvard Bul.* 19 March 2/2 Practice for the outfielders on the University baseball squad was held outdoors on March 13 for the first time. The rest of the squad will leave the cage as soon as the ground is dry enough. **1935** *N.Y. Times* 8 July 20/6 Mike wandered a bit from the batting cage. **1948** *Gary* (Ind.) *Post-Tribune* 1 July 24/8 The big guy . . . went up to take his licks in the batting cage, the spot he loves best of all.

2. Used attrib. with reference to basketball.

1907 SMITH *Basket Ball Guide* 25 The cage game has for the first time been recognized and provided for. **1922** *Ardmore* (Okla.) *D. Press* 14 Jan. 1/2 The Ardmore cage-crew moves on to Lawton for the final game of the jaunt with the high school team of that city. **1946** *Grizzly Growl* (Yampa, Colo.) 20 Dec. 2/1 The Hayden Tigers won in a fast cage game over the Bears last Friday night.

Hence * **cager,** a basketball player.

1922 *Ardmore* (Okla.) *D. Press* 1 Jan. 1/6 Loco High School will return to Wilson next Friday when a game with the Wilson High cagers will occur. **1947** *L.A. Times* 18 Jan. 7/2 The Pomona College cagers defeated Caltech 47–33 last night in a Southern California Conference game.

cagey 'kedʒɪ, *a.* [Cf. dial. *cadgy,* gay, cheerful.] Sly, cautious, cunning. *Slang.*

1893 *Standard.* **1909** *Sat. Ev. Post* 1 May 5/3 See, he's cagey about going to 'em, but when a good medium gets him in front of her he swallows it all, lock, stock and barrel. **1948** *Chi. Tribune* 9 March 9/5 Those cagey political chaps May put your notion to the test.

Hence **cagily,** *adv.*

1934 WEBSTER. **1948** *Time* 25 Oct. 81/1 The Yankee management had timed things cagily.

Cahokia kə'hokɪə, *n.* [App. native name of unknown significance.] A roving tribe of the Illinois confederacy of Indians now consolidated under the name Peoria. — **1770** PITTMAN *Present State* 51 The principal Indian nations in this country are, the Cascasquias, Kaoquias, Mitchimamias, and Peoryas. **1946** FOREMAN *Last Trek* 204 The confederacy known as the Illinois Indians, now reduced to a weak remnant of former powerful tribes, was composed of the Kaskaskia, Peoria, Michigamea, Cahokia, and Tamaroa Indians.

cahoo, see **cahot.**

cahoole kə'hul, *v.* [Origin unknown.] (See quot.) *Obs.* — **1851** HALL *College Words* 40 Cahoole, at the University of North Carolina, this word in its application is almost universal, but generally signifies to cajole, to wheedle, to deceive, to procure.

cahoot kə'hut, *n.* [Origin obscure. F. *cahute,* Du. *kajuit,* G. *kajüte,* have been suggested but there is no evidence of connection with any of these.]

1. *In cahoot(s)* (*with*), in partnership, company, league (with). *Slang.*

1829 S. KIRKHAM *Eng. Gram.* 207/1 Hese in cohoot with me. **1844** *St. Louis Reveille* 14 June 2/1 Several different tribes, the Chayennes, . . . Kiawas, and others, as is supposed, were scouring the plains (in cahoot). **1948** *Green Bay* (Wis.) *Press-Gazette* 12 July 7/5 Working in cahoots with a minor official of the insurance company, he would inspect a house, examine the locks, doors and burglar alarms.

Also *to go in cahoot with, to go (in) cahoots*, to colleague with. *Slang.*

1846 CORCORAN *Pickings* 136 I'd have no objection to go in *cahoot* vith a decent feller for a character. **1855** *N.Y. Herald* 22 Nov. 4/5 This being a rather fat sop, one or two men, as they may settle between themselves, will be selected from each party, and, as they say down South, go 'cahoots,' that is to say, share the spoils. **1862** G. K. WILDER *MS Diary* 14 May, Mc wished me to go in cahoots in a store.

b. cahoot business, partnership. *Rare.*

1845 HOOPER *Suggs* (1928) 29 I'd make a *cahoot* business with old man Doublejoy, get the money from him and enter that mill-shoal with the twenty-foot fall.

2. A confederate or associate. *Rare.*

1869 *Cong. Globe* 6 April 538/3 Fisk and his 'cahoots' have got at cross purposes, and he has been put out of bed.

cahoot kəˈhut, *v.* [f. prec.] *intr.* To go into partnership, consort *with. Slang.*

1857 *N.Y. Herald* 20 May (B.), They all agree to cahoot with their claims against Nicaragua and Costa Rica. **1886** S. W. MITCHELL *R. Blake* 261 The women ken cohoot together down at the old house, and me and you, we'll go a'-fishin'. **1948** *Chi. Tribune* 1 Aug. (Comics) 6 Why don'tcha feud fa'r an' squar'—with shootin' arns instead o' gossip thet he's cahooting with speerits?

cahot kəˈho, *n.* Also **cahoo.** [F., a jerk, jolt.] A ridge of snow in the road, a "thank-you-ma'am." Chiefly Canadian.

1807 HERIOT *Travels* 269 After a heavy fall of snow, the loaded slays which pass along in the vicinity of the towns, alternately take up in their front, and deposit a quantity of snow, and thus form in the roads furrows and ridges in a transverse position, which are called *cahots;* until these are filled up, travelling becomes fatiguing and unpleasant. **1874** *Vt. Bd. Agric. Rep.* II. 659 The highways leading to our larger villages . . . are frequently so full of pitchholes or 'cahoos' as to render them totally unfit for travel. **1883** W. G. BEERS *Over the Snow* 36 There leaping in the air the toboggan bounds over a cahot, or ground-swell, as if thrown from a catapult.

Cahuilla kɑˈwiljə, *n.* "The name, of uncertain derivation, of a Shoshonean division in s. California, affiliated linguistically with the Aguas Calientes, Juaneños, and Luiseños" (Hodge). In full **Cahuilla Indians.**

1862 HAYES *Pioneer Notes* (1929) 275 The black and fiercer Cahuillas, whose name means *Master* or *The Great Nation*, who twenty years before filled every habitable spot, had left here a petty village of fifty beings on a little rise of ground at the edge of the present City. **1888** LINDLEY *Calif. of South* 384 It is also interesting to the ethnologist to study the language, habits, and religion of the Cahuilla Indians, who live here. **1896** *Land of Sunshine* Aug. 106 A wild trail through narrow passes led the Coahuias into the mountain valley which bears their name. **1940** JAEGER *Desert Wild Flowers* 9 Both the thin, sweet, outside pulp and the hard, horny, pea-sized seed of the palm fruits were eaten by the Cahuilla Indians.

* **Cain,** *n.* In colloq. phrases: (1) *by Cain*, as an expletive; (2) *to raise Cain*, to create a disturbance; (3) *what in Cain*, what in creation, what on earth.

(1) **1819** A. PEIRCE *Rebelliad* 40, I swear by Hadley, and by Cain, You ne'er shall taste my wine again. **1852** CONWAY *Hiram Hireout* 11 (We.), Sweet as a butterfly's breath, by Cain. — (2) **1840** *St. Louis Pennant* 2 May (Th.), Why have we every reason to believe that Adam and Eve were both rowdies? Because . . . they both raised Cain. *c*1849 PAIGE *Dow's Sermons* I. 247 They will feel that they have been raising Cain and breaking things. **1948** *Chi. D. News* 15 Sep. 12/6 The grasshoppers are raising cain in the city's residential districts. — (3) **1854** M. J. HOLMES *Tempest & Sunshine* 172 It had been there two weeks, and he didn't know what in cain to do with it. **1855** *Knickerb.* XLVI. 83 What in Cain did you play that for?

* **caisson,** *n.*

1. caisson disease, a disease caused by too rapid decrease in air pressure, as upon coming out of caissons, etc., characterized by neuralgic pains and sometimes resulting in death or various paralyses. Cf. **bend,** *n.*[2]

1873 A. H. SMITH (*title*), The effects of high atmospheric pressure, including the caisson disease. **1911** *Scientific Amer. Supp.* 21 Oct. 270/1 Attention was first called to caisson disease or compressed-air sickness in the middle of the last century. **1948** *Reader's Digest* Jan. 78/2 The Roeblings, father and son, and the workmen who got caisson disease were not the only casualties of the Bridge.

2. caisson fever, =prec.

1900 *Everybody's Mag.* Jan. 51/1 They took many precautions to prevent attacks of caisson fever, a dangerous and lingering form of paralysis due to working in the heavy atmospheric pressure of the air-chambers.

Cajan ˈkedʒən, *n.* Also **Cajun.** Colloquial form of **Acadian, 'Cadian.** Also attrib. or as adj.

1868 *Putnam's Mag.* II. 54 Among them were Creoles, Cagians, the descendants of the old Acadians, and a few mulattoes. **1885** *Outing* Feb. 337/1 The Cajan fisherman will gladly teach you his art of catching trout. **1948** *Democrat* 23 Sep. 4/5 The Cajans of Washington County proudly claim today that some of their ancestors were sailors under the notorious buccaneer, Jean Lafitte.

cajon kɑˈhon, *n. W.* [Sp. *cajón* in Amer. Sp. sense shown here.] (See quots.)

1862 HAYES *Pioneer Notes* (1929) 276 For midsummer, the wind was bleak that blew down through the Cajon. *Ib.* 278 The woods of Lytle Creek are a verdant thread coming from the Cajon and broken as it bends toward Jurupa. **1900** *Amer. Geog. Soc.* XXXII. 34 Cajon: A box canyon. Local in Southwest. (Sp., meaning 'box.') **1909** *Cent. Supp.* 185/3 Cajon. . . . In *phys. geog.*, a small basin inclosed on nearly all sides by steep hills or mountains. [Southwestern U.S.]

attrib. **1948** *Southwestern Rev.* Winter 33/2 The old walls of Picurin pueblo were of cajón or 'box' construction, a use of large blocks of adobe rather than bricks.

* **cake,** *n.* In combs.: (1) **cake cutter,** (see quot. 1874); (2) * **eater,** one who is effeminate and addicted to ease and pleasure, *slang;* (3) **sugar,** (see quot. 1835); (4) **tobacco,** plug tobacco, *obs.;* (5) **urchin,** (see quot.); (6) **walk,** see as a main entry; (7) **walker,** one who participates in a cakewalk *q.v.*

(1) **1874** KNIGHT 422/2 Cake-cutter. A device for cutting sheets of dough into round or ornamental forms, as heart-shaped, etc. **1879** MRS. WHITNEY *Just How* 226 Little strips of paste, cut with notched edges, by a wheel cake-cutter, may be laid across the tops. — (2) **1922** *Dly. Ardmoreite* (Ardmore, Okla.) 6 Jan. 10/4 He calls us 'lounge lizards, tea drinkers, cake eaters and all that.' **1931** *K.C. Star* 20 Nov. 38 An Emporia cake-eater . . . believes that a fair recompense for a date with a Manhattan beauty would be for her to pay all the expenses, plus a reasonable hourly stipend. — (3) **1835** AUDUBON *Ornith. Biog.* III. 440 It takes ten gallons of sap to produce a pound of fine-*grained sugar;* but an inferior kind in lumps, called *cake-sugar*, is obtained in greater quantity. **1844** GREGG *Commerce of Prairies* I. 173 When short of means they often support themselves upon only a *real* each per day, their usual food consisting of bread and a kind of coarse cake-sugar *piloncillo* to which is sometimes added a little crude ranchero cheese. [**1882** *Vermont Agric. Rep.* VII. 65 Dr. Cutting referred to a very fine sample of caked sugar.] — (4) **1852** *Knickerb.* XL. 191 [The store's] contents made a curious *mélange.* Printed calicoes crowded cake-tobacco. **1867** DIXON *New America* I. 157 He finds it pays better to sell cake-tobacco for chewing at six dollars a pound. (5) **1889** *Cent.* 757/1 A flat sea-urchin; a sand-dollar . . . *Mellita quinquefora* and *Echinarachnius parma* are common United States cake-urchins. — (7) **1898** WILLIAMS & WALKER in J. W. Johnson *Black Manhattan* 105 We, the undersigned world-renowned cake-walkers, . . . hereby challenge you to compete with us in a cake-walking match. **1947** DEVOTO *Across Wide Missouri* 322 Everything is orderly again when the procession nears the Company camp—column of files, lances and painted war shields at salute, the dignity of a Nazi sub-führer or a minstrel-show cake-walker swelling the noble chests and making the noble faces solemn.

b. In phrases: (1) *cake and caudle visit*, a brief formal visit at which one partakes of cake and caudle, *rare;* (2) *cake-and-peanut girl*, ?a girl selling cakes and peanuts, *rare;* (3) *hurry up the cakes*, to hasten matters, *colloq.;* (4) *cake and beer wagon*, a wagon from which cakes and beer are sold.

(1) **1787** TYLER *Contrast* (1790) v. ii, Half my visits are cake and caudle visits. — (2) **1845** *Knickerb.* XXVI. 367 A cake-and-peanut girl, with a clean, sweet face, came along. — (3) **1848** BARTLETT 186 *Hurry up the cakes*, i.e. be quick; look alive. **1897** ROBINSON *Uncle Lisha* 68 Go ahade and hurry up yo' cakes, foh I'll be bound Baker and his man's thah with the boat foh now. — (4) **1851** *Polly Peablossom* 45 'Cake and beer' wagons were doing a brisk business.

As the last term in **angel, angel('s) food, ash, batter, black, boiled, Boston cream, buckwheat, butter, cider, coffee, corn, cottonseed, drop, election, fire, fish, fried, guess, handy, hoe, hominy, Hoosier, horse, hot, ice cream, imperial, inauguration, Indian, jelly, journey, lady, layer, loaf, Long Island, maple sugar, marble, molasses, New Year, nimble, nut, pan, root, saleratus, Saratoga corn, seed, shanty, shingle, shovel, split, stir, sunshine, turn, Washington, wheat cake.**

* **cake,** *v. tr.* To entertain with cakes. *Rare.* — **1861** J. B. JONES *Rebel War Clerk's Diary* I. 33 [The ladies of Richmond] wine them and cake them—and they deserve it.

cakea kɑˈkiə, *n.* [?Imitative.] Probably the poor-will, *Phalaenoptilus nuttalli*, the note of which is really three-syllabled and has been variously interpreted. *Obs.*

1873 MILLER *Amongst Modocs* xxx. 341, I heard the call of the *cakea*, or night bird. **1887** J. HAWTHORNE *Fort. Fool* xxii, The call of the cakea sounded by night from hillside to hillside. **1906** *Amer. Folk-Lore* XIX. 142 Yokuts [Indian] names. . . . Many names had no known significance, but others denoted animals, objects, sounds, or tribes. . . . Kukuya, the cry of the mountain quail [was the name of a man].

cakewalk ˈkekˌwɔk, *n.*

1. Orig. a parade or walk-around, poss. first indulged in by Negroes, in which the reward for the fanciest steps was a cake. Now a walk in which those participating pay for the privilege of walking to music on a numbered floor, each one hoping that when the music stops he will be on a lucky number and thus receive a cake as a prize. Also attrib.

1879 *Harper's Mag.* Oct. 799/1 Reader, didst ever attend a cake walk given by the colored folks? **1930** *Randolph Enterprise* (Elkins, W. Va.) 18 Dec. 1/1 After the supper a cake walk program was carried out. **1948** *Lisle* (Ill.) *Advertiser* 21 Oct. 5/1 A fortune teller, fish pond, cake walk, country store, spook house, and refreshment room—that's a list of the many things to happen on the night of November 5.

b. *transf.* and *fig.*

1863 in *Mont. Hist. Soc. Contrib.* III. (1900) In the center of the lodge there was a bush planted,—the medicine bush—and around and around that bush we went. At last their curiosity was satisfied. . . . We had a good laugh over our cake walk. **1894** MARK TWAIN in *Critic* 7 July 8/1 This Shelley biography . . . is a literary cake-walk. **1904** in *Birds of Amer.* (1917) I. 79 Speaking of the peculiar dance of the Albatrosses, Mr. Fisher says, 'The old birds have an innate objection to idleness, and so for their diversion they spend much time in a curious dance, or perhaps more appropriately a "cake-walk."' **1948** *New Yorker* 25 Sep. 24/1 Among such old songs are . . . 'Who Dar!' (a cakewalk).

2. A dance, sometimes as a stage performance, in which some of the steps and figures are adapted from the earlier form of cakewalk.

1895 *N.Y. Dramatic News* 19 Oct. 16/1 On Thursday, Friday and Saturday nights a cake walk will take place in conjunction with the regular performance, open to all comers. **1902** HARBEN *A. Daniel* 53, I was doing the cake-walk with that fat Howard girl. **1947** PAUL *Linden* 336 The members of the Wenepoykin Bicycle Club agreed to give a blackface minstrel show with an olio featuring a prize cake-walk after intermission.

cakewalk ˈkekˌwɔk, *v. intr.* To perform a cakewalk. Also transf. — *a*1909 O. HENRY *Roads of Destiny* xx. 341 The plumed knights were cake-walking in the banquet-halls above. **1946** *Chi. D. News* 1 July 31/2 If the Yankees had our pitching staff they'd cake walk to the pennant.

Hence **cake-walking,** *a.* — **1898** [see **cakewalker**]. **1948** *Chi. Maroon* 27 Feb. 8/1 Coulter House dances tonight in Judson Library to the Cake Walking Babies' theme of Riverboat Shuffle.

cala kɑˈlɑ, *n.*[1] *La.* [African *kala* (Bambara), with same meaning.] A rice cake. Also attrib.

1880 CABLE *Grandissimes* 133 Frowenfeld entered after him, *calas* in hand. **1882** BUEL *Metropolitan Life Unveiled* 521 The door was opened, and we were received by an aged negress, whose face was familiar to me as that of the 'cala-woman,' from whom I had often bought that dainty. **1947** *Chi. Tribune* 1 Nov. 14/8 I'll also have for you a recipe for a famous New Orleans specialty, calas or hot rice fritters.

Cala ˈkælə, *n.*[2] (See quot. 1910 and cf. **California ham.**) Chiefly *pl.*

1910 L. D. HALL *Market Classes . . . of meat* 281 Picnics or *Calas* (formerly termed California hams) are cut 2½ ribs wide, . . . They . . . are sold almost entirely as sweet-pickled, smoked and boiled meats. The lighter averages (4 to 8 pounds) are sometimes termed Boston Shoulders . . . but Chicago and other western packers now trim them like Calas and designate both as Picnics. **1945** *Chi. D. News* 6 Sep. 18 (*advt.*), Values for Friday and Saturday. . . . Juicy 'Miracle' Cooked Callies . . . for wonderful dinners or sandwiches. **1947** *Chi. Times* 22 July 11/4 Ready-to-eat shankless Callies 8 to 10 lbs. Whole or half. 41c.

* **calabash,** *n.*

1. A person's head. *Slang. Obs.* See also **black calabash.**

"A humorous name for the head, generally implying emptiness" (B. '59). "By far the most frequent use made of the word is, as a cant term, for a weak and empty head" (De Vere 121).

1723 *Boston News Letter* 27 June 2/2 You have in the cavity of your Callabash a viscid juice. **1852** *Alta California* (S.F.) 6 Apr. 2/3 Brady says his wife struck him over the calabash with a brass candlestick. **1856** C. WHITE *Oh, Hush!* 8 Come, no prevarication, or I'll smash dat calabash.

2. calabash banjo, a banjo made of a calabash. *Rare.*

1843 CARLTON *New Purchase* I. 200 The merry rascals were dancing away to a cornstalk fiddle and a calabash banjo.

calabaza ˌkɑləˈbɑsə, *n. W.* [Sp. in same sense.] (See quots.) — **1897** *Land of Sunshine* Dec. 17 Three ribbons of cultivated land extend from the acequia, . . . planted in rows of corn, beans, oats, and chile, with the wild *calabazas* (gourds) scattered about. **1937** NICHOL *Natural Vegetation Ariz.* 208 The soft gourd (*Cucurbita foetidissima*) and the calabasa (*C. digitata*) are widespread throughout all desert types and extend into the grasslands, chaparral, and piñon-juniper.

calabazilla ˌkɑləbəˈsiljə, *n.* [Sp. *calabacilla*, dim. of *calabaza*, in Amer. Sp. sense shown here.] A wild squash, *Cucurbita foetidissima.*

1885 HAVARD *Flora W. & S. Texas* 522 *Cucurbita perennis*, Gray. (Calabacilla.) . . . The pulp of the green fruit is used with soap to remove stains from clothing. *c*1892 *D.N.* I. 188 (Texas) Calabacilla: a gourd with round fruit the color of an orange. **1925** JEPSON *Flowering Plants Calif.* 660 Calabazilla [is] . . . also called Chili Coyote and used by Spanish-Californians, the root as a cleanser, the leaves medicinally.

calaboose ˈkæləˌbus, *n.* Chiefly *S.* [Sp. *calabozo*, dungeon.] A jail, a prison. Also attrib. Cf. **calabozo, village calaboose.**

1792 J. POPE *Tour S. & W.* 43 Their Fate will be confinement . . . in the Callibouse at Mobille. **1866** *Eastern Slope* (Washoe, Nev.) 13 Oct. 1/6 Now he is a poor drunkard, and earns barely a . . . living as a calaboose shyster. **1898** *Dly. Ardmoreite* (Ardmore, Okla.) 15 July 3/3 Workmen are busy erecting the calaboose for the city. **1948** *Chi. Tribune* 9 March 9/5 Once you turned me loose, Freed me from the calaboose.

calaboose ˈkæləˌbus, *v. tr.* To imprison. *Obs.* — **1840** *N.O. Picayune* 30 Oct. 2/3 He calaboosed him— . . . Charley took him in. **1857** *Cin. Commercial* (B.), Col. Titus . . . was calaboosed on Tuesday for shooting at the porter of the Planters' House.

calabozo ˌkæləˈboso, *n.* Also **calaboza, calaboz.** *S.* [Sp., cf. **calaboose,** *n.*] = **calaboose.**

1826 FLINT *Recollections* 208 The commandant, a priest, a file of soldiers, and a calaboza made up the engine of government. **1911** S. CODY *Heroes of Plains* (Bentley), They were occasionally threatened with imprisonment in the Calabozo of St. Louis. **1948** *Chi. Tribune* 4 Feb. 22/6 Now I must go to the calabozo and stay a long time, since my offense is most serious.

* **calamity,** *n.*

1. (See quot. 1914.)

1871 *Winnebago Co.* (Wis.) *Press* 3/2 We learn that our people have given Mr. Riggs a wide berth and that he has packed his 'calamities' and left town. **1884** HILL *Colo. Pioneers* 282 A crop-eared, one-eyed mule, a few battered cooking utensils, a few rations of 'grub,' and a corresponding amount of 'traps and calamities,' comprised the outfit. **1914** *D.N.* IV. 153 Calamity, old stuff, such as is bought at an auction.

2. (See quot.)

1891 *N. & Q.* VIII. 64, I do not know that any of the dictionaries have the word *calamity* in the sense of a rude vehicle. In the State of Maine, or in some parts of it, a cheap, homemade wagon, often of the rudest description, is known as a *calamity*, probably from the idea of a *tumble-down* affair.

3. In slang combs. used to denote a noisy pessimist or one who predicts calamity, as **calamity howler, prophet, shouter.** Also **calamity howling.**

1892 *Cong. Rec.* 2 March 1654/1 We had some 'calamity howlers' here in Washington as well as in Kansas. **1892** in *Rep. Camp. Text Bk.* (1894) 229 The calamity prophets of both parties. **1892** *Cong. Rec.* 17 March 2160/2 [They] were of the stripe of calamity-shouters whose occupation is gone unless they can prove that calamity stalks abroad. **1948** *Time* 5 April 94/2 After months of financial calamity-howling, the seven major studios last week found that in 1947 . . . they had netted (after taxes) about $96,000,000.

calamityite kəˈlæmətiˌaɪt, *n.* One who predicts calamity. *Rare.* — **1894** *Rep. Camp. Text Bk.* 229 Bad for calamityites.

Calapooya kɑləˈpujə, *n.* [Native name of unknown significance.] (See quot. 1907.) Usu. *pl.*

1814 LEWIS & CLARK *Exped.* II. 227 It is inhabited by a nation called Calahpoewah, a very numerous people whose villages, nearly 40 in number, are scattered along each side of the Multnomah. **1849** ROSS *First Settlers Ore.* (1923) 253 This year another party . . . spent some months in that quarter among the Collappohyeaass. **1881** NASH *Two Yrs. Ore.* (1882) 187 There were plenty in the valley, Klick-i-tats and Calapooyas—these last were a mean set at that. **1907** HODGE *Amer. Indians* I. 187 Calapooya. The name, properly speaking, of a division of the Kalapooian family formerly occupying the watershed between Willamette and Umpqua rs., Oreg. **1914** APPLEGATE *Recollections Boyhood* (1934) 128 We found a tribe of Kalapooyas living along the river at this place.

b. In full **Calapooya Indians.**
1838 PARKER *Exploring Tour* 164 The methodist church of the United States have established a mission among the Calapooah Indians.

calash kəˈlæʃ, *v. intr.* To drive in a calash. *Rare.* — **1732** B. LYNDE *Diary* 29 Dined at Justice Gardner's, and afterward rode and calash'd to Mr. Jas. Coffin's.

calashed kəˈlæʃt, *a.* Provided with a calash or hooped hood. *Rare.* — **1807–8** IRVING *Salmagundi* ii. 40 Our ladies in stays . . . well calash'd without, and well bolster'd within, . . . were shaped like a pail.

calaverite ˌkæləˈveraɪt, *n.* "A rare tellurid of gold, occurring massive, of a bronze-yellow color and metallic luster, first found in Calaveras county, California" (*Cent.*).
1868 DANA *Min.* 795 (Supp.) Calaverite is frequently associated with petzite. **1874** *Amer. Phil. Soc. Proc.* XIV. 229 Calaverite . . . is associated with sylvanite and quartz. **1917** *Amer. Mineralogist* Oct. 125 To make the matter more certain, the mineral exhibited what appeared to be an excellent cleavage (calaverite normally showing none).

* **calculate,** *v.*

1. *tr.* and *intr.* To think, "reckon," to purpose *to* do something, to plan *upon* doing a thing. *Colloq.*
"*Calculate*, used frequently in an improper sense, as reckon, guess" (1815 Humphrey's *Yankee* 104). "This use of the word . . . is not sanctioned by English usage" (W. '47). "Its use is confined to the illiterate of New England" (B. '48). "The Yankee calculates, and pretty shrewdly also, while the Southron allows" (1853 P. PAXTON *Yankee in Texas* 116).
1805 PIKE *Sources Miss.* II. 152 We had reason to calculate, that they had good guides. **1836** R. WESTON *Visit* 59, 'I calculate upon doing so' is used by a Yankee, while we say 'I intend to do so.' **1917** *D.N.* IV. 390 Cowc'late [is] . . . used by people who would recognize ca'clate as illiterate. . . . 'I cowc'late to be there.'

2. To depend upon, make due allowance *for.*
1825 *Austin Papers* (1924) II. 1201 One of the Boats that I calculated for the Trip I found on examination was worm eaten. **1878** MRS. STOWE *Poganuc People* 186 Ye hain't calkerlated for the heft o' them fellers; governors and colonels and ministers weighs putty heavy.

* **calculation,** *n.* **a.** Some kind of gambling game or trick. *Obs.* **b.** Judgment. *Colloq.* — **(a) 1851** GREEN *Twelve Days* 115 The Dr. frequently amused the passengers with several games, particularly one called 'Calculation.' — **(b) 1870** *Putnam's Mag.* V. 80/2 Though neighbor Vale has the best heart in the world, he hasn't a mite of kalkerlation; and none of the Vales never had, as ever I heerd on.

* **Caleb,** *n.* [App. the personal name.] (See quot.) *Obs.* — **1833** CATLIN *Indians* I. 71 All eyes were turned at once upon *Caleb* (as the grizzly bear is familiarly called by the trappers in the Rocky Mountains—or more often 'Cale,' for brevity's sake).

* **calendar,** *n.* (See quot. 1914.) Also attrib. Cf. **senate calendar.**
1839 *Cong. Globe* 25 Jan. 146/2 On the first and third [changed to fourth] Friday of each month, the calendar of private bills shall be called over. **1914** MCLAUGHLIN & HART *Cyclo. Amer. Govt.* I. 202 A calendar is a register containing a list of the bills which have been reported from committees and which are ready to be considered in their turn. . . . The state legislatures all have their calendars, the number and kind varying among the different states. *Ib.*, Calendar Wednesday is the day set apart . . . for the consideration of public bills, excepting those that are privileged under the rules.

* **calf,** *n.*

1. The young of the buffalo.
1824 G. W. RAUCK *Boonesborough* 166 A number of buffaloes . . . made off . . . others loping slowly and carelessly, with young calves playing, skipping and bounding through the plain. **1897** INMAN *Old Santa Fe Trail* 218 The buffalo cow . . . is as dangerous with a calf by her side as a she-grizzly with cubs. **1917** *Mammals of Amer.* 41 To his very great astonishment, the doctor now saw that the central and controlling figure of this mass was a poor little calf, so newly born as scarcely to be able to walk.

2. Attrib. in the sense of immature or crude. *Colloq.*
1851 *Harper's Mag.* June 37/1 He's a Calf preacher—a young bottle-nosed Gospeller. **1909** WASON *Happy Hawkins* 203 A prep-school is a sort of a calf college.

3. In combs.: (1) **calf brander,** *W.* one who brands calves, also **calf branding;** (2) **corral,** *W.* a corral in which calves are branded; (3) **crop,** *W.* the calves born in one season; (4) **herd,** in colonial times, the group of calves belonging to a particular colony; (5) **keeper,** one in charge of a colonial calf herd, *obs.;* (6) **kill,** any one of various plants whose foliage is, or is thought to be, poisonous to calves; (7) **kneed,** knock-kneed; (8) **pasture,** a pasture for calves; (9) **rope,** *fig.* a cry of surrender, *colloq.;* (10) **roping,** *W.* lassoing calves; (11) * **'s-head,** the pitcher plant, *Darlingtonia californica*, of California; (12) **time,** the season when buffalo calves are born, *rare;* (13) **wrestler,** *W.* one who throws calves for branding, also **calf wrestling.**
(1) 1881 ROMSPERT *Western Echo* 179 Sometimes, however, the mother and offspring get together again before they have entirely forgotten their *relations;* and then a calf of one brand is following a cow of another. This is very undesirable to the calf-brander. **1882** *Lippincott's Mag.* May 430/1 Then the calf-branding begins. — **(2) a1918** G. STUART *On Frontier* I. 184 Laid foundation for calf corral. — **(3) 1912** BOWER *Flying U.* 184 The calf crop is going to be good, if this weather holds on another two weeks or so. **1936** *Univ. Ariz. Gen. Bul.* No. 3, 184 Periodic droughts account for a low average calf crop throughout the state. — **(4) 1652** *Southampton Rec.* I. 84 The calf herd shall be kept for the ensueing year at Sagaponack. **1662** [see **calf keeper**].
(5) 1657 *Hempstead Rec.* I. 17 All men in this towne that will have Calves kept by the Calfe keeper to give in thare number. **1662** *Ib.* 126 The Calfe-keeper went forth with the Calfe heird. — **(6) 1859** BARTLETT 64 Calf-kill . . . [is] so called from its poisonous properties. **1871** DE VERE 413 Calfkill is the absurd name given in the North to one of the most beautiful flowering shrubs of North America. **1909** *Cent. Supp.* 188/1 *Calf-kill*, . . . 2. *Leucothoë Catesbæi*, a shrub of the southern Alleghanies, poisonous to cattle and sheep. . . . 3. The velvet-grass, *Holcus lanatus.* — **(7) 1894** *Vt. Agric. Rep.* XIV. 119 The chest should be full, . . . forearms long, . . . knees strong, neither calf-kneed nor sprung. — **(8)** [**1639** *Boston Rec.* 1 Two Accres . . . of Broken up ground in the Calues pasture.] **1656** *Suffolk Deeds* III. 255 The Land in the Orchard And Calfe Pasture, together with the meadow & other Land belonging therevnto. **1775** FITHIAN *Journal* II. 144 Mrs. Brown . . . rode with us three miles on our way to the calf-pasture. **1897** *Outing* XXX. 245/2 Mounting, we left her far behind as we sped down the Calf Pasture. — **(9) 1906** *D.N.* III. 129 Calf-rope, *n.* I give up, I surrender. 'I'll give it to him till he yells *calf-rope.*' [Ark.] **1946** *Boston Transcript* Sep. 7/1 'Holler calf rope!'
(10) 1914 *World's Work* Feb. 445/1 Lassoing or rope throwing has its many styles, such as horse roping, steer roping, calf roping, and fancy roping, each an art in itself. **1948** *Denison* (Tex.) *Herald* 2 July 9/3 Three cowpokes by way of Fort Worth walked away with all honors in the calf roping event. — **(11) 1889** *Cent.* 764/1 Calf's-head [is so called] . . . in allusion to the ventricose hood at the summit of the leaf. — **(12) 1848** RUXTON in *Blackw. Mag.* LXIII. 713 'Twas about 'calf-time,' maybe a little later. — **(13) 1888** ROOSEVELT in *Cent. Mag.* April 861/2 The calf-wrestlers, grimy with blood, dust, and sweat, work like beavers. **1927** *Frontier* VIII. 46 The following day was devoted to branding calves born during the exodus, and signalized my introduction to 'calf-wrestling.'

b. *No one knows the luck of a lousy calf*, no one knows how well an unpromising boy or girl may succeed. *Colloq.*
1836 CROCKETT *Adventures* 13 It is a true saying that no one knows the luck of a lousy calf.

As the last term in **box, buffalo, dogie, feeder, finback, necked calf.**

* **Calhoun-.** Used in expressions now obsolete in allusion to John C. Calhoun (1782–1850) a well-known Democratic statesman and supporter of States' rights, as (1) **Calhounery,** (see quot. 1858); (2) **Calhounism,** the political principles of the Calhounites; (3) **Calhounist,** a political supporter of John C. Calhoun; (4) **Calhounite,** =prec.
(1) 1837 *Russellville* (Ky.) *Advt.* 19 Oct. 2/4 This looks preciously like 'Calhounery.' **1858** *N.Y. Tribune* 12 July 6/4 Certain crimes unknown to the common law, and which we know by the general title of Calhounery. These crimes are stuffing ballot boxes, giving false returns, and permitting illegal votes to be cast. — **(2) 1839** *N.Y. Semi-Wkly. Express* 14 Dec. 2/4 Mr. Rhett has escaped from a Lethonian fog,—or from a denser darkness, the mistifications of Calhounisms. **1900** *Kansas Hist. Colls.* VI. 378 He was the ablest representative of Calhounism in the Southwest. — **(3) 1848** *N.Y. Wkly. Tribune* 13 May 5/4 The Calhounists of South Carolina will not be represented at the Baltimore Convention. — **(4) 1824** J. Q. ADAMS *Diary* (1929) 319 A Calhounite transferred to Jackson. **a1882** WHITMAN *Specimen Days* 261 A resolute and arrogant determination on the part of the extreme slaveholders, the Calhounites, to carry the states rights' portion of the constitutional compact to its farthest verge.

calibogus kæləˈbogəs, *n.* [Origin unknown.] A beverage made of rum, spruce beer, and molasses. Chiefly Canadian.

1758 N. Ames in *Dedham Hist. Reg.* I. 16 Calabogus Club begun. **1785** Grose *Dict. Vulgar Tongue. Calibogus,* rum and spruce beer, American beverage. **1832** J. M'Gregor *British America* I. 221 Spirits are frequently mixed with spruce beer, to make the drink named Callibogus. **1895** *Amer. Folk-Lore* VIII. 38 Still there are a few words in use which seem to have come in that way, for example *callibogus,* a mixture of spruce beer and rum; a *scalawag,* a scamp. **1947** Downey *Lusty Forefathers* 3 He seemed bent on drinking right down the list posted beside the bar. 'Alicante . . . Calibogus . . . Constantia . . . Ebulum . . . Flip.'

caliche kɑˈlitʃə, *n. S.W.* [Sp. in Amer. Sp. sense shown here.] A crusty formation of calcium carbonate that forms within or on top of the soil in arid or semiarid regions of the Southwest. (See quot. 1941.) Also attrib.

1885 *Santa Fe W. New Mexican* 22 Oct. 4/6 By digging down on the vein through this caliche, you strike the mineral. **1929** *San Antonio Express* 2 June (Bentley), Truck load after truck load of crushed rock, followed by caliche gravel, was dumped into ruts in order to make them passable. **1941** *Harper's Mag.* Oct. 497/1 Casa Grande is now a national monument and the government has protected the four-storey edifice made of *caliche* (an Arizona adobe) and is ready and willing to answer all your questions.

***calico,** *n.*

1. A cheap cotton cloth printed on one side, usu. with a figured pattern. See also **curtain calico, sunflower calico.**

1779 *R.I. Commerce* II. 82 Good handsome purple and white Calicho to make her two Gowns. **1830** S. H. Collins *Emigrant's Guide* 176 Calico is called muslin, and prints are called calicoes here. **1947** *Reader's Digest* Oct. 154/2 Her dress was calico, with an apron over it.

b. (See quot.) *Rare.*

1867 Scott *Partisan Life* 241 It must be remembered that calico, with Mosby's men, is a generic for all dry goods.

2. A member of the Calico Club. *Obs.*

1743 *Boston News-Letter* 14 July 2/2 This is to inform the most worthy and hospitable Society of Calico's . . . that there will be a Meeting of said Society at the Bunch of Grapes on Tuesday. . . . [signed] Calico.

3. *ellipt.* **a.** (See quot.) *Rare.* **b.** A dress or garment made of calico. *Colloq.* **c.** A calico horse or mare. *Colloq.*

(a) 1842 *Nat. Hist. N.Y., Zoology* IV. 304 The New York Sole, *Achirus mollis.* . . . They abound on the shallow flats on the Jersey shore opposite New York, where they are called Calico and Coverclip. — **(b) 1850** Lewis *La. Swamp Dr.* 51 Thar war Mam, fust on one side, then on t'other, her new caliker swelled up round her like a bear with the dropsy. **1944** Holton *Yankees* 7 If they ran out on errands they would be wearing their morning calicos. — **(c)** *a***1861** Winthrop *Canoe & Saddle* 203 A hundred horses, roans, calicos, sorrels, . . . were nipping bunch-grass on the plain. **1907** Mulford *Bar-20* 261 How is it yore ridin' th' calico?

4. A girl or woman. Also attrib. *Jocular.*

1848 *Glance at N.Y.* 28 Only come up to-night, and I'll show you as gallus a piece of calico as any on de floor. . . . He said something about a piece of gallus calico. . . . Ha! ha! ha! you unsophisticated mortal, he means his sweetheart! **1909** *Sat. Ev. Post* 9 Jan. 9/1 What air you calicoes thar a-blubberin' about? **1947** *Westerners' Brand Book* 120 Bill had a bad case of 'calico fever,' or, in other words, was woman crazy.

5. *attrib.* or *adj.:* Of or pertaining to horses or cows of a piebald or spotted appearance, as **calico animal, cow, horse, mare, mustang, pony.**

1861 Newell *Orpheus C. Kerr* I. 195 Another fine calico animal of the stud . . . previous to losing his teeth he was sold to a western dealer in hides for three dollars. — **1878** I. L. Bird *Rocky Mts.* 263 On Mr. K. going out, he found, instead of our 'calico' cow, a brindled one. — **1867** Scott *Partisan Life* 412 Well, I must have him back, and the calico horse too, that we got in the Fairfax raid. **1946** Woodard *Word-List* 8 Calico horse: *n.* A reddish horse with irregular stripes. Pamlico. Common. — **1809** Irving *Knickerb.* VII. iii, His doughty trumpeter Van Corlear, mounted on a broken winded, wall eyed, calico mare. — **1892** Bret Harte *Col. Starbottle's Client* 250 The man she most despised . . . mounted on a 'calico' mustang . . . dashed among them. — **1891** Garland *Main-travelled Roads* (1922) 283 The stranger drove a jaded-looking pair of calico ponies. **1927** Benét *J. B.'s Body* 17 They drag their skies and sunsets after them Like calico ponies on a rawhide rope.

6. In special combs.: (1) **calico ball,** a charity ball at which the ladies wore calico dresses that were later given to the needy, *obs.* or *hist.;* (2) **bally,** (see quot.), *obs.;* (3) **betty,** a kind of card game, *obs.;* (4) **Club,** ?a students' club at Harvard, *obs.;* (5) **counter,** a counter in a store at which calicoes are sold; (6) **course,** (see quot.), *obs.;* (7) **hop, party,** =**calico ball,** *obs.;* (8) **rock,** a rock formation of variegated coloration, *obs.;* (9) **stamp,** an insigne, usu. of paper, placed upon a bolt of calico, *rare.*

(1) 1859 A. Van Buren *Sojourn in South* 192 They . . . came home late this evening from the 'calico ball,' . . . In this ball the ladies all wore calico dresses. **1889** Farmer 116/1 The popular *calico-balls* [are] now as well known here [=England] as across the water [=U.S.], whence they were introduced. **1934** Emma G. Sterne (*title*), The Calico Ball. — **(2) 1889** Barrere & Leland 220 Calico-bally (American), a frequenter of calico-balls. About fifty years ago in Philadelphia it was usual to speak of balls frequented by factory girls as 'slewers,' and the commoner kind of grisettes as *calico* or dollar balls; hence *calico-bally* has come to signify, when applied to a young gentleman dissipated or fast, one who goes anywhere for amusement. —**(3) 1775** Fithian *Journal* II. 126 In our dining room companies at cards, Five & forty, Whist, Alfours, Callico-Betty etc. — **(4) 1761** N. Ames in *Dedham Hist. Reg.* I. 145 White, Hunt, Bliss & Honyman rusticated from College for being in the Calico Club, Comm[encemen]t Night.

(5) 1869 Alcott *Little Women* II. 332 She . . . covered herself with confusion by asking for lavender ribbon at the calico counter. — **(6) 1902** Clapin 93 'A calico course' [is] a course frequented by women students. — **(7) 1875** *Chi. Tribune* 21 Nov. 3/2 The Skinner Club . . . held a calico hop Tuesday. — **1855** *Harper's Mag.* X. 553/2 Did you go to the Calico Party, gentle reader? **1876** *L.A. Wkly. Review* 5 Aug. 3/2 Don't forget the Calico Party to be given by the ladies of East Los Angeles. — **(8) 1807–8** Irving *Salmagundi* xviii. 413 They display their singular drollery in bantering nature . . . representing her tricked out in . . . calico rocks. **1835** Martin *Descr. Virginia* 27 The carved or calico rock of Kanawha. — **(9) 1835** Hoffman *Winter in West* I. 219 Handling his feet the while much after the manner of the rampant unicorn on a calico stamp.

b. In the names of plants and animals: (1) **calico angler,** an angler fish with markings suggestive of calico, *rare;* (2) **back,** (*a*) the ruddy turnstone, (*b*) the harlequin cabbage bug; (3) **bass,** a variegated fresh-water fish, *Pomoxis sparoides,* found chiefly in the streams of the Mississippi Valley; (4) **bug,** =**calico back** (*b*); (5) **bush,** (see quots.); (6) **corn,** (see quots.); (7) **flower,** =**calico bush;** (8) **salmon,** *W.* the dog salmon; (9) **spider,** (see quot.), *rare;* (10) **tree,** =**calico bush.**

(1) 1818 *Amer. Mag.* II. 326/1 Calico Angler—*Lophius calico.* — **(2)** (*a*) **1872** Coues *N. Amer. Birds* 246 *Strepsilas.* . . . Turnstone. Brant Bird. Calico back. **1917** *Birds of Amer.* I. 268. (*b*) **1890** Webster 204/3 *Calicoback,* . . . [is] called also calico bug and harlequin cabbage bug. **1895** Comstock *Man. Insects* (1923) 145 The Harlequin Cabbage-bug or Calico-back . . . is very destructive to cabbages, radishes, and turnips in the Southern States. — **(3) 1884** Goode *Nat. Hist. Aquatic Animals* 406 The Calico Bass, *Pomoxys sparoides.* **1947** *Downtown Shop. News* (Chi.) 28 May 4/2 There are other species of bass to be found in fresh water; the White bass or White croppie, the Calico bass or Black croppie, the Warmouth bass and the Northern rock bass. — **(4) 1890** [see **calico back** (*b*)].

(5) 1814 Pursh *Flora Amer.* I. 297 *Kalmia latifolia,* . . . a shrub from three to eight feet high, very elegant when in flower; called Laurel or in the mountains Callico-bush. **1943** Peattie *Great Smokies* 260 On above Brevard at the village of Pisgah Forest, mountain laurel, that dainty 'calico bush' of New England, grows three high in the 'pink beds.' — **(6) 1849** Emmons *Agric. N.Y.* II. 264 Calico corn. Color remarkably variegated. . . . It is cultivated mostly as a curiosity, or for popping. **1892** *Amer. Folk-Lore* V. 105 *Zea mays,* . . . yellow kernels, striped with red; calico corn. Ill. — **(7) 1802** J. Drayton *S. Carolina* 69 Calico flower, wild ivy, or laurel, . . . is a beautiful flowering ever green; whose flowers of red and white, grow in such large clusters together; as to give the whole plant at a small distance, the appearance of having a bit of calico thrown over it. **1897** Sudworth *Arborescent Flora* 315 Mountain Laurel. . . . Common names [include] . . . Calico Bush, . . . Calico-tree (Tenn.), Calico Flower (Tenn.). — **(8) 1909** *Cent. Supp.,* Calico salmon. Name in Alaska for dog-salmon, *Oncorhynchus keta,* named for mottled coloring in summer. **1944** Ross *Westward* 179 Cracklings from the pork were also cooked with dog or 'calico' salmon (inferior to the Chinook) in a big pot with boiled potatoes. — **(9) 1899** *Animal & Plant Lore* 40 The bite of the 'calico spider,' a large yellow and black species, is supposed to be deadly poison. Eastern Mass.

(10) 1804 Michaux *Voyage à L'Ouest* 48 Quelques-uns désignent encore ce dernier arbrisseau, sous le nom de Calico tree. **1897** [see **calico flower**].

c. (See quots.) *Colloq.*

1916 *D.N.* IV. 313 *Calico side, on the,* 'a courting.' **1943** *Nat. Geog. Mag.* May 623/2 When soldier boys swung their country girls clear off the floor in an old-time square dance, they called it 'making the calico crack.'

calico ˈkæləˌko, *v.* [Cf. ∗**calico,** *n.* **4.**] *intr.* To court the ladies. *Jocular.* — **1887** *Lippincott's Mag.* July 102 For it very frequently happens that the best students do a good deal of 'calicoing.' **1915** *D.N.* IV. 181 He's out a *calicoin'* every Sunday. (Va.)

calicoist ˈkæləˌko·ɪst, *n.* (See quot.) *Rare.* — **1887** *Lippincott's Mag.* July 102 He soon makes the acquaintance of most of the young ladies in the neighborhood, if he is a 'calicoist' (which implies a greater lover of the fair sex than of his studies).

∗**California,** *n.*

1. Used attrib. or as adj.

The expressions of this kind are quite numerous. Only a few typical ones are given here.

a. In the names of, or with reference to, animals: (1) **California condor,** =**California vulture;** (2) **gray,** =**gray whale;** (3) **hare,** any one of various large hares of western North America; (4) **horse,** a small, wiry, half-wild horse found in California in early times, *obs.;* (5) **jay,** a jay, *Aphelocoma californica,* resembling the eastern blue jay but having no crest; (6) **lion,** the puma or cougar, *Felis concolor;* (7) **mustang, nag,** =**California horse;** (8) **nuthatch,** a subspecies of the white-breasted nuthatch; (9) **pony,** =**California horse,** *obs.;* (10) **quail,** a glossy crested quail, *Lophortyx californica,* found along the California coast; (11) **sardine,** a sardine, *Sardinia caerulea,* found on the coast of California; (12) **sicklebill,** the California thrasher, *Toxostoma redivivum;* (13) **vulture,** a large vulture, *Gymnogyps californianus,* found in the coastal mountainous regions of southern California; (14) **widgeon,** (see quot.); (15) **woodpecker,** a woodpecker, *Balanosphyra formicivora,* that has the habit of boring holes in trees, often dead redwoods, and filling them with acorns.

(1) **1889** *Cent.* 1176/2 California condor, the large vulture of California, *Cathartes* or *Pseudogryphus californianus.* **1948** *Sierra Club* (So. Calif. Chap.) *Sched.* 127, 45 Welcome to the San Cayetano Mountains, the stronghold of the California Condor. — (2) **1857** Hayes *Pioneer Notes* (1929) 234 The whales of this present ground are called California Grays, and Devil-fish too, for, says Capt. Co., 'they are the devil sometimes!' — (3) **1869** *Proc. Calif. Acad. Sci.* IV. 63 Lepus californicus *Gray,* California Hare. — (4) **1846** in *Calif. Hist. Soc. Quart.* V. 380 Several Horses gave out to day and from the appearance of many others I begin to conclude that californea Horses are not a hardy race of animals. **1891** *Harper's Mag.* June 4/2 The California horse is small—fourteen and a half to fifteen hands.

(5) **1853** Sitgreaves *Exped. Zuni & Colo. Rivers* 34 There were quite a number of birds among the cedars, among them the California jay, (*Cyanocorax Californicus*). **1948** *Pacific Discovery* Mar.–Apr. 18/1 The raucous call of the California jay rises from the cypress tree. — (6) **1850** *Deseret News* (Salt Lake City) 29 June 17/2 It is reported that the *California lion* has been seen, yes killed, in this valley, but who can show us one, or even a stuffed skin? **1914** Applegate *Recollections Boyhood* (1934) 168 The deep basso growl of the gray mountain wolf was heard at nights, as also the scream of the prowling panther, cougar, and California lion. — (7) *a*1918 G. Stuart *On Frontier* I. 150 The horses used were California mustangs, noted for their surefootedness, speed, and endurance. — **1877** J. S. Campion *On Frontier* 304 We set out . . . well-mounted on unshod California nags. — (8) **1858** Baird *Birds Pacific R.R.* 378 *Sitta pygmaea,* California nuthatch. **1878** Hinton *Handbook Ariz.* 238 The California nuthatch abounds in the mountains. — (9) **1876** Crofutt *Transcontinental Tourist* 91 Terms heard on the Plains . . . 'Bronco,' California or Spanish pony.

(10) **1831** Beechey *Voyage* II. 81 The California quail (*tetrao virginianus*), . . . afforded amusement to our sportsmen. **1944** *Nat. Geog. Mag.* June 694/2 Chestnut-backed chickadees, hermit thrushes, . . . and kinglets live almost side by side with such hot-country birds as mocking birds, . . . California quail, wren-tits, and road-runners. — (11) **1884** Goode *Nat. Hist. Aquatic Anim.* 569 The California Sardine—*Clupea sagax.* — (12) **1881** *Amer. Naturalist* XV. 210 The California sickle-bill (*Harporhynchus redivivus*), a thrush . . . is a resident by no means rare in Southern California. — (13) **1858** Baird *Birds Pacific R.R.* 5 *Cathartes californianus.* . . . The California Vulture. . . . The largest rapacious bird of North America . . . inferior in size only to the gigantic condor. **1882** *Cent. Mag.* Aug. 521/2 The vultures follow, represented by two species: the turkey-buzzard and the great California Vulture. — (14) **1891** *Cent.* 6921/1 The green-headed widgeon [is] also called locally . . . southern widgeon, California widgeon, [etc.].

(15) **1859** S. F. Baird *Cat. N. Amer. Birds* 95 *Melanerpes formicivorus,* Bonap. California Woodpecker. **1944** *Nat. Geog. Mag.* June 696/1 Near Mount Diablo we located a nesting tree of the California Woodpecker that was convenient for study.

Also *California brown towhee, buzzard, egg-bird, gray whale* (see **gray**), *grouse, jack* (the jackrabbit), *mocking bird, partridge, pompano* (see **pompano**), *sage sparrow, shell, squirrel hawk* (see **squirrel hawk**), *thrasher,* etc.

b. In the names of, or with reference to, plants: (1) **California bay,** =**California laurel;** (2) **bayos,** (see quot.), *rare;* (3) **buckeye,** a small tree, *Aesculus california;* (4) **bulrush,** a marsh sedge, *Scirpus californicus;* (5) **fan palm,** a southern California fan-leaved palm, *Washingtonia filamentosa,* named for George Washington; (6) **grape,** (see quot.); (7) **holly,** the evergreen toyon of the Pacific Coast; (8) **laurel,** the mountain laurel, *Umbellularia californica,* of the Pacific Coast; (9) **lilac,** (see quot. 1881); (10) **nutmeg,** an evergreen, *Torreya californica,* the fruit of which resembles a nutmeg; (11) **pea,** a pea of a variety supposed to have been introduced from California; (12) **pitcher plant,** =**calf's-head;** (13) **poppy,** the yellow-flowered *Eschscholtzia californica;* (14) **rose bay,** (see quot.); (15) **strawberry,** ?a spice-bush, *Calycanthus occidentalis;* (16) **walnut,** a black walnut, *Juglans californica,* found in California.

(1) **1887** *Overland Mo.* Aug. 153/1 The California bay, or laurel, which may be called a tree from its size, though usually growing in bushy form, is beautiful in color, and is a favorite because of its fragrance. **1897** *Land of Sunshine* Apr. 224 There are . . . the magnolia grandiflora, the California bay-tree and scores of trees the very names of which are unfamiliar to the general reader. — (2) **1855** *N.Y. Herald* 12 Dec. 2/4 Beans.—Sales of 175 sacks California bayos at 6 1/2c, and 20 do. do. red at 4 1/2c. per lb. — (3) **1893** *N.A. Fauna* VII. 297 The handsome California Buckeye, which grows to be a small tree, was in full bloom . . . on the west slope of the Sierra Nevada between Kernville and Walker Basin. — (4) **1899** *Land of Sunshine* Apr. 244 These first school-houses were of logs, unhewn; roofed with shakes or with *tule* [toó-ly] or California bulrush, scirpus lacustius.

(5) **1900** *Land of Sunshine* Sep.–Oct. 235 The first of many objects of interest was to see the California Fan Palm (*Neowashingtonia filamentosa*) growing in its native home—narrow Palm Cañon. **1946** *So. Sierran* Nov. 2/3 Among these, the California fan palm (*Washingtonia filifera*), our only native palm, holds first place. — (6) **1862** *Rep. Comm. Patents: Agric.* 479 The California grape (*Vitis Californica* of Bentham) completes the list of species of grape which are known to be natives of North America north of Mexico. — (7) **1884** Sargent *Rep. Forests* 84 *Heteromeles arbutifolia.* . . . California Holly. **1888** Lindley *Calif. of South* 332 Later still the heather of the uplands, *Adenostoma,* is in full flower, also *Heteromales* [*sic*], or California holly, bearing heavy crops of scarlet berries from Christmas to Easter. — (8) **1871** *Colo. Gazeteer* 117 It will be recalled, on this occasion, that the last tie laid was manufactured from California laurel, with silver plates bearing suitable inscriptions. **1946** *Sierra Club Bul.* Dec. 21 Vigorous sprouts growing from the crowns of shrubs . . . were seen in . . . California laurel, . . . toyon, service berry. — (9) **1853** Winthrop *Letters* 14 Apr., Of these the only interesting one is the California lilac so called, bearing a pretty bluish flower. **1881** *Amer. Cyclo.* XII. 312/2 *Ceanothus thyrsiflorus* is a small tree producing an abundance of light blue flowers, and known as the 'California lilac.' **1946** R. Peattie *Pac. Coast Ranges* 55 The most characteristic chaparral plants are the gnarled tree-shrubs, numberless in species and variously called wild or California lilac or blue blossom.

(10) **1908** Sudworth *Forest Trees Pac. Slope* 191 California nutmeg is a rare tree of small size. It is called nutmeg from the fancied resemblance of its seed-kernel to the nutmeg of commerce. **1911** Chase *Yosemite Trails* 125 It is the California nutmeg-tree . . . a slender, spiry tree with grey bark, and leaves much like those of the white fir. **1947** Peattie *Sierra Nevada* 144 California nutmeg, a member of the yew family, another evergreen native found in only a few places in California, occurs occasionally in this zone. — (11) **1854** Davis *Farm Bk.* 55 Planted a few California peas in the hills in the M. Jones field. — (12) **1915** *Nat. & Science on Pac. Coast* 153 Mention can be made only of the California pitcher plant (*Darlingtonia californica*). — (13) **1911** Richter *Honey Plants of Calif.* 991 Friedrich Huck's 'Unsere Honig und Bienenpflanzen,' a German work on honey plants, has listed the California poppy as an introduction from California, and as a source of pollen for the bees. **1948** *Chi. Tribune* 18 Apr. VII. 9/1 The orange yellow of the California poppy grows in clusters. — (14) **1915** *Nat. & Science on Pac. Coast* 154 The California rose bay (*R. californicum*) is partial to rugged mountain sides and grows as far north as British Columbia.

(15) **1862** *Rep. Comm. Patents: Agric.* 190 *Fragaria lucida,* California strawberry. — (16) **1888** Lindley *Calif. of South* 335 The California walnut is a vigorous grower wherever there is moisture.

Also *California bluebell, coffee* (*tree*), *cottonwood, maple, oak, redwood, sidesaddle flower* (see **sidesaddle flower**), *slippery elm,* etc.

2. In special combs.: (1) **California battalion,** the American insurgents who in 1846 raised the Bear flag (*q.v.*) in California, *obs.;* (2) **blanket,** a type of superior blanket much used formerly in California; (3) **clipper,** a clipper ship engaged in the California trade, now *hist.;* (4) **diamond,** a very small diamond or diamond-like crystal found in California, also attrib.; (5) **fashion,** the fashion characteristic of California, *obs.;* (6) **fever,** (*a*) (see quots.), (*b*) extreme desire to go to California, *obs.;* (7) **gold,** gold obtained from California, also attrib.; (8) **gold-finder,** a device allegedly efficacious in locating gold deposits, *obs.*, cf. **gold monkey;** (9) **ham,** =**Cala;** (10) **hat,** (see quot. 1853, and cf. **California cut** in **b.** below); (11) **jack,** a variety of seven-up suitable for two players; (12) **pants,** a kind of superior riding breeches popular in California about 1870; (13) **prayer book,** a pack of cards, *jocular;* (14) **saddle,** a light, high-horned, single-girth saddle having covered stirrups, cf. **center-fire,** (b) 1933 example; (15) **toothpick,** a bowie knife, cf. **Arkansaw toothpick;** (16) **wagon,** a wagon used by one moving to California, *obs.;* (17) **widow,** (see quot. 1877), *obs.* [cf. "American widow" in *EDD s.v. Widow* 2, for a woman whose husband had gone to America].

(1) 1848 *Calif. Claims* (Senate Rep. 23 Feb.) 35 On the fifth [of July] we organized the 'California battalion,' adopting the 'grizly bear' as our emblem. **1850** Garrard *Wah-To-Yah* xx. 247 Lieutenant Talbot, California Battalion, and several men dressed in California costume. — **(2) 1878** I. L. Bird *Rocky Mts.* 25 A luxurious bed ... with ... costly California blankets. **1936** Barnard *Rider* 22 Two pairs California blankets ... $20.00. — **(3) 1854** Simms *Southward Ho!* 439 The sails of a California clipper. **1947** *Chr. Sci. Monitor* 15 Jan. 8/2 When you think of the California clippers, the name which first flashes across your mind is *Flying Cloud.* — **(4) 1865** *Dly. Constitutionalist* (Augusta, Ga.) 25 Oct. 1/4, 10,000 California Diamond Rings $3 to $10. **1872** Richardson *Wonders of Yellowstone* 107 Its shores are paved with volcanic rocks, sometimes in masses, sometimes broken and worn into pebbles of trachyte, obsidian, chalcedony, cornelians, agates and bits of agatized wood; and again, ground to obsidian-sand and sprinkled with crystals of California diamonds.

(5) 1840 Dana *Two Years* xiv. 109 The captain made it harder for us, by telling us that it was 'California fashion' to carry two [hides] on the head at a time. **1887** *Overland Mo.* Aug., In August we found the red and yellow columbine, just as it grows on New England hill-sides; ... except that, in true California fashion, they grow much larger. — **(6)** (*a*) **1840** Dana *Two Years* xxi. 216 Their children are brought up Spaniards, in every respect, and if the 'California fever' (laziness) spares the first generation, it always attacks the second. **1849** Wierzbicki *California* 83 The diseases that may be said to be incident to the climate are tractable, and we had the good fortune to lose not a single case ... be it diarrhoea ... or what may be called California fever—a confused type of all fevers. (*b*) **1849** Charles Welford *MS Lett.* 28 June (J. C. Brown Library), The California Fever is rather up again. **1899** *Land of Sunshine* April 241 In the beginning of the 'California Fever,'—due mostly to Frémont's wonderful journeys ... the Isbells left Mt. Pleasant, Ia., April 17, 1846. — **(7) 1849** *Pacific News* (S.F.) 31 Dec. (Supp.) 1/4, I recommend that collectors be authorized to receive the taxes in California gold, at the usual rate of sixteen dollars per ounce, Troy. **1857** *Hutchings Mag.* Mar. 398/2 The first night's encampment on the prairie was spent till bed time by the young 'hopefuls' singing California gold songs with a glee and hilarity. — **(8) 1849** Sherwood *Pocket Guide* ii, Bruce's Hydro-Centrifugal Chrysolite, or California Gold-Finder. — **(9) 1876** *Santa Barbara* (Calif.) *D. Index* 10 Aug. 4/3 California plain Hams, 14 @ 15c; Eastern Hams, 16½ @ 18½c. **1910** [see **Cala**].

(10) 1849 M. F. Ward *Letters from Three Continents* (2 ed.) 322 An effort seems to be making [in London] to introduce the brown *California* hats, as we call them in America, with feathers, but they are as yet very few. **1853** Felt *Customs New Eng.* 119 They were at first called *sombreros*, the Spanish for hats, *slouches*, and *California hats,* because fashionable in the modern Ophir, but latterly, by some, the *Paris felts.* — **(11) 1882** Steele *Frontier Army* (1883) 50 Here is the down-east Yankee ... turning his native cunning to account at poker and California jack. **1921** Mulford *Bar-20 Three* 39 For two hours they sat and played California Jack in plain sight of the street. — **(12) 1927** Russell *Trails* 2 Maybe he'd wear California pants, light buckskin in color, with large brown plaid, sometimes foxed, or what you'd call reinforced with buck or antelope skin. **1939** Abbott-Smith *We Pointed* 8 Striped or checked California pants made in Oregon City, the best pants ever made to ride in. — **(13) 1852** W. Kelly *Diggings of Calif.* 57 But by far the greater number were engaged in the study of the 'California prayer-book.' **1942** Lillard *Desert Challenge* 143 Friends asked forgiveness after violent disagreements and proposed a congenial session with a 'California prayer book.' — **(14) 1849** Wierzbicki *California* 69 The materials entering into the construction and trimming of a California saddle, are as few and as simple as possible. **1927** Russell *Trails* 3 There ain't no prettier sight for my eyes than one of those good-lookin', long-backed cowpunchers, sittin' up on a high-forked, full-stamped California saddle with a live hoss between his legs.

(15) 1856 Simms *Eutaw* xiii. 142 His ... hunter-knife ... [was] a most formidable weapon only inferior in size and weight to the modern 'California toothpick.' **1942** Lillard *Desert Challenge* 142 Men cut each other with 'California toothpicks.' — **(16) 1843** in *Miss. Val. Hist. Rev.* VI. 107 In company with one California Waggon & 5 Oregon waggons Came up. **1855** Boynton & Mason *Journey through Kans.* 29 Having provided ourselves with two horses, and a light California wagon, in which we could sleep, if necessary. — **(17) 1851** *Ore. Statesman* 23 May 2/1 A California widow publishes the following in a San Francisco paper: Husband Wanted—Whereas my husband has lately left my bed and board without provocation on my part, I hereby advertise for a suitable person to *fill the vacancy.* **1877** Bartlett 261 'California widow' ... came into use during the rush to California, 1850 to 1860, when the new-found treasures of that country separated so many husbands from their wives.

b. In less frequent combs., usu. rare or obs.; (1) **California adieu,** the name of a drink; (2) **bank note,** (see quot. and cf. **California shinplaster**); (3) **cut,** (see quot. and cf. **California hat**); (4) **gridiron,** (see quot.); (5) **lantern,** (see quot.); (6) **plan,** (see quot.); (7) **revolver,** a revolver of a type once common in California; (8) **road,** the road or trail to California; (9) **shinplaster,** (see quot. and cf. **California bank note**); (10) **sight,**

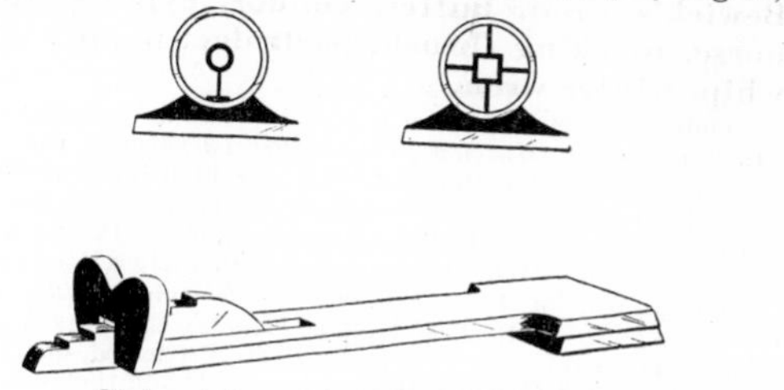

Globe sights and California sight

(see quot.); (11) **team,** a California wagon and the animals drawing it; (12) **trail,** see **trail 1. b;** (13) **treasure-ship,** a ship having a large amount of California gold aboard; (14) **tree,** the frame of a California saddle; (15) **wine,** wine made from California grapes.

(1) 1850 *Calif. Courier* (S.F.) 23 Aug. 2/4 'Pine Apple Julips, Cherry Cobblers, Cuba Punches, and California Adieus.'—What's them? — **(2) 1840** Dana *Two Years* xiii. 98 [Mexicans] at Monterey ... have no circulating medium but silver and hides—which the sailors call 'California bank notes.' — **(3) 1850** in *Pub. Col. Soc.* XXVII. 241 Then there are the steerage passengers & crew forward, hard, sun brown men with Hoosier rig on, a tan colored short frock and trows, heavy soled boots or bare-foot as the case may be, with the round slouch hat California cut—all colors, white, red, green, brown, black & dun. — **(4) 1850** Ryan *Adventures* I. 129 The 'California gridiron' now came into active and general use. It is a straight stick cut from a tree, stripped of its bark, and whittled to a sharp point. Several pieces of beef are 'speared' upon this; and, whilst one point rests on a piece of wood yet unburnt, and is held by one of the cooks, another turns the meat until the slices are done.

(5) 1948 Johnston *Gold Rush* 50/1 He groped his way through the darkness by the light of a 'California lantern,' which consisted of a candle inserted into a bottle from which the bottom had been broken. — **(6) 1888** J. D. Billings *Hardtack* 301 The hospital tents in the Army of the Potomac were heated, for the most part, by what was called, for some reason, the *California Plan.* This consisted of a pit, dug just outside of the hospital door, two and a half feet deep, from which a trench passed through the tent [etc.]. — **(7) 1881** *N.Y. Tribune* (D) 1/2 It was a large California revolver of large calibre. — **(8) 1857** T. H. Gladstone *Englishman in Kansas* 176 Or, from Kansas city, the traveller may take the more frequented 'California Road,' in order to trace upward the Kansas river, and see the towns and settlements which have risen so rapidly upon its banks. — **(9) 1848** *Californian* (S.F.) 12 Apr. 2/3 The good old Governor has been retrenching the expenses of the military and the fountain head of the golden fountain being stopped has left the glittering stream to dry up, and vessels dealing in California shin plasters (bullock hides) have brought that stock 50 per cent. below par.

(10) 1884 KNIGHT *Supp.* 154 *California Sight,* a hind sight for a gun; capable . . . of adjustment for ranges of varying distance. — (11) 1850 *Birmingham Emig. Co. Jrnl.* 19 Apr., Here we learned that about 60 California teams had crossed at this place the day before we did. — (13) 1862 MOORE *Rebellion Rec.* V. II. 145, I directed that an armed revenue cutter should proceed to sea to afford protection to . . . the California treasure-ships. — (14) 1876 CROFUTT *Trans-continental Tourist* 53 The best [saddle of the plains] now in use is made with what is known as the 'California Tree.'

(15) 1872 in BLAIR *Amer. Humor.* (1937) 434 On Forty-sixth street met lady who had some nice California wine.

Californiaite ˌkælə'fɔrnjəˌaɪt, *n.* An emigrant to California. *Rare.* — 1850 in *Mo. Hist. Rev.* XXX. 222 (*advt.*), California Wagons, manufactured at Jefferson City . . . are warranted, and we advise Californiaites to give them a call.

Californiaized ˌkælə'fɔrnjəˌaɪzd, *a.* Rendered Californian in sentiment or character. *Obs.* — 1847 in *Amer. Sp.* XXI. (1946) 116/1 It is illustrative of the predominant passion in Californiaized Yankees however. 1873 BEADLE *Undevel. West* 156 Most of the business men were 'Californiaized Jews,'—an improved variety of the race.

*** Californian,** *n.* and *a.*

1. *n.* A native of what is now California, a citizen of the state of California.

1789 MORSE *Amer. Geog.* 479 The characteristics of the Californians, are stupidity and insensibility. 1848 *Californian* (S.F.) 19 April 2/2 Two Californians had also discovered silver ore in the neighborhood of the town. 1893 K. SANBORN *S. Calif.* 18 Some one says that Californians 'irrigate, cultivate, and exaggerate.' 1947 *Chi. D. News* 17 Dec. 22/5 For some time the Californian has had only one real defender.

2. *a.* Of or pertaining to California, as **Californian Bewick's wren, butter, condor, cypress, herring, horse, mocking thrush, partridge, poppy, vulture, whip, winter wren.**

Only a few representative terms of this kind are included here. 1878 *U.S. Nat. Museum Proc.* I. 402 *Thryomanes bewicki* [var.] *spilurus.*—Californian Bewick's Wren. — 1850 RYAN *Adventures* I. 228 A large bladder of lard—or Californian butter, as the Yankees jestingly call it. — 1833 BONAPARTE *Ornithology* IV. 15 The wings are three feet nine inches long . . . as in the closely related species the Californian Condor. 1891 *Cent.* 6795/3 *Californian vulture,* the Californian condor. — 1850 B. TAYLOR *Eldorado* I. vii. 47 A few miles west of the Pueblo there is a large forest of redwood, or Californian cypress. — 1873 *Cassell's Mag.* Jan. 245 About the time of Gold discoveries some one applied the term Californian to these. The word was appropriate and Californian such highly-coloured herrings are called to this day. — 1848 RUXTON *Adventures* 106 Two or three days before the one appointed for the marriage, the father with his eight sons made their appearance, their gallant figures, as mounted on stout Californian horses they entered the hacienda, exacting a buzz of admiration from the collected rancheros. 1869 BREWER *Rocky Mt. Lett.* 18 Hoffman rode beside me, each of us with a barometer, as of old, and as if to complete the illusion, he rode a Californian horse. — 1873 *Amer. Naturalist* VII. 327 Next, we have the Californian Mocking-Thrush (*Harporhynchus redivivus*). — 1806 LANGSDORFF *Voyages* (1817) 441 Many of these baskets, or vessels, are ornamented with . . . the black crest feathers of the crested Californian partridge, *tetraonis cristati.* 1839 AUDUBON *Ornith. Biog.* V. 152 Californian Partridge, *Perdix Californica,* . . . was discovered in the course of the voyage of *La Perouse.* — 1845 FRÉMONT *Exped.* 249 The Californian poppy, of a rich orange color, was numerous to-day. 1912 *Out West* Apr. 220/1 Here, in the land of their nativity, the Californian poppy lifts its golden chalice to the sun, violet lupines make *parterres* of brave color between the lichened boulders. — 1839 AUDUBON *Ornith. Biog.* V. 240 Californian Vulture, *Cathartes Californianus,* . . . inhabits the valleys and plains of the western slope of the continent, and has not been observed to the eastward of the Rocky Mountains. 1891 [see **Californian condor**]. — 1850 RYAN *Adventures* II. 69, I made use of the usual Californian leather whip, which was attached to the end of the bridle, to fasten the reins to a tree. — 1878 *U.S. Nat. Museum Proc.* I. 403 *Troglodytes hyemalis,* [var.] *pacificus,* Californian Winter Wren.

Californianism ˌkælə'fɔrnjənˌɪzəm, *n.* A term typical of California. *Obs.* — 1868 WHYMPER *Alaska* 177 We sat down to a repast—to use a Californianism—of a high-toned and elegant nature.

californite ˌkælə'fɔrnaɪt, *n.* [*California* +*-ite.*] (See quot. 1909.) — 1909 *Cent. Supp.* 188/2 Californite. . . . A compact, massive variety of vesuvianite, of an olive-green to grass-green color, resembling some kind of jade. It is found in California and has been used as an ornamental stone. 1917 *Amer. Mineralogist* Jan. iv/1 Californite, oval and round, . . . each 15c.

calinda kə'lɪndə, *n. La.* [Amer. Sp. in same sense.] A dance formerly popular among Negroes and Creoles (see quot. 1931). In full **Calinda dance.**

1763 in *Amer. Sp.* XX. (1945) 47 Under pretence of *Calinda* or the dance, they [the Negroes] sometimes get together to the number of three or four hundred, and make a kind of *Sabbath.* 1880 CABLE *Grandissimes* 121 There our lately met *marchande* . . . led the ancient Calinda dance. 1889 WARNER *Studies So. & West* (1904) VIII. 81 He seized then a bunch of candles, plunged them into the bowl, held them all up flaming with the burning brandy, and, keeping his step to the maddening 'Calinda,' distributed them lighted to the devotees. 1931 READ *La.-French* 120 Calinda, *m.* An immodest African dance, in which the men formed in one line and the women, facing them, in another. The *calinda* and other voodoo dances were banished from Congo Square by the city of New Orleans about 1843.

calisthenium ˌkæləs'θinɪəm, *n.* [f. *calisthen*ics and *-ium.*] A place for exercising in calisthenics. *Obs.* — 1871 *Scribner's Mo.* II. 344 Besides the College [at Vassar] we find the Calisthenium. 1883 *N.Y. Tribune* 25 Dec., After the play the calisthenium was thrown open and the girls danced until supper-time.

*** calk,** *n.* (See quots.) Cf. *** creeper 2, toe calk.**

[1805 *Naval Chron.* XIII. 113 In Canada it is customary during the winter season . . . to wear on the feet a sort of patten, called *caulks.*] 1874 KNIGHT 430/1 The calk . . . attached to a boot consists of a plate with spurs, which project a little below the heel. 1948 *Chi. Tribune* 6 July 1. 1/4 They also wear shoes with metal calks on the sole to prevent slipping on the smooth white pine log.

Hence **calk-booted,** *a.*

1948 *Popular Western* June 60/1 We ain't caulk-booted loggers our ownselves, but it didn't take me an' Red here long to see Janson was pilin' these spruces deliberate.

*** call,** *n.*

1. (See quot. 1864.) *Obs.* Cf. **call spring.**

1838 in BASSETT *S. Plant.* 109 He said he had not the calls, and could not make a deed until I sent them to him, which I intend doing. 1864 WEBSTER 186/2 *Call,* . . . [in] Land Law, an object, course, distance, or other matter of description in a survey or grant requiring or calling for a corresponding object, &c., on the land.

2. *Poker.* A demand that the hand of a player or players be shown. Also fig.

1850 LEWIS *La. Swamp Dr.* 123 A gambler who has staked his whole pile, and found at the call that he has been bluffing up against a greenhorn with 'three white aces.' 1887 *Courier-Journal* 24 Jan. 2/4 Then they [the poker players] put up their railway shares in good-sized blocks, until when the call was made a controlling interest in each railroad was represented in the pot. 1946 MOREHEAD & MOTT-SMITH *Penguin Hoyle* 132 Every player who is 'in on the call' must expose his full hand face up on the table in the showdown.

b. A demand made upon a bank by an authorized official for a statement of its condition.

1910 *Sat. Ev. Post* 13 Aug. 14/2 'How much money have we, Bill?' 'Three thousand one hundred and sixty-five the last time the comptroller issued a call.'

3. **=moosecall.**

1860 *Harper's Mag.* March 442/1 'Tom, can you call moose?' . . . Stripping a sheet of bark from a birch-tree, Jenks quickly fashions a 'call,' and . . . raises the bark to his lips. 1920 *Outing* Oct. 6/3 Some guides use string or tacks to bind a call, said Bert, but it's best to use cedar roots for that gives the instrument a better tone.

4. One who responded to a "call" or inner prompting to preach. *Rare.*

1880 ROLLINS *N.E. Bygones* 155 Laymen left their ploughs and became exhorters; and the genuine 'call' often developed rare power to control minds.

5. A strike summons.

1905 *N.Y. Ev. Post* 6 Sep. 2 The ranks of the striking house painters were augmented to-day, when the Painters' District Council issued a call, making the strike general in all branches of painting.

6. *On* (or *upon*) *call,* on demand, immediately available.

1848 *N.Y. Wkly. Tribune* 4 March 8/4 On call, money is 7 per cent. with occasional loans at 6 per cent. 1889 MARK TWAIN *Conn. Yankee* xlii. 532 He bought about twice as much more [stock], deliverable upon call.

7. In combs., in some of which the first term has verbal force: (1) **call board,** in a stock exchange, a board for posting information concerning transactions, prices, etc.; (2) **box,** a post-office box from which mail can be withdrawn only by a patron calling for it; (3) **court,** a "called" or specially summoned court, *obs.;* (4) **loan,** a loan of money repayable on call or demand, also attrib.; (5) **meeting,** a meeting specially summoned, cf. *** called,** *a.* **1;** (6) **number,** a number assigned to a library book, to be used in calling for it; (7) **out,** (see quot.); (8) **room,**

a room in a stock exchange where "calls" are made; (9) **slip,** a slip for noting the number, title, etc., of a library book desired by a borrower; (10) **spring,** a spring established by surveyors as a call, cf. **1** above.

(1) **1880** *Bradstreet's* 1 Sep. 1/2 On the call board the caller refused to call a trade. — (2) **1887** *Courier-Journal* 23 Jan. 12/5 The post-office there [Corinth, Miss.] is not provided with lock-boxes, but uses what are known as call-boxes, with ordinary glass fronts. **1900** E. Dix *Deacon Bradbury* 40 The plain glass of the call-boxes. — (3) **1779** in L. Summers *Ann. S.W. Virginia* (1929) 730 To the Sheriff for summoning a Call Court on Robert Carr. — (4) **1852** *N.Y. Wkly. Tribune* 10 April 8/4 The rates are 4 @ 4 1/2 on Government Stocks, 5 @ 6 on general call loans. **1859** *Banking Mag.* (N.Y.) July 77 The call loan system. **1940** Wright *How & When to Buy & Sell Securities* 149 A call loan can be called for payment or paid up at any time the holder or the borrower desires.

(5) **1904** Harben *Georgians* 31 That afternoon they held a call meeting of Republicans in the parlor. **1909** A. C. Rice *Mr. Opp* 112 There's a call meeting of the Turtle Creek Land Co. for this morning at eleven at Your Hotel. — (6) **1876** *Public Libraries U.S.* (Bureau of Educ.) I. 626 Users of the [decimal] scheme . . . will find it of great practical utility . . . in determining the character of any book simply from its call number. **1915** Fay & Eaton *Use of Books* 108 This number distinguishes the book from other books in the library. It is known as the 'call number' of the book. — (7) **1916** *D.N.* IV. 269 *Call-out,* n. 1. An invitation to dance with a masker. 2. A lady who has received an intimation that she will be called out, and is assigned to a special section of seats. 'Those seats are there for the *call-outs.*' — (8) **1886** *Harper's Mag.* July 213/1 The Call Room daily presents an impressive spectacle of the traffic in grain. — (9) **1881** *A.L.A. Papers* 4/1 All books are to be asked for on call-slips made out from the catalog. **1947** *Prairie Schooner* Winter 454 He got the call slip for his book from the girl at the main desk.

(10) **1786** *Md. Hist. Mag.* XIX. 267 He has seen Wm. Rogers and Nicholas Gay surveyor of the Country run a line of Eagers Land and stopped at the call spring now called Cloppers Spring.

As the last term in **close, cow, dinner, moose, party, riot, shop, telephone, turkey, water call.**

* **call,** *v.*

1. *tr.* To decoy game (a turkey, moose, etc.) with a caller.

1831 Audubon *Ornith. Biog.* I. 12 During spring, Turkeys are *called,* as it is termed, by drawing the air in a particular way through one of the second joint bones of a wing of that bird, which produces a sound resembling the voice of the female, on hearing which the male comes up, and is shot. **1860** *Harper's Mag.* March 442/1 'Tom, can you call moose?' **1947** Brown *Outdoors Unlimited* 152 After considerable calling, I coaxed two drakes and a hen to drop to a lower level.

2. In poker, to ask for a show of hands after putting into the pool a sum equal to the largest bet made by any preceding player. Also fig. and absol.

1844 J. Cowell *Thirty Years* 94 The young lawyer . . . looked at the money staked, and then his hand again, and lingeringly put his wallet on the table and called. **1898** Page *Red Rock* 493 'Called your hand, rather, didn't he?' **1921** Mulford *Bar-20 Three* vii. 87 He pushed the money out onto the table. 'I calls,' he grunted.

b. With personal object. Also transf.

1845 *St. Louis Reveille* 2 May 2/1, I *go* it—and—call you. **1876** *Ventura Free Press* (San Buenaventura, Calif.) 8 Jan. 2/3 One man puts his money on three aces, and then the other man takes out a revolver and calls him. **1896** *Cong. Rec.* 23 May 5634/1 Mr. Milliken. . . . I do not know how great the amount of our saving might be, if . . . [Mr. Cummings] should consult all of his . . . colleagues on this floor. Mr. Cannon . . . Do you think we had better 'call' him? **1931** *K.C. Star* 14 Sep., Fully 6,000 people were . . . able to 'call' the writer on the proposition as to whether or not this paper knows who the probate judge is.

3. (See quot. and cf. **call,** *n.* **1.**) *Obs.*

1864 Webster 186/1 *Call,* . . . [in] Land Law, to require, as objects, courses, or distances, to answer or correspond with a description in a survey, or grant, of land.

4. *Baseball.* In various significations: **a.** To declare a game ended.

1865 *Wilkes' Spirit of Times* 5 Aug. 381/1 The last inning was played when it was nearly dark, but the Empires in a manly way declined to have the game called for such a reason, although they probably lost the game in consequence. **1948** *P.C.C. Chronicle* (Pasadena, Calif.) 7 May 4/5 The game was called at the end of four and one-half innings because of rain.

b. To start a game.

1867 *Ball Players' Chron.* 13 June 1/4 The game was called at 4 o'clock, the Ontarios at the bat. **1899** *Chi. D. News* 27 May 6/1 That Sunday game with the same Senators will be called at 2:30 o'clock sharp.

c. To pronounce a pitched ball a "strike" or a "ball."

1867 *Ball Players' Chron.* 20 June 6/2 McNally in a very few cases had balls called on him, but generally delivered them fair to the bat. **1948** *Pauls Valley* (Okla.) *D. Democrat* 4 July 4/5 How often do you see even an armpit-high pitch called a strike?

d. To determine when a pitcher's motions constitute a balk *q.v.*

1867 *Ball Players' Chron.* 5 Sep. 5/3 The umpire kept both nines up to a strict observance of the rules, . . . calling a balk, too, on a ball which was delivered with a step forward. **1948** *Pauls Valley* (Okla.) *D. Democrat* 2 July 4/4 Umpire Milt Shoffner had called a 'balk' on Blues pitcher Bill Woop in the third inning.

e. To pronounce a struck ball a "fair hit" or a "foul."

1868 Chadwick *Base Ball* 61 The umpire must call foul balls and balks without being asked. **1947** R. Smith *Baseball* 165 One umpire, the *Herald* reported, called a ball fair, then foul, then fair again, with two runs hanging in the balance.

f. To rule that a runner is "out" or "safe."

1912 Mathewson *Pitching* 194 The Chicago team at last won the game when Clarke was called out at third base on a close play. **1948** *Green Bay* (Wis.) *Press-Gazette* 12 July 15/2 Fischer . . . was ejected by Umpire Harding in the sixth inning for arguing too hot and too long after being called out trying to steal third.

g. To decide a close play for or against one side.

1912 Mathewson *Pitching* 174 Most clubs try to keep an umpire from feeling hostile toward the team because . . . he is likely to call a close one against his enemies, not intending to be dishonest. **1948** *Duncan* (Okla.) *D. Banner* 2 July 5 Though onlookers may jeer or call the game against us we rest assured that the Cosmic Umpire will understand and will call our plays with fairness.

5. In colloq. and slang phrases: (1) **To call off,* to name over, enumerate; (2) *to call to the book,* to take to task, call to account; (3) **to call out,* (*a*) to single out an actor or actress for special applause, (*b*) to summon members of a labor union to strike, (*c*) (see quot.); (4) *to call to the chair,* to elect or designate as the presiding officer or chairman of a meeting; (5) *to call one's* (or *the*) *bluff,* to accept one's challenge or dare, to demand a showdown, *slang;* (6) *to call down,* to reprimand severely, take issue with; (7) **to call for,* (see quot.); (8) *to call the turn,* see **turn,** *n.;* (9) *to call one's hand,* to block one's "game," to demand a reckoning of one, *slang,* cf. (5) above.

(1) **1840** Cooper *Pathfinder* xii, Name them? It is no easy matter to call off the stars, for the simple reason that they are so numerous. — (2) **1867** *Cong. Globe* 16 March 138/2 We are calling to the book men who have been in arms against us. — (3) (*a*) **1870** O. Logan *Before Footlights* 306 It has been the custom when an actor or actress was 'called out' as the phrase is, that they should come out before the curtains. (*b*) **1895** Robinson *Men Born Equal* 284 Ugly threats, moreover, were being made by the strikers that the members of other labor organizations would be 'called out.' (*c*) **1916** *D.N.* IV. 268 Call out, . . . at a carnival ball, when one is masked, to invite (a lady) to dance [New Orleans]. — (4) **1875** *Chi. Tribune* 25 Aug. 8/2 Mr. Henry J. Goodrich was called to the chair.

(5) [**1876** Bret Harte *Two Men of Sandy Bar* 17 But suppose that he sees that little bluff, and calls ye.] **1896** *Cong. Rec.* 26 March 3248 Where shall we be when the bluff is called? **1948** *Southwestern Rev.* Summer 267/2 One prominent Texas sheepman, C. C. Doty, established his rights by calling a cowman's bluff. — (6) **1896** Ade *Artie* 27 (We.), I didn't want to call her down. **1923** R. Herrick *Lilla* 74 She boxed this boy's ears when he was impudent, 'called down' a snippy upper class girl. — (7) **1912** Thornton *Amer. Gloss.* I. 138 A deed is said to 'call for' so many acres of land. — (9) **1857** *S.F. Call* 25 Mar. 1/1 Finally, after floating through a mist of metaphors, his good nature gets the better of him; and he concludes to 'call our hand,' and go several natural curiosities . . . better. **1898** Page *Red Rock* 493 'Called your hand, rather, didn't he?' **1948** *Dly. Ardmoreite* (Ardmore, Okla.) 4 Apr. 1/1 Some time, and very soon, something to call the Russian hand will have to be done.

callalou ˌkæləˈlu, *n.* Also **cullaloo.** [Amer. Sp. *calalú* in senses similar to those here shown. See Read, 119 f.] (See quots.) *Obs.* — **1810** F. Cuming *Tour* 297 Mr. Green made me observe some ginger in a thriving state, and the cullaloo or Indian Kail [in his garden near Natchez, Miss.]. **1892** Harris *Plantation* 122 And then there was Callalou—a mixture of collards, poke salad, and turnip greens boiled for dinner and fried over for supper.

callamink ˈkæləˌmɪŋk, *n.* Also **callemink.** [Du. *kalamink.*] Calamanco, a kind of woolen cloth. *Colloq.* — **1795** B. Dearborn *Columbian Grammar* 134 Improprieties, commonly called Vulgarisms, [include] . . . Callemink for Calamanco. **1901** Jewett *Tory Lover* xii. 106, I dove into my pockets an' come upon this old piece o' callamink I'd wrapped up some 'baccy in.

* **called,** *a.*

1. Of meetings: Specially summoned. Cf. **call meeting.**

1849 CHAMBERLAIN *Ind. Gazetteer* 52 At a called meeting of the Board, . . . the Central Medical College of Indiana was made a part of the University. **1889** *Cent.* 766/2 Called session, a special session of a legislative body summoned by the executive.

2. In baseball, applied to a pitched ball ruled by the umpire a "ball."

Since all "balls" are "called balls," this expression is app. obs. On the other hand, **called strike** (see below) makes a useful distinction and is still in use.

1868 *N.E. Base-Ballist* 20 Aug. 10/1 It is not necessary for a ball to be returned to pitcher except on 3rd called ball, when players are entitled to one base same as on a balk. **1880** *S.F. Globe* 12 July 1/5 Nolan took first on called balls. **1887** *Courier-Journal* 26 May 2/6 He . . . held the big batter of the Brooklyn Club down to five small hits, two of which were bases on called balls.

b. called strike, a pitched ball judged a "strike" by the umpire, regardless of other considerations.

1887 *Outing* Jan. 406/1 The batsman is now decided out when the ball after the third called strike is not struck at or hit. **1922** *Montgomery* (Ala.) *Advertiser* 6 Oct. 3/4 He issued three straight balls to Pipp . . . walked Meusel, and fanned Ward on a called strike. **1948** *Time* 21 June 6/3 He went down on called strikes.

* **caller,** *n.* **1.** (See quot.) *Obs.* **2.** One who calls moose with a moosecall. **3.** One who calls out offers of sale in the produce exchange. **4.** (See quot.) **5.** *Railroad.* One who calls men to report for work. **6.** An official who announces the result of a vote in a legislature.

(1) **1842** *Knickerb.* XX. 6 The head-waiter . . . or 'Caller' as he was designated. — (2) **1866** W. R. KING *Sportsman in Canada* iii. 52 [Moose-hunting] The caller . . . retires with a reserve gun, to the rear of the sportsmen. **1948** *Sat. Ev. Post* 9 Oct. 12/3 Most users of calls, however, discover that being a good caller takes a bit of doing. — (3) **1886** *Harper's Mag.* LXXIII. 213/1 William L. Eichell, caller of grain, presides. — (4) **1893** M. PHILIPS *Making of a Newspaper* 212 No reporter . . . can watch a field of six or more horses through a race, and then from memory write a correct account of it. . . . He does not trust his memory, but summons to his aid an assistant, who is known as a 'caller.'

(5) **1898** HAMBLEN *Gen. Manager's Story* 72 When it became known that Joe's fireman was sick, all the others made it a point to be away from home when the caller made his rounds with orders to call the first man he found off duty. — (6) **1911** *Okla. Session Laws* 3 Legisl. 227 When callers announce a vote, the enumerators shall call the numbers aloud, keeping check on each other.

Also **caller-out,** one who announces the changes in steps in a dance.

1882 *Cent. Mag.* Oct. 878/2 The 'caller-out,' though of less importance than the fiddler, is second to no other. He not only calls out the figures, but explains them at length to the ignorant, sometimes accompanying them through the performance.

As the last term in **dance, deer, turkey caller.**

* **calling. 1. calling card,** (see quot. 1946). **2. calling down,** a reprimand, a "call down." *Slang.*

(1) **1905** *N.Y. Times* 7 Feb. 5 (*advt.*), We'll execute calling cards to your order in conformity with the very latest requirements of fashion. **1946** WILSON *Fidelity* 163 These calling cards were in no sense what their name implies, for they were given away to one's friends and preserved thereafter just like other mementos. . . . The name was hidden under a lovely wreath or picture, glued down at one end. . . . The name was in script or print. — (2) **1909** WASON *Happy Hawkins* 219 'Well, James gets an awful callin' down,' sez Bill. **1923** WATTS *L. Nichols* 63 He thought that he would never forget the calling down one of the myrmidons earned.

calliope kəˈlaɪəpɪ, *n.* [f. Gr. *kalliopē*, the beautiful-voiced.]

1. A musical instrument consisting of a series of steam whistles operated from a keyboard. Cf. **musical steam engine.**

The spelling in quot. 1927 is indicative of the common pronunciation [ˈkælɪˌop.]

1858 J. COOK *Letters* (1946) 19 Sep. 45 On board the *Armenia* . . . is a Calliope, or an instrument resembling an organ & played in connection with the engine. **1863** RUSSELL *Diary* I. 265 On the metal roof was a 'musical' instrument called a 'calliope,' played like a piano by keys, which acted on levers and valves, admitting steam into metal cups, where it produced the requisite notes—high, resonant, and not unpleasing at a moderate distance. **1927** SANDBURG *Songbag* 349 The last wagon in the parade, [was[the steam 'kallyope.' **1948** *Newsweek* 30 Aug. 18/1 To the accompaniment of exploding fire-crackers and a calliope's groaning, [he] hailed Dewey.

2. calliope hummingbird, a hummingbird, *Stellula calliope*, of the western U.S. and Mexico.

1878 *U.S. Nat. Museum Proc.* I. 426 *Stellula calliope.*—Calliope Humming-bird.

calliopean ˌkælɪəˈpiən, *a.* Of or pertaining to a calliope. — **1860** *Harper's Mag.* Dec. 135/1 An ass on the opposite side of the ring began one of those grand, imposing, thrilling *caliopean* overtures to a concert for which he is so famous.

* **Callirrhoë,** *n.* A small genus of North American herbs of the mallow family. Also (not *cap.*) a plant of this genus. — **1860** GRAY *Botany* 66. **1914** BAILEY *Cyclo. of Horticulture* 629/2 The callirhoës are of the easiest culture, and deserving of a much greater popularity. **1939** *Nat. Geog. Mag.* Aug. 229/1 Callirhoe (Callirrhoë), the musical Greek name of the poppy mallow . . . , is the same as that borne by a nymph of the sea.

callithump ˈkæləˌθʌmp, *n.* Also **cowthump.** [Poss. shortened from **callithumpian,** *q.v.*] **1.** A **callithumpian band. 2. =shivaree.** *Colloq.*

(1) **1856** HALL *College Words* (ed. 2) 342 The band [=Pandowdy, noise-making band of Bowdoin] corresponds to the *Calliathump* [*sic*] of Yale. **1871** DE VERE 589 *Callithump* . . . represents the French *charivari*, the German *Katzenmusik*. — (2) **1941** *Ling. Atlas* Map 409 'Our minister married his third wife; we had a pretty good cowthump out of that.' [Southbury, Conn.] 'Nowadays we call it serenade; we always used to call it callithump.' [New Milford, Conn.]

callithumpian ˌkæləˈθʌmpɪən, *n.* and *a.* [See note.]

1. *n.* A member of a callithumpian band. *Obs.*

The precise origin of this term is difficult to make out. It may be a fanciful formation f. Gr. *kalli-* (cf. **calliope**) +*thump*, "beautiful thump." Cf. also *EDD Gallithumpians*, a society of social reformers, also applied to disturbers of order at Parliamentary elections.

*c***1830** FURMAN *Customs* 17–18 The streets of the City that night were absolutely thronged with watchmen so that it was impossible for the Callithumpians to effect any meeting, although some of them attempted it in the early part of the evening, and were arrested. **1836** HILL *Yankee Stories* 9 (We.), He said it was the *callathumpians*, (or some such *Dutchiffed* [*sic*] name,) that always went round New Year to kick up a sort of jollification. **1879** *Atlantis* (Glendale, Mont.) 28 Dec. 3/1 We have to return thanks to the Calathumpians for their serenade on Christmas day. **1881** *Reinbeck* (Iowa) *Times* 30 June 3/1 All who wish to join the calithumpians are requested to meet at Cremer's blacksmith shop Friday night.

2. *a.* Designating a band of discordant instruments (see quot. 1848).

*c***1830** FURMAN *Customs* 16 A celebrated detachment of these Rioters has long assumed the name of the 'Callithumpian Band,' and has been distinguished for being more noisy and uproarious than the others. **1848** BARTLETT 61 *Callithumpians*. . . . This party is called the *Callithumpians* or the *Callithumpian Band*. **1904** *N.Y. Times* 25 May 1 The calithumpian band had kept up the music without interruption all night. **1941** *Ling. Atlas* Map 409 Callithumpian band, jocular name for the serenaders. [Northfield, Mass.]

b. Of or pertaining to such a band. *Obs.*

1856 *N.Y. Herald* 9 Jan. 5/1 In the evening, occasional unearthly sounds, provided from tin horns and several Calathumpian accompaniments, filled the air. **1886** *Harper's Mag.* July 213/2 The call [on the exchange] lasts ten or fifteen minutes, and occasionally has the accompaniment of callithumpian discord. **1889** *Cent.* 931/3 *Charivari*. . . . Serenades of this sort . . . are still occasionally heard in the United States, where they are also known as Callithumpian concerts. *a***1897** *Phil. Hartmann & the Boys* (B. & L.), Hartmann's neighbours thought it would be a bright thing to give him a calliathumpian serenade.

callyhooting kæləˈhutɪŋ, *adv.* [App. related to **scallyhoot** *q.v.* Cf. "carahojing" in 1900 quot. *s.v.* **carajo,** *v.* and see Wentworth *s.v. tarryhoot*.] In an unrestrained, rapid, reckless manner. *Colloq.*— **1880** HARRIS *U. Remus* (1884) 190 Dey tells me dish yer train goes a callyhootin'. **1883** ——— *Nights* (1911) 132 Bimeby Brer Rabbit come a-cally-hootin' back des a-hollerin'.

calochortus ˌkæləˈkɔrtəs, *n.* [Gr. *kalo-* +*chortus*, "beautiful grass, fodder."] An herb or (*cap.*) genus of herbs of the lily family found in the western U.S. and Mexico.

1869 MUIR *First Summer in Sierra* (1911) 22 Found a lovely lily (*Calochortus albus*) in a shady adenostoma thicket near Coulterville. **1903** AUSTIN *Land of Little Rain* 147 Farther south on the trail there will be . . . singly, peacock-painting bubbles of calochortus blown out at the tops of tall stems. **1937** *Range Plant Handbook* W47 The species of *Calochortus* are not native to the eastern United States, ranging only from Nebraska west to the Pacific, north into Canada, and south to Mexico.

*calomel, *n.* In rare or obs. combs.: (1) **calomel doctor,** (see quot.); (2) **school,** a medical school. *Contemptuous.* — **(1) 1872** E. EGGLESTON *End of World* xxxii. 208 Every morning, Dr. Dibrell, a 'calomel-doctor'—not a steam doctor—rode by the house on his way to Andrew's. — **(2) 1876** in GUILD *Old Times* (1878) 405 Old man Eatherly of Wilson county, took a notion to send his son John to a calomel school.

calopogon ˌkæləˈpogən, *n.* [Gr. *kalopōgōn,* "beautiful beard."] An American grass pink or genus of bulbous orchids having bearded flowers.

1857 GRAY *Botany* 450 Calopogon, *C. pulchellus,* . . . [grows in] bogs; common. July. Flowers 1′ broad, pink-purple, fragrant. **1894** TORREY *Fla. Sketch-Book* 125 Here I picked a goodly number of novelties . . . [among which was] a calopogon, quite as pretty as our Northern *pulchellus.* **1940** DEAM *Flora Indiana* 347 Calopogon . . . grows in the open in both peaty and marly springy places, in tamarack bogs, and in a moist, prairie habitat.

* **caloric,** *n.* Designating a type of heated-air engine invented by John Ericsson (1803–89) or a ship driven by such an engine. *Obs.*

1853 in *Amer. Phil. Soc. Proc.* V. 305 The experimental trial of the caloric-engine vessel. **1853** *Hunt's Merch. Mag.* XXVIII. 164 We gave . . . a description of Ericsson's Caloric ship. **1866** LOWELL *Biglow P.* 2 Ser. 33 They go it like an Ericcson's ten-hoss-power coleric ingine.

calumet ˌkæljəˈmɛt, *n.* [Dial. F. *calumet,* applied by the French in Canada to various plants having stems suitable for pipestems, and to the Indian pipe.]

1. A ceremonial pipe used by North American Indians in their councils, peace-makings, etc. Cf. **eagle calumet.**

[**1678** MARQUETTE in *La. Hist. Coll.* IV. (1852) 21 These pipes for smoking are called in the country calumets, a word that is so much used, that I shall be obliged to employ it in order to be understood, as I shall have to speak of it frequently.] **1698** tr. HENNEPIN *New Discovery* 74 This *Calumet* is the most mysterious Thing in the World among the Savages of the Continent of Northern America; for it is us'd in all their important Transactions: However, it is nothing else but a large Tobacco-Pipe made of Red, Black, or White Marble. **1836** IRVING *Astoria* xvi. 232 The Ponca chief then, . . . arrayed his beautiful daughter in her finest ornaments, and sent her forth with a calumet to sue for peace. **1880** CABLE *Grandissimes* 21 The father . . . had so outsmoked . . . their 'Great Sun,' as to find himself, as he finally knocked the ashes from his successful calumet, possessor of a wife. **1948** *C.A. Jrnl.* June 123 The missionary . . . watched them smoking the calumet (the pipe of peace) ere evening closed.

b. Also **calumet pipe, calumet (pipe) of peace.**

1705 HARRIS *Navigantium atque itinerantium* II. 907/2 We then sent three Men to buy Provisions with the *Calumet* of Peace. **1751** GIST *Journals* 50 We might smoak the Calamut Pipe of Peace with them. **1884** SWEET & KNOX *Through Texas* 54 The Muscogees sitting on a decayed log, smoking the calumet of peace. **1948** *Indiana Mag. Hist.* Sep. 245 Among the aborigines, wampum, like the calumet pipe, was a symbolic present whose mysterious connotations were never fully understood by the whites.

2. Short for **calumet dance.**

[**1698** tr. HENNEPIN *Voyage* 211 This Dance of the *Calumet* is a solemn ceremony amongst the Savages, which they perform upon important Occasions, as to confirm an Alliance, or make Peace with their Neighbours.] **1823** *Niles' Reg.* XXIII. Supp. 64/2 A part of my nation . . . came to my village three times . . . to dance the *calumet,* (make presents), and triumph at the expense of the whites whom they plundered.

3. In combs. now obs. or hist.: (1) **calumet bird,** = **calumet eagle;** (2) **dance,** among some of the Plains Indians a ceremonial and invocative dance with, or in honor of, the calumet; (3) **eagle,** an eagle, as the golden eagle or bald eagle, the feathers of which were used by the Indians to adorn the calumet; (4) **party,** a party of Indians on a peaceful mission; (5) **song,** an Indian ceremonial song in which the calumet was used.

(1) 1805 LEWIS in Biddle *Lewis & Clark Exped.* (1814) II. 504 The beautiful eagle or calumet-bird, so called from the circumstance of the natives decorating their pipe-stems with its plumage. **1814** BIDDLE *Ib.* I. 112 Our chief tells us that the calumet-bird lives in the holes formed by the filtration of the water from the top of these hills through the sides. — **(2)** [**1678** MARQUETTE in *La. Hist. Coll.* IV. (1852) 35 The calumet dance . . . is performed only for important matters, sometimes to strengthen a peace or to assemble for some great war.] **1778** CARVER *Travels* 268 The Indians have several kinds of dances which they use on different occasions, as the Pipe or Calumate Dance. **1809** KENDALL *Travels* II. 293 The *poigan, poagan,* pipe or calumet-dance is a dance introduced from among Indians of the south. — **(3) 1806** CLARK in *Lewis & C. Exped.* (1905) IV. 158 The Calumet Eagle is sometimes found on this side of the Rocky Mountains. **1826** *N. Amer. Rev.* Jan. 118 The bird itself is called the Calumet Eagle. . . . They are very rare, and killed with difficulty. **1833** CATLIN *Indians* I. 68 This bird has often been called the calumet eagle . . . from the fact, that the Indians almost invariably ornament their Calumets or pipes of peace with its quills. — **(4) 1842** *S. Lit. Messenger* VIII. 462/2 In the spring of '14, a calumet party of about twenty Grand Pawnees paid them a visit in their villages.

(5) 1730 *Miss. Prov. Arch.* Fr. Dom. I. (1927) 66, I learned that the Natchez had gone to the Choctaws to sing the calumet-song, which confirmed my belief that the warning that had been given me to beware of the Choctaws, was only too true.

calycanthus ˌkælɪˈkænθəs, *n.* [Gr. *kalyx,* calyx +*anthus,* flower.] The Carolina allspice or strawberry shrub. Also attrib.

1814 MITCHILL in *Mineral. Jrnl.* I. 213 The persimmon, the papeflora, the calycanthus, and the papaw, strike their roots through the sands of the shore. **1851** LINCOLN *Botany* 262 *Calycanthaceæ,* the Calycanthus Tribe. **1901** MOHR *Plant Life Ala.* 518 *Butneria fertilis* (Walt.) . . . Smooth Calycanthus. Mountain Spice-wood. *Ib., Butneria florida* (L.) . . . Calycanthus. Carolina Allspice.

calzoneras kalsonˈerəs, *n. W.* [Amer. Sp. (< Sp. *calzón*) in same sense.] Trousers buttoned at the sides.

1844 GREGG *Commerce of Prairies* I. 211 A curiously shaped article called *calzoneras,* intended for pantaloons, with the outer part of the legs open. **1850** B. TAYLOR *Eldorado* (1862) xiii. 122 A handsome young Californian, dressed in blue calzoneros. **1910** J. HART *Vigilante Girl* 196 She had replaced their calzonera, or riding-breeches, with a divided skirt of doeskin.

camass ˈkæməs, *n.* Also **camas, commas, kamas,** etc. [Chinook Jargon, f. *chamas,* sweet, in the Nootka language of Vancouver. Cf. Hodge and see **passhico.**]

1. The quamash, *Camassia esculenta,* or related species, whose sweet, nutritious bulbs are eaten by Indians of the Northwest and of western Canada. Also attrib. See also **poison camass.**

1805 ORDWAY in *Journals of Lewis & O.* 290 These natives have a large quantity of this root bread which they call commass. The roots grow in these plains. **1832** WYETH *Journal* 172 [The] Indians . . . dig the Kamas root. *Ib.* 202 Kamas in bloom. The Indians are taking large quantities of it. **1868** WHYMPER *Alaska* 24 He has subsisted for twelve days on fern and 'gamass,' or lily roots, and a few berries. **1945** MACDONALD *Egg & I* 104 Camas and starflowers carpeting the woods.

2. Designating areas where this plant is found, as **camass field, flat, ground, meadow, plain, prairie.**

1847 *Sangamo Jrnl.* (Springfield, Ill.) 22 Apr. 1/2 Kamas fields begin to appear plentiful, where swine can range and fatten. **1855** in *Reports of Explor. & Surveys* XII. I. (1860) 199 The Indians were collecting their horses to go out to the kamas fields northward of Snake river. — **1806** ORDWAY in *Journals of Lewis & O.* 414 A number of Indians went across this commass flat on horseback to another prarie or flat to the north. — **1855** in *Reports of Explor. & Surveys* XII. I. (1860) 200 We came to . . . the Coeur d'Aléne kamas grounds. At these kamas grounds there were twenty-five lodges of Coeur d'Alénes, and about 250 Indians. **1880** BURNETT *Old Pioneer* 150 Every succeeding fall they found . . . our settlements . . . encroaching more and more upon their pasture and camas-grounds. — **1884** *Cent. Mag.* May 139 We encamped in a prairie dotted with clumps of cottonwood trees and camas meadows. — **1843** in *Overland to Pacific* VII. (1938) 297 The Grand Round . . . is a large Kamsh plain. — **1842** DE SMET *Letters* (1843) 182 The summit once attained, we proceeded to cross a smiling little plain, called the Camash Prairies, where the Flat Heads come every spring to dig up that nourishing root. **1927** WALGAMOTT *Remin. Early Days* II. 40 There are many camas prairies in the west.

b. (1) **camass eater,** (see quot.); (2) **pocket gopher,** =next; (3) **rat,** a pocket gopher, also **camass pouched rat.**

(1) 1865 STUART *Montana as It Is* 58 It is very abundant in Oregon, and was an important article of food to the first settlers. Hence, they derived their 'sobriquet' of 'camus eaters,' 'camus' being the name that the root is known by among the whites. — **(2) 1936** BAILEY *Mammals & Life Zones Ore.* 225 If the big camas pocket gopher (*Thomomys bulbivorus*) were twice its present size its longer tail would be the only convenient means of distinguishing the two. — **(3) 1849** *Sk. Nat. Hist., Mammalia* IV. 96 The Camas pouched rat is common in N. America, on the banks of the Columbia river. **1868** WOOD *Homes without Hands* 35 The Camas Rat (*Pseudostoma borealis*). . . . The name is derived from its food, which consists chiefly of quamash root. **1936** BAILEY *Mammals & Life Zones Ore.* 250 The original name of camas rat was undoubtedly based on their fondness for the bulbs of the camas.

cambric tea. [See quot. 1891.] A drink, esp. for children, consisting of weak tea to which milk and sugar have been added. Cf. **hot water tea.**

1888 *Union Signal* (Chicago) 21 Jan. 3 [She] offered me tea, cambric tea to be sure, but in a beautiful cup. **1891** *N. & Q.* VI. 174 Cambric Tea . . . is so called because it is thin, white and weak. **1903** BURNHAM *Jewel* 225 'Is there going to be some cambric tea for this baby?' inquired Dr. Ballard. **1944** *Greeley* (Colo.) *D. Tribune* 28 Sep. 6/4 Many children dearly love cambric tea, which is made by pouring about two tablespoons of weak tea into a cup of hot milk and adding a dash of sugar.

Cambridge Platform. A system of church government drawn up by a synod (Congregationalist) which met at Cambridge, Mass., in 1648. Now *hist.*

1770 STILES *Lit. Diary* (1901) I. 59 Here I saw the original MS. of the Cambridge Platform in the writing of Mr. Rd. Mather, the principal compiler. **1832** WILLIAMSON *Maine* I. 379 A code of ecclesiastical rules, or articles of discipline, among the churches, which. . . consisted of 17 chapters, and have been denominated 'The Cambridge Platform';—being subsequently the ecclesiastical constitutions throughout the New-England churches. **1923** *Pub. Col. Soc.* XXV. 239 Cf. the reprint of the Cambridge Platform in W. Walker's Creeds and Platforms of Congregationalism (1893), p. 203.

Camden and Amboy. (See quot. 1948.)

1856 *Spirit of Times* 13 Sep. 29/1 All the horses in this 'snap' were from the 'State of Camden and Amboy,' and 'a *soft* snap' it proved to be. *Ib.* 4 Oct. 78/3 Riding in a foreign country, out of the United States, the 'State of Camden and Amboy,' if you please, the settlement of the match was arranged between themselves—'heads I win, tails you loose [*sic*]!' **1948** MENCKEN *Supp.* II. 602 *Camden and Amboy State* . . . harks back to the time when the promoters of the Camden and Amboy Railroad ran the politics of the State [i.e., New Jersey].

***camel,** *n.*

1. (See quots. 1855 and 1903.) Also attrib.

1855 WELD *Vacation Tour* 240 The locomotives used for the purpose are colossal machines, called 'camels,' and enormously powerful. The weight of the engine in running order is thirty tons and its length twenty-eight feet. **1877** E. MARTIN *Hist. Great Riots* 337 The strikers were quiet and orderly at first, the only violence being the throwing of a man from a camelback engine for attempting to start the fires. **1903** E. JOHNSON *Railway Transportation* 44 Ross Winans . . . brought out the first 'camel' type of engine, so named because the engine-driver's cab is placed above the middle part of the boiler.

2. camel cricket, an insect of the genus *Mantis* having a long thorax suggestive of the elongated neck of a camel. Also a cave cricket.

1859 BARTLETT 356 *Rear Horse,* the vulgar name, at the South, for the orthopterous insect called the Mantis, Camel Cricket, or Johnny Cock-Horse. **1889** *Harper's Mag.* June 45/2 The camel-cricket is another active destroyer of injurious insects.

3. (See quot.) *Obs.*

1882 G. A. SALA *America Revisited* II. 317, I subsequently discovered, by the aid of a comic illustrated paper, that a 'camel' was the popular name for that addendum to the feminine toilette which in England is known as a 'dress improver,' and which in the days of the Hottentot Venus used to be called a 'bustle.'

4. camel walk, a dance so called.

1921 *Frontier* May 16 The morbid minded may read them as openly as they danced the shimmy and the camel-walk a year ago. **1943** S. J. PERELMAN *Keep It Crisp* 31 The Lady, her wrists trailing the piano keys, is bent backward in an arc recalling the Camel Walk of 1922.

camerist ˈkæmərɪst, *n.* A photographer. See also **hand camerist.**

1890 *Internat. Ann., Anthony's Photog. Bul.* III. 19 Theoretically, all camerists believe in a good negative. **1900** *Boston Ev. Transcript* 23 Feb. 12/6 When a high wind is encountered, the cloth at one end can be buttoned . . . around the head or face of the camerist. **1906** *Suburban Life* July 15/1 And away goes Miss Summer Camerist, probably saying: 'The hateful fool! I just know he spoiled my films on purpose!'

camino real. *S.W.* [Sp., highway.] "In Spanish and southwestern English it is used to signify the main highway and implies a highway built by the state or the king" (Bentley).

1840 D. TURNBULL *Travels in West* 176 In traveling along the neglected highway or Camino real . . . I thought I had observed . . . indications of coal. **1910** *Scribner's Mag.* Oct. 503/2 We might, by continuing along the Camino Real, visit the remainder of Fray Junipero's churches. **1941** *Amer. Sp.* Oct. 179 As a *camino real,* it was the chief commercial artery in the Southwest during the eighteenth century.

camisa kəˈmisə, *n. S.W.* [Sp. in same sense. An Amer. borrowing.] A shirt, undershirt, or chemise.

1829 PATTIE *Narrative* 285 The Indian women were all clad in blue petticoats, and cotton *camisas,* with bosom and sleeves ruffled. **1845** GREEN *Texian Exped.* 320 Any sergeant's wife in the castle would trust him for the washing of his camisa. **1939** VESTAL *Old Santa Fe Trail* 264 The women wore a skimpy *camisa,* loose, abbreviated sleeves, short red skirts, gay shawls, and slippers.

camote kaˈmotə, *n. S.W.* [Amer. Sp. (< Nahuatl) in sense 1.] **1.** A sweet potato. **2.** A parasitic plant, *Ammobroma sonorae,* formerly much used as food by Papago Indians.

(1) [**1772** ULLOA *Noticias Americanas* 99 Allí prevalecen el *Maiz,* las *Batatas,* que llaman *Camotes,* . . . y muchas especies de simientes.] **1895** *Amer. Folk-Lore* Jan.–Apr. 56 There are also added slices of *Camotes* (sweet potatoes) and *Calabazas,* or pumpkins. — (2) **1925** BRYAN *Papago Country* 27 Their principal vegetable food was the camote (*Amnobroma sonorae*), an edible root found in the sand dunes. **1931** DAYTON *Western Browse Plants* 154 White bur-sage [is] . . . one of the two chief host plants of the curious, parasitic, lennoaceous plant sandroot (*Ammobroma sonorae*), known also as sandfood and camote.

***camp,** *n.*

1. The "quarters" on a slave plantation. *Obs.*

1763 in *Amer. Sp.* XX. (1945) 47, I went that very evening to the camp of the *Negroes,* and from hut to hut. **1839** F. A. KEMBLE *Journal* 18 There are four settlements or villages (or, as the negroes call them, camps) on the island, consisting of from ten to twenty houses.

2. (See quots.) *Obs.*

1789 in CIST *Cincinnati* (1841) 204 We raised what in this country is called a camp, by setting two forks of saplings in the ground, a ridge-pole across, and leaning boat-boards . . . one end on the ground and the other against the ridge pole. **1835** ABBOTT *New England* 17 About eight miles from the camp which they erected, a few settlers had commenced operations. . . . [*footnote*], This name is given to a rude hut erected for some temporary purpose in the forest. **1866** *Beadle's Mo.* June 490/1 Some fifty log cabins had been built, huts and 'camps,' covered with pine boards were very numerous.

3. A sugar camp.

1823 COOPER *Pioneer* xx, The sugar-boiler . . . was busy in his 'camp.' **1848** in DRAKE *Pioneer Life Ky.* 85 There were but few sugar trees on father's land, and he rented a 'camp,' as the grove was called. **1898** N. E. JONES *Squirrel Hunters of Ohio* 18 There are a few of the older crop of sugar trees still remaining; but the great 'camps' that furnished sweets in abundance have, with other varieties of timber, fallen victims to the woodman's ax.

4. A group of buildings or temporary structures erected as living quarters for miners, lumberers, etc., also a town that has sprung up around or near a mine or group of mines.

1836 COX *Baptists* 350 They construct *camps* of various descriptions, made of logs notched into each other, and planted where the trees are thickest. **1877** WM. WRIGHT *Big Bonanza* 27 This was a little hamlet of a dozen houses of all kinds. . . . In this little town or 'Camp,' as such places are usually styled in mining countries. **1946** *Trail & Timberline* May 74/2 Leadville, by this time the leading camp in the state, fortunately had some gold mines.

b. One or more buildings, freq. situated near a lake or in the woods or mountains, forming a temporary residence, esp. in summer.

1880 SWEETSER *Picturesque Maine* 62 Here and there, on the rocky knolls of the mainland, . . . are commodious buildings for the entertainment of sportsmen, still preserving, in their generic name of 'camps,' the memory of earlier, less elaborate shelters. **1881** *Harper's Mag.* May 873/1 An Adirondack Camp may seem cut off from the busy world. **1906** *N.Y. Ev. Post* 16 June (Resort Sec.) 4 The word 'camp' is ambiguous as applied to abodes in the Adirondack forest, for it may be used to designate a snug little cabin, with its modest half-acre of territory, or it may apply to an extensive establishment that represents the outlay of thousands of dollars, standing in the midst of a royal estate of 50,000 acres. **1948** *Kankakee* (Ill.) *D. Jrnl.* 5 June 12/5 The first scouts will be residents in the camp beginning June 20 and continuing until July 24.

5. The place where a camp meeting is held (see also quot. 1911).

1843 CARLTON *New Purchase* II. 136 The camp was furnished with several stands for preaching, exhorting, jumping, and jerking. **1888** CRADDOCK *Broomsedge Cove* 37, I hev seen ye, a-many-a-time—a preachin' . . . at the church-house, and at camp, too. **1911** C. HARRIS *Eve's Husband* 175 Some friends of Clancy Drew's pitched what they called a 'camp' two miles from town and invited every colored voter . . . to come and have a good time.

6. (See quots. 1880 and 1909.)

1880 TOURGEE *Invisible Empire* 415 Sometimes several 'camps' or 'dens' [of the Ku-Klux Klan] would, independently of each other, direct a warning to be sent to the same individual. **1904** HARBEN *Georgians* 132 The general is invited to address nearly all the veteran camps over the State when the badges of honor are presented once a year. **1909** WEBSTER 316/1 A lodge or local division of certain patriotic societies connected with past wars; as, a *camp* of the Sons of Veterans. *U.S.* **1947** LUMPKIN *Southerner* 113 Each state had its division of the parent organization [United Confederate Veterans], and each division its multitude of 'camps' honeycombing the counties.

7. In combs.: (1) **camp bird,** =**camp robber;** (2) **boss,** one in charge of a camp, esp. a lumber camp; (3) **cabin,** a cabin serving as a camp, *obs.;* (4) **cook,** one who cooks for a group of campers; (5) **cot,** a portable cot suitable for use in a camp; (6) **cure,** a cure effected by living an outdoor life in a camp, *obs.;* (7) ***fire,** a social gathering of members of a post or posts of the Grand Army of the Republic, as if around a campfire; (8) **ground,** (*a*) the place where a camp meeting is held, (*b*) a camping ground; (9) **house,** a house in which one lives somewhat as in a camp; (10) **hunt,** a hunt by a group of hunters who "camp out"; (11) **keeper,** one in charge of a camp; (12) **keeping,** living accommodations provided in a camp, *rare;* (13) **kit,** a box containing cooking and mess utensils; (14) **meeting,** see as a main entry; (15) **out,** an occasion of camping out, *rare;* (16) **preacher,** a preacher who takes part in a camp meeting, *obs.;* (17) **robber,** any one of various birds, as the Canada jay, that steal provisions from camps; (18) **rustler,** *W.* (see quot.); (19) **stove,** a light, portable stove suitable for use in a camp; (20) **tender,** =**camp rustler.**

Camp stove

(1) 1914 CLEMENTS *Rocky Mt. Flowers* 64 The 'camp-bird,' the Rocky Mountain jay, is a resident. — **(2)** *a***1904** WHITE *Blazed Trail* ii. 22 Especially is it true of the camp boss, the foreman. **1931** *New Republic* 8 April 202/2 The following morning after the prisoners left for the swamp the camp boss whipped me as I lay on the mattress on the floor. — **(3) 1886** Z. F. SMITH *Kentucky* 4 The ends of the poles . . . rested against, or on top of, the fallen tree, thus forming a frame-work for the side of the camp-cabin. — **(4) 1881** ROMSPERT *Western Echo* 185 There is a great difference in camp-cooks; and some make nice doughnuts and puddings for the boys, while others get nothing but bread and meat, and sometimes beans and potatoes. **1945** *Reader's Digest* Sep. 110/2 'They ought to be good,' said the erstwhile camp cook, 'I had about 20,000 head to pick from.'
(5) 1850 ENOS CHRISTMAN *One Man's Gold* (1930) 107, I have made a camp cot to carry with me to the mines. **1943** GEIST *Hiking* 143 There is an inexpensive folding camp cot which is made of wood and canvas. — **(6) 1878** I. L. BIRD *Rocky Mts.* 47 Consumptives . . . trying the 'camp cure' for three or four months. — **(7) 1882** G. A. SALA *America Revisited* I. 148 The 'Grand Army of the Republic' informed me that they would hold 'a grand camp fire' at the Academy of Music. **1898** *Buffalo* (N.Y.) *Express* 18 Dec. 18/7 The members of the 74th regiment will participate in a campfire to be given in the Armory, on Thursday evening. — **(8) (*a*) 1805** L. DOW *Travels* Wks. 1806 II. 94, I viewed the Camp-ground, and preparations making for the meeting. **1900** C. WINCHESTER *W. Castle* 103 Pastor Castle . . . started for the camp ground, with a one-horse load of baggage and provisions. (*b*) **1816** U. BROWN *Journal* II. 360 Their Pilot mist his way, & never could find their Camp ground. **1944** *Nat. Geog. Mag.* June 698/1 We heard our first sierra grouse tooting from the top of a red fir near one of the campgrounds. — **(9) 1897** *Outing* XXX. 374/2 The permanent camp . . . , of course, is more of a house than a camp, and may be roughly built of large logs [etc.]. . . . This style of camp-house has proved thoroughly useful for its purpose and has many friends. **1948** *Capital-Democrat* (Tishomingo, Okla.) 24 June 1/3 Surrounding camp houses, empty most of year, are the center of family life at annual summer revival meetings

(10) 1841 *Spirit of Times* 25 Dec. 506/3 (We.), I learned . . . that there was in contemplation a camp hunt. **1889** *Cong. Rec.* 19 Jan. 1010/2 He enjoyed no recreation as much as he did the 'camp hunts' for deer, which in his day, as now, were in vogue in Louisiana. — **(11) 1825** *Austin Papers* (1924) II. 1206 Mr. Dixon . . . understood surveying on the Brazos and Kilpatrick accompanied him as Camp-keeper. **1871** PINE *Beyond West* 276 Then follow the pack animals, each bearing three packs, snugly fastened, so as not to slip in traveling. These are in charge of men called camp-keepers. — **(12) 1837** IRVING *Bonneville* I. vii. 91 In return for this protection, and for their camp keeping, they [=free trappers] are bound to dispose of all the the beaver they take, to the trader who commands the camp, at a certain rate per skin. — **(13) 1864** *Rep. Comm. Patents* (1866) I. 992 Camp Kit.—December 20, 1864.—This invention consists in the arrangement of two plates forming a case, in which the cooking and eating utensils for a soldier or traveller may be conveniently packed and carried. **1880** *Harper's Mag.* Aug. 400/2 The camp kit . . . must be compact as well as light. **1882** HUBBARD *Moosehead Lake,* Guides who render the above-named prices furnish a canoe and the necessary camp 'kit,' except blankets.

(15) 1879 STOCKTON *Rudder Grange* 120 If it gives you a good camp out, I don't mind. — **(16) 1845** JUDD *Margaret* I. xvi. 152 In the midst of all . . . might be heard the voice of the Camp-preacher. **1851** *Harper's Mag.* July 218/2 A camp preacher . . . thundered forth the evil consequences of not listening to what he was saying with reverence. — **(17) 1893** *Outing* Sep. 424/1 Our scavengers, the 'camp robbers,' were on hand too, waiting their turn. They are pretty little gray-and-black plumaged birds, the size of a pigeon, but with a dismal squawk which they keep up incessantly. They will carry off anything from a biscuit to an iron spoon, and are useful if they confine their depredations to refuse and garbage. **1946** R. PEATTIE *Pac. Coast Ranges* 208 With shy boldness the soft-voiced camp robber, or Oregon jay, glides in on level wings for plunder. — **(18) 1913** W. C. BARNES *Western Grazing Grounds* 380 Among stockmen . . . 'Camp Tender, Camp Rustler' [is] a man who accompanies the sheep herd, looks after the packs, locates camp and relieves the herder from such matters. — **(19) 1862** T. J. JACKSON in *Memoirs* (1892) 363 Last night was very cold, but my good friend . . . secured a camp-stove for me. **1948** *Mazama* July 1/2 The chores will be kept to a minimum by use of gasoline camp stoves, . . . disposable plates, cups, etc. — **(20) 1913** [see **camp rustler**].

b. In phrases: (1) *At long camps,* (see quot.), *obs.;* (2) *to make camp,* to camp; (3) *to take into camp,* to appropriate, defeat, *colloq.*

(1) 1837 IRVING *Bonneville* I. xvii. 176 He turned his back upon the swamp and its muskrat houses, and followed on at 'long camps,' which, in trapper's language, is equivalent to long stages. — **(2) 1846** SAGE *Rocky Mt. Life* (1859) 58 We made camp late in the afternoon at the head of the right fork of Blue. **1850** GARRARD *Wah-To-Yah* xxi. 256 We made camp in a bottom opposite the mouth of the Purgatoire. **1902** WISTER *Virginian* xvi, Well, suppose you're camping out, and suppose it's a hot night, or you're in a hurry, and you've made camp late. — **(3) 1866** *Wilkes' Spirit of Times* 10 Feb. 381/1 After the grease had been pretty well absorbed, the tired porker was taken into camp by an individual who looked as if highly pleased by the thought that he had proved himself more active and tenacious than the rest. **1930** *Randolph Enterprise* (Elkins, W.Va.) 16 Jan. 5/1 Elkins High School took another contender into camp last Thursday night when Philippi came up here to tackle Frank Wimers tame tigers.

As the last term in **bark, branding, brush, coal, construction, contraband, convict, cook, cow, dry, gold, grading, half-faced, hay, hide, hunting, line, log, logging, lumber, lumbering, maple sugar, miners', mining, mixed ale, Osage, out, outside, parole, placer, prospect, prospecting, shearing, sheep, sign, signal, silver, Siwash, squaw, station, sugar, summer, timber, trading, training, turpentine, veteran, wagon, water, wood camp.**

***camp,** *v.*

1. (See quot.) *Obs.*

1852 MRS. ELLET *Pioneer Women* 164 Large parties of old and young, male and female, . . . assembled and bivouacked, or 'camped,' to use their own phrase, in the woods near the grove of [sugar-]maples, which were soon notched and pierced.

2. In phrases: (1) *To camp down*, (*a*) to form a camp, settle down for a time, (*b*) to lie or sit down, *colloq.;* (2) *to camp out*, to spend the night outdoors, to live in the open in a tent or camp, also transf.; (3) *to camp on the trail of*, see **trail.**

(1) (*a*) **1781** in G. POWERS *Hist. Sk. Coos* (1841) 197 Camped down on the River Lamoille this night. *a***1889** *Spirit of Times* (F.), They . . . when day broke took to the bush, camped down a smart piece off the trail. (*b*) **1850** W. COLTON *3 Years Calif.* 310, I have seen this *savan* camp down and snore soundly through the night. **1869** ALCOTT *Little Women* II. 100 I'll be hanged if I camp down before her table afterward. — (**2**) **1748** WASHINGTON *Writings* I. 3 We camped out in the field this night. **1835** LONGSTREET *Ga. Scenes* 9 The old gentleman and his lady had consented to *camp out* for a day. **1948** *Dly. Ardmoreite* (Ardmore, Okla.) 10 June 6/4 He has camped out in a tent in sub-zero weather, so cold eggs would freeze before they could be scrambled.

* **campaign,** *n.*

1. Political activity before an election, marked by organized action in attempting to influence voters. Cf. **4.** below.

1809 *Steele Papers* II. 601 The electioneering campaign having become much warmer than I had anticipated. **1890** NORTON *Polit. Americanisms* 26 *Campaign*, a political contest. . . . 'Its specific application to politics appears to be mainly American, though this usage has been to some extent adopted in England' (*vide Pall Mall Gazette, et al.*). **1946** *Democrat* 6 June 1/7 Among the things Folsom promised in his campaign were [etc.].

2. The period in which new members are sought and pledged by students belonging to college organizations. Also attrib.

1871 BAGG *At Yale* 72 The . . . members of the initiation committee are also chosen on the night of the campaign. . . . Besides attending to the initiation when it comes, they are supposed to take the lead beforehand in electioneering, and pledging sub-Freshmen to the society. Gamma Nu elects a . . . 'campaign committee.' **1887** *Lippincott's Mag.* Nov. 741 The most able and influential men are chosen for societies . . . and the 'campaign' as the annual struggle for recruits is called, often becomes very exciting. . . . As a rule . . . election is the result of work at 'campaign' time.

3. The period during which a furnace is in continuous operation.

1871 *Amer. Inst. Mining Eng. Trans.* I. 98 By their corrosive action on the lining . . . they shorten a campaign or run to a few days. **1874** RAYMOND *6th Rep. Mines* 393 A campaign lasts six months; but the men are changed frequently, as . . . the work is . . . very unhealthy.

b. Also with reference to a cannery.

1894 *Irrigation Age* April 172/2 The Chino, California, factory will also start out in its '94 campaign with a capacity of 1,000 tons of beets per day, being on an even footing with the Watsonville factory.

4. In sense **1.** in numerous combs., as (1) **campaign badge,** (2) **biographer,** (3) **biography,** (4) **book,** (5) **button,** (6) **document,** (7) **fund,** (8) **paper,** (9) **song,** (10) **songster,** (11) **textbook,** (12) **year.**

(**1**) **1868** *Harper's Wkly.* 15 Aug. 528/4 Campaign Badges in great variety, at the lowest prices. — (**2**) **1884** *Critic* 2 Aug. 49/1 Honest excuse for praise is at least desirable in such cases, as the campaign biographer well knows. — (**3**) **1879** H. JAMES *Hawthorne* 136 The 'campaign biography' . . . consists of an attempt, more or less successful, to persuade the many-headed monster of universal suffrage that the gentleman on whose behalf it is addressed is a paragon of wisdom and virtue. **1944** *Newsweek* 11 Sep. 104/3 This is not a typical buttery campaign biography of a Presidential candidate. — (**4**) **1904** *Omaha Bee* 16 Aug. 4 The republican campaign book stands upon . . . a record of promises made good.

(**5**) **1900** *Cong. Rec.* 8 March 2670/2 A social condition that dictates to a man what kind of button he shall wear . . . makes a man want to stick campaign buttons all over him. **1948** *Aurora* (Ill.) *Beacon-News* 7 Nov. 5/6 Truman campaign buttons which threatened to glut the market in pre-election days hit a sudden boom today. — (**6**) **1871** *Cong. Rec.* 2 June 3543/1 It is said that we get all our campaign documents from the public printer. **1904** *N.Y. Ev. Post* 1 Nov. 3 It does not appear that any effort will be made to prevent the distribution of the pamphlet as a campaign document. — (**7**) **1905** *McClure's Mag.* 49 They . . . gave the seat for which he had sacrificed so much to . . . the largest contributor, in the new public service crowd, to the Democratic campaign fund. **1948** *Omaha World-Herald* 5 July 3/2 He also helped Mr. Roosevelt collect campaign funds in 1936. — (**8**) **1844** *Talladega* (Ala.) *Dem. Watchtower* 12 June 2/6 We issue our Campaign Paper to meet the wants of numerous Associations. **1855** *S. Lit. Messenger* XXI. 2 A new campaign-paper was established at Jackson, called the True Issue. — (**9**) **1868** *Nation* 10 Sep. 207/2 We have now before us some thirty or forty of the campaign songs of this Presidential contest. **1948** *This Week Mag.* 13 June 5/2 Campaign songs have declined in importance.

(**10**) **1856** (*title*), Republican Campaign Songster. **1880** *Nation* 21 Oct. 285/2 We must, in conclusion, say a word in favor of the superior political excellence and spontaneity, slight as they are, of the casual newspaper bard over those of the 'Campaign Songster.' — (**11**) **1909** PARKER *G. Cleveland* 121, I had for more than seven weeks, in 1888, at the office in the White House, prepared the Democratic Campaign Text-Book. **1914** MCLAUGHLIN & HART *Cyclo. Amer. Govt.* I. 363/1 The Spanish American War created an entirely unexpected situation which the congressional committee met in its campaign text book. — (**12**) **1929** *Randolph Enterprise* (Elkins, W. Va.) 21 Nov. 4/2 If we have no turkey to eat we will kill the old rooster as this is not a campaign year anyhow.

Also *campaign club, committee, contribution, editorial, expense, literature, manager, medal, meeting, orator, season, sheet, speech*, etc.

As the last term in **barrel, coon, lumber, presidential, primary, schoolhouse, squaw, stump campaign.**

* **campaign,** *v.*

1. *intr.* To conduct a political campaign. Also **campaigning,** *n.*

1876 *Cattaraugus* (N.Y.) *Union* 31 Aug. 1/8 Lincoln and Douglas were campaigning it for Congress. **1923** R. HERRICK *Lilla* 181 Gordon made various short tours in the state giving addresses. . . . All this was indirect campaigning. **1948** *Sat. Ev. Post* 3 July 16/2 He campaigned with force but dignity, as if running for a lodge office.

2. *tr.* To exploit. *Rare.*

1888 *Boston W. Globe* 28 March (F.), The new owner sold the steed for 800 dollars to James Gray, . . . who after campaigning him on the track for a couple of years, . . . sold him to Bonner.

* **campaigner,** *n.* One who takes active part in a political campaign.

1856 *N.Y. Herald* 16 Jan. 1/6 That old campaigner, Mr. Bennett, fought political battles in General Jackson's early start, 30 years ago. **1876** *Pacific Appeal* (S.F.) 9 Sep. 1/4 Mr. Tilden is a shrewd campaigner. **1948** *Time* 21 June 23/2 Appearing on a CBS television program, he proved himself the best campaigner yet on the newest communications medium to reach into the U.S. home.

Campbellism ˈkæmḷ ɪzəm, *n.* The doctrines or religious principles of the Campbellites. Now *hist.*

1843 J. L. SCOTT *Jrnl. Western Tour* (1843) 94, I listened to a preacher . . . of Campbellism. **1872** MORRELL *Flowers & Fruits* 272 Campbellism and the anti-mission element gave us the principal troubles up to this time. **1947** *S. Folklore Quart.* Sep. 176 The Baptist . . . publicist [was] . . . at one time 'suspected of a tendency to Campbellism.'

Campbellite ˈkæmḷˌaɪt, *n.*

1. A popular designation or nickname for a member of the denomination known as Disciples of Christ, so called from Alexander Campbell (1788–1866), one of the founders of the sect.

1830 *Mass. Spy* 22 Dec. (Th.), Elder Rigdon . . . is described as having been a Campbelite leader of some notoriety. **1834** PECK *Gaz. Illinois* 91 The Campbellites or 'Reformers' . . . have several traveling, and a number of stationary preachers. **1908** PHILLIPS *Old Wives* 7 We're Christians . . . Disciples of Christ. Some . . . call us Campbellites. **1948** *Crusader* May 15/1 No longer called 'Campbellites'—they remained in the Baptist fellowship until 1830.

attrib. **1844** FEATHERSTONHAUGH *Excursion* 55, I was told afterwards that the party was given to a lady on her marriage to a preacher of the *Campbellite* persuasion. **1847** PALMER *Rocky Mts.* 23 A Campbellite preacher, named Foster, was reading a hymn, preparatory to religious worship.

2. =**crappie.** *Colloq.*

1872 *Harper's Mag.* July 315/2 'What do you call those fish?' 'Campbellites,' promptly responded the boy. 'Why do you call them Campbellites?' 'Because they spoil so quick after I get them out of the water.' **1885** *Stand. Nat. Hist.* III. 235 The names new-light and Campbellite are due to the fact that it became abundant and the subject of observation when the religious denomination bearing those names originated. **1906** *D. N.* III. 129 Campbellite, n. A fish resembling the perch.

Campeachy hat. A broad-brimmed hat of a type obtained from Campeche, Mexico. *Obs.* — **1858** *Texas Almanac* (*advt.*), We are constantly receiving a general assortment of . . . campeachy hats. **1888** CABLE *Bonaventure* 11 Broad-brimmed Campeachy hat of Sosthène.

* **camper,** *n.*

1. One who sets up a temporary abode near a camp meeting so as to attend the services. *Obs.*

1805 L. DOW *Travels* Wks. 1806 II. 61 We held Quarterly-meeting on Clarke's creek; some supposed I would get no campers. **1883** *Ad-*

vance 16 Aug., At the Sabbath services none but the regular campers were in attendance—the gates being closed to outsiders.

2. camper out, one who "camps out."

1856 KANE *Arctic Explor.* II. ix. 92 As ingeniously . . . crowded together as the campers-out in a buffalo-bag. **1891** *Fur, Fin, & Feather* March 207 Not one sportsman in a hundred, old camper out though he may be. **1901** THOMPSON *In Maine Woods* 62 For the camper-out Moosehead is the most important place on the map of Maine.

***camphor,** *n.*

1. Spirits of camphor. Also **camphor bottle.**

1834 C. A. DAVIS *Lett. J. Downing* 261 When it gits hold, kamfire and lodnum stand no chance with it! **1852** STOWE *Uncle Tom* xxix, Marie sobbed, . . . and called Mammy . . . to bring her the camphor-bottle, and to bathe her head. **1857** C. VAUX *Villas* 85 One almost expects to see the lady of the house walk in with a bottle of camphor in her hand, to prevent infection.

2. In special combs.: (1) **camphor chest,** a clothes-chest containing camphor as a protection against moths; (2) **ice,** (see quots.); (3) **trunk,** =**camphor chest;** (4) **weed,** (see quot.); (5) ***wood,** (see quot. 1879), also attrib.

(1) **1861** MRS. STOWE *Pearl Orr's Isl.* I. viii. 59 That ar shawl your mother keeps in her camfire chist. **1889** MRS. ROSE T. COOKE *Steadfast* v. 59 Mrs. Dennis was packing away blankets in the camphor chest upstairs. — (2) **1881** A. A. HAYES *New Colorado* 197 In alkali regions, glycerine, or what is called 'camphor ice,' should be used on face and hands. **1907** *Sears Cat.* (ed. 117) 796/1 Camphor Ice. A salve of remarkable healing qualities. — (3) **1869** STOWE *Oldtown Folks* 34 Mrs. Major had a real *Ingy* shawl up in her 'camphire' trunk. **1895** *Cent. Mag.* July 323/2 Cedar-chest and camphor-trunk and flowered bandbox have been called upon to disgorge their treasures. — (4) **1915** ARMSTRONG *Western Wild Flowers* 454 *T. [richostema] lanceolatum* is called Camphor Weed, because of its strong odor.

(5) **1859** STOWE *Minister's Wooing* xii., Mrs. Katy, Mary, and . . . the dressmaker, might have been observed sitting in solemn senate around the camphor-wood trunk. **1879** DALL in Morris *Pub. Service Alaska* 110 The wood [near Sitka] . . . consists particularly of a noble thuja (*T. excelsa, C. nutkænsis*). . . . From its agreeable perfume, it is known to the Russians as *dushnik*, or scented wood. This is the wood formerly exported to China, and returned to us as 'camphor-wood,' &c., famous for excluding moths.

camping out. The action or an occasion of living in the open in a camp or tent. Also attrib.

1834 *Western Mo.* II. 664 All the taverns and houses of entertainment are crowded with strangers of another class— . . . families who are not accustomed to 'camping out.' **1873** BAILEY *Life in Danbury* 218 It is here the picnic and camping-out parties gather. **1948** *Dly. Oklahoman* (Okla. City) 16 May E. 3/4 The state has . . . innumerable camping-out places in the piney woods of the east or in the rugged regions of the west.

camp meeting.

1. An assemblage, usu. of Methodists, for holding in the woods or other retired spot a series of religious meetings. See also **general, Negro camp meeting.**

Meetings of this kind, often lasting for several weeks, arose in Kentucky in 1799, and were popular for nearly a century.

1803 L. DOW *Travels* Wks. 1806 II. 21 We went on to the camp-meeting which I had appointed last August. **1883** *Harper's Mag.* Aug. 483/2 A great camp-meeting had been going on for more than a week among the negroes. **1929** E. W. HOWE *Plain People* 6 In addition to his circuit riding, every summer father held camp meetings, where collected people from a large territory.

2. Used in combs., as **camp meeting district, ground, hymn, season, singing.**

1910 J. HART *Vigilante Girl* 121 Those chronic backsliders in the camp-meeting districts. — **1804** *Phila. Gazette* 28 Sep. 3/2, 38 Carts were counted on the camp-meeting ground on Sunday last. — **1863** B. TAYLOR *H. Thurston* 286 Melinda at once strode away, . . . muttering fragments of camp-meeting hymns. **1900** *Musical Courier* 30 May 20/2 A camp meeting hallelujay hymn . . . reeks of the forests of equatorial Africa. — **1882** *N.Y. Tribune* 7 Aug. 4/3 The camp-meeting season has set in with vigor so far as the crowds in attendance are concerned. — **1947** *Democrat* 17 July 8/2 Everyone shall enjoy these services, filled with camp meeting singing, and soul stirring messages.

Also *camp meeting day, gathering, inclosure, revival, song, standard,* etc.

campoody ˌkæmˈpodɪ, *n. S.W.* [Paiute, f. Sp. *campo,* camp.] An Indian hut or village.

1850 JACKSON *Forty-niner* (1920) 10 There is an Indian campoody up on the ridge above Brush Creek, where about two hundred Digger Indians are camped. **1887** *Rep. Indian Affairs* II, Many live in comfortable board or log houses, and others in 'campoodies' (huts) made of puncheons, pieces of boards, &c. **1903** AUSTIN *Land of Little Rain* 63, I sniffed the unmistakable odor of burning sage. It is a smell that . . . indicates usually the nearness of a campoodie.

b. A white man's hut or cabin.

1856 *Butte Record* (Oroville, Calif.) 6 Sep. 2/2 We took a little walk . . . and brought up with a round turn and an invitation at John Davis' Campoda.

campo santo. *S.W.* [Sp. in same sense.] A burial ground or cemetery.

1836 PARKER *Trip to the West* 272 (Bentley), Then all the graves in the campo santo are brave with tapers. **1877** *Field & Forest* July 10 The Pueblos have their regular 'campos sanctos,' or else bury in the floors of their churches. **1943** HEWITT *Mission Monuments N.M.* 217 A stone terrace was reconstructed, as were the walls of the *campo santo*

campus ˈkæmpəs, *n.* [L., field, theater of action, arena.]

1. The principal grounds of a university, college, or other school, the open space between or around the buildings. See also **back, college, university campus.**

First used at Princeton and probably introduced by President Witherspoon. See A. Matthews in *Pub. Col. Soc. Mass.* III. 431–37.

1774 in J. F. HAGEMAN *Hist. Princeton* (1879) I. 102 Having made a fire in the Campus, we there burnt near a dozen pounds [of tea]. **1835** *Vade Mecum* (Phila.) 10 Jan. 3/3 'Between the hours of recitation,' says a pedagogue's circular, 'the pupils may recreate themselves on the *campus!*' **1898** *Mo. So. Dakotan* I. 6 He donated ten acres of valuable land for the university's site and campus. **1946** *Sat. Ev. Post* 3 Aug. 16/3 The place where he stopped was a corner from which the whole campus spread out before and below him.

b. A field for athletic sports. *Obs.*

Cf. *OED* †*Campo* in this sense.

1887 *Lippincott's Mag.* Sep. 453 The Campus, or play-ground, is several miles off. **1897** A. MATTHEWS in *Pub. Col. Soc. Mass.* III. 433 At twenty of these [colleges] . . . Campus is applied to an athletic field alone. **1902** CLAPIN 94 *Campus*, a student's word meaning the college grounds; also, the athletic field.

2. A place of action, a battleground. *Obs.*

1835 LONGSTREET *Ga. Scenes* 73 She brought her hands to the campus this time in fine style. **1840** *Cong. Globe* App. 17 Jan. 144/1 We are told that the Abolition battle must be fought at the North; that we must deal kindly here, to afford a campus for their chivalry at home.

***can,** *n.*

1. A glass jar in which fruits, vegetables, etc., are put up in the home.

1884 MRS. OWENS *Cook Book* 319 Fill your cans, as many as will stand in your wash boiler. . . . Pack the jars full.

2. can opener, a kitchen utensil for opening cans of fruit, meat, etc.

1874 KNIGHT 452 Can-opener. . . . The illustration shows several forms. **1948** *Democrat* 23 Sep. 3/3 It is easy to cut with a can-opener.

3. *To rush the can,* to drink freely at a bar or in a saloon. Also transf. *Slang.*

1930 *Chi. Ev. Post* 19 May 1/5 As many as 1,500 customers a day . . . come to 'rush the can.' **1948** *Milwaukee Jrnl.* 18 July (Ed. Sect.) 2/3 You rushed the growler, the can or the pitcher.

As the last term in **ash, fruit, garbage, kerosene, oyster, tomato can.**

can kæn, *v.*

1. *tr.* To preserve (meats, fruits, etc.) in properly sealed cans or jars. Also absol.

1861 *Ill. Agric. Soc. Trans.* IV. 511 Good fruit . . . is always marketable in large cities . . . and much will be dried, or canned, for export. **1883** *U.S. Museum Bul. 27* 110 The process of canning Crabs is somewhat similar to that for lobsters, as practiced on the New England coast. **1902** LORIMER *Lett. Merchant* 24 The boys drive a bunch of steers toward him, or cows maybe, if we're canning. **1944** *Democrat* 10 Feb 2/5 Housewives who wish to can early fruit now may obtain five extra pounds of sugar.

2. To expel (a student) from school, to discharge (an employee). *Slang.*

1905 *D.N.* III. 73 Jim was up before the faculty and got canned for two weeks. **1913** *Industrial Worker* (Spokane) 21 Aug. 1/2 For writing that editorial, the editor was 'canned.' **1944** *Chi. D. News* 22 Nov. 6/3 The new management . . . did not 'can' the notable foreign editor.

3. To stop, leave off (something). *Slang.*

1911 LEWIS *Apaches N.Y.* 20 'Can that black-jack guff,' he retorted. **1926** *Ladies' Home Jrnl.* July 26 Can the bud stuff, Blank verse, old dear.

* **Canada,** *n.*

1. The Canada goose.

1871 Lewis *Poultry Book* 90 The America Wild Goose is identical with the Canada. **1894** *Outing* XXIV. 74/2 We see four old Canadas winging their way diagonally toward us. **1922** Bigelow *Scatter-gun Sk.* 109 The old Canada came down in a heap.

2. In combs., chiefly in the names of animals: (1) **Canada distemper,** (see quot.), *obs.;* (2) **flycatcher,** = **Canada warbler;** (3) **grouse,** the spruce partridge; (4) **honker,** the Canada goose; (5) **jay,** the whisky jack, *Perisoreus canadensis,* cf. **venison bird, camp robber;** (6) **line,** the boundary between the U.S. and Canada; (7) **lynx,** the loup-cervier, *Lynx canadensis;* (8) **patriot,** (see quot. 1846), *obs.;* (9) **porcupine,** a porcupine, *Erethizon dorsatus,* found in northeastern America; (10) **rat,** a pocket gopher; (11) **robin,** = **cedar waxwing;** (12) **soldier,** (see quot.); (13) **sparrow,** the tree sparrow, *Spizella arborea,* of Canada and the northern U.S.; (14) **warbler,** a flycatching warbler, *Wilsonia canadensis,* of Canada and the northern U.S.

(1) 1802 J. Drayton *S. Carolina* 63 A malignant fever called the Yellow Water, Canada distemper, &c. . . . has carried off numbers of the horses in the United States. — **(2) 1811** Wilson *Ornithology* III. 100 [The] Canada Flycatcher, *Muscicapa Canadensis,* . . . is a solitary, and in the lower parts of Pennsylvania, rather a rare species. **1858** Baird *Birds Pacific R.R.* 294 Canada Flycatcher . . . [inhabits] eastern United States to the Mississippi. — **(3) 1839** Audubon *Ornith. Biog.* V. 563 Spotted or Canada grouse, *Tetrao Canadensis,* . . . is also plentiful on the Rocky Mountains and the plains of the Columbia. **1874** Coues *Birds N.W.* 395 The Canada Grouse is chiefly a boreal bird, reaching but a little way over our border. — **(4) 1907** W. Lillibridge *Trail* 126 The swelling, diminishing note . . . of the grey Canada honker. **1946** *Reader's Digest* Jan. 40/1 An eagle's egg is smaller than the Canada Honker's and only half the size of a whistling swan's.

(5) 1811 Wilson *Ornithology* III. 33 The Canada Jay, *Corvus Canadensis* . . . inhabits the country extending from Hudson's bay . . . to the river St. Lawrence. **1948** *Reader's Digest* March 145/1 Canada jays, or camp robbers, as the Alaskans call them, carried on their never-ending three-ring circus. — **(6) 1776** *Vt. Hist. Soc. Coll.* I. 16 That part of America being situated south of Canada line . . . commonly called . . . the New Hampshire Grants. — **(7) 1840** Emmons *Mass. Quadrupeds* 33 The Northern or Canada Lynx presents a very striking resemblance to the cat. **1942** Rich *We Took to Woods* (1948) 40 The answer is illusion:—jam into bear's blood, bobcat into Canada lynx, vaccination scar into dagger wound. — **(8)** *c***1845** Paulding *Madmen All* 192 Green-horns, Canada Patriots, Loafers. **1846** Mansfield *Winfield Scott* 287 The flame of insurrection was kindled in Canada. . . . The frontier inhabitants of the United States . . . enrolled themselves as Canada patriots or sympathizers . . . capable of bearing arms, . . . professed friends and abettors of the Canadian movement. — **(9) 1826** J. Godman *Nat. Hist.* II. 150 The Canada Porcupine. *Hystrix Dorsata.* . . . In some parts of the Western states, . . . they are found in great abundance, and are highly prized by the aboriginals, both for the sake of their flesh and their quills.

(10) 1821 in *Amer. Jrnl. of Science* IV. (1822) 184 In these drawings, the sacs are delineated as distended like two blown bladders, giving the Canada Rat, as he is called, a very grotesque appearance. — **(11) 1844** *Nat. Hist. N.Y., Zoology* II. 44 This well known bird [*Bombycilla Carolinensis*] has various popular names. . . . In Massachusetts, it is called Canada Robin. — **(12) 1925** *Smithsonian Inst. Ann. Rep.* 271 Our arrival happened to coincide with that of the well-known annual pest of mayflies or "Canada soldiers," which come suddenly, remain a week or less, and as suddenly depart. — **(13) 1869** Burroughs in *Galaxy* VIII. 173 The fox-sparrow . . . comes to us in the fall, from the north, where it breeds likewise the Tree or Canada-sparrow. **1884** Burroughs in *Cent. Mag.* Dec. 220 In winter, especially, they sweep by me and around me in flocks,—the Canada sparrow, . . . the shore-lark, . . . the red-poll, the cedar-bird. — **(14) 1868** *Amer. Naturalist* II. 176 The Canada Warbler (*Myiodioctes Canadensis*) . . . arrives about the middle of May. **1945** *Mass. Audubon Soc. Bul.* Feb. 18 The Bay-breasted and orange Blackburnian were glimpsed last spring on their way north along with the more abundant Magnolia and Canada Warblers.

b. In the names of plants: (1) **Canada balsam,** the transparent aromatic resin exuded from the balsam fir, also the tree itself; (2) **blueberry,** a species of *Vaccinium* found in northeastern North America; (3) **bluegrass,** (see quot. 1901); (4) **corn,** an early-maturing variety of yellow corn, *obs.;* (5) **lily,** the meadow lily of the eastern states; (6) **nettle,** = **wood nettle;** (7) **plum,** a wild plum, *Prunus nigra;* (8) **rice,** = **wild rice;** (9) **snake-root,** the wild ginger, *Asarum canadense;* (10) **thistle,** the cursed thistle, *Cirsium arvense,* introduced from France into Canada and thence into the U.S.; (11) **violet,** (see quot. 1891).

(1) 1818 *Mass. H. S. Coll.* 2 Ser. VIII. 170 We have . . . spruce, hemlock, and silver fir, from the last of which the Canada balsam is obtained. **1916** Seton *Woodcraft Man.* 270 Balsam Tree or Canada Balsam (*Abies balsamea*) Evergreen; famous for the blisters on its trunk, yielding Canada balsam which makes a woodman's plaster for cuts or a waterproof cement; and for the exquisite odor of its boughs, which also supply the woodman's ideal bed. Its *flat* leafage is distinctive. — **(2) 1858** Thoreau *Maine Woods* 95 Many plants . . . grew abundantly between the rails,—as Labrador tea, Kalmia glauca, Canada blueberry. *a***1862** Thoreau *Maine Woods* 311 At camps and carries [I saw]: raspberry, *Vaccinium Canadense* (Canada blueberry). — **(3) 1901** Mohr *Plant Life Ala.* 826 *Poa compressa,* Canada Blue Grass. Prairie region and north, [cultivated] for pasture. **1937** *Range Plant Handbook* G99 In the southern United States, particularly the Southwest, Canada bluegrass occurs in the higher mountains, and on irrigated lawns and pastures where abundant moisture is supplied artificially. — **(4) 1837** Colman *Mass. Agric. Rep.* (1838) 82 This is what we call Canada corn; a kind I never planted here before. **1848** C. L. Fleischmann *Nordamerikanische Landwirth* 113 Canada Corn, oder Eight Rowed Yellow Small Corn. . . . Eine veredelte Abart davon, zwölfzeilig, führt den Namen Browne Corne. **1917** Will & Hyde *Corn Among Indians* 72 By Canada corn he probably means flint corn, as that name was usually applied to the most popular varieties of that type in the eastern states.

(5) 1909 *Cent. Supp.* 729/1. **1943** Peattie *Great Smokies* 196 The splendid Canada lily was abundant all over this meadow. — **(6) 1817–18** Eaton *Botany* (1822) 500. **1859** Bartlett 5 *Albany Hemp,* . . . Canada nettle, so called from the use made of its fibrous bark. — **(7) 1848** *Knickerb.* XXXI. 31 We add the Hawthorn, Poplar, . . . Larch and Canada-Plum. **1897** Sudworth *Arborescent Flora* 236 Canada Plum [is the common name in] Mass., N.Y., Mich., Ont. — **(8) 1848** Bartlett 62 Canada Rice. (*Zizania aquatica.*) A plant which grows in deep water along the edges of ponds and sluggish streams, in the Northern States and Canada. **1890** *Cent. s.v. Rice,* Indian rice . . . [is] also called Canada or wild rice, and Indian oats or water-oats. — **(9) 1832** Williamson *Maine* I. 122 Canada Snakeroot, . . . the aromatic flavour of its root has rendered it a fit and wholesome substitute for ginger. **1847** Darlington *Weeds & Plants* 269 The Canada Snake-root . . . is common in rich woodlands.

(10) 1799 *Mass. Spy* 31 July (Th.), A torvous, stubborn, and vexatious weed, known by the name of the Canada Thistle. **1897** *Chi. Tribune* 6 July 12/1 You are hereby notified . . . to cause all Canada thistles to be cut down. **1948** *Lisle* (Ill.) *Eagle* 21 Oct. 4/3 Noxious weeds are defined by law as Canada thistle, perennial sow thistle, European bindweed, leafy spurge, Russian knapweed and hoary cress. — **(11) 1821** *Jrnl. Science* III. 274 Floral . . . calendar for Plainfield, Mass. . . . May 3. Lombardy poplar and Canada violet in blossom. **1891** *Cent.* 6761/3 Canada violet, *Viola Canadensis,* a species common northward and in the mountains of eastern North America, having an upright stem a foot or two high, and white petals purplish beneath.

Also *Canada bean, border, cap, crane, fly, hat, hypericum, Indian, oak, owl, pony, stove, trader,* etc.

cañada kænˈjædə, *n.* Also **canada.** *S.W.* [Sp. in same sense.] A small canyon, a glen, narrow valley.

1836 C. J. Latrobe *Rambler in Mexico* 64 We considered the scenery of the Cañada superior to any we had ever seen. **1923** Saunders *So. Sierras Calif.* 114 Into this *cañada* we turned, following a trail which led across the outer range of the Sierra Madre. **1933** *Amer. Sp.* Oct. 8/2 *Cañada* describes the wide shallow mouth of a canyon, and *cañoncito* is a little canyon.

* **Canadian,** *a.*

1. *absol.* A Canadian horse. *Obs.* Cf. **2. d.**

1831 *Boston Transcript* 9 Aug. 2/1 The driver descending from his lofty eminence on the cotton bales, . . . the whole constituting a load for six stout Canadians, commenced torturing the poor beasts with the lash. **1876** *Vt. Bd. Agric. Rep.* III. 132 The result of the cross of the Morgan upon this Canadian has been a great improvement to the Canadian.

2. In combs.: (1) **Canadian band,** (see quot.), *obs.;* (2) **barge,** (see quot.), *obs.;* (3) **French,** (*a*) French Canadians, (*b*) the variety of French spoken by Canadians; (4) **Frenchman,** a Canadian of French descent; (5) **railway,** (see quot.), *obs.;* (6) **shoe,** a kind of Indian shoe resembling a moccasin, *obs.;* (7) **voyageur,** a Canadian serving as a voyageur; (8) **zone,** one of the six life-zones or horizontal bands into which American flora and fauna are grouped according to a system devised by C. H. Merriam, also **Canadian life zone.**

(1) **1846** TAYLOR *Narrative* 67 On an evening, when a number of them [tree toads] are together, the harmony they produce is quite melodious, and has entitled them to the distinction of the Canadian band. — (2) **1827** *Spirit of Seventy-Six* (Frankfort, Ky.) 24 May 2/3, I remember the day when the arrival of a Canadian barge (as the St. Louis boats were called at the head of the Ohio) was an important event in the transactions of a year. — (3) (*a*) **1845** FRÉMONT *Exped.* 105 My party consisted principally of Creole and Canadian French. **1880** HEARN *Creole Sks.* (1924) 145 The Canadian French have, nevertheless, been among the most thrifty, energetic, and enterprising pioneers in the world. (*b*) **1846** M'KENNEY *Memoirs* I. 62 These dexterous Canadians . . . enlivening the scene . . . with their boat songs, and a jabbering of their Canadian French. — (4) **1817** E. P. FORDHAM *Personal Narrative* 144 The owner is a Canadian Frenchman. **1915** YOUNG *Hard Knocks* 124 On the fourth day he was six hours behind him at a ranch kept by a Canadian Frenchman, a friend of Boswell's.

(5) **1836** T. POWER *Impressions of Amer.* I. 229, I encountered my first sample of a corduroy-road, or, as it is sometimes facetiously termed, a Canadian railway. — (6) **1806** LEWIS in *L. & Clark Exped.* (1905) V. 114 One of our party had previously made him a present of a pair of Canadian shoes or shoe-packs. **1868** *Putnam's Mag.* II. 363 The unwieldy raw-hide network, known as the 'Canadian shoe,' is seldom used, the Norwegian pattern having proved more acceptable and less cumbersome. — (7) **1846** SAGE *Scenes Rocky Mts.* iii, We were further increased by the accession of two Canadian *voyageurs* — French of course. — (8) [**1859** COOPER *Distribution Forests & Trees No. Amer.* 274 Passing into the Canadian region we find seventeen species of trees suddenly added as characteristic, and towards its southern border many of those of the Apalachian Province begin to appear.] **1894** *Nat. Geog. Mag.* 29 Dec. 236 The distinctive temperatures of the three Boreal Zones (Arctic, Hudsonian and Canadian) are not positively known. **1903** *Mich. Ornith. Club Bul.* June 47 This section of country is a part of the Canadian Life Zone of Lower Michigan. **1946** R. PEATTIE *Pac. Coast Ranges* 71 On we go, through the so-called Canadian zone, with its mountain hemlock and western white pine, up to the Hudsonian zone, where the trees, all of them conifers now, become smaller and smaller.

b. In the names of plants: (1) **Canadian balsam,** =**Canada balsam;** (2) **coffee,** (see quot.), *obs.;* (3) **goldenrod,** (see quot.); (4) **holly,** (see quot.); (5) **ivy,** (see quot.); (6) **pine,** (see quot. 1916); (7) **puccoon,** (see quot.); (8) **thistle,** =**Canada thistle;** (9) **yew,** the ground hemlock, also **Canadian yew-tree.**

(1) **1806** LEWIS in *L. & Clark Exped.* (1905) IV. 46 This [fir] tree affords considerable quantities of a fine clear arromatic balsam in appearance and taste like the Canadian balsam. **1853** STRICKLAND *Twenty-Seven Yrs.* I. 162 A fair mixture of this species of trees is best, with here and there a large pine, and a few Canadian balsams scattered among the hard-wood. — (2) **1851** JOHNSTON *Notes* I. 268 *Canadian Coffee* . . . is a species of pea growing in a small inflated pod. It has the flavour of a pea, with a bitterish after-taste, and when roasted, has much of the odour and taste of coffee. — (3) **1836** LINCOLN *Botany* App. 140 *Solidago canadensis*, (Canadian goldenrod). — (4) **1785** MARSHALL *Amer. Grove* 64 *Ilex canadensis*. Canadian, or Hedge-hog Holly.

(5) **1832** TRAILL *Backwoods* 56 His eye will be attracted by fantastic bowers, which are formed by the scarlet creeper (or Canadian ivy). — (6) **1803** LAMBERT *Descr. Genus Pinus* 50 Canadian Pine, *P. Canadensis*, bears a great resemblance to the Common Yew. **1916** SETON *Woodcraft Man.* 267 Red Pine, Canadian Pine, or Norway Pine (*Pinus resinosa*) Evergreen; somewhat less than the White Pine . . . Range . . . Minnesota and Manitoba to Nova Scotia and Pennsylvania. — (7) **1802** J. DRAYTON *View of S.-C.* 72 Canadian puccoon (*Sanguinaria Canadensis.*) . . . The root dies a bright red, with which the Indians used to paint themselves. — (8) **1836** R. WESTON *Visit* 102 What are called Canadian thistles, . . . emigrate to the Southern States in great numbers. **1853** STRICKLAND *Twenty-Seven Yrs.* I. 32 In consequence of their inexperience, half the clearing was quite overrun with raspberries and Canadian thistles. (The latter weed is far more troublesome to eradicate than any other I know. It is the same as the common corn-thistle, or *Serratula arvensis*, so well known to English agriculturists.) — (9) **1785** MARSHALL *Amer. Grove* 151 *Taxus canadensis*. Canadian Yew-Tree . . . is a beautiful evergreen shrub, capable of being formed into any shape. **1860** *Ill. Agric. Soc. Trans.* IV. 462 An Evergreen Vine on the Fox River. . . . Mr. Edwards believes it the Canadian Yew.

c. In the names of animals: (1) **Canadian cuckoo,** (see quot.), *obs.;* (2) **flycatcher, flycatching warbler,** =**Canada flycatcher;** (3) **lynx,** =**Canada lynx;** (4) **rat,** =**Canada rat,** *obs.;* (5) **woodpecker,** (see quot. 1891).

(1) **1846** TAYLOR *Narrative* 63 A bird, called Whip-poor-will, is called the Canadian cuckoo. It receives its name from the very distinct manner in which it pronounces the words. — (2) **1874** COUES *Birds N.W.* 80 *Myiodioctes Canadensis*. . . . Canadian Fly-catching Warbler. . . . *Hab.* . . . West to the Lower Missouri. **1892** TORREY *Foot-Path Way* 16 A hurried search showed black polls . . . [and] one Canadian flycatcher (singing lustily). — (3) **1841** GURNEY *Journey* 230 'The Canadian lynx,' is a handsome creature. — (4) **1821** in *Amer. Jrnl. of Science* IV. (1822) 185 Sometime ago, a small quadruped was brought to me from the country beyond Lake Superior, which I immediately knew to be the *Canadian Rat*, with large pouches on the sides of his neck.

(5) **1839** AUDUBON *Ornith. Biog.* V. 188 Canadian Woodpecker. *Picus Canadensis* . . . is more plentiful . . . in the State of New York. **1891** *Cent.* 6968/1 Canadian woodpecker, the large northern form of the hairy woodpecker (which see), formerly *Picus canadensis* (Gmelin, 1788), and before that *Picus leucomelas* (Boddaert, 1783).

d. Denoting horses of a breed raised in Canada. *Obs.*

1816 SCENE PAINTER *Emigrant's Guide* 23 Canadian horses (a small but hardy race). **1834** BRACKENRIDGE *Recoll.* 126 A youth . . . on a stout Canadian poney, issuing from the busy town. **1841** *S. Lit. Messenger* VII. 219/1 The vivacity of a little rough-coated, bob-tailed chunk of a Canadian poney. **1882** *Wheelman* I. 14/1 Like a racking Canadian horse, with his head down and forward, he rocked from side to side.

Also *Canadian blackbird, blueberry, cherry tree, dogwood, elder, goods, goose, hemlock, hemp, holly, moonseed, nettle, pine, poplar, sparrow*, etc.

canaigre kəˈnegɚ, *n. S.W.* [Amer. Sp. in same sense. See Santamaría *s.v. canagria.*] A species of dock, *Rumex hymenosepalus*, having roots rich in tannin; the tannin obtained from these. Also attrib.

1878 *Rep. Agric.* (1879) 119 In many respects cañaigre root resembled rhubarb. **1894** H. TRIMBLE *Tannins* II. 106 The use of canaigre in tanning has passed the experimental stage. *Ib.* 107 The Canaigre plant is from one to three feet in height. **1938** GOODDING *Native & Exotic Plants* 56 Outside of possible commercial use [for its high tannin content] the Canaigre is valueless.

* **canal,** *n.*

1. *S.W.* A large irrigation ditch.

1808 Z. PIKE *Sources of Miss.* 223 Both above and below Albuquerque, the citizens were beginning to open the canals, to let in the water of the river. **1890** *Stock Grower* 31 May 6/3 In our great southwest are many relics of ancient basins and canals, showing that the pre-historic people had a flourishing agriculture in the regions. **1930** in *Today's Literature* (1935) 511 Two storage reservoirs, one behind the big dam and one fed by a big canal.

2. A long canal-like arm of a sea or sound. Often in proper names.

1900 SPURR *Yukon Diggings* 25 The lights of Juneau soon dropped out of sight, as we steamed up Lynn Canal under the shadow of the giant mountains. **1946** R. PEATTIE *Pac. Coast Ranges* 206 From between the bases of these peaks a row of streams races down to Hood Canal, a long arm of Puget Sound. **1948** *C.A. Jrnl.* June 84 Early explorers called many of these inlets 'canals' because of their trench-like forms.

3. In combs.: (1) **Canal boys,** name of a gang of ruffians formerly active in New York City, *obs.;* (2) **canal commissioner,** a state official concerned with the construction or regulation of a canal or canal system; (3) **department,** a department in a state government having supervision of canals; (4) **driver,** one who drives canal-boat horses; (5) **extra,** (see quot.), *rare;* (6) **grant,** a granting of land for canal purposes; (7) **land,** land ceded to a state or set aside by it for canal purposes; (8) **map,** a map showing canals; (9) **packet, packet boat,** a packet boat used on a canal; (10) **policy,** a policy of state government relative to canals; (11) **scrip,** scrip issued for canal construction; (12) **shovel,** a shovel of a type especially suitable for use in canal work, *obs.;* (13) **thief,** one of a group of corrupt politicians and contractors who just after the Civil War conspired to defraud New York in connection with repairs to the canal system of the state; (14) **zone,** (see quot.).

(1) **1872** BRACE *Dangerous Classes N.Y.* 89 'Canawl-boys' . . . seem to drift into the city every winter, and live a vagabond life. — (2) **1817** *N.Y. Herald* 9 April 2/1 The next subject of discussion, was a power given the canal commissioners, to purchase the interest of the Western Inland Lock Navigation Company. **1883** T. WEED *Autobiography* 204 (We.), Canal commissioners, engineers, and invited

guests . . . were received with great rejoicing. — (3) **1832** *Am. R.R. Jrnl.* I. 516/3, I have kept as strict an eye over . . . the Canal department. **1914** McLaughlin & Hart *Cyclo. Amer. Govt.* I. 218 Six indictments followed and the suspension and final removal of the auditor of the canal department. — (4) **1840** *Niles' Reg.* 29 Aug. 404/1, 18 dead bodies [were found, including that of] . . . a canal driver. **1882** Thayer *From Log-Cabin* 187 Jim, you've too good a head on you to be . . . a canal driver.

(5) **1847** Robb *Squatter Life* 90 'Take it cool, gentlemen,' shouted a westerner, from a top berth, 'these are the canal extras [=extra services].' — (6) **1849** Chamberlain *Ind. Gazetteer* 204, 50,000 acres of the vacant land were selected for the canal grant. — (7) **1845** *Ill. Rev. Statutes* 108 Purchasers of school or canal lands or town lots, may . . . transfer and assign all right and title to the lands or lots purchased. **1874** *Ill. Rev. Statutes* (1883) 183 Said commissioners . . . shall have authority . . . to lease from time to time any of the canal lands or lots owned by the State. — (8) *Am. R. R. Jrnl.* III. 592/3 (*caption*), Railroad and Canal Map. — (9) **1830** *Williams's N.Y. Ann. Reg.* 133 Lines of Canal Packet Boats. **1864** T. L. Nichols *Amer. Life* I. 116 There were two modes of reaching Buffalo—the mail-coaches and the canal-packets.

(10) **1827** Drake *Cincinnati* 14 In February, 1825, the Legislature . . . adopted what is now denominated the Canal Policy. — (11) **1844** *Ind. Senate Jrnl.* 85 Treasury notes and canal scrip. — (12) **1854** *Penn. Agric. Rep.* 394 Canal Shovels. — (13) **1881** *Nation* 10 March 160/2 The suits brought by the State against the 'canal thieves.' — (14) *a***1931** Jameson *Dict. U.S. Hist.* 81 Canal Zone. A strip of land granted to the United States by Panama in accordance with the treaty of February 26, 1904, the compensation being $10,000,000 with annual payments of $250,000 in addition.

As the last term in **beaver, boat, Erie, irrigating, Pacific, Panama, ship, state, steamboat canal.**

canal kəˈnæl, *v. tr.* To cut a canal across (land), to dig a canal around (falls). Also *intr.*

1819 E. Dana *Geog. Sks.* 20 The operation of canalling and locking the falls has lately been commenced. **1828** *Deb. Cong.* 9 April 2251 To canal across lofty mountains must be considered as a physical impossibility. **1870** Emerson *Society & Solitude* 144 What of the grand tools with which we engineer, . . . canalling the American Isthmus?

canaller kəˈnælɚ, *n.* Also **canaler. 1.** One who works or lives on a canalboat. **2.** A canalboat. *Rare.*

(1) **1830** *Germantown* (Pa.) *Telegraph* 14 July 4/1 A Canawler asked his captain 'what A.M. stood for after a man's name?' **1884** *S.F. Chronicle* Aug., These clusters of canal-boats are substantially floating villages. The 'canaler's' family is seen on deck. **1893** *Outing* Sep. 465/2 The 'canalers' were found to be a good-natured and kind-hearted set of men. — (2) **1887** *Cent. Mag.* Aug. 487 Near the bow of each canaler was a lantern of uncertain hue.

***canalling,** *n.* Travel or transportation by canalboat. — **1834** *Boston Post* 8 Aug. 2/3 Canalling Extraordinary. . . . A small boat containing a family of 12 souls . . . passed through . . . on the Erie Canal. **1889** K. Munroe *Golden Days* 85 For leisurely travelling this beat canalling all hollow.

Canaliño ˈkænəˈlinjo, *n.* [Sp., an inhabitant of a channel region.] An Indian of a now extinct tribe once numerous on the coast of the Santa Barbara Channel, Calif. Also the culture represented by this tribe. — **1929** Rogers *Prehistoric Man Santa Barbara Coast* 367 By the time of the arrival of the Canalino in our vicinity, the climate had assumed practically the same semi-arid phase with which we are familiar today. **1933** Harrington *Gypsum Cave, Nev.* 118 They were found in the deepest and oldest graves of the site which belonged to a culture intermediate between the 'Hunting People' and the 'Canaliño' or latest Indian culture.

canary slip. An official form used by the federal Pension Office (see quot.). *Obs.* — **1894** *Cong. Rec.* App. 3 March 624/2 The slips . . . instead of giving [the applicant's] military history, gave simply the date of enlistment, muster in, and the date of discharge. . . . These slips have an office nomenclature. They are called 'canary slips,' in distinction from full record slips.

***cancer,** *n.*

1. cancerroot, any one of various root parasites, as squawroot.

1714 *Phil. Trans.* XXIX. 64 To this [=boar thistle] they add a Root, call'd the Cancer Root. **1901** Mohr *Plant Life Ala.* 731 *Thalesia uniflora*. . . One-flowered Cancer Root. . . . Mountain region. Dry gravelly hillsides. **1947** *Midland Naturalist* July 58 Cancer-root [is] occasional in bottomland forest.

2. cancerweed, a plant popularly believed to be a remedy for cancer, esp. a sage, *Salvia lyrata.*

1802 Drayton *S. Carolina* 60 Cancer weed. (*Salvia Lyrata, et Mexicana.*) **1931** Clute *Plants* 123 A number of the ancient plant names recall afflictions which have happily gone quite out of style, if not out of the physician's vocabulary. . . . In the list are salt-rheum weed, itch-weed, . . . and cancer weed (*Salvia lyrata*).

canchalagua ˌkɑntʃəˈlɑgwə, *n. local.* [Amer. Sp. in same sense.] A gentianlike plant of the genus *Centaurium,* used medicinally.

[**1772** Ulloa *Noticias Americanas* 109 La *Calaguala,* yá *Canchalagua,* más conocidas yá por sus virtudes en *Europa* que ahora viente años, son producciones de aquellos inhabitables pinaculos de la cordillera.] **1848** E. Bryant *California* (1849) 452 There is another plant in high estimation with the Californians, called canchalagua, which is held by them as an antidote for all the diseases to which they are subject. **1922** Smiley *Weeds of Calif.* 153 This is but one of several 'canchalaguas' growing within the state, though it is the handsomest.

candelabrum cactus. (See quot. 1904 and cf. **cholla.**)

1878 Hinton *Handbook Ariz.* 343 To what age the candelebra cactus attains is a matter of mere conjecture, their growth being exceedingly slow. **1892** Bourke *On the Border* 53 And the majestic 'pitahaya,' or candelabrum cactus, whose ruby fruit had long since been raided upon and carried off by flocks of bright-winged humming-birds. **1904** Wooton *Native Ornamental Plants N.M.* 32 The Cholla or Candelabrum Cactus (*Opuntia arborescens*), . . . and several species of *Cereus* are to be had for a desert garden.

***candidate,** *n.* As the last term in **bourbon, caucus, floating, Free Soil, gold standard, labor, log cabin, nullification, prohibition, squatter, stump, Tammany candidate.**

candidate ˈkændəˌdet, *v. intr.* To be a candidate, esp. of clergymen who preach trial sermons with a view to settlements. Also **candidating,** *n.*

1848 Lowell *Bigelow P.* I. viii. 108 The can'idatin' line, you know, 'ould suit me to a T. . . . So I'll set up ez can'idate fer any kin' o' office. **1884** *Cent. Mag.* June 308 Let him put the question to some [choir-singers] who every spring have to candidate for a situation. **1887** *N.Y. Evangelist* 17 Nov., But the church refuses to call without a hearing. 'Thanks,' says Mr. Man; 'I am quite happy here, and do not care to candidate.' **1919** Cady *Rhymes of Vt.* (1923) 256 We bless the Lord that we are through With candidating in Vermont.

***candle,** *n.* In combs.: (1) **candle alder,** the common smooth alder, *Alnus rugosa;* (2) **berry,** the fruit of the wax myrtle, or the shrub producing this, also attrib.; (3) **berry myrtle,** the wax myrtle; (4) **berry tree,** =prec.; (5) **box returns,** fraudulent election returns, *rare;* (6) **bush,** =next; (7) **cactus,** =**ocotillo;** (8) **dipper,** a device for making dip candles; (9) **factor,** one who makes or sells candles, *obs.;* (10) **fish,** the eulachon, or the beshow, *Anoplopoma fimbria,* cf. **black candlefish;** (11) **hunting,** hunting deer at night by shining their eyes with candles, *obs.;* (12) **of the Lord,** =**Our Lord's Candle;** (13) **tree,** (see quot. 1889); (14) **wick,** designating an unbleached cotton bedspread the pattern of which is of wicking; (15) ***wood,** (*a*) a resinous wood, as pitch pine, the splinters of which are burned to provide light, make tar, etc., (*b*) the ocotillo, *Fouquieria splendens,* of the southwestern states.

(1) **1837** Darlington *Flora Cestrica* 525 Common Alder. Candle Alder. **1847** Darlington *Weeds & Plants* 328 Common Alder. Candle Alder. . . . [Grows in] swamps and margins of rivulets: throughout the United States. . . . This shrub is of little or no value. — (2) **1738** Byrd *Dividing Line* 27 In that moist Soil . . . grew that kind of myrtle which bears the candle-berries. **1892** *Amer. Folk-Lore* V. 103 *Myrica cerifera,* candle-berry, Worcester Co., Mass. **1912** *Comrade* 6 Jan. 3 Our grandmothers used to make candles out of these bay-berries, and thus it has its name, candleberry bush. **1948** *Times-Picayune Mag.* (N.O.) 19 Dec. 8/1 Miss Hooper goes picnicking for candle berries with her 60 Indian school children—and any grownups who care to go. — (3) *c***1730** Catesby *Carolina* I. 13 The broad-leaved Candle-berry Myrtle. *Ib.* 69 The narrow-leaved Candle-berry Myrtle. **1880** Cable *Grandissimes* 34 The northern shore of Biloxi Bay was rich in candleberry-myrtle. — (4) **1753** *Chambers' Cyclo. Supp.*, Candle berry tree, . . . an aromatic evergreen . . . also called the Virginia myrtle. **1828** Webster, Candle-berry Tree, . . . a shrub common in North America, from the berries of which a kind of wax or oil is procured, of which candles are made. . . . In popular language, this is called bay-berry tallow. **1911** *Boston Transcript* 27 May II. 7 The early English settlers called this plant the 'Candleberry tree,' and the Swedes called it the 'tallow-shrub.'

(5) **1858** *Cong. Globe* 15 March 1122/1 Cincinnati directories and candle box returns have been infinitely more potent than the real votes of the inhabitants. — (6) **1906** *Out West* Jan. 36 That they do both may be well illustrated by examining some features of the reaction of the single species, the ocotillo or candle bush. — (7) **1901** *Scientific Amer.* 9 Mar. 149/1 Here is the large candle cactus so common on the Mexican and Arizonian deserts. — (8) **1874** Knight 442

The candle-dipper shown is intended to give a determinate weight to any number of candles. **1911** FERBER *Dawn O'Hara* 207 The simple woman told the story of each precious relic, from the battered candle-dipper on the shelf, to the great mahogany folding table. — **(9) 1864** MARK TWAIN *Sketches* (1926) 122 John Smith, Soap Boiler and Candle Factor. **1865** STOWE *House & Home P.* 222 We buy . . . candles of the candle-factor.

(10) 1881 *Nature* XXIV. 39/2 Oolachan oil . . . is obtained from a fish called by the North American Indians 'Oolachan,' or 'candle-fish,' from the fact that when dried the fish itself can be used as a torch or candle. **1946** R. PEATTIE *Pac. Coast Ranges* 32 The candlefish yielded an oil essential to the rounding out of their diet. — **(11) 1842** *Amer. Pioneer* 47 Besides the common modes, they often practice candle hunting. . . . Deer come to the rivers to eat a kind of water grass, to get which they frequently immerse their whole head and horns. They seem to be blinded by light at night, and will suffer a canoe to float close to them. — **(12) 1948** *Nat. Hist.* April 180 The 'Candle of the Lord' sends up its triumphant banner to tell the desert traveler that spring has come. — **(13) 1889** *Cent.* 789/1 candle-tree. . . . In the United States, the *Catalpa bignonioides*, from its long round pods. **1907** HODGE *Amer. Indians* I. 213 The two species native in the United States are the common catalpa, bean-tree, Indian bean, or candle-tree (*Catalpa catalpa*) and the western catalpa. — **(14) 1930** *Sears Cat.* Fall 357 Candlewick Embroidery is a popular vogue in needlework. A candlewick tufted bedspread is an article you would be proud to own. **1935** *Montgomery Ward Cat.* (ed. 123) 326 Cut six inches longer, so these allover hand tufted Candlewick Spreads really cover your pillows! **1944** *Reader's Digest* August 100 Catherine Evans, a Georgia farm girl, built a business at home by copying a family heirloom—a candlewick bedspread.

(15) (*a*) **1634** WOOD *N. Eng. Prospect* I. v. 17 Out of these Pines is gotten the candlewood that is so much spoken of, . . . but I cannot commend it for singular good, because it is something sluttish, dropping a pitchie kinde of substance where it stands. **1700** *Springfield Rec.* II. 357 No Stranger or any that are not proper Inhabitants of the Town shal . . . draw any Candell wood for Tarr from tyme to tyme. **1935** *Col. of Conn.* 14 Candlewood used for tar making was prohibited if gathered within 6 miles of the Connecticut River. (*b*) **1889** *Cent.* 789/1 candlewood. . . . The genus *Fouquiera* of northern Mexico and the adjacent United States, including several species with erect, slender, very resinous, and often leafless stems, and large bright-scarlet flowers. **1939** PICKWELL *Deserts* 65/2 One of the commonest is 'candlewood,' the name of the family; another is 'coachwhip.'

b. *snuffing the candle*, a frontier amusement in which riflemen at night snuffed candles with bullets as a test of marksmanship.

1838 GOSSE *Letters* 131 'Snuffing the candle' is performed in the night. [**1877** WM. WRIGHT *Big Bonanza* 361 To snuff a candle with a pistol or rifle has always been a great feat. **1948** DICK *Dixie Frontier* 143 So skillful did some of these marksmen become that they did unbelievable stunts. One of these was to snuff a candle without putting it out.]

As the last term in **bayberry, car, Confederate, Our Lord's, star candle.**

* **candy,** *n.* In combs.: (1) **candy bar,** a piece of candy in the shape of a small bar; (2) **braid,** a twist of candy, *rare;* (3) **bucket,** a large wooden bucket in which candy is shipped; (4) **butcher,** =**butcher 2;** (5) **cane,** stick candy resembling in shape a small walking cane; (6) **factory,** an establishment where the business of making candy is carried on; (7) **grass,** the stink grass naturalized in the U.S.; (8) **kitchen,** a place where candy is made and sold at retail; (9) **maker,** one who makes candy; (10) **marble,** hard candy in the shape of a marble; (11) **saloon,** =**candy store;** (12) **shop,** =**candy store,** also attrib.; (13) **stand,** a place or station occupied by a candy vendor; (14) * **stick,** (see quot.); (15) **store,** a store or shop in which candies are sold.

(1) 1943 CROW *Amer. Customer* 158 The total coinage of the country would buy a five cent candy bar for only four-fifths of the people! **1948** *Democrat* 30 Sep. 1/7 The stand sold uncounted hundreds of candy bars. — **(2) 1870** EMERSON *Society & Solitude* vii. 143 Why need I speak of steam, . . . which . . . can twist beams of iron like candy-braids? — **(3) 1931** DOBIE *Coronado* 49 The doctor had made copies of the stone and plates on some wooden lids of old-fashioned candy buckets, but when the Kirkpatrick home burned they burned also. **1944** WILSON *Passing Inst.* 111 By the time the last piece was said, the boys returned with a candy bucket. — **(4) 1940** MENCKEN *Happy Days* 232 The candy-butcher . . . carried a basket containing oval boxes of figs, little red railroad lanterns full of candy pills, gumdrops in red, white and green, [etc.], and my father was always good for a sale. **1946** *Time* 23 Dec. 84/3 He went to school in Jamestown, N.Y., worked as a candy butcher on trains, then as a dress salesman.

(5) 1936 BARNARD *Rider* 3 All went well for a while, but at Christmas time I was given one of those candy canes. **1944** *Nat. Geog. Mag.* Sep. 351 The little miss at the far end of the table is working hard on a candy cane. — **(6) 1851** CIST *Cincinnati* 260 [Cincinnati industries include] Sarsaparilla, cough candy factories. **1948** *Confectioner* June 48/1 (*advt.*), Male Help Wanted—18 years or over, for general work in candy factory located in Milwaukee. — **(7) 1894** *Amer. Folk-Lore* VII. 104 *Eragrostis major* . . . stink-grass, Neb. candy-grass; Central Neb. **1901** MOHR *Plant Life Ala.* 380 Candy Grass . . . [is] a frequent garden weed. — **(8) 1911** H. P. FAIRCHILD *Greek Immigration* 127 The line in which the Greeks have made their greatest success is the fruit stores, candy kitchens and ice cream parlors. — **(9) 1880** (*title*), The Candy-maker, or Confectioner's Handbook, 137 recipes and other valuable matter. **1896** *Godey's Mag.* Feb. 145/2 Why do you haunt me with your supernatural tooth-aches? Go haunt the candy-maker, or the cook.

(10) 1938 DAMON *Grandma* 49 Alice bought outright for cash in Deacon Parker's store one hundred candy marbles—ten for a cent they came, all colors. — **(11) 1857** *Phoenix* (Sacramento) 30 Aug. 2/3 On Washington street there kept a candy saloon, a handsome and fair damsel. — **(12) 1845** *Knickerb.* XXV. 424 Candy-shop keepers, washer-women and tailors, all have a harvest to reap. **1903** C. L. BURNHAM *Jewel* 103 Next door was a candy shop with alluring windows. — **(13) 1913** CATHER *O Pioneers!* 179 Why had she seemed pleased when all the French and Bohemian boys, and the priest himself, crowded round her candy stand? — **(14) 1894** in *Smithsonian Rep.* 1123 This is the only species of Elaps I have found in south Florida, where it is rather common. It is known under several names, as 'coral snake,' 'American cobra,' 'garter snake,' and 'candy stick.'

(15) 1884 *N.Y. Herald* 27 Oct. 7/6 Girl to learn to attend bakery, lunch room or candy store. **1943** OTTLEY *New World* 155 In every street either a candy store, barber shop, beauty parlor, or tavern is a collection headquarters.

b. Denoting social gatherings of young people to make candy, esp. molasses candy, as (1) **candy bee,** (2) **breaking,** (3) **party,** (4) **pull(ing),** (5) **stew.**

(1) 1845 in *Amer. Sp.* April 106 But the distinguished festival of Podunk is the *candy bee*. Were you ever present at one of these? — **(2) 1932** RANDOLPH *Ozark Mts.* vii, I have recorded the tales that were told to me . . . at frolics and candy-breakin's and play-parties in the Ozark Mountain country. — **(3) 1845** *Lowell Offering* V. 268 We used to have sewing parties, tea parties, candy parties. **1876** *Wide Awake* 279/2 Well enough, Nan, for you to give your invitations for that candy-party. — **(4) 1850** *Jrnl. Birmingham Emig. Co.* 22 Apr., We had a pleasant evening and of course made a candy-pulling to pass of the time. **1862** in *Calif. Hist. Soc. Quart.* X. (1931) 377 In the evening went to Col Hoge's with Warfield had a candy pull a good dance &c. **1946** PARTRIDGE & BATTMANN *As We Were* 13 Candy pulling was one of those things that went on before the young swains, dropping in of an evening, brought what has now become the conventional box of candy.

(5) *c***1870** BAGBY *Old Va. Gentleman* 11 Of parties of all kinds, from candy-stews and 'infairs' up to the regular country balls at the county seat. **1887** *Courier-Journal* 30 Jan. 13/3 A supper in addition to a 'candy-stew' was an unheard-of luxury.

As the last term in **barley, cactus, cotton, cough, cream, ice cream, maple, maple-sugar butternut, molasses, motto, nut, peanut, peppermint, popcorn, stick, store candy.**

* **cane,** *n.*

1. A tract overgrown by cane. *Obs.*

1833 *Life of Crockett* 53 The 'gentleman from the *cane*' was soon known to every member of both houses. **1836** J. HALL *Stat. West.* 27 The inhabitants drive their cattle to the cane in the autumn. **1853** in *Amer. Sp.* XIX. 43 Having squeezed through a thick piece of cane, we came suddenly upon as pretty a scene of confusion.

2. In combs., chiefly *S.:* (1) **cane bottom,** (*a*) low land, frequently along a stream, overgrown with cane, also attrib., (*b*) used attrib. with *chair* in the sense of "cane bottomed"; (2) **brake,** see as a main entry; (3) **branch,** a branch or small stream along which cane grows in abundance; (4) **country,** a region where cane grows abundantly; (5) **cutter,** a local name for the swamp rabbit, in full **cane-cutter rabbit,** cf. **c.** (4) below; (6) **grass,** a reed-like grass of the genus *Arundinaria;* (7) **knife,** a knife for cutting cane in canebrake regions, cf. **c.** (7) below; (8) **land,** land upon which wild cane grows in abundance; (9) **marsh,** a marshy area overgrown with cane; (10) **pole,** a cane stem, a fishing pole; (11) **rack,** a game popular at fairs, carnivals, etc., in which walking canes serve as prizes; (12) **rush,** (see quot.

1890); (13) **seat,** cane-seated, also absol.; (14) **soil,** extremely fertile soil as indicated by the growth of cane or reeds on it; (15) **spree,** =**cane rush,** also **canespreeing;** (16) **swamp,** a swamp overgrown with cane.

(1) (*a*) **1819** E. DANA *Geog. Sk.* 188 The river cane bottom land . . . may average in width a half or three-quarters of a mile. **1837** A. WETMORE *Gaz. Missouri* 289 Joplin reached his old haunts, in a cane-bottom on Flat Creek. (*b*) **1843** *Knickerb.* XXI. 150 His apartments . . . were adorned with . . . a sufficient allowance of cane-bottom chairs. **1948** *Democrat* 7 Oct. 1/1 Real cane bottom chairs. — (**3**) **1772** D. TAITT in *Travels Amer. Col.* 497 We encamped at a Cane branch runing NW by W into Weoka or Little Scambia. **1775** ADAIR *Indians* 266 When they came to a boggy cane-branch, they strove to persuade him to alight. — (**4**) **1800** W. TATHAM *Agriculture & Commerce* 65 In the cane countries and poccosins it is equally so in the winter. **1824** G. W. RAUCK *Boonesborough* 163 We arrived at the commencement of a cane country, traveled about thirty miles through thick cane and reed.

(**5**) **1941** YEAGER *Mammalogy* XXII. 377. **1944** CLARK *Pills* 128 For a whole week during the Christmas season hillbilly and cane-cutter rabbits lived in misery. — (**6**) **1827** *Western Mo. Rev.* I. 209 Wild rice . . . very accurately resembles the cane grass of the vast swamps and savannahs on the gulf of Mexico. **1845** SIMMS *Wigwam & Cabin* 1 Ser. 15 A swamp-bottom, the growth of which consisted of . . . dense thickets of low stunted shrubbery, cane grass, and dwarf willows. — (**7**) **1798** A. ELLICOTT in *Life & Lett.* 159 [The country] could only be explored by using the cane knife and hatchet. — (**8**) **1786** in *Mag. Amer. Hist.* I. 312 On the North Fork of Licking, where we passed, is some fine cane land. **1831** HOLLEY *Tex. Lett.* (1833) 51 When a colonist wishes to describe his land as first rate, he says it is all peach and cane land. **1886** Z. F. SMITH *Kentucky* 59 The old yearning for the 'caneland' came over them. — (**9**) **1788** SCHÖPF *Reise* II. 242 Finden sich überall [in North Carolina] Sümpfe . . . und am gewühnlichsten längst den Flüssen und Bächen, die Rohrsümpfe (Cane-Marshes), wohin auch die Savannah's zu rechnen sind. **1790** *N.C. Gazette* 13 Dec., It is computed that one third of this Tract is of valuable Tide swamp, or cane marsh and meadow.

(**10**) **1816** *Niles' Reg.* X. 225/2 More mud is added, until a surface is formed above the water, and then a growth of canepoles spring up. **1888** GRIGSBY *Smoked Yank* xii. (1891) 100, I saw some starving men with long willow or cane poles . . . trying to kill food, swallows [etc.]. — (**11**) **1896** *Chicago Rec.* 14 Feb. 1/4 Delegate Hutchinson . . . defended the cane rack and declared that the agriculturists and fair officials of his country had decided that it was a game of skill and not of chance. **1948** *Neb. Munic. Rev.* June 37/2 It shall be unlawful for any person to maintain . . . any slot machine, . . . cane-rack, knife-board, . . . pin-ball machine, or any drawing by chance through which a prize is offered. — (**12**) **1890** *Cent.* 5277/3 *Cane-rush,* a rush between the freshmen and sophomores of an American college or academy for the possession of a cane, carried in defiance of custom by one on the freshmen. **1902** L. BELL *Hope Loring* 109 Brewster, or our class, who saved the day for us in the cane rush. — (**13**) **1851** CIST *Cincinnati* 205 Cane-seat and rocking-chairs, are made to a considerable extent. **1873** BAILEY *Life in Danbury* 116 He never could sit on a 'cane seat.' **1887** *Courier-Journal* 20 Feb. 3/7 At Auction . . . Cane-seat chairs and Rockers. — (**14**) **1847** *De Bow's Review* III. 553, I found the specific gravity of the Cane soil. **1858** *Texas Almanac 1859* 76 The three soils mentioned above, namely, stiff black, peach, and cane-soils, are the principal soils in this portion of the country.

(**15**) **1879** *Princeton Book* 384 [The] cane-spree, that annual expression of the innate and inalienable superiority of Sophomores to Freshmen. **1895** WILLIAMS *Princeton Stories* 13 'Now, that is cane-spreeing,' said the junior casually. — (**16**) **1709** LAWSON *Carolina* 10 Some Sewee Indians [were] firing the Canes Swamps, which drives out the Game. **1800** B. HAWKINS *Sk. Creek Country* 23 The Alabama is margined with cane swamps.

b. In less frequent combs., often rare or obs.: (1) **cane barrel,** a section of a canestalk; (2) **beer,** beer made from the skimmings from sugar cane juice being boiled into molasses; (3) **brush,** the tops and leaves of cane; (4) **cactus,** (see quot. 1911); (5) **house,** a bear den in a canebrake; (6) **meadow,** a canebrake; (7) **raised,** raised on cane; (8) **region, ridge,** =**cane land;** (9) **rocker,** a rocking chair made of canes; (10) **tackey,** (see quot.); (11) **vine,** a variety of greenbrier, *Smilacina lanceolata.*

(**1**) **1883** SHIELDS *S. S. Prentiss* 63 The bursting of the pent-up air from the cane-*barrels* [as the cane burned] sounded like the rattle of musketry upon a battle-field. — (**2**) **1938** MATSCHAT *Suwannee River* 131 Freeman was busy skimming the boiling syrup and putting it carefully to one side: cane beer, with a sweet-sour taste, would be made from the fermented skimmings and, later, would form excellent 'buck' for a wildcat still. — (**3**) **1848** *Rep. Comm. Patents 1847* 454 Cane brush is the best for them [silkworms] to wind in. — (**4**) **1909** LONGYEAR *Rocky Mt. Wild Flower Studies* 51 The name 'Cane cactus' often applied to this plant is derived from the fact that canes are sometimes made from the old stems that have made a straight growth. **1911** *Smithsonian Inst. Ann. Rep.* 449 The cane cactus (*Opuntia arbuscula*) bears heads of large blossoms.

(**5**) **1834** in CODY *Story of Wild West* 211 They [bears] go into their holes in large hollow trees, or into hollow logs, or their cane-houses, or the harricanes, and lie there till spring, like frozen snakes. — (**6**) **1791** BARTRAM *Travels* 233 Cane meadows, so called by the inhabitants of Carolina, &c. *Ib.* 377 There are extensive cane brakes or cane meadows spread abroad round about. — (**7**) **1853** PAXTON *Yankee in Texas* 121, I rode an all fired chunk of a pony—real Creole, cane raised. — (**8**) **1842** *Spirit of Times* 29 Jan. 566/2 (We.), On a cane ridge bordering the swamp. **1850** LEWIS *La. Swamp Dr.* 112 The land between the tillable or cane ridges, was low swamp, almost quagmire, never thoroughly dry. **1852** J. REYNOLDS *Hist. Illinois* 195 Above the cane region, the rushes grew on the sandy margins of the Mississippi. — (**9**) **1900** E. A. DIX *Deacon Bradbury* 5 The deacon dropped into his large cane rocker, and put on his glasses.

(**10**) **1850** *Rep. Comm. Patents 1849: Agric.* 161 Some planters breed the largest sized 'cane-tackeys,' as they are called, or native ponies of Spanish origin, to well bred but small stout horses. — (**11**) **1831** AUDUBON *Ornith. Biog.* I. 23 In Louisiana, it is called the *Cane Vine.* It bears a small white flower in clusters. The berries are bitter and nauseous.

c. In combs. of obvious meaning relating to sugar cane: (1) **cane beer,** see **b.** (2) above, (2) **carrier,** (3) **cart,** (4) **cutter,** cf. **2.** (5) above, (5) **field,** (6) **fodder,** (7) **knife,** cf. **2.** (7) above, (8) **mill,** (9) **plantation,** (10) **tops,** (11) **wagon,** (12) **yard.**

(**2**) **1833** SILLIMAN *Man. Sugar Cane* 31 The canes are brought up to the mill by means of a machine called the Cane carrier. **1848** *Hunt's Merch. Mag.* XVIII. 337 It is brought into a shed, where the cane-carrier is situated. — (**3**) **1858** *Texas Almanac* (*advt.*), Axles, suitable for Cane carts. **1887** *Cent. Mag.* Nov. 108/2 The great cane-carts carrying the plant cane to the freshly tilled fields. — (**4**) **1843** in *Index of Patents* (1874) I. 198 Cane-cutter [invented by] J. P. Bryan [of] Princeton, Ky. July 8, 1843. **1850** LEWIS *La. Swamp Dr.* 200 The cane that would conceal my bones would be falling before the knife of the cane-cutter. **1886** *Harper's Mag.* June 80/2 Cane-cutters first slice the cane diagonally . . . in pieces three or four inches long [in making sugar].

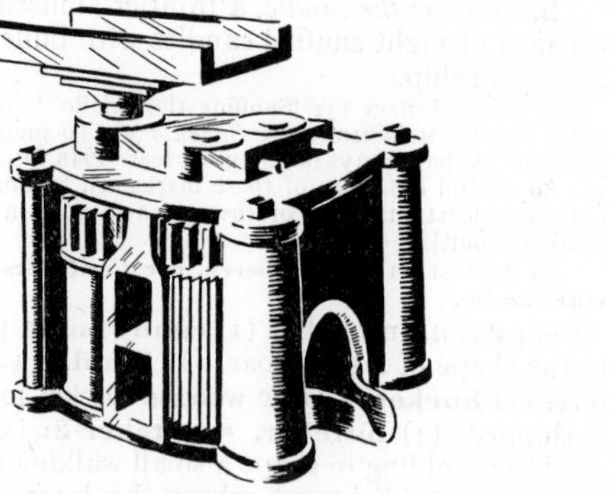

One form of cane mill or grinding mill

(**5**) **1833** SILLIMAN *Man. Sugar Cane*, A cane field planted in the open manner. **1916** W. A. DU PUY *Uncle Sam* 83 The handling of the raw sugar that came from the canefields of Louisiana.— (**6**) **1851** *Fla. Plant. Rec.* 422, 1 [slave] hawling Cain fodder in the Lot. **1932** W. KELLEY *Inchin' Along* 6 In Lige's sugar cane patch he could see a couple sitting close together on a bed of cane fodder. — (**7**) **1944** *Sat. Review* 2 Sep. 23 Young second-wife of Southern planter slain with cane-knife. — (**8**) **1833** SILLIMAN *Man. Sugar Cane* 30 The Cane mill consists of three cast iron cylinders. **1946** *Democrat* 22 Aug. 4/2 For Sale —Small cane mill, horse drawn, in good condition. — (**9**) **1850** S. F. COOPER *Rural Hours* 29 A very great proportion comes from the cane plantations of Louisiana.

(**10**) **1826** J. BRADFORD *Ky. Notes* 11, I ordered Jamie to make us a shelter, which he did by erecting forks and poles, and covering them with cane tops, like a fodder house. **1833** SILLIMAN *Man. Sugar Cane* 12 A part of the planting is done with cane tops, or that portion of the Cane which is rejected in cutting it for the mill. **1853** *Harper's Mag.* Nov. 756/1 These leaves and cane-tops really form a large proportion of the gross vegetation of the annual product of the soil. — (**11**) **1853** *Harper's Mag.* VII. 761/1 The stalks . . . on the ground [are] soon . . . placed in the cane-wagons which, with their four gigantic muleteams, have just come rattling on to the scene of action. — **(12) 1862** *Rep. Comm. Patents: Agric.* 302, I should say two acres would be sufficient for cane-yard and sheds. The mill should be situated at one end of the cane-yard.

As the last term in **candy, Chinese, Creole, fishing, gentleman's, ice cream, maiden, mutton, Niagara, Otaheite, Philippine, plant, purple, red, reed, ribbon, seed, stubble, sugar, switch, virgin cane.**

canebrake ˈkenˌbrek, *n.* Also **-break.** *S.*

1. A thicket of canes, a region overgrown with canes. Also attrib. See also **Mississippi, prairie canebrake.**

1769 in *Amer. Sp.* XV. 162/1 As we ascended the brow of a small hill, a number of Indians rushed out of a thick cane brake. **1796** B. Hawkins *Letters* 41 Here commence large swamps and between them and the river are some rich flat canebrake land. **1876** in Guild *Old Times* (1878) 391 These cane-brake women always manage their husbands. **1946** *Chi. D. News* 24 June 16/2 Mob violence is no less reprehensible on a Northern picket line than it is in a Georgia canebrake.

b. Designating the banded rattlesnake, *Crotalus horridus*, of the southern states. Cf. **Seminole, 1. b.**

1933 Ditmars *Reptiles of World* 260 This variety lives along the coastal region and is called the Cane-Brake Rattlesnake. **1944** *Sat. Ev. Post* 9 Sep. 13/2 Big diamond rattlesnakes as thick as a man's arm, and the bright-colored canebrake rattlers or 'Seminoles,' [are] as beautiful as they are deadly.

2. Used to name particular regions once noted for canebrakes, esp. that portion of Alabama of which Uniontown, Demopolis, and Faunsdale are the leading towns. Also attrib.

1850 in Boyd *Alabama* 129 (*title*), *Canebrake Female Institute Catalogue, 1850.* *c***1850–8** O'Neall-Chapman *Annals* 51 The parts of Newberry first occupied and settled by the white man, were as follows: the Dutch Fork in 1745: . . . the Canebrake, on Enoree, (Pennington's grant,) 1751, or possibly earlier. **1884** *True Democrat* 19 March 3/2 Canebrake roads are still very bad. *c***1898** Christian *Days* 79 There were no Railroads in the Canebrake at that time.

canee ˈkeˌni, *n.* An affected variant of "cane." *Obs.* — **1795** *Tablet* (Bost.) 18 Such gentlemen as carry small canes, in modish language termed *canees*, ought to put them in a horizontal position under their right arm. **1815** in Kittredge *Old Farmer* (1904) 220 [To] brandish a canee, . . . and smoke segars, are not the most essential qualifications for a schoolmaster.

***Canfield,** *n.* The name by which the card game known as Klondike was originally copyrighted about 1905, the supposition being that a famous New York gambler, Richard Canfield, invented it. Cf. **Klondike 2.** — **1912** *Sat. Ev. Post* 6 July 3/1, I write when I am not raising my children, shopping for the house, . . . or playing double Canfield with my husband. **1946** Morehead & Mott-Smith *Penguin Hoyle* 175 Here one could buy a pack of cards for $50 and play a game of Canfield under the watchful eye of the croupier.

***canker,** *n.* In combs.: (1) **canker lettuce,** the false wintergreen; (2) **rash,** (see quot. 1828); (3) ***worm,** either of two species of measuring worm. See also **fall, spring cankerworm.**

(1) 1890 *Cent.* 4875/3 *P. rotundifolia*, the larger wintergreen, . . . has been called Indian lettuce and canker-lettuce. *c***1895** *D. N.* I, 385 *Canker lettuce*, . . . [is] said to be a cure for 'canker.' Mass. w. — **(2) 1803** *Med. Repository* 341 A bilious malignant fever made its appearance, and continued till August, when the cholera and canker-rash commenced, and continued through the year. **1828** Webster, *Scarlatina*, the scarlet fever; called in popular language, the 'canker rash.' **1862** *Harper's Mag.* June 138/1 Here lies, till the general resurrection, William . . . who, after nine days' violent seizure of a canker rash, calmly resigned his infant life to the King of Terrors. — **(3)** *c***1680** J. Hull *Diary Occurr.* 203 The canker-worm hath, for the four years, devoured most of the apples in Boston. **1793** *N.Y. State Soc. Arts* I. 187 The canker-worm, only destroys the leaves and fruit for the season. **1865** Sala *Diary* I. 218 These trees are, one and all, infested by a horrible little reptile known commonly as the 'measuring worm,' the 'canker worm,' or the 'pace-maggot.' **1934** *Nat. Geog. Mag.* LXVI. 127 They [birds] find trees infested with cankerworms . . . of which they seem to be very fond.

Cann kɑn, *n.* [Origin unknown.] A variety of winter apple. *Obs.* — **1817** W. Coxe *Fruit Trees* 132 Cann Apple . . . is cultivated in West-jersey as a fine cider fruit. **1859** Elliott *Western Fruit Book* 129 Cann. American. Fruit . . . 'very good.' October 10 December.

Cannacker kəˈnɑkɚ, *n.* [Cf. **Canuck, Kanaka.**] A Canadian. *Obs.* — **1835** N. Wyeth *Journal* 235, I today dispatched Capt Thing to Fort Hall Having 19 men viz 4 Kanackas, 10 white men, and him self a fur man and three Nez Perces in all. **1846** W. G. Stewart *Altowan* I. vii. 191 The Cannackers, as they were commonly called, set themselves quietly about reviving the fire.

canned kænd, *a.*

1. Of foodstuffs: Put up and sealed in a can for preservation.

1859 R. B. Marcy *Prairie Traveler* 31 Canned vegetables are very good for campaigning. **1888** Lindley *Calif. of South* 358 As to canned peaches, there is a good market in the East and Europe. **1944** *Chi. D. News* 13 July 21/1 Of course, only meat from fresh-caught crabs is used, but heretic souls in less favored sections say that the trick can be done with canned crabmeat, and some say they use chopped cooked shrimp.

b. canned heat, a kind of solid alcohol, Sterno. Also attrib.

1917 *Rep. State Mineralogist Calif.* 42 A small 'sterno,' or a 'Canned Heat' outfit, is very compact and convenient for a quick lunch. **1947** *Chi. Tribune* 2 Nov. (Grafic Mag.) 7/5 When supper time came he lighted the canned heat and he cooked himself some lima beans and ham.

2. *fig.* Artificially built up or preserved. Also, stereotyped. *Slang.*

1893 *Harper's Mag.* LXXXVI. 969/2 Many 'canned' reputations have been destroyed, and many maligned characters have been uplifted to honour. **1908** *St. Louis Globe-Democrat* 1 July 6/6 Chicago preachers are to leave canned sermons behind while they are on their summer vacations. **1931** *K. C. Times* 8 Sep., Canned editorials give the subscribers, if any, a break.

b. Of music: recorded.

1917 *Lit. Digest* 25 Aug. 29/1 That was canned jazz, but you didn't know it then. **1948** *Chi. Maroon* 23 April 9/3 Two [*sic*] much stuff is canned, syndicated out of New York or Chicago and used throughout the country.

3. Having a can tied to the tail; cashiered, dismissed. *Slang.*

1903 A. Adams *Log Cowboy* iii. 37, I was half a mile in the lead, burning the earth like a canned dog. **1911** Quick *Yellowstone N.* 37 Did you get canned for letting me in?

canner ˈkænɚ, *n.*

1. One who cans meat, fruit, etc. Cf. **vegetable canner.**

1878 Bishop *Voy. Paper Canoe* 120 The canners take a large portion. **1899** *Bulletin U.S. Fish Comm.* XVIII. 6 In the opinions of the canners, the coho should rank next after the king salmon in food value. **1948** *Calif. Citrograph* April 177/3 In a short time a lot of peach growers went out of business and the canners were short of peaches.

b. Also an implement used in canning.

1948 *Capital-Democrat* (Tishomingo, Okla.) 3 June 6/4 This canner is the quickest, easiest, and most positive seal of any.

2. An animal fit only for canning.

1890 *Stock Grower* 11 Jan. 5/2 A large proportion of the offerings were fit only for canners and feeders. **1892** *Pall Mall Gaz.* 8 Dec. 2/1 'Canners,' which is the designation of all animals collected at the Chicago and other markets that are refused by the butchers as unfit for their trade. **1911** Quick *Yellowstone N.* 303 A collection of skips an' culls an' canners that was sure a fraud on the Injuns.

cannery ˈkænərɪ, *n.* An establishment where meats, fruits, etc., are canned.

1870 *Dept. Agric. Rep. 1869* 600 Aside from the canneries about one hundred men are engaged in salmon fishing, . . . who have their own nets, [etc.]. **1883** R. Rathbun in *U.S. Nat. Museum Bul. No. 27* 115 In 1880, there were twenty-three canneries in Maine, . . . giving employment to about 650 factory hands and 2,000 fishermen. **1948** *Green Bay* (Wis.) *Press-Gazette* 13 July 14/5 She said the Green Bay cannery was getting only 60 per cent of a normal yield.

As the last term in **crab, fish, fruit, oyster, salmon, sardine cannery.**

canning ˈkænɪŋ, *n.* The process or business of preserving meats, vegetables, etc., in cans or jars. Also attrib. Cf. **salmon canning.**

1874 in *Ore. Hist. Quart.* XXXIV. 244 Capt. West . . . has adventured into the canning of beef and mutton. **1875** *Dept. Agric. Rep. 1874* 279 In 1873 there were in Maine thirty-three canning-factories. *Ib.*, The canning establishment of Mr. William Archdeacon . . . occupies 13 acres of land. **1905** *Chi. D. News* 1 July 12/4 Common to good canning cows 1.40 @ 2.00. **1948** *Milwaukee Jrnl.* 18 July 2/2 Compared with the 1947 production, the canning pea crop this year was smaller.

***cannon,** *n.*

1. A pistol. *Slang.*

1901 Flynt *World of Graft* 137 The thief had him covered with his 'cannon' before he could do any damage.

2. cannon car, (see quot.).

1895 Wait *Car-Builder's Dict.* 64 Gun-car or cannon-car. A specially heavy car for transporting ordnance, often having sixteen wheels.

3. cannon cracker, a large firecracker.

1871 Bagg *At Yale* 297 A party of carousers insist upon . . . firing off cannon-crackers in the entries. **1912** Dreiser *Financier* 26 Uncle Seneca . . . brought some great cannon-crackers out on the evening of July the Fourth.

4. cannon stove, (see quot. 1923). Also **cannonball stove.**

1764 *Pa. Gazette* 26 April 3/3 The esteemed Cannon-stoves are yet sold by him. **1923** J. L. Rosenberger *Pa. Germans* 52 About the middle of the eighteenth century cannon or upright cylindrical heating-stoves made their appearance, and were first used principally in large rooms frequented by the public, and in churches. All burned

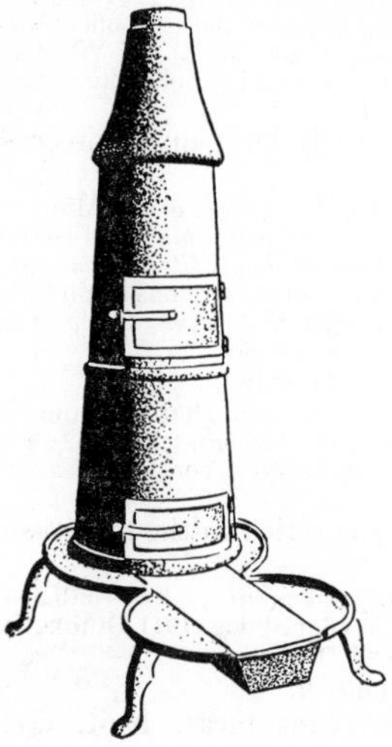

Cannon stove

wood. **1947** Beebe *Mixed Train Dly.* 83 The agent . . . maintained his premises at Turkish-bath temperature through the agency of a cannon-ball stove which glowed red all over though it was still early October.

***canoe,** *n.* In combs.: (1) **canoe awl,** a form of awl used in sewing a birchbark canoe; (2) **bark,** the bark of the canoe birch; (3) **birch,** =**paper birch;** (4) **cedar,** the western red cedar, *Thuja plicata;* (5) **deposit,** a place where canoes are kept or cached, *obs.;* (6) **gum,** a substance used for calking the seams of a canoe; (7) **Indians,** Indians that make great use of canoes; (8) **load,** the amount which can be carried in a canoe; (9) **maker,** one who makes canoes; (10) **man,** a voyageur, one who operates a canoe; (11) **place,** a place at which canoes are kept or can be used, *obs.;* (12) **trapper,** a trapper who uses a canoe in his work, *rare;* (13) **tree,** a tree of which a canoe can be made, *obs.;* (14) **wood,** any one of various trees, esp. the tulip tree or its wood, used in making canoes; (15) **yoke,** any one of various devices for assisting one in carrying a canoe.

(1) **1836** Thorpe *Life on Lakes* II. 185 With this waatap, by help of the canoe-awl, the canoe was sewed up every nicely in about two hours. — (2) **1903** White *Forest* xiii. 172 A cache in the forest country is simply a heavily constructed rustic platform on which provisions and clothing are laid and wrapped completely about in sheets of canoe bark. — (3) **1810** Michaux *Arbres* I. 25 Canoe birch (*Bouleau à cannot*). **1917** Eaton *Green Trails* 16 The trunks of the great canoe birches are green with age and moss. — (4) **1884** Sargent *Rep. Forests* 177 *Thuya gigantea* . . . Red Cedar. Canoe Cedar. **1946** R. Peattie *Pac. Coast Ranges* 70 Nothing can express the density or the unbroken extent of primeval grandeur of these Sitka spruces, western hemlocks, giant canoe cedars.

(5) **1807** Gass *Journal,* They had got to the canoe-deposit on the 8th instant. — (6) **1902** White *Conjuror's House* xii. 168 At noon the squaws set out to gather canoe gum on the mainland. — (7) **1921** *Outing* July 157/1 The Ojibways . . . were 'canoe Indians' as the Indians or the Plains were 'horse Indians.' **1940** *Mt. Hood Guide* 26 The principal food of the canoe Indians was the salmon, supplemented by roots, berries and some game. — (8) **1691** *Annals Albany* (1850) II. 115 The def[endan]t accused him of stealing $\frac{1}{2}$ canoe load of water millions. **1753** Washington *Diaries* I. 46 They were sent from New-Orleans with 100 men, and 8 Canoe-Loads of Provisions. **1880** *Harper's Mag.* Dec. 31 Indians brought in canoe-loads of fine full jacketed potatoes. — (9) **1805** Pike *Sources Miss.* (1810) 36 Killed a number of pheasants and ducks, while visiting my canoemaker.

(10) [**1683** Hennepin *Louisiana* (1880) 58 The Sieur de la Salle . . . has trained his men so well to manage canoes in the most frightful rapids, that they are now the most skillful canoemen in America.] **1755** L. Evans *Anal. Map Colonies* 17 The River is full of Falls and Rifts for forty Leagues, where the Canoe Men are often obliged to carry over Land, and to wade in several Places. **1897** *Outing* June 228/1 The ability to carry sail in such a light contrivance, depends entirely upon the skill of the canoeman. — (11) **1653** *Southampton Rec.* I. 94 John Cooper Sen shall send forth men to . . . bring to the towne what cattell they can meete with beyond the canoe place. **1766** in W. Smith *Bouquet's Exped.* (1868) 145*n.*, To the canoe place. 6 miles. — (12) **1828** in Sullivan *Travels Jedediah Smith* (1934) 55, 2 of the 4 Canoe trappers came in . . . the river . . . had overflowed its banks so that there was no chance for trapping. — (13) **1638** *Springfield Rec.* I. 164 It shall be lawfull for any inhabitant to fell any Cannoe trees and work them for his owne use. **1640** *Ib.* 167 No man shall fall any Cannoe tree that shall be within the bounds of the Plantation. — (14) [**1649** *Pa. Archives* V. 2 Ser. 133 Timber is very abundant here (New Netherland) . . . two sorts of canoe wood, ash, birch, (etc.).] **1762** Clayton *Flora Virginica* 83 *Polyandria Polygynia. Liriodendrum.* . . . White-wood & Canoe-wood-tree nostratibus. **1916** Seton *Woodcraft Man.* 287 Tulip Tree, White-wood, Canoe Wood, or Yellow Poplar (*Liriodendron Tulipifera*) One of the noblest forest trees, ordinarily 100 feet, and sometimes 150 feet high. Noted for its spendid clean, straight column; readily known by leaf, 3 to 6 inches long, and its tulip-like flower.

(15) **1879** Bishop *4 Months in Sneak-Box* 21 He would need a canoe light enough to be easily carried upon the shoulders of one man, with tha aid of the canoeist's indispensable assistant—the canoe-yoke. [**1880** *Harper's Mag.* LXI. 401/1 With a yoke resting in braces on deck at a point nearly midships, the canoe may be carried with comparative ease.]

b. *To paddle one's (own) canoe,* see **paddle,** *v.*

As the last term in **bark, bastard, big, birch, birch bark, cedar, Chinook, decked, dugout, flag, gold, leather, log, northern, oyster, paddling, pine, poplar, scoop shovel, skin, tobacco, trapping canoe.**

canoe kəˈnu, *v.*

1. *intr.* To paddle a canoe, to go in a canoe. Also *to canoe it.*

1732 B. Lynde *Diary* (1880) 30 March 24, I canoed to C. H. and bro't son's horse to go to Boston next day. **1841** Cooper *Deerslayer* xix, What say you, Sarpent, shall you or I canoe it? **1884** Mark Twain *H. Finn* Wks. XIII. (1923) xli. 385 Come along, let Sid foot it home, or canoe it. **1948** *Nat. Geog. Mag.* Aug. 213/1 'Did you ever canoe through a rock garden?' he asked.

2. *tr.* To transport or convey in a canoe.

1794 Asbury *Journal* II. 229, I got two men to canoe me across the river. **1850** *Knickerb.* XXXV. 21 We descended their tortuous slope to 'South Bay,' across which we were canoed.

canoeable kəˈnuəbl̩, *a.* Affording passage for canoes. *Obs.* — **1755** L. Evans *Anal. Map Colonies* 28 [The branch] is canoable about twenty miles farther. **1756** J. Maury in Winsor *Miss. Basin* 216 The navigable, or rather canoeable parts of the rivers which empty themselves into the sea.

canoeing kəˈnuɪŋ, *n.* Paddling or journeying in a canoe. Also attrib.

1752 P. Stevens in *Travels Amer. Col.* 306, [I] lodged at the canoeing place from said lake to the drowned land. **1886** *Leslie's Pop. Mo.* XXII. Dec. 642/1 Canoeing was introduced here over fifteen years since. **1897** *Outing* June 227/1 The occasional sailor . . . is apt to adopt that method of canoeing which affords him the most fun at the least expenditure of effort.

canoer kəˈnuɚ, *n.* A canoeist. *Rare.* — **1898** *Outing* June 269/1 Not so long ago the Adirondacks and New England were almost unthought of as fields for the summer camper, canoer and angler.

cañon, see **canyon.**

cañoned ˈkænjənd, *a. S.W.*

1. Inclosed or confined in a canyon.

1846 in W. H. Emory *Notes Mil. Reconnoissance* (1848) 443 We reached the 'Ocate'; as it is a [*sic*] cañoned, that is, is enclosed with high rocky walls, we were forced to go two miles up stream in order to reach the crossing. **1861** Newberry *Geol. Rep.* 103 None of the area traversed by the Santa Fe road at all deserves the name of desert, or is comparable in dryness and sterility with the cañoned country west of the mountains.

2. Cut by canyons.

1848 Bryant *California* 342 On the southern side the shore is hilly, and *cañoned* in some places. **1886** J. S. Diller in *8th Ann. Rep. Geol.*

Survey I. 426 The long, gentle slope . . . is . . . deeply cañoned by numerous streams.

cant kænt, *n.* [Bense regards this as f. LG. *kanthout*, Du. *canthout*, in sense here shown.] A log slabbed on one or more sides. — **1877** *Lumberman's Gaz.* 24 May, A cant or square-edged timber. **1879** *Ib.* 5 Nov., The cheapest and most effective means yet devised for holding the cant in place.

***cantab,** *n.* Short for next. *Rare.* — **1834** *Knickerb.* III. 301 Nick was made a cantab at Harvard.

***Cantabrigian,** *n.* A person living in Cambridge, Mass., or attending Harvard University. Also as adj. — **1887** *Harper's Mag.* March 589/1 Mrs. Saintsbury was Boston-born, . . . and was a Cantabrigian by marriage. **1893** W. K. Post *Harvard Stories* 26 The New Haven men struggled to the Cantabrigian twenty-yard line.

cantaque ˌkɑnˈtɑk, *n.* Also **cantac.** (See quot. 1931.) — **1806** in *Ann. 9th Cong.* 2 Sess. 1107 *n.*, The cantac, occasionally used by the hunters [of the Black River region, La.] for food, . . . has a bulbous root, ten times the size of a man's fist. **1931** Read *La.-French* 84 Cantaque, *m.* Smilax—*Smilax laurifolia* L., or perhaps *Smilax Bona-nox* L.; its large tuber served as food for the Indians and early settlers. These tubers were reduced to powder and mixed with cornmeal or flour. *Cantaque* is still known to some of the older French natives of Southwest Louisiana. This word is derived from Choctaw *kantak*, smilax.' Compare Choctaw *kantak pâska* 'brier-root (smilax) bread.'

cantico ˈkæntəko, *n.* [f. *gintkaan*, to dance, in Delaware dial. of Algonquian.] A dance or dancing party, a social gathering or jollification.

"The word, spelled also cantica, canticoy, kantico, kanticoy, kintacoy, kintecaw, kintecoy, kintekaye, kinticka, was in great use among the Dutch and English colonists in the region between New York and Virginia from the latter part of the 17th to the 19th century, nor is it yet entirely extinct in American English" (Hodge).

1670 D. Denton *Descr. N.Y.* (1902) 50 At their Cantica's or dancing Matches, . . . all persons that come are freely entertain'd, it being a Festival time. **1683** Penn *Works* (1782) IV. 309 Their worship consists of two parts, sacrifice and cantico. *Ib.*, The other part is their cantico, performed by round dances, sometimes words, sometimes songs, then shouts. **1701** Wolley *Journal N.Y.* (1860) 37 Their Kin-tau Kauns, or time of sacrificing is at the beginning of winter. **1866** Whittier *Writings* V. 144 [An Indian girl] told us that they did still hold their Kentikaw, or Dance for the Dead.

cantico ˈkæntəko, *v.* Also **kenticoy.** [See **cantico,** *n.*] *intr.* To hold a cantico. *Obs.* — **1663** in *N.Y. State Hist. Assoc. Proc.* VI. (1906) 138 The Indians thereabout on the river side [made] a great uproar every night, firing guns and Kintecaying, so that the woods rang again. **1867** in *L.I. Hist. Soc. Mem.* I. 275 These Indians had *canticoyed* (*gekintekayt*) there to-day, that is, conjured the devil, and liberated a woman among them, who was possessed by him, as they said.

cantina kænˈtinə, *n. S.W.* [Sp. in sense **1**; Amer. Sp. in sense **2.**]

1. (See quots.)

1844 Gregg *Commerce of Prairies* II. 99 A pack-mule to carry his *cantinas* (a pair of large wallets or leathern boxes). **1913** G. D. Bradley *Story of Pony Express* 58–9 The *mochila* had four pockets called *cantinas* in each of its corners—one in front and one behind each of the rider's legs. These *cantinas* held the mail.

2. (See quot. *c*1893.)

*c***1893** *D. N.* I. 245 *Cantina*, bar-room. Of frequent use [in Texas]. Often found on signs of Mexican bar-rooms. **1923** W. Smith *Little Tigress* 153 (Bentley), In a few steps they were at the cantina called the Spring of the Golden Dreams. **1946** *Desert* Jan. 5/2 It was a village of adobe huts, cantinas and dirty streets.

***canton,** *n.*

1. A nation or tribe of Indians. *Obs.*

1688 *Pa. Archives* I. 104 The late attempt . . . made by the French upon the five Nations or Cantons of Indians. **1820** *Amer. Antiq. Soc. Coll.* 64 We desired them to give notice to the five cantons of their nation.

2. A division or unit of a society.

1885 *Revised Odd-Fellowship* (1891) 282 The name of the Degree is changed to 'Patriarchs Militant,' and the name of Canton substituted for Uniform Camp, as a unit of organization. **1906** *Springfield Republican* 7 Feb. 10 Lieut-Col. E. E. Gilson of Canton Athol has been elected colonel of the 5th regiment of Odd Fellows, department of Massachusetts. This regiment includes a number of cantons in the middle and western part of the state.

cantsloper ˈkæntˌslopɚ, *n.* [See note.] An overcoat or greatcoat. *Obs.*

From now obs. Du. *schansloper*. East Anglian *consloper*, a greatcoat (see *EDD*) is app. f. the same source. May, the only real authority for the use of **cantsloper,** mentions having met some Dutch at Pittsburgh.

1788 J. May *Jrnl. & Lett.* (1873) 54 At 11 A.M. paid the visit to our Governor, wrapped in my cantsloper. **1876** *N.E. Hist. & Geneal. Reg.* Jan. 44 'Cantsloper' . . . is found again in [the Journal] . . . of '89 and also in a copy of the Journal made by the original writer's oldest daughter, Abby; but it is spelled . . . '*Kentsloper, khansloper.*' The suggestion is ventured that it was a slopper, or outside garment, for rough and wet weather, named, possibly, after the county of Kent in England . . . or . . . after the khan.

Cantum ˈkæntəm, *n.* [f. **cant, n.* or *v.*] (See quot.) *Rare.* — **1781** S. Peters *Hist. Conn.* 280 Some travellers have called the fanatical sects of Connecticut . . . Cumguntums, Cantums, &c. because they groan and sing with a melancholy voice their prayers, sermons, and hymns.

Canuck kəˈnʌk, *n.* Also **Kanu(c)k.** [Origin obscure. In B. '77, p. 778, said to be a corruption of *Connaught*, a nickname given by the French Canadians to the Irish.]

1. A Canadian, esp. one of French extraction.

1835 H. C. Todd *Notes* 92 Jonathan distinguishes a Dutch or French Canadian, by the term *Kanuk.* **1840** *Boston Transcript* 7 Feb. 2/1 The French-Canadian—or *Conuck*, as Her Majesty's provincial subjects of English and American extraction sometimes call him—can never, by any means be induced to lay 'aside the adominable practice' [of smoking and chewing in church]. **1884** *Harper's Mag.* June LXIX. 125 The crews were carefully chosen; a 'Kentuck,' or Kentuckian, was considered the best man at a pole, and a 'Kanuck,' or French Canadian, at the oar or the 'cordelle,' the rope used to haul a boat up-stream. **1947** DeVoto *Across Wide Missouri* 197 They chattered . . . and mingled with the halfbreeds of all tribes and their dear friends the Yankees, Canucks, Mexicans, and Kanakas.

Hence, *jocular*, **Canuckia,** Canada. *Rare.*

1889 *Outing* Mar. 505 (*heading*), Snowshoeing in Canuckia.

b. The language of the "Canucks."

1904 Day *Kin o' Ktaadn* 145 'Roule, roulant, ma boule roulant,' It's all Canuck but a good old song. [**1947** Paul *Linden* 54 His Canuck brogue, in contrast with the Irish inflections of Hal Kingsland and Ginger, . . . gave the Massasoit a mildly cosmopolitan atmosphere.]

2. A Canadian horse. Also attrib. or as adj.

1860 Holland *Miss Gilbert's Career* ii. 29, I'll hang on the tail of it and try legs with that little Kanuck of his. **1862** *Cong. Globe* 29 April 1867/3 They went . . . from St. Louis to Canada to buy the little Canuck ponies at $130 apiece. **1888** C. D. Ferguson *Exp. Forty-niner* ii. 23, I have often since thought it would be a good way to advertise horses . . . for certainly no frontier town ever saw a grander sight than those four Canucks.

canutillo ˌkɑnuˈtiljo, *n. W.* and *S.W.* [Sp. *cañatilla*, "little reed" in the Amer. Sp. sense shown here.] Any one of various plants of the genus *Ephedra*.

1912 Lumholtz *New Trails* 247 The only wood available consisted in old stumps of the curious canutillo. **1913** Wooton *Trees & Shrubs N.M.* 24 Canatillo . . . grow[s] on the sandy mesas and to some extent on the foothills of the drier mountains. **1931** Dayton *Western Browse Plants* 12 All the species are known also as Mormon-tea, canatillo, Brigham tea, teamsters' tea, shrubby horsetail, and by other local names. **1934** *N.M. Agric. Exp. Sta. Press Bul. 714* 1 It has many common names, such as canatillo and Mormon tea.

***canvas,** *n.* In combs.: (1) **canvasback,** see as a main entry; (2) **backed,** (*a*) denoting a canvasback duck, (*b*) of a wagon, having a canvas cover or top, *rare;* (3) **duck,** a canvasback duck; (4) **ham,** (see quot. 1944 and cf. **canvassed ham**), also attrib. and transf.; (5) **house,** a house or abode made largely of canvas; (6) **lodge,** a lodge or dwelling place chiefly of canvas; (7) **mail,** mail conveyed in strong canvas bags; (8) **man,** one who works at putting up and taking down a circus tent; (9) **moccasin,** a moccasin of canvas; (10) **top,** a wagon having a canvas top or cover.

(2) (*a*) **1841** H. Playfair *Papers* I. 289 The roasted fowls, and canvass-backed ducks, were all admirable. **1870** *Amer. Naturalist* III. 639 Canvas-backed Duck . . . is much less common in New England than several authors represent. (*b*) **1856** N. H. Parker *Iowa As It Is* 56 Our ferry is busy all hours in passing over the large canvas-backed wagons, densely populated with becoming Iowaians. — (3) **1814** Paulding *Sc. Fiddle* v. 102 Twelve canvas ducks, at morning play, By that discharge all found their grave. — (4) **1831** *Louisville Pub. Adv.* 12 Nov., There is a party in Arkansas ycleped the '*Canvas Ham Party.*' [**1869** Mark Twain *Innocents Abroad* xxxvii. 394 A canvas-covered ham.] **1944** (H. Swift in letter to the editor) Canvas hams . . . were prepared largely for export and southern domestic shipment, by covering the hams with a cloth and dipping them into what was known as 'whitewash,' which consisted of a mixture of flour, glue, water, etc. . . . Improvement in merchandising eliminated canvas hams some twenty or thirty years ago.

(5) **1850** in *Calif. Hist. Soc. Quart.* VIII. 25 The Alcadas office is held in [a] Canvas house about 15 feet by 12; this [Eliza City] is cer-

tainly a rum place, but a good situation. **1877** Wm. Wright *Big Bonanza* 24 As early as 1851, there were erected a few temporary structures, principally canvas houses. — **(6) 1885** *Rep. Indian Affairs* 33 A large portion of them is still living in canvas lodges instead of permanent habitations. — **(7) 1894** Searight *Old Pike* 168 There was a 'Lock mail' in leather pouches, and a 'Canvass mail,' the latter very frequently called 'the second mail,' carried in alternate months by the respective lines. — **(8) 1886** in M. R. Warner *P. T. Barnum* (1923) 356 Subscriptions amounting to $125 raised by canvasmen for a youth who was injured in the Youngstown 'adventure.' **1948** *Minneapolis Morning Tribune* 28 Sep. 6/6 And who is this head canvas man? He's an artist, a prima donna, a technician, a craftsman, a weather man—and a boss. — **(9) 1856** Kane *Arct. Expl.* II. xvi. 167 Canvas moccasins . . . for every one of the party. — **(10) 1901** S. E. White *Westerners* xix. 174 Molly was by now . . . used to the narrow confines of her canvass-top.

* **canvasback,** *n.*

1. A wild duck or species of duck, *Nyroca valisineria,* so called from the color of the back. In full **canvasback duck.** Cf. **Washington canvasback.**

1782 Jefferson *Virginia* vi. 77 Besides these [birds], we have The . . . Widgeon, Sheldrach, or Canvas back. **1791** Maclay *Deb. Senate* 282 Canvass back ducks, ham, and chickens, . . . all amazingly fine, were his constant themes. **1835** in M. B. Smith *Forty Yrs. Washington Soc.* (1906) 359 After the soup, Ma'am, boil'd fish, and after the Fish, canvas-backs, the Bouilli to be removed. **1944** Footner *Rivers of East. Shore* 155 The most highly prized is of course the canvasback; the most plentiful the black duck, no mean substitute.

b. canvasback grass, = **tape grass.**

1839 in Audubon *Ornith. Biog.* V. 137 The food they are most partial to, is the canvass-back grass (*Valisneria Americana*), . . . and shell-fish.

2. A sailing vessel as contrasted with a steamship. *Colloq.*

1930 Cutler *Greyhounds* 137 A few barnacled old captains stuck to their guns, but on the whole the year started badly for the 'canvas backs.' **1938** Albion *Square-Riggers* 256 They lured away from the sailing liners most of the transportation of passengers, of specie, and of some of the fine freight, but enough heavy freight was left to keep the 'canvasbacks' busy right down to the Civil War.

* **canvass,** *n.*

1. An official scrutiny of the votes cast in an election.

1828 Webster *s.v.,* A canvass of votes. **1839** *Maysville* (Ky.) *Eagle* 11 Dec. 2/5 We publish in our paper of to-day the official canvass, by the canvassers, of the votes for Senators in the several districts. **1888** Bryce *Amer. Commonw.* II. App. 682 If all the returns have not been received, the canvass must be postponed. **1948** *Ill. Munic. Rev.* May 73/2 A newly elected alderman to fill a vacancy may take office immedately upon the canvass of the returns.

2. Personal solicitation of a district for custom or sale.

1871 *Colo. Gazeteer* 304 To agents who will make a thorough canvass, we will allow a liberal commission upon copies sold. **1887** *Courier-Journal* 8 May 10/6 Mr. A. H. Perry . . . is now making a canvass of the city, and the demand for this remarkable book will doubtless be very great.

b. A survey to determine the sentiment for or against a candidate or a cause.

1898 *K. C. Star* 18 Dec. 4/2 The efforts of the advocates of an extra session of the Fifty-sixth Congress . . . have not been fruitful. The canvass of the House . . . has been far from satisfactory. **1919** *Harvey's Wkly.* 22 Nov. 11/2 Ohio, the home of . . . the W.C.T.U., after a particularly searching canvass of the people, has repudiated its Legislative ratification of the Prohibition Amendment.

* **canvass,** *v.*

1. *tr.* To scrutinize (an election) closely, to count or recount (votes).

1791 *Mass. Mag.* Sep 590/1 General Jackson is canvassing the election of General Wayne. **1872** *Ill. Revised Statutes* (1883) 510 The county clerk or his deputy . . . shall proceed to open, canvass and publish the return from each precinct or election district. **1947** *Chi. D. News* 17 Jan. 14/2 When the popular votes for governor are canvassed by the legislature only a candidate with a majority of all the votes shall be qualified.

2. To test or determine prevailing sentiment.

1859 Stowe *Minister's Wooing* xiv. 182 D—— must canvass the Senate thoroughly.

3. To solicit (a district) for custom or sale. Also **canvassing,** *n.*

1876 *Mt. Messenger* (Downieville, Calif.) 10 June 3/1 Mr. Reed, of San Juan, is now canvassing the county for 'Bancroft's Native Races' and other books. **1887** *Courier-Journal* 22 Jan. 4/5 After obtaining the proper license, [he could] proceed with his canvassing. **1892** *Irrigation Age* 1 May 30/1 The writer canvassed the city of Cheyenne for subscribers to *The Age.*

b. To push or promote the sale of a book.

1907 Mark Twain *Christian Science* II. 253 In the profane subscription trade, it costs the publisher heavily to canvass a three-dollar book. **1916** Eastman *From Deep Woods,* 69 I canvassed for a book, I think it was the 'Knights of Labor,' published in Boston.

canvassed (ham). (See quot. 1830, and cf. **canvas ham.**) *Obs.* — **1830** *Castigator* (Georgetown, Ohio) 6 July 1/5 These *canvassed* delicacies were readily manufactured by covering the more indifferent hams, as they were brought from the smoke house, with coarse *tow* cloth, and then applying a white-wash brush, to cover them with a coat of lime. Such, a 'canvassed ham' is understood to be. **1882** *Black Hills Pioneer* (Deadwood, Dakota Terr.) 1 Jan. 16/5 Hams, sugar cured, canvassed.

* **canvasser,** *n.* One who officially examines the return of votes at an election, often *State Board of Canvassers.* Cf. **county canvasser.**

1792 in Jay *Correspondence* III. 428 This reference was understood by us all as intended to procure a cloak for the canvassers to cover their villainy in rejecting the votes of Otsego. **1877** *Colo. General Laws* 377 The state board of canvassers shall meet at the office of the secretary of state. **1904** *Newark Ev. News* 25 Nov. 5 Governor Murphy has appointed . . . the State Board of Canvassers . . . The board will . . . officially determine the number of votes which were cast for the different candidates.

canvassing board. A board which certifies the results of an election. — **1875** *Chi. Tribune* 11 Nov. 5/3 The Canvassing Board continued their operations yesterday afternoon in the County Building. **1906** *Indian Laws & Tr.* III. 187 An election commissioner . . . shall distribute all ballots and election supplies, . . . and deliver the same to the canvassing board herein named.

* **cany, caney,** *a.* Abounding with canes, usu. in place-names.

1797 Morse *Amer. Gazetteer, s.v.,* Cany Fork, in the state of Tennessee, is a short navigable river. **1831** M. A. Holley *Texas* (1833) vi. 57 Cane-break creek or Caney, as it is usually called, winds its way through this tract. **1859** Bartlett 66 *Caney Fork* or *Branch* is a frequent name for streams in Kentucky and Tennessee, undoubtedly from canes having grown there formerly.

canyon ˈkænjən, *n.* Also †**cañon, kanyon, kenyan,** etc. *S.W.* [Sp. *cañón* in same sense.]

1. A deep gorge, ravine, or valley, having steep sides. Cf. **dalle.**

1834 Pike *Sketches* 20 Between these three points two cañons ran up into the bosom of the ridge. **a1842** O. Russel *Journal* (1921) xv. 65 This stream ran through a tremendous mountain in a deep, narrow canyon of rocks. **1946** *Nat. Geog. Mag.* Jan. 33/2 Its slopes and high pine-studded canyons form a delightful resort from summer heat and a snow playground in winter.

transf. and *attrib.* **1913** Eaton *Barn Doors & Byways* 99 The wonder of these buildings soon wears off for those who fly up and down in their elevators or dash about in the cañon slits between them. **1914** Brininstool *Trail Dust* 77, I want to git out where the breezes Ain't smothered by canyons of brick. **1947** *L. A. Times* 16 Feb. II. 1/3 Downtown Los Angeles' haze-filled canyons have nothing on the little town of Dominguez, huddled in the lee of four gasoline refineries and a huge chemical plant, when it comes to smog.

2. In combs.: (1) **canyon bed,** the bed or lowest part of a canyon; (2) **finch,** (see quot.); (3) **flat,** a region of flat or level land in or near a canyon; (4) **gap,** a water gap suggestive of a canyon; (5) **live oak,** an evergreen oak, *Quercus chrysolepis,* found in California above the 1,000 foot contour and extending into Oregon, northwest Arizona, and Mexico; (6) **spring,** (see quot.); (7) **squirrel,** the bushy-tailed ground squirrel, *Otospermophilus grammurus,* found in the Rockies from central Colorado to Mexico; (8) **wall,** the side of a canyon; (9) **wren,** a wren, *Catherpes mexicanus,* found in the southwestern U.S.

(1) 1872 Mark Twain *Roughing It* xii. 101 The simple rivulet . . . plodding its patient way down the mountainsides, and canyon-beds. **1907** White *Ariz. Nights* 18 Our way led first through a canon-bed filled with rounded boulders and rocks, slippery and unstable. Big cottonwoods and oaks grew so thick as partially to conceal the cliffs on either side of us. — **(2) 1881** *Amer. Naturalist* XV. 212 There are two other species of the same genus . . . which I afterwards found breeding in Arizona, the Abert's finch (*Pipilo aberti*) and the canon finch (*Pipilo mesoleucus*). — **(3) 1869** Muir *First Summer in Sierra* (1911) 38 Bruin's favorite feeding-grounds are groves of the California oak in park-like cañon flats. — **(4) 1845** Frémont *Exped.* 147 A canon gap in the mountains.

(5) 1908 Sudworth *Forest Trees Pac. Slope* 295 Canyon live oak is an evergreen oak, with the soft, scaly trunk bark of a white oak. **1946** R. Peattie *Pac. Coast Ranges* 55 Even the noble canyon live oak and the aristocratic California laurel, demean themselves, as it were, with stunted replicas in the chaparral. — **(6) 1902** *Science* n.s. XV. 86/1 From beneath the lava stream or from a porous layer, numerous powerful springs issue along the side of the canyon below Shoshone Falls. These may be called 'canyon springs,' a new term introduced in the classification of springs. — **(7) 1907** Mearns *Mammals of Mex. Boundary* 317 This species, in Arizona designated as the 'rock-squirrel' or 'canyon-squirrel,' is both widely known and held in general disfavor. — **(8) 1873** Muir *John of Mts.* (1938) 78 Oftentimes in climbing canyon walls I come to polished slopes that seem too steep to venture on. — **(9) 1878** Coues *Birds of Colo. Valley* 165 Such rifts of solid rock alone are entirely to the liking of the Cañon Wren. **1945** McAtee *John and Joe* 12, I can hardly neglect to comment on his fantasy about the white breast of the canyon wren.

As the last term in **box, Grand, pocket, redwood, side canyon.**

canyon 'kænjən, *v. S.W. intr.* Of a stream: To enter or flow into or through a canyon.

1851 Wm. Kelly *Across Rocky Mts.* 134 Five or six miles beyond our camp it [Sweetwater River] canons through a perpendicular fissure, called Devil's Gate, where it rushes with great noise and velocity through its pent-up channel. **1868** Bowles *Colorado* (1869) 85 Nearly all the rivers of Colorado and Utah run for brief distances, from one to twenty-five miles, through these gorges of rock; or they 'canyon,' as, by making a verb of the Spanish noun, the people of the country describe the streams as performing the feat of such rock passages. **1911** Chase *Yosemite Trails* 208 Above it 'cañons' to the long gorge that is known as the Grand Cañon of the Tuolumne.

Hence **canyoned,** *a.*, cut or formed into canyons.

1846 Bryant *California* (1848) 342 On the southern side the shore is hilly, and *cañoned* in some places. **1878** I. L. Bird *Rocky Mts.* 195 Below them lay broken ravines of fantastic rocks, cleft and canyoned by the river. **1944** *Christian Sci. Monitor* 26 Dec., But the great inland rivers of America, as wide as the Missouri and as canyoned as the Colorado, called for a more ample nomenclature.

b. *canyon up,* (see quot.).

1893 Roosevelt *Wilderness Hunter* 303, I was following a stream which at last 'canyoned up,' that is, sank to the bottom of a canyon-like ravine impassible for a horse.

caouane kə'wan, *n.* [F. in same sense.] (See quots.) — **1884** Goode *Fisheries* 153 The southern species, *Macrochelys lacertina,* known as the 'Alligator Turtle,' or 'Loggerhead,' is found in western Georgia, and in all the States bordering on the Gulf, from Florida to Texas. It also occurs in Missouri, where it is said to receive the name 'Caouane.' **1931** Read *La.-French* 136 The name *caouane* is applied to the fresh-water alligator snapping turtle (*Macrochelys lacertina* Schweigger), which ranges from western Texas to western Florida and as far north as Missouri.

∗**cap,** *n.*[1]

1. *Mining.* (See quots.)

1871 *Colo. Gazeteer* 160 These veins . . . pinch up and widen out, and, sometimes, are nearly or completely closed by the 'cap,' and lost by a fault. **1878** Fossett *Colorado* 177 To use common phrases, they 'widen out' at one point or 'pinch up' at another—discover a 'pocket, ore chimney or bonanza,' or 'go into cap.' **1884** Knight *Dict. Mech.* Supp. *s.v.*, A vein is 'in the cap' when it is much contracted. **1931** Willison *Here They Dug Gold* 122 Most of the hard-rock mines are in cap.

2. In combs.: (1) **cap and ball,** denoting a percussion cap firearm shooting a single ball; (2) **berry,** = **salmon berry,** *rare;* (3) **corn,** a now obsolete variety of corn; (4) **gun,** a toy gun using paper percussion caps; (5) **pistol,** a toy pistol for exploding paper percussion caps; (6) **rock,** *W.* in mining, barren vein matter supposed to overlie ore, also, a relatively resistant rock stratum which forms the summits of many buttes and mesas, also attrib.; (7) **shooter,** (see quot.); (8) **wire,** ?wire for making cap frames, *obs.*

(1) 1924 in Henry *Conquer. Plains* 280 It must be remembered that in those days the old cap and ball pistol was the weapon in use, as there were no metallic cartridges used until about 1872, and possibly it was later than that. **1947** *True* Nov. 30/1 The original Colt cap-and-ball revolver was patented in 1836. — **(2) 1917** Eaton *Green Trails* 79 The cap-berry was perhaps the most conspicuous, a large shrub with numerous blossoms not unlike small white roses in appearance. — **(3) 1850** *N. Eng. Farmer* II. 175 The Canada corn, and the small cap corn, will bear near planting. — **(4) 1931** *K.C. Star* 22 July, They had bought two ice cream cones, a cap gun, two rolls of caps, and each had half a bottle of pop.

(5) 1920 I. Ostrander *How Many Cards?* 8, I found a gat on him that's like a toy cap pistol compared to that gun lying there. **1947** *Sat. Ev. Post* 13 Sep. 174/1 He rose . . . as if he were a boy who had tried to hold up a bank with a cap pistol. — **(6) 1867** Hollister *Mines of Colo.* 64 The quartz and cap or wall-rock together paid them tolerably well for a few weeks. *Ib.* 65 The cap was one hundred and thirty feet deep in one end of the mine. **1918** Visher *So. Dakota* 39 The steep-sided character of the buttes, which in no little degree is responsible for their conspicuousness, is the result of the cap rock, infrequent rains, and wind work. **1948** *Popular Western* June 24/2 He let the two riders increase their lead, to vanish in a fold of the hills below the caprock formation which had given the town its name. — **(7) 1917** *D.N.* IV. 409 cap-shooter, n. A gun with percussion lock.—cap-shooting, adj. 'Sure as a cap-shootin' gun. — **(8) 1711** *Springfield Rec.* II. 41 A peice of smal cap wire, 1 shilling. **1775** in E. Singleton *Social N.Y.* 247 Henry Wilmot, in Hanover Square, sells . . . cloak trimmings, skeleton and cap wires. **1784** *Mass. Centinel* 26 June 3/3 For Sale, a Variety of Goods, by wholesale, amongst which are . . . Cap Wire, Pile Beavers, Washing Buff, Herring Bone, [etc.].

b. In colloq. phrases: (1) *To burst a cap,* (see quot.), *obs.;* (2) *to pop a cap,* to fire.

(1) 1846 *Spirit of Times* 18 April 91/2 You often hear this or that acquaintance speak of the misfortune of having '*bursted a cap*' at a fine buck or other valuable game, meaning thereby, that the percussion cap on their gun exploded without igniting the powder in the barrel. — **(2) 1906** Ridley *Battles* 454 Govan's men hallooed out: 'Lie down, Mr. Bate, Mr. Govan is gwine to pop a cap.'

As the last term in **back, bed, bishop's, black, blanket, bottle, breakfast, chimney, coonskin, eye, fox skin, frosh, hay, Indian, Jo Johnson, legal, McClellan, Methodist, night, red, Scotch, Shaker, thunder, Turk's, white cap.**

Cap kæp, *n.*[2] Short for "Captain." *Colloq.*

1840 *Spirit of Times* 17 Oct. 391/3 The old cap. wanted to kill one o' them varmints. **1886** Harte *Snow-bound* 90, I reckoned I had the right to a little fun on my own account, cap. **1926** Cooper *Oklahoma* 132 'Cap' Cooper, the first engineer . . . held the proud position at the throttle.

∗**cap,** *v.* **1.** *tr.* To free (strawberries) of bractlets. **2.** *To cap the vortex,* variant of "to cap the climax." *Rare.* — **(1) 1906** H. D. Pittman *Belle of Blue Grass C.* ix. 129 Close beside her sat a great basket of fresh strawberries which must be capped before she could set out for church. — **(2) 1901** O. Henry *Heart of West* 52 To-day he caps the vortex.

∗**cape,** *n.*

1. A piece of timberland projecting into a prairie. *Obs.*

1831 Peck *Guide for Emig'ts* II. 110 The traveller is surrounded by timber; his eye never loses sight of the deep green outlines, throwing out its capes and headlands. **1836** J. Hall *Statistics of West* vi. 83 The forest has pushed long capes or points into the prairie.

2. In combs.: (1) **Cape Ann,** see as a main entry; (2) **catboat,** a type of catboat developed at Cape Cod for use as a fishing and pleasure boat; (3) **Cod,** see as a main entry; (4) **Codder,** a native of Cape Cod, Mass.; (5) **cape fever,** (see quot.) *obs.;* (6) **Cape fishing,** fishing in the Cape Cod region, *obs.;* (7) **Cape Floridan,** one living in the region of the Florida capes, *rare;* (8) **grape,** a variety of wine grape, *obs.;* (9) **Cape Horner,** a vessel on a voyage around Cape Horn; (10) **May,** see as a main entry; (11) **race(r),** the red-throated loon, *Gavia stellata,* often observed near Cape Race, Newfoundland; (12) **Cape wheat,** a variety of wheat, *obs.*

(2) 1935 Lincoln *Cape Cod Yesterdays* ix, What has become of the old Cape catboats? — **(4) 1825** J. Neal *Bro. Jonathan* III. 281 Tongues an' sounds! that's a Cape Cod-er, you know. **1947** Coffin *Yankee Coast* 320, I say this at peril of my life, for many of my friends are Cape Codders.

(5) 1856 Olmsted *Slave States* 220 So among sailors and soldiers, when men suddenly find themselves ill and unable to do their duty in times of peculiar danger, or when unusual labor is required, they are humorously said to be suffering under an attack of the powder fever, [or] the cape-fever. — **(6) 1673** *Plymouth Laws* 167 One halfe of the excise due to the Country on the Mackerell to be caught att the Cape bee . . . abated; . . . except any shall come in before the next Court and rent the said privilidge of Cape fishing. **1689** *Ib.* 216 Ordered . . . that the magistrates of the County of Barnstable or any two of them be a Committee to dispose and manage the Cape fishing. — **(7) 1775** Adair *Indians* 152 Though they could never settle out of their garrisons in West-Florida . . . , yet the Cape-Floridans were only Spanish mercenaries, shedding blood for their maintenance. — **(8) 1826** Flint *Recoll.* 60 They . . . cultivated a blue grape which, I think, they called the 'cape grape.' **1856** Fergusson *America* 272 Those which are chiefly cultivated are . . . the Cape, now called the Schuylkill grape. — (9) **1840** DANA *Two Years* xxxv. 444 No merchant vessel looks better than an Indiaman, or a Cape Horn-er, after a long voyage. **1851** MELVILLE *Moby Dick* iii. 12 The picture represents a Cape-Horner in a great hurricane.

(11) **1835** AUDUBON *Ornith. Biog.* III. 24 In the neighbourhood of Boston, and along the Bay of Fundy, they are best known by the names of 'Scape-grace' and 'Cape-racer.' **1875** *Fur, Fin, & Feather* 119 The smaller species of loon I have heard variously called the spike-bill, the cape-race, [etc.]. **1917** *Birds of Amer.* I. 15. — (12) **1786** WASHINGTON *Diaries* III. 4 The Cape Wheat which (on the 30th of November) was cut. **1787** *Ib.* 210 The Cape wheat at Dogue run is forwarder than the common Wheat. **1855** BROWNE in *Trans. Amer. Inst. N.Y.* 590 Cape wheat, from the Cape of Good Hope . . . doubtless produces an excellent flour. It will probably do much better in the South than in the North, if sown in autumn.

* **Cape Ann.** [Name of a cape in n.e. Mass.] **1. Cape Ann turkey, = Cape Cod turkey. 2.** *in the Cape Ann stage,* (see quot.). *Obs.*

(1) **1844** *Knickerb.* XXIV. 470, I had left a real gobbler at home, to come here and dine on a 'Cape-Ann turkey'! Of all articles tolerated . . . I most abominate boiled salt fish. **1947** BEROLZHEIMER *Regional Cookbook* 72 Salt Codfish (Cape Ann Turkey). — (2) *a***1856** in HALL *College Words* (ed. 2) 460–1 Various words and phrases which have been in use . . . to signify some stage of inebriation: Over the bay, . . . a passenger in the Cape Ann stage, [etc.].

cape bonnet. A form of poke bonnet having an ample cape-like border on the bottom.

Cape bonnet

[**1799** WELD *Travels* 89 There is a kind of bonnet very commonly worn [in Va.], which, in particular, disfigures them amazingly; it is made with a caul, fitting close on the back part of the head, and a front stiffened with small pieces of cane, which projects nearly two feet from the head in a horizontal direction.] **1836** C. GILMAN *Recoll.* (1838) xix. 131, I perceived . . . a young girl . . . dressed in homespun, with a *cracker*, or cape bonnet of the same material. **1896** POOL *In Buncombe County* 21 A woman in a very deep cape bonnet, a bonnet which makes a face look as if it were at the far end of a cavern,—pushed her way up.

* **Cape Cod.** [Name of a peninsula in s.e. Mass.] Used attrib., chiefly colloq. and humorous, as **Cape Cod chowder, clergyman, cottage, measure, protection, style, trousers, turkey** (see quots.).

1886 POORE *Reminisc.* I. 384 She could make a regal Cape Cod chowder. **1935** LINCOLN *Cape Cod Yesterdays* 46 If you expect a quahaug soup with tomatoes in it to taste like a Cape Cod clam chowder, you will be even more [disappointed]. — **1846** LOWELL *Biglow P.* 1 Ser. ii. 30 They might have been permitted . . . to take some few sculpins, . . . known in the rude dialect of our mariners as Cape Cod Clergymen. — **1923** W. NUTTING *Massachusetts* 22 The Cape Cod cottage has achieved the distinction of receiving this specific name. . . . This cottage is . . . uniformly found at the Cape. **1945** BAKER *Party Line* 266 New Cape Cod cottages and a few modernistic bungalows, however, filled the vacant lots where once Kenneth and I stomached through deep spring grass. — **1881** MCLEAN *Cape Cod Folks* i, We call it four miles, more or less. That's Cape Cod measure—means most anythin' lineal measure. — **1844** *Lexington Observer* 27 Nov. 1/3 A raw boned yankee made his appearance with a knife and a pine stick in one hand, and a Cape Cod protection, alias a cake of gingerbread in the other. — **1945** *Grant Co.* (Wis.) *News* 12 Apr. 5/1 The new home is Cape Cod style. — **1804** W. AUSTIN *Lett. from London* 68 After thinking a moment what would be least likely in New England to find its way to Rag Fair, I asked for a pair of *Cape Cod trowsers.* — **1865** C. NORDHOFF *Lett.* 1 May (F. & H.), A salted cod fish is known in American ships as a Cape Cod turkey. **1901** GREENOUGH & KITTREDGE *Words & Their Ways* 331 'Welsh rabbit' is merely a joke, like 'Cape Cod turkey' for codfish. **1946** HIBBEN *Cookery* 71 'Cape Cod Turkey' (Stuffed Codfish).

***capelin,** *n.* (See quot. 1884). — **1884** GOODE *Nat. Hist. Aquatic Animals* 456 The Green Smelt of the Connecticut coast *Menidia notata,* [is] also called . . . by the boys about Boston the 'Capelin.' [**1946** PEASE *Sequestered Vales* 93 Herring-like fishes called caplin [were] spread out in the dooryards to dry before being placed raw on the table as an appetizer.]

capellina ˌkɑpeˈljinə, *n. W.* [Sp. in same sense.] (See quots.) — **1874** KNIGHT 455 *Capellina,* the *bell* or cover of the pile of amalgam bricks in the Spanish process of separating the mercury from the metal. **1889** *Cent.* 803/1 capellina. . . . In the western mining districts of the United States, a vessel employed in separating the quicksilver from the amalgam.

* **Cape May.** [The most southerly point in N.J.]

1. An oyster from the Cape May region.

1876 *Harper's Wkly.* 15 Apr. 307/2 'Brigantines,' while of better flavor to those who prefer salt oysters, are invariably lean compared to their transplanted rivals, as are also the 'Cape Mays.'

2. In combs.: (1) **Cape May diamond,** (see quots.), *obs.;* (2) **goody,** the lafayette, *Leiostomus xanthurus;* (3) **warbler,** a handsome American warbler, *Dendroica tigrina.*

(1) **1846** *Dollar Newspaper* (Phila.) 12 Aug. 3/5 Occasionally a pure crystal of quartz, disfigured and despoiled of its natural beauty and proportions by the action of the waves, is found, and this is the famed Cape May diamond, so eagerly sought for, and so highly prized when found. **1856** *Spirit of Times* 1 Nov. 149/1 In Cape May diamonds or genuine pearls, I care not what you have on. **1866** W. REID *After the War* 81 Others [of the Negroes] . . . were dressed in broadcloth, with flashy scarfs and gaudy pins, containing paste, or Cape May diamonds. — (2) **1855** S. F. BAIRD in *9th Rep. Smithsonian Inst.* 329 The 'Cape May Goody' of the Jersey coast, so called from its great abundance at Cape Island, is very rarely taken in winter. **1935** *Old Salt* (Atlantic City) 9 Aug. 3/2 Years ago I used to catch a small pan fish known as the "Cape May goodie." Are they still around? . . . Yes. It is the spotfish. — (3) **1812** WILSON *Ornith.* VI. 99 [The] Cape-May Warbler, *Sylvia Maritima,* . . . was discovered in a maple swamp, in Cape May county. **1825** BONAPARTE *Ornith.* I. 33 The female Cape-May warbler may be very easily mistaken for an imperfect *Sylvia coronata.* **1939** LINCOLN *Migration* 88 The Cape May Warbler is an excellent example.

Caper ˈkepɚ, *n.* A resident of Cape Cod. *Colloq.* — **1907** LINCOLN *Old Home House* 121 Her opinion of the Cape and Capers, 'specially me, was decided.

caper juice. Whisky. *Slang. Rare.* — **1888** *Portland Transcript* 29 Feb. (F.), Say, fellers, let's take a leetle mo' uv the caper juice.

capias ˈkepɪəs, *v. tr.* To take into custody on a writ of capias. *Rare.* — **1868** *N.Y. Trib.* 17 July 2/4 It appeared that Bright was indebted . . . and it became desirable to get Bright into the state of Illinois to *capias* him. . . . As soon as he arrived in Chicago he was *capiased* and thrust into jail on the debt.

***capital,** *n.* As the last term in **bank, maple sugar, political, share capital.**

capitalistic ˌkæpətlˈɪstɪk, *a.* Of or pertaining to capitalists or capitalism.

1873 in COMMONS *Doc. Hist. Amer. Indust. Soc.* (1910) IX. 371 The growth of capitalistic association and monetary institution. **1889** D. A. WELLS *Recent Econ. Changes* 399 The natural and necessary growth of what has been termed the 'capitalistic system.' **1910** C. W. ELIOT *Future of Trades-Unionism* 3 The invention of the corporation with limited liability . . . was . . . the starting point of the tremendous expansion of capitalistic association.

* **capitalization,** *n.* Using capital letters in printing or writing.

1864 WEBSTER 194/2. **1913** SLATER *Freshman Rhetoric* 2 Strict obedience . . . to custom, in all matters of spelling, . . . capitalization, and other formal details. **1949** *Manual of Style* (Index).

* **capitalize,** *v.*

1. *tr.* To begin (a word) with a capital letter, to print in capitals. Also **capitalizing.**

1864 *Acct. College N.J.* 25 All these compositions . . . are critically examined with respect to the language, orthography, pointing, capitalizing, with other minutiae. **1809** W. CUNNINGHAM *Corr.* (1823) 165, I capitalized the prophetic parts of the letter, . . . and italicized the Latin. **1937** *Manual of Style* 29 Do not capitalize 'war' when used in the phrase 'the war,' without a distinguishing epithet.

2. To make capital out of, turn to account. Often *capitalize on.*

1869 *Kansas Hist. Coll.* (1900) VI. 164 Its only purpose [i.e., of opening the Cherokee Strip] seems to have been to capitalize this land in the hands of speculators. **1926** *Publishers' Weekly* 22 May 1701 The book-stores and the libraries can capitalize on that same interest. *Ibid.* 29 May 1795 The publishers . . . do not intend to capitalize the publicity. **1948** *Railroad Yardmaster* Jan.–Feb. 34/1 Capitalizing on this newly discovered secret, Church planted more grapes.

3. To incorporate on the basis of capital, to invest with capital.

1870 MEDBERY *Men Wall St.* 11 The variations of its [*sc.* Wall St.'s] share market affect the whole volume of capitalized indebtedness the country through. **1895** *Denver Times* 5 March 8/4 The I. X. L. Candy company . . . is capitalized, and has 100 shares of stock. **1948** *Chi. Tribune* 18 Aug. III. 5/5 The Canadian unit, Visking, Ltd., will be capitalized at 5,000 shares of $100 par value stock.

capitalizer ˈkæpətḷˌaɪzɚ, *n.* A capitalist, one who invests capital for increase. — **1880** *Atlantic Mo.* Dec. 848/2 The administrator of capital and labor is not a mere middleman; he is a capitalizer. **1882** W. B. WEEDEN *Soc. Law Labor* 28 Small farmers . . . are almost always capitalizers.

Capitalonian ˌkæpətəˈlonɪən, *n.* A resident of a capital, as Washington, D.C. Also as a title. — **1840** (*title*), *Capitalonian* (Harrisburg, Pa.). **1869** *New No. West* (Deer Lodge, Mont.) 17 Sep. 2/5 Ecstasy was spread over the faces of the Capitalonians like apple butter on the dinner of a country school boy.

capitan ˌkæpɪˈtæn, *n. S.W.* [See note.] A captain, chief, or leader.

An Amer. borrowing of the Sp. *capitán* in the sense here shown, but the spelling in the 1834 quot. suggests the corresponding French word, *capitaine*, which McDermott records as a "term or title often used for an Indian chief as recognized by the French authorities."

[**1604** GRIMSTON tr. *Natvrall Hist. Indies* 273 Maguey is a tree of wonders, whereof the Notaries or *Chapetons* (as the *Indians* call them) are wont to write wonders. **1685** JOUTEL *Journal* (1719) 118 They [Indians of Texas region] spoke some Words of broken *Spanish*, as *Capita*, instead of *Capitan*, a Captain.] **1834** LEONARD *Narrative* (1839) 64/2 These Indians appear quite different from those more convenient to the Spanish settlements, and call themselves Pagans, their chief Capetaine, and have names for several things nearly the same as we have. **1844** GREGG *Commerce of Prairies* I. 77 The 'capitanes,' or head men of the whites and Indians, shortly after met, and again smoking the calumet, agreed to be friends. **1919** J. S. CHASE *Calif. Desert Trails* 173 Arrived at Toro, I sought an interview with the *capitan*. **1947** *Westerners' Brand Book* 111 The Sheriff notified the Indian leaders that they must pay their taxes but the *capitanes* sent back word they would not pay.

* **capitol**, *n.*

1. "In some states, the State-house, or house in which the legislature holds its sessions; a government house" (W. '28).

See A. Matthews' article in *D.N.* II. 199–224, and cf. **state capitol, statehouse, summer capitol.**

1699 *Va. Assembly Acts* (1727) I. 205 An act directing the Building the Capitol and the City of Williamsburgh. **1772** WASHINGTON *Diaries* II. 57 Spent the Evening at the Burgesses' Ball in the Capitol. **1834** C. D. ARFVEDSON *United States* I. 318, I visited one day the Capitol, as it is called, or Statehouse occupied by the Legislature of the state. **1943** *Chi. D. News* 12 June 6/6 These suckers agreed to provide the State of Texas with a new capitol.

2. The building in which Congress meets at Washington.

1793 JEFFERSON *Writings* IX. 18 Dr. Thornton's plan of a capitol has . . . captivated the eyes and the judgments of all. **1845** LEWIS *Impressions* 71 The Capitol, so called from that of Rome, is the principal object of attraction in Washington. **1927** BENÉT *J. B.'s Body* 155 Muddy Washington, with its still-unfinished Capitol, [is] sprawling, badly-paved. **1947** *Newsweek* 8 Sep. 22/3 The capitol belongs to the public, not to architects and not to art groups.

3. In combs.: (1) **Capitol commission,** a commission for locating a state capitol; (2) **Hill,** the eminence in Washington, D.C., on which the Capitol is built; (3) **square,** a square occupied in part by a capitol.

(1) **1910** *Okla. Session Laws* 3 Legisl. 8 The Executive Mansion shall be located in the vicinity of the said capitol grounds on a site consisting of one-half block, the same to be selected by the Capitol Commission. — (2) **1804** *Fredericktown* (Md.) *Herald* 7 April 3/3 On Capitol Hill in the City of Washington. **1840** F. HALL *Letters* vi, Who knows but 'Capitol Hill' will, one day, become the crater of a physical, instead of a political volcano. **1946** *Nation* 10 Aug. 141/2 The Congressional Reorganization Bill . . . aims at increasing efficiency on Capitol Hill by decreasing the number of standing committees. — (3) **1835** *S. Lit. Messenger* I. 258 A superb monument to the memory of Washington on the capitol square.

Also *capitol building, grounds, landing, site, wall,* etc.

caporal ˌkæpəˈræl, *n. S.W.* [Sp. in Amer. Sp. sense shown here. An Amer. borrowing.] The boss or manager of a ranch.

*c***1892** *D. N.* I. 245 (Texas words), *Caporál:* overseer, man who directs the work, but does not pay the laborers. **1936** *Ariz. Univ. Gen. Bul. No. 3* 194 A subforeman, *caporal*, is employed to keep in direct touch with the needs of the different bands and is in immediate charge during the absence of the owner. **1941** FERGUSSON *Southwest* 177 Under him came a caporal to supervise three vaqueros, watch for disease, seek strayed or stolen sheep, and supervise the moving of the flocks to other pastures.

capote kəˈpot, *n.* Also **cappo, capot.** [F., an Amer. borrowing.] A long cloak, properly one having a hood. Also attrib.

1799 JAMES SMITH *Acc. Captivity* 10 They gave me a new ruffled shirt, . . . also a tinsel laced cappo. **1805** PIKE *Sources Miss.* (1810) 31 Found a small red capot hung upon a tree; this my interpreter informed me was a sacrifice by some Indian to the *bon Dieu*. **1847** in H. HOWE *Ohio Hist. Coll.* 131 On the day of the battle, St. Clair . . . wore a coarse cappo coat and a three-cornered hat. **1901** *Everybody's Mag.* Sep. 285/1 Always, the man in the *capote* travelled at the heel of Markovitch, watching. **1941** DORSEY *Master of Miss.* 31 There were . . . ordinary townsmen known as *habitants*, dressed much as the boatmen were, in a *capot* made of a Mackinaw blanket, invariably white, with *capuchon* attached.

* **capper,** *n.* A decoy or confederate for a gambler, gambling house, etc. *Slang.* See also **bottle, white capper.**

1853 *Alta California* (S.F.) 25 Apr. 1/7 Each shop has a glib-mouthed auctioneer and at least two cappers, puffers, or decoy-ducks. **1906** WOOLRIDGE *Grafters of Amer.* 238 Cappers are sent out to bring in the rural visitors. **1941** ASBURY *Gem of Prairie* 73 In 1860 . . . he became a roper and capper for a small faro bank.

* **captain,** *n.*

1. As a courtesy title. *Colloq.*

1746 *London Mag.* XV. 324 Wherever you travel in Maryland (as also in Virginia and Carolina) your Ears are constantly astonished at the number of Colonels, Majors, and Captains, that you hear mentioned. *c***1855** ROBERTSON *Few Months* 107 This reminds me, that in the South and West, nearly all tall men are called generals, stout men judges, and men of middling proportions, captains or colonels! **1881** MARSHALL *Through Amer.* (1882) 240 To be called 'boss,' 'captain,' 'judge' (pronounced jidge) or 'colonel' by the people you meet when you are travelling in the United States, is all very well.

b. One who excels. *Colloq.*

1917 *D. N.* IV. 409 'He's a *captain* on the floor to dance.' 'He's a *captain* to tell a tale.' (N.C.) Also Kan., Ky.

2. (See quots.) *Colloq.*

1807 C. SCHULTZ *Travels* I. 167 Here the master of every boat, should she even be no larger than a canoe, is always a 'captain.' **1833** SHIRREFF *Tour* (1835) 49 Captain is a general title for stage drivers. **1867** LATHAM *Black and White* 97 Presently the guard, here called 'the Captain of the train,' came to a coloured gentleman, and asked for his ticket. **1889** FARMER 123 The conductor or guard of a train. This official, on whom devolves the chief responsibility for the safety . . . of a train, is, in America, often addressed as *captain*. **1895** HOWELLS *Recollections* 149 When the husking party had assembled, they were all called out into line, and two fellows, mostly ambitious boys, were chosen captains. These then chose their men, each calling out one of the crowd alternately, till all were chosen.

3. *Polit.* A minor party official in an election district or precinct.

1914 *Cyclo. Amer. Govt.* I. 229 The captain wields a good deal of power in his small district.

4. In combs., sometimes in possessive: (1) **Captain-General,** the chief commander of the militia of a colony or state; (2) **Captain Lynch,** in allusive use, cf. **Lynch law;** (3) **Captain's beat,** (see quot.), *obs.;* (4) **captain's clerk,** the clerk of a sea captain, *obs.;* (5) **Captain's walk,** =**widow's walk.**

(1) **1653** *Va. House of Burgesses* 86 He could . . . command Lieut. Coll. Cornelius Loyd and . . . his General meaning the Governor who is stiled Captain General of Virginia. **1747** *N.J. Archives* 1 Ser. VII. 11 The Council then administered to his Excellency . . . the usual oath for the due Execution of his Office of Captain General and Governor of this province. **1889** *Cent.* 811/1 The governor of Rhode Island is by title captain-general and commander-in-chief of the military and naval forces of the State. — (2) **1841** FOOTE *Texas* II. 16 Being cut off from all opportunity of bringing the offender to

justice through the regular legal tribunals . . . they resolved to have recourse . . . to that well-known arbiter vulgarly yclept Captain Lynch. — (3) **1859** BARTLETT 68 Captain's Beat. The limits within which the members of a military company reside. Within the same limits the votes are received on election days. Southern. — (4) **1794** *Ann. 3rd Congress* 1426 The following petty officers . . . shall be appointed by the captains of the ships . . . two master's mates, one captain's clerk. **1796** *Ann. 4th Congress* 2 Sess. 2786 Pay of the officers, seamen, and marines [per month]: . . . 2 Captain's Clerks, $13. — (5) **1935** LINCOLN *Cape Cod Yesterdays* 43 When he sighted it, he would come down from his 'Cap'n's walk,' go out to the barn, hitch his horse to the truck-wagon, and cart an empty keg over to the packet landing. **1940** EARLY *N. Eng. Sampler* 178 Then he invited everyone in town—and watched the proceedings from the Captain's Walk, on top of his house.

b. *Captain of* (1) *finance*, etc., (2) *industry*, (3) *the caravan*, (see quots.).

(1) **1905** *McClure's Mag.* 353 His fellow culprits are American captains of finance, law and politics. — (2) **1887** *Harper's Mag.* May 973/2 The modern captain of industry guides and protects the productive forces of society. **1948** *Time* 6 Sep. 93/1 The slightest expression of intolerance on the part of a captain of industry is regarded as incipient Fascism. — (3) **1844** GREGG *Commerce of Prairies* I. 45 A gentleman by the name of Stanley . . . was unanimously proclaimed 'Captain of the Caravan.' **1880** A. A. HAYES JR. in *Harper's Mag.* LXI. 187/2 In such a caravan there would be, perhaps, one hundred wagons, and a 'captain of the caravan' would divide them into four divisions, with a lieutenant to each. **1918** CONNELLEY *Hist. Kansas* I. 140 When the traders had all arrived at Council Grove . . . there was elected a Captain of the Caravan, whose duty it was to direct the order of travel and select the camping-places.

As the last term in **bell, block, cornstalk, doughboy, great, Mingo war, mining, police, precinct, scrub, steamboat, sucker, war captain.**

captainize ˈkæptɪnˌaɪz, *v. intr.* To act as captain. *Rare.* — **1840** *Bentley's Misc.* VII. 625 Shall I captainise over my troops one day, and put up with such a 'tarnal confounded insult as this the day after?

∗**caption,** *n.*

1. The heading or title of a document, section, chapter, etc.

"*Caption* is often used in the U.S. in the sense of preamble, or head of a chapter or discourse" (Worc. '46); "but this use is not sanctioned by good writers" (*Ib.* '60).

1789 J. MADISON *Writings* (1904) V. 355 In the Caption of the address . . . we have pruned the ordinary stile of the degrading appendages of Excellency, Esqr. &c. **1888** *Cong. Rec.* 14 July 6295/1, I send to the clerk's desk a letter which I ask that he will read, including the printed caption at its head.

2. The title or heading of an article, story, etc.

"This legal term is used in the newspapers in cases where an Englishman would say *title, head*, or *heading*" (B. '59). "In this sense, the word is an Americanism, but is not used by our best writers" (W. '64).

1823 G. A. MCCALL *Lett.* (1868) 124 The caption of the article was in large capitals and in these words. **1919** H. L. WILSON *Ma Pettengill* ii. 43 The caption says of Vida Sommers. 'Her Love Has Turned to Hate.' **1937** *Manual of Style* 137 Captions for the columns of open tables and boxheads for ruled tables should ordinarily be set in 6 point.

3. A legend beneath a picture. Also **captionless.**

*a***1904** WHITE *Blazed Trail* iv. 58 Under each [picture] was an appropriate caption, such as Surprise, Grief. **1944** JOHNSON *As I Dare* 151 You can't have a picture without a caption. **1944** *Newsweek* 25 Sep. 102 This captionless effort . . . is from a collection of cartoons.

caption ˈkæpʃən, *v. tr.* To furnish with a caption or title.

1901 *Science* XIV. 22 Nov. 808/1 An effective poem . . . captioned 'The Song of the Innuit.' **1912** LONDON *Son of Sun* vii. 246 It means the feathers of the sun. Thus does the base interloper caption himself. **1945** *Christian Cent.* 4 April 428/1 Another ad [is] captioned, 'The World's Best Seller—The Book of Disunity.'

∗**captive,** *n.* **1. captive line,** a line or cord used by Indian pack carriers. *Obs.* Cf. **tumpline. 2. captive mine,** a coal mine which does not produce for the open market but for a steel mill, railroad, etc., which owns and operates it. See *Amer. N. & Q.* Dec. 1946, 135 f.

(1) **1754** *N.H. Hist. Soc. Coll.* I., There was next to their skin tied a number of small metump lines . . . a collar of a length about sufficient to go round a man's neck . . . what is called captive lines. — (2) **1922** *Mineral Resources U.S.* II. 546 It was not possible, however, to distinguish in the value of 'coal loaded at mines for shipment' between the output of commercial mines and the output of the 'captive mines' owned or controlled by consumers. **1948** *Chi. Tribune* 26 June II. 5/3 The United States Steel corporation and other firms with 'captive' mines, continue to refuse to meet the Lewis terms.

capulin ˌkɑpuˈlin, *n. S.W.* [Amer. Sp. *capulín*, in sense **1.**] **1.** The Mexican cherry, *Prunus capuli*. **2.** (See quot.)

(1) **1806** WEBSTER 43/1 Capulin, *n.* The Mexican cherry. *c***1893** *D. N.* I. 245 (Texas words), *Capul, -es*, a tree or shrub of southwestern Texas, not identified, with small, blackish-red or deep yellow edible berries, called *capules*. [**1899** H. B. CUSHMAN *Hist. Indians* 228 In case of sores they applied a poultice, then carefully washed the afflicted parts with the resin of the capal-tree.] — (2) **1893** *Stand.* 282/3 *capulin*, . . . a species of ground-cherry *Physalis pubescens;* strawberry-tomato . . . *capuli*.

∗**car,** *n.* [Sense **3.** is app. from *corf*, basket.]

1. A railroad vehicle for carrying freight or passengers.

1826 *Mass. Statutes* 4 March, The conveyance of stone and other property in their cars and vehicles on said railways. **1903** E. JOHNSON *Railway Transportation* 123 The conductor of the freight train by which the car is moved. **1948** *Chi. D. News* 17 Aug. 1/3 The eight cars at the back of the train remained on the tracks.

b. *The cars*, a railroad train. *To take the cars*, to set off on a railroad journey.

1831 *Niles' Reg.* XLI. 21 The cars now leave Schenectady at a little after 12 M. **1850** HOUSTON *Hesperos* I. 55 We . . . then 'took the cars' (the favourite term here) for Boston. **1938** DAMON *Grandma* 286 Up the little private road in front of the house the 'car-team' was heard coming, that ancient hack that always took everyone who was about to make a railway journey, to the 'cars.'

2. A carload.

1867–8 *Ill. Agric. Soc. Trans.* VII. 446 A farmer had far better send . . . one car of good sheep in the twelve months, than six cars . . . of bad breed. **1905** A. H. RICE *Sandy* 41 A car of live stock . . . was on its way to a great exposition in a neighboring city. **1948** *Green Bay* (Wis.) *Press-Gazette* 30 June 23/4 Receipts were: wheat 38 cars, corn 83, oats 34 and soybeans 9.

3. (See 1st. quot.)

*a***1870** CHIPMAN *Notes on Bartlett* 69 Car, . . . a square box in which, floating, are preserved live fish. — New England and Middle States. This is clearly ='cauf.' **1947** COFFIN *Yankee Coast* 137, I could see cars full of lobsters and baskets of clams down there at the shallow end of our sea-cellar.

4. The cage of an elevator.

1870 *Gold Hill* (Nev.) *News* 25 Aug., The cable fell, coiled among the debris of the broken platforms, upon the car and cage. **1916** W. A. DU PUY *Uncle Sam* 204 The operator obeyed instantly and some excuse was made to the passengers on the car. **1943** BAKER *Trio* (1946) 113 When leaving car, close car gate and landing door, otherwise elevator becomes inoperative.

5. In combs.: (1) **car agent,** a representative of a shipper who accompanies a shipment on a railroad to protect and deliver it; (2) **barn,** a building that houses streetcars, equipment, etc.; (3) **bell,** the bell of a streetcar; (4) **carriage,** a railroad car, *obs.;* (5) **conductor,** one in charge of a horsecar or other streetcar; (6) **hook,** an iron hook used by the driver of a horsecar for controlling the whiffle-trees, also attrib., *obs.;* (7) **house,** a building in which railroad cars are housed; (8) **load,** see as a main entry; (9) ∗**man,** a railroad brakeman; (10) **train,** a railroad train made up of engine and passenger cars, *obs.*

(1) **1839** *Amer. R.R. Jrnl.* IX. 175 Superintendant [*sic*], clerk, and car agents. — (2) **1880** *Chi. Tribune* 10 May 1/7 An hour and a half passed before the well-tutored delegation from the car-barns . . . had cast their votes. **1944** KAHN *Cable Car Days* 60 Stut was the engineer in charge of setting up the machinery in the carbarn. — (3) **1863** M. HARLAND *Husks* 20 The tinkle of the car-bell, three blocks off, arose to her window. **1902** HARBEN *Abner Daniel* 297 We git our pay for our land in bein' glad an' heerin' car-bells an' steam-whistles in the middle o' the night. — (4) **1854** *S. Lit. Messenger* XX. 725/1 An easy and commodious car-carriage whirls the Baltimorian through in half a day.

(5) **1876** *Scribner's Mo.* April 911/2 There were addresses . . . relating to the . . . car-conductor. — (6) **1873** *N.Y. Tribune* 29 Jan. 1/2 The last duty of the courts with regard to the car-hook murderer, Wm. Foster, was performed on Friday. **1876** *Cong. Rec.* 5 Aug. 5209/1 Is it fair to charge crime upon the whole people of N.Y.: of the Nathan murder or the car-hook murder? — (7) **1833** *Amer. R.R. Jrnl.* II. 481/3 A cotton shed and car house have been erected. **1872** HUNTINGTON *Road-Master's Assistant* 32 Notice the kegs and barrels full of bent and broken spikes . . . around every car-house, shop or depot. — (9) **1881** *Rep. Ala. R.R. Comm.* I. 53 Conductor, two car men and myself were all.

(10) **1855** *Amer. Inst. N.Y. Trans.* 164 Who does not fail to see, from the car trains in their daily and weekly transit, . . . all the low places? **1886** LOGAN *Great Conspiracy* 84 What with special car trains, and weighty deputations, and imposing processions, . . . his [Douglas'] political journey through Illinois had been more like a Royal Progress than anything the Country had yet seen.

b. In combs. of obvious meaning or sufficiently explained in the quots., as (1) **car builder,** (2) **candle,** (3) **coupler,** (4) **coupling,** (5) **-fare,** (6) **ferry,** (7) **inspector,** (8) **knocker,** (9) **line,** (10) **lot,** (11) **mile,** (12) **mileage,** (13) **seal,** (14) **seat,** (15) **shed,** (16) **shop,** (17) **starter,** (18) **stove,** (19) **works.**

(1) **1883** J. D. FULTON *Sam Hobart* 165 Car Builders' Dictionary. **1894** CARWARDINE *Pullman Strike* 81 Car builder . . . $13.00. — (2) **1895** WAIT *Car-Builder's Dict.* 23 A special kind of large diameter called *car-candles* are used for lighting passenger-cars and burned in *candle-lamps*. . . . The best car-candles are made of paraffin and *hydraulic pressed*. — (3) **1901** *Sci. Amer.* 9 Nov. 299/2 Since these essentials may be of some interest to prospective inventors of car-couplers we give them for what they are worth. — (4) **1847** *Index to Patents* (1874) I. 210 Car-coupling [patented by] W. C. Bussey, Rockgrove, Ill., July 17, 1847. **1883** J. D. FULTON *Sam Hobart* 170 A Division Superintendent came into our rooms, who was interested in a car-coupling arrangement. I suppose there are hundreds of different kinds of car-couplings.

(5) **1870** F. FERN *Ginger-Snaps* 182 What troubles me most is, whether I am to pay six cents for car-fare. **1947** *Life* 3 March 104/2 He . . . carried his lunch . . . and . . . walked to and from work to save carfare. — (6) **1880** H. HALL *Census of 1880* VIII. 221 Side-wheel car-ferry Transport, iron, of 1595 tons and 2000 nominal horse-power . . . with three railroad tracks on deck. **1948** JACOBS *We Chose the Country* 6 If we were in luck, one of the gigantic car ferries which shuttle freight cars across the lake would pass within a stone's throw. — (7) **1839** *Amer. R.R. Jrnl.* IX. 175 Car inspectors. **1882** *Rep. Ala. R.R. Comm.* II. 62 Chas. Askins, car inspector [was] killed at Birmingham. — (8) **1931** *Illinois Central Mag.* June 30/2 A car inspector is known far and wide as a 'car-knocker,' 'cartoad,' and 'carpeck,' because he is always 'knocking' or 'pecking' on the cars, in making repairs. — (9) **1890** H. PALMER *Stories Base Ball Field* 222 Cincinnati, Hamilton & Dayton R.R. [is] . . . the favorite through Car Line Cincinnati to St. Louis. **1919** CUNNINGHAM *Chronicle* 118 They turned up the hill, then down, the cutter gliding over the street toward the car line and past Mrs. Erksen's bay.

(10) **1900** NELSON *ABC Wall St.* 133 Car lots. The number of cars of various grains received and inspected daily at the leading grain centres. **1948** *Sat. Ev. Post* 10 July 12/3 It took the combined efforts of all the Spartanburg growers to scrape together enough peaches for a carlot shipment. — (11) **1940** *Quiz* [Quest.] 219 . . . The transportation of a car one mile, known as a 'car-mile,' is the unit of a car movement employed in computing train service costs and efficiency. — (12) **1903** E. JOHNSON *Railway Transportation* 174 If each car carrying the mails be taken as a unit, the 'annual travel' or car mileage aggregated 302,613,325. — (13) **1889** *Cent.* 835/2 *Car-seal*, . . . a clasp of soft metal designed to bind the ends of a wire passed through the lock of a freight-car. **1940** *Quiz* [Quest.] 242 . . . The car seal is used to prevent or to detect illegal entry into a car. Each seal is numbered and bears the name of the railroad by which it is applied. A record is kept of each seal issued. — (14) **1852** *Rep. Comm. Patents 1851* 158 What we claim as new . . . is the mode . . . of reversing the back of car seats. **1874** KNIGHT 482/1 Car-seat Arm-lock. (Railway.) A lock attached to the bar of a seat-back, to prevent its being reversed by unauthorized persons. **1876** INGRAM *Centen. Expos.* 179 The back of the settee reversed like a car seat.

(15) **1880** HARRIS *Uncle Remus* 204 (We.), In de kyar-shed. **1944** BROWN *Yankee from Olympus* 296 (We.), I'll meet you in the car shed on the square. — (16) **1852** *Chi. Tribune* 6 May 1/6 They have recently erected a spacious Car Shop and a Foundry, in addition to their former Steam Engine and Machine Works. **1903** *Sci. Amer. Supp.* LV. 22934/1 The following general classification of railway shops may be made: First, machine, erecting, and car shops; second, paint shops; third, round houses. — (17) (*a*) **1874** KNIGHT 484/1 Car-starter. (Railway.) A device to assist in starting a street-car from the dead stop. **1889** *Cent.* 835/3 Car-starter, . . . a device by which the momentum of a street-car is utilized in overcoming its inertia in starting again. (*b*) **1876** *Scribner's Mo.* Apr. 911/2 The stockholders and directors, the 'car-starters' and 'spotters,' . . . were all embalmed in verse. **1889** *Cent.* 835/3 *Car-starter*, . . . a car- or train-dispatcher.— (18) **1874** KNIGHT 484/2 Car-stove. (Railway.) One specifically adapted for railway cars, having certain means of securing in place, prevention of scattering of fire in case of upsetting, or arrangements for the induction of outside air. — (19) **1884** HOWELLS *S. Lapham* xx, The Great Lacustrine & Polar Railroad . . . 's going to build car-works right by those mills.

Also *car building, chair, detention, door, door-lock, mate, route, spittoon, steps, ticket, time, track(s), wheel, whistle, window,* etc.

As the last term in **accommodation, advertising, baggage, balloon, barrel, bell, boarding, bobtail, boudoir, box, buffet, bunk, burden, cabin, caboose, café, cannon, cattle, chair, club, coach, coal, colored, conductor's, construction, crank, day, dining, dirt, dormitory, drawing room, drawing room sleeping, drover's, dummy, electric, emigrant, emigrant sleeping, express, fish, flat, flume, freight, fruit, gondola, gravel, grip, gun, hand, hay, hog, honeymoon, hopper, hopper-bottom, horse, horse-rail, hotel, house, ice, inspection, iron, Jim Crow, kitchen, ladies, life, lodging, log, luggage, lumber, mail, Mann boudoir, milk, mixed, motor, mule, Negro, observation, oil, ore, owl, palace, palace day, palace drawing, palatial, parlor, passage, passenger, pay, paymaster's, platform, pleasure, plow, postal, post office, private, provision, prowl, Pullman, push, rail, railroad, railway, reclining-chair, refreshment, refrigerating, refrigerator, restaurant, sailing, second class, service, silver palace, single-decked, slab, slat cattle, slave, sleeping, smoking, special, squad, stable, stake, steam, stock, stock palace, stone, straight, street, surface, tank, through, tip, tourist, tow, trail, train, transportation, trolley, way, wood, wrecking car.**

caracara ˌkarəˈkarə, *n.* [Amer. Sp. in same sense.] A vulture-like hawk, *Polyborus cheriway auduboni*, found in the Southwest. Also **caracara eagle.** Cf. **Audubon's caracara.**

1839 AUDUBON *Ornith. Biog.* V. 351 Caracara Eagle. *Polyborus Braziliensis.* Nests of the Caracara found in the Floridas . . . were placed on the highest branches of the tall trees in the pine barrens. **1895** *Yearbook Dept. Agric. 1894* 211 Among the birds may be mentioned the white-crowned pigeon, Zenaida dove, . . . and caracara eagle. **1942** *Nat. Pks. Service Fading Trails* 261 Caracaras . . . are not as timid as most of the hawk tribe and consequently are easy prey for man.

carajo kaˈrɑho, *n. S.W.* [Sp., the virile member.] An ox driver, "mule skinner," any base fellow. Also as an interj.

1844 GREGG *Commerce of Prairies* I. 298 Then you shall die first, carajo! **1856** *Iroquois Republican* (Middleport, Ill.) 18 Dec. 1/4 'Carrajo' is less delicate . . . the shibboleth of the vulgar. **1870** DUVAL *Big-Foot Wallace* 240 Carrajo! what red hair that fellow's got! **1932** in ADAMS *W. Words* 29 Shouting 'Carajo' . . . ! An exclamation used by mule skinners, cowboys, and other outdoor workers.

b. The tall upright stem of the maguey or similar plant. Also such a stem or pole used as an ox goad.

1880 F. L. OSWALD *Summerland Sk.* 293 He had . . . finally strayed to Sisal and exchanged the spit for a muleteer's goad,—vulg., 'caracho-pole.' **1901** *Kansas Hist. Colls.* (1902) VII. 52, I hurried him [an ox] along by repeated punches with my *carajo* pole. **1902** *Out West* Oct. 452 He showed her the *mescal*, and . . . told her the many aliases of *maguey*, '*carajo* poles,' *palmilla*, . . . bear grass, Spanish dagger or bayonet.

transf. **1910** BRONSON *Remin. Ranchman* 287 An' thar was . . . th' boss music-maker on a perch in th' middle of th' bunch, shakin' a little *carajo* pole to beat hell out of any of th' outfit that wa'n workin' to suit him.

carajo kaˈrɑho, *v.* Also **caraho.** *S.W.* [f. prec.] *intr.* To shout "carajo!" *Obs.*

1844 *N. O. Picayune* 26 Aug. 222/3 Mr. L., informed of the case, again approached, in no pleasant humor, it may be supposed, cursed, *sacre'd* and *carahoo'd*. **1850** GARRARD *Wah-To-Yah* iv. 65 At other times, he *sacre*-ed in French, *caraho*-ed in Spanish-Mexican. **1900** SMITHWICK *Evolution of State* 53 They gave chase, *carajoing* and firing their carbines.

caramba kəˈrɑmbə, *interj. S.W.* [Sp.] An exclamation of vexation, admiration, etc.

1838 *N.Y. Mirror* 6 Jan. 217/2 *Carramba*, why do you speak thus. **1870** DUVAL *Big-Foot Wallace* 240 Carrambo! look at that fellow's teeth, will you! **1947** *Time* 20 Jan. 75/2 '*Caramba*,' he muttered.

carau kəˈrɑu, *n.* [?Imitative.] The crying bird, *Aramus giganteus*, found in Florida and the Greater Antilles.

1858 BAIRD *Birds Pacific R.R.* 657 *Aramus Giganteus*, . . . Carau; crying bird; Courlaw. **1889** *Cent.* 1311/1 Courlan, . . . also called *carau, crying-bird,* and *limpkin*. **1917** *Birds of Amer.* I. 201.

*** caravan,** *n.*

1. A train of wagons, or string of pack-mules. See also **Missouri caravan.**

1817 S. BROWN *Western Gaz.* 77 General Harrison . . . was accompanied in his march through the wilderness by a caravan of waggons! **1819** *Niles' Reg.* XVI. 238/2 A *caravan*, consisting of eleven covered waggons, drawn by two, three, or four horses each, . . . [bound] for the state of Illinois. **1905** VALENTINE *H. Sandwith* 3 Caravans of pack-mules followed lone Indian trails.

2. A traveling show or circus or a vehicle forming part of this.

1824 IRVING *T. Trav.* I. 272 Several caravans containing wild beasts, and other spectacles. **1845** SOL. SMITH *Theatr. Apprent.* 176 He is one person today and another to-morrow— . . . some people say he is as good as a caravan! **1877** JEWETT *Deephaven* viii. 125, I am sure she never looked forward to an Easter Oratorio with half the pleasure she did to this 'caravan,' as most of the people called it [a circus].

attrib. **1841** COOPER *Deerslayer* xiv, The Otsego is a favorite place for the caravan-keepers to let their elephants bathe.

* **caravanserai,** *n. W.* Grandiloquent for a frontier tavern or inn. *Obs.*

1826 FLINT *Recoll.* 211, I have seen two of the latter [handsome houses] which were not content with the title of 'hotel,' . . . but which carried on their signs the still more fashionable term 'caravanserai.' *a***1861** WINTHROP *Canoe & Saddle* 312 They sleep in an Americanized caravansary. **1888** *Kansas Hist. Colls.* (1890) IV. 246 Lawrence, a rude town of some forty or fifty log and rough board cabins with a 'caravansary' for immigrants, built of sod walls and cloth roof.

* **caraway,** *n. attrib.* Designating cakes, cookies, etc., flavored with caraway seeds.

1805 *Pocumtuc Housewife* (1906) 33 [Recipes] for Caraway Cookies . . . Doughnuts . . . Rye Doughnuts. **1832** L. M. CHILD *Frugal Housewife* 73 Caraway Cakes. Take one pound of flour [etc.]. **1898** I. H. HARPER *S. B. Anthony* I. 14 Doughnuts, caraway cakes and other toothsome things which little ones love.

* **carbonate,** *n.* "The common term in the West for ores containing a considerable proportion of carbonate of lead. They are sometimes earthy or ochreous (soft carbonates), sometimes granular and comparatively free from iron (sand carbonates) and sometimes compact (hard carbonates)" (Raymond, *Mining Glossary*). Also attrib. or as adj.

1876 *Kern Co. W. Courier* (Bakersfield, Calif.) 8 Jan. 2/3 The galena is very tough and hard to work; the carbonates, on the contrary, may be easily picked down. **1880** *Dly. Southwest* 9 June 3/1 It is really a 'carbonate' camp, and the little Mexican furnace now in operation there, is proving the exceeding richness of the ores. **1936** MCKENNA *Black Range* 285 When the rich carbonates were discovered in Leadville Tabor was clerkin' in a grocery store.

carbonated warbler. (See quot. 1891.)

1831 AUDUBON *Ornith. Biog.* I. 308 The Carbonated Warbler[s] *Sylvia Carbonata* were both busily engaged in searching for insects along the branches and amongst the leaves of a Dog-wood tree. **1858** BAIRD *Birds Pacific R.R.* 288 The Carbonated Warbler is known only by the description and figure of Mr. Audubon, taken from two specimens killed at Henderson, Kentucky, in 1811. **1891** *Cent.* 6819/3 Carbonated Warbler, an American warbler so named by Audubon in 1831, and never since identified. More fully called *carbonated swamp warbler*, also *dusky-warbler*

Carborundum ˌkɑrbəˈrʌndəm, *n.* [*carbon*+*corundum*.] A trade-mark for certain abrasives, as silicon carbide. Also (not *cap.*) the product bearing this trade-mark. Also attrib.

1892 *Official Gazette U.S. Patents* LIX. 1914/1 [Trade-mark registered by] The Carborundum Company, Monongahela City, Pa. *Ib.*, Trade-marks registered June 21, 1892 [include] Carborundum. **1900** *Sci. Amer.* 16 June 378/1 The cross section of a carborundum furnace now presents a remarkable appearance. **1943** GEIST *Hiking* 149 A carborundum sharpening stone is convenient on a long tour where your instruments may require sharpening.

carcage kɑrˈkɑhə, *n. S.W.* [Sp. *carcaj, -cax,* in same sense.] (See quot.) *Obs.* — **1844** GREGG *Commerce of Prairies* I. 90 Swung upon the shoulder of each buffalo hunter hangs his *carcage* or quiver of bow and arrows.

carcajou ˈkɑrkəˌdʒu, *n.* [Can. F. f. Algonquian.] The wolverine.

1744 A. DOBBS *Hudson's Bay* 40 The Beavers have three Enemies, Man, Otters, and the Carcajon [*sic*], or Queequehatch. **1832** WILLIAMSON *Maine* I. 133 The Wolverine, (Carcajou) is as large as a wolf and of like colour. **1917** KEPHART *Camping* I. 262 The wolverine, also called glutton, carcajou, skunk bear, and Indian devil, is the champion thief of the wilderness. **1947** DEVOTO *Across Wide Missouri* 165 To them the 'carcajou' was literally demoniac: he had an infernal ancestor.

b. (See quots.)

1831 CUVIER *Supp. to Buffon* I. 267. **1864** WEBSTER 197/1 *Carcajou*, . . . the American badger (*Meles Labradorica*), found in the sandy plains or prairies of North America. **1895** GERARD in *N.Y. Sun* 30 July, Carcajou, a name properly belonging to the wolverine, but erroneously transferred by certain writers to the American badger, and by old hunters of northern New York to the lynx.

carcel ˈkɑrsəl, *n. S.W.* [Sp. *cárcel*, in same sense.] A prison.

1840 TURNBULL *Travels in West* 57 (Bentley), The survivor, for safe keeping merely, was sent to the carcel. **1910** *Sat. Ev. Post* 8 Oct. 5/1 The general and the chief of police . . . had carted off four *carreta* loads of my machinery to the *carcel.* **1932** BENTLEY *Spanish Terms* 116 carcel. . . . This word is heard occasionally along the border by English-speaking people and is encountered no more frequently in writings of this region.

***card,** *n.*[1] A currycomb. *Obs.* — **1820** *Columbian Centinel* 8 Jan. 4/3 Wool, Cotton, and Cattle Cards. **1858** *Rep. Comm. Patents* (1859) I. 346 Improvement in Cards for currying Cattle. **1860** OLMSTED *Back Country* 246 He picked up a piece of corn cob and began scraping him. 'Hadn't he got a curry comb or card?'

* **card,** *n.*[2]

1. A number of candies or buttons arranged on a pasteboard card.

1758 *Essex Hist. Coll.* XLV. 344 The following Goods are stolen. Viz. . . . sundry Bundles of Sleeve Buttons, Glass sett in Brass, one Card Bristol Stone sett in Silver [etc.]. **1899** WILKINS *Colonial Times* 107 I'll buy you a whole card of peppermints. **1920** LEWIS *Main Street* 39 And Axel Egge's, like home, lots of Swedes and Norskes in there, and a card of dandy buttons, like rubies.

2. "A note published by some one in the papers, containing a brief statement, explanation, request, &c." (W. '47).

1769 *Boston News-Letter* 2 Feb. (Th.), A Card from the London and British Merchants to the American Merchants. **1856** PHILLIPS *Kansas* 380 At St. Louis Governor Shannon was stopped by General Smith, who advised him to go back again. This he did, publishing a card in the city denying the report of his intended resignation. **1945** *Bristol* (N.H.) *Enterprise* 15 Feb. 4/1 (*advt.*), Births, marriages and death notices inserted free. Card of thanks, $1.00.

3. A flat cake (or "sheet") of gingerbread; a "pan" of biscuits, etc. Also attrib.

1823 COOPER *Pioneers* ix, With 'cards of gingerbread.' **1835** BALDWIN *Flush Times* 160 He had ravished himself from the supper table, scarcely eating any thing—three or four cups of coffee, . . . a card of spare-ribs and one or two feet of stuffed sausages. **1871** *Atlantic Mo.* Nov. 574 Through clouds of smoke and steam . . . sprang the cooks . . . dropping a card of biscuits and picking them up again in their fists. **1897** ROBINSON *Uncle Lisha* 287 There were numerous booths where refreshments of mead, spruce beer, and great cards of good old-fashioned yellow gingerbread were temptingly displayed.

b. (See quot.)

1884 PHIN *Dict. Apiculture* 20 Card, a frame filled with honey comb, a sheet of honeycomb.

4. (See quot. 1940.) *Obs.* or *hist.*

1847 *Farmers' Almanac* (N.Y.) 9/1 A man got up the other night and took, as he supposed, a card of matches, and began to break off one by one, trying to light a lamp, until the whole card was used up,

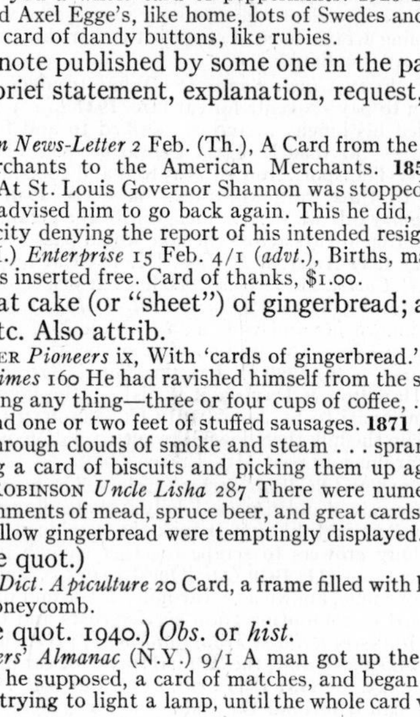

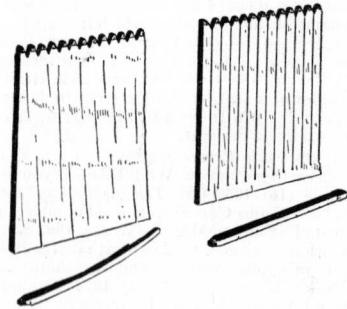

Cards of friction matches

without accomplishing his object, when he discovered that he had used up his wife's comb! **1870** O. OPTIC *Field & Forest* 65 Mr. Mellowtone gave me a card of matches. **1940** *Amer. Sp.* 449/2 A *card of matches* in the nineteenth century was a piece of wood, I should say about a tenth of an inch thick and two and a half inches square, divided into matches by slits which ran from the edge to within about half an inch of the opposite edge.

5. An attraction or advertisement.

1866 *Wilkes' Spirit of Times* 16 June 246/1 The chief card of the week, in the base-ball line, was a game between the famous Eckfords and the equally well-known Union Club. **1887** *Courier-Journal* 1 May 12/1 The festival of last year was quite a card for Louisville. **1947** *Westerners' Brand Book* 94 It was a great card and all San Francisco turned out.

6. In combs.: (1) ∗**cardboard,** a railroad pass, *rare;* (2) ∗**case,** (see quot.); (3) **catalogue,** a catalogue, usu. of the books in a library, made out on cards; (4) **end,** (see quot.); (5) **index,** an alphabetical index formed by entries on cards, also attrib. and fig.; (6) **press,** a small press for printing cards; (7) **receiver,** a card tray; (8) **sharp,** a "cardsharper"; (9) **waybill,** (see quot.).

(1) **1887** *Courier-Journal* 8 May 15/4 People who have life passes over the railroads seem to be numerous. Most of them want to know if the Interstate Commission can . . . force the railroads to honor their own cardboard. — (2) **1909** *Cent. Supp.* 201/3 Card-case, . . . a case of drawers in which catalogue-cards are arranged. — (3) [**1853** *Rules Public Library Boston* 10 He shall make and keep, on uniform cards . . . a complete alphabetical catalogue of the Library.] **1854** *Boston City Doc. No. 74* 12 The Alphabetical Card Catalogue, which contains a full title of each book on a separate card. **1948** *Vt. Quart.* 42 The function of the librarian is . . . to introduce newcomers to them by way of the card catalogue. — (4) **1841** Park *Pantology* 475 The cotton after being picked or batted into a light, uniform mass, and then twice carded, . . . comes . . . in continuous rolls, called card ends.

(5) **1849** *Rep. Comm. Patents* (1850) 344, I also claim the card index formed with the shoulder *b*, to suspend the card in the slit of the plate or false bottom *a*. **1900** *Engineering Mag.* XIX. 767 Those who desire to clip the items for card-index purposes. **1911** H. S. Harrison *Queed* vi. 67 She had touched the spring of the automatic card-index system, known as his memory. **1948** *Tenn. Hist. Quart.* March 31 He has even been called the party manager of Jackson's administration, the father of the card-index system of the modern machine politician. — (6) **1847** *De Bow's Review* III. 278 His 'card press' . . . is of superior character. **1851** Cist *Cincinnati* 232 This establishment has also just completed a new and improved card press. — (7) **1861** *Vanity Fair* 16 March 129/1 She undertook this morning to wash my Sévres card receiver and vases. *c*1903 *Sears Cat.* (ed. 113) 98 Card Receiver, very fancy. — (8) **1884** Harte *On Frontier* 273 We ain't takin' this step to make a card sharp out of him. **1910** *Cosmopolitan* June 14/1 It's a kyard-sharp by the name of Frosty who puts himse'f in nom'nation to extricate the professor. — (9) **1903** E. Johnson *Railway Transportation* 123 This way-bill either accompanies the freight or is forwarded by mail. In the latter case the agent makes out a 'card way-bill,' which is given to the conductor of the freight train.

b. *To give cards and spades,* to give a liberal advantage, in allusion to scoring in cassino. *Colloq.*

[**1888** *Grip* (Toronto) May (F.), He found a Chinaman . . . who could give him cards and spades and beat him out.] **1898** *N.Y. World* 3 Sep. 2/5–6 The calentura can give cards and spades to yellow fever in the game of death.

As the last term in **ball, business, calling, case, catalogue, cattle, conversation, dance, dancing, dead, dinner, drawing, gumming, hock, horse, machine, postal, rate, report, score, shade, short, side, soda, tally, three, time, trip, union, wafer, way, wine, withdrawal, working card.**

∗**card,** *v.*[1] *tr.* To dress or curry (a horse, ox, etc.) with a card or currycomb. Also absol. Cf. ∗**card,** *n.*[1]

1851 J. S. Springer *Forest Life* 82 In the morning, . . . his faithful visits are repeated to hay . . . and card, and yoke up. **1864** *N.Y. Tribune* 3 May 5/1 Often they do abound in lice, and their owners try all remedies, anxious to learn which one is effective. The best thing is to card thoroughly every day, for in carding thousands will drop off. **1888** *Vt. Agric. Rep.* X. 35 [He] spoke favorably of carding heifers and cows, and thinks it will pay.

∗**card,** *v.*[2]

1. *tr.* To send a message to (a person) on a postal card. Also **carding,** *n. Obs.*

1830 *Cin. Chronicle* 15 May 1/3 Of all the labor-saving devices that have been discovered, there is none which exceeds what . . . is called carding. *Ib.* 1/4 The expedient of carding was then resorted to, which is simply dropping a card with those whom you do not care a sixpence about, without the trouble of carding a man with your own hands. **1875** in *Newspaper* Fulcitus carded almost daily his friend Ruisseaux. **1880** (*from a letter*) Will you card to me here an answer to my friend the professor's question?

b. (See quot.) *Rare.*

1844 Poe *Oblong Box* Works III. 233, I observed that his name was carded upon *three* staterooms.

2. To provide a library book with record cards.

1893 *Stand.* 284/3 In library usage, the carding of books is distinguished from 'cataloguing,' which includes the determination of the form of entry and all necessary bibliographic details.

∗**cardinal,** *n.*

1. The redbird or cardinal grosbeak, *Richmondena cardinalis.*

1687 tr. Joutel *Journal* 191 There is a sort of Bird, all red, which for that Reason is call'd the Cardinal; this they often tame and teach to sing like a *Canary Bird.* **1756** P. Browne *Jamaica* 467 The Cardinal. This bird is frequently imported from South Carolina. **1885** M. Thompson *By Ways & Bird Notes* 159 In the region of Tallulah Falls I met with an old man whose chief business was snaring red-birds (cardinals) for the sake of their skins. **1947** *Chi. Tribune* 16 Feb. (Grafic Mag.) 8/5 The cardinal is a former summer visitor who decided to stay here the year around.

2. =**cardinal flower.**

1838 *S. Lit. Messenger* IV. 318/2 The little noisy brook . . . steals off among the flowers it nourishes, the brilliant cardinals and snow-white Clematis. **1881** *Harper's Mag.* Sep. 585/1 The fragrant clethra, whose prim fingers of creamy bloom made a good foil to the cardinals.

3. In combs.: (1) **cardinal bird,** =**cardinal 1;** (2) **flower,** the scarlet lobelia, *Lobelia cardinalis,* or its showy red flower; (3) **grosbeak,** =**cardinal 1;** (4) **lobelia, plant,** =**cardinal flower.**

(1) [**1678** Ray *Willughby's Ornithol.* II. ii. 245 The Virginian Nightingale . . . Mercurialis affirms, that by the Portugues it is commonly called, The Cardinal bird, because it is of a scarlet [purpurei] colour, and seems to wear on its Head a red hat.] **1786** Franklin *Writings* IX. 503 It is rare that we see the Cardinal Bird so far north as Pennsylvania. **1889** *Cent.* 820/2 Cardinal-bird . . . is sometimes called the *Virginia nightingale*, on account of its song. — (2) [**1629** Parkinson *Paradisus* 356 The rich crimson Cardinals flower. This braue plant, from a white roote spreading diuers wayes vnder ground, sendeth forth many greene leaues.] **1705** Beverley *Virginia* II. 24 The Cardinal-Flower, so much extoll'd for its Scarlet Colour, is almost in every Branch. **1913** Stratton-Porter *Laddie* i. 11 On either side of the entrance he had planted a cluster of cardinal flower that was in full bloom. **1947** *Midland Naturalist* July 60 Cardinal-flower [is] occasional (locally common) in river swamps. — (3) **1783** Latham *Gen. Synops. Birds* II. i. 118. **1802** Bingley *Anim. Biog.* (1813) II. 161 The Cardinal Grosbeak . . . is an inhabitant of several parts of North America. **1885** *Cent. Mag.* March 682 The brown thrushes, the cardinal grosbeaks, and the cat-birds were singing in the hedges. — (4) **1839** *Boston Wkly. Mag.* 3 Aug. 377/1 The cardinal lobelia gleams like the flower of a brighter clime around the borders of the rivulets. **1869** *Amer. Naturalist* III. 211 Many of the fern-like mosses . . . do perfectly well if planted in a very small quantity of soil upon this top stone. . . . The red cardinal plant (*Lobelia cardinalis*), seem[s] especially adapted for this purpose.

As the last term in **Arizona, bloody, Kentucky, Mexican, Virginia cardinal.**

∗**care,** *n. In care of,* in the address of a letter or package: In the charge or oversight of, "care of." — **1917** Merwin *Temperamental Henry* 256 If you care to write a good-bye, address me in care of the ship. **1940** Stuart *Trees of Heaven* 62 Write me a letter, send it by mail, Send it in care of Greenupsburg jail.

carear ˌkareˈɑr, *n. Texas.* [Sp. *carear, v.*, to tend a herd of cattle, etc.] A herd of cattle. *Obs.* — **1857** Stacey *Journal* 61 Yesterday afternoon the trail of a large carear was discovered heading across the road in a northerly direction.

∗**career,** *n.* The profession of one who makes special preparation for, and takes up as a permanent calling, an office in a diplomatic or consular branch of the U.S. Foreign Service. Also attrib.

1927 *Lit. Digest* 25 June 14/2 The foundation of any sound Foreign Service must consist of 'career men' who have become experienced. **1930** Nevins *Henry White* 2 He illustrated better than any other American of the time the possibilities of skilled service by a diplomatist of career. **1947** *Sat. Ev. Post* 17 May 24/1 His day is fairly typical for a United States Foreign Service career officer, and he himself is typical of the new blood being transfused into the overseas arteries of the State Department.

b. Also attrib. in the sense of "professional."

1931 F. J. Stimson *My U.S.* 190, I think the career professors look somewhat askance at one who comes in from the outside world. **1947** *Chi. Tribune* 25 May (Mag.) 18/4 He's hoping instead for an attractive career gal in the magazine, newspaper, or advertising field, he says.

∗**careless,** *a.* Denoting any one of various weeds of the genus *Amaranthus.* Also absol.

1807 J. Scott *Md. & Del.* 26 Common and white plantain, . . . Jameson, careless, poke root. **1849** C. C. Cox in *S. Hist. Quart.* XXIX. 206 Traveled to the second watering place . . . grass short, but plenty of *Careless Weed* of which our Animals seemed very fond. **1900** *Land of Sunshine* Nov. 320 A species of chenopodium, called 'careless weed' by freighters and cattle men, exceeds ten feet in height. **1941**

STUART *Men of Mts.* 152 The pig . . . likes ragweeds, pulsey, careless and horseweeds.

carencia kɑ'rɛnsɪə, *n. S.W.* [Sp. *querencia*, in sense shown here.] A favorite place of resort, a haunt. *Obs.* — **1856** HAYES *Pioneer Notes* 19 Aug., He thought they would be more apt to stay on this pasturage, as the seaside had been their *carencia*. **1898** *Land of Sunshine* Mar. 184 Should one of them attempt to stray from her 'carencia,' . . . the luckless odalisque is sure to receive a severe punishment.

carette kɑr'ɛt, *n.* [*car*+*ette*, as in *wagonette*.] A form of streetcar having wooden spoked wheels and not requiring rails. Also a motor vehicle entered from the rear and having seats on the sides of the body. *Obs.* — **1896** *Columbus* (O.) *Dispatch* 1 July 9/5 The carette rumbling on its way to the north side was half-filled. **1903** *Chi. Record-Herald* 1 May 3/5 An ancient carette has been doing yeoman service on the South Side, carrying carpets and rugs.

Carey's sedge. *local.* A variety of sedge grass. *Obs.* — **1843** TORREY *Flora N.Y.* II. 409 *Carex Careyana* . . . Carey's Sedge . . . Shady dry woods, Auburn (*J. Carey, Esq.*) This handsome species has been found also in Ohio.

carga 'kɑrgə, *n. W.* [Sp. in same sense. An Amer. borrowing.] A load or weight varying according to locality.

1844 GREGG *Commerce of Prairies* I. 181 The *carga*, if a single package, is laid across the mule's back. **1876** RAYMOND *8th Rep. Mines* (1877) 7 A carga is a Mexican load of cleaned ore, ready for the furnaces, weighing 300 pounds avoirdupois. **1897** INMAN *Old Santa Fe Trail* 57 The *carga* is then hoisted on top of the saddle if it is a single package.

cargador ˌkɑrgə'dɔr, *n. W.* [Sp., in similar senses.]

1. A porter or carrier. *Obs.*

1811 tr. HUMBOLDT *Political Essay* I. 39 The existence of these valleys prevents the inhabitants from travelling except on horseback, afoot, or carried on the shoulders of Indians, (called *cargadores*). **1844** GREGG *Commerce of Prairies* II. 103 The *cargadores* who were carrying my packages were no doubt as much frightened as myself. **1888** J. J. WEBB *Memoirs* 168 These 'cargadores' performed the labor and took the place of our draymen in transporting goods from place to place in the cities all through Mexico. **1912** LUMHOLTZ *New Trails* 139 My attendant was a *cargadore* (carrier) whose business may best be described as that of moving goods which he carries on his own back.

2. (See 1st quot.)

c1893 *D. N.* I. 245 Cargador, the man in charge of the packs, in a pack train. **1897** INMAN *Old Santa Fe Trail* 57 Two arrieros, or packers, place the goods on the mule's back, one, the *cargador*, standing on the near side, his assistant on the other. **1923** J. H. COOK *On Old Frontier* 153 One of these was Arthur Sparhawk, an expert cargador or mule-packer.

cargo 'kɑrgo, *v. tr.* To load or supply with a cargo. Also fig. *Colloq.* — **1892** *Cong. Record* 18 March 2188/1 Pelts and peltries, and anything else the teamster may be cargoed with. **1909** WASON *Happy Hawkins* 253 He slouched into the office purty consid'able cargoed up with conflictin' emotions.

carhunk, see **cohonk.**

caribou 'kɑrəˌbu, *n.* Also **caribo, carraboo, carriboo,** etc. [F., from Algonquian source.]

1. Any one of various North American species or varieties of reindeer. Also attrib. Cf. **mountain, woodland caribou.**

[**1610** in *Jesuit Relations & Allied Doc.* I. 82 Ilz pechent les Castors, dont ilz vivēt, & d'autres chasse, comme Ellans, Caribous, Cerfs, [etc.].] **1672** J. JOSSELYN *N. Eng. Rarities* 20 The *Maccarib, Caribo*, or *Pohano*, a kind of Deer, as big as a Stag. **1778** CARVER *Travels* 110 Buffaloes, carrabou, and moose deer, are numerous in these parts. **1868** WHYMPER *Alaska* 23 He had, when in pursuit of a Cariboeuf deer, wandered far from the camp of his companions. **1948** *Sierra Club Bul.* Mar. 15 Wolves seldom kill sheep when caribou are available.

2. In special combs.: (1) **caribou bog,** a bog frequented by caribou; (2) **fly,** prob. a deer fly or black fly; (3) **moss,** reindeer moss, *Cladonia rangiferina;* (4) **plain,** =**caribou bog;** (5) **road,** a road or trail made by caribou; (6) **shanks,** (see quot. 1888).

(1) **1850** JOHNSON *Notes* I. 23 It rises very gently and very slightly till it reaches an immense bog—called in these provinces a Carriboo bog or Cariboo plain—which is the water-shed from which flow both the Cornwallis river and that of Annapolis. — (2) **1835** AUDUBON *Ornith. Biog.* III. 586 Where musquitoes, although plentiful enough, are not accompanied by carraboo flies. — (3) **1904** S. E. WHITE *Silent Places* xiii. 137 The foundation he made of caribou-moss, gathered dry from the heights. — (4) **1831** FOWLER *Journal* 271 Barren or Cariboo plains bear on the peat, which is often many feet in depth, a few scattered spruces and creeping cranberries. **1850** [see **caribou bog**].

(5) **1895** *Outing* XXVII. 218/1 Here we found the caribou roads at least six inches deep, and evidently used daily to and from water. — (6) **1887** *Harper's Mag.* Feb. 458/2 The hunter . . . covers his feet with . . . a pair of moose or caribou shanks, with the hair outside. **1888** *Ib.* Sep. 510/2 The skin from the hind legs of some caribou . . . worn with the hair outside, are 'caribou shanks.'

cariole 'kærɪˌol, *n.* [F. *carriole*, an Amer. borrowing.] A kind of dog sled formerly used in the Northwest, chiefly in Canada. See **dog cariole.**

1801 in GATES *Fur Traders* 152 Dannis finished a sort of Cariole he has made for me . . . [*footnote*], A cariole was a kind of dog sled that was used to a considerable extent in the Northwest. It was made of oak or birch boards planed smooth and turned up at the front, and was fitted with parchment sides and a comfortable back. **1806–8** PIKE *Sources Miss.* 71 He presented me with his dogs and cariole, valued in this country at two hundred dollars. **1848** BALLANTYNE *Hudson Bay* (1890) 188 The cariole is in form not unlike a slipper bath, both in shape and size. It is lined with buffalo robes, in the midst of a bundle of which the occupant reclines luxuriously, while the dogs drag him slowly through the soft snow, and among the trees and bushes of the forest. **1948** *Canadian Alpine Jrnl.* June 123 Early in March, in a cariole drawn by four dogs, he turned again west, and the third day reached Fort Assiniboine.

carioling 'kærɪˌolɪŋ, *n.* Riding in a cariole or sleigh. *Obs.* — **1806** T. ASHE *Travels in Amer.* 30 In winter, carioling or sleying predominates. **1831** BOUCHETTE *Brit. Domins.* I. 409 The chief pleasures of the inhabitants consist at this time of *carioling* and visiting each other.

carload 'kɑrˌlod, *n.*

1. A load for a railroad car. Also attrib., sometimes in the sense "brought in or sold by the carload."

1854 THOREAU *Walden* 130 This car-load of torn sails is more legible and interesting now than if they should be wrought into paper and printed books. **1879** *Bradstreet's* 17 Dec. 1/3 Packers are paying $4.35 to $4.50 for car-load hogs, and $4 to $4.35 for wagon hogs. **1884** *Rep. N.M. Terr.* 75 Other herds were slaughtered in the woods and the dressed meat shipped by car-load lots. **1945** *Tracks* June 56/1 Thus the section foreman who ordered a carload of cross-ties had his message rendered 'carload of lies.'

b. As a measure of quantity (see quots.).

1875 *Chi. Tribune* 16 Sep. 8/7 Nominally a car-load is 20,000 pounds. **1889** *Cent.* 826/1 Car-load, . . . a customary unit of measure in the United States, equal to 70 barrels of salt, 90 barrels of flour, 9,000 feet of boards, 340 bushels of wheat, 430 bushels of potatoes, etc. **1893** *Stand.* 287/2 [A] car-load . . . varies on different railroads . . . , and . . . also with different substances. **1948** *Capital-Democrat* (Tishomingo, Okla.) 17 June 1/6 Sufficient quantity of sawdust, shipped by the carload, and sodium fluosilicate can be ordered by next week.

2. *fig.* A large number or quantity. *Colloq.*

1867 *Ball Players' Chron.* 11 July 1/1 The large majority of these were visitors from the city, . . . the car loads which came up from Harlem, . . . contributing the greater portion. **1882** SWEET & KNOX *Texas Siftings* 16 It is estimated that one first-class conductor has more sense than a car-load of legislators. **1934** *Reader's Digest* August 103 Here I am with a smoker's throat and a hacking cough which the ads tell me there is not one in a carload of.

carloading 'kɑrˌlodɪŋ, *n.* The amount of freight loaded into freight cars in a given period. Usu. pl. with reference to the number of freight cars so loaded as an index of business activity.

1913 *Wall St. Jrnl.* 4 Oct. 7/2 (*heading*), New York Central Carloading. **1925** *Ib.* 14 Jan. 4/1 Freight car loadings for the first 27 days [were] 4,161 under the total for the same month in 1923. **1948** *Alva* (Okla.) *Review-Courier* 2 July 5/4 Carloadings over the state climbed 6.8 per cent in volume during May.

carne 'kɑrnɪ, *n. S.W.* **1.** Short for chile con carne *q.v. Rare.* **2. carne seca,** (see quots.).

(1) **1852** in *Old Santa Fe* III. (1916) 198 Told them [app. Mexicans] that . . . if they did not kill themselves, eating carne, pan, coffee and sugar, they need not fear any thing else. — (2) **1894** *Scribner's Mag.* May 603/1 Lucky indeed will be the guest who shall be invited to partake of 'carne seca' (jerked beef) broken up and fried in grease. **1936** MCKENNA *Black Range* 52 To make jerky, or *carne seco*, which we could always sell to the Mexicans, we cut the meat from the bones in long, thin strips and hung it over a line to dry.

Carnegiea kɑr'negɪə, *n.* [Andrew *Carnegie* (1837–1919).] A genus of cacti of which the giant cactus, *Carnegiea gigantea*, is the only species.

1908 BRITTON & ROSE in *N.Y. Bot. Gard. Jrnl.* IX. 188 *Carnegiea gigantea.* **1937** NICHOL *Natural Vegetation Ariz.* 204 Dense stands of the giant cactus or saguaro (*Carnegiea gigantea*) may dwarf the woody forest. **1940** PRESTON *Rocky Mt. Trees* 251 The state flower of Arizona . . . *Carnegiea gigantea.*

Carnegie library. A library provided by the philanthropy of Andrew Carnegie (1835–1919), a wealthy American steel manufacturer and philanthropist.

1901 *World's Work* May 776/1 The Carnegie Library, of Pittsburgh, has just issued a catalogue of such of its books as are recommended for the schools of that city. **1902** *Out West* Aug. 225 The inexpensive pleasure of peppering the map of the United States with Carnegie Libraries is probably the brightest thought that ever befell the mind of Rapid-Fire Benevolence. **1948** *Dly. Ardmoreite* (Ardmore, Okla.) 31 Mar. 5/7 She had been associated with the Carnegie library in Ardmore for the past seven months.

* **Carolina,** *n.*

1. *pl.* An inclusive term for North and South Carolina.

1766 *Lett. to Earl of Dartmouth* 27 June (Dartmouth MSS), They are a lawless set of rascalls on the frontiers of Virginia, Maryland, the Carolinas, and Georgia. **1809** FRENEAU *Poems* II. 205 *n.*, A shrub leaf very commonly used in the Carolinas, as a substitute for tea. **1893** POST *Harvard Stories* 15 If the governors of the Carolinas had been with them, those celebrated dignitaries, I suspect, would have experienced none of their proverbial trouble. **1947** *This Week Mag.* 4 Oct. 27/1 In the Carolinas and Virginia, they prefer them plain.

2. In the names of plants and trees: (1) **Carolina allspice,** the sweet shrub; (2) **ash,** the water ash, *Fraxinus caroliniana;* (3) **bean,** the Lima bean; (4) **beech drop,** the sweet pinesap, *Monotropsis odorata*, a rare herb found in the southeastern U.S.; (5) **buckthorn,** the yellow buckthorn, *Rhamnus caroliniana;* (6) **groundnut,** the peanut; (7) **hemlock,** an evergreen, *Tsuga caroliniana*, found in the southeastern states; (8) **jasmine, jessamine,** the yellow jessamine; (9) **kidney-bean tree,** (see quot.), *obs.;* (10) **moonseed,** a vine, *Cocculus carolinus*, of the moonseed family, or a related plant; (11) **moss,** the Spanish moss of the southern states, *obs.;* (12) **pink, pinkroot,** the American wormroot, an herb of the genus *Spigelia*, or a vermifugal preparation made from this; (13) **poplar,** the cottonwood, *Populus deltoides;* (14) **potato,** the common sweet potato, also **Carolina,** *obs.;* (15) **rice,** gold-seed rice, a variety of rice grown along the Atlantic Coast, the ripe husk of which is of a yellowish color; (16) **rose,** the Cherokee rose; (17) **silver-bell tree,** (see quot.); (18) **tea,** the Appalachian tea, *Ilex vomitoria*.

(1) **1789** *Amer. Philos. Soc.* III. p. xxi, The barks of young Sassafras, and of *Calycanthus Floridus* . . . called Carolina allspice much resemble cinnamon. **1868** GRAY *Field Botany* 131 *Calycanthus*, Carolina allspice or sweet-scented shrub. . . . Fl. spring and all summer. **1931** CLUTE *Plants* 70 We may add . . . the Carolina allspice (*Calycanthus Floridus*) with no close associations with the tropical spice of that name. — (2) **1785** MARSHALL *Amer. Grove* 50 *Fraxinus americana*. Carolina or Red Ash. — (3) **1829** EATON *Botany* (ed. 5) 326 *Phaseolus lunatus*, Carolina bean, lima bean. — (4) **1861** WOOD *Botany* 495 Carolina Beech-drops, . . . *Schweinitzia odorata*, Ell. [grows in] rich shady soils, Md. to N. Car.

(5) **1813** H. MUHLENBERG *Cat. Plants* 24 *Rhamnus Carolinianus*, Carolina Buckthorn. **1883** HALE *Woods & Timbers N.C.* 150 Carolina buckthorn (*Frangula Caroliniana*) A thornless shrub . . . the berry is blackish, of the size of a small pea. **1901** MOHR *Plant Life Ala.* 133 The lime-loving Carolina buckthorn. — (6) **1792** IMLAY *Western Territory* 212 The Carolina ground-nut grows low down on the Mississippi. — (7) **1905** *Bureau Forestry Bul. No. 60* 16 The typical trees are red spruce, Fraser fir, and Carolina hemlock. **1943** PEATTIE *Great Smokies* 260 When you reach Cashiers near High Hampton the Carolina hemlocks are giant size. — (8) **1831** AUDUBON *Ornith. Biog.* I. 114 It [Florida jessamine] is also named *Carolina Jessamine* and *Yellow Jessamine*. **1890** *Cent.* 2478/3 The plant . . . known in the United States as the wild, yellow, or Carolina jasmine. **1941** R. S. WALKER *Lookout* 56 Of the creeping and climbing wild vines that grow on Lookout Mountain, Carolina jasmine is one of the earliest flowering kind. — (9) **1818** NUTTALL *Genera No. Amer. Plants* II. 116 This shrub has received the common name of 'Carolina Kidney-bean tree' [i.e., *Wisteria speciosa* (*Glycine frutescens*. Willd.)].

(10) **1785** MARSHALL *Amer. Grove* 86 *Menispermum carolinum*. Carolinian Moonseed. This is much smaller and weaker than the other [*M. canadense*], scarcely becoming shrubby. **1901** MOHR *Plant Life Ala.* 517 *Cebatha carolina*. . . . Carolina Moonseed. — (11) **1835** INGRAHAM *South-West* II. 16 The long black moss, well known at the north as 'Carolina moss,' hangs in immense fringes. **1843** DAUBENY *Journal* 151 Nor were the trees covered as heretofore with festoons of Carolina moss. — (12) **1779** *N.J. Archives* 2 Ser. IV. 21 To be sold, . . . Carolina pink root. **1789** *Amer. Philos. Soc.* III. p. xviii, Carolina pink; a southern plant: it will destroy the worms; but caution in the dose is requisite. **1871** DE VERE 309 The Pink-root . . . is quite generally known as Carolina Pink also. — (13) **1860** in HALE *Woods & Timbers N.C.* 120 Carolina poplar (*Populus angulata*). . . . The wood does not appear to be used. **1931** MATTOON *Forest Trees Okla.* 25 The cottonwood, or Carolina poplar, is found along streams throughout the State. — (14) **1775** ROMANS *Nat. Hist. Florida* 123 The varieties, in an ascending scale for goodness, [are] 1st. Spanish, . . . 2d. Carolina, little superior to the first. 3d. Brimstone. **1819** SCHOOLCRAFT *Mo. Lead Mines* 34 The sweet, or Carolina potatoe was raised last year in considerable perfection. **1884** *Cent. Mag.* XXVII. 442/1 The sweet potato was adopted from the aborigines in all the Southern colonies, and it is yet known in the market as the 'Carolina.'

(15) **1787** JEFFERSON *Writings* VI. 194 The objection to the Carolina rice then, being, that it crumbles in certain forms of preparation. **1868** *Rep. Comm. Agric.* 174 In this article I will confine my attention chiefly to what is known as golden or Carolina rice. — (16) **1802** J. DRAYTON *S. Carolina* 72 Carolina rose. (*Rosa Caroliniana*.) Grows on clayey soils, near water: and adjacent ditches. *a***1858** WARDER *Hedges & Evergreens* 33 A great many shrubs and trees have been used for the formation of hedges, but none is better adapted to this purpose than the Cherokee or Carolina Rose. — (17) **1901** MOHR *Plant Life Ala.* 89 The Carolina silver-bell tree (*Mohrodendron* (*Halesia*) *carolinum*) also makes its appearance here. — (18) **1891** *Cent.* 7008/3 Yapon [is] an evergreen shrub or small tree of the holly kind . . . *Ilex Cassine;* . . . also called cassena, and Appalachian, Carolina, and South Sea tea. **1907** HODGE *Amer. Indians* I. 150/1 Black drink ('Carolina tea' Catawba yaupon).

Also *Carolina azolla, black gum, boxthorn, cane, cotton, cypress, globe tree, grass, indigo, ironwood, laurel, live oak, nightshade, orange, privet, red bay, red bud, red oak, walnut*, etc.

b. In the names of birds and other animals: (1) **Carolina bat,** a native American bat, *Vespertilio subulatus;* (2) **dove,** the mourning dove; (3) **duck,** (see quot. 1896); (4) **junco,** a species of junco found in the southern Allegheny region; (5) **parakeet,** =next; (6) **parrot,** a handsome parrot, *Conuropsis carolinensis*, now believed to be extinct; (7) **pigeon,** =**Carolina dove,** *obs.;* (8) **rail,** the short-billed sora, *Porzana carolina*, found in the marshes along the Atlantic Coast; (9) **turtledove,** =**Carolina dove;** (10) **waxwing,** the cedar waxwing; (11) **wren,** a large wren, *Thryothorus ludovicianus*, characterized by its loud clear song, also **great Carolina wren.**

(1) **1823** JAMES *Exped. Rocky M.* I. 261 *Vespertilio Carolinus*, Geoff.—Carolina bat. **1842** *Nat. Hist. N.Y., Zoology* I. 10 The Carolina Bat is found along the Atlantic States from Georgia to Connecticut. — (2) **1874** COUES *Birds N.W.* 389 *Zenædura Carolinensis*, . . . Carolina Dove; Common Dove. **1894** B. TORREY *Fla. Sketch-Book* 147 Herons in the usual variety were present, with ospreys, an eagle, kingfishers, ground doves, Carolina doves, [etc.]. — (3) **1784** in C. ASPINALL-OGLANDER *Admiral's Widow* 115 Many winged families of most respectable size and beautiful feather, especially Carolina ducks, which I judged to be the Summer duck, so rare and beautiful. **1896** NEWTON *Dict. Birds* 1 Acorn-duck, a name given in some parts of North America to the Carolina or Wood-Duck, *Æx sponsa*. — (4) **1898** *Atlantic Mo.* Oct. 492/2 But if this is true of the Carolina junco, I failed to satisfy myself of the fact. **1943** PEATTIE *Great Smokies* 275 The Carolina juncos ('Snowbirds') may be incubating eggs under a snow-covered canopy of rootlets and dried plant remains.

(5) **1850** S. F. COOPER *Rural Hours* 426 It is well known that we have in the southern parts of the country a member of the Parrot tribe, the Carolina Parakeet. **1917** *Birds of Amer.* II. 123 The Carolina Paroquet is to-day nearly, if not quite, extinct, no record of its appearance having been made for several years. **1945** MATHEWS *Talking* 104 Every time I stop in the field to pull cocklebурs . . . I think of the Carolina parakeet. — (6) **1811** WILSON *Ornith.* III. 97 The Carolina, or Illinois Parrot, (for it has been described under both these appellations) is thirteen inches long. **1857** *Rep. Comm. Agric. 1856* 147 The Carolina parrot, or parrakeet, is the only one of the two hundred species of its genus, which has been found in the United States. — (7) **1812** WILSON *Ornith.* V. 91 Carolina Pigeon, or Turtle Dove: *Columba Carolinensis.* **1828** BONAPARTE *Synopsis* 119 The Carolina Pigeon. . . . Inhabits the United States during summer; common; wintering chiefly in the southern states. — (8) **1831** WILSON & BONAPARTE *Amer. Ornith.* III. 110 *Rallus Carolinus*, Linnaeus and Wilson,—Carolina Rail. **1917** *Birds of Amer.* I. 207. — (9) **1812** [see **Carolina pigeon**]. **1831** AUDUBON *Ornith. Biog.* I. 91 The Carolina Turtle Dove. *Columba Carolinensis*. . . . The roosting places which the Carolina Turtles prefer are among the long grasses found growing in abandoned fields. **1867** *Amer. Naturalist* I. 54 Carolina Turtle Doves.

(10) **1874** COUES *Birds N.W.* 93 *Ampelis Cedrorum*, . . . Cedar Bird; Cherry Bird; Carolina Waxwing. **1917** *Birds of Amer.* III. 94. — (11) **1810** WILSON *Ornith.* II. 61 [The] Great Carolina Wren, *Certhia Caroliniana*, . . . is frequently seen, early in May, along the shores of the Delaware. **1948** *Bird-Banding* July 101 When choosing a nest the Carolina Wren shows a decided preference for some type of receptacle or ledge to support and protect the roofed, side-entrance nest.

c. In miscellaneous obs. combs.: (1) **Carolina gouger,** a gouger, *q.v.*, living in Carolina; (2) **race horse,** a razor-back hog, *humorous;* (3) **swamper,** (see quot.).

(1) **1840** HALIBURTON *Clockm.* 3 Ser. ix, Regular built bruisers too; claw your eyes right out, like a Carolina gouger. — (2) **1862** E. KIRKE *Among Pines* 212 We call them Carolina race-horses, said the Colonel, as he finished an account of their peculiarities. — (3) *c***1812** in JOHN BERNARD *Retrospections* (1887) 250 A 'Pennsylvania hurricane,' like a 'Caroliny swamper,' was, indeed, a common term nearer home, for a sublime Munchausenism—vulgarly speaking a long lie.

Carolinian ˌkærəˈlɪnɪən, *a.* and *n.*

1. *n.* A native of North or South Carolina. Cf. **North, South Carolina.**

1707 J. ARCHDALE *Descr. of Carolina* 15 After a very mature Deliberation, and by the Encouragements of several Carolinians then in England my Going was concluded for. **1793** DRAYTON *Tour through Eastern States* (1794) 5 Presenting a variety of prospect, which with a Carolinean accustomed to a level country, was particularly pleasing. **1861** *Richmond* (Va.) *Examiner* 5 Dec. 2/2 The Western people are as brave as the Carolinians. **1948** *Sat. Ev. Post* 17 July 57/1 James Edward Oglethorpe . . . founded this 'cradle of Georgia' in 1733, as a protective buffer for the Carolinians against the Spaniards in Florida.

2. *a.* Of or pertaining to North or South Carolina.

1706 PENN in *Penn-Logan Corr.* (1872) II. 105 Lord Cornbury had but £600 pr. ann. . . . for salary, . . . and for Colonel Dudley, . . . they have not allowed him more, or very little, and the Carolinian Lords, not so much. **1775** ROMANS *Hist. Florida* 174 In the article of beef, cattle can hardly yield profit where the *Carolinian* or *Georgian* method of killing at two, three, and four years old obtains. **1851** *S. Lit. Messenger* XVII. 26/1, I determined to try my fortune among the . . . stirring pursuits of the Carolinian gold country.

b. In biogeography, designating the humid subdivision of the Upper Austral zone, including most of the eastern U.S. and extending west to the 100th meridian. Cf. **Canadian zone.**

1859 COOPER *Distribution Forests & Trees No. Amer.* 268 The regions in which *trees* are found (indicated by letters on the map) are: . . . G. *Carolinian*, with eighteen characteristic and *seven* peculiar. **1894** *Nat. Geog. Mag.* 29 Dec. 237 The Upper Austral Zone comprises two principal subdivisions: an eastern Carolinian area and a western or Upper Sonoran area. **1906** DICKERSON *Frog Book* 37 The eastern wooded portions of the austral zones, counting from north to south, are known as the Alleghenian, Carolinian, and Austroriparian faunas, respectively. **1945** *Mass. Audubon Soc. Bul.* Feb. 18 In some of its southerly-exposed slopes facing Boston there is always the possibility of finding more southern forms usually relegated to the Carolinian life zone.

Widely used in the names of, or with reference to, plants, trees, insects, etc., as *Carolinian allspice, ash, bay-tree, catchfly, cedar, cherry, cranesbill, glasswort, holly, ironwood, lime tree, red bud, vine,* etc.

Carolinite ˌkærəˈlaɪnaɪt, *n.* A native of Carolina. *Rare.* — **1775** *N.C. Gazette* (Newbern) 24 March, Now it came to pass that the Carolinites of the North . . . had heard all these sayings.

Carolus doubloon. (See quot.) *Rare.* — **1891** S. M. WELCH *Recoll. 1830–40* 168 The gold coins most popular in circulation [in upper New York] were the 'Carolus Doubloons,' standard value $16.

carom ˈkærəm, *v.* [f. **carom*, a stroke in billiards.] *intr.* To glance, rebound. Also fig.

1860 HOLMES *Professor* iii. 88 She glanced from every human contact, and 'caromed' from one relation to another. **1911** MULFORD *Bar-20 Days* iv. 45 The table skidded through the door on one leg and carromed off the bar at a graceful angle. **1948** *Newsweek* 3 May 71/3 The ball caromed to Peewee Reese, the Brooklyn shortstop.

***carp,** *n.* As the last term in **American, buffalo, scale carp.**

***carpenter,** *n.* In combs.: (1) ***carpenter bee,** any one of various solitary bees of the genus *Xylocopa*, esp. *X. virginica;* (2) **bird,** the California woodpecker; (3) **shop,** the workshop of a carpenter; (4) **'s leaf,** (see quot.); (5) **weed,** (see quot.).

(1) **1838** GOSSE *Letters* 143 Those species which thus drill round holes in wood, for the purpose of obtaining a secure and commodious nidus for their young, are appropriately called Carpenter-Bees. **1867** *Amer Naturalist* I. 157, I send specimens in alcohol of the pupa of *Xylocopa Virginica*, the Carpenter Bee. **1909** *N.J. State Museum Rep.* 698 The large carpenter bee [is] common throughout the State. — (2) **1858** *Atlantic Mo.* Dec. 870/1 The little Hair-Bird . . . is called the 'Chipping-Sparrow,' as if he were in the habit of making chips, like the Carpenter-Bird. [**1947** BUMP *Ruffed Grouse* 274 Called the 'carpenter bird' by certain Indian tribes, the bird has since been aptly dubbed 'the kettledrum of Nature's orchestra.'] — (3) **1866** *Rep. Indian Affairs* 83 The carpenter shop is not sufficiently large for the repairing of large wagon beds. **1948** *Red Book* (Chi.) March 280/1 (*advt.*), Van Buren Carpenter Shop. — (4) **1814** PURSH *Flora Amer.* II. 446 Galax rotundifolia. . . . In the Virginia mountains this plant is known by the name of Carpenter's-leaf, being used in healing all kinds of wounds and cuts. — (5) **1891** *Amer. Folk-Lore* IV. 148 Carpenter Weed was our only name for *Brunella vulgaris*.

Carpenteria ˌkɑrpənˈtɪrɪə, *n.* [Wm. M. *Carpenter* (1811–48), an Amer. physician.] A showy, white-flowered shrub of California, a member of the saxifrage family, discovered by John C. Frémont.

1850 TORREY *Plantae Fremontianae* 12 Carpenteria Californica. . . . This genus is named in memory of . . . the late Professor Carpenter of Louisiana. **1908** WEBSTER *Flowering Trees & Shrubs* 26 The Carpenteria is nearly related to the Mock Orange. **1942** VAN DERSAL *Ornamental Amer. Shrubs* 209 In its native locale carpenteria grows in the sun. **1947** PEATTIE *Sierra Nevada* 103 California's carpenteria . . . has been in cultivation for over forty years.

***carpet,** *n.* In combs.: (1) **carpetbag,** see as a main entry; (2) **bagged,** having a carpetbag, ruled or dominated by carpetbaggers, *obs.;* (3) **bagger, baggery, bagging,** see as main entries; (4) **bagism,** the principles and practices of carpetbaggers, *obs.;* (5) **chair,** a folding chair with back and seat of carpet; (6) **hive,** (see quot.), *obs.;* (7) **house,** a store that specializes in the sale of carpets; (8) ***knight,** during the Civil War a term applied to a member of the State or National Guard, *obs.;* (9) **sack,** a carpetbag; (10) **satchel,** =prec., *rare;* (11)

Carpet sack or satchel

store, a store in which carpets are sold; (12) **sweeper,** a household appliance for sweeping or cleaning carpets; (13) **wool,** (see quot.).

(2) **1857** *Harper's Mag.* Sep. 558/1 Brown and Rogers, carpet-bagged and duster-clad . . . set foot once more . . . upon the solid pavement. **1872** *Chi. Tribune* 10 Oct. 4/6 Repudiation there, and in other carpet-bagged States, is, we fear, but a question of time. — (4) **1870** CHIPMAN *Notes on Bartlett* 69 *Carpet-bagism.* Political rule, &c. of carpet-baggers. **1872** *N.Y. Herald* 16 Dec. 5/1 Carpet-Bagism in Alabama and in New Orleans. **1911** H. S. HARRISON *Queed* iv. 45 The morning *Post* . . . had crucified carpet-baggism.

(5) **1882** HOWELLS *Modern Instance* xx, She had done what could be done with folding carpet chairs to give the little room a specious air of luxury. **1886** ——— *Minister's Charge* 152 There were bright folding carpet-chairs. — (6) **1870** *Rep. Comm. Agric. 1869* 332 The carpet hive was patented in 1868, and is composed of a skeleton frame or trellis, from which the textile covering is to be removed during warm weather. . . . As the weather grows cold the carpet is to be thrown over the trellis. — (7) **1867** *Atlantic Mo.* March 338/2 Now it is a gorgeous and enormous carpet-house that arrests his attention; now a huge dry-goods store, or vast depot of groceries. **1887** *Courier-Journal* 7 May 3/6 This supplies a long-felt want of this city—an exclusive Carpet House at popular prices. —(8) **1862** in MCCLELLAN *Own Story* 281 There is a prodigious cry of 'On to Richmond!' among the carpet-knights of our city, who will not shed their blood to get there. **1880** *Harper's Mag.* May 916/2 These 'carpet knights,' as they were called, spent [days of terrible suspense] in building bridges. — (9) **1855** *Herald of Freedom* 30 June 2/6 Risking our precious bodies, trunks, carpet-sacks, and 'hoss pistols,' without insurance, on the . . . Missouri river. **1901** CHURCHILL *Crisis* 402 He had contrived to be rid of the carpet-sack in which certain precious letters were carried.

(10) **1856** COZZENS *Sparrowgr. Papers* xiii. 183, I found them with their new carpet-satchels all ready for the morning. — (11) **1865** STOWE *House & Home P.* 85 They proceed to the carpet-stores, and there are thrown at their feet by obsequious clerks velvet and Axminsters. **1868** MRS. WHITNEY *P. Strong* 128, I . . . ran up into the carpet store. — (12) **1859** *Rep. Comm. Patents 1858* II. 444 This invention has reference to that description of carpet or floor sweepers in which a revolving brush . . . is made to take up and deposit the sweepings in a case covering the brush. **1947** *Democrat* 16 Oct. 2/3 His free hand gestured out over wash tubs, kraut shovels, and toil-worn carpet sweepers. — (13) **1889** *Secy. of Agric. Rep.* 245 About seven-tenths of the entire importation of the last ten years has been admitted under the third class as 'carpet wools,' a designation very inexact, as it includes the wool of all the races of sheep in the world, improved and unimproved, merino and English only excepted.

Early (*c*1858) form of carpet sweeper

b. In the names of plants, insects, etc.: (1) **carpet fly,** (see quot.), *rare;* (2) ***grass,** any one of various grasses, as *Axonopus compressus,* a pasture and lawn grass (see quot. 1901); (3) **pink,** a catchfly, *Silene acaulis,* of western North America; (4) **shell,** (see quot.); (5) **weed,** the Indian chickweed, *Mollugo verticillata,* which forms a carpet-like mat on the ground.

(1) **1869** *Amer. Naturalist* II. 592 The Carpet-fly, *Scenopinus pallipes* . . . in the larva state, is found under carpets, on which it is said to feed. — (2) **1882** A. M. MACY in E. K. Godfrey *Nantucket* 36 The carpet-grass and the orange-grass . . . were eagerly sought for at that period. **1901** MOHR *Plant Life Ala.* 120 Carpet grass (*Paspalum compressum*) a West Indian species most probably introduced. **1948** *Holland's* March 50/3 All three are good grasses—and of course there are those old favorites, Bermuda and carpet. — (3) **1938** THOMPSON *High Trails* 85 The carpet pink flourishes early, and old man's whiskers, and blue beardtongue. — (4) **1893** *Stand.* 289/1 *Carpet-shell,* a small clam (*Tapes staminea*) extensively used as food in California.

(5) **1784** CUTLER in *Mem. Academy* I. 407 Carpet-weed. . . . Blossoms greenish white. **1817–8** EATON *Botany* (1822) 355 *Mollugo verticillata,* carpet weed generally grows in gardens among purslain. **1947** *Midland Naturalist* July 42 Carpetweed [is] common (locally abundant) in cultivated fields.

b. In colloq. phrases: (1) *To come on the carpet,* to put in an appearance, (2) *to be (out) on the carpet,* (see quot.).

(1) **1888** *Cent. Mag.* XXXVI. 552/2 She certain' have been more dressy and pink in the face since—since you come on the carpet. — (2) **1909** *D. N.* III. 355 (Out) on the carpet, said of one who is a candidate for matrimony. 'They say Widow Jones is out on the carpet again.'

As the last term in **ingrain, log cabin, rag, squaw, strip carpet.**

***carpetbag,** *n.*

1. *attrib.* In allusion to those who travel with little or no baggage, as **carpetbag adventurer, emigration, gentry, merchant, scrub.**

1846 *Ga. Messenger* 24 Dec., [It] may be traced to some of those carpet-bag gentry, who are wandering through upper Georgia. **1856** PHILLIPS *Kansas* 265 The larger portion of these carpet-bag adventurers were reckless characters, from the vilest purlieus of society; men who had been robbers and gambling loafers, and whose lawless character well suited them for the task they were to perform. **1857** *Herald of Freedom* (Lawrence, Kansas) 19 Sep. (Th.), Early in the spring several thousand excellent young men came to Kansas. This was jokingly called the carpet-bag emigration. **1884** *Kingston* (N.M.) *Clipper* 8 Mar. 1/5 An effort is being made to remove more of the jobbers, bloodsucks, and renegade carpet bag scrubs from our territory. **1944** CLARK *Pills* 25 It was a lucrative field for economic exploitation for the 'fly-by-night' carpetbag merchant.

2. With reference to the Reconstruction period in the South just after the Civil War, as (1) **carpetbag corruption,** (2) **days,** (3) **element,** (4) **era,** (5) **government,** (6) **member,** (7) **senator,** (8) **state,** (9) **Yankee.**

(1) **1886** Z. F. SMITH *Kentucky* 795 Instead of the twelve years of carpet-bag corruption and spoliation, . . . there might have been . . . a reconstruction. — (2) **1887** *Courier-Journal* 29 Jan. 5/5 During the carpet-bag days he was the friend of the South. — (3) **1895** CHAMBLISS *Diary* 300 These rowdies are not Mississippians. They belong to the carpet-bag element. — (4) **1888** *Chicago Inter-Ocean* (F.), One of the most vulnerable men who figured in Southern politics in the carpet-bag era. **1944** *Harper's Mag.* March 363/1 The carpetbag era was over, but the farmers—and they were the great majority—were in the grip of perpetual hard times.

(5) **1871** *Cong. Globe* App. 3 March 273/2 The favorite name applied to our southern governments by our Democratic friends is that of 'carpet-bag governments.' **1938** ASBURY *Sucker's Prog.* 238 Afterward [he] became an important figure in the carpet-bag government of Louisiana. — (6) **1870** in TOURGEE *Invisible Empire* (1880) xii. 504 As to the carpet-bag members of the Convention . . . they were thirteen in number. — (7) **1870** *Nation* 6 Jan. 6/1 No one expects high political morality from carpet-bag senators. — (8) **1873** BEADLE *Undevel. West* xxiii. 471 If a State, this would be a most complete 'rotten borough'—the worst 'carpet-bag' State in the Union. **1943** HICKS *Amer. Dem.* 511 Finally Congress decided to refer the double returns received from the carpet-bag states to an Electoral Commission of fifteen. — (9) **1881** *Georgians* 123 They would do very well if they were not haunted and harangued by a set of carpet-bag Yankees.

b. In modern use applied to any exercise of authority by an outsider or an outside government.

1902 *Out West* Feb. 146 The other [Hawaiian political party] is the 'American' or 'Carpet Bag' party, made up of late comers, who care nothing for these or similar traditions. **1944** *Chi. D. News* 9 Dec. 4/5 During the last week we have read that carpetbag administrations in Greece and Belgium, with the support of the Churchill government, are beating the brains out of the people who led the underground fight against the Nazis.

carpetbag ˈkɑrpɪtˌbæg, *v. intr.* To go to a new environment motivated entirely by selfish and unworthy motives, to act as a carpetbagger. *Colloq.*

1872 *Ill. Dept. Agric.* 266 Almost the entire force of our common schools tends to . . . send [our young men] . . . 'carpet bagging,' down South. **1882** *Nation* 17 Aug. 121/1 They had served in Congress together, and had lived not far from each other before Dorsey 'carpet-bagged' from Ohio to Arkansas. **1890** *Cong. Rec.* 4 June 5598/2 Mr. McDuffie carpet-bagged from somewhere down into Alabama. **1948** *Sat. Ev. Post* 17 July 57/1 You keep expecting a boy in gray to step out from behind a tree and begin playing Dixie on a fife—a kind of Pied Piper who will lead all improper and carpetbagging spirits to the river and march them in.

carpetbagger ˈkɑrpɪtˌbægɚ, *n.*

1. One of the poor northern adventurers who, carrying all their belongings in carpetbags, went south to profit from the social and political upheaval after the Civil War.

1868 ROSE *Great Country* 181 Many of them are what the Southerners call 'carpet-baggers,' men travelling with little luggage and less character, making political capital out of the present state of affairs. **1885** *Cent. Mag.* April 956/1 The carpet-baggers, who so largely assumed its command, despite some honorable exceptions, were for the most part unprincipled men. **1948** *Green Bay* (Wis.) *Press-Gazette* 30 June 20/3 It was an old law passed after the civil war to create unwonted voting power for carpetbaggers in Negro areas, where the white man was disenfranchised.

2. A term of contempt or humor applied to a stranger, foreigner, transient, etc.

1869 *Republican D. Jrnl.* (Lawrence, Kans.) 3 Nov., Fifty loaded teams between Burlington and Emporia [included] coaches heavily loaded with passengers, besides several *carpet-baggers* on foot. **1901** CHURCHILL *Crisis* II. xviii. 279 There's lots of those military carpet-baggers hanging around for good jobs. **1948** *Chi. Tribune* 3 April I. 2/6 They have brought swarms of out-of-state orators and carpet-baggers to tell us in Wisconsin how to vote next Tuesday.

carpetbaggery ˈkɑrpɪtˌbægərɪ, *n.* Corrupt political rule by nonresident demagogues. *Obs.*

1872 *Cin. Commercial* 22 May. (Supp.) 2/4 They had pretty much lost confidence in the old Democratic party, . . . and were ready to take any road out of their misgovernment, carpet-baggery, and skull-duggery. **1874** in FLEMING *Hist. Reconstruction* II. 146 The real author of carpetbaggery (Uncle Sam) stepped upon the stage. **1884** *Milnor* (Dakota) *Teller* 30 July, My talk on Dakota before the house committee on territories . . . led to the introduction of a bill by Mr. Tillman of South Carolina, to abolish this infamous system of territorial carpet-baggery.

carpetbagging ˈkɑrpɪtˌbægɪŋ, *n.*

1. Traveling with a carpetbag or other light baggage.

1869 *Atlantic Mo.* XXIII. 747 After three weeks' delightful Carpet-Bagging.

2. The practice of carpetbaggery *q.v.* Also attrib.

1870 *Clipping from periodical,* The Rev. Carpetbagging Thief and Cadetship-peddler has arrived in Washington, and has had a long interview with Ben Butler. **1888** BRYCE *Amer. Commw.* II. 621 Negro suffrage produced, during the few years of 'carpet-bagging' and military government which followed the war, incredible mischief. **1945** MARSHALL *Santa Fe* 216 He had saved Galveston in '72 when years of carpetbagging rule had nearly ruined it.

carrel, see **corral.**

carreta kəˈretə, *n. W., S.W.* [Sp. in same sense.] A crude wagon or cart.

Carreta of the Southwest

1844 GREGG *Commerce of Prairies* I. 96 Large parties of New-Mexicans, some provided with mules and asses, others with *carretas* or truckle-carts and oxen, drive out into these prairies to procure a supply of buffalo beef. **1888** LINDLEY *Calif. of South* 83 There was a Mexican *carita,* drawn by two oxen. **1941** FERGUSSON *Southwest* 79 He carried with him, enshrined on her own carreta, an image of the Virgin, La Conquistadora, to whom he prayed for success.

carretela ˌkɑreˈtilə, *n. W.* and *S.W.* [Sp. *carretilla,* in Amer. Sp. sense shown here.] =prec. *Obs.*

1846–7 MAGOFFIN *Down Santa Fé Trail* (1926) 86 He is eternally singing, even when he is driving *la carratela* (carriage) over the worst kind of . . . roads. **1854** BARTLETT *Personal Narrative* II. xxxvi. 375 As my carratella (little wagon) was quite light. **1856** WHIPPLE *Explor. Ry. Route* I. 30 The carretela which carries the [surveying] instruments was again upset, and another barometer broken.

* **carriage,** *n.* In combs.: (1) **carriage boot,** (*a*) a waterproof cover or apron to protect the driver of a carriage from rain and mud, (*b*) a boot or shoe made specially for wear in a carriage, both *obs.;* (2) **house,** a building for housing a carriage; (3) **place,** a portage, *rare;* (4) **porch,** a porch at or under which a carriage may conveniently be stopped; (5) **shop,** a carriage maker's shop; (6) **weight,** a weight to which is attached a rein for preventing a carriage animal from going away.

(1) (*a*) **1868** *Rep. Comm. Patents 1867* I. 481/2 Carriage Boot.—[patented] January 15, 1867. The apron is combined with a dash cover. (*b*) **1907** M. C. HARRIS *Tents of Wickedness* II. iv. 266 When she was ready, carriage-boots and all, she went drearily out of the door. — (2) **1761** in *Notes on Old Gloucester County, N.J.* I. 316 Their fine carriage house is finished and painted. **1803** *Steele Papers* I. 395 A Carriage House 16 feet square. **1900** C. WINCHESTER *W. Castle* v. 90 On the table stood a lighted lantern, ready to guide his steps to the carriage-house and stable. — (3) **1775** J. MELVIN *Journal* (1857) 10 The carriage-place is about a mile in length. — (4) **1857** C. VAUX *Villas* 303 A carriage porch leads to a vestibule and octangular hall. **1861** WINTHROP *Open Air* 268 The old villa serves us for headquarters. . . . Four granite pillars . . . make a carriage-porch. (5) **1847** H. HOWE *Ohio* 126 Chagrin Falls contains . . . 1 carriage, 2 tin, 3 harness and 3 cabinet shops. **1887** *Trial H. K. Goodwin* 49 There is a harness shop and then a carriage shop. — (6) **1923** E. F. WYATT *Invis. Gods* III. iii. 119 He threw out the carriage weight [from the buggy] and started toward the house.

As the last term in **baby, car, close, depot, electric, ladies, land, log, mill, pleasurable, riding, rockaway, sail carriage.**

* **carrier,** *n.* As the last term in **cane, cash, chain, hod, lumber, mail, moccasin, paper, stone carrier.**

* **carrion,** *n.* In combs.: (1) * **carrion bird,** the Canada jay; (2) * **flower,** a species of cat brier whose flowers have an offensive smell; (3) **vine,** =prec.

(1) **1784** J. BELKNAP *Jrnl. Tour* (1876) 10 The Dr. saw a blue bird, with a white head, which is said to be a *saw-whetter,* alias *carrion-bird.* **1844** *Nat. Hist. N.Y., Zoology* II. 130 The Canada Jay. *Garrulus Canadensis.* . . . Its food consists of berries, caterpillars, eggs of other birds, and even carrion, from whence it derives one of its popular names of Carrion Bird. — (2) **1837** DARLINGTON *Flora Cestrica* 567 Herbaceous Smilax. *Vulgo*—Carrion-flower. **1947** *Midland Naturalist* July 37 Carrion-flower [is] rare in seepage swamps, terrace forest, hedgerows, and wood margins. — (3) **1938** DAMON *Grandma* 70 The graceful way a carrion vine has of arching, even the glossy varnish on poison-ivy foliage pleased her.

carrizo kɑˈriso, *n. S.W.* [Sp. in same sense.] A reed of any one of various species.

1884 *Harper's Mag.* Oct. 750/2 Crates of the carrizo cane. **1912** WOOTON & STANDLEY *Grasses N.M.* 116 The mud or adobe of which the roof is composed rests on the reeds of the Carrizo and is prevented from falling through. **1933** *Amer. Sp.* Oct. 9/1 If a pool or spring is well grown with reeds, it is called *carrizal* (place of reeds) from *carrizo,* a reed.

carrot ˈkærət, *n.* [App. f. earlier F. *carote, carotte,* in same sense.] A roll of leaf tobacco. *Obs.* or *hist.*

1772 D. TAITT in *Travels Amer. Col.* 537 Others took the cock off his riffle and Sixteen carrots of Tobacco. **1812** STODDARD *Sketches La.* 227 Carottes of tobacco are still made by the French of Missouri and Louisiana. The leaves, after the large stem has been removed, are laid together lengthwise and compressed; then the bundle is covered with a cloth and tightly wrapped from end to end with a cord, making the tobacco into an almost solid mass from twelve to eighteen inches long and tapering almost to a point at each end. **1857** *Ill. Agric. Soc. Trans.* II. 360 The Creoles manufactured the tobacco into carrots, as they were called. A carrot is a roll of tobacco twelve or fifteen inches long. **1890** *Cong. Rec.* 27 Aug. 9213/2, I have here some carots [*sic*] of Cuban tobacco. **1941** McDERMOTT *Glossary* 43 carotte, n. f. Leaves of tobacco twisted or rolled into the shape of a carrot—the common form in which tobacco was stored and sold in the Mississippi Valley.

* **carrotweed,** *n.* The ragweed, *Ambrosia elatior.* — **1907** LYONS *Plant Names* 30 A[mbrosia] artemisiæfolia . . . Tassel-weed, Stick-weed, Carrot-weed, Bastard Wormwood. **1944** *New Yorker* 16 Sep. 28/3 Now she made out the individual weeds, and she saw that . . . here, in her enclosure, flourished only the most virile, the most virid, the most weedlike weeds, the coarse growers— . . . Queen Anne's lace; the crawlers—carrotweed, Jill-run-over-the-ground, [etc.].

* **carrousel,** *n.* A merry-go-round.

1889 *Cent.* 834/2. **1909** *Sat. Ev. Post* 13 March 64/1 We make everything in the Riding-Gallery line from a hand-power Merry-Go-Round to the highest grade Carousselles. **1947** BEEBE *Mixed Train Dly.* 54 McLean was proprietor of a dance pavilion and carousel.

* **carry,** *n.*

1. =**carrying place.**

1838 in C. T. JACKSON *Second Rep. Geol. Mass.* 53–4, I continued up the west branch to the lower carry into that lake . . . the upper carry is about eight miles above the lower. **1889** *Outing* May 124/2 Each man is expected to carry his own clothing over *carries,* as the guides have enough to do with taking care of the camp equipage and stores. **1947** *Nat. Geog. Mag.* July 68/2 [There] is the site of brave old Fort Stanwix, most famed of the pre-Revolutionary forts built to guard the crucial carry.

2. The carrying of a canoe, goods, etc., over a carry, usu. *to make a carry.*

1861 WINTHROP *Open Air* 28 A bateau cannot climb through breakers over boulders. We must make a 'carry,' an actual portage. **1899** JEWETT *Queen's Twin* i. 5 It belonged to the up-country Indians when they had to make a carry to the landing here to get to the out' islands. **1913** EATON *Barn Doors & Byways* 52 The current seemed to widen, grow more sluggish, promising perhaps a mill pond, the excitement of a 'carry,' the thrill of a strange village!

3. In combs.: (1) **carry-log,** *S.* (see quot. 1899); (2) **man,** a man who works at a carrying place, *rare;* (3) **path,** a path at a carrying place.

(1) **1781** *Virginia St. P.* I. 569 [Capt. Allen] is in want of waggons and a carry-log. **1862** *N.Y. Tribune* 27 Feb. (Chipman), The only carry-log we could obtain broke in attempting to transport the first gun. **1899** GREEN *Va. Word-Bk.* 79 Carry-log, *n.* A set of very tall wheels for carrying timber. — (2) **1858** THOREAU in *Atlantic Mo.* June 6/1 At the north end of the carry, . . . there was a log camp of the usual construction, with something like a house adjoining, for the accommodation of the carry-man's family. — (3) *a***1862** THOREAU

Maine Woods 287 The carry-paths themselves were more than usually indistinct.

∗ **carry,** *v.*

1. *intr.* To pass over or traverse a carry *q.v.*

1755 L. Evans *Anal. Map Colonies* 20 The same River conducts them again to the great Carrying-place; where . . . they are obliged to carry over Land four or eight Miles, to Wood Creek. **1869** W. Murray *Adventures* 10, I have boated up and down that [=Adirondack] wilderness, going ashore only to 'carry' around a fall.

2. *tr.* To set in motion, operate. *Rare.*

1831 Peck *Guide for Emigrants* 199 There is a spinning machine [etc.] . . . of one hundred and sixty spindles, and one . . . of one hundred and twenty-six spindles. They are carried by ox power on an inclined plane.

3. To hold (stock) without selling, in expectation of a rise; to keep merchandise on hand or in stock.

1848 W. Armstrong *Stocks* 10 It is nominally considered that the stock is meanwhile 'carried' or possessed by the seller. **1905** *Chi. D. News* 29 July 10/2 Unless the market broadened and became active he could not market even his 36,000 shares at one price, and he probably was 'carrying' other stocks elsewhere. **1907** *Pearson's Mag.* Jan. (*advt.*), [Book-cases] carried in stock by agents in over 1,200 cities.

4. (See quot.)

1859 *Harper's Mag.* Nov. 729/1 The beautiful grain [rice] falls. . . . The reaper usually 'carries' or takes a sweep of three rows at a time.

5. To take a leading part in singing; to bear or sustain (a part or melody).

1868 G. G. Channing *Recoll. Newport* 73 Four of the congregation, with the leader already referred to, volunteered as a *quintette* to '*carry* the singing.' **1890** *Harper's Mag.* Dec. 147/1, I carried the toon. Peleg sung a real sweet second. **1903** Wiggin *Rebecca* 27 She 'carried' the alto by the ear.

6. To keep up or provide with financial support.

1879 *Bradstreet's* 8 Oct. 4/4 He is forced to pay on loans necessary to 'carry' the farmer. **1914** *Collier's* 10 Jan. II. 58/2 I'm afraid we're carrying you now for as much as our custom allows. **1931** *K. C. Star* 8 Oct., The banks are carrying more people than the railroads are.

7. Of newspapers and magazines: To print.

1926 *Publishers' Weekly* 22 May 1676/1 There are many towns in which the newspapers do not carry book reviews.

8. In colloq. phrases: (1) *To beat the devil and carry a rail,* see **rail;** (2) *to carry one high (and dry),* to tease one immoderately; (3) *carry me out,* (see quot.).

(2) **1887** E. B. Custer *Tenting on Plains* v. 169 He used to carry me high and dry about them little roads leading off to folks he said I was a-feedin'. — (3) **1889** Barrere-Leland I. 228 Carry, carry me out! (American), an expression of incredulity or affected disgust.

carryall ˈkærɪˌɔl, *n.* [In sense **1.** from F. *carriole,* but in **2.** app. based on the verb ∗ *carry.*]

1. Orig. a light one-horse vehicle, later used of a large, heavy carriage as well.

1714 J. Stoddard in *N.E. Hist. & Gen. Reg.* V. 27 Mr. Longuille sent a carryall for us, which carried us to Montreal. **1811** *Colonial Centinel* 5 June 3/1 For sale a Carryall, that is very convenient to carry five or six persons to their places of visitation. **1897** Terhune *Old Field* 170 Mr. Grigsby had come to the landing in a blue-bodied "carryall." A plank laid across the front served him for a seat. Two splint-bottomed chairs were set for the children, leaving room behind them for their trunks. **1945** F. Rowe *Chapin Sisters* 6 The stage . . . was little more than an elongated carry-all.

2. A bag or other receptacle for carrying a miscellaneous assortment of things. Also transf. and attrib.

1884 H. Habberton *My Friend Moses* 216 A haversack; could he find one of these carry-alls. **1912** *Nation* 27 June 641/3 There are frequent lapses due to over-hasty condensation which reduces the sentence to a disparate carry-all. **1945** *Chi. D. News* 12 Feb. 6 For youngsters who tote huge conglomerations of unrelated matter . . . there are some attractive little canvas carryall bags in navy blue.

∗ **carrying,** *n.*

1. The process of transporting over a carry *q.v. Obs.*

1857 *Knickerb.* L. 495 This was my first experience in 'carrying,' the generic word for this sort of business.

2. In obs. combs.: (1) **carrying belt,** a belt used in carrying packs, baggage, etc., cf. **head strap, tumpline;** (2) **ground,** =**carrying place;** (3) **horse,** a baggage horse; (4) **path,** the path at a carrying place, cf. **Indian carrying path;** (5) **place,** a place where canoes, goods, etc., have to be carried overland around barriers in a stream or from one stream or lake to another, also attrib., cf. **carry, Indian carrying place.**

(1) **1809** A. Henry *Travels* 150 On the bark was laid the body of the child, accompanied with an axe, . . . its own string of beads, and—because it was a girl—a carrying belt and a paddle. — (2) **1784** in *Amer. Sp.* XV. 162/2 To have the Carrying Ground oppened from the navigation of S'd River to the nearest Branch of the New River. — (3) **1758** in *Lett. to Washington* II. 351, I suppose that you may provide them w[i]th the necessary Carrying Horses for their Tents. **1788** Franklin *Autobiog.* 398 With Two hundred and fifty-nine carrying horses, [they] were on their march for the camp. — (4) **1756** in R. Rogers *Journals* (1765) 17 This night we lodged on the mountain, and next morning marched to the Indian carrying-path, that leads from Lake George to Lake Champlain.

(5) **1689** *Mass. H. S. Coll.* 4 Ser. V. 221 Then we marched down to . . . several of the carrying-places. **1795** Sullivan *Hist. Maine* 32 The carrying place from boatable waters in it, to boatable waters in the Chaudiere, is only five miles over. **1832** Williamson *Maine* I. 48 It then passes the 'carrying place rips,' half a mile in length. **1948** *Sci. Mo.* July 42/1 The French . . . called it the 'Grand Portage' or 'Long Carrying Place,' because of its length (8–9 miles).

As the last term in **chain, gun carrying.**

∗**cart,** *n.* As the last term in **board, box, cane, cider, clam, cotton, dirt, dump, dumping, express, hand, hog, ice, Jersey, junk, mud, peanut, pembina, plantation, prairie, road, Shaker, timber, Yankee cart.**

∗ **carter,** *n.* (Also *cap.*) [App. f. proper names.]

1. A variety of potato. In full **carter potato.** *Obs.*

1847 *Rep. Comm. Patents* (1848) 356 The mercers and carters, two favorite varieties, suffered most. **1849** Emmons *Agric. N.Y.* II.45 Carter Potato. . . . This is esteemed as a rich variety. **1855** *Amer. Inst. N.Y. Trans.* 209 One member . . . raised last year 300 bushels of carter potatoes on an acre.

2. Carter's oats, (see quot.). *Colloq.*

1908 *D. N.* III. 297 Carter's oats, n. phr. Usually in expressions of exaggerated comparison. 'We had more whisky than *Carter had oats.*' The story goes that Carter of Georgia, in bragging of the yield of a certain oat-field, claimed that the oats were so thick that he had to move the fence to find room to stack the bundles.

∗**Carthouse,** *n.* [?f. proper name.] A variety of apple. *Obs.* — **1818** *Amer. Mo. Mag.* II. 428/2 Table Apples [include] . . . 25. Carthouse, December. **1851** Barry *Fruit Garden* 289 [Winter apples] *Carthouse* (Gilpin, Red Romanite) . . . cultivated rather extensively in some parts of the south.

cartoon kɑrˈtun, *v.* [f. the noun.] *tr.* To portray or caricature in a cartoon.

1884 A. A. Putnam *10 Years Police Judge* 194 They make bold to cartoon . . . the goodly profession of the law. **1911** R. D. Saunders *Col. Todhunter* 130 It's you they ought to cartoon, if they've got to cartoon somebody. **1945** *Reader's Digest* July 46/1 The Mexican Indian you have seen so often cartooned, sitting with his head on his knees, his sombrero over his eyes, isn't sleeping at all.

Hence **cartooning,** *n.*

1948 *Chi. Tribune* 23 June III. 3/6 Dewitt Coulter, a bruising tackle, sees no reason why he can't pursue two careers at once—football and cartooning.

∗**cartridge,** *n.* In obs. or rare combs.: (1) **cartridge class,** a class or group engaged in making cartridges for military purposes; (2) **frolic,** a shooting affray. — (1) **1863** Russell *Diary* I. 218 The hall was filled with little round rolls of flannel. 'These,' said he, 'are cartridges for cannon of various calibres, made by the ladies of Mrs. Lawton's "cartridge class."' — (2) **1856** Phillips *Kansas* 321 The house was to be burned down that night; so the captain sent out to invite his neighbors to a cartridge frolic.

∗ **cart wheel.** A large coin, esp. a silver dollar. *Colloq.*

[**1855** Barnum *Life* 21 Talk of 'cart wheels,' there was never one half so large as that dollar looked to me.] **1873** Miller *Amongst Modocs* 38, I gave you a whole cart-wheel, did I not? a clean twenty dollar, and told you to keep the change. **1899** T. Hall *Tales* 242 My buckskin cayuse agin two hundred an' fifty cart-wheels. **1927** Eubank *Horse & Buggy Days* 24 Today it's the dollar that is Almighty; it's the 'cart wheel' that is the block and tackle which lifts the ill-bred bore into high society.

attrib. **1908** *Sat. Ev. Post* 22 Aug. 21/2 In the South much silver, especially the 'cart-wheel dollars,' as they are termed by the negro cotton hands, is employed.

∗**carver,** *n. W.* (See quot.) — **1913** W. C. Barnes *Western Grazing Grounds* 381 Cutting Horse.—A horse used especially for the work of cutting out; a 'carver,' a 'chopper,' chopping horse.

Carver chair. A chair similar in design to one owned by John Carver, first governor of the Plymouth Colony, and characterized particularly by having in the back three horizontal and three vertical spindles.

1924 Nutting *Furniture Pilgrim Cent.* 299 This great Carver chair has a back superior to any other that we have seen, in its massiveness, and the character of its turnings. **1937** Langdon *Everyday Things* 32 From Plymouth Colony mostly there has come a type of chair, or two similar types of chair which are indeed instinct with dignity and a certain formality but not so repellent in their magnificence. These are the Carver Chair and the Brewster Chair. [**1944** ADAMS *Album Amer. Hist.* I. 51 John Carver, the first Governor of Plymouth Colony, brought a chair with him which is still preserved, and it has given the name Carver to this type.]

carving horse. *W.* (See quot.) Cf. ∗**carver,** *n.* — **1920** HUNTER *Trail Drivers Texas* I. 297 The specially trained horses used [to cut out cattle] . . . are called '*carving horses.*'

Cary plow. Also **cary plow.** A plow of a now indefinable type. *Obs.*

1819 *Va. Herald* (Fredericksburg) 19 May 1/1,50 Cary Ploughs Just received and for sale by the subscriber, from No. 1 to 4—price $6.50, to $8.50. **1840** *Ill. State Reg.* (Springfield) 18 Jan. 1/5 The Subscribers are now manufacturing and offer for sale, at the Springfield Foundery, Jewett's newly invented Cary Ploughs. **1852** JOHN REYNOLDS *Hist. Illinois* 49 A small piece of iron was on the front part, covering the wood, which in some manner resembled our cary **ploughs** of the present day.

Carver chair (*c*1660) with splint bottom

casa ˈkɑsɑ, *n. S.W.* [Sp.]

1. A dwelling house. Also in proper names.

1844 FARNHAM *Travels Calif.* 57 We took our leave of the illustrious dignitary under a running salute from his dog, and repaired to el casa del goubernador [*sic*]. **1894** *Harper's Mag.* Feb. 354/2, I 'led out' for the casa at a rate of speed which the boys afterwards never grew weary of commending. **1945** *Pueblo* (*Colo.*) *Star-Journal* 3 June 8/3 The property was named 'El Pomar' because of the many apple trees in the garden, but the building itself has been named 'Casa Maria.'

2. casa grande, a large or extensive pueblo. Also attrib.

1811 tr. HUMBOLDT *Political Essay* I. xlvii, Fray Pedro Font visited also the site of the ruins called *las Casas grandes.* **1846** ABERT *Exam. N.M.* 75 We are struck with the great similarity between the 'casa grande,' and the buildings at 'Acoma' and the 'Pueblo de Taos.' **1881** MORGAN *Houses Amer. Aborigines* 133 What are supposed to be the oldest remains of architecture in New Mexico, such as the *Casas Grandes* of the Gila and Salinas rivers, are of adobe brick. **1948** *Ill. State Arch. Soc. Jrnl.* April 1/2 The Casa Grande ruins are along the roadside on the principal highway between Tucson and Phoenix.

b. The home or dwelling of the owner of a ranch. Cf. ∗**big house 5,** (*a*).

1912 FEWKES *Casa Grande, Ariz.* 153 A hostile faction bent on pillage came into this region from east or west and drove the agriculturists out of their casas grandes. **1930** LYMAN *John Marsh* 210 (Bentley), Of the three buildings found there, the largest, called the casa grande, was occupied by . . . a sailor.

casaba kəˈsɑbə, *n.* [f. the place, *Kassaba,* in Asia Minor, whence this melon was introduced.] Any one of various sweet winter melons having a yellow rind.

1889 *Oregonian* (Portland) 12 Oct. 3/1 Melons of all kinds, watermelons, cassabas, muskmelons, nutmeg melons, continue to arrive in considerable quantities. **1929** *Ladies' Home Jrnl.* July 89/2 The next melon in similarity to these two [honeydew and honeyball] is the casaba. **1941** LOFBERG *Sierra Outpost* 17 Out in the shed's insulation were . . . a box of oranges and grapefruit, a crate of casabas with stems paraffined so they would keep.

cascara kæsˈkɛrə, *n.* [See **3.**]

1. Short for **cascara sagrada.** Also attrib.

1903 *Sears Cat.* (ed 113) 279/1 We guarantee our Cascara Cathartic Tablets to give satisfaction. **1935** *Montgomery Ward Cat.* (ed. 123) 507 Quinine reduces the feverish condition associated with head colds, cascara aids prompt elimination.

2. (See quots. and cf. next.)

1931 DAYTON *Western Browse Plants* 113 Cascara buckthorn [is] . . . locally known as cascara sagrada, chittim, coffee berry, . . . and shittimwood. **1946** R. PEATTIE *Pac. Coast Ranges* 68 Cascara trees (really a kind of buckthorn) are still stripped, in summer, by seasonal labor, . . . and you see signs in the woods, advertising for cascara barkers, at the peak of the employment period.

3. cascara sagrada, *W.* [Sp. *cáscara sagrada,* lit. "sacred bark," used in Mexico for the bearberry]. The bearberry or cascara buckthorn, *Rhamnus purshiana,* of the Pacific Coast. Also the dried bark of this used as a mild laxative.

1902 CHESNUT *Plants Used by Indians* 298 It was most probably through the agency of the Mendocino County Indians that the use of cascara sagrada (*Rhamnus purshiana*) was introduced, not only throughout the State, but throughout the United States, where it is an official remedy. **1946** R. PEATTIE *Pac. Coast Ranges* 68 The Spanish padres learned at an early date to appreciate a related species, and it was really they who named it *cascara sagrada,* or 'sacred bark.'

cascaron ˌkæskəˈron, *n. W.* [Sp. *cascarón,* eggshell, in Amer. Sp. sense shown here.] (See quots.) — **1879** *Scribner's Mo.* Aug. 615/1 The cascarones looked very pretty. . . . They were egg-shells, emptied of their contents by means of a small hole in one end. **1910** J. HART *Vigilante Girl* 226 They call them cascarones; the eggshells are emptied, and filled — sometimes with these colored papers or confetti, and sometimes scented waters. It is a carnival custom you find among all the Latin races.

∗**case,** *n.*[1]

1. The condition of leaf tobacco when soft and pliant.

1640 *Md. Archives* 98 Bad Tobacco shall be judged ground leafes Second Crops leafs notably brused . . . frost bitten . . . in the house sooty wett or in too high Case. **1724** JONES *Virginia* 40 When it [=tobacco] is in proper Case, (as they call it) . . . they *strike* it, or take it down. **1864** *Agric. Soc. Ret. Maine* 162 The fires should be suffered to go out and the tobacco be suffered to come in case, or get soft again. **1944** *D.N.* Nov. 65 case, in: adj. phr. In proper condition—cured and having the correct amount of moisture to ensure handling without injury or loss. (Same as *in order.*)

2. A person peculiar or remarkable in some way. *Colloq.* Cf. **hard case.**

1833 *Life of Crockett* 20 In the slang of the backwoods, one swore . . . he would never be 'a case'—that is flat, without a dollar. **1884** *Harper's Mag.* May 922/2 There was a little wheat in all that chaff of a man. . . . But the wife is a case. **1944** PYLE *Brave Men* 182 Any time his name was mentioned among higher officers, they would nod and say, 'Yes, Sheehy is a case.'

b. A case or instance of being in love. *Slang.*

1852 *Harper's Mag.* V. 338/2 Young America sipping cobblers, and roving about in very loose and immoral coats, voted it 'a case.' The elderly ladies thought it a 'shocking flirtation.' **1928** F. N. HART *Bellamy Trial* iii. 73 Everyone knew they had a terrible case on each other.

As the last term is **gone, groundhog case.**

∗**case,** *n.*[2]

1. In faro, the last card of any denomination remaining in the dealing box. In full **case card.**

1856 *Harper's Mag.* Dec. 69/1 He has no great faith in 'cases,' but believes in betting on three cards at a time. **1938** ASBURY *Sucker's Prog.* 14 Case card—The last card of each denomination.

2. Used attrib. in the sense of "dollar." *Slang.*

1885 *Santa Fe W. New Mexican* 30 July 4/6 Captain Hoover furnished him street car fare to the extent of two five case notes. **1908** K. MCGAFFEY *Show-Girl* 196 He gives me a twenty case note and the card. **1921** *Collier's* 15 Jan. 20/4 He takes out his wallet and removes a hundred case note.

3. In special combs. and phrases, orig. with reference to faro: (1) *To keep cases,* to have charge of the cue-box, *transf.,* to keep a close watch over; (2) **case-keeper,** (see quot. 1938); (3) *to come* (*get*) *down to cases,* to come to the point, *colloq.*

(1) **1856** *S.F. Bulletin* 4 Dec. 2/2 He was sitting in front, keeping the 'cases.' He had some thousand or twelve hundred dollars in 'checks,' before him. **1896** G. ADE *Artie* iii. 24, I could see that a Johnny-on-the-spot with a big badge marked 'Committee' was tryin' to keep cases on her. **1920** MULFORD *J. Nelson* xiv. 144, I'm keepin' cases on these cattle. — (2) **1867** *Terr. Enterprise* (Virginia, Nev.) 18

Aug. 3/1 A man who is a 'case keeper' . . . at a game kept on C street, and known as Charley, . . . was badly cut in the face by another 'sport' named James Miller. **1891** QUINN *Fools of Fortune* 201 A record of the game is kept by means of an implement known as a 'case-keeper.' **1938** ASBURY *Sucker's Prog.* 14 Case-keeper—A device for keeping a record of the cards as they were drawn. Also, the man who operated the device. — **(3) 1918** C. E. MULFORD *Man from Bar-20* ii. 21 Comin' down to cases, you ain't really a cow-puncher. **1948** *Time* 19 July 87/3 Then he got down to cases.

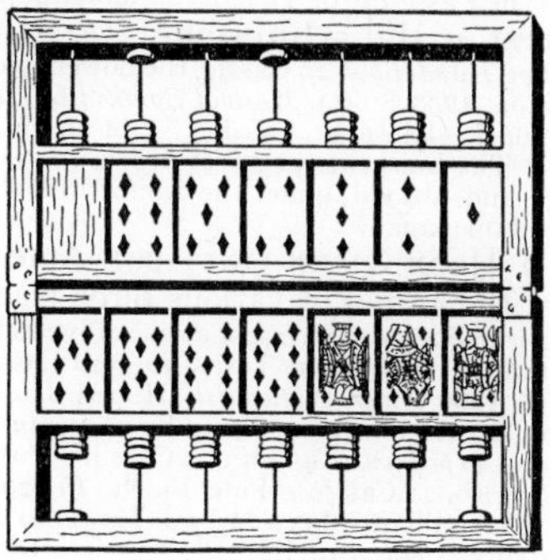

One form of case-keeper

b. In other combs.: (1) **case cat,** formerly in the fur trade a lynx, because that animal was often "cased" or skinned somewhat as a stocking is turned, leaving the fur inside, *obs.;* (2) ***caseknife,** a variety of bean, in full **caseknife bean,** *obs.*

(1) 1820 in MORSE *Rep. Indian Affairs* (1822) II. 37 Their [Fond du Lac Indians'] game is moose, bear, marten, mink, muskrat, case cat, (lynx) [etc.]. — **(2) 1790** S. DEANE *New-Eng. Farmer* 20/1 The caseknife bean is so called, because the pod is shaped like that instrument. **1857–8** *Ill. Agric. Soc. Trans.* III. 503 There are many varieties of pole beans. The early Dutch caseknife is excellent, both as a snap and shell bean. **1941** *L.A.* Map 259.

As the last term in **bridge, burial, card, cellar, cigar, double, dressing, dry-goods, half, hunter's, overnight, sample, slave, soul, splint letter-, ticket case.**

***cash,** *n.*

1. *Stock exchange.* (See quots. 1870, 1900.)

1870 MEDBERY *Men. Wall St.* 49 Cash, in broker's language, means that the contract entered upon shall be fulfilled by payment and delivery of stock, at or before 2.15 P.M. of the day of sale. **1875** *Chi. Tribune* 13 Sep. 6/1 A large Premium on Cash Pork, Wheat and Corn. **1900** S. A. NELSON *A B C Wall St.* 133 Cash grain. Grain for immediate delivery, or to be delivered during the current month. **1902** NORRIS *Pit* (1922) ix, Jadwin sold, . . . a tremendous load of 'cash' wheat at a dollar and sixty cents a bushel.

2. Short for "cashboy" or "cashgirl." *Colloq.*

1876 *Scribner's Mo.* Feb. 600/1 Then she rapped on the counter and called out 'cash!' **1886** A. DALY *After Business Hours* 20, I say—ain't she a tip-topper? . . . I knowed her when I was cash at Lord & Taylor's.

3. In special combs.: (1) **cash article,** an article for which money can readily be obtained, also transf.; (2) **carrier,** (see quots.); (3) **crop,** a crop, as cotton, tobacco, that is readily salable; (4) **down,** in ready money, cash, *colloq.;* (5) **drugstore,** a drugstore that does not extend credit; (6) **register,** a mechanical device for recording cash receipts; (7) **store,** (see quot. 1835).

(1) 1835 *S. Lit. Messenger* I. 339 A man was a cash article there. **1858** HOLMES *Autocrat* ii. 29 You are wasting merchantable literature, a cash article. — **(2) 1889** *Cent.* 843/2 [The] cash-carrier . . . usually consists of a car or receptacle traveling upon an overhead track or wire extending from the counters to a central office or desk. **1903** G. ADE *In Babel* 18 He had thought out an overhead cash-carrier of the kind used in retail stores. — **(3) 1868** *Dept. Agric. Rep.* (1869) 18 Wheat is a cash crop, and demands a small outlay of labor. **1948** *Time* 9 Feb. 63/1 Cotton is normally America's largest cash crop. — **(4)** [**1722** Calvert Papers in *Md. Hist. Soc. Pub.* No. 34 (1894) 31 A Reserve was made of Allmost all the Lands upon the Western shore, for the Value of £120 Cash paid downe. **1771** *N.C. Morav. Rec.* II. (1925) 616 To a man who can pay one half or one third, cash down, possession of the land is given, with the promise that a Deed will be made as soon as the balance is paid.] **1911** L. J. VANCE *Cynthia* 222 They bought this vessel . . . for a song, paying part cash down.

(5) 1810 *Wash.* (D.C.) *Chronicle* 17 Nov. 2/2 (*advt.*), Cash Drug Store. — **(6) 1879** *U.S. Pat. Off. Gazette* XVI. 847/1 [Patent No.] 221,360. Cash Register and Indicator. . . . Filed Mar. 26, 1879. **1947** *Sierra Club Bul.* March 3/1 The campaign between men of vision and the cash-register has been long. — **(7) 1811** *Raleigh* (N.C.) *Star* 7 Mar. 1/2 Cash Store. S. Bond having taken in a partner, the business in future will be conducted under the firm of *Bond & Jones.* **1835** H. C. TODD *Notes* 67 At Utica, I was struck with the words *Cash Store,* over many of its shops. I found they denoted, that money would be paid for all things bought, and also required for all goods sold there. **1929** E. W. HOWE *Plain People* 313 Why should not Cash Stores everywhere be sued for refusing credit?

b. In colloq. phrases: (1) *equal to cash,* (see quot. 1889), *obs.;* (2) *cash (down) on the nail,* immediate or spot cash; (3) *cash and carry,* used with reference to cash stores that do not deliver purchases made at them; (4) *cash on the barrel head,* =*cash on the nail.*

(1) 1836 HALIBURTON *Clockm.* 1 Ser. xvi, Though I say it, that shouldn't say it, they [the U.S. Americans] fairly take the shine off creation—they are actilly equal to cash. **1889** FARMER 126 Equal to Cash —Of undoubted merit. An idiom, no doubt allusive to the fact that paper currency is largely the medium of exchange. — **(2) 1855** HALIBURTON *Nat. & Hum. Nat.* II. 111 What's the price . . . cash down on the nail? **1867** *Beadle's Mo.* May 430/2 As true as you're alive, and cost four-and-ten pence a yard, cash on the nail. **1892** A. C. GUNTER *Miss Nobody of Nowhere* xvi. 185 These horse dealers are cash-on-the-nail chaps, so I gave 'em my check. — **(3) 1921** *D.N.* V. 112 cash-and-carry, n. 'No credit and no deliveries' is a motto. **1948** *Denison* (Tex.) *Herald* 1 July 16/2 Now She Shops 'Cash and Carry' Without Painful Backache. — **(4) 1932** *K.C. Times* 7 April 22 No more divorces in Holt County until there is cash on the 'barrel head,' is the edict. **1948** *Reader's Digest* Feb. 3/1 Our 1947 trading balance will be almost a billion dollars in the neighbor's favor, but payable as cash on the barrelhead in American currency.

As the last term in **clean, spot cash.**

***cash,** *v.*

1. *To cash down, over,* to supply cash, to pay or settle at once. *Colloq.*

1854 M. J. HOLMES *Tempest & Sunshine* xvi. 227 Tempest is in a desput hurry to know whether I'm goin' to cash over and send her to market in New Orleans. **1882** SWEET & KNOX *Texas Siftings* 41 Cash down, quick, or I'll bounce you off at the next station we come to.

2. *To cash in,* in poker, faro, etc., to hand in (one's checks, chips, etc.) and get cash for, to convert into cash. Also fig. *Colloq.*

1896 G. ADE *Artie* v. 46 If you're stuck on him I'll cash in right here and drop out of the game. **1899** ——— *Doc' Horne* xxi. 232, I lost back to $2,500 and cashed in. **1945** *Somerset News* 19 April 1/1 Later will come memoirs from those who will try to cash in on whatever New Deal limelight they were permitted to enjoy.

b. To pass away, die. Also without *in. Slang.*

1888 *Amer. Humorist* 11 Aug. (F., p. 134). Do you and each of you solemnly sw'ar that you will . . . cling to each other through life till death calls upon you to cash in your earthly checks? **1908** MULFORD *Orphan* xix. 250 The Orphan not only saved me but also some of them, for I'd a gotten some of them before I cashed. **1948** *Sat. Ev. Post* 10 July 88/2 Cashing in or shipping out, it made no difference as long as you didn't watch them die.

cashaw, see **cushaw.**

cashier's check. (See quot. 1881.)

1867 *Comm. & Fin. Chron.* 29 June 807 Mr. Hulburd, it will be remembered, condemns in his letter the use of 'cashiers' cheques.' **1881** *Bradstreet's* III. 305 Cashiers' checks, or checks issued by the cashier or president upon the bank itself. **1948** *Capital-Democrat* (Tishomingo, Okla.) 10 June 4/4 A Certified or Cashier's Check in the amount of $1,700.00 shall be submitted with the proposal.

***casing,** *n.*

1. *Mining.* (See quot. 1881.)

1869 J. R. BROWNE *Adv. Apache County* 525 They are all true fissure veins, with well-defined casings. **1873** *Alaska Herald* (S.F.) 9 July 5/2 The vein which contains the silver is sandwiched in between casings of granite. **1881** RAYMOND *Mining Gloss.* 18 Casings are zones of material altered by vein-action, and lying between the unaltered country rock and the vein.

b. Also **casing-rock.**

1872 MARK TWAIN *Roughing It* xxix. 160 The wall or ledge of rock . . . maintained a nearly uniform thickness . . . away down into the bowels of the earth, and was perfectly distinct from the casing-rock on each side of it.

2. The framework about a door or window. Cf. **window casing.**

1873 F. Roe *Army Lett.* 143 We draped them from the casing of one window to the casing of the next. **1913** Stratton-Porter *Laddie* (1917) 38 All the casings were oiled wood, and the walls had just a little yellow.

3. An iron pipe, esp. as used in oil and gas wells.

1875 *Chi. Tribune* 6 Nov. 2/5 The gas was flowing through a 5⅝ inch casing, the full size of the well, at a pressure of 100 pounds to the square inch. **1948** *Petroleum World* May 41/2 A string of 7-inch casing has been cemented at 946 feet, at the top of the oil sand.

b. A water jacket around the barrel of a gun.

1888 *Cent. Mag.* XXXVI. 889/1 By means of this casing, or water-jacket, it is impossible to overheat the gun by firing.

c. casinghead gas, gasoline, (see quot. 1926).

1926 *Rep. La. Dept. Conservation 1924–26* 40 The policy of the department of conservation has been to grant no permits for burning gas into carbon black except . . . when casing-head (gas produced incidental to the production of oil) gas or gas that would otherwise go to waste, is used for that purpose. **1948** *Dly. Ardmoreite* (Ardmore, Okla.) 30 Mar. 10/4 The plant produces liquid petroleum and casing head gasoline.

4. The outer rubber covering of an automobile tire.

1902 *Sci. Amer.* 1 March 150/1 The inner tube is protected by an outer tube or casing having a U-shaped cross-section and made of interlaid rubber and fabric. **1948** *Sat. Ev. Post* 17 July 69/4 Even the smallest hole in a casing will 'suck in' dirt and moisture, causing fabric rot which leads to serious blowouts.

5. *pl.* Intestines of hogs, etc., prepared for use as containers for sausage.

1904 *Encycl. Amer., s. v. Packing Industry,* The intestines are cleansed and salted and used for sausage casings in their own sausage factories. **1947** Berolzheimer *Regional Cook Book* 288 Stuff cleaned casings with sausage meat, tie ends securely and smoke with green hickory or apple wood for 3 to 4 days.

∗**cask,** *n.* The weight formerly allowed or estimated for the cask or hogshead in which tobacco was marketed. Cf. **lager beer, tobacco cask.**

1642 *Md. Archives* I. 123 Every freeman or freewoman & every Servant . . . shall pay the said Tobacco with Cask (or allow for Cask after the rate of 10£: p hundred). **1705** *N.C. Col. Rec.* I. 617 A Plea of Debt for Four Hundred Forty and Three pounds of good Merchantable Tobacco & Cask. **1731** *Md. Hist. Mag.* XIX. 285, I have never received the Acct. Sales you mention of three hogshead & Cask.

∗**cask,** *v.* **1.** *tr.* To put or pack (tobacco) in a cask. **2. casked tobacco,** tobacco packed in a cask. Both *obs.*

(1) **1639** *Md. Archives* I. 70 Tobaccos shall be struck and casked. **1644** *Ib.* IV. 270, 200 lb. tob for 2. tonne of cask provided & used by him for the casking of the said tobacco. — (2) **1650** *Md. Archives* I. 321 Hee demanded twelve thowsand pounds of Casked Tobacco. **1669** *Ib.* 220 Two thousand pounds of Casked Tobacco.

∗**casket,** *n.*

1. A coffin. Also attrib. Cf. **burial casket.**

1863 Hawthorne *Our Old Home* (1879) 101 'Caskets'! — a vile modern phrase, which compels a person . . . to shrink . . . from the idea of being buried at all. **1931** *Randolph Enterprise* (Elkins, W.Va.) 23 April 3/2 Many casket boxes and steel vaults she helped to haul. **1948** *Atlantic Mo.* Sep. 87/2 Shrouds have long since become slumber robes, and coffins caskets.

2. casket girl, (see quot. 1904).

1880 Cable *Grandissimes* iv. 30 Clotilde, the Casket-Girl, . . . was one of an heroic sort. **1904** McClellan *Dress* 384 Casket-girls.—Name given to the girls sent out by the French Government to Louisiana, each provided with a small trunkful of clothing.

∗**Cass,** *n.* Used attrib. with reference to those who agreed with the political views, esp. as regards popular sovereignty, of Lewis Cass (1782–1866). *Obs.*

1848 *Gem of Prairie* (Chi.) 25 March 5/2 The Democrats of Detroit . . . proceeded to nominate a regular Cass ticket for city offices. **1848** *Field Piece* (Chi.) 28 June 2/4 The above is an accurate representation of the whole of the 'straight out' Cass men in the city. **1859** Bartlett 190 The Hards embrace the Cass Hunkers of 1848, of the National school of politics; while the softs are composed of the remnants of the Van Buren and Adams party of 1848.

b. Also **Cassism, Cassite.** *Obs.*

1848 *Field Piece* (Chi.) 16 Aug. 2/5 It makes the Cassites feel so bad. *Ib.* 20 Sep. 2/1 The meeting of a few discontents in New York City to nominate Henry Clay for the Presidency, has given what little life there is to Cass-ism in that State. **1852** *Hutsonville* (Ill.) *Jrnl.* 12 June 2/5 Cassites suspect Maryland delegates are inclined to go over to Douglas on grounds of expediency.

casse tête. [F.] (See quots.) *Obs.*

[**1687** Joutel *Journal* (1713) 214 Il y en avoit qui avoient des massues qu'ils appellent Cassetétes. **a1716** Perrot *Mémoire des Sauvages de l'Amérique* (1864) 132 Tout son monde estant assemblé, il envoya presenter le casse-teste aux Saulteurs, Missisakis et autres nations.] **1778** Carver *Travels* 294 Those . . . who have not an opportunity of purchasing these kinds of weapons, use bows and arrows, and also the Cassé Tête or war club. **1819** Nuttall *Travels Ark.* (1821) 138 A lofty blue ridge appears to the south, called by the French hunters the Cassetête or Tomahawk mountain.

cassie ˈkæsɪ, *n.* [F.] = **huisache.**

1876 Hobbs *Bot. Hand-Book* 20 Cassie, the flowers yield a perfume, Acacia Farnesiana. **1933** Small *Manual Southeastern Flora* 654 Vachellia . . . Popinack. Hinsach. Cassie. Sweet-acacia. **1937** *Range Plant Hdbk.* B-1 The huisache, or sweet acacia . . . is widely cultivated at home and abroad, under the (unfortunately misleading) names cassie and opopanax.

∗**Cassin,** *n.* [John *Cassin* (1813–69), Amer. ornithologist.] Used in the names of various birds (see quots.).

1858 Baird *Birds Pacific R.R.* 174 Cassin's Flycatcher . . . Valley of Gila, eastward to Pecos river, Texas. *Ib.* 340 Cassin's Vireo. . . . Fort Tejon, Cal. **1869** *Amer. Naturalist* III. 184 The first specimen collected was a Cassin's Kingbird (*Tyrannus vociferans*). **1874** Coues *Birds N.W.* 106 *Carpodacus Cassini* . . . Cassin's Purple Finch. *Ib.* 140 *Pencœa Cassini* . . . Cassin's Pine Finch. *Ib.* 209 Blue Crow; Cassin's Jay; Maximilian's Jay. *Ib.* 238 *Tyrannus vociferans,* . . . Cassin's Flycatcher. **1945** *Auk* July 382 Cassin's Kingbird has become less common here than it was formerly.

cassine kəˈsinə, *n.* [F., "black drink" *q.v.*, f. the name given the drink by a now extinct Timucuan Indian tribe of Fla. See Read, pp. 84 ff.]

1. The yaupon. Also **cassine yaupon.**

1587 Hakluyt tr. Laudonnière *Notable Hist. Fla.* in *Voyages* III. (1600) 307 Baskets full of the leaues of Cassine, wherewith they make their drinks. **1765** J. Bartram *Diary* 19 Sep., I saw here several of true evergreen casseena which ye creek indians generaly plant in all their settlements making much use of it dayly. **1806** in *Ann. 9th Congress* 2 Sess. 1128 The cassina yapon, . . . grows here along the banks of this stony creek. **1947** *Sports Afield* Dec. 19/2 The islands are clothed in lush, semitropical dress of oak and pine and magnolia, with an understory of palmetto and cassena.

2. A drink prepared from the leaves of this plant. Cf. **black drink.**

1587 Hakluyt tr. Laudonnière *Notable Hist. Fla.* in *Voyages* III. (1600) 307 The King . . . commaundeth Cassine to be brewed, which is a drinke made of the leaues of a certaine tree: They [=Fla. Indians] drinke this Cassine very hotte. **1791** W. Bartram *Travels* 236 The king conversed, drank Cassine and associated familiarly with his people and with us. **1931** Read *La.-French* 85, I have not met any Creoles or Acadians who are familiar with *cassine,* or who brew the drink that the word denotes.

cassinette ˌkæsɪˈnɛt, *n.* [Origin obscure.] A light mixed cloth having a cotton warp and a filling of fine wool or wool and silk. Also attrib.

1813 *Austine Papers* (1924) I. 231, 3 yds. Casinitte. **1846** *Indiana Mag. Hist.* XXIII. 447, I have known him . . . wear . . . cassinet pantaloons. **1881** *Echo* 2 Feb. 1/5 Scarlet woollen blankets pay 51 per cent. on their value . . . cassinetts, 135 per cent.

∗**caster,** *n.* Also **castor.** A cruet-stand. In full **caster-stand.**

1819 *N.Y. S. Advertiser* 6 Apr. 4/5 (*advt.*), Castors & Liquor Stands. **1853** Felt *Customs N. Eng.* 21 Castor—as a frame of wood or metal, it holds small bottles with various condiments. . . . Now it is seen in most families with comfortable means of support. **1881** *Harper's Mag.* May 853/2 This caster . . . held instead of the ordinary pepper and mustard, various liquids and spices of mysterious nature. **1906** O. Henry *Four Million* 251 On each table is a caster-stand containing cruets of condiments and seasons.

Castilleja ˌkæstɪˈlijə, *n. W.* [Amer. Sp. in 2nd sense.] A genus of plants of the figwort family. Also (not *cap.*) a plant of this genus. — **1888** Muir *Picturesque Calif.* 25 Daisies star the sod about the margin of it, and the center is lighted with tall lilies, castilleias, larkspurs and columbines. **1937** *Range Plant Hdbk.* W-49 Species of Castilleja, especially the reddish hued ones, are generally known as paintbrush or Indian paintbrush in the West.

∗**casting,** *n.* A coin. *Slang. Obs.* — **1846** Corcoran *Pickings* 18 He slipped a Mexican casting into the hand of Fournier. **1851** *Polly Peablossom* 41 A substantial farmer, . . . by years of toil, had accumulated a tolerable pretty pile of castings.

cast-iron dog. The Mexican hairless dog. *Colloq. Obs.* — **1853** Brewerton *With Kit Carson* (1930) 208 One of those hairless, rat-tailed New Mexican curs, which the Americans are in the habit of designating as 'cast-iron dogs.' **1882** Sweet & Knox *Texas Siftings* 60 The stranger . . . calls him a cast-iron dog.

***castle,** *n.* [In those examples having a New York provenience, f. Du. *kasteel.*] (See quot. 1906.) Now *hist.* See also **adobe, wolf castle.**

*a***1649** WINTHROP *Hist.* I. 3 When we came before the town, the castle put forth a flag. **1762** *Newport Mercury* 6 Dec. 3/1 He was left only an old Big Coat to cover him until he got to a Castle belonging to the Six Nations. **1826** COOPER *Mohicans* v. 25 Every Indian who speaks a foreign tongue is an Iroquois, whether the castle of his tribe be in Canada, or be in York. **1906** RUTTENBER *Indian Names* 132 The traditionary word 'castle,' in early days of Indian history, was employed as the equivalent of town, whether palisaded or not.

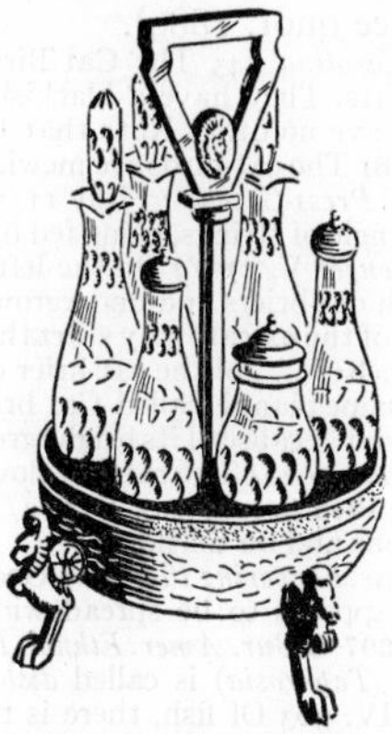

Caster or caster-stand

***castor,** *n.*

1. The gland or musk bag of the beaver. *Obs.*

1712 BYRD *Secret Diary* (1941) 488 The castor . . . is not the stones of the beaver but two glands just above the genitals. **1765** R. ROGERS *Acc. N. America* 255 The musk bags or castor taken from these animals [beavers] is of great use among druggists. **1806** LEWIS in *L. & Clark Exped.* (1905) III. 319 The male beaver has six stones, two of which contain a substance much like finely pulverized bark of a pale yellow colour . . . these are called the *bark stones* or castors.

2. Formerly in the fur trade a unit of value, presumably that of a good beaver skin, or a wooden counter representing this. Now *hist.* Cf. **beaver,** *n.* **1. c.**

1848 BALLANTYNE *Hudson Bay* (1890) 61 Trade is carried on with the natives by means of a standard of valuation, called in some parts of the country a *castor.* This is to obviate the necessity of circulating money. **1892** *Harper's Mag.* March 496/2 An Indian who came in with furs threw them down, and when they were counted received the right number of castors—little pieces of wood which served as money. **1904** S. E. WHITE *Silent Places* i. 11 He got his 'debt' at the store up two hundred castors.

3. In combs.: (1) **castor bean,** the seed of the palma Christi, or the plant itself; (2) **oil bean,** =prec.; (3) **pomace,** the crushed seed of the castor oil plant used as fertilizer, *obs.;* (4) **tree,** a species of magnolia; (5) **wood,** =prec.

(1) **1819** *Balt. Morn. Chronicle* 23 Apr. 4/5 Physical herb seed . . . palma christi or castor bean. **1947** SESSIONS *Cities of America* 57 Many a time the Commodore spent his last dollar for sweet-potato slips or castor beans . . . to hand out among the Valley people. — (2) **1814** PURSH *Flora* II. 603 Ricinus communis. . . . Frequent in old plantations in Virginia and Carolina . . . Introduced by the Negroes. Known by the name of Castor-oil Bean. **1901** C. MOHR *Plant Life Ala.* 594 *Ricinus communis,* Castor Oil Bean. — (3) **1877** *Conn. Bd. Agric. Rep.* (1878) 395 In some [fertilizers], castor pomace, leather scraps, and other cheaper materials are used. — (4) **1871** DE VERE 208 The Beaver-tree (Magnolia glauca) is so called in the West, while elsewhere it is more generally known as Castor-tree. — (5) **1859** BARTLETT 27 *Beaver-tree,* . . . called also Beaver-wood, and sometimes Castor-wood.

caswellite ˈkæzwəlˌaɪt, *n.* [Named after J. H. *Caswell,* a N.Y. mineralogist.] A form of biotite found in Franklin, N.J. — **1894** A. H. CHESTER in *Trans. N.Y. Acad. Sci.* XIII. 49. **1896** *Chem. Soc. Jrnl.* LXX. II. 309 It is supposed that the caswellite has been derived by the local action of water containing manganese and calcium on this biotite.

***cat,** *n.*

1. Short for **catfish.**

1705 BEVERLEY *Virginia* II. 32 Conger-Eels, Perch, and Cats, &c. **1765** J. BARTRAM *Diary* 27 Dec., 'Tis full of large fish, as cats, garr, mullets, and several other kinds. **1892** LUMMIS *Tramp Across Continent* 11 One of the most expert of these diver-fishermen hooked a 'cat' too big for him, and was dragged down and drowned. **1948** *Capital-Democrat* (Tishomingo, Okla.) 24 June 10/3 Cobb, on another trip, caught four ten-pound cat on one line.

Hence **catfisherman, catfishing.**

1944 *Country Gentleman* Aug., The least publicized, least expensive or pretentious, and one of the participant sports most widely enjoyed by Americans, is catfishing. **1948** *Capital-Democrat* (Tishomingo, Okla.) 24 June 3/4 Kenny DeBusk, State game and fish director, has been urging catfishermen to take more of the flatheads from the Oklahoma waters.

2. A lynx.

1791 in *Pub. Champlain Soc.* XXI. 526 No Catts on the East side where the Beaver are. **1897** INMAN *Old Santa Fe Trail* 293 There was tremendous cat in the Walnut them days, and by noon we'd ketched five big beauties. **1947** *Democrat* 16 Oct. 1/7 The cat, which was on display . . . measured 36 inches from tip of nose to the tip of her stump tail.

b. The skin of a lynx. *Obs.*

1800 in GATES *Fur Traders* 148 Collin come back, he brought 19 wolves & 14 Beavers, 7 Catts.

3. Short for **one old cat.** *Colloq.*

*c***1866** BAGBY *Old Va. Gentleman* 49 He must now learn to cut jackets, play hard-ball, choose partners for cat and chermany. **1948** *Dly. Ardmoreite* (Ardmore, Okla.) 6 July 8/4 'Cat' could be played with as few as three players; pitcher, catcher and batter. There were but two bases. The player hit the ball at home plate and attempted to get to the other base and back. If he made it he kept on batting until he made an out.

b. (See quot.)

1947 R. SMITH *Baseball* 28 Two-hole cat had a parent called 'cat' (short for 'catapult') in which a small stick named a 'cat' was catapulted out of a circle while the boy who was 'it' hastened after it and other boys scrambled varying distances, depending on how long it took 'it' to recover the stick.

4. In checkers, a failure to reach an opponent's king row (see also quot. 1889). *Colloq.*

1889 *Cent.* 852/3 Cat, . . . the occurrence [in faro] of two cards of the same denomination out of the last three in the deck. **1931** *K.C. Times* 16 July, H. C. Fewell . . . got a 'cat' in checkers at the City Square last Saturday afternoon.

5. (See quot.) *Obs.*

1893 EGGLESTON *Duffels* 189, I broke into my stock of school-boy stories of the jokes about the 'cat,' or roll pudding we had twice a week.

6. (See quot. 1930.) *Colloq.*

1930 *D.N.* VI. ii. 86 cat, a caterpillar tractor (not confined to this section [Upshur, West Virginia]; heard also in Nebraska.) **1948** *Hungry Horse News* (Columbia Falls, Mont.) 24 Sep. 1/3 At the present time they have six 'cats' working, and expect to have 30 in operation next spring.

b. cat skinner, one who operates a machine of this kind.

1947 *Time* 16 June 27/1 Into Fairbanks alone last week Pan American was flying 2,500 laborers, cat skinners, carpenters. **1948** *Chr. Sci. Monitor* 22 April 14/6 Strategies fail for various reasons—because a maniacal cat-skinner disables one of two cats, because the men stampede at a critical time.

7. In special combs.: (1) **cat-and-rat rifle,** a small-caliber rifle for shooting rats, birds, etc.; (2) ***face,** a partially healed-over scar, esp. one made by boxing or chipping, on the trunk of a pine; (3) ***hole,** a hole in a stream or swamp such as catfish might frequent, also transf.; (4) **hook,** a fishhook suitable for catching catfish; (5) **swamp,** ?a swamp frequented by wildcats, cf. **cattail swamp.**

(1) **1940** MENCKEN *Happy Days* 140 We had an air-rifle, but wanted a cat-and-rat rifle, which used real cartridges, and our father's harsh and profane prohibition of it only made us want it the more. — (2) **1879** *Lumberman's Gazette* 3 Dec. (Th. Supp.), Logs that have cat faces or burnt places. **1946** *Democrat* 26 Dec. 1/1 The southern fusiform rust which causes swelling and cat-faces on pine trees should be controlled. — (3) **1857** *Mich. Agric. Soc. Trans.* IX. 578 The very important work of draining our swamps, marshes and 'cat holes,' has been fairly commenced. **1923** ADAMS *Pioneer Hist.* 180 One mile east we pass the corner—Young's Corners—it is called, and then for a mile or two we have hills galore, clay knolls and cat-holes, until we come to the log house. — (4) **1850** LEWIS *La. Swamp Dr.* 112 Whenever the levees proved insufficient, or happened to break, chickens and garden-tools fell to a discount, and ducks and cat-hooks rose to a premium. — (5) **1704** *Providence Rec.* IV. 178 Bounded . . . on the

southeasterne Corner with a white oake tree marked, standing a little way in the cat swamp.

b. In combs. (sometimes rare) of obvious meaning or sufficiently explained in the quots., as (1) ∗**cat cry,** (2) **doze,** (3) **fit,** (4) **-gut church,** (5) **haul(ing),** (6) **hop,** (7) **Indians,** (8) **luck,** (9) **nap,** (10) **Nation,** (11) **piece,** (12) **rig,** (13) **rigged,** (14) ∗**-'s foot,** (15) **sleep,** (16) **stick,** (17) **stitch,** (18) **stitching,** (19) **stones.**

(1) 1898 DELAND *Old Chester Tales* 53 The audience came stamping and scuffling in, . . . [with] much loud, good-natured raillery, and some cat-cries. — **(2) 1847** in H. HOWE *Ohio* 199 [He] slept cat-dozes in an upright position. — **(3) 1905** *D.N.* III. 60 catfit, catnip-fit, *n.* Same as *conniption fit.* **1907** W. LILLIBRIDGE *Trail* 110 Mary'd have a cat-fit if she knew. — **(4)** *c***1770–1800** FISHER *Olde N.-Eng. Psalm-Tunes* (1930) p. vii, The churches that used stringed instruments were known as 'cat-gut churches.'

(5) 1824 SINGLETON *Lett. South & West* 79 The cat-haul . . . is, to fasten a slave down flatwise . . . and then to take a huge fierce tom-cat by the tail backward, and haul him down along the . . . bare back, with his claws clinging into the quick all the way. **1847** *Chamber's Misc.* XVI. No. 149, 17, I saw [in Maryland] a slave punished by *cat-hauling*. The cat was placed on the bare shoulders, and forcibly dragged by the tail down the back and along the thighs of the prostrate slave, tearing the skin and flesh with its claws and teeth. **1867** D. R. LOCKE *Swingin' Round* 118 Let me ketch yoo at it, . . . and I'll give you sich a cat-haulin ez yoo never—. — **(6) 1891** QUINN *Fools of Fortune* 195 If, on the other hand, two of the three cards are of the same denomination, only three arrangements are possible, . . . which is technically called a 'cat hop.' **1909** *Cent. Supp.*, Cat-hop, in faro, two cards of the same denomination left in the dealing-box for the last turn. — **(7) 1752** in J. WINSOR *Miss. Basin* (1895) 267 Cat Indians or Flat Heads. **1757** WM. SMITH *Hist. Province of New York* (1792) 57 The Hurons on the north side of the lake Erie, and the Cat Indians on the south side, were totally conquered and dispersed. — **(8) 1716** CHURCH *Philip's War* (1867) II. 160 The said Edee turning him over, generally had Cat luck, falling on his feet. — **(9) 1823** COOPER *Pioneers* xxxii, I just closed my eyes in order to think the better with myself. . . . It was only some such matter as a cat's nap. **1899** *Atlantic Mo.* LXXXIII. 753/1 This submissive aspect was . . . merely a cat nap before a fierce awakening.

(10) 1906 HODGE *Amer. Indians* I. 430/2 The Jesuit Relation for 1653, speaking of L. Erie, says that it 'was at one time inhabited toward the s. by certain peoples whom we call the Cat Nation.' **1940** *Dict. Am. Hist.* II. 223 Lake Erie . . . was named after the Eries (or Cat Nation). — **(11) 1905** *Forestry Bur. Bul.* 61 Catpiece. A small stick in which holes are made at regular intervals, placed on the top of uprights firmly set in floating booms. — **(12) 1867** F. LUDLOW *Little Bro.* 96 The cat-rig boat . . . carries a main-sail only and is a favourite on the Shrewsbury river. **1877** BARTLETT 106 Cat-Rig, a boat-rig with one mast near the bow with only one sail, and that one a boom-sail. — **(13) 1882** GODFREY *Nantucket* 360 Nantucket can boast of a very fine fleet of small yachts. The majority of them are cat-rigged, and are usually sailed by their owners. **1886** *Outing* IX. 14/1 The building of open yachts, sloop and cat-rigged, was immensely stimulated by the action of the Centennial Commission. — **(14) 1877** BARTLETT 778 Cat's Foot! An exclamation of disbelief. New England. **1927** *Amer. Sp.* III. 138 A thing too absurd to be believed was greeted by 'The cat's foot!'

(15) 1837 SEDGWICK *Live & Let Live* (1876) 65 Roused from her cat-sleep by the unwonted noise. — **(16) 1832** *Boston Transcript* 7 Jan. 2/1 He 'dropt into' the cellar to survey his wood-pile; . . . he found that the faithful fellow had thrown down the large logs *whole*, sprinkled them over with sawed cat-sticks. **1859** BARTLETT 72 Cat-stick; . . . In Pennsylvania, Maryland, and further south, the term is applied to small wood for burning. **1899** *Boston Transcript* 14 Jan. 12/2 The 'Caton chimney' of Kentucky is doubtless an emigrant from the Atlantic coast, with tobacco stalks substituted for catsticks. — **(17) 1906** K. H. WATSON *Handbook of Dress* (1915) 116 The cat stitch . . . is an alternate slanting back stitch, the needle being placed first to the right and then to the left. . . . It is used to finish flannel seams and hems, fasten down linings, opened seams, and canvas facings and featherbone. . . . The *catch* stitch is a variation of the cat stitch. . . . The cat stitch is worked *from* the worker. — **(18) 1871** STOWE *Pink & White Tyranny* 40 There were all sorts of . . . cat-stitching and hem-stitching going on. — **(19) 1936** MORSE *Furniture* 325 About 1750 the hob-grate was invented. . . . The bars, of course, are of iron for holding coal, and the sides of the grate are of brass. These were at first called 'cat-stones' to distinguish them from 'fire-dogs,' but later they were named 'hob-grates.'

8. In the names of plants and animals: (1) **cat-bird,** the black-capped thrush, *Dumetella carolinensis*, one of whose calls resembles the mewing of a cat; (2) **brier,** any one of several species of *Smilax*, also attrib.; (3) ∗**claw,** *S.W.* any one of several prickly plants, as *Acacia greggi* [poss. a trans. of Amer. Sp. *uña de gata*, a common name for various plants, esp. acacias and mimosas, see Santamaría and cf. ∗**cat's claw**]; (4) ∗**fish,** see as a main entry; (5) ∗**gut,** (see quots.); (6) ∗**head,** (*a*) =**catfish,** *obs.*, (*b*) (see quot. 1817), *obs.*; (7) **nip,** see as a main entry; (8) ∗**o' nine tails,** ?a catfish, also **cat o' sixty-nine tails;** (9) **owl,** (see quot. 1916); (10) **pine,** *local* the white spruce; (11) ∗**-'s claw,** =**cat claw;** (12) **spruce,** *local* the black or hemlock spruce; (13) ∗**squirrel,** ∗**tail,** see as main entries; (14) **thrasher,** (see quot. 1889).

(1) 1709 LAWSON *Carolina* 143 The Cat-Bird . . . makes a Noise exactly like young Cats. They have a blackish Head, and an Ash-coloured Body, and have no other Note that I know of. **1850** S. F. COOPER *Rural Hours* 81 The cat-birds are mewing about the grounds. **1948** *Green Bay* (Wis.) *Press-Gazette* 13 July 11/5 They found an adult catbird caught in a tangle of strings, being fed by another catbird. — **(2) 1839** *S. Lit. Messenger* V. 375/2 On the left was a large bay-gall . . . thickly beset with cat-briers and undergrowth. **1888** *Outing* XII. 483/2 The first rattle of the ox-cart may start them [=quail] from the stubble-field to the shelter . . . of the cat-brier coppice. **1943** SHIMER *Plant Names* 19 The same plant is called Cat briar for its sharp stout prickles, and Green briar because of its bright green bark. — **(3) 1893** CANFIELD *Maid of Frontier* 204 The catclaw flowered into white after each infrequent rain. **1946** *So. Sierran* Dec. 2/3 The cat-claw . . . is common in the canyons and on hillsides.

(5) 1840 DEWEY *Mass. Flowering Plants* 65 Goat's Rue . . . popularly called catgut . . . appears to be spread widely over the United States and Canada. **1897–8** *Bur. Amer. Ethnol. Rep.* I. 425 The catgut or devil's shoestring (*Tephrosia*) is called *distaíyĭ*. — **(6)** (*a*) **1683** PENN *Works* (1782) IV. 303 Of fish, there is the sturgeon, herring, rock, shad, catshead, sheepshead, [etc.]. **1809** HENRY *Travels* 252 We took pouts, cat-fish, or cat-heads, of six pounds weight. (*b*) **1817** W. COXE *Fruit Trees* 138 Cathead. This is a very large round apple; flattened at the ends. **1856** *Rep. Comm. Patents: Agric.* 295 The autumn varieties of apples are the 'Gravenstein,' . . . 'Belle-fleur,' 'Fall Pippin,' 'Cat Head,' and 'Pound.' — **(8) 1791** J. BREVARD *MS Diary* 18 July (N.C. Univ.), The Fish called the Cat o' nine Tails. *a***1841** W. HAWES *Sporting Scenes* II. 54 What a husband she would have had in that usher, with his cat-o'-sixty-nine-tails swinging from his long, lean, foul-nailed fingers! — **(9) 1792** IMLAY *Western Territory* 225 [Birds in south central U.S. include] night hawk, cat owl, screech owl, [etc.]. **1916** SETON *Woodcraft Man.* 306 Great Horned Owl or Cat Owl (*Bubo virginianus*). This is the largest of our Owls. About twenty-four inches long and four feet across the wings.

(10) 1894 *Amer. Folk-Lore* VII. 99 *Picea alba* . . . cat-pine, Buckfield, Me. — **(11) 1849** AUDUBON *Western Jrnl.* (1906) 73 Every tree, shrub and plant is thorny to a degree no one can imagine until they have tried a thicket of 'tear-blanket' or 'cat's claw.' **1940** JAEGER *Desert Wild Flowers* 97 Cat's-claw is a spreading deciduous shrub or small tree, of rocky desert hillsides and washes. — **(12) 1894** *Amer. Folk-Lore* VII. 100 *Picea nigra*, . . . cat-spruce, Penobscot Co., Me., yew-pine, spruce-pine, West Va. **1948** *Sat. Ev. Post* 6 Nov. 36/2 Seal Island is small and lean and low, covered with wind-bitten cat-spruce trees. — **(14) 1888** GOODE *Amer. Fishes* 394 Around the Gulf of Maine this species is also known by the names 'Kyack' or 'Kyauk,' 'Saw-belly,' and 'Cat-thrasher.' **1889** *Cent.* 865/3 Cat-thrasher, a clupeoid fish, *Clupea æstivalis*. (Maine, U.S.)

9. In colloq. and slang phrases: **a.** *Spry as a cat*, quite spry, nimble.

1922 in *N.J. Almanac 1823*, (Yankee Phrases) I late was *as fat as a doe*. And playsome and *spry as a cat*.

b. *Like a cat in a strange garret*, ill at ease, timorous.

Cf. Du. *Kijken (zich voelen) als een kat in een vreemd pakhuis*.

1824 *Woodstock* (Vt.) *Observer* 16 March (Th.), 'What was King Caucus like?' said an old gentleman. 'Why, like a cat in a strange garret, frightened at every step it took.' **1900** *Atlantic Mo.* LXXVI. 157 And next Sunday Mis' Tolland come walkin' into our meeting, but I must say she acted like a cat in a strange garret.

c. *Cat in the meal* (*tub*), something hidden or sinister, also in allusive contexts.

No doubt in allusion to the story, widely known through Webster's "blue-backed speller," of the cat and the rats.

1839 *Diplom. Corr. Texas* (1908) I. 412 They say there is a cat in [the] meal, by his retirement. **1865** *Cin. D. Commercial* 3 Oct. 3/7 The Convention can not more effectually vitiate its good actions than by passing this ordinance. That meal tub has a cat in it. **1880** *Cong. Rec.* 10 May 3193/1 Is this the cat in the meal-tub of refunding?

d. *Dog my cats*, hang it, darn it. *Colloq.*

1839 *Spirit of Times* 23 March 30/1 (We.), Dog my cats if such an ugly set of customers can be found. **1843** *St. Clair Banner* (Belleville, Ill.) 12 Dec. 1/3 Dog my cats, if I can't flog any man on that boat, for fist fight or for rough and tumble! **1893** MARK TWAIN *P.*

Wilson iii, Dog my cats if it ain't all I kin do to tell t'other fum which. **1941** STUART *Men of Mts.* 51 'Dog my cats,' says Thorny, . . . 'if I don't believe I'm dreaming.'

e. *To poke a dead cat at somebody*, to insult or revile someone.

*a***1846** *Quarter Race Ky.* 87, I only thought he might be a pokin his dead cat at somebody what lives in this holler.

f. *As high as a cat's back*, exceedingly, excessively.

1848 J. MITCHELL *Nantucketisms* 42 'Dust as high as a cat's back.' Quite a row.

g. *Cat and monkey trick*, app. an allusion to the story, often formerly included in school readers, of the monkey that acted as a judge for two cats, robbing them both, but cf. *cat's paw* in *OED*.

1856 OLMSTED *Slave States* 494 So successfully was this cat-and-monkey trick performed, that multitudes of Carolina Indians were exported, as slaves, to the West Indies, where they were exchanged for rum, which thereby became very cheap in the Colony, and made drunkenness very common.

h. *That cat won't fight*, that plan will not work. (Cf. ∗*that cock won't fight*, in same sense.)

1869 MARK TWAIN *Innocents* iv, First I thought I would leave France out and start fresh. But . . . the governor would say, 'Hello, here—didn't see anything in France?' *That* cat wouldn't fight, you know.

i. *To look like the cat after it had eaten the canary*, to look smug, eminently pleased. Also in allusive context.

1871 F. ROE *Army Lett.* 26, I . . . forced myself to be halfway pleasant to the four men who were there, each one looking precisely like the cat after it had eaten the canary! **1948** *Milwaukee Jrnl.* 18 July (Ed. Sec.) 6/1 In almost every instance when mine host in restaurant or hotel has bid me adieu, he has assumed the appearance of a very smug cat while I cannot escape the feeling that I resembled the ill fated canary.

j. *Cats and dogs*, (see quots. 1900, 1947).

1879 *Bradstreet's* I Nov. 4/1 Mr. So-and-so is reported to be buying largely of 'cats and dogs' stock. **1900** S. A. NELSON *A B C Wall St.* 133 Cats and dogs. Worthless securities. **1947** *Chi. Tribune* 29 June II. 10/2 Instead he bought the so-called 'cats and dogs' or low priced, highly speculative stocks and 'gambled away' the money.

k. *Cat and bull story*, a fanciful, euphemistic variant of "cock and bull story."

1902 HARBEN *Abner Daniel* 237 I'll believe my part o' that cat-an'-bull story when I see.

For *to skin a cat*, see ∗**skin,** *v.*

As the last term in **ash, bear, black, bob, brown, case, channel, civet, coon, copy, duck bill, eel, fisher, flannel-mouthed, four-cornered, gay, hill, Job's, maltese, moose, mountain, mud, one-eyed, one old, ring-tail, ring-tailed, savagerous wild, she, silver, spotted, store, swinge, three-cornered, tiger, two hole, wild cat.**

∗**cat,** *v. intr.* To fish for catfish. *Colloq.*

1834 CARUTHERS *Kentuckian* II. 217, I'm jist now like I've been at times when I've been out catting. **1835** *Vade Mecum* (Phila.) 24 Jan. 2/3 To use a vulgarism, when the Buncombe people 'go a catting,' they *go* a catting.' **1865** *Wilkes' Spirit of Times* 19 Aug. 387/3 When we goes a catting, we goes a catting, and throws trout back into the water to pay 'em for their imperdence of biting.

cataded, -did, see **katydid.**

Catalan ˈkætlən, *n.* [Sp., an Amer. borrowing.] (See quots.) *Obs.* — **1805** *Amer. Pioneer* II. 231 The retail groceries are generally kept by Spaniards, who are called Catalans, (from Catalonia, I suppose). [**1828** BERNARD *Reise* I. 100 Als Louisiana spanische Colonie wurde, kamen viele Catalonier nach N.O., und etablirten dort Schenken. Seit dieser Zeit benennt man dort alle Schenkwirthe mit dem eigenthümlichen Namen catalans.]

Catalina cherry. [f. Santa *Catalina* Island.] An evergreen cherry, *Prunus lyoni*, found on islands off the coast of California. — **1923** *Stand. Plant Names* 384/1 [Prunus] lyoni . . . Catalina Cherry. **1942** VAN DERSAL *Ornamental Amer. Shrubs* 150 Catalina cherry is a robust, rapid-growing plant of excellent appearance either as a specimen or back-ground plant.

catalo ˈkætəˌlo, *n.* Also **cattalo.** [See quot. 1899.] A hybrid or cross between the American buffalo or bison and domestic cattle. Cf. **half-bison.**

[**1856** *Spirit of Times* 4 Oct. 81/1, I would cross these cattle with the buffalo, and continue to cross with proper selections of the progeny among each other, . . . until I obtained all the desirable qualities of both the original stocks.] **1894** *S.F. Midwinter Appeal* 10 Feb. 3/3 Grand Exhibit of Buffaloes and Cattleos. **1899** C. J. JONES in H. Inman *Buffalo Jones' 40 Yrs. Adv.* 243 To these crossbreeds I have given the name 'Catalo,' from the first syllable of *cattle* and the last three letters of *buffalo.* **1906** *Harper's Mag.* April 798 [The buffaloes] are now reduced to a few scattered remnants, and captives sinking to slow extinction in the hybrid cattelo with his mongrel name. **1948** *Chi. Tribune* 2 Mar. II. 4/4 The breeders say they still are a long way from getting cattalo capable of reproducing.

∗**catalogue,** *n.*

1. Originally a list of college or university students, officers, alumni, etc., now a volume or booklet issued by a college or university containing announcements, regulations, etc.

For information about early catalogues at Harvard see *Proc. Mass. Hist. Soc.* VIII. 9–75, and *Proc. Amer. Antiquarian Soc.* XXIV. 264–304.

1682 *Mass. H.S. Coll.* 4 Ser. VIII. 311, I lately received . . . a catalogue of Harvard's sons. **1786** in J. MACLEAN *Hist. Coll. N.J.* (1877) I. 344 Ordered, That a complete catalogue of the graduates of this college be prepared and published at the expense of the present Senior Class. **1860** W. H. COOK *Letters* (1946) 17 June 65, I send inclosed letters and term bills that I have fowarded money to pay. I cannot make this bill correspond with the catalogue. **1946** *Newsweek* 1 July 76/2 Bucknell's first catalogue cautioned parents to restrict students to one or two dollars in spending money.

2. Short for mail order catalogue *q.v.*

*c***1873** [M. WARD & Co.] It is with great pleasure that we present you with our Catalogue. **1946** THOMPSON *Amer. Daughter* 55 The catalogue is the farmer's Bible.

3. catalogue card, one of the cards making up a card catalogue *q.v.*

1908 *A.L.A. Catalog Rules* p. v, One of the first matters to be considered by the Publishing Board was the means of introducing more uniformity into the size and style of type, the size and quality of catalog cards. [etc.]. **1948** *New Yorker* 25 Sep. 24/3 The Library of Congress . . . supplies a standard form of catalogue card to libraries.

As the last term in **card, college, dictionary, form, garden, mail order, price, seed, title, triennial, union catalogue.**

catalpa kəˈtælpə, *n.* ["W. R. Gerard says that catalpa is derived from *kutuhlpa*, signifying 'winged head,' in reference to its flowers, in the Creek language" (Hodge).] Any one of various trees of the genus *Catalpa* belonging to the trumpet-creeper family. Also attrib. See also **common, western catalpa.**

*c***1730** CATESBY *Carolina* I. 49 The Catalpa Tree . . . was unknown to the inhabited parts of Carolina, till I brought the seeds from the remoter parts of the country. . . . It is become an ornament to many of their gardens. **1785** WASHINGTON *Diaries* II. 347 Planted . . . two catalpas (large) West of the Garden House. **1876** *Field & Forest* II. 27 Can anybody living in southeast Illinois render account concerning the above considerable quantity of Catalpas split for rails? **1945** *Prairie Farmer* 8 Dec. 4/2 Hedge, Catalpa, red cedar, chestnut, and black locust are most durable woods for fence posts.

b. catalpa worm, a worm found in the early summer on the leaves of the catalpa and valued as fish bait.

1908 *D.N.* III, 297 catawba, n. 1. Catalpa. 2. The catalpa worm. 'We fished with *catawbas*.' (Cf. patalpa, D.N. ii, 324.) **1948** *Democrat* 4 Nov. 1/3 He opened its stomach and found inside two large catalpa worms.

∗**catamaran,** *n.* **1.** (See quot. 1884.) **2.** (See quot.)

(1) **1848** COOPER *Oak Openings* II. xiv. 202 It only remained to get sail on the catamaran . . . in order to keep ahead of the sea. **1884** KNIGHT *Supp.* 178/1 Catamaran. . . . . The name has been applied to other craft, especially used on the Hudson River, and in New York harbor. These vessels have twin hulls united, and carry a cloud of canvas, being remarkably staunch. **1886** *Outing* IX. 17/2 The Providence entry was the famous catamaran *Amaryllis.* — (2) **1905** *Forestry Bur. Bul.* No. 61, 33 Catamaran, a small raft carrying a windlass and grapple, used to recover sunken logs.

catamingo ˈkætəˌmɪŋgo, *n.* [Origin unknown.] (See quots.) *Obs.* — **1842** *Nat. Hist. N.Y., Zoology* I. 37 The New-York Ermine . . . is called, in some parts of the State, the Catamingo, and the White Weasel. **1850** S. F. COOPER *Rural Hours* 500 The Ermine of New York is a small creature. . . . Our people sometimes call it the Catamingo.

∗**catamount,** *n.* Any one of various wild animals of the cat family, esp. the cougar or lynx.

1698 *Springfield Rec.* II. 348 Voted to allow Wm. Mackcranny twenty shillings outt of the Rates for his killing four Cattamounts. **1765** R. ROGERS *Acc. N. Amer.* 261 The Catamounts and Wild-Cats are great enemies to the elk. *c***1837** HAZLITT *Diary* I. 49 Once while we were there, an animal they call a cat-a-mount [or puma] made its appearance near Falmouth. It was said to be five feet long; besides, the tail was as much more; and it could mount trees, whence its name. **1944** *Birmingham News* 21 Nov. 4/7 When that old catey-mount yowls near our house it just makes my hair stand plumb straight up.

cataract curl. (See quot. 1864.) — **1864** SALA in *Daily Tel.* 10 June 11. 18o An elastic pipe must have passed through one of her 'Niagaras' or 'cataract curls'—the name given to the shower of true or false ringlets the ladies are in the habit of wearing at the back of their heads. **1865** SALA *Diary* I. 357 By fifties and hundreds came the young ladies in hoop skirts, lace shawls, bright-coloured dresses, with parasols, and streaming 'cataract curls.'

catawampously ˌkætəˈwɑmpəslɪ, *adv.* Also **catawampishly, catawamptiously.** [f. **catawampus,** *a.*] Savagely, fiercely, eagerly. *Colloq. Obs.*

1846 *N.Y. Herald* 17 June, On Taylor came and met the foe All marshall'd forth so pompously, And there he's slain two thousand men, All chaw'd up catawampously. **1852** *Calif. Express* (Marysville) 25 Aug. 1/5 Oh, what a treat would be . . . to sit a deep marble bowl within And champagne gurgling around your chin . . . Till you open your mouth and down it goes; Gulp by gulp, and sup by sup, Till you 'cattawampishly chaw it up.' **1857** F. DOUGLASS *Speech* (B.), Where is the wealth and power that should make us fourteen millions take to our heels . . . for fear of being catawamptiously chawed up? **1889** FARMER 128/1 Catawamptiously, with avidity; fierce eagerness.

catawampus ˌkætəˈwɑmpəs, *n.* and *a.* [Of fanciful formation.]

1. *n.* A bogy, sprite, hobgoblin. Used jocularly of a person. *Colloq.*

1843 CARLTON *New Purchase* I. 265 The tother one what got most sker'd, is a sort of catawampus. **1866** C. H. SMITH *Bill Arp* 54 It is a thing that plots and plans and schemes for a few weeks and then suddenly pokes its head out like a catawampus and says 'Booh!' **1947** *Westerners' Brand Book* 122 Hiyah Zeb, y'u ole catawampus.

b. Also as an interjection.

1938 MATSCHAT *Suwannee River* 19 At her refusal, he drank deeply. 'Catawumpus! Kin lick my weight in wildcats, after that.'

2. *a.* Spiteful, askew, wrong. *Colloq.*

[**1844** DICKENS *Martin Chuzzlewit* xxi, There air some catawampous chawers in the small way too, as graze upon a human pretty strong.] **1884** CRADDOCK *Where Battle Was Fought* 405, I kin prove ter ye that ye air all cat-a-wampus on that p'int. **1931** *Nat. Geog. Mag.* Dec. LX. 734 A new fence post, set out of line, is 'catawampus' or 'wapper-jawed.' **1947** SESSIONS *Cities of Amer.* 19 Blaring, blatant Broadway, an individualist to the last, runs catawampous from one end of the island to the other, and everything meets head on in the West Forties.

catawampussed ˌkætəˈwɑmpəst, *a.* Confounded, "bodaciously used up." *Colloq.* or *slang. Obs.* — **1839** *N.O. Picayune* 8 Mar. 2/4 Things have been a goin' on in a catawompussed fix for a long time, nary party ownin' the land yet both makin' jest as free as though they had it reg'larly deeded over to 'em. **1880** P. DEMING *Adirondack Stories* 31 May I be cat-a-wampussed if he won't swaller all the soap that old coot is a mind to give him!

Catawba kəˈtɔbə, *n.* Also **catawba.** [Choctaw *Katâpa*, separated (from other Siouan tribes).]

1. =**Catawba Indian,** often pl. as a tribal designation. Also attrib.

1716 *N.C. Col. Rec.* II. 252 The false Representation of the Virginians in England . . . wherein is asserted that the Cattabas are in their Government. **1831** *American* (Harrodsburg, Ky.) 4 Mar. 1/5 Look at the Catawbas, sir; between seventy and one hundred Indians, wretched and depraved beyond description. **1895** *Cent. Cyclo. of Names* 563 Kataba or Catawba. . . . The few survivors of this people are on the Kataba reservation in York County, South Carolina. **1946** *Nat. Geog. Mag.* Jan. 54/1 It was spoken by . . . a number of eastern tribes, such as the Cheraw and the Catawba of the Carolinas.

b. The language or dialect used by the Catawba Indians. Also attrib. *Obs.*

1809 *Steele Papers* II. 589 The Lord's prayer in the Catawba dialect w[oul]d be useful to me. **1858** *S.C. Hist. Soc.* II. 327 The difficulty of the Catawba is increased by the fact, that . . . many words are lost.

2. =**catalpa.** Also attrib.

1832 D. J. BROWNE *Sylva* 126 In the Carolinas and in Georgia the catalpa is called Catawbaw Tree, from a tribe of Indians by that name who inhabited that part of the country. **1876** HOBBS *Bot. Hand-Book* 21 Catawba tree, Catalpa tree, Bignonia Catalpa. **1931** MATTOON *Forest Trees Okla.* 109 This tree, often miscalled 'catawba,' is native to the central Mississippi River basin.

b. (See quot. and cf. **catalpa worm.**)

1947 DALRYMPLE *Panfish* 153 'Catawbies' is a local name in Ohio for the larvae of a butterfly. . . . The fisherman who taught me to use them would shake them from the trees on which they naturally feed—the catalpa tree (from which the name 'catawbies' grew).

3. =**catawba grape.** (See also quot. 1907.)

1846 *Knickerb.* XXVII. 419 A trellis . . . with a snaky-looking vine trailed over it, from which glorious bunches of Catawbas and Isabellas may be gathered. **1907** HODGE *Amer. Indians* I. 216 Catawba. . . . This grape is a cultivated variety of the northern fox-grape (*Vitis labrusca*) and is said to have been named by Maj. Adlum, in 1825, after the Catawba tribe and r. of North Carolina. **1945** *Vaughan's Gardening Illust.* (1946) 99 Catawba (Red). Large bunches of coppery-red fruit. Late bearing; excellent for grape juice.

4. Wine made from these grapes. In full **Catawba wine.**

1851 CIST *Cincinnati* 256 Good Catawba commands six dollars per dozen bottles. **1867** *Atlantic Mo.* Aug. 241 Twelve varieties of American wine. . . . The cheapest is the Ohio Catawba, one dollar a bottle. **1889** *Cent.* 857/2 Both still and sparkling Catawba wines are made. **1907** HODGE *Amer. Indians* I. 216 Catawba—A grape, or the wine produced from it, made famous by Longfellow in one of his poems.

5. In special combs.: (1) **catawba cobbler,** an iced drink the chief ingredient of which is catawba wine, *obs.;* (2) **grape,** a native American grape bearing red fruit, said to have been first domesticated along the Catawba River in the Carolinas; (3) **Indian,** an Indian of a Siouan tribe formerly occupying a part of the Carolinas, *obs.;* (4) **laurel,** =**catawba rhododendron;** (5) **nation,** the tribe of Catawba Indians, *obs.;* (6) **rhododendron, rosebay,** a species of handsome pink-flowered rhododendron found in the southern Allegheny region.

(1) **1859** *First Impressions of the New World* 207 It was served . . . in the form of Catawba cobbler which I thought improved it. **1876** M. F. HENDERSON *Cooking* 341 Sherry, Claret, or Catawba Cobblers. — (2) **1831** *Boston Transcript* 22 Sep. 2/1 Zebedee Cook, Jr., Esq., Dorchester; [contributed] . . . Constantia, Catawba and Isabella Grapes. **1898** E. C. HALL *Aunt Jane* 171 Concord and Catawba grapes loaded the vines on the rickety old arbor. — (3) **1715** *Virginia State P.* I. 178 Two of our Traders . . . were among the Catawba Indians at ye breaking out of this War. **1858** *S.C. Hist. Soc.* II. 327, I had as a camp servant, a Catawba Indian. — (4) **1813** MUHLENBERG *Cat. Plants* 43 Catawba Rosebay, or Catawba laurel (*Rhododendron Catabiense*).

(5) **1757** in *Lett. to Washington* II. 54 There came to my House twenty Six Indians of the Catawbas Nation. **1858** *Ib.* 327 It is known that the Catawba nation at present numbers but fifty human beings, men, women and children. — (6) **1813** MUHLENBERG *Cat. Plants* 43 Catawba Rosebay. **1868** GRAY *Field Botany* 216 *R. Catawbiense*, Catawba Rose-bay. High Alleghanies from Virginia s[outhward]. **1890** *Cent.* 5157/1 The ordinary species of American outdoor plantations is *Rhododendron Catawbiense*, the Catawba or Carolina rhododendron. **1943** PEATTIE *Great Smokies* 197 Mountain folk call this growth a 'bald'—meaning that compared with the densely forested peaks, the knobs covered with Catawba rhododendron appear close-cropped.

* **catch,** *n.*

1. A place where something is obtained or caught. *Colloq.*

1850 MITCHELL *Lorgnette* 81 Went the other night to take supper at Dobson's—a very scholarly sort of a catch. **1920** HUNTER *Trail Drivers Texas* I. 98 Our camp was the catch and cut-out for all the other bosses.

2. A lurking or easily overlooked consideration. *Colloq.*

1855 BARNUM *Life* 120 The old farmer, who was pretty 'cute, was sure that there was some 'catch' in this offer. **1948** *Chi. Tribune* 20 June (Comics) 14, I thought there was a catch in it!

3. *Agric.* A stand of small grain, grass, etc., sufficient to obviate the necessity of sowing again. *Colloq.* Cf. * **catch,** *v.* **1.**

1868 G. BRACKETT *Farm Talk* 128 'Seed this down this year?' 'Yes, that's one reason why I sowed the field to barley,—so as to get a good catch.' **1888** *Vt. Agric. Rep.* X. 48 Wheat gives a good catch, barley next, and oats poorest, of all. **1941** WHITE *One Man's Meat* 238 He had a dream lately telling him what to do about my newly laid down field, where I didn't get a very good catch of grass.

As the last term in **fair, fly, running catch.**

* **catch,** *v.*

1. *intr.* To germinate or sprout. *Colloq.* Cf. * **catch,** *n.* **3.**

1843 OLIVER *Eight Months* 95 There is a practice mentioned by Mr. Newell, and highly recommended by others, of putting in hayseed without ploughing the ground; this is done by burning the prairie grass in the spring and harrowing the seed. The seed catches quick and grows well. **1868** G. BRACKETT *Farm Talk* 128 Sow oats thin, and fix the ground as well as for barley, and grass will catch well enough.

2. *tr.* Short for * *to catch on, q.v. Colloq.*

1883 NYE *Baled Hay* 19 She . . . has been seen trying to catch the combinations to the safes of several of our business men. **1896** *Godey's*

Mag. April 406/2, I am a child myself. Do you catch? We ought all to be children. **1948** *Sat. Review* 15 May 28/2 Why, Dad, are you tired on April first? . . . Because you've had a March of thirty-one days! Catch?

3. In baseball, to catch (the balls) thrown by the pitcher, to serve as catcher. Usu. in ellipt. contexts.

1865 *Wilkes' Spirit of Times* 8 July 301/1 Wansley caught behind in a handsome manner and batted well. **1887** *Courier-Journal* 26 May 2/6 Young Love Cross caught Ramsey in fine style, and Greer also handled Porter's delivery as well as could be desired. *Ib.* 27 May 2/4 O'Brien caught a poor game, and his six passed balls were all costly.

4. In noun combs.: (1) **catchall,** see as a main entry; (2) * **basin,** a reservoir for catching and impounding the surface water over an extensive area; (3) **boom,** (see quot.); (4) **crumb,** (see quot.), *rare;* (5) * **fly,** designating a marsh grass, *Leersia lenticularis,* found in the southern states; (6) **rope,** *W.* a lariat, *rare;* (7) **up,** (see quots. and cf. **5** (2) below), *obs.;* (8) **water drain,** a small stream or rivulet, *rare.*

(2) **1884** *Science* III. 372/1 It may fairly be questioned . . . whether any extension of forests, or system of catch-basins or reservoirs, could possibly retain or mitigate to any considerable extent such general and overwhelming floods. **1889** *Secy. of Agric. Rep.* 268 The building of numerous catch-basins throughout the plains to save the rain-fall which is wasted . . . will add greatly to the supply. — **(3) 1905** *Forestry Bur. Bul. 61* A boom fastened across a stream to catch and hold floating logs. — **(4) c1837** Catlin *Indians* II. 198 One of his little fair enamoratas, or 'catch crumbs,' . . . fixed her eyes and her affections upon his beautiful silk braces.

(5) 1829 Eaton *Botany* (ed. 5) 273 *Leersia lenticularis,* catch-fly grass. **1845** Lincoln *Botany* App. 118/2. **1894** Coulter *Bot. W. Texas* III. 512 *H[omalocenchrus] lenticularis.* (Catchfly grass.)—Not yet reported from Texas, but it may be expected in the eastern half of the State. — **(6) 1881** Romspert *Western Echo* 174 Each boy has a half-inch catch-rope, about forty feet long, and made out of sea-grass, leather, or raw-hide. — **(7) 1844** Gregg *Commerce of Prairies* I. 50 The 'Catch up'—Breaking up of the Encampment [etc.]. **1846** Stewart *Altowan* I. iii. 109 The sunset came, and the 'catch up' sounded on the camp. — **(8) 1817** *Ann. 14th Congress* 2 Sess. 1008 The Pungo branch of North river is the nearest body of water to it, (except mere catchwater drains).

5. Combined with adverbs in colloq. expressions: (1) * *To catch on,* to understand or comprehend, to grasp an opportunity quickly and turn it to advantage; (2) * *to catch up,* to catch and harness horses, oxen, etc., preparatory to beginning a journey; (3) * *to catch up with,* to detect and bring to justice, to be entirely through with.

(1) **1883** Peck *Bad Boy* 62 Don't he ever catch on, and find out you have deceived him? **1948** *McAlester* (Okla.) *News-Capital* 1 July 4/1 Often it takes many years to train a civil servant thoroughly in the art of bureaucracy, but once in a while one comes along who catches on fast. — **(2) 1843** T. J. Farnham *Travels Prairies* I. 57 After this, we 'caught up' and went on with the intention of encamping with the Santa Féäns. **1946** *Sierra Club Bul.* Dec. 64 Then we'd have to catch up the mules, take off up over the bank and around the end of the [fallen] log. — **(3) 1902** Harben *Abner Daniel* 73 You are a-axin' that beca'se you think I'll be ketched up with, . . . but I tell you the' ain't no man on the face o' the earth that could find my still now. **1924** *Scribner's Mag.* Dec. 649/2 I'm all caught up with this army. Get me? I'm through, resigned, quit.

To catch goss, hail Columbia, the larks, see the nouns.

catchall ˈkætʃˌɔl, *n.*

1. A box, bag, closet, nook, etc., used as a receptacle for various articles.

1841 *Knickerb.* XVII. 327 It is as much as I can do to keep things clean that are in sight, without cleaning out every dirty hole. There must be some *catch-all.* **1924** Mulford *Rustlers' Valley* 62 The gallery leading from the ranchhouse to the summer kitchen was far from being the customary catch-all of riding gear and general miscellany. **1944** Wilson *Passing Inst.* 26 Did you ever see a ketch-all? We had one in our 'clean-clothes' closet.

attrib. **1874** Howells *Foregone Conclusion* xviii. 246 They hunted out Ferris's property from a catch-all closet in the studio of a sculptor with whom he had left them. **1916** Bower *Phantom Herd* 236 The boys . . . trailed off to bed, in the ketch-all cabin.

2. In fig. and transf. uses (see quots.).

1838 *Cong. Globe* App. 16 April 275 [The party includes] old Federalists, . . . Antimasons, and Abolitionists. They have, sirs, been a kind of catch-all, or omnium gatherum. **1859** Stowe *Minister's Wooing* viii, All but this dead grind, and the dollars that come through the mill, is by them thrown into one waste 'catch-all' and labeled romance. **1892** *Harper's Mag.* Feb. 373/2 This is the mere catch-all for the furs got at posts farther up the coast. **1948** *Gainesville* (Tex.) *D. Register* 3 July 2/2 The [Congressional] Record's appendix . . . seems to be a 'catch all' for remarks the nation's lawmakers wish to record for the benefit of their constituents.

attrib. **1947** *Reader's Digest* Jan. 71/2 This party is in fact a catchall party, the first large-scale, political cooperative effort between Protestants and Catholics in Europe.

* **catcher,** *n.*

1. Short for **cowcatcher.** *Obs.*

1850 *Quincy* (Ill.) *Whig* 2 July 1/7 On examining the catcher, on the arrival at the depot, the interstices were found filled with fragments of a wagon body.

2. = **mail catcher.** Also attrib.

1875 *Chi. Tribune* 18 Sep. 5/3 The 'catcher' is known as Ward's patent. **1887** *Postal Laws* 253 'Catcher' pouches must not under any circumstances be sent out upon any stage or horseback routes, or used for any other purpose than to exchange mails where trains do not stop. **1890** *Railways of Amer.* 313 On one side was a postman . . making a mile or two an hour; and on the other a representation of the fast mail train, the 'catcher' taking a pouch from the 'crane' as it passes at the rate of fifty miles an hour.

3. In baseball, a player stationed behind the home plate to catch the balls thrown by the pitcher. Also **catcher out.**

1856 *Spirit of Times* 8 Nov. 165/1 The 'Excelsior's' fielding was rather loose, with the exception of Mr. Stagg (catcher), who filled his position admirably. **1868** *N.E. Base-Ballist* 6 Aug. 1/1 Instead of two sides of nine men each, half the time, five, would suffice for a game, with one at the bat, a catcher out, giver and a chaser or two, the fun would continue for hours. **1948** *Chi. Tribune* 1 Feb. II. 3/4 In 1939 he was exclusively a catcher but moved to first base the following year.

b. catcher's mask, mitt, a mask or mitt for protecting the catcher's face or hand from pitched balls.

1903 *Sears Cat.* (ed. 113) 479/3 Baseball Catchers' Masks. **1909** *Collier's* 15 May 15/2 Immediately the big catcher's mitt, claimed by two or three different inventors, became a feature of the game. **1938** White *One Man's Meat* 1 You open a closet door and there in the half-dark sit a catcher's mitt and an old biology notebook.

As the last term in **ant, bee, bug, clam, cow, dog, fly, fool, frog, mail, mail bag, Negro, possum, salt, slave, Yankee catcher.**

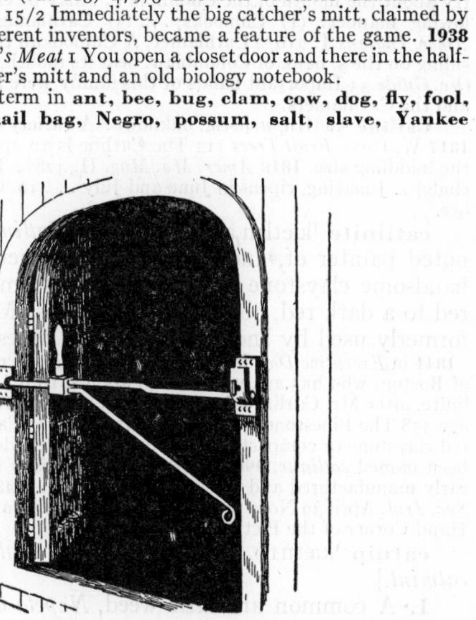

Catcher or mail catcher

catching up. (See quot. 1848 and cf. **catch,** *v.* **5** (2).) *Colloq.* — **1846** W. Stewart *Altowan* I. iv. 115 The hunters however, were to take the opportunity of the general catching up. **1848** E. Bryant *California* iii. 32 The scene of 'catching up' as the yoking and attaching of the oxen to the wagons is called in emigrant phraseology, is one of great bustle and confusion.

* **caterpillar,** *n.* A type of tractor which travels on two jointed steel bands, one on each side of the machine. — **1915** *Lit. Digest* 4 Sep. 467/1 Government road-building throughout the interior has paved the way for automobiles, caterpillars and traction-engines. **1948** *Minneapolis Morn. Tribune* 28 Sep. 6/6 Then the caterpillars drag the [circus-] wagons down on the lot and they start all over again.

As the last term in **buttonwood, cotton, false, forest tent, grass, salt marsh, slug, tent, yellow-necked, zebra caterpillar.**

* **catfish,** *n.*

1. Any one of various common fresh-water fishes of North America having some fancied resemblance to a cat,

1612 SMITH *Virginia* 15 Of fish we were best acquainted with . . . Rockfish, Eeles, Lampreyes, Catfish, Shades. **1709** LAWSON *Carolina* 160 Cat-Fish are a round blackish Fish, with a great flat Head, a wide Mouth, and no Scales. **1819** THOMAS *Travels* 211 There are three kinds of Cat-fish: the Mississippi cat, the mud cat, and the bull head. **1943** *Duval Co. Facts* (San Diego, Tex.) 19 Oct. 2/3 De cat fish bitin' in de ribber right now!

2. a. catfish hole, a hole in a stream or swamp such as a catfish might be found in, cf. **cat hole. b. cat soup,** a soup of which catfish is the chief ingredient.

(a) **1934** CRAMER *Stars Fell* 95 Big Branch still runs through Persimmon Bottom down to the catfish hole. **1948** *Durant* (Okla.) *D. Democrat* 4 July 2/2 Old Blue still ranks as the cat fish hole of the southwest. — (b) **1834** BRACKENRIDGE *Recoll.* 21 Coarse black bread, a kind of catfish soup, hot with pepper, and seasoned with garlick, was almost the only food they gave me. **1947** *Chi. Sun* 22 June 24/3 Another good old back country dish that is seldom encountered except on the rivers of Missouri and Arkansas is catfish soup.

As the last term in **black, blue, flathead, mud, stone, white, yellow catfish.**

cat-foot ˈkætˌfʊt, *v. intr.* To go stealthily in the manner of a cat. Also *tr. Colloq.* — **1916** H. L. WILSON *Somewhere in Red Gap* iii. 119 Mebbe it's a Blackhander's camp, I think; so I didn't yell any more. I cat-footed. **1948** *Popular Western* June 69/2 Patrolling the area, a cocked gun ready, Grif Maunder cat-footed the area topside.

cat-haul ˈkætˌhɔl, *v. tr.* To subject (one) to a cat-haul. Also fig. *Colloq.* — **1840** *Cong. Globe* App. 12 Jan. 99/2 White people of the South . . . hunting slaves with dogs and guns, cat-hauling slaves, &c. **1881** *Cong. Rec.* 28 Feb. 2202/2 You begin to ransack and examine and cat-haul the whole navy, big and little.

Cathlamet ˈkæθləˌmɛt, *n.* [Native word of unknown significance.] (See quot. 1907.)

1845 DUNN *Ore. Terr.* 83 The Cathlamets . . . live on the north sides of the river, and around Baker's Bay and other inlets. **1849** ROSS *First Settlers Ore.* (1923) 95 All the Indian tribes inhabiting the country about the mouth of the Columbia . . . may be classed in the following manner: (1) Chinooks; . . . (3) Cathlamux. **1907** HODGE *Amer. Indians* I. 216/2 Cathlamet. A Chinookan tribe formerly residing on the s. bank of Columbia r. near its mouth, in Oregon. **1940** *Ore. Guide* 33 Important bands of this family were the Clatsops . . . and the Cathlamets.

Catline ˈkætlɪn, *n.* [Orig. unknown.] A variety of apple. *Obs.* — **1817** W. COXE *Fruit Trees* 114 The Catline is an apple rather below the middling size. **1818** *Amer. Mo. Mag.* II. 428/2 Table Apples [include] 1. Junating, ripens in June and July . . . 10. Catline, September.

catlinite ˈkætlɪnˌaɪt, *n.* [George *Catlin* (1796–1872), noted painter of, and writer about, Amer. Indians.] A handsome claystone varying in color from pale grayish-red to a dark red, obtained in southwest Minnesota and formerly used by Indians for making pipes. Also attrib.

1841 in *Executive Doc. No. 237* 17 According to Professor Jackson, of Boston, who has analysed it, and applied to it the name of catlinite, after Mr. Catlin, it is composed of [etc.]. **1857** DANA *Mineralogy* 358 The Pipestone of the North American Indians was in part a red claystone or compacted clay from the Coteau de Prairies. It has been named *catlinite.* **1907** HODGE *Amer. Indians* I. 613 The Iowa early manufactured and traded catlinite pipes. **1948** *Ill. State Arch. Soc. Jrnl.* April 39 Note the Siouan Catlinite pipe at the Upper Left Hand Corner of the Picture.

catnip ˈkætnɪp, *n.* [*cat*+*nip, nep, dial.* and *obs.* for *catmint.*]

1. A common aromatic weed, *Nepeta cataria*, of the mint family.

1712 *Essex Inst. Coll.* X. 94 He boiled tansy, sage, hysop, and catnip in some of ye best wort. **1839** *S. Lit. Messenger* V. 752/1 Neighboring cats . . . would root up her catnip with unsparing effrontery. **1931** CLUTE *Plants* 99 Catnip or catmint (*Nepeta cataria*) is so called because cats are fond of it, not merely the house-cat, but also the great cats of warmer regions.

b. Short for next.

1809 IRVING *Knickerb.* VII. x, A whole army of old women . . . were bent upon driving the enemy out of his bowels . . . with catnip and penny royal. **1856** M. J. HOLMES *Homestead on H.* 229 Miss Lucy . . . was much given to drinking catnip.

2. catnip tea, tea made from the leaves of catnip.

1837 J. C. NEAL *Charcoal Sk.* (1838) 160, I go about doing little jobs for a fip or a levy, so's to get my catnip tea and bitters regular. **1863** MRS. WHITNEY *F. Gartney's Girlhood* viii., Any old woman can make gruel, and feed a baby with catnip tea. **1948** *Hoosier Folklore* March 6 Snakeroot and catnip tea are good, also pennyroyal tea.

catogan ˈkætəgən, *n.* [F., in similar sense.] (See quots.) Also attrib.

1823 BELTRAMI *Pilgrimage* (1828) II. 182 The [Sioux] women, in imitation of the Saukis, wear the *catogan.* **1885** *N.Y. Weekly Sun* 29 April 3/5 To dress the hair on the top of the head and form it into a catogan loop in the nape of the neck, as ultra-fashionable women are arranging their coiffure at this moment. **1888** CABLE in *Cent. Mag.* Dec. 258/1 For driving or for evening they [=ladies of New Orleans] placed on top of the high, powdered hair what they called a *catogan,* a little bonnet of gauze or lace trimmed with ribbons. **1923** WYATT *Invisible Gods* II. i. 38 Her hair neatly arranged in what was called a 'Catogan queue,' and tied with white hair ribbons.

Caton chimney. A cat-and-clay or stick-and-dirt chimney in which tobacco stalks are substituted for the wooden sticks. *Rare.* — **1899** *Boston Transcript* 14 Jan. 12/2 The 'Caton chimney' of Kentucky is doubtless an emigrant from the Atlantic coast, with tobacco stalks substituted for cat-sticks.

Catskillian ˌkætsˈkɪlɪən, *n.* A native or inhabitant of the Catskill region in New York. *Rare.* — **1883** *Harper's Mag.* Sep. 524/1 The lore which all old Catskillians cling to.

* **cat squirrel.**

1. (See quot. 1943.)

1826 J. GODMAN *Nat. Hist.* II. 129 The Cat-Squirrel, *Sciurus Cinereus,* . . . is found in great abundance throughout the oak and chestnut forests of this country. **1890** *Cent.* 5882 Fox- or cat-squirrels are several large red, gray, or black species of North America. **1943** W. J. HAMILTON *Mammals* 225 Gray Squirrel. Cat Squirrel. *Sciurus carolinensis.* . . . A large tree squirrel, with long, somewhat flattened bushy tail, the upper parts of the body grayish.

2. The southern gray squirrel, *Sciurus carolinensis carolinensis.*

1884 J. C. HARRIS *Mingo* 171 The cat-squirrels . . . occasionally scamper across the crumbling shingles. **1908** *D.N.* III. 297 Cat-squirrel. . . . The gray squirrel in distinction from the red or fox-squirrel. **1933** *Amer. Sp.* Feb. 48 Cat-squirrel, n. The grey squirrel as distinguished from the larger reddish fox squirrel, which is also common in the Ozarks.

3. (See quot. 1889.)

1889 *Cent.* 865/3 cat-squirrel. . . . A name of the ring-tailed bassaris, *Bassaris astuta.* Southwestern U.S. **1917** *Animals of Amer.* 109/1 Dr. Coues speaks of it as the Bassarisk; and the reader may find other references to it as the 'Bassaris,' 'Cat Squirrel' (so called in Texas). **1933** GRINNELL *Mammal Fauna Calif.* 99 Bassariscus astutus raptor (Baird) *Synonyms* . . . Civet Cat; . . . Ring-tail; . . . Mountain Cat; Cat Squirrel.

* **cattail,** *n.*

1. cattail millet, any one of several varieties of sorghum.

1889 VASEY *Agric. Grasses* 30 *Pennisetum spicatum,* . . . (Pearl Millet; Cat-tail Millet; Egyptian Millet), . . . is best adapted for cultivation in the South. **1901** MOHR *Plant Life Ala.* 135 Cattail millet, Hungarian grass and the so-called Johnson grass . . . furnish green forage and hay crops throughout the summer. **1945** *Democrat* 6 Sep. 4/1, I have plenty of good hay. Cattail millet, crab grass, Brussel No. 1 hay.

2. cattail pine, =**hickory pine.** *Rare.*

1878 *Cherry Creek* (Nev.) *Independent* 18 Jan. 2/2 Mr. Carey intends bringing the water into town through wooden pipe, made from cattail pine.

* **catted,** *a.*

1. Of a chimney: Furnished with cat-sticks. *Obs.*

1665 *Southampton Rec.* I. 154 Post is agreed with to build a watch house of 15 foot square, 7 foot gice over it, a chimney catted and fit for daubing. **1889** *Cent.* 853/1 A chimney well catted.

2. catted chimney, a stick-and-dirt or cat-and-clay chimney.

1639 in J. B. FELT *Annals of Salem* 119 He is to build a meeting house, . . . one catted Chimney of 12 feet long and 4 feet in height. **1684** I. MATHER *Providences* pref. 15 A violent flash . . . of Lightning . . . broke and shivered one of the Needles of the katted or wooden Chimney. **1899** *Boston Transcript* 14 Jan. 12/2 The 'catted chimney' was quickly and easily made of cat-sticks and clay.

* **cattle,** *n.*

1. In miscellaneous combs.: (1) **cattle brand,** a brand or mark of ownership made on cattle; (2) **chute,** a narrow structure through which cattle are driven in loading or unloading them in shipping, cf. **stock chute;** (3) **drive,** *W.* the entire number of cattle offered for sale in a year, also livestock of the cow kind driven over trail or the action of driving them; (4) **fever,** =**Texas fever,** also attrib.; (5) **grub,** a warble fly; (6) **guard,** (*a*) one or more persons who watch over cattle, (*b*) a structure in a line of fence crossed by a road or railroad preventing cattle from getting into or out of a field; (7) **path,** a path made by cattle; (8) **range,** see as a main entry; (9) **rustling,** cattle stealing, also transf.; (10) **scales,** platform scales suitable for weighing cattle, also attrib.; (11) **spinach,** a saltbush common in arid regions of the West; (12) **tick,** a species of cow- or fever-tick; (13) **town,** *W.* a town dependent for its importance on the cattle trade; (14) **trail,** *W.* a route or way along which great herds of cattle are driven; (15) **war,** *W.* (*a*) the disturbance in the cattle country attendant upon the buying up and fencing by private individuals of vast areas that had con-

Cattle scales or hay scales

stituted a free range, cf. **fence war,** (*b*) fierce rivalry over cattle and cattle-raising.

(1) 1915 *Amer. Mag.* March 52/1 How would you like the job of remembering cattle brands and how would you like to have established the reputation of knowing more than fifteen thousand brands? **1948** *Omaha World-Herald* (Mag.) 20 June 7/3 Montana is the only state that has more registered cattle brands than Nebraska. — **(2) 1897** *Outing* XXIX. 548/1 The . . . scow headed for one of the cattle-chutes that straddle the dreary shore of Lakeside. **1946** *Chi. D. News* 28 Aug. 1/1 It looks something like a combination of a guillotine, cattle chute and Noah's Ark. — **(3) 1878** *Caddo* (Ind. Terr.) *Free Press* 28 June 6/1 The cattle 'drives' from Texas each year represent a good deal of money. **1945** *Everybody's Digest* Aug. 85 Since before the great cattle drives, starting north from Texas in 1866, the cowhand . . . has been making and speaking a lingo of his own. — **(4) 1909** *Westm. Gaz.* 6 Sep. 7/3 The cattle-fever epidemic. **1944** Barbour *Eden* 137 The cattlemen . . . accused the deer of being hosts of a tick which carries cattle fever.

(5) 1926 *U.S. Dept. Agric. Bul.* 1369 (*title*), The Cattle Grubs or Ox Warbles, Their Biologies and Suggestions for Control. **1947** *Time* 27 Jan. 19/1 There were bills to . . . authorize federal funds for fighting cattle grubs. — **(6)** (*a*) **1757** in *Pa. Archives* 2 Ser. II. 685 This day, at 10 A.M., three partys of Indians surrounded the Cattle Guard, killed 4, & wounded 5 men of the party, & 4 men escaped, one being shott through the hatt. **1862** *Harper's Mag.* Sep. 449/2 An opening some twenty-five feet in width, left vacant [in a caravan train] to enable the cattle-guard, in case of an alarm, to drive in their charge. (*b*) **1843** in Edwards *Chancery Cases* III. 489 The first cattle guards he saw were in one thousand eight hundred and thirty six. **1948** *Calif. Citrograph* April 261/1 Cattle guards have been placed across some of the roads. — **(7) 1838** Hawthorne *Note-Books* I. 194 Turning off towards the south village, followed a cattle-path till I came to a cottage. **1887** *Outing* X. 117/2 The bank was worn away on the other side by a cattle-path just wide enough for one. — **(9) 1907** S. E. White *Arizona Nights* 272 Cattle rustling so near the Mexican line was an easy matter. **1948** *Railway Carmen's Jrnl.* June 133/2 American labor is still in its frontier days, as far as political cattle rustling is concerned.

(10) 1854 *Penna. Agric. Rep.* 395 Best Hay and Cattle Scales. **1881** *Rep. Indian Affairs* (1872) 121 Agency Buildings at Poplar River are agent's house, . . . cattle-scale house. — **(11) 1929** Chalfant *Death Valley* 80 *Atriplex polycarpa*—Cattle spinach. **1940** Jaeger *Desert Wild Flowers* 51 The common name, 'cattle spinach,' was given because of its high value as a browse plant. — **(12) 1869** *Amer. Naturalist* III. 51 The Cattle Tick[s] . . . drop from the cattle in the woods, and more frequently along the cattle paths. **1948** *Sat. Ev. Post* 10 July 84/2 He had an iron jaw and no more brains than a cattle tick. — **(13) 1880** *Scribner's Mo.* March 768/1 New Sharon . . . was known out West as 'a cattle-town.' **1938** Asbury *Sucker's Prog.* 310 The invasion reached its peak with the rise of the frontier cattle towns and mining camps and the building of the trans-continental railroads. — **(14) 1872** *Overland Mo.* VIII. 326/1 Bewildered in the maze of cattle-trails out of all whooping, and losing even my familiar and helpful Number Nip, 'the shod-horse tracks,' to which the trail hunter clings as to life . . . I remember all these things. **1947** *Sierra Club Bul.* Nov. 48 United States Cavalry troops cleared and improved many of the cattle trails by use, and located some new trails.

(15) (*a*) **1892** *Irrigation Age* 15 Sep. 224/2 Largely as a result of the unfortunate cattle war, the political control of Wyoming has been changed by the recent election. **1902** O. Wister *Virginian* xxxvi. 503 The herds were driven away to Montana. Then, in 1892, came the cattle war. (*b*) **1934** *Rocky Mt. News* (Denver) 31 Jan. II. 7/3 (*heading*), Cattle wars waged over branding irons.

b. In less frequent combs.: (1) **cattle bird,** (see quot.); (2) **chip,** a piece of dried cattle dung; (3) **corn,** corn destined for cattle; (4) **fly,** (see quot.); (5) **gap,** =**cattle guard** (*b*); (6) **horse,** a horse used in hunting or rounding up cattle; (7) **issue,** a government issue of cattle to reservation Indians in compliance with treaties, cf. **issue cattle;** (8) **lick,** (see quot.); (9) **mill,** a mill operated by animal power, *obs.;* (10) **paper,** *W.* notes, mortgages, etc., based upon cattle as a security; (11) **pass,** a way by which cattle are enabled to cross a railroad safely; (12) **poor,** possessing many cattle when they are cheap and money is scarce, cf. **land poor;** (13) **sense,** sense or judgment that comes from long experience with cattle; (14) **sign,** evidence of the recent presence of cattle; (15) **snap,** a bargain in cattle, *rare;* (16) **stop,** a structure designed to stop cattle, as from getting on a railroad; (17) **test,** a test for determining the pulling ability of oxen; (18) **trade,** *W.* trade or dealing in cattle; (19) **wire,** wire sufficient in size and strength to use in fencing against cattle; (20) **yell,** *W.* a yell used by cowboys in driving cattle herds.

(1) 1837 *Brit. Cyclo. Nat. Hist.* II. 158 Cow-bunting or Cattle-bird (*Molothrus pecoris* Swainson). . . . The American cattle-bird . . . is a small bird about the size of the European sky-lark. — **(2) 1903** A. Adams *Log Cowboy* 210 We were frequently forced to resort to the old bed grounds of a year or two previous for cattle chips. — **(3) 1887** *Courier-Journal* 27 Jan. 7/7 Cattle Corn. Z. T. Smith, Ballard county, first [prize].— **(4) 1892** V. Kellogg *Kansas Insects* 116 The cattle pest from Europe that bids fair to extend itself over the whole United States, and be as troublesome as its nearly related pest, the well-known Stable Fly, or Cattle Fly.

(5) 1942 Rawlings *C. Creek* 183 No one came to meet me as my car crossed the cattle-gap. — **(6) 1878** I. L. Bird *Rocky Mts.* 152 These trained cattle-horses keep perfectly cool; . . . mine jumped aside at the right moment, and foiled the assailant. — **(7) 1915** Young *Hard Knocks* 130 In addition to this cattle issue, we had a commissary issue once a month. On this day we issued flour, bacon, beans, coffee, sugar, molasses and corn. — **(8) 1887** *Harper's Mag.* Feb. 349/1 Large blocks of it [*sc.* salt] are sent to the Western Plains for 'cattle licks.' — **(9) 1848** *De Bow's Review* VI. 273 *Cattle mills* are still very generally seen in many of the colonies. The animals usually employed are mules.

(10) 1924 in Dale & Rader *Okla. Hist.* (1930) 590 Thus there grew up in the West that large class of securities known as 'cattle paper.'— **(11) 1850** *Hunt's Merch. Mag.* XXIII. 353 Every railroad . . . shall make and maintain all necessary cattle guards, cattle passes, and farm crossings. — **(12) 1892** *Scribner's Mag.* June 732/2 Stock was neglected as valueless. Men were 'cattle-poor,' and it was a time of discouragement. — **(13) 1874** McCoy *Cattle* 177 One who is blessed with that rare quality called 'Cattle sense'—an article quite rare among bankers. — **(14) 1900** Drannan *Plains & Mts.* 394 Three days' ride from the fort I struck plenty of cattle sign.

(15) 1890 *Stock Grower & Farmer* 6 Sep. 5/1 J. A. Johnson, . . . whose eyes are always open to nab 'cattle snaps,' took today's train for the east. — **(16) 1867** J. N. Edwards *Shelby* 385 Telegraph poles, wires, cattle-stops, bridges, trestle-work, . . . and heavy timbers were given to the flames. — **(17) 1919** Cady *Rhymes of Vt.* (1923) 265 The sight our fambly liked the best Was what they called the 'cattle test'; It made your heart-throbs pause To hear a great long whiplash crack, And see them oxen take up slack, And haul a mountain forth and back And leave it where it was. — **(18) 1873** *Newton Kansan* 3 April 3/4 She hopes for a large cattle trade this year and next. — **(19) 1904** *Indian Laws & Tr.* III. 89 Forty thousand dollars, or as much thereof as may be necessary, shall be expended by the Secretary of the Interior in fencing the Crow reservation, said fence to be built of six strands of galvanized barbed cattle wire.

(20) 1912 Bower *Flying U.* 219 He fired again and again, and gave the range-old cattle-yell; the yell which had sent many a tired herd over many a weary mile.

2. Designating one or more persons having to do with dealing in or raising cattle, as (1) **cattle baron,** (2) **broker,** (3) **buyer,** (4) **czar,** (5) **detective,** (6) **feeder,** (7) **guard,** see **1.** (6) (*a*) above, (8) **herder,** (9) **hunter,**

(10) **inspector,** (11) **king,** (12) **man,** (13) **puncher,** (14) **queen,** (15) **rancher,** (16) **ring,** (17) **rustler,** (18) **thief.**

(1) 1898 CANFIELD *Maid of Frontier* 129 Having been used to the cattle baron or his immediate underling, they would have gone far and fared hard for him. **1947** *Sierra Club Bul.* May 37 Since those high and far-off days the range has never been capable of supporting anything like the number of cattle it could have supported if the cattle barons had not maimed it. — **(2) 1866** *Internal Revenue Guide* 69 Cattle brokers, whose annual sales do not exceed ten thousand dollars, shall pay ten dollars. . . . Any person whose business it is to buy or sell, or deal in cattle, hogs, or sheep, shall be considered as a cattle broker. **1927** SIRINGO *Riata* 59 Cape Willingham . . . at this writing is a prosperous cattle broker in El Paso, Texas. — **(3) 1853** HAYES *Pioneer Notes* (1929) 92 They were hung, in like manner, not long before, for the horrid murder of two young American cattle-buyers. **1947** *Chi. Tribune* 14 Oct. 1/5 Their firm flesh convinced the cattle buyer of Wilson & Co. they were worth $36.35 a hundredweight. — **(4) 1930** HENRY *Conquer. Plains* 185 The cattle czars now loudly foretold disaster on our Plains.

(5) 1912 RAINE *Brand Blotters* 53 Norris . . . was the cattle detective of the association and for a year now the rustlers had outgeneraled him. — **(6) 1868** *Rep. Comm. Agric.* 337 An experienced cattle-feeder could not so easily fatten stock on grass raised on newly seeded grounds. **1948** *Dly. Ardmoreite* (Ardmore, Okla.) 30 April 12/2 Cattle feeders are not refilling their feed lots. — **(8) 1847** RUXTON *Adv. Rocky Mts.* (1848) 184 A new settlement of San Antonio [is] a little hamlet of ten or twelve log-huts, inhabited by pastores and vaqueros—shepherds and cattle-herders. **1883** ZEIGLER & GROSSCUP *Alleghanies* 315 A huge flat rock near the summit of the mountain, whereon the cattle-herders used formerly to place the salt brought by them to the stock which range the summit meadows. — **(9) 1708** *Boston News-Letter* 17–24 May 2/2 We shall have . . . 1000 good Negroes that knows [*sic*] the Swamps and Woods, most of them Cattle-hunters. **1740** W. STEPHENS *Proc. Georgia* 613 Seven or eight of our most expert Cattle-Hunters were sent out on Horseback to scout about.

(10) 1891 O'BEIRNE *Leaders Ind. Territory* 52/2 He . . . was appointed by Governor Cooke as Cattle Inspector for Northern Texas. — **(11) 1874** *Chi. Times* 2 Jan. 5/4 They are, in fact, 'the cattle kings' of the United States and consequently the world. **1948** *Ore. Hist. Mag.* March 22 Of the 'cattle kings' and the 'sheep kings' of this region, not much has been written. — **(12) 1864** *Ohio Agric. Rep.* XVIII. 150 Our 'cattle men' have not been derelict in endeavoring to improve the character of their herds. **1947** *Steamboat* (Colo.) *Pilot* 13 Feb. 8/5 Cattle men and sheep men are not any too friendly. — **(13) 1928** *Collier's* 18 Aug. 19/1 We wasn't horse breakers; we was cattle punchers. — **(14) 1876** *Bedrock Democrat* (Baker, Ore.) 23 Aug. 3/2 Mrs. Nash, of Corpus Christi . . . [is] fairly entitled to the name of the 'Cattle Queen of Texas.' **1927** SIRINGO *Riata* 56 Here we had the pleasure of a genuine cattle-queen's presence.

(15) 1945 *This Week Mag.* 14 July 15/1 Actually, Miss Loy is a Montana girl, the daughter of a cattle rancher. — **(16) 1885** *Santa Fe W. New Mexican* 10 Sep. 4/7 Rev. Sligh's Interpreter asserts the existence of a cattle ring in New Mexico whose motto is, 'The man with the water hole must go.' — **(17) 1903** A. ADAMS *Log Cowboy* vii. 42 The stampede . . . was the work of cattle rustlers. **1948** *Democrat* 10 June 1/3 Cattle Rustlers Nabbed by Patrol. — **(18) 1862** T. F. DEFOE *Market Book* 172 These 'Rangers' were organized in New York, principally from the refugees, as a foraging party, under the command of the city's former Governor (Tryon), who made himself quite extensively known as a 'Cattle Thief,' and was one of the most efficient in supplying the city with fresh provisions. **1916** C. A. EASTMAN *From Deep Woods* 117/2 This was a golden opportunity for the white horse and cattle thieves in the surrounding country.

3. Pertaining to the raising of cattle or to a region where they are raised: (1) **cattle country,** (2) **ground,** (3) **growing,** (4) **hunt,** (5) **land,** (6) **ranch,** (7) **ranching,** (8) **range,** see as a main entry.

(1) 1886 ROOSEVELT in *Cent. Mag.* July 340/1, I had to leave the East in the midst of the hunting season to join a round-up in the cattle country of western Dakota. **1943** *Collier's* 28 Aug. 11/1 Do not miss the opening of this stirring tale of the cattle country. — **(2) 1626** in *Amer. Sp.* XV. 163/1 Or fence their cattle ground as the pasture & field of the cattle bee not taken from them. — **(3) 1860** GREELEY *Overland Journey* 327 Cattle-growing was the chief employment of the Californians of other days. **1862** *Rep. Comm. Patents: Agric.* 444 We mention this importation . . . as being the first step in an improved agriculture that was to revolutionize our large cattle-growing districts. — **(4) 1839** J. K. TOWNSEND *Narrative* 206 Our visitors . . . had mounted their horses . . . for a cattle hunt on the hills. **1878** I. L. BIRD *Rocky Mts.* 145 We were to have had a grand cattle-hunt yesterday, beginning at 6.30, but the horses were all lost.

(5) 1902 WISTER *Virginian* 282 Days look alike, and often lose their very names in the quiet depths of Cattle Land. — **(6) 1857** OLMSTED *Journey through Texas* 160 Some live upon the produce of farms and cattle-ranches owned in the neighborhood. **1946** *Ill. State Arch. Soc. Jrnl.* July 32/1 She owns and operates a large cattle ranch near Fairfax, Okla. — **(7) 1888** ROOSEVELT in *Cent. Mag.* Feb. 500 Cattle-ranching can only be carried on in its present form while the population is scanty. **1936** *Univ. Ariz. Gen. Bul.* No. 3, 184 Cattle ranching in Arizona is typical of the more extensive type.

4. Designating structures or conveyances for keeping or conveying cattle, as (1) **cattle barn,** (2) **car,** (3) **corral,** (4) **scow,** (5) **train,** (6) ***yard.**

(1) 1850 *N. Eng. Farmer* II. 46 The most fitting place to keep laying hens over winter is in the stable, or cattle-barn. **1924** H. CROY *R.F.D. No. 3* 148 I'm going to put up the finest cattle barn in the state. — **(2) 1863** BROWNE *Four Years in Secessia* (1865) 256 We were . . . greatly fatigued, on reaching what *was* the Rebel capital, from riding in box, platform, hog and cattle cars. **1948** *Southwestern Rev.* Winter 61/2 With a rush and a rumble of hooves they stampeded up the loading chute and into the cattle car. — **(3) 1877** *Rep. Indian Affairs* 62 A cattle-corral, 150 by 300 feet, has been built by the agency employes. **1913** CATHER *O Pioneers!* 20 There it lay outside his door. . . . To the south, his plowed fields; to the east, the sod stables, the cattle corral, the pond. — **(4) 1897** MARK TWAIN *Following the Equator* xxxii. 301 (R.), The Flora is about the equivalent of a cattle-scow. . . . They smuggle her into passenger service, and 'keep the change.'

(5) 1850 *Snow's Pathfinder* Jan. 55 A cattle train leaves Wells River and Montpelier each Tuesday morning for Brighton cattle-market. **1948** *Southwestern Rev.* Winter 62/2 The cattle train did get moving along in the morning with a cowboy sitting on top of each cattle car. — **(6)** [**1767** *N.C. Morav. Rec.* I. (1922) 18 Sep. 353 After dinner the Governor and the gentlemen walked about a bit, saw our stable, farm, brewery, and cattle-yard.] **1889** *Secy. of Agric. Rep.* 237 The Missouri River cattle-yards promise to rank above Chicago.

As the last term in **agency, anchor, beef, black, buffalo, grass, gulf, immigrant, Indian, issue, Kentucky, maroon, mustang, prairie, range, she, Sioux, stock, Texas, timber cattle.**

cattle range.

1. An unsettled or sparsely settled region over which cattle graze. Used esp. of the prairie regions of the West.

1640 *Essex Inst. Coll.* V. 170/1 Ordered that none of the land within the cattle range shall be granted . . . to any man. **1882** *Cent. Mag.* Aug. 510/1 The ground between the buttes is fertile, and the whole region is an excellent cattle-range. **1948** *Southwestern Rev.* Summer 272 They were in sheep country, but had passed across a forbidden cattle range to get there.

2. (See quots.) *Obs.*

1835 HOFFMAN *Winter in West* II. 130 We entered at once upon a large and beautiful park or chase. [*footnote*], Called 'a cattle-range,' if I mistake not, in Kentucky. **1889** FARMER 129/1 Cattle-range. Parks, even those attached to country-residences, are so called in Kentucky; this State is famous for its pasture and grazing lands.

***catty,** *n.* =**catfish.** *Obs.* — **1836** *Franklin Repository* (Chambersburg, Pa.) 4 Oct. 1/3 If you don't sashay as I said before I'll fetch you up like a catty on a corn [*sic*] line—jerk? **1856** *Spirit of Times* 4 Oct. 71/2 When I fish for catties I want catties, and don't want nothin' else.

catydid, see **katydid.**

caucus ˈkɔkəs, *n.* [See note.]

1. A meeting of political leaders for making plans, agreeing upon candidates, etc.

App. correctly derived in the *Cent.* (1889) f. Med. L. *caucus* (<Med. Gk. *kaukos*), a drinking vessel "in allusion to the convivial or symposiac feature" of the Caucus Club (see quot. 1763 below). No other equally plausible explanation has so far been made. Derivations from Virginian *caucauasu*, elder, counselor, or *caulkers'* (meeting), or from the initial letters of the names of six men (see *Amer. Sp.*, April 1943, p. 130) appear unlikely or impossible. The isolated use of West-Corcus in quot. 1745 below appears to be without significance, but cf. the spelling "corkusmen" in **3. b.** below.

[**1745** *Boston Ev. Post Supp.* 19 Aug. 1/1 Whereas the Association of Lay-Brethren, lately convened at Boston, to take into their serious Consideration the Conduct of those reverend Clergymen, who have encouraged the Itineration of Mr. George Whitefield, whereby the Liberties of the Laity have been invaded, [etc.]. . . . It is accordingly proposed, that there be such a general Meeting, and that it be held . . . at West-Corcus in Boston. **1763** J. ADAMS *Diary* Wks. II. 144 This day learned that the Caucus Club meets, at certain times, in the garret of Tom Dawes, the Adjutant of the Boston Regiment.] **1773** J. ADAMS *Works* IX. 334 This no doubt, was concerted last Saturday, at Neponset Hill, where Brattle and Russel dined, by way of caucus, I suppose. **1804** *Fredericktown* (Md.) *Herald* 28 Apr. 3/2 The democratic members of both houses met in *caucus* to agree on the nomination of a President and Vice-President. **1948** *Chi. Tribune* 20 June I. 2/1 The first caucus of the delegation of 56 . . . will provide the first real test of where the delegates stand on candidates.

2. (See quots.) *Obs.*

1828 COOPER *Notions* II. 35 Directly under the dome [of the Capitol at Washington] is a gloomy vaulted hall, that I have heard called the 'caucus'; more, I believe, from its fancied fitness for the political meetings that are thus termed, than from the fact that it has ever actually been appropriated to such an use. **1835** H. C. TODD *Notes* 33 Under the dome is a gloomy vaulted hall, called the *Caucus;* the soubriquet of an electioneering committee, being a corruption of calker-meeting, which originated amongst the shipping interest of Boston. **1837** COOPER *Gleanings in Eng.* II. 48 The room . . . reminded me of the apartment beneath the rotunda of the Capitol; that which is called the *caucus.*

3. In special, usu. obs., combs.: (1) **caucus candidate,** a candidate for President or Vice-President, etc., nominated by the members of his party in Congress; (2) **nomination,** a nomination for President or Vice-President made by the members of Congress belonging to a particular political party; (3) **President,** a President nominated by a congressional caucus; (4) **system,** the system of nominating candidates for President and Vice-President by congressional caucuses.

(1) **1816** *Ann. 14th Congress* 2 Sess. 352 They were pledged before they were chosen to vote for the caucus candidate, and no man doubts they have redeemed the pledge. **1910** *Aurora* (Ill.) *D. Beacon* 8 Sep. 1/3 If Joseph G. Cannon is the Republican caucus candidate for speaker will you vote for him? — **(2) 1816** *Ann. 14th Congress* 2 Sess. 352 In Virginia the legitimacy of caucus nomination has been fully sanctioned. **1888** *Chicago Inter-Ocean* 3 Jan. 6/4 In the lower house all the caucus nominations were confirmed without a scratch. — **(3) 1809** *Ann. 10th Congress* 2 Sess. 1421 We are to meet to-morrow here to attend the registering of the election of a caucus President. — **(4) 1846** MACKENZIE *Life Van Buren* 186 Because he differed a little from Van Buren's party caucus system, the senate rejected Governor Yates's nomination. **1948** *Tenn. Hist. Quart.* March 14 The partial breakdown of the caucus system of nomination made political orthodoxy less important than in the period of the Virginia–New England Dynasty.

b. caucus man, a man taking part in a caucus. *Obs.*

1762 *Mass. H. S. Proc.* XX. 48 We daily see many of your predictions accomplished respecting the connections & discords of our politicians, corkusmen, plebeian tribunes, &ca.

Also *caucus army, committee, company, convention, influence, loan, management, meeting, monger, non-intercourse, party, proceeding, speech, tribe,* etc., often with derogatory implications.

As the last term in **Congress, congressional, Democratic, house, king, kitchen, legislative, primary, Republican, sub caucus.**

caucus ˈkɔkəs, *v. intr.* To meet or assemble as a caucus. Also **caucusing,** *n.*

1788 W. GORDON *History Independence U.S.* 365 The word *caucus,* and its derivative *caucussing* are often used in Boston. The latter answers much to what we stile parliamenteering or electioneering. **1848** *Rough & Ready* (Louisville) 1 Jan. 2/2 No caucusing—no wire-working—no bickering or strife will be visible. **1948** *Time* 14 June 15/2 Favorite-son backers who know they have no chance caucus endlessly, listening for the first rumble of a bandwagon.

b. Also, rarely, *tr.*

1893 *Dly. Ardmoreite* (Ardmore, Okla.) 12 Nov. 1/1 By the tariff revision talk now raging Culberson and Bland want the matter caucused.

caucuser ˈkɔkəsɚ, *n.* One active in caucuses. *Rare.* — **1823** *Niles' Reg.* XXV. 101 The danger of a choice in the house of representatives would not be dreaded, even by Messrs. Gales and Seaton, the great caucussers of the day.

cauliflower ear. An ear so deformed as the result of an injury, usually in boxing or wrestling, as to suggest a cauliflower. Also **cauliflowered,** *a.*

1909 *Sat. Ev. Post* 1 May 31/2 It was the 'cauliflower ear' of pugilism. **1947** *Time* 27 Jan. 60/2 His dress was sharp, his nose potato-shaped, his ears cauliflowered. **1947** *Chi. Sun* 26 Dec. 5/3 Cauliflower ears attest to his earlier ring career about the time of Jeffries and Britton.

***cause,** *n.* As the last term in **abolition, colonization, lost, Oklahoma, union cause.**

* **caution,** *n.*

1. A person, thing, action, etc., that provokes admiration, astonishment, etc. *Slang.*

1835 HOFFMAN *Winter in West* I. 197 The way in which the icy blast would come down the bleak shore of the lake 'was a caution.' **1870** M. COLLINS *Vivian* III. ii. 26 His wife was what the Yankees call a 'caution.' **1948** *Sat. Ev. Post* 17 July 60/3 She was just a little thing, Babe was, but it was a caution how just having her near could brighten the general drabness of life.

b. Often *a caution to* (something, somebody). *Slang.*

1834 *Knickerb.* III. 34 The way I'll lick you will be a caution to the balance of your family. **1861** NEWELL *Orpheus C. Kerr* I. 230 The way that gal squealed when we struck a rut, was a caution to screech owls. **1864** *Sacramento Union* 8 Jan. 2/4 The whole company was ordered to the mountains, and the way the wood came down was a caution to Mormon. *a***1904** S. E. WHITE *Blazed Trail* 206 The way he [=a horse] climbed up through that dark gorge was a caution to thoroughbreds.

2. *W.* (See quot.) *Obs.*

1857 T. H. GLADSTONE *Englishman in Kansas* 171 On a piece of paper nailed to a tree, appear the words, . . . 'This is Jim Barton's claim; and he'll shoot the first fellow as comes within a mile of it.' Such an announcement is technically called a 'caution.'

cavallada, see **caballada.**

cavallard, see **caballada.**

cavallo, see **caballo.**

cavalrist ˈkævl̩rɪst, *n.* A cavalryman. *Rare.* — **1898** *Boston Herald* 19 June 17/1 He leads the life alternately of a cavalrist, infantrist, engineer, artillerist and staff officer.

***cavalry,** *n.* As the last term in **black horse, foot, mule, mustang cavalry.**

* **cave,** *v. cave down,* to undermine, to collapse, or to cause to collapse. *Colloq.*

1761 S. NILES *Indian Wars* II. 340 But Providence prevented them by sending a great rain, and caved down the sides of their trench. **1851** CIST *Cincinnati* 344, I obtained permission to open a sand-pit, which had long been closed for fear of caving down a house, by further excavation. **1857** *Hutchings Mag.* July 13/1 The most efficient manner of washing down these banks is by undermining them near the bed rock, when large masses—frequently many tons in weight—'cave down.'

* **caveat,** *n.* Formerly a notice filed at the Patent Office by an inventor to prevent the possible granting of a patent to another for the same invention. Also **caveator.**

1836 in *Sci. Amer.* (1846) 24 Oct. 35/1 Any citizen of the United States . . . may, on paying to the credit of the Treasury, in manner as provided in the ninth section of this act, the sum of $20, file in the Patent Office a caveat, setting forth the design and purpose, and its principle and distinguishing characteristics, and praying protection of his right, till he shall have matured his invention. **1847** WEBSTER 184/2 [A] caveat . . . [is] lodged in the office before the patent right is taken out. **1881** *Sci. Amer. Circular,* After a Caveat has been filed the Patent Office will not issue a patent for the same invention to any other person without giving notice to the Caveator. **1945** ADAMS *Album Amer. Hist.* II. 291 In 1837, after five years of experimentation, Samuel F. B. Morse, an artist, filed at the Patent Office a caveat for a magnetic telegraph.

caviya, see **caballada.**

cavort kəˈvɔrt, *v.* Also **cauvaut, cavault, covault.** [Origin obscure. Poss. f. *ca-* (*q.v.*)+*vault.* Cf. *EDD kaivan, kaiving,* rearing, plunging.] *intr.* To act up, prance, cut didos (see also quots. 1829, 1830). Also fig. *Colloq.*

1793 *Steele Papers* I. 106 The Hon. J—e 'cauvauted,' don't laugh at the expression, it suits the idea I meant to convey. **1829** *Va. Lit. Museum* 16 Dec. 419 Cavault or Cavort ranting, highflying.—West. **1830** ROYALL *Lett. fr. Ala.* 122 Covault is of Tennessee birth. . . . It signifies an unruly or ungovernable man; also an untame horse, or anything that cannot be controuled. **1873** BAILEY *Life in Danbury* 97, I could no more get hold of the fearful agony that was cavorting around in me [etc.]. **1914** BRININSTOOL *Trail Dust* 197 Ev'ry bronco is cavortin' in the chilly autumn air. **1947** *Harper's Mag.* April 331/2 Then with your mind's eye, you begin to see the earth, the horizon and the sky, and your own airplane cavorting in it.

cavorter kəˈvɔrtɚ, *n.* One who cavorts. *Colloq.* — **1835** LONGSTREET *Ga. Scenes* 21, I could see nothing in it [*sc.* the crowd] that seemed to have anything to do with the cavorter.

cavorting kəˈvɔrtɪŋ, *n.* and *a.*

1. *n.* Kicking, plunging, ranting, extravagant behavior or conduct. *Colloq.*

1831 *Boston Transcript* 8 Apr. 1/1 I'm a ring-tail roarer, all the way from Salt River. So, none of your cockloftical cavorting about me, or I'll be into you like a streak of lightning. **1859** GRATTAN *Civilized Amer.* II. 383 Accustomed to attack rampant bears at home, the cavortings of the British lion seemed much less terrible to him than to some of his more civilized countrymen. **1946** *Chi. D. News* 4 Nov. 14/3 The little girl is all dirtied up from cavorting with the squirrels.

2. *a.* That cavorts. *Colloq.*

1839 HOFFMAN *Wild Scenes* 30, I had . . . expected of course to see one of those roystering, 'cavorting,' rifle-shirted blades that I have seen upon our western frontier. *a***1909** O. HENRY *Roads of Destiny* 103 Did Hot Tamales fancy he saw a steer, red and cavorting, that should be headed off and driven back to herd?

cavortish kəˈvɔrtɪʃ, *a.* Inclined or given to cavorting. *Colloq.* —

1835 LONGSTREET *Ga. Scenes* 28 Bullet [a horse] became more and more *cavortish*.

cavvy ˈkævɪ, *n. W.* Short for "cavy-yard" for which see **caballada.**

1913 W. C. BARNES *Western Grazing Grounds* 380 Following is a list of definitions of words and expressions in common use among stockmen: . . . Cavvyard, Cavvy. (Spanish). A bunch of horses. **1947** *Trail Riders Bul.* Feb. 20/1 The ranch was gittin' a shipment of mustangs from Oklahoma, so the boss sends us out tuh run up a corral big 'nough tuh hol' the new cavvy.

b. cavvy wrango, =wrangler.

1925 WILL JAMES *Drifting Cowboy* 80 (Bentley), The cavy-wrango had brought the horses in, and they were all there to pick from one another day's riding.

cavy-yard, see **caballada.**

cawcawwassough ˈkɔkɔˌwɔsu, *n.* [Algonquian, in same sense.] (See quot.) *Obs.* Cf. **caucus** and **cockarouse.** — **1612** SMITH *Virginia* 5 In all these places is a severall commander, which they call Werowance, except the Chickhamanians, who are governed by the Priests and their Assistants of [*read* or] their Elders called Cawcawwassoughes.

cayac ˈkaɪæk, *n.* [Read explains La. F. *kaïc* (a big, powerful fellow, a roughneck), app. the same word, as coming f. standard French *gaïac*, the lignum-vitae tree.] (See quots.)

*c***1850** in FRIEDERICI (1947) 338/1 Seven buffalo bulls on the road leading to Fort Clarke. . . . With our telescope we could note their age; they were, according to the current expression, *cayacs*. That means they were thrust out by the young bulls and nevermore allowed to approach any herd of cows. Such animals, excluded from the herd, range in small groups by themselves; their flesh is not used for food. **1931** READ *La.-French* 141 Kaïac . . . . This word signifies a 'big, powerful fellow,' a 'roughneck,' according to my friends at French Settlement.

Cayenne ˌkeˈen, *n.* **=K.N.** *Obs.* — **1855** *N.Y. Wkly. Tribune* 10 Feb. 2/6 The Cayennes may have seen 'Sam,' but they have not seen the beginning of the end of the new Order or League of Freedom. **1855** *Louisville Times* 15 Aug. 2/3 And *Cayenne* said: 'Americans America shall rule.'

cayote, see **coyote.**

Cayuga keˈjugə, *n.* [Iroquoian place-name.] An Indian of an Iroquoian tribe formerly occupying the region around Cayuga Lake, N.Y. Also attrib.

1744 *Col. Rec. Pa.* IV. 722 The several Nations had drawn for the performance of the Ceremony and the *Lot* falling on the Cayogo Nation [etc.]. **1792** *Affecting Hist. F. Manheim* 34 A number of . . . Cayugas will commence hostilities. **1827** WEST *Journal* 288 These Indians, with the Cayugas', who are the most numerous of the six nations, on the above station, keep many feasts, and particularly one at the time of planting their corn. **1947** *Dly. Oklahoman* (Okla. City) 21 Sep. 5-D/1 A beating was taken by the Seneca, Oneida, Tuscarora, Onondaga, Mohawk and Cayuga tribes who sold about one-third of northwestern Pennsylvania and the western one-sixth of New York.

b. Cayuga black, (see quot.). *Rare.*

1871 LEWIS *Poultry Book* 84 The Cayuga Black. This is a variety of our duck tribe well worthy of cultivation, and the best of the dark ducks.

Cayuse kaɪˈjus, *n.* [f. the tribal name.]

1. (See quot. 1907.) Also **Cayuse Indians.**

1825 MCLOUGHLIN *Letters* (1941) I. 7 We had an account of a Battle between the Cai-ouses, Nez Perces, and Snakes. **1838** PARKER *Journal* 126 We called at encampment of Cayuse Indians of about a dozen lodges. **1850** HINES *Voyage* 12 The merits of the different portions of the country were considered, the Flat Heads, the Nez Perces, the Kayuses, and other tribes. **1907** HODGE *Amer. Indians* I. 224 Cayuse. A Waiilatpuan tribe formerly occupying the territory about the heads of Wallawalla, Umatilla, and Grande Ronde rs and from the Blue mts. to Deschutes r. in Washington and Oregon. **1948** *Pac. Northwest Quart.* April 100 The Whitmans took up their mission work among the Cayuse Indians.

b. (See quot.)

1927 WALGAMOTT *Remin. Early Days* II. 50 Most squaw-men were French or Canadian-French, sometimes called Cayuse French.

2. (not *cap.*) *W.* Orig. an Indian pony, many of which were bred by the Cayuse Indians, later used colloquially for any horse. Also attrib.

1867 *Territorial Enterprise* (Virginia, Nev.) 31 Jan. 2/4 Jane . . . was mounted behind her lover and away, nor bated they the noble cayuse till many a league was passed. **1901** M. E. RYAN *Montana* 27 The 'cayuse' bell sounded nearer and nearer, and directly from the dense forest a packhorse came stepping with care over the fallen logs. **1948** *Chi. Tribune* 27 May II. 2/6 Life atop a cayuse in the professional arenas . . . is no easier than one astride a bronco on the college rodeo field.

b. Also **cayuse horse, nag, plug, pony.**

1839 FARNHAM *Great Western Prairies* (1841) 157 But as Skyuse horses never make such disagreeable mistakes, we rode the steeps in safety. *a***1918** G. STUART *On Frontier* I. 158 In the fall of 1860, Frank L. Worden and Captain C. P. Higgins came up from Fort Walla Walla with a pack train of cayuse horses. — **1854** *Oregonian* (Portland) 11 Nov. 1/5 Of sports, there are the races of Cayuse nags, as fiercely contested as horse flesh and Indian enterprise can make them. — **1880** NYE *B. Nye & Boomerang* 17 He jabs the Mexican spurs into the foamy flank of his noble cayuse plug. — **1864** MARK TWAIN *Sketches Sixties* (1926) 127 When we got pretty close to it, the island shrunk into a fish . . . and the mastodon dwindled down to a Cayuse pony. **1944** ROSS *Westward* 112 Many eager men thought nothing of riding their Cayuse ponies right up to the doors of respectable Portland houses.

c. cayuse performance, a rodeo. *Rare.*

1877 *Palouse Gazette* (Colfax, Wash.) 13 Oct. 1/3 Did you see the cayuse performance the other day?

3. *W.* A cold east wind, the opposite of a Chinook *q.v. Colloq.*

1905 G. E. COLE *Early Oregon* v. 77 The weather turned very cold, a Cayuse or East wind prevailing.

cayuseship kaɪˈjusˌʃɪp, *n.* The quality or state of being a cayuse. *Rare.* — **1894** *Outing* XXIV. 150/2 The only method of procedure on the part of his cayuseship consisted in a series of mad plunges ahead.

C.C.C. Abbreviation for "Civilian Conservation Corps." Also attrib.

1933 *Time* 17 April 12/2 By authority of last fortnight's relief act, he issued an order creating the C.C.C. and providing it with $10,000,000 as a starter. **1934** *Nat. Geog. Mag.* LXV. 676 Gangs of men, many of them C.C.C. crews, were toiling to straighten curves and improve the road. **1946** *Okla. Dly.* (Norman) 2 Aug. 1/1 The former CCC camp on the shores of Lake Murray near Ardmore, recently leased by the school of geology, is the setting.

ceanothus ˌsiəˈnoθəs, *n.* [Gr. *keanōthos*, a kind of thistle.] Any one of various American shrubs of the buckthorn family, esp. abundant on the west coast, and sometimes cultivated. Cf. **American ceanothus.**

1785 MARSHALL *Amer. Grove* 27 American Ceanothus, or New-Jersey Tea-Tree. **1903** AUSTIN *Land of Little Rain* 86 South the land rises in very blue hills, blue because thickly wooded with ceanothus and manzanita. **1948** *So. Sierran* Feb. 2/2 On the January 18 trip to Griffith Park the hills were already covered with blooming Ceanothus.

attrib. **1869** MUIR *First Summer in Sierra* (1911) 76 It led far up the ridge into an open place surrounded by a hedge-like growth of ceanothus chaparral.

* **cecropia,** *n.* A large silkworm, *Samia cecropia*, native to the eastern states.

1868 *Amer. Naturalist* II. 313 It is not a soft, flossy cocoon, like that of Cecropia. **1885** *Harper's Mag.* Apr. 777/2 The *Attacus prometheus*, and the *A. polyphemus*, though inferior in size to the *cecropia*, are far better adapted to this purpose than the Chinese worm. **1947** DUBKIN *Enchanted Streets* 152 The Cecropia is predominantly purple and orange, with two white crescents on the hind wings.

attrib. **1884** *Amer. Naturalist* XVIII. 1046 Poison Glands in the skin of the Cecropia caterpillar. **1885** *Ib.* XIX .1142 The anatomy of the Cecropia moth. **1947** DUBKIN *Enchanted Streets* 148 The Cecropia caterpillar is lazy and does not relish any unnecessary climbing.

* **cedar,** *n.*

1. *attrib.* Designating places, areas, etc., where cedar is the prevailing growth, as (1) **cedar barren,** (2) **bluff,** (3) **bottom,** (4) **brake,** (5) **branch,** (6) **glade,** (7) **hammock,** (8) **island,** (9) **knob,** (10) **lick,** (11) **lot,** (12) **swamp,** (13) **thicket.**

(1) **1824** *Catawba Journal* 26 Oct., A residence on cedar or pine barrens during the summer, has been efficacious in pulmonary cases. **1893** LELAND *Memoirs* 291, I never shall forget the dismal appearance of the Cedar Barrens. The soil was nowhere more than two inches deep, and the trees which covered it by millions had all died as soon as they attained a height of fifteen or twenty feet. — (2) **1779** in RAMSEY *Tennessee* (1853) 202 We have found a few log cabins which have been built on a cedar bluff above the Lick. **1807** GASS *Journal* 30 We passed cedar bluffs on the north side, a part of which were burning. — (3) **1807** GASS *Journal* 42 We again went on, having . . . a cedar bottom on the south side. — (4) **1830** DEWEES *Lett. from Texas* 124 The night was very dark, and our course lay over mountains of rock and through cedar brake. **1948** *Popular Western* June 90/1 He was in the cedar brakes along a chain of foothills that marched off to dim, blue mountains in the west.

(5) **1665** in *Amer. Sp.* XV. 163/2 To a Cedar branch on the North side of the Land of Saml Taylor. — **(6) 1901** MOHR *Plant Life Ala.* 82 Large supplies of the valuable timber of the cedar . . . are drawn every year from the cedar glades. — **(7)** *Ib.* 102 These cedar hammocks once formed detached tracts extending over many square miles. — **(8) 1633** in *Amer. Sp.* XV. 163/2 Abutting Eastwardly upon a Cedar Island. — **(9) 1805** SIBLEY in *Ann. 9th Congress* 2 Sess. 1104 From the Panis towns to Santa Fe, . . . all the country [is] prairie, a few scattering cedar knobs excepted. **1838** DRAKE *Tales & Sk.* 33 He was a full grown Kentuckian, born on the cedar knobs of the Blue Licks.

(10) 1781 in *Amer. Sp.* XV. 280/2 A branch of Salt river 4 miles North of the Cedar licks. — **(11) 1813** *Mass. Spy* 14 April 4/4 To be sold . . . two Cedar Lots, lying in the Great Cedar Swamp. — **(12) 1636–7** *Plymouth Col. Rec.* I. 51 A parcell of land is graunted vnto Mr Thomas Prence, lying betweene the two cedar swamps at Iland Creeke Pond. **1712** in *Amer. Sp.* XV. 163/2 To a white Oake Standing Near the Side of the Cedar Swamp Poquoson. **1942** WEYGANDT *Plenty of Penna.* 15 Such [hunters] will tell you . . . of white egrets wandering in long lines through the green glooms of cedar swamps. — **(13) 1841** *Spirit of Times* 6 Feb. 579/3 Cedar thicket. **1923** J. H. COOK *On Old Frontier* 45 The country was rough and broken, and here and there were large cedar thickets or brakes.

2. Designating things made of cedar: (1) **cedar canoe,** (2) **chest,** (3) **closet,** (4) **post,** (5) **rail,** (6) **shell,** (7) **shingle.**

(1) 1762 in *N.J. Archives* 1 Ser. XXIV. 60 Run away. . . . A Servant Lad . . . in an old Cedar Canoe, with her Sides broke. **1892** *Outing* July 272/2 We had but one boat of our own, a light cedar canoe. — **(2)** [**1588** HARIOT *Briefe & True Report* B2v Cedar, a very sweet wood & fine timber, whereof if nests of chests be there made, or timber thereof fitted for sweet & fine bedsteads, tables, desks, lutes, . . . will yeeld profite.] **1775** *Essex Hist. Coll.* XIII. 178 A Pane of Looking Glass in the same Trunk or the Cedar Chest. **1948** *Aurora* (Ill.) *Beacon-News* 7 Nov. (Supp.) 12/2 Not only brides, therefore, enjoy cedar chests. — **(3) 1860** in *Diary of Mrs. S. Cowell* 69 We notice a . . . cedar closet, lined with shelves, wherein to keep clothing free from moths. **1866** HALE *If, Yes & Perhaps* (1868) 256, I was up in the cedar closet one day, looking for an old parade cap of mine. — **(4) 1726** BENJAMIN LYNDE *Diary* (1880) 15, I went thro' the woods a mile and a half more directly to Edw. Esty's, where I rested, dined and had account of my shingles . . . also rails, cedar posts and clapboards. **1904** E. W. PRINGLE *Rice Planter* 77, I have already bought the wire . . . and had the cedar posts got out, so that it will not cost so much to get the fence put up.

(5) 1730 BENJAMIN LYNDE *Diary* (1880) 16 Charged him (Edward Esty) . . . to cart as much of the 1000 best cedar rails as he can himself by the beginning of October. **1856** OLMSTED *Slave States* 151 A great many rough poles of the juniper, under the name of 'cedar-rails,' are sent to New York. — **(6) 1867** *Ball Players' Chron.* 25 July 5/1 Their boat is a cedar shell, 51 ft. 6 in. in length, 19 inches wide. — **(7) 1673** *R.I. Hist. Soc. Coll.* XXIV. 80 Shipped . . . Newport to Barbados . . . one barll aples & five hundred of Ceder chings. **1884** CRADDOCK *Where Battle Was Fought* 100 A moment later the cedar shingles that roofed the gin-house were blazing timorously.

3. In the names of, or with reference to, plants and trees: (1) **cedar apple,** a hard, somewhat spherical excrescence formed on cedar trees by various rusts; (2) **ball,** =prec.; (3) **berry,** the fruit of the red cedar, *Juniperus virginiana;* (4) **elm,** (see quots.); (5) **pine,** (see quots.).

(1) 1846 LYELL *Second Visit* (1849) II. 244 The cedar . . . is often covered at this season with what is termed here the cedar apple . . . supposed by many of the inhabitants to be the flower or fruit of the tree itself. **1948** *Holland's* March 46/2 When these 'cedar apples' do erupt, your apple trees, flowering crabs and many other ornamentals will be infected. — **(2) 1889** *Cent.* 875/3 Cedar-apple . . . [is] also called *cedar-ball.* **1909** *D.N.* III. 297. — **(3)** [**1709** LAWSON *Carolina* 90 The Cedar-Berries are infused, and made Beer of, by the Bermudians.] **1737** BRICKELL *N. Carolina* 38 The following are made in Country . . . Ceder-Beer, made of Ceder-Berries. **1884** BURROUGHS in *Cent. Mag.* Dec. 220 In winter, especially, they [wild birds] sweep by me and around me in flocks, . . . feeding upon frozen apples in the orchard, upon cedar-berries, [etc.]. — **(4) 1884** SARGENT *Rep. Forests* 122 *Ulmus crassifolia.* . . . Cedar Elm. **1931** MATTOON *Forest Trees Okla.* 60 Cedar Elm (*Ulmus crassifolia* Nutt.) . . . is found in the southeastern part of the State.

(5) 1884 SARGENT *Rep. Forests* 201. **1894** COULTER *Bot. W. Texas* III. 554 *Pinus glabra.* A tree 24 to 30 m. high. . . . Extending into Eastern Texas from the Gulf states. 'Cedar pine.' **1897** SUDWORTH *Arborescent Flora* 27 *Pinus virginiana.* Scrub Pine. Common names [include] . . . Short-leaved Pine (N.C.), Cedar Pine (N.C.).

4. In miscellaneous combs.: (1) **cedar bird,** =**cedar waxwing;** (2) **cooper,** (see quot.), *obs.;* (3) **quarry,** (see quot.), *obs.;* (4) **waxwing,** the cherry bird, *Bombycilla cedrorum,* common throughout temperate North America.

(1) 1791 BARTRAM *Travels* 288 *Ampelis garrulus,* crown bird or cedar bird. These birds feed on various sorts of succulent fruit. **1892** TORREY *Foot-Path Way* 33, I saw that the ground was already preëmpted by a company of cedar birds. **1942** PEATTIE *Friendly Mts.* 208 A party of cedar birds in their somber but sleek plumage give their lisping notes. — **(2) 1832** BROWNE *Sylva* 148 The superior fitness of this wood [*sc.* white cedar] for various household utensils, has given rise, in Philadelphia, to a distinct class of mechanics called cedar coopers. —**(3) 1839** *Amer. R.R. Jrnl.* VIII. 351 Cedar quarries.—On asking a friend from Oswego, the other day, who used this term, what it meant, he informed us that much of the cedar which comes from Lake Ontario is absolutely dug out of the soil. . . . Generation has apparently succeeded generation of this timber, and fallen, and been successively covered with earth, and is now dug out for railroads, fence posts, etc. and in a perfectly sound state. — **(4) 1844** *Nat. Hist. N.Y., Zoology* II. 44. **1948** *Green Bay* (Wis.) *Press-Gazette* 30 June 4/1 A letter . . . came to me recently about the smart actions of a cedar waxwing in trying to conceal its nest.

As the last term in **Alaskan, canoe, giant, ground, incense, Indian, Monterey, Oregon, Port Orford, post, red, salt, stinking, swamp, Washington, white, yellow cedar.**

ceja ˈsehɑ, *n. S.W.* [Sp., eyebrow, also summit.] (See quot. 1909.)

1834 A. PIKE *Sketches* 44 In the course of fourteen days we should arrive at a descent, or falling off of the prairie to the east, and . . . there (rising out of this ceja, or eyebrow, as they called it) we should find the rivers. **1844** GREGG *Commerce of Prairies* I. 277 The still existing Pueblo of Acoma also stands upon an isolated mound whose whole area is occupied by the village, being fringed all around by a precipitous *ceja* or cliff. **1909** *Cent. Supp.* 215/1 Ceja, . . . in phys. geog., the brow or cliffed margin of a mesa or upland. (Southwestern U.S.)

b. (See quot.)

1893 *D.N.* I. 245 Ceja, eyebrow. In Texas, a long and narrow strip of *chaparral.*

cekwik ˈsiˌkwɪk, *n.* [Fanciful spelling of "see quick."] (See quot.) — **1873** *Seaside Oracle* (Wiscasset, Maine) 25 Jan. 1/5 My boys would play a game with an Icelandic name—they called it Cekwik. One boy arranges ten or twelve things in the passage, by the door—say a mat, a boot, [etc.]. . . . Then, ten or fifteen other boys form in one rank, single file, and trot 'double-quick' past the open door, to see what they can see. Some see only two, others ten things; trot by the door again, and so learn to play Cekwik.

celandine poppy. (See quot. 1891.) — **1857** GRAY *Botany* 25 *Stylophorum.* Celandine Poppy. . . . Perennial herb, with . . . pinnately divided leaves like Celandine. **1891** *Cent.* 6013/2 *Stylophorum diphyllum* is the celandine poppy or yellow poppy of the central United States, formerly classed under *Meconopsis.*

* **celerity,** *n.* (See quots. 1858, 1930.) In full **celerity coach, celerity wagon.** Now *hist.*

Celerity coach or wagon

1858 *Leslie's Wkly.* 23 Oct. 327/3 The vehicles are not unlike a Jersey wagon, they are of the description known as a celerity wagon, being similar . . . to the common Troy coach. **1859** in *So. Calif. Hist. Soc. Pub.* 17, 104 The vehicles used upon the road from Fort Smith westward are of the description known as Celerity Coaches. **1930** BANNING *Six Horse* 147 The 'Celerity' was a type of 'mud-wagon.' . . . It was adapted especially for use on heavy roads, or for rugged, mountainous country. **1947** CONKLING *Butterfield Overland Mail* I. 133 The 'celerity' wagon was an innovation on the part of Butterfield to provide a lighter and faster type of vehicle for use on the rougher sections of the route.

celery (-leafed, -leaved) crowfoot. (See quots.)

1817–8 EATON *Botany* (1822) 424 *Ranunculus sceleratus,* celery crowfoot. **1840** DEWEY *Mass. Flowering Plants* 26 Celery-leafed

Crowfoot . . . grows in wet places, and flowers in June. **1901** MOHR *Plant Life Ala.* 514 Celery-leaved or Cursed Crowfoot . . . [grows] throughout Atlantic North America west to British Columbia and Arizona.

* **cellar,** *n.*

1. *Baseball.* The lowest position in league rank.

1922 *N.Y. Times* 1 July 9/2 Red Sox Are Up Again. Leave Cellar to Athletics by Taking Final of Series, 4 to 1. **1948** *Dly. Ardmoreite* (Ardmore, Okla.) 19 Apr. 6/2 Last year the Braves, after hovering near the first division until mid-season, took a tail-spin which landed them in the cellar.

2. In combs.: (1) **cellar boss,** *transf.* a contemptuous designation for an inconsequential person, *rare;* (2) * **case,** *local* (see quot. 1890); (3) **kitchen,** a kitchen in a cellar or basement [cf. Du. *kelderkeuken*]; (4) **lot,** a lot upon which there is a cellar, *rare;* (5) **way,** a way to or through a cellar.

(1) **1902** LORIMER *Lett. Merchant* 108 One of those fellows . . . who goes around and makes the boys give up their lunch money to buy flowers for the deceased aunt of the cellar boss' wife. — (2) **1890** *D.N.* I. 18 Cellar-case, outside entrance to a cellar, with a sloping door. In Eastern Massachusetts 'bulkhead' is invariably used. **1895** A. BROWN *Meadow-Grass* 161 Caleb saw that she had prepared for her return by leaving the doors of the cellar-case open, and laying down a board over the steps. — (3) **1830** J. F. WATSON *Philadelphia* 202 Cellar Kitchens, now so general, are but of modern use. **1846** CHILD *Fact & Fiction* 247 She was mostly confined to the cellar kitchen, from which she looked out upon stone-steps and a brick wall. **1856** *Rep. Comm. Patents: Agric.* 223 My place of keeping [sweet potatoes] is a cellar-kitchen. — (4) **1665** *Hempstead Rec.* I. 162, I the a fors'd John Smith have sold on to my soninlaw Samuell Denton the afore saide seller and seller lotte.

(5) **1761** S. NILES *Indian Wars* II. 512 Two or three were found lying on that part of the floor which was left, and in the cellar-way. **1863** S. C. MASSETT *Drifting About* 50 The stage entrance was through a cellar-way in Broadway. **1922** R. PARRISH *Case & Girl* 181 His fingers explored the edge of this opening cautiously, revealing a cellar-way, leading down into the basement.

As the last term in **bank, barn, beer, cyclone, dance, dugout, ice, lager beer, Negro, oyster, storm cellar.**

Celluloid ˈsɛljəˌlɔɪd, *n.* Also **celluloid.** [f. *cellulose*+ *-oid,* like.] A trade-mark for an artificial substance with a cellulose base used in place of ivory, coral, etc., in the manufacture of many small objects. Also attrib.

1871 *Amer. Dental Assn. Trans.* XI 152 We have many so-called cheap materials . . . : rubber, celluloid, pyroxyline, porcelain base, aluminum, and the alloys of tin. **1882** SWEET & KNOX *Texas Siftings* 9 He is usually swung to a satchel containing a comb and brush, . . . a clean celluloid collar, and a newspaper. **1903** *Sears Cat.* (ed. 113) 635/1 Celluloid Waterproof Collars for Men and Boys, 11 Cents. **1947** *Atlantic Mo.* Oct. 52/2 Celluloid . . . was discovered by John Wesley Hyatt as the accidental and undesired result of his effort to produce from wood pulp a substitute for ivory billiard balls.

b. *transf.* Used attrib. with reference to motion pictures.

1922 *Frontier* Nov. 18 As the celluloid hero flashed his impartial smile across the screen—it was the stolid Indian who stamped, whistled, and clapped, while the white man sat in half-bored silence. **1947** *Redbook* July 20/1 The difference between celluloid fame and oblivion is foot-upon-foot of motion-picture film lying discarded and forgotten in the cutting-room barrel.

* **cement,** *n.* "Gravel firmly held in a silicious matrix, or the matrix itself" (Raymond, *Mining Gloss.*).

1856 *Butte Record* (Oroville, Calif.) 29 Nov. 3/4 A hard substance, called by the miners 'cement,' is found in many places at depths varying from 16 to 30 or 40 feet, on which a deposit of 'pay dirt' is lodged. **1869** BRACE *New West* 170 It is said that there are several hundred miles of this cement in the State, 'ranging from one thousand feet to several miles wide, and from one hundred to one thousand feet deep, all of which is rich in gold.' **1873** LAWRENCE *Silverland* 181 An adit-level, or tunnel, has been driven in upon the hard bed-rock itself; whence is extracted 'cement' so hard and tough as only to be worked in a steam-mill. **1947** CHALFANT *Gold, Guns, & Ghost Towns* 36 Good evidence exists that such red cement rich in gold as that described was found in 1862 during Dr. Randall's search.

b. cement rock, (see quot.).

1918 VISHER *So. Dakota* 25 The gold bearing ores are found in considerable quantities in . . . 'cement' rocks or conglomerate of Cambrian age.

cenizo seˈniso, *n. S.W.* [Sp. in Amer. Sp. sense shown here.] A shrub, *Atriplex canescens,* having silvery-gray foliage.

1907 LYONS *Plant Names* 62 A[triplex] canescens. . . . S. Dakota to Mexico and California. Bushy Atriplex, Cenizo. **1931** DAYTON *Western Browse Plants* 28 Other names in more or less common use are chamiza (New Mexico), cenizo, buckwheat shrub, bushy atriplex, salt sage. **1941** FERGUSSON *Southwest* 5 Olive-green cedars, dusty gray cenizo, light and feathery mesquite, and cactus, gray and thorny.

* **censor,** *n.* A census enumerator. *Rare.* — **1837** *Mass. Statutes* 12 April, The said census shall be taken in the several cities by censors appointed by the mayor and alderman.

* **censurate,** *n.* Censorship. *Rare.* — **1898** *Boston Globe* 24 April 8/4 The censurate of the press is now stricter than ever.

* **census,** *n.* **1. census marshal,** (see quot. 1890). **2. census taker,** one who collects data for a census. Cf. **state census.**

(1) **1885** *Harper's Mag.* Aug. 355/2 He told him that the 'census marshal' was coming, and that unless he told that functionary just who he was, he would be put in prison. **1890** *Cent.* 3639/2 The officers who take the State census in certain States are called *marshals* or *census marshals.* — (2) **1840** *N.O. Picayune* 25 Aug. 2/2 The following took place between a census taker and a married lady. **1911** ROLT-WHEELER *Boy with Census* 1 Since I'm going to be a census-taker, I think I'd like to apply for this district.

* **cent,** *n.*

1. A coin usu. made partially or entirely of copper and having a value of one-hundredth of a dollar. Also attrib.

Congress in 1781 instructed Robert Morris to devise a system of national coinage. He proposed a small silver coin as the unit of value. Jefferson, however, proposed the dollar as the unit, and that the smallest coin in value should be one of copper, 200 (later 100) of these to have the value of a dollar.

1782 MORRIS in Sparks *Life G. Morris* (1832) I. 275 One hundred [units] would be the lowest silver coin, and might be called a *Cent.* **1848** THOREAU *Maine Woods* 16 One of the party commenced distributing a store of small cent picture-books among the children. **1944** *Chi. D. News* 10 Jan. 10/2 The price is 739 one hundred thousandths of a cent.

Hence **center,** a cigar selling for one cent. Also **centapee** (i.e., "cent-apiece") **cigar.** *Obs.*

1857 *Spirit of Times* 147/1, I plunged my hand into my pocket, and pulled out four or five 'centers.' *Ib.* 310/1 Had supper down in the bottom of said boat, smoked a centapee cigar, and went to bed.

b. *fig.* The smallest amount, often in the phrase *not worth a cent.*

1803 J. DAVIS *Travels* 389 But I never wronged Master of a cent. **1830** S. SMITH *Major Downing* 23 They don't seem to rip up worth a cent. **1900** GEORGE ADE *More Fables in Slang* 37 They did not Mocha and Java worth a Cent.

2. In special combs.: (1) **cent shop,** a small shop in which articles are sold for a cent; (2) **Cent Society,** =**mite society.** Both *obs.*

(1) **1851** HAWTHORNE *Seven Gables* ii, Reduced now, in that very house, to be the huckstress of a cent-shop! — (2) **1817** in H. M. BROOKS *Gleanings* 137 The Annual Meeting of the Boston Cent Society will be holden . . . on Tuesday, April 8th, at 11 o'clock A.M. **1822** *Missionary Herald* XVIII. 14 Received seven boxes of clothing; . . . one from Female Cent Societies in Barnet, Vt.

As the last term in **bungtown, Connecticut, copper, Franklin, fugio, half, nickel, red, ten, thirty, three, two cent.**

* **centennial,** *n.*

1. An exposition or celebration commemorating the one-hundredth anniversary of the signing of the Declaration of Independence. Also attrib. or as adj.

1873 *Dept. Agric. Rep.* (1874) 10 The approaching Centennial Exposition affords an additional argument for the preparation of such a collection of our forest specimens. **1876** HOWELLS in *Atlantic Mo.* July 92/1 The Centennial is what every one calls the great fair now open at Philadelphia. **1876** *Humboldt Times* (Eureka, Calif.) 10 June 2/4 The new Centennial stamped envelop has made its appearance. **1945** TRYON *Poor Man* 47 The invention had been introduced at the time of the Centennial, over twenty years before.

2. centennial plant, =**century plant.** *Obs.*

1831 *Boston Transcript* 9 July 2/4 *Yuca Filamentosa* . . . is in appearance somewhat like the Aloes or Centennial plant.

3. Centennial State, Colorado, which was admitted to the Union in 1876.

1878 BEADLE *Western Wilds* 489 Whether in material or moral greatness, we may be justly proud of our Centennial State. **1889** *Secy. of Agric. Rep.* 265 The settler . . . is growing a better crop of maize in all the eastern counties of the Centennial State than is the farmer of Michigan. **1948** *Democrat* 15 Jan. 4/3 The Centennial State flower is the Rocky mountain columbine.

centennialism sen'tenɪəlˌɪzəm, *n.* The practice of holding centennials. *Rare.* — **1874** *N.Y. Tribune* 14 Sep. 7/1 Centennialism is the order of the day, and if anything has the least twang of a dead century, it is pretty sure to succeed.

***center,** *n.*

1. A place or region centrally located, or ranking first in population, industry, social influence, etc.

1729 in *N.H. Hist. Soc. Coll.* VII. 351 It was decided that 'ye place called ye centre' should be the place for the meeting house. **1788** *N.H. Town Papers* XI. 276 The lands aforesaid are . . . so remote from the Centers of the respective towns to which they belong that we have hitherto found the greatest inconvenience in attending public worship and ordinary Town meeting. **1856** *Ill. State Reg.* (Springfield) 19 June 3/1 The Democracy of the centre will meet in mass meeting . . . to ratify the nomination of Buchanan and Breckenridge. **1948** *Pauls Valley* (Okla.) *D. Democrat* 4 July 1/5 Garvin county has developed into an oil county as well as an agricultural center.

b. In place-names.

1791 *N.H. State P.* XXII. 206 The fourth [post route] from Portsmouth to . . . Sandwich Center harbour Plymouth. **1844** in S. F. SMITH *Hist. Newton* 491 A new road, wide and nearly level, . . . leads from the West Newton Centre direct to Watertown Bridge. **1889** R. T. COOKE *Steadfast* 292 Tempy Hopkins had come down in the chaise with Parson Dyer from Pickering Centre.

2. *Baseball.* Short for **center field, fielder.**

1866 *Wilkes' Spirit of Times* 23 June 262/3 Edwards, as centre, is decidedly the best fielder in the nine. **1867** *Ball Players' Chron.* 8 Aug. 6/3 The nine will be as follows: Martin pitcher; . . . Waterman, left; Dick Hunt, center. **1899** *Chi. D. News* 2 June 6/1 Mertes made . . . a great catch in the seventh of a long line hit to center. **1948** *Green Bay* (Wis.) *Press-Gazette* 12 July 15/1 He traveled to second on Fischer's single to center.

b. In basketball, one of the two opposing players who at the start of play occupy the center circle.

1909 *Cent. Supp.*, center. In . . . basket-ball . . . and other games, the one who plays in the middle of the forward line. **1948** *P.C.C. Chronicle* (Pasadena, Calif.) 31 Mar. 4/4 Dick, although shorter than most of his opposing centers, . . . was a consistent high scorer for the Bullpups.

3. In combs.: (1) **centerboard,** a keel that may be raised or lowered as occasion demands, also attrib.; (2) **boarder,** a vessel having a centerboard; (3) **driving,** *a.* denoting a rifle sufficiently accurate to "drive the center," *rare;* (4) **field,** in baseball, (*a*) that portion of the outfield contiguous to second base, (*b*) = next, (*a*); (5) **fielder,** (*a*) a baseball player who covers center field, (*b*) a hit to this location; (6) **fire,** (*a*) (see quot.), (*b*) (see quots.); (7) **jam,** (see quots.); (8) **rush,** the center or snapper-back on a football team; (9) **rusher,** =prec.; (10) **shot,** a marksman capable of hitting the center of a target.

(1) **1849** *Rep. Comm. Patents* 221 What I claim . . . as my invention . . . is suspending in a jointed frame a centre board composed of one or more pieces capable of being turned with either their edges or sides to the bottom of the vessel. **1856** *Spirit of Times* 13 Sep. 27/2, I have at least proved to the English, that a centre-board boat is a sea boat. **1945** *Nat. Geog. Mag.* Sep. 276 At eight or nine boys and girls are racing in small, wide centerboard boats known as 'brutal beasts.' — (2) **1886** *Outing* VIII. 58/1 The boats are necessarily of light draught and center-boarders. **1897** *Ib.* XXX. 337/1 The slippery bilge of an eggshell centreboarder. — (3) **1907** MARK TWAIN *Christian Sc.* II. ii. 117 (R.), Is there a long-range, center-driving, up-to-date Mauser-magazine for elephants? — (4) (*a*) **1865** *Sun. Mercury* (Phila.) 3 Sep. 3/5 Dick McBride struck a ball over to centre field. **1948** *Miami* (Okla.) *D. News-Record* 4 July 4/4 For sensational catches in centerfield you can't beat him. (*b*) **1857** *Spirit of Times* 29 Aug. 404/3 Enterprise Club. Maxfield, catcher; . . . England, third base; Bleecker, centre field. **1867** *Ball Players' Chron.* 18 July 1/4 The other positions [were] . . . very well played, especially that of the second base, short stop, and centre field.

(5) (*a*) **1866** CHADWICK *Base-Ball Player* 30 The Center Fielder should always be in readiness to back up the second base, and should always go to long field in cases where a hard-hitter is at the bat. **1948** *Dly. Ardmoreite* (Ardmore, Okla.) 30 Mar. 6/4 Russell is a fair center-fielder. (*b*) **1867** *Chi. Times* 26 July 5/2 Barker struck a safe centre fielder, which gave Spaulding his tally. — (6) (*a*) **1874** KNIGHT 510/2 Center-fire cartridge, one in which the fulminate occupies an axial position, instead of being around the periphery of the flanged capsule. (*b*) **1907** WHITE *Ariz. Nights* 251 He was a quiet-appearing young fellow, rather neatly dressed in the border costume, rode a 'centre fire,' or single-cinch, saddle, and wore no chaps. **1933** *Amer. Sp.* Feb. 28 Center-Fire. California saddle with only one cinch, attached in center of the saddle. The *center-fire* was no good for hard riding, for it would not stay on the horse. **1948** ROLLINSON *Wyo. Cattle Trails* 37 The center-fire rig was difficult to keep in place on a horse's back. — (7) **1905** *Forestry Bur. Bul.* 61 Center Jam. A jam formed on an obstacle in the middle of a stream, and which does not reach either shore. **1926** RICKABY *Ballads* 234 Centre jam. A log jam which forms free of the banks of the stream, usually upon some rock or obstruction amid stream. — (8) **1887** *Cent. Mag.* XXXIV. 891/1 The 'center rush,' kicks the ball backward, or 'snaps it back,' to the quarter-back. **1905** *McClure's Mag.* June 121 Greene . . . returned to Philadelphia with two promising Exeter football players, Henry R. Bankart, the centre-rush, and Edward J. Hart, a half-back. — (9) **1890** *Cent.* 5726/3 Snap-back, in foot-ball, the act of a center rusher in putting the ball in play by pushing it with his foot [etc.]. **1893** W. CAMP *College Sports* 99 As he usually stood in the middle, he was called the center-rusher. This name has since given place almost entirely to 'snap-back.'

(10) **1842** *Amer. Pioneer* I. 225 And as to the use of the rifle, he was said to be one of the quickest and surest centre shots to be found. **1883** ZEIGLER & GROSSCUP *Alleghanies* 215 Their fame as 'center shots,' with the rifle, was well known to the British regulars, who feared to meet them.

b. In phrases: (1) *To catch on center*, of a steam engine, to stop where neither a backward nor forward impulse can be effective, to be on dead center, *fig.* in quot.; (2) *to come to the center*, to come out openly, take a prominent stand, *slang;* (3) *to set on centers*, in building, to place posts, rafters, etc., at a given distance from center to center; (4) *to drive the center*, see **drive,** *v.* Cf. **off center,** *s.v.* ***off,** *prep.*

(1) **1869** MARK TWAIN *Innocents Abroad* iv. 45 He had no one to blame but himself when his voice caught on the centre occasionally, and gave him lockjaw. — (2) **1873** MILLER *Amongst Modocs* 38 Haven't got the tin. Can't come to the centre! Haven't got the dust. *Ib.* 75 Whenever my man comes to the centre, I will call him, see if I don't. — (3) **1897** MOORE *How to Build* 21 The extra cost of using timber three inches thick and twelve inches wide for floor-beams, set sixteen inches on centers (i.e., sixteen inches from center to center or thirteen inches apart) will be fully justified by the stiffness of the floor.

As the last term in **community, head, left, money, off, packing, shipping, wampum center.**

***central,** *a.* and *n.*

1. *n.* A telephone exchange or an operator employed in this.

1889 MARK TWAIN *Conn. Yankee* xv. 184, I used to wake . . . and say 'Hello, Central!' just to hear her dear voice. **1910** *Out West* Jan. 28, I called up my wife on the 'phone and had the usual trouble with central. **1948** *Chi. Sun-Times* 7 Sep. 47/3 He thought all those other rings were somebody calling 'central.'

2. A large grinding and boiling plant where sugar is made from cane grown in the region. Also **sugar central.**

1904 *Nation* LXXVIII. 29 The excursion on the Mississippi, with stops at Chalmette and at a great sugar 'central.' **1925** *Wall St. Jrnl.* 10 Jan. 15/4 There are now 138 centrals grinding cane.

3. *a.* In combs.: (1) **central committee,** a political committee having a position of rank or leadership; (2) **Central Military tract,** (see quot.), *obs.;* (3) **central office,** a telephone central; (4) **standard time,** the time on the 90th meridian fixed as standard in the central time zone by the Interstate Commerce Commission; (5) **Central State,** (see quot. 1888); (6) **central states,** the states now or formerly regarded as being in the central part of the U.S.; (7) **time,** =**central standard time.**

(1) **1840** *Niles' Reg.* 4 July 295/1 We are requested by the central committee of the democratic party of Virginia [etc.]. **1892** *Courier-Journal* 1 Oct. 8/1 (*caption*), Democratic State Central Committee Prepared for a Red-Hot Canvass From Now On. — (2) **1856** FERGUSON *America* 416 From this . . . we pass through a district of country [in Ill.] called the Central Military-tract, from its having been assigned to the soldiers who served in the various wars of the States. — (3) **1880** *Chi. Tribune* 20 May 12/5 Hello! . . . Is this the Central Office? **1895** *Critic* 6 April 263/2 The awful nuisance of the central [telephone] office, and . . . what is familiarly known as the 'hello-girl.' — (4) **1931** *Durant* (Okla.) *D. Democrat* 28 July 1/4 Clyde Pangborn and Hugh Herndon left . . . at 4:19 o'clock, central standard time. **1947** *Chi. D. News* 21 June 4/6 Some of the legislators at Springfield would put Chicago back on Central Standard Time.

(5) **1886** D. W. WILDER in *Kansas Hist. Coll.* III. 405 The Central State will 'get there.' **1888** *Harper's Mag.* June 39/1 When they think of . . . her geographical situation, then Kansas is the 'Central State.' — (6) **1800** W. TATHAM *Agric. & Commerce* 45 To what Circumstance is it owing, that eight Bushels of Wheat, raised by dear Labour, are a profitable Crop in the central States? **1876** CROFUTT *Trans-*

continental Tourist 33 Nebraska, so lately opened up to the world, and so lately considered one portion of the 'wild West,' forms now one of our central States. — (7) **1883** *Cent. Mag.* Sep. 796/2 The western limit of the ninetieth meridian, or 'central time' system, is fixed at points on the great transcontinental lines. **1945** *Chi. D. News* 14 Sep. 7/1 The voters . . . voted . . . in favor of Central Time with summer daylight saving.

centralism ˈsɛntrəlˌɪzəm, *n.* The centralization of the powers of government. *Obs.* — **1831** *Cong. Deb.* 2 Feb. 51 A system of centralism, hostile to the federative principle of our Union, encroaching upon the wealth and power of the States. **1871** *Cong. Globe* 13 April 651/1 Nor am I deterred from this conclusion by any cry of centralism, or it may be of imperialism.

centrifugal sɛnˈtrɪfjʊgl, *n.* [f. the adj.] **1.** A centrifugal machine, or a drum in such a machine, for drying sugar. **2.** Sugar freed from molasses by such a machine.

(1) **1883** Mark Twain *Life on Miss.* xlviii, You heave your cane into the centrifugals and grind out the juice. **1887** *Cent. Mag.* XXXV. 114/2 Next the 'masse cuite' falls into the 'centrifugals,' which are small drums holding about 120 pounds of sugar. — (2) *Ib.* 119/1 Centrifugals [ranged in price] from 4-5/8 for 'seconds' to 6-1/4 cents.

centurially sɛnˈtʃʊrɪəlɪ, *adv.* By centuries. *Rare.* — **1799** in *Hist. Mag.* (1858) Jan., In reckoning centurially we adopt a different phraseology from that which is used in all other accounts of time.

***centurion,** *n.* One who has made a ride of one hundred miles on a bicycle. *Obs.* Cf. ***century 2.** — **1897** *Outing* XXX. 346/1 There are long-distance riders, too, galore in the N.Y.A.C. and not a few centurions. **1898** *N.Y. Journal* 15 Aug. 8/3 Walter McGrath, the boy champion centurion of Philadelphia, . . . has a record of more than a score of one hundred miles rides.

***century,** *n.*

1. (See quot. 1859.) *Slang.*

1859 Matsell *Vocabulum* 18 Century. One hundred dollars. **1909** *Sat. Ev. Post* 16 Jan. 7/3 'A century each way on Bologna,' he directed.

2. A ride of one hundred miles on a bicycle. Cf. **centurion.**

1898 *N.Y. Journal* 8 Sep. 11/1 His wonderful one hundred miles ride of today . . . completed two hundred and fifty consecutive centuries. **1943** Powell *Home Again* 227, I had made my century on a bicycle—quite a feat, considering that it was over fisherman's trails and sandy roads.

3. In combs.: (1) **century blooming,** with reference to the century plant, blooming (reputedly) every hundred years; (2) **note,** a hundred-dollar bill, *slang*, cf. **C note;** (3) **plant,** any one of various commonly cultivated species of *Agave* which flower only once and then die (see also quot. 1948); (4) **ride, run,** = ***century 2.**

(1) **1846** Child *Fact & Fiction* 60 The century-blooming aloe is luxuriantly growing. **1865** Mrs. Whitney *Gayworthys* xxiii. 219 Say . . . would not have been a palm or an aloe, or a cereus, or any grand and solitary, century-blooming thing, if she had known of such. — (2) **1908** K. McGaffey *Show-Girl* 70 The whole blooming city didn't have change for a century note. **1948** *Sat. Ev. Post* 31 July 22/3 The murdered gambler was clutching a penny matchbox into which somebody had stuffed a century note. — (3) [**1764** *N.C. Morav. Rec.* II. (1925) 572 Century Plant grows abundantly here on the Uplands. The people who have come hither from Europe use it much as a tea for fever.] **1847** Wood *Botany* 539 *Agave Americana.* American Aloe, Century Plant. . . . It is a popular notion that it flowers but once in a hundred years. **1948** *Woodlawn Booster* (Chi.) 12 May 14/1 Some varieties of the century plant flower every year. — (4) **1893** *Outing* Oct. 57 (*title*), A Century Ride. **1897** *Outing* XXX. 349/1 The more enthusiastic indulge in century runs.

b. Used to denote a **discourse, lecture, sermon,** delivered on the hundredth anniversary of the founding of a church or colony. *Obs.*

1815 in *Mass. Col. Soc. Pub.* XXVI. 418 In 1815 the Rev. Manasseh Cutler published at Salem, 'A Century Discourse, delivered in Hamilton.' **1729** in *Pub. Col. Soc.* XXVI. 406–7 On Wednesday the 6th of *this* Instant, was celebrated here, the 1st Century Lecture in the Meeting House of the 1st Church here. . . . The Century Lecture Began with Singing Psal. CXXII. **1738** *Ib.* 295 Mr. Dexter's Century Sermon, on the Public Thanksgiving November 23, 1738. **1814** M. Cutler in *Life Jrnls. & Corr.* (1888) 349 Proposed to the people a meeting on Thursday afternoon at 2 o'clock, with a view of delivering a century sermon, being 100 years since the foundation of this church and society.

***cereal,** *n.* =**breakfast cereal.** Also attrib.

1899 *Chi. D. News* 9 May 7 Free with 6 packages of Hazel Cereals, any assortment, a handsomely decorated tea canister. **1944** Stafford *Boston Adv.* 57 My ugly 'bob' was fashioned to the uncompromising lines of a cereal bowl. **1948** *Green Bay* (Wis.) *Press-Gazette* 13 July 24/4 For breakfast, the scouts are apt to find tomato juice, cereal, toast and milk on the menu.

cerne sɜn, *n. W.* [F., an Amer. borrowing.] In hunting buffalo, an encircling of the entire herd. *Obs.* — **1839** C. A. Murray *Travels* I. 336 A 'cerne' or 'surround,' in this part of the wilderness, requires a great deal of arrangement to render it successful. **1843** Frémont *Exped.* 29 It had been a large herd when the cerne commenced, probably three or four hundred in number.

***ceroon,** *n.* "The American mode of spelling Seroon, a bale or package made of skins" (Simmonds *Dict. Trade*, 1858).

1824 *Shipping & Commercial List* 31 July (Pettigrew P.), A sale of 30 ceroons of Cuba [tobacco], was made, by auction, at 13½ a 14¼ cents, 60 days. **1832** *Louisville Pub. Adv.* 3 March, 8 puncheons Jamaica rum; 2 ceroons indigo. *a***1861** T. Winthrop "Chitrés," *Isthmiana*, A young ragamuffin . . . had come into town on a nag between two hide ceroons, full of mami apples.

cerro ˈsɛro, *n. W.* [Sp. in same sense.] A hill or butte. Also in proper names.

1828 Pattie *Narrative* (1839) 297 The principal mountains coast Rio del Norte, following its western banks. Some peaks, or *cerros*, are to be distinguished. **1861** Newberry *Geol. Rep.* 99 From this volcano rise the volcanic cones of the 'Cerrilos.' **1946** *So. Sierran* Oct. 3/3 Cerro Gordo, Inyo Mountains, elevation 9217 feet, was climbed Monday by twelve persons.

***certificate,** *n.* A title to land or a statement about ownership. *Obs.*

1694 *N.C. Col. Rec.* I. 405 Ordered that a certificate thereto be made to the Secretary's office. **1780** W. Fleming in *Travels Amer. Col.* 631 The Court having finished the business rose at nine Oclock in the Evening, having in the course of this business granted certificates for 1,096,650 acres. **1872** *Rep. Indian Affairs 1871* 171 The Omahas [on a reservation in Nebraska] have received certificates—a kind of possessory title—which secures the land to them and their heirs.

As the last term in **donation, flour, gold, land, land office, loan, loan office, pre-emption, silver, soldier's, tax certificate.**

***certificate,** *v.* (See quot.) *Obs.* — **1828** Webster, Certificate, *v. t.* or *i.*, to give a certificate; to lodge a certificate with the proper officer, for the purpose of being exempted from the payment of taxes to support the ministry, in a parish or ecclesiastical society. *New England.*

***certification,** *n.* The act of guaranteeing the payment of a check. — **1870** Medbery *Men Wall St.* 263 Whispers . . . of certifications of checks to the amount of twenty-five millions by one bank alone . . . lent color to the rumor. **1876** *West Coast Star* (Mendocino, Calif.) 15 June 1/2 Vethman . . . soon after obtained certification of a check for $1,275.

***certified,** *a.* In combs.: (1) **certified (public) accountant,** an accountant who holds a state certificate of competency in accounting, often abbreviated C.P.A.; (2) **check,** a bank check certified as valid by the bank upon which it is drawn, also transf.; (3) **copy,** a copy attested by the proper persons as being a correct reproduction of an original.

(1) **1913** *Indian Laws & Tr.* III. 565 To enable the Secretary of the Interior to employ a chartered and certified accountant, . . . $10,000. **1948** *Woman's Day* March 18/3 George is a certified public accountant. — (2) **1849** *Hunt's Merch. Mag.* XXI. 353 The system of certified or marked checks, does not prevail here [London]. **1906** O. Henry *Four Million* 198 The bride is the certified cheque among the wedding presents that the gods send in when man is married to mortality. **1948** *Chi. Tribune* 2 May I. 6/4, I used to carry a couple of million in my pockets, in certified checks and cash. — (3) **1902** Pidgin *Quincy A. S.* 301, I hold in my hand three documents. The first one is a certified copy of the war record of Wallace Stackpole.

***certify,** *v.*

1. *tr.* To transfer or deed (land). *Rare.*

1845 Hooper *Simon Sugg's Adv.* vi. 71 He told his wife that her father must 'certify' his land to him.

2. Of a bank or bank official: To sign or stamp (a check) as valid.

1818 *N.Y. Ev. Post* 30 Sep. 2/5 The rogue . . . drew a check for the sum, and got the cashier to certify on the back—*Good for the within sum.* **1892** Van Schaack *Law of Bank Checks* 88 If the bank only accepts or certifies the check, the holder can demand its payment at any time thereafter. **1911** *Cosmopolitan* Jan. 236/1 We'll go there first and get the checks certified.

cerulean warbler. A wood warbler, *Dendroica cerulea*, of the eastern states, chiefly west of the Alleghenies. — **1828** Bonaparte *Synopsis* 85 The Caerulean Warbler, *Sylvia caerulea*, . . . inhabits the northern and middle states in summer: rare in the Atlantic states: common in the western. **1917** *Birds of America* III. 133 It is mainly in swampy woodland from the Genesee and Monongahela valleys west to the lower Missouri valley that the Cerulean Warbler is common.

chachalaca ˌtʃɑtʃəˈlɑkə, *n.* [Amer. Sp. (< Nahuatl) in same sense.] The Texan guan, *Ortalis vetula macalli*, or a bird related to this.

1851 *Acad. Nat. Sci. Proc.* V. 222 [Sandpipers] were exceedingly numerous about Matamoros, during the following winter, and were served on the tables of the Hotels and Restaurants very prodigally, as well as the Chiac-chia-lacca. **1894** *Scribner's Mag.* May 697/2 Through the dense foliage of mesquite . . . sounds the harsh cackle of the toothsome 'chachalaca.' **1947** Edminster *Ruffed Grouse* 1 Four families of this order are found in North America . . . the curassows, guans, and chachalacas.

***chaff,** *n.* As the last term in **apple, golden, hay, red chaff.**

chaff-seed ˈtʃæfˌsid, *n.* (See quots.) — **1817–8** Eaton *Botany* (1822) 450 *Schwalbea americana*, chaff-seed. **1857** Gray *Botany* 294 Chaff-Seed, . . . [an] upright herb, with leafy simple stems, terminated by a loose spike of rather large dull purplish-yellow flowers.

***chafing dish.** A small portable stove used for cooking. Also attrib.

1893 Post *Harvard Stories* 99 You get your chafing-dish, Dick. **1909** Stratton-Porter *Girl of Limberlost* 451 They . . . made chafing-dish tea. **1920** Lewis *Main Street* 2 She played tennis, gave chafing-dish parties.

***chain,** *n.*

1. A series of rocks in a river. *Obs.*

1823 James *Exped.* I. 44 The Ohio would also admit of a bridge at the chains. **1828** *Western Mo. Rev.* I. 512 The circumstances, that change the aspect and current of the river, are denominated, in the vocabulary of the watermen, chutes, races, chains, sawyers . . . and cypress bends.

2. A number of banks, theaters, etc., owned and operated by one person or company.

1846 Mackenzie *Van Buren* 208 Is it not evident that Throop was secretly selected . . . as a convenient instrument for regulating future state elections through a chain of banks, controlled by county juntos of greedy politicians? **1895** *N.Y. Dramatic News* 14 Dec. 6/2 A chain of eleven theatres to be run in connection with the Bijou circuit. **1910** *Sat. Ev. Post* 15 Oct. 15/1 The chain-of-stores system for the sale of cigars, candy, men's hats, clothes and furnishings is spreading fast. **1926** *Pittsburgh Gazette Times* 7 Feb. II. 4/5 Mr. Hacket . . . is the featured artist tonight in the Atwater Kent Radio Hour, which will be broadcast over WEAF and chain at 9:15 o'clock. **1943** Menefee *Assignment* 225 In Toledo, a chain of grocery stores stuffed handbills advertising for women workers into every shopping bag.

b. *attrib.*

1933 *Time* 17 April 13/2 Householders found 3.2% beer at most chain groceries. **1945** *Nation* CLX. II. 17 March 303/2 The Independent Bankers' Association, an organization of small and medium-sized banks opposed to chain-banking, has issued a statement. **1947** *Chri. Sci. Mon.* 16 Jan. 3/7 The union claims the big chain grocers are making enough profit to absorb the increase.

Esp. **chain store.**

1910 *Sat. Ev. Post* 10 Sep. 76/2 At first there were loud declarations of war from the manager of the association that buys goods for retail grocers fighting the chain stores. **1914** *Printer's Ink* 10 Sep. 6/1 It appears to me that eventually the chain stores will drive the department stores out of business. **1948** *Dly. Ardmoreite* (Ardmore, Okla.) 20 Apr. 3/2 He sells chain stores and his sales reach out to every state of the union and to Alaska and Hawaii.

3. *pl.* Any one of various arrangements of chains or chains and bars suitable for attaching to the tires of motor vehicles to increase traction, usu. on wet, icy, or snowy roads.

1914 *Country Life* Dec. 201/1 When the snow came chains were added to the rear wheels on top of the treads. **1948** *Spokesman-Review* (Spokane, Wash.) 23 Sep. 13/4 The state department of highways reported that four inches of packed snow had fallen . . . and advised motorists to carry chains on that route to the Coast.

4. In special combs.: (1) **chain bearer,** one who carries the measuring chain in surveying; (2) **belt,** a belt symbolizing a "covenant chain," *rare;* (3) **carrier,** = **chain bearer;** (4) **carrying,** the carrying of a surveyor's chain; (5) **gang,** a number of prisoners chained to each other, or wearing chains, while working; (6) **ganger,** a member of a chain gang, *rare;* (7) **harrow,** (see quot.); (8) **lightning,** see as a main entry; (9) **man,** = **chain bearer;** (10) **pickerel,** the ordinary pickerel, *Esox niger;* (11) **snake,** = **king snake.**

(1) **1736** *Va. State Papers* I. 226 Take three Chain-bearers, to be duly sworn according to the Laws of this Country. **1869** *Overland Mo.* III. 248 The only way for the chain-men to work along these cliffs . . . was by being suspended by ropes from above, the chain-bearers signaling to those holding the ropes. — (2) **1754** *Mass. H.S. Coll.* 3 Ser. V. 41 We return you all our grateful acknowledgements for renewing and brightening the covenant chain. This chain belt is of very great importance to our United Nations. — (3) **1702–3** *Penn-Logan Corr.* (1870) I. 174 Neither surveyors nor chain-carriers will go thither. **1867** G. W. Harris *Sut. Lovingood* 98 While yu am waitin' fur yer chain-kerriers. — (4) **1798** in *Ann. 10th Congress* 1 Sess. II. 2739 The surveying at present is done by Mr. Gillespie, the chain-carrying by Mr. Ellicott and Mr. Walker. *a***1909** O. Henry *Roads of Destiny* 93 I'll . . . go back to chain-carrying for the county surveyor. (5) **1835** Ingraham *South-West* II. 185 This galley-looking procession . . . was what is very appropriately termed the 'Chain gang.' **1946** *Chi. Sun* 23 Dec. 8/1 His fondness for Georgia's infamous chain-gang-peonage and whipping post system . . . [was a] symptom of the backwardness of his administration. — (6) **1860** *Marysville* (Calif.) *Appeal* 3 Feb. 3/1 John Smith has got to assume the duties of a chain ganger in San Francisco. — (7) **1870** *Rep. Comm. Agric. 1869* 322 Only one patent was taken out during the year of the class known as

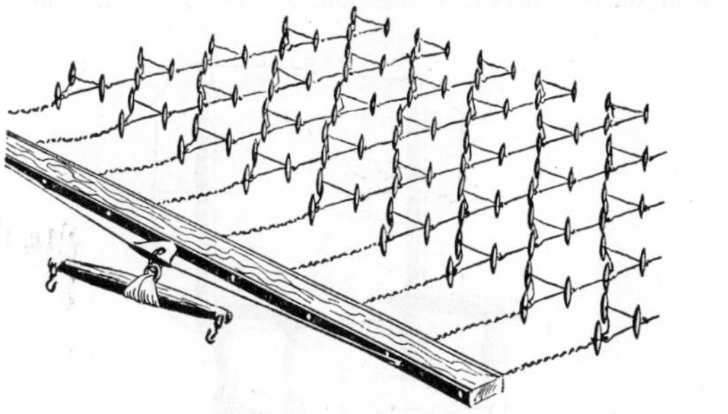

Chain harrow

'chain' harrows, *i.e.*, composed entirely of iron chains, no beams whatever being employed. — (9) **1714** in *Mass. H.S. Coll.* 6 Ser. V. 299 The survayer and chainmen being under oath. *c***1945** Hopkins *Okefenokee* 15 Through a prairie the work was the chainmen's work. (10) **1905** Fowler *Fishes N.J.* 177 Esox reticulatus Le Sueur. Pike, Chain Pickerel. Pickerel. Common Eastern Pickerel. **1947** Dalrymple *Panfish* 273 Our next largest Pike is the Eastern, or Chain, Pickerel. — (11) **1736** Catesby *Carolina* II. 52 As it wanted a Name, the best I could think of was, that of *Chain-Snake*, from some Resemblance of a Chain that seems in many Places to environ the Body, tho' these Marks extend but half Way round. **1875** *Field & Forest* I. 31 Careful measurements show the length of [an immature specimen of] the Chain snake to be 27 inches.

b. In phrases: (1) *To brighten the chain, fig.* to renew friendship; (2) *chain and ball,* = *ball and chain,* also fig.

(1) **1754** [see **chain belt**]. **1846** *Spirit of Times* 18 April 96/2 At Petersburg, he had brightened the chain with his old friend Dr. Minge, one of nature's noblemen. — (2) **1867** Devens *Pictorial Bk.* 154 The extreme penalty, however, was commuted by the President to one year's hard labor with chain and ball. **1904** Rives *Castaway* 213 What had he, George Gordon, dragging the chain and ball of a life sentence of desperation, to do with her in her purity?

As the last term in **ball and, covenant, fifth, fluke, fob, hog, jack, log, logging, mill, safety, tail, wrapper chain.**

chain lightning.

1. Lightning which appears to move rapidly in a zigzag course. Often fig.

1834 C. A. Davis *Lett. J. Downing* 37 I'm goin there like a streek of chain-lightning. **1882** Howells *Modern Instance* xxx, Those of his following considered him as smart as chain-lightning and bound to rise. **1918** Mulford *Man from Bar-20* 141 He's dangerous, chain-lightnin' with his guns.

2. Inferior whisky. Also attrib. *Slang.*

1843 Haliburtcn *Attaché* 1 Ser. xv, The drinks ain't good here [= in England]; they hante no variety in them nother: no white-nose, apple-jack, stone-wall, chain-lightning, rail-road [etc.]. **1890** D'Oyle *Notches* 8 'Fine Old Rye Whiskey' . . . was the . . . title which Old Hank was wont to affix to his bottles of 'Chain-lightning.'

***chair,** *n.*

1. Short for **electric chair.**

1922 *Ardmore* (Okla.) *D. Press* 5 May 1/3 As he was strapped in the chair, he said: 'I will be with you in heaven.' **1948** *Chi. Tribune* 14 Mar. I. 45/1 Gangsters consider 'the chair' just another professional risk.

2. In combs.: (1) ***chair back,** a tidy or antimacassar, *obs.;* (2) **board,** a board running horizontally along the wall of a room to prevent injury to it by the backs of chairs [cf. Du. *stoelplank*], *obs.;* (3) **car,** (see quot. 1895); (4) **lady,** a woman who presides as chairman, *facetious;* (5) **post,** one of the main uprights in a chair; (6) **road,** a road suitable for light-wheeled traffic, *rare;* (7) **table,** (see quots.).

(1) **1880** *Harper's Mag.* Oct. 656/1 She . . . carries home an embroidered 'Chair-back'—the more dignified name that she gives nowadays to her 'tidy.' **1881** *Art Interchange* (N.Y.) 27 Oct. 90/1 Coverings for sofa cushions, . . . chair-backs with lace falling from the edges. — (2) **1854** *S. Lit. Messenger* XX. 559/2 The wainscoting [is] of walnut, and extending unbroken around the whole apartment to the height of what is called the chair-board. **1899** VANDERBILT *Flatbush* 67 A wooden molding, called a 'chair board,' often . . . extended around the room, about three feet from the surbase. — (3) **1882** G. A. SALA *America Revisited* I. 208 The Pullman Parlour Car—commonly termed a 'chair' car—is a decided boon to railway travelers in America. **1895** WAIT *Car-Builder's Dict.* The names *parlor-car,*

Chair table (*c*1700)

drawing-room car and *chair-car* are all used somewhat indiscriminately, but *chair-car* ordinarily refers to a parlor-car with adjustable or reclining chairs, for riding in which no extra fare is charged. **1947** LUMPKIN *Southerner* 211 It brought us sleepers and chair cars, meals on diners. — (4) **1931** *Atlantic City News* 7 Aug. 10/4 Mrs. Joseph Foy is chairlady of the card party.

(5) **1788** *Amer. Museum* IV. 519/1 The snake was . . . about the thickness of a common chair-post. **1872** *Cong. Globe* App. 578/2 They went out and got big long brushes, as big as these chair posts. **1911** *Roxboro* (N.C.) *Courier* Nov., The snake was as large around as a chair post. — (6) **1781** *Royal Ga. Gaz.* 4 Jan. (Th.), There is a good chair road from Savannah. — (7) **1909** *Cent. Supp.* 1314/2 table-chair. . . . An old English or Colonial piece of furniture which was used as a table or chair, the top turning back to a vertical position on a hinge. Also *chair-table.* **1937** LANGDON *Everyday Things* 25 Convenience was furthered by a clever improvement. The large broad back was pivoted on to the arms where they joined the back-posts. It could then be tipped forward and the settle became on occasion a good broad table, often called quite simply and naturally a chair-table.

As the last term in **barrel, Brewster, carpet, Carver, death, dental, education, electric, extension, flag, gubernatorial, Hitchcock, ice, invalid, Italian, lady, opera, presidential, rawhide-bottomed, revolving, rocking, rolling, roundabout, rush-bottom, Shaker, Shaker rocking, shuck-bottomed, sleeping, splinter-bottomed, splinter-bottomed arm, split-bottom arm, split-seated, stick, stick back, swivel, walking-cane chair.**

chairmaker's rush. A tall, coarse rush, *Scirpus americanus,* used for chair bottoms. — **1843** TORREY *Flora N.Y.* II. 352 *Scirpus triqueter*. . . . Chairmaker's Rush. . . . Swamps and wet meadows, both salt and fresh: common. **1847** DARLINGTON *Weeds & Plants* 361 Sharp-pointed Scirpus. Chair-maker's Rush.

***chaise,** *n.* As the last term in **Boston, buggy, Italian, landeritt, sleigh chaise.**

chalchuite ˈtʃæltʃuit, *n. S.W.* [Amer. Sp. *chalchihuite* (< Nahuatl), in same sense.] A kind of turquoise found in New Mexico, the green variety being the most esteemed.

[**1716** VELARDE *Relación* (1926) 308 Sólo estiman las pedrezueles llamadas chalchiguites, que tanto preciaban los mexicanos [etc.].] **1861** NEWBERRY *Geol. Rep.* 99 The Cerrilos furnished a great part, if not all, the *chalchuitl,* so much worn for ornament. **1888** WALLACE *Land of Pueblos* 75 Though by no means costly as Shylock's turquoise, the *chalchuite* still holds its repute among the various tribes of the red race.

chalice cup. The western pasqueflower, *Anemone occidentalis.* — **1917** EATON *Green Trails* 91 The moist little meadow is as intimate and peaceful as a cloistered garden, and in mid-July, when we were there, was carpeted with chalice cups.

***chalk,** *n.* [Sense **1.** is possibly from a different word.]

1. A quarter of a dollar. *Obs.*

1796 B. HAWKINS *Letters* 451, I gave the account to Mr. Barnard to show you; it amounts to 130 chalks. **1798** *Ib.* 304 Christian Russel . . . is willing to give 200 chalks and a rifle gun for the negro. **1805** Dow *Journal* 10 Jan., A girl . . . asked one dollar, and three quarters, which they call seven chalks.

2. The real or proper thing, also *the clear chalk. Slang. Obs.*

1840 HALIBURTON *Clockm.* 3 Ser. 203, I have had liberal offers from the sect here, for whatever is the go to Europe will soon be the chalk here. **1843** STEPHENS *High Life N.Y.* II. 202, I tell you what, it was the clear chalk, the ginuine thing.

3. In combs.: (1) ***chalk-line,** the small green heron; (2) **rag,** a rag used to erase a blackboard, *colloq.;* (3) **talk,** a talk or lecture which the speaker illustrates by means of a blackboard and chalk, also **chalk-talker.**

(1) **1844** *Nat. Hist. N.Y., Zoology* II. 224 The Poke, chalk-line, Fly-up-the-creek . . . is a southern species. [**1945** MCATEE *Nomina Abitera* 25 As other names of herons indicate, the birds are able when flushed to lay a 'chalk-line.'] — (2) **1854** M. J. HOLMES *Tempest & Sunshine* 29 Then she would resolve . . . not to pin any more chalk rags to the boys' coats. — (3) **1881** *Christian Misc.* V. 40 His inimitable 'chalk talk.' **1888** in FARMER 132/2 The celebrated chalk-talker entertained a fair-sized audience this evening on prohibition. **1948** *Newsweek* 30 Aug. 53 Top figures in the comics and cartoon world stepped forward to demonstrate their art and give quick chalk talks in the old war-time fashion.

b. In phrases: (1) *chalk and water,* stuff, nonsense, *obs.;* (2) *to be a chalk above,* to be considerably above or superior to, *obs.;* (3) *to come up to* (*the*) *chalk,* to begin again, come up to the mark, be satisfactory, *slang;* (4) *to toe the chalk,* to toe the mark, *rare;* (5) *to walk a chalk* (*line*), *fig.* to act strictly in an indicated manner, *colloq.*

(1) **1834** C. A. DAVIS *Lett. J. Downing* 179 Some on you say it ain't right to pay interest to foreigners. . . . Well, that's all chalk and water. — (2) **1836** HALIBURTON *Clockm.* 2 Ser. xxii. (1837) 228 They reckon themselves here, a chalk above us Yankees. — (3) **1836** CROCKETT *Adventures* 73 He soon recovered himself and came up to the chalk again. **1871** DE VERE 318 The President, in whom he is disappointed for one reason or another, does not *come up to chalk.* — (4) **1862** LOWELL *Biglow P.* II. ii. 61 That 'ere's most frequently the kin' o' talk Of critters can't be kicked to toe the chalk.

(5) **1835** *Vade Mecum* (Phila.) 14 Feb. 3/2 Walk a crack, or you must walk your chalk before the Mayor. **1948** *Time* 2 Aug. 12/2 The Communists, their fellow travelers and their stooges—many of whom deny that they are Communists but all of whom walk the Communist chalk line—were there before him.

***chalk,** *v.*

1. *tr.* To mark (one's hat) with chalk as a sign of leave to travel free of charge. *Colloq. Obs.* or *hist.*

1823 QUITMAN *Life & Corr.* 78, I shall be able to say, 'Come and see me,' and I will 'chalk your hat' for the journey. **1881** HAYES *New Colorado* 149 Twenty-five seedy, second-class ruffians, who proposed to travel, as they say in the West, 'with their hats chalked,' or free. **1928** STARR *100 Yrs. Amer. Railroading* 76 The practice out there was called 'chalking the hat,' from the custom of the conductor in placing a white mark or ticket on the 'stove-pipe' or other headgear of the free passenger.

b. To mark as an indication that the object has been passed or directed officially. *Obs.*

1866 MRS. WHITNEY *L. Goldthwaite* iii, Stooping to examine the trunk . . . [he said,] 'These things is chalked all right for Littleton.' **1875** MILLER *Amongst Modocs* 38 A tall fine-looking man stepped ashore, . . . and said, 'chalk that.' **1892** MARK TWAIN *£1,000,000 Bank-note* 258 He was going to try to bribe the postman to chalk it through.

2. To set down as, to estimate, figure on. *Colloq.*

1835 BIRD *Hawks of Hawk-H.* II. 78 He chalked me down like a fool, me and Tom Staples. **1874** *Vt. Bd. Agric. Rep.* II. 618 The farmers on that committee were outwitted, for while they chalked from $25,000 to $30,000, others chalked from $150,000 to $200,000.

3. In colloq. and obs. phrases: (1) *To chalk off*, to stalk off; (2) **to chalk up*, to mark up, raise the price of, also to add or mount up; (3) *to chalk the lamp post*, (see quot.); (4) *to chalk on a barn door*, to calculate roughly.

(1) **1840** in *Wyo. Hist. and Geol. Soc. Proc.* XV. (1917) 169 Mr. Jordan gave me a package containing some two thousand dollars to carry home (Philadelphia) for him . . . at last agreed to do so, and chalked off to bed, meditating on robbers, etc. etc. — (2) **1834** C. A. Davis *Lett. J. Downing* 83 Tell the folks Kolery is comin, and they go at it mixin Paragoric and Kamfire, and chalk it up like gold dust. **1878** Stowe *Poganuc People* 36 But who's going to pay for it all? These 'ere sort of things chalk up, ye know. **1948** *Green Bay* (Wis.) *Press-Gazette* 30 June 23/1 Smaller advances were chalked up for U.S. Rubber, Western Union, Warner Brothers and J. I. Case.

(3) **1857** *Boston Post* 5 March (F. & H.), Chalking the lamp post. The term for bribery in Philadelphia. — (4) **1880** *Cong. Rec.* 19 April 2478/2 [The Geneva arbitrators] took the two statements, . . . went up into a mountain and chalked on a barn door, and split the difference.

chalked hat. A hat marked with chalk as an indication of a free pass; a person wearing a hat so marked. *Obs.* (See ***chalk,** *v.* **1.**)

1846 *Spirit of Times* 16 May 133/1 The chalked hats were 'numerous' on the occasion. *Ib.* 4 July 217/3, I would also take this opportunity of hinting to the directors of some Rail Roads and Steamboats . . . when a gentleman calls on them, by request, for a 'chalked hat' [etc.]. [**1855** in *Wis. Hist. Soc. Coll.* V. 317 We . . . spent the night with Col. E. Brigham [from Massachusetts]. . . . He treated us very kindly, and told us 'our hats were chalked.']

***challenge,** *n.* (See quot. 1847.)

1829 *Ill. Rev. Laws* (1833) 346 (*marginal note*), Challenges. **1847** Webster 190/1 Challenge, . . . In elections, an exception to a person as not legally qualified to vote. (United States.) **1889** *Mich. Gen. Statutes* III. 2827 [If] the challenge, is not withdrawn, one of the inspectors shall tender to him . . . one of the following oaths.

***challenge,** *v. tr.* "In elections, to object to a person as not qualified to vote" (W. '47). Also to question the validity of (a ballot or vote) cast by such a person.

1829 *Ill. Rev. Laws* (1833) 246 If his vote shall be challenged by any elector . . . , the judges of the election shall tender to such person an oath. **1851** *Iowa Code* 46 Any person offering to vote may be challenged, as unqualified. **1911** *Okla. Sess. Laws* 3 Legisl. 230 The other envelope shall be sufficiently large to hold all challenged and mutilated ballots. **1948** *New Yorker* 25 Sep. 25/3 One of the principal duties of a watcher is to challenge would-be voters whom the Association suspects of being fraudulently registered.

***challenger,** *n.* One who challenges the right of another to vote. — **1853** *Knickerb.* XLII. 653 He was shrewdly suspected of not being 'right' by a man who winked at a 'challenger,' who 'thus then' interposed: 'Are you naturalized?' **1911** *Okla. Sess. Laws* 3 Legisl. 78 Every person desiring to vote at such special election, after having passed the challengers [etc.].

chalupa tʃəˈlupə, *n. S.W.* [Sp. in Amer. Sp. sense shown here.] A small, somewhat boat-shaped corncake, often toasted and having some condiment on the inside. — **1895** *Amer. Folk-Lore* Jan.–Apr. 61 There were enchiladas, chaloupas, fried chicken, cold turkey, and I dare not say what else. **1947** Berolzheimer *Regional Cook Book* 583 Taos salmon chalupas with Spanish onion rings set a high mark for unusual piquant flavor.

cham-chack ˈtʃæmˌtʃæk, *n. local.* [Imitative.] The red-bellied woodpecker. — **1932** Howell *Florida Bird Life* 307 *Centurus carolinus* . . . Zebra Woodpecker; Guinea Sapsucker; Cham-chack. **1938** Matschat *Suwannee River* 26 'Good God' woodpeckers, with black and white wings and scarlet crests, and two other woodpeckers, called 'white-shirts' and 'cham-chacks,' work with a continuous *r-r-r-rat-a-tat-tat-tat.*

***chamber,** *n.* A lock on a canal, a confined part of a stream.

1829 A. Royall *Pennsylvania* I. 151 The Union canal is eight feet wide, . . . and the locks or chambers, as they are called, are very long and narrow. **1872** Flagg *Good Investment* iv. 222/1 He entered the chamber of Lower Twin, and followed that in its descent. **1890** *Cent.* 3497/2 When a vessel is descending, water is let into the chamber of the lock till it is on a level with the higher water.

As the last term in **barn, bed, bridal, kitchen, representative, senate, shed, snag chamber.**

***chamber,** *v.*

1. *tr.* Of a shotgun: To receive (a certain number of buckshot) in the barrel in one compact layer, to test (buckshot) to find out the number needed to form such a layer. Also *intr.* of shot, to form most nearly such a compact layer.

1839 *S. Lit. Messenger* V. 97/2 My father's big gun . . . would chamber five buckshot. **1884** *Forest & Stream* XXII. 225 One should be careful to chamber the buckshot at the choke of the gun, and to choose the size that most nearly chambers.

b. Of a rifle: To receive (a cartridge) properly in the firing chamber.

1902 White *Blazed Trail* xx. 141 Wallace's rifle chambered the .38 Winchester cartridge.

2. Of a mining vein: To spread out.

1873 Beadle *Undevel. West.* 335 The miner starts with a vein a foot or more wide . . . ; then it suddenly 'chambers' to some size, then 'pinches' to the thickness of a knife blade.

chambray ˈʃæmbre, *n.* [*Cambrai*, France.] A kind of cotton cloth with a linen finish woven with colored warp and white filling yarns; also a dress of this. Also attrib.

1814 *Niles' Reg.* V. 317/2 Twenty-four cases cotton and woollen goods, cloths, ginghams, chambrays, shirtings, [etc.]. **1915** D. R. Campbell *Proving Va.* 90 'We haven't any cards, or'—she glanced down at her pink chambray—'party clothes.' **1948** *Dly. Ardmoreite* (Ardmore, Okla.) 1 April 4/4 Her classic chambray dress has a ruffled front, like grandfather's shirt.

***chameleon,** *n.* Also ***camelion.**

1. *S.* A popular name for various small American lizards of the genus *Anolis.* Cf. **American chameleon.**

[**1738** Mortimer in *Phil. Trans.* XL. 346 *Lacertus viridis Carolinensis.* The green *Lizard* of *Carolina.* These Creatures are quite harmless, and suffer'd to go about the Houses: They will from green, by Cold, change to brown.] **1796** Morse *Amer. Geog.* I. 218 We have . . . the green lizard, or little green cameleon of Carolina . . . ; [it] has the faculty of changing its colour. **1827** J. L. Williams *W. Florida* 28 The chameleon is the least ugly of the species; he is very frequently seen. **1934** *Nat. Geog. Mag.* LXV. 609 The . . . display of the green lizard, or 'chameleon,' is less energetic, but calls forth even greater admiration.

2. (See quot.)

1844 Gregg *Commerce of Prairies* I. 195 Another indigenous reptile is the horned-frog of the Prairies, known here by the name of *camaleon* (or chameleon), of which it is probably a species, as its color has been observed to vary a little in accordance with the character of the soil it inhabits.

chamisal ˌtʃamiˈsal, *n. S.W.* [*chamiso* + *-al*, a Spanish suffix to denote "a grove of."] A dense growth or thicket of chamiso *q.v.* Cf. **chemise brush.**

1853 *H. Repr. Ex. Doc.* 91 (Bentley), Traveling . . . is rendered very trying by . . . patches of dense masses of shrubbery known as the chemizal. **1902** *Bureau Plant Industry Bul.* No. 12, 31 These chaparral areas . . . have become landmarks, the word chamisal, sometimes corrupted into chemisal . . . being adopted as a local name. **1931** Dayton *Western Browse Plants* 53 Chamiso is especially characteristic on long steep slopes where it forms a chamisal, or dense impenetrable thicket.

attrib. **1867** Harte *Condensed Novels* 244 Except the occasional pattering of a squirrel, or a rustling in the chimisal bushes, there were no signs of life.

chamise lily. *Calif.* (See quot. 1925.) Cf. **chaparral lily.**

1915 Armstrong *Western Wild Flowers* 28 In California they are often called Chamise Lily. **1917** Saunders *Western Flower Guide* 28 The bulbs of the Chamise Lily are edible and were used to some extent by the Northern California Indians. **1925** Jepson *Flowering Plants Calif.* 245 L[ilium] rubescens. . . . Near the coast called Redwood Lily; towards the interior Chaparral or Chamise Lily.

chamiso tʃəˈmiso, *n.* Also **chamise.** *W.* [Amer. Sp. in same sense.] A shrub, *Adenostoma fasciculatum*, found on the dry coast ranges and foothills in California. Also a semidesert shrub, *Atriplex canescens*, of New Mexico. Cf. **Adenostoma, cenizo.**

1846 Emory *Military Reconn.* 77 In one view could be seen clustered, the . . . green wood acacia, chamiza, . . . and a new variety of sedge. **1869** Brace *New West* 94 The chaparral, with which we made such a disagreeable acquaintance, is generally a thorny, impervious shrubbery, made up of the Chinquapin . . . and the Chamiso. **1947** *So. Sierran* May 4/2 As we passed through the foothill area we noted: lavender bush lupine, . . . creamy-panicled chamise and elderberry.

champ tʃæmp, *n.* Short for **champion. Slang.*

1868 *N.E. Base-Ballist* 6 Aug. 2/4 The 'Champs' enjoyed themselves in various ways during the morning. **1929** *Liberty* 30 Nov. 44/1 The sailor gave the champ a battle that might easily have been called a draw. **1948** *Chi. D. News* 16 Aug. 10/6 So to emulate champ FDR's militant liberalism, . . . Mr. Truman should do these things.

Champlain ʃæm'plen, *n.* [Lake *Champlain.*] Used in obs. or rare combs., with **black oak, minnow, pickering, willow.**

1801 Michaux *Histoire des Chênes* 7 Chêne quercitron à feuilles anguleuses. *Great Black Oak*, or *Champlain Black Oak.* **1842** *Nat. Hist. N.Y., Zoology* IV. 220 The Champlain Minnow. *Hydrargira atricada.* **1842** *Ib.* 16 The Champlain Pickering. *Pileoma semifasciatum.* **1810** Michaux *Arbres* I. 41 *Champlain willow*, nom donné par moi.

Champneya ˌtʃæmp'nejə, *n.* [John *Champney*, a florist of Charleston, S.C.] Any one of a number of roses derived from crossing the China rose and the moss rose. — **1823** D. Douglas *Journal* (1914) 26 Called on Messrs. Landreth: obtained the trees with . . . roses Champneya, Cherokee, and two others. **1829** *Amer. Advertiser* (Phila.) 29 July 4/2 His present stock of plants, consists of several hundred of the most choice kinds of Roses, among which are the White Cabbage, Red Cabbage, Chamney, Nosette.

* **chance,** *n.* In colloq. uses, chiefly *S.*

In early Maryland land records (1667–1700) also frequent with personal names to denote a person's "lot" of land, as James Chance, Oglesbyes Chance, Dixsons Chance, Hollis his Chance, etc. See the *Md. Hist. Mag.* XIX–XXI.

1. A quantity or number (*of* something).

Used with various adjs., esp. *smart, right smart, powerful, mighty,* or *fine*, to denote a (fairly or very) large number or quantity. Similarly in senses **2.** and **3.**

1805 Ordway *Journal* 316 (Criswell), The men returned with a fine chance of Elk meat. **1818** in *Rhode Island Hist.* I. (1942) 133 Dan returned from Vincennes about a fortnight since with a (smart chance of, as the Kentuckians say) of fruit trees . . . together with currionts & goosebury bushes and grape vines. **1822** J. Woods *Eng. Prairie* 345 You have a powerful chance of plunder on your creature. What are you going to do with it? **1842** *Knickerb.* XX. 491 There's a mighty chance of lawyers' lies in the papers. **1888** Craddock *Broomsedge Cove* 250, I've been huntin' guinea-hens' aigs. . . . I fund a right smart chance of 'em. **1939** *These Are Our Lives* 68, I have a nice chance o' chickens, and my hens lay right good.

2. A sample or specimen.

1830 Royall *Southern Tour* I. 62 The Postmaster—is a poor *chance*, a rough course looking creature. **1888** *Kansas Hist. Coll.* IV. 245 We found Chicago then, as I first heard the expression—'a right smart chance of a place.'

3. A distance or space of time. *Rare.*

1840 Simms *Border Beagles* 98, I can't tell you [how far it is to Benton]—it's on the other road, and a smart roundabout chance to get to it. **1845** ——— *Wigwam & Cabin* I. 45 There I stood a pretty considerable chance.

4. * *To take chances, a chance*, etc., to run the risk of. *Colloq.*

1902 S. G. Fisher *True Hist. Amer. Revolution* 311 Washington thought himself justified in taking the chances rather than abandon New York without a blow. **1935** Horwill *Amer. Usage* 61/2 Hence to *take a chance* (or *chances*), a common expression in Am., means something rather different from the Eng. expression *take one's chance.* The Am. expression emphasizes the element of risk or danger, whereas the Eng. suggests nothing more than the uncertainty of the result.

As the last term in **Chinaman's, fighting, logging, long, white man's chance.**

* **chancellor,** *n.* In some states, a judge, esp. the presiding judge, in a court of chancery or equity.

1732 in *Amer. Sp.* XX. (1945) 270 And that the present President hath since declined taking the oaths as Chancellor [New York]. **1789** *Ann. 1st Congress* I. 26 The oath . . . would be administered by the Chancellor of the State of New York. **1856** *Harper's Mag.* XIII. 844/1 The Convention created upward of sixty chancellors, or judges, with the full attributes of that office. **1889** *Cent.* 919/2 Chancellor. . . . In Delaware, New Jersey, and some others of the United States, a judge of the Court of Chancery or Equity. In Alabama, Mississippi, and Tennessee there are district chancellors chosen by popular vote. **1948** *Highway Traveller* Dec. 15/1 Washington in a dazzling coach drawn by six white horses was taken to the city hall, where the oath was administered by Chancellor Robert R. Livingston of New York State.

chancer 'tʃænsɚ, *v.* Short for **chancery,** *v.*

Apparently confined to N. Eng. and now obsolete or obsolescent. See A. Matthews in *Nation* 74 (1902) p. 12.

1671 in *Pub. Col. Soc.* XXIX. 4 Dat the 30th of Sept 1671 . . the Jurie . . . found for the plt the forfeiture of the bond & costs of Court & on ye Request of the defendt ye Court chancired it to one hundred pounds in spetie according to bond ye Debt beeing ninety pounds. **1719** *Conn. Col. Records* (1872) VI. 127 An arbitration bond . . . might be chancered. . . . The said bond is hereby chancered and reduced to that sum. **1798** Root *Law Rep.* I. 114 The Court is of opinion that the case is within the statute and that said note be chancered to £3. 15. 3. **1902** A. Matthews in *Nation* 74, 12 Mr. John Noble . . . tells me that *to chancer* is still heard in Massachusetts, though the verbal noun *chancering* is more common.

chancerable 'tʃænsərəbḷ, *a.* Capable of being chancered. *Obs.* — **1726** *Conn. Col. Records* (1872) VII. 74 It is resolved, that the aforesaid note is chancerable.

chancering 'tʃænsərɪŋ, *n.* The action of adjusting judicially. — **1684** *Mass. Court of Assist. Rec.* I. 261 The plaintiff and defend[an]ts pleas as to the Chancering of the bond. **1740** W. Douglass *Discourse* 7 England, France and Holland have tacitly allowed their several American Colonies . . . by Chancerings in their Courts of Judicature . . . to depreciate . . . the value of their original Denominations. **1902** [see **chancer,** *v.*].

chancerize 'tʃænsəˌraɪz, *v. tr.* =**chancery,** *v. Obs.* — **1707** in *R.I. Col. Rec.* IV. 26 This Assembly . . . do order and enact, that the said bonds be by the Governor and council truly chancerized. **1722** *Ib.* 320 This assembly do adjudge and decree that the judgment . . . is hereby chancerized down to twenty shillings.

* **chancery,** *n.* Adjustment of a sum or matter in dispute as by a court of chancery. *Obs.*

1679 *Mass. Court of Assist. Rec.* I. 154 After ye Court had heard ye partjes pleas [for?] a chancery of ye bond they Judged it meet [etc.]. **1699** Sewall *Diary* I. 495 The Jury brings in their verdict for Madam Usher. Mr. Leverett and Newton crave a Chancery. **1706** *Ib.* II. 167 Mr. Blagrove is cast, Asks a Chancery in writing.

chancery 'tʃænsərɪ, *v.* [f. the noun.] *tr.* To adjust or settle equitably, after the manner of a court of chancery. *Obs.* — **1674** *Mass. Court of Assist. Rec.* I. 21 The Court . . . chanceried the dammage additional to 40 s. only. **1684** *Ib.* 261 The plaintiff desired his bond might be chanceried. The Court . . . did chancery it to sixty-eight pounds.

* **change,** *n.*

1. Conversion to a religious state, or to a different frame of mind, usu. **change of heart.** *Colloq.*

1828 Webster, Conversion, in a theological or moral sense, a change of heart, or dispositions. *c***1847** F. M. Whitcher *Widow Bedott P.* xi. 108 'Do you mean to insiniwate that ye've met with a change?' said the Widow Bedott to Jim Clarke, the peddler. **1924** Mulford *Rustlers' Valley* xiv. 167 A Los Altos bum only has to see Baldy to get a change of heart an' a yearnin' for home.

2. Short for **change pitcher.** *Obs.*

1880 *Chi. Tribune* 25 April 7/6 The Baltimore Club has a one-armed pitcher, and he was batted so severely by the Troys that big Brouthers had to go in as change.

3. In combs., chiefly obs.: (1) **change note,** =**exchange note;** (2) **partner,** app. a game played at parties; (3) **pitcher,** in baseball, an alternate pitcher.

(1) 1852 Gouge *Fiscal Hist. Texas* 244 She [Texas] issued her securities in every variety of form . . . notes with interest and notes without, 'red backs,' and star notes, and change notes. — **(2) 1833** Greene *Dod. Duckworth* I. 30 There was no obstruction to the pleasant games of . . . change-partners. — **(3) 1868** Chadwick *Base Ball* 36 Your change pitcher should occupy the position of short-stop. *Ib.* 160 Of the Atlantics, Zettlein occupies the regular position, with Pratt as change pitcher. **1947** R. Smith *Baseball* 65 The right fielder, Miller, as the 'change' pitcher—that is, the man who would come in and toss the ball up if the regular pitcher wobbled or tired.

b. *Change of base*, see * **base,** *n.* **2. d,** quots. 1862, 1919.

1870 O. Logan *Before Footlights* 219 [The room had] recently been occupied by an officer of rank whose brother officers . . . required the most minute explanation in regard to his sudden change of base. **1903** Stiles *Four Years* 79 It would not be well for him to seriously interfere with or molest us in our 'change of base,'—or 'retreat' if one prefers this latter term.

As the last term in **loose, short change.**

changeable hare. The American varying hare, *Lepus americanus. Rare.* — **1814** Brackenridge *Views* 57 The changeable hare (*lepus variabilis*) a beautiful animal, gray in summer, and white in winter is seen in this country.

* **channel,** *n.*

1. channel bass, the branded drum, *Sciaenops ocellata.*

1889 *Cent.* 921/3. **1947** *Sports Afield* Dec. 43 Surf fishing for channel bass, with the tide tugging at your knees and pounding the white beach behind you, adds fun to a coastal holiday.

2. channel cat(**fish**), a catfish of the genus *Ictalurus* found in the streams of the Mississippi Valley and Gulf States.

1836 Kirtland in *Ohio Geol. Survey* 169 *Pimelobus pallidus* . . . Channel cat-fish. **1913** Cather *O Pioneers!* 29 Twice every summer she sent the boys to the river, twenty miles to the southward, to fish for channel cat. **1948** *Capital-Democrat* (Tishomingo, Okla.) 17 June

9/3 They . . . came in with 6 black bass weighing from 2½ to 4 lbs. and 1 channel cat 4 lbs. caught on plugs.

3. Channel City, Santa Barbara, California, from its early importance with reference to the Channel Islands off the southern coast of California.

1894 *Land of Sunshine* Nov. 113/2 In 1887 the Southern Pacific made its way into the Channel City. **1938** *L.A. Times* 12 Aug. 12/1 Here were only simple red men of a far-off day, living in simple ease on the site of what was later to be the Channel City.

As the last term in **river channel, ship channel.**

***chanticleer,** *n.* The rooster as the emblem of the Democratic party. *Obs.* — **1851** *S.F. Herald* 26 Aug. 2/4 'Coons and Chanticleers, the cherished emblems, the distinctive badges by which friend may be told from foe—will be in great demand.

***chap,** *n.* A child. Also **chappie.** *Colloq.*

1881 in CYRIL CLEMENS *Mark Twain* (1932) 37 (R.), There's a new baby down stairs [Jean, born 1880]. . . . Little chaps like that can't be comfortable on a long journey, you know. **1907** *D.N.* III. 221 chap, *n.* A baby; a child; a boy until he is eight or nine years old. Used almost wholly by men. **1942** RAWLINGS *C. Creek* 71 Somewhere in the family blood was a strain that should not, eugenically, have been perpetuated. Yet all of the Widow Slater's brood, the 'chappies' as she called them, Carolina fashion, had a luminous quality.

As the last term in **abolition chap, ward chap.**

chaparajos ˌtʃæpəˈrehos, *n.* Also **chaperajos, chaparejos.** Variants of **chaparreras.**

Perhaps the result of a confusion of *chaparreras* and *aparejos*, the pl. of *aparejo*, meaning gear, equipment.

1887 *Outing* X. 115/1 We had all discarded our *Chaparajos*, and the horses were lightly blanketed. **1888** ROOSEVELT in *Cent. Mag.* Feb 505/2 The broad hat, huge blunt spurs, and leather *chaperajos* of the riders. **1927** RUSSELL *Trails* 3 Their chaparejos were made of heavy bullhide, to protect the leg from brush an' thorns, with hog-snout tapaderos. **1939** ROLLINS *Gone Haywire* 13 Concealed within the right leg of his chaparejos there was always a knife, long-bladed and very sharp.

chaparral ˌtʃæpəˈræl, *n. S.W.* [Sp. in Amer. Sp. sense as shown in **1.**]

1. (See quots. 1846, 1911.) Cf. **mesquite chaparral.**

1845 T. J. GREEN *Texian Exped.* vi. 59 Suddenly the head of the line was turned . . . into a dense and most difficult chaparral. **1846** *Davenport* (Iowa) *Gazette* 25 June 2/4 Chapporal . . . is a term applied to a species of evergreen thicket, composed of the musquit bush matted with vines, growing about six or seven feet long. **1911** PLUMMER *Chaparral* 8 Chaparral. An area whose permanent and mature crop is a mixed forest of stunted trees, resulting from certain climatic conditions which produce sclerophyllous or hard-leafed dwarfs. **1941** FERGUSSON *Southwest* 22 He loathes that town as a rattler loathes a chaparral.

b. *transf.* and *fig.*

1851 in *Pioneer* (S.F.) (1854) Feb. 94 Sometimes we were compelled to cross broad plains, acres in extent, called *chaparrals*, covered with low shrubs. **1870** MARK TWAIN *Sketches* 153 (R.), Her hair was frizzled into a tangled chaparral. **1878** *Cong. Rec.* App. 15 June 453/2 They see in every democratic Representative upon this floor a Mexican bandit skulking in the political chaparrel.

2. Close-growing, tangled, or thorny shrubs such as form a chaparral. Cf. **mock chaparral.**

1850 B. TAYLOR *Eldorado* (1862) x. 94 The road passed between low hills, covered with patches of chapparal. **1910** J. HART *Vigilante Girl* 325 On the mountains was a scanty growth of greasewood, scrub, and chaparral. **1948** *So. Sierran* Mar. 1/3 Chaparral is a folk name derived from 'chaparro,' early Spanish name for the scrub oak Quercus dumosa, one of its dominant species.

3. In combs.: (1) **chaparral berry,** the berry of the chaparral shrub, also attrib.; (2) **bird,** =next; (3) **cock,** =**road runner;** (4) **deer,** app. a sub-species of the mule deer, *rare;* (5) **lily,** (see quot. 1942 and cf. **chamise lily**); (6) **pea,** a thorny shrub, *Pickeringia montana*, found in chaparral regions; (7) **shrub,** the buffalo berry, *Shepherdia argentea;* (8) **tea,** (see quot.).

(1) **1881** in *Annals of Wyoming* XIV. (1942) 119 Gazelle and Ma made some Chapparel berry pies and cookies. **1920** HUNTER *Trail Drivers Texas* I. 134, I walked all day with nothing to eat but chapparal berries. — (2) **1941** FERGUSSON *Southwest* 15 A chaparral bird can scare a rattler stiff and peck it to death. — (3) **1853** SITGREAVES *Exped. Zuni & Colo. Rivers* 92 The Paisano or Chaparral Cock [is] common in western Texas, frequenting barren and brushy plains. **1946** R. PEATTIE *Pac. Coast Ranges* 97 The bird is also called chaparral cock and snake killer. — (4) **1886** VAN DYKE *So. Calif.* 80 One of them, the little chaparral deer, is almost extinct, and never was abundant.

(5) **1917** SAUNDERS *Western Flower Guide* 5 A somewhat similar lily, with rather smaller and more erect flowers, is . . . *Lilium rubescens*, Wats., popularly known as Chaparral Lily. **1942** *Stand. Plant Names* 334/2 Lilium rubescens (*L. washingtonianum r.*) Chaparral Lily. — (6) **1909** *Cent. Supp.* 956/2 Chaparral pea, a spiny leguminous bush, *Xylothermia montana*, of high altitudes in the Coast range of middle and southern California. **1946** *Sierra Club Bul.* Dec. 21 Other shrubs were sending up suckers from roots or underground stems: wild rose, chaparral pea, . . . and snowberry. — (7) **1855** in *Calif. Pion. Soc. Quart.* V. 17 July 11 The suburbs of the city (San Francisco) are exceeding wild. A few chaparral shrubs, a little tansy, & some life everlasting, were all I saw growing, except two little flower gardens which are irrigated. — (8) **1885** HAVARD *Flora W. & S. Texas* 514 Encenilla; Chaparral Tea. . . . An infusion of the flowering tops, either green or dried, makes excellent tea.

Also *chaparral bush, flora, leaf, thicket, walled*, etc.

chaparralish ˌtʃæpəˈrælɪʃ, *a.* Crabbed, cantankerous. *Rare.* — **1910** O. HENRY *Strictly Business* 17 Helen Grimes, chaparralish as she can be, is goaded beyond imprudence.

chaparreras ˌtʃæpəˈrɛrəs, *n. pl.* Also **chaparreros.** *S.W.* [Amer. Sp. in same sense.] Leather trousers worn to protect the legs while riding through chaparral. Cf. **chaps.**

1861 TYLOR *Anahuac* 335 Chaparreros, over-trousers of goatskin with the hair on, used in riding. **1865** *Atlantic Mo.* XV. 61 Don had insisted on my assuming . . . Mexican riding-costume: cool linen drawers, cut Turkish fashion; over these . . . the leathern chapareros or overalls. *a***1909** O. HENRY *Roads of Destiny* 95 Lonny is one of them, a knight of stirrup and chaparreras.

chapote tʃəˈpotɪ, *n. S.W.* [Amer. Sp. (< Nahuatl) in same sense.] (See quot. 1846.)

1846 GREGG *Diary & Letters* (1941) I. 239 Among other wild fruits of this vicinity, that called by Mexicans chapote and generally by Americans, black persimmon (or Mexican or Mustang persimmon) a black fruit about half the bulk of the common persimmon, much the same shape, and of very pleasant sweet flavor, when ripe. **1885** HAVARD *Flora W. & S. Texas* 523 Mexican Persimmon; the Chapote of the Mexicans. Shrub or small tree 10 to 20 feet high. **1937** PARKS *Valuable Plants Texas* 95 The plant received the name of Capote as the Mexican women use the ripe persimmon in making a hair dye.

chapped tʃæpt, *a.* [f. **chaps.**] Wearing chaps. —**1914** *World's Work* Feb. 442/2 Chapped and booted cowboys . . . passed frequently to the jingle of chain and spur.

chapping ˈtʃæpɪŋ, *n. W.* (See quot. 1926.) — **1910** W. M. RAINE *B. O'Connor* 60 A chapping would sure do him a heap of good. **1926** BRANCH *Cowboy* 31 The rest of the outfit might avenge the dignity of their calling by a 'chapping'—a laying on of leather after the manner of ancient disciplinarians, the offender's own pair of chaps sometimes the instrument.

chaps tʃæps, *n. pl. W.* Short for **chaparajos,** or **chaparreras.**

1844 W. SHEPHERD *Prairie Exper.* 41 The cow-boys, with their *schaps*, i.e. leather-leggings and flopping wide-brimmed hats, are trooping off. **1884** NYE *Baled Hay* 139 'Chaps,' as they are vulgarly called, . . . are made of leather with fronts of dog-skin with the hair on. . . . The seat of the garment has been postponed *sine die.* **1948** *Time* 26 Jan. 20/2 In the summer, he donned chaps and a big hat, and tooted his brass on horseback with traveling Wild West shows.

***chapter,** *n.*

1. A branch of an organization or society, as a college fraternity. Cf. **graduate chapter.**

1815 DRAKE *Cincinnati* 166 A Chapter of Royal Arch Masons was established in this place. **1887** *Lippincott's Mag.* Nov. 739 These are houses owned by the Amherst chapters of the various Greek fraternities. **1948** *Dly. Ardmoreite* (Ardmore, Okla.) 7 April 5/3 Beta Rho chapter of Beta Sigma Phi observed annual founders' day with a banquet at the Hotel Ardmore.

2. chapter house, room, the building or room used as a meeting place by a chapter, esp. of a college fraternity.

1851 CIST *Cincinnati* 160 The furniture of the chapter room is of mahogany. **1888** *Cent. Mag.* XXXVI. 755/1 The wealthy chapter-houses of the East are furnished with all the luxury and refined taste of the highest modern art. **1945** *Reader's Digest* July 28/1 The big event . . . was an evening party at the chapter house where candidates were given a final once-over by the members.

***chaptered,** *a.* Of a college fraternity: Having chapters in different localities. *Rare.* — **1871** BAGG *At Yale* 110 There are other important chaptered fraternities existing in American colleges.

chaqueta tʃɑˈketə, *n.W.* [Sp., jacket.] (See quots.) — **1902** CLAPIN *Americanisms*, tchah-ket-ah (sp.) In Texas, a jacket, and, more specifically a jacket made of leather or very heavy cloth, worn by cowboys as a protection against thorns of the chaparral. **1909** *Cent. Supp.*, Chaqueta, a jacket, particularly a leather jacket, worn by cow-boys as a protection when traveling through the chaparral (Western and south-western U.S.).

characterology ˌkærɪktəˈrɑlədʒɪ, *n.* The science dealing with the study of character. — **1903** *Amer. Jrnl. Psychol.* July–Oct. 356 An iconoclastic attitude towards all attempts at practical characterology. **1920** L. H. McCormick (*title*), Characterology; an Exact Science.

charbon ˈʃɑrbən, [?F.] (See quot.) *Rare.* — **1836** *Niles' Reg.* 8 Oct. 96/3 A disease termed *charbon* is causing great mortality among the stock of Louisiana—some carried off by it, and in many instances it has proved fatal to man. Sulphur, flour of sulphur and brimstone, it is said, will effect a speedy cure.

charco ˈtʃɑrko, *n. S.W.* [Sp., pool or puddle.] (See quot. 1942.)

1890 *Stock Grower* 9 Aug. 4/3 In a day or so the rain came and the water holes and the 'charcos' were again filled. **1925** Bryan *Papago Country Ariz.* 121 Charcos are found as single pools or a series of pools along streams that deposit fine-grained material, usually sandy clay or adobe. **1942** Castetter & Bell *Pima & Papago Agric.* 42 Often there were natural water holes or pools of standing water of variable size along channels where flood waters spread out over adobe flats and washes, in which case they were known as *charcos*, usually three to five feet deep.

∗**charcoal,** *n.*

1. (See quots.) *Obs.*

*a*1877 *Exchange Paper* (B. 397), The members of the [Missouri] Legislature are divided into charcoals, Clay-banks, White-legs [etc.]. . . . The 'Charcoal' believes slavery a moral enormity. **1915** W. B. Stevens *Missouri* I. 333 The Radicals, as the Charcoals had come to be . . . called, carried Missouri in the general elections of 1864.

2. a. charcoal nigger, (see quot.). **b. charcoal road,** (see quot. 1846). Both *obs.*

(a) 1870 Macrae *Americans* II. 35 To call him 'a charcoal nigger' was the blackest insult of all, making him the furthest removed from the nobility of whiteness. — **(b) 1846** *Sci. Amer.* 10 Oct. 18/2 The citizens of Yazoo, Miss., have determined to make a charcoal road over the valley swamp of that place. Sixty hands cutting timber will burn and spread the charcoal over two miles in 30 days—the embankments being already thrown up. **1850** *N. Eng. Farmer* n.s. II. 240/2 We had an opportunity last week of passing over a portion of the charcoal road between this place and Oconomowoc.

∗**charge,** *n.* As the last term in **bird, fixed, pan, trackage charge.**

∗**charge,** *v.tr.* In library work, to make a record of (the lending of a book). — **1893** *Library Bureau Catalog* 95 Call Slips. Plain manilla, white or colored paper, cut into small slips, . . . used for charging loans, memo., etc. **1925** Arnett *Elements of Library Methods* 165 This method of charging books is known as the Newark system.

charge account. A credit account at a store. — **1909** O. Henry *Options* (1916) 96 I've got more power here than . . . a charge of dynamite, and a charge account at Tiffany's combined. **1948** *Dly. Oklahoman* (Okla. City) 28 Dec. 8/1 Stores are seeking new charge accounts . . . because the charge customer will buy more at a time, but less often, which is an advantage to the retailer.

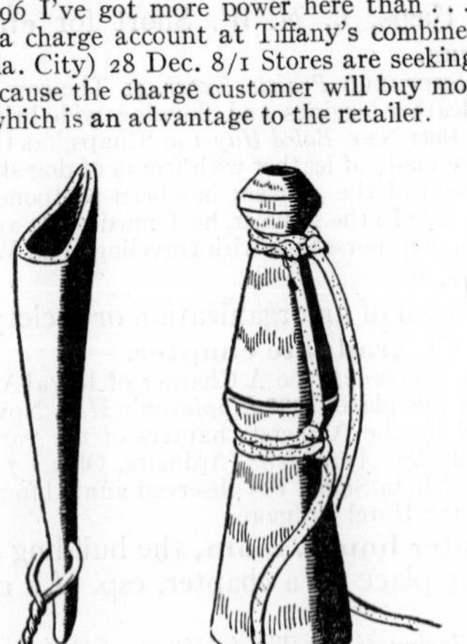

Charger or loader and deer bleat

∗**charger,** *n.* A small container holding the proper amount of powder for charging a muzzle-loading firearm. Cf. ∗**loader.**

1709 Lawson *Carolina* 128 The teeth of this Creature [*sc.* an Alligator], when dead, are taken out to make Chargers for Guns, being of several Sizes, fit for all Loads. **1837** A. Wetmore *Gaz. Missouri* 325 We made a few powder-horns, and highly-finished 'chargers,' and new wiping-sticks. **1874** Long *Wild-Fowl* 37 A quick-loading flask, *i.e.*, one having a large feed hole to the charger, should also be used.

chargéship ˌʃɑrˈʒeʃɪp, *n.* The office or appointment of chargé d'affaires. *Obs.* — **1830** Mackenzie *Life Van Buren* (1846) 260 A Senator high in his confidence pressed me to accept the Charge-ship to Sweden at Somerville's death. **1858** Lincoln in Logan *Great Conspiracy* 74 They have seen in his round . . . face, . . . Marshalships, and Cabinet appointments, Chargéships and Foreign Missions.

∗**chariot,** *n.* **1. chariot-berlin,** a chariot-like berlin. *Rare.* **2.** ∗**chariot-wheel,** (see quot.). *Obs.* — **(1) 1732** *S.C. Gaz.* 2 Dec., A good Chariot-Berlin, with the Harness.— **(2) 1800** Rollins *N. Eng. Bygones* 213 They wore mittens of blue and white, striped, or knit in a curious pattern, called 'chariot wheels,' by the housewives.

chariotee ˌtʃærɪˈti, *n.* A light, covered four-wheeled pleasure carriage. *Obs.* — **1825** *Catawba Journal* 17 May, A coachee, chariotee, phaeton, panneled and stick gigs [etc.]. **1867** Lackland *Homespun* I. 50 An open wagon, set on the old-fashion 'thorough-braces,' comes as near to a coupé, chariotee, or barouche as you can ordinarily discover.

∗**charitable,** *n.* In the names of organizations founded for benevolent purposes. *Obs.*

1792 N. Webster in Ford *Notes* I. 362 Forming a Constitution for a Charitable Society. *Ib.*, At evening a number of Gentlemen convened at the Court House & formed themselves into a 'Charitable Society.' **1795** Bentley *Diary* II. 140 Went to Boston & in the afternoon was entertained at the King's Chapel by the Address of Judge Minot to the Charitable Fire Society. **1839** A. Lawrence *Diary & Corr.* 172, I will give to the Charitable Mechanic Association ten thousand dollars. **1898** Page *Red Rock* 271 She has had some correspondence with him on behalf of her charitable society for the freedmen.

charivari, see **shivaree.**

Charleston ˈtʃɑrlztən, *n.* [*Charleston*, S.C.] A form of dance in which the knees touch and the heels are lifted alternately out and back. — **1925** *N.Y. Times* 26 July 23/2, I have no objection to a person dancing their feet and head off, . . . but I think it best that they keep away from the Charleston. **1944** *Chi. Tribune* 14 Nov. 10 1/2 Gradually it [the Lindy Hop] picked up the steps of Mooch, Sugar, Charleston, Shag, and Suzy-Q.

Charlestonian ˌtʃɑrlzˈtonɪən, *n.* A native of Charleston, S.C.

1828 Mrs. Basil Hall *Aristocratic Journey* (1931), 214, I must do the Charlestonians the justice to say that I have not seen any chewing amongst them nor spitting. **1860** *Charleston* (S.C.) *Mercury* 6 Nov. 1/1 A salute of thirteen guns greeted the approach of the Charlestonians. **1947** *Sat. Ev. Post* 8 Feb. 70/3 America's only original contributor to the study of evolution, William Charles Wells, was a Charlestonian.

Charley horse. [Origin unknown.] Stiffness in an arm or leg, usu. from overexercise or muscular strain, often of baseball or football players. *Colloq.*

1889 *Cin. Comm. Gazette* 17 March 15/1 Toward the close of the season Mac was affected with a 'Charley-horse' and that ended his ball-playing for 1888. **1913** *Amer. Mag.* July 68/1 Everybody got jov'al, and the barkeep at Sierra Joe's got a charley-horse tryin' to keep up with his orders. **1947** *Sooner Mag.* Nov. 14/2 The day before the first scheduled game with Oklahoma City he suffered a charley-horse.

∗**charter,** *n.*

1. Designating an election held in accordance with the charter of a city or borough. Also **charter office.**

1834 P. Hone *Diary* I. 94 Our only hope lies in the elections in New York and Pennsylvania, particularly our charter election. **1839** Marryat *Diary in Amer.* II. 221 On the 9th, 10th, and 11th instant, a local election for mayor and charter-offices was held in this city. **1900** C. Winchester *W. Castle* 209 At the next charter election, after the revival, a live Christian man was elected Mayor.

2. Charter Oak, a large oak in Hartford, Conn., in which the charter of the colony was allegedly hidden in 1687 when Sir Edmund Andros, Governor General of New England, came to get it.

1831 *Boston Transcript* 10 Oct. 2/1 The 'Charter Oak' still lives and flourishes, enjoying a green old age. **1868** Beecher *Norwood* 327 What of that famous Boston Common Elm, which is to Massachusetts what the Charter Oak was to Connecticut? **1947** *Sat. Ev. Post* 8 Mar. 118/2 Capt Joe Wadsworth was the man who saved the Charter, guaranty of Connecticut liberties, from the British governor, by hiding it in the Charter Oak.

b. Also **Charter Oak City, cooking stove, grape.**

1859 *Ladies' Repository* XIX. 51/1 Hartford, Connecticut, is the 'Charter Oak City,' from the old oak-tree so famous in our colonial history. — *a*1918 in G. Stuart *On Frontier* (1925) I. 258 James bought a Charter Oak cooking stove No. 8. — **1849** *N. Eng. Farmer* I. 320 Any information from Mr. C., concerning the Charter Oak grape, will be very acceptable. **1856** *Rep. Comm. Patents: Agric.* 308

Several gentlemen, of this vicinity, have vines of the 'Charter Oak' grape, said to be a native of Connecticut, the fruit of which grows almost as large as a plum.

*__chartered,__ *a.* Superior, excelling. *Slang. Obs.* — **1834** *Amer. R.R. Jrnl.* III. 304/2 Why she's chartered! She's a ra'al one, I assure you. [Praising a horse.] **1853** *Weekly Advertiser* (Fredericksburg, Va.) 12 Feb. 1/2 The half-breeds, loafers and 'chartered fighters,' as they call themselves, held a caucus.

*__chase,__ *v.* **1.** *tr.* To follow (a drink) with a chaser *q.v.* **2.** *To chase oneself,* to go away, "beat it." *Slang.*

(1) **1941** Daniels *Tar Heels* 255 They had been drinking corn whisky and chasing it down with near beer. — (2) **1896** Ade *Artie* 119 (We.), Aw, go chase yourself. **1921** R. D. Paine *Comr. Rolling Ocean* xii. 206 Let him rest, Kid. You chase yourself below and look things over.

*__chaser,__ *n.* A small quantity of water or other mild beverage taken after a drink of liquor. Also fig. *Colloq.*

1897 *Daily News* 30 Aug. 2/1 Everything was 50 cents. a drink, no mixed drinks, and no water for a chaser. *a***1906** O. Henry *Trimmed Lamp* 169 Eagerly gulping down the strong black headlines to be followed as a chaser by the milder details of the smaller type. **1946** *Nat. Geog. Mag.* Sep. 298/2 It's even rumored that some older hill men, after a moonshine snort, take a goat's milk chaser!

As the last term in **Negro, rainbow chaser.**

*__chasing,__ *n.* As the last term in **ambulance, dollar, rainbow chasing.**

chasing tune. (See quot.) *Obs.* — **1897** Terhune *Old-field School* 37 The three were singing one of Moore's Melodies arranged as a fugue, or, as unmusical people used to call it, 'a chasing tune.'

*__chasm,__ *n.* Short for **bloody chasm.** *Rare.* — **1879** *Chi. Tribune* 14 May 6/3 Never, no, never—will we shake hands across the awful chasm until these things come to pass, both in letter and spirit. *a***1909** O. Henry *Roads of Destiny* xxi. 352 Don't reopen the chasm, Doc. Any Yankeeness I may have is geographical.

*__chat,__ *n.* A large warbler, *Icteria virens,* of eastern North America. Cf. **yellow-breasted chat.**

1808 Wilson *Ornithology* I. 92 While the female of the Chat is sitting, the cries of the male are still more loud and incessant. **1869** *Amer. Naturalist* III. 295, I obtained there also . . . [the nest] of the Chat (*Icteria viridis*), with four eggs. **1946** Hausman *Eastern Birds* 538 The Chat conceals itself in the top of a bush, and from this hidden stage pours forth its surprising vocal performance.

chatteldom ˈtʃætldəm, *n.* The institution or condition of slavery. *Obs.* — **1858** *N.Y. Tribune* 12 April 3/2, I insisted upon the propriety of placing the hand of chattledom on 'small farmers and greasy mechanics,' to prevent the impertinence of their wanting to associate with gentlemen's body-servants.

chattelism ˈtʃætl̩ˌɪzəm, *n.* The system of holding human beings as chattels or slaves. *Obs.* Cf. **human chattelism.**

1865 W. Phillips in *Commonwealth* (Boston) 18 Feb., To grind the negro without restoring chattelism. **1875** *Scribner's Mo.* Dec. 275/2 The system of human Chattelism does not enter here. **1879** Tourgee *Fool's Errand* 336 That transition period which comes between Chattelism . . . and absolute individual autonomy.

chattelization ˌtʃætl̩əˈzeʃən, *n.* The action of converting (persons) into chattels. *Obs.* — **1854** A. L. Stone *Boston Oration* 4 July 25 A system of human chattelization.

chattelized ˈtʃætl̩aɪzd, *a.* Converted into chattels. *Obs.* — **1878** *N. Amer. Rev.* CXXVII. 251 This system of chattelized humanity rested upon that false relation . . . which is the life of every form of oppression.

chattelizing ˈtʃætlaɪzɪŋ, *a.* Reducing persons to the state of chattels. *Obs.* — **1863** in Logan *Great Conspiracy* 530 This Amendment . . . would . . . 'obliterate the last lingering vestiges of the Slave System; its chattelizing, degrading, and bloody codes.'

chattel mortgage. A mortgage on the chattels, in contrast to the real estate, of the mortgagee. — **1860** M. J. Holmes *Maude* xxi. 213 There was a heavy mortgage upon the farm, and even a chattel-mortgage upon the furniture. **1898** E. N. Westcott *D. Harum* 193 They've got wind o that chattel morgedge.

*__chattering,__ *a.* **1. chattering flycatcher,** =**chat. 2. chattering plover,** the killdee or killdeer, *Oxyechus vociferus.*

(1) **1858** Baird *Birds Pacific R.R.* 248 Yellow Breasted Chat. . . . Chattering flycatcher. . . . Eastern United States to the Missouri, south to Guatemala. — (2) *c***1730** Catesby *Carolina* I. 71 *Pluvialis vociferus.* The Chattering Plover. This is about the size of the larger Snipe. In Virginia they are called Kill-deers, from some resemblance of their noise to the sound of that word. They abide in Carolina and Virginia all the year. **1917** *Birds of Amer.* I. 259.

Chautauqua ʃəˈtɔkwə, *n.* [See note.]

1. The name of a town (also of a lake and county) in western New York State used attrib. with reference to meetings of a religious and educational nature the first of which were held at Chautauqua, N.Y.

This word stems from a Seneca Indian place-name variously represented in early, chiefly French, writings and maps, as *Tchadakoin, Chautaughque, Chataconit,* etc. Various meanings have been assigned to it but Hodge gives it as "one has taken out fish there" referring to Lake Chautauqua. See *Amer. Sp.* Oct. 1934, 232 f., and Read, *La. Place-Names* 21.

1873 (*title*), The Chautauqua Lake Journal, published for the Chautauqua Lake Camp Meeting Association. **1881** *N.Y. Herald* 23 Aug. 10/2 The Chautauqua assembly exercises closed this morning and the people are leaving in large numbers. **1948** *Nat. Geog. Mag.* March 296/1 They helped wreck vaudeville and Chautauqua entertainment.

b. Chautauqua salute, (see quots.).

1886 J. H. Vincent *Chautauqua Movement* 278 The 'Chautauqua Salute' was introduced for the first time [in 1877] on the occasion of the charming pantomimic lecture delivered at the old auditorium. The waving of white handkerchiefs by the people, in expression to the deaf man of the high appreciation of his silent lecture, was remarkable, brilliant, and effective. **1910** *Springfield W. Republican* 15 Dec. 9 The men cheered and the many women gave a Chautauqua salute, so far as they could make their handkerchiefs show above the crowd.

Also *Chautauqua contract, convention, grounds, lecturer, movement, spirit, system, tent, town,* etc.

2. An assembly for religious and educational purposes, orig. used of that at Chautauqua, N.Y., and later of similar ones elsewhere. Also latterly a selected group of educators and entertainers sent out on circuit to hold meetings, often in the open air or in tents.

1884 *Dakota Mission Conf. of M. E. Ch.* 5 Sess. 64½ Religious Summer Resort, The Great Chautauqua of the West, Big Stone Lake, Dakota. **1920** Lewis *Main Street* 236 She turned to the Chautauqua as she had turned to the dramatic association, to the library board. **1948** *Time* 9 Feb. 102/3 During the peak year of 1924, Chautauqua visited 12,000 U.S. towns and villages.

Chautauquan ʃəˈtɔkwən, *n.* A member of a Chautauqua. Also transf.

1878 J. H. Vincent *Chautauqua Movement* 80 Now, let every Chautauquan present and absent read Dr. Vincent's lecture. **1880** *Chautauquan* I. 40 This is the first number of volume one of 'The Chautauquan.' **1947** *Newsweek* 2 June 58/2 McConnell was an ex-Chautauquan when he first squeezed his bulk behind a microphone.

*__chaw,__ *v.*

1. (See quot. 1909.) *Slang.*

1842 *Dartmouth* IV. 117 Yesterday, a Junior cracked a joke on me, when all standing round, shouted in great glee, 'Chawed! Freshman chawed'! . . . I didn't understand, when a fellow is used up, he is said to be chawed. **1909** *D.N.* III. 298 *Chaw,* v. tr., . . . to hack or guy one.

2. **To chaw up,* to demolish, defeat, "use up," often in fig. contexts. *Slang.*

[**1830** *Painesville* (O.) *Telegraph* 15 June 1/5 *Chewed up*—Having an ear, nose and lip bit off.] **1837** Haliburton *Clockm.* (B. & L.), I felt as if I could chaw him right up, I was so mad. **1884** Hill *Colo. Pioneers* 198, I went *in quest* of him, and I just chawed him up. **1901** White *Westerners* xxxiii. 305 They agreed that they'd be tee-totally chawed up.

3. In combs.: (1) **chawback,** a fictitious animal alleged to devour tobacco, *rare;* (2) **tobacco,** chewing tobacco, *obs.;* (3) **wax,** (see quot.).

(1) **1851** *Polly Peablossom* 115 You'll see . . . the infernal Chawbacks—that's what we call 'em—a settin' up in a crotch, a chawin' what is cured, and squirtin' ambeer all over the country. — (2) **1834** Caruthers *Kentuckian* I. 103, I'll be bound you'd look at some body else's pretty cheeks more nor you would at the parson's chaw-tobacco. **1858** *Ubiquitous* (Sacramento) 11 Apr. 2/2 The mother Magigos, is the color of a 'chaw-tobacco.' — (3) **1940** Wilson *Wabash* 250 Had they stayed longer, they might also have acquired the universal feminine habit of chewing burgunday pitch—one of the precursors of modern American chewing gum, or 'chaw-wax,' as it is still called in some parts of Indiana.

chawed rock. (See quots.) — **1843** *Nat. Hist. N.Y., Geology* IV. 162 The calcareous matter is soon dissolved out from weathering, leaving the hornstone in jagged and irregular projecting points, from which it receives the local name of 'chawed rock.' **1846** Emmons *Agric. N.Y.* I. 182 It weathers out into extremely rough masses, so that persons who have occasion to work the rock generally call it chawed rock.

chawing gum, see **chewing gum.**

chayote tʃɑˈjotə, *n.* [Sp. (<Nahuatl) in same sense.] The succulent edible fruit of a tropical vine, *Sechium edule* (see also quot. 1909). — **1909** *Cent. Supp.* 230/3 Chayota. . . . A genus of dicotyledonous plants which belong to the family *Cucurbitaceae.* **1947** Berolz-

HEIMER *Regional Cook Book* 648 Wash chayote, cut in half and scoop out, using potato ball cutter.

∗**cheap,** *a.* In combs.: (1) **cheap cutter,** (see quot.), *colloq.;* (2) **Cheap John Congress,** a derogatory term for Congress, *rare;* (3) **cheap skate,** a contemptible, stingy person, *slang;* (4) **cheap (ware) store,** a store where articles were actually or allegedly sold at or below wholesale prices, originally such a store operated (*c*1820) by a British agent attempting to regain for British manufacturers dominance of the American market, *obs.;* (5) **wit,** a weak-witted person, *slang.*

(1) **1929** *Amer. Sp.* V. 118 One who was shallow-pated, pretentious, and probably dishonest was a 'cheap cutter.' [In Maine.] — (2) **1930** HENRY *Conquer. Plains* 186 Another chapter, gents, in the hist'ry of that air crazy institution, to wit an' namely, Uncle Sam's Cheap John Congress. — (3) **1896** *Chicago Record* 1 Feb. 13/1 A few 'cheap skates' who don't even belong to the club, called a meeting at the Hotel. **1948** *Railway Clerk* May 260/1 A feller that's a born deadbeat and cheapskate hates to keep remindin' his own self of it. — (4) **1822** GALL *Auswanderung* II. 286 Das Wenige was noch übrig geblieben war, wanderte nun vollends in die Kassen der Importers und der Cheap-Store-Keepers und von da nach Europa. **1855** BÜCHELE *Land* 472 Tritt man in einen dieser Schoppen, der sich gewöhnlich durch seinen Umfang und die Inschrift: *'Cheape ware store'* auszeichnet, so stellen sich alle Bedürfnisse der civilisirten Welt bunt durch einander ausgestapelt dar. — (5) **1890** JEWETT *Strangers* 249, I think them wanderin' cheap-wits likes the fun on't.

∗**cheat,** *n.* A now indefinable form of dance. *Obs.* See also **York cheat.** — **1886** B. P. POORE *Reminisc.* I. 74 The 'basket dance,' and, on exceptional occasions, the exhilarating 'cheat,' formed the staple for saltatorial performance.

cheatage 'tʃitɪdʒ, *n.* Income derived from illegal conduct of a public office. *Obs.* — **1839** MARRYAT *Diary in Amer.* I. 195, I afterwards found that it was a common expression in the States to say a place was worth so much besides cheatage. **1856** *Hutchings Mag.* July 45/2 'Cheatage' is considered one of the most profitable perquisites of office, as well as the main stay in political tactics.

Chebacco ʃə'bæko, *n.* Also **chebacco.** [Obs. name of a region and river in Essex Co., Mass.] **Chebacco boat,** a type of fishing boat formerly built in Chebacco, Mass. Now *hist.* or *obs.* Cf. **Jebacco boat.**

Chebacco boat

1823 COOPER *Pilot,* The *Naval Ency.* . . . defines *chebacco-boat* as a boat employed in the Newfoundland fisheries. **1860** BABSON *Hist. Gloucester* 569 At the commencement of the Revolutionary War, eighty schooners and a large number of Chebacco boats were engaged in the fisheries. **1902** *Amer. Folk-Lore* 242 Certain fishing-boats, used in the Newfoundland trade, were called, from Chebacco, the name of a place near Ipswich, Mass., where they were fitted out, *'chebacco-boats.'* Through corruption, or by jesting alteration of the name, they were also known as *'tobacco*-boats.' **1930** *Old-time N. Eng.* April 187 These found ready market in all ports of the northern coast, being widely known as 'Chebacco boats,' and were immediately progenitors of the pinky schooner later so numerous upon this coast.

b. Also **chebacco man, chebacco schooner.**

1823 COOPER *Pilot* I. i. 13, I was born on board a chebacco-man. **1926** GABRIEL *Pageant of Amer.* III. 300 Any morning in the late eighteenth-century Gloucester might see the bright red sterns of the little 'chebacco' schooners as they made for their mooring spars.

chebec ˌtʃi'bɛk, *n.* [Imitative.] =**least flycatcher.** — **1917** *Birds of Amer.* II. 210/2 The Chebec's habits are very like those of the other members of its family. **1941** SETON *Trail of Artist-Naturalist* 185 Whoever would credit the chebec, a flycatcher, with singing a song?

chebog 'tʃiˌbɑg, *n.* (See quots.) — **1895** GERARD in *N.Y. Sun* 30 July Chebog, a name for the fish called the mossbunker, or menhaden: from one of the Algonquian dialects of the Eastern States. **1902** *Amer. Folk-Lore* 242 Chébog. One of the names for the *menhaden* (q. v.). Probably from Narragansett.

chechinquamin tʃə'tʃɪŋkəmɪn, *n.* [Algonquian.] =**chinquapin.** *Obs.*

1612 SMITH *Virginia* 11 They haue a small fruit growing on little trees, husked like a Chesnut, but the fruit most like a very small acorne. This they [=Va. Indians] call Chechinquamins, which they esteeme a great daintie. **c1618** STRACHEY *Virginia* 72 They plant their fields and sett their corne, and live after those monthes most of acrons [*sic*], walnutts, chesnutts, chechinquarinns, and fish. **1705** HARRIS *Navigantum atque itinerantium* I. 842/2 The *Chechinquamins* are a Fruit in much esteem amongst the Natives.

∗**check,** *n.*[1]

1. *Agric.* The point at which furrows at right angles cross. Also the rectangle marked off by such furrows.

1787 WASHINGTON *Diaries* III. 194 In each of these checks or crosses a root, when it was large and looked well, was put. **1856** DAVIS *Farm Bk.* 19 Began to plant corn in the mill cut—5 feet rows by 3½ dropped in checks. **1864** *Rep. Agric. Soc. Maine* 160 It [land] is then to be laid off with a plow . . . & a small hill made in or on the check . . . for the reception of the plant.

2. A square section of land. *Rare.*

1795 J. SULLIVAN *Hist. Maine* 195 The method of regular settlement by lots, checks, and ranges is quite a modern contrivance in the District.

3. In some methods of irrigation, an area to which the water is confined by levees or embankments.

1894 *Irrigation Age* March 115/1 The primitive irrigators differed much in their ways of making their checks and running the water into them. **1902** NEWELL *Irrigation* 187 This flooding in rectangular checks is practised most largely by the Mexicans living along the Rio Grande in New Mexico and in adjacent portions of the Southwest. **1915** FORTIER *Use of Water in Irrig.* 91 Cross levees are constructed to break up some of the larger checks, making the average size of each compartment 1 acre or less in extent.

attrib. **1899** *U.S. Geol. Surv. Water Supp. Paper 19* 22 These check levees are usually made too steep to permit of their being crossed at random by farming implements.

∗**check,** *n.*[2]

1. *checks and balances,* political or constitutional principles, policies, etc., designed to prevent administrative power from being carried to excess.

1787 J. ADAMS *Def. Const. U.S.* (1794) I. p. i, The checks and balances of republican governments have been in some degree adopted by the courts of princes. **1866** *Cong. Globe* App. 16 June 254/2, I have heard it said that this is a world of checks and balances. **1948** *Chi. Sun-Times* 18 Mar. 35/4 The first step in our American system of checks and balances to knock out the silly clause has now been taken.

2. =**baggage check.**

1845 *Hunt's Merch. Mag.* XIII. 581 The conductor . . . hands the owner a tin check. **1913** STRATTON-PORTER *Laddie* viii, So one afternoon father took her trunk to the depot and bought the tickets and got the checks.

Early (*c*1850) form of check or baggage check

3. (See quot. 1889.)

1845 HOOPER *Simon Sugg's Adv.* v. 57 He called for 'Twenty, five-dollar checks.' . . . The dealer handed him the red checks. **1889** FARMER *Americanisms,* Checks, money; cash. A term derived from poker where counters or *checks* bought, as one enters, at certain fixed rates, are equivalent to current coin.

b. *To pass* (or *hand*) *in one's checks*, to die. Also to give up, surrender. *Colloq.* Cf. **cash,** *v.* **2. b.**

1857 *Spirit of Times* 7 Mar. 6/1 Was it not enough to make one sigh, since those days have passed away, and those noble and peril-loving souls have nearly all 'handed in their checks.' **1865** *Republican Banner* (Nashville, Tenn.) 27 Sep. 3/2, I began to feel as though I had played away four years in a game of Political Faro, and 'handed in my checks' to old Time the remorseless dealer. **1938** Asbury *Sucker's Prog.* 336 Thompson finally passed in his own checks on the night of March 11, 1884, when he and King Fisher, . . . were shot down in a variety theater in San Antonio.

4. A bill at a restaurant or dining room.

1868 A. D. Whitney *P. Strong* 128, I let her settle for the dinner checks at Vinton's, while I finished my ice-cream. **1910** O. Henry *Strictly Business* 192 Through an arched opening at the bottom you thrust your waiter's check and the money. **1948** *Chi. Tribune* 23 June II. 7/4 When it came time to pay the checks, the gunman menaced the cashier, . . . and robbed him of $50.

5. In combs., many of which are based on the verb rather than the noun stem but which are included here for convenience of reference: (1) ***check clerk,** (see quots.); (2) **letter,** a letter of the alphabet serving as a mark of identification or control; (3) **list,** (*a*) a list of names, titles, etc., so arranged as to form a ready means of reference, comparison, or verification, (*b*) a list of qualified voters on which the names of these may be checked as they vote at an election; (4) **master,** a railroad official having charge of baggage; (5) **off,** an arrangement whereby a labor union receives the dues, fees, etc., of its members directly from the employer who withholds them from wages, also attrib.; (6) **protector,** a device for preventing the raising of checks; (7) **raiser,** one who tampers with checks so as to increase the amount they are made out for, also **check raising;** (8) **room,** a room in a railroad station, hotel, etc., where baggage is checked and temporarily kept; (9) **row,** one of the rows in a cornfield so plowed as to form a check pattern, also attrib.; (10) **rowed,** of corn, planted in check rows; (11) **rower,** (see quots.); (12) **set,** the device on a checkrower that governs the dropping of the seed; (13) **stand,** a place where baggage is checked; (14) ***strap,** (see quots. 1887, 1889, 1909), also transf. and attrib.; (15) **stub,** the counterfoil of a check; (16) **up,** a careful examination; (17) **word,** the key word of a cipher, *rare.*

(1) 1889 *Cent.* 940/3 Check-clerk, a clerk whose business it is to check the accounts of others, their time of attendance at work, etc. **1889** Farmer 134/1 Check clerk, the clerk in charge of a cloak-room, or one employed in the office at hotels, to allot rooms to visitors, and to book their names in the hotel register. — **(2) 1776** *Journals Cont. Cong.* 15 Nov. 955 That each denomination [of the certificates] have a check letter corresponding with a letter in the margin to be left in the book. **1851** *Ann. 5th Congress* 708 There was also a check-letter in the books and on the certificates which rendered forgery almost impossible. — **(3)** (*a*) **1853** (*title*), Check list of periodical publications received in the reading-room of the Smithsonian Institution. **1948** *Pac. Northwest Quart.* April 177 The University of Washington Library is taking steps to compile a supplement to Charles W. Smith's checklist, *Pacific Northwest Americana.* (*b*) **1885** Merriam *Life S. Bowles* II. 107 The use of the check-list as a protection against fraud was voted, but was almost ignored; although twelve hundred votes were cast, only a hundred and twenty names were checked. **1888** Bryce *Amer. Commw.* II. II. xii. 433 The composition of a primary is determined by the roll or 'check list,' as it is called, of ward voters entitled to appear in it. — **(4) 1874** B. F. Taylor *World on Wheels* I. 63 The tremendous voice of the check-master tolls like a bell, '4689 Cleveland'! . . . and the baggage-car is as lively with all sorts of baggage as corn in a corn-popper.

(5) 1922 *Tom Mooney's Mo.* (S.F.) Nov. 4/4 The miners were on strike against a cut in wages [and] abolition of the 'check-off' system. **1947** *Time* 17 March 24/1 They . . . abandoned the fight to get a closed shop, compulsory check-off, or maintenance of membership. — **(6) 1903** *Sears Cat.* (ed. 113) 354/5 Check Perforators . . . Check Protectors. — **(7) 1894** *Dly. Ardmoreite* (Ardmore, Okla.) 27 April 2/3 The accomplished check-raiser while here cut a very wide swath. **1903** *N.Y. Ev. Post* 19 Oct. 2 (*caption*), Notorious Check Raiser Jumps from Train. **1948** Chaplin *Wobbly* 252 Middleton was a commercial artist, a full-blooded Negro, and a 'four-time loser' at check-raising. — **(8) 1900** George Ade *More Fables in Slang* 154 After he had gone past, on his way to the checkroom, she would put some camphor on her handkerchief. **1948** *Mus. Sci. & Ind.* (Chi.) *Exhibit Finder* 2 Near the checkroom is the *Museum Mart,* where visitors may purchase a variety of articles identified with the Museum exhibits. — **(9) 1858** *Rep. Comm. Patents* (1859) I. 474 The seed may . . . be distributed from either hopper, and sown either in drills or check-rows. **1861** *Ill. Agric. Soc. Trans.* IV. 312 Most of the corn is now planted with drills, or check row machines. **1888** *Vt. Agric. Rep.* X. 26 He puts the crop in check rows, to be able to cultivate thoroughly both ways.

(10) 1888 *Sci. Amer.* n. s. LVIII. 298/1 Particularly for use on growing check-rowed and listed corn. — **(11) 1882** *Belleville* (Ill.) *Advocate* 9 June 4/4 (*advt.*), Haworth Check Rowers, with Wire or Cord. **1884** Knight *Supp. s. v. Check Rower.* 1. A corn planter. 2. An attachment to a corn planter by which it is made automatically to drop the seed corn at regular intervals of distance across a field [etc.]. — **(12) 1861** *Ill. Agric. Soc. Trans.* IV. 248 He must have a boy to tend the check-set of the corn-planter. — **(13) 1886** E. W. Howe *Moonlight Boy* 102 My friend left his own baggage at a check stand. **1904** F. Lynde *Grafters* 31 The train was in, and the porter had fetched Loring's hand-bag from the check-stand. — **(14) 1887** *Scribner's Mag.* Oct. 508/1 'I'll put a check-strap on him, if he won't do it!' a little chap exclaimed . . . using a phrase drawn from the training of horses; for the 'check-strap' in cow-boy parlance, controls the bit in the horse's mouth. **1889** *Cent.* 941/3 check strap. . . . In a harness, a strap passing between the fore legs of a horse and connecting the collar with the belly-band, designed to prevent the collar from riding up when the horse backs. **1906** F. Lynde *Quickening* 130 At the Woodlawn gates she pulled the old-fashioned, check-strap signal, and Scipio reined in his horses. **1909** *Cent. Supp.* 231 check strap. . . . A leather strap, extending from the bottom of the body of a carriage to the perch, to check the upward movement of the body.

(15) 1911 H. Quick *Yellowstone N.* ix. 234 Smythe made him admit that he had bought the tools, and had no check-stub of the payment. **1945** Gardner *Golddigger's Purse* 174 The last check stub in the book . . . is a check stub bearing the same date as the day of the murder. — **(16) 1944** *Sat. Review* 2 Sep. 31/1 A check-up in red pencil follows to be sure that all numbers have been used and no one number used twice. **1948** *Capital-Democrat* (Tishomingo, Okla.) 17 June 10/3 Complete auto check-ups to see if county motorists have their autos in good driving condition will be made in a safety lane in the county soon. — **(17) 1807** *Ann. 10th Congress* 1 Sess. I. 561 Take the following for the catchword or checkword, and you may very readily decipher the figures.

As the last term in **baggage, bank, cashier's, certified, cold, counter, furniture, gold, memorandum, overdrawn, pay, pin, rain, rubber, season, side, sight, train, traveler's check.**

***check,** *v.*[1] *tr.* To mark off (corn ground) preparatory to planting. Cf. **check,** *n.*[1]

[*a*1676 John Winthrop in *Philos. Trans.* No. 142 (1678) 1066 The *English* have now taken to a better way of Planting by the help of the Plough; in this manner; In the Planting time they Plough single Furrows through the whole Field, about 6 feet distant, more or less, as they see convenient. To these, they Plough others across at the same distance. Where these meet they throw in the Corn, and cover it either with the Howe, or by running another Furrow with the Plough.] **1768** Washington *Diaries* I. 265 At the first and last of which [plantations I] just began to check Corn G[roun]d. **1871** *Ill. Agric. Soc. Trans.* VIII. 239 After the field has been thoroughly prepared . . . proceed to check it off from east to west with a three-rowed marker. **1945** Botkin *My Burden* 168 And checking corn is running a straight row clean 'cross the field both ways, and it makes a check 'bout two feet square.

***check,** *v.*[2]

1. *intr.* To write or draw checks *for* (an amount), *against* (an account), etc.

1809 *Ann. 10th Congress* 2 Sess. 416 The money . . . is deposited in the Treasury as in a bank, to be checked for, whenever that commerce . . . shall be again reopened. **1869** *Atlantic Mo.* Sep. 376/1 This gentleman can check for much more than fifteen millions. **1912** Mulford *Buck Peters* 221 That beastly German had the cheek to get away with the money after all. He chequed against the blessed lot yesterday forenoon.

b. *tr.* To draw (money) from a bank by check.

1879 B. F. Taylor *Summer-Savory* 210, I am not quite sure it would not be a luxury to put a dollar into some bank just for the sake of checking it out. **1916** Du Puy *Uncle Sam* 28 In this way a depositor who never had a thousand dollars in the bank eventually checked out $50,000.

2. To consign (baggage) on a railroad, etc., receiving an identification check therefor. Also with *in, through.*

1846 *Dly. Ev. Traveller* (Boston) 16 July 3/2 Passengers . . . will consult their comfort and convenience by being particular to have their Baggage 'checked.' **1907** M. C. Harris *Tents of Wickedness* I. 89 She felt vaguely comforted that she should not have to buy the tickets nor to check her trunk. **1944** *Chi. D. News* 2 Nov. 1/1 Just been checking in the baggage since 7:30 this morning.

fig. **1860** *Richmond Enquirer* 6 Nov. 1/5 (Th.), Douglas men, will you follow Little Sandy Rives into Black Republicanism, for he has taken his ticket and checked his baggage through. **1884** SWEET & KNOX *Through Texas* 16 Phil Parker was pointed out to strangers as a gambler, and a man who had checked several of his acquaintances through to the other world.

b. To leave (articles) in charge of someone in return for a check.

1897 *Westminster Gaz.* 25 Feb. 10/2 Here are some . . . extracts from the programmes of the Chicago theatres. . . . 'Remove your hats during the performance. You can check them with the maid.' **1948** *Mus. Sci. & Ind.* (Chi.) *Exhibit Finder* 2 A charge of ten cents will be made for checking coats and hats.

3. To take or give a check for (articles left in charge).

1871 HOWELLS *Wedding Journey* i. 8 The ticket-seller was there, and the lady who checked packages left in her charge. **1888** *Amer. Humorist* 21 July (F.), Turning to the man who checks umbrellas and canes. **1948** *Time* 28 June 15/3 Mrs. Lawlor had quit work as a hat-check girl. 'After all, there's nothing to check in the summer,' she said.

4. *To check up*, to examine closely, count up, compare.

1889 *Kans. Times & Star* 15 Mar., He says Willis checked them up closely and discovered nearly 600 saloons here, and only 400 paying a license. **1920** *Cosmopolitan* Oct. 134/2 He checked up very carefully all promissory notes, particularly the unsecured ones and those overdue. **1948** *Omaha World-Herald* 20 June 1/2 The buyer of the used car (owner No. 4) decided to check up on its mileage.

5. *To check in*, *fig.* to die. *Colloq.* Cf. **check,** *n.*² **3. b.**

1912 RAINE *Brand Blotters* 338 They couldn't take me alive at all, and I reckon before I checked in a few of them would.

6. *intr.* To agree upon being compared.

1928 *Publisher's Wkly.* 22 Dec. 2491/2 One of the sheets . . . checked closely with fiction which was found in the Gottschalk store.

***checked,** *a. checked and balanced,* (see quot. and cf. *checks and balances*). — **1796** *Gazette U.S.* 5 Nov. (Th.), The checked and balanced government that Mr. Adams so much admires.

***checker,** *n.* [In sense **1.** possibly a different word.]

1. *The checker*, the very thing. *Colloq.*

*c***1850** WHITCHER *Widow Bedott P.* 324 'That's the checker,' said Teeters. **1854** M. J. HOLMES *Tempest & Sunshine* ix. 122 'By Jupiter!' said Mr. Middleton, 'that's just the checker. No wonder I like you so well.' **1911** H. QUICK *Yellowstone N.* 97 When I hadn't but four sections I thought 'twas about the checker f'r a man with three sons.

2. *pl.* (See quot.)

1920 *Sears Cat.* (ed. 140) 634 Cracker Jack or Checkers. The popular popcorn, peanut and molasses confections.

3. In combs.: (1) **checker-back loon,** the common loon, *Gavia immer;* (2) **bee,** an occasion upon which a group engages in playing checkers; (3) **belly,** (see quot.); (4) **berry,** see as a main entry; (5) ***board,** (see quot.); (6) **man,** a piece used in the game of checkers; (7) **up,** one who inspects or examines carefully, cf. ***check,** *v.* **4.**

(1) **1893** ROOSEVELT *Wilderness Hunter* 132 Now and then great checker-back loons drifted buoyantly by; stopping with bold curiosity to peer at the white tent gleaming between the tree-trunks. — (2) **1919** CADY *Rhymes of Vt.* (1923) 176 The jiff the prison guards was free They'd start a guardroom checker bee. — (3) **1930** PHILLIPS & LINCOLN *American Waterfowl* 287 white-fronted Goose (*Anser albifrons albifrons*) *Other names:* Brant, Speckle-belly, Checker-belly, . . . California Goose.

(5) **1909** *Cent. Supp.*, Checker-board. . . . In American foot-ball, a term sometimes applied to the field of play. — (6) **1883** E. E. HALE in *Harper's Mag.* Jan. 278/2 He had built up a little tower of checker-men. **1893** *Outing* Feb. 95/1 Last winter, however, he worked out no less than sixty tricks, using checker-men for players, and had them diagramed . . . for the use of the Harvard eleven. — (7) **1911** ROLT-WHEELER *Boy with Census* 251 A checker-up compares them with the original schedules, and if incorrectly punched, punches a new card. **1920** C. R. COOPER *Under Big Top* 8–9 To say nothing of the 'checkers up' who inspect the work of the various cars.

As the last term in **lumber checker.**

***checkerberry,** *n.* Any one of several red berries or the plants bearing these, as the foxberry or bearberry, the partridge-berry, the creeping wintergreen, etc. Also attrib.

1776 in *Pa. Mag. of Hist* I. (1877) 173 Some families [had] no other bread but patatoes for sometime, which with Checkerberry tea was seen the only food for a woman with a Sucking Child at her Breast. **1784** CUTLER in *Mem. Academy* I. 444 *Arbutus.* . . . Foxberry. Checkerberry. . . . The berries are rather of an agreeable taste, and are sometimes eaten by children in milk. **1843** *Amer. Pioneer* II. 125 In descending the Alleghany, the children and girls were much delighted at seeing the sides of the road covered with the vivid green leaves and bright scarlet berries of the 'Partridge bush,' or 'Checkerberry.' **1891** *Amer. Folk-Lore* IV. 149 Gaultheria procumbens seems to have an almost endless variety of epithets. . . . We [in New Hampshire] also knew the name *Checkerberry.* **1947** BEROLZHEIMER *Regional Cookbook* 54 Candy, in the limited varieties then made, one being a large checkerberry medal stamped with a head, was also plentiful.

checkered adder. =**milk snake.** Cf. **chequered.** — **1839** STORER *Mass. Reptiles* 227 *Coluber eximius.* Chicken snake; milk snake; and chequered adder. **1843** STEPHENS *High Life N.Y.* II. 172, I say, par, did you ever see a checkered adder a charmin a bird?

***checking,** *n.*

1. The consigning of baggage in return for a check. Cf. **check,** *v.*² **2.**

1870 W. F. RAE *Westward by Rail* 77 Excited passengers are rushing about in quest of the luggage which, despite the system of 'checking,' is often going astray or getting out of sight. **1886** B. P. POORE *Reminisc.* I. 41 Baggage checks and the checking of baggage were then unknown.

2. a. checking account, a bank account against which checks may be drawn. **b.** ***checking room,** =**check room.**

(a) **1926** *Springfield W. Republican* 19 Aug. 10 She preferred the more generous way, and they had a joint checking account. **1948** *So. Bend* (Ind.) *Tribune* 15 Aug. I. 4/2 An additional $800,000 cash was in her personal checking account. — (b) **1910** *N.Y. Ev. Post* 13 Dec. 7 Mr. Spottford arrived at the station carrying a small grip, and asked Charles where the checking-room was.

cheechako tʃiˈtʃɑko, *n. Alaska* and *N.W.* [f. Chinook Jargon.] A newcomer, tenderfoot. Also attrib.

1897 *Chi. Record* 2 Mar. 4/4 Many a 'Checaco' (tenderfoot) on his way to the mines, with a pack on his back, has thrown down his pack and struck back for town, . . . cursing the country and its mosquitoes. **1904** ROBINS *Magnetic North* II. 118 It is curious to see how soon travellers get past that first cheechalko meeting feeling that it is a little 'nervy' . . . to walk into another man's house uninvited. **1945** *Sky Line Trail* June 21/1 Cheechakos are advised, however, not to attempt to skin a . . . [raccoon] more than four times, as it has a bad effect on its . . . disposition.

cheer leader. One who leads the cheering, esp. at college athletic events.

1909 *Dly. Maroon* (Chi.) 2 Oct. 4/3 The cheer leaders for the year will take the student body in hand and will give it the first training of the year in yelling and singing. **1918** *Chi. Herald-Examiner* 2 Oct. 11/3 (*heading*), Cheer Leaders. **1946** *Life* 18 Nov. 114/2 Cheerleader Aldreda Young, 16, calls for a 'Hey, gang, are we gonna win!' during football game with Shaw college.

***cheese,** *n.*

1. (See quot.) *Obs.*

1841 DE SMET *Letters* (1843) 120 To preserve the [buffalo] meat it is cut in slices, thin enough to be dried in the sun; sometimes a kind of hash is made of it, and this is mixed with the marrow taken from the largest bones. This kind of mixture is called Bull or Cheese, and is generally served up and eaten raw.

2. In combs.: (1) **cheese apple,** [cf. Du. *kaas-*, *kaasjeappel*], a variety of flat, cheese-shaped apple, *obs.;* (2) ***box,** a term of derision used by the Confederates for Ericsson's "Monitor," and other armor-clad vessels of similar design, also attrib.; (3) **Cheesedom,** "a name facetiously applied to the cheese-producing part of the Western Reserve" (Th. Supp.), *obs.;* (4) **cheese factory,** [cf. Du. *kaasfabrick*], a place where cheese is made on a large scale; (5) **house,** [cf. Du. *kaashuis*], a house or room in which cheese is made or stored; (6) **tub,** =**cheesebox,** *obs.*

(1) **1709** LAWSON *Carolina* 109 We have . . . the long Apple . . . Flattings, Grigsons, Cheese-Apples, and a great number of names. **1867** WARDER *Pomology* 427 Flat Apples . . . Cheese. This fruit was received from . . . Grass Hills, Gallatin County, Kentucky. — (2) **1862** *N.Y. Tribune* 10 June, Where is the Monitor? We have not heard a word of the little cheese-box since the repulse in James River until yesterday. **1863** KETTELL *Hist. Rebellion* II. 466 Her singular and diminutive appearance . . . was described by the enemy as that of a 'cheese-box upon a plank.' **1871** *Harper's Mag.* XLIII. 482/1 Ericsson's 'cheese-box' monitors. — (3) **1867** *Cong. Globe* 14 Feb. 1253/3, I am very sorry that my colleague and friend is not here to defend his butter and cheese, representing as he does what in Ohio we call 'Cheesedom.' — (4) **1868** *Mich. Agric. Rep.* VII. 228 The cheese factory of Rufus Baker & Son . . . received the past season the milk of 600 cows. **1896** *Vt. Agric. Rep.* XV. 23 We believe the dairymen of

Vermont are making a mistake in not establishing more cheese factories.

(5) **1759** in CAROLINE HAZARD *College Tom* (1894) 79 Had in ye Cheese House 46 Cheeses new milk with them in ye Press & 8 Cheeses made every other day at first. **1868** *Mich. Agric. Rep.* VII. 252 You know better than I can tell you whether your cheese-houses are encumbered to any extent with surplus or unsaleable stock. — (6) **1867** HEADLEY *Farragut & Nav. Commanders* 519 Worden in his 'cheese-tub,' as the rebels called her, was crowding all steam to overtake his powerful adversary.

As the last term in **American, cottage, factory, filled, full cream, full milk, Goshen, hand, head, hog's, hog's head, pineapple, pot, store, white oak cheese.**

cheesery 'tʃizərɪ, *n.* A cheese factory. — **1883** *Harper's Mag.* Apr. 692/2 From the upper stories of these cheeseries were long wooden gutters leading to the ships.

cheeweeh 'tʃiˌwi, *n.* =**chewink.** *Obs.* — **1796** MORSE *Amer. Geog.* I. 210 [Birds of the United States include] Towhe Bird, Pewee, Cheeweeh. **1832** WILLIAMSON *Maine* I. 143 The Pewit, or Cheeweeh, lives in the summer months about barns and out buildings.

Chehalis tʃə'helɪs, *n.* [Native word of unknown significance.] A name used collectively for several Salishan tribes on Chehalis River and its tributaries in the state of Washington. Also the language of these Indians.

1844 LEE & FROST *Oregon* 103 The remainder they take prisoners, and convey them to the north, and sell them to their Clatsop, Chenook, or Checalish neighbors. **1849** ROSS *First Settlers Ore.* (1923) 95 All the Indian tribes inhabiting the country about the mouth of the Columbia ... may be classed in the following manner: (1) Chinooks; ... (9) Multnomas; and (10) Chickelis. **1894** *Amer. Anthrop.* July 300 All these languages—the Nootka, Nisqually, Chinook, Chihailish, and others—were alike harsh in pronunciation. **1940** SMITH *The Puyallup-Nisqually* 19 Most of the informants were familiar with the Chehalis.

***chelone,** *n.* =**turtlehead.** Cf. **turtle chelone.**

1784 CUTLER in *Mem. Academy* I. 464 *Chelone*.... Chelone. Fish-head. Snake-head. Blossoms in spikes; white. **1875** *Amer. Naturalist* IX. 388 With these charming plants are found ... white chelone. **1943** PEATTIE *Great Smokies* 199 The most brilliant flower in bloom was the great lavender-purple turtlehead, *Chelone Lyoni*, named, of course, for the John Lyon who died at Black Mountain.

Chemehuevi ˌtʃemə'wevə, *n.* [Native word of unknown significance.] "A Shoshonean tribe, apparently an offshoot of the Paiute, formerly inhabiting the E. bank of the Rio Colorado from Bill Williams fork to the Needles and extending westward as far as Providence mts., Cal." (Hodge). Also attrib.

1858 IVES *Colo. River* (1861) 54 A small party belonging to a tribe called the Chemehuevis came into camp this evening. **1884** *Davenport Acad. Nat. Sci. Proc.* IV. 109 As the Chemehuevi Indians formerly visited the new settlements, it is more than probable that they were the authors of the drawings. **1903** JAMES *Indian Basketry* 67 The Chemehuevis live on a reservation on the California side of the Colorado River not far from the town of Needles. **1940** JAEGER *Calif. Deserts* 120 The Chemehuevi, perhaps the most miserable Indians in the West, were undoubtedly victims of their environment. **1948** *Desert Mag.* Aug. 22/2 The Indians in this village were probably of the Chemehuevi tribe.

b. (See quot.)

1925 BRYAN *Papago Country* 108 The younger alluvium, of Chemehuevis age, forms a well-defined terrace.

chemise brush. =**chamisal.** — **1897** *Outing* XXX. 552/1 The deer's favorite browse is chemisal—'chemise brush' it is commonly called.

chemuck tʃə'mʌk, *n.* *N.W.* [Cf. Shasta dial. *si-hi-mik*, acorn mush.] (See quots.)

1853 *S.F. Alta California* 22 April 1/7 The warrior partook heartily of an abundant lay-out of *chemuk*, composed of pulverized acorns, grass seed and preserved worms. **1868** *Dispatch & Vanguard* (S.F.) 5 Dec. 4/7 His warriors will saw wood and beg biscuit and gambol upon the square (and likewise upon an old blanket for chemuck and short bits and apparel). **1888–90** BARRERE-LELAND I. 241 Che-muck (American), food; taken from the Indians of the North-West, and now current among the miners.

chenango tʃə'næŋgo, *n.* [App. f. Seneca *ochenango*, large bull thistles.] A variety of potato. *Obs.* — **1838** COLMAN *Mass. Agric. Rep.* 34 The Chenango, sometime called the Mercer, or Pennsylvania Blue. *c***1887** in *Amer. Sp.* (1948) April 112/2 In 1828 the Chenango came around, a large clouded variety (of potato).

cheniere 'ʃɪnərɪ, *n.* Also **chinnery.** [La. F. *chênière*.] A liveoak forest or grove. Cf. **shinnery.**

1847 *De Bow's Review* III. 257 They have acquired the name of the chenaies. **1885** *Outing* Feb. 337/2 In the intervening hours, however, you can fish from the bank, seated on some *chênière* in the shade of umbrageous oaks, between which long vistas extend. **1908** *Sat. Ev. Post* 24 Oct. 11/1 The moon shone down kindly ... on a tiny figure ... racing along the trail ... across a stretch of 'chinnery' where the sand was deep and the gallant old mare labored direfully.

***chequer,** *v. tr.* To lay off (land) in squares or rectangles preparatory to planting. Cf. **check,** *v.*[1]

1788 WASHINGTON *Diaries* III. 378 At Muddy hole, One plow ... was employed in chequering ... the three feet ridges which had been plowed for Pease. **1800** TATHAM *Agric. & Commerce* 56 It is also to be remembered, that a crop of maize is constantly ploughed and hoed, from the time of breaking up the ground, and *checquering* it. *c***1836** CATLIN *Indians* II. 158, I have seen the rich Louisianian chequering out his cotton and sugar plantations.

***chequered,** *a.* and *adv.*

1. *a.* Denoting snakes and bugs having checks or checkered markings. Cf. **checkered adder.**

1675 JOSSELYN *Two Voyages* 112 The Checkquered snake, having as many colours within the checkquers shadowing one another, as there are in a Rainbow. **1827** J. L. WILLIAMS *West Florida* 29 The garter, riband, green, chequered, and glass snakes, make up the account of this species, in West Florida. **1838** GOSSE *Letters* 210 A pretty, but offensive bug, the Chequered Bug (*Hammatocerus Purcis?*), is found crawling on plants, in gardens, &c.

2. *adv.* (See quot.) *Rare.*

1852 BRISTED *Upper Ten Th.* i. 33 The team are greys and chestnuts ... driven chequered: that is, the horses of the same color diagonally.

chequet, see **chickwit.**

Cheraw 'tʃirɔ, *n.* [Native word of unknown meaning.] (See quot. 1907.) In full **Cheraw Indians.**

1739 in A. GREGG *Hist. Old Cheraws* (1867) 9 On Saturday last ... arrived in this town eleven of the chief men among the Catawbas and Cheraw Indians. **1907** HODGE *Amer. Indians* I. 244/2 Cheraw. An important tribe, very probably of Siouan stock, formerly ranging in central Carolina e. of the Blue ridge, from about the present Danville, Va., southward to the neighborhood of Cheraw, S.C. **1943** PEATTIE *Great Smokies* 17 DeSoto ... calls this country Xuali (in English rendered Sualla), which is probably the Indian word Suwali, one of the names for the Cheraw Indians.

cherimoya ˌtʃɛrɪ'mojə, *n.* [Amer. Sp. *chirimoya* in same sense. An Amer. borrowing.] A small tropical American tree, *Annona cherimolia*, or the sweet juicy fruit of this.

[**1772** ULLOA *Noticias Americanas* 99 En esta clase sentran lo *Chirimoyas, Aguacates*, 6 *Paltas, Guabas*, 6 *Pacaes, Nísperos, Guayabos*, ... y *Plátanos*.] **1825** H. PAULDING *Journal of Cruise* (1831) 51, I prepared the ground and made quite an extensive plantation of orange, lemon, cheromoya, apricot ... and a variety of other fruits. **1872** MARK TWAIN *Innoc. at Home* xviii. (1882) 375 We had an abundance of fruit in Honolulu, of course, Orange, pine-apples, bananas, ... and a rare and curious luxury called the chirimoya, which is deliciousness itself. **1928** BAILEY *Cyclo. Horticulture* 737/2 The cherimoya is considered by many to be the finest of the subtropical fruits.

cherioni ˌtʃɛrɪ'onɪ, *n.* *S.W.* [App. native name.] A soapberry, *Sapindus marginatus*, found in the Southwest. Also attrib. and as a proper name. — **1925** BRYAN *Papago Country* 44 Cherioni is popularly thought to be an unfailing indicator of water, a tradition derived from the Papagos. *Ib.* 182 The site of Cherioni Well was chosen because of the presence of a large cherioni tree.

chermany 'tʃɜmənɪ, *n.* [Origin unknown.] (See quot. 1889.)

*c***1866** BAGBY *Old Va. Gentleman* 49 He must now learn to cut jackets, play hard-ball, choose partners for cat and chermany. **1889** *Cent.* 948/3 Chermany, ... in the southern United States, a variety of the game of base-ball. **1904** M. D. CONWAY *Autobiog.* I. 35 Our recess games were chiefly chermany and handy.

Cherokee 'tʃɛrəˌki, *n.* ["The tribal name is a corruption of Tsálăgĭ or Tsárăgĭ, the name by which they commonly called themselves, and which may be derived from the Choctaw *chiluk-ki*, 'cave people'" (Hodge).]

1. An Indian of a powerful tribe once occupying the entire southern Allegheny mountain region, often in pl. as a tribal designation.

[**1699** in W. J. RIVERS *Hist. S.C.* (1856) 449 If he were impowered ... he would forthwith ... take with him 50 White men and 100 of the Chirakues Indians to be his Guard.] **1721** in *N.C. Col. Rec.* II. 422 The remaining 3800 Indians are the Cherokees, a Warlike Nation. **1789** *Ann. Congress* I. 22 Aug. 68 Treaties were formed by the United States with the Cherokees. **1865** *Memphis D. Commercial* 24 Sep. 1/2 The work of reconciliation seems to be completed among all the tribes, except among the Cherokees. **1947** *Democrat* 11 Sep. 4/3 The word 'Cherokee' is derived from the Choctaw word 'Chilukki,' meaning 'cave people.'

b. White Cherokee, see ***white.**

2. The language of the Cherokees, usu. as a symbol of remote learning or of something unintelligible.

1788 ATKINSON *A Match* 52 This is all Cherokee to me—I don't understand a word of your simile. **1835** B. D. WINSLOW [*Harvard*] *Class Poem* 14 He peruses Persian, Hebrew, Greek Or dips for pleasure into Cherokee. **1852** *Harper's Mag.* V. 395/2 The boys listened in silent awe to the eloquent appeal of the 'Luminary of the West,' but it was all Cherokee to Billy.

3. a. A Cherokee way or custom. **b.** =**Cherokee pony.** Both *rare.*

(a) 1834 CARUTHERS *Kentuckian* I. 220 We might show them fellers a little of the real Cherokee. — **(b) 1839** *Knickerb.* XIII. 245 Never do I feel more vividly the pride of existence, than when . . . mounted on my swift-footed Cherokee.

4. In combs.: (1) **Cherokee agent,** an Indian agent stationed among the Cherokees, *obs.;* (2) **alphabet,** the syllabary devised by the celebrated Cherokee half-breed, Sequoya (d. 1843); (3) **claimant,** a claimant to land assigned to the Cherokees in the West to secure their removal from their homes east of the Mississippi; (4) **hedge,** a hedge of Cherokee roses; (5) **laws,** the tribal laws of the Cherokee Indians as collected and printed in the characters invented by Sequoya, cf. **Cherokee alphabet;** (6) **medicine,** vegetal medicine allegedly similar to that used by the Cherokees, *obs.;* (7) **Nation,** the Cherokee tribe of Indians; (8) **outlet,** see as a main entry; (9) **plum,** =?**Chickasaw plum,** *obs.;* (10) **pony,** (see quot.), *obs.;* (11) **rose, strip,** see as main entries; (12) **turkey,** (see quot.), *rare.*

(1) 1821 NUTTALL *Trav. Arkansa* 130, I had again the pleasure of seeing the brother of the late governor Lewis, now Cherokee agent. — **(2) 1845** *Cherokee Advocate* (Tahlequah, Okla.) 6 Mar. 3/2 Recently intelligence has been received, which renders it highly probable that the Inventor of the Cherokee Alphabet, has not, as is generally supposed, been gathered to his fathers, but is still among the living. **1947** *St. Louis Globe-Democrat* 30 Mar., Among them was the famous Sequoya, inventor of the Cherokee alphabet, who has been called the most gifted man ever produced by the Indian race. — **(3) 1845** *Cherokee Advocate* (Tahlequah, Okla.) 9 Jan. 3/1 The attention of Cherokee claimants is invited to the Notice of the *Honorable Commissioner,* inserted in another column. — **(4) 1836** GILMAN *Recoll.* (1838) 89 It was his delight to . . . enter the avenue where the Cherokee hedge shut out the view. **1888** *Harper's Mag.* May 867/1 Their only exit lay at the end of the Cherokee hedge.

(5) 1831 *American* (Harrodsburg, Ky.) 11 Mar. 1/1 Would the House have a specimen of these Cherokee laws? — **(6) 1865** SALA *Diary* I. 230 Nothing is left of the Cherokees, but disgusting mural advertisements of 'Cherokee Medicines.' **1867** W. H. DIXON *New America* II. 96 These people say, they want no Cherokee medicines, no plantation bitters, no Bourbon cocktails. — **(7) 1741** *S.C. Hist. Soc. Coll.* IV. 20 The General acquainted his Honr . . . that he had sent up an officer into the Cherokee Nation. **1946** FOREMAN *Last Trek* 218 Forty went to the Cherokee Nation. — **(9) 1781–2** JEFFERSON *Notes* (1787) 36 Cherokee plumb. *Prunus sylvestris fructu majori.* **1842** BUCKINGHAM *Slave States* I. 180 The Cherokee plum, now putting forth its blossoms, was like the black-thorn of England in May, and produces a small, round, harsh, and sour fruit, like the sloe.

(10) 1834 SIMMS *Guy Rivers* II. 138 The reader has already heard something of the Cherokee pony. . . . They are a small, but compactly made and hardy creature. — **(12) 1893** *Columbus* (O.) *Dispatch* 30 Nov., We . . . beg leave to present you with the accompanying 'Cherokee turkey,' alias bald eagle, in time for approaching Thanksgiving festival.

c. Used as an adj. in the predicate. *Obs.*

1765 J. HABERSHAM *Letters* 36 Our clear Creek Leather is now rather esteemed better than Cherokee. **1844** *Sucker* (Pittsfield, Ill.) 19 July 3/4 The Cherokee Advocate will be printed on an imperial sheet with new type, both English and Cherokee, every week, at *Three Dollars* per annum. **1878** RUEDE *Sod-House Days* 211 Sam Hoot has a pair of oxen; one Texan, thin as a board—the other Cherokee, with warbles, i.e., worms in the flesh under the skin.

Also *Cherokee bead, cattle, chief, country, expedition, grape, language, mission, people, tongue, town, treaty, tribe, woman,* etc.

Cherokee ˈtʃɛrəˌki, *v.* **1.** *tr.* Of women: To arrange (the hair) in the manner of Cherokee women. *Obs.* **2.** *out-cherokee,* to excel greatly. *Rare.*

(1) [**1709** LAWSON *Carolina* 191 The Hair of their [*sc.* Cherokee women's] Heads is made into a long Roll like a Horses Tail, and bound round with *Ronoak,* or *Porcelan,* which is a sort of beads they make of the Conk-Shells.] **1765** in *Amer. Hist. Mag.* July (1890) 16 Married ladies in New York go constantly to the Assembly, and the girls don't Cherokee their hair. **1771** *Mass. Spy* 21 March (Th.), An old fashioned lady, with a foretop of hair Cherokeed, to imitate the Indian dress. — **(2) 1834** CARUTHERS *Kentuckian* I. 217, I wish I may be tetotally smashed in a cider-mill if that don't out-cherokee old Kentuck.

Cherokee outlet. A strip of land about fifty-seven miles wide extending westward from the 96th to the 100th meridian in the northwestern part of the present state of Oklahoma, granted by the U.S. in 1828 to the Cherokees as a western outlet from their lands to the buffalo hunting grounds. Sometimes regarded as identical with the Cherokee strip, sense **1.**

[**1828** in J. B. THOBURN *Hist. Okla* IV. (1916) 30 The United States further guarantees to the Cherokee Nation a perpetual outlet, west and free and unmolested use of all the country lying west of the western boundary of all the above described limits, and as far west as the sovereignty of the United States and their right of soil extend.] **1900** *19th Ann. Rep. B. A. Ethnol.* 142 The western outlet . . . being what was afterward known as the cherokee strip or outlet plus the two-mile strip extending westward along the south line of Kansas. **1942** DALE *Cow Country* 157 This reservation lay in the western part of the Territory just south of the Cherokee Outlet.

Cherokee rose. A Chinese climbing rose, *Rosa laevigata,* naturalized in the southern states. Also attrib.

1823 D. DOUGLAS *Journal* (1914) 26 Called on Messrs. Landreth: obtained the trees with two species of *Phlox* from Georgia . . . also roses Champneya, Cherokee, and two others. **1895** MUIR *John of Mts.* (1938) 339 Three dozen Cherokee rose bushes arrived today from Oakland. **1947** *Nat. Geog. Mag.* July 6/2 Apparently the Cherokee rose originally was taken overland from China to Persia, there to be picked up by the Arab Moslems and carried along with them when they planted their gardens in Spain. The Spaniards later brought it to the gardens of their settlements in Florida, from whence it escaped to become perhaps the most common and most celebrated 'wild' rose in parts of the South.

Cherokee strip.

1. A strip of land about three miles wide along the northern boundary of the Cherokee outlet but included in what is now the state of Kansas. Also, by confusion, the Cherokee outlet *q.v.*

1869 *Cong. Globe* 8 Dec. 29/2 Settlers on certain lands within the State of Kansas known as the 'Cherokee Strip.' **1936** BARNARD *Rider* 131 The distinction between the Cherokee Strip and the Cherokee Outlet having now been pointed out, the lands heretofore designated as the Cherokee Outlet will be called the Cherokee Strip. **1944** *U. of C. Mag.* May 4 Her father rode a race horse at the opening of the Cherokee Strip from the Kansas border to near the present town of Perry, which he later laid out as a park-studded community.

attrib. **1930** FERBER *Cimarron* 222 After all, a hundred other men in Osage were going to make the Cherokee Strip Run. **1945** M. JAMES *Cherokee Strip* 24 Dick Yeager was any Cherokee Strip youngster's ideal of what an outlaw should be and do.

2. In the House Chamber at Washington, that portion of the rear of the Republican (or Democratic) side of the chamber occupied by members of the opposite party when such a seating arrangement is made necessary by a preponderance of members of one of the two parties.

1905 *Baltimore American* 7 March 4 On the boundary of what is known as the 'Cherokee Strip,' or, in other words, the section on the Democratic side occupied by Republican Senators who cannot find desks on the Republican side. **1919** *Speech of J. L. Slayden in House of Representatives* 15 Jan. 7, I sat in the 'Cherokee strip,' now abolished.

cherridary ˈtʃɛrɪˌdɛrɪ, *n.* Also **cherryderry.** [Of E. Indian origin.] (See quot. 1904.) Usu. attrib. *Obs.*

1712 *Boston News-Letter* 11–18 Aug. 2/2 A Spanish Indian man . . . [wearing] a Cheridary Wastcoat. **1723** HEMPSTEAD *Diary* 132 Cuz Fox made my Cherryderry breaches. **1737** *Virginia Gazette* 30 Dec., Two pieces of striped blew and white Cherryderry. **1904** MCCLELLAN *Dress* 384 Cherridary.—An Indian cotton stuff like gingham. (1712 and after.)

***cherry,** *n.* In combs.: (1) **cherry birch,** the sweet birch, *Betula lenta;* (2) **bird,** =**cedar waxwing;** (3) **bug,** the rose beetle or bug; (4) **cobbler,** a cobbler (*q.v.*) made of cherries; (5) **cranberry,** (see quot.); (6) **currant,** a variety of red currant; (7) **land,** land upon which some variety of wild cherry grows; (8) **sawfly,** (see quot.); (9) **stone (clam),** a small round clam or quahog; (10) **tomato,** a variety of tomato bearing a small fruit, cf. **strawberry tomato.**

(1) **1810** MICHAUX *Arbres* I. 26 (*Betula lenta*). Black birch, cherry birch. **1901** MOHR *Plant Life Ala.* 72 In this valley the hemlock is accompanied by the sweet or cherry birch, . . . at home in the same northern life zone. — (2) **1805** LEWIS *Journal* VI. ii 187 (Criswell), This day a flock of cherry or cedar birds were seen. **1939** LINCOLN *Migration* 102 This species is the well-known 'cherry bird' that sometimes takes a heavy toll of small fruit. — (3) **1854** EMMONS *Agric. N.Y.* V. 79 The rosebug, or cherrybug, as it is called, is very destructive. — (4) **1946** *Sat. Ev. Post* 11 May 16/3 She went back to the desserts and picked out two cherry cobblers.

(5) **1874** *Dept. Agric. Rep. 1873* 445 The American cranberry is divided by growers and writers into three different varieties, viz., the Bell cranberry, . . . the Bugle cranberry, . . . the Cherry cranberry, which is similar in size, shape, and color to the cherry. — (6) **1855** *Chicago Times* 19 July 4/3 We were shown on Saturday a noble specimen of fruit called the 'cherry currant.' . . . Except for its transparency, the fruit might pass for grapes. It is a new variety. **1868** *Mich. Agric. Rep.* VII. 429 Currants—Red Dutch, Cherry, White Grape, and Black Naples. — (7) **1783** FLEMING in *Travels Amer. Col.* 663 Travelling through poor indifferent green cherry land. — (8) **1862** *Harper's Mag.* Nov. 743/2 The *Lyda cerasi*—'Cherry Saw-Fly'—is of the family of *Tenthredinida.* — (9) **1880** MARK TWAIN *Tramp Abroad* 574, I have selected a few dishes and made out a little bill of fare . . . as follows. . . . Cherry-stone clams. **1947** COFFIN *Yankee Coast* 294 Quahaugs, or round clams. Cherrystones, littlenecks to the outside world.

(10) **1847** DARLINGTON *Weeds & Plants* 251 The small round kind, known as 'Cherry Tomato,' is probably *L. Cerasiforme.* a**1870** CHIPMAN *Notes on Bartlett* 181 Ground Cherry. . . . Sometimes called Winter Cherry, and, of late, Cherry Tomato. **1892** COULTER *Bot. W. Texas* II. 297 *Lycopersicum esculentum.* (Cherry tomato.) . . . Introduced from tropical America.

As the last term in **Bing, bird, black, bunch, cabinet, choke, chunk, English, fire, ground, hollyleaf, Indian, Jerusalem, May, mountain, pigeon, pin, red, rum, sand, small, small red, whisky cherry.**

* **Chesapeake,** *n. attrib.* Denoting a large dog bred from a Newfoundland and a nondescript retriever, as **Chesapeake Bay (retriever), Chesapeake water dog.**

1873 *Forest & Stream* 16 Oct. 151/1 The Chesapeake water dog is a magnificent animal. **1921** *Outing* June 141/2 FOR SALE—Chesapeake Bay Retriever. . . . High class dog $250.00. **1946** *Time* 23 Dec. 63/3 Against him in the national championship last week at Herrin, Ill. were the 19 best retrievers—Labradors, Goldens and Chesapeake Bays—in the U.S. **1948** *Sat. Ev. Post* 24 Jan. 43/2 He greets the Bates Chesapeake Bay retriever.

ellipt. **1915** *Outing* Nov. 171/2 The Chesapeake will fetch anything on earth that it is within his physical powers to move or handle.

b. Short for *Chesapeake oyster.*

1910 *Sat. Ev. Post* 8 Oct. 29/3 Now—oyster lovers *everywhere,* can have their favorite variety of the *world's best oysters . . . Blue Points, . . . Cape Cods, Chesapeakes* or *Gulfs.*

***cheshire,** *n.* (See quot. 1909.) — **1890** *Cent.* 6113/2 Cheshires and Victorias are white swine, originating in New York State, which do not represent distinct breeds. **1909** F. D. COBURN *Swine in America* 58 The Cheshire originated in Jefferson county, New York, about the middle of the nineteenth century. It has also been known as the Jefferson County hog, or Jefferson County White, and is supposed to be the result of crossing a Yorkshire boar upon native sows having considerable Suffolk blood. The Cheshire is always white, with a pinkish skin.

chessy ˈtʃɛsɪ, *a.* Full of chess. *Rare.* — **1842** C. M. KIRKLAND *Forest Life* I. 153 My wheat was unaccountable chessy, though I turned water upon it and kept it moist all summer.

* **chest,** *n.*

1. chest protector, a padded or inflated protective piece of equipment worn on the front of the body by a baseball catcher or plate umpire.

1889 *Cin. Comm. Gazette* 17 March 7/2 [When] he sprained the bosom of his pants . . . it was worth a gold medal to see Jim shift his chest protector around to his rear. **1948** *This Week Mag.* 1 May 14/2 [He] rubbed his chest protector and glanced up.

2. chest-(up)on-chest, an article of furniture so made as to resemble two chests of drawers placed one upon the other.

1819 NOAH *She would be a Soldier* I. i, I had put my house in such nice order—painted my walls—got a new chest upon chest. **1930** *Old Time N. Eng.* Oct. 87/1 An even richer chest-on-chest in the same style is privately owned.

As the last term in **camphor, cedar, community, hope, ice, war chest.**

* **Chester,** *n.*

1. Chester line, Ball, a type of draft horse presumably developed in Chester County, Pa. *Obs.*

1825 KEATING *Exped. St. Peter's River* I. 24 There are several appelations by which the different breeds of this useful animal are distinguished in Pennsylvania, such as the Conestoga, the Chester line, &c. but these are principally of a local import. **1839** in OMWAKE *Conestoga Teams* (1930) 91 The best model of the heavier kind of farmer's or wagoner's horse is the Suffolk Punch. It strongly resembles the famous Chester Balls and the Conestoga horses of Pennsylvania.

2. Chester White, a breed of large white hogs said to have been developed in Chester County, Pa. Also attrib.

1856 *Rep. Comm. Patents: Agric.* 61 The best breed of swine which we rear is the 'Chester White.' **1925** BRYAN *Memoirs* 34 My first experience with hogs was with a Chester White boar. **1948** *Capital-Democrat* (Tishomingo, Okla.) 17 June 1/1 The organization is emphasizing the Chester White breed by maintaining a boar to be used by the youths and adults of south central Oklahoma.

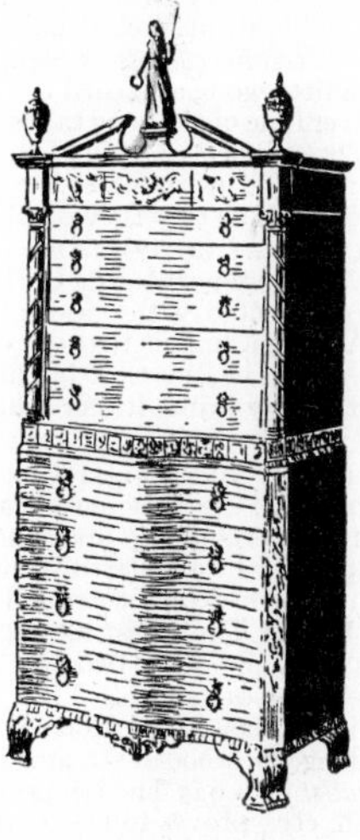

Chest-on-chest

chesterlite ˈtʃɛstɚˌlaɪt, *n.* (See quot. 1889.) — **1850** DANA *Mineralogy* (ed. 3) 678 Chesterlite. . . . Triclinic and resembling Albite. . . . Occurs at Poorhouse Quarry, Chester Co., Pa., implanted on dolomite either in single or clustered crystals. **1889** *Cent.* 951/1 chesterlite. . . . A variety of potash feldspar, occurring in small white crystals implanted on dolomite, from Chester county, Pennsylvania.

chestily ˈtʃɛstɪlɪ, *adv.* [f. **chesty,** *a.*] In a chesty manner. *Slang.* — **1908** G. H. LORIMER *J. Spurlock* iii. 59 So I explained rather chestily to Horton. **1931** *K.C. Times* 26 June, A Clinton man chestily announces that he does not fear divorce.

chestiness ˈtʃɛstɪnɪs, *n.* [f. **chesty,** *a.*] The action of being chesty. *Slang.* — **1910** OWEN JOHNSON *The Varmint* xiii. 181 'Sit down, Doc, and pay attention.' 'Why so much chestiness?' said Doc puzzled. 'I haven't sold anything to any of you have I?'

* **chestnut,** *n.*

1. A story, joke, etc., that has been often told or used. *Colloq.* Cf. **chestnut bell, chestnut planter, chestnutty.**

The numerous accounts of the origin of this use are all incapable of proof. A writer in *Notes & Queries* (1889) VII. 52 stated: "I first heard the word in 1882, in a theatrical chop-house (Brown's) in New York."

1883 in JOSEPH HATTON *Henry Irving's Impressions of America* I. 290 [*footnote*], The stock of last year's 'chestnuts' is being worked off; and I have one, a little shop-worn, which I have dusted for the occasion. . . . In America 'chestnut' is a slang phrase for an old story. **1886** *Boston Herald* June, One of the peculiar tidal waves of popularity having brought the term 'chestnut,' as applied to everything jocular and antediluvian, into prominence, its origin is being discussed. **1948** *Time* 5 April 106/2 He has omitted such chestnuts as *The Raven* and *O! Captain! My Captain!*

2. In combs.: (1) **chestnut-backed chikadee,** the American brown-backed chickadee, *Penthestes rufescens;*

(2) **bell,** (see quot. 1886 and cf. **1.** above), *obs.;* (3) **blight,** a blight, introduced from China, caused by a fungus, *Endothia parasitica*, which has virtually exterminated the American chestnut; (4) **coal,** see as a main entry; (5) **collared (lark) bunting,** =next, *rare;* (6) **collared longspur,** a longspur of the great plains; (7) **hangnest,** =**orchard oriole;** (8) **lamprey,** a chestnut-colored lamprey, *Ichthyomyzon castaneus*, sometimes found in streams in the Mississippi Valley; (9) **leaved oak,** the chestnut oak of the eastern states; (10) **oak,** see as a main entry; (11) **planter,** a retailer of stale jokes, *rare;* (12) **rail,** a fence rail made from a chestnut tree; (13) **rail worm,** (see quot.), *rare;* (14) **sided,** denoting a warbler, *Dendroica pennsylvanica*, found in the eastern states; (15) **weevil,** (see quots.); (16) **white oak,** an oak, *Quercus bicolor*, found chiefly in the eastern states.

(1) 1874 Coues *Birds N.W.* 22 Chestnut-backed Chickadee. . . . The centre of abundance of this species appears to be in Washington Territory. **1948** *Pacific Discovery* Mar.–Apr. 15/1 Of all the birds living in the court, the chestnut-backed chickadees seem to have priority. — **(2) 1886** *Detroit Free Press* 25 Sep., The now well-known chestnut bell. This is a little gong attached to the vest, and when an old story is told the silver tone of the gong takes the place of the words 'chestnut' or 'rats.' **1928** *Chi. Tribune* 8 Oct. 28/6 Chestnut bells were sold on the street corners and worn under the coat by many jokers, who would greet the telling of a story they considered a bit ancient by tinkling the 'chestnut bell.' — **(3) 1912** *Amer. Lumberman* 13 April 51/2, I am required by law to report to you that I have found on your premises chestnut trees infected with chestnut blight. **1948** Boyce *Forest Pathology* 498 A foreign fungus that does find a congenial host may do to it exactly what the chestnut blight fungus has done to American chestnut, or it may injure it more than any native fungus could.

(5) 1839 Audubon *Ornith. Biog.* V. 44 Chestnut-Collared Lark-Bunting, *Emberiza Ornata*, . . . is by no means a common bird; keeps in pairs, and appears to live exclusively upon the ground. **1858** Baird *Birds Pacific R.R.* 435 Chestnut-collared bunting. . . . A chestnut band on the back of the neck extending round on the sides. — **(6) 1917** *Birds of Amer.* III. 22 The Chestnut-collared Longspur (*Calcarius ornatus*) differs from the other two species in having the tail much shorter. — **(7) 1874** Coues *Birds N.W.* 192 Chestnut Hangnest . . . is abundant in the eastern portions of the Missouri, and of common occurrence along the wooded streams of the mountains. — **(8) 1885** *Amer. Naturalist* Sep. 925 The lamprey eel of Kansas, parasitic on the buffalo-fish, etc., proves to be usually the chestnut lamprey. — **(9) 1785** Marshall *Amer. Grove* 125 *Quercus Prinus.* Chesnut-leaved Oak. . . . The timber somewhat approaches toward that of Chesnut in appearance.

(11) 1890 *Harper's Mag.* Sep. 594/4 A fallow field for the chestnut planter. — **(12) 1783** *Huntington Rec.* III. 99, 1300 Chestnut Rails which fenced the above Trees at 3s per 100. **1945** *Sat. Review* 5 May 7/2 Chestnut rails where blue hawberries Scatter clouds, forbidden kiss Taunting merrily. — **(13) 1854** Emmons *Agric. N.Y.* V. 261. (Index), Chestnut-rail worm. [*Ib.* 118 *Clytus campestris.* . . . The larva is injurious to fallen chestnut timber, damaging it for rails.] — **(14) 1810** Wilson *Ornithology* II. 99 The Chesnut-Sided Warbler, *Sylvia Pennsylvanica* . . . is one of those transient visitors. **1945** *Nat. Geog. Mag.* June 742 Chestnut-sided Warblers build rather flimsy nests in low bushes in clearings or near woods from southern Canada to northern United States east of the Rockies.

(15) 1862 *Rep. Comm. Patents: Agric.* 604 The 'chestnut weevil,' found abundantly upon chestnut and chincapin trees, about the time the burs break out and expose the fruit in early autumn. **1891** *Cent.* 6870/2 Chestnut weevil, *Balaninus caryatripes*, a very long-nosed weevil whose larva is the common chestnut-grub of the United States. — **(16) 1708** Sewall *Diary* II. 222 Southward of the Swamp is a small Chestnut White-Oak. **1859** A. L. Hillhouse *Michaux's Sylva* I. 44 In Pennsylvania this species . . . is called Chestnut White Oak, Swamp Chestnut Oak, [etc.].

b. Denoting regions where chestnut is the prevailing growth, as **chestnut bottom, country, land, ridge.**

1842 in *Amer. Sp.* XVIII. 121, I know that you can distinguish walnut from chestnut bottom. — **1817** U. Brown *Journal* II. 372 Thence 21 Miles through a poor thin Chestnut Country without farmers. — **1755** L. Evans *Anal. Map Colonies* 28 Consisting in general of low dry Ridges of White-Oak and Chestnut Land. **1796** B. Hawkins *Letters* 18, [I] continue thro' rich uneven chestnut land for 5 miles. — **1754** in Chalkley *Scotch-Irish Settlement Va.* III. 323, 155 acres on a chestnut ridge in Beverley Manor. **1778** T. Hutchins *Topog. Description Va.* 1 They consist chiefly of *White Oaks*, and *Chestnut* ridges.

As the last term in **acorn, horse, lowland chestnut.**

chestnut coal. (See quot. 1924.) Also ellipt. and attrib.

1815 T. B. Hazard *Nailer Tom's Diary* (1930) 456/2 Paul Mumford sent me 80 Bushels of Chusnut Coal. **1858** *Rep. Comm. Patents* (1859) I. 105 The next screen contains the 'nut' and its successor the 'chestnut' size. **1924** Shurick *Coal Industry* 149 Anthracite coal is separated into seven common sizes, which have been standardized as follows: . . . chestnut, ¾ to 1⅜ inches; stove, 1⅜ to 2 inches [etc.]. **1947** *Black Diamond* 16 Aug. 55/4 Ten-cent-a-ton increases have been made in the cost of stove coal and a chestnut and pea mixture.

chestnut oak. Any one of several American oaks or species of oak having leaves resembling those of the chestnut, esp. the common southern species, *Quercus prinus*. Cf. **rock chestnut oak.**

1708 Sewall *Diary* II. 222 By the Stump grows up a fine little Chestnut Oak. **1709** Lawson *Carolina* 91 Chestnut-Oak, is a very lofty Tree, clear of Boughs and Limbs, for fifty or 60 Foot. They bear sometimes four or five Foot through all clear Timber; and are the largest Oaks we have, yielding the fairest Plank. . . . They are call'd Chesnut, because of the Largeness and Sweetness of the Acorns. **1832** Williamson *Hist. Maine* I. 109 The Chesnut Oak is found in the western parts of the State. **1941** Stuart *Men of Mts.* 22 Here are the graves—two graves dug under the chestnut-oaks—twin graves—side by side.

attrib. **1703** *Providence Rec.* V. 176 The Northwest Cornner is a Chessnut Oake Tree. **1835** *Survey of Property* Nov., *Pettigrew P.* (N.C. Univ.), Beginning at a big chuznut oak corner Tree. **1847** in H. Howe *Ohio* 27 They . . . collect the chestnut-oak bark from the neighboring hill tops.

chestnutting ˈtʃɛsˌnʌtɪŋ, *n.* Gathering chestnuts.

1775 Patten *Diary* 349 David and I went Chesnuting and we got a bushell. **1907** M. C. Harris *Tents of Wickedness* II. i. 113, I know I would apostatise for a chestnutting in Frost's woods on a mellow September afternoon. **1946** *Yankee* Sep. 30/2 There are still many of us living who remember with delight those joyous occasions when we went 'chestnutting' in the crisp October days.

chestnutty ˈtʃɛsˌnʌtɪ, *a.* [f. **chestnut,** *n.* **1.**] Of the nature of a chestnut, *n.* **1;** old and well known, stale. *Colloq.* — **1884** *Detroit Free Press* 14 May 2/1 Excitement about it soon dies away, and references to it are regarded as chestnutty in the press and in the pulpit. **1887** *Chi. Tribune* 27 Nov. 27/6 Ha! ha! laughed a Dearborn-street clerk as his employer told a story with a very ancient and chestnutty smell.

chesty ˈtʃɛstɪ, *a.* Conceited, self-assertive, self-important in demeanor. *Slang.* — **1899** George Ade *Fables in Slang* 90 All during the seventeen years Zoroaster and Zendavesta continued to walk chesty and tell people how good they were. **1948** *Time* 5 April 44/3 The Yankees walloped his Red Sox two for one, and pulled into Sarasota last week chestier than ever.

chevals ʃəˈvælz, *n.* Reduced form of **sherryvallies,** riding breeches. *Rare.* — **1803** L. Dow *Journal* 28 Oct., My pantaloons were worn out; my riding chevals were worn through in several places.

chevreuil ʃɛˈvril, *n.* [F., a deer.] A term applied to various deer (see quots.). *Obs.*

*c***1795** in McDermott *Glossary* 51 The dwarf Deer of the United States of which there is an abundance also in the Illinois Country and which the French of these countries call Chevreuil. **1832** R. Cox *Adv. Columbia R.* xxix. 319 The jumping deer, or chevreuil, together with the rein and red-deer, frequent the vicinity of the mountains in considerable numbers, and in the summer season they oftentimes descend to the banks of the rivers and the adjacent flat country.

chewallop tʃəˈwɑləp, *adv.* [Imitative.] With a flop or splash. *Colloq.* Cf. **ca-.**

1836 *Public Ledger* (Phila.) 27 July (Th.), Down I came chewhallop right on Deb's bonnet and her fixups, and overset the chair. **1840** Haliburton *Clockm.* 3 Ser. ii, I was on the edge of a wharf, and only one step more [and I] was over head and ears chewallop in the water. **1893** Russell *Americanisms* 29 Chewallop (or Kerwallop). A bow-wow word (onomatopoesis) to express the sound of a falling body. Generally spelled with 'ker'; but the other has the authority of Judge Haliburton.

* **chewing,** *n. attrib.*

1. chewing gum, a preparation of vegetable gum or resin, esp. chicle, sweetened and flavored, used for chewing. Also transf.

For an account of the beginning of the chewing gum industry in this country see *Amer. N. & Q.* June, 1945, 35–39.

[**1763** Mark Catesby *Hortus* 9 From between the wood and the bark [of the sweet gum tree] there issues a fragrant gum, which trickles from the wounded tree, and by the heat of the sun congeals into transparent resinous drops; which the Indians chew, esteeming it a preservative of the teeth.] **1850** *Chi. D. Democrat* 25 Oct. (*advt.*), Chewing Gum! A new and superior preparation of Spruce Gum. **1882** *Chi. Advance* 6 April 219 They are the 'chewing-gum' of literature, offering neither savor nor nutriment, only subserving the mechanical process of mastication. **1947** *Time* 3 Feb. 23/3 He was fond of chewing gum.

2. chewing tobacco, tobacco prepared for chewing.
1789 *Mass. Sentinel* (Boston) 28 Oct. 4/3 Also, Chewing Tobacco of various kinds, which he will sell as low as can be purchased at any Manufactury in Boston. **1835** Martin *Descr. Virginia* 175 A dark greyish soil . . . which produces the best chewing tobacco in the state. **1948** *Dly. Ardmoreite* (Ardmore, Okla.) 3 May 4/1 But cigarettes, chewing tobacco, and snuff stretch our generosity just a little too far.

b. chewing-tobacco tag, a small piece of metal, stamped with a brand name or other advertising matter, placed on plug tobacco by the makers.
1940 Mencken *Happy Days* 130 They found a pocket-knife, a couple of sea-shells, three or four nails, two cigarette pictures, a dozen chewing-tobacco tags, a cork, a slate pencil, an almost fossil handkerchief, and three cents in cash.

chewink tʃɪˈwɪŋk, *n.* [Imitative.] = **towhee.**
1794 *Philos. Soc. Trans.* IV. 110 This bird was the chewink, or ground-robin. **1858** *Atlantic Mo.* Dec. 865/1 The Chewink (*ringilla erythrophthalma*) is a very constant singer during four months of the year, from the middle of April. **1945** *Democrat* 21 June 2/3 The joree, also called towhee and chewink, one of the finch family, is getting more plentiful in Montgomery.

Cheyenne ʃaɪˈɛn, *n.* ["From the Sioux name *Shahi'yena*, *Shai-ena*, or (Teton) *Shai-ela*, 'people of alien speech,' from *sha'ia*, 'to speak a strange language'" (Hodge).] One of the most important warlike plains tribes of the Algonquian Indians; an Indian of this tribe.
1813 *Mo. Gazette* 15 May 1/2 Finding an inland tribe of indians calling themselves Shawhays, but known among the whites by the appellations of Cheyen-nes, we procured from these people an accession of forty horses. **1857** Gove *Letters* 28 The messenger reports 840 head of cattle stampeded about 30 miles beyond Kearney by the Cheyennes (pronounced as though written Shy-ans). **1946** Foreman *Last Trek* 296 Colorado troops attacked the Cheyenne in May.
attrib. **1804** Clark in *Lewis & C. Jrnls.* I. (1904) 175 We passed the . . . River Chien (or Dog River) (Chayenne). . . . (So called from the Chayenne Indians who live on the heads of it.) **1843** T. Talbot *Journals* 30 It consisted of about 20 Lodges of the Sheyenne nation. **1897** Inman *Old Santa Fe Trail* 279 The susceptible young hunter fell in love with a very pretty Cheyenne squaw. **1946** *New Yorker* 18 May 31/1 That was in August, '74, when all that Cheyenne trouble was brewing which ended in the Custer massacre of '76.

b. (See quots.)
1907 Mulford *Bar-20* ix. 94 He sat in his Cheyenne saddle like a centaur. *Ib.* xxv. 237 The saddle, a famous Cheyenne and forty pounds in weight, was black, richly embossed, and decorated with bits of beaten silver.

chia ˈtʃiə, *n. S.W.* [Amer. Sp. *chía* (< Nahuatl), in same sense.] Any one of various species of *Salvia*, or the seeds of this used in making a beverage. Also **chia seed.**
1896 W. R. Gerard in *Garden & For.* IX. 262 Chia—the Aztec name, according to Molina (*Vocab. Mexic.*) for the 'oily seeds' of some plant. **1919** J. Smeaton Chase *California Desert Trails* 78 The nourishing properties of chia seed should be better known. **1947** *Desert Mag.* May 28/3 Until the middle of June visitors will find . . . mimulus, chia, . . . mallow . . . in the Valley of Fire and other rocky areas.

* **chic,** *n.* and *a.* Stylishness; clever, neat, well-appearing. *Colloq.*
1889 Howells *Hazard of New Fortunes* I. ii. iv. 169 Where a girl doesn't seem very strong . . . no amount of *chic* is going to help. **1892** *N.Y. Tribune* 13 Mar. 16/6 It was very chic . . . for him to have preferred to resign the chief magistracy of the Republic . . . rather than to affix his signature. **1948** *This Week Mag.* 16 Oct. 29/2 One of them Hollywood flowered shirts is right chick on the right rooster.

Chicago ʃəˈkɑgo, *n.* Also **chicago.** [An Indian term variously explained as meaning skunk, wild onion, etc.]

1. (See quots.)
[**1817** in Haines *Amer. Indian* (1888) 718 The River Chicago (or, in the English, 'Wild Onion River').] **1867** Richardson *Beyond Miss.* 121 Passed beds of the wild onion many acres in extent. 'Chicago' is an Indian name for this plant. **1901** *Harper's Wkly.* 5 Oct. 291/2 The blue-flowered wild onion (chicagou) disputes inch by inch with the subdivider's sidewalks of artificial stone.

2. (*cap.*) In baseball, a defeat in which the losing team fails to score. Cf. **Chicago,** *v.*
1871 *N.Y. Herald* 5 July 3/4 They yesterday suffered a defeat which of all others is considered the most degrading which a first class club can meet with, viz.—a Chicago. **1874** *Field & Stream* 29 Oct. 183/2 As it was however, the Fly Aways managed to secure three runs during the last inning, thus saving themselves from a Chicago. **1947** R. Smith *Baseball* 73 For many years a shutout was officially designated, in the yearly guides, as a 'Chicago.'
attrib. **1886** *Chi. Tribune* 8 May 5/4 The Washington ball-players received a 'Chicago' defeat at the hands of the New York team at the polo grounds today. **1886** *Outing* July 488/2 It will be seen that three games were marked by 'Chicago' scores, and a majority of the contests were won by single-feature scores.

3. A form of card game otherwise known as *Newmarket* and *Michigan.*
1934 Webster. **1946** Morehead & Mott-Smith *Penguin Hoyle* 153 Michigan has many other names: Newmarket, Boodle, Chicago, Stops, etc.

4. In obs. combs. with reference to the well-known city: (1) **Chicago construction,** (see quot.); (2) **fever,** (see quot.); (3) **method,** (see quot.); (4) **platform,** (*a*) the platform adopted by the Republicans at their convention in Chicago in May, 1860, (*b*) the free-silver platform of William Jennings Bryan adopted at Chicago in 1896; (5) **syllabub,** (see quot.).
(1) **1901** *Black Scaffolding* 69 This furore for what is known in America as Chicago construction—viz., the erection of abnormally lofty buildings, was initiated more than a decade back by Mr. W. L. B. Tenny, of Chicago. — (2) **1869** Henry Deedes *Sketches South & West* 65 Immense fortunes have been made, many of them by the purchase and sale of building lots—so much so, that this traffic has earned for itself the appellation of the 'Chicago fever.' — (3) **1892** *Harper's Mag.* Feb. 427/1 They have adopted what they call 'the Chicago method.' . . . This plan is to construct the actual edifice of steel framework, to which are added thin outer walls or brick or stone masonry, and the necessary partitions of fire-brick, and plaster laid on iron lathing. — (4) (*a*) **1860** *Cin. Commercial* 29 Dec. 3/2 The Chicago Platform was framed with a view to recognizing the admissibility of a doctrine of absolute non-intervention. **1863** *Cong. Globe* 7 Feb. 801/1 You are ready [to vote for] a proposition . . . in violation of the Chicago platform, which your President [*sc.* Lincoln] declared was a law unto him. (*b*) **1896** *Chi. Tribune* 13 July 6/1 We do not feel that the Detroit Tribune loves the Chicago platform any better than it does the St. Louis platform. — (5) **1878** *Amer. Home Cook Book* 180 Chicago Syllabub. . . . Sweeten a pint and a half of sherry with the loaf of sugar in a bowl, and add nutmeg. Milk into it from the cow about two quarts of milk.

b. *Chicago of the South,* (see quot.).
1947 *Time* 27 Jan. 50/3 Houston calls itself the Chicago of the South, and indeed there are resemblances.

Chicago ʃəˈkɑgo, *v.* (See quots.) *Obs.* Cf. **Chicago,** *n.* **2.**
1891 Maitland *s.v.*, Chicagoed (Am.), the equivalent of 'skunked' or beaten out of sight. Some years ago Chicago had a baseball team which met with phenomenal success. Other competing clubs which ended the game without scoring were said to have been 'Chicagoed.' **1894** *Life* 5 July 11/2 Chicagoed: (*Der.* The name of an ancient city once the site of a world's fair.) Anything which has sunk into oblivion and is of no importance; hence, a blank score at any game or sport. **1909** *Cent. Supp.* 234/2 chicago . . . v.t. [In allusion to the assumed meaning of *Chicago*, namely, 'skunk' (it really means 'at the place of the skunk or skunks').] In *card-playing* and other games, to 'skunk' or 'whitewash' (an opposing side); that is, to prevent it from scoring any runs or points. [Slang, U.S.]

Chicagoan ʃəˈkɑgəwən, *n.* A native or inhabitant of Chicago, Ill.
1861 in M. W. Disher *Cowells in America* (1934) 378 At this time there are several thousand Zouave organizations in this section and the West, all dating their organization since the tour of the Chicagoians. **1882** *Advance* (Chicago) 27 July, A nervous, train-weary Yankee or Chicagoan. **1947** *Chi. Tribune* 27 June 17/4 As rash as the Chicagoan who discards his long underwear before June.

Chicagoese ʃəˈkɑgoˌiz, *a.* Characteristic of, spoken in Chicago. Also as a noun, = next. — **1855** *Knickerb.* XLVI. 315 Anything that offers a speculation is called in the Chicagoese language 'a good thing.' **1897** *Land of Sunshine* Oct. 205 The *Chap-Book* is . . . Chicago of the Chicagoese, [yet] it is far enough West to try to think for itself.

Chicagonese ʃəˌkɑgoˈniz, *n.* Used collectively for Chicagoans. — **1867** *Atlantic Mo.* March 335/2 The inconvenience to which they [draw-bridges] subject the busy 'Chicagonese' . . . must be seen to be understood. **1886** *Harper's Mag.* July 217/1 This bold statement . . . gave no small offense to the Chicagonese.

chicalote ˌtʃikəˈlotə, *n. S.W.* [Amer. Sp. (<Nahuatl) in same senses.] (See quots.)
1889 *Cent.* 954/1 chicalote. . . . A Mexican name given in southern California to a species of thorn-poppy. **1922** Smiley *Weeds of Calif.* 151 A native species with pure white flowers (*A. platyceras* var.

hispida Prain), known as 'Chicalote,' ranges from Lake County to San Diego. **1939** PICKWELL *Deserts* 47/1 The Mexicans call this plant the 'Chicalote.'

chicaric ˈtʃɪkərɪk, *n.* [Echoic.] The turnstone. — **1877** HALLOCK *Sportsman's Gazetteer* 164 The names Chicaric and Chickling have reference to their rasping notes.

chicharron ˌtʃitʃəˈron, *n. S.W.* [Sp. *chicharrón*, in same sense.] A crackling. — **1856** WEBBER *Tale of South Border* 48 (Bentley), Chicharrones are cracklings, and are one of the greatest delicacies the Mexicans know! **1932** BENTLEY *Sp. Terms* 120 *Chicharrones* are relished as a food by the poorer Mexicans but are eaten by Americans also.

chichicoe ˈtʃitʃəko, *n.* [f. native name.] A rattle of a gourd or small drum, used by Indians as a musical instrument. *Obs.*

1778 CARVER *Travels* 268 The music of the drums and chichicoues, make an agreeable harmony. **1818** EASTBURN *Yamoyden* (1834) IV. xiv. 266 With a rattling Chichicoe he led Or swift, or slow, their measured tread. **1840** *Knickerb.* XV. 405 The drum beat, the chiciqua rattled, and the song rose in the Mandan village.

chickadee ˈtʃɪkəˌdi, *n.* [Imitative.] Any one of various titmice, esp. the black-capped titmouse.

1839 AUDUBON *Synopsis* 79 *Parus atracapillus*, . . . Black-cap Tit.—Black-cap Titmouse, or Chicadee. . . . Never [seen] in the southern parts. **1904** WALLER *Wood-Carver* 73 The chicadees are fairly singing somersaults over one another. **1948** *Reader's Digest* March 148/1, I would busy myself about the cabin, feeding the chickadees that came to the tray on the windowsill.

transf. **1860** HOLLAND *Miss Gilbert* 62 When a feller gets tied to a wife and has a lot of little chickadees around him. **1889** K. MUNROE *Golden Days* XXV. 272 Ain't he just a chick-a-dee-dee with the cheek of a government mule!

As the last term in **brown-capped, chestnut-backed, Labrador brown-capped, Mexican, mountain chickadee.**

Chickahominy ˌtʃɪkəˈhɑmənɪ, *n.* [f. native name, app. meaning "hominy people."] "A tribe of the Powhatan confederacy, formerly living on Chicahominy r., Va." (Hodge).

1629 JOHN SMITH *Virginia* II. (1819) 16 Besides this, by the meanes of *Powhatan*, we became in league with our next neighbours, the *Chichahamanias*, a lustie and a daring people, free of themselves. **1688** *Cal. Va. St. Papers* I. 22 Petition of 'Herquapinck,' 'Paucough' and Hearseeque—'Monguys and Cheif Rulers of the poore and distressed Remnant' of Chickahominy Indians. **1800** JEFFERSON *Notes* 98 The *Chicahominies* removed about the year 1661, to Mattapony river.

Chickamauga ˌtʃɪkəˈmɔgə, *n.* [Native name, app. given by the Shawnees, Creeks, or Chickasaws.] "The name given to a band of Cherokee who espoused the English cause in the war of the Revolution and moved far down on Tennessee r. . . . in the neighborhood of the present Chattanooga" (Hodge). Also attrib.

1784 FILSON *Kentucke* 87 The Chicamawgees live about ninety miles down the Tenese from the Cherokees, at a place called Chicamawgee. **1794** P. MCDONALD & A. M'LEOD *Acct. Captivity* 3 We were fired on by a party of about 20 Indians of the Chickkemogga nation. **1943** PEATTIE *Great Smokies* 64 When Sevier finished his campaign there was no fight left in them, except for the cruel, depraved Chickamauga band of mongrels and outlaws down on the Tennessee.

chickaree ˈtʃɪkəˌri, *n.* [Imitative.] The American red squirrel.

[**1804** *Md. Hist. Mag.* IV. 9 These squirrels are exceedingly active and the mountaineers call them the Chiparee squirrel.] **1829** J. RICHARDSON *Fauna Bor. Amer.* I. 187 *Sciurus Hudsonius* (Pennant). The Chickaree. **1888** ROOSEVELT in *Cent. Mag.* June 211 Occasionally a chickaree or chipmunk scurried out from among the trunks of the great pines. **1948** *Sierra Club Bul.* Mar. 11 Every Sierra camper has looked up from his sleeping bag to see a scolding chickaree dropping pine cone scales from a tall tree.

b. The note of this creature.

1894 *Outing* Feb. 396/2 On top of this snow-covered log a chipmunk has jerked his nervous, impulsive little body along, with a sharp *chic-a-ree* at each convulsive motion.

Chickasaw ˈtʃɪkəˌsɔ, *n.* [See quot. 1927.]

1. *pl.* An important warlike tribe of Muskhogean Indians related in customs and language to the Choctaws, formerly occupying much of the present Mississippi and Alabama but now citizens of Oklahoma.

1722 COXE *Descr. Carolana* 14 Above 200 Miles up this River to the South East, is the great and powerful Nation of the Chicazas. **1770** PITTMAN *Present State* 6 The Chicashaws formerly were very troublesome to them. **1854** BENTON *30 Years' View* I. 626/1 The Chickasaws, Creeks, and Choctaws having previously agreed to remove. **1927** READ *La. Place-Names* 22 Chickasaw. The meaning of this name has been lost. Perhaps *Chickasaw* signifies 'rebellion,' the term referring to the separation of the Chickasaws from the Creeks and the Choctaws.

b. Short for **Chickasaw horse.** *Obs.*

1801 DAVIS *Travels* (1803) 210, I have, Sir, in Mr. *White's* stable the prettiest *Chickasaw* that ever trod upon four pasterns. **1824** SINGLETON *Letters* 76 The toughest and long-lived field horses [in Va.] are said to be the Chickasaws, or small calico-coloured ponies; often serving for thirty years.

c. Applied to a variety of grape, also short for **Chickasaw plum.**

1861 *Ill. Agric. Soc. Trans.* IV. 97 A new seedling which is called the Chickasaw, which is a very delicious grape. **1892** LYON *Fruits* 26 The disease known as plum pockets which, last year, attacked a few trees of *Chicasas*, has appeared again this season in a very few cases.

d. The language of these Indians.

1893 *Dly. Ardmoreite* (Ardmore, Okla.) 27 Dec. 3/1 Salus populi, suprema est lex, which, in Chickasaw, means, 'The people are first bidden to the feast.'

2. In combs.: (1) **Chickasaw float,** see **float;** (2) **horse,** (see quot. 1784), *obs.;* (3) **pea,** a now unidentifiable variety of pea, *obs.;* (4) **plum,** see as a main entry; (5) **rose,** =**Cherokee rose;** (6) **tea,** (see quot.), *obs.*

(2) **1779** in *Amer. Hist. Rev.* I. 94 The Pawné and Chicasa horses are very good and some of them delicate, but the common breed in this country [near Fort Henry] is triffling as they are adulterated. **1784** SMYTH *Tour* I. 139 Whilst I remained at this place I met with a very singular occurrence: having purchased a beautiful Chickasaw horse, named so from a nation of Indians who are very careful in preserving a fine breed of Spanish horses they have long possessed. — (3) **1837** J. L. WILLIAMS *Florida* 112 The cow pea, lady pea, and chickasaw pea, produce excellent crops during the heat of summer.

(5) **1835** C. J. LATROBE *Rambler in N.A.* II. 8 The Chickasaw-rose, a beautiful briar with snow-white expanded flowers and yellow stamina, was abundant near the plantations. **1887** *Harper's Mag.* Feb. 350/1 Along one side of his home . . . runs a superb hedge of Chickasaw roses. — (6) **1813** MUHLENBERG *Cat. Plants* 59 Chicasa tea. *Bignonia capreolata.*

Also *Chickasaw brave, country, fellow, Indian, land, language, man, nation, scalp, tribe, warrior,* etc.

Chickasaw plum. A native American plum from which several cultivated varieties have been developed.

[**1760** in FRIES *N.C. Morav. Rec.* I. (1922) 229 The wagon came back from Springhill, on the Cape Fear River, loaded with . . . rosemary, chickesaw plums and a kind of pine with very long leaves.] **1827** *Western Mo. Review* I. 323 The Chickasaw plum is common from 34° to the gulf of Mexico. **1942** VAN DERSAL *Ornamental Amer. Shrubs* 149 *Prunus angustifolia*, the chickasaw plum, is a thicket-forming twiggy shrub or small tree 4 to 10 feet high. **1948** *Dly. Ardmoreite* (Ardmore, Okla.) 18 July 4/4 Redbud trees, Chickasaw plums, . . . and cherries grow wild in the Arbuckles.

chickberry ˈtʃɪkˌbɛrɪ, *n.* =**checkerberry.**

1859 BARTLETT 76 Chequer berry, . . . also called Chickberry. **1871** DE VERE 402 It is also known as *chequer*-berry, and in New England occasionally as *chick*-berry. **1889** *Cent.* 954/3 Chickaberry. . . . A corruption of *checkerberry* [U.S.].

* **chicken,** *n.*

1. *W.* =**prairie chicken.**

1812 J. C. LUTTIG *Jrnl. Exped. Upper Mo.* (1920) 14 Oct. 85, 4 Men went out to hunt . . . got this Day 21 Chickens. **1866** in *Annals of Iowa* 3 Ser. XIV. 258 Killed a fine lot of Chickens & had a Pot Pie. **1901** WHITE *Westerners* XX. 189 The careful attention necessary for the destruction of the wily 'chicken' or experienced squirrel.

2. A barnyard fowl of any age.

1827 *Harvard Reg.* May 84 How in days of yore his Satanic Majesty rung the college bell at midnight, when some students were 'hooking' chickens. **1887** *Scribner's Mag.* May 622/1 The farm people had all retired with the chickens long before. **1944** HOLTON *Yankees* 173 Our man Holmes had a good-sized flock of chickens which Mrs. Holmes helped him tend.

3. (See quots.) *Slang.*

1846 H. N. MOORE *Fitzgerald and Hopkins* 141 'Them's the queerest chickens I ever seed in my life any how!' he remarked to himself, as he commenced concocting the juleps. **1888** J. D. BILLINGS *Hardtack* 52 A Marblehead man called his chum his 'chicken,' more especially if the latter was a young soldier. **1890** *Cong. Rec.* 21 April 3637, I saw an admirable illustration of the affection which a sailor will lavish on a ship's boy to whom he takes a fancy, and makes his 'chicken' as the phrase is.

4. (See quot.) *Obs.*

1925 E. FRASER & J. GIBBONS *Soldier & Sailor Words* Chicken, The: the U.S. Army colloquial term for the national 'Eagle' badge worn on caps and uniform.

5. In miscellaneous combs.: (1) * **chicken bone,** (see quot. 1908), *colloq.;* (2) **calling contest,** a contest in calling chickens; (3) **dispute,** a cockfight, a term of mock modesty app. used in an effort to evade prosecution under the law forbidding cockfighting, *obs.;* (4) **farm,** a farm upon which chickens are raised on a large scale, also **chicken farming;** (5) **feed,** see as a main entry; (6) **fight, fighter,** a cockfight, one who patronizes cockfighting, cf. **b.** (6) below; (7) **fixings,** see as a main entry; (8) **flip, flutter,** names of dances, *obs.;* (9) **gumbo,** gumbo in which chicken is a principal ingredient, also attrib.; (10) **house,** a poultry house; (11) **livered,** chicken-hearted, *colloq.;* (12) **man,** (*a*) a census taker, *humorous, obs.,* (*b*) one who deals in chickens; (13) **pull, pulling,** the sport of pulling a loosely buried live chicken from the ground in dashing past him on horseback; (14) **ranch,** *W.* a large chicken farm, hence **chicken rancher;** (15) **salad,** a salad in which chicken is the chief ingredient; (16) **shooting,** the shooting of prairie chickens; (17) **thief,** see as a main entry; (18) **wire,** wire fencing of a mesh sufficiently small to restrain chickens; (19) **yard,** an inclosed area for chickens.

(1) 1842 in THOMPSON *M. Jones* (1872) 88 You come under little sister's chicken bone, and I do believe she know'd you was comin when she put it over the dore. **1908** *D.N.* III. 298 chicken-bone, *n.* Specifically the wish-bone. — **(2) 1930** *Dixon* (Ill.) *Ev. Telegraph* 24 Sep. 2/7 There were many entries in the hog and chicken calling contests last evening. — **(3) 1844** *N.O. Picayune* 4 Mar. 17/2 There will be a *Chicken Dispute!* on the Troy Road, at the Half-way House, on Wednesday. **1849** *Ib.* 3 June 2/4 *Mr. E. P. S.* was the next witness called, a perfect 'bird' in his way, and who can't be beat, at 'heeling' in a 'chicken dispute.' — **(4) 1887** I. R. *Ranche Life Montana* 56 The worst of chicken farming here is, that in summer there is a glut of eggs, about 6d a dozen. **1895** *Outing* XXVI. 452/1 Wilson . . . owned a prosperous chicken farm. **1945** *Reader's Digest* Aug. 76 My sister, who runs a chicken farm in upper New York state, hires a handy man.

(6) 1839 *Spirit of Times* 18 May 126/2 (We.), *Col. Pete Whetstone* . . . lately 'got a hard fall' on 'a chicken fight.' **1845** HOOPER *Simon Sugg's Adv.* ii. 21 Don't you know that all . . . chicken-fighters . . . go to hell? **1865** MARK TWAIN *Jumping Frog,* If there was a chicken-fight, he'd bet on it. — **(8) 1835** *S. Lit. Messenger* I. 550 Horse-galloping dances . . . chicken flutter . . . for gentlemen. **1838** *Ib.* IV. 637/1 The then fashionable style of 'chicken-flutter and cross-shuffle,' required quadruple the strength which similar articles now do. **1912** *Boston Journal* 25 Nov. 1/4 Boston's elect danced the grizzly bear and the chicken flip in the Grand Salon. — **(9) 1867** *Common Sense Cook Book* 61 [Recipe:] chicken gumbo. **1908** LORIMER *J. Spurlock* 207 First there was a chicken gumbo soup, and then cold boiled Virginia ham.

(10) 1853 *Harper's Mag.* VII. 753/1 You notice that the 'chicken-house' seems to be in excellent condition; its inhabitants are thrifty and well-conditioned. **1945** *Chi. Tribune* 12 Aug. VII. 1/1 We looked at her house, barn, and chicken house standing like three Babes in the Woods. — **(11) 1872** MARK TWAIN *Roughing It,* Many a notorious coward, many a chicken-livered poltroon, coarse, brutal, degraded, has made his dying speech without a quaver in his voice. **1908** S. E. WHITE *Riverman* iii. 23 What's the matter with the chicken-livered bunch, anyway? — **(12)** (*a*) **1845** HOOPER *Suggs* (1928) 105 In some portions of the country the excitement against the unfortunate officers—who were known as the '*chicken men*'—made it almost dangerous for them to proceed with the business of taking the census. (*b*) **1890** *Harper's Mag.* Feb. 353/2, I am a-goin' to see Pete Jones, the chicken man. — **(13) 1928** BREAKENRIDGE *Helldorado* 84 On Sunday afternoons it was customary to have horse-races and chicken-pullings. **1941** FERGUSSON *Southwest* 344 Horse and foot-races and 'chicken pulls' are nearly inevitable. To pull a live chicken out of soft dirt, where it has been buried and its head dodges helplessly, may look savage, but it's fun for the boys. — **(14)** [**1855** *N.Y. Herald* 12 Dec. 2/2 At Chicken Ranch [in Calif.] James Bennett & Co. have just struck good paying dirt at a distance of some three hundred feet in their tunnel.] **1876** *Gold Hill* (Nev.) *News* 5 Oct. 3/5 'Old Kentuck,' the well known chicken rancher of the Sutro road, will leave shortly for Sacramento. **1887** I. R. *Ranche Life Montana* 55, I hope we may do pretty well with the chickens . . . as Jem says this is a very good chicken ranche. **1948** *Chi. Tribune* 5 Dec. (Grafic Mag.) 14/1 He had purchased a chicken ranch near Glenview.

(15) 1841 in *Md. Hist. Mag.* XXXVI. 52 We had two tureens, terrapins at each end, chicken salad, oysters, brought up hot, [etc.]. **1948** *Chickasha* (Okla.) *D. Express* 30 June 12/3 He was a great druggist, . . . but don't you think he made his chicken salad a little too salty? — **(16) 1865** *Wilkes' Spirit of Times* 29 July 339/3 'Chicken' shooting commencing directly after this, I did not go down after ducks that fall. **1890** *Outing* Aug. 341/1 My first chicken shooting of any consequence was enjoyed in the beautiful Badger State, longer ago than I care to think about now. — **(18) 1920** *Outing* June 164/2 It is a very good idea to take along a roll of chicken wire. **1948** *Dly. Ardmoreite* (Ardmore, Okla.) 31 Mar. 5/2 Crumpled chicken wire pushed into the vase makes a sturdy holder for flower arrangements. — **(19) 1853** *Harper's Mag.* VII. 759/1 Every one [of the Negroes] has his pigs and his poultry; for all adults have not only the chicken-yard, but also their garden. **1923** R. HERRICK *Lilla* 257 Down beyond the new barn, . . . were the chicken yards.

b. In the names of, or with reference to, plants and animals: (1) **chicken-berry,** the partridge berry; (2) **cock,** a rooster; (3) **corn,** a variety of sorghum; (4) **dog,** a dog trained to hunt prairie chickens; (5) **eater,** (see quot.); (6) **fight, fighter,** (see quots. and cf. (6) above); (7) **grape,** =**frost grape;** (8) **plover,** a local name for the turnstone, *Arenaria interpres;* (9) **shad,** (see quots.); (10) **snake,** any one of various non-poisonous snakes, as the milk snake, supposedly destructive to young chicks and eggs.

(1) 1832 WILLIAMSON *Maine* I. 130 Chicken-berry, (Mitchella Repens). — **(2) 1859** BARTLETT 524 Head and tail up, like chicken-cocks in laying-time. **1865** MARK TWAIN *Jumping Frog* (1875) 33 (R.), Well, thish-yer Smiley had rat-terriers and chicken-cocks. — **(3) 1856** *Cong. Globe* 17 April 960/2 Chinese sugar cane is nothing more than what we call chicken corn down in Georgia, and is of no sort of value. **1948** *Scientific Mo.* May 387 But the grain they will yield In the seedgrower's field. . . . Makes no chicken corn, cow feed, or hog mash. — **(4) 1876** *Fur, Fin, & Feather* Sep. 95 You can always find good 'chicken dogs' wherever there are chickens.

(5) 1870 GILLMORE tr. *Figuier's Reptiles & Birds* 578 The Peregrine Falcon . . . inhabits North America, where it is frequently called the Chicken-eater. — **(6) 1891** *N.Y. Herald* 29 Mar. 14/4 We found . . . wild lettuce and 'chicken fighters' or wild violets, which are so misnamed because children catch two blossoms together at the curves in their stems and with a quick jerk break off the poor little blue heads. **1942** WARNICK *Dialect Garrett Co., Md.* 5 Chicken-fights, n., violets (chicken-fighters, Colloquial U.S.). — **(7) 1807** SCOTT *Md. & Del.* 112 [This is] a middle sized grape, of a purple colour, growing in clusters, like the chicken grape. **1892** *Amer. Folk-Lore* V. 94 *Vitis cordifolia,* chicken grapes. Chestertown, Md. — **(8) 1870** in *Fur, Fin, & Feather* (1872) 72 Nothing in this section shall be held to apply to Wilson's snipe . . . or chicken plover. **1917** *Birds of Amer.* I. 268. — **(9)** *a***1873** *Dept Agric. Rep. 1873* 452 The 'chicken-shad,' as they are called among the pound-fishermen, instead of being a distinct species are the yearlings of the *praestabilis.* **1884** ROE *Nature's Story* (1885) 197 The males will come back next spring, and these young males are called 'chicken shad' on the Connecticut.

(10) 1709 LAWSON *Carolina* 134 The Egg or Chicken-Snake is so call'd, because it is frequent about the Hen-Yard, and eats Eggs and Chickens. **1948** *Nat. Hist.* April 185/2 Chicken snakes are among the few that enter poultry houses or barns in search of eggs or young birds.

c. In less frequent combs.: (1) **chicken dance,** a kind of dance performed by Indians; (2) **fit,** a sudden or violent fit, *colloq.;* (3) **gaff,** an artificial spur for a fighting cock; (4) **ground,** an area frequented by prairie chickens; (5) **lifter,** one who steals chickens, *slang;* (6) **money,** money for purchasing chickens, or that obtained by a housewife from the sale of chickens; (7) * **pie,** (see quot.), *rare;* (8) **season,** the open season on prairie chickens; (9) **stamping ground,** used with reference to prairie chickens (see quot.).

(1) 1899 CUSHMAN *Hist. Indians* 499 Then followed the fun-making dances, such as chicken dance, horse dance. — **(2) 1845** J. J. HOOPER *Simon Sugg's Adv.* iii. 31 Hoop-ee! won't they roll over the floor, and have chicken-fits, a dozen at a time! — **(3) 1834** H. J. NOTT *Novellettes* I. 19 He brought forth a dice-box, several dice, a pair of chicken gaffs, and various other utensils. — **(4) 1876** *Fur, Fin, & Feather* Sep. 96 The best chicken ground is undoubtedly to be found in Iowa.

(5) 1877 HARTE *Story of Mine* 305 Ye ain't one of them chicken-lifters that raided Henderson's ranch? — **(6) 1853** SIMMS *Sword & Distaff* 266 Did you suppose that the widow, . . . would go to the country and take no money with her—even if it were only a stocking full of shillings for chicken money. **1856** STOWE *Dred* II. 156 Drinking up all my chicken-money down to 'Bijah Skinflint's. — **(7) 1871** DE VERE 264 A curious term has, of late, sprung up in the South, to designate the necessary expenses for purchasing legislative votes and newspaper influence. . . . These are called Chicken-pie. — **(8) 1893** *Outing* Aug. 365/1 The 'chicken' season then opened on the fifteenth, and there were plenty of birds that year. — **(9)** *Ib.* Apr. 40/1 Their ball-rooms, which are known as 'chicken stamping grounds' in the West, can be readily recognized by the way in which the grass and low shrubbery are trampled down, and the numerous runways in the adjoining bushes.

As the last term in **Creole, fried, frying, Maryland, meadow, pheasant, prairie, sage, Saratoga, secesh, spring chicken.**

chicken feed.

1. Feed for chickens.

1865 R. H. KELLOGG *Rebel Prisons* 109 The rations . . . were slightly varied in the shape of two buckets of mush for ninety men. 'Chicken feed,' the boys called it. **1886** *Cent. Mag.* May 44/1 All the refuse [of the wheat] is sold for chicken-feed. **1945** *Chi. Tribune* 12 Aug. VII. 1/7 She can order flour at the same time she orders goat and chicken feed and have it brought out on the same truck.

transf. **1945** *Reader's Digest* Dec. 103/1 The candy, of course, sold for a penny. There was butter-corn, or 'chicken feed,' a favorite confection.

2. Small change. *Slang.*

1836 CROCKETT *Exploits* 78, I stood looking on, seeing him pick up the chicken feed from the green horns. **1930** FERBER *Cimarron* 114 I'll bet neither the Kid nor his father before him ever saw a nickel or a dime. They wouldn't have bothered with such chicken feed. **1946** *Chi. D. News* 14 March 1/4 The average tavern keeper doesn't want to be bothered with minors. They're worth chicken feed at best.

chicken fixings. Chicken prepared as food, as contrasted with less-esteemed food. *Colloq.*

1838 FLAGG *Far West* II. 72 [It is said] that the first inquiry made of the guest by the [Illinois] village landlord is: 'Well, stran-ger, what'll ye take? wheat-bread and chicken fixens, or corn-bread and common doins?' **1885** CRADDOCK *Prophet* 178 Brother Jake Tobin sets mo' store on chicken fixin's than on grace. **1927** BENÉT *J. B. 's Body* 137 There's goin' to be mixin's and mighty doin's, Chicken-fixin's and barbecuin's.

fig. **1854** M. J. HOLMES *Tempest & Sunshine* v. 78 We don't have any of your chicken fixings nor little three-cornered handkerchiefs laid out at each plate. **1870** DUVAL *Big-Foot Wallace* 302 The Mexican war had ended, and that chap with the gold epaulets on his shoulders and the 'chicken-fixings' on his coat-sleeves had mustered us out of the service and paid us off. **1914** *D.N.* IV. 70 Chicken-fixin's, . . . anything fancy, in food, dress, or otherwise.

chicken thief. [Cf. Du. *kiekendief.*]

1. One who steals chickens.

1883 *Harper's Mag.* June 162/2 Dar's moah den forty chicken thieves in Austin. **1944** CLARK *Pills* 74 Some of them had the distinction of being pointed out as the biggest chicken thieves in their respective states.

2. A river trading boat the presence of which encouraged the stealing of chickens to sell or barter. *Colloq. Obs.*

1819 DEWEES *Lett. from Texas* 11 The vessels upon this river consist . . . mostly of upper country flat boats, (generally called broad-horns), and chicken thieves. **1856** OLMSTED *Slave States* 675 He had lately caught one of his own negroes going towards one of the 'chicken thieves,' (so the traders' boats are called) with a piece of machinery.

chickerberry ˈtʃɪkɚˌbɛrɪ, *n.* =**checkerberry.** *Obs.* — **1821** COOPER *Spy* xxix. 'They will not think of such a thing,' the returned the pedler, picking the chickerberries that grew on the thin soil where he sat. **1823** ——— *Pioneer* ix. Is the poor devil to . . . put them in his pocket, . . . as you would a handful of chestnuts, or a bunch of chicker-berries?

chickery ˈtʃɪkərɪ, *n.* A chicken house. *Rare.* — **1859** *Harper's Mag.* Sep. 502/1 The physician's widow . . . laments over the hard necessity which has rebuilt her barns, changed a tumble-down wood-shed into a model chickery, thoroughly repaired her fences (etc.).

chick wintergreen. The starflower, *Trientalis americana.* Also **chickweed wintergreen.**

1814 BIGELOW *Florula Bostoniensis* 88 Trientalis Europaea. *L. Chickweed* Wintergreen. **1840** DEWEY *Mass. Flowering Plants* 155 *Trientalis Americana.* Ph. Chick Wintergreen. . . . It is little different from the European; grows in open woods, and blossoms in May. **1843** TORREY *Flora N.Y.* II. 11 *Trientalis Americana.* . . . Chickweed Wintergreen. . . . Low shady woods, and in sphagnous swamps. **1868** GRAY *Field Botany* 224 *Trientalis americana,* American Chickweed-wintergreen or Starflower. In open low woods; . . . a pretty plant.

chickwit ˈtʃɪkwɪt, *n.* [See note.] (See quots.) *Obs.*

"Trumbull (*Natick Dict.*, 21, 1903) cites the forms *chequit* and *checout*, and suggests a derivation from *chohki*, signifying, 'spotted,' in the Massachuset dialect of Algonquian" (Hodge). It has not been possible to verify the reference in *Century* 957/2 to a form *chigwit* in Harriott 1590.

*a***1870** CHIPMAN *Notes on Bartlett* 37 [The Weak-fish, or Squeteague] or Chickwit. **1877** BARTLETT, Chequet. An Indian name of the *Labrus squeteague*, or weak fish, retained in parts of Connecticut and Rhode Island. **1884** GOODE *Aquatic Animals* 362 The Squeteague—*Cynoscion regale.* . . . 'Squitee,' and 'Chickwit' are doubtless variations of this name in different ancient and modern dialects. **1892** *Outing* Apr. 54/1 He did say where it be called the 'gray trout,' 'sun trout' and 'shad trout,' the 'chickwit,' 'squit,' 'succoteague' and 'squitee.'

chicle ˈtʃɪkl, *n.* [Amer. Sp. (<Nahuatl) in same sense.] (See quot. 1889.) In full **chicle-gum.**

1889 *Cent.* 955/2 chicle-gum. . . . An elastic gum obtained from the naseberry, *Achras Sapota*, a sapotaceous tree of tropical America. It is used as a masticatory. **1907** WISTER *Simple Spelling Bee* 36 He again removed his chicle and placed it on the window-sill. **1947** *Chi. Tribune* 17 May 10/1 People of all ages placed a resilient material known as chicle in the mouth in the form of a wafer which was chewed until the fight had gone out of it, and was then spewed forth.

chico ˈtʃiko, *n. S.W.* [Amer. Sp. *chicalote* (<Nahuatl), used of various thorny plants.] =**greasewood.** Also attrib.

1913 WOOTON *Trees & Shrubs N.M.* 64 Greasewood (*Sarcobatus vermiculatus*) . . . is often called *chico* bush in the northwestern part of the State. **1929** A. ELLIS *Life* 26 He galloped his horses over the chico until they looked like waves. **1931** DAYTON *Western Browse Plants* 34 Greasewood (*Sarcobatus vermiculatus*), sometimes called 'black greasewood,' also 'chico' by Spanish-speaking people, is a shrub 2 to 10 feet high with a bark that in young plants is whitish.

chicopee ˈtʃɪkəˌpi, *n.* [?f *Chicopee* Falls, Mass.] A kind of cloth. goods. Also attrib. *Obs.* — **1843** *Knickerb.* XXI. 496 A small lot of 'Chickopees' were knocked down in the Forum this morning. **1871** W. M. GROSVENOR *Protection* 132 The manufacturer made Chicopee brown sheetings at 10⅞ cents in 1841.

chicot tʃiˈko, *n.* [F., snag, stump.]

1. (See quots.) *Obs.*

1821 NUTTALL *Journal* 68 We continued at the same rate, floating along without any labour, except that of occasionally rowing out from the shore, or avoiding submerged trunks of trees, called snags or sawyers, as they are either stationary or moveable with the action of the current; by the French they are called *chicos.* **1873** *Forest & Stream* 11 Dec. 273/2 A fire is kindled on some logs from an old chicot, and we are soon enjoying a hearty meal. **1941** DORSEY *Master of Miss.* 15 The French boat-hands called them *chicots*, the teeth of the rivers.

2. The Kentucky coffee tree, *Gymnocladus dioica.*

1832 BROWNE *Sylva* 167 In the winter when its leaves are fallen, the fewness of its branches . . . give it a peculiar appearance somewhat resembling a dead tree. This is probably the reason of its being called *Chicot*, stump tree, by the French Canadians.

***chief,** *a.* (*cap.*) In combs.: (1) **Chief engineer,** the head of an engineering department, usu. of a railroad; (2) **Executive,** the President of the U.S. or the governor of a state, also attrib.; (3) **magistracy,** the office of the President of the U.S.; (4) **magistrate,** the President of the U.S., cf. **first magistrate;** (5) **signal officer,** the officer in charge of the signal service.

(1) **1832** *Amer. R.R. Jrnl.* I. 563/3 They have also received . . . the report of their Chief Engineer. **1944** *Chi. Tribune* 26 Oct. 33/8 (*advt.*), Chief engineer. — (2) **1833** in *Speeches & Doc. Amer. Hist.* II. (1944) 91 But when the Chief Executive Magistrate is, by one of the most important branches of the Government in its official capacity . . . declared guilty of a breach of the laws and Constitution [etc.]. **1873** BEADLE *Undevel. West* 805 My first duty was to call upon the Chief Executive, Governor E. Y. Davis. **1948** *Dly. Ardmoreite* (Ardmore, Okla.) 15 July 6/1 You will be criticized and your qualifications sharply questioned to serve as chief executive of the nation. — (3) **1790** *Steele Papers* I. 60 The vice-President by virtue of his present appointment would take the chief Magistracy untill the 4th. March 1793. **1909** *Forum* Dec. 522 If the candidate for the chief magistracy of the nation should die before the assembling of the electoral colleges on the second Monday of January, how should they vote? — (4) **1788** A. HAMILTON *Federalist* No. 68, 14 March, The chief magistrate of the United States. **1884** CURTIS in *Cent. Mag.* Nov. 128 The very men from among whom the Presidential electors ought to select a chief magistrate for the nation.

(5) **1871** *Harper's Mag.* Aug. 414 The chief signal officer has . . . thoroughly organized and equipped a system. **1880** LAMPHERE *U.S. Govt.* 147/2 The Chief Signal Officer has charge, under the direction of the Secretary of War, of all signal duty, military telegraphs, sea-coast service [etc.].

b. In phrases: (1) *chief cook and bottle washer,* and variants [see quot. 1946], one having charge of things in general, a factotum, *colloq.;* (2) *Chief of Police,* one in charge of the police force of a city.

(1) **1840** *Magician* (Harrisburg, Pa.) 29 Aug. 2/3 Taking it for granted that the Kitchen Orator will be appointed 'Chief Cook and Bottle Wash' at the White House, he hopes, no doubt, to receive a sub-appointment as a reward. **1865** *Republican Banner* (Nashville,

Tenn.) 3 Oct. 3/2 Burk, as chief cook and bottle-washer of 'the machine,' was making himself hilariously disagreeable as the autocrat of the melee. **1946** *N. & Q.* June 41/1 Old Salem logs occasionally hold this listing: 'Chiff chark and bottle washer.' ('Chiff chark' is, I understand, a name for a variety of Russian wine glass.) I wonder if 'chief cook and bottle washer' is a derivative of this expression. [*Ib.* Dec. 140/1 The Russian word *chara* means 'cup,' 'glass,' or 'goblet.' I understand also that the *chara* was used by the Boyars in old Russia for drinking purposes.] — (2) *c***1849** JUDSON *B'hoys of N.Y.* 42 (We.), Chief of police. **1851** J. H. ROSS *In New York* 28 The 'Chief of Police' has his office at the City Hall. **1948** *Kankakee* (Ill.) *D. Jrnl.* 5 June 2/4 A team of pistol sharpshooters representing the Kankakee city police department will compete . . . , Chief of Police Dan Bergan announced today.

As the last term in **big, fire, head, Indian, medal, medicine, Miami, Mingo, Mohawk, principal, rebel, Sac, Seneca, Sioux, sub, war chief.**

chiefess ˈtʃifɪs, *n.* Among the Indians, a female chief. *Obs.* — **1778** J. CARVER *Travels* 41 This heroine was ever after treated by her nation as their deliverer, and made a chiefess. **1848** ALLEN *Ten Years in Ore.* 46 Next him came the chiefs and chiefesses (as they are called) of blood, the most respectable of foreign residents, missionaries; and in the rear followed an immense concourse of the common people.

chienté ʃænˈte, *n.* Variant of **shanty,** in allusion to the view that Can. F. is the source of shanty. *Obs.*

[**1829** COOPER *Wish-ton-wish* (1859) xvii. 243 *Shanty*, or *Shantee*, is a word much used in the newer settlements. . . . The only derivation which the writer has heard for this American word, is one that supposes it to be a corruption of *Chienté*, a term said to be used among the Canadians to express a dog-kennel.] **1841** ——— *Deerslayer* xix, There isn't a jail in the colony that has a more lock-up look about it than old Tom's *chiente.* **1848** ——— *Oak Openings* I. ii. 33 The supper was finished, . . . the whole party left the chienté, to enjoy their pipes.

chifforobe ˈʃɪfəˌrob, *n.* [f. *chiff*onier + ward*robe*] An article of furniture consisting of a chest of drawers and a wardrobe. — **1908** *Sears Cat.* (ed. 117) 419 The chifforobes as illustrated on this page are a modern invention, having been in use only a short time. **1948** *Democrat* 4 Nov. 5/5 Chifforobes, $39.50 up.

chigger ˈtʃɪgɚ, *n. S.* The larval form of certain mites, esp. the red bug, *Trombicula irritans.* Cf. ***jigger,** *n.*[1]

The Amer. usage of this term may stem from its use by Negro slaves and not from a continuation of the earlier British use. Turner finds the word in various of the African languages. The first two quots. may refer to the flea.

[**1743** CATESBY *Carolina* App. p. xxxvii, The particular genus's I observed in Carolina [include] . . . Fleas. Chego. The Louse. **1780** ASBURY *Journal* I. 384, I cannot go into the woods, there are so many ticks, chiegoes, and such insects at this season upon the ground.] **1824** SINGLETON *Letters* 62 In the sultry months, the underbrushwood is powdered with *chiegoes*, minim insects, too minute to be inspected, but which get into the skin, and sting like nettles. **1917** KEPHART *Camping* I. 253 The *moquim* mentioned above answers the description of our own chigger, jigger, red-bug, as she is variously called. **1947** *Chi. D. News* 14 June 6/3 Wallace has been getting under the presidential skin like chiggers from the tall grass.

b. chigger flower, weed, (see quots. 1899).

1899 *Animal & Plant Lore* 117 *Anthemis colula* is called 'chigger-weed' because it is supposed to harbor chiggers. Indiana. *Ib.* 118 *Asclepias tuberosa*, the butterfly milkweed, is called 'chigger flower,' from the belief that insects known as chiggers harbor in it. Southwestern Missouri. **1931** CLUTE *Plants* 59 The dog-fennel (*Anthemis cotula*), which bears several other names of a derogatory nature, may as well have chigger-weed added to the list.

Chihuahua tʃɪˈwɑwɑ, *n.* [Amer. Sp. in sense **1.** Cf. *Chihuahua*, a state and city in Mexico.]

1. A small dog native in Mexico believed to antedate Aztec civilization in that region.

1858 VIELE *Following Drum* 185 The Chihuahua are rare, even here in such close vicinity to Mexico. **1948** *Dly. Ardmoreite* (Ardmore, Okla.) 1 June 7/7 Here's the new claimant to the world's smallest-dog crown. This chihuahua from McAllen, Texas, weighs one and three-quarter ounces, and likes to take naps on a lemon.

2. (See quots.)

1889 H. H. MCCONNELL *Five Yrs. a Cavalryman* 187 The 'Chihuahua' wagon is much like the old 'Conestoga' wagon . . . of the East. **1925** J. B. GILLETT *Six Yrs. with Texas Rangers* 89 At that time each frontier post had its chihuahua or scab town, a little settlement with gambling halls, saloons, etc., to catch the soldiers' dollars. **1939** ROLLINS *Gone Haywire* 110 Th' hombres that skedaddled jus' now musta bin sheepherders, for two o' 'em was wearin' only one spur, an' the rowels was Chihuahuas. . . . What do I mean by Chihuahuas? Why, big rowels like th' Mexicans mostly uses.

chikamin ˈtʃɪkəmɪn, *n. N.W.* [Nootka.] Money, cash.

1881 FARROW *Mt. Scouting* App. 29/2 Money, check-a-min. **1914** *Sunset* Feb. 396/2 You ketchum me dog, me ketchum you chikamun. **1948** *Sat. Ev. Post* 28 Aug. 24/1 By the chikamin in front of him, he was cleaning up as usual.

Chilcat ˈtʃɪlkæt, *n.* ["Said to be from *tcĭl-xăt*, 'storehouses for salmon'" (Hodge).] A tribe of Indians about the head of Lynn Canal in Alaska, noted for their manufacture of the blankets which bear their name. Also an Indian of this tribe. Also attrib.

1845 DUNN *Ore. Terr.* 193 A little to the northward of this there is a tribe called the Chilkasts. **1896** *Land of Sunshine* June 3 Together with other Indian relics—totem poles, pipes, medicine charms and several handsome blankets of the Navajo and Chilcat weaves—it fills a good-sized room. **1915** *Nat. & Science on Pac. Coast* 195 This art receives perhaps its highest expression in the weaving of certain blankets or robes composed of cedar-bark string and the wool of the mountain goat. These fabrics are usually called Chilcat blankets, from the name of one of the tribes in southern Alaska. **1936** REICHARD *Navajo Shepherd & Weaver* 168 The yellow yarn of the Chilkat blanket was dyed by boiling a lichen in the *fresh urine of children.*

chilchipin ˌtʃɪltʃəˈpin, *n. S.W.* [Amer. Sp. *chiltipiquín* (<Nahuatl) in same sense.] A plant of the genus *Capsicum, C. frutescens baccatum*, or the berry of this.

1894 *Amer. Anthrop.* July 299 The mescal . . . has added to it several kinds of roots and berries, the most important being chilchipin, said to be the basis of the fiery Tabasco sauce. **1895** *Amer. Folk-Lore* Jan.–Apr. 46 The *chilchipin* is the fiery berry forming the basis of Tabasco sauce. **1942** CASTETTER & BELL *Pima & Papago Agric.* 121 Papago made expeditions to secure *chiltepiquin;* they pulled up the entire plant which they brought home for drying, then picked the fruit and stored it in a sealed olla.

***child,** *n.*

1. **this child*, used by a speaker in jocular allusion to himself. *Colloq.*

1839 *N.O. Picayune* 24 Mar. 2/2 Neba min; you'll hab a chance to catch dis child some oder time. **1892** DUVAL *Young Explorers* 91 No, dat he ain't, . . . dis chile too smart for dat, and I clum out'n de way like a squirl. **1930** WITTKE *Tambo & Bones* 169 De debble kotch ye, shoa! but bress de lam', he habn't cotch dis child yet!

2. In combs.: (1) **child board,** the board to which an Indian baby is strapped, *rare;* (2) **Child Health Day,** (see quots.).

(1) **1823** KEATING *Narr.* 182 At the time he approached us he had a child-board on his back. — (2) **1930** *Boston Herald* 10 April 3/2 Congress . . . has authorized and requested the President of the United States of America to proclaim annually that May day is Child Health Day. **1933** *Survey* May 116/1 The American Child Health Association . . . has served as the lighthouse for Child Health Day.

b. *child of the forest*, an Indian.

1818 *Lynchburg* (Va.) *Press* 7 Aug. 2/6 The benevolent *Penn* . . . treated these children of the forest in an honorable way. **1880** NYE *B. Nye & Boomerang* 247 They were as fine looking children of the forest as I ever saw.

As the last term in **corncob child.**

***children,** *n.* As the last term in **fresh air, Mohawk, red, white children.**

Children's warbler. (See quots.) — **1831** AUDUBON *Ornith. Biog.* I. 180 Children's Warbler. *Sylvia Childrenii.* . . . I have named it after my most esteemed friend, J. G. Children, Esq. of the British Museum. **1891** *Cent.* 6819/3 Children's warbler, the female or young summer yellow-bird, *Dendrœca æstiva.*

chile mill. (See quot. 1890.) Also **Chilian mill.**

1849 *Pacific News* (S.F.) *Supp.* 4/5 One perfect Chilian mill . . . arranged to be worked by horse, water or steam power, adapted for grinding gold or silver ores. **1856** *S.F. Bulletin* 6 June 1/2 Chile mills, with various modified forms of construction, the *ball* process, 'with little balls chasing big ones' and different grinding processes have each been in turn adopted and discarded. **1890** *Cent.* 3764/1 Chilian mill, a form of mill consisting of two heavy wheels or rollers, set parallel on a horizontal shaft. The rollers travel in a vat or other suitable receptacle, and scrapers are usually provided to keep the material in the path of the wheels. This form of mill, which is of much antiquity, is now used especially for grinding oleaginous seeds, nuts, fruits, etc.

chilhowee lily. Prob. a local name for the Atamasco lily. — **1888** CRADDOCK *Broomsedge Cove* 166 A vague vision of vast multiplied fields of the Chilhowee lily was before his eyes.

chili ˈtʃɪlɪ, *n.* Also **chile.** Orig. *S.W.* [Amer. Sp. *chile* (<Nahuatl), used of various species of *Capsicum.* An Amer. borrowing.]

1. Red or cayenne pepper or the pod yielding this.
1836 PARKER *Trip to the West* 271 (Bentley), You will have for a holiday dinner . . . soup with meat balls and chile in it, chicken with chile, rice with chile, fried beans with more chile. **1865** *Atlantic Mo.* XV. 60 We had . . . an infinity of Mexican hashes and stews seasoned with chiles or red-pepper pods. **1874** BOURKE *Journal* 13 Oct., Chili is also one of their vegetables.

b. *ellipt.* A dish or sauce seasoned with chili.
1846 in EMORY *Mil. Reconn.* (1848) 40 Chile the Mexicans consider the chef-d'oeuvre of the cuisine. . . . It was red pepper, stuffed with minced meat. **1891** *N. & Q.* VII. 299 Chile, or Chilly, as the name of a sauce, and a very familiar word at this season, is in none of the dictionaries.

2. Short for **chile con carne.**
[**1900** F. NORRIS *Blix* 167 The two sat, pretending to eat their chili peppers, their hearts in their throats, hardly daring to raise their eyes from their plates.] **1927** EUBANK *Horse & Buggy Days* 177 My old friend Ike McHenry. . . . I found serving the boys with iced tea and chili a la mode. **1947** *Steamboat* (Colo.) *Pilot* 2 Jan. 3/5 If the kids come to your house after a game, give them chili, bread and butter, a bowl of fruit.

3. In combs.: (1) **chili cojote,** *W.* a species of gourd, *Cucurbita foetidissima,* also known as "chilicothe," cf. **chilicote;** (2) **colorado,** see as a main entry; (3) **con carne,** a Mexican dish containing meat and kidney beans flavored with chili; (4) **joint,** a restaurant where foods seasoned with chili are served; (5) **sauce,** a sauce the principal ingredients of which are pepper, tomatoes, and onions; (6) **verde,** (see quots.).
(1) **1893** *Amer. Folk-Lore* VI. 142 *Cucurbita perennis,* Chili cojote; calabazilla. So. **1940** JAEGER *Desert Wild Flowers* 253 Called 'Chili Cajote' by the early Californians; they held the crushed root in high esteem as a cleansing agent in washing clothes. — (3) **1857** S. COMPTON SMITH (*title*), Chile Con Carne, or The Camp and the Field. **1948** *Life* 15 March 130/2 She even had a hot supper waitin' for me one night. Chili con carne. — (4) **1927** EUBANK *Horse & Buggy Days* 31 We made the round trip in less than three hours, scouted a couple of oil wells and ate dinner in a Wichita chili joint. **1941** FERGUSSON *Southwest* 339 Le's figure on a junta for nooning at the chile joint.
(5) **1882** F. E. OWENS *Cook Book* 90. **1948** *Calif. Citrograph* April 223/2 Chili sauce is a favorite partner for peanut butter. — (6) **1844** GREGG *Commerce of Prairies* I. 153 Chile verde (green pepper), not as a mere condiment, but as a salad, served up in different ways, is reckoned by them one of the greatest luxuries. **1896** *Land of Sunshine* June 28 Chile verde con queso. (Green Peppers with Cheese.)

Chilian clover. (See quot. 1855.) *Obs.* — **1855** BROWNE in *Trans. Amer. Inst. N.Y.* 618 Chilian Clover, or Alfalfa (*medicago sativa*) from Chili, a perennial variety of lucerne, which succeeds well in our middle and southern States. **1906** *Out West* April 337 It is of the clover family and is sometimes called Chilean clover.

chili colorado. *S.W.*

1. Red or cayenne pepper, or the pod yielding this.
1844 KENDALL *Santa Fe Exped.* II. 160 Seated upon the ground, a female might be seen with a few chiles colorados, or red peppers, for sale. **1884** HILL *Colo. Pioneers* 283 The scarlet ribbons in her dark hair rivaled in brilliancy the wreathes of 'chili-colorado' that festoon the walls of a Mexican plaza in the Indian summer time. **1910** O. HENRY *Strictly Business* 25 There [=El Refugio] only will you find a fish . . . baked after the Spanish method. . . . Chili colorado bestows upon it zest, originality and fervour.

2. A dish seasoned with chili, as chile con carne *q.v.*
1869 BROWNE *Adv. Apache Country* 78 We had Chili colorado and onions and eggs, and wound up with preserves and a peach-cobbler. **1888** J. J. WEBB *Memoirs* 19 Our bill of fare was the usual dishes of Chili Colorado, beans, atole, tortillas, &c. Americanized by the addition of bacon, ham, coffee, and bread.

chilicote ˌtʃɪlə'kotə, *n.* Also **chilicothe.** [See note.]
Santamaría lists *chilicote* in sense **2.** below, and *chilicoyote* (<Nahuatl) in sense **1.** Both these forms appear to be from a native word, given in *Cent. Supp.* as *chicayote.*

1. The California bigroot, *Echinocystis fabacea.*
1898 A. M. DAVIDSON *Calif. Plants* 66 In the valleys of Southern California one can always find the chilicothe in flower before Christmas. . . . The plant is often called big-root or man-root; roots two feet long and half as thick are common. **1915** ARMSTRONG *Western Wild Flowers* 518 Chilicothe, Wild Cucumber. *Micrampselis fabacea* (*Echinocystis*). **1917** SAUNDERS *Western Flower Guide* 215 They called the plant Chilicothe—a form apparently of the Aztec *chilacoyote,* wild cucumber.

2. (See quots.)
1909 *Cent. Supp.* 235/2 chilicote. . . . A name in northern Mexico of *Erythrina coralloides,* a small thorny trifoliate tree belonging to the *Fabaceae,* the hard scarlet seeds of which were formerly strung into necklaces by the Indians. **1931** DAYTON *Western Browse Plants* 86 Western coralbean (*Erythrina flabelliformis*), often called chilicote by Mexicans and ranchers, is the only species of the large tropical-subtropical coraltree genus (Erythrina) occurring in the West.

∗**chill,** *n.* In combs.: (1) **chill day,** the day on which one has (or expects to have) a recurrent chill; (2) **plow,** (see quot. 1909), also **chilled plow;** (3) **tonic,** any one of various tonics taken for chills.
(1) **1879** STOCKTON *Rudder Grange* 166 It was his chill-day, an' he didn't take his quinine. **1884** SWEET & KNOX *Through Texas* 102 'Can't do it,' said Bud; 'to-morrow is my chill day.' — (2) **1886** *York Herald* 23 Aug. 3/6 There are several imitations of the original American chill plow in the market. **1909** *Cent. Supp.* 1022/1 Chilled plow, a plow which has the point and edges of the share of chilled steel or of chill-hardened steel. It is made in many forms. — (3) **1935** CASON *90°* 33 A practice is made of 'advancing' such things as fat meat, sugar, snuff, fertilizer, stick candy, denim, calico, kerosene, chill tonics, kidney pills. **1944** CLARK *Pills* 235 Chill tonics returned almost as much money as the cotton crops.

b. *chill and fever,* fever and ague *q. v.*
1773 *Pa. Mag. Hist.* V. 198 To-day very unwell with a chill and fever. **1835** P. SHIRREFF *Tour* 393 To the west of the Alleghanies, the most common complaint is bilious fever, in every variety of type, passing by the names of 'ague,' 'chill and fever,' and many etceteras. **1907** C. C. ANDREWS *Recoll.* 103 Malaria had been unusually prevalent, and I had already begun to feel indications of chills and fever.
As the last term in **congestive, dumb, grave, sinking, swamp chill.**

∗**chill,** *v. intr.* To suffer from chills. *Colloq.*
1869 *Overland Mo.* III. 130 Jones, are you chilling it much this winter? **1881** *Harper's Mag.* Jan. 319/1 Well, they do a powerful heap of *chilling* in some spots. **1929** J. PARKER *Old Army* 24 Mr. Smith, how are you today? . . . Oh pretty well, I'm chillin' today.

∗**chilly,** *a.* In the colloq. phr. *a chilly day,* "a facetious way of expressing extreme infrequency of occurrence" (Th. Supp.). — **1893** *Cong. Rec.* 16 Dec. 290/1 It is a chilly day when a Congressman goes to the Pension Office now.

∗**chimney,** *n.*

1. A natural rock formation suggestive of a chimney.
1832 N. J. WYETH *Journal* (1899) 9 June 155 Arrived at the Chimney or Elk Brick the Indian name this singular object looks like a monument about 200 feet high. **1858** D. K. BENNETT *Chronology N.C.* 84 Winding our way along the margin of this most wild and restless foaming river, we reach . . . what are called the 'chimneys.

2. "A body of ore, usually of elongated form, extending downward within a vein" (Raymond).
1860 *S.F. News Letter* 20 Jan. 5/1 Silver ore is found in what are termed chimneys, and at every foot the miner is liable to lose the lead, it dropping sometimes two or three thousand feet, and sometimes turning short to the right or left. **1891** *Union Pac. R.R., Utah* (ed. 4) 38 A single chimney of ore in a contact along the east base of Grampian Mountain . . . turned out 90 tons of ore a day for four years, realizing to its owners more than $13,000,000. **1931** DOBIE *Coronado* 172 One thing is certain: granting there are two deposits, there is no lead to either of them; each is a 'chimney,' or 'spew.'

3. In combs.: (1) **chimney bird,** ?a chimney swift, *rare;* (2) **cap,** [cf. Du. *schoorsteenkap*], a rotating top or cowl for a chimney; (3) **cloth,** see as a main entry; (4) **pink,** (see quot.); (5) **place,** [cf. Du. *schoorsteenplaats*], an open fireplace or hearth; (6) **rock,** see as a main entry; (7) **scraper,** a device for cleaning a chimney, *rare;* (8) **shelf,** a mantel-shelf; (9) ∗**swallow,** =**chimney swift;** (10) ∗**sweeper,** (see quots.); (11) **swift,** a small American swift, *Chaetura pelagica,* that nests in chimneys; (12) **viewer,** [cf. Du. *schoorsteenschouw*], in colonial times in New England an official appointed to inspect chimneys.
(1) **1789** MORSE *Amer. Geog.* 59–60 The following catalogue [of American birds] is inserted. . . . The Chimney bird. — (2) **1846** *Rep. Comm. Patents* (1847) 221 What I claim, therefore, as my invention . . . is a ventilator or chimney cap. **1889** *Cent.* 961/3. — (4) **1893** *Amer. Folk-Lore* VI. 138 *Saponaria officinalis,* Boston pink . . . chimney pinks. N. H.
(5) **1800** *Raleigh* (N.C.) *Register* 18 March, Having left fire burning in the chimney place. **1929** SHELTON *Salt-box House* iv. 29 The wide chimney-place called them to her burning heart. — (7) **1819** *Plough Boy* I. 183, I was induced a few days since to attend the exhibition in this city, of Hall's patent chimney scrapers. — (8) **1881** MCLEAN *Cape Cod Folks* 293 The bare, shining floor, the unpainted table, the chimney-shelf. — (9) **1789** MORSE *Amer. Geog.* 60 [Birds of the United States include:] The . . . Red winged Starling, Swallow, Chimney do., Snow bird [etc.]. **1948** *Dly. Ardmoreite* (Ardmore, Okla.)

23 July 7/1 Other very interesting birds to watch are the chimney swifts or chimney swallows.

(10) **1849** *Rep. Comm. Patents: Agric.* (1850) 393 The sooty powder on the flowering parts of corn-plants, called smut, chimney-sweepers, and dust-brand, is formed of the spores of another uredo. **1908** *D.N.* III. 298 chimney-sweeper. . . . The chimney-swift. The latter is rarely or never heard [in Ala.]. — **(11) 1849** AUDUBON *Western Jrnl.* (1906) 129, I saw fifteen or twenty swifts, about double the size of our common chimney swift at home. **1948** [see **chimney swallow**]. — **(12) 1684** *Conn. Hist. Soc. Coll.* VI. 212 The Chimney veiwers . . . shall make presentments of what defects they find in chimneys & want of ladders, to the next authority to be fined. **1922** KIMBALL *Domestic Arch.* 26 In Connecticut chimneys of wood and clay were in use in 1639, and may have persisted until 1706 when the last chimney-viewer of Hartford was elected.

As the last term in **board, caton, catted, crawfish, ground, ore, pay, stick-and-clay, stick-and-dirt, wood, wooden chimney.**

chimney cloth. [Cf. Du. *schoorsteenkleed, -val.*] A valance placed round a chimney piece or mantel as a decoration, or to retain the smoke. *Obs.*

1744 FRANKLIN *Fire-places* 7 A Chimney-cloth was look'd upon as essential to a Chimney. **1885** EGGLESTON in *Cent. Mag.* April 879/2 But fire-places so open did not always draw well, on which account a 'chimney-cloth' had to be used at times to close the upper part of the fire-place and keep the smoke from escaping into the room. **1926** A. M. EARLE *Col. Days in N.Y.* 125 In the house of Mayor Rombouts in 1690 were fine chimney-cloths trimmed with fringe and lace, . . . and humbler checked chimney-cloths.

chimney rock.

1. An isolated column of rock resulting from weathering. Also (*cap.*) as the name of particular formations of this kind.

1847 in *Utah Humanities Rev.* (April, 1948) 125 Chimney Rock was still visible down the River at the towering heights of the long range of Black Hills above us. **1850** *Western Journal* IV. 359 The sides of these buttes are . . . covered with grass. This is the formation of which . . . the Chimney rocks of the Platte river are composed. **1876** APPLEGATE *Day With Cow Column* (1934) 8 We are not yet in sight of the grander but less beautiful scenery (of the Chimney Rock, Court House, and other bluffs, so nearly resembling giants castles and palaces).

2. A form of rock or limestone suitable for building chimneys.

1870 *Cong. Globe* App. 26 March 225/2 The marbles of our western border have heretofore served as 'chimney rock' for the cabin of the luxurious border farmer.

* **chin,** *n.*

1. A talk, also reduplicating **chin-chin.** *Slang.* Cf. * **chin.** *v.* **2.**

1894 P. L. FORD *P. Stirling* 14 I'll wait till I've graduated, and had a chin with my governor about it. Perhaps he'll make up my mind for me. **1918** E. M. ROBERTS *Flying Fighter* 289, I went back and resumed the 'chin-chin' with Kerr and the other boys. **1928** T. GANN *Discov. & Adv. Central Amer.* 106 Whenever three or four of them came together for a 'chin.'

2. In combs.: (1) **chin-chin artist,** one who is quite a talker, *slang;* (2) **fly,** (see quot. 1909), also fig.; (3) **stuff,** talk, loquacity, *slang;* (4) **whiskers,** beard on the chin, also **chin-whiskered.**

(1) **1896** *Voice* (New York) Aug. 27 1/5 Chauncey M. Depew, the chin-chin artist of the New York Central Railway. — **(2) 1867** in CARPENTER *6 Mo. at White House* 129 You were brought up on a farm, were you not? . . . Then you know what a *chin fly* is. *Ib.* 130 If Mr. ——— has a presidential chin fly biting him, I'm not going to knock him off. **1909** *Cent. Supp.* 236/2 Chin-fly a horse bot-fly. *Gastrophilus nasalis,* possibly so called because its eggs are laid about the horse's mouth. — **(3) 1919** *Detective Story Mag.* XXVIII. Nov. 60 All we got to do is to frame up a good spiel to make him bite. And that's your little job. You always were there with the chin stuff. Go to it. — **(4) 1868** WHYMPER *Alaska* 283 [In California] beards are termed 'chin whiskers,' and our 'whiskers' are distinguished as 'side whiskers.' **1904** O. HENRY *Heart of West* iv. 42 A chin-whiskered man in Walla-Walla . . . had grubstaked us. **1948** *Sat. Review* 24 July 5/1 Book publishers no longer sprout chin whiskers.

b. *To take it on the chin,* to bear up resolutely under adversity. *Colloq.*

1932 *Blue Valley Farmer* (Okla. City) 18 Feb. 8/6 Millions of small children, sturdy lads and bonnie lasses, must 'take it on the chin.' **1948** *Duncan* (Okla.) *Dly. Banner* 1 July 2/4 It took real courage and fight to do a comeback after taking it on the chin for so many games.

* **chin,** *v.*

1. *tr.* To grasp an overhead bar and draw (oneself) up by the arms until the chin is above the bar. Also fig.

1871 MARK TWAIN *Screamers* 77 When I stood before the 'Republican' office and looked up at its tall unsympathetic front, it seemed hardly *me* that could have 'chinned' its towers ten minutes before. **1906** O. HENRY *Four Million* 74 He wore a dress suit, and could chin the bar twice with one hand. **1931** *K.C. Star* 29 July, He brought a breath with him that a 6-year-old boy could have chinned himself on.

2. To address, talk to (a person), also *intr.,* to talk, gossip. Also **chin-chin.** *Slang.* Cf. **chinning,** *n.*

1883 HAY *Bread-Winners* 161 You haven't done a———thing but lay around on the grass and eat peanuts and hear Bott chin. **1893** GUNTER *Miss Dividends* 247, I heard one of them call another 'Constable' and the other chinned him as 'Sheriff.' **1947** *Chicago Sun* 4 June 16 Let's go to the coffee joint and chin-chin!

* **China,** *n.* Also **china.**

1. = **Poland China.** Also attrib.

1838 H. COLMAN *Mass. Rep. Agric.* 74 A cross with some of our small boned breed, such as the Byfield or the China. **1856** *Rep. Comm. Patents: Agric.* 63 [In Beaver County, Penn.] the 'China' breed is the most prevalent, though some keep the 'Russian.' **1871** EGGLESTON *Hoosier Schoolm.* xxvi. 180 You can't make nothin' else out of him, no more nor you can make a china hog into a Berkshire.

b. Short for **china tree.**

1847 *Knickerb.* XXIX. 197 The China is the favorite shade-tree of this and many of the southern towns. **1848** *Ib.* XXXI. 545 One long winding street, flanked by rows of stately poplar and button-wood trees, with a sprinkling of sycamores and chinas.

2. In special derivatives and combs.: (1) **chinaberry,** the soapberry, *Sapindus saponaria,* found in the southern states, or the china tree *q.v.,* also the fruit of one of these, also attrib.; (2) **brier,** = **bull brier;** (3) **bug,** (see quot.), *rare;* (4) **cracker,** a firecracker, *rare;* (5) **-dom,** = **Chinatown,** *obs.;* (6) **house,** *Calif.* (see quot. 1924), *obs.;* (7) **-man's chance,** see as a main entry; (8) **pump,** app. a form of pump improvised by early gold miners in the West, *obs.;* (9) **stone,** (see quot.), *obs.;* (10) **store,** a store that specializes in chinaware; (11) **town,** a place or district, esp. in a city, inhabited by Chinese; (12) **tree,** the pride of China tree, *Melia azedarach,* extensively planted as a shade tree in the South; (13) **wedding,** (see quot.); (14) **wheat,** "a spring wheat grown in the United States, said to have been derived from a grain found in a tea-chest" (*Cent.*); (15) **wood,** the soapberry, *Sapindus saponaria.*

(1) 1890 *Harper's Mag.* Dec. 106 The high gray towers . . . were crowned with ornaments like the berries of the chinaberry-trees. **1907** COOK *Border & Buffalo* (1938) 166 Their meat was bitter and sickening, from eating china-berries (the fruit of *Sapindus marginatus,* or soapberry trees). **1944** HARPER *Weeds* 141 M. Azedarach L. Chinaberry. A medium-sized tree, very commonly cultivated for shade in the South, and often escaping to edges of fields, partly cleared woods, etc., mostly in the coastal plain. — **(2) 1745** *Itinerant Observ.* 14 The good Indians regaled us, and for greens, boiled us the Tops of China-Briars, which eat almost as well as Asparagus. **1909** *Cent. Supp.* 165/1 China brier, a thorny vine, *Smilax glauca,* which causes trouble in agricultural land from Pennsylvania to Tennessee. — **(3) 1849** *Rep. Comm. Patents: Agric.* (1850) 137 Wheat is at best a delicate and uncertain crop subject to two great disasters, rust and mildew: and also the Hessian fly and china bug. — **(4) 1860** HOLMES Professor (1902) 259 [Women] . . . are like China-crackers on the morning of the fifth of July.

(5) 1856 *Sacramento Union* 15 July 3/1 Jean Detremont and Wm. Mills found themselves in the dock yesterday for disturbing the peace in Chinadom. **1883** *Harper's Mag.* May 831/1 The cemetery seemed to me the most curious of all the sights connected with Chinadom in San Francisco. — **(6) 1850** in *Calif. Hist. Soc. Quart.* VIII. 173, [He] showed me a small American house 19×16 feet . . . then got two pieces of china house and started off to Hock Farm. **1924** in *Calif. Pion. Soc. Quart.* I. No. 2, 27 They [special guards] were to evict the occupant of what was known as a 'China House,' a portable affair imported from the Orient, and quite common in those days [c1848–58]. — **(8) 1872** RAYMOND *Mines* 100 All the tailings, after leaving the agitators, flow into a tank from which they are raised by a China pump to a second tank. **1899** *Mo. So. Dakotan* I. 173 With the aid of our home made china pump we succeeded in reaching a high point of the bed rock in one place from which eighteen or twenty dollars was taken in coarse gold, from only a few pans of gravel some of the nuggets weighing as high as $1.25. — **(9) 1838** F. HALL *Letters* (1840) 5 About three miles before I reached this city, I came to the *China* *stone quarry*, so called, I suppose, on account of the feldspar it furnishes, having been employed at New York and abroad, in the manufacture of china or porcelain ware.

(10) 1860 S. MORDECAI *Virginia* xxii. 247 An occasional appendage to the Swan was a house nearly opposite to it, . . . where a large China store now stands. **1948** WESTON *Mother Lode* 70 The little 'China store' was a favorite with children. — **(11) 1857** *Butte Record* (Oroville, Calif.) 31 Jan. 2/7 The uncouth sounds welling up from Chinatown at intervals within the last eight and forty hours show most conclusively Chinatown was wild with joy. **1948** JOHNSTON *Gold Rush* 14/2 In common with other camps of the period, Coulterville had a Chinatown of considerable proportions. — **(12) 1819** E. EVANS *Pedestrious Tour* 315 Here grew the China tree, of a beautiful appearance, and bearing fruit of an inviting aspect, but of an unpleasant taste. **1896** HARRIS *Sister Jane* 191 The bird . . . flew wildly to the top of the big China tree on the sidewalk. **1948** WESTON *Mother Lode* 94 The quaint little building with ancient 'China' trees sprouting through the front-porch roof, was once a candy shop. — **(13) 1888** *St. Louis Globe-Democrat* 30 March (F.), The occasion was the twentieth anniversary, or China wedding of Mr. and Mrs. Pope. — **(14) 1852** REGAN *Emigrant's Guide* 255, I find a variety of seed called the China wheat, does well. **1856** *Rep. Comm. Patents: Agric.* 199 But little wheat is sown in this county [Bennington, Vt.], except the spring varieties. That known as the 'China' wheat, has been the most productive.

(15) 1907 COOK *Border & Buffalo* (1938) 91 There was a thicket of stunted hackberry and palodura, hard poles of chinawood, close to where the old campfire had been.

As the last term in **American, Boston, Poland, wild China.**

Chinaman's chance. An extremely poor chance. *Colloq.*

This expression originated in California, poss. in the days of the "Forty-niners." It may have stemmed from the practice by Chinese miners of working over tailings left by white miners where their chances of gain were regarded as meager, see 1st. quot. below. Or it may have grown out of the early intense hostility against Chinese that developed in that region.

[**1928** FOY & HARLOW *Clowning Thro' Life* 154 Chinese had picked up small fortunes around mining camps by working over the 'tailings' or refuse heaps which the white miners considered beneath their notice.] **1939** *News Letter & Wasp* (S.F.) 10 March 9 There were not many who gave the Chinese a Chinaman's chance when the Japanese commenced their invasion of China. **1946** *Democrat* 25 July 2/3 Mr. Talmadge wasn't given a 'Chinaman's chance' for success by more than 90 percent of Georgia's newspapers.

chincapin, see **chinquapin.**

chinch bug. Also **chintz bug.**

1. A small hemipterous insect of the genus *Blissus*, destructive to wheat and corn. See also **false chinch bug.**

1785 in *S. Lit. Messenger* XXVIII. 38/1 The devastation of the Chintz bug, which since harvest have infested the Indian Corn. **1786** WASHINGTON *Diaries* III. 97 Examined the low and sickly looking corn in several parts of this field and discovered more or less of the Chinch bug on every stalk between the lower blades and it. **1873** *Winfield* (Kans.) *Courier* 3 July 4/1 The Chinch bug is making fearful ravages in the late sown wheat. **1948** *Norman* (Okla.) *Transcript* 1 July 14/1 Grasshoppers and chinch bugs have damaged crops in many localities.

2. A bedbug, a chinch.

1819 *Plough Boy* I. 79, I will inform her, as a good housewife, how she can keep her beds and bed-rooms clear of vermin, vulgarly called chinch bugs.

chincomen, see **chinquapin.**

chinee tʃaɪ'ni, *n.* [f. *Chinese*, taken as a pl.] A Chinese. *Colloq.* Cf. **heathen Chinee.** — **1871** R. SOMERS *Southern States* 163 The Chinée, who struts even here with a celestial sort of air, must have his tent all nicely fixed up and provided for him. **1910** MULFORD *Hopalong Cassidy* 142 That cross between a nigger an' a Chinee is in Davy Jones' locker, is he?

∗**chinese**, *n.* and *a.*

1. A form of ornamental railing. *Obs.*

1771 in *Copley-Pelham Lett.* 130 A pattern of Chinese for the Top of the house I will send you. **1771** *Ib.* 170, I don't think the Chinese you sent by Smith is so hansome as Mr. Vassell's.

2. In combs.: (1) **Chinese berry,** the berry of the China tree; (2) **cane, = Chinese sugar cane;** (3) **houses,** (see quots.); (4) **laundry,** a laundry operated by Chinese; (5) **policy,** a governmental policy of political and commercial isolation, *obs.;* (6) **quarter,** a part of a city where Chinese people live; (7) **sugar cane,** any one of several varieties of sorghum from the juice of which sugar and sirup are made; (8) ∗**wheel,** a pin wheel, a form of fireworks.

(1) 1864 CATE *Two Soldiers* 27 To a half bushel of Chinese berries, picked from the stems, add three gallons of water. — **(2) 1856** *Spirit of Times* 15 Nov. 182/2 The chief advantages of the Chinese cane as a sugar-plant . . . is the facility of its cultivation and the easy treatment of its juice. **1863** *Rep. Comm. Agric.* 131 The Chinese cane has a very lofty and well-proportioned stalk. — **(3) 1915** ARMSTRONG *Western Wild Flowers* 488 Chinese Houses. *Collinsia bicolor.* **1920** RICE *Calif. Wild Flowers* 113 Very popular are the little Chinese Houses, *Collinsia bicolor* (there are 15 or more species), quite common throughout California, one variety of which is called Innocence. — **(4) 1904** *Grand Rapids Press* 25 Nov. 5 Men raided Chinese Laundry.

(5) 1808 *Deb. Congress* Nov. 598 Are we now, without warning, to break up all our institutions heretofore, and declare for a Chinese policy. — **(6) 1869** *Atlantic Mo.* Dec. 744/2 Every California town has its Chinese quarter. **1900** *Oriental & Occidental Press* (S.F.) 9 June 1/3 It is claimed by the Board of Health that this awful malady has been hibernating in the Chinese quarter since the 7th of last March. — **(7) 1847** DARLINGTON *Weeds & Plants* 412 The genus Sorghum has acquired a considerable importance within a few years, on account of the introduction of some species or varieties as a sugar-producing plant, under the names of Chinese Sugar Cane, Sorghum, Sorgho, Imphee, &c. **1901** MOHR *Plant Life Ala.* 68 Broad fields of which alternate with . . . patches of the Chinese sugar cane or sorghum (*Sorghum saccharatum*). — **(8) 1844** KENDALL *Santa Fe Exped.* II. 98, I have little doubt he was very officious among [such fireworks as] squibs, India crackers, Chinese wheels.

∗**chink**, *n.* A strip of wood suitable for filling up a crevice in the wall of a log cabin. *Obs.*

1804 ORDWAY in *Journals Lewis & O.* 166 We raised the roof of the meat & Smoak house bringing it up with Timber cross drawing in, So as to answer with chinks & dobbing. [**1824** DODDRIDGE *Notes* 137 In the mean time masons were at work. With the heart pieces of the timber of which the clapboards were made, they made billets for chunking up the cracks between the logs of the cabin and chimney; a large bed of mortar was made for daubing up those cracks.] **1944** W. BLAIR *Tall Tale America* 66 In the spring when the dogwood came out, they'd knock away the chinks so that light and air could come into the cabins.

∗**chink**, *v. tr.* To fill up the chinks or crevices in the walls of a log cabin or log house with sticks, mud, etc.; to finish off a wall or house in this way.

1748 in CHALKLEY *Scotch-Irish Settlement Va.* I. 35 Presentment vs. Court House . . . built of logs, chinked with mud, but cracks 4 to 5 inches wide. **1843** CARLTON *New Purchase* I. 60 The interstices of the log-wall were 'chinked.' **1920** HUNTER *Trail Drivers Texas* I. 376 Most of our houses were built of logs . . . and the cracks 'chinked' with sticks and mud.

transf. a**1859** *Spirit of Times* (B.), Perhaps you would like to have it to use for chinking in among your election returns.

b. Used with ∗*daub.*

1829 T. FLINT *G. Mason* 10 They knew infinitely better than he did how to 'daub and chink' a log cabin. **1883** SHIELDS *S.S. Prentiss* 18 The school-house was a hewn-log house, chinked and daubed with cat and clay. **1947** *Dly. Ardmoreite* (Ardmore, Okla.) 27 July 9/4 When we came to Ardmore there were just a few log cabins all chinked and dobbed with mud.

c. Also with *up.*

1887 in *Amer. Sp.* XV. (Oct., 1940) 326 As the shanty was only 'chinked up' they had plenty of 'port holes' to fire through. **1929** F. E. MCCLINCHEY *Joe Pete* 46 He chinked up the holes between the logs in the walls of the second, smaller room.

∗**chinker**, *n.* (See quot.) *Obs.* — **1857** *Spirit of Times* 3 Jan. 294/2 The farmer calls the pebbles used to fill these spaces between the big blocks, 'chinkers.'

∗**chinking**, *n.* The wooden strips, mud, etc., used in closing the crevices in the walls of a log house. Also the process of filling such crevices.

1791 JILLSON *Dark & Bloody Ground* 107 It has a dirt floor pounded hard and no chinking in the walls. **1824** BLANE *Excursion* 181 This operation is called chinking; and before it has been performed the cabin, in winter, would be uninhabited from the cold. **1912** WASON *Friar Tuck* 175 We had hard work thawin' out the clay for chinkin', an' we didn't get the cabin as tight as we'd a' liked. **1947** *Sierra Club Bul.* May 92 The chinking is perfect so that not a trace of snow or draft comes in through the sides.

transf. **1835** LONGSTREET *Ga. Scenes* 197 [In dressing up as Daniel Lambert] Billy required the aid of at least eight pillows, with some extra chinking, as we say in Georgia. **1888** *Amer. Missionary* April 108 She wore one of the smallest thimbles with a bit of cloth inside for 'chinking' to keep it on.

chinning 'tʃɪnɪŋ, *n.* [f. ∗**chin,** *v.*] Talk, chatter. *Colloq.*

1876 *Santa Cruz* (Calif.) 28 July 1/5 'Shoot the chinning,' cried the President, 'Will you never tumble?' **1920** LEWIS *Main Street* 42

Next to Nat is Chet Dashaway. Great fellow for chinning. He'll talk your arm off.

chinny ˈtʃɪnɪ, *n.* Talkative. *Colloq.* — **1883** HAY *Bread-Winners* 81 He hated these 'chinny bummers,' as he called them, who talked about 'State help and self-help' over their beer. *Ib.* 100, I forgot about the old lady, though she was more chinny than the young one.

Chinook tʃɪˈnuk, *n.* Also **chinook.** ["From *Tsinúk*, Chehalis name" (Hodge).]

1. An Indian of a well-known tribe of the Chinookan family formerly living along the lower Columbia River, often pl. as a tribal designation.

1831 R. COX *Adv. Columbia R.* I. 299 He was rescued when in a state of great exhaustion by two Chinooks. **c1836** CATLIN *Indians* II. 110 The Chinooks, Inhabiting the lower parts of the Columbia, are a small tribe, and correctly come under the name of Flat Heads. **1907** HODGE *Indians* I. 272 The Chinook were first described by Lewis and Clark, who visited them in 1805, though they had been known to traders for at least 12 years previously. **1948** JOHNSTON *Gold Rush* 48/1 My party consisted of three white men, one Delaware, one Chinook, and about sixty Indians from the Sacramento Valley.

attrib. **1805** CLARK in *Lewis & C. Exped.* (1905) III. 294 The Chinnook womin are lude and carry on sport publickly. **1841** WILLIAMS *Tour to Ore.* (1921) 51, I started in a canoe down the Willamette River, in company with some Chenook Indians.

2. The language of these Indians. Also the Chinook Jargon *q.v.* Also attrib. Cf. **Oregon Jargon.**

1824 in *Wash. Hist. Quart.* III. 212 The woman speaks and understands the Chenook language pretty well and is to interpret to the men. **1828** in DALE *Ashley-Smith Explor.* (1918) 266 Two Inds., who speak Chinook, came to our camp. **1865** STUART *Montana as It Is* 83 In travelling through that 'illahe' it is necessary to have a Chinnook dictionary in your pocket or an interpreter. **1945** SERVICE *Ploughman* 231 Understands Latin and Greek. Speaks French, German and Chinook.

3. "A name applied to certain winds of N.W. United States and British Columbia. According to Burrows (*Yearbook Dept. Agric.*, 555, 1901) there are three different winds, each essentially a warm wind whose effect is most noticeable in winter, that are called chinooks" (Hodge). Cf. **Wallawalla Chinook.**

1876 *Silver City* (Ida.) *Avalanche* 18 March 2/2 In winter however it is somewhat blustery, the wild, yet balmy chinook, sweeping with intense force from the open south and west country. **1890** *Silverton* (Colo.) *Miner* 1 Feb. 3/1 A 'chinook' prevailed all day Saturday and Sunday, cutting most of the snow on the sidewalks into slush. **1947** *Time* 20 Jan. 40/3 Cameron, who entered the valley in 1936, explained the mild climate; chinooks (warm winds) keep the air balmy and moist.

b. In full **Chinook wind.**

1860 in *Pac. N.W. Quart.* XXXI. 347 Pleasant warm weather, high winds from S.W., they call it the Chinook wind. **1947** *Denver Post* 3 March 1/4 A warm but gusty Chinook wind, straight out of Alaska and Canada, brought rising temperatures and clearing weather to Denver Monday.

4. Used ellipt. for: **a. Chinook canoe, b. Chinook salmon, c. Chinook dog.**

(a) 1869 *Harper's Mag.* Nov. 798/1 Having . . . exchanged our 'Chinook,' or salt-water canoe, for two small shovel-nosed canoes. **1943** *Sat. Ev. Post* 1 May 29/2 Ahead of the Chinook lay a barge carrying a pile driver. — **(b) 1889** *Oregonian* (Portland) 4 Nov. 5/1 He . . . landed after a most exciting fight, a chinook or chisel-mouth of large size. **1947** *Sports Afield* Dec. 28/3 The spring runs of Chinooks . . . spawn as far as 600 miles inland. — **(c) 1945** *Nat. Geog. Mag.* Sep. 261 (*caption*), With seven 100-pound Chinooks hitched to his sled, he traveled 502 miles across the Maine snows in 90 hours.

5. In special combs.: (1) **Chinook canoe,** a large canoe such as the Chinook Indians use; (2) **dog,** = **husky 2;** (3) **Jargon,** a trade language or jargon in use in the Pacific northwest, composed of elements from Chinook proper, Nootka, English, French, and other sources; (4) **licorice,** a lupine found in the Pacific Coast region; (5) **salmon,** quinnat salmon; (6) **State,** (see quot. 1890); (7) **wawa,** the Chinook language.

(1) 1890 *Aberdeen* (Wash.) *Herald* 2 Oct. 1/2 The trip to the lake is made in Chinook canoes of about a ton capacity. — **(2) 1942** PEATTIE *Friendly Mts.* 293 The largest Chinook dog ranch is at Wonalancet, New Hampshire, and the largest Eskimo dog ranch in North Woodstock, in the same state. — **(3) 1855** H. R. SCHOOLCRAFT *Hist. Indian Tribes* V. 548 A jargon of Indian words in Oregon and Washington mixed with English, French, and Spanish, . . . called the Chinook Jargon. **1946** *Mazama* (Portland, Ore.) Dec. 1 Nesika klataw sahale [is] Chinook jargon for 'We Climb High.' — **(4) 1893** *Amer. Folk-Lore* VI. 140 *Lupinus littoralis*, Chinook liquorice. Washington, D.C.

(5) 1851 *S.F. Picayune* 15 Oct. 2/5 We notice that P. B. Macy & Co. have received a supply of Chenook salmon, by the Sea Gull. **1947** *Field & Stream* June 66/1 The chinook salmon is monarch of Alaskan waters and he'll smash your tackle to prove it. — **(6) 1890** *Brighton* (Colo.) *Register* 11 Jan. 4/1 Washington is the 'chinook State.' **1924** *Amer. Mercury* Jan. 50/2 (*heading*), Hurrying on the Kingdom in the Chinook State, as reported by the Editor and Publisher. — **(7) 1892** *Kamloops* (B.C.) *Wawa* 8 May 112 (heading), *Chinook Wawa.* **1914** APPLEGATE *Recollections Boyhood* (1934) 124 We learned to speak the Chinook Wa-Wa that winter.

chinook tʃɪˈnuk, *v.* [f. the noun.] *intr.* (See quot. 1922.) — **1890** in *Oreg. Hist. Quart.* XLI. 105 We worked three days getting the sheep to ground part clear of snow; they done well for two days, but it chinooked for a few hours and then froze a heavy crust. **1922** *D.N.* V. 181 chinook, verb, intr. To blow warm (an impersonal verb like it rains, from the noun chinook). 'We were going for a sleighride, but it chinooked and the snow went off.' Oregon, Washington, Idaho.

Chinookan tʃɪˈnukən, *a.* and *n.*

1. *a.* Of or pertaining to the Chinook Indians.

1893 PILLING *Bibliography of the Chinookan Language.* **1908** BOAS *Amer. Ind. Languages* 563 The Chinookan stock embraces a number of closely related dialects which were spoken along both banks of the Columbia river from the Cascades to the sea, and some distance up the Willamette valley. **1940** *Mt. Hood Guide* 25 This language is identified as the Upper Chinookan or Kikct dialect.

2. *n.* = **Chinook,** *n.* **1.**

1940 *Ore. Guide* 33 On the north side of the Columbia, from its mouth to the Cascades, the Chinookans held sway.

chinquapin ˈtʃɪŋkəpɪn, *n.* [See note.]

1. The dwarf chestnut or a tree related to this. Also the small edible nut of such a tree. Also attrib.

"Such forms as chincomen and chechinquamin, found in early writings, make plausible the supposition that a *p* was later substituted for an *m* in the last syllable of the word, which would then represent the widespread Algonquian radical *min*, 'fruit,' 'seed.' The first component of the word, according to Hewitt, is probably cognate with the Delaware *chinqua*, 'large,' 'great' " (Hodge).

1615 R. HAMOR *True Discourse Virginia* 23, I know no one Country yeelding without art or industry so manie fruites, . . . many groues of *Chincomen trees* with a huske like vnto a Chesnut, rawe or boyled, luscious and harty meate. **1676** GLOVER *Acc. Va.* in *Phil. Trans.* XI. 629 Beside these [nuts], here is another called a Chincopine, which is like a Chesnut, with a Burry husk, but lesse by far. **1799** *Farmer's Reg.* (Greensburg, Pa.) 30 Nov. (Th.), She remembered chinquoimines, chesnuts, walnuts, &c., where the principal buildings in Philadelphia now stand. **1814** PURSH *Flora Amer.* II. 625 Castanea pumila. . . . This small tree, or rather shrub, grows to the height of thirty feet and upwards in the southern regions, but to the north it seldom exceeds seven or eight feet. The fruit is very sweet and agreeable to eat, and is generally known by the name of Chinquapin. **1948** *Galveston* (Tex.) *News* 14 June 11/2 Among the 150 crops are those with such exotic names as anise, . . . chinquapin, a nut, . . . and jujubes.

2. In special combs.: (1) **chinquapin business,** (see quot.), *colloq.;* (2) **oak,** any one of various chestnut oaks, esp. *Quercus muhlenbergi*, also **chinquapin scrub oak;** (3) **perch,** (see quots.).

(1) 1905 JOHNSON *Highways* 341 Merchants [in Fla.] who lack capital to sell on long credits are said to do a 'chinquapin business,' and they look with envy on their more fortunate competitors with the big per cents rolling in. — **(2) 1785** MARSHALL *Amer. Grove* 125 *Quercus Prinus humilis.* Dwarf Chesnut or Chinquepin Oak. This generally rises with several shrubby, spreading stalks, to the height of two or three feet. **1916** SETON *Woodcraft Man.* 281 Yellow Oak, Chestnut Oak, or Chinquapin Scrub Oak (*Quercus Muhlenbergii*). A great forest tree; up to 160 feet high; . . . It is much like the chestnut oak but its leaves are narrower, more sharply saw-edged, and its acorns much smaller. **1931** MATTOON *Forest Trees Okla.* 55 Chinquapin Oak . . . occurs throughout the eastern part of the State. — **(3) 1884** GOODE *Aquatic Animals* 407 The Crappie—*Pomoxys annularis* . . . [is] called . . . 'Chinquapin Perch' in the Lower Mississippi. **1947** DALRYMPLE *Panfish* 84 Here, my friend, are the various names by which you would address that little gamester, the Crappie, depending on where you happened to be at the moment: Bachelor, . . . Chinquapen, Chinquapen Perch, Crapet, . . . Sand Perch.

Also *chinquapin bush, log, nut, post, switch, time,* etc.

As the last term in **golden-leaf, water, western chinquapin.**

***chip,** *n.*

1. = **buffalo chip.** Usu. *pl.*

1848 BRYANT *California* 80 The 'chips' are an excellent substitute for wood. **1903** ADAMS *Log Cowboy* 210 We had begun to feel the scarcity of wood for cooking purposes. . . . These chips were a poor substitute. **1948** *Southwestern Rev.* Summer 237/2 The cowboys made fires of the 'chips.'

2. (See quot.) *Obs.*

1889 Barrere-Leland I. 244 Chip (American journalism). Local items in newspapers are called chips, and sometimes the term is applied to the reporter who collects them.

3. The "box" or scarified surface made on the trunk of a pine in securing turpentine from it. Cf. **chipping,** *n.*

1896 *Pop. Sci. Monthly* Feb. 470 The chip has reached a height of six or eight feet. *Ib.* 478 He makes a small chip about three inches wide, an inch and a half high, and only two fifths of an inch deep near the foot of the tree. **1904** *D.N.* II. 395 chip, n. A term used in the turpentine industry. 'At intervals of three or four weeks the resin from the boxes . . . known as the *chip*, is taken out with a flat metal

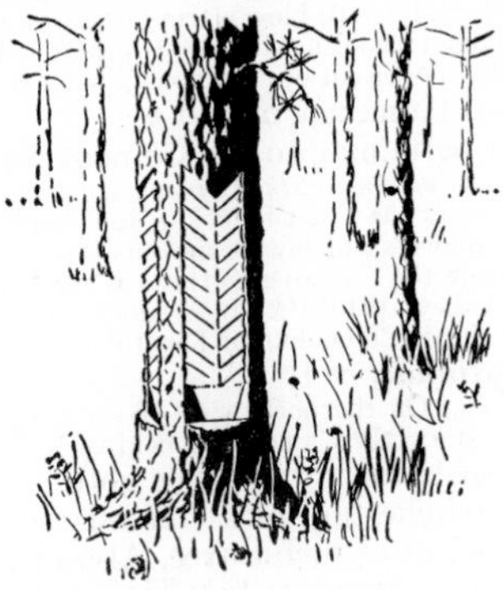

Chip (sense **3**), cat face, and turpentine box on pine

spoon and placed in a bucket, which in turn is emptied, after filling, into a barrel.' *Evening Post,* June 1, 1903.

4. In combs.: (1) **chip basket,** a basket for fragments of wood resulting from chopping, fig. in quot.; (2) **boat,** a toy boat made of or consisting of a chip, *rare;* (3) **bridge,** ?a flimsy wooden bridge, a toy bridge; (4) **day,** (see quots.), *obs.;* (5) **dirt,** soil scraped from a chipyard for use as fertilizer; (6) **dung,** =prec., *obs.;* (7) **manure,** =prec., *obs.;* (8) **stuff,** refuse from milled grain, *obs.;* (9) **yard,** an area in which wood is cut and which consequently is littered up with chips, also attrib.

(1) 1856 Stowe *Dred* I. 22 [She] throws you into her chip-basket of beaux and goes on dancing and flirting as before. — **(2) 1809** Irving *Hist. N.Y.* (1927) II. i. 71 He was a countryman and schoolfellow of that great Hudson, with whom he had often played truant and sailed chip boats, when he was a little boy. — **(3) 1669** *Essex Inst. Coll.* V. 274/1 A popler tree . . . standing by a way through a swampe or bridge called the chip bridge. **1870** Emerson *Society & Sol.* 34 From his [=a child's] first pile of toys or chip bridge to the masonry of Minot Rock Light-house of the Pacific Railroad. — **(4) 1847** Wells & Davis *Sk. Williams Coll.* 79 They give us, near the close of the second term what is called 'chip day,' when we put the grounds in order, and remove the ruins caused by the winter's siege on the wood-piles. **1873** in Tyler *Hist. Amherst Coll.* (1895) Each spring we had our 'chip day,' when the students in mass turned out to scrape and clear up the grounds near the buildings.

(5) 1849 *Rep. Comm. Patents: Agric.* 103 Shallow ploughings given annually, liquid manure, chip-dirt, road scrapings, . . . have been turned in with marked advantage. **1944** Wilson *Passing Inst.* 6 Chip dirt was also attractive to fishing worms. — **(6) 1804** in J. Roberts *Penn. Farmer* 137, I ploughed it five times more, then put on twenty loads of chip, and ten loads of yard dung. — **(7) 1821** *Mass. H.S. Coll.* 2 Ser. IX. 139, [I] filled up the cavity, around the roots, with chip manure. — **(8) 1849** *Rep. Comm. Patents: Agric.* (1850) 102 These cows are fed with shorts or chip-stuff, together with roots and slops from the kitchen. — **(9) 1850** *Knickerb.* XXXVI. 73, I first let down her bars, crossed her chip-yard, and stood before her habitation. **1879** B. F. Taylor *Summer-Savory* 110 Thus a number of residents of La Porte, Indiana, went and camped out for a week in plain sight of the city! It was a sort of chipyard picnic. **1939** in E. Taggard *Here We Are* (1941) 21, I threw down my books in the chipyard.

b. In colloq. phrases: (1) *To have a chip on one's shoulder,* and variants, to be in a belligerent attitude or frame of mind; (2) *the chip doesn't fly far from the stump,* "like father, like son"; (3) *to pass in one's chips,* to die; (4) *the bug under the chip,* see ∗**bug,** *n.* **3.** (4).

(1) 1830 *L.I. Telegraph* (Hempstead, N.Y.) 20 May 3/5 When two churlish boys were *determined* to fight, a *chip* would be placed on the shoulder of one, and the other demanded to knock it off at his peril. **1870** *Terr. Enterprise* (Virginia, Nev.) 23 Aug. 3/1 He could not well do otherwise than plead guilty, even though Napoleon did knock the 'chip off his shoulder.' **1947** *Time* 3 Mar. 20/2 We dare not present to the world a picture of Uncle Sam with a chip on each shoulder and both arms in a sling. — **(2) 1886** Page in *Cent. Mag.* 192/2 She wuz standin' by her ma, I tell you; dee bofe had de same sperit,—de chip don' fly fur fum de stump. — **(3) 1884** Hill *Colo. Pioneers* 160 He one day passed in his chips and the box he had so long used with economy was now utilized for himself. **1936** McKenna *Black Range* 56 But we kept alive, and we learned afterwards that we had been lucky, for several cowboys passed in their chips in that snowstorm.

As the last term in **blue, Boston, buffalo, bull, cattle, cow, ox, poker, potato, prairie chip.** Cf. also **Saratoga chips.**

chip tʃɪp, *a.* Short for ∗**chipping,** *a.,* in combs.: (1) **chip bird,** =**chipping bird;** (2) **sparrow,** =**chipping sparrow;** (3) **squirrel,** =**chipping squirrel.**

(1) 1824 *Mass. Yeoman* 28 April (Th.), The destruction of a robin, chip, blue, or black bird is not all. **1869** Lowell *Study Windows* (1871) 15 The only bird I have ever heard sing in the night has been the chip-bird. — **(2) 1852** Stowe *Uncle Tom's Cabin* xvi. 191 Then she sat on his knee like a chip sparrow, still laughing. — **(3) 1839** Webber *Old Hicks* (1848) 49 [Sand rats] look something like the common chip squirrel, except that their bellies are broader, and their forepaws formed very short and strong for burrowing. **1884** J. C. Goldsmith *Himself Again* 5 A little chip-squirrel, no thicker than one's finger.

∗**chip,** *v.*

1. *tr.* To cut or scarify (the surface of a pine) in securing turpentine from it. Cf. ∗**chipping,** *n.*

1788 Schöpf *Reise* II. 221 Und eben so oft werden die Boxes wieder nachgehackt oder angefrischt (re-chip'd). **1904** *D.N.* II. 395 chip, v. In the turpentine industry, the scarification of the pine.

2. ∗*chip in(to),* in various colloq. uses: **a.** To contribute money, usu. for a benevolent purpose.

1861 *Winsted* (Conn.) *Herald* 22 Nov., An idea seems very generally to prevail that the printer should 'chip in' to every charitable and religious operation. **1903** *N.Y. Sun* 15 Nov., Nevertheless they all chipped in for the benefit of Simpson's widow and little child next day. **1948** *Dly. Ardmoreite* (Ardmore, Okla.) 22 April 14 Maybe if all of us chipped in, we could buy what we need!

b. In poker, to place a chip or counter in the pool. Fig. in quots.

1876 Harte *G. Conroy* VI. ii, You've jest cut up thet rough with my higher emotions thet, there ain't enough left to chip in on a ten-cent ante. **1904** W. H. Smith *Promoters* 101 If he got a rake-off on the game he'd have to chip into the play.

c. To join with others in an enterprise.

1872 Mark Twain *Roughing It* l. 356 Mind you, I don't object to trying him, if it's got to be done to give satisfaction; and I'll be there and chip in and help, too. **1947** Paul *Linden* 217 Will you ask the men I've listed here to chip in?

chiparee, see **chickaree.**

chipmunk 'tʃɪpmʌŋk, *n.* [f. Algonquian. Cf. Chippewa *atchitamon,* "head first," from the way the animal descends trees.] Any one of various small, striped, squirrel-like rodents of the family Sciuridae.

1832 Traill *Backwoods* 86 The shrill whistling cry of the little striped squirrel, called by the natives 'chitmunk.' **1857** *Rep. Comm. Patents: Agric.* 71 The chipmuck exists throughout the Eastern, Middle, as well as in some of the Western States, and as far north as latitude fifty degrees in the British Possessions. **1948** *Sierra Club Bul.* Mar. 11 Who has not paused at a turn in the trail . . . to watch a nervous chipmunk jerking its tail as it chatters on a stump?

As the last term in **antelope, Gila, Missouri, prairie, sage chipmunk.**

∗**chipped,** *a.* Of meat, esp. beef: Smoked and cut in very thin slices, esp. **chipped beef.**

1819 *Mass. Spy* 18 Aug. (Th.), No vapid tea, or cold toast, and greasy butter, and chipped meat. **1833** Hall *Harpe's Head* 214 A little farther up were venison steaks, then fried ham; then there was cold ham, and chipped beef, and sausages. **1859** *Knickerb.* LIV. 406 Such waffles, chipped beef, sweetmeats, melon. **1948** *Field & Stream* July 116/3 Dried or chipped beef is excellent.

Chippewa 'tʃɪpə,wɑ, *n.* [A popular adaptation of **Ojibway** *q.v.*] A member of a large Algonquian tribe of Indians formerly living in the Great Lakes region. Often pl. as a tribal designation. Cf. **woods Chippewa.**

1671 in *N.Y. State Col. Hist.* IX. 803 St Mary of the Falls, the place where . . . the Indian nations called Chipoës, Malamechs, Noquets and others do actually resided [*sic*]. **1772** *N.Y. Gazette* 16 Nov. 3/1 Phineas Pond (an English Trader) with his two Battoemen, were murdered by the Chippewas. **1880** *Harper's Mag.* Dec. 43 The guttural ejaculations of the Chippewas who came to her door. **1948** *Scientific Mo.* July 31/2 The Sioux then became Plains Indians, and the Chippewas continued to be forest dwellers.

attrib. **1773** *N.Y. Gazette* 26 Dec. 3/1 The Chippawa Indians, near Saguiny Bay, on Lake Huron, are making great Concessions for the murder of Phineas Bond. **1831** *Boston Transcript* 30 Dec. 1/1 The Chippewa tribe formerly inhabited the regions around Lake Superior.

b. Designating or pertaining to the language of these Indians.

1778 CARVER *Travels No.-Amer.* 416 The Chipéway tongue is not incumbered with any unnecessary tones or accents. **1799** JAMES SMITH *Acc. Captivity* 37, I could not, at this time, talk Ottawa or Jibewa well. **1833** *Advocate* (Shelbyville, Ky.) 7 Sep. 2/6 It is well printed, presenting the *Chippewa* words in our ordinary type, . . . as there is no Chippewa alphabet. **1948** *Green Bay* (Wis.) *Press-Gazette* 30 June 8/2 An expert ventriloquist . . . would go out on the ice to a fishing Indian and make the trout address the fisherman in the most approved Chippewa dialect.

c. The name of a proposed territory (see quot.). *Obs.*

1860 *N.Y. Tribune* 19 May 5/2 Chippewa includes the northern half of Nebraska and Dakota, extending from Washington Territory to Minnesota.

d. A variety of Irish potato.

1945 *N. Eng. Homestead* 13 Oct. 11/2 The first tubers are brought to Maine and planted in test plots at Highmoor Farm, Monmouth, beside a row of Chippewas. **1948** *Minn. Morning Tribune* 28 Sep. 19/1 Potato Market . . . Wisconsin Chippewas U.S. No. 1 size A washed, $3.25.

Chippewan ˈtʃɪpəwən, *a.* Also **Chippewayan.** Used with **Mountains** as a name for the Rocky Mountains. *Obs.*

1815 DRAKE *Cincinnati* 91 North America is traversed by two ranges of high mountains—the Allegheny and Chippewan. **1829** *Va. Lit. Museum* 146/1 A slope, or inclined plane, extending from the rocky or Chippewayan mountains, towards the Pacific Ocean. **1838** *Knickerb.* June 513 The indications that the entire country between the Alleghany and Chippewan or Rocky Mountains, was once covered by an immense ocean, are without number.

Chippewayan ˌtʃɪpəˈweən, *n.* The language of the Chippewa Indians. *Obs.* — **1861** *Ladies' Repository* XXI. 354/1 It was in monotonous Chippewayan, and to our ears the burden of the song is lost.

* **chipping,** *n.*

1. The action of scarifying the trunk of a pine in securing turpentine from it; the surface resulting from this.

1832 BROWNE *Sylva* 232 The chippings extend the first year a foot above the box. **1859** PERRY *Turpentine Farming* 61 Consequently, I commenced with five chippings. **1896** *Pop. Sci. Mo.* Feb. 469 The turpentine season does not really open till spring, when the sap starts to flow in the trees and chipping begins.

2. chipping station, a place where Indians made stone arrowheads, axes, etc.

1928 V. C. REELING *Evanston* 55 Chipping stations or workshops were situated for miles along the lake shore. **1942** *Chi. Tribune* 24 Nov. 12/3 The chipping station was probably just outside the burying ground, for there is evidence of an Indian cemetery to the north of the hospital.

* **chipping,** *a.* In combs.: (1) **chipping bird,** =next; (2) **sparrow,** the hairbird, *Spizilla passerina*, one of the best known of American sparrows; (3) **squirrel,** =**chipmunk,** also attrib.

(1) **1791** BARTRAM *Travels* (1792) 289 *Passer domesticus;* the little house sparrow or chipping bird. **1869** BURROUGHS in *Galaxy Mag.* Aug. 139/2 The social-sparrow, . . . *alias* 'red-headed chipping-bird,' is the smallest of the sparrows. — (2) **1810** WILSON *Ornithology* II. 127 [The] Chipping Sparrow . . . *Fringilla Socialis* . . . inhabits, during summer, the city, in common with man. **1948** *Chi. Tribune* 20 Apr. II. 4/4 The singing of chipping and song sparrows convinced us spring is marching right along. — (3) **1800** *Raleigh* (N.C.) *Register* 1 July, An Advertisement was lately published in several papers, offering a generous price for 10,000 chipping squirrel skins, for exportation. **1889** *Cent.* 965/1 The hackee or chipping-squirrel of the United States, *Tamias striatus*.

chippy ˈtʃɪpɪ, *n.*

1. Any one of various small birds, esp. the chipping sparrow, characterized by a low chirping note. Also attrib.

1864 WEBSTER, *Chipping-bird* . . . also *chippy*. **1880** *Harper's Mag.* June 76 [The] dear little eggs of chippies in their horse-hair bed. **1913** STRATTON-PORTER *Laddie* iii, In the hollow of a rotten rail a little chippy bird always built a hair nest.

2. A girl or woman of loose habits, a prostitute. *Slang.*

1890 *Saguache* (Colo.) *Sentinel* 2 Jan. 4/4 The leading dudes and chippies of Europe had [the influenza] and pulled through all right. **1948** *Time* 19 July 102/3 Lulu Belle . . . was a spicy play featuring Lenore Ulric as a colored chippy.

chiquito tʃəˈkito, *n.* and *a.* *S.W.* [Sp. dim. of *chico*, small.] Used of children or of a thing small of its kind. Also **chica,** a term of endearment for a little girl. *Colloq.*

1857 IVES *Colo. River* (1861) 39 We found a large party of Cocopas . . . waiting on the bank, with grinning faces, for the arrival of the 'chiquito steamboat,' as they call our diminutive vessel. **1859** REID *Scouting Exped.* 108 (Bentley), Beneath you, sporting in the limpid element, you behold men and boys, and women with their chiquitos. **1903** O. HENRY *Heart of West* 38 (Bentley), But if you'll run in, chica, and throw a pot of coffee together. . . . I'll be a good deal obliged.

Chiricahua ˌtʃɪrɪˈkawə, *n.* [Apache, "great mountain."] An Indian of an important division of the Apache formerly occupying a mountainous region in southeastern Arizona.

1885 *Weekly New Mexican* 4 June 2/3 Any Indian, Chiricahua, Mescalero or Navajo, caught on a raiding or stealing expedition should be sent to the happy hunting ground. **1893** *Outing* June 189/1 A grand dance was to be given by the Chirricahuas. **1948** *Range Riders Western* May 91/1 No Chiricahua could have been more still and lifeless seeming than he was for minute after minute.

attrib. **1878** HINTON *Hdbk. Ariz.* 45 The Apaches were, under Gen. Howard's policy, first congregated on the Chiricahui Reservation, occupying the southeastern portion of the territory. **1882** *L.A. Times* 8 Feb., Seventeen Indians were seen and are supposed to be from the San Carlos Reservation, en route to join the Chiricahua Apaches.

chiropractic ˌkaɪrəˈpræktɪk, *n.* [See note.] A drugless curative system based upon the manual adjustment of the joints, esp. those of the spine. Also attrib. or as adj.

"The name chiropractic was suggested for the new science by the Rev. Samuel H. Weed of Bloomington, Ill., an early patient. The name (Greek *cheir*, hand, and *praktikos*, efficient) was freely translated by Palmer as 'done by hand' " (*Dict. Amer. Biog.* XIV. 177/1).

1898 *Stone's Davenport* (Iowa) *City Directory* 384 Dr. Palmer Chiropractic School & Cure, Daniel D. Palmer propr. **1908** *U.S. Cong.* April 6 A bill to regulate the practice of chiropractic, to license chiropractic physicians, [etc.]. **1947** *Denver Post* 2 Mar. C. 3/3 The other (amendment) was a 'chiropractic' amendment which would have given the chiropractors about the same status as medical doctors.

chiropractor ˈkaɪrəˌpræktɚ, *n.* A practitioner of chiropractic. — **1913** DORLAND *Med. Dict.* (ed. 7). **1947** *Time* 17 Mar. 65/1 The modern chiropractor does not use the strenuous adjustments of the past any more than the modern medical doctor practices bloodletting.

* **chisel,** *n.* As the last term in **blind, full, ice chisel.**

chiselmouth. (See quot. 1909.)

1889 *Oregonian* (Portland) 4 Nov. 5/1 He . . . landed after a most exciting fight, a chinook or chisel-mouth of large size. **1896** JORDAN & EVERMANN *Fishes of N.A.* 207 Achrocheilus, Agassiz. (Chisel-mouths.) . . . A single species, American. **1909** *Cent. Supp.* 238/1 chiselmouth. . . . A cyprinoid fish, *Acrocheilus alutaceus*, found in the lower Columbia river and its tributaries, as far up as Shoshone and Spokane Falls. Also called *chiselmouth jack*.

Chisholm Trail. The most famous of the western cattle trails, leading from San Antonio, Tex., to Abilene, Kans., so named for Jesse Chisholm (*c*1806–68), a celebrated scout and plainsman.

1874 *Forest & Stream* 15 Jan. 359/2 In 1872 there were four hundred and fifty thousand cattle driven . . . up the famous 'Chisholm trail.' **1926** COOPER *Oklahoma* 18 Long-horned cattle still raised the dust of the Chisholm Trail on their tedious journey from Texas to the shipping points of Kansas. **1948** *Dly. Oklahoman* (Okla. City) 16 May E. 3/2 Many freight-hauling and cattle-driving trails were blazed and used until the middle 80's, these including the Chisholm trail, the Jones and Plummer trail, . . . and others.

chispa ˈtʃispə, *n.* *W.* [Sp., "spark," also "small particle."] A speck or small nugget of gold. *Obs.*

1853 *S.F. Alta California* 29 April 1/7 During the week two more 'chispas' were taken out, . . . one weighing twelve and the other ten ounces. **1862** *S.F. Bul.* 22 Sep. 1/1 The miners, with scarce an exception, have well filled purses, or rather as some of the miners express it, the 'chispas.' **1923** SAUNDERS *So. Sierra Calif.* 94 A glitter of something yellow caught his eye, and his fingers closed on some of the little gold nuggets that the Spanish people call *chispas*.

*****chit, *n.* **a.** The small end of a cigar. *Obs.* **b.** *pl.* A grade of rice consisting of small grains. — **(a) 1846** *Yale Lit. Mag.* XII. 71 (Th.), But, Doctor, you have not bitten off the chit. — **(b) 1856** OLMSTED *Slave States* 477 In the Carolina mills the product is divided into 'prime,' 'middling' (broken), 'small' or 'chits,' and 'flour' or 'douse.'

chittamwood ˈtʃɪtəmˌwʊd, *n.* [Origin obscure. Web. '34 suggests a Muskhogean Indian origin and cites Choctaw *shitimmi*, to puff, puffy. Poss. a euphemism for * *shittimwood.*] (See quots.) Also **chittam.**

1843 N. BOONE *Journal* 4 July (App.), Marched 4 miles E.S.E. and encamped on a pretty grove of Elm, hackberry, Tallow trees, and chittim (wood) with good grass and water. **1890** *N. & Q.* IV. 8 March 238 *Chittim-Wood* (Vol. ii, p. 151).—There are two or three species of tree in the United States which, with their wood, are known as chittim or chittam-wood. **1938** GOODDING *Native & Exotic Plants* 117 *Bumelia rigida*, or Chittimwood, . . . is a small tree with very stiff branches and vicious stiff thorns.

chittediddle. ˈtʃɪtɪˌdɪdl̩, *n.* Var. of **katydid,** representing a different appreciation of the sound. *Rare.* — **1804** LEWIS in *L. & Clark Exped.* (1905) VI. 127 The green insect known in the U' States by the name of the sawyer or chittediddle, was first heard to cry on the 27th. of July.

Chiv ʃɪv, *n.* (See quot. 1860, and see next.) *Colloq. Obs.*

1860 B. TAYLOR *At Home & Abroad* 3 Ser. (1888) 322 How long, I wondered, before these *Chivs* (the California term for Southerners—an abbreviation of Chivalry) start the exciting topic [slavery]. **1881** *City Argus* (S.F.) 2 July 1/5 The 'chivs' will have to take a back seat in the future. **1910** J. HART *Vigilante Girl* 293 These Chivs have been bullying us Northern Democrats long enough.

* **chivalry,** *n.* (See quot. 1888.) Cf. **Palmetto, Southern Chivalry.**

1842 *Liberator* (Boston) 21 Jan. 10/6 Such freedom was not to be tolerated by the 'chivalry' of Maryland. **1888** M. LANE *Pol. Catch-Words* 27 Sep. 15 Chivalry. — A cant name for the Southern people, that was much in use about the time of the breaking out of the Civil War. The idea was that Southern emigration had been largely from the Royalist or Cavalier population of England, while the Northern emigration had been largely of the Roundhead or Puritan part. Hence the South was supposed to represent the blue blood or chivalrous portion of the country. **1947** *Amer. Sp.* April 93/1 Observe that Northern use of the term is usually with a shade of contempt, with reference to the 'chivalry.'

*****chock, *v.*[1] *absol.* To fill in as packing. *Colloq.* — **1868** *Putnam's Mag.* June 668/2, I found afterward she had all her clothes and mine in the truck and then she'd chock'd in all around with maple sugar.

chock tʃɑk, *v.*[2] [Imitative.] *intr.* To enter with a slight shock or knock. *Colloq.* — **1913** MULFORD *Coming of Cassidy* ii. 31 Skinny's smoking gun chocked into its holster. *Ib.* xiii. 218 Towne's gun chocked back in the scabbard as its owner . . . went down.

* **chocolate,** *n.*

1. Used to denote soils of a color or texture resembling chocolate.

1819 E. DANA *Geog. Sks.* 188 Next to the river swamp . . . we enter upon an extensive body of level, rich land, of fine black or chocolate-coloured soil. **1821** NUTTALL *Travels Arkansa* 99 Everywhere I observed the chocolate or reddish-brown clay of the salt formation, deposited by southern freshets. **1827** A. SHERWOOD *Gaz. Georgia* 87 This has been one of the most fertile counties in the State; the real chocolate soil. **1869** *Overland Mo.* III. 130 Texas is notable for the number of its soils . . . there is the 'chocolate' prairie, and the 'mulatto.'

2. In special combs.: (1) **chocolate cooky,** a chocolate-flavored cooky or one with a chocolate coating; (2) **corn,** (see quots.); (3) **flower,** local name for a species of geranium; (4) **Friday,** a frozen food or drink of which chocolate is an ingredient, *rare;* (5) **fudge,** fudge made of chocolate; (6) **marble,** marble colored somewhat like chocolate, *rare;* (7) **plant,** *N. Eng.* the water avens, also, *ellipt.*, **chocolate;** (8) **root,** (see quot.); (9) * **soda,** short for "chocolate ice cream soda," a drink the ingredients of which are ice cream, chocolate sirup, and carbonated water; (10) **sundae,** a sundae over which chocolate is poured.

(1) **1909** FARMER *Boston Cook Book* 491 German Chocolate Cookies. **1943** *Sat. Ev. Post* 1 May 28/3, I just finished a batch of cookies. Chocolate cookies. — **(2) 1847** DARLINGTON *Weeds & Plants* 412 It [i.e., Chinese Sugar Cane, Sorghum, Sorgho, etc.] was introduced into Pennsylvania forty years ago under the name of 'Chocolate Corn'; and the seeds were roasted by the farmers' families, as a substitute for coffee. **1890** *Cent.* 3765/3 Indian millet [or] African millet, . . . *Sorghum vulgare*, . . . is sometimes called coffee- or chocolate-corn, because of its attempted use as a substitute for coffee. — **(3) 1892** *Amer. Folk-Lore* V. 93 *Geranium maculatum*, chocolate-flower. Stratham, N.H. — **(4) 1904** DERVILLE *Other Side of Story* 277 Cool off for the night with 'chocolate Fridays,' 'strawberry Sundays,' and other popular concoctions.

(5) **1897** *Confectioner's Price List*, Chocolate fudge. — **(6) 1798** WILLIAMSON *Descr. Genesee* ii., In one of the creeks, . . . there was . . . discovered a fine body of chocolate marble, which has been found to bear a good polish, and the blocks sufficiently large for any sort of building ornament. — **(7) 1832** WILLIAMSON *Maine* I. 121 The Chocolate plant . . . flourishes luxuriantly in woods. . . . Its root, when boiled, makes a drink in taste and goodness like chocolate. **1893** *Amer. Folk-Lore* VI. 141 *Geum rivale*, chocolate. Buckfield, Me.; Franconia, N.H. — **(8) 1890** *Cent.* 2504/3 The roots of . . . the water-avens, *Geum rivale*, . . . from their reddish-brown color are sometimes known by the names of chocolate-root and Indian chocolate. — **(9) 1945** *This Week Mag.* 19 May 18/3 Sarah Milton was at the other end of the counter, drinking a chocolate soda.

(10) 1922 TARKINGTON *Gentle Julia* 184, I'll take a chocolate sundae. **1945** MAXWELL *Folded Leaf* 191 Chocolate sundae is only fifteen [cents].

As the last term in **peanut chocolate.**

Chocorua plague. (See quots.) *Obs.*

1877 *Vt. Dairym. Assn. Rep.* V. 51 The 'Chocorua Plague' or 'cripple ail,' which prevails in New Hampshire near the foot of the White Mountains, arises from this cause [=lack of phosphate]. [**1907** HODGE *Amer. Indians* I. 287/8 Chocorua. The legendary last survivor of a small tribe of Indians who, previous to 1766, inhabited the region about the town of Burton, N.H. He was pursued by a white hunter to the mountain which bears his name and driven over the cliffs or shot to death. Before dying he is reported to have cursed the English and their cattle.]

Choctaw ˈtʃɑktɔ, *n.* [f. *Chata*, an ancient tribal designation the meaning of which is now unknown.]

1. An Indian of a tribe of the Muskhogean stock formerly occupying portions of the present states of Alabama and Mississippi, often pl. as a tribal designation. Cf. **White Choctaw.**

[**1700** IBERVILLE in Margry *Déc.* IV. 463 Je crois que vous pourrés . . . destacher . . . quatre hommes, pour aller dans le dedans du pays et jusqu' aux Chaqueta, et voir ce que c'est que cette nation, dont les autres Sauvages parlent tant.] **1722** COXE *Descr. Carolana* 25 This mightier Nation of the Chattas consisting of near 3000 Fighting Men, live chiefly about the Middle of the River. **1789** *Ann. 1st Congress* 22 Aug. I. 68 It will appear that, in the latter end of the year 1785, and the beginning of 1786, treaties were formed by the United States with the Cherokees, the Chickasaws, and Choctaws. **1882** *Amer. Naturalist* XVI. 222 The two thousand Choctaws still living in their ancestral homes in Mississippi, retain, in all their pristine vigor, many of the usages of their ancestors. **1948** *Dly. Ardmoreite* (Ardmore, Okla.) 21 April 7/5 Doc is half Choctaw along with a mixture of English and Irish.

b. In full **Choctaw Indians.**

1738 W. STEPHENS *Proc. Georgia* 82 The Choctaw Indians in the French Interest, had . . . come in a great body.

c. The language of these Indians, in full **Choctaw language.** Also used as a type of any unknown or difficult tongue.

1796 MORSE *Amer. Geog.* I. 669 The Chickasaw and Choctaw languages. **1839** *N.O. Picayune* 1 Mar. 2/4 Even admitting a person understands French and pronounces the name of a dish correctly, its all Hebrew or Choctaw to the waiter. **1921** *Outing* July 167/2 He became eloquent on such terms as 'batter,' 'dough,' 'rising,' and 'setting,' which were mainly Choctaw to me. **1948** *Dly. Ardmoreite* (Ardmore, Okla.) 8 July 10/2 Half of the paper was printed in the Choctaw language.

d. (See quot.) *Obs.*

1861 *The Crisis* (Columbus, O.) 31 Jan. 3/4 A correspondent of the New York *Times*, dating from Georgia, a short time ago, wrote that there 'is a secret society called the Choctaws, numbering 25,000 men, who are sworn to secession or revolution.'

e. A fancy figure in ice skating consisting of a forward stroke on the edge of one skate and then a backward stroke on the opposite edge of the other.

1907 G. H. BROWNE *Handbook Figure Skating* 20 American Skating and Competitions . . . 1862 About this time, or earlier, were skated the figures subsequently named Mohawks, Choctaws and Cross-cuts, (Edw. Brady, E. B. Cook). **1948** *Time* 2 Feb. 51/2 Whatever she tried—from difficult double Salchows to simple open Choctaws—was carefully and beautifully done.

2. In special combs.: (1) **Choctaw ball game,** the game of chunky or Indian ball as engaged in by the Choctaws, *obs.;* (2) **float,** see **float;** (3) **log,** an improvised log raft, *obs.;* (4) **nation,** the Choctaw tribe regarded as a nation; (5) **nut,** (see quot.), *obs.;* (6) **pony,** a pony such as the Choctaw Indians used, *obs.*, cf. **Cherokee pony;** (7) **purchase,** an area of land purchased by the government from the Choctaw Indians, *obs.;* (8) **root,** (see quot.); (9) **'s mile,** ?a short distance, *rare.*

(1) **1894** *Outing* XXIV. 215/2 The game lasted five hours and a half, and we all agreed that few if any of the outdoor sports equaled in excitement, skill and picturesqueness a Choctaw ball game. — (3) **c1875** in HUDSON *Humor* (1936) 229 These impromptu rafts were known by the name of 'Choctaw Log,' the early settlers having learned their construction and utility from roving bands of Choctaw hunters. — (4) **1764** H. GRACE *Captivity* 41 We next visited the Chactaws Nation. **1860** CLAIBORNE *Sam. Dale* 104 Captain Cassity certified that he received similar information from John Walker, a white man residing in the Choctaw nation. **1947** *Dly. Oklahoman* (Okla. City) 5 Nov. 5/8 A flood of ballots from members of the Choctaw and Chickasaw Nations has been pouring into the offices of the Five Civilized Tribes here.

(5) **1838** FLAGG *Far West* II. 178 Of the nuts, the pecan or Choctaw nut, the hickory, and the black walnut, are chief. — (6) **1830** *Boston Transcript* 26 Nov. 3/1 Two gentlemen and a lady, mounted each on a Choctaw poney, and evidently from far-famed Chickasha. — (7) **1834** *Richmond* (Ind.) *Palladium* 18 Jan. 1/1, I settled down in the Cane on the Chuctaw purchase. — (8) **1931** CLUTE *Plants* 29 A familiar plant, still used for basket-making and similar purposes, and commonly called Indian hemp (*Apocynum cannabinum*), was once known as Choctaw root. — (9) **1840** W. G. SIMMS *Border Beagles* II. 101 Why here, you blue-bottle, here in Cane Castle, hard by, within a Choctaw's mile.

Also *Choctaw boy, chief, country, horse, hunter, territory, treaty, tribe, warrior,* etc.

chogset ˈtʃɑgsɪt, *n.* ["Trumbull . . . derives *chogset,* in Pequot *cachauxet,* from *chohchohkesit* in the Massachuset dialect, signifying 'spotted' or 'striped' " (Hodge).] (See quots.)

1842 *Nat. Hist. N.Y., Zoology* IV. 173 The Bergall has various popular names [including] . . . Chogset, a name derived from the Mohegan dialect, but its purport unknown. **1895** GERARD in *N.Y. Sun* 30 July, Chogset, an eastern Algonquian name for the blue perch or burgall. The word apparently means 'that which is flabby,' referring to the soggy flesh of the fish. **1902** *Amer. Folk-Lore* 243 Chogset. This name current in parts of New England for fish (*Ctenolabrus Cæruleus*), known also as 'blue perch,' 'cunner,' 'nibbler,' etc., is derived from some eastern (probably Narragansett or Massachusets) dialect.

* **choice,** *n.* A spot or location chosen for settlement, often in place-names. *Obs.*

1667 *Md. Hist. Mag.* XX. 24 Phillips Choice. **1678** in *Ib.* XIX. 344 Benjamins Choice. **1698** *Ib.* 367 Parkers Choice. **1707** *Ib.* I. 7 That . . . a town should be erected on a tract on the same River . . . called Taylor's Choice. **1834** H. BRACKENRIDGE *Recoll.* ii. 19 In ten days we reached the encampment of General Wayne, at a place called Hopson's choice, now a part of the city of Cincinnati.

As the last term in **fielder's, ladies', sailor's choice.**

choicy ˈtʃɔɪsɪ, *a.* Choosy, fastidious. *Colloq.* — **1909** R. A. WASON *Happy Hawkins* 208, 'I ain't nowise choicy,' sez I, 'call me anything you want.'

* **choke,** *v.*

1. *choke in, up,* to refrain from speaking, hold one's tongue. *Colloq.*

1843 STEPHENS *High Life N.Y.* I. ii. 19 Cousin John looked at her so eternal cross that she was glad to choke in. **1907** MULFORD *Bar-20* ix. 105 'Why, about eight years ago I had business—' 'Choke up,' interposed Red.

2. In combs.: (1) **chokeberry,** any one of various shrubs of the genus *Aronia,* or the small astringent fruit of this, also the chokecherry *q.v.,* also attrib.; (2) **bow,** ?a form of yoke used on a horse going at large to prevent its getting into inclosures, *obs.;* (3) **cherry,** any one of various American wild cherries of the genus *Padus,* also attrib.; (4) * **dog,** (see quot.), *obs.;* (5) **huckleberry,** =**chokeberry;** (6) * **pear** =**chokeberry;** (7) **tater,** (see quot.), *colloq.;* (8) * **weed,** used allusively for hemp such as a hangman's rope is made of, *rare;* (9) **whortleberry,** a variety of whortleberry.

(1) **1778** CARVER *Travels* 511 The Choak Berry. The shrub thus termed by the natives grows about five or six feet high, and bears a berry about the size of a sloe, of a jet black. **1832** WILLIAMSON *Maine* I. 117 The Prune genus embraces . . . the Choke-cherry, or as some may call it the choke-berry, of two varieties. **1938** MATSCHAT *Suwannee River* 207 Chokeberry bushes and blackberry vines were in full bloom. — (2) **1811** *Mass. Spy* 26 June (Th.), Strayed, a Bay Mare . . . had on a Choke Bow, tied with a string. — (3) **1784** CUTLER in *Mem. Academy* I. 449 Choke Cherry. A low shrub. . . . The Red Choke Cherry. A shrub. **1929** DICKSON *Across Plains* 151 She set out choke-cherry 'butter' and plum jelly which she had made. **1943** HOWARD *Montana* 16 The Indians chewed the dried roots of the chokecherry. **1948** *Nat. Hist.* Dec. 434/2 One-fourth pound of the leaves of young shoots in the closely related chokecherry was determined . . . to be fatal to sheep. — (4) **1821** COOPER *Spy* xxi, Replenishing the mug with a large addition of the article known to the soldiery by the name of 'choke-dog,' she held it towards the peddler.

(5) **1931** CLUTE *Plants* 69 One taste . . . is enough and will serve to indicate why the aronias are often called choke-huckleberries. — (6) **1892** *Amer. Folk-Lore* V. 95 *Pyrus arbutifolia* . . . choke-pear. Washington Co., Me. — (7) **1893** *Voodoo Tales* 145 The choke-taters or artichokes (not the green vegetable rosettes served to 'white folks,' but the tubers of the great 'Jerusalem sunflower' . . .) were buried in the ashes. — (8) **1812** *Aurora* (Phila.) 23 Dec. (Th.), These gentry should remember that we have plenty of choak-weed in America, and enough willing to see it used, when the safety of the country is in danger. — (9) **1784** CUTLER in *Mem. Acad.* I. 439 The Choke Whortleberry.

* **choker,** *n.* (See quot. 1925.) Also attrib.

1905 *Forestry Bureau Bul.* 61 B. **1925** *Amer. Sp.* Dec. 136/1 The short cables, each with a steel loop in one end and a steel hook in the other, which were set around the logs were called 'chokers.' **1944** BINNS *Timber Beast* 22 To assist this giant in picking up the logs, there were six 'choker men' who noosed short cables around the logs which were to be brought in.

choking snake. (See quot.) *Rare.* — **1795** in S. WILLIAMS *Nat. Hist. Vt.* (ed. 2) I. App. 485 In a field in Connecticut. . . . I approached with caution within twenty feet of a black snake, about seven feet long, having a white throat, and of the kind which the people there call runners or choking snakes.

* **cholera,** *n.* **1.** =**hog cholera. 2. cholera infantum,** a disease of children that occurs in summer and is characterized by vomiting and diarrhea. See also **anti-, mountain cholera.**

(1) **1879** *Diseases of Swine* 178 Cholera in Kansas and Nebraska seems to attack preferably the Berkshire. — (2) **1829** B. HALL *Travels N. Amer.* III. 389 Our researches, . . . were all cut short . . . by the illness of our little girl, whose long exposure to the noxious air of the great rivers, had given her a complaint very fatal to children in that country, and called by the ominous name of Cholera Infantum. **1895** *Outing* XXVI. 405/2 You are forced to wish that cholera-infantum had been more prevalent sixty years ago.

cholla ˈtʃojə, *n. S.W.* [Sp. in Amer. Sp. sense shown here.] Any one of several species of spiny cacti, esp. *Opuntia cholla.* In full **cholla cactus.** Cf. **deer bush** (*b*). See also **jumping, staghorn, tree cholla.**

1856 *Wide West* (S.F.) Oct. 4/6 There is a shrub called . . . the *Choya,* . . . and other species of the Cacti family. **1874** in *Amer. Plants* (1909) II. 409 In Cholla valley, the most remarkable of these protected localities, the cholla cactus (Opuntia prolifera) attains a height of six feet. **1948** *Pacific Discovery* Mar.–Apr. 8/2 Or a small gray desert fox will be a sharp-eared shadow behind the moonlight-haloed knobs of the Cholla cactus, now there, then gone.

chonk tʃɔŋk, *v.* [Imitative. Cf. **champ,* **chomp.*] *intr.* To chew vigorously, to "chomp." *Colloq.* — **1843** STEPHENS *High Life N.Y.* I. 50 But there sot the old man a chonking an apple. **1908** *D.N.* III. 298 You chonk like a horse.

chonking ˈtʃɔŋkɪŋ, *n.* A small piece or fragment nibbled away or pared off. *Colloq.* — **1882** *Cent. Mag.* XXV. 299/1 The ground . . . [was] covered with the 'chonkings' of the frozen apples, the work of the squirrels in getting at the seed. **1895** *D.N.* I. 385 Chankings, parings of apples and other fruits, or the core and other rejected parts of an apple. Me., Vt., Mass., Conn.

choosy ˈtʃuzɪ, *a.* Particular, fussy. *Colloq.* — **1862** *Harper's Mag.* Dec. 100/2 But so I'm sure enough thar at last, I'm noways choosy about the road. **1948** *Chi. Tribune* 11 July (Grafic Mag.) 18/1 Gerold Gray was choosy about his rooming houses.

* **chop,** *n.*

1. A cut or notch made in a tree.

1662 *Va. Statutes* II. 101 The surveighors being for the most part careles of seeing the trees marked, . . . in a small time the chopps being growne up, or the trees fallen, the bounds become as uncertaine as at first. **1750** T. WALKER *Journal* 54 Besides several Trees blazed Several ways with 3 Chops over each blaze. **1832** *Louisville Directory* 106 Jacob Sodowsky . . . was the first man who shewed a method of identifying the chops which were made on the line and corner trees of old surveys.

2. (See quots.) Cf. **corn, Indian, oat chop(s).**
1830 COLLINS *Emigrant's Guide* 132 When it [rye] is ground only (as it is used for bread in England) they here call it 'chop,' and give it to cattle. **1877** RUEDE *Sod-House Days* 49 Send me a recipe for making johnny cakes. The corn-meal here is what you call chop—hulls an all. **1922** *Outing* July 184/3 When the cow had licked up the last bit of chop, she looked around at the milker.

3. In combs.: (1) **chop feed,** =**chop,** *n.* **2;** (2) **grass,** ?=**crab grass,** *rare;* (3) **log,** a log upon which things are chopped.
(1) 1852 *Mich. Agric. Soc. Trans.* III. 151 Chop feed is good for them in small quantities, say half a pint to a sheep. **1871** *Rep. Indian Affairs* 529, I have added . . . a hay-cutter for preparing 'chop-feed.' — **(2) 1871–3** *Texas Almanac* 12 No labor . . . is better bestowed than that which is applied to drawing the heavy cover of crab or chop-grass . . . into the water-furrow. — **(3) 1867** T. LACKLAND *Homespun* I. 124 There is an indiscriminate spirting of fresh blood all around the chop-log.

* **chop,** *v.*

1. *tr.* To begin clearing (land) by felling and trimming the timber.
1821 W. DALTON *Travels U.S.* 82 Farms are called improved, when the settler, having chopped a few acres, has piled up into the form of a dwelling-house, a number of logs. **1868** S. SMITH *Autobiog.* 10 My brother Josiah chopped twelve acres for a Mr. Wildman, his compensation being a yoke of oxen. 'Chopping' consists of felling the trees, cutting them into logs 12 feet long, and piling the brush!

b. (See quot.) *Colloq.*
1899 GREEN *Va. Word-book* 85 Chop, *v.* To mark a tree by making three chops with an axe on each side, showing the boundary between tracks [*sic*] of land. Line-trees are chopped every three years by law.

2. To cut down or clear away (weeds, etc.); to break up (land). *Obs.*
1770 WASHINGTON *Diaries* I. 394 The Ground here was tolerably clean and in Good Order, the Grass and Weeds being Choped over. **1859** *Harper's Mag.* Nov. 727/1 Just before planting [rice] the ground is first chopped or broken rudely.

b. *To chop in,* to plant (small grain) by hoeing it into the soil. *Obs.*
1787 WASHINGTON *Diaries* III. 198 Women putting up the New fence but ordered them to chop in Oats in the low parts w[hi]ch had been hoed.

3. To thin young cotton plants and clear the drill of grass and weeds with a hoe. Also with *out.*
1820 in *Henderson's N.C. Almanack* (1823) 25 The hands may begin to thin by chopping out the cotton with their hoes. **1852** *Florida Plant. Rec.* 65, I have choped out a Little Cotton. **1948** *Ada* (Okla.) *Ev. News* 4 July 6/3 They instructed their three children to chop cotton.

Hence **chopping out.**
1842 in TURNER *Cotton* (1865) 55 The . . . useless operations of *bar-shearing, scraping* and *chopping out* are saved.

* **chopped,** *a.* Of waves: Choppy.
1849 N. KINGSLEY *Diary* 26 Oweing to the winds shifting, and causeing heavy chopped seas, many of them come aboard of us. **1860** ABBOTT *South & North* 61 A stern norther rose in the night, blowing . . . and raising that short, chopped sea, as the sailors term it. **1880** WALLACE *Ben-Hur* 12 Here chopped waves, there long swells.

* **chopper,** *n.*

1. A wood-chopper, one who cuts down trees.
1785 A. ELLICOTT in *Life & Lett.* (1908) 44 My Brother Joseph at Present runs the guide Line for the Choppers. **1860** HOLLAND *Miss Gilbert's Career* ix. 146 In the yards of the quiet dwellings the sturdy chopper's axe was swung. **1932** *Old-Time N. Eng.* Jan. 144/1 There were twenty or twenty-five choppers, altogether, and he could throw any one of them.

b. =**cotton chopper.**
1947 LUMPKIN *Southerner* 25 Don't let your choppers cut the roots by careless hoeing, for then the plants will shed their precious bolls.

2. One who operates a ticket box, as at a subway station.
1899 *N.Y. Journal* 7 Feb. 4/2 The ticket agents and 'choppers' are shivering in their shoes. At several of the down stations where the traffic is light at night, the services of both the old agents and 'choppers' have been dispensed with. **1904** *N.Y. Ev. Post* 26 Nov., I asked policemen, ticket-sellers and choppers if they had seen a lady in a gray dress with two valises pass through.

3. *W.* (See quot.) Cf. **chopping horse.**
1913 W. C. BARNES *Western Grazing Grounds* 381 Cutting Horse. A horse used especially for the work of cutting out; a 'carver,' a 'chopper,' chopping horse.

As the last term in **cotton, feed, hay, herring, master, ticket, tie, wood chopper.**

* **chopping,** *n.*

1. A tract upon which the trees have been (or are being) felled. (See also quot. 1839.) *Obs.*
1817 *Mass. Spy* 11 June (Th.), A. S., in a piece of chopping that he was clearing, fell a tree across a stump. **1839** HOLMES *Explor. Aroostook River* 54 Some prefer to let the '*chopping,*' or trees that are felled, lie until the next spring, before they burn them. **1846** *Knickerb.* XXVIII. 343, I succeeded. . . to get the whole of my 'chopping' logged and cleared. **1937** WILSON *Aroostook* 137 In the preparation the state of Maine had paid for a 'chopping' of five acres on each of the hundred-acre lots, built for each lot a log cabin eighteen by twenty-six feet.

2. Short for **chopping bee.**
1893 T. D. PRICE *MS Diary* 20 April, A. Jones made a chopping for Wolcott.

3. In combs.: (1) **chopping ax,** an ax for chopping as distinguished from one for hewing; (2) **bee,** a gathering of neighbors to assist someone in clearing land, chopping wood, etc.; (3) **frolic,** =prec.; (4) **horse,** (see quot.); (5) **squad,** a squad of men assigned to do chopping.
(1) 1778 *Pa. Archives* 6 Ser. XII. 247 Sold at Public Vendue . . . one Chopping Ax—£1 6s. **1925** HEMING *Living Forest* 156 It was done with a three-an'-a-half pound 'choppin' ax'—the kind a hunter wouldn't carry.' — **(2) 1809** *Mass. Spy* 12 July (Th.), At Bristol (Ver.), June 7, at a chopping-bee, a limb of one of the falling trees struck one of the men. **1943** DAMON *Sense of H.* 10 They . . . used ter hev choppin' and buildin' bees' ter help each other turn and turn abaout. — **(3) 1853** RAMSEY *Tennessee* 720 Weddings, military trainings, house-raisings, chopping frolics, were often followed with the fiddle, and dancing, and rural sports. — **(4) 1920** HUNTER *Trail Drivers Texas* I. 297 The specially trained horses used [to cut out cattle] . . . are called . . . chopping horses. — **(5) 1864** GRIGSBY *Smoked Yank* xxi. (1891) 181 There are fifty-two in the chopping squad, including the captain of the squad and myself.

As the last term in **cotton, pork, wood chopping.**

chop suey ˈtʃɑpˈsuɪ, *n.* [Chinese *tsa-sui,* odds and ends.] A food first served in Chinese restaurants, consisting of a mélange of various ingredients, particularly bean sprouts, vegetables, chipped or sliced meat, and flavored with sesame or peanut oil, or with soy sauce.
1928 ASBURY *Gangs of N.Y.* 301 The tongs are as American as chop suey—the latter is said to have been invented by an American dishwasher in a San Francisco restaurant, while the first tong was organized in the Western gold fields about 1860. **1947** *Democrat* 7 Aug. 8/1 Chop suey, unknown in China, was originated in New York City by an American chef. The word chop suey in Chinese means 'hash.'

attrib. **1903** G. ADE *People You Know* 16 The next Picture that came out of the Fog was a Chop Suey Restaurant and everybody breaking Dishes. **1936** MCKENNA *Black Range* 220 Every time I went into a chop suey joint in the Southwest, the owner would give me the glad hand.

* **choral,** *n.* A choral hymn, esp. one such as the Negroes in the South sing. — **1875** E. KING *Southern St. N. Amer.* 613 Listening to the singing of 'Dust an' Ashes,' one of the sweetest and sublimest chorals ever improvised.

chore boy. A boy who does chores, a cook's helper on a ranch or in a lumber camp.
1848 *Knickerb.* XXXII. 230, I afterwards saw Betty . . . laughing with the gardener and 'chore-boy.' **1893** *Scribner's Mag.* June 711/2 For a crew of sixty men, the cook has a helper, called in camp parlance the 'cookee,' and a 'chore-boy' to fetch wood and water and help wait on table. **1932** *DAB* VIII. 30 Galusha had the usual life of a chore boy with a little schooling in the winter and the activities of his grandfather's tavern for variation.

* **chorister,** *n.* One who leads the congregation of a church or a choir in singing.
1769 *Plymouth Church Rec.* I. 332 To choose one or more Persons (since our dear Brother John May is taken from us by death who was our former Chorister) to lead in singing in the publick Worship. **1841** *Knickerb.* XVII. 33 A New-Hampshire Yankee . . . wants to set up a singin'-school in Tinnecum, where I have been chorister for these ten years past. **1930** W. R. MOODY *D. L. Moody* 141 A short time before Moody had engaged a young man, Ira D. Sankey, to be chorister in his church and Sunday school.

choupique ˈʃupɪk, *n.* Also **choupic.** *S.* [Choctaw Indian *shupik* in same sense.] (See quot. 1931.)
1763 in *Amer. Sp.* XX. (1945) 48 The *Choupic* is a very beautiful fish; many people mistake it for a trout. **1885** *Outing* Feb. 336/2 For the rest, there are gais, own cousins to the alligator, buffalo, *gaspergoos,* . . . and *choupics.* **1931** READ *La-French* 88 The Bowfin (*Amia calva* L.). *Choupique* is almost the only name given in Louisiana to this fish even by those who cannot speak French. **1945** *Amer. Sp.* Feb. 48

Choupic. . . . As a pre-school boy in New Orleans this word was as familiar to me as 'green-trout' (black bass), 'gaspergou,' or perch. It is pronounced by the English-speaking natives 'shoepick.'

*** chouse,** *v. W. tr.* (See quot. 1920.)

1920 HUNTER *Trail Drivers Texas* 313 The round-up boss would let no one ride through the herd and 'chouse' or unnecessarily disturb them. **1931** DOBIE *Coronado* 116 One morning while they were 'chousing' a bunch of outlaw cattle, Russel caught a hurried glimpse of two very old Mexicans. **1948** *Sat. Ev. Post* 10 July 84/1 When you chowse 'em around they lose weight.

chow tʃaʊ, *n.* [f. **chowchow.**] Food, or the time when food is served. Also **chow line.** *Slang.* Cf. *** chuck,** *n.*[1]

1856 *Spirit of Age* (Sacramento) 27 Nov. 2/2 Ah Chow—*ah* in the Celestial lingo means *Mr. Chow,* something good to eat,—we may, therefore, say Mr. *Grub* was found guilty of peddling tea without a license. **1921** *Montanan* Feb. 14 After 'chow' that evening I heard the details of what took place after my departure. **1948** *Lawton* (Okla.) *Constitution* 2 July 1/6 The pair argued over their place in the breakfast chow-line.

chowchow ˈtʃaʊˌtʃaʊ, *n.* [Said to be prob. f. pidgin English. App. first used in Calif.] A relish of various things, esp. chopped mixed pickles. — **1850** B. TAYLOR *Eldorado* xii. (1862) 117 The grave Celestials serve up their chow-chow and curry. **1944** MENCKEN in *New Yorker* 30 Dec. 18/3 With it they threw in a dozen cases of dill pickles, chowchow, mustard, and mincemeat.

chowder ˈtʃaʊdɚ, *n.* [F. *chaudière.*]

1. A stew or thick soup composed of game, fish, or clams, together with salt pork, onions, potatoes, crackers, milk, etc. Cf. **clam chowder.**

1751 *Boston Ev. Post* 23 Sep. 2/1 Directions for making a chouder. **1868** ROSE *Great Country* 247, I found out, on enquiry, that it was one of the excursions that are made daily, during the summer, from Providence to Rocky Point, one of the attractions being 'clams' and 'chowder.' **1945** COLCORD *Sea Lang.* 53 Chowder is made with milk in Maine and Massachusetts, with water and added tomatoes in Rhode Island and further south.

transf. **1870** *Cong. Globe* 22 Dec. 281/2 This [amnesty] bill may be called a 'chowder' of rare and varied ingredients. **1918** in *Liberty* 11 Aug. (1928) 8/2 Battery D found the straw pile first, and that led to a tired cat and dog fight. We won, and retired in a variety of straw chowder.

b. *By chowder!* a mild imprecation. *Colloq.*

1827 *Nat. Gazette* (Phila.) 13 Oct. 4/1 Once in our Bay, I vum by chowder The Tea was made of good Gunpowder.

c. *To run a chowder mill,* (see quot.). *Colloq.*

1874 *Atlantic Mo.* Sep. 300/2 All keeping beach hotels, . . . with the collateral occupation of 'running a chowder mill,' as the phrase goes here [at Coney Island].

2. A social gathering at which those present partake of chowder, in full **chowder party.**

1826 FLINT *Recoll.* 354 We had public chowder-parties, where sixty people sat down under grape-vine arbours, to other good things beside fish. **1848** BARTLETT 82 Nearly 10,000 persons assembled [at a political mass-meeting] in Rhode Island, for whom a clambake and chowder were prepared. **1906** *N.Y. Ev. Post* 6 Nov. 8 The Bowery . . . went about the business . . . with as much good nature as if it were 'Big Tim's' annual 'chowder.'

As the last term in **bear, Cape Cod, clam, corn, egg, fish, Manhattan clam, potato, Yankee chowder.**

chowder ˈtʃaʊdɚ, *v. tr.* (See quots.)

1732 in *Amer. Sp.* XV. 227/1 'Dined on a fine chowdered cod.' **1806** WEBSTER, Chowder, *v. t.* to make a chowder. **1947** COFFIN *Yankee Coast* 295 Steamed, chowdered, stewed, broiled, or fried bare, or in a good thick egg-batter, clams are always in season and in good taste.

chow mein ˈtʃaʊˈmen, *n.* [Chinese in similar sense.] A thick stew of chicken, mushrooms, onions, fried noodles, etc. Also attrib.

1927 *Ladies' Home Jrnl.* Nov. 143/1 Chow mein is another one-dish main course that is popular in Chinese restaurants, and chicken chow mein is one of the most often selected of this variety. **1943** *Copper Camp* 116 Nothing was left for John Chinaman but his 'long-noodle—all pork,' chop suey and chow mein eating houses. **1948** *Woodlawn Booster* (Chi.) 12 May 4/3 Sprinkle with salt and serve with chow mein, creamed eggs or chicken a la king.

Christadelphians ˌkrɪstəˈdɛlfɪənz, *n. pl.* [*Christ*+Gr. *adelphos,* brother.] A small religious sect organized in 1844 by John Thomas, M.D., a seceder from the Campbellites. Also known as **Brothers of Christ** and **Thomasites.**

1869 *(title), Who Are the Christadelphians.* **1894** A. H. NEWMAN *Baptist Churches U.S.* 503 Most Plymouth Brethren and Christadelphians . . . agree with Baptists in rejecting infant baptism. **1919** *Census of Religious Bodies: 1916* II. 189/2 In polity the Christadelphians are thoroughly congregational. **1943** *Yearbk. of Amer. Churches* 19.

*** Christian,** *n.*

1. A white colonist or settler as distinguished from an Indian. *Obs.*

1622 MOURT *Relation* 22 We found the remainder of an old Fort, or Palizide, which as we conceiued had beene made by some Christians. **1723** *N.Y. State Doc. Hist.* (1849) I. 717 The Language of those Indians is not understood by any Christian among us. **1838** *S. Lit. Messenger* IV. 800/2 Cassena . . . is still used by the 'Christians' or whites wherever it grows.

2. A member of any one of various religious sects, as the Stoneites, Republican Methodists, the Christian Connection, and the Campbellites.

In early use often pronounced with the vowel sound in *Christ.*

1805 E. SMITH (ed.) The Christian's Magazine, Reviewer, and Religious Intelligencer. **1815** in MILLS & SMITH *Missionary Tour* 19 There was even a man of the New England sect of *Christ*-ians [*Footnote:* The sect of Elias Smith] preaching and distributing books in this [=Missouri] and the adjacent Territory. **1859** BARTLETT 81 Christian, . . . a name assumed by a sect which arose from the great revival in 1801. **1944** WILSON *Passing Inst.* 197 The Methodist, the Baptists, and the Christians were our three denominations.

3. In special combs.: (1) **Christian Church,** the Christian Connection *q.v.,* also the Disciples of Christ; (2) **Connection,** a denomination having the Bible as its only authoritative rule of faith and practice, resulting from various independent secession movements in the Methodist, Baptist, and Presbyterian churches, and since 1931 united with the Congregational Church under the name of Congregational and Christian Church; (3) **Endeavor,** a group of young people organized in any one of various Protestant churches to do Christian work, also attrib.; (4) **Indians,** any one of various groups of Indians who have accepted some form of Christianity; (5) **Perfectionist,** those composing the Oneida Community *q.v., obs.;* (6) *** Science,** see as a main entry; (7) **Scientist,** one who adheres to the teachings of Christian Science.

(1) **1824** R. H. BISHOP *Hist. Church Ky.* 130 They have assumed to themselves the exclusive name of 'The Christian Church.' They have usually been called 'New Lights, or Stoneites.' **1849** CHAMBERLAIN *Indiana Gazetteer* 72 The Christian Church.—Owing to the fact that this denomination of Christians have neither Conferences, Associations or Synods, it is found difficult . . . to do more than approximate to their number. **1948** *Crusader* May 15/1 They were jointed in 1832 by Barton W. Stone and 10,000 members of 'The Christian Church.' — (2) **1844** RUPP *Relig. Denominations* 167 Sometimes in speaking of themselves as a body, they use the term Christian Connexion. **1889** P. BUTLER *Recoll.* 210 Geo. W. Hutchinson had been a preacher in what was known as the 'Christian Connection' in the New England States. — (3) **1893** *Chi. Tribune* 10 July 3/3 Twelve years after the first Christian Endeavor society was organized at Portland, Me., its founder . . . has planted and visited Christian Endeavor societies in Australia, China, Japan, India, and along the highways where Paul planted the first Christian churches in Europe. **1900** NICHOLSON *Hoosiers* 144 He then retired finally from the ministry; but the phrase, 'Christian Endeavor,' first applied by Dr. Eggleston to his Brooklyn church, is widely known as the name of a society of young people. **1931** F. L. ALLEN *Only Yesterday* 92 Dr. Francis E. Clark, the founder and president of the Christian Endeavor Society, declared that the modern 'indecent dance' was 'an offense against womanly purity.' — (4) **1827** JEDEDIAH SMITH in Browne *Min. Resources West* (1867) 296, I understand, through the medium of one of your Christian Indians, that you are anxious to know who we are. **1853** *S.F. Herald* 21 Jan. 5/6 The Christian Indians, a peculiar and interesting band once resident in Canada, whence they emigrated from Ohio, are now located on the lands of the Wyandotts, who consider them intruders and desire their removal. **1942** WEYGANDT *Plenty of Penna.* 40 A son of my first Weygandt ancestor in America . . . visited Heckewelder's Christian Indians in Ohio.

(5) **1867** *N.Y. Tribune* 19 June 7/2 Four miles from Oneida, Madison County, N.Y., a class calling themselves Christian Perfectionists, 20 years ago organized a community. — (7) **1876** B. ALCOTT *Journals* 465 They take the name of 'Christian Scientists' and find in the Christian Records the foundation of their faith, the gift of healing as practised by Christ being their central doctrine. **1945** STEINBECK *C. Row* 17 A good half of the girls are Christian Scientists.

b. *To make a Christian out of,* to force one to a desired action or attitude. *Slang.*

1943 *Reader's Digest* Dec. 111/1 But it sure made Christians out of the others.

As the last term in **Revengeless, Weaponless Christian.**

* **Christiania,** *n.* [Former name of the capital of Norway.] Also **christiania.** A "swing" in skiing used to stop short. In full **Christiania swing.** Cf. **christy.**

1913 *Outing* Jan. 499/2 The beginner when he tries to make the Christiana swing will find that when he comes rushing down the hill not only will he hesitate to throw his weight forward, but his feet will be so close together that in attempting to turn one of the ski will cross the other and he will fall. **1922** *Ib.* Jan. 161/2, I always could make a Christiania swing more easily to the left than to the right. **1947** *Sierra Club Bul.* Nov. 90 The candidate should demonstrate four linked christianias as an additional gauge of proficiency and good form in the turn.

* **Christian Science.** A religion and system of healing, founded by Mary Baker Eddy in 1866, based upon the teaching that all cause and effect is mental and that a full understanding of Jesus' healing and teaching will result in abolishing sin, sickness, and death. Also attrib.

*c***1867** EDDY *Science of Man* (MS) 10 Jehovah cannot be understood so as to demonstrate Christian Science when interpreted through a belief or doctrine. **1895** *Outlook* 19 Jan., A great Christian Science church was dedicated in Boston on Sunday, the 6th inst. **1914** *N. Eng. Mag.* April 59/1 Perhaps the most prominent factor in promoting the growth of Christian Science is the healing work accomplished by the Christian Science practitioner. **1947** *Chr. Sci. Mon.* 1 Mar. 3/4 He withdrew from private business in 1929 to become a Christian Science practitioner in Chicago.

* **Christmas,** *n.*

1. A Christmas gift. Also *collect. Colloq.*

1857 in EASTERBY *S.C. Rice Plant.* (1945) 136 Joe and Will went to Waverly to see Christmas given out to the negroes there. **1895** *D.N.* I. 386.

2. In combs.: (1) **Christmas berry,** see as a main entry; (2) **cactus,** the crab cactus of South America, which has red flowers, also attrib.; (3) **fern,** an evergreen fern used as a winter decoration; (4) * **gift,** (see quot. 1908); (5) **gifting,** giving presents at Christmas, *rare;* (6) **gun,** (see quot.), *obs.;* (7) **stocking,** a stocking hung up, usu. beside the fireplace, to receive the presents left by Santa Claus on Christmas Eve; (8) **tree,** see as a main entry.

(2) **1921** *Frontier* Nov. 23 She stooped to inhale the fragrance of a hyacinth, and caress the smooth green Christmas cactus leaves. **1943** DAMON *Sense of H.* 65 The Christmas cactus on a little bracket at the side punctually justifies its name. — (3) **1880** J. ROBINSON *Flora Essex Co., Mass.* 135 *Aspidium acrostichoides, Sw.* (Christmas fern.) Rocky woods. Common. **1947** *Midland Naturalist* July 26 Christmas Fern [is] occasional (locally common) in seepage swamps. — (4) **1844** *Knickerb.* XXIII. 16 Threatening to catch him for a Christmas gift next morning, [she] disappeared up the stairs. **1908** *D.N.* III. 298 Christmas gift, a greeting on Christmas morning. The person who is caught, i.e., who is greeted first, is expected to give a present to the one who catches him. The custom is passing away. **1947** LUMPKIN *Southerner* 40 The game was to catch each other at 'Christmas gift!' (5) **1853** KANE *Grinnell Exped.* 270 But even here that kindly custom of Christmas-gifting was not forgotten. — (6) *c***1898** CHRISTIAN *Days* 25, I have spoken of the boys preparing their 'Chrismus guns,' by this I do not mean real guns, as it was not considered safe for slaves to own firearms, but they invented various things to make a noise with, as noise was what they desired. — (7) **1853** SUSAN & ANNA B. WARNER *Christmas Stocking* (1854) 3 Little Carl always hung up his stocking, and generally had it filled. **1883** *Harper's Mag.* Dec. 15/2 The saint who generously filled the Christmas stocking.

As the last term in **white Christmas.**

Christmas berry. 1. (See quot.) **2.** (See quots. and cf. **toyon.**)

(1) **1932** C. C. LOVELL *Golden Isles Ga.* 58 The grounds were enclosed by hedges of *Ilex cassine*, or Christmas berry. — (2) **1946** *Chi. Tribune* 23 Dec. 14/3 Other specimens in the holiday arboretum are: The Christmas berry, also called toyon, a shrub native to California; the pepper or Christmas-berry tree, widely planted in California, and the Christmas flower, which is the Mexican name for the poinsettia. **1948** *Pacific Discovery* Mar.-Apr. 30/2 The common toyon or Christmas berry is probably a relict since it has relatives . . . in the Orient.

Christmas tree. A small evergreen, usu. a spruce or fir, set up at Christmas and ornamented with lights, tinsel, etc., and bearing Christmas gifts or presents.

The 1855 quot. below refers to the practice in Germany. The custom may have been introduced here by Germans. See "Our First Christmas Tree" in *Reader's Digest* Dec. 1944, 31-34.

1838 H. MARTINEAU *Retrospect of Western Travel* II. 178, I was present at the introduction into the new country of the spectacle of the German Christmas-tree. **1855** *Rural New Yorker* 49/1 The last thing attended to is the selection and adornment of the Christmas tree. **1856** *S.F. Call* 25 Dec. 2/1 Who can think . . . of the anxious children gathered round the Christmas tree—the fabulous visits of Santa Claus . . . without feeling that man has other ends than those that characterize every day life? **1864** *Alta California* (S.F.) 7 Feb. 1/7 [In Philadelphia,] as in California, the stocking-hanging system has exploded in favor of the Christmas tree, and the churches were lighted and brightened by green boughs and young faces, awaiting for the kindly remembrances of older and richer people. **1948** *Reader's Digest* March 153/1 We cut a Christmas tree and decorated it with pieces of red string and rabbits' fur tassels.

transf. **1947** *Time* 27 Jan. 76/1 In oil fields . . . a 'Christmas Tree' means a series of pipes, valves and fittings. It is mounted on top of a well and meters the flow of oil.

christy ˈkrɪstɪ, *n.* Short for **Christiania.** Also as a verb. *Colloq.* — **1942** PEATTIE *Friendly Mts.* 300 On the same hill well-to-do brokers, indigent college students, and automobile mechanics 'herring bone' and 'christie' together. **1947** *Trail & Timberline* April 60/2 Our chins were up, and we were really swinging into some neat but gaudy christies.

Christy's Minstrels. A troupe of Negro minstrels originally organized by George Christy of New York. Now *hist.* — [**1857** *Spirit of Times* 19 Dec. 256/3 George Christy and Wood's Minstrels.] *Ib.* 26 Dec. 272/2 They are located at Mechanics' Hall, formerly the habitation of the original Christy's Minstrels.

chromo ˈkromo, *n.* Short for chromolithograph. Also attrib.

"It is claimed that the word 'chromo' was coined in Boston, in 1864, by our honored fellow-citizen, Mr. Louis Prang" (C. W. Ernst in *Bostonian Soc. Proc.* XVI. 26).

1869 *Republican Jrnl.* (Lawrence, Kans.) 20 March, Chromos, paintings, engravings and everything which adds to the ornamenting of a parlor are to be found at their store. **1913** CATHER *O Pioneers!* 9 There he was, turning over a portfolio of chromo 'studies' which the druggist sold to the Hanover women who did china-painting. **1948** *Sierra Club Bul.* March 75 A chromo by Prang was within the reach of almost every lover of nature.

b. *To take (contest) the chromo*, to "take the cake," to vie *with. Colloq.*

1893 MARK TWAIN *£1,000,000 Bank-Note*, etc. 93 The full name . . . will be Mrs. Ambulinia Valeer Elfonzo. It takes the chromo. *Ib.* 255 With Chicago it contests the chromo for flatness of surface.

chromo ˈkromo, *v. tr.* To reproduce in a chromo. *Rare.* — **1877** HARTE *Story of Mine* ix. 111 Something that could be afterwards lithographed, or chromoed.

chronicle song. A ballad of a historical nature. *Colloq.* — **1853** BALDWIN *Flush T. Shipp* 149 He was the merriest, jovialest feller you ever see, and can sing more chronicle songs than one of these show fellers.

chrono-thermalist. App. a medical practitioner using a system involving time and heat. *Rare.* — **1864** T. L. NICHOLS *Amer. Life* I. 364 There are also physicians of every school. There are . . . hydropaths mild and heroic; chrono-thermalists, Thompsonians, [etc.].

* **chub,** *n.*

1. *local.* Any one of various American fishes as the tautog, black bass, etc.

[**1716** in *Memoirs of a Huguenot Family* (1872) 288 We catched a dish of fish, some perch, and a fish they call chub.] **1842** *Nat. Hist. N.Y., Zoology* IV. 193 The Brilliant Chubsucker, *Labeo oblongus*, . . . is . . . familiarly known under the name of Chub, and Chub-sucker. **1855** BAIRD in *Smithsonian Rep.* 340 The tautog, smooth black fish or chub, . . . [is] caught off the steep banks, in the channel-ways and the thoroughfares. **1890** MCALLISTER *Society* xxiii. 311 Menu of an old-fashioned Southern dinner. . . . Boiled fresh water Trout (known with us at the North as Chub).

2. (*cap.*) A Texan. *Rare.*

1869 *Overland Mo.* III. 129 For the Texan soubriquet 'Chub' I know of no explanation, unless it be found in the size of the Eastern Texans.

3. (See quot.)

*a***1870** CHIPMAN *Notes on Bartlett* 81 Chub. . . . A round squash. Conn.

4. In combs.: (1) **chub eel,** (see quot.); (2) **mackerel,** a small mackerel, *Pneumatophorus grex*, found in warm seas; (3) **sucker,** either of two American suckers of the genus *Erimyzon* found in the central and eastern states.

(1) **1884** GOODE *Fisheries* I. 236 The burbot . . . is called 'Chub-eel' . . . in Mohawk River, New York. *Ib.*, 'Chub-eel' is a mere off-hand name given to the species by a fisherman who supposed it to be a hybrid between an eel and a catfish. — (2) **1814** MITCHILL *Fishes N.Y.* 422 Thimble eyed, bull eyed, or chub mackerel. *Scomber grex.* . . . Comes occasionally in prodigious numbers to the coast of New-York, in autumn. **1884** GOODE *Fisheries* I. 303 The Chub Mackerel . . . closely resembles in general appearance the common Mackerel. — (3) **1817** C. A. LE SUEUR in *Acad. Nat. Sci. Phila. Jrnl.* I Ser. I. 93 C[*atostomus*] *gibbosus*. . . . This species I discovered in the river Connecticut, near Northampton, where it is named Chub Sucker. **1884** in GOODE *Fisheries* I. 614 The 'Chub Sucker' . . . is one of the most abundant and widely diffused of the Suckers.

As the last term in **day, gold, Indian, Negro, river, Roanoke, salt-water chub.**

***chuck,** *n.*[1]

1. A meal or mealtime. Cf. **chow.**

1865 *Harper's Mag.* Feb. 325/1, [I] finished chuck on twelve o'clock. **1890** RYAN *Told in Hills* 302 'Past chuck?' On being informed that the midday meal had been ended two hours before, [etc.]. **1925** *Cent. Mag.* Oct. 358/2 We've just finished chuck, but there's Java on the fire, dip in.

2. In combs.: (1) **chuck box,** a box or box-like container for carrying provisions, esp. as used on a chuck wagon; (2) **horrors,** (see quot.); (3) **house,** a cookhouse, a commissary; (4) **tender,** a camp cook or his helper; (5) **wagon,** *W.* a wagon carrying provisions, cooking equipment, etc., for cowboys, also attrib. and transf.

(1) **1905** *Outlet* 16 A carpenter was then at work building chuckboxes for each of the six commissaries. **1947** *Westerners' Brand Book* 71 We had college men and high school graduates, but they didn't hang their sheepskins on the chuck box. — (2) **1926** J. BLACK *You Can't Win* iv. 39 New arrivals . . . had not yet acquired the 'chuck horrors,' that awful animal craving for food that comes after missing half a dozen meals. — (3) **1910** *Sat. Ev. Post* 1 Oct. 74/2 About fifty tons of flour, twenty-five barrels of coffee and fifty half-barrels of salt fish are used in the chuck houses on the farm each year. — (4) **1897** F. NORRIS *Third Circle* (1909) 57 Over at the 'Big Dipper' mine a chuck-tender named Kelly had been in error as regards a box of dynamite sticks.

(5) **1890** *Gate City Herald* (Deep Creek Falls, Wash.) 23 Oct. 1/4 At eleven o'clock the . . . majority of the rounders galloped away toward the 'chuck' wagon for dinner. **1947** *Nat. Geog. Mag.* June 745/2 The special event at Calgary is the chuck-wagon race. **1948** *Newsweek* 27 Sep. 19/1 Rival Truman delegations from the bolting counties . . . had been waiting outside around loudspeakers and a chuck-wagon.

b. *W. To ride the chuck line*, etc., (see quot. 1942). Hence **chuck line rider.** Cf. **grub liner.**

1903 A. ADAMS *Log Cowboy* xviii. 280 He was riding the chuckline all right. **1906** —— *Cattle Brands* 27 Sometimes there might be ten men at a camp, and only two men on the pay-roll. These extra men were called 'chuck-line riders.' **1942** DALE *Cow Country* 122 Some men out of a job for the winter would merely ride from camp to camp throughout a wide area spending a night or so at each. This was commonly called 'riding the chuck line,' but such visitors were always gladly received. **1948** *Popular Western* June 36/1 You can't believe these fiddle-footed chuck line riders!

chuck tʃʌk, *n.*[2] Short for woodchuck, also *chuck of the wood.*

1781 PETERS *Hist. Conn.* (1829) 189 The woodchuck, . . . when eating makes a noise like a hog, whence he is named Woodchuck, or chuck of the wood. **1809** *Mass. Spy* 8 Nov. (Th., p. 952), Then if to go further I was put in doubt By a Chuck at the mouth of a hole. **1948** *Outdoor Life* July 19/1 In all the years I've hunted chucks I've never had a farmer turn me down.

chuck-a-luck ˈtʃʌkəˌlʌk, *n.* [App. f. *chuck*, throw + *luck.*] A banking gambling game played with dice, the players betting on how the dice will fall. (See also quot. 1906.)

1836 *Quarter Race Ky.* (1846) 24, I thought I'd make a rise on chuck-a-luck, but you prehaps never saw such a run of luck. **1882** *Cent. Mag.* April 884/2 He had the faculty of losing his money, and other people's . . . at all games of chance, from chuck-a-luck to brag. **1906** *Suburban Life* July 22/2 There is a new game, on the principle of the old bean-bag game, called 'chuckaluck,' sold for two dollars. **1938** ASBURY *Sucker's Prog.* 52 Chuck-a-Luck is one of the oldest of dice games, and in England was originally called Sweat-Cloth. . . . About 1820 it began to be known in some sections of the country as Chucker-Luck and Chuck-a-Luck. In recent years it has often been called Bird Cage.

attrib. **1845** HOOPER *Suggs* (1928) 78 In spite of the excitement of . . . the occasional exhibition of a chuck-a-luck table . . . time at last began to hang heavily upon the hands of the inmates of Fort Suggs. **1890** *Portland* (Ore.) *Examiner* 1 Dec. 4/1 Have the police yet found those dozen and one Chinese and other chuck-a-luck games? **1944** *Harper's Mag.* June 53/1 On the first floor were about six 26 games; upstairs were at least two roulette wheels and several crap tables and chuck-luck layouts.

chuckaway ˈtʃʌkəˌwe, *n.* [An extension of **chuck,** *n.*[1]] *W.* Chuck, food, provisions. — **1873** *Newton Kansan* 20 Feb. 3/4 An Indian scout . . . asked first for chuckaway. **1936** BARNARD *Rider* 67 Lockridge refused to give any, and told him he would give them some chuck-away, but if so many of them ever came again he would give them nothing.

***chucklehead,** *n.* (See quot.) *Rare.* — **1784** CUTLER in *Mem. Academy* I. 473 *Trifolium*. . . . The indigenous species of this genus [include] . . . the woolly-headed clover, or chuckle-head.

chuckwalla ˈtʃʌkˌwɑlə, *n. S.W.* [See note.] A large herbivorous lizard, *Sauromalus ater*, found in the desert regions of the Southwest and used by the Indians as food.

The word is prob. from the language of the Cahuilla Indians in southeastern California. Those familiar with the lizard often call it the "chuckawalla," and our quots. reflect this usage. The first quot. shows the word used with reference to the Chuckawalla Mts.

[**1869** *Overland Mo.* Aug. 139/1 All who have crossed the upper arm of the Colorado Desert, from San Bernardino *via* San Gorgonio Pass, Toros, Dos Palmas and Chucolwalla, to the Colorado River, will remember the ragged volcanic rift in the southern side of the Glacier Mountains.] **1893** *N.A. Fauna* VII. 174 The 'chuck-walla,' by which name this remarkable lizard is universally known to both Indians and whites (except the Mormons), inhabits many of the Lower Sonoran Desert ranges in the southern part of the Great Basin. **1914** BRININSTOOL *Trail Dust* 103 Let me see the chuckawalla and the Gila monster too. **1947** *Southern Sierran* Apr. 4/1 It was a rare treat to find three chuckwallas, one of which posed for repeated portraits with all the patience of a Powers' model.

In full **chuckwalla lizard.**

1942 LILLARD *Desert Challenge* 248, I reckon my critics never drank alkali water and lived on whang leather and Chuckawalla lizards.

b. chuckwalla's delight, a plant of the sunflower family, so named because these animals are fond of eating its flowers.

1940 JAEGER *Desert Wild Flowers* 286 Chuckwalla's delight *Bebbia juncea aspera*. **1947** *Desert Mag.* May 28/3 Other species expected are . . . Ghost Flower, . . . Chuckawalla's Delight, . . . Desert Dandelion.

chuck-will's-widow. [Imitative.] The largest of the American goatsuckers, *Antrostomus carolinensis*, found in the eastern states.

1791 BARTRAM *Travels* 154 *Caprimulgus rufus* called chuck-will's widow, from a fancied resemblance of his note to these words. **1871** *Harper's Mag.* July 188 At one time there were several species of hawks, a flock of butcher-birds, whip-poor-wills, chuck-will's-widows, and a host of smaller birds. **1945** MATHEWS *Talking* 52 The first notes of the chuck-will's-widow come plaintively from the east ridge as the moon rises.

chufa ˈtʃufə, *n.* [Sp.] The earth almond, *Cyperus esculentus*, producing small edible tubers; also one of these tubers.

1855 in *Amer. Inst. N.Y. Trans.* 605 Earth Almond, or Chufa . . . from the south of Spain. . . . The tubers resemble in taste a delicious chestnut or cocoa nut, and like them, may be eaten raw or cooked. **1879** *Home & Farm* (Louisville, Ky.) 15 My hogs had no corn. They had abundance of chufas with the run of potato pinder & pea fields. **1944** HARPER *Weeds* 77 *C. esculentus* L. Chufa. . . . It is sometimes cultivated as food for hogs, and children sometimes eat the tubers, which have a nutty flavor.

chug tʃʌg, *n.*[1] Prob. = **cholla.** *Rare.* — **1856** WHIPPLE *Explor. Ry. Route* 100 To-day we have found a new species of cactodendron, called *chug*. It grows in extensive patches to the height of eight to ten feet; a confused mass of angular joints, whose sheathed spines at a distance glisten beautifully in the sun.

chug tʃʌg, *n.*[2] [Onomatopoeic.] **1.** A sudden dull or muffled sound. **2. chug wagon,** an automobile. *Slang. Obs.*

(1) **1866** *Harper's Mag.* Jan. 271/2 The ponderous brother came down upon the floor with a 'chugg' that shook the house. **1904** M. E. WALLER *Wood-carver* 106 Aunt Lize is churning, and Tag's tail whacks in time to every *chug-chug* of the dasher. — (2) **1909** *Boston Herald* 29 July 3/1 A big chug wagon jumped away from the Senate office building late this afternoon and snorted off toward Fort Myer. **1910** E. S. FIELD *Sapphire Bracelet* 35 Besides, your chug-wagon wears a New York number.

chug tʃʌg, *v.* [Onomatopoeic.] **1.** *tr.* To spur *up* or urge (a horse) forward. *Colloq.* **2.** *intr.* To go with a puffing or explosive noise. Also **chug-chug.**

(1) **1887** CUSTER *Tenting on Plains* 384 Come on, old lady! Chug up that old plug of yours; I've got one orderly. — (2) **1907** FIELD *Six-Cylinder Courtship* 59 An automobile chugged up to the station-house and stopped before the door. **1948** *Railway Clerk* June 334/1 The Pioneer will chug-chug for an estimated 2,000,000 visitors to the Fair's Pageant of Transportation Progress.

chum tʃʌm, *n.* [Poss. the same word as dial. *chum*, food, provisions.]

1. (See quot. 1889.)

1857 *Spirit of Times* 7 Nov. 150/1 So we would take no more than one in fifty, of those, too, which proved by their breaking for our chum, that they were ready to bite. **1889** *Cent.* 993/2 *Chum*, a bait, consisting usually of pieces of some oily fish, as the menhaden, commonly employed in the capture of bluefish. **1947** COFFIN *Yankee Coast* 50 He cuts up the dead ones, and scatters this wash-bait, the 'chum,' on the deep.

attrib. **1876** *Fur, Fin, & Feather* Sep. 131 He carries a basket with . . . a 'chum-thrower' which may be described as a shovel with all the edges turned up.

2. The remains of menhaden after the oil has been pressed out.

1859 *Me. Bd. Agric. Rep.* IV. 182 Pogies will be caught for the chum and not for the oil. **1879** *Bureau of Fisheries Rep.* V. 219 The fish-refuse enters our markets in several conditions. The following have come under my observation: 1. 'Crude stock,' 'green scrape,' 'chum,' [etc.].

3. =**dog salmon.**

1908 *Pop. Sci. Mo.* Dec. 169 The dog Salmon (*Oncorhyncus Keta*) is known also as calico salmon and *chum*. **1948** *Scientific Mo.* April 283/1 The commercially important species of salmonid fishes of the Columbia Basin are the chinook, silver, chum, and blueback salmon.

chum tʃʌm, *v. tr.* and *intr.* To fish with chum, to attract fish by means of chum.

1857 *Spirit of Times* 7 Nov. 150/1 After chumming our fishing-place, and watching the bits of chum that floated upon the surface of the surf, we would see a break made by a large bass. **1876** *Fur, Fin, & Feather* Sep. 131 The chummer's principal duty is to 'chum.' This performance consists in throwing out quantities of chum from the stand to the particular spot in the water where the fisherman will cast his line. **1921** *Outing* Feb. 207/2 The fishermen 'chummed' industriously from the sterns.

Hence **chumming,** *n.*

1882 *Forest & Stream* XIX. 363 Chumming is much more sport, the fish then being captured with rod and reel.

chummer ˈtʃʌmɚ, *n.* One who uses chum in fishing. — **1876** *Fur, Fin, & Feather* Sep. 131 The chummer cuts up bait . . . and thus manufactures the chum. **1932** MILLER *I Cover Waterfront* 33 He was the chummer. This meant he had to stand on the edge of the bait tank and throw out live sardines to start the tuna biting.

chumpa ˈtʃʌmpə, *n.* [The Choctaw verb meaning "to buy for cash," mistaken by white people for a noun. See C. Byington, *Dict. of the Choctaw Language* (1915) *s.v.*] A bundle or faggot of pine kindling. Also **chumpa girl.** *Obs.*

1851 E. S. WORTLEY *Travels in U.S.* 131 This morning we had a visit from two Indian chumpa girls. They are called so from carrying little fagots of pine-wood for sale. *Ib.* 136 Saw numbers of the chumpa girls returning from the pine woods (which are a good many miles off) so laden with the chumpa (pine) that they could hardly move. **1857** A. B. MEEK *Romantic Passages* 322 All are familiar with the soft quick, petitionary voice in which they exclaim 'chumpa,' as they offer their cheap burdens for sale. *Ib.* 330 Let who will hereafter experiment upon Choctaw character, to discover whether these Chumpa-girls have not like affections with other people. **1859** MACKAY *Tour* I. 290 The [Choctaw Indian] women, young and old, are often seen in Mobile, with bundles of firewood on their backs, which they sell in the streets, crying, with a melancholy intonation, 'Chumpa! Chumpa!' the only word resembling English which they speak, and somewhat more musical than 'chumps,' which it signifies.

***chunk,** *n.*

1. A horse, esp. a small stocky one (see quot. 1909).

1818 PALMER *Journal* 131 The other words and sayings that are peculiar to the United States . . . are as follows . . . *Chunk*, a small horse. **1829** *Western Mo. Rev.* III. 180 It is a usage, not wholly disallowed, for the candidate to ride a race on a Kentucky 'chunk' for the amusement of the spectators. **1909** *Cent. Supp.* 248/1 Chunk, specifically, a range-bred horse of the western United States, suitable for draft purposes.

2. *chunk of fire*, a small firebrand. *Colloq.*

1834 A. PIKE *Sketches* 30, I threw away my chunk of fire. **1876** MARK TWAIN *Tom Sawyer* vi. 63 Mary, get me a silk thread, and a chunk of fire out of the kitchen. **1942** WARNICK *Dialect Garrett Co., Md.* 5 Chunk of fire, n. phr., burning end of a chunk of wood. 'Can I borrow a chunk of fire?'

3. In the colloq. phrase *chunk of a* . . . : (1) With *boy, lawyer, Negro, woman*, a well-grown or promising specimen, a fair sample; (2) with *horse, pony*, a thick, compact horse; (3) with *fight*, a considerable encounter or fray; (4) (see quots.).

(1) **1821** DODDRIDGE *Backwoodsman & Dandy*, I was then a thumpin chunk of a boy, may be ten or a dozen years old. **1866** C. H. SMITH *Bill Arp* 115, I want to buy a nigger, and I had just as lief buy a chunk of a free nigger as any other sort. **1894** *Cong. Rec.* 13 July 7445/1 You are a lawyer, Mr. Kilgore:—Yes, a chunk of a lawyer. **1900** G. ADE *More Fables* 6 Next Morning, at the Hotel he spotted a stylish little chunk of a Woman who kept the Cigar Case.

(2) **1827** *Western Mo. Rev.* I. 386 Himself ambling by her side upon a 'chunk' of a poney. **1845** SIMMS *Wigwam & Cabin* 2 Ser. 83 He was . . . riding a short, heavy chunk of a horse. **1892** DUVAL *Young Explorers* 196, I wanted . . . to be 'over the hills and far away' . . . and (thanks to a pretty good 'chunk of a pony' . . .) I was *there* in less than ten minutes.

(3) **1833** J. HALL *Leg. West* 50 If a man got into a chunk of a fight with his neighbour, a lawyer would clear him for half a dozen muskrat skins. **1873** HAYCRAFT *Elizabethtown, Ky.* 39 He . . . by way of a change in his amusements now and then took a chunk of a fight.

(4) **1822** J. WOODS *English Prairie* 185 A hog of two hundred lbs. weight is here called a fine chunk of a fellow. **1883** ZEIGLER & GROSSCUP *Alleghanies* 88 He lives in a poor chunk of a cabin over in them woods, close enough now to fire-wood, shore.

4. In combs.: (1) **chunk apple,** a variety of apple, *obs.;* (2) **bottle,** *S.* a stout, squat bottle; (3) **cherry,** ?=**chokecherry,** *obs.;* (4) **head,** a copperhead snake, also transf.; (5) **yard,** [cf. **chunky**], the court upon which Indians played chunky (see quot. 1791), also transf., *obs.*

In these expressions the first element is obviously from various sources, not in every case easy to discover. They are all grouped here for convenience.

(1) **1896** HASWELL *New York* 251 They were [*c*1830] as well known as Mrs. Dominy's 'chunk apple' and clam pot-pies at Fire Island. — (2) **1845** SIMMS *Wigwam & Cabin* 2 Ser. 146 Returning towards night-fall to the camp, Mingo brought with him a 'Chunk-bottle' of Whiskey. **1852** *Florida Plant. Rec.* 70 Poor of a Chunck [*sic*] bottle full of the solution and drench your Mule with it While it is warm. — (3) **1886** ROOSEVELT in *Outing* May 134 We descended . . . into a smooth open valley, through whose bottom extended a dry water course, filled up with a dense growth of wild plums, ash and chunk cherries. — (4) **1818** *Jrnl. Science* I. 84 *Scytalus Cupreus* or Copper-head Snake . . . is known by a variety of names in different parts of the State of New-York: . . . *copper-head, copper-snake, chunk-head,* [etc.]. **1863** in *Pub. Col. Soc.* XX. 232 If we add that our political Copperheads, like their reptile type, as so 'slow and clumsy in their motions' that they deserve the additional cognomina of 'Chunk-heads' and 'Deaf-adders,' and that 'a very slight blow' makes an end of them, we shall have made the analogy complete.

(5) **1791** BARTRAM *Travels* 520 Chunk yard, a term given by the white traders, to the oblong four square yards, adjoining the high mounts and rotundas of the modern Indians. **1860** THOREAU *Letters* (1865) 189 That memorable stone 'chunk yard.' **1865** LUBBOCK *Prehist. Times* (1869) 259 The 'chunk-yards' . . . are sometimes from 6 to 9 hundred feet in length. **1873** JONES *Antiq. So. Indians* 345 Instead of calling them chunk-yards, we ought properly to denominate them chungke-yards.

b. *To extinguish one's chunk*, to kill (one). *Slang.*

1852 MARK TWAIN in *Hannibal* (Mo.) *Jrnl.* 16 Sep., He resolves to 'extinguish his chunk' by feeding his carcass to the fishes of Bear Creek.

chunk tʃʌŋk, *v.* [f. **chunk*, *n.*]

1. *tr.* =**chink.** *Colloq. Obs.*

1782 in L. SUMMERS *Ann. S.W. Va.* (1929) 761 Ordered that the Clerk of this Court hire some persons to chunk and daub the Court-house. **1818** BIRKBECK *Letters* 30 This cabin is built of round straight logs, about a foot in diameter, lying upon each other, and notched in at the corners, forming a room eighteen feet by sixteen; the intervals between the logs 'chuncked,' that is, filled in with slips of wood. **1843** OLIVER *Eight Months* 237 The logs are not laid quite close, an interval of two or three inches being left between each, which is afterwards *chunked* and *daubed*, i.e., filled up with bits of wood, and plastered with clay or mortar; the two hewn sides thus forming the outer and inner surfaces of the wall.

2. *fig.* To cut or break into chunks. *Rare.*
1834 C. A. DAVIS *Lett. J. Downing* 166 I'll give you my notions . . . and leave you to slice it or chunk it as best suits you.

3. *S.* To throw at or pelt with, or as with, chunks of wood. Also with *down* and *out.*
1835 SIMMS *Partisan* 425 His dog stole my bacon . . . and when I chunked the varmint, the nigga gin me sass. **1841** *S. Lit. Messenger* VII. 40/2 Uncle Daniel, there's Louis chunking down the haws. **1906** F. LYNDE *Quickening* 253, I didn't believe hit that night when he r'ared and took on so to me and 'lowed to chunk me with a rock.

4. *S.* To feed (a fire) with chunks of wood; to mend, to rake up or bring together the embers of (a fire).
1840 *S. Lit. Messenger* VI. 398/2 Chunk the fire, Charles, and see if you cannot make it burn better. **1850** GARRARD *Wah-To-Yah* iv. 65 Smith kept the squaws of the lodge 'chunking' up the fire. **1902** A. MACGOWAN *Last Word* 15 The fire in the engine was, in Southern parlance, 'chunked up.'

5. (See quot.)
1905 *Forestry Bureau Bul.* No. 61, 33 Chunk, to clear the ground with engine or horses, of obstructions which can not be removed by hand. To chunk up, to collect and pile for burning the slash left after logging.

chunked tʃʌŋkt, *a. Colloq.* **1.** Plump, chunky. **2.** *S.W.* Impudent. *Obs.* **3.** Plastered, chinked. *Obs.*
(1) **1843** STEPHENS *High Life N.Y.* I. 115 She had on a great loose . . . gown, that made her seem twice as chunked as she used to. **1906** H. FITZGERALD *Sam Steele's Adv.* 220, I was gettin' altogether too chunked and fat. — (2) **1853** P. PAXTON *Yankee in Texas* 227 By Ned, says he, if it aint that owdacious critter of Miss Mash's, a helpin' hisself in broad daylight; . . . that's putty chunked. **1859** BARTLETT 82 Any person who is impudent or bold, at the South-west, is said to be chunked. — (3) **1857** D. H. STROTHER *Virginia Illust.* 206 The old homestead, with its chunked and daubed walls.

chunker ˈtʃʌŋkɚ, *n.* (See quots.) — **1887** *Cent. Mag.* XXXIV. 488/1 The majority were empty coal-boats,—'chunkers' from Mauch Chunk, or 'Skukers' from 'Schuylkill Haven.' **1893** *D.N.* I. 329 Chunker, coal boat used on the canal.

chunky ˈtʃʌŋkɪ, *n.* Also **chunkey.** [Catawba *chenco* (see quot. 1709).] (See quot. 1907.) Also attrib.
[**1709** LAWSON *Carolina* 57 These *Indians* are fortify'd in, as the former, and are much addicted to a Sport they call *Chenco,* which is carry'd on with a Staff and a Bowl made of Stone, which they trundle upon a smooth Place like a Bowling-Green, made for that Purpose, as I have mentioned before.] **1775** ROMANS *Nat. Hist. Florida* 77 When

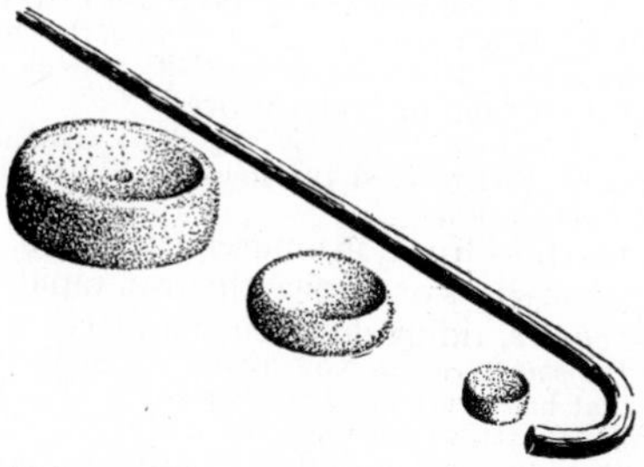

Articles used in the Indian game of chunky

growing up, they use wrestling, running, heaving and lifting great weights, the playing with the ball two different ways, and their favourite game of *chunkè,* all very violent exercises. **1907** HODGE *Indians* I. 298/1 *Chunkey,* the name commonly used by the early traders to designate a man's game formerly popular among the Gulf tribes and probably general in the S., E. of the Mississippi. It was played with a stone disk and a pole which had a crook at one end. The disk was rolled ahead, and the object was to slide the pole after it in such a way that the disk would rest in the curve of the crook when both came to a stop. **1947** MARTIN *Indians* 38 Discoidals, sometimes called 'chunkeystones,' are circular disks of stone, ranging in size from one to eight inches in diameter and from one to six inches in thickness. *Ib.* 39 Others may have been used in a game called *chungke, chenco,* or *chunkey* (the traders' name for this game). Chunkey was a man's game played with a stone disk and a long-forked pole.

chuparosa ˌtʃupəˈrosə, *n. S.W.* [Amer. Sp. *chuparrosa* as a plant name.] A low shrub of the acanthus family, found in deserts of southern California and Arizona.
1912 LUMHOLTZ *New Trails* 207 As we followed the fairly distinct Indian trail, . . . I observed the chuparosa (*beleperone californica*), the flowers of which are eaten by the Papago. **1940** JAEGER *Calif. Deserts* 172 Its tubular flowers are often visited by humming birds for the nectar, hence its Spanish name, 'chuparosa,' meaning 'sucking rose.' **1946** *Desert Mag.* April 28/3 Great patches of Chuparosa may show their bright red flowers.

* **church,** *n.*

1. A building in which religious services are regularly held.

The use in this country of "church" with reference to all places of worship has been often commented upon by British travelers, and in former times was a matter of some concern to certain Protestant sects as shown by the first group of quots. See quot. 1925.

(1) **1810** LAMBERT *Travels* III. 90 The churches [in N. Eng.], or as they are oftener termed, meetings, are constructed of similar materials. **1835** TODD *Notes* 39 All places of public worship, in New York State, are called churches, but in most others, meeting-houses or chapels, in which *woman* is pronounced after its ancient orthography of *womman.* **1868** G. G. CHANNING *Recoll. Newport* 70 It was considered by Congregationalists, Baptists, &c., a concession to Romanism to call places of worship 'churches.'

(2) **1640** *Bay Psalm Book* (*title-page*), The necessity of the heavenly Ordinance of singing Scripture Psalmes in the Churches of God. **1705** *Boston News-Letter No. 56* 14 May 2/1 The Enemy finding that they could not take the Fort and Castle, They burnt all the houses here but 5 and the Church, and went back to the Southward burning and demolishing all where they came. **1849** E. DAVIES *Amer. Scenes* 118 Three 'churches,' with their neat and graceful spires, rising above the other buildings, were conspicuous in the distance. **1925** KRAPP *Eng. Lang.* I. 146 In America the word *church* has not the specialized meaning which permits it to be applied in England only to the established church. In American usage the difference between a church and a chapel, as the words are ordinarily used, is that a chapel is a smaller building than a church. **1943** M. FLAVIN *Journey in the Dark* 6 Two of the three churches were of this side of the Square—the Baptist and the Methodist.

2. In combs.: (1) **Church-Amish,** (see quots. and cf. **Amish**); (2) **burner,** see as a main entry; (3) **fair,** a festival at which articles are sold for the benefit of a church; (4) **house,** (see quot.); (5) **Indian,** an Indian who has embraced Christianity, *obs.;* (6) **letter,** a written statement given by the proper authority in a church to a member to enable him more easily to become a member of another church; (7) **lot,** see as a main entry; (8) **Church of Christ, Scientist,** the official name of the Christian Science Church founded by Mary Baker Eddy, cf. **First Church of Christ, Scientist;** (9) **Church of (Jesus Christ of) Latter-day Saints,** the official name of the Mormon Church; (10) **Church of the Self-Savers,** (see quot.), *obs.;* (11) **sociable,** a social gathering of church members and their friends; (12) **social,** a church sociable or a church supper; (13) **South,** the Methodist Episcopal Church, South, *rare;* (14) **supper,** a supper given by the members of a congregation, esp. one to raise funds.

(1) **1938** HARK *Hex Marks Spot* 103 The Amish way of dressing never varies. Flat-crowned, broad-brimmed hats for the men, coats with plain, straight collars and either buttons or hooks and eyes, according to whether they're Church or House Amish. **1940** *Sat. Ev. Post* 30 March 40/4 Here, again, we run into the difference between the most conservative, the house-Amish, and the less conservative, the church-Amish. — (3) **1872** *Newton Kansan* 5 Sep. 4/1 At a certain church-fair, a set of Cooper's works was promised to the individual who should answer a set of conundrums. **1947** PAUL *Linden* 333 It had to be her luck to accept the chairmanship of the committee to stage the Congregational Church Fair on the year it was held in Associate Hall. — (4) **1889** *Cent.* 995/1 Church-house. . . . A building in which to rest, keep warm, eat lunch, etc., between the services of the church on Sunday; a Sabbath-day house. (U.S.)

(5) **1878** DENNIS in Morris *Pub. Service Alaska* (1879) 7 The 'church Indians' . . . concluded to make an example of somebody; therefore they marched to the Russian's house, seized his still and liquor, and, with him in custody, marched to the ranch. — (6) **1900** C. WINCHESTER *W. Castle* x. 202 The pastor did nothing but write church letters all that day. **1906** L. BELL *C. Lee* 228 I'd leave the Presbyterian Church and join the Christian Scientists so quickly my church letter would be torn by the way I'd snatch it. — (8) **1899** M. B. EDDY *Church Manual* 15 In the spring of 1879, a little band of earnest seekers after Truth went into deliberations over forming a church without creeds, to be called the 'Church of Christ, Scientist.' They were members of evangelical churches, and students of Mary Baker Eddy in Christian Science, and were known as 'Christian Scientists.' — (9) **1838** S. WOOD *Lett. from U.S.* 10 The Church of the Latter-day Saints originated in 1830, with a man of the name of Joseph Smith.

1905 *Out West* Sep. 243 By virtue of the sacred keys thus given, the Church of Jesus Christ of Latter-day Saints was organized at Fayette, Seneca county, New York, on the 6th day of April, 1830. **1948** *Time* 18 Oct. 76/3 It teaches that true salvation is found only in the Church of Jesus Christ of Latter-Day Saints.

(10) 1882 *Advance* (Chi.) 16 March, The 'Church of the Self-Savers,' a new Socialistic organization, held service Sunday in this city. — **(11) 1876** MARK TWAIN *Tom Sawyer* v, At church 'sociables' he was always called upon to read poetry. **1947** *Chi. Sun* 30 June 3/1, I never did see the beat of Jim at a church sociable or a wedding. — **(12) 1882** *Harper's Mag.* Jan. 318/2 At a church 'social' . . . the faithful shepherd of the flock observed . . . some simple devices for the entertainment of the young people present. **1946** R. PEATTIE *Pac. Coast Ranges* 256 She was taken to quilting parties and church socials. — **(13) 1846** *Dollar Newspaper* (Phila.) 6 May 3/3 Bishop Soule was present, but . . . he does not geographically belong to the Church South. — **(14) 1913** CATHER *O Pioneers!* 212 Emil had returned only the night before, and his sister was so proud of him that she decided at once to take him up to the church supper. **1947** *N. & Q.* Aug. 73/2, I should like to know something of the history of church suppers in America.

As the last term in **branch, Christian, community, frame, free, French, Indian, Jim Crow, log, Manifesto, Methodist Episcopal, Mormon, Mother, Pilgrim, second church.**

* **church,** *v. tr.* To subject to church discipline. *Colloq.*

1829 *Western Mo. Rev.* III. 114 It is notorious, that a woman was churched there [*sc.* in N. Eng.], for cutting off the ends of the fingers of her gloves, and exposing the tips of her dainty and delicate fingers. **1902** WILSON *Spenders* xii. 132 They'd have her up and church her, sure. **1946** *Chi. Sun* (Bk. Week) 21 April 5/4 Without much compunction, the parishioners formed a posse to church the whole family.

b. *To church-maul,* (see quot.). *Obs.*

*a***1870** CHIPMAN *Notes on Bartlett* 83 Church-maul, To. — To call to account, to discipline, by ecclesiastical methods. N.E., vulgar.

church burner. One of a group of Philadelphia rowdies who burned several Catholic churches in Philadelphia in July, 1844, during riots between members of the Native American party and the Irish. Also **church burning party.** Now *obs.* or *hist.*

1844 *Quincy* (Ill.) *Herald* 26 July 2/4 The Native American Whigs have a new name; they are now called the church burning party, from their sacking and burning so many churches in Philadelphia recently. *Ib.* 13 Sep. 2 Hold ye men who attempt to justify the church burners of Philadelphia, lest the stones should cry out. **1856** *Cong. Globe* 9 Jan. 187/1 We see the good-natured gentleman from Philadelphia voting . . . with those whom he has called 'Church-burners.' **1946** *Amer. Sp.* April 116/2.

Churchers 'tʃɜtʃəz, *n.* [Origin obscure.] "A body of Indians living E. and N.E. of the white settlements in New England in 1634. . . . Not the Praying Indians, as the period is too early" (Hodge). — **1634** WOOD *N. Eng. Prospect* II. i. 56 The Indians to the East and North east, bearing the name of Churchers, and Tarrenteenes.

church lot. A lot or parcel of land owned by a church.

1646 *Suffolk Deeds* II. 147 Sayd lot & parcell of land lyeth betweene the Church lot yt was once Mr. Tillyes [etc.]. **1754** *Ga. Col. Rec.* VI. 436 The Lotts will be One hundred and twenty by eighty Feet, except . . . the Church Lotts, which will be One Hundred and eighty by two-hundred feet. **1846** WILEY in *Indiana Mag. Hist.* XXIII. 327 A valuable addition to the church lot for a site on which to build a parsonage. **1857** C. VAUX *Villas* 302 The bay-window in the library . . . would give a desirable relief to the straight, uninteresting wall adjoining the church lot.

churro 'tʃuro, *n. S.W.* [Sp.] The coarse-wooled sheep of Mexico. — **1889** *Cent.* 996/3 [The] *churro,* . . . used extensively in crossing with the merino, in Texas, northern Mexico, California, etc.

chute ʃut, *n.* Also †**schute.** [See note.]

1. A fall or rapid in a river; a narrow, rocky, or precipitous channel or passage.

F. *chute,* through voyageur influence, early began to displace earlier *shoot* in sense **1,** and has been extended as the evidence shows. Cf. **2.** below and see ***shoot,** *n.*

1804 DUNBAR *Life* 260 We had a good observation about 4 miles below the 'Chutes' (falls). **1812** MARSHALL *Kentucky* 74 [The falls are] rendered still more alarming and dangerous by the irregularity of the schutes. **1908** WHITE *Riverman* iv. 30 Immediately below Reed's dam ran a long chute strewn with boulders, which was alternately a shallow or a stretch of white water according as the stream rose or fell. **1947** *So. Sierran* Oct. 4/1 We stayed in this chute until we reached what seemed like the back of the mountain, avoiding all chutes leading to the right.

b. A road, path, or way. Also *to take the chute,* often in fig. use.

1834 *S. Lit. Messenger* I. 142, I can tell you a chute that's a heap shorter than the road you talk of taking. **1860** *Baltimore Patriot* Sep., The Douglas and Breckinridge men . . . are rushing to Lincoln with a perfect stampede. Besides this, the Bell men are also taking the same chute every day. **1873** BEADLE *Undevel. West.* 564 On the steepest part he took the wrong chute, pulling up his burro just in time to avoid his plunging head first into a ravine.

c. (See quot. 1890.)

1862 *Lett.* in *N.Y. Tribune* 11 June, When we came to a bayou or chute, the Fleet would divide, part going the irregular way, and part keeping the direct course. **1890** *N. & Q.* V. 54 A *chute,* in river-men's parlance, is a half-silted, abandoned channel—especially one that affords passage at higher stages of water. **1941** *Chr. Sci. Mon.* (Weekly Mag. Sec.) 3 May 11, I miss chute in the Lower Mississippi sense of a bayou or side channel usually behind an island, though the word is often used in that sense by Mark Twain and others.

2. An inclined plane, trough, or slide used in conveying grain, ore, etc., to a lower level. (Earlier * *shoot.*)

1829 *Amer. Advertiser* (Phila.) 29 July 2/3 At the upper end of the town, the *chute* of the Railway extends from the side of a mountain to the bed of a river, a distance of about 750 feet, descending about 34 feet in the hundred. **1872** MARK TWAIN *Roughing It* lii. 380 Under the bins are rows of waggons loading from chutes and trap-doors in the bins. **1931** *K.C. Star* 3 Sep., I've got a good joke on an elevator man. He paid me for sixty bushels of wheat, but I dumped seventy into the chute.

3. A sluice, trough, or flume by means of which logs are passed through a dam or down a precipitous descent. Cf. **shoot,** *n.* **2.**

1830 *Wellsborough* (Pa.) *Phenix* 31 July 2/2 The comb at the head of the schute should be made at a right angle with the side walls. **1878** *Lumberman's Gaz.* 18 Dec., 426 The [gates of the dam] are opened, the logs are run through the chute, and sufficient water is furnished to carry them below. **1903** WHITE *Forest* viii. 95, A dozen rivermen, one after the other, would often go through a chute of a dam standing upright on single logs.

b. A structure enabling fish to pass a dam in a stream.

1871 *Ohio Laws* LXVIII. 15 An act to provide for the erection and maintenance of 'chutes' for the passage of fish over the dams. **1875** KNIGHT 874/2 It may consist of a chute with a sinuous track for diminishing the velocity and assisting the passage of the fish to the level above the dam.

4. *W.* A branding chute *q.v.* or a narrow passageway similar to this. Also **chute-branding.** Cf. * **shoot,** *n.* **3.**

1881 *Rep. Indian Affairs* 8 The contractor puts the cattle . . . in a chute, where they are branded. **1911** MULFORD *Bar-20 Days* 197 Chute-branding robbed them of the excitement . . . which they always took from open or corral branding. **1945** *Casper* (Wyo.) *Tribune-Herald* 29 July 1/3 Wild broncs erupt rapidly from the chutes, calves and ropers race across the arena, and specialty acts fill in between.

5. *Mining.* A vein or body of ore.

1882 C. KING *Rep. Prec. Metals* 111 The chute exposed is 20 feet, but neither end has been reached. It is found in three levels, the upper being 30 feet from the lower.

6. chute-the-chute, in amusement places, a descent down which one slides or rides with great rapidity. Hence *shooting the chutes,* riding down such a place.

1895 *N.Y. Dramatic News* 30 Nov. 17/4 Shooting the Chutes, the latest craze that has struck the town. **1922** *N.Y. Times* 9 July VI. 14/3 Scores of little attractions were combined: small shows brought under one tent, so to speak, with their own bathing pools, 'dip-the-dips,' scenic railways, chute-the-chutes, and all the rest. **1943** GEIST *Hiking* 56 It was like Coney island without the chute-the-chutes.

As the last term in **branding, brush, cattle, counting, loading, log, ore, slaughter, stock chute.**

chute ʃut, *v. tr.* To send through a chute, to inclose or confine in a chute. — **1884** *Harper's Mag.* May 872/1 Logs . . . are often chuted down from the lofty ridges. **1920** MULFORD *J. Nelson* 234 Anybody knows that chutin' em [cattle] and stampin' on th' brand is easier.

chuza 'tʃusə, *n. S.W.* [See note.] App. the Sp. *juego de boliche,* or pigeon-holes, a game played with balls on a concave table. *Obs.*

Santamaría gives various senses of this word. With reference to a game, he says it designates in Amer. Sp. a stroke in bowls or billiards which knocks down all the pins.

1844 GREGG *Commerce of Prairies* I. 240 Among the multitude of games which seem to constitute the real business of life in New Mexico, that of *chuza* evidently presents the most attractions to ladies. . . . It is played with little balls, and bears some faint resemblance to what is called *roulette.* **1885** *Santa Fe Wkly. N. Mexican* 10 Sep. 3/6 [At the Isleta festival] the game of chuzas was a favorite pastime, no less than ten tables being in operation.

cibola 'sibəla, *n.* [Amer. Sp. f. a native term in the Southwest for "buffalo."]

1. (*cap.*) A fabled region of great wealth searched for in vain in Mexico by early Spanish explorers, and finally identified with seven pueblos in western N. Mexico occupied by the Zuñi Indians. Cf. **Seven Cities.**

[**1540** CORONADO *Letter* 3 Aug.] **1677** HEYLYN *Cosmography* IV. 103/2 Frier Marco de Niza . . . had been informed of a large and wealthy province called Cibola, a Months journey thence; wherein were seven great Cities under the Government of one Princess, the Houses of which were built of Stone, many Stories high, the Lintels of their Doors adorned with Turquoises. **1873** S. W. COZZENS *Marvellous Country* 30 The treasure came from a country known as Cibola. **1945** STEWART *Names on the Land* 17 Coronado, far in the Southwest, searched for Cíbola and Quivira, and found an endless plain. . . . During a full century Cíbola and Quivira were as well-known names as Florida and California, and then they slowly disappeared.

b. A name suggested for what is now the state of Colorado. *Obs.*

1878 FOSSETT *Colorado* 103 Accordingly steps were taken to form a Territory and State, to which the names of Jefferson, Cibola—the Spanish for buffalo—and Colorado were all proposed.

2. An American buffalo. Also attrib.

1698 TONTI *LaSalle's Latest Discoveries* 106 We saw . . . four Footed Creatures all sorts, especially one large sort of Oxen, which they [Indians] call *Cibola's;* these are much larger than any hath been meantion'd, and are raised like a Cammel from the Chine to the middle of the Back; they feed among the Canes, and go together sometimes no less in number than Fifteen Hundred. **1722** COXE *Descr. Carolana* 53 Every Year in the Season, are Multitudes of the wild Kine call'd *Cibolas.* **1846** ABERT *Exam. N.M.* 73 'Cibolo,' . . . at the present day, is used to mean buffalo. **1945** MARSHALL *Santa Fe* 4 The Indians, learning to ride, hunted farther afield; they could follow the *cibola* herds and the antelope.

Cibolan ˈsibəˌlən, *n.* [f. prec.] An early inhabitant of Cibola.

1881 MORGAN *Houses Amer. Aborigines* 205 The Mound-Builders . . . wore skin garments, and possibly woven mantles of cotton, as the Cibolans of New Mexico did at the time of Coronado's expedition. **1883** PRINCE *Hist. N.M.* 157 They had been so long (forty years) among the Cibolans that they had nearly entirely forgotten their original language. **1893** DONALDSON *Moqui Pueblo Indians* 20 The Cibolans could give no very exact information concerning them.

cibolero ˌsibəˈlero, *n. S.W.* [See **cibola.**] A buffalo hunter. Now *hist.*

1844 GREGG *Commerce of Prairies* I. 96 A word concerning the *Ciboleros.* . . . Every year, large parties of New Mexicans . . . drive out into these prairies to procure a supply of buffalo beef. . . . *Ib.* 105 The bottom being of solid rock, the ford is appropriately called by the ciboleros, *el Vado de Piedras.* **1941** FERGUSSON *Southwest* 326 Ciboleros in leather jackets and breeches and flat straw hats wore quiverfuls of bows and arrows and carried steel-tipped lances fluttering with silken tassels.

* **cider,** *n.*

1. In combs., chiefly obs.: (1) **cider beggar,** (see quot.); (2) **brandy,** (see quot. 1859); (3) **cake,** a cake somewhat similar to pound cake in making which cider is used; (4) **cart,** (see quot.); (5) **fixings,** cider-making apparatus, *colloq.*; (6) **frolic,** a social gathering at which cider is drunk, *colloq.*; (7) **pap,** (see quot.); (8) **toast,** toast having cider poured over it.

(1) **1851** *Knickerb.* XXXVII. 557 In olden times there was a distinct class of itinerants in New England, who were called 'cider-beggars.' — (2) **1800** *Columbian Centinel* 22 Jan. 4/4 For Sale, A quantity of Cider-Brandy and Gin. **1859** BARTLETT, Apple Brandy, a liquor distilled from fermented apple-juice; also called Cider brandy. — (3) **1832** CHILD *Frugal Housewife* 71 Cider cake is very good, to be baked in small loaves. **1939** WOLCOTT *Yankee Cook Bk.* 261. — (4) **1877** *So. Hist. Soc. P.* III. 17 The passage of a cider-cart (a barrel on wheels) was a rare and exciting occurrence.

(5) **1848** BURTON *Waggeries* 10 He was gettin' his cider fixins ready in the fall. — (6) **1766** HILTZHEIMER *Diary* (1893) 24 Jan. 10 Attended a cider frolic at Greenwich Hall. **1844** *S. Lit. Messenger* X. 529/2 A 'cider frolic,' in which the Green Mountain boys especially delight. — (7) **1708** E. COOK *Sot-Weed Factor* 5 Homine and Syder-pap, (Which scarce a hungry dog wou'd lap). . . . Syder-pap is a sort of Food made of Syder and small Homine, like our Oatmeal. — (8) **1898** I. HARPER *S. B. Anthony* I. 15 The pride of the children's lives was to eat cider toast out of them [*sc.* porringers].

2. In the phrase: *all talk and no cider,* much talk but no results, "much cry and little wool." Hence *more cider and less talk. Colloq.*

1807 IRVING *Salmagundi* vii. 79 The people, in fact seem to be somewhat conscious of this propensity to talk, by which they are characterized, and have a favorite proverb on the subject, viz. 'all talk and no cider.' **1849** N. KINGSLEY *Diary* 50 Fine stories are cold comfort, when it is as they say 'All talk and no cider.' **1862** BROWNE *A. Ward His Book* (F.), What we want is more cider and less talk.

As the last term in **boiled, buffalo, hard, Jersey, milk-and-, Ohio apple, sap cider.**

ciderish ˈsaɪdərɪʃ, *a.* Somewhat like cider in flavor. *Rare.* — **1854** THOREAU *Walden* 277 There where grow still the apple-trees, . . . their fruit still wild and ciderish to my taste.

cienaga ˈsɪnɪgə, *n. S.W.* [Sp. *ciênaga,* marsh, swamp.] A small marshy or miry area, often less than an acre in extent, generally located on sloping ground where a spring issues from a mountainside or where there are seepages.

1846 ABERT *Exam. N.M.* 45 After a short march we reach 'Cienaga,' a very well watered place, as its name denotes. **1866** MELINE *Two Thousand Miles on Horseback* (1867) 58 You hear, too, of *chenegays* (one or more springs together; a corruption of the Spanish *cien aguas*—one hundred fountains). **1888** LINDLEY *Calif. of South* 236 The waters emerge from the side of low lime-hills, and, filtering through the earth, form a sort of limited *cienaga* or marsh. **1939** *Jrnl. Mammalogy* 14 Nov. 434 The largest area was the San Simon Cienega, located on the Arizona-New Mexico State line in the middle of the valley.

* **cigar,** *n.*

1. *S.W.* = **shuck cigar.** *Rare.*

1848 J. S. ROBINSON *Santa Fe Exped.* 49 The Spanish Mexicans use no chairs, but sit upon the floor on a mat or carpet, beneath which is always kept a quantity of corn-shucks, which are used for making cigars.

2. The seed pod of the catalpa. *Colloq.* Cf. **cigar tree, devil's cigar.**

1876 *Field & Forest* Sep. 51 Some of the boys in my youth took their first lessons, in smoking, by using the 'beans' or 'cigars' of the Catalpa I refer to above.

3. In combs.: (1) * **cigar case,** a showcase in which cigars are kept on display in a cigar or other store; (2) **drummer,** a drummer who sells cigars; (3) **fish,** a small, cigar-shaped tropical fish of the genus *Decapterus;* (4) **lamp,** a small lamp or other lighting fixture used in lighting a cigar, *obs.*; (5) **leaf,** a tobacco leaf such as is used in making cigars; (6) **lighter,** a twist of paper for lighting a cigar, a pocket or other mechanical apparatus for lighting

One form of cigar lamp (*c*1880)

a cigar (see quot. 1874); (7) **-sign Indian,** a wooden Indian used as a sign before a cigar store, cf. **cigar store Indian;** (8) **stand,** a stall or counter where cigars are sold; (9) **store,** see as a main entry; (10) **tree,** the catalpa; (11) **wagon,** ?a wagon from which cigars, cigarettes, etc., are sold, *rare.*

(1) **1897** BRODHEAD *Bound in Shallows* 14 Alexa inclined herself idly against the rim of the small cigar-case. **1900** G. ADE *More Fables* 6 Next Morning, at the Hotel he spotted a stylish little chunk of a Woman who kept the Cigar Case. — (2) **1909** O. HENRY *Options* 69 A manner . . . that not even a cigar-drummer would intrude upon. — (3) **1888** GOODE *Amer. Fishes* 230 The Round Robin, *Decapterus punctatus,* called at Pensacola 'Cigar-fish.' — (4) **1898** WESTCOTT *D. Harum* 62 Mr. Lenox reached over for the cigar-lamp.

(5) **1863** *Ill. Agric. Soc. Trans.* (1865) V. 669 Tobacco of this description should be . . . prized lightly in the casks so as to admit of a free and open leaf, such being mostly required for cigar leaf. — (6) *c***1845** W. THOMPSON *Chron. Pineville* 49 'Cigar-lighter,' added a mischievous fellow on the opposite side, with a wink to the crowd. **1874** KNIGHT 553/1 Cigar-lighter, a little gas-jet suspended by an elastic tube. **1932** *K.C. Times* 5 Mar. 26 What shall it profit a man to rise in the world's eyes and then have a cigar lighter that won't work? — (7) **1895** *N.Y. Dramatic News* 30 Nov. 3/2 In the next act Gaylor prevents a murder by masquerading as a cigar-sign Indian. — (8) **1880** *Bradstreet's* 19 May 8/1 A cigar stand is kept as a part of the establishment. **1938** ASBURY *Sucker's Prog.* 322 As late as 1891, according to the reformed gambler John Philip Quinn, 'all the cigar stands along Market Street have back rooms for Poker parties.'

(10) **1876** *Field & Forest* Aug. 28 It is occasionally, though not often, called 'Indian Bean' or 'Cigar Tree.' **1933** SMALL *Southeastern Flora* 1241 Catalpa. . . . Indian-beans. Indian-cigars. Cigar-trees. Smoking-beans. Catalpas. Catawbas. — (11) **1861** *Vanity Fair* 9 Feb. 63/1 The senior Mr. Primpenny then hailed a stage passing up the true Broadway, Mr. Kineboy remarking . . . he thought it was a yaller soda-water or cigar wagon.

As the last term in **cabbage, devil's, five-cent, grapevine, Indian, oak-leaf, opera, seed, shuck, stogie, sweet fern cigar.**

cigarette ˌsɪgəˈrɛt, *n.* [F.] A small quantity of finely cut tobacco in a cylindrical envelope, usu. of thin paper, open at both ends. Also attrib.

From the evidence at present available it appears that this word may have come into American and British use independently. The earliest British evidence in the *OED* is of 1842. The scene of the 1835 quot. below is Russia.

1835 in W. R. ALGER *Life Edwin Forrest* I. (1877) 287 After dinner some of the ladies smoked cigarettes, and others played cards. **1884** *Boston Jrnl.* 30 Sep. 2/3 He was taking out his cigarette case while waiting on the sidewalk for an opportunity to cross a crowded street. **1948** *Tishomingo* (Okla.) *Capital-Democrat* 17 June 5/3 The average American smoked 115 packs of cigarettes in 1946.

b. cigarette picture, (see quot. 1944).

1940 MENCKEN *Happy Days* 130 They found a pocket-knife, a couple of sea-shells, three or four nails, two cigarette pictures, a dozen chewing-tobacco tags, a cork, a slate pencil, an almost fossil handkerchief, and three cents in cash. **1944** JOHNSON *As I Dare* 23 This collection yielded place to cigarette pictures. Every package of cigarettes contained a picture, and by begging at the doorways of tobacco shops and by trading among friends I might boast a full set of flags, or baseball players, or especially actresses and thus be exalted above my fellows.

cigarito sigəˈrito, *n. S.W.* [Sp. *cigarrito*, little cigar.] A small cigar or a cigarette.

1834 in *Calif. Hist. Soc. Quart.* VIII. 147, I heartily cursed our guide, while listening to his singing of the *petenera*, and seeing him strike the steel to light his cigarita. **1848** *Calif. Star* (S.F.) 18 Mar. 2/2 Deliberately drawing from his vest pocket, his worn and soiled *machero*, he applies fire to a cigarito, which he thrusts in his mouth. **1910** J. HART *Vigilante Girl* 348 But there was no sign of activity; the bandits were lolling around their fire, smoking cigaritos.

cigar store.

1. A shop that specializes in the sale of cigars and smoking accessories.

1848 E. JUDSON *Mysteries N.Y.* II. 23 Are you going back to that hateful cigar store? **1948** *Chi. D. News* 17 Nov. 26/1 The retailer and the buyer in the cigar store, however, are operating in a 'free economy.'

2. cigar-store Indian, an Indian figure, usu. carved of wood, often used as a sign before a tobacco shop. Cf. **wooden Indian.**

1937 MITCHELL *Horse & Buggy Age* 32, I concluded that it must have been given to a cigar store Indian in search of a mount. **1948** *Ill. State Arch. Soc. Jrnl.* April 37/1 The old type of Cigar Store Wooden Indian is rapidly vanishing from the American scene! **1949** *This Week Mag.* 9 Jan. 4/4 A cigar-store Indian was chosen justice of the peace in Allentown, N.J., some years ago.

cimline ˈsɪmlɪn, *n.* [Origin obscure.] (See quot.) — **1880** *Scribner's Mo.* Aug. 492/2 The top cord or line of the [drift] net is called a 'cimline' [in N.Y.].

cimarron ˈsɪməˌron, *n. S.W.* [Amer. Sp. *cimarrón*, wild, feral.] The bighorn or Rocky Mountain sheep.

[**1844** GREGG *Commerce of Prairies* I. 194 The *carnero cimarron* or bighorn of the Rocky Mountains—the *berrendo* or antelope and the *tuza* or prairie dog of the plains—hares, polecats, and other animals of lesser importance, may also be considered as denizens of these regions.] **1849** MARCY *Account Reconnaissance* 201 The big-horn, or cimarron, . . . cropping the short herbage which grows upon them. **1907** MEARNS *Mammals Mex. Boundary* 233 *Ovis mexicanus* . . . *Pang'-wŭh* of the Hopi Indians of northeastern Arizona. *Cimarron* of the Mexicans.

cinch sɪntʃ, *n.* Also †**sinch.** Orig. *W.* [Sp. *cincha* in sense **1.**]

1. A strong girth for a saddle, often of braided horsehair. Also attrib.

1859 G. A. JACKSON *Diary* 521, [I] nailed shoes on Old Chief to-day, and Black Hawk and I made Hackamore and sinche. **1889** *N. & Q.* III. 47 There are no buckles on the belly-band, and their place is supplied by two rings through which is passed the cinch-strap, which is tied by the cinch-knot. **1947** *Trail Riders Bul.* May 9/1 He was always on hand to adjust a stirrup here and there and see to it that the cinches were tightened.

b. *fig.* A sure or easy thing, often in phrases. *Slang.*

1888 *Chicago Inter-Ocean* 2 Feb. (F.), Black and blue thinks the Dwyers have a cinch on both the great events. **1907** MULFORD *Bar-20* 60 Yu won't have no cinch ridin' home with that leg. **1947** *Dly. Ardmoreite* (Ardmore, Okla.) 14 Nov. 1/1 It sounds like a cinch—and it is a cinch, too, in one way.

2. A card game derived from and resembling auction pitch.

Usu. taken as of a different origin from **1**, but prob. merely an extension.

1889 (Amer. newspaper), I found that sinch is the great Northwestern game of cards, a recent invention, and played everywhere and by everybody. . . . It is a variation of High, Low, Jack. **1938** ASBURY *Sucker's Prog.* 323 At first the Nevadans used the room principally as a place in which to play Cinch, a variation of All-Fours which was also known as Double Pedro or High Five, but after a few years it was devoted almost entirely to Poker. **1946** MOREHEAD & MOTT-SMITH *Penguin Hoyle* 57 Cinch, a partnership game for four players, is the aristocrat of the high-low-jack games.

3. In special colloq. or slang combs.: (1) **cinch bet,** a bet on a sure thing; (2) **bill,** a proposed legislative bill designed to "put the cinch" on a company or corporation who, it is hoped, will bribe the legislators to kill the bill, *rare;* (3) **binder,** one who is crafty or cunning [see quot. 1878 *s.v.* **cinch,** *v.* **1.**]; (4) **game,** a game the outcome of which is certain.

(1) **1944** *Democrat* 14 Aug. 15/3 GI's 'Cinch Bet' Was Newsweek Boner. — (2) **1887** *S.F. News Letter* 29 Jan. 20/2 The 'cinch' bill which is aimed at the gas companies . . . is a measure of such a barefaced nature that no one can plead ignorance in regard to it. — (3) **1916** H. L. WILSON *Somewhere in Red Gap* v. 180, I had another aunt named Patience, only she proved to be a regular cinch-binder. — (4) **1895** CHAMBLISS *Diary* 172, I suppose the Parvenucracy would consider it 'bad form' if I were to call this a 'cinch game.'

As the last term in **double, hair, lead pipe cinch.**

cinch sɪntʃ, *v.* Also †**sinch.** Chiefly *W.* [f. **cinch,** *n.*]

1. *tr.* to fasten (a saddle) by a cinch, to saddle (a mule or horse). Also intr. or absol.

1873 BEADLE *Undevel. West* 273 With all set and everything tightly 'cinched,' we took the start. **1878** E. B. TUTTLE *Border Tales* 36 All [mules] soon learn to swell themselves out when being sinched. **1947** *Trail & Timberline* May 77/2 Put muscle into the pull on the front cinch on the pack saddle, the original pull to cinch up the pack rope and the final pull on the pack rope before it is tied.

b. Used fig., esp. in the sense "to make sure or certain." *Slang.*

1902 *Harper's Mag.* 468, I spoke awful good English to him most of the time. . . . I can, yu' know, when I cinch my attention tight on to it. **1910** RAINE *B. O'Connor* 25 That extra hour and a half cinches our escape. **1944** *Chi. D. News* 22 July 3/1 The nomination had been cinched with an unofficial majority for the Missourian. **1946** MOREHEAD & MOTT-SMITH *Penguin Hoyle* 59 If no higher trump has been played, third hand must usually *cinch* a trick by playing some higher trump than the five.

2. To bring into difficulties, to "spoil one's game." *Slang.*

1875 *Scribner's Mo.* X. 277/1 [At San Francisco] a man who is hurt in a mining transaction is 'cinched.' **1910** ROOSEVELT in *Outlook* 3 Sep. 2/1 If the rich man strives to use his wealth to destroy others, I will cinch him if I can.

cincha ˈsintʃɑ, *n. W.* [Sp. in same sense.] =**cinch,** *n.* **1.** Also transf.

1876 BOURKE *Journal* 27 Feb., This is made double in the middle of its length by a 'cincha,' or belt of canvas passing around the girth. **1884** NYE *Baled Hay* 138 The full . . . swell and broad cincha of the chaparajo have given place to the tight pantaletts. **1927** SIRINGO *Riata* 67 The cinchas on these saddles being broad, and in the center of the saddle, it is difficult to keep the saddle tight on the pony's back.

Cincinnati ˌsɪnsəˈnætɪ, *n.* [f. *Cincinnatus*, Roman dictator.]

1. Used in the name of a patriotic and benevolent organization formed in 1783 by those who had been officers in the Revolution. Cf. **Loyal Legion.**

Officers and their direct, sometimes collateral, descendants were eligible for membership in this organization of which Washington was the first president. State societies were formed, all of which, through failure of heirs, had disintegrated by 1900. A revival of the general organization, however, was effected in 1902.

1783 *N.H. Hist. Soc. Coll.* VI. 279 The officers of the American Army . . . possess high veneration for the character of that illustrious Roman, Lucius Quintus Cincinnatus, and being resolved to follow his example . . . they think they may with propriety denominate themselves The Society of the Cincinnati. [**1784** J. ADAMS *Wks.* IX. 524, I am sorry you have any marks of an order of Cincinnatus, which is the first step taken to deface the beauty of our temple of liberty.] **1838** *S. Lit. Messenger* IV. 792/1 One declared object of the Cincinnati Society, was 'to preserve the memory of the American Revolution.' **1948** *Chi. Tribune* 29 Feb. 1. 24/6 The Revolutionary officers attempted to form an aristocracy hereditary in the eldest of the male line, calling itself the Order of the Cincinnati.

b. Those composing this organization. *Obs.*

1798 J. ADAMS *Wks.* IX. 223 When the Cincinnati of South Carolina pledge their lives, their fortunes, and their sacred honor, I believe no man will doubt their integrity.

2. Whisky made at Cincinnati, Ohio. *Obs.*

Cincinnati, at first known as Losantiville, was renamed in honor of the Society of that name in 1790.

1847 ROBB *Squatter Life* 57 What'll you take Missus? shall I sweeten you a little of about the best Cincinnati rectified that ever was toted into these 'ere parts? **1858** *Nat. Intelligencer* 10 July (B.), A citizen of St. Paul . . . says a barrel of the 'pure Cincinnati,' . . . is a sufficient basis upon which to manufacture one hundred barrels of 'good Indian liquor!'

3. (See quot.)

1908 *D.N.* III. 299 Cincinnatti [*sic*], n. The name of a game of marbles. [East Alabama].

4. In special combs., now obs.: (1) **Cincinnati Bullion,** (see quot.); (2) **cracklings,** (see quot.); (3) **doubloon,** (see quot.); (4) **oration,** app. an oration dealing with the Cincinnati Society; (5) **oysters,** (see quot.); (6) **quail,** (see quot.).

(1) **1845** *Cincinnati Misc.* I. 240 Cents or Coppers are generally known in the West as, 'Cincinnati Bullion.' — (2) **1864** *Harper's Mag.* Sep. 433/1 Here is the list: . . . 200 pounds Borden's meat biscuit; 20 pounds 'Cincinnati cracklings'—pork scraps. — (3) **1858** in *Kans. Hist. Coll.* XIV. 99 There is one curious fact about the currency here . . . nothing smaller than five-cent piece is in circulation. A cent they call a 'Cincinnati doubloon' and a three-cent bit is totally disregarded. — (4) **1838** *S. Lit. Messenger* IV. 792/1 It is therefore our purpose to make 'The Cincinnati Oration' one of the standing exercises at the college commencements.

(5) **1938** ASBURY *Sucker's Prog.* 271 For some forty years hogs and Cincinnati were so nearly synonymous in the public mind that pigs-feet were called 'Cincinnati oysters,' and in many places were so listed on restaurant menus. — (6) **1884** in *Amer. Sp.* XX. (1945) Feb. 71/1 'Cincinnati quail—have it fat,' was the next order. The cook cut off a large slice of fat pork and put it on a plate.

Cincinnatian ˌsɪnsəˈnætɪən, *n.* and *a.*

1. *n.* A citizen of Cincinnati, Ohio.

1831 J. H. ATHERTON in *Filson Club Hist. Quart.* XVI. 213 The opinion of all the Cincinnatians to the contrary notwithstanding there is much more business done here (Louisville) than there in proportion to the population. **1899** *Commercial Tribune* (Cincinnati) 5 Aug. 12/5 Cincinnatians who go East hear of him frequently. **1947** *Dly. Racing Form* (Chi.) 3 Nov. 36/3 The Cincinnatian is a stickler for 'class in the dam.'

2. *a. Geol.* Pertaining to formations of the Lower Silurian age.

1899 *Science* X. 877 Probably in no other region is the succession of these [Lorraine and Richmond] faunas so complete as about Cincinnati, and this fact justifies the recognition of the term Cincinnatian. **1906** CHAMBERLIN & SALISBURY *Geol.* II. 310 Cincinnatian (Neo-Champlainic): Richmond beds, Lorraine beds, Utica shales.

***cinder,** *n.*

1. cinder cone, *Geol.* (see quot. 1889).

1889 *Cent.* 1003/1 cinder-cone. . . . A formation resulting from the deposition of successive eruptions of fine material, ash lapilli and scoriae, from a volcano. **1902** *Out West* Aug. 174 The heavier material fell about the orifices and built up the so-called cinder cones. **1948** *Sierra Club* (So. Calif. Chap.) Sched. 127, 69 Camp Friday night on the desert near cinder cone north of Little Lake.

2. cinder hole, (see quot. 1852).

1852 *Harper's Mag.* V. 151/2 A cinder hole is a small cavity left in the iron at the time of the manufacture of it. **1861** *Army Regulations* 469 Musket barrels . . . [are] rejected for defects [like]: . . . Interior cinder-holes, . . . Exterior cinder-holes.

Cinderella slipper. (See quots.) *Obs.* — **1810** *Columbian Centinel* 17 Jan. 3/1 Thomas Wiley . . . has just received a specimen of the new invented Gold and silver Cinderrella Slippers, designed for Balls and Assemblies. [**1874** ALDRICH *P. Palfrey* xvii, Sitting . . . with her feet thrust into a pair of satin slippers of the Cinderella family.]

***cinnamon,** *n.*

1. Short for **cinnamon bear.**

1855 MARRYAT *Mts. & Molehills* 253 The cinnamon's weight was quoted at 400 lbs. **1892** LUMMIS *Tramp Across Continent* 59 A cinnamon dies hard; and before the hunter could reload . . . the brute was upon him. **1946** R. PEATTIE *Pac. Coast Ranges* 82 Some of the bears formerly called cinnamons were undoubtedly grizzlies.

2. In combs.: (1) **cinnamon bear,** a dark-brown variety of the black bear (see also quot. 1946 in **1.** above, and cf. **cinnamon grizzly**); (2) **fern,** a large fern, *Osmunda cinnamomea*, so called from the color of its fronds, also **cinnamon-colored fern;** (3) **grizzly,** a grizzly bear; (4) **honeysuckle,** an azalea, *Azalea viscosa*, found in swamps in the eastern states; (5) **teal,** the red-breasted teal, *Querquedula cyanoptera*, found in the western U.S.

(1) **1829** J. RICHARDSON *Fauna Bor. Amer.* I. 15 The Cinnamon Bear of the Fur Traders is considered by the Indians to be an accidental variety of this species (*Ursus americanus*). **1945** MATHEWS *Talking* 164 This great cinnamon bear had taken his sheep. — (2) **1847** WOOD *Botany* 634 Cinnamon-colored Fern. . . . This is among the largest of our ferns, growing in swamps and low grounds. **1917** BAILEY *Sand Dunes Indiana* 156 The brakes and cinnamon ferns are hip high. — (3) **1872** *Harper's Mag.* LXVI. 20 The sportsman looks to his rifle as he sees the monstrous tracks of the cinnamon grizzly. — (4) **1894** *Amer. Folk-Lore* VII. 93 *Rhododendron viscosum* . . . Gray, cinnamon honeysuckle, West Va. **1901** MOHR *Plant Life Ala.* 653 *Azalea viscosa glauca*. . . . Cinnamon Honeysuckle. . . . Mountain region. Rocky banks of brooks.

(5) **1891** *Cent.* 6206/1 Cinnamon teal, *Querquedula cyanoptera*, of western North America . . . , [is] so called from the color of the under parts of the adult male. **1948** *Green Bay* (Wis.) *Press-Gazette* 12 July 22/7 Improvements [were] noted among mallards, gadwalls, shovellers, cinnamon teal and Canada geese.

CIO ˈsiˌaɪˈo, *n.* Also **C.I.O.** [Orig. abbrev. for Committee for Industrial Organization; see quot. 1938.] Abbrev. for Congress of Industrial Organizations, one of the two great labor organizations of the U.S., organized on a permanent basis in 1938, at which time the present name was officially adopted. Also attrib.

1935 *Nation* 11 Dec. 665/1 The job that John L. Lewis and his fellow-members of the Committee for Industrial Organization have set for themselves . . . seems difficult. **1936** *Ib.* 27 May 662/1 The organization of the C.I.O. have already waived any jurisdictional claims. **1938** *Time* 28 Nov. 11/3 John L. Lewis and 518 other delegates to a constitutional convention assembled in Pittsburgh to bury the three-year old Committee for Industrial Organization. In its stead they erected a permanent organization, whose full official title is 'Congress of Industrial Organizations (CIO).' **1948** *Chi. Tribune* 10 May 11. 3/3 The raise was rejected by the CIO United Packinghouse Workers union.

***cipher,** *n.*

1. The zero mark on a thermometer. *Obs.*

1788 NOAH WEBSTER in Ford *Notes* I. (1912) 226 Mercury at 6 below cypher. **1815** *Ib.* 177 The Thermometer fell to 12 below cypher in Boston. **1815** DRAKE *Cincinnati* 94 From nine years observations, at Cincinnati, it appears that the thermometer falls below cypher twice every winter.

2. cipher dispatch, a dispatch in cipher, esp. with reference to one of the telegraphic communications in cipher sent by friends of Samuel J. Tilden in an effort to secure his election as President in 1876.

1874 in MCPHERSON *Hand-Book Politics* (1876) 27 Two cipher dispatches received. **1878** *N.Y. Tribune* 12 Nov., The history of the electoral crisis in November and December, 1876 . . . [is] disclosed by the cipher dispatches of the Democratic leaders. **1901** JAMESON & BUEL *Encycl. Dict. Amer. Ref.* I. 148 Cipher Dispatches . . . were sent by friends of Tilden, . . . and purported to arrange for the payment of certain moneys to ensure the carrying of South Carolina and Florida.

***cipher,** *v.* **1.** *To cipher out*, to work out (as if) by calculating, to think or study out. *Colloq.* **2.** (See quot.)

(1) **1825** NEAL *Bro. Jonathan* I. 172 (Th.), Let each man [figuratively] take a slate and cipher it out. **1898** WESTCOTT *D. Harum* 154 S'posen you come 'round to my place tomorro' 'bout 'leven o'clock, an' mebee we c'n cipher this thing out. — (2) **1889** *Cent.* 1005/3 Cipher, v. 2. In fox-hunting, to hunt carefully about in search of a lost trail; said of a dog. (New Eng.). 3. To run on three legs: said of a dog (Kentucky.).

***ciphering,** *a.* Designing, calculating. *Colloq.* — **1825** J. NEAL *Bro. Jonathan* I. 154 A . . . cool, keen, cyphering, thrifty temper.

***circle,** *n.*

1. *W.* Attrib. with reference to brands used by cattle ranchers. Often *cap.*

1903 A. ADAMS *Log Cowboy* ii. 12 We were in honour bound to accept everything bearing the 'circle dot' on the left hip. **1910** RAINE *B. O'Connor* 219 We're after them for rustling a bunch of Circle 33 cows. **1942** DALE *Cow Country* 144 Jim Collins, of the Half Circle H, once went to a wedding in company with one of his chums.

2. *W.* A group of cowboys engaged in circle riding *q.v.*, also the act of circle riding.

1927 JAMES *Cow Country* 82 We was just catching horses for the second circle of the day when the two rode up. **1930** RAINE & BARNES *Cattle* 300 Half an hour after the circle starts down the prong one can see for miles small bunches of cattle in motion.

3. In special combs.: (1) **circle hunt,** a hunt in which a large number of men and boys surround an area and move in, driving all the game to the center, now *hist.*; (2) **rider,** *W.* a cowboy engaged in rounding up cattle by circle riding; (3) **riding,** *W.* (see quot.).

(1) **1924** DILLIN *Ky. Rifle* 10 Even as late as 1818 these slaughters, or 'Circle Hunts,' as they were called were still held in communities where wild animals were so plentiful as to be a menace to the meager crops and herds of the pioneer farmer. — (2) **1888** ROOSEVELT in *Cent. Mag.* April 860/1 As soon as . . . the last circle-riders have come in . . . we begin to work the herd. **1926** BRANCH *Cowboy & Interpreters* 56 In rough country where each little ravine must be searched and each knoll circled, each group of 'circle riders' would be smaller than groups in unbroken plains country. — (3) **1888** ROOSEVELT in *Cent. Mag.* April 857/2 This morning work is called circle riding. . . . As the band goes out, the leader from time to time detaches one or two men to ride . . . making the shorter, or what are called inside, circles, while he keeps on; and finally . . . makes the longest or outside circle himself.

b. *To ride circle*, to do the work of a circle rider on a ranch; *to swing round the circle*, see ***swing,** *v.*

1943 HOWARD *Montana* 176 Where once you rode circle and I night wrangled, a gopher couldn't graze now.

As the last term in **benevolence, cooking, fairy, family, golden, improvement, Knights of the, parquet, prayer, praying, second, sewing, squared circle.**

***circling,** *n. W.* (See quot.) *Obs.* — **1878** BEADLE *Western Wilds* 536 The savages attacked in the manner known as 'circling'—that is, riding round and round the whites, hanging on the opposite side of their horses so as to be shielded.

***circuit,** *n.*

1. An association of baseball teams from various cities that play among themselves for the league championship. Also attrib.

1889 *Sporting Life* (Phila.) 3 July 4/1 St. Louis is a played-out base ball city and, all things considered, the weakest point in the Association circuit. **1898** *K.C. Star* 18 Dec. 3/1 Little was heard to-day of changes in the league circuit, the prime movers in the scheme preferring to work in the dark. *Ib.*, The advocates of a reduced circuit have little intention of buying any one out at lofty prices. **1948** *Chickasha* (Okla.) *D. Express* 4 July 11/4 Lawton, the Cinderella club of the circuit, is in second place with 38 wins, 25 losses and a .603.

2. In special combs.: (1) **circuit breaker,** a device which breaks or interrupts an electric circuit; (2) **clerk,** the clerk of a circuit court; (3) ***court,** see as a main entry; (4) ***judge,** a judge who presides over a federal or state circuit court; (5) **preacher,** a minister having charge of one or more churches in a circuit; (6) **rider,** a minister serving churches in a circuit; (7) **riding,** serving as a minister who rides a circuit, also fig.

(1) **1872** *U.S. Patents Official Gazette* II. 140/1 Claim . . . [includes] the combination of two batteries with a circuit and a circuit-breaker. **1879** G. PRESCOTT *Speaking Telephone* 251 A delicate circuit-breaker, attached to the membrane, was arranged to break the circuit of a telegraph line at the vibration. — (2) **1848** *S. Lit. Messenger* XIV. 648/1 One of the proprietors went immediately to the circuit clerk, and complained on oath against the authors of, and actors in, this riot. **1891** O'BEIRNE *Leaders Ind. Territory* 51/2 In 1879 he was appointed circuit clerk under Judge Loring Folsom. — (4) **1801** *Ann. 6th Congress* 9 Jan. 902 His travelling expenses were trifling compared with those of the Circuit Judges. **1948** *Chi. Tribune* 11 July 29/1 The original law creating the appeals circuit provided for three circuit judges.

(5) **1830** *William's New-York Ann. Reg.* 291 Other towns [of Franklin County, N.Y.] have no settled ministers—Supplied by circuit and other preachers. **1931** SWEET *Religion* 46 The circuit preacher frequently formed his circuit by riding up one side of the stream and down the other. — (6) **1837** WETMORE *Gaz. Missouri* 333 When Patsy gets her eye on the greyhound, she'll feel a heap gladder than when the circuit-rider comes round! **1946** ADAMS *Album Amer. Hist.* III. 14 In the sparsely settled regions of the west and south, the circuit rider served the religious needs of the people. — (7) **1904** *N.Y. Ev. Post* 1 Nov. 6 A careful political observer, who has been 'circuit riding' for the Kansas City Star throughout Missouri, writes [etc.]. **1929** E. W. HOWE *Plain People* 6 In addition to his circuit riding, every summer father held camp meetings.

As the last term in **judicial circuit.**

***circuit court.**

1. Prior to 1911, a federal court presided over by a justice of the Supreme Court, a special circuit judge and the judge of the district court, or by any two of these.

1789 *Statutes at Large* I. 93 All writs and processes issuing from a supreme or a circuit court. **1807** *Ann. 10th Congress* 1 Sess. I. 424 The annexed statement . . . as given in the circuit court of the United States for the fifth circuit and Virginia district [etc.]. **1910** HART *Vigilante Girl* 308 Mark my words, . . . if this case gets into the circuit court somebody is going to get hurt.

2. In some states, a court having jurisdiction in matters of state cognizance. Also attrib.

1836 *Diplom. Corr. Texas* (1908) I. 162 The Supreme Court consisting of a chief justice and the Judges of the Supreme or Circuit Courts as his associates. **1877** *Mich. Gen. Statutes* (1882–3) I. 93 There shall be published of the volume containing the public acts of each session . . . a sufficient number of copies to supply the following persons . . . prosecuting attorneys, circuit court commissioners [etc.]. **1948** *Pauls Valley* (Okla.) *D. Democrat* 1 July 1/7 The judge urged an appeal so that the circuit court would rule on his position, however.

3. *Circuit Court of Appeals*, an appellate federal court immediately below the Supreme Court, established in 1891.

1891 *U.S. Session Laws* XXVI. 827 There is hereby created in each circuit a circuit court of appeals. **1905** *Indian Laws & Tr.* III. 158 Hereafter all appeals and writs of error shall be taken from the United States courts in the Indian Territory . . . to the United States circuit court of appeals for the eighth circuit.

***circular,** *n.* App. a long, full, loose-fitting cloak. In full **circular cloak.** *Obs.* — **1837** *S. Lit. Messenger* III. 225 A huge umbrella under . . . which was an . . . urchin . . . carrying home some gentleman's new circular cloak. **1883** PECK *Bad Boy* 125 Ma . . . got the doctor to prescribe a fur lined circular.

As the last term in **specie circular.**

circularization ˌsɜkjələrɪ'zeʃən, *n.* The sending out of circulars. — **1928** *Publishers' Weekly* 16 June 2450 If . . . the Guild advertising or circularization should be considered contrary to the spirit of this agreement.

***circumstance,** *n.* In colloq. expressions: (1) *not a circumstance to*, nothing in comparison with; (2) *a mere* (or *remote, poor*) *circumstance*, a person or thing of little or no consequence; (3) (see quot.).

(1) **1836** *Crockett's Yaller Flower Almanac* 19 Orson the wild man of the woods, is nothing to him—not a circumstance. **1869** *Sitka* (Alaska) *Times* 6 Aug. 3/2 The whooping of the Indians or wailing of the cayotes is no circumstance in comparison. **1927** *Haldeman-Julius Quart.* July–Sept. 10/2 Hamlet without the ghost would not be a circumstance to it.

(2) **1838** FLAGG *Far West* I. 145 The race of John Gilpin or of Alderman Purdy were, either or both of them, mere circumstances to ours. *c*1840 Florida newspaper (Th. 969), I'm a small specimen, as you see, a remote circumstance, a mere yearling; but cuss me if I ain't of the true imported breed. **1899** MARK TWAIN *How to Make . . . Dates Stick* (1917) 155 (R.), Next comes King John, and he was a poor circumstance.

(3) **1889** FARMER 148 To whip something into a circumstance.

***circus,** *n.*

1. A noisy dispute, row, uproar, a lively time. *Colloq.*

1869 MARK TWAIN *Innocents Abroad* 358 (R.), Constantinople was —well, it was an eternal circus. **1885** *N.Y. Mercury* 23 May (Ware), Coghill found out that he had paid Lafayette just three times too much for the Louisiana lands. . . . Then there was a circus. **1909** WARE *Passing English* 78 He made a desperate fight, but there was no 'circus' this time.

b. (See quot.) *Slang.*

1928 ASBURY *Gangs of N.Y.* 178 Women habitues danced the cancan and gave exhibitions similar to the French peep shows. The descriptive title of 'circus,' which is now generally applied to such displays in this country, is said to have originated in the Haymarket.

2. a. *To play circus*, to go around in circles. **b.** *To see the circus*, to face trouble, to "see the sights." Both *colloq.*

(a) 1867 *Atlantic Mo.* May 589/1, I believe we are playing circus here. **1876** HABBERTON *Jericho Road* 11 The West wasn't made fur blunderin' shadders to play circus in. — **(b) 1891** THANET *Otto the Knight* 106 Best Billy says, 'No, sir; it has been Atherton and Temple too long for that; we'll see the circus together.' **1898** ATHERTON *Californians* 13 He was persuaded by Polk to take a trip into the San Joaquin valley to 'see the circus,' as the Yankee phrased it.

As the last term in **flea, road circus.**

cisatlantic ˌsɪsətˈlæntɪk, *a.* Of or pertaining to this side of the Atlantic. ?*Obs.*

1782 JEFFERSON *Notes Va.* 118, I only mean to suggest a doubt, . . . whether nature has enlisted herself as a Cis- or Trans-Atlantic partisan. **1835** *Vade Mecum* (Phila.) 6 June 3/2 In serenading, it seems it likewise bears off the palm from all cis-atlantic rivals. **1879** HOLMES *Motley* xvii, 107 What can I say to you of cis-Atlantic things?

cisco ˈsɪsko, *n.* Also **sisco.** Short for **siscowet.**

1848 BARTLETT 81 Cisco, the popular name of a fish of the herring kind which abounds in Lake Ontario. **1875** *Amer. Naturalist* IX. 135, I received . . . a collection of deep-water 'Siscoes' taken in Lake Tippecanoe, Kosciusko Co., Indiana. **1947** DALRYMPLE *Panfish* 333 The Ciscoes come swarming up from the deep water and greedily tak e the flies.

attrib. **1872** in *Fur, Fin, & Feather* 200 Cisco fishing at Geneva Lake, Wis. . . . Their coming is heralded by the cisco-fly. **1892** *Outing* Jan. 305/1, I had been invited to spend a morning with two mutual friends in their cisco shanty upon the then frozen waters of beautiful upper Nashota Lake.

ciscoette, ciscovet, see **siscowet.**

ciscoist ˈsɪskoˌɪst, *n.* One who fishes for cisco. *Rare.* — **1872** *Fur, Fin, & Feather* 200 The lucky ciscoist is he (or she) who brings to this classic shore a sixteen-foot rod.

* **cistern,** *n.*

1. * **cistern bottoms,** (see quot. 1833). Also attrib. in sing.

1833 SILLIMAN *Man. Sugar Cane* 41 On draining off the molasses cisterns, a greater or less deposit of sugar, called cistern bottoms, is found in these vessels. **1848** *De Bow's Review* VI. 457 Adding the cistern bottom sugars . . . the crop of 1844–5 exceeded 200,000 hogsheads. **1856** *Rep. Comm. Patents: Agric.* 278 Some of our planters have not, perhaps, made so much molasses of late years, while others have made a greater quantity than they did last season, more particularly those who rolled a good portion of their crop into syrup or molasses, which, I am satisfied, must give them a larger quantity of cistern bottoms.

2. cistern sugar, (see quot.).

1835 INGRAHAM *South-West* I. 240 When all the molasses is removed from the cistern, an inferior kind of sugar is re-manufactured, which is called cistern-sugar, and sold at a lower price.

3. cistern water, water stored in a cistern.

1858 *Texas Almanac* Cistern water is used for culinary purposes. **1884** SWEET & KNOX *Through Texas* 636 Some thought it was thunder, and thousands of respectable people went out for the purpose of fixing the pipes to catch cistern-water.

As the last term in **wagon cistern.**

***citation,** *n. Mil.* Mention in an official dispatch. — **1918** E. S. FARROW *Dict. Mil. Terms.* **1930** *Publishers' Weekly* 5 July 11 [He] holds the Congressional Medal of Honor, nine citations and the highest decorations of the Allied Governments.

***citess,** *n.* (See quot. 1816.) *Obs.* — **1796** *British Critic* VII. 367 The Americans have coined the term *Citess*, which is better [than Citizeness]. **1816** PICKERING 61 *Citess.* This word, as well as citizenness, was used in America during the first years of the French Revolution, as a translation of the Revolutionary title *Citoyenne;* but it has for several years been wholly disused.

citified ˈsɪtɪˌfaɪd, *a.* Accustomed to or suggestive of the city. *Colloq.*

1828 *Yankee and Boston Lit. Gazette* 16 July I. 227 There is a deal more comfort in playing with a country lass . . . than with a cityfied girl. **1902** HARBEN *Abner Daniel* 254, I reckon you've got too citified for us. **1945** *La Junta* (Colo.) *Tribune-Democrat* 14 Feb. 2/1 Roger Lewis and Frankie O'Connor found the escalators great fun in Denver when they went up there for the stock show and it bothered them not a bit when a citified dame gave them the cool once over and said . . . 'hicks.'

citify ˈsɪtɪˌfaɪ, *v. tr.* To make citylike or more refined. *Rare.* — **1865** *Atlantic Mo.* XV. 501 I'd take an' citify my English.

* **citizen,** *n.*

1. (See quot.) *Obs.*

1868 *Putnam's Mag.* II. 46 The freedmen [in Port Hudson, La., in 1863–64] were still called 'contrabands,' to their own great wonderment; but as their ideas crystallized, they began to call each other 'citizens,' and before the close of the war any one speaking of their 'camps' in terms less respectful than the 'citizens' quarters,' was not considered friendly to the colored man.

2. In combs.: (1) **citizen soldier,** a civilian who in an emergency serves as a soldier; (2) **soldiery,** a military force of citizen soldiers; (3) **-s' ticket,** a ticket made up and endorsed by the more respectable element in both the Republican and the Democratic parties when neither party has put up desirable candidates.

(1) [**1843** PRESCOTT *Mexico* (1850) II. 310 The citizen-soldiers of Villa Rica.] **1948** *Sat. Ev. Post* 10 July 80/3 In the days just before Pearl Harbor our citizen soldiers weren't always too highly regarded. — **(2) 1837** *S. Lit. Messenger* III. 643 In addition to the ordinary engine, hose and axe companies there is a detachment of citizen soldiery . . . always on what is called alarm duty. **1876** INGRAM *Centennial Expos.* 658 One of the largest, most imposing, and, in all respects, most complete displays of the citizen-soldiery of Pennsylvania. — **(3) 1855** *N.Y. Herald* 18 Dec. 3/1 One of the gentlemen on the citizens' ticket, in Boston, . . . had expressed himself not only in favor of the introduction of slavery into Kansas, but of introducing it into Massachusetts. **1889** *Metropolitan* (Hyde Park, Ill.) 5 Nov. 4/1 He wasn't elected on a Citizen's ticket, so he knows just what is expected of him.

b. Designating Indians or groups of Indians who become or desire to become citizens and give up their tribal identification, esp. **citizen band, party, Potawatomi.**

1871 *Rep. Indian Affairs* (1872) 513 There is much feeling on the part of the 'citizen party,' as they are called. **1906** *Indian Laws & Tr.* III. 232 That the Secretary of the Interior be, and he is hereby, authorized, . . . to allot the lands covered thereby to some member or members of the Citizen Band of Pottawatomie Indians. **1907** HODGE *Amer. Indians* I. 300/2 Citizen Potawatomi. A part of the Potawatomi who, while living in Kansas, withdrew from the rest of the tribe about 1861, took lands in severalty and became citizens,but afterward removed to Indian Ter. **1946** FOREMAN *Last Trek* 342 The 'citizen' and Indian members of the Wyandot tribe began to unite.

citizening ˈsɪtəzənɪŋ, *n.* Admitting to citizenship. — **1890** *Home Missionary* (N.Y.) April 528 The citizening of the five tribes [in Indian Territory, U.S.] and statehood are inevitable.

citrange ˈsɪtrɪndʒ, *n.* [f. *ci*trus *tri*foliata or*ange*.] A hybrid citrus plant or its fruit produced by crossing the common sweet orange with the trifoliolate orange.

1904 H. J. WEBBER in *Yearbk. U.S. Dept. Agric.* 227 The Citrange, a new group of Citrus plants. . . . It . . . becomes necessary to refer these hybrids to a new group of citrus fruits, and it is proposed to call them 'citranges.' **1928** BAILEY *Cyclo. Horticulture* 778/2 The citranges are very cold-resistant if in a dormant condition, being able to stand temperatures as low as 15° or even 10° F. without injury. **1948** *Calif. Citrograph* May 299/2 Tangelo, citrange, and many others have not yet been proved . . . as a first-class citrus rootstock.

citron melon. *n.* A kind of small watermelon having a rind esp. suitable for preserving.

1806 CLARK in *Lewis & C. Exped.* (1905) IV. 175 The substance is about the consistancy of the rind of the citron Mellon and 3/4 of an inch thick, yellow celindrick, and regularly tapering. **1876** HOBBS *Bot. Hand-Book* 24 Citron melon, variety of watermelon, Citrullus vulgaris. **1877** BARTLETT 122 Citron melon, the sort of melon employed for the purpose [of making imitation citron].

* **citrus,** *n.* **1. citrus fair,** an exhibition of citrus fruits. **2. citrus fruit,** fruit obtained from any tree of the genus *Citrus* and allied genera, or from hybrids of these.

(1) 1883 *Cent. Mag.* Oct. 810/1 At a citrus fair in the Riverside colony in March, 1882, in a building . . . built of redwood planks. **1899** *Land of Sunshine* May 322 Two of them were brought into bearing, and the fruit first brought to general notice at a citrus fair in Riverside in 1879. — **(2) 1882** *Harper's Mag.* Dec. 59/2 The lands suitable for the cultivation of the 'citrus fruits,' too, are limited in extent. **1948** *Calif. Citrograph* June 331/1 It seems desirable to discuss this and other aspects of the industry related to the major problem of marketing citrus fruit.

***cits,** *n.* Civilian clothing. *Mil. slang.* — **1829** in OLIVER E. WOOD *West Point Scrap Book* (1871) 47 My uniform I've taken off, My 'cits' I've just put on, And silk I've substituted for The leather stock I've worn. **1937** KENDALL BANNING *West Point Today* 294 Cadet Lingo. . . . Cits, n. Civilian clothing.

* **city,** *n.*

1. A grandiose or anticipatory designation for a mere hamlet or village.

"It is strange that the name of city should be given to an unfinished log house, but such is the case in Texas. . . . This city mania is a very extraordinary disease in the United States" (1843 Marryat *Travels M. Violet* xxii).

1747 *N.J. Archives* 1 Ser. VII. 66 After weighing all things I have pitcht upon this City [Burlington] (as call'd tho' but a village of 170 houses) for the place of my residence. *c***1826** STANLEY *Journal* 279 In the course of the last two days we passed several *cities*—some of them however almost invisible, and one or two litterally in the condition of Old Sarum. **1883** J. LAWRENCE *Silverland* 68 We reached Alta city—all mining camps are cities hereabouts. **1946** *St. Louis Globe-Democrat* 11 Aug. In one group of six western counties there are more than 20 'cities' not one of which today has as many as 100 citizens.

2. In combs.: (1) **City Associators,** see ***associator,** *obs.;* (2) **attorney,** see as a main entry; (3) **block,** a regular division of a city bounded by streets or other thoroughfares, the distance along one side of this; (4) **boss,** one at the head of a political machine in a city; (5) **collector,** a tax collector for a city; (6) **council,** a board of elected officials having partial or complete charge of the government of a city; (7) **dads,** used jocosely for **city fathers,** also **city daddies;** (8) **docket,** a docket of cases pending before a city court; (9) ***editor,** the editor in charge of collecting and editing local news in a city newspaper, also **city editor-in-chief,** cf. **night city editor;** (10) **fathers,** those in charge of the municipal affairs of a city; (11) **feller,** a man who lives in a city, *jocose;* (12) **hall,** see as a main entry; (13) **item,** (see quot.); (14) **jay,** =**city feller;** (15) **limits,** the boundaries of a city; (16) **lot,** see as a main entry; (17) **manager,** see as a main entry; (18) ***marshal,** a city official having charge of the police force; (19) **park,** a park within a city and under its management; (20) **recorder,** =**recorder 2;** (21) **school,** a school maintained by a city, also attrib.; (22) **scrip,** used collectively for the certificates of indebtedness issued by a city; (23) **slicker,** a man of slippery character who lives in a city, also jocular.

(3) 1884 *Cent. Mag.* May 64/2 It was no easy task to take such a site —only a city block—and yet secure such ample accommodation and illumination. **1907** LILLIBRIDGE *Trail* 131 He was within half the distance of a city block of the latter [sentinel]. **1948** *Durant* (Okla.) *D. Democrat* 1 July 1/4 But now I wouldn't walk around a city block. — **(4) 1944** *Evanston Review* 12 Oct. 8/2 The entire convention, he asserted, was dominated by 'what would be acceptable to the Big Chief—and to Sidney Hillman and the city bosses.' **1948** *Time* 19 July 24/2 Some of the big city bosses thought Barkley was too old.

(5) *c***1870** BAGBY *Old Va. Gentleman* 263 'Well,' said I, 'if you will turn a city collector into a courting man, I can't help it.' **1875** *Chi. Tribune* 21 Sep. 8/2 The City Collector announces that delinquents on city taxes have but a few more days of grace. **1897** *Ib.* 14 July 5/3 The City Collector . . . estimates there are 300,000 bicycles in [Chicago]. — **(6) 1789** MORSE *Amer. Geog.* 428 The intendant and wardens form the city council. **1945** *Chi. D. News* 12 July 12/5 Three cheers for the City Council. — **(7) 1881** *Pacific Censor* (Vancouver, Wash.) 26 Jan. 3/1 It was . . . rumored that the 'city dads' were meditating the passage of a dog law. **1946** *New Yorker* 18 May 17/1 The city daddies have been working for we don't know how many years to solve the subway-fare problem. — **(8)** *c***1826** STANLEY *Journal* 301 The Judge showed me the City Docket, of a similar nature, amounting to above 700 cases. — **(9) 1870** MAVERICK *Raymond & N.Y. Press,* The City Editor, directs the work performed by the reporters, whose duty is to gather all the local intelligence of the day. **1877** *Harper's Mag.* Dec. 52/1 The city editor-in-chief divides his staff into five or six squads. **1947** *True* Nov. 61/1 Not long after I got a telegram from my city editor.

(10) 1845 *St. Louis Reveille* 19 Jan. 2/4 Allow me to call the attention of our 'City Fathers' to the importance of erecting public hydrants on the Levee. **1948** *Dly. Ardmoreite* (Ardmore, Okla.) 30 Mar. 1/1 The city fathers who designed our town must have forgotten the need of playgrounds and parks. — **(11) 1944** *Chi. D. News* 5 July 10/2 The tassels are corn tassels, but a lot of 'city fellers,' raised on the farm, will be curious about this detasseling stuff. — **(13) 1889** *Cent.,* City item, in American newspapers, an item of local or city news, as distinguished from foreign or general news. — **(14) 1896** *Chi. Tribune* 27 July 7/1 To the 'city jay' the twelve-hour day is a severe strain. **1923** *Nation* 12 Dec. 688/1 The Holstein is the cow to raise for producing milk to be sold to the city jay.

(15) 1841 *Louisville Journal* 6 May 2/1 There are in the city proper but ten watchmen, and one in Portland, making in all eleven for the city limits. **1948** *Sat. Ev. Post* 26 June 23/1 At the city limits on the west, . . . the New Bedforder can go out into a countryside of rare charm along the shores of Buzzards Bay. — **(18) 1817** *N.Y. Herald* 12 April 1/6 A man . . . taking his stand at the Whitehall-slip, accompanied by two of the city marshalls, waited for the arrival of the ferry-boat. **1948** *Dly. Ardmoreite* (Ardmore, Okla.) 28 July 1/1 Sometime, surely between 1893 and 1898, there were changes in the men who served as city marshals. — **(19) 1885** *Cent. Mag.* Oct. 911 It would seem that the primary purpose of a city park . . . is to furnish a free bath of fresh air for lungs doomed to inhale some fluid which is not always fresh nor over cleanly. **1948** *L.A. Times* 30 July II. 1/8 At the City Park in Orange 1200 people turned out for the program.

(20) 1865 *Republican Banner* (Nashville, Tenn.) 17 Oct. 3/2 The City Recorder sent him to jail to await trial before the Criminal Court. — **(21) 1849** CHAMBERLAIN *Ind. Gazetteer* 298 The public buildings in the City are the Court House . . . [and] two fine buildings for City Schools. **1904** *Forum* Oct. 257 The most comprehensive and in many ways the best all-around American city school exhibit. — **(22) 1838** *Observer & Reporter* (Lexington, Ky.) 11–12 May 3/1 The *Five Years City Scrip* is now redeemed with bank notes upon presentation to . . . the Committee of Ways and Means of the City Council. **1916** THOBURN *Hist. Okla.* II. lxxii. 782 The alley . . . was vacated, with forty feet off of the lots on either side, at a cost of $16,000, which sum was paid in city scrip. — **(23) 1924** *Cosmopolitan* Nov. 104/2 You reckon I'm a goin' tew give that city slicker back his option money? **1948** *Seventeen* June 71/1 That was a lot of money and I couldn't take a chance on some city slicker getting it.

b. Often used in designations of various cities: (1) *City of Brotherly Love,* Philadelphia, Pa.; (2) *of Churches,* Brooklyn, N.Y.; (3) *of Corruption,* San Francisco, Calif., in the days of the vigilance committees; (4) *of Elms,* New Haven, Conn.; (5) *of Fair Colors,* Short Creek, Ariz., where an experiment in communal living was tried early in the twentieth century; (6) *of Lakes,* (see quot.); (7) *of Loving Brothers,* (see quot.); (8) *of Magnificent Distances,* (*a*) Washington, D.C., (*b*) Solano, Calif., *rare;* (9) *of Monuments,* Baltimore, Md.; (10) *of Mud,* (see quot.), *rare;* (11) *of Notions,* Boston, Mass.; (12) *of Rocks,* Nashville, Tenn.; (13) *of Spindles,* Lowell, Mass.; (14) *of Squares,* Philadelphia, Pa., *rare;* (15) *of the Angels,* Los Angeles, Calif.; (16) *of the Bluffs,* Natchez, Miss.; (17) *of the Hills,* Richmond, Va.; (18) *of the Lakes,* Chicago, Ill.; (19) *of the Plains,* (see quot.); (20) *of the Saints,* Salt Lake City, Utah; (21) *of the Straits,* Detroit, Mich.; (22) *of White Sand,* Pensacola, Fla., *obs.*

(1) 1793 PRIEST *Travels* (1802) 13, I told him, that more likely the sins of the *quakers* had drawn down this judgment on the city of *brotherly love.* **1855** *Knickerb.* XLV. 216 A recent gossippy letter from a genial friend in the 'city of brotherly-love.' **1948** *Reader's Digest* May 132/1 These incidents all occurred in Philadelphia—the City of Brotherly Love. — **(2) 1850** *S.F. Herald* 6 Sep. 1/5 At Brooklyn, the storm was terrible in the city of churches. **1857** *Spirit of Times* 20 June 245/2 Verily Brooklyn is fast earning the title of the 'City of Base Ball Clubs,' as well as the 'City of Churches.' — **(3) 1856** *Town Talk* (S.F.) 22 May 4/2 The dish-water journals of the 'city of corruption' are crying 'peace, peace, let the law (?) take its course!' — **(4) 1843** *Yale Lit. Mag.* VIII. 328 Some inconsiderate hard-hearted beauty, that was supposed to reside somewhere in the 'City of Elms.'

(5) 1942 STEGNER *Mormon C.* 218 The City of Fair Colors, even during the years of its boom when Barlow and others were proselytizing through Utah and Nevada and California, was not a completely idyllic place. — **(6) 1866** *Harper's Mag.* Apr. 675/2 Any one who has visited . . . our beautiful 'City of Lakes' (Madison, Wisconsin) must surely have known . . . one Liab Dean. — **(7) 1844** *Nauvoo* (Ill.) *Neighbor* 24 July 2/4 Appalling as it is, we have to give more particulars of mobbery in the once good city of Loving brothers—Philadelphia. — **(8)** (*a*) **1834** FEATHERSTONHAUGH *Slave States* (1844) 11 Any one who has endured . . . that caravansary called *Gadsby's Hotel* at Washington, the city of 'magnificent distances,' will feel exceedingly rejoiced when, after a short interval of two or three hours, he finds himself transferred by rail-road to Barnum's at Baltimore. **1846** *Hancock Eagle* (Nauvoo, Ill.) 17 April 3/3 It was the eccentric John Randolph, who styled Washington 'the city of magnificent distances.' (*b*) **1857** *S.F. Call* 18 Mar. 2/3 The editor of Solano Herald has taken a *pasear* from the 'city of magnificent distances' to Suisun. — **(9) 1836** T. POWER *Impressions of Amer.* I. 89 Several domes of considerable magnitude, a tall column or two, various towers and spires . . . have gained for it the title of the City of Monuments.

(10) **1844** *Nauvoo* (Ill.) *Neighbor* 24 July 4/2 Some sixteen years ago, I was 'a prentice boy' in the 'City of Mud,' now the goodly city of Rochester [N.Y.]. — **(11) 1841** *N.O. Picayune* 18 Feb. 4/1 There are more things, gentle reader, in the little city of Notions, than is dreamt of in thy philosophy. **1856** *Spirit of Times* 27 Sep. 64/3 He holds the father and daughter in durance vile until he can obtain a satisfactory proof from the City of Notions. — **(12) 1857** *Spirit of Times* 20 June 252 Never, since I have been an inhabitant of this 'city of rocks,' have I had the pleasure to behold a larger attendance. — **(13) 1875** *Chambers's Jrnl.* 13 March 172/1 Lowell, Mass., [is] the City of Spindles. — **(14) 1836** T. POWER *Impressions of Amer.* I. 102 Back to Philadelphia, on my way to New York—will pass this night in the City of Squares.

(15) 1845 SUTTER in *Hancock Eagle* (Nauvoo, Ill.) (1846) 10 April 1/7 In our late campaign, while we were in the 'City of the Angels,' . . . the physician of my division, Dr. Townsend, received an offer of $1,200 by subscription . . . on condition of his staying there. **1947** *Chi. Tribune* 21 July 14/3 Like the City of the Angels, its palm-fronded twin of the Alamo exudes the fragrance of braised brake linings. — **(16) 1841** *Miss. Free Trader* (Natchez) 4 Mar. 1/2, I have noticed, during the last week, a sweet belle from the north . . . but, alas! for us in the 'Crescent City,' she was absorbed, appropriated, by a young counsellor of modest yet noble bearing from your 'City of the Bluffs.' — **(17) 1867** *Ball Players' Chron.* 13 June 2/4 They will take their batteries down to Richmond to engage in the pastime of giving the clubs of the City of Hills a sound drubbing. — **(18) 1850** *Quincy* (Ill.) *Whig* 30 April 3/2 Although I have been in the 'City of the Lakes' nearly three weeks, I have seen but little of it. — **(19) 1920** *Outing* May 67/1, I looked under Denver and discovered that its nickname was 'City of the Plains.'

(20) 1943 *Quincy* (Ill.) *Herald* 14 July 2/2 The Missouri Mail also left our wharf with a large party of Missourians and Illinoians, for the City of the Saints. **1901** *World's Work* Oct. 1263/2 Hence the cup of joy runneth over in 'the City of the Angels' and 'the City of the Saints.' — **(21) 1845** *Detroit Jrnl.* 12 Aug., Ithaca Hook and Ladder Co. No. 3 [has] . . . complimented us by a visit to the 'City of the Straits.' **1848** *Gem of Prairie* (Chi.) 25 March 5/2 The election in this old 'City of the Straits,' on Monday, resulted in a *total defeat* and *annihilation* of Mexican anti-war whiggery. **1879** *Chi. Tribune* 5 Feb. 4/6 It is believed that Detroit is called the City of 'Straights' to commemorate the abstemious habits of Mr. Zachariah Chandler. — **(22) 1848** *Oquawka* (Ill.) *Spectator* 20 Sep. 1/4 On his arrival at the 'city of White Sand,' his first inquiry was, 'Where does Mr. Navy live?'

As the last term in **banner, bluff, boom, Classic, cliff, Convention, dog, Elm, Empire, Falls, Federal, Flour, Flower, Forest, Fountain, Garden, Gate, ghost, Golden, Green Mountain, Gulf, hill, Holy, Iron, Island, Key, Keystone, lithograph, log, Monument, Monumental, Morgan, Mound, packing, Palmetto, paper, Phoenix, Pilgrim, Pork, prairie, prairie-dog, rag, railroad, reserve, Rose, sister, Smoky, Spindle, stump, village, Windy, Witch City.**

city attorney. (See quot. 1914.)

1887 *Courier-Journal* 2 Feb. 3/2 Mr. William Baird, the well-known city attorney . . . is lying in a most critical condition. **1914** *Cyclo. Amer. Govt.* I. 276 The city attorney or corporation counsel is the chief legal officer of the American municipality. He is sometimes chosen by the city council, but more often appointed by the mayor. His term of office is usually from two to four years. . . . He is the legal adviser of the mayor, the city council, and all municipal boards or officers. . . . In addition, he has general charge of the city's interests in all litigation before the courts or in all pending state legislation. **1948** *Dly. Ardmoreite* (Ardmore, Okla.) 29 July 9/3 He was city attorney at the time, some 30 years ago.

city hall. The headquarters of the municipal government of a city. Also, esp. in colonial times, a capitol or state house.

1675 ANDROS in Easton *Indian War* 106 There was at the City Hall an order of the last Gen[er]all Court of Assizes. **1889** BRAYLEY *Boston Fire Dept.* 183 The old State-House, or City Hall, as it was then called, was badly damaged. **1948** *Dly. Ardmoreite* (Ardmore, Okla.) 13 July 1/1 Finally I decided to contact the city hall and find out just how much water had been poured into the city reservoir.

attrib. **1836** HONE *Diary* I. (1889) 198 (We.), In the vicinity of City Hall Park. **1872** BRACE *Dangerous Classes N.Y.* 28 These youthful ruffians . . . live on . . . City-Hall places and pot-houses.

city lot. A lot or specified area or portion of land within a city or a proposed city.

1683 PENN *Works* (1726) II. 706 Your City-Lot is a whole Street, and one side of a Street, from River to River, containing near one hundred Acres. **1862** COLT *Went to Kans.* 53 Some are building their cabins on their city lots. **1923** R. HERRICK *Lilla* 19 'Put it into city lots around Chicago,' he replied superiorly.

city manager. An administrator employed by a city to manage its affairs. Also **city manager plan.**

1913 *Amer. City* Dec. 525/2 The city manager plan has been in force in Abilene, Kans., for a number of months. **1925** *City Manager Plan of City Govt.* 10 Mar. 10 The progress of the City-Manager plan has been steady since its first adoption by Staunton, Virginia in 1908. **1948** *Alva* (Okla.) *Review-Courier* 2 July 1/6 He is to take over as city manager of Ponca City on August 1.

* **civet cat.** = **cacomistle.** See also **tree civet.**

1852 MARCY *Explor. Red River* (1854) 200 *Bassaris Astuta.* Licht. Civet cat. [Found at] Cross-Timbers. **1917** *Animals of Amer.* 108 The name Civet Cat applied to this animal is really a misnomer, as the Civet Cats are found only in the Old World, but this name has been used locally in the West in place of the more proper one of Ring-tailed Cat. **1948** *Desert Mag.* Aug. 29/3 The civet cat saw the fox and raised up on her front paws and began to wave her tail in the air.

civic center. The headquarters of various welfare agencies in a community or municipality. Also the headquarters of a municipality, usu. situated at or near its center. — **1915** *Amer. City* April 334/1 This is the first civic center to be undertaken in Westchester County. **1946** *Covina* (Calif.) *Argus-Citizen* 8 Dec. 1/7 (*heading*), West Covina Asks Residents' Help in Zoning for Business District and Civic Center.

civics ˈsɪvɪks, *n.* The science of the rights and duties of citizenship, esp. as the subject of a school course. Hence **civics class.**

"In 1885 he [Henry R. Waite] founded the American institute of civics, of which he has since been president. He was the first to employ the term 'civics' to designate those branches of science that pertain to the elevation of citizenship" (*Appleton's Cyclo. Biog.* VI. 318).

1886 *Citizen* (Boston) Dec. 5 Shall Civics be taught in the public schools? **1916** *Amer. City* Feb. 154/1 You will find girls in charge of the civics class. **1948** *Dly. Ardmoreite* (Ardmore, Okla.) 30 Mar. 3/1 The civics class recently made a tour of Murray county offices here to get an insight into government.

Civilian Conservation Corps. Those engaged in conservation work in accordance with a plan undertaken by the federal government in 1933 to combat unemployment by providing jobs at public expense for many of those on relief rolls. Cf. **C.C.C.** — **1933** *Newsweek* 15 April 6/1 The first twenty-five thousand of the Civilian Conservation Corps, the administration's expeditionary force against unemployment, started toward various army camps this week. **1946** *Longmont* (Colo.) *Times-Call* 21 June 1/2 During recent years the Civilian Conservation Corps provided fire fighters, and many war prisoners and conscientious objectors were used in the forests.

* **civilize,** *v.* **1.** *S. tr.* (See quot. 1864.) *Colloq.* **2. civilize up,** to spruce up in dress. *Rare.*

(1) *c*1845 *Big Bear Ark.* 98 Arter howd'ying and civerlizin' each other I sot down. **1864** NICHOLS *Amer. Life* I. 387 When people salute each other at meeting, he [the Southerner] says they are howdyin' and civilizin' each other. — **(2) 1920** HUNTER *Trail Drivers Texas* 442 We would civilize up a bit when we went to a dance, that is, we would take off our spurs and tie a clean red handkerchief around our neck.

civilizee ˌsɪvlaɪˈzi, *n.* One who is civilized. *Colloq.* — **1848** *N.Y. Observer* (B.), The barbarian likes his seraglio; the civilizee admires the institution of marriage. The barbarian likes a roving, wandering life; the civilizee likes his home and fireside. **1897** *N. Eng. Mag.* Dec. 407 The members [of Brook Farm, *c*1837] looked upon the outside world as in some degree barbarian, and spoke of its people with a tone of contempt as civilizees.

civil rights.

1. The rights for all citizens, esp. Negroes, contemplated in the 13th and 14th Amendments to the Constitution. Also attrib.

1874 FLEMING *Hist. Reconstruction* II. 201 The mere mention of civil (negro) Rights has almost destroyed the public schools and colleges in some of the Southern States. **1875** *Statutes at Large* XVIII. 335 An Act to protect all citizens in their civil and legal rights. **1948** *Time* 17 May 25/2 Thirteen were pledged to bolt the convention if a civil-rights plank were adopted.

2. civil rights bill, any one of various bills passed by Congress in 1866, 1870, and 1875, in an effort to secure equal rights for all citizens.

1866 A. JOHNSON in Fleming *Hist. Reconstruction* I. 225 The Civil Rights bill was more enormous than the other. **1867** in *Ib.* II. 15 Who gave us the Civil Rights Bill? **1875** *43d Congress* 2 Sess. H. R. Rep. No. 262, 1262 The thieving crew known as carpet-baggers . . . regardless of the . . . consequences to ensue from the passage of said odious civil-rights bill. **1876** *Pacific Appeal* (S.F.) 9 Sep. 2/1 The party passed the defective Civil Rights Bill.

civil service.

1. Civil Service Commission, a commission of three members appointed by the President to have control, through proper means, of appointments and promotions in the classified civil service, also a similar commission in a state or city. Hence **Civil Service Commissioner.**

1872 *Atlantic Mo.* Feb. 254 The report of the Civil-Service Commission was immediately sent to Congress. **1916** *Amer. Academy Annals* LXIV. 155 Private business has much to learn from civil service commissions in selecting employees fit to do particular jobs. **1945** *Reader's Digest* Nov. 97/1 By no means does all the blame for the defects of Civil Service rest on the Civil Service Commissioners.

2. civil service reform, (see quot. 1885). Also attrib.

1872 *Atlantic Mo.* March 384 The President had three times declared himself in favor of civil service reform. **1885** *Mag. Amer. Hist.* Jan. 99/2 *Civil Service Reform.*—The correction of abuses in the public service, or more specifically, the adoption of a system which shall not permit the removal of good and faithful officers for partisan reasons, and which shall prevent appointment to office as a reward for partisan services. **1944** Johnson *As I Dare* 73 The Civil Service Reform Association began at a meeting in his home.

* **Civil War.** The war between the Southern Confederacy and the federal government (1861–65).

1862 Longfellow in *Life* (1886) II. 382 Of the Civil War I say only this. It is not a revolution. . . . It is Slavery against Freedom. **1894** *Harper's Mag.* LXXXVIII. 273/1 The economic changes produced in the country by the civil war . . . have attracted little attention compared with the social, financial, and political changes. **1948** *Chi. D. News* 1 March 10/7 Some 80 years later, conflicts in economic interest brought on the Civil War.

clabber ˈklæbɚ, *v. intr.* (See quot. 1879.) *Colloq.* — **1879** Webster *Supp.* 1549 *Clabber,* . . . to turn thick in the process of souring—said of milk. **1920** Alsaker *Eating for Health* 47 Clabbered milk and buttermilk are easily digested.

Clackama ˈklækəmə, *n.* [App. native name.] (See quot. 1907.) Also **Klackamus (Clackamas) Indians.**

1841 Williams *Tour to Ore.* (1921) 52 Brother Waller preached to a few of the Klackamus Indians. **1849** in *Sen. Ex. Doc.* 52, *31st Cong.* 1 Sess. (1850) 171 The *Clackamas* Indians live upon a river of that name, which empties into the Wallammette one mile below Oregon city. **1907** Hodge *Amer. Indians* I. 302/1 Clackama. A Chinookan tribe formerly occupying several villages on Clackamas r., in Clackamas co., Oreg. **1940** *Mt. Hood Guide* 24 Small bands of the Clackamas tribe inhabited the area drained by the river that today bears its name.

claco, see **tlaco.**

***clad,** *n.* As the last term in **bloomer, cotton, tin clad.**

* **claim,** *n.*

1. A tract of public land the ownership of which is applied for by a prospective settler.

1792 *Ann. 2nd. Congress* 1036 Within these triangles, however, are the following claims of citizens, reserved by the deed of cession, and consequently forming exceptions to the rights of the United States. **1856** Brewerton *War in Kans.* 325 [They] had, as we have already hinted, very kindly offered to direct us in the path which led to Peirson's 'Claim' (the word 'Claim,' by the way, is generally used in Kansas in referring to a settler's residence, that being the title by which he holds his land). **1945** M. James *Cherokee Strip* 3 The rim was about my favorite place on the whole claim.

fig. **a1861** Winthrop *J. Brent* 18 If he throws me and breaks my neck I get a claim in Paradise at once. **1884** Nye *Baled Hay* 55 The servant girl . . . has 'a claim' in the promised land.

2. *W.* A piece of land claimed by a miner in accordance with mining law.

1850 Kingsley *Diary* 144 We got the claim ready to go to work on to morrow with a quicksilver machine. **1904** *Churchman* 22 Oct. 711 The white miners had come back to the towns from the scattered claims upon which they had been working. **1948** *Newsweek* 19 April 46/3 They staked out about 80 claims in the rocky hills around the town.

3. In Christian Science terminology, an imaginary disturbance which "claims" to be an ailment.

1898 *Westm. Gaz.* 26 March 3/1 Ailments were referred to as 'claims.' . . . Soon after this, the mother herself was attacked by a claim of influenza. **1903** Mark Twain *Mrs. Eddy in Error* 508 (R.), In Christian Science terminology, 'claims' are errors of mortal mind, fictions of the imagination.

4. In combs.: (1) **claim agency,** the business of a claims agent; (2) **agent,** an attorney or representative who handles claims; (3) **Claim Association,** (see quot.); (4) **cabin,** a cabin erected by a settler "proving up" his claim to public land, *obs.;* (5) **holder,** *W.* the holder of a mining claim; (6) **jumper,** *W.* one who takes unlawful possession of another's claim of land, also transf.; (7) **jumping,** *W.* seizing another's claim by violence; (8) **notice,** (see quot.); (9) **record book,** (see quot.); (10) **shack,** =next; (11) **shanty,** a hut, often very flimsy, erected on a land claim in order to fulfill legal requirements; (12) **stake,** a stake used in marking out the bounds of a claim, also **claim staking.**

(1) **1864** *Harper's Mag.* Nov. 692/1 My claim agency at Washoe, and the bankruptcy . . . were but the prices paid for that valuable experience. — (2) **1860** *Wilkes' Spirit of Times* 10 March 14/3 (We.), Claim agent and broker. **1903** *N.Y. Ev. Post* 6 Oct. 6 Our pension policy has furnished an enormous incentive to claims agents and Congressmen. — (3) **1914** *Cyclo. Amer. Govt.* I. 291 Claim Associations for Public Lands. Claim Associations or land clubs were extra-legal frontier political organizations established by the pioneers of the Middle West for the protection of *bona fide* settlers on the public lands. — (4) **1857** H. E. Bishop *Floral Home* 310 We occasionally passed, or were in sight of, a claim cabin, but no token of human life was any where visible.

(5) **1862** in *Pac. N.W. Quart.* XXXIV. 41 A party of 16 tried to jump the claims & it was agreed to fight it out . . . every one of the claim holders whipping his man & retaining his claim. **1891** Garland *Main-travelled Roads* (1922) 137 He was of German parentage, a middle-sized, cheery, wide-awake, good-looking young fellow—a typical claim-holder. — (6) **1839** in *Annals of Iowa* 3 Ser. X. 430 To Claim Jumpers. . . . This is therefore to forbid all persons entering or trespassing upon said (land) claim under the penalty of the law. . . . Royal C. Gilman. **1945** M. James *Cherokee Strip* 4 You know what a claim-jumper a cowbird is—laying its eggs in other birds' nests and all. **1948** Johnston *Gold Rush* 34/1 Occasionally, a claim jumper was hailed into court; but as the practice of locating another man's ground became distinctly hazardous, it did not occur with the frequency that many writers of western fiction would have us believe. — (7) **1846** *Ore. Spectator* 29 Oct. 2/3 In regard to 'claim-jumping,' he very correctly observes [etc.]. **1928** Foy & Harlow *Clowning Thro' Life* 136 Claim-jumping and lot-jumping had brought the community almost to a state of Civil War. — (8) **1889** *Cent.* 1023/2 Claim-notice. . . . A notification posted by a miner or other settler upon a piece of public land [etc.]. — (9) **1898** *Mo. So. Dakotan* I. 14 During the stay of the Holman party at Yankton, they opened a regular claim record book, in which were recorded the names of claimants, and a description of the land claimed by prospective residents.

(10) **1916** Bower *Phantom Herd* 149 We learned our little lessons when we were building claim-shacks for ourselves. **1940** Baber & Walker *Longest Rope* 34 He had just finished building his claim shack and had planned to be married soon. — (11) **1860** *Harper's Mag.* Aug. 299/2 Claim-stakes and claim-shanties speck the road from one end of the [Sauk] river to the other. **1941** Wilder *Little Town on Prairie* 14 Now that the corn was planted, Pa built the missing half of the claim shanty. — (12) **1860** [see **claim shanty**]. **1946** *Nat. Geog. Mag.* Jan. 1/2 They found gold, gold enough not only to make a good living but to cause a local flurry in claim staking. **1948** Johnston *Gold Rush* 34/1 Respect my claim stakes driven by the rules of Douglas Bar.

Also *claim hunting, locator, owner, robber, seeker,* etc.

c. *To jump a claim,* see ***jump,** *v.* **2. b.**

As the last term in **banner, bar, bottom, coal, creek, desert, discovery, donation, floating, gold, gravel, gulch, hill, hog, homestead, Indian, land, mineral, mining, placer, pocket, prairie, pre-emption, Price Raid, river, silver, sluicing, sod house, soldier's, timber, tomahawk, tree, upland, water, wild-cat claim.** Also in the pl. **Alabama Claims, Court of claims, Creek claims.**

* **claim,** *v. tr.* To take up, enter, possess as one's own (public land, a stream, spring, etc.).

1835 *Ind. Mag. Hist.* IV. 70 He will perhaps lay the foundation of a cabin, is 'claimed' or located, and no person will interfere or presume to settle upon it without first purchasing the first claimant's right. **1889** K. Munroe *Golden Days* 291 The thirsty travellers . . . dared not drink . . . without first obtaining permission of the man who had thus 'claimed' [the spring]. **1935** *Denver Post* 4 June 7B/8 Then came the humble 'nesters' who homesteaded the soil, claimed the streams.

***claimant,** *n.* As the last term in **Cherokee, Connecticut, New Hampshire, occupying claimant.**

***claimer,** *n.* One who claims or pre-empts public land. *Obs.* — **1769** *Col. Soc. Pub. Mass.* VI. 30 . . . He never knew of any of the Inhabitents . . . being Disturbed by any Claimer whatsoever. . . . **1780** W. Fleming in *Travels Amer. Col.* 645 Each claimer [is] to make his entries according to the number drawn to his name.

Clallam ˈklæləm, *n.* (See quot. 1907.) Also **Clallam Indians.**

1843 Thos. J. Farnham *Travels* 111/2. **1889** *Amer. Anthrop.* Oct. 334 These clubs were obtained among the Clallam and Skokomish Indians. **1907** Hodge *Amer. Indians* I. 302/2 Clallam ('strong people'). A Salish tribe living on the s. side of Puget sd., Wash. **1946** R. PEATTIE *Pac. Coast Ranges* 301 In August the Clallam Indians come from the strait of Juan de Fuca, as they have done for centuries of Augusts, only now they come in cars.

***clam,** *n.*

1. The quahog, or the long clam.

1624 EDWARD WINSLOW *Good Newes from N.-Eng.* 21 This Riuer yeeldeth . . . Oysters, Muscles, Clams, and other shell-fish. **1716** CHURCH *Philip's War* 27 There were a great many Indians gone down to Wepoiset to eat Clams. **1903** *Atlantic Mo.* Sep. 326 A shrewd Yankee came and saw the abundance of clams in the long stretches of beach at low tide, and began shipping them away by barrowfuls to Boston and New York. **1944** *New Yorker* 25 Nov. 30/2 One bed is about as big as R.I. itself, tons of clams, mountains of clams.

2. A close-mouthed or dull person. *Slang.* Cf. **clam critic.**

1866 MARK TWAIN *Screamers*, 'Travelling Show' 150 That lets you out, you know, you chowder-headed old clam! **1889** ——— *Conn. Yankee* xii. 155 These innumerable clams had permitted it so long that they had come . . . to accept it as a truth.

3. The mouth. *Slang. Obs.* Cf. **clamshell, clam trap.**

1825 NEAL *Bro. Jonathan* I. 143 Shet your clam, our David. **1833** ——— *Down-Easters* I. 93 Shet your clam!—like that better?—hold your yop!

4. In combs.: (1) **clam bait,** clams used as bait, esp. in catching cod and haddock, also *a.*, **clam baited;** (2) **bake,** an outdoor gathering at which clams are baked and eaten, also attrib. and transf.; (3) **baker,** one participating in a clambake, *rare;* (4) **bank,** a bank upon which clams abound; (5) **bluff,** ?a bluff at which clams are abundant, *rare;* (6) **butcher,** (see quot.); (7) **cart,** a cart for hauling clams; (8) ***catcher,** (see quots.); (9) **chowder,** a chowder in which clams are the chief ingredient, a social gathering at which this dish is served, cf. **chowder,** *n.* **1** and **2,** and see also **Coney Island, Manhattan clam chowder;** (10) **cod,** (see quot. 1889); (11) **critic,** a dull or stupid critic, *slang,* cf. **2.** above; (12) **farm,** an area of cultivated clam beds; (13) **fritter,** a fritter made with clams; (14) **fry,** a meal of fried clams; (15) **horn,** a horn used by an itinerant clam vendor to announce his wares, cf. **b.** (2) below; (16) **humper,** (see quot.); (17) **opening,** (see quot.); (18) **pancake,** =**clam fritter;** (19) **pot-pie,** a pot-pie of clams; (20) ***shell,** see as a main entry; (21) ***trap,** the mouth, *slang, obs.*

(1) **1838** *Mass. Stat.* 17 April, An Act to regulate the Inspection of Clam Bait. **1894** *Outing* XXIV. 263/1 Then we cast forth our clam-baited hooks and waited. — (2) **1835** *Vade Mecum* (Phila.) 5 Sep. 2/1 A Clam Bake.—Our curiousity [*sic*] has been gratified, as to the nature of the festival understood by this term. **1890** MCALLISTER *Society* 186 All pronounced this kind of clambake picnic a species of *fête* not to be indulged in knowingly a second time. **1945** *Chi. D. News* 31 March 4/1, I suffer from the suspicion that the big United Nations clambake at San Francisco will be operated like a hod-carriers' convention. — (3) **1907** LINCOLN *Old Home House* 68 By two o'clock 'twas so bad that I . . . telephoned to the Setuckit Beach life-saving station to find out if the clambakers had got there right side up. — (4) **1634** WOOD *N. Eng. Prospect* (1865) 47 The Bay . . . will be all flatts for two miles together, upon which is great store of Muscle-banckes, and Clam bancks. **1871** DE VERE 69 The clam of Boston is the *Mya arenaria* of the clam-banks.

(5) **1841** *S. Lit. Messenger* VII. 854/2 Its boundaries . . . run thus: . . . in a direct line along the shore over the clam bluff as it stood before the tide washed it away. — (6) **1889** BARRERE & LELAND I. 253/2 Clam butcher (American), a man who opens clams. — (7) **1838** *N.Y. Advertiser & Exp.* 14 Feb. 3/5 A couple of long shorers . . . hitched an old broken winded horse . . . to the skeleton of a vehicle which they distinguished by the appellation of 'clam cart.' **1856** *Spirit of Times* (N.Y.) 6 Sep. 4/1 Get out of there with your old clam-cart. — (8) **1845** *St. Louis Reveille* 14 May 2/4 The inhabitants of . . . New Jersey [are called] Clam-catchers. **1888** WHITMAN *Nov. Boughs* 70 Those [soldiers] from . . . New Jersey . . . [were called] Clam Catchers. — (9) **1836** *Harvardiana* III. 36 A dish of untasted clam-chowder. **1898** HAMBLEN *Gen. Manager's Story* 131 The engineers had a clam chowder. **1947** *Chr. Sci. Mon.* 15 Jan. 14/2 And, to their way of thinking, clam chowder should be forever freed from the tomato introduced by the burghers of Old New York and traitorously adopted by Rhode Island.

(10) **1888** GOODE *Amer. Fishes* 339 These are called 'Shoal-water Cod,' . . . 'Worm-cod,' 'Clam-Cod.' **1889** *Cent.* 1082/2 Clam-cod, inshore cod which feed on clams. — (11) **1889** *Phila. Times* 15 July, Don't bother about clam critics. — (12) **1870** *Scribner's Mo.* I. 60 His oyster and clam farms, in which he had at last become master and director of other men. — (13) *c***1852** S. J. HALE *New Book of Cookery* (ed. 5) 64 Clam Fritters. . . . Drop the batter by table-spoonful in boiling lard; let them fry gently, turning them when done on one side. **1935** LINCOLN *Cape Cod Yesterdays* 60 Clam fritters used to be called 'clam cakes' when we were young. — (14) **1905** *N.Y. Ev. Post* 10 June 6 'Fish dinners' and clam fries are to be had at any number of eating-houses at the river's mouth.

(15) **1866** *Eastern Slope* (Washoe, Nev.) 28 July 2/5 The clam horn's notes were far surpassed By the accents of that fearful blast—Excelsior! — (16) **1889** *N. & Q.* III. 77 Maryland is the 'Monumental [State],' and the inhabitants are 'clam-humpers.' — (17) **1880** LUDLOW *Dramatic Life* 680 It was 'a clam opening,' which meant, in the theatrical slang, that he opened and closed on the same night. — (18) **1863** WEBSTER *Improved Housewife* 73 Clam Pancakes. — (19) **1896** HASWELL *New York* 251 They were as well known as Mrs. Dominy's 'chunk apple' and clam pot-pies at Fire Island.

(21) **1800** *Aurora* (Phila.) 8 April (Th.), Otis shut up his clam trap.

b. In colloq. phrases: (1) *as happy as a clam,* and variants, well pleased, quite contented; (2) *toot your horn if you don't sell a clam, fig.* to proceed even though without success; (3) *to take up a clam ranch,* (see quot.).

(1) **1834** *Harvardiana* I. 121 He could not even enjoy that peculiar degree of satisfaction, usually denoted by the phrase 'as happy as a clam.' *a***1870** CHIPMAN *Notes on Bartlett* 523 *Happy as a clam* (*in the mud at high water*). Both forms are used. The latter form is a learned appendix added kindly from condescension to wits somewhat dull. **1875** HOLLAND *Sevenoaks* 436 The two fellers . . . as happy as two clams in high water. **1907** *N.Y. Ev. Post* (semi-weekly ed.) 20 June 5 Now I'm in business and happy as a clam at high tide. **1911** LINCOLN *Cap'n Warren's Wards* 244, I was as happy as a clam at highwater.

(2) **1863** *Gold Hill* (Nev.) *News* 2 Nov. 3/1 Awake, Mark! arise and toot your horn if you don't sell a clam. **1872** MARK TWAIN *Roughing It* xlvii. 334 Just go in and toot your horn, if you don't sell a clam.

(3) **1882** *Standard* 26 Sep. 2/1 'To take up a clam-ranch' is a proverbial expression [in Oregon] to express the last stage of hard fortune.

As the last term in **beach, cherrystone, dipper, flat razor, fresh-water, hard, hard-shelled, hen, hog, little neck, long, razor, Rockaway, round, sea, soft, soft-shell, squirt, stem, surf, tea clam.**

clam klæm, *v.*

1. *intr.* To dig for or collect clams.

1676 *Mass. H.S. Coll.* 3 Ser. I. 71 His father and mother were taken by the Pequts and Monhiggins about ten weeks ago, as they were clamming . . . at Courwesit. **1716** CHURCH *Philip's War* 29 They came near the bank, and saw a vast company of Indians, . . . some catching Eels & Flat-fish in the water, some Clamming. **1769** *Huntington Rec.* II. 505 Liberty to Hunt Gun fish or clam within the Limmits of ye s[ai]d Town. **1948** *Outdoor Life* June 14/3 It is necessary to have a license to clam.

b. Of hogs: To root for clams.

[**1636** *Dorchester* (Mass.) *Rec.* 5 July, Provided they leave stiles and gates for persons and cattle, when persons are disposed to travell or drive Cattle or swine that way to Clamming.] **1641** *Dorchester* (Mass.) *Rec.* 1 Jan., If there be any Liuinge neare vnto any Clam bankes where they would haue their hogges to Clam.

2. *To clam up,* to become silent. *Slang.*

1916 H. L. WILSON *Somewhere in Red Gap* vi. 237 When I ask for details he just clams up. **1948** *Dly. Ardmoreite* (Ardmore,Okla.) 14 May 1/1 He always clammed up and denied any memory.

clammer ˈklæmɚ, *n.* **1.** A clamboat. **2.** One who gathers clams.

(1) **1864** *Harper's Mag.* Feb. 311/1 Before us . . . loomed in view above the low horizon the clammers. **1888** *Cambridge* (Mass.) *Press* 15 Sep. 1/7 Clammers call in daily at the Neck, on their way up to Ipswich. — (2) **1883** GOODE *Fish. Indust.* 47 The fishery is not an expensive one, the whole outfit of the 'clammer' not requiring an expenditure of over $150. **1897** *Outing* XXX. 213/1 [Picture of] The little clammers.

clamming ˈklæmɪŋ, *n.* The gathering of clams. Also attrib.

1675 *Wyllys Papers* 217 A party of Ninecrafts men sent out in Canooes to keepe ye enemy from fishing & claming. **1774** *Huntington Rec.* II. 526, I will Not Hinder any Person whatsoever from fishing oystering claming or gunning anywhere in the mill pond. **1894** *Youth's Companion* 22 Nov. 562/3 The bulk of the eeling and quahaug clamming as well as the lobstering was done in its vicinity. **1947** *Denver Post* 2 Mar. A. 8/2 It is causing serious damage to the clamming industry, while clam diggers can't even resort to a little duck hunting on the side.

***clammy,** *a.* In combs.: (1) **clammy honeysuckle,** =**swamp azalea;** (2) **locust,** a small locust, *Robinia viscosa,* having clammy twigs; (3) **rice,** (see quot.), *obs.*

(1) **1860** *N.C. Geol. Survey: Botany* 98 Clammy Honeysuckle (*A[zalea]viscosa*).... The flowers are white or flesh-colored and very fragrant. — (2) **1817–18** Eaton *Botany* (1822) 431 *Robinia viscosa*, clammy locust; ... flowers approaching from white to red. Cultivated. **1892** Apgar *Trees Northern U.S.* 94 Clammy Locust.... A small tree, 30 to 40 ft. high; native south, and has been quite extensively cultivated north. — (3) **1802** Drayton *S. Carolina* 127 A third kind was called clammy rice, as adhering, when boiled, into one glutinous mass.

***clamp,** *n.* (See quot.) *Obs.* — **1774** Fithian *Journal* I. 252 Sometimes they get sticks & splinter one end of them for Brushes, or as they call them here *Clamps*, & spitting on part of the floor, they scrub away with great vigor. [In Virginia, referring to the way the children in their play did what their parents did.]

***clamshell,** *n.*

1. The jaws or mouth, usu. *pl. Slang.*

1833 *Polit. Examiner* (Shelbyville, Ky.) 23 Mar. 2/1 Shut up your clack, or I'll knock your clam-shells together pretty quick. **1860** Holland *Miss Gilbert* 95 All those opposed will shut their clam-shells. **1903** *D.N.* II. 424 clam-shell, *n.* Mouth. 'When I told him that he shut up his *clamshell*.' [Cape Cod.]

2. A quilt pattern shaped somewhat like the shell of a clam. In full **clamshell pattern.**

1861 Mrs. Stowe *Pearl Orr's Island* II. xv. 128 A pattern [for a quilt] denominated in those parts clam-shell. *Ib.* 130 She stuck a decisive needle into the first clam-shell pattern.

3. Designating various objects suggestive in whole or in part of a clamshell, as (1) **clamshell bucket,** (2) **crane,** (3) **dredge,** (4) **padlock.**

(1) **1947** *Chr. Sci. Mon.* 12 April 15/6 One 'bite' of a gigantic clamshell bucket on a new type steamshovel used in handling of coal would furnish the average home with a two-year supply of fuel. [**1948** *Sat. Ev. Post* 4 Dec. 20/1 Chocked securely on the trailer was a giant earth-moving machine, a steam-powered, clam-bucket rig.]—(2) **1947** *Time* 27 Jan. 79/2 The clamshell crane is no clam. It speaks up for a variety of jobs. — (3) **1874** Knight *Dict. Mech.* 746/1 The 'clam-shell' dredge ... consists of a pair of scoops which are hinged to an axis and close upon the load. **1877** *Encycl. Brit.* VII. 465/1 Dredging in Canada and the United States is done by what are called *Dipper* and *Clam-shell* dredges. — (4) **1859** Bartlett 85 The padlock now used on the United States mail-bags is called the 'Clam-shell padlock.'

b. clamshell hoe, a crude hoe, used by Indians, made of a clamshell. *Obs.*

1634 Wood *N. Eng. Prospect* II. xix. 95 An other work is their [=Indians'] planting of corne, wherein they exceede our English husband-men, keeping it so cleare with their Clam shell-hooes, as if it were a garden rather than a corne-field.

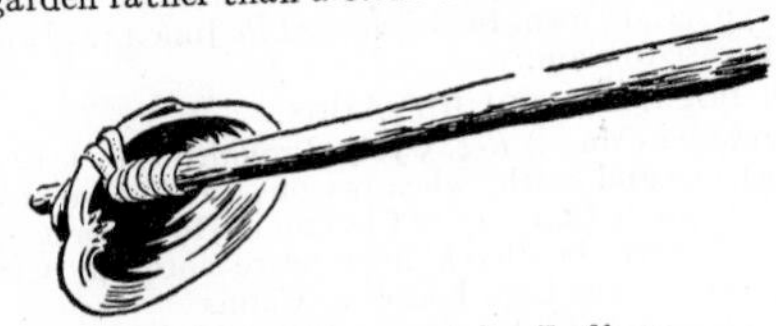

Clamshell hoe used by Indians

***clapboard,** *n.*

1. A riven board, often thinner at one edge than at the other, used in making the sides, roof, etc., of a house.

1632 in Shurtleff *Log Cabin* (1939) 37 Governor Winthrop writes: Mr. Oldham had a small house near the wear at Watertown, made all of clapboards, burnt down by making a fire in it when it had no chimney. **1705** *Boston News-Letter* 12 March 2/2 The Meeting-house was built of Timber 60 Foot long, 25 Foot wide, & 18 Foot studd ceiled with Clapboards. **1800** Tatham *Tobacco* 32 Clap-boards are thin pieces of four feet long, riven generally out of white oak, and one edge thicker than the other. **1943** M. Flavin *Journ. in Dark* 8 Jim was busy in the back, nailing loose clapboards on the house.

2. In combs. in the sense "made of or covered with clapboards," as (1) **clapboard house,** (2) **hut,** (3) **roof,** (4) **shutter,** (5) **tenement.**

(1) **1640** *Suffolk Deeds* I. 16 The little Claboard howse. **1757** *Lett. to Washington* II. 174 The rest of the Town is indifferently improved, many very bad low clapboard Houses upon their Principal Streets which are in general narrow & confined. **1945** Maxwell *Folded Leaf* 195 Professor Severance lived with his mother in a large white clapboard house which had been built in the 'eighties. — (2) **1739** *Ga. Col. Rec.* IV. 677 A certain Number of other Soldiers were employ'd in building Clap-board Huts. — (3) **1770** Summers *Ann. S.W. Virginia* (1929) 77 A log cabin ... with a clapbord roof. **1880** Burnett *Recoll. Old Pioneer* 29 (Th.), A log cabin ... with chinked cracks, clapboard roof, and puncheon floor. **1927** Sandburg *Songbag* 129 Some live in a cabin with a huge log wall, ... Clapboard roof and a button door. — (4) **1843** Carlton *New Purchase* I. 108 [The] window ... being occasionally shut at first with a blanket, afterwards with a clapboard shutter. — (5) **1943** M. Flavin *Journ. in Dark* 164 [There were] the stockyards and the hunkies in their clapboard tenements.

b. clapboard tree, (see quot. 1939).

1646 *Cambridge Rec.* 8 June, To fell two clapboard trees. **1676** *Jamaica* (L.I.) *Rec.* I. 182 They are to have Liberty to take any timber ... in our commons exsept Clappborde trees and Rayle trees under eightene inches. **1939** Shurtleff *Log Cabin* 38 The comparative scarcity of cedar in New England resulted in several efforts to conserve 'clapboard-trees,' as cedars suitable for clapboards were often called in that section.

clapboard ˈklæbəd, ˈklæpˌbord, *v. tr.* To cover with clapboards. Also **clapboarded,** *a.*

1637 *Plymouth Col. Rec.* XII. 26 The house to be ... clap boarded within ... and a partition to be made of clap board. **1701** *Boston Town Records* XI. 10 Capt Andrew Belcher his Petition to omit Rough Castings his ware house for the Space of six foot next the ground, & to board & Clapboard that Space approved. **1835** *S. Lit. Messenger* II. 53 We behold the low log-cabin of a school-house—the clap-boarded roof but indifferently tight. **1947** Coffin *Yankee Coast* 89 A clapboarded Maine house fits beautifully in with conical treetops which splinter the light and make embroidery of every skyline.

clapboarding ˈklæbərdɪŋ, ˈklæpˌbordɪŋ, *n.* **1.** The putting on of clapboards. *Obs.* **2.** A facing, or other part of a structure, made of clapboards.

(1) **1637** *Dedham Rec.* III. 32 It is agreed concerning Clapboarding of houses yt it shalbe at liberty vntill midsomer day next. **1740** *Boston Rec.* 273 For Clapboarding the Backside and other Repairs. — (2) **1767** *Boston Ev. Post* 15 June (Th.), The lightning fell in a perpendicular direction, ripping the clapboarding and plaistering as it fell. **1905** H. Garland *Tyranny of Dark* 59 The paint was blistering and peeling from the clapboarding on the sunny side of the main building.

***clape** klep, *n.* [Imitative.] (See quot. 1844.) — **1844** *Nat. Hist. N.Y., Zoology* II. 192 The Clape, or Golden-Winged Woodpecker. *Picus Auratus* ... is called High-hole, Yucker, Flicker, [etc.] **1917** *Birds of Amer.* II. 164 Another person hearing the loud one-syllable call across the fields or the swamp lot has named the bird the Clape.

clapmatch, see **clockmutch.**

***Clapp,** *n.* **Clapp('s) favorite,** a pear introduced by T. Clapp about 1860.

1890 Lyon *Fruit Testing* 29 For smaller plantations the following will afford a partial succession of vigorous, productive varieties, of fair quality: Summer Doyenne, Clapp's Favorite, Bartlett. **1930** Bailey *Cyclo. Horticulture* 2516/2 Clapp Favorite is sold as an 'Early Bartlett,' and a Winter Bartlett, an Oregon seedling, has been planted to carry the same style of pear as late as possible. **1938** Damon *Grandma* 82 Their sparse elderly fruit the robins always got, There were pears: Bartlett, Seckel, and Clapp's Favorite.

clapper rail. A large rail, *Rallus longirostris crepitans*, found in salt marshes along the Atlantic Coast—prob. so named from its note.

1813 Wilson *Ornithology* VII. 112 The Clapper Rail, or, as it is generally called, the Mud Hen, soon announces its arrival in the salt marshes, by its loud, harsh and incessant cackling. **1870** *Amer. Naturalist* III. 48 Off the coast of Cape Charles, Va., I found the nest of the Clapper-rail ... built in a bush. **1947** *Sports Afield* Dec. 20/2 The principal game bird of the marshes is the clapper rail.

***Clark,** *n.* Also ***Clarke.** [Wm. *Clark* (1770–1838), Amer. general and explorer.] Used chiefly in the possessive in the names of birds: (1) **Clark's crow,** a grayish-white bird, *Nucifraga columbiana*, found in coniferous forests in the western states; (2) **grebe,** *Podiceps occidentalis*, now regarded as the same as the western grebe, *Aechmophorus occidentalis;* (3) **nutcracker,** =**Clark's crow.**

(1) **1811** Wilson *Ornithology* III. 29 Clark's Crow, *Corvus columbianus*, ... inhabits the shores of the Columbia, and the adjacent country, ... frequenting the rivers and sea shore, probably feeding on fish. **1947** *Mazama* Dec. 20/2 A dozen Clarks crows were busy as bees feeding on helgramites. — (2) **1874** Coues *Birds N.W.* 728 Clarke's Grebe. Bill about as long as the head. — (3) **1915** *Nat. & Science on Pac. Coast* 107 The curious Clarke nutcracker shows obvious interest in the wayfarer, for he expects to find forage about the camping places. **1946** R. Peattie *Pac. Coast Ranges* 208 Cawing inquisitively, Clark's nutcracker flashes like a small white airplane directly over your head.

Clarkia ˈklɑrkɪə, *n.* [See prec.] A small genus of plants, natural order Onagraceae, natives of the U.S. west of the Rocky Mountains. Also a plant of this genus.

1857 *Spirit of Times* 11 April 90/3 To the above may be added the Clarkias, white and rose colored, the Celosia, . . . and several others. **1863** *Horticulturist* XVIII 155 The Clarkia grows about two feet high. The color is mostly rosy red. It is a very pretty plant for the border. **1882** *Cent. Mag.* June 223/1 Here were bahia, madia . . . etc., . . . blending finely with the purples of clarkia, orthocarpus, and oenothera. **1947** *Nat. Geog. Mag.* July 60/2 Clarkia (*Clarkia elegans*): This excellent annual now comes in several shades and also in . . . double forms.

Clarksville tobacco. (See quot.) *Obs.* — **1863** *Ill. Agric. Soc. Trans.* V. (1865) 669 Those heavy descriptions of tobacco known in Virginia as heavy shipping leaf, and in the West as Clarksville tobacco.

* **class,** *n.* [See **classis,** from which "class" in sense **1.** may have developed.]

1. *Educ.* A group of high school or college students of the same academic standing who, normally, enter at the same time, pursue their courses together, and at the end of four years graduate together.

1671 SEWALL *Letter-Book* I. 19 Remember me kindly to all our Class; jointly and severally named. **1766** CLAP *Ann. Yale College* 81 Under-graduate Students . . . are divided into four Classes; according to the respective Years in which they were admitted. **1899** E. E. HALE *Lowell & Friends* 180 The class of youngsters who entered Harvard College in 1856, when Lowell began his work there, graduated in 1860. **1947** *Time* 19 May 42/2 Secretary of State George C. Marshall became an honorary member of the Class of '48 at Wellesley College.

2. In combs.: (1) **class album,** (see quots.); (2) **baby,** (see quots.), *obs.;* (3) **book,** see as a main entry; (4) **cup,** (see quot. 1856); (5) **day,** see as a main entry; (6) **mate,** see as a main entry; (7) **-mating,** the seeking of favors from classmates, *rare;* (8) **poem,** a poem designed to be read before one's classmates; (9) **ring,** a ring of a design adopted by the members of a school class; (10) **secretary,** the secretary of a school class; (11) **tutor,** (see quot. 1856), *obs.*

(1) 1871 BAGG *At Yale* 476 Lithographic title-pages of various designs, for the class albums, are issued every year. **1944** *Letter to Editor* 'Class album' . . . refers to the predecessor of the present day Class Book. From 1822 to about 1850 autograph albums were circulated among the members of the graduating class. Each member of the class wrote his name and possibly a verse or statement for the owner of the book—his classmate. Many of these class albums are in the Yale Library. — **(2)** [**1863** *Harper's Mag.* Nov. 787/1 The first boy born to any member of the class . . . is henceforth known as the 'class-boy.'] **1902** CLAPIN 120 Class-baby. In college slang, the first child born to a member of a class after graduation. Also, the youngest member of a class. — **(4) 1854** *Presentation Day Songs* (Yale) 14 June, Each man's mind was made up To obtain the 'Class Cup.' **1856** HALL *College Words* (ed. 2) 68 *Class cup.* It is a theory at Yale College, that each class appropriates at graduating a certain amount of money for the purchase of a silver cup, to be given . . . to the first member to whom a child shall be born.

(7) 1774 J. ADAMS in *Fam. Lett.* (1876) 10 You know I never get or save anything by cozening or classmating. — **(8) 1835** B. D. WINSLOW (*title*), Class Poem, delivered in the University Chapel, July 14, at the Valedictory Exercises of the Class of 1835. **1897** FLANDRAU *Harvard Episodes* 181, I was thinking of all the horrible Class Poems and Odes and Baccalureate Sermons and ghastly Memorial Day orators that are allowed to go on. — **(9) 1895** KING *Fort Frayne* 309 Of course it wasn't my class ring. **1948** *Lawton* (Okla.) *Constitution* 2 July 4/6 A visitor from Iowa . . . would always have a warm spot in her heart for Lawton if the person who found her class ring in the business district area yesterday would return the prized possession.

(10) 1851 HALL *College Words* 44 The book [Class Book] is then deposited in the hands of the Class Secretary, whose duty it is to keep a faithful record of the marriage, birth of children, and death of each of his classmates. **1871** BAGG *At Yale* 536 One of these [on the committee] is chosen 'class secretary,' and on him the greater part of the burden falls. — **(11) 1856** *College Words* (ed. 2) 466 *Class Tutor.* At some of the colleges in the United States, each of the four classes is assigned to the care of a particular tutor, who acts as the ordinary medium of communication between the members of the class and the Faculty. **1860** *Harvard Orders & Regul.* ii, The Class Tutors grant leave of absence from church and from town on Sunday.

b. Used with reference to the classification of baseball leagues (see quot. 1912).

1889 *Sporting Life* (Phila.) 17 July 1/6 All other professional leagues and associations to be divided into say four classes known as Class A, B, C and D. **1912** *Amer. Mag.* June 200/2 'Organized baseball', that is, leagues belonging to the National agreement, are classified on a general population basis for purposes of fixing salaries and prices of players. The classes are the Major leagues (American and National), and Class AA, A, B, C, D, and E. **1948** *Dly. Ardmoreite* (Ardmore, Okla.) 14 July 8/1 Why don't you go back to that Class 'D' League where you came from?

Also *class average, cane, cap, committee, crew, dance, dinner, election, eleven, history, marshal, meeting, oration, oratorship, pin, president, prophet, race, reunion, room, rush, sing, song, spirit, stamp, supper, system, teacher, tree,* etc.

As the last term in **Bible, cartridge, confirmation, cooking, cyclone, dancing, dictionary, first, first reader, fourth, freshman, graduating, junior, primer, second, senior, sonder, sophomore, spelling, third class.**

class book. Orig. a class album *q.v.*, but now an annual volume produced by high school and college students, usu. by seniors, and known by a particular name.

1838 *Harvardiana* IV. 368 The 'Class Book' is a large volume, in which autobiographical sketches of the members of each graduating class are recorded. **1851** HALL *College Words* 44 Every graduating class [at Harvard] procures a beautiful and substantial folio of many hundred pages, called the Class Book, and lettered with the year of the graduation of the class. **1944** *Rockford College Bul.* 60 The students of the College publish . . . a junior class book, the *Cupola.*

class day. A day set aside for social and memorial functions by a college class shortly before its graduation. Also attrib.

See A. Matthews "A Search for Origins" in the *Harvard Graduates Mag.* XXII. (1913–14), 580–81.

1833 F. A. WHITNEY in *Harvard Bk.* (1875) II. 165 Our Class Day, glorious summer weather. **1851** HALL *College Words* 186 Class day [is] . . . the day on which the members of that class finish their collegiate studies, and retire to make preparations for the ensuing Commencement. **1948** *Reader's Digest* May 156/2 My function on the Class Day program was to predict in telling gibes what each of the boys would probably turn out to be.

classhood ˈklæshʊd, *n.* The condition of having social classes. *Rare.* — **1878** *Cong. Rec.* 7 March 1551/2 [Free labor in America] eliminated classhood in society and made opportunities for advancement socially, politically, and financially equal among men.

Classic City. (See quot. 1871.) *Obs.* — **1859** *Ladies' Repository* XIX. 51/1 Boston is the 'Classic City,' the 'Modern Athens,' and the 'Literary Emporium,' from its acknowledged pre-eminence in the literary and fine-art pursuits. **1871** DEVERE 662 Boston, in Massachusetts, . . . is called the Classic City, in appreciation of the high culture of her inhabitants.

* **classified,** *a.*

1. classified (civil) service, originally those positions in the federal service which had been classified or graded according to salary, now commonly used for that part of the public service subject to competitive examinations under civil service laws.

1889 in *Wks. T. Roosevelt* (1926) XIV. 92, I expect from the President an extension of the classified service. **1912** *Statutes at Large* XXXVII. 555 No person in the classified civil service of the United States shall be removed therefrom except for such cause as will promote the efficiency of said service. **1920** *Civil Service Comm. 37th Rep.* 14 (*caption*), Statutes affecting the classified service.

2. Designating or with reference to newspaper ads grouped according to their nature.

1909 O. HENRY *Options* 6, I know every end of the business from editing to setting up the classified ads. **1927** *New Masses* May 13/4 She was looking into the classified columns. **1948** *Sat. Ev. Post* 3 July 104/3 The classified-ad columns in the newspapers are not generally regarded as the place to look for a renaissance of the pioneer American spirit.

classis ˈklæsɪs, *n.* Also **classes.** [L., an Amer. borrowing.]

1. = **class 1.** *Obs.*

1642 J. ELIOT *N. Eng. First Fruits* II. iv. The Students of the first Classis that have beene these foure yeeres trained up in University-Learning. **1673** *Harvard Rec.* I. 56 Mr Daniell Gookin . . . is forthwith to take upon him the charg of a classis. **1723** *Ib.* 483 After his taking the Care of the Classis to the End of this Year. **1851** HALL *College Words* 49 *Classis.* Same meaning as Class.

2. A list of books confined to one class or subject, contained in a case or alcove in a library. *Obs.*

1736 in *Pub. Col. Soc.* XV. 133 If any Book or Books be given to ye Library, they shall be brought into ye Library with ye knowledge & consent of ye President & Resident Fellows of the Corporation, and an exact account thereof both in ye College Book, and in ye classes hanging before ye Library Books, shall be taken, & kept from time to time by ye Library Keeper.

classmate ˈklæsˌmet, *n.* A student who is in the same class with another. Cf. **college classmate.**

1713 SEWALL *Diary* 5 June, He had spoken for my Classmate Capt. Saml. Phipps to the Gov[erno]r. **1895** WILLIAMS *Princeton Stories* 81, I thought I was coming to my own room—. . . I mean my classmate's room. **1948** *Chi. Tribune* 26 June II. 1/2 Memories That Linger. . . . Class mates assembled for the last time on commencement day.

Clatsop ˈklætsɑp, *n.* (See quot. 1907.) Also attrib.

1806 LEWIS in *L. & Clark Exped.* (1905) III. 311 The Clatsops, . . . the Chinnooks and others residing in this neighborhood . . . are great higlers in trade. **1829** *McLoughlin Letters* (1941) I. 71 The day previous he had seen the Chief of the Clatsop village. **1907** HODGE *Amer. Indians* I. 305 Clatsop. (*Lä'k!ĕlak*, 'dried salmon.'—Boas). A Chinookan tribe formerly about C. Adams on the s. side of the Columbia r. and extending up the river as far as Tongue pt and s. along the coast to Tillamook Head, Oreg. . . . In 1875 a few Clatsop were found living near Salmon r. and were removed to Grande Ronde res. in Oregon. **1946** *This Week Mag.* 7 Sep. 19/1 He joined up with some Chinooks of the Clatsop variety.

clatterwacking ˈklætəˌwækɪŋ, *n.* [Imitative.] A rattling, clattering noise. *Colloq.* — **1851** *Polly Peablossom* 148, I hearn the darndest clatter-wacking and noise.

clattery ˈklætərɪ, *a.* Characterized by a rattling noise. *Rare.* — **1880** MARK TWAIN *Tramp Abroad* xxxii. 341 There was a small piano in this room, a clattery, wheezy, asthmatic thing.

∗**clause,** *n.* As the last term in **basket, dummy, director, elastic, grandfather clause.**

∗**claw,** *n.* In combs.: (1) **claw balk,** (see quot.); (2) ∗**foot,** a piece of furniture the feet of which are carved to resemble claws, also attrib.; (3) ∗**footed,** *a.* of furniture, having the feet carved to resemble claws, also fig.; (4) **Claw-thumper,** app. erroneous for Craw-thumper *q.v.*; (5) **-toed,** =**clawfooted,** see **lowboy.**

(1) **1884** *Cent. Mag.* XXIX. 280/1 Each two men carrying a claw-balk, or timbers fitted with a claw, one of which held the gunwale of the boat, the other the shore abutment. — (2) **1867** LOWELL *Biglow P.* 2 Ser. No. 6, 153 But the old chist wun't sarve her gran'son's wife. . . . An' so ole clawfoot, from the precinks dred O' the spare chamber, slinks into the shed. **1881** *Harper's Mag.* March 528/1 About 1700 the claw-foot side-boards, sofas and tables were generally used. — (3) **1847** PARKMAN in *Knickerb.* XXX. 229 On the Platte one may sometimes see the shattered wrecks of ancient claw-footed tables. **1851** MELVILLE *Moby Dick* xvi, With an old-fashioned claw-footed look about her. **1889** COOKE *Steadfast* 167 A claw-footed table, round, and shining with beeswax and rubbing. — (4) **1863** *Walla Walla* (Wash.) *Statesman* 6 June 1/7 The inhabitants of Maryland are called Claw Thumpers. **1888** WHITMAN *Nov. Boughs* 70 Those [soldiers] from . . . Maryland [were called] Claw Thumpers. — (5) **1886** MITCHELL *R. Blake* (1895) 58 Claw-toed chairs with carved scroll and shell work backs.

As the last term in **blue, cat, cat's claw.**

∗**clay,** *n.* In combs.: (1) ∗**claybank,** see as a main entry; (2) **bluff,** a bluff composed largely of clay; (3) **colored bunting,** =next; (4) **colored sparrow,** (see quot. 1917); (5) **dauber,** =**dirt dauber;** (6) **dog,** (see quot.); (7) **eater,** one who eats clay, used esp. of southern poor whites of the "cracker" type; (8) **eating,** *a.* characterized by the eating of clay; (9) **gall,** a spot of clayey soil rendered barren by erosion; (10) **hole,** [cf. Du. *kleigat*], a hole washed or dug in a clay bed; (11) **lick,** see **lick;** (12) **pigeon,** a saucer-like object of baked clay tossed in the air as a target in trap shooting; (13) **pinch,** a narrow, steep, or otherwise difficult part of a road or way in a clay formation; (14) **rock bluff,** a rocky bluff in a clay soil or clayey formation; (15) **root,** *S.* the root or network of roots of a tree in clayey soil exposed when the tree is blown down; (16) **slip,** (see quot.); (17) ∗**stone,** see **clay dog.**

(2) **1804** CLARK in *Lewis & C. Exped.* (1904) I. 48 We passed a high land, & clay bluff on the S.S. called the Snake bluff. **1833** CATLIN *Indians* I. 69 We stopped at the base of some huge clay bluffs. *Ib.*, This group of clay bluffs, which line the [Missouri] river for many miles. — (3) **1889** *Cent.* 722/2 Clay-colored bunting . . . [is] a small bird closely resembling the chipping-sparrow. — (4) **1869** *Amer. Naturalist* III. 299, I saw . . . the Clay-colored Sparrow. **1917** *Birds of Amer.* III. 43 The Clay-colored Sparrow (*Spizella pallida*) very much resembles an immature Chippy. It is found on the great plains of North America from the eastern base of the Rocky Mountains to the prairie districts of the upper Mississippi valley. **1945** *Auk* July 392 Clay-colored Sparrows are more common in the park region than has been believed.

(5) **1851** *De Bow's Review* XI. 56 *Mason wasp* or clay dauber [occurs]. — (6) **1892** *N.J. State Geologist Rep.* 138 The low plain [south of Morristown is] . . . equally rich in concretions, which are locally known as 'clay-stones,' 'clay-dogs,' 'stone-dogs,' etc. — (7) **1841** SIMMS *Scout* xiv. He was a little, dried up, withered atomy,—a jaundiced 'sand-lapper' or 'clay-eater' from the Wassamasaw country. **1932** LEWINSON *Race* 7 Ground between these two millstones were the proletarian 'poor whites,' 'hillbillies,' 'red-necks,' and 'clay-eaters.' — (8) **1863** E. KIRKE *Southern Friends* 47 It was fortunate for the clay-eating feminine that her conversation had disgusted us. **1888** *Fort Smith Tribune* Feb. (F.), He came originally from the clay-eating and turpentine district of South Carolina. — (9) [**1832** C. VIGNOLES *Florida* 91 In the pine lands, the early courses of the creeks and streams are through two sorts of channels, *bay galls* and *cypress galls.* . . . Clay is often found in both these kinds of galls.] **1898** HARRIS *Tales of Home Folks* 25 Where the ridge and the hunt entered the woods there was what is known as a 'clay gall,' a barren spot, above two acres in extent. **1944** *D.N.* Nov. 7 Clay gall . . . Clay land from which the good soil has been washed.

(10) **1812** in *Amer. Hist. Rev.* XXXVII. (1931) 74 The road is full of . . . Clay holes [which] cannot be avoided. In many places they run across the road, in others small so that the traveller can drive around them. **1860** COX *Recoll. Wabash Valley* 10 One of the Indian women, after remaining in the water in the clay-hole amongst the dead bodies of her slaughtered relatives for two days and nights, was taken out alive. **1948** *Chi. Tribune* 23 June I. 20/2 An abandoned clayhole in Glenview is being used for disposal of garbage from the city and a dozen suburbs. — (12) **1888** *Outing* Sep. 501 Doubtless he had broken innumerable glass balls and 'clay pigeons' at a trap. **1948** *Life* 21 June 44 The President also fished and shot at clay pigeons. — (13) **1797** in *Amer. Sp.* XV. 164/2 To two chesnut Oaks near the Clay pinch. **1857** *Ib.*, To a white oak and 2 Chestnuts on the top of the Clay pinch. — (14) **1860** GREELEY *Overland Journey* 176 A range of such precipitous clay-rock bluffs as I have tried to describe.

(15) **1916** MASSEY *Reminisc.* 35 There were many old 'clay roots' in that vicinity, showing that it had once been visited by a cyclone. — (16) **1882** WORTHEN *Econ. Geol. Ill.* II. 18 This coal-seam is subject to some irregularities, such as 'clay-slips' or 'horse-backs,' sometimes called 'faults' by the miners, which consists in a thickening of the roof shales, thus cutting off or pinching the coal-seam to one-half or three-fourths of its usual thickness.

As the last term in **adobe, beauty, blue, paint, potato, wheat, white-face(d), white oak clay.**

∗**Clay,** *n.* [f. proper name.]

1. A breed of trotting horses. *Obs.*

1893 G. W. CURTIS *Horses* 66 Sources of trotting blood [include] . . . the Clays, who take the family name from Henry Clay, a son of Andrew Jackson.

2. *Hist.* In derivatives and combs. relating to Henry Clay (1777–1852), Amer. politician and statesman, as: (1) **Clay ball,** (2) **Clay club,** (3) **Clay dinner,** (4) **Clayism,** (5) **Clayite,** (6) **Clay man,** (7) **Clay party.** Cf. **Henry Clay.**

(1) **1896** HASWELL *New York* 402 Early in this year the movement to nominate Mr. Clay for the Presidency took form, and the 'Clay balls,' which were a notable feature of the campaign of 1844, began to be given. — (2) *c***1845** W. T. PORTER *Big Bear Arkansas* 105 Our Jack got his finger cut with a steal trap catchin of a koon for a Clay Club. — (3) **1827** *U.S. Telegraph* (Wash., D.C.) 7 Aug. 2/4 Those who attended the Clay dinner at Noble's, declared there were three times as many at the Jackson dinner. — (4) **1831** *American* (Harrodsburg, Ky.) 22 July 3/4 We find the Legislature acting under the influence of 'Clayism,' wasting one hundred and thirty thousand dollars, in order to saddle the Turnpike Tollgates more surely on the people. **1848** *N.Y. Wkly. Tribune* 19 Feb. 3/5 Talk about Taylorism, or any other *ism* but Clayism, you must go somewhere else.

(5) **1830** *Village Herald* (Princess Anne, Md.) 27 July 2/5 The Clayites got up a meeting, recently, in Nicholasville, Ky. **1868** GREELEY *Autobiog.* 212 All that we Clayites achieved was the substitution of Millard Fillmore as Vice-President for Abbott Lawrence, of Boston. — (6) **1830** *Boston Transcript* 18 Sep. 2/4 Tariff and Anti-Tariff, Masonic and Anti-Masonic, Jackson-men and Clay-men, Workies and Idlers—let us agree to suspend all our differences, till we meet again at the next Centennial Celebration. *c***1849** PAIGE *Dow's Sermons* I. 130 My unfortunate accomplices in political rascality, the Clay-men, are hopping about like peas upon a hot shovel. — (7) **1831** *American* (Harrodsburg, Ky.) 25 Mar. 2/5 The Clay party in this county, have been very busily engaged in trying to caucus out candidates for their opponents. **1832** *Polit. Examiner* (Shelbyville, Ky.) 26 May 3/1 We are requested to inform the voters of the Clay party in Shelby county, that a meeting will take place at the Court-House. —

∗**claybank,** *n.*

1. A yellowish color; usu. attrib. or as adj. with reference to a horse. Also **claybank colored.**

1851 REID *Scalp Hunters* xxiii, [A mare] of that dun-yellowish colour known as 'clay-bank.' **1855** *Putnam's Mag.* Feb. 188, I mounted a claybank colored nag and rode to the hunt. **1896** POOL *In Bun-*

combe County 48 The woman caught the clay bank horse without any difficulty. **1906** O. HENRY *Rolling Stones* (1912) 30 An elegant gentleman of a slightly claybank complexion sitting in an upholstered chair. **1910** —— *Strictly Business* 68 'Keep that awhile for me, mister,' he said, chewing at the end of a virulent claybank cigar.

b. An animal, esp. a horse, of this color.

1853 *Oregonian* (Portland) 5 Nov. 1/6 Well, ses he, getting off an' hitching his ole clay-bank to a swinging limb, 'count me *in*.' **1896** POOL *In Buncombe County* 40 The steed was a 'clay bank.' **1939** ROLLINS *Gone Haywire* 56 Ace-in-the-Hole was a claybank.

2. *pl.* (*cap.*) A nickname for the members of a faction of the Missouri legislature. *Obs.*

1863 *N.Y. Tribune* 14 Nov. 6/2 They might have succeeded by dropping him and presenting some one of similar principles but personally less obnoxious to the 'Claybanks.' *a***1877** in BARTLETT 397 The Missourians have quite a penchant for curious characterization. The members of the Legislature are divided into Charcoals, Clay-Banks, White-legs, [etc.]. **1905** HUME *Abolitionists* 159 The Claybanks, or Conservatives, at the outset enjoyed a decided advantage in having the State government on their side.

Claytonia klə'tonɪə, *n.* [f. John *Clayton* (1693–1773), Amer. botanist.] A genus of herbs of the purslane family found chiefly in North America. Also (not *cap.*) a plant of this genus.

17— LINNAEUS *Species Plantarum* (1764 ed. 3) I. 294 Claytonia virginica. **1818** *Mass. H.S. Coll.* 2 Ser. VIII. 168 Among our herbaceous wild plants, the first that appear are the delicate claytonia, the graceful three-lobed hepatica, [etc.]. **1880** *Scribner's Mo.* May 101/2 A good sample of our native purslane is the Claytonia, or spring beauty. **1941** SETON *Trail of Artist-Naturalist* 41 We found that overnight someone had planted throughout the woods the little spring flowers we called the 'beauties' (*claytonias*), and we gathered them with eager fingers.

***clean,** *a.*

1. After Indian phraseology: Not stained by bloodshed, free from strife. *Rare.* Cf. ***bloody, *a.* 1.**

1802 DRAYTON *S. Carolina* 14 The path over this mountain has been crooked and straight, bloody and clean; (according to the Indian talks).

3. In combs.: (1) **clean cash,** clear or actual cash, *colloq.;* (2) **cotton,** ginned cotton, *rare;* (3) **out,** an appliance for cleaning drains, *rare;* (4) **shot,** in basketball (see quot.); (5) **ticket,** (see quot. 1859); (6) **title,** a clear title; (7) **up,** see as a main entry.

(1) **1855** *Knickerb.* XLVI. 97, I think . . . if all my debts were paid I should be worth three hundred dollars clean cash! **1875** *Chi. Tribune* 21 Nov. 2/6 'In clean cash, right in the savings bank,' answered Jim. — (2) **1857** D. BRAMAN *Texas* 24 The land is quite fertile, producing, on an average, one bale, or 500 lbs. clean cotton per acre. — (3) **1888** *Boston newspaper* (*advt.*), Patent Traps and cleanouts for drains. — (4) **1916** BANCROFT *Handbook* 113 Clean-shot. A shot that sends the ball through the goal without first touching the backboard or rim of basket.

(5) **1848** *N.Y. Wkly. Tribune* 10 June 4/5, I go with my friend, Mr. Van Buren, for a clean ticket. [**1855** *N.Y. Herald* 6 Nov. 4/6 Every party man who believes that the salvation of the constitution depends upon the success of his party, should vote a clean party ticket.] **1859** BARTLETT 86 Clean Ticket, the entire regularly nominated ticket at an election; a ticket without any erasures. 'He went the clean ticket on the Whig Nominations.' — (6) **1898** PAGE *Red Rock* 337 Leech, it was reported, had come up from town, given a clean title and prepared a deed which was to be delivered on a certain day.

b. *Baseball.* Indicating something done or made without error or benefit of error, as (1) **clean fielding,** (2) **hit(ting),** (3) **home run,** (4) **score,** (5) **single.**

(1) [**1893** *Chi. Tribune* 28 April 7/3 The fielding of the Washingtons was clean and effective.] — (2) **1868** *N.E. Base-Ballist* 17 Sep. 26/2 They secured no less than 102 bases on clean hits. **1884** *Chi. Tribune* 2 May 6/1 Clean hitting was the order at first, but when Weidman got down to his work the run-getting of the home club ceased. **1948** *Sat. Ev. Post* 9 Oct. 47/2 The hitter came up and swung on the bad ball, chopping it into right for a clean hit. — (3) **1865** *Wilkes' Spirit of Times* 29 July 348/2 The first time he went to the bat, he made a clean home run by a powerful and safe hit. **1876** *Chi. Tribune* 4 Aug. 5/2 The features of the game were the wonderful catching of Brown, . . . and Manning's clean home run in the sixth. — (4) **1860** in *Amer. Sp.* XXII. 201/1 Remember that you must have 'a good bat' and strike a 'fair ball' to make a 'clean score' and a 'home run.' **1867** *Ball Players' Chron.* 13 June 2/1 Lotilda at the first base, played admirably in the field, and showed the only clean score in the match. — (5) **1948** *N.Y. Times* v. 5/6 Peanuts Lowery socked a clean single to right center.

c. *The clean thing,* the honest, manly, straightforward course or action. *Colloq.*

1835 CROCKETT *Tour* 193, I don't like it. It isn't the clean thing. **1873** *Newton Kansan* 19 June 3/2 Let patriots everywhere . . . prepare to do the clean thing by Uncle Sam.

d. *To come clean,* see ***come, *v.***

***clean,** *v.*

1. *tr.* To gin (cotton). *Obs.*

1827 SHERWOOD *Gaz. Georgia* 116 At three or four gin-houses much of the cotton raised in the vicinity, and in Burke, was cleaned. **1841** *Hunt's Merch. Mag.* March 223 We behold a vegetable production [cotton] cleaned from its seeds by machinery. *Ib.* 217 The species derives its name . . . from the mode of cleaning it.

2. To defeat decisively, to clean out. *Slang.*

1869 DUMONT *Benedict's Songster* 49, I can beat old Uncle Snow, the best way he can go, I will clean the whole caboodle, then ye people watch my step. **1931** *K.C. Star* 28 Oct., Seven boy orators representing as many nations met in a contest at Washington Saturday night. The Dutch boy cleaned them. **1948** *Houston* (Tex.) *Post* 14 June 10/1 Old Joe . . . finished the cleaning job on Truman at Potsdam.

b. Of a batter in baseball: To free (bases) of runners by a hit that enables them to score. Also with *up.*

1870 *Cin. Commercial* 14 May 4/6 Gould cleaned the bases, taking first himself. **1947** R. SMITH *Baseball* 9 The best batter ought to be the fourth man up to bat, so that he could clean up the bases with a solid, long hit, if the first three had been lucky enough to reach base.

3. **To clean out,* to defeat or "use up" (an adversary) completely. *Slang.*

1858 in *Kans. Hist. Coll.* XIV. 99, I allow that I could clean you out quicker than greased lightning would pass a funeral. **1909** O. HENRY *Roads of Destiny* 92 The man who cleaned out the horse thieves.

b. To empty or rid (a place) of its occupants by violence. *Slang.*

1858 *Kans. Hist. Coll.* (1896) V. 567 These same men attacked Barnesville . . . and literally cleaned it out, both of inhabitants and property. **1902** WHITE *Blazed Trail* 175 He invaded the enemy's camp, attempted to clean out the saloon with a billiard cue single handed.

4. **To clean up,* to gain, acquire. Also absol. *Colloq.*

1831 PECK *Guide* 147 He gave a friend one measured acre . . . and cleaned up thirty-five bushels and eight quarts [of wheat]. **1908** WHITE *Riverman* 254 We ought to clean up five dollars a thousand on our mill. **1947** *Sierra Club Bul.* June 2/2 The West today knows many a ghost town where men of too much enterprise cleaned up and cleared out.

b. *W.* (See quot. 1872.) Cf. **clean-up, *n.* 1.**

1851 JACKSON *Forty-niner* 84 Last week was an off week, but we are going now to put in steady work until we clean up our ground. **1872** MARK TWAIN *Roughing It* xxxvi. 255 At the end of the week the machinery was stopped and we 'cleaned up.' That is to say, we got the pulp out of the pans and batteries and washed the mud patiently away till nothing was left but the long-accumulating mass of quicksilver, with its imprisoned treasures. **1910** HART *Vigilante Girl* 51 What a life to lead! . . . To 'clean up' on Saturday a few ounces of gold dust, to take their dust to the town on Saturday night and spend it for whiskey.

c. To beat or vanquish, to rid (a region) of undesirables. *Slang.* Cf. ***cleaning 3. b. *house, *n.* 9. b.**

1888 SHERIDAN *Memoirs* I. 47 As the regular troops up there were of no account, the citizens . . . intended cleaning up the hostiles. **1925** MULFORD *Cottonwood Gulch* 188 Colonel Hutton will make a good judge, an' our friend Dangerfield [sheriff] will clean up this cursed country like a new broom. **1948** *Sat. Ev. Post* 3 July 16/3 The amateur's confidence that he could clean up Chicago sounded pretty naïve.

d. *W.* (See quot.)

1888 ROOSEVELT in *Cent. Mag.* April 860/1 He becomes a good brand reader and is able to really 'clean up a herd'—that is, be sure he has left nothing of his own in it.

e. To settle one's affairs.

1920 *Cosmopolitan* Oct. 134/2, I must hustle back to Iowa and clean up.

***cleaning,** *n.*

1. (See quot.)

1905 *Forestry Bureau Bul.* 61 Cleaning. A thinning made in a stand [of trees] which has not yet reached the small-pole stage. Its main object is to remove trees of undesirable form and species.

2. A fortune, a "killing." *Slang.*

1932 *K.C. Times* 28 Mar. 18 We'd like to be a real detective for a year, make a 'cleaning' and then retire.

3. ***cleaning up,** in gold mining, collecting the products of value that have accumulated over a period in a stamp mill, riffle box, etc.

1857 *Hutching's Mag.* July 8/1 These sluices are sometimes 'run,' as it is termed, for many days together before 'cleaning up.' **1873** G. A. LAWRENCE *Silverland* 177 The cleaning up . . . consists in removing the pavement and blocks from the bed of the sluice, gathering the precious compost, and replacing or renewing the blocks or stones of the pavement.

b. The act of reforming a bad or scandalous state of things. *Slang.*

1916 DUPUY *Uncle Sam* 170 The cleaning up of the customs scandals in the port of New York was a most complicated task. **1924** MULFORD *Rustler's Valley* i 235 That town needs cleanin' up.

clean-up ˈklinˌʌp, *n.*

1. *W.* In mining, the process of periodically separating the valuable mineral from the gravel and rock which have collected in the sluices or at the stamping mill.

1866 *Cong. Globe* 18 June 3231/1 When what they technically call in mining the clean-up comes, very often the clean-up exhibits the lofty sum of nothing, while thousands have been expended in the effort. **1876** BOURKE *Journal* 8 Sep. 22 In speaking of the 'clean-up,' the Deadwooders always said so many 'pounds,' in other 'diggings,' the word 'ounces' is used. **1936** *Colo. Mag.* July 139 One hundred and twenty-five pounds of quicksilver was required for the cleanup, which usually netted about 50 pounds of coarse, 'shot' gold.

2. An exceptional financial success; a big "haul." *Colloq.*

1878 HART *Sazerac Lying Club* 21 (We.), At the same time make a nice little clean-up for himself. **1907** WHITE *Arizona Nights* 181 He and Simpson had made a pretty good clean-up, just enough to make them want to get rich. **1928** *Sat. Ev. Post* 4 Feb. 121/3 This development project ought to be a clean-up for us.

***clear,** *n.* **1.** An area above the tree line. **2.** A clearing. Both *obs.* — **(1) 1784** CUTLER in *Life & Corr.* I. 102 This kind of walking did not extend above sixty or seventy rods before we came into the clear, as it is called, which is above the trees. — **(2) 1834** AUDUBON *Ornith. Biog.* II. 499 If a 'clear' or 'cutting place' should lie in the course, the birds may be confidently expected to have alighted there.

***clear,** *a.*

1. Of lumber: Free from knots or other imperfections.

1739 HEMPSTEAD *Diary* 356, I bot 3050 foot of white pine bords . . . & one bord 47 foot clear stuff a wide & thick one for Table Leaves. **1832** *N.H. Hist. Soc. Coll.* III. 204 Great quantities of excellent clear boards have been sawed at the several mills in town. **1865–6** *Ill. Agric. Soc. Trans.* VI. 645 Clear flooring, rejected on account of thickness, shall be classed with common flooring. **1900** BRUNCKEN *N. Amer. Forests* 80 The various grades [of lumber] are known by technical names, such as clear, select, culls, and the like.

2. Of unmixed breed, full-blooded. *Obs.*

1797 *Mass. H.S. Coll.* V. 264 All the Indians, both clear and mixed, in all New-England, do not probably exceed one thousand. **1834** C. A. DAVIS *Lett. J. Downing* 25 Though I tell'd 'em down south my father was an Irishman, and my mother, too, I am as clear a Yankee . . . as the Major himself.

3. (See quot. 1889.)

1834 THOMPSON *Adv. T. Peacock* 91 These Dutch minxes . . . are clear pepper-pots for grit. **1851** CIST *Cincinnati* 214 Pig-iron, and one thousand tons Tennessee clear blooms. **1889** *Cent.* 1037/2 Without admixture, adulteration, or dilution: as, a fabric of clear silk; clear brandy; clear tea.

b. clear home run, =clean home run.

1865 *Sun. Mercury* (Phila.) 3 Sep. 3/5 None of the Athletics had obtained a clear home run up to the ninth innings.

4. In combs.: (1) **clear grit,** see **grit;** (2) **mess,** (see quot.), *obs.;* (3) **nosed ray,** (see quot. 1814); (4) **pork,** (see quot. 1867); (5) **sides,** =prec.; (6) **stone,** designating a freestone peach; (7) **swing,** free range, unhampered space, *colloq.;* (8) **weed,** richweed, *Pilea pumila,* a low-growing herb of the nettle family having shining pellucid stems.

(2) 1852 FLEISCHMANN *Wegweiser* 206 Das gesalzene Schweinefleisch wird im Handel als *Clear Mess, Mess,* und *Ordinary Mess,* als *Prime, Prime ordinary* und *Rumps* gesondert. *Clear Mess* besteht aus den Seitestücken ohne Rippen. — **(3) 1814** MITCHILL *Fishes N.Y.* 478 Clear-nosed Ray. *Raja diaphanes.* The snout which is lengthened toward an acute angle, is semi-transparent almost to the eyes, and its clearness allows a finger or a pen to be distinguished through it tolerably well, almost as high up as the eyes. **1842** *Nat. Hist. N.Y., Zoology* IV. 366 Clear-nosed Ray . . . are caught along with codfish, and are eaten by the poorer classes. — **(4) 1831** *Boston Transcript* 1 Feb., 30 bbls. Clear Pork, (very thick). **1867** DE VOE *Market Ass't* 98 When the rib-bones are taken out of the thick side-pork, it is generally called 'clear pork'; that is also corned or salted. [**1945** *Chi. D. News* 28 June 1/6 Fat back and clear plate pork will be two points higher in July.]

(5) 1865 *Cin. D. Commercial* 3 Oct. 4/1 Bacon Clear Sides sold at 24c, loose. **1930** *San Antonio* (Texas) *Light* 31 Jan., Clear Sides Salt Bacon. — **(6) 1819** *Patterson's Alman. 1820* (Pittsburgh) 19 A small clearstone peach, the skin a greenish yellow, the flesh of the same colour; dry without much flavour. **1941** *L.A* Map 267. — **(7)** *a***1859** *N.Y. Tribune* (B.), We expect to see . . . a clear swing and ample reward granted to labor and intelligence. **1908** *D.N.* III. 299 Give him a clear swing, and he'll beat you every time [Eastern Ala.]. — **(8) 1821** *Mass. H.S. Coll.* 2 Ser. IX. 157 Plants which are indigenous in the township of Middlebury [Vermont, include] . . . Urtica pumila, Clearweed. **1939** *Nat. Geog. Mag.* Aug. 220/2 Such are the wood and false nettles . . . or the lowly bedstraws, clearweeds, pellitories, and three-seeded mercury.

***clear,** *v.* In phrases.

1. *To clear outward(s)*, of a vessel, to sail away from a port. *Obs.*

1708 *Boston News-Letter* 11–18 Oct. 4/2 Cleared Outward *Downing, Presbury* and *Walter* for Connecticut. **1715** *Boston News-Letter* 10 Jan. 2/2 Cleared Outwards Jacob Parker for Piscataqua. **1719** *Weekly Mercury* 22 Dec. 2/2 Cleared Outwards, Dan. Wait, Jos. Jackson, and Tho. Miller for Piscataqua.

2. *To clear a docket*, to dispose of all the cases on a docket. Also fig.

1822 *Ann. 17th Congress* 1 Sess. I. 271 Mr. J. said the docket of congress was never cleared but once. **1866** LOWELL *Biglow P.* 2 Ser. xi. 236 Did he put thru the rebbles, clear the docket, An' pay th' expenses out of his own pocket? **1899** TARKINGTON *Gentleman from Ind.* ii, The court had cleared up the docket by sitting to unseemly hours of the night.

3. **To clear out*, to drive out, send packing. *Colloq.*

1877 HARTE *Story of Mine*, etc. 338, I reckon he'll clear out that yar Sacramento counter-jumper. **1888** ——— *Argonauts N. Liberty* 198, I'll push on and clear him out.

***clearance,** *n.* **1.** A clearing *q.v.*, an area from which the trees and undergrowth have been removed. *Obs.* **2.** (See quot.)

(1) 1800 J. MAUDE *Niagara* 100 Passed three clearances; . . . Soil excellent. **1857** GLADSTONE *Englishman in Kansas* 170 Often, in riding over the prairie, the traveller meets with a small clearance, sufficient, at least, to show that some one has been there. — **(2) 1900** NELSON *A B C Wall St.* 134 Clearances. Freight shipped by water for interior or coast ports.

***clearing,** *n.*

1. A piece of forest land cleared of trees for cultivation.

1678 in *Amer. Sp.* XV. 165/1 A bottom on ye lower side of the clearing of John Rabon. **1724** *Ib.*, At the Mouth of a Small Branch below his Clearing. **1812** MELISH *Travels* II. 282 A little beyond Grand river we came to a *clearing*, and looking into it, saw a handsome house about 500 yards distant. **1947** *Chr. Sci. Mon.* 1 Mar. III. 7/3 On up past an abandoned farmhouse in its small clearing.

b. (See quot. 1929.)

1859 TALIAFERRO *Fisher's R.* 218 Nor could a man clear a piece of ground without inviting his neighbors, and having a 'clearin'.' **1929** *Amer. Sp.* V. 17 clarin', n. A social gathering, the real purpose of which is to clear the host's land of timber and underbrush. People bring axes and saws and work hard all day, while the owner's part is to provide good food, and perhaps some whiskey for the frolic in the evening. [Ozark Mts.]

2. *W.* A clean-up, *q.v.*, in mining. *Obs.*

1851 KINGSLEY *Diary* 168 We kept the machine running on the top dirt in the last clearing and got 13 ounces 11 dollars in amalgam. *Ib.* 172 This begins to pay as we anticipated the whole clearing would.

3. clearing sale, a sale for disposing of merchandise preparatory to getting in a new stock.

1891 *Memphis Appeal-Avalanche* 26 April 3/1 We begin tomorrow (Monday), the most extraordinary clearing sales of silks ever offered. **1899** *Chi. D. News* 30 May 5/3 Clearing Sale Jackets and Suits.

As the last term in **dead, hill, swamp, turpentine clearing.**

Cleavelandite ˈklivlәndˌaɪt, *n.* [Named for Parker *Cleaveland* (1780–1858). See quot. 1822.] (See quot. 1837.) — **1822** H. J. BROOKE in *Annals Philos.* (May, 1823) 381, I have, therefore, preferred adopting the term *Cleavelandite* to denote the species, out of respect to the Professor of Natural Philosophy in Bowdoin College, United States. **1837** DANA *Mineralogy* 297 The variety [of Albite] from Chesterfield [Mass.] was denominated Cleavelandite, in compliment to Prof. Cleaveland, by Mr. Brooke, who supposed at the time that it was a distinct species.

Cleaveland stone. =?prec. *Obs.* — **1835** HOFFMAN *Winter in West* I. 104 The appropriation by government for its erection had not been large enough to have permitted the beautiful Cleaveland stone . . . to be substituted for the perishable looking material of which the building is now constructed. **1871** L. H. BAGG *At Yale* 159 The light yellow Cleveland stone is the chief material of which it is composed.

***clerk,** *n.*

1. An assistant to a storekeeper, esp. one who waits on customers in a store.

1771 FRANKLIN *Autobiog.* 286 He propos'd to take me over as his clerk, to keep his books, in which he would instruct me, copy his letters, and attend the store. **1835** H. C. TODD *Notes* 10 The city has 6,000 clerks, chiefly natives, exclusive of *shop-men,* who are here and in Canada also, universally called clerks. **1948** *Chi. D. News* 8 Sep. 1/7 A clerk . . . was charged with taking . . . cash she was carrying to a bank.

2. The purser of a steamboat.

1845 F. N. MOORE *Diary* (1946) 39 The clerk went in with the yawl, and brought from the town some stores. **1864** CUMMING *Hospital Life* 157/1, I had a little girl with me, for whom the clerk of the boat had charged full price.

3. In hotels, etc., an employee who assigns rooms or sleeping quarters to guests.

1879 R. J. BURDETTE *Hawkeyes* 62 Abou Tamerlik came to the city of Bagdad, threw his gripsack on the counter, and, as he registered, spake cheerfully unto the clerk. **1892** DUVAL *Young Explorers* 198 A little while afterwards the clerk came up to my room and asked if I wished for supper. **1947** BASKINS *Dr. Has Baby* 180 We followed the clerk to our room, followed in turn by the bellhop with our bags.

As the last term in **baggage, bill, captain's, check, circuit, county, day, district, drug, dry goods, enrolling, entry, grocery, hotel, Indian, mailing, mud, night, postal, room, routing, senate, sergeant, settling, shoe, shop, soda, stated, steamboat, store, third, trading, under clerk.**

***clerk,** *v. intr.* To work as a clerk in a store. Also **clerking,** *n.*

1848 RUXTON in *B. Mag.* LXIII, 715 Young Sublette comes up, and he'd been clerking down to the fort on Platte, so he know'd something. **1887** *Harper's Mag.* Jan. 220/2 Ef she was in your place and wanted to go to clerking, she'd believe she'd go further from home.

Also *to clerk it. Colloq.*

1862 BROWNE *A. Ward His Book* 231 Sarah's father use to keep a little grosery store in our town, and she used to clerk it for him in busy times. **1889** *Harper's Mag.* July 314/1 He . . . then 'clerked it' in a drug-store.

Hence ***clerkship,** a position as clerk in a store.

1891 O'BEIRNE *Leaders Ind. Territory* 137/2 After his marriage Alonzo started stock-raising and farming, and took a clerkship with John D. Hardin, a merchant of Atoka.

Clevelander 'klivləndɚ, *n.* One who lives in Cleveland, Ohio. — **1870** *Cin. Commercial* 14 May 4/5 The splendid playing of the Clevelanders . . . greatly pleased all who witnessed it. **1948** *Ohio State Arch. & Hist. Quart.* Jan. 68 Abraham Lincoln in Cleveland was of interest to Clevelanders.

cleverly 'klɛvəlɪ, *a. local.* In health, well. *Obs.*

1784 A. ADAMS *Letters* (1848) 210 She is cleverly now, although she had a severe turn for a week. **1816** PICKERING 63 In answer to the common salutation, How do you do, we often hear [in New Eng.], I am cleverly. **1834** C. A. DAVIS *Lett. J. Downing* 82, I've been amost sick for a week. . . . But I'm getting cleverly now.

***click,** *v. intr.* To walk pertly or sprightly. *Obs.* See also **lickety click.** — **1824** FORD *Notes N. Webster* II. 271 You wou'd smile to see how alert I am, with a little quilted hood on my head—*clicking* (to use an Amherst expression) over the green, & back again before the girls have miss'd me.

***cliff,** *n.* In combs.: (1) **cliff brake,** one or other species of fern of the genus *Pellaea,* esp. *P. atropurpurea;* (2) **city,** *S.W.* a large group or city of cliff dwellings, *rare;* (3) **dweller,** (*a*) *S.W.* an Indian belonging to one of the tribes that made their homes in caves or upon ledges in canyon walls, (*b*) one who lives in an apartment house, *slang;* (4) **dwelling,** *S.W.* the abode of an Indian cliff dweller; (5) **limestone,** a form of limestone occurring in the upper Mississippi Valley region in massive abrupt cliffs and precipices, *obs.;* (6) **plum,** (see quot.), *rare;* (7) **stone,** =**cliff limestone,** *rare;* (8) **swallow,** =**eave swallow,** cf. **jug swallow, mud swallow.**

(1) 1867 GRAY *Lessons in Bot.* 659 *Pellae.* Cliff-brake. . . . *P. atropurpurea.* . . . [Grows on] dry calcareous rocks: not common, but of wide range. **1941** R. S. WALKER *Lookout* 56 Purple cliffbreak finds congenial homes in the limestone ledges. — **(2) 1873** BEADLE *Undevel. West* 517 Farther west are the 'Cliff cities' of Cañon de Chelley. **1878** —— *Western Wilds* 257 We should reach the celebrated 'cliff cities' which have made this cañon so famous. — **(3)** (*a*) **1881** *Rep. Indian Affairs* 137 The peach trees are supposed to have been originally planted by a superior race or by ancient explorers, possibly by the cliff-dwellers. **1948** JOHNSTON *Gold Rush* 46/2 Like the cliff dwellers of the Southwest, the men who worked in those diggin's have vanished. (*b*) **1893** FULLER *Cliff-Dwellers* 5 It will be unnecessary for us to go afield either far or frequently during the present simple succession of brief episodes in the lives of cliff-dwellers. **1916** *Amer. Mag.* April 31/2 You cliff-dweller on Manhattan, what would you do without Michigan? — **(4) 1888** *Science* XI. 258/1 Some cliff-dwellings in Walnut Cañon, about twelve miles southeast of Flagstaff, Arizona, were examined. **1947** *Sierra Club* (So. Calif. Chap.) Sched. 126, 75 The natural cave containing Betatakin is larger than the famous Rainbow Natural Bridge, which we will visit on leaving the cliff dwellings.

(5) 1840 *Mich. Agric. Soc. Trans.* V. 289 Its place is higher in the series than the blue limestone . . . and without doubt is equivalent in position to the 'cliff limestone' of Indiana. **1857** DANA *Mineralogy* 278 They abound in what has been called 'cliff limestone,' in the states of Missouri, Illinois, Iowa, and Wisconsin. — **(6) 1819** *Western Rev.* I. 93 Plants peculiar to this region [=Ky.] and giving a decided character to its vegetation [include]: . . . *Prunus pendula,* Cliff plumb. — **(7) 1851** CIST *Cincinnati* 20 The superincumbent cliff-stone . . . is developed into a stratum of six-hundred feet in height. — **(8) 1825** BONAPARTE *Ornithology* I. 65 The Cliff Swallow advances from the extreme western regions, annually invading a new territory farther to the eastward. **1939** LINCOLN *Migration* 79 A study of the spring migrations of the Black-poll Warbler and the Cliff Swallow affords an interesting comparison of the flights of day and night migrants.

climate 'klaɪmɪt, *v.* [App. short for **acclimate.*] *tr.* To acclimate or acclimatize. *Obs.*

1849 KINGSLEY *Diary* 92 Relinquishing the idea of going to the diggings this winter [to] get ourselves climated ready for spring. **1852** STOWE *Uncle Tom* x, If he stands the fever, and 'climating, he'll have a berth good as any nigger ought ter ask for. **1863** E. KIRKE *Southern Friends* 61 It gits a feller's stumac used to Tophet 'for the rest on him is 'climated.

climate-struck, *a.* (See quot.) *Obs.* — **1724** JONES *Virginia* 48 This easy Way of Living, and the Heat of the Summer makes some very lazy, who are then said to be Climate-struck.

***climber,** *n.*

1. One who seeks to advance himself unduly in society or in business. Also attrib.

1833 *Knickerb.* I. 179 But with all her meanness as a climber, what a glorious leader of fashion she'd make. **1911** HARRISON *Queed* 301 He was of the climber type, a self-made man in the earlier and less inspiring stages of the making. **1920** OSTRANDER *How Many Cards?* 89, If by the Fords you mean Lonsdale Ford and his wife, they're climbers; never heard of until a few years ago.

2. A device, as a spurred boot or detachable sharpened steel rod or bar for strapping to the leg, to give assistance in climbing telegraph poles, trees, etc.

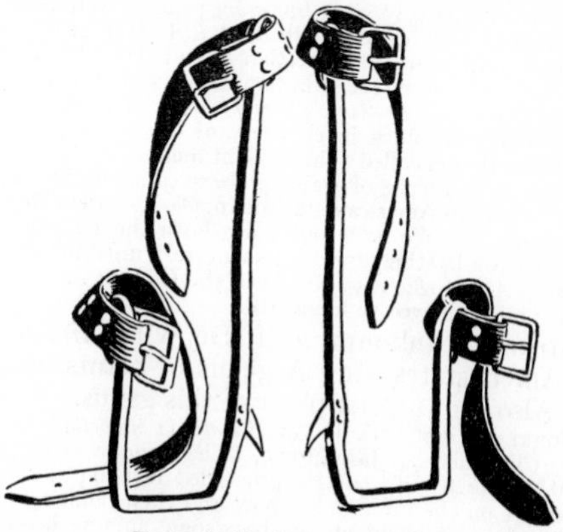

Pair of climbers (sense 2)

1874 KNIGHT 566 Climber, A boot provided with spurs, by which a person is enabled to climb telegraph-poles to make repairs or additions to the wires or insulators. **1894** *Outing* XXIII. 355/2 A pair of such steel climbers as linemen fasten to their feet when about to climb telegraph poles. **1948** *Sat. Ev. Post* 24 Jan. 48/2 I'd go up, using climbers and a safety rope around the tree.

***climbing,** *n.* **1.** (See quot.) *Obs.* **2. climbing fern,** a delicate decorative North American fern, *Lygodium palmatum.* See also **Hartford climbing fern.**

(1) **1851** HALL *College Words* 50 It was customary [at Dartmouth] for each one of these four [best scholars] to treat his classmates, which was called 'Climbing,' from the effect which the liquor would have in elevating the class to an equality with the first scholars. — (2) **1817–8** EATON *Botany* (1822) 345 [The] climbing fern . . . generally climbs to the height of about 3 or 4 feet. **1938** SMALL *Ferns Southeastern States* 339 Besides climbing-fern, it is known as creeping-fern, Hartford-fern, and Windsor-fern.

* **clinch,** *n.* A rough and tumble combat characterized by clinching. Also attrib.

1849 LANMAN *Alleghany Mts.* 50 He found the wolf alive, when a 'clinch fight' ensued and the hunter's knife completely severed the heart of the animal. **1860** HOLMES *Professor* iii. 64 Both rolled together, and the Conflict terminated in one of those inglorious and inevitable Yankee clinches. **1881** *Family Her.* 12 March 304 A citizen who met with a mishap in a bar-room 'clinch.'

transf. **1944** *Chi. D. News* 2 Dec. 3/2 Crum asked Hall to demonstrate the embrace with his lawyer, Grant Cooper. The two grinning six-footers went into a clinch. **1948** *Dly. Ardmoreite* (Ardmore, Okla.) 2 May 14/6 The visitors got plenty of hits—12—but couldn't produce in the clinches.

b. *pl.* ?Clutches. *Rare.*

1850 C. MATHEWS *Moneypenny* 10 Somehow or another we never could get our clinches on you.

* **clinch,** *v. intr.* Infighting or wrestling, to grapple and struggle at close grips. *Colloq.*

The general sense occurs in early modern English (1652) but the modern technical use is American. See quot. 1863.

1828 *Yankee* May 174/3 A native Yankee . . . would never be the first to strike a blow, nor hardly ever the first to clinch, as he calls it. **1863** in MILES *Pugilistica* (1906) III. 516 The Yankee again 'clinching'—we must borrow an Americanism which expresses more than our word 'closing'—succeeded in once more putting on the 'hug' and throwing King heavily. **1948** *Sat. Ev. Post* 3 July 77/1 The champ . . . came in and clinched.

* **cling,** *n.* A clingstone or clingstone peach, usu. with a qualifying word. Also **cling peach.**

1845 DOWNING *Fruits Amer.* 494 The Catherine cling is a very fine, old English variety. **1872** *S.F. Wkly. Bul.* 27 Sep. (Hoppe), Cling peaches are moderately plentiful. **1947** *Downtown Shop. News* (Chicago) 13 Feb. 6/4 Canned cling peaches are recommended to be included in children's menus.

clingjohn ˈklɪŋˌdʒɑn, *n.* (See quot.) *Obs.* — **1866** LOWELL *Biglow P.* 2 Ser. p. lviii, I subjoin a few phrases not in Mr. Bartlett's book which I have heard: . . . *Cling-john;* a soft cake of rye.

clingstone ˈklɪŋˌston, *n.* A peach or variety of peach in which the flesh adheres closely to the stone. In full **clingstone peach.**

1705 BEVERLEY *Virginia* IV. 78 The best sort of these [=peaches and nectarines] cling to the Stone, and will not come off clear, which they call Plum-Nectarines, and Plum-Peaches, or Cling-Stones. **1831** *Boston Transcript* 23 July 1/1 *Cling-stone* peaches were exhibited, of high flavor and sound healthy flesh. **1941** *L.A.* Map 267.

Clinker right men. Early settlers in and about Elizabethtown, N.J., who held land by virtue of Indian grants and purchases. *Obs.* — *a*1752 WM. DOUGLASS *British Settlements* II. 280 Complaints dated April 13, 1745, were filled in chancery of the Jerseys, against the Elizabeth proprietors called Clinker right men.

* **Clinton,** *n.* A species of grape, prob. so called for De Witt Clinton (1769–1828), an American statesman. *Obs.* — **1849** *Rep. Comm. Patents: Agric.* 188 We have put down both the Isabella and the Clinton in cotton-batting, and kept them fresh until February. **1868** *Rep. Comm. Agric. 1867* 155 Not even the Clinton . . . will make a good wine unless allowed to hang late.

Clintonia klɪnˈtonɪə, *n.* [f. De Witt *Clinton* (1769–1828), Amer. statesman.] A genus of plants of the lily family. Also (not *cap.*) a plant of this genus.

1843 TORREY *Flora N.Y.* II. 301 *Clintonia umbellata*. . . . Small-flowered Clintonia. . . . Jamestown, Chautauqua county. **1858** THOREAU *Maine Woods* 114 He proceeded rapidly, . . . looking to right and left on the ground, . . . now and then pointing in silence to a single drop of blood on the handsome shining leaves of the Clintonia Borealis. **1948** *Green Bay* (Wis.) *Press-Gazette* 13 July 11/4 Such wildflowers as twinflowers, clintonia, bunchberry and others grow out of the soft spongy moss.

Clintonian klɪnˈtonɪən, *n.* and *a.*

1. *n.* A political supporter of George Clinton (1739–1812), Vice-President under Jefferson and Madison, or of his nephew De Witt Clinton (1769–1828), Governor of New York. *Obs.* Cf. **anti-Clintonian.**

1792 JEFFERSON *Writings* VI. (1895) 89 The Clintonians again tell strange tales about these votes of Otsego. **1829** VAN BUREN in Mackenzie *Life* 206 The only personal objection that was made to Mr. Butler, was his conduct last winter in regard to the Clinton Bill, and I believe that every Clintonian in both houses voted against him. **1872** *Harper's Mag.* May 842/1 The Clintonians' political capital consisted of their support of an internal improvement policy.

2. *a.* Pertaining or politically loyal to De Witt Clinton. *Obs.*

1802 *Balance* (Hudson, N.Y.) 10 Aug. 250 (Th.), Parody by a Clintonian Burrite. Burrites! Clintonians! Democrats! hear me for my family. **1812** *Mass. Spy* 23 Nov. 3/3 The Madisonian ranks at Washington are thrown into utter consternation by the certain information that the Clintonian electoral ticket had prevailed in Ohio, by a majority of 547. **1882** COOPER *Amer. Pol.* I. 19 An address was issued by his friends, August 17th, 1812, which has since become known as the Clintonian platform, and his followers were known as Clintonian Democrats.

Clintonianism klɪnˈtonɪənˌɪzəm, *n.* The political philosophy of the Clintonians. *Obs.* — **1812** *Mass. Spy* 2 Dec. 3/3 Federalism, weak of itself, has called disaffection and Clintonianism to its aid. **1827** *Spirit of Seventy-Six* (Frankfort, Ky.) 12 July 3/3 Jacksonianism and Clintonianism, it intimates, compose a draught too bitter for any Republican to swallow.

clintonite ˈklɪntənaɪt, *n.* [f. De Witt *Clinton* (1769–1828).] (See quot. 1889.) — **1831** *Science* XIX. 159 Dr. Torrey presented bronzite (Clintonite) from Orange Co. **1889** *Cent.* 1048/2 clintonite. . . . A micaceous mineral of a reddish-brown to copper-red color, occurring in brittle foliated masses at Amity in New York. Also called *seybertite*.

Clinton's ditch. A derisive nickname for the Erie Canal in allusion to the prominent part De Witt Clinton took in its construction.

1835 H. C. TODD *Notes* 64 The Erie canal—here called c*anol*—was at first attempted to be laughed down, under the cognomen of The Big, and Clinton's Ditch. **1879** *Cong. Rec.* 22 Jan. 629/2 Clinton's ditch, as it used to be called, was sneered at when it was an experiment. **1945** ADAMS *Album Amer. Hist.* II. 163 'Clinton's Ditch' . . . was the derisive name applied to the dream of DeWitt Clinton—a canal to connect Lake Erie with the sea.

* **clip,** *n.* A single stroke or time, a "fell swoop." *Colloq.*

1801 BROOKS *Gleanings* 64 Twenty per Cent was struck off at one clip, from those kind of Shoes, which are mostly worn. **1853** *S. Lit. Messenger* XIX. 218/1 Why, for contempt at ten dollars a clip—that was old Ramkat's tariff. **1909** WASON *Happy Hawkins* 12 A man can drink an' fight an' carry on for a year at a clip.

As the last term in **fall, fighting clip.**

clippable ˈklɪpəbl̩, *a.* Of items in a newspaper: Suitable for being clipped out. *Rare.* — **1889** *Voice* (N.Y.) 29 Aug. A half column of short paragraphs wherein we can find nothing clippable.

* **clipper,** *n.*

1. A sailing vessel designed primarily for speed, first built at Baltimore. Cf. **Baltimore clipper.**

1823 COOPER *Pilot* I. 26, I have seen a little clipper, in disguise, outsail an old man-of-war's-man in a hard chase. **1891** *Scribner's Mag.* X. 267 In 1845 the American clippers, long, low, of good beam, . . . set a greater spread of canvas in proportion to their tonnage than any ship hitherto sailed. **1947** *Sat. Ev. Post* 84/2 From his yards came the great clippers—bigger, swifter, lovelier than any sailing vessels had ever been before.

b. Attrib. with **bark, brig, brigantine, fleet, schooner, ship.**

1849 *Pacific News* (S.F.) 2 Oct. 3/3 The new, fast sailing clipper bark Tonro, coppered and copper fastened [is for sale.] — *c*1849 JUDSON *B'hoys of N.Y.* 70 (We.), A beautiful clipper brig lay at anchor off the battery. — **1855** *N.Y. Herald* 15 Nov. 2/3 They sailed the day after their arrival in the clipper brigantine Vaquero, for Sydney. — **1948** *American Fabrics No. 6* 65/1 Her clipper fleet was developed and the greyhounds of the sea visited every Asiatic port in the quest for silk. — **1842** HALE *If, Yes, & Perhaps* 97 He immediately took measures for the charter of two little clipper schooners. — **1845** *St. Louis Reveille* 21 Mar. 2/4 The clipper ship Houqua, Captain Palmer, . . . arrived at New York on the 10th, in the remarkably short passage of 90 days from Canton. **1947** *Chi. D. Tribune* 2 Nov. 22/3 America had the carrier trade of the world in the clipper ships until the Alabama, built in England for that purpose, drove them from the sea.

Also **clipper-built,** *a.*

1834 HOFFMAN *Winter in West* (1835) II. 72 Another [section of St. Louis] will present you only with the clipper-built brick houses of the American residents,—light as a Baltimore schooner, and pert-looking as a Connecticut smack. **1873** BEADLE *Undevel. West* 70, I then observed . . . a peculiar sort of clipper-built fly. **1886** *Leslie's Mo.* XXI. 303/1 [A] more clipper-built craft never left Gloucester Harbor.

2. (See quot.) *Rare.*

1832 WATSON *Hist. Tales N.Y.* 36 Their most frequent diet was clams, called clippers.

3. In special combs.: (1) **clipper fever,** enthusiasm for building and operating fast-sailing clipper ships, esp. in the China and India trade, *obs.;* (2) **mill,** a miniature windmill in connection with a weather vane, *rare;* (3) **plow,** (see quot. 1854), *obs.;* (4) **sled,** a low-bodied coasting sled having round spring runners.

(1) **1852** MACKINNON *Atlantic Sks.* I. 63 Since the above was written, the clipper-fever in the United States is quite over; and well it may be. — (2) **1879** TAYLOR *Summer-Savory* 125 The clipper mill on the top of the woodshed that runs at the wind's will, and faces about to catch it. — (3) **1854** *S.F. Chronicle* 7 Jan. 4/5 L. E. Morgan & Co. exhibited in the Hall a most superb and highly finished clipper or prairie plow, cutting a 16-inch furrow. **1861–4** *Ill. Agric. Soc. Trans.* V. 507 With our clipper plows, two-horse cultivators and iron rollers. — (4) **1883** *Harper's Mag.* Dec. 146/2 A large . . . sled . . . twice as wide and twice as long as your clipper-sled.

As the last term in **Baltimore, California, coupon, land, opium, prairie, wire clipper.**

* **clipping,** *n.*

1. An item cut out from a newspaper or magazine. Cf. **newspaper clipping.**

1865 *Lafayette* (Ind.) *D. Courier* 27 Sep. 2/2 We give below a few clippings from our exchanges concerning the condition of the crops in the various localities. **1948** *Carpenter* May 16 A Philadelphia correspondent sent us the following clipping from the help-wanted columns of the Inquirer.

2. clipping bureau, an organization that supplies to customers clippings from newspapers and magazines. Cf. **press clipping bureau.**

1910 *Sat. Ev. Post* 30 July 6/2 The latter has been posted on Antioch affairs by the girl who runs the clipping bureau. **1948** *This Week Mag.* 14 Aug. 18/3 One of America's oldest clipping bureaus, Allen's in San Francisco, was founded by Will Clemens in 1888. Helping him get a start was his cousin Sam, who did some writing—under the name of Mark Twain.

* **clique,** *n.* A group of speculators who pool their efforts and resources to regulate the price of stocks or commodities. Also attrib. Cf. **Erie clique.**

1855 *N.Y. Herald* 5 Dec. 3/5 Thousands of shares are held by a small clique of speculators. **1867** *Comm. & Finan. Chron.* V. 588/2 On the clique stocks falling below a certain point the combination are prompt buyers. **1901** MERWIN & WEBSTER *Calumet 'K'* 285 The Clique of speculators who held the floor were buying.

***cliqued,** *a.* (See quot. 1881.) — **1881** *Bradstreet's* IV. 26 Nov. 344/1 Banks are just now in a state of extreme distrust in regard to 'pooled' or 'cliqued' stocks; that is, stocks which are mainly held by combinations of speculators. **1885** *Graceville* (Minn.) *Transcript* 3 Jan. 6/3 Indian corn has been higher, under cliqued holding of light stocks.

* **cloak,** *n.*

1. cloak fern, a small fern of the genus *Notholaena.*

1925 JEPSON *Flowering Plants Calif.* 27 N. parryi Eat. Parry Cloak Fern. **1940** JAEGER *Calif. Deserts* 163 Four species of cloak ferns occur in the shelter of rocks.

2. * **cloakroom,** in the Capitol at Washington, an anteroom not open to the public to which Senators, Congressmen, etc., may retire to leave their wraps, confer, rest, telephone, etc.

1868 ROSE *Great Country* 129 Will no voice be heard . . . given with a roar . . . and a rush to the cloak room amid the shouts and laughter of the House? **1912** NICHOLSON *Hoosier Chron.* 535 Senators who had been smoking in the cloakroom, or talking to friends outside the railing, became attentive. **1947** *Chi. D. News* 12 Dec. 18/7 The cloakrooms of Congress resounded with a lurid account of what General Eisenhower there proposed as a solution.

attrib. **1880** LAMPHERE *U.S. Govt.* 265/1 Appointed by the door-keeper: . . . pages, laborers, and cloak-room men.

As the last term in **Boston, circular, Shaker cloak.**

* **clock,** *n.* In combs.: (1) **clock factory,** a factory in which clocks are made; (2) **game,** (see quot. 1944); (3) **peddler,** one who travels about selling clocks, also **clock peddling,** *obs.;* (4) **picture,** a picture used as an ornament in the lower front of a large clock, *obs.;* (5) **reel,** a reel which gives out a loud clack or knock when a given length of yarn has been wound upon it, *obs.;* (6) **room,** the room of a house in which the clock is kept, *obs.;* (7) **watcher,** an employee who wastes time watching the clock in anticipation of quitting time, *colloq.*

(1) **1820** FLINT *Lett. from Amer.* 213 Ivory and wood clock factory, [employs] 14 [men]. **1902** *Harper's Mag.* May 991 The great centre of clock-manufacture was then in Thomaston and Bristol, Connecticut, where are still some of the largest clock-factories. — (2) **1897** *Chi. Tribune* 15 July 5/5 The bucket shops, clock games, and slot machines must go. **1944** *Lett. to Editor* 9 Dec. The 'Clock Game' was extant around and just before the year 1900. It was offered to the public by small brokerage offices with little or no reputation. It gave the public a chance to guess the price of a stock at any agreed hour, with a wager as to the accuracy of the guess. The deciding factor was the ticker tape running through at the time designated. — (3) **1833** *Trial E. K. Avery* 64 A clock pedlar took tea that night. **1853** *Harper's Mag.* VII. 708/2 He first tried clock-peddling; but his instruments . . . were returned. **1883** EGGLESTON *Hoosier School-Boy* 99 Wanderers from New England, who had grown tired of clock-peddling. — (4) **1842** MRS. KIRKLAND *Forest Life* II. xlv. 199 She lost no opportunity of instilling . . . the idea that nothing but dress was wanting to make her 'a real beauty—handsome enough for a clock-picter!'

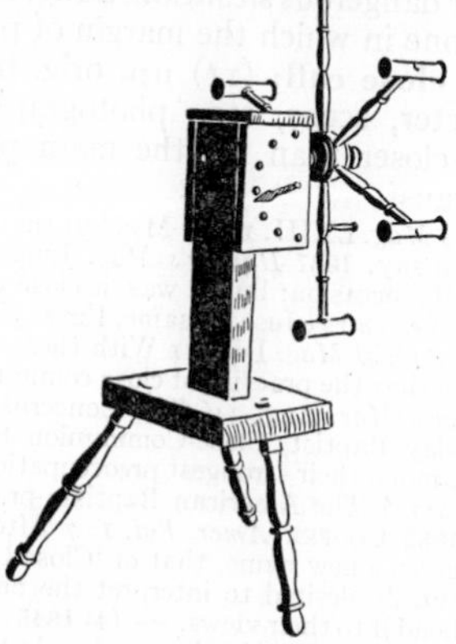

Clock reel

(5) **1843** *Lowell Offering* III. 141 Married Orlando Y. and Mary W; for which received a clock-reel, two wheel pins, and a press board. — (6) **1885** JEWETT *Marsh Island* viii. 98 Doris came with her sewing to sit . . . outside the clock-room. **1899** A. BROWN *Tiverton Tales* 209, I set down in my clock-room, about three in the arternoon, an' there I set. — (7) **1918** M. B. OWEN *Typewriting Speed* 106 Clock watchers and hurry-home people, who have both these habits to the detriment of their work. **1948** *Chi. Tribune* 4 Oct. 4/7 You weren't wrong when you told me Klinker wasn't a clock watcher.

As the last term in **banjo, concert, corner, electric, timber, time, wall-sweep, wooden, Yankee clock.**

* **clocker,** *n.* One who times, often surreptitiously, race horses in their private training runs. Cf. **railbird** (*b*).

1909 *Sat. Ev. Post* 16 Jan. 7/3 I've nosed into the paddock and made a lifetime hit with stable boys, jockeys, trainers, clockers and even owners, but every time they handed me a sure one I got burned. **1910** WILSON *Chicago Cess-Pool Infamy* 44 Three hundred dollars had been placed to win upon a 'clocker's tip' in that day's last race in Louisville. **1948** *Dly. Racing Form* 29 June 2/2 Almost all training trials come under the view of competent and impartial clockers.

clockmutch ˈklɑkmʌtʃ, *n.* Also **clapmatch.** (See quots.) *Obs.* — **1848** BARTLETT 86 Clockmutch. (Dutch, *klapmuts,* a night-cap.) A woman's cap composed of three pieces,—a straight centre one, from the forehead to the neck, with two side pieces. A New York term. *Ib.* 125 Clapmatch. . . . A kind of woman's cap.

***clod,** *n.* **1.** * **clod-breaker,** a farm implement for breaking clods. **2.** * **clod crusher,** (see quot.). Both *rare.* — (1) **1849** *Rep. Comm. Patents* 523 There is no difficulty in combining the effect of the plough, harrow and pulverizer, or clod-breaker, in the same machine. — (2) **1888–90** BARRERE-LELAND I. 256 Clod-crushers (American), an epithet used by Americans to describe the large feet which they believe to be the characteristics of Englishwomen as compared with those of their own country.

***clog,** *n.* Short for "clog dance." Also attrib. *Colloq.* — **1869** *Atlantic Mo.* July 74/1 This was, I think, the first introduction of clogs as a drawing-room entertainment. **1887** *Courier-Journal* 19 Feb. 8/1 The clog led by Mr. Willis Pickett is a novelty, and is very finely done, Mr. Pickett himself holding the championship as a clog dancer. His clog solo was much applauded.

* **close,** *a.* and *adv.*

1. Used of a *county, district,* or *parish* in which political strength is almost equally divided between or among rival parties.

1874 *Cong. Rec.* 30 Jan. 1042/1 In 1870 it [=St. Helena parish] gave 30 democratic majority. It is considered a very close parish. **1887** *Ib.* 20 Jan. App. 50/1 Mr. Goff: What do you mean by doubtful counties? Mr. Grosvenor: Close counties, like some of those in the State of my friend from West Virginia. **1904** *Forum* July 17 In the last Congressional election there were comparatively few close districts.

2. In special substantival combs.: (1) **close call,** a narrow escape, also *a close call for Sunday, colloq.;* (2) **communion,** among Baptists, participation in the Lord's Supper restricted to those of the same faith and order, to immersed members of other Protestant churches, or sometimes, to members of the same local organization, also attrib.; (3) **constructionist,** =**strict constructionist;** (4) **cut,** a way more direct than the usual one, *colloq.;* (5) **fence,** (see quot.); (6) **fit,** a crisis or pinch, *slang;* (7) **hug,** =**Indian hug,** *obs.;* (8) **papers,** *fig.* a difficult or dangerous situation, *slang, obs.;* (9) **price,** a low price or one in which the margin of profit is slight; (10) **shave,** =**close call;** (11) **up,** orig. in motion pictures a character, scene, etc., photographed with the camera much closer than for the main portion of the picture, also transf.

(1) 1881 *Harper's Mag.* LXIII. 118/1 My! but that was a close call, 's Mr. M. used to say. **1887** *Harper's Mag.* June 160/1 A sudden swoop . . . saved the occasion; but it was 'a close call' for Sunday. **1920** MULFORD *J. Nelson* 123 Just th' same, I'm sayin' we had a close call. — **(2) 1824** *Baptist Mag.* IV. 411 With these views of catholicism we do not see that the practice of close communion at all interferes. **1880** *Harper's Mag.* Aug. 346 The Concerns of the meeting-houses—Seventh-day Baptist, Close-Communion Baptist, and Adventist . . . were among their strongest preoccupations. **1883** SCHAFF *Relig. Encycl.* I. 211/1 The American Baptists practise close communion. — **(3) 1882** COOPER *Amer. Pol.* I. 7 After this the Anti-Federalists were given a new name, that of 'Close Constructionists,' because they naturally desired to interpret the new instrument in such a way as to bend it to their views. — **(4) 1845** SIMMS *Wigwam & Cabin* 2 Ser. 79, I was busy in adjusting my foot in the stirrup . . . to find my way by a close cut.

(5) 1852 G. W. L. BICKLEY *Hist. Tazewell Co., Va.* 204 The garden was about sixty yards from the house, and as no sawmills were in existence at that day in this county, slab-boards were put up in the manner called 'wattling' for palings. These were some six feet long, and made what is called a close fence. — **(6) 1884** MARK TWAIN *H. Finn* xxix. 305 Stead of being fixed so I could take my own time—and have Mary Jane at my back to save me and set me free when the close-fit come, here was nothing in the world betwixt me and sudden death. — **(7) 1828** *Yankee* May 174/3 If he [a Yankee] finds after two or three attempts that he cannot get a grab at you at close-hug or rough-and-tumble, the fight is over, and he goes off. — **(8) 1877** WRIGHT *Big Bonanza* 94 When them boys finally got convalescent and riz up and come for me, it was close papers for a time. — **(9) 1887** *Courier-Journal* 8 May 8/6 We are in the field armed to the teeth with closest prices ever given to the world.

(10) 1834 C. A. DAVIS *Lett. J. Downing* 13, I did not so much as get my feet wet when the bridge fell, though it was a close shave. **1946** *Okla. Dly.* (Norman) 22 Aug. 2/4 [The] barber had a close shave when a truck crashed the front window of his shop and rammed into the rear room. — **(11) 1913** E. P. SARGENT *Technique of Photoplay* 16 A bust is a portrait showing the head and shoulders only, but bust is more definite than close up, which is sometimes used. **1932** *Blue Valley Farmer* (Okla. City) 25 Feb. 2/4 James . . . gives us a close-up on matters political. **1946** *New Yorker* 18 May 85/2 Snap close-ups of friendly bears, deer and mountain sheep.

b. Of or pertaining to situations in baseball where it is difficult for a player to know what to do, or for an umpire to rule justly. *Colloq.*

1896 *Chi. Tribune* 2 July 8/1 Keefe worked on the base lines, and had only one close decision, which he gave in favor of Chicago. — **1912** MATHEWSON *Pitching* 174 Most clubs try to keep an umpire from feeling hostile toward the team because, even if he means to see a play right, he is likely to call a close one against his enemies, not intending to be dishonest. **1922** *Ardmore* (Okla.) *D. Press* 6 May 3/3 His size, . . . and his ability to judge close ones . . . make him an ideal leadoff man. — **1896** *Chi. Tribune* 23 Aug. 7/4 It was a close play, but Childs was out. **1948** *Norman* (Okla.) *Transcript* 1 July 6/1 He slid in safely on a close play at home after Right-fielder Fred Herford's infield out.

c. In verbal expressions: (1) **close herd,** (see quot. 1887), also transf. and as adv.; (2) **hoe,** to hand-hoe, *rare.*

(1) 1874 McCOY *Cattle* 348 Like other extensive Colorado ranchmen, he outrides the country instead of close herding his stock. **1887** *Scribner's Mag.* Oct. 508/2 A friend tells me he has heard a sheriff talk of 'close-herding' several prisoners in his charge. On the plains it means the difficult art of keeping cattle in a compact body, close together. **1947** *Time* 1 Dec. 25/3 He rode close herd on the Marshall plan from the start. — **(2) 1865** TURNER *Cotton* 51 A greater proportion of labor is bestowed on the cotton crop than any other, particularly on large plantations, where it is usual to plough four times, and close hoe at least three, and in some years oftener.

* **close,** *v.*

1. In noun combs.: (1) **close carriage,** a carriage in which the occupants are inclosed on all sides; (2) **down,** a stoppage of work in a factory, etc., cf. **2.** (1) (*c*) below; (3) **out,** an instance of closing out, as by a sale, also attrib., cf. **2.** (4) below; (4) **range,** (see quot.); (5) **sleigh,** a sleigh in which the occupants are inclosed on all sides; (6) **stove,** a stove the firebox of which is inclosed on all sides; (7) **time,** the time when certain animals cannot be taken legally, *obs.*

(1) 1845 SOL. SMITH *Theatr. Apprent.* 64 My friend came to the door, with a close carriage, into which we got. **1898** PAGE *Red Rock* 562 The next moment a close carriage, with a good pair of horses, drove quickly by them in a cloud of dust. — **(2) 1889** *Voice* (N.Y.) 5 Sep., Interfere with the unrestricted manufacturing interests of our country by forced 'close-downs,' lockouts, &c. — **(3) 1926** *Amer. Wool & Cotton Reporter* 8 July 66 At the season's close there are frequent close-outs at prices which show no relation to cost. **1945** *Ledger-News* (Antonito, Colo.) 19 July 1/2 Farm Auction close out sales are exempted from the tax imposed on other occasional sales. **1948** *Dly. Ardmoreite* (Ardmore, Okla.) 1 April 4/6 (*advt.*), Special Closeouts! On All Gifts We Think Have Been in Stock Too Long But May Be Just What You Want. — **(4) 1881** CHASE *Editor's Run* 93 Those who are able are buying land along water courses, enclosing their purchases, and as much government land back of it as they desire, with wire fences. This is 'close range.'

(5) 1767 *Mass. Gaz.* 12 Feb. 4/2 A close sleigh or booby-hutch, to go with either one or two horses. **1779** *Boston Gaz.* 13 Dec. 3/3 A second-hand Chariot with harness compleat . . . two neat close sleys. — **(6) 1775** in *N.J. Archives* 1 Ser. XXXI. 144 Manufactured at Batsto Furnace, in West New-Jersey . . . open and close stoves of different sizes. — **(7) 1878** in HUBBARD *Moosehead Lake* (1882) 186 The 'close-time' for mink, beaver, sable, otter, and fisher, is from May 1st to October 15th.

2. With adverbs in phrases: (1) * *To close down,* (*a*) to come down upon, (*b*) of night, to approach, draw on, (*c*) to stop the operation of; (2) *to close in on,* to come to grips with, *colloq.;* (3) *to close on,* in baseball, to catch, *colloq.;* (4) * *to close out,* (*a*) to sell off (goods), wind up or finish (a business, transaction, etc.), (*b*) hence *closing out sale;* (5) * *to close up,* (*a*) to cease talking, *slang,* (*b*) to finish off, wind up.

(1) (*a*) **1869** MARK TWAIN *Innocents* xxiv. 254 They have set a gunboat to watch the vessel night and day, with orders to close down on any revolutionary movement in a twinkling. (*b*) **1883** ——— *Life on Miss.* liv. 536 The night presently closed down. (*c*) **1903** *N.Y. Ev. Post* 18 Sep. 2 President Shields has issued orders to close down all of the operations of the company. — **(2) 1901** G. ADE *40 Modern Fables* 7 This is a Tall Problem for a 20-year-old Girl to close in on. — **(3) 1880** BROOKS *Fairport Nine* 184 Jake Coombs and Eph Mullett, hit high balls to Pat Adams, at third base, and he closed on them, and umpire Dunbar declared them out. — **(4)** (*a*) J. M. LETTS *California* 159 We offered him [a mule] to Mr. Priest for six dollars. . . . He offered two, at which we 'closed him out.' **1891** O'BEIRNE *Leaders Ind. Territory* 59/1 In 1879 he opened business in Audubon, Wise county, but closed out in 1883, arriving in Caddo the following year. **1917** CAHAN *Rise David Levinsky* 334 Please tell Mr. Huntington I have a job to close out, a seventeen-dollar garment for seven fifty. (*b*) **1865** *Memphis D. Argus* 19 Nov. 3/2 Best quality calicoes are 25 cents, at R. J. Dalton & Company's great closing out sale. **1877** *Deseret News* (Salt Lake City) 30 Aug. 2/5 On Tuesday, the 16th inst., Z.C.M.I. will commence their annual closing out sale of Summer Goods.

(5) (*a*) **1856** *Spirit of Times* 6 Sep. 4/1 If they didn't 'close-up' there'd be another 'clam-cart' after them. (*b*) **1898** WESTCOTT *D. Harum* 137, I guess 't won't take him long to close up his matters. **1923** R. HERRICK *Lilla* 39 The Porters, the Lawndale addition having finally been 'closed up' at a handsome profit, had planned a trip to Europe.

* **closed,** *a.* In combs.: (1) **closed gentian,** a North American gentian the flowers of which never open; (2) **season,** a season when certain kinds of game cannot legally be killed, also attrib.; (3) **shop,** a shop in which

only union members are employed, or, sometimes, one in which union members are not employed.

(1) **1857** GRAY *Botany* 346 *Gentiana Andrewsii*. . . . Closed Gentian. . . . [Grows in] moist rich soil; common, especially northward. **1942** PEATTIE *Friendly Mts.* 209, I find more of the gentians, and also of the closed gentians, in the thicket beyond. — (2) **1914** *Collier's* 10 Jan. 37/2 He wouldn't know whether there was a bounty on them or whether they came under the closed-season law. **1929** J. PARKER *Old Army* 24 There was no closed season then for game. **1948** *Green Bay* (Wis.) *Press-Gazette* 12 July 15/7 The possibility of a closed season on ducks this fall is not too remote. — (3) **1904** *N.Y. Ev. Post* 15 Aug. 1 An increase in wages, recognition of the union, and 'closed shops' are demanded. **1948** *Chi. D. News* 24 Aug. 18/3 A 'closed shop' violates the fundamental rights of the individual—his right to work wherever he pleases.

***closet,** *n.* As the last term in **cedar, gun, ice, pot, telephone closet.**

***cloth,** *n.* As the last term in **army, ax, bale, baling, breech, broad, burying, cadet, chimney, enameled, factory, file, forestry, India rubber, lodge, mummy, Negro, over, pilot, roller, Salem, slave, squaw, sweat, tow, truck, Virginia, wash cloth.**

***clothes,** *n.* In combs.: (1) **clothespin,** a forked peg or clamp used to fasten washed clothes on a line; (2) **pole,** a pole for propping up a clothesline; (3) **post,** (see quot.); (4) **room,** [cf. Du. *kleedkamer*], a room in which clothes are kept; (5) **slice,** a battling stick, *rare;* (6) **yard,** a plot of ground devoted to the drying of clothes.

(1) **1846** *Hunt's Merch. Mag.* XV. 108 Among the articles now exported largely to England, are clothes-pins. **1944** *Democrat* 29 June 3/4 Clothespins that have had the heads dipped in white paint are easily found when dropped in grass. — (2) **1865** *Atlantic Mo.* XV. 659 She never conjectures to what base uses a clothes-pole may come. — (3) **1935** BAILEY *Standard Cyclo. Horticulture* I. 652 Clothes-post. . . . A post set in the ground to support a clothes-line. — (4) **1857** VAUX *Villas* 137 In the attic . . . a space for lumber is marked on the plan; but this might be used as a clothes-room. **1865** A. D. WHITNEY *Gayworthys* xviii. 176 She vanished up the end staircase, and hid herself away in the old clothes-room.

(5) **1899** A. BROWN *Tiverton Tales* 6 With two russets for balls and the clothes-slice for a mallet . . . Della . . . played her first game [of croquet]. — (6) **1856** M. J. HOLMES *Rice Corner* vi, I suspected nothing when Sally's white dress was bleached on the grass in the clothes-yard for nearly a week. **1866** A. D. WHITNEY *L. Goldthwaite* iii, The windows looked out from one side into a village street, and from the other into stable and clothes yards! **1945** *Reader's Digest* Aug. 86 The cedar poles were in a clearing back of the clothesyard.

As the last term in **glad, meeting, old, store, Sunday-go-to-meeting clothes.**

***clothier,** *n.*

1. (See quot. 1806.) *Obs.*

1751 CHALKLEY *Scotch-Irish Settlement Va.* I. 45 Joseph Love, clothier, has leave to build a fulling mill on Roan Oak. **1806** WEBSTER 54/1 *Clothier,* one who fulls and scours cloths. **1816** PICKERING 64 Although we use *clothier* for *fuller,* yet the place, where the cloth is cleansed and dressed, is called a fulling-mill.

2. clothier general, formerly an officer in the Continental and U.S. Army, a quartermaster general. Hence **clothier's department.**

1777 *Jrnls. Cont. Congress* VIII. 426 *Resolved,* That the clothier general furnishes each non-commissioned officer and soldier . . . with the articles of cloathing enumerated by a resolution of Congress. **1778** *Ib.* X. 23 *Resolved,* That the cloathier general be directed to deliver . . . as much linen and as many blankets as can be spared. **1797** *Ann. 5th Congress* 704 All persons having unliquidated claims against the United States, pertaining to the . . . Hospital, Clothier's, or Marine Department, should exhibit particular abstracts of such claims.

As the last term in **state, sub-clothier.**

clothing store. A store in which clothing is sold.

1829 *Va. Herald* (Fredericksburg) 28 Feb. 3/1 He was then keeping a Clothing Store in Cincinnati, Ohio. **1865** *Atlantic Mo.* XV. 616 The clothing-store . . . paying so little that every tailor's working woman seeks . . . opportunity of changing her employment. **1945** *Jefferson Co. Republican* (Golden, Colo.) 26 Dec. 1/2 He worked for the Hudson's Men's Clothing Store for nine more years.

attrib. **1869** MARK TWAIN *Innocents* xxvi. 278 The clothing-store merchant wished to consume the corner-grocery man with the envy. **1940** MENCKEN *Happy Days* 101 They made no more impression upon him than if they had addressed a clothing-store dummy.

As the last term in **bed, overall clothing.**

***cloud,** *n.*

1. *fig.* The shadow of war, strife, or violence, in Indian speech or with reference to this. *Obs.*

1777 *Virginia State P.* I. 292 The Dragging Canoe in some part of the Treaty said . . . that there was a dark cloud over that country. **1778** *Ib.* I. 315 What did you understand by the Expression of the Indians at the Treaty 'that a black cloud hung over the Country they were selling said Henderson.' *Ib.,* Was the Metaphor Black Cloud ever interpreted to relate to the Cherokees' right to the soil in that Country? Answer, No.

2. cloudburst, a sudden, violent, and heavy fall of rain. [Cf. G. *Wolkenbruch.*]

[*a***1817** DWIGHT *Travels* III. 249 This deluge, which they call the bursting of a cloud, took place in Oct. 1784.] **1869** MUIR *First Summer in Sierra* (1916) 48 These floods may occur in the summer, when heavy thunder-showers, called 'cloud-bursts,' fall on wide, steeply inclined stream basins furrowed by converging channels. **1948** *Galveston* (Tex.) *News* 14 June 4/8 Seasonal thundershowers and occasional cloudbursts . . . sent small rivers surging upwards again.

***clout,** *n.* A long, hard hit in baseball. *Colloq.* — **1934** WEBSTER. **1948** *Dly. Ardmoreite* (Ardmore, Okla.) 20 July 8/4 In addition to his two circuit clouts, each with one man on base, Martin connected for a double.

***clout,** *v. tr.* In baseball, to hit (the ball). *Colloq.*

1910 *Aurora* (Ill.) *D. Beacon* 8 Sep. 4/3 By the by, the Tigers can certainly clout the ball. **1948** *Gainesville* (Tex.) *D. Register* 2 July 6/3 Ted Williams . . . may make good his prediction, before the season got under way, that he'd clout .400 or better this year.

Hence ***clouter,** *n.*

1914 *Chi. Tribune* 6 Aug. 15/1 Eddie staved off the famous clouters by means of his cunning and his spit ball. **1946** *Senior Scholastic* 15 April 34/2 The Giants own a raft of clouters.

clove klov, *n. local.* [Du. *klove, kloof,* in same sense.] A ravine or valley, chiefly in place-names.

1777 *N.J. Archives* 2 Ser. I. 433 The other Part [of Washington's army is] to be commanded by Mr. Green, at the Clove, and Parts adjacent. **1828** WEBSTER, . . . *Clove,* . . . This word, though properly an appellative, is not often used as such in English; but it is appropriated to particular places, that are real clefts, or which appear as such; as the Clove of Kaaterskill, in the state of New-York, and the Stony Clove. It is properly a Dutch word. **1869** A. B. STREET *Indian Pass* 136 Shortly, I found myself entering the 'Whiteface Clove.' **1930** *Amer. Sp.* V. 158 *Clove,* the usual Dutch word for *ravine* or *valley;* it has only survived in a few cases. There are a number in the Catskills.

attrib. **1821** *Niles' Reg.* XXI. 29 The Falls [in the Catskill Mts.], the Clove Passage, the view from the Pine Orchard, . . . are objects worthy of regard. **1884** ROOSEVELT *Amer. Backlogs* 16 Twenty long miles lay between us and our destination, including . . . passing through a steep and precipitous canyon, or 'clove-road' as it was called in the vernacular. **1902** TOMPKINS *Hist. Rec. Rock. Co., N.Y.* 86 A highway through the Highlands from Haverstraw to the Skunemunk clove road.

clove currant. *local.* = **buffalo currant.** — **1892** *Amer. Folk-Lore* V. 96 *Ribes aureum*. . . . Clove currant. Cambridge, Mass.

***clover,** *n.* In combs. now obs.: (1) **clover eater,** a nickname for a Virginian; (2) **huller,** a machine for freeing clover seed from the hull; (3) **lick,** ?a salt lick where wild clover abounds; (4) **tea,** (see quot.).

(1) **1869** *Overland Mo.* III. 129 For no particular reason that I am aware of, a Virginian is styled a 'Clover-eater.' — (2) **1841** C. CIST *Cincinnati (advt.),* Agricultural Machinery, . . . including . . . Clover Hullers. **1854** *Pa. Agric. Rep.* 80 William Kirkpatrick, Lancaster city . . . 1 clover huller and cleaner. — (3) **1746** in *Amer. Sp.* XV. 280/2 To a spanish oak a Hickory and a Black Oak on the side of a Ridge near the Clover Lick. **1786** *Ib.,* Sixty acres . . . on the North fork of the South branch of Potowmack near the great Clover lick. — (4) **1841** CIST *Cincinnati* 166 Clover tea, . . . under the name of Pouchong, &c. is now the fashionable article of modern times.

As the last term in **bear, bird foot, Bokhara, broom, buffalo, bur, bush, Chilian, Florida, French, Japan, Kentucky, Mexican, owl's, pin, prairie, rabbit-foot, redtop, sour, Spanish, spiked, stone, trailing, winter clover.**

Clowwewalla ˈklowəˌwɑlə, *n.* [Native word of unknown significance.] (See quot. 1907.) — **1838** PARKER *Exploring Tour* 162 We arrived at the falls of the Willamette at one o'clock in the afternoon and hired eight Clough-e-wall-hah Indians to carry the canoe by the falls. **1907** HODGE *Amer. Indians* I. 313/1 Clowwewalla. A branch of the Chinookan family formerly residing at the falls of Willamette r., Oreg. They are said to have been originally a large and important tribe, but after the epidemic of 1829 were greatly reduced in numbers.

***club,** *n.*

1. The bill for the beverages of a meal, as distinct from the food. *Obs.*

1793 *Mass. H.S. Coll.* 3 Ser. V. 111 Care is also taken to keep out of your way small beer and cider, so that your club at dinner amounts to more than the dinner itself. **1799** Brown *A. Mervyn* iii, 'Tis our custom to charge dinner and club; but, as you drank nothing, we'll let the club go.

2. Short for "baseball club."

1855 *N.Y. Herald* 30 Nov. 1/2 All the clubs were out yesterday, and in spite of the cold played their games out. **1870** *Cin. Commercial* 13 May 5/1 The Red Stockings . . . have about done with such effete clubs as they met on their Southern tour, and must now prepare to meet men of bone and muscle. **1944** *Chi. D. News* 21 Oct. 11/1 The club . . . has been given a three-year pact.

3. In combs.: (1) **club car,** (see quots.); (2) **raiser,** one who induces a group or club to subscribe to a newspaper or magazine; (3) **sandwich,** a sandwich of many ingredients as chicken, lettuce, tomato, mayonnaise, etc., also transf.; (4) **shoe,** a coarse, heavy shoe, *rare;* (5) **skates,** skates that may be fastened to ordinary shoes; (6) **squash,** ?a kind or variety of squash suggestive of a club, *obs.;* (7) **tail,** *local* (see quot.); (8) **wheat,** (see quot. 1909); (9) **woman,** a woman who is a member of a club, esp. one active in club work, also transf.

(1) **1895** Wait *Car-Builder's Dict.* 31 Club car. . . . A buffet-parlor car built and owned by railroad companies but kept expressly as a private car for members of a club, which members live in the suburbs of a large city. **1948** *New Yorker* 25 Sep. 27/1 The new Twentieth Century club car has a shower, a barber, a valet, a service bar, card tables, a radio telephone, which is operative over the four hundred and thirty-five miles between New York and Buffalo, and a secretary, who will take dictation at no extra cost. — (2) **1872** *Newton Kansan* 26 Sep. 4/5 If agents and club-raisers want to make it 'pay,' try this. **1887** *Courier-Journal* 2 Feb. 3/6 Weekly, to clubs of eight, with extra copy to club-raiser (nine copies one year) . . . $8.00. — (3) **1925** Witwer *Roughly Speaking* 168 He put the coffee down on a bench and with great care selected a club sandwich for me and one for himself. **1945** *New Yorker* 25 Aug. 14 This is a club-sandwich sort of story, combining a hotel, a secretary, and an electric fan. — (4) **1830** Royall *Lett. from Ala.* 175 They come running into the Rotunda with their muddy club shoes.

(5) **1868** *Mich. Agric. Rep.* VII. 356 E. T. Barnum, Detroit, [exhibited a] display of club skates. **1887** *Courier-Journal* 5 Jan. 6/3 As to the ponds, they are filled with people from the type of grace and beauty displayed in the cut above, fitted out with seal-skin cap and the latest club skates, to the urchin who ties his runners on with a string. — (6) **1817–8** Eaton *Botany* (1822) 257 *Cucurbita verrucosa,* club squash. E[xotic]. **1854** *Pa. Agric. Rep.* 206 David S. Hoffman, for one club squash. — (7) **1842** *Nat. Hist. N.Y., Zoology* IV. 257 The American Shad. *Alosa praestabilis.* . . . On the coast of Carolina, the fatter ones have the tail swollen, and are called Club-tails. — (8) **1849** Emmons *Agric. N.Y.* II. 142 Club wheat, Pennsylvania wheat. . . . Heads short. **1909** *Cent. Supp.* 1442/2 Club wheat, a group of wheats (sometimes distinguished as *Triticum compactum*) characterized by a short, dense head and short, stiff straw: also called *square-head wheat* from the shape of the ear. — (9) **1895** Susan Hale *Lett.* 294 She . . . is a 'club-woman,'—and she early secured me to 'attend a meeting' of her club. **1944** *Amer. Poetry Mag.* XXV. 18 *Though I Am Blind* (from the Kansas Clubwoman).

As the last term in **Ananias, ball, baseball, bean, booster, bully, calico, Clay, coon, country, dancing, devil('s), eating, Empire, fire, Four H, German, golden, home, hunt, Kiwanis, lynch, mudsill, night, OK, pig, press, reform, rifle, Rotary, Saber, sand, sappy, spelling, Toe, war, ward, watch club.**

clubbing ˈklʌbɪŋ, *n.* Subscription to a periodical by each of a group of people, or to a group of magazines by a single subscriber, at a reduced rate. Also attrib.

1856 Derby *Phoenixiana* 123 Inducements For Clubbing. Twenty copies furnished for one year, for fifty cents. **1880** *Boston Journal Chem.* (*O.E.D.*), The clubbing price of any American or foreign periodical not on the list will be furnished on application. **1907** *Pearson's Mag.* Jan. (Contents-page), The face value of a subscription bill may be applied to any combination or clubbing offer advertised.

* **clump,** *n.*

1. A heavy, cumbrous ship or vessel. Hence **clump-built.** Also attrib. *Obs.*

1808 *Columbian Centinel* 17 Feb. 3/1 A clump black looking brig, ashore, with her foremast gone, was seen 9th inst. **1809** Irving *Knickerb.* VI. v, The mariners are busily prepared, hoisting the sails of yon top sail schooner, and those two clump built Albany sloops. **1830** S. Breck in *Recollections* 139 Our brig was a clump, and made but small way.

2. A group *of* houses.

1870 Hawthorne *Eng. Note-Books* I. 121 The clump of village houses. **1898** Page *Red Rock* 519 The two rescuers . . . dismounted behind a clump of buildings.

clumsy-cleat ˈklʌmzɪˈklit, *n.* (See quot.) — **1874** C. M. Scammon *Marine Mammals* 224 About three feet from the stern is the 'clumsy-cleat,' a stout thwart with a rounded notch on the after side, in which the officer or boat-steerer braces himself by one leg against the violent motion of the boat, caused by . . . the efforts of the whale.

* **cluster,** *a.* With *diamond, pin, ring,* in sense: Having precious stones set in a cluster.

1872 Mark Twain *Roughing It* xlviii. 339 The cheapest and easiest way to become an influential man . . . was to stand behind a bar, wear a cluster-diamond pin, and sell whisky. **1873** Mark Twain & Warner *Gilded Age* xxxiii. 301 He wore a diamond cluster-pin and he parted his hair behind. *a***1906** O. Henry *Trimmed Lamp,* 173 She wore a cluster ring of huge imitation rubies. **1945** *Democrat* 29 March 4/2 Lost—Diamond cluster ring, one big stone surrounded by 12 small ones.

clutter-buck, *n.* A term of derision or contempt. *Colloq.* — **1887** *Courier-Journal* 24 Jan. 4/3 The difference between a wide-awake city at the head of the procession and a sleepy-headed old clutter buck which stumbles along at the tail end.

cluttery ˈklʌtərɪ, *a.* Somewhat cluttered. *Rare.* — **1904** Susan Hale *Lett.* 388 At Bowbridge we rested the horses in a cluttery little town.

co-, see **ca-.**

* **coach,** *n.*

1. A railroad passenger car, often a day coach as opposed to a sleeper or Pullman.

1832 *Amer. R.R. Jrnl.* I. 193/3 Arrived 7 coaches, with 77 passengers. **1856** *N.Y. Herald* 11 Jan. 1/3 My train was composed of four coaches, two baggage cars and two engines. **1948** *Chi. D. News* 17 Aug. 1/3 Three coaches, three sleepers and a diner left the tracks.

2. (See quots.)

1874 Scammon *Marine Mammals* 75 Next to and above the bone of the upper jaw [of a whale] (which is termed the 'coach' or 'sleigh'). **1935** Mitchell *America* 41 The Fifth Avenue coach (euphemism for bus) costs a dime if you go one block only and a dime if you go all the way.

3. In combs.: (1) **coach car,** a railway coach, *rare;* (2) * **house,** (see quot.), *obs.;* (3) **station,** *W.* a regular stopping place for a stagecoach, *obs.;* (4) * **whip,** see as a main entry.

(1) **1873** *Newton Kansan* 27 Feb. 3/2 About twenty couple . . . chartered a coach car and special engine and attended Grand Masonic and Odd Fellows ball. — (2) **1838** Cooper *Homeward Bound* 12 Mr. Effingham led his daughter into the hurricane-house—or, as the packet-men quaintly term it, the coach-house. — (3) **1881** *Rocky Mt. Sk.* in *Sunday at Home* Sep. 567/2 Asking . . . [a minister to] go to a coach station some fifteen miles over the mountains, and hold a preaching service.

As the last term in **accommodation, baby, baggage, day, drawing room, head, hotel, mail, old family, overland, palace, sleeping, stage, treasure, Troy coach.**

coachee ˌkoˈtʃi, *n.* A surrey-like pleasure carriage, usu. for four persons, somewhat longer and of lighter construction than a coach, and having a top. Now *hist.*

1790 *Pa. Packet* 11 Oct. 4/2 A light Waggon or Cochee to be sold. Very elegant, and as good as new. **1832** Va. Act in *Statutes at Large* IV. 657 For every chariot, coach, coachee, stage, or phaeton with two horses, [a toll of] twelve and a half cents [shall be collected]. **1948** Rittenhouse *Amer. Horse-Drawn Vehicles* 37 Coachee. This example, shown in the U.S. National Museum, had C-springs made of hickory.

* **coachwhip,** *n.*

1. Any one of various long, slender, harmless snakes found in the southern states. In full **coachwhip snake.**

1736 Mortimer in *Phil. Trans.* XXXIX. 256 The Coach-whip Snake; so called from its being very long and slender like a Coach-whip. **1827** Williams *West Florida* 29 The coach-whip is most frequently seen in the pine barrens; he resembles a coach-whip, with a black handle; but is very innocent. **1943** *Democrat* 12 Aug. 2/2 He was a coach-whip, which measured 72 inches in length.

2. = **ocotillo.** In full **coachwhip cactus.**

1913 Wooton *Trees & Shrubs N.M.* 125 The plant is sometimes called Coach Whip Cactus, but this is a very decided misnomer, because the plant is in no way related to the cacti. **1931** Dayton *Western Browse Plants* 115 Only one species of this family occurs in the United States, viz., ocotillo (*Fouquieria splendens*), frequently called candlewood and coachwhip. **1939** Pickwell *Deserts* 65/2 One of the commonest is 'candlewood,' the name of the family; another is 'coachwhip.'

coakum ˈkokəm, *n.* Also **cocum.** [App. a variant of **skoke,** *n.*[1]] = **pokeweed.** — **1814** Bigelow *Florula Bostoniensis* 112 Poke. Cocum. . . . One of the most common and conspicuous plants in waste grounds, by road sides, &c. **1896** *Garden & Forest* IX. 262/2 Coakum, . . . with its variants Cocum and Cunicum, is a word of Indian (Tarascan) origin, but not of Indian application. . . . The colonists of Massachusetts . . . formed the word through a corruption of Mechoacan.

*__coal__, *n.* In combs.: (1) **coal bank,** an exposed seam of coal; (2) **baron,** the owner of a rich coal mine or mines; (3) ***breaker,** "A building containing the machinery for breaking coal with toothed rolls, sizing it with sieves, and cleaning it for market" (Raymond, *Mining Glossary*); (4) **camp,** the quarters or place occupied by men engaged in mining coal; (5) **car,** a car designed to carry coal, esp. a railway car for this purpose; (6) **claim,** a piece of land having, or thought to have, valuable coal deposits on it, and legally claimed by one seeking to own it; (7) **county,** a county in which the chief industry is mining coal; (8) **digging(s),** a place where coal is or may be dug;

Coachee (*c*1800)

(9) **dump,** a place where coal is dumped for future use; (10) **elevator,** a building in which coal is raised and stored preparatory to loading on cars, ships, etc.; (11) **flat,** a coal barge; (12) **flour,** =**cold flour;** (13) **handler,** one who loads or unloads coal; (14) **hill,** a hill composed of or containing coal; (15) ***hole,** see as a main entry; (16) **king,** =**coal baron;** (17) **land,** land upon which there are coal deposits; (18) **lateral,** ?a railroad that parallels a coal road; (19) **oil,** see as a main entry; (20) **passer,** *naut.* one who brings coal from the bunkers to the furnaces; (21) ***pit,** (see quot.), *rare;* (22) **prospector,** one who prospects or seeks for evidence of coal; (23) **road,** see as a main entry; (24) **tipple,** =**tipple;** (25) **train,** a train loaded with coal.

(1) **1805** COLLINS *Kentucky* I. 408 A coal bank is within three hundred yards. There are also five valuable coal banks near the river. **1886** *Harper's Mag.* June 62/2 A gentleman who wanted a coal bank opened engaged for the work a man passing along the road. — (2) **1887** GLADDEN *Applied Christianity* 18 The coal barons must not be permitted to enrich themselves by compelling the miners to starve at one end of their lines and the operatives to freeze at the other. **1945** *Nation* 31 March 353/1 He recites his picturesque polemics against the coal barons. — (3) **1863** *Harper's Mag.* Sep. 459/2 A tall slender structure is erected, usually called a 'coal breaker.' **1889** *Cent.* 1068/1 Coal-breakers were first used in the Pennsylvania anthracite regions in 1843. — (4) **1917** SINCLAIR *King Coal* 3 A number of branch railroads ran up into the canyons, feeding the coal-camps.

(5) **1858** *Pa. R.R. Ann. Rep.* 14 The rolling stock . . . consisted . . . of . . . 92 Four-wheeled Coal cars. **1906** LYNDE *Quickening* 99 He . . . had handled the levers of the great steam-hoist that shot the coal-cars from the mine to the coal-yard bins. — (6) **1891** O'BEIRNE *Leaders Ind. Territory* 75/2 He has also a good coal claim. — (7) **1917** SINCLAIR *King Coal* 116 We'll show 'em a trick from the coal-counties! — (8) **1882** WORTHEN *Econ. Geol. Ill.* II. 173 Shelton's coal-digging . . . supplies the country for miles around with its blacksmith coal. **1918** VISHER *So. Dakota* 72 Vegetation in such zones is fairly conspicuous, and has been used often in locating 'coal diggings.' — (9) **1882** *Nation* 21 Dec. 526/3 There are great new piers, storehouses, and coal-dumps at Newport News.

(10) **1887** *Courier-Journal* 6 May 6/4 An ordinance was passed granting to the Winefrede Coal Company the right to erect a coal elevator on a piece of land belonging to the city. **1895** *N.Y. Dramatic News* 16 Nov. 4/4 Speedy dived off a South Boston coal elevator Monday. — (11) **1851** *Knickerb.* XXXVII. 182 The river is dark as night; but we see, every now and then, 'broad-horns' and coal-flats, with a twinkling light. **1887** *Courier-Journal* 1 May 14/6 The current was so swift at this point that their boat was thrown in between two coal-flats, and while trying to get clear of them, the skiff was upset. — (12) **1860** CLAIBORNE *Sam Dale* ii. 36 Our accoutrements were a 'coonskin cap, bearskin vest, short hunting-shirt, . . . a wallet for parched corn, coal flour or other chance provisions. **1942** in *Amer. Sp.* XIX. 71 'And he'd look for other powerful, simple food,' Mr. Travis goes on, 'such as *rockahominy*, or *pinole* or *coal-flour.* Under whatever name, it's corn, parched in clean ashes until it bursts, then sifted and blown clean and pounded to a coarse flour. — (13) **1887** *Courier-Journal* 31 Jan 1/7 Matters were comparatively quiet among the striking coal-handlers. **1888** *Nation* 12 Jan. 22/1 There had been a similar difficulty brewing for some time among the coal-handlers at Port Richmond. — (14) **1781–2** JEFFERSON *Notes Va.* (1788) 27 Another coal-hill on the Pike run of Monongahela has been a-fire ten years; yet it has burnt away about twenty yards only. **1891** *Cent. Mag.* March 738 This is the marsh and that is the coal hill.

(16) **1887** *Courier-Journal* 20 Jan. 4/3 If the correspondent will look around Washington, . . . he will find plenty of kings—lumber kings, coal kings, iron kings, etc. **1893** M. HOWE *Honor* 166 The Earl of Blankshire . . . asks to have the famous coal king pointed out. — (17) **1750** WALKER *Journal* 21 June, Deer are very scarce on the Coal Land. **1917** *Cyclo. Amer. Govt.* I. 299 The first act specifically dealing with coal lands in the public domain was that of July 1, 1864, which fixed the minimum price at $20.00 an acre. — (18) **1878** PINKERTON *Strikers* 318 All the coal shipped . . . also by the 'coal laterals,' is forwarded through Reading to the great markets of the East beyond.

(20) **1866** W. DAVIDGE *Footlight Flashes* 123 He was once a coal passer in 'the Cunard service,' but [was] dispensed with by the company for idleness and dissipation. **1887** *Courier-Journal* 15 Feb. 2/5 An attempt to cause trouble among the firemen and coal-passers on some of the coastwise lines . . . proved a failure. — (21) **1828** *Yankee* July 227/1 Then they all repair to the house, or the refreshment is brought out to them, where a motherly quantity of lusty pumpkin and coalpit or two-story apple platter pies are provided. — (22) **1888** LEE *Plains to Peaks* 59 An old coal prospector says the outcroppings of the veins extend across the whole of Garfield County and into Utah. — (24) **1894** *Current Hist.* IV. 138 The excited mob burned coal cars and coal tipples. **1931** *Randolph Enterprise* (Elkins, W.Va.) 23 April 1/4 The State Federation of Womans Clubs met with an accident at the coal tipple in Harding.

(25) **1861** *Chi. Tribune* 26 May 1/6 Governor Letcher has detained the coal trains and hands belonging to them. **1885** *Cent. Mag.* XXX. 285/2 These coal trains passed Harper's Ferry at all hours.

As the last term in **block, bony, buckwheat, chestnut, egg, English, lump, mesquite, pea, peach orchard, Pennsylvania bituminous, Pittsburgh, prairie, rock, steamboat, Virginia coal.**

*__coalers__, *n. pl.* Shares of stock in coal-carrying railroads. *Colloq.* — **1892** *Daily News* 16 Feb. 6/6 Readings and other stocks reacted under realizations, but 'coalers' then gradually lost their prominence. **1909** *Daily Chron.* 17 April 2/1 Coalers were again the best stocks in the Yankee market.

*__coalhole__, *n.*

1. A hole in a sidewalk, covered by a lid, leading into a coalbin or coal cellar.

1854 SHILLABER *Mrs. Partington* 56 Keep part of an eye directed to earth, and avoid the coal-holes and cellar-ways that are open for your unwary feet. **1895** *N.Y. Dramatic News* 23 Nov. 4/3 Some of the dramatis personæ disappear as quickly as if they had fallen through a coal hole.

b. A jail or prison. *Slang. Obs.*

1835 *Vade Mecum* (Phila.) 14 Mar. 3/7 Not so fast—You're cotched, and must toddle along to the coal hole—so come along.

2. (See quot. 1865.) Also attrib. *Obs.*

1863 *Harper's Mag.* July 282/2 The 'coal-hole' gentry were bulling and bearing the 'leading fancy'' a day or two ago. **1865** *Harper's Mag.* April 621/1 At that time dealings in gold were confined to the Board of Brokers and the outside Board, popularly known, from the dinginess of its apartments, as the 'Coal-hole.'

*__coaling__, *n.* A place where charcoal is burned. *Rare.* — **1905** VALENTINE *H. Sandwith* 268 Dave . . . drove off with him as far as Custard's, a lonely inn not far from the coalings.

coal oil.

1. Petroleum or a refined oil, esp. kerosene.

1858 *Rep. Comm. Patents* I. 126 This lamp . . . is more especially designed for burning coal oil and similar substances that are rich in carbon. *c*__1908__ F. M. CANTON *Frontier Trails* 166 Even our coal oil would freeze partially. **1946** WILSON *Fidelity* 19, I drew molasses or vinegar or coal-oil from the barrels in the side room.

b. coal oil lamp, a lamp designed to burn coal oil.

1858 *U.S. Patent* 25 May, Coal oil and other lamps. **1947** *Southwestern Jrnl.* Fall 33 The old coal-oil lamps were replaced by electric wiring and incandescent lights.

2. Coal Oil Johnny, Tommy, (see quots.). *Colloq.*

1877 *Alta California* (S.F.) 13 May. 1/2 Clemens was by no means a Coal Oil Tommy—he drank for the pure and unadulterated love of the ardent. **1902** McKee *Land of Nome* 195 Two very small and very light-draft stern-wheelers, referred to as 'coal-oil Johnnies,' plied intermittently between White Mountain and Council, as the condition of the streams allowed. **1943** Crow *Amer. Customer* 168 'Coal Oil Johnny,' a figure who was rich today, broke tomorrow, and rich again next day, became a favorite character.

coal road. A railroad engaged chiefly in transporting coal. Also a railroad on which coal-burning locomotives are used.

1887 *Courier-Journal* 8 Jan. 4/1 In the last sixteen years the combination coal roads have sustained the rate of transportation at 1¾ cents per ton per mile. **1903** *Cin. Enquirer* 2 Jan. 1/4 If the coal roads would compel all independent mining companies to live up to their contracts and would take more than half their output to be sold at $5 a ton at tidewater, I have no doubt prices would be lower. **1947** *Time* 29 Dec. 56/2 Though diesels comprise only 10% of all locomotives, they have already begun to invade coal roads like the Pennsylvania.

∗ **coarse,** *a.*

1. coarse gold, *W.* gold in large grains as distinguished from gold dust. Also **coarse-quartz gold.**

1848 Mason in Bryant *California* App. 458 In the bed of small streams or ravines, now dry, a great deal of coarse gold has been found. **1882** C. King *Rep. Prec. Metals* 79 The gold is a coarse-quartz gold, very little washed, and often connected with its original quartz matrix. The sources from which this quartz comes are evidently ledges in the immediate vicinity. **1947** *Beaver* June 11/1 They had come out the year before, bringing with them coarse gold from somewhere in that vast country—perhaps from the Flat River.

2. coarse hand, a large, clumsy kind of handwriting. *Colloq.*

1845 Kirkland *Western Clearings* 154 'What should I want coarse-hand for?' said the disciple [in penmanship] with great contempt. **1884** Mark Twain *H. Finn.* xviii. 169 She asked me if I could read writing, and I told her 'no, only coarse-hand.'

∗ **coast,** *n.*

1. A slope down which one may coast on a sled; also, an act of sliding or gliding down.

1775 *Mass. Hist. Soc. Proc.* VIII. 398–9 Some of our school lads—who as formerly in this season improv'd the Coast from Sherburn's hill down to School street. General Haldimand, improving the house that belongs to Old Cook, his servant took it upon him to cut up their coast and fling ashes upon it. **1866** *Harper's Mag.* Feb. 355/2 She . . . watched his first successful coast down the street on his new sled. **1897** *Outing* Feb. 461/1 The road outside the town afforded a most delightful coast, and down we flew [on bicycles] without any exertion.

2. The land bordering immediately upon the lower Mississippi River, app. short for **German Coast.** *Obs.* Cf. ∗ **coast,** *v.* **2.**

1814 Brackenridge *Views La.* 175 The dwellings on the Coast are generally frame, of one story in height. The Coast may be said to begin at Pointe Coupée. From this to La Fourche, two-thirds of the banks are perfectly cleared. **1835** Ingraham *South-West* II. 24 *note.* The banks of the Mississippi are termed 'the coast' as far up the river as Baton Rouge. **1892** Duval *Early Times in Tex.* 15 The next day we came to the 'coast,' a strip of country so called, extending along the river for more than a hundred miles above the city of New Orelans.

attrib. **1851** Hall *Manhattaner* 124 The shadows of the dancers and masquers at that 'coast ball,' will be among my most pleasurable reminiscences of the South. **1851** Cist *Cincinnati* 282 Flat-boats . . . take down more or less bacon for the coast trade. **1887** *Cent. Mag.* March 673/1 There would not be . . . so many strapping youths sent, all unlettered, to the sugar-kettles of the coast plantations.

b. (See quots.)

1852 Stansbury *Gt. Salt Lake* 29 A range of small hills of a sandy reddish clay, with a sharp outline toward the river, forming the 'coast of the Nebraska.' **1867** J. Meline *Santa Fe & Back* 18 It is the summit of the dunes or sand-hills. . . . These sand-hills form a line of bluffs sometimes called 'Coast of the Nebraska.'

3. Short for: **a. Barbary Coast. b. Pacific Coast.**

(a) 1880 Edmund Leathes *Actor Abroad* 173 During my sojourn in the city [San Francisco], and years previous to it, any one who was sufficiently daring to approach the vicinity of the 'Coast' between midnight and daylight might constantly hear the pop of the revolver. — **(b) 1866** *Dly. Morning Chronicle* (Wash., D.C.) 5 Feb. 1/1 Oregon is the land of pretty girls and big red apples. . . . there are enough around to supply the whole coast. **1947** *Chi. Sun* (Book Week) 13 July 2/2 He was . . . defeated, it is true, but a big figure on the Coast.

4. In special combs.: (1) **coast fever,** a fever that prevails along a coast (see also quot. 1856); (2) **fox,** a small gray fox, weighing about four and a half pounds, found on San Miguel and Santa Barbara Islands, Calif.; (3) **gunner,** one who shoots birds along a coast; (4) **live oak,** the California live oak; (5) **Coast Range,** a range of mountains along the Pacific Coast of the U.S.; (6) **states,** states which border on the coast of the Atlantic or the Gulf of Mexico; (7) **survey,** see as a main entry; (8) **surveying,** *a.* engaged in a coast survey.

(1) 1841 Dana *Two Years* 247 A captain . . . murdered a lad from Boston who went out with him before the mast to Sumatra, by keeping him hard at work while ill of the coast fever, and obliging him to sleep in the close steerage. (The same captain has since died of the same fever on the same coast.) **1856** Olmsted *Slave States* 200 So among sailors and soldiers, when men suddenly find themselves ill and unable to do their duty in times of peculiar danger, or when unusual labor is required, they are humorously said to be suffering under an attack of the powder-fever, the cape-fever, the ice-fever, the coast-fever, or the reefing-fever. — **(2) 1870** *Amer. Naturalist* III. 186 The Coast Fox (*Vulpes littoralis*), if really distinct from the gray, does not occur northward. **1890** *Cent.* 2355/2 [The] genus *Urocyon* . . . , to which the coast-fox of California (*U. littoralis*) also belongs. — **(3) 1874** Long *Wild-Fowl* 63 Coot are uncommonly foolish ducks, so much so that 'silly as a coot' has become a frequent expression of the coast-gunners when speaking of a light-headed or tipsy person. — **(4) 1884** Sargent *Rep. Forests* 147 Enceno. Coast Live Oak. **1916** *Iowa Acad. Sci. Proc.* XXIII. 500 Coast Live Oak [is], . . . a tree sometimes seventy feet high with a short trunk and spreading branches.

(5) 1844 Frémont *Exped.* 252 The Indians . . . make frequent descents upon the settlements west of the Coast Range. **1948** *Sierra Club Bul.* Mar. 11 In parts of the Coast Ranges, the abundance of quail is determined by summer water supply. — **(6) 1885** *Cent. Mag.* April 955/1 The 'black belt' thus takes in all the Coast States from the Potomac to the Mississippi, and Louisiana beyond. — **(8) 1852** *Harper's Mag.* VI. 121 The Coast Surveying party continues its operations.

b. In phrases: (1) *On the coast,* (see quots.); (2) *coast to coast,* from the Atlantic to the Pacific Coast.

(1) 1848 Mitchell *Nantucketisms* 40 'On the coast.' Near. **1859** Bartlett 303 *On the coast,* near, close at hand. A nautical expression, in common use in Nantucket. **1871** De Vere 341 A gallant lover will assure his lady-love that if she will only fix the day, 'he'll be sure to be on the coast with the parson.'

(2) 1911 *Chi. D. News* 23 Sep. 1/1 Aviator Robert G. Fowler, coast to coast aviator . . . resumed his flight at 6:43 a.m. to-day. **1926** *Collier's* 19 June 5/3 I've already made arrangements for my future, just in case, being president of 'Ye Tiffin Shoppe, Inc.'—a coast-to-coast chain of nobby tea parlors. **1947** *Time* 19 May 68/2 Her research project turned into a coast-to-coast lecture tour, with radio dates and extra speeches thrown in.

As the last term in **Barbary, German, Gold, Golden, Pacific, sugar, West Coast.**

∗ **coast,** *v.*

1. *intr.* To glide down a snow-covered slope on a sled.

1836 *Boston Pearl* 9 Jan. (Th.), Skate, if you like; 'coast,' if you are boy enough. **1898** *N. Eng. Mag.* June 455/1 How well do I remember how we boys used to coast down this hill in the full of the moon. **1947** *Chi. D. News* 2 Jan. 1/4 (*heading*), Coasts Despite Warning, Is Killed.

b. (See quot.)

1889 *Amer. Folk-Lore* II. March 64 *Coast,* . . . the word was common in my boyhood,—passed in Wayne and neighboring counties of New York State,—though the sense was usually the riding over fences, etc., upon the hard crust formed upon the surface of snow.

c. To glide by momentum, as on a bicycle or in an automobile. Said also of birds on the wing. Also fig.

1889 *Cent.* 1070/2. **1904** *Sci. Amer. Supp.* LVII. 23663/3 When the wings are motionless, the great birds are 'coasting.' . . . That coasting in the air . . . is possible is readily proved. **1948** *Dallas Morning News* 2 May 11. 1/4 From then on it was no contest. He coasted home.

2. (See quot.) Cf. ∗ **coast,** *n.* **2.**

1894 Eggleston in *Cent. Mag.* XLVII. 856 To 'coast' in flat-boatman's phrase is to peddle a cargo to the French planters on the lower Mississippi.

∗ **coastal,** *a.* **coastal marsh, plain,** (see quots.). — **1900** *Amer. Geog. Soc.* XXXII. 34 Coastal marsh: One which borders a seacoast and is usually formed under the projection of a barrier beach. *Ib.*,

Coastal plain: Any plain which has its margin on the shore of a large body of water.

***coaster,** *n.*

1. One who coasts, also a sled used for coasting.

1881 *Our Little Ones* 72 Tomorrow the hills All over the town Will be lively with coasters That race up and down. **1888** *Battle Creek Moon* 2 Jan., The Deadly Coaster. Pittsburgh, Pa. . . . A bob-sled on which a party of half a dozen young men were coasting struck a carriage. **1911** White *Bobby Orde* 195 The centre of the street was entirely given over to the coasters darting down. **1943** M. Flavin *Journ. in the Dark* 17 Tom had a coaster—a long, low, sleek one, with shiny runners anchored to the frame.

2. A footrest on a bicycle for use in coasting.

1897 *Outing* Feb. 463/2 Having gleefully perched my feet up on the coasters, I . . . shot forward like an arrow. **1902** *Sears Cat.* (ed. 112) 356/1 Adjustable Foot Rests or Coasters.

b. coaster brake, a brake on a bicycle which is applied by backward pressure on the pedals and released when the pedals are stationary, thus permitting coasting down slopes.

1901 *World's Work* Aug. 1079/2 The coaster brake has done away with the sudden stops, and the wear and tear of both wheel and nervous system which were part of the old wheel brake system. **1933** Cheley *Camping Out* 439 The wheel should be equipped with a reliable coaster brake.

3. *W.* (See quot. 1929.) Also **coaster horn.** Cf. **Texas coaster.**

1890 *Stock Grower* 19 Apr. 7/2 There are lots of big old-fashioned 'coaster' horns among them. **1929** Dobie *Vaquero* 20 The 'coasters,' or 'sea lions,' as people sometimes called the longhorned cattle of the coast country, could swim like ducks and were as wild. **1930** Ferber *Cimarron* 80 The steers was long-legged coasters—and run! Say, they come through between us like scairt wolves, and I lost the count.

4. Short for roller coaster *q.v.* Also attrib.

1910 *Sat. Ev. Post* 9 July 5/1 Ten years ago, if a coaster 'dropped' ten feet, it was a 'thriller.' **1910** *Sat. Ev. Post* 9 July 29/2 He laid out a plan for a coaster railway that would run by gravity and got basic patents on it.

5. coaster wagon, a small wagon used by children, often for coasting.

1911 *Sears Cat.* (ed. 122) 866 A celebrated make of Coaster Wagon improved and fitted with brake. **1948** *Minneapolis Star* 17 Sep. 8/3 A new red coaster wagon, given to him by a married couple with no children of their own, restored happiness today to Jackie.

As the last term in **Pacific, roller coaster.**

***coasting,** *n.*

1. The sport of sliding down a snow-covered slope.

1775 J. Eliot in *Belknap P.* III. 77 The General at first did not understand what they meant by the term coasting. When informed of its meaning, he . . . ordered his servant to go & throw water on the place sufficient to rectify the damage caus'd by the ashes. **1849** *Boston Bee* 23 Jan. 1/1 The New Bedford young people say there is 'no enjoyment equal to'—*coasting.* **1909** *N.Y. Ev. Post* 28 Jan. (Th.), Coasting is fun for everybody. . . . In the frosty night, grown men and women fill the flying 'bobs' that go whizzing down the icy incline.

attrib. **1775** J. Eliot in *Belknap P.* III. 77 One of his servants . . . had spoiled their sport by tossing a quantity of ashes over a spot of ground which they & their fathers before them had taken possession of for a coasting-place. **1879** *Atlantis* (Glendale, Mont.) 28 Dec. 5/1 The hard dry snow on the streets tempted the little children to get their little sleds and have a coasting spree down the hill. **1914** *Country Life* Dec. 188/2 Coasting-days come as spring approaches and crust forms on the snow.

2. Of a bicycle, railroad car, or other vehicle: The action of gliding from the force of gravity.

1883 *Wheelman* I. 337 On such a road, with a brisk wind . . . 'coasting' was indulged in for a number of miles. **1909** *Cent. Supp.* 265/1 Coasting, in railroading, the act of allowing a train or a car to run upon a down grade by its own gravity, without steam or electric power [U.S.]. **1921** Hall *Yosemite Nat. Park* 308 Many drivers have the habit of coasting with their gears out of mesh.

coasting coat. App. a heavy coat. *Obs.* — **1677** *New Castle Court Rec.* 104 Hee . . . did by force . . . detayne from Mr Thomas Morse, one sandy browne Coasting Coate to ye vallue of fyve lb then in his Custodie. **1678** *Ib.* 350, 1 Coasting Coat.

coast survey. A survey of a coastal region. Also (*cap.*) the government agency set up for conducting surveys of this kind (see quot. 1944).

1832 *Cong. Deb.* 30 May 3187 The coast survey . . . will not be completed . . . under sixty years. **1879** *Supt. Coast & Geodetic Survey Rep.* (1881) 7 The work of the Coast and Geodetic Survey depends on the aggregation of certain varieties of fact, formulated to obtain unity of results. **1944** *U.S. Govt. Manual* 375/6 A survey of the coast of the United States was authorized by act of Congress of Feb. 10, 1807. . . . The act of June 20, 1878 . . . changed the name of this agency from Coast Survey to Coast and Geodetic Survey. **1948** *Spokesman-Review* (Spokane, Wash.) 23 Sep. 13/2 Good progress is being made by the coast and geodetic survey in the work of mapping Lake Roosevelt.

***coat,** *n.* As the last term in **beaver, blanket, blue, bob, bobtail, Boston, gray, great, gum, high water, house, Joseph's, Indian, mackinaw, match, moon, over, papoose, pea, pigeon-tailed, Prince Albert, rain, rifle, rubber, scratch, shad belly, Shanghai, Siwash, spiketail, spiketailed, sport, swallow tail, tear, tin, tuxedo coat.**

coatee ˌkoˈti, *n.* A short, close-fitting coat, orig. a military coat. *Obs.* Cf. **cadet coatee.**

1757 *N.Y. Mercury* 31 Jan. 3/1 My coat, when coatees flourished, was reduced to the size of a dwarf's, and then again increased to the longitude of a surtout. **1800** *Lancaster* (Pa.) *Journal* 20 Sep. (Th.), A Negro Man named Isaac . . . took with him a home-made lincy coattee. **1889** *Cent. Mag.* Jan 462/1 Several years before I had seen those wonderful coatees with their forty-four buttons of shining brass.

***cob,** *n.*[1]

1. The central spine or axis on which the kernels of an ear of corn grow in rows.

1684 I. Mather *Providences* 159 Then Nicholas Desborough . . . was strangely molested by stones, pieces of earth, cobs of Indian corn, &c. **1776** Romans *Concise Hist.* 188 Afterwards exposed upon a hurdle in a small hut to the smoak of the inner part of the cars of corn, which is properly the receptacle of the seed, and called the *cobs.* **1852** Regan *Emigrant's Guide* 321 As a general rule the corn is never *shelled* or taken off the *cob* till wanted for use. **1946** *Reader's Digest* Jan. 111/2 The cobs were good fuel in a land where trees were few.

b. Short for **cob pipe.** *Colloq.*

1857 *Spirit of Times* 4 July 275/3 Tonight, it happened to be a pipe. Not a 'dudeen,' nor a 'cob'—'cobs' are good, though—nor a 'chip'; no, neither of these, but a real, genuine 'meerschaum.'

2. In combs.: (1) **cob corn,** corn in the ear; (2) **crusher,** a machine for crushing corncobs; (3) **fashion,** a method of arranging logs, etc., so that the ends interlock, as in a child's cob house; (4) **house,** see as a main entry; (5) **meal,** meal obtained by grinding the entire ear of corn, including the cob, cf. **cobish meal;** (6) **pipe,** a tobacco pipe whose bowl is made from a section of corncob; (7) **work,** a structure made somewhat in the fashion of a child's cobhouse *q.v.*

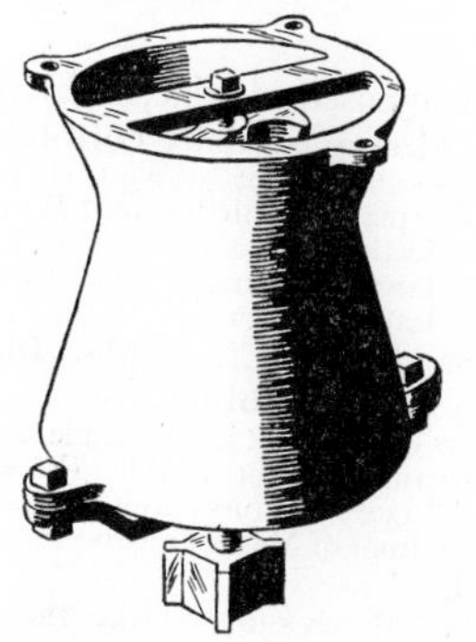

One form of cob crusher (*c*1840)

(1) 1864 in Easterby *S.C. Rice Plant.* (1945) 304 Boath Parsels only measured 365 bushels of Cob Corn, which Gives only $182\frac{1}{2}$ bushels of Sheld Corn. — **(2) 1841** *Spirit of Times* 6 Nov. 429/1 (We.), Corn and Cob Crusher. **1905** *Sears Cat.* (ed. 115) 565/2 We consider this one of the best cob crushers and feed grinders made. — **(3)** *a***1862** Thoreau *Maine Woods* 193 They had got a young moose, . . . confined in a sort of cage of logs piled up cob-fashion. **1888** Billings *Hardtack* 49 By far the most common way of logging up a tent was to build the walls 'cob-fashion,' notching them together at the corners.

(5) 1833 *Amer. R.R. Jrnl.* II. 488/2, I have also made further discovery of the use of cob meal. **1882** *Maine Bd. Agric. Rep.* XXVI. 255 Cob meal or middlings might be substituted for clear corn meal and not materially alter the effect of the ration. — **(6) 1847** in Drake *Pioneer Life Ky.* 63 Father [was] meanwhile quietly smoking a cob pipe in the corner. **1944** CLARK *Pills* 68 They smoked cob pipes, twirled corncob walking canes and wore festoons of cobs on their wide-brimmed wool hats. — (7) **1845** JUDD *Margaret* I. 158 A great fire . . . a large green forestick, and a high cob-work of crooked and knotty refuse-wood.

b. *To confess the cob*, a humorous variant of *to confess the corn*, see * **corn.** *Obs.*

1853 PAIGE *Dow's Sermons* IV. 127 (Th.), He might as well have confessed the cob.

* **cob,** *n.*[2]

1. cob gold, gold in roughly coined or uncoined form, allegedly of Spanish origin. *Obs.*

1789 *Md. Jrnl.* 2 Jan. (Th.), The public are hereby cautioned against taking a certain kind of cob-gold, which is now in circulation. **1860** S. MORDECAI *Virginia* 276 Also a portion of Cob gold and silver in irregular uncoined pieces.

2. cob money, early Spanish American coins, usu. of silver. *Obs.*

1793 *Mass. H.S. Coll.* III. 120 At times to this day, there are King William and Queen Mary's coppers picked up, and pieces of silver, called cob money. *a***1862** THOREAU *Cape Cod* 148 Pieces of silver called cob-money. **1868** LOSSING *Hudson* 80 The old silver coins occasionally found at Fort Edward are called 'cob-money' by the people.

cobbed roof. ?A roof formed by placing timbers cob-fashion, gradually drawing them closer to a ridge or peak. *Obs.* — **1816** D. THOMAS *Travels Western Country* (1819) 119 But a great proportion are scattered back from the road, formed of hewn logs with a *cobbed* roof, one story high and one room on a floor.

cobbings ˈkɑbɪŋz, *n. pl.* (See quot.) *Obs.* — **1805** PARKINSON *Tour* 328 Otherwise [i.e., unless the suckers are removed] the corn will not grow in the ear to its proper length or size, but grow short—what they call '*cobbings*.'

cobble ˈkɑbl̩, *n. local.* [App. f. G. *Kobel*, a cliff or hill.] A rounded hill. Chiefly in place-names. — **1890** M. TOWNSEND *U.S.* 135 *Cobble.* From the German, *koble*, meaning 'rocks.' Name applied to a hill or other moderate elevation whose sides have a covering of loose or cobble-stones. *Cobble Hill* (Adirondacks), N.Y., *Cobbleskill*, N.Y. (In the Catskills.) The word is local with Massachusetts and New York. **1930** *Amer. Sp.* V. 158 *Cobble*, a hill, not much used, though widely dispersed in the northern part of the district [i.e., of the eastern part of New York] as Rattle Snake Cobble (Glen Falls), etc.

* **cobbler,** *n.*

1. A drink composed of wine, sugar, fruit juices, and crushed ice. Cf. **sherry, whisky cobbler.**

1839 *Spirit of Times* 26 Oct. 397/3 (We.), He has since taken . . . three coblers and two pig and whistles. **1887** WHITMAN *Nov. Boughs* (1888) 437 My recollection of the 'cobblers' (with strawberries and snow on top of the large tumblers,) . . . help the regretful reminiscence of my New Orleans experiences.

2. (See quot. 1859.) Cf. **apple, blackberry, Catawba, cherry, peach cobbler.**

1859 BARTLETT 90 Cobbler . . . a sort of pie, baked in a pot lined with dough of great thickness, upon which the fruit is placed. **1947** *Reader's Digest* April 130/2 Cobblers came to the table in long black pans and were put in front of Mama on two asbestos mats.

3. (See quot.)

1869 *Harper's Mag.* March 540/1 During the fall we were sorely afflicted with scurvy, or, as the whalers call it, 'the cobbler.'

cob house.

1. A toy house built of cobs, a structure of sticks or other material laid criss-cross.

1774 J. BELKNAP in *Life* (1847) 68 They have a neat poultry house, built of sawed strips of wood, in the form of a cob-house, with four compartments. **1881** *Harper's Mag.* Nov. 824 George builds a cob house of chips and is soon rewarded with a blaze. **1923** ADAMS *Pioneer Hist.* 242 A stone fireplace, with a hearth of flat stone, and a chimney constructed of sticks laid up cob-house fashion and plastered with mud inside and out, served as a range and heater.

attrib. **1859** *Harper's Mag.* March 485/1 Long golden bars of 'diet-bread' piled up, cob-house fashion. **1882** THAYER *From Log-Cabin* i. 20 It was twenty by thirty feet, made of unhewn logs, notched and laid one upon another, in what boys call the 'cob-house' style. **1932** *Old-Time N. Eng.* July 8 Here jackscrews and cob-house piles of railway ties were used to get the building up to the road level.

2. *fig.* An insecure, unstable scheme; a "house of cards." Also attrib.

1834 *Cong. Deb.* 26 Feb. 736 With the first shock in the commerce or credit of the country, the whole cob-house fabric must tumble. **1854** HAMMOND *Hills, Lakes,* etc. 261 The fifteen or sixteen States went on increasin' to twenty, and then twenty-five, and so on till Texas came in, and there was a talk about the cob-house goin' down agin. **1913** *Ev. Post* (N.Y.) 5 June 6/3 (Th. Supp.) Mayor Gaynor made a statement, comparing the 'Curran Scandal committee' to a 'cobhouse of sensationalism, lying, and scandal. All cobhouses (he added) fall down at the first jar.'

cobia ˈkobɪə, *n.* [Origin unknown.] The sergeant fish, *Rachycentron canadus.* — **1873** *Forest & Stream* 258/1. **1884** GOODE *Aquatic Anim.* 444 The Cobia or crab-eater, *Elacate canada*, . . . is considered one of the most important food-fishes of Maryland and Virginia.

cobish meal. (See quot. and cf. **cob meal.**) *Rare.* — **1824** *N. Eng. Farmer* II. 262 By 'cobish meal,' we believe our correspondent means the produce of Indian corn ground or broken with the cob, without shelling it before it was submitted to the operation of the mill.

Coburger ˈkoˌbɜgɚ, *n.* An army or navy officer who secures an easy assignment by underhand means, reputedly so called from the royal house of Coburg in England. *Obs.* — **1886** *Pall Mall Gaz.* 15 June 14/1 There are quite a number of naval officers in Washington, comprehensively classed as Coburgers.

coca ˈkokɑ, *n.* [Sp. (Aragon and Valencia), a small round cake. Cf. Santamaría *de coca* "gratis," "free."] (See quot.) *Obs.* — **1889** *N. & Q.* II. 9 March 223, I remember, when a child, in St. Augustine, Fla., that our Minorcan bakers always gave with their loaves, as 'contra,' a small, hard-baked biscuit, something like the German zwie-back which was known to us as a 'coca,' and may serve as an illustration of the saying [i.e., a baker's dozen].

Coca-Cola ˈkokəˈkolə, *n.* [A trade-mark.] A popular soda-fountain and bottled drink, so called to suggest certain of its ingredients.

1887 *Ev. Jrnl.* (Atlanta) 30 June 1/4 Drink the brain tonic and intellectual soda fountain beverage Coca-Cola. **1900** *Atlanta Jrnl.* 12 June 1/2 About how many glasses of Coca-Cola were sold at Soda Fountains in Atlanta during the month of April, 1900? **1947** *Reader's Digest* June 33/1 Coca-Cola, the world's best known commercial product, is older than nine out of ten Americans.

attrib. **1934** CARMER *Stars Fell* 184 The first thing anybody knew Henry Wilkinson . . . picked up a Coca-Cola bottle and hit Tom over the head with it.

cocash kəˈkæʃ, *n.* ["From one of the eastern dialects of the Algonquian language, signifying 'it is rough to the touch,' in reference to the stem of the plant." (Hodge).] (See quots.) — **1877** BARTLETT 129 Cocash and Squaw-weed. Names given to *Erigeron Canadense* (and other species of the genius), used by the Northern Indians for medicine. **1907** HODGE *Amer. Indians* I. 316/2 Cocash. A name of the red-stalk or purple-stem aster (*Aster puniceus*), known also as swan-weed, early purple aster, etc.

coch kɑk, *n.* Short for cochleaureatus *q.v.* Hence **cochship.** *Obs.* — **1871** L. H. BAGG *At Yale* 131 The Delta Phi men attended the class meeting, and voted for the three Cochs and two Editors whom they had—without hope of success—nominated in the usual way. *Ib.* 422 It was announced that DKE had ordered that none of its members should accept cochships.

cochleaureatus ˌkɑklɪɔrɪˈɑtəs, *n.* [L. *cochlea*, a snail shell or spoon, + *laureatus*, crowned with laurel.] (See quots.) *Obs.*

1853 *Songs of Yale* 37 Now give in honor of the spoon, Three cheers, long, loud, and hearty, And three for every honored June In *coch-le-au-re-a-ti.* **1856** HALL *College Words* (ed. 2) 81 At Yale College, the wooden spoon is given to the one whose name comes last on the list of appointees for the Junior Exhibition. The recipient of this honor is designated *cochleaureatus.* **1871** BAGG *At Yale* 407 At first, when all the non-appointment men were called Cochleaureati, the Cochs were expected to be most chosen from their number.

Cochranism ˈkɑkrənˌɪzəm, *n.* (See quots.) Also **Cochranite.** *Obs.*

1819 H. M. BROOKS *Gleanings* 103 (*advt.*), Cochranism Delineated, Or a description of, and specific for, a religious Hydrophobia, which has spread & is spreading in . . . the counties of York and Cumberland, District of Maine—price 12 1-2 cents—for sale at the Bookstore of Henry Whipple. [**1853** *Me. H.S. Coll.* III. 165 In 1816 the religious movement under Jacob Cochran commenced in this town [Scarborough], and some of those concerned in it remain at the present time amongst his followers.] **1871** DE VERE 242 The *Cochranites* of the New England States held public exhibitions of so gross a character that the civil authorities were more than once compelled to intervene, for the vindication of public decency.

cocina koˈsinɑ, *n. S.W.* [Sp. in same sense.] A kitchen. *Obs.* — **1844** KENDALL *Santa Fe Exped.* II. 253 The chain was tightly riveted to his right ankle, and whenever he left his cot for the cocina or kitchen, he was obliged to drag it after him. [**1846** MAGOFFIN *Down Santa Fe Trail* 103 We have four rooms including *la cochina* (the kitchen).]

cocinero kosiˈnero, *n. S.W.* [Sp. in same sense.] A cook. Also **cocinera,** a woman cook. *Obs.*

1844 GREGG *Commerce of Prairies* I. 242 Respecting fandangos, . . . from the grandest señora to the cocinera—all partake of this exhilarating amusement. **1845** GREEN *Texian Exped.* 258 When not presiding as chief cocinero (cook) much of my time was employed at the desk.

1944 ADAMS *W. Words* 39/2 Borrowing from the Spanish, the Southwest cow country called the cook *cocinero*, and from this came the common nickname *coosie*.

***cock,** *n.*

1. A cock or representation of a cock as the emblem of the Democratic party. *Obs.*

1844 *Republican Sentinel* (Richmond, Va.) 31 Aug. 2/5 Before the November elections are over, his graceful figure will appear in a *recumbent* position, and the Democratic Cock will crow at least one note of triumph over the prostrate Coon. **1844** *St. Louis Reveille* 26 Nov. 2/3 Among the most striking objects connected with it [a parade], were several pictures of the American eagle, having in his talons a coon and a cock, favorite emblems in the late struggle. **1845** *St. Louis Reveille* 1 Jan. (Supp.) 1/1 The Coons stop a chink And the Cock won't crow!

2. In the names of various birds: (1) *cock of the mountains*, =next; (2) *cock of the plains*, =**sage cock;** (3) **cock of the woods*, the pileated woodpecker; (4) *cock-robin duck*, (see quot. 1889).

(1) 1841 DESMET *Letters* (1843) 54 Often the traveller sees the prairie hen and the cock of the mountains start up from the midst of the heath. — **(2) 1805** LEWIS in *L. & Clark Exped.* (1904) II. 384 Capt. C. killed a cock of the plains or mountain cock. It was of a dark brown colour with a long and pointed tail. **1886** *Stand. Nat. Hist.* (1888) IV. 209 The sage-cock, or cock-of-the-plains . . . is the largest grouse found in America. — **(3) 1816** PAULDING *Letts. from South* I. 154 Of living objects, we sometimes saw a covey of partridges, a cock of the woods, or a ground squirrel. **1886** VAN DYKE *So. Calif.* 139 The large black, red-headed woodpecker, sometimes called 'cock-of-the-woods,' or, by some rustics, 'woodcock,' is missing. **1946** RICHTER *Fields* 143 They were going to have fine weather, for the cock of the woods flew around screeching. — **(4) 1856** *Spirit of Times* 13 Dec. 242/2 Of the mergansers and goosanders, known as shell-drakes, and, in some places, as 'Cock-robin ducks,' we do not deign to speak. **1889** *Cent.* 1789/1 Cock-robin duck, the hooded merganser. (New Jersey, U.S.)

As the last term in **chaparral, chicken, fountain, game, lock, log, May, prairie, sage, timber, wood cock.**

***cockade,** *n.* As the last term in **black, blue, palmetto, union cockade.**

cock-a-nee-nee ˈkɑkəˌnini, *n.* [Origin unknown.] (See quots.) *Obs.* — **1807** IRVING *Salmagundi* x. 229 Boil your molasses to a proper consistency. . . . This manufacture is called by the Bostonians *lasses candy*, by the New Yorkers, *cock-a-nee-nee*—but by the polite Philadelphians, by a name utterly impossible to pronounce. **1855** BARNUM *Life* 21 My stock in trade consisted of a gallon of molasses, boiled down and worked into molasses candy, called in those times [1820–25] 'cookania.'

cockarouse ˈkɑkəraʊs, *n.* Also †**caucorouse,** †**coccorous.** [f. Algonquian Indian.] A chief or leader among the Indians. Also transf.

1624 SMITH *Virginia* II. 38 They haue . . . few occasions to vse any officers more then one commander, which commonly they call Werowance, or Caucorouse, which is Captaine. **1705** BEVERLEY *Virginia* II. 33 That man was counted a Cockarouse, or brave Fellow, [who would not lose his hold of a Sturgeon]. **1743** CATESBY *Carolina* App. p. xi, The Indians [of Carolina deem] . . . it ignominious for a *Coccorous*, that is a war-captain, or good hunter, to do mechanick works except what relates to war or hunting. **1944** FOOTNER *Rivers of East. Shore* 327 Rising men, such as overseers, redemptioners and so forth, were always pressing close on the heels of these extravagant cockerouses. 'Cockerouse' was Maryland slang for an important man.

***cocked-hat,** *n.* (See quot. 1889.)

1858 *S. Lit. Messenger* XXVII. 351/1 His great strength compelled him to use the largest balls, even when playing 'Cocked-Hat.' **1889** *Cent.* 1078/1 Cocked-hat. . . . A variety of the game of bowls in which three pins, placed at the angles of a triangle, are used. **1907** MARK TWAIN *Chaps. from Autob.* 335 (R.), Next we started cocked hat—that is to say, a triangle of three pins.

***cockle,** *n.*[1]

1. *cocklebur, any one of various coarse annual weeds of the genus *Xanthium*, or the troublesome prickly seed pod of this. Also attrib.

1804 CLARK in *Lewis and Clark Expedition* I. (1904) 79, I saw wild Timothy, lambs-quarter, Cuckle burs, & rich weed. **1845** HOOPER *Daddy Biggs' Scrape* 196 They was as thick all round me, as cuckle-burrs in a colt's tail. **1947** CROY *Corn Country* 183 The next day was cocklebur cutting.

b. Used in an exclamation. *Rare.*

1850 LEWIS *La. Swamp D.* 45 Murder! Hingins! h——l and kuckle-burs! Oh! Lordy!

2. cockle-machine, separator, ?a machine for separating the seeds of cockle from wheat. *Obs.*

1887 *Amer. Miller* XV. 211 (*advt.*), Kurth's Cockle separator. *Ib.* 301 Two double-cylinder cockle-machines, French system.

***cockle,** *n.*[2] A small shell-shaped sweetmeat made of sugar and flour and having a motto or couplet rolled inside it. *Obs.* Cf. **motto.** — **1851** HAWTHORNE *Twice-told T.* I. viii. 149 And those little cockles . . . much prized by children for their sweetness, and more for their mottoes. **1893** HALE *N. Eng. Boyhood* 159 She frosted it [a cake] herself, and dressed it with what in those days they used to call 'cockles' of sugar. These cockles generally had little scraps of poor verses, which were supposed to be entertaining.

cocktail ˈkɑkˌtel, *n.* [Origin unknown.]

For an enumeration and discussion of some of the theories that have been advanced to account for this term see Mencken, *Supp.* I. 256 ff.

1. A well-mixed iced drink composed of spirituous liquor and various flavoring ingredients, sometimes including bitters.

1806 *The Balance* (Hudson, N.Y.) 13 May 146 *Cock tail*, then, is a stimulating liquor, composed of *spirits* of any kind, *sugar*, *water*, and *bitters*—it is vulgarly called *bittered sling*. . . . It is said, also, to be of great use to a democratic candidate: because, a person having swallowed a glass of it, is ready to swallow any thing else. **1882** *Cent. Mag.* April 884/2 His morning meal was a simple Kentucky breakfast—'three cocktails and a chaw of terbacker.' **1948** *New Yorker* 6 Nov. 64/2 Cocktails are now so numerous that no bartender, however talented, can remember how to make all of them, or even the half of them.

fig. **1948** *Dly. Ardmoreite* (Ardmore, Okla.) 30 April 6/5 To me the Sioux seem a racial cocktail—a people stoical as the Japanese, as independent and happily irresponsible as the Irish, as cynically subtle as the French.

attrib. **1928** *Collier's* 1 Sep. 49/2, I found twelve styles of cocktail glasses in silver, twenty-three styles in glass. **1948** *Chi. D. News* 4 March 1/3 Sign in a Los Angeles cocktail bar: 'Our cocktails make you see double and feel single.'

2. *W.* In cowboy usage, the last watch of the night. Also attrib.

1891 *Outing* Mar. 411/1 Half-past 2 and the boys are counting the minutes before calling the 'cocktail guard' that relieves them. **1927** JAMES *Cow Country* 37 No songs was heard during 'cocktail' that evening. **1948** ROLLINSON *Wyo. Cattle Trails* 205 We . . . returned to camp about 5 A.M., called the cook, and aroused the boys who were to come out on herd. We called this 'the cocktail relief.'

3. In special combs.: (1) **cocktail lounge,** in a hotel, club, etc., a room furnished with easy chairs, sofas, etc., where patrons may obtain and partake of cocktails; (2) **oyster,** a small oyster suitable for serving with cocktails; (3) **powder,** ?a powder from which cocktails may be prepared, *obs.*; (4) **shaker,** (see quot. 1868). [The 1868 example is from a British source, but it is not likely that the expression is of British origin.]

(1) 1940 MENCKEN *Happy Days* 237 Today the influence of the cocktail lounge has brought in blue glass, chrome fixtures, and bars of pale and puny woods. **1948** *Time* 8 Mar. 22/1 They call it progress, this metamorphosis of the old-fashioned corner saloon into the modern, glittering cocktail lounge. — **(2) 1945** MACDONALD *Egg & I* 85 We could gather both the large soup oysters and the tiny cocktail oysters by the bucketful. — **(3) 1856** *Reader* 8 July 30 Advertisements of quack medicines, patent skirts, cock-tail powders, plantation bitters. — **(4) 1868** in *Amer. Sp.* XXI (1946) 212, I never possessed a pair of 'cocktail-shakers' myself, but a young officer in the Blues, a fellow-passenger in a Cunard steamer in which I crossed the Atlantic in 1865, did possess, and was very proud of, a brace of tall silver mugs in which the ingredients of the beverage known as 'cocktail' (whiskey, brandy or champagne, bitters and ice) are mixed, shaken together and then scientifically discharged. **1948** *Chi. D. News* 6 Nov. 6/3 Somebody sent me a cocktail shaker made up as a fire-extinguisher.

Also *cocktail dress, hour, mixer, napkin, party*, etc.

As the last term in **ale, brandy, fruit, gin, Manhattan, Martini, prairie, rum, soda, whisky cocktail.**

cocktailed ˈkɑkˌteld, *a.* Under the influence of cocktails. *Rare.* — **1856** *Harper's Mag.* Dec. 66/1 The Virginian Editor. . . . Cocktailed past the point of nervousness and remorse, he dresses himself.

cockup hat. The queen's delight, *Stillingia sylvatica. Obs.* — **1765** J. BARTRAM *Diary* 15 Aug., A curious plant called in north carolina Cockup hat common all ye way. **1830** *Huntingdon* (Pa.) *Courier* 15 Sep. 4/5 American remedies wanted. . . . Yaw Weed or Cock-up-Hat, (Stilingia sylvatica).

***coco,** *n.* Also ***cocoa.**

1. A person's head. *Slang.*

This meaning may not have originated in the U.S. The *OED* lists *cocoa-nut* "head" in slang (British) use 1873——. Santamaría lists a similar use of Sp. *coco* "in various countries."

1835 *Vade Mecum* (Phila.) 31 Jan. 3/5 Take care or you will crack his cocoa. **1890** *The Road* (Denver) 24 May 8/1 What put that thought into your cocoa? **1922** R. PARRISH *Case & Girl* 185 We'll slip out and leave Mike to explain how he got his coco cracked.

2. Short for **coco grass.** Also attrib. Cf. **Mexican cocoa.**

1873 *Dept. Agric. Rep.* (1874) 269 Even the hardy and noxious gramineal plant, commonly called 'coco' in Louisiana, is destroyed after two seasons of broadcast cultivation. **1897** STUART *Simpkinsville* 43 A heavy dew . . . hung in glistening gems upon the blades of bright green cocoa spears that had shot up between the drier clods. **1947** *Jrnl. Wildlife Management* Jan. 54/1 Muddy peats subject to admixture of clay from storm tides are taken over by 'coco' marsh, an association of 'coco' or salt-marsh bulrush, saltgrass, and 'wire-grass.'

3. coco grass, the nut grass, *Cyperus rotundus*, found chiefly in the southern states.

1837 COMMONS *Doc. Hist.* I. 221 Cutting coco grass on the 22d. **1902** GORDON *Recoll. Lynchburg* 111 The floods, the irrepressible cocoa-grass, the poisonous vegetable exhalations are in his way.

* **coconut,** *n.* Also * **cocoanut.**

1. A variety of squash, in full **coconut squash.** *Obs.*

1834 *Amer. R.R. Jrnl.* III. 152/2 The cocoanut squash . . . is found to be fully equal to them. **1857–8** *Ill. Agric. Soc. Trans.* III. 509 The Lima cocoanut, long and blue, is [an] excellent [variety of squash].

2. *attrib.* Designating **cake, candy, pudding,** of which coconut is an ingredient.

1828 E. LESLIE *Receipts* 17 Cocoa-nut Pudding. **1830** *York* (Pa.) *Gazette* 6 July 1/3 He has just received a complete and general assortment . . . consisting of . . . Mint Drops, Cocoanut Cake, and Lady Fancy's, &c. **1877** *Harper's Mag.* April 603/1 He didn't get me any cocoa-nut candy. **1891** CHASE & CLOW *Industry* II. 145 There were tiers of cocoanut cakes, some baked to a delicate brown.

cocoonery kəˈkunərɪ, *n.* A place where silkworms are raised. *Obs.* Cf. **multicaulis.**

1839 *S. Lit. Messenger* V. 753/1 She . . . even went to the expense of having a neat little cocoonery erected in the centre of the lot. **1856** *National Mag.* Jan. 26/1 The bushes, resembling enormous cabbages which are seen at the right and left of the cocoonery, form a plantation of mulberry-trees. **1885** *Boston Jrnl.* 7 Sep. 2/4 A cocoonery that will protect a million worms.

Cocopa ˈkokəˌpɑ, *n.* [Native term of unknown meaning.] An Indian of a Yuman family living in the valley of the Rio Colorado. Usu. pl. with reference to the tribe.

1857 IVES *Colo. River* (1861) 31 If our two visitors are fair specimens of the Cocopas the latter are much inferior to the other Colorado tribes. **1901** VAN DYKE *Desert* 46 Branches of the Yuma Indians, like the Cocopas, overran all the country when the Padres first crossed the desert. **1911** WRIGHT *Winning Barbara Worth* 93 He was interrupted by the return of Abe, who was followed by an old, grizzly-haired Cocopah. **1947** *Westerners' Brand Book* 44 These Indians were mostly Mojaves, Yumas and Cocopahs.

Also **Cocopa Indian.**

1907 *Amer. Geog. Soc. Bul.* 10 According to the traditions of the Cocopah Indians, a member of the tribe accused of sorcery, or other serious crime, was sent back to his evil master by the simple process of dropping him into a pool of boiling mud—an obvious entrance to his abode below. **1908** HORNADAY *Camp Fires on Desert* 352 The town . . . is garnished with loafing Co'capaw Indians that are spelled Cocopah.

C.O.D. Abbreviation of "cash on delivery," "collect on delivery," directing payment to be made to the carrier on receipt of goods.

1859 *N.Y. Tribune* 22 Jan. 2/4 C.O.D. and P.O.D. The Principle On Which We Do Business Is P.O.D. and C.O.D. Which literally means Pay On Delivery and Collect On Delivery. **1865** *Chi. Tribune* 29 Sep. 3/4 Send me one thousand plants, best sort, strawberries, C.O.D., per express. **1947** *Redbook* Oct. 35/1 The C.O.D. charges are much more than the pen is worth.

fig. **1904** *Grand Rapids Press* 24 May 4 According to later returns it appears that instead of having carried Michigan Mr. Hearst has merely arranged to have it sent C.O.D.

* **cod,** *n.* **1. cod-meadow,** a feeding ground of cod. **2. cod-ocracy,** =**codfish aristocracy.** Both *rare.* — **(1) 1877** *U.S. Fish Comm. Rep.* (1879) 541 The 'fishing grounds,' 'cod-meadows,' have an extent of about 200 geographical miles in length, and 67 miles in breadth. — **(2) 1861** *Walsh's Humorist* (S.F.) 17 Aug. 5/3 For several years past the *cod*-ocracy of Massachusetts have been celebrated as seekers for pedigrees, as well as for the adoption of crests and coats of arms.

As the last term in **blue, buffalo, Cape, clam, cultus, inshore, pine-tree, rock, shoal, shoal water, shore, tom, water cod.**

codder ˈkɑdɚ, *n.* A person or vessel engaged in codfishing. Cf. **dory codder, rock codder.** — **1846** *Knickerb.* XXVII. 513 There's a school of 'em, as sure as I'm a living codder. **1893** *Harper's Mag.* April 726/2 'We should lie in the track of some ships,' said the captain. . . . 'There's the codders and the herring-busses.'

codding ˈkɑdɪŋ, *n.* (See quot. 1859.) Also attrib.

1714 in *Amer. Sp.* XV. 227/1, I Lent Ensign Harris my Pockitt Compass to go a Codding. **1859** BARTLETT 90 Codding, fishing for codfish. A common term in New England seaports, where vessels are fitted out for the purpose. **1891** CHASE & CLOW *Industry* II. 122 The grandest codding station in the world is Newfoundland.

* **code,** *n.* As the last term in **black, bloody, Eaton, Missouri, Morse, slave code.**

* **codfish,** *n.*

1. =**buffalo cod.**

1884 GOODE *Fisheries* 267 Cultus Cod . . . is universally called 'Codfish' where the true cod is unknown.

2. In combs.: (1) **codfish aristocracy,** orig. in Massachusetts, a class made wealthy by the codfisheries; in later use, the newly rich; (2) **aristocrat,** a member of the codfish aristocracy, *contemptuous;* (3) **ball, cake,** codfish and potato molded into a small sphere or cake and fried; (4) **chowder,** chowder of which codfish is an ingredient; (5) **gentility,** =**codfish aristocracy;** (6) **Codfish State,** Massachusetts, a nickname, *obs.*

(1) 1849 *Rainbow* (Bellville, Ohio) 30 Nov. 2/4 That evil is the instigation or giving rise to what is called Codfish Aristocracy a class of persons who wish to appear before the public as though they were worth thousands. **1897** *Cong. Rec.* 7 July 2444/1 Just the other day England was the richest nation. To-day Uncle Sam could buy the whole of the tight little island . . . and hold it as a summer resort for our codfish aristocracy. **1943** MENEFEE *Assignment* 12 They hate the 'codfish aristocracy,' who looked down their noses at the upstart Irish as long as they could. — **(2) 1943** *Democrat* 4 Nov. 2/3 Decent people can eat their meals in a decent place undisturbed by codfish aristocrats. — **(3) 1845** *Knickerb.* XXVI. 462 Wonder if they had any 'codfish-balls' or 'bread-puddings?' **1944** *Vogue* July 70, I come home and renew acquaintance with . . . baked beans and codfish cakes. **1948** *Richmond* (Va.) *News Leader* 6 May 31/3 Bacon and eggs, sausage, fish roe, codfish balls, . . . are ingredients which you will have to reconsider. — **(4) 1840** *Knickerb.* XV. 186, No one who has ever eaten fried tongues and 'sounds' at Siasconset, can ever long for any other dish, unless it be a codfish chowder, served up at the same place.

(5) *c***1850** WHITCHER *Bedott P.* 305 I've noticed that yer codfish gentility always dew [feel uneasy]. — **(6) 1850** *Quincy* (Ill.) *Whig* 30 April 1/6 He had all the tact and shrewdness of the Codfish State.

b. *To make codfish of,* to beat decisively. *Rare.*

1776 *Battle of Brooklyn* I. ii, Did he not make codfish of them all at Boston!

As the last term in **dun, George's codfish.**

* **codling,** *n.* Any one of various codlike fishes of *Phycis, Urophycis,* and allied genera. — **1814** MITCHILL *Fishes N.Y.* 372 Codling. *Gadus longipes.* . . . Weighs sometimes as heavy as eighteen pounds. . . . This is the hake of the New-York fishermen. **1842** *Nat. Hist. N.Y., Zoology* IV. 291 The American Codling *Phycis americanus.* . . . American Hake. Storer. *Ib.* 292 The Spotted Codling *Phycis punctatus.* . . . This is an exceedingly rare but distinct species. It occurs from the coast of New York to the gulf of St. Lawrence.

co-ed ˈkoˌɛd, *n.* A female student in a coeducational institution, usu. a college. Also attrib.

1889 *Pueblo* (Colo.) *Opinion* 21 July 2/2 A Newport Story, a 'Co-Ed.' Story . . . are some of the attractions of *Demorest Monthly Magazine* for August. **1900** *D.N.* II. 28 Co-ed, a woman studying at a co-educational college or university. Used generally. **1946** THOMPSON *Amer. Daughter* 182, I hear you've been elected one of the seven most athletic coeds on the campus.

b. Often attrib., frequently in the sense of **coeducational,** of which it may be a shortening.

1895 *Bachelor Arts Mo.* May 113 There is even danger that soon 'co-ed' institutions will degenerate into mere matrimonial agencies. **1913** *Ladies' Home Jrnl.* Nov. 19/2 In the teeming life of a big 'coed'-university the members of the sororities and fraternities form the interlocking directorates of social life. **1947** *Chi. D. News* 16 Jan. 1/2 (*heading*), Ohioan Is Indicted In Coed Kidnaping.

coeducate koˈɛdʒəket, *v.* [Back formation f. **coeducation.**] *tr.* and *intr.* To educate (students of both sexes) together.

1855 *Pa. School Jrnl.* III. 201 Another enumerates the great number of schools where the sexes are co-educated. **1894** *Forum* July 585 The men who have been 'co-educated' bear the marks of it through life, I believe, in their attitude towards women. They respect them far more, they unconsciously treat them as equals. **1923** *Forum* LXX. 2050 This sympathetic attitude is naturally based on the belief that coeducation coeducates.

coeducation ˌkoɛdʒəˈkeʃən, *n.* The education of male and female students jointly at one institution.

1852 *Pa. School Journal* Jan. I. 9 Co-education of the sexes. The instruction of males and females in the same room and in the same class, is supposed by many to be an evil; and, as such, it is avoided in large towns, by the separation of the sexes into different schools. **1870** Macrae *Americans* II. 395 The effect of co-education on the female students is not so easily determined. **1947** *Democrat* 6 Nov. 4/4 Auburn was the first institution in the state [i.e., Alabama] to provide for co-education and the second in the entire South.

coeducational ˌkoɛdʒəˈkeʃənl, *a.* Permitting the attendance of students of both sexes in the same classes.

1881 *Williamsport* (Pa.) *Sun & Banner* VIII. No. 3, 1 It is a coeducational school. **1902** *Chi. Record-Herald* 7 Sep. II. 4/3 Under these circumstances it is probable that the coeducational system may be continued at the Northwestern without any danger of the institution being converted into a female seminary. **1948** *Time* 21 June 60/2 Japan's new coeducational schools . . . are warmly encouraged by the U.S.

Hence **coeducationalist,** =next.

1909 *D. Maroon* (Chi.) 13 Oct. 1/1 In addition to criticising the prejudice against co-educationalists at Cornell, Mr. Slosson says the university is old-fashioned.

coeducationist ˌkoɛdʒəˈkeʃənɪst, *n.* One who favors coeducation. — **1855** *Pa. School Jrnl.* III. 202 The term child no longer exists with the co-educationist. *Ib.* 214 The co-educationist complains that no Yale or Harvard opens its doors to females. Let us imagine that a change has come over society. That the co-educationists have triumphed.

***coercionist,** *n.* One who favored forcing the southern states to remain in the Union by the use of coercive measures. *Obs.* — **1861** *Crisis* (Columbus, O.) 7 Feb. 7/2 If there is any good christian reader of your paper who is a coercionist, let me ask him to read the following sentiments. **1861** *Cin. Commercial* 7 May 2/4 (*heading*), Letter from a Coercionist in Eastern Tennessee.

Coeur d'Alêne ˈkɜdəˈlen, *n.* [See note.] The Skitswish tribe of Indians of northern Idaho.

"The name Coeur d'Alène (French 'Awl-heart'), by which they are popularly known, was originally a nickname used by some chief of the tribe to express the size of a trader's heart" (Hodge II. 594).

1838 Parker *Tour* 290 We came to villages of Indians who understood the Spokein language, but belonged to another tribe, probably to the Cœur d'Alene. **1849** in *Sen. Ex. Doc. 25, 31st Cong.* 1 Sess. (1850) 170 The *Coeur d'Helene*, or *Pointed Hearts*, live between the Spokane and Colespin. **1918** Rees *Ida. Chronology* 65 It was set apart for the Cœur d'Alenes and southern Spokanes and other fragmentary bands. **1938** *Amer. Anthrop.* XL. 436 The Shoshones of southern Idaho were the means of furnishing horses to the Cayuse, Walla Walla, Yakima, Palouse, Nez Perce, Coeur d'Alene, Flathead, Blackfeet . . . and many other tribes before horses were common among the Sioux and the northeastern Assiniboin.

* **coffee,** *n.*

1. The seeds of the Kentucky coffee tree. *Rare.*

1784 J. Filson *Kentucke* 23 The coffee-tree greatly resembles the black oak, . . . and also bears a pod, in which is enclosed good coffee.

2. In combs.: (1) **coffee ball,** a light perforated metal ball used for making coffee, cf. **tea ball;** (2) **boiler,** a vessel in which coffee is made; (3) **cake,** [cf. G. *Kaffeegebäck*], a breakfast cake, usu. twisted and glazed with melted sugar; (4) **cooler,** *fig.* one who shirks or idles, *slang;* (5) **essence,** (see quot.), *obs.;* (6) **granite,** (see quot.), *obs.;* (7) **-house loafer,** a loafer who frequents coffeehouses; (8) ***mill,** (see quot.), *obs.;* (9) **sack,** a sack of strong, closely woven material in which green coffee is shipped; (10) **saloon,** ?a coffee shop, *obs.;* (11) **shell,** a gastropod, *Melampus coffeus,* found along the Florida coast.

(1) 1903 *Sears Cat.* (ed. 113) 355/1 Coffee Balls. **1905** *Ib.* (ed. 115) 490/3 Tea or Coffee Balls. . . . Put the tea or coffee in the ball and drop it into the pot and boil in the usual way. — **(2) 1851** A. O. Hall *Manhattaner* 18 Bachelor bread-toasters, coffee-boilers, and the like, are soon picked up from neighboring shops. **1904** Glasgow *Deliverance* 58 Here a cheerful blaze made merry about an ancient crane, on which a coffee-boiler swung slowly back and forth. — **(3) 1885** *Cuisine Creole* 161 Coffee Cake. **1948** *Chi. Sun-Times* 18 Mar. 29/3 The coffee cake may be purchased at the bakery or home made. — **(4) 1876** in *Mont. Hist. Soc. Contrib.* II. (1896) We are assured that we shall easily fill up the complement in spite of the cold water cast upon our efforts by the 'coffee-coolers' as the shiftless, superannuated loungers about camp are very aptly termed. **1939** Abbott-Smith *We Pointed* 177 The government . . . drawed up a treaty fixing the new boundaries for the Sioux reservation, . . . and they got some of these coffee-coolers to consent to it. . . . [Footnote defines coffee-coolers as "Yesmen among the Indians who would do anything for a cup of coffee."]

(5) 1877 Ruede *Sod-House Days* 99 To give the beverage [i.e., rye coffee] a ranker flavor, what is known as 'coffee essence' is used. . . . This essence is a hard, black paste put up in tins holding some two ounces, with a red or yellow wrapper on which is printed in bold black type the figure 5000. . . . It is probably made of bran and molasses. — **(6) 1887** *N.Y. Tribune* 7 April 2/2 Granites . . . are a rough kind of sorbets. They are sometimes called rock punch and rock ice-cream, and are made of fruit juice, sugar and water. . . . For coffee granite put half a cup of coffee in a French coffee-pot. —**(7) 1839** *N.O. Picayune* 23 April 2/1 The coffee-house loafers in Mississippi are said to suffer unaccountably since the 'gallon law' went into effect. — **(8) 1887** H. L. Williams *Buffalo Bill* 10 One of the old-pattern Colts, with the barrels revolving, the ancient 'coffee-mill' or 'pepper-box,' laughed at all over the West in the present day. — **(9) 1850** Garrard *Wah-To-Yah* xxiii. 272 We carried charcoal from the pit to the intended 'shop.' With coffeesacks on our shoulders, we lifted until our appearance would have well vied with that of a city *charbonnier.* **1882** Peck *Sunshine* 103 The drummer wiped the perspiration from his face with a coffee sack.

(10) 1877 *S.F. Spark* 28 July 1/3 At five o'clock she walked nervously into a Kearny street coffee saloon. — **(11) 1870** *Amer. Naturalist* III. 403 Many snails . . . can be collected and the Coffee-Shell . . . is close at hand.

b. In the names of plants (1) **coffee bean (tree),** (*a*) =**Kentucky coffee tree,** (*b*) a legume, *Glottidium vesicarium,* poisonous to cattle; (2) ***berry,** see as a main entry; (3) **corn,** (see quots.), *obs.;* (4) **fern,** (see quot. 1909); (5) **nut,** see as a main entry; (6) **pea,** the chickpea, *Cicer arietinum,* allied to the vetch; (7) **plant,** (*a*) in California, a species of buckthorn, (*b*) the evening primrose; (8) **tree,** =**Kentucky coffee tree;** (9) **weed,** a wild plant of the genus *Cassia* producing a small brown berry, cf. **Florida coffee.**

(1) (*a*) **1821** Nuttall *Trav. Arkansa* 41 Among the trees, we still continue to observe the coffee-bean (*Gymnocladus canadensis*). *Ib.* 178 In this elevated alluvion I still observe the Coffee-bean tree. **1848** *Cultivator* n.s. V. 213, I will remark . . . that . . . two young coffee bean trees are in a thrifty condition. **1897** Sudworth *Arborescent Flora* 255 *Gymnocladus dioicus.* . . . Common names [include] . . . Coffee Bean. (Ill., Kans., Nebr.). Coffee Bean Tree (Ky., Ark.). (*b*) **1948** *Miami* (Okla.) *D. News-Record* 30 June 8/2 Farmers call it bladderpod, coffeebean and castle-bean. — **(3) 1817–8** Eaton *Botany* (1822) 471 *Sorghum vulgare,* indian millet, coffee corn. . . . Var. *bicolor.* **1840** Dewey *Mass. Flowering Plants* 252 Coffee Corn. Grand Millet. Sometimes cultivated in gardens as a curiosity, or for feeding hens, etc.; not considered of great value. . . . Its tops are used also for brooms. — **(4) 1909** *Cent. Supp.* 466/3 Coffee-fern, *Pellaea andromedaefolia,* of Arizona and California, so called in allusion to the resemblance of the revolute-margined leaf-segments to kernels of coffee. **1940** Jaeger *Calif. Deserts* 163 The coffee fern . . . and the bird's foot, . . . so common in the southern California foothills, reach the desert borders.

(6) 1816 *Gales's N.C. Almanac* 25 There is a kind of pea . . . much covered with a fine downy or hairy substance. It is known by various names, but mostly by the name of *Coffee Pea.* **1868** Gray *Field Botany* 111 Common Chick-Pea, . . . [is] called Coffee-Pea at the West, there cultivated for its seeds, which are used for coffee. — **(7)** (*a*) **1890** *Cong. Rec.* 12 June 5992/1 [The wild silk-worm] . . . subsists upon an indigenous plant found on the coast, the common name of which is 'coffee plant.' (*b*) **1893** *Amer. Folk-Lore* VI. 142 *Oenothera biennis,* scurvish . . . fever-plant; coffee-plant. Eastern States. — **(8) 1784** Filson *Kentucke* 23 The coffee-tree greatly resembles the black oak, grows large, and also bears a pod, in which is enclosed good coffee. **1931** Clute *Plants* 41 The coffee-tree (*Gymnocladus dioica*) was much too harmful to be used as a substitute for coffee, but its hard brown seeds, about the size of coffee beans, make the name appropriate. — **(9) 1933** Small *Southeastern Flora* 661 D[itremexa] occidentalis (L.) Britton & Rose. [*Cassia occidentalis* L.] —coffee-weed. Coffee-senna. Nigger-coffee. Styptic-weed. **1945** *Democrat* 20 Sep. 2/3 The coffee weed which has a small potato matted in its roots has given us hope.

c. In phrases: (See quots.) *Rare.*

1828 Royall *Black Bk.* II. 132 The English do not like the Western Country; our coffee is too strong for them. **1858** Gove *Letters* 164, I hope the government will have sense enough to declare the Territory in rebellion. If they do that we will settle their coffee very soon.

As the last term in **barley, Boston, burnt wheat, Canadian, corn, crumb, crust, dandelion, Demerara, domestic, Florida,**

iced, Illinois, Indian, Jeff Davis, Kentucky, Lincoln, malt, polecat, potato, rye, seed tick, Spanish, sweet potato, wheat, wild coffee.

coffee ˈkɔfɪ, *v.* **1.** *intr.* To drink coffee. **2.** *tr.* To serve (a person) with coffee.

(1) **1851** CURTIS *Nile Notes* xiii. 100 He coffeed and smoked, and would leave a duck for dinner, gave us all the last news, &c. **1885** W. J. HORNADAY *2 Years in Jungle* 277 Rose very early, coffeed in haste, and . . . set out. — (2) **1868** S. HALE *Letters* 48 The Colonel, who coffeed us the day before.

* **coffeeberry,** *n.*

1. = **Kentucky coffee tree.**

1822 J. WOODS *English Prairie* 224 On the creek bottoms, [there grow] coffee-berry, poplar, pecon, white walnut, [etc.].

2. = * **coffee plant** (*a*). Also attrib.

1886 VAN DYKE *So. Calif.* 33 The *madroña*, the coffee-berry, the manzanita, the wild mahogany, . . . form what is called the chaparral. **1946** LINSDALE *Calif. Ground Squirrel* 253 A squirrel watched on an afternoon early in September had its cheek pouches full of coffee-berry fruits.

3. (See quot.)

1942 CASTETTER & BELL *Pima & Papago Agric.* 26 On the lowest, drier level adjoining the desert are thickets of *jojoba* or coffeeberry (*Simmondsia californica*).

coffee nut. The coffee tree or its fruit. Also **coffee nut tree.**

1797 in *Filson Club Hist. Quart.* II. (1928) 166 The natural fruit is . . . beachnut, Coffee nut & Buck eye, this last resembles the Chestnut, but is as large as a hickory nut of the largest Size. **1804** CLARK in *Lewis & C. Exped.* (1905) I. 95 The Groves contain Hickory, Walnut, coffee nut & Oake in addition. **1817** BROWN *Western Gaz.* 25 Sugar maple . . . coffee-nut tree, and sycamore, are found in their congenial soils [in Ill.]. **1884** SARGENT *Rep. Forests* 58 *Gymnocladus Canadensis* . . . Kentucky Coffee Tree. . . . Coffee Nut.

* **coffin,** *n.*

1. A large shoe. Hence **coffin-clad,** *a. Slang.*

1851 HALL *College Words* 51 Coffin. At the University of Vermont, a boot, especially a large one. **1880** MARK TWAIN *Tramp Abroad* xlvii. 547 In the seat thus pirated, sat two Americans, greatly incommoded by that woman's majestic coffin-clad feet.

2. In special combs.: (1) **coffin boat,** (see quot. 1871), *obs.;* (2) **canoe,** a canoe shaped like a coffin, *obs.;* (3) **carrier,** the great black-backed gull; (4) **handbill,** see as a main entry; (5) **meat,** a corpse, *slang, rare;* (6) **nail,** a derogatory term for a cigarette, also attrib.; (7) **tack,** = prec.; (8) **varnish,** (see quot.), *slang;* (9) **warehouse,** a store where coffins are sold, *obs.*

(1) **1851** E. J. LEWIS *Hints to Sportsmen* 189 The Surface-boat, Coffin-boat, or Battery. **1871** DE VERE 334 A *battery* is the odd name given in Chesapeake Bay to a heavy boat, not unlike a coffin in shape, and hence also known as *coffin-boat*, used in duck-shooting. — (2) **1851** MELVILLE *Moby Dick* cx, Like a whaleboat these coffin-canoes were without a keel. — (3) **1872** COUES *N. Amer. Birds* 312 Great Black-backed Gull. Saddle-back. Coffin-carrier.

(5) **1837** BIRD *Nick of Woods* II. 105 He ar'n't hurt much to speak on, for all of his looking so much like coffin-meat at the first jump. — (6) **1901** A. G. ROBINSON *Philippines* 263 For a package containing thirty 'coffin-nails' the price was three and a half cents, American money. **1948** *Chi. D. News* 4 Dec. 4/7, I am a little hurt at the irritable stand taken by the *Journal* . . . concerning the vitamin-enriched copy of the coffin-nail advertisements. — (7) **1897** *Chi. Tribune* 15 July 3/2 (*headline*), Unconscious from cigaret smoke. George Decker of Jersey City succumbs to an excessive use of 'coffin tacks.' **1944** CLARK *Pills* 151 At Durham, North Carolina, in 1881, Washington Duke and Sons were producing the immoral 'coffin tacks,' and the South was off on a new trail of vice. — (8) **1945** *Everybody's Digest* 86 'Coffin varnish' for whisky was once in frequent popular use and is occasionally heard today. — (9) **1833** T. HAMILTON *Men & Manners* I. 17 'Coffin Warehouse,' however, was sufficiently explanatory of the nature of the commerce carried on within. **1851** MELVILLE *Moby Dick* (1926) i. 1, I find myself involuntarily pausing before coffin warehouses.

As the last term in **bark, devil's, ice, Job's coffin.**

coffin handbill. (See quot. 1914.)

*c*1828 in PRAY *Mem. J. G. Bennett* 97 They print cheap tracts, circulate cheap pamphlets, get up cheap coffin-hand bills, scrape together cheap barbecues, and all to put down Jackson. **1846** M'KENNEY *Memoirs* I. 202, I am told . . . that you took an active part in distributing under the frank of your office, the 'coffin hand-bills.' **1914** *Cyclo. Amer. Govt.* I. 308 Coffin Hand-bills. Handbills issued during the campaign of 1828 by Binns, editor of the Democratic Press of Philadelphia, an Adams supporter, narrating the lawless deeds of Jackson, especially his execution of a number of militiamen as deserters in the Florida campaign. These hand-bills were bordered with woodcuts of coffins, hence the name 'coffin hand-bills.'

Also, rarely, as a verb.

1828 in JAMES PARTON *Life of Andrew Jackson* (1866) III. 147*n.* 'Well, then,' says Harry, 'coffin-hand-bill him.' 'I have,' says Binns, 'but he won't stay coffin-hand-billed.'

coffle ˈkɔfl, *v. tr.* To fasten (slaves, etc.) together. Also **coffled,** *a. Obs.* — **1859** J. DOY *Narr.* (1860) 128 Berkeley was afterwards sold for jail fees, and his new owner started with him for the Southern market. He was coffled with a huge $1200 chattel. **1865** *Atlantic Mo.* XV. 752 Millions now of Confederate promises to pay, which the hurrying multitude and that coffled gang were treading under foot.

* **cog,** *n.*

1. cog mill, a mill in which the driving power is transmitted by a cogwheel. *Obs.*

1802 J. DRAYTON *S. Carolina* 121 Three kinds of rice mills, called pecker, cog, and water mills, are used in this state. **1837** PECK *New Guide* 127 A cog-mill is formed by constructing a rim, with cogs upon the shafts, and a trundle head to correspond. Each person furnishes his own horses to turn the mill.

2. cog rail, a cogged center rail that enables a locomotive equipped with a cogwheel to go up steep ascents. Also **cog-railway.**

1896 *Vt. Bd. Agric. Rep.* XVI. 126 We cannot boast of a Mt. Washington with its cog-railway. **1944** JOHNSON *As I Dare* 281 Ask a tourist for the highest mountain in Colorado and he is likely to say 'Pike's Peak,' because he has heard it oftenest, and he will tell you there is a cog-rail to the top.

3. *To miss* (*slip*) *a cog,* of the heart: To miss or skip a beat. *Colloq.*

1903 A. H. LEWIS *The Boss* 206 More 'n once I've felt my heart slip a cog. **1909** R. A. WASON *Happy Hawkins* 293, I threw some water in his face. That's about all the rule I know for any one who is missin' cogs.

cohab koˈhæb, *n.* [f. * *cohab*itation.] A Mormon guilty of illegal cohabitation. Also attrib. *Colloq.*

1888 *Ogden* (Utah) *Union* 11 June 2/5 The general verdict of returning cohab convicts is, 'Had a good time, good usage, good fare, etc.' **1890** *Ogden* (Utah) *Commercial* 25 Oct. 1/4 (*headline*), Cohabs in Trouble. **1948** *Amer. Folk-Lore* Jan.–Mar. 29 A 'cohab' . . . left in such haste that he didn't even get into his trousers.

Cohee, see **Coohee.**

coho ˈkoˌho, *n.* [Origin obscure.] The silver salmon, *Oncorhynchus milktschitsch*, of the northern Pacific Coast. — **1898** *Fish Comm. Bul.* No. 18, 6 In the opinions of the canners . . . the coho should rank next after the king salmon in food value. **1948** *Field & Stream* June 83/1 Apropos of threadlining for coho—or steelhead, for that matter—always check the last few feet of your line for wear.

cohoes koˈɑs, *n.* Also **cohos, cowass,** etc. [See note.]

From a Du. rendering of Algonquian *koowa, koaaes,* pine, small pine trees, in the locative "at the place of the pines." See Ruttenber, *Indian Names,* 200 f., and cf. quot. 1907 *s.v.* **Coos.**

1. An area originally overgrown with pines, pine land. Usu. (*cap.*) as a place-name.

1768 in F. CHASE *Hist. Dartmouth College* (1891) I. 104 From thence I travelled to Cohos, on Connecticut River. **1781** PETERS *Hist. Conn.* 110 In its [*sc.* the river's] northern parts are three great bendings, called cohosses. **1809** KENDALL *Travels* III. 191 Above and below the Fifteen-mile Falls, in the Connecticut, are tracts of country, called respectively the Upper and the Lower *Coos* or *Cohoss,*—which term implies, according to some, a fall in a river; according to others, a Bend in a river; and according to a third party, a parcel of meadow-land. But the true interpretation is *pine land.* **1888** J. Q. BITTINGER *Hist. Haverhill N.H.* 363 The Indian names which were given to the territory of Haverhill and its rivers have been retained in part. The country was known in earliest times as Cowass, Kohass and Cohas or Cohos. . . . *Cohos* it is said means *crooked*, and was borrowed from the Cohasaukes, a part of the St. Francis tribe, *uck* or *auke* meaning *river* or *place*, and was applied to the territory of Haverhill, on account of the crooked course of the river and the consequent large bends of the land.

2. (See quot. 1828.) Often as a proper name. Cf. *Cohoes,* N.Y.

The presence of *hoos,* Dutch for "water-spout," in the Dutch rendering of the Algonquian source word app. occasioned the development of this sense.

1798 MORSE *Amer. Ga.* 106 Cohoez, or the *Falls* in Mohawk R. between 2 and 3 miles from its mouth, and ten miles northward of Albany, are a very great natural curiosity. **1828** WEBSTER, *Cohoes,* or *Cohoze,* a fall of water, or falls; a word of Indian origin in America. **1854** GREATREX *Whittlings* 366 From Schenectady I went to view the Cohos, or falls of the Mohawk river. **1913** JAMES (tr.) *Danckaerts Jrnl.* (1679–80) 213 There are no fish in it except trout, sunfish, and other kinds peculiar to rivers, because the Cohoes stops the ascent of others, which is a great inconvenience for the *menage* and for bringing down the produce. [**1947** *Nat. Geog. Mag.* July 110/2 To the north the widening river flows eastward to the falls of Cahoes and the locks of Waterford.]

cohog, see **quahog.**

cohogle kəˈhogl, *v.* [Of fanciful origin.] *tr.* and *intr.* (See quot. 1829); also, to associate. *Jocular. Obs.* — **1829** *Va. Lit. Museum* 16 Dec. 419 To *cohogle.* 'To bamboozle.' Kentucky. **1855** *Olympia* (W. T.) *Pioneer* 6 July (Th.), Now the question is, will it pay to cohogle with these owls any longer?

cohoke ˈkoˌhok, *n. Va.* [App. f. Amer. Indian.] (See quots.) — **1657** in *Amer. Sp.* XV. 166/1, 500 acres of marshland commonly called Cohoke. **1928** *Ib.*, Just below the reservation is an extensive marsh and forested swamp known as Cohoke, a name of fixed usage applied both to the grassy marsh and to the swamp which is picturesquely 'Cohoke lowground.' Cohoke is clearly the original native district name.

cohonk kəˈhɔŋk, *n.* [Imitative.] The Indian name for the Canada goose, *Branta canadensis.* Also as a measure of time. *Obs.*

*c*1655 FORCE *Tracts* III. No. 10, 28 It [the sun] is all the clock they have for the day, as the coming and going of the *Carbunks* (the geese) is their almanack or prognostick for the winter and summer seasons. **1705** BEVERLEY *Virginia* III. 43 They reckon the Years by the Winters, or *Cohonks,* as they call them; which is a Name taken from the Note of the Wild Geese. **1728** W. BYRD *Writings* (1901) 146 The Indians call these Fowl Cohunks, from the hoarse Note it has, and begin their year from the Coming of the Cohunks, which happens in the Beginning of October. **1841** *S. Lit. Messenger* VII. 219/1 Cohonk. . . . Indian term for Winter.

cohosh ˈkohɑʃ, *n.* [Algonquian. Cf. Massachusetts *kôshki,* "it is rough."] (See quot. 1907.) Usu. with defining terms, as *red, white cohosh.* Cf. also **black, false cohosh.**

1796 MORSE *Amer. Univ. Geog.* I. 189 Among the native . . . plants of New England, the following have been employed for medicinal purposes: . . . Cohush (*Actaea spicata*). This is a valuable plant. **1907** HODGE *Amer. Indians* I. 321 Cohosh. The common name of several plants; written also cohush. . . . White cohosh is white baneberry (*Actaea alba*); red cohosh is red baneberry (*A. rubra*).

b. Esp. **blue cohosh, =squawroot.**

1821 *Mass. H.S. Coll.* 2 Ser. IX. 148 Plants which are indigenous in the township of Middlebury [Vt.], include . . . *Caulophyllum thalictroides,* Blue cohosh. **1939** *Nat. Geog. Mag.* Aug. 220/1 These giants of the springtime tower above their humbler companions in the form of wandlike blue larkspurs, blue cohosh [etc.]. **1942** PEATTIE *Friendly Mts.* 193 Along fence rows are now noted purple trilliums, wild ginger, blue cohosh, and wild oats.

c. Tea prepared from cohosh.

1948 *Chi. D. News* 26 Feb. 16/3 (*caption*), Ever Take A Nip of Cohoosh?

coin notes. Government notes to be paid in coins. *Rare.* — **1876** *Cong. Rec.* 25 July 4866/1 The first section of this bill requires coin-notes to be paid out, and consequently it involves the . . . necessity of redeeming those coin-notes.

cojinillo kohiˈniljo, *n.* Also **coginillo.** *S.W.* [Dim. of Sp. *cojín,* saddle pad.] (See quots.) *Obs.* — **1808** PIKE *Sources Miss.* (1810) III. 218, I soon found that the old soldier . . . was fond of a drop of the cheering liquor, as his boy carried a bottle in his cochmelies [*sic*] (a small leather case attached to the saddle for the purpose of carrying small articles). **1844** GREGG *Commerce of Prairies* I. 214 The *corazas* [=covers] of travelling saddles are also provided with several pockets called *coginillos*—a most excellent contrivance for carrying a lunch or bottle.

Coke kok, *n.* Also **coke.** Short for **Coca-Cola.** *Colloq.*

1909 *Coca-Cola Bottler* (Phila.) Nov. 17/1 The words are painted in crude characters upon a piece of a goods box and if you go in and asked to be served with 'Ice Cold Cokes' you will be presented with a very good bottle of carbonated Coca-Cola. **1927** BENÉT *Wild Goslings* 201 When the others ordered coke little Nan swung a Moxie. **1948** *Chelsea* (Mass.) *Record* 30 Nov. 4/6 A diet of chocolate creams and cokes won't do anybody any good.

attrib. **1941** DANIELS *Tar Heels* 261 The result is that many of those who eat out in North Carolina have become little more than sandwich munchers and coke drinkers. **1944** HOLTON *Yankees* 110 If there were not hot-dog stands and coke machines, there were other indigestible articles enough on sale. **1945** *Las Cruces* (N.M.) *Citizen* 15 Feb. 5/6 Mrs. Ted Nelson entertained with a 'coke' party at her home Tuesday morning.

cola ˈkolə, *n.* Any one of various soft drinks the names of which terminate in "cola." *Colloq.* — **1938** MATSCHAT *Suwannee River* 238 All the trails converged upon the crossroads store . . . with . . . its flyspecked window, and the bottles of Cola and cherry phosphate on a counter inside. **1948** *Family Circle* June 85/1 She ordered a cola and sipped it idly, watching her reflection in the mirror.

colchon kolˈtʃɑn, *n.* [Sp. *colchón.*] A mattress.

1856 DAVIS *El Gringo* 179 The females in particular, prefer the easy *colchon*—folded mattress—to the straight and stiff-backed chairs and settees. **1926** *Cent. Mag.* Nov. 25/2 No doubt before the arrival of the American rocking chair the *colchón* contributed to comfort in the best houses as it still does in humble homes. **1936** POE *Buckboard Days* 142 I'd like for you to mention among the girls that I've bought two new sheepskins for my *calchon.*

* **cold,** *a.* and *adv.*

1. In combs.: (1) **cold check,** a bogus or fraudulent check, *slang;* (2) **deck,** a specially prepared pack of cards surreptitiously introduced into a game, also fig., *slang;* (3) **decker,** a cheat, *slang;* (4) **drop,** a sure advantage, *slang;* (5) **fact,** absolute, unbiased fact, *colloq.;* (6) **feet,** the loss of courage, one who has lost his spirit, cf. **2.** (5); (7) **flour,** (see quots., and cf. **coal flour**); (8) **footer,** one excessively timid, a coward, *slang;* (9) **frame,** a boxlike structure with glass at the top, in which plants are protected; (10) * **lead,** a bullet or bullets, *slang;* (11) **max,** (see quots.), *slang;* (12) **nose,** (see quot. 1892), also attrib.; (13) **plague,** ?influenza, *obs.;* (14) **scald,** "a double misfortune, as of a person who should be at once frozen and scalded" (B. '77), *obs.;* (15) **setting,** in dairying, the process of cooling milk preparatory to removing the cream; (16) **shake,** (see quot.), *obs.;* (17) **shut,** (see quot.), *obs.;* (18) **snap,** a spell of severely cold weather; (19) **tack,** app. a tack cut from cold metal, *obs.;* (20) **timberline,** (see quot. 1925); (21) **turkey,** extreme matter-of-fact plainness, usu. attrib. or as adv., *slang;* (22) * **water,** see as a main entry.

(1) **1927** *Cleveland Press* 2 Feb. John Horan, wanted in connection with a 'cold' check passed three weeks ago. **1939** *These Are Our Lives* 304 Lots of cold checks is passed and we have to run them down. — **(2) 1857** *S.F. Call* 3 April 4/2 He's got the thing all set to ring in a 'cold deck.' **1880** *S.F. Globe* 12 July 1/6 The Santa Rosa Club wrung in a 'cold deck' on the Pataluma Ball Club on the 5th instant [by employing skilled professionals]. **1946** *Chi. D. News* 17 July 14/7 The boys in the back room can't deal us a cold deck when the voters bring their own cards to the game. — **(3) 1920** MULFORD *J. Nelson* XV. 163 I've had all th' visitin' I want with a bunch of cold-deckers. — **(4) 1909** S. E. WHITE *Rules of Game* V. xii, What do you do, then, when a man gets the cold drop on you?

(5) 1855 *N.Y. Wkly. Tribune* 17 March 1/1 The *Delta* of the 24th ult. has, among the cold facts and speculations of its Money Articles, the following statement. **1946** T. JONES *Skinny Angel* 26 Mother had found out the cold facts about the library. — **(6) 1900** *Kansas Hist. Coll.* VI. 136 The regiment developed but two or three cowards, two or three pairs of weak knees—two or three pairs of 'cold feet,' as the soldiers expressively term the complaint. **1916** *Boston Journal* 5 April 8/1 Hot-heads and cold-feet (—rioters and cowards). — **(7)** [**1753** DUMONT *Mémoires Historiques sur la Louisiane* (Paris) I. 33 On en [*sc.* du mahi] fait du pain, de la bouillie, de la farine froide, de la farine grolée, [etc.].] **1859** BARTLETT 91 Cold Flour, a preparation made of Indian corn (maize) parched and pulverized, mixed with one third its quantity of sugar. Two or three teaspoonfuls of this compound stirred in a glass of water will answer for a meal when food is scarce. **1916** THOBURN *Hist. Oklahoma* I. 262 Corn was . . . ground into a fine powder, which was called 'cold flour.' — **(8) 1920** HUNTER *Trail Drivers Texas* 429 Two of my men stayed with me, and the third, a 'cold-footer,' crossed on the bridge. — **(9) 1857–8** *Ill. Agric. Soc. Trans.* III. 503 The seed for early summer cabbages can be planted in a cold frame early in September. **1885** *N.H. Forestry Comm. Rep.* June 82 The common cold frame used by market gardeners—six feet wide, and as long as may be desired—will be found convenient.

(10) 1809 FESSENDEN *Pills Poetical* 32 Our spouting democrats. . . . When they can't reason with a Fed, In logick substitute cold lead. **1890** M. E. RYAN *Told in Hills* 332 [The message] belongs to the command, and I may get a dose of cold lead before I could deliver it. — **(11) 1871** O. E. WOOD *West Point Scrap Book* 339 A Vocabulary of the Expressions and Phrases used in the Corps of Cadets. . . . To make a cold max.—To make a perfect recitation. **1937** KENDALL BANNING *West Point Today* 294 Cadet Lingo. . . . Cold, *a.* Absolutely without error, as 'a cold max' (meaning a cold maximum mark in recitation). — **(12) 1836** C. GILMAN *Recoll.* (1838) 210 After driving about for sometime, Bounce, a cold-nose dog, struck a trail. **1892** HARRIS *Plantation* 35 He had what is called a 'cold nose,' which is a short way of saying that he could follow a scent thirty-six hours old, and yet he was a very shabby-looking dog. — **(13) 1819** E. DANA *Geog. Sk.*

35 The diseases vulgarly called the *spotted fever*, and *cold plague*, . . . in the severest seasons of winter cold, at the northwest, have occasionally made dreadful ravages. **1878** GUILD *Old Times* 110 In 1816 a disease prevailed in and about Nashville called the cold plague, which was more fatal than cholera. — **(14) 1839** *Spirit of Times* 4 May 108/1 (We.), It was indeed 'a cold scald.' **1845** *St. Louis Reveille* II. 18 June 1/6 That really was a 'cold scald' for us, when these persecuted Saints, driven from the free State of Missouri, took shelter in the bosom of Illinois.

(15) 1888 *Vt. Bd. Agric. Rep.* X. 14 Mr. Parker, of Georgia, who runs two cream separators at Westford, cold setting at Georgia and also at Jeffersonville, thought there was but little difference in quantity of milk to pound of butter. *Ib.* 15 When cream was raised in a large can by deep cold setting more inches of cream would be indicated at the end of four hours. — **(16) 1888–90** BARRERE-LELAND I. 263 Cold shake (American), a cold period of weather, also used sometimes in reference to fever and ague. As a figure of speech it is applied to cold and reserved conduct. 'It gives me the *cold shakes* just to look at her—she's so frozen up an' dignerfied.' — **(17) 1887** *Scribner's Mag.* II. 304/2 Out West the same [bear-] trap is used, but instead of pinning it to the ground a long chain is attached, and the end of this chain is made fast around a log, with a 'cold-shut' or split-ring, such as you put your pocket-keys on, and which can be fastened by hammering. — **(18) 1776** T. SMITH *Jrnl.* (1849) 279 A dismal cold snap of weather. **1948** *Reader's Digest* March 157/1 Each day, as the cold snap gradually wore off, I went out to hunt. — **(19) 1816** *Mass. H.S. Coll.* 2 Ser. VII. 119 *Cold Tacks*, so termed from the manner in which they are made, have become an article of important manufacture in this town [Abington, Mass.].

(20) 1903 *Amer. Geol. Soc. Bul.* XIV. 556 On the mountains of central Idaho, the cold timberline is sharply drawn at an elevation of about 10,000 feet, while the dry timberline, equally well defined, has an elevation of about 7,000 feet. **1925** BRYAN *Papago Country* 375 The cold timber line, at which the growth of trees is prohibited by low temperature, is not found in this part of Arizona even on the highest summits. — **(21) 1916** W. A. DU PUY *Uncle Sam* 90 He had gone to Henry Gottrell 'cold turkey,' and with authority from the department. **1944** *New Yorker* 16 Sep. 19/3 Just cold-turkey business, you lousy faker!

2. In colloq. and slang phrases: (1) *Cold as a wagon tire*, quite cold or dead; (2) *to lay* (or *knock*) *cold*, to knock unconscious; (3) *to throw cold*, (see quot.), *rare;* (4) *cold as bones*, (see quot.); (5) *to have* (or *get*) *cold feet*, to be excessively timid, to lack courage; (6) *to turn down cold*, to refuse flatly; (7) *to get* (one) *cold*, to have a decided advantage over one; (8) *to quit cold*, to quit entirely and absolutely.

(1) 1832 J. HALL *Legends of West* (1885) 264 Here's the Speckled Snake as cold as a wagon tire. **1836** *Quarter Race Ky.* (1846) 18 Oh! my Grapevine! tear the hind sights off him!—you lay him out cold as a wagon-tire. — **(2)** *a***1846** *Ib.* 45 He picked up an ole axe helve an gin me a wipe aside the hed that laid me cole fur a while I tell you. **1899** *Chi. D. News* 1 May 7/1 The ball . . . laid him out cold for a minute. **1942** RICH *We Took to Woods* (1948) 53 One hunter . . . went running through the woods at top speed, smacked into a tree, and knocked himself cold. — **(3) 1848** RUXTON in *Blackw. Mag.* LXIV. 24 They indulged their appetites—or, in their own language, 'throw'd' the meat 'cold.' — **(4) 1854** in *Minn. Farmer's Diaries* (1939) 115 *Cold as 'bones'* Regular Northwester.

(5) 1896 ADE *Artie* 108 He's one o' them boys that never has cold feet. **1946** *This Week Mag.* 9 Feb. 12/4 Then they were herded down to the hairdresser to be shorn. Some girls got cold feet at the last moment. — **(6) 1905** REX BEACH *Pardners* iii. (1912) 79 We were liable to get turned down cold if we didn't have some story. — **(7) 1924** MULFORD *Rustlers' Valley* xix. 213 What you doin'? I got you cold. — **(8) 1947** *Westerners' Brand Book* 125, I gets plumb peeved and quits. Yessir, quits 'em cold.

Coldenia kɑl'dinɪə, *n.* A genus of plants of the borage family, named for Cadwallader Colden (1688–1776), an Amer. botanist, physician, politician, and correspondent of Linnaeus. Also as the name of a plant of this genus.

1758 in *Scientific Mo.* 1948 July 18/2 Her father has a plant called after him Coldenia. **1893** COVILLE *Death Valley Exped.* 163 This plant has passed currently under the name of *Coldenia palmeri.* **1940** JAEGER *Desert Wild Flowers* 207 Shrubby Coldenia. *Coldenia canescens.*

* **cold water.**

1. *attrib.* Of or pertaining to total abstinence.

1830 *Cong. Deb.* 25 Feb. 584/1 It may be expedient to make our sailors cold water drinkers [=temperance men]. **1848** W. E. BURTON *Waggeries* 20 You oughter be the commodore of all them cold water clubs, and perpetual president of all temp'rance teetotallers. **1906** *Springfield Republican* 16 Aug. 1 Another [case in point] comes in the action of the prohibition state executive committee in Pennsylvania. . . . The cold water convention there nominated William H. Berry.

2. cold-water regime, the administration of President Hayes (1877–81), who served no spirits at his table. *Obs.*

1884 *Cent. Mag.* April 807/2 The cold-water regime lasted four years, and has left behind an interesting souvenir in the fine portrait of Mrs. Hayes, by Huntington, which stands in the Green Room.

colear kolɪ'ɑr, *v. S.W.* [Sp. in Amer. Sp. sense shown here.] *tr.* To "tail" (an animal). Cf. * **tail,** *v.*

[**1844** J. GREGG *Commerce of Prairies* 242 Among the vaqueroes, and even among persons of distinction, el coleo (tailing) is a much nobler exercise.] **1847** in BENTLEY *Sp. Terms* 126 Not a ranchero . . . could more dexterously colear a bull. **1932** *Ib.*, The use of *colear* is restricted to those engaged in or familiar with the cattle business.

colemanite 'kolmən,aɪt, *n.* [After W. T. *Coleman*, leader of one of the San Francisco vigilance committees.] A hydrous borate of calcium, the most common source of borax and boracic acid in the U.S.

1915 *Nat. & Science on Pac. Coast* 242 There appears to be no limit to the quantity of colmanite mineral. **1929** CHALFANT *Death Valley* 106 The decomposition of mountains of tufa and the natural washing down into the valley left over the surface of Death Valley . . . a reprecipitation of the decomposed colemanite . . . of the hills. **1942** LILLARD *Desert Challenge* 100 Colemanite, a former source of borax, was deposited in the muddy mountains.

coleslaw 'kolslɔ, *n.* [Du. *kool sla*, cabbage salad.] A salad of sliced or shredded cabbage.

1794 *Mass. Spy* 12 Nov. 4/2 A piece of sliced cabbage, by Dutchmen ycleped cold slaw. **1867** DE VOE *Market Ass't* 325 There is also the 'early dutch,' 'flat dutch,' which the Dutch commonly slice and call it kohl-slaw, or salat, meaning simply cabbage salad; but the progress here has corrupted it to be cole or cold slaw. **1941** *Yankee* Dec. 19/2 The tables were set with bowls of pickles and salad and coleslaw.

* **colic,** *n.* In combs.: (1) **colicroot,** any one of various herbs reputed to be efficacious in cases of colic, as (*a*) butterfly weed, (*b*) star grass, *Aletris farinosa* and *aurea*, (*c*) wild ginger, *Asarum canadense*, and closely related plants; (2) **weed,** any one of various herbs, as dutchman's breeches, squirrel corn, and the yellow-flowered *Corydalis flavula* of the eastern states.

(1) (*a*) EATON *Botany* (ed. 6) 33 *Asclepias tuberosa*, butterfly-weed, colic-root, pleurisy-root, white root. . . . Cathartic, diaphoretic, expectorant. (*b*) **1840** DEWEY *Mass. Flowering Plants* 208 *Aletris farinosa*. False Aloe. Colic Root. . . . The root is very bitter, and in small quantities used as a tonic and stomachic. **1843** TORREY *Flora N.Y.* II. 310 Star-grass. Colic-root. . . . Dry woods and thickets, sometimes in dry swamps. **1889** *Cent.* 136/3 The two species, *A. farinosa* and *A. aurea*, . . . are called colic-root from their medicinal reputation. (*c*) **1894** *Amer. Folk-Lore* VII. 97 *Asarum canadense*, . . . coltsfoot, N.Y. Colic-root. West Va. **1901** MOHR *Plant Life Ala.* 481 Colic Root [grows in] Alleghenian and Carolinian areas. — **(2) 1817–8** EATON *Botany* (1822) 253 *Corydalis cucullaria*, colic weed. **1821** *Mass. H.S. Coll.* 2 Ser. IX. 149 Plants, which are indigenous in the township of Middlebury, [Vt., include] . . . *Corydalis* . . . *glauca*, Colic-weed. **1840** DEWEY *Mass. Flowering Plants* 40 Colic Weed . . . blooms in May, along hedges and light woods.

colin 'kɑlɪn, *n.* [Amer. Sp. *colín* (<Nahuatl), in same sense.] The American quail or bobwhite.

[**1678** RAY (tr.) *Willughby's Ornith.* 393 Those of New Spain call Quails *Colin.* **1753** CHAMBERS *Cyclo. Supp. Colin*, . . . the name of an American bird, called by most authors a quail.] **1871** *Mich. Gen. Statutes* (1882–3) I. 583 No person shall kill or destroy, or attempt to kill or destroy, any colin or quail, [etc.]. **1897** *Ann. Rep. Comm. Fisheries* 317 American quail; Virginia quail; partridge or colin.

* **collapse,** *v.*

1. *To collapse a flue*, (see quot. 1833). Also transf. *Obs.*

1833 E. T. COKE *Subaltern's Furlough* v, I . . . used often to imagine what a hurry and scuffle there would be in the cabin, if the vessel 'collapsed its flue'— . . . or, in plain old English burst its boiler. **1847** ROBB *Squatter Life* 146, I do feel as ef I wur about to collapse a flue, or bust my biler, for the fact of the marter is, Marie, . . . ef I git caught here thar'll be suthin' broke. **1896** HASWELL *New York* 170 A flue of the boiler of this boat, on June 21, collapsed while she was landing at Poughkeepsie, and three persons were killed.

2. *tr.* To close or fold up into a smaller compass.

1921 MULFORD *Bar-20 Three* 229 Far back . . . a Mexican collapsed his telescope. **1944** *New Yorker* 16 Dec. 13/2 On the plextex wall behind them is a motto, . . . and next to it a booklet containing instructions for collapsing the premises.

∗**collar,** *n.*

1. *fig.* A collar for the neck as a symbol of subserviency to a political party or leader. *Obs.*

1834 *Boston Transcript* 5 April 2/1 Dennis Doyle . . . handed round a paper to obtain signatures to denounce the patriot Macneven, for refusing to wear a collar! **1836** *Cong. Globe* App. 9 May 337/1 Sir, I . . . am proud to wear the collar of such a man as Andrew Jackson, whose collar is the collar of Democracy. **1866** *Ib.* 6 April 1802/2 The Senator from O. has suggested that I have taken upon myself the collar of the President of the U.S.

b. Attrib. with **dog, man, press, representative.** *Obs.*

1833 *Niles' Reg.* XLIV. 146/2 Almost every generally accepted principle laid down in the proclamation may be clearly traced in Mr. Webster's 'federal,' or 'blue light' speech, as many of the 'collar presses' bawled out that it was. **1834** *Louisville Pub. Advertiser* 7 June, 'Collar-men' 'collar presses' and 'collar-representatives' are terms very much used by the opposition. **1836** *Cong. Deb.* 9 May 3552 Those who composed the Jackson party are denounced by the new-born whigs, as 'collar dogs.' . . . Sir, I am a party man, and one of the true collar dogs. **1840** *Log Cabin Song Book* 49 Van Buren's collar men . . . , They soon will fly their courses.

2. In special combs.: (1) **collar button,** a detachable button-like device used to fasten a collar to a shirt, also attrib.; (2) **paper,** paper used for making collars, also attrib.

(1) **1886** Stapleton *Major's Christmas* 253 Poor old Funk, he never has anything—a silver fruit knife and a collar button. They were all he had. **1946** *This Week Mag.* 28 Dec. 8/2, I will put a dime in the collar-button box on my dresser. — (2) **1867** *Atlantic Mo.* March 370/2 They learned that Columbia wears about her neck annually nearly as many reams of paper as she uses to write upon, and that this collar-paper may be made of stock much inferior to that employed for letter-paper. *Ib.*, In the Collar-paper Manufactory, . . . the pulp, when first drawn from the stuff-chest, is carried into a large trough.

b. *To fill one's collar,* to perform one's duties well. *Colloq.*

1898 Westcott *D. Harum* 195, I seen right off that you was goin' to fill your collar, fur's the work was concerned.

As the last term in **assassin, buggy, falling, flag, high, husk, portage, root, rush, sand, shuck, shuck horse, white collar.**

∗**collateral,** *n.* Anything given as collateral security.

1832 *Cong. Deb.* App. 62/2 May 13, 15 Days $20,000 collateral. **1911** Saunders *Col. Todhunter* 112 The Todhunter farm is as pretty a piece of collateral for a three-thousand-dollar loan as old Shylock himself would have the heart to ask. **1948** *Chi. Tribune* 20 June (Grafic Mag.) 23/2 Elliott had put up stock in the chain as collateral for the loan. *attrib.* **1865** *Boston Post* 28 July 2/5 The supply of currency was ample for commercial . . . paper at 6 per cent. up, for prime collateral loans.

collateral kəˈlætərəl, *v. tr.* To provide collateral security for (a loan). *Rare.* — **1907** *Sun* (N.Y.) 18 Dec. 4/1 Using the stock of the last purchase to collateral a loan with which to buy the new.

collect ˈkɑləkt, *n. local.* [In sense **1.** an Anglicizing of Du. *kolk*, a pit, or *kalk*, lime. Sense **2.** is a rare use of the ordinary English word.]

1. (*cap.*) Orig. a pond, later a region about this, in New York City near the present Tombs Prison. Also attrib.

1809 Irving *Hist. N.Y.* (1927) 1 My wife . . . would needs put him in her best chamber, which commands a very pleasant view of the new grounds on the Collect. **1896** Haswell *New York* 14 The Collect —that is, the pond that had been bounded by White, Bayard, Elm, Canal, and Pearl streets, which naturally had discharged into the East River through 'Wreck Brook,' across the region still known as 'The Swamp,' but had been diverted into the North River through a drain cut on the line of Canal Street, passing under the Stone Bridge —was but partly filled in. **1947** *New Yorker* 1 Mar. 24/3 That's the site of the Collect Pond, where people used to throw pieces of broken pottery and so on.

2. A depression in which water collects. *Rare.*

1839 in *Mich. Agric. Soc. Trans.* VII. 386 These sinks derive their name from the fact of their being collects for the waters of the surrounding region.

∗**collect,** *v.*

1. *tr.* To take or pick up from a place of deposit (see also quot. 1895). *Colloq.*

1875 C. James *Yoke of Freedom* 53 Jack went down the great marble staircase, . . . collected his hat and cloak, [etc.]. **1895** *Neb. St. Jrnl.* 23 June 5/5 To 'collect' an old ram requires good lungs, good legs, good judgment, and good shooting. **1928** F. N. Hart *Bellamy Trial* ii. 30, I was to collect the keys under the doormat at the gardener's cottage.

2. Used adverbially or as adj. to indicate that something sent, as a telegram, is to be paid for on delivery, in full *collect on delivery.* Cf. **C.O.D.**

1893 K. D. Wiggin *Polly Oliver* xv. 165 In an hour another message marked 'Collect,' followed the first one. **1913** *U.S. Postal Laws & Reg.* § 489 Collect-on-delivery service. *Ib.*, A collect-on-delivery parcel. **1948** *Time* 19 July 85 Please reserve two rooms for our representatives. . . . Confirm by wire collect.

∗**collector,** *n.* As the last term in **city, county, gold collector.**

∗**college,** *n.*

1. One of a group of buildings occupied by a college.

On this sense see O. F. Emerson in *Nation* LXI. 293 ff., *D.N.* IV. 299–300; and A. Matthews in *D.N.* II. 91–114 and *Mass. Col. Soc. Pub.* XV. cxxviii–cxxxi.

1654 *Harvard Inventory* in *Nation* LXI 346/1 Another house called Goffes colledge, & was purchased of Edw. Goffe. conteyning five chambers. **1712** in *D.N.* II. 99 Wee are of Opinion with respect to the Old College, That the best way is to take off the Roof. **1894** *Harvard Rec.* I. p. xxx. (*note*), I was born close to the colleges. **1916** *D.N.* IV. 300, I remember especially the night of the tornado which blew down the buildings of the college near our time of graduation,—the first report along the street was 'the colleges are down.'

2. A divisional unit in some universities.

1870 *Rep. Comm. Agric. 1869* 455 The university embraces a college of science, literature, and art; an agricultural and mechanical college, a college of the Bible; a normal college; a college of law; and a college of medicine. **1948** *Chi. Tribune* 27 June III. 6/3 The other [convocation was] . . . for the 749 students who received bachelor's degrees from the college of the university.

3. In combs.: (1) **college catalogue,** a pamphlet or book issued, usu. annually, by a college, and containing information, chiefly about departments and courses, of special interest to students; (2) **faculty,** the teaching staff of a college; (3) **farm,** a farm owned by a college, esp. one upon which experiments in agriculture are carried out; (4) **glee,** a song such as is popular with glee clubs made up of college students; (5) **Indian,** an Indian who has attended the schools provided by the white man, *rare;* (6) **journalism,** the business of writing for, editing, managing, etc., student publications in college; (7) **magazine,** a magazine brought out by college students; (8) **nine,** a college baseball team; (9) **periodical,** a periodical issued by college students; (10) **scrip,** land scrip issued and sold to establish a college or colleges; (11) **shark,** a college student who does brilliant work; (12) **store,** a store that specializes in supplies for college students; (13) **township,** a township of public land set aside for the benefit of a college; (14) **widow,** a young woman in a college town who year after year is popular with successive classes of college boys; (15) **yard,** at Harvard, and later at Yale, the grounds adjacent to the main building or buildings of a college, a campus; (16) **yell,** a yell adopted by college students, esp. for use in athletic contests.

(1) **1877** *Harper's Mag.* April 695/1 The number of names on a college catalogue affords . . . no means of estimate of the actual character of the instruction given by its authority. **1948** *Ponca City* (Okla.) *News* 4 July 9/5 Answers to most other individual questions or problems will be found in the college catalog. — (2) **1848** N. Ames *Childe Harvard* 141, I do conjure you, that ye suffer not Contempt of College Faculty to go Unpunished! **1945** *Grant Co.* (Wis.) *News* 12 April 1/6 College faculty and students will entertain visiting forensic contestants and friends. — (3) **1674** *Harvard Coll. Rec.* I. 60 Ordered that the treasurer . . . cause to be measured out the bounds of the Colledg farm near Pacatuck river in the Colony of Connecticut. **1874** *Dept. Agric. Rep. 1873* 307 Professor Goessman . . . gives the results of experiments made in 1872 on the college farm. — (4) **1897** Brodhead *Bound in Shallows* 86 'Ma,' she expostulated, 'how you go on! Just because Mr. Dillon gets me to play him college glees now and again.'

(5) **1724** Jones *Virginia* 19 The Northern and Southern Nations might be managed by Missionaries from the Society, and the College Indians. — (6) **1890** *N. & Q.* IV. 29 March 257 College journalism originated at Dartmouth, in 1800, with Daniel Webster as one of the editors. After a space of nine years, the *Literary Cabinet* was established at Yale, followed shortly afterwards by the *Fioriaa* at Union, and *Harvard Lyceum* at Harvard. — (7) **1836** *Harvardiana* III. 163

Embarrassments [are] to be met in conducting a college magazine. — **(8) 1882** *Nation* 30 Nov. 458/2 All the 'athletic sport' that the great majority of the students get consists in the payment of money to the 'College eight,' or 'College nine,' as the case may be. — **(9) 1836** *Harvardiana* II. 387 Evidently, a college periodical has . . . higher pretensions.

(10) 1869 *Cong. Globe* 4 Feb. 874/2 The proposition of the Senator from New York is to give to this college scrip a very considerable increased value. **1880** Lamphere *U.S. Govt.* 199/2 A homestead settler may . . . pay for it with cash, warrants, or college scrip, or private land scrip. — **(11) 1819** Peirce *Rebelliad* 60 He found already muster'd there . . . all the other college sharks. — **(12) 1850** Thaxter *Poem before Iadma* 19 Arrived at Harvard, straightway he adopts the bulletin's advice, And buys his books at the College Store. — **(13) 1803** *Cong. Deb.* (1851) 1330 No grant or promise of an academy or college township was inserted. — **(14) 1871** Bagg *At Yale* 523 A 'college widow' is the unfortunate young woman, who, having been the pet of several college generations without making a single permanent capture, at last finds herself deserted of admirers, and with faded charms falls out of sight and memory. **1907** *Nation* 26 Dec. 591/1 The professor's wife of this type is, we suppose, almost as well recognized in such an atmosphere as the 'college widow.'

(15) 1639 *Harvard Records* (1925) I. 172 The frame in the Colledge yard & digging the cellar, carriage & setting it up [£] 120. **c1764** in Woolsey *Hist. Disc. Yale* (1850) 55 The Freshmen are forbidden to wear their hats in College-yard . . . until May vacation. **1904** *N.Y. Ev.Post* 3 May 7 Sever Hall, one of the largest buildings in the college yard [at Harvard]. — **(16) 1923** E. F. Wyatt *Invis. Gods* II. iii. 62 Will Halliday seemed more and more the zenith of manly perfection . . . in college yells.

b. In combs. of obvious meaning or sufficiently explained in the quots., as (1) **college belle,** (2) **Bible,** (3) **boy,** (4) **campus,** (5) **classmate,** (6) **fraternity,** (7) **girl,** (8) **lot,** (9) **president,** (10) **settlement,** (11) **town.**

(1) 1882 Howells *Modern Instance* iii, These college-belles . . . were inferior to Marcia Gaylord, too, in looks and style. — **(2) 1850** Thaxter *Poem before Iadma* 14 The Student cons the College Bible with eager, longing eyes. **1851** Hall *College Words* 52 The laws of a college are sometimes significantly called *the College Bible.* **1855** *Harvard Mag.* I. 414 Whatever the College Bible tells us to do,—if we except nine tenths of it which is a dead letter,—that we usually do with all our might. — **(3) 1825** in *W. & M. Coll. Quart.* 2 Ser. VIII. 82 A Young Oxonian . . . with all the frankness of a 'College boy' told me he 'saw I was a stranger & would be happy to go the rounds with me.' **1925** Bryan *Memoirs* 97, I was still a college boy in 1880. — **(4) 1834** Simms *Guy Rivers* I. xv. 219 Ralph . . . acted . . . precisely as he might have done in the College Campus, with all the benefits of a fair field and a plentiful crowd of backers. **1943** *Nat. Geog. Mag.* April 407/2 Hanover is Dartmouth and Dartmouth is Hanover. Town common and college campus, deep and elm-shaded, are one and the same.

(5) 1877 *Harper's Mag.* Dec. 110/1 Mr. Daly was a college classmate of mine. — **(6) 1888** *Cent. Mag.* Sep. 759/1 The constitutions of many college fraternities are now open to the inspection of faculties. **1943** Menefee *Assignment* 40 The 'Forty Thieves' draw their membership from older boys and once maintained a house—something like a college fraternity, with jungle ethics their major study.—**(7) 1882** *Nation* 13 July 22/3 College boys and college girls fresh from their books could stand a better examination than people who had practical experience. **1944** *Chi. Tribune* 10 Dec. (Grafic Mag.) 3 Its president . . . clings fast to her belief 'that the college girl doesn't do anything better for being dirty or sloppy while she does it.' — **(8) 1871** Bagg *At Yale* 534 The 'College lot' is quite near the entrance of the same [New Haven Cemetery], and many tutors as well as undergraduates of all classes have been laid there side by side. — **(9)** [**1835** Ingraham *South-West.* I. xxii. 233 The lady of a living collegiate president is of the élite, decidedly.] **1845** *Knickerb.* XXV. 182 The writer gives the reply of a fellow-student to a question of a college president. **1941** Lee *Stagecoach North* 51 He looked more like a college president than a backwoods lawyer.

(10) 1909 Webster 438/1 College settlement, a social settlement in charge of an organization of college students or graduates. — **(11) 1852** *Harper's Mag.* V. 334/2 It was in one of those quiet college towns which are the pleasantest spots in New England. **1945** *Nat. Geog. Mag.* May 541 Wayne, where a State Teachers College is located, is a pretty college town.

As the last term in **business, commercial, country, electoral, fresh-water, Indian, junior, land grant, log, manual labor, metaphysical, Orleans, senior, state, state teachers', teachers', war college.**

colleger 'kɑlɪdʒɚ, *n.* A student at college. — **1827** *Harvard Reg.* (1828) 214, I guess as how, if we get fore-handed enough we'll send him to be a Colledger, and make a Parson of him. **1927** J. Freeman *When West Was Young* 345 You don't need to git rough, you young colleger!

∗**collegiate,** *a.* (See quots.) *Obs.* — **1818** J. Bristed *Resources U.S.* 413 There is, however, in some of our cities, a custom, which diminishes their usefulness; namely, the collegiate system which makes three or four churches common to as many, or more clergymen. . . . The essence of the collegiate system is, not to suffer the same clergyman to preach twice successively in the same church. **1864** Webster 251, Collegiate church, . . . a church which is united with others under the joint pastorate of several ministers. (U.S.)

Collins ax. An ax so named from its manufacturer (see quot. 1943).

[**1848** C. L. Fleischmann *Nordamerikanische Landwirth* 306 Es giebt viele Fabriken welche sich mit Anfertigung von Aexten beschäftigen, worunter die von Collins die besten und dauerhaftesten liefert; sie werden von verschiedener Grösse, Schwere und Form gemacht.] **1850** *Quincy* (Ill.) *Whig* 12 Nov. 3/1 Collins, Hunt, & Simmons axes, for sale by the dozen . . . at St. Louis prices. **1864** *Harper's Mag.* Oct. 574/1 One went with a necklace of mattocks around his neck and those Collins axes in his girdle. [**1943** Crow *Amer. Customer* 65 Samuel W. Collins was a Connecticut hardware dealer

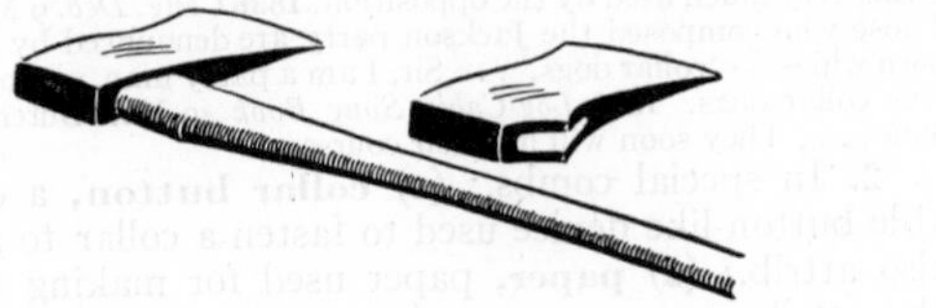

Typical Collins axes used for chopping

who noted the universal demand for axes and the generally poor quality of those supplied and decided to go into the business of manufacturing them. After running a small shop in Hartford,Connecticut, for a few years, he later built a factory on the Farmington River which for more than a hundred years has been the world's largest producer of axes.]

Collinsia kə'lɪnzɪə, *n.* [f. Zaccheus *Collins* (1764–1831), a Philadelphia botanist.] A genus of annual or biennial herbs of the figwort family, or a plant of this genus.

1821 Nuttall *Trav. Arkansa* 127 The acclivity, through a scanty thicket, rather than the usual sombre forest, was already adorned with violets, and occasional clusters of the parti-coloured Collinsia. **1845** Wilkes *U.S. Expl. Exped.* IV. 307 Among them were to be seen Ranunculus, Scilla, Lupinus, Collinsia, and Balsamoriza. **1857** Gray *Botany* 285 Collinsia. . . . Rich shady places, W. New York to Wisconsin and Kentucky. May, June. **1917** Saunders *Western Flower Guide* 193 Collinsia is a North American genus which preserves in its name the memory of an excellent botanist of a century ago, Zaccheus Collins of Philadelphia.

colloquian kə'lokwɪən, *n.* One who engages in a colloquy *q.v. Obs.* — **1871** G. R. Cutting *Student Life at Amherst Coll.* 40 For the Exhibition, four orators are now chosen in each society from the Senior class, instead of three as formerly, and the colloquians of each society unite in the composition of an original 'colloquy.'

∗**colloquy,** *n.* A college exercise consisting of a prepared conversation. Also attrib. *Obs.* — **1860** *Yale Lit. Mag.* XXV. 399 (Th.), Some cue that will enable colloquy men to save an inglorious fizzle. **1861** *Ib.* XXVI. 80 (Th.), He has just succeeded in getting a Colloquy appointment. **1871** [see **colloquian**].

colloquy 'kɑləkwɪ, *v. intr.* To converse, to engage in a colloquy. *Obs.* — **1868** Hawthorne *Note-Books* I. 135 Then they colloquied at much length about the various peculiarities and merits of the new invention. **1871** *Cong. Globe* 16 March 126/1, I saw the Speaker colloquying with the Democrats.

∗**cologne,** *n.* A toilet water composed of alcohol and aromatic oils. Also attrib. See also **log cabin cologne.**

1832 Kennedy *Swallow Barn* I. 125 She would like to have some Cologne of a particular kind. **1851** Hall *Manhattaner* 36 His cologne bottle and flesh brush will find active employment in the duties of the toilet. **1946** *Chi. D. News* 5 Aug. 13/6 (*heading*), Soap, Cologne Combine To Wash Heat Away.

Also **cologne water.**

1814 *Boston Indep. Chronicle* 20 Jan. 4/4 (*advt.*), Cologne Water. **1838** Hawthorne *Note-Books* I. 119 Cologne-water is among the essences manufactured though the bottles have foreign labels on them. **1939** Brownell *Horse & Buggy Philos.* 51 If a skunk bathed in cologne water every morning he would still be a skunk.

colonche ko'lontʃe, *n.* Also †**calinche.** *S.W.* [Amer. Sp. in same sense.] (See quots.)

1846 Bryant *California* (1848) 376 A juicy fruit is produced by the prickly-pear, named *tuna,* from which a beverage is sometimes made called *calinche.* **1895** *Amer. Folk-Lore* Jan.-Apr. 58 The pink *colonche* or cider of the tuna, . . . is an exceptionally good drink. **1911** Wooton

Cacti in N.M. 25 *Colonche* (Co-lone-chay) is a fermented drink made from these fruits [i.e., tunas].

colonel, *n. A title of respect but without military associations. *Colloq.*

1744 A. HAMILTON *Itinerarium* (1907) 94 Had it been a rattlesnake I should have been entitled to a colonel's commission for it is a common saying here that a man has no title to that dignity until he has killed a rattlesnake. **c1855** ROBERTSON *Few Mos.* 107 This reminds me, that in the South and West, nearly all tall men are called generals, stout men judges, and men of middling proportions, captains or colonels! **1896** HARRIS *Sister Jane* 11 His title of colonel . . . was purely a title of respect, a mark of the esteem in which he was held by his friends and neighbors, a tribute to his moral and business qualities. **1939** WELLMAN *Trampling Herd* 81 Auctioneers, by virtue of their office, were colonels in the west.

As the last term in **Kentucky, rattlesnake, secesh colonel.**

colonial, *n. A kind of drink. *Rare.* — **1900** H. LAWSON *Over Sliprails* 70 'Wal, I reckon you can build me your national drink. I guess I'll try it.' A long colonial was drawn for him.

colonial, *a.

1. Belonging to, or characteristic of, the period of the colonies, esp. of architecture.

1776 *Boston Rec.* 240 How many Persons belonging to this Family are now in the Service? Is it Continental, or Coloniel? Is it by Sea, or by Land? *Ib.* 242 The Question [was] accordingly put—Whether holding any military Commission in the Continental or Colonial Army is not incompatable [*sic*] with holding any Civil Trust? **1836** *S. Lit. Messenger* II. 284 The Colonial Legislature claimed the supreme power as residing within itself. **1886** *Harper's Mag.* Oct. 668/1 The building has rather a colonial character with its long corridors and pillared piazzas. **1946** *Negro Digest* Aug. 51/1 The Man Bilbo relaxes confidently in his Dream House, near Poplarville. . . . The Dream House, a brick colonial mansion built during his last term as governor.

2. *Colonial Dames of America,* either of two national organizations of American women of colonial descent, for the purpose of collecting and preserving documents, relics, etc.

1897 (*title*), Officers and Members of the Massachusetts Society of the Colonial Dames of America. **1905** *Mass. Soc. Col. Dames America Reg.* 13 The Society of Colonial Dames of America has been formed . . . to do honor to the virtues of their forefathers [etc.]. **1918** *Encycl. Amer.* VII 286/2 Colonial Dames of America, The National Society of. An ancestral and patriotic organization of American women, founded 19 May 1892, and composed of one Colonial Society from each of the 13 original States, one society from the District of Columbia and one associate society from each of the non-colonial States.

b. (See quot.)

1948 *Vt. Quart.* April 49 Vermont has its own organization of Colonial Dames.

***colonialism, *n.* 1.** A condition characteristic of the colonial period in American history. **2.** The policy of acquiring overseas dependencies, imperialism.

(1) **1884** *Boston Journal* 30 Dec. 2/4 The Anglomaniacs are delighting their small souls with this remnant of the spirit of colonialism. **1904** *N.Y. Times* 9 May 9 Through the southern part of Maryland to the Potomac, a region of old families, old prejudices, sleepy Colonialism, and the colored brother. — (2) **1904** *Topeka D. Capital* 2 June 4 McKinley, Root, Roosevelt and Taft have all at one time or another declared for eventual independence of the Philippines. Probably few Americans hope to see colonialism perpetuated.

colonies, *n. pl. As the last term in **middle, thirteen, thirteen united, United colonies.**

colonist ˈkɑlənɪst, *n.* [**colony*+*-ist.*]

1. A settler in one of the American colonies prior to 1776.

1701 J. LOGAN in *Pa. Hist. Soc. Mem.* IX. 68 If good colonists were brought into them, . . . there might be raised some thousands of pounds. **1823** COOPER *Pioneers* ii, Mr. Effingham had, from the commencement of the disputes between the colonists and the crown, warmly maintained what he believed to be the just prerogatives of his prince. **1853** in WINTHROP *Hist.* (1908) I. 1 (*note*), Endicot and the first colonists of Massachusetts demand our gratitude for the Abigail.

b. An early settler from the U.S. in Texas before its admission to the Union, or one of those who went to Kansas to take part in the struggle over slavery there in 1854–58. *Obs.*

1838 C. NEWELL *Revol. Texas* 203 A large portion of our population, usually denominated 'the Colonists,' and composed of Anglo-Americans, have been greatly calumniated before the Mexican government. **1877** JOHNSON *Anderson Co., Kans.* 209 Spriggs and Heflin opened a store at a little town . . . where they kept such articles as were most needed by the colonists. **1901** DUNCAN & SCOTT *Allen & Woodson Co., Kans.* 69 His sympathies were against the Abolition Colonists, and as he had the reputation of backing his opinion with his revolver, he was a terror to the 'Yankee Colonists.'

c. One who takes up government land with the intention of transferring it to another individual or company. *Obs.*

1910 WHITE *Rules of Game* 534 'The "colonists,"' said Bob, 'took up this land merely for the purpose of turning it over to the company.'

2. A settler in the West from one of the older states.

1871 *Colo. Gazeteer* 130 The Greeley colonists will broaden in their sympathies and views of life, after inhaling the mountain atmosphere of this region for a few years. **1948** *Sat. Ev. Post* 26 June 6/3 As he pushed his Great Northern across plains and mountains, he dropped off colonists from boxcars wherever the rails ended and built up communities.

b. *attrib.* Designating railroad passenger cars provided for such colonists. Cf. **emigrant train.**

1889 *Union Pac. RR. Ore. & Wash.* 80 In addition to the above the Company also run free Colonist Cars between Portland and Chicago. **1890** H. PALMER *Stories Base Ball Field* 218 Pullman Sleepers, Dining Cars, And Free Colonist Sleepers On Express Trains Daily. **1948** *Sat. Ev. Post* 4 Sep. 21/3 He often rode colonist cars from Nelson, British Columbia, to Montreal—three nights and two days—on an outlay of seventy-five cents.

3. A person who moves temporarily into a polling district to participate in an approaching election.

1868 *Nation* VI. 282 When every town and city in the United States is voting on the same day, and 'colonists' and 'repeaters' are needed at home, and each State is reduced for its voters to its own citizens. **1909** *Daily Chron.* 3 Nov. 1/6 It is more than likely that thousands of their 'colonists' have voted in some of the districts.

4. A member of a group united by a common bond of cultural, political, or other interests. *Rare.*

1893 J. AULD *Picturesque Burlington* 32 Wilcox and his disciples . . . entered into their socialistic scheme under the name of Dawn Valcour Community. The colony was hardly settled before dissensions arose and the colonists divided themselves into two camps, one on either end of the island.

5. A resident at a summer resort.

1903 *N.Y. Tribune* 27 Sep., The younger colonists [at Tuxedo] joined in a paper chase through the park this afternoon on horseback.

As the last term in **Oklahoma, Shalam, Yankee colonist.**

colonization, *n.

1. (See quot. 1914.) Cf. **colonist, *n.* 3.**

1842 *Cong. Globe* App. 31 May 471/2 Could it even be hoped, while the street of a compact city should be made the boundary between congressional districts, that 'colonization' and 'pipe-laying' would be effectually prevented? **1892** *Boston Journal* 7 Nov. 7/4 My attention was directed to the alleged cases of false registration or colonization in this morning's Herald. **1914** *Cyclo. Amer. Govt.* III. 629 In crowded city wards colonization of voters is sometimes attempted. Groups of voters transferred from a 'safe' precinct to a 'doubtful' one get a show of legal residence for a few days necessary before the election. . . . More often illegal colonization is practiced; men without even this brief residence in the district are registered and voted.

2. Attrib. with **cause, company, society,** with reference to the colonization of Negroes from the U.S. in Africa or elsewhere. Cf. **National Colonization Society.**

1817 *Niles' Reg.* XIII. 82/2 It is contemplated, by the present plan of the American colonization society, to find each colonist with food for one year, after his arrival in Africa. **1818** J. BRISTED *Resources U.S.* 150 The intention, at present, on the part of the Colonization Company, is to settle as many free blacks as they can induce to go. **1833** in *Cent. Mag.* XXX. (1885) 784/2 [Wm. Lloyd Garrison] has only since 1830 turned against the Colonization cause. **1947** *Tenn. Hist. Quart.* Dec. 296 He fully approved of the American Colonization Society's plan to send the Negroes back to Africa.

colonizationism ˌkɑlənɪˈzeʃənɪzəm, *n.* The principles of colonizationists *q.v.* *Obs.*—**1831** *Liberator* I. 174/1 It is the intention of the writer of this article to discuss the subject with some fair and able . . . advocate of Colonisation-ism. **1832** in *Life W. L. Garrison* (1885) I. 327 Here I am now in the hot-bed of Colonizationism.

colonizationist ˌkɑlənɪˈzeʃənɪst, *n.* An advocate of ameliorating the condition of Negro slaves in the U.S. by establishing them in colonies elsewhere, chiefly in Africa. Also attrib. *Obs.*

1831 *Liberator* I. 174/1 Why do Colonizationists generally shrink from a fair contest on the merits of their system? **1854** in C. ROBIN-

SON *Kans. Conflict* (1892) 94 So it is with the colonizationist societies and their dupes they send to abolitionize Kansas. **1881** JOHNSON *Garrison & Times* 100 A colored man from Liberia, a man of intelligence as well as wealth, and highly esteemed by Colonizationists, being on a visit to Boston, took the opportunity of making the acquaintance of the Abolitionists. **1905** HUME *Abolitionists* 130 It completely unmasked the pretended friendship of the Colonizationists for the negroes, free or slave.

* **colonize,** *v.*

1. *tr.* To place or register (hired political supporters) in doubtful districts where their votes may decide a closely contested election. Also transf. and absol. Hence **colonizing,** *n.*

1842 *Cong. Globe* App. 31 May 471/1 So far as he was informed, the practice of colonizing had its origin, as connected with the elections of the people in our country, in the city of New York. **1885** *Cent. Mag.* Feb. 636 All the political rascality of the country stands ready to contribute its services. . . . Arrangements are made for colonizing voters from the neighboring States. **1903** *N.Y. Tribune* 13 Sep., The attempt to colonize in the Third Ward by a faction of the Democratic party was frustrated to-day. **1948** *New Yorker* 25 Sep. 26/1 Floaters are retainers of po itical organizations, and it's still common practice to 'colonize' doubtful districts with them.

2. *W.* To secure (public land or mining claims) in excess of the legal maximum by employing others to take out individual claims.

1910 WHITE *Rules of Game* 366 'This bunch of prospectors files on the claims, and gets them patented. Then it's nobody's business what they do with their own property. So they just sell it to me.' 'That's colonizing,' objected Bob. *Ib.* 534 It appears as though the lands were 'colonized.' *Ib.* 559 They believe that we did actually colonize the lands.

* **colonizer,** *n.* One who "colonizes" (voters). Cf. * **colonize,** *v.* **1.**

1892 *Nation* LV. 274/3 With the New York cheats, bullies, receivers, colonizers, . . . he can have but a very slight acquaintance. **1904** *N.Y. Ev. Post* 7 Nov. 1 The superintendent of elections is authority for the statement that there are gangs of colonizers and repeaters in the city. **1935** PEEL *Political Clubs N.Y. City* 35 As fast as the Whigs could import colonizers, they were beaten back by the stalwart Democrats.

* **colony,** *n.*

1. (See quots.) Cf. **colonist,** *n.* **3; colonization,** *n.* **1; colonize,** *v.* **1.**

1900 FLYNT *Itinerant Policeman* 191 In large cities like New York, Chicago, Philadelphia, and San Francisco, and during fiercely fought political struggles even in some of the smaller towns, they [tramps] are collected into colonies by unscrupulous electioneering specialists, and paid to vote as they are told. **1900** *Chi. Times-Herald* 2 May 5/2 One of the Carter canvassers in the Twelfth ward claims to have discovered an anti-Carter 'colony' in the Chicago Dental College.

2. In obs. combs.: (1) **colony agent,** (*a*) before the Revolution one who represented an American colony in Europe, (*b*) an agent of a land company interested in settling a particular area; (2) **bill,** a form of paper money issued by one of the American colonies; (3) **excursion,** an excursion promoted by a land company in its efforts to secure settlers for a particular region; (4) **line,** the boundary line of a colony; (5) **scheme,** a plan or scheme of a land company for settling an area in which they are interested.

(1) (*a*) **1774** *Jrnls. Cont. Cong.* I. 104 Resolved, That the address to the King, be enclosed to the several colony agents. **1775** *Ib.* II. 24 The inclosed Packet, containing . . . a Letter to our Colony Agent, Benjamin Franklin, Esqr. [etc.]. (*b*) **1878** BEADLE *Western Wilds* 388 [Duluth] was lively with immigrants, colony agents, real estate speculators, travelers and freighters. — (2) **1740** W. DOUGLASS *Discourse* 7 Some are . . . in Paper Money called Colony or Province Bills of public Credit. **1767** FRANKLIN *Wks.* (1887) IV. 86 Their being payable in cash, upon sight, by the drawer, is indeed a circumstance that cannot attend the colony bills. — (3) **1889** *Whitewater* (Wis.) *Reg.* 25 Oct. Ho! For California. All who desire can join the colony excursions going there and get homes and wealth in that mild and healthful climate. — (4) **1690** *Conn. Col. Rec.* IV. 40 Neer the northeast corner of the Colony line. **1816** *Mass. H.S. Coll.* 2 Ser. VII. 118 Some of the water of the great pond in Weymouth, will flow southerly, which shews that the colony line is, in this part of it, on the height of land. — (5) **1871** *Colo. Gazeteer* 128 Scarcely a State east of the Mississippi but has had its colony scheme and colony excitement. **1883** *Cent. Mag.* Aug. 524/1 The colony scheme has been completed; the [San Jacinto] valley has been divided up.

Also *colony law, prison, record, road, seal, servant, treasury,* etc.

As the last term in **bay, bread, colored, gopher, muskrat, northern, Old, paper-money, tent, tobacco colony.**

colonyite ˈkɑlənɪˌaɪt, *n.* A member of a colony sponsored by a land company. *Rare.* — **1873** *Newton Kansan* 12 June 2/3 The Syracuse colonyites are stampeding for Barton county.

***colophon,** *n.* A publisher's imprint. — **1930** *Publishers' Weekly* 19 April 2113/1 The publishers must cut their lists and have their colophons stand for a particular quality which, in time the bookseller will recognize and consider in his buying. **1948** *Chi. Tribune* 27 June IV. 5/1 The Wilson company uses the lighthouse for its colophon and declares it symbolizes the guidance which the firm gives to those seeking their way thru the maze of books and periodicals.

* **color,** *n.*

1. *Western mining.* A mere trace of metallic gold.

1851 L. A. CLAPPE *Lett. from Calif.* 92 There is a deep pit in front of our cabin, and another at the side of it, though they are not worked, as, when 'prospected,' they did not 'yield the color.' **1910** J. HART *Vigilante Girl* 51 Sometimes riffles would be clogged with coarse gold; . . . often there was nothing in them but 'the color'—ghostly flakes of gold set in black sand. **1948** *Pacific Discovery* Mar.–Apr. 19/2 It was hard work, this moving gravel into new piles, . . . panning out the residue for the little specks of color.

fig. and *transf.* **1868** HARTE *Luck of Roaring Camp*, 'Is that him?' 'mighty small specimen'; 'hasn't mor'n got the colour.' **1873** MILLER *Amongst Modocs* 43 'Are you really dead-broke?' 'Skinned clean down to the bedrock. Haven't got the colour.' **1947** *Harper's Mag.* March 228/1 Without attempting immediately to assay the Wheeler 'color' and determine whether that glittering stuff was gold or just iron pyrites [etc.].

b. In pl., or with *a*, where "a color" is conceived of as a particle of gold.

1859 G. A. JACKSON *Diary* 5 Jan., Panned out two cups, nothing but fine colors. **1874** RAYMOND *9th Rep. Mines* 18 Each sample or pan so taken showed one or more 'colors' to the pan. In no case was there a failure to obtain a color. **1947** *Desert Mag.* Feb. 6/2 Shorty would follow a mirage if in it were reported to be some 'colors.'

2. In combs.: (1) **color dirt,** dirt showing only a trace of the presence of gold; (2) **line,** see as a main entry.

(1) **1944** *Nat. Geog. Mag.* June 673/2 When the placer miner quit the worked-out claims of early days, many a roystering town, like Roosevelt, became a ghostly place of echoes, visited only occasionally by patient Chinese who earned a good living from panning color dirt cast aside by white men.

As the last term in **bacon, off color.**

Coloradan ˌkɑləˈrɑdən, *a.* and *n.* Also **Coloradian, Coloradoan.** [f. **Colorado** *q.v.*]

1. *n.* A native or resident of Colorado.

1863 in *Mont. Hist. Soc. Contrib.* III (1900) 329 Drove to Rocky Point. There we met a train of Coloradians. **1871** *Colo. Gazeteer* 130 In time they may teach the recklessly extravagant Coloradans a wholesome lesson of saving and economy. **1879** WILLIAMS *Pacific Tourist* 79/1 Why, Coloradoans are the most disappointed people I ever saw. Two-thirds of them came here to die, and they *can't do it.* **1947** *Trail & Timberline* Feb. 15/1 Many Coloradoans have shown interest in the recreational possibilities of Alaska.

b. The speech regarded as characteristic of Coloradans.

1880 *Harper's Mag.* Mar. 544/2 The latter, with a lofty superiority, stigmatized us as 'tender-feet' (Coloradoan for new-comers).

2. *a.* Pertaining to or characteristic of Colorado.

1868 BOWLES *Colorado* (1869) 82 Long's Peak . . . is the prominent north-eastern mountain of the Coloradian series, . . . and is fourteen thousand feet high. **1879** TAYLOR *Summer-Savory* 33 There is yet another cough, which may be called the cough colloquial and Coloradan.

Colorado ˌkɑləˈrɑdo, *n.* [Sp. *colorado*, red, used first of the river and later of the state.] The name of a river and state used in combs.: (1) **Colorado bee plant,** the Rocky Mountain bee plant; (2) **beetle,** =**Colorado potato beetle,** also attrib.; (3) **blue grass,** (see quot.); (4) **blue spruce,** a decorative evergreen spruce, *Picea pungens;* (5) **blue stem,** (see quot.); (6) **bug,** =**Colorado potato beetle;** (7) **grass,** (see quot.); (8) **potato beetle,** a beetle, *Leptinotarsa decemlineata*, very destructive to the leaves of the potato; (9) **potato bug,** =prec.; (10) **raven,** the American raven, *Corvus corax;* (11) **turkey,** =**wood ibis;** (12) **white fir,** =**white fir.**

(1) **1938** GOODDING *Native & Exotic Plants* 62 *Cleome serrulata* is the common Colorado Beeplant, readily recognized by its large bunches of pink flowers. — (2) **1868** *Mich. Agric. Rep.* VII. 181 A plant . . . of the night-shade family . . . was well covered with the Colorado

beetle and its slugs. **1948** *Chi. Tribune* 15 Feb. I. 30/6 An import license was refused because of the danger of Colorado beetle infestation. — **(3) 1894** *Amer. Folk-Lore* VII. 103 *Agropyrum glaucum* . . . slough-grass, pond-grass, Colorado blue-grass. — **(4) 1897** Sudworth *Arborescent Flora* 40 *Picea pungens*. . . . Common names [include] Colorado Blue Spruce (Colo.). **1933** *Colo. Agric. Coll. Bul.* 326-A 11 Since the chief purposes of tree distribution by the State Forester are for windbreaks, shelterbelts and groves, rather than for ornamentation, the Colorado Blue Spruce is no longer offered by him.

(5) 1894 Coulter *Bot. W. Texas* III. 549 *Agropyron repens*.—(Colorado Blue-stem.) . . . High plains, western Texas and northward. — **(6) 1867** *Mich. Agric. Rep.* VI. 72 The Colorado bug is a native of Colorado, and . . . was confined there till the potato was brought thither, which, suiting its taste better than its original food, it commenced its fearful ravages, moving eastward sixty miles a year, destroying the entire potato crop in its course. **1868** *Rep. Comm. Agric.* 64 Specimens of . . . the 'Colorado bug' have reached the Department, and prove to be merely varieties of the *Cantharis*, or potato bug of the eastern States. — **(7) 1889** Vasey *Agric. Grasses* 25 *Panicum Texanum* (Texas Millet). . . . It is frequently called Colorado grass, from its abundance along the Colorado River in that State. — **(8) 1868** *Mich. Agric. Rep.* VII. 165 In the report of 1867, quite a lengthy account was given of the Colorado potato beetle—(*Doryphora 10-lineata*) of Say. **1946** *Reader's Digest* Sep. 10/1 The notorious Japanese beetle is a DDT casualty, and so are the Colorado potato beetle, the gypsy moth, . . . and the Oriental fruit moth. — **(9) 1870** *Cin. Commercial* 16 May 7/2 It is the Colorado potato bug which, in 1868, appeared in Ohio, and as far east as Western Virginia. **1876** *Field & Forest* Sep. 44 A closer examination showed the destructive agent to be the Colorado potato-bug.

(10) 1858 Baird *Birds Pacific R.R.* 563 *Corvus cacolotl*, Wagler. Colorado Raven. *Ib.* 564 The general appearance is that of the Colorado raven. — **(11)** *Ib.* 682 *Tantalus loculator*, Linn. Wood ibis . . . is said to be abundant on the Colorado river, especially about Fort Yuma, and to be there called Colorado turkey. **1917** *Birds of Amer.* I. 178. — **(12) 1897** Sudworth *Arborescent Flora* 55 *Abies concolor*. . . . Common names [include] . . . Colorado White Fir (Col. lit.).

* **colored,** *a.* Used in combs. with reference to things for, or made up of, Negroes, as (1) **colored car,** (2) **colony,** (3) **gallery,** (4) **league,** (5) **school,** (6) **suffrage.**

(1) 1885 *Cent. Mag.* XXX. 685/1 The 'ladies' car' of the morning trip became the 'colored car' on the return, afternoon trip. — **(2) 1872** *Newton Kansan* 3 Oct. 2/2 A colored colony lost very heavily, and many others. — **(3) 1851** *Polly Peablossom* 104 The yellow tickets are for parquette and boxes, the blue ones for third tier, and the white for the coloured gallery. — **(4) 1887** *Courier-Journal* 8 May 11/2 The National Colored League season was formally opened yesterday at the Louisville Base Ball Park.

(5) 1829 *Yankee* April 127/2 The primary schools—colored schools— . . . are now so good in themselves, [etc.]. **1944** *Democrat* 27 Jan. 2/4 (*heading*), Colored school raises $52.00 at rally. — **(6) 1878** *N. Amer. Rev.* CXXVI. 387 State governments are opposed to colored suffrage.

Also *colored church, circle, citizen, class, congregation, domestic, gentleman, laborer, lady, man, people, person, population, regiment, society, student, troops*, etc.

c. colored supplement, a section of a newspaper devoted to colored pictures, transf. in quot.

1912 C. Mathewson *Pitching* xi. 236 'The necktie,' he explained that night at dinner, and pointed to the three-sheet, colored-supplement affair he was wearing around his collar.

color line.

1. *Mil.* A line of stacked rifles at which the colors rest.

1861 *Army Regulations* 75 The colors are then planted at the centre of the color line, and the arms are stacked on the line. **1888** Billings *Hardtack* 73 . . . Each company of a regiment should pitch its tents in two files . . . at right angles with the color-line of the regiment.

2. The line of social and political distinctions between Negroes and white people.

1875 in Fleming *Hist. Reconstruction* II. 396 The 'color-line' means that the whites of this State have become satisfied that it is useless further to attempt to coalesce with the negroe element in voting. **1897** Howells *Open-eyed Conspiracy* xi., I was glad to find that the good taste and the correct fashion were without a color-line; there were some mulatto ladies present as stylish as their white sisters, or stepsisters. **1948** *Chi. Tribune* 29 Aug. I. 20/1 The Supreme court, in cases dealing with educational opportunities in states which maintain color lines in schools, has not ordered the color line abolished.

b. *To draw the color line*, to make distinctions on the basis of color. Also *to cross the color line*, to act without making such distinction.

[**1878** *N.Y. Herald* 12 Dec. 3/6 In saying this he did not raise a color line, but rather he sought to destroy it.] **1885** *Cent. Mag.* XXX. 274/2 The negro is quick to draw the color-line. **1894** Cable *J. March* xxii., 'I'd marry you ef you wuz pyowhite!' . . . 'You wouldn' be afeared evm to cross de color line?' **1905** N. Davis *Northerner* 67 You have endangered the 'Caucasian supremacy of the White Hosts of the American continent' by your 'incendiary action in crossing the color-line.' Alec's strong on the color-line! He makes copy of it whenever he is short of locals. **1948** *Chi. D. News* 3 March 20/2 Would you Southern Democratic rebels draw the color line if the convention should nominate a dark horse?

colorphobia ˌkʌlɚˈfobɪə, *n.* Dislike of Negroes.

1841 in Joseph Sturge *Visit to U.S.* (1842) cxl, On board the cars Colorophobia again began to rage; but the agent soon quelled it. **1847** W. L. Garrison in Garrison *W. L. Garrison* III. 200 A genuine specimen of American democratic, Christian colorphobia. **1886** *Boston Jrnl.* 23 Oct. 6 Colorphobia in Chicago. A colored Congregational preacher . . . began suit to-day for $5000 against Robert J. Mossop, a restaurant keeper on West Madison street, and his head waiter James Hughes. The charge against the defendants is that they refused to allow Smith to take a meal in the restaurant.

Hence **colorphobist,** *n. Obs.*

1870 *Cin. Commercial* 13 May 4/5 Both sets of delegates, the colorphobists and the philanthropists retained their place upon the floor.

* **Colt,** *n.* A firearm of a type invented by Samuel Colt (1814–62). Often in the possessive or as attrib.

1838 in Easterby *S.C. Rice Plant.* (1945) 84 Have you seen any of Colts patent repeating rifles? **1861** *Harper's Wkly.* 6 July 430/1 Each is armed with a pair of Colt's navy revolvers, a rifle, a Texan bowie-knife, and a lasso. **1948** *Range Riders Western* May 16/1 Desperately, the rancher tried to trigger his Colt again.

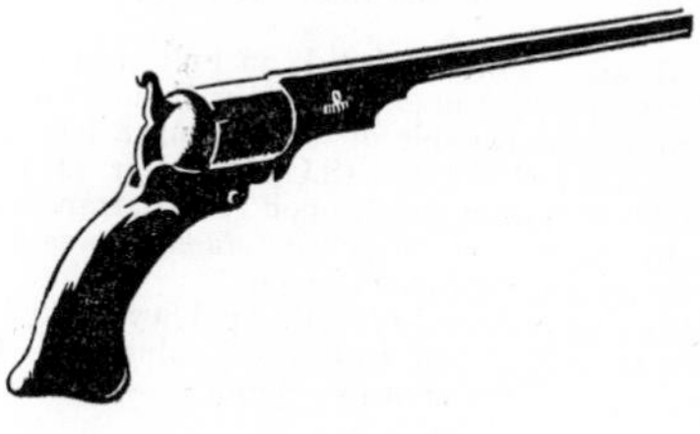

Early model Colt

b. Esp. **Colt's revolving pistol.** *Obs.* Cf. **revolving pistol.**

1840 *Spirit of Times* 5 Sep. 319/1 (We.). If you have any of Colt's revolving pistols take that along. **1844** *Lexington Observer* 24 July 3/4 The doctor, drawing a pair of Colt's revolving pistols, prepared to receive his excellency.

As the last term in **frontier, Judge, kicking, Morgan, mustang, old field, woods colt.**

* **colt's-tail,** *n.* (See quot.). *Obs.* — **1829** *Mass. Spy* 13 May (Th.), It has been the uniform custom, at our courts, to break in the new members of every Grand Jury, by requiring them to pay what is called a colt's tail—or in other words a treat.

Columbia kəˈlʌmbɪə, *n.* [f. *Columbus*, the Latinized name of the discoverer of America.]

1. A name for the U.S., esp. in poetical or oratorical contexts.

1775 Wheatley in *Pa. Mag.* (1776) April 193 Columbia's scenes of glorious toil I write. **1846** *N.Y. Tribune* 5 Jan. 1/4 We propose that our country shall take to herself the name Columbia, in honor of the great Discoveror of this continent. **1910** O. Henry *Strictly Business* 28, I don't know where this country of yours is, but I'm for it. I guess it must be a branch of the United States, though, for the poetry guys and the schoolmarms call us Columbia, too, sometimes. **1947** *St. Louis Globe-Democrat* 7 Sep., Perhaps Columbia was too poetical a name for our practical-minded people; or perhaps Freneau was not quite a great enough poet.

2. A special type of passenger locomotive having two pilot-truck wheels, four driving wheels and two trailing-truck wheels.

1861 *Remin. Life Locomotive Engineer* 110 As Hi was Passing the curve one day, running at full speed, some slight obstruction caused the Columbia to leave the track.

3. Columbia formation, (see quot. 1909).

1896 Clendenin *Fla. Parishes E. La.* 187 Both Lafayette and Columbia formations are well developed in the Florida parishes. **1909** *Cent. Supp.* 491/3 Columbia formation, in *geol.*, a subdivision of the Quarternary formation of the Atlantic coastal plain and the Mississippi valley, consisting of a series of subestuarine and submarine deltas and associated delta-deposits.

4. Used attrib., chiefly with reference to the Columbia River region, in the names of birds: (1) **Columbia grouse,** =**sage grouse;** (2) **jay,** Collie's magpie-jay, *Calocitta colliei*, a bird of western Mexico, erroneously thought by Audubon to be from the "woody portions of North California," *rare;* (3) **partridge,** ?the Oregon ruffed grouse, *Bonasa umbellus sabini.*

(1) **1855** Ross *Fur Hunters Far West* (1924) 144 The other was a wild turkey-cock, or what we call the Columbia grouse, a bold and noble bird. — (2) **1831** Audubon *Ornith. Biog.* I. 483 The Columbia Jay. *Corvus Bullockii.* — (3) **1814** Brackenridge *Views of Louisiana* 59, I have seen a specimen of the Columbia partridge, of the most beautiful plumage. **1819** E. Dana *Geog. Sk.* 53 The plumage of the Columbia Patrtidge is very beautiful.

b. *Columbia River smelt,* (see quot.).

1923 Ward *Encycl. Food* (1941) 190 Euchalon, or candle-fish, or 'Columbia River Smelt,' a rich, delicious, slender little fish of the North Pacific coast, which reaches a maximum length of about twelve inches. It is placed on the market fresh, smoked, brined, kippered, and canned.

Columbiad kəˈlʌmbɪæd, *n.* Also **columbiad.** [f. **Columbia.**] A long-chambered cannon, especially thick at the breech and thin at the muzzle, designed particularly for shooting at high angles of elevation. Also attrib. Now *hist.*

"About 1812, Colonel Bomford, U.S.A., introduced a chambered gun called by him the Columbiad. These were made thicker at the breech and thinner at the muzzle than was then customary" (Knight, 447).

1818 J. M. Duncan *Travels U.S.* I. 36 Fulton also intended that she should carry upon her upper deck four Columbiads, as they are called, enormous guns capable of discharging a ball of a hundred pounds weight. **1861** *Charleston* (S.C.) *Mercury* 24 Jan. 3/5 Two Columbiad guns are now mounted upon Fort Barrancas. **1947** *Amer. Sp.* Dec. 241 By the War of 1812 even *Columbiad* was reduced to the level of a name for a newfangled cannon.

fig. **1865** Hamilton *Skirmishes* vii. 84 They looked upon them [preachers] all as a kind of ecclesiastical columbiad. **1872** *Newton Kansan* 3 Oct. 3/2 A Republican columbiad was fired at Newton last night.

Columbian kəˈlʌmbɪən, *a.* and *n.* [f. **Columbia.**]

1. *n.* An American, esp. a native of the U.S.

1789 S. Low *Politician Outwitted* II. ii, As the East is to the West . . . or the Aborigines of America to the Columbians of this generation, so is that line to this line. **1815** W. Thornton *Outlines Const. for Columbia* 1, I was born in America, between the tropics, and being a Carib by birth, I feel an unspeakable attachment to the whole race of the Columbians. **1947** *St. Louis Globe-Democrat* 7 Sep., His [Freneau's] . . . happy coinage at first appealed to his fellow countrymen as a welcome substitute for the awkward United States of America. Now they could call themselves Columbians instead of Americans, an invidious term that covers too much territory.

transf. **1868** Rose *Great Country* 260 The most celebrated of these waters [at Saratoga, N.Y.] is known by the name of 'Congress,' and there are others called 'Empire,' 'Columbian,' 'High Rock,' 'Excelsior,' [etc.].

b. (See quots.) *Obs.* or *hist.*

1800 in *Old-Time N. Eng.* April (1928) 176 Superfine Columbians and common playing cards per groce, dozen or single pack. Sold by Thayer and Furber, No. 30 Union St. **1928** *Ib.*, The American card makers advertised their cards as 'Columbians' and 'Eagles' and stoutly invited comparison with the 'Moguls,' 'Merry Andrews' and 'Harry the Eights' of their English competitors.

2. *a.* Of or pertaining to Columbia or the U.S. *Obs.*

1784 Freneau *Poems* (1809) II. 197 Who would be sad, to leave a sultry clime, Where true Columbian virtue is a crime. **1786** *Broadside Verse* (1930) 195 Succeeding ages will your virtues tell, . . . Columbian Daughters' skill extends so wide. **1797** C. Prentiss *Fugitive Ess.* 49 The Columbian muse is leading her sons to the pinnacle of poetical excellence. **1818** Fessenden *Ladies Monitor* 116 'Tis said indeed among Columbian fair, A lady-gambler is extremely rare.

b. In the names of organizations, as **Columbian Benevolent Society, Columbian Order.**

1811 Mease *Philadelphia* 277 Columbian Benevolent Society [was] instituted 1804. All well known, healthy citizens of Pennsylvania are eligible. **1813** *Niles' Reg.* IV. 25/2 *(caption)*, Tammany Society or Columbian Order. **1928** *Amer. Mercury* Sep. 1/2 The Tammany Society, or Columbian Order, is a fraternal society.

c. In the names of inventions, as **Columbian press, Columbian steam engine.** *Obs.*

1816 *Niles' Reg.* X. 213/2, I then discovered the principles of my Columbian Steam Engine. **1818** J. M. Duncan *Travels U.S.* I. 201 The Columbian press, invented by a person of the name of Clymer a native of Philadelphia, appears to be in many respects very superior to any other that I have yet seen.

d. Of or pertaining to a size (16 point) of type. Fig. in context.

1844 *Sucker* (Pittsfield, Ill.) 15 Feb. 2/3 *Public Schools—Columbian fount cases* from which the rising generation can *take sort.* May they *prove capitals* and never *run short.*

e. Of or pertaining to the time of the discovery of America by Columbus.

1885 *Harper's Mag.* Jan. 224/1 They [skulls] could not have been ante-Columbian, because we turned up a bit of rusted iron, the fragment of a knife. **1948** *Southwestern Jrnl. Anthro.* Spring 53 Some pre-Columbian civilizations used gourd shells in a manner comparable to china or crockery of the present day.

3. Designating the region of the Columbia River.

1845 Dunn *Ore. Terr.* 228 They are found in considerable numbers west of the Rocky Mountains, in the Columbian region.

b. In the names of, or with reference to, birds found in the vicinity of the Columbia River, as **Columbian jay, owl, sharp-tailed grouse.**

1839 Audubon *Ornith. Biog.* V. 271 Little Columbian Owl. *Strix Passerinoides.* **1849** —— *Western Journal* (1906) 128 The Ultramarine takes its [*sc.* Stellar's Jay's] place, and I hope in a few days to see the Columbian; a few ravens are to be seen. **1917** *Birds of Amer.* II. 28 The Columbian Sharp-tailed Grouse (*Pedioecetes phasianellus columbianus*) is much paler in tint.

c. Columbian ground squirrel, a ground squirrel, *Citellus columbianus*, found from Montana north to Alaska.

1912 *Outing* Dec 304/2 Scattered over the meadow were the subterranean burrows of the Columbian ground squirrel. **1948** *Trail Riders Bul.* June 22/2 Columbian ground squirrels, being social in habit, are usually found living in small colonies numbering from ten to twenty inhabitants.

4. Columbian Exposition, an international exposition held in Chicago May 1 to Oct. 30, 1893, to celebrate the 400th anniversary of the discovery of America by Columbus. See also **World's Columbian Exposition.**

1904 *Amer. Almanac* 291/2 The Columbian Exposition, held in Chicago in 1893, to commemorate the 400th anniversary of the discovery of America, was another magnificent enterprise. **1946** *Dly. Ardmoreite* (Ardmore, Okla.) 15 Dec. 5/1 The Columbian Exposition, Chicago, 1893 . . . was held in Jackson Park.

***columbo,** *n.* =**American columbo.** Also attrib. with **root.**

1803 *Lewis & Clark Exped.* (1905) VII. 244, ½ lb. Columbo Rad. [$]1. **1817** S. Brown *Western Gaz.* 53 Upon the spurs of the hills, and the poorest soil, is found the wild columbo root. **1855** *Mich. Agric. Soc. Trans.* VI. 149 The plants on the uplands are columbo, sundial, indigo root.

Columbus Day. Oct. 12th, observed as a holiday in most of the states to commemorate the discovery of America by Columbus in 1492.

[**1892** *Lit. Digest* V. 668/2 This complete and fervid American sentiment . . . at this Columbus celebration . . . is even more striking.] **1893** *N.-Eng. Hist. & Gen. Reg.* XLVII. 164 The following paper is a portion of an article which was prepared by the author, apropos of the approach of Columbus day. **1948** *Chi. D. News* 15 Sep. 3/3 (*heading*), Truman Asks Columbus Day Observance.

***column,** *n.* As the last term in **baseball, patent, social, want column.**

columnist ˈkɑləmɪst, ˈkɑləmnɪst, *n.* A writer who conducts a special department, usu. one column wide, in a newspaper. — **1920** *Blackw. Mag.* Aug. 146/1 The 'colyumist' of a New York paper. **1948** *Time* 21 June 96/2 Last week Columnist Hedda Hopper, in a patient, motherly tone, read the movie-makers a mild warning.

comadre koˈmadre, *n.* *S.W.* [Sp. in same sense.] A term used by mother and godmother with reference to each other; "co-mother," a close woman-friend of a family.

1834 A. Pike *Sketches* 105 We have been brought up together; our mothers are comadres, (sponsors) and you can never know me better than you do now. **1899** *Out West* Nov. 324 The *compadres* and *comadres* who stand for them do not look unworthy of their charges. **1948** *Southwestern Jrnl. Anthro.* Spring 43 Each compadre and comadre must be greeted individually even when several are together in one group.

comal koˈmɑl, *n.* Also **comalli.** *S.W.* [Amer. Sp. (<Nahuatl) in same sense.] (See quots.) — **1844** Gregg *Commerce of Prairies* I. 153 This is afterwards spread on a small sheet of iron or copper, called *comal* (*comalli*, by the Indians), and placed over a fire. **1912** Lum-

HOLTZ *New Trails* 191 The ordinary *comal,* made of earthen-ware, is of course useless for travel.

Comanche kəˈmæntʃɪ, *n.* [Origin unknown.]

1. (See quot. 1907.) Also an Indian of this tribe.

1806 WILKINSON in Pike *Sources Miss.* 109 You will also receive a . . . large one [=belt] for the Tetaus or Comanches. **1836** CROCKETT *Exploits* 157, I beheld in the distance about fifty mounted Cumanches, . . . dashing toward the spot where I stood. **1907** HODGE *Amer. Indians* I. 327 Comanche. One of the southern tribes of the Shoshonean stock, and the only one of that group living entirely on the plains. Their language and traditions show that they are a comparatively recent offshoot from the Shoshoni of Wyoming, both tribes speaking practically the same dialect and, until very recently, keeping up constant and friendly communication. **1948** *Southwestern Rev.* Summer 234/2 We would be company, as well as protection in case of an attack by the Comanches.

b. The language used by these Indians.

1874 *Forest & Stream* 13 Aug. 1/2 It is in fact the *Court* language, all councils with Kiowas and Plain Indians being held in Comanche. **1948** *Popular Western* June 84/1 Billy Bates spoke many Indian languages, among them Comanche.

2. Often in transf. and fig. use.

1831 HOLLEY *Texas* 90 To denote the greatest degree of degradation, they [the Mexicans] call a person a Comanche. **1836** EDWARD *Hist. Texas* 109 To pass the highest praise on an American's horsemanship, is to say, he rides like a Comanche! **1876** in GUILD *Old Times* (1878) 390 The man who does not appreciate her is a beast—a Comanche, and should be driven to the far West, where he belongs. **1946** *Reader's Digest* March 144/2, I won't have you looking like a Comanche.

3. Comanche yell, an especially blood-curdling yell characteristic of the Comanches.

1897 INMAN *Old Santa Fe Trail* 332 He gave a series of war-whoops which discounted a Comanche yell. **1945** MATHEWS *Talking* 45 He would get up from his chair, wave his great black hat, and do a buck-and-wing on the pine flooring, giving a Comanche yell as he finished.

Also *Comanche brave, charge, country, horse, Indian, moccasin, tongue,* etc.

Comanche kəˈmæntʃɪ, *v. pass.* To be attacked by the Comanches. *Rare.*—**1887** E. B. CUSTER *Tenting on Plains* 446 'Injuns!' replied Brigham, who knew by many an experience how wagons were Apached, Comanchied, or otherwise aboriginated.

comandante ˌkomanˈdantɪ, *n. S.W.* [Sp. in same sense.] A commanding officer.

1844 KENDALL *Santa Fe Exped.* II. 119 Colonel Velasco . . . took his leave, at the same time introducing the commandante of our new guard. **1897** *Outing* XXX. 74/2 In the old adobe . . . Resánoff dined with the comandante. **1904** O. HENRY *Cabbages & Kings* 12 The *comandante* . . . wrote in his secret memorandum book the accusive fact that Señor Goodwin had on that momentous date received a telegram.

***comb,** *n.* As the last term in **dressing, fine-tooth, shell, side, tuck comb.**

***comb,** *v.*

1. *intr.* Of a wave: To roll over and break with a foamy crest.

1807 J. BARLOW *Columbiad* I. 412 The stream ungovernable foams with ire, Climbs, combs tempestuous. **1838** POE *A. G. Pym* Wks. (1902) III. 9 Whenever we rose from a plunge forward, the sea behind fell combing over our counter, and deluged us with water. **1881** W. C. RUSSELL *Sailor's Sweetheart* II. vi. 321 The waves combed over the vessel in green seas.

2. (See quot.) *Rare.*

1854 THOREAU *Walden* 321 Ice has its grain as well as wood, and when a cake begins to rot or 'comb,' that is, assume the appearance of honey-comb, . . . the air cells are at right angles with what was the water surface.

3. *To comb up,* to make oneself neat by combing one's hair. *Colloq.*

1884 MARK TWAIN *H. Finn* vi. 38, I didn't see how I'd ever got to like it so well at the widow's, where you had to wash, and eat on a plate, and comb up, and go to bed and get up regular.

4. *tr.* To search closely, to examine, as with a fine-toothed comb.

1904 O. HENRY *Cabbages & Kings* iv. 80 Goodwin himself led the searching party which combed that town as carefully as a woman combs her hair; but the money was not found. **1922** PARRISH *Case & the Girl* 330 Say I combed that pier, believe me, West, and finally I ran across a kid who put me wise.

***comber,** *n.*

1. A wave that breaks with a foamy crest; a breaker.

1840 DANA *Two Years* ix. 71 The heavy swell of the Pacific was setting in, and breaking in loud and high 'combers' upon the beach. **1921** PAINE *Comr. Rolling Ocean* 84 A thundering comber fell on deck forward with a crash of splintered woodwork. **1947** *Time* 17 Mar. 41/2 Miles of broad beaches . . . great combers to jump in.

2. (See quot.)

1874 KNIGHT 597/2 Comber, a ledge around the well or passenger portion of a sail-boat to keep back spray and waves which 'comb' over the deck.

comb-grain pine. (See quot.) — **1897** MOORE *How To Build* 21 Where comb-grain pine is specified (so named because the grain is straight and in appearance like the artificial graining done by the grainer's comb) the best results may be secured as to wear and appearance.

***combination,** *n.*

1. A lock the mechanism of which is controlled by one or more dials. In full **combination lock.** Also the series of movements required to open such a lock.

[**1845** CIST *Cincinnati Misc.* 194 The locks which are on the combination principle, not only defy picking, but cannot be opened, even by their own keys, unless in the owner or maker's own hands.] **1875** *Chi. Tribune* 29 July 2/2 They [robbers] succeeded in getting the hinges off and partly removing the combination [of the bank door]. **1880** MARK TWAIN in *Atlantic Mo.* XLVI. 228/2 They commanded him to reveal the 'combination,' so that they could get into the safe. **1887** *Courier-Journal* 6 Feb. 3/6 For Sale-Safes-Hall's Combination Lock, Fire-proof safe. **1947** *Science Illustr.* July 93/1, I want a door-knob with a combination lock fitted into it.

fig. **1906** L. BELL *C. Lee* 271 What did you do about praying while changing your idea of a personal, corporeal God to one of spirit? Why, Carolina, I've lost the combination!

2. A theatrical company which travels with one or more plays, or which offers mixed vaudeville and dramatic performances. Also attrib. and transf.

1866 *Charleston Courier* 10 May, The Hibernian Hall. The Southern Combination Troupe: Comic, Irish Singing, Fancy Dresses, and Negro Performances. **1868** *Charleston Courier* 28 Dec., Stone and Murray's Combination Circus, starring John Henry, Equestrian and Thaumaturgic Artiste, at The Citadel Green. **1896** *N.Y. Dramatic News* 4 July 17/3 Proctor's Leland Opera House, Albany, N.Y. Open Time For Stars And Combinations.

3. A union of corporations for establishing a monopoly. Also attrib.

1883 *Harper's Mag.* Nov. 938/1 By combinations and traffic agreements forced on other companies they [=the Union Pacific and Central Pacific railroads] have come to control the traffic of the State [of California]. *Ib.* 942/2 Combinations and consolidations, though tending to form monopolies, are not unmixed evils. **1887** *Courier-Journal* 8 Jan. 4/1 In the last sixteen years the combination coal roads have sustained the rate of transportation at 1¾ cents per ton mile. **1903** *Chi. Chronicle* 11 April 2 Attorney General Knox is already preparing to bring suit against a number of combinations which he considers unlawful as being in restraint of trade.

4. A railroad car carrying both passengers and baggage. In full **combination car.** Also **combination train.**

1896 *N.Y. Tribune* 7 Sep. 1/3 The baggage-car, a combination and a passenger coach were overturned [in the wreck]. **1903** C. T. BRADY *Bishop* xv. 227 We were the only passengers in the combination-car—half-baggage, half-passenger. **1906** *N.Y. Ev. Post* 26 Nov. 1 Between Slater and Armstrong, Mo., a masked man, single handed, robbed twenty passengers in three cars of the fast eastbound combination Chicago and Alton–Chicago, Burlington and Quincy passenger train.

5. A number of magazines that may be subscribed for together at reduced rates.

1907 *Pearson's Mag.* Jan. (Contents-page), The face value of a subscription bill may be applied to any combination or clubbing offer advertised.

6. In special combs.: (1) **combination report,** a summary of news items from various parts of the country, published and distributed to subscribers by a central news bureau; (2) **store,** a general store, where many kinds of commodities are sold.

(1) **1877** *Harper's Mag.* Dec. 57/2 Each of these Southern cities is interested in the news of the others, and to supply them with it a summary of all that has been received at Washington is included in the combination report, which, being delivered at all points, gives back to each city some of its own news. — (2) **1897** *Outing* XXIX. 583/2 There was a little 'combination-store'; hats and calico on one side, canned goods and coffee on the other, and a post-office at the back.

***combine,** *n.*

1. An alliance or combination by organizations or individuals to further personal interests, often by corrupt means. Cf. **hog combine.**

Said in the *Cent.* to have been first used in this sense in the trial of a New York alderman for bribery in 1886.

1887 *Courier-Journal* 8 Jan. 4/1 A writer in the *North American Review* shows how the Pennsylvania coal monopoly illustrates the public benefits of 'monopolistic combines.' **1917** J. F. DALY *Life A. Daly* 82 The citizen in question . . . had been engaged in a campaign for municipal reform in his town, and had conceived the ingenious idea of representing the wicked 'combine' of the local 'boodlers' on the stage. **1948** *Time* 31 May 26/2 SCAP seemed to be trying not only to break up the big combines but to atomize the Japanese economy as well.

2. A machine which heads, threshes, and cleans grain, esp. wheat, in the harvesting process.

[**1857** *Ill. State Register* (Springfield) 15 July 3/2 In the afternoon, the combined mower and the Illinois mower were put upon trial, in a beautiful field of timothy. **1858** *Southern Cultivator* XVI. 163 Improved combined thresher and winnower.] **1926** *K.C. Star* 23 June, Hundreds of combines will be in the fields in southern, central, and western Kansas by Wednesday. **1948** *Miami* (Okla.) *D. News-Record* 4 July 3/5 The big job is getting enough combines working all at the same time to catch up with the delay caused by the rains.

combine ˈkɑmˌbaɪn, *v.* [f. the noun.] *tr.* To harvest (grain, esp. wheat) with a combine. Hence **combiner,** *n.*

1926 *K.C.* (Mo.) *Star* 23 June, The first wheat combined in this vicinity was from the 100-acre field of A. E. Rudd. **1948** *Chi. Tribune* 26 June 1. 6/2 The grain is beginning slowly to turn color and it won't be too long before it is time to combine it. *Ib.* 11 Aug. 6/2 The wheat that can't be handled by that fleet is moved to storage by 28 smaller trucks owned by contract combiners.

* **come,** *v.*

1. With prepositions and adverbs in colloq. and slang uses: **a.** **To come across with,* to hand over, contribute.

1910 *Sat. Ev. Post* 13 Aug. 8/1, I knew pull was required, . . . but I hadn't learned that I'd have to come across with the price as well. **1922** *Outing* Jan. 160/2 You have done a lot of talking and it's about time that you gave us a rest or else come across with the goods. **1948** *Holland's* March 10/2 This situation was relieved when a tardy subscriber came across with a four-dollar check for his season ticket.

b. *To come at,* to imply, mean.

1872 MARK TWAIN *Roughing It* xxviii. 156 Here—what you mean? What are you coming at? Is there any mystery behind all this? *Ib.* xxxi. 172 Is that your idea? Is that what you're coming at? **1894** WILKINS *Pembroke* 52 What I was comin' at was—I'd been kind of wrong in my reasonin'.

c. **To come back,* to make a smart or fitting retort. Cf. **3** (4) below.

1896 G. ADE *Artie* vi. 54 Did you ever get the worst of it in such a way that you couldn't come back at the time? **1928** F. N. HART *Bellamy Trial* i. 12, I was thinking of something really bright to come back with.

d. **To come by,* see **by.**

e. **To come down,* to become ill *with* (a disease).

1895 WOOD *Yale Yarns* 77 (We.), The good Deacon almost feared he was about to come down with a fever. **1911** LINCOLN *Cap'n Warren* 147 The housekeeper felt sure he was coming down with some disease or other.

f. **To come in,* (1) to score a run in baseball, (2) in poker, to enter a game after the deal, to join those already playing, also fig. Cf. **3.** (7) below.

(1) **1867** *Ball Players' Chron.* 6 June 2/2 He came in finally on a called ball passing the catcher. *Ib.* 2/3 Have his run he would, and he finally came in amidst loud cheers. — (2) **1887** KELLER *Draw Poker* 23 If he comes in, he must make good the ante and deposit in the pool a sum equal to the raise, if there be any, of the preceding player. **1922** T. A. MCNEAL *When Kansas was Young* 187 'That need not stand in the way of a pleasant evening,' remarked the Major, 'you have plenty of cattle. Suppose we make the ante a steer and two steers to "come in." '

g. **To come off,* (1) of a hen, to finish hatching a brood, (2) to desist, quit, usu. imperative.

(1) **1878** RUEDE *Sod-House Days* 225 Another hen is sitting on 15 eggs. She will come off in a week. — (2) **1892** *N.Y. Mercury* Feb. (Ware), 'How much does yez ax for this book?' 'Six dollars' replied the smiling clerk. 'Six dollars! Oh, come off!' **1904** W. H. SMITH *Promoters* 293 '[It] makes one conscious of his own superiority to call some one else down.' 'Oh, come off!' Goldsby replied.

h. **To come out,* (see quot. 1871).

*c***1847** WHITCHER *Bedott P.* 108, I experienced religion . . . at one o' brother Armstrong's protracted meetin's. . . . Them special efforts is great things—ever sence I come out I've felt like a new critter. **1871** DE VERE 231 A person proposing to join a church is expected first openly to come out, that is to say, to profess his religion.

i. **To come through,* (1) to experience religious conversion, (2) to make a clean breast, to confess.

(1) **1881** PIERSON *In the Brush* 172 They could scarcely speak for hoarseness—enjoyed seeing them 'come through' (the vernacular for conversion). **1947** *Democrat* 3 July 4/2 The prospect would usually 'come through' after this performance. — (2) **1916** W. A. DU PUY *Uncle Sam* 169 The man that the Government wanted usually came through with all he knew. **1916** SANDBURG *Chicago Poems* 63, I ask you to come through and show me where you're pouring out the blood of your life.

j. **To come to,* to be due or owed to (one).

1793 *Md. Hist. Mag.* VI. 356, I am satisfied that there is something considerable comming to me in the Limekills account. **1891** *Harper's Mag.* Nov. 888/2 He decides upon his own responsibility whether they have sufficient money coming to them to meet the accommodation. **1921** PAINE *Comr. Rolling Ocean* 44 You had it coming to you.

k. **To come up,* (1) of a playing card, to turn up as the card just dealt, (2) in baseball, to take one's turn at bat.

(1) *a***1846** *Quarter Race Ky.,* etc. 79, I took the two dollars up and let him make another turn when I replaced the bet, and the queen came up in my favour. — (2) **1880** N. BROOKS *Fairport Nine* xiv. 182 'Another blank for the White Bears!' cried Ned Martin, exultingly, as he came up to the bat. **1914** *Outing* July 446 It happened that later in the game Clarke again came up, with Byrne again on first base.

l. **To come up with,* to outwit, get the better of.

1856 *Harper's Mag.* XII. 710/1 One of our smart young lawyers was well come up with the other day. **1901** WHITE *Westerners* 78 Revenge with him seemed to be . . . in the victim's realization that he was being come up with.

2. In colloq. phrases: (1) *To come the camp-meeting touch,* to preach or speak in the manner of delivering a camp-meeting sermon, *rare;* (2) *to come out of that,* to cease meddling with, desist; (3) *to come right down to,* to get down to fundamental facts; (4) *to come clean,* to confess fully; (5) *to come snake-eye,* of dice, to show the "snake-eye" or two when thrown, *rare;* (6) *to get one's come-uppance,* to get one's deserts.

(1) **1851** GREEN *Twelve Days* 120 Git up here and gin us a sprinkling of brimstone; stir up these old ironsides on board—give 'em an extra lick, and come the camp-meeting touch. — (2) **1869** MARK TWAIN *Innocents* iii. 35, I saw a long spy-glass on a desk . . . and reached after it. . . . 'Ah, Ah, hands off! Come out of that!' — (3) **1891** BUNNER *Zadoc Pine* 74 'Oh, Popper Leete,' remonstrated his wife, 'tain't so bad as that!' 'Well,' Mr. Leete insisted, . . . 'tain't much better, when you come right down to it.' — (4) **1926** J. BLACK *You Can't Win* iv. 33 Come on, out with it. If you want any help here you've got to come clean. **1943** LAURA V. HAMNER *Short Grass & Longhorns* 155 The next morning he went up to the White House to 'come clean.'

(5) **1931** *K.C. Star* 3 Dec. 32 The department has . . . a pair of dice with a predilection for coming snakeye. — (6) **1869** *Harper's Mag.* Jan. 277/1 Dennis once got his 'come-up-ance.' **1912** W. L. PHELPS *Teaching in School & College* 59, I thereafter learned that Aristides got his come-uppance six lines from the bottom of the left-hand page. **1946** *Newsweek* 26 Aug. 73/1 There she ran up against the Georgia peach . . . and finally got her come-uppance.

For other phrases see the words in boldface: *to come the* **giraffe** *over; to come the* **gum** *over; to come the* **gum game** *over; to come the* **possum** *over; to come up* **missing;** *to* **get** *what's coming to one; to* **have** *it coming.*

3. In noun and adj. combs.: (1) ***come again,** persevering, recuperative, *rare;* (2) **-as-you-come,** (see quot.); (3) **-at-ye,** (see quot.), *obs.;* (4) ***back,** (*a*) a prompt, suitable retort, an effective countermeasure, *slang,* cf. **1. c** above, (*b*) a recovery, a return to a former state of efficiency, *slang;* (5) ***down,** a drop in social esteem or position; (6) **hither,** lure, attraction, *slang;* (7) ***in,** the amount put up by a player who comes late into a poker game, cf. **to come in;* (8) ***off,** a derogatory term for a thing or creature; (9) **on,** one who inveigles others into gambling ventures, also attrib., *slang;* (10) ***out,** capacity for improvement or development; (11) **-outer,** see as a main entry.

(1) **1868** WOODRUFF *Trotting Horse* 299 People forget the wonderful constitution and come-again qualities of Flora. — (2) **1877** BARTLETT 779 Come-as-you-come. The name of a popular fireside amusement, wherein one person gives the others present the initial letter or letters of some object there visible, by which to guess to what object

he refers. — (3) **1889** *N. & Q.* III. July 6, 119 American soldiers on the frontier once called the Apache and Comanche tribes *Up-at-ye* and *Come-at-ye.* — (4) (*a*) **1896** G. Ade *Artie* 59, I never will be able to give him the right kind of a hot come-back for what he done to me. **1936** McKenna *Black Range* 173 'Some people have no ear for music,' was Pete's come-back. (*b*) **1908** K. McGaffey *Show-Girl* 224 But it is a good thing to have a bank account to flash, so that the boob will think he will get a comeback if he does lose. **1947** *Hyde Park Herald* (Chicago) 29 May 2/4 In his comeback last year, he ran up a string of 23 straight victories.

(5) **1840** Dana *Two Years* xxviii, This was indeed a come-down from the highest seat in the synagogue to a seat in the galley. [**1870** *Rocky Mt. Herald* (Denver) 16 July 4/2 The spotless and immaculate characters of Republicanism were playing the 'come down' game of Zachariah.] **1944** Fast *F. Road* 117 Seems a sure enough come down for an uppity nigger.—(6) **1932** *Screenland* April 81/1 The latest of the ace Broadway actresses to succumb to Hollywood's 'come-hither' is Helen Gahagan. — (7) **1901** G. Ade *40 Modern Fables* 153 It was only a measly little Child's Game with a Come In of Two call Five. — (8) **1934** Vines *Green Thicket World* 181 They were all *purty*-looking come-offs. — (9) **1905** *N.Y. Ev. Post* 28 Jan 2 The general appearance of the man caused the officer to become suspicious, and he soon learned that Dates was a 'come-on'. **1905** *N.Y. Times* 24 Feb. 1 Detectives yesterday arrested two men on a charge of participating in a clever 'come-on' game. **1948** *Time* 17 May 38/2 The Alberta government was spending $179,900 on radio programs, advertisements and glossy come-ons.

(10) **1853** *S. Lit. Messenger* XIX. 669/2 It is astonishing, Frank, what come-out there is in men! **1892** Duval *Young Explorers* 153, I tell you, . . . there's a heap of come out in a Spanish mule, ef a feller only knows how to git it out'n him.

comedy drama. Serious drama in which comedy is interspersed and sometimes stressed. — **1885** *Boston Journal* 8 Dec., This [*Living for Show* by A. Daly] is what has of late been known as a comedy drama.

come-outer ˌkʌmˈaʊtɚ, *n.*

1. (See quot. 1917.)

1840 Longfellow in *Life* (1891) I. 373 Not long after, came up from Cape Cod a new sect called the 'Come-outers,' who formed a holy alliance with the Transcendentalists. **1860** Greeley *Overland Journey* 187 We met several wagon-loads of come-outers from Mormonism on their way to the states. **1917** *Cyclo. Amer. Govt.* I. 330 Comeouter. The name originally applied to certain religious dissenters or radical religious reformers who separated themselves from an established organization. Such a group flourished in New England, about 1840, including that group of non-resistance Abolitionists who advocated 'coming-out' from the church and the state because of the attitude of both toward the slavery question. Also applied to ultra-radical reformers, particularly in political and religious matters.

2. Hence **come-outerism, come-outism.** *Obs.*

1844 *Liberator* (Boston) 12 Jan. 5/1 Friend Garrison thinks the present dying freaks of come-outism is a kind of second, great reformation. **1847** W. L. Garrison in *Life* (1889) III. 202 A good deal of prejudice is cherished against me on account of my 'infidelity' and 'come-outerism.' **1896** Leonard *Cent. of Congregationalism in Ohio* 47 Comeouterism then [1840–50] flourished, which called upon the elect [ultra-abolitionists] . . . to break loose from the Laodicean churches.

* **comer,** *n.* An animal or person that shows promise of development. *Colloq.* See also **first, old, over, up-comer.**

1879 *St. Nicholas Mag.* Nov. 84/2 He [a crab] eats everything he gets hold of, which, of course, fattens him up some. Then he is called a 'comer.' **1901–2** *Kansas State Bd. Agric. Rep.* 202 He . . . still shows that remarkable looseness and elasticity of hide that indicates a 'comer' when he is put next to the feed-box. **1947** *Denver Post* 2 Mar. 1/2 Richard isn't quite that smart but he is a comer if his boorish behavior doesn't get the better of him.

b. comer-out, =**come-outer.** *Rare.*

1841 Emerson *Miscell.* (1855) 267 Mysticism . . . forms the sole thoughts of some poor Perfectionist or 'Comer out.'

* **comfort,** *n.*

1. =**comforter.**

1844 *Rep. Comm. Patents* (1847) 35 It [cotton] has already been employed in what are variously called 'comforts' and 'comfortables.' **1913** Stratton-Porter *Laddie* xi. 211 Laddie had filled the kitchen oven with bricks and hung up a comfort at four o'clock to keep the Princess warm. **1945** Botkin *My Burden* 112 Then a great big mattress full of goose feathers and two-three comforts as thick as my foot with carded wool inside!

2. comfort-bag, (see quot. 1870). *Obs.*

1866 Moore *Women of War* 586 The little child diligently sewing with tiny fingers upon the soldiers 'comfort-bag.' **1870** Macrae *Americans* I. 79 They made tens of thousands of little house-wives—'comfort-bags,' as the soldiers called them—with buttons, needle and thread, comb, cake of soap, and above all, a little tract or Testament.

3. comfort room, station, a public toilet or place of ease.

1910 *Aurora* (Ill.) *D. Beacon* 8 Sep. 6/1 A public comfort room . . . would pay the city of Aurora a profit every year. **1934** *Amer. Sp.* April 113/2 Near the camps and at the oil stations are the comfort stations for ladies and for gents. **1948** *Fargo* (N.D.) *Forum* 28 Sep. 8/2 Stage III includes construction of 31 residences, an apartment building, bus and comfort station.

See also **western, Yankee comfort.**

* **comfortable,** *n.* =**comforter.** *Colloq.* Cf. **winter comfortable.**

1842 in Buckingham *E. & W. States* III. 434 Still Mr. Van Buren was not content; he longed for the 'Turkish divan' and the 'French comfortable.' **1906** Freeman *By Light of Soul* 437 She did not get into bed, but took a silk comfortable off, and wrapped it around her. **1945** Tryon *Poor Man* 96, I threw back most of the voluminous quilts, comfortables and sheets.

* **comforter,** *n.* A warm bed cover, usu. made of gay-colored fabric filled with down or wool and either scroll-stitched or tacked with wool thread. See also **tow comforter.**

1832 S. G. Goodrich *Univ. Geog.* 107 The females also have similar meetings called 'quilting bees,' when many assemble to work for one, in padding or quilting bed coverings or comforters. **1913** A. B. Emerson *R. Fielding at Snow Camp* 28 Later Aunt Alvirah made up the couch with plenty of blankets and thick, downy 'comforters.' **1947** *Chi. D. News News-Views* 29 March 5/2 Country activities for the Mrs. includes a quilting bee with neighbors. . . . It's a pleasant way to spend an afternoon as well as finish a comforter.

* **comic,** *a.* and *n.*

1. *n. pl.* That part of a newspaper given over to comical drawings and comic strips. Cf. **funny, funny paper.** See also **Sunday comic.**

[**1911** *Survey* 15 April 103/1 Beginning with the object of entirely suppressing the comic, this body found not only that this plan was impracticable, but that it was undesirable, as the comic sheet responds to a real demand on the part of the public, both young and old.] **1923** *Nation* 21 Nov. 571 They gave their new paper a sporting page, a women's column, comics, 'colyums.' **1948** *Time* 3 May 22/3 He found out that most readers preferred comics to the front page.

b. Short for **comic valentine.** *Rare.*

1931 *Randolph Enterprise* (Elkins, W.Va.) 12 Feb. 4/2 Saturday is Valentine day and the stores are full of enough comics to set the whole neighborhood fighting.

2. In combs.: (1) **comic artist,** one who draws comics; (2) **book,** a small paper-backed booklet made up of comic strips; (3) **page,** the page of a newspaper which has the comics; (4) **paper,** a newspaper devoted largely to pictures and jokes; (5) **section,** the part of a newspaper which contains the comics; (6) **strip,** a series of drawings, usu. in a newspaper, presenting an adventure, often of a humorous kind, cf. **funny, funny paper;** (7) **supplement,** a part of a newspaper devoted to comics, also attrib.; (8) **valentine,** a valentine having a picture or printed matter designed to be humorous.

(1) **1910** *Bookman* May 291/1 One peculiar feature of this series is that it reverses the scheme followed by most of the comic artists. — (2) **1945** *New Yorker* 24 Mar. 38 They cast their looks on comic books. **1948** *Chi. Tribune* 20 June IV. 11/3 He doesn't like to read comic books, doctor. — (3) **1920** *Collier's* 20 March 41/1 It's a good thing you ain't runnin' the comic page.—(4) **1865** *Cin. D. Gazette* 3 Aug. 1/7 The fourth number of the new comic paper overflows with jokes. **1867** *Harper's Wkly.* 30 Mar. 199/3 He also said he thought the New York *Citizen* was a good comic paper.

(5) **1904** *St. Louis Globe-Democrat* 3 July (*heading*), Comic and Children's Section. — (6) **1920** Sandburg *Smoke & Steel* 47 And the comic strips in the papers. **1948** Mathews *Southernisms* 28 The use of the word in the name of the principal character in a comic strip . . . is also worthy of mention. — (7) **1900** *Everybody's Mag.* Nov. 230/2 The comic supplements alone are estimated to have increased the circulation of those Sunday editions which carry them by fifty thousand a week. **1909** *Sat. Ev. Post* 16 Jan. 7/1 It's a nice comic-supplement name. **1911** *Outlook* 15 April 802/2 With the great majority of illustrated comic supplements it is impossible to associate the idea of fun, of humor, or of manners. — (8) **1855** M. Thompson *Doesticks* 195 It seems to be a time which many a man takes advantage of to revenge some fancied slight from a scornful lady, by sending her one of those scandalous nuisances, misnamed 'comic Valentines.' **1948** *Sat. Ev. Post* 11 Sep. 56/4 Launcelot knifed him by mailing comic valentines to the board of directors from the fellow's suburb.

comida koˈmidə, *n.* [Sp., food, dressed victuals.] (See quot.) *Rare.* — **1898** CANFIELD *Maid of Frontier* 212 Pancho's mother . . . had 'comida,' too, which is bread stewed in rich goat's milk with pepper.

coming-home stretch. =**home stretch.** *Obs.* — **1839** *N.O. Picayune* 19 April 2/2 Finding all right—that he had the foot of him—[the jockey] hauled in a little and let Richard cut out the work until the coming-home stretch. *Ib.*, On the coming-home stretch the tug commenced. **1841** *Ib.* 21 Mar. 2/2 Grey Medoc . . . reached Altorf at the fourth turn, and swung into the coming home stretch dead locked.

commandancia ˌkomɑnˈdɑnsɪə, *n. S.W.* [Sp. *comandancia,* in same sense.] The office or authority of a commandant. *Rare.* — **1848** BRYANT *California* (1849) 283 The village of Branciforte, . . . on account of the smallness of its population, is subject to the commandancia of Monterey.

***commander,** *n.* An overseer of slaves. *Rare.* See also **lieutenant commander.** — **1842** *McDonough Papers* 65, I was in the habit of never retiring to rest at night until seeing my commander, and knowing that the people had come in from their work.

***commandery,** *n.* (See quot. 1874.) — **1867** *Mich. Gen. Statutes* (1882–3) I. 1147 Any ten or more residents of this state being members either of any commandery of knights templars, council, chapter of royal arch masons, [etc.]. *Ib.*, The name and location of the commandery, council or chapter of which they are members. **1874** MAKEY *Encycl. Free-masonry* 175/2 In the United States all regular assemblies of Knights Templars are called Commanderies. . . . These Commanderies derive their warrants of Constitution from a Grand Commandery, or . . . from the Grand Encampment of the United States.

commandment sin. An immoral act contrary to one or more of the Ten Commandments. *Colloq.* — **1900** DIX *Deacon Bradbury* 29 As the deacon would afterward constantly say to his wife, it was no 'Commandment sin.'

***commerce,** *n.* As the last term in **dry goods, interstate, Secretary of Commerce.**

***commercial,** *a.* In combs.: (1) **commercial agency,** an organization that furnishes its subscribers information about the standing of commercial firms; (2) **agent,** an agent who attends to commercial interests; (3) **college,** a business college, esp. in the names of such schools; (4) **convention,** (see quot.), *obs.;* (5) **course,** a course of study in a commercial school; (6) **emporium,** a grandiloquent term for a city or would-be city; (7) **fertilizer,** a material prepared on a large scale and sold commercially as a fertilizing agent; (8) **lumberman,** one who is interested in lumber as a commercial product; (9) **note-paper,** (see quot.); (10) **state,** a state whose inhabitants are interested chiefly in commerce; (11) **tourist,** (see quot. 1894).

(1) **1897** *Bouvier's Law Dict.* I. 357/2 Commercial Agency. — (2) **1877** *Encycl. Brit.* VI. 317/1 The United States commercial agents, although appointed by the president, receive no exaequatur. **1882** *Cent. Mag.* April 884/1 Our domestic jocosity, . . . reserving for its most palpable hits the bully, the visionary speculator, the gamester, and the commercial agent. — (3) **1858** *Hunt's Merch. Mag.* XXXIX. 412 Commercial colleges . . . are peculiar institutions, which have sprung but lately into vigorous life in response to a general and widely-felt want. **1944** *Chi. Classified Tel. Directory* 772 Chicago Commercial College Secretarial and Business Courses. — (4) **1860** MORDECAI *Va.* 43 These 'Commercial Conventions,' as they are called, composed more of planters, lawyers and politicians than of merchants, assemble to discuss subjects of which few of them have any practical knowledge. They would regulate not only our own trade, but that of Europe, and dictate to the nations there, how they should relinquish one of their most important sources of revenue, for our benefit.

(5) **1939** *These Are Our Lives* 39 She took the commercial course at the Wayboro school two years ago, but because of a change of teachers in mid-season she claims the course did her little good. **1945** *Somerset News* 15 March 2/2 Those eager young faces you are seeing around town in the business district are Washington High School seniors taking a commercial course. — (6) **1835** HOFFMAN *Winter in West* II. 65 The ancient city of St. Louis, the capital and metropolis, though not yet the commercial emporium, of the grand valley of the Mississippi. **1837** *S. Lit. Messenger* III. 178 The way I looked down on the 'aristocracy of wealth' . . . as I strutted through the Broadway of the 'Commercial Emporium' . . . was truly 'a sin.' — (7) **1888** *Vt. Agric. Rep.* X. 32 If half the money spent each year for commercial fertilizer was spent annually in preventing the waste of the valuable properties of manure, . . . the crops would increase in value. **1944** *Democrat* 29 June 1/3 During the 12 months just ended the fertilizer plants of the country have delivered the farmers the largest tonnage of commercial fertilizers and fertilizer materials in the nation's history. — (8) **1944** *Nat. Geog. Mag.* June 668/1 Beside the Payette Lakes a friend of mine, a commercial lumberman, lets choice timber live on to protect the beauty of the resort. — (9) **1879** WEBSTER *Supp.* 1550 *Commercial note-paper,* a small size of writing-paper, usually about 5 by 7½ or 8 inches.

(10) **1781** *N.H. Comm. Safety Rec.* 247 Money has never been so plenty here as in the Commercial States. **1789** *Ann. 1st Congress* I. 211 The impost must come from the commercial States. — (11) **1887** *Courier-Journal* 8 Feb. 3/4 The highest compliment that can be paid Mr. Lane is to say that those who have seen commercial tourists en route will recognize him at a glance. **1894** *Cong. Rec.* 14 Feb. 2186/1 The 'commercial tourists,' as I believe they are called now,—down in my country we call them drummers.

***commissary,** *n.*

1. A government officer with indicated duties (see quots.). *Obs.*

1772 in *Amer. Sp.* XX (1945) 270 In 1766 he acted as commissary of Indian affairs and settled the trade of the Indian country. **1778** in *Hist. MSS Comm.* 15th Rep. App. VI. 407 Also to the Superintendant General of the Port of N.Y. and the Commissaries of Prisoners, to be by them occasionally distributed among the people. **1830** *William's N.Y. Ann. Reg.* 307 Government of the United States. War Department. . . . George Gibson, Commissary of subsistence. *Ib.*, Government of the United States. War Department. . . . George Bomford, Commissary of ordnance.

2. A store in which all or most of the articles sold are for people engaged in a particular kind of work, as lumbering, mining, railroading, etc.

1882 *Rep. Indian Affairs* 1 Sep. 151 Two new buildings . . . have been constructed; a commissary with offices, and a council-house. **1905** *Forestry Bureau Bul.* No. 61, 33 *Commissary,* a general store for supplying lumbermen. **1938** NIXON *Forty Acres* 4 The store in which I grew up served as commissary, office and general clearing house for the plantation.

b. Attrib. with **building, bureau, butter, store, wagon.**

1851 GLISAN *Jrnl. Army Life* 81 The buildings will be arranged in . . . a paralelogram . . .—the commissary and quartermaster buildings at one end. — **1892** *Harper's Wkly.* 9 Jan. 42/1 General Meigs's plan of reorganization for the Quartermaster's Department was also adopted in the Commissary Bureau. — **1873** BEADLE *Undevel. West* 528 For the last three days we lived on Navajo bread, coffee, and 'commissary butter,' straight. — **1780** R. PUTNAM in *Memoirs* 154 Either a commesary store should be keept here or some extra provition should be lodged here for the supply of such small parties. **1862** O. W. NORTON *Army Letters* 116 Artillery is being loaded up every night, commissary stores are going. — **1848** J. S. ROBINSON *Santa Fe Exped.* 10 If we cannot overtake the commissary wagons we shall have nothing to eat. **1865** BOUDRYE *Fifth N.Y. Cavalry* 92 Long trains of forage and commissary wagons may be seen passing to and fro.

3. Food, supplies of food, esp. for use on a military expedition.

1883 *Cent. Mag.* Sep. 672 This enforced idleness reduced our commissary to an alarming minimum. **1929** PARKER *Old Army* 337 The Spanish ship Salvadora arrived with commissaries.

b. (See quot. 1865.) *Obs.*

1865 *Harper's Mag.* June 131/1 Very fond of 'commissary,' as the poor substitute for whisky furnished the army is called. **1869** *Ib.* Nov. 932/1 A bountiful supply of that exhilarating army beverage ycleped 'Commissary.'

4. A commissary wagon. *Rare.*

1905 A. ADAMS *Outlet* 245 A wagon-way could be easily cut in the bank and the commissaries lowered to the river's edge with a rope to the rear axle.

***commission,** *n.* In combs.: (1) **commission government,** a system of municipal government first adopted in Galveston, Texas, in 1901, in which executive and legislative powers are vested in a small elective board, also **commission form of government;** (2) **house,** a business firm which deals for its customers in return for a percentage of the profits; (3) **store,** a store in which goods are sold on commission for a factor, *obs.*

(1) **1908** H. B. RICE *Commission Form of Govt.* 1 The subject of my discussion is the commission form of government in Houston, Texas, and how it works. **1911** *Amer. Acad. Pol. Sci. Annals* Nov. 56 The commission government movement has made greater progress in the West . . . than it has in all the other and more conservative parts of the United States. **1914** *World Almanac* 188 Commission government of cities in United States . . . instead of by a Mayor and other city officials, was first instituted in Galveston, Tex., in 1901. — (2) **1831** PECK *Guide* 148 A commission house in St. Louis showed me letters

from New York substantiating the fact. **1922** T. A. McNeal *When Kansas Was Young* 187 The Major had established his commission house at Kansas City, in the early eighties. — (3) **1820** Flint *Lett. from Amer.* 212 The enumeration of houses, made in March, 1819, was as follows: . . . Auction and commission stores, 5.

b. *To put out of commission,* to make unable to function. *Colloq.*

1904 Stratton-Porter *Freckles* 181, I'll play and you'll sing, and we'll put the birds out of commission. **1930** *Randolph Enterprise* (Elkins, W.Va.) 2 Oct. 4/3 A snow storm put our boys out of commission and they lost the game 21 to 13.

As the last term in **capitol, Civil Service, county, Electoral, emigrant, fish, highway, Interstate Commerce, oyster, Price Raid, railroad, roving, Sanitary, state, state textbook commission.**

***commissioner,** *n.*

1. =**county commissioner.**

1844 *Belleville* (Ill.) *Advocate* 11 July 2/5 A commissioner or his representative should repair to the spot, be the first to travel the road, and remain on the ground with power and means to put the road in such repair that strangers may travel without risk of life. **1865** *Evansville* (Ind.) *D. Jrnl.* 26 Sep. 2/1 John Houge is a candidate for reelection to the office of Commissioner of Vanderburgh County. **1948** *Alva* (Okla.) *Review-Courier* 2 July 1/1 When we consider the record of our present commissioners we are assured of their good faith as public officials.

b. (See quot.)

1899 Green *Va. Word-Bk.* 94 Commissioner, *n.* A justice of the peace.

2. commissioners' court, a court composed of commissioners (see also quot. 1933).

1684 Sewall *Diary* I. 50 May 6, Commissioners Court. **1844** *Ind. Senate Jrnl.* 107 The petition of . . . citizens of the county of Randolph, praying for the passage of an act to extend the time of holding the commissioners' court in said county. **1933** *Pub. Col. Soc.* XXIX. xx, Although the County Court was the usual court of first jurisdiction, there was also a series of Commissioners' Courts in every town for causes not involving a debt or damage greater than forty shillings. A Commissioners' Court consisted of a single magistrate, or, in a town where no magistrate resided, three commissioners appointed by the General Court and sworn into office before a County Court.

3. In the titles of public officials having duties of an indicated kind: (1) *Commissioner for* (or *of*) *Indian Affairs,* (2) *of the land office,* and variants, (3) *of the canal fund,* (4) *of emigration,* (5) *of police,* (6) *of labor.*

(1) **1700** in J. W. Lydekker *Faithful Mohawks* (1938) 10 Extract of what was said by the Sachems of the Praying Indians of Canada . . . to the Commissioners for the Indian Affairs in Albany. **1946** *Sat. Review* 8 June 38/1 John Collier, who as Commissioner of Indian Affairs took a leading part in setting up these studies, is no longer in charge of the Indian Service. — (2) **1830** *Williams's N.Y. Ann. Reg.* 229 Commissioners of the Land Office. **1840** *Niles' Reg.* 4 April LVIII. 69 From the annual report of the commissioner of the general land office it appears . . . the quantity of public land sold amounted to 3,414,907 acres. **1846** Polk *Diary* (1910) II. 108 Mr. Buchanan . . . seemed to be deeply concerned at the removal of a clerk . . . by Mr. Piper, the acting commissioner of the Public Lands. **1911** *Okla. Session Laws* 3 Legisl. 242 The Commissioners of the School Land Office shall cause the land to be appraised by three disinterested freeholders of the state. — (3) **1830** *Williams's N.Y. Ann. Reg.* 229 Commissioners of the Canal Fund. Lieut. Governor, Comptroller, Secretary of State, Surveyor General, Treasurer, and Attorney General, ex officiis. — (4) **1851** Quentin *Reisebilder* I. 52 So kann ich, in Beantwortung dieser Frage, nur demjenigen beistimmen, wasin einer 'Bekanntmachung der Commissioners of Emigration vom November 1848' treffend gesagt worden ist. **1872** Brace *Dangerous Classes N.Y.* 60 The success of . . . the Commissioners of Emigration in their 'Labor Exchange,' indicate what might be accomplished.

(5) **1888** *Chi. Inter-Ocean* 2 Jan. 1/4 In the former [saloon] was the Hon. Pat Mealey, Commissioner of Police of this city. — (6) **1898** *K.C. Star* 18 Dec. 2/2 Addresses will be made by Samuel Gompers, president of the American Federation of Labor; . . . S. J. Kent, commissioner of labor of Nebraska [etc.].

As the last term in **bank, canal, county, election, emigrant, fire, fish, forest, forestry, highway, Indian, jury, police, railroad, reserve, road, school, street, water commissioner.**

***committee,** *n.*

1. In the names of various (legislative) committees of a more or less institutional nature.

a. Committee of Correspondence, during the Revolutionary period, a committee appointed by a town or colony to communicate and coördinate measures variously taken toward redress of grievances.

1766 in Franklin *Works* (1847) VII. 318 On the 10th we had the pleasure of finding that thou hadst wrote a letter to the Committee of Correspondence, which at once stopped the virulence of the proprietary party. **1823** Tudor *Otis* 22 He [Gen. Warren] was the author of the scheme for forming Committees of Correspondence, which he communicated to Samuel Adams, in 1773, who was making him a visit. **1906** in *Pub. Col. Soc.* XI. 31 When, on 2 November, 1772, the Town of Boston adopted Samuel Adams's proposal to create a Committee of Correspondence to consist of twenty-one persons, Dr. Young was appointed a member of it.

b. Committee of the whole, (see quot. 1914).

1775 *Jrnls. Cont. Congress* III. 307 The Congress resolved itself into a Com[mitt]ee of the whole, to take into their farther consideration the state of the trade of the confederated Colonies. **1829** B. Hall *Travels in N.A.* II. 32 This led to a warm discussion by four or five members, none of whom spoke above a few minutes, excepting one gentleman, who addressed the House, now in 'Committee of the whole,' as it is called, no less than five times. **1914** *Cyclo. Amer. Govt.* I. 355 Committee of the Whole. This is a device for avoiding the formalities of rigid debate, used by Congress, and many of the state legislatures The Speaker commonly calls to the chair a member of the house, and debate proceeds in the national House by five minute speeches. Amendments can be more freely offered here than in the regular House. At the end of the discussion the committee of the whole through its chairman, reports to the House the action of the committee.

c. Committee of the States, under the Articles of Confederation, a committee with a semblance of executive power when Congress was not in session.

1777 *Jrnls. Cont. Congress* IX. 923/1 The committee of the States, or any nine of them, shall be authorized to execute in the recess of Congress, such of the powers of Congress as the United States in Congress . . . shall . . . think expedient.

d. Committee of Observation, one of the early local committees of the Revolution. *Obs.*

1775 *Md. Hist. Mag.* X. 302 A meeting of the Freemen of the middle district of Frederick County at the Court House on the 12th of September 1775, . . . the following Gentlemen were chosen a Committee of Observation.

e. Committee of Seventy, see ***seventy 1.** (b).

2. Committee of Vigilance, a vigilance committee *q.v. Obs.*

1830 *Central Watchtower* (Harrodsburg, Ky.) 3 July 1/3 Mr. Knapp, . . . either of his own motion, or more probably at the instance of others, laid it before the 'Committee of Vigilance.' **1832** *Boston Transcript* 24 Mar. 1/2 *Resolved,* That a Committee of Vigilance be appointed, . . . whose duty it shall be to collect and publish facts respecting the condition of laboring men, women and children, and abuses practiced on them by their employers. **1851** *S. F. Herald* 13 June 2/6 The Committee of Vigilance have nothing secret in their proceedings.

3. committee of one (or **two**), one or two persons. Usu. humorous.

1848 *N.Y. Wkly. Tribune* 26 Feb. 4/1 *Resolved,* That the Chair appoint a Committee of one from each Congressional district. **1880** *Harper's Mag.* Dec. 91 She slept in that 'grand committee of two' which is the strength and comfort of a happy marriage. *a***1889** Farmer 161 To use an American expression he was an investigating committee of one, that had to be continually lubricated. **1922** *Dly. Ardmoreite* (Ardmore, Okla.) 10 Jan. 5/3 The [spelling] bee . . . was referred to a committee of one composed of W. R. Burnitt.

As the last term in **appointment, block, central, county, executive, grand, joint, judiciary, lecture, national, prudential, reception, school, Senate, smelling, state, state central, steering, vigilance, ward committee.**

***common,** *a.* and *n.*

1. *n. N. Eng.* A public pleasure-ground or park.

This use developed from "common" in the old sense of land held in common by a community as shown in first example.

[**1634** *Watertown Rec.* 1 No man shall fell or cut down any timber trees upon the Common.] **1818** Palmer *Journal* 195 The Salem ancient artillery corps had a field-day. . . . The place where they went through their evolution is called a common, but it is very handsome, and might, with propriety, be called a park. **1879** M. Blake *Hist. of Franklin* 67 The improvement of the Common, by planting shade trees, laying out walks, etc., is in the hands of a voluntary association. **1945** McLean *Moment of Time* 16 Then, at the edge of the common, he stepped abruptly behind the trunk of the larger elm.

2. *pl.* Pasture lands. *Obs.* Cf. **cow, ox, sheep common.**

1857 *Lawrence Republican* 18 June 1 Two-thirds of her [Virginia's] soil that was formerly fertile and productive has been exhausted and much of it thrown into commons. **1857** D. Braman *Texas* iii. 51 The rich prairies of this county afford free commons to any number of herdsmen.

3. A vacant lot.

1865 *Atlantic Mo.* XV. 474/1 There lay numerous open lots or commons, all of which afforded abundant evidence of the extent to which this public wastefulness was carried. **1901** H. ROBERTSON *Inlander* 26 The three [boys] . . . became . . . friendly with the young barbarians on the commons.

4. *a.* Used in the names of birds and trees regarded as the most familiar or widespread, as **common buckeye, catalpa, crow-blackbird, dove, hickory, wintergreen.** Chiefly *obs.*

1815 DRAKE *Cincinnati* 77 The botanical resources of this . . . Forest of the Miami country [include] . . . *Aesculus flava,* Common or fœtid buckeye. — **1897** SUDWORTH *Arborescent Flora* 334 *Catalpa catalpa.* . . . Common Catalpa. — **1825** BONAPARTE *Ornithology* I. 42 Common Crow-Blackbird. *Quiscalus Versicolor.* — **1858** BAIRD *Birds Pacific R.R.* 604 *Zenaidura Carolinensis,* Carolina, or Common Dove. — **1814** PURSH *Flora* II. 638 Juglans tomentosa. . . . This is known under the name of Mocker Nut, White-heart Hickory or Common Hickory. The wood is excellent for mechanical purposes, and particular esteemed as fire-wood; but the nuts are very hard, with but little kernel in them. — **1791** *Amer. Philos. Soc. Trans.* III. 105 Both the Indians and the white inhabitants of this country are acquainted with the blistering property of other indigenous vegetables: such are the *Common-Wintergreen* . . . some species of the genus *Ranunculus,* or *Crow-foot,* &c.

5. Denoting schools or education available to all children. Cf. **common school.**

1831 PECK *Guide* 244 The influx of emigrants . . . is producing a rapid change in common education. **1837** H. MARTINEAU *Society* III. 335 A fund was also accumulating, which was to be applied whenever its income would support a common free-school in every district of the State, for two months in the year. **1849** CHAMBERLAIN *Ind. Gazetteer* 204 Common English schools are kept from three to six months in the year, but no higher branches are taught. *Ib.* 262 Many private and common district schools are also to be found in most parts of the city.

6. In special combs.: (1) **common cracker,** *N. Eng.* (see quot.); (2) **doings,** formerly in frontier lingo, plain, ordinary food, also transf., *obs.;* (3) **school,** see as a main entry; (4) **wheel,** an ordinary supporting wheel in contrast to a drive wheel, *rare.*

(1) **1939** WOLCOTT *Yankee Cook Bk.* 127 The crackers should be the round 'Boston' crackers—they called them 'common crackers' when I was a boy. Split them, you understand, and put a few in the chowder and add a few dry halves to float on top just before serving. — (2) **1838** E. FLAGG *Far West* II. 72 Well, stranger, what'll ye take: wheat-bread and chicken fixens, or corn-bread and common doins? **1850** *Knickerb.* XXXVI. 575 O, ye editors of the *'Pacific News'* of San Francisco, answer us; is that a specimen of your 'common-doin's' in agriculture, in your soil? **1852** REGAN *Emigrant's Guide* 66 What'll you hev, strangers? Chicken fixin's or common doin's.' — (4) **1852** *Hunt's Merch. Mag.* XXVI. 641 The common wheels . . . revolve about eight times.

b. Commons House of Assembly, (see quot.). *Rare.*

1783 STOKES *View* 28 In some of them [i.e., Amer. colonies], the House of Representatives was called 'the Commons House of Assembly.'

common school.

1. A public elementary school, a district school.

"*Primary school,* a school for instructing children in the first rudiments of language and literature; called also *common school,* because it is open to all the children of all the inhabitants in a town or district" (Web. '41, *s.v. school*).

*a***1656** BRADFORD *Hist. P. Plantation* (1899) 194 Indeeds, we have no comone schoole for want of a fitt person, or hithertoo means to maintaine one; though we desire now to begine. **1795** in R. BOESE *Public Educ. in City of N.Y.* (1869) 21 The establishment of Common Schools throughout the state is happily calculated to remedy this inconvenience. **1851** *Mich. Constitution* vi. The general assembly shall . . . secure a thorough and efficient system of common schools throughout the state. **1902** *Rep. Comm. Education* p. x, A comparative summary showing the increase in what are called common schools, including under this designation schools of the elementary and secondary grades supported from public funds.

b. The building in which such a school is carried on.

1835 J. MARTIN *Descr. Va.* 153 It contains several dwelling houses, . . . a mercantile store, and a common school.

2. Attrib. with **district, education, intelligence, law, system.**

1849 CHAMBERLAIN *Ind. Gazetteer* 152 The common school districts are generally organized and support schools from three to ten months in the year. **1948** *Gainesville* (Tex.) *D. Reg.* 3 July 1/6 Spring Creek is common school district No. 45, while Era is consolidated independent school district No. 54. — **1818** *Boston D. Advertiser* 21 April, Have they not a right to a good bringing up, and to a common school education? — **1881** *Harper's Mag.* April 640/2 Every reputable person . . . knows that the state [Vt.] has the same . . . common-school intelligence as the rest of New England. — **1945** *Amer. Sp.* April 98. A threefold language culture began to fade out with the passing of the common school law in 1834. — **1831** PECK *Guide* 245 A complete common school system must . . . be organized.

Also *common school fund, house, instruction, learning, purpose, teacher,* etc.

***Commonweal,** *n. Hist.* A movement or organization of the unemployed who, in the depression following the panic of 1893, sought by a march upon Washington to induce Congress to enact a public works program. Also attrib. Cf. **Coxey's army.**

1894 *Columbus* (O.) *Dispatch* 4 April, It begins to look as though the commonweal will go through to Washington. If the commonwealers under Frye . . . succeed in effecting a union with the Coxeyites the general army will be a formidable thing. **1894** *Chautauquan* XIX. 335/1 Carl Browne saw in this the spirit of the reincarnated Christ abroad in the army, but to mere mortals it appeared to be due to the military organization of the Commonweal and to the strict discipline enforced by the next in rank to Browne. **1900** *Ohio Archæol. & Hist. Pub.* IX. 163 The organizers . . . tempered their appeal with the hope that no one in ill health would join the Commonweal.

b. Commonweal Army, =**Coxey's Army.** *Obs.*

1894 *Harper's Wkly.* 31 Mar. 308/2 Jacob Sechler Coxey . . . and Carl Browne . . . are the sole proprietors and managers of the great Commonweal army, scheduled to proceed overland on Easter Sunday to Washington. **1900** *Ohio Archæol. & Hist. Pub.* IX. 166 The day brought a number of recruits for the Commonweal Army.

Commonwealer ˈkamənˌwilɚ, *n.* One who participated in the Commonweal movement, a member of Coxey's Army. *Obs.*

1894 *N.Y. Herald* 20 April 9/6 The Commonwealers left Harrisburg last night twenty-five stronger than they entered. **1894** *Dly. Ardmoreite* (Ardmore, Okla.) 24 April 3/1 Frye, Kelley and the rest of the Commonwealers are worked up along the toe path. **1929** D. L. McMURRY *Coxey's Army* 89 The bitterness of the Commonwealers at the police restrictions was matched by the resentment of their sympathizers. . . . The arrests were made not for good cause, but because the men were Commonwealers.

***commonwealth,** *n.*

1. One of the states of the U.S.

But specifically, "Massachusetts, Pennsylvania, Virginia, and Kentucky are officially styled commonwealths" (*Cent.*).

1779 *Pa. Gaz.* 24 March 4/3 All the best whigs in the commonwealth. **1865** LOWELL in *N. Amer. Rev.* C. 161 The sturdy commonwealths which have sprung from the seed of the Mayflower. **1947** *Chr. Sci. Mon.* 16 Jan. 7/4 The Court also decreed: 'That the Governors of the said Commonwealth for all time to come be officially responsible for the safe custody of the said Manuscript Book.'

2. A form of money or credit once current in Kentucky. Also attrib. *Obs.*

1825 *Constitutional Advocate* (Frankfort, Ky.) 26 Oct. 2/1 The people prefer giving $1.25 in silver, equal to $1.37 Commonwealth, for United States land, rather than live in Kentucky and let the Legislature regulate their private contracts. **1833** *Polit. Examiner* (Shelbyville, Ky.) 15 June 3/1 Kentucky has tried her 'Commonwealth' credit, and when it began to flag she undertook to keep it up by a sort of legislative force.

b. Esp. with **paper.** *Obs.*

1822 *Mirror* (Russellville, Ky.) 20 April 4/5, I shall offer for sale at public auction to the highest bidder . . . for ready money (Commonwealth's and Kentucky Bank paper) [etc.]. **1825** *Constitutional Advocate* (Frankfort, Ky.) 26 Oct. 2/1 One dollar in Commonwealth's paper is the minimum price of the land west of the Tennessee river. **1845** SOL SMITH *Theatr. Apprent.* 121, I asked him at what rate he took Commonwealth paper?

comote kəˈmot, *v. tr.* To put into commotion, disturb. *Obs.* — **1852** HAWTHORNE *Blithedale Rom.* xvi. 165 An unfriendly state of feeling could not occur between any two members, without the whole society being more or less commoted and made uncomfortable thereby. *a***1864** ——— *Dr. Grimshawe's Secret* 334 The Warden, greatly commoted for the nonce, complied with the maiden's fantasy.

***communism,** *n.* As the last term in **Bible, Oneida communism.**

communitary kəˈmjunəˌterɪ, *a.* Pertaining to community interest or welfare. Hence **communitariness.** *Rare.* — **1895** *Advance* (Chicago) 14 March 846/1 The societies in which they [*sc.* Harvard and Yale] were placed were characterized by a communitariness of blood, belief, interest and character. *Ib.*, No communitary instinct pervades and unifies society [in the Western States].

* **community,** *n.*

1. A socialistic or communistic society such as that at Brook Farm *q.v.* Also attrib. *Obs.* Cf. **Oneida, Shaker community.**

1828 in *Amer. Sp.* XVIII. 122 Mr. Owen has published the Constitution, which is to be adopted by the community. **1841** THOREAU *Jrnl.* 3 March, As for these communities, I think I had rather keep bachelors hall in hell than go to board in heaven. **1900** ESTLAKE *Oneida Community* 70 Jealousy I never knew. It was contrary to the Community spirit.

2. In special combs.: (1) **community center,** a place where those living in a community assemble to participate in social, recreational, and cultural activities; (2) **chest,** a fund made up of individual donations to meet the needs for charity and social welfare work in a community, also attrib.; (3) **chorus,** a group of singers in a community, organized and under the direction of a leader; (4) **Christmas tree,** a Christmas tree, frequently in a church or schoolhouse, about which those in a community gather, usu. on Christmas eve; (5) **church,** (see quot.); (6) **high school,** a high school serving the needs of an entire community; (7) **house,** a building in which the social activities of a community take place, and from which the social welfare program is administered; (8) **sing,** an occasion of singing by the members of a community; (9) **singing,** singing engaged in regularly by the members of a community.

(1) **1921** *Outing* June 133/1 A Community Center and an organization which pays attention only to such organized athletics as named above would be missing an opportunity if not derelict in its duty. **1948** *Lisle* (Ill.) *Eagle* 21 Oct. 2/1 It is an easy matter for local people to see how the money is being used for the Community Center. — (2) **1921** *Rural Organization* 103 We may be able to work out some form of county-wide *community chest.* **1947** *Dly. Ardmoreite* (Ardmore, Okla.) 14 Nov. 1/4 Coffee and doughnuts will be served to the workers . . . preliminary to the first annual Community Chest drive in Ardmore. — (3) **1929** *Encycl. Brit.* VI. 139/1 The community chorus movement in the United States was launched in Rochester, N.Y., in 1912 by Harry Barnhart. — (4) **1915** *Co. League Advisor* (Chicopee Falls, Mass.) 11 Mar. 1/1 Last Christmas a community Christmas tree was enjoyed at the Common at Huntington.

(5) **1935** HORWILL *Mod. Amer. Usage* 76/1 A *community church* is a church composed of members of various denominations who unite in a single organization instead of grouping themselves in several separate churches. — (6) **1921** *Rural Organization* 118 The 'Community' high and consolidated schools of Illinois. — (7) **1915** *Co. League Advisor* (Chicopee Falls, Mass.) 11 Mar. 1/1 Two pianos . . . have been placed in community house and there is seldom a time when they are not in use. **1948** *Reader's Digest* Sep. 128/2 If [it is] in the autumn, come to the husking bee back of Community House. — (8) **1930** *Randolph Enterprise* (Elkins, W.Va.) 6 Nov. 3/6 The writer was permitted to attend the Community Sing. — (9) **1922** LEWIS *Babbitt* 74 Ryland wore spats, he wrote long letters about City Planning and Community Singing. **1948** *Dly. Ardmoreite* (Ardmore, Okla.) 4 July 1/6 Old-timers and their families are expected to crowd the courthouse lawn today and participate in the church services, community singing, and visiting of the old-time get-together.

* **commutation,** *n. attrib.*

1. Pertaining to the payment of Revolutionary officers in accordance with a resolution of the Continental Congress of March 22, 1783, commuting the half pay promised them upon disbanding into a lump sum equal to five years' full pay, to be discharged in certificates bearing 6% interest. *Obs.*

1787 R. TYLER *Contrast* (1920) 46 And so, brother, you have come to the city to exchange some of your commutation notes for a little pleasure. **1790** in *Jrnl. Wm. Maclay* (1927) 240 It was meant as the stock to ingraft some mischief on with respect to the commutation pensions and half-pay of the old army.

2. commutation money, = **head money.** Also **commutation fund.** *Obs.*

1846 BROMME *Reisebuch* 329 Das amerikanische Kopfgeld *'Commutation Money'* genannt, welches die Kommune am amerikanischen Landungsplatze erhebt, wird in Bremen zugleich mit dem Ueberfahrtsgelde bezahlt. **1851** QUENTIN *Reisebilder* I. 45 Der Ertrag dieses Vergleichsfonds (Commutation fund) ausdrücklich zu andern Zwecken nie verwendet werden soll.

3. Designating passengers who travel regularly between certain places, or with reference to the business of serving them.

1856 W. H. SWIFT *Mass. Railroads* 14 Commutation or season passengers, so called. **1903** E. JOHNSON *Railway Transportation* 148 The 'resort' traffic and suburban traffic, or what is frequently called the commutation business, is zealously stimulated by reduction in fares and by offering an attractive service. **1912** *Out West* April 260/2 Alhambra . . . is seven miles to the northeast from the business center of Los Angeles, . . . commutation fare seven and one-half cents. **1948** *N.Y. Star* 30 June 3/1 The railroad . . . argued that its prospective deficit made a permanent 25 per cent commutation fare increase imperative.

b. commutation ticket, a passenger ticket good for several rides issued at a reduced rate; also a meal ticket issued at a reduced rate.

1849 *Pathfinder* Nov. 50 (Ernst). **1899** F. NORRIS *McTeague* 290 Trina had lied again both as to the want of oil for the stove and the commutation ticket for the restaurant. **1945** *Reader's Digest* March 104/1 An art director, who commutes from Westchester to New York City, carried a New York Central commutation ticket, complete with photograph.

* **commute,** *v. intr.* To travel regularly by public conveyance between two points, as between one's suburban residence and the city.

1865 [implied in **commuter**]. **1889** *Cent.* 1139 Commuter, one who commutes. **1948** *Chickasha* (Okla.) *D. Express* 30 June 5/6 He wears out himself and his pocketbook commuting to his job in the city.

commuter kəˈmjutɚ, *n.* [f. prec.] One who commutes.

1865 *Atlantic Mo.* XV. 82 Two or three may be styled commuters' roads, running chiefly for the accommodation of city business-men with suburban residences. **1898** *Harper's Weekly* 26 Feb. 205/3 Of all criminally good-natured individuals the New York commuter is the worst offender. **1947** *Chi. D. News* 14 Oct. 1/3 Commuters . . . were delayed briefly this morning when a metal rim on one of the locomotive's wheels became loosened.

compadre komˈpɒdre, *n. S.W. & W.* [Sp. in same sense.] An intimate male companion or associate, esp. used as a familiar term of address.

1834 A. PIKE *Sketches* 99 Nay, compadre, an American cannot steal. **1902** *Out West* Sep. 355 And what does it appear to you, *compadre?* **1948** *Chi. Tribune* 4 Feb. 22/5 You, Francisco, are not only my compadre and my brother, you are the omen of my good fortune as well.

compañero ˌkompəˈnjero, *n. S.W. & W.* [Sp. in same sense.] A male companion, a "pardner." Also **compañera,** a female companion, a mistress.

1844 KENDALL *Santa Fe Exped.* II. 342 That the good padres of that country have their compañeras, or female companions, is well known. **1845** FRÉMONT *Exped.* 256 Four *compañeros* joined our guide at the pass. **1931** *N.Y. Herald-Tribune* 5 July (Bentley), The young Communist . . . compañero and understudy of Siqueiros, has just written an exciting book.

* **company,** *n.* Attrib. in the sense: Belonging to, employed by, or serving the interests of a business company, as **company doctor, house, spotter, store, union.**

1930 *These Are Our Lives* 82 It seems to me that a coal mining company ought to have men at the head of it who have sense enough to hire a good company doctor. — **1935** CASON *90°* 28 It costs them less to do those things than to keep the people in food at the company houses. **1948** *Sat. Ev. Post* 4 Dec. 159/1 The . . . lights in the company houses were turned off at nine P.M. — **1917** SINCLAIR *King Coal* 34 Red-faced feller, Gus. Look out for him—company spotter. — **1872** *Harper's Mag.* Nov. 841/1 This arrangement is a much better one than that of a 'company store,' which is so common elsewhere, especially with joint-stock companies. **1945** MACDONALD *Egg & I* 20 We had heard from Mother that Hennessy's, the company store, also sold Paris gowns. — **1917** R. F. HOXIE *Trade Unionism* 51 There are virtually no 'company' unions in Great Britain. **1935** HORWILL *Amer. Usage* 77/2 In Am. the term *company union* denotes a union 'instigated and practically dominated by the employers, organized and conducted for the purpose of combating or displacing independent unionism.' **1948** *Time* 29 Nov. 27/1 Harry Bridges has long accused Beck of running company unions for the benefit of the employer.

As the last term in **artillery, bank, boom, bridge, colonization, critter, electric, Emigrant Aid, engine, express, family, fire engine, fish, flume, fluming, hook and ladder, hose, hydrant, ice, improvement, independent, Indian, ladder, land, land emigrating, land grant, library, logging, lumber, mining, mountain, news, Ohio, oil, operating, packing, phono-**

graph, pre-emption, ranging, road, settlement, slab, snap, stock, telegraph, town, transfer, trapping, trust, wagon, wrecking company.

*comparison, *n.* (See quot.) *Obs.* — 1828 *Yankee* Sep. 288/1 Comparison is very amusing for a still play; in playing this, one of the company leaves the room; in his or her absence, someone names a subject; the absent person is then called in, who asks them all separately what it is like [etc.].

***compass,** *n.*

1. A homemade measuring contrivance shaped somewhat like a huge pair of dividers, its two pointers being at a fixed distance apart. *Obs.*

1854 DAVIS *Farm Bk.* 42 Planted [corn] at 2 feet by a compass.

2. compass flower, plant, any one of several plants, as the rosinweed, *Silphium laciniatum,* having leaves or branches which show polarity. Cf. **polar plant.**

[1843 N. BOONE *Journal* 191 The polar plant, a rosin weed. This plant is a tall plant, perhaps 7 feet high, and a few [*sic*] shaped leaf which ranges, generally, north and south, affording a tolerable compass to the traveler over the prairies.] 1847 LONGFELLOW *Evangeline* line 1219 This is the compass-flower, that the finger of God has planted. 1851 GLISAN *Jrnl. Army Life* 70 There is a very useful plant, called the compass-plant. 1939 *Nat. Geog. Mag.* Aug. 220/2 The most familiar being the black-eyed Susan, those intelligent giants the compass plants, . . . coreopsis and the closely related bur marigolds.

***compensation,** *n.* Payment for services, salary, esp. with reference to government employees. Also attrib.

1787 *Constitution* i. § 6 The Senators and Representatives shall receive a compensation for their services to be ascertained by law, and paid out of the Treasury of the U.S. 1816 *Niles' Reg.* X. 415/1 The 'compensation law' is doing wonders. 1924 C. A. BEARD *Amer. Govt.* 627 The salaries of judges are usually rather low in comparison with the compensation afforded to judicial officers in Europe.

comper ˈkɑmpɚ, *n.* [?Fanciful f. *compeer.] (See quot.) *Obs.* — 1836 *Yale Lit. Mag.* I. 26 (Th.), Any fracas or tumult, like the Calethump of Christmas eve memory, would be styled a 'comper.' *Ib.* 27 What pen can describe the 'comper' which this excited!

***complaint,** *n.* **1. complaint book,** [cf. G. *Beschwerdebuch*], (see quot.). **2. complaint department,** an office or department of a business where complaints are heard and acted upon. **3. complaint desk,** a desk at which complaints are received.

(1) 1856 D. MACLEOD *F. Wood* 201 Two qualities suggested and produced the Compaint-Book. The public were notified through the press that such a book was open at the Mayor's office, wherein might be registered complaints of dereliction from duty on the part of any corporation officers, of violated ordinances, of illegal incumbrances, of nuisances. — (2) 1926 *N.Y. Times Magazine* 15 Aug. 6 Complaints were routed past the complaint department to the President's office. — (3) 1905 *Chi. D. News* 1 July 1/6 (*heading*), Objects to Complaint Desk.

As the last term in **breast, summer complaint.**

complected kəmˈplɛktɪd, *a.* Complexioned, usu. preceded by a qualifying term. *Colloq.*

1806 LEWIS in *L. & Clark Exped.* (1905) III. 315 They are generally low in stature, proportionably small, rather lighter complected and much more illy formed than the Indians of the Missouri. *c*1847 WHITCHER *Bedott P.* 74 She was a dark complected woman. 1863 B. TAYLOR *H. Thurston* 52 He a'n't blacker 'n I'd be now, if I was complected like him. 1939 P. G. PERRIN *Writer's Guide & Index to English* (1942) 449 *Complected* in such phrases as 'He is a dark-complected man' is vulgate or local for 'a dark-complexioned man.'

composuist kəmˈposjuɪst, *n.* [Irreg. f. *compose, v.*] A composer. *Obs.*

1800 J. ELLIOTT and S. JOHNSON *Dict.* 42 Com posˈ u ist, s. one who writes pieces. 1816 PICKERING 64 This extraordinary word has been much used at some of our colleges, but very seldom elsewhere. It is now rarely heard among us. 1851 HALL *College Words* 77 *Composuist,* a writer; composer. . . . The word is not found, I believe, in any dictionary of the English tongue.

***compote,** *n.* A dessert dish having a stem or support, a comport. — *a*1904 in A. HAYDEN *Chats Eng. China* 160 Dessert service . . . consisting of one tall compôte, seven oval dishes [etc.]. 1926 *Chi. Tribune* 11 June, Compotes. . . . These may also be used as mayonnaise or bonbon dishes.

***compound,** *n.* **1. compound basis,** *S.* the basis of being of the white race and possessed of property, used to determine the right of franchise. **2. compound interest note,** (see quot.). Both *obs.* — (1) 1830 *Va. Lit. Museum* 477/2 By the compound basis, the West would have forty three, the east, seventy seven [delegates]. — (2) 1870 *Nation* Feb. 86 One of the means of raising money, adopted during the war pressure, was the issue of a large amount of what were called compound-interest notes, or legal-tender greenbacks bearing interest.

***compress,** *n.* A machine for compressing bales of cotton, or the building in which compressing is carried on. Also attrib. Cf. **cotton compress.**

1868 *Rep. Comm. Patents* II. 257/2 The table or platen of a compress is so constructed that with it cotton and other goods that have been . . . put up in bales, can be again compressed without removing the hoops. 1879 *Harper's Mag.* Oct. 718 Compress rates are paid by transportation companies or ship captains, who charge freight by the bale, and are large gainers by the compress system. 1943 *Amer. Sp.* April 123/1 The only separate pressing establishments are compresses, where bales are repressed for export.

***compressed,** *a.* **1. compressed burbot,** (see quots.). **2. compressed yeast,** (see quot.).

(1) 1842 *Nat. Hist. N.Y., Zoology* IV. 285 Compressed Burbot. . . . Eel-pout. 1870 *Amer. Naturalist* IV. 251 The Compressed Burbot or Eel Pout. . . . My first acquaintance with this rare fish was early in the spring of 1859. — (2) 1891 CHASE & CLOW *Industry* II. 98 Yeast is the froth that rises to the top of malt liquor. It is thick, like cream, and after being taken off, is partly dried, pressed, washed and then cut into little blocks. Then it is called *compressed yeast,* and you have seen how it comes to us in those little blocks, rolled up in tin-foil.

***compressing,** *n.* Pressing cotton bales into smaller compass to facilitate shipping. — 1841 *Hunt's Merch. Mag.* June 563 Compressing—Cotton, per bale, 75 cents; cotton intended to be compressed, 12½ cents for the first month. 1879 *Harper's Mag.* Oct. 717 Considerably more than a million dollars is paid for the item of compressing.

***Compromiser,** *n.* A nickname for Henry Clay (1777–1852), who often reconciled Northern and Southern interests before the Civil War. Also **Great Compromiser.** — 1886 WILLEY *Hist. Antislavery Cause* 102 Henry Clay, the leader of the Whig party and aspirant for the presidency, the 'compromiser,' in 1839 offered a petition from people in the District [of Columbia]. 1913 BASSETT *Short Hist. U.S.* 454 It appealed to his [=Henry Clay's] imagination that 'the Great Compromiser,' as he was called, should finish his career with another compromise.

***compromit,** *v. tr.* To compromise, involve in difficulty, imperil. Prob. *obs.*

1787 JEFFERSON *Writings* VI. 136 The public reputation is, every moment, in danger of being compromitted with him. 1843 *Amer. Pioneer* II. 209 Men of property and influence, who had become compromitted in the destruction of general Neville's house, exerted themselves to involve the whole country in open resistance to the laws. 1879 H. C. WOOD *Therapeutics* (ed. 3) 521 Mucus may so accumulate in the lungs . . . as seriously to embarrass, or even fatally compromit, respiration. 1919 MENCKEN *Amer. Lang.* 36 The colonial pedants denounced *to advocate* as bitterly as they ever denounced *to compromit* or *to happify.*

Comptonia ˌkɑmpˈtonɪə, *n.* [After Henry *Compton* (1632–1713), an English prelate.] The North American sweet fern, *Comptonia asplenifolia,* having fern-like leaves.

1823 CRABB *Technol. Dict. s.v.,* Fern-leaved Comptonia, a shrub, native of New England. 1889 *Cent.* 1157/1 *Comptonia.* . . . The only species, *C. asplenifolia,* is the sweet-fern of the United States. . . . It is said to be tonic and astringent, and is a domestic remedy for diarrhea. 1942 TEHON *Native Ill. Shrubs* 59 Comptonia . . . has the general characteristics of the family.

***Comstock,** *n.* [Henry Tompkins Paige *Comstock* (1820–70), Amer. prospector who located (1859) on the site of the famous Comstock lode but sold his claim for a small amount.]

1. =**Comstock lode.**

1867 *Terr. Enterprise* (Virginia, Nev.) 2 Feb. 3/1 The real out and out Washoe miner can be found away down in the bowels of the Comstock. 1926 *Collier's* 30 Oct. 19/2 As a superintendent he had access to all the mines of the Comstock. 1947 *Time* 27 Oct. 106/2 Ambitious men moved in, capable of trying to dominate the entire Comstock.

attrib. 1876 *Nevada State Jrnl.* (Reno) 12 Aug. 3/1 He . . . began to insult a peaceable citizen who came in for a drink, calling him the vilest names in the vocabulary of Comstock slang. 1895 *Voice* (N.Y.) 23 May 6/3 It was at the end of the huge but demoralizing Comstock 'boom.' 1946 *Nat. Geog. Mag.* Jan. 19/1 Here Comstock kings banqueted on iced oysters from the coast, costly squab, and imported champagne.

2. Comstock lode, a fabulously rich lode of silver and gold discovered in 1859 at the present Virginia City, Nev.

1866 *Beadle's Mo.* Aug. 102/1 The Comstock Lode proved the richest vein of silver ever found. 1948 JOHNSTON *Gold Rush* 35/1 Thus was the fabulous treasure of the Comstock Lode revealed.

Comstocker ˈkʌmˌstɑkɚ, *n.* One associated with the famous Comstock lode mines at Virginia City, Nev.

1876 *Gold Hill* (Nev.) *News* 7 Dec. It would be hard to find a jury of generous Comstockers who would convict them. **1877** Wright *Big Bonanza* 356 A Comstocker . . . dropped in at a chop-house where about a dozen newcomers had just settled in a flock, at two or three adjoining tables. **1948** *Nev. Highways* July–August 4/2 Comstockers even grew fearful that production would upset the world's monetary balance.

comstockery ˈkʌmˌstɑkərɪ, *n.* [f. Anthony *Comstock* (1844–1915), Amer. reformer.] Excessive censorship of immoralities occurring in books, newspapers, pictures, etc.; prudery.

1911 Schroeder *'Obscene' Lit. & Constit. Law* 101 There is no organized force in American life which is more pernicious or more productive of moral evil in the domain of sex, than the very work which has come to be known as Comstockery. **1946** Mencken *The Gods* 251 On the theological level . . . it gave us such indecencies as comstockery, Prohibition, and the laws against the teaching of evolution as a biological fact.

Also **Comstockism.**

1915 *Survey* 6 Nov. 128/2 Let us trace precisely the way in which liberalism in public affairs may become Comstockism in morals.

con kɑn, *n.* Short for "confidence," used in **con game, con man;** see **confidence game, confidence man.** *Slang.*

1903 *N.Y. Sun* 30 Nov. 7 Two sailors say he worked the 'con' game on them. **1945** *Nation* CLX. 31 March 359/2 The present hollering for sixty million jobs is a con game, pure and simple. — **1889** *Portland* (Ore.) *Mercury* 29 June 1/7 It does not take an unsophisticated countryman to get swindled by the 'con man.' **1948** *Chi. Tribune* 25 June 16/6 A petty con man fleeced a hard working girl on an apartment deal.

Also *con racket, speech, talk,* etc.

con kɑn, *v.* [f. prec.] *tr.* To swindle, dupe. *Slang.*

1896 G. Ade *Artie* iv. 35 Don't try to con me with no such talk. **1917** Mathewson *Sec. Base Sloan* xiv. 196 Don't let anyone con you into signing a contract. **1944** *N. & Q.* Nov. 116/2 Con. To inveigle an individual (either a criminal or an informant) into doing something by verbal trickery.

* **con-.** Used in various euphemisms for "damned," as **condarned, condemned, condigned.** *Colloq.* or *slang.* Cf. **contwisted,** *a.*

1839 *N.O. Picayune* 8 Mar. 2/4 I'll be condarned if I know which is the smartest. — **1861** Winthrop *Open Air* 249 'But I took a big cold,' the diver continued, 'and I'm condemned hoarse yit.' **1921** Paine *Comr. Rolling Ocean* 140 Bless my soul, what sort of a condemned rum-shop have I stumbled into? — **1902** White *Blazed Trail* xiv. 95 And now this condigned jobber ties us up for a million and a half.

***Conant,** *n.* (See quots.) — **1905** *Springfield W. Republican* 22 Dec. 11 The standard silver coins being used in the Philippines are known as "Conants," having been named for Charles A. Conant, who was sent to the islands to prepare a coinage system. **1906** Mrs. C. Dauncey *Englishw. in Philippines* iii. 20 The money here is a dollar currency called Conant, which is worth 2s. 1d.—half the American dollar. *Ib.* iv. 27 The Mexican dollar, which is only about two-thirds of the Conant unit.

conbobberation kənˌbɑbəˈreʃən, *n.* [Of fanciful origin.] Disturbance. *Colloq. Obs.* — **1835** Kennedy *Horse Shoe Robinson* I. 65 What are you making such a conbobberation about! **1845** Hooper *Daddy Biggs' Scrape* 194 There was somethin' a flouncin' and sloshin', and makin' a devil of a conbobberation at the end of the line.

concageer ˈkɑnkəˌdʒɪr, *n.* [Origin unknown.] (See quot.) *Obs.* — **1859** Bartlett *Concageer,* a name applied to the small lizards and salamanders of the United States.

* **concede,** *v. tr.* To acknowledge, admit, grant that an election has terminated in an indicated manner.

1824 *Commentator* (Frankfort, Ky.) 2 Oct. 3/1 This state is generally conceded to General Jackson. **1891** *N.Y. Herald* 1 Mar. 15/5 An Independent Canvass Concedes the Victory to Him, but Reduces His Majority from 41 to 9. **1946** *Pueblo* (Colo.) *Chieftain* 27 June 1/7 J. B. Bridston Wednesday night conceded the North Dakota republican senatorial nomination to U.S. Senator William Langer as additional returns boosted Langer's lead.

concededly kənˈsidɪdlɪ, *adv.* Admittedly.— **1882** *N.Y. Tribune* 22 March, The present Executive Mansion . . . is concededly not what it ought to be. **1930** *Randolph Enterprise* (Elkins, W.Va.) 25 Dec. 1/2 Volume of December retail buying well up to year ago but value concededly less.

* **concert,** *n.*

1. The first part of a minstrel show. *Obs.*

1856 *Porter's Spirit of Times* I. 32/3 George Christy & Wood's Minstrels. . . . Concert commences at 8 o'clock. **1857** *Ib.* 344/3 Buckley's Serenaders.— . . . The nightly concert which precedes the burlesque is also highly entertaining.

2. concert clock, a musical clock. *Obs.*

1797 *Boston Chronicle* 19 Dec., Exhibition of Concert Clocks. *Ib.* The above Concert Clocks have been exhibited in New-York. **1797** in *Old-Time N. Eng.* (1926) July 43 Mr. Bowen informs the Public, that he has purchased Mr. Paff's much admired Exhibition of Concert Clocks.

3. concert saloon, a public hall or room where music is played. Also attrib. *Obs.*

1861 in M. W. Disher *Cowells in America* (1934) Niblo's Garden . . . has succumbed to the pressure of the times, and closed, last night. So did Wallack's and several of the Concert Saloons. **1867** A. Daly *Under Gaslight* II. 16 Nina, what's she, concert-saloon girl? **1936** Asbury *French Quarter* 320 The concert-saloon, forerunner of the modern night club, provided a dance-floor upon which pleasure-seekers might kick up their heels to the music of a tinny piano and a squeaky fiddle.

As the last term in **gift, leaf, old folks', promenade, sacred concert.**

* **concession,** *n.* A small area or place made available to someone for a lunch shop, hot-dog stand, etc.; the right to carry on such a business. Also attrib.

1910 *Sat. Ev. Post* 9 July 5/3 A third of this goes to the park, for it is a concession, and in addition it must pay rent. **1913** *Collier's* 6 Dec. 12/2 Who is managing the 'concessions' of the Panama-Pacific Exposition? **1948** *Miami* (Okla.) *D. News-Record* 4 July 11/4 He has operated the concession stand in the Miami postoffice for the last four years.

concessioner kənˈseʃənɚ, *n.* One who has secured a concession at a ball park, fair ground, etc.

1910 *Sat. Ev. Post* 15 Oct. 18/2 My friends, the concessioners, . . . naturally wanted me to hang on so they could continue their blessed graft. **1938** Thompson *High Trails* 131 Then came the development of an aesthetic consciousness on the part of the National Park Service, and they began regulating the practices of concessioners. **1948** *Denison* (Tex.) *Herald* 1 July 1/7 A California bait company wanted names of the principal concessioners with an idea of supplying them with lures.

* **conch,** *n.* Also **Conch.** A low-class white person, esp. one living along the southern coast of Fla., or in N.C. Also attrib. Cf. **concher,** and see **horse conch, rebel conch.**

This nickname was app. introduced from the Bahama region. See quots. and note that Santamaría lists *concho* as used in Costa Rica for a country hick.

1852 *N.Y. Wkly. Tribune* 1 May 7/3 Nearly one half of all residents [of Key West] are natives of the Bahama Islands. They are called Conch-men or *Conchs,* by reason of their skill in *diving.* **1870** J. S. Bradford in *Lippincott's Mag.* (Nov.) VI. 458 The North Carolina conch is unquestionably the lowest specimen of the race known. He has absolutely no virtues, and is dirtier, if possible, than the negro. But he is not so lazy. **1948** Mencken *Supp.* II. 137 The dialect of the Conchs, as they are called, who inhabit the Florida Keys, has been reported on by Thomas R. Reid, Jr.

attrib. **1942** Rawlings *C. Creek* 52 She . . . promised to send medicine to one, quilt scraps to another, and a pound of little conch pea seed to yet another.

b. (See quot.)

1877 Bartlett Koncks or Conks. Wreckers are so called, familiarly, at Key West; and the place they inhabit is called Koncktown.

concha ˈkontʃə, *n.* Also **concho.** *S.W. & W.* [Sp., shell or shell-shaped object.] (See quots.) Also attrib.

1887 *Scribner's Mag.* II. 512/1 And listen to the *conchas,* the silver ornaments outside the spur, as they jingle and ring to the broncho's tread! **1936** Barnard *Rider* 15 The Indians had blankets of bright colors, and wore buckskin leggings with fringe below the knee and silver conchos on the side, and their moccasins were brightly beaded. **1947** *N.M. Quart. Rev.* Autumn 314 His scallop shell, or concha, made in silver for pilgrim's wear, is the probable ancestor of the silver concha belt worn by Navaho horsemen.

concher ˈkɑŋkɚ, *n.* =**conch.** *Obs.* — **1873** De Vere *MS Notes* 45 *Conch* of Fla., conchers, mostly from Key West, fr[om] large shellfish (*Strombus gigans*) on which it is pretended they subsist.

Concho grass. =**Texas millet,** prob. so called from the Conchos (Indians). — **1884** Vasey *Agric. Grasses* 36 It . . . has been called Concho grass in some parts. **1889** *Cent.* 1165/2 Concho-grass . . . is now cultivated in the southern United States and found to yield a large amount of valuable forage.

concoa ˈkɑŋkə, *n. local.* (See quot. a1870.) *Obs.* — **a1870** Chipman *Notes on Bartlett* 93 *Concoa,* the butter-nut. So called (or oftener pronounced as the word conquer), and thus written and printed in Essex County, Mass. The word may be of Indian origin (or que. Portuguese?). **1877** BARTLETT 136.

* **Concord,** *n.*

1. A type of coach first made in Concord, N.H., about 1827, in which thorough-braces were used for the first time. In full **Concord coach.** Now *hist.*

1853 *Shasta Courier* (Redding, Calif.) 12 Mar., The Proprietors of the above line . . . have placed upon this route their splendid stock of American Horses and elegant Concord Coaches. **1908** MULFORD *Orphan* 38 Bill Howland emerged from the . . . office of the . . . Stage Company and strolled down the street to where his Concord stood. **1948** RITTENHOUSE *Vehicles* 47 Concord coaches weighed 2,500 lbs., and sold for $1,250 or more. They carried nine passengers inside and as many more as could cling to the roof.

attrib. **1902** MCFAUL *Ike Glidden* 89 As they approached Squirmtown they saw numerous teams,—some of the two-seated 'Democrat' type, others of the Concord pattern. **1930** BANNING *Six Horses* 359 The most important function of Concord thorough-braces has already been explained.

Concord coach

b. Also **Concord buggy, hack, spring wagon, stage, wagon.**

1902 *Sears Cat.* (ed. 112) 364/2 Our $37.95 Concord Buggy. — **1860** in *N.D. Hist. Quart.* VI. (April, 1932) 233 Started at 6.30 a.m. in a covered vehicle (generally known as a Concord wagon or hack) on leather slings and rather comfortable. — **1941** FERGUSSON *Southwest* 100 The North raged about the 'horseshoe' or 'ox-bow' route. But Mr. Butterfield bought a hundred Concord spring wagons and square-bodied coaches. — **1855** *Wide West* (S.F.) 24 June 1/3 On shore we scramble and to the tops of the 'Concord stages' that are waiting. **1948** *Popular Western* June 29/1 Later, with the two Concord stages drawn up in front of the main grandstand, the crowd gave an enthusiastic ovation to the rival drivers, Tex Grant and Monte Fargin. —**1853** *Deseret News* (Salt Lake City) 14 May 1/1 A man calling himself Wm. McClafflin hired of the subscriber, a grey horse and Concord wagon, for the purpose of going to Kingston. **1947** *Steamboat* (Colo.) *Pilot* 16 Jan. 2/7 The stage firm had invested $250,000 in building stage stations, hiring drivers and station keepers, buying the finest string of draft mules in the West, and purchasing 52 'Concord wagons' as the stagecoaches were called.

2. A superior variety of grape, producing large, sweet, bluish-black fruit. In full **Concord grape.**

1858 *Mich. Agric. Soc. Trans.* X. 217 Mr. Prince thought it a better grape than the Concord. **1913** STRATTON-PORTER *Laddie* xi. The newly-opened bottles of grape juice filled the house with the tang of concord and muscadine. **1946** HOLBROOK *Lost Men* 129 Here [in Sleepy Hollow Cemetery, Concord, Mass.] lies Ephraim Bull, originator of the Concord grape, America's first great contribution to horticulture.

* **concourse,** *n.* A place through which a large number of people pass, as a boulevard or the lobby of a large railway station.

1862 *Harper's Mag.* Dec. 42/1 One Saturday afternoon in June a group of cavaliers had assembled on the 'Concourse' at the Central Park. **1935** HORWILL *Amer. Usage* 79/1 Concourse . . . denotes the large open space, or main hall, in the centre of a station of the modern type. **1948** *Chi. Tribune* 3 Apr. I. 5/6 There are nine other moving stairways operating in Rockefeller's concourse.

* **concur,** *v. tr.* To approve (a bill or resolve). *Obs.* — **1815** in *Amer. Sp.* XXII. 277 Concur [is] used with us in a manner so strange I can hardly understand or explain it—for instance the house has passed a *resolve* or bill, it wont be concurred by the Senate.

* **condemn,** *v. tr.* To declare (property) to be taken for public use, under the right of eminent domain.

1833 *Niles' Reg.* XLIV. 192/2 All expenses to be incurred, in condemning, or purchasing ground . . . shall be . . . at the proper cost of the rail road company. *Ib.* 263 In the case of the Chesapeake and Ohio canal company *vs.* George Lefever, . . . being a proceeding to condemn land for the canal, the jury returned an inquisition of $6,500 damages. **1909** *Indian Laws & Tr.* III. 385 To condemn any of said lands necessary for the purpose of reclamation. **1948** *Ill. Munic. Rev.* May 75/1 The city may condemn the property and acquire title by court action if no agreement can be reached.

* **condemnation,** *n.* The seizure of property for public use, or for the payment of a debt that is due. Also attrib.

1852 DUNLAP *Book Forms* (1857) 853 Schedule or Inquisition of Real Estate levied upon by Fi. Fa., for Condemnation. **1903** *Mont. Supreme Ct.* XXIX. 155 Condemnation proceedings are special proceedings provided for by the statute. **1947** *Sat. Ev. Post* 8 Feb. 96/4 Owens Valley property had been condemned for the purpose, and residents claimed that they had received too little compensation under the condemnation awards.

condensed milk. Milk that has been evaporated and sweetened to preserve it and make it easier to transport.

1863 NORTON *Army Lett.* 177 We buy condensed milk of the sutlers. **1876** *Avalanche* (Silver City, Ida.) 25 April 3/2 When the waiter handed around 'condensed milk' put up in Maine, to go into my tea, I was dumfounded. **1947** *Chi. Tribune* 4 July 5/1 Milk powder plants erected in the south could ship powdered or condensed milk to northern areas cheaper than when produced here.

condensery kənˈdɛnsərɪ, *n.* A place where milk is condensed. Cf. **milk condensery.**

1921 *Ladies' H. Jrnl.* May 39/2 At these condenseries the milk from these herds [etc.]. **1940** CUMMINGS *American & His Food* 67 Gail Borden . . . opened his first big condensery just after the outbreak of the conflict. **1947** *Chi. Tribune* 2 July 7/1 Prices paid to milk producers at the condensaries are expected to increase this month following a recent increase in the price of butter.

condensing company. A business firm engaged in manufacturing condensed milk. — **1878** *Ill. Dept. Agric. Trans. 1876* XIV. 293 The condensing company are particular in all respects; they take only good milk, and make only a good product.

* **condition,** *n.*

1. *Educ.* The requirement that a student do additional work in order to obtain "credit" in a subject; the subject in which such a requirement is made.

1832 in *Atlantic Mo.* Oct. (1887) 434/1 She straightway got a tutor, and prodded Ralph night and day to make up the conditions. **1833** *Ib.* 443/2 Ralph is . . . actually gone back to Cambridge to make up his conditions. **1851** HALL *College Words* 78 The branches in which he [an entering student] is deficient are called conditions. **1907** *Scribner's Mag.* LXI. 506/1 At the end of sophomore year it became imperative for him to work off his accumulated conditions in the science he loathed. **1942** *Univ. of Wisconsin Bul.* 43 The usual way of removing a condition is by a successful final examination.

2. condition powders, medicinal powders designed to keep stock in good condition. *Colloq.*

1884 THOMAS HUGHES *Gone to Texas* 189 You ought to have a few packages of 'condition powders' for stock and chickens.

* **condition,** *v. Educ. tr.* To grant a student a certain status on the condition that he attain proficiency in a given subject by a specified time (see quot. 1900).

1832 in *Atlantic Mo.* Oct. (1887) 434/1 On his examination at Cambridge last Fall, he was heavily conditioned. **1863** *Harper's Mag.* Nov. 785/2 The professors and tutors speedily question them as to their attainments, and either 'admit' or 'condition' them. **1900** *D.N.* II. 29 Condition, v.t. (Of an instructor) to mark a student deficient in a subject.

Hence * **conditioning,** *n.*

1897 *Educ. Rev.* XIII. 8 [Some students] get through by much coaching and conditioning.

condolence council. "A tribal council of the Iroquois, held after the death of a sachem" (Th. Supp.). *Rare.* — **1890** *Smithsonian Rep.* 49 He . . . successfully made special effort to obtain the chants and speeches used in the condolence council of the league.

* **conduct,** *n.* **1. conduct book,** in school or in the navy, a book in which a record of behavior is kept. **2. conduct law,** (see quot.). *Obs.*

(1) **1856** COZZENS *Sparrowgrass P.* xiii 185 A conduct-book! There was G. for good boy, and R. for reading, and S. for spelling and so on. **1889** *Cent.* 1177 Conduct-book, . . . a book kept on board of United States men-of-war, in which the conduct and ability of each man of the crew is noted. — (2) **1882** COOPER *Amer. Pol.* Bk. I. 178 Since reconstruction . . . some of the States, notably Georgia . . . passed

class laws, which treat colored criminals differently from white, under what are now known as the 'conduct laws.'

* **conduct,** *v. N. Eng. intr.* To act, behave. *Colloq.*

"By a customary omission of the pronoun, to *conduct*, in an intransitive sense, is to behave; to direct personal actions" (W. '28). "This offensive barbarism is happily confined to New England, where it is common both in speech and writing. Like many other expressions in the same predicament, it has received the tacit sanction of Dr. Webster, himself a New England man" (B. '48).

1754 EDWARDS *Works* (1843) II. 17 *n.*, I say not only doing, but conducting; because a voluntary forbearing to do, sitting still, keeping silence, &c., are instances of persons' conduct, about which Liberty is exercised. **1786** J. BELKNAP in *Belknap P.* (1877) I. 432 How does *fulmen eripuit* [i.e., Franklin] conduct, and how is he approved in his curule department? **1871** *Binghamton Republ.* 17 Jan. (De Vere), Mr. Schutt said to him, How strangely you have conducted!

conducta kən'duktə, *n. S.W.* [Sp. in same sense.] A caravan or escorted party. *Obs.*

1836 HOLLEY *Texas* vi. 117 There are already heavy capitalists located there, and one conducta has arrived from Chihuahua with three hundred thousand dollars. **1871** DE VERE 105 The caravan is quite at home in New Mexico and Sonora, although frequently called there by its Spanish name, conducta. **1910** BRONSON *Redblooded Heroes* 234 It was a point at which conductas were often attacked.

conductment kən'dʌktmənt, *n.* The action of directing, command. — **1757** *Lett. to Washington* II. 128 A Return of Provisions &c for the Cherokee Indians commanded by the Young Warrior under my conductment from Winchester . . . to Wassers Fort. **1868** in *Autobiography of Matthew Vassar* (1916) 11, I dont believe in erecting a 'Monument' to my everlasting Shame by a failure in Judgement in its conductment.

* **conductor,** *n.*

1. =**lightning rod.** Also attrib. *Obs.*

1764 in N. F. MOORE *Hist. Sk. Columbia Coll.* (1846) 49 Ordered, that a conductor be fixed to the cupola of the college, as a security against lightning. **1846** *Dollar Newspaper* (Phila.) 12 Aug. 2/3 The conductor on a building at the corner of Baltimore street and Tripolett's alley, was also struck. **1852** *Knickerb.* XL. 191 Soon a large and ancient plain brick building, with conductor-protected gables, rises upon the view.

2. One who has charge of mail, etc., in a stagecoach. *Obs.* or *hist.*

1790 *Independent Chron.* 4 March 4/2 A person to go through with the mail to take Care of it. . . . This conductor shall transact all . . . business committed to him. **1872** MARK TWAIN *Roughing It* ii. 25 By the side of the driver sat the 'conductor,' the legitimate captain of the craft; for it was his business to take charge and care of the mails, baggage, express matter, and passengers. **1930** BANNING *Six Horses* 400 A *conductor* was a traveling official (unknown to the later 'shotgun messenger' days), who, usually as a ranking driver, was responsible for the welfare of passengers and cargo of a vehicle, or a train of vehicles, over long stretches of certain overland lines.

3. A railroad employee who has charge of a train.

1832 *Amer. R.R. Jrnl.* I. 721 Seat for the conductor. **1882** E. A. FREEMAN in *Longman's Mag.* I. 90 It is otherwise when one word is used rather than another under the notion of its being finer. This is plainly the case with 'depôt,' and I suppose it is also with 'conductor' for 'guard.' **1944** *Reader's Digest* March 17 All five of the great unions which operate our railroad trains—engineers, firemen, conductors, trainmen, switchmen—deny membership to Negroes.

Hence **conductor's car,** (see quot.).

1895 WAIT *Car-Builder's Dict.* 22 Caboose-car. . . . A car attached to the rear of all freight trains, for the accommodation of the conductor and trainmen. . . . Also, but rarely, called *conductor's car* or *train-car.*

b. An agent furthering the escape of slaves over the Underground Railroad. Now *hist.*

1869 T. J. MAY *Recoll. Anti-Slavery Conflict* 297 Even after I came to reside in Syracuse I had much to do as a station-keeper or conductor on the Underground Railroad. **1941** BUCKMASTER *Let My People Go* 69 He gave them a meal, allowed them to rest, and put them in charge of a conductor.

As the last term in **car, freight, lightning, milk, Pullman, railroad, railway, train, yard conductor.**

* **cone,** *n.*

1. A cone-shaped edible biscuit-like container filled with ice cream.

1920 *Outing* July–Aug. 246/2 Ray licked the ice cream from out his dripping cone. **1948** *Chi. Tribune* 28 March (Comics) 10 He's cryin' because I'm eatin' this cone—an' won't give him any!

2. coneflower, any one of various plants of the genus *Rudbeckia,* so named from the cone-like disk of the flower head. Cf. **purple coneflower.**

1817–8 EATON *Botany* (1822) 436 *Rudbeckia laciniata,* cone-flower, cone-disk sunflower. **1918** VISHER *So. Dakota* 85 Abundant species with resin include the cone-flower, gum-weed, and Psoralea. **1939** *Nat. Geog. Mag.* Aug. 256/2 The stout stems of the coneflower stand stiffly here and there.

Conestoga ˌkɑnə'stogə, *n.* [See note.]

1. *pl.* An important Iroquoian tribe of Indians formerly living along the Susquehanna River and its tributaries, the last survivors being murdered by the whites in 1763. In full **Conestoga Indians.**

This name is regarded as coming from *Kanastóge,* a translation by the Huron Indians of the Delaware Indian river name, *Susquehanna,* both words meaning roily or muddy river or water. See *Sixth Report of the U.S. Geographic Board* (1933) 13–14.

1699 in *N.Y. Doc. Col. Hist.* IV. (1854) 579 When the English heard you were coming against the Canastogues, they instead of assisting those who were their friends came and joyned with you and killed them and destroyed their Castles. **1764** in *Mass. Hist. Soc. Coll.* 4 Ser. X. (1871) 508 Since then the Connastago Indeans were all killed. **1831** A. S. WITHERS *Chron. Border Warfare* 78 The Canestoga Indians, to the number of forty, lived in a village, in the vicinity of Lancaster. **1938** HARK *Hex Marks Spot* 65 They led me to the fair and rolling meadows of the Conestoga valley, where in olden times had dwelt the Conestoga Indians, 'people of the forked roof poles.'

2. A heavy freight wagon of a type first built in Conestoga Valley, Pa. In full **Conestoga wagon.** Now *hist.* Cf. **scoop wagon.**

1781 in *Pa. Mag. Hist.* LXIV. 222, I cannot say I will follow your Advice respecting marrying a Dutch Girl, with a good Plantation & a Conostoga Waggon. **1808** *Balance* (Hudson, N.Y.) 16 Feb. 28 (Th.), The throng of Pittsburg and Conestoga waggons. **1901** CHURCHILL *Crisis* 11 After many years the streams began to move again, . . . by white conestogas threading flat forests and floating over wide prairies. **1945** MENCKEN *Supp.* I. 233 The *Conestoga-wagon* survived until my own boyhood. I have seen whole fleets lined up in Howard street, Baltimore, laden with butter and eggs from the Pennsylvania German country.

Conestoga wagon

b. Conestoga Wagon, the name of a Philadelphia tavern. Now *hist.*

1750 *Pa. Gazette* 26 Feb., Just imported and to be sold very cheap for ready money by Thomas White, at his house in Market Street, almost opposite the sign of the Conestoga Waggon. **c1782** in W. GORDON *Hist. Amer. Revol.* (ed. 2) III. 329 A small dirty room in the Philadelphia tavern called the Canastoga-waggon. **1949** *Pa. Dutchman* 25 Aug. 1/4 The Conestoga Wagon Inn mentioned by Washington was located on Market Street, Philadelphia, above Fourth Street, and was the same tavern mentioned as 'The Sign of the Dutch Wagon' in the Pennsylvania Gazette early in 1750.

3. A large draft horse developed by Pennsylvania-German farmers from English stock. In full **Conestoga horse.** Now *hist.*

1825 WILLIAM H. KEATING *Narrative Expedition to St. Peter's River 1823* II. 24 There are several appellations by which the different breeds of this useful animal are distinguished in Pennsylvania, such as the Conestoga. **1839** E. HOOPER *Practical Farmer* 474 [The] Suffolk Punch . . . strongly resembles the famous Chester Balls and the Canestoga horses of Pennsylvania. **1942** WEYGANDT *Plenty of Penna.* 83 Plain clothes folk, when there were many of them about, could resist cards and dancing . . . more easily than they could a tight little Morgan . . . or a team of great Conestogas.

b. Conestoga breed, the breed of these horses.

1929 *Randolph Enterprise* (Elkins, W.Va.) 14 Nov. 1/2 Slick, powerful horses of the Conestoga breed were used by prosperous teamsters.

4. *pl.* (See quot.)

1896 *D.N.* I. 229 Kentucky Words: . . . Conestogas . . . brogans.

5. Short for **Conestoga cargo plane.**

1946 *Reader's Digest* March 19/2 Although the Conestogas are intended primarily for freight, they are fitted with folding canvas chairs for passengers.

6. In other combs.: (1) **Conestoga bonnet,** a bonnet having a crown suggestive in shape of the covers used on Conestoga wagons, *obs.;* (2) **cargo plane,** a large airplane for carrying freight; (3) **cigar,** (see quot.), *obs.*, cf. **stogy;** (4) **trail,** (see quot.); (5) **wagoner,** the driver of a Conestoga wagon, *obs.*

(1) **1843** in THOMPSON *M. Jones* (1872) 147, I was monstrous glad Mary was settin right behind a big tall woman what had a great big conestoga bonnet on, so she couldn't see the outlandish thing. — (2) **1946** *Reader's Digest* March 17/2 Bob Prescott handed it all to the Surplus War Property Board as down payment on 14 big twin-motored Conestoga cargo planes built for the Navy. — (3) **1894** SEARIGHT *Old Pike* 144 To meet this demand [for a cheap cigar], a small cigar manufacturer in Washington, Pennsylvania, whose name is lost to fame, started in to make a cheap 'roll-up' for them at four for a cent. They became very popular with the drivers, and were at first called Conestoga cigars; since, by usage, corrupted into 'stogies' and 'tobies.' — (4) **1930** OMWAKE *Conestoga Teams* 13 One hundred years ago wagoning was at its height, and on the Conestoga trail—the road from Philadelphia to Pittsburgh, which was the gateway to the Ohio country—were fleets of the great white-topped wagons. There were said to be three thousand daily, on this road alone.

(5) **1788** FRENEAU *Misc. Works* 88 Plain Johan Shovelshoes, the Conestogoe waggoner, immagines the soul to be a thin airy substance. **1863** *Harper's Mag.* Feb. 423/1 The Conestoga wagoners, like the chimney-sweepers, have nearly faded from the remembrance of the oldest inhabitants.

Coney Island. [A place, formerly an island, on the southwestern part of Long Island, noted as a pleasure resort.] *attrib.* Designating things characteristic of Coney Island, as **Coney Island barker, chute-the-chutes, clam chowder, maze.**

1895 *Outing* XXVII. 238/2 Curried mussel . . . in aroma and taste is not unlike a Coney Island clam chowder. **1904** *N.Y. Ev. Post* 24 Oct. 7 Such a fort . . . is worse than a Coney Island maze. **1921** *Outing* Dec. 111/2 It became a profitable commercial enterprise, something of a forerunner to the Coney Island 'Chute the Chutes.' **1947** *True* Nov. 71/2 He looked like a cross between a Coney Island barker and a costermonger.

b. *transf.* A place likened to Coney Island in its attractions.

1889 *Sporting Life* (Phila.) 10 July 3/6, I took advantage of an opportunity offered me on last Sunday, and 'did' 'the Coney Island of Philadelphia' thoroughly. **1947** *Sierra Club Bul.* Nov. 1 The Coney Islands are on the increase.

* **confectionery,** *n.* Also **-ary.**

1. A store in which candy and other sweets are sold. In full **confectionery store.**

1803 E. S. BOWNE *Life* 156, I never go by a toy shop, or confectionery without longing to have them [children] here. **1887** *Courier-Journal* 11 Jan. 3/4 Annie Heinrich . . . clerked for . . . proprietress of an ice-cream and confectionery store. **1948** *Sat. Ev. Post* 11 Sep. 113/1 Brandon braked the car to a stop in front of the Palace Confectionery Store.

2. (See quot. 1859.) *Obs.*

1836 *Quarter Race Ky.* (1846) 24, I went to town last night to the confectionary, (a whiskey shop in a log pen fourteen feet square). **1846** *Dollar Newspaper* (Phila.) 4 Mar. 1/7 The Court House was a certain groggery, grocery, or confectionary, as the case may be, at the Cross Roads. **1859** BARTLETT 94 Confectionary, in the South-west and some parts of the West, a bar-room.

Confed kən'fɛd, *n.* and *a.* [Short for ***Confederate.**] **1.** *n.* =**Confederate 1. 2.** *a.* Designating the currency issued by the Confederate States. Also absol. Both *obs.*

(1) **1861** *N.Y. Tribune* 7 Feb. The Confeds seemed to like the liquors hugely. **1895** *N.Y. Dramatic News* 23 Nov. 3/3 What became of that comedy of yours which I produced under the title of Feds and Confeds? — (2) **1865** BOUDRYE *Fifth N.Y. Cavalry* 259 For one dollar greenbacks, we can get from five to ten dollars Confed. **1888** GRIGSBY *Smoked Yank* xxii. 193, I had nothing to offer as a bribe, except a few dollars in confed., as we called the rebel money.

* **Confederacy,** *n.*

1. The union of the American states under the Articles of Confederation. *Obs.*

1777 *Jrnls. Cont. Congress* IX. 907/1 The stile of this confederacy shall be, 'The United States of America.' **1781** HAMILTON *Works* (1886) VIII. 34 The accession of Maryland to the Confederacy will be a happy event if it does not make people believe that the Confederacy gives Congress power enough. **1881–5** MCCLELLAN *Own Story* 31 The right of secession would virtually have carried us back to the old Confederacy.

2. The U.S. regarded as a political unit. *Obs.*

1804 *Guardian of Freedom* (Frankfort, Ky.) 21 July 2/1 Were the several members of the Confederacy unconnected, perpetual jealousies would arise. **1846** POLK in *Pres. Mess. & P.* IV. 457 Mail facilities [are] . . . indispensable . . . for binding together the different portions of our extended Confederacy. **1859** *Democratic Age* April 489 New Jersey . . . beheld Washington more months in the Revolution, than any other State that now lives in the Confederacy.

3. The Confederate States of America. Also attrib. Now *hist.*

[**1829** *Va. Herald* (Fredericksburg) 18 Feb. 2/3 To the purpose of party leaders, intending to accomplish the dissolution of the Union and a new Confederacy, two postulates are necessary.] **1860** in KETTELL *Hist. Rebellion* II. 44 In the opinion of South Carolina the constitution of the United States will form a suitable basis for the Confederacy of the Southern States withdrawing. **1861** *Charleston* (S.C.) *Mercury* 14 March 2/3 (*heading*), Hoisting the Confederacy Flag. **1945** *Chi. D. News* 8 Jan. 6/1 Critics of the Confederacy made plenty of trouble for Jeff Davis with their speeches and guns.

As the last term in **cotton, Creek, Gulf, Miami, Pacific, Southern Confederacy.**

confederal kən'fɛdərəl, *a.* Of or pertaining to the U.S. before the Constitution was adopted. *Obs.* — **1782** *Independent Ledger* 4 Feb. 3/2 May the confederal armies, be always mindful of the end for which they drew their swords. **1866** H. PHILLIPS *Amer. Paper Curr.* II. 94 On the 15th of September [1778] a report . . . was communicated; . . . such portions as related to a confederal fund . . . were referred to . . . Messrs. Duer, Gerry and A. Adams.

* **Confederate,** *a.* and *n.*

1. *n.* A citizen of the Southern Confederacy. Usu. *pl.*, the forces of the South during the Civil War. Now *hist.*

1861 *Boston Transcript* 14 May, The capture of the President by the doughty Confederates. **1862** in F. MOORE *Rebellion Rec.* V. II. 228 An apparently interminable train, loaded, as was afterward learned, with nearly three thousand confederates, was just about departing south. **1948** *Green Bay* (Wis.) *Press-Gazette* 12 July 25/6 Son William, who also volunteered, was captured by the Confederates and imprisoned at Andersonville, Georgia.

transf. **1948** *Chi. D. News* 15 July 9/1 The Confederates . . . had been trying to hang Mr. Truman on the gallows of racial differences.

b. (See quot.). *Obs.*

1864 CUMMING *Hospital Life* (1866) 122/2 They have a very nice oil, distilled from pitch, called Confederate, which is a great improvement on the 'pine-knot' lights.

2. *a.* Democratic, in allusion to the popularity of that party in the South.

1876 *Chi. Tribune* 5 Aug. 4/6 We have never counted on West Virginia going Republican this fall, but have set her down as Confederate and Bourbon to the backbone. **1941** FERGUSSON *Southwest* 85 In the Civil War, El Paso went Confederate with Texas, though with some doubt.

b. (See quot.) *Obs.*

1869 *Overland Mo.* III. 128 When a Texan wishes to express the strongest possible approval of some sentiment, he will exclaim 'You're mighty Confederate!'

3. In obs. or hist. combs. relating or alluding to the Southern Confederacy and to the Civil War: (1) **Confederate beef,** a facetious designation for mule meat, cf. **Confederate duck;** (2) **brigadier,** a member of Congress who had formerly been an officer in the Confederate army, also transf.; (3) **candle,** (see quot.); (4) **cotton,** in the South, cotton which had been prevented from reaching a market by the federal blockade of southern ports during the Civil War; (5) **Democracy,** democracy such as prevailed in or was characteristic of the South; (6) **duck,** (see quot.); (7) **flag,** =**stars and bars;** (8) **gray,** the gray uniform worn by Confederate soldiers, also transf.; (9) **gray-back,** [cf. **greenback**], a legal-tender note of the Confederate government; (10) **jasmine,** the star jasmine, extensively cultivated in the South; (11) **layer,** a kind of layer cake; (12) **Memorial Day,** see **Memorial Day;** (13) **paper,** (see quots.); (14) **pintree,** a local name for the honey locust; (15) **scrip,** scrip issued by the Confederate government; (16) **shinplaster,** a derogatory term for Confederate money; (17) **stamp,** a postage stamp issued by the Confederate government; (18) **States,** the states composing the Southern Confederacy, in full **Confederate States of America.**

(1) **1863** *Vicksburg* (Miss.) *Citizen* 2 July 1/1 We are indebted to Major Gillespie for a steak of Confederate beef *alias* meat. — (2) **1879** *Chi. Tribune* 27 Jan. 4/1 Let the Confederate Brigadiers rave their fiercest at the hostility their schemes of plunder have excited in their own party ranks. **1919** J. L. SLAYDEN *Speech* in House of Rep. 15 Jan. 7, I have seen the end of . . . the Confederate brigadiers, whose coming to Congress in the seventies caused so much unjustified alarm in the North. **1948** *Time* 11 Oct. 24/2 Appearing in Baltimore, in the border state of Maryland, he was met by a college student dressed in the full regalia of a Confederate brigadier. — (3) **1888** *Cent. Mag.* XXXVI. 770/2 Another light in great vogue was the 'Confederate,' or 'endless' candle. It was constructed by dipping a wick in melted wax and resin and wrapping it around a stick, one end of the wick being passed through a wire loop fastened to the end of the stick. — (4) **1916** MASSEY *Reminisc.* 220 Those who had cotton of their own sold it and bought some new clothes. Many who had none took some ('Confederate cotton' they called it) and followed the fashion.

(5) **1865** *Indianapolis D. Jrnl.* 14 Sep. 2/1 The Confederate Democracy of the Northern States have some curious ways of illustrating their curious principles. **1889** *Cin. Comm. Gazette* 17 March 1/3 The record . . . shows him in Congress and out of Congress . . . the mouth-piece of the Confederate Democracy and their tool. — (6) **1888** *Cent. Mag.* XXXVI. 766/2 A rare and famous dish of those days [1861–65] was 'Confederate duck.' . . . This peculiarly named fowl was no fowl at all, but a tender and juicy beefsteak rolled and pinioned around a stuffing of stale bread crumbs. — (7) **1861** *Charleston* (S.C.) *Mercury* 18 April 2/5 When a telegram announced that the Confederate flag was raised upon Sumter, a salute was fired. **1947** *N.Y. Times* 12 Oct. v. 1/7 More than 24,000 fans, some of them waving Confederate flags, watched with glee as Virginia started pouring it on for two touchdowns in the first period. — (8) **1864** in CHESNUT *Diary* 301 The bridesmaids were dressed in black, the bride in Confederate gray, homespun. **1866** in FLEMING *Hist. Reconstruction* I. 47 No armed foe being in the field, the great armies of the North waged active and honorable warfare against Confederate grey and its brass buttons. **1947** *Atlantic Mo.* Aug. 70/2 [My] Alabama and Texas grandfather . . . wore the Confederate gray. — (9) **1875** *Chi. Tribune* 2 Nov. 4/5 The Confederate graybacks became valueless, simply because they will never be redeemed.

(10) **1897** R. M. STUART *Simpkinsville* 49 He turned . . . to see the . . . edge of a woman's skirt as it disappeared behind the hedge of Confederate jasmine. **1927** MOWRY *Ornamental Vines* 220 Confederate Jasmine . . . is one of the few vines bearing very fragrant flowers. — (11) **1893** *Harper's Mag.* Feb. 457 The centre table fairly groaned beneath its burden of cakes: 'White Mountain,' 'Lady Washington,' 'Confederate layer,' 'Marble,' 'Dolly Varden,' 'General Lee,' and a score of others. — (13) **1865** in CHESNUT *Diary* 344 A change has come o'er the spirit of my dream. Dear old quire of yellow, coarse, Confederate home-made paper, here you are again. **1906** *Ib.* xxi, The Diary, as it now exists in forty-eight thin volumes, of the small quarto size, is entirely in Mrs. Chesnut's hand-writing. She originally wrote it on what was known as 'Confederate paper,' but transcribed it afterward. — (14) **1897** SUDWORTH *Arborescent Flora* 254 *Gleditsia triacanthos*. . . . Common names. . . . Confederate Pintree (Fla.).

(15) **1863** in F. MOORE *Rebellion Rec.* V. I. 27 Hereafter the dealing in and passage of currency known as 'confederate scrip' or 'confederate notes' is positively prohibited. **1891** *Harper's Mag.* Dec. 46/1 This suit of clothes cost me twelve hundred dollars in Confederate scrip. — (16) **1889** MARK TWAIN *Conn. Yankee* xxxi. 396 In the North a carpenter got three dollars; . . . in the South he got fifty—payable in Confederate shinplasters worth a dollar a bushel. — (17) **1861** *Charleston* (S.C.) *Mercury* 1 June 2/5 All letters of single rate must then be paid five cents in money, or Confederate stamps. — (18) **1861** in *Official Rec. Rebellion* 4 Ser. I. 426 The said Confederate States . . . and the Creek Nation . . . have agreed to the following articles. **1861** *Charleston* (S.C.) *Mercury* 12 Feb. 3/1 To-day I witnessed the election by the Congress in the Capitol, of Jefferson Davis, of Mississippi, as President of the Confederate States of America. **1946** *Chi. D. News* 20 Nov. 18/4 It is not necessary to set up a Confederate States of America in order to engage in rebellion or insurrection against the authority of the United States.

Also *Confederate army, authorities, bill, bond, cipher, colonel, colors, Congress, cruiser, currency, finance, fleet, government, guard, gunboat, hat, leader, lines, mail-carrier, money, navy, note, president, prisoner, raider, service, sick, soldier, steamer, times, vessel, veteran,* etc.

Confederated States.

1. The states making up the U.S., often used before the Civil War in allusion to the theory of state sovereignty under the Constitution. *Obs.*

1777 in BUCKINGHAM *Newspaper Lit.* I. 251 Which [interest with Britain] the Grand Council of these Confederated States, in their Wisdom, have seen fit for ever to dissolve. **1834** JACKSON in *Pres. Mess. & P.* III. 65 States . . . magnanimously sacrificed domains which would have made them the rivals of empires, only stipulating that they should be disposed of for the common benefit of themselves and the other confederated States. **1847** POLK in *Ib.* IV. 564 It is difficult to estimate the 'immense value' of our glorious Union of confederated States.

2. = **Confederate States of America.** *Obs.*

1861 *Crisis* (Columbus, O.) 21 Feb. 1/5 Stephens, who clung to the Union with the devotion of a hero, is Vice President, of the Provisional Government of the confederated States. **1861** in LOGAN *Great Conspiracy* 143, I look for nothing else than that the Commissioners from the Confederated States will be received here and recognized by Abraham Lincoln.

* **Confederation,** *n.* The agreement under which the American states united during the Revolutionary War, the Articles of Confederation. Cf. **New England Confederation.**

1784 in *S. Lit. Messenger* XXVIII. 35/1, I think it would be wise in Congress to recommend to the States the calling a Convention for the sole purpose of amending the Confederation. **1821** JEFFERSON *Autobiog.* Writings I. 77 A majority of the States, necessary by the Confederation to constitute a House even for minor business, did not assemble until the 13th of December. **1948** *Chi. Tribune* 1 Aug. 1. 22/3 The day before the Constitution's adoption, the Confederation, the previous form of government, created the Northwest Territory.

confederationist kən͵fedəˈreʃənɪst, *n.* A supporter of the Confederate States of America *q.v. Rare.* — **1861** *Louisville Jrnl.*, The confederationists may be of one bone with their new President.

Confederatism kənˈfedərət͵ɪzəm, *n.* The doctrine and practice of the supporters of the Confederate States of America. *Rare.* — **1870** E. MULFORD *Nation* xvii. 340 Confederatism, in its attack upon the nation, is in league with hell.

conferee ͵kɑnfəˈri, *n.* [f. * *confer, v.*+*-ee.*] One chosen to confer on some matter. Also **fusion, tariff conferee.**

1771 J. BOUCHER *Causes Amer. Revol.* (1797) 238 By some logic of their own, their conferees have found out, that 'none of our parishes are so inconsiderable but that the worst is too good for the worst clergymen.' **1794** *Ann. 4th Congress* 2 Sess. 2804 One of the conferees then inquired whether the President could not suspend the execution of the excise acts. **1903** *N.Y. Ev. Post* 11 Sep., Mr. Grout is still in Europe and has not communicated with the Fusion conferees. **1909** *Westminster Gaz.* 30 July 7/4 The Tariff conferees have accepted the President's demands and signed the report.

* **conference,** *n.*

1. conference meeting, a gathering for prayer and religious discussion.

1670 I. MATHER *Life R. Mather* 79 The last private Conference-Meeting which he was at in Dorchester, he had prepared to speak. **1835** REED & MATHESON *Visit* II. 15 Conference or Inquiry Meetings.—These are instituted for those persons who have become anxiously concerned for their salvation. **1881** *Harvard Coll. Ann. Rep.* 67 General Exercises [of the Divinity School include] conference meeting, conducted by students.

2. An organization of athletic teams within a particular area. Also attrib.

1910 FISHER *Coll. Basket Ball Guide* 37 Chicago started the season with . . . five of the squad that won the Conference Championship last year. **1916** *Outing* Jan. 411/1 In the Middle Western Conference Illinois and Minnesota played a tie game and defeated all other opponents. **1948** *Dly. Ardmoreite* (Ardmore, Okla.) 15 Jan. 6/3 The Ardmore Douglass high school Dragon cagers will meet the Lawton Lions in their second conference game of the season.

As the last term in **district, general, Northern, quarterly conference.**

* **confidence,** *n. attrib.* Designating swindlers and swindling operations in which advantage is taken of the victim's confidence, as (1) **confidence game,** (2) **line,** (3) **man,** (4) **operator,** (5) **sharp,** (6) **woman.** Cf. **con,** *n.*

(1) **1856** *Spirit of Age* (Sacramento) 14 Mar. 4/1 G. W. Meylert's now about town, playing the confidence game and making grand attempts at swindling. **1947** *Steamboat* (Colo.) *Pilot* 9 Jan. 1/8 It was decided not to press confidence game charges in district court. — (2) **1910** O. HENRY *Strictly Business* 29 Jimmy Dunn . . . was an artist in the confidence line. — (3) **1849** *N.O. Picayune* 21 July 1/4 'Well, then,' continues the 'confidence man,' 'just lend me your watch till to-morrow.' **1948** *Dly. Racing Form* (Chi.) 29 June 2/3 He had a reputation and justly so, for keeping touts, confidence men and other undesirables off the race tracks. — (4) **1856** *Chicago W. Times* 31 Jan. 4/2 Benjamin Greer, one of the most shrewd and successful

'confidence' operators ever known in this country, was arrested in Broadway, New York, on Wednesday. **1872** *Chi. Tribune* 19 Oct. 8/4 Robert H. Young, . . . a noted swindler and confidence operator.
(5) **1886** Howells *Minister's Charge* 43 'Beats? I don't know what you mean,' said Barker. 'Confidence sharps, young feller. They're 'round everywhere, and don't you forget it.' — (6) **1887** *Courier-Journal* 25 Jan. 3/5 A noted thief and confidence woman, . . . was arrested by Officer Stevens yesterday morning.

confidence ˈkɑnfədəns, *v.* [f. the noun.] *tr.* To victimize (a person) by some confidence scheme. *Slang.* — **1875** *Chi. Tribune* 1 Oct. 4 In a back room of some large building . . . they are 'confidenced' of what money they may have about them. **1888** *Missouri Repub.* 15 Feb. (F.), Detectives . . . arrested Lawrence Stanley . . . on a charge of confidencing Henry Mueller.

* **confirmation,** *n.* **1. confirmation class,** a group, usu. of children, preparing for confirmation. **2.** Used with **grant, line,** with reference to the dispute over land claims by New Hampshire and New York. *Obs.*
(1) **1902** *Harper's Mag.* May 925 You remember your first confirmation class? **1902** G. M. Martin *Emmy Lou* 174 Rebecca and Gertie and Rachel must thereafter be excused on certain days at an early hour for attendance at Confirmation Class. — (2) **1755** *Huntington Rec.* II. 424 A certain piece of Land Lying Between ye old pattent Line and the confirmation Line. **1798** I. Allen *Hist. Vermont* 20 Some leading characters on the east side, by yielding up their New Hampshire Grants, had new or confirmation grants from New York in paying half fees.

* **confiscation,** *n. attrib.* Designating a congressional *act* or *bill* providing for the appropriation of the property of persons supporting the Southern cause during the Civil War. *Obs.*
*c*1862 Grant in Penniman *Tanner-Boy* 108 The interpreting of confiscation-acts by troops themselves has a demoralizing effect. **1864** *Harper's Mag.* March 559/1 The confiscation Act, passed July 17, 1862, apparently provided for the confiscation of the entire rights of property of all persons in rebellion. **1863** Russell *Diary* II. 274 The Confiscation Bill, for the emancipation of slaves and the absorption of property belonging to rebels, has, indeed, been boldly resisted in the House of Representatives; but it passed with some trifling amendments.

confisticate kənˈfɪstɪˌket, *v. tr.* (See quot. 1781.) *Obs.*
1781 Witherspoon *Druid P.* No. 7, *Confisticate,* for *confiscate.* The most ignorant of the vulgar only use this phrase. **1795** B. Dearborn *Columbian Grammar* 134 Improprieties, commonly called Vulgarisms, . . . [include] Confisticated for Confiscated. **1864** Trowbridge *Cudjo's Cave* xxxiv. 334 The prop'ty of these yer durned Union-shriekers is all gwine to be confisticated.

conflab ˈkɑnflæb, *n.* A colloquial variant of "confab." — **1873** *Winfield* (Kans.) *Courier* 7 Aug. 3/1 'Conflabs' lively among the lawyers. **1887** *Saginaw Ev. Jrnl.* 7 Dec., Don has always come out ahead in his conflabs with the Michigan delegation.

conflabber ˈkɑnˌflæbɚ, *v.* [Cf. prec.] *intr.* To jabber, converse. *Colloq.* — **1843** *Yale Lit. Mag.* IX. 76 Beg your pardon, Miss Orra, but I can't help it—conflabberin' away with a white man, never mind who that was.

conflutement kənˈflutmənt, *n.* A frill or curlicue. *Colloq.* — **1842** in Thompson *M. Jones* (1872) 55 Why, sich other cog-wheels, cranks, and conflutements I never did see—and then they's so spiteful, and makes the fire fly so. **1896** J. C. Harris *Sister Jane* 168 Your Aunt Prue had saw some new-fangled bonnet . . . an' pictur'd out to your Aunt Sally ev'ry flower an' folderol an' all the conflutements that the consarn had on it.

Congaree ˌkɑŋgəˈri, *n.* (See quot. 1907.)
1709 Lawson *Hist. Car.* (1937) 25 The Congerees are kind and affable to the English, the Queen being very kind, giving us what Rarities her Cabin afforded. **1884** *Cent. Mag.* Jan. 442/1 The Lenni Lenape on the Delaware grew peaches before Penn came, and the Congarees in Carolina, about 1708, had the art of drying peaches. **1907** Hodge *Amer. Indians* I. 338 Congaree. A small tribe, supposed to be Siouan, formerly living in South Carolina.

congenial kənˈdʒinjəl, *n.* A congenial person. *Rare.* — **1908** S. E. White *Riverman* xxi. 185 A small coterie, among whom Carroll soon found two or three congenials.

congeree ˌkɑŋgəˈri, *n.* Local variant of "conger eel." *Obs.* — **1884** in Goode *Fisheries* I. 629 This species [*Sidera mordax*] . . . is always known as 'Conger Eel' or 'Congeree.' . . . Its flesh . . . is very palatable when fried.

* **congestive,** *a.* Of or pertaining to congestion, as **congestive chill, fever.**
1834 in Bassett *South. Plant.* 76 She is gettinge better Jim and enykey all have had the congestif fever. **1848** Bryant *Calif.* (1849) 37 Of late years, in the winter season, the congestive fever prevails. **1871** Eggleston *Queer Stories* 108 His father died of a congestive chill.

* **congo,** *n.*
1. A Negro, originally one from the Congo region in Africa. Also **Congo Negro, slave, woman.** *Obs.*
1810 Lambert *Travels U.S.* II. 443 All the papers are well stocked with advertisements, among which, prime Congo, Gambia, and Angola slaves for sale at Gadsden's wharf, were very conspicuous. **1855** *Chi. Times* 5 July 1/2 A number of native Congoes—real Guinea negroes—arrived in Salem, Massachusetts, a few days ago. . . . Congo, showing his ivory, tumbled into the ship's boat. **1860** Olmsted *Back Country* 439 If all the slaves in the United States were 'real Congo niggers,' which not one in one thousand is. **1880** Cable *Grandissimes* 89 A dwarf Congo woman, as black as soot, had ushered her in. **1922** Cady *Rhymes* (1926) 17 My! such a peaceful, fambly day, It makes you Congos Quakers.

b. The language of such a Negro. *Obs.*
1880 G. W. Cable *Grandissimes* xxviii. 221 His name . . . he by and by condescended to render into Congo.

c. Congo Minstrels, Negro minstrels. *Obs.*
1855 *Putnam's Mo.* Jan. 79/2 Then Ethiopian Serenaders, and Congo Minstrels will draw crowded houses at three dollars a seat, and one dollar for a promenade ticket. **1896** Haswell *New York* 411 At Apollo Hall there was presented the performance of the 'Congo Minstrels,' later known as the 'Negro Minstrels.'

2. *S.* A kind of dance performed originally by Negroes but later by white people. Originally attrib. with **dance, minuet.** Also *to dance Congo.*
1803 J. Davis *Travels* 380 There was nobody that could face him at a Congo Minuet. **1823** Holmes *Acc. U.S.* 332 In Louisiana, and the state of Mississippi, the slaves have Sunday for a day of recreation, and upon many plantations they dance for several hours during the afternoon of this day. The general movement is in what they call the Congo dance. **1835** Longstreet *Ga. Scenes* 128 Except the minuet, which was introduced only to teach us the graces, and the congo, which was only to chase away the solemnities of the minuet, it was all a jovial, heart-stirring, foot-stirring amusement. **1936** Asbury *French Quarter* 242 Sometimes there were almost as many white spectators surrounding the square to watch the slaves 'dance Congo' as there were black dancers.

b. A kind of song or chant used in voodoo ceremonies.
1889 Warner *Studies So. & West* (1904) VIII. 82 Before this point had been reached the chant had been changed for the wild *canga,* more rapid in movement than the *chanson africaine.*

3. A bluish-black snakelike amphibian having two pairs of inconspicuous limbs, and found in the southeastern states. In full **Congo snake.**
1835 Audubon *Ornith. Biog.* III. 90 The Congo snake and water-moccasin glide before you as they seek to elude your sight. **1888** Cable *Bonaventure* 284 A large moccasin—not of the dusky kind described in books, but of that yet deadlier . . . black sort, an ell in length, which the swampers call the Congo—came up the anchor-rope. **1947** *Chi. Tribune* (Grafic Mag.) 21 Dec. 9/3 There were malaria and typhus in the swamps, and many snakes: rattlers, moccasins, copperheads, and the Congo, a blue black eel, most feared of all.

* **congregation,** *n.* As the last term in **Indian, Mohawk, place congregation.**

congregationalism ˌkɑŋgrɪˈgeʃənḷˌɪzəm, *n.* A system of organization of a religious body by which each local church has full control of its own affairs.
1716 I. Mather *Disq. Eccl. Councils* 6 Mr. [Wm.] Bradshaw, an eminent Nonconformist Minister, . . . was the Author of that Judicious Script [*English Puritanism,* 1605]. It is perfect Congregationalism. **1767** Chauncy *Lett.* (1768) 26 Zealous endeavours to make converts from Presbyterianism and Congregationalism to Episcopacy. **1870** Bancroft *Hist. U.S.* (ed. 23) I. 359 The three great principles of congregationalism; a right faith attended by a true religious experience as the requisite qualifications for membership; the equality of all believers, including the officers of the church; the equality of the several. **1948** *Chi. Tribune* 23 June II. 6/3 American Congregationalism was founded on the autonomy and complete independence of the local church.

* **congress,** *n.*
1. (*cap.*) The national legislative body of the U.S. Cf. **national legislature.**
From 1774 to 1781 this referred to the Continental Congress, from 1781 to 1789 to the Congress under the Articles of Confederation, and after 1789 to that under the Constitution. It is here conceived as a continuing body. The Constitution, Art. 1, sec. 4, provides that Congress meet on the first Monday in December, but the 20th Amendment, effective since Oct. 15, 1933, changed the time of meeting to Jan 3.
1774 *Jrnls. Cont. Cong.* I. 104 The Congress resumed the consideration of the address to his Majesty. **1789** *Ann. 1st Congress* I. 207 Resolved, That this House will, on Friday next, proceed by ballot to

the appointment of a Chaplain to Congress on the part of this House. **1838** *S. Lit. Messenger* IV. 209 The Committee was then appointed by Congress to draft the Declaration. **1948** *Chi. D. News* 26 Aug. 11/1 Authorization was voted for joint technical staffs . . . to begin framing the program in the 81st Congress.

b. *collect. Obs.*

1775 FITHIAN *Journal* II. 60 The hon. Congress are yet sitting, & have published to the world reasons for our taking up arms against Britain. **1788** JEFFERSON *Writings* V. 16 Congress, by the Confederation, have no original and inherent power over the commerce of the States. **1794** S. WILLIAMS *Hist. Vermont* 235 Congress have not been prevailed on to assist in dismembering a state.

c. As a proper name or appellative. *Obs.*

1776 *Jrnls. Cont. Cong.* IV. 250 A petition from P. Moore, in behalf of the owners of the sloops *Congress* and *Chance*, privateers, for 400 lb. of powder . . . was presented and read. **1807** J. R. SHAW *Life* (1930) 91 From Carlisle we were ordered to Lancaster, in order to relieve the Congress-regiment, and to do duty over the prisoners who were taken with Cornwallis. **1813** J. ADAMS *Works* X. 27 That immortal mortar, which was called the Congress, . . . finally drove the British army out of Boston. **1819** *Niles' Reg.* XVII. 63/2 The Congress frigate, captain Henley, having on board Mr. Graham, our minister to the court of Brazil, has arrived at Rio Janerio [*sic*], all well.

d. The legislative body of other political units whose territory is now within the U.S., as Texas and the Confederate States. *Obs.* or *hist.*

1836 in SAYLES *Early Laws Texas* I. 217 An act authorizing the printing and publishing the laws of . . . the present congress. **1848** POLK in *Pres. Mess. & P.* IV. 596 By an act of the Congress of Texas passed in December, 1836, her western boundary was declared to be the Rio Grande [etc.]. **1861** *Const. Confederate States* i. § 9 The importation of negroes of the African race, from any foreign country other than the slave-holding States or Territories of the United States of America, is hereby forbidden; and Congress is required to pass such laws as shall effectually prevent the same. **1923** *Southern Hist. Soc. P.* XLIV. 4 The regular Congress of the Confederate States was elected in November, 1861.

e. The lower house of Congress.

1842 *Niles' Reg.* 28 May 208/2 Election for Congressman. The election for a member of congress . . . took place in Washington county. **1881** *Harper's Mag.* March 538/2 The 'old Patroon' was a member of the Congress that elected John Quincy Adams President. **1888** LOWELL *Independent in Politics*, Members of Congress must be residents of the district that elects them.

2. The body of senators and representatives for each term of two years for which representatives are elected.

1774 *Jrnls. Cont. Cong.* I. 102 Resolved, as the Opinion of this Congress, that it will be necessary, that another Congress should be held on the tenth day of May next. **1873** *Newton Kansan* 30 Jan. 1/6 There are from 5,000 to 6,000 bills per Congress. **1944** *Cong. Directory* 28 He was elected to the Seventy-fifth Congress and to each succeeding Congress.

3. Ellipt. for **Congress shoe, Congress water.** *Obs.*

1868 ROSE *Great Country* 260 The most celebrated of these waters is known by the name of 'Congress,' and there are others called 'Empire,' 'Columbian,' 'High Rock,' 'Excelsior,' and by many more high-sounding titles. **1899** A. BROWN *Tiverton Tales* 109 Her shoes—congress, with world-weary elastics at the side—were her own, inherited from an aunt.

4. In combs.: (1) **Congress beef,** beef provided by Congress, *rare;* (2) **boot,** (see quot. 1853); (3) **brand,** *La.* a brand placed upon cattle of unknown ownership sold at auction for the public benefit, *obs.;* (4) **caucus,** =**congressional caucus,** *obs.;* (5) **gaiter,** =**Congress boot;** (6) **land,** public land controlled by Congress, *obs.;* (7) **man,** see as a main entry; (8) **money,** paper money authorized by the Continental Congress and by the U.S. Congress during and after the panic of 1837, *obs.;* (9) **note,** a note issued by the Continental Congress, *obs.;* (10) **price,** a price established by Congress, esp. for the sale of public land, *obs.;* (11) **shoe,** =**Congress boot;** (12) **slipper,** a form of house slipper; (13) **Spring,** a mineral spring at Saratoga, N.Y. (see quot. 1841); (14) **Sunday,** (see quot.), *obs.;* (15) **water,** water obtained from Congress Spring; (16) **woman,** a woman elected as a Representative to Congress.

(1) 1777 MACKENZIE *Diary* I. 184 Deluded Hessians . . . are invited by their own brethren who have deserted from Slavery, and are now enjoying the inestimable sweets of freedom, and living on fat, fresh Congress Beef in Plenty. — **(2) 1847** *Semi-Wkly. News* (Fredericksburg, Va.) 12 Aug. 3/1 (*advt.*), Congress Boots and Shoes. **1853** FELT *Customs N. Eng.* 90 Six years ago, Congress Boots, for both sexes, were introduced. They come up so as to cover the foot neatly and closely by means of India rubber cloth inserted in the leather, on each side, wide enough to cover the ankles. **1938** DANIELS *Southerner* 156 An open collar showed a white throat. He wore congress boots with elastic sides. — **(3) 1857** F. L. OLMSTED *Journey through Texas* 393 The 'Congress brand,' or mark of the parish. — **(4) 1803** B. AUSTIN *Constitutional Republicanism* 87 If a Congress Caucus is to decide, we have only to inquire who the man is in whom they have agreed, and notify him of his appointment. **1854** BENTON *30 Years' View* I. 86/1 Congress caucuses for the nomination of presidential candidates fell under the ban of public opinion.

(5) 1852 *S.F. Herald* 5 Oct. 3/4 (*advt.*), Gents' fine patent leather Congress gaiters. **1943** *Copper Camp* 278 A pair of baggy trousers surmounted a pair of Congress gaiters, usually with holes cut in them to relieve pressure on corns and bunions. — **(6) 1806** T. ASHE *Travels in A.* 89 The great part then of this land being obtained by Congress

Congress boots, gaiters, or shoes

from the Indians by an imposition, called by the fallacious name of a legal purchase, is known by the name of 'Congress Lands.' **1886** *Cent. Mag.* Nov. 34/2 They cut the timber, with frontier innocence, from 'Congress land,' and soon had a serviceable craft afloat. — **(8) 1776** *N.C. Morav. Rec.* III. (1926) 1066 The best part of his trip was that he used the £180 Congress money there (Cross Creek); but nearly as much more has accumulated in the store here (Salem) during the time. **1841** *Knickerb.* XVII. 384 Some hay, oats for your horse, wheat, rye, wood, butter, and cider for yourselves, etc., to be paid for in congress money. — **(9) 1776** *Battle of Brooklyn* I. iv, Gives him a handfull of Congress notes. **1776** in SERLE *Journal* 98 A Flag of Truce came from the Town this Afternoon, with Letters, Cloaths, & Money (hard Cash, not *Congress Notes*) for some of the Rebel Prisoners.

(10) 1776 A. ADAMS in *Fam. Lett.* (1876) 183, I find you have licensed tea, but I am determined not to be a purchaser unless I can have it at Congress price. **1849** CHAMBERLAIN *Ind. Gazetteer* 281 Digby had bought the town site at the United States land sale, at a little more than Congress price. — **(11) 1847** see [**Congress boot**]. [**1899** A. BROWN *Tiverton Tales* 109 Her shoes—congress, with world-weary elastics at the side—were her own, inherited from an aunt.] **1944** CLARK *Pills* 213 For men with ancient feet scarred in miles of travel on sandy soil behind plows there were the relatively soft 'Congress' shoes which gave some freedom and protection. — **(12) 1944** *Harper's Mag.* March 373/1 She sat so quietly, her hands folded, her knees together, and her feet in Congress slippers side by side on the floor. — **(13) 1817** *N.Y. Herald* 13 Aug. 1/1 Some individuals cannot reside at Ballston, but are obliged to resort to Saratoga, and drink the Congress Spring, which contains about three times as much purgative salt. **1841** BUCKINGHAM *Amer., N. States* II. 430 In 1792 . . . the second spring was discovered by Mr. John Taylor Gilman, . . . at that time a member of Congress. It was this which caused it to be called the 'Congress Spring.' **1884** L. DE COLANGE *Nat. Gazetteer* 902/1 The most celebrated [springs at Saratoga] are the Congress, Empire, . . . [and five other] Springs. — **(14) 1776** *N.C. Col. Rec.* X. 457 This being a day of humiliation, fasting and prayer (or in vulgar language Congress Sunday), [etc.].

(15) 1833 J. STUART *Three Years N.A.* I. 192 The quantity of gas is such, that a very nice sort of breakfast bread is baked with Congress water, instead of yeast. **1880** *Amer. Punch* Jan. 4/1 Some were talking of . . . the cooling and invigorating influences of 'iced tea,' 'congress water,' and the like. **1930** WILLIAMSON *Amer. Hotel* 242 'Dr.' Clarke refused to ship Congress water to rival places. — **(16) 1928** *N.Y. Times* 8 Nov. 28/3 The increasing number of 'Congresswomen' is but another indication of the larger part their sex is taking in the public life of the nation. **1948** *Time* 26 July 65/2 Jean Arthur [plays the rôle of] a visiting Congresswoman.

Also *Congress bill, chamber, commissary, financier, hall, paper money, resolves, sale,* etc.

As the last term in **Continental, coon, Indian, Jacksonian, lame duck, Old, press, provincial, rump, Secretary of, Southern congress.**

congressional kən'grɛʃənl, *a.* [See note.]

1. Of or pertaining to a congress, esp. (*cap.*) to the Congress of the U.S.

The *OED* derives this term from **congression* (an old word meaning "congress")+*al.* Webster regards it as based upon *congress.*

1775 Edmund Quincy in *N.E. Hist. & Gen. Reg.* II. 166 A happy effect indeed, then, of the First American Congressional Appointment of ye kind. **1799** in Joel Barlow *Lett. from Paris* (1800) 54 This congressional institution, notwithstanding its solemn pretensions of confederating the states of Greece, was more detrimental than beneficial. **1865** Banner (Cleveland, Tenn.) 21 Oct. 2/1 The North Carolina Convention, among its other business, redistricted the State for Congressional representatives. **1948** *McAlester* (Okla.) *News-Capital* 3 July 1/8 The third district congressional race will be on the ballots Tuesday, too.

2. In special combs.: (1) **congressional biography,** a biography appearing in the Congressional Directory; (2) **bummer,** see **bummer 2. c;** (3) **caucus,** see as a main entry; (4) **convention,** a congressional caucus, or a political meeting of party delegates within a congressional district for selecting a candidate for the House of Representatives in Congress, *obs.;* (5) **Directory,** a directory containing information about members of Congress; (6) **district,** a division in a state which elects a representative to the lower house of Congress; (7) **districting,** dividing a state into congressional districts; (8) **election,** an election every two years at which members of the lower house of Congress are chosen; (9) **Globe,** the name of Congressional Record *q.v.* from 1834 to 1873; (10) **knife,** (see quot.), *rare;* (11) **library,** the Library of Congress; (12) **mess,** see **mess,** *n., obs.;* (13) **Record,** the publication which records the proceedings in Congress; (14) **school,** a school supported by income derived from the townships that Congress set aside for school purposes, *obs.;* (15) **test oath,** just after the Civil War, an oath of loyalty required by the federal government of congressmen from the former Confederate States, *obs.;* (16) **township,** (see quot. 1914), also attrib.

(1) **1946** *Negro Digest* Aug. 48/1 His [Rankin's] Congressional biography is one of the longest in the directory. — (4) **1824** *Nat. Intelligencer* 17 Feb. 1/3 Mr. Markey . . . felt that a Congressional Convention to nominate candidates, should be as numerously attended, as it was practicable that it would be. **1872** *Newton Kansan* 22 Aug. 3/1 A Republican County Convention will be held . . . to select delegates to attend . . . the Republican Congressional Convention. **1883** *Harper's Mag.* June 162/2 Austin was crowded with strangers in attendance on the Democratic Congressional Convention.

(5) **1842** F. Wood in MacLeod *Biog.* 99 The honorable chairman (Mr. Saltonstall) has, in the two counties which he is set down in Congressional Directory as representing, 19,567 persons engaged in manufactures and trades. **1948** *Democrat* 2 Dec. 7/2 The main historical clue . . . is found in the . . . Biographical Congressional Directory. — (6) **1812** *Ann. 12th Congress* 1 Sess. II. 1436 The proceedings of a public meeting of the Republican citizens of the First Congressional district of Pennsylvania. **1944** *Democrat* 27 April 1/5 My brother . . . is a candidate for Delegate to the National Democratic Convention from this Congressional District. — (7) **1889** *Voice* (N.Y.) 9 May, Congressional districting and gridironing, such as has been attempted in New Jersey, . . . is a great danger to our country. — (8) **1804** *Guardian of Freedom* (Frankfort, Ky.) 21 April 2/1 The congressional election coming on in August, it is a respect I owe to the district I represent to say a word on that subject. **1948** *Dly. Ardmoreite* (Ardmore, Okla.) 25 July 20/6 He sought out Dr. Bean for a forecast on the off-year congressional elections. — (9) **1861** *Crisis* (Columbus, O.) 21 Feb. 1/1 We publish from the *Congressional Globe* a very pretty little piece of sparring in Congress among our Ohio members. **1948** *Ohio State Arch. & Hist. Quart.* Jan. 14 Hundreds of pages of the *Congressional Globe* were filled with the bitter denunciations of the angry congressmen.

(10) **1898** *K.C. Star* 18 Dec. 15/1 Going to his desk the aged clerk took from a drawer a small pearl-handled penknife of the sort a generous government furnishes to senators and representatives—a 'congressional knife,' in fact. — (11) **1801** *Ann. 7th Congress* 2 Sess. 1292 To place on each book some proper mark or marks, to designate it as belonging to the Congressional library. **1947** *Chi. Tribune* 15 June 2/6 It is recorded in the Congressional library in Washington that 120 years ago the Fox Indians, whose maize crops failed one season, subsisted 'on the root of the lotus plant that grew in abundance in the Fox lake region.' — (13) **1831** *Cong. Deb.* 3 Feb. 606 We might go through the whole congressional record, and we should find Mr. Randolph . . . equally hostile to the administration of Mr. Madison. **1948** *Chi. Tribune* 25 June 8/3 He recently used the Congressional Record as an advertising medium. — (14) **1838** *Indiana H. Rep. Jrnl.* 126 Resolved, That the committee on education be instructed to inquire into the expediency of so amending the law regulating Congressional schools, as to repeal said act.

(15) **1865** *Bolivar* (Tenn.) *Bulletin* 19 Oct. 1/7 The Congressional test oath will not be repealed. — (16) **1838** *Indiana H. Rep. Jrnl.* 98 Resolved, that the committee on Education be instructed to inquire into the expediency of repealing the fifteenth section of an act entitled An act incorporating congressional townships. **1845** *Ind. Senate Jrnl.* 362 No. 114. A bill to authorize the borrowers of the congressional township fund to secure their loans by lands within the proper congressional townships. **1914** *Cyclo. Amer. Govt.* III. 546 The rectangular areas thus formed, containing thirty-six sections of 640 acres each, are known as the 'geographical,' 'original-surveyed,' or 'congressional' townships.

b. Congressional Medal of Honor, a decoration in the name of Congress awarded to one in military service who distinguishes himself beyond the call of duty. Cf. **Medal of Honor.**

1900 *Everybody's Mag.* Dec. 544/1 A soldier won the Congressional Medal of Honor. **1948** *Reader's Digest* March 48/1 Framed on the wall was the blue-ribboned gold star of the Congressional Medal of Honor.

congressional caucus. Formerly a meeting of those members of Congress who were of one party, for the purpose of selecting presidential and vice-presidential candidates, a function now discharged by party conventions.

"The congressional caucus naturally divides into two periods: (1) the period of development, or mixed congressional caucuses, extending from 1788 to 1804; (2) the period of purely congressional caucuses or the reign of the caucus, 1804–1824" (McLaughlin & Hart *Cyclo. Amer. Govt.* I. 233).

1803 B. Austin *Const. Republicanism* xx. 88 If they [=the people] mean to be led by Congressional or Legislative Caucusses, it is best the business should be openly acknowledged. **1884** *Harper's Mag.* June 128/2 The Presidential candidates were . . . nominated by Congressional caucus. **1948** *Sat. Ev. Post* 10 July 19/1 This, the so-called congressional caucus, broke down in the 1820's under public criticism of its undemocratic, ingrown and intrigue-ridden character.

congressman ˈkɑŋgrəsmən, *n.* A member of Congress, esp. a member of the House of Representatives. See **ex-, silver congressman.**

The tendency to restrict this term to members of the House of Representatives (see quot. 1897 below, and cf. Bryce, *Amer. Commonwealth* I, 197 note) grows out of the fact that before the adoption (May 31, 1917) of the seventeenth amendment people did not vote directly for senators and hence tended to associate the term "congressmen" with the representatives in Congress for whom they voted.

1780 *Amer. Times* iii. 28 Ye coxcomb Congressmen, declaimers keen, Brisk puppets of the Philadelphian scene. **1832** Ferrall *Ramble through U.S.* 180 Here you may see tradesmen, 'nigger traders,' farmers, 'congress men,' captains, generals, and judges, all seated at the same table, in true republican simplicity. **1897** *Nation* LXV. 496/2 Allow me to enter a plea in behalf of the accurate use of the word Congressman. . . . The tendency to restrict its application to Representatives is to be regretted. **1947** *Newsweek* 28 July 11/1 A record number of free committee junkets are planned by congressmen during the summer recess.

b. congressman-at-large, a member of the House of Representatives elected from a state as a whole rather than from a single congressional district.

1882 *Nation* 12 Oct. 298/1 On Tuesday the New York Republican State Committee nominated Mr. Howard Carroll for Congressman-at-large, to fill the vacancy. **1948** *Chi. Tribune* 29 Feb. III. 7/3 He was nominated for congressman-at-large.

c. congressman-elect, a man who has been elected to the House of Representatives, but whose term has not yet begun.

1847 *Whig Almanac 1848* 6 Henry Nicoll, the Congressman elect from the lower District, . . . [was] one of the Vice-Presidents [of a mass meeting]. **1883** *Boston Advertiser* 9 Nov., Congressman-elect Andrew, in his capacity as president of the Algonquin, stands in the centre of the large reception room on the second floor.

coniacker ˈkonɪˌækɚ, *n.* [Origin unknown.] (See quot.) *Obs.* — **1848** Bartlett 396 *Coniacker,* a counterfeiter of coin.

Conjeprezion ˌkɑndʒəprəˈzaɪən, *n.* Also **Conjeprezite.** ["From *Con*gregation of *Je*hovah's *Pre*sbytery of *Zion*" See *Annals of Iowa* 2 Ser. III. 17.] (See quot.) *Obs.* — **1858** *N.Y. Tribune* 2 Nov. 3/3 This town [Preparation, Iowa] is the Zion of a new body of religious enthusiasts, who call themselves 'Conjeprezites,' and their system of religion or religious organization 'the Conjeprezion.'

*** conjure,** *v.* In combs. denoting persons and means involved in conjuring or hoodooing, esp. among Negroes, as

(1) **conjure bag,** (2) **bottle,** (3) **charm,** (4) **doctor,** (5) **man,** (6) **woman,** (7) **worker.**

(1) [**1863** E. KIRKE *Southern Friends* 153 The conjurer's bag of the Africans . . . is called 'waiter' or 'kunger' by the Southern blacks, and is supposed to have the power to charm away evil spirits, and do all manner of miraculously good things for its wearer.] **1942** RAWLINGS *C. Creek* 276 'I wisht I could find me a good root man, to find out is something buried under my house.' 'A conjur bag?' 'Yessum.' — (2) **1899** *Animal & Plant Lore* 14 A 'conjure-bottle' is an article that creates much terror among superstitious negroes. . . . Alabama. — (3) **1891** THANET *Otto the Knight* 83 One of us—no matter which—took a foreign coin out of her purse, saying, 'That is my own private conjure charm, Jerry.' — (4) *Ib.* 64 Thanks to a gifted 'conjure doctor,' Uncle Rufe Lemew, no one had died. **1944** CLARK *Pills* 85 They produced a concoction only slightly less revolting than those made by neighborhood 'conjure doctors.'

(5) **1909** *Sat. Ev. Post* 29 May 16/1 His mammy used to scare him with tales of the potent 'conju'-man' who came down in this very swamp and changed skins with the devil. — (6) **1899** CHESNUTT (*title*), The Conjure Woman. **1938** MATSCHAT *Suwannee River* 237 So he went off . . . leaving her to learn the lore of El Rio from . . . his sister, Aunt Sue, a 'conjure' woman much revered in the colored community. — (7) **1900** H. ROBERTSON *Red Blood & Blue* 92 Wingate's Lane was a brier-grown byway that led through weeds and thickets to . . . the hut of old Dru Wingate, the conjure-worker.

* **conk,** *n.* (See quots.) Also attrib.

1851 SPRINGER *Forest Life* 99 There is a cancerous disease peculiar to the Pine-tree, to which lumbermen give the original name of 'Conk' or 'Konkus.' **1902** *Forestry Bureau Bul.* No. 33, 15 The conk or bracket seen on affected trees is the fruiting organ. *Ib.*, Conk spores never enter through the bark, but usually through the scars of broken branches. **1905** *Ib.* No. 61, 33 Conk . . . [is] the decay in the wood of trees caused by a fungus. **1948** BOYCE *Forest Pathology* 403 The large annual conks with a reddish shiny lacquerlike upper surface and usually with a short thick lateral stalk are conspicuous on logs, stumps, and standing or fallen dead trees.

* **connect,** *v. intr.* Of trains, boats, etc.: To meet at such times as will enable passengers to go directly from one to the other and so continue their journey. Also said of persons who make transportation connections.

1852 *Chi. Tribune* 6 May 1/3 Leave Chicago, Dearborn street, at 7½ o'clock, A.M., connecting with St. Charles Branch R.R. at 10 o'clock A.M. **1865** *Nashville Dispatch* 30 Aug. 2/1 The passenger train arrives from Chattanooga at 5:50 P.M., in time to connect with the evening train for Louisville. **1874** B. F. TAYLOR *World on Wheels* I. 106 His chronic mania is to 'connect.' He didn't 'connect' yesterday. **a1925** THORNTON in *D.N.* VI. 190 When the first conveyance is delayed, he [the traveler] may fail . . . to 'connect.'

Connecticotian kəˌnɛtɪˈkatɪən, *n.* An inhabitant of Connecticut. *Rare.* — **1702** C. MATHER *Magnalia* (1853) I. 82 The confusions then embarrassing the affairs of the English nation, hindred our Connecticotians from seeking any further settlement.

Connecticut kəˈnɛtɪkət, *n.* [f. Mahican *quinnitukqut*, "at the long tidal river" (Hodge).]

1. *pl.* Indians belonging to any one of various tribes living along the Connecticut River. Also (*sing.*) attrib. *Obs.*

1634 WOOD *N. Eng. Prospect* II. i. 56 Those [Indians] who are seated West-ward be called Connectacuts, and Mowhacks. **1638** UNDERHILL *Newes from Amer.* 15 The Conetticot company having with them three-score Mohiggeners, whom the Pequeats had drove out of their lawful possessions, these Indians were earnest to join with the English.

2. A breed of horses. *Obs.*

1857 *Spirit of Times* 31 Jan. 347/2 'Great' horse that Yankee, for one standing only fourteen hands high: half Canadian-pony, half Connecticut, he was on the whole 'Kanuck.'

3. The name of a N. Eng. colony or state, used in combs.: (1) **Connecticut cent,** a bronze coin of small value minted by Connecticut, *obs.;* (2) **claimant,** one holding a title to land on the basis of Connecticut's claim of jurisdiction over it, *obs.;* (3) **Jonathan,** a country bumpkin from Connecticut, *rare;* (4) **lottery,** a lottery sponsored by Connecticut to raise money for colonial expenses, *obs.;* (5) **peddler,** a peddler from Connecticut, cf. **Yankee peddler;** (6) **Reservation, Reserve,** (see quots.); (7) **river pork,** (see quot. and cf. next); (8) **shad,** shad found in Connecticut waters; (9) **six,** a cigar made from Connecticut tobacco, *obs.;* (10) **stone,** (see quot. 1809); (11) **tobacco,** tobacco grown in Connecticut; (12) **warbler,** the tamarack warbler, *Oporornis agilis,* found chiefly in the eastern U.S.; (13) **wooden clock,** a clock of wood made in Connecticut; (14) **Yankee,** a Yankee from Connecticut, usu. regarded as particularly sharp and cunning.

(1) **1888** *Western Reserve Hist. Soc.* II. 71 These pieces, or Connecticut cents, . . . were to weigh forty to the pound, and it is known that during the first three years [1785–88] at least 28,944 pounds were coined. — (2) **1787** *Pa. Laws* (1803) III. 201 An Act for ascertaining and confirming to certain persons, called Connecticut claimants, the lands by them claimed in the county of Luzerne. — (3) **1833** *Polit. Examiner* (Shelbyville, Ky.) 9 Feb. 4/2 A Connecticut Jonathan, in taking a walk with his *dearest*, came to a toll bridge. — (4) **1754** *Md. Gazette* 6 June, Tickets for the Connecticut Lottery (set on Foot by the Legislature of that Government), . . . are to be sold.

(5) **1830** *National Aegis* (Worcester, Mass.) 28 April 1/5 There is not a more curious specimen of human nature in existence than the genuine Connecticut pedler. **1843** *Knickerb.* XXII. 2 Its execution [i.e., of a thought] would have done honor to a Connecticut pedler. — (6) **1798** in *Western Reserve Hist. Soc. Pub.* No. 96, 175 We the Subscribers are severally interested in the tract of Land called the Connecticut Reserve. **1812** MELISH *Travels* II. 257 We now entered into the *Connecticut Reservation*, at the 41st degree of latitude. **1901** JAMESON & BUEL *Encycl. Dict. Amer. Hist.* II. 50 The jurisdiction over this part [of W. Ohio] was ceded to the United States by Connecticut in 1786, but the ownership of the lands was retained by that State, which gave rise to the name, 'The Connecticut Reservation,' or 'Western Reserve.' — (7) **1907** *Springfield W. Republican* 21 March 13 Shad were formerly so plenty in this region as to be known as 'Connecticut river pork.' — (8) **1824** *Shipping & Comm. List* 31 July (Pettigrew P.), Shad, Conn't Mess. **1880** MARK TWAIN *Tramp Abroad* xlix. 574, I have selected a few dishes and made out a little bill of fare, which will go home in the steamer that precedes me, and be hot when I arrive—as follows: . . . Connecticut shad. — (9) **1870** C. D. WARNER *Summer in Garden* viii. Indeed, I offered him a Connecticut six; but he wittily said that he did not like a weed in a garden.

(10) **1771** in *Copley-Pelham Lett.* 153 Connecticut Stone hearths I think will be best. **1809** KENDALL *Travels* I. 90 A mile or two above the city, on the opposite bank, is a quarry of free-stone, of a coarse garnet-coloured grit, commonly called Connecticut-stone. — (11) **1768** JOHN LEES *Journal* (1911) 10 A good deal of Connecticut Tobacco is also sent from this place [Providence, R.I.] to New York, from which it is afterwards exported to Newfoundland [etc.]. — (12) **1812** WILSON *Ornithology* V. 64 [The] Connecticut Warbler . . . is a new species, first discovered in the state of Connecticut. **1941** SETON *Trail of Artist-Naturalist* 218, I found the nest and eggs of the Connecticut warbler, and sent them safely to the Smithsonian, where they are now to be seen. — (13) **1843** *Knickerb.* XXII. 5 [A planter asked] while pointing to a Connecticut wooden clock which stood upon a shelf. — (14) **1851** GREEN *Twelve Days* 116 This seemed to please the Connecticut yankee very much, and made him more anxious to bet. **1943** *Harper's Mag.* (New Bks.—first page), Just how does a Connecticut Yankee differ from other Yankees?

Also *Connecticut bill, bottom, cider, claret, clock, man, paper, road, sloop, tin wagon,* etc.

Connecticutter kəˈnɛtɪkətɚ, *n.* A native or inhabitant of Connecticut. — **1897** *Land of Sunshine* Dec. 28 All the gates the *Courant* can put up will not keep the steady stream of Connecticutters from migrating to California. **1947** *Amer. Sp.* Dec. 251 The Public Printer's decisions that a citizen of Connecticut is a *Connecticuter*, . . . and one of Massachusetts a *Massachusettan* are not endorsed in those states, either officially or by common consent.

* **connection,** *n.* **1.** The means or arrangement for continuing a journey by transferring to another train, stage, etc., at a junction point, usu. *to make* (*miss*) *connections.* **2.** (See quot.) *Obs.*

(1) **1856** *N.Y. Herald* 10 Jan. 4/6, I found that the ticket agents were not selling through tickets by this route to St. Louis. I was informed that 'the connection was broken.' **1865** *Dly. Age* (Phila.) 28 Sep. 4/3 Passengers taking the 8 A.M. train for New York will have time to dine in Baltimore and make connections. **1944** *Santa Fe Time Table* 12 Nov. 63 We hate late trains, too— . . . and we are sorry if they have caused you to miss a connection or important meeting. — (2) **1851** HALL *College Words* 297 Take up one's connections. In students' phrase, to leave college. Used in American institutions.

As the last term in **Christian, railroad, stage, water connection.**

conniption kəˈnɪpʃən, *n.* [Cf. *EDD canapshus*, ill-tempered, captious.] A fit of rage, passion, etc. In full **conniption fit.** *Colloq.* Cf. **cat fit.**

1833 S. SMITH *Major J. Downing* 209 Ant Keziah fell down in a conniption fit. **1859** *Harper's Weekly* 19 Nov. (Th.), She went into a conniption at the sight of poor Snap. **1948** *Sat. Review* 19 June 4/3

The idea sounded fine on paper and gave story editors of rival studios conniption fits, but did not work out in practice.

b. conniption bug, (see quot.).

1948 *Field & Stream* July 42/2 Various stages of the dobson are known as conniption-bugs, chippers, water grampus, . . . and hell-divers.

conquedle kɑnˈkwidl̩, *n. N. Eng.* [Imitative.] (See quots.)

1778 *Letters fr. Sir Chas. Blagden* (1903) 431 The Quongquéedle of Rhode Island, Bob of Lincoln in New England, seems to be *Emberiza oryzivora.* **1778** MACKENZIE *Diary* I. 281, I shot a bird here [Newport, R.I.] this day, which is called here, The Quamquidle, or Bob-o'-Lincoln; but properly the Rice bird. **1858** *Atlantic Mo.* Oct. 601 The Bobolink, or Conquedle, has unquestionably great talents as a musician.

Conquer John ˈkɑŋkɚˌdʒɑn, *n.* A local name for Solomon's seal. Cf. **John the Conqueror root.** — **1893** MARY A. OWEN *Old Rabbit* 67 Er chunk ob er root ob Conquer-John. **1894** *Amer. Folk-Lore* VII. 102 *Polygonatum biflorum* . . . conquer-John, Mo.

* **conscience,** *n.*

1. conscience fund, money wrongfully acquired or withheld restored to relieve the conscience. Also attrib.

1867 *Harper's Mag.* Aug. 333/1 The history of the 'Conscience Fund' is not without interest and entertainment. The account was opened in 1861, . . . and on the receipt of the sum of $6000 . . . accompanied by a statement that the restitution which had long been due the Government was promoted by conscience. This gave the account its name. **1948** *Sat. Ev. Post* 3 July 72/3 The city's conscience fund has hit an all-time high.

2. Conscience Whig, a member of the Whig party who refused to compromise with regard to slavery. Now *hist.*

1848 *Free Soil Minstrel* 20 For conscience whigs and liberty men, And every true barnburner, Here join to stay proud slavery's curse, And from free soil to spurn her. **1943** DEVOTO *Yr. of Decis.* 478 They had already lost the 'Conscience Whigs'—those who were not wrapped in the cotton thread which Emerson said held the nation together.

conscript kənˈskrɪpt, *v.* [f. the noun.] *tr.* To compel one to enter military service.

1813 *Conn. Courant* 23 Nov. 3/5 State troops which had been remanded to their homes by the Governor [of Vermont] had been conscripted under the orders of the former Captain General. **1907** ANDREWS *Recoll.* 180 General Steele had made arrangement for a Union Citizen who had been conscripted into the confederate service to go north the next day. **1945** *Chi. D. News* 13 Jan. 4/1 Many businessmen and industralists are against conscripting men to work as well as fight.

* **consequential,** *n.* A person of importance. *Rare.* — **1817** ROYALL *Lett. from Ala.* 5, I suspect they must be some of the consequentials of the neighborhood.

consequentiousness ˌkɑnsəˈkwenʃəsnɪs, *n.* The quality of being "consequential." *Rare.* — **1862** *N.Y. Herald* 26 April, He rides at the State's expense upon steamboats and railroad cars, seeking in all places to impress upon beholders an idea of his consequentiousness.

* **Conservative,** *n.* In the pl. as the name of certain political parties or factions. Now *obs.* or *hist.*

a. The branch of the Democratic party which opposed the Treasury Bill of 1837, and continued, for a short time, as an independent force.

1838 *Democratic Rev.* I. 2 No little uncertainty prevailed as to the course that would be pursued by . . . the friends of the Administration to whom the specific name of 'Conservatives' had been applied. **1842** BUCKINGHAM *Slave States* II. 354 A new party is rising up, however, called by themselves Conservatives, who will not ally themselves to either. By both the old parties, however, these Conservatives are called 'Impracticables.' **1914** MCLAUGHLIN & HART *Cyclo. Amer. Govt.* I. 566 A proposal to establish an independent, or subtreasury system [in 1837] . . . was passed by the Senate but twice rejected by the House, a Democratic faction known as Conservatives uniting with the Whigs to defeat it.

b. The conservative wing of the New York Democratic party opposed to the Barnburners.

[**1847** *Semi-Wkly. News* (Fredericksburg, Va.) 21 Oct. 2/2 The Hunkers are the conservatives, who have long been accustomed to rule the party, and enjoy the offices.] **1848** *N.Y. Wkly. Tribune* 3 June 2/2 In New York the Barnburners were known as Democrats,—the Hunkers were known as Conservatives. **1888** M. LANE in *America* 27 Sep. 16 *Conservatives,* a name self-given to that wing of the New York Democracy known as Hunkers. The name of Hunkers was accepted and the other was not.

c. (See quot. 1914.)

1865 *Cin. D. Gazette* 3 Oct. 2/2 A very wise and safe reference, but one, we predict that will not result as the Conservatives over the river desire. **1914** *Cyclo. Amer. Govt.* I. 402 The Conservatives or Johnson men were the adherents of President Johnson in his contest with Congress over the question of reconstruction. . . . The Conservatives played a rather important part in the South, where for a time they took the old name of 'Constitutional Unionists,' and their opponents the term 'Radicals.'

Also attrib. or as adj.

1865 *New Era* (Fredericksburg, Va.) 23 June 1/3 In the great Conservative party, which is to finish the work of restoring the Union, there will be room for the good men of all parties and creeds. **1865** *Memphis D. Argus* 14 Oct. 2/1 A majority of . . . the friends who elected him are themselves Conservatives—Conservative Republicans—who approve of his whole policy. **1941** BUCKMASTER *Let My People Go* 342 Their assumptions were based on Johnson's reconstruction plan and the fine support which conservative papers in the North were giving to them both.

* **conservatively,** *adv.* According to a moderate estimate. — **1904** *S.F. Chronicle* 12 July 7 Wearing a diamond pin, conservatively valued at $75. **1943** MENEFEE *Assignment* 298 The Department of Labor estimates conservatively that we will have 12 million unemployed six months after the war is over.

* **conservator,** *n.* (See quots.)

1828 WEBSTER *s.v., Conservator,* in Connecticut, a person appointed to superintend idiots, lunatics, &c., manage their property, and preserve it from waste. **1874** in *Ill. Rev. Statutes* (1883) 735 Whenever any idiot, lunatic or distracted person has any estate . . . [etc.], it shall be the duty of the court to appoint some fit person to be the conservator of such person. **1921** *Gen. Laws of Mass.* Sec. 16 cci, If a person by reason of advanced age or mental weakness is unable to properly care for his property, the probate court may . . . appoint a conservator to have charge and management of his property, subject to the direction of the court.

Conserve-slavery party. A political party favoring the continuance of slavery. *Obs.* — **1862** *N.Y. Tribune* 13 May 6/1 Several of the members of the new Conserve Slavery Party [in the House] did not vote with their friends of the Caucus upon the bill excluding Slavery from the . . . Territories.

* **considerable,** *a.* Absol. in various colloq. uses.

a. *considerable of,* a fair or large number or amount of something.

1685 *Mass. H.S. Coll.* 4 Ser. V. 132 One more, of Long Island, [who hath] . . . lost considerable of wheat and Indian corn. **1778** I. ANGELL *Diary* (1899) 8 There was a Considerable of firing between the sentries. **1903** K. D. WIGGIN *Rebecca* 132 Rebecca took her scolding . . . like a soldier. There was considerable of it.

b. Much, a good deal, often *by considerable.*

1722 *Lancaster Rec.* 200 He promising to Leve the hiway there Wider by Considerable then five Rods. **1837** MARTINEAU *Society* I. 340 She has a widowed mother to support, and she 'gets considerable' by sewing. **1900** E. A. DIX *Deacon Bradbury* 245 It's cost 'em consider'ble, an' they was so sure o' gittin' back half or more. **1903** *N.Y. Sun* 22 Nov., The new seal is not Nellie, not yet, by considerable; but it is already a great attraction.

c. *considerable of a(n),* something of considerable size, magnitude, etc.

1766 CUTLER in *Life & Corr.* I. 10 This morning about 6 o'clock considerable of a shock of an earthquake was felt in Boston. **1779** *N.H. Hist. Soc. Coll.* VI. 311 The water is carried under ground down the hill and through the bottom of the river, to a considerable of an eminence on the opposite side.

Used also of persons.

1781 WITHERSPOON *Druid P.* No. 7, He is considerable of a surveyor, considerable of it may be found in that country. This manner of speaking prevails in the northern parts. **1852** BRISTED *Upper Ten Th.* 142 He is really worth knowing and considerable of a man, as we say—no fool at all. **1909** A. C. RICE *Mr. Opp* 97, I was considerable of a performer at one time.

consigneeship ˌkɑnsaɪˈniʃɪp, *n.* The state of being a consignee. *Rare.* — **1876** BANCROFT *Hist. U.S.* (rev. ed.) VI. 503/1 [A Boston] town-meeting adopts the Philadelphia resolves, and invites the Hutchinsons to resign their consigneeship.

* **consociation,** *n.* "A convention of pastors and messengers of churches" (W. '06); a council of churchmen.

"It is usually composed of the pastors of the Congregational churches of the district represented and one lay delegate from each" (*Cent.*).

1781 PETERS *Conn.* (1829) 162 This quarrel continued till 1764, when it subsided in a grand continental consociation of ministers. **1844** RUPP *Relig. Denominations* 209 In Rhode Island, an evangelical association of ministers was formed in 1808. The next year the name was changed to that of the 'Evangelical Consociation,' by which it is now known. **1869** STOWE *Oldtown Folks* 451 The Consociation was another meeting of the clergy, but embracing also with each minister a lay delegate.

consociational kən‚sosɪ'eʃənl, *a.* Having to do with a consociation. *Obs.* — **1806** WEBSTER *Consociational*, pertaining to a consociation. *a***1817** T. DWIGHT *Travels* IV. 320 The Clergyman . . . attends every associational, and consociational, meeting within his district.

consociationism kən‚sosɪ'eʃənɪzəm, *n.* The system of ecclesiastical organization in which independent churches coöperate by means of a confederation. — *a***1840** in E. A. PARK *Memoir N. Emmons* (1861) 163 Associationism leads to Consociationism; Consociationism leads to Presbyterianism. **1884** *Advance* (Chicago) 11 Dec., They now sought a middle way between Presbyterianism and Congregationalism. That middle way was Consociationism.

consolidarian kən‚sɑlə'dɛrɪən, *n.* One who believes in consolidating. *Rare.* — **1788** *Mass. Spy* 16 April 2/2 The cause of the contest I found to be, that the people of Exeter were high Consolidarians, and lent every possible aid to those of their own party in convention.

* **consolidated,** *a.* In combs.: (1) **consolidated engine,** = **consolidation 2;** (2) **milk,** = **condensed milk,** *rare;* (3) **note,** an interest-bearing treasury note to replace other bills of credit, esp. in the states or colonies before the Constitution, also **consolidated state note,** *obs.;* (4) **school,** a school resulting from the bringing together of two or more schools, also attrib.; (5) **ticket office,** (see quot.).

(1) **1887** *Sci. Amer.* n.s. LVI. 3/2 The locomotive was one of the heaviest kind known as a consolidated engine, having four drive-wheels on a side, and weighing 106,000 pounds. — (2) **1861** BERKELY *Sportsman* 261 An excellent breakfast of very good and very hot coffee . . . with some of the 'consolidated milk' brought in the sealed cans from Mr. Duncan's store in New York, to mix with our coffee. — (3) **1784** *Mass. Centinel* 10 July 1/1 Lost . . . a leather pocket-book, containing . . . five Consolidated State Notes. **1832** WILLIAMSON *Maine* II. 539 For which [land] they gave £3,000 in consolidated notes. — (4) **1911** *Okla. Session Laws* 3 Legisl. 245 All the lands and funds that have heretofore been or may hereafter be derived from the sale thereof, . . . shall be set aside and credited to a fund which is hereby created to be known as the 'Union Graded or Consolidated School District Fund.' **1945** *N. Eng. Homestead* 8 Dec. 26/4 The success story . . . came to light at the Dublin, N.H., Consolidated School. — (5) **1924** F. J. HASKIN *Amer. Govt.* 393 Instead of a separate ticket office in cities for each railroad, consolidated ticket offices, where a ticket for any train on any road could be purchased, were established.

* **consolidation,** *n.* **1.** A company formed by the merging of two or more companies. **2.** A powerful low-speed freight locomotive having two pilot-truck wheels and eight drivers, in full **consolidation locomotive. 3.** *Educ.* The combining of two or more schools into one, esp. in rural areas.

(1) **1882** C. KING *Rep. Prec. Metals* 74 The consolidation owns about 35 miles of ditches. — (2) **1877** FORNEY *Catechism of the Locomotive* 432 Consolidation locomotives, . . . which have eight driving-wheels, are employed almost exclusively for traffic over heavy mountain grades. **1882–83** KNIGHT *Mech. Dict.* 555/2 The original 'Consolidation' locomotive was built in 1866 from the plans of Wm. Alexander Mitchell, at the Baldwin Works in Philadelphia. **1947** BEEBE *Mixed Train Dly.* 67 Its motive power is all drawn from the ranks of the Southern's ten-wheelers and Consolidations. — (3) **1901** LONGSDORF (*title*), The Consolidation of Country Schools, and the Transporting of the Scholars by Use of Vans.

consolidationist kən‚sɑlə'deʃənɪst, *n.* A believer in a strong central government. *Obs.* Cf. **State rights.** — **1833** WEBSTER *Works* (1860) I. 295 For one, I repel all such imputations. I am no consolidationist. **1883** *American* VI. 202 Would it not unite the consolidationist and the advocate of states rights?

* **constitution,** *n.*

1. (*cap.*) The principles of government for the U.S. drawn up at Philadelphia in 1787, or the document embodying these principles.

[**1775** JOHN ADAMS in *Jrnl. Nicholas Cresswell* (1925) 148 When 50 or 60 men have a constitution to form for a great Empire.] **1787** *Constitution,* We the people of the United States, . . . do ordain and establish this Constitution for the United States of America. **1856** D. MACLEOD *F. Wood* 69 Hasty legislation, either in the enactment of laws or their repeal, is objectionable. . . . To guard against it, the framers of the Constitution devised many ways. **1946** *Chi. D. News* 23 Nov. 6/1 Give the vice-president greater responsibilities than were originally contemplated in the Constitution.

b. ?A social gathering to arouse interest in the anticipated Constitution of 1787. *Obs.*

1772 WINSLOW *Diary* 15, I told you . . . that I was going to a constitution with Miss Soley. . . . [It was] a very genteel and well regulated assembly.

2. The body of fundamental laws of one of the states in the U.S.

1780 CUTLER in *Life & Corr.* I. 78 Attended town-meeting for receiving the Constitution. **1865** *Detroit Tribune* 30 Sep. 4/1 The proposed new Constitution of South Carolina is framed in accordance with these principles. **1948** *Milwaukee Jrnl.* 18 July 1/5 When it came time for Wisconsin to cease being a territory and grow into a state, a constitution was needed.

3. a. Constitution-shrieker, (see quot.). *Obs.* **b. Constitution State,** (see quot. 1943).

(a) **1867** *N.Y. Tribune* 21 Dec. 4/5 Some of the Democratic organs . . . have noisily earned the designation of Constitution-shriekers, by their eternal harping upon that much-abused instrument. — (b) **1935** *Col. of Conn.* 3 Connecticut thus offers one of the most interesting illustrations of self-government of all the States of the Union, and derives its title of 'The Constitution State.' **1943** *World Almanac* 297/1 The Fundamental Orders, adopted in 1639 by these early settlements, was the first written constitution of an autonomous government and the forerunner in many respects of the constitution of the United States; hence, the title 'Constitution State' for Connecticut.

As the last term in **Federal, Lecompton, state, Wyandotte constitution.**

* **constitutional,** *a.* Often *cap.*

1. Of or pertaining to the U.S. Constitution.

1789 CUTLER in *Life & Corr.* I. 197, I addressed them on the nature of our Constitutional Government. **1872** *Atlantic Mo.* April 515 The 'constitutional' question has intruded itself at every step into politics. **1946** HOLBROOK *Lost Men* 105 Thousands of us today speak of this or that as being 'constitutional' without knowing what it means.

2. In special combs.: (1) **constitutional amendment,** an amendment to the federal Constitution or to the constitution of a state; (2) **construction,** the interpretation placed upon the federal Constitution; (3) **convention,** a body of delegates who meet to draw up a constitution; (4) **democrat,** a democrat according to the provisions of the federal Constitution; (5) * **law,** law having to do with the interpretation and construction of the Constitution of the U.S. or of a state; (6) * **lawyer,** (*a*) a lawyer versed in matters pertaining to the Constitution of the U.S., (*b*) (see quot.); (7) **post,** the mail service of the revolting colonies as distinguished from that of the British government or "ministerial post," *obs.;* (8) **right,** a right possessed by a citizen, state, etc., under the provisions of the Constitution of the U.S.; (9) **Union,** see as a main entry; (10) **Unionist,** (see quot.), *obs.*

(1) **1854** BENTON *Thirty Years' View* I. 122/2 In the meantime, the friends of popular election should press the constitutional amendment. **1947** *Dly. Oklahoman* (Okla. City) 5 Nov. 2/1 First returns from statewide voting Tuesday on a constitutional amendment to pay Ohio veterans of World War II $300 millions in bonuses disclosed a big margin in favor of the proposal. **1948** *This Week Mag.* 16 Oct. 5/1 Congress is pondering a Constitutional amendment. — (2) **1860** in E. D. FITE *Pres. Campaign of 1860* (1911) 254 The conflict of constitutional construction is indeed a mere incident of the great struggle, a mere symptom of the crisis. — (3) **1843** (*title*), Journal of the Constitutional Convention of Vermont. **1948** *Chi. Tribune* 29 Feb. I. 24/5 Yet, after returning to private life, he became the leading critic of the Confederation and was the leader in calling the Constitutional Convention. — (4) **1865** *Memphis D. Argus* 14 Oct. 2/1 President Johnson is at perfect liberty . . . to stand forth as he is, and as he always was, a Conservative, Constitutional Democrat.

(5) **1886** ALTON *Among Law-Makers* 249 [The] 'plea to the jurisdiction' raised an important question of constitutional law. **1948** *Dly. Ardmoreite* (Ardmore, Okla.) 1 July 6/6 Under this amendment the state was forced by constitutional law to balance its budget. — (6) (*a*) **1830** *Cong. Deb.* 75/2 The venerable Connecticut senator is a constitutional lawyer, of sound principles, and enlarged knowledge. **1936** WILLIS *Const. Law of U.S.* (1936) 10 Marshall was the greatest judge and one of the two greatest constitutional lawyers the United States has ever produced. (*b*) **1910** *N.Y. Ev. Post* 26 Oct. 8 'Constitutional lawyer' . . . in Indiana, . . . signifies a member of the bar who was admitted to practice without any except the constitutional qualifications. — (7) **1775** *Jrnls. Cont. Cong.* III. 488 A constitutional post is now established from New Hampshire to Georgia. *Ib.*, Deane is for a recommendation to the people to write by the constitutional post. — (8) **1831** P. HONE *Diary* I. 38 [Men] should

have protested and seceded from the convention when a proposition so monstrous as the denying to Congress the constitutional right to pass these laws was about to be adopted. **1892** M. A. Jackson *Gen. Jackson* 143 It was for her constitutional rights that the South resisted the North. **1947** *Chi. D. News* 10 June 12/4 The bill takes away our constitutional rights.

(10) 1914 *Cyclo. Amer. Govt.* I. 402 The Conservatives (President Johnson's supporters) played a rather important part in the South where for a time they took the old name of 'Constitutional Unionists,' and their opponents the term 'Radicals.'

* **constitutionalist,** *n.*

1. In Pennsylvania politics from about 1780 to 1800, an opponent of change in the state constitution. *Obs.*

1782 J. Adams *Works* III. 353 Vaughan has a brother in Philadelphia, who has written him a long letter about the Constitutionalists and the Republicans. **1796** Morse *Amer. Geog.* I. 564 This party was styled republicans; the other, constitutionalists [in Pennsylvania]. **1890** W. G. Sumner *Hamilton* 136 The constitutionalists,—that is, supporters of the Constitution of Pennsylvania—were the opponents of the Federal Constitution.

2. One holding a particular view concerning the U.S. Constitution. *Obs.*

1802 Cutler in *Life & Corr.* II. 100 It is most probable we may sit a week longer. The Constitutionalists say little; it only wastes time. **1833** *Niles' Reg.* XLIV. 1/1 State-rights men or constitutionalists—tariffites or anti-tariffites, &c. &c. have been so jostled that no party knows exactly where is its own present location. **1834** *U.S. Telegraph* 2 Jan. Whatever dispute remains between the Constitutionalists of the North and the quondam Nullifiers, may be settled when the common enemy [Jacksonism] is overthrown. **1949** *Time* 28 Feb. 20/1.

constitutionality ˌkɑnstəˌtjuʃənˈælətɪ, *n.* The quality of being in harmony with the Constitution of the U.S. or with a state constitution.

1787 A. Hamilton *Works* VII. 9, I pass now to an examination of the constitutionality of the measure proposed by the bill. **1865** *Memphis D. Argus* 19 Nov. 2/6 Judge Underwood will maintain the constitutionality of the test oath. **1948** *Chi. D. News* 18 Sep. 6/1 Let the challenged constitutionality of the Taft-Hartley act be resolved by the Supreme Court.

* **constitutionally,** *a.* By virtue of the U.S. Constitution. — **1804** *12th Amend. Constitution* § 3 But no person constitutionally ineligible to the office of the president shall be eligible to that of vice president of the United States.

Constitutional Union. Used attrib. to designate certain political groups or factions having conservative tendencies.

1. A party formed in 1850 by Georgians who opposed disunion. *Obs.*

1852 in A. C. Cole *Whig Party in South* 240 Let the Constitutional Union party be firm, and the South will be safe.

2. A party of southern Whigs and other conservative elements who ignored the slavery issue in the presidential campaign of 1860 and favored the continuance of the Union.

1860 *Polit. Text-Book 1860* 29 As representatives of the Constitutional Union men of the country . . . we hereby pledge ourselves [etc.]. **1900** *Miss. Hist. Soc. Pub.* III. 77 A tabular view of the convention . . . shows that it was composed of 100 delegates [among which were] . . . 3 Reconstructionists, . . . 2 Constitutional Union, 2 Union Conservatives, . . . 2 Henry Clay Whigs, 4 Old Whigs. **1948** *Chi. Tribune* 4 Jan. I. 4/4 Douglas and Breckenridge headed opposing Democratic factions while Bell ran on the Constitutional Union ticket.

3. (See quot.)

1870 W. W. Holden *Proclamations* 31 For be it known to your honor that there is a widespread and secret organization in this State, partly political and partly social in its objects; that this organization is known, first, as 'The Constitutional Union Guard,'—secondly, as 'The White Brotherhood,'—thirdly, as 'The Invisible Empire.'

* **construction,** *n.* In combs.: (1) **construction camp,** the camp or headquarters of workmen engaged in building something; (2) **car,** a railroad car carrying materials used in building a railroad; (3) **gang,** a group of workmen engaged in construction work; (4) **stock,** (see quot.), *obs.;* (5) **train,** a railroad train which carries equipment and supplies used in building a railroad.

(1) 1884 *Cent. Mag.* Oct. 843 Adventurers who had followed the construction camps on the Northern Pacific Railroad, and had been left stranded when that highway was completed, drifted into the new diggings. **1948** *C.A. Jrnl.* June 106 Eventually a trail beginning near an abandoned construction camp was selected as possible. — **(2) 1873** Beadle *Undevel. West* 397 We went over on the first locomotive which crossed: hitherto construction cars had been shoved across singly by hand. **1947** Beebe *Mixed Train Dly.* 298 The club car 'Julia Bullette' of the romantic Virginia and Truckee . . . was originally built as a construction car. — **(3) 1932** Grayson *Leaders* 436 He had hundreds of men working for him, and for years his construction gangs were busy at widely separated points throughout the northwestern states. — **(4) 1853** *Mich. Gen. Statutes* (1882–3) I. 915 Any such company may create and issue shares of guaranteed stock, to be denominated 'construction stock.' — **(5) 1869** Brace *New West* 184 Every stick of fuel, every railroad tie, and beam for trestle-work, must be carried on construction-trains from these mountains. **1911** Wright *Winning Barbara Worth* 318 A line of stakes led one way to the town of Barba and the other way in the direction to meet the construction train working out from the junction with the S. & C. at Deep Well.

As the last term in **Chicago, Constitutional, liberal construction.**

* **constructive,** *a.* **1. constructive blockade,** (see quot.). **2. constructive mileage,** (see quot. 1888).

(1) 1809 *Ann. 10th Cong.* 2 Sess. 392 The second head of dispute regards the practice of constructive blockades. The complaint on this subject was, that blockades were formed by proclamations, and that neutrals were compelled to consider ports blockaded before which no force was stationed. — **(2) 1848** Bartlett 224 Many of the Senators, in 1845, when Mr. Polk was inaugurated, refused to pocket their constructive mileage, holding it to be an imposition on the public. **1888** M. Lane *Pol. Catch-Words* 18 Oct. 15 Mileage.—An allowance to legislators of so much a mile for the distance from their homes to the place of assemblage. Constructive mileage is where they are supposed to have gone home and returned, and is merely an extra bonus of the amount of money that they would have been entitled to, if they had really gone home and returned.

Consular Seal. A brand of wine. *Rare.* — **1870** R. Tomes *Decorum* 140 All smacking of the lips, even over your host's finest Tokay, Consular Seal, or Burgundy, is but a barbarous mode of expressing an appreciation of vinous excellence.

* **consulary,** *a.* ?Acting as consuls or agents for trading companies. *Obs.* — **1718** Sewall *Diary* III. 196 Col. Pynchon and Mr. Cooke Consulary Men were there. **1720** *Ib.* 249 Gov[erno]r Dudley is buried. . . . Councillours and Ministers had Scarvs, and Consulary men.

Consul's man. (See quot.) *Rare.* — **1824** W. N. Blane *Excursion U.S.* 2 In addition to our crew, we had on board several 'Consul's men,' as they are called. An American seaman, if in distress in a foreign country, has only to inform his Consul that he wishes to return home; and is immediately sent on board some American vessel, returning to the United States. The government allows ten dollars for his passage; and at that price every vessel is obliged to take a certain number of these men.

consumption root. App. the false wintergreen, *Pyrola americana. Obs.* — **1784** Cutler in *Mem. Academy* I. 444 *Pyrola.* . . . Consumption-Root. Blossoms white; in woodland. July. **1795** Winterbotham *Hist. View* III. 398 Among the native and uncultivated plants of New-England, the following have been employed for medical purposes: . . . Bistort, . . . Spice wood, or feverbush, . . . Consumption root.

* **contact,** *n.* In mining, the plane of rock lying between layers of dissimilar rock. Also attrib.

1871 Raymond *3rd Rep. Mines* 262 It is . . . a contact vein, porphyry forming the hanging and syenite the foot wall. **1899** Norris *McTeague* 404 Here's a 'contact' and here is it again, and there, and yonder. . . . That's grano-diorite on slate. **1923** Bower *Parowan Bonanza* 13, I'm hoping it'll run into higher values when I hit the contact.

* **contact,** *v. tr.* To "get in touch with" (a person). Also absol. *Slang.*

1929 L. F. Carr *America Challenged* 61 Mr. Dickey contacted every family in three representative agricultural counties. **1931** Ira L. Reeves *Ol' Rum River* 47, I tried on several occasions to get in touch with the local units. . . . But we never seemed to be able to contact. **1948** *Capital-Democrat* (Tishomingo, Okla.) 24 June 4/3 It is my desire to contact each and every voter of this county and ask for their vote.

contador kontaˈdor, *n. S.W.* [Sp., accountant or auditor.] An accountant or collector. *Obs.* — **1803** in *Ann. 8th Congress* 2 Sess. 1521 The Contador, Treasurer, and Interventor, are officers subordinate to the Intendant. The first . . . keeps all accounts and documents respecting the receipt and expenditure of the revenue; and is, therefore, a check upon the Intendant. **1809** F. Cuming *Western Tour* 312, I returned to my friend Egan's, who accompanied me to the house of Don Gilbert Leonard, the contador (or collector).

* **contest,** *n.* As the last term in **baby, baseball, beauty, presidential, shearing contest.**

contestee kɑntɛsˈti, *n.* One against whom a contesting claim is brought, esp. in a contested election.

1870 *Cong. Globe* 16 Feb. 1349/3 So many voted for the contestant and so many for the contestee in that ward. **1888** *Troy D. Times* 4 Feb. (F.), O'Ferral of Virginia spoke in support of the majority resolution, and contended that the contestee, James B. White, had failed utterly to make proof of his naturalization. **1896** *Cong. Rec.* 9 June 6333/1 Two hundred and twenty votes were found to be there for the contestee.

Conthieveracy kən'θivərəsı, *n.* An abusive name for the Southern Confederacy inspired by the South's seizure of U.S. property within its borders at the outbreak of the Civil War. *Obs.* — **1861** *N.Y. Tribune* 15 July, A boat . . . communicated to the officers of the Preble all the particulars of the depredations of the piratical craft, named after the President of the Southern 'Conthieveracy.' **1867** *Atlantic Mo.* March 278/1 Across the level marshes there came a nasal sound, as of the 'Conthieveracy' in its slumbers.

* **continent,** *n.*

1. The territory occupied by the North American colonies, or the colonists themselves. *Obs.*

1760 *N.J. Archives* XX. 514 Now we the Subscribers, and Creditors of the said Myer Levy, do hereby request the Assistance of all and every well disposed Person, either on the Continent, or in the West India Islands, to apprehend the said Myer Levy. **1774** MORRIS in Sparks *Life G. Morris* I. 27 Uniting the whole continent in one grand legislature. **1789** *Ann. 1st Congress* I. 161, I believe we have only to try the experiment [of taxing salt], to be convinced it would have a similar effect throughout the Continent. **1798** ALLEN *Hist. Vermont* 56 The battle of Lexington, threw the whole continent into a ferment.

2. A collective name for the general government over the colonies and states during the Revolution, as distinguished from the individual states and from the British authorities. *Obs.*

1775 J. ADAMS *Works* IX. 363, I am to inquire what number of seamen . . . would probably enlist in the service, either . . . in the pay of the continent or in the pay of the province. **1781** JEFFERSON *Writings* IV. 174 There are some collections of forage and provisions belonging to the Continent, and some to the State.

* **continental,** *n.*

1. A soldier or former soldier in the Continental Army.

1777 *Md. Hist. Mag.* V. 210 Perhaps it would be in your Excellency's power to spare 3 or 400 Continentals. **1823** J. THACHER *Journal* 93 Colonel Whitcomb with a party of continentals was ordered to pursue the Indians. **1897** *Outing* XXIX. 472/1 Sally . . . sewed garments and picked lint for the Continentals, thinking the while of her two lovers. **1947** COFFIN *Yankee Coast* 237 Our Continentals came home free men, went back to fishing, and started building ships.

b. Any supporter of the American cause, as contrasted with a loyalist.

1781 *Independent Ledger* 24 Dec., Come all Continentals, who Washington love, The pride of Columbia, the fav'rite of Jove.

c. *pl.* The uniform worn by a soldier in the Continental Army. *Obs.*

1887 *Scribner's Mag.* (F.), The Englishman . . . will know one thing, the Yankee, who contemplates his grandfather in continentals above the chimney-piece, will know another.

2. *ellipt.* Currency issued by the authority of the Continental Congress. Also *pl. Obs.* Cf. **old continental.**

1821 COOPER *Spy* xvi, If it's silver or goold . . . it's but little I have, though I've a trifling bit of the continental. **1835** BIRD *Hawks of Hawk-H.* I. 246 Were I a rebel, you would have found naught but a roll of beggarly continentals. **1845** COOPER *Chainbearer* ii, I had provided myself with a little silver . . . and some thirty or forty thousand dollars of 'continental,' to defray my traveling expenses.

b. *Not to give* (or *care*) *a continental,* to have no regard. *Colloq.*

1872 MARK TWAIN *Roughing It* xlvii. 334 He didn't give a continental for anybody. **1907** M. C. HARRIS *Tents of Wickedness* III. vii. 326 He did not care a continental what they thought.

* **continental,** *a.* Often *cap.*

1. Pertaining to the North American continent.

1760 FRANKLIN *Writings* IV. 47, I entirely agree . . . that we are in North America 'a far greater continental as well as naval power.' **1855** in HAMBLETON *H. A. Wise* 247 The stranger who consults the chart of our Continental Republic, hardly discovers our State amid her leviathan sisters. **1948** *Sat. Ev. Post* 26 June 79/2, I began to press him for the job of United States judge of the Virgin Islands. The occupant of that office had always been a continental white man.

2. Of or pertaining to the colonies or states collectively during the Revolution or to the general government formed by them.

1774 in J. ADAMS *Works* IX. 344 There is an opinion . . . that the Massachusetts gentlemen . . . do affect to dictate and take the lead in continental measures. **1776** in JOHNSTON *N. Hale* 155, I proposed going with Dudley, who is appointed to Comm[a]n[d] a Twenty Gun Ship in the Continental Navy. **1893** THANET *Stories* 182 He recalled how, as a boy, he had gone to a fancy-dress ball in Continental small-clothes, so small that he had been strictly cautioned . . . not to bow.

3. Denoting or having reference to the currency and securities of the Confederation. *Obs.* Cf. **4.** (8) below.

1776 *Jrnls. Cont. Congress* V. 432 Colonel Roberdeau, . . . having tendered to Congress the moiety belonging to them, in exchange for continental dollars [bills of credit]. **1784** *Mass. Centinel* 4 Sep. 3/2 Bought, Sold, and Negotiated, at the Land Office, . . . Continental Certificates, and every other kind of publick securities. **1790** *Steele Papers* I. 65, I am well informed that six millions of our Continental Securities are now in the hands of persons living in Holland. **1865** H. PHILLIPS *Amer. Paper Curr.* II. 49 The Virginia convention had made the continental bills a legal tender.

b. Hence in expressions of disparagement on account of the depreciation and repudiation of the Continental money (see quots.). Cf. * **continental,** *n.* **2. b.**

1841 SIMMS *Kinsmen* I. 98, I wouldn't give a continental copper for the safety of your skin. **1851** *S.F. Sun. Dispatch* 10 Aug. 4/4 Look o' here, stranger, that clock you sold me aint worth a continental cuss. 'T wont go at all! **1874** EGGLESTON *Circuit Rider* 148, I tole him as how I didn't keer three continental derns fer his whole band. **1890** *N. & Q.* V. 169 'A Tinker's Dam' is equivalent to the expression, 'A Continental Damn.' The latter expression arose when Continental money had become so utterly worthless towards the end of the Revolution, as the Confederate notes did at the end of the Civil War.

4. In special combs.: (1) **Continental Army,** the army raised by the Continental Congress at the outbreak of the Revolution; (2) **backbone,** =**Continental Divide;** (3) **bank,** the first bank of the U.S. chartered by Congress in 1791, *rare;* (4) **Congress,** either one of the two congresses held in Philadelphia during the Revolution and made up of delegates from the colonies; (5) **Convention,** the Constitutional Convention which assembled in Philadelphia in May, 1787, *obs.;* (6) **Divide,** the divide which separates the watersheds of the Pacific from those of the Atlantic; (7) **fast,** a fast recommended by Congress for the nation in dedication to the principles of the Revolution; (8) **money,** a currency of paper notes issued by the Continental Congress; (9) **tea,** =**Jersey tea,** or **Labrador tea,** these plants having allegedly been used for tea during the Revolution; (10) **thanksgiving,** a day of thanksgiving decreed by the Continental Congress, app. because of the victory at King's Mountain and other local American successes; (11) **wagon,** (see quot. 1778), *obs.*

(1) **1775** DUNMORE *Correspondence* 2 Aug., They [the General Congress] have ordered an Army to be immediately raised (stiled the Continental Army). **1947** *Newsweek* 14 July 21/1 Symbolically, they wore the blue-and-buff uniforms and tricorn hats of the Continental Army. — (2) **1891** *Scribner's Mag.* X. 215 The road . . . re-crossed the main range, the highest ridge of the continental backbone. — (3) **1798** W. MANNING *Key of Liberty* 56 The free circulation of money arose prinsaply from the State banks which were erected to oppose the parshality of the Continental Banks. — (4) **1774** *Boston Rec. Comm.* XVIII. 176 The result of a continental Congress. **1871** *Scribner's Mo.* I. 234 Charles Thompson, first and long the confidential secretary of the Continental Congress. **1948** *Pa. Mag. Hist.* April 113 The papers of the Continental Congress have never been properly catalogued, let alone published.

(5) **1787** CUTLER in *Life & Corr.* I. 254 Members of the Continental Convention, now convened in this city for the purpose of forming a Federal Constitution. — (6) **1868** W. J. PALMER *Surveys Across Continent* 171 The great Continental Divide at Arkansas Pass. **1948** *Hungry Horse News* (Columbia Falls, Mont.) 24 Sep. 1/4 September's first snows Thursday touched the high peaks of the continental divide with fresh white. — (7) **1775** FITHIAN *Journal* II. 47 A number of the town gentlemen proposed, if my appointments will allow me, to preach in this town on the day of the Continental Fast. **1780** CUTLER in *Life & Corr.* I. 77 Continental Fast and Annual for this State [Massachusetts]. Preached. — (8) **1775** *Jrnls. Cont. Congress* II. 207 That each gentleman who signs the continental money, be . . . paid out of the continental treasury, one Dollar and one third of a dollar for each and every thousand bills signed and numbered by him. **1844** UNCLE SAM *Peculiarities* II. 209 My old grandmother has a hundred thousand dollars of the revolutionary continental money, which Uncle Sam never paid. — (9) **1830** *Huntingdon* (Pa.) *Courier*

15 Sep. 4/5 American Remedies Wanted.... Continental Tea, leave of, (Ceanothus Americanus). **1906** A. HENKEL *Wild Medicinal Plants* 41 Labrador tea; continental tea; James-tea.

(10) 1780 THOMAS SMITH *Journals* (1821 ed.) 113 December 7. Continental thanksgiving, I preached; Mr. Deane (whose turn it was) not coming down. **1780** SAMUEL DEANE *Diary* (1849) 348 December 7. Continental Thanksgiving. — **(11) 1778** BERKENHOUT *Excursion* 579 On this road we passed a number of continental waggons (so they are called) with flower and Rum for Washington's army. They have five thousand of these Waggons, the drivers of which, being taught the use of arms, act in the double capacity of Waggoners, or Soldiers as occasion may require. **1782** *Ann. S.W. Virginia* 774 Richard Trimbel produced satisfactory proof... that he ought to be paid the sum of £27 for drawing a Continental waggon twelve months.

Also *Continental colonel, concern, currency, debt, flour, frigate, infantry, officer, paper money, service, soldier, tax, treasurer, troops, uniform*, etc.

continentaler ˌkɑntəˈnɛntlɚ, *n.* **1.** A soldier in the Continental Army. **2.** A gun of a type used during the Revolution. Both *obs.*

(1) 1775 in *Harper's Mag.* LXII. 639/2 Come out ye Continentallers! We're going for to go To fight the red-coat enemy. **1850** H. C. WATSON *Camp Fires Revol.* 41 The continentallers... were ordered to march to Bunker Hill. — **(2) 1857** *Mag. of Travel* I. 179 [An Iowa pioneer is speaking:] I don't want none of yer brass and German fixens round my old Continentaler.

***continentalist,** *n.* An advocate of a federal government for the revolting colonies after the Revolution. *Obs.* — **1781** A. HAMILTON (*title*), The Continentalist. (A series of essays published by London's New York Packet Company.)

continentally ˌkɑntəˈnɛntəlɪ, *adv.* **1.** With reference to American as opposed to British interests. *Obs.* **2.** *fig.* With wide views or extensive sympathies. — **(1) 1783** HAMILTON in Sparks *Corr. Revol.* IV. 22 They are the men who think Continentally. — **(2) 1883** *Amer. Home Missionary Soc. 45th Rep.* 100 If there ever was a time when Christians needed to accustom their minds to larger things, when they needed to think 'continentally,' it is now.

continued story. A story that runs through more than one issue of the periodical in which it is printed, a serial story. — **1881** RITTENHOUSE *Maud* 7 Elmer brought me the Sunday Bulletin with that sweet continued story in it.

***continuity,** *n.* In motion pictures, a scenario worked out in detail. — **1921** *Collier's* 25 June 26/3 It is a hobby of mine never to pay no attention to a continuity, as it only gets a man balled up. **1947** *Time* 20 Oct. 12/3 The continuity contained a double-meaning statement so obvious that we considered it vulgar.

***contour,** *n.* **1.** *fig.* General appearance, prospect. *Rare.* **2. contour plow,** a plow used in giving a desired contour to a piece of ground. Hence **contour plowing.**

(1) 1904 *Charlotte D. Observer* 21 Aug. 1 Mr. Blackburn is jubilant over the contour of things, and says he is confident of election. — **(2) 1941** S. V. BENÉT *Listen to the People* (1942) 479 People whose contour-plows bring back the grass To a dust bitten and dishonored earth. **1941** FERGUSSON *Southwest* 148 In the same region, farmers who had tried rotation of crops and contour plowing found their fields secure after torrential spring rains. **1945** *Reader's Digest* Nov. 27/2 They... learn modern farm methods such as terracing and contour plowing.

***contraband,** *n.* A Negro who had been a slave, taken during the Civil War under the protection of the U.S. Government. *Obs.* or *hist.*

1861 *Richmond* (Va.) *Examiner* 2 Dec. 3/4 For a long time 'contrabands' have been arriving in Philadelphia by divers ways, from Virginia, Delaware and Maryland. **1863** *N.Y. Tribune* 3 Jan. 1/6 Several contrabands came into camp to-day, and were received in accordance with the proclamation. **1906** *Springfield W. Republican* 15 Feb. 8 At one time he had under his charge 150,000 of 'contrabands'; many of these he placed on abandoned plantations, and 70,000 of these able-bodied men were enlisted as soldiers.

b. In full **contraband of war.**

1861 B. F. BUTLER in J. PARTON *Butler in New Orleans* (1864) 127 These men are Contraband of War; set them at work. **1947** LUMPKIN *Southerner* 225 They even hit upon the strange name of 'contraband of war' in their anxiety to seem legal in not returning 'property,' when thousands upon tens of thousands of slaves poured out of their old habitats into Union Army camps and over Union lines.

c. Attrib. with **camp, hue, slave.** *Obs.*

1865 SCHURZ in *39th Congress* 1 Sess. Sen. Ex. Doc. No. 2, 15 The government was feeding the colored refugees, who could not be advantageously employed, in the so-called contraband camps. **1867** *Atlantic Mo.* Nov. 609/1 After the play, Rice, having shaded his own countenance to the 'contraband' hue, ordered Cuff to disrobe, and proceeded to invest himself in the cast-off apparel. **1886** LOGAN *Great Conspiracy* 381 The Contraband-Slave question, however, continued to agitate the public mind for many months.

***contract,** *n. fig.* An enterprise or undertaking. *Colloq.*

1881 HAYES *New Colorado* 87 A person should carefully study his temperament and possible disabilities before he takes a contract to go into a deep shaft. *Ib.* 159 Here, too, was Armijo to have annihilated General Kearny, but for the unfortunate circumstance of his troops declining, as they say in the West, 'to take the contract.' **1891** E. ELLIS *Check No. 2134* 50 Any person might well shrink from the contract of corraling a couple [of such men].

As the last term in **beef, tie, yellow-dog contract.**

contracting agent. (See quot.) *Obs.* — **1859** *Harper's Mag.* Aug. 425/2 The freight lines represented in New York employ a small army of freight solicitors, or, as they delight to call themselves, 'contracting agents.'

***contraction,** *n.* The reduction of the volume of currency in circulation.

1838 *Speeches of D. Barnard* 209 We are informed that all our alarms about expansions and contractions are quite useless, because the precious metals have been found to be more fluctuating than any thing else ever used as money. **1875** *Nation* XXI. 113/1 A decision in favor... of inflation that will be the same thing as contraction,... will certainly bring about one of the most tremendous financial catastrophes ever witnessed. **1892** *Ib.* LV. 19 The anxiety of the advocates of free coinage... is... due to a fear that this would result in a contraction of the currency.

contractionist kənˈtrækʃənɪst, *n.* One who advocates or supports the policy of reducing the volume of currency. *Obs.* Cf. **gold standard contractionist.**

1875 *Nation* XXI. 112/2 As regards the Republican party, its own desire is to please everybody—both contractionist and inflationist, the solvent and insolvent, the creditor and the debtor. **1890** *Cong. Rec.* 12 July 7208/1 This bold confession is made... by this distinguished Senator and contractionist. **1892** *Ib.* 30 June 5658/1 It was the duty of Senators to return here when a bill of this kind was pending; but they can defeat the will of the people and serve the gold-standard contractionists; they can serve Lombard and Wall streets by being absent.

***contractor,** *n.* As the last term in **beef, Indian cattle, land, wood contractor.**

contribution box. A box in which contributions are received, esp. a wooden box with a long handle passed among the pews of a church for the collection.

No British evidence is available for this expression, but it is such an obvious formation that it may well be old in the language. The article described in quot. 1930 (also note "bag" in quot. 1835) is suggestive of Du. *kerkezakje* for a similar contrivance utilizing a bag, usu. of velvet, on a handle.

1666 *Cambridge Proprietors' Rec.* (1896) 211 Whether the Inhabitants, who are Assessed to pay the Ministers Salary, and put the same into the contribution Box, Shall either put their money in papers... or Shall Mark their Money. **1835** INGRAHAM *South-West.* I. 215 The contribution-box or bag makes its begging tour among the pews. **1899** *Chi. Record* 2 Aug. 4/4 [The Conductor] reaches out the box... just as a church deacon passes the contribution box. **1930** *Amer. Sp.* V. 419 contribution-box: a wooden box with a long handle in which the church collection was taken. [Rural N. Hampshire.] **1948** *Sat. Ev. Post* 7 Aug. 76/3 These boys... stole fruit from stands and light-fingered the China Relief money out of the contribution boxes.

***contrive,** *v. local. tr.* To carry or transport. *Obs.*

"*Contrive*.... I doubt whether this strange expression is ever used at the present day. I never heard it myself, nor have I found any person that has heard it from any class of people in this country" (Pickering 70).

1781 WITHERSPOON *Druid P.* No. 5, I wish we could contrive it to Philadelphia. The words *to carry it, to have it carried*, or some such, are wanting. **1791** in JILSON *Dark & Bl. Ground* 74 When they had contrived the wounded within, they confined themselves to the defence of the fort.

contwisted kənˈtwɪstɪd, *a.* [Of fanciful origin.] Dratted, doggoned, dad-blamed. *Colloq. Obs.* — **1834** CARUTHERS *Kentuckian* I. 23, I wish I may be contwisted. **1845** C. M. KIRKLAND *Western Clearings* 71 His father... tore his boot almost off with what he called 'a contwisted stub of the toe.'

contwistification kənˌtwɪstəfəˈkeʃən, *n.* Bickerings, disturbance, quarrel. *Colloq. Rare.* — **1835** KENNEDY *Horse Shoe Robinson* I. 77 We hold in despise all sorts of contwistifications—either by laying of tongue-traps, or listenings under eaves of houses.

conundered kəˈnʌndɚd, *a.* [App. based on **conundrum.*] Perplexed, confounded. Hence **conunderment.** *Colloq. Rare.* — **1865** A. D. WHITNEY *Gayworthys* 320 Mrs. Hopeley avowed herself 'conundered' to tell. *Ib.* 325 'Well, if I ain't conundered, now!' she exclaimed. *Ib.* 385 This solution of what 'had been, verily, her main conunderment.'

***convention,** *n.*

1. Any one of various conventions, as the Albany Convention of 1754, the first concerted effort of the colonies for political unity, and the Hartford Convention *q.v. Obs.* Cf. **Nashville Convention, Southern Convention.**

1754 FRANKLIN *Writings* III. 207 Plan of Union Adopted by the Convention at Albany; with the Reasons and Motives for Each Article of the Plan. **1814** *Niles' Reg.* VII. 155 Against the resolution proposing a convention of delegates from the New-England states [at Hartford], and the resolutions connected therewith, the undersigned feel bound . . . most earnestly to remonstrate. *Ib.* 257 It is said, in Baltimore, by those disposed to put the most favorable construction on the intended proceedings of the convention at *Hartford*, that they will only propose some amendments to the constitution.

b. An assembly of specially authorized or chosen delegates for forming, ratifying, or amending the federal Constitution or a state constitution.

1776 FITHIAN *Journal* II. 194 Towards evening we were also honoured with the company of Messrs. Hugg, & Leaming two delegates in the New-Jersey Convention. **1783** MORRIS in Sparks *Life G. Morris* (1832) I. 256 Have a convention of the states to form a better constitution. **1910** *New Mex. Const. Convention Proc.* 10 Delegate Catron moved that this Convention extend its sympathy to the family of Mrs. Sargent. **1945** *Christian Cent.* 24 Jan. 116/3 He has proposed a convention to revise the state constitution, suggesting a reapportionment of congressional and senatorial districts.

c. Among the southern states, a meeting of elected delegates for the purpose of formally seceding, or considering secession, from the Union. *Obs.*

1860 in W. R. SMITH *Alabama Convention Hist. & Deb.* 34 The General Assembly at its last session passed . . . resolutions requiring the Governor, in the event of the election of a Black Republican [as president of the U.S.], to order elections to be held for the delegates to a Convention of the State. **1861** *Texas Secession Convention Jrnl.* (1912) 194 It is the sense of this Convention that the jurisdiction of the federal courts of the Confederate States shall be so defined and restricted by law as to avoid a repetition of such abuses.

d. Such a meeting in the southern states to consider ways and means of returning to the Union at the close of the Civil War. *Obs.*

1865 *Nashville Dispatch* 30 Aug. 1/7 The Mississippi Convention has solicited the President, by memorial, to withdraw all colored soldiers from Mississippi. **1865** *Detroit Tribune* 6 Oct. 1/1 A resolution to repeal the ordinance of secession was brought up in the North Carolina Convention yesterday.

2. An extra-legal meeting of delegates, or members, of a political party, usu. for the purpose of selecting candidates for public office, or for drawing up resolutions.

a. As applied to local or state conventions.

1808 *Independent Chron.* (Bost.) 29 Feb. 2/3 A convention of republican delegates from the several towns in the county of Essex. **1840** *Niles' Reg.* 4 July 276/2 The whigs of Maine, through their delegates, assembled in convention at Augusta. **1862** in F. MOORE *Rebellion Rec.* V. I. 8 A Convention of Unionists was held at Nashville, Tennessee, this day.

b. As applied to a congressional caucus. *Obs.*

1808 in M. CAREY *Olive Branch* (1818) 441, I deem it expedient, for the purpose of nominating suitable characters for the president and vice-president of the United States, . . . to call a convention of republican members, to meet at the senate Chamber. **1816** *Niles' Reg.* X. 59/2 *Resolved*, That the practice of nominating candidates for the offices of president and vice president of the United States, by a convention of senators and representatives in congress, is inexpedient and ought not to be continued. **1824** *Nat. Intelligencer* 17 Feb. 1 Heretofore conventions of the Republican Members of Congress, for the nomination of candidates for President and Vice President, have been held upon the presumed approbation of their constituents only.

3. In special combs.: (1) **convention ball,** a ball held in connection with a convention, esp. a ball following the convention which framed the state constitution of California in 1849; (2) **bonnet,** (see quot.), *rare;* (3) **city,** a city in which many conventions are held; (4) **sermon,** a sermon preached in connection with the holding of a convention, *obs.;* (5) **system,** a system of which a convention is a feature, specif. the system by which political parties now nominate candidates for President and Vice-President.

(1) **1889** MUNROE *Golden Days* 347 The great convention ball came to an end. — (2) **1830** ROYALL *Southern Tour* I. 36 These silly women, . . . when the Convention was about to meet, fabricated these large umbrella bonnets, which they named Convention-bonnets. — (3) **1887** C. B. GEORGE *40 Yrs. on Rail* v. 92 Chicago . . . is the greatest railroad center on the globe, [and] is the chief . . . convention city of America. **1912** in *D.N.* VI. 192 Although Baltimore is best known as the 'Monument City,' it long ago achieved a wide distinction as the 'Convention City.' In fact, it can really be said to be the birthplace of the convention system for Presidential nominations. — (4) **1780** CUTLER in *Life & Corr.* I. 78 The Rev. Mr. McCarty . . . [is] to preach the next Convention Sermon. — (5) **1880** *Harper's Mag.* Aug. 470 Meanwhile progress has been made in defining the convention system. **1944** *Chi. D. News* 5 Aug. 7/5 The convention system and electoral college should be abolished and president and vice-president nominated by direct vote of the people.

b. Attrib. with **army, regiment, soldier, troops,** with reference to the British soldiers who surrendered according to the "Convention of Saratoga" in 1777. *Obs.* Cf. * **conventioner.**

"Burgoyne . . . at Saratoga, October 17, . . . surrendered his army, the conditions being that the troops should march to Boston, whence they might return to England with the understanding that unless they were exchanged they were not to serve again in North America during the war" (Bassett *Short Hist. U.S.* 197–98).

1778 in *Amer. Sp.* XX. (1945) 270 A Flagg came up with money for the Convention Troops, and was soon dismissed. **1780** *Heath Papers* 136 Many Convention soldiers get to New York. **1781** WASHINGTON *Diaries* II. 222 The 46th and 86th Regim[en]ts—the first of them being a convention Regim[en]t and the other not in America. **1781** H. HAMILTON in *Hist. MSS Comm.* 9th Rep. App. III. II. 240 The same evening, halting at the house of a rebel, Colonel Lewis, we had the good fortune to see two officers of the Convention Army. **1849** H. HOWE *Hist. Coll. Va.* 165 The British and German prisoners taken at Saratoga in the revolution and known as the 'Convention troops' were sent to Charlottesville in the beginning of the year 1779.

As the last term in **bone, border, commercial, congressional, Constitutional, Continental, county, Democratic, Democratic National, education, federal, Fish Kill, Free Democratic, Hartford, Joint, kangaroo, Kodak, labor, mass, Mississippi reconstruction, mixed, national, nominating, open, party, peeled stick, political, presidential, primary, Republican, rump, secession, silver, snap, soft shell, southern, state, tariff, ward convention.**

convention kən'venʃən, *v. tr.* To establish religious conventions in a region. *Rare.* — **1824** MARSHALL *Kentucky* I. 268 The mighty project, for conventioning the western country, . . . exhibited but the fantasy of an abortion.

* **conventionalist,** *n.* A member or supporter of a constitutional (or similar) convention. *Obs.* Cf. **Hartford convention(al)ist.**

1824 W. N. BLANE *Excursion* 171 Those who have been the cause of this convention [to adopt a state constitution], are the men who have come from the slave-holding States. On their success in getting the votes of two-thirds of the legislature, the Conventionalists assembled at two or three public dinners. **1901** JAMESON & BUEL *Dict. Amer. Hist.* I. 180 *Conventionalists*, in the Pennsylvania politics of 1804–1808, the name assumed by those extreme Democrats who desired to see a new convention called, to modify the Constitution of the State in a radically democratic sense.

* **conventioner,** *n.* **1.** One of the British soldiers surrendered at Saratoga. *Obs.* Cf. * **convention 2. b. 2.** A member of the Constitutional Convention of 1787. Both *rare.* — (1) **1786** in CHALKLEY *Scotch-Irish Settlement Va.* I. 384 Defendants, pretending to have . . . authority to take up and secure any of the . . . soldiers in the British service, commonly called conventioners [etc.]. — (2) **1842** *Supreme Court Rep.* XLI. 638 Let it be remembered, that the conventioners who formed the Constitution, were the representatives of equal sovereignties.

conversation cards. (See quot. 1794.) *Obs.* — **1794** *Balt. D. Intelligencer* 27 Sep. 3/3 Just Published, And for sale . . . (*Price, One Quarter of a Dollar per Pack,*) a new and elegant Edition of the much admired Conversation Cards: Containing a variety of amusing, entertaining, and innocent *Questions* & *Answers* in the art of courtship. Each pack contains 64 cards, 32 questions in black and 32 answers in red. **1827** *Balt. Comm. Chronicle* 9 Aug. 1/1 (*advt.*), Conversation Cards.

* **convict,** *n.* In combs.: (1) **convict camp,** a camp serving as the temporary headquarters of a group of convicts working on roads, levees, etc.; (2) **lease system,** the practice of leasing convicts to a contractor, who uses their labor in a specified manner, usu. in work gangs outdoors; (3) **lessee,** a contractor who leases convicts; (4) **servant (man),** a convict serving time as an indentured servant, *obs.*

(1) **1884** *Cent. Mag.* Feb. 593/2 One can turn again only to leased prisons elsewhere, to find numbers with which to compare the ghastly mortality of some of these Texas convict camps. **1899** CHESNUTT *Wife of His Youth* 317 In the shifting life of the convict camp

they [*sc.* letters] had long since ceased to reach him. — **(2) 1885** *Cent. Mag.* XXX. 687/1 The popular mind has been seduced by the glittering temptations of our Southern convict-lease system. **1911** *Jrnl. Crim. Law & Criminology* March 949 The convict lease system is not only a crime against downfallen humanity, but as a business proposition it is a failure. — **(3) 1887** *Courier-Journal* 19 Feb. 2/3 The Governor . . . ordered the convict lessee to depart his presence. — **(4) 1751** *Virginia Gaz.* 1 Aug. 3/2 Ran away from the Subscriber, last night, a Convict Servant Man, Named Edward Sutton. **1759** *Newport Mercury* 16 Oct. 2/3 Whoever takes up the said Convict Servant, and returns him to his Master, shall have Fifteen Pistoles Reward. **1761** *Pa. Gazette* 8 Oct. 4/3 Run away . . . an English Convict Servant Man.

* **convicted,** *a.* Overcome by the consciousness of sin. *Colloq.*

1822 in MRS. M. B. SMITH *Forty Yrs. Washington Soc.* (1906) 159 A Methodist hymn, sung amidst the groans and sobs of the newly converted, or convicted as they call them. **1845** HOOPER *Suggs* x. 124 By this time it had come to be generally known that the 'convicted' old man was Captain Simon Suggs, the very 'chief of sinners' in all that region. **1885** CRADDOCK *Prophet* 5 'The boys air convicted, then?' he asked. . . . 'The boys hev got thar religion, too,' she faltered.

* **convocation,** *n.* A meeting or organization of the clergymen of part of a diocese.

"The analogue in England is a conference of the clergy of an arch-deaconry or rural deanery" (*OED*).

1692 SEWALL *Diary* I. 367 A bill is sent in about calling a Fast, and Convocation of Ministers, that may be led in the right way as to the Witchcrafts. **1747** D. NEAL *Hist. N.-Eng.* (ed. 2) I. 155 There was no such Thing as a Synod or Convocation in the Country [New England], till the Year 1637. **1906** *Churchman* 20 Oct. 585 The thirty-second annual convocation of the missionary district of Sacramento was held in Trinity church, Sacramento.

convulsion root, weed. Local names for the Indian pipe. — **1876** HOBBS *Bot. Hand-Book* 26 Convulsion weed, Ice Plant, American, Monotropa uniflora. **1891** *Amer. Folk-Lore* IV. 148 Grandmother called *Monotropa uniflora* Convulsion Root. (New Hampshire.)

* **cony,** *n.*

1. A hat made of rabbit fur, instead of beaver. *Rare.*

1855 BARNUM *Life* 99 If a 'peddler' wanted to trade with us for a box of beaver hats . . . he was sure to obtain a box of 'coneys.'

2. The little chief hare, *Ochotana princeps,* of the northern Rocky Mountains region.

1872 *Harper's Mag.* Dec. 32/2 They are said to be a true cony, however, and no marmot, and consequently cannot hibernate like the common woodchuck. **1914** CLEMENTS *Rocky Mt. Flowers* 110 In slide rock and in bouldery moraines up as high as 13,000 feet, one finds the pika, or cony. **1938** THOMPSON *High Trails* 130 The conies are well protected from both the severe weather and attacks from numerous enemies.

3. (See quot. 1889.)

1888 GOODE *Amer. Fishes* 51 The Coney of Key West, *Epinephelus apua,* the Hind of Bermuda, is an important food-fish. **1889** *Cent.* 3990 Nigger-fish . . . is found . . . along the coast of Florida. It is one of the groupers, and is also called . . . cony. **1945** SERVICE *Ploughman* 429 They had little flavour; their flesh was soft and I left most of my catch on the bank. They were what was known as 'coneys.'

Coody ˈkudɪ, *n.* (See quot. 1914.) *Obs.* Cf. **Coot,** *n.*[2]

1814 DE W. CLINTON in Hammond *Hist. Polit. Parties* I. 398 [Coody, alias Verplanck,] has become the head of a political sect called the Coodies, of hybrid nature, composed of the combined spawn of federalism and Jacobinism. **1829** in MACKENZIE *Van Buren* (1846) 218 With all the adroitness peculiar to that family, [Hoffmann] rakes up old prejudices, enlists Duer, who is attached to young Hoffman, with all the coodies, high minded, and Clintonians. **1914** *Cyclo. Amer. Govt.* I. 467 Coodies. The name of a political faction in New York state which sprang up in 1814 under the leadership of Gulian C. Verplanck whose political articles appeared in the New York papers over the name 'Abimaleck Coody.'

Coodyitism ˈkudɪəˌtɪzəm, *n.* The doctrines of the Coodies. *Rare.* — **1815** *Columbian Centinel* 12 April 2/3 Ipswich. Our votes have fallen off; but there have been no converts to Coodyitism.

Coohee ˈkohi, *n.* Also **Cohee.** [See quots. 1834, 1899.] An inhabitant of the mountains of western Virginia and Pennsylvania. Usu. *pl.*

1817 PAULDING *Let. from South* I. 112 The people of whom I am now writing call those east of the mountain Tuckahoes, and their country Old Virginia. They themselves are the Cohees, and their country New Virginia. **1834** CARUTHERS *Kentuckian* II. 192 In Virginia, the inhabitants east of the Blue Ridge are called *Tuckahoes,* and those on the west *Cohees;* as some allege, from the Scotch-Irish phrase '*quo'he*' (quoth he). **1860** *Harper's Mag.* Aug. 350/1 My father often declared that this rough raking from the old Cohee, . . . finally determined him to execute a scheme, . . . of throwing up his commission. **1899** GREEN *Va. Word-book* 96 Coohees, *n. pl.* Of Scotch origin 'Quo'he.' *Coohees* was the nickname applied to people in western Virginia, while those in the east were called 'Tuckahoes.'

* **cook,** *n.* In combs.: (1) **cook-all,** (see quot.), *obs.;* (2) **book,** [cf. G. *kochbuch,* Du. *kookboek*], a book in which recipes for preparing food are given; (3) **camp,** in a logging camp, a building in which food is prepared; (4) **car,** a commissary car on a railroad work train; (5) **fire,** [cf. Du. *kookvuur*], an open-air fire suitable for cooking; (6) **kettle,** [cf. Du. *kookketel*], a cook pot; (7) **oven,** (see quot.); (8) **range,** =**cooking range;** (9) **shack,** a shack in which the cooking is done for a group of cowboys, lumbermen, etc.; (10) **shanty,** =prec.; (11) **stove,** a cooking stove; (12) **tent,** a tent, as with armies, circuses, and other traveling groups, in which food is cooked; (13) **wagon,** a wagon carrying a cook's supplies and equipment, used chiefly on cattle ranges in the West.

(1) 1819 W. FAUX *Memorable Days* 311 Some three families cook and bake in one iron skillet, called the cook-all. — **(2) 1809** R. TYLER *Yankey in London* 179, I can send you an assortment of culinary reviews, vulgarly called cook-books. **1903** *Cin. Enquirer* 2 Jan. 4/4 The cook book is the first aid to dyspepsia. **1946** *This Week Mag.* 17 Aug. 19/1 He isn't satisfied just collecting old cookbooks. — **(3) 1893** *Scribner's Mag.* June 703/2 There is . . . a cook camp, which is a large dining-room and kitchen combined. **1929** F. E. MCCLINCHEY *Joe Pete* 37 Carried . . . to the cook camp where Mabel worked. — **(4) 1910** *Sat. Ev. Post* 23 July 8/2 And quite as important as the crane is the cook-car—generally some old-time coach or sleeper descended to humble service on the road.

(5) 1852 STANSBURY *Gt. Salt Lake* 148 Numbers of the latter tribe hung around the camp, crowding the cook-fires. **1894** WISTER in *Harper's Mag.* LXXXIX. 518/1 Sergeant Keyser . . . had adopted the troop cook fire for his camp guard after the cooks had finished their work. — **(6) 1863** E. KIRKE *Southern Friends* xxi. 215 A large iron pot . . . serving for both washtub and cook-kettle. — **(7) 1926** J. BLACK *You Can't Win* 171 The spots most favored in Chinatown by the hypos and small beggars were the 'cook ovens,' places built back of Chinese lodging houses where the occupants did their cooking on the community plan. — **(8) 1866** *Rep. Indian Affairs* 182 One cook stove, August 14, 1861. One cook range, August 21, 1861. **1924** SHEPHARD *P. Bunyan* 160 The cook-range in Paul's new cook-house was of blue steel and was twenty-four blocks long. — **(9) 1909** WASON *Happy Hawkins* 38. I felt a sting in the left shoulder, spun around and fell, but jumped up just as Jabez changed directions for the cook shack. **1948** *Durant* (Okla.) *D. Democrat* 2 July 1/4 Mr. Smith will speak from his local Bryan County headquarters, a converted cook-shack, located on the Northeast corner of the square.

(10) 1895 *Outing* XXVI. 393/1 It was a blazing bonfire of hemlock bark in a deep hole, which threw a flickering warm light on the side of the cook-shanty. **1921** *Outing* April 19/3 There are, of course, no facilities in the hotel, but arrangements may be made in the cook shanty outside where there are a stove and other amenities. — **(11) 1824** T. B. HAZARD *Nailer Tom's Diary* (1930) 625/1 Sett up the Cook Stoe in the west Room. **1948** *Durant* (Okla.) *D. Democrat* 4 July 2/4 One state senatorial race [is] getting as hot as a $5 cookstove, and the race so unpredictable that little money is being bet by either side. — **(12) 1885** E. B. CUSTER *Boots & Saddles* 53 We looked out, to find the cook-tent blown flat to the ground. **1946** *Trail Riders* Oct. 2/1 That evening the tepees clustered on the edge of the Panther river were a welcome sight, not to mention the smoke from the cook tent. — **(13) 1900** GARLAND *Eagle's Heart* 162 On the ground, scattered among the tents, and in the shade of the cook wagon, were some twenty or thirty herders. **1907** MULFORD *Bar-20* 119 Two cook wagons were stalled a short distance from the corral.

As the last term in **bull, camp, land cook.**

cookage ˈkʊkɪdʒ, *n.* The process of cooking. *Rare.* — **1896** *Columbus* (O.) *Dispatch* 18 July 7/3 Dr. Weber further says that the offensive stench is caused by escaping steam from the cookage of garbage.

cookee ˈkʊkɪ, *n.* [dim. of * *cook, n.*] A camp cook or cook's helper. *Colloq.*

1846 *Spirit of Times* 4 July 218/2 We embarked . . . in company with . . . a cookie who was lord and master of the culinary department. *a***1904** S. E. WHITE *Blazed Trail* i. 12 A fat cook, two bare-armed cookees, . . . were the only human beings in sight. **1944** W. BLAIR *Tall Tale America* 174 Paul always gave any cook as many cookees to help as he needed.

cookeite ˈkʊkaɪt, *n.* [f. J. P. Cooke of Harvard.] A variety of lithium mica. — **1866** *Amer. Jrnl. Sc.* 2 Ser. XLI. 246 On cookeite, a new mineral species. **1868** DANA *Min.* 489 Cookeite. . . . Occurs with tourmaline and lepidolite at Hebron and Paris, Maine.

* **cooking,** *n.* and *a.* In combs.: (1) **cooking book,** =**cookbook,** *rare;* (2) **circle,** a group of women who

meet to cook, usu. for some charitable cause; (3) **class,** a class composed of those learning to cook; (4) **furnace,** =?**bake oven,** *obs.;* (5) **range,** an apparatus for cooking more elaborate than a cookstove, usu. having more than one side oven and a top well supplied with holes having removable covers for pots, pans, etc.; (6) **stove,** a stove designed for use in cooking.

(1) **1891** *N. & Q.* VII. 299 I find 'Chile Sauce' in a cooking book published at San Francisco in 1879.—(2) **1882** M. HARLAND *Eve's Daughters* 321, I enjoy—nobody more—the fun of salad-clubs and cooking-circles. — (3) **1881** *Harper's Mag.* April 667/1 The cooking class under a teacher who has had charge of the 'North End Mission' cooking school in Boston, is a favorite 'branch.' — (4) **1826** *Va. Herald* (Fredericksburg) 30 Aug. 3/5 Agent for sale of Gunpowder, Shot, Stone Ware and Cooking Furnaces.

Cook stove or cooking stove (*c*1835)

(5) **1846** *Boston Herald* 14 Oct. 1/3 Dodd & Wilson . . . now offer one of the best assortments of . . . grates, furnaces, cooking ranges. **1883** *Cent. Mag.* May 76/1 Four suites of rooms, in different quarters of the city, were procured and fitted with counters, tables, crockery, cooking-ranges and furniture. — (6) **1823** R. B. THOMAS *Farmer's Almanack* Jan. 7/2, I have procured me one of Rich's cooking stoves, and think I save half my wood by it nearly. **1894** P. L. FORD *P. Stirling* 55 Four bottles, with the corks partly drawn, were on the cold cooking stove.

cooky ˈkukɪ, *n.* Also **cookie.** [f. Du. *koekje*, little cake. An Amer. borrowing.]

1. A small, flat, sweet cake.

1703 in JUDD *History of Hadley* (1905) 241 The Dutch in New York provided for funerals, rum, beer, gloves, rings; and in 1703, at a funeral, '800 cockies, (cookies or cakes) and one and a half gross of pipes' were furnished. **1784** in VAN SCHAACK *Life Peter Van Schaack* (1842) 360 Little Cornelius is her favorite; she convinces him of her affection by giving him a small present, as Indian sugar, cookies, etc. **1819** J. M. DUNCAN *Travels U.S.* II. 286 He did not remain long enough to eat his cookie, as the little round cake provided for the occasion is called. **1944** *This Week Mag.* 7 Oct. 18 On the square is the way to cut baking-powder biscuits and cookies.

b. Attrib. with **cutter, jar, sheet, shop, tin.**

1903 *Sears Cat.* (ed. 113) 355/2 Cookey Cutters. **1948** *This Week Mag.* 9 Oct. 28/3 With a cooky cutter, Mrs. Wilson removed a circle from each slice. — **1945** *Chi. Tribune* 8 Jan. 13/1 (*advt.*), The lid of my cookie jar . . . will always be open to your drivers! **1947** *Chi. Tribune* 2 Nov. VII. 10/1 Little Willie had been scolded many times for getting into the cookie jar between meals. — **1929** *Ladies' Home Jrnl.* Oct. 110/2 Drop it on a buttered cooky sheet from the end of a spoon. **1944** *Sears Cat.* (ed. 189) 739 Cookie Sheets. For any type of oven. — **1888** BILLINGS *Hardtack* 131 Their culinary skill—or lack of it—was little appreciated by men within easy reach of home, friends, and cooky shops. — **1947** *Nat. Geog. Mag.* Feb. 142/2 A cooky tin produced pleated, ribbonlike strips.

c. *To bet* (or *wager*) *a cooky*, to express assurance by pretending to wager a small amount. *Colloq.*

1843 STEPHENS *High Life N.Y.* II. 37 But look a here, I'll bet a cookey you can't turn that into fust rate English as soon as I can. **1874** ALDRICH *P. Palfrey* vi, I'd wager a cookey, now, young Dent has ben settin' up to that Palfrey gal, an' there's ben trouble. **1944** *Reader's Digest* Aug. 108, I'll bet a cookie the safety valve is tied down right now.

2. Applied to a person, often disparagingly. *Slang.*

1920 *Collier's* 6 March 42/3 That girl friend of yours is a cookie—hey, what? **1928** *Chi. Tribune* 7 Oct. (Comics) 2 What a swell bunch of cookies you turned out to be. **1948** *Atlantic Mo.* Jan. 27/2 The private dick is a very tough cookie indeed, who can break a man's wrist without a quiver of distaste.

As the last term in **chocolate, drop, ginger, molasses, New Year, seed cooky.**

* **cooler,** *n.*

1. =**water cooler.**

1838 *N.Y. Mirror* 13 Jan. 229/1 The peculiar philosophical effect of this cooler . . . we are unable to explain; but of its cooling properties no doubt can exist. **1888** *Cent. Mag.* XXXVI. 771/2 A car, that had . . . its painted tin cooler with the refreshing liquid ice-water. **1905** F. H. SMITH *At Close Range* 250, 'I'll go to the cooler and wash up what I can . . .' she said . . . as she . . . made her way to the wash-basin.

2. App. some kind of coat or tunic. *Obs.*

1848 *Knickerb.* XXXII. 227 What if his waistcoat boasted but two . . . buttons, and his ill-fitted cooler came but half-way down to the bend of his knee in a spare 'swallow-tail' behind? **1880** N. BROOKS *Fairport Nine* 25 In summer time he wore a parti-colored tunic, or cooler.

3. A jail or prison. *Slang.*

1884 *Milnor* (Dak.) *Teller* 8 Aug., Two Milnor bloods were . . . arrested on the charge of drunkeness [*sic*] lodged in the cooler over night and then fined $5 in the morning. **1947** *Time* 3 Feb. 20/3 Judge Moore just gave him twelve months in the cooler.

b. *To put in the cooler*, to shelve or put aside. *Colloq.*

1906 *N.Y. Ev. Post* 30 Jan. 1 This is taken to indicate that, to use the legislative phrase, the resolution will be 'put in the cooler' for the time, and only released if public pressure gets too strong.

As the last term in **coffee, ice, milk, water cooler.**

cooley, variant of **coulee.**

Coolidge tube. A tube devised by Wm. David Coolidge, an American physicist, for generating X rays. — **1915** *Nature* 15 April 195/2 The Coolidge tube is based on the discharge of independent electrons. **1925** *Wall St. Jrnl.* 12 Jan. 10/1 He showed the great contribution of the General Electric research laboratories . . . in the invention of the Coolidge X-ray tube, fused quartz and the Mercury boiler.

coolieism ˈkulɪˌɪzəm, *n.* The system of importing coolies to secure cheap labor. *Obs.* — **1870** *Cong. Globe* 21 Jan. 654/1 [To seek to produce manufactures] by reductions on labor alone, . . . is to depress labor, not to protect it. To seek it by Chinese immigration in the form of coolieism is still worse. **1879** *Calif. Constitution* Art. xix, § 4 Asiatic coolieism is a form of human slavery, and is forever prohibited in this State.

Hence **coolieite,** designating one who is friendly to coolieism. *Rare.* — **1876** *L.A. Wkly. Herald* 12 Aug. 2/2 He can't be very sincere, however, or he would abandon his coolieite political bed-fellows.

cooling board. A board or slab upon which a corpse is placed during preparation for burial. — **1853** SIMMS *Sword & Distaff* 224 He wouldn't care ef I was on my cooling board to-morrow. **1896** J. C. HARRIS *Sister Jane* 19 I'm old and ugly, but I don't want to be put on my cooling-board on account of driving a new set of nails in the front palings.

coolweed ˈkulˌwid, *n.* The clearweed or richweed, *Pilea pumila.* — **1843** TORREY *Flora N.Y.* II. 223 *Adike pumila.* . . . Richweed. Coolweed. . . . Moist shady places, particularly in cool ravines. **1889** *Cent.* 1250 Coolweed, . . . so called from its succulent pellucid stems and its habit of growing in cool places.

* **coolwort,** *n.* **1.** The false miterwort, *Tiarella cordifolia.* **2.** The bishop's cap or miterwort, genus *Mitella.*

(1) **1848** BARTLETT 90 Coolwort (*Tiarella cordifolia*), the popular name of an herb, the properties of which are diuretic and tonic. It is prepared by the Shakers. **1850** S. F. COOPER *Rural Hours* 85 The white cool-wort is mingled in light and airy tufts with the blue and yellow violets. **1891** *Cent.* 6326 *Tiarella cordifolia*, native from Canada to Virginia, is called false miterwort and coolwort. — (2) **1891** *Amer. Folk-Lore* IV. 148 Our name for *Mitella diphylla* was Coolwort.

coon kun, *n.* [See **aracoun.**]

1. =**raccoon.**

1742 HEMPSTEAD *Diary* 388 Josh . . . kiled another Coon to Day. **1857** *Lawrence* (Kan.) *Republican* 11 June 4 Ben and his master had many a tiresome tramp through the woods after coons. **1948** *Bangor* (Me.) *D. News* 28 July 2/1 In New York, a coon came out second in their contest for occupancy of a trail shelter.

b. Used as food.

1852 J. REYNOLDS *Hist. Illinois* 205 They hunted, marched slow, and lived well, in comparison to the time they ate the coon. **1898** DUNBAR *Folks from Dixie* 7 Scouring the woods . . . hunting for that venison of the negro palate,—'coon.

2. A fellow, usu. of a rustic, frontier type. *Colloq.* Cf. **old coon.**

1832 *Polit. Examiner.* (Shelbyville, Ky.) 8 Dec. 4/1, I was always reckoned a pretty slick koon for a trade. *a***1855** KELLEY *Humors* 317

Did you ever see a real, true, unadulterated specimen of *Down East*, enter a store, or other place of everyday business, for the purpose of 'looking around,' or *dicker* a little? They are 'coons,' they are, upon all such occasions. **1897** THANET *Missionary Sheriff* 13, I tell you the coons that say you never must hit a woman don't know anything about that sort of women.

b. *Polit.* A picture or representation of a coon used as a party emblem by the Whigs during the presidential campaign of 1840. Hence a nickname for a Whig. Cf. **old coon.**

1842 *Washington Globe* 1 Nov. 3/4 The Coons have heretofore sailed under colors belying their principles. **1859** GRATTAN *Civilized Amer.* I. 305 The word Coon was, on the other hand, applied by the Democratic party to the Whigs, because some stuffed skins of that animal (the racoon) had been hoisted by them as emblems of hunting prowess, during the Presidential contest in 1840, and because of a ludicrous fable (the point of which consisted in a racoon calling out to a marksman who levelled his rifle at it, 'I'm a gone coon!'). **1892** W. S. WALSH *Literary Curiosities* 190 In American politics, coon was a nickname for a Whig, first applied during the Presidential campaign of 1836.

c. A Negro. *Slang.*

1862 *Songs for the Times* 3 Play up, Pomp, you yaller coon. **1903** *Cin. Enquirer* 2 May 11/5 What is called in New York a 'coon' is in St. Louis a 'shine.' **1948** *Chi. Defender* 23 Oct. 7/2 A lot of us are referred to as 'nigger,' 'coon,' 'darky,' etc., right to our faces and can't do anything about it if we want to keep our jobs, our credit, our property, or life and limbs.

d. Short for **coon oyster.**

1944 HARNETT T. KANE *Deep Delta Country* 101 The oysters overcrowd and starve each other until they become 'coons.'

3. In colloq. combs.: (1) **coon cat,** =**cacomistle;** (2) **country,** a region where coons are plentiful; (3) **dog,** a dog especially good at hunting coons; (4) **dog principle,** the principle that a person, etc., must be good for a certain purpose because he is assuredly not good for anything else; (5) **fashion,** in the fashion or manner of a coon, cf. **coon,** *v.* **1;** (6) **grape,** the bluish, grape-like but inedible fruit of a vine, *Ampelopsis cordata*, found in the southeastern states, also the fox grape, *Vitis labrusca;* (7) **heel,** (see quot.); (8) **hound,** =**coon dog;** (9) **hunt,** a hunt for coons, also **coon hunter, coon hunting;** (10) **oyster,** (see quots.); (11) **root,** (see quot.); (12) **'s age,** a very long time (cf. *EDD* "crow's age" in same sense); (13) **skin,** see as a main entry; (14) **tail,** the hornwort, *Ceratophyllum demersum*, also attrib.

(1) **1918** *Nat. Geog. Mag.* May 482/2 In the United States it is known by several other names, including 'civet cat,' 'coon cat,' and 'band-tailed cat.' **1947** CAHALANE *Mammals No. Amer.* 166 The other common names [of the cacomistle] arose from the bicolored tail: coon cat, band-tailed cat, and ringtail.— (2) **1941** WHITE *One Man's Meat* 269 The best coon country is always far away. — (3) **1833** J. HALL *Harpe's Head* 230 An old 'coon dog, has a face covered with scars. **1945** BOTKIN *My Burden* 176 She a mightly good possum and coon dog. — (4) **1878** BEADLE *Western Wilds* 173 On the Hoosier's 'Coon-dog principle,' [the region] ought to be rich in mines.

(5) **1863** *Ladies' Repository* XXIII. 89 A large tree from each side is felled, that enables us to place poles from one to the other. Upon these we crawl over in what is called the 'coon fashion.' — (6) **1941** LYON *Hills* 252 They's possum grapes, coon grapes, and fox grapes, all mixed up! — (7) **1881** E. INGERSOLL *Oyster Industry* 243 *Coon Heel.*—A long, slim oyster (Connecticut.) — (8) **1920** *Outing* April 59/3 For Sale—a few as good Coon Hounds and mixed hunters as live. **1947** *Sports Afield* Dec. 87/1 Airdale terriers, hounds, collies, or a mixture of breeds, are coon 'hounds' as long as they're able to find and follow a coon's trail and have sense enough to sit and yap under whatever tree the coon finally climbs. — (9) **1835** AUDUBON *Ornith. Biog.* III. 235 With your leave, then, Reader, I will take you to a 'Coon Hunt.' **1840** *S. Lit. Messenger* VI. 386/1 He is fond of possum, rabbit, and coon-hunting. **1946** *Illinois Conservation* Winter 26/1 A damp breeze probably aroused more than a few 'coon hunters.

(10) **1870** *Amer. Naturalist* III. 460 The small oysters . . . are not generally eaten except by the racoons, hence the common name for them of 'coon oysters.' **1946** WOODARD *Word-List* 10 coon oyster: *n.* A long, narrow sharp-shelled oyster found in marshes. Usually in clusters, sometimes a dozen to a cluster. Pamlico and Carteret counties, 1900–46. Common. — (11) **1893** *Amer. Folk-Lore* VI. 137 *Sanguinaria Canadensis* . . . puccoon root. Anderson, Ind. coon-root. West Va. — (12) **1843** in THOMPSON *M. Jones* (1872) 129 Mary soon got over her skare, but the way she's mad at cousin Pete won't wear off in a coon's age. **1948** *Okla. City Times* 14 June 1/2 Haven't had so much fun in a coon's age. — (14) **1915** MCATEE *Wild-Duck Foods* 24 The seeds of coontail are eaten by practically all wild ducks, but the foliage by a much smaller number and less frequently. **1947** BROWN *Outdoors Unlimited* 48 Gone are the coon-tail moss . . . and other aquatic naturals which once fed the migrations.

b. In obs. expressions alluding to Whigs and their presidential campaigns, as (1) **coon campaign,** (2) **club,** (3) **Congress,** (4) **-dom,** (5) **singer,** (6) **song,** [This early use of "coon song" is app. not related to the much later use shown in **c.** below]; (7) **tavern.**

"The Democratic editors are doubling the 'o' in such words as the following: Convention, *Coon*vention,—Congress, *Coon*gress,—Consistency, *Coon*sistency."—*Quincy* (Ill.) *Herald*, 1843, 17 Jan. 2/3.

(1) *c***1887** *Scribner's Mag.* May 621/1 The venerable Mr. Pratt . . . remained clean-shaven in pious memory of Henry Clay and the coon campaign. — (2) **1844** *Louisville Pub. Advertiser* 17 Feb. 1/3 The Richmond Whig hoists over the notices of the meeting of the coon club in that city the picture of a bare-head, bare-footed boy on a bob tailed horse. — (3) **1844** *Republican Sentinel* (Richmond, Va.) 13 April 2/2 The last Congress was a Coon Congress. — (4) **1848** *N.Y. Wkly. Tribune* 1 April 5/4 The universal kingdom of Koondom is just now in a deplorable fix. **1848** *Field Piece* (Chi.) 13 Sep. 4/1 The Locofocos are designating the Taylor party as the Kingdom of Coondom.

(5) **1844** *Republican Sentinel* (Richmond, Va.) 10 Aug. 3/3 Mr. Duffield, (the Coon Singer,) was there, and aided by the Glee Club, made a powerful impression. — (6) *Ib.* 4 May 3/3 We had the pleasure of listening to some exquisite airs in front of the Governor's House, and forcibly contrasted their influence with the absurd and degrading 'Coon Songs,' which have so often filled the Clay Cabins. — (7) **1844** BROWN in *Edin. Jrnl.* I. 264 It now possessed three meeting-houses, a loco-foco and a 'coon' tavern, and a temperance house.

c. Denoting or relating to Negroes in slang expressions, as **coon baby, barber shop, bellhop, shouter, slugger, song, town, whelp.**

1905 N. DAVIS *Northerner* 153 Isn't she a dream of a coon baby? — **1901** HARRIGAN *Mulligans* 110 That's fine stuff to read in a coon barber shop! — **1912** COBB *Back Home* 224 He's got every coon bellhop around the place fighting for a chance to wait on him. —**1945** *Newsweek* 26 March 108/2 She sang first in the German Village, a big, old-fashioned beer garden. Then she became a black-faced coon shouter. — **1877** in H. ASBURY *Underworld of Chicago* (1941) 80 Prospect of a Prize Fight Between Two Noted Coon Sluggers. — **1896** *N.Y. Dramatic News* 18 July 11/4 Caroline Hull has met with success in singing Thomas LaMark's new coon song, 'Black Baby Mine.' **1948** MENCKEN *Supp.* II. 644/1 This was broadcast in 1900 by Just Because She Made Dem *Goo-goo* Eyes, a coon-song by Hughie Cannon (words) and Johnny Queen (music). — **1898** *K.C. Star* 18 Dec. 4/6 A Tremendous Hit, The Comedy Success, A Trip to Coontown! — **1837** BIRD *Nick of Woods* I. 223 You half-niggurs! you 'coon-whelps! you snakes! you varmints!

d. In colloq. phrases: (1) *To tree the coon*, to solve a problem, to corner a sought-after person; (2) *to skin* (or *hunt*) *the same old coon*, etc., to defeat the Whigs again (cf. sense **2. b.**), also to do a thing again and again; (3) in comparisons of obvious meaning; (4) *to go the whole coon*, (see quot.), *rare;* (5) *to be coon*, to be wise, alert, or "fly," *obs.*

(1) [**1834** CARUTHERS *Kentuckian* I. 96 You see he has the rogue in the city like a coon when he's treed; an old dog's better than a young one in such a fix.] **1840** *Kentucky Rifle* 31 Oct., They've treed the coon. **1852** STOWE *Uncle Tom* xvii, Well, Tom, yer coons are farly treed.

(2) **1842** [see **coonism**]. **1848** LOWELL *Bigelow P.* 1 Ser. v, The perfection o' bliss Is in skinnin' thet same old coon,' sez he. **1865** *Wilkes' Spirit of Times* 11 March 23/1 In the fifth, sixth and eighth innings, they clung also to that 'same old coon,' in the shape of an O. **1879** LOWELL *Poetical Wks.* 384 Meanwhile I inly curse the bore of hunting still the same old coon.

(3) **1846** CORCORAN *Pickings* 47 To use his own words, 'he dropped on him like a catamount on a coon.' **1847** ROBB *Squatter Life* 106, I slid atween 'em [snags and sawyers], sarpentine fashion, and got over clar as a pet coon. **1874** E. EGGLESTON *Circuit Rider* iv. 48 You're cross as a coon when it's cornered. **1910** in HODGE *Amer. Indians* II. 348 To be 'as forlorn as an unmated coon' is to be extremely wretched.

(4) **1892** W. S. WALSH *Literary Curiosities* 190 *Coon, Go the whole*, an American equivalent for 'go the whole hog.'

(5) **1852** *Calif. Sun. Dispatch* (S.F.) 18 Jan. 1/5, I know it's a humbug afore I commence: cause that ere Barnum lays the hose of the whole concern. . . . May be he aint coon!

As the last term in **gone, old, Zip Coon.**

coon kun, *v.* [f. the noun.]

1. *intr.* To go slowly, clumsily, stealthily, in the manner of a coon (see quot. 1917). *Colloq.*

1834 A. PIKE *Sketches* 77 (Th.), Irwin was obliged to straddle the log, and, as they quaintly call in the west 'coon it across.' **1886** *Cent.*

Mag. Nov. 16/2, (*footnote*) In trying to 'coon' across Knob Creek on a log, Lincoln fell in. **1917** KEPHART *Camping* II. 44 Don't be ashamed to get down and straddle the log, and 'coon it,' hunching yourself along with hands and thighs.

b. *To coon a fence, log, pole,* to go hesitatingly or in a clinging manner along a fence, log, or pole. *Colloq.*

1835 CYRUS P. BRADLEY *Journal* (1906) 245 'Cooning the fence'—that is . . . clinging to the fence-rails with fingers and toes and worming along the best manner the case will admit of. **1835** SIMMS *Partisan* 320 That sort of locomotion which, in the South and West, is happily styled 'cooning the log.' **1926** LORD *Frontier Dust* 190, I would show her how a Yankee could coon a pole.

2. *tr.* To steal. *Slang.*

1890 *Rockford* (Wash.) *Enterprise* 23 Aug. 3/1 One of our lads while 'cooning' apples in town this week was caught and badly scared. **1916** WILSON *Red Gap* 92, 'I found 'em,' pleaded the bad man. . . . 'Cooned 'em, you mean!' thundered the judge. 'You cooned 'em from Buck or Sandy.' **1948** *Antioch Rev.* Autumn 160 Nearly every man that had cooned a horse in the county was in cahoots with them.

coona ˈkunə, *n. S.W.* [Sp. *cuna* in Amer. Sp. sense shown here.] A kind of dance.

1846 EMORY *Military Reconn.* 43 This cold and formal dance soon gave way to the more joyous dances of the country, the Coona, the Bolero, and the Italiana. **1902** *Out West* Sep. 283 The favorite dance of Old California [was] the Cuna, or 'Cradle-Waltz.' **1939** VESTAL *Old Santa Fe Trail* 272 The Mexicans did most of the prancing, engaged in such 'lascivious' dances as the waltz, or in some of their charming folk dances such as the *cuna*.

cooncan ˈkunˌkæn, *n.* [Variant of ∗*conquian* (Sp. *con quién,* with whom), in sense shown here.] =**rummy 2.** — **1889** *Cent. Mag.* April 905/1 The men got out a pack of Mexican cards and gambled at a game called 'Coon-can' for a few nickels and dimes. **1944** *Pocket B. of Games* 60 Derived from a Spanish game, known as Con Quien?, it is scarcely fifty years old. The original name was corrupted in the English-speaking countries to Coon-Can, and was named Rum, or Rummy—meaning odd, or queer—by the English.

coonee-lattee ˈkunɪˌlætɪ, *n.* [?Amer. Indian.] The mockingbird. *Rare.* — **1835** SIMMS *Yemassee* I. 73 The Catawba . . . speaks with the trick-tongue of the Coonee-lattee. [Note] The mocking bird. *Ib.* 169 The Coonee-latee, or Trick-tongue of the Yemassees—together with the gleesome murmur of zephyr and brook, gave to the scene an aspect of wooing and seductive repose.

cooner ˈkunɚ, *n.* One who hunts coons, sense **1.** *Rare.* — **1900** BACHELLER *E. Holden* 5 He was what they call in the north country 'a natural cooner.' After nightfall, . . . he spoke in a whisper and had his ear cocked for coons.

coonery ˈkunərɪ, *n.* The doctrines of the Whig party. *Obs.* Cf. **coon,** *n.* **2. b.** — **1843** *Missouri Republican* 21 March (Th.), The beggary which Whiggery (or, to adopt the latest alias, Coonery) has brought upon the Government. *a***1859** *Boston Post* (B.), Democrats, . . . we must achieve a victory— . . . coonery must fall with all its corruptions and abominations.

Cooneyite ˈkunɪ·aɪt, *n.* (See quot.) *Rare.* — **1856** *Spirit of Times* 4 Oct. 70/3 Those dwellers of the old dominion [=Virginia] are here [in Washington, D.C.] nick-named 'Cooneyites,' and are the greatest drinkers of bad whiskey extant.

cooniness ˈkunɪnɪs, *n.* The quality of being sly and furtive, like a coon. *Rare.* — **1944** *Harper's Mag.* June 44/1 Mr. Dewey began to be a candidate a good many years ago and has conducted himself with such a professional sagacity, not to say cooniness, that not much is known about him.

cooning ˈkunɪŋ, *n.* **1.** The hunting of coons. Also attrib. **2.** Creeping in the manner of a coon. Cf. **coon,** *v.* **1,** quot. 1917. Both *colloq.*

(1) **1830** *Palladium of Brit. No. Amer.* (Toronto) 29 Aug. 244/1 [He] jumps into a dug out and goes a coonin'. **1876** BURROUGHS *Winter Sunshine* 85 At this time, cooning in the remote interior is a favorite pastime. *Ib.* 86 Then follows a pell-mell rush of the cooning party up the hill. **1934** LOMAX *Amer. Ballads* 252, I met Colonel Davy, and he was goin' a-coonin'. — (2) **1883** SHIELDS *S. S. Prentiss* 27 The crossing of such a [log] bridge, in Western parlance, is styled *cooning*.

coonish ˈkunɪʃ, *a.* Like a coon. Also with reference to the Whigs. *Obs.* — **1840** HALIBURTON *Clockmaker* 3 Ser. ii, I thought I should a-died for shame one minit, and the next I felt so coonish I had half a mind to fly at the Speaker and knock him down. *Ib.* xiv, The old women began to whisper and look coonish, and, at last . . . I got a notice to make myself scarce from Judge Lynch. **1843** *Quincy* (Ill.) *Herald* 24 Jan. 2/3 Coming as it does directly upon the heels of the great Coonish change of 1840, it presents many gratifying peculiarities.

coonism ˈkunɪzəm, *n.* A term formerly used for the Whigs collectively or their doctrines and practices. *Obs.* Cf. **coon,** *n.* **2. b.** — **1842** *Spirit of Times* 9 Oct. (Th.), Ohio has gone most unexpectedly for Democracy,—has skinned the coons, and repudiated Coonism, Federalism, Clayism, and every other species of Whiggism. **1844** *Republican Sentinel* (Richmond, Va.) 22 June 3/4 You must gather under the banner of Polk and Dallas, and free yourselves from all such humbugs as Log Cabins, Clayism, Coonism, Federalism, and all such nonsense.

coonjine ˈkunˌdʒaɪn, *n.* [Origin unknown.] (See quot. 1941.) Also as a verb. *Slang.*

1896 *The Bully* (A song), I coonjined in the front door, the coons were dancing high. **1933** *Amer. Sp.* Dec. 77/2 Coonjining is the peculiar gait or shuffle that darkies of more than fifty years ago sometimes indulged in, especially along the shores of the Mississippi. **1941** *Chr. Sci. Mon.* (Wkly. Mag. Sec.) 3 May 11 Coonjine, a word used originally on the river for the waddling run of Negro rousters with freight across the stage or gangplank. . . . There's almost as much side as forward motion to it. From the gait the word got to mean the songs and jingles to the singing of which the Negro rousters jerked themselves along. **1944** W. BLAIR *Tall Tale America* 211 At work, he'd joke and sing his songs,—coonjine, and he was a good worker. **1948** *Sat. Review* 26 June 15/1 The wagoners who drove the six-horse teams across the Alleghenies, the Negro roustabouts who coonjined freight up and down the stage planks of our river steamers . . . have gone with the Conestoga wagons and the gleaming side-wheel packets.

coonjiner ˈkunˌdʒaɪnɚ, *n.* One who coonjines. *Slang.* — **1907** C. D. STEWART *Partners* 87 There was Blue and Red, which was our best coonjiners.

coonship ˈkunʃɪp, *n.* The state of being a coon in the sense of a Whig. *Obs.* — **1842** *Spirit of Times* (Phila.) 20 Oct. (Th.), 'Twas there his coonship sat in state, a-watching of the moon, O the instant you'd lay eyes on him, you'd know that same Old Coon. **1844** *Republican Sentinel* (Richmond, Va.) 15 June 1/5 There grew around his *tale* a bright, white ring, which so beautified his Coonship, that the Republicans fell in love with him.

coonskin ˈkunˌskɪn, *n.*

1. The skin of a raccoon. Also attrib.

[**1624** *Smith Generall History* III. ii. 48 *Powhatan* . . . sat covered with a great robe, made of *Rarowcun* skinnes.] **1818** A. ROYALL *Lett. from Ala.* 103 He . . . axed Marchant if he didn't want to trade for some coonskins. **1895** *Cent. Mag.* Aug. 620/2 The darkies used to drag a coon-skin through the woods, and run mongrels after it. **1947** *Sports Afield* Dec. 31/3 Coon fur is not as valuable as it was in the heyday of the coonskin coat.

b. Used as a party symbol by the Whigs, esp. in the presidential campaign of 1840. Also attrib. *Obs.*

1840 *Niles' Reg.* 14 March 21/2 The delegation from Fairfield county . . . came, carriages, horsemen, music; . . . then the 'Mad river trappers' in their lodge, . . . 'coon skins' nailed on the sides. **1841** *Cong. Globe* 3 Feb. 147 The log cabins and coon skin banners, which you used so successfully in the late contest; will not avail you now. **1846** CORCORAN *Pickings* 154 If I find they are locofocos, I damn coon skins, log cabins, and hard cider. **1885** *Harper's Mag.* Oct. 743/1 This law grew out of the 'log-cabin, hard-cider, and 'coonskin' campaign of 1840.

2. coonskin cap, a round cap made of the skin of a coon or coons, usu. with the tail of the animal hanging down the wearer's back. Hence **coonskin-capped.**

1836 SIMMS *Mellichampe* i, He gathered up his rifle, drew the 'coonskin cap over his eyes, and at once fell in procession with the rest.

Coonskin cap

1881 *Harper's Mag.* April 712/1 As for . . . plains-men and coon-skin-capped hunters . . . of the 'West,' . . . you see no more of them. **1948** *Chi. D. News* 9 Aug. 10/2 Kefauver posed for campaign pictures wearing a coon-skin cap.

coonskinner ˈkunˌskɪnɚ, *n.* A supporter of the Whig party, whose symbol was a coonskin. *Obs.* Cf. **coon,** *n.* **2. b.** — **1842** *Cong. Globe* App. 9 July 650/1 What can be a more protective tariff? Why, there is not a tariff in the world half so dear to a coonskinner.

coontie ˈkuntɪ *n.* [Seminole *kunti,* coontie flour.] Any one of various tropical woody plants of the genus *Zamia,* or a kind of arrowroot obtained from its roots and stems. Also attrib.

1791 W. BARTRAM *Travels* 241 A very agreeable, cooling sort of jelly, which they [Indians in Florida] call conte, . . . is prepared from the root of the China briar. **1800** B. HAWKINS *Sk. Creek Country* 21

This [China] briar is called *Coonte*, and the bread made of it . . . is an important article of food among the hunters. **1837** WILLIAMS *Florida* 33 The inhabitants living principally on fish, turtle, and coonti. **1944** BARBOUR *Eden* 49 The basis of the *sofkee* used to be the arrowroot-like starch which is made from the coomtie [*sic*] plant. But the coomtie does not grow abundantly where the Indians are now forced to live, and grits is the ordinary substitute.

coony ˈkunɪ, *a.* Sly and cunning, like a coon. *Slang.* — **1903** *Springfield* (Mass.) *Republican* 29 Aug., The coony Vickers allowed but two hits, and only one of the 'Reds' crossed the plate. **1947** *Time* 27 Jan. 20/2 Ezell ran a coony eye over the new Georgia constitution.

∗ **coop,** *n.* **1.** A place in which voters are assembled and held. *Obs.* Cf. ∗ **coop,** *v.* **2.** *To fly* (or *clear*) *the coop,* to depart without notice, escape, elope. *Slang.*

(1) **1889** *Pall Mall Gaz.* 18 Feb. 6/2 They were made to vote the ticket of the party that controlled the 'coop.' Our coop was in the rear of an engine-house on Calvert-street. — (2) **1839** in *Amer. Sp.* XXI. (1946) 116/2 A tin pedlar has cleared the coop, hook and line, bob and sinker, without being able to square his accounts! **1901** LIMERICK *Toothsome Tales* 68 (We.), Then he'd fly the coop. **1947** *Chi. Sun* 26 Dec. 38/2 The first thing you know they will all fly the coop.

As the last term in **fish, marquee, sweating coop.**

∗ **coop,** *v. tr.* (See quot. 1885.) *Obs.*

1844 *Lexington Observer* 16 Oct. 2/3 He is said to have been 'cooped' by the locofocos. **1885** *Mag. Amer. Hist.* XIII. 99/2 Coop, to 'coop voters' is to collect them as it were in a coop or cage, so as to be sure of their services on election day. **1889** *Pall Mall Gaz.* 18 Feb. 6/2 Four of us, including [E. A.] Poe . . . were nabbed by a gang of men who were on the look out for voters to 'coop.'

coop-and-seek. The game of hide-and-seek. *Rare.* — **1884** *Advance* (Chi.), And then we play at coop and seek.

cooped voter. (See quot.) *Rare.* — **1888** M. LANE in *America* 27 Sep. 15 Cooped voters, a lot of voters, collected and kept under a kind of guard, so that the other side cannot get at them. They are usually well fed and liquored, and on election day are taken to the polls and voted, being carefully watched to see that no one tampers with them.

∗ **Cooper,** *n.*[1] **1. Cooper's hawk,** a large American hawk, *Accipiter cooperi.* **2. Cooper's sandpiper,** (see quot.). **3. Cooper tanager,** a western form of the summer tanager *q.v.*

(1) **1828** BONAPARTE *Ornithology* II. 1 Cooper's Hawk. *Falco Cooperii. Ib.* 9 The Male Cooper's Hawk is eighteen inches in length. **1948** *Pacific Discovery* Mar.–Apr. 18/2 The Cooper hawk [is] sulking among the shrubs at the back of the Aquarium. — (2) **1874** COUES *Birds N.W.* 491 Cooper's sandpiper.—*Tringa cooperi,* . . . *Hab.*—Long Island. The type specimen remains unique. — (3) **1915** *Nat. & Science on Pac. Coast* 112 The Lucy warbler, . . . Cooper tanager, . . . and a score of other species, are but summer visitants.

∗**cooper** ˈkupɚ, *n.*[2] [f. the verb.] One who assembles and holds voters in order to vote them on a particular side. *Obs.* — **1885** *Mag. Amer. Hist.* XII. 99/2 Liquor dealers are the usual 'coopers,' for obvious reasons.

∗**cooper,** *v. tr.* To understand. *Rare.* — *a***1889** in BARRERE-LELAND I. 270 Why on earth nature made you in the shape she did is more than I can cooper.

∗ **coöperationist,** *n.* Formerly in South Carolina, one favoring coöperation with the federal government in its efforts to deal with slavery. *Obs.* Cf. next.

1851 *Harper's Mag.* IV. 120/1 The following table shows the relative strength of each party in the State—those in favor of the Union as it is, of course, voting with the Co-operationists. *Ib.* III. 557/2 A letter . . . was also read, reflecting in severe terms upon the spirit manifested by the 'actionists' toward the 'co-operationists.' **1852** *Whig Almanac* (N.Y. 1867) 43/2 The Co-Operationists . . . carried six districts; and the Secessionists . . . carried one. **1861** *Charleston* (S.C.) *Mercury* 8 Jan. 3/4 Ninety-two, out of one hundred and thirty-two counties, thus far heard from, have elected 142 secessionists, and 68 co-operationists.

coöperation party. A party in South Carolina made up of those desirous of coöperating with the federal government and thus avoiding civil strife over slavery. *Obs.* — **1851** in EASTERBY *S.C. Rice Plant.* (1945) 109 He is one of the Cooperation party, and is of course of the majority.

coöperative apartment. An apartment building owned jointly by those occupying units in it. — **1932** WASHBURN & DELONG *High & Low Financiers* 86 He purchased a fourteen-room cooperative apartment . . . for one hundred and forty-eight thousand dollars. **1948** *Time* 28 June 13/1 It provided only for a government secondary market for G.I. mortgages, authorized veterans cooperative apartments.

Coos koˈus, *n.* [See **cohoes** and quot. 1907 below.] (See quots.)

1797 in *D.N.* II. 350 The Ct. House . . . commands a pleasing prospect of . . . the Great Ox-bow of Connecticut River, where are the rich intervale lands called the Little Coos. *a***1817** DWIGHT *Travels* II. 135 Lancaster and Northumberland in New Hampshire, and the towns opposite to them in Vermont, compose a tract, long known in New England by the name of the *Upper Coos.* **1881** *Amer. Naturalist* XV. 426 The country [in N.E. Vermont] . . . was called by the Indians 'Coos,' which word in the Abenaqui language is said to signify 'the Pines.' **1907** HODGE *Amer. Indians* I. 342 Coosuc (from *koash* 'pine,' *ak* 'at:' 'at the pine'). A small band, probably of the Pennacook, formerly living about the junction of the Upper and Lower Ammonoosuc with the Connecticut.

∗ **coot,** *n.*[1] Any one of various surf ducks or scoters of the genus *Oidemia.*

1791 BARTRAM *Travels* 118 The laughing coots with wings half spread were tripping over the little coves. **1870** *Amer. Naturalist* III. 226 Myriads of seaducks from the Northern seas . . . which are so absurdly designated by fishermen and gunners as 'Coots.' **1917** *Birds of Amer.* I. 152 By sunrise the companies of Coots will begin to pass. They fly swiftly and the man who secures many must be a good shot. **1948** *Milwaukee Jrnl.* 18 July (Sports Sec.) 6/3 The coot (mud hen) bag limit will be reduced from 25 to 15.

As the last term in **box, ivory billed, mud, patch-head, patch polled, spectacle, white winged coot.**

Coot kut, *n.*[2] = **Coody.** *Obs.* — **1833** GREENE *Fibbleton's Travels* 162 From Coots [they] presently assumed the name of, Highbinders, Highminders, or Highfliers.

cootch kutʃ, *n.* Short for **hootchy-kootchy.** Also attrib.

1930 *Variety* 3 Sep. 77/3 Sheriffs refuse to stand for cooch dancers. **1943** *Copper Camp* 274 A gal called 'Round the World' Showed . . . the forty-seven movements Of the dance known as the kootch. **1947** *Denver Post* 20 Feb. 18/2 An attractive 'girl' of 17 . . . had been . . . a carnival kootch dancer.

cooter ˈkutɚ, *n.* [See note.] A turtle, as the Carolina box turtle, or a terrapin. *Colloq.*

This word may have been introduced by Negro slaves. Turner records it in use among the Gullahs and cites West African (Bambara, Malinké) *kuta;* Central African (Congo basin) *nkudu.* But W. L. McAtee in *Nomina Abitera* (1945) 21, points out that the noun may well be from the verb *coot* (of unknown origin) denoting the unusual method of copulation followed by turtles. The *OED* records the verb from 1667.

1832 T. COOPER *Memoirs of Nullifier* (1860) 24 It was a large cooter, that . . . rose to the surface, only a few feet distant. **1859** MACKAY *Tour* I. 324 The greatest novelty was the small turtle called the 'cooter,' similar to but smaller than the 'terrapin,' so well known and esteemed in Baltimore, Philadelphia, and Washington. **1945** MCATEE *Nomina Abitera* 21 Nothing would be more natural than to call cooters those who coot.

transf. **1868** in EASTERBY *S.C. Rice Plant.* (1945) 242, I am not surprised, because he is a 'coota' generally and loves inaction for its own sake, and because he is an obstinate creature prone to take the reverse side of almost any question presented to him.

b. Preceded by a qualifying word as **alligator, Florida, hard-backed, soft-shell cooter.**

1884 GOODE *Fisheries* 155 *Pseudemys concinna,* the 'Florida Cooter,' is found in all the Southern States. **1934** *Nat. Geog. Mag.* LXV. 612 The Florida terrapin, known in the local vernacular as the 'hard-backed cooter,' is the species most frequently seen basking on logs projecting above the water. **1942** RAWLINGS *C. Creek* 226, I am especially enthusiastic about our turtles, especially the soft-shell cooter. *Ib.* 227 The alligator cooter is the most highly prized of all inland turtle meats. He is very dangerous, a virulent fighter encased in a ridged, scaly shell from which he takes his name, with a fierce hooked beak at the end of his head and long neck that can make mincemeat of an enemy.

c. *Drunk as a cooter,* quite drunk. *Colloq.*

1827 *Mass. Spy* 22 Aug. (Th.), A few jolly topers, who wallowed in the sand, 'as drunk as a cooter.' **1851** *Polly Peablossom* 45, I can manage to have him as drunk as a cooter by dark. **1908** *D.N.* III. 307.

cooter ˈkutɚ, *v.* [f. the noun.] *intr.* To loiter, idle. *Colloq.* — **1913** KEPHART *So. Highlanders* 203 Yes, I'm jest cooterin' around. **1948** *Chi. Tribune* 9 May (Comics) 7 I'll cooter over to Sally's jest like thar's been no quarrel!

∗**cop,** *n.*[1] As the last term in **fly, motorcycle, speed, traffic cop.**

Cop kɑp, *n.*[2] (See quot. 1875.) *Obs.* — **1865** *Carson* (Nev.) *Appeal* 17 Oct. 2/3 The 'Cops' are quite confident of success. **1875** *Chambers's Jrnl.* 13 March 172/2 During the rebellion, the Peace party, being suspected of favouring the South, were nicknamed Copperheads or Cops.

∗ **cop,** *v. To cop out,* to win (a girl or woman) as a sweetheart or wife. *Slang.*

1896 ADE *Artie* 91 There's no need of a man goin' nanny just because he's copped out a nice girl all for himself. **1909** O. HENRY

Options 254 'Why don't you cop the lady out?' asked Mack. **1910** McCUTCHEON *Rose in Ring* 197 Oh, I'm not asking you to give her up, kid—not for a minute. Cop her out if you can.

copa de oro. (See quots.)

1912 *Out West* June 396 Never yet have they seen good, or anything like real representations in artificial creations of California's most distinctive flower, the golden poppy, or as the poetic Spaniards called it, *copa de oro*. **1915** ARMSTRONG *Western Wild Flowers* 164 The State flower of California . . . has many poetic Spanish names, such as Torosa . . . and Dormidera, besides Copa de Oro, meaning 'Cup of gold.' **1947** *Desert Mag.* July 22/1 The Copa de Oro is an extremely variable species, and some botanists have named as many as 40 varieties.

copalm ˈkoˌpɑm, *n.* [Prob. f. Amer. Sp. *copal* (<Nahuatl) in senses shown here.] The sweet gum tree or its resin.

[**1758** DUPRATZ *Histoire Louisiane* II. 27 Le Copalm réunit deux grandes qualités; l'une, d'être extrèmement commun, l'autre de donner un baume dont les vertus sont infinies.] **1775** ROMANS *Florida* 336 Live oak abound here, intermixed with copalm and other timbers. **1889** *Cent.* 3474 In hot regions it [the tree] exudes a gum, sometimes called copalm . . . or copal-balsam, used in the preparation of chewing-gum, and to some extent in medicine as a substitute for storax.

* **Copenhagen,** *n.* **1.** (See quot. 1889.) **2.** Used attrib. in the sense of "for the purpose of seizure." *Rare.* Cf. next.

(1) 1848 in HAMMOND *Remembrance of Amherst* (1946) (We.), The mysteries of Copenhagen. **1865** *Indianapolis D. Jrnl.* 14 Sep. 1/4 The 'tournament' . . . has not half so much sense in it as the game which little boys and girls play, called Copenhagen. **1889** *Cent.* 1253 *Copenhagen*, . . . a children's game in which the players form a circle with their hands on a rope, and one inside the circle tries to touch the hands of any other player and kiss that one before he or she can get inside the rope. **1916** *Amer. Mag.* March 29/1 She's the one he kisses when they play 'Post-office' and 'Copenhagen' at parties. — **(2) 1813** *Boston Gaz.* 11 Feb. (Th.), Letters from Georgia say the 'Copenhagen' expedition against the Floridas goes on swimmingly, anything in the laws of the U.S. to the contrary notwithstanding.

* **Copenhagen,** *v. tr.* To seize or capture, as the English under Nelson did Copenhagen, Denmark, in 1801. *Obs.* Cf. **Burgoyne,** *v.*, **Cornwallis,** *v.*

1810 *Raleigh* (N.C.) *Reg.* 5 July 3/5 Fort Griswold, the scene of the massacre of the 6th of September, 1781, was full in view, and the ruins of houses and marks of the conflagration of that day, when the town was *Copenhagen'd* by Arnold and his British myrmidons, were to be seen on every hand. **1811** *Mass. Spy* 13 Feb. (Th.), Hints are given that a plan was organized to 'Copenhagen' Canada.

* **copper,** *n.*

1. =**copperskin.** *Rare.*

1772 in *Travels Amer. Col.* 523 He said there would be Copers and White people present at the meeting.

2. =**cent,** *n.* **1.**

Between 1785 and 1788 several of the states coined cents or coppers on their own account (see first quot.).

1785 in J. H. HICKCOX *Amer. Coinage* (1858) 102 All Coppers by him coined, shall be in pieces of one third of an ounce. **1835** H. C. TODD *Notes* 7 The word coppers designates cents. **1944** KAHN *Cable Car Days* 70 A well-known lady living on Nob Hill . . . boarded a California Street cable car and produced five coppers in payment of her fare.

b. As the type of a small amount of money, usu. with a negative. Cf. *not a penny.*

1788 JEFFERSON *Writings* VII. 40 Neither had a wish to lay up a copper. **1832** KENNEDY *Swallow Barn* II. 91 The daughter . . . looking as innocent as if she wa'nt worth one copper. **1904** GLASGOW *Deliverance* 40 The old gentleman hadn't a red copper to his name.

c. (See quot. 1917 under **copperhead 3.**) *Rare.*

1863 *Chi. Tribune* 1 May 2/3 The heavy coinage of 'nickels' still continues, the number last week made at the mint in Philadelphia being 53,000. When the people . . . discover that they have no intrinsic value over thirty-seven or forty cents a pound, . . . they will let the coppers loose in such loads as to make them a nuisance.

3. A copperhead snake. *Obs.*

1832 TROLLOPE *Domestic Manners* II, Doubting in our ignorance if he were indeed the deadly copperhead we had so often heard described, a farmer joined us, who exclaimed, 'My! if you have not got a copper. That's right down well done, they be darnation beasts.'

4. *pl.* (See quot. 1900.)

1899 *Boston Globe* 28 April 9/5 The largest owners of 'coppers' know of no investment that will be as safe and give as large returns as 'coppers.' **1900** S. A. NELSON *A B C Wall St.* 135 Coppers, copper mine stocks. **1925** *Wall St. Jrnl.* 12 Jan. 11/2 There would seem to be sound basis for reasoning that 'coppers' as a class are very much behind the market.

5. In combs.: (1) **copper-bellied snake,** =**copperhead 1,** *obs.;* (2) **belly,** see as a main entry; (3) **camp,** an encampment of those engaged in mining copper; (4) **cent,** =**cent 1;** (5) **head,** see as a main entry; (6) **headed,** *a.* having the attributes of a copperhead snake, (see **copperhead 2.**), *obs.;* (7) **headed snake,** =**copperhead 1;** (8) **headism,** the beliefs and practices of the copperheads (sense **2**), also transf., cf. **northern copperheadism;** (9) **Johnny,** =**copperhead 2,** *rare;* (10) **journal,** *local,* a cheap, sensational journal, so called because under the dominance of Anaconda Copper Co.; (11) **picker,** a petty thief who steals copper fixtures, *rare;* (12) * **plate,** (see quot. 1935), also attrib.; (13) **skin,** an Indian, also **copperskinned;** (14) **skipper,** (see quot.), *rare;* (15) **snake,** =**copperhead 1,** also attrib. and transf.; (16) **toed,** *a.* denoting shoes or boots the toes of which are protected by copper, hence **copper-toes.**

(1) 1705 BEVERLEY *Virginia* IV. 64 The black Viper-Snake, and the Copper-bellied Snake, are said to be as venemous [*sic*] as the Rattle-Snake. **1789** MORSE *Amer. Geog.* 61 Of the Snakes which infest the United States, are the following, viz. . . . The Copper-bellied Snake [etc.]. — **(3) 1881** *Tombstone* (Ariz.) *W. Epitaph* 27 June, G. W. Marsh, United States Deputy Collector, . . . returned Tuesday from an official visit to the great copper camp of Cochise county. **1906** *Out West* Feb. 89 A copper 'camp' is a city, and the typical copper-camps of Arizona are among her most thriving towns. — **(4) 1800** *Deb. Congress* (1851) 1256/2 There has been coined and issued from the Mint . . . 9,106 dollars and 68 cents, in copper cents. **1901** MONTGOMERY *Reminiscences* 17, I reckon the old fellow liked me chiefly because I was free with my dimes and quarters, and did not put him off with copper cents.

(6) 1853 SIMMS *Sword & Distaff* 446 It is sich a little mean copper-headed son of a skunk, that has the impudence to come here and to seize the rightful property of a gentleman. **a1861** WINTHROP *Canoe & Saddle* 248 The copper-headed, snaky beguiler continued his solicitations. **1865** *Mo. State Times* (Jefferson City) 24 Nov. 2/2 With all the copper-headed assiduity in heralding forth his slightest transgression, the conduct of the negro has been surprisingly good. — **(7) 1806** ASHE *Travels* II. 287 We called the following at least to our attention. Rattle Snake, Yellow Ditto, . . . Two Headed Ditto, Copper Headed Ditto. **1847** in DRAKE *Pioneer Life Ky.* 25 The copper-colored man, and the copper-headed snake [were] then extremely common. — **(8) 1863** *N.Y. Tribune* 11 March, The celebrated People's Regiment—44th New York—has spoken out in the matter of Copperheadism. **1893** T. MORSE *Lincoln* II. 182 Many causes conspired to induce an obstreperous outbreak of 'Copperheadism' in the spring of 1863. **1945** *Chi. D. News* 8 Jan. 6/1 Because a few lame ducks in Washington and a couple of double-tongued radio commentators snipe at the United States' participation in the anti-Axis war, is no reason to assume that there is any considerable Copperheadism here today. — **(9) 1872** *Newton Kansan* 10 Oct. 2/3 Such a course reminds me of the inconsistency of the Democratic, late 'copper-Johnny' party in espousing the lost cause.

(10) 1920 *S.F. Rank & File* 1 May 1/1 The yellow journals, which here [Butte] are appropriately called 'copper journals' began featuring imaginary stories of violence and terror. — **(11) 1872** BRACE *Dangerous Classes N.Y.* 94 The Eleventh Ward and 'Corlear's Hook,' where the 'copper-pickers,' and young wood-stealers, and the thieves who beset the ship-yards congregated. — **(12) 1790** *Columbian Centinel* 29 Sep. 19 [For sale,] Mahogany Chairs, . . . dining and card Tables, one suit of purple and white copper-plate Bed Curtains. **1871** *Harper's Mag.* Dec. 116/1 Anna glanced in, and saw straw matting, painted pine, copper-plate counterpane and curtains. **1935** DOW *Every Day Life* 73 *Copper plate.* A closely woven cotton fabric on which patterns, landscapes, pictorial representations have been printed from engraved copper plates; much in fashion during the eighteenth and early nineteenth centuries. — **(13) 1840** HOFFMAN *Greyslaer* II. 26 'Go on, go on, Kit; d'ye say a dozen Injuns?' 'Yes, uncle, not a Copperskin less.' **1904** WHITE *Silent Places* 72 What the hell do we care for a lot of copper-skins from Rupert's House! **1907** COOK *Border & Buffalo* (1938) 115 Come on, you copper-skinned devils; I'm good for the whole Cheyenne tribe! — **(14) 1867** *Amer. Naturalist* I. 221 The mature larva of another much smaller butterfly, the little Copper Skipper (*Chrysophanus Americanus*), so abundant at this time, may sometimes be found on the clover.

(15) [**1764** *N.C. Morav. Rec.* II. (1925) 580 Copper Snake is not so brown as the Rattlesnake, and I have not seen large ones.] **1765** TIMBERLAKE *Mem.* 46 The copper-snake, whose bite is very difficult to cure. **1849** J. B. JONES *Wild West Scenes* 86 It's that copper-snake, traitor, skunk, water-dog, lizard-hawk, horned frog. **1891** RYAN *Pagan* 62 He rode on, . . . crossing the summit that divides the copper-snake's range on the west side from the domain of its more honest relative. — **(16) 1872** HOLMES *Poet* 54 She was ashamed to let her little boy go out in his old shoes, and copper-toed shoes they was too. **1902** C. MORRIS *Stage Confidences* 292 [They swore] they would kick with their copper toes any one who tried to kiss them. **1937** LUTES *Home Grown* 77 His copper-toed boots squshing through seeping Michigan sand or sopping roadside grass, Jodie covered the flat, uninteresting distance between his home and the schoolhouse in record time.

b. In phrase (see quot.). *Colloq.*

1856 A. CARY *Married* 131 He is . . . the closest man I ever worked for—mean enough to steal the coppers off the eyes of a dead man.

As the last term in **barrel, bungtown, half, two copper.**

***copper,** *v.*

1. *tr.* To appropriate or embezzle, also *to copper one's pocket. Slang.*

1832 T. HAMILTON *Men & Manners* II. 387 One member of Congress . . . was charged with selling franks at twopence apiece, and thus coppering his pocket at the expense of the public. **1884** (U.S. Newspaper) Aug., He's been in office for a long while an' never coppered a d——n cent.

2. (See quot. 1864.) Also fig. *Slang.*

1856 *Dem. State Jrnl.* (Sacramento) 25 July 2/3 It is a safe bet to 'copper' all that comes from the immaculate [Vigilance] Committee. **1864** W. B. DICK *Amer. Hoyle* (1866) 277 Coppering a Bet.—If a player wishes to bet that a card will lose (that is, win for the bank), he indicates his wish by placing a cent . . . upon the top of stake. It is called 'coppering,' because coppers were first used to distinguish such bets. **1939** ROLLINS *Gone Haywire* 48 Feelin' sort o' mistaken sorry fer th' ol' tightwad. . . . I coppered a bet fer 'im.

***copperas,** *n. attrib.* Denoting the color or hue imparted to goods in the dyeing of which copperas is used as a fixative.

1840 *Spirit of Times* 7 March 8/2 (We.), Copperas trowsers; Copperas breeches. **1850** H. C. LEWIS *La. Swamp D.* 46 I'll never let on you cuddent tell copperas breeches from bar-skin. **1878** GUILD *Old Times* 40 They were clothed at home by their honest labor; the boys in their jeans and copperas cotton, and the girls in their beautiful stripes of cotton and linsey. **1900** J. C. HARRIS *On the Wing* 65 He wore brogans of undressed leather, his copperas-colored breeches short enough to show his woolen socks.

b. copperas-coloreds, trousers made of cloth in the dyeing of which copperas was used. *Rare.*

1851 *Polly Peablossom* 29 The first step upon arriving in the city was to lay aside their 'copperas-coloureds.'

copper belly. 1. A harmless red-bellied water snake, *Natrix sipedon*, also **copper-belly snake. 2.** = **copperhead 1.**

(1) 1736 CATESBY *Carolina* II. 46 *Anguis ventre cuprei coloris.* The Copper-belly Snake. . . . They are of a brown Colour, except their Bellies, which are of a muddy Red or Copper Colour. **1791** BARTRAM *Travels* 276 There are many other species of snakes in the regions of Florida and Carolina, as the . . . copper belly, ring neck and two or three varieties of vipers. **1871** SCHELE DE VERE *Americanisms* 387 The true Copperbelly (*Nerodia erythogaster*) is perfectly harmless and of aquatic habits. — **(2)** [**1788** SCHÖPF *Reise* I. 485 Ich habe mich überall nach der Klapperschlange und dem Kupferbauch (Copper belly, auch Mocсoson-Snake genannt,) deren Biss eben so gibtig ist, erkundiget.] **1842** *Nat. Hist. N.Y., Zoology* III. 54 The Copper-head . . . has various popular names in different districts; the most common of these are, in this State [N.Y.], Copper-head, Red Adder, and Dumb Rattlesnake. In other districts, it is called Copper-belly, Red Viper, Deaf Adder and Chunk-head. **1871** DE VERE (1872) 387 The Copperhead (Trigonocephalus contortrix) . . . is known as Copper-belly and Chunkhead.

copperhead 'kɑpɚ,hɛd, *n.*

1. A poisonous snake, *Agkistrodon mokasen*, coppery brown in color with dark markings, found in the eastern states. In full **copperhead snake.**

1775 FITHIAN *Journal* II. 54 The snake that wounded her they call a 'Copper-head.' **1788** J. MAY *Jrnl. & Lett.* (1873) 70 One of Colonel Stacey's men bit by a copperhead snake. **1819** THOMAS *Travels* 126 Our host . . . had been bitten by a *copper-head* some months ago, and was scarcely recovered. **1949** *Scientific Mo.* Jan. 55/1 Thus, the belief goes, whenever one sees a copperhead, a rattlesnake may appear on its trail.

b. (See quot. 1848.) *Obs.*

1809 IRVING *Knickerb.* VI. iv, These were the men who vegetated in the mud along the shores of Pavonia, being of the race of genuine copperheads. **1848** *Ib.* (rev. ed.) VII. i, The Yankees sneeringly spoke of the round-crowned burghers of the Manhattoes as the 'Copperheads.'

c. An Indian. *Obs.*

1838 *S. Lit. Messenger* IV. 295/1 He said . . . it would be a sin to kill one, but if he was to go he should want to kill one of the damned copper-heads. *a***1861** T. WINTHROP *Canoe & Saddle* X. 149 Meanwhile those five copperheads watched me, as I have seen a coterie of wolves . . . watch a wounded buffalo.

d. *fig.* A hostile or vindictive person.

1853 SIMMS *Sword & Distaff* 446 'Come, copper-head! march!' and Millhouse, planting himself on one side of the captive.

2. During the Civil War, a Northerner who sympathized with the South. Now *hist.* Cf. **Peace Democrat.** Cf. **northern copperheadism.**

For further quotations and discussion, see Albert Matthews "Origin of Butternut and Copperhead," in *Mass. Col. Soc. Pub.* XX. 205–37.

1862 *Lawrence* (Kans.) *Republican* 11 Sep. 4/1 That faction of the Democracy who sympathise with the rebels are known in Ohio as 'Vallandinghamers,' in Illinois as 'guerrillas,' in Missouri as 'butter-nuts,' in Kansas as 'jayhawkers,' in Kentucky as 'bushwackers,' and in Indiana as 'copperheads.' **1917** B. MATTHEWS *These Many Yrs.* 62, I was only twelve, but . . . I promptly responded, 'I won't be a copperhead anyhow!' **1948** *Ohio State Arch. & Hist. Quart.* Jan. 25 Congressman Clement L. Vallandigham of Ohio, later the notorious Copperhead, . . . suggested that Brown had been affected by the atmosphere in which he had lived.

attrib. **1862** *Cin. Gazette* 30 July, The Copperhead Bright Convention meets in Indianapolis today. **1865** *Indianapolis D. Jrnl.* 14 Sep. 2/1 If the Copperhead party is suffered to gain the assembly, it will not be adopted. **1947** *Newsweek* 17 Feb. 68/2 He used the copperhead label freely on those who disagreed with him.

b. A Negro. *Obs.*

1865 *Republican Banner* (Nashville, Tenn.) 17 Oct. 3/1 The Judge 'coppered' him with a fine of five dollars in default of which the diminutive copper-head was sentenced to drive the 'copper-ation' cart for two weeks. **1867** *Fredericksburg* (Va.) *News* 2 July 3/2 Then the copperhead or copper colored President called for a vote of thanks &c.

c. Any traitorous, disloyal person. Also attrib.

1902 *Out West* March 309 Even the newspaper mind no longer suffers epilepsy about 'copperheads.' **1945** *Nation* CLX. II. 17 March 292/2 The copperhead press, which slyly apologised for Nazi aggression, is now weeping crocodile tears over 'poor Poland.'

3. A badge worn as an emblem by the Copperheads (sense **2.**), (see quot. 1917). *Obs.*

"The . . . Copperheads had been so called for nearly six months before there is any trace of their wearing a badge" (A. Matthews in *Mass. Col. Soc. Pub.* XX. 220). Some of these badges were made of the coins mentioned in quot. 1917 below.

1863 in *Mass. Col. Soc. Pub.* XX. 224 By 'Copperheads,' politicians must not be understood, but a sort of copper badge, representing the head of Washington for example. **1865** *Sun. Mercury* (Phila.) 3 Sep. 4/2 The best thing Bill Kelly could do would be to open a junk shop, and buy up all the material for making Copperheads. **1917** *Amer. Jrnl. of Numismatics* 54 *Copperheads*, a name commonly applied to the tokens issued during the Civil War in the United States (1862–1865). In the latter part of the year 1862 the first of these copper tokens were issued in Cincinnati, Ohio, and other western cities. Many of them have on the obverse the Indian head copied from the United States cent, and this feature probably gave them their name.

***coppery,** *a.*

1. Sympathetic to the Copperheads (sense **2.** above). *Obs.*

1864 *Aurora* (Ill.) *Beacon* 15 Feb. 1/6 Josh. Allen, of Illinois [is] one of the most coppery of all the Copperheads **1866** F. KIRKLAND *Bk. Anecdotes* 63 In old Eastern Massachusetts . . . resides a certain Dr. ———, whose loyalty was commonly reputed as rather 'coppery.' **1906** *Nation* LXXXII. 179/2 The Rev. Ambrose Converse . . . made his pro-slavery *Christian Observer* so 'coppery' during the civil war that Seward suppressed it and arrested him.

2. coppery iris, (see quot.); **coppery-tailed trogon,** a trogon, *T. ambiguus*, found in the Southwest; **coppery whipsnake,** the coachwhip snake.

1831 AUDUBON *Ornith. Biog.* I. 80 The Coppery Iris, or Louisiana Flag. . . . Found on the banks of the Mississippi near New Orleans. Flowers of a beautiful copper colour, veined with purple. — **1917** *Birds of Amer.* II. 132 The Coppery-tailed Trogon utters its call in the manner of the Peacock, sitting bolt upright on a limb, its long tail hanging straight down, and its bill pointed at the zenith. **1944** *Nat. Geog. Mag.* June 689/2 The first authentic nest of the Coppery-tailed Trogon in the United States had been discovered. — **1870** *Amer. Naturalist* III. 187 A few of the former [reptiles] are not known north-ward, viz., . . . the Coppery Whipsnake (*Drymobius testaceus*).

cop-stock 'kɑp,stɑk, *n.* [Du. *kapstok* in the same sense.] (See quot.) *Obs.* — **1889** MELLICK *Story Old Farm* 240 Household articles were distributed about the walls of this farm-kitchen, hung on cop-stocks—wooden pegs, driven into the beams of the low-studded ceiling.

* **copy,** *n.* In combs.: (1) **copy boy,** in a newspaper office, a boy who takes copy, proof, etc., from one desk or office to another; (2) **cat,** an imitator, *colloq.;* (3) **desk,** the desk of a copyreader, also transf.; (4) **editor,** =**copy-reader;** (5) * **holder,** one who assists a proofreader by reading copy aloud; (6) **press,** a copying press; (7) **reader,** in a printing office or publishing house, one who edits copy for printing.

(1) **1894** SHUMAN *Steps into Journalism* 21 Now we have reached the bottom of the list—unless we include the copy boy. **1947** *Chi. Tribune* 8 June (Grafic Mag.) 14/1 Accept the job as copy boy on the local sheet to pick up experience, even tho it pays less than other jobs you might land. — (2) **1896** JEWETT *Pointed Firs* xiii. 102, I ain't heard of a copy-cat this great many years . . . ; 'twas a favorite term o' my grandmother's. **1948** *Dly. Ardmoreite* (Ardmore, Okla.) 25 May 4/1 In Soviet Russia today it is radio day, in honor of the invention of radio by the Russian scientist Popov. That Italian fellow Marconi was a copycat. — (3) **1932** *Atlantic Mo.* CXLIX 570 He knows how to put labels on men, on merchandise, on ideas, on events, and march them properly in front of the reporters and in view of the copy desk. **1946** *Democrat* 24 Jan. 1/1 Headlines that will be 'easy for the copy desk to write.' — (4) **1899** J. L. WILLIAMS *Stolen Story* 24 The copy-editors began gathering in now.

(5) **1888** *Cong. Rec.* 24 Jan. 666/1 Persons employed in the Printing Office under the names of proof-readers and copy-holders receive already . . . as much as or more than the 25 per cent. **1949** *Newsweek* 7 Feb. 4/2 He . . . had the proofs read successively by seventeen different proofreaders with copy holders. — (6) **1911** L. V. VANCE *Cynthia* 46 The lines of typewritten words, blurred and befogged with purple by the copy-press. — (7) **1892** *Harper's Wkly.* 9 Jan. 42/4 Upon the taste, the good judgment, and discretion of these copy-readers the character of the paper very greatly depends. **1947** *True* Nov. 61/1 Give thanks we have a copy reader who didn't go to college.

As the last term in **certified, drop, hard, state copy.**

Coquimbo koˈkimbo, *n. S.W.* [Sp., name of a river and province in Chile.] **Coquimbo owl.** (See quots.) — **1844** GREGG *Commerce of Prairies* II. 230 This has been called the Coquimbo owl. Its note, whether natural or imitative, much resembles that of the prairie dog. **1867** J. MELINE *Santa Fe & Back* 276 The prairie owl found among them is the burrowing owl (*Strix cunicularia*), sometimes called the Coquimbo owl.

coquina koˈkinə, *n.* [Sp., a shellfish.] A soft stone, consisting of marine shells bound together by calcareous cement, used as a building material. Also attrib.

1837 WILLIAMS *Florida* 44 The quarries of Coquina stone are extensive. *Ib.* 52 This river being choked up by the Coquina formation . . . the waters were driven laterally into the St. Lucia. *Ib.* 118 [The court house] is built of coquina stone. **1883** SHIELDS *Rustlings in Rockies* 178 The old Spanish residences are built of coquina, a species of shell-rock. **1932** C. C. LOVELL *Golden Isles Ga.* 11 The material used for this building was coquina, or tabby, a mixture of crushed oyster shells and cement, poured into moulds and tamped down. **1942** *Amer. Philos. Soc. Trans.* XXXIII. 58/1 Beds of fossiliferous rocks (coquina) . . . may be seen near high-tide mark at Hurl Rock Beach.

Corahism ˈkorəˌɪzəm, *n.* [f. *Korah,* name of a leader in revolt, Numbers xvi.] (See quot.) *Rare.* — **1702** C. MATHER *Magnalia* (1853) II. 495 *Corahism;* or that litigious and levelling spirit, with which the separation has been leavened.

* **coral,** *n.* In combs.: (1) * **coral bean,** (see quot.); (2) **begonia,** (see quot.); (3) **berry,** (see quot. 1944); (4) **honeysuckle,** =**trumpet honeysuckle;** (5) * **snake,** =**harlequin snake;** (6) **sumac,** the poison tree, *Metopium linnaei.*

(1) **1885** HAVARD *Flora W. & S. Texas* 500 *Sophora secundiflora,* Lag. Frijolillo; Coral Bean. Stout ornamental shrub, with deep green foliage, common from the Gulf Coast to the Pecos. — (2) **1892** *Amer. Folk-Lore* V. 96 *Begonia* sp. (similar to *B. maculata,* but not spotted), coral begonia. Bedford, Mass. — (3) **1859** BARTLETT 99 Coral Berry. (*Symphoricarpus vulgaris.*) The Indian Currant of Missouri. **1944** HARPER *Weeds* 211 S[ymphoricarpos orbiculatus] . . . (Coral-berry.) A medium-sized shrub, presumably native on dry limestone rocks in the Tennessee Valley, and also common on roadsides in that region, and occasionally in the neighboring regions which are not calcareous. — (4) **1864** *Harper's Mag.* Dec. 43/1, I stepped up on the shaky old wooden porch, coverd with the same coral honey-suckle. **1941** R. S. WALKER *Lookout* 58 Trumpet, or coral honeysuckle with its scarlet and yellow flowers that open in April and May, is one of the most popular wild flowers in the mountain.

(5) **1883** *Harper's Mag.* Oct. 708/1 None of venomous acquaintances, whether . . . black-snake, whip-snake, coral-snake, or viper, has ever . . . [sprung] off the ground at me. **1948** *Nat. Hist.* April 187/2 Venomous relatives of the cobra, coral snakes in the United States have the red bands bordered by yellow, in contrast to the false coral (king) snakes, which have the red bordered by black. — (6) **1884** SARGENT *Rep. Forests* 54 *Rhus Metopium.* . . . Poison Wood, Coral Sumach, [etc.].

As the last term in **staghorn, tree coral.**

* **cord,** *n.*

1. Designating a boat's carrying capacity. *Obs.*

1758 *N.J. Archives* XX. 303 A convenient Wharf lately built, sufficient to stow 500 Cord of Wood, from which Place a ten Cord Boat at any common Tide, may go loaded. **1777** *Ib.* 2 Ser. I. 356 A wharf or landing place belonging to said place, where a 12 cord boat may load.

2. A large number or great amount. *Colloq.*

1834 C. A. DAVIS *Lett. J. Downing* 167 Now just see about the Bank. There it stands . . . with its hundred cord of specie, and its cart load of books. **1847** *Knickerb.* XXX. 394 From childhood we had been told that there were 'cords' of snakes in the southern country. **1902** LORIMER *Lett. Merchant* 108 It just naturally sold cords of papers.

3. A measure of barnyard manure.

1837 COLMAN *Mass. Agric. Rep.* 21 We use from four to ten cords of manure, average eight cords per acre. **1848** *Cultivator* n.s. V. 185 Before plowing I spread over one-third of the ground about ten cords of common barn-yard manure per acre. **1884** *Vt. Agric. Rep.* VIII. 14 [He] would not put on more than twelve loads, or four or five cords of manure, to the acre.

As the last term in **alarm, bell, shade cord.**

cordeau kɔrˈdo, *n.* =next. *Rare.* — **1817** J. BRADBURY *Travels* 103 On the instant of my arrival, Mr. Lisa came to borrow a *cordeau,* or towing-line, from Mr. Hunt.

cordelle kɔrˈdɛl, *n.* [F.] A rope or line used in towing a boat. Also **cordelle rope.** Now *hist.*

1811 BRACKENBRIDGE *Louisiana* 214 Continued until eleven, with cordelle, or towing line—the banks being favorable. **1863** *Washoe* (Nev.) *Times* 11 July 1/5 Seven of the deck hands went out in a yawl to adjust the cordell rope to a tree. **1946** RICHTER *Fields* 281 Several hands jumped out in the water with the cordelle and pulled it to the bank.

cordelle kɔrˈdɛl, *v. tr.* To tow a boat by means of a cordelle. Also absol. Now *hist.*

1812 J. C. LUTTIG *Jrnl. Exped. on Upper Missouri* (1920) 62 Departed early cloudy and head wind cordelled all Morning. **1838** PARKER *Tour* xxiii. 307 We passed the Cascades by hiring Indians to Cordelle the canoe down them. **1940** HATCHER *Buckeye Country* 5 He . . . trudged along the bank . . . 'cordelling,' . . . his pirogue up-stream.

Hence **cordelling,** *n.* Also attrib.

1816 H. KER *Travels* 36 After getting above their cordaling ground, in swift water they make use of their warp. **1870** NOWLAND *Indianapolis* 27 The Wabash and White Rivers were ascended by what is called 'cord-elling.' **1941** BALDWIN *Keelboat Age* 65 When the bottom of the river was too soft for poling, and the shores on both sides were unsuitable for cordelling, resort was made to warping.

* **corder,** *n.* In colonial times, a town official whose duty was to pile merchantable wood into standard cords. *Obs.* Cf. **wood corder.**

1654–5 *Boston Rec.* 123 Att a meething this Day—was Chosen—for Corders of Wood, Tho. Leader, Rich. Tayler. **1733** *Phila. Council Minutes* (1847) 326 The Question was Putt whether Peter Cahoun, one of the present Corders of Wood, should be Removed. **1811** MEASE *Philadelphia* 94 He [the mayor] appoints the city commissioners, the high constables, watchmen, the corders of wood at the public landings, etc.

cordillera kɔrdɪlˈjɛrə, *n. W.* [Sp. in same sense. An Amer. borrowing.] A range or system of mountains, often *pl.*

[**1808** PIKE *Sources Mississippi* (1810) 1. App. 56 But we must cross (what is commonly termed) the Rocky Mountains, or a spur of the Cordeliers, previous to our finding the waters, whose currents run westward, and pay tribute to the western ocean.] **1857** E. STONE *Life of Howland* 285 Under easy sail she crossed the entrance to Mount Hope Bay, and doubling Popasquash point, the Tiverton cordillera was lost from sight. **1946** R. PEATTIE *Pac. Coast Ranges* 329 Here at last is discovered the greatest break through the western cordilleras leading from the slopes of Los Angeles and the Pacific coast into the interior wilderness.

Also **cordilleran,** *a.*

1891 *Scribner's Mag.* Oct. 465/1 We might think of our Cordilleran system as a great plateau, of unequal height in different parts, and everywhere bearing upon its surface a system of mountain ranges small or large. **1915** *Nat. & Science on Pac. Coast* 246 True Alpine climbing may be found in America only among the great Cordilleran

Ranges of the West. **1946** *Mazama* Dec. 1 The mountain goat . . . makes its home high among the pinnacles and glaciers of the cordilleran range of Western America. **1948** *Pacific Discovery* July–Aug. 19/2 The deep Cordilleran ice mass blanketed the mountains of Alaska and western Canada and extended down among the higher mountains of the United States.

* **corduroy,** *n.*

1. =**corduroy road.** Also the material for making such a road. Now *hist.*

1828 Mrs. BASIL HALL *Aristocratic Journey* (1931) 284 The drivers universally drive smack along through holes, over stumps and stones, up hills, and across long pieces of corduroy. **1874** B. F. TAYLOR *World on Wheels* 241 Bounce over the 'Corduroy,' went the old road. **1894** *Outing* Mar. 437/2 About midway the dogs feathered for an instant on the corduroys of the road, and then dashed eagerly into the bush. **1944** CLARK *Pills* 58 Short split pine poles were laid down in long panels of corduroy and then buried beneath a slushy covering of mud. *attrib.* and *transf.* **1834** CARUTHERS *Kentuckian* I. III, Oh! The comforts and blessings of a corduroy turnpike. **1881** NASH *Two Yrs. Ore.* (1882) 130 We dug, and graded, and moved logs, and built bridges, and laid corduroy crossings over wet places. *a***1900** in NICHOLSON *Hoosiers* 42 The kind o'-sort o' fiddlin' that the folks calls 'cordaroy' [*sic*].

2. In special combs.: (1) **corduroy bridge,** (see quot. 1842), now *hist.*, cf. **gridiron bridge;** (2) **road,** a road across swampy or marshy places consisting of tree trunks laid beside each other transversely, also fig., cf. **ground bridge.**

Corduroy road, bang-up, or ribbed road

(1) [**1822** J. WOODS *English Prairie* 71 Along a rough road with many log-bridges; but some of my fellow passengers, from the state of Kentucky, called them corderoy.] **1842** BUCKINGHAM *Slave States* I. 237 A corduroy bridge, composed of round trunks of trees with the bark on, laid side by side, sometimes close to each other, but often with spaces of two or three inches between them. **1946** ADAMS *Album Amer. Hist.* III. 132 *Opposite* we see the Union troops crossing the Chickahominy on a corduroy (log) bridge. — (2) [**1780** *N.C. Morav. Rec.* IV. (1930) 1894 We crossed marshy ground on a corduroy road half a mile long, to drive over which would certainly be good medicine for a hypocondriac.] **1824** BLANE *Excursion* 147 A Corderoy Road consists of small trees, stripped of their boughs, and laid touching one another, without any covering of earth. **1944** LANKS *Alaska* 31 Where the highway ran through a swampy area, a corduroy road was first laid.

corduroy ˈkɔrdəˌrɔɪ, *v. tr.* To lay (soft, swampy, or muddy stretches of a road) with logs or poles placed transversely.

1861 *Md. Hist. Mag.* V. 313 We have mapped out the woods with new roads, and corduroyed the swamps for miles. **1887** *Cent. Mag.* Oct. 933 We were compelled to corduroy the roads before our trains could be moved. **1948** *C.A. Jrnl.* June 97 In most places the trail had to be corduroyed.

corduroying ˈkɔrdəˌrɔɪ·ɪŋ, *n.* The material used in making a corduroy road. *Obs.* — **1861** *S.F. Herald* 22 Apr. 1/5 All that it needs is a few small bridges and some corduroying to make an excellent wagon road of it. **1876** BOURKE *Journal* 945 The road travelled had much 'corduroying' upon it, and heavy excavations and grading.

core drill. To drill with a core drill which removes a cylindrical core from the object penetrated. Also **core drilling.**

1903 *Sci. Amer.* 18 July 44/1 Core drilling is indispensable in a great variety of engineering and mining enterprises, affording, as it does, a means for drilling out a sample core or column of rock. **1927** EUBANK *Horse & Buggy Days* 116 They geologized it and they core drilled it, and reported 'no trace of oil and no structure.' **1948** *Sat. Ev. Post* 28 Aug. 68/4 During the last winter the Atlantis spent two months core-drilling the Gulf of Mexico.

coreopsis ˌkorɪˈɑpsɪs, *n.* [f. Gk. *koris*, bug+*-opsis*, appearance, in allusion to the bug-like shape of the seed. The word as a genus name was first used by Linnaeus.] Any one of various American plants of the natural order Compositae, some of which are cultivated for their flowers.

1766 J. BARTRAM *Journal* 3 Jan. 21 Saw . . . many alligators, tho' so very cold that it had froze the great convolvulus and coreopsis. **1857** *Spirit of Times* 11 April 90/3 The Coreopsis, is a showy yellow flower. **1913** CATHER *O Pioneers!* 34 The golden coreopsis grew up out of the clear water, and the wild ducks rose with a whirr of wings. **1947** *Chi. Tribune* 29 June VII. 1/8 Everything from shy Quaker Ladies to sought after velvets, golden coreopsis, . . . blooms with utter abandon.

* **Corinthian,** *n.* An amateur yachtsman. Also attrib. or as adj.

1874 *Forest & Stream* 13 Aug. 6/3 The decision to postpone the Corinthian race set for Saturday, the 8th, was unquestionably a wise one. **1883–4** *Forest & Stream* XXI. (*Cent.*), It is to canoeists . . . that the yachtsman may look for some of the most valuable additions to the ranks of Corinthians, as those who follow canoeing do so from pure love of sport. **1948** *N.Y. Times* 23 May v. 7/2 The Unqua Corinthian Yacht Club at Amityville will open for 1948 on Sunday afternoon.

* **cork,** *n.*

1. a. (See quot.) *Slang. Obs.* **b.** Burnt cork used by actors in making up as Negro minstrels. Also attrib.

(a) 1851 HALL *College Words* 85 *Cork, calk.* In some of the Southern colleges, this word, with a derived meaning, signifies a *complete stopper.* Used in the sense of an entire failure in reciting. — **(b) 1858** *Spirit of Times* 20 Feb. 400/2 This talented company of 'cork artists,' still continue to draw crowded audiences. **1867** *Atlantic Mo.* Nov. 611/1 Between acts the extravanganzaist in cork and wool would appear, and . . . command . . . full share of admiration in the arena.

2. Erroneous for * **calk,** *n.*

1902 WHITE *Blazed Trail* XXVII. 187 His face and flesh were ripped and torn everywhere by the 'corks' on the boots. **1944** NUTE *Lk. Superior* 210 A man on the drive wore special spiked, or calked, boots, and the adjective soon degenerated into 'corked' boots. Nothing would have been so abhorrent to a river hog as true cork on his boots.

3. In combs.: (1) **cork dobber,** a piece of cork, as the stopper of a jug, used as a dobber on a fish line; (2) **elm,** =**rock elm;** (3) **opera,** =**Negro minstrelsy;** (4) **pine,** the white pine, *Pinus strobus*, also attrib.; (5) * **screw,** (see quot.), cf. **devil's corkscrew.**

(1) **1889** MELLICK *Story Old Farm* 5 Again we are boys, with cork dobbers, buckshot sinkers and hickory poles, angling in the pond above for the slippery catfish. — (2) **1813** MUHLENBERG *Cat. Plants* 29. **1849** EMMONS *Agric. N.Y.* II. 323 Cork Elm (*Ulmus racemosa*). . . . The structure of this wood is singular and beautiful. **1931** CLUTE *Plants* 26 The plant usually regarded as the true wahoo, is the plant often called the burningbush . . . but . . . the cork elm (Ulmus racemosa), and the basswood . . . also bear the name. — (3) **1857** *Spirit of Times* 19 Dec. 256/3 The new, elegant, and most comfortable Hall . . . of The Cork Opera . . . continues to be crowded nightly. **1869** *Atlantic Mo.* July 79/1 Mitchell, poor fellow, like Lynch and Sliter and so many of my old associates in the cork-opera, has passed away. — (4) **1873** *Michigan Atlas* pref. 20 The soft or cork-pine, [is] so called from the resemblance in softness and texture of its wood to the cork of commerce. **1902** WHITE *Blazed Trail* 119 Often in the hollows it shaded gradually into the rough-skinned cork pine. — (5) **1905** *Forestry Bureau Bul.* No. 61, 33 *Corkscrew,* a geared logging locomotive. (P[acific] C[oast] F[orest]).

* **corker,** *n. Baseball.* (See quot. 1868.) *Colloq.*

1867 *Ball Players' Chron.* 20 June 1/1 Clyne hit a 'corker' to right field which bottled up Ketchum, Johnny securing his third by the hit. **1868** CHADWICK *Base Ball* 137 Smith then hit a 'corker'—a ball that flies from the bat like a cork from a champagne bottle. **1900** *Chi. Times-Herald* 4 May 4/3 Barret capped the climax by swiping a corker to left field that only stopped when it hit the fence.

corker plum. A local variant of "coco plum." — **1896** W. R. GERARD in *Garden & For.* IX. 263 Hickok. *Chrysobalanus Icaco.* Through Carib-Span., from *ikákoo*, the name of the plum-like fruit in the female dialect of the Caribs of the Lesser Antilles. Cocoa, in the name Cocoa-plum (Corker-plum in Fla.), is a variant of the word.

Corkonian kɔrˈkonɪən, *n.* An Irishman from Cork (see also 1st quots. and cf. **Fardown**). *Obs.*

1834 *Amer. R.R. Jrnl.* III. 21 June 384/1 The parties arrayed against each other are known as the *Fardowns* and the *Corkonians.* **1857** *Spirit of Times* 21 Feb. 405/2 After a due devotion to the crathur, they formed into two hostile factions, called Corkonians and Far-Downers, and held a regular pitched battle. **1905** VALENTINE

H. Sandwith 180 The 'Corkonians' employed on the Dunkirk branch of the Pennsylvania and Erie Canal [in 1856] became more notorious.

corky white elm. =**rock elm.** — **1857** GRAY *Botany* 396 *Ulmus racemosa*, Corky White Elm. . . . River-banks, W. New England, New York, and Michigan. April.

Corliss engine. [f. G. H. *Corliss* (1817–88), Amer. engineer.] (See quot. 1874.) — **1874** KNIGHT 624/2 *Corliss-engine*, a form of steam-engine having a variable and automatic cut-off of peculiar character. **1881** *Harper's Mag.* April 665/2 A sixty-horsepower Corliss engine . . . supplies the power to these shops and to a saw-mill.

***cormorant,** *n.* As the last term in **double-crested, Florida, Townsend cormorant.**

***corn,** *n.*

1. Indian corn or maize, *Zea mays.*

1608 J. SMITH *Works* (1884) 9 Shortly after it pleased God (in our extremity) to moue the Indians to bring vs Corne, ere it was halfe ripe, to refresh vs. **1705** BEVERLEY *Virginia* II. 40 None of the Toils of Husbandry were exercised by this happy People; except the bare planting a little Corn, and Melons. **1818** PALMER *Journal* 17 Corn always means maize. Wheat, oats, &c. are called grain by way of distinction. **1947** *Democrat* 16 Oct. 2/1 For the United States as a whole in the last few years, average corn yield was a little over 30 bushels to the acre.

2. Short for **corn whisky.** *Colloq.*

1820 *Chillicothe* (O.) *Supporter* 5 July, If we go to town, . . . we are invited to try a little corn as usual. **1845** HOOPER *Suggs* v. 54 Let me git one o' these book-larnt fellers over a bottle of 'old corn.' **1931** BRADFORD *John Henry* 27 So he sang: 'Sell my cotton, Drink my cawn, 'n' Haul my ashes ev'y mawnin'.' **1948** *Democrat* 4 Nov. 4/3 Those who habitually associate 'corn' with snakes may read some significance into this incident.

3. (See quots. 1937, 1948.) *Slang.* Cf. ***corny,** *a.*

1937 *Amer. Sp.* Oct. 180 Unexciting music is called 'corn.' **1947** *Time* 20 Jan. 69/3 What is finally thrown together is a hack job of comedy, corn, melodrama and sex. **1948** *Chi. Tribune* 20 June (Grafic Mag.) 8/2 Corn . . . is sentiment, sincere, and unashamed; corn is the familiar, the tried, and the true. Corn is the joke about the penny-pinching Scotsman.

4. In combs. designating implements used in raising or handling corn: (1) **corn and cob crusher,** etc., see **8.** (7) below; (2) **basket,** a basket for holding corn; (3) **cracker,** see as a main entry; (4) **crusher,** a mill or machine for crushing or grinding corn; (5) **cultivator,** a tool or implement for use in cultivating corn; (6) **cutter,** (see quot. 1877); (7) **drill,** an implement for planting corn in rows; (8) **dropper,** an implement for dropping corn at regular intervals in a row, fig. in context; (9) **grinder,** (*a*) =**metate,** (*b*) a mill for grinding corn, also transf.; (10) **hoe,** a hoe suitable for use in cultivating corn; (11) **husker,** a machine for husking corn, cf. **6. b.** (6); (12) **husker's peg,** =**husking pin;** (13) **knife,** a knife used for cutting down corn; (14) **marker,** a device for laying off corn rows; (15) ***mill,** (*a*) a mill for grinding corn, (*b*) = **corngrinder** (*a*); (16) **muller,** *archaeology* (see quot. and cf. **mano**); (17) **picker,** a machine for harvesting corn, cf. **6. b.** (7) below; (18) **planter,** see as a main entry; (19) **plow,** a plow used in cultivating corn; (20) **popper,** an implement used in popping popcorn; (21) **separator,** =next, *rare;* (22) **sheller,** a machine for removing grains of corn from the cob, cf. **box cornsheller, patent cornsheller;** (23) **shelling machine,** =prec., *obs.;* (24) **sled,** (see quot. 1922).

(2) **1648** *Conn. Public Rec.* I. 487 Inventory [includes] . . . 1 spade . . . a corne baskitt . . . a Howse at Hartford, with the homelott. **1871** STOWE *Sam Lawson* 66 Hand me that corn-basket; we'll put that over him. — (4) **1841** *Spirit of Times* 6 Nov. 429/1 (We.), Corn and Cob Crusher. **1845** in BOUCHER & BROOKS *Correspondence to Calhoun* (1930) 305 The corn crusher will be . . . 35 dolls. . . . This I consider cheap. **1862** *Rep. Comm. Patents: Agric.* 308 The granulating mill is simple, like a bark-mill or corn-crusher.

(5) **1840** *Ann. 26th Cong.* 1 Sess Sen. Doc. No. 111, 3 Cultivator, corn. [Patented by] John B. Smith . . . [on] April 15 [1839]. **1852** *Mich. Agric. Soc. Trans.* III. 101 Best corn cultivator. **1945** *Dly. Sentinel* (Grand Junction, Colo.) 27 Nov. 9/3 For sale . . . two-way plow, corn planter, corn cultivator. — (6) **1877** BARTLETT 780 *Corn-Cutter*, a machine for cutting up the stalks of Indian corn for the food of cattle. **1946** RICHTER *Fields* 189 He'd just as soon carry the corn cutter. Will Beagle made it and said you could lay an Indian's guts on the ground with it. — (7) **1853** *Mich. Agric. Soc. Trans.* IV. 84 Corn drill, an excellent article. **1874** KNIGHT 624/2. — (8) **1877** J. M. BEARD *K.K.K. Sketches* 45 Dick Shuttail . . . testified that the raiders were mounted on elephants or camels; . . . and that these beasts were branded on the side with three corn-droppers (K.K.K.), or, more probably (as suggested by a hearer), one corn-dropper three times. — (9) (*a*) *c*1824–38 G. FURMAN *Antiquities L.I.* 97 At Maspath Kills, in Queens County, Indian corngrinders . . . have been frequently ploughed up. **1854** BARTLETT *Personal Narr.* II. 245 Several broken metatees, or corn-grinders, lie about the pile. (*b*) **1841** *Knickerb.* XVII. 234 Improved coffee-mills . . . corn-grinders . . . and a thousand other half-completed plans. **1843** STEPHENS *High Life N.Y.* II. 197, I . . . grinned jest enough to show my corn-grinders. **1944** *Story Parade* Dec. 45, I have an old corn grinder And I grind, grind, grind.

(10) **1790** *Pa. Packet* 14 April 3/2 William Perkins, Blacksmith, Makes and sells. . . . A Quantity of the best kind of corn or tobacco hoes. **1869** BROWNE *Adv. Apache Country* 63 A third [Indian], one of

One form of cornplanter (sense 3)

the unbreeched multitude, wore a frying-pan in front by way of an apron, and a corn-hoe behind. — (11) **1858** *Rep. Comm. Patents* I. 358, I claim an improved corn-husker. **1876** *Vt. Bd. Agric. Rep.* III. 609 The corn harvest may now be greatly accelerated by the use of the corn husker, driven by horse power. **1945** *E. Colo. Leader* (Limon) 20 July 7/2 WPB announced restrictions had been taken off a large list of rubber-tired equipment including . . . combines, hay balers, corn pickers, . . . threshers and corn huskers. — (12) **1872** TALMAGE *Serm.* 162 Corn-husker's peg never ripped out fuller ear. — (13) **1856** *Mich. Agric. Soc. Trans.* VII. 54 D. O. & W. S. Penfield . . . [exhibited] six corn knives. **1948** *Chi. D. News* 9 Oct. 3/3 Others suggested anything from a machete to a hatchet or corn knife. — (14) **1857** *Ill. Agric. Soc. Trans.* III. 62, I lay off my ground with a corn-marker . . . into checks of three feet three inches square.

(15) (*a*) **1637** *Dedham Rec.* 27 Abraham Shawe is Resolved to erect a Cornemill in our towne of Dedham. **1703** *Providence* (R.I.) *Rec.* IV. 54 His Corne Mill now standing on said River. **1882** *Rep. Indian Affairs* 31 Aug. 4 Nearly every family has a corn mill. **1922** KEPHART *So. Highlanders* 30 Medlin itself comprised two little stores built of rough planks and bearing no signs, a corn mill, and four dwellings. (*b*) **1846** EMORY *Military Reconn.* 80 These could be nothing else than the corn-mills of long extinct races. — (16) **1881** *Smithsonian Rep.* 612 The stone, with a hole in the center, which is called a corn-muller, I found about 80 yards from the grand mound. — (17) **1944** *Reader's Digest* Oct. 78/1, I came across an example—a corn-picker costing $200 which sold at $600. **1947** *Democrat* 8 May 2/7 The mechanical corn picker is rated the most dangerous of farm machines. — (19) [*c*1774 CRÈVECOEUR *Sk. 18th-Cent. Amer.* (1925) 140 We have, besides (the cross-plow), a smaller sort, called the corn-plough with which we till through the furrows.] **1830** *Cortland Observer* (Homer, N.Y.) 2 July 1/3 They also make . . . a large assortment of ploughs, heavy and light, . . . from the large breaking-up or greensward ploughs, to the small light corn ploughs. **1947** *Chi. Tribune* 4 July 4/3 They are able to get into the fields with their corn plows.

(20) **1874** B. F. TAYLOR *World on Wheels* I. viii. 63 The baggage-car is as lively with all sorts of baggage as corn in a corn-popper. **1946** *Reader's Digest* Jan. 60/1 The Boy would have the cornpopper waiting. — (21) **1864** *Ohio Agric. Rep.* XVIII. 67 Higley's Corn Separator. — (22) **1813** in *Mem. Phila. Soc. for Promoting Agric.* III. (1814) 250 (*caption*), Description of the Corn sheller. . . . One bushel of corn in the ears, may with ease be shelled in five minutes. **1946** *Democrat* 30 May 4/4 For Sale—One rolling chair and one corn sheller. — (23) **1813** in *Mem. Phila. Soc. for Promoting Agric.* III. (1814) 249 The inventor of the corn shelling machine . . . is John Haven, of Montgomery county [Penna.]. **1858** *Rep. Comm. Patents* I. 359 Improvement in Corn-Shelling Machine. **1933** *Old-Time N. Eng.* July 8/1 A number of corn-shelling machines, including the very early type consisting of a hollowed-out tree trunk with wooden rods passing through to form a grating. — (24) **1922** R. E. BELL *Kansas Vocabulary* (Thesis) 48 corn-sled. . . . A rude implement for cutting corn, since displaced by the corn-binder. It was a wooden sled, having a knife on either, and sometimes both, sides of the sled. **1944** *Greeley* (Colo.) *D. Tribune* 30 Sep. 2/5 Public Auction . . . 14 ft. trailer, made of Ford chassis; corn sled; McCormick mower.

b. Denoting structures used for storing corn: (1) **corn barn,** (see quot. 1852); (2) **crib,** a crib for storing corn, cf. **log corncrib;** (3) * **house,** a house in which corn is stored, also attrib.; (4) **pen,** a pen, usu. of rails, for storing corn, *obs.;* (5) **shade,** a light shelter under which corn is kept temporarily, *obs.*

(1) **1780** Ebenezer Parkman *Diary* (1899) 16 Oct. 278 Dr. Hawes . . . took the whole care of husking the Corn, & carrying it into the Corn Barn. **1852** *Harper's Mag.* April 590/2 A corn-barn is a small square building standing upon high posts at the four corners. **1888** Billings *Hardtack* 237 [The task of foragers] was to go out with wagons in quest of the contents of smoke-houses or barns or corn-barns. — **(2) 1687** *Brookhaven Rec.* 51 I, Hannah Huls, Through inadvertance and pasion, defamed Nathanell Norten, of this towne, by saying he had stollen Indian corn out of my fatther daiton's his corn cribb. **1874** *Vt. Bd. Agric. Rep.* II. 514 My corn crib, on the south side of the barn, is divided into two. **1948** *Democrat* 11 Nov. 8/4 Insects in corn cribs do tremendous damage. — **(3) 1699** J. Dickenson *God's Protecting Providence* 82 The People had . . . large Cropps of Corn, as We could tell by their Corn-houses. **1772** Taitt in *Travels Amer. Col.* 555 Some other Chiefs were Smoking and talking with me on a Cornhouse Scaffold. **1945** Botkin *My Burden* 211 Start to set the cornhouse afire, but my ma say: 'Please sir, don't burn the cornhouse.' — **(4) 1860** Claiborne *Life of Dale* 26 We ran to the corn-pen, pulled down the rails, and let the high pile of corn slip down on the blazing shucks. **1864** Cate *Two Soldiers* 47, I moved our lodging for the night from Sweet Gum Hotel to a corn pen in order to keep dry in case of falling weather. — **(5) 1773** *Doc. Hist. N.Y.* (1851) IV. 848 The rioters . . . burnt five Houses, two Corn Shades and one Stack of Hay.

5. In combinations denoting foods: (1) **corn ball,** see as a main entry; (2) **battercake,** a griddlecake made of corn meal; (3) **bread,** bread made of corn meal, see **8.** (5) below; (4) **cake,** a hoecake or johnnycake, cf. **Saratoga corn cake;** (5) **chop,** corn ground coarsely as food for stock; (6) **dodger,** a small cake, usu. hard baked, of cornbread; (7) **doings,** see **doings;** (8) **dumpling,** a dumpling of corn meal boiled with vegetables; (9) **flakes,** a popular breakfast cereal made of corn in the form of crisp flakes suitably seasoned; (10) **flour,** (see quot. 1851); (11) **fodder,** the blades of corn cured for use as forage, also corn sown broadcast and cut for feed before maturity, also attrib.; (12) **fritter,** a fritter made with corn or corn meal; (13) **hominy,** =**hominy,** *obs.;* (14) * **meal,** meal made from corn, also attrib.; (15) **muffin,** a muffin made of corn meal; (16) **mush,** (see quot. 1920); (17) **oyster,** (see quot. 1877); (18) **pone,** *S.* bread of corn meal hand shaped into a flat loaf, usu. rectangular, cf. **gritted, hominy corn pone;** (19) **pudding,** (see quot. 1848); (20) **sirup,** a thick light-colored sirup made usu. of cornstarch and used as a sweetening agent; (21) **soup,** soup the principal ingredient of which is green corn; (22) **starch,** starch made from corn, esp. in the form of a fine white flour used for puddings, etc., also attrib.; (23) **starch pudding,** a pudding made of cornstarch; (24) **stover,** stalks of corn suitably cured and used as food for stock.

(2) **1833** *Md. Hist. Mag.* XIII. 319 The servant will bring you hot muffins and corn batter cakes every 2 minutes. **1884** Mrs. Owens *Cook-Book* 163 Recipe for Corn Batter Cakes. — **(3) [1750** Beauchamp *Cen. N.Y. Morav. Jrnls.* (1916) 92 We went with him (Oneida chief) to his hut, and he set before us a meal of bear meat and corn bread.] **1775** in Schaw *Jrnl. Lady of Quality* (1923) 171 And vast quantities of pork, beef and corn-bread were set forth. **1945** *Chi. Tribune* 13 May VII. 1/8 Can't have greens without cornbread. And none of your sweetened stuff either! — **(4) 1791** Bartram *Travels* 38 It is . . . an ingredient in most of their cookery, especially homony and corn cakes. **1903** *N.Y. Sun* 1 Nov., Corn cakes as a substitute for bread are popular in the South. **1944** *Chr. Sci. Mon.* 25 April (Editorial), Anybody that ever ate spoon bread, corn cakes, or pones below Mason and Dixon's line knows that white corn is for folks and yellow for critters.

(5) **[1773** *N.C. Morav. Rec.* II. (1925) 768 Toll (at mill) . . . one-eighth for corn-meal, one-tenth for flour, corn chops and rye chops, and one-twelfth for malt chops.] **1933** T. Williamson *Woods Colt* 78 Even when he fetches the horse, a-packin' in *corn chop,* he don't do no more than mash down a fern. — **(6) 1834** H. C. Kimball *Jrnl.* in *Prophet* (N.Y.) (1845) 15 Mar. (Th.) We sometimes had to live mostly on johnny-cake and corn-dodgers. **1945** Wallace *Barington* 69 I'll take my sewing, bake a ham, and stir up a corn dodger whenever I get hungry. — **(8) 1880** *Harper's Mag.* Feb. 330/1 Here were they 'lustily entertained' . . . feasting on 'corn dumplings,' venison, and hominy. **1939** *These Are Our Lives* 352 She'd cook up a big pot of greens with corn dumplin's, fix sausage and gravy to eat with the yams, and maybe bake a sweetcake, if she had time, or pies. — **(9) 1908** *Sat. Ev. Post* 31 Oct. 55/3 There are 13 imitations of Kellogg's Toasted Corn Flakes. **1948** *Woodlawn Booster* (Chi.) 12 May 2/2 A good breakfast combination is corn flakes with apple sauce and stewed raisins.

(10) 1674 in *S.C. Hist. Soc. Coll.* V. 458 Two fatt turkeys to helpe out with our parcht corne flower broth. **1791** W. Bartram *Travels* 456 They fast seven or eight days, during which time they eat or drink nothing but a meagre gruel, made of a little corn-flour and water. **1851** *Rep. Juries Gt. Exhibition* (1852) 55 Maize-flour, commonly called . . . 'corn-flour' in the U.S. . . . is extensively used for puddings and other purposes in that country. — **(11) [1752** A. G. Spangenburg *Diary* (1887) 26 Sep., Hay they have none for there are no meadows, & corn fodder & tops do not go far.] **1870** McClung *Minnesota* 105 Corn fodder is raised by sowing the corn broadcast or drilling, and from four to eight tons per acre may be gathered. **1945** *Farmington* (N.M.) *T. Hustler* 16 Feb. 5/5 For Sale—250 large shocks Corn Fodder in fine condition. — **(12) 1862** Stowe *Pearl Orr's Isl.* xxix, A very minute account which Mrs. Kittridge was giving of the way to make corn-fritters, which should taste exactly like oysters. **1903** *N.Y. Ev. Post* 26 Sep., Corn is . . . becoming somewhat hard and tough. Corn fritters may be made of this hard corn. **1941** *L.A.* Map 289. — **(13) 1811–14** Brackenridge *Journal* 202 Their food consists of lied corn homony for breakfast. **1830** *Boston Transcript* 5 Nov. 1/3 There's great many ways to kill poor nigger . . . some eat too much corn homany—swell and kill 'em; therefore hab mercy on us, and no let this homany swell too much. — **(14) [1749** Peter Kalm *Travels N. Amer.* II. (1937) 629 There was the same perpetual evening meal of porridge made of corn meal.] **1782** J. Holt in *Va. Hist. Mag.* IV. 400 The wheat . . . will do to mix with Corn meal for My Servants. *a***1853** Wm. Whitteker in *W. Va. Hist.* I. 212 We also have corn meal mush twice a week for Breakfast. **1948** *Scientific Mo.* May 384 Make it into succotash, corn meal, corn flakes, and syrup.

(15) 1844 in Thompson *M. Jones* (1872) 189 When we got in the dinin room, thar the old woman was, keeled over in her cheer, with her eyes sot in her head and a corn muffin stickin in her mouth. **1947** Croy *Corn Country* 200 She is especially famous for her corn muffins. — **(16) 1846** J. S. Griffin in *Calif. Hist. Soc. Quart.* XXI. (1942) They (horse drovers) had nothing to eat but penolas & corn mush—no shelter. **1920** R. L. Alsaker *Eating for Health* 131 Corn mush: Cook corn meal in plain water until it is done, using moderate amount of salt. — **(17) 1847** *Carolina Housewife* 101 Corn Oysters. Grate corn, while green and tender, with a coarse grater, in a deep dish. **1877** Bartlett 148 *Corn-oyster,* a fritter to which the combined effects of grated Indian corn (not quite ripe) and heated butter impart a taste like that of oysters. **1947** Berolzheimer *Regional Cook Book* 104. — **(18) 1859** Bartlett 100 *Corn Pone,* a superior kind of corn-bread, made with milk and eggs and baked in a pan. **1948** *Dly. Ardmoreite* (Ardmore, Okla.) 11 April 12/3 He is Beaumont, Texas, reared and eats blackeyed peas and corn pone. — **(19) 1848** J. Mitchell *Nantucketisms* 40 *Corn-pudding,* corn pounded or grated with milk, eggs, & sugar & baked. **1944** Holton *Yankees* 236, I don't believe corn pudding was a unique delicacy, but I never seem to have eaten it anywhere except at Grandmother's, and I have rarely heard of it since her day.

(20) 1903 *U.S. Dept. Agric. Circular No. 10* 8 *Glucose sirup* or *corn sirup* is glucose unmixed or mixed with sirup or molasses. **1948** *Milwaukee Jrnl.* 18 July 10/3 Substitution of light corn sirup should not be increased beyond two cups or the results will not be up to standard. — **(21) 1847** *Carolina Housewife* 45 Corn Soup. Take young corn and cut the ears across, then grate them in water—two ears to a pint. **1891** *Wide Awake* Christmas issue, All the guests were invited to partake of the old-time national dish,—the corn soup, and its accompanying relish, the delicious hulled-corn boiled bread. — **(22) 1853** *S.F. Whig* 28 July 1/4 (*advt.*), Farina and corn starch. **1868** *Ballou's Mag.* Nov. 396/1 [Recipe:] Cornstarch Cake. **1948** *Calif. Citrograph* June 374/4 Mix cornstarch, sugar, peel and orange juice. — **(23) 1876** M. F. Henderson *Practical Cooking* 323 Cornstarch and rice puddings are explained among the regular receipts for puddings. **1942** Rich *We Took to Woods* (1948) 93, I use it to take the lumps out of gravy or chocolate cornstarch pudding or cream sauce. — **(24) 1863** *Maine Bd. Agric. Rep.* 18 In the above trial, the stock was full-fed mostly largely upon corn stover. **1888** *Vt. Agric. Rep.* X. 27 Mr. Pike says that on his farm he can get corn stover on one acre that will be equal in value to a ton and a half of hay and have the ears of corn in addition.

b. In less frequent combs. of this kind, usu. obs.: (1) **corn ashcake,** =**ashcake;** (2) **biscuit,** (see quots.), *obs.;* (3) **chowder,** chowder in which corn is the principal ingredient; (4) **flipper,** see **flipper;** (5) **grits,** grits made of corn; (6) **johnnycake,** =**johnnycake;** (7) **loaf,**

=**corn pone,** *obs.;* (8) **slap jack,** =**corn fritter;** (9) **stick,** a stick-like piece of crisp corn bread cooked in a special form of griddle; (10) **sugar,** dextrose made from corn; (11) **tortilla,** =**tortilla.**

(1) **1839** *Jeffersonian* 26 Jan. 399 (Th.), Fellows whose richest loaf is corn ash-cake. — (2) **1847** *Carolina Housewife* 23 Corn Biscuits. Six table-spoonfuls of soft hommony, half a pint of corn meal, a large table-spoonful of lard, half a pint of milk. **1889** *N. & Q.* IV. 60 Johnny-cake . . . was a rough, coarse, corn cake. . . . A better quality, and among better people, was dignified by the name of 'corn biscuit.' **1927** in *Amer. Sp.* XIII. 23 'What eber you do doan you neber dot your cawn biskits.' The slave women of Virginia brought this injunction, always solemnly impressed, to the new States. Nobody seems to have known its exact meaning. — (3) **1944** *Chi. D. News* 13 July 21/2 It's corn chowder and this grand popcorn Yankee one-piece dinner or supper ought to be cooked in an iron pot right in the middle of the garden, with friends from all the surrounding gardens.

(5) **1839** KEMBLE *Journal* 18 A small shed, which they call the cook's shop, and where the daily allowance of rice and corn grits of the people is boiled. — (6) **1855** SIMMS *Forayers* 330 There were some fragments of chicken; a plate of corn johnny-cake. — (7) **1809** in SMITH *Forty Years Washington Society* (1906) 83 A most excellent Virginian breakfast—tea, coffee, hot wheat bread, light cakes, a pone, or corn loaf—cold ham, nice hashes, chickens, etc. **1829** T. FLINT *George Mason* 11 The repast of smoking corn loaf, sweet potatoes, and fried bacon were arranged on it. — (8) **1843** CARLTON *New Purchase* II. 58 That emboldened us to trot on very fast, in the comfortable assurance of rapidly approaching a snug breakfast of chicken fixins, eggs, ham-doins, and corn slap-jacks. — (9) **1944** FAST *F. Road* 44 She piled a dish high with the stuff and threw in two corn sticks for good measure.

(10) **1850** S. F. COOPER *Rural Hours* 29 Probably some beet and corn sugar in small quantities may be included in the calculations. — (11) **1948** *Ariz. Republic* (Phoenix) 29 Feb. 1. 6/1 Every picturesque quality of western life, from saddle-making to cooking corn tortillas, will be shown.

See also *corn on the cob, corn bread and common doings, corn and molasses cake* in **8.** below.

c. Denoting drinks: (1) **corn beer,** beer made from corn; (2) **coffee,** coffee made of parched corn; (3) **juice,** whisky, esp. that made from corn; (4) **liquor,** =prec.; (5) **spirits,** =**corn whisky;** (6) **whisky,** whisky made from corn.

(1) [*c***1662** J. WINTHROP in *N.E. Quarterly* X. (1937) 131 The English have found out a way to make very good Beere of this Graine which they doe either out of Bread made of it, or by Maulting of it.] **1891** *Cent. Mag.* March 706, [I] carried with me some of the corn beer brewed in the camp. — (2) **1844** FEATHERSTONHAUGH *Slave States* 114 The supper consisted of . . . coffee made of burnt acorns and maize. . . . He laughed at our fastidiousness, and advised us to drink some of the corn-coffee. **1894** ROBLEY *Bourbon Co., Kansas* 68 The menu consisted of cornbread, bacon, fried potatoes and corn coffee with 'long sweetnin'.' — (3) *a***1846** *Quarter Race Ky.*, etc. 83 He . . . only axes a 'fip' for a reel, and two 'bits' fur what corn-juice you suck. **1936** MCKENNA *Black Range* 38 No, and I'll never miss my jug of corn juice. — (4) **1927** BENÉT *J. B.'s Body* 71 They keep the beechwood-fiddle and the salt Old-fashioned ballad-English of our first Rowdy, corn-liquor-drinking, ignorant youth. **1945** *Chi. D. News* 6 Jan. 4/5 They never said whether this feller could shoot a rifle good or make corn licker with a nice head on it.

(5) **1764** J. INGERSOLL *Lett. relating to Stamp-Act* (1766) 7 They . . . have erected Works for the Distilling of Corn Spirits. — (6) **1843** CARLTON *New Purchase* I. 210 Candidates were perpetually . . . making licentious speeches, treating to corn whiskey, violating the Sabbath [etc.]. **1948** *Sat. Review* 28 Aug. 12/3 Chism himself teaches eleven-year-old Jarvis to drink corn whiskey.

6. In the names of plants and animals: (1) **corn bird,** the common jay, *Cyanocitta cristata*, cf. ∗**corn thief;** (2) **borer,** the larva of a European moth, *Pyrausta nubilalis*, a serious corn pest in parts of the U.S., also attrib.; (3) **broom,** =**broomcorn,** *rare,* cf. **7.** (1) below; (4) **chinch bug,** =**chinch bug,** *rare;* (5) **ear worm,** the bollworm, which is injurious to corn, tomatoes, etc.; (6) **eater,** a corn weevil, *rare,* cf. **b.** (4) below; (7) **grub,** the cutworm, *rare;* (8) **lily,** the American hellebore, *Veratrum viride;* (9) **louse,** (see quot. and cf. **cornroot louse**); (10) **moth,** the grain moth, *Tinea granella,* also **corn emperor moth** (see quot. 1854); (11) **root louse,** (see quot. 1892); (12) **root worm,** (see quot.); (13) **scaup,** (see quot.), *obs.;* (14) **silk moth,** =**corn moth;** (15) **snake,** *S.* a large, harmless snake, *Elaphe guttata,* often found in cornfields; (16) ∗**thief,** the red-winged blackbird, also the northern bluejay, cf. **corn bird;** (17) **worm,** = **corn-ear worm.**

(1) **1857** *Rep. Comm. Patents: Agric.* 140 The blue-jay or 'Corn Bird,' as it is called in some localities. — (2) **1934** WEBSTER. **1948** *Calif. Citrograph* April 207/2 Corn borer larvae were found in a lot of Illinois popcorn being carried in a suitcase. — (3) **1836** C. GILMAN *Recoll.* (1838) 225 My silk rustled like a patch of corn-broom in a breeze. — (4) **1788** *Amer. Museum* III. 177/1 Premiums . . . for preventing damage to crops by insects; especially . . . the corn chinch-bug or fly; a gold medal: a silver medal for the second best.

(5) **1889** *Secy. of Agric. Rep.* 360 The Corn Ear-worm (*Heliothis armigera*) has done considerable damage to the ears of field corn. **1928** BAILEY *Cyclo. Horticulture* 850/1 The corn-ear worm, known South as the cotton-boll worm, is especially injurious to sweet corn. — (6) **1854** EMMONS *Agric. N.Y.* V. 265 Index, *Calandra,* or Corneater: . . . *Calandra granaria.* — (7) **1817** *Nat. Intelligencer* 7 June 1/5 What modes of previous preparation of the soil have been found to prevent the Corn Grub. — (8) **1947** *So. Sierran* Aug. 2/2 Two miles beyond this point the Baden-Powell group descended 500 feet to Lily Springs (8060 feet) where ice cold water, masses of corn lilies . . . made the side trip worth while. — (9) **1892** V. KELLOGG *Kansas Insects* 21 Corn-louse (*Aphis maidis*). . . . Very small, soft-bodied, apple-green insects; body elliptical or slightly ovate in outline.

(10) **1850** in TURNER *Cotton* (1865) 158 The P. Zea, or corn-moth, is of a pale yellow or a shining ash color. **1854** EMMONS *Agric. N.Y.* V. 231 *Saturnia maia.* Corn Emperor moth. *Ib.* 232 *Saturnia io.* Corn Emperor Moth. . . . These caterpillars feed upon the leaves of the elm, poplar, dogwood and sassafras, and also upon clover and indian corn. **1889** *Cent.* 1271/3 Corn-moth . . . [is] exceedingly destructive to grain-sheaves in the field, and to stored grain. — (11) **1862** *Ill. Agric. Soc. Trans.* V. 492 These honey-tubes are sufficiently plain in the corn-root louse. **1892** V. KELLOGG *Kansas Insects* 20 Corn-root louse (*Aphis maidi-radicis*). . . . The Corn-root Louse appears as a wingless, soft-bodied, bluish-green, sub-ovoid insect; or it may have four transparent membranous wings. — (12) **1892** V. KELLOGG *Kansas Insects* 17 Western corn-root worm (*Diabrotica longicornis*) . . . The worm is from one-fourth to one-half inch long, six legged, soft, and white, with a small brown head. — (13) **1856** *Spirit of Times* (N.Y.) 25 Oct. 129/1 Blue-winged teal, dusky duck, and corn-scaup—more commonly known as broadbills—are very abundant on the Jersey rivers. — (14) **1861** *Harper's Mag.* Aug. 322/2 [The] *Tinea Maisinia—'Corn-silk Moth'* . . . feeds only on the efflorescence or silk of the corn.

(15) **1676** T. GLOVER *Phil. Trans.* XI. 631 There is another sort called the *Corn-Snake,* because he is usually found in Corn-fields; this is near as big as the *Rattle-Snake.* **1736** CATESBY *Carolina* II. 55 *Anguis e rubro & abbo varius.* The Corn Snake. . . . It is all over beautifully marked with red, and white, which seems to have given it the Name of Corn-Snake; there being some Maize or Indian Corn much resembling this Colour: they are Robbers of Hen-Roosts, otherwise they are harmless. **1896** P. A. BRUCE *Econ. Hist. Va.* I. 129 Other varieties of snake were common, such as the puff adder, the moccasin, the corn, . . . and the horn. — (16) **1844** *Nat. Hist. N.Y., Zoology* II. 141 The Red-winged Blackbird [*Icterus phoeniceus*] is equally well known in every part of the State under the names of Swamp Blackbird and Corn-thief. **1917** *Birds of Amer.* II. 217. — (17) *c***1758** in WOODWARD *Ploughs* (1941) 306 Their Enemies are the worm abt 1 inch long & black like the Indian corn worm & a small vermin wch makes a hole thro ye Stalk of them about as big as a pin. **1849** *Rep. Comm. Patents: Agric.* 333 They are, I believe, called 'White corn-worms.' **1898** CUSHMAN *Hist. Indians* 272 The corn-worms were usually numerous and were committing great depredations upon their fields of green corn.

b. Denoting persons having to do with corn: (1) **Corn Belter,** one who lives in the corn belt; (2) **cracker,** see as a main entry; (3) **detasseler,** one who removes the tassels from corn in producing improved varieties; (4) **eater,** (see quot. 1907), cf. (6) above; (5) **general,** one of the two leaders in charge of rival groups of huskers at a husking bee, *obs.,* cf. quot. 1882 *s.v.* **cornshucker;** (6) **husker,** =**husker,** also (*cap.*) with reference to an athletic team from the Cornhusker State, see **7.** (3) below and cf. **4.** (11) above; (7) **picker,** one who harvests corn, cf. **4.** (17) above; (8) ∗**planter,** see as a main entry; (9) **priest,** (see quot. 1920); (10) **shucker,** a cornhusker.

(1) **1945** *New Yorker* 10 Feb. 32/3 All his education and social mixing out in the world has failed to disguise the fact that he is a jolly Corn Belter at heart. — (3) **1944** *Chi. D. News* 14 July 9/1 El Paso, Ill. . . . is due for a lively two weeks when 90 Chicago girl corn detasselers descend upon it. — (4) **1844** EMERSON *Experience* Ess. 2 Ser. 64 Nature . . . is no saint. The lights of the church, the ascetics,

Gentoos and corn-eaters, she does not distinguish by any favor. **1907** Hodge *Amer. Indians* I. 85 In the sign language the Arikara are designated as 'corn eaters,' the movement of the hand simulating the act of gnawing the kernels of corn from the cob.

(5) 1882 *Cent. Mag.* XXIV. 874 Imagine a negro man standing up on a pile of corn, holding in his hand an ear of corn and shouting the words on the next page, and you will have pictured the 'corn gin'r'l.' — **(6) 1872** [see **cornhusker's peg** in **4.** (12) above]. **1947** *Chi. Tribune* 18 Oct. 19/3 The last argument took place at Lincoln, Neb., in 1925 and the Cornhuskers took that one by a neat 17 to 0 margin. — **(7) 1944** W. Blair *Tall Tale America* 211 He was a roustabout for a while, a deckman on a steam boat for a while, a cornpicker for a while. — **(9) 1917** Will & Hyde *Corn Among Indians* 87 Scattered Corn, an elderly Mandan matron, whose father was the last Mandan corn priest, . . . gives the following information on Mandan planting. **1920** Cushing *Zuni Breadstuff* 523 The wise men of the tribe style their people 'the flesh of flesh,' and themselves the 'Corn Priests of Earth.'

(10) 1882 *Cent. Mag.* XXIV. 874 Two 'gin'r'ls' are chosen from among the most famous corn-shuckers on the ground, and these proceed to divide the shuckers into two parties. **1947** Croy *Corn Country* 222 In 'the old days' every neighborhood used to have a champion corn-shucker.

7. In miscellaneous combs.: (1) **corn broom,** a broom made from the panicles of broomcorn, cf. **6.** (3) above; (2) *** -fed,** see as a main entry; (3) **Cornhusker State,** Nebraska, cf. **6. b.** (6); (4) **money,** (*a*) corn used as currency, *obs.*, (*b*) a form of scrip or certificates once used locally in Iowa for purchasing corn and so aiding business, *rare;* (5) **pay,** corn paid in as taxes, *obs.;* (6) **payment,** a payment made in corn, *obs.;* (7) **pile,** a pile of corn, esp. one made in preparation for a husking bee; (8) **pit,** the part of a stock exchange devoted to trading in corn; (9) **popping,** the act of roasting popcorn to cause it to pop or burst, cf. **b.** (7) below; (10) **right,** (see quot.), *obs.;* (11) **shelling,** removing the grains of corn from the cob, an occasion of shelling corn; (12) **shock,** a number of stalks of corn placed upright and tied in a somewhat conical stack; (13) **song,** (see quot. 1882); (14) **specie,** corn used as a medium of exchange, *obs.;* (15) *** stealer,** the hand, *slang, obs.*

(1) *a***1817** Dwight *Travels* IV. 485 [Manufactures of Mass. include] Straw bonnets, Brushes, Corn Brooms. **1935** *Col. of Conn.* 11 Corn brooms: . . . These were made about 1798. — **(3)** [**1930** in Shankle *State Names* (1934) 131 The name 'Cornhuskers' arose within the past thirty years as an epithet for the University of Nebraska football team, and it was extended to include the state.] **1948** *Dly. Racing Form* (Chi.) 29 June 36/2 Racing in the cornhusker state will shift to Madison for the forthcoming Madison Downs session which will get away on Thursday, July 8. — **(4)** (*a*) **1691** *Mass. Bay Currency Tracts* 31 Do not our Brethren at Connecticut find Corn-mony will do their business for them? (*b*) **1933** *Arkansas Gazette* 26 Feb. 11/3 The price paid—25 cents in 'corn money'—was almost three times the current market price.

(5) 1677 *Braintree Rec.* 18 Twenty shillings a year out of the corne pay. — **(6) 1685** *Springfield Rec.* II. 188 Said Persons as make the Corne Payment of ye money Rate. — **(7) 1865** in *Kans. Hist. Quart.* VII. (1938) 32 Clear the snow off the corn pile and cover it with canvas. **1883** Harris *Nights* (1911) 400 He had been the captain of the corn-pile, the stoutest at the log-rolling. — **(8) 1891** *Boston Journal* 20 Nov. 8/3 For a time this morning there was a panic in the corn-pit, and the November option of that cereal sold up 7 cents from the closing price of yesterday. **1902** Norris *Pit* i, There's the Board of Trade Building, where the grain speculating is done,—where the wheat pits and corn pits are. — **(9) 1881** McLean *Cape Cod Folks* 171, I was amused to follow, with my ear, the old gentleman's progress in the successive stages of his corn-shelling and corn-popping.

(10) 1831 A. S. Withers *Chron. Border Warfare* 49 The lands [in Va.] taken up by them [=adventurers], were held as 'corn rights'—each acquiring a title to an hundred acres of the adjoining land, for every acre planted in corn. — **(11)** *a***1849** Ruxton *Life Far West* 62 Better for him had he minded his corn-shelling alone. **1881** [see **corn popping**]. — **(12) 1857** *Rep. Comm. Patents: Agric.* 80 They have been found hibernating under piles of rails, and in corn-shocks. **1945** *Chi. D. News* 31 Jan. 3/3 The snow was so deep on level land that only the tops of corn shocks could be seen. — **(13) 1834** Caruthers *Kentuckian* II. 24 Here was the sooty patent-sweeper, with our southern corn-songs converted into the monotonous twang of business. **1882** *Cent. Mag.* Oct. 874/2 The corn-song is almost always a song with a chorus. . . . These songs are kept up continuously during the entire time the work [of corn-shucking] is going on, and though extremely simple, yet when sung by fifty pairs of lusty lungs, there are few things more stirring. — **(14) 1721** in *Pub. Col. Soc.* III. 4 In our most happy times (as in our fondness we call them) we allowed our Governor an Hundred per annum &c and when the Salary was changed from Corn-Specie to money, there was a muttering and grumbling in the country, as tho' they were going into a mutiny.

(15) 1827 *Mass. Spy* 24 Oct. (Th.), Give us a shake of your corn-stealer; why, you look out in sorts, Dorcas. **1880** *Cong. Rec.* 22 Jan. 488/1 His phalangers or metacarpus, or, rather, corn-stealers, are bigger than those of any other member.

b. With reference to gatherings, festivals, or ceremonies associated with the harvesting, eating, etc., of corn: (1) **corn boiling,** a festive gathering at which green corn is boiled and eaten, *rare;* (2) **dance,** (*a*) a ceremonial or religious dance or festival held by American Indians in connection with the planting or harvesting of corn, cf. **new corn dance,** (*b*) a dance indulged in by Negroes at the time of planting corn, *rare;* (3) **fair,** a fair for exhibiting corn and corn products; (4) **feast,** a feast held by Indians at the time of ripening of green corn; (5) **festival,** (see quot.); (6) **husking,** see as a main entry; (7) **popping,** a social gathering at which popcorn is popped and eaten, cf. **7.** (9) above; (8) **roast,** a party at which green corn is roasted and eaten; (9) **shucking,** =**corn husking,** a festive occasion for this purpose, also attrib.

(1) 1929 *Randolph Enterprise* (Elkins, W.Va.) 26 Sep. 1/1 Tygart Lodge of the Knights of Pythias had a most enjoyable corn boiling and weiner roast last Thursday night. — **(2)** (*a*) **1725** Chicken in *Travels Amer. Col.* 155 At Little Terriquo where was mett together at the corn dance several of the head men. **1836** *Knickerb.* VIII. 154 Sometimes, by . . . remaining away until the corn dances take place, they are forgiven at that jubilee. **1903** White *Forest* 128 Belts of bead-work, yellow and green, for the Corn Dance. (*b*) **1840** Hoffman *Greyslaer* III. 185 De boys . . . has gone to de village to hold corn-dance for seedtime. — **(3) 1888** *Boston Journal* 24 Nov. 2/4 Portsmouth, Ohio, is to have a corn fair. — **(4) 1826** Cooper *Mohicans* xxii, Had they held their corn-feast—or can you say anything of the totems of their tribe?

(5) 1904 *Brooklyn Eagle* 31 Aug. 4 Corn festivals in Kansas are public celebrations in recognition of good crops. — **(7) 1884** *Harper's Mag.* Sep. 610/2 What romps they would have! what corn-poppings! **1887** *Courier-Journal* 6 Feb. 11/3 The corn popping, given by the Pastor's Helpers at East Baptist Church, was in every way a pleasing success. — **(8) 1905** *Denver Republican* 6 Sep. 6/2 Loveland's annual corn roast will be held for the last three days of this week. **1944** Holton *Yankees* 256 Eating clams is the only act more messy than gnawing corn off the cob at a corn roast, but to my mind it is more satisfying. — **(9) 1819** W. Faux *Memorable Days* 211 My host had a large party of distant neighbours assembled to effect a corn shucking, something like an English hawkey, or harvest home. **1898** Harris *Tales* 93, I back de canoe out in de light, en fetched one er dem ol'-time corn-shuckin' whoops. **1944** Duncan *M. Graham* 181 Almira had had her share of merrymakings: apple stirrings and parings, corn shuckings, and fulling bees.

c. Designating parts of the corn plant: (1) **cornhusk,** the coarse axile leaves or bracts that inclose an ear of corn, also attrib.; (2) **silk,** the cluster of glossy, silky styles at the end of an ear of corn; (3) **stock,** a cornstalk; (4) **tassel,** "the graceful feathery flower of the maize plant" (F.); (5) **top,** the part of a corn stalk above the ear, formerly much used as forage; (6) **trash,** (see quot. 1894).

(1) 1712 *N.H. Probate Rec.* I. 693 He shall give unto his mother in law ellener the sixth part of the produce of the hole farm the corn husks and the grain. **1819** *Amer. Farmer* I. 55 Plough Gier. We have seen in use, in a particular neighborhood in this state, wooden hames or collar, as a substitute for the leathern or corn-husk collar. **1947** B. Haile *Prayer Stick Cutting* 91 These are knotted in a cornhusk which the singer places inside, wraps the blades with the yucca strips and lays the tap aside. — **(2) 1861** [see **cornsilk moth**]. **1878** B. F. Taylor *Between Gates* 259 Let the fellow's hair turn the color of corn-silk in the sun. **1948** *Life* 13 Sep. 36/1 With the corn silk turning a dry dark brown over firm ears, the Brewsters . . . must have looked at each other with a wild surmise. — **(3) 1768** Washington *Diaries* I. 262 Finishd cutting down Corn Stocks at all my Plantations. **1900** C. Winchester *W. Castle* ii. 30 Cutting and binding corn-stocks. **1939** *L.A.* Map 126. — **(4) 1871** De Vere (Index). **1904** Glasgow *Deliverance* 288 He ain't got no fancy for corn-tassels and blue ribbons. **1948** Jacobs *We Chose Country* 192 We inhaled the wonderful sweetness of the corn-tassel odors.

(5) 1733 Hempstead *Diary* 265 Stacked our Corn Tops & Husks. **1828** W. Cobbett *Treatise on Corn* Sec. 17 When I came to see the topping of the corn in America, and heard the upper part of the plant called the corn-top, I saw that it must always have been the universal practice to 'cut off the tops of the corn.' [**1941** *L.A.* Map 262.] — (**6**) **1803** R. C. DALLAS *Hist. Maroons* I. 119 (B. '77), The beds with which they provided their guests were not of feathers, but of wholesome fine picked corn-trash, with clean sheets. **1894** *Cent. Mag.* XLVII. 850 In a limited region farther south the infelicitous word 'corn-trash' is sometimes used for shucks.

See also as main entries **corn blade, cob, shuck, stalk.**

d. Designating places or areas where corn is grown: (1) **corn belt,** the region in the central portion of the U.S. where corn is extensively grown; (2) **bottom,** a piece of bottom land suitable for corn; (3) ***field, hill,** see as main entries; (4) **hole,** ?a cornhill, *rare;* (5) ***land,** land used or suitable for growing corn; (6) **lot,** an area or patch where corn is or may be grown, *obs.;* (7) **patch,** a small field of corn.

(**1**) **1882** *Nation* 13 July 24/3 Crop reports from the West still continue favorable, though there are some discouraging accounts of the prospects in the 'corn belt.' **1948** *Life* 23 Aug. 96 Small farmers, or owners of hundreds of acres of some of the most valuable land in the corn belt, they all wear the same work clothes. — (**2**) **1843** *Ind. Mag. Hist.* III. 193 We are gaining meadows, and corn bottoms, and green hillsides, and town plots, by an utter extermination of the forest. — (**4**) **1763** WASHINGTON *Diaries* I. 183, 190 Corn holes.

(**5**) **1654** JOHNSON *Wonder-w. Prov.* 41 Their Corne Land in Tillage in this Towne is about 1200. Acres. **1838** H. W. ELLSWORTH *Valley N. Wabash* iv. 39 The lands, that we call first rate corn-lands, are generally alluvial bottom lands. **1948** *Downers Grove* (Ill.) *Reporter* 21 Oct. 11/3 (*advt.*), 40 acres mostly level, black corn land, 2⅜ miles from Fairview station. — (**6**) **1640** *R.I. Col. Rec.* I. 75 It is ordered that the hoggs [be driven] away out of the corne lotts. **1642** *Portsmouth Rec.* 12 It is ordered that all the hogges [be kept] awaye out of the corne lotts. — (**7**) **1784** W. WALTON *Captivity B. Gilbert* 53 His Employ was to fence and secure the Corn-patch. **1946** *Nat. Geog. Mag.* Aug. 266/1 A few miles farther on we saw a family cultivating their corn patch.

Also *corn bed, boat, breaker, carrier, chamber, cleaner, colored, country, crop, crust, district, drier, gatherer, ground, grower, growing, harrow, harvester, heap, hoeing, laden, leaf, loft, middle, parching, planting, plowing, pounder, rack, raiser, raising, row, sack, setting, shovel, silage, sloop, stand, state, stubble, toll, year,* etc.

8. In phrases: (1) *Corn on the cob,* green corn suitable for boiling or roasting, also ear corn, unshelled corn; (2) *corn in the ear, shuck,* unshelled or unhusked corn; (3) *corn in the milk,* corn in the soft or roasting-ear stage; (4) *to acknowledge the corn,* and variants (see quot. 1948); (5) *corn bread and common doings,* (see quots.), *obs.;* (6) *as flat as a corn and molasses cake,* quite flat, *obs.;* (7) *corn and cob crusher, grinder, mill,* (see quot. 1859); (8) *all for corn,* (see quot.), *obs.*

(**1**) [**1753** *N.C. Morav. Rec.* II. (1925) 19 Sep. 522 Noon meal . . . a kettle full of corn on the cob, salt, and afterwards water-melons.] **1867** DE VOE *Market Ass't* 414 What usually makes a bushel: Sixty pounds of *wheat, Irish Potatoes, Beans,* or *clover-seed;* . . . seventy pounds of *corn on the cob.* **1944** *Nat. Geog. Mag.* Jan. 95 An American captain, together with the French owner of the plantation, inspects corn on the cob to be served at Army messes.

(**2**) **1784** PATTEN *Diary* 478, I bot a parcel of corn in the Ear supposed to be between 4 and 5 bushels for 13/6. **1834** in BASSETT *South. Plant.* 59 Beanland has got your crop gathered: made 25 bales of cotton, has about one of the cribs full of corn in the shuck, about 4 stacks of fodder, killed 4000 pounds of pork.

(**3**) **1817** J. BRADBURY *Travels* 131 Sweet corn is corn gathered before it is ripe, and dried in the sun: it is called by the Americans green corn, or corn in the milk.

(**4**) **1839** *N.O. Picayune* 15 April 2/1 We were certain it was not Dutch, and was in error in saying it was Scotch, and 'acknowledge the corn.' **1861** *Harper's Mag.* July 280/2 Sure enough it was his own house. . . . He 'owned the corn,' flung Cæsar a dollar to pay for the information, and passed the remainder of the night at home with his guests. **1882** *Tomahawk* (Buffalo) No. 2, 1/2 'The editor of the Clipper admits the corn,' says a correspondent in the Vigilant. **1948** FUNK *Hog on Ice* 38 To acknowledge the corn . . . means to admit the losing of an argument, especially in regard to a detail; to retract; to admit defeat.

(**5**) **1838** FLAGG *Far West* II. 72 What'll ye take: wheat-bread and chicken fixens, or corn-bread and common doins? by the latter being signified bacon. **1842** DICKENS *Amer. Notes* 67 He had ordered 'wheat-bread and chicken fixings,' in preference to 'corn-bread and common doings.'

(**6**) **1840** *Picayune* 20 Sep. 2/2 A blow . . . laid him as flat . . . as a corn and molasses cake.

(**7**) **1848** *De Bow's Review* VI. 133 Rice thrashers, Fanning Mills, Corn Shellers, Smut Machines, Corn and Cob Crushers. **1854** *Pa. Agric. Rep.* 363 Corn and cob grinder, Thomas H. Wilson, a good article. **1859** BARTLETT 99 Corn and Cob Mill. A mill for grinding the entire ear of Indian corn.

(**8**) **1877** BARTLETT 147 *All for corn.* Honest, well-meant, sincere. 'He took it all for corn'; i.e. he believed it to be true.

As the last term in **Baden, barley, boat, boiled, bread, broom, brown, butter, calico, Canada, cattle, chicken, chocolate, coffee, cracked, crow, Day, dent, Dutton, dyeing, eared, early, Egyptian, English, field, fired, flint, fodder, German, golden, Golden Sioux, gourd, great, green, Guinea, hog, hominy, hot, hulled, Illinois, Indian, Jerusalem, June, Kentucky, King Philip, lady finger, long, low, lyed, Mandan, May, Mohawk, mutton, old field, Oregon, Otaheite, papoon, parched, parching, Pennsylvania, pied, Polk, pop, popped, popping, rareripe, Ree, rent, rice, roast, roasted, round, sea, seed, she, shelled, shock, shocked, short, sod, soft, soiling, southern, spiked Indian, squaw, squirrel, steamer, store, stump, sweet, tree, tucket, turkey, upland, Virginia, Wabash, white, yellow corn.**

***corn,** *v. tr.* To plant with corn. — **1886** *Consular Rep.* No. lx. 40 Those hundreds of thousands of acres of once valuable Southern lands, corned to death, and now lying to waste in worthless sage grass. **1940** STUART *Trees of Heaven* 129 I'd corn this land three years, then I'd sow it in wheat and orchard grass.

corn ball.

1. a. A corn pone or corndodger. **b.** (See quot.) Both *rare.*

(**a**) **1843** CARLTON *New Purchase* I. 64 Nanny remained near the dutch oven to keep us supplied with red-hot pones, or corn-balls. — (**b**) **1917** WILL & HYDE *Corn Among Indians* 160 There were several varieties of corn balls. One was made of pounded sugar corn mixed with grease. . . . Another kind of corn ball was made of pounded corn, pounded sunflower seed, and boiled beans.

2. (See quot. 1877.)

1873 E. S. PHELPS *Trotty's Wedding* i, They were eating a corn-ball at recess. **1877** BARTLETT 779 Corn-Balls. Balls made of pop-corn and molasses, of which children are very fond. **1943** FARMER *Boston Cook Book* 704 *Corn Balls:* 5 quarts popped corn, 2 cups sugar. . . . Make into balls, let stand in cold place until brittle.

corn blade. The leaf of corn, esp. as cured and used as forage. Usu. *pl.*

1688 CLAYTON *Acc. Va.* in *Phil. Trans.* XVII. 947 Their Indian Corn-blades, which they gather for their Fodder. **1775** ADAIR *Indians* 407 The women . . . knead both [chestnuts and corn] together, wrape them up in green corn-blades of various sizes, about an inch-thick, and boil them well. **1843** *Amer. Pioneer* II 233 Horses here are very small and spirited; they live chiefly on cornblades, brought every day to market in bundles for six cents. **1926** ROBERTS *Time of Man* 43 The cornblades were brown and hard.

corncob ˈkɔrnˌkɑb, *n.*

1. The axis on which the grains of Indian corn grow.

1787 in MENCKEN *Supp.* I. (1945) 506 The Adventures of Jonathan Corncob (title) [An English book brought out in London.] **1793** J. BARLOW *Hasty Pudding* III, The dry husks rustle, and the corn-cobs crack. **1808** PIKE *Sources Miss.* App. II. 175 [We] ascended the river, both sides of which were covered with old Indian camps, at which we found corn cobs. **1946** *Chi. D. News* 22 Nov. 1/5 A large corn milling plant operated today on a fuel mixture of coal and corn cobs.

b. (See quots.) *Obs.*

*c***1844** R. H. COLLYER *Amer. Life* 7 Almost every house or room has in one corner a bar where the various evil spirits of rum, gin and brandy, and various fancy mixtures called, 'Toenails, Bowel Ploughers, Corn Cobs, Eye Snappers,' are retailed. **1852** BENNETT *Mike Fink* 66/1 I'll set [him] aginst the best among ye any day, fur a gallon o' the rale corn-cob.

c. Short for **corncob pipe.** *Colloq.*

1892 *Outing* Sep. 441/1, I were settin' on de po'ch yender, smokin' m' ole corncob. **1945** MARSHALL *Santa Fe* 79 Oldtimers describe him as wearing a cowboy hat over city clothes and smoking a corncob with great nonchalance during the ceremonies.

2. An entire ear of boiled or roasted green corn.

1813 J. LAMBERT *Travels* I. 132 They [=Canadians] are extravagantly fond of the corn cobs boiled or roasted, and rubbed over with a little butter and salt. **1885** PHILLIPS-WOLLEY *Trottings of Tenderfoot* 5 (F.), We . . . gazed in terror at the pretty jewelled fingers and white teeth opposite making short work of a very buttery corn-cob.

3. In combs.: (1) **corncob bowl,** the bowl of a corncob pipe, *rare;* (2) **child,** =**corncob doll,** *rare;* (3) **crusher,** a machine for crushing or grinding corncobs; (4) **doll,** a doll made of a corncob; (5) **fire,** a fire made of corncobs; (6) **oil,** =**corn whisky,** *jocose* and *obs.;* (7)

pipe, a pipe the bowl of which is made from a corncob; (8) **shell,** (see quot.), *rare;* (9) **soup,** soup made from the cobs of tender green corn, *colloq.;* (10) **stopper,** a bottle stopper consisting of a corncob or piece of corncob.

(1) **1856** *Yale Lit. Mag.* XXI. 145 (Th.), He was employed in whittling a corn cob bowl into a pipe. — (2) **1865** MRS. WHITNEY *Gayworthys* i. 16 Say could . . . admonish and discipline, dress and array, her indefinite family of corn-cob children. — (3) **1852** FLEISCHMANN *Wegweiser* 213 In Bezug auf den Getreidebau gibt es besondere Maschinen . . . für das Zerquetschen der Maiskolben (*corn cob crushers*), indem die letzteren als Viehfutter dienen. **1936** *Sears Cat.* (ed. 173) (Index), Corn Cob Crushers. — (4) **1937** COFFIN *Kennebec* 239 There are corncob dolls, with husk dresses and beads for eyes. **1944** DUNCAN *M. Graham* 108 She made Almira corncob dolls.

(5) **1929** E. W. HOWE *Plain People* 50, I recall the luxury of a corn-cob fire to dress by in the dark winter mornings. — (6) **1856** *Town Talk* (S.F.) 13 June 1/2 The old man had gone out to procure some 'corn-cob oil' wherewith to regale his guest. — (7) **1832** KENNEDY *Swallow Barn* II. 246 He stood in the group, with his corncob pipe. **1945** *N. Eng. Homestead* 27 Oct. 12/3 But husbandmen continued to smoke corncob pipes contentedly in their ancient autumn lodge. — (8) **1888** in FARMER 170/1 Soon after that disgrace, a party of the boys prepared a lot of grenades—corn-cob shells they called them—and determined to storm head quarters. — (9) **1946** HIBBEN *Cookery* 39 Corncob Soup (Tennessee). . . . Put the cobs in a soup kettle with cold water, bring to a boil, and simmer, covered, 1 hour.

(10) [**1801** *Spirit Farmer's Museum* 236 Jotham, get the great case bottle, Your teeth can pull its corn cob stopple.] *c***1866** BAGBY *Old Va. Gentleman* 49 He must now go to old-field school, and carry his snack in a tin bucket, with a little bottle of molasses, stopped with a corn-cob stopper. **1912** COBB *Back Home* 286 'Business pretty good, ain't it Squire?' 'It's good,' the Squire would say, licking off the corn-cob stopper of a molasses jug.

corncracker, *n.*

1. (*cap.*) A nickname given to the inhabitants of various southern states, esp. Kentucky. Also attrib. Cf. **Kentucky, lynching corncracker.**

1835 *Western Review* June 342 There is neither wit nor meaning in the terms *Hoosier, Sucker, Corncracker,* and *Buckeye,* which have become so current; and it is not without mortification that we hear strangers inquiring the origin and meaning of these names. **1880** *Scribner's Mo.* Oct. 914/1 A medley of legends and anecdotes was then served up for us in Corn-cracker vernacular. **1940** HATCHER *Buckeye Country* 298, I never in my life heard a Buckeye get into his voice that quiver of ecstasy that is second nature to a Corncracker when he mentions his bluegrass and his mountains and his folks.

b. Corncracker State, a nickname for Kentucky.

1927 EUBANK *Horse & Buggy Days* 12 Old Jack Bedford is as good an old soul as ever left the Corn Cracker state.

2. A mill for grinding or cracking corn.

1844 LEE & FROST *Oregon* 134 At the mission we had a small cast-iron corncracker, in which we ground wheat after a fashion. **1900** SMITHWICK *Evolution of State* 76 There was a saw mill with a corn cracker attached. **1948** *N.W. Ohio Quart.* April 84 They built a dam and millrace and the little corncracker began to turn.

b. (See quot.)

1946 RICHTER *Fields* 139 Some said they would a deal rather have a hominy block. A corn cracker, they called it.

3. (See quot.)

1884 GOODE *Aquatic Animals* 666 Of the Eagle Ray family, *Myliobatidae,* . . . only one [species] seems to be found in Florida and the Gulf; this is the 'Whipparee' or 'Corn-cracker' of the South (*Rhinoptera quadriloba*).

***corned,** *a.* **1. corned beef hash,** a hash the principal ingredient of which is corned beef. **2. corned willie,** corned beef or corned beef hash. Also attrib. *Slang.*

(1) **1902** LORIMER *Lett. Merchant* 94 After he had schemed out ten different combinations, the other ninety turned out to be corned-beef hash. **1939** WOLCOTT *Yankee Cook Bk.* xv., Corned beef was equally at hand for corned beef hash. — (2) **1918** in *Liberty* 11 Aug. (1929) 8/2 Spare time . . . was filled with hard-tack, corned willie . . . and lectures. **1925** *Scribner's Mag.* Sep. 242/1 The men are building breast-works out of corned willy cans, sir!

***cornel,** *n.* As the last term in **low, silky cornel.**

Cornellian kɔr'nɛlɪən, *n.* A student at Cornell University. — **1897** *Outing* XXX. 475/1 It certainly is not going beyond the limits of veracity to say that most rowing men, except Cornellians, desired the success of Harvard. **1898** *Buffalo* (N.Y.) *Express* 18 Dec. 10/2 The team set to work and after three practices went against the beefy well-trained Cornellians.

***corner,** *n.*

1. A tree that designates the junction of two boundaries of a surveyed tract, a stake or marker set up at such a point or contemplated junction.

1699 *Derby* (Conn.) *Rec.* 202 The southered corner is an ash tree. **1746** *N.H. Probate Rec.* III. 453 A tree spotted on four sides . . . is the North East Corner of the Lot. **1816** U. BROWN *Journal* II. 221 If the old original white oak Corner Cannot be found Establish a Corner there in Lieu & in place of said White Oak. **1947** *Harper's Mag.* July 82/1 The early surveyors blazed or spotted the trees along these lines, and for corners set posts, marked trees, or piled up stones.

2. The place at which two panels *of* a rail fence join.

1711 *Boston Town Rec.* VIII. 86 [List of landmarks.] 25. A White Stump on ye Corner of a fence. *c***1845** W. T. PORTER *Big Bear Arkansas* 125 You see, the young cub was standin' in the corner of the fence eatin' roastin' ears.

3. *N. Eng.* In various colloquial uses (see quots.).

1825 J. NEAL *Bro. Jonathan* II. 10 They continued watching him until he came to the 'corner,' the west end of every Yankee village, or settlement. **1841** GURNEY *Journey* 216 The small villages in New England are often called *corners.* **1892** *Vt. Agric. Rep.* XII. 130 Each town has a small village or 'Corners,' where the Churches, post-office, store, and various shops are located. **1942** RAWSON *N.H. Borns a Town* 15 To the east of these falls and spreading out as though sown by some generous hand certain little villages today lie comfortably among the breathing hills where they were given birth one hundred and eighty years ago as 'clearings,' 'hollows' 'notches,' or 'corners.'

4. On the stock exchange, a condition produced by operators who secure all or practically all of a stock.

[**1841** JACKSON *Week in Wall St.* 52 It has been said that he could shoot round a corner; but that is a slander upon the truth, and arose only from his dexterity in always providing a corner, round which he *can* escape, whenever his favorite weapon throws wide of the mark.] **1869** J. B. BROWNE *Great Metropolis* 44 'Corners' are the ambition and dread of all. **1947** *Time* 27 Oct. 106/2 One of his exploits was the 'Hale & Norcross corner' in 1868, by which he got control of an important mine.

transf. **1873** MILLER *Amongst Modocs* 45, I may state that four aces in a game of poker make a 'corner' that cannot be broken.

5. In combs.: (1) **corner ball,** =**bull pen 2,** *obs.;* (2) **biscuit,** (see quot.), *rare;* (3) **bound,** a tree or other marker at the corner of a tract of land or surveyed area; (4) **boy,** one who lounges about street corners, a street loafer, *obs.;* (5) **clock,** a clock designed to stand in a corner; (6) **drugstore,** a drugstore at a street corner; (7) **grocery,** a grocery store situated at a street corner, a saloon or barroom similarly located, also attrib.; (8) **groggery,** a grogshop on a street corner; (9) **lot,** a lot or division of a block in a city or proposed city having frontage on two streets, also attrib.; (10) ***man,** (see quot. 1905); (11) **mark,** a stake, post, or similar marker set up at the corner of a tract of land; (12) **marked,** *a.* of a tree, marked in such a way as to designate the corner of a surveyed tract of land, *obs.;* (13) ***post,** a stake or post that designates the corner of a piece of land; (14) **stake,** a stake that marks the corner of a piece of land; (15) **store,** a store located where two streets corner; (16) **tree,** a tree that marks the corner of a surveyed tract of land.

(1) **1848** in DRAKE *Pioneer Life Ky.* 149 This was the case with that admirable game, a favorite at all country schools, corner ball. **1857** *Spirit of Times* 14 Mar. 28/2 A great match at 'Corner Ball' came off at Strasburg on a recent Saturday afternoon . . . between Lampeter and Strasburg. — (2) **1876** MRS. WHITNEY *Sights & Insights* I. ii. 9 And corner biscuits. . . . She had some little pans made . . . to hold four breakfast biscuits, because she thinks a biscuit is good for nothing without a corner. — (3) **1669** *Essex Inst. Coll.* VI. 175/2 The corner bound between Mr. Endecots & Mr. Reads land. **1723** *Providence Rec.* XVI. 223 A heape of stones which is a Corner bound of a Lott of Land. — (4) **1855** D. C. MITCHELL *Fudge Doings* (N.Y.) II. 47 (Th.), Presently the corner-boy, Jerry, comes in. He is a short-haired, half-Irish boy [etc.].

(5) **1863** BOOTH *N.Y.* 182 About 1720, the corner-clocks, consisting of cases reaching from the floor to the ceiling, with the dial at the top and the pendulum swinging almost at the bottom were introduced. These were all imported, nor were any manufactured in the country until within a comparatively recent date. — (6) **1871** *Cin. Commercial* 30 Aug. 3/2 A gentleman . . . stopped at a corner drug store and asked for a glass of soda water. **1948** *Sat. Ev. Post* 3 July 15/2 There used to be 1500 bookie joints, all illegal, of course, but as open as the corner drugstore. — (7) **1849** in ADAMS *Pioneer Hist.* 149 A little old 'corner grocery' building occupied the corner where Pratt &

Millspaugh's block now stands. **1852** *Knickerb.* XXXIX. 106 What's the use-t of Sabbath, if our young men must frequent corner groceries and a bowling saloon? **1932** *Atlantic Mo.* CL. 141 If one should be lacking, she telephones to the corner grocery. — **(8) 1864** *Cong. Globe* 19 Jan. 270/1 (Th. Supp.), The hungry wife . . . complains not of taxation, but that her wretched husband loiters in the school-house of modern Democracy,—the corner groggery. — **(9) 1702** *Penn-Logan Corr.* (1870) I. 129, I have sold the corner lot next the Meeting-House for £115. **1868** *Putnam's Mag.* III. 24 No corner-lot banditti, Or brokers from the city. **1897** F. NORRIS *Third Circle* (1909) 104 Incidentally corner lots are desirable [in San Diego].

(10) [**1823** *N. Eng. Farmer* 7 June 354/2, I was at the raising [of a log barn], [and] did the chopping at one corner.] **1905** *Forestry Bureau Bul.* 61 *s.v.* Corner man. In building a camp or barn of logs, one who notches the logs so that they will fit closely and make a square corner. **1941** ALLEY *Random Thoughts* 466, I deny his statement that 'the mountain home of today is the log cabin of the American pioneer —a pen that can be erected by four 'corner men in a day.'—**(11) 1690** *Duxbury Rec.* 71 A stake & a heap of stones for the north east corner, where was the former corner mark of said land. **1710** *Ib.* 84 A stone set in the ground, which is his North West corner mark. **1898** [see **corner post**]. — **(12) 1676** *N.Y. State Col. Hist.* XII. 547 From the head of the branch to a corner mark't Spanish Oake. **1681** *New Castle Court Rec.* 503, 40 perches to a corner marked swamp oake. — **(13) 1650** *Rowley Rec.* 67 [The fence belonging to] Thomas Dickinson begins at Cornerpost Twelue Lengths ends at XVI. **1785** A. ELLICOTT in *Life & Lett.* 41 Joseph went with some Hands to enlarge the Pile of Stones about the Corner Post. **1898** C. C. POST *10 Yrs. Cowboy* 167 Phil and two others shouldered their guns and started out with them to find a corner post or mark of some kind. — **(14) 1678** *Oyster Bay Rec.* I. 114 A lott of Land, . . . rainging from ye corner stake [etc.]. **1739** *Southampton Rec.* III. 16 They both of them accepted of ye division where they set ye corner stakes. **1891** *Scribner's Mag.* X. 471 At each corner of his ground, ranging in extent from twenty to twenty-five acres, every individual captain directed these stakes to be forced down as far as possible. Such were called 'corner-stakes.'

(15) 1817 *Cape-Fear Recorder* 5 April, Having removed from the red corner store at Mud Market. **1946** *Progress* March 30/1 Let's drop in some afternoon at a corner store, particularly one near a school, and observe a group of girls. — **(16) 1661** *Portsmouth Rec.* 108 That ye lotters are to run the line . . . from Corner tree to Corner tree. **1791** BARTRAM *Travels* 45 Next morning we marked the corner tree. **1922** KEPHART *So. Highlanders* 346 Do you consider it consistent with his profession as a minister of the Gospel to forge corner-trees?

b. In phrases: (1) *To turn the double corner,* (see quot.), *rare;* (2) *at loose corners,* at loose ends, *rare;* (3) *to carry (up) a corner,* (see quots. and cf. **corner man**); (4) *to trim one's corners,* to venture as far as the situation will permit, *colloq.;* (5) *to cut corners,* to take a short course across a corner, hence to take reckless advantage.

(1) 1821 in KITTREDGE *Old Farmer* (1904) 275 Bob Raikins and Jo Jakins, with 6 or 8 more, *turning the double corner,* as they call it; or, to use a military term, firing off sling and punch from *right to left.* — **(2) 1850** N. KINGSLEY *Diary* 135 Shall now be working at loose corners until the canvass comes. — **(3) 1878** GUILD *Old Times* 160 The principal workmen in making notches in the logs (carrying up corners), were Hon John Bell and Dr. Boyd McNairy. **1944** WILSON *Passing Inst.* 47 It took skill to carry a corner. Only the most agile young men could do this. The rabble could tote logs and push them up the skids. — **(4) 1904** STRATTON-PORTER *Freckles* 157 Freckles was trimming his corners as closely as he dared. — **(5) 1931** *K.C. Times* 7 Nov. The careless driver . . . cuts corners or tries to pass another car at the top of a hill.

As the last term in **Amen, fence, grain, Negro, outside, pigsfoot, pine, post-office, section, trim, wheat, witness corner.**

* **corner,** *v.*

1. *intr.* To meet or converge at a corner.

1821 *Boston Selectmen* 189 A point where said fence and his other fence join cornering on said streets. **1885** in *Wis. Hist. Soc. Coll.* X. 82 Still more notable was the post where sections fourteen, fifteen, twenty-four and twenty-three corner. **1913** STRATTON-PORTER *Laddie* i, The Big Elm . . . stood where four fields cornered. *Ib.*, She was . . . one of those new English people who had moved on the land that cornered with ours on the north-west.

b. To deepen the "box" on a turpentine tree and thus accentuate its corners. *Rare.*

1893 *Outing* Jan. 269/2 Then he 'cornered' the old 'boxes' in the pines, and 'chipped' with a vengeance till they ran full of turpentine.

2. *tr.* To drive or force into a corner.

[**c1835** CATLIN *Indians* II. 67 Their enemy, who had cornered them up in such a way that there was no other possible mode for their escape.] **1849** LANMAN *Alleghany Mts.* 77 When we came near the falls, one of the Hyatts and myself stopped fishing, and went to work to corner the buck.

fig. **1834** *Crockett Narr. Life* 28, I commenced a close courtship, having cornered her from her old beau. **1948** *St. Paul Dispatch* 17 Sep. 1/3 When a neighborhood pup cornered the mother skunk every kid in the neighborhood went to the dog's aid.

b. To get or place in an embarrassing or difficult position, also with *up. Colloq.*

1824 *Mass. Spy* 21 April (Th.), Cornered up so unexpectedly, she candidly confessed. **1894** MARK TWAIN *P. Wilson* xv, Wilson detected it in his hand, by palmistry, and charged him with it, and cornered him up so close that he had to confess.

3. *Stock exchange.* To subject (a person) to financial difficulties by manipulating the market. *Obs.*

1836 *Knickerb.* VII. 42 He has been cornered by the brokers on the — stock, and has lost all his fortune. **1848** *Ib.* XXXII. 273 Something had gone wrong in Wall-street. Suspect he'd been 'cornered.'

b. To secure control over (stocks or commodities). Also absol.

1849 *Hunt's Merch. Mag.* XXI. 119 To corner successfully, requires a little more confidence in one another than is found now-a-days. **1879** *Harper's Mag.* Oct. 717 During the Cuban war a number of resident capitalists 'cornered' all the beef in the market. **1948** *Sat. Ev. Post* 26 June 47/2 The New Bedford whaling firm, . . . set out to corner the whalebone market.

cornerer ˈkɔrnərɚ, *n.* One who secures a corner on a particular stock or commodity. — **1849** *Hunt's Merch. Mag.* XXI. 110 If the game is well played, the cornerers will make as much in selling out as they have in buying in. **1904** O. HENRY *Cabbages & Kings* (1916) 192 'My name is Pinkney Dawson,' said the cornerer of the cockleburr market.

* **cornering,** *n.* **1.** Embarrassing or confronting with difficulty. *Rare.* **2.** Securing a commercial corner on stocks, etc., also attrib. **3.** (See quot. and the examples given *s.v.* **corner man.**)

(1) a1836 CROCKETT in Watterson *Oddities* (1883) 247 Pay to-day and trust to-morrow. Now that idea . . . was a sort of cornering in which there was no back out. — **(2) 1841** *Week in Wall St.* 27 No cornering, I hope. **1848** W. ARMSTRONG *Stocks* 15 The first and principal move in a cornering operation is to create a demand for particular Stocks, and at the same time cause a scarcity of the articles. **1872** TALMADGE *Abominations Modern Soc.* 116 The broker guilty of 'cornering' as well knows that he is sinning against God and man. — **(3) 1852** REGAN *Emigrant's Guide* 311 When the logs were hauled on to the ground two of the most expert would superintend the 'cornering,' in which a notch was cut out of the end of one log a foot from the extremity, and the end of the next which was to lie in this notch was shaped to fit it.

cornetist kɔrˈnɛtɪst, *n.* One who plays a cornet.

1881 *Musical Standard* 29 Jan. 72/1 In the *Musical Record* (Boston, U.S.) mention is made of a young lady cornetist. **1916** WILSON *Red Gap* 233 Ed was known far and wide as the world's challenge cornetist. **1948** *News-Palladium* (Benton Harbor, Mich.) 14 Aug. 3/1 Sunday's municipal band concerts will be based on sacred music with Bill Glines, cornetist, as soloist.

* **corn-fed,** *a.*

1. Fed on Indian corn.

1787 in T. F. DEVOE *Market Book* 181 As I have travelled thro' all the States, I will furnish the *Bill of Fare: . . . North Carolina,* corn-fed pork and peach brandy. **1845** *Knickerb.* XXVI. 511 A pair of spring chickens . . . [which had] been corn-fed for some time. **1865** *Atlantic Mo.* XV. 450 Mine, bein' corn-fed, ought to bring half a cent more.

2. (See quot. 1877.) *Colloq.*

1809 IRVING *Knickerb.* III. vi, They grew up a . . . hardy race of . . . strapping corn-fed wenches. **1877** BARTLETT 148 *Corn-fed,* stout, plump, spoken of a woman. **1916** WILSON *Red Gap* 111 There was a corn-fed hussy in a plush bonnet with forget-me-nots, two hundred and thirty or forty on the hoof.

b. Used also of men and boys.

1840 in BUCKINGHAM *E. & W. States* (1842) I. 454 A well corn-and-pork fed Western Buckeye. **1948** *Chi. Tribune* 20 June (Grafic Mag.) 8/5 He looks like a corn-fed boy, as he should.

c. (See quot.) *Obs.*

1870 MACRAE *Americans* I. 191 When reduced to Indian corn for food, they expressed the difference between themselves and their more fortunate antagonists by contracting 'Federal' and 'Confederate' into 'Fed ' and 'Co(r)nfed.'

* **cornfield,** *n.*

1. A field in which Indian corn is grown.

The earliest example may not refer to a maize field.

1608 SMITH *Newes from Va.* Wks. 1884 I. 32 His next course South, where within a quarter of a mile, the riuer diuideth in two, the neck a plaine high Corne field. **1634** *Md. Plantation Rel.* 13 Yet doe they daily relinquish their houses, lands, and Corne-fields, and leaue them to us. **1709** LAWSON *Carolina* 70 We saw several Plots of Ground clear'd by the *Indians,* after their weak manner, compass'd round with great Timber Trees, which they are no-wise able to fell, and so keep the Sun from Corn-Fields very much; yet nevertheless, we saw as large Corn-stalks, or larger, than we have seen any where else. **1865** GRIGSBY *Smoked Yank* xxvi. (1891) 235, I left my horse and crawled along on the inside of a corn-field fence. **1948** *Chi. D. News* 12 Jan. 1/1 The farmer . . . coveted his neighbor's wife across the cornfields.

2. In combs.: (1) **cornfield bean,** *S.* prob. the cowpea; (2) **darky,** =**cornfield Negro;** (3) **duck,** a local name for the black-bellied tree duck, *Dendrocygna autumnalis,* or the fulvous tree duck, *D. bicolor;* (4) **Negro,** a Negro accustomed to field work rather than to housework, also transf.; (5) **pea,** =**cowpea;** (6) **shuffle,** a kind of shuffling dance, *obs.*

(1) **1939** HARRIS *Purslane* 129 Jessie farmed about as he pleased, planted cabbage in the cotton rows, corn-field beans among the corn. — (2) **1881** *Georgians* 95 That infectious, good-natured, 'corn-field darky' laugh arose again. **1883** *Cent. Mag.* Nov. 132/1 Spencer . . . had the manners of a cornfield darky. — (3) **1878** *U.S. Geol. & Geog. Survey Bul.* IV. 62 By the inhabitants it is called 'Corn-field Duck,' from its habit of frequenting corn-fields for the grain. **1878** *Nat. Museum Proc.* I. 170 *Dendrocygna fulva.* . . . Like the Corn-field Duck, it is a summer visitant. — (4) **1851** *Polly Peablossom* 117 We worked like a cornfield nigger. **1948** MENCKEN Supp. II. 124/1 The late W. J. Cash . . . noted . . . a tendency among educated Southerners to drop, on informal and especially jovial occasions, into what he termed *cornfield nigger.*

(5) **1820** *Western Carolinian* 1 Aug. He will find its component parts to consist of corn field peas. **1902** *Everybody's Mag.* Jan. 70/1, I dun et 'bout two quarts uv cawnfiel' peas cooked right greasy wid er poun' er two er bac'n. — (6) **1846** *N.O. Picayune* 31 Aug. 648/2 In slang parlance he was great on 'Virginia hoedowns' and 'old corn-field shuffles.'

corn hill. The spot or portion of ground where one or more stalks of corn are or may be grown.

[**1622** MOURT *Relation* 30 We marched to the place where we had the corne formerly, which place we called Corne-hill.] *a***1676** JOHN WINTHROP in *Philos. Trans.* No. 142 (1678) 1066 Where the Ground is bad or worn out, the Indians used to put two or three of the forementioned Fishes, under or adjacent to each Corn-hill, whereby they had many times a Crop double to what the Ground would otherwise have produced. **1873** *Newton Kansan* 1 May 1/5 Rhode Island farmers will plant miniature torpedoes in their corn-hills as a substitute for scare-crows. **1948** *New World* (Chi.) 2 July 13/3 Indian corn hills or 'squaw hills' as they are sometimes called, are plainly visible in the park.

cornhusking ˈkɔrnˌhʌskɪŋ, *n.*

1. A social gathering of neighbors to husk the corn belonging to the one at whose home they meet.

[**1786** *N.C. Morav. Rec.* V. (1941) 2144 In Friedland M. R. and J. H. had a fight at a corn-husking and wounded each other.] **1818** WEEMS *Drunkard's Looking Glass* 4 He does not trouble his head about asking the Fool where he has been, whether at a Funeral . . . or a Cock-fight, a Corn-husking. **1943** DEVOTO *Yr. of Decis.* 324 The fiddles were playing a hoedown at a corn husking back home.

2. The husking and gathering of corn. Also attrib.

1890 *Lordsburg Californian* 4 Sep. 5/3 Corn husking has begun. **1913** CATHER *O Pioneers!* 37 Ivar hired himself out in threshing and corn-husking time.

***cornice,** *n.* **cornice rock, cliff,** (see quots.). — **1836** J. HALL *Statistics of West* iii. 49 The cornice rocks, are great curiosities. **1838** FLAGG *Far West* II. 219 The Mississippi now rolls through a broad, deep valley, bounded by an escarpment of cliffs upon either side; and wherever these present a bold façade to the stream, they are grooved, as at the cornice-rocks, by a series of parallel lines. *Ib.* 208 Beyond the stream (Mississippi), stretching away to the northwest, the range of heights you view are the celebrated cornice-cliffs above Herculleaneum.

cornplanter ˈkɔrnˌplæntɚ, *n.*

1. (*cap.*) *attrib.* Designating a division of Seneca Indians under the influence of a celebrated half-breed Seneca chief named Cornplanter.

[**1794** *Gazette of U.S.* 20 June (Th., p. 930), Corn-planter [sends commodities to Lt. Polhemus]]. **1824** BUCHANAN *Sketches* I. 55 Cornplanter's Letter Allegheny River, 2d mo. 2d, 1822. [Speech of Cornplanter to the Governor of Pennsylvania.] **1834** H. BRACKENRIDGE *Recoll.* vii. 74 The arrival of Cornplanter Indians, on the bank of the Alleghany. **1907** HODGE *Amer. Indians* I. 338/2 Both villages belonged to the division of the Seneca known as Cornplanter's band.

2. One who raises Indian corn.

1832 *Cong. Deb.* 9 Feb. 339 The corn planter and wheat grower understand their interests. **1845** SIMMS *Wigwam & Cabin* 2 Ser. 104 One of a tribe [*sc.* crows], of which the corn-planter has an aversion.

3. A machine or device for planting corn. Cf. **hand cornplanter.**

1839 BUEL *Farmer's Companion* 151 Some of them, under the name of corn-planters, are employed in planting Indian corn. **1948** *Democrat* 28 Oct. 3/2 Two-Row Corn Planter. . . . This machine could plant 15 to 20 acres per day if the area previously had been marked by cross-plowing.

corn shuck. =**cornhusk.** Also attrib.

1784 *N.C. Morav. Rec.* V. (1941) 2390 (Disbursements, Penna. cur.) . . . corn-shucks—3s. $1\frac{1}{2}$d.] **1834** *Amer. R.R. Jrnl.* III. 251/2 Corn-shuck mattresses. *c***1845** *Big Bear Ark.,* 21 You can have . . . a wildcat-skin, pulled off hull, stuffed with corn-shucks, for a pillow. **1884** THOMAS HUGHES *G.T.T. Gone to Texas* 190, I had a . . . present . . . in the shape of a corn shuck hat. **1947** *Chr. Sci. Mon.* 20 Dec. III. 12/3 Visitors are cordially invited inside, where they see handwoven window curtains, . . . corn-shuck mats and numerous other articles that delight the eye.

cornstalk ˈkɔrnˌstɔk, *n.*

1. The stem or stalk of Indian corn.

1645 *New Haven Col. Rec.* 157 Itt was ordered thatt no pson or psons shall kindle a fire to burne leaves, straw cornestalks or any kinde of rubbish. **1777** *Jrnls. Cont. Cong.* IX. 929 Resolved, That a committee of three be appointed to collect and digest the late useful discoveries for making molasses and spirits from the juice of corn stalks. **1899** WYETH *Forrest* 444 For thirty days so little rain had fallen in this section that the earth was parched, the blades on the corn-stalks were twisted, the leaves were withering, the highways were filled with dust, and the wet-weather streams and branches were now as dry as the road-beds. **1948** *Ponca City* (Okla.) *News* 4 July 16/4 Corn stalks stripped of their leaves are all that remain after grasshoppers destroyed this corn field near Bassfield, Miss.

b. (See quot. 1816.) *Obs.*

1726 S. PENHALLOW *Indian Wars* (1824) 110 On the Monday after, they killed Jabez Coleman of Kingston, with his son, as they were gathering corn stalks. **1779** T. SMITH *Jrnl.* (1821) 147 Cut our corn stalks. Never was the corn so forward. **1816** PICKERING 71 *Corn-stalks.* (Used generally in the plural number.) The farmers of New England use this term, and more frequently the simple term, *stalks,* to denote the upper part of the stalks of Indian corn (above the ear) which is cut off while green, and then dried to make fodder for their cattle.

2. In combs.: (1) **cornstalk borer,** =**corn borer;** (2) **captain,** see **cornstalk drill, cornstalk militia,** *rare;* (3) **cutter,** (see quots.); (4) **disease,** (see quot. 1900); (5) **drill,** (see quot.), *obs.;* (6) **ground,** ?ground upon which there are cornstalks, *rare;* (7) **harvester,** a

One form of cornstalk cutter

machine for harvesting cornstalks, *rare;* (8) **lawyer,** (see quot.), *obs.;* (9) **militia, militiaman,** (see **cornstalk drill**), *obs.;* (10) **mill,** a mill for extracting the juice from cornstalks, *obs.;* (11) **pine,** the loblolly pine of the southern states.

(1) [**1882** *Comm. Agric. Rep.* 142 The smaller stalk-borer works throughout the entire summer and fall, and, as late as October, cuts the toughened stalks of the late corn to such an extent that they are easily blown to the ground.] **1902** *Dept. Agric. Yearbook* 729 Corn stalk-borer, larger (*Diatræa saccharalis* Fab.) . . . [was] reported in 1902 as occasioning considerable injury in Virginia, in some portions of which it is known as the 'shatter worm.' — (2) **1898** *Cong. Rec.* 23 April 4216/1, I was a tin soldier—a kind of cornstalk captain—but I have had . . . [some] experience. — (3) **1852** *Mich. Agric. Soc. Trans.* III. 29 Best corn stalk cutter. **1939** GILBERT *Forty Yrs.* 2 We had an old cornstalk cutter on the farm. You turned a crank, and with its curved knives it drew in the stalks if you gave them a start. — (4) **1900** *Dept. Agric. Yearbook* 307 The cornstalk disease . . . is a strange, little-understood malady of cattle, due to the eating of dry cornstalks in the field after harvest. **1945** *Prairie Farmer* 8 Dec. 4/2

Horses may die from the so-called cornstalk disease if they are turned into husked cornfields following damp, rainy weather. (5) **1896** ROOSEVELT *Winning of West* IV. 245 Such musters were often called, in derision, cornstalk drills, because many of the men, either having no guns or neglecting to bring them, drilled with cornstalks instead. — (6) **1754** HEMPSTEAD *Diary* 627 In the afterno[on] I rid out to crossm[an's] lot & diged Stones among the Cornstalk ground. — (7) **1891** *Atlantic Mo.* June 808/1 Represented among the patents are an improved gridiron, a locomotive smokestack, a cornstalk harvester, . . . and a telephone transmitter. — (8) **1836** W. F. GRAY *Diary* (1909) 113 He is called here [in Texas] a *cornstalk* lawyer which is explained to be equal to a *quack* among physicians. — (9) [**1801** *Washington Federalist* 12 Feb., The militia of the latter, untrained and farcically performing the manual exercise with *cornstalks* instead of muskets, burdened besides with a formidable internal foe, . . . what, may it be asked, would be the issue of the struggle?] **1839** *Knickerb.* XIV. 107 Your vagabond has his occupation, his trade, his standing in society. He falls into his place as scientifically as a cornstalk militia-man. **1913** O. A. ROTHERT *Hist. Muhlenberg Co.* (Ky.) 168 Those who had no firearms to bring, or who had forgotten them, would enter the drills with a trimmed sapling or a cornstalk—consequently the name, the Cornstalk Militia.

(10) **1847** L. COLLINS *Kentucky* 547 He had the misfortune to lose his arm; from a severe wound received while attending a corn stalk mill. — (11) **1897** SUDWORTH *Arborescent Flora* 26 Pinus taeda . . . Loblolly Pine. . . . Common Names. . . . Cornstalk Pine (Va.).

b. In the names of things made or consisting of cornstalks: (1) **cornstalk bow,** a bow made of a cornstalk for playing on a cornstalk fiddle, *rare;* (2) **coffin measure,** a cornstalk upon which the measurements for a coffin are indicated, *rare;* (3) **fiddle,** a child's plaything

Cornstalk fiddle with bow

made of a joint of a cornstalk by loosening a part of the fiber and placing a support at each end; (4) **fodder,** (see quot. 1816 in **1. b.** above), *obs.;* (5) **horse,** a cornstalk used by a child as a horse, *rare;* (6) **viol,** a cornstalk fiddle.

(1) **1858** D. K. BENNETT *Chron. N.C.* 102 'Gourd fiddles' were then in vogue, 'puncheon floors,' and 'corn-stalk bows!' — (2) **1889** RILEY *Pipes o' Pan* 14 The countryman from 'Jessup's Crossing,' with the cornstalk coffin-measure, loped into town. — (3) **1824** *Historical Colls.* (Concord, N.H.) May 159 And there they'd *fife away like fun,* And play on cornstalk fiddles. **1892** M. A. JACKSON *Gen. Jackson* 21 At school, one day, during recess, he became absorbed in making a cornstalk fiddle. **1943** HOLT *Carver* 18 Little boys made cornstalk fiddles the same way little girls made rag dolls. — (4) **1868** WOODRUFF *Trotting Horse* ii. 50 If anybody thinks to follow the old starving, cornstalk fodder, fed-in-the snow system, . . . he must go to the devil on his own road.

(5) **1886** POORE *Reminisc.* I. 175 'What! unwhig me? Me, who was a Whig when you gentlemen were riding cornstalk horses in your fathers' barnyards?' — (6) **1819** PEIRCE *Rebelliad* 72 He saw Bat Fuller's corn-stalk viol.

c. In the obs. or rare names of products secured from cornstalks, as (1) **cornstalk juice,** (2) **liquor,** (3) **meal,** (4) **molasses,** (5) **paper,** (6) **sugar,** (7) **whisky.**

(1) **1777** CUTLER in *Life & Corr.* I. 63 Boiled some cornstalk juice into molasses. — (2) **1777** CUTLER in *Life & Corr.* I 63 Boiled cornstalk liquor. — (3) **1894** *Vt. Agric. Rep.* XIV. 44 A sample of 'cornstalk meal' was shown, made from weatherworn butts. — (4) **1825** NEAL *Bro. Jonathan* I. 77 A spoonful or two of 'turrible good' cornstalk molasses. **1853** RAMSEY *Tennessee* 718 The pith of the matured stalk of the corn is esculent and nutritious, and the stalk itself compressed between rollers, furnishes what is known as corn-stalk molasses.

(5) **1944** *N. & Q.* IV. 57 George M. Rommel's *Farm Products in Industry* . . . announced as a book printed on cornstalk paper, was actually printed on paper containing only twenty-five percent cornstalk fiber. — (6) **1843** ELLSWORTH *Improvements in Agric.* 21 While the temperance reformation is so greatly lessening the consumption of corn in the manufacture of whiskey, the introduction of this manufacture of cornstalk sugar promises to furnish a much more profitable as well as salutary application. **1848** *Hunt's Merch. Mag.* XIX. 491 The manufacture of beet or corn-stalk sugar . . . might be effected. — (7) **1780** *N.J. Archives* 2 Ser. IV. 671 His corn-stalk whiskey for his grog.

* **Cornwallis,** *n.* (See quot. 1848.) *Obs.*

1847 LOWELL *Biglow P.* I. 17 Recollect wut fun we hed . . . Up there to Waltham plain last fall, along o' the Cornwallis? **1848** *Ib.* 143 *Cornwallis,* a sort of muster in masquerade; supposed to have had its origin soon after the Revolution, and to commemorate the surrender of Lord Cornwallis. **1881** *Harper's Mag.* Jan. 260/2 The annual muster of the militia . . . brought together all the boys of the county to see . . . the hilarious sport called a 'Cornwallis.'

Cornwallis kɔrnˈwɔlɪs, *v. tr.* To force to capitulate. *Obs.* — **1799** *Farmer's Reg.* (Greensburg, Pa.) 28 Dec. (Th.) (*caption*), The Duke of York Cornwallis'd and Burgoyn'd in Holland.

Cornwallisade kɔrn,wɔlɪsˈed, *n.* An event such as that at Yorktown when Cornwallis surrendered. *Obs.* — **1908** A. MATTHEWS in *Proc. Amer. Antiq. Soc.* XIX. 27 The surrender of Burgoyne at Saratoga, of Lincoln at Charleston, and of Cornwallis at Yorktown, had given rise to the words 'Burgoynade,' 'to Burgoyne,' 'Lincolnade,' and 'Cornwallisade.'

***corny,** *a.* Over-sentimental, trite. Also of poor quality. *Slang.* Cf. ***corn,** *n.* **3.** — **1933** *Time* 10 April 30/1 Songs will become a little simpler, or 'corny,' meaning more homey. **1948** *Sat. Ev. Post* 17 July 10/2 The line he takes is corny, but good, you know.

* **corporal,** *n.*

1. a. = **fallfish. b.** Erroneous for caporal *q.v.*

(a) 1888 GOODE *Amer. Fishes* 427 The name Corporal seems to have been derived from the Dutch or German settlers of the Middle States. — **(b) 1920** HUNTER *Trail Drivers Texas* I. 229 Gilly Henson was our corporal or boss.

2. corporal's guard, (see quot. 1914).

[**1844** *Niles' Reg.* LXVI. 135/3 When John Tyler came into office he possessed the confidence of the whole party. He suddenly abandoned his principles; and did that party follow him? No, sir; with all the patronage of the government in his hands, he could not carry off a 'corporal's guard.'] **1886** POORE *Reminisc.* I. 280 The 'Corporal's Guard' who sustained Mr. Tyler were all on hand and prominently seated to hear him abuse the Whigs. **1914** *Cyclo. Amer. Govt.* I. 470 Corporal's Guard. The small coterie of Senators and Representatives who supported the administration of President John Tyler, (*see*), 1841–45, while the majority of the Whig members under Clay's leadership . . . opposed the administration.

corporate limits. The outermost bounds of an incorporated area. — **1851** CIST *Cincinnati* 269 Farther north, is Fairmount, a north-western suburb immediately adjoining our corporate limits. **1896** J. C. HARRIS *Sister Jane* 17 Their place, indeed was something of a plantation, . . . just outside the corporate limits of the village.

* **corporation,** *n.*

1. (See quots.) *Obs.*

1844 *Lowell Offering* IV. 145 The driver carried me to the 'corporation,' as it is called; and which, so far as I can describe it, is a number of short parallel streets with high brick blocks on either side. **1845** *Ib.* V. 11 On one of the corporations of this city, about eight years ago, might have been seen, on a summer evening, a company of four or five young females, who through the day had labored at their several employments in some one of the factories connected with the corporation.

2. In combs.: (1) **corporation attorney,** an attorney employed by an incorporated town; (2) **bill,** (see quot.), *obs.;* (3) **council,** a body of men chosen to direct the governing of an incorporated town or city; (4) **counsel,** an attorney who is the chief legal officer of a municipality; (5) **dinner,** in N.Y. City, a dinner given in honor of or under the auspices of the governing body of the city; (6) **hole,** formerly in N.Y. City, a derisive term for a pothole, mudhole, etc., in the city streets, *obs.,* cf. **corporation pudding;** (7) **lawyer,** a lawyer employed by a corporation of business men; (8) **limits,** = **corporate limits;** (9) **line,** the boundary line of an incorporated area; (10) **pudding,** (see quot. 1896), *obs.;* (11) **stop,** (see quot.).

(1) **1830** *Williams's N.Y. Ann. Reg.* 282 City Governments. Common Council of Albany. . . . John E. Lovett, Corporation Attorney. — (2) **1834** THORBURN *Forty Years* 186, I put two one-penny corporation-bills in the plate . . . [footnote:] Paper money, then in circulation in New York before the United States had established a mint. — (3) **1854** THORPE *Master's House* 51 He gave vent to his wrath at the occasional agitation in the Corporation Council of New Orleans. — (4) **1863** *N.Y. Times* 14 July 1/6 The real object of the meeting was to authorize the Corporation Counsel to associate such eminent counsel with him as he might choose, and take steps to test the constitutionality of the National Enrollment Act, under which the draft is being

made. **1915** *Highland Park* (Ill.) *Press* 17 June 1/6 Corporation Counsel Holmes made a statement on the C. & M.E. situation and other important matters.

(5) **1809** Irving *Hist. N.Y.* (1927) III. ii. 122 It being their duty to . . . hunt the markets for delicacies for corporation dinners. — (6) **1860** *Harper's Mag.* Sep. 570/1 The plaintiff, in a suit against the city, had been injured by a fall caused by what is termed 'a Corporation hole.' — (7) **1893** Thanet *Stories* 215 He went away for an interview with the corporation lawyer. **1945** *Nation* 7 April 386/2 After graduation he became a corporation lawyer with offices at 25 Broad Street, across the street from the New York Stock Exchange. — (8) **1847** C. Lanman *Summer in Wild.* iv. 30 When this city was in its glory . . . the corporation limits were uncommonly extensive. **1912** *Amer. Mag.* May 119/1 Baseball on Sunday was not permitted within the corporation limits of St. Paul, and a Sunday park had been erected outside the city's jurisdiction. — (9) **1841** Cist *Cincinnati* 29 Between Main street and the corporation line.

(10) **1896** Haswell *New York* 168 Frequently parties, suffering from the neglect by the accumulation of filth in the streets, would pile it up in a great mass and then label it 'Corporation Pudding.' **1938** Hart *New Yorkers* 15 There was a pleasant fiction current that these mounds of offal (known to the jocular citizenry as 'Corporation Pudding') were to be removed by cartmen in the employ of the city. — (11) **1889** *Cent.* 1275/3 corporation-stop. . . . A stop in a gas- or water-main for the use of the gas- or water-company only.

As the last term in **domestic, moneyed, public service corporation.**

corporosity ˌkɔrpəˈrɑsɪtɪ, *n.* [L. *corpus*+*-osity.*]

1. Bodily bulk. Also as a humorous title after *his excellency*, etc. *Obs.*

1837 J. C. Neal *Charcoal Sketches* (F.), His corporosity touches the ground with his hands in a vain attempt to reach it. **1870** Olive Logan *Before Footlights & Behind Scenes* 174 The manager presently came bustling in—a gentleman endowed with an ample corporosity, and a little hard of hearing.

2. Often used in the grandiose greeting shown in the quots. *Humorous.*

1890 *Amer. Folk-Lore* III. 64 How does your corporosity sagatiate? **1945** *Sat. Review* 27 Jan. 15/2 The polysyllabic pomposities of the 1840's which blackface minstrelsy exploited—*How does your corporosity segashuate this evening?*—were strutty and dry.

*__corps__, *n.* As the last term in **advance, drum, Engineer, Marine, Signal Corps.**

corpse plant. (See quot.) — **1857** Gray *Botany* 262 *Monotropa uniflora*, Indian Pipe, Corpse-plant. . . . Dark and rich woods.

corral kəˈræl, *n.* Orig. *W.* [Sp. in same sense. An Amer. borrowing.] An inclosure for horses, cattle, etc. Also attrib.

1829 *Amer. Turf Reg.* Oct. 101 They procure from a great distance, and by almost incredible labour, a quantity of wood palisades, with which they form a *corral*, of great size. **1928** Breakenridge *Helldorado* 24 With the help of the corral boss I got the pick of the saddle horses in the corral. **1947** *Reader's Digest* Oct. 111/1 He roared to the cowboys at the corrals.

fig. **1890** Ryan *Told in Hills* 336 He first led us out of that corral in the hills. **1946** *Progress* March 30/1 When the draft all but depleted the male element, the possibility of meeting some vulnerable lad at the drugstore corral became an all-important motive.

As the last term in **adobe, calf, cattle, count, feed, government, horse, log, picket, pig, rope, shearing, sheep, side, stock corral.**

corral kəˈræl, *v.* Orig. *W.*

1. *tr.* To confine (horses or cattle) in, or as in, a corral.

1847 Ruxton *Adv. Rocky Mts.* xxvii. During their stay [i.e., of a band of Arapaho Indians] the animals were all collected and corraled. **1873** Miller *Amongst Modocs* 18 They [Indians] . . . assisted to bring in and corral the horses. **1945** *This Week Mag.* 28 July 5 He and the native Indians on his payroll bucked a savage spring gale . . . to finish the roundup, butchering 75, and corralling the rest.

absol. and *transf.*

1860 *Knickerb.* LV. 100, I want to 'corel' you for a little chat. **1869** *Overland Mo.* III. 126 At night they 'round up' or 'corral' ('corral,' in Texas, means also to herd without an inclosure, on the open prairie). **1944** *Newsweek* 26 June 17 When Allied armies approach Paris the Nazis will corral all mature males in the Luxembourg, Buttes-Chaumont, and Vincennes parks, which have already been turned into concentration camps.

2. (See quot. 1848.)

1848 Bryant *Calif.* (1849) 19 The wagons, in forming the encampment, were what is called corraled, an anglicised Spanish word, the significance of which, in our use of the term, is that they were formed in a circle. **1876** *Denver Times* 6 May 1/6 They made a strong defense, . . . corralling the wagons and fighting from behind the wagons and teams. **1928** Stansbery *Passing of 3D Ranch* 13 We coralled our wagons and kept our horses in it that night.

corregidor kəˈrɛgəˌdɔr, *n.* *W.* [Sp. An Amer. borrowing.] The chief magistrate of a town formerly in Spanish territory.

1836 D. B. Edward *Hist. Texas* vii. 149 Those Ayuntamientos of the towns that of themselves, or with a population that does not exceed five thousand souls, shall consist of one alcade, . . . two corregidors. **1876** Harte *Gabriel Conroy* xviii, It is *that* has made you and your colleagues dear to us—dear to those who have been the helpless victims of your courts—your *corregidores.* **1948** *N.M. Quart. Rev.* Summer 238 He accepts without question or comment the standard but inconclusive categorization of gobernadores, alcaldes mayores, and corregidores.

corrupt bargain. *Hist.* A reputed collusion between J. Q. Adams and Henry Clay in the presidential election of 1824 by which the former was to become President and the latter Secretary of the Treasury. Also transf. and attrib.

1827 Clay *Speech* 12 July, Every circumstance was then fresh; the witnesses all living and present; the election not yet complete; and therefore the imputed corrupt bargain not fulfilled. **1913** Bassett *Short Hist. U.S.* 382 The Jackson-Calhoun group . . . voted against the confirmation of Clay, and returned to their homes full of scorn at what they proclaimed a corrupt bargain to obtain the presidency. **1913** A. C. Cole *Whig Party in So.* 254 Renneau of Georgia resented this charge of a 'corrupt bargain' as applied to the delegates from his section. **1948** *Tenn. Hist. Quart.* March 21 Jackson's outburst of anger was taken up by his political band, and the corrupt bargain charge became the shibboleth of the campaign.

*__corsage__, *n.* A bouquet worn by a woman, orig. at the waist, now usu. pinned just below the shoulder.

[**1886** *Amer. Garden* Jan. 8/3 An enterprising florist who has imported Water-Lilies from Florida for a week past, selects twenty expanded ones for a bouquet de corsage.] **1911** Harrison *Queed* 105 On her rounded breast nodded his favor, a splendid corsage of orchid and lily-of-the-valley. **1946** *Sterling* (Colo.) *Advocate* 10 June 3/3 The bride chose an aqua blue afternoon dress with black accessories and a corsage of white gardenias.

*__corsair__, *n.* A species of rockfish found on the California coast. — **1884** Goode *Aquatic Animals* 265 Corsair (*Sebastichthys rosaceus*) . . . is known to the Portuguese fishermen at Monterey by the name of 'Corsair.'

*__Cortland__, *n.* A variety of apple introduced in 1915 by the N.Y. State Experiment Station. — **1945** *Bristol* (N.H.) *Enterprise* 15 Feb. 1/1 Apples Pinnacle Farm New Hampton, N.H. McIntosh Cortland Baldwins Delicious Northern Spies. **1945** *Greeley* (Colo.) *D. Tribune* 15 Mar. 10/6 Apples: Transparent, Anoka, . . . Cortland, Prairie Spy.

cortlandtite ˈkortləndˌaɪt, *n.* [*Cortlandt* Township, N.Y.] (See quot. 1909.) — **1895** *Standard Dict.* **1903** Geikie *Text-bk. Geol.* (ed. 4) 241 Cortlandtite . . . so named from its occurrence in the 'Cortlandt series' of eruptive rocks on the Hudson River. **1909** F. H. Hatch *Text-Bk. Petrol.* 243 Cortlandtite = olivine + hornblende + hypersthene . . . Name suggested by G. H. Williams.

corvina kɔrˈvinə, *n.* [Sp., a kind of fish.] Any one of various sea fish related to the croaker or weakfish. — **1842** *Nat. Hist. N.Y., Zoology* IV. 74 The Silvery Corvina. *Corvina argyroleuca.* . . . This fish . . . is frequently called Silvery Perch by the fishermen. *Ib.* 77 The Sharp-Finned Corvina. *Corvina oxyptera.* . . . Pectoral fins long and pointed. **1888** Goode *Amer. Fishes* 121 *Cynoscion parvipinne*, is usually known as the 'Corvina' or 'Caravina.'

cosmic ray. A term first applied by Robert A. Millikan to any one of many very penetrating rays of extremely high frequency, apparently resulting from nuclear transformations, and reaching the earth with equal intensity day and night. Also attrib. —**1925** Millikan in *Science* 20 Nov. 447/1 The experiments with the sounding balloons indicates [*sic*] that the frequencies of these cosmic rays do not extend over into the X-ray region of frequencies. **1948** *Time* 5 July 44/3 A whole galaxy of cosmic ray experts gathered last week . . . to honor Nobel Prizeman Dr. Robert A. Millikan, 80, principal discoverer and namer of cosmic rays.

Cosnino ˈkɑsˌninə, *n.* [Native name of unknown significance.] An Indian of a small isolated Yuman tribe in Colorado and Arizona. Usu. *pl.*, as a tribal designation. Also attrib.

1854 J. R. Bartlett *Narrative* II. 178 On the eastern side, the same missionaries notice the *Tehuas*, *Cosninas*, and *Moquis.* **1893** Donaldson *Moqui Pueblo Indians* 62 They were Apaches, Utes, Piutes, Navajos, and Cojoninas. **1903** James *Indian Basketry* 89 In similar fashion the Havasupais, or Kohoninos, do not dye their willows black, but use, instead of willows, the peeled pod of the martynia, which is jet black. **1907** Hodge *Amer. Indians* I. 538/1 In this connection it is of interest to note that the Cosnino caves on the upper Rio Verde, near the n. edge of Tonto basin, central Arizona, were named from this tribe, because of their supposed early occupancy by them.

* **Cossack,** *n.*

1. *pl.* (See quots.) *Obs.*

1832 R. Cox *Adv. Columbia River* 266 Last June they received a mortal blow from the Cossacks of Red River. [*footnote:*] A *nom de guerre* given by the writer to the sons of white men by Indian wives. **1848** J. Mitchell *Nantucketisms* 40 *Cossacks,* the name of a local party, opposed to the mixture of blacks & whites in the public schools.

2. (See quots.) Also **Pennsylvania Cossacks.**

1928 *Collier's* 29 Dec. 9/4 Remember the state constabulary of Colorado, the so-called 'Cossacks' who were so bitterly complained of by striking miners. **1933** H. O'Connor *Mellon's Millions* 208 The operators had already formed the Coal and Iron Police, that private army, clothed with the police power of the state, which has long been infamous in labor history as the Pennsylvania Cossacks. **1948** Chaplin *Wobbly* 139 The strike committee notified the commander of the constabulary that the life of a 'Cossack' would be taken in retaliation for every steel worker killed.

3. Cossack outpost, in a military organization, an outpost consisting of four men, one of whom is always on guard.

1895 F. Remington *Pony Tracks* 203 The 'Cossack outposts' are another feature much insisted on, and, strange to say, this arrangement was first invented in America, despite its name.

cossas ˈkɑsəz, *n. pl.* [Hindu *khāssah*]. Plain cottons and muslins imported from India. Also attrib. *Obs.*

1790 *Pennsylvania Packet* 19 Oct. 3/2 Richard and James Potter are rapidly disposing of their Fall Importation. . . . Two yard pullicats Cossacs. **1795** *Columbian Centinel* 10 Jan. 3/3 An extensive assortment of fresh India and other goods consisting of three thousand pieces India Cottons, such as Tandas, Cossahs, Gurrahs, [etc.]. **1800** *Ib.* 29 Jan. 3/3 India Cottons. For Sale . . . 1 bale Tandah Cossas.

Costa('s) hummingbird. A species of hummingbird, *Calypte costae,* found in the Southwest, and named in 1839 in honor of Louis Marie Pantaléon Costa (1806–64), an enthusiastic student of hummingbirds.

1860 Baird in *Ives's Rep.* V. 5 *Atthis costæ,* Reich., Coste's humming bird. Colorado river. **1898** *N.Y. Observer* 14 July 34/2 Costa's Humming-bird, he says, is a rare summer resident. **1940** Jaeger *Desert Wild Flowers* 302 Sagebrush is also a favorite nest site for the . . . Costa hummingbird.

costal kosˈtɑl, *n. S.W.* [Sp., a sack.] A sack or large bag. *Obs.* — **1870** *Republican Review* (Albuquerque, N. Mex.) 3 Dec. 4/1 Albuquerque Market Prices . . . Corn, per costal 1 25. **1872** *Ib.* 6 Jan. 2/1 We suggest that a law . . . making the costal a lawful measure; stating its length, width, and the kind of material it should be made of.

* **co-state,** *n.* A state allied or associated with the others in the Federal Union. *Obs.*

*c*1798 Jefferson *Writings* XVII. 389 This commonwealth does therefore call on its co-states for an expression of their sentiments. . . . The rights and liberties of their co-states will be exposed to no dangers. **1852** *Harper's Mag.* V. 256/2 The wrongs sustained by the State . . . amply 'justify that State . . . in dissolving at once all political connection with her co-States.' **1854** Benton *30 Years' View* I. 349 Virginia exercises the right that pertains to a State . . . in . . . declaring her views, and inviting the like action of her co-States.

costive ˈkɔstɪv, *a.* [f. * *cost*+*ive.*] Expensive, costly. *Colloq.*

1848 *Oquawka* (Ill.) *Spectator* 6 Dec. 4/1 I can't do it all at once, as my women folks are going costive and expensive on me every year. **1870** *Rocky Mt. Herald* (Denver) 20 July 4/2 Now comes into court one 'sister' Pettis who pays her two dollars for a [license]; sweet little poodle but pretty cost-ive. **1878** *Caddo* (Indian Terr.) *Free Press* 11 Oct. 5/2 A scarcity of ice has been a great hardship heretofore, and to ship it from Denison, made it very costive.

cost mark. Code letters or symbols placed upon articles kept for sale to indicate the price paid for them. — **1872** *Chi. Tribune* 9 Oct. 3/3 We are determined to reduce our stock of these goods and will positively sell all fine laces by the cost mark instead of the selling mark. **1877** in Appel *Biog. Wanamaker* (1930) 93 Our cost-mark is Dont Give up. *Ib.,* As we give you our cost-mark any person can look at our tickets and find the exact cost of every item in our store.

costumer ˈkɑstjumɚ, *n.*

1. One who deals in costumes or dresses.

1864 Webster. **1887** *Lippincott's Mag.* Aug. 295 Costumers from New York are employed, and much time is spent in rehearsing for the presentations. **1948** *So. Bend* (Ind.) *Tribune* 15 Aug. (Comics) 3 Who's your costumer?

2. =**hat tree.**

1926 *Sears Cat.* 863. **1935** *Montgomery Ward Cat.* 484 Made of solid Oak in Golden finish . . . this costumer should last for years.

* **cot,** *n.*

1. A sofa. *Obs.*

1800 J. Boucher *Glossary* xlix, A *Cot;* a sopha. **1835** *S. Lit. Messenger* IV. 89/2, I should not like to occupy one of those settees or cots as they call them, all conglomerated as they are into a dense mass.

2. cotbed, a narrow, easily portable single bed. Also **cot bedstead,** the frame of such a bed. Cf. **camp cot.**

1838 Ingraham *Burton* II. 175 A narrow cott bed, with a military cloak thrown over it, constituted the sole furniture of the warrior's abode. **1849** *Rep. Comm. Patents* 289 What I claim . . . is the construction of a folding cot bedstead. **1856** *Spirit of Times* 15 Nov. 172/3 A roaring wood fire at one end of the room, three or four Chairs, an old wooden table, a cot bedstead . . . and you have a sugar-house interior. **1892** Gunter *Miss Dividends* 177 She goes up to her room, where she finds a clean cot-bed.

cotbetty ˈkɑtˌbɛtɪ, *n.* [An extension of *cot* in the same sense.] (See quots.) *Obs.* — **1859** Bartlett 102 *Cotbetty,* a man who meddles in the woman's part of household affairs. North and East. It is probably of English origin. Halliwell and Wright give both *cot* and *cot-quean* with the same meaning. **1870** *Nation* 4 Aug. 73/1 'Cot-betty,' not 'cot,' was what our old cook called us when we bothered her in the kitchen.

cote kot, *n.* [f. F. *côte,* in similar senses.] (See quots.) *Obs.*

1817 S. Brown *Western Gaz.* 167 There are [at Detroit] about three hundred buildings of all descriptions, exclusive of the suburbs, or 'Cotes.' **1846** J. W. Webb *Altowan* I. ii. 42 At this moment, through an open that showed them the côte above, they discovered two buffalo bulls. [footnote to *côte:*] Small hills. French terms are become vernacular, in many instances, among the trappers. **1867** Latham *Black & White* 166 They had their houses in New Orleans, and their houses on the 'cote.' [Bank of the Mississippi.]

coteau kəˈto, *n.* [F.] An upland area.

1825 Keating *Exped. St. Peter's River* II. 220 The Coteau des Prairies is a very remarkable feature in the aspect of this region. **1839** *Boston Wkly. Mag.* 12 Jan. 143/2 This strange ledge or wall breaks out on the summit of the *coteau* or dividing ridge, between the head waters of the St. Peter's and the Missouri rivers. **1918** Visher *So. Dakota* 36 Topographically the coteaus may be considered as extensive mesas standing some 500 to 700 feet above the Dakota Valley which separates them. **1937** Hyde *Red Cloud's Folk* 8 Riggs came across the coteau to Fort Pierre.

* **cottage,** *n.*

1. A summer residence with or without pretentiousness, usu. at a health or pleasure resort.

1876 *Cattaraugus* (N.Y.) *Union* 31 Aug. 3/5 Fair Point . . . contains about 250 cottages, some of them very nice. **1948** *Nat. Geog. Mag.* Aug. 160/1 America's empire builders competed in the splendor of multimillion-dollar 'cottages.'

2. In combs.: (1) **cottage cheese,** cheese made of drained, and usu. pressed, milk curd; (2) **pudding,** a form of pudding consisting of a plain cake covered with sweet sauce.

(1) 1848 Bartlett 314 *Smear-Case,* a preparation of milk made to be spread on bread, whence its name, otherwise called cottage-cheese. **1945** *Pueblo* (Colo.) *Chieftain* 18 June 5/4 Now you get a paper cup of cottage cheese to smear on your bread. — **(2) 1909** O. Henry *Options* 266 We had browsed . . . on local topics, and then parted, after . . . Irish stew, . . . cottage-pudding, and coffee. **1943** Farmer *Boston Cook Book* 545 Cottage Pudding: ¼ cup butter, ½ cup sugar. . . . Serve with Vanilla Sauce . . . , Hard Sauce . . . , Lemon Sauce . . . or with strawberries . . . stewed blueberries, or peaches.

As the last term in **boarding, Cape Cod, frame, log house, prairie, summer cottage.**

* **cottager,** *n.* One who occupies a summer residence at a resort.

1882 *Nation* 7 Sep. 196/2 The 'Cottagers,' or persons who when they go to the country live in their own houses, will stay. **1890** Howells *Shadow of Cream* I. ii, They have no acquaintance among the other cottagers. **1948** *Chi. Tribune* 20 June VII. 12/4 In too many areas that are the summer stamping grounds of cottagers, campers, and fishermen there are no civic facilities for a mass DDT on the pesky things.

* **cotton,** *n.*

1. Short for **cottonwood.** *Rare.* Cf. **cotton timber.**

1804 Clark in *Lewis & C. Journals* I. (1904) 54 The Countrey and Lands on each Side of the river . . . may be classed as follows . . . the low or overflown points or bottom land, of the groth of Cotton & Willow. **1806** *Ib.* V. (1905) 297 The bottoms of the Bighorn river are extencive and Covered with timber principally Cotton.

2. In combs. designating implements, receptacles, or structures, etc., used in cultivating, gathering, or processing cotton: (1) **cotton bag,** a bag into which cotton is packed for transport, also attrib.; (2) **basket,** a large basket for cotton, esp. one used by cotton pickers; (3) **compress,** an establishment where cotton bales are compressed for further shipment; (4) **hook,** an implement consisting of a piece of metal curved at one end and provided with a handle at the other, used in handling bales of cotton; (5) **machine,** a machine for ginning or spinning cotton; (6) **pen,** a temporary structure for storing cotton as it is picked, *obs.;* (7) **picker,** a machine for picking cotton, cf. **4. b.** (10) below; (8) **planter,** =**cottonseed planter,** cf. **4. b.** (11) below; (9) **shed,** a shed, esp. at a shipping point, where cotton bales are stored temporarily; (10) **sweep,** (see quot. 1891).

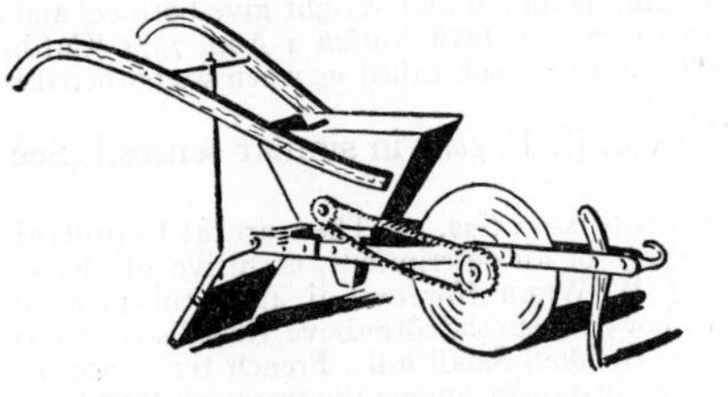

Cotton planter

(1) 1826 in *Amer. Sp.* XXII. 201/2 So Packenham he made his brags, If he in fight was lucky, He'd have their girls and cotton bags, In spite of old Kentucky. **1861** in CHESNUT *Diary* 42 They had cotton bag bomb-proofs at Fort Moultrie, and when Anderson's shot knocked them about some one called out 'Cotton is falling.' — **(2) 1852** STOWE *Uncle Tom* xix, Poor, shiftless dogs put stones at the bottom of their cotton-baskets to make them weigh heavier. **1939** *These Are Our Lives* 381, I remember distinctly mother takin' me to the fields when I was just a little fellow and placin' me on a blanket or in the cotton basket while she worked. — **(3) 1879** *Bradstreet's* 22 Oct. 2/2 Following the successful establishment of the 'cotton compress' comes a unanimous demand for a public grain elevator. **1948** *Dly. Ardmoreite* (Ardmore, Okla.) 28 April 2/4 He knows that when the famous Billie Bryan came to Ardmore, that he made his speech in the cotton compress. — **(4) 1841** *Niles' Reg.* 27 Feb. 404/2 A law has been passed providing for the inspection of bale rope and bagging, and one prohibiting the use of cotton hooks. **1887** *Courier-Journal* 16 Feb. 2/7 One of the men was cut under the eye by a cotton hook.

(5) 1795 ELI WHITNEY in *Amer. Hist. Rev.* III. 102, I found my property all in ashes!—My shop, all my tools, material and work equal to twenty finished cotton machines all gone. **1843** *Hunt's Merch. Mag.* IX. 271 In 1841 the plaintiff let the cellar . . . for the purpose of driving a cotton machine on the first floor. — **(6) 1856** DAVIS *Farm Bk.* 64 Made 1 cotton Pen of rails. **1867** DEVENS *Pictorial Bk.* 415 My officers were crowded into cotton pens with my brave soldiers. — **(7) 1833** *Cong. Deb.* 26 Jan. 1363 To save this cost [i.e., of picking cotton by hand], a cotton picker has been invented. **1949** *Reader's Digest* Feb. 119/2 The development of International Harvester's cotton picker was stymied for more than three years. — **(8) 1858** *So. Cultivator* XVI. 226 (*advt.*), Washburn's patent cotton and corn planter will work well any where. **1944** *Chi. D. News* 1 May 1/3 He also stated that the firm handled . . . corn and cotton planters and other kinds of farm equipment. — **(9) 1833** *Amer. R.R. Jrnl.* II. 481/3 A cotton shed and car house have been erected. **1883** S. BONNER *Dialect Tales* 120 Then he walked irresolutely toward a cotton shed.

(10) 1848 *De Bow's Review* VI. 132 The Cotton Sweep Cultivator is made expressly to take the place of the cotton sweep. **1891** *Cent.* 6106/2 Sweep. . . . A form of light plow or cultivator used for working crops planted in rows, as cotton or maize; a cotton-sweep.

b. In similar but less frequent combs.: (1) **cotton baling press,** =**cotton press;** (2) **chopper,** a machine for chopping out or thinning young cotton plants, cf. **4.** (4) below; (3) **gimblet,** a tool used by a cotton sampler in securing a sample from a bale of cotton; (4) **harvester,** a machine for harvesting cotton; (5) **hoe,** a hoe designed for use in cultivating cotton; (6) **knife,** ?a knife for cutting cotton stalks; (7) **pickery,** a place where cotton is picked over or sorted into piles according to its grade; (8) **scaffold,** a scaffold upon which wet cotton is dried; (9) **scraper,** a kind of plow suitable for the shallow cultivation of cotton; (10) **screw,** a screw press for baling cotton; (11) **shovel,** a simple form of plow used in cultivating cotton; (12) **warehouse,** a storage place for bales of cotton.

(1) 1815 *Niles' Reg.* IX. 187/1 We beg to inform you that we make a very complete Cotton Baling Press. — **(2) 1946** *Science Digest* Aug. 94/1 Mechanical cotton-choppers and beet-thinners have been invented, but they have the weakness of being entirely mechanical. — **(3) 1841** *Hunt's Merch. Mag.* 274 Resolved, That the factors in the city be requested to direct their clerks, or others employed to sample cotton, to cut the bale sufficiently only to draw from them a fair sample with a cotton gimblet. — **(4) 1849** *Rep. Comm. Patents* 459 The Cotton Harvester is a new machine so far as is known to the office.

(5) 1869 *Overland Mo.* III. 11 Seventy huge, clumsy cotton-hoes rose and fell in thoughtless machine-work. — **(6) 1832** *Louisville Pub. Advt.* 3 March, John D. Thorpe . . . is . . . opening a general-assortment of Hardware . . . among which are . . . a great variety of thick back Cotton knives. — **(7) 1840** *N.O. Picayune* 8 Oct. 2/5 A petition from Alexander Jackson, asking permission to build a shed in a yard . . . used as a cotton pickery, was read. — **(8) 1855** DAVIS *Farm Bk.* 219 Making cotton scaffold with 4 hands. — **(9) 1858** *Rep. Comm. Patents* I. Improvement in Cotton Scrapers.

(10) 1858 *So. Cultivator* XVI. 38/1 The subscriber has thoroughly tried . . . his wrought iron cotton screw. — **(11) 1854** *Florida Plant. Rec.* 104, I have had the plowes put away . . . corn plowes 20, cotton shovels 22, etc. — **(12) 1827** in COMMONS *Doc. Hist.* I. 284 They have cotton warehouses there [=Augusta, Ga.] covering whole squares.

For **cotton gin, house, press, sack,** see as main entries.

c. Denoting conveyances used for transporting cotton, as (1) **cotton boat,** (2) **cart,** (3) **droger,** (4) **float,** (5) **packet,** (6) **wagon.**

(1) 1891 THANET *Otto the Knight* 240, I was a wild young man running a cotton-boat. **1942** HEREFORD *Old Man River* 82 The cotton boats, with extra large guards, were being groomed for service. — **(2) 1858** *Harper's Mag.* Dec. 2/1 There were cotton carts and covered wagons, carrying from one to half a dozen bales. — **(3) 1848** BARTLETT 123 *Droger,* lumber droger; cotton droger, etc. A vessel built solely for burden, and for transporting cotton, lumber, and other heavy articles. — **(4) 1879** HEARN *Creole Sketches* (1924) 79 Without, cotton-floats might rumble, and street-cars vulgarly jingle their bells. **1883** *Cent. Mag.* Nov. 40/1 Where marsh lands used to swelter under the sun, pavements of block stone had been laid, enduring as Roman causeways, though they will tremble a little under the passing of cotton-floats.

(5) 1887 *Courier-Journal* 6 Feb. 2/6 The New Orleans and Memphis Cotton packet Helena . . . will continue on to St. Louis. — **(6) 1840** DANA *Two Years* xxix. 334 She was a good substantial ship . . . and wall-sided and kettle bottomed, after the latest fashion of south-shore cotton and sugar wagons. **1944** CLARK *Pills* 43 Cotton wagons bumping long miles over Georgia, Mississippi and South Carolina hill roads carried brown-stone liquor jugs buried in seed cotton.

3. In the names of, or with reference to, animals: (1) **cotton army worm,** =**cotton worm;** (2) **boll weevil,** =**boll weevil;** (3) **boll worm,** =**corn-ear worm;** (4) **caterpillar,** a caterpillar or some similar larva injurious to cotton, *obs.;* (5) **fish,** some unidentified fish or kind of fish, *rare;* (6) **fleahopper,** a fleahopper injurious to cotton; (7) **louse,** a plant louse injurious to cotton; (8) **moth,** the cotton worm in its adult stage; (9) **mouth** (*a*) the poisonous water moccasin, *Agkistrodon piscivorus,* so called from the whitish interior of its mouth, which it opens when excited, also attrib., (*b*) also known as **cotton mouth(ed) moccasin;** (10) **rat,** a burrowing rat, *Sigmodon hispidus,* that frequents cotton fields; (11) **red-bug,** =next; (12) **stainer,** a small red bug, *Dysdercus suturellus,* which stains the fiber of cotton; (13) **tail,** the common American rabbit, *Lepus sylvaticus,* having a cotton-like tuft on the under side of its tail, also attrib., cf. **Molly Cottontail;** (14) **worm,** a larval cotton pest hatched from the eggs of a moth, *Alabama argillacea.*

(1) 1855 *Rep. Comm. Patents: Agric.* 71 The leaves of the [cotton] plant are sometimes entirely devoured by what is commonly known to planters as the . . . 'cotton army-worm.' **1870** RILEY *Mo. Rep. Insects* 37 (Th. Supp.), The cotton-worm . . . is very generally known by the name of Cotton Army worm, in the South. — **(2) 1901** F. W. MALLY (*title*), Mexican Cotton-Boll Weevil. **1948** *Calif. Citrograph* April 207/2 One lot of cotton bolls being carried in a hatbox as souvenirs by a lady who had been touring in the south, were found to be infested with Cotton boll weevil. — **(3) 1870** *Amer. Naturalist* III. 168 Will our Southern friends as the season opens remember that we want specimens of the Cotton Ball [*sic*] Worm and Army Worm in all their stages. **1928** [see **corn-ear worm**]. — **(4) 1846** *De Bow's Review* II. 278 Cotton Caterpillar. **1856** *Rep. Comm. Patents: Agric.* 66 If it or any similar method should lead to the destruction of the cotton caterpillar and boll-worm, . . . it will be of incalculable benefit.

(5) 1851 *De Bow's Review* XI. 56 Gaspagon; Cotton Fish; Trout [occur]. — **(6) 1946** *Science News Letter* 30 March 302/3 The new material killed also more cotton leafworms, plant bugs, cotton flea-hoppers, and cotton aphids. **1948** *Okla. Cotton Grower* 15 April 2/6 Chlorinated camphene gives good to excellent control of the boll weevil, bollworm, cotton fleahopper and leafworm. — **(7) 1846** *De Bow's Review* II. 141 The insects, we are most troubled with, are the '*cotton lice*.' **1856** *Rep. Comm. Patents: Agric.* (1856) 68 When the cotton-plant is very young and tender, it is particularly subject to the attacks of the cotton-louse. — **(8) 1843** in *Rep. Comm. Patents: Agric.* (1856) 73 That the cotton-moth survives the winter is nearly certain. **1860** *Harper's Mag.* June 41/1 The *Oblinita*, . . . another cotton moth, is said to have this same kind of sucker. — **(9)** (*a*) **1832** G. A. McCall *Lett. from Frontiers* (1868) 259 On reaching the spot, I found a large *moccason* or *cotton-mouth* snake writhing on the ground, with his head crushed and his upper jaw broken . . . but there it stood perpendicular and disclosing the whole of the interior of his immense dead-white, or, as it is well named, 'cotton-mouth.' **1947** *Chi. D. News* 15 April 1/3 Among the snakes captured were a half dozen deadly cottonmouths. (*b*) **1879** *Scribner's Mo.* Oct. 882/1 A wilderness of briars, vines and young forest trees; affording shelter to innumerable rabbits, opossums, raccoons, catamounts, rattlesnakes and 'cotton-mouth' moccasins. **1947** *Prairie Schooner* Winter 433 A cotton-mouthed moccasin lay on the sand.

(10) 1831 Audubon *Ornith. Biog.* I. 298, I have never seen them [Red-shouldered hawk] chase any other small birds than those mentioned, or quadrupeds of smaller size than the *Cotton Rat*. **1948** *N.Y. Times* 12 Sep. E. 9/6 A dormant virus . . . attacks the muscle-controlling nerves of the cotton rat. — **(11) 1868** *Rep. Comm. Agric.* 71 They hybernate in the perfect state concealed beneath bark, under brush-heaps, or stones, like the cotton red-bug. — **(12) 1856** *Rep. Comm. Patents: Agric.* 103 The Red-Bug, or Cotton-Stainer . . . is found by millions in East Florida, on the cotton plantations, where it does immense damage by staining the fibre of the cotton in the bolls. — **(13) 1869** Muir *First Summer in Sierra* (1911) 11 Cotton-tail rabbits are running from shade to shade among the ceanothus brush. **1875** *Fur, Fin, & Feather* 136 To those who are fond of sport with 'cotton tails,' we can say that we know of none more exhilarating. **1948** *Chi. D. News* 8 Dec. 63/2 Thousands of hunters will be searching the fields and coverts for cottontails. — **(14) 1847** *Rep. Comm. Patents* 170 There has been some complaint respecting the cotton worm in the early part of the season. **1890** *Boston Journal* 7 March 4/1 An average annual loss of $30,000,000 has been occasioned in the South by the cotton-worm alone.

b. In similar expressions sufficiently explained in the quots.: (1) **cotton aphis,** (2) **crane fly,** (3) **eater,** (4) **mule,** (5) **span worm.**

(1) 1909 *Cent. Supp.* 304/2 cotton-aphis. . . . A plant-louse, *Aphis gossypii*, occurring commonly on the cotton-plant in the southern United States, especially in the early summer. — **(2) 1862** *Harper's Mag.* Nov. 741/1 The *Ctenophora xylena*—'Cotton Crane-Fly'. . . . This crane-fly . . . deposits her eggs on the cotton-seed. — **(3) 1851** *De Bow's Review* XI. 57 They were supposed by some to be the *Cotton Eater* (*Ophiusa Xylina*). — **(4) 1908** *U.S. Dept. Agric. Farmers' Bul. 334*, 24 Cotton mules are lighter boned than miners and not so compactly built. **1909** Webster 511/3 cotton mule. A comparatively small mule in distinction from a large one, or *sugar mule*. *Southern U.S.* **1948** *Southwestern Rev.* Winter 29/2 He couldn't ride a cotton mule. — **(5) 1855** *Rep. Comm. Patents: Agric.* (1856) 91 The Small Cotton Span-Worm, a very small looper-caterpillar, or span-worm.

c. Also in the names of, or with reference to, plants: (1) **cotton bloom,** the flower of the cotton plant; (2) **boll,** the seed pod, esp. when unopened, of the cotton plant; (3) **grass,** see **red cotton grass;** (4) **gum,** a tupelo, *Nyssa aquatica*, a large tree found in southern swamps; (5) **root,** a medicinal product obtained from the roots of certain cultivated varieties of cotton; (6) **rose,** the Confederate rose, *Hibiscus mutabilis* (see also quot. 1889 and cf. **German cotton rose**); (7) **seed,** see as a main entry; (8) **square,** =**square 3;** (9) **timber,** short for **cottonwood timber,** *rare;* (10) **tree,** =**cottonwood,** cf. **Mississippi cotton tree;** (11) **weed,** (*a*) any one of various wild plants somewhat resembling cotton, (*b*) the stalks and branches of the cotton plant as distinguished from the bolls or "fruit"; (12) **wood,** see as a main entry.

(1) 1854 *Harper's Mag.* VIII. 454/1 The 'cotton bloom,' under the matured sun of July, begins to make its appearance. **1862** *Cong. Globe* 23 April 1792/2 [The South] that land of sunshine and flowers, where the cotton-bloom whitens their broad acres. — **(2) 1820** in *Henderson's N.C. Almanack* (1823) 27 A half grown cotton bowl, at or about which time the worm attacks it, is full of juice. **1858** *Texas Almanac 1859* 85 The frosty nights now opening the cotton-bolls with great rapidity. — **(4) 1860** Curtis *Woody Plants N.C.* 62 104 Cotton gum. . . . As it does not split and is very easily worked, it is manufactured into light bowls and trays. **1884** Sargent *Rep. Forests* 93 Large Tupelo. Cotton Gum. Tupelo Gum.

(5) 1904 *Indian Laws & Tr.* III. 103 It shall be unlawful for any person, from or after the passage of this act, to retail any of the following poisons, except as follows: . . . ergot, cotton root, cantharides, . . . and their pharmaceutical preparations. — **(6) 1831** Audubon *Ornith. Biog.* I. 104 Large-flowered Hibiscus, Cotton Rose, or wild Althaea. **1857** Gray *Botany* 229 *Filago*, Cotton-rose . . . annual, low branching woolly herbs. **1889** *Cent.* 2211/1 The cotton-rose or herb impious of Europe . . . is also naturalized in the United States. — **(8) 1842** in Bassett *Plantation Overseer* 163, I have cotten squairs too and three on a stalk. **1948** *Okla. Cotton Grower* 15 March 4/7 Boll weevil insecticides should be applied when cotton squares have a 25 percent or more infestation of the pest. — **(9) 1805** John Ordway in *Wis. Hist. Coll.* XXII. (1916) 257 Passed bottoms covered with cotton Timber.

(10) 1602 Brereton *Relation* 12 Walnut trees great store. Elmes. Beech. Hollie. Haslenut trees. Cherry trees. Cotten trees. Other fruit trees to us unknowen. **1763** in *Amer. Sp.* XX. (1945) 46 The Cotton-tree (a poplar) is a large tree which no wise deserves the name it bears, unless for some beards that it throws out. **1898** Cushman *Hist. Indians* 228 For fresh wounds they made a poultice of the root of the cotton-tree which proved very efficacious. — **(11)** (*a*) **1815–16** *Niles' Reg.* IX. Supp. 189/1 The circumstance of a young school girl effecting a cure of one by rubbing it every day, . . . with the juice of Milk or Wild Cotton Weeds which finally destroyed the wen. (*b*) **1854** *Florida Plant Rec.* 92 The cotton weed is verry Low but is full of boles.

4. In combs. referring to people: (1) **cotton agent,** one who purchases cotton for another whom he represents; (2) **broker,** a broker who deals in cotton and cotton stocks; (3) **buyer,** one who buys cotton; (4) **chopper,** one who chops out or thins young cotton plants, cf. **2. b.** (2) above; (5) **factor,** =**cotton agent;** (6) **head,** a small child having hair suggestive of cotton, also **cotton headed,** cf. **towhead;** (7) **rebel,** a southerner during the Civil War, *rare;* (8) **Senator,** a U.S. Senator representing a cotton state.

(1) 1866 in Fleming *Hist. Reconstruction* I. 29 The time has arrived, as I think, when this Cotton business should be wound up and the entire lot of cotton agents withdrawn from the South. **1891** O'Beirne *Leaders Ind. Territory* 27/1 In 1865 he was chosen cotton agent for the Creek Indians. — **(2) 1836** Wm. F. Gray *Diary* (1909) 69 Augustin Slaughter . . . is in reduced circumstances. Has just come to New Orleans, and opened an office as cotton broker. **1909** O. Henry *Roads of Destiny* 292 The transient master of Charleroi, who, to-morrow, would be again the clerk of a cotton broker. — **(3) 1932** W. Kelley *Inchin' Along* 82 The cotton buyer . . . had been an earl or a duke or something in England. **1945** Easterby *S.C. Rice Plant.* 422 Malloy . . . had been a merchant and cotton buyer in Cheraw since 1835 — **(4) 1874** Knight *Dict. Mech.* I. 543/2 The cotton-chopper straddles the row, and chops wide gaps, leaving the plants in hills. **1892** Harris *U. Remus & Friends* 196 De overseer lean his chin on de fence, And lissen at de cotton-choppers sing.

(5) 1827 in Commons *Doc. Hist.* I. 284, I was there boarding with about one hundred cotton factors, cotton merchants, and cotton planters. **1948** *Sat. Ev. Post* 17 July 54/3 Here the buildings, once occupied by cotton factors, sit at river-bank level and rise to the top of the forty-foot bluff. — **(6) 1861** *Harper's Mag.* Feb. 292/1 John . . . was the father of a thriving little family of 'cotton-heads.' **1884** Cable *Dr. Sevier* (1885) 417 [He] fed his ague-shaken wife and cotton-headed children. — **(7) 1861** *Vanity Fair* 4 May 208/1 If there's anything Civil between us and the Cotton Rebels, we don't exactly see it. — **(8) 1947** *Reader's Digest* March 79/1 Thus there are 'silver Senators' and 'cotton Senators' and 'wheat Senators' and 'labor Senators' and 'big business Senators'—and too few United States Senators.

b. In similar combs. of obvious meaning: (1) **cotton black,** (2) **farmer,** (3) **fellow,** (4) **grower,** (5) **hand,** (6) **maker,** (7) **manies,** (8) **Negro,** (9) **operator,** (10) **picker,** cf. **2.** (7) above; (11) **planter,** cf. **2.** (8) above, (12) **raiser,** (13) **sampler,** (14) **slave,** (15) **speculator,** (16) **-tot,** (17) **Whig.**

(1) 1862 E. Kirke *Among Pines* 289 We give our'n meat and whiskey ev'ry day, but them articles is skarse 'mong th' cotton blacks, an' the rice niggers never get 'em. — **(2) 1882** *Cent. Mag.* Feb. 572/2 How could the white cotton farmer . . . master in one or two decades the true methods acquired of necessity by Northern farmers? **1948** *Nation's Agric.* June 5/2 The move helped to scuttle OPA and resulted in an additional $40,000,000 in income to cotton farmers late in 1946. — **(3) 1847** Robb *Squatter Life* 136 Some cotton fellar here bid sixty dollars. — **(4) 1824** *Ann. 18th Congress* 1 Sess. 635 With respect to the home market for our raw material, I deny that the cotton-growers have yet derived any material advantage from that source. **1917** *Wall St. Jrnl.* 10 Feb. 1/4 Cotton growers are optimistic over the outlook.

(5) 1870 *Nation* 12 May 296/1 Chinese laborers—of whom, as 'cotton hands,' glowing accounts were given—are to be called into the rice districts. — **(6) 1822** in *Life & Corr. Quitman* I. 76 Ministers . . . become the most rigorous task-masters and cotton-makers. — **(7) 1845** *St. Louis Reveille* 14 May 2/4 The inhabitants of . . . Tennessee [are called] Cotton-manies. **1886** *Chi. W. News* 29 April 4/3 Tennessee is the Big Bend state, from the circular course of its main river, but its people are Cotton-Manies. — **(8) 1942** Rawlings *C. Creek* 84 The Ogeechee River is tidal and its salt tongue licks far into Georgia. The Negroes of the region, cotton niggers, sugar niggers, rice or tobacco niggers, the sons and daughters of slaves, are of a special African tribe and have kept their identity. — **(9) 1856** D. Macleod *F. Wood* 80 Mr. James Depeyster Ogden—not a banker, it is true, but a cotton operator—or, in other words, a cotton speculator.

(10) 1850 H. C. Lewis *La. Swamp Dr.* 35 Behold me, then, a student of medicine, but yesterday a cotton-picker. **1937** Coolidge *Texas Cowboys* 15 Eastern Texas, according to the punchers, is given over to cotton and corn, and their favorite term of reproach is to call a man a cotton-picker. — **(11) 1808** *Ann. 10th Cong.* 2 Sess. 658 What say the cotton planters, than whom none are more interested in foreign commerce? **1945** Adams *Album Amer. Hist.* II. 318 From South Carolina and Georgia, cotton planters moved westward into Alabama, Mississippi and Louisiana. — **(12) 1825** *Catawba Journal* 28 June, Even if we had boating to the heads of our rivers, we should have to wagon or drive our produce for the cotton raisers, to their doors, or sell at a reduced price. — **(13) 1846** *Knickerb.* XXVII. 268 'Cotton-samplers' are seen winding their way, now stopping before a bale and boring down to the very heart of it, . . . then despatching their boys to the office with samples. — **(14) 1862** E. Kirke *Among Pines* 288 The rice-negro seldom lives to be over forty, and the cotton slave very rarely attains sixty.

(15) 1856 [see **cotton operator**]. — **(16) 1893** *Chi. Tribune* 21 April 4/1 Southern planters who persist in devoting all their energies to raising cotton and neglecting other crops are known by their neighbors as cottontots. — **(17) 1851** K. Quentin *Reisebilder* 104 Seine [D. Webster's] letzte berühmte Rede in Faneuil-Hall hat ihn auch mit einem Theile der Hunkers, oder, wie sie von ihren Gegnern wohl genannt zu werden pflegen, den Cotton-Whigs entzweit. **1891** *Cent.* 6898/3 Cotton-Whig. in *U.S. hist.*, in the last days of the Whig party, one of those northern Whigs who were disposed to regard the compromise of 1850 as a final settlement of the slavery question, so called from their supposed partiality to the cotton interest. **1941** Buckmaster *Let My People Go* 159 'Conscience' Whigs were in revolt against 'Cotton' Whigs.

5. Denoting places, regions, etc., where cotton is grown, or where it is the principal crop, as (1) **cotton area,** (2) **belt,** (3) **country,** (4) **county,** (5) **estate,** (6) **farm,** (7) **field,** (8) **ground,** (9) **growing state,** (10) **kingdom,** (11) **land,** (12) **patch,** (13) **plantation,** (14) **Plantation State,** (15) **region,** (16) **state,** (17) **swamp.**

(1) 1874 *Dept. Agric. Rep. 1873* 378 The following is given as the 'cotton area' of the State [=Calif.] . . . 20,519,920 [acres]. — **(2) 1871** R. Somers *Southern States since War* 257 In many other parts of the 'Cotton Belt.' **1948** *Ga. Review* Spring 10 To the people of the Cotton Belt and the country, the mechanization of cotton means progress. — **(3) 1671** *S.C. Hist. Soc. Coll.* V. 297 The winter here doth prove something sharpe and colde, soe that I feare this will not prove a Cotton Country. **1843** *Knickerb.* XXII. 4 As you . . . begin to enter the Cotton Country, the scenery is completely changed. — **(4) 1910** *World's Work* Dec. 13757/1 At Waxahachie, Tex., the county-seat of the greatest cotton county of the state, the leading doctor shuts up his house every fall because all his servants desert him for the cotton-fields.

(5) 1847 *De Bow's Review* IV. 252 We are indebted to a cotton planter of Onachita . . . for a copy of a very valuable paper [on] the management of a successful cotton estate. — **(6) 1818** *Albany Argus* 3 Nov. 3/2 Good cotton farms usually sold from forty to one hundred dollars per acre. — **(7) 1796** Morse *Amer. Geog.* (ed. 3) I. 699 Several indigo planters have converted their plantations into cotton fields. **1935** Wolfe *Of Time & River* (1944) 367 On a dusty sand-clay road between some cotton fields they stopped the car, and walked out into the field. — **(8) 1834** in Bassett *South. Plant.* 66, I have got all of my old ground broke aupe and my coten ground boded aup but about 40 acres. — **(9) 1821** *Ann. 16th Cong.* 2 Sess. 1565 There is scarcely a currency left, except in the cotton-growing States.

(10) 1861 Olmstead (*title*), Journeys and Explorations in the Cotton Kingdom. **1945** *Christian Cent.* 29 Aug. 987/2 The Allis Chalmers company . . . promises the cotton kingdom a mechanical picker that will work. — **(11) 1825** in Commons *Doc. Hist.* I. 252 This tract contains . . . about 300 acres clear, and some of it under fence, of excellent cotton and provision land. **1941** Daniels *Tar Heels* 63 Between me and the window and the flat cotton lands outside it, the rich Scotchman in politics sat most of the time almost grimly silent. — **(12) 1760** Washington *Diaries* I. 134 The Pocoson at Cotton Patch Point. **1812** Melish *Travels* II. 140 We saw a very handsome field of cotton, called here a cotton patch. **1948** *Miami* (Okla.) *D. News-Record* 2 July 8/7 Their hoes were stacked like rifles in the cotton patch. — **(13) 1803** in *Ann. 8th Cong.* 2 Sess. 1502 Their banks have the best soil, and the greatest number of good cotton plantations. **1893** *Harper's Mag.* Feb. 383/2 There are other fertilizer companies using potash, cotton seed meal, and phosphate to make a product that is used on the cotton and sugar plantations. — **(14) 1889** *N. & Q.* III. 77 Alabama is the 'Cotton Plantation' State. Its inhabitants are called 'lizards.'

(15) 1846 *De Bow's Review* 1 Jan. 23 The route intersects centrally, and crosses the cotton region. **1880** Tourgee *Bricks* 11 The plantation was just upon that wavy line which separates the cotton region of the east from the tobacco belt. — **(16) 1844** *Whig Almanac 1845* 5/1 Coming before the People those of the Cotton States were assured that Mr. Polk was a genuine Free Trader. **1890** M. Townsend *U.S.* 66 Alabama is called the Cotton State because it is the central State of the Cotton Belt. **1948** *Ga. Review* Spring 12 Mississippi, one of the 'big three' cotton states, produced a higher yield of wheat per acre than any major wheat state. — **(17) 1901** Churchill *Crisis* 37 But seven years in a cotton swamp,—seven years it takes; that's all.

6. In miscellaneous combs.: (1) **cotton bale,** a closely packed bale of ginned cotton now weighing about 500 lbs.; (2) **batting,** carded cotton in the form of thin rolls or sheets; (3) **blockade,** during the Civil War the federal

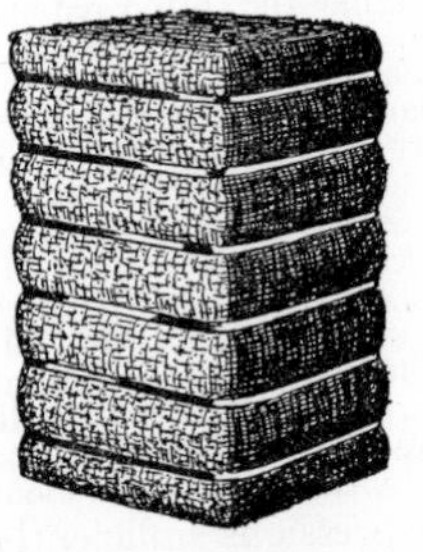

Cotton bale

blockade of the South preventing the shipping of cotton abroad, *obs.;* (4) **book,** a book for recording the weight of cotton gathered; (5) **brag,** an overseer's boast of having harvested the largest cotton crop with a given number of slaves, *obs.;* (6) **candy,** candy of a light fluffy form made by spinning melted granulated sugar brought to a high temperature, also attrib. and fig.; (7) **Centennial Exposition,** an exposition or fair opened in New Orleans in Dec., 1884, designed originally to commemorate the one-hundredth anniversary of the first exportation of cotton from America; (8) **chopping time,** the time when cotton is "chopped" or thinned; (9) **clad,** *a.* during the Civil War, a vessel protected or "armored" with cotton bales, cf. **cotton gunboat;** (10) **Confederacy,** the Southern Confederacy, *obs.;* (11) **domestic,** =**domestic;** (12) **exchange,** a place or institution where transactions involving cotton are carried on; (13) **gunboat,** a river boat hastily armored, chiefly with cotton bales, and used by the Confederates in the defense of New Orleans during the Civil War, *obs.;* (14) **-mouth thirst,** thirst such as causes one "to spit cotton," see **7.** (3) below; (15) **picking,** see as a main entry; (16) **spool,** a small spool on which cotton thread is wound; (17) **stalk hemp,** a hemp-like product obtained from cotton stalks, *rare;* (18) **yard,** (*a*) a yard or open area where wet cotton is spread out to dry, *obs.*, (*b*) a lot where cotton bales are stored temporarily while awaiting shipment.

(1) *c*1807 in *Tenn. Hist. Mag.* 1 Ser. V. 59 Just at the moment when about to begin the raft of cotton bales, (we) descried two persons . . . who seemed approaching towards us (near New Madrid). **1883** *Cent. Mag.* Nov. 40/1 Even before I had left the steam-boat my imagination had already flown beyond the wilderness of cotton-bales. *Ib.* Feb. 566 He . . . hid himself among the cotton bales that were piled on the forward part of the boat. **1942** [see **cotton pattern** in **b.** below]. — (2) **1827** *Hartford* (Conn.) *Mirror* 31 Dec. 1/2 (*advt.*), Irish Linens—Cotton batting old price 10 cts lb. **1947** *Denver Post* 9 Jan. 10/1 All I want to know is what the freight rate on cotton batting is going to be. — (3) **1865** *Atlantic Mo.* XV. 651 Enormous stock which the cotton blockade enabled him to work off. — (4) **1851** *Florida Plant. Rec.* 437 Paid 75 cts. for a cotton book. **1856** in COMMONS *Doc. Hist.* I. 126 The cotton to be weighed every night and the weights set down in the Cotton Book.

(5) **1839** WELD *Slavery As It Is* 134 The southern newspapers, at the crop season, chronicle carefully the 'cotton brag,' and the 'crack cotton picking,' and 'unparalleled driving.' *Ib.*, We recollect the . . . editor of a religious paper at Natchez, Miss. in which he took care to assign a prominent place, and capitals to the 'cotton brag.' — (6) **1926** *Springfield* (Mass.) *Union* 4 March How much profit is made on cotton candy sold at fairs and the like. **1947** *Time* 2 June 44/2 The Rose prose, with a base of carnival-barker shrewdness and a pink topping of cotton-candy poetry, has caught the crowd like an inspired midway pitch. **1948** *Democrat* 30 Sep. 1/7 The stands sold . . . cotton candy, popcorn, peanuts, etc. — (7) **1885** *Cent. Mag.* May 14/1 It is time something should be said about cotton in a description of a Cotton Centennial Exposition. — (8) **1927** J. D. FREEMAN *When West Was Young* 316 It was cotton-chopping time when the long rows of thickly planted stalks had to be thinned out with hoes. **1947** LUMPKIN *Southerner* 41 In a general way he could have told when it was cotton chopping time, and when cotton picking. — (9) **1867** J. N. EDWARDS *Shelby* xxviii. 485 The five steamboats were carefully cotton-clad. **1919** DUNN *Indiana* II. 612 He was in command of the 'tin-clad' Indianola at Vicksburg; and after running the batteries there was engaged single-handed with two Confederate rams and two 'cotton-clad' steamers.

(10) **1861** in *Annals of Iowa* 3 Ser. XXIV. 32 The Cotton Confederacy seems pretty well organized and they are making preparations for war on rather a large scale. **1866** RICHARDSON *Secret Service* v. 74 Five or six Union members . . . denouncing unsparingly the plan of the cotton Confederacy. — (11) **1869** MARK TWAIN *Innocents* xxvii. 286 Then you stretch a great sheet of 'cotton domestic' from the point where the joists join the hillside down over the joists to the ground. — (12) **1885** *Cent. Mag.* May 5/1 Pledges of about $225,000 were obtained, . . . chiefly from the railroad companies, the banks, and the Cotton Exchange. **1948** *Okla. City Times* 14 June 11/8 This year's first bale of cotton reached the Houston cotton exchange at 12:50 a.m. Monday. — (13) **1884** CABLE *Dr. Sevier* 368 The cotton gun-boats and the rams were building. **1885** ——— in *Cent. Mag.* April 919/1 There had been a great hammering, and making of chips, and clatter of railroad iron, turning these tow-boats into iron-clad cotton gun-boats. — (14) **1907** S. E. WHITE *Arizona Nights* xiii. 194 We were both old hands at the business, had each in our time suffered the 'cotton-mouth' thirst.

(16) **1842** L. M. CHILD *Lett. New York* 173 The portraits of Victoria on our cotton-spools, are graceful in comparison. **1866** A. D. WHITNEY *L. Goldthwaite* xiii, She used from her own cotton-spools and skeins of silk. — (17) **1865** TURNER *Cotton* 247 The Cotton Stalk Hemp is, in my opinion, worthy of the highest consideration. It has the color of the Gunny or East India bagging, and the fibre is as strong as that of the hemp. It is prepared by knocking off the lateral limbs of the cotton stalk, then cutting down the stalk and burying it in a plough furrow in the field. — (18) (*a*) **1828** in *Amer. Sp.* XVIII. 123 The cotton [is] put into round baskets, which when filled are brought into the cotton yard, and spread along planks, for the purpose of drying. (*b*) **1881** *Bradstreet's* 18 June 374/4 The other remaining railroads . . . already have their wharfs and cotton yards. **1885** *Cent. Mag.* April 919/2 The . . . cotton-yards were full of cotton.

b. In other combs. of this sort of obvious meaning or sufficiently explained in the quots.: (1) **cotton bat,** (2) **bed,** (3) **blue,** (4) **bond,** (5) **boom,** (6) **brokerage,** (7) **business,** (8) **futures,** (9) **growing,** (10) **harvest,** (11) **interest,** (12) **pattern,** (13) **rock,** (14) **row,** (15) **sampling,** (16) **stone.**

(1) **1844** *Rep. Comm. Patents* (1847) 35 These are nothing more than a thick layer of cotton, carded in what are called at the north 'cotton bats.' **1904** T. WATSON *Bethany* 21 From the basket on the floor she takes the filmy cotton 'bat.' — (2) **1816** *Niles' Reg.* X. 28/2 In the first place, beds are made (such as would be called flat cotton beds) four or five feet apart. **1858** WARDER *Hedges & Evergreens* I. ii. 34 Break up the soil deeply . . . , and throw up the dirt in the same manner as if preparing a cotton-bed. — (3) **1889** *Cent.* 1295/1 cotton-blue. . . . A coal-tar color similar to soluble blue, used in dyeing. — (4) **1865** *Morning Star* 6 Feb., What do you mean by Cotton Bonds? Witness: Certificates of the Confederate Government representing say twenty bales of cotton worth so much money.

(5) **1880** *Bradstreet's* 24 Nov. 2/4 Keeping pace with the extraordinary cotton boom, this . . . city . . . is really branching out. — (6) **1936** ARTHUR *Old New Orleans* 136 [They] came to New Orleans from France to make their fortune, which they did in the cotton brokerage business. — (7) **1818** *Austin Papers* (1924) 333 When you get to Red River you can decide whether you will enter into the Cotton business or not. — (8) **1884** CRADDOCK *Where Battle Was Fought* 44 He speculates heavily in cotton futures. **1948** *Jrnl. Commerce* (N.Y.) 6 July 1/5 Prospects for a new large crop served to put cotton futures prices down 3 to 14 points. — (9) **1868** *Rep. Comm. Agric.* 425 A correspondent enthusiastically claims . . . that fruit culture will displace cotton-growing [in La.]. **1884** CRADDOCK *Where Battle Was Fought* 264 Give up this wealth for . . . the fourth of a scanty crop on somebody's acres exhausted with fifty years of cotton-growing?

(10) **1842** in *Amer. Sp.* XVIII. 122 It was in the midst of the cotton-harvest. **1943** *Ib.* 122/2 Cotton Harvest. The season or the activity of cotton picking. . . . Writing in 1909, Professor Leonidas Payne noted that in Alabama *cotton picking* is the usual term, with *harvest* restricted to small grains; and this is my observation also. — (11) **1846** *De Bow's Review* II. Sep. 139 First, the determined opposition of all the cotton interests in New Orleans and Mobile to the use of hoops. — (12) **1942** *Democrat* 3 Dec. 2/3 The 1943 cotton-bagging-for-cotton-bales program, calling for the manufacture and sale of up to 8,000,000 cotton 'patterns,' or bale covers, to encourage the use of domestic cotton. — (13) **1856** SWALLOW *Geol. Missouri* (B.), Cotton Rock, a variety of Magnesian limestone, of a light buff or gray color, found in Missouri. It is very soft when fresh from the quarry. — (14) **1846** *De Bow's Review* II. 135, I make my cotton rows about five feet apart.

(15) **1844** JOE COWELL *Thirty Yrs. Among Players* 98 It was a glorious relaxation from the perils of the sea and toils of cotton sampling for the jolly Yankee captains and honest deacons' sons. — (16) **1796** HILTZHEIMER *Diary* (1893) 18 Oct. 235 Drove down the Chester Road to Richard Tutton's, and dug up in his field near the house what is called cotton stone. When it is washed and dried it looks white and fuzzy, and if laid in oil will burn like a candle for a long time, and fire will not consume it.

7. In colloq. and slang phrases: (1) *Too high for picking cotton*, slightly drunk; (2) *Cotton is king*, an expression referring to the supremacy of cotton in the agriculture of the South, cf. **King Cotton;** (3) *to spit cotton*, to spit only with difficulty because of thirst or embarrassment, also fig., cf. **6.** (14) above.

(1) [**1818** WEEMS *Drunkard's Looking Glass* 4 The patient goes by a variety of nicknames . . . such as . . . cut in the craw—high up to picking cotton (Georgia.)] **1829** *Maysville Eagle* 8 April, I have been . . . most too 'high for picking cotton.' — (2) **1855** D. CHRISTY *Cotton is King* 11 The very things necessary to the overthrow of American Slavery, were left undone, . . . so that, now, after nearly a 'thirty years' war,' we may say, emphatically, Cotton is King, and his enemies are vanquished. **1894** *Harper's Mag.* LXXXIX. 133/1 Cotton was still King. Webster's apostasy had not cost him the admiring allegiance of his own State. **1947** *Democrat* 23 Oct. 4/1 Cotton no longer is king, but all three county banks are bulging with deposits. — (3) **1866** LOWELL *Biglow P.* 2 Ser. p. xlvii, To *spit cotton* is, I think, American. **1899** GREEN *Va. Word-Book* 354 When one is very thirsty and his mouth dry the spittle white and sticky he is said to 'spit-cotton.' **1947** *Chi. D. News* 14 June 6/3 The Kansas City vote frauds . . . have Attorney General Tom Clark spitting cotton, they believe.

As the last term in **absorbent, bale, blockade, Boston, bumblebee, bunch, clean, Confederate, copperas, darning, Demerara, factory, flax, Forsythe, Georgian, green seed(ed), Gulf, highland, indigo, inland, island, King, long, long staple, mastodon, Mexican, Molly, Negro, okra, sandy, sea board, sea island, sea shore, short, short staple(d), small boll, spool, spot, stone, storm, Tennessee, Texas, upland, yellow cotton.**

Cottondom 'kɑtn̩dəm, *n.* The southern states. *Obs.* — **1856** *S.F. Bulletin* 3 May 1/1 There is . . . glad jubilation throughout the whole realm of Cottondom. **1894** *Amer. Missionary* (N.Y.) Nov. 379 If I understand what 'mine eyes behold,' whiskey is king in 'cottondom.'

cotton gin. A machine for separating the fiber of the cotton plant from the seed.

1796 *Amer. Hist. Rev.* III. (1897–98) 93 (*caption*), Improvement in the Cotton Gin. **1797** E. WHITNEY in *Amer. Hist. Rev.* (1897–98) III. 108, I have been so long and so continually placed in the very vortex of error and prejudice, of complaints and abuse respecting our unfortunate cotton gins. **1835** H. C. TODD *Notes* 9 Eli Whitney, inventor of the celebrated American cotton gin, died at Whitneyville, near New Haven, Jan. 8, 1825. **1946** WILSON *Fidelity* 112 We could . . . wonder at the uses of the abandoned machinery of the cotton gin.

cotton house. A house in which cotton is stored.

1796 B. HAWKINS *Letters* 30, I viewed his cotton house, the staple of the cotton [being] good. **1864** CATE *Two Soldiers* 51 But I spent my night's rest, such as it was, in a cotton house beneath the cotton. **1945** BOTKIN *My Burden* 231 The fire burn up the ginhouse full of cotton and the cotton-house, too, and the corncrib.

Cottonia kəˈtonɪə, *n.* = **Cottondom.** *Rare.* — **1862** *Cincinnati Times* April (B.), The Confederates having determined to abandon all the Border States, and make a stand in Cottonia proper.

***Cottonocracy,** *n.* "A term applied to the Boston manufacturers, especially by the 'Boston Whig' newspaper" (B. '48). *Obs.*

cotton picking.

1. A social gathering of friends and neighbors for removing the seed from cotton or for harvesting cotton.

1795 J. & E. PETTIGREW *MS Lett.* 3 Oct. (N.C. Univ.), One of the students was banished; it was for going to a cotton picking after eight at Knight. **1880** BURNETT *Old Pioneer* 12 What were called 'cotton pickings' were then [*c*1820] very common. **1945** BOTKIN *My Burden* 92 We didn't have no kind of cotton-pickings 'cept just pick our own cotton.

2. The gathering or harvesting of cotton. Also attrib.

1845 *Knickerb.* XXV. 426, [I'm] no more sick than a spring alligator on a sunny mud-bank, or a lazy nigger in cotton-pickin'-time. **1850** H. C. LEWIS *La. Swamp Dr.* 34, [I] resumed my cotton-picking, feeling but little disappointed. **1884** SWEET & KNOX *Through Texas* 239 They were to quit shooting each other and to turn their attention to agricultural matters until after the cotton-picking season was over.

cotton press.

1. A press for packing ginned cotton into bales.

1806 DUNBAR *Life* 349 This was burnt down with my cotton mill, two cotton presses, a corn magazine contiguous. **1815** *Niles' Reg.* IX. 187/1 The following notice of an improved cotton press, is handed to us by an intelligent friend. **1900** *Cong. Rec.* 3 Feb. 1477/2 Every article of commerce is produced there, from a paper bag to the huge ice plants and cotton and sugar presses scattered everywhere.

2. The building in which one or more of such presses are operated.

1828 in *Amer. Sp.* XVIII. 123 The cotton press formerly belonged to a German commission merchant. **1885** *Cent. Mag.* April 919/2 The cotton-presses and cotton-yards were full of cotton, but there it all stuck.

cotton sack. (See quot. 1908.)

1850 H. C. LEWIS *La. Swamp Dr.* 201 The strap of the cotton-sack, galling my shoulder, recalled me to myself. **1908** *D.N.* III. 301 cotton-sack, n. A bag with a strap for hanging over the shoulder, used in picking cotton. [**1948** *Sat. Ev. Post* 23 Oct. 33/1 On the rare occasions when he gets a piece of ice, he wraps it—and it keeps well—in an old cotton-picking sack.]

***cottonseed,** *n.* In combs.: (1) **cottonseed cake,** the solid matter or residuum remaining after the oil is pressed from cottonseed; (2) **meal,** a meal, high in protein value, and used as a feed and as fertilizer, made from cottonseed after the removal of the hulls and oil; (3) **oil,** a pale yellow oil extracted from cottonseed, also attrib.; (4) **planter,** an agricultural implement for planting cotton.

(1) **1869** *Rep. Comm. Agric.* 286 The cotton-seed cake, and the phosphated cotton-seed cake, were received after the cotton came up. **1883** SMITH *Geol. Survey Ala.* 544 The cottonseed-cake is not much used either alone or mixed, for crops, probably because of the cost. **1946** R. PEATTIE *Pac. Coast Ranges* 126 Range cattle look their worst now, and it is time to put out cottonseed cake or corn stalks or hay. — (2) **1858** C. FLINT *Milch Cows* 197 Cotton-seed meal . . . is obtained by pressing the seed of the cotton plant, which extracts the oil, when the cake is crushed or ground into meal. **1945** *N. Eng. Homestead* 22 Sep. 30/3 A concentrate ration . . . is fed, generally using common farm grains plus linseed oil meal and cottonseed meal. — (3) **1833** *Niles' Reg.* XLIV. 222/1 An extensive factory of cotton seed oil has been established at Natchez. **1862** *Rep. Comm. Patents: Agric.* 135 My practice has been to feed three times a day—. . . at noon with one of the following articles: Swedish turnips, . . . Indian meal, cotton-seed oil-cake. **1947** *Science News Letter* 6 April 219/2 Improved Methods for Extracting Cottonseed Oil. — (4) **1848** *De Bow's Review* VI. 133 Cotton seed planter. **1858** *Rep. Comm. Patents* I. 438 Improvement in Cotton Seed Planters.

cottonwood ˈkɑtn̩ˌwʊd, *n.* Any one of various species of American poplars, or a tree of such a species, having seeds surrounded by a substance resembling cotton.

1802 ELLICOTT *Journal* 123 A boat may at all times come to with safety at . . . any of the points that are covered with young cotton wood. **1851** *Polly Peablossom* 123 My 'shipmate' . . . remarked to me that he believed 'some d—— cuss was prowling around the cotton woods.' **1945** WALLACE *Barington* 1 There is no fragrance on earth like the incense of burning cottonwood.

b. Attrib. with **ball, bark, borer, bottom, cabin, salve, timber, town, tree.**

1942 STEGNER *Mormon C.* 3 She saw the cottonwood balls hanging like clusters of grapes, and beyond them, on the flat profile of the mountain, the pines. — **1824** in *Mo. Hist. Soc. Coll.* (1928) VI. 6 April 60 Nothing for horses to eat, except cotton wood bark. **1857** *Kit Carson's Own Story* (1926) 22 Their horses were very poor, having been fed during the winter on cottonwood bark. — **1884** *Rep. Comm. Agric.* 336n The first of these, the Cottonwood Borer (*Saperda calcarata* Say) we shall not treat at this time. — **1893** *Outing* Mar. 466/1 He can sail up the river, past the willow and cottonwood 'bottoms,' as far as Marysville. — **1872** *Kans. Mag.* Jan. 15 His residence was one of the conventional structures of the period: a cottonwood cabin of two rooms. — **1947** *Reader's Digest* Oct. 165/1 She gave me a little jar of cottonwood salve. . . . They made it by crushing the green buds of cottonwood trees and boiling them with moose grease. — **1826** in MARICE S. SULLIVAN *Travels of Jedediah Smith* (1934) 10 The place we had selected for winter quarters was . . . in a situation well calculated for the supply of . . . Cotton wood timber. **1832** in KENNEDY *Texas* (1841) I. 188 We encamped on a creek, . . . with a rich bottom, with some cotton-wood timber on it. — **1856** PHILLIPS *Kansas* 126 It is a cotton-wood town of the 'great futurity' school. — **1787** CUTLER in *Life & Corr.* I. 214 The side next the lots of interval lined for two miles with the tallest and straightest cotton-wood trees I ever saw. **1948** *Chr. Sci. Monitor* 8 April 6 Buds on the cottonwood trees and the willows burst open.

c. *To have the cottonwood on one,* to have the advantage. *Rare.*

1888 *Detroit Free Press* 3 Nov. (F.), I jess reckoned she was blowin' around, an' yere she had de cottonwood on me all de time!

As the last term in **big, bitter, river, swamp, sweet, sweet-bark, valley cottonwood.**

cottony maple scale. A scale insect injurious to maple trees. — **1905** *Chi. D. News* 26 July 3/1 Chicago is in danger of losing its soft maple trees, box elders and ornamental shrubs if measures are not taken to stop the ravages of the pulvinaria innumerabilis, commonly known as the cottony maple scale. **1913** ESSIG *Injurious & Beneficial Insects Calif.* 110 Cottony Maple Scale . . . can be easily recognized in early summer by the large white cottony egg-sacs which are posterior to the brown female bodies.

***couch,** *n.* As the last term in **field couch, studio couch.**

***cough,** *n.*

1. cough candy, a sweetish medicinal preparation for relieving a cough.

1842 *S. Lit. Messenger* VIII. 199/2 An intelligent operative at Lowell has actually extracted an excellent cough candy from the devil's own turnip. **1882** *Harper's Mag.* Aug. 345/1 Some freaky confectioner's device made of opaque, light brown cough candy. **1947** *This Week Mag.* 15 March 15/2 At that time [*c*1850] the product was known as 'cough candy.'

2. cough root, any one of various plants (see quots.) thought to be beneficial in curing coughs.

1876 HOBBS *Bot. Hand-Book* 27 Cough root, Beth root, Trillium pendulum. **1937** *Range Plant Hdbk.* W-106 Two Rocky Mountain species of [*Ligusticum*] are called cough-roots because of their medicinal uses.

As the last term in **graveyard cough.**

***cough,** *v.* *To cough up:* **1.** To give up, hand over. **2.** To tell, divulge. Both *slang.*

(1) **1894** *S.F. Midwinter Appeal* 27 Jan. 2/4 Cough up a nickel, read the paper, and get the latest of camp doings. **1904** W. H. SMITH *Promoters* vii. 122 I'll cough up the stock and bonds all right. *a***1909** O. HENRY *Roads of Destiny* xix. 324 Everybody cough up what matches he's got. — (2) **1896** G. ADE *Artie* xi 95 And I cough up to you because I know that you're a good fellow. **1948** *Time* 29 Mar. 27/3 The operators were not going to cough up.

coulee ˈkulɪ, *n.* [See quot. 1931.] A small stream, or the bed of such a stream when dry.

1807 in *Amer. State P., Pub. Lands* (1832) I. 313 Bounded in front by the river Detroit, and in rear by a *coulee* or small run. *Ib.* 346 Bounded . . . above by a creek (or coulee) called *ventre de boeuf.* **1881** *Chi. Times* 14 May (*O.E.D.*), These 'coolies' are dry during the summer season, but are flooded in the spring of the year. **1931** READ *La.-French* 166 *Coulée,* a substantive from the feminine past participle of Fench *couler,* 'to flow,' is generally used in Louisiana of a small stream that may become dry in summer. *Coulée* is also written *coulee, -ie, coolie, -ey,* as an English word. **1948** *Kananaskis Ranch Cat.* 3 They may be huddled together down in a sheltered couley, out of the wind, waiting the storm out.

Coulter pine. The big-cone pine, *Pinus coulteri,* of southern California, named in honor of its discoverer, Dr.

Thomas Coulter, an Englishman (or Irishman) who travelled extensively in California about 1830.

1888 LINDLEY *Calif. of South* 333 On the southern spurs of the great snowy range are . . . Coulter pines with enormous cones. **1906** *Out West* Mar. 175 The cones . . . of the Coulter Pine often weigh eight to ten pounds. **1923** SAUNDERS *So. Sierras Calif.* 30 On the hillside along this trail a pine began to appear which finds its best development at an altitude much higher—the Coulter pine, one of the characteristic conifers of the Southern California mountains.

* **council,** *n.* In combs.: (1) **council bag,** a bag taken by an Indian to a council, *rare;* (2) **camp,** a camp agreed upon for a council between whites and Indians, *obs.;* (3) **chief,** an Indian chief representing his tribe in a council, *obs.;* (4) **district,** a district entitled to elect a member of a territorial council, *obs.;* (5) **fire,** among Indians, a ceremonial fire made in connection with the holding of a council, cf. **Seven council fires;** (6) **ground,** a place at which Indians were accustomed to hold councils; (7) **lodge,** an Indian lodge in which councils are usu. held; (8) **pipe,** a pipe used by those in attendance at an Indian council, *obs.;* (9) **ring,** a circular area marked out with stones as the site of an Indian council, also the council itself; (10) **square,** a square where an Indian council meets, or is to meet.

(1) 1748 O. WEISER *Journal* 43 Scaishady & the half King . . . had nothing in their Council Bag . . . either to recompense a Messenger or to get Wampum to do the business. — **(2) 1870** KEIM *Sheridan's Troopers* iv. 30 They met many of the chiefs and headmen of the Kiowa and Comanche tribes at the Council camp. — **(3) 1826** FLINT *Recoll.* 144 They were the select men, that is the warriors, and council-chiefs of their tribes. — **(4) 1849** E. S. SEYMOUR *Sks. of Minn.* 53 The number of persons authorized to be elected having the highest number of votes in each of the said council districts for members of the council shall be declared by the governor to be duly elected. **1901** DUNCAN & SCOTT *Allen & Woodson Co., Kansas* 19 Bourbon, Allen, McGee, Dorn, Woodson and Wilson counties formed the 12th council district.

(5) 1753 WASHINGTON *Diaries* I. 57 At this Place a Council Fire was kindled, where all their Business with these People was to be transacted. **1898** CUSHMAN *Hist. Indians* 315 He calmly gazed upon the throng whose faces shone with the light of the blazing council fire. **1947** *Chi. Tribune* 6 July 1. 3/1 He is an Oneida Indian from Wisconsin, serving his second term as president of the Indian Council Fire. — **(6) 1842** *Diplom. Corr. Texas* I. 629 Urge upon the President . . . the appointment of the commissioners immediately; . . . and their early departure for the Council ground. **1946** FOREMAN *Last Trek* 49 He carried also a request that the eastern Indians arrange a council at the Wapakoneta council ground. — **(7) 1806** CLARK in *Lewis & C. Exped.* (1905) V. 289 On this Island I observ[e]d a large lodge the same which Shannon informed me of a fiew days past. This Lodge (is) a council lodge, it is of a Conocil form 60 feet diameter at its base. **1817** J. BRADBURY *Travels* 117 The news was carried through the village by heralds, who stood at the door of the council-lodge. **1948** *Chi. D. News* 18 March 20/7 They are depending on us to decide which of them will sit for the next four years in the council lodge. — **(8) 1760** G. CROGHAN *Journal* 104 We then put ashore shook hands and smoked with them [Ottawas] out of their Council Pipe. — **(9) 1913** EATON *Barn Doors & Byways* 173 It is an old Indian trail. Follow it, and presently you may come upon a ring of stones—the old Narragansett Council Ring. **1948** *Green Bay* (Wis.) *Press-Gazette* 30 June 16/4 The earliest democracy on the North American continent was the Indian pow-wow and council ring where the Great Chief was chosen.

(10) 1846 M'KENNEY *Memoirs* I. 82 The council square . . . was covered with boughs of evergreen, resting on a frame-work of timber, supported by posts inserted in the ground.

b. *Council of Censors,* (see quots.).

1776 *Pa. Constitution* § 47 There shall be chosen . . . two persons in each city and county . . . to be called the Council of Censors. **1794** S. WILLIAMS *Vermont* 349 A council of censors, to consist of thirteen persons to be elected by the people every seventh year. The duty assigned to them is to inquire whether the constitution has been preserved inviolate. **1841** *Niles' Reg.* 19 June 256/3 The council of censors of this state [Vermont] are in session, and propose several amendments to the constitution. **1873** *Harper's Mag.* XLVI. 575 The septennial Council of Censors, which until recently existed under the Constitution of Vermont (and which was borrowed from the first Constitution of Pennsylvania), [etc.].

c. *Council of revision,* (see quot.).

1834 PECK *Gaz. Illinois* 63 The governor and judges of the supreme court constitute a council of revision, to which all bills that have passed the assembly must be submitted.

As the last term in **bay, bucktail, city, corporation, executive, family, governor's-, grand, Indian, legislative, national, select, state, war council.**

council ˈkaʊnsl, *v.* [f. the noun.] *intr.* To hold a council, used esp. with reference to Indians. Also **councilling,** *n.* ?*Obs.*

In the *OED* "counciling," with quot. 1870 below, is called a nonce word, "as if from a verb **council* to hold a COUNCIL."

1770 WASHINGTON *Diaries* I. 423 After much Counceling the overnight, they all came to my fire the next Morning. *Ib.* 424 The tedious ceremony which the Indians observe in their Councelings and speeches detained us till 9 Oclock. **1787** in RAMSEY *Tennessee* (1853) 470 The whole town, . . . had been councilling three days, at the instigation of a principal Creek chief. **1804** CLARK in *Lewis & C. Exped.* (1904) I. 129 The Chiefs retired to a Bourey (Bowray) made of bushes by their young men too Divide their presents and Smoke eate and Council. **1870** BRYANT *Iliad* I. II. 51 Shall all our councillings and all our cares Be cast into the flames?

councilmanic, ˌkaʊnslˈmænɪk, *a.* Pertaining to a council or councilman.

1861 *N.Y. Tribune* 16 Nov., Fifth Councilmanic District—Delegates nominated. **1888** *Phila. Press* 29 Jan. (F.), There is less interest taken in the councilmanic elections, perhaps, than has been known for some years past. **1911** HARRISON *Queed* 197 He read enormously with expert facility and a beautifully trained memory; read history, . . . councilmanic proceedings, [etc.].

* **count,** *n.*

1. (See quots.)

1881 E. INGERSOLL *Oyster Industry* 243 *Count,* . . . method of selling oysters in Philadelphia and New York, by enumeration instead of measurement. *Ib., Count,* . . . in respect to terripins, one of full size, i.e., six inches long; two or three small ones will make a *count.* (Savannah.) **1883** GOODE *Fisheries* 47 'Count' Clams, the largest size, . . . sell for $3 per barrel, wholesale. It takes 800 'counts' to make a barrel.

2. count corral, *W.* a corral for counting cattle.

1871 *Rep. Indian Affairs* (1872) 377 The probable cost of new buildings for agency, employés, stable, corral for public animals, and count-corral, etc., would not be less than thirty or thirty-five thousand dollars.

As the last term in **book, New York, presidential, winter count.**

* **count,** *v.* In colloq. phrases.

1. *To count in,* to count upon (one) as being a participant or well-wisher. Cf. **2. c.**

1857 *Knickerb.* XLIX. 185, 'I propose that we all just empty our pockets and show what we've got.' 'Good,' says Hiram, 'count me in.' **1859** *Harper's Mag.* Dec. 76/1, I received . . . an answer from Dr. Benjamin Brightyse . . . [who] desired a personal interview. . . . I put into decent English the very shameful equivalent thereof which I had in my mind—to wit, 'Count me in, old hoss.'

b. To secure the election or nomination (of a candidate) by a fraudulent count of the votes, or by other improper means. Cf. **2. b.**

1875 *Chi. Tribune* 4 Nov. 4/2 Two of [the commissioners] . . . were unquestionably 'counted in' by held-back returns from certain city precincts. **1886** LOGAN *Great Conspiracy* 658 Soon they actually began, themselves, to believe, that President Hayes had been 'counted in,' by improper methods!

2. *To count out,* to eliminate from a fight (a contestant) who fails to resume the contest before the expiration of an allotted time.

1808 *Repertory* (Boston) 2 Aug. (Th.), The judges were proceeding to 'count out' his antagonist [a fighting cock].

b. To defraud (a candidate) of his right in an election by a dishonest count of the votes. Also fig.

1875 *Chi. Tribune* 4 Nov. 1/3 Commissioners Nelson and Jones Counted Out of an Election. **1906** *Churchman* 17 Nov. 743 We are ignored and counted out in the efforts of the common people to secure a fair chance. **1931** ADAMS & ALMACK *Hist.* 494 In 1838 he ran for Congress but was 'counted out' by five votes after fifty ballots had been thrown out because the voters had spelled his name 'Duglas' and not 'Douglas.'

c. To excuse from being present or from being a participant.

1854 *Knickerb.* XLIII. 643 When it comes to hunting grizzlies on a pony, jist 'count me out.' **1863** *Cong. Globe* 23 Feb. 1227/3 Perhaps . . . [he thought I wanted] to immortalize myself by coupling my name with so distinguished a person as himself! If that is the gentleman's idea I beg him to count me out.

d. *W.* Of a herd of cattle: To turn out or prove to be when counted.

1903 A. Adams *Log Cowboy* 13 Just so the herd don't count out shy on the day of delivery.

3. *W. To count over,* to count (a cattle herd) in relinquishing it to another.

1920 Hunter *Trail Drivers Texas* I. 67 We counted the old herd over to the ranch boss.

For *to count coup,* see **coup.**

∗**counter,** *n.*[1] Formerly in Virginia, one appointed to count the tobacco plants within a parish or district. — **1724** *Bristol Vestry Book* 17 All below the s'd Roads to the Extent of the P'ish & south side of Nottoway River the lower precinct, Instance Hall and John Mays are appointed Counters for the same. **1728** *Ib.* 41 In obedience to an act of assembly for the better Improveing the Staple of tobo it is ord'red that the parrish be Devided into precincts for Counting tobo plants. . . . James pitillo and henry Wyatt are appointed and ord'red Counter for yt precinct.

∗**counter,** *n.*[2] [In **1.** short for ∗*countertenor.*]

1. In singing, a part between tenor and treble. *Colloq.*

1871 Stowe *Sam Lawson* 129, I 'member I used to lead the singin' in them days, and Miry she used to sing counter. **1878** ——— *Poganuc People* vii. 56 Ben . . . beating and roaring, first to treble and then to counter and then to bass.

2. In combs. in which the first element is from sources other than that of ∗**counter 1.** above, but listed here for ease of reference: (1) **counter-brand,** (see quot. 1889 and cf. **counterbrand,** *v.*); (2) **burning,** the burning of a protective strip against an approaching fire; (3) **check,** a blank check, obtainable at a bank, of a kind designed to be cashed immediately by the person drawing it; (4) **scales,** a weighing device for use on a counter in a store.

(1) **1889** *Cent.* 1302/2 counter-brand. . . . A mark put on branded cattle, effacing the original brand. **1941** Seton *Trail of Artist-Naturalist* 322 Didn't you invent that slick counterbrand? — (2) **1882**

Counter scales

Baillie-Grohman *Camps in Rockies* 37 So, to have any chance with what is here called counter-burning, we had to begin several hundred yards or so ahead. — (3) **1856** *Mich. Agric. Soc. Trans.* VII. 61 S. S. Barrows, . . . [exhibited] common and counter check. **1931** *Durant* (Okla.) *D. Democrat* 24 Nov. 6/3 (*advt.*), Counter checks. — (4) **1851** Cist *Cincinnati* 227 W. G. Groves . . . manufactures platform and counter scales, beams, trucks, skids, and truck-wagons. **1857** *Lawrence Republican* 28 May 3 Counter and Platform Scales, of all sizes and patterns, furnished to order by Allen & Gilmore. **1935** *Montgomery Ward Cat.* (Index), Scales, Counter.

As the last term in **bargain, calico, drugstore, false, grocery, lunch, notion, pie, ribbon, soda, store counter.**

counterbrand ˈkaʊntɚˌbrænd, *v. W. tr.* (See quots.)

1859 Bartlett 103 To *Counter-brand,* to destroy a brand by branding on the opposite side. **1874** McCoy *Cattle* 8 When a stock is purchased it is usual, if it be not very large, that each animal is counter branded; i.e., the first brand burned out and the purchaser's brand burned on instead. **1944** Adams *W. Words* 41.

∗**counterfeit,** *a.* and *n.*

1. counterfeit Democrat, a Democrat who is not entirely loyal to the party. *Rare.*

1838 *Cong. Globe* App. 16 April 275 Counterfeit Democrats, National Republicans, Anti-masons, and Abolitionists.

2. counterfeit detector, a publication listing and describing worthless and counterfeit money as an aid in its detection. Cf. **bank note detector.**

1826 (*title*), Day's New-York Bank Note List, Counterfeit Detector and Price Current. **1849** *Ill. Reveille* (Bloomington) 27 Nov. 2/5 They can place but little reliance in Counterfeit Detectors, while the publishers of one of them offer to buy the paper of an imaginary bank at one per cent. discount. **1860** *Harper's Mag.* May 859/1 'Counterfeit Detectors' are henceforth at a discount, and magnifying glasses below par. **1949** *Chi. Tribune* 30 Jan. 1. 4/4 The National Counterfeit Detector has been published once a month since 1907.

∗**counting chute.** *W.* (See quot.) — **1913** W. C. Barnes *Western Grazing Grounds* 381 Counting Chute.—A V-shaped fence into which the sheep are crowded and as they escape through a small opening at the point can be readily counted.

∗**country,** *n.* and *a.*

1. *Navy.* A passageway or open space near staterooms and messrooms.

1853 Kane *Grinnell Exp.* cxi. (1856) 25 The area . . . which is known to naval men as 'the country,' seemed completely filled up with the hinged table.

2. In combs.: (1) **country distemper,** (*a*) (see quot.), (*b*) a disease of sheep; (2) **Country Gentleman corn,** a variety of sweet corn, also attrib.; (3) **highway,** = **country road 1,** *obs.;* (4) **land,** land granted to one of the New England colonies, *obs.;* (5) **mill,** ?a mill whose products are designed for local sale or consumption, *obs.,* cf. **country work** and see **merchant mill;** (6) **party,** (see quot. 1909 and cf. **court party** (*b*)); (7) **rate,** formerly in New England, a tax assessed on property, *obs.;* (8) **treasurer,** formerly in New England, the treasurer of a colony or province, *obs.;* (9) **way,** a road or highway constructed at the expense of a colony or province, *obs.,* cf. **country road 1;** (10) ∗**work,** ?work done for local patrons, *obs.,* cf. **country mill.**

(1) (*a*) **1709** Lawson *Carolina* 18 For I never could learn, that this Country-Distemper, or Yawes, is begun or continu'd with a Gonorrhoea. (*b*) **1811** *Agric. Museum* I. 23 The principal disease from which I have suffered, and from which I did suffer sorely for several years, after I began to raise this stock, my people called *the country distemper.* — (2) **1899** *Chi. D. News* 21 June 7/4 Country Gentleman corn—regular price 12c—per doz. $1.15; per can 10c. **1942** Weygandt *Plenty of Penna.* 96 We planted, for an early crop, a few rows of black Mexican, and then a dozen rows of shoepeg or Country Gentleman, and then the rest of the patch with Stowell's Evergreen. — (3) **1656** *Braintree Rec.* 7 Turning out of the country highway. **1702** *Conn. H.S. Coll.* VI. 266 A high way leading from the bank by Joseph Eastons house to the Country High way. — (4) **1683** *Conn. Col. Rec.* III. 117 To use utmost endeavoures to suit them with a sufficient tract of land, which if they can procure by exchang of country lands they may, or by setleing them on some country land, or on some unimproved land. **1706** *Ib.* 540 Two hundred acres of countrie land.

(5) **1819** *Plough Boy* I. 8 This Furnace is furnished with a general assortment of Patterns, among which are Patterns of latest improvement for Merchant and Country Mills. **1850** *Hunt's Merch. Mag.* XXII. 28 All the *country* [cotton] mills in New England . . . have wholly or partially failed. — (6) **1812** H. Marshall *Kentucky* 382 At the head of this party, were Colonel Thomas Marshall [and others], . . . sometimes distinguished, by the appellation of the *country party;* in contradistinction to the *court party,* an epithet bestowed on their opponents, on account of their leaders being members of the bench, or barr, of the Supreme Court. **1909** R. M. McElroy *Kentucky* 136 In opposition to this party [Court Party] and its principles, stood 'the Country party,' loyal, and determined to preserve the integrity of the United States by a legal and constitutional separation, and admission into the Union. — (7) **1640** *Conn. Public Rec.* I. 61 It is Ordered, that Country Rates yet behind vnpayd, shall be accepted. **1692** *Suffield Doc. Hist.* 115 The Towne made choice of, and impowered thaire trusty freinds; Ensigne John Pengilly, and Serj David Winchill, to . . . ask in ye Townes behalfe for some easement of the Countrey rate. — (8) **1654** *Mass. Records* III. 341 The secritary . . . of the Court shall . . . returne a true transcript . . . [of fines and dues],—to be payd into the country Treasurer. **1690** *Manchester Rec.* 37 The s[ai]d constable is forthwith to Colect and pay to the Country Treasurer tweelve pounds. — (9) **1640** *Braintree Rec.* 8 To lay out the Country way. **1672** *Essex Inst. Coll.* LVI. 299 William Sargent . . . conveyed to Isaac Green . . . about 2 acres salt marsh on east side of country way towards Hampton.

(10) **1777** *N.J. Archives* 2 Ser. I. 299 There is also on said premises a large frame mill with two pair of stones, the one pair sopes, the other cullen, one pair for merchant and the other for country work, with four boulting cloths, all in good order.

b. In combs. of obvious meaning in which rural people, things, etc., are referred to, as (1) **country college,** (2) **cracker,** (3) **cured ham,** (4) **dinner,** (5) **home,** (6) **jake,** (7) **jay,** (8) **paper,** (9) **produce,** (10) **sausage,** (11) **sugar,** (12) **trader.**

(1) **1881** *Harper's Mag.* April 644 The peddler engaged a young man who had just graduated from some country college. — (2) **1865** in Chesnut *Diary* 401 Everybody in our walk of life gave Milly a help-

ing hand. She was a perfect specimen of the Sandhill 'tackey' race, sometimes called 'country crackers.' **1908** *D.N.* III. 301 country-cracker, *n.* A backwoodsman, a rustic. The term *cracker* is specifically applied to a Georgian. — **(3) 1944** *Chi. Tribune* 6 Aug. VII. 1/4 It was a lunch such as country women would prepare, a crockful of potato salad, country cured ham, meat loaf [etc.]. — **(4) 1940** MENCKEN *Happy Days* 76 At intervals of a mile or so along the road there were old-time coaching inns, and they were still doing a brisk trade in 25-cent country dinners and 5-cent whiskey.

(5) 1852 MITCHELL *Dream Life* 268 The country-home, where lived the grandfather of Frank, gleams kindly in the sunlight of your memory. **1925** BRYAN *Memoirs* 85 The precinct in which our country home near Lincoln was located. — **(6) 1884** MARK TWAIN *H. Finn* xx, These country jakes won't ever think of that. **1899** ADE *Fables* (1902) 81 Brother Lyford had continued to be a rude and unlettered Country Jake. **1939** BROWNELL *Horse & Buggy Philos.* 186 Look at the Country Jake and his cowhide boots. — **(7) 1899** A. H. QUINN *Pa. Stories* 45 Well, you all know what a country jay Dutch was when he came to college. — **(8) 1846** *Bankers Mag.* 1 Aug. 65 The result is, a uniform circulation, known to and by everybody, not subject to those variable and uncertain values which we find attached to country paper in other cities. — **(9) 1722** in *Pa. Arch.* 8 Ser. II. (1931) 1394 The Petition . . . praying . . . that all importer of Servants and Goods may be enjoined to take Country Produce for Pay . . . was read, and ordered to lie on the Table. **1872** *Newton Kansan* 22 Aug. 3/6 Highest cash prices paid for country produce.

(10) 1902 LORIMER *Lett. Merchant* 7 Does it pay to feed in pork trimmings at five cents a pound at the hopper and draw out nice, cunning, little 'country' sausages at twenty cents a pound at the other end? — **(11) 1872** EGGLESTON *End of World* xvi. 110 A feller don't like to eat up all his country sugar to wunst. — **(12) 1714** *Mass. Bay Currency Tracts* 139 Some are not able, and others take the opportunity to defraud the Country Trader, and he of Consequence is not able to pay the Merchant in Boston. **1825** NEAL *Bro. Jonathan* II. 136 He knew not how cautioned your 'country trader' is, when he gets into a large tavern.

c. Also **country docket, fever, millstone, potato,** (see quots.). All *obs.*.

*c***1826** STANLEY *Journal* 301 On the second day, the Court [in Charleston, S.C.] was occupied with what is called the Country Docket; chiefly trifling causes of debt from the country, to which no defence was made, and which the debtor had only put upon the list to gain the time which would elapse before the cause came on. — **1822** *Christian Observer* XXII. 630 Their apprehensions being confined to what they term the 'country fever' and 'fever and ague.' **1882** G. C. EGGLESTON *Wreck of Red Bird* 6 'What's country fever?' asked Jack. . . . 'It's a very severe and fatal form of bilious fever, which one night's exposure—or even a few hours' exposure after sunset—brings on.' — **1834** *S. Lit. Messenger* I. 97 Loose rocks— . . . of the species of agglomerated quartz familiar to the west under the name of country mill-stone. — **1787** WASHINGTON *Diaries* III. 255 At Muddy hole finished late in the Afternoon and ditch round the Barn, and Dug the Irish Potatoes in the half Acre of experimental ground (adjoining the ½ Acre of Sweet or Country Potatoes).

For **country club, mark, pay, road, store,** see as main entries.

As the last term in **ant, back, beaver, brush, bush, cane, cattle, chestnut, coon, cotton, cow, creek, Digger Indian, down, fur, God's, gold, Indian, loco, logging, lumber, Miami, mosquito, mountain, Navaho, oil, old, Oregon, overmountain, panhandle, parish, park, Pawnee, pea, pine hill, plains, prairie, prairie-dog, sage, sagebrush, sand-hill, sawdust, settled, snake, snowshoe, southern, steerage, stock, stump, sunk, tall, tobacco, turpentine, west, western, wheat, white man's, wooden country.**

country club. A club having its headquarters in or near the country and composed of town or city people interested in outdoor sports, games, etc. Also the club building and adjacent grounds. Also attrib.

[**1867** *Ball Players' Chron.* 20 June 1/2 They wanted us to accompany them in order to show us what a terrific thrashing they were going to give the 'country club.'] **1894** *Harper's Mag.* LXXXIX. 16/1 The Country Club is either very restful and bucolic, or very athletic and exciting, just as one chooses. **1916** WILSON *Red Gap* 195 Wilbur Todd had once endeavoured to hold her hand out on the porch at a country-club dance. **1948** *Ada* (Okla.) *Ev. News* 4 July II. 1/1 A special program has been arranged for country club members.

country mark.

1. In colonial times, a mark or brand used on stock to indicate the colony to which it belonged. *Obs.*

1664 in *Records E.-Hampton* I. 218 Beniamine Price marked a filey of a year old wth the Cuntry marke.

2. A mark or scar identifying a slave as being from a particular part of Africa. Now *hist.*

1754 *S.C. Gazette* 22–29 Jan. 3/3 Run Away, . . . Duke a black well made fellow, about 6 feet high, with several of his country marks down each side of his face. **1790** *N.C. Chronicle* 10 May, Ran away, an outlandish negro fellow, named Toby—; . . . has his country mark on both sides of his face. **1940** E. M. COULTER *T. Spalding* 82 Many of them bore their 'country's marks' which they had acquired in Africa.

country pay. (See quots. 1809, 1946.) Now *hist.*

1643 *Essex Inst. Coll.* L. 319 Seaven years after my decease shall pay vnto my daughter Ellen sixteene pounds in Cuntry paye. **1713** *N.C. Col. Rec.* II. 21 [I] am promised twenty barrels pork . . . and most of the remainder in country pay, pork and corn being very scarce. **1809** KENDALL *Travels* I. 193 In those parts of the United States to which the present pages are confined [i.e., New Eng.], the dollar is estimated at six shillings currency, or as it is now called in the country, *lawful money*. For this, the ancient phrase is, *country pay*. **1946** *Yankee* Sep. 15 'Country pay' is the colloquial term for products given in exchange for services or goods. The expression goes back to before the Revolution.

country road.

1. A road built by or at the expense of one of the New England colonies. *Obs.* Cf. **country highway.**

1669 *Essex Inst. Coll.* VI. 175/2 The higheway . . . to range up straight to the Country Roade. **1775** *Essex Inst. Coll.* XIII. 191, I have . . . got a very commodious House . . . about 2 miles from the grand country road.

2. A road passing through a rural district.

1846 *Hunt's Merch. Mag.* XIV. 29 Commencing with a noble system of town and country roads, she early embarked on turnpikes. **1948** *Dly. Ardmoreite* (Ardmore, Okla.) 27 June 16/3 Strawn began driving about the town of Wagoner, venturing now and then onto the country roads where the centers weren't too high.

country store.

1. A store situated out in the country.

1741 in *N.J. Archives* 1 Ser. XII. 92 To be sold. . . . Three Hundred Acres of Land . . . with a very good Landing Place, and well situated for keeping a Country Store. **1889** MELLICK *Story Old Farm* 9 The small structure on the corner, opposite the tavern, is that magazine of wonders, a country store. **1946** *This Week Mag.* 17 Aug. 18/2 In this old country store she bought her food from bins and barrels.

b. country storekeeper, one who keeps such a store.

1742 *Pa. Gazette* 13 Jan. [Franklin offers his goods to] country storekeepers. **1840** *Hunt's Merch. Mag.* II. 532 The country store-keepers all keep open accounts with the large dealers in Havana. **1945** *This Week Mag.* 1 Dec. 2/3 Then there is Walt, who left a showy advertising job in New York to become a country storekeeper.

* **county,** *n.*

1. The largest division of a colony or state for purposes of local government.

Such a political division is known as a county in all the states, except Louisiana, where "parish" is used. Formerly in South Carolina the term "district" was used.

1635 *Watertown Rec.* 2 Agreed that the charges of the new meeting house . . . shalbe levied as other generall Levies are for the County. **1705** BEVERLEY *Virginia* IV. 8 The Method of bounding the Counties is at this time, with respect to the convenience of having each County limited to one single River, for its Trade and Shipping. **1880** *Hist. Columbia Co., Wis.* 495 Abstract offices . . . contain a complete and perfect history, so far as it is possible to obtain it, of every piece of land in the county. **1945** *Somerset News* 15 Feb. 3/3 Force counties with substandard clinks to pay board and lodging to the b-ho-ys in Annapolis.

2. In combs. referring to officials or official groups within a county: (1) **county assessor,** an official who, for purposes of taxation, establishes the valuation of property within a county; (2) **attorney,** the prosecuting officer of a county; (3) **board,** a body having charge of the political administration of a county, or of some specified county interest; (4) **collector,** a county tax collector; (5) **commission,** a group of persons charged with the performance of some task having reference to a county; (6) **engineer,** an engineer employed by a county to have supervision over county roads, bridges, etc.; (7) **judge,** in some states, the highest judicial officer in a county; (8) **justice,** a magistrate, as a justice of the peace, having jurisdiction in minor legal matters in a county; (9) **lieutenant,** the chief military officer of a county, *obs.*; (10) **manager,** a nonpolitical executive officer selected to have charge of the administrative affairs of a county;

(11) **recorder,** (see next); (12) **register,** in some counties, an official who records public documents; (13) **superintendent,** an official who has charge of administering the public schools situated in the villages, small towns, or rural districts of a county; (14) **surrogate,** =**surrogate;** (15) **surveyor,** a surveyor authorized to make official surveys within a county; (16) **warden,** a warden, esp. a game warden, having jurisdiction within a county.

(1) **1877** JOHNSON *Anderson Co.* (Kansas) 219 [He] was elected county assessor in 1860, and was elected engrossing clerk of the Territorial Legislature in the winter of 1861. **1911** *Okla. Session Laws* 3 Legisl. 331 The office of the county assessor is hereby created. — (2) **1873** *Harper's Mag.* XLVI. 799 The county attorney, H. W. Paine, had prepared himself to conduct the case for the State. **1948** *Capital-Democrat* (Tishomingo, Okla.) 24 June 4/3 In 1946 I was elected your County Attorney as which I am now serving. — (3) **1839** *Indiana H. Rep. Jrnls.* 539 The several county boards shall, for purposes of county revenue . . . fix any per centum . . . deemed necessary. **1876** *Chi. Tribune* 3 Aug. 7/3 May I ask . . . why the indicted members of our County Board of Commissioners are not made to stand aside and stop transacting the county business until they prove themselves innocent men? **1946** *Ill. Taxpayer* Aug.–Sep. 7/2 The County Board of Supervisors can prevent the possibility of large salary increases for County Clerks by holding down their salaries under the Constitutional salary provisions. — (4) **1817** DWIGHT *Travels* I. 241 The taxes are collected by County Collectors, by warrant from the County Treasurer.

(5) **1920** *3rd Nat. Country Life Conf. Proc.* 109 By far the most effective remedy in this connection has been the creation of the county commission. — (6) **1862** *Cin. Commercial* 26 Aug. 3/6 J. W. Gilbert, County Engineer, reported the bridge across the canal at Carthage is in a dangerous condition. **1911** *Okla. Session Laws* 3 Legisl. 222 County engineers of the several counties of this state, . . . may hereafter have by law, authority over the public highways. — (7) **1819** NOAH *She Would Be a Soldier* I. i, I'm a squire, and a county judge, and a *brevet* ossifer in the militia besides. **1948** *McAlester* (Okla.) *News-Capital* 3 July 1/8 The county judge's race is one in which not much interest is being shown. — (8) **1831** *Ind. Mag. Hist.* XXII. 62 David Miller . . . proposed Goshen and the county justices, of whom I was one, agreed unanimously to call it by that name. — (9) **1750** *Va. State P.* I. 244 We have neither County Lieutenant, nor any other Military officer amongst us & Consequently no Soldiers. **1812** MARSHALL *Kentucky* 288 Representations had been made by some of the county Lieutenants, to the executive authority of the commonwealth.

(10) **1898** PAGE *Red Rock* 214 She should not apply for one of the schools under the new county-managers. **1948** *Norman* (Okla.) *Transcript* 4 July B. 1/4 The county manager form has been tried in one or more states and is now in the trial and error stage. — (11) **1844** *Ind. Senate Jrnls.* 41 The expediency of so amending the eighth chapter of the Revised Statutes, prescribing the duties of county recorders, as to exempt them from indictment. **1947** *Pasadena* (Calif.) *Star-News* 9 Sep. 16/2 When County Recorder Mame Beatty introduces her new photo-recording machines on Sept. 20 she also will display some new price lists for services rendered by her office. — (12) **1726** *Boston Selectmen* 148 The free-holders also are to be warned that at the same time & place they are to vote for County Regester. **1855** *Mich. Gen. Statutes* (1882–3) I. 1060 Before any corporation . . . shall commence business, the president or directors . . . shall cause said articles of association to be recorded at length in the county register's office. — (13) **1846** *Ind. Hist. Soc. Pub.* III. 417 Let us have county superintendents, whose duty it shall be to examine teachers, visit schools, and report to the superintendent of the state. **1947** *Democrat* 6 Nov. 1/7 Much interest was shown in our program by the County Superintendent, the teachers of the various schools and the general public. — (14) **1852** *N.Y. Wkly. Tribune* 28 Feb. 8/1 Hugh J. Hastings, Editor of *The Knickerbocker*, Orville H. Chittenden, County Surrogate, and two others entered their recognizances in the sum of $1,500 for the appearance of the prisoners before the next Grand Jury.

(15) **1844** *Ind. Senate Jrnls.* 276 Resolved, That the committee on elections be directed to enquire into the expediency of . . . altering the present law . . . for electing the county surveyors. **1945** *Greeley* (Colo.) *D. Tribune* 13 Aug. 4/4 He was also county surveyor [of] Gilpin for several years. — (16) *a***1800** in STOWE *Key* (1853) 253 All [such] horses, cattle, hogs, or sheep . . . shall be seized and sold by the county wardens. **1857** *Maine Rev. Statutes* 269 The county wardens . . . may recover the penalties for unlawfully hunting and killing moose and deer.

b. In similar combs. of more obvious meaning or explained in the quots.: (1) **county canvasser,** (2) **committee,** (3) **junto,** (4) **marshal,** (5) **officer,** (6) **physician,** (7) **sheriff,** (8) **supervisor.**

(1) **1838** in ADAMS *Pioneer Hist.* (1923) 119 The board of county canvassers under this act shall consist of one of the presiding inspectors of said election from each township. **1846** *Mich. Gen. Statutes* (1882–3) I. 138 The several inspectors appointed by the inspectors of election in townships and wards, to attend the county canvass, shall constitute the board of county canvassers. — (2) **1689** *Huntington Rec.* II. 33 It is thought convenient that . . . two men, out of every town be upon the twentieth Instant to meet at Southampton as a County Committee. **1904** *N.Y. Sun* 9 Aug. 3 To-night Mr. Woodruff's boom for the Governorship is to get a strong boost at the meeting of the county committee. — (3) **1846** MACKENZIE *Van Buren* 208 Is it not evident that Throop was secretly selected . . . as a convenient instrument for regulating future state elections through a chain of banks, controlled by county juntos of greedy politicians? — (4) **1685** *Plymouth Laws* 296 It is Ordered, that there be a County Marshall, who shall always attend said Courts, who are impowered to serve all Warrants, Attachments or Summons.

(5) **1818** FLINT *Lett. from Amer.* 64 To-day the inhabitants of Pennsylvania elect their Representatives in Congress, members of the State Assembly, and County Officers. **1901** DUNCAN & SCOTT *Allen & Woodson Co., Kansas* 19 Watson Stewart was elected to the council . . . with the following county officers; . . . probate judge; . . . sheriff; [etc.]. — (6) **1945** *Hardin* (Mont.) *Tribune-Herald* 15 Feb. 7/2 Said services were rendered without the knowledge of the County Physician. — (7) **1689** *Plymouth Laws* 210 Also to accompt with the Treasurer and the late County Sheriffs or County Treasurers with respect to rates or fines. — (8) **1830** *Williams's N.-Y. Ann. Reg.* 249 The board of County Supervisors is composed of the Supervisors of the several towns. **1947** *L.A. Times* 28 Feb. II. 2/1 Willis . . . was also asked to explain why the jury had failed to return indictments . . . on complaints filed by County Supervisor Charles P. Salzer.

For **county agent,** ***clerk,** ***commissioner, convention,** ***court,** ***treasurer,** see as main entries.

3. Designating roads, institutions, etc., maintained by a county, as (1) **county bridge,** (2) **farm,** (3) **Health Center,** (4) **home,** (5) **hospital,** (6) **house,** (7) **jail,** (8) **poor farm,** (9) **poor house,** (10) ***road,** (11) **school.**

(1) **1668** *Boston Rec.* 7 The Countie Bridge at Muddy River being presented as defective the Court ordered . . . a Committee to order the substantial erecting of a Bridge there. **1797** *Mass. H.S. Coll.* V. 253 From the county-bridge at the lower falls, . . . to Cambridge line. — (2) **1871** *Mich. Gen. Statutes* (1882–3) 496 It shall be the duty of the superintendents of the poor of each county . . . to report . . . the value of county farms, including buildings: . . . and the income received from the county farm. **1948** *Denison* (Tex.) *Herald* 1 July 1/3 Mar-Lang Construction Co. of Sherman was the successful bidder on the erection of a new county farm home to replace the one destroyed by fire. — (3) **1920** *3rd Nat. Country Life Conf. Proc.* 210 A California county has worked out a 'County Health Center.' — (4) **1911** *Okla. Session Laws* 3 Legisl. 30 The board of county commissioners of the respective counties of this state may . . . purchase land for a county home.

(5) **1868** A. B. CONDICT *P. Eckert* 122 It was deemed advisable . . . to remove him at once to the county hospital. **1903** *Chi. Chronicle* 11 April 1/2 He died in an ambulance on the way to the county hospital. — (6) **1731** *Rec. of Providence R.I.* IX. 59 To bound out the highway that Leads up into the Neck by the County house. **1853** A. BUNN *Old Eng. & New Eng.* 231 Jonathan having a 'notion' that it will never do to be poor and seem poor at the same time, has christened these buildings 'County Houses.' **1900** BACHELLER *E. Holden* 5 Some were for sending me to the county house, but they decided, finally, to turn me over to a dissolute uncle, with some allowance for my keep. — (7) **1699** *N.J. Archives* 1 Ser. III. 480 Capt[ain] Isaac Whitehead was . . . examined about the breaking the prison at Woodbridge being the County Goal [*sic*] for the County of Middlesex. **1889** in SALMONS *Burlington Strike* 435 Members of the Brotherhood of Locomotive Engineers . . . [were] locked in the county jail, under bonds of $5,000 each. **1945** *Somerset News* 15 Feb. 3/3 The Sun's recent exposé of county jail conditions suggests another one. — (8) **1921** *Frontier* May 29 The other day a story appeared . . . telling of the death of an old miner at the county poor-farm. **1945** *This Week Mag.* 14 April 2/2 A Russian family moved in . . . behind the county poor farm. — (9) **1841** *Knickerb.* XVII. 395 The youth had been sent to that den of filth and abomination, the county Poor-House. **1948** *Sat. Ev. Post* 10 July 21/1, I can always go to the county poorhouse, but you're too young.

(10) **1691** *Essex Hist. Coll.* V. 93/1 All the housing & lands on the northerly side the county rode. **1773** PATTEN *Diary* 307 Jamey and Bob worked at the County Road bridge. **1948** *This Week Mag.* 9 Oct. 7/1 Tim Travers turned off the highway onto the county road. — (11) **1812** *Niles' Reg.* I. 361/2 The legislature . . . also appropriated . . . 25,000 per annum for the supporting of county schools. **1905** *Forestry Bureau Bul.* No. 62, 36 Of these latter grants there are four classes—public school lands, university lands, asylum lands, and county school lands. **1923** HERRICK *Lilla* 132 He could play god . . . [to] the teachers and janitors of the county schools.

4. In miscellaneous combs.: (1) **county building,** a building in which the administrative affairs of a county are carried on; (2) **clerkship,** the official position of a county clerk; (3) **judgeship,** in some states, the position held by the highest judicial officer in a county; (4) **levy,** a tax levied upon property within a county; (5) **line,** the boundary line of a county; (6) **option,** the right granted by a state government to the people of a county to legislate for themselves in certain matters, esp. with reference to the sale of liquor within the county; (7) * **rate,** a tax levied on county property for county purposes; (8) **right,** the proper authorization secured by an agent to sell a particular commodity in a county; (9) **scrip,** certificates of indebtedness issued by a county; (10) **seat,** a town in which the administrative offices and buildings of a county are located, also attrib.; (11) **seatship,** the state of being a county seat, *rare;* (12) **site,** =**county seat;** (13) * **town,** =**county seat;** (14) **warrant,** a bond or other acknowledgment of indebtedness issued by a county to raise money.

(1) **1815** Drake *Cincinnati* 48 No permanent county buildings have yet been erected. **1923** Herrick *Lilla* 132 He had an office in the County building with his own clerks and stenographers. — (2) **1773** *Carrol P.* in *Md. Hist. Mag.* XV. 285 The County Clerkships in Virginia are filled by young Gent[leme]n who Serve an Apprenticeship in the Secretaries Office. **1887** *Courier-Journal* 15 Feb. 6/5 The indictments against Messrs. Stickrod and Kleinhaus are based upon a $1,000 bet on the result of the Webb-Newman race for the County Clerkship last year. — (3) **1887** *Courier-Journal* 2 Feb. 8/4 W. P. Winfree, the Democrat who has twice been awarded the county judgeship of the strong Republican county of Christian. **1910** J. Hart *Vigilante Girl* 127 Yes, I was elected Alcalde of this town a few days after I came here. . . . After that I got a county judgeship. — (4) **1705** Beverley *Virginia* iv. 9 The County Levies are such as are peculiar to each County, and laid by the Justices upon all Tithable Persons, for defraying the Charge of their Counties. **1830** *Va. Lit. Museum* 776/2 [Roads] the cost of which may be defrayed out of the county levy.

(5) **1797** *Wilmington* (N.C.) *Gazette* 5 Sep., 1110 acres on the east side of Black river, joining the county line, at a lightwood post. **1948** *Capital-Democrat* (Tishomingo, Okla.) 24 June 2/3 He discovered he had stepped over the county line into Coal county. — (6) **1910** *Cosmopolitan* Nov. 774/2 In Ohio fifty-seven of the eighty-eight counties are dry (nominally) under the county-option law. **1925** Bryan *Memoirs* 205 Have you heard that Billy has come out for county option? **1947** *Democrat* 3 July 1/1 It will probably put racing on the county option basis. — (7) **1665** *Dorchester Town Rec.* IV. 129 The Cuntry and County Rate for this yeare is . . . 80. **1703** *Mass. H.S. Coll.* 4 Ser. II. 237 The other proposal is that the town of Deerfield may be freed from Countey Rates during the time of the war. — (8) **1839** *Knickerb.* XII. 344 He was then on a journey through the state of New-York, for the purpose of disposing of what he called 'county rights'; or, in other words, to sell the privilege of catching rats, according to his patent trap. — (9) **1856** Derby *Phoenixiana* 41 A Justice of the Peace . . . fines any accused person whom he thinks has any money—(because if he don't he has to take his costs in County Scrip). **1873** *Winfield* (Kansas) *Courier* 18 Sep. 2/3 City Scrip is selling for 80 cents, County Scrip 80 cents, and School Bonds at 90 cents.

(10) **1803** in B. H. Young *Jessamine Co., Ky.* (1898) 84 We have succeeded . . . in locating our county seat. **1872** Eggleston *End of World* 208 A physician from the county-seat village went by. **1948** *Norman* (Okla.) *Transcript* 4 July B. 2/1 Mail from Whitesburg, the county seat, has been brought in by muleback since the settlement first approved of its name. — (11) **1882** *Cent. Mag.* Oct. 872/1, I saw the rival villages of Pomeroy and Pataha City fighting each other at a distance of three miles for the honor and profit of the county-seatship of the new county of Garfield. — (12) **1828** A. Sherburne *Mem.* 186 The town of Cornish appointed me as their delegate, but restricted me with respect to the county site. **1851** *Polly Peablossom* 98 A queer old customer . . . used to visit the county site regularly on 'General Muster' days and Court Week. — (13) **1670** *Connecticut Rec.* II. 140 Waightes and measures . . . [are] to be preserued and kept in the county townes as standards for the respectiue countyes. **1853** *Knickerb.* XLIII. 537 A meeting was held at the county-town, where all the candidates were to appear and make speeches. **1905** Valentine *H. Sandwith* 36 The Sandwith Meeting House stood . . . on the edge of the county town of Dunkirk. — (14) **1944** Clark *Pills* 187 No longer were teachers paid with county warrants.

b. In similar combs. of more obvious meaning, as (1) **county bank,** (2) **bar,** (3) **Democracy,** (4) **fair,** (5) **paper,** (6) **tax,** (7) **treasury,** (8) **trot,** (9) **wide.**

(1) **1910** O. Henry *Strictly Business* 37 The crop of farmers is never so short out there but what you can get a few of 'em to sign a petition for a new post office that you can discount for $200 at the county bank. — (2) **1912** Cobb *Back Home* 88 She hired . . . the most silvery tongued orator of all the silver tongues at the county bar, to defend her nephew. — (3) **1893** Jameson *Dict. U.S. Hist.* (1931) 123 County Democracy, a faction of the Democratic party in New York City, which opposed Tammany Hall, especially before 1886, since which time it has been of little importance. — (4) **1856** W. H. Cook *Letters* (1946) 21 Sep. 34 Charley & myself have been up to the county fare the past week. **1948** *Reader's Digest* Dec. 145/2 'Land of Goshen,' said Granny, 'it never entered my head to show my weavin' at a county fair.'

(5) **1828** in *Amer. Sp.* XVIII. 123, I read the issue of the trial . . . in the county paper. **1904** M. E. Waller *Wood-Carver* 34 Then there's the semi-weekly county paper that Uncle Shim used to take. — (6) **1721** *Mass. H. Rep. Jrnls.* III. 127 A Petition Signed by the Select-men . . . praying to be eased from the County Tax. **1799** in *Ann. 7th Congress* 2 Sess. 1437, I was going to deliver up to him my county-tax papers. **1871** *Mich. Gen. Statutes* (1882–3) I. 320 The state taxes contained in such apportionment of the auditor general and shall be levied in the same manner as, and become a portion of, the county taxes of the same year. — (7) **1830** *Williams's N.-Y. Ann. Reg.* 179 Containing a statement of the amount of taxes paid into the county treasuries by the several banking insurance and other incorporated companies within this state. **1911** *Okla. Session Laws* 3 Legisl. 27 Seventy-five per cent of the fees . . . collected . . . shall be paid into the county treasury. — (8) **1912** Cobb *Back Home* 38 Saturday was the last day of the county fair and the day of the County Trot. — (9) **1921** *Rural Organization* 94 There were the following county-wide organizations existing in the county. **1936** *Young Democrat* (Okla. City) IV. No. 10, 5/3 Harden Ray was speaker at countywide meeting held in Woodward.

Also *county bond, boundary line, charge, debt, enterprise, exhibition, flag, hunt, money, nomination, revenue, show, society,* etc.

As the last term in **agricultural, back, banner, black, close, coal, cow, doubtful, frontier, Garden, home, iron, panhandle, Pike, river county.**

county agent. An agent whose activities are limited to one county, esp. one employed by a state to promote agriculture in a county.

1705 *Va. State P.* I. 96 It is proposed. . . . That in every County a person of good reputation and Knowledge in the tobacco trade be appointed, under the name of the County Agent, to view . . . all tobacco paid away for discharge of publick or private Debts in that County. **1894** *Dept. Agric. Yearbook* 55 State and County Agents. A fundamental objection to the present system of gathering agricultural statistics in the United States is the fact that correspondents, who are expected to furnish reliable data, are paid nothing for their work. **1949** *Democrat* 10 Feb. 1/3 County Agent Advises Early Planting For Hog Grazing.

* **county clerk.** In some counties, an official who acts as clerk of the county court, secretary of the county board, and may also perform other duties.

1692 *Watertown Rec.* II. 51 The Rates . . . wear vpon fille in the countie clarks hand. **1773** *Carrol P.* in *Md. Hist. Mag.* XV. 285 How unqualified are most of our County Clerks. **1945** *Hardin* (Mont.) *Tribune-Herald* 15 Feb. 7/1 The Board met this day in regular session, the following members being present: . . . together with the County Clerk.

* **county commissioner.** In some states, an officer elected to have administrative oversight of various county interests, esp. roads.

1668 *Mass. Rec.* IV. ii. 364 And for county commissioners, this Court doe nominate & appoint Capt[ain] Hopestill Foster & Ensigne Daniel Fisher for Suffolke [etc.]. **1865** *Cairo* (Ill.) *D. Democrat* 4 Oct. 1/1 A new County Commissioner will also be appointed at the Convention. **1945** *Somerset News* 15 Feb. 1/2 We elect judges and county commissioners.

county convention. A meeting of delegates from various parts of a county to nominate candidates for county offices and elect delegates to district and state conventions.

1784 *Mass. Centinel* 31 March 3/2 By a gentleman from Worcester we are informed, that one of those nuisances to society, a County Convention, lately met there. **1848** *Knickerb.* XVIII. 514 We have met for the purpose of appointing delegates to a county convention. **1948** *Sat. Ev. Post* 10 July 112/1 This self-anointed kingmaker . . . had never attended so much as a county convention in his life.

* **county court.**

1. A court having jurisdiction within the limits of a county. Also attrib.

1639 *Md. Archives* 47 An Act for the Erecting of a County Court. **1788** in Ramsey *Tennessee* (1853) 406 That the Sheriff take into custody the County Court docket of said county. **1948** *New World*

(Chi.) 2 July 10/7 After an adverse ruling in a county court, the appeal to the state's high court was made by Mr. and Mrs. Yelte Visser.

b. (See quot.)

1906 *N.Y. Ev. Post* 4 Dec. 11 In Missouri counties, the county court, a body of three men elected by districts, is not a court in the commonly accepted definition of the term. It is more properly a board of supervisors. The men comprising the court are usually not lawyers but business men, chosen to attend to certain important branches of the county business. They try no cases either civil or criminal.

2. A session of such a court. Also **county court day.**

1708 *Maryland Hist. Mag.* XVII. 217 The Country being sencible that too many and frequent County Courts were not only burthensome but chargeable. **1832** *Polit. Examiner* (Shelbyville, Ky.) 3/1, I have discovered, in your last paper, a notice to the voters of Shelby county, to meet at the Courthouse in Shelbyville, on the 18th inst. (being County Court day). **1927** Eubank *Horse & Buggy Days* 94 They all come to town on county court day.

3. county courthouse, the building in which county courts are held and county business is transacted.

1743 Franklin *Poor Rich 1744* 21 Two are held yearly at the respective County Court-Houses. **1881** *Harper's Mag.* April 711/1 The County Court-house is a handsome . . . structure. **1948** *Dly. Ardmoreite* (Ardmore, Okla.) 4 May 3/2 The third party presidential candidate spoke on the county courthouse lawn

***county treasurer.** An official having charge of the financial affairs of a county.

1654 *Mass. Rec.* III. 341 That the county Treasurer shall once every yeare present his acco[unt] to the County Court. **1817** Dwight *Travels* I. 241 The taxes are collected by County Collectors, by warrant from the County Treasurer. **1945** *Chi. D. News* 2 Feb. 14/1 This appears to be the first time since the memory of man runneth not to the contrary that the 'L' was square with the county treasurer.

coup ku, *n. W.* [F., in Amer. sense shown here.] Among plains Indians, a personal deed of daring and victory, esp. the first blow or wound given an enemy. Now *hist.*

1832 Catlin *Indians* I. 27 Each one took a smoke of the pipe, and recited his exploits, and his 'coups' or deaths. **1897** Grinnell *Indian* 2 Some of the lodges are painted in gay colours with odd angular figures which tell in red, black, or green, of the coups of the owner. **1939** Vestal *Old Santa Fe Trail* 243 His rating in the tribe depended on his proven *coups*.

b. coup stick, (see quot. 1876).

1876 Bourke *Journal* 15 June, Making 'coup' sticks, which are long willow branches, about 12 feet from end to end, stripped of leaves and

Coup stick such as the Crow Indians used

bark and having each some distinctive mark in the way of feathers, bells, [etc.] . . . in dividing the spoil, each man claims the animals first struck by his 'coup' stick. *a***1918** G. Stuart *On Frontier* II. 122 Some Indian has scratched a crude picture of an Indian with a war bonnet on and a 'coup' stick in his hand seated on a horse.

c. *To count coup*, to be the first to strike an enemy with an object held in the hand, to recount one's exploits. Now *hist.*

[**1742** in Friederici (1947) 216/1 Ces Sauvages n'avoient mis que deux nuits à se rendre de l'endroit où ils avoient fait coup.] **1831** *Illinois Mo.* July 459 The visiters were smoked as usual, feasted on fat dogs; and then they danced and counted their *coups*. **1876** Bourke *Journal* May 10 We have our way of fighting. We will run in and count 'coo' (corruption of the French 'coup' = blow or stroke) 'and the soldiers can do the fighting.' **1947** DeVoto *Across Wide Missouri* 81 War chief: any brave who had counted enough coups to entitle him to lead a war party on his own.

coup ku, *v. W.* [f. the noun.] *intr.* To make a coup. *Rare.* — **1895** Remington *Pony Tracks* 48 Woe to the Sioux if the Northern Cheyennes get a chance to *coup!*

coupon clipper. One who clips or cuts coupons from bonds, a person of wealth. — **1887** *Nation* 2 June 460/3 The select few of the coupon-clippers may escape it [i.e., being in debt]. **1892** *Courier-Journal* 4 Oct. 6/3 A feeling of unrest, depression and apprehension . . . pervades all classes and every business of the country, except the business of that class known as the coupon-clippers, the money-lenders and the protected manufacturer.

cource kurs, *n.* [Origin unknown.] *W.* (See quot.) *Obs.* — **1887** *Scribner's Mag.* II. 511 Sometimes there is a *cource* (Indian?), or leather cover, to protect the saddle in wet weather.

coureur de bois. [F.] A French or half-breed hunter, trader, boatman, etc., of the northern and western U.S. and Canada. Now *hist.*

For an account of the history and meaning of this term in French, see R. M. Saunders, "Coureur de Bois: A Definition," in *Canadian Hist. Rev.* XXI. (1940) 123–31.

[**1672** in *Doc. Col. Hist. N.Y.* (tr.) IX. (1855) 90 Importance of clearing and sowing lands—Necessity of securing the country against the incursion of the Iroquois and the disorders of the Coureur de bois.] **1700** in *N.Y. Col. Docs.* IV. 749 Severall of the French Coureurs de Bois or hunters . . . refuse to obey the Governor of Canada's orders to come to Canada. *c***1806** Pike *Sources Miss.* App. I. 35 A few desperate adventurers, whose mode of life . . obtained for them the appelation of 'Coureurs des Bois.' **1948** *Scientific Mo.* July 46/2 The most interesting class of the fur-trading days were the *coureurs de bois*.

transf. **1837** Peck *New Guide* 335 Along to east and north of the Four lakes [Wisconsin], are alternate quagmires and sand ridges, for fifty miles or more, called by the French coureurs du bois.

***course,** *adv.* Of course. *Colloq.* — **1901** Merwin & Webster *Calumet K* 13 'Have you tried to get any of it here in Chicago?' 'Course not. It's all ordered and cut out up to Ledyard.' **1917** McCutcheon *Green Fancy* 158 Course I couldn't tell her what I told the sheeny, seein' as she's a female.

***course,** *n. course of sprouts*, a flogging, drubbing, or course of severe discipline, usu. *to put through a course of sprouts. Colloq.*

1851 M. Reid *Scalp-Hunters* ii, See that he be put through a 'regular course of sprouts.' **1869** Barnum *Struggles* 409 'Putting Barnum through a course of sprouts' . . . meant an examination . . . compelling him to disclose everything with regard to his property. **1897** *Outing* XXIX. 484/1 He put . . . [the dogs] through a course of sprouts which ultimately developed brilliant though erratic working qualities.

As the last term in **calico, commercial, double major, double minor, graduate course.**

***course,** *v.*

1. *tr.* To follow the course or slope of (a stream or valley).

1725 *Lancaster* (Mass.) *Rec.* 238 We . . . corsed three stremes that Run into Contocook and then Campt. **1779** W. Fleming in *Travels Amer. Col.* 621 The River when the Channel is coursed is 3/4 of a mile broad. **1894** J. Winsor *Cartier to Frontenac* 6 An expanse of water which had already coursed another great continental valley.

2. To trace (a bee) to its hive by following its observed direction of flight.

1831 M. A. Holley *Texas* v. 42 There are persons here, who have a peculiar tact in coursing the bee, and of thus discovering these deposits of the luscious store. **1877** McDanield & Taylor *Coming Empire* 240 We . . . were trying to course some bees that came there to get water. **1900** Smithwick *Evol. of State* 292 An expert had no difficulty in following [the bees] to their hive. . . . This was called 'coursing.'

3. (See quot.) ?*Obs.*

1857 *Mich. Agric. Soc. Trans.* VIII. 165 As we are on the subject of dipping or coursing sheep, it may not be amiss to consider the best way of washing them.

***court,** *n.*

1. (See quot. 1809.)

1800 Dunbar *Life* 111 You will be pleased to present to the court, a few of the bills which may be first found. **1809** E. A. Kendall *Travels* III. 251 The court consisted only in the person of one of the magistrates, his bare-headed companions being but assistants in courtesy.—This use of the words *court* and *honourable court* had often misled me. **1923** in Horwill 88 It is not for the Court to say that he will not in any case enforce capital punishment as an alternative.

1948 *Chi. D. News* 18 Dec. 5/2 The defendant cannot think that the court is bound to enter judgment according to those recommendations.

2. (See quot. 1848, and cf. **general court.**)

1639 *Conn. Fundamental Orders* i, It is Ordered, sentenced and decreed, that there shall be yerely two generall Assemblies or Courts. **1662** *Mass. Laws* (1814) 211 It is ordered by this court . . . [that all writs shall be made] in his majesty's name. **1683** *Ib.* 187 This court doth order and enact that every Town, consisting of more than five hundred families . . . , shall set up . . . two grammer schools. **1848** BARTLETT 95 *Court.* In New England this word is applied to a legislative body composed of a House of Representatives and a Senate; as, the *General Court* of Massachusetts.

3. In various expressions designating a tribunal *of* a specified character or jurisdiction: **a.** * *court of appeal(s)*, in some states, the state supreme court.

1777 *Journals Cont. Cong.* VIII. 607 Resolved, That Thursday next be assigned to take into consideration the propriety of establishing a court of appeals. **1825** *Harbinger* (Frankfort, Ky.) 25 May 1/2 The court of appeals shall consist of three judges, two of whom shall be sufficient to constitute a court. **1948** *Owensboro* (Ky.) *Inquirer* 22 Oct. 3/3 The court of appeals is to hear arguments today on whether vaccination of school children can be required by law.

b. * *court of assistants*, (see quot. 1933).

1629 in NOBLE *Records* I. v, The Court, as such, was as old as the Colony itself. The first record, which is headed with the formal title, 'At a Court of Assistants,' is that of the 18th of May, 1629. **1691** SEWALL *Diary* I. 354 The marriage of Hanna Owen with her husband's brother, is declar'd null by the Court of Assistants. **1933** *Pub. Col. Soc.* XXIX. xx–xxi, Immediately superior to the County Court was the Court of Assistants, consisting of the Governor, Deputy-Governor, and the other annually elected Assistants or Magistrates. The Court of Assistants was the institutional ancestor of the Superior Court of Judicature of the Province of Massachusetts Bay, and of the Supreme Judicial Court of the Commonwealth; it also had the functions of an upper house of the legislature and a governor's council.

c. * *court of claims*, (see quot. 1889).

1889 *Cent.* 1313 Court of Claims. (*a*) a United States court, sitting in Washington, for the investigation of claims against the government. (*b*) In some States, a county court charged with the financial business of the county. **1891** O'BEIRNE *Leaders Ind. Territory* 161/2 He was commissioned as a member of the committee on the court of claims. **1948** *Sat. Ev. Post* 26 June 81/2 He won his case overwhelmingly, both in the Court of Claims and in the Supreme Court of the United States.

d. * *court of common pleas*, (see quots.).

1809 KENDALL *Travels* I. 178 The courts of the state are . . . *county-courts*, which belong to the counties respectively, and which are otherwise called *courts of common pleas*. **1828** WEBSTER *s.v.* Common, *a.* In some of the American states, a court of common pleas is an inferior court, whose jurisdiction is limited to a county, and it is sometimes called a county court. **1914** *Cyclo. Amer. Govt.* I. 503/1 In the United States, courts of common pleas are now to be found in New Jersey, Pennsylvania, Delaware and Ohio, one or more counties forming a judicial district for such courts.

e. *court of election*, = **election court.** *Obs.*

*a***1649** WINTHROP *Hist. N. Eng.* 3 The court of election was at Boston, and Thomas Dudley, Esq. was chosen governor. **1651** *Mass. H.S. Coll.* 4 Ser. VI. 362, I shalbe glad to see you att the Court of Election. **1678** *Conn. Public Records* III. 1 A court of election held at Hartford, May 9th.

f. *court of errors*, a court empowered to consider error proceedings (see quot. 1914).

1809 R. TYLER *Yankey in London* 35 More absurd than the court of errors in the state of Connecticut, where the council of that state, composed generally of plain farmers, correct the judgments of their supreme court, [etc.]. **1866** *Harper's Mag.* May 812/1 You can take it up to the Court of Errors, and have the decision reversed. **1914** *Cyclo. Amer. Govt.* III. 395/2 At the apex of the hierarchy of state courts stands one appellate court of last resort in every state, in forty states known as the supreme court, in the other eight as the court of appeals, court of errors, or the court of errors and appeals.

g. *court of* (*general*) *sessions*, any one of various state courts of original criminal jurisdiction.

1705 *Boston News-Letter* 3 Sep. 2/2 The Court of General Sessions of the Peace for the County of Suffolk, Held at Boston the 13th of August last. **1724** *New-Eng. Courant* 2–9 Nov. 2/2 At an Adjournment of a Court of General Sessions of the Peace, now holden at Boston, for and within the County of Suffolk. **1894** P. L. FORD *P. Stirling* 69 A special commission . . . made Peter a deputy of the Attorney-General, to prosecute in the Court of Sessions.

h. *court of impeachment*, the Senate of the U.S., or the upper house of a state legislature, acting as a tribunal for the trial of public officers of the government.

[**1788** HAMILTON in *Federalist* II. 211 The supreme court would have been an improper substitute for the senate, as a court of impeachments.] **1798** *Ann. 5th Congress* II. 2245 On this day the Senate formed itself into a High Court of Impeachment, in the manner directed by the Constitution. **1868** *Cong. Globe* 4 March 1644/2 The organization of the Senate as a court of impeachment . . . should precede the actual announcement of the impeachment on the part of the House. **1872** *Atlantic Mo.* XXIX. 386/2 The high court of impeachment being now ready for the trial of the case.

i. *court of Indian offenses*, a temporary tribunal having jurisdiction over legal matters involving Indians.

1883 *Rep. Indian Affairs* p. xii, On the 10th of April last you gave your official approval to certain rules governing the 'Court of Indian offenses.' **1946** FOREMAN *Last Trek* 235 Later, without legal authorization, the Commissioner of Indian Affairs established 'courts of Indian offenses.'

j. *court of pardons*, a court or board concerned with pardons.

1904 *N.Y. Ev. Post* 14 June 1 The delegation requested that the Court of Pardons [in New Jersey] be recommended to commute the death sentence to life imprisonment.

4. In combs.: (1) **court beaver,** ?the best or choicest kind of beaver, *rare* [cf. *EDD court-faggot*, the best kind of faggot]; (2) **house,** see as a main entry; (3) **interpreter,** one appointed to interpret in court proceedings; (4) * **party,** (*a*) a group in the first U.S. Congress who favored Hamilton's financial plans for the federal government, *obs.*, (*b*) in Kentucky (*c*1786–1789), a party allegedly favoring secession from Virginia, the establishment of an independent government, and the negotiation of a treaty with Spain for navigation of the Mississippi, *obs.*, cf. **country party, New court party, Old court party;** (5) **reporter,** one whose duty is to report what occurs in a court; (6) **stenographer,** (see quot.); (7) **week,** the week during which a county court is in session.

(1) *a***1649** WINTHROP *Hist. N. Eng.* I. 64 He gave the governour two large skins of court beaver. — (3) **1896** *N.Y. Dramatic News* 11 July 3/1 Even the hardened court interpreter fled trembling to the nearest Raines hotel and the courtroom flies fell off the ceiling in a dead faint. — (4) (*a*) **1789** MACLAY *Deb. Senate* 115 He gave me a short history of the court party, which (as might be expected) is gaining ground. **1790** *Ib.* 191 Hence appears plainly how much the assumption of the State debts made a point of by the court party. (*b*) **1812** [see **country party**]. **1824** *Ky. Reporter* 12 July 2/2 This same modest candidate said, that his opponent (meaning Tompkins) was brought out by the Court Party to sustain court power. **1909** R. M. MCELROY *Kentucky* 135 The party of which Wilkinson was leader . . . was known as the Court party, on account of the fact that the leaders, Brown, Sebastian and Innis, were all members of the Supreme Court of the District.

(5) **1894** SHUMAN *Steps into Journalism* 82 With the amanuensis and court reporter we all know that it [shorthand] is worth more than the knowledge of any foreign language. — (6) **1930** G. R. SHERRILL *Criminal Procedure in N.C.* 155 A number of counties have regular court stenographers whose business it is to take down the proceedings of the court. — (7) **1724** *Essex Inst. Coll.* XXXVI. 332 Jan. 2 Court Week. **1896** HARRIS *Sister Jane* 161, I used to ride his horse to water court-week. **1944** DUNCAN *M. Graham* 13 But this was only during court week. Greensburg may have been gay during court week, but education was its hobby.

As the last term in **auto-, call, circuit, county, district, election, federal, general, hog, Indian, juvenile, kangaroo, levy, lynch, March, May, miners', mustang, orphans', Palatine's, parish, precinct, prerogative, primary, probate, provincial, purchased, select, squatter, state, state supreme, superior, supreme, surrogate's court.**

courtesy of the Senate. (See quot. 1889.)

1888 BRYCE *Amer. Commw.* (1889) I. vi. 58 By this system, which obtained the name of the Courtesy of the Senate, the President was practically enslaved as regards appointments. *Ib.* The 'Courtesy of the Senate' would never have attained its present strength but for the growth . . . of the so-called Spoils System. **1889** *Cent.* 1314/1 *Courtesy of the Senate*, in the Senate of the United States, special consideration required by custom to be shown to the wishes of individual members or former members of the Senate on certain occasions.

* **courthouse,** *n.*

1. Chiefly *S.* = **county courthouse.** Cf. **log courthouse.**

1683 *Md. Hist. Mag.* I. 5 Ordered that Mr. Miles Gibson . . . have power and authority to employ carpenters for repairing the Court house. **1711** *N.C. Coll. Rec.* I. 808 The sherifs of the several Countys are required forthwith to signify this order to the respective Indian Traders, and to publish the same at the Courthouse. **1865** *Evansville* (Ind.) *D. Jrnl.* 26 Sep. 2/2 We invite attention to the call for a Railroad meeting at the Court House to-night. **1948** *Democrat* 23 Sep. 1/1 We examined and inspected the court house and premises.

b. The county seat in which such a building is located.

1804 *Guardian of Freedom* (Frankfort, Ky.) 14 Sep. 3/4 Extract of a letter from a gentleman at Wythe Court-house (Virginia) to his friend in Frederick Town, (Md.) dated July 30, 1804. **1888** *Nation* 27 Oct. 331 The word court-house for county-seat is probably of Southern origin, though there are at least two county-seats in Ohio that still retain this designation. **1948** *Chi. Tribune* 5 Dec. I. 24/3 Greene, however, crossed into North Carolina . . . , offering battle at Guilford courthouse.

2. In combs.: (1) **courthouse fight,** a fight or brawl in a county seat on the occasion of a session of court, *colloq.;* (2) **square,** a square plot of land upon which a courthouse is located, cf. **square 1;** (3) **town,** a county seat; (4) **yard,** the grounds about a courthouse.

(1) **1827** Cooper *Prairie* iii, Their natures have greatly changed if they too are not both dreaming of a turkey-hunt or a court-house fight at this very moment. — (2) **1826** *Constitutional Advocate* (Frankfort, Ky.) 31 Mar. 1/2 Part of a lot on Main street, in Georgetown, facing the court house square, improved, mortgaged by R. J. Ward to the bank, and purchased at sale foreclosure. **1927** Eubank *Horse & Buggy Days* 17 In a county seat town the hitch rack was generally around the court house square. — (3) **1866** F. Kirkland *Bk. Anecdotes* 638 Baker and his party proceeded to Bowling Green, a small court-house town in Caroline County. — (4) **1898** B. H. Young *Jessamine Co., Ky.* 139 The platform was erected in the court-house yard. **1899** Tarkington *Gentleman from Ind.* 2 Here stood the old red-brick court-house, loosely fenced in a shady grove of maple and elm . . . called the 'Court-House Yard.' **1905** N. Davis *Northerner* 160 There have been five men hung by mobs right here in Adairville—in the court-house yard, in the very center of town.

* **courting,** *n.* In combs.: (1) **courting flute,** a flute used by Indian youths in love-making, *obs.;* (2) **frolic,** an excursion chiefly for love-making, *colloq.;* (3) **horse,** (see quot.), *colloq.;* (4) **stick,** a long wooden tube, alleged-

Indian courting flute

ly used in colonial New England by courting couples to secure privacy in the presence of others, *obs.;* (5) **suit,** (see quot.); (6) **tacky,** = **courting horse.**

(1) **1833** Catlin *Indians* I. 243, I often and familiarly heard . . . the Winnebago courting flute. **1846** L. M. Child *Fact & Fiction* 263 The maiden understood very well why his courting-flute was heard about the wigwam till late into the night. — (2) **1847** Robb *Squatter Life* 59 A pacel of fellers . . . that looked as nice, all'ays, as if they wur goin' to meetin' or on a courtin' frolic. — (3) **1887** *Harper's Mag.* LXXIV. 354/1 The gallants train their little horses to prance; . . . these are called 'courtin' horses,' and are used when a young man goes courting. — (4) **1884** *Proc. Cent. Celeb. of Longmeadow* (Mass.) 235 Most curious of all, a long, slender wooden tube, about six feet in length and an inch in diameter, octagonal at one and round at the other and fitted at either end for ear and mouth pieces now, however missing, which has for generations been known as the 'Courting Stick.' **1948** *So. Folklore Quart.* March 108 A random sampling will immediately show . . . the wholesome readiness of the editor to recognize as folklore much that has not hitherto been so regarded: the poetry on samplers . . . ; cider-mills and courting-sticks and lobster stews.

(5) **1845** *Lowell Offering* V. 143 He wore a black coat and pants, with a white vest and cravat; thick shoes, and blue socks. This was his Courting Suit. — (6) **1944** Harnett T. Kane *Bayous of Louisiana* 283 There developed a 'courting tacky,' a particular kind of prairie pony.

***cousin,** *n.* As the last term in **British, rattlesnake's, secesh, ship's cousin.**

cousin trout. A local name for a cyprinoid fish resembling a trout.

1839 Storer *Mass. Fishes* 91 *Leucisus pulchellus.* . . . In some portions of the State it receives the name of 'Cousin Trout.' **1848** Thoreau *Maine Woods* 53 We cast our lines . . . [and] instantly a shoal of white chivin (*Leucisci pulchelli*), silvery roaches, cousin-trout, . . . fell upon our bait. **1888** Goode *Amer. Fishes* 428 In Massachusetts it is often called the 'Cousin Trout' in allusion to its trout-like habits.

* **cove,** *n.*

1. Flood land or meadow land adjoining an inlet. *Obs.*

1637 *R.I. Col. Rec.* I. 45–6 The grasse upon the rivers and coves about Kitickamuckqutt. **1704** *Providence Rec.* XIV. 279 The one halfe of that Salt Cove. . . . Called the Round Cove Jt. being a piece of Ground which beareth a sort of salt Grass which is Called Thatch and Each Tide the said Cove is flowed with a salt water. **1765** J. Bartram *Diary* 21 Nov., There is many coves & very rich low swamps up ye coves.

2. (See quots.)

1859 Bartlett 104 *Cove,* a strip of prairie extending into the woodland. **1871** De Vere 511 *Notch,* a narrow passage through the mountains, . . . is in the Catskill mountains represented by *cove.* **1917** Eaton *Green Trails* 237 Sometimes the current has even laid a sand bar completely across the opening, converting the ancient bed into a swamp or stagnant pond. In some parts of our country these old channels are known as coves, in other parts as swales.

3. (See quot. 1881.) In full **cove oyster.**

1876 *Harper's Wkly.* 15 April 307/2 The 'Morris Coves' of Philadelphia, while very insipid, are the plumpest bivalves brought to market. **1881** E. Ingersoll *Oyster Industry* 243 The packer, by cove-oysters, simply means steamed oysters in hermetically sealed cans. . . . The oysterman means the single oysters scattered through the bays and creeks. **1946** Wilson *Fidelity* 89 Many old-timers would prefer the grocery, such as one of ours at Fidelity, with its cheese and crackers, its cove oysters and pepper sauce.

b. cove plant, a bedded cove oyster.

1867 *Harper's Wkly.* 25 May 330/2 Among the noble works of art that hang upon his walls may be mentioned the following . . . 'No Smoking,' a noble work of art; . . . also 'Cove Plants' and 'Lager Beer.'

As the last term in **Mosquito, thatch cove.**

coveite ˈkovaɪt, *n.* One who lives in a cove. *Colloq.* or *slang.* — **1895** *Cent. Mag.* May 155/2 Dialect stories dealing with the homely country folk of the Cotton States, the 'crackers' of Georgia, the 'Coveites' of Tennessee, etc. **1897** *Scribner's Mag.* XXII. 377/2 These fine folks don't ax folks like weuns in the front do'; weuns ain't nothin' but 'Covites come to peddle.'

covena kəˈvinə, *n. W.* [?Indian name.] A plant of the genus *Brodiaea,* the bulbs of which were eaten by the Pima and Papago Indians. Cf. **Brodiaea.**

1912 Lumholtz *New Trails* 213 There is a certain tuberous plant growing on the plains called *covena,* which forms a further food supply. **1915** Armstrong *Western Wild Flowers* 16 Covena is the Arizona name. **1942** Castetter & Bell *Pima & Papago Agric.* 60 Bulbs of *covenas* or Papago blue bells (*Brodiaea capitata* var. *pauciflora*) were of less importance, usually eaten raw in early spring before other foods were available.

***covenant,** *n.* As the last term in **halfway, National, restrictive covenant.**

covenant chain. In colonial times, a chain belt symbolizing the bond of peace between colonists and Indians, usu. in fig. contexts. *Obs.* Cf. **chain 4. b.** (1), **chain belt.**

1696 *Doc. Hist. N.Y. State* (1849) I. 342 We underwritten have mett & considered about the properest methods for . . . renewing with them and the rest of the Five Nations the Covenant Chain. **1715** *Boston News-Letter* 22 Aug. 2/1 His Excellency our Governour is this Week bound for Albany to meet our Five Nations of Indians, to renew the Covenant Chain. **1745** *Pa. Col. Rec.* V. 14 We are all united with You in the same Covenant Chain, which as long as we preserve it free from Rust must remain impregnable. **1754** *Mass. H.S. Coll.* 3 Ser. V. 41 We return you all our grateful acknowledgements for renewing and brightening the covenant chain. This chain belt is of very great importance to our United Nations.

***cover,** *n.* As the last term in **forest, lodge, wagon, yellow cover.**

* **cover,** *v.*

1. *tr.* (See quot.) *Obs.*

1818 Harris *Remarks* 44 The agent of government interfered [one Indian having killed another], assembled the principal chiefs of the tribes with the relations of the deceased, and then offered to cover (as they term it) the body, that is, by placing near it presents of cloth, silks, and various articles, till they were decided to be equivalent to the loss sustained.

2. *Stock exchange.* To buy stock previously sold short to protect one's self when the market rises. Also *to cover shorts* or *short sales.*

1868 *Comm. & Fin. Chron.* VI. 358/2 The decline in values will enable him to cover his sales at a profit. **1870** MEDBURY *Men Wall St.* 134 'Cover,' to 'cover one's shorts.' Where stock has been sold and the market rises, the seller buys where he can, in order to protect himself on the day of delivery. This is 'covering short sales.' **1885** *Harper's Mag.* Nov. 842/1 He . . . 'covers,' or 'covers his shorts,' by buying stock to fulfill his contract on the day of delivery. *Ib.* 842/1 This [buying stock to fulfill contract on the day of delivery] is a self-protective measure, and is called 'covering short sales.'

3. To secure and write up for a newspaper an account of (an event, meeting, or other item of interest).

1893 in PHILIPS *Making of a Newspaper* 6 [The news editor] has been preparing to 'cover' such important events as are 'in sight.' **1944** ROSS *Westward* 26 Narcissa would have proved good copy for roving journalists had there been any around to cover the first overland journey of white women.

4. *To cover into the treasury,* (see quot. 1889).

1868 *Cong. Globe* 17 Feb. 1211/3 They [=covering warrants] are drawn in this way and receipted by the Treasurer. And that is technically called covering money into the Treasury. **1884** *Harper's Mag.* June 53/2 The bribe was 'covered into the Treasury.' **1889** FARMER 176/1 *Covered into the Treasury,* a cant official phrase, expressive of the transfer of an unexpected balance of an appropriation back into the Treasury, and the final balancing and cancelling of the account. The phrase was originally 'covering [the item in a balance-sheet] by a transfer of the amount into the Treasury.' The words 'by a transfer of the amount' were gradually eliminated, leaving the phrase as it stands—a puzzle to many. **1892** *Public Ledger* (Phila.) 7 Jan., The work was done for $1900 less than the appropriation, and that amount was covered into the State Treasury.

coverage ˈkʌvərɪdʒ, *n.* **1.** The aggregate of risks covered by an insurance policy. Also attrib. **2.** The act of covering or reporting, esp. for a newspaper, an event, situation, etc. Cf. **news coverage.**

(1) **1912** *Agents' Record* (Hartford, Conn.) 17 June, There will be nineteen policyholders disillusionized and disgusted with the limited coverage contract. **1929** *New Yorker* 17 Aug. 12/1 Coverage is for mortality only, not accidents. **1949** *Nat. Underwriter* 7 Jan. 6/3 Casualty coverages may be written on both employers and employes associations. — (2) **1931** *K.C. Star* 19 Nov. 22 You must admit that it gives its readers thorough coverage on animal news. **1948** *Time* 26 July 52/1 The picture coverage of the Democratic Convention, and the G.O.P. Convention before it, was the most complete in journalistic history.

cover charge. In some dining places, a charge made for service and accommodations over and above the cost of the food served. Also attrib.

1921 *Nation* 21 Sep. 320/2 As levied here, the cover charge is a compulsory blanket assessment for nothing in particular; it commonly includes bread and butter, but the supply is meager. **1932** *Variety* 22 Mar. 1/3 Cover charge places have virtually disappeared from Broadway. **1948** *Miami* (Okla.) *D. News-Record* 4 July 20/3 The night clubs of Manhattan are like a thousand other night clubs throughout the land—smoky second-hand air sold with a cover charge.

coverclip ˈkʌvəˌklɪp, *n.* [Origin obscure.] (See quots.)

1842 *Nat. Hist. N.Y., Zoology* IV. 304 The New-York Sole, *Achirus mollis,* . . . is common in our waters. . . . They abound on the shallow flats on the Jersey shore opposite New York, where they are called Calico and Coverclip. **1884** GOODE *Aquatic Animals* 177 The nearest relative of the Sole is often called the American Sole, *Achirus lineatus,* and is known on the coast of New Jersey as the Hog-choker, Cover-clip, or Cover. **1945** MCATEE *Nomina Abitera* 20 American Sole (Achirus fasciatus) . . . DeKay . . . notes this as being called 'cover-clip' . . . in New Jersey.

* **covered,** *a.* In combs.: (1) **covered bridge,** a bridge protected from the weather by a shed or cover, also **covered wooden bridge;** (2) **buggy,** =**top buggy;** (3) **dish,** designating a group meal consisting of food brought in covered dishes by individual members of the group; (4) **money,** (see quot.); (5) **rice,** (see quot.); (6) **sled,** (see quot.), *obs.;* (7) **sleigh,** a sleigh having a cover; (8) **wagon,** a wagon having a removable cover, also transf.

(1) **1824** in *Ind. Hist. Soc. Pub.* IV. 51 A good covered wooden bridge (near Pittsburgh) crosses each river. **1883** RILEY *Old Swimmin'-Hole* 44 Thare ust to stand the tavern that they called the 'Travelers' Rest,' And thare, beyent the covered bridge, 'The Counterfitters' Nest.' **1949** *Democrat* 13 Jan. 7/4 Covered bridges . . . are still an important factor in our country's transportation system. — (2) **1857** ERASMUS BEADLE *To Nebraska in '57* (1923) 26 Went to the shop and up to Florence, Six miles, in a covered buggy. — (3) **1931** *Durant* (Okla.) *D. Democrat* 3 June 4/5 The ladies of the Durant country club enjoyed a covered dish luncheon Thursday. **1946** *Cobleskill* (N.Y.) *Times* 14 March 5/6 Covered dish supper will be served by the following committee. — (4) **1890** *Cent.* 3832/1 Covered money, a technical phrase used in United States legislation and administration for money which has been deposited in the Treasury in the usual manner, and which can be drawn out only to pay an appropriation made by Congress.

(5) **1868** *Rep. Comm. Agric.* 176 The first system, or 'covered rice,' is where the grain is covered up in the soil two or three inches deep, as fast as it is drilled in, which thus protects it from birds, floating away, &c. — (6) **1826** FLINT *Recoll.* 14 Then there are what the people call 'covered sleds,' or ferry-flats, and allegany-skiffs, carrying

Covered bridge

from eight to twelve tons. — (7) **1808** ISAIAH THOMAS *Diary* (1916) 66 Sat off . . . in a covered Sleigh for Boston. **1881** M. J. HOLMES *Madeline* 274 Drive back to Aikenside as fast as possible, and change the carriage for a covered sleigh. — (8) **1745** in J. S. MCCLENNAN *Louisburg* (1918) 163 That the commander in chief now in Garrison shall have liberty to send off covered waggons to be inspected only by one officer of ours. **1876** MILLER *First Families* 226 The two covered wagons [i.e., poke bonnets] were poked up close against each other. **1948** *Dly. Oklahoman* (Okla. City) 16 May E. 28/1 A sizeable percentage of the nation's population . . . believes that in Oklahoma the people still live in sod houses, travel in covered wagons, bathe in the creek.

* **cow,** *n.*

1. *W.* A cow buffalo. Also attrib.

[**1723** in MERENESS *Travels Amer. Col.* (1916) 61 We put to shore and killed a cow.] **1821** J. FOWLER *Journal* 25 The Hunters killed two Fatt Cows . . . these anemels [buffaloes] Being very plenty Heare. *a***1842** O. RUSSEL *Journal* (1921) 102 Off they started and returned at night with their animals loaded with cow meat. **1947** *Denver Post* 15 Feb. 9/7 Wyoming's mislabeled 'bow-and-arrow buffalo hunt' turned out . . . an ugly . . . slaughter of four magnificent animals, three bulls and a gentle old cow.

b. Used also of the female of the moose and elk.

1857 *Spirit of Times* 31 Jan. 353/2 The moose . . . left his yard, as the place is termed, in which he passes the winter—one old bull generally having three or four cows, with the calves. **1941** SETON *Trail of Artist-Naturalist* 359 Then I got out pencil, paper, and foot rule, and sketched the three beds in the snow. This evidenced that the cows had been there all night.

2. (See quot.) *Obs.*

1843 MARRYAT *M. Violet* 254 A cow is a kind of floating raft peculiar to the western rivers of America, being composed of immense pine trees tied together, and upon which a log cabin is erected.

3. Often pronounced "keow" in N. England, and hence during the trouble in Kansas over slavery used to test those suspected of being from that area and consequently abolitionists.

1856 in *Kansas Hist. Soc.* IX. 337 We knew him first by his talk; secondly by his eyes; and thirdly, by his eyelashes. He could not say *cow.* **1866** *Beadle's Mo.* Oct. 283/2 During the early Kansas troubles, the Missourians posted a guard at the ferry on the great river, and, when an immigrant sought to cross into the new, convulsed Territory, asked him to say 'cow.' If he pronounced it 'keow,' he was voted a Yankee . . . and was not permitted to enter the desired paradise.

4. *W.* (See quots.) *Colloq.*

1869 *Overland Mo.* III. 127 The 'cow-whip' . . . is used only in driving the herd, which is often called 'the cows.' **1884** SHEPHERD *Prairie*

Exp. 22 The cows, which in cow-boy language include all sexes and sizes, split up into bunches and take possession of some small valley or slope where water is procurable at no great distance. **1930** RAINE & BARNES *Cattle* 60 Property rights in stock were rather casual, since cows, as all cattle were called regardless of age or sex, were an investment which traveled on the hoof unwatched and unguarded.

5. In obs. combs. in allusion to colonial times: (1) **cow common,** see as a main entry; (2) * **grass,** an area allotted to a colonist sufficient for the pasturage of a cow, also * **cow's grass** [cf. *OED* "cow's grass," 1824——, and Du. *koe(ien)gras*, as a measure of land]; (3) **keep,** =next; (4) * **keeper,** a person employed by a town or village to look after the pasturing of the cows of the inhabitants; (5) * **keeping,** the occupation of a cow-keeper, also as adj.; (6) * **pasture,** in colonial New England, a cow common; (7) **rate,** a tax upon cows; (8) **walk,** =**cow common.**

(2) **1638** *Charlestown Land Records* 23 Six acres of land in the east feilde bought of mr. Ruck with some oulde houseing upon it, and three Cowes grasse at wilsones point. **1645** *Suffolk Deeds* I. 61 Mr John Cotton teacher of Boston granted unto Thomas Whitamore a parcell of Meddow counted two Cowe grasses. — (3) **1641** *Boston Rec.* 61 Our brother John Davies and our brother Tho. Buttolph shall agree with a Cowe keep for the towne for the present summer. **1643** *Plymouth Rec.* 13 John Smyth shalbe the Cowe Keep for this yeare to keep the Townes Cowes. — (4) **1619** in *Mass. Hist. Soc. Coll.* 4 Ser. IX. 12 Our cowekeeper here of James citty on Sundays goes . . . in freshe flaming silke. **1739** W. STEPHENS *Proc. Georgia* 313 The last who went off . . . was caught by the Cow-keeper at old Ebenezer.

(5) **1652** *Md. Council Proc.* 281 These are . . . to prohibit every Inhabitant . . . to give any of the said Indians here any entertainment . . . except any Indian Cowkeeping Youth. **1654** *East-Hampton Records* I. 57 It is ordered yt every cowe in the heard shall pay 6d to the owners of the bulls and to be set of in the Cowe keepinge. **1663** *Hempstead Town Rec.* I. 137 The foresaid townesmen do ingage themselves to the said William Oseburne, to pay or cause to bee paid to him (for and in consideration of his cow-keeping) fourteen shillings a weeke. — (6) **1636** *Springfield Rec.* I. 156 Every one that hath a house lot shall have a proportion of the Cowpasture. **1800** *Mass. H.S. Coll.* VI. 218 The Neck contains one hundred and forty-six acres, of which the greater part are in a town pasture, annually rented to the inhabitants as a cow pasture. — (7) **1661** *Hempstead Town Rec.* I. 97 Thomas Langdone shall . . . have heare after fower bushelles and a hallf of Indian corne to bee paide when the cowe ratte is paid. — (8) **1652** *Suffolk Deeds* I. My three divisions in the Cow walke of Dorchester. **1658** *Hempstead Town Rec.* I. 42 And it is hereby prohibited unto any manner of person . . . to plant or plow within the said boundes, southward of the said line, and within the cowes-walkes.

6. In combinations alluding chiefly to cattle-raising in the West: (1) **cow brand,** a brand placed upon a cow to denote ownership; (2) **business,** cattle-raising on a large scale; (3) **call,** a call used to cattle; (4) **camp,** a camp of cowboys, also attrib.; (5) **country,** (see quot. 1927); (6) **game,** the cattle business, *colloq.;* (7) **hunt,** a roundup; (8) **hunting,** *a.* taking part in a cow hunt or roundup; (9) **lick,** (see quot.); (10) **lodge,** (*a*) =**park,** *n.* **4,** *obs.,* (*b*) a place where cattle are kept or pastured; (11) **punching,** herding cattle on a ranch; (12) **ranch,** a ranch where cattle are raised; (13) **range,** the plains over which cattle range; (14) **saddle,** a heavy saddle suitable for use in roping and holding range stock, having a steel fork and usu. provided with double cinches; (15) **sense,** such sense as is needed for success in cattle-raising, good common sense; (16) **town,** a town in a cattle-raising district, esp. one from which large shipments of cattle are made; (17) **trail,** (*a*) a trail or path made by cattle, (*b*) *W.* the route over which large herds of cattle are driven; (18) **village,** =**cow town;** (19) **work,** the work of caring for cattle on a ranch (see also quot. 1929).

(1) **1928** *Nat. Geog. Mag.* June 659 The story of the economic growth of Texas is told by cow brands. — (2) **1907** S. E. WHITE *Arizona Nights* v. 94 The boss assigns him two or three broncos to break in to the cow business. **1947** *Westerners' Brand Book* 55 No man ever learned the cow business easily or quickly. — (3) **1907** S. E. WHITE *Arizona Nights* 106 We indulged in a great variety of the picturesque cow-calls peculiar to the cowboy. — (4) **1873** in *Annals of Wyoming* VIII. (July, 1931) 495 Had supper with them and learned that . . . Mr. Richards . . . has a cow camp (on Red Creek) three miles north. **1945** M. JAMES *Cherokee Strip* 8 Mr. Howell knew a cow-camp cook in Colorado who was bitten on the thumb by a rattler.

(5) **1881** CHASE *Editor's Run* 160 There is no excuse in a cow country like this for a landlord to set before his guests oleomargarine or condensed milk. **1927** JAMES *Cow Country* vii, When we speak of cow country out here, we mean range country—a country where cattle run loose in open territory and are identified by brands and earmarks, not by names and spots. **1945** *Reader's Digest* Sep. 109/1 With nearly all its cattle behind wire, the ranch junked the oldest and most revered custom of the cow country. — (6) **1912** BOWER *Flying U* 13 I'll gamble that's a spot higher than he stacks up in the cow game. **1940** BABER & WALKER *Longest Rope* 41, I must say he knew the cow game. — (7) **1853** P. PAXTON *Yankee in Texas* 108 Everything in the shape of a man . . . had left the settlement, and engaged in a general 'cow-hunt.' **1929** DOBIE *Vaquero* 13 When we gathered cattle, we said that we were on a 'cow hunt,' a 'cow work,' a 'work,' or a 'cow drive,' or maybe we said we were out 'running cattle.' — (8) **1898** H. S. CANFIELD *Maid of Frontier* 132 The ordinary immense Texas affair, intended only for cow-hunting males. — (9) **1924** J. M. FRANKS *Seventy Yrs. in Texas* 74 From cowlicks or places where cattle would eat out great holes in the branches [i.e., streams].

(10) (*a*) **1844** in *Pub. Col. Soc. Mass.* VII. (1906) 389 The Indian name for it signifies '*cow lodge,*' of which our own may be considered a translation; the enclosure, the grass, the water, and the herds of buffalo roaming over it, naturally presenting the idea of a park. **1845** FRÉMONT *Exped.* 282 The New Park—a beautiful circular valley. . . . The Indian name for it signifies 'cow lodge.' (*b*) **1872** *Amer. Naturalist* VI. 68 The Utes use these parks during the summer as cow lodges, but as winter approaches the herd is driven down to the plain. — (11) **1881** ROMSPERT *Western Echo* 189 Some of them have been cow-punching—as it is called—for many years, and know every water for hundreds of miles around. **1934** LOMAX *Amer. Ballads* 417 He's sold him his saddle, his spurs and his rope, And there's no more cow-punching, and that's what I hope. — (12) **1881** ROMSPERT *Western Echo* 98 We came upon an old picket *cow-ranch* among the hills, and concluded to stop there until morning. **1948** *Southwestern Rev.* Summer 234/1 At that time there were no settlers, cow ranches, or people except buffalo hunters living in Texas west and northwest of Wichita. — (13) **1920** HUNTER *Trail Drivers Texas* I. 230, I . . . got my first experience on the cow range in 1876. — (14) **1895** REMINGTON *Pony Tracks* 1, I inspected the horses, and saw that one had a 'cow saddle.' **1903** *Forest & Stream* 21 Feb. 147 A bit farther on we saw some cow-punchers, or what seemed such, for they sat in cow saddles and wore *chaparejos.*

(15) **1903** A. ADAMS *Log Cowboy* xx. 309 The wisdom of mounting us well for just such an emergency reflected the good cow sense of our employer. **1943** HOWARD *Montana* 150 It is hoped they will absorb enough cow sense to go out on the range and eat. — (16) **1885** *Santa Fe W. New Mexican* 3 Dec. 4/1 St. Louis is the biggest cow-town on earth just at present. **1947** *Time* 3 Feb. 82/2 His father was a well-fixed cattleman, banker and hotel proprietor in the little cow town of Canadian. — (17) (*a*) **1853** P. PAXTON *Yankee in Texas* 100 He will see them pouring in from every imaginable direction, by every possible road, . . . wagon roads, main road, 'cow trails,' and 'blazes.' **1913** LONDON *Valley of Moon* III. xxii, He started back down the cow trail. (*b*) **1920** HUNTER *Trail Drivers Texas* I. 123 My first experience on the cow trail was in 1872. *Ib.* 151 All the Texas outfit . . . took the cow trail for Texas. — (18) **1904** O. HENRY *Heart of West* 192 He moodily shot up a saloon in a small cow village on Quintana Creek. — (19) **1886** ROOSEVELT in *Cent. Mag.* July 341/1 It is even more laughable to see some young fellow from the East or from England, . . . attempt in his turn to do cow-work with his ordinary riding or hunting rig. **1929** DOBIE *Vaquero* 13 When we gathered cattle, we said that we were on a 'cow hunt,' a 'cow work,' a 'work,' or a 'cow drive,' or maybe we said we were out 'running cattle.'

See also **cow brute, dog, horse, pony,** in **7.** below.

b. Designating those having to do with cattle-raising in the West, as (1) **cow boss,** (2) * **boy,** see as a main entry; (3) **girl,** (4) **hand,** (5) **hunter,** (6) **man,** (7) **outfit,** (8) **people,** (9) **poke,** (10) **prodder,** (11) **puncher,** (12) **waddy,** (cf. **waddy**).

(1) **1900** GARLAND *Eagle's Heart* 156 We'll ride over to the round-up to-morrow, and I'll introduce you to the cow boss, and you can go right into the mess. — (3) **1884** *Boston Journal* 28 Nov. 2/3 A beautiful cowgirl lives near Murkel, Taylor county, Neb. She owns some stock, which she personally looks after. **1916** WILSON *Red Gap* 208 Her pretty hair all neated under the La Parisienne cowgirl hat. **1946** *Fort Collins Coloradoan* 16 June 2/3 Mrs. Creed, world champion cowgirl and trick rider, will be the timer. — (4) **1886** *Outing* VIII. 3/1 Though a first rate cow hand he very shortly proved himself to be wholly incapable of acting as head. **1948** *Range Riders Western* May 17/1 The rider looked like an ordinary cowhand.

(5) **1863** *Harper's Mag.* March 536/1 It had the reputation of being the resort of fugitives and cow-hunters. **1920** HUNTER *Trail Drivers Texas* I. 175, I remember the many times that cowhunters rode up to my father's house. — (6) **1881** ROMSPERT *Western Echo*

165 There are many fine, large, branded horses, which have escaped from the *hunters, cow-men, emigrants,* and the *Government,* now running with the wild herds. **1948** *Popular Western* June 34/1 The other cowmen . . . disliked to deal with Amos. — **(7) 1881** ROMSPERT *Western Echo* 186 It is quite pleasing to see a cow-outfit taking dinner upon the wide, level prairie. **1946** *Chicago Sun* 29 Nov. 1/7 They ought to go out to some of these cow outfits and get on the tails of a bunch of mustang during a horse roundup. — **(8) 1927** RUSSELL *Trails* 1 Up to a few years ago there's mighty little known about cows and cow people. — **(9) 1928** *Lariat Mag.* Jan., I camped there once, and a cowpoke told me why they were named that. **1948** *Denison* (Tex.) *Herald* 1 July 9/2 Due to the size of the entry list, the cowpokes have just been allowed to enter one event each night.

(10) 1930 HENRY *Conquer. Plains* 51 For the cowprodders, and sometimes the drovers, to go about fully armed, presumably ready to shoot men on sight, soon grew to be the well-known disposition in this unorganized, humming, little universe. — **(11) 1878** in *Colo. Mag.* XVI. (1939) 152 At Hugo the cow-punchers were assembling for the round-up. **1948** *Popular Western* June 20/1 The big room was jammed with cowpunchers and gamblers. — **(12) 1923** J. H. COOK *On Old Frontier* 19 Trouble would come to the 'cow waddie' who had caused it.

7. In the names of, or with reference to, birds and other animals: (1) **cow alligator,** a female alligator, cf. **bull gator;** (2) **bay,** a kind of oyster, *obs.;* (3) **bird,** (*a*) any one of various small birds, esp. *Molothrus ater,* which frequently perch on cattle in search of parasites, (*b*) the yellow-billed cuckoo, cf. **red-eyed cowbird;** (4) **blackbird,** =**cowbird** (*a*); (5) **boarder,** in a dairy herd, a cow that is unprofitable; (6) **brute,** a euphemism for "bull," also, in the West, a full grown range cow or steer never handled since calfhood, hence wild and difficult to manage, cf. Wentworth, *Dial. Dict.;* (7) **buffalo,** a female buffalo; (8) **bug,** (see quot.), *obs.;* (9) **bunting,** =**cowbird** (*a*); (10) **crab,** (see quot.); (11) **critter,** a cow or steer, *colloq.* or *humorous;* (12) **dog,** ?a dog trained to assist in handling cattle; (13) **fly,** a gadfly or breeze fly that annoys cattle [cf. Du. *koevlieg,* in same sense]; (14) **horse,** *W.* a horse trained for use in hunting or handling cattle; (15) **killer (ant),** a large velvet ant, *Dasymutilla occidentalis,* found in the Southwest, also a wasp of the family Mutillidae; (16) **moose,** a female moose; (17) **nose(d ray),** a sting ray, genus *Rhinoptera,* found on the eastern coast of the U.S.; (18) **pony,** *W.* a pony used by a cowboy in his work on a cattle ranch; (19) **snake,** =**bull snake;** (20) **sucker,** any one of various harmless snakes erroneously thought to milk cows; (21) **troopial,** =**cowbird** (*a*), *obs.*

(1) 1880 CABLE *Grandissimes* xxviii. 237 In dimmer recesses the Cow alligator, with her nest hard by. — **(2) 1881** MARSHALL *Through Amer.* (1882) 34 Mr. Burns set before me a large plateful of Cow Bays. — **(3)** (*a*) **1801** WILSON *Ornithology* II. 40, I placed a young unfledged cow-bird (the *Fringilla pecoris* of Turton) . . . in the same cage with a Red-bird, which fed and reared it with great tenderness. **1945** *Chi. D. News* 2 Feb. 14/6 He was chirping as merrily as a cowbird in a robin's nest. (*b*) **1810** WILSON *Ornithology* II. 145 The American Cuckoo (*Cuculus Carolinensis*) is by many people called the Cow-bird, from the sound of its notes resembling the words cow, cow. **1903** *N.Y. Ev. Post* 24 Oct., The cowbird is not aggressively intrusive, like the sparrow. — **(4) 1810** WILSON *Ornithology* II. 151 Hence they [Cow buntings] have pretty generally obtained the name of Cow-pen birds, Cow-birds, or Cow Blackbirds. **1886** *Harper's Mag.* Nov. 874/2 Who ever heard of a cow-blackbird that did not manage somehow to find its feathered nest?

(5) 1896 *Vt. Agric. Rep.* XV. 65 There is less excuse for keeping 'cow-boarders' now than before Dr. Babcock's invention. — **(6) 1828** *Cherokee Phenix* (New Echota, Ga.) 24 April 1/3 Any person or persons finding a dead cow brute and skinning the same, such person or persons shall receive from the owner of such beast, the sum of fifty cents. **1943** L. V. HAMNER *Short Grass* 181 Never let a cow brute take a backward step. . . . Graze cattle in the direction they are to go. — **(7) 1751** GIST *Journals* 56 At Night I killed a fine barren Cow-Buffaloe. **1890** HARTE *Waif of Plains* 105 He was dimly conscious that Jim had wildly thrown his hatchet at a cow-buffalo pressing close upon his flanks. — **(8) 1880** *New Virginians* I. 103 There is [in Va.] a black one nearly 2 in. long . . . and nearly an inch across . . . with yellowish spots on its back, which they call—I know not why—the cow-bug. — **(9) 1810** WILSON *Ornithology* II. 145 [The] Cow Bunting, *Emberiza Pecoris,* . . . winters regularly in the lower parts of North and South Carolina. **1903** *N.Y. Ev. Post* 24 Oct., Flocks of redwinged blackbirds, with an occasional cow-bunting and perhaps a rusty grackle.

(10) 1879 *St. Nicholas* Nov., Probably some of the boys would like to hear how crabs grow. The mother is called a 'cow Crab.' — **(11) 1865** *Atlantic Mo.* XV. 671 He knowed I was apt to buy cow-critters along in the spring. **1923** J. H. COOK *On Old Frontier* 111 If the steer succeeded in goring the horse, . . . rider, horse, and cow-critter were likely to get into a tangled mess. — **(12) 1929** DOBIE *Vaquero* 200 It was at this Dog Town, where cow dogs hemmed up cowboys . . . that I settled in the fall of 1880. — **(13) 1851** *De Bow's Review* XI. 56 *Cow Fly, Tabani*—Large black. **1879** *Diseases of Swine* 208 Ticks, screw-worm, and the large horse or cow fly have destroyed many animals. — **(14) 1853** P. PAXTON *Yankee in Texas* 97 The dogs that had returned were cared for, the very best cow horses . . . selected. **1945** MATHEWS *Talking* 156, I appreciate the feeling which inspires a cowhorse to buck on a frosty morning.

(15) 1889 *Cent.* 1321/1 Cow-killer ant . . . [is] so called from the popular belief that these wasps, which superficially resemble ants, kill cattle by their stinging. **1899** *Animal & Plant Lore* 63 Cow-killer, cow-killer ant, *Mutilla, Clerus,* or *Trichodes,* South. *Ib.* 93 A hymenopterus insect, which somewhat resembles a red ant, is known as 'cow-killer,' from the (imaginary) effects of its sting upon cattle. Alabama and Texas. **1940** JAEGER *Calif. Deserts* 58 Those furry-backed insects which so energetically wander about on the sands, and which are known as fuzzy ants or cow-killers, are really solitary, parasitic wasps. — **(16) 1839** HOFFMAN *Wild Scenes* 59 A yard with three moose in it, an old cow-moose and two yearlings, was discovered. **1946** STANWELL-FLETCHER *Driftwood Valley* 194 When the cow moose is alarmed, it is not uncommon for her to desert her calf. — **(17) 1814** MITCHILL *Fishes N.Y.* 479 Cow-nosed Ray. *Raja bonasus.* With a blunt snout resembling the nose of an ox. *Ib.,* A shoal of cow-noses roots up the salt waterflats as completely as a drove of hogs would do. **1842** *Nat. Hist. N.Y., Zoology* IV. 375 The Cow-nosed Ray . . . is an exceedingly common species about New York in the autumn. — **(18) 1874** J. G. MCCOY *Cattle Trade* 126 A few short weeks after the opening of the cattle trade . . . every stall—fully one hundred or more—would be full of cow ponies. **1947** *Denver Post* 15 Feb. 9/5 An excited cow pony took the bit in its teeth and bucked into the staggering animal. — **(19) 1804** LEWIS in *L. & Clark Exped.* (1905) VI. 124 This snake is vulgarly called the cow or bull snake from a bellowing nois which it is said sometimes to make resembling that anamal. **1946** STUART *Plum Grove Hills* 27 I ran upstairs and killed two cow-snakes restin' on the wall plate.

(20) 1904 CONWAY *Autobiog.* I. 22 Any deficiency of milk in a cow was ascribed to the 'cowsucker' (black snake). **1948** *Atlantic Mo.* Feb. 88/1 To the last, though, the little cowsucker would coil and vibrate his tail and strike savagely but harmlessly at our hands. — **(21) 1839** *Penny Cyclo.* XV. 307/1 The Cow-Pen Bird, Cow Blackbird, Cow Troopial, and Cow-Bunting of the American colonists. **1891** *Cent.* 6499 American blackbirds (*Icteridæ*) which go in flocks . . . [include] the cow-troopial.

8. In the names of plants: (1) ***cowberry,** a local name for the partridge berry, *Mitchella repens;* (2) **-horn squash,** prob. a crookneck squash; (3) **-itch (vine),** =**trumpet creeper;** (4) **lily,** any one of several yellow-flowered plants, esp. the marsh marigold, *Caltha palustris;* (5) **mint,** a local name for some plant or plants having mint-like properties, *obs.;* (6) **oak,** the common white oak, *Quercus michauxi,* found chiefly in the Gulf States; (7) **pea,** a leguminous plant of the genus *Vigna,* widely cultivated in the South, the seed of this; (8) **plant,** (see quot.); (9) **poison vine,** ?poison ivy, *obs.;* (10) ***-slip,** the marsh marigold, *Caltha palustris,* cf. **American, Brandywine, Virginia, Virginian cowslip.**

(1) 1892 *Amer. Folk-Lore* V. 98 *Mitchella repens,* . . . cow-berry. Ulster Co., N.Y. — **(2) 1866** *Eastern Slope* (Washoe, Nev.) 15 Dec. 1/2 His nose is just like dad's, crooked as a cowhorn squash. — **(3) 1933** SMALL *Southeastern Flora* 1241 The leaves of this plant are often mistaken for those of *Toxicodendron,* whence the name 'cow-itch.' **1941** R. S. WALKER *Lookout* 57 It is known by the undignified name of cow-itch vine. — **(4) 1862** LOWELL *Biglow P.* II. iv. 112 There was a pool . . . spotted with cow-lilies garish. **1931** CLUTE *Plants.*

(5) *Western Rev.* I. 93 The following are some of the trees and plants peculiar to this region [=Ky.] and giving a decided character to its vegetation. . . . *Synandra grandiflora,* Cow mint. — **(6) 1884** SARGENT *Rep. Forests* 141 *Quercus Michauxii.* . . . Basket Oak. Cow Oak. **1901** MOHR *Plant Life Ala.* 61 North of the maritime belt, cow oak (*Quercus michauxii*), Texas oak (*Quercus texana*) [etc.], . . . prevail. — **(7) 1776** in *W. & M. Coll. Quart.* XVII. 17 The ground . . . must be got ready . . . as soon as it is run over with the cow-pease. **1865** SALA *Diary* II. 327 At Macon the prisoner's ration was one pint of coarse Indian meal, one-third of a pound of bacon, rancid, and often full of worms, a handful of 'cow-peas' and rice, and a little salt. **1948** *Capital-Democrat* (Tishomingo, Okla.) 17 June 3/4

Mr. Smith plans to continue his test with crotalaria as a soil building crop in comparison with cowpeas. — **(8) 1894** *Amer. Folk-Lore* VII. 93 *Rhododendron maximum*, . . . cow-plant, Montpelier, Vt. — **(9) 1851** *De Bow's Review* XI. 46 Cow Poison Vine grows short and jointed.

(10) 1839 BRYANT *Poetical Wks.* (1903) 187 Children Gathered the glistening cowslip from thy edge. **1943** DAMON *Sense of H.* 109 Cowslips cooked in a very little spring water make a banquet . . . fit for the gods.

9. In miscellaneous combs.: (1) **cow barn,** a barn for cattle; (2) **bay,** a place occupied by a prostitute, *slang,* cf. ∗**crib,** *n.* **4;** (3) **catcher,** (*a*) a strong inclined frame on the front of a locomotive for catching or thrusting aside cattle or other obstructions on the tracks of a railroad, cf. **cow guard, cow lifter, cow remover,** (*b*) a similar contrivance for use on streetcars, *rare;* (4) **chip,** dried cow or buffalo dung, usu. *pl.;* (5) **fodder,** *S.* the leaves of corn cured as food for cows; (6) **guard,** =**cowcatcher** (*a*), *rare;* (7) **linter,** a "lean-to" where cows are sheltered, *obs.;* (8) **lot,** an inclosure for cattle, cf. **hay**

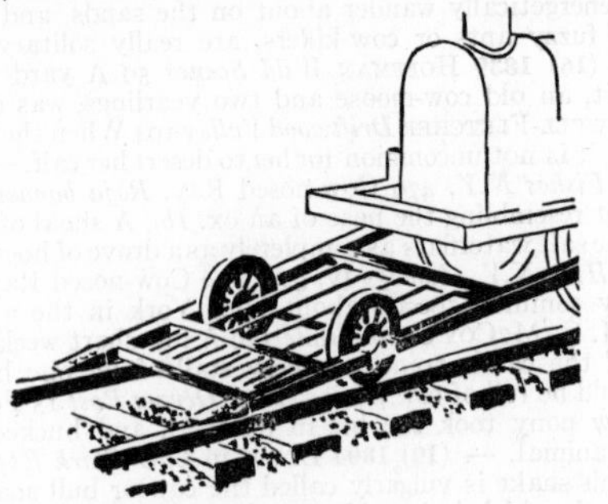

Early (c1840) form of cowcatcher

cow lot; (9) **pond,** a pond for collecting water for cows, also in proper names; (10) **pot,** ?a large pot in which food for cows is cooked, *obs.* [cf. Du. *koepot* in this sense]; (11) **remover,** a device on the front of a locomotive for removing cattle from the track, *obs.*, cf. **cowcatcher;** (12) ∗**-skin,** =∗**cowhide,** *n.* **1;** (13) **-skin horse,** a tough, wiry horse, *rare;* (14) **track,** =**cowpath,** *obs.;* (15) **whip,** (see quots.); (16) **wood,** =**cow chips.**

(1) 1885 M. D. WOODWARD in *Checkered Yrs.* (1937) 66 Our buildings shelter somewhat on the northwest—a large granary, a horse barn, and a cow barn lie in that direction. **1947** *Reader's Digest* June 128/1 His pulpit is a corner of a barley field, a desk in a country schoolhouse, the cleared end of a cow barn, or the rostrum of a once-deserted country church. — **(2) 1851** J. H. ROSS *In New York* 96 It takes one more than ten years to find out all the nokes and corners and cow-bays in this modern Sodom. — **(3)** (*a*) **1838** *Railway Mag.* March 185 This machine is used . . . in the United States and is termed a 'cow or horse catcher.' **1944** *Reader's Digest* March 90 But the front of the locomotive was the crowning touch, being covered with luminous aluminum paint from cowcatcher to smokestack. (*b*) **1884** *Phila. Times* No. 3041, 2 Cow-catchers for street cars. — **(4) 1866** in *Annals of Iowa* 3 Ser. XIV. 260 Weather cool cloudy damp & unpleasant laying on the open Prairie (near Nebraska City) with but cow chips for a fire. **1948** *Southwestern Rev.* Summer 237/2 Cow chips soon became an economic factor in the development of the short grass country.

(5) 1855 DAVIS *Farm Bk.* 233 Fixed a straw covering over my cow fodder. — **(6) 1878** I. L. BIRD *Rocky Mts.* 3 First came two great gaudy engines. . . . with great, solitary, reflecting lamps in front above the cow-guards. — **(7) 1794** R. B. THOMAS *Farmer's Almanack* Sep. 5 See to your corn stalks; cut them, and after they are wilted, bind and carry them into your cow linters. — **(8) 1645–6** *Charlestown Land Rec.* 69 Alsoe three cow lotts gras: being by estimation three Akers, more or lesse. **1836** SIMMS *Mellichampe* xlvii. 393 Da's some of you sodger bin . . . breck down de gate of de cow-lot. **1948** *Dly. Ardmoreite* (Ardmore, Okla.) 18 July 4/2 A soldier boy was through here Friday who said the roads to the cowlots in Wisconsin were better than the highways in Oklahoma. — **(9) 1664** *Groton Rec.* 11, The Towne have granted unto John. Shadock . . . the vse of two [acres] of meadow lying upon Cowpond Brooke. **1893** *Harper's Mag.* Feb. 465 Three of 'em, you know, 's been out to Mr. Jakes's farm all day a-spyin' dug-up things with a spy-glass. Mr. Jakes is diggin' a new cow-pond, an' they do say he's dug up enough to undo the whole Bible.

(10) 1856 *Rep. Comm. Patents: Agric.* 282, I boiled it in a deep, old-fashioned 'cow-pot,' and . . . obtained 32 quarts of tolerable syrup. — **(11) 1848** *Amer. Railroad Jrnl.* 13 May 305 This apparatus is said, by the inventor, to answer for a *snow-plough* as well as *cow-remover*.— **(12) 1738** FRANKLIN *Poor Richard's Alm. 1739* 19 A good cowskin, crabtree or Bulls pizzle may be plentifully bestow'd on your outward man. **1864** W. WHITBY *Amer. Slave* 187 The man who wields the blood-clotted cow-skin during the week, fills the pulpit on the Sunday. **1947** *West. Pa. Hist. Mag.* March–June 34 Tarleton avoids this scheme by attacking Pentland and giving him a chastisement with a 'cowskin.' — **(13) 1887** *Outing* X. 119/1 If I only had that cow-skin horse now what I used ter own back in old Missouri. — **(14) 1678** *Duxbury Rec.* 30 There being a great rock in the river, and a cow track going over the said river. **1857** OLMSTED *Journey through Texas* (1861) 93 Our road was little better than a cow-track.

(15) 1853 P. PAXTON *Yankee in Texas* 93 The rest relied for offence and defence upon their long cow-whips—an implement consisting of a short eighteen inch handle, to which a very heavy lash from twelve to eighteen feet long is attached. **1869** *Overland Mo.* III. 127 The 'Cow-whip' is a very long lash with a very short stock, and is used only in driving the herd, which is often called 'the cows.' — **(16) 1850** GARRARD *Wah-To-Yah* ii. (1927) 27 We huddled around the miserable 'cow wood' fires.

b. In combs. of this kind of obvious meaning or sufficiently explained in the quots.: (1) **cow county,** (2) **driver,** (3) **fat,** (4) **flop,** (5) ∗**hide,** see as a main entry, (6) **juice,** (7) **land,** (8) **lane,** (9) **lifter,** (10) **path,** (11) ∗**pen,** see as a main entry, (12) **thief.**

(1) 1850 in *Amer. Sp.* XXI. (1946) 116/2 The last spell of rain and wind, lasting some thirty days, has brought the subject home to every man's mind in the 'cow counties.' [Calif.] **1946** *Ib.* Cow County. . . . Phrase still used in Calif., referring to rural districts in general, 'the sticks.' — **(2) 1771** *Carroll P.* in *Md. Hist. Mag.* XIV. 136, I have order'd Squires to go downe tomorrow with the Cowdriver. **1856** WILLIS *Convalescent* 112 With no accomplishments except for his own pleasure—no rat-catcher, no cow-driver, no pig-chaser—he loved me! **1932** W. KELLEY *Inchin' Along* 211 The ox drivers—'cow drivers,' they were called. — **(3) 1846** *Spirit of Times* 6 June 170/2 Were not the calls for cow fat (butter) and white salt, melodious in the extreme! — **(4) 1940** MENCKEN *Happy Days* 136 Even in the city a popular ginger-and-cocoanut cake, round in contour and selling for a cent, was called a cow flop, and little girls were supposed to avoid it at least in the presence of boys.

(6) 1846 *Spirit of Times* 6 June 170/2 And wasn't the *cow juice* (milk) in requisition! — **(7)** [**1855** BUCHELE *Land und Volk* 148 Viehzucht findet grössere Pflege als in einem der anderen südlichen Staaten, besonders im Norden und, neben der Baumwollencultur, im sogenannten Kuhlande im Südosten.] **1902** O. WISTER *Virginian* xviii. 216 No small trick in cow-land could be more offensive than this taking another man's rope. — **(8) 1891** S. M. WELCH *Recoll. 1830–40* 64 From Virginia to Goodell . . . was then a driveway or cow-lane. — **(9) 1840** A. M. MAXWELL *Run through U.S.* II. 21 Nor is the engine provided with what some have, and all should have, a machine denominated a *cow-lifter*, which is placed in front, and which trips a cow, sheep, or calf off its legs, and suspends the animal in mid-air until the engine can be stopped. **1863** RUSSELL *Diary* I. 130 Piggy is occasionally whipped of his legs by the cowlifter, and hoisted volatile into the ditch at one side. **1948** *Chi. Tribune* 8 Aug. 1/6 The term 'cowcatcher' . . . was 'cowlifter' and 'horselifter' before some one hit on the happy combination that stuck.

(10) 1674 *Md. Archives* II. 353 A Tract of Land Lyeing . . . upon a Hill by a greate Swampe neare a Cow Path. **1851** J. H. ROSS *In New York* 14 The lower part of the city has a few narrow zig-zag cow-path streets. **1897** BRODHEAD *Bound in Shallows* 162 He fetched up breathless in the ragged cow-path. — **(12) 1781** in R. PUTNAM *Memoirs* 184 Your favor of the 25, with the cow-thieves, arrived safe. **1903** A. ADAMS *Log Cowboy* 95 I think you're common cow thieves.

c. In colloquial phrases of obvious meaning. For *To salt the cow to catch the calf*, see ∗**salt,** *v.*

1894 P. L. FORD *P. Stirling* 17, June twenty-ninth will see chum and me at the Shrubberies 'if it kills every cow in the barn.' **1945** *Sat. Review* 27 Jan. 14/3 Surely the colloquial contraction in *darker'n the inside of a nigger's pocket* makes it a mite blacker than *dark as the inside of a cow.*

As the last term in **American, beef, bell, buffalo, butter, calico-colored, Creole, fat, grass, hunting, kill, moose, red, Texas, wild cow.**

cowallop kəˈwɑləp, *adv.* [Imitative.] Suddenly, abruptly. Also **cowhalloping,** *n.*, a beating. *Colloq.*

1843 STEPHENS *High Life N.Y.* II. 88 It didn't seem more than half a jiffy when we drew up co-wallop right afore Jase's house. **1851** *Polly Peablossom* 60 The pop-eyed feller looked as ef he thought he was about to ketch the orfullest cowhallopin he'd ever seed. **1859** TALIAFERRO *Fisher's R.* 205 So I jist hipped him, and throwed him co-wollup—a desput fall on the hard yeth.

Cowbellian ˈkauˌbelrən, *n.* (See quots.) *Obs.*

1841 *N.O. Picayune* 12 May 2/1 They were assisted by a regular tin-pan and cowbellion accompaniment from without. **1842** TASISTRO *Random Shots* I. 235 The only other association I intend to notice is that of the 'Cowbellians,' an appellation in which I never could find either sense or reason. . . . The members of this club generally turn out during the Christmas holydays, and every new year witnesses the imbodying forth of some beautiful conception, consisting of faithful representations of the costumes and manners of different nations. **1857** *Spirit of Times* 21 Mar. 44/2 Mardi-Gras night . . . compared very favorably with the far-famed Cowbellions of Mobile.

In full **Cowbellian de Rakian.** *Obs.*

1856 *Mobile Advertiser* 1 Jan., The first to appear and the most anxiously looked for, was the renowned and venerable society of Cowbellions de Rakin. **1934** CARMER *Stars Fell* 237 While Mobile waited the coming of the new year, 1833 . . . a band of young men . . . descended upon a hardware store, accoutered themselves with rakes and cowbells, and turned the night into a bedlam. Thus the society of *Cowbellian de Rakian* was born.

* **cowboy,** *n.*

1. During the Revolutionary War, a member of one of the Tory guerrilla bands that operated between the American and British lines near New York. Now *hist.* Cf. **skinner.**

1779 in *Geo. Clinton Papers* (1900) IV. 502 Your whig Militia below have as great an Itch for plundering, as the Cow Boys. **1823** J. THACHER *Military Jrnl.* 285 These shameless marauders have received the names of cow-boys and skinners. **1898** N. BROOKS *Boys of Fairport* xiii. 176 The cowboys were the worst kind of Tories; they went around in the bushes armed with guns and tinkling a cow-bell so as to beguile the patriots into the brush hunting for cows.

2. *W.* On a ranch, a mounted employee who assists in handling cattle. Also an actor who demonstrates on the stage the skills of a cowboy. See Adams, *Western Words.*

1866 *Wilkes' Spirit of Times* 21 April 130/3 Three or more determined cow-boys, mounted on active ponies and armed with severe cow-whips, will almost always succeed in driving the bunch, including the stallion, into the corral. **1874** J. G. MCCOY *Cattle Trade* 10 The young man who has long been a cow boy has but little taste for any other occupation. **1944** *Chi. D. News* 10 Jan. 9/6 The students were treated to entertainment by several 'cowboys' from a Loop theater who gave lariat demonstrations, and sang. **1947** *This Week Mag.* 10 May 13/1 The cowboy turned to the driver of the sedan.

3. In combs.: (1) **cowboy boots,** a type of high-heeled, often ornamented boots worn chiefly by cowboys; (2) **pool,** a form of pool played with a cue ball and three object balls and characterized by a complicated system of scoring, viz., exactly 90 points by caroms and by pocketing the object balls numbered 1, 3, and 5, 10 points by caroms alone, and a final single point by pocketing the cue ball after contact with the number one object ball; (3) **Cowboy President,** (see quot.); (4) **cowboys and Indians,** a game played by children acting out their conceptions of conflicts between cowboys and Indians.

(1) **1912** *Out West* March 180/2 He acknowledged the introduction scarcely in keeping with the sombrero he held in his hand, or his cowboy boots and spurs. **1948** *Sat. Ev. Post* 10 July 90/1 He was a lean, sunburned individual who had Texas written on him as plainly as if he'd been wearing cowboy boots. — (2) **1907** HOYLE *Games* 305 (*heading*), Cow-Boy Pool. **1921** *Cleveland Enterprise* 18 June 2/3 The game of Cowboy Pool . . . calls for the best skill of the artists of the cue. — (3) **1914** *Cyclo. Amer. Govt.* I. 317 Cowboy President. A name sometimes applied to Theodore Roosevelt . . . in consequence of his experience as a North Dakota ranchman 1884–1886, and his subsequent interest in 'cowboy' life. — (4) [**1887** *N.Y. Herald* 21 Feb. 9/1 A Chinaman . . . was passing through City Hall Park . . . yesterday afternoon when a mixed lot of 'cowboys and Injuns' swooped down upon him.] **1949** *Chi. Tribune* 17 July (Comics) 4 We'll play cowboys and Indians.

b. Also **cowboy dandyism, hat, land, levis** (cf. **levis**), **movie, reunion, saddle, song, suit, tournament, town.**

1887 T. ROOSEVELT *Ranch Life in Mont.* 6 In swaggered two men, dressed to the highest pitch of cowboy dandyism. — **1903** ADE *In Babel* 251 To see 'em cavortin' around town here in their cowboy hats and gassin' in front of every store [etc.]. **1944** *Reader's Digest* May 117/2, I found tents, guns and canoes, cowboy hats and blacksnake whips. — **1897** HOUGH *Story of Cowboy* 52 A tight coat, 'a biled shirt,' or a buttoned waistcoat are things not recognized in cowboyland. — **1948** *Range Riders Western* May 13/2 She was dressed in her riding clothes—plain cowboy levis and flannel shirt. — **1945** *New Yorker* 10 Feb. 16/2 Villa-Lobos is almost equally enthusiastic about cowboy movies. — **1899** *Caddo* (Okla.) *Herald* 22 Sep. 4/2 The cowboy reunion at Plainview, Tex. — **1881** ROMSPERT *Western Echo* 173 The average cow-boy saddle weighs forty pounds, and *some* weigh *sixty-five* pounds. — **1937** COOLIDGE *Texas Cowboys* 81 That is all right for poetry and cowboy songs, but saddles make very poor pillows and the Cherrycow men had to sleep. **1948** *McAlester* (Okla.) *News-Capital* 1 July 12/8 He was featured in Life Magazine as knowing 3,000 cowboy songs by heart. — **1942** DALE *Cow Country* 235 It is significant that Rotarians purchase from mail-order houses cowboy suits for their offspring. **1945** *Democrat* 22 Feb. 1/5 While attempting to put out a broomsedge fire, the fringe of a cowboy suit he was wearing became ignited. — **1889** *Phoenix Arizonan* 7 April 3/2 Fully from 1200 to 1500 people attended the

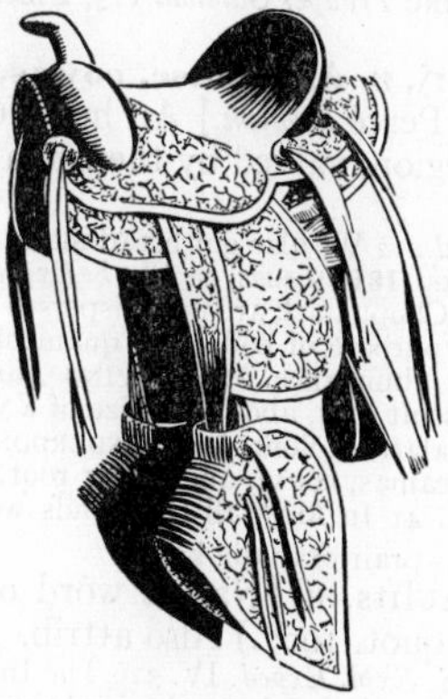

Cowboy saddle

cow-boy tournament at the fairgrounds yesterday. **1927** SIRINGO *Riata & Spurs* 118 Caldwell put on her Sunday clothes and held a grand cowboy tournament at the fair grounds. — **1920** HUNTER *Trail Drivers Texas* I. 50 This was a typical cowboy town.

As the last term in **mail order, Mormon, Pennsylvania, Texas cowboy.**

cowboyism ˈkaubɔɪˌɪzəm, *n.* (See quot.) *Obs.* — *a***1870** CHIPMAN *Notes on Bartlett* 104 *Cowboyism.* Spirit and practices of the cowboys. Applied, Aug. 1861, in Fairfield Co., Ct. [Conn.], to semi-Secessionists there and elsewhere in N.E.

cow common. In colonial times, public land set aside for pasturing cows, sheep, etc. Also a share in such lands sufficient for the keeping of one cow, hence **cow's common.** *Obs.*

1639 *Cambridge Prop. Rec.* 57 A roade of Land vpon the Cow Common. **1791** *Mass. H.S. Coll.* III. 154 Each share is subdivided into lesser parts, called cows' commons, which give the proprietor a privilege to turn out as many cows or other cattle, as he owns of such parts in common or other stock, in the proportion of one horse or sixteen sheep in two cows' commons. **1809** KENDALL *Travels* II. 209 Shares, or portions of shares, called cow's commons, entitle the holder to the pasturage of a certain number of sheep, or of sheep, oxen, cows, or horses, in proportion.

* **cowhide,** *n.*

1. A severe whip made of one or more thongs of cowhide, twisted or plaited; often painted. Cf. **cowskin,** *n.*

1818 M. BIRKBECK *Lett. from Illinois* 90 The enraged barrister with a hand-whip, or cow-hide, as they are called, . . . actually cut his jacket to ribbons. *c***1862** DAVIS *Farm Bk.* 4 It is my rule that all discipline . . . shall be inflicted by a broad leathern flail or strap and not by whips, switches or cow-hides. **1908** *D.N.* III. 315, I'll take a cowhide an' give you bringer if you don't mind.

2. *pl.* Cowhide boots or shoes.

1841 *Spirit of Times* 6 Feb. 583/1 Inch-soaled cowhides on a pine flooring. **1859** *Harper's Mag.* Nov. 856/1 [The Doctor] stopped suddenly in his discourse . . . and awaited the appearance of the wearer of the cow-hides. **1919** CADY *Rhymes of Vt.* (1923) 22 Each boy was taught a-what to do To make his cowhides winter through.

3. Attrib. in the sense: Made of or resembling cowhide, with (1) **boot,** (2) **shoe,** (3) **tail,** (4) **whip.**

(1) **1838** TITTERWELL *Yankee Notions* 116 (We.), I have even known a ghost in cow-hide boots. **1947** PAUL *Linden* 210 He had a plug hat . . . and cowhide boots without buttons or laces. — (2) [**1659** *Pa. Archives* 2 Ser. V. 336, 250 pairs of farmers' cowhide shoes, including some women and childrens' shoes—@ 32 stivers, fl. 400.] **1825** JOHN

NEAL *Bro. Jonathan* II. 46 He wore . . . cowhide shoes—newly greased. **1887** WILKINS *Humble Romance* 73 Wa'al I guess it's on account of dresses half way up to your knees and them cowhide shoes. — **(3) 1895** *Cent. Mag.* Aug. 623/2 The old Kentucky foxhound was of every color, loose in build, with open feet and a cowhide tail. — **(4) 1819** W. FAUX *Memorable Days* (1823) 305 One man then bound him to a tree and lashed him with a cow-hide whip.

cowhide ˈkaʊˌhaɪd, *v. tr.* To flog or beat (a person) with a cowhide.

Recorded in *EDD* but with only an 1890 quot.

1794 *Kentucky Gazette* (photostat) VII. 1 Mar. 2/3 In November 1792 . . . a justice of the peace was cited to appear before the house of Delegates . . . some he had horse-whipped; others he had cow-hided. **1818** FLINT *Lett. from Amer.* 116 The happy Kentuckian slave lives under the danger of being cow-hided . . . for the slightest . . . offence. **1899** C. KING *Trooper Galahad* 115, I mean to cowhide him tonight.

cowish ˈkaʊɪʃ, *n.* Also **couse, cowas, cows.** [Native name. Cf. Nez Percé *kowish.*] An herb, *Cogswellia cous,* of the Oregon region, valued by the Indians for its edible roots.

1807 GASS *Journal* 212 We also got bread made of roots, which the natives call Co-was. **1814** *Lewis & Clark Exped.* (1893) 958 The greater part of the Chopunnish are now dispersed in villages through this plain, for the purpose of collecting quamash and cows, which grow here in great abundance. **1837** IRVING *Bonneville* II. 99 The cowish, also, or biscuit root, about the size of a walnut; which they reduce to a very palatable flour. **1885** ONDERDONK *Idaho* 134 Their favorite roots are camas, couse, and bitter root. **1911** CURTIS *No. Amer. Indian* XII. 41 In May all the bands would congregate at Tipahlíwan (Camas prairie) to dig kouse.

Cowlitz ˈkaʊlɪts, *n.* [Native word of unknown significance.] (See quot. 1907.) Also attrib.

1845 WILKES *U.S. Expl. Exped.* IV. 316 The Indians belong to the Klackatack tribe, though they have obtained the general name of the Cowlitz Indians. **1892** BOSTON TILICUM *Puyallup Indians* 17 He is a Cowlitz and half-breed Kanaka. **1903** JAMES *Indian Basketry* 51 Inland, south of Mt. St. Helen's, are the Klikatats, belonging to the Sahaptin family and north are the Kowlitz, another tribe of the Salish family. **1907** HODGE *Amer. Indians* I. 355/2 Cowlitz. A Salish tribe formerly on the river of the same name in s.w. Washington. . . . They are no longer known by this name, being evidently officially classed as Chehalis.

cowology kaʊˈɑlədʒɪ, *n.* The science of cattle-raising. *Rare.* — **1845** T. J. GREEN *Texian Exped.* 265 Jake . . . has followed cattle long upon the Texian prairies and was deeply versed in cow-ology.

* **cowpen,** *n.*

1. Formerly in the southeastern states, a large inclosure in the forest capable of holding entire herds of cattle. *Obs.* [Cf. quot. 1855 *s.v.* **cowland.**]

1735 in *Ga. Hist. Soc. Coll.* II. 20 A Savannah, . . . which is exceeding good for a stock of cattle, and on which they frequently settle their cow-pens. **1775** *S.C. Hist. Soc. Coll.* II. 61 He had thoughts of sending for three or four of the principal head men [of the Creek Indians] to meet him . . . at his cowpen. **1851** JOHNSON *Traditions* 144 Large flocks of cattle were kept at that time all over South-Carolina, in settlements called cow pens; very much as still practiced by the Spaniards south of us. **1884** *Cent. Mag.* Jan. 443/2 The ranch system had its beginning in Virginia and the Carolinas and among the Spaniards of Florida. 'Cowpens,' as they were then called, were established on lands not yet settled, and cattle were herded in droves of hundreds or thousands. **1893** TURNER *Signif. Frontier in Amer. Hist.* 14 Travellers of the eighteenth century found the 'cowpens' among the canebrakes and peavine pastures of the South, and the 'cow drivers' took their droves to Charleston, Philadelphia, and New York.

2. In combs.: (1) **cowpen bird,** =**cowbird** (*a*); (2) **bunting,** =**cowbird** (*a*); (3) **full,** a large number, *colloq.* [cf. *EDD gowpen,* a great quantity, large store, and *OED gowpenful,* double handful]; (4) **ground,** ground that has been a cowpen; (5) **keeper,** one in charge of a cowpen (sense **1.** above), *obs.;* (6) **Spanish,** (see quot.); (7) **tobacco,** tobacco grown upon cowpenned land, *obs.*

(1) 1731 CATESBY *Carolina* I. 34 *Passer fuscus.* The Cowpen Bird. . . . They delight much to feed in the Pens of Cattle, which has given them their name. **1887** C. C. ABBOTT *Waste-Land Wand.* 55 The cowpen-bird, which is never mated, and for several months in the year deposits fertile eggs in the nests of other birds. — **(2) 1857** *Rep. Comm. Patents: Agric.* 129 Associating partially with reed-birds, grackles, and cow-pen buntings, . . . they [red-winged starlings] move to the Southern States in such dense flocks as almost to cloud the air. — **(3) 1886** POORE *Reminisc.* I. 263 I feel fully able, with my bow and arrow, to run through a 'cow-pen full' of such cock robins as he is. — **(4) 1786** in *Pub. Col. Soc.* XVIII. 39 Sowed Turnip Seed on the Cowpen ground which had been just plowed, harrowed them in, at the home house adjoining the clover.

(5) 1739 W. STEPHENS *Proc. Georgia* 287 Five of the Steers that broke away . . . [were] picked up as far off as Old Ebenezer by the Cow-Pen Keeper there. **1741** *Ga. Col. Rec.* VI. 19 Joseph Barker the Cowpen Keeper at Ebenezer. — **(6) 1931** DOBIE *Coronado* 117 The Texans talked 'Mexican,' or 'cowpen Spanish,' as fluently as though they were natives, and after supper the ancient strangers, evidently feeling at ease, asked if anyone present could tell where the old 'War Crossing' on the Nueces was. — **(7) 1724** H. JONES *Virginia* 39 Land when hired is forced to bear Tobacco by penning their Cattle upon it; but Cowpen Tobacco tastes strong. **1809** IRVING *Hist. N.Y.* (1927) III. iv. 146 One of true delft manufacture and furnished with a charge of fragrant Cow-pen tobacco.

cowpen ˈkaʊˌpɛn, *v.* [f. the noun.] *tr.* (See quot. 1899.)

1688 JOHN CLAYTON in *Phil. Trans.* XVII. 979 So that after they have cleared a fresh piece of Ground out in the Woods, it will not bear Tobacco past two or three Years, unless Cow-pen'd. **1786** WASHINGTON *Diaries* III. 131 [I] plowed a poor ½ acre to Cowpen on. **1787** *Ib.* 183 About an acre was sown in my Meadow, part of which had been cowpened. **1899** GREEN *Va. Word-Book* Cow-pen, *v.* To manure land by penning cattle on it.

b. Hence **cowpenned land.**

1800 W. TATHAM *Tobacco* 6 Cow-penned land is that which is manured by removing the cattle about upon it. . . . This is effected by means of moveable fences.

cowpenning ˈkaʊˌpɛnɪŋ, *n.* The penning of cattle upon land to enrich it.

1688 JOHN CLAYTON in *Phil. Trans.* XVII. 984 Hitherto, as I have said, they have used none [i.e., no system of fertilizing] but that of Cowpenning. **1782** CRÈVECOEUR *Letters* 125 They have however, . . . by bringing a variety of manure, and by cow-penning, enriched several spots. **1871–3** *Texas Almanac* 12 Cow-penning, in successive lots, . . . is a good plan for manuring.

cowskin ˈkaʊˌskɪn, *v.* [f. the noun.] *tr.* To whip or beat (a person) with a cowskin. Also **cowskinning,** *n.*

1799 *Aurora* (Phila.) 20 May (Th.), I am a constable, and may therefore kick, cuff, beat, bruise, cowskin, or kill any man I please. **1802** BRACKENRIDGE *Mod. Chivalry* II. vii. 259 Taking advantage of the humiliated state of mind in which the bog-trotter now was, from the late cowskinning he had received. **1856** SIMMS *Charlemont* 285 That William Hinkley should have cowskinned Stevens would have been much more gratifying to him could he have been present. **1947** *West. Pa. Hist. Mag.* Sep.–Dec. 132 The 'cowskinning' incident, with its attendant excitement, was the final blow.

* **Coxey,** *n. attrib.* Of or pertaining to J. S. Coxey. *Obs.* Cf. **Coxey's Army.** — **1894** *Nation* LVIII. 323/2 What we are now witnessing, both in the Populist movement and in the Coxey marches, has been predicted. **1894** *Harper's Mag.* LXXXIX. 316/1 In Montana a collision occurred between Coxey troops, who had seized a Northern Pacific train, and the State authorities. *Ib.* 478/2 Fifteen members of the 'Coxey Industrial Army' were drowned in the Platte River near Brighton, Colorado.

Coxeyism ˈkɑksɪˌɪzəm, *n.* The political teachings or practices of J. S. Coxey. *Obs.* Cf. **Coxey's Army.** — **1894** *Nation* LVIII. 358/1 Protection leads straight to socialism, of which Coxeyism is simply a filthy eruption. **1929** D. L. MCMURRY *Coxey's Army* 262 So far as any immediate realization of its program was concerned, Coxeyism was a failure.

Coxeyite ˈkɑksɪˌaɪt, *n.* A follower or adherent of J. S. Coxey. *Obs.* Cf. **Coxey's Army.** — **1894** *Columbus* (Ohio) *Dispatch* 4 April, If the commonwealers under Frye who are now in St. Louis succeed in effecting a union with the Coxeyites the general army will be a formidable thing. **1929** D. L. MCMURRY *Coxey's Army* 89 A parade through the streets of Allegheny was called off because the route mapped out by the police differed essentially from that planned by the Coxeyites.

Coxey's Army. [See note.] A group of several hundred unemployed who in 1894, chiefly under the leadership of J. S. Coxey, marched to Washington, D.C., in an effort to secure relief through legislation. Also **Coxey's men.** Now *hist.*

Jacob Sechler Coxey of Massillon, Ohio, b. 1854, led a group of 500 unemployed into Washington, D.C., on May Day, 1894. He demanded that Congress enact certain bills drawn up by him, one of which called for the issuance of $500,000,000 in irredeemable paper money for road construction. Carl Browne led a second "army" from California.

1894 *N.Y. Herald* 17 April 7/1 When the second Los Angeles delegation of Coxey's army arrived here last night the Fire Department was called out and the tramps were drenched with cold water and driven from the freight train which they had captured. **1894** *Life* 10 May 300/1 Men and generals between them have made up 'Coxey's army,' and a very misty, queer, mixed-up lot they certainly are. **1948** *Time* 26 April 40/1 Jacob Sechler Coxey, who 54 years ago led 'Coxey's Army' of unemployed to Washington, . . . reached 94 in Massillon, Ohio.

coyote ˈkaɪot, kaɪˈotɪ, *n.* Also †**cuiota, cayota, kiote,** etc. *W.* [Amer. Sp. (<Nahuatl).]

1. The prairie wolf, *Canis latrans.*

1759 *tr.* VENEGAS *Nat. Hist. Calif.* I. 37 The coyotes are scarce. This is a Mexican word, and in New Spain the name of a peculiar species of wild dog, in some particulars resembling the foxes of Spain, especially in their arts and stratagems; though their figure is very different. **1831** BEECHEY *Voyage* 79 Wolves and foxes are numerous, and the *cuiotas*, or jackalls, range about the plains at night, and prove very destructive to the sheep. **1850** *Calif. Courier* (S.F.) 29 July, Cayotas are to be employed to search the hills and valleys for sheep. **1948** *Denison* (Tex.) *Herald* 2 July 12/7 If all coyotes were killed, Texas farms and ranches would abound with crop-destroying rabbits. *attrib.* **1850** GARRARD *Wah-To-Yah* i. 12 We were serenaded by the coyote wolf. **1908** VISSCHER *Pony Express* 39 There was little delay in these changes of horses, as the rider gave the 'coyote yell' half a mile away, and, day or night, the station men had the pony ready. **1948** *Dly. Ardmoreite* (Ardmore, Okla.) 28 April 2/3 At $2.50 a head, the coyote pups meant $22.50 in bounties.

b. Used of persons. *Slang.*

1872 POWERS *Afoot & Alone* 277 Many slouching fellows make that pretense [i.e., pretend to be looking for government lands], while they are really squatters or 'coyotes.' **1890** *Chi. Advance* 20 Nov., Some Indians, some Mexicans, many 'coyotes,' as the Mexicans call the half breed population. **1948** *N.M. Quart. Rev.* Summer 198 Often *coyote* is used as a synonym for *native*, and is applied to Indians and *mestizos* (mixed bloods), as readily as to plants.

c. (See quot.) *Obs.*

1898 *Mo. So. Dakotan* I. 65 Thenceforward the Dakotans were called 'kiotes,' a nick-name which will probably last.

d. A horse of the color of a coyote.

1903 A. ADAMS *Log Cowboy* 14 It was my good fortune to get a good mount of horses,—three sorrels, two greys, two coyotes, a black, a brown, and a *grulla*. [**1939** ROLLINS *Gone Haywire* 56 He was a purebred of the Spanish strain known in the Southwestern ranges as *bayo coyote*.]

2. In special combs.: (1) **coyote days,** early days in the settlement of the West when coyote houses (see (4) below) were not uncommon; (2) **dog,** a dog related closely to coyotes or possessing traits of these, *obs.;* (3) **gold,** gold obtained from coyote excavations, *obs.;* (4) **house,** (see quot.); (5) **melon,** =**calabazilla;** (6) **thistle,** any one of several species of *Eryngium;* (7) **tobacco,** (see quot. 1942); (8) **well,** a water hole.

(1) **1885** H. H. JACKSON *Zeph* i., Especially lucky were those who came in the beginning, in the 'tent and coyote' days, as they were called, and had seen the lots they bought then for hundreds of dollars boom up into value rated by thousands. — (2) **1868** WHYMPER *Alaska* 20 These people appeared to be very bare of provisions, and disputed with their wretched 'cayota' dogs anything that we threw out of camp, in the shape of bones, bacon rind, or tea leaves, and similar luxuries. — (3) **1850** SAWYER *Way Sketches* (1926) 119 The Coyota gold is very fine dust, almost as fine as black sand. — (4) **1871** PINE *Beyond West* 307 A coyote house is a small cellar dug in the ground with a few boards placed up over the hole as a roof.
(5) **1907** MEARNS *Mammals Mex. Bdry.* 474 This rat also feeds upon the seeds of a large gourd known by the name of 'Coyote melon.' **1948** *N.M. Quart. Rev.* Summer 198 A desert gourd common to the Southwest as well as Mexico is called coyote melon and is said to be eaten by coyotes. — (6) **1922** SMILEY *Weeds of Calif.* 160 This is but one of several so-called 'coyote thistles' found in California. — (7) **1912** LUMHOLTZ *New Trails* 52 The name for tobacco . . . used for certain sacred purposes, is . . . coyote tobacco. **1942** CASTETTER & BELL *Pima & Papago Agric.* 108 The first tobacco smoked by the Papago and Pima was *Nicotiana trigonophylla* Dunal, known as 'Coyote's tobacco.' — (8) **1933** JAEGER *Calif. Deserts* 29 Even the insects are aware of the location of these 'coyote wells,' as they are often called, and several times when in need of water I have located such places by watching converging lines of thirsty bees.

b. In terms referring to mining in which excavations suggestive of those of coyotes are made, as (1) **coyote diggings,** (2) **hole,** (see also quot. 1906), (3) **placer,** (4) **shaft.**

(1) **1850** *S.F. Picayune* 31 Aug. 3/1 There are Coyoto Diggings, near this place, from which, at the depth of from 17 to 25 feet, $23,000 have been taken out in two days. **1948** *N.M. Quart. Rev.* Summer 199 In mining lingo of early California, derived from the Mexicans, 'coyote holes' or 'coyote diggings' were small drift tunnels. — (2) **1851** *Sacramento Transcript* 1 May, He noticed one coyote hole where the miners had sunk the shaft through a strata . . . of ashes. **1889** K. MUNROE *Golden Days* 111 Between the very wet and very dry diggings came the 'coyote holes' . . . sunk in bottom-lands formed . . . by the deposits of some running stream. **1906** *N.Y. Ev. Post* 12 Sep. 7 Drilling coyote holes is the name applied by railroad contractors to drilling blast holes in grade-running cuts through hills. — (3) **1851** *S.F. Picayune* 4 Dec. 1/6 The experience of every succeeding day seems to develop the fact that river mining is less productive, in the aggregate, than the dry, or 'cayote' placers. — (4) **1851** *S.F. Picayune* 14 Oct. 2/4 The beds of the streams have proved very rich, the banks richer, the cayote shafts richest of all.

coyote ˈkaɪot, *v. W.* [f. the noun.] *Mining. intr.* (See 1st quot. and quot. 1920.) Also **coyoting,** *n.*

1851 *S.F. Picayune* 1 Oct. 3/2 In some instances, where peculiar facilities exist . . . the miner is enabled to sink his hole at once, and *coyote* (i.e., dig smaller holes), in every direction, around the bottom of it. **1860** *Harper's Mag.* April 607/2 'Coyoteing' or drifting . . . has been superseded by the improvement of tunneling. [It] received its name from its fancied resemblance to the subterranean burrowing of a . . . 'coyote.' **1920** A. T. JACKSON *Forty-niner* 43 *note*, 'Coyoting' was a local descriptive term of a mining method which meant the sinking of shafts, and running small drifts from the bottom in the bedrock in all directions [etc.]. **1948** *N.M. Quart. Rev.* Summer 199 'To coyote' was to dig in coyote fashion.

b. To "vamoose," to dig one's way *out. Colloq. Obs.*

1857 *Phoenix* (Sacramento) 13 Sep. 1/3 And I, why I *cayotied*. **1861** STONE *Pacific Song Book* 21, I did as I had done before, Coyoted out from 'neath the floor.

c. (See quots.) *Colloq.*

1948 *N.M. Quart. Rev.* Summer 199 Nowadays in the Southwest, 'coyoting around' means drifting loosely from one place or occupation to another, without anchor or responsibility. *Ib.*, At the same time, to 'out-coyote' another man means little more than to outsmart, to excel at the trickster's own game.

Coyotero ˌkojəˈtero, *n.* [Amer. Sp. in same sense.] An Indian of any one of various Apache bands whose principal home was formerly in eastern Arizona, often pl. as a division or tribal designation. Also attrib.

[**1776** *Franciscan Journal* tr. in W. R. HARRIS *Catholic Church in Utah* (1909) 134 This afternoon we were overtaken by a Coyote Indian and a half-breed from Abiquiú.] **1829** R. W. H. HARDY *Travels in Mex.* 430 The neighbourhood of this hill is inhabited by a tribe of the Apache Indians, called Coyotéros, from the circumstance of its being believed that they feed upon the flesh of the coyote (jackal). **1844** GREGG *Commerce of Prairies* I. 290 By far the greatest portion of the [Apache] nation is located in the west, and is mostly known by the sobriquet of *Coyoteros*, in consequence, it is said, of their eating the *coyote* or prairie-wolf. **1943** WOOD *W. Reed* 120 The few Coyotero Apaches who, with their women and children, lived there were peaceable folk.

* **crab,** *n.* [See note.]

Words from different sources are treated together here for ease of reference. The application in sense **1.** may have originated as a jocular understatement; **crab schooner** suggests Du. *krabschuit*, a boat used for war purposes; **crab wood** is a modification of "carap(a) wood."

1. A horse valued for his speed, usu. **fast crab.** *Obs.*

1839 *Spirit of Times* 27 July 246/1 (We.), A pair of very 'fast crabs' will command from $1200 to $1800. **1849** G. G. FOSTER *N.Y. in Slices* 46 [The b'hoy comes] calling with whip and voice upon his 'crab' to 'go it or break a leg!' **1861** *Vanity Fair* 5 Jan. 4/2 There is literally nothing that I care to do, . . . except to smoke good cigars . . . drive my own fast crab, and keep a bachelor establishment.

2. =**crawfish 1.**

1890 *Manti* (Utah) *Sentinel* 28 Nov. 1/2 We call crawfish 'crabs' in Penn Yan [N.Y.]

3. In combs.: (1) **crab cactus,** (see quot. 1930); (2) **cannery,** a place where crab meat is canned; (3) **eater,** any one of various fishes said to eat crabs; (4) **grass,** see as a main entry; (5) **gumbo,** (see quot.); (6) **lantern,** (see quot. 1908); (7) **orchard,** a place where crab-apple trees abound, also as a place-name; (8) **schooner,** "the sort of vessel otherwise termed *Crab, Grab?*" (B. '77), *obs.;* (9) **wood,** (see quots.).

(1) **1900** L. H. BAILEY *Cyclo. Amer. Horticulture* 536. **1942** WEYGANDT *Plenty of Penna.* 172 They love whitewash on the dooryard palings; wrens in bird boxes by the back stoop; crab cactuses in the south windows. — (2) **1888** *U.S. Museum Bul.* No. 27, 110 In 1880, there were three Crab canneries in the United States. — (3) **1814** MITCHILL *Fishes N.Y.* 491 Crab-eater. *Centronotus spinosus*. . . .

On dissecting this fish, the most remarkable occurrence was the stomach distended with food, consisting of twenty spotted sand-crabs that were entire enough to be counted. **1842** *Nat. Hist. N.Y., Zoology* IV. 113 The Northern Crab-eater. *Elacate atlantica*.... It is a rare and probably a solitary fish. *Ib.* 114 The Crab-eater ... was captured in a seine in the harbour of Boston. **1888** GOODE *Amer. Fishes* 144 The Cobia or crab-eater, *Elacate canada*, ... is considered one of the most important food-fishes of Maryland and Virginia.

(5) **1936** *Chi. D. News* 4 Feb. 10 The Creole cook prepares many different kinds of gumbos, but the most popular is crab gumbo, composed of hard-shell crabs, shrimp and ham (or chicken) and the whole mixed and seasoned with okra, onions, garlic, parsley and green peppers. — (6) *c***1770** J. BOUCHER *Glossary* I. 50 At night crab-lanthorn and fried cucumbers; Or milk and peaches mash'd, and roasting-ears. **1801** in *W. & M. Coll. Quart.* 2 Ser. VI. 183 Had some peaches stewed in order to make Crab Lanterns for dinner. **1908** *Dialect Notes* III. 302 *Crab-lantern*, a half-moon pie made of dried fruit and fried. — (7) **1738** in *Amer. Sp.* XV. 291/1 Beginning at a place called the Crabb Orchard near the Ridge of Mountains on the head Springs of Shennando. **1788** *Ib.*, Thence ... to a double white oak and black oak by a Crab Orchard & Sinkhole. **1856** P. CARTWRIGHT *Autobiog.* 20 When we came within seven miles of the Crab Orchard, ... it was nearly night. — (8) **1862** *N.Y. Tribune* 14 June (B.), The 'Reliance,' a vessel belonging to our Potomac flotilla, has captured a crab-schooner named the 'Monitor.' — (9) **1884** SARGENT *Rep. Forests* 121 *Sebastiana lucida*.... Crab Wood. Poison Wood. **1897** SUDWORTH *Arborescent Flora* 271 *Gymnanthes lucida*. Crabwood (Fla.).

b. *To turn* (or *bend*) *the crab*, (see quot. 1936).

1867 HARTE *Condensed Novels* 173 He had been observed ... amusing himself by going through that popular youthful exercise known as 'turning the crab.' **1936** *Amer. Mercury* Feb. 176 In the playground we performed an exercise called 'Bend the crab,' raising the arms over the head, inclining backwards until the palms were flat to the ground and the body arched.

As the last term in **blue, box, cow, fiddler, horsefoot, Jonah, kelp, king, land, red, rock, sand fiddler, sea horsefoot, shedder, silk, soft, soft-shelled, sow, spirit, squeaker, stone, Virginia crab.**

***crab grass.**

1. Any one of various grasses, esp. of the genus *Digitaria*, having creeping stems that root freely at the nodes.

1743 CLAYTON *Flora Virginica* 134 Panicum spicis alternis oppositisve [etc.] ... Crab-grass. **1781–2** JEFFERSON *Notes Va.* (1788) 40 Our grasses are lucerne, ... greensward, blue grass, and crab grass. **1948** *Holland's* June 47/3 If permitted to grow high enough, Bermuda grass will shade out crab grass and protect it from gaining much headway.

2. Yard grass, *Eleusine indica*. Cf. **sprouting crab grass.**

1857 GRAY *Botany* 554 *Eleusine*. Crab-grass. Yard-grass. **1878** KILLEBREW *Tenn. Grasses* 231 *Elusine Indica*, Crab grass, yard grass.... It forms very good and lasting picking for all stock. **1883** VASEY *Grasses U.S.* 33 *Eleusine Indica*, ... Yard-grass, Crab-grass. Extensively naturalized.

crack, *n.

1. A small opening between two floor boards, often *to walk a crack*, as a test of soberness, also fig.; *to toe a crack*, to stand with one's toes on a crack, also fig., to toe the mark, "come up to the scratch." *Colloq.*

1825 PAULDING *J. Bull in Amer.* vii. 81, I had qualified myself by being able to walk a crack after swallowing half a gallon of whiskey. **1869** STOWE *Oldtown Folks* 483 Your minister sartin doos slant a leetle toward the Arminians; he don't quite walk the crack. **1875** STOWE *We & Our Neighbors* 100 Any boy that don't toe the crack gets it. **1892** HARRIS *U. Remus & Friends* 183 Tinktum Tidy wait twel eve'ybody got still, en den he got up en drapt de corn thoo de crack er de floor. **1944** DUNCAN *M. Graham* 235 On his good days he read to the children or marshaled them to toe the cracks in the kitchen floor close to the stove while he gave out spelling words.

b. A narrow valley. *Rare.*

1863 S. JUDD *Hist. Hadley, Mass.* 435 This figure is intended to represent the shape of the mountain, ... with its slopes both gentle and steep, between the valleys called cracks.

c. crack-loo, crack-a-loo, (see quot. 1946). *Colloq.*

*c***1845** *Big Bear Ark.* 176 It may be crack-loo, poker, brag, or set-back-euchre. **1904** O. HENRY *Heart of West* 120 In those times cattlemen played at crack-loo on the sidewalks with double-eagles. **1946** WOODARD *Word-List* 10 crack-a-loo: *n.* A game played with pennies, nickels, or dimes. The coin is pitched against the ceiling and falls to the floor. The person whose coin comes to rest on or nearest a chosen crack wins. Pamlico.

d. *On the crack*, of a door: Slightly open.

1892 HARRIS *U. Remus & Friends* 143 When he got little nigher, he tuck notice dat de front door wuz on de crack. **1911** R. D. SAUNDERS *Col. Todhunter* 161 Then the front door was opened on the crack.

2. crack shot, a shot that hits the center of the target, a marksman capable of firing such shots. *Colloq.*

1888 CODY *Story of Wild West* 542 Major Brown declared it was a crack shot, because it broke the plate. **1932** *K.C. Times* 20 April 20 A certain Jefferson City lawyer ... is also a crack shot of the local gun club.

3. A cutting remark, a wisecrack *q.v. Slang.*

1902 A. H. LEWIS *The Boss* 120 This is exec'tive session, an' that crack about bein' a taxpayer is more of a public utterance. **1948** *Sat. Ev. Post* 17 July 38/4, I ought to kill you for a crack like that!

crack, *v.

1. *To be what it's cracked up to be*, to come up to report or expectation, usu. in the negative. *Colloq.* or *slang.*

1835 CROCKETT *Van Buren* 20 Martin Van Buren is not the man he is cracked up to be. **1945** *Chi. D. News* 5 Feb. 8/6 Despite the lurid headlines, vice in Chicago is not what it's cracked up to be by the local Purity Leaguers.

2. *intr.* Of day: To break. *Rare.* Cf. **day crack.**

1845 C. M. KIRKLAND *Western Clearings* 123 'When did you get home?' pursued the inquirer. 'Just as the east was cracking for daylight.'

3. crack down, to take stern measures. *Slang.*

[**1933** *Newsweek* 21 Oct. 8/1 The 'cracking down' phase of the Blue Eagle's career opened last week.] **1947** *Time* 25 Aug. 34/3 If one of the 21 American republics were attacked, all of them would go into a huddle, and if two-thirds of them agreed to crack down on the aggressor, all 21 would have to go along.

Also as a noun.

1947 *Chi. Times* 29 Aug. 22/1 (*heading*), Shape crackdown on 2 death streets. **1948** *Chi. Sun-Times* 3 Nov. 43/3 Chicago's steadily improving traffic control methods and the current safety crackdown are beginning to ease congestion on downtown streets.

crackajack, variant of **crackerjack.**

crack-buster, *n.* (See quot.) — **1879** *St. Nicholas Mag.* Nov., He [=young crab] still keeps on eating and gets bigger still, and then cracks a little, and is called a 'Crack-buster.'

cracked corn. Corn that has been cracked into coarse bits.

[**1785** *N.C. Morav. Rec.* V. (1941) Sep. 2393 (Expenses of journey from Bethlehem to Salem) ... 5 bu. cracked corn, 22/6.] **1833** J. BOARDMAN *America* 16 It may be requisite to inform my readers, ... that homony is a preparation of maize; cracked corn is broken maize. **1945** *Mass. Audubon Soc. Bul.* Feb. 5 Cracked corn is appealing to many species.

cracker, *n.

1. Orig. a frontier outlaw and braggart, later applied to a "poor white" of the southern states, esp. Georgia and Florida. Cf. ***conch,** ***n.***

This sense derives from **cracker* in its old meaning of a boaster, braggart, liar. See quot. 1766.

1766 *Lett. from Gavin Cochrane to Earl of Dartmouth*, 27 June (Dartmouth MSS), I should explain to your Lordship what is meant by Crackers; a name they have got from being great boasters; they are a lawless set of rascalls on the frontiers of Virginia, Maryland, the Carolinas, and Georgia, who often change their places of abode. **1836** *Knickerb.* VII. 453 It is the killing of the cattle of the 'crackers'— as the southern back-woodsmen are called—that is the most fruitful source of disputes. **1891** *Cent. Mag.* Feb. 488 As the cracker neither adds nor multiplies, it is only by being refused further credit he is made to realize that his supplies depend upon his own efforts. **1948** *Good Housekeeping* Jan. 103/1 She was about sixteen going on seventeen—and fated to be what the Crackers down our way call 'a good breeder.'

attrib. **1886** IZA D. HARDY *Oranges and Alligators* 186 Distinguishable at a glance from the 'cracker' cottage is the home of the Northern settler. **1946** *Chi. Sun* (Book Week) 21 April 5/5 His detailed background of Crackerland folklore ... and his over-sized characterizations ... offer unusually robust entertainment.

b. cracker bonnet, a bonnet such as cracker women wear. *Obs.*

1836 C. GILMAN *Recoll.* (1838) 131, I perceived a tall, sallow-looking man ... speaking to a young girl ... dressed in homespun, with a cracker or cape bonnet of the same material.

c. Cracker State, Georgia, a nickname. Also attrib.

1871 DE VERE 659 Georgia ... little deserves the name of Cracker State, by which it is occasionally designated. **1948** *Chi. Tribune* 27 June IV. 8/1 Without doubt this Cracker state Claghorn is concerned that The Tribune is against demagogs.

Also *cracker funeral, home, house, life, man, planter, woman,* etc.

2. A machine for crushing anthracite coal.
*c*1870 CHIPMAN *MS Notes on Bartlett* 105 A boy employed about the crackers.

3. In special combs.: (1) **cracker anniversary,** the Fourth of July, *rare;* (2) **barrel,** see as a main entry; (3) **berry,** (see quots.); (4) **box,** (*a*) a box such as crackers are shipped in, (*b*) used attrib. with reference to those designated under **cracker barrel b;** (5) **boy,** (see quot.), cf. **2** above; (6) **factory,** a place where crackers are made.
(1) **1829** *N.Y. Journal of Commerce* 4 July 4/2 Not a cracker-anniversary passes without causing some serious accident, either to property, life or limb.—(3) **1867** DE VOE *Market Ass't* 393 The common low-bush blueberry or *huckleberry*, is commonly known among the Jersey pickers or gatherers as the 'cracker-berry,' as they crack or snap in the mouth on account of their tough skin. **1931** CLUTE *Plants* 42 One might be puzzled to know why one species of huckleberry (*Gaylussacia baccata*) is called crackers, cracker berry, and black-snaps, until in eating the fruit he finds the seeds cracking between his teeth. — (4) (*a*) **1857** *Harper's Mag.* July 149/1 Their instruments consisted of a couple of drums made of hollow logs with hide stretched over one end, and a Boston tin cracker-box. **1947** *Westerners' Brand Book* 121 One described a city man as 'wearin' one o' them stiff collars so high he'd have to stand on a cracker box to spit out.' (*b*) **1911** HARRISON *Queed* 230 Republican cracker-box orators were trying somehow to make capital of the thing. **1925** J. R. TANDY (*title*), Crackerbox philosophers in American humor and satire.
(5) **1862** *Independent* 13 March, Young boys—*cracker*-boys they are called—whose duty it is to pick out and throw away the bits of slate and other impurities which come whirling along with the coal. — (6) **1887** *Courier-Journal* 12 Jan. 3/4 Capt. Frank Carroll . . . has quit the river business to accept a position with a wholesale Cincinnati cracker factory as drummer. **1894** ROBLEY *Bourbon Co., Kansas* 62 Already foundations for future cities were being laid, which in the near future were to become 'busy marts of trade,' . . . vote bonds, and have a macadam tax, and a cracker factory.
As the last term in **Boston, cannon, China, corn, country, fire, Florida, Georgia, Giant, graham, Jackson, lynching corn, milk, mud, New York, nut, oyster, pilot, popping, rifle, shell, shooting, soda, water cracker.**

cracker barrel. A large barrel in which crackers are shipped. Also fig.
1905 *Springfield W. Republican* 15 Sep. 12 Dr. Hall puts on no 'lugs,' and is not above sitting on a cracker barrel in a country grocery for a chat with old acquaintances. **1948** *Chi. Tribune* 7 March I. 38/4 St. Louis, in those early days of western expansion, became the cracker-barrel for gun fanciers. **1948** *Chi. D. News* 1 May 2/2 The boys are sitting around the cracker barrel.

b. Used attrib. with reference to rustic wiseacres who often gather at country stores and discuss any and all subjects. *Colloq.*
1938 *Time* 31 Oct. 26/3 On the air and in print the Burns character is that of a cracker-barrel philosopher. **1947** *Chi. D. News* 14 Oct. 14/5 The old 'cracker barrel' forums are back even if there are no cracker barrels any more.

crackerdom ˈkrækɚdəm, *n.* The region occupied by crackers (sense 1). *Rare.* — **1902** HARBEN *Abner Daniel* 296 We are glad to welcome amongst us a sort of second savior in our Sodom an' Gomorry of crackerdom.

crackerjack ˈkrækɚˌdʒæk, *n.* Also **crackajack.** [App. of fanciful origin.]

1. An especially fine thing or person. Also attrib. or as adj.
1896 *N.Y. Herald* 2 April 7/4 There are so many crackajacks in the lot that it is going to be very hard to make up the regular team, because some good men will have to sit on the bench and wait for a chance. **1911** SAUNDERS *Col. Todhunter* 123 You've given me a cracker-jack talk on Missouri politics. **1948** *Dallas Morn. News* 2 May II. 1/7 Except for one end and center he has lost a crackerjack line-up among last season's letter men.

2. (*cap.*) A manufacturer's trade-name for a confection composed of popcorn, and sometimes peanuts, glazed with molasses. Also attrib.
1902 *Sears Cat.* (ed. 112) 20/3 Cracker Jack. . . . Price, per case of 100 packages 2.85. **1944** *Nat. Geog. Mag.* June 680/1 At noon they stopped . . . [and] ate Forestry K rations—a palatable, sustaining meal out of a heavily waxed carton the size of a Cracker Jack box. **1947** BASKINS *Dr. Has Baby* 131 She dangled a red balloon, ate popcorn, peanuts and Cracker Jacks.

* **crackling,** *n.* **1.** Used depreciatingly of a person. *Rare.* **2. crackling bread,** *S.* corn bread interspersed with cracklings, also attrib.
(1) **1834** CROCKETT *Life* 198, I looked like a pretty cracklin ever to get to Congress! — (2) **1842** in THOMPSON *M. Jones* (1872) 70, I haint eat nothin but back-bone and turnips, and spare-ribs, and sassingers, and cracklin-bread ever sense the killin commenced. **1902** W. S. GORDON *Recoll. Lynchburg* 122 Be it remembered, those were days of crackling-bread epicureanism. **1946** THOMPSON *Amer. Daughter* 84 There was the rendering of lard that brought on crackling bread.

cracky ˈkrækɪ, *n.*[1] Used as an exclamation, usu. *by cracky. Colloq.*
1830 *Painesville* (Ohio) *Telegraph* 15 June 3/2 Oh! Crackee what luck! **1856** M. J. HOLMES *L. Rivers* vi. 66 That's so, by cracky. You've hit her this time, granny. **1946** *Sat. Ev. Post* 11 May 21/1 There will be some changes made, by cracky.

cracky ˈkrækɪ, *n.*[2] [LG. *krakewagen*, a wagon that constantly squeaks.] (See quots. 1890, 1940.) In full **cracky wagon.**
1890 *D.N.* I. 60 *Cracky-wagon*, a one-horse wagon, without springs. Western Pennsylvania. **1893** *Kansas Hist. Coll.* V. 75 He was in what was then known as a 'cracky wagon.' **1940** *Amer. Sp.* XV. 83/1 In isolated mountain communities along the Pennsylvania-West Virginia border. . . . I once heard . . . *cracky*, a small, light wagon, sometimes called a 'spring wagon.'

* **cradle,** *n.*

1. *Mining.* A rocker or boxlike apparatus that may be vigorously agitated by hand in washing out gold-bearing earth. Also fig. *Obs.* Cf. **long tom.**

Cradle (sense 1) or gold rocker

1824 OLMSTEAD *N.C. Geology* 35 Having arrived at the proper stratum . . . he removes it with a spade into the *cradle*. This is a semi-cylinder laid on its side (like a barrel bisected longitudinally and laid flat-wise,) and made to rock with two parallel poles of wood. By rocking the cradle rapidly, the water is thrown over-board, loaded with as much mud as it is capable of suspending. **1848** B. B. MASON *Official Rep.* 17 Aug., About 200 men were at work in the full glare of the sun, washing for gold—. . . the greater part had a rude machine known as the cradle. This is on rockers six or eight feet long, open at the foot. **1852** MOTLEY *Letters* (1889) I. 146, I don't know whether I shall at last find a few grains of pure gold in my cradle, to reward me for my labors. **1948** JOHNSTON *Gold Rush* 23/2 Improvements in the art of recovering gold were manifested in the cradle, the long tom, and, finally, in the sluice.

2. Short for *Cradle of Liberty*, in allusion to Faneuil Hall. Cf. **5.** below. *Obs.*
1844 *N.O. Picayune* 4 Mar. 22/1 On the 4th of March the members of the Clay Club are going to rock the old cradle with a magnificent *shindy*.

3. A kneading trough. *Rare.*
1874 B. F. TAYLOR *World on Wheels* I. 90 The big wooden cradle wherein they kept the dough warm till it 'rose' like any other member of the family.

4. In combs.: (1) **cradle bath,** (see quot.), *rare;* (2) **heap, hill,** a hillock, as of a fallen tree, forming an obstruction in a road, *obs.;* (3) **hole,** (see quot. 1889); (4) **knoll,** (see quot. 1905); (5) **ride,** (see quot.), *obs.;* (6) **rocker,** =**rocker 1,** *obs.;* (7) **shell,** a variety of sea shell; (8) **snatcher,** one who keeps company with or marries one of the opposite sex who is quite young or relatively young, *slang;* (9) **spit,** a form of spit for cooking, *obs.*
(1) **1841** GURNEY *Journey* 181, I well remember the daily pleasure which I enjoyed before breakfast, at Lynn, in the use of the cradle bath, as it was called by the people. It is a hollow in one of the rocks by the sea coast, which nature fills every day with fresh sea water. —

(2) **1830** GALT *Lawrie Todd* I. 186 It was then but the mere blazed line of what was to be a road; stumps and cradle heaps, mud-holes and miry swails, succeeded one another. **1855** HALIBURTON *Nature & Human Nat.* II. 374 The stanhope is in the coach-house, but the bye-road was so full of stumps and cradle-hills, it was impossible to drive in it. — (3) **1840** *Spirit of Times* 1 Feb. 582/1 (We.), Cradle Holes. **1889** *Cent.* 1327/1 cradle-hole.... A rut or slight depression in a road; specifically, such a depression formed in snow which covers a road.... A spot in a road from which the frost is melting. — (4) **1897** ROBINSON *Uncle Lisha* 32 There were moss-covered cradle-knolls and ... mats of sphagnum. **1905** *Forestry Bureau Bul.* No. 61, 34 *Cradle knolls*, small knolls which require grading in the construction of logging roads. (North Woods, Lake States.)

(5) **1871** L. H. BAGG *At Yale* 65 The Freshmen ... could be given a 'cradle ride,' in a vehicle, much like a reversed hen-coop mounted on wheels, which might be dragged swiftly across the stage over the rough clumps of wood carefully placed in its way. — (6) **1889** *Cent.* 1326/3 [The] machine ... resembles in form a child's cradle, and, like it, has rockers; hence also called a *rocker*, and sometimes a *cradle-rocker*. — (7) **1882** E. K. GODFREY *Nantucket* 34 [There are] the 'money' shells, the 'cradle' shell, the 'razor' shell, the many varieties of conch and mussels. — (8) [**1925** *N.Y. Times* 8 Sep. 28/2 'Cradle Snatchers' [the name of a play] is concerned with the activities of three wives.] **1944** HOLTON *Yankees* 10, I can't imagine Father as a cradle snatcher. — (9) **1814** *Niles' Reg.* V. 318/1 Improved and-irons with trevits, do. chafing dishes, do. gridirons and pye pans, cradle spits.

5. Used in phrasal nicknames of various places, as *Cradle of the Confederacy*, *of Liberty*, *of New England*, *of the Revolution*, (see quots.).

1945 *Ala. Hist. Quart.* Spring 70, I could not write a paper on Alabama without talking a bit about Montgomery, 'The Cradle of the Confederacy.' — **1808** J. QUINCY in *Ann. 10th Congress* 2 Sess. 545 It has been asked, ... 'will not Massachusetts, the cradle of liberty, submit to such privations?' **1833** *Niles' Reg.* XLIV. 223/2 Here is true 'chivalry'—within the sound of a halloo from Faneuil Hall, the 'cradle of liberty,' or Bunker's Hill. **1946** *Times-Herald* (Washington, D.C.) 28 Dec. 2/2 Within view of historic Faneuil Hall—'the cradle of liberty'—New England's first treason case since the Revolutionary War opened today. **1947** *Chi. Tribune* 2 Nov. 1. 1/2 You have shown that Philadelphia is still the cradle of liberty and will demonstrate to prevent Russian sympathizers from taking over. — **1809** A. ABBOT *Discourse* (1810) 3 It is with no common emotions, my respected auditors, that I have come to the cradle of New-England [i.e., Plymouth] on this occasion. — **1814** *Niles' Reg.* VI. 1/2 Little did that great man believe that in ten or fifteen years after his death, men in Boston, the 'cradle of the revolution,' should coldly sit down and calculate a separation of the states. **1820** W. TUDOR *Lett. Eastern States* 307 It is natural that the citizens of a town, whose hall for public meetings has been called 'the cradle of the Revolution,' ... should feel a pride in belonging to it.

As the last term in **bark, birchbark, grapevine, Indian, log, mourning cradle.**

* **cradle,** *v. W. Mining. tr.* To wash (gold-bearing earth or gravel) in a cradle. Hence **cradling,** *n. Obs.*

An 1853 example of "cradling" used of the gold-mining operations in Australia has been found in C. Clacy, *Visit to Gold Diggings of Australia*, 117. The verb in the sense shown here may have been first so used in Australia, though the noun, *q.v.*, was in use in the North Carolina gold region as early as 1824.

1858 HOLMES *Autocrat* (1883) 50 Most lives drop a few ... grains of wisdom.... Oftentimes a single cradling sets them all. **1867** W. H. DIXON *New America* II. 14 The White Man ... appears to be the master in every zone ... cradling gold in the Sacramento valleys, ... talking buncombe in Columbia, writing leaders in New York. **1922** *Frontier* May 8 There's just as much gold here as below, but I have to cradle it.

fig. **1860** HOLMES *E. Venner* xvi, When you ask me to cradle for it, I tell you that ... I can do something better than hunt for the grains of truth among their tricks and lies.

***craft,** *n.* As the last term in **ax, plains, sternwheel craft.**

* **cram,** *v. tr.* To fill in (cracks) between logs of a building with mud, to chink. Also absol. *Obs.*

1781 *Cal. Va. State P.* I. 560 [He] has received no assistance from the latter except in 'cramming between the loggs.' **1837** *S. Lit. Messenger* III. 217 A plain building of sawed logs, *crammed*, as we say in Virginia, with mud. **1839** *Ib.* V. 113/1 There ... is the log-hovel, its interstices crammed with reddish earth.

cramberry ˈkræmˌbɛrɪ, *n.* [See note to **cranberry.**] Variant of **cranberry.**

1670 DENTON *Descr. N.Y.* 4 The Fruits natural to the Island are ... Huckelberries, Cramberries. **1758** J. WILLIAMS *Hist. Captivity* 16 They ... gave me the best they had, ... Cramberries, but no Bread. **1901** HEGAN *Mrs. Wiggs* 24, I think I wouldn't 'a' minded so much, ... ef they hadn't 'a' sent the cramberries, too!

attrib. **1671** *Norwalk Rec.* 60 The hill by the path that goes to Cramberry plain. **1685** *Providence Rec.* IV. 227 His meaddow, called cramberry Meaddow. **1808** W. TUDOR *Miscellanies* (1821) 21 Cranberry Sauce [is] vulgarly called cramberry sauce.

* **cramp,** *n.*

1. cramp bark, the bush cranberry, *Viburnum opulus*, the bark of which is used as an antispasmodic.

1848 BARTLETT *Cramp-bark* ... the popular name of a medicinal plant; its properties are anti-spasmodic. It bears a fruit intensely acid. **1942** VAN DERSAL *Ornamental Amer. Shrubs* 109 It is frequently listed as *Viburnum americanum*, and called cramp-bark, highbush cranberry, pembina, and wild guelder-rose.

2. cramp colic, colic accompanied by cramp.

1857 *Harper's Mag.* Nov. 860/2 Jack hath eaten four large potatoes, three big drop dumplings. one boiled fowl, and bread according; ... it was fair to conclude that Jack was dead from cramp-cholic. **1911** R. D. SAUNDERS *Col. Todhunter* 86 Th' ain't none of us Todhunters can eat cucumbers without bein' doubled up with cramp colic. **1944** CLARK *Pills* 236 One of the mortal diseases of the South was 'cramp colic.'

As the last term in **snowshoe, whisky cramp.**

* **cramp,** *v. tr.* To force (a steamboat) in a desired direction. Also transf.

1875 MARK TWAIN *Old Times* iii. 52 Stand by—wait—wait—keep her well in hand. Now cramp her down! *Ib.* iv. 67 Cramp her up to the bar! What are you standing up through the middle of the river for? *Ib.* 70 Twenty times a day we would be cramping up around a bar. **1883** ——— *Life on Miss.* xviii, I told you not to cramp that reef. **1919** CADY *Rhymes of Vt.* (1923) 50 They cramp and back and cramp again And out a-come the helper men.

cranberry ˈkrænˌbɛrɪ, *n.* [See note.]

1. The bright red berry of any one of various plants of the genus *Vaccinium*, or the plant itself.

Regarded in the *OED* as an early American borrowing of LG. *Kraanbere*, but the earliness of the American evidence, together with the presence of the word, and its variant *cramberry*, in British dialect in our sense **1.** leaves this in doubt.

1647 ELIOT *Day-breaking* 11 Why are Strawberries sweet and Cranberries sowre? **1705** BEVERLEY *Virginia* II. 15 Cranberries grow in the low Lands, and barren sunken Grounds, upon low Bushes, like the Gooseberry. **1870** *Rep. Comm. Agric. 1869* 205 Observation shows that the cranberry usually chooses a peaty, or a silicious, moist soil. **1948** *Reader's Digest* Sep. 109/2 We children sometimes gathered cranberries on the salt-marsh.

b. The color of the fruit. Also attrib.

1873 E. S. PHELPS *Trotty's Wedding* xxviii, 'The cranberry tablecloth!' said I. *Ib.*, Alta and I bought eleven rolls of the gray-and-cranberry stripe [wallpaper]. **1877** ——— *Story of Avis* 13 The color was that called variously and lawlessly by upholsterers cranberry, garnet or ponso; known to artists as carmine.

2. In special combs.: (1) **cranberry bean,** (see quot. 1790), *obs.*; (2) **bog,** a low, wet area in which cranberries abound; (3) **field,** a field in which cranberries grow; (4) **gatherer,** a cranberry rake; (5) **marsh,** =**cranberry bog;** (6) **meadow,** a meadow in which cranberries grow; (7) **potato,** (see quot.), *obs.*; (8) **pudding,** a pudding of cranberries; (9) **rake,** an implement used in gathering cranberries; (10) **sauce,** stewed cranberries; (11) **State,** (see quot.); (12) **swamp,** a swamp in which cranberries abound; (13) **tart,** a tart containing cranberries; (14) **tree,** the high or bush cranberry, *Viburnum opulus;* (15) **worm,** =**fireworm.**

(1) **1790** S. DEANE *N.-Eng. Farmer* 20/1 The cranberry-bean is so called from the resemblance it bears, when ripe, to that fruit. **1941** *L.A.* Map 259 Cranberry beans ... [are] speckled, smaller and more round than lima beans. — (2) **1807** *Mass. H.S. Coll.* 2 Ser. III. 94 They annually sell a hundred or two hundred bushels of craneberries, which grow in great plenty in their craneberry bogs. **1948** *Sat. Ev. Post* 4 Dec. 70/3 Caleb got lost and wandered down The bottom land to the cranberry bogs. — (3) **1870** *Rep. Comm. Agric. 1869* 205 There are cultivated cranberry fields in Maine, Massachusetts, Connecticut, and New Jersey. **1906** *Country Life* Nov. 72 It would be a difficult matter to determine the cost of transforming these swampy tracts into producing cranberry fields. — (4) **1874** KNIGHT 642/1 [The] cranberry-gatherer ... [is] adapted to catch below the berries on the stalk, and collect them in a bag or box attached to the rake-head.

(5) [**1748** ELIOT *Field-Husb.* i. 4 There are three Kinds, viz. Thick Swamp, Boggy Meadow, and smooth, even, shaking Meadow; this last sort is called Cramberry Marsh.] **1832** *Boston Transcript* 21 Jan. 1/1 She had a harsh face, like a cranberry marsh all spread with spots of white and red, as if she had the measles. **1924** DEAM *Shrubs of Indiana* 278 We have records of cranberry marshes as far south as

Warren County. — (6) **1749** ELIOT *Field-Husbandry* ii. 35 The way to get out of this Difficulty . . . is by clearing and dreining Swamps, Cran-berry and Bog Meadows. **1892** B. TORREY *Foot-Path Way* 197, I walked down the bay shore of Cape Cod . . . meaning to look into a large cranberry meadow. **1939** *L.A.* Map 29, 30. — (7) **1790** SAMUEL DEANE *N.-Eng.Farmer* 224/2 We have had. . . . A long red potatoe. . . . A large white potatoe, a great bearer, known by the name of flour-potatoe. . . . Cranberry potatoe, and winter white. — (8) *c***1795** in *Ore. Hist. Quart.* XXVIII. 268 For the last month . . . the people (on board the Ruby anchored in Columbia River) has had three fresh Dinners in a Week with the addition of Cranberrie Pudding on Sundays. **1832** L. M. CHILD *Frugal Housewife* 64 Cranberry Pudding. A pint of cranberries stirred into a quart of batter [etc.]. — (9) **1849** *Cultivator* n. s. VII. 52, I have used a wooden machine, made like a cranberry rake, . . . to gather my clover-seed this season. **1913** *Country Life* April 140/3 A 'blueberry rake' . . . is an implement similar to the cranberry rake in use on Cape Cod.

(10) **1767** J. ADAMS *Diary* 8 April, Tufts . . . determined to go over and bring [them] . . . to dine upon wild goose, and cranberry sauce. **1948** *Reader's Digest* March 147/2 We were winding up a huge supper of moose, roast grouse, cranberry sauce. — (11) **1870** MCCLUNG *Minnesota* 150 The extent of the growth of this fruit in Minnesota is wonderful—so remarkable that formerly we were called 'The Cranberry State.' — (12) **1664** *Norwalk Rec.* 51, 3 parcells of meadow, and called Cranbury Swamp. **1891** RYAN *Pagan of Alleghanies* 183, I've seen the light on the cranberry-swamp myself. — (13) **1711** WILLIAM BYRD *Secret Diary* (1941) 436, I said my prayers and ate some cranberry tart for breakfast. **1875** STOWE *Deacon Pitkin's Farm* 38 You seem to have nothing on your mind but the responsibility for all those pumpkin pies and cranberry tarts. — (14) **1814** PURSH *Flora* I. 203. **1847** DARLINGTON *Weeds & Plants* 163 Cranberry-tree. Bush, or High Cranberry. **1892** APGAR *Trees Northern U.S.* 114 Fruit in peduncled clusters, light red and quite sour (whence the name 'Cranberry-tree').

(15) **1871** *Amer. Naturalist* IV. 685 The yellow cranberry worm . . . of the New Jersey cranberry fields.

Also *cranberry bush, cove, crop, culture, district, farm, farmer, grower, jelly, juice, land, picker, picking, pie, plain, raising, separator, vine*, etc.

As the last term in **bugle, bush, cherry, high, hog, mock, mountain, tree, upland cranberry.**

cranberrying ˈkræn͵berɪ·ɪŋ, *n.* The picking of cranberries. — **1830** in *N. Eng. Mag.* 1895 Nov. 319/2 Oct. 17. Acranberrying with Rebecca, tired. **1881** MCLEAN *Cape Cod Folks* 275 She hires a room, and Beck she's saved a little money cranberryin'.

***crane,** *n.*

1. A structure beside a railway from which a mail pouch is suspended to be taken by the mail catcher of a passing train.

1875 *Chi. Tribune* 18 Sep. 5/3 For the use of this fast mail train it has been necessary to erect a crane at every post office on the line of the road. **1890** *Railways of Amer.* 313 On the other [side was] a representation of the fast mail train, the 'catcher' taking a pouch from the 'crane' as it passes at the rate of fifty miles an hour! **1946** *Colo. School Jrnl.* Dec. 2/2 Even when a train rushes past a station without stopping, a metal arm reaches out and sweeps in a mail sack suspended from a track-side crane.

2. In obs. combs.: (1) **crane dance,** (see quot.); (2) ***neck squash,** prob. the crook-neck squash; (3) **potato,** (see quot. and cf. **cranberry potato**), *obs.*

(1) **1858** WILKIE *Davenport* 29 Our [Sac] women plant the corn, and as soon as they get done, we make a feast, and dance the *crane* dance in which they join us, dressed in their best. . . . At this feast our young braves select the young woman they wish to have for a wife. — (2) **1778** CARVER *Travels* 525 Of these there is the round, the crane-neck, the small flat, and the large oblong Squash. — (3) **1820** in MORSE *Rep. Indian Affairs* (1822) II. 34 The crane potatoe is another article of food, called by them the Sitch-auc-waub-es-sec-pin.

As the last term in **blue, brown, clamshell, great blue, hooping, large brown, prairie, sand-hill, sandy hill, Savannah, white, whooping, wrecking crane.**

crank kræŋk, *n.*[1] [?f. ***cranky,** *a.*] One having a crotchet or mental twist, one mentally unbalanced on some subject.

Regarded in *OED* (and thence in *DAE*) as an Americanism, but late evidence for it occurs in *EDD q.v.* Its use became general at and after the trial of Charles Guiteau in 1881. Thornton (mainly in the *Supp.*) gives eleven examples between 1882 and 1910.

1833 in DUNN *Indiana* (1919) II. 1124 Uncle Sam's 'old Mother Bank' Is managed by a foreign crank. **1881** in HAYES *Guiteau* 275 Thus you will see that a man may be here who has been styled a crank or off his balance and even partially insane and yet may be abundantly responsible for crime. **1947** *Time* 3 Feb. 46/3 Audiences used to be largely record collectors and cranks who also liked folk dancing because it was pure and sexless.

attrib. **1948** *Dly. Ardmoreite* (Ardmore, Okla.) 21 April 1/3 He gets a lot of crank letters and these I threw away.

***crank,** *n.*[2] **1. crank box,** a signaling device consisting of a box provided with a crank. **2. crank car,** a car drawn by a cable which is wound on a fixed axle. Both *rare.* — (1) **1873** in *43d Congress* 1 Sess. H.R. Ex. Doc. No. 190, 3 The old time 'crank-boxes,' upon which we rely in great part for our alarms, . . . are entirely unfit for the purpose. — (2) **1833** *Amer. R.R. Jrnl.* II. 325/2 [There are] 4 crank cars.

***cranked,** *a.* Mentally unbalanced. *Rare.* — **1881** *N.Y. Herald* 9 Dec. 4/3 He thought I was badly cranked about my book.

crankism ˈkræŋkɪzəm, *n.* The attitude or behavior characteristic of a crank *q.v. Obs.*

1882 *Cong. Rec.* 13 February 1106/2 Such mathematics is contaminated with congenital infirmity. . . . It is crankism applied to figures. **1888** *Nation* 22 March 236/2 It may indeed be looked upon as a pyrotechnic illustration of crankism. **1890** *Troy D. Times* 15 Nov. 2/3 The epidemic of crankism which has prevailed.

***crape,** *n.* **1. crape myrtle,** an ornamental shrub, *Lagerstroemia indica*, common in the southern states. Also attrib. **2. crape tree,** =prec.

(1) **1850** B. TAYLOR *Eldorado* i, The houses of the planters . . . are buried among orange trees, acacias and the pink blossoms of the crape myrtle. **1893** *Harper's Mag.* Feb. 464 Sonny slep' in a crape-myrtle tree ev'ry night for a week once-t. **1948** *Dly. Ardmoreite* (Ardmore, Okla.) 18 April 16/2 Ardmore folk became crape myrtle conscious a few years ago and this city has many lovely crape myrtles as a result. — (2) **1910** C. HARRIS *Eve's Husb.* 113 We were sitting upon a bench near a flowering pink crape tree.

crappie ˈkræpɪ, *n.* Also **croppie.** [App. f. F. dial. *crape*, or LG. *krape*.] A name applied to several North American fresh-water fishes of the Great Lake and Mississippi Valley region, esp. *Pomoxis annularis* and the related calico bass *q.v.*

1856 *Spirit of Times* 20 Sep. 43/1 Our best fish are the pike and salmon, . . . striped, rock and black bass, croppy, and the common sunfish. **1889** FARMER 184/2 Croppie, a local name for a species of green bass found in Lake Minnetonka. **1948** *Denison* (Tex.) *Herald* 1 July 1/4 He was pretty disgusted with his catch of seven tiny crappie.

b. crappie bass, (see quot.).

1947 *Collier's* 29 Mar. 93/1 All these following 'bass' also are sunfish: Redeye bass, warmouth bass, rock bass, crappie bass, calico bass and blue bass.

craps kræps, *n.* Also **crap,** esp. in attrib. use. [See note.]

The *OED* records *crabs*, the lowest throw at the game of hazard, as early as 1768. This form was taken over into French in the form *crabs, craps*, as the name of the game of hazard. From French in the New Orleans area *craps* in our sense **1** passed into American use. See H. Asbury, *Sucker's Progress*, 40 ff.

1. A gambling game played with dice, being a simplified form of the much older game of hazard.

1843 J. H. GREEN *Expos. Gambling* 88 The Game of Craps . . . is a game lately introduced into New Orleans, and is fully equal to faro in its . . . ruinous effects. **1893** *Chi. Tribune* 2 April 37/3 Finally a negro condescended to accommodate the gentleman from Iowa with a game of craps. **1944** *Chi. D. News* 19 Dec. 8/6, I was amazed to discover how much of our language comes from craps.

b. (See quots.)

1891 QUINN *Fools of Fortune* 277 The numbers 7 and 11 are called 'craps.' **1909** WEBSTER *s.v.* craps, The caster throws or 'shoots' the dice, and wins if the throw is 7 or 11 (called a *nick* or *natural*), but loses if it is 2, 3, or 12 (called a *crap*). **1946** MOREHEAD & MOTT-SMITH *Penguin Hoyle* 218 He loses if it is 2, 3, or 12 (*craps*); he has a *point* to make if it is 4, 5, 6, 8, 9 or 10.

c. (See quots.) *Obs.*

1859 MATSELL *Vocabulum* 111 Craps or Props. A game peculiar to Boston. Sometimes it is played with shells, and sometimes with coffee-beans, but more generally the former, as they can be loaded. . . . It is a substitute for the dice. [**1938** ASBURY *Sucker's Prog.* 47 Except among Negroes who had come up from the South, Craps was almost unknown in the East until the 1890's, although in the 1850's a game was played in Boston which was occasionally called by that name. More often, however, it was known as Props.]

2. In combs. of obvious meaning, as (1) **crap board,** *obs.*, (2) **game,** (3) **house,** (4) **roller,** (5) **shooter,** (6) **shooting,** (7) **table.**

(1) **1887** *Courier-Journal* 19 Feb. 6/5 The contrivance aforesaid was what is commonly called a 'crap' board and dice. — (2) **1891** QUINN *Fools of Fortune* 539 The 'clock,' policy playing, 'crap' games, and the sale of lottery tickets run on as though there were no let or

hindrance imposed by State law. **1948** *Chi. D. News* 6 Jan. 10/7 He took some $18,000 off the track that day, and doubled it that night in a crap game. — **(3) 1888** *Mo. Republican* Feb. (F.), When arrested he was in the negro crap-house kept by Alex Wells. — **(4) 1891** QUINN *Fools of Fortune* 277 He dropped $10 to the 'crap' roller, expressed himself as satisfied, and we returned to the cabin.

(5) 1895 *Westm. Gaz.* 13 Aug. 8/1 Most of the orders come from the Southern negro 'crap-shooters.' **1948** *Time* 12 April 25/2 When the Boss needed money, his boys put a deeper bite on the brothel-keepers, bookies and crap-shooters. — **(6) 1885** *Boston Journal* 6 June 1/8 Dallas, Texas. . . . 250 negroes are being tried for 'crap-shooting,' a game played with dice. **1946** MOREHEAD & MOTT-SMITH *Penguin Hoyle* 218 There is little to skilful play in crapshooting other than knowing the odds concerned in various bets. — **(7) 1857** J. H. GREENE *Gambling Exposed* 205 Ask many of the merchants what has resulted to them in consequence of their clerks being decoyed to the craps table. **1948** *Omaha World-Herald* 20 June 1/5 Business at the roulette wheels and crap tables has been restored to pre-primary election levels.

b. *To shoot craps*, to play craps.

1891 *N. & Q.* VIII. 41 There is a sort of gambling game, called *crap*, or 'shooting crap,' much played by newsboys, bootblacks and negroes. . . . Can any correspondent describe the game? **1948** *Ariz. Republic* (Phoenix) 29 Feb. I. 3/3 They may be just shootin' craps!

***crash,** *v. tr.* To gain admittance without having the proper credentials. *Slang.* Cf. **gate crasher.** — **1925** WITWER *Roughly Speaking* 124 Even the discovery of Jerry Murphy and Pete Kift, who were sitting in back of us and declared they had crashed the gate, failed to depress me. **1944** JOHNSON *As I Dare* 341 He got away for a trip to Denver, crashed his way into a big gambling game, sank all his roll, and practically broke the bank.

crate kret, *v.* [f. the noun.] *tr.* To pack in a crate for transportation (see note).

The first quot. refers to the frontier amusement of turning a strong crate over a drunken person and weighting it down so as to imprison him.

1871 EGGLESTON *Hoosier Schoolm.* xi. 99 The boys thought 'twas funny to crate me. **1897** *Outing* XXX. 366/1 Crated and swathed in white clothes, it appeared like a mummy. **1945** *Readers' Digest* June 11/1 There time is required to crate and load the equipment.

crate wheat. A now unidentifiable variety of wheat. *Obs.* — **1849** EMMONS *Agric. N.Y.* II. 140 Velvet-beard or Crate wheat . . . has been cultivated about twenty years in Western New-York. **1849** *Rep. Comm. Patents: Agric.* (1850) 104 The kinds of wheat heretofore most highly approved were 'red-chaff,' 'crate' and 'Hutchinson.'

cravat goose. The Canada goose, *Branta canadensis.* — **1889** *Cent.* 1336/1 Cravat-goose . . . [is named] from the white mark on the throat. **1917** *Birds of Amer.* I. 158 Canada Goose. . . . Other names [include] Wild Goose; Common Wild Goose; Cravat Goose [etc.].

crawdad ˈkrɔˌdæd, *n. local.* [Of fanciful formation.] A crawfish.— **1905** *D.N.* III. 76 crawdad *n.* Crawfish [nw. Ark.] **1948** *Dly. Ardmoreite* (Ardmore, Okla.) 21 April 7/5 Most boys of that age are content with crawdads but Leonard's specialty is bream.

Hence **crawdadding.** — **1933** T. WILLIAMSON *Woods Colt* 138 Mighty small taters an' few in the hill, I says to him, so don't you go to crawdaddin.'

* **crawfish,** *n.*

1. A fresh-water crustacean belonging to any one of numerous species of the genus *Cambarus.*

1624 SMITH *Gen. Hist. Va.* v. 175 Great craw-fishes . . . they have taken in great quantity. **1709** LAWSON *Carolina* 163 Craw-Fish, in the Brooks, and small rivers of water, amongst the Tuskeruro Indians, . . . are found very plentifully. **1814** BRACKENRIDGE *Views* 177 An immense quantity of water finds its way through the embankment, mostly through holes made by crawfish. **1948** *Capital-Democrat* (Tishomingo, Okla.) 17 June 8/3 They had . . . several nice size catfish caught on jug-lines baited with cut carp and crawfish.

2. In combs.: (1) **crawfish band,** an Indian tribe, allegedly having originated from crawfish, speaking a Choctaw-Chickasaw dialect and formerly living on the Yazoo River in Mississippi, *obs.;* (2) **chimney,** the mud tower at the entrance to a crawfish hole; (3) **hole,** a hole made by a crawfish; (4) **land,** (see quot. and cf. **crawfishy,** *a.*); (5) **plan,** (see **crawfish,** *v.*); (6) **soil,** (see quot. and cf. **crawfish land**).

(1) *c***1836** CATLIN *Indians* II. 128 Our people have amongst them a band which is called, the *Craw-fish band.* They formerly . . . lived under ground, and used to come up out of the mud. — **(2) 1940** WILSON *Wabash* 201 There he is—old Mr. Coon—running along the bank as solemn and intent and as spry as a little, old man. He is inspecting crawfish chimneys; and, when he finds one that suits him, he pushes it over and, with great deliberation, runs his arm down into the hole. — **(3) 1889** RILEY *Pipes o' Pan* 79 But the sun, hit blazed away, Till I jest clumb down in a crawfish-hole. — **(4) 1905** *D.N.* III. 132 Crawfish land. . . . Low, watersoaked ground. [nw. Ark.]

(5) 1875 *Cong. Rec.* 12 Jan. 397/1, I cannot consent to 'turn back.' . . . I am not constructed upon the craw-fish plan. My way must be on. — **(6) 1857** OLMSTED *Journey through Texas* 360 Having a wet, sandy or 'craw-fish' soil.

crawfish ˈkrɔˌfɪʃ, *v.* [f. the noun.] *intr.* To move or crawl backwards. Usu. fig. in the sense of to back out or withdraw from a position or agreement. *Colloq.*

1842 in THOMPSON *M. Jones* (1872) 22, I crawfished out of that place monstrous quick, you may depend. **1850** *Quincy* (Ill.) *Whig* 12 Nov. 1/5 The council met the next day and 'craw-fished'—withdrawing the resolutions by an almost unanimous vote. **1888** J. KIRKLAND *McVeys* 302 Reach your years? I like that! I should have to 'crawfish' to achieve that. **1948** *Range Riders Western* May 79/2 I'd hate to be in your shoes, Lafe, when Frank hears you crawfished.

Hence **crawfisher,** one who crawfishes; **crawfishing,** a backing out or unmanly withdrawing. *Colloq.*

1873 *Winfield* (Kansas) *Courier* 31 July 2/2, I apprehend that readers of our articles can easily see that you have been guilty of what the boys would call 'crawfishing.' **1901** G. ADE *40 Modern Fables* 209, I have got you to the Point from which there can be no Craw-fishing. You could not Weaken now. **1912** *Out West* Jan. 77/2 If you know anything about a crawfisher's life, you know that he has a lot of time for monkeying around after pulling his pots in the morning.

crawfishy ˈkrɔˌfɪʃɪ, *a.* (See quot. 1859.) Cf. **crawfish land, soil.** — **1859** BARTLETT 107 *Crawfishy*, a term applied to wet land, because inhabited by crawfish. **1883** SMITH *Geol. Survey Ala.* 363 In wet lowlands there is much . . . 'crawfishy' land, which is worthless unless improved; but by thorough ditching . . . the crawfishy character disappears.

***crawl,** *n.* **a.** (See quot.) *Obs.* **b.** *W.* An act on the part of a hunter of creeping up on buffalo. *Obs.* Cf. next. — **(a) 1838** AUDUBON *Ornith. Biog.* IV. 46 We discovered a well-beaten path . . . , very much resembling those made by the Beaver, to which hunters give the name of 'crawls.' — **(b) 1850** GARRARD *Wah-To-Yah* i. 24 The immense herds feeding and running near camp enticed the men to many a 'crawl' that evening, and more than one greenhorn took his first trembling and unsuccessful shot.

* **crawl,** *v.*

1. *W. intr.* To advance *on* or *upon* (one's quarry) in a stealthy manner.

1820 DEWEES *Lett. Texas* 18 We crawled up to them and succeeded in creasing a fine, large horse. **1844** GREGG *Commerce of Prairies* II. 218 A dextrous hunter will sometimes 'crawl upon' a gang of buffalo, on a perfectly level plain. **1875** *Fur, Fin, & Feather* 105 The ladies can sit in the wagon and see 'pa' or 'Augustus' running the buffalo or 'crawling on' the antelope.

2. *tr.* To mount or manage (a horse). *Slang.*

1893 REMINGTON in *Harper's Mag.* Dec. 75/1 Anything and everything is his [the administrator's] work, from the negotiation for the sale of five thousand head of cattle to the 'busting' of a bronco, which no one else can 'crawl.'

3. crawl out, *n.*, a backdown. *Colloq.*

1903 A. H. LEWIS *The Boss* 184 That's a crawl-out, . . . an' it aint worthy of you.

***crawler,** *n.* (See quot. 1889.) Cf. **night crawler.** — **1884** *Standard Nat. Hist.* II. 156 They [*Corydalus cornutus*] are called by fishermen 'crawlers,' 'dobsons,' and sometimes . . . 'hellgrammites.' **1889** *Cent.* 1285/2 The hellgrammite . . . is much used for bait by anglers, who call it *dobson* and *crawler.*

***Craw-thumper,** *n.* [f. its derisive application to Roman Catholics.] A nickname for an inhabitant of Maryland. *Obs.* Cf. **Claw-thumper.** — **1845** *St. Louis Reveille* 14 May 2/4 The inhabitants of . . . Maryland [are called] Craw-thumpers. **1948** *Dly. Ardmoreite* (Ardmore, Okla.) 11 July 21/5 Nebraskans have been dubbed 'Bug Eaters'; Marylanders as 'Craw Thumpers.'

* **crayfish,** *n.* = **crawfish,** *n.*

1784 T. HUTCHINS *Top. Descr. La.* 30 Cray-fish abound in this country. **1883** MARK TWAIN *Life on Miss.* xlix, In his suite was a tall pyramid of scarlet crayfish. **1948** *Chr. Sci. Mon.* 6 March 8/3 If one wasn't catching crawdads (the South's affectionate term for the crayfish) he fished for sunfish.

crayfishing ˈkreˌfɪʃɪŋ, *n.* The catching of crayfish. *Rare.* — **1835** INGRAHAM *South-West* I. 174 Others were engaged in the delicate amusement of cray-fishing.

* **crazy,** *a.*

1. *absol.* One who is crazy. *Colloq.*

1867 GOSS *Soldier's Story* 30, I was addressed as 'old crazy' by my companions, and told to keep still. **1889** *Harper's Mag.* Oct. 702/1 The doctor from the crazies . . . tried all kinds o' brainy tricks on her but her head was 's sound as their own.

2. In combs.: (1) **crazy bait,** prob. the plant, devil's shoestrings, *Tephrosia virginiana,* which when bruised and placed in a stream stupefies fish and renders them easy to take (see *Amer. Sp.*, April, 1942, pp. 133–4), *obs.;* (2) **bone,** see as a main entry; (3) **mother,** (see quot.); (4) **patchwork,** patchwork of pieces of cloth of irregular shapes, colors, and sizes; (5) **quilt,** a quilt made of pieces of cloth of various sizes, colors, and shapes, also transf. and attrib.; (6) **set,** *a.* foolishly bent, *rare;* (7) **stitch,** any one of various fancy stitches used in making a crazy quilt; (8) **weed,** *W.* =**loco-weed.**

(1) 1867 *Penna. Laws* 1068 Any person, or persons, found guilty of throwing crazy bait, cocculus indicus, lime, or any other poisonous drug, or substance, into any of the streams aforesaid shall . . . pay a fine of forty dollars. — **(3) 1890** *Amer. Jrnl. Psych.* Jan. 66 In some games like 'crazy mother,' younger children are commanded, or older ones stumped or dared, to do dangerous things. — **(4) 1885** *Harper's Mag.* March 531/2 Here . . . is an autograph portière with alternate stripes of 'crazy patchwork' embroidered on crimson turcoman.

(5) 1886 *Harper's Wkly.* 13 Mar. 174/3 To Embroider Crazy Quilts [etc.]. **1888** *Boston Ev. Jrnl.* 20 June, A Washington letter gives a clever sketch of the conversation which recently took place at the house of a matron who receives a hundred or two of people on the afternoon of 'her day.' 'Crazy quilt conversation,' the hostess declared it to be. **1948** *Time* 29 Mar. 42/2 There were many other pieces in the political crazy quilt. — **(6)** *c***1849** PAIGE *Dow's Sermons* I. 49 All of you [who] are so crazy-set for this new El Dorado will find, eventually, that you must dig for potatoes as well as for gold. — **(7) 1886** *Harper's Wkly.* 13 Mar. 174/3 Designs for 100 styles of Crazy Stitches enclosed in each package. — **(8) 1889** *Cent.* 1337 Crazy-weed . . . [being eaten] by horses and cattle produces emaciation, nervous derangements, and death. **1939** *Nat. Geog. Mag.* Aug. 247/1 This is eminently true of this section of the pea family, known as 'locoweeds' or 'crazyweeds,' for death by slow poison lies in wait for man or beast that may be inclined to feast upon the foliage.

b. In phrases: *Crazy as a bed-bug, crazy as a loon,* see the nouns.

crazy bone. The funny bone. Also transf.

1876 A. D. WHITNEY *Sights & Insights* I. 148 Do you remember the old 'Boston days?' When we went into the city shopping . . . holding on to . . . our accumulated packages with our 'crazy-bones?' **1878** B. F. TAYLOR *Between Gates* 204 There were about fifty elbows to that grade [of the road], and the horses . . . struck 'the crazy-bone' and George reined them in just in time—it was a crazy-bone pretty much all the way. **1887** *Courier-Journal* 16 Jan. 16/6 When Loto scrambled up out of that drawer, with lame ankle and aching shoulder, and a stinging 'crazy bone,' she felt very sickly indeed.

***cream,** *n.*

1. Short for ***creamer.** *Obs.*

1800 *Independent Chronicle* (*advt.*) XXXII. 2–6 Jan. 4/4 Staple Goods. . . . Silvered Tea Urns; with Coffee Pots, Tea Pots, Sugars and Creams to match. **1819** *Detroit Gazette* (*advt.*) II. 2 July 3/3 Crockery. Coffee and Tea cups. . . . Sugars and Creams.

2. Short for **ice cream.** Cf. **cream-freezer.**

1851 W. K. NORTHALL *Curtain* 113 The old temple being consecrated to bad music and excellent cream. **1898** WESTCOTT *D. Harum* 222 'Don't gi' me but jest a teasp'nful o' that ice cream. . . .' He took a taste of the cream and resumed. **1910** *Sat. Ev. Post* 13 Aug. 35/3 It makes a smoother, better grade of cream than ordinary freezers.

3. In combs.: (1) **cream biscuit,** a biscuit in the making of which cream is used; (2) **candy,** a hard, white pulled candy, or one having a foundation of fondant; (3) **Cream City,** (see quot. 1868); (4) **cup,** any one of several California annuals of the poppy family; (5) **-freezer,** an ice cream freezer; (6) **pie,** a pastry shell or layer cake with creamy filling; (7) **pitcher,** a small pitcher for cream; (8) ***pot,** a breed of cattle developed *c*1820 in Massachusetts, also attrib., *obs.;* (9) **soap,** (see quot.), *obs.;* (10) **soda,** (see quot.); (11) **soup,** soup in the making of which milk or cream is used; (12) **tartar,** cream of tartar, also attrib.; (13) **toast,** toast over which cream or cream sauce has been poured, cf. **milk toast.**

(1) 1863 A. D. WHITNEY *F. Gartney* xiv, I'll make some cream biscuits like Aunt Faith's. **1898** I. H. HARPER *S. B. Anthony* I. 44 Later when visiting her brother-in-law, . . . she made some especially nice cream biscuits for supper. — **(2) 1855** M. THOMPSON *Doesticks* xiv. 116, I couldn't eat anything for a fortnight but oranges, cream candy, and vanilla-beans. **1886** *Harper's Mag.* June 94/1 Cream or soft candies are made in a simple way, from sugar mixed with cream of tartar to prevent crystallizing. **1901** CHURCHILL *Crisis* 151 They were chewing cream candy in unison. — **(3) 1867** *Chi. Times* 27 July 6/2 The game was opened by the Cream City club going to bat. **1868** HANKINS *Dakota Land* 443 The peculiar color of brick and stone almost exclusively used in building up Milwaukee, led to its being fitly sobriqueted the 'Cream City.' **1902** *Sears Cat.* (ed. 112) 787/1 Cream City Flour Bin and Sifter. — **(4) 1888** LINDLEY *Calif. of South* 328 Two weeks later rank patches, with open, bright-yellow flowers, appear in company with blue *Nemophilas*, nodding cream-cups, purple *Calendrinias*, and yellow violets. **1946** R. PEATTIE *Pac. Coast Ranges* 53 One could go on to speak of . . . dainty creamcups and tidytips, of little Johnny-tuck.

(5) 1861 HOLMES *E. Venner* vii, The Colonel . . . had agitated a quantity of sweetened and thickened milk in what was called a cream-freezer. — **(6) 1805** *Pocumtuc Housewife* (1906) 25 [Recipe for] Cream Pie. **1876** M. F. HENDERSON *Cooking* 300 Cream Cake or Pie . . . is an excellent dessert cut as a pie, or it may be served as a cake for tea. **1898** S. HALE *Letters* 337 An excellent dinner soon steamed on the table,—roast beef, salad, cream-pie. — **(7) 1838** [in the plant-name *devil's cream-pitcher, q.v.*]. **1860** HOLMES *E. Venner* xxi, The Widow shall have the credit of her well-ordered tea-table, also of her bountiful cream-pitchers. **1905** VALENTINE *H. Sandwith* 50 She approved of her cream pitchers—silver cows with curled tails and noses that gurgled milk—since they afforded her boarders polite amusement. **1944** *Sears Cat.* (ed. 189) 611. — **(8) 1862** *Rep. Comm. Patents: Agric.* 433 Colonel Jaques . . . succeeded in establishing a tribe of cattle possessing a certain similarity which he called 'Cream Pots,' and which attained a degree of local reputation. **1867** *Rep. Comm. Agric. 1866* 291 The original dam of the 'Cream Pot' breed of stock was a large, light roan short-horn cow. — **(9) 1857** *Lawrence* (Kans.) *Republican* 28 May 4 Take it [vessel] off, and in a few hours you will have some nice hard or 'Cream Soap.'

(10) 1889 FARMER, Cream soda, a favorite drink of American women. It is composed of ice cream mixed with soda water. — **(11) 1888** L. HARGIS *Graded Cook Book* 13 Amber Cream Soup. . . . One pint cream, one pint milk, pinch of salt, pinch of cinnamon, three eggs. **1904** *Delineator* Aug. 290 Cream soups, bouillons or chowders are made in the morning and warmed for dinner. — **(12) 1790** *Pa. Packet* 1 Jan. 4/1 A fresh . . . assortment of drugs and medicines, among which are . . . cream tartar, jalap [etc.]. **1857** COLLINS *Great West. Cook Book* 59 Cream Tartar Biscuit. **1879** A. D. WHITNEY *Just How* 14 Two teaspoonfuls of cream-tartar to one of soda. — **(13) 1856** M. J. HOLMES *L. Rivers* xxvi. 285 On entering the kitchen she found Aunt Milly preparing a rich cream toast. **1891** *Harper's Mag.* Dec. 49/2 My cousin Flagg, with his mind undistracted by relays of cream toast, could give his entire attention to the Lost Cause.

As the last term in **ice, Neapolitan (ice), scuppernong ice cream.**

***creamer,** *n.* A small pitcher used for cream.

1877 PHELPS *Story of Avis* 237 That rose-curlew on the creamer is like a singing leaf. **1893** THANET *Stories Western Town* 215 She re-

A cream or creamer

membered the silver service, the coffee-pot, . . . the creamer, . . . the sugar-bowl. **1948** *Dly. Ardmoreite* (Ardmore, Okla.) 30 Mar. 3/6 Consists of 6 dinner plates, . . . 2-piece covered sugar and 1 creamer.

creamery ˈkrimərɪ, *n.*

1. A small building in which milk is stored. *Rare.*

1858 *Harper's Mag.* June 44/2 Come down with me to the creamery, and we'll cool off before dinner.

2. A place where milk, butter, and cheese are prepared for market. Also attrib.

1872 *Vt. Bd. Agric. Rep.* I. 164 Mr. Bliss spoke of the creameries in New York. **1881** *Bradstreet's* 26 Nov. 349/2 Creamery butter sold at 30 @ 32c. **1948** *Land o' Lakes News* Jan. 5/2 Farmer Bill delivered his Milk to the Private Creamery.

b. A specially made tank in which milk is stored to allow the cream to rise.

1902 *Sears Cat.* (ed. 112) 798/2 In this manner of operating The Peerless Creamery, capacity for storing two milkings must be provided; in other words, order a creamery of double the capacity that you would were you intending to use ice.

3. Ellipt. for "creamery butter."

*a*1877 *N.Y. Bulletin* (B.), In the general features of the butter market there is no change. The fine creameries are considered well sold at 23 cts.... Western creamery, 22 cts. **1881** *Chi. Times* 14 May, The current makes of creamery are already beginning to show a good deal of grass flavor and color. **1902** *Boston Ev. Globe* 18 Feb. 4/5 Reworked or ladle butter, 14 to 17 cents, imitation creamery, 17 to 19 cents.

* **crease,** *v. W. tr.* To stun (a wild horse, steer, etc.) by the impact of a bullet, orig. with reference to capturing wild horses by shooting them in the crest of the neck. Now *hist.* Cf. next.

1808 Pike *Sources Miss.* 159 We fired at a black horse, with an idea of creasing him, but did not succeed. **1839** *Knickerb.* XIII. 247 In hunter's parlance, I had 'only creased him' [i.e., a stag]. **1913** Mulford *Coming of Cassidy* 119 The drawing bar-tender, ... dazed from shock of a ball that 'creased' his head. **1943** DeVoto *Yr. of Decis.* 59 Encountering some wild horses, he tried to crease one but broke its neck.

* **creasing,** *n. W.* Shooting a wild horse in the crest of the neck to stun and so capture it.

1820 W. B. Dewees *Lett. from Texas* (1852) 18 We discovered a large herd of Mustangs searching for water ... crawled up to them and succeeded in creasing a fine, large horse. **1844** Gregg *Commerce of Prairies* II. 208 The mustang is sometimes taken by the cruel expedient of 'creasing,' which consists in shooting him through the upper *crease* of the neck, above the cervical vertebræ. **1923** J. H. Cook *On Old Frontier* 69 A third method of capture is by 'Creasing.'

* **creation,** *n.*

1. Used as an interjection. *Colloq.*

1843 Haliburton *Attaché* II. ix. 159 'Creation, man,' said Mr. Slick, 'I have done it ... and you didn't know it.' **1847** Robb *Squatter Life* 90 'Cre-*a*-tion and the deluge" shouted Jonathan. *Ib.* 138 Cre-*a*-tion, how tough he war. **1922** *D.N.* V. 265.

2. A large number, a multitude. *Colloq. Obs.*

1852 Watson *Nights in Block-House* 28 We saw a whole swarm of the red-skins comin' down on us, yellin' like a whole creation of wild-cats. *Ib.* 50 He fought like a creation of wild-cats.

3. *all creation,* everyone or everything, esp. *in* (or *like*) *all creation,* with intensive force. Also *to beat* (or *lick*) *all creation.*

1825 Neal *Bro. Jonathan* I. 257 Giving out his challenge ... in a loud voice, for 'Indian hug' ... or 'close hug'—to 'all creation.' **1834** S. Smith *Sel. Lett. Downing* 14 But when in all creation any of 'em will be finished I guess it would puzzle a Philadelphy lawyer to tell. **1853** *Knickerb.* Sep. 122 (Th.), 'Heavenly marcies!' sez she, 'if that don't beat creation!' **1891** Farmer *Slang s.v. creation, To beat* or *lick creation* (American), to overpower; excel; surpass; to be incomparable. **1917** H. T. Comstock *The Man* 347 This out-of-door stuff costs like all creation.

* **creature,** *n.*

1. *S.* In colloq. use, esp. in the form "critter," a horse.

1782 *Md. Journal* 30 July (Th.), Stolen, the following creatures, viz. one a bay Horse, the other a half blooded black Mare. **1842** Buckingham *Slave States* II. 292 Horses are called 'critturs.' ... 'There is no getting a crittur for love or money: they are all employed hauling oats.' **1868** Beecher *Norwood* 338 Hiram Beers ... had general oversight of all the 'critters,' as Deacon Marble styled the horses.

2. critter company, (see quot. 1889). *Obs.*

1866 F. Kirkland *Bk. Anecdotes* 482 Up comes Captain Forrest with his crittur company (cavalry). **1884** Cable *Dr. Sevier* liv, Compliments that flew back and forth from the 'web-foots' to the 'critter company,' and from the 'critter company' to the 'web-foots.' **1889** *Cent.* 1497/3 'A critter company' is a cavalry company. (Prov. U.S.)

* **credit,** *n.*

1. *Educ.* A unit of academic work counting toward graduation.

1904 E. G. Dexter *Hist. Educ. U.S.* 288 On the basis of 'credits,' one credit representing a subject pursued daily ... for one year in the secondary schools, forty-five credits is the usual requirement. **1948** *Miami* (Okla.) *D. News-Record* 4 July 10/1 It is imperative that the student have his transcript of credits ... sent to the dean of administration as early as possible.

2. In combs.: (1) **credit man,** an employee who determines the amount of credit customers are allowed; (2) **mobilier,** see as a main entry; (3) **state,** a state the finances of which rest on a credit basis; (4) **union,** an organization whose members secure loans on the collective credit of the group, or an association which makes small loans on easy terms to its members, also **credit unionism.**

(1) **1880** *Bradstreet's* 28 Feb. 2/3 The credit-man of a large dry goods jobbing house stated that ... not one in five hundred gave them notes. **1915** *Lit. Digest* 21 Aug. 377/3 Big order comes in from Jones & Co. Everybody pleased—except that office kill-joy, the credit man. — (3) **1802** Cutler in *Life & Corr.* II. 97 All the New England States are credit states. **1809** *Essex Inst. Coll.* XXXIX. 324 Massachusetts is a credit state, to a larger amount than any other.— (4) **1915** *Survey* 6 Feb. 475/2 Most students of credit unionism agree that credit unions should be a spontaneous expression of co-operative spirit on the part of those forming them. **1945** *Christian Cent.* 8 Aug. 916/3 'The finest credit union in the United States,' is how Roy F. Bergengren ... describes the Light of Tyrrell credit union at Columbia, N.C. **1948** *Railway Clerk* June 336/1 His activities in the credit union movement began in 1927.

As the last term in **advanced, bank of, fall, state, traveler's credit.**

credit mobilier. [F. *crédit,* credit + *mobilier,* personal.] An institution that makes loans secured by personal property, also (*cap.*) a Pennsylvania corporation which in 1867 became the construction company for the Union Pacific Railroad but which soon collapsed as a result of the scandal caused by its alleged bribery of certain congressmen. Also attrib.

1861 *Charleston* (S.C.) *Mercury* 19 Feb. 1/4 The Republicans want to open a *credit mobelier* and get Yankee laborers to take stock from ten cents upwards. **1872** *N.Y. Sun* 4 Sep., The King of Frauds; How the Credit Mobilier bought its way through Congress. **1873** *Ill. Dept. Agric. Trans.* X. 149 Just so many of our railroads have each a stump speech, a parasite, one or two or three 'credit mobiliers,' in the shape of express companies. **1948** *Sat. Ev. Post* 9 Oct. 168/2 The exposure of the Crédit Mobilier racket seventy-five years ago was entirely due to the work of the Wilson Committee and the Poland Committee.

* **creek,** *n.*

1. A stream larger than a brook but smaller than a river, orig. a tributary to a larger stream or body of water.

This sense is usu. regarded as an extension of the word in the sense of an inlet or arm of the sea, but Bense thinks Du. *kreek* may account for this Amer. sense. See also *Amer. Sp.* V. (1930) 158–9.

1622 in Shurtleff *Log Cabin* (1939) 155 Creeks and Swamps as they call them ... offer all aduantages to their ... enimys. **1724** Jones *Present State* 34 Into these Rivers run abundance of great Creeks or short Rivers, navigable for Sloops, Shallops. **1894** Robley *Bourbon Co., Kansas* 63 The stage ... made the trip once a week; that is, when the creeks were not up and there was no other preventing providence. **1945** *Democrat* 4 Jan. 2/2 He found the creek and decided that the logical thing to do was to follow it.

b. *N. Eng.* An artificial inlet or short canal. ?*Obs.*

1631 *Mass. Bay Rec.* I. 89 There shalbe levyed ... thirty pounds for the makeing of the creek at the new towne. **1656** *Charlestown Land Records* 141 A plott of ground [was] given to mr. Garrett in the marsh to cutt a creek with convenientcy of Landing about it.

c. (See quot.) *Rare.*

1808 in *Niles' Reg.* XV. 48/2 *Creeks,* properly so called, which rise below the falls of the first rivers, or rather collect the water of the level land below the falls, and discharge it into the tide waters.

2. (*cap.*) A Creek Indian. Often pl. with reference to the tribe or the confederacy (see quot. 1907). Cf. **Lower Creeks, Upper Creeks.**

1725 G. Chicken in *Travels Amer. Col.* 106, I hope your Honour will be speedy to me in your Expresses, Especially in your answer to me when you have heard from the Creeks. **1830** in M'Kenney *Memoirs* I. (1846) ix. 215 It appears the entire cost of removing each Creek, and supporting him, has been fifteen cents per day, or fifty-four dollars per year. **1907** Hodge *Amer. Indians* I. 362 *Creeks.* A confederacy forming one of the largest divisions of the Muskhogean family. They received their name from the English on account of the numerous streams in their country. **1948** Mathews *Southernisms* 45 In the treaty of Fort Jackson, in 1814, it was stipulated that those Creeks west of the river should return to the eastern side.

b. The language of these Indians.

1922 Kephart *So. Highlanders* 193 He spoke Creek (or was it Choctaw?) and Navaho and Seminole.

3. Used (sense **1**) in combs.: (1) **creek bottom,** level land along a creek, also attrib.; (2) **broadbill,** the lesser scaup duck; (3) **claim,** *W.* a mining claim along a creek, *obs.* (cf. **Creek claims** below); (4) **diggings,** *W.* a place by a creek where shallow mining for gold is carried on, *obs.;* (5) **duck,** a local name for the gadwall; (6) **farm,** a farm beside a creek; (7) **fish,** (see quot.); (8) **grass,** a reed or grass found growing in or near creeks; (9) **line,** a dividing line formed by a creek (cf. **Creek line** below); (10) **plum,** a variety of plum which thrives along the courses of creeks, rivers, etc., of the Southwest; (11) **stuff,** a grass, *Spartina cynosuroides,* found along creeks and salt marshes; (12) **thatch,** any grass of the genus *Spartina,* also attrib.; (13) **trout,** (see quots.).

(1) **1822** J. WOODS *Residence in English Prairie* 224 On the creek bottoms, [there grow] coffee-berry, poplar, pecon, white walnut, &c. &c. **1883** SMITH *Geol. Survey Ala.* 231 The creek-bottom lands in the Tennessee Valley are of varying degrees of fertility. *Ib.* 418 Analyses of . . . gravelly creek-bottom soils from Madison. **1947** *Newsweek* 24 Feb. 30/1 The car rumbled over an embankment and smashed into a creek bottom. — (2) **1844** *Nat. Hist. N.Y., Zoology* II. 324 This Creek Broadbill . . . appears to prefer the creeks and smaller streams of the interior. **1917** *Birds of Amer.* I. 136. — (3) **1865** in *Frontier* VIII. 131 A Creek claim shall be two hundred feet up or down the said creek (Elk Creek, Deer Lodge Co., Mont.) and shall extend from the rise of the rim rock on each side of the said creek. **1897** *U.S. Consular Rep.* Oct., Creek and river claims shall be 500 feet long, measured in the direction of the general course of the stream. — (4) **1850** L. SAWYER *Way Sketches* 118 In this region there is two classes of mines, the Coyota and the ravine and creek diggings. **1852** *N.Y. Wkly. Tribune* 22 May 8/2 They are creek and ravine diggings.

(5) **1917** *Birds of Amer.* I. 118. **1935** *U.S. Dept. Agric., Biol. Survey Poster* 31 Aug., Local names [of migratory game birds] . . . Gadwell.—Gray duck, redwing, creek duck. — (6) **1871** W. J. FLAGG *Good Investment* ii, These he judged to be sufficient, considering the light and friable soil of the creek farm. **1886** P. G. EBBUTT *Emigrant Life Kansas* 199 Creek farms are always more or less infested with them [sandburrs], but they are comparatively scarce on the prairie. — (7) **1884** GOODE *Fisheries* I. 614 The 'Chub Sucker,' 'Sweet Sucker,' or 'Creek-fish' is one of the most abundant and widely diffused of the Suckers. — (8) **1665** *Southold Rec.* I. 366 Thomas Hutchinson and Edward Pety . . . weare to have . . . all the common meadow and land whereon Creeke grass groweth. **1695** *Rec. of Providence R.I.* IV. 192 Haveing . . . purchassed of the said Towne of Providence a certaine Cove of Creeke Grass or Thatch. — (9) **1881** *Harper's Mag.* Feb. 435/1 Your conversation tonight is about as crooked and uncertain as the creek line. **1885** *Cent. Mag.* April 843 In a hill region the number is limited of those who can live persistently, without any hurt to friendly neighborhood, on opposite sides of a creek-line.

(10) **1885** HAVARD *Flora W. & S. Texas* 512 *Prunus rivularis,* Scheele. (Creek Plum) Small shrub, not uncommon on the Colorado and its tributaries, bearing excellent red plums in August and September. **1891** COULTER *Bot. W. Texas* I. 102 Creek plum. . . . The fruit is said to be excellent. — (11) **1669** *Essex Inst. Coll.* XXXVII. 219 On aker more for Capt. Gardner & Thomas Mary . . . for the mill and creek stuff proportionable. **1807** *Mass. H.S. Coll.* 2 Ser. III. 51 Another kind of grass, called creek stuff, grows on the borders of the ponds, and the greatest part of it in the water. — (12) **1673** *Essex Inst. Coll.* XXXVII. 220 [The town made the following grant to him] . . . 2 acres meadow, and his proportion of creek thatch. **1682** *Southold Rec.* I. 195 A parcell of Creek thatch meadow lying between Hallocks Neck and Saugures Neck. **1794** *N.Y. State Soc. Arts* I. 143 He informed me that he gave the horse no grain of any kind, but kept him in a very poor pasture adjoining a creek where creek-thatch grew on sand-flats. — (13) **1820** *Western Rev.* II. 177 Alleghany Trout. *Salmo Alleganiensis.* . . . It is found in the brooks of the Alleghany mountains falling into the Alleghany and Monongahela. It has the manner of the small Brook-trouts, and is called Mountain-trout, Creek-trout, &c. **1842** *Nat. Hist. N.Y., Zoology* IV. 236 The Red bellied Trout. *Salmo erythrogaster.* Creek Trout?

b. In sense **2:** (1) **Creek claims,** lands or areas in Alabama and Georgia claimed by the Creek Indians, *obs.;* (2) **confederacy,** the confederacy made up of various Indian tribes formerly occupying chiefly northern and eastern Alabama and parts of Georgia, *obs.;* (3) **country,** the area, chiefly in Alabama and Georgia, formerly occupied by the Creeks, *obs.;* (4) **headman,** a chief among the Creeks, *obs.;* (5) **Indian,** an Indian belonging to the Creek confederacy, usu. pl. as a collective designation; (6) **land,** land in Georgia and Alabama once occupied by the Creek Indians, *obs.;* (7) **language,** the language of the Creeks; (8) **leather,** a kind of leather prepared by the Creeks, *obs.;* (9) **line,** the boundary line of the Creek lands, esp. the line which separated these lands from those of the Choctaws, *obs.;* (10) **Nation,** the Indian nation made up of the Creek Indians; (11) **War,** (see quot. 1907), now *hist.*

(1) **1817** S. BROWN *Western Gaz.* 13 The eastern boundary of the Creek claims is pine land. — (2) **1873** BEADLE *Undevel. West* 378 Traders penetrating their country from Pensacola named it, from the number of streams, the Creek Country, and gave the Muscokee Nation the title of Creek Confederacy. **1946** *Nat. Geog. Mag.* Jan. 53/2 Typical Muskhogean-speaking peoples were the tribes comprising the great Creek confederacy, which occupied the territory now constituting Georgia and Alabama. — (3) **1873** [see **Creek confederacy**]. — (4) **1761** *Pennsylvania Gaz.* 1 Oct. 2/3 The French Officers at Albama, invited the Creek headman to a talk at that fort.

(5) **1732** *Calendar St. Papers Amer. & W. Indies* 217 They [the Spanish] have a party among the Creek Indians as well as we. **1832** *Boston Transcript* 19 April 2/1 This is the same Gov Houston who so unaccountably resigned his gubernatorial functions, and joined the Creek Indians, by whom he was adopted as a son. **1948** *Dly. Ardmoreite* (Ardmore, Okla.) 26 May 2/3 Tulsa was first called 'Tulsey Town' for the Creek Indians, who belonged to the Tallassee or Tulsey community. — (6) **1845** HOOPER *Suggs* (1928) 28 There he was, as jolly as Bacchus, with a pretty large family and considerable experience, but without funds—a speculator in Creek lands. **1854** BENTON *30 Years' View* I. 59/1 It did not cede the whole of the Creek lands in Georgia. — (7) **1725** G. CHICKEN in *Travels Amer. Col.* 120 Do you understand the Creek Language? **1893** *Dly. Ardmoreite* (Ardmore, Okla.) 1 Nov. 1/2 Some of the Creek language is very beautiful and easy to learn. — (8) **1765** J. HABERSHAM *Letters* 36 Our clear Creek Leather is now rather esteemed better than Cherokee. — (9) **1797** B. HAWKINS *Letters* 92, I have judged proper to postpone the running of the Creek line till we run the Cherokee line.

(10) **1732** *Calendar St. Papers Amer. & W. Indies* 217 Two of our Indian traders having been killed near the Creek nation in their way thither. **1946** FOREMAN *Last Trek* 163 They were recorded as part of the Creek Nation, their chiefs participating in the Creek general councils. — (11) **1898** CUSHMAN *Hist. Indians* 406 Eli Crowder secured for himself, in the Creek War, the name of Creek-Killer. **1907** HODGE *Amer. Indians* I. 363/2 The only serious revolt of the Creeks against the Americans took place in 1813–14—the well-known Creek war, in which Gen. Jackson took a prominent part.

Also (sense **1**) *creek bank, bed, land, mud, prairie, side, timber, water;* (sense **2**) *Creek tomahawk, war-whoop, word.*

As the last term in **beaver, cross, dry, eel, falling, fresh, fresh-water, gold, goose, hay, mill, Mosquito, mud, pay, pine, salt, sand, spring creek.**

creeker ˈkrikɚ, *n.* (See quot.) *Obs.* — **1872** W. J. FLAGG *Good Investment* iv, A *'creeker'*—as they [people along the Ohio R.] called backwoodsmen.

∗**creep,** *v. intr.* Of railroad rails: To move slightly under pressure or as a result of expansion and contraction. Cf. **creeping track.** — **1872** HUNTINGTON *Road-Master's Ass't* 29 The rails in creeping have a tendency to move towards the foot of the grade. **1885** *Science* V. 344/2 In some places the rails move longitudinally, or 'creep.' . . . On long inclines or grades the track may creep down hill.

∗ **creeper,** *n.*

1. The trumpet creeper or the Virginia creeper.

1802 ELLICOTT *Journal* 288 Many of the trees in the low grounds are loaded with a variety of vines, the most conspicuous of which are the

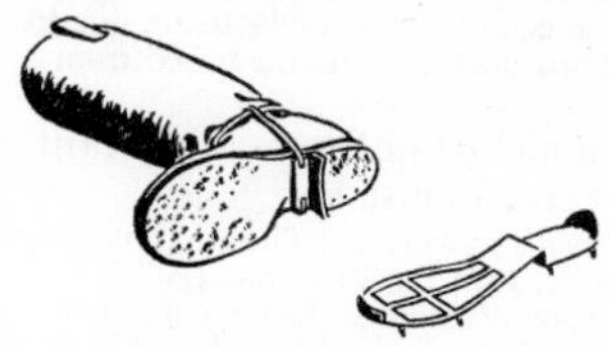

Types of creepers

creeper, or trumpet flower, (*begnonia radicans,*) and common poison vine, (*rhus radicans*). **1878** WHITMAN *Specimen Days* (1882) 123 Perennial blossoms and friendly weeds I have made acquaintance with hereabout [New Jersey, include]: Creeper, trumpet-flower. **1885** CRAWFORD *Amer. Politician* 281 On the walls of Beacon Street the great creepers have burst into blossom.

2. *pl.* (See quot.) Cf. ∗**calk.**

1859 BARTLETT 107 *Creepers,* pieces of iron, furnished with sharp points and strapped under the feet, to prevent one falling when walking upon ice.

3. (See quot. 1877.) Cf. ∗**spider 1.**

1877 BARTLETT 159 *Creeper,* a shallow iron dish used in frying; a spider. New England. **1888** J. D. BILLINGS *Hardtack* 133 These fry-pans—Marbleheadmen called them *Creepers*—were yet comparatively light. **1939** *L.A.* Map 132.

As the last term in **American, brown, finch, pine, Sierra, trumpet, Virginia, Virginian creeper.**

*__creeping,__ *a.* In combs.: (1) **creeping cucumber,** (see quots.); (2) **greenhead,** a bluet, *obs.;* (3) **snowberry,** a slender, woody, evergreen plant, *Chiogenes hispidula,* bearing white berries; (4) **track,** see ***creep,** *v.*

(1) 1836 LINCOLN *Botany* App. 116 *Melothria pendula,* (small creeping cucumber). **1889** *Cent.* 1388/2 [The] creeping cucumber . . . is a delicate low cucurbitaceous climber of the southern United States, bearing oval green berries. — **(2) 1847** WOOD *Botany* 306 *H[oustonia] glomerata.* Creeping Green-head . . . N.Y. to La. — **(3) 1856** GRAY *Man. Bot.* 250 *Chiogenes,* Creeping Snowberry. **1871** DE VERE *Americanisms* 404 The queen of them all is said to be the lovely, creeping *snowberry* (Chiogenes hispidula). — **(4) 1872** HUNTINGTON *Road-Master's Ass't* 29 Much damage has been done by expansion, from improper treatment of 'creeping track.'

creepy ˈkripɪ, *n.* (See quots.) *Obs.* — **1854** *Pa. Agric. Rep.* 163 The Committee on Poultry report, that they have been agreeably surprised at the variety of poultry exhibited . . . comprising, in the tribe of barn-yard fowls, . . . the Frizzle; the Creely and the Creepy. **1871** DE VERE 380 A tailless fowl is in Pennsylvania called a *bunty,* and a small speckled kind a creepy (S. S. Haldeman).

cremationism krəˈmeʃənˌɪzəm, *n.* The practice of, or preference for, cremating the dead. *Rare.* — **1884** *Fargo Argus* Feb., We are not restricted for cemetery room, and cremationism is on the increase.

*__crematory,__ *n.* A furnace or incinerator for garbage and other waste. — **1889** *Oregonian* (Portland) 5 Dec. 7/1 Castendiech said he had visited the crematory and found it working well, and all the garbage was burned up except the tin cans, etc. **1896** *Chi. Tribune* 18 Aug. 6/2 In New York the crematory is located on an island in the harbor and the garbage is hauled to the river front at convenient points and taken away in scows.

*__creole,__ *n.* Usu. *cap.*

1. A person of mixed blood, esp. a white person descended from French or Spanish settlers in Louisiana and the Southwest.

This term is and has been used with various significations; it cannot be defined with precision. Friederici has an extensive and valuable account of the word and its significations.

1792 J. POPE *Tour S. & W.* 22 He is a Creole of French Extraction. **1811** *Niles' Reg.* I. 272/1 There was some severe fighting between the creoles of Texas and the Spanish troops. **1867** LATHAM *Black & White* 159 A Creole of Louisiana is one who traces back through one parent or another to the colonists; and the colonists were those who dwelt in the land at the time Louisiana was sold by France to the United States in 1803. **1945** *Reader's Digest* March 77/1 With 20,000 other Creoles, Cajuns, Isleños, Dalmatians, Sabines—the mixed folk of south Louisiana—Alcée is going to trap muskrats.

b. (See quots.)

1839 *N.O. Picayune* 17 April 2/1 The negro man is described as a creole, speaking rather bad English. **1846** LYELL *Second Visit* (1849) II. 93 The word creole is used in Louisiana to express a native-born American, whether black or white, descended from old-world parents, for they would not call the aboriginal Indians creoles. **1859** BARTLETT 108 *Creole* Great offence has been given [in N. O.] by strangers applying the term to a good-looking mulatto or quadroon. **1889** *Cent. Creole,* a native born negro, as distinguished from a negro brought from Africa.

c. Used as a nickname for an inhabitant of Louisiana. Also **Creole State,** Louisiana.

1845 *St. Louis Reveille* 14 May 2/4 The inhabitants of . . . Louisiana [are called] Cree-*owls.* **1871** DE VERE 660 Louisiana . . . also appears as the Creole State, on account of the large number of its inhabitants who are descendants of the original French and Spanish settlers. **1893** *Outing* Feb. 364/1 Let him who doubts enter the cane and palmetto jungle of the Creole State . . . and he will never doubt again.

d. In Alaska, one born of Russian and native Indian parents.

1867 *N.Y. World* 13 Nov. 1/5 A large concourse of people had assembled, composing Americans, Russians of all classes, Creoles and Indians. **1877** WHITE in Morris *Pub. Service Alaska* (1879) 127 The Indians and creoles (or half-breed Russians) easily distil [liquor] from either molasses, sugar, potatoes, or the various kinds of wild berries. **1924** NICHOLS *Alaska* 105 The Creoles, being tenacious Greek-Catholics, resented Protestant religious opening exercises.

e. The language used by the Creoles in Louisiana.

1879 HEARN *Creole Sketches* (1924) 54, I explique myself to her, and she tell me in Creole—[etc.]. **1885** *Harper's Wkly.* 10 Jan. 27/3 Creole is the maternal speech; it is the tongue in which the baby first learns to utter its thoughts.

2. A variety of domestic fowl. Also **Creole chicken.** *Obs.* Cf. **Creole egg.**

1849 *N. Eng. Farmer* I. 386 Creoles were shown by D.M. Robertson. **1854** *Pa. Agric. Rep.* 205 C. T. Campbell for best pair Creole chickens. **1856** *Porter's Spirit of Times* 4 Oct. 81/1 I have another breed [of chickens] called the Creoles, which excels them all.

3. A horse or pony of a type common among the Creoles of Louisiana. In full **Creole horse, Creole pony.** (See also quot. 1946.)

1841 *N.O. Picayune* 16 April 2/5 There are nineteen entries, among them some of the first 'Creoles of Louisiana.' *Ib.* 1/6 He got on to a creowl hoss that never'd ben rid much, and was as fiery as a rattlesnake. **1853** P. PAXTON *Yankee in Texas* 378 Planters and stockraisers in Texas keep many horses, but they are usually of the small breed of Louisiana Creole ponies, or those of the Spanish kind. **1946** W. A. READ in Letter to the editor 25 April, The French of Louisiana use the term *Créole* in the sense of 'excellent,' or 'superior.' *Un cheval Créole,* though small and unattractive, possesses remarkable stamina. Creole tomatoes, or onions, or peas are so named because they are the very best.

b. Also **Creole donkey.**

1852 GAYARRE *Louisiana* 45 Baby . . . was mounted on a small creole donkey.

4. In special combs., now obs.: (1) **Creole ball,** a ball given by Creoles; (2) **cane,** a variety of sugar cane the stalks of which are esp. soft and of a light green color; (3) **egg,** an egg laid by a Creole hen; (4) **party,** a political party in Texas.

(1) 1856 OLMSTED *Slave States* 646, I attended a Creole ball, while at Washington. — **(2) 1827** in COMMONS *Doc. Hist.* I. 214 Most of the plant cane, and also stubbles of Creole cane in new land mark the row. **1856** *Rep. Comm. Patents: Agric.* 275 The cane called 'Creole' originated in Malabar or Bengal. It is believed to have passed through Arabia, Egypt, Sicily, Spain, the Canary Islands, and the West Indies, before it reached this country, in 1751. — **(3) 1840** *N.O. Picayune* 3 Oct. 2/3, 'I sell tobacco, creole eggs, mackerel and other fixings,' said Clements. **1864** NICHOLS *Amer. Life* I. 186 Everything is brought you hot and fresh, from creole eggs to oysters. — **(4) 1836** EDWARD *Hist. Texas* 125 The Creole party is divided into several factions.

b. In combs. of obvious meaning, as **Creole aristocracy, city, contact, cow, dish, French, loaferism, rice, show, Spanish, spring.**

1851 HALL *Manhattaner* 93 The well-brushed heads about, principally belong to scions of Creole aristocracy. — **1880** HEARN *Creole Sketches* (1924) 121 We doubt whether this book, in spite of its delicate merit, will become a favorite with residents of the Creole city. — **1883** *Cent. Mag.* July 421/1 Creole contact had been felt. — **1840** *N.O. Picayune* 15 Sep. 2/6 Strayed or Stolen — From the subscriber on the 7th instant, a black (small) creole Cow. — **1936** *Chi. D. News* 4 Feb. 10 What are Creole dishes? That question was answered for Chicagoans today. **1946** THOMPSON *Amer. Daughter* 195 There were the smells again: barbecue, fried shrimp, creole dishes, and a new thing from the stockyards. — **1867** *Beadle's Mo.* May 392/2 It is said that over twenty thousand of the inhabitants may be classed as 'transient'; perhaps the Creole French only can be called permanent. **1900** STOCKTON *Afield & Afloat* 47 He spoke to them in broken Creole-French, in broken English, and in Negro-French. — **1851** HALL *Manhattaner* 17 So it [the St. Louis Hotel in New Orleans] will long remain . . . the headquarters of Creole loaferism. — **1854** *N.O. Delta* 28 May, Another specimen of Creole rice may now be seen at the Reading Room of the Exchange. — **1895** *N.Y. Dramatic News* 12 Oct. 5/3 The Creole show is at the Gaiety theatre, New York. — **1852** STOWE *Uncle Tom* xlii. 42 Cassy was dressed after the manner of the Creole Spanish ladies. — **1880** CABLE *Grandissimes* xii. 77 It was getting well on into the Creole spring and approaching the spring of the almanacs.

As the last term in **French, Spanish Creole.**

*__Creolism,__ *n.* A Creole term or expression. *Rare.* — **1895** G. KING *New Orleans* 43 He calls these blocks, therefore, 'Islands; Isles,' which is the origin of the Creolism 'Islet' for street or square.

*__creosote,__ *n.* A resinous evergreen shrub, *Covillea mexicana,* found in the Southwest. In full **creosote bush, plant.** Cf. **hediondilla.**

1846 in EMORY *Mil. Reconnoissance* (1848) 612 The vegetation on the jornada is the creosote bush, the mesquite, the Fremontia [etc.]. **1853** SITGREAVES *Exped. Zuni & Colo. Rivers* 34 Up the Rio Grande . . . the vegetation alters but little, the timber being principally . . . the creosote plant, (*Larrea Mexicana,*) . . . and various species of artemisia. **1908** AUSTIN *Land of Little Rain* 10 If you have any doubt about it, know that the desert begins with the creosote. This immortal shrub spreads down into Death Valley and up to the lower timber-line, odorous and medicinal. **1947** *So. Sierran* May 4/2 On the desert we noted . . . the creosote bushes with their many small yellow blossoms.

***crescent,** *n.*

1. a. (*cap.*) Short for Crescent City. *Rare.* **b.** The state flag of South Carolina. *Rare.* **c.** A small crescent-shaped roll of bread.

(a) **1851** A. O. HALL *Manhattaner* 64, I advise you . . . not to throw either topic in the teeth of your true blooded Crescent citizen. — (b) **1861** in MOORE *Rebellion Rec.* I (1862) 37/2 We've torn the hated banner down, And placed the Crescent there. — (c) **1886** *Cent. Mag.* XXXII. 939 At noon I bought two crisp 'crescents,' which I ate sometimes at a shop counter.

2. Crescent City, New Orleans.

1835 INGRAHAM *South-West* I. 91, I have termed New Orleans the Crescent city . . . from its being built around the segment of a circle formed by a graceful curve of the river. **1909** *Springfield W. Republican* 11 March 1 Secretary Meyer . . . never was in New Orleans, and . . . the president was in the Crescent City about a month ago. **1949** *N.O. Times-Picayune* (Mag.) 2 Jan. 10/3 During the War of 1812, the land forces had little to brag about up until the battle in the Crescent City.

b. *Crescent City of the Northwest,* (see quot.). *Rare.*

1871 DE VERE 663 Galena in Illinois . . . is indebted to its remarkably quick growth for the familiar name of Crescent City of the Northwest.

***crested,** *a.* (1) **crested flycatcher,** a flycatcher, *Myiarchus crinitus,* of the eastern states, also **great crested flycatcher,** cf. **Arizona crested flycatcher;** (2) **partridge,** the valley quail of California; (3) **titmouse,** the tufted titmouse, *Baeolophus bicolor,* found in the eastern U.S., cf. **black crested titmouse.**

(1) *c*1730 CATESBY *Carolina* I. 52 The crested Fly-Catcher. . . . It breeds in Carolina and Virginia, but retires in Winter. **1810** WILSON *Ornithology* II. 75 The Great Crested Flycatcher, *Muscicapa Crinita,* . . . arrives in Pennsylvania early in May, and builds his nest in a hollow tree deserted by the Blue-bird or Woodpecker. **1948** *Green Bay* (Wis.) *Press-Gazette* 13 July 11/4 Birds that sang in the afternoon were the . . . scarlet tanager, indigo bunting, red-eyed vireo and crested flycatcher. — (2) **1806** VON LANGSDORFF *Voyages* (1817) 453 We often amused ourselves with shooting the crested partridges and the rabbits which abound upon the sand hills near the shore. — (3) *c*1730 CATESBY *Carolina* I. 57 The crested Titmouse. . . . They breed in and inhabit Virginia and Carolina all the year. **1831** AUDUBON *Ornith. Biog.* I. 200 The Crested Titmouse is of a rather vicious disposition, which sometimes prompts it to attack smaller birds. **1917** *Birds of Amer.* III. 206.

creston kresˈton, *n. S.W.* [Sp. *crestón* in similar senses.] A ridge running across a slope (see also quot. 1909). — **1890** BANDELIER *Delight Makers* 466 To the north the plain rises gradually, traversed only by the north *creston,* until it merges into the plain of Santa Fé. **1909** *Cent. Supp.* 313/3 creston. . . . In *mining geol.,* the outcrop of a vein: used along the Mexican boundary.

crevalle krəˈvælə, *n.* [Variant of **cavalla.*] Any one of various fishes of the *Caranx* or related genera. Cf. **horse crevalle.**

1897 BRICE *Fishes Indian River, Fla.* 14 The crevallé is probably common in Indian River at all times, but is not highly esteemed by commercial fishermen. **1937** PEARSON *Adv. In Bird Protection* 332 From the results I have no hesitancy in recommending it to other anglers who desire to fish for the larger-sized cravalle. **1947** DALRYMPLE *Panfish* 264 Most of the time these fishermen take small Jack (Crevalle) of two or three pounds.

crevasse krəˈvæs, *n.* [F. in the La. F. sense shown here.] A break in a levee, usu. with reference to the lower Mississippi.

1813 *Pittsburgh Alman. 1814* 57 The numerous crevasses (breaks) above, are supposed to have added to the safety and perhaps prevented the city from experiencing inundation. **1891** *Scribner's Mag.* Oct. 465 Every crevasse that bursts a levee is an effort of the river to escape from the high-lying channel to which man would confine it. **1941** BALDWIN *Keelboat Age* 77 A similar danger was the crevasse, formed in time of high water when the river broke through a levee.

transf. **1850** *Cong. Globe* App. 149/2 A moral crevasse has occurred: fanaticism and ignorance . . . have accumulated into a mighty flood.

***crevice,** *v. W. intr.* To work or explore crevices in rocks for gold.

1853 *Ore. Statesman* 6 Dec. 1/2 One claim thou may'st own, and then drive your stake. And coyote and crevice till you make or you break. **1856** M. TAYLOR *Gold Digger's Song Book* 27, I have drifted, I've washed, I've creviced and dug.

Hence **crevicing,** *n.* Also attrib.

1851 *Alta Californian* 17 July, The early adventurers in the gold-diggings required simply . . . a strong sheath-knife for crevicing. **1855** *S.F. Golden Era* 21 Jan. 2/5 Indian lover hard by—approaches miner with a drawn crevicing-knife. **1948** JOHNSTON *Gold Rush* 41/2 As crevicing was better up the fork, they broke camp, and moved to Zumwalt Flat.

***crew,** *n.* As the last term in **baling, branding, driving, logging, notion-peddling, rear, saw, scrub crew.**

***crib,** *n.*

1. = **corncrib.** Also attrib. Cf. **log crib** (*b*).

1701 C. WOLLEY *Jrnl.* (1860) 42, I . . . ordered my Negro boy about 12 years old to tye them [i.e., bear cubs] under the Crib by my Horse. **1749** HEMPSTEAD *Diary* 524 The minister & people here are very modist in their apparel & in their houses, mostly Log houses Cribb fashion. **1847** *Florida Plant. Rec.* 254 Sam [is] getting crib logs. **1948** *Democrat* 15 July 1/4 During the next few weeks cribs should be well cleaned of all old shucks and corn.

transf. **1833** S. SMITH *Major Downing* 166 All the presidents and cashiers, and clerks, and money counters about the crib. **1839** *Chicago American* 26 Oct., He finds on Saturday that there is no money in the crib to pay off the hands.

2. A raft of planks or timber.

1776 C. CARROLL *Journal* (1845) 47 The smaller rafts are called *cribs.* **1814** *N.Y. Sup. Ct. Rep.* (Johnson) X. 237 Light cribs of boards would float over the dam in safety. **1880** *Lumberman's Gaz.* 28 Jan., Cribs are formed of about 20 sticks of timber fastened between two logs called 'floats.' **1926** RICKABY *Ballads* 234 Crib. A raft.

3. A structure, originally of logs, anchored under water and used to form a pier or dam or intake for water. Also attrib.

1815–6 *Niles' Reg.* IX. Supp. 164/2 These dams are built with timber, in the manner of crib dams, secured to the rocks below with iron bolts. **1867** *Harper's Wkly.* 20 April 252/4 When they had succeeded in this dangerous undertaking the flood-gates of the 'crib' were opened, and the waters went down with a roar like that of an infant Niagara. **1948** *Chi. D. News* 30 Jan. 14/7 Supplying water to Chicago homes is a task of constant vigil, a trip to the crib three miles off Wilson av. revealed.

4. A saloon, low dive, or house of prostitution. *Slang.* Cf. **cow bay, cribbey.**

1848 B. A. BAKER *Glance at N.Y.* 23 Let's take a drink; there's a crib open. **1901** FLYNT *World of Graft* 219 *Crib,* gambling dive. **1948** *Newsweek* 30 Aug. 19/2 Patrons entering the courtyard found a string of two-room apartments or 'cribs.'

5. The inclosure for trapped fish in a pound-net.

1873 *Rep. U.S. Fish Commission* I. 264 The pound-nets . . . have several parts, termed the 'leader,' the 'heart,' the 'pot,' or 'crib,' and the 'tunnel.' **1884** KNIGHT *Dict. Mech.* Supp., *Crib* (Fishing), the bowl or pound of a Pound Net.

As the last term in **corn, framed corn, government, log, Negro, panel, public crib.**

***crib,** *v.*

1. *tr.* To store (corn) in a crib.

1719 HEMPSTEAD *Diary* 93, I went to Stonington & Stephen to Cribb the Corn. *a*1805 *Steele Papers* II. 864 Anderson sold 9000 W cotton—& 2000 W Tobo. and cribbed 40 waggon Loads of corn. **1939** *These Are Our Lives* 256 Why, the buyers would crib eight and ten thousand bushel of wheat and corn.

2. To arrange logs into rafts.

1876 *Minn. Laws* 100 Any person who may do . . . any manual labor in cutting, . . . cribbing or towing any logs, or timber in this state, shall have a lien thereon. **1905** *Forestry Bureau Bul.* No. 61, 34 *Crib logs, to,* to surround floating logs with a boom and draw them by a windlass on a raft (a *crab*), or to tow them with a steamboat. (N[orth] W[oods], L[ake] S[tates].)

cribbey ˈkrɪbɪ, *n.* (See quot.) *Obs.* — **1848** E. JUDSON *Mysteries N.Y.* I. 113 *Cribbeys,* blind alleys, dark narrow ways.

***cricket,** *n.* As the last term in **camel, gopher hole, Jerusalem, Mormon, prairie, sand, savanna, tree cricket.**

***crime,** *n.*

1. *Crime of 1873* (see quots.).

1893 *Fortnightly Rev.* LIII. 765 The Silver party in the United States insists . . . that the legislation of 1873 was smuggled through Congress by corrupt practices, and so . . . widespread is this conviction that every Western schoolboy connects the currency crisis of today with what is now termed the 'Crime of 1873.' **1914** *Cyclo. Amer. Govt.* I. 519 'Crime of '73.' A term applied to the demonetization of silver in 1873, by a statute which extremists of the silver party later claimed to have been covertly put through by a legislative plot. **1942** LILLARD *Desert Challenge* 49 This so-called 'Crime of '73' legislated away the contemporary importance of Nevada.

2. crime wave, a sudden and widespread increase of crime.

[**1910** *Sat. Ev. Post* 29 Oct. 46/2 A good many 'waves of crime' occur in the imagination of newspapers.] **1923** *Nation* 11 July 42/2 The United States is in the throes of . . . 'crime waves.' **1948** *Ada* (Okla.)

Ev. News 4 July 4/6 Why were nine billion, six hundred million dollars spent last year in America for alcohol to increase the crime wave?

criminal lawyer. A lawyer who specializes in criminal law.

1869 TOURGEE *Toinette* ii. 19 They knew the weak point of the old man, his repute as a criminal lawyer. **1889** *Cent. Mag.* Feb. 634/1 The failure of criminal justice, . . . and the evolution of a class of 'criminal lawyers' whose perfect flower was the royal type of 'jury fixer,' were antecedent circumstances sufficient to show that a heavy responsibility belongs to the public men who had permitted criminal law to break down. **1947** *True* Nov. 69/1 Criminal lawyers did not keep charts and graphs of their acquittals.

crimmy ˈkrɪmɪ, *a. local.* Cold, chilly. — **1886** E. L. BYNNER *A. Surriage* 58 Ye're crimmy wi' th' fog Job. Ye'd best get some grog. **1891** *Amer. Folk-Lore* IV. 159 Words from the dialect of Marblehead. . . . *Crimmy,* chilly. An old fisherman says: 'Ain't it too crimmy to go sailen'?'

∗**crimp,** *n.*

1. (See quot. 1863.)

1863 H. S. RANDALL *Pract. Shepherd* vii. 75 That combination of appearances which indicates choice wool—viz., fineness, . . . regularity and distinctness of 'crimp'—that curved and graceful form and arrangement of the locks and fibers in the sheared fleece which indicate extreme pliancy. **1874** *Vt. Bd. Agric. Rep.* II. 410 Fineness of fiber can be judged by its appearance to the eye, by its feeling when touched and by its fineness of crimp. *Ib.* 411 Style of wool is judged by its crimp; the number of crimps to an inch in length of very fine wool is from twenty-seven to twenty-nine.

b. A fold or crease.

EDD has *crimple* in this sense.

1922 SANDBURG *Slabs Sunburnt West* 10 If these bother respectable people With the right crimp in their napkins, . . . forgive us.

2. *pl.* An artificial waviness of the hair, crimped or curled hair.

1866 A. D. WHITNEY *L. Goldthwaite* vi, 'I've brushed out half my crimps,' she said again; 'and my ruffle is basted in wrong side out.' **1891** WILKINS in *Cent. Mag.* Feb. 501 She watched them as they . . . adjusted their lace veils over their crimps.

3. *To put a crimp in* (or *into*), to thwart or block. *Slang.*

1896 ADE *Artie* 106 They'll put a crimp in him if things come their way. **1911** HARRISON *Queed* 321 They never forgive a man who puts a crimp into the party. **1931** *K.C. Times* 17 July, Cigarettes went up to 15 cents a package, which . . . put a crimp in its jubilation.

∗**crimple,** *n.* A curl or ringlet of hair, a crimp *q.v. Obs.* — **1844** *Lowell Offering* IV. 148 My paper is full, and I can only say ribbons, bows, plumes, ruffles, fringes, wimples, and crimples. **1881** McLEAN *Cape Cod Folks* vi. 131 Teacher, . . . how shiny those crimples in your hair look, with that streak of sun lighting on 'em!

∗**crimson,** *a.* In the names of birds: (1) **crimson finch,** =**purple finch;** (2) **fronted finch,** the house finch, *Carpodacus mexicanus;* (3) **linnet,** =**purple finch;** (4) **necked bullfinch,** =**crimson-fronted finch.**

(1) **1858** *Atlantic Mo.* Oct. 596/2 Among the earliest songsters of spring . . . is the Crimson Finch or American Linnet. — (2) **1874** COUES *Birds N.W.* 109 The Crimson-fronted Finch is only an occasional visitor to Clear Creek County, Colorado. — (3) **1839** PEABODY *Mass. Birds* 330 The Purple Finch, *Fringilla purpurea.* . . . The crimson linnet, as it is sometimes called, has a rich and varied warble, clear as the softest tones of a flute. — (4) **1825** BONAPARTE *Ornithology* I. 50 The Crimson-necked Bullfinch was procured by Long's party, near the Rocky Mountains.

crinkle-root ˈkrɪŋklˌrut, *n.* An American variety of toothwort, *Dentaria diphylla.* — **1847** *Knickerb.* XXIX. 377 Sassafras is 'coming good' now too in the woods; and so is 'crinkle-root.' **1899** VAN DYKE *Fisherman's Luck* 74 Crinkle-root is spicy, but you must partake of it delicately, or it will bite your tongue.

cripple ˈkrɪpl̩, *n.* Also **creuple.** [f. Du. *kreupel* in such combs. as *kreupelbosch, -hout.* Cf. also G. *krüppelbaum, -busch.*] A swamp or low-lying tract of land overgrown with trees or shrubs. Cf. **mussel cripple.**

1675 *N.J. Archives* I. 115 The sd . . . land lyeth between two Small gutts or Run's, and streatches into the woods as far as the great Swamp or Cripple wch backs the said two Necks of land. **1676** *N.Y. State Col. Hist.* XII. 556 Martin Garritson was Imployed by Mr. Hans Block (Deceased) to make a way from his Plantation over the valley & Creuple, into his Backward Land which Lyeth behinde the Sayd Valley & Creuple. **1720** *Pa. Col. Records* III. (1852) 111 Then south 16 Degrees Lat through the Swamp and Cripple. **1890** *N. & Q.* 17 May V. 30 In parts of Connecticut even the low *swale,* or wet land about the backset, is sometimes called a *creek;* near Philadelphia it would be called a cripple. **1942** in WENTWORTH 144/2 The site was protected from intrusion by 2 spungs & a cripple on the west & north.

attrib. **1769** R. SMITH *Tour Four Great Rivers* (1906) 12 A Quantity of low cripple Land may be seen . . . & this reaches 4 miles to the Kaatskill. **1778** *Mass. H.S. Coll.* 2 Ser. II. 445 [We] proceeded as far as Jacob Truaxes cripple Bush, 11 miles from Albany. **1866** *Cong. Globe* 6 June 2995/2 In 1690 the London Land Company acquired title to League Island, known in the language of the day as 'cripple land,' signifying land which is in part covered by the tide, and in part overgrown with sturdy oaks and other trees of the forest.

cripple ail. [*EDD* has *cripple* in this sense.] (See quot.) — **1877** *Vt. Dairym. Ass. Rep.* V. 51 The 'Chocorua Plague' or 'cripple ail,' which prevails in New Hampshire near the foot of the White Mountains, arises from this cause [=lack of phosphate].

∗**crippled,** *a.* (See quot.) *Slang. Obs.* — **1869** J. H. BROWNE *Great Metropolis* 44 All stratagems are deemed fair in Wall Street. The only crime there is to be 'short' or 'crippled.'

crissal thrasher, thrush. A thrasher, *Toxostoma crissalis,* found in the Southwest.

1872 COUES *N. Amer. Birds* 75 Crissal Thrasher. **1878** HINTON *Hdbk. Ariz.* 338 The song of the crissal thrush . . . is said to be 'in sweetness of tone and modulation, almost unrivaled.' **1940** JAEGER *Desert Wild Flowers* 96 The shreddy bark of the screw bean is often sought by the crissal thrasher as lining material for the coarse-twigged nest which it builds.

∗**crisscross,** *n.* (See quots.) *Obs.* — **1848** BARTLETT 90 *Criss-cross,* a game played on slates by children, at school. **1893** W. CAMP *College Sports* 120 The criss-cross or double pass is another excellent example of a disguised play, the ball being passed by the quarter to one of the backs.

∗**Crittenden,** *n. attrib.* Of or pertaining to the Constitutional amendments and the resolutions relating to slavery proposed in Congress in 1860 by J. J. Crittenden (1787–1863) of Kentucky.

1860 *Bloomington* (Ill.) *D. Pantograph* 21 Dec. 2/2 Senator Douglas has decided to support Crittenden's proposition for restoring the Missouri compromise Line. **1863** *Cong. Rec.* 1166/1 [Senator Wilson] says the President has faithfully carried out the Crittenden Resolution. **1941** BUCKMASTER *Let My People Go* 283 The country had let the Crittenden Compromises lie joyfully in its mind as an alternative to bloodshed.

∗**critter,** see ∗**creature.**

∗**croaker,** *n.* Also †**croker,** †**crocus.** Any one of various fishes that make croaking noises (see quot. 1871).

1676 T. GLOVER *Virginia* in *Phil. Trans.* XI. 625 In the Creeks are great store of small fish, as Perches, Crokers, Taylors, Eels. **1772** in PHILLIPS *Notes on B. Romans* (1924) 123 It Abounds here in fish of all kinds, . . . the Hog Fish, the Croaker, the Glen Fish. **1871** *Amer. Naturalist* IV. 694 Croker (*Micropogon undulatus* Cuv.). A southern fish of the perch family; in form, deep like the sheepshead; color, silvery; takes clam bait eagerly; weight, from one to two pounds; a good table fish. **1947** DALRYMPLE *Panfish* 26 He stood on the beach at Santa Monica, California, watching the surf fishermen scramble for Yellowtail, Sand Sharks, and Croakers.

attrib. **1945** *Reader's Digest* Nov. 126/2 A croaker chorus is like the roar of a machine shop.

Croatan kroˈtæn, *n.* [Name of a village and formerly of an island off the coast of North Carolina.] *pl.* A group of several thousand people evidently of mixed Indian and white blood, found in eastern N.C., esp. in Robeson County. Also **Croatan Indians.**

"In 1911 the legislature, at the insistence of the mixed-bloods, struck out the word 'Croatan,' and the official name of the group became 'Indians of Robeson County N.C.' " (*Amer. Sp.*, April 1947, 86).

1907 HODGE *Amer. Indians* I. 365/2 About 20 years ago their claim was officially recognized and they were given a separate legal existence under the title of 'Croatan Indians,' on the theory of descent from Raleigh's lost colony of Croatan. **1923** LINDQUIST *Red Man in U.S.* 108 The Croatans may not in the strictest sense be classed as Indians. **1947** *Time* 3 Nov. 24/3 A 33-year-old member of the Croatan Indians was jailed for slashing two of his fellow tribesmen and drinking their blood.

∗**crockery,** *n.* **1. crockery crate,** a crate or case in which crockery is shipped. **2. crockery store,** a store in which crockery is sold. Both *obs.*

(1) **1849** FOSTER *N.Y. in Slices* 4 Nothing could more effectually stamp you as vulgar than to be seen stumbling over the crockery-crates . . . of the shilling pavement. **1869** BROWNE *Adv. Apache Country* 368 For a bed in a . . . crockery-crate, with straw, $7.50. — (2) **1844** NORRIS *Directory* 27 Burley, A. G. & Co. crockery store. **1863** MASSETT *Drifting About* 114, I . . . went with him to the office, . . . at about where Genella's crockery store now stands.

* **Crockett,** *n. A sin to Davy Crockett,* a frontier expression denoting anything of an exceptional or extraordinary sort, in allusion to David Crockett (1786–1836), the noted frontiersman. *Obs.*

1833 *Polit. Examiner* (Shelbyville, Ky.) 22 June 4/1 Now Penn says we ar' gone fawn skins, and that the way we'll get lamb'd is a sin to Davy Crockett. **1834** FEATHERSTONHAUGH *Slave States* (1844) 62 Any magnificent steamer, built upon a larger plan than usual, is called 'A sin to Crockett.' **1848** *New Negro Forget-me-not Songster* 90 De way I used 'em up was a sin to Davy Crockett.

* **crocodile,** *n.* The alligator, *Alligator mississipiensis,* of the southern states. *Obs.*

1587 HAKLUYT tr. Laudonnière *Notable Historie* 2r There is such aboundance of Crocodiles that often times in swimming men are assayled by them, of Serpents there are many sortes. **1682** ASH *Carolina* 32 In the mouths of their rivers, or lakes near the sea, . . . [is] the alligator or crocodile, whose scaly back is impenitrable. **1770** PITTMAN *Present State* 30 [Fish] abound here all the year, which accounts for the vast number of crocodiles that are continually on the banks of this river. **1864** WEBSTER 314/3 The American crocodile is properly an alligator. **1948** *Highway Traveler* Dec. 8/2 This is he only home of the American crocodile.

crocus ˈkrokəs, *n.* Also **crocos, crokass, croker.** [See note.]

The origin of this term is obscure. The *OED s.v. crocus,* the plant name, has a British example of 1710 of "Two Bales of Crocus," and under sense 5, "Crocus Ginger-bag" occurs taken from the same source as our 1699 quot. below. These quots. suggest that as the name of a material the term may not have been first used in this country, though the *OED* does not recognize such a sense.

1. "A coarse stuff worn by slaves and working people" (McClellan, *Dress,* 385).

1689 *Maine Doc. Hist.* IV. 458 Here is great want of . . . Some beds or Crocos to make Straw beds. **1764** in A. E. BROWN *J. Hancock, His Book* 44 Please to send . . . a Bale of crocus for Bread Bags, 7 or 800 yds., yd. wd.

2. Attrib. with **apron, bag, breeches, ginger-bag, shirt.** Chiefly *obs.*

1699 J. DICKENSON *God's Protecting Providence* 35 He gott some Canvass and Crocus ginger-baggs, which they had gott out of the Vessell. **1704** *Boston News-Letter* 13 Nov. 2/2 Ranaway on Wednesday last, the 8th. Currant from his Master in Boston, a Sirranum Indian: . . . has on a black broad Cloath Jacket, . . . a Crocus Apron, [etc.]. **1733** *N.J. Archives* XI. 322 Taken up . . . a New-Negro Man, . . . he had on nothing but a crocus Shirt. **1738** *Virginia Gaz.* 22 Sep., Ran away . . . Mulatto Slave . . . had on an old Felt Hat, a Canvas Shirt, a Cotton Jacket, and a Pair of Crocus Breeches. **1790** in CHALKLEY *Scotch-Irish Settlement Va.* I. 509 [After dissecting the body they] did sew him up in a crokass bag and put him in the cave within mentioned. **1904** STERLING *A Belle* 233 We therefore collected the silver, piece by piece, secreting it in 'crocus' bags.

b. crocus sack, croker-sack, (see quot. 1908).

1908 *D.N.* III. 302 croker-sack, n. A bag made of burlap or coarse brown hemp. Universal. The first element was doubtless originally *crocus,* the final *s* being absorbed by the initial *s* of sac. **1942** RAWLINGS *C. Creek* 103 As I came to the door, he held up one hand in command, unfurled a crocus sack, and with great drama rolled a large king snake onto the grass.

Crokinole ˈkrokəˌnol, *n.* The trade-mark for a game resembling squails, or the game itself. Also attrib.

1898 M. LEONARD *Big Front Door* 14 Just when we wanted to play Crokonole! **1902** *Sears Cat.* (ed. 112) 1136/1 Felt Lined Crokinole board, made of oak, highly polished. **1939** GILBERT *Forty Yrs.* 58, I had charge of the boys' club, and we played Crokinole and Barnyard, a game that is hard on the chairs.

cronk kraŋk, *n.* and *a.* A drink said to have been named from its inventor (see quot. *a*1856). *Obs.* — **1855** BESTE *Wabash* I. 319, I saw [near Indianapolis] a printed bill recommending a beverage it called 'Cronk.' I had seen this advertised in every village we had passed, and highly puffed. *a***1856** *Burlington Sentinel* in HALL *Coll. Words* (ed. 2) 461 We give a list of a few of the various words and phrases which have been in use, at one time or another, to signify some stage of inebriation: Over the bay, . . . swipy, slewed, cronk.

cronker ˈkraŋkɚ, *n.* [Imitative.] A wild goose. *Rare.* — **1888** *Portland Transcript* (F.), After a half-hour's wait, a flock of the wild cronkers, numbering several thousand, flew down near the spot and began devouring the corn.

cronocko krəˈnɑko, *n.* (See quots.) *Rare.* — *c***1618** STRACHEY *Virginia* 50 He [the weroance] and his cronoccoes, that is councellours, and priests. *Ib.* 60 The liuetenant of the blockhowse . . . overreached one of the cronockoes or chief men, and, closing with him, overthrew him.

* **crook,** *n.* and *a.*

1. A swindler or thief. *Colloq.*

1879 *Chi. Tribune* 6 Feb. 5/2 The *Times* still continues its attacks upon the Government officials in the interest of the Pekin and Peoria crooks. **1896** FRANCIS *Frauds of Amer.* (1902) 364 That class of circus followers outside the pale of the law, such as pickpockets, gamblers and short-change men, are titled 'crooks' or 'grafters.' **1948** *Green Bay* (Wis.) *Press-Gazette* 13 July 5/2 The detective went in and subdued the crook with the butt-end of his pistol.

2. In combs.: (1) * **crook-back,** a contemptible person, *rare;* (2) **knife,** ?a knife having a crooked blade, *obs.;* (3) **neck,** a squash of a variety characterized by crooked necks, in full **crook neck squash,** cf. next, and see **crooked neck(ed), summer crookneck;** (4) **-necked squash,** =prec.

(1) *c***1828** PRAY *Mem. J. G. Bennett* 105 We have called Jackson a murderer, an adulterer, a traitor, an ignoramus, a fool, a crook-back, a pretender and so forth. — (2) **1866** *Rep. Indian Affairs* 292,200 buckskin needles, 100 awls, 6 crook-knives. — (3) [**1756** KALM *Resa* II. 439 Crocknecks eller Krumhalsar kallades et slags Pumpor, som äro krokote på ändan, samt eljest nog aflånga.] **1812** in *Amer. Sp.* XXI. (1946) 117/1 A crookneck or winter squash pudding. **1830** *Westchester* (N.Y.) *Village Rec.* 23 June, The captain takes a darnd great yaller thing just like a crook neck squash, and puts it to his mouth and bawls through it. **1948** *Chi. Tribune* 16 July 23/2 The most familiar squashes, white scallop or patty pan, yellow crookneck, and zucchini are all cooked in the same way. — (4) **1818** *Mass. Spy* 11 Nov. (Th.), Upwards of ten tons of the best crook-necked & winter Squashes. **1831** *Working-man's Gazette* (Woodstock, Vt.) 19 Jan. 190/3 Joe Gawky . . . stooped in his chest like a crook-necked squash. **1945** *N. Eng. Homestead* 27 Oct. 3/2 They are shaped much like a banana and the size of a summer crooknecked squash.

* **crook,** *v.tr.* To steal, cheat, defraud. *Slang.* — **1882** C. B. LEWIS *Lime-Kiln Club* 216 But for a jury of six good men he would once have gone to jail on the charge of 'crooking' six hens. **1948** *L.A. Times* 19 Dec. (Comics) 1, I didn't crook his brother. He paid me in counterfeit dough.

* **crooked,** *a.*

1. Dishonest, unscrupulous, unlawful. *Colloq.*

1876 *S.F. Dly. Examiner* 10 Oct. 4/5 Aside from 'crooked' official ways there might be more said, but enough for the present. **1891** ROBERTS *Adrift America* 196 If you are not too good to do a little crooked business I can put you in the way of living more comfortably than you seem to be doing at present. **1948** *Duncan* (Okla.) *D. Banner* 1 July 8/7, I was never involved in any crooked work.

2. In combs.: (1) **crooked fence,** (see quot.), for **crooked rail fence** see **rail fence;** (2) **neck(ed),** *a.* having a crooked neck or stem, usu. with **squash;** (3) * **stick,** (see quot. 1923); (4) **whisky,** whisky on which the payment of tax or license has been evaded.

(1) **1909** *D.N.* III. 410 Crooked fence, n.phr. A Virginia fence. — (2) **1784** *Mass. Spy* 22 April 1/1 Garden Seeds [include]. . . . Crooked neck squash; early dwarf kidney, and six week beans. **1870** WARNER *Summer in Garden* viii, He said the summer squash . . . was nearly all leaf and blow, with only a sickly crooked-necked fruit after a mighty fuss. **1908** *D.N.* III. 297 *Cashaw,* a large crooked-necked pumpkin or squash with dappled, greenish stripes. — (3) **1848** LOWELL *Biglow P.* 1 Ser. ix. 124 So, ez I ain't a crooked stick, . . . I'll go back to my plough. **1923** *D.N.* V. 234 crooked stick. . . . A man who has turned out to be more or less a failure in life. No dishonesty of character is implied. 'She was very partikler who she was goin' to marry, but she finally picked up a crooked stick.' [sw. Wis.] — (4) **1875** *Chi. Tribune* 25 Aug. 2/2 The United States authorities seized 350 barrels of crooked whisky at the warehouse of the Chicago Canal and Dock Company. **1883** HOWELLS *Woman's Reason* xvii, Lots of people make a living by selling crooked whisky.

b. *Crooked as a dog's hind leg,* (see quot. 1903 and cf. **1.** above). *Colloq.* Cf. **hell-western crooked.**

1903 *D.N.* II. 310 crooked as a dog's hind leg, *colloq. phr.* Very crooked. [se. Mo.] **1920** LEWIS *Main Street* 166 Terry is crooked as a dog's hind leg.

* **crookedness,** *n.* Dishonesty. *Colloq.*

1876 *Wkly. Jimplecute* (Jefferson, Tex.) 5 April 4/1 Our friend Moise Kahn has been charged with a little 'crookedness' in his whiskies. **1896** FRANCIS *Frauds of Amer.* (1902) 296 If they do it is accepted as an indication of crookedness, and the suspected points are at once put under the closest espionage. **1947** R. SMITH *Baseball* 231 In the earliest days of the game the gamblers had won such a hold that crookedness was almost taken for granted.

* **crop,** *n.*

1. The time at which agricultural crops are gathered. *Obs.*

1623 in NEILL *Virginia Carolorum* 69 Mr. Bolton shall receive for his salary . . . ten pounds of tobacco, and one bushel of corn, for every planter and tradesman, above the age of sixteen years, alive at the crop. **1678** *Brookhaven Rec.* 49 Forty five pound to be payd in good tobackoe, in hogsheds, at three pence a pound in duch weight, to be delivered at yourk fery, the next ensueing crop.

2. In combs.: (1) **crop book,** (see quot.), *obs.;* (2) **grass,** =**crab grass** (*a*); (3) **hogshead,** (see quots.), *obs.;* (4) **lien law,** *S.* a law giving to one who advances food and supplies to a farmer a lien on the crop; (5) **master,** one in charge, usu. as owner, of a growing crop, *obs.;* (6) **mortgage,** a mortgage on a crop; (7) **note,** (see quot. 1937); (8) **report,** a report on the condition of crops; (9) **reporter,** one who reports on the condition of crops in a given area; (10) **reporting service, system,** a service or system whereby the federal government secures and distributes information about crops; (11) **tobacco,** ?tobacco used in filling crop hogsheads, *obs.;* (12) **writer,** one who writes about crops.

(1) **1800** W. TATHAM *Tobacco* 79 The crop book is the most important concern: it contains a regular entry, in columns, of every single hogshead of *crop* tobacco. — (2) **1775** ROMANS *Nat. Hist. Florida* 128 The artificial grasses found here are 1st. That kind of grass known in the islands by the name of dog grass, and in Carolina and Georgia by that of crop grass. **1944** HARPER *Weeds* 62 When this [*Syntherisma sanguinale*] first came to the notice of English speaking people it was called 'crop grass.' — (3) **1784** SMYTH *Tour* II. 138 The weight of each hogshead must be nine hundred and fifty pounds neat, exclusive of the cask, for less a note will not be given under the name of a Crop hogshead. **1800** W. TATHAM *Tobacco* 85 The standard weight of a shipable, or, what is commonly termed, a *crop*, hogshead. — (4) **1935** CASON *90°* 35 Up and down the Cotton Belt southern states after 1865 vied with one another in passing crop lien laws.

(5) **1800** W. TATHAM *Tobacco* 100 The *crop master* is generally the proprietor of the land which he cultivates. **1850** in TURNER *Cotton* (1865) 42, I do not regard some of our large crop-masters as worthy of imitation—they make eight, ten, aye, twelve bales per hand, but it is by working negroes, and wasting land. — (6) **1939** *These Are Our Lives* 121 When land is rented a crop mortgage is taken. — (7) **1769** *Md. Hist. Mag.* X. 135 Nathan Hammond delivers to the Vestry Two Crop notes for their Tobacco cropt last Fall, which were given to the Treasurer to sell for them. **1937** LANGDON *Everyday Things* 313 In Virginia, for example, after about 1734 there were public warehouses to which planters could send tobacco and receive in return therefor certificates, usually called crop-notes, in various amounts large and small. These certificates stated the value not in money but in pounds of tobacco. These could be passed as money and were accepted as such. — (8) **1876** *Stockton* (Calif.) *W. Herald* 5 Aug. 1/2 (*heading*), The Crop Report in Chicago. **1940** BABSON *Business Barometers* 9 Government *Crop Reports* are important to the businessman. — (9) **1947** *Chi. Tribune* 18 Oct. 1/7 They have no place for the sheep and are dumping them on the market at substantial losses, crop reporters said. **1948** *Norman* (Okla.) *Transcript* 4 July 4/2 A. W. Erickson, Minneapolis crop reporter, found many stalks with double and triple heads in the southwest from 1942 through 1945.

(10) **1873** *Dept. Agric. Rep.* 10 The crop-reporting system, though an unpaid service, is more efficient and reliable than any other means employed to ascertain the condition of growing crops. **1911** *Amer. Acad. Pol. Sci. Annals* Sep. 93 The crop reporting service has been evolved and enlarged into the Bureau of Statistics of the Department of Agriculture. — (11) **1780** *Cal. Va. St.Papers* I. 385 Balance due Carter Braxton £23758, 12. 0, payable in Crop Tobacco @ £65 pr: 100 wt. **1800** [see **crop book**]. — (12) **1897** *U.S. Dept. Agric. Yearbk.* 67 (*Cent. Supp.*), Educated and practically trained meteorologists, crop writers, printers, and messengers are on duty.

As the last term in **banner, calf, cash, ditch stone, hide, hog, ice, Indian corn, knee, log, maple, money, over, over half, peanut, provision, sale, sandy, share, slip, sod, stem, tobacco, top, truck, vigintial, volunteer, war crop.**

***crop,** *v. intr.* To work as a farmer. *Colloq.*

*a*1847 in H. HOWE *Ohio* 357 Among the first settlers . . . was John Knoop . . . he came down the Ohio to Cincinnati, and cropped the first season on Zeigler's stone house farm. **1885** CRADDOCK *Prophet* 33 They an' thar sons rooted up the wilderness. They crapped. **1903** *D.N.* II. 310 crop . . . cultivate. 'I am *cropping* with Mr. Brown this year.' [se. Mo.]

croppie, see **crappie.**

***cropping,** *n.* As the last term in **green, share, Virginia cropping.**

***cross,** *n., a.,* and *adv.*

In some of the following combs. the 1st element has verbal force, but the terms are grouped together for convenience of reference.

1. In combs.: (1) **cross-buck saddle,** *W.* a pack saddle resembling a small sawbuck, cf. **cross tree;** (2) **creek,** either of two creeks the mouths of which are opposite each other on different sides of the stream they flow into; (3) **cut,** see as a main entry; (4) **fox,** (see quot. 1917); (5) **handed,** *adv.* in a manner which involves the crossing of one's hands, esp. in rowing; (6) **haul,** (see quots. 1905 and 1926), also **cross hauling,** also attrib.; (7) ***legged,** *a.* designating articles of furniture the legs of which are crossed; (8) **line,** a transportation line that crosses another or that connects others, also attrib.; (9) **log,** a log used in making one of the ends of a log cabin, *obs.;* (10) **lots,** *a.* and *adv.* extending or going across a field, meadow, etc., across the fields, as a short cut, *colloq.;* (11) **over,** a portion of railroad track that joins two main lines or roads, also attrib.; (12) **post,** a mail route that connects certain places or main routes, *obs.;* (13) **road,** see as a main entry; (14) **tag,** (see quot. 1891); (15) **tie,** a transverse railroad sleeper, cf. **railroad crosstie;** (16) **Cross Timbers,** see as a main entry; (17) **town,** (*a*) *a.* extending or going across a town or city, (*b*) *adv.* across a town or city; (18) **tree,** (see quots. and cf.

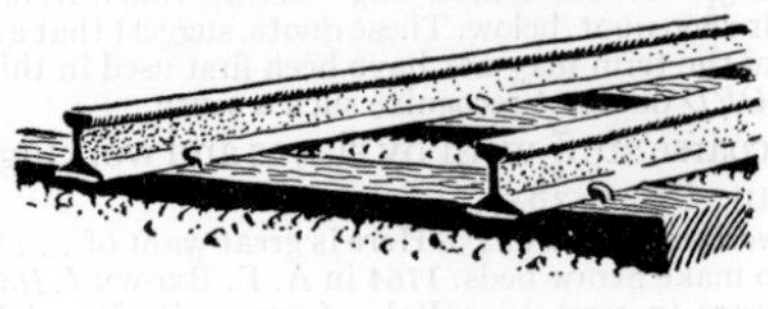

Crosstie and T rails

cross-buck saddle); (19) **vine,** a woody vine, *Bignonia capreolata,* of the southern states; (20) ***way(ing),** a causeway, *obs.*

(1) **1922** P. A. ROLLINS *Cowboy* 153 The West employed two types of pack-saddle, respectively designated as the 'cross-buck saddle' and the 'aparejo.' **1947** *Trail & Timberline* May 75/1 You will need . . . a wooden cross-buck pack saddle, a pad and a saddle blanket. — (2) **1635** in *Amer. Sp.* XV. 169/1 Soe coming down the river to a Crosse Creek. **1770** *Ib.* 169/1 We came to two other cross Creeks that on the West side largest. **1942** RAWLINGS (*title*), Cross Creek. — (4) [**1792** CARTWRIGHT *Labrador Jrnl.* 374 Cross-fox. A fox which is bred between a silver and yellow.] **1897** LEONARD *Gold Fields Klondike* 80 The beautiful silver or black fox, the red fox, cross fox, and, on the coast, the white fox, are among the most valuable of the fur animals. **1917** *Mammals of Amer.* 75 The Cross Fox gets its name from the large cross-mark formed by two dark stripes; one across the shoulders, and the other running down the middle of the back. . . . It occurs . . . occasionally in the northwestern States.

(5) **1836** IRVING *Astoria* I. 110 The merchant fishermen . . . passed the objects of traffic, as it were, crossed-handed; trading away part of the wares received from the mountain tribes to those of the river and the plains, and *vice versa.* **1882** *Cent. Mag.* Sep. 708/1 The gaunt women bring their stuff to 'trade' at the village stores, rowing 'cross-handed.' — (6) **1905** *Forestry Bureau Bul. 61* Cross haul. . . . The cleared space in which a team moves in cross hauling. (N.F.) **1924** SHEPHARD *P. Bunyan* 80 He sent Bud to Ashland over forty miles away to get a crosshaul, and the kid didn't know no better than to start out to go after it. **1926** RICKABY *Ballads* 234 Cross-haul. A line (chain) used in the early days in loading logs. Cross-haul loading, in spite of the fact that it has been superseded by the modern (but less romantic) steam loaders, served the shanty-boy long and well. — (7) **1854** M. S. CUMMINS *Lamplighter* v. 34 I've got a very good little cross-legged bedstead . . . and I will lend it to you. **1869** TOURGEE *Toinette* xvii. 185 The low, cross-legged table, which we kept clean and white. — (8) **1803** *Fredericktown* (Md.) *Herald* 30 April 4/4 There are several cross lines, viz. One from Baltimore by the way of Frederick-Town to Hager's Town, one from Baltimore by the way of Petersburg and Gettysburg to Chambersburg. **1918** VISHER *So. Dakota* 114 Cross-line railroads have not been built, and several of the young towns are so nearly equal in size that it is quite uncertain which will attain leadership. — (9) **1822** J. WOODS *English Prairie* 275 They continue till the building is nine or ten logs high on each side, when the two last cross-logs are laid on three or four feet longer than the other cross ones; this is to form a sort of eaves to drip the logs. **1881** TOURGEE *'Zouri's Christmas* ii, There was no second story; only some loose boards laid upon the cross-logs on one side.

(10) 1825 J. NEAL *Bro. Jonathan* I. 138 They could push on, a pooty, tedious, clever bit furder, cross lots — they could. 1873 MARK TWAIN & WARNER *Gilded Age* xxi. 199 The Montague dwelling, where Ruth lived, the cross-lots path she traversed to the Seminary. 1922 A. BROWN *Old Crow* 469 They might even go over to Mountain Brook by the path 'cross lots.' — (11) 1884 *Harper's Mag.* July 272/2 The incoming trains approach the city on the western track until they reach the 'cross-over,' which throws them to the eastern track. 1898 HAMBLEN *Gen'l Manager's Story* 123 An eighth of a mile beyond the bridge was a cross-over switch. 1947 BEEBE *Mixed Train Dly.* 236 Thirsty colored folk and parched but hopeful hillbillies are forever dreaming that one of its cars, awash with barrels of wonderful, expensive bonded whisky, may roll down an embankment or come to grief at the Southern crossover at Georgetown. — (12) 1791 *State P.* (1819) I. 28 The establishment of additional cross posts . . . cannot fail to be of material utility. 1796 in R. PUTNAM *Memoirs* 414 Marietta may be accommodated with a cross Post to connect with the route from Wheeling to Limeston. — (14) 1891 *Amer. Folk-Lore* IV. 223 Cross Tag. The player who is 'it' selects one of the others whom he will chase. The pursued is given a short start, and, while both are running, another player will try to cross between them. If successful, he becomes the object of pursuit. 1894 WISTER in *Harper's Mag.* LXXXVIII. 782/1 'What could they have been after, do you think? . . . 'Playing cross-tag,' said Mart.

(15) [1813 *Niles' Reg.* III. 323/1 The three large ribs are preserved in their proper relative situations by fifty-four crossties.] 1833 in COMMONS *Doc. Hist.* I. 219 Begun laying cross-ties of plantation railroad. 1948 *Democrat* 23 Sep. 1/2 The following forest production figures were reported . . . cross ties and switch ties, 1,146,305. — (17) (*a*) 1894 *Cong. Rec.* 28 May 5413/1, I do not believe that on the L street, or, as it is called, this cross-town road, it is possible for a cable or electric motor to be successfully used. 1947 *Time* 3 Nov. 112/3 It straddles Manhattan in the manner of a crosstown bus. (*b*) 1906 O. HENRY *Four Million* (1916) 165 The crowd in the gutter scattered, and the fine hansom dashed away 'cross-town. 1916 WILSON *Red Gap* 401 Then up a little way we catch sight of a regular old-fashioned horse-car going cross-town. — (18) 1913 *Outing* Jan. 425/1 The crosstree or sawbuck, however, is used almost exclusively by forest rangers, cowboys, prospectors and pack travelers generally. 1933 CHELEY *Camping Out* 462 The packing that we shall consider here will be with the cross-tree type. 1943 GEIST *Hiking* 128 The load is carried on the pack animal by means of alforjas (saddlebags) and panniers, or the sawbuck or crosstree saddle for the carrying of duffel bags. — (19) 1785 MARSHALL *Amer. Grove* 21 *Bignonia crucigera.* Cross-vine. This rises with slender trailing stalks, which must be supported, . . . being impatient of much cold. 1838 GOSSE *Letters* 114 There are other plants which climb up trees. . . . There is one which is named the Cross Vine, from the singular circumstance of its stem, on the stripping off of its bark, spontaneously dividing into four parts, as if split crosswise into quarters. 1944 HARPER *Weeds* 204 In Small's Manual it is made the type of *Bignonia*, a name long used for our well-known native cross-vine.

(20) 1794 E. DENNY *Journal* 199 But there does not appear to have been any cross-way done. *Ib.* 201 Indeed in many places where the cross-waying is, the ground does not appear to want it. 1879 BISHOP *4 Months in Sneak-Box* 93, I had frequently built crossways over treacherous swamps.

b. In less frequent combs., often rare or obs.: (1) ***cross-bill,** see as the last term in **European, red, white-winged crossbill;** (2) **brander,** *W.* ?a brand-blotter or cattle thief, cf. **cross brand,** *v.;* (3) **chains,** (see quot.); (4) **cleavers,** the wild licorice; (5) **gig and saddle,** a certain combination of numbers in the game of policy; (6) **-hop,** (*a*) =**cross-jump,** cf. **crosscut,** (*b*) a term used in card playing, *obs.* in both senses, cf. **double cross-hop;** (7) **jump,** in dancing, a frolicsome leap into the air during which the performer's legs are crossed and uncrossed, cf. **double cross-hop,** and G. *kreuzsprung* in the same sense; (8) **middlings,** a grade of flour; (9) **pins,** pushpin; (10) **roader,** (*a*) one who lives in a crossroads village, (*b*) (see quot.), *rare* in both senses; (11) **saddle,** designating a certain combination of numbers in the game of policy; (12) ***shot,** a view from another position to calculate a desired location; (13) **shuffle,** a step in dancing; (14) **staked pole fence,** (see quot.).

(2) 1912 R. A. WASON *Friar Tuck* xl. 269 There must be at least fifteen crossbranders in the neighbourhood and probably more. — (3) 1905 *Forestry Bureau Bul. 61* Cross chains. Chains connecting the front and rear sleds of a logging sled. (N.F.) — (4) 1814 BIGELOW *Florula Bostoniensis* 37 *Galium brachiatum.* Cross Cleavers. . . . Found in woods. . . . Fruit a little burr.

(5) 1847 C. WHITE *Policy Players* (1874) 3, I want 8, 5, and 14 in a cross gig and saddle, for ten cents in each. — (6) (*a*) 1835 A. B. LONGSTREET *Ga. Scenes* (1843) 17 Jake Slack went to make a cross-hop just now, and tied his legs in a hard knot, and i stop'd to help him untie them. (*b*) 1838 *S. Lit. Messenger* IV. 328 'Let me look at your hand.' 'Won't you take a cross-hop?' — (7) 1842 in *Amer. Sp.* XVIII. 123 But you frightened Mrs. Strong with your cross-jumps, and Frencher-capers. — (8) 1818 *Niles' Reg.* XIV. 359/2 *Petersburg, Va. inspections,* for April, May, and June, 1818—7541 *bbls* superfine; 331 do. fine; 660 do. cross middlings. — (9) 1866 WHITTIER *Snowbound* 445 He teased the mitten-blinded cat, Played cross-pins on my uncle's hat.

(10) (*a*) *c*1870 BAGBY *Old Va. Gentleman* 278 [He] dismissed the case, and sent the Madison Cross Roaders home, grumbling and dissatisfied. (*b*) 1889 BARRERE-LELAND I. 283 Cross-roader (American), a man whose ways are doubtful or dishonest. . . . For the simple purpose of being introduced to the club, there to 'fleece the suckers,' who never suspect they are playing against a cross-roader.—Chicago Tribune. — (11) 1847 C. WHITE *Policy Players* (1874) 6 Give me 10, 32, 9, and 25. I want them in a cross saddle combination for twenty cents in each. — (12) 1944 *New Yorker* 7 Oct. 38/3 The ranger . . . immediately called another lookout and asked for what foresters call a cross shot at the smoke. — (13) 1835 *S. Lit. Messenger* I. 550 Horse-galloping dances . . . for gentlemen . . . cross shuffle . . . for ladies.— (14) 1880 *Scribner's Mo.* Feb. 502/2 There were also cross-staked pole fences, in which the fence was laid straight, each pole being upheld by two stakes crossing the one beneath, their lower ends being driven into the ground.

c. *Without a cross,* having no racial mixture. *Colloq. Obs.*

[1826 COOPER *Mohicans* viii. 98 What might be right and proper in a red-skin, may be sinful in a man who has not even a cross in blood to plead for his ignorance.] 1849 M'LEAN *Notes* I. 211 In their physiognomy and personal appearance they exhibit all the characteristic features of the genuine aboriginal race; and that party certainly appeared, one and all, to be 'without a cross.'

2. In verbal expressions: (1) **cross-brand,** *W.* (see quot. and cf. **vent,** *v.*); (2) ***cut,** to take a short cut across (country); (3) **hoe,** to hoe (ground) across the line followed in a previous breaking, *obs.;* (4) **pile,** to pile (lumber) so that the pieces in successive layers are at right angles to each other; (5) **way,** to render (a place) passable by means of a causeway, *obs.*

(1) 1877 COZZENS *Crossing the Quicksands* 302 Each animal purchased must be 'cross-branded,' i.e., the seller re-brands upon the shoulder, as a sign that his title to the animal has passed. — (2) 1903 A. ADAMS *Log Cowboy* 49, I cross cut the country and was soon on another trail of our stampeded cattle. — (3) 1788 WASHINGTON *Diaries* III. 324 The women at this place began to cross hoe the gr[oun]d they had broke up in the lower end of the Ho. Meadow. — (4) 1878 *Lumberman's Gaz.* 25 Dec. 446 The amount of lumber now cross-piled on the several mill docks . . . is . . . about seventy two million feet. — (5) 1794 E. DENNY *Journal* 199 Near five miles was cross-way'd, and no road can be had from the lake to French creek with less.

As the last term in **Saint Andrew's, Southern, top, widow's cross.**

***cross,** *v.a.* **to cross out,* (see quot.). **b.** *to cross off corn land,* (see quot.). Both *obs.* — (a) 1883 E. EGGLESTON *Hoosier School-Boy* i. 12 The ball thrown between a batter and the base to which he was running 'crossed him out.' — (b) 1927 *Florida Plant. Rec.* 586 *Crossing off corn land:* running furrows in a checker-board pattern preparatory to planting corn. Liability to erosion in the South confines this practice to level lands.

***crosscut,** *n.*

1. a. =**cross jump.** *Obs.* **b.** A crosscut saw. **c.** A way of cutting cards.

(a) 1842 DICKENS *Amer. Notes* (1850) 62/2 Single shuffle, double shuffle, cut and cross-cut. — (b) 1853 P. PAXTON *Yankee in Texas* 89 Far more congenial to my feelings than felling trees, handling cross-cuts, rolling blocks. 1942 RICH *We Took to Woods* (1948) 55 Excellence on a two-man cross-cut has nothing to do with size and strength. — (c) 1903 *Cin. Enquirer* 3 Jan. 11/5 Well, they kep' up the cross-cut for two or three draws, and finding they couldn't scare Jennings out, Foster dropped his hand.

2. In combs.: (1) **crosscut heel,** (see quot.), *obs.;* (2) **saw,** a saw for cutting across the grain of wood, as contrasted with a ripsaw; usu. from five to seven feet long, for use by two men.

(1) 1853 FELT *Customs N. Eng.* 84 By 1714, such heels had lost some of their altitude. Still they were common until fifty-two years ago, under the name of *cross-cut* heels. Small girls, as well as women, wore them. — (2) 1645 *Conn. Rec.* I. 467 If my sonne shall liue to the age of eighteene yeares . . . he shall haue my gunne, . . . and my long crosscutt sowe. 1880 *Lumberman's Gaz.* Jan. 728 The trees are cut

into logs by a long 'crosscut' saw. **1948** *Milwaukee Jrnl.* 18 July (Sports Sec.) 6/1 My old man celebrated his eighty-sixth birthday by . . . rehanging two doors, filing one crosscut hand saw.

b. *To saw a crosscut,* ?to saw a cut across a log. *Rare.*
1861 *Cong. Globe* 2 March 1354/2 In the West . . . we sometimes do what we call 'sawing a cross cut.' It always requires two to perform the operation well.

crosse krɔs, *n.* Also **cross.** [f. **lacrosse.**]

1. =**lacrosse.** *Obs.* Cf. **bagataway, ball play.**
1763 in F. B. HOUGH *Siege of Detroit* (1860) 29 We were inform'd, that the 2d June the Chippawas were playing at Cross at Michilimackinac. **1806** PIKE *Sources Miss.* (1810) I. 100 This afternoon they had a great game of the cross on the prairie, between the Sioux on the one side, and the Puants and Reynards on the other.

One form of crosscut saw

2. (See quots.)
1867 *Ball Players' Chron.* 20 June 5/4 It is played with a 'crosse,' each player carrying one, and a sponge rubber ball. *Ib.* 24 Oct. 7/2 This 'Crosse' is a hickory stick, about four feet long and bent at the end, and over the crooked part a network of deerskin is stretched, on which the ball is caught and carried until knocked out by an opponent. **1916** BANCROFT *Handbook* 374 Crosse. The netted stick used in lacrosse. The terms 'crosse' and 'stick' are used interchangeably.

b. In full **crosse stick.** *Obs.* Cf. **ball stick.**
1806 PIKE *Sources Miss.* (1810) 100 The ball is made of some hard substance and covered with leather, the cross sticks are round and net work, with handles of three feet long.

***crossing,** *n.* A place where a river or other body of water is crossed. In full ***crossing place.** Cf. **buffalo crossing.**
1753 GIST *Journals* 82 This day we travelled to the big crossing, about fifteen miles. **1763** WASHINGTON *Diaries* I. 193 A common causay through at the crossing place woud. most certainly lay all that Arm dry. **1848** RUXTON in *Blackw. Mag.* LXIII. 717 Probably he would . . . have struck the big river, and leaving at the 'Crossing' the waggons destined for Santa Fé, have trailed us up the Arkansa to Bent's Fort. **1930** *Denver Post* 22 June II. 9/3 When I sent the riders out, I told them we would bunch the cattle at the crossing on Troublesome [Creek].

b. A place in a river where steamboats seeking the safest channel cross from one side to the other. Also attrib.
1875 MARK TWAIN *Old Times on Miss.* iii. 51 By and by even the shoal water and the countless crossing-marks began to stay with me. *Ib.* v. 89 If you go on until you know every street crossing, the character, size and position of the crossing-stones. **1942** ROBERT A. HEREFORD *Old Man River* 109 At a 'crossing' where the channel which had been following one side of the river suddenly shifted to the other.

c. crossing log, =**foot log.**
c1845 *Big Bear Ark.,* etc. 130 I'll go to the Cypress crossin' log. **1858** D. K. BENNETT *Chron. N.C.* 24 In a hot pursuit by Indians they were once compelled to seek shelter under the 'crossing log' over a creek.

As the last term in **blind, buffalo, farm, grade, Indian, log crossing.**

***crossroad,** *n.* Often used in combs. (frequently in *pl.*) with derogatory implications of smallness, cheapness, etc., as (1) **crossroads grocery,** (2) **politician,** (3) **store(keeper),** (4) **town.**
(1) **1868** *Putnam's Mag.* I. 715 Now and then an enterprising specimen of the breed set up a 'crossroads grocery,' and prosecuted his nocturnal trade with the blacks on a large scale. **1944** *Reader's Digest* July 108 An excellent place to encounter the shantyboater, in the southernmost tributaries, is the floating store or fish docks—to the river dweller what the crossroads grocery is to the rustic on land. — (2) **1869** *Champaign Co.* (Ill.) *Gazette* 26 May 1/2 Then work for the man and defer the payments we may have promised to Cross-roads politicians until the recurrence of an election fraught with less interest. **1905** *Forum* April 485 Mr. Cleveland was the first President with the moral courage to place an obstacle in the way of the cross-roads politicians. — (3) **1845** *S. Lit. Messenger* XI. 586/1 Let the country merchant and cross-road store-keeper go to the importer and pay him for the goods. **1944** CLARK *Pills* 11 Crossroad stores frequently marked the beginnings of towns. They stood at important points on highways and railroads, and by process of accretion villages and towns grew up about them. — (4) **1882** *Rep. Ala. R.R. Comm.* II. 20 Merchants at poor markets in a few cross-roads towns . . . sell goods. **1916** THOBURN *Hist. Oklahoma* III. 784 Oklahoma City was in those days known as 'the cross roads town.'

Also *crossroads highschool, hotel, idea, log cabin, schoolhouse, settlement, tavern, village,* etc.

Cross Timbers. (See quot. 1834.) Now *hist.*
1820 DEWEES *Lett. Texas* 15, I joined a party of about thirty men, who were going up Red river to the Cross Timbers on a buffalo hunt. **1834** A. PIKE *Sketches* 13 These Cross Timbers are a belt of timber, extending from the Canadian, or a little further north, to an unknown distance south of Red River. The belt is in width from fifteen to fifty miles, composed of black-jack and post oak, with a thick undergrowth of small bushy oak and briers. **1924** F. R. BECHDOLT *Tales of Old-Timers* 224 It was July 21 when they came to the Cross Timbers. This belt of woodlands, which stretched half-way across the State of Texas, marked the western limit of the territory that was known to the white man.

b. (See quot.)
1945 MATHEWS *Talking* 22 As a matter of fact, they [blackjacks] go by any number of names, such as scrub-oak, jack-oak, and Cross Timbers.

crotalism ˈkrotḷˌɪzəm, *n.* [f. *Crotal*aria + *-ism.*] (See quot.) — **1900** *U.S. Dept. Agric. Yearbook* 308 (*Cent. Supp.*), The diseases resulting from plant poisoning known as locoism and *crotalism,* which prevail in some parts of the West and Northwest, are caused, respectively, by the continued eating in the field of some one of the several locoweeds (Astragalus and Aragallus species) and by the eating of the rattleweed or rattlebox (Crotalaria sagittalis) either in the field or in hay.

Crotalus ˈkrotələs, *n.* [NL. based on Gk. *krotalon,* rattle.] The genus consisting of the typical American rattlesnakes. Also (not *cap.*) a snake of this genus.
1792 *Mass. Mag.* IV. 249 The Crotalus Horridus, or Rattle Snake, in zoology, a genus belonging to the order of Amphibiae Serpenter. **1816** J. BIGELOW in *N.-Eng. Jrnl. Med. & Surgery* V. 338 We were told by the people in Bartlett and Conway, that the rattlesnake (*crotalus horridus*) infests the rocks and sides of the hills in great numbers. **1866** *Beadle's Mo.* Feb. 153/1 The Prairie Dog's . . . size and fearlessness make him an easy prey to owl, crotalus and cayota. **1933** DITMARS *Reptiles of World* 255 The typical rattlesnakes—genus *Crotalus*—have the top of the head covered with small scales, except, with a few species, a few crowded plates directly over the snout.

***crotch,** *n.*

1. A V-shaped cut made in the ears of cattle to denote ownership. *Rare.*
1653 *Plymouth Rec.* 2 The marke of his cattle is a croch on the left eare.

2. The area immediately above the junction of two rivers, the bifurcation of a river.
1698 *Conn. Probate Rec.* I. 574, I give him a certain parcell of Land lying in the Crotch of the River. **1725** *Lancaster Rec.* 240 We marched to ye crotch of ye River. **1845** SIMMS *Wigwam & Cabin* 280 The Forks of Edisto—a part of the country thus distinguished as it lies in the crotch formed by the gradual approach of the two branches of Edisto River.

3. The place at which a road forks, or where roads meet or separate.
1752 *Duxbury Rec.* 311 The New Meeting house at the Northerly corner of John Chanlers 2d Homestead by the crotch of the ways. **1780** E. PARKMAN *Diary* 204 Mr. Andrews and Mr. Gale . . . have got to ye crotch of ye Road. **1857** HOLLAND *Bay-Path* xxii. 265 I'm standing right in the crotch of the roads.

4. crotch tongue, (see quot.).
1905 *Forestry Bureau Bul. 61* Crotch tongue. Two pieces of wood in the form of a V, joining the front and rear sleds of a logging sled. (N.W., L.S.)

Croton ˈkrotṇ, *n.* [See note.]

Hodge says "Tooker considers the word a personal name and drives it from *kloltin,* in the Delaware dialect of Algonquian, signifying 'he contends.'" The word is app. not **Croton,* a genus of plants.

1. Short for **Croton water.** Also attrib.
1843 *Knickerb.* XXII. 94 Anon flooding his doors, windows and blinds with hissing streams of Croton. **1882** *Harper's Mag.* April 721/2 Ogla-Moga looked at the innocent glass of Croton that was handed him with undisguised disdain. **1905** *N.Y. Ev. Post* 16 Dec. 8 The headquarters where nothing stronger than a Croton cocktail can be obtained. **1927** SANDBURG *Songbag* 272 It was old jerked beef, croton coffee, and sour bread.

2. Short for **Croton (water) bug.** *Obs.*
1876 *Billings' Farmer's Allminax* 12 Thare is only one sure way to git the krotons out ov a house, burn up the house.

3. In special combs.: (1) **Croton (water) bug,** a small, winged cockroach, *Blatella germanica,* that became common in New York shortly after the city was supplied with Croton water; (2) **water,** water from the Croton River in Westchester County, New York, first utilized as a water supply by New York City in 1842.
(1) **1857** T. B. GUNN *N.Y. Boarding-Houses* 53 The buckwheat cakes . . . sometimes had insects (known as Croton-water bugs) in them. **1894** *Life* 19 April 254/2 What is the difference between a Croton bug and a cockroach. . . . None; the former term is used by the landlord, the latter by the tenant. **1907** HODGE *Amer. Indians* I. 367/1 Croton-bug. The water cockroach (*Blatta germanica*), from Croton, the name of a river in Westchester co. — (2) **1837** GREENE *Glance at N.Y.* 185 The Croton water is found, by chemical analysis, to be exceedingly pure. **1842** *Boston Transcript* 5 Oct. 2/3 The Croton water of New York is supplied yearly at twelve and five dollars, according to the size of the house. **1948** *Newsweek* 30 Aug. 81/3 Coming of Croton Water . . . awakening the city to the need for an adequate water-supply system, led to the building of the Croton reservoir aqueduct.

croup kettle. "A small kettle and alcohol lamp for quickly raising a steam for inhalation in cases of croup" (Knight *Supp.*). — **1889** MARK TWAIN *Conn. Yankee* xl. 516, I rousted out the croup-kettle myself; for I don't sit down and wait for doctors.

crouter ˈkraʊtɚ, *n.* [App. suggested by *sauerkraut,* but cf. G. *kraut* in similar sense.] A Dutch or German person. *Rare.* — **1856** MARK TWAIN in *Keokuk Sat. Post* 1 Nov. 3, I was a settin in the parlor of my Dutch boardin house in Fourth street (I board among the crouters so as to observe human natur in a forren aspeck).

* **crow,** *n.*

1. (*cap.*) (See quot. 1907.) In full **Crow Indians.** Usu. *pl.* except in attrib. use.
1804 CLARK in *Lewis & Clark Journals* I. (1904) 189 The Chien . . . or Dog Indians . . . [are] at war with the Crow Indians. **1812** J.C. LUTTIG *Jrnl. Exped. Upper Mo.* (1920) 78 Lecomte . . . asked them what Nation they were, they answered Crows. **1907** HODGE *Amer. Indians* I. 367/2 Crows. (trans., through French *gens des corbeaux,* of their own name, *Absároke,* crow, sparrowhawk, or bird people). A Siouan tribe forming part of the Hidatsa group, their separation from the Hidatsa having taken place, as Matthews (1894) believed, within the last 200 years. **1948** *N.M. Quart. Rev.* Spring 25 DeVoto admits to having written 'not only twenty-one Arapaho, but also thirty-eight Crow and even, God help us, one hundred and two Blackfoot.'

b. The language used by these Indians.
1846 W. STEWART *Altowan* I. viii. 207 The language used was Crow. **1932** LINDERMAN *Red Mother* 39 How much I wished that I could speak Crow!

Crow (sense 2) worn by a Pawnee dancer

2. (See quots.) Also **crow-belt, crow dance.**
1823 LONG *Exped.* I. 235 Hashea . . . wore a handsome robe of white wolf skin, with an appendage behind him, called a *crow.* This singular decoration is a large cushion, made of the skin of a crow, stuffed with any light material, and variously ornamented; it has two decorated sticks projecting from it upward, and a pendant one beneath; this apparatus is secured upon the buttocks by a girdle passing round the body. **1947** *Primitive Man* July 40 It is very similar in character to the present day Arapaho crow-dance. *Ib.* 41 The Assiniboine gave crow-belts (feather bustles) to each of two men.

3. A Negro. Cf. **Jim Crow.**
1823 COOPER *Pioneers* xvii, Shut your oven, you crow! Where is the man that can hit a turkey's head at a hundred yards? **1924** *Amer. Mercury* Feb. 130/1, I wish I was black like you. . . . No you don't. Dey'd call you Crow, den—or Chocolate—or Smoke.

4. *fig.* An extremely distasteful or unpalatable dish. Also **boiled crow.** Also in allusion to next. *Colloq.*
1872 *Daily News* (London) 31 July, Both General Grant and Mr Horace Greeley appear to be what is called, in the curious slang of American politics, 'boiled crow' to their adherents. **1880** *Scribner's Mo.* Feb. 622/1 They may find a Grant who will grow lukewarm in their favor, or a Conkling to cook crow for his own party. **1888** *Cong. Rec.* 14 July 6314/2 Other representatives of the Democracy from Ohio are taking this enforced 'dish of crow.'

b. *To eat crow,* or *boiled crow,* (see quots. and cf. prec.). *Colloq.*
[**1851** *S.F. Picayune* 3 Dec. 1/6 The bet was made, the crow was caught and nicely roasted, but before serving it up, they contrived to season it with a good dose of Scotch snuff. Isaac sat down to the crow, he took a good bite, and began to chew away. 'Yes, I kin eat a crow! . . . *I kin eat a crow, but I'll be darned if I hanker after it.*'] **1877** *N. & Q.* 5 Ser. VIII. 186/1 A newspaper editor, who is obliged by his 'party' . . . to advocate 'principles' different from those which he supported a short time before, is said to 'eat boiled crow.' **1885** *Mag. Amer. Hist.* XIII. 199 'To eat crow' means to recant, or to humiliate oneself. To 'eat dirt' is nearly equivalent. **1949** *Democrat* 13 Jan. 4/1 It's our time to eat crow.

5. In special combs.: (1) **Crow agency,** an agency for the Crow Indians; (2) **bait,** a poor, worthless horse, *colloq.;* (3) **bar,** an iron or steel bar having a wedge-shaped end used as a pry or lever, also fig., cf. **stone crowbar;** (4) **bill blackbird,** =next, *rare;* (5) **-blackbird,** any one of various large American grackles, as the purple grackle, cf. **rusty crow blackbird;** (6) **corn,** the colicroot, *Aletris farinosa;* (7) **duck,** the American coot or mud hen, *Fulica americana;* (8) **fish,** (see quot.), *rare;* (9) **foot violet, =bird's-foot violet;** (10) **head,** a contemptible, insignificant thing, *rare;* (11) **headed,** having a head like a crow, *rare;* (12) **hop,** *W.* (see quot. 1944); (13) **poison,** fly poison, also a small plant, *Nothascordum bivalve,* poisonous to stock; (14) **roost,** a place where crows in great numbers roost; (15) * **-'s foot,** (see quot. 1851); (16) * **track,** a wrinkle in the corner of the eye suggestive of the track of a crow.
(1) **1876** in *Mont. Hist. Soc. Contrib.* II. (1896) 220 Some of our own scouts . . . had for some reason left Custer's command and were returning to the Crow agency. **1916** C. A. EASTMAN *From Deep Woods* 143 At the Crow agency I met a Scotchman. — (2) [**1857** *Spirit of Times* 14 Feb. 382/1 He had a ole ball-face, bob-tail rip, jest' 'bout fit for crow-bait, which he was proud as fury on—sech a hoss!] **1860** *Marysville* (Calif.) *Appeal* 25 March 2/1 For many moments did the excited teamster 'cuss' and belabor his crow-baits, but they wouldn't budge an inch. **1948** *Sat. Review* 28 Aug. 5/1 He and some cronies spotted an actor in a general's dress uniform with a bear cub in his arms, leading a crow-bait white horse. — (3) **1748** *N.J. Archives* 1 Ser. VII. 208 Men, armed with clubs, axes & crow bars, came. **1890** *Cent. Mag.* Feb. 623/1 But tobacco, tobacco—what rude crowbar is that with which to pry into the delicate tissues of the brain! **1948** *Chi. D. News* 23 April 1/1 Three vandals armed with rocks and a crowbar smashed . . . store windows. — (4) **1737** *Duxbury Rec.* 249 There shall be paid out of said town's treasury to any and all persons, Three pence for each and every Crow-bill Black bird that shall be Killed.
(5) **1778** CARVER *Travels* 473 The crow blackbird . . . is quite black, and of the same size and shape of those in Europe. **1811** WILSON *Ornithology* III. 46 Every industrious farmer complains of the mischief committed on his corn by the Crow Blackbirds, as they are usually called. **1947** *Collier's* 29 Mar. 92/2 There is the purple grackle which is most frequently known as the blackbird or as the crow blackbird, the marsh blackbird, and the red-winged blackbird. — (6) **1889** *Cent., Crow-corn.* . . . The mealy white flowers . . . somewhat resemble kernells of grain. — (7) **1792** in *Pub. Champlain Soc.* XXI. 476 This day we took some eggs of the Crow duck its a large black kind of duck with a beak like a crow and lives upon fish. **1925** E. H. FORBUSH *Birds of Mass.* 369 Coot. Other names: Blue Peter; Blue Marsh-Hen; Crow Duck. — (8) **1807** *Mass. H.S. Coll.* 2 Ser. III. 57 The black fish, called the crow fish at Nantucket, is caught in the Sound and harbours in May and June. — (9) **1933** SMALL *Southeastern Flora* 886 V[iola] pedata. . . . Bird's-foot violet. Crowfoot-violet. Pansy-violet. Johnny-jump-up. **1942** WEYGANDT *Plenty of Penna.* 270, I think of the pike-side over the Welsh Mountain blue with crowfoot violets.

(10) **1834** CROCKETT *Tour* 191 It would be but a few years until America would be a crow-head. — (11) **1929** *Randolph Enterprise* (Elkins, W.Va.) 14 Feb. 3/2 All thin, undersized, scrawny 'crow headed' birds should be discarded. — (12) **1903** *Wide World Mag.* 548 The ways they try to throw their riders may be classed under three heads. The first is known as the crow-hop. **1944** ADAMS *W. Words* 45 crow hop. When a horse jumps about with arched back and stiffened knees at a pretense of bucking. — (13) **1837** H. MARTINEAU *Society* I. 290 The ground was gay with violets, may-apple, buck-eye, blue lupin, iris, and crow-poison. The last is like the white lily, growing close to the ground. Its root, boiled, mixed with corn, and thrown out into the fields, poisons crows. If eaten by cattle, it injures but does not destroy them. **1938** MATSCHAT *Suwannee River* 216 Black Ben looked at the orchids clustered at the base of the bee tree. . . . Along the borders of the marsh crow poison opened tall racemes of tiny lilly-like bloom. — (14) **1811** WILSON *Ornithology* IV. 82 The most noted Crow roost with which I am acquainted is near Newcastle, on an island in the Delaware. **1946** *Okla. Game & Fish News* March 4/1 They located crow roosts in the shinnery motts west of Elk City.
(15) **1828** *Harvard Reg.* Feb. 377 The freshman . . . crawls back to watch the starting of some one blessed with a *crows-foot,* to act as a van-guard. **1830** HOLMES *Myst. Visitor* 64 What if the creature should arise . . . and swallow down a sophomore, Coat, crow's-foot, cap, and all! **1851** HALL *College Words* 88 *Crows-foot,* at Harvard College a badge formerly worn on the sleeve, resembling a crow's foot, to denote the class to which a student belongs. — (16) **1856** M. J. HOLMES *L. Rivers* xxxviii. 416 To her utter dismay Carrie has discovered a 'crow track' in the corner of her eye. **1857** ——— *Meadow-Brook* xi, The crow-tracks around her eyes were now decidedly deep-cut wrinkles.

Also (sense **1**) *Crow chieftain, country, dancer, language, nation, robe, tribe, war-party,* etc.

As the last term in **blue, Clark's, eel, fish, Jim, mountain, rain, water crow.**

* **crowd,** *n.* A set, clique, or "ring." *Colloq.*

1840 *Cong. Globe* App. 2 April 376/2, I became satisfied that Democracy had but few charms for that crowd. **1881** *Nation* XXXII. 398 [Grant] does not seem to entertain that dread of 'Monopolists' which characterizes some of his 'Crowd' in Albany. **1932** GRAYSON *Leaders* 418 He had a good thing to sell, he was not particularly anxious to part with it, and he intended to extract the last million from the Morgan crowd.

b. (See quot.)

1929 DOBIE *Vaquero* 12 The 'crowd'—as a cow outfit was then generally called—contained twenty or twenty-five vaqueros, nearly all of them cattle owners and as live a bunch of real cowmen as ever joined in a cow hunt.

c. A single individual. *Rare.*

1884 SWEET & KNOX *Through Texas* 13 They said that he 'always went heeled, toted a derringer, and was a bad crowd generally.'

* **crowd,** *v.*

1. *tr.* To embarrass financially, to dun (a person) for money. *Colloq.*

1775 *N.H. Hist. Soc. Coll.* IX. 88, I have Several Debts that crowd much. **1776** *Ib.* 97, I am crowded for money beyond what I can well discribe. **1853** B. YOUNG in *Jrnl. Discourses* I. 340 (Th.), [I have never] distressed a man for what he owes me, or crowded any person in the least.

2. *To crowd through* or *on,* to force or compel (something) to go through, to hasten or forge on. *Colloq.*

1852 E. BENNETT *Mike Fink* i. 13/2 But crowd her through, my beauty, for I'm in a hurry. *a***1861** WINTHROP *John Brent* 53, I might perhaps make it a new story; but I crowd on now to the proper spot where this drama is to be enacted. *Ib.* 209 He crowded on, more desperately, . . . as a lover rides for love. **1876** MARK TWAIN *Tom Sawyer* xxxv. 272 If she'll let up on some of the roughest things, I'll smoke private, and cuss private, and crowd through or bust.

3. *To crowd up,* to surge or well up, to force higher.

1858 HOLMES *Autocrat* 353 The great maternal instinct came crowding up in her soul. **1910** *Springfield W. Republican* 6 Jan. 1 The price of cotton is being crowded up higher than conditions of supply and demand warrant.

4. In phrases: (1) *To crowd one's feelings,* to impose upon one's feelings, *rare;* (2) *to crowd the mourners,* to exercise undue pressure, to push or hurry in an unseemly way, *colloq.;* (3) *to crowd the rhetoric,* to say more than the facts warrant, *rare;* (4) *to crowd to the wall,* to force into utter subserviency; (5) *to crowd one off a wire,* to send a telegraphic message too fast for another to receive, *colloq.*

(1) **1851** J. J. HOOPER *Widow Rugby's Husb.* 128 Dad drat my upper leather ef any man shall crowd my feeling's that way. — (2) **1848** *N.Y. Wkly. Tribune* 1 Jan. 5/3 He rather 'crowded the mourners' in his historical illustrations. **1859** BARTLETT 282 *'Crowding the mourners,'* in political slang, means adding some further embarrassment to politicians laboring under difficulties. **1923** *D.N.* V. 205 crowd the mourners, v. phr. To be in a hurry, premature. 'Keep ca'm now, an' don't crowd the mourners,' *i.e.* don't be precipitate. [Mo.] — (3) **1874** B. F. TAYLOR *World on Wheels* I. xvii. 124 We are apt to crowd the rhetoric sometimes, and say that railroads have taken America. — (4) **1871** *Rep. Indian Affairs* 362, I for one do not believe that it is necessarily the destiny of all the Indians to be 'crowded to the wall.' — (5) **1901** S. MERWIN & WEBSTER *Calumet K* vi. 108 It takes a pretty lively man to crowd me off the end of a wire.

* **crowder,** *n.*

1. A variety of cultivated pea the fruit of which grows as if crowded in the pod. In full **crowder pea.**

1787 WASHINGTON *Diaries* III. 161 Number of Grains Crowder Pease . . . 1600 in the lb . . . 97,600 in the Bush. **1859** TALIAFERRO *Fisher's R.* 143 But as all on us . . . was mighty fond o' peas, I were mighty pertic'ler to plant a mighty good share uv them; and to make a bully crap o' Crowders. **1948** *Democrat* 6 May 1/7 This sheller does not shell crowder peas satisfactorily.

b. Also **gray, mountain, white crowder.**

1797 IMLAY *Western Territory* (ed. 3) 240 The white crowder, and many others, are undoubtedly at least as good [as the European]. **1855** DAVIS *Farm Bk.* 188 First next the ditch are the Harper peas to a peach tree and then come the gray crowder or poor mans pea. *Ib.*, The peas here are the Mountain crowder—2d the white crowder and then the gray crowder.

2. A horse of superior speed. *Slang. Obs.*

1839 *N.O. Picayune* 17 Mar. 2/1 Two of the nags are known to be 'crowders,' while the other is said to be faster than the general run. **1856** *Spirit of Times* 11 Oct. 100/3 We must not omit to mention in this connection, such 'crowders' as Jim Bell, Sarah Bladen, Reel, . . . Grey Medoc, Altorf, and a score of other names, which are illustrious in the annals of the American turf.

3. A great success. *Rare.*

1841 *N.O. Picayune* 17 Jan. 2/4 The little fellow's benefit at the St. Charles last night was a 'crowder.'

4. A V-shaped drag for making head ditches in the check system of irrigation.

1893 *Standard* 445/2 crowder . . . in southwestern California, an implement somewhat like a snow-plow, to run along a narrow ragged ditch to clear and widen it and compact its sides. **1915** FORTIER *Use of Water in Irrig.* 73 One of the most servicable home-made implements for making head ditches is the crowder.

crowdy ˈkraudɪ, *a.* Beset or occupied by crowds. *Rare.* — **1827** COOPER *Prairie* i, There is country left, it is true . . . but to my taste, it is getting crowdy.

***crowfoot,** *n.* As the last term in **celery, kidney-leaved, water crowfoot.**

crow-hop, *v.* *W. intr.* To hop like a crow (see quot. 1897). *Colloq.* Cf. **crow-hop,** *n.* — **1897** *Chi. Tribune* 25 July 15/2 Crow Hop, to 'crawfish.' 'Leedy has crow hopped out of the special session of the Legislature.' **1939** ROLLINS *Gone Haywire* 57 Both Ace-in-the-Hole and Skookum might crowhop or pussy-back a bit when first mounted on frosty mornings.

* **crown,** *n.*

1. a. (See quot.) **b.** ?The cured head of a hog. Both *obs.*

(a) **1687** *Doc. Hist. N.Y. State* I. 255 We have the news of Keman that the Indians have taken 8 men 1 woman and 8 crowns or scalpes. — (b) **1852** in EASTERBY *S.C. Rice Plant.* (1945) 115, I enquired for bacon today for plantation rations. Mary look'd & told me there were but 2 crowns (I gave one to Thomas yesterday, & have used none myself) and 6 chines.

2. In combs.: (1) **crownbeard,** any plant of the genus *Phaethusa;* (2) **bird,** (see quots.); (3) **cap,** a metallic cork-lined stopper designed to be crimped over the top of a bottle by a device or machine for the purpose; (4) **Crown City,** (see quot. and cf. (8) below); (5) **fire,** a forest fire which burns down from the tops of the trees, cf. * **crown,** *v.;* (6) **pin,** a pin securing the body of a Concord coach to the frame of the vehicle, *obs.;* (7) **Crown Point bill,** (see quot.), *obs.;* (8) **Crown of the Valley,** =**Crown City.**

(1) **1857** GRAY *Botany* 222 Crownbeard, . . . *Verbesina Siegesbeckia.* . . . Rich soil, W. Penn. to Illinois, and southward. . . . [Also] *V. Virginica.* Dry soil. **1947** *Desert Mag.* April 12/3 April possibilities: . . . prickly pear, brittle bush, apricot mallow, . . . and crownbeard. — (2) **1791** BARTRAM *Travels* 288 *Ampelis garrulus,* crown bird, or cedar bird. These birds feed on various sorts of succulent fruit. **1808** WILSON *Ornithology* I. 112 In some parts of the country they [cedar birds] are called Crown-birds; in others Cherry-birds, from their fondness for that fruit. — (3) **1928** *Collier's* 1 Sep. 47/1 The great Woolworth chain deals heavily in this business, and has a

special department for corks, bottle cappers, tubing, crown caps, etc. — (4) **1916** *Amer. City* Feb. 182/2 Pasadena is the 'Crown City,' Glendale is the 'Jewel City,' and so on.

(5) **1921** *Outing* Dec. 109/2 If the fire is a crown fire there is little that the canoe crews can do toward putting it out. **1948** *Highway Traveler* Sep.–Oct. 22/1 If the fire is nearby, and not of the 'crown' variety, usually the fast trucks can transport men, firefighting equipment and pack mules close enough to the fire to do the job. — (6) **1852** CASEY *Two Yrs.* 160 There is also a provision made for the said probabilities, which provision is in the shape of an iron pin, called a crown pin, which keeps the body of the coach in its position on the frame under all ordinary oscillations. — (7) **1756** in *Amer. Sp.* XX. (1945) 271 The first proceedings relate to the Act for calling in and sinking bills of credit emitted by this Colony [Rhode Island] called Crown Point Bills. — (8) **1897** *Land of Sunshine* Dec. 43 Ten years before the road was built, a stage coach afforded sufficient accommodation for the travel between Los Angeles and the 'Crown of the Valley.'

***crown**, *v. intr.* Of a forest fire: To burn rapidly in the tops of trees rather than along the ground. Cf. **crown fire.** — **1916** *Outing* Jan. 406/2 Burning rapidly up hill in the dry ground cover and windfalls, the fire was threatening every minute to crown. **1947** *Time* 3 Nov. 26/1 The fire crowned into the tops of trees and leaped forward 'as fast as a race horse could run.'

***crowner**, *n.* Something which "caps the climax," sometimes applied to the most ridiculous or unexpected of a series of conditions or events. *Colloq.*

1815 *Mass. Spy* 31 May (Th., 146), This is the crowner, the capsheaf. **1854** M. CUMMINS *Lamplighter* xiii. 97 But her goggles were the crowner; such immense, horrid-looking things I never saw! **1922** ALICE BROWN *Old Crow* xxvii. 320 Isn't that a joke, Rookie? Charlotte would say it's the crowner.

crude krud, *n.* [f. the *adj.*] Short for "crude oil," or "crude petroleum," Cf. **Pennsylvania crude.** — **1916** T. J. HOOVER *Concentrating Ores* 123 Russian crude. **1925** *Wall St. Jrnl.* 31 Jan. 1/3 Humble Oil & Refining Co. has advanced Currie, Powell and Richland crudes 30 cents a barrel to $1.80.

cruellist ˈkruəlɪst, *n.* One who exercises cruelty. *Rare.* — **1893** *Amer. S.P.C.A. 27th Rep.* 34 The horse was unharnessed . . . while the cruellist was taken before Justice Casey, who fined him twenty dollars.

cruellize ˈkruəlˌaɪz, *v. tr.* To subject to cruel treatment. *Rare.* — **1846** L. M. CHILD *Fact & Fiction* 199 They don't all cruellize their slaves.

cruelsome ˈkruəlsəm, *a.* Cruel, unfeeling. *Rare.* — **1853** SIMMS *Sword & Distaff* 511 It would certainly . . . be a most cruelsome thing that she shouldn't hev' the man she wanted.

***cruise**, *n.* A survey or estimate of the amount of timber on a particular area. — **1911** J. F. WILSON *Land Claimers* viii. 112, I finished the cruise today. **1948** *Sat. Ev. Post* 31 July 86/2 Boss wants you to look over this cruise on some timber.

***cruise**, *v. intr.* (See quots.)

1879 VIVIAN *Wanderings in Western Land* 53 About the month of October experienced men are sent out into the forests exploring, or to use their own term 'cruising'; their object being, in the first place, to find suitable lumber for chopping; and, secondly, that it shall be in such a locality as to make it remunerative to get it to a market. **1895** *Outing* XXVII. 218/2, I found he was off 'cruising' (*i.e.*, hunting up good timber tracts). **1905** *Forestry Bureau Bul.* No. 61, *Cruise*, to estimate the amount and value of a standing timber.

Also *tr.*

1919 T. K. HOLMES *Manfr. Tall Timber* 40 Si and me cruised a part of this timber before ever you fellers come down from Blainesburg. **1947** *Sierra Club Bul.* Oct. 4/2 Logging companies, however, are now cutting on the edges and have already cruised the heart of the virgin forest.

***cruiser**, *n.*

1. (See quot. 1900.) Cf. **landlooker** (*b*), **timber cruiser.**

1893 *Scribner's Mag.* June 695/1 My first day's experience as a 'Cruiser' or 'Landlooker.' **1900** E. BRUCKEN *N. Amer. Forests* 81 This has given rise to a peculiar class of people variously known as woodsmen, cruisers, landlookers, whose business it is to give information as to the existence of pine timber, its location, amount, value. **1946** R. PEATTIE *Pac. Coast Ranges* 232 With his cruiser's eye, he could measure the quantity and the quality of the timber from the water's edge.

2. A high-topped laced boot such as timber cruisers often wear.

1902 WHITE *Blazed Trail* 131 They were . . . dressed in broad hats, flannel shirts, coarse trousers tucked into high laced 'cruisers.' **1946** *Sat. Ev. Post* 11 May 41/1 He was wearing Tillamook light cruisers from Portland.

3. A police squad car or prowl car.

1929 *Sat. Ev. Post* 7 Dec. 68/2 The cruisers are high-powered seven-passenger touring cars manned by a crew of four.

cruller ˈkrʌlɚ, *n.* Also †**crull.** [See note.]

This word is clearly from the Du. In *WNT s.v. krul* (cf. our quot. 1831) a form *krulle* is listed, the definition being "Eene soort van gebak van gekromden vorm." Bense cites M. Du. *krulle-koken* and LG. *krull-koken*, but failed to come upon *krul*, *krulle*.

Any one of variously shaped sweet cakes made from rich egg batter and fried in deep fat.

1805 *Pocumtuc Housewife* (1906) 34 [Recipe for making] Crullers, Matrimony or Love Knots. **1831** PECK *Guide* 152 The Yankee . . . tell us of their pies, doughnuts, crulls. **1842** *Boston Transcript* 14 Dec. 2/3 The *ole-kocken*, *krullers* and *cookies* were of a quality that proved the skilful hand of some genuine Dutch housewife in the manufacture. **1946** *This Week Mag.* 8 June 6/3 First, let us start with her coffee cake and her crullers.

b. cruller baby, ?a cruller having the shape of a baby. *Rare.*

1882 *Cent. Mag.* July 344/2 Miss Petty use to fetch out some sweet flag or some cruller babies or somethin' or other she'd laid by for her.

***crumb**, *n.*

1. A body louse; a low character. *Slang.*

Hotten, *Dict. Slang*, lists *crummy-doss*, lousy bed.

1863 O. W. NORTON *Army Letters* 175 Fortunately, I am not troubled with the 'crumbs' now. **1898** *Scribner's Mag.* XXIII. 440/1 And just then I felt something crawling on my neck. It was a crumb. **1918** RIDEOUT *Key of Fields* 236 A couple of crumbs want to kill you. Sit quiet. I won't let them.

2. crumb coffee, (see quots.). *Obs.* Cf. **crust coffee.**

[**1866** Goss *Soldier's Story* 83 Sometimes we made coffee of burned bits of bread, by boiling them in a tin cup, which was greedily drank, without sweetening or milk.] **1938** Letter to M. M. Mathews 11 April, We didn't have 'crumb coffee' during the Civil War. Some did,—parched crumbs, bran, meal, chipped sweet potatoes and parched rye. My mother used parched rye.

***crummy**, *n.* =**caboose.** Also **crummy car.** *Slang.*

1934 *Amer. Sp.* April 74/1 There was a hundred and thirty *rattlers* and a *crummy* on that thing and you should have heard the old *hog* wheeze as we went down to the station. **1946** R. PEATTIE *Pac. Coast Ranges* 279 Gone is the 'crummy' car that used to bring loggers into town on Saturday night. **1948** *Sat. Ev. Post* 25 Dec. 22/2 Most railroad men call it simply 'the crummy,' but the caboose has other loving titles.

***crush**, *n.*

1. The object of one's ardent affection. Also a sudden infatuation. Often *to get* or *have a crush on. Slang.*

1884 RITTENHOUSE *Maud* 338 Wintie is weeping because her crush is gone. **1914** G. ATHERTON *Perch of Devil* I. 31 Some of the younger married women . . . get a crush on some other woman's husband. *Ib.* 186 To be jealous you've got to have a fearful crush. **1920** LEWIS *Main Street* 2 For all her enthusiasms, for the fondness and the 'crushes' which she inspired, Carol's acquaintances were shy of her.

2. A crowd. *Colloq.*

1924 A. J. SMALL *Frozen Gold* i. 40 Any one of that crush would do murder for no more than 500 dollars reward.

***crusher**, *n.* As the last term in **clod, cob, corn, corncob, feed, jaw, rock crusher.**

***crust**, *n.*

1. The frozen surface of snow.

1809 A. HENRY *Travels* 146 The stag is very successfully hunted . . . the crust upon the snow, cutting his legs . . . to the very bone. **1867** *Beadle's Mo.* March 277/1 The surface of the snow often thaws during the day, and freezes again at night; it is this hard covering that causes the crust. **1948** JACOBS *We Chose Country* 110 This is the period when we especially love sunshine after a snowstorm—the beautiful sunshine that puts a crust on top the new-fallen snow.

2. In combs.: (1) **crust coffee,** (see quot. 1939); (2) **hunter,** one who practices crusting *q.v.*; (3) **hunting,** =**crusting 1.**

(1) **1853** STRICKLAND *Twenty-seven Yrs.* I. 251 To wash down this elegant repast, a dish of crust coffee without either milk or sugar. **1863** *Ladies' Repository* XXIII. 90/1 For supper we had fried sweet potatoes, a little crust coffee, and venison. **1939** I. WOLCOTT *Yankee Cook Bk.* 187 A beverage called Crust Coffee was made from the hard crusts from brown bread. Hot water was poured over the crusts and the resulting liquid was served as a coffee substitute. — (2) **1889** *Forest & Stream* XXX. 47/1 Thus eluding . . . the . . . crust-hunters as well as the hound. **1893** *Harper's Weekly* Xmas 1211/3, I begrudge using the word sport . . . when the crust hunter . . . is the subject under discussion. — (3) **1885** *Forest & Stream* XXIV. 425 Advocates of January crust-hunting. **1887** *Harper's Mag.* Feb. 458/1 Crust hunting is based on this characteristic [of the moose]. *Ib.* 458/2 In March . . . the time for crust hunting has come.

As the last term in **boiled pie, graham, pie, upper crust.**

*** crusted,** *a.* Of snow: Having the surface hardened by freezing.
1809 A. HENRY *Travels* 146 February, in the country and by the people where and among whom I was, is called the Moon of Hard or Crusted Snow; for now the snow can bear a man, or at least dogs, in pursuit of animals of the chase. **1835** *Liberator* (Boston) 5 Dec. 196/5 The full moon looks down upon the crusted snow. **1892** *Outing* Dec. 193/2, I am not dealing now with the method of calling moose in the rutting season, or of the execrable practice of running them down in deep-crusted snow.

cruster ˈkrʌstɚ, *n.* =**crust hunter.**
1885 *Forest & Stream* XXIII. 468/1 If Maine could . . . keep down dogs and crusters, . . . her forests would not be thinned of deer. **1893** *Harper's Weekly* Xmas 1211/3, I have no toleration of 'crusters,' except where an empty camp-kettle has made meat a necessity. **1905** *N.Y. Ev. Post* 4 Dec. 6 After the season for killing deer closed, more than 100 deer were killed by crusters.

crusting ˈkrʌstɪŋ, *n.* **1.** (See quot. 1837.) **2.** The action of forming a crust on snow.
(1) 1837 *N.Y. Mirror* 28 Oct. 140/3 'Crusting' is the term applied to taking large game amid the deep snows of winter, when the crust of ice which forms upon the surface after a slight rain, is strong enough to support the weight of a man, but gives way at once to the hoofs of a moose or deer; while the animal, thus embarrassed, is easily caught and despatched with clubs. **1902** *Nation* LXXIV. 493 There are still many deer killed by the very noxious and illegal methods of 'crusting.' — **(2) 1945** McATEE *Pheasant* 41 Excessive snowfall, followed by heavy crusting may seal in some of the birds.

*** crusty,** *a.* Of snow: Having a crust. *Rare.* — **1772** WASHINGTON *Diaries* II. 54 The Snow was so deep and crusty, even in the Tract.

*** cry,** *n.* **1.** Among Indians, a ceremonial lamentation. *Obs.* **2.** A screaking noise made by the wheel of a vehicle. *Rare.* See also **cat, wood cry.**
(1) 1853 J. H. EAGLE *Corr.* (Huntington Lib.) 27 May 2 They were to have another cry after dinner, but we got tired and did not wait to see it. **1856** *Spirit of Age* (Sacramento) 1 April 1/1 In consequence of the unusual mortality among the Diggers during the last winter, a general order was issued . . . for the assembly of the tribes . . . to meet in this city to hold a 'cry,' for the purpose of propitiating the Great Spirit in their behalf. — **(2) 1873** BEADLE *Undevel. West* 57 The coach drags heavily, the wheels often causing a disagreeable 'cry' in the sand and soda.

*** cry,** *v.*
1. *To cry back,* of animals in breeding: to revert to an earlier type. Also **crying back.**
1850 D. J. BROWNE *Amer. Poultry Yard* 81 Animals will, after many cross-breedings, 'cry back.' **1850** D. J. BROWNE *Amer. Poultry Yard* 229 The cases, in which white birds are produced from colored parents, are only a breaking out of mixed blood, the 'crying back,' in fact, to a cross some generations past. **1868** G. BRACKETT *Farm Talk* 43 If a native-bred bull be used, be he never so well-formed and fine an animal, his offspring are likely to 'cry back' to his scrub parentage.
2. **to cry off,* to sell at auction.
1723 *Brookhaven Rec.* 114 Itt was cryed off to him att twenty one shilling per acre. **1784** *Huntington Rec.* III. 124 Whosoever shall have said Ferry cryed of on their bid. **1847** ROBB *Squatter Life* 135, I . . . was comin' along, slow and easy, by the St. Louis Exchange, when I heerd Major Beard cryin' off a lot of field hands.

cry-baby, *n.* An opprobrious appellation for one who cries easily or complains at circumstances.
1851 A. CARY *Clovernook* 274 You had better be still, cry-baby, or he will beat you to death. **1876** MARK TWAIN *Tom Sawyer* xvi. 137 Well, we'll let the cry-baby go home to his mother, won't we, Huck? **1948** *Dly. Ardmoreite* (Ardmore, Okla.) 7 April 1/6 First graders are no cry babies.
Hence **cry-baby,** *v. intr.*
1902 O. WISTER *Virginian* vii. 85 I am not crybabying to the Judge.

crying-bird ˈkraɪ·ɪŋˌbɜd, *n.* =**limpkin.** — **1791** W. BARTRAM *Travels* 49 The crying-bird, another faithful guardian, screaming in the gloomy thickets, warns the feathered tribes of approaching peril. *Ib.* 147 There is inhabiting the low shores and swamps of this river . . . a very curious bird, called by an Indian name (*Ephouskyca*) which signifies in our language the crying bird. **1948** *Outdoor Life* July 72/2 The limpkin, or crying bird, of Florida and points south, has a weird, desolate cry.

cryist ˈkraɪ·ɪst, *n.* One who cries easily. *Rare.* — **1887** *Courier-Journal* 16 Jan. 16/4 Loto was not what might be called a 'cryist.' Few people ever witnessed her sparse tears.

*** crystaline,** *n.* A variety of sugar cane. *Obs.* — **1849** *Rep. Comm. Patents: Agric.* 168 It was invoiced 'crystaline'; a very large proportion of the eyes of this cane had been rubbed off by the rolling of the casks. **1856** *Ib.* 273 The varieties of cane which have hitherto been most cultivated in Louisiana [include] . . . 'Crystaline,' or 'Malabar'; the 'Otaheite'; the 'Purple.'

*** crystallize,** *v. tr.* ?To preserve (fruit) by coating it with sugar. Also ***crystallizing,** *n.* — **1888** LINDLEY *Calif. of South* 363 The best fruits for crystallizing are the orange, apricot, nectarine, cherry, fig, muscat grape, pear, and plum. *Ib.*, Their crystallized apricots are perfectly splendid in taste as well as appearance. **1947** BEROLZHEIMER *Regional Cook Book* 237 Fruitcake . . . 2 cups currants 2 cups crystallized cherries.

C.S. =next. *Obs.* — **1865** *New Era* (Fredericksburg, Va.) 30 June 3/1 All mules and horses branded 'U.S.' or 'C.S.' are to be taken from their present owners by the Government.

C.S.A. Abbreviation for Confederate States of America. Also attrib.
1861 *So. Enterprise* (Thomasville, Ga.) 19 June 3/2 We have taken a through ticket, and checked our baggage for the C.S.A. **1862** LOWELL *Biglow P.* 2 Ser. iv. 126 Nice paper to coin into C.S.A. specie. **1888** GRIGSBY *Smoked Yank* (1891) vi. 48 There was a large quantity of C.S.A. cotton (cotton purchased by the Confederate Government branded C.S.A.) concealed in a swamp six or seven miles above his camp. **1948** *Range Riders Western* May 83/2 Cy Hawkins himself had been a colonel, only he had worn the letters CSA on the collar of his gray uniform instead of USA.

cuartel kwɑrˈtɛl, *n.* Also **quartel.** *S.W.* [Sp. in same sense.] Barracks or quarters for soldiers.
1832 DEWEES *Lett. from Texas* 142 Seven hundred Mexicans . . . were at the quartel or barracks. **1890** *Outing* Oct. 8/1, I saw you, too, at the *cuartel* at Tucson. **1923** W. SMITH *Little Tigress* 58 (Bentley), At the iron gate of the cuartel, Don Roberto begged to be excused.

*** cub,** *n.*
1. A child. *Colloq.*
1780 J. MAY in *N.E. Hist. and Gen. Reg.* XXVII. (1873) 16 Am exceedingly glad the little cubs are better. Hope their health, as well as the others and yours, may be continued. **1889** K. MUNROE *Golden Days* xi. 119 The cubs [Indian children] would grow up to be trouble-some before long. **1893** MARK TWAIN *P. Wilson* iii, She put her cub in Tommy's elegant cradle.
b. cub-headed, *a.* foolish. *Obs.*
1840 BIRD *Robin Day* 61 Here came two cursed cub-headed school-boys.
2. An apprentice pilot on a river steamboat. Also transf.
1875 MARK TWAIN *Old Times on Miss.* ii. 25 The 'off-watch' was just turning in, and I heard . . . such remarks as 'Hello, watchman! an't the new cub turned out yet?' *Ib.* v. 79 The pilot not on watch takes his 'cub' or steersman . . . and goes out in the yawl. *Ib.* 81 Nothing delights a cub so much as an opportunity to go out sounding. **1883** ——— *Life on Miss.* xviii, A cub had to take every thing his boss gave, in the way of vigorous comment and criticism. **1903** *N.Y. Sun* 29 Nov. 20 These men were all cubs back in that Congress which met first in the summer of 1893.
b. *Attrib.* in the sense of an apprentice or novice.
1875 MARK TWAIN *Old Times on Miss.* i. 14 The boys . . . learned to disappear when the ruthless 'cub'-engineer approached. **1903** *N.Y. Times Sat. Rev.* 24 Oct. 758 The recorder of the experiences and emotions of a cub pilot on the Mississippi. **1908** A. RUHL *Other Americans* ii. 9 The mere gringo feels like a cub reporter at the office of a campaign committee.

*** Cuba,** *n.*[1]
1. Short for **Cuba tobacco.** *Obs.*
1824 *Shipping & Commercial List* 31 July (Pettigrew P.), A sale of 30 ceroons of Cuba was made, by auction, at 13½ a 14½ cents, 60 days.
2. In combs.: (1) **Cuba grass,** =**Johnson grass;** (2) **Six,** a kind of cigar imported from Cuba, *obs.;* (3) **tobacco,** a kind of tobacco derived from Cuba, also **Cuban tobacco.**
(1) 1885 HAVARD *Flora W. & S. Texas* 530 Johnson-Grass, or Cuba-Grass, . . . a tall, perennial broom-corn, quick to spread by its root-stocks, very nutritious and productive . . . but most difficult to eradicate. — **(2) 1849** D. NASON *Journal* 46 Those luscious cigars, 'Cuba Sixes,' are twirls of the Sabbath day. — **(3) 1837** J. L. WILLIAMS *Florida* 106 The Cuba Tobacco stands next to sugar, in the estimation of our small farmers. **1890** *Cong. Rec.* 27 Aug. 9213/2, I have here some carots of Cuban tobacco.

cuba ˈkubə, *n.*[2] [Poss. an error for **cougar.*] (See quot.) *Rare.* — **1781** PETERS *Conn.* (1829) 190 The Cuba I suppose to be peculiar to New-England. The male is of the size of a large cat, has four long tushes, sharp as a razor.

Cubana kjuˈbænə, *n.* [App. f. *Cuba* + *Havana.*] A Cuban cigar *Rare.* — **1851** *Polly Peablossom* 105 Our friend . . . had taken his seat and was smoking a pleasant Cubana.

Cuban pine. A slash pine, *Pinus caribaea,* found along the coast of the southern states. — **1883** SMITH *Geol. Survey Ala.* 289 Toward the Gulf coast the . . . tree-growth consists of the long-leaf pine and the so-called Cuban pine. **1901** MOHR *Plant Life Ala.* 131 Open groves of Cuban pines cover the flats behind the dunes, merging frequently into the pine meadows of the coast plain.

***cubeb,** *n.* A medicated cigarette containing the crushed and dried fruit of *Piper cubeba.* In full **cubeb cigarette.** Also **cubeb smoker.**

1880 *Diary of a Daly Débutante* 110 Mr. Daly . . . asked whether we ever smoked cubeb cigarettes. *Ib.*, Two or three had used them for colds or sore throat and the rest of us said we didn't mind trying them; so a package of cubebs were sent for. **1896** MOE *Hist. Harvard* 14 He had just taken his morning's morning and smoked a cubeb cigarette. **1901** H. ROBERTSON *Inlander* 285, I was in the same room once with a cubeb smoker, and I reckon I can manage to worry along now on what I got of that smoke.

***cuckold,** *n.* Also ***cuckle.**

1. Any one of various species of beggar-ticks, esp. *Bidens connata.*

1784 CUTLER in *Mem. Academy* I. 478 *Bidens.* . . . Harvest-Lice. Cuckold. Blossoms yellow. In cornfields. September. **1840** DEWEY *Mass. Flowering Plants* 137 *Bidens frondosa.* L. Common Beggar Ticks or Cuckold, or, more elegantly Burr Marygold. . . . Only careful cultivation will eradicate this troublesome weed; no beauty, and no obvious use; August. **1894** *Amer. Folk-Lore* VII. 91 *Bidens frondosa,* . . . cuckles, Concord, Mass.

2. cuckold's horns, =**unicorn plant.**

1820 S. H. LONG *Expedition* III. 239 The unicorn plant, (Martynia proboscidea, Ph.) . . . is sometimes cultivated in gardens, where it is known by the name of cuckold's horns. **1846** EMORY *Military Reconn.* 49 We found to-day lycium in great abundance, senecis longilobus, martynia proboscidea, (*cuckold's horns,*) and a small shrub with flower like convolvulus.

***cuckoo,** *n.* A North American bird belonging to any one of several species of the genus *Coccyzus.*

1709 LAWSON *Carolina* 143 The Cuckoo of Carolina may not properly be so call'd, because she never uses that Cry; yet she is of the same Bigness and Feather. **1871** BURROUGHS *Wake-Robin* (1886) 23 The cuckoo is one of the most solitary birds of our forests. **1917** *Birds of Amer.* II. 130 Mr. Burroughs mentions three instances in which Robins have actually killed Cuckoos; in one case the Robins caught the robber in the very act, and so pecked and mauled him that he died of his injuries.

b. *transf.* Used contemptuously for one who fails to follow the orthodox leaders of his political party. Also attrib.

1895 *Cong. Rec.* App. 4 Jan. 65/1 Who did it? Grover Cleveland, with his brigade of cuckoos. How? By the corrupt use of patronage. *Ib.* 28 Dec. 388/1 You cuckoo Democrats are against it because the President has sent down his order for you to be against it. **1898** *Ib.* App. 6 Jan. 4/2, I call the attention of the distinguished gentleman from Massachusetts, who suddenly was born into the kingdom of the personal cuckoo party. **1917** *N.Y. Times* 7 Aug., Which would you rather be, a cuckoo or a copperhead?

As the last term in **black-billed, Canadian, ground, Maynard, Maynard's, yellow-billed cuckoo.**

***cucumber,** *n.*

1. Short for **cucumber tree.**

1797 F. BAILY *Tour* 178 They are generally found on the richest land, and frequently in stony ground, and mixed with . . . elm, oak, cucumber, and other trees. **1835** A. PARKER *Trip to Texas* 47 The timber consists of the various kinds of oak, . . . bass wood, . . . cucumber, [etc.]. **1919** CUNNINGHAM *Chronicle* 283 We cut down cucumbers and white woods and split 'em and hollowed 'em out with an adz.

2. In combs.: (1) **cucumber beetle,** any one of various leaf beetles of the genus *Diabrotica* which as larvae and in the adult form are injurious to various vegetables and fruit trees; (2) **bug,** =prec.; (3) **flea beetle,** a black beetle, *Epitrix cucumeris,* that attacks the leaves of the cucumber and other plants; (4) **magnolia,** =**cucumber tree;** (5) **patch,** a small area in which cucumbers are grown; (6) **root,** the Indian cucumber (see quot. 1931); (7) **tree,** any one of various magnolias producing a fruit resembling a small cucumber, cf. **large-leaved, long-leafed, white cucumber tree;** (8) **wood,** the wood of a cucumber tree.

(1) **1856** *Rep. Comm. Patents: Agric.* 90 Among the remedies suggested for destroying the striped cucumber-beetle, (Galereuca vittata,) Dr. B. S. Barton . . . recommends 'sprinkling the vines with a mixture of red pepper and tobacco.' **1948** *Ada* (Okla.) *Ev. News* 2 July 4/4 [It] is a powerful insecticide that will kill such stubborn pests as Cucumber Beetles, yet is perfectly harmless to humans. — (2) **1838** *Mass. Zool. Survey Rep.* 100 The cucumber-bug . . . is called *Galeruca vittata.* At first sight it appears much like the potato-insect. **1861** *Ill. Agric. Soc. Trans.* V. 432 This insect . . . comes so near in its colors and markings to the *Diabrotica vittata,* or 'Cucumber-bug' that care must be taken to prevent mistake. — (3) **1877** *Rep. Vermont Board Agric.* IV. 154 The Cucumber Flea Beetle, . . . a little black beetle . . . sometimes attacks the raspberry. — (4) **1850** S. F. COOPER *Rural Hours* 476 The Cucumber Magnolia grows in rich woods in the western part of our State. **1943** PEATTIE *Great Smokies* 240 In the mountains you see . . . an astonishing array of flowering trees and shrubs such as azaleas, . . . Judas tree or red-bud, and the cucumber magnolia or cucumber tree.

(5) **1880** NYE *B. Nye & Boomerang* 188, I think he will run, as I may say, like a bay steer in the cucumber-patch. — (6) **1814** BIGELOW *Florula Bostoniensis* 85 *Medeola Virginica.* Cucumber root. . . . In low woods and swamps. June, July. **1931** CLUTE *Plants* 41 The cucumber-root (*Mediola Virginica*) was more accurately named, for the underground root-stock has a strong flavor of cucumber. — (7) **1781–2** JEFFERSON *Notes Va.* (1788) 38 Cucumber-tree. *Magnolia acuminata.* **1895** CRADDOCK *Myst. Witch-Face Mt.* 56 A cucumber tree with its great, broad green leaves and its deep red cones . . . gave the only touch of color. **1943** PEATTIE *Great Smokies* 155 The chestnut oak is equally tall, and even the cucumber tree soars up, in some of the rich coves, to 90 feet. — (8) **1904** O. HENRY *Cabbages & Kings* 161 Johnny Atwood . . . prated feebly of cool water to be had in the cucumber-wood pumps of Dalesburg.

As the last term in **creeping, Indian, Jerusalem, one-seeded bur, one-seeded star, seed, single-seeded, star cucumber.**

***cud,** *n.* [*EDD* has *cud,* an ass, stupid fellow.] (See quot. 1890.) — **1868** G. BRACKETT *Farm Talk* 65 The Captin is a 'hard cud' to trade with: couldn't beat him down a cent. **1890** *Amer. Folk-Lore* III. 311 'He's a tough *cud,*' *i.e.* a hard case. Maine.

***cudbar,** *n.* [Var. of **cudbear,* a purple or violet powder used for dyeing.] A violet or purple color. Also attrib. — **1895** A. BROWN *Meadow-Grass* 12 Her petticoats were dyed of a sickly hue known as cudbar, and she wore heavy woollen stockings of the same shade. *Ib.,* Polly . . . ran hither and thither on her sturdy cudbar legs.

cuddy hole. [Poss. a variant (by confusion) of **cubby-hole.*] A close, snug place, a cubby hole.

1844 *St. Louis Reveille* 22 Dec. 1/6 Tophet was Siberia, compared to that cuddy-hole—'twould have sweated a salamander to death! **1851** *Polly Peablossom* 107 If he would come out of his cuddy hole, he would get the most allfired cowollaping he ever hearn talk of. **1871** *Ku Klux Conspiracy* VI. 2 He went and looked in the cuddy-hole where I was.

***cue,** *n. attrib.* In faro (see quots.).

1864 W. B. DICK *Amer. Hoyle* (1866) 205 Another mode of keeping the game, common in the Northern States, is by a 'cue-box,' by which the different stages of the game are correctly noted by one of the players, or by a regular 'cue keeper,' who is usually attached to the bank. **1892** QUINN *Fools of Fortune* 196 As each card is dealt the player denotes the denomination on his 'cue card.' **1913** MULFORD *Coming of Cassidy* vii. 115 Why weren't there cue-cards, so the players could keep their own tally of the cards instead of having to depend on the cue-box kept by the case-keeper.

cuesta ˈkwestə, *n. S.W.* [Sp., hill, slope.] (See quots.) — **1899** W. DAVIS *Phys. Geog.* 133 An upland of this kind may be called a cuesta, following a name of Spanish origin used in New Mexico for low ridges of steep descent on one side and a gentle slope on the other. **1918** VISHER *So. Dakota* 14 The Hog-back-rim (a cuesta) [owes its form] to the outcropping of resistant sandstones. *Ib.* 44 The outermost [zones] are the hog-back ridges (cuesta) which form the foothills.

Cuff kʌf, *n.* [See **Cuffy.**]

1. Short for Cuffy, *q.v.*

1755 HEMPSTED *Diary* 656 An Indian freewoman wife to Mr. Tilley's Negro Cuff died. **1867** *Atlantic Mo.* Nov. 600/1 After the play, Rice, having shaded his own countenance to the 'contraband' hue, ordered Cuff to disrobe.

2. =**Cuffy b.** *Colloq.*

1814 BRACKENRIDGE *Louisiana* 211 They chased a she bear into a hollow tree. . . . The chopping was renewed; madam Cuff again appeared, and was saluted as before. **1831** *Illinois Mo.* July 452 The moon was now shining brightly, and Cuff being able to see his enemies, and satisfied of his own safety, began to act on the offensive.

Cuffy ˈkʌfɪ, *n.* Also **Cuffee.** [f. *Kofi,* used by natives on the Gold Coast as a name for a boy born on Friday.] A Negro.

1713 SEWALL *Diary* II. 386, I press'd him, and came away with some hope; obliged Cuffee to call for him. **1858** *Salem* (Ill.) *Advocate* 2 July 1/4 The Cuffee who was robbed exclaimed with great emphasis, 'he broke my box open and took de dollar out.' **1947** LUMPKIN *Southerner* 63 Give me cuffee, and I can give you cotton.

Also **Cuffeedom,** *n. Obs.*

1859 *Kirk Anderson's Valley Tan* (Salt Lake City) 19 April 3/3 Two girls, the slaves of Thos. S. Williams, Esq. are the reigning ebony belles of Great Salt Lake City, and at their shrine the cringing knees of all cuffeedom bow down.

b. A bear. *Colloq.*

1824 DODDRIDGE *Notes* 21 When the bear approached him, he sprang out, and hallooed at him; but cuffee, instead of running off as he expected, jumped at him with mouth wide open. **1892** DUVAL *Young Explorers* 123 There ain't but one way to git cuffy out'n that hole, and that is to smoke him out.

cuidado kwi'dado, *interj. S.W.* [Sp. in same sense.] Look out! Be careful! — **1855** HARRY GRINGO *Tales for Marines* 139 (Bentley), Qui-dow! marm! don't make lub to de baby. *Ib.* 276 O cuidado! Screamed the pastor. Beware it is certain death. **1903** MARY AUSTIN *Land of Little Rain* 265 (Bentley), There are still some places in the West where the quails cry 'cuidado.'

cui-ui 'kwi,wi, *n.* [App. an Indian name. The spelling *kuyui* is found, and in Jordan & Evermann's *Fishes of N.A. couia* occurs.] A rather slender, round-bodied, black-skinned fish, *Chasmistes cujus*, about twenty inches long, found in Pyramid Lake, or a gray-skinned variety found in Winnemucca Lake.

1877 *Territorial Enterprise* (Va. City, Nevada) 27 Dec., There is found in the waters [of Pyramid Lake] fish the like of which has never been seen in any other part of the world. This is what is called by the Indians the 'Coo-ee-waa.' It has a tremendous head, with a sucker mouth, and is so covered with ugly, shaggy fins that the fish must be trimmed of them—sheared, as it were—before being sent to market. **1917** *U.S. Bur. Fisheries Bul.* 35 Doc. 843, In former times the coming of the 'cui-ui' was a great event. **1942** LILLARD *Desert Challenge* 104 Far outnumbering them are ten thousand or so white pelicans, which stay during the warmer half of the year and eat tons of chub, minnow, suckers, and quee-wee.

culheag kəl'heg, *n.* [?Amer. Indian.] (See quots.) *Obs.* — **1784** J. BELKNAP *Tour to White Mts.* (1876) 13 Along this road yesterday and this morning we saw the culheags, or log-traps, which the hunters set for sables. **1792** —— *Hist. N.H.* III. 90 The culheag or log-trap, is used for taking wolves, bears and martins.

***cull,** *n.*

1. Lumber that is defective, or a log not suitable for lumber. Also attrib.

1829 J. MACTAGGART *Three Years* I. 245 The refuse wood is called *culls*, and brings an inferior price. **1850** *Western Journal* IV. 97 There is less loss on the rejected, or 'cull' planks of 12 feet, than of 8 feet. **1865–6** *Ill. Agric. Soc. Trans.* VI. 647 Culls are a quality manufactured from winding, worm-eaten, shaky or dry-rot timber, badly manufactured, or less than sixteen (16) inches in length. **1929** F. E. MCCLINCHEY *Joe Pete* 174 The man sent by the lumber company arrived. He told Jaakkola that they had too much cull stuff in the piles.

2. (See quot.)

1881 E. INGERSOLL *Oyster Industry* 243 *Culls*, culled-out oysters; the next to the poorest grade, 4 to 5 years old. (New York and East river.)

cullaloo, see **callalou.**

***culler,** *n.* Formerly a town official appointed to inspect fish, staves, etc., offered for sale. *Obs.*

1663 *Boston Rec.* 15 Francis Hudshon and Ralph Sammies are made choice of by the Select-men for to be Cullers of fishe. **1781** *Baltimore Rec.* 43 Jacob Dawson appointed Garbler, Culler of Staves. **1832** WILLIAMSON *Maine* II. 683 There are in each town about 20 town officers, *viz.*—1. Selectmen; . . . 17, inspectors of lime, where lime is burned; 18, cullers of fish [etc.].

b. (See quots.)

1849 *Rep. Comm. Patents: Agric.* 322 When the tobacco is taken down, the 'cullers' take each plant and pull off the defective and trashy ground and worm-eaten leaves. **1881** E. INGERSOLL *Oyster Industry* 243 *Culler*, one who picks over oysters, or *culls* out the worthless and smaller ones; usually a boy.

***cultivate,** *v.* (See quots.) *Obs.*

*a***1870** CHIPMAN *Notes on Bartlett* 110 *Cultivate*, to use the implement named cultivator;—as a verb tr. & intr. Ordinary word in Eastern Conn. **1886** P. G. EBBUTT *Emigrant Life* 90 Growing very rapidly, [the corn] is soon ready for 'cultivating.' This consists of going over it twice at right angles with a horse-hoe or 'cultivator,' cutting up the weeds, and throwing the earth up to the roots.

***cultivator,** *n.* As the last term in **buggy, corn, duck foot, shovel, walking, wheel cultivator.**

***culture,** *n.* As the last term in **beauty, bee, Boston culture.**

cultus 'kʌltəs, *a.* [Chinook, worthless.] (See quot. 1945.)

1851 *Ore. Statesman* 28 Mar. 2/3 They did not award him the work—a work which he is just as incompetent to perform as though he was not possessed of a *cultus* old printing establishment. **1894** WISTER in *Harper's Mag.* LXXXVIII. 784/1 He can't bile water without burnin' it. . . . He's jest kultus, he is. **1945** *Senior Scholastic* 23 April 19/3 *Cultus*—Worthless. A degree of worthlessness not expressed by English. For example, a 'cultus siwash' is the last word in no-accountedness.

b. cultus cod, buffalo cod.

1884 GOODE *Fisheries* 267 Cultus Cod . . . is universally called 'Codfish' where the true cod is unknown. **1907** HODGE *Handbook* I. 371 *Cultus-cod*, a name of the blue, or buffalo, cod (*Ophiodon elongatus*), an important food fish of the Pacific coast from Santa Barbara to Alaska; so called from cultus, signifying 'worthless.'

c. cultus potlatch, (see quot. 1909). Also a potlatch *q.v.*

1865 STUART *Montana as It Is* 114 Present (gift) Cul-tes pot-latch. **1909** SHAW *Chinook Jargon* 4/2 Cultus potlatch,—a present or free gift; a benefaction. **1930** HAEBERLIN & GUNTHER *Puget Sound Indians* 60 The sagwē' gwe' or cultus potlatch was held in the old times by the following tribes: Chehalis, Cowlitz, Skykomish, Klallam, Snohomish.

Culver('s) physic, root. A tall herb, *Leptandra virginica*, or its root, said to have been so named from a Dr. Culver who employed it in medicine.

1716 C. MATHER in *Mass. Hist. Soc. Colls.* 4 Ser. VIII. 420 There is a fine plant, in your vicinity at Lebanon, known by the name of *Culver's Root;*—Famous for the cure of Consumptions. **1829** EATON *Botany* (ed. 5) 275 *Leptandra virginica*, Culver's physic . . . var. *purpurea*, Ph. flowers purple. . . . *S.* **1840** DEWEY *Mass. Flowering Plants* 162 Culver's Physic. Culver Root. Grows in alluvial meadows; . . . July. Root bitter and offensive. **1901** MOHR *Plant Life Ala.* 724.

cumaro 'kumero, *n.* Also **cumero, cumaru.** *S.W.* [See note.] (See quot. 1925.)

The form of this word suggests Sp. *cumarú*, used of a Central American tree, but its meaning is the same as that of Amer. Sp. *cumbro*.

1869 J. R. BROWNE *Adv. Apache Country* 274 The country is well wooded in this vicinity, abounding in fine specimens of cumero, a tree resembling the hackleberry. **1913** WOOTON *Trees & Shrubs N.M.* 62 The Elm Family (*Ulmaceae*) is represented in New Mexico by a single species of Hackberry or Cumaro (*Celtis reticulata*). **1925** BRYAN *Papago Country* 46 A smaller species, *Celtis reticulata*, is included under the popular name hackberry or cumaru.

cumbe kumbə, *n. S.W.* [Sp. *cumbé*, in same sense.] A Negro dance. *Obs.* — **1846** ABERT *Exam. N.M.* 32 The principal ones [waltzes] are the 'cumbe,' and the 'Italiano.' *Ib.* 70 They danced the 'cumbe,' they waltzed, and danced again.

***Cumberland,** *n.*

1. *pl.* Cumberland Presbyterians. *Obs.*

1834 *Biblical Repertory* VI. 347 This accounts for the name 'Cumberland Presbytery,' at first given to that section of our Synod, and subsequently adopted by the present Cumberlands, as they are generally called.

2. Cumberland Presbyterian, a member of a Presbyterian sect which arose in 1810 in the Cumberland region of Tenn. and Ky. Also attrib.

1821 in A. ROYALL *Letters from Ala.* (1830) 122 Here is a new sect called Cumberland presbyterians. **1890** DORCHESTER *Christianity in U.S.* 487 The *Cumberland Presbyterian* body was organized in Tennessee in 1810. It was a split from the Presbyterian Church, principally because of a refusal to set aside the rule of that denomination which required a classical education as a qualification for license to preach the Gospel. **1945** *Christian Cent.* 21 March 378/1 Cumberland Presbyterians are celebrating the 135th anniversary of the formation of their denomination.

3. Cumberland road, a road built by the federal government from Cumberland, Maryland, to Ohio and eventually on into Illinois. Now *hist.*

1816 *Ann. 14th Congress* 2 Sess. 21 Except the Cumberland road, the United States possesses neither roads nor canals, on which to legislate. **1854** BENTON *30 Years' View* I. 22/1 The Cumberland road, and the Cheseapeake and Ohio canal, were the two prominent objects discussed. **1906** *Springfield W. Republican* 16 Aug. 2 The old National road, often referred to as the Cumberland road, was the main highway of traffic across the Alleghany mountains in the first quarter of the 19th century.

4. Cumberland spice, (see quot.). *Obs.*

1817 W. COXE *Fruit Trees* 134 Cumberland Spice. This apple was brought from Cumberland county, New-Jersey.

cum laude. [L., with praise.] Used in, or with reference to, diplomas given students who have done superior work. Also **magna cum laude, summa cum laude,** indicating grades of superior work.

1893 POST *Harvard Stories* 274 Jack . . . lost a *cum laude* and had to 'take his A.B. straight.' **1925** *Harvard Quinquennial Cat.* 257 From

1872 to 1879 inclusive there were two grades of distinction at graduation, summa cum laude and cum laude. *Ib.* 277 Since 1880 there have been three grades of distinction at graduation, summa cum laude, magna cum laude, and cum laude. **1946** *Reader's Digest* March 168/1 There is a message for all Americans in the last thoughts of this brilliant and sensitive youth—a graduate *summa cum laude* from Yale.

transf. **1946** *Chi. D. News* 24 April 14/2 It should go further and make him a motorman cum laude.

Cunarder kəˈnɑrdɚ, *n.* [Sir Samuel *Cunard* (1787–1856).] One of a fine class of ocean steamships composing the Cunard Line.

1850 *Knickerb.* XXXVI. 574 We thought of the gradual progress to elegance and profuse luxury of our river-steamers; . . . then of the 'Cunarders.' **1902** *Out West* May 504 Within a week Tom was . . . beaming over the side of a Cunarder with his bride beside him. **1947** *Time* 29 Dec. 11/1 Ambassador Panyushkin was one of 1,164 passengers aboard the luxury Cunarder *Mauretania.*

cunner ˈkʌnɚ, *n.* [App. variant of ∗*canoe.*] (See quots.) *Obs.*

1877 *Harper's Mag.* April 706/2 An unpainted dirty dugout, known in the vernacular of the district [=Chesapeake Bay] as a cunner, and by persons of education called a canoe. **1881** E. INGERSOLL *Oyster Industry* 243 *Cunner,* a canoe (Chesapeake). **1893** *Outing* XXII. 94/2 We embarked in the keeper's large 30-foot 'cunner'—the local pronunciation of canoe, so called on account of its being constructed from the hollowed trunks of three large trees joined together somewhat in the form of a canoe or dugout.

∗**cunning,** *a.* Dainty, neat, attractive. — **1843** STEPHENS *High Life N.Y.* I. 220 'Why, that pair,' sez she, . . . a burying her hands . . down in the pocket of her cunning short apron, 'I'll put them to you at twelve dollars.' **1916** WILSON *Red Gap* 29 I've just counted nine, all leading out of town to the cunningest mountains and glens that would make you write poetry hours at a time.

∗**cup,** *n.*

1. *W.* =**treaty cup.** *Obs.*

1859 G. A. JACKSON in F. Hall *Hist. Colo.* II. App., Panned out two cups; nothing but fine colars.

2. (See quot. 1935.)

1859 *Amboy* (Ill.) *Times* 13 Oct. 4/1 Add one teacup of sugar, two cups of sour cream, flour to make a stiff batter. **1935** HORWILL *Mod. Amer. Usage* 94 In Am. cooking recipes *cup* is a definite measure, denoting half an Am. pint. **1948** *Good Housekeeping* Jan. 124/1 Add 1 cup chili sauce or catchup to liquid in pan.

3. In combs.: (1) **cupcake,** orig. a cake the ingredients of which were measured by cupfuls (cf. *poundcake*), now a cake baked in a small cup or muffin tin; (2) **custard,** custard baked and served in cups; (3) **defender,** a yacht defending America's cup, an international yacht-racing trophy first won by the schooner "America" in 1851; (4) **plant,** a tall, coarse, square-stemmed plant, *Silphium perfoliatum,* the base leaves of which form a cuplike cavity; (5) **towel,** a dishcloth or dish towel.

(1) **1828** E. LESLIE *Receipts* 61 [Recipe for making] Cup Cake. **1911** FERBER *Dawn O'Hara* 109 There were little round cup cakes made of almond paste that melts in the mouth. **1948** *Hungry Horse News* (Columbia Falls, Mont.) 24 Sep. 4/1 Refreshments were served including individual birthday cup-cakes complete with candles. — (2) **1853** *S.F. Whig* 28 July 1/4 (*advt.*), Washington Cake, Jelly Cake, Cup Custard, Molasses Cup Cakes. **1948** *Okla. Cotton Grower* 15 April 7/4 Recipes. . . . Cup Custard. — (3) **1895** *Bachelor Arts Mo.* Sep. 557 Had Mr. Williams insisted on his rights *Vigilant* would be the only available cup defender, *Defender* resting at the bottom of the sea. **1901** *World's Work* Sep. 1141/2 The Herreshoff's latest cup-defender, *Constitution,* is a better boat than *Columbia* in light weather. — (4) **1847** WOOD *Botany* 336 *Silphium perfoliatum.* . . . Cup-plant . . . A coarse, unattractive plant. **1870** *Amer. Naturalist* IV. 580 Another species of the same genus, called the cup plant . . . is common in the moist ravines. — (5) **1904** E. GLASGOW *Deliverance* 267 Cynthia, standing at the kitchen window with a cup-towel slung across her arm, watched the three chatting merrily in the sunshine.

As the last term in **Adam's, chalice, class, Davis, eye, fruit, Indian, mossy, over, painted, squirrel, treaty cup.**

∗**Cupid,** *n.* **1. Cupid's chariot wheel,** (see quot.). *Obs.* **2. Cupid's cup,** a kind of fern. **3. Cupid's delight,** the wild pansy.

(1) **1812** MELISH I. 142 The most of them had large, three inch diameter sort of rings in their ears, called by some of the students [at Princeton, N.J.], not inaptly, 'Cupid's chariot wheels.' — (2) **1880** *Harper's Mag.* Sep. 559 Love's torch, they call it rather, Or Cupid's cup, if maidens pluck and gather. — (3) **1892** *Amer. Folk-Lore* V. 92 *Viola tricolor.* . . . Cupid's delight. Salem, Mass.

cuppen ˈkʌpən, *n. S.* Cowpen. *Colloq.* — **1823** *Nat. Intelligencer* 1 May 1/4 *Cuppen, s.* The enclosure within which milch-cows are kept. **1859** TALIAFERRO *Fisher's R.* 61 Molly and the childering had jist got home from the cuppen with the milk of seven master cows. **1946** NIXON *Va. Words.*

cura ˈkurɑ, *n. S.W.* [Sp., in same sense.] A priest. *Obs.* — **1836** LATROBE *Rambler in Mexico* 63 Four or five leagues higher up, shortly after the traveller has passed a large Hacienda belonging to a wealthy *cura* on the left bank, it [=a valley] contracts. **1867** *Wkly. New Mexican* 15 June 2/2 They took up the line of march for the residence of the greatly venerated cura Padre Baca.

∗**curb,** *n.*

1. a. Orig. the curbstone or sidewalk as the place of operation of curb brokers, now often transf., esp. in phr. *on the curb.* **b.** Used collect. for the body or group of curbstone brokers.

(a) **1890** BIFF HALL *Turnover Club* 208, I will post the quotations at to-morrow's opening, and I don't think there will be any sold on the curb. **1948** *Salt Lake Tribune* 29 June 20/8 Eleven stocks closed off, four even and five up as 85,907 shares changed hands, including 16,200 on the curb. — (b) **1903** *Nation* LXXVI. 446 The Stock Exchange and the 'curb,' in cutting down their bid . . . gave pretty plain evidence what their opinion was.

2. In combs.: (1) **curb broker,** (see quot. 1900), cf. **curbstone broker;** (2) **hop,** one employed in a drugstore or soft drink stand to serve customers who drive up to the street curb in cars, *slang;* (3) **market,** a stock market conducted after a nearby exchange has closed, orig. on the street or sidewalk, or dealing in securities not listed on the exchange; (4) **prices,** prices on the curb market; (5) **service,** service given patrons of a drugstore, soft drink shop, etc., as they remain in their cars at the street curb; (6) **stock,** stock dealt in by a curb market; (7) ∗**stone,** see as a main entry.

(1) **1900** S. A. NELSON *A B C Wall St.* 130 Curb Broker.—One who deals in the curb market only. **1910** O. HENRY *Strictly Business* 12 Bob Hart, as well as any other normal actor, grocer, newspaper man, professor, curb broker, and farmer, has a play tucked away somewhere. — (2) **1939** *These Are Our Lives* 342 The first job I had when I came to Memphis was being curb hop for a drugstore. — (3) **1900** S. A. NELSON *A B C Wall St.* 10 Within this area . . . are . . . the curb market, with its swarm of brokers, and the offices of the corporation lawyers required to guide the tremendous interests involved. **1929** E. C. STEDMAN *Story of Wall Street* 343 The New York Curb Market . . . was conducted in the open air on Broad Street. — (4) **1930** *San Antonio* (Texas) *Light* 31 Jan., Closing curb prices.

(5) **1931** *K.C. Star* 25 Aug., The hoppers sit on the curb in front of the drug store, honk and attack the curb service boys when they come out. **1948** *This Week Mag.* 16 Oct. 1/3 A curb-service café on one of the highways leading to a West Coast race track hangs out this sign. — (6) **1915** *World's Work* (N.Y.) Oct. 691 Unlisted (Curb) Stocks.

∗**curbstone,** *n. attrib.* Designating one, not a member of the stock exchange, who carries on stock transactions, orig. on the sidewalk, as (1) **curbstone agent,** (2) **broker,** (3) **operator.**

(1) **1884** *Cent. Mag.* Aug. 629/2 Both of whom have carried stock-gambling to the depth of peddling 'privileges' to small speculators through curb-stone agents. — (2) **1848** W. ARMSTRONG *Stocks* 7 This class comprehends . . . all those petty operators and non-descripts, who have neither a local habitation or, scarcely, a name, that are dignified by the title of curb-stone brokers. **1904** W. H. SMITH *Promoters* 360 I've had hundreds of circulars from curbstone brokers and promoters of all sorts of things. — (3) **1861** *Knickerb.* LVII. 635 All sorts of brokers from the leading houses down to the curbstone 'operator.' **1870** MEDBERY *Men Wall St.* 162 He was a curbstone operator before 1862.

∗**cure,** *n.* As the last term in **camp, faith, gold, Keeley, pole, prayer, sure, wilderness cure.**

∗**cure-all,** *n.* A medicine or remedy reputed to cure all diseases. Also transf. Cf. **king's cure-all.**

1821 *Lancaster* (Pa.) *Journal* 26 Jan. (Th.), Popular Remedies against External and Internal Fogginess . . . [include] Cure-all, rum and brandy, [etc.]. **1909** WASON *Happy Hawkins* 50 Dock, ol' Monody here is a cure-all himself; he give me the best salve ever I see for my own shoulder. **1948** *Denison* (Tex.) *Herald* 2 July 1/8 The new insecticides, 'although possessing some superior qualities over the old, should not be considered as miraculous cure-alls.'

attrib. **1931** *K.C. Times* 3 Oct., The cure-all doctors haven't anything on the photographer who advertises, 'Have Your Picture Taken and Live Forever.'

∗**cured,** *a.* As the last term in **country, field, fire, sugar cured.**

∗**curer,** *n.* One who has charge of the curing of tobacco. *Obs.* Cf. **bacon, beef curer** and see **faith curer.** — **1880** Tourgee *Bricks* 25 So: you're the curer at Knapp-of-Reeds, I believe? **1881** ——— *'Zouri's Christmas* iii, So he made him his 'curer,' and gave him the cabin across the ford.

∗**curing house. a.** In sugar-making, a house in which newly-made sugar is placed to drip and harden. **b.** A house in which leaf tobacco is cured.

(**a**) **1672** W. Hughes *Amer. Physician* 33 The Sugar-house, or Curing-house, (as they term it). **1834** in Commons *Doc. Hist.* I. 281 The sugar is then formed, and is removed into the curing-house. **1891** Chase & Clow *Industry* II. 137 They were put into hogsheads in the curing-house, and the molasses drained away from the crystals into tanks. — (**b**) **1864** *Maine Agric. Soc. Ret.* 162 After remaining on the scaffold a few days it [tobacco] becomes yellow, it must then be carried to the barn or curing house.

∗**curl,** *n.*

1. *local.* A bend in a river. Also as a place-name. *Colloq.*

1638 in *Amer. Sp.* XV. 169/2 Within the four Mile Creek near Curles. **1899** Green *Va. Word-Book* 108 Curles, n. Name of a place on the James river from the '*Curles* of the river,' 1612. From an Indian word meaning 'a sinuous tidal estuary;' 'the *curls* of the river.' **1929** in *Amer. Sp.* XV. 169/2 These bends are often called the Curles of the River, and in olden times this section was also often called The Corkscrew. So nearly completely circular are some of these 'curles' that to go the six miles from City Point to Farrar's Island the river takes a sinuous course of sixteen miles.

2. In combs.: (1) **curl leaf,** a disease of potatoes, *obs.;* (2) **curl-leaf (mountain) mahogany,** (see quots. and cf. **mountain mahogany**), also **curl-leaf thicket,** a thicket of this shrub; (3) **curl maple,** =**curled maple,** *obs.*

(**1**) **1886** *Harper's Mag.* July 283/1 Foreign varieties and their hybrids are sometimes afflicted with the curl-leaf. — (**2**) **1931** Dayton *Western Browse Plants* 45 Curlleaf mountain-mahogany (*C. ledifolius*), frequently known simply as curlleaf or mountain-mahogany, is much the commonest, most widely distributed, and best known of the narrow-leaved and hard-leaved species. **1937** *Range Plant Handbook* B50 Curlleaf mountain-mahogany, also known as curlleaf and desert mahogany, is usually a shrub from 3 to 15 feet high, but it may become a small tree, occasionally becoming 40 feet in height. **1940** Jaeger *Desert Wild Flowers* 92 Go into the curl-leaf thickets when you will during summer, and you will always find them much frequented by birds. — (**3**) **1818** Fearon *Sketches* 24 Curl maple, a native and most beautiful wood, is also much approved. **1832** Williamson *Maine* II. 703 Our indigenous cherry, black-birch, and curl maple, which received so fair a polish in the service of our grandmothers, were shoved from the parlour and setting room, to admit articles of foreign mahogany.

As the last term in **blue, bull, cataract, peach, peach-leaf-, saliva, spit curl.**

∗**curled,** *a.* **1. curled leaf,** (see quot.). *Obs.* **2. curled maple,** a variety of sugar maple, a tree belonging to this variety, or wood obtained from such a tree. Also attrib. Cf. **bird's-eye maple, curl maple.**

(**1**) **1856** *Rep. Comm. Patents: Agric.* 298 The peach, in this county, has been affected with a disease, known as the 'curled leaf,' which threatens to destroy the trees.... Some think it is owing to cold, wet weather, and recommend shortening all the limbs as a remedy. — (**2**) **1778** in *Pa. Archives* 6 Ser. XII. 860 Invantary.... A Curl'd maple Teatable—£1 2s. 6d. **1787** Sargent in *Mem. Academy* II. I. 157 Curled Maple, to five feet diameter. **1817** Paulding *Lett. from South* I. 142 Let fashion change as it may, his ... old oaken chest and clothes-press of curled maple, with the Anno Domini of their construction upon them, ... still stand their ground. **1916** Seton *Woodcraft Man.* 290 Sugar Maple, Rock Maple, or Hard Maple (*Acer saccharum*) A large, spendid forest tree, 80 to 120 feet high; red in autumn.... Bird's-eye and curled Maple are freaks of the grain.... Its sap produces the famous maple sugar.

∗**curlew,** *n.* As the last term in **brown, Eskimo, long-billed, red, short-billed, sicklebill, Spanish, stone, white curlew.**

∗**curly,** *a.* In combs.: (1) **curly head,** a species of clematis, *Clematis ochroleuca,* of the eastern states; (2) **maple,** maple wood having fibers that run in wavy lines, also attrib.; (3) **mesquite,** a valuable pasture grass, *Hilaria belangeri,* of the Southwest; (4) **top,** a virus disease esp. destructive to sugar beets but also affecting tomatoes, beans, and squash; (5) **wolf,** a mean or contemptible person, *slang.*

(**1**) **1851** *De Bow's Review* XI. 49 *Curly head,* a vine resembling the other [Morning Glory]. — (**2**) **1909** Mrs. Stratton-Porter *Girl of Limberlost* xi. 218 In an expressed crate was a fine curly-maple dressing table. **1942** Weygandt *Plenty of Penna.* 29 Curly maple is hard to come by and is jealously husbanded in what cabinet making shops have the luck to have a supply of it. — (**3**) **1877** McDanield & Taylor *Coming Empire* 100 There are several varieties of mesquite grass in Texas, inhabiting various localities, best suited to their various natures. They are all rich and sweet, but the curly mesquite ... excels them all. **1937** *Range Plant Handbook* G69 Curly-mesquite cures well on the ground and is highly palatable to all classes of livestock for both winter and summer use. — (**4**) **1901** *Yearbook U.S. Dept. Agric.* 671 Sugar beets ... suffered severely from leaf spot. In Utah, Colorado, Nebraska, ... the disease known as 'curly top' was prevalent and injurious.

(**5**) **1919** *Amer. Mag.* Nov. 69/3 Alex was a curly wolf, they's no question about that. **1948** *Popular Western* June 69/2 I'm well ahead of schedule, in spite of everything the Prescott curly wolves have done to block us.

∗**currant,** *n.* **1.** *local.* The fruit of the barberry. **2. currant leaf,** any one of various plants of the genus *Mitella.*

(**1**) **1891** Coulter *Bot. W. Texas* I. 10 *Berberis trifoliata* [grows] on gravelly slopes and foothills.... The red berries ripen in May, are often called 'currants,' and are used for tarts, jellies, etc. — (**2**) **1821** *Mass. H.S. Coll.* 2 Ser. IX. 152 Plants which are indigenous in the township of Middlebury, [Vt., include] ... *Mitella diphylla,* Currant leaf. **1882** *Harper's Mag.* Dec. 126/2 The old man drank his store tea in triumph, offering no objections to the currant-leaf beverage with which his wife and daughter saw fit to regale themselves.

As the last term in **buffalo, cherry, flowering, Indian, Missouri, skunk, squaw currant.**

∗**currency,** *n.*

1. That which serves as money, a medium of exchange. Also attrib.

This term has been applied esp. to paper money, but it has not been restricted to that form of money.

1729 Franklin *Writings* II. 149 We must distinguish between Money as it is Bullion, which is Merchandize, and as by being coin'd it is made a Currency. **1733** *Conn. Rec.* VII. 422 Whosoever shall presume to strike or emit any bills of credit ... to be used and improved as a general currency ... shall be subject to the same pains and penalties as those that are guilty of forging. [**1755** Johnson *Dict.,* Currency.... The papers stamped in the English colonies by authority, and passing for money.] **1896** C. W. Ernst in *Proc. Bostonian Soc.* 25 The popular word for paper money was 'currency,' duly entered as an American coinage in Johnson's Dictionary of 1755, and unduly neglected by our own lexicographers. **1947** *Sat. Ev. Post* 14 June 166/2 Suddenly, and for no particular reason, ... there was a great rush of currency to the front office.

attrib. **1931** *Blue Valley Farmer* (Okla. City) 10 Sep. 6/3 This was intensified by the 'currency panic' of 1907.

b. A circulating medium of an indicated origin. *Obs.*

1757 *General Orders* 121 Who Shall Apprehend & bring them [escaped prisoners] to Albany Shall Receive 20 £ N. York Currancy Emediately paid. **1780** *N.J. Archives* 2 Ser. IV. 531 The lowest price 100l. York currency. **1788** *Kentucky Gaz.* 15 Nov. 2/2 Whereas I gave my note under seal for 20£ Virginia currency of the 12th of August last to Mr. Vivin Goodlow payable on demand.

2. Currency Bureau, the office or bureau under the control of the U.S. Comptroller of the Currency.

1864 *Statutes at Large* XIII. 100 There shall be assigned to the comptroller of the currency ... suitable rooms in the treasury building for conducting the business of the currency bureau. **1914** *Cyclo. Amer. Govt.* I. 367/2 This officer is head of the Currency Bureau of the Treasury Department.

3. currency exchange, a place, other than a bank, where, for a liberal fee, checks are cashed.

1945 *Chi. D. News* 14 Sep. 6/4 [She] said today she would give grand jury testimony against her former sweetheart ... on charges of embezzling $8,800 from the currency exchange where she worked. **1948** *Chi. Tribune* 17 Oct. (Grafic Mag.) 20/4 Banks and currency exchanges work in close cooperation with the police department in apprehending bogus check writers.

4. currency sixes, (see quots.).

1890 *Cent.* 5662 *Currency sixes,* six per cent. bonds issued by acts of 1862 and 1864, and made redeemable in United States Treasury notes or any other currency which the United States might declare a legal tender. **1895** *Cong. Rec.* 31 Jan. 1594/1 Certain bonds ... bearing 6 per cent interest, and ... known in Treasury parlance as the 'currency sixes.'

As the last term in **devil's, federal, fractional, Georgia, hard, mixed, New York, Pennsylvania, postage, postage-stamp, postal, rubber, small note, soft, Virginia, wildcat currency.**

*current, n. As the last term in **Alaska, under current.**

currental electricity. Current or dynamical electricity. *Rare.* — **1858** *N.Y. Tribune* 26 Oct. 6/4 The 'machine' to which your correspondent refers in its inceptional state, looks to the gathering of currental electricity with a view of producing vibratory motion.

current pay. A commodity or personal note commonly accepted as a medium of exchange. Also **current country pay.** *Obs.*

1653 *Boston Rec.* 11 They may make it up out of my owne estate in currant pay answerable to money. **1653** *Plymouth Laws* 98 That the publicke officers wages bee paied in such pay as is marchantable and current countrey pay and not in warmpwampeag. **1683** *Braintree Rec.* 21 He doth here bind his heires and successors to pay vnto the said Towne of Braintrey the above mentioned rent in current pay as corne or cattle. **1691** *Mass. Bay Currency Tracts* 15 'Tis strange that . . . another Gentlemans Bills in the Western Parts for as many or more years should gain so much Credit as to be current pay, among the Traders in those places.

Currier and Ives. *attrib.* Designating prints of scenes and events in the U.S. in the middle and latter part of the nineteenth century produced by Nathaniel Currier (1813–88) and James Merritt Ives (1824–95), American lithographers. Also absol.

1935 LINCOLN *Cape Cod Yesterdays* 217 There are antique hooked rugs on the floor and Currier and Ives prints on the walls. **1948** *Sat. Review* 11 Sep. 37/2 He could not believe it when he saw Tom's and Huck's Mississippi, with steamers just like those in the Currier and Ives in my room. **1948** *Washington Post* 5 Dec. 19M/2 An illustrated lecture on Currier and Ives prints will be delivered.

***curtain,** *n.* **1.** The sheet of descending water at Niagara Falls. **2. curtain calico,** calico suitable for making curtains, also attrib. **3. curtain paper,** (see quot.). All *obs.*

(1) **1854** GREATREX *Whittlings* 358 It is a customary thing for everybody who can muster the necessary amount of nerve, to go once behind what is termed 'the curtain.' — (2) **1835** LONGSTREET *Ga. Scenes* 57 'Have you any curtain calico?' said Mrs. D. **1884** MARK TWAIN *H. Finn* xx. 194 He got out two or three curtain-calico suits. **1893** MARK TWAIN *P. Wilson* iii, She had caught sight of her new Sunday gown—a cheap curtain-calico thing. — (3) **1858** SIMMONDS *Dict. Trade Products* 118 *Curtain-paper,* a peculiar kind of paper-hangings made in the Western States of America, . . . used as substitutes for roller blinds by a large class of people.

As the last term in **advertising, bonnet, fire, foot, mosquito curtain.**

***curve,** *n.*

1. *Baseball.* A ball so pitched as to deviate sharply from the line or course which gravity would cause it to take. Also attrib. Cf. **down, out, snake curve.**

1879 *De Witt's Base-Ball Guide* 24 The great difficulty in curve pitching is to obtain the required command of the ball. **1887** *Chi. Tribune* 10 May 2/3 Nearly all the Boston players found Ferguson's curves too much for them. **1947** *Dly. Ardmoreite* (Ardmore, Okla.) 11 Aug. 6/4 The gritty curveballer, currently pitching the best ball of his career, was the big man in the Cards' twin victory over the Pittsburgh Pirates.

b. The ability to throw such a ball.

1879 *De Witt's Base-Ball Guide* 24 A pitcher without 'the curve' was nowhere in the estimation of club directors and managers in 1878. **1910** *Amer. Mag.* April 787/2 Young pitchers with wonderful curves, and weird control, shoot the ball recklessly around heads worth $25,000 each to the big League clubs.

2. a. curve-billed thrasher, =next. **b. curve-billed thrush,** a thrush, *Toxostoma curvirostre,* of the Southwest, having a curved bill.

(a) **1881** *U.S. Nat. Museum Bul.* No. 21, 12 *Harporhynchus curvirostris*. . . . Curve-billed Thrasher. **1898** APGAR *Birds U.S.* 64 The Curve-billed Thrasher . . . of Mexico and New Mexico has been found in Texas. **1917** *Birds of Amer.* III. 182 In the same part of the United States [=s.e. Texas] . . . is the Curve-billed Thrasher. — (b) **1873** *Amer. Naturalist* VII. 328 We have the Curved-billed Thrush (*H. curvirostris*) in which . . . the bill is much less curved than in either of the last two. **1881** *Amer. Naturalist* XV. 217 Before leaving Tucson I found nests and eggs of . . . the curved-billed thrush.

***curve,** *v. Baseball. tr.* To throw or pitch a curve.

[**1856** *Spirit of Times* 6 Dec. 229/1 It is questionable, however, whether his style of pitching is most successful, many believing a slow ball curving near the bat, to be the most effective.] **1878** *De Witt's Base-Ball Guide* 35 With a view of settling the vexed question as to whether a pitcher can or cannot curve a ball, practical experiments were made at Cincinnati, O., on Saturday. **1896** *Chi. Tribune* 2 July 8/1 Kittredge curved the first two balls over the plate and deceived the batter, who hit weakly and was out. **1905** *Chi. D. News* 17 July 4/1 His curved ball was breaking much better for him too.

curver ˈkɜvɚ, *n. Baseball.* A ball pitched so as to curve. *Rare.* — **1878** *De Witt's Base-Ball Guide* 36 He, too, succeeded in sending a curver that swung around the middle barrier.

cush kʊʃ, *n.* Also †**cushie** *S.* [See note.] (See quots.) *Colloq.*

An African (orig. Arabic) word brought into this country by slaves. Cf. Gullah *kush, kushkush,* cornmeal dough sweetened and fried, and Hausa *kusha,* a thin cake made from ground-nuts, *kuskus,* a wheaten food. See *Couscous* and *Cuscus*[1] in *OED.*

*c***1770** J. BOUCHER *Glossary* p. l, *Cushie;* a kind of pancake, made of Indian meal. *Ib.,* At dinner, let me [have] that best *buck-skin* dish of *Cushie,* and *dough-boys,* and small *homony.* **1869** *Overland Mo.* III. 129 In an attempt to vary their everlasting pork and corn-bread, when the latter waxed old, they crumbled it fine and fried it in grease, . . . a mess which they called 'cush.' **1909** *Cent. Supp.* 329/1 *Cush,* (origin obscure) in North Carolina, the crumbs and scrapings of cracker or meal-barrels, fried with grease. **1948** MATHEWS *Southernisms* 123 Turner records that in Gullah the term *cush,* and also the fuller form *cushcush,* occur in the sense of cornmeal dough sweetened and fried.

cushaw kəˈʃɔ, *n.* [See note.]

The origin of this word is somewhat obscure, but it is prob. f. an American Indian term. Hodge is slightly in error in ascribing to Hariot the form *escushaw.* See quot. 1588 below.

A winter crookneck squash, *Cucurbita moschata,* or a variety of this.

1588 HARIOT *Briefe & True Report* C4ᵛ *Coscushaw,* some of our company tooke to bee that kinde of roote which the Spaniards in the West Indies call *Cassauy.* **1698** G. THOMAS *Pa. & N.J.* 21 Cucumbers, Coshaws, Artichokes, with many others; . . . besides what grows naturally Wild in the Country. **1763** tr. DUPRATZ *Hist. Louisiana* (1758) II. 8 The *Cushaws* are a kind of pompion. There are two sorts of them, the one round, and the other in the shape of a hunting horn. **1868** W. N. WHITE *Gardening for South* 214 The best variety [of squash] for family use is the Cashaw, a long, cylindrical, curved variety. **1947** *Democrat* 11 Sep. 1/7 Grover states that he has also had cushaws and an ample supply of vegetables.

***cushion,** *n.* As the last term in **buggy, strawberry, tomato cushion.**

cushion scale. (See quot. 1889.)

1886 *Comm. Agric. Rep.* 466 The Cottony Cushion-scale is found only in California, Australia, South Africa and New Zealand. **1889** *Cent.* 1411/3 *Cushion-scale,* a very common scale-insect, *Icerya purchasi,* injurious to the orange. **1947** *Calif. Citrograph* Dec. 50/4 Cottony cushion scale has built up rapidly in the absence of the predator and some trees were pretty messy.

cusie ˈkusɪ, *n. S.W.* (See quot. 1944.) *Colloq.* — **1903** A. ADAMS *Log Cowboy* x. 69 How soon will supper be ready, Cusi? **1944** ADAMS *W. Words* 39/2 Borrowing from the Spanish, the Southwest cow country called the cook *cocinero,* and from this came the common nickname *coosie.*

cusk kʌsk, *n.* [See note.]

This term is puzzling. That it originated in this country as early as the date of our first quot. may well be doubted, though it has not been found elsewhere. Another name, **tusk,* for the fish of sense **1,** is recorded by the *OED s.v.* **Torsk,* but only as early as 1707. The two names, *tusk* and *cusk,* used of the same fish, app. have a relationship, but one not easy to make out.

1. A large sea fish, *Brosmius brosme,* resembling the cod. Also **cusk fish.**

1616 SMITH *N. Eng.* 17 And scarce any place, but Cod, Cuske, Holybut, Mackerell, Scate, or such like, a man may take with a hook or line. **1724** *Essex Inst. Coll.* I. 72.2 *n.,* At 4 this morning sounded, found 65 fathom . . . sand, got a cusk, saw two shallops & one Skooner. **1843** D. WEBSTER *Priv. Corr.* (1857) II. 178, I will bring you a cusk if there shall be one in our market. **1948** *Dly. Ardmoreite* (Ardmore, Okla.) 21 Mar. 8/5 The cusk fish lays more than 2,000,000 eggs in a season.

2. (See quot. 1867.)

1839 HOLMES *Explor. Aroostook River* 33 The large lake trout . . . abound here—also the kusk, a fish somewhat similar in appearance to the salt water kusk. **1867** *Amer. Naturalist* I. 165 The donation of two species of fish from Lake Winnipisiogee, one the *Lota maculosa* (Ling, or freshwater Cusk), and the other a species of Lake Trout. **1906** *N.Y. Ev. Post* 2 June 8 The breeding season of the black bass, pike, perch, and cusk is past.

As the last term in **lake, red cusk.**

cuspadorian ˌkʌspəˈdɔrɪən, *n.* One who cleans cuspidors. *Rare.* — **1884** *Cent. Mag.* March 652/1 The official register contains the names of nearly fifteen thousand persons, beginning with President and ending with 'cuspadorians,' who serve the United States in the city of Washington.

cuspidor ˈkʌspəˌdɔr, *n.* [See note.] A spittoon.

The earliest Amer. evidence at present available for this term is in the application papers filed Oct. 10, 1871, by E. A. Heath of N.Y. City, in connection with patents numbered 119,705 and 119,706. These papers use the spelling "cuspadore." The word was probably based upon Du. *kwispedoor, kwispeldoor*, used of a spitbox, and derived in the East Indies f. Portuguese *cuspidor*, spitter. The *OED* shows that in 1779 a British traveler in New Guinea recorded *cuspadore* meaning a spit-basin, but the word never caught on in British use.

1871 [see note above]. **1875** MARK TWAIN in *Atlantic Mo.* Feb. 220/2 Here [on a Miss. steamboat] . . . bright, fanciful 'cuspadores' instead of a broad wooden box filled with sawdust. **1891** DUNCAN *Amer. Girl in London* 125 The British Government does not provide cuspidores for its legislators. **1947** *Field & Stream* June 35/2 He ran me out of the office with a bust of Walton, a cuspidor, and a string of invectives which has left me permanently bald.

* **cuss,** *n.*

1. A good-for-nothing fellow or creature, usu. with a qualifying word, and often applied good-naturedly or humorously. *Colloq.* Cf. **bobtail cuss.**

1775 *Narrag. Hist. Reg.* III. 263 A man that . . . was noted for a damn cuss. **1845** *Cincinnati Misc.* 226, I gave the child to its mother, and taking my rifle down, started out after the old cuss [a bear]. **1883** *Harper's Mag.* Oct. 706/2 The 'horned toad' is distinctly an 'amoosin' cuss.' **1932** *K.C. Times* 18 March 18 Some up-to-the-minute newspaper man tell a dern ignorant cuss of a country editor why.

b. *To take the cuss off*, to improve matters somewhat. *Colloq.*

1843 STEPHENS *High Life N.Y.* II. 55 The men begun to stream into the theatre like all possessed, with a small sprinkling of the feminine gender, jest enough to take the cuss off and no more.

2. cuss word, a profane word, an oath. *Colloq.*

1872 MARK TWAIN *Roughing It* xlvii. 334 He didn't give a continental for anybody. Beg your pardon, friend, for coming so near saying a cuss-word. **1911** *Chi. D. News* 23 Sep. 9/4 'What is it that Col. Goethals ain't going to allow to be used in the digging of the Panama canal?' 'Cuss words,' said Sandow.

* **cuss,** *v. to cuss out*, to curse (someone or something) soundly and thoroughly. *Colloq.*

1881 in *N. & Q.* 6 Ser. V. 65/1 Cuss out, to subdue by overwhelming severity of tongue. 'He cussed that fellow out,' i.e. he annihilated him verbally. **1887** *Cent. Mag.* April 844/2 He had even mounted a dry-goods box, and, as the boys expressed it, 'cussed out the town.' **1901** WHITE *Westerners* 134 Clearly he could not . . . 'cuss out' the delinquents as they deserved.

* **custard,** *n.* In combs.: (1) * **custard apple,** the North American papaw; (2) **pie,** custard baked in a pie tin lined with pastry; (3) **squash,** a variety of squash especially suitable for making custards; (4) **tree,** = **custard apple.**

(1) **1785** MARSHALL *Amer. Grove* 9 *Annona.* Papaw Tree, or Custard Apple. . . . The Seed-vessel a very large berry or fruit. **1896** *Nat. Geog. Mag.* Dec. 390 The virgin forest is composed of the wild lemon, . . . the dogwood, the custard-apple, and prickly ash. — (2) **1832** L. M. CHILD *Frugal Housewife* 68 It is a general rule to put eight eggs to a quart of milk, in making custard pies. **1894** *McClure's Mag.* IV. 83/2 Why, we've got corn' beef . . . an' watermelon perserves. An' you can make a custard pie. — (3) **1945** *N. Eng. Homestead* 27 Oct. 3/2 Custard squashes are grown in abundance; and yield a profit. — (4) **1808** T. ASHE *Travels in Amer.* 85 One was called Custard island, in consequence of its abounding with the papaw, which is vulgarly known by the name of the Custard tree. The fruit of the papaw when ripe, exactly resembles in taste the flavour, composition and colour, a custard of the best quality.

As the last term in **cup, rice custard.**

* **Custer,** *n. attrib.* Of or pertaining to the annihilation by a large force of Sioux Indians of the U.S. forces under Gen. George A. Custer (1839–76) at the battle of the Little Big Horn, in Montana, June 26, 1876.

1876 *Nation* XXIII. 21/2 The Custer tragedy has nothing new or unusual about it. **1891** *Cosmopolitan* XI. 302 General Terry never came under accusation . . . in connection with the Custer affair in 1876. **1898** *McClure's Mag.* XI. 444, I have come to hear your story of the Custer battle.

custodary kʌsˈtodərɪ, *n.* Also **custodiary.** A person or bank having charge of public funds. *Obs.* — **1838** CLAY *Speeches* (1842) 355 Every custodary of the public funds provided by the bill is a creature of the executive. **1840** KENNEDY *Quodlibet* 197 The State Banks were the safest of all possible custodiaries of the people's money.

* **custom,** *n.* In combs.: (1) **custom garment,** a garment that is custom-made; (2) **hatching,** the hatching of eggs furnished by customers; (3) **made,** made according to order or measure as distinguished from ready-made; (4) **master,** a collector of customs, *obs.*; (5) **ore,** = next; (6) **rock,** *W.* rock or ore sold to a crushing mill or smelter by small operators who do not have facilities for treating it; (7) **shop,** a shop at which custom-made articles are produced; (8) **smelter,** *W.* a smelter that is dependent upon custom rock or ore; (9) **tailor,** a tailor who makes garments for customers; (10) **work,** work done to order for customers.

(1) **1905** *Washington Star* 24 Nov. 5 (*advt.*), Double or Single-Breasted Sacks, as perfect-fitting as the finest custom garments. — (2) **1932** *Blue Valley Farmer* (Oklahoma City) 28 Jan. 6/3 Custom hatching 2½ cents. — (3) **1855** *Chi. W. Times* 16 Jan. 1/2 [There] may be found a large and splendid assortment of custom made boots and shoes. **1948** *Sat. Ev. Post* 3 July 71/1 The members tried to give him a custom-made automobile as a present. — (4) **1658** *Mass. Rec.* IV. 325 To aid the costome masters of wines, &c. in helping them to breake open any place, cellar, &c. **1665** *Conn. Rec.* II. 15 The Treasurer together with the Deputies of Hartford are impowred to farme out ye Customes that are to be receaued by the Customasters. **1675** *Ib.* 256 The custom masters shall be alowed for all such wine and liquors as he enters, for every single barrell twelve pence.

(5) **1876** RAYMOND *8th Rep. Mines* 181 The company has bought all the custom-ores it could get. — (6) **1871** RAYMOND *3rd Rep. Mines* 294 The following mills were running in Gilpin County, mainly on custom-rock. — (7) **1851** CIST *Cincinnati* 176 Two-thirds of these [shoes] at least, are made here, wholesale, or at custom shops. — (8) **1880** G. INGHAM *Digging Gold* 268 There is at Galena a small custom smelter. — (9) **1903** *N.Y. Times* 26 Sep. 6 (*advt.*), Custom tailors charge for suits like these $35.

(10) **1830** *Williams's N.-Y. Ann. Reg.* 163 In the town of Orange there are no manufactories of cotton or woollen but such as are used for custom work. **1891** *Harper's Mag.* June 56/2 His steady business brought in enough—Lynn work and custom work together—to pay for their house.

b. Also **custom-booted, built.**

1931 *K.C. Times* 24 Nov. 20 He passed around the business section today giving the boys the correct time from his custom-built watch. **1932** *Tulsa D. World* 17 Feb. 3/5 No pink-coated, custom-booted hunters ride smartly to the hounds. **1948** *Duncan* (Okla.) *D. Banner* 2 July 6/3 Their argument is that the Republican-controlled Congress already has provided the Democrats with two custom-built campaign issues.

customers' man or **woman.** One employed by a broker to encourage customers to trade.

1932 WASHBURN & DELONG *High & Low Financiers* 71 Lore was 'customers' woman,' super-salesman, office manager and general helpmeet in her husband's office. **1940** WRIGHT *How & When to Buy & Sell Securities* 260 Formerly known as 'customers' men' they now prefer to be called 'customers' brokers' and have formed an association to promote a higher ethical standing for their profession. **1945** MENCKEN *Supp.* I. 577 The surviving customers' men in the offices of the New York stockbrokers formed an Association of *Customers' Men.*

* **cut,** *n.*

1. A cultivated field or portion of one, often preceded by a designating term.

1765 WASHINGTON *Diaries* I. 216 Finished sowing Wheat at the Mill—viz 19 Bushels. in ye large cut within the Post and Rail fence and 6 B. in ye small cut. **1855** DAVIS *Farm Bk.* 160 The Hoes worked in the crab apple cut & got through it & began in the church cut. **1898** *Mo. So. Dakotan* I. 87 Lamoure had stopped his team on the north side of the cut next to the slough and was down on his knees tinkering at the pitman of the mower.

2. A light lunch or snack. *Obs.*

1770 WASHINGTON *Diaries* I. 383 Had a cold Cut at Mrs. Campbell's. **1773** *Ib.* II. 102 Mr. Hoops and a Mr. Warton calld here, but would not stay dinner, taking a Cut before it. **1827** *Cin. Enquirer* 15 Aug. 2/5 A dinner at Buffalo, a snack at Black Rock, a cold cut at Utica, and a duck at Albany.

3. A piece of a tree trunk cut off for splitting into rails, clapboards, etc. Cf. **butt cut, rail cut.**

1774 PATTEN *Diary* 328, I got leave of Matthew Little to cut Rail stuff on his land that we began to cut on and the boys cutt one or 2 cuts more. **1823** in SWEET *Religion* 166 It was usual to get from three and four, to seven and eight cuts of rails from a tree. **1936** KROLL *Share-cropper* 83 Between the crop chores Darius would send Soddy and me to the woods with the light saw to saw limbs, or maybe cuts for hickory stave bolts.

4. (See quots.) *Colloq.*

1851 HALL *College Words* 90 *Cut.* An omission of a recitation. **1856** *Ib.* (ed. 2) 147 *Cuts.* When a class [at Bowdoin College] for any reason become dissatisfied with one of the Faculty, they absent themselves from his recitation, as an expression of their feelings. **1915** *D.N.* IV.

233 cut, *n.* Unexcused absence from class. Also at Harvard an hour when no class is held because the instructor 'cut,' i.e. is absent with or without previous notification. . . . Also applied as noun or verb to non-academic appointments.

5. *Mining. W.* (See quot. 1877.)

1856 *S.F. Bulletin* 16 Oct. 1/2 The 'cuts' there are paying from $800 to $1,800 per week, the 'Gold Cut' making the highest yield. **1877** W. WRIGHT *Big Bonanza* 56 When her pan of dirt was being handed up out of the cut (i.e. the open drift run into the lead), he stepped forward to receive it. **1947** CHALFANT *Gold, Guns, & Ghost Towns* 33 The chief landmark of the old camp site is a long and deep gash in the earth, known as 'the Sinnamon cut,' from which it was said the owner hydraulicked $90,000 worth of gold.

6. (See quot. 1905.)

1877 *Lumberman's Gaz.* May 24 The balance of the cut will be effectually hung up until we have rain. **1905** *Forestry Bureau Bul.* No. 61, *Cut*, n. A season's output of logs. **1948** *Popular Western* June 69/1 The best you can hope for is a long jerkline haul of your entire cut, if you can get permission to make trail through the T-Slash.

b. Of a sawmill: actively sawing. *Rare.*

1853 *Frontier Journal* (Calais, Me.) 28 June 2/1 Yankee like, the logs are made to follow one after another in quick succession, keeping about twelve saws continually in the 'cut.'

7. A reduction in price, rates, wages, etc.

1881 *Chi. Times* 17 June, Before noon of yesterday this 'cut' had been supplemented by a still further 'cut' of two cents. **1910** *N.Y. Ev. Post* 29 Nov. 2 President Taft informed his Cabinet officers, after scrutinizing the final draft of the estimates, that there must be a further and deeper cut in them. **1948** *Chi. Tribune* 26 June I. 3/1 Gov. Warren supported universal military training and restoration of congressional cuts in European aid.

8. *W.* A group of cattle separated from the main herd as for shipping, branding, etc. Cf. ***cut,** *v.* **4,** and see **cut herd** in **18. b.** (4) below.

1884 ALDRIDGE *Life on Ranch* 89 One of our party goes in, and whenever he sees an animal bearing one of our brands he runs it out, continuing until we have collected a little bunch of cattle, which a second man herds, to prevent them straying off and mixing with the other 'cuts.' **1947** *Westerners' Brand Book* 53 These brand-readers were used as a rule in the 'cut.'

9. A share of booty or plunder. *Slang.*

1928 *Lariat Mag.* Jan. 59 'What's eating you?' growled one of the others. 'You're getting your cut, ain't you?' **1948** *Sat. Ev. Post* 10 July 28/3 At the big local estates you often had to deal with the kind of servant who demands a 10 per cent cut from the grocer and the druggist.

10. a. double cut, (see quot.). **b.** *To jump the cut,* to manipulate the cut at cards to the advantage of the dealer. Both *slang.*

(a) **1898** HAMBLEN *Gen'l Manager's Story* 87 He undertook to make a 'double cut,' that is, to cut off two sections of the moving train, and send each into its own proper switch without stopping. — (b) **1887** *Orange Journal* 16 April (F.), If he lets the light of day strike his operations he is no more a first rate crook than a card sharper, who is detected, can really be called a good hand at jumping the cut.

As the last term in **big greasy, butt, California, close, crab apple, cross, dead, dirt, eel, fine, first, half, huckleberry, inside, lickety, log, mill, over, peach, plug, rail, railroad, rock, saw, short, through, under cut.**

***cut,** *v.*

1. *tr.* (See quot.) *Colloq.*

1869 *Overland Mo.* III. 130 When a Texan driver wishes to mend any part of his wagon underneath, he often has to 'cut' it, *i.e.* throw the fore wheels out of alignment with the others.

2. In voting, to "scratch" (a candidate or party ticket), to vote against (a party candidate).

1881 M. J. HOLMES *Madeline* 10 Accordingly, with no definite idea as to what was expected of him, except that he was to . . . 'cut one or two of the first candidates.' **1904** *N.Y. Ev. Post* 6 Sep. 2 Information . . . indicated that Mr. Bell, the Republican nominee for governor, was being cut by the farmers of Chittenden County because of his policy. **1906** *Ib.* 6 Nov. 1 In the country towns the Republicans are not cutting their State ticket in any particular.

3. *Baseball.* To pitch a ball so that it passes over (the home plate). Also said of a ball.

1899 *Chi. D. News* 22 May 6/1 When he wanted to steady and cut the plate while the batter was waiting he ripped in one high. **1917** MATHEWSON *Sec. Base Sloan* 248 Another offering that would have cut the outer corner of the plate knee-high had not Manager Milburn's bat been ready for it.

4. *W.* To reduce (a herd) in size by removing certain cattle from it. *Colloq.* Cf. ***cut,** *n.* **8.**

1882 *Lippincott's Mag.* May 432/2 The great herd is to be 'cut,'—that is, the cattle classified according to their several ages and corresponding value. **1937** COOLIDGE *Texas Cowboys* 88 With a big herd they cut from both sides atonce.

5. Short for **To cut out*, **e.** below. *Slang.*

1907 FIELD *Six-Cylinder Courtship* 54 'My dear fellow—' I began. 'Cut it!' he commanded.

6. To dilute (whisky) with water or some other cheap liquid. Cf. **cut liquor.**

1931 COL. IRA L. REEVES *Ol' Rum River* 207 The quantity of their monthly withdrawals of alcohol and whiskey if 'cut' and converted into the usual bootleg whiskey, had an estimated retail value of something like $400,000.

7. *To cut behind,* to move quickly behind, to "hitch on to," (see quot. c1890).

1848 *Popular Songs* 36 Another calls out 'cut behind.' **1860** HOLMES *Professor* viii. 279 Here is a boy that loves to . . . chalk doorsteps, 'cut behind' anything on wheels or runners. **c1890** *D.N.* I. 212 The expression *cut, cut behind,* was used [in N. Eng.] to call the attention of a driver to boys running behind his wagon. [**1904** DARROW *Farmington* 161 Sleigh-riding . . . wasn't half so much fun as hitching to cutters or jumping on sleds.]

8. **To cut down,* to cut up (pork) into pieces small enough for salting. *Obs.*

1843 *Knickerb.* XXI. 436 His property . . . *cut up* very handsomely (to borrow the common figure . . . derived from the cutting down of pork for the winter).

b. To become depressed. Cf. **18. b.** (1) below.

1881 R. T. COOKE *Somebody's Neighbors* 198 He cuts down dredful; the consolation of religion wa'n't of no account to him.

c. Of a pistol or revolver: To come down level from an upright position. Also of a person: To shoot.

1918 MULFORD *Man from Bar-20* 90 He wheeled like a flash, his upraised gun cutting down swiftly. *Ib.* 96 Bein' in a pocket made by them fool boulders I couldn't get out, so I had to cut down on you with both hands.

9. **To cut in,* to connect (an instrument, as a telephone) with a line of communication.

1904 W. H. SMITH *Promoters* 348 That telephone is 'cut in,' and I have a number of friends . . . who are listening through it.

b. To interrupt a dancing couple to take the place of one of them. Cf. **to cut out.*

1921 R. D. PAINE *Comr. Rolling Ocean* 135 Excuse me, but may I cut in? Miss Crozier wants to see you right away. **1922** TARKINGTON *Gentle Julia* 163 Nobody else has got a right to cut in and dance with you more than the one you go with.

10. **To cut loose,* to act, shoot, or speak without restraint. *Colloq.*

1809 WEEMS *Marion* (1833) 217 The enemy . . . all at once cut loose upon them with a thundering clap. **1931** *K.C.Times* 30 Oct., You could get on the other side of the fairway where he could not hear and cut loose.

11. **To cut off,* in baseball, to put out a player, or foil a run, by a judicious throw. Cf. **cut-off,** *n.*, as a main entry.

1867 *Ball Players' Chron.* 6 June 2/2 Wilder led off in this innings, but Shaw cut him off in his prime, Willard fielding a hot ball to 1st base in style. **1883** *Chi. Tribune* 3 July 6/5 Purcell's and Ferguson's errors were serious, the former failing to cut off the tieing run at home plate. **1948** DIMAGGIO *Baseball for Everyone* 77 The usual infield alignment has the first baseman and third baseman in on the grass to cut off the run.

12. **To cut on,* to act up. *Rare.*

1887 WILKINS *Humble Romance* 405 Why, what air you cuttin' on so fur?

13. **To cut out,* (see quots.). Cf. **to cut in* **b.**

1775 A. BURNABY *Travels* 21 After some time, another lady gets up, and then the first lady must sit down, she being, as they term it, cut out: the second lady acts the same part which the first did, till somebody cuts her out. **1775** CRESSWELL *Journal* 53 Betwixt the Country dances they have what I call everlasting jigs. A couple gets up and begins to dance a jig (to some Negro tune) others comes and cuts them out, and these dances always last as long as the Fiddler can play. **1944** DUNCAN *M. Graham* 109 They danced three- and four-handed reels and jigs, and cut out partners to make the dance last longer.

b. To renew or dress out the grooves of a rifle barrel. *Obs.*

1806 CLARK in *Lewis & C. Exped.* (1905) IV. 254 My small rifle . . . wanted cutting out. *Ib.* 257 John Shields cut out my small rifle.

c. *W.* To separate (an animal) from a herd.

1869 *Overland Mo.* III. 126 Another rides in, selects a stray brand, and 'cuts it out,' by chasing it out with his horse. **1948** *Sat. Ev. Post* 10 July 84/4 Well, I reckon we better cut him out of your *remuda* and leave him here for a few days.

d. (See quot.)

1881 E. INGERSOLL *Oyster Industry* 243 *Cut-Out*, . . . in respect to scallops, to open them, or remove the edible part from the shells (Rhode Island.) *Ib., Cut-Out*, . . . to open oysters. (Providence river.)

e. To stop doing something. *Slang.* Cf. **cut-out,** *n.*, as a main entry.

1903 ADE *People You Know* 82 (We.), Cut it out! **1943** *Collier's* 28 Aug. 12/2 The shorter man said, 'Cut that out, Bill.'

14. *To cut over*, to fashion anew.

1904 E. W. PRINGLE *Rice Planter* 73 We . . . watch with interest the successful and ingenious remodelling of sleeves—I being the only recalcitrant who will not cut over sleeves.

b. To cut and remove the timber from (an area). Cf. **18.** (9) below.

1917 *Birds of Amer.* II. 154 When found they are usually in regions of original forest growth, rarely being seen where the woods have been once cut over.

15. *To cut round*, (see quot. 1889). *Colloq.* Cf. next.

*c***1847** WHITCHER *Bedott P.* ix. 91 They say she cut round and hollered and laffed and tried to be wonderful interestin.' **1879** STOCKTON *Rudder Grange* viii. 86 He [the dog] was only cuttin' 'round because he was so glad to get loose. **1889** FARMER 188/2 *To cut round*, to make a display.

16. * *To cut up*, to show off, make merry, act friskily. Cf. **18** .(15) below.

1847 FIELD *Drama in Pokerville* 198 One of them fellers that tumbles! —seen 'em once, more'n half naked, cuttin' up down to Madison! **1869** BARNUM *Struggles & Triumphs* 598 Well she has been cutting up one of the greatest pranks you ever heard of. **1947** R. SMITH *Baseball* 44 During a game, George used to love to make the spectators howl by cutting up on the base lines.

b. To cut (stalks of corn) close to the ground.

1839 BUEL *Farmer's Companion* 251 With proper implements . . . two smart men will cut up and stook two acres, in a day. **1891** WHITMAN *Good-bye My Fancy* 35 How mellow, crisp Autumn days, . . . and gathering the corn—'cutting up,' as the farmers call it.

17. With nouns in colloq. or slang phrases: (1) *To cut an appearance*, to cut a figure, *rare;* (2) *to cut a* (*big*) *swath*, to make a great show, appear important; (3) *to cut a gash*, =prec.

(1) **1789** DUNLAP *Father* I. i, I may cut a very decent appearance yet. — (2) **1843** STEPHENS *High Life N.Y.* I. 136 Gracious me! how he was a strutting up the side-walk—didn't he cut a swath! **1887** FREDERIC *Seth's Brother's Wife* xxiv, Chaps from Rhode Island or Floridy puttin' on airs, and pretendin' to cut as big a swath as New York did. **1904** *N.Y. Globe* 30 March 7 It is not likely that the new concern will cut much of a swath in the commercial world during the present generation. — (3) **1903** ADE *People You Know* 188 They might be up at Headquarters cutting more or less of a Gash.

For to *cut the bag open, cut corners, cut dirt, cut an eye, cut an eye-tooth, cut one's own fodder, cut grit, cut ice, cut across lots, cut the mustard, cut a rusty, cut a shine, cut (a) sign, cut a string, cut a trail*, see the nouns.

18. In combs. with nouns and adverbs: (1) **cut back,** (see quots.); (2) **bank,** (see quot. 1932), also attrib.; (3) **bluff,** a bluff on the outer bank at the bend of a stream, *obs.;* (4) **feed,** feed for cattle that has been chopped up in a feed cutter; (5) **horse,** *W.* a cutting horse; (6) **in,** (*a*) a sub-title introduced into the sequence of a moving picture, (*b*) a share or interest, *slang;* (7) **leaf,** in the names of various trees (see quots.) having leaves more incised than usual; (8) **lips,** (*a*) the stone toter, *Exoglossum maxillingua*, (*b*) the sucker, *Lagochila lacera;* (9) **over,** cleared of timber by cutting, also absol.; (10) **plug,** smoking tobacco cut, or apparently cut, from a plug; (11) **price,** a reduced price, also attrib.; (12) **rate,** a rate less than the usual one, also attrib.; (13) **rock,** *W.* (see quots.), *obs.;* (14) **silver,** (see quot. 1849 and cf. **cut money**), *obs.;* (15) * **up,** (*a*) the act of making practical or verbal jokes, *rare*, (*b*) one who frequently makes such jokes or plays pranks; (16) * **water,** the black skimmer, *Rhynchops nigra.*

(1) **1909** *Sat. Ev. Post* 5 June 19/1 Why don't you buy cut-backs (these are the cattle that at Kansas City, are found to be unfit for killing), or Texas stock, and feed 'em? **1918** V. O. FREEBURG *Photoplay Making* 248 That device, known in the studios as the 'cut-back,' is the instantaneous shifting from one plot or set of actions to another parallel plot or set of actions. **1933** *Amer. Sp.* Feb. 29/2 Cutback. An inferior animal left after those worthy of selling have been *cut out.* — (2) **1819** *N. Amer. Rev.* VIII. 11 A level was then taken . . . to the Nottoway at Cut Bank Bridge. **1932** *D.N.* VI. 228 Cutbank. This word (variously spelled *cutbank, cut-bank*, and *cut bank*) is often used for the outer bank at the bend of a stream, the bank which the stream cuts into, leaving the opposite side flat. **1947** *Sierra Club Bul.* May 72 The fisherman hopes to land his fish from the cutbanks of the creek that meanders through the meadow. — (3) **1805** LEWIS in *L. & Clark Exped.* (1904) I. 329, I asscended to the top of the cutt bluff this morning. **1812** STUART *Narratives* 137, 4 miles NW brought us to a part of the River where the mountains on the right and cut Bluffs on the left made us apprehensive of Rapids impassable for our craft. — (4) **1858** C. FLINT *Milch Cows* 118 The best course is, to feed in the morning . . . with cut feed. **1863** D. G. MITCHELL *My Farm* 136 The cattle are withdrawn to their winter quarters, for their dietary of cut-feed, oil-cake, occasional bran and roots.

(5) **1927** RUSSELL *Trails* 164 Then these punchers rope out their fast or 'cut' hosses, saddle and ride to the herd. **1948** ROLLINSON *Wyo. Cattle Trails* 119 There were . . . half a dozen extra-fine cut horses, and four or five well-trained rope horses. — (6) (*a*) **1918** V. O. FREEBURG *Photoplay Making* 19 The devices of leaders, cut-ins, close-ups, flash-backs, visions, dissolving views, fade-outs, fade-ins, double-exposures, dual roles, etc., have a strong appeal of novelty. (*b*) **1931** COL. IRA L. REEVES *Ol' Rum River* 182 Others within the organization will think they are entitled to a cut-in should the brewery attempt at any time to make anything other than near-beer. — (7) **1897** SUDWORTH *Arborescent Flora* 261 *Robinia pseudacacia dissecta.* . . . Cutleaf Locust. **1900** GARLAND *Eagle's Heart* 97 In the swales blue joint grew rank. The only trees were cottonwoods and cutleaf willow. **1923** WYATT *Invisible Gods* 16 Mountain ash and cut-leaf birch flickered their light foliage in summer. — (8) (*a*) **1880** GÜNTHER *Introd. to Study of Fishes* 596 From the fresh waters of North America . . . *Exoglossum* (the 'Stone Toter' or 'Cut-lips'). **1888** GOODE *Amer. Fishes* 427 The 'Cut-lips,' 'Day Chub,' or 'Nigger Chub,' *Exoglossum maxillingua*, has but a narrow distribution. (*b*) **1889** *Cent.* 1417/1 Cutlips. . . . The hare-lipped sucker. (Mississippi valley.) — (9) **1899** *Westminster Gaz.* 6 Jan. 10/2 At least 90 per cent. of the cut-over lands [on the Pacific Coast] are of absolutely no value for agricultural purposes. **1922** TITUS *Timber* vi. 60 If we had known we could have gone north . . . into the hardwood cutover and made a go of it. **1947** *Sierra Club Bul.* June 4/1 It would seem more desirable . . . at this time to acquire Federal ownership to these private properties (cut over though they may be).

(10) **1897** A. H. LEWIS *Wolfville* 108 The Old Cattleman . . . securing his pipe, beat the ashes there-out and carefully reloaded with cut plug. **1947** COFFIN *Yankee Coast* 60 He *manufactures* up—that's his word also—about his weight in cut-plug in a year. — (11) **1910** *Sat. Ev. Post* 10 Sep. 76/2 Tricky cut-price operators, getting a stock of goods by questionable methods, selling below living prices, and turning their profits by going into bankruptcy, demoralized prices. **1929** E. W. HOWE *Plain People* 122 There was always one source of ready money: job printing, and this I solicited and got out at night, at cut prices. — (12) **1881** *Chi. Times* 12 March, The New York Central . . . has been meeting the cut rate made via Baltimore. **1947** *Steamboat* (Colo.) *Pilot* 2 Jan. 6/6 Some of you will starve to death while others will go to New York and wear a long linen duster with the price of cut-rate tickets down their backs. — (13) **1837** IRVING *Bonneville* II. 48 All these basaltic channels are called cut rocks by the trappers. **1839** TOWNSEND *Narrative* viii. 270 These [fissures] are what are called the cut-rocks, the sides of which are in many places as smooth and regular as though they had been worked with the chisel. — (14) **1844** *Cincinnati Misc.* 6 As late as 1806 . . . the business house in Philadelphia in which I was apprentice, received over one hundred pounds of cut silver. **1849** CHAMBERLAIN *Indiana Gazetteer* 120 Even *cut silver*, which was, in general, an attempted division of a dollar into five quarters, disappeared.

(15) (*a*) **1843** CARLTON *New Purchase* II. 209 Art and tact . . . are requisite for the cut-up. . . . If the affair is not done up to the point—it is teasing; if beyond—it is horse-play. *Ib.* The cut-ups were usually in wet weather. (*b*) **1901** ADE *40 Modern Fables* 106 These Town Cut-Ups had only one Accomplishment. **1931** *K.C. Times* 6 Aug., Cut out the cutup's cutout. — (16) **1731** CATESBY *Carolina* I. 90 *Larus Major Rostro in sequali.* The Cut Water. . . . These Birds frequent near the Sea-coasts of Carolina. **1844** *Nat. Hist. N.Y., Zoology* II. 297 The . . . Razor-bill, Cutwater, . . . Flood Gull, . . . for it [Black Skimmer] is known under all these names, reaches our coast from Tropical America in May. **1917** *Birds of Amer.* I. 73 Black Skimmer. . . . Other Names.—Cutwater; Scissorbill; Shearwater; Storm Gull.

b. In less frequent combs., often rare or obs.: (1) * **cut down,** troubled, distressed, *colloq.*, cf. **8. b.** above; (2) **half-bit,** a half-bit resulting from cutting a coin, *obs.;* (3) **hay,** hay that has been cut into short lengths;

(4) **herd,** *W.* a herd made up of cattle that have been cut out of a larger herd; (5) **liquor,** adulterated liquor; (6) **point,** (see quot.); (7) **round,** a round fragment of wood sawed from a larger piece; (8) **skull,** designating one who is stupid, *rare;* (9) **sugar,** (see quot.); (10) **tack,** a tack made by cutting, *rare,* cf. **cut nail;** (11) **ticket,** (see quot.).

(1) **1847** Field *Drama in Pokerville,* etc. 117 Sure enough, there was no mistake about it, till, finally, terribly cut down, he was obliged to say: 'Well, gentlemen, it *is* here, by gracious!' — (2) **1838** *S. Lit. Messenger* IV. 294 We had no money—not even a cut half-bit. — (3) **1786** Cutler in *Life & Corr.* II. 264 Fowl meadow-grass . . . makes good cut-hay for cows. — (4) **1907** White *Ariz. Nights* 117 Occasionally some particularly enterprising cow would conclude that one or another of the cut-herds would suit her better than this mill of turmoil.

(5) **1938** Asbury *Sucker's Prog.* 343 Suckers . . . paid exorbitant prices for cut and adulterated liquor. — (6) **1763** Du Pratz *History of Louisiana* (1758) I. 208 The *Great Cut-point* is about forty leagues below the river of the Arkansas: This was a long circuit which the *Mississipi* formerly took, and which it has abridged, by making its way thro' this point of land. — (7) **1903** Wiggin *Rebecca* vi. 74 It had been hard . . . labour to take armfuls of 'stickins' and 'cutrounds' from the mill to this secluded spot. — (8) **1839** Royall *Southern Tour* I. 73 One cut-scull clerk was quite a fool. — (9) **1891** *Cent.* 6046/2 Cut sugar, a commercial name for loaf-sugar cut into prismatic form, generally cubes.

(10) **1880** Burnett *Old Pioneer* 362 On one occasion one man went around San Francisco, and brought up all the cut tacks in the city. — (11) **1914** *Cyclo. Amer. Govt.* I. 537 Cut Ticket. A ticket or ballot made up of candidates from two or more parties. Before the adoption of the Australian ballot . . . it was the regular party ticket modified by 'scratching' or by the use of 'pasters'. . . . Under the Australian ballot system, one votes a 'split ticket' when he fails to vote a straight party ticket.

For **cut money, nail, off, out, throat, under,** see as main entries.

cutaway harrow. A disk harrow having disks parts of which have been cut out to enable the remaining parts to penetrate more deeply. — **1902** L. H. Bailey *Cyclo. Amer. Horticulture* 1969 After breaking, two harrowings, one with a cutaway, the other with an Acme harrow, should follow. **1939** Gilbert *Forty Yrs.* 103 Then I got . . . a cutaway harrow and even a barrel in which to salt down shad from the Connecticut River.

cute kjut, *n.* = ∗**cuteness.** *Obs.* — **1850** Garrard *Wah-To-Yah* xix. 219 This hos doesn't see the cute of them notions; he's fur examinin'. **1871** Eggleston *Hoosier Schoolm.* 110 The cute they was in the head of the master.

∗**cute,** *a.* Especially attractive, dainty, artful. *Colloq.*

1838 Jonathan's Visit in *Poor Will's Almanac,* And *gals!* all as *cute* as a whistle! **1857** D. H. Strother *Virginia Illust.* ii. 166 'What cute little socks!' said the woman. **1948** *Nat. Geog. Mag.* March 292/2 She knows she's cute.

b. cute curve, a sharp curve. *Rare.*

1881 A. A. Hayes *New Colorado* vii. 97 By the way that Smart Aleck hollered when we swung round some of them 'cute' curves, he'd seen something new this trip.

∗**cuteness,** *n.* The quality of being attractive or pretty. — **1903** *Booklovers Mag.* Dec. (*advt.*), The illustration gives but a faint idea of the beauty and cuteness of the calendar itself.

cutey, cutie ˈkjutɪ, *n.* A smart, cute girl. *Slang.* — **1921** R. D. Paine *Comr. Rolling Ocean* viii. 130 Her friends thought she was a cutey for turning the trick. **1927** J. Barbican *Confess. Rum-Runner* xiv. 149 He goes about with a high-stepping cutie who's ace-high on the face and figure.

Cutlerite ˈkʌtlɚˌaɪt, *n.* A member of a sect within the Mormon Church. *Obs.* — **1851** *Ore. Statesman* 23 Dec. 1/5 The Cutlerites, reformers, settled on Silver Creek, Mills county, Iowa. **1870** Beadle *Utah* 124 Most of the other aspirants took off various sects, known in the Brighamite church as 'Gladdenites,' 'Strangites,' 'Brewsterites,' 'Cutlerites,' 'Gatherers,' etc.

Cutler's willow. (See quot.) *Rare.* — **1843** Torrey *Flora N.Y.* II. 213 *Salix Cutleri.* . . . Cutler's Willow. . . . Summit of Mount Marcy, Essex county. Also on Whiteface.

cut money. (See quots. 1816, 1824.) *Obs.*

1809 *Kentucky Statutes* IV. (1814) 45 When any collector of public money shall be about to pay cut money into the public treasury, [etc.]. **1816** D. Thomas *Travels Western Country* (1819) 110 In this district [Ky.] *cut money* is very common. If change cannot be made, the chisel and mallet are introduced. . . . One fifth is often palmed off on the traveler for a quarter. **1824** W. N. Blane *Excursion U.S.* 257, I was obliged to cut a silver dollar, into quarters, and even into eighths; a practice so common in the Western States, that the *cut-money,* as it was called was the only change that could be had in Missouri. **1874** R. H. Collins *Kentucky* I. 26 Feb. 8 [1809]—Act providing for exchange of 'cut money' at three per cent. discount.

cut nail. A nail cut from a nailrod or a nail plate as distinguished from a wrought one. Also attrib. See **scratch awl.**

[**1791** *Mass. Statutes* 10 March The manufacture or sale of nails which shall be cut from cold iron.] **1795** Jos. Scott *Gazetteer* 1288/2, 3 nail manufactories for cut nails. **1817** S. Brown *Western Gaz.* 316 Also, nine mercantile stores, . . . one cut nail factory. **1945** *Amer. Sp.* April 115, I have lately seen cut nails called 'square nails' by somebody who evidently did not know their right name.

∗**cut-off,** *n.*

1. A piece of land that is cut off or separated from a larger body. *Obs.*

1647 *Watertown Rec.* 13 Those that have theare Land in liew of the cut of by the Great Dividents. **1821** Nuttall *Journal* 144 We now passed an island or cut-off two miles long, and forming a point four or five miles round.

2. A direct road or way between two points, a short cut. Also transf.

1773 *Georgia Acts* (1881) 300 The commissioners or Surveyors . . . are hereby Impowered and required to make any such cut off as shall be thought necessary from River to River . . . in such Cuts off and Clearing. **1806** Pike *Sources Miss.* (1810) 64 Observed Mr. Grant's trackes going through it; found his mark of a cut off, (agreed on between us) took it, and proceeded very well. **1943** DeVoto *Yr. of Decis.* 180 Do not try a cutoff, do not try anything but the known, proved way.

attrib. **1944** Duncan *M. Graham* xxvi, Tramping a 'cutoff trail' through the wilderness, he had come upon Harrod's Fort and had been welcomed for his knowledge of Shawnee, Delaware, Maumee, and Kickapoo Indian tongues. **1948** *Dly. Ardmoreite* (Ardmore, Okla.) 26 April 1/1, I have had that experience myself on cut-off roads.

b. A channel, sluggish stream, bayou, slough, etc., resulting from a river's changing its course. Chiefly *S.* Cf. **oxbow cut-off.**

1814 Brackenridge *Louisiana* 229 This name originated in the circumstance of a trader . . . being in the river at the very moment that this cut-off was forming. **1890** M. Townsend *U.S. Index* 137 Cutoffs are applied to lakelets on the banks of the Mississippi and of the Red River, formed of the parts of the river left by the change in the channel, which gradually become insulated through the deposit of silt. **1947** *Chi. Tribune* 17 July 12/4 The Buffalo Rock channel cutoff, which eliminates three sharp bends in the Illinois waterway three miles below here, was opened to barge traffic today.

3. *W.* A number of cattle cut out from a herd. *Rare.*

1895 Remington *Pony Tracks* 87 Fresh horses are saddled . . . but before high noon the work is done, and the various 'cut offs' are herded in different directions.

∗**cut-out,** *n.*

1. An opening or hole cut in a floor. *Rare.*

1851 A. O. Hall *Manhattaner* 30 Above the bar and post-office (the former . . . looked down upon through a wide cut-out in the floor) are the . . . reading-rooms of the merchants.

2. *W.* The action of cutting out cattle from a herd, an animal so cut out or the place where such animals are temporarily kept. Also attrib.

1874 J. G. McCoy *Cattle Trade* 81 In the beginning of the cut-out, a few gentle cows or working oxen are driven a short space from the round-up and held, to form a nucleus, to which those cut out gather. **1890** *Gate City Herald* (Deep Creek Falls, Wash.) 23 Oct. 1/4 All this time the 'cut-out' experts leading these extra horses came up leisurely in the rear. **1907** Mulford *Bar-20* 120 In this contest Hopalong Cassidy led his nearest rival, Red Connors . . . by twenty cut-outs. **1920** Hunter *Trail Drivers* 98 Our camp was the catch and cut-out for all the other horses.

3. In canal or road construction, a place where a cut is made.

1898 *Engineering Mag.* XVI. 116/1 The dredge by which the cut-outs were excavated and the embankments constructed.

4. A piece of cardboard, paper, etc., cut out (or intended to be cut out) in a certain figure or design.

1905 Calkins & Holden *Art of Modern Advertising* 10 The grocer must be supplied with attractive counter slips, 'hangers,' window-cards, 'cut-outs,' posters and other forms of lithographed matter. **1927** *Ladies' Home Jrnl.* Dec. 68/3 It would be easy enough to adapt for the purpose the various animal cut-outs and illustrations.

5. A section excised from a play or motion-picture film, as by censorship.

1918 *America* (N.Y.) 20 July 352/1 A list of the cut-outs is marked on the permit so that an inspector visiting the theater can see whether those parts are omitted.

cuttage ˈkʌtɪdʒ, *n.* (See quot.) *Rare.* — **1898** S. B. Green *Forestry in Minn.* 294 *Cuttage.* The practice or process of multiplying plants by means of cuttings.

cuttanimmons kəˈtænɪmənz, *n.* Prob. the arrow arum *q.v.* *Rare.* — **1705** Beverley *Virginia* III. 15 They make Food of another Fruit call'd *Cuttanimmons*, the Fruit of a kind of Arum, growing in the Marshes: They are like Boyl'd Peas, or Capers to look on.

***cutter,** *n.*

1. A light sleigh, usu. drawn by one horse. Also fig.

1804 Fessenden *Terrible Tractoration* 80 Guide my wild Parnassian pony, Till our aerial cutter runs Athwart 'a wilderness of suns!' **1852** Regan *Emigrant's guide* 372 The riding sleighs or *cutters* are very tastefully made with iron runners, and *sleigh ridding* [*sic*] is a fashionable amusement in the winter season. **1948** *Highway Traveler* Dec. 20/2 There are dog team races as well and cutters or sleighs for travel in the more romantic mode.

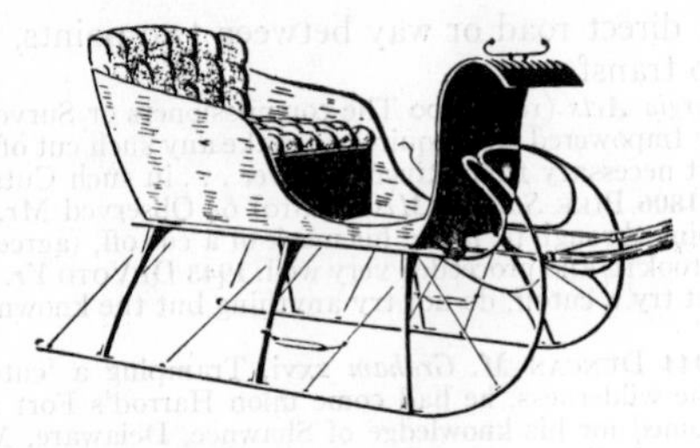

Cutter (sense 1)

2. A device for checking a wagon going downhill. *Obs.*

1894 Searight *Old Pike* 121 When there was ice, and there was much of it in the winter, they had to use rough locks and cutters, and the wagon would sometimes be straight across the road, if not the hind end foremost.

3. A beef animal of an inferior grade, or the beef obtained from such an animal.

1905 *Chi. D. News* 3 July 7/7 Canners and cutters were rather slow, as packers did not care to secure them, to-morrow being a holiday. **1947** *Chi. Tribune* 17 July 23/1 Canners sold steady and losses in cutters ranged up to 50 cents.

4. *W.* (See quots.)

1913 W. C. Barnes *Western Grazing Grounds* 381 *Cutter.*—Slang for six-shooter. **1944** Adams *W. Words* 47 cutter A slang name for the pistol, one engaged in cutting out cattle, a good cutting horse; also the man who cuts earmarks during branding.

5. A fine fellow, a jim-dandy. *Colloq.*

1930 Vines *River Goes with Heaven* 215, I was a young cutter then, Jake.

6. cutter-out, *W.* One who cuts out cattle from a herd.

1910 C. E. Mulford *Hopalong Cassidy* iii. 28 Each of the cutters-out rode after some calf. **1920** —— *J. Nelson* xxv. 259 There was only one pair of ropers . . . and only three cutters-out.

As the last term in **belly, cake, cane, cheap, cooky, corn, cornstalk, dust, ensilage, feed, fence, fodder, fog, ice, leaf, log, lumber, nail, phlegm, pocket, Portland, road, sky, stalk, tie, tobacco, trail, under, wire, wood cutter.**

***cutthroat,** *n.* and *a.*

1. A game of chance played with 24 numbered balls one of which was thrown to each player, the one receiving the ball with the highest number being the winner. Also used of a card game. *Obs.* Cf. **3. b.** below.

1823 I. Holmes *Account* 353, I have seen at least twenty boys surrounding a billiard table, playing at a sort of game of chance they call cut-throat. **1853** *Knickerb.* XLII. 453 The cards were produced by Doem, and the three sat down to 'cut-throat.'

2. (See quot.) *Obs.*

1848 E. Bryant *California* ix. 137 The Sioux, in the Snake language, when translated into ours are called 'cut-throats' and the sign for their name is a motion with the hand across the throat.

3. a. Of securities or business practices: Yielding no return on an investment, difficult or impossible to compete against, satisfy, or escape.

1848 W. Armstrong *Stocks* 31 It [*sc.* Harlem Railroad stock] is generally considered to be most essentially a 'cut-throat stock.' **1881** *Bradstreet's* 16 April 237/4 The three great objects . . . are . . . to avoid cut-throat competition. **1894** *Cong. Rec.* 19 March 3083 This system . . . we in the East have the fashion of calling cutthroat mortgages.

b. Of games of chance: Difficult or impossible to win. Also absol. Cf. **1.** above.

1870 Duval *Bigfoot Wallace* 247 Just as soon as I can learn to play poker and cut-throat loo, . . . I have some hopes the fraternity will admit me as a member. **1873** Beadle *Undeveloped West* 95 This game [=rondo coolo], like keno, has less of the 'cutthroat' about it than the others. **1878** —— *Western Wilds* 104 There flourished every form of 'cut-throat' gambling known . . . 'Cut-throat' games were the rule. **1946** Morehead & Mott-Smith *Penguin Hoyle* 27 The deal is as in Cutthroat Bridge.

4. =mustang grape.

1877 McDanield & Taylor *Coming Empire* 43 It deserves the name Cut-Throat from the acrid juice lying between the skin and the pulp. **1878** C. Hallock *Sportsman's Gazetteer* (1883) iv/1 Cut-throat, the mustang or wild grape of Texas, so-called from its acrid taste.

5. cutthroat (trout), (see first quots.).

1891 *Cent.* 6503/3 *Cutthroat trout*, the Rocky Mountain brook-trout. **1897** *Outing* XXX. 163/2 The father of all the Pacific trout, the black-spotted or 'cut-throat' (*Salmo mykiss*) with the scarlet splotch on his lower jaw, was most in evidence. **1946** *Mazama* Dec. 33/2 At the proper seasons steelhead trout and sea-run cutthroat trout provide capital sport for fishermen.

***cutting,** *n.*

1. A crop of indigo, grain, etc.; a quantity that has been cut.

1778 T. Hutchins *Topogr. Descr. Va.* 43 Indigo may likewise be successfully cultivated—(but not more than two cuttings in a year). **1797** Imlay *Western Territory* (ed. 3) 249 If the season be any thing favourable, it [indigo] will afford five cuttings between March and November. **1904** E. W. Pringle *Rice Planter* 121 Monday's cutting is tied up and put in little cocks in the field.

b. A quantity (of timber) that may be cut, or a place where the timber has been cut.

1902 S. E. White *Blazed Trail* 191 It's a fine country, . . . with a great cutting of white pine. **1942** Rich *We Took to Woods* (1948) 131 If we . . . scramble up a steep, spruce-covered slope to the foot of the pumpkin pine, we'll come out in an old, overgrown birch cutting.

2. *W.* The action of separating cattle from a herd.

1903 O. Henry *Rolling Stones* (1912) 88 Saunders had assigned him to a place holding the herd during the cuttings.

b. Usu. attrib. or as adj., as **cutting ground, horse, pony, shute, work.**

1907 White *Arizona Nights* 121 We shook our hats free of water, and drove the herd back to the cutting grounds again. — **1881** Romspert *Western Echo* 177 Each firm has particular horses trained for this business, and they are called 'cutting horses.' **1948** *Norman* (Okla.) *Transcript* 4 July 4/3 In his prime, old Lightfoot was one of the best cutting horses on the range. — **1887** F. Francis *Saddle & Moccasin* (Lentzner), I had been furnished with a trained cutting pony, reported to be one of the best in the valley. — **1920** Hunter *Trail Drivers Texas* I. 297 When fences became more common the calves were cut out through a *cutting shute*. — **1893** Roosevelt *Wilderness Hunter* 24 The men roped fresh horses, fitted for the cutting-work round the herd, with its attendant furious galloping and flash-like turning and twisting.

3. cutting out, (see quot. 1824). Also attrib.

1824 Doddridge *Notes* 131 The jigs were often accompanied with what was called cutting out; that is, when either of the parties became tired of the dance, on intimation the place was supplied by some one of the company without any interruption of the dance. **1831** *Boston Transcript* 17 Aug. 2/2 Every body else in Downingville was trying the double shuffle and the cutting out jig.

b. = ***cutting 2.** Also attrib.

1882 *Lippincott's Mag.* May 431/1 It is only when some refractory animal is to be headed off, or a herd divided into two or more parts by the operation known as 'cutting out,' that bursts of speed are necessary or indulged in. **1887** R. E. Strahorn *Hand-Book Wyoming* 35 Our artist has given a very fair representation of the 'cutting out' scene. **1946** *Reader's Digest* Dec. 129/2 After dinner we start the cutting out.

4. cutting up, the action of behaving mischievously.

1843 Carlton *New Purchase* II. 209 Cutting up . . . consists in cracking nuts and jokes—racing one another, and slamming doors [etc.]. **1883** Macon *Uncle Gabe Tucker* 162 De perlicemen nebber would 'a' let John de Baptis' do any sich cuttin'-up as dat.

As the last term in **beaver, rate, tobacco, watermelon, wood cutting.**

Cuttyhunk ˈkʌtɪhʌŋk, *n.* [*Cuttyhunk* Island, Mass.] An exceptionally strong linen fishing line. Also attrib.

1916 *Outing* Oct. 110/2 A spool of the Cuttyhunk was sent me with the request that I give it a thorough try-out. **1933** Cheley *Camping*

Out 447 A reel that will hold at least 900 feet of No. 12 cuttyhunk line is needed. **1947** *Atlantic Mo.* Sep. 36/2 The next morning I . . . again began fly-casting, this time with about 40 yards of nine-thread Cuttyhunk salt-water line.

cut-under ˈkʌtˌʌndɚ, *n.*

1. Underselling. *Rare.*

1851 CIST *Cincinnati* 313 The next effect will be a general reduction on the margin of profit in commercial operations—a system of cut-under, will be pursued.

2. A carriage having the body cut out so that the front wheels turn under the body. In full **cut-under run-about, surrey, trap.** See **runabout.**

1887 A. HAYES *Jesuit's Ring* 61, I have chartered a cut-under. Jump in. **1907** *Chi. Tribune* 8 May 19 (*advt.*), Can be bought cheap—a hand-some light cutunder 2-seated trap and cutunder family surrey. **1948** RITTENHOUSE *Vehicles* 13 Cut Under Runabout. City driving required sharp turns into driveways and alleys, and this necessitated the 'cut under' construction which gave clearance to the front wheels when turning in a small radius.

***Cuvier,** *n.* [Georges *Cuvier* (1769–1832), French naturalist.] Formerly used in the possessive in names of the golden-crowned kinglet, *Regulus satrapa.* — **1831** AUDUBON *Ornith. Biog.* I. 288 Cuvier's Regulus. *Regulus cuvierii.* . . . Charles Lucian Bonaparte . . . proposed naming it *Regulus Carbunculus.* **1858** BAIRD *Birds Pacific R.R.* 228 Cuvier's Golden Crest. *Regulus cuvieri.* . . . It is only known by the figure and description of Audubon. . . . The specimen was killed in June, 1812, on the banks of the Schuylkill river, in Pennsylvania.

***cyclamen,** *n.* = **American cowslip.** — **1887** *Overland Mo.* Aug. 152/1 Then, if we could have been there, we should have seen the beautiful 'shooting stars,' or wild cyclamens. **1946** R. PEATTIE *Pac. Coast Ranges* 52 The whole sod may be covered with a fall of shooting stars, our New-World cyclamens, that leap away from the earth on fine stems as if they spurned it.

cyclery ˈsaɪklərɪ, *n.* A bicycle shop.

1897 *Trans-Mississippian* (Council Bluffs, Ia.) 20 April (*advt.*), Council Bluffs Cyclery. **1899** FRASER *Round World on Wheel* xxxvii. 484 There is a cyclery—that's an American word—where machines are hired out at a shilling an hour. **1912** *Out West* April 271 Neal Sorenson, Owner Alhambra Cyclery. **1936** MENCKEN *Amer. Language* 176 In Pasadena, Calif., there is a *hattery,* in South Pasadena a *cyclery.*

***cyclone,** *n.* In combs:. (1) **cyclone cellar,** a cellar prepared for shelter during a cyclone, also transf.; (2) **class,** (see quot.), *rare;* (3) **movement,** a figure in dancing; (4) **pit,** = **cyclone cellar.**

Cyclone cellar

(1) **1887** CUSTER *Tenting on Plains* 652 Those women who take refuge in these days in their cyclone-cellar . . . will know. **1904** LORIMER *Old Gorgon Graham* 125 This was one of those holy moments . . . when an outsider wants to pull his tongue back into its cyclone cellar. **1946** *Reader's Digest* March 135/1 In the winter it was snug and cozy; and in summer-time as cool and nice as our cyclone cellar. — (2) **1896** CHADWICK *Spalding's Base B. Guide* 59 This change for the better in pitching methods resulting in sending most of the old 'cyclone' class of pitchers to the rear—fellows who had not a single idea of what scientific work in the box was, and who relied solely upon a wild, intimidating speed in delivery for success in the position. — (3) **1891** SLOAN *Fogy Days* 127 We are just getting down properly to our knitting in what is called the cyclone movement, when the music suddenly ceased. — (4) **1889** *Cent.* 1423/2 Cyclone-pit[s] . . . on the prairies and plains of the western United States.

cyclonish ˈsaɪˌklonɪʃ, *a. fig.* Caused by, or having the nature of, a cyclone. — **1884** *Harper's Bazaar* in *Advance* (Chicago) 1 Jan. (1885), A wee-toddler . . . burst noisily in upon us while at breakfast, giving the door a cyclonish bang. **1893** *Nation* 13 July 32/3 She is altogether of the . . . cyclonish, Western type—a good-tempered girl with no end of go.

***Cyclops,** *n.* An officer in the Ku-Klux Klan, often with a preceding term, as **Exalted, Grand, Great Grand Cyclops.**

1867 *41st Cong.* 2 Sess. H.R. Misc. Doc. No. 53, 315 The officers [of the Ku-Klux Klan] . . . shall consist of a Grand Wizard of the Empire . . . ; a Grand Dragon of the Realm . . . a Grand Cyclops of the Den. **1880** TOURGEE *Invisible Empire* 412 The person, through the Cyclops of the order of which he is a member, can make application to the Great Grand Cyclops . . . in which case execution of the sentence can be stayed. **1923** S. FROST *Challenge of Klan* 36 The individual Klan [a single local chapter] . . . is headed by an Exalted Cyclops. **1946** *Coronet* Oct. 3/1 The Cyclops and his twelve Terrors may burn a fiery cross on your lawn.

***cylinder,** *n.*

1. The part of a revolver which contains the chambers for the cartridges.

1862 WINTHROP *Canoe & Saddle* 27 Pleasant, well oiled click that cylinder has. **1908** VISSCHER *Pony Express* 45 When I had adjusted my Spencer rifle, which was a seven-shooter and my Colt's revolver, with two cylinders ready for use in case of emergency, I started. **1945** MATHEWS *Talking* 65 I held the muzzle of my Smith & Wesson to his head and emptied the cylinder.

2. A phonograph record of a cylindrical shape, in full **cylinder record.** Also fig.

1893 *Harper's Mag.* Jan. 214/2 It's just a phonograph. . . . It don't seem to be exactly in order. Perhaps the cylinder's got dry. **1894** O. HENRY *Rolling Stones* (1912) 171 'One moment, Mr. President,' I interrupted; 'would you mind changing that cylinder?' **1907** *Pearson's Mag.* Jan. (*advt.*), You cannot get the best results from any talking machine without using Columbia Disc or Cylinder Records.

3. In special combs.: (1) **cylinder churn,** a churn the container of which is cylindrical, *obs.;* (2) **glass,** glass

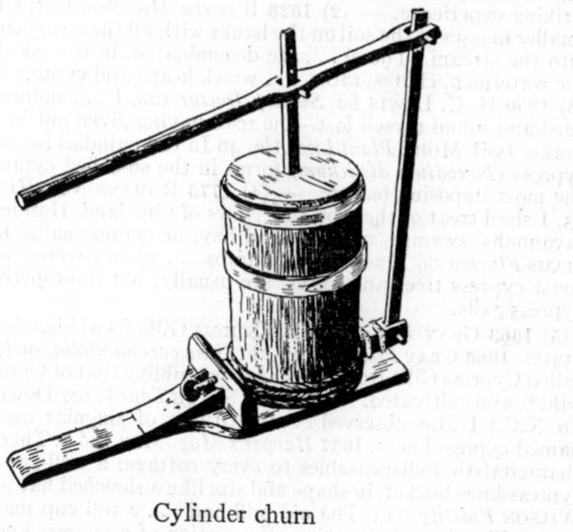

Cylinder churn

blown into a cylindrical shape and then cut and pressed into flat sheets; (3) **press,** a printing press in which a cylinder either carries the type or gives the impression; (4) **saw,** ?a band saw, *obs.*

(1) **1854** *Pa. Agric. Rep.* 396 Best Cylinder Churn, . . . Best Washing Machine. **1858** C. FLINT *Milch Cows* 227 The cylinder churn is very simply constructed, and capable of being easily cleaned.—(2) **1819** SCHOOLCRAFT *Mo. Lead Mines* 187 In the manufacture of common window glass, technically called *cylinder glass* in the United States, sands are frequently employed. — (3) **1851** J. H. ROSS *In New York* 212 But the climax of all presses for quick work, is the 'Cylinder Press.' **1924** *Publishers' Weekly* CVI. 188/1 *cylinder press*—A printing press with a rotating impression cylinder under which a bed containing the type or plates moves forward and backward. Most books are printed on such presses. — (4) **1851** CIST *Cincinnati* 181 They are . . . fed to a cylinder saw, which cuts them into staves of the proper thickness and curve.

cymbal, see **simball.**

cymbling, see **simlin.**

***cypress,** *n.*

1. Any one of various American evergreen trees allied to or confused with the true cypress, also the wood of such a tree.

It is impossible to identify precisely the trees meant in all the quots. here given.

1587 HAKLUYT tr. Laudonnière *Notable Historie* 2r There is great store of Ceders, Cypresses, Bayes, Palme trees, Hollies, and wilde Vines. **1612** SMITH *Virginia* 10 There is a kinde of wood we called Cypres, because both the wood, the fruit, and the leafe did most resemble it. **1728** BYRD in *N.C. Col. Rec.* II. (1886) 752 The ground . . . was overgrown with Gall bushes and the trees which grew here & there amongst them were generally Cypresses. **1898** ATHERTON *Californians* 221 Magdalena sat down by the open window where she could smell the cypresses. **1939** MCATEE *Wildfowl Food Plants* 9 Only the cypresses of this group are of consequence in producing wildfowl food.

2. In combs.: (1) **cypress bay,** =**cypress pond;** (2) **bend,** (see quot.), *obs.;* (3) **brake,** a thicket or dense growth of cypress trees; (4) **gall,** a piece of poor land or swamp on which cypress trees grow; (5) **gilia,** (see quots.); (6) **knee,** one of the large, hollow, conical excrescences that grow from the roots of the bald cypress, also attrib.; (7) * **moss,** =**Spanish moss;** (8) **nubbin,** =**cypress knee,** *rare;* (9) **pond,** (see quot. 1934); (10) **powder,** (see quot.), *obs.;* (11) **shingle,** a shingle made of cypress wood, also **cypress heart shingle;** (12) **slash,** a slash in which there are many cypress trees; (13) **spurge,** a European spurge found as a weed in the eastern states; (14) **swamp,** a swamp in which there are many cypress trees; (15) **timber,** a large piece or slab of cypress wood, a forest or standing growth of cypress trees, also attrib.; (16) **vine,** any one of various twining vines, esp. *Quamoclit pennata,* also attrib.

(1) 1934 *Nat. Geog. Mag.* LXV. 602 To pass from the sparkling sunshine of the prairies into the gloom of the adjoining cypress bays is a striking experience. — **(2) 1828** *Western Mo. Rev.* I. 512 Larger or smaller masses of the soil on the banks with all the trees, are plunged into the stream. [These] . . . are denominated, in the vocabulary of the watermen, chutes, races, . . . wreck heaps and cypress bends. — **(3) 1850** H. C. LEWIS *La. Swamp Doctor* 108, I . . . suddenly awakened and found myself lost—the road having given out in a cypress brake. **1901** MOHR *Plant Life Ala.* 46 In the paludial forest, . . . the cypress (*Taxodium distichum*) forms in the so-called cypress brakes the most imposing feature. — **(4) 1775** ROMANS *Nat. Hist. Florida* 15, I shall treat of them by the names of pine land, Hammock land, savannahs, swamps, marshes, and bay, or cypress galls. **1837** WILLIAMS *Florida* 89 Pine barren swamps . . . when covered with small coast cypress trees and knees, are usually, but improperly, termed cypress galls.

(5) 1863 GRAY *Botany* p. lxx, Cypress Gilia [is a] biennial, from S. States. **1868** GRAY *Field Botany* 261 *Gilia coronopifolia,* or *Ipomopsis,* called Cypress Gilia from the foliage resembling that of Cypress-Vine: wild S. and cultivated. — **(6) 1784** SMYTH *Tour* I. 107 Down this way [in N.C.] I also observed . . . multitudes of singular excrescences, named cypress knees. **1857** *Harper's Mag.* May 746/1 There are four characteristic indispensables to every cottage: a well-sweep with a cypress-knee bucket, in shape and size like a slouched hat [etc.]. **1946** WILSON *Fidelity* 113 The old mill had . . . a toll cup made into a bucket-like shape by cutting off a section of a cypress knee. — **(7) 1847** *Knickerb.* XXIX. 331 Another curiosity of the southern forest is the cypress moss, which abounds in the swamps. . . . In the vicinity of the Gulf of Mexico it hangs from the branches. **1862** E. KIRKE *Among Pines* 211 We passed . . . now and then a horned animal browsing on the cypress-moss where it hung low on the trees. — **(8) 1850** H. C. LEWIS *La. Swamp Doctor* 94, I tuck a stick and puncht at one of them [the cypress knees] . . . to see if it war a real cypress nubbin. — **(9) 1708** in *Amer. Sp.* XV. 170/1 Beginning at a Cyprus in the Cyprus pon. **1800** B. HAWKINS *Sk. Creek Country* 20 The eastern boundary of the creek claims, is poor pine land, with cypress ponds and bay galls. **1934** *Nat. Geog. Mag.* LXV. 604 Especially interesting to the naturalist wandering in the pine lands are numerous cypress ponds—shallow depressions, generally filled with a foot or two of water and supporting typical swamp trees, such as cypress, black gum, slash pine, yaupon, and sweetbay.

(10) 1784 CUTLER in *Mem. Academy* I. 487 The root [of Arum, i.e., cuckoopint] is sold (dried and powdered) at a high price under the name of Cypress Powder. — **(11) 1724** *Md. Hist. Mag.* VI. 1 [The house] was well shingled with good cypress shingles. **1732** *Bristol* (Va.) *Vestry Bk.* 146 Ordered . . . the Roofe to be first Covered with plank and Shingled on that with Good Cypress heart Shingles. **1828** *Cong. Deb.* 2 April 2112, 60,000 Cypress Shingles, estimated in the calculation of freight, at six shingles for one stave or foot of other lumber, at $1[.]50. — **(12) 1912** I. COBB *Back Home* 301 It was all deep timber—oak barrens in the high ground and cypress slashes in the low. — **(13) 1857** GRAY *Botany* 388 *Euphorbia Cyparissias,* Cypress Spurge. . . . Escaped from gardens to roadsides, in a few places in New England. **1890** *Cent.* 5870/1 Cypress spurge, a common garden plant, . . . is a native of Europe, running wild in the eastern United States. **1931** CLUTE *Plants* 133 Associated with toad-flax and soapwort along many a roadside is the cypress spurge (*Euphorbia cyparissias*). It is a close-set little plant, much resembling an evergreen, and country housewives used to delight in planting it in some out-of-the-way corner. — **(14) 1641** in *Amer. Sp.* XV. 170/1 Upon the maine head of the Lower baye Creek called Cypress Swamp. **1765** J. BARTRAM *Diary* 20 July, Rode over great variety of savana Cypress and bay swamps. **1948** *Ga. Review* Spring 72 It circled in a deep pool and flowed on to the gum and cypress swamp.

(15) 1775 ROMANS *Hist. Florida* 200 A comfortable house of square cypress timber, dove tailed. **1803** in *Ann. 8th Congress* 2 Sess. 1507 The land [near New Orleans] . . . abounds with cypress timber, which is sawed by mills. **1890** *Boston Journal* 3 Nov. (*advt.*), A valuable tract of hard pine and cypress timber land in the State of Florida for sale. — **(16) 1819** A. PETTIGREW *Lett.* 7 Jan. (Pettigrew P.), I hope you will not forget my flowers in the box also two passion vines, & inquire of Sam for the cypress vine seed which I forgot to bring with me. **1853** P. PAXTON *Yankee in Texas* 57 The cypress vine, with its dazzling gem-like blossoms, whose form is said to have suggested the pentagonal star of the Texan flag. **1944** HARPER *Weeds* 182 Q. vulgaris Choisy (*Ipomoea Quamoclit* L.), the cypress vine, is more commonly cultivated, on account of its attractive feathery foliage, but less frequently escaped.

As the last term in **Alaska, American, bald, black, Californian, Lawson's, Monterey, Nootka, pecky, pond, red, red bank, Spanish, standing, white, yellow cypress.**

cypriere ˌsiprɪˈɛr, *n.* (See quots.) — **1832** BROWNE *Sylva* 144 In Louisiana those parts of the marshes where the cypress grows almost alone are called Cyprieres, cypress swamps, and they sometimes occupy thousands of acres. **1931** READ *La.-French* 35 Cyprière *f.* Cypress forest or swamp: formed from La.-Fr. *cypre,* 'cypress,' with the aid of the suffix *-ière.* Cf. *chênière,* 'live oak forest,' *pacanière,* 'pecan grove,' *pinière,* 'pine forest.'

* **Czar,** *n.* A nickname for T. B. Reed (1839–1902) of Maine, from his rigid application of parliamentary rules while Speaker of the House of Representatives. *Obs.*

1893 *McClure's Mag.* I. 375, I remember asking the ex-Speaker [T. B. Reed of Me.] how he felt . . . when he was being held up as 'The Czar'—a man whose iron heels were crushing out American popular government. **1895** *Munsey's Mag.* XX. 418 When Mr. Reed put through the rules which have come to be known by his name he was . . . denounced furiously as 'czar,' as 'tyrant.' **1896** *Cong. Rec.* 23 Jan. 936/1 In . . . 1890, . . . the whole Democratic party were railing against our benign and amiable 'Czar.'

Hence **Czarism.**

1892 *Cong. Rec.* 27 Jan. 600/1 We have heard it here time and again . . . that we are here as a protest against the czarism of Mr. Reed, of the last Congress.

D

∗**D,** *n.*

1. An abbreviation for Drunkard or Drunkenness, used as a badge or symbol which, in colonial New England, those convicted of drunkenness were condemned to wear. Now *hist.*

1634 in A. M. EARLE *Curious Punishments* 89 Robert Coles, for drunknenes by him comitted at Roksbury, shalbe disfranchised, weare about his necke . . . a D. made of redd cloth & sett vpon white. **1636** in *Pub. Col. Soc.* III. 57 To stand att the nexte Genall Court one houre in publique vewe with a white sheete of pap on his brest, haveing a greate D made vpon it. **1895** *Amer. Antiq. Soc. Proc.* April 112 He was also ordered to wear the D outwards and was enjoined to appear at the next general Court. **1947** DOWNEY *Lusty Forefathers* 123 *D* was the stigma for drunkards who must wear it a year and might in addition be disenfranchised, forbidden to hold office, flogged and given a term in a work gang.

2. Abbreviation for Dollar or Dollars. *Obs.*

1791 JEFFERSON in *Harper's Mag.* LXX. 535/1 Recd. from Fra. Hopkinson an order on in the bank for 120D. *Ib.*, A pound of tea making 126 cups cost 2 D. **1885** *Harper's Mag.* LXX. 534 It will be observed that the modern symbol of the dollar was not then in use, a capital D being uniformly used by Jefferson.

3. (See quot.) *Rare.*

1867 DEVENS *Pictorial Bk.* 203 [In] branding deserters . . . in Richmond . . . the culprit was fastened to a large table, with his face downward, and a large 'd' scarred upon his posteriors.

4. Used as a grade or mark in school. Also attrib. Cf. **A, B, C.**

[**1890** in M. L. SMALLWOOD *Exams. & Grading Systems* 53 In each of their courses students are now divided into five groups, called A, B, C, D, E. . . . To graduate a student must have passed in all his courses, and have stood above the group D.] **1897** *Mount Holyoke Faculty Minutes* 7 Feb., [Mount Holyoke's plan of marking:] D—80–84; E—75–79; F—Failed. **1945** *Beloit College Bul.* June 11 It is my conviction that no team with D grades will ever win a championship.

∗**dab,** *n.* As the last term in **Indian, rusty, sand, smack dab.**

∗**dabchick,** *n.* Also **dobchick, dopchick.** Any one of various small American grebes, esp. the pied-billed grebe, *Podilymbus podiceps.*

1731 CATESBY *Carolina* I. 91 The Pied-Bill Dopchick. . . . These Birds frequent fresh water-ponds in many of the inhabited parts of Carolina. **1839** PEABODY *Mass. Birds* 377 The Pied-Billed Grebe, or Dobchick, *Podiceps Carolinensis* . . . dive with great quickness, and use their wings under the water. **1946** HAUSMAN *Eastern Birds* 68 Pied-billed Grebe . . . Dive-dapper, Dipper, . . . Dabchick, Hell-diver.

∗**Daboll,** *n.* [Nathan *Daboll* (1750–1818), author of arithmetics and almanacs.] Short for "Daboll's arithmetic." *Obs.* — **c1849** PAIGE *Dow's Sermons* I. 63 More requires more, (according to Daboll and the devil,) the last more requires most. **1853** F. TOWNSEND *Fun & Earnest* 265 (Th.), Do make some distinction between your Bible and your Daboll, your Shakespeare and your City Directory.

Daboll ˈdebl, *v. intr.* (See quot. and cf. prec.) *Obs.* — **1855** *Knickerb.* XLVI. 100 'How does it Daboll, Mr. Flipkins?' 'The three columns are equal, they foot up precisely the same!'

∗**dace,** *n.* A small American fish belonging to any one of several genera of the family Cyprinidae. See also **horned dace, red dace, roach dace.**

1654 JOHNSON *Wonder-w. Prov.* 79 Salmon and Daice cannot come up by reason of the Rocky falles. **1709** LAWSON *Carolina* 160 Dace are the same as yours too. **1884** GOODE *Fisheries* I. 616 The species of this family [Cyprinidae] known as 'Minnows,' 'Chubs,' 'Shiners,' and 'Dace' literally swarm in all of the fresh waters of the United States. **1947** CARPENTER & SIEGLER *Fishes N.H.* 31 Carp, goldfish, chubs, dace, fallfish, shiners, and minnows are all members of the Minnow Family.

∗**dad,** *n.* A euphemistic deformation of *God* used colloq. in participial and imperative verbal expressions in some such sense as "confound(ed)," as (1) **dad-blamed, dad-blame it,** (2) **dad-blasted,** (3) **dad-burned,** (4) **dad-burn (it, me),** (5) **dad-fetch,** (6) **dad-gum, -gummed, dad-gum it.**

(**1**) **1844** in THOMPSON *M. Jones* (1872) 189 Fun's fun; but I'm dad blamed if there's any fun in any sich doins. **1884** MARK TWAIN *H. Finn* xxxviii. 391, I doan' want no rats. Dey's de dadblamedest creturs to 'sturb a body. **1946** *Chi. D. News* 23 Nov. 1/2 Dad blame it, I've taken all I can from you. — (**2**) **1890** *Cent. Mag.* Dec. 249 You're two of the confoundest, dad-blastedest old eejits that ever was! **1901** HARBEN *Westerfelt* 134, I waited till I wus in my sixty-fifth year . . . 'fore I started out huntin' fer a dad-blasted woman. — (**3**) **1884** CRADDOCK *Tenn. Mts.* 141 No man ez treats his wife like that dad-burned scoundrel Ike Peel do oughter be let live. **1921** GREER-PETRIE *Angeline at Seelbach* 3 He's agwine to be on the lookout fur these here resolvin' doors fur the dad burned things air shore tricky. — (**4**) **1839** *Spirit of Times* 18 May 129/1 (We.), If I don't now, dad burn me. **1901** HARBEN *Westerfelt* 300 Yes, dad burn it; you know she loves you.

(**5**) **1839** *Spirit of Times* 28 Dec. 512/1 (We.), Dad fetch him, the minit I started he jumped right in to me. **1912** I. COBB *Back Home* 32 He said to himself in a tone of feeling that he [would] be dad-fetched. — (**6**) **1887** *Scribner's Mag.* (F.), His mule shied. . . . 'Dad-gum ye!' cried Jeff, irritabily, 'whut—by grabs, hit's a human critter!' **1912** RAINE *Brand Blotters* 62 Dad gum it, I was aimin' to do that assessment work. **1944** CLARK *Pills* 156 There was a sentiment that 'a dad-blamed hog and a dad-gummed cow were the most aggravating things that ever made tracks on a piece of cotton land.'

b. Also in more occasional expressions (see quots.).

1834 CARUTHERS *Kentuckian* I. 216, I'll be dad shamed if it ain't all cowardice. **1844** *S. Lit. Messenger* X. 47/1 No body better not tell me . . . that I'll sell my vote; or I'll be dad seized if I don't fling a handful o' fingers right in his face. **1866** C. H. SMITH *Bill Arp* 47 I'll be dad-swamped if the Commissary didn't keep his flour in 'em. **1869** *Overland Mo.* Aug. 131 When he wishes to express a peculiarly fierce and inexorable resolve, a Southwesterner [says] . . . 'dad-snatched if you can.'

∗**daddy,** *n.*

1. An appellation used of or to an elderly man to express familiarity or affection. *Colloq.*

1774 FITHIAN *Journal* I. 202, I saw her at Daddy Gumby's. **1836** GILMAN *Recoll.* (1838) 33 *n.* The terms daddy, maumer, uncle, aunty, broder and titer (brother and sister) are not confined to connexions among the blacks, they seem rather to spring from age. **1889** P. BUTLER *Recollections* 34 Well, old Daddy, how did you like the preaching?

2. a. daddy bug, a daddy-longlegs or harvester. **b. daddy nut,** a variety of American linden. **c. daddy sculpin,** (see quot.).

(**a**) **1859** *S. Lit. Messenger* XXIX. 416/1 There were . . . long-legged daddy-bugs striding over the ground. — (**b**) **1893** *Amer. Folk-Lore* VI. 139 *Tilia* sp., daddy-nuts. Madison, Wis. — (**c**) **1884** GOODE *Fisheries* I. 258 On our Atlantic coast are found several species of this family [the Cottidae], generally known by the name 'Sculpin,' and also by such titles as 'Grubby,' 'Puffing-grubby,' 'Daddy Sculpin,' 'Bullhead,' [etc.].

daddyism ˈdædɪ·ɪzəm, *n.* (See quots.) *Obs.* — **1871** *Harper's Bazaar* Aug. (F.), 'His grandfather was a distinguished man.' 'Was he?' replied the man of Chicago. 'That's of no account with us. There's less daddyism here than any part of the United States. What's he himself?' **1902** CLAPIN 151 *Daddyism*, a recent word, made to represent slavish adulation of high parentage or noble birth.

∗**dagger,** *n.* As the last term in **mesquite, smeared, Spanish, T dagger.**

Dago ˈdego, *n.* Also **dago.** [Sp. *Diego*, James].

1. Originally a Spaniard; now, contemptuously, a person of Spanish, Portuguese, or (most commonly) Italian origin. Also attrib. *Slang.*

[**1723** BUMSTEAD in *N.E. Hist. & Gen. Reg.* (1861) XV. 199 Ye negro Dago hanged for fiering Mr. Powell's house, 7 Mr. Cooper preacht ye lecture on that occation; from Job 7 & 20. **1832** E. C. WINES *Two Years & Half in Navy* I. 145 These Degos [of Minorca,] as they are pleasantly called by our people, are a great pest.] **1882** BAILLIE-GROHMAN *Camps in Rockies* 372, I waited until a lot of Dago emigrants passed. **1946** *Negro Digest* Aug. 51/1 Berate as Red anyone who disagrees, humiliate the Jews and the 'Dagoes.'

b. (See quot. 1900.) Also semi-adverbial. *Slang.*

1900 *D.N.* II. 31 Dago, n. 1. The Italian language. 2. Professor of Italian. 3. One studying Italian. 4. An uncouth person. **1923** Watts *L. Nichols* 290 He don't talk so dago now.

2. dago red, cheap red wine. *Slang.*

1910 Walcott *Open Door* xii. 146 You know I'm . . . pleased when the meal can be washed down only with diluted 'dago red.' **1945** Service *Ploughman* 209 Me, I'll eat turkey an' wash it down with dago-red.

dagon ˈdegən, *n.* [Origin obscure.] **1.** (See quot.) *Obs.* **2. Dagon cooter, plow,** an obsolete form of plow not now definable.

(1) 1895 *D.N.* I. 378 dagon: a single ox yoked to a cart. Common in negro settlements along the south shore of N.S. Sometimes used metaphorically; 'my old woman is a faithful old *dagon.*' — **(2) 1818** *Norfolk* (Va.) *Herald* 22 July 4/4 The Subscriber has for sale at his store East side of the Market, A large stock of Dagon Ploughs. **1833** *Tarborough Free Press* 22 Jan. (*advt.*), For making Dagon plows of sheet iron. **1859** Taliaferro *Fisher's R.* 103 There came into the neighborhood [in N.C.] a valuable plow called the Dagon Cooter [? = Scooter].

* **Dahlgren,** *n.* A smoothbore gun, shaped somewhat like a bottle, invented in 1856 by Lt. J. A. Dahlgren of the U.S.N. Now *hist.*

1862 in Kettell *Hist. Rebellion* II. 471 An inspection just made shows that the rebels abandoned . . . four nine-inch Dahlgrens. **1901** Churchill *Crisis* 427 The Parrots and the Dahlgrens roared. **1910** *Sat. Ev. Post* 30 July 27/3 They're big fellows—those Dahlgrens and Columbiads.

b. Also **Dahlgren battery, gun, howitzer.**

1861 *Charleston* (S.C.) *Mercury* 13 April 2/5 Major Anderson is concentrating his fire on the Floating Battery and the Dahlgren Battery. **1861** *Humorist* (S.F.) 14 Sep. 7/1 Dahlgreen [*sic*] gun.—Im-

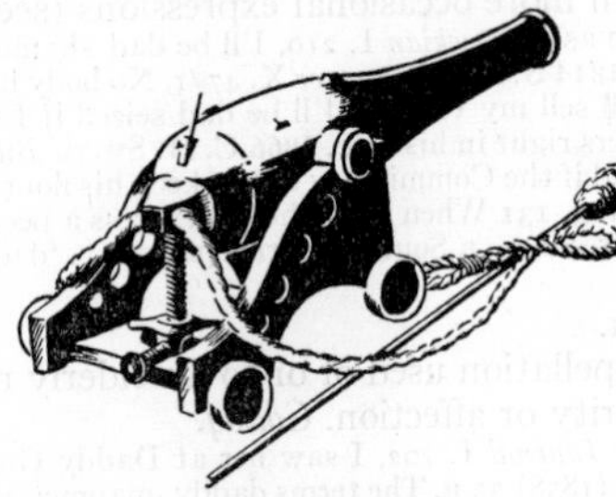

Dahlgren gun

proved cannon, named for the inventor. **1863** F. Moore *Rebellion Rec.* V. I. 71 The steamer W. B. Terry, with two Dahlgren howitzers on board . . . was captured by a body or rebel guerrillas.

dahoon dəˈhun, *n.* [See note.]

"*Dahoon,* a word first used by Catesby (1722–6). It has been supposed to be Indian, but it cannot now be referred to any language formerly spoken in the Southern States" (W. R. Gerard in *Garden & Forest* IX. (1896) 263).

A species of small evergreen trees or shrubs, *Ilex cassine;* a tree of this species. Also **dahoon holly.**

c1728 Catesby *Carolina* I. 31 The Dahoon Holly. This Holly usually grows erect, sixteen feet high. . . . This is a very uncommon plant in Carolina. **1884** Sargent *Rep. Forests* 35 *Ilex Dahoon.* . . . Dahoon. Dahoon Holly. **1942** Van Dersal *Ornamental Amer. Shrubs* 162 The single native evergreen species with berries that are sometimes yellow is *Ilex cassine,* officially known as dahoon, but also as dahoon holly and yaupon.

daily ˈdelɪ, *n.* [f. the adj.] A newspaper issued every day or every day except Sunday. Cf. **grapevine, penny, war daily.**

[**1823** D. Webster *Priv. Corr.* I. 333, I am glad to see that you publish, in the Daily [i.e., the *Boston Daily Advertiser*], your narrative.] **1823** Paulding *Westward Ho!* I. xxi. 190 'Make out an estimate of the cost of establishing a paper.' 'A daily, sir?' 'Ay, a daily, if you wish.' **1945** *Jefferson Co. Republican* (Golden, Colo.) 3 Oct. 4/3 The large and many small dailies deliver the bulk of their circulation by carrier.

* **dairy,** *n.*

1. The products of a dairy. *Rare.*

1882 *Narragansett Hist. Reg.* I. 226 Farmers used to sell their dairy in the Boston market.

2. In combs.: (1) **dairy lunch,** (see quot. 1912), in full **dairy lunch restaurant, room;** (2) **ranch,** *W.* a ranch which produces, on a commercial scale, milk and milk products.

(1) 1904 *World's Work* VII. 4458/1 He [Horace Fletcher] eats his meals at dairy-lunch restaurants. *Ib.* 4458/2 This time we did not go to the dairy lunch. **1912** Schoch and Kron *Little Yankee* 38 A dairy lunch room . . . is no place to get a 'square meal': the foods to be had are such things as cold meats, baked beans, spaghetti, sandwiches, pie and coffee. **1945** *New Yorker* 31 Mar. 26 But they go alone to eat at the Dairy Lunches. — **(2) 1879** Vivian *Wanderings in Western Land* 143, I once stopped at a dairy ranche. **1906** *Out West* April 347 On the dairy ranches there are also hens.

As the last term in **spring, winter dairy.**

* **daisy,** *n.*

1. The American whiteweed or oxeye daisy, *Chrysanthemum leucanthemum,* or any one of various native weeds or flowers resembling this. Also attrib.

1784 Cutler in *Mem. Academy* I. 483 *Chrysanthemum.* White Weed. Goldens. Daisie. The young leaves may be eaten as sallad. **1896** Wilkins *Madelon* 324 This Dorothy . . . could no more develop into aught towards which she herself inclined not than a daisy plant out in the field could grow a clover blossom. **1944** *Sat. Rev. Lit.* 23 Sep. 27/2 Has pulling the petals of a daisy, one by one, to find out what kind of husband you are going to have gone out of fashion?

2. In special combs.: (1) **daisy beggar ticks,** (see quot.); (2) **fleabane,** any one of various white-rayed American species of *Erigeron,* a plant belonging to such a species; (3) **hat,** (see quot.), *obs.*

(1) 1817–8 Eaton *Botany* (1822) 205 *Bidens chrysanthemoides,* daisy beggar-ticks. . . . Flowers large. — **(2) 1857** Gray *Botany* 198 *Erigeron . . . annuum,* Daisy Fleabane. Sweet Scabious. . . . *E. strigosum,* Daisy Fleabane. **1872** *Vt. Bd. Agric. Rep.* I. 279 *E*[*rigeron*] *annuum,* and *E. strigosum,* Daisy Fleabanes, acrid plants, mingle their coarse stalks quite too freely with the hay from newly seeded land. **1931** Clute *Plants* 131 'Kiss-me-and-I'll-tell-you' replied an attractive native of the Southern States when asked the name of that plant which people of colder climes know as the daisy fleabane. — **(3) 1878** Guild *Old Times* 46 Now we have the daisy, the sundown, the riverside, and the gipsey hat, costing from twenty-five to fifty dollars each, and which do not cover two inches of the crown, and two must be had for every season, making eight per year.

As the last term in **English, New England, oxeye, prairie, Shasta, western, yellow daisy.**

Daisy Millerism. [See quot. 1944.] Bold or unconventional behavior on the part of women. *Obs.* or *hist.*

1885 Howells *S. Lapham* i, His wife—one of those women who . . . seem born to honor the name of American Woman, and to redeem it from the national reproach of Daisy Millerism. [**1944** *N. & Q.* April 12 The publication, in 1879, of Henry James's novelette *Daisy Miller* roused much discussion, for his characterization was considered an insult to American womanhood. 'For thirty years,' writes Arthur Hobson Quinn, 'American girls were called "Daisy Millers" by Europeans.' The term was similarly used in America.]

Dakota dəˈkotə, *n.* Also **Dahcotah.** [f. a native word, said to mean "allies."]

1. An Indian of the largest and best-known tribe within the Siouan family of Indians; *pl.,* the tribe of such an Indian.

1804 Lewis and Clark *Journals* (1904) I. 132 This Great Nation who the French has given the Nickname of Suouex, Call themselves *Dar co tar.* . . . Those *Dar ca ter's* or Suoux inhabit or rove over the country on the Red river. **1827** Cooper *Prairie* iv, The Dahcotah bade his companions remain where they lay. **1870** O. Optic *Field & Forest* 24 They may be wandering Dakotahs, who do not stay long in one place. **1944** Nute *L. Superior* 20 There they also learned of a new tribe of Indians who dwelt about the western end of Lake Superior—the Dakota, or Sioux.

b. *pl.* An inclusive term for North and South Dakota.

1894 *Chi. D. News* 17 July 1/1 Thunder-showers will occur during the next twenty-four hours in Montana, Wyoming, the Dakotas, Minnesota and perhaps Nebraska. **1949** *Chi. Sun-Times* 5 Jan. 72/1 Old timers in the Dakotas said the storm was the worst since 1872.

2. In combs.: (1) **Dakota beadwork,** (see quot.); (2) **Indian,** an Indian of the Dakota tribe; (3) **Nation,** the Dakota tribe; (4) **tongue,** (see quot.); (5) **turnip,** = **tipsinah.**

(1) 1906 H. Quick *Double Trouble* 25 A glimpse of an interior hung with Navajo blankets, Pueblo pottery, Dakota beadwork, and barbaric arms. — **(2) 1846** Lanman *Summer in Wild.* (1847) 56 Here it was I first saw an extensive encampment of Sioux or Dacotah Indians.

1850 TAYLOR in *Pres. Mess. & P.* IV. 26 A treaty concluded with the half-breeds of the Dacotah or Sioux Indians for them. — (3) 1841 TYLER in *Pres. Mess. & P.* IV. 62 They are divided into bands, which have various names, the generic name for the whole being the Dahcota Nation. — (4) 1881 *Harper's Mag.* Feb 472/1 The story is told by . . . the author of a grammar and dictionary of the Dakota tongue. (5) 1910 HODGE *Amer. Indians* II. 760 *Tipsinah.* . . . This plant is also known as the Dakota turnip.

b. With reference to North and South Dakota, as **Dakota cyclone, governor, settler, Territory.**

1882 *Cent. Mag.* XXIV. 509 Perhaps in course of time, after the Dakota settlers have obtained their titles from the Government, the manifest advantages of coming together in groups of families for social pleasures and for the protection of homes by barriers of trees against the fierce winds, will lead them to adopt the village mode of life. 1884 *Milnor* (Dakota) *Teller* 21 March, Pat Donan is mentioned as a possible Dakota governor. 1884 M. D. WOODWARD in *Checkered Yrs.* (1937) 21 Now I am old, my husband is dead, and I am called to live on the Dodge farm in Dakota Territory, just fifty years later. 1888 MUIR *Picturesque Calif.* 37 No wind less than a Dakota cyclone could have power to lift them from their places. 1941 WILDER *Little Town on Prairie* 9, I don't want you to eat the only bug in the whole of Dakota Territory.

c. *Geol.* Of or pertaining to the lowest subdivision of the (Upper) Cretaceous in the western part of North America.

1876 DODGE *Black Hills* 36 The Cretaceous formation is formed at its base of a series of yellowish and reddish sandstones, the Dakota group, more or less massive, capping the cordon or escarpment of foot-hills that surrounds the Black Hills proper. 1918 VISHER *So. Dakota* 17 The great source of flowing wells is the Dakota sandstone, from which nearly all the great flows come. 1945 *Craig* (Colo.) *Empire-Courier* 25 July 1/5 Topped Dakota sand and is now drilling below 5600 feet. 1948 *Scientific Mo.* July 55/2 The streams, in their upper reaches, had cut down enough to begin to expose the Dakota sandstone that covers broad areas all along the east side of the Rockies.

Dakotan dəˈkotn̩, *n.* A native or inhabitant of the Dakota Territory or of one of the Dakotas. Also attrib. or as adj.

[1861 (*title*), Weekly Dakotian.] 1884 M. D. WOODWARD in *Checkered Yrs.* (1937) 32 The Dakotan of the next generation should be an educated person. 1898 *Mo. So. Dakotan* I. 5 Here the judge first inculcated the principles of Dakotan jurisprudence. *Ib.*, A special train conveyed nearly one hundred sorrowing Dakotans to the spot where the last sad rites were rendered. 1947 *Amer. Sp.* Dec. 249 *Dakotan* now prevails in both Dakotas.

Dalea ˈdelɪə, *n. W.* [Named for Samuel *Dale* (1659–1739), an English botanist and pharmacologist.] A genus of herbs and shrubs of the pea family, confined to prairies and desert regions. Also (not *cap.*) a plant or shrub of this genus.

1893 COVILLE *Death Valley Exped.* 85 A leafless *Dalea*, which I take to be this species, was seen in January in Paradise Valley. 1917 SAUNDERS *Western Wild Flowers* 102 The most magnificent of the Pacific coast daleas is a small tree, *D. spinosa*, gray, practically leafless, which grows in the same desert and eastward to Arizona. 1947 *Desert Mag.* April 12/2 There are bushes of golden senna and the purple bloom of California dalea.

dalle dæl, *n.* [F., trough, gutter. An Amer. borrowing.] Usu. *pl.* The rapids of a river, or the region where a river flows turbulently in a relatively narrow channel through a rock formation, used (*cap.*) esp. of the Columbia River. Cf. **dells.**

1793 in GATES *Fur Traders* 85 After passing a narrow Racy rapid named the Dalles we saw an Island on which . . . the Irroquois . . . tried to cut off a strong Brigade of trading canoes. 1825 D. DOUGLAS *Journal* (1914) 129 Six miles below the Falls the water rushes through several narrow channels, formed by high, barren, and extremely rugged rocks about two miles long. It is called by the voyageurs *The Dalles*. 1948 *Chi. Tribune* 25 July VII. 16/2 Interstate park, at St. Croix falls, hangs on the cliffs above the dalles of the St. Croix river.

b. *To run the dalle,* to navigate a boat down such a rapids. Cf. ***run,** *v.* 3.

1839 TOWNSEND *Narrative* xv. 358 Here Mr. M'Leod and myself debarked, and the men ran the dall.

c. Dalles Indians, (see quots.).

1842 MACVICKAR ed. *Lewis & Clark Exped.* II. 386 n. The whole number of those enumerated he estimates at about 32,000, without including the Falls and La Dalle Indians, and other tribes north and south of the Falls, which would, he thinks, more than double that number. 1907 HODGE *Amer. Indians* I. 380 *Dalles Indians.* The Chinookan tribes formerly living at The Dalles, Oreg., and on the opposite side of Columbia r. While tribes of other stocks, notably Shahaptian, frequently visited The Dalles during the summer, they were not permanent residents. Of the Chinookan tribes the Wasco were important, and the term is sometimes limited to that tribe.

Dallis grass. Also **Dallas grass.** A tall water or marsh grass, *Paspalum dilatatum*, of the southern states. Also attrib.

1923 *Stand. Plant Names* 358/2 Paspalum dilatatum Dallis Grass. 1943 *Democrat* 12 Aug. 4/4 Spend some time and gather Dallas grass seed to be planted in your pastures this fall. 1948 *Ponca City* (Okla.) *News* 4 July 16/4 In the background is what is left of a field of clover and Dallis grass.

Dall sheep. An entirely white species, *Ovis dalli*, of mountain sheep, named for Wm. Healey Dall (1845–1927), prominent naturalist in Alaska.

1916 *Nat. Geog. Mag.* Nov. 449/2 The only variation in the pure white coat of the Dall sheep is a mixture of a few black hairs on the rump. 1947 *Beaver* June 9/2 These alplands in wintertime provide feed for the Dall Sheep. 1948 *Sierra Club Bul.* Mar. 14 This naïve thought . . . would require the National Park Service to kill the wolves at McKinley, purportedly to save the Dall mountain sheep from local extinction.

dally ˈdælɪ, *n. W., S.W.* [See **dally welta.**]

1. (See quots.)

1930 RAINE & BARNES *Cattle* 313 To avoid strain the man using a reata never tied his rope to the saddle horn, but with about half its length in his left hand took a dozen turns or 'dallies' . . . around his saddle horn and then let it slowly slip as the strain came, thus easing the effect of the jerks. 1937 COOLIDGE *Texas Cowboys* 57 One of them took a 'dally' around the post and his new grass-rope popped like a pistol as it broke.

2. dally man, roper, a cowboy who upon roping an animal gives his rope a turn around the horn of his saddle.

1937 *D.N.* V. 621 Instead of saying 'give it a turn,' the Mexicans say *da le vuelta;* and Texans have compromised by calling this type of *roper* or *rope-thrower* a *dally man.* 1948 ROLLINSON *Wyo. Cattle Trails* 39 Though there were some Northern cowpokes that were 'dally' ropers, yet there were many Wyoming and Montana riders who roped as did most Texans 'tying hard and fast,' or making the open or home end of the rope fast to the saddle horn.

dally ˈdælɪ, *v. S.W.* [See **dally welta.**] *tr.* and *intr.* (See quots. and cf. **dally,** *n.*) — 1921 *Outing* Mar. 246/3 When working with your rope loose (not tied to the saddle), the high horn is easier to 'dally' on; that is to wind a few turns of the end after you have thrown. 1948 *Popular Western* June 26/2 He would have felt easier if he could have roped his prisoners' horses together and dallied the hackamore to his own saddle horn.

dally welta ˈdælɪˈwɛltə, *n. W., S.W.* Variously spelled. [Sp. *dale vuelta*, give it a twist (imperative).] (See quots.)

1932 BENTLEY *Dict. Sp. Terms* 132 dale vuelta. . . . An expression often used by cowboys when ordering someone to wrap a lasso rope around the horn of a saddle, a post, or the like. From a command it has been adapted to a noun phrase in such an expression as 'he gave it a *dally welta.*' 1939 ABBOTT-SMITH *We Pointed* 45 Davis was a dally welter, and he lost his rope.—[*note to dally welter:*] A roper who wraps the end of his rope around the saddle horn, Oregon style, instead of tying it fast the way the Texans do.

b. *To take one's dally welta(s),* (see quot. 1930).

1929 JOHN A. LOMAX *Cowboy Songs* 382 Take your dolly weltas. 1930 HUNTER *Trail Drivers Texas* I. 298 If a cowboy ropes a cow without hitching the rope to the saddle, 'he takes a *dolly welter.*'

Dalton plan. A method of individual instruction in public schools in which students complete work at their own speed in instalments, so called in allusion to Dalton (Mass.) High School, where the plan was first used.

1922 HELEN PARKHURST *Educ. on Dalton Plan* ii. 15 The Dalton Laboratory Plan provides that means by diverting his energy to the pursuit and organization of his own studies in his own way. 1944 *Vogue* 1 Oct. 175 Miss Parkhurst, originator of the progressive Dalton plan, is now conducting a research project in the education of children of from one to three years.

Hence **Daltonians, Daltonism, Daltonize.**

1924 A. J. LYNCH *Individual Work & Dalton Plan* 47 Convinced Daltonians recognise at once that assignments are the heart and centre of the plan. 1927 ALDOUS HUXLEY *Proper Studies* 133 These ancient seats of learning [*sc.* Oxford and Cambridge] were Daltonized long before Daltonism was invented.

***dam,** *n.* A rubber shield or guard to exclude saliva, placed by a dentist around a tooth upon which he is working.

1872 L. P. MEREDITH *Teeth* (1878) 117 By the use of the rubber-dam inconvenience and unsuccessful operations may be avoided. 1898 *Philistine* March 144 He had completed the job and was removing the Dentist Damn. [*sic*]. 1948 LUFKIN *Hist. Dentistry* 277 With the advent of the rubber dam (1862) a practical method of aseptic root canal procedure was developed.

As the last term in **beaver, brush, feeder, fish, flood, horse, rolling, storm, tumbler, wing dam.**

* **Dame,** *n.*

1. A member of one of various patriotic organizations, as Colonial Dames of America, Dames of the Revolution.

[1897 (*title*), Officers and Members of the Massachusetts Society of the Colonial Dames of America.] 1899 *N.Y. Journal* 27 June 3/6 'You are a "National Dame," are you not?' asked Colonel Bartlett. 1917 *Mass. Soc. Col. Dames of Amer.* 7 [She] invited the Dames to luncheon at her house in Harvard.

2. A member of an organization, originating at Harvard in 1896, for wives, mothers, and sisters of graduate students. Also **Dames Club.**

1944 *Wis. State Jrn* . 12 Nov., The neighborhood groups of the University of Wisconsin Dames club will meet on Tuesday. 1948 *Democrat* 22 July 8/5 A total of 223 out of the 315 women in the Yale Dames responded to the questionnaire.

damned Yankee. Also **damyankee.** A term of contempt for an American, esp. one from New England, much used since the Civil War by Southerners for an inhabitant of the northern states. Also attrib. Now *jocular*.

1812 *Niles' Reg.* III. 45/1 Take the middle of the road or I'll hew you down, you d'—d Yankee rascal. 1865 *N.Y. Ev. Post* 28 Sep. 1/1 They swore to some men of a cavalry patrol camped across the river, that they would shoot the first d——d Yankee who tried to cross the bridge. 1909 O. HENRY *Options* 95 You've had to go to work just as we 'damyankees,' as you call us, have always been doing. 1949 *Democrat* 13 Jan. 4/1 Our balmy Southern climate has refused to be dominated by the damyankee type of weather.

* **dampen,** *v. Magnetism. tr.* To muffle or stop the vibrations of a diaphragm or plate. — 1879 G. PRESCOTT *Speaking Telephone* 36 The object in using the rubber is to dampen the movement of the disk.

dampsome ˈdæmpsəm, *a.* (See quot.) *Rare.* — 1798 W. DUNLAP *André* I. ii, Rest all content upon the dampsome earth.

damster ˈdæmstɚ, *n.* (See quot.) *Obs.* — *a*1861 T. WINTHROP *Life in Open* (1863) 24 Hardly less important is the Damster. To him it falls to conserve the waters at a proper level. At his dam, generally below a lake, the logs collect and lie crowded.

danaite ˈdenə·aɪt, *n.* [J. F. *Dana* (1743–1827), Amer. chemist.] (See quot.) — 1833 *Jrnl. Science* XXIV. 386 Danaite, a new ore of cobalt and iron.

danalite ˈdenəlaɪt, *n.* [J. D. *Dana* (1813–95), Amer. mineralogist.] (See quot. 1889.) — 1866 *Jrnl. Science* 2 Ser. XLII. 72 On Danalite, a new Mineral Species. 1889 *Cent.* 1450/2 *Danalite*, a rare mineral, a silicate of iron, zinc, manganese, and glucinum, containing about 6 per cent of sulphur, found in eastern Massachusetts, in grains and isometric crystals in granite.

danburite ˈdænbəraɪt, *n.* [f. *Danbury*, Conn.] A yellowish or white silicate of lime.

1839 *Jrnl. Science* XXXV. 137 Danburite, a new Mineral Species. 1890 KUNZ *Gems & Precious Stones* 139 Danburite has been found . . . in considerable abundance at Russell, N.Y. 1889 *Cent.* 1450/2 *Danburite*. . . . A borosilicate of calcium, of a white to yellowish color, occurring in indistinct embedded crystals at Danbury in Connecticut; also in fine crystals resembling topaz at Russell in St. Lawrence county, New York, and in Switzerland.

* **dance,** *n.* In combs.: (1) **dance caller,** one who calls by way of direction the different figures of a square dance; (2) **card,** (see quot. and cf. **dancing card**); (3) **cellar,** a disreputable dance hall; (4) **ground,** the place where Indians are accustomed to hold ceremonial dances, *obs.;* (5) **hall,** a public hall or room in which dances are held, also attrib.; (6) **house,** a house, esp. a disreputable one, in which public dancing is carried on [cf. Du. *danshuis*, G. *tanzhaus*]; (7) **lodge,** an Indian lodge for dancing; (8) **party,** a dancing party; (9) **record,** a phonograph record of dance music; (10) **violin,** a violin that is used in making the music for a dance, *rare.*

(1) 1936 BARNARD *Rider* 114 The dance-callers were Jim Thorn and George Hall. — (2) 1895 WILLIAMS *Princeton Stories* 199 You will here meet several of those whose names you have on your dance-card, and you may make up your mind whether to remember that fact or not. — (3) 1855 *Knickerb.* XLV. 363 This is the dance-cellar of notorious Jim Poole! 1856 OLMSTED *Slave States* 136 No place better than a filthy, tobacco-impregnated bar-room or a licentious dance-cellar; . . . for a stranger . . . to pass the hours unoccupied by business. — (4) 1858 THOS. S. WOODWARD *Reminiscences* (1939) 34 And could the perpetrators of those crimes escape and lay out until their green-corn dance, and then reach the dance-ground undiscovered, they would go unpunished.

(5) 1858 *Mass. Acts & Resolves* 125 Any person who shall offer to view . . . any . . . show, concert, or dance-hall exhibition of any description . . . shall be punished by a fine. 1905 GARLAND *Tyranny of Dark* 7 The strains of a saloon band rose to vex the girl's poetic soul with repugnant remembrances of the dance-hall. 1948 WESTON *Mother Lode* 129 More than ten thousand dollars in gold was mined from the ground within this ruin after its abandonment as a dance hall. — (6) 1848 *Western Boatman* June 133 That afternoon I wrote a letter to a friend of mine in Natchez, who was a woman that kept a dance-house. 1946 FOREMAN *Last Trek* 256 His forsaken wife, Comes-at-Rain, sprang through the window of the dance house. — (7) 1893 *Outing* Oct. 9/2 The middle of the camp was marked by a big dance-lodge. — (8) 1884 *Cent. Mag.* Nov. 154 An occasional dance-party, where the fiddle and the jug of crooked whisky, with its corn-cob stopper, produce something faintly resembling gayety. — (9) 1922 *Ardmore* (Okla.) *D. Press* 10 Jan. 2/1 With these swell new dance-records on the phonograph we can all learn to dance! 1931 *Sears Cat.* Spring (Index).

(10) 1908 HANDSAKER *Pioneer Life* 20 Some of the boys enjoyed their Christmas greatly by having a 'stag dance' to the music of a squeaky dance violin.

As the last term in **adoption, antelope, barbecue, barn, basket, bear, beggar's, begging, black, boasting, bran, buffalo, bull, calumet, chicken, corn, dead, devil, discovery, dog, eagle, eagle tail, feather, fire, fish, ghost, grass, gun, horse, Indian, juba, kitchen, maize, medicine, new corn, Osage, Osage buffalo, peace, physic, pipe, platform, polecat, posy, prisoner's, sacred, scalp, scalping, set-out, Shaker, shell, smoke, snake, snowshoe, song and, Spanish, spear, squaw, stag, straw, sun, tea, tomahawk, turkey, virgin, voodoo, war, wolf dance.**

* **dance,** *v.*

1. *tr.* Among American Indians, to triumph or gloat over (a scalp) in a dance. *Obs.*

[1814 in *Coll. State Hist. Soc. of Wis.* IX. 279 Delivered to the Renard, 'Dancing the Scalp,' [name of an Indian] 2 one and one-half point blankets.] 1820 in MORSE *Rep. Indian Affairs* (1822) II. 131 The whole party then paint themselves, and approach the village with the scalps stretched on small hoops. . . . The Chiefs in council then determine, whether they shall dance the scalps (as they term it) or not. 1846 SAGE *Scenes Rocky Mts.* x, Rarely did we return empty-handed from the foeman's land—without . . . scalps to dance.

2. In phrases: (1) *To dance Indian*, to dance like an Indian, *obs.;* (2) *to dance Juba*, see **Juba;** (3) *to dance in the hog trough*, (see quot. and cf. *EDD*, *to dance in the half-peck*, in a similar sense).

(1) 1850 GARRARD *Wah-To-Yah* xvii. 208 This coon wants to dance Injun when he hides that [brandy] in his meatbag. — (3) 1942 WARNICK *Dialect Garrett Co., Md.* 6 Dance in the hog trough, v. phr., when a younger sister or brother married before an older one, the latter was said to have to 'dance in the hog trough.'

* **dancing,** *a.* and *n.* In combs.: (1) **dancing card,** a card upon which to write the names of those with whom one is to dance; (2) **class,** a group receiving instruction in dancing; (3) **club,** a dancing party, *rare;* (4) **exercise,** a kind of spasmodic nervous affliction induced by religious excitement, *obs.*, cf. * **exercise 2;** (5) **jack,** a jumping jack; (6) **party,** a social party for dancing; (7) **Quaker,** =**Shaker,** *obs.;* (8) **reception,** a ball, *obs.;* (9) **saloon,** a large room or hall for dancing, *obs.*

(1) 1897 HOWELLS *Open-eyed Conspiracy* xv, She looked by and by at her dancing-card — (2) 1870 A. S. STEPHENS *Married in Haste* xxxi. 172 Constance had never felt . . . pleasure in departing for her dancing classes. 1897 FLANDRAU *Harvard Episodes* 207 Billy . . . hadn't told John where he was going after the dancing-class. — (3) 1902 G. M. MARTIN *Emmy Lou* 277 'There's to be a dancing club on Friday evenings,' she explained, 'and I'm invited.' — (4) *c*1843 B. W. STONE *Biography* 40 The dancing exercise. This generally began with the jerks, and was peculiar to professors of religion. The subject, after jerking awhile, began to dance, and then the jerks would cease. 1847 H. HOWE *Hist. Coll. Ohio* 46 This revival was attended with the phenomena of 'bodily exercises,' then common in the west. They have been classified by a clerical writer as . . . the *Dancing* exercise [etc.].

(5) 1860 M. J. HOLMES *Maude* ii. 21 Half a dozen dolls, as many pounds of candy, a dancing jack and a mewing kitten, were promised. — (6) 1852 J. REYNOLDS *Hist. Illinois* 52 They arrange all things necessary for the dancing party. 1898 PAGE *Red Rock* 131 For they

say, Larry, there's going to be a dancing-party. — **(7) 1823** THACHER *Military Jrnl.* 169 They are called Shaking Quakers, or dancing Quakers, though they have no affinity either in principle or character to the established order of Quakers. — **(8) 1891** S. M. WELCH *Recoll. 1830–40* 384 Mrs. Coe sent out cards to all her friends, inviting them to a series of three balls or dancing receptions. — **(9) 1835** *S. Lit. Messenger* I. 545 The upper story is occupied as a dancing saloon. **1875** STOWE *We & Neighbors* 381 We turned a corner, and entered a dancing-saloon.

b. *dancing on the carpet,* (see quot.). *Slang. Obs.*

1890 *Railways of Amer.* 386 The mortification of being called into the superintendent's office to explain some dereliction of duty is disguised by referring to the episode as 'dancing on the carpet.'

As the last term in **buck, ghost, spook dancing.**

dancing ˈdænsɪŋ, *adv.* Thoroughly, utterly, esp. with *drunk* and *mad. Colloq.*

1808–14 WILSON *Ornithology* I. 92 Descending, as he [the yellow-breasted chat] rose, by repeated jerks, as if highly irritated, or as is vulgarly said 'dancing mad.' **1831** AUDUBON *Ornith. Biog.* I. 315–16 At this juncture both [owls] might be said to be dancing mad. **1884** CRADDOCK *Tenn. Mts.* 166, I wish these dancin'-drunk fellows could be sent to the state-prison.

***dandelion,** *n.* In combs.: (1) **dandelion coffee,** a coffee substitute prepared from dandelion roots; (2) **fleet,** (see quot.), *obs.;* (3) **greens,** the tender leaves of young dandelions suitable for use as potherbs.

(1) [**1711** BYRD *Secret Diary* (1941) 387, I slept very well . . . which I imputed to the drink made of the root of dandelion and whey.] **1852** MOODIE *Roughing It* 89, I met with an account of dandelion coffee published in the *New York Albion,* given by a Dr. Harrison, of Edinburgh, who earnestly recommended it as an article of general use. **1886** *Harper's Mag.* Sep. 578/2 If you'd asked pleasanter, I should just as soon told you that we use dandelion coffee. — **(2) 1889** *Cent.* 2264/3 Dandelion fleet, a name formerly given to the vessels sailing from Gloucester, Massachusetts, which did not engage in winter fishing, and were said not to start in the spring until the dandelions were in bloom. — **(3) 1887** WILKINS *Humble Romance* 234 There were . . . two old women . . . searching for dandelion greens among the short young grass. **1945** *New Yorker* 26 May 60 With the shad came a dish of dandelion greens in a tart sauce.

***dandy,** *n.* and *a.* In combs., often obs. or rare: (1) **dandy darky,** (see quots.); (2) **Dandy Jim,** the name for a fictitious "dandified" stage darky (see prec., 1889), [?origin of jim dandy *q.v.*]; (3) **keg, rig, trap,** (see quots.).

(1) 1889 *Harper's Mag.* June 138/2 Rice was the author of many of his own farces, . . . and he was the veritable originator of the *genus* known to the stage as the 'dandy darky,' represented particularly in his creations of 'Dandy Jim of Caroline' and 'Spruce Pink.' **1930** WITTKE *Tambo & Bones* 29 Rice was equally successful . . . in his portrayal of the 'fancy Negro,' or 'dandy darky.' — **(2) 1845** *St. Louis Reveille* 5 Jan. 2/3 'Dandy Jim of Caroline' come the extras, with a considerable finish, and indeed a spirit of genuine hilarity animated the company. **1930** WITTKE *Tambo & Bones* 29 Rice was equally successful in the rôle of a . . . 'fancy Negro,' . . . whom he depicted in such numbers as 'Dandy Jim of Carolina' and 'Spruce Pink.' — **(3) 1827** *Western Mo. Rev.* I. 448 He wore excellent broadcloth, high heeled shoes, and a corset—or as Violetta called it, . . . a dandy keg. — **1888–90** BARRERE-LELAND I. 294 Dandy-rig (West American), fashionable attire. — **1889** FARMER *Americanisms* 192 Dandy trap. A loose stone which tilts when trodden on, and, in wet weather, throws up the mud under it, to the great detriment of the clothes of the victim.

As the last term in **jim, joe, prairie, Yankee-Doodle Dandy.**

danger line. The line or boundary between safety and danger. Also fig. — **1890** *Cong. Rec.* 5 June 5654/2, I believe the good sense of our law-makers will still hold us inside 'the danger line of peril.' **1902** *Mo. Weather Rev.* 3/1 The December floods of the Tennessee . . . continued considerably above the danger lines for the first few days.

dangleberry ˈdæŋglˌbɛrɪ, *n.* [App. f. **dangle*+ **berry.*] The blue tangle or blue huckleberry, *Gaylussacia frondosa.*

1833 EATON *Botany* (ed. 6) 380 *Vaccinium stamineum,* squaw whortleberry, deer berry, dangle berry. **1889** FARMER 192/1 *Dangle berry,* a species of the blue whortleberry. **1947** *Midland Naturalist* July 54 Dangleberry [is] common (locally abundant) in pine-oak forest and upland oak forest.

dangnation ˌdæŋˈneʃən, *n.* and *interj.* Euphemism for *damnation. Slang.* Cf. **dingnation.** — **1863** E. KIRKE *Southern Friends* v. 80 What a dangnation fool I was. **1889** FARMER 192/1 Dangnation! —A comforting exclamation for those whose consciences will not allow them to say 'damnation!'

dangue, see **dengue.**

Danite ˈdænaɪt, *n.* [In allusion to Gen. xlix. 17 "Dan shall be a serpent by the way, an adder in the path," etc.] A member of a secret order allegedly organized within the Mormon Church, *c*1838. Now *hist.* Cf. **Big Fan, Daughters of Zion,** ***fan,** *v.* **2.**

"While the Church of Jesus Christ of Latterday Saints was passing through some of its most fiery trials in Missouri, in the autumn of 1838, one Sampson Avard undertook to organize a band of devotees, placing them under oaths and terrible penalties for violation of such secrecies as he enjoined upon them for the purpose of obtaining power and to take spoil during the mob violence that was being perpetrated, and thus becoming a bandit, to rule and plunder without regard to law or order. These he called Danites" (1891 *Amer. Notes & Q.* VI. 183).

1838 *Test* (Rushville, Ill.) 12 Dec. 3/4 There, Patton, one of the bloodiest of the Danites, directed two of his bands. **1870** BEADLE *Life in Utah* 389 The Church has often used an order of secret police, popularly known as 'Danites.' This order was first instituted during the troubles in Missouri; it was remodeled in the third or fourth year of their residence at Nauvoo, and has been continued since. **1948** *Amer. Folk-Lore* Jan.–Mar. 20 See those dreadful Danites how they lynch many lives.

b. Also **Danite Band, Society.**

1838 in HUNT *Hist. Mormon War* (1844) 196 Instruction was given to the Danite band by Joseph Smith, junior, that if any of them should get into a difficulty, the rest should help him out, . . . right or wrong. **1882** BUEL *Metrop. Life Unveiled* 365 The Mormons organized defense corps, which they called the 'Danite Band.' — **1838** in HUNT *Hist. Mormon War* (1844) 201 Some months ago, I received orders to destroy the papers concerning the Danite society. **1858** *Cong. Globe* 15 June 3056/1 The Committee on Territories . . . brought to light . . . a small pamphlet containing the ritual of the secret military organization [in Kansas], commonly called the 'Danite Society.'

Danver's winter sweet. [?*Danvers,* Mass.] (See quot. 1847.) *Obs.* — **1847** IVES *New Eng. Fruit* 43 *Danvers Winter Sweet.*—This apple is of medium size; the form a little oblong, tapering to the eye. **1863** *Horticulturist* XVIII. 262 Of Apples, we may mention . . . Danver's Winter Sweet.

D.A.R. Abbreviation for Daughters of the American Revolution. Also a member of this organization. Also attrib. Cf. ***Daughters.**

1906 *Washington Post* 29 April 44 Two D.A.R.'s attending the local convention were waiting for the elevator to take them to their meeting rooms. **1944** *Democrat* 14 Dec. 4/3 The Elizabeth Bradford Chapter of the D.A.R. held its regular meeting at the home of Mrs. L. R. Tucker. **1947** *N. & Q.* July 55/2 Collection of American Revolutionary documents circulated among D.A.R. societies.

dark dɑrk, *n.* =**darky.** *Obs.* — **1862** *N.Y. Tribune* 4 March, They [slaves] were assisted by two venerable old darks who were sitting cross-legged on the floor. **1903** S. HALE *Letters* 384 Two darks are lying on their back on the sunny curbstone.

***dark,** *a.* and *adv.* In combs.: (1) ***dark blue,** a blue stocking, *rare;* (2) **-bodied shearwater,** the sooty shearwater, black hag, or black hagdon, *Puffinus griseus;* (3) **complected,** see **complected;** (4) ***day,** May 19, 1780, when an unexplained darkness (perhaps caused by forest fires) extended over New England, now *hist.,* cf. **yellow day;** (5) ***horse,** *fig.* a political candidate who enters a contest or receives a nomination unexpectedly, esp. one selected as a compromise by a convention split up into various factions; (6) **Dark Lantern,** used attrib. and in the pl. with reference to the Know-Nothings, also transf.; (7) **Dark Lanternism,** =**Know-Nothingism,** *obs.;* (8) **Dark Lanternites,** (see quot.), *obs.;* (9) **meat,** meat of a relatively dark color, such as is found on the legs of fowls, alleged to have originated out of prudishness to avoid using "leg" regarded as immodest; (10) **Darktown,** a Negro section or district and its inhabitants, used in titles of plays, songs, organizations, etc.; (11) **dark woodmouse,** any of various white-footed mice, *rare.*

(1) 1830 *Collegian* 120, I addressed a little conversation to her, and was convinced by her every phrase that she was most decidedly a *dark blue.* — **(2) 1887** RIDGWAY *Man. N.A. Birds* 61. **1917** *Birds of Amer.* I. 83 Dark-bodied Shearwater. . . . Occurs in summer on the Pacific coast from southern Alaska to Lower California, and on the Atlantic coast from Gulf of St. Lawrence to South Carolina. **1946** HAUSMAN *Eastern Birds* 70 Sooty Shearwater. . . . Dark-bodied Shearwater, Black-bodied Shearwater, . . . Mutton Bird. — **(4) 1806** *Mass. Hist. Soc. Coll.* I. 95 Dr. Tenney's Letter on the Dark Day, May 19, 1780. **1942** RAWSON *N.H. Borns a Town* 153 The folks of

The Town always bracketed that event with 'the Dark Day'. . . . An hour before noonmark the darkness of night had wrapped itself about the day world and held it in its clutches until three in the afternoon. (5) [1847 JAMES BUCHANAN in *Tenn. Hist. Mag.* 1 Ser. III. 261 If the war were over and Taylor nominated by the Whigs, he would be a hard horse to beat.] **1865** *Nashville D. Union* 25 Nov. 2/1 Major Gen. John Pope is said to have an eye open for the slim chance of a 'dark horse' winning. **1947** *Steamboat* (Colo.) *Pilot* 2 Jan. 2/1 There will be no dark horse coming up from behind as was the case when Warren G. Harding broke the deadlock between Leonard Wood and Governor Lowden. — **(6) 1856** *N.Y. Herald* 2 Jan. 1/5 It will be necessary to have a little legislation to more thoroughly clip the wings of the arrogant dark lantern gents. **1858** *N.Y. Tribune* 1 April 4/5 Mr. Fernando Wood is the chief of these Democratic Dark Lanterns. **1903** *Cin. Enquirer* 3 Jan. 2/2 (*heading*), James D. Black Issues a Card, in Which He Refers to Dark-Lantern Practices. — **(7) 1856** *Dem. State Journal* (Sacramento) 1 Nov. 3/1 Propositions for fusion had been made by two . . . professors of Dark Lanternism above named, who are high 'Muck-a-Mucks' in the County Council. — **(8) 1902** *Kansas Hist. Colls.* VII. 401 The cohorts of slavery in Missouri . . . at length . . . combined under a secret organization, called 'dark-lanternites,' and several murders were committed by them before the free-state men retaliated. — **(9) 1859** GRATTAN *Civilized Amer.* II. 55 And some of them would scarcely hesitate to ask for the breast of a chicken, though almost all call it the 'white meat,' in contradistinction to the 'dark meat,' as all ladies and gentlemen designate the legs of poultry. **1948** *Savings News* Jan. 15/2 Turkey . . . steak includes white and dark meat, liver and gravy makings, sells for about $1 a pound—and you won't have to buy 20 pounds of turkey at once.

(10) 1884 in *Amer. Sp.* XXII. 202/1 The Darktown Fire Brigade—Saved! **1885** *Ib.*, Lawn Tennis at Darktown. **1948** *Dly. Ardmoreite* (Ardmore, Okla.) 1 April 14/6 A play 'The Darktown 13 Club' has been combined with a pie supper for presentation at 7:30 Friday evening at Lone Grove. — **(11) 1869** *Amer. Naturalist* III. 476 Dark Woodmouse (*Hisperomys austerus?*), before found only in Washington Territory, but undistinguishable by descriptions.

b. Dark and Bloody Ground, a designation given to Kentucky because of the early strife over its hunting grounds; formerly thought to be a translation of its Indian name. Also transf.

[1777 *Va. State P.* I. 283 When the said Henderson & Co. proposed purchasing the lands below the Kentucky, the Dragging Canoe told them it was the bloody Ground, and would be dark, and difficult to settle it.] **1784** FILSON *Kentucke* 8 The fertile region, now called Kentucke, then but known to the Indians, by the name of the Dark and Bloody Ground, and sometimes the Middle Ground. **1891** THANET *Otto the Knight* 226 Years ago Arkansas in very truth was a 'dark and bloody ground.' **1948** MENCKEN *Supp.* II. 627 *Dark and Bloody Ground* alluded, not to battles between Indians and the first white settlers, but to contests between Northern and Southern tribes of Indians.

c. dark and bloody, short for prec. *Obs.*

1848 *Campaign Flag* (Maysville, Ky.) 24 Mar. 2/2 Whiggery is in the ascendant in the 'dark and bloody.'

***darky,** *n.* A Negro. Also attrib. *Colloq.*

1775 in MOORE *Songs Amer. Revol.* (1856) 100 The women ran, the darkeys too; and all the bells, they tolled. **1829** *N.Y. Morning Courier* 15 June 1/6 The Negroes keep their jubilee; While Cuffee, with protruding lip, *Bravuras* to the darky's skip. **1847** LOWELL *Biglow P.* 1 Ser. ii. 24, I'd an idee thet they were built arter the darkie fashion all. **1948** *Hungry Horse News* (Columbia Falls, Mont.) 24 Sep. 8/1 The ladies of the local congregation have been sanding and oiling the new church floor which now shines like a darkey's heel after a foot bath.

Hence **darkydom.** *Rare.*

1861 *Humorist* (S.F.) 24 Aug. 2/1 The 'colored' keeper of the brothel, . . . if he or she have cash, can send the young scions of 'Darkydom' to Oberlin, and place them side by side with the *white trash*.

As the last term in **cornfield, dandy, field, plantation, stage darky.**

Darlingtonia ˌdarlɪŋ'tonɪə, *n.* [See quot. 1850 and cf. next.] A genus of insectivorous plants found in California. — **1850** TORREY (*title*), On the Darlingtonia californica, a New Pitcher-Plant from Northern California. *Ib.* 3, I take great pleasure in dedicating it to my highly esteemed friend Dr. William Darlington [1782–1863], of West Chester, in Pennsylvania, whose valuable botanical works have contributed so largely to the scientific reputation of our country. **1928** BAILEY *Cyclo. Hort.* 965/1 As greenhouse plants, darlingtonias require the same treatment as their allies, sarracenias, dioneas and droseras.

Darlington oak. *local.* The laurel oak, so called in honor of Wm. Darlington (1782–1863), an American botanist. — **1897** SUDWORTH *Arborescent Flora* 175 *Quercus laurifolia*. . . . Common names [include] Darlington Oak (S.C.), Willow Oak (Fla., S.C.), [etc.].

darnation dɑr'neʃən, *n.* [f. **darn, v.*, after **damnation.*] Damnation, tarnation; used as a mild imprecation or in imprecatory expressions. *Slang.*

1825 WOODWORTH *Forest Rose* I. iii, Darnation take the garlic, I say. **1840** *S. Lit. Messenger* VI. 508/2 'O, darn it to darnation,' muttered Joe. **1878** STOWE *Poganuc People* iii. 33 If I didn't hold on to him he'd have us all to the darnation in five minutes.

b. As *a.* and *adv.*

1798 *Aurora* (Phila.) 14 Aug. (Th., *s.v. nation*), It seems as if the Irish are as incorrigible as the darnation Bostonians. **1828** *N.Y. Mirror* 2 Aug. 26/3 'New-York,' said he—and Jonathan was a frequent visiter here to sell his onions and wooden dishes—'would be a darnation fine place, if they ever got it done.' **1859** A. CARY *Country Life* i. 8 It's a darnation sight easier.

***darning,** *n.* **1. darning cotton,** cotton thread suitable for use in darning. **2. darning gourd,** a small gourd used as a darning egg.

(1) **1850** S. WARNER *Wide, Wide World* iv, Here are tapes, and buttons, and hooks and eyes, and darning cotton, . . . silk-winders. **1936** *Sears Cat.* 422 240 Yds. of Darning Cotton 12 balls . . . 9c. — (2) **1899** GREEN *Va. Word-Book* 111 Darning-gourd. . . . A small, smooth gourd over which an article to be darned is drawn. **1944** WILSON *Passing Inst.* 181 After supper, that busy time for Mother, the darning gourd was inserted into the worn stockings and the holes mended.

***darter,** *n.*

1. The American snakebird or water crow or water turkey (*qq.v.*), *Anhinga anhinga.*

1813 WILSON *Ornithology* IX. 82 Female Black-bellied Darter. . . . They commonly sit on a stump, which rises out of the water, in the mornings of the spring, and spread their wings to the sun, from which circumstance they have obtained the appellation of Sun-birds. **1917** *Birds of Amer.* I. 93 The Darters . . . include four species, and are generally distributed throughout the tropic and semi-tropic regions of both hemispheres. **1946** HAUSMAN *Eastern Birds* 92 The Darters, or Water Turkeys, are odd-looking birds with thin heads; long, slender, pointed bills; long, snake-like necks; long tails . . . , and webbed feet.

2. Any one of various small fresh-water fishes closely related to the perches.

1855 BAIRD in *Smithsonian Rep.* 328 Darter. *Boleosoma fusiforme.* **1884** GOODE *Fisheries* I. 417 'Darters' or *Etheostomatidae* . . . are found in all fresh waters of the United States east of the Rocky Mountains. **1947** CARPENTER & SIEGLER *Fishes N.H.* 74 The perches reach eating size whereas the darters seldom exceed 3 inches.

As the last term in **blue, joe, rainbow, tessellated darter.**

***dash,** *n.* (See quot. 1881.)

1856 *Spirit of Times* 27 Sep. 60/1 They each stripped in fine order, except Rosabel, who was evidently drawn a 'few shades too fine' for a four mile dash. **1881** *Standard* (London) 7 Sep. 5/2 They [=the Americans] have certainly coined . . . the word 'dash' to signify a race run in one heat. **1948** *P.C.C. Chronicle* (Pasadena, Calif.) 31 Mar. 4/5 Anderson took a third in the open 100 yard dash.

***data,** *n.* Facts, news. *Colloq.*

"The word sometimes = *facts* or *news* without any suggestion that this information is to be the basis of an argument or calculation" (Horwill, 96).

1902 TOMPKINS *Hist. Rec. of Rock. Co., N.Y.* 46 There is but little data to estimate Indian populations. **1948** *Dly. Ardmoreite* (Ardmore, Okla.) 6 Aug. 2/2 Data on Oklahoma's areas will be combined with that from all other producing states to provide an up-to-date study . . . for every area in the nation.

***date,** *n.*

1. (*pl.*) Newspapers, news dispatches. *Obs.*

1845 *N.Y. Tribune* 7 July, By the United States Steamer *Princeton* . . . we have Texas dates to the 23d of June. **1876** *Fur, Fin, & Feather* Sep. 134 After reading the latest dates from the States we retired to our quarters. **1887** *N.Y. Herald* 20 Feb. 14/3 (*heading*), Detroit Dates.

2. An address, a date line.

1881 *Harper's Mag.* June 118/2 It was really surprising how big a mail sometimes went out of letters bearing in one corner the odd date 'At Pettengill's.' **1904** *Indianapolis News* 5 Sep. 5 Writing to the Chicago Chronicle under an Indianapolis date, F. E. Sullivan says [etc.].

3. An appointment, ordinarily of a social nature, and now usu. between opposite sexes. Also attrib. *Colloq.*

1885 E. W. HOWE *Mystery of Locks* 187 If he'll make a date with me, I'll exchange stories with him. **1899** ADE *Fables in Slang* (1902) 138 Her Date Book had to be kept on the Double Entry System. **1948** *Good Housekeeping* Jan. 161/2, I was fond of them and took them on many a pleasant date.

b. A person of the opposite sex with whom such an appointment is made. *Colloq.*

1944 *Chi. D. News* 24 June (Pict. Sect.) 7 His date this night was K. T. Stevens. **1948** *Kankakee* (Ill.) *D. Jrnl.* 5 June 11 My date stood me up tonight.

4. In combs. and derivatives in some of which the first element is **date* in the sense of a fruit: (1) **date fish,** any one of various bivalve mollusks of the genus *Pholas;* (2) ***-less,** without social engagements, *colloq.;* (3) ***line,** a line, or part of one, giving the date of issue of a newspaper or the date and place of origin of a dispatch, letter, etc.; (4) **plum,** the persimmon tree or its fruit.

(1) **1838** *Knickerb.* XI. 446 Each separate raisin therein embedded, bearing much resemblance to the date-fish in his rock. **1884** *U.S. Nat. Museum Bul.* No. 27, 263 Date Fish . . . [is found on] northwest coast of America to California, Puget Sound, Vancouver Island, San Diego, and San Pedro. — (2) **1923** *N.Y. Tribune* 25 April, The young men at Northwestern University have agreed to join the young women of that institution in observing three dateless nights each week. **1944** *Chi. Tribune* 10 Dec. (Grafic Mag.) 4 Sometimes that mood indigo comes up briefly on a dateless Friday night.— (3) **1888** *Mo. Repub.* 24 March (F.), The telegraph man, who has edited Mulhatton's yarns before, and knows a fake from a barn-door, by the date-line alone. **1947** *Chi. D. News* 10 April 30/2 Came the Sunday paper with a yarn bearing a London dateline about a specialist. — (4) **1785** MARSHALL *Amer. Grove* 40 Diospyros. The Date Plum, or Persimmon Tree. **1931** CLUTE *Plants* 41 The persimmon (*Diospyros Virginiana*) was a new fruit to the pioneers, but they did the best they could under the circumstances and called it date plum.

As the last term in **blind, Indian, sailing date.**

***date,** *v. intr.* To make a social appointment with a person of the opposite sex. Also *tr.*

1928 *Collier's* 5 May 36/3 Well, I be doggone. . . . Dat fool gal datin' wid me and wawkin' off wid dat money man. **1932** *K.C. Star* 20 May 34 An Emporia girl who 'dates' a wrestler telephoned her boss the other day that she could not be at work because she had sprained her arm. **1947** *Chi. Tribune* 25 May (Comics) 4 Is 'wolf in sheep's clothing West' dating the slick chick *or* is the slick chick dating West?

datil ˈdɑtəl, *n. S.W.* [Sp. *dátil,* a date.] =**Spanish bayonet.**

1882 *Atlantic Mo.* Oct. 549/2 The somewhat sweet fruit of the datila, or Spanish bayonet, is rendered sweeter by a like process. **1913** WOOTON *Trees & Shrubs N.M.* 33 The Datil (*Yucca baccata*) is a species closely resembling the preceding, but almost stemless. **1948** *Southwestern Rev.* Summer 246/2, I saw a heap, a whole bunch, of the *datiles* turn themselves loose from the stem on which they grew and fall right at the coyote's mouth.

daub duck. (See quot. 1917.) — **1888** G. TRUMBULL *Names & Portraits of Birds* 111 Mr. Henry P. Ives, of Salem, Mass., a gentleman who is well acquainted with this species, tells me of hearing it [the ruddy duck] commonly called the Daub-Duck at Rangely Lake, Me. **1917** *Birds of Amer.* I. 152 Ruddy Duck . . . *Erismatura jamaicensis* (*Gmelin*). . . . Other names.—Dumpling Duck; Daub Duck; Deaf Duck; [etc.].

***dauber,** *n.* =**dirt-dauber.** Cf. **clay, mud dauber.** — **1838** GOSSE *Letters* 238, I watched with much interest the proceedings of a Dauber in building her mud-cells. **1871** DE VERE 391 *Yellow-jacket* is the familiar and descriptive name of . . . the Sand-wasp (*Ammophila*), one of whose cousins is familiarly known by the name of *Dauber*, from the manner in which he builds his nest.

***Daughters,** *n. pl.* In the names of various women's organizations: (1) *Daughters of Liberty,* a society of women, formed in Boston in 1769–70, who pledged each other not to patronize British importers and shopkeepers, now *hist.;* (2) *of Rebekah,* a secret order for women formed in Indiana in 1851 and designed to supplement the work of the Odd Fellows; (3) *of Temperance,* a women's temperance organization; (4) *of the American Revolution,* (see quot. 1893), and cf. **D.A.R.;** (5) *of the Confederacy,* a patriotic, social, and benevolent organization of southern women formed in Nashville, Tenn., in 1894, and composed of those descended from one who served, or gave loyal aid to, the Southern cause during the Civil War; (6) **of Zion,* the name, based upon Micah 4:13, of an organization of Mormon women, alleged to have served as a personal bodyguard for Joseph Smith and as a kind of task force, *obs.,* cf. **Danite.**

(1) **1769** *Boston Gazette* 16 Oct. 1/3 And as true Daughters of Liberty, they made their Breakfast upon Rye Coffee, and their Dinner was partly made of that sort of Venison called Bear. **1945** *Mademoiselle* Jan. 127 The Daughters of Liberty, in the American Revolution, threatened to use the same method for the opposite purpose. — (2) **1930** *Randolph Enterprise* (Elkins, W.VA.) 16 Jan. 5/4 The Odd Fellows and Daughters of Rebekah of Belington had a banquet last night at their lodge room attended by about 125. — (3) **1852** *N.Y. Wkly. Tribune* 7 Feb. 1/5 [Among them were] thirteen two-horse sleighs, mainly with 'Daughters of Temperance,' and other ladies. **1855** BARNUM *Life* 333 We could see that . . . the Daughters of Temperance . . . had discharged their mission of peace and love. — (4) **1890** (*title*), Daughters of the American Revolution Constitution and By-Laws. **1893** JAMESON *Dict. U. S. Hist.* (1931) 132 *Daughters of the American Revolution,* a society of the female descendants of distinguished soldiers, sailors and patriots of the Revolution, organized at Washington, October 11, 1890. **1948** *Chi. D. News* 1 May 6/3 Purposeful females . . . with orchids . . . denote the annual invasion of the Daughters of the American Revolution.

(5) **1894** *Confederate Veteran* II. 180/1 Daughters of the Confederacy are also organized as auxiliary to the association, with county organizations like the veterans, and their roll has about 1,000 members including the floral roll. **1911** R. D. SAUNDERS *Col. Todhunter* i. 4 Working the Daughters of the Confederacy as a political proposition. — (6) **1838** in HUNT *Hist. Mormon War* (1844) 196 About four months ago, a band called the Daughters of Zion, since called the Danite band, was formed of the members of the Mormon church, the original object of which was to drive from the county of Caldwell all those who dissented from the Mormon church. **1942** STEGNER *Mormon C.* 95 The formation of the Host of Israel was paralleled by the formation of the secret police known at first as the Daughters of Zion.

b. Members of one of these organizations.

1911 SAUNDERS *Col. Todhunter* 5 You couldn't any more keep from campaigning among the Daughters than a yearling colt can keep from kicking up its heels in the pasture, and you know it. **1941** FERGUSSON *Southwest* 54 All our national and sectional Daughters are there and active, and even more patriotic Daughters of Texas' founders, fighters, signers, or early arrivals.

Also *Daughters of America, of the Cincinnati, of the Revolution, of the Utah Pioneers,* etc.

***davenport,** *n.* A large upholstered sofa. Also attrib. — **1902** *Sears Cat.* (ed. 112) 621 This Davenport Bed Couch is 6 feet long and 21 inches wide, with the added feature of one wing or side forming a divan back. **1948** *So. Sierran* May 6/2 She received guests from the Sierra Club as she reclined on a davenport.

***David,** *n.* (See quot.) *Obs.* — **1878** *N. Amer. Rev.* CXXVII. 230 The Confederates were the first to use the torpedo-boat, and began by launching several cigar-shaped vessels, each about fifty feet long, propelled by steam, and carrying a torpedo on the end of a boom, which could be run out, lowered under a ship's bottom, and fired. These vessels were called 'Davids.'

Davis Cup. [f. Dwight F. *Davis* (1879–1945), Amer. statesman who instituted the custom in 1900.] A cup presented as a national trophy to that country whose team of four players wins in an international championship contest in lawn tennis. Also attrib. — **1901** *Outing* June 320/1 Another challenge has now been received from them and accepted, and a second attempt to 'lift' the Davis Cup will be made this season. **1948** *New Yorker* 25 Sep. 52/2 The Davis Cup will remain in the United States . . . practically forever.

Davis Cup

Davisdom ˈdevɪsdəm, *n.* "The so-called C.S.A. at the head of which is Jefferson Davis" (Chipman). *Obs.* — **1861** *N.Y. Tribune* 19 Aug. (Chipman), Political parties loyal to Davisdom.

dawbug ˈdɔˌbʌg, *n.* =**dorbug.** — **1812** *Mass. Spy* 1 July 4/1 At gentle hour of evening grey, A Daw bug o'er thy neck I'd creep [*Note:* Better known by this name to the good people of New England than to Linnaeus or Buffon.] **1843** *Lowell Offering* III. 183, I helped the daw-bug dig his hole, And burrowed for the poor blind mole.

*day, *n.*

1. In combs.: (1) **day boarder,** one who obtains meals at a boarding house but does not room there; (2) **chub,** (see quot.); (3) **Day corn,** (see quot.), *rare;* (4) **crack,** daybreak, *colloq.;* (5) ***flower,** a plant of the genus *Commelina,* having ephemeral petals; (6) **herd,** *W.* a herd of cattle kept together by day; (7) ***light,** see as a main entry; (8) **lighted,** open, honest; (9) **nursery,** a nursery in which small children are cared for during the day; (10) **-times,** *adv.* by day, in the daytime, *colloq.*

(1) **1858** *S. Lit. Messenger* XXVII. 32/1 As to the day-boarder . . . its mind is never sound. **1861** *Chi. Tribune* 26 May 1/8 Two single gentlemen can be accommodated with Board. . . . Also a few day boarders. — (2) **1884** GOODE *Fisheries* I. 618 The Cut-lips—*Exoglossum maxillingua.* The 'Cut-lips,' 'Day Chub,' or 'Nigger Chub,' . . [is] found in abundance only in the basin of the Susquehanna. It reaches a length of six or eight inches, and has no economic importance. — (3) **1867** *Rep. Iowa Agric. Soc.* (1868) 168 Corn.—The leading variety is . . . known as 'Day corn' owing to its having been brought into this country by Timothy Day. — (4) **1851** T. A. BURKE *Polly Peablossom* 51 As soon as day-crack he hollered up his puppies, an' put! **1897** *Outing* XXX. 27/2 You wake up at day-crack stimulated, clarified.

(5) **1688** R. HOLME *Amoury* II. 99/2 The Virginian Spiderwort . . . may be called the Day Flower, for it opens in the day, and closes in the night. **1901** MOHR *Plant Life Ala.* 430 *Commelina communis.* Asiatic or Common Day-flower. . . . Grows [in] Carolinian and Louisianian areas. Adventive and naturalized. Southern New York and New Jersey to Florida and Louisiana. **1947** *Midland Naturalist* July 36 Common Dayflower [is] rare in hedgerows, wood margins, and cultivated fields. — (6) **1884** R. ALDRIDGE *Life on a Ranch* 89 In the meantime two other round-ups have been proceeding, and our 'cuts' from them are brought along and all thrown together, forming the nucleus of what we call our 'day-herd.' **1929** DOBIE *Vaquero* 16 Of course it has always been the boy's job to stand day-herd. — (8) **1887** WILKINS *Humble Romance* 124 Everything, down to his love-making was prompt, and earnest, and day-lighted with John Elliot. **1889** *Cent.* 1466/3. — (9) **1883** *Cent. Mag.* May 76/2, I should be glad . . . to . . . tell you about our Employment Agency, our Industrial School, our Kindergartens, and our Day Nursery. **1945** *Springfield* (Mass.) *Union* 13 March 5/3 The Day Nursery also receives some funds for child care.

(10) **1854** CUMMINS *Lamplighter* xvii. 135 Willie was very busy daytimes, but was always with them in the evening. **1916** PORTER *David* 62 If you've only heard them daytimes, you don't know a bit what pine trees really are.

b. Designating persons or groups who perform indicated duties during the day, as (1) **day clerk,** (2) **editor,** (3) **force,** (4) **guard,** (5) **herder,** (6) **marshal,** (7) **scout,** (8) **wrangler.**

(1) **1855** HOLBROOK *Among Mail Bags* 103 By the aid of a reliable day clerk. . . . I learned the name and general standing of the physician. **1882** SWEET & KNOX *Texas Siftings* 25 The night clerk is not so gorgeous or inclement as the day clerk. — (2) **1873** MATHEWS *Getting on in World* 218 Mr. Brooks . . . acting as leading editor, reporter, day editor, night editor, and even type-setter. **1877** *Harper's Mag.* Dec. 53/2 The day editor [puts] . . . news relating to art in the hands of the art editor. — (3) **1886** *Cent. Mag.* May 42/2 The day force had left the big Washburn Mill. — (4) **1844** GREGG *Commerce of Prairies* I. 83 Our wagons were regularly 'formed,' and the animals turned loose to graze at leisure, with only a 'day-guard' to watch them. **1846** SAGE *Scenes Rocky Mts.* iii, The day-guard consisted of only two persons upon duty every other day.

(5) **1902** *Out West* Oct. 446 He had been night-wrangler, horse-wrangler, day-herder, bog-rider, water-mason, full hand, bronco buster, outside man. — (6) **1915** YOUNG *Hard Knocks* 60 Pete Hicks . . . was day marshal; his brother Bill, night marshal. — (7) **1758** ROGERS *Jrnls.* 83 We halted two miles west of those guards, . . . that the day-scout from the fort might be returned home before we advanced. — (8) **1890** D'OYLE *Notches* 34 The 'day-wrangler' brought up the horses. **1927** JAMES *Cow Country* 82 There was the main herd which couldn't be let go night or day, not mentioning the *remuda,* which needed a night-hawk and a day wrangler.

c. Designating or referring to conveyances that operate by day, or that are not provided with sleeping accommodations, as (1) **day boat,** (2) **car,** (3) **coach,** (4) **line,** cf. **evening line,** (5) **steamer,** (6) **train.**

(1) **1838** HONE *Diary* I. (1889) 300 A nice little day-boat . . . starting today. **1917** J. F. DALY *Life A. Daly* 128 The opening scene was one of those 'fashionable resorts,' the upper deck of an Albany day-boat on its way to the metropolis. — (2) **1872** *Harper's Mag.* XLIV. 875/1 He had in one train a day car, in which he and his companions could sit at ease, read, write, or amuse themselves as in a parlor. **1901** CHURCHILL *Crisis* iv. 147 All that Stephens saw was a regular day-car on a side-track. — (3) **1873** *Winfield* (Kans.) *Courier* 11 Jan. 2/7 Elegant Day Coaches, [etc.] . . . are some of the modern improvements used on this Line. **1948** *Reader's Digest* Dec. 150/1 Stiff-starch proud in their Sunday-go-to-meeting finery, but shy as woods mice in that elegant day coach. — (4) **1838** *N.Y. Mirror* 21 April 343/3 The day-line of the Hudson River Association will commence running on the first of May. **1948** *Time* 22 Nov. 29/1 The Day Line steamers were one of the last relics of a garish, opulent, but less hurried day.

(5) **1881** *N.Y. Herald* 23 Aug. 2/5 Niagara Falls, Thousand Islands, . . . and Montreal via the New American line of palace day steamers on the St. Lawrence. — (6) **1846** *Hunt's Merch. Mag.* XV. 245 A result which would, doubtless, have been still larger if the night train had been converted into a day train, and continued. **1917** McCUTCHEON *Green Fancy* 345 Three days later he and 'Miss Jones' said farewell to the strollers and boarded a day train for New York City.

Early (*c*1840) type of day coach

2. In phrases: (1) *between two days,* overnight; (2) *day after, day before,* (see quot. 1935); (3) *day in court,* (see quot. 1914).

(1) **1861** *Harper's Mag.* Dec. 133/2 He balanced cash one Saturday for the last time, and left between two days. **1902** McFAUL *Ike Glidden* 12 Hadn't been 't he left town 'tween two days he'd be good way on the road to the pen'tentiary now. — (2) **1886** S. W. MITCHELL *R. Blake* 292, I saw a man at the Cape wharf day before yesterday inquirin' about Mrs. Wynne. **1905** *N.Y. Ev. Post* 20 May 4 Day before yesterday the President was again in a state of terrific determination. *Ib.* 26 Sep. 6 Day after election people will want to know [etc.]. **1935** HORWILL *Amer. Usage* 96 An Am. idiom is the omission of *the* before *day after, day before.* — (3) **1914** *Cyclo. Amer. Govt.* I. 541 Day in Court. A phrase denoting the right of every person, both natural and corporate, to have his claims decided upon by a court; also the general principle that every one has the right to be heard. It came into general currency in the debate over the Hepburn railroad rate bill in 1906. **1948** *Time* 9 Aug. 16/1 Tall, Dartmouth-bred William Remington had his day in court.

As the last term in **admission, all, alumni, banner, bargain, bird, buncombe, Child Health, chill, chip, class, dark, Decoration, dining, Discovery, dough, election, Emancipation, Evacuation, Exhibition, fast, field, Flag, Forefather(s'), Frontier, German, glorious, gravel, groundhog, hanging, hiring, inauguration, Independence, Independent, issue, Jackson, Jefferson, King's Mountain, Labor, ladies, land, landing, loaf, mail, Memorial, missionary, Mother's, mountain, moving, National, Old Defenders', Patriots', picking, Pilgrim's, Pioneer, Pope, private bill(s), public, Saint Patrick's, salary, sale, scrub, Siwash, soap, steamer, sugar, tag, Thanksgiving, Turkey, watermelon, yellow day.**

Also (*pl.*) as last term in **broken, carpetbag, freshman** (see **freshman week**), **powwowing, thirty days.**

dayherd ˈdeˌhɜd, *v. W. tr.* (See quot. 1944.) Also transf. — **1928** *Sat. Ev. Post* 12 May 193/2 Here they was out day-herding onions! **1944** ADAMS *W. Words* 49 day herd: To stand guard over cattle in the daytime while they graze.

***daylight,** *n.*

1. (See quots.)

1884 GOODE *Fisheries* I. 177 The Spotted Turbot . . . in New Jersey is called Window-pane, or Daylight, because it is so thin that when held to the light the sun can be seen through its translucent flesh. **1893** *Stand.* 470/3 *Daylight,* (Local U.S.) The sand-flounder or windowpane . . . : named from its translucency.

2. In colloq. combs.: (1) **daylight down,** sundown; (2) **end,** (see quot.); (3) **in,** (see quot.).

(1) **1769** PATTEN *Diary* 234, I went to Lieut Moors Mill and got above a bushell of corn ground and we took notice of a blazeing star in the west about an hour high at daylight down. **1858** *N.Y. Tribune* 9 Oct. 3/3 It was e'en as much as I could do to git 'em into the wagon

agin, and as it was, it was daylight-down before we got ten Crawford's. — (2) **1774** FITHIAN *Journal* I. 100 In the Evening, (for here they call the time between Dinner and daylight-End Evening) He & Mrs. Carter shewed me their house. — (3) **1787** CUTLER in *Life & Corr.* I. 214, I arrived in General Parsons' before daylight-in, but it was too dark to make any observations on the city.

Dayton wagon. A wagon forming part of the equipment of a fire-fighting force. *Obs.* — **1887** *City of Balt. Half Century's Progress* 59 Two new engines had been built and placed in service, also one hose carriage, one Dayton wagon for the telegraph, one Concord wagon for chief engineer.

∗**D. B.** (See quots. 1871, 1892.)

1871 BAGG *At Yale* 32 For the first time the corporation conferred the degree of D.B. (Bachelor of Divinity) upon those who had completed the three years' course. **1892** *Brigham Young Acad. Circular* 15 Candidates for graduation, who have successfully completed any of the four years' courses, and who receive the vote of the Principal and of two thirds of the members of the faculty, will be recommended to the General Board of Education for the degree of Bachelor of Didactics (D.B.). **1943** *Univ. of Chi. Cat.* 190 (*caption*), The Department of New Testament and Early Christian Literature—Officers of Instruction: . . . Edgar Johnson Goodspeed, D.B., Ph.D., D.D.

deac dik, *n.* Also **dea.** Abbreviation of "deacon." *Colloq.* or *slang.*

1742 in *Coll. N.H. Hist. Soc.* VII. 362 Deac. Campbell, Thomas Wells and Joshua Prescott were appointed a committee to prevent the killing of deer 'contrary to the law in that case made and provided.' **1821** *Mass. Spy* 28 Feb. (Th.), Deac Josiah Bridge. *Ib.* 4 April, Dea. Ebenezer Read. **1913** *Sat. Ev. Post* 1 Feb. 34/3 Look at 'er, deac!

∗**deacon,** *n.*

1. (See quots. 1923, 1944.) *Colloq.* Cf. ∗**deacon,** *v.* **3.** below.

1873 *Chi. Tribune* 2 Jan. 6/2 Hides . . . deacons, 50 @ 65¢. **1898** WESTCOTT *D. Harum* xvii, 'I guess you got a "deakin" in that lot. . . . You didn't never kill that calf. . . . That calf died, that's what that calf done.' **1923** *D.N.* V. 234 *deacon, . . . n.* A calf of veal age; the hide or skin of such a calf. 'That hide ain't worth much; it's only a deacon.' **1944** ADAMS *W. Words* 49 deacon: A small, runty calf.

2. In combs., sometimes possessive: (1) **deacon bench,** =**deacon seat 2;** (2) **hide,** (see quot. 1923 under **1.** above); (3) **like,** sanctimonious, *colloq.;* (4) **meeting,** (see quots.); (5) **seat,** see as a main entry; (6) **veal,** veal unfit for use because killed too young, *colloq.*

(1) **1922** TITUS *Timber* xiv. 124 Sitting on the deacon's bench in the men's shanty, John opened them. *Ib.* 176 Joe was on the deacon bench filling his pipe. — (2) **1932** *Atlantic Mo.* CL. 36 Last winter I sold a similar cowhide for one and a half cents a pound, and deacon hides for thirty-five cents. — (3) **1869** LOWELL *Writings* (1890) III. 209 The hostility of all smaller birds makes the moral character of the crow, for all his deaconlike demeanor and garb, somewhat questionable. — (4) (*a*) **1870** CHIPMAN *Notes on Bartlett* 115 Deacon's Meeting.—one, in pastor's absence, conducted by a deacon. **1881** PIERSON *In the Brush* 282 The hardy Puritan pioneers, in the absence of a minister, had what were called 'deacon-meetings,' the schoolmaster, or whoever was regarded as the best reader in the settlement, reading a sermon.

(6) **1923** *D.N.* V. 234 *deacon, . . .* Belonging to such a calf [*sc.* of veal age]. *Deacon veal* is an equivalent of bob-veal.

∗**deacon,** *v.*

1. *tr.* To read aloud (a psalm or hymn) a line at a time, the congregation singing each line as soon as read. Usu. with *off. Colloq.*

[**1823** *Mass. Spy* 8 Oct. (Th.), Some fifty years ago, it was the province of one of the Deacons, after the Psalm had been read from the pulpit, to repeat it line by line.] **1831** *Boston Transcript* 27 Aug. 2/1 In the olden times, it was a custom in many parts of New-England to sing the psalms and hymns by 'deaconing' them, as it was called, that was, by the deacon's reading each line previous to its being sung. **1867** *Atlantic Mo.* Jan. 25 A deacon he, you saw it in each limb, And well he knew to deacon-off a hymn.

2. *local.* To kill (a calf).

1839 *Mass. Agric. Rep. 1838* 53 In this case some calves were raised; but most of them were killed at four days old. Throughout the county of Berkshire this mode of dealing with the calves is termed 'deaconing' them. **1925** ARNOLD *Hides and Skins* 8–9n 'To deacon' was to play a shabby trick—thence, as one of several strained metaphors, to kill a calf while still very young.

3. To fill (a container) with fruit so that only the finest specimens are visible; to pack (fruit) with the finest and best on top. *Colloq.*

1855 *Harper's Mag.* XI. 857/1 The only change it was known to produce in the farmer's practice was to make him careful afterward to 'deacon' both ends [of the barrel]. **1869** ALCOTT *Little Women* I. 168 The blanc-mange was lumpy, and the strawberries not as ripe as they looked, having been skilfully 'deaconed.' **1922** A. BROWN *Old Crow* 47 The old-fashioned men at Wake Hill used to read their Bible Sunday . . . and go out early Monday morning to carry the apples to market all deaconed on top.

b. Also transf. and fig. *Colloq.*

*a***1870** CHIPMAN *Notes on Bartlett* 115 To 'deacon' land is to extend one's fence so as to include a portion of the highway.—Middle-Haddam, Ct. **1904** LORIMER *Old Gorgon Graham* 210 When you catch a fellow off guard who seemed all right, you may find that he has deaconed himself for your benefit, and that all the big strawberries were on top.

deaconish ˈdikənɪʃ, *a.* Suggestive of or resembling a deacon, sanctimonious. Also absol.

1793 *Mass. Spy* 8 Aug. 1/1 A deaconish story, and fair promises. **1794** *Mass. Spy* 22 May (Th.), I should hate to have a deaconish fellow for a sweetheart, much more for a husband. **1861** *Boston Sunday Herald* 12 April 4/2 Shed, the defaulter, affected the deaconish in speech and dress.

deacon seat. Also **deacon's seat.**

1. A seat in church reserved for deacons, usu. immediately in front of the pulpit.

1667 *Dorchester Rec.* IV. 146 [Men] to take care about ordering the worke about the gallery and likewise a table before the Deacons

Deacon's seat (sense 1)

Seate. **1687** SEWALL *Diary* I. 178 Mr. Danforth sat in the Deacon's Seat. **1857** *Atlantic Mo.* I. 96/1 This important functionary was accustomed . . . to take his place in the deacon's seat.

2. A long bench in front of the fire in a log cabin or in front of the sleeping bunks in a lumber camp. Also transf.

1851 SPRINGER *Forest Life* 71 Directly over the foot-pole, running parallel with it, and in front of the fire, is the deacon seat. **1868** *Harper's Mag.* March 412/2 At the foot of the bed . . . was a long, flat beam, called the 'Deacon's Seat.' This Deacon's Seat is one of the representative places in a lumberman's camp. **1947** *Harper's Mag.* July 81/1 At the opening of the tent we had a bench made from saplings, or from a board if we had one, which Mr. Teare called the 'deacon seat.'

∗**dead,** *a.* and *n.*

1. *n.* A complete failure in a recitation. *College slang. Obs.*

1827 *Harvard Reg.* Nov. 287 And sad it is to take a *screw* Or *dead* in recitation, As our best scholars sometimes do. *Ib.* Dec. 312, I have a most instinctive dread Of getting up to take a *dead.* **1851** HALL *College Words* 92 It was formerly customary in many colleges, and is now in a few, to talk about 'taking a dead'.

2. In combs., sometimes with adverbial force: (1) ∗**dead ball,** a ball lacking resilience; (2) **broke,** bankrupt, without money, *colloq.;* (3) **card,** in faro, a card which is the only one of its denomination left in the deal-box, also transf., *slang;* (4) ∗**duck,** *fig.* a person or a thing that has become utterly played out or worthless, *slang;* (5) **furrow,** the last or finishing furrow left in the center of "lands" in plowing, also fig.; (6) **giveaway,** a complete betrayal, *colloq.*, cf. **giveaway;** (7) ***line,** (*a*) a line around or within a prison the crossing of which is punishable by death, also transf., cf. **Sheriff's Deadline,** (*b*) a time by which some task has to be completed; (8) **load(s),** a great abundance, *colloq.;* (9) **oodles,** =prec., *colloq.;* (10) **pan,** an expressionless countenance, usu. attrib. or adj., *slang;* (11) **ringer,** a person or a thing which closely resembles another, *slang;* (12) ***run,** a run at full speed without any let-up; (13) **sure,** absolutely sure; (14) **wagon,** a wagon used for carrying corpses, *colloq.*

(1) 1870 *N.Y. Herald* 22 July 5/6 A dead ball was used, and again it was clearly demonstrated that this is the proper kind to play with. **1876** *Chi. Tribune* 6 Aug. 7/2 A heavy shower . . . rendered the grounds very muddy and slippery, and this, together with the very dead and mushy ball that was used, accounts in a measure for the weak hitting. — **(2) 1851** KELLER *Trip Across Plains* 43 They are passionately fond of gambling, and never quit the game, until one of the parties is *dead broke.* **1931** *K.C. Star* 29 Sep., Chet Shore came back from his honeymoon dead broke. — **(3) 1901** ADE *40 Modern Fables* 23 They preferred that it should be some Dead Card who wore Congress Gaiters and Throat Warmers. **1908** LORIMER *J. Spurlock* ix. 226 But as far as Miss Roby goes, you will consider yo'self on a dead card. **1938** ASBURY *Sucker's Prog.* 8 The card thus exposed [in the dealing box] was dead. . . . The dead card began the farthest pile, on which all winning cards were placed. — **(4) [1829** *N.Y. Courier* 15 June 2/1 There is an old saying 'never waste powder on a dead duck;' but we cannot avoid flashing away a few grains upon an old friend, Henry Clay.] **1844** in JAMES *Andrew Jackson* (1937) 481 (We.), Clay [is] a dead political duck. **1948** *N.M. Quart. Rev.* Spring 79 Any politician that does not come out 100 per cent against the proposed dams . . . will be a 'dead duck' politically.

(5) 1838 *Mass. Agric. Rep. 1837* 68 It [=the side hill plough] saves considerable time in turning at the corner of a field, and it avoids a dead furrow in the center. **1858** *Chi. Press* 12 March 2/2 Yet trace them here on the map through the State and they are found to be of importance, great 'dead furrows' in the wide sweep of prairies. **1894** *Irrigation Age* Jan. 34/2 With the same cultivator, with the discs straddling the dead furrow, the ridges of dry earth are thrown down over the water furrow as soon as it is dry enough for the teams to travel over it. — **(6) 1882** PECK *Sunshine* 83 A piece of that dog as big as a finger would ruin a butcher. It would be a dead give away. **1948** *Sat. Ev. Post* 21 Aug. 109/2 The language itself was a dead giveaway. — (7) (*a*) **1864** in *Cong. Rec.* 12 Jan. (1876) 384/1 A railing around the inside of the stockade, and about twenty feet from it, constituted the 'dead line,' beyond which the prisoners are not allowed to pass. **1909** O. HENRY *Roads of Destiny* 59 Not even a whitelead drummer or a fur importer had ever dared to cross the dead line of good behaviour in her presence. (*b*) [**1920** *Chi. Herald & Examiner* 2 Jan. 10/4 Corinne Griffith . . . is working on 'Deadline at Eleven,' the newspaper play.] **1946** *Sierra Club Bul.* Dec. 113 For a total of thirty-two years he has been harassing *Bulletin* authors with deadlines. — **(8) 1869** MARK TWAIN *Innocents* lvii. 616 Oh, certainly; the old man's got dead loads of books. **1902** CLAPIN 154 Dead load, a great quantity of anything. — **(9) 1869** *Overland Mo.* III. 131 A Texan never has a great quantity of any thing, but he has 'scads' of it or 'oodles,' or 'dead oodles,' or 'scadoodles,' or 'swads.' **1884** SWEET & KNOX *Through Texas* viii. 100 When I kem here in '46 thar was deadoodles of game all around here.

(10) 1929 *Variety* 17 April 51/3 They clicked better at the Palace where the intimacy heightened the dead-pan comic's expression. **1948** *Calif. Acad. Sciences News Letter* Oct. 2 The ground squirrel . . . provides a deadpan comedy act with his four days' struggle to solve a hardboiled egg. — **(11) 1909** O. HENRY *Roads of Destiny* 67 'Isn't Ida's a dead ringer for the lady's head on the silver dollar?' **1945** *Sat. Review* 4 Aug. 22 The magnate had an accountant who was a dead ringer for the detective in every stage play. — **(12) 1889** MUNROE *Golden Days* xii. 130 He . . . started on a dead run back over the trail. **1920** MULFORD *J. Nelson* 199 Leaping into the saddle, he wheeled around the store and rode at a dead run for the cover of an arroyo several hundred yards beyond. — **(13) 1857** *Spirit of Times* 7 Nov. 149/1 The latter had received such accessions since their first game, that it was considered a *dead sure thing.* **1886** *Chi. Tribune* 11 May 3/5 The reporter was willing if it was dead sure, but wanted a full explanation of the scheme first. — **(14) 1894** *Outing* XXIV. 7/1 Dead wagons, hospital ambulances and sanitary corps vehicles were the most prominent objects in the streets. **1943** *Amer. Sp.* XVIII. 153/1 *Dead wagon* in upper South Carolina . . . usually means 'hearse' or (more correctly, as an informant pointed out) a light truck in which bodies are carried to an undertaker's.

b. In less frequent combs., usu. rare or obs.: (1) **dead bubble,** (see quot.); (2) **cake,** a cake made for a funeral; (3) **clearing,** (see quots.); (4) **dance,** a dance by Indians on the occasion of a death; (5) **face,** the scarred surface on a pine that has ceased to be productive of turpentine; (6) **lights,** the eyes, *slang;* (7) **must,** see **must;** (8) **pole,** (see quot.); (9) ***rent,** (see quot.); (10) **rope,** a rope marking or serving as the dead line *q.v.* about prison grounds; (11) **rush,** (see quot.), *slang;* (12) **settlement,** an abandoned homesite; (13) **shot,** =**forty rod liquor;** (14) **shout,** a shout given by Indians to announce the capture or death of an enemy; (15) **sneak,** (see quot.); (16) **tar,** tar obtained from dead, as distinguished from that obtained from green, wood; (17) ***timber,** *fig.* worthless material, *colloq.*

(1) 1846 THORPE *Myst. Backwoods* 35 The arrow-fisherman will tell you they [=large bubbles of light gas] come from an old stump, and are denominated dead bubbles. — **(2) 1857** *Harper's Mag.* March 462/2 Sanders Lansing . . . particularly excelled in making 'Dead Cakes,' as they were called, for funerals. — **(3) 1837** *N.Y. Mirror* 16 Dec. 193/1 The forest had already closed over the little domain that had been briefly rescued from its embrace, and the place was now, what, in the language of the country, is called a 'dead-clearing.' **1839** HOFFMAN *Wild Scenes* 20 'A dead clearing.' That is, when thickets and briers so overrun the land, and spread their roots and tendrils through the soil, that they become more difficult to eradicate than the original forest growth, which yields at once to the axe of the woodsman. — **(4) 1791** J. LONG *Voyages* 35 The dances among the Indians are many and various, . . . [including] the dead dance.

(5) 1859 G. W. PERRY *Turpentine Farming* 96 Several causes may be enumerated as contributing to produce what is called 'dead faces.' — **(6) 1877** MARK TWAIN in *Atlantic Mo.* XL. 446 Well, sir, his deadlights were bugged out like tompions. — **(8) 1898** *Land of Sunshine* April 215 These dead-poles are different from the totem poles, in that they chronicle no history of events, but are merely decorated with emblems of the tribe—a raven, bear, or whale. — **(9) 1883** *Cong. Rec.* 9 Feb. 2352/2 Never was there a fitter phrase than dead-rent. I was then informed . . . that those salt-works had been stopped by the action of the New York companies . . . and were paid so much income not to make salt.

(10) 1865 SALA *Diary* II 326 This was called the 'dead rope,' and the sentinels had orders to shoot any prisoners [i.e., northern prisoners in southern areas] who should touch it. — **(11) 1877** BARTLETT 543 A *rush* is a glib recitation, but to be a *dead rush* it must be flawless, polished, and sparkling like a Koh-i-noor. — **(12) 1835** C. F. HOFFMAN *Far West* II. 182 We were glad to reach, about mid-day, what in the language of the country [Kentucky] is called 'a dead settlement.' — **(13) 1865** *Republican Banner* (Nashville, Tenn.) 28 Oct. 3/2 Bob Kaneere [is] proprietor of a negro saloon on Cherry street, where dead-shot is retailed to African independence by the rod. — **(14) 1758** EASTBURN *Captivity* 12 They frequently every Day gave the dead Shout, which was repeated as many Times, as there were Captives and Scalps taken! **1790** T. BROWN *Suff. & Deliverance* 9 [This 'Live-shout' is] different from the Shout they make when they bring in scalps, which they call a Dead-Shout.

(15) 1899 BREEN *Thirty Years* 86 So well was the object of the measure cloaked that Phelps concluded he could run it through the Legislature on what the wide-awake members called 'the dead sneak'—a term which they applied to the passage of any bill which had 'business' in it, but for which no 'business' was transacted. — **(16) 1788** SCHÖPF *Reise* II 222 Dieses zum Therbrennen bestimmte todte Holz heisst Lichtholz (Light-wood); und der davon bereitete Ther wird todter Ther (dead Tar) genannt, zum Unterschied von grünen Ther (green Tar) welcher aus frischgefällten Baumen, die man vorher einige Jahre auf Terpentin benuzt hatte, erhalten wird. — **(17) 1910** *Mass. Labor Laws* (?1911) To pile up a great bulk of legislation which includes much dead timber.

3. In colloq. and slang phrases: (1) *dead as a salmon*, quite dead; (2) *dead to rights*, assuredly, positively; (3) *to give a dead cut*, to forsake, leave entirely out of account; (4) *on the dead*, confidentially.

(1) 1807 IRVING *Salmagundi* vi. 143 When a man is mortally stabbed, he ought to take a flying leap of at least five feet, and drop down 'dead as a salmon in a fishmonger's basket.' — **(2) 1881** *City Argus* (S.F.) 2 July 4/4 'Jimmy,' as he is familiarly called by the 'fly cop,' attempted to get into Banker Sather's cash-box—was caught 'dead to rights,' and now languishes in the city Bastile. **1947** FAIR *Fools Die on Friday* 189 We've got her this time dead-to-rights. — **(3) 1897** BRET HARTE *Three Partners* 187 When he found you'd given the dead-cut to the railroad . . . he loped over to Boomville after you.— **(4) 1896** G. ADE *Artie* i. 7 On the dead, I don't believe any o' them people. **1908** G. H. LORIMER *J. Spurlock* iii. 50 Give your poor Aunt Julia's savings to the union! On the dead, Spur, that's carrying it too far.

For **dead beat, *-fall, *-head, -heading, *man, Dead Rabbit, *-set, *-wood,** see as main entries.

***dead,** *v. tr.* and *intr.* To fail or cause to fail in a recitation. *College slang. Obs.* Cf. ***dead,** *a.* and *n.* **1.** and **dead rush.**

1837 *Harvardiana* III. 255 Have I been *screwed*, yea, *deaded* morn and eve. **1847** HALL *College Words* (1856) (Th.), In fact, he'd rather dead than dig; he'd rather slump than squirt. **1884** J. HAWTHORNE in *Harper's Mag.* LXIX. 386/2 Was it Dr. Peabody, whose . . . inquiry, 'What is ethics?' had deaded so many a promising . . . student?

Hence **deading,** *n.*

1827 *Harvard Reg.* Sep. 194 And what with *ticking, screwing*, and *deading*, [I] am candidate for a piece of parchment to-morrow, certifying that I am admitted to be by all A.B!' **1876** TRIPP *Student-Life* 72 It was my day to be called up, and I didn't relish the idea of deading.

***dead beat.**

1. A worthless person, a loafer, sponger. Also attrib. *Slang.* Cf. **beat, political dead beat.**

1863 *Cornhill Mag.* Jan. 94 'Beau' Hickaman [was] a professional pensioner, or, in the elegant phraseology of the place 'a deadbeat.' **1875** *Chi. Tribune* 13 Oct. 4/4 The eagerness of our local officials to avail themselves of every opportunity to go on a dead-beat spree. **1948** *Newsweek* 30 Aug. 16/1 He . . . later broke with him because he was a dead beat and no good.

Hence **dead-beatism,** *n.*, worthlessness. *Slang.*

1869 J. H. BROWNE *Great Metropolis* 192, I have known men of fine talents, with excellent opportunities and beginnings, fall to the under plane of dead-beatism. **1882** *Cong. Rec.* 25 Jan. 615/1 [Are we] going to put a premium on judicial trumpery and dead-beatism?

b. ?A complete failure. *Rare.*

1869 *New North West* (Deer Lodge, Mont.) 9 July 1/2 The Pacific Circus gave its closing performance last night. It was a dead beat.

c. A period of idleness and indolence. *Slang.*

1881 STODDARD *E. Hardery* 108 It's comfortin' . . . to know he won't hev to work. It'll be just one long dead beat for him.

2. (See quots.) *Obs.*

1871 BAGG *At Yale* 138 In sophomore year, Beta Xi men are called 'Dead Beats,' or simply 'Beats,' by those of Theta Psi. **1877** BARTLETT 170 Dead-beat, a mixture of ginger-soda and whiskey, taken by hard drinkers after a night's carousal.

***deadbeat,** *v. intr.* and *tr.* To loaf, to make (one's way) by cheating or sponging. *Slang.* — **1881** STODDARD *E. Hardery* 177 He's dead beated on you. **1888** *Boston Jrnl.* (F.), No party can dead-beat his way on me these hard times.

***deaden,** *v.*

1. *tr.* To kill (trees or timber) by girdling or cutting through the bark all around. Also **deadened,** *a.*

1775 ADAIR *Indians* 405 They deadened the trees by cutting through the bark. **1822** J. FLINT *Lett. from Amer.* 303 The shipping viewed in the direction of the line that it forms along the wharfs, has something like the appearance of a thick forest of deadened pine-trees. **1859** A. VAN BUREN *Sojourn in South* 96 A house was half erected, and some fifty acres of the timber 'deadened.' **1948** *N.O. Times-Picayune* (Mag.) 24 Oct. 6/4 These trees have been deadened.

b. To open up or clear (land) in this way.

1855 W. SARGENT *Braddock's Exped.* 84 A good woodsman will soon deaden a number of acres, which by the next seed-time will be ready for cultivation.

2. (See quot.) *Obs.*

1859 BARTLETT 115 A political candidate at the West *deadens* his competitor's votes in a district by doing away with false impressions, misstatements, etc., originating with the other party.

***deadener,** *n.* One who deadens trees by girdling them (see also quot. 1905). — **1905** *Terms Forestry & Logging* 34 *Deadener*, a heavy log or timber, with spikes set in the butt end, so fastened in a log slide that the logs passing under it come in contact with the spikes and have their speed retarded. **1948** *N.O. Times-Picayune* (Mag.) 24 Oct. 6/4 'Deadeners' go into the section after it has been surveyed for cutting.

***deadening,** *n.* An area where the trees have been killed by girdling (see also quot. 1823). Also the process of girdling.

1785 in *Amer. Sp.* XV. 170/2 1000 Acres commonly called the poplar level and Including a pawpaw deadening. **1823** JAMES *Exped.* II. 94 Large bodies of timber are so frequently destroyed in this way [by the burning of weeds nearby], that the appearance has become familiar to hunters and travelers, and has received the name of *deadening*. **1880** BURNETT *Old Pioneer* 14 The large trees were belted around with the axe, by cutting through the sap of the tree, which process was called 'deadening' **1947** BROWN *Outdoors Unlimited* 105 Coupled with the fact that its waters are usually shallow, progress through the deadening is almost impossible.

***deadfall,** *n.*

1. A saloon or low gambling dive. *Slang.*

1837 WETMORE *Gaz. Missouri* 337 At a small pot-house grocery or dead-fall of the village . . . there was a lingerer. **1874** in FLEMING *Hist. Reconstruction* II. 318 A 'Dead-fall' is simply a small shop or store where for a few pounds of stolen cotton or a measure of corn, white thieves give whiskey to black ones. **1941** ASBURY *Gem of Prairie* 51 The little nest of gamblers dominated by the patrician John Sears had become, in 1857, a large and discordant colony of deadfalls and skinning joints, with a few square houses struggling desperately for survival.

2. An area in a forest encumbered with blown-down trees; also a tree that has fallen across a trail.

1884 *Cent. Mag.* Dec. 195 We spent more than three days in getting through the woods, intersected as they were by bits of burnt forests and numerous extensive 'dead-falls' of trees thrown pell-mell over, under, and astraddle. **1947** *Mazama* Mar. 2/1 On this trip we want to do a little work on the trail removing deadfalls, making a bridge or two across the creek, and plant a few more trees.

***deadhead,** *n.*

1. A person admitted free to theaters, public conveyances, etc. Also transf. and attrib. *Colloq.* Cf. **D.H.**

1841 *Spirit of Times* 23 Jan. 564/1 The house on Tuesday was filled as far as $300 could fill, barring 'the dead heads.' **1863** *Me. Bd. Agric. Rep.* 15 The milch cow which barely pays the expense of keeping and care is a 'dead head,' yielding no profit. **1904** DERVILLE *Other Side of Story* 143 Even unsophisticated Jetty Downing knew that the circular forbidding the seeking of outside influence was a 'deadhead.' **1948** *Time* 23 Aug. 63/3 Rickenbacker thinks he knows what is wrong with the industry: too many carriers, too low fares, too many deadhead services.

Hence **deadheadism,** the practice of deadheading or admitting deadheads. *Colloq.*

1857 *N.Y. Tribune* (B.), As I had never experienced the blessed privilege of deadheadism, I could not naturally resist the opportunity of enjoying so new a sensation. **1873** *Chi. Tribune* 4 May 5/2 (*heading*), Dead-headism Dead. Western Railroad Managers Determined to Abolish Free Riding.

2. A camp follower or hanger-on. *Colloq.*

1867 EDWARDS *Shelby* xxviii. 470 And even the real fighting men did little injury, sneaks and dead-heads being the principal plunderers.

3. (See quot. 1905.) Also **deadhead log.**

1902 WHITE *Blazed Trail* 380 He was enabled to catch the slanting end of a 'dead head' log whose lower end was jammed in the crib. **1905** *Forestry Bureau Bul.* No. 61, 34 Deadhead, a sunken or partly sunken log.

4. Attrib. in the sense: Costing or paying nothing. *Colloq.*

1869 BREWER *Rocky Mt. Lett.* 11 We had quite a train—some congressmen who have dead-head tickets over the road. **1873** *Winfield* (Kans.) *Courier* 27 May 1/6 A couple of lads in Portage City, Wis., climbed a tree outside the tent to get a 'dead-head' view of Forepaugh's circus. **1892** *Cong. Rec.* App. 31 May 385/1 The free-delivery service is burdened by the collection and delivery of thousands of dead-head matter under the 'penalty postage system.'

b. deadhead engine, a railway locomotive pulling a string of empty freight cars.

1945 *Greeley* (Colo.) *D. Tribune* 15 Dec. 1/7 Four train crewmen . . . were killed and two others were injured seriously today in the headon collision of a deadhead engine and a 37-car freight train.

deadhead ˈdɛdˌhɛd, *v.*

1. *tr.* To give (a person) permission to ride on a train without paying; to obtain (entrance) into. Also absol. *Colloq.*

1858 *Olympia* (Wash.) *Pioneer* 27 Aug. (Th.), The conductor concluded that it was the intention of the trio to dead-head one party through. **1860** E. COWELL *Diary* 220 This line and two others have entered into a compact not to 'dead head.' **1907** STEWART *Partners* 263 She could 'a' dead-headed her way into a show without half trying.

b. *transf.* and *fig.*

1854 LOWELL in *Atlantic Mo.* LXX. 746/2, I will not be deadheaded. **1871** *N.Y. Tribune* March, (F.), In Pittsfield, recently, he is reported to have advertised that he would furnish a free pass to glory, but very few of the unrighteous population seemed anxious to be deadheaded on this train.

2. *intr.* To sponge, to play the parasite. Also *to deadhead it. Colloq.*

1855 *Chi. W. Times* 6 Sep. 1/3 The 'fast boys' of Chicago prefer to be members of the police force, by virtue of which they 'dead head' at all the unlicensed taverns. **1877** E. MARTIN *Hist. Great Riots* 124

Mr. Layng himself could not have deadheaded it over the road without a pass countersigned by Robert Ammond. **1910** *World's Work* Dec. 13748 The two brothers 'deadheaded' around the state (for in those days a pass was a privilege and not a crime). **1945** *Chi. D. News* 31 March 4/2 Did it ever enter your noggin that you must . . . stop kicking about taxes, because you cannot deadhead in a democracy?

3. Of logs: To meet with an obstacle, to jam.

1922 Titus *Timber* viii. 79 Your hardwood will begin dead-heading in a hurry. *Ib.* x. 89 If the raft goes to pieces and that one log deadheads.

deadhead ˈdɛdˌhɛd, *adv.* Without paying. Also, of a railroad train or car, without passengers (cf. **deadhead engine**). *Colloq.*

1873 Mark Twain & Warner *Gilded Age* xxx. 275 Senators and Representatives . . . always traveled 'dead-head' both ways. **1908** Phillips *Old Wives* 219 Probably Murdock, with his special car, was traveling deadhead. We other people paid our fare. **1945** *Greeley* (Colo.) *D. Tribune* 9 Aug. 1/6 The engine and caboose running deadhead to Dawson, were overturned by the impact.

deadheading ˈdɛdˌhɛdɪŋ, *n.* [f. **deadhead,** *v.*] The practice of giving free to certain individuals favors or privileges for which payment is customarily exacted; acting or playing the part of a deadhead.

1873 *Newton Kansan* 27 Feb. 3/4 Railroads occasionally complain of the deadheading, but no institution suffers so much from it as the press. **1885** *Harper's Mag.* March 542/1 Mr. Jefferson was not in the habit of dead-heading at hotels. **1903** G. C. Eggleston *First of Hoosiers* 263 Edward, throughout his life objected, on principle, to all 'dead-heading' of the clergy, and to all 'discounts' made to preachers on the ground of their calling.

∗**dead man.**

1. (See quot. 1905.)

1867 Hosmer *Trip to States by Way Yellowstone & Mo.* 61 After they had found the spars would do no good, the mate and four men went ashore and made a 'dead man.' **1905** *Terms Forestry & Logging* 34 Deadman, a fallen tree on the shore, or a timber to which the hawser of a boom is attached. **1948** *Sat. Ev. Post* 4 Dec. 66/4 A gasoline motor began to clatter out there, cables running from the corners of the barge to deadmen anchored in the canyon rock, grew taut, and the whole equipment began to lurch toward the bank.

2. dead man's hand, (see quots.).

1909 *Cent. Supp.* 564/3 Dead-man's hand, in poker, two pairs, jacks and eights. **1944** Adams *W. Words* 49 Throughout the West the combination of aces and eights is known as the *deadman's hand.* This superstition was handed down from the time Jack McCall killed Wild Bill Hickok in Deadwood, South Dakota, while he sat in a poker game holding this hand.

Dead Rabbit. A member of a gang of criminal ruffians in New York City; a ruffian in general. Often pl. with reference to the gang. Now *hist.*

Typical Dead Rabbit

1857 *Harper's Mag.* Aug. 402/1 A gang of thieves and desperadoes, known as the 'Dead Rabbits,' made an attack upon a few policemen on duty. **1880** *Cong. Rec.* 12 April 2327/1 We should protect the ballot-box from violence, . . . from the 'short boys' and '*dead rabbits,*' of this country. **1946** Adams *Album Amer. Hist.* III. 61 On the night of July 4, 1857, the 'Dead Rabbits' and the 'Bowery Boys,' competing gangs of hoodlums, staged a memorable battle.

Also **Dead Rabbit Club.** *Obs.*

1857 *Spirit of Times* 11 July 301/3 Towards sundown, however, a fight commenced in the Sixth Ward, between a party known as the Dead Rabbit Club, and the Bowery Boys.

Hence **Dead Rabbitism.** *Obs.*

1858 *N.Y. Tribune* 14 June 3/2 More Dead Rabbitism—Another outrage was committed in Mulberry street . . . this morning.

∗**dead set,** *n.* and *a.*

1. *n.* A complete failure in a recitation. *Slang. Obs.*

1819 A. Pierce *Rebelliad* 52 See the front of Logic tower; Screws, dead-sets, and fines. **1837** *Knickerb.* IX. 123 The next week came Greek. I knew nothing of the Grammar—I took *dead set* after *dead set,* that is, I was set down. **1861** in *Pub. Col. Soc.* XXVII. 69 I've dealt them dead setts, tho they've scrap'd till I'm sore.

2. *a.* Resolved, determined, intent on. *Colloq.*

1848 J. Mitchell *Nantucketisms* 41 Dead set, determined. **1889** *Cin. Comm. Gaz.* 17 March 15/1 He is dead set on the club's pulling down the Association pennant. **1946** *Sat. Ev. Post* 11 May 41/2 Pop's dead set on me being a forest engineer.

∗**deadwood,** *n.*

1. In tenpins, a pin that has been knocked down and lies in the alley in front of those remaining.

1858 *S. Lit. Messenger* XXVII. 351/1 He . . . sent his ball . . . straight to the left quarter of the Centre-Pin, and never left any dead wood on the alley. **1947** *Time* 17 Mar. i, This is the 'impossible' done with a vengeance—an automatic bowling pin spotter that sets up pins . . . removes dead wood . . . returns the ball . . . and even calls fouls!

b. *To get* (or *have*) *the deadwood on,* (see quot. 1867). *Colloq.*

1851 Clappe *Lett. from Calif.* 84 If they ask a man an embarrassing question, or in any way have placed him in an equivocal position, they will triumphantly declare that they have 'got the dead-wood on him.' **1867** A. D. Richardson *Beyond Miss.* xi. 134 Another and more significant barbarism is 'the deadwood'— from the game of 'tenpins,' in which a fallen pin sometimes lies in front of the standing ones so that the first ball striking it will sweep the alley. 'I have the dead wood on him' was used familiarly meaning: 'I have him in my power.' **1909** *Denver Republican* 2 Feb., Cactus Center's got the deadwood on that measley Spotted Pup.

2. (See quots.)

1855 *Golden Era* (S.F.) 1 July 1/3 Others were ensnared and relieved of many an ounce by his counterfeiting intoxication and recklessly tossing his money around, and exhibiting 'dead-woods' (certainties of winning) to their temptation. **1875** G. P. Burnham *Three Years* v, Dead-Wood, the material for certain conviction.

b. As an intensive. *Colloq.*

1876 Mark Twain *Tom Sawyer* 289 Are you in real dead-wood earnest, Tom?

3. The block of a buffer at the end of a railroad track.

1882 *Ala. R.R. Comm. Rep.* II. 76 Yard man . . . got his fingers caught between pin and deadwood.

4. A person or thing regarded as useless, unprofitable, or constituting an impediment. Also attrib.

1887 *Sci. Amer.* 1 Oct. 209/1 The commissioner [of patents] has made some effort . . . to cut the deadwood out of the examining and clerical forces left him as a legacy by his predecessor. **1928** *Dly. Express* 11 Aug. 9/5 These papers do not receive any advertising support from us unless they make a price which we consider is adequate when you cut out their dead-wood circulation. **1948** *Sat. Ev. Post* 4 Sep. 72/4 He made enemies in his housecleaning of entrenched relatives and other deadwood.

∗**deaf,** *a.* In combs.: (1) ∗**deaf adder,** any one of various harmless American snakes, esp. the hognose snake; (2) **and dummy,** a person who is deaf and dumb, *colloq.*; (3) **duck,** the ruddy duck, *Erismatura jamaicensis rubida.*

(1) **1842** *Nat. Hist. N.Y., Zoology* III. 52 The Hog-nosed Snake, *Heterodon platyrhinos* . . . is also called Deaf Adder, Spreading Adder, Hog-nose and Buckwheat-nose. **1848** Bartlett 34 *Blauser,* the name given by the Dutch settlers to the hog-nosed snake. . . . The other popular names in New York are Deaf-adder and Buckwheat-nosed. — (2) **1896** Mark Twain *Tom Sawyer Detective* viii. 521 (R.), Tom said it would take him days to get so he wouldn't forget he was a deef and dummy sometimes, and speak out before he thought. — (3) **1888** G. Trumbull *Names & Portraits of Birds* 111 Others at Detroit, and the 'punters' of St. Clair Flats, refer to the species [the ruddy duck] still as Fool-Duck, Deaf-Duck, and Shot-Pouch. **1917** *Birds of Amer.* I. 152 Ruddy Duck. . . . Other names [include] Dumpling Duck; Daub Duck; Deaf Duck [etc.].

Deak dik, *n.* Also **Deke.** [f. ΔKE.] A collegiate name for a member of the Delta Kappa Epsilon fraternity.

1871 Bagg *At Yale* 138 DKE men are often called 'Deaks' by the others, but as this word is somewhat akin to an epithet it is not employed in their presence. **1900** *D.N.* II. 14 The same names are also given to a member of such a society, as 'He's a *Deke.*' **1935** *Amer. Mercury* June 225/1 It is inconceivable that any obligation lies on the state to exempt benevolent institutions such as the Y.M.C.A., or fraternal ones such as Odd Fellows or Dekes.

*****deal,** *n.* A transaction or arrangement, esp. one involving secret, conniving, or disreputable machinations. Cf. **new, square deal.**

1882 *Nation* 3 Aug. 87/1 The various halls in which they arrange the 'deals' by which our municipal system is carried on. **1889** *Cent. Mag.* Feb. 633/1 Give us something like the Australian system of voting, so that the resulting legislature will represent the state's business interest, and not a series of 'deals,' 'dickers,' 'trades' and bargains. **1945** *Nation* CLX. II. 17 March 300/1 The kind of deal the British have in mind is not, therefore, totally inconceivable later on.

*****dealer,** *n.* As the last term in **dry goods, free, fur, hickory, ice, junk, lumber, monte, Negro, New, policy, real estate, sidewalk dealer.**

dealing box. (See quot.) — **1938** Asbury *Sucker's Prog.* 9 Dealing boxes were an American innovation, and made their appearance about 1822, when a Virginia gambler named Bayley constructed the first one and put it into a game at Richmond. It was of brass, about half an inch wider than a pack of cards.

*****dean,** *n. Educ.* Used in the titles of administrative officers who have general supervision over students, or who serve as liaison officers between the president of a university and the heads of the departments, as **dean of men, of women, of the faculty, of social sciences,** etc. Cf. **junior dean.**

1892 *Chicago Univ. Quarterly Calendar* 6 Julia E. Bulkley, Associate Professor of Pedagogy, and Dean (of women) in the Academic Colleges. **1921** *Outing* Nov. 66/2 The present Dean of Men in the same school dates back as far as does Huff. **1943** *U. of Chi. Announcements* 5 President Harper . . . was succeeded by Harry Pratt Judson, who had been closely associated with him as Dean of the Faculties. **1945** *New Yorker* 10 Feb. 28/3 Ruml was . . . Professor of Education and Dean of the Social Sciences at the University of Chicago. **1948** *Miami* (Okla.) *D. News-Record* 4 July 10/1 It is important that the student have his transcript of credits . . . sent to the dean of administration as early as possible.

*****Dearborn,** *n.* [Prob. f. Gen. Henry *Dearborn* (1751–1829).] A light four-wheeled carriage, usu. covered and provided with side-curtains. Often with **carriage, cart, wagon.**

1818 Hall *Travels* 115 Perhaps the change from a dusty jolting stage to an open easy waggon, or Dearborn, as they are called in this State [N.Y.], disposed us to regard the landscape with more than usual complacency. . . . They obtained the name of Dearborn, from the General's taking the field in one. **1820** *Mass. Spy* 15 March (Th.), I don't live extravagantly—I keep a little Dearborn wagon, and now and then take a side box at the theatre. **1825** Weems *Letters* III. 358 It might be well to set Jesse out with a coarse little dearborn cart. **1844** Gregg *Commerce of Prairies* I. 24 This company . . . owned twenty-five wheeled vehicles, of which one or two were stout road-wagons, two were carts, and the rest Dearborn carriages. **1912** Dawson *Pioneer Tales* 20 Smith, Sublette, and Jackson chose one that practically became the Oregon Trail, from starting point to terminus, hauling ten wagons and two Dearborns in the year 1829.

Dearborn's seedling. [?Name of originator.] A variety of pear. *Obs.* — **1847** Ives *N. Eng. Fruit* 59 *Dearborn's Seedling.* This fine and beautiful pear originated at Brinley Place, Roxbury. **1863** *Rep. Comm. Agric. 1862* 182 Dearborn's Seedling. . . . This variety originated at Roxbury, Massachusetts.

*****death,** *n.* In combs.: (1) **death baby,** a local name for a species of fungus of the genus *Ithyphallus;* (2) **camass,** a common western plant, *Zygadenus venenosus,* poisonous to stock; (3) **chair,** =**electric chair;** (4) **dose,** a fatal potion, *rare;* (5) **-head button,** a button resembling or suggesting a death's-head, *obs.;* (6) **horse,** (see quot. 1877); (7) **hug,** designating a cry serving as a summons to a supreme effort, *rare;* (8) **-of-man,** (see quots.); (9) **trap,** a building or structure where the fire-risk is great; (10) **tube,** a gun, *obs.*

(1) 1892 *Nation* LV. 107/1 A certain fungus called 'death-baby,' . . . is fabled to foretell death in the family. **1899** *Animal & Plant Lore* 107 An offensive toadstool (*Phallus sp.*) is called 'death-baby.' . . . They are thought to foretell death. Salem, Mass. — **(2) 1889** *Cent., s.v. camass.* **1906** Parsons *Wild Flowers of Calif.* 9 Our Northern Indians call it 'death camass,' while the farmers in the Sierras call it 'lobelia.' **1937** *Range Plant Handbook* W209 The more virulent species of deathcamas cause the majority of sheep losses from poisonous plants on the early spring and summer ranges. — **(3) 1890** *N.Y. Tribune* 7 Aug. 2/1 Kemmler stepped into the death-chair. **1911** in Lewis *Apaches N.Y.* 5 You will express amazement as you read that they carry so slight an element of Sing Sing and the Death Chair. — **(4) 1852** Watson *Nights in Block-House* 307 Well, as soon as these red men receive their death-dose, or are whipped into keepin' quiet, you will have free range again.

(5) 1784 *Mass. Centinel* 4 Sep. 3/3 To be sold . . . a general assortment of European goods, consisting of . . . kerseymeres, . . . best Death-head Buttons, scarf twist, . . . kenting handkerchiefs. — **(6) a1859** Ramsay *Poetical Picture Amer.* 166 (B.), Locusts, tobacco-worms, and slugs, Death-horses, or the hard-shell bugs. **1877** Bartlett 172 *Death-Horses,* an insect, perhaps the 'death's head moth.' — **(7) 1850** Lewis *La. Swamp Doctor* 169 Hopping to the door . . . he gave a death-hug rally to his dogs. — **(8) 1876** Hobbs *Bot. Hand-Book* 30 Death of man, Poison hemlock, Cicuta maculata. **1909** *Cent. Supp.*, death-of-man. . . . The American water-hemlock or spotted cowbane, *Cicuta maculata:* so called from the poisonous properties of its root. **1931** Clute *Plants* 134 Several other plants in our flora serve to remind us of life's vicissitudes. . . . The water hemlock (*Cicuta maculata*) is death-of-man. — **(9) 1862** *N.Y. Tribune* 13 March (*Cent.*), A wooden man-of-war is now as worthless as an eggshell; more so, for it is a death-trap. **1888** *Boston Journal* 4 Aug. 3/4 Destruction of a Death-Trap in the Bowery, New York City. **1949** *Chi. Tribune* 27 Feb. III. 2/3 Beyond that, he sees a death trap in every overcrowded public place—and there are many of them—because of insufficient exits.

(10) 1851 Melville *Moby Dick* cxxiii. 507 He placed the death-tube in its rack, and left the place. **1864** Norton *Army Letters* 284 Thirteen glittering death tubes were aimed at his [*sc.* a deserter's] breast, there was a flash [etc.].

b. *To be death on,* to be especially effective against. *Colloq.*

1842 *Spirit of Times* (Phila.) 10 March (Th.), We need not say that this medicine is death on colds. **1863** E. Kirke *Life in Dixie's Land* 191 [The Carolina swine] have their uses; they make excellent bacon, and are 'death on snakes.' **1948** *Sat. Ev. Post* 30 Oct. 112/2 The American people probably would be death on a candidate who gave the impression he was too 'good' or too busy to drop around and visit them during the quadrennial battle royal.

c. In expressions relating to Indians: (1) **death feast,** (see quot.), *obs.;* (2) **fit,** an obstinate determination on the part of an Indian to die, *rare;* (3) **halloo, hallow,** a whoop or shout uttered by Indians to announce the death of an enemy; (4) **mall,** (see quot. 1779), *obs.;* (5) **song,** among Indians, a song sung just before death, or to commemorate the dead; (6) **whoop,** =**death halloo.**

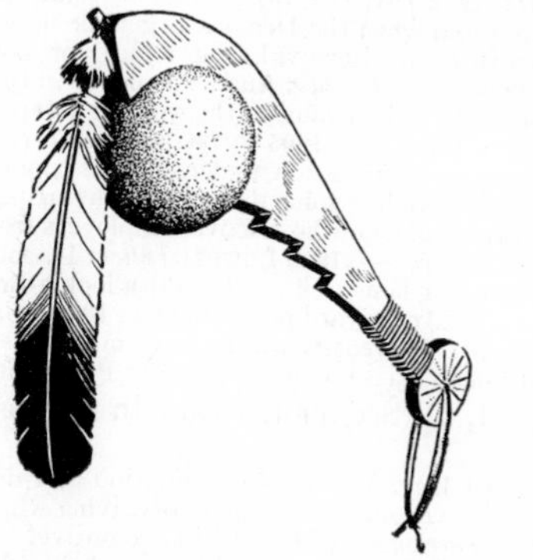

Death maul of a type used by Sioux

(1) 1911 Curtis *No. American Indian* VIII. 49 Following a chief's demise a great death-feast was held, to which in some instances were invited the people of all the Nez Percé bands, as well as the Umatillas, the Wallawallas, and even the Cayuses. — **(2) 1823** Cooper *Pioneers* xxxviii, 181 'Tis useless to talk to an Indian with the death-fit on him, lad. — **(3) 1765** Timberlake *Mem.* 91 While we were again preparing for our departure, the Death Hallow was heard from the top of Tommotly town-house. **1826** Cooper *Mohicans* xxiii, The startling sounds that Duncan had heard were what the whites have, not inappropriately, called the 'death-halloo'; and each repetition of the cry was intended to announce to the tribe the fate of an enemy. — **(4) 1779** in *R.I. Hist. Tracts* VII. 39 An inhabitant showed me an Indian weapon called a death mall. The handle was unwieldy, the ball about the bigness of a three pounder, curiously cut out of a maple knot. **1796** MORSE *Univ. Geog.* I. 97 On their head they [*sc.* Indians] wore a cap . . . commonly wove double, the better to secure them against a mortal blow from the death-mall.

(5) **1778** CARVER *Travels* 337 They are then bound to a stake . . . and obliged . . . to sing their death-song. **1892** DUVAL *Young Explorers* 232 When the burial was finished the warriors walked slowly around the grave in a circle, singing the 'death song,' and a most lugubrious wailing it was. **1947** DEVOTO *Across Wide Missouri* 84 Some of the Gros Ventres began to sing their death songs. — **(6) 1725** T. FITCH in *Travels Amer. Col.* 201, I Went Back to the Tallapoopes where I Mett the Death hoop. **1800** HAWKINS *Sk. Creek Country* 78 He gives the death whoop.

deb dɛb, *n.* Short for ∗*débutante.* Also attrib. *Colloq.* Cf. **sub deb.** — **1926** *Ladies' Home Jrnl.* July 26 One of my deb cousins makes a transcendent cocktail. **1947** *Chi. D. News* 14 Nov. 29/7 The preceding day the deb will get the feel of festivity.

debbie 'dɛbɪ, *n.* =**deb.** *Colloq.* — **1927** *N.Y. American* 6 Sep. (*heading*), Society Plans for 'Debbies.'

Deb's apron strings. *local.* (See quot.) — **1892** *Amer. Folk-Lore* V. 106 *Laminaria Longicruris,* . . . Deb's apron-strings. Portland, Me.

Debsism 'dɛbzɪzəm, *n.* The political philosophy of Eugene Debs (1855–1926) and his followers. *Obs.* See next. — **1896** *Chi. Tribune* 11 July 12/2 This is an endorsement of Debsism—that is, to seize railroad tracks and burn trains. *Ib.* 13 July 6/2 He is for Debsism and the revolutionizing of the Supreme Court.

Debsite 'dɛbzaɪt, *n.* A follower of or sympathizer with Eugene Debs (1855–1926), a well-known American socialist. *Obs.* — **1894** *Nation* 12 July 19/3 He despatched a posse of deputies to the place where a lot of Debsites had seized a mail train.

∗**debt,** *n.* As the last term in **deferred, domestic, registered, state, store, tobacco debt.**

debunk di'bʌŋk, *v.* [f. *de*+**bunk,** *n.*[3]] *tr.* To show that (something) is "bunk" or nonsense. *Slang.*

1923 in *Word Study* XX. (Dec., 1944) 5/1 De-bunking means simply taking the bunk out of things. **1948** *Sat. Review* 26 June 13/1 In dealing with military reputations the author neither glorifies nor debunks.

Hence **debunker, debunking.**

1923 *Nation* 10 Oct. 398/1 Michael, after drifting round the globe, becomes a debunking expert, a pricker of bubbles. **1948** *Time* 17 May 6/3 A little debunking of the Toscanini legend would be a healthy thing for this country. *Ib.* 18 Oct. 115/1 Dr. Freeman, though no debunker, is too conscientious a historian to duck any ugliness that must out.

∗**decapitate,** *v. tr.* To remove from office for political reasons. *Colloq.*

1850 HAWTHORNE *Scarlet Letter* i, The Posthumous Papers of a Decapitated Surveyor. **1871** DE VERE 265 When the poor office-holder . . . is superseded by a successor, he is, in political language, *beheaded* or *decapitated.* **1872** *Dly. Telegraph* (London) 5 Jan. Republicans . . . will be decapitated when the Democrats get the upper hand again.

∗**decapitation,** *n.* Removal from office for political reasons. *Colloq.* — **1869** *N.Y. Herald* 5 Aug., The clerks in the Treasury Department began to feel anxious, as the work of decapitation will soon make an end of them also. **1905** PHILLIPS *Plum Tree* 144 He made a bitter fight against decapitation, and, as he was popular with the people of his district, we had some difficulty in defeating him.

∗**decapitator,** *n.* One who removes employees from office for political reasons. *Colloq.* — **1885** LOWELL *Letters* II. 296, I was to have gone to Washington last week . . . to take a look at my decapitators, but the illness of Mr. Bayard prevented me. **1892** *Columbus* (O.) *Dispatch* 2 Feb., Mr. Stevenson will be remembered as the official decapitator of fourth-class postmasters under President Cleveland.

∗**decapod,** *n.* (See quot. 1909.) In full **decapod locomotive.**

1888 *Scribner's Mag.* Aug. 183 Consolidation and decapod types of engines, which have four and five pairs of driving-wheels. **1909** FOWLER *Locomotive Dictionary* 32 Decapod Locomotive. . . . A locomotive having a two-wheel front truck and ten-coupled [*sic*] driving wheels, but no trailing truck. Used for heavy freight service on steep grades. **1947** BEEBE *Mixed Train Dly.* 276 Big-business short lines such as the Winston-Salem Southbound, the Akron, Canton and Youngstown or the Nevada Northern boast Decapods and other classifications with 250-pound engine pressure.

∗**decennial,** *n.* (See quot. 1889.) — **1889** *Cent.* 1482/3 decennial. . . . A decennial anniversary. . . . A celebration of a decennial anniversary. **1904** *Nation* LXXVIII. 85/2 How far his [i.e., W. R. Harper's] experiments have succeeded, how far they must fail, may better be judged at his second decennial than at his first.

decenter di'sɛntɚ, *v. tr.* To deprive (something) of its position as the center. *Rare.* — **1895** *Advance* (Chicago) 304 If the home is left to us at all it is much decentered, and for this reason has lost the fragrance of charming sanctity.

décharge ˌde'ʃarʒ, *n.* [F., the act of relieving of a charge or load.] (See quots.) — **1825** KEATING *Exped. St. Peter's River* II. 84 In the afternoon, we passed in the river several rapids and falls, which occasion what is called by the voyagers the 'Dechargés' and the 'Portages.' The former term is applied whenever the obstruction is but a partial one, in which case the canoe is lightened and either paddled or towed over the rapids. **1941** MCDERMOTT *Glossary* 65 décharge, demi-charge. . . . In the North, the lightening of canoes preparatory to the passage of the boats over the shallow waters of the rapids. A carrying of the goods or freight in contrast to the carrying of goods and canoe at a portage.

∗**deck,** *n.*

1. The roof of a railroad car or a stagecoach.

1853 B. F. TAYLOR *Jan. & June* 58 Did you ever creep gingerly . . . up to the deck of a railway Car, when the train was moving? **1873** W. S. TYLER *Hist. Amherst College* 185 The driver [of the stage-coach], opening the door, asked if any passenger would resign his seat for one 'on the deck,' in favor of a lady. **1908** LONDON *Road* 59, I am on top of the train—on the 'decks,' as the tramps call it.

b. A compartment of a freight car for transporting hogs or sheep.

1879 *Chi. Tribune* 14 May 7/4, I also learned that sixty or eighty good-sized hogs were loaded in each deck of the car. **1947** *Denver Post* 15 Jan. 23/1 Around twelve decks of hogs were billed direct to Denver packers; no through shipments were received up to noon.

2. In combs.: (1) **deck hand,** a common sailor or laborer employed aboard a vessel esp. a river steamer; (2) **head,** (see quot.); (3) **passage,** the privilege of traveling on the deck of a vessel—the cheapest passage obtainable; (4) **passenger,** one who takes a deck passage on a vessel, also used of passengers on stagecoaches; (5) **trumpet,** a boatswain's whistle.

(1) 1844 *Knickerb.* XXIII. 88 On board of one of the steam-boats on the Mississippi, I encountered a deck-hand, who went by the name of Barney. **1947** *Coronet* July 122/1 One deck hand, certain that the situation was utterly hopeless, knelt and prayed. — **(2) 1864** W. B. DICK *Amer. Hoyle* (1866) 60 Deck-Head. The card turned up as trump. — **(3) 1828** in *Amer. Sp.* XVIII. 121 The great difference of fare between a cabin and a deck passage . . . contributes to establish a distinction in this assemblage of people. **1901** STILLMAN *Autobiog. Journalist* I. 48 We went by train to Albany, where we took deck passage on a towing steamer for New York. — **(4) 1824** OWEN *Diary* 57 Here the steerage, or as they are called deck passengers, sit, eat and sleep. As they have a stove upon deck it was very comfortable. **1860** HOLLAND *Miss Gilbert* xix. 346 He landed and commenced the passage up the valley as a 'deck passenger' of the slow coach. **1938** ASBURY *Sucker's Prog.* 201 Deck passengers on even the finest steamboats were herded like cattle among the freight, were required on many vessels to furnish their own food and bedding, and were otherwise accorded the treatment which their poverty and lowly estate deserved. — **(5) 1839** COOPER *Home as Found* (1878) ii. 37 Pierre offered . . . a capital watch . . . and a deck trumpet, in solid silver.

b. In colloq. phrases: (1) *two decks and a passage,* see **two;** (2) *on deck,* (*a*) in baseball, ready to bat next, (*b*) present, on hand, still in the ring.

(2) (*a*) **1867** *Ball Players' Chron.* 26 Sep. 5/4 Well, I went on deck and took up a bat. **1893** *Stand.* 476/1 On deck . . . [in] Baseball, standing next in batting order. **1945** COLCORD *Sea Lang.* 64 In baseball, the man next in batting order is on deck. (*b*) **1884** PECK *Peck's Boss Book* (1892) 179 (We.), The boy is on deck for business the next morning. **1948** *Hungry Horse News* (Columbia Falls, Mont.) 24 Sep. 8/1 We hope to be on deck to greet you when you visit your brother.

As the last term in **berth, boiler, cold, full, half, hurricane, promenade, Texas deck.**

∗**deck,** *v.*

1. *tr.* To pile (logs) on a skidway. Also with *up.* Cf. **decking chain.**

1901 *Munsey's Mag.* XXV. 392/1 Other men pile—technically 'deck'—them [logs] exactly as in the woods. **1948** *N.O. Times-Picayune* (Mag.) 24 Oct. 7/1 Logs are 'decked' in neat piles, first out along one side of the track, then back down the other side.

2. To clamber to the deck or roof of a railway car. *Slang.*

1908 LONDON *Road* 59 Only a young and vigorous tramp is able to deck a passenger train.

deckaneer ˌdɛkə'nɪr, *n.* A deck hand or roustabout. *Obs.* — **1840** in RABB *Tour* (1920) 23, I resumed our observations of the 'deckaneers,' as the men are called who handle the freight.

decked canoe, *n.* (See quot.) *Obs.* — **1885** *Cent. Mag.* XXX. 500 There is something peculiarly fascinating in the modern decked canoe. It is a miniature yacht, compact, finished, ready for smooth weather or rough, portable by one man and yet able to stand, when rightly managed, very severe gales. . . . Its decks and minion masts offer places for lanterns.

*decker, *n.* One who rolls logs upon a skidway. See also **cold, double, single decker.** — **1902** S. E. WHITE *Blazed Trail* viii. 57 He decided to advance Bob Stratton to the post, that 'decker' having had more or less experience the year before.

Deckhard rifle. (See quot.) *Obs.* — **1853** RAMSEY *Tennessee* 228 All were well mounted, and nearly all armed with a Deckhard rifle. . . . This rifle was remarkable for the precision and distance of its shot. It was generally three feet six inches long, weighed about seven pounds, and ran about seventy bullets to the pound of lead. It was so called from Deckhard, the maker, in Lancaster, Pa.

decking chain. A long chain used in decking logs. — **1901** *Munsey's Mag.* XXV. 392/1 A decking chain more than three hundred feet long is required to roll the logs to their places. **1902** S. E. WHITE *Blazed Trail* xi. 83 A shout of surprise or horror would have stopped the horse pulling on the decking chain.

*** declaration,** *n.*

1. (*cap.*) The public announcement by the Continental Congress that the American colonies were free and independent of Great Britain. Also the document approved by the Continental Congress July 4, 1776, embodying this.

The first example is anticipatory.

[**1774** THOMAS HUTCHINSON *Diary and Lett.* (1883) 181 His Lordship [*sc.* Lord North] immediately said, that the behaviour of the Council and House had been such for some time past as to render it necessary there should be a change, and that it ought to have been done the last Session, upon the Declaration of Independence, both by the Council and House.] **1776** JEFFERSON *Writings* IV. 258 If any doubts has [*sic*] arisen as to me, my country will have my political creed in the form of a 'Declaration' &c. which I was lately directed to draw. **1837** *Knickerb.* X. 444 He was a distinguished man: . . . read 'the Declaration' on every Fourth-of-July. **1948** *Green Bay* (Wis.) *Press-Gazette* 30 June 8/7 The great crowd heard John Nixon, prominent Philadelphian, read the entire Declaration.

attrib. **1821** JEFFERSON *Writings* XV. 329, I think he [*sc.* Mr. Adams] will outlive us all, I mean the Declaration-men, although our senior since the death of Colonel Floyd. **1902** LORIMER *Lett. Merchant* 234 He located his claim on Beacon Hill, between a Mayflower descendant and a Declaration Signer's great-grandson.

2. In full *Declaration of (American) Independence.*

1776 in J. ADAMS *Works* II. 291 Then you will have nothing to do but convince them that the present time to make a final Declaration of Independence is the best. **1836** *S. Lit. Messenger* II. 271 The Declaration of American Independence, the Constitution of the United States . . . form altogether a mass of political learning not to be surpassed in any other country. **1948** *Chickasha* (Okla.) *D. Express* 4 July 16/1 By spending a few minutes in reading the Declaration of Independence, good Americans on this day ought to shake themselves a little, mentally.

transf. **1852** STOWE *Uncle Tom* xvii. 17 George stood out in fair sight, on the top of the rock, as he made his declaration of independence. **1871** L. H. BAGG *At Yale* 160 In the Yale Banger of 1845 . . . is a burlesque of the Keys cut, representing the Scroll as a 'Declaration of Independence from the Scull and Bone.'

b. Also *Declaration of Independency. Obs.*

1776 *Mass. Spy* 17 July 3/2 On Wednesday last the Declaration of Independency was read at the head of each brigade of the Continental Army posted at and near New York, and everywhere received with loud huzzas, and the utmost demonstrations of joy. **1790** WASHINGTON *Diaries* IV. 135 This day being the Anniversary of the declaration of Independency the celebration of it was put off until tomorrow.

c. A document in which the representatives of a state or a proposed state declare it to be free of another state or governing power. *Obs.*

1806 in MARSHALL *Kentucky* (1812) 347 Accordingly we find Mr. Brown recommending a declaration of independance, that is, a separation of Kentucky from the parent state, and from the federal union. **1838** C. NEWELL *Revol. Texas* 76 Notwithstanding the reasons for a Declaration of Independence, the popular mind in Texas was not yet prepared for that measure. **1845** *Liberator* (Boston) 17 Jan. 10/3 All persons, (Africans, and the descendants of Africans and Indians excepted,) who were residing in Texas on the day of the Declaration of Independence, shall be considered citizens of the republic.

Decoration Day. = **Memorial Day.**

"The thirtieth day of May, 1868, is designated for the purpose of strewing with flowers, or otherwise decorating, the graves of comrades who died in defense of their country during the late rebellion. . . . In this observance, no form of ceremony is prescribed, but posts and comrades will in their own way arrange such fitting services and testimonials of respect as circumstances may permit" (1868 Logan *G. A. R. Gen. Order* No. 11).

1871 *Mich. Gen. Statutes* (1882) I. 445 The thirtieth day of May, commonly called decoration day, . . . shall . . . be treated and considered as the first day of the week, commonly called Sunday. **1947** *Chi. Sun* 30 May 17/1 The graves are pretty on Decoration Day.

decoyment dɪˈkɔɪmənt, *n.* Decoying. *Rare.* — **1841** FOOTE *Texas & Texans* I. 59 Abominable treachery [was] practised for the decoyment of the confiding Montezuma into captivity.

*deed, *n.* As the last term in **gift, Indian, tax, warranty deed.**

*** deed,** *v. tr.* To transfer (property, esp. land) by deed. Also absol.

"We sometimes hear this word used colloquially; but rarely, except by illiterate people" (Pickering). "A popular use of the word in America" (W. '28).

1806 WEBSTER 79 Deed, to give or transfer by deed. **1845** COOPER *Chainbearer* vii, Old Andries found out that the man who deeded to us had no deed to himself, or no mortal right to the land. **1902** HARBEN *Abner Daniel* 33 The farm you was going to deed to Alan? . . . You didn't include that?

Hence **deeded land.**

1872 *Newton Kansan*, 29 Aug. 3/3 (*advt.*), City Property exchanged for farms, homesteads or deeded lands. **1900** DRANNAN *Plains & Mts.* 575 A man . . . had a ranch for sale, consisting of three hundred and twenty acres of deeded land.

deedie ˈdidɪ, *n.* [?Imitative.] (See quot. 1902.) *Colloq.* — **1885** CRADDOCK *Prophet* 275, I jes' tole him 'twar ez safe ez a unhatched deedie in a aig. **1902** CLAPIN 155 *Deedies,* in the South, a common name for chickens or young fowls.

*** deep,** *a.* In combs.: (1) **deep milker,** a cow that produces a large amount of milk, *rare;* (2) **sea flounder,** the summer flounder or plaice, *Paralichthys dentatus;* (3) **South,** an area of vaguely defined limits embracing esp. the most southerly parts of Georgia, Alabama, Mississippi, and Louisiana, and regarded as being most typically southern and conservative.

(1) **1853** *Mich. Agric. Soc. Trans.* IV. 117 The cows are not deep milkers. — (2) **1884** GOODE *Fisheries* 178 On the bills of fare in Boston and New York hotels it [the plaice] is often called the Deep-sea Flounder. — (3) **1938** MATSCHAT *Suwannee River* 285 After a trip to the Deep South I spoke with Dr. Small regarding the various local names in use for the same plants. **1948** *N.O. Times-Picayune* (Mag.) 5 Dec. 24 The Deep South outdoors lovers sometimes feel slighted that their fall and winter don't produce the wildly bizarre colorings in trees and shrubs.

*** deer,** *n.* In combs.: (1) **deer beat,** (see quot.), *obs.;* (2) **bed,** (see quot. 1835); (3) **bleat,** (see quot. 1897–98 and cf. next); (4) **caller,** = prec.; (5) **face,** a contemptible person, *obs.* [prob. inspired by doeface *q.v.*]; (6) **fly,** (*a*) any one of various flies, esp. of the genus *Chrysops,* that molest deer, horses, etc., (*b*) designating a fever or disease now known as tularemia *q.v.;* (7) ***foot,** (see quot.); (8) **gun,** a gun suitable for use in hunting deer; (9) **inspector,** (see quot.), *obs.,* cf. **deer reeve;** (10) **lick,** a place to which deer and other animals resort on account of the salt or salt springs found there; (11) **mouse,** any one of various American mice of the genus *Peromyscus,* as *P. leucopus* of the eastern states, cf. **desert deer mouse;** (12) **path,** a path or runway made by deer; (13) **reeve,** = **deer inspector,** now *hist.;* (14) **runway,** a way or path frequented by deer; (15) **shut,** (see quot.), *rare;* (16) **sign,** evidence of the presence of deer; (17) ***skin,** designating a hunting shirt made of deerskin, *obs.;* (18) **skin sifter,** (see quot.), *obs.;* (19) **slayer,** a gun used in shooting deer, *rare;* (20) **trace,** a path or track made by deer; (21) **yard,** a place in the forest where deer herd in winter for feeding and protection.

(1) **1838** *Knickerb.* XII. 293 The deer . . . treading the snow from around its branches, as often as it falls during the season. This spot is called the deer or moose beat, by the hunters. — (2) **1835** W. IRVING *Tour on Prairies* 82 Numerous 'deer beds' where those animals had couched the preceding night. **1897** *Outing* XXX. 556/1 On making the ascent of a pine-tipped steep, we came upon a couple of deer-beds—two oval depressions, each about three feet long. — (3) **1852** MARCY *Explor. Red River* (1854) 54 We saw in advance of us a herd of antelopes quietly feeding among some mezquite trees, when the idea occurred to me of attempting to call them with a deer-bleat. **1897–8** *Bur. of Amer. Ethnol. Rep.* I. 426 The bruised root [of a certain plant], from which a milky juice oozes, is rubbed upon the deer bleat . . . with which the hunter imitates the bleating of the fawn. — (4) **1898** CUSHMAN *Hist. Indians* 197 Thus the hunter, with his deer-caller, easily enticed his game within range of his rival.

(5) **1845** HOOPER *Suggs* (1928) 18, I do wish to God he'd bust wide open, the durned old deer-face! *Ib.* 65 Keep your jaw, you slink . . . you durned, little, dirt-eatin' deer-face! — **(6)** *(a)* **1853** J. BENWELL *Travels* 127 Dusky-looking deer-flies constantly alighted on our faces and hands, and made us jump with the severity of their bites. **1947** *Hygeia* Nov. 837/2 Man acquires the disease either by direct contact with sick animals or through insects, such as deer flies or ticks, which have fed on them and then bitten him or been crushed on his skin. *(b)* **1937** EDWARD FRANCIS in *Public Health Reports* LII. 22 Jan. 1 This name [tularaemia] was given to the disease by the writer in 1920 after establishing the identity of the California rodent disease and 'deer-fly fever' in man. — **(7)** **1905** *Forestry Bureau Bul. 61* Deer foot. A V-shaped iron catch on the side of a logging car, in which the binding chain is fastened. — **(8)** **1834** *S. Lit. Messenger* I. 157 Their arms were of divers descriptions, double barreled guns, deer guns, ducking guns. **1857** *Porter's Spirit of Times* 3 Jan. 295/2 *(advt.)*, Always on hand, a full line of bird, duck, and deer guns,which I sell very low, and warrant to suit the purchaser. — **(9)** **1742** in *Coll. N.H. Hist. Soc.* VII. 362 Deac. Campbell, Thomas Wells and Joshua Prescott were appointed a committee to prevent the killing of deer 'contrary to the law in that case made and provided'; afterward these officers were regularly chosen by the town, and called 'Deer inspectors.'

(10) [**1776** *N. C. Morav. Rec.* III. (1926) 1089 At a place called Lichtenfels, . . . two and a half miles from Salem, there is a large deer-lick.] **1778** *Md. Journal* 2 June (Th.), I never saw a Deer-lick. Hunters have told me that Deer frequent those Places for the Mud. **1932** WILDER *Little House in Big Woods* 169 A deer-lick was a place where the deer came to get salt. When they found a salty place in the ground they came there to lick it, and that was called a deer-lick. — **(11)** **1833** CATLIN *Indians* I. 194 One of the spectators saw this strange animal catching and devouring a small 'deer mouse,' of which little and very destructive animals their lodges contained many. **1945** MCATEE *John and Joe* 14 Comparable examples among the mammals are deer mice and meadow voles. — **(12)** **1823** COOPER *Pioneers* xxi, Following a deer-path, [I] rode to the summit of the mountain. **1911** WHITE *Sec. Bk. No. Shore* 59 One of its leading thoroughfares [of Lake Forest, Ill.] preserves in its title its former significance. Deerpath Avenue was an old hunting trail, while the Deerpath Inn occupies the former site of a hunter's cabin. — **(13)** **1760** *Records of Amherst, Mass.* (1884) 22 Noah Dickinson Elijas Baker Moses Dickinson Dearifs. **1762** in *Coll. N.H. Hist. Soc.* II. 106 Among the town officers chosen this year was a clerk of the market, and a deer reif. . . . It was the duty of the latter to enforce the laws against killing deer in the spring. **1942** RAWSON *N.H. Borns a Town* 65 A 'deer reve' was named 'to inspect the Killing Deer.' — **(14)** **1835** HOFFMAN *Winter in West* I. 169 The numerous deer-runways, . . . and innumerable tracks of racoons, wolves, and bears, showed us that we were upon a favourite hunting ground of the Pottawattamies.

(15) **1674** in *Mass. H.S. Coll.* I. 153 The men [Christian Indians] . . . do use turkey or eagle's feathers, stuck in their hair, as it is traced up in a roll. Others wear deer shuts, made in the fashion of a cock's comb died red, crossing their heads like a half moon. — **(16)** **1827** COOPER *Prairie* xii, Buffalo-signs and deer-signs are plenty. — **(17)** **1829** T. FLINT *George Mason* 6 Their hearts revolted from the outlandish and foreign aspect of the tall planters, dressed in deerskin hunting-shirts. **1836** IRVING *Astoria* II. 62 Each had a good buffalo or deer skin robe; and a deer skin hunting shirt and leggins. — **(18)** **1899** GREEN *Va. Word-Book* 113 Deerskin sifter. . . . A sifter for separating the husk from the meal, made by punching small holes in a tanned deerskin, for lack of the wire gauge. — **(19)** **1843** CARLTON *New Purchase* I. 223 Our hunter would have made many a dive for the rescue of his 'deer slayer.'

(20) **1897** J. L. ALLEN *Choir Invis.* ii. 13 Beyond which he struck a narrow deer-trace, and followed that. — **(21)** **1849** LANMAN *Alleghany Mts.* viii. 58, I discovered a large spot of bare earth, which I took to be a deer-yard. **1880** *Adirondack Region Survey 7th Rep.* 159 We reached an open forest plateau on the mountain, where we were surprised to find a 'deer-yard.' Here the deep snow was tramped down by deer into a broad central level area. **1948** *Chi. Tribune* 29 Sep. III. 3/3 We have visited deer yards in winter to see how tough it is for animals to find enough browse in overcrowded areas.

b. In the names of plants: (1) **deer berry,** any one of several ericaceous plants, esp. the dangleberry *q.v.;* (2) **brush,** *W.* the cholla *q.v.;* (3) **bush,** *(a)* the deer laurel, *Rhododendron maximum,* *(b)* =**cholla;** (4) **feed,** =**deer brush;** (5) **grass,** any one of various species of *Rhexia,* or of *Muhlenbergia;* (6) **horn cactus,** the night-blooming cereus (see quot. 1911); (7) ∗**tongue,** the wild vanilla, *Trilisa odoratissima;* (8) **tongued laurel,** =**deer bush** *(a)*; (9) **weed,** a bushy herb of the genus *Lotus* found in southern California.

(1) **1814** PURSH *Flora* I. 285 Vaccinium stamineum. . . . In the mountains they are known by the name of Deer-berries. **1947** *Midland Naturalist* July 54 Deerberry [is] occasional (locally common) in pine-oak forest and upland oak forest. — **(2)** **1883** *Harper's Mag.* March 502/2 The 'deer brush' resembles horns. **1937** *Range Plant Handbook* B44 Deerbrush is one of the most valuable browse plants of the West, and in California it provides more forage than any other browse species. — **(3)** *(a)* **1869** W. MURRAY *Adventures* 123 Forcing our way along through spruce and balsam thickets, and heavy undergrowth of deer-bush, which flapped their broad flat leaves, loaded with water, into our eyes, we came upon a giant pine. *(b)* **1904** BURDICK *Mystic Mid-Region* 38 In some places the deer-bush thrives; this plant is so named because of the resemblance of its branches to the horns of a deer. — **(4)** **1871** *Harper's Mag.* Sep. 493 Barberry, stunted cedar and pine, and masses of 'deer-feed' vary the monotony of this sandy desert.

(5) **1785** *Narr. John Narrant* 17, I . . . saw at some distance bunches of grass, called deer-grass. **1938** *Range Plant Handbook* G87 Spike muhly, a tufted perennial grass, is also known as . . . wild-timothy, and deergrass. — **(6)** **1911** WOOTON *Cacti in N.M.* 53 Deerhorn Cactus (*Peniocereus gregii*) . . . is a species to please the cactus fancier. **1946** *Desert Mag.* May 28/3 Commonest flowers blooming in April in the Palm Spring region were . . . deerhorn, beavertail, and barrel cactus. — **(7)** **1861** WOOD *Botany* 413 Deer's-Tongue. . . . The fleshy leaves exhale a rich fragrance . . . even for years after they are dry, and are therefore by the southern planters largely mixed with their cured tobacco, to impart its fragrance to that nauseous weed. **1945** *Chi. Tribune* 13 May VII. 1/4 When they found deer tongue, I gave scarcely a look to the thick spotted leaves that had shot straight out of the ground. — **(8)** **1891** RYAN *Pagan* 23 The deer-tongued laurel raises grotesque antlers above the azalias. — **(9)** **1911** RICHTER *Honey Plants of Calif.* 997 *Lotus glaber* Greene. Wild Alfalfa. Deerweed. **1947** *Chr. Sci. Monitor* 15 Jan. 8/1 They graze their way up our stony mountain, sample all the bunch-grass, clovers, and deerweed in Sky Valley.

As the last term in **big-eared, blacktail, black-tailed, burro, chaparral, desert mule, Florida Whitetailed, jumping, moose, mountain, mule, red, spruce, tow head, Virginia, Virginian, white-tailed deer.**

∗**defecator,** *n.* An apparatus for purifying cane juice in the manufacture of sugar. — **1874** KNIGHT 683 Defecators for sorghum partake of the character of filters. **1886** *Harper's Mag.* June 82/2 We are in the defecating-room, fitted with banks or ranges of square tanks about six feet high, which are the 'defecators.'

∗**defective,** *n.* One who is mentally deficient. — **1881** G. S. HALL *German Culture* 267 She [Laura Bridgman] is not apt, like many defectives, to fall asleep if left alone or unemployed. **1941** ATTERBERRY, AUBLE & HUNT *Intro. to Soc. Science* 257 Mental defectives have some social intelligence, especially the imbeciles and the morons.

defectless dɪˈfɛktlɪs, *a.* Having no defect. *Rare.* — **1883** MARK TWAIN *Life on Miss.* xlviii, An absolutely defectless memory.

∗**defense,** *n.* The defendant and his legal counsel. Also attrib. — **1898** *K.C. Star* 19 Dec. 1/2 Contrary to all precedent Judge Wofford brushed both the state's and defense's request for trial aside. **1948** *Spokesman-Review* (Spokane, Wash.) 23 Sep. 2/3 A defense motion challenging the trial jury was denied as was a defense motion for a change of place of trial.

deferred debt. That part of the domestic debt incurred during the American Revolution and assumed by the federal government, so that it bore no interest until 1801. *Obs.*

"Refunding [of the debts of the Revolution] . . . was a slow process. . . . Of the domestic debt . . . 24.3 per cent was at 6 per cent with interest payments deferred until 1801." (1913 J. S. Bassett *Short Hist. U.S.* 260).

1792 HAMILTON *Works* II. (1885) 330 The 1st of January, 1802, when the deferred debt will become redeemable. **1797** *Ann. 5th Congress* I. 689 Mr. Nicholas called up for decision the resolution . . . directing the Committee of Ways and Means to report a plan for raising a sufficient revenue to meet the Deferred Debt, which becomes payable to the year 1801.

defibrator dɪˈfaɪbretɚ, *n.* [f. postulated *defibrate*+*-or.*] In sugar-making, a machine for shredding sugar cane in an effort to extract the maximum amount of juice. — **1886** *Harper's Mag.* June 80/1 There have been attempts to extract a greater proportion of juice by purely mechanical means, as by defibrators, shredding the cane into pulp. **1891** *Cent.* 6046/1 The process of manufacturing cane-sugar generally begins with extracting the juice of the canes . . . by the use of raspers or 'defibrators.'

deflagrator ˈdefləˌgretɚ, *n.* [f. ∗*deflagrate*+*-or.*] An instrument or apparatus for producing intense heat. *Rare.* — **1824** LONGFELLOW *Life* (1891) I. v. 51 The last [lecture] was upon the galvanick heat produced by Professor [Robert] Hare's deflagrator.

defoliage dɪˈfolɪ·ɪdʒ, *v. tr.* To deprive of foliage. *Rare.* — **1879** *Scribner's Mo.* XVIII. 402 [Caterpillars, *Dryocompa senatoria*] sometimes completely defoliage the trees.

deforestation dɪˌfɔrɪsˈteʃən, *n.* Also **deforestration.** The process of removing the forest from land. — **1874** *Vt. Bd. Agric. Rep.* II. 501 But now, because of these early clearings and succeeding deforestations, the lowlands have become drier and warmer. **1920**

LEWIS *Main Street* 116 [He] expects to reform everything from deforestration to nosebleed by saying phrases like 'surplus value.'

deforested dɪˈfɔrɪstɪd, *a.* Cleared or stripped of forests. — **1879** *Harper's Mag.* LIX 371 These deforested Eastern lands are . . . famous for seasons of blinding storms. **1887** *Scribner's Mag.* I. 568 [Channels] often, on the deforested surface, increase one hundred fold in their length.

deforester dɪˈfɔrɪstɚ, *n.* One who removes or clears away forests. *Rare.* — **1880** *Scribner's Mo.* XIX. 502 Most speculating deforesters go to the bad pecuniarily.

defy dɪˈfaɪ, *n.* [f. the verb.] A defiance or challenge. *Colloq.* — **1897** *Harper's Mag.* Jan. 231 He sent out the last defy to the enemy in 1800. **1910** in *W. James' Mem. & Studies* (1911) 396 Roaring my fierce defy.

* **degradation,** *n. Educ.* The action of punishing a student by degrading him. Now *hist.* Cf. * **degrade,** *v.*

1734 in *Pub. Col. Soc.* XV. 136 And If Such scholars shall not reform after being privately Admonished, he shall be further punished by public Admonition, degradation, or Expulsion. **1851** HALL *College Words* 94 Degradation consisted in placing a student on the list, in consequence of some offence, below the level to which his father's condition would assign him. **1925** *Pub. Col. Soc.* XV. cxli, Next to expulsion, 'degradation' was the highest punishment. . . . As the students appeared on all private and public occasions—at lectures, recitations, prayers, Commencement exercises, and in the meeting-house—and received their degrees, in the order in which they had been placed, 'degradation' was not only a punishment to the student himself but was a blow at family pride.

degrade dɪˈgred, *n.* [f. F. *dégrader*, in the voyageur sense of being detained by bad weather.] A stop in a journey caused by bad weather. *Obs.*

1793 in GATES *Fur Traders* 103 When the Canadians were forced by adverse winds to land and wait for more favorable sailing conditions, they were said to have made a 'degrade.' **1836** THORPE *Life on Lakes* I. 167 A perfect gale of wind, blowing up the river, still detains us; but *the degrades* has lost all its horrors. *Ib.* II. 95 Still *degrades* (what an expressive term) at White Fish Point. [**1857** *Spirit of Times* 5 Dec. 209/3 The wind rose so much in the night, that we found ourselves, July 13, what our boatman, Pierre, calls '*degradé*,' and compelled to lay over for the day.]

* **degrade,** *v. tr.* Formerly at Harvard, to reduce (a student) to a rank beneath the one originally assigned him in accordance with his family's social standing (see also quot. 1915). Also fig. Now *hist.*

1712 in *Pub. Col. Soc.* XV. 402 George Hussey being Convict of Dressing himself in Women's apparell and walking the Street in that Scandalous dress, was publickly admonish'd, and made A publick Confession, and degraded. **1748** *Ib.* XVI. 790 That when any Damage is done to a Library-book by taking any Cutts out of it by any Undergraduate He shall pay treble Damages & be Degraded. **1799** *Ib.* XVIII. 66 May Jacobinism still remain degraded to the very bottom of the class of American society. **1915** *Pub. Col. Soc.* XVIII. 68 With the abolition of this system after 1769 and its total disappearance in 1772, one might naturally conclude that the punishment of degradation fell with the system. But . . . the authorities showed some ingenuity in retaining it by degrading a student below his alphabetical place.

* **degree,** *n.* A particular grade of crime, esp. with reference to homicide. See also **second degree, third degree.**

1796 in *Statutes of Va.* (1835) II. 5/6 All murder which shall be perpetrated by means of poison, or by lying in wait, or by any other kind of wilful, deliberate and premeditated killing . . . shall be deemed murder of the first degree; and all other kinds of murder shall be deemed murder of the second degree. **1845** *Quincy* (Ill.) *Whig* 25 Nov. 2/4 The jury found a verdict of guilty of manslaughter in the 4th degree. **1886** *Starry Flag* (S.F.) May 5/1 Doctor J. Milton Bowers . . . was convicted on April 23rd of murder in the first degree. **1947** *This Week Mag.* 8 March 10/2 According to the experts, Britain will have a system of degrees of murder before another year has passed.

dehorn diˈhɔrn, *v.*

1. *tr.* To remove the horns from (cattle). Also fig.

1888 *Voice* 12 Jan. 2 [H. H. Haaff] is the champion of dehorning cattle. **1914** *Boston Ev. Transcript* 6 June III. 2/1 Four years ago they dehorned the speaker. **1948** *Democrat* 11 March 4/6 Calves can best be dehorned when they are young.

Hence **dehorning, dehorning clipper(s).**

1888 *Missouri Republican* 15 Feb. (F.), Dehorning is performed when the calf is young, and the tips of horns movable. **1903** *Sears Cat.* (ed. 113) 501/2 Leavitt's V-shape Blade Dehorning Clipper, cuts all around horn as handles are closed. **1913** BARNES *Western Grazing Grounds* 180 This is easily done by either throwing or snubbing them up to a strong post or fence and taking the points off with a pair of dehorning clippers or an ordinary meat saw.

2. (See quot.)

1905 *Forestry Bureau Bul.* No. 61, 35 Dehorn, to saw off the ends of logs bearing the owner's mark and put on a new mark.

dehorner diˈhɔrnɚ, *n.* One who dehorns cattle, or an instrument used for this purpose.

1888 H. H. HAAFF (*title*), Haaff's Practical Dehorner or Every Man His Own Dehorner. **1907** *Sears Cat.* (ed. 117) 477/2 This style Dehorner in the large size will clip any size horn from cattle of any age, smooth and clean. **1935** *Montgomery Ward Cat.* (ed. 123) 642 Safe Cattle Dehorners.

Deke, see **Deak.**

* **Delaware,** *n.*

1. *pl.* A tribe of Algonquian Indians, the Lenape or Leni-Lenape group, formerly occupying the basin of the Delaware River. Also Indians belonging to this tribe.

1721 *N.Y. Doc. Col. Hist.* (1855) V. 623 On the other hand all the English . . . have . . . in Jersey & Pennsylvania, their own or home nations, called Delawares, [who] are exceedingly decreased. **1832** FERRALL *Ramble thro' U.S.* 46 The Lenni Lenape, or Delawares, as they were called by the English, from the circumstance of their holding their great 'Council-fire' on the banks of the Delaware river. **1876** BANCROFT *Hist. U.S.* V. iv. 379 In this manner ten minutes were gained so that the Delawares with their prisoners . . . succeeded in reaching the creek. **1907** HODGE *Amer. Indians* I. 385/1 The English knew them as Delawares, from the name of their principal river.

In full **Delaware Indians.**

1761 NILES *Indian Wars* II. 430 Two bateaux of Frenchmen, with a large party of Delaware Indians . . . were to join Captain Jacobs. **1872** R. G. MCCLELLAN *Golden State* 88 Fremont [in 1845] . . . arrived with his faithful guide and escort, Kit Carson, and his men, (six of whom were Delaware Indians) . . . within a hundred miles of Monterey. **1946** FOREMAN *Last Trek* 17 History, however, seems to single out the Delaware Indians to introduce the discussion.

b. The language of these Indians. Also attrib.

a1772 WOOLMAN *Journal* 201 The interpreters . . . found some difficulty, as none of them were quite perfect in the English and Delaware tongues. **1826** COOPER *Mohicans* viii, Hawk-eye and the Mohicans conversed earnestly together in Delaware for a few moments, when each quietly took his post. **1866** *Beadle's Mo.* Oct. 283/2, I know English . . . and have picked up a smattering of French, Spanish, Choctaw and Delaware.

2. Used attrib., as **Delaware chief, district, reserve.**

1838 *N.Y. Mirror* 27 Jan. 245/3 Yesterday five Delaware chiefs, who had gone from the main army to the stronghold of the hostiles, reappeared with four Indians. **1857** in *36th Congress* 1 Sess. H.R. Rep. 648 You are hereby instructed to repair immediately to Doniphan, in the 'Delaware district,' in Kansas. **1857** GIHON *Geary & Kansas* 19 Immediately above the Wyandot begins the Delaware reserve.

3. An American grape, red or reddish in color, growing in compact bunches; the vine bearing this grape.

1861 WILLIS *Subscribers Directory* 340 New Hardy Grape Vines . . . Delaware; Concord; Hartford Prolific. **1862** *Rep. Comm. Patents: Agric.* 476 My two '*Delawares*' grew well, but made very slender wood. **1929** BAILEY *Cyclo. Horticulture* 1380/2 Delaware is in good demand because of its quality when well grown.

4. Delaware line, a military unit or organization in the Revolutionary army made up of soldiers from the state of Delaware. *Obs.*

1809 *Ann. 10th Congress* 2 Sess. 981 Mr. Van Dyke presented a memorial of sundry late officers in the Delaware line of the late Revolutionary army.

* **delegate,** *n.* As the last term in **House of Delegates, walking delegate.**

delegateship ˈdɛləgɪtˌʃɪp, *n.* The position or office of a delegate to Congress or to a political party convention. — **1863** *Walla Walla* (Wash.) *Statesman* 27 June 2/2 The Washington *Standard* is pitching into some one of the candidates for the Delegateship, styling him an imported webfoot. **1892** *Columbus* (O.) *Dispatch* 23 March, Federal office holders in the South are being put forward for delegateships.

* **delegation,** *n.* The body of delegates chosen to represent a political unit in an assembly, legislature, or convention.

1775 *Jrnls. Cont. Cong.* II. 16 We, the subscribers, do . . . signify our assent to, and approbation of, the above Delegation. **1815** *Niles' Reg.* IX. 110/2 The delegation from the several counties of this state to the general assembly, . . . are federal by a majority of one-fifth of the whole number. **1848** *N.Y. Wkly. Tribune* 27 May 5/6 The news of the preliminary triumph of the Hunker Delegation . . . was received here with intense interest. **1884** *Cent. Mag.* March 644/1 It was therefore arranged . . . [that] Jefferson . . . should persuade the

Virginia delegation to vote for assumption, while Hamilton was to induce the New York delegation to yield their preferences concerning the capital. **1948** *Newsweek* 27 Sep. 19/1 Rival Truman delegations from the bolting counties . . . had been waiting outside around loud-speakers and a chuck-wagon.

b. A bloc, a combining of members of different political parties for a common purpose.

1932 Grayson *Leaders* 377 It was not long before a strong silver delegation was formed in Congress.

delicatessen ˌdɛləkəˈtɛsn̩, *n.* [G., dainties, f. F. *délicatesse.*]

1. *pl.* Prepared foods, such as cooked meats, cheese, pickles, baked goods, and canned products.

1893 Howells *Coast of Bohemia* 261 He really went . . . to the shop of an old German . . . who dealt in delicatessen. **1948** *Chi. D. News* 28 April 15 (*advt.*), Delicatessen and Cheese.

2. *sing.* A store or shop in which such foods are sold. Also attrib.

1913 Cather *O Pioneers!* 123 When one of us dies . . . our landlady and the delicatessen man are our mourners. **1923** *New Republic* 25 April 235/2 In the delicatessen across the street he noted two fat women. **1948** *Seattle Sun. Times* 26 Sep. 4/1 There is a Swede, who has been running a delicatessen in the city for many years.

b. In full **delicatessen shop, store.**

1893 *Harper's Mag.* April 660 They [*sc.* Germans in Brooklyn] maintain . . . their delicatessen shops and pork-butchers, their beer saloons and summer gardens. **1898** *N.Y. Journal* 17 Aug. 14/6 Four Jersey City lawyers and one Police Court Justice will on Thursday decide the question of constitutional rights as applied to a delicatessen store dog with no tail. **1948** *Sat. Ev. Post* 17 July 38/3 He didn't want no delicatessen store.

transf. **1905** *N.Y. Ev. Post* 13 Nov. 7 Next week's opening of Mr. Conried's operatic delicatessen store on Broadway.

∗**Delicious,** *n.* A variety of late, dark-red eating apple of delightful flavor introduced in 1881 by J. Hiatt of Peru, Iowa. Also attrib.

1906 *Suburban Life* July 29/1 Among the newer sorts, I am best pleased with Black Ben, Delicious and King David. **1928** Bailey *Cyclo. Horticulture* 319/2 The newer plantings are mostly Stayman Winesap, McIntosh, Delicious, and Northern Spy. **1948** *Nat. Geog. Mag.* March 357/2 The widely known Delicious apple was a chance seedling.

∗**delight,** *n.* As the last term in **lady's, sheep herder's, traveler's delight.**

∗**delinquent,** *a.* Of taxes: Not paid in due time. Cf. **back tax.**

1868 *Harper's Mag.* Aug. 372/2 The auctioneer . . . was knocking down Hardin Bogg's farm for delinquent taxes. **1905** *Omaha Bee* 10 Jan. 3 In many cases the property is not worth as much as the delinquent taxes against it. **1948** *Chesterton* (Ind.) *Tribune* 28 Oct. 13/4 The second auction of county property taken for delinquent taxes last week yielded $5,265.00.

∗**deliver,** *v. Polit. tr.* To bring (votes, political leaders) to the support of a particular cause or candidate. *Collcq.*

1893 *Nation* 16 Nov. 365 No man is so fierce in his Americanism as . . . a boss who has 'delivered' the vote of his district as per contract. **1904** *Brooklyn Union* 3 June 6 The basis of the break is said to have been a charge that Shevlin 'delivered' Boss McLaughlin in some deal without the latter's knowledge. **1948** *Sat. Ev. Post* 3 July 71/3 They have to deliver the vote or out they go.

∗**delivery,** *n.* As the last term in **desk, free, general, range, special delivery.**

delivery wagon. A wagon used in delivering supplies, express parcels, etc.; a delivery truck. Cf. **express wagon** (*a*). — **1879** Peck *Peck's Fun* (1882) 88 (We.), Smith took [the goods] out to put them in the delivery wagon. **1923** Watts *L. Nichols* 199 Driving a delivery wagon connoted helping to load and unload it, often a back-breaking task.

Dells dɛlz, *n. pl.* [Variant of "Dalles."] The rapids of a river, or the place where these are occasioned by a stream's cutting through a rock formation, used esp. of the Wisconsin River. Cf. **Dalle.**

1846 *Quincy* (Ill.) *Whig* 16 April 2/5 The wagons can come as far as the Delles, then by water the balance of the way. **1884** *Among the Dells* 5 The Dells of the Wisconsin river are known as one of the attractive summer resorts of the Northwest. They are about five miles in length, and are formed by the converging of the river's banks, through which the broad expanse of water above is forced with great rapidity. **1945** Gray *Pine, Stream & Prairie* 15 It has spectacular moments when it passes through the Dells between high rocky cliffs full of curious formations to which the prosy poets of our times have given such names as 'the devil's punchbowl.'

Del Mar Pine. *local.* (See quot.) — **1897** Sudworth *Arborescent Flora* 19 Pinus torreyana Parry. Torrey Pine. . . . Common Names [include] . . . Del Mar Pine (Cal.).

Delmarva dɛlˈmɑrvə, *n. local.* [f. *Del*aware+*Mar*yland+*Vir*ginia.] The Delaware peninsula. Also attrib. — **1933** *Amer. Sp.* Dec. 57/2 Perhaps the most old-fashioned varieties of Delmarva speech are current on the islands of the Chesapeake and off the Atlantic coast. **1948** Mencken *Supp.* II. 136 In the lower reaches of Delmarva . . . he found that the influence of Tidewater and General Southern was rather more marked.

∗**Delmonico,** *n.* The name of Alonzo Delmonico (1813–81), a New York restaurateur, used of, or in allusion to, restaurants. Also **Delmonican,** *a.*

1848 *N.Y. Wkly. Tribune* 5 Aug. 6/3 There are three distinct classes of eating-houses and each has its model or type. Linnæus would probably class them as Sweenyorum, Browniverous and Delmonican. **1880** *Harper's Mag.* Mar. 551/2 Eschewing the flesh-pots of the hotels and the 'Delmonicos of the West,' . . . he may procure tent and general 'outfit' . . . and proceed to camp out. **1893** *Outing* April 19/2, I am ashamed to say that we could not induce them to accept more than a quarter of a dollar apiece for it all—and Delmonico could not have suited us better.

attrib. **1941** Farmer *Boston Cook Book* 461 Delmonico Tomatoes (Stuffed with Sweetbreads).

b. (See quot.)

1890 *Railways of America* 244 The first dining-car was named the 'Delmonico,' and began running on the Chicago & Alton Railroad in the year 1868.

∗**delta,** *n.*

1. (*cap.*) (See quots.) *Obs.*

1823–7 *Tour through College* 13 We should assemble on a neighboring green, the *Delta*, since devoted to the purposes of a gymnasium. **1842** *Knickerb.* XIX. 433 A question that is settled by a game of football in the delta, a large enclosure near the college, fenced in the shape of the Greek letter of that name. **1856** Hall *Coll. Words* (ed. 2) 155 *Delta.* . . . A plat of Bowdoin College, of this shape, and used for similar purposes [to those of the *Delta* at Harvard], is known by the same name.

2. delta-plain, plateau, (see quot. 1903). Cf. **Mississippi delta.**

1892 R. D. Salisbury *Geol. Surv. New Jersey* 101 (*Cent. Supp., s.v. Delta plain*). **1903** *Amer. Geol.* Sep. 163 For such topographic forms Professor Davis long since proposed the name of delta-plain or delta-plateau, instead of sand-plain.

∗**delusion,** *n.* A penchant *for* (something). *Rare.* — **1901–2** *Kans. St. Bd. Agric. Rep.* 52 (*Cent. Supp., s.v. Dished*), There was a time when swine-breeders had a delusion for 'dished faces' and heavy jowls.

Dem dɛm, *n.* Also **Demmy.** A jocular shortening of "Democrat."

1840 Bird *Robin Day* 12 We had dubbed our parties Feds and Demies—that is, Federalists and Democrats. **1869** *Champaign Co.* (Ill.) *Gaz.* 21 April 1/2 For the very reason that Demmys and ex-Confeds don't like him, all good, true, and loyal men, do. **1948** *Chi. D. News* 11 June 16/5 The Dems figure that the next president . . . faces tough going.

demagoguery ˈdɛməˌgɑgərɪ, *n.* The practices and principles of a demagogue; demagogism.

1855 *Georgetown* (Ky.) *Herald* 14 June, He is too familiar with the tricks of demagoguery and too loose in his political principles. **1865** *Louisville Jrnl.* 30 Sep. 2/1 One of the natural and inevitable efforts of this spirit of demagoguery, on elective judiciary is the frightful and extensive prevalence of crime which the papers are everywhere chronicling. **1935** *Amer. Mercury* July 293/2 Demagoguery has ever flourished in what our forefathers were wont to call 'hard times.'

∗**Demerara,** *n. attrib.* Designating or pertaining to coffee and cotton coming from, or in some way associated with, Demerara County, British Guiana. *Obs.* — **1800** *Columbian Centinel* 8 Jan. 3/3 For Sale . . . 11,000 wt. Demarary Coffee. **1856** *Rep. Comm. Patents: Agric.* 227 In the following June, there were received there a supply of cotton seeds of the 'Upland Georgia,' 'Sea Island' and 'Demarara' varieties.

∗**demerit,** *n.* A mark placed on a student's record to denote a fault, esp. in conduct. Also attrib.

1862 Strong *Cadet Life W. Point* 150 The more immediate penalty is the demerit. **1877** Burdette *Rise of Mustache* 311 Got three demerit marks for drawing a picture of her [=teacher]. **1947** *Chr. Sci. Mon.* 21 May 9/2 The demerit system, patterned after the one in effect at the United States Military Academy, is designed to insure discipline and respect without regimentation.

∗**demerit,** *v. tr.* To reduce (a person) in rank or standing. — **1895** *Cent. Mag.* Oct. 843/2 He stands a fair chance of being demerited and punished until his hope of release before he is of age is almost extinguished.

demit dɪˈmɪt, *n.* Also **dimit.** (See quots.) — **1856** R. Morris in A. G. Mackey *Encycl. Freemasonry* (1879) 221/2 A 'demit,' technically considered, is the act of withdrawing, and applies to the Lodge and not to the individual. **1879** *Ib.* 220/1 The granting of 'a dimit' does not necessarily lead to the conclusion that the Mason who received it has left the Lodge. He has only been permitted to do so. *Ib.* 221/2 'A demit' is . . . an Americanism of very recent usage.

Demo ˈdɛmo, *n.* A Democrat. *Jocular.*

1793 *Steele P.* I. 108 Mr. Smiley—a man who was very Popular in the State assembly, he is a great Demo(crat) and taulks tolerable well. **1821** *Niles' Reg.* 24 Nov. XXI. 198 (*note*), One most momentous affair . . . greately agitated the mind of the fashionable world at Washington nearly the whole of last winter, and divided the people thereof into two parties, as hot against each other as the *Demos* and *Feds* used to be. **1948** *Chesterton* (Ind.) *Tribune* 28 Oct. 12/3 The program chairman kept peace between GOP and Demos by allowing a spokesman for each party to talk about its candidates, without referring to specific issues.

b. Also **Demo-Confed(erate),** a southern Democrat. *Obs.*

1879 *Chi. Tribune* 5 Feb. 4/5 The Demo-Confeds, who will be in control of both Houses, will undoubtedly resume their revolutionary proceedings. *Ib.* 15 March 4/6 It will be a striking warning of the dangers of a Demo-Confederate oligarchy gaining control of the National Congress.

***democracy,** *n.* (Usu. *cap.*) The principles of the Democratic party, the Democratic party, or its members collectively.

1803 *Wash. Federalist* 4 Feb. 1/1 The Republicans in the United States will know how to give credence to the bold assertions of the democrats that this state is fast hastening to join the phalanx of democracy. **1814** *Ann. 13th Cong.* 1576 Federalism and Democracy have lost their meaning. **1838** *Chi. Democrat* 21 Nov. 1/2 Thousands of Claymen turn swiftly from Clay, Before the full glare of Democracy's day. **1937** *Baltimore Sun* 30 Nov., The word in question is used with a capital when it refers to Democracy as 'the principles of the Democratic party,' to quote the unabridged dictionaries; but this does not refer to our Government as such.

As the last term in **barefooted, county, Equal Rights, Jacksonian, Northern, Swallow Tail, tadpole, War, Young democracy.**

***Democrat,** *n.* Also ***democrat.**

1. Originally a member of the old Democratic-Republican party (see quot. 1810); in later use a member of the Democratic party *q.v.*

1798 Washington *Writings* XIV. 105 You could as soon scrub the blackamore white as change the principle of a profest Democrat. **1810** Cuming *Western Tour* 69 There are two parties, which style themselves Federal republicans, and Democratick republicans, but who speaking of each other, leave out the word *republican*, and call each other Federalists and Democrats. **1839** T. Brothers *United States* 134 The duty of each of . . . [these 'block'] committees is to organise and drill all the whigs, or democrats . . . that live in a certain number of houses adjoining each other. **1947** *Chi. D. News* 17 Dec. 22/5 Democrats generally will be glad to see his back.

transf. **1830** *Bell's Life in N.Y.* 14 Sep. 1/1 The lady, who had more zeal than either patience or skill, . . . succeeded only in taking a few of those that are called *democrats*, or rock bass, . . . a species that abound in the waters of that romantic lake [George].

2. A light wagon, usu. having two seats. In full **democrat wagon.** Also attrib. Cf. **democratic wagon.**

1871 *Harper's Mag.* Aug. 382 There were two teams running a race, and presently a white horse and green-bodied democrat wagon hove in sight. **1902** McFaul *Ike Glidden* 89 As they approached Squirmtown they saw numerous teams,—some of the two-seated, 'Democrat' type, others of the Concord pattern. **1947** *Trail Riders Bul.* May 3/1 He drove them around in an old fashioned democrat.

As the last term in **anti-, boll weevil, border state, bourbon, counterfeit, Douglas, Dumb, Free, funder, Gold, Gold Standard, hardshell, hook and ladder, Hunker, Independent, Jackson, Jacksonian, Jeffersonian, Mugwumpian, northern, Patent, Peace, silver, Southern, swamp, War, Whisky Democrat.**

***Democratic,** *a.*

1. Pertaining or belonging to the old Democratic-Republican party, or to the Democratic party.

1803 *Fredericktown* (Md.) *Herald* 30 April 3/3 Major Stevenson was the Federal candidate, and Osborne Sprigg Esq. . . . was the democratic candidate. **1841** in MacLeod *Biog.* 77 It is not now with the Kentucky Senator as it was when pressed upon by the Democratic Senator of New-York. **1944** *Chi. D. News* 10 Jan. 4/2 Today this country is Republican rather than Democratic.

2. In special combs.: (1) **Democratic campaign textbook,** a campaign book *q.v.* prepared in behalf of the Democratic party in a particular campaign; (2) **caucus,** a meeting of Democratic leaders to nominate candidates for local offices or to elect delegates to a party convention; (3) **convention,** a meeting of Democratic delegates held for the purpose of nominating party candidates for an approaching election, cf. **Free Democratic convention;** (4) **donkey,** (see quot.); (5) **Greenback,** participated in or achieved by members of the Democratic and the Greenback parties, *obs.;* (6) **National Convention,** a meeting of Democratic delegates for the purpose of nominating presidential and vice-presidential candidates; (7) **party,** see as a main entry; (8) **Republican,** a member of a political party made up of those who opposed the old Federalist party, also **Democratic-Republican party,** now *hist.;* (9) **Society,** a local society or group made up of Democrats, now *hist.;* (10) **ticket,** a ballot with a list of Democratic candidates for office printed upon it, *fig.* (esp. in later use) the group of Democratic candidates at a particular election; (11) **wagon,** =**democrat wagon;** (12) **Whig,** =**Whig.**

(1) **1909** Parker *G. Cleveland* 121, I had for more than seven weeks, in 1888, at the office in the White House, prepared the Democratic Campaign Textbook. — (2) **1804** Cutler in *Life & Corr.* II. 164 You have seen doings of the Democratic caucus here. — (3) **1865** *Cairo* (Ill.) *D. Democrat* 4 Oct. 1/1 A Democratic Convention of Delegates . . . will assemble at the Court House . . . for the purpose of nominating a candidate for the office of County Clerk. **1872** *Newton Kansan* 22 Aug. 4/3 Greeley, being now to all intents and purposes a Democrat, nominated by a regular Democratic convention, . . . must make up his cabinet . . . with Democrats. — (4) **1914** *Cyclo. Amer. Govt.* I. 564 Democratic Donkey. A symbol representing the Democratic party, originated by Thomas Nast in his cartoon of January 15, 1870: "A Live Jackass Kicking a Dead Lion," which represented the Democratic press attacking Edwin M. Stanton . . . after his death. This was the first instance of the use of the donkey to represent Democratic sentiments.

(5) **1882** Cooper *Amer. Pol.* Bk. I. 195 This was the second Democratic-Greenback victory in Maine. — (6) **1847** *Semi-Wkly. News* (Fredericksburg, Va.) 1 Nov. 2/5 Another resolution suggested a State Convention to be held on the 22d of February, 1848, for the appointment of delegates to the Democratic National Convention. **1944** *Harper's Mag.* March 307/1 In all those ten years his name had appeared in the *New York Times* just once—on the list of Ohio delegates to the Democratic National Convention of 1924. — (8) **1810** [see ***Democrat,** *n.* **1**]. **1811** *Niles' Reg.* I. 3/1 The intended publisher is, in the common language of the day, a 'democratic republican.' **1936** *Pittsburgh Post-Gazette* 26 Sep. 1. 5/1 The advent of Jefferson's Democratic-Republican party found enthusiastic, if not numerous, adherents here **1948** *Time* 14 June 15/1 In 1812 the Federalists summoned party delegates to a New York City convention and nominated De Witt Clinton (defeated in the election by the Democratic-Republicans' James Madison). — (9) **1795** *Pittsburgh Gazette* 13 June 3/1 A member of Congress blamed the Democratic Societies. *a*1821 C. Biddle *Autobiog.* iv. 252 Shortly after this, there was formed in the city a Democratic Society. **1948** *Wm. & Mary Quart.* Oct. 480a The earliest known anti-Jefferson cartoon . . . shows Jefferson (with the gavel) presiding over the Philadelphia 'Democratic' Society.

(10) Fearon *Sketches* 147 Persons in the interest of the parties have written on their hat or breast, 'Federal Ticket,' or 'Democratic Ticket,' soliciting citizens as they approach the polls 'to vote their ticket.' **1945** *Sat. Review* 24 Feb. 8/3 Earl Browder's alignment with him in the Roosevelt camp brought a greatly intensified bombardment of the Democratic ticket from the editorial howitzers. — (11) **1889** *Cent.* 1527/1 *Democrat*, a light wagon without a top, . . . [was] originally called *democratic wagon.* (Western and Middle U.S.) — (12) **1842** *Whig Almanac 1843* 14/2 The other party take the name of Democratic Whigs, or in some States simply Whigs. *Ib.* 16/1 It is the cardinal conviction of those known as Whigs, ('Democratic' or 'Federal' Whigs, as you please,) that Government need not and should not be an institution of purely negative, repressive usefulness and value.

Democratico-Slavic, *a.* Designating the Democratic party, and suggesting that party's attitude toward slavery. *Rare.* — **1862** *Independent* 10 April 5/1 The politicians . . . are now endeavoring to reconstruct the Democratico-Slavic party.

Democratic party. One of the two strongest political parties in the U.S. Cf. **Free, National Democratic party.**

The present Democratic party had its origin during the political realignment and party reorganization of 1825–29. Before that time the term was used with reference to the old Republican or Democratic-Republican party. Cf. **anti-federalist.**

*c*1800 Twining *Travels* (1894) 51 [Gallatin] was one of the principal members of the opposition, or of the anti-federal or democratic party, as opposed to the federal system, of whom General Washington was the head. **1829** *Morning Courier* (N.Y.) 4 Nov. 2/1 Men who have long passed current as genuine and faithful . . . have aspired to break down the Regular Nominations of the Democratic party. **1846** Polk *Diary* (1929) 63, I called to their recollection that the Democratic party were in a decided majority in both houses of Congress. **1948** *Chi. Tribune* 1 Aug. IV. 7/1 Hamilton's death ended the power of the Federalists to challenge Jefferson's newly formed Democratic party.

***demoiselle,** *n.* **= Louisiana heron.** — **1903** Coues *Key N.A. Birds* II. 878 H[ydranassa] tricolor ruficollis . . . Louisiana Egret Demoiselle. **1946** Hausman *Eastern Birds* 105 Its names Demoiselle and Lady-of-the-Waters suggest that it is considered the most graceful of all the heron tribe.

demoralization dɪˌmɔrələˈzeʃən, *n.* [f. **demoralize,** *v.*+-*ation.*] The act of demoralizing or state of being demoralized.

1806 Webster 81/1 Demoralization, *n.* the destruction of morality. **1813** S. Grellet *Memoirs* (1860) I. 216, I felt deeply for . . . the deplorable state of ignorance and demoralization into which many of them [*sc.* the poor of London] are sunk. **1948** *Chi. D. News* 11 June 16/7 The most serious sign of irresponsibility and demoralization is the action of the House in slashing the foreign relief appropriation.

demoralize dɪˈmɔrəlˌaɪz, *v.* [See note.] *tr.* To weaken the moral principles of, to destroy temporarily the courage or spirit of (a person), to upset the normal functioning of.

Noah Webster first used this word, in the form "demoralizing" (see quots. 1794, 1841 below). In his dictionary of 1828 he etymologized it as being derived from *de* and *moralize* or *moral.* The usual derivation from F. *démoraliser* is erroneous.

1806 Webster 81/1 Demoralize, . . . to corrupt, undermine or destroy moral principles. **1841** Lyell *Travels* I. 65 When the lexicographer, Noah Webster, whom I saw at Newhaven, was asked how many new words he had coined, he replied one only 'to demoralize,' and that not for his dictionary, but long before in a pamphlet published in the last century. **1903** *Cin. Enquirer* 2 May 9/4 The hog market has been greatly demoralized. **1948** *Chi. D. News* 11 June 16/7 On their side of the aisle, the Democrats are demoralized.

Also **demoralizing,** *a.*, tending to weaken moral principles.

1794 Webster *Revol. in France* 32 All wars have, if I may use a new but emphatic word, a demoralizing tendency. **1943** *This Week Mag.* 28 Aug. 4/2 It is . . . demoralizing in world affairs to let systematic cruelty and crime go unpunished.

demoralizer dɪˈmɔrəlˌaɪzɚ, *n.* A person or thing that demoralizes. — **1934** Webster. **1944** *Chi. D. News* 29 May 6/5 Rather than being morale boosters, I would label them demoralizers.

demote dɪˈmot, *v.* [By analogy with **promote.*] *tr.* To reduce to a lower grade or class in school or in office.

*c*1891 in *Stand.* 489/2 The school children in Senator Wilson's District of Iowa 'use the word *demote* as an antithesis of promote, and . . . it is so used generally in that section of the country.' **1911** L. Witmer *Special Class for Backward Children* 91 Because no improvement occurred, he was demoted to second grade B. **1948** *Democrat* 3 June 3/3, I have legal protection and can not legally be demoted either in salary or position.

Hence **demotion,** *n.* (See quot.)

1911 Monroe *Cyclo. Educ.* II. 295/1 *Demotion,* a term sometimes used to signify the opposite of promotion. It designates the placing of a pupil in a class below that in which he happens to be, and with which he is unable to keep pace.

***den,** *n.* A local unit of the Ku-Klux Klan. *Obs.* — **1868** in *Doc. & Sp. in Amer. Hist.* III. (1943) 79 The Empire shall be divided into four departments. . . . The fourth department to be styled the Den. **1898** Page *Red Rock* 352, I myself organized a band of Ku Klux regulators—'a den,' as we called it, in this County.

As the last term in **beaver, penny poker, rattlesnake, snake den.**

***den,** *v.*

1. *tr.* To track (a bear) to its den. *Rare.*

1861 *Harper's Mag.* April 604/2 We . . . could see where it [the bear] would go into den after den of rocks, in and out. Followed on till near dark, when we 'denned' it.

2. *den up,* of bears, snakes, etc.: To hibernate, to go into a den for the winter. Also transf.

1843 *Amer. Pioneer* II. 171 In that climate [Canada] the bears usually den up in the winter, and lie in something of a torpid state. **1894** *Home Missionary* Jan. 463 Our people . . . are inclined to 'den up' in the hot weather, as certain animals . . . do in the cold season. **1929** W. Heyliger *Builder of Dam* 214 The animal had seemed bursting with fat. 'Getting ready to den up early,' said Ricky.

dengue ˈdɛŋgɪ, *n.* Also **dangue.** [Sp. in same sense.] An epidemic tropical fever, accompanied by characteristic pains in the limbs and joints; breakbone fever. Also attrib.

1828 *Charleston Courier* 15 July, The Dengue. This . . . epidemic exists at the time in our city. **1828** *Free Press* (Tarboro, N.C.) 29 Aug., The *Dangue Fever,* which has raged so generally in Charlestown, has spread to other parts of the country. **1889** *Times* (London) 28 Dec. 7/3 Dengue, also known as 'break-bone,' . . . was first described in Philadelphia in 1780. **1944** *Sat. Review* 14 Oct. 70/1 He was sent to help in a study and eradication of the mosquitoes that carry dengue.

***denim,** *n.* A strong cotton cloth used for coverings, hangings, overalls, aprons, etc. Also attrib.

1850 Judd *R. Edney* viii. 117 A pair of denim over-hauls mated it on the other; . . . he looked more closely at them . . . for he wanted a pair. **1864** Webster 354/1 Denim, a coarse cotton drilling used for overalls, etc. **1944** Clark *Pills* 221 Overalls and jumpers made of blue denim finally took the place of jeans and coarse cassimere.

denominationalize dɪˌnɑməˈneʃənəlaɪz, *v. tr.* To bring in line with or convert to some religious denomination. *Obs.* — **1869** *Nation* VIII. 190/2 The religious sentiment but not too much denominationalized, to coin a word. **1892** *Advance* (Chicago) 8 Dec., We believe our brethren are conscientiously seeking to meet absolute need, rather than to denominationalize the frontier.

***dent,** *n.* A variety of corn, the kernels of which have a characteristic dent or depression. In full **dent corn.** Cf. ***horsetooth,** and **white dent.**

1853 *Mich. Agric. Soc. Trans.* V. 125 The land . . . was planted . . . with the 'Indian Yellow Dent.' **1872** *Vt. Bd. Agric. Rep.* I. 53 We cannot grow the Baldwin . . . with more success than we could grow the dent, or the horse-tooth corn of the south and west. **1947** *Annals Mo. Bot. Garden* Feb. 14 There is abundant evidence that the varieties of the United States corn belt originated by repeated hybridization between the northern flints and soft-textured southern dents.

***dental,** *a.* In combs.: (1) **dental chair,** a specially constructed chair for the use of those having dental work done; (2) **operator,** a grandiose term for a dentist, *rare;* (3) **parlor,** formerly a commercial establishment where dentistry was practiced by non-professional men, frequently at exorbitant prices; (4) **surgeon,** a dentist, cf. **surgeon dentist;** (5) **surgery,** dentistry.

(1) **1880** Mark Twain *Tramp Abroad* xxiii. 222 About five hundred soldiers gathered together in the neighborhood of that dental chair waiting to see the performance. — (2) **1863** Dicey *Six Months* II. 126 The inns are houses or halls, the butcher's is the meat market, the dentist calls himself a dental operator, the shops are stores, marts, or emporiums, and the public-houses are homes, arcades, exchanges, or saloons. — (3) **1894** *Chi. D. News* 16 July 8/2 (*advt.*), Boston Dental Parlors. **1943** *Harper's Mag.* Dec. 47/1 A series of State laws passed after 1916 finally brought decent standards to the dental profession, and by 1921 the last of the dental parlors in New York City took down its gilded tooth and closed its doors. — (4) **1840** *Amer. Jrnl. Dental Science* I. 157 The objects of this Society [the Amer. Soc. of Dental Surgeons] are to promote union and harmony among all respectable and well-informed Dental Surgeons. **1940** Black *From Pioneer to Scientist* 66 Although a national dental organization seems to have been in contemplation since 1817, it did not take form until 1840, when the 'American Society of Dental Surgeons' was organized. (5) **1826** L. Koecker (*title*), The Principles of Dental Surgery. **1940** Black *From Pioneer to Scientist* 65 Drs. Chapin A. Harris and Horace H. Hayden . . . organized a dental school in 1839 (the first dental school in the world) and graduated its first class in 1840. It was called The Baltimore College of Dental Surgery, and is still in existence.

Denverite ˈdɛnvəraɪt, *n.* A native or inhabitant of Denver, Colorado. — **1866** Meline *Two Thousand Miles on Horseback* (1867) 57 Even after the Pacific Railroad reaches it (and that it soon may, every true Denverite makes the doxology of his morning and evening prayer) the terminus must long remain at the foot of the range. **1947** *Denver Post* 2 March A. 6/6 Less well-to-do Denverites inclined strongly toward the municipal bond issue.

depance deˈpɑns, *n.* [F. *dépense,* a place where provisions are stored.] (See quot.) *Obs.* — **1845** Dunn *Ore. Territory* 108 The blacksmiths are busily engaged making beaver-traps for the trappers—. . . the clerk in charge of the provision-store (generally called, after the French, *depance*), packing their provisions for them, to last until they get into hunting-ground.

*department, *n.*

1. A division of a military organization or the region over which this operates or exercises rule. Also attrib.

1775 WASHINGTON *Writings* II. 489 The other Officers in the higher departments are not yet fixed therefore I cannot give you their names. **1861** *Army Regulations* 126 The proceedings of garrison and regimental courts-martial will be transmitted . . . to the department head-quarters for the supervision of the department commander. **1922** PARRISH *Case & Girl* 22 Once possessed of your name and army rank, the department records at Washington furnished all further information. **1948** *Sat. Review* 26 June 12/2 There was the sizzling imbroglio between General B. F. Butler, commissioned by Lincoln as head of the 'Department of New England' . . . and Governor Andrew of Massachusetts.

2. **department store,** a large urban retail store, handling a wide assortment of goods, esp. dry goods, clothing, and house furnishings, grouped into appropriate departments. Also attrib.

[**1847** *Hunt's Merch. Mag.* (N.Y.) XVII. 442 From this desk run tubes, connecting with each department of the store, from the garret to the cellar, so that if a person in any department . . . wishes to communicate with the employer, he can do so without leaving his station.] **1887** in F. PRESBREY *Advertising* (1927) 314 H. Heyn's Department Store. **1947** *Chi. D. Times* 28 Nov. 44/2 A year ago she was notably shy in the presence of department store Santas and could scarcely bring herself to express her Christmas wants.

3. In the names of divisions of the executive branch of the U.S. Government presided over by a cabinet member, usu. with the title of Secretary: (1) **Department of Agriculture,** (2) **Commerce,** (3) **Foreign Affairs,** (4) **Justice,** (5) **Labor,** (6) **State,** (7) **the Interior,** (8) **War.**

(1) **1870** *N.Y. Herald* 15 June 4/4 The Department of Agriculture is engaged in ascertaining by experiment which of these products can be raised within the United States. **1948** *Washington Post* 5 Dec. 23M/3 The Agriculture Department acted yesterday to oppose a requested 8 per cent emergency freight increase.—(2) **1903** *Cin. Enquirer* 14 Feb. 1/7 The President is considering the appointment of Prof. Jeremiah W. Jenks, of Cornell, as the head of the new Bureau of Corporations created by the Department of Commerce. **1943** MENEFEE *Assignment* 298 By 1946, according to a Department of Commerce study, our labor force will have increased by two and one-half millions. — (3) **1789** *Abr. Debates of Cong.* (1857) 94/1 Resolved, That it is the opinion of this committee that there ought to be established. . . . A Department of Foreign Affairs, at the head of which shall be an officer to be called Secretary to the United States for the Department of Foreign Affairs, removable by the President. **1892** HART *Formation of Union* 144 The first executive department to be established was the Department of Foreign Affairs, of which the name was a little later changed to the *Department of State*. — (4) **1870** *N.Y. World* 24 June 1/6 The President concluded, after all, not to veto the act creating the Department of Justice, and reorganizing under it the attorney-general's office and various law offices of the other departments. **1948** *Time* 16 Aug. 17/1 There was strong suspicion that Department of Justice lawyers had not been overanxious to produce evidence which would reflect on a Democratic administration.

(5) **1913** *Boston Transcript* 4 Mar. 2/2 For the new Department of Labor, William Bauchop Wilson of Blossburg, Pa., is a natural choice. **1948** *Time* 1 Nov. 79/1 The Department of Labor reported that food prices dropped 0.6% from mid-August to mid-September. — (6) **1789** WASHINGTON in S. K. Padover *Jefferson* (1942) 169, I was determined . . . to nominate you for the Department of State. **1946** *Chi. D. News* 5 March 8/6 There is a real, imperative need of vigorous leadership and firm statesmanship in the Department of State and the White House to assume moral leadership. — (7) **1849** *U.S. Statutes at Large* IX. 395 There shall be created a new executive department of the government of the United States, to be called the Department of the Interior. **1946** *Chi. D. News* 13 Feb. 5/1 The Department of the Interior must always be on guard against any association of money with politics. — (8) **1789** *Ann. 1st Congress* I. 78, I nominate, . . . for the Department of War, Henry Knox.

As the last term in **canal, complaint, detective, executive, fire, graduate, gulf, health, Home, immigration, Indian, Interior, mountain, Navy, pay, Post-Office, preparatory, shoe, State, state game, Subsistence, Treasury, War, women's department.**

*deposit, *n.*

1. Supplies, provisions, etc., stored for future use; a cache. *Obs.*

1758 WASHINGTON *Writings* II. 68 Lastly, if we advance on both roads by deposites, we must double our number of troops over the mountains. *Ib.* 70 Our next deposite probably will be at Salt Lick. **1837** IRVING *Bonneville* I. 98 Having no established posts and magazines, they [mountain traders and trappers] make these caches or deposits at certain points.

2. a. **deposit bank,** one of the state banks in which funds accruing to the government were deposited by the Secretary of the U.S. Treasury after Pres. Jackson's quarrel with the second U.S. Bank in 1832. *Obs.* b. **deposit slip,** a receipt given one who makes a deposit in a bank.

(a) **1834** C. A. DAVIS *Lett. J. Downing* 101 He is however plaguy wrathy with the deposit banks in New-York makin money so plenty there. **1854** BENTON *30 Years' View* I. 424/2 The deposit banks above all were selected for pressure. — (b) **1938** MENCKEN *Amer. Lang.* 244 An Englishman hasn't a bank-account, but a banking-account. His deposit slip is a paying-in-slip.

As the last term in **blanket, canoe, safe, special, time deposit.**

***deposit,** *v. tr.* To place (food supplies, etc.) where they will be needed later. *Obs.* Cf. ***deposit,** *n.* **1.** — **1805–8** PIKE *Sources Miss.* 54 Deposited one barrel of flour. **1807** GASS *Journal* 184 The Commanding Officer thought that would be sufficient to serve the party, until we should arrive at the Missouri where there is some deposited.

***depositary,** *n.* A depository bank. In full **depositary bank.** — **1886** *Secy. Treas. Rep.* I. 88 One hundred and sixty national banks acted as depositaries during the year, receiving the moneys from collecting officers of the Government. *Ib.*, A number of failures have taken place among the depositary banks. **1918** AGGER *Organized Banking* 219 It was not until recently . . . that payments on government account were made by checks directly drawn on depositary banks.

***depository,** *n.* **1.** =**deposit bank. 2. depository bank,** a bank in which the Treasurer of the United States deposits government funds. — (1) **1838** *United States Mag.* I. 396 The large amounts of public money of which the use was enjoyed by the few banks employed as depositories, excited a general feeling of dissatisfaction. — (2) **1899** in *Cong. Rec.* 1. Feb. (1900) 1383/2 Transfers may be ordered from time to time into the Treasury from depository banks now holding the sum of $80,000,000 of the public moneys.

*depot, *n.*

1. A railroad station.

1832 *22d Cong.* 2 Sess. H.R. Doc. No. 101, 171 The graduation and masonry of the Baltimore and Ohio railroad have been completed as far as to Frederick city, 60 miles . . . from the depôt at Baltimore. **1842** LONGFELLOW in *Life* (1891) I. 415 To borrow the expression of a fellow-traveller, we were 'ticketed through to the depot' (pronouncing the last word so as to rhyme with *teapot*). **1948** CHAPLIN *Wobbly* 43 He coveted the more profitable territory in front of the Western Indiana Depot at Sixty-third and Wallace streets.

2. In combs.: (1) **depot agent,** an employee of a railroad company who has charge of a depot; (2) **carriage,** a carriage used to convey persons to and from a depot; (3) **hotel,** a hotel adjacent to a depot; (4) **master, officer,** =**depot agent;** (5) **platform,** a platform at a depot for facilitating the handling of freight; (6) **wagon,** a

Depot wagon

vehicle used to transport persons and goods to and from a depot.

(1) **1843** *Hunt's Merch. Mag.* VIII. 193 Regulations For The Government of Depot-Agents. **1945** PEARSON *Country Flavor* 20 A good depot agent knows as much news as the R.F.D. man and spreads it around impartially. — (2) **1876** SCUDDER *Dwellers* vi. 93 The Rev. Mr. Lovering had seen the depot carriage stop. — (3) **1878** PINKERTON *Strikers* 142 Engineers, firemen, and off-time baggage-men . . . met mysteriously in little groups at the depot hotel, the machine-shops, . . . and in other localities. — (4) **1862** BROWNE *A. Ward His*

Book 199 'What time does this string of second-hand coffins [the cars] leave?' I inquired of the depot master. **1948** *Time* 1 Nov. 28/1 Depending on who's around, the depot master is mayor, or I am. — **1878** PINKERTON *Strikers* 315 Two of the depot officers mounted the tank, and, drawing their revolvers, threatened the crowd.

(5) **1874** B. F. TAYLOR *World on Wheels* I. xx. 145 Then one money-purse of a mail-bag will be thrown off from a passing train upon the depot platform. — (6) **1906** R. W. CHAMBERS *Fighting Chance* 3 The motor steamed out, honking hoarsely; the depot-wagon followed, leaving the circle at the end of the station empty of vehicles. **1948** RITTENHOUSE *Vehicles* 19 Rockaway or depot wagon. The name of this wagon indicates its customary use.

b. In other combs. of obvious meaning, as **depot building, grounds, house, lands, loafer, lot.**

1881 *Chi. Times* 16 April, The company is constructing a depot building . . . at Leaf River. — **1881** *Mich. Gen. Statutes* I. (1882) 860 When any part of the land of any railroad company in this state, in or adjacent to its depot grounds is not in actual use for depot or other purpose pertaining to the operation of a railroad, [etc.]. — **1833** *Amer. R.R. Jrnl.* II. 164/1 Depot house, car house, and stables. **1880** CABLE *Grandissimes* xxvi. 199 The yellow depot-house of Westwego. — **1839** *Amer. R.R. Jrnl.* VIII. 234 Suitable and convenient *Depot Lands* for the Stations have been secured. — **1930** FERBER *Cimarron* 144 The group had stepped off the passenger coach of the Katy at the town of Wahoo arrayed in such cinder-strewn splendor as to cause the depot loafers to reel. — **1832** *Amer. R.R. Jrnl.* I. 804/2 A small portion of the second and third tracks [are] laid in the depot lot.

As the last term in **emigrating, freight, locomotive, news, passenger, railroad, railway, slave, trading, trapping, union, watering depot.**

dépouille deˈpujə, *n.* Also **depuis.** *W.* [F., a hide.] (See quots.) *Obs.*

1800 COUES *Henry and Thompson Journals* (1897) I. 62 They were waiting for me, with the flesh of two fat cows, whose dépouilles [layers of fat under the skin] were about two inches thick. **1846** DE SMET *Life and Travels* (1905) II. 564 These preparations completed, our meal (dinner and supper the same time), consisting of flour, camas roots, and some buffalo tallow, called *dépouille* by the Canadian mountaineers, is thrown into a large kettle nearly filled with water. **1852** STANSBURY *Gt. Salt Lake* 247 For the first time witnessed the operation of cutting up a buffalo . . after these the 'fleece,' the portion of flesh covering the ribs; the 'depuis,' a broad, fat part extending from the shoulders to the tail.

***depreciate,** *v. intr.* To decrease in value or esteem, orig. and usu. with reference to currency.

1740 W. DOUGLASS *Currencies* 32 If bills were to depreciate after a certain rate, justice might be done. **1780** *Heath P.* 115 The simple resolves of the Court . . . have depreciated in a twofold proportion to the circulating medium. **1874** *Atlantic Mo.* April 440/2 As might have been expected, with the authorization of the new issues the notes began to depreciate. **1889** *Cent.* 1547/1 Real estate is depreciating.

depreciation dɪˌpriʃɪˈeʃən, *n.* A decline or fall in value. Also attrib.

1740 W. DOUGLASS *Currencies*, Depreciations are uncertain. **1788** *Md. Journal* 26 Feb. (Th.), Wanted at said office, Finals, Depreciation Certificates, and every other kind of Paper retaining any kind of value. **1865** *Atlantic Mo.* XV. 190 Bounties had been promised to induce them to disband peacefully, and to compensate them for the depreciation of the currency.

***deputy,** *n.* In combs.: (1) **deputy governor,** one chosen to assist the governor of one of the American colonies, *obs.;* (2) **marshal,** one who assists or acts for a marshal, esp. in later use an assistant to the chief executive officer of a federal judicial district; (3) **president,** an assistant to the president of an American colonial council, *obs.;* (4) **searcher,** an assistant customs officer empowered to search ships, *obs.*

(1) **1629** *Mass. Charter* (1853) 10 There shalbe one Governor, one Deputy Governor, and eighteene Assistants of the same Company. **1781** S. PETERS *Conn.* (1829) 78 By authority of the charter, the freemen choose annually, in May, a Governor, a deputy-Governor, a Secretary . . . and twelve Assistants. — (2) **1791** in IMLAY *Western Territory* (ed. 3) 461 The return made by the deputy-marshal of New-York, shews . . . the precise number of inhabitants that have made settlements in these lands. **1894** ROBLEY *Bourbon Co., Kansas* 84 The existence of this rival court was not to be tolerated by Judge Williams . . . , and . . . he ordered Deputy Marshal Little to organize a posse and dissolve it. — (3) **1648** *Me. Hist. Soc. Coll.* I. 540 The whole assembly referred the examination . . . unto . . . Georg Cleeve, gent., deputy presid[en]t [etc.]. **1698** CHAMBERLAIN *Lithobolia* (1914) 66 The noise of this brought up the Deputy-President's Wife. — (4) **1683** *N.H. Hist. Soc. Coll.* VIII. 159 Edward Randolph did constitute and appoint this deponent deputy-searcher of his Majesty's customs. **1685** *Ib.* 260 Thomas Thurton, Province marshal, and deputy searcher of his Majesty's customs in the said province.

***derail,** *n.* = **derailer.** — **1940** *Quiz* [quest. 81] A derail or derailer is a device designed to guide cars, locomotives and other rolling stock off the rails at a selected location to avoid collisions or other accidents. **1947** *Chi. Tribune* 15 June (Grafic Mag.) 14/4 The derail functioned perfectly, but too late for the three cars and caboose that had cleared it.

derailer diˈrelɚ, *n.* (See quot. 1940.) — **1894** *Columbus* (O.) *Dispatch* 5 Sep., He was about ten feet from the derailer when the cars passed him going toward the Union station like a whirlwind. **1940** [see **derail**].

***derange,** *v. tr.* To remove from office or position. *Obs.* — **1796** MORSE *Univ. Geog.* I. 244 The officers who have been deranged by the several resolutions of Congress, upon the different reforms of the army. **1828** WEBSTER *s.v.* (citing W. H. Sumner), When a general officer resigns or is removed from office, the personal staff appointed by himself are said to be deranged.

***derby,** *n.* A stiff felt hat with a dome-shaped crown and a narrow stiff brim. In full **derby hat.**

1870 *Harper's Bazaar* 5 Nov. 707 The Derby roundcrown felt hat also, with the D'Orsay curve, is worn negligee. **1878** in MARSHALL *Through Amer.* (1881) 255 Many [English tourists wear] various modifications of the Derby, with long, light veils draped thereon with studied carelessness. **1947** *True* Nov. 72/1 He had a huge head . . . usually covered by a derby.

Hence **derbyed, derby-hatted.** *Colloq.*

1905 HOWELLS in *Harper's Mag.* Mar. 560 One of the few cylindered or derbyed heads in the swarming processions of Piccadilly. **1948** CHAPLIN *Wobbly* 22 Later came daring derby-hatted dandies with their first 'high-wheelers,' defying the ridicule of scoffing bystanders.

***derelict,** *a.* and *n.* Remiss in the performance of one's duty, one who has neglected his duty.

1864 *Daily Tel.* (London) 13 Sep., Probably you will think that United States Commissioner Newton was very 'derelict' in his duty. **1872** MARK TWAIN *Sk., Cannibalism in Cars*, The committee has been derelict in its duty. **1888** *Voice* (N.Y.) 3 Jan., The Republicans re-nominated and triumphantly re-elected the derelicts. **1915** HAY in Thayer *Life & Lett. J. Hay* ii. 225 Various other gentlemen think that we are derelict in our duty.

***derrick,** *n.* A towerlike structure erected over a deep bored well, esp. one for oil, in the process of boring it.

Derrick over a well

1861 *Dly. Dispatch* (Richmond, Va.) 30 April 1/4 At the time of the explosion, everything in the neighborhood—sixty or seventy rods—took fire, and shanties, derricks, engine-houses, and dwellings, were at once enveloped in flames. **1909** RICE *Mr. Opp* 11 We'll sink a test well, get up a derrick and a' engine, and have the thing running in no time. **1948** *Time* 21 June 1/2 When they finish drilling an oil well, they ordinarily dismantle the derrick, move it piece-meal to a new location.

b. derrick house, a house in connection with, and adjacent to, a derrick.

1901 *Munsey's Mag.* XXV. 743 The hillsides along Oil Creek were thickly dotted with derrick houses.

derringer ˈdɛrɪndʒɚ, *n.* Also †**Deringer, Derringer.** [f. Henry *Derringer*, its inventor.] A short pistol of large caliber for use at close quarters. In full **derringer pistol.** Also attrib.

1853 Brewerton *With Kit Carson* (1930) 188 Upon the board was displayed . . . a preventive to interference . . . in the shape of Bowie knives, 'Derringers,' and 'six-shooters.' **1854** Bartlett *Personal Narr.* I. iii. 48 My carriage driver carried a pair of Deringer pistols. **1948** *Chi. Tribune* 7 March 1. 38/6 As delicate as the ladies who once casually carried them in hand muffs are the small single shot derringers, developed by Henry Derringer, of Philadelphia.

derringer 'dɛrɪndʒɚ, *v. tr.* To shoot. *Rare.* — **1907** S. E. White *Arizona Nights* 167, I mighty near derringered him as he lay.

One form of derringer

***descender,** *n.* (See quot.) *Rare.* — **1813** *Niles' Reg.* V. Add. 11/2 Jonathan Ellicott . . . had invented several ways of conveying wheat, flour or other substance . . . by the substance to be removed, falling on the top of a band, revolving on rollers or pullies, which was turned by the gravitation of such substances, which he called a descender.

***description,** *n.* A brief account of the exact location and the boundaries of a piece of land; also the land itself. *Colloq.* — **1857** Gove *Letters* 101 I enclose you a list of my lands, and have learned to show the machinery of descriptions; don't you think I have made it plain? **1902** White *Blazed Trail* xix, The investors would become possessed of certain 'descriptions' lying in this country, all right enough. *Ib.* xxili, I have some descriptions I wish to buy in.

deseret 'dɛzəˌrɛt, *n.* [A word coined in the *Book of Mormon.* See quot. 1830.]

1. A honeybee.

1830 *Book of Mormon* (1920) Ether ii. 3 And they did also carry with them deseret, which, by interpretation, is a honey-bee; and thus they did carry with them swarms of bees. **1934** Shankle *State Names* 149 The word Deseret, meaning *the honeybee,* is taken from the *Book of Mormons* [*sic*]. **1947** [see next].

2. (*cap.*) Utah Territory, or Salt Lake City.

1849 *Whig Almanac 1850* 51 If Congress ratifies the Constitution of Deseret, two Senators and a Representative will soon be chosen from there. **1883** *Harper's Mag.* Oct. 705/1 What a strangely interesting city it is, this 'Deseret' of the Latter-Day Saints, which ordinary men and women who live outside the Utah territory, call Salt Lake City! **1947** *This Week Mag.* 18 July 5/1 'Deseret,' the Mormons called their Promised Land in the West. In the Book of Mormon, it means 'honey-bee'—a symbol of the selfless, co-operative industriousness by which the Saints managed to sustain themselves while spreading the gospel.

b. *State of Deseret,* Utah Territory as organized in 1850 (see quot. 1947).

1850 *Deseret News* (Salt Lake City) 15 July 7/1 The Mormons . . . give to their new dominions the name of 'The State of Deseret,' a mysterious appellation derived from their religious dialect and signifying the land of the honey-bee or of industry and all kindred virtues. **1947** *Time* 21 July 20/2 The Mormon State of Deseret, which encompassed Utah, a corner of California and a piece of Wyoming, prospered.

3. Deseret alphabet, (see quot. 1857).

1857 *Alameda Co. Gaz.* (San Leandro, Calif.) 10 Oct. 1/2 In order to circumvent the enemies of the Saints, Brigham has invented a new

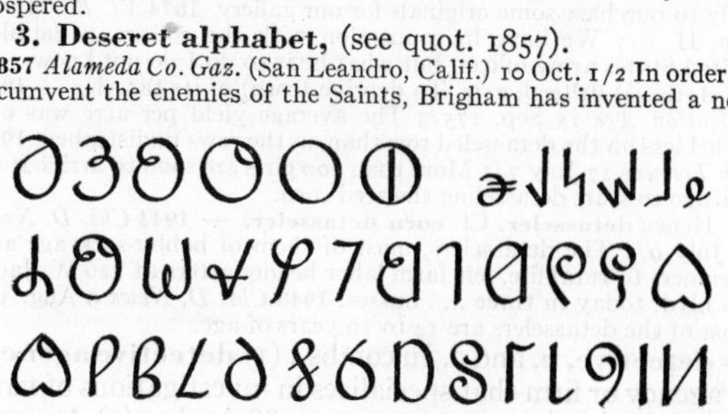

Deseret alphabet

alphabet, which he terms the 'Deseret Alphabet.' It contains forty-one characters, which are entirely new to the outside world. **1860** *Mountaineer* (Salt Lake City) 25 Feb. 106/6 The regents were instructed to visit the schools throughout the Territory . . . recommending everywhere attention to the Deseret Alphabet. **1944** *Utah Hist. Quart.* Jan.–Apr. 99 It appears to be well established that George D. Watt, an English convert to Mormonism, was the man chiefly responsible for the Deseret Alphabet.

Deseretian ˌdɛzə'riʃən, *n.* An inhabitant of Deseret, a Mormon. *Obs.* — **1850** *Deseret News* (Salt Lake City) 10 Aug. 66/1 The bees save honey, & the wise virgins keep oil in their lamps: so Deseretians, live by the golden rule. *Ib.* 16 Nov. 156/2 The Deseretians would willingly lend a hand to help his excellency.

***desert,** *n.* In the names of birds and other creatures found in desert regions: (1) **desert ant,** (2) **black throat,** (3) **brush rat,** (4) **deer mouse,** (5) **gray fox,** (6) **mule deer,** (7) **pocket rat,** (8) **quail,** (9) **song sparrow,** (10) **sparrow,** (11) **sparrow hawk,** (12) **tortoise,** (13) **woodrat.**

(1) **1878** Beadle *Western Wilds* 250 All the hillocks made by the desert ants are found to be dotted with garnets. — (2) **1917** *Birds of Amer.* III. 48 The western race is named justly the Desert Sparrow or Desert Black-throat (*Amphispiza bilineata deserticola*). — (3) **1917** *Mammals of Amer.* 225 Desert Brush Rat.—*Neotoma desertorum.* Merriam. Pelage very soft; tail short, brownish buff above with mixture of black hairs. California, Nevada, Oregon, Utah, Colorado in desert areas. — (4) **1917** *Mammals of Amer.* 239 Desert Deer Mouse. —*Peromyscus eremicus eremicus* (Baird). Size medium; tail very long, longer than head and body; colors pale. Desert regions of southeastern California eastward to western Texas.

(5) **1917** *Mammals of Amer.* 80 Desert Gray Fox.—*Urocyon cinereoargenteus texensis* Mearns. Paler than the Eastern Gray Fox; ears longer; tail longer. Texas. [**1948** *Pacific Discovery* March–April 8/2 A small gray desert fox will be a sharp-eared shadow behind the moonlight haloed knobs of the cholla cactus, now here, now there, then gone.] — (6) **1917** *Mammals of Amer.* 15 Desert Mule Deer.—*Odocoileus hemionus eremicus* (Mearns.) Very pale, large, with heavy horns. Western Desert Tract of the United States. — (7) **1917** *Mammals of Amer.* 259 Desert Pocket Rat.—*Dipodomys deserti deserti* Stephens. Very large and pale; total length, 13.5 inches Mojave and Colorado Deserts, California. — (8) **1877** J. S. Campion *On Frontier* 251 On going to the water holes in the morning we see flocks of the pied or desert quail coming to the puddles. — (9) **1917** *Birds of Amer.* III. 52 The slender bill of the Desert Song Sparrow (*Melospiza melodia fallax*) is like that of the Mountain Song Sparrow.

(10) **1917** [see **desert black throat**]. — (11) **1917** *Birds of Amer.* II. 91 The Desert Sparrow Hawk (*Falco sparverius phalæna*) is larger than the stock form, with longer tail. — (12) **1933** Harrington *Gypsum Cave, Nev.* 10 The desert tortoise was fairly abundant. **1947** Carr *Desert Parade* 57 The desert tortoise does not thrive in captivity. — (13) **1908** Bailey *Harmful & Beneficial Mammals* 18 The desert wood rat is a native of the arid region and is the only species found in the valleys of western Nevada.

b. In the names of plants found in desert regions: (1) **desert almond,** (2) **bush,** (3) **catalpa,** (4) **cedar,** (5) **flowering willow,** (6) **holly,** (7) **juniper,** (8) **lily,** (9) **mistletoe,** (10) **oak,** (11) **peach,** (12) **tea,** (13) **trumpet,** (14) **weed,** (15) **willow.**

(1) **1913** *Agric. Research Jrnl.* Nov., [These] small downy fruits with thin dry flesh have won for them the local names 'wild almond' in the Great Basin region, wild peach or desert almond for another form in the Mohave Desert. **1925** Jepson *Flowering Plants Calif.* 507 P[runus] fasciculata Gray. Desert Almond. — (2) **1897** Sudworth *Arborescent Flora* 225 *Parkinsonia microphylla* . . . Desert Bush, (Ariz.). — (3) **1940** Jaeger *Calif. Deserts* 188 In the late spring and summer days the desert catalpa or so-called desert willow (*Chilopsis linearis*) cheers the wayfarer with its pendant green leaves and its wealth of gay, pink, tubular flowers. — (4) **1910** Jepson *Silva of Calif.* 63 The 'Desert Cedar' of the Colorado Desert is *Adenostema sparsifolium* Torr., a shrub of the Rose Family.

(5) **1875** *Amer. Naturalist* IX. 139 Along the course of this sandy bed, the 'desert flowering willow' (*Chilopsis linearis*) was abundant. — (6) **1915** Armstrong *Western Wild Flowers* 536 Desert Holly [is] an odd little desert plant, only two or three inches high, with stiff, smooth, dull bluish-green leaves, with prickly edges. **1948** *Desert Mag.* July 35/1 Joshua trees, . . . smoke trees, desert holly and indigo bush are protected under the ordinance. — (7) **1897** Sudworth *Arborescent Flora* 98 *Juniperus californica utahensis.* . . . Common Names [include] . . . Desert Juniper. — (8) **1917** Saunders *Western Wild Flowers* 4 The deep-seated bulbs of the Desert Lily used to form an item of importance in the diet of the Desert Indians. **1946** *Desert Mag.* March 30/1 In the Cronise area . . . a fairly mild and moist winter already has assured that locality of its usual fine display of desert lilies. — (9) **1946** *Desert Mag.* April 28/3 Among the most conspicuous were Rock Hibiscus, . . . Desert Tea (Ephedra), Desert Mistletoe, Desert Holly, Burro Weed and creosote Bush.

(10) **1894** *Amer. Folk-Lore* VII. 99 *Quercus Wislizeni,* . . . desert oak, S.E. Cal. — (11) **1925** Jepson *Flowering Plants Calif.* 507 P[runus] andersonii Gray. Desert Peach. **1942** Van Dersal *Ornamental Amer. Plants* 155 Highly ornamental in full bloom and probably

one of the best shrubs in the United States is the desert peach. — (12) **1946** [see **desert mistletoe**]. — (13) **1917** SAUNDERS *Western Flower Guide* 42 The inflated stalks, swelling upward gradually like a musical horn, explain the popular designation Desert Trumpet. **1937** *Range Plant Handbook* w69 Desert-trumpet (*E[riogonum] inflatum*), sometimes called Indianpipe weed, is another interesting annual, which ranges from Colorado and New Mexico to California. — (14) **1873** BEADLE *Undevel. West* 639 Our horses were hungry enough to chew sand-burrs and desert weed.

(15) **1884** SARGENT *Rep. Forests* 116 *Chilopsis saligna* . . . Desert Willow. **1946** *So. Sierran* Dec. 2/3 The desert willow . . . is noticeable for its flower, a large, fragile, orchid-like blossom, white marked with lavender and yellow, with crinkled edges of petals.

c. In miscellaneous combs.: (1) **desert claim,** a claim to public land in the semi-arid regions of the West; (2) **Indians,** (see quot.); (3) **Land Act,** an act of Congress, passed in 1877, permitting individuals who agreed to expend a specified amount per acre for irrigation and reclamation to purchase larger amounts of government land in the semi-arid regions than had previously been possible; (4) **land entry,** the filing of a claim for desert land; (5) **Land Law,** =**Desert Land Act;** (6) **pavement,** *W.* (see quots.); (7) **polish,** (see quot. and cf. **desert varnish**); (8) **rat,** a person who has lived in desert regions for a long time; (9) **varnish,** (see quot. 1904 and cf. **desert polish**).

(1) **1911** WRIGHT *Winning Barbara Worth* 195 To prove up on these desert claims the government compels them to have the water. — (2) **1885** JACKSON *Century of Dishonor* 506 The Indians known as the Desert Indians are chiefly of the Cahuilla tribe, and are all under the control of an aged chief named Cabezon. — (3) **1887** *Courier-Journal* 20 Feb. 2/5 On the bill repealing the pre-emption, timber-culture and desert-land acts, reported a continued disagreement. **1943** HOWARD *Montana* 110 Homestead laws were flagrantly violated, often with the aid of corrupt local officials, especially the Desert Land Act. — (4) **1908** *Indian Laws & Tr.* III. 381 If any person making homestead or desert-land entry shall fail to comply with the law and the regulations under which his entry is made, or shall fail to make final proof, . . . he shall forfeit all money which he may have paid on the land. **1914** *Cyclo. Amer. Govt.* 586 Desert land entries on coal lands are limited to 160 acres

(5) **1880** MCELRATH *Yellowstone Valley* 81 Under the Desert-Land law an entry may be made by any person of requisite age, a citizen, or who has filed his declaration to become one. — (6) [**1901** VAN DYKE *Desert* 39 Beyond Yuma on the Colorado there are thousands of acres of mosaic pavement . . . so hard that a horse's hoofs will make no impression upon it.] **1939** PICKWELL *Desert* 41/2 With the wind's help, this same gravel is bedded down in places with rain into the interesting and strikingly level desert 'pavements.' — (7) **1903** GEIKIE *Text-bk. Geol.* (ed. 4) 436 On the sandy plains of Wyoming, Utah . . . surfaces even of such hard materials as chalcedony are etched into furrows and wrinkles, acquiring at the same time a peculiar and characteristic glaze ('desert polish'). — (8) **1907** *Putnam's Mo.* July 482/2 This [is] the camp that had . . . lured . . . desert rats, dusty prospectors, mysteriously called as by some scent to this new ground of gold. **1947** *So. Sierran* April 4/1 The Sierra Club desert rats appropriated Mule Canyon for 'basecamp' and Odessa Canyon for maneuvers. — (9) **1904** *U.S. Geol. Survey* Monograph 47, 547 In arid regions the hardened film has frequently been smoothed by the wind-blown sand, so as to present a polished surface. Such polished hardened films are known as 'desert varnish.' **1925** BRYAN *Papago Country* 85 Many of the granite boulders have a brown or blackish color from the so-called 'desert varnish.'

As the last term in **alkali, American, Great, Nevada, sage, sagebrush, sand, western desert.**

***designation,** *n.* The authoritative allotment of ground for oyster culture. — **1881** INGERSOLL *Oyster Industry* 66 The first designation [in the vicinity of New Haven] was made in April, 1864, and all the suitable ground in West river and in the harbor was soon set apart.

***desk,** *n.*

1. The department of a newspaper in which copy is edited. Also attrib.

1927 U. SINCLAIR *Money Writes* 18 The reporters who write up the sensational event—each one is hoping to attract the attention of the 'desk.' **1932** *Dict. Amer. Biog.* IX. 147 For a time he was in complete editorial charge but in 1857 he sold out his financial interest and ceased to hold a regular desk position, though he continued as a contributor.

2. In combs.: (1) **desk clerk,** =**clerk 3;** (2) **delivery,** delivery at or across a desk; (3) **mate,** the boy or girl who shares a desk in school with another; (4) **room,** space for a desk in a business office, also transf.; (5) **secretary,** (see quot. 1935); (6) **sergeant,** the police officer serving at the headquarters desk.

(1) **1947** *Prairie Schooner* Winter 459 My desk clerk says he registered her in around eight o'clock last night. — (2) **1887** *Postal Laws* 393 If the addressee is a box-holder all of his registered mail should be held for desk delivery. — (3) **1902** G. M. MARTIN *Emmy Lou* 83 Hattie, Emmy Lou's desk-mate, watched the door. — (4) **1868** KIMBALL *Undercurrents* 9, I occupied an office—no, I had 'desk-room' in a basement office. **1919** CADY *Rhymes of Vt.* (1923) 19 The town lot booster only needs A little deskroom in his hat.

(5) **1907** *Springfield W. Republican* 7 Nov. 16 C. F. Atkins has been appointed desk secretary at the central Young Men's Christian Association. **1935** HORWILL *Mod. Amer. Usage* 101 In Am. *desk secretary* denotes a secretary whose duties lie wholly within the office, as distinct from a *field secretary*. — (6) **1908** MCGAFFEY *Show-Girl* 89 All he got was a clout on the head from the desk sergeant. **1948** *Miami* (Okla.) *News-Record* 4 July 19/1 'Ask the desk sergeant,' said the turnkey.

As the last term in **copy, sacred desk.**

deskism ˈdɛskɪzəm, *n.* The manner or bearing of one who sits at a desk. *Rare.* — **1840** POE *Man of Crowd* Wks. (1914) II. 64 Setting aside a certain dapperness of carriage, which may be termed *deskism* for want of a better word.

desperadoism ˌdɛspəˈredoˌɪzəm, *n.* The acts of desperadoes or a condition brought about by desperadoes. — **1872** MARK TWAIN *Roughing It* xlviii. 343 My idea, when I began this chapter, was to say something about desperadoism in the 'flush times' of Nevada. **1896** *Atlantic Mo.* Jan. 66 Do not thrust desperadoism upon them.

destitute rations. Rations for those who are destitute, esp. such rations issued by the federal government to those in the South whom the Civil War left without resources. *Obs.* Cf. **draw day.** — **1865** *Nation* I. 209 And this seems to be plainly shown by the reports, drawn up by Government officials, of the issue to citizens of what are known as 'Destitute Rations.'

***destroying,** *a.*

1. ***Destroying Angel,** a member of an alleged secret militant organization among the Mormons; *pl.* the society composed of such members. Now *hist.* Cf. **Danite, Mormon Destroying Angel.**

1838 *Peoria* (Ill.) *Reg.* 24 Nov. 1/5 Among many other things, they had assembled them into three different societies, called Danites, Gideonites, and the destroying Angels, consisting of about 150 men altogether. **1843** *Nauvoo* (Ill.) *Times & Seasons* 15 April 167 'Oh,' says he, 'he is one of Joe Smith's "destroying angels"; my life is not safe here.' **1943** DEVOTO *Yr. of Decis.* 83 So in 1842 O. P. Rockwell, one of the Sons of Dan (the 'Destroying Angels' of ten-cent fiction), crept up to a window in Boggs's house and shot him—not quite fatally.

2. Destroying Band, (see quot. and cf. prec.). *Obs.*

1838 *Test* (Rushville, Ill.) 12 Dec. 3/3 In order to make the stubborn or honest part of the Mormons conform to this rule, the band of Danites, the band of Gideon, and the Destroying Band were organized by Jo. Smith and Rigdon.

***detail,** *v. tr.* To designate or appoint (a soldier) for some special duty. Also transf.

1703 *N.H. Prov. Papers* (1868) II. 404 Ordered, that sixty men be detailed out of the several towns of this Province, to be improved for the destroying and suppressing of the French and Indian enemy. **1838** HALIBURTON *Clockmaker* 2 Ser. xi. 161 We propose detailing you to Italy to purchase some originals for our gallery. **1874** *Vt. Bd. Agric. Rep.* II. 617 We have in connection with the college, a detailed United States army officer, but what he is to do I do not know.

detassel dɪˈtæsl, *v. tr.* To deprive (corn) of its tassels. — **1892** *Irrigation Age* 15 Sep. 175/3 The average yield per acre was one bushel less on the detasseled row than on the rows undisturbed. **1947** *Chi. Tribune* 17 July 7/3 More than 100 girls are soon to arrive from Chicago to start detasseling the seed corn.

Hence **detasseler.** Cf. **corn detasseler.** — **1944** *Chi. D. News* 14 July 9/1 The detasselers, most of them of bobby-sock age and foreigners to rural life, left farm labor headquarters at 226 W. Jackson blvd. today in three . . . busses. **1948** *Chi. D. News* 9 Aug. 3/2 Most of the detasselers are 14 to 16 years of age.

***detective,** *n.* and *a.* In combs.: (1) **detective agency,** an agency or firm that specializes in investigations of various kinds; (2) **camera,** (see quot. 1889), *obs.;* (3) **department,** a department of a police force that does detective work; (4) **force,** a police force made up of detectives; (5) **story,** a story telling of detective work, also transf.

(1) **1872** CRAPSEY *Nether Side N.Y.* 56 All the large commercial cities are now liberally provided with 'Detective Agencies,' as they are called. **1904** O. HENRY *Cabbages & Kings* (1916) 241 Shorty O'Day, of the Columbia Detective Agency, lost his position. — (2)

1887 *Cent. Mag.* XXXIV. 723/1 After being assured by excellent authorities that the idea was absurd, Mr. William Schmid, of Brooklyn, N.Y., made the first of the 'detective' cameras. **1889** *Harper's Mag.* Jan. 291/2 In special cameras, designed to be carried about in the hand, and commonly called 'detective cameras,' shutters of high speed are generally employed. — **(3) 1892** *Rocky Mt. Celt* (Globeville, Colo.) 27 Aug. 2/7 There are gentlemen in the detective department, but they were few and far between during the conclave. — **(4) 1849** *Alta California* (S.F.) 24 Dec. 3/3 The badge is of such a character that, when it becomes necessary to employ any of them [policemen], as a detective force, they can be removed. **1854** *Pioneer* (S.F.) Dec. 330 The advantages of such a plan in giving efficiency and celerity to the services of a Detective Force are too manifest to require at our hands any lengthy exposition.

(5) 1883 Anna K. Green (*title*), X Y Z, a Detective Story. **1948** *Fargo* (N.D.) *Forum* 28 Sep. 6/2 Griffith . . . has branded the accusations as a 'detective story.'

As the last term in **cattle, house, store detective.**

* **detector,** *n.* =**counterfeit detector.**

1832 *Boston Transcript* 26 July 2/1 It is stated in Bicknell's Detector, that the city was well supplied with apples, pears [etc.]. **1850** *Quincy* (Ill.) *Whig* 12 Nov. 4/2 The clerk looked at the bill, examined one of Presbry's Detectors, and then found his twenty fully described as a well known counterfeit! **1893** *Cong. Rec.* 25 Aug. 936/2 Every man had to carry a detector with him. **1949** *Chi. Sun. Tribune* 30 Jan. 1. 4/4 The Detector described in complete detail every United States and Canadian counterfeit known or believed to be in current circulation. It also describes bogus issues of more ancient date.

As the last term in **bank-note, lie detector.**

Detroiter dɪˈtrɔɪtɚ, *n.* A native or inhabitant of Detroit, Mich. — **1886** *Chi. Tribune* 9 May 11/1 The Detroiters played a remarkably pretty fielding game. **1947** Perry *Cities of America* 120 Detroiters, just like other people, enjoy a frolic now and then.

detur ˈditɜ, *n.* [L., "let there be given."] (See quots. 1797, 1943.)

1797 C. Prentiss *Fugitive Ess.* 90 By the will of a gentleman of fortune some time since deceased, a number of books were to be distributed, with impartiality, to a few of the best scholars in the two senior classes: which books have obtained the name of *Deturs.* **1836** Lowell *Letters* I. 10 The 'deturs' have been given out, and I have got Akenside's Poems. **1943** *Off. Reg. Harvard Univ.: Expenses and Financial Aids* 31 July 45 Deturs. Part of the income of a bequest from Edward Hopkins, a London merchant who came to America in 1637, is used in the purchase of books called 'Deturs,' one of which is given to every student in Harvard College who wins for the first time a scholarship in the First Group.

* **develop,** *v.* **1.** *intr.* To come into sight. *Rare.* **2.** *tr.* and *intr.* To become or make known or manifest.

Horwill, *Amer. Usage* 102, says sense **2.** is found in Jane Austen, but is now obs. in Eng.

(1) 1859 *Harper's Mag.* Aug. 311/1 In due time the stage, a very barbarous cart, developed, and we disappeared. — **(2) 1864** Webster 366/1 The plans of the conspirators develop. **1900** *Publishers' Circular* 15 Dec. 617/2 The inquiry did not develop any new facts. **1930** *Durant* (Okla.) *Democrat* 30 Dec. 6/6 It has developed that James Lucey, cobbler-philosopher, received five double eagles for Christmas in an unmarked package that contained no cord.

* **devil,** *n.*

1. The cougar, *Felis concolor. Rare.*

*a***1862** Thoreau *Maine Woods* (1894) 381 He answered with a mysterious air, and in a half whisper, 'Devil [that is, Indian Devil, or cougar] lodges about here—very bad animal.'

2. In combs.: (1) **devil-dance,** among Indians, a dance regarded as inspired by evil spirits; (2) **dog,** (see quots.); (3) **Devil's Backbone,** a name applied to various ridges (see quots.); (4) **'s coffin,** (see quot.), *obs.;* (5) **'s corkscrew,** a very large fossil, erect and spiral, found in the Bad Lands; (6) **'s currency,** (see quot.), *obs.;* (7) **'s dye,** (see quot.), *obs.;* (8) **send,** something regarded as having been sent by the devil, *rare;* (9) **'s fire,** will-o'-the-wisp, *rare;* (10) **'s food,** a rich, dark chocolate cake, usu. attrib., cf. **angel cake,** * **angel('s) food (cake)**; (11) **'s footsteps,** (see quot.), *obs.;* (12) **'s house,** (see quot.), *obs.;* (13) **'s lane,** (see quot. 1888), *colloq.;* (14) **'s oven,** (see quots.), *obs.;* (15) **'s slide,** (see quot. 1869); (16) **'s tea-table,** (see quot.); (17) **wagon,** an automobile or locomotive.

(1) 1883 Wright *Among Alaskans* 133 The converted Indians, at other times so bold, shrank from intermeddling with the madness of a devil-dance, and warned her to desist from a hopeless errand. **1937** *Southwestern Lore* Sep. 34 The Apaches in their Devil Dance are a whirl of diabolical frenzy, in sharp contrast to the deliberate and fanciful figures of the Evergreen Dance in which deer, buffalo, and sheep are apparently trying to evade the watchful eyes of hunters armed with bows and arrows. — **(2) 1919** Mencken *Amer. Lang.* 333 *Teufelhunde* (*devil-dogs*), for the American marines, was invented by an American correspondent; the Germans never used it. **1936** Mencken *Amer. Lang.* 574 The term *devil-dogs,* often applied to the Marines during the World War, was supposed to be a translation of the German *teufelhunde.* During the fighting around Chateau Thierry, in June and July, 1918, the Marines were heavily engaged, and the story went at the time that the Germans, finding them very formidable, called them *teufelhunde.* But I have been told by German officers who were in that fighting that no such word was known in the German army. — **(3) 1876** *West Coast Signal* (Eureka, Calif.) 12 July 3/3 The 'Devil's Backbone' was a ridge which ran parallel with the river for several miles and was vertebrated—that is, had a succession of high points and depressions, alternately. **1924** Deam *Shrubs of Indiana* 271 Grimes collected his specimen from the dry ledge at the 'Devil's Backbone' along Sugar Creek. — **(4) 1882** D. Kemp *Yacht Sailing* xvi. (1884) 258 The home of the sneak-boat, or sneak box, or devil's coffin, and the contrivance is indifferently termed, is Barnegat Bay.

(5) 1892 [*Nebraska*] *University Studies* I. 303 Notwithstanding its inelegance, the name 'Devil's corkscrew,' bestowed by the ranchmen, is appropriate and descriptive. **1909** *Cent. Supp.* 341 Daimonelix, though known for years to the cowboys and ranchmen as the *devil's corkscrew* was first definitely described by Erwin H. Barbour, State geologist of Nebraska, in 1891. — **(6) 1943** Crow *Amer. Customer* 153 The New Englanders, . . . were greatly shocked by this chicanery and advised the Indians not to accept the steel-drilled wampum, which they called 'devil's currency.' — **(7) 1863** E. Kirke *Southern Friends* 49 The latter region . . . was absolutely packed with thirsty neighbors imbibing certain fluids known at the South as 'blue ruin,' 'bust-head,' . . . and 'devil's dye,' at the rate of a 'bit' a glass. — **(8)** *a***1861** Winthrop *Canoe & Saddle* 11 There had come . . . a devilsend of a lumber brig, with liquor of the fieriest. — **(9) 1876** M. Twain *Tom Sawyer* IX. 88 (R.), 'Look! See there!' whispered Tom. 'What is it?' 'It's devil's fire. Oh, Tom, this is awful.'

(10) 1905 *Granville Centennial Cook Bk.* 51. **1945** *Chi. D. News* 11 Jan. 19/6 9″ Devilsfood cakes Ea. 59c. **1948** *Minneapolis Morn. Tribune* 28 Sep. 10/5 Don't bother with fussy devils food recipes! — **(11) 1860** Holmes *Professor* viii. 235 The first was a series of marks called the 'Devil's footsteps,' These were patches of sand in the pastures where no grass grew. — **(12) 1809** Weems *Marion* (1833) 47 If there was a devil's house (a dram shop) hard by, you might be sure to see *that* crowded. — **(13) 1872** Eggleston *End of World* iii. 27 His refusal to join fences had resulted in that crooked arrangement, known as a 'devil's lane' on three sides of his farm. **1888** *Cent. Mag.* XXXVI. 82/2 Where two of their fields joined without an intervening road they had not been able even to build a line fence together; but each man laid up a rail fence on the very edge of his own land, and the salient angles of the two hostile fences stood so near together that a half-grown pig could not have passed between. This is what is called, in the phrase of the country, a 'devil's lane,' because it is a monument of bad neighborhood. — **(14) 1826** Flint *Recoll.* 95 Opposite 'the Tower' is another bold bluff, on the Illinois shore, called the 'Devil's oven.' **1843** [see **devil's mare** in **4.** below].

(15) 1869 Muir *First Summer in Sierra* (1911) 202 Narrow slot-like gorges extend across the summit at right angles, which look like lanes, formed evidently by the erosion of less resisting beds. They are usually called 'devil's slides,' though they lie far above the region usually haunted by the devil. **1948** *Sierra Club Bul.* March 127 The other [accident occurred] during a regularly scheduled Sierra Club trip to Devils Slide, San Mateo County. — **(16) 1893** Leland *Memoirs* 304 Very often the summits of the hills were crowned with round towers. On the Ohio River there is a group of these shaped like segments of a truncated cone, and 'corniced' with another piece reversed. . . . These are called 'Devil's Tea-tables.' — **(17) 1904** *N.Y. Ev. Post* 26 Aug. 6 The name of 'devil wagon' in itself has done something to change the attitude of the man on the street toward the automobile. **1906** *Out West* Feb. 101 Several Indians were made permanently 'good' before they decided to let the 'devil-wagon' go on its way unmolested.

3. In the names of plants: (1) **devil club,** =**devil's club;** (2) **grass,** any one of various troublesome, rapidly spreading grasses, as joint grass, couch grass, etc.; (3) **'s apron,** any one of several varieties of kelp having leaves shaped somewhat like an apron; (4) * **'s bit, bite,** a popular name for various plants such as blazing star, button snakeroot, etc.; (5) **'s bread,** a shelf fungus; (6) **'s claw,** (*a*) (see quot.), (*b*) =**unicorn plant;** (7) **'s club,** (*a*) the spiny shrub, *Oplopanax horridus,* of the western states, (*b*) a Hercules'-club, *Aralia spinosa,* of the eastern states; (8) **'s cream pitcher,** prob. the pitcher plant *q.v.;* (9) **'s lettuce,** some now unidentifiable plant, *obs.;* (10) * **'s walking stick,** =**devil's club** (*b*); (11)

('s) weed, used locally for any one of various troublesome weeds, as the king devil, wild lettuce, the nailrod; (12) **wood,** a tree the wood of which is exceptionally difficult to cut or split, esp. the American olive, *Osmanthus americanus*, cf. **bois de diable, vine maple.**

(1) **1944** *New Yorker* 7 Oct. 38/2 It's a jungle, a trackless forest of Douglas fir with a ground of devil clubs, chinquapin and other brush. — (2) **1870** WARNER *Summer in Garden* vii, To sow the lawn with interlacing snake-grass (the botanical name of which, somebody writes me, is devil-grass). **1872** *Vt. Bd. Agric. Rep.* I. 289 *Triticum repens.* Its various English names, *Couch*, . . . *Witch* and *Devil Grass*, attest how widespread it is becoming. — (3) **1858** HOLMES *Autocrat* 190 As I don't want my wreck to be washed up on one of the beaches, in company with devil's-aprons, bladder-weeds . . . and bleached crab-shells, I turn about. **1948** YOUNGKEN *Pharmacognosy* 71 The kelp *Laminaria saccharina* or Devil's Apron [is] a source of iodine and algin. — (4) **1736** *N.J. Archives* XI. 446 To drink give a decoction of Devil's bitt or Robbins plantain. **1894** *Amer. Folk-Lore* VII. 92 *Liatris scariosa*, . . . Devil's bite, Concord, Mass. **1931** CLUTE *Plants* 82 Our own *Aletris farinosa* is one of the few devil's bits still used in medicine.

(5) **1907** *St. Nicholas* July 846/1 'Shelves,' often called 'devil's bread,' . . . grow on woodland stumps and trees and logs. — (6) (*a*) **1897** SUDWORTH *Arborescent Flora* 250 *Acacia greggi*. . . . Common names [include] . . . Devil's Claws. (Nev.). (*b*) **1912** LUMHOLTZ *New Trails* 353 The pods of the *martynia* (devil's claw), split in two, furnish the black part of the texture. **1948** *Chr. Sci. Mon.* 22 April 3/3 The decorative pattern is achieved by weaving in unbleached fibers of natural green, or perhaps black fibers from the devil's claw-pod. — (7) (*a*) **1885** *Cent. Mag.* April 836 A noticeable plant, called the devil's club from the brier-like character of its stem, spread out leaves as large as a Panama hat. **1948** *Field & Stream* July 54/1 You don't really appreciate solid earth until you've slogged daylong across seemingly endless muskegs broken only by dense thickets and garnished with devil's-club. (*b*) **1931** CLUTE *Plants* 83 Another thorny species is the devil's walking-stick or devil's club (*Aralia spinosa*). — (8) **1838** *S. Lit. Messenger* IV. 318/2 Often, in learning the common name of a flower or plant, we learn something of its character or use, 'bitter sweet,' 'devil's cream-pitcher,' or 'fever-bush,' for example. — (9) **1843** OLIVER *Eight Months* 71 Anything very singular in nature is ascribed to the devil, as 'devil's oven,' 'devil's lettuce,' [etc.].

(10) **1928** BAILEY *Cyclo. Horticulture* 344/1 *A*[*ralia*] *spinosa*, Linn. Angelica Tree. Hercule's Club. Devil's Walking-stick. **1942** TEHON *Native Ill. Shrubs* 211 The Devil's-Walkingstick . . . is a large, erect shrub up to 20 feet high with stems covered with tight bark and many strong, straight, or curved spines. — (11) **1731** J. SECCOMB *Father Abbey's Will* x, Some Devil's Weed, And Burdock Seed, To season well your Porridge. **1877** *Vt. Bd. Agric. Rep.* IV. 138 The pimpernel . . . in some States grows in old fields, and among grain, where I have heard it called 'devil weed.' **1894** *Amer. Folk-Lore* VII. 91 *Aster diffusus*, . . . white devil, wire-weed, devil weed, . . . West Va. *Ib.* 92 *Lactuca Canadensis*, . . . Horse-weed, Devil's iron-weed, Devil's weed. West Va. — (12) **1832** BROWNE *Sylva* 225 The wood . . . when perfectly dry is excessively hard and very difficult to cut and split: hence is derived the name of Devil Wood. **1938** VAN DERSAL *Native Woody Plants* 175 Devilwood . . . [is] usually a large shrub to small tree or rarely a large tree; evergreen; often occurs in sandy soil.

b. In similar combs. sufficiently defined in the quots., as (1) ∗**devil's apple,** (2) **ear,** (3) **fig,** (4) **grandmother,** (5) **hopvine,** (6) **horns,** (7) **ironweed,** (8) **paintbrush,** (9) **pincushion,** (10) **shoestrings,** (11) ∗**snuffbox.**

(1) **1793** *Columbian Centinel* 26 Oct., Several children have very much injured themselves, by eating the seeds of Stramonium, or Thorn-Apple, commonly called Devil's Apple. **1876** HOBBS *Bot. Hand-Book* 31 Devil's apple, the fruit of Datura Stramonium. **1931** CLUTE *Plants* 84 The devil's apple is often reputed to be the plant which we call the mandrake (*Podophyllum peltatum*). This, however, is a case of mistaken identity. Our plant, though quite harmless, happens to resemble the poisonous mandrake of Europe (*Mandragora*) and thus bears the disparaging name. — (2) **1845** S. JUDD *Margaret* i. 5 It was a wake-robin, commonly known as dragon root, devil's ear, or, Indian turnip. **1907** LYONS *Plant Names* 50 A[*risaema*] triphyllum . . . Jack-in-the-pulpit, . . . Brown-dragon, Devil's ear. — (3) **1876** HOBBS *Bot. Hand-Book* 31 Devil's fig, Prickly poppy, *Argemone Mexicana.* **1931** CLUTE *Plants* 84 The plant we call the prickly poppy (*Argemone Mexicana*) is the species often known as devil's fig. — (4) **1894** *Amer. Folk-Lore* VII. 92 *Elephantus tomentosus*, . . . tobacco weed, devil's grandmother, W.Va. **1931** CLUTE *Plants* 83 But how the elephant's food (*Elephantopus tomentosus*) deserves the name of devil's grandmother is hard to conjecture.

(5) **1931** CLUTE *Plants* 83 The thorny *Smilax rotundifolia* is commonly known as the devil's hop-vine. — (6) **1931** CLUTE *Plants* 83 The unicorn plant (*Martynia Louisiana*), whose fruits end in two curved hooks, is the devil's horns. — (7) **1894** *Amer. Folk-Lore* VII. 92 *Lactuca Canadensis*, . . . Horse-weed, Devil's iron-weed, Devil's weed. West Va. *Lactuca integrifolia*, . . . Devil's iron weed. W.Va. — (8) **1907** LYONS *Plant Names* 233 *H*[*ieracium*] *aurantiacum* . . . Grim-the-collier, Devil's Paint-brush, Flora's Paint-brush. **1947** *Midland Naturalist* July 64 *Hieracium aurantiacum* (Devil's-Paintbrush). One station in abandoned field. — (9) **1903** JAMES *Indian Basketry* 85 A stout, horny cactus spine from the devil's pincushion (Echinocactus polycephalus), set in a head of hard pitch, furnished the needle. **1911** WOOTON *Cacti in N.M.* 47 The 'Devil's Pincushion' (*Echinocactus texensis*) . . . is a rather striking plant that comes into the eastern part of the state from Texas.

(10) **1860** CURTIS *Woody Plants N.C.* 91 Hobble-Bush. Tangle-Legs. (*V. lantanoides*, Michx.) — A small straggling shrub . . . [also called] *American Wayfarer's Tree* and the *Devil's Shoestrings.* **1941** STUART *Men of Mts.* 50 Thorny looks up at Bud standing half the time above him and peck-pecking away, moving slowly with a row of corn through the crab-grass and devil-shoestrings. — (11) **1892** *Amer. Folk-Lore* V. 105 *Ustilago Maydis* (the smut of Indian corn), Devil's snuff-box. Chestertown, Md. **1902** CHESNUT *Plants Used by Indians* 300 The common puffball, or devil's snuffbox, . . . was observed growing very plentifully on the ground after a prolonged rain storm in May, 1898.

4. In the names of fishes and other creatures: (1) ∗**devilfish,** *local*, the gray or Californian whale; (2) **-jack-diamond fish,** a garfish; (3) **'s horse,** the praying mantis (see also quot. 1843); (4) **'s mare, rear horse, riding horse,** the praying mantis.

(1) **1860** *Merc. Marine Mag.* VII. 213 They [California gray whales] have a variety of names among whalemen, as . . . 'Hard-head,' 'Devil-fish.' **1888** *Amer. Naturalist* XXII. 511 Of all the known species of whales, this is the most cunning, courageous and vicious. . . . Few whalemen would court an encounter with it, and it early received the name of the Devil Fish. — (2) **1843** BUCKINGHAM *E. & W. States* III. xi. 203 The Devil-jack-diamond fish, or *litholepis adamantinus*, is another of these river monsters, which is as voracious as the alligator-gar, and, like it, has scales which, when dry, will strike fire with steel. **1944** V. BROOKS *World of Wash. Irving* 146 Audubon told Rafinesque about the devil-jack diamond fish whose bullet-proof scales would strike fire with flint. — (3) **1843** *Amer. Pioneer* II. 233 Very large, black grasshoppers, called cheval du diable, or devil's horses, burrow in all the ground. They are, I believe, the same thing as craw-fish, or the shrimps which they use for food. **1884** SWEET & KNOX *Through Texas* xliv. 629 Another of the most peculiar and interesting insects in Texas is called the 'devil's horse.' **1931** READ *La.-French* 25. — (4) **1843** OLIVER *Eight Months* 71 Anything very singular in nature is ascribed to the devil, as 'devil's oven,' 'devil's lettuce,' 'devil's mare,' (the last a singularly shaped insect). **1899** *Animal & Pl. Lore* 63 Devil's riding horse, praying prophet, praying mantis, *Phasmomantis carolina.* Fort Worth, Tex. **1932** READ *La.-French* 25 Other English names for this insect are 'Soothsayer,' 'Mule Killer,' 'Devil Horse,' and 'Devil's Rear Horse.'

5. In phrases: (1) *To whip the devil* (*a*)*round a stump*, to avoid or overcome a difficulty by roundabout means; (2) *the World, the Devil, and the Flesh*, (see quot.); (3) *to find the devil's golden tooth*, (see quot.).

(1) **1786** *Belknap Papers* I. 427 What the Virginians call 'whipping the devil round a stump.' **1891** *Cong. Globe* 13 Feb. 2606/1 In some instances there has been what the boys used to call 'whipping the devil around the stump,' and copyright given when the residence [abroad] has been very slight indeed. — (2) **1870** MACRAE *Americans* II. 372 The New York journals still hold the foremost place in the country. Three of the most prominent are the *Tribune* (Radical), the *Herald* (rotatory), and the *World* (Democratic)—otherwise distinguished from each other as the World, the Devil, and the Flesh. — (3) **1888–90** BARRERE-LELAND I. 306 'One would think he'd found *the devil's golden tooth*,' a common saying in Massachusetts. Founded on a story to the effect that Kidd, the pirate, once obtained from the devil his eye-tooth, which had the power of changing all metals into gold.

As the last term in **blue, horse, Indian, kill, king, mud, red, spit, white devil.**

∗**devil,** *v. tr.* To worry (someone) excessively; to annoy or vex. *Colloq.*

1823 FAUX *Mem. Days* 216 Go . . . tell our great Father, the President, how we are deviled and cheated. **1884** SWEET & KNOX *Through Texas* iii. 47 They devilled the poor fellow almost to death. **1944** *Chi. Tribune* 6 Aug. VII. 1/6 Aunt Lizzie knew every flower and plant, the smelly Indian turnip which young fellas used to carry to 'devil' each other.

Devonshire shovel. (See quot.) *Obs.* — **1815** *Niles' Reg.* IX. 94/2 Iron and steel shovels (called Devonshire shovels) and ditching shovels [were manufactured in Amer.]

* **dew,** *n.* In combs.: (1) * **dewdrop,** (*a*) an ornamental glass bead resembling a drop of dew, (*b*) (see quot.); (2) * **lap,** (see quots.); (3) **mink,** prob. the chewink, *Pipilo erythrophthalmus, rare;* (4) **poison,** a breaking-out or rash thought to have been caused by dew, *colloq.;* (5) **skimmer,** a boat of very light draft.

(1) (*a*) **1880** *Harper's Mag.* June 31/1 'Grass-work' consists in the fastening of small glass beads or 'dew drops' to the artificial blades. (*b*) **1893** *Amer. Folk-Lore* VI. 141 *Dalibarda repens,* dew drop. N.Y. — (2) **1887** *Scribner's Mag.* II. 508/2 Words used in connection with . . . life on the plains include . . . *dewlap,* a cut in the lower part of the neck. **1944** Adams *W. Words* 49 *dewlap* A mark of ownership made on the underside of the neck or brisket of an animal by pinching up a quantity of skin and cutting it loose, but not entirely off. When the wound is healed, it leaves a hanging flap of skin. Some marks are slashed up and called *dewlaps up,* others are slashed down and called *dewlaps down.* — (3) **1781** S. Peters *Hist. Conn.* (1829) 193 Larks, humilitys, whipperwills, dewminks. *Ib.,* The dewmink, so named from its articulating those syllables, is black and white, and of the size of an English robin. — (4) **1912** I. Cobb *Back Home* 110 He couldn't even go barefooted in summer, because if he did his legs would be broken out all over with dew poison. — (5) **1927** Lewis R. Freeman *Waterways of Westward Wandering* 300 The craft which plied up and down these . . . log-choked shallows must have been veritable 'dew-skimmers.'

As the last term in **honey, prairie dew.**

Dewey Decimal System. A library classification system first put into use by its originator, Melvil Dewey, in the Amherst College Library in 1873. Also **Dewey system.**

1879 *Library Journal* IV. 139 The books on the shelves were numbered and arranged according to the 'Dewey system.' **1885** *Ib.* X. 26 At first sight the scheme looks like a modification or improvement of the Dewey Decimal System. **1942** *Amer. Sp.* Dec. 261 Furthermore, Berrey and Van den Bark attempt the same Dewey-decimal-system completeness of classification.

b. Also **Dewey decimal number.**

1944 *Sat. Review* 9 Dec. 15/2 Shall I write another book, And will it here, too find a nook? With Dewey decimal number, letter, Or other marking, clearer, better.

* **D.H.,** *n.* (See quot.) *Obs.* — **1874** B. F. Taylor *World on Wheels* I. xv. 112 'D.H.' Everybody knows what D.H. is. He sees it on the telegram that costs him nothing. He sees it in the glass when he looks at himself, if he rides free upon the train—Dead Head.

D hoe. A hoe, shaped like a **D**, designed for use by thrusting or pushing; a Dutch hoe. *Obs.* — [**1797** I. Thomas *N. Eng. Farmer* 95 Dutch Hoe, sometimes called a *Scuffle;* an iron instrument, with a sharp steeled edge, nearly in the shape of the letter D.] **1825** Lorain *Pract. Husbandry* 191 The scuffle (or D hoe as it is sometimes called,) will destroy weeds growing on a level surface. *Ib.* 397 The D hoe, together with the hoe and tined harrows, used as before directed, will keep the soil free from the foliage growing on them.

* **dialect,** *n.* As the last term in **Bay State, Texas, trap, Yankee dialect.**

dial telegraph. (See quot.) *Obs.* — **1860** Prescott *Telegraph* 160 The dial telegraphs are those in which a needle traverses a dial, upon the margin of which are placed the letters of the alphabet.

* **diamond,** *n.*

1. *Baseball.* The infield or square formed by the lines connecting the four bases; loosely, the entire playing field. Also attrib.

1875 *Cin. Enquirer* 6 July 4/5 In the last seven innings the ball hardly got outside the diamond. **1880** *Phoenix* (Ariz.) *Gazette* 27 Nov. 3/1 The Norvall Base Ball Club . . . have signified their willingness to meet our boys on the diamond field. **1948** *Pauls Valley* (Okla.) *D. Democrat* 1 July 5/2 That diamond is no place for a professional baseball game.

2. Short for **diamond hitch.**

1904 White *Mountains* 50 The Diamond is good because it holds firmly, is a great flattener, and is especially adapted to the securing of square boxes. **1947** *Trail & Timberline* May 77/1 The single diamond is the simplest and most practical tie for this type of load.

3. In combs.: (1) * **diamondback,** see as a main entry; (2) **boom,** a boom in the diamond business; (3) **flounder,** *local,* a food fish, *Hypsopsetta gutulata,* found in the Pacific Ocean, esp. in the bays of southern California; (4) **half,** (see quot.), *obs.;* (5) **hitch,** *W.* a hitch, used in fastening a pack on a horse, in which the rope used forms a diamond-shaped quadrilateral on top of the pack, also transf., cf. **Kit Carson hitch;** (6) **horseshoe,** the dress circle in a theater; (7) **pack,** a pack fastened with a diamond hitch; (8) **rattler,** = **diamondback 2;** (9) **rattlesnake,** = **diamondback 2;** (10) * **snake,** = prec.; (11) **Diamond State,** Delaware, app. so called from its small size.

(2) **1897** M. Twain *Following Equator* lxix. 700 (R.), The South African diamond-boom began. — (3) **1884** Goode *Fisheries* I. 185 South of Point Concepcion [in s. Calif.] the name Diamond Flounder is in use. . . . As a food-fish it ranks high. — (4) **1885** *Santa Fe W. New Mexican* 15 Oct. 2/5 A new pattern in silk quilts is taking the place of the crazy work so long popular. The pattern is called the 'diamond half,' the pieces having that shape.

(5) **1869** *New No. West* (Deer Lodge, Mont.) 8 Oct. 2/3 We took certain comprehensive and exhaustive lessons in that packing mystery known as the 'diamond hitch.' **1877** Stanley *Rambles in Wonderland* 52 When the load is arranged on the animal's back a rope is securely lashed about it and fastened by an ingenious loop known as the 'diamond-hitch.' **1944** *Sat. Ev. Post* 9 Sep. 107/2 He sat in the original game, not with a fruit tree, but with the cash capital of one snake, and now he had half the world grabbed and a diamond hitch on the other half. — (6) **1945** *Chi. D. News* 19 May 4/5 Ferdinand, . . . then a boy of 9, sat in a box with his mother in the 'Diamond Horseshoe' of the magnificent auditorium that his father had built. **1947** *Time* 10 Mar. 6/3 Change the boards of the symphony into young, active organizations, not figureheads of the diamond horseshoe. — (7) **1936** Barnard *Rider* 25 A diamond pack which held my bedding and supplies was put on him. — (8) **1889** *Cent.* 1592/3. **1908** Ditmars *Reptile Book* 449 Pine swamps and hummock lands are the abodes of the Diamond Rattler. — (9) **1835** Featherstonhaugh *Slave States* (1844) 152, I found that Mr. Cook was a collector of natural curiosities, the stuffed skins of three extraordinarily thick *Diamond rattle-snakes* being hung up on the porch. **1944** *Sat. Ev. Post* 9 Sep. 13/2 Big diamond rattlesnakes as thick as a man's arm, and the bright-colored canebrake rattlers or 'Seminoles,' [are] as beautiful as they are deadly.

(10) **1873** Beadle *Undevel. West* 231 One farmer told us of a diamond snake biting his horse so badly that the animal fell dead. — (11) **1869** *Cong. Globe* 20 Dec. 262/2 Pass this bill [for the reconstruction of Georgia], and you strike down the sovereignty of the States, . . . and my own little 'Diamond State' is crushed. **1934** Shankle *State Names* 107 Delaware gets the nickname, the *Diamond State,* from the fact that it is small in size but great in importance.

As the last term in **baseball, California, Cape May, nine diamond.**

* **diamondback,** *n.*

1. A turtle of a variety found along the Atlantic Coast having diamond-shaped markings on the shell. In full **diamondback terrapin.**

1877 Bartlett 699 *Terrapin,* (*Palustris*), a name given to a species of tide-water tortoise, common in Connecticut and the Atlantic States south of New York, and considered an article of luxury. . . . The most celebrated is the diamond-back. **1887** *Lippincott's Mag.* Sep. 456 Baltimore, . . . the home of the soft-shell crab, the diamond-back terrapin, and the canvas-back duck. **1947** Sessions *Cities of Amer.* 52 There are few sections that would dare to claim a greater understanding of what to do with a diamond-back terrapin.

2. A rattlesnake of a species, *Crotalus adamanteus,* having diamond-shaped markings on the back. In full **diamondback rattler, rattlesnake.**

1894 Cable *J. March* xxvii, Di'mon'-back rattlesnake hisself cayn't no mo' scare me 'n if I was a hawg. **1908** Ditmars *Reptile Book* 449 The flattened trails of the big Diamond-backs across the dry sandy roads . . . were as straight as the course of a wheel. **1948** *Popular Western* June 27/1 A diamondback rattler, sunning himself on the rocks there, buzzed its lethal warning as it snapped itself into a coil.

* **Diana,** *n.* **1.** An early variety of N. Eng. grape. In full **Diana grape. 2. Diana's paintbrush,** (see quot.).

(1) **1849** *N. Eng. Farmer* I. 84 We are pleased to learn that the Diana Grape is so early. **1866** *Rep. Comm. Agric. 1865* 187 The Diana improves by being left upon the vine until after pretty severe frosts. . . . It was grown from seed of the Catawba by Mrs. Diana Crehore, Milton, Massachusetts. **1892** Lyon *Fruits* 32 As a long keeper either Agawam or Diana will be found satisfactory. — (2) **1931** Clute *Plants* 55 When the reddish dandelion-like blossoms of this immigrant [orange hawkweed] began to paint our roadsides, the poetically minded called it Diana's paintbrush.

* **Diarbekr,** *n.* (See quot.) *Obs.* — c**1770** John Randolph, Jr. *Gardening* (1924) 30 There is a rough, knotty Melon, called the Diarbekr, from the province belonging to the Turkish empire in Asia, . . . most exquisite of all Melons, which have been brought to great perfection here (Va.).

* **dicer,** *n.* A stiff hat. *Slang.* — **1890** Biff Hall *Turnover Club* 162 These hats, in aggregation, might have served to illustrate the

evolution of the modern silk tile from the much-abused accordeon . . . until the manager appeared with a fairly good and presentable 'dicer.'

dicho ˈditʃo, *n. S.W.* [Sp. in same sense.] A saying or proverb.

1892 LUMMIS *Tramp Across Continent* 185 This trick, of course, is never played on ladies, whose forfeits are generally no more severe than the recitation of a *dicho* (a Spanish epigrammatic verse). **1910** *Sat. Ev. Post* 13 Aug. 3/2 'The lands of the sun expand the soul.' . . . This *dicho* of our Latin neighbors seems the likeliest solution. **1930** SAUNDERS & O'SULLIVAN *Capistrano Nights* (Bentley), These stories, fables, dichos, form a unique contribution to the folklore of California.

*** **dick,** *n.* A detective. *Slang.* Cf. **house dick.**

1911 LEWIS *Apaches* (1912) 95 Still, those plain-clothes dicks did not despair. **1923** *Jrnl. Amer. Inst. Crim. Law & Criminology* Aug. 308 The boy on the road does not take the 'dicks' seriously. **1948** *Time* 3 May 19/3 Last week every cop, private dick, stool pigeon and neighborhood snoop in Detroit was working overtime.

As the last term in **Negro, Silver Dick.**

dickcissel dɪkˈsɪsl, *n.* [See quot. 1917.] The black-throated bunting or little meadowlark, *Spiza americana.*

1887 R. RIDGWAY *Manual N.A. Birds* 452 Dickcissel, . . . dark grey, becoming whitish on belly and lower tail-coverts. **1917** *Birds of Amer.* III. 75 The Dickcissel is so named from the simple song with which he makes cheery the fence-rows and bushy corners of the prairies. **1945** MCATEE *John and Joe* 12 Was it change in conditions that impelled the dickcissel practically to desert the eastern part of its range?

dicker ˈdɪkɚ, *n.* [Prob. f. the verb *q.v.*]

1. *collect.* Goods, commodities, etc., exchanged in trading or bartering. *Obs.*

1823 COOPER *Pioneers* xiv, 'I am told you have sold your betterments to a new settler. . . . Was it cash or dicker?' . . . 'Why, part cash, and part dicker.' **1880** *Harper's Mag.* May 907/2 'I don't believe he has a cent in the world,' I remarked. 'No matter: I'll take "dicker."'

2. The action of trafficking by exchange, haggling, petty bargaining; a trade or exchange effected in this way. *Colloq.*

1831 *Boston Transcript* 22 Dec. 1/1 His 'dicker' was begun, And by aid of solemn face, He closed a bargain soon. **1887** *Chi. Tribune* 5 May 2/3 A compromise was effected, he was reinstated and the Pittsburg club got him, but had to release Milt Scott to Baltimore to complete the dicker. **1945** WILLIAMS *It's a Free Country* 101 The first pay day, he drove to Eutaw and made a dicker with Dave Purvis.

b. =**dickering.**

1863 E. KIRKE *My Southern Friends* iv. 64 And when I git 'bout a hun'red [Negroes] together, take 'em ter Orleans, and auction 'em off. Thar's no fuss and dicker 'bout thet, ye knows. **1923** ADAMS *Pioneer Hist.* 367 The few citizens dealt with each other by making exchanges, one thing for another. Father said they would speak of this as 'dicker.'

c. *Polit.* A deal or bargain.

1888 *Cent. Mag.* XXXVII. 313/2 We should be rid at one stroke . . . ; of the nomination of notoriously unfit candidates, of 'deals' and 'dickers' and 'trades' at the polls. **1910** *Springfield W. Republican* 8 Dec. 8 Trade and dicker beween the two leading political parties.

3. (See quot. 1908.) *Colloq.*

1904 HARBEN *Georgians* 108 They soon had half a dozen cabins built accordin' to the latest dicker up North. **1908** *D.N.* 304 dicker, n. Plan, fashion. 'They got it up accordin' to the latest *dicker.*' *Rare.*

dicker ˈdɪkɚ, *v.* [See note.]

It has been suggested (see *OED*) that this verb is from **dicker, n.*, in the sense of hides or skins, and came first into use on the North American frontier among traders who may have used it in the sense "to deal by the dicker, to deal in skins." Conclusive evidence for such an origin is not at present available.

1. *tr.* To dispose of (an article or commodity) by exchange or bartering.

1836 DUNLAP *Mem. Water Drinker* I. 56 He trudged off, determined to give, or sell, or dicker, the fish at his friend Spiffard's. **1902** MCFAUL *Ike Glidden* 69 I'm ready to dicker any horse I've got, at any time.

2. *intr.* or *absol.* To bargain, traffic, haggle.

1848 COOPER *Oak Openings* I. ii. 32 The white men who penetrated to those semi-wilds, were always ready to 'dicker' and to 'swap,' and to 'trade' rifles, and watches. **1887** J. HAWTHORNE *Great Bank Robbery* xiii, I didn't come here to dicker. **1945** *La Junta* (Colo.) *Tribune-Democrat* 15 Feb. 2/2 In pre-war days. . . . I could always talk the dealers out of enough to supply us for the session, but they won't dicker any more.

b. *Polit.* To try to arrange matters, or come to terms, by mutual bargaining.

1904 CRISSEY *Tattlings* 134 [Gunshoe and the Yankee] dickered and haggled up to the last minute before the bill was to come up for third reading. **1910** *N.Y. Ev. Post* 6 Oct. (Th.), [Governor Hughes of New York] would not dicker or bargain. He would not help his bills through the Legislature by either log-rolling or patronage.

3. *To dicker after, for, on, over, with,* to try to obtain (someone or something) by petty endeavorings, haggling, or bargaining; to carry on such dealings about (a commodity) or with (someone).

1824 *Woodstock* (Vt.) *Observer* 15 June 4/5 (Th.), The subscriber has for sale the following property which he wishes to dicker for. **1854** M. J. HOLMES *Tempest & Sunshine* vii. 46 You'd better scratch gravel for home, and if I catch you here again dickerin' after Fanny, I'll pull every corn-coloured har out of your head! **1878** BEADLE *West. Wilds* 510 Fifteen minutes after the German had poisoned the ox, some Indians . . . dickered with him for it. **1921** MULFORD *Bar-20 Three* 54 Give him a chance to dicker over a herd an' he's happy for a week or more. **1927** RUSSELL *Trails* 21 We're in Blood Lance's lodge, smokin' an' dickerin' on this swap. **1948** *News-Dispatch* (Michigan City, Ind.) 3 April 1/1 Painters, at the moment, are dickering for a $2 scale, up 25 cents.

b. *To dicker at,* to dabble at, to work at in a superficial manner.

1856 M. J. HOLMES *L. Rivers* xxxviii. 415, I've given her such a sum as will bear your expenses, and leave you more than you can earn dickerin' at law for three or four years.

dickerer ˈdɪkərɚ, *n.* One who dickers. — **1891** *Columbus* (O.) *Dispatch* 2 April 48 Bargains that would do credit to London East End dickerers. **1902** MCFAUL *Ike Glidden* viii. 62 Dunno as you would call 'em horse trades, b'cause some of the dickerers round here don't trade fair.

dickering ˈdɪkərɪŋ, *n.* and *a.* Bargaining, swapping, haggling.

1802 *Port Folio* II. 268*n.*, In the gibberish of Connecticut horse jockies, . . . *Dickering* signifies all that honest conversation, preliminary to the sale of a horse, where the parties very laudably strive in a sort of gladiatorial combat of lying, cheating, and overreaching. **1848** COOPER *Oak Openings* I. ii. 32 But, we should be doing injustice to le Bourdon, were we . . . to confound him with the 'dickering' race. **1889** *Harper's Mag.* June 93/2 A prompt bargain is distasteful to him; he desires the disputation of dickering and the excitement

b. Political conniving, planning, arranging.

1880 *Ill. State Jrnl.* (Springfield) 20 May 5/1 He is attending strictly to his business as bookkeeper . . . and is not engaged in any 'trading or dickering,' but has active friends who are determined to present his name to the Convention as a candidate. **1910** *N.Y. Ev. Post* 28 Nov. 1 Gov.-elect Wilson entertains no thought of parcelling out the patronage he will control in political dickering.

*** **dickey,** *n.*[1] **1.** A shirt collar. Also **dickey cravat.** *Colloq.* **2.** (See quot.)

(1) **1830** *Collegian* 40 After taking off his coat, stock, and dickie. **1843** STEPHENS *High Life N.Y.* I. i. 4 There was a chap . . . with the edge of his dickey turned over his stock—like an old-fashioned baby's bib. **1902** HARBEN *Abner Daniel* 191, I don't know but I'd move down to Atlanta an' live alongside o' Bill, an' wear a claw-hammer coat an' a dicky cravat fer a change. — (2) **1884** GOODE *Fisheries* I. 224 The Haddock is often called 'Dickie' by Connecticut fishermen.

*** **Dickey,** *n.*[2] [See quot. 1946.] =**Deak.** Also attrib. *Student slang.*

The explanation in quot. 1887 is apparently facetious.

1887 *Harper's Mag.* March 591/1 'What in the world is the "Dickey"?' 'It's the society that the Freshmen [at Harvard] are the most eager to get into. They're chosen ten at a time, by the old members, and to be one of the first ten—the only Freshmen chosen—is something quite ineffable.' **1905** *N. Eng. Mag.* Nov. 318/1 The Delta Kappa Epsilon, known as the Dickey, is the great Sophomore secret society. **1946** *Sat. Review* 14 Sep. 6 As a sophomore I had been active in the production of the Dickey (ΔKE) Christmas theatricals.

Dictaphone ˈdɪktəˌfon, *n.* [f. *dicta*te+-*phone.*] A trade-mark identifying a certain make of dictating machines and other sound recording and reproducing equipment. Also (not *cap.*) sometimes incorrectly used to describe these machines generally. — **1907** *Dly. Chron.* 3 July 3/5 The 'dictaphone,' an adaptation of the phonograph. **1945** *New Yorker* 24 Feb. 69 (*advt.*), The word *Dictaphone* is the registered trade-mark of Dictaphone Corporation, makers of dictating machines and other sound recording and reproducing equipment bearing said trade-mark.

dictatee ˌdɪktəˈti, *n.* One who is dictated to. *Rare.* — **1896** *Nation* 28 June 486/2 Dictation implies knowledge on the part of the dictator and dictatee.

*** **dictionary,** *n.* In combs.: (1) **dictionary catalogue,** a catalogue of books giving in one alphabetic arrangement the authors, titles, and subjects of the books listed; (2)

class, formerly in elementary schools, esp. in country schools, a spelling class in which a dictionary was used as a textbook, now *hist.;* (3) **paper,** (see quot.).

(1) **1876** C. A. CUTTER (*title*), Rules for a printed dictionary catalogue. **1915** FAY & EATON *Use of Books & Libraries* 112 All the cards in the catalogue are arranged alphabetically by their headings, like the words in a dictionary, and the catalogue is therefore called a dictionary catalogue. — (2) **1853** RICHARDS *V. Life* 32 In dictionary class I got up sixth, although I had not studied my lesson very much. **1946** WILSON *Fidelity* 138 In one school we had a dictionary class, in which we spelled the words; gave diacritical markings, parts of speech, definitions, synonyms, and antonyms. — (3) **1904** *Chi. D. News* 23 Feb. 21 Dictionary papers, so named because they look like the figured paper linings that were once almost the trademark of books of erudition, are frequently used for [lamp] shades.

dictograph ˈdɪktəˌgræf, *n.* Also **dictagraph.** [Irreg. f. L. *dictum*, thing said, +*-graph*.] (See quot. 1907.) — **1907** *U.S. Patent 843, 186* 5 Feb., Our invention relates to what we shall term a *dictograph*, being a telephonic system or apparatus by which a person—for example, the manager of an office—may dictate letters to any of his corps of stenographers without requiring them to leave their place at their own desks. **1916** W. A. DUPUY *Uncle Sam* 209 Billy Gard sat patiently with the headpiece of the dictagraph securely in place.

*** didapper,** *n.* The Carolina or pied-billed grebe, *Podilymbus podiceps*, or a small bird resembling this.

1616 SMITH *N. Eng.* 16 Turkies, Diue-doppers, and many other sorts, whose names I knowe not. **1781–2** JEFFERSON *Notes Va.* (1788) 77 Besides these [birds], we have . . . [the] Didapper, or Dopchick. *c*1845 *Big Bear Ark.* 41, I aimed a sockdollager at him. . . . He can dodge like a diedapper. **1946** *Democrat* 12 Sep. 2/3 It even looked like a bird in flight—some kind of a didapper or small grebe.

diddle, *n.* A slight, graceful movement. *Rare.* — **1835** LONGSTREET *Georgia Scenes* 13 Always giving two or three pretty little perch-bite diddles, as she arose from a coupee—Nancy Ware was her very self.

diddledees, *n. pl. local.* (See quots.) — **1889** *Amer. Folk-Lore* II. 64 Diddledees. . . . At Hyannis [Mass.], in my boyhood, it was the universal name for the fallen pine-needles that carpet the ground in the woods. **1942** Newspaper Filler (Wentworth), What you call pine leaves all depends on the section of the country in which you live. They are known as needles, spills, pins, twinkles, diddledees, straws, tags, and shats.

*** die-.** The verb stem used in combs.

1. dieback, a disease affecting trees causing them to die from the top downward. Also attrib.

1886 in S. FALLOWS *Supp. Dict.* **1895** *Dept. Agric. Yrbk. 1894* 199 Die-back manifests itself by a number of striking characters. The foliage becomes very dark green [etc.]. *Ib.* 200 Finally a reddish brown resinous substance exudes on the twigs, forming the so-called die-back stain. *Ib.* 201 Die-back appears to be a form of indigestion, due to an overfed condition of the plant. **1948** *Calif. Citrograph* April 229 (*caption*), Stubborn disease, chlorosis and curling of leaves, dieback of twigs and multiple buds.

2. dieup, the dying off of cattle from disease, starvation, etc., on a large cattle ranch.

1904 D. H. BIGGERS *Cattle Range* (1944) 52 The first big die-up occurred . . . in that portion of western Texas [in 1884]. **1943** L. V. HAMNER *Short Grass*, Things went well with them until the 'big dieup' in January, 1886.

Diegueño djəˈgenjo, *n.* [Amer. Sp. in same sense. See quot. 1907.] (See quot. 1907.) Also attrib.

1858 *S.F. Bulletin* 5 Nov., The true native American of the wild forests—such as the Yumas, Cocopas, Dieguiños, . . . predominate. **1885** JACKSON *Century of Dishonor* 492 An intelligent young Indian living there had recently been elected as general over the Dieguino Indians in the neighborhood. **1907** HODGE *Amer. Indians* I. 390/1 Diegueños. A collective name, probably in part synonymous with Comeya, applied by the Spaniards to Indians of the Yuman stock who formerly lived in and around San Diego, Cal., whence the term; it included representatives of many tribes and has no proper ethnic significance. **1947** *Westerners' Brand Book* 112 The tax assessments were levied principally against the Luiseno, Diegueno and Cupeno tribes.

*** diet,** *n.* In combs.: (1) *** diet bread,** sponge cake; (2) **kitchen,** (see quot. 1889); (3) **list,** a list of available or desirable foods.

(1) **1830** *Huntingdon* (Pa.) *Gazette* 15 Sep. 4/5 [Recipes] Diet Bread. Sponge Cake. Dough Cake. **1913–17** *D.N.* IV. 239 diet bread, Sponge cake. — (2) **1866** MOORE *Women of War* 233 We had been all the morning in the 'diet kitchen,' and the dinner for our large family of over three hundred, on special diet, was well under way. **1889** *Cent.* 1608/1 Diet-kitchen, an establishment, usually connected with a dispensary or with the outdoor department of a hospital, for preparing and dispensing suitable diet for invalids, especially among the poor. **1945** *Athol* (Mass.) *D. News* 26 May 6/2 Every possible comfort, such as nurses, special diet kitchen and facilities for babies, will be supplied on their trans-Atlantic voyage. — (3) **1856** KANE *Arctic Explor.* I. 19 A very moderate supply of liquors . . . made up the diet-list. **1866** MOORE *Women of War* 224 As we had no 'diet list,' we took down on a slip of paper every afternoon what articles of food each man thought he could eat.

dietitian daɪəˈtɪʃən, *n.* [f. *diet*+phys*ician*.] One skilled in the application of principles of nutrition to the feeding of individuals and groups. — **1905** *Springfield W. Republican* 29 Dec. 16 Miss Ruth Montague has accepted a position as dietitian at the Massachusetts state sanitarium. **1947** *Coronet* April 6/2 The dietitian persuaded her to toss the candy overboard, while the skimpy meals were replaced by three balanced ones.

diff dɪf, *n.* [App. a variant of biff *q.v.*] A blow or stroke. *Colloq.* — **1877** BURDETTE *Rise of Mustache* 208 The dog, looking up, misunderstood the motion and thought his master was going to hit him a diff with that hat. **1889** HARRIS *Balaam & Master*, He got a big scyar [=scar] on de side er his neck now what somebody hit 'im a diff.

*** different,** *a.* Used absolutely of one who is unusual, odd, eccentric, etc. *Colloq.* — **1885** PHELPS *Old Maids* II. 8 Corona was used to these little lapses in the line of human sympathy which come of solitary living with some one who is 'different.' **1938** DAMON *Grandma* 120 But Grandma didn't care what the neighbors said, partly because she enjoyed being different.

*** differential,** *a.* and *n.*

1. *n.* A difference, agreed upon by the railroads, in the rates to a certain point by different routes or to different points by roads competing for the same traffic, a preferential rate.

1890 *Spectator* 20 Sep. 383 The morality of American Railway Companies as regards . . . differentials and commissions. **1903** E. JOHNSON *Railway Transportation* 236 The Joint Executive Committee endeavored . . . to fix the rates (or the 'differentials') which Philadelphia and Baltimore should have as compared with New York and Boston on the Western business. **1946** *Democrat* 21 Feb. 2/3 We don't believe there is any justification whatsoever for such a differential in favor of the Northern growers.

2. *a.* Of or pertaining to a differential.

1882 *Nation* 27 July 66/3 The report of the Railroad Advisory Commission on the subject of 'differential rates' between the West and the seaboard. **1898** *Boston Herald* 23 Jan. 14/4 When the Southern Pacific established its tourist line out of Washington it was found that the regular rate of $69.75 and $67.40 over the differential lines, on California business had been lessened $2. by the new competitor, under a claim that it was entitled to a differential.

3. differential grasshopper, locust, a large destructive grasshopper found in the western states.

1892 KELLOGG *Kansas Insects* 42 Differential locust (*Melanoplus differentialis*). . . . This locust . . . is about 1½ inches long and its wings, expanding 2½ inches, and is of a general bright yellowish-green color. **1913** ESSIG *Injurious & Beneficial Insects Calif.* 17 The Differential Grasshopper . . . is one of the larger hoppers, averaging five and one eighths inches from front to the tip of the tegmina or wing covers.

*** diffusion,** *n. attrib.* Of or pertaining to a process or apparatus used in sugar-making. — **1886** *Harper's Mag.* June 80 The 'diffusion' process is used somewhat in cane and commonly in beet-sugar making. *Ib.*,These slices go to the diffusion 'battery,' a series of ten or a dozen tanks. *Ib.* 92/1 The diffusion process now replaces crushing.

*** dig,** *n.* A hard-working student, a "grind." *Colloq.* — **1830** *Collegian* 231 Wishing that I could see . . . the many honest digs who had in this room consumed the midnight oil. **1911** D. S. JORDAN in *Nature* LXXXV. 355 This single case is typical of the attitude into which our fellowship system . . . throws the young digs who arise in our various colleges.

*** dig,** *v.*

1. *intr.* To study hard. *Colloq.*

1827 *Harvard Reg.* Dec. 303 Here the sunken eye and sallow countenance bespoke the man who dug sixteen hours 'per diem.' **1894** FORD *P. Stirling* 14 Peter dug at his books all the harder, by reason of Watts's neglect of them.

b. **To dig in*, to burrow in or hold tenaciously, to work hard. *Colloq.*

1851 *Knickerb.* XXXVIII. 183 [The crab] pinched, scratched, 'dug in,' and 'held on.' **1884** MARK TWAIN *H. Finn* xxxviii, We got to dig in like all git-out. **1948** *Dly. Ardmoreite* (Ardmore, Okla.) 28 July 3/3 Despite this paralyzing disaster, Ardmore residents dug in and refused to give up.

c. **To dig* (*out*), to run rapidly, to depart hastily. *Colloq.*

*a*1855 KELLEY *Humors* 384 Mad and furious, the young chaps made a general onslaught on the people present, who 'dug out' very quick, leaving the bacchanalians to their glory. **1910** MCCUTCHEON *Rose in*

Ring 334 If it wasn't for you, Davy, I'd cut it in a minute and dig for the wooly West. **1917** MATHEWSON *Sec. Base Sloan* xiii. 183 Wayne circled and dug out for second.

2. *tr.* (See quot.) Cf. ***digger 2,** ***digging 3.**

1877 BARTLETT 176 To *dig* is used among the lower classes at the South for the act of *dipping* or rubbing snuff. A friend informs me that *to dig* is more common than *to dip* snuff.

3. **To dig up*, to bring to light, produce, often of money and sometimes absol. *Colloq.*

1888 *N.Y. W. Times* 28 March (F.), Senator Sherman digs up the past and screams over the ancient relics. **1910** W. M. RAINE *B. O'Connor* 21 Dig up, Mr. Pullman, go way down into your jeans. *Ib.* 192 If it's a show-down he'll dig the dough up.

For examples of *to dig up the hatchet* see **hatchet 4. c.**

***digger,** *n.*

1. (*cap.*) (See quot. 1907.) Cf. **Ute Diggers.**

1834 in *Ore. Hist. Soc. Quart.* XVII. 247 Camped on the Snake Falls and near a band of the Snake Indians called the Diggers. They . . . live chiefly on fish and roots hence their name Diggers. **1907** HODGE *Amer. Indians* I. 390 *Digger.* Said by Powell to be the English translation of Nuanuints, the name of a small tribe near St. George, s.w. Utah. It was the only Paiute tribe practising agriculture, hence the original signification of the name, 'digger.' In time the name was applied to every tribe known to use roots extensively for food and hence to be 'diggers.' . . . As the root-eaters were supposed to represent a low type of Indian, the term speedily became one of opprobrium. **1948** *Pacific Discovery* Nov.–Dec. 16/1 California Indians — 'Diggers' because the earth provided their living, not the chase—stocked their larders with these cones, eating them green and eating their 'nuts.'

attrib. **1836** in *Overland to Pacific* VI. (1936) 232 Kentuc . . . was offended with Mr. McLeod, about some beaver trading which he made with a Diggar Indian. **1856** *Trinity Journal* (Weaverville, Calif.) 12 April 1/2 The only instance in which we recall having 'viewed her in her natural state' was the accidental, and altogether undesigned surprisal of a Digger woman pounding acorns. **1859** *S.F. Telegram* 16 Feb. 1/3 The Coroner had a *post mortem* examination made on the remains of Capt. John, the old Digger Chief, who was yesterday found dead in a vacant house. **1882** HARTE *Flip* 85 If that's too much to do for your old dad, ye might do it to please that digger squaw as a Christian act. **1946** *So. Sierran* Aug. 1/2 J. H. Johnson from Tulare, and five comrades were guided across the pass by a Digger Indian named Sampson.

b. The language spoken by the Digger Indians. *Rare.*

1869 MARK TWAIN *Innocents Abroad* 205 It is Indian, and suggestive of Indians. They say it is Pi-ute—possibly it is Digger. I am satisfied it was named by the Diggers.

2. (See quot.) *Obs.* Cf. ***dig,** *v.* **2, digging 3.**

1860 in M. W. DISHER *Cowells in Amer.* (1934) 66 The practice [of snuff-chewing] is called 'digging' instead of 'dipping' and those slaves to it are called 'diggers.'

3. (See quot.)

1934 SHANKLE *State Names* 132 Diggers, Miners, and Sagebrushers are sobriquets applied to the inhabitants of Nevada.

4. In special combs.: (1) **Digger Indian country,** the country inhabited by any Indians known as "Diggers"; (2) **pine,** a California pine so called from the use of its nuts as food by the Digger Indians; (3) **roast,** a roast cooked in a hole dug in hot ashes and then filled in with hot coals, *rare.*

(1) **1849** in *Soc. Calif. Pion. Quart.* II. 102 We are now coming into the Digger Indian country. — (2) **1884** SARGENT *Rep. Forests* 195 *Pinus Sabiniana* . . . Digger Pine. Bull Pine. **1948** *Pacific Discovery* Nov.–Dec. 15/2 The Digger pine, so unimposing, so seemingly worn and frayed by the winds and paled by the sun, produces in great numbers enormous cones, heavy, hooked, and filled with 'nuts.' — (3) **1897** *Outing* XXX. 555/2 That night for a late supper, we had deer meat in another form—a 'digger roast,' as the boys called it.

As the last term in **gold, money, muscle, Oregon gold, peanut, potato, root, sang digger.**

***digging,** *n.*

1. The action or habit of studying or working hard. *Colloq.* Cf. ***dig,** *v.* **1.**

1827 *Harvard Reg.* Dec. 194, I've . . . always despised digging, you know. **1873** W. MATHEWS *Getting On* xv. 226 Men of genius have seldom revealed to us how much of their fame was due to hard digging.

2. *pl.* Region, neighborhood, district. *Colloq.*

1834 SIMMS *G. Rivers* 70 He's been at this business in these diggings now about three years. **1866** C. H. SMITH *Bill Arp* 26 What makes cotton sell at sixty-seven cents a pound in your diggins? Is it not awful scarce? **1945** *N. Eng. Homestead* 22 Sep. 18/2 They came forth with a crop such as never was before in these particular diggings.

3. (See quots.) *Obs.*

1860 [see **digger,** *n.* 2]. **1887** *Chi. Tribune* 2 April 5/6 Neither mind, health, self-respect, love for husband, children or friends can give her sufficient resolution to abstain from 'digging' or 'dipping,' as snuff-chewing is called.

4. digging machine, a machine for digging. *Obs.* Cf. **excavator.**

1853 *Harper's Mag.* VI. 424 A Mr. Evans, who had a contract with the city for filling up 'the Flats' on the 'Neck,' invited the city government to examine his road and his famous digging-machine.

As the last term in **coal, gold, graveyard, money, placer, river, seam, tail digging.**

Also *pl.* in **ancient, bank, bar, coyote, creek, drift, dry, gold, gravel, gulch, hill, hydraulic, pocket, poor man's, prospecting, seam, surface, Washoe, wet diggings.**

***digging,** *a.* **1.** (See quot.) **2.** Dear or costly. Also transf. Both *colloq.*

(1) **1800** TATHAM *Tobacco* 12 The *narrow* or *hilling* hoe follows the operation of the sprouting hoe. . . . It can be set more or less digging (as it is termed), that is on a greater or less angle with the helve, at pleasure. — (2) **1820** MEAD *Travels* 62, I have often been amused with the manners and language of the lower class of people in the south. In Georgia anything a little uncommon is said to be 'too digging.' **1852** in THOMPSON *M. Jones* (1872) 239 'Don't you think that's a little too digin, Mrs. Rogers, to make me pay sixteen dollars for a basket what aint no bigger than my fist.'

***dignify,** *v. tr.* (See quot. 1898.) Also **dignification,** *n. Obs.* or *hist.* — **1730** in G. SHELDON *Hist. Deerfield, Mass.* (1895) I. 482 Voted to leave it to ye seaters to dignify the pews and seats [in the meeting house]. **1753** *Ib.* 484 That the Dignification of the Seats in the meeting house be Intirely set aside. **1898** J. R. TRUMBULL *Hist. Northampton, Mass.* I. 516 It became customary to 'dignify the meeting,' that is to give to those seats in one portion of the house equal rank with others in different locations.

dike daɪk, *n.* [f. the verb *q.v.*] (See quots.) *Colloq.* — **1871** DE VERE 597 *Dike*, denoting a man in full dress, or merely the dress, is a peculiar American cant term, as yet unexplained. To be *out on a dike* is said of persons, mainly young men, who are dressed more carefully than usual, in order to pay visits or to attend a party. **1908** *D.N.* III. 305 Dike, a display of dress. 'He's on a big dike, today.'

dike daɪk, *v.* [Origin obscure. Cf. **dight* and Eng. dial. *dick*, to deck, adorn.] (See quot. 1902.)

1851 HALL *College Words* 100 At the University of Virginia, one who is dressed with more than ordinary elegance is said to be *diked out.* **1902** CLAPIN 159 Dike, to attire oneself faultlessly for social purposes. Diked out, to be dressed up, with connotation of being one's in best clothes. **1948** *Sat. Ev. Post* 14 Aug. 83/1 Here in the path she could feel a dress and apron she knew, but the body diked out in them lay stiff and cold.

b. Also **dike up.**

1912 *Sat. Ev. Post* 20 July 3/1 Was you goin' to a show last night, Lisette, when I seen you pass our window all diked up so elegant?

dill pickle. A pickle flavored with dill. Also attrib.

1904 O. HENRY *Heart of West* 224 No more long hairs in the comb or dill pickles lying around in the cigar tray. **1940** EARLY *N. Eng. Sampler* 279 Alice Longworth denied that she said the President [Coolidge] was weaned on a dill pickle, but it was a good line anyhow. **1948** *Fargo* (N.D.) *Forum* 19 Sep. 19/7 Little did she guess what the result would be when she tried a new dill pickle recipe.

***dime,** *n.*

1. A silver coin of the U.S. worth ten cents. Cf. **half, thin dime.**

1786 in *Amer. Museum* (1789) II. 182 Dimes, the lowest silver coin, ten of which shall be equal to the dollar. **1890** KENDALL *Travels* I. xvii. 193 Dimes or tenth parts are mentioned by writers, but never enter into accounts. **1948** *Calif. Citrograph* April 224/4 A dime is a dollar after the taxes are taken out.

2. *pl.* Money; financial gain. *Colloq. Obs.*

1845 SOL. SMITH *Theatr. Apprent.* 7, I, in search of 'the dimes,' acted plays in newly-built theatres. **1871** *Harper's Mag.* June 37/2 Among the excursionists there would be . . . such as travel to gather ideas rather than dimes.

3. In combs.: (1) **dime bank,** a child's toy bank in which to save dimes, also transf.; (2) **dreadful,** = **dime mystery thriller,** cf. **penny dreadful;* (3) **edition,** an edition of a book selling for ten cents; (4) **museum,** a place charging ten cents admission which exhibits freaks, monstrosities, etc.; (5) **mystery thriller,** an exciting, improbable mystery story published in an edition selling for ten cents; (6) **novel,** see as main entry; (7) **show,** a show, freq. of a vulgar sort, to which the admission is ten cents; (8) **social,** a social, a social gathering, usu. for charitable purposes, to which the admission is ten cents; (9) **songbook,** a songbook selling for ten cents, orig. put out by the publisher of the first dime novels *q.v.;* (10) **store,** a store, usu. one of a chain, which retails articles of moderate price, the maximum price orig. being ten cents, cf. **five and ten cent store.**

(1) **1902** *Sears Cat.* 1126/2 The Little Gem Dime Savings Bank. . . . Opens automatically when $5.00 in dimes have been deposited. Price, each . . . 6c. **1944** HALSEY *Best Friends* 90 The worst of it was that I have been secreting wampum in my dime bank with the idea of buying a War Bond. — (2) **1910** *Outing* Dec. 281/1 It [Boy Scout movement] brings together all the romance of the frontier, the great Northwest, our own West as it is handed down in history, . . . anything the boys would otherwise obtain out of the dime dreadfuls. — (3) **1861** *Vanity Fair* 26 Jan. 38/2, I invested in the dime editions of startling narratives, and made an occasional dash at comic publications. — (4) **1883** *Chi. Morning News* 13 Sep. 6 Kohl & Middleton's New Palace of Amusements. South Side Dime Museum. . . . Thirteen Living Human Curiosities. **1946** PARTRIDGE & BETTMANN *As We Were* 164 The Dime Museums existed only by preying upon the gullibility of their patrons.

(5) **1943** *Chi. D. News* 23 Sep. 1/4 The Fillmore st. police today were investigating a fantastic story that might have been lifted from a dime mystery thriller. — (7) **1886** *Harper's Mag.* Dec. 147/2 It was more fun than the dime show. **1892** *Dly. News* (London) 29 March 2/5 The nuisance of 'dime shows' as they are called in America. — (8) **1907** *Springfield W. Republican* 13 May 4 An interesting program has been prepared for the dime social of the woman's auxiliary of the Young Men's Christian association. — (9) **1864** *N. Amer. Rev.* July 304 Over 350,000 copies of the Dime Song Book No. 1 have been sold. **1877** BARTLETT 177 There is also a great variety of song books, known as 'Dime Song Books.'

(10) **1931** *K.C. Star* 23 Oct., Twin girls, age 4, rendered a program as blues singers at a dime store in Emporia. **1948** *Redbook Mag.* April 90/3 You can shop for these trinkets all the way from the dime stores to the jewelers', letting your bank balance be your guide.

b. *dime a dozen,* said of anything quite plentiful or cheap. *Colloq.*

1930 TERRETT *Only Saps Work* 188 These are mere dime-a-dozen rackets, compared with the truly big-time stock market swindles. **1948** *Galveston* (Tex.) *News* 14 June 7/7 Sunday night at the cocktail party and buffet supper, choice fishing stories were a dime a dozen.

dime novel. A novel, often of a trashy, ephemeral sort, costing ten cents or less; cheap sensational literature in general.

Erastus F. and Irwin P. Beadle began publication of the Dime Book Series in 1860 with Ann S. Stephens' *Malaeska; the Indian Wife of the White Hunter* as the first dime novel. Orig. the series included songbooks and biographies as well as novels. Although the novels were not the best literature, they were not considered detrimental to youth.

1864 *N. Amer. Rev.* July 304 A Dime Novel is issued each month, and the series has undoubtedly obtained greater popularity than any other series of works of fiction published in America. **1940** MENCKEN *Happy Days* 121 They never got any further along the road to debauchery than reading dime-novels and smoking cigarettes. **1947** *Denver Post* 23 Feb. A. 7/2 Called dime and half-dime novels, they left the stands at a nickel a toss.

attrib. **1882** *L.A. Times* 2 April, The cowboy gang . . . are the most reckless of the dime novel description. **1887** *Courier-Journal* 4 Feb. 5/3 Henry White . . . has led a life that would qualify him for a dime-novel hero. **1889** *Valley Bul.* (Solomonville, Ariz.) 27 Dec. 1/4 Dick Blye uttered a creditable imitation of the war-whoop of a dime-novel Indian.

b. Also **dime-novelish, -ism, -ist, -ly.**

1887 *Scribner's Mag.* July 120/1 He had a suspicion that it was a trifle boyish, and 'dime-novelish.' — **1887** *Courier-Journal* 6 Feb. 16/3 He swore, according to the accepted canons of dime-novelism. — **1879** *Amer. Punch* April 40/1 Read the following voluntary testimonials, (written to order by the hundred, by a Dime novelist in New York,) which speak for themselves. **1930** BANNING *Six Horses* 346 Capricious ghost-writers and press agents—dime-novelists, in fact, . . . were given liberties with many names not their own. — **1915** *Amer. Mag.* Dec. 62/3 All the emotional poignancy and human profundity of Hardy's story were lost in their poor, trashy, dime-novelly canned drama.

***dimension,** *n. attrib.* Designating lumber sawed to specific sizes and length. — **1864** THOREAU *Cape Cod* vii. 156 The modern houses built of what is called 'dimension timber,' imported from Maine, all ready to be set up. **1905** *Forestry Bureau Bul.* No. 67, 71 The ranchmen in the vicinity of the proposed reserve are dependent upon it for fuel, fencing, and house logs, and also, to a small extent, for dimension stuff.

* **diner,** *n.* = **dining car.** Also transf.

1890 *Commercial Gaz.* 29 June, One coach, the chaircar, sleeper and diner . . . overturned. **1935** *Amer. Mercury* July 311/2 The diner was back from the sidewalk, under a couple of big trees. **1948** *Chi. D. News* 17 Aug. 1/3 Three coaches, three sleepers and a diner left the tracks.

dinero diˈnero, *n. S.W.* [Sp. in same sense.] Money, treasure. *Colloq.*

1856 *Butte Record* (Oroville, Calif.) 29 Aug. 2/6 They pungled the dinero, and observed that, as it was cheap, they had a mind to play the 'balance of the day out.' **1941** FERGUSSON *Southwest* 339 Then while you wrangle your dudes, I'll see what I can round up for the baile at night. Got enough dinero? **1948** *Popular Western* June 99/1, I could use some extra dinero.

* **dinette,** *n.* A small dining room, usu. in an alcove of a small apartment. Also a set of furniture suitable for use in this.

1930 *Ladies' Home Jrnl.* Jan. 38/3 On the opposite east wall were two clumsy, heavy French doors between the living room and the dinette. **1931** *Sears Cat.* Spring 622 (*heading*), Stylish Dinette at Bigger Savings. **1948** *L.A. Times* (Home Mag.) 8 Aug. 9/1 The small dinette off the kitchen, papered in blue morning-glories, substituted very nicely for the former large dining room.

dingbat ˈdɪŋbæt, *n.* Any one of various things (see quots.), often a dingus *q.v. Colloq.*

1861 *New Haven Palladium* 27 Dec., It has been found necessary to expend the 'dingbats' to put something more substantial on the 'fly' [= in motion]. **1877** BARTLETT 177 Dingbat, a bat of wood that may be thrown (dinged); a piece of money; a cannonball; a bullet. **1895** *D.N.* I. 387 ding-bat. Mr. Philip Hale, of the *Boston Journal,* has been collecting information through that paper concerning this word. The following [8] definitions appear. **1923** *Montanan* May 10 Explain just why that blasted 'ding bat' of a Ford, as Stub calls it, just naturally stood on its hind legs, down there in the middle of the road and turned a flip-flop. **1934** LOMAX *Amer. Ballads* 24 A dingbat [i.e., a low-class tramp] sat on a rotten tie.

dingbusted ˌdɪŋˈbʌstɪd, *a.* A euphemism for "damned." *Slang.* — **1884** MARK TWAIN *H. Finn* xiv. 123 Well, now, I be dingbusted!

***dinge,** *n.* Also **dingy.** A Negro. *Slang.* — **1909** O. HENRY *Roads of Destiny* 134 These dingies will cheat you out of the gold in your teeth if you don't understand their ways. **1929** *Sat. Ev. Post* 7 Dec. 130/2, I found that no-good dinge who cooks for us sleeping off a jag on the back porch.

* **dingle,** *n.* (See quots.)

1889 *Cent.* 1624 Dingle, the protecting weather-shed built around the entrance to a house. **1895** *D.N.* I. 387 Dingle, a storm-door, built by standing spruce or fir poles close together in front of the camp door. Me. lumbermen. **1905** *Forestry Bureau Bul.* No. 61, Dingle, the roofed-over space between the kitchen and the sleeping quarters in a logging camp, commonly used as a storeroom. **1944** NUTE *Lk. Superior* 208 At the other end was the 'dingle,' or passageway into the kitchen.

* **Dingley,** *n. attrib.* Designating a highly protective tariff provided for in a congressional act of 1897 drawn up by Representative Nelson Dingley of Maine.

1902 BANKS *Newspaper Girl* 294 A kind, good man, and the typical American gentleman, was Mr. Dingley, of Dingley Tariff fame. **1914** *Cyclo. Amer. Govt.* I. 588 The Dingley tariff was in effect twelve years, longer than any tariff since 1828.

b. Dingleyism, (see quot.). *Obs.*

1906 *Churchman* 21 July 92 Protection, whether good or bad, is not necessarily Dingleyism.

dingnation ˌdɪŋˈneʃən, *n.* A euphemism for "damnation." *Slang.* See **dangnation.** — **c1845** W. T. THOMPSON *Chron. Pineville* 167 You've skinned my leg all to flinders, dadfetch your everlastin picter to dingnation. **1884** MARK TWAIN *H. Finn.* xiii. 114 Who in the dingnation's a-going to pay for it?

dingus ˈdɪŋgəs, *n.* [See note.]

No doubt from Du. *dinges* in the same sense as that here shown. The S. Afr. use 1898 shown in the *OED Supp.* is clearly from the Dutch in that region, the Amer. usage representing an independent borrowing made in this country.

A thing the proper name of which is unknown or momentarily forgotten. *Slang.* Cf. **dingbat.**

1876 *Pioche* (Nev.) *D. Jrnl.* 23 Sep. 3/1 The latest thing in the way of a soul-warmer that the youths of Pioche have got up is a dingis made thusly. **1933** T. WILLIAMSON *Woods Colt* 80 Aw, thar was a little safety catch somewhar, some kind of a little dingus you have to push. **1944** HOLTON *Yankees* 81 There was a funny dingus called a telephone coming into use, but most of us knew about it only by hearsay.

dining, n. In combs.: (1) **dining car,** a car or coach in which railroad passengers can secure meals; (2) **day,** (see quot. 1902); (3) **house,** a house on a farm for dining, a public place where meals are served.

(1) 1838 *Amer. R.R. Jrnl.* VII. 328 Nothing now seems to be wanting to make railroad travelling perfect . . . except the introduction of dining cars, and these we are sure will soon be introduced. **1948** *New Yorker* 25 Sep. 27/1 The dining car, which is serviced from a kitchen car, . . . has a continuous serpentine leather sofa. — **(2) 1805** CUTLER in *Life & Corr.* II. 190 If I had time I would give some history of a dining day, of the table and its furniture. **1902** G. C. EGGLESTON *D. South* 272 We'll have a 'dining day,' as a dinner party is queerly called here in Virginia. — **(3) 1854** BROMWELL *Locomotive Sk.* 37 Nearly every large farm has a cluster of buildings . . . around which are scattered wagon and carriage-sheds, corn-cribs, spring-house, wash-house, summer dining-house, etc. **1888** E. BELLAMY *Looking Backward* xiv, I myself served as a waiter for several months in this very dining house.

* **dinkey,** *n.* **1.** A boat, prob. a "dink," a small boat used in duck shooting. **2.** A small locomotive for switching, logging, etc.

(1) 1849 *Pacific News* (S.F.) 27 Nov. 4/2 Picked up adrift, in San Pablo bay, a small copper Dinkey. — **(2) 1874** *Kalama* (Wash.) *Beacon* 20 Jan. 4/2 The passenger train from Tacoma . . . passed the Des Chuttes bridge . . . an hour or two previous to the 'dinkey.' **1948** *Milwaukee Jrnl.* 18 July 6/3 The huffing and puffing steam dinkeys . . . still see service when traffic is heavy.

* **dinner,** *n.* In combs.: (1) **dinner alarm,** a dinner gong; (2) **bell,** a bell rung as a summons to dinner; (3) **bucket, = dinner pail;** (4) **call,** a formal call upon one's host or hostess after a dinner engagement; (5) **card,** a card indicating the seat one is to occupy at a formal dinner, a place card; (6) **horn,** on a farm or plantation, a horn blown to announce dinner to those working in the fields, cf. **hummingbird's dinner horn;** (7) **pail,** see as a main entry; (8) **pot,** a pot in which food is cooked (see also quot. 1893); (9) **ring,** a finger ring with an elaborate setting, usu. with brilliants, designed to be worn with evening dress; (10) **speech,** a speech made on the occasion of a dinner; (11) **station,** a place at which a public conveyance stops regularly so that the passengers may dine; (12) **stop,** a stop made by a train so that the passengers may dine.

(1) 1851 CIST *Cincinnati* 172 Bells of all sizes, from a dinner alarm to the largest class of church bells. — **(2) 1809** in M. B. SMITH *Forty Yrs. Washington Soc.* (1906) 70 The dinner bell rings twice. **1947** *Chi. Tribune* 8 June v. 9 The 'dinner bell' is a time-honored reminder of delicious home-cooked meals. — **(3) 1901** *Scribner's Mag.* XXIX. 404/2 Billy put on his coat, took his dinner-bucket. **1949** *Sat. Ev. Post* 15 Jan. 27/2 Today, miners hang their dinner buckets in the butlers' pantries of the millionaires' homes. — **(4) 1895** WILLIAMS *Princeton Stories* 263 It's two years now, and it's not good form to let a dinner call go more than two years in Princeton. **1898** C. KING *Trooper Galahad* 43 She was so honored that he should call when he must be having so many claims on his time, so many dinner-calls to pay.

(5) 1883 *Harper's Mag.* July 306/2 Such delicate decorative work as refined and accomplished women may be able . . . to do, such as painting dinner cards. **1907** M. C. HARRIS *Tents of Wickedness* I. iii. 35 His dinner-card lay on the side of the cloth next her, and she . . . glanced at it. — **(6) 1836** GILMAN *Recoll.* (1838) 51 The business was scarcely settled, when the dinner-horn sounded. **1946** *Reader's Digest* Jan. 142/1 My wife blew the dinner horn. — **(8) 1775** FITHIAN *Journal* II. 68 Tea . . . is boild in a common dinner-pot, of ten or fifteen gallons, & from thence poured out in tin cups. **1890** RYAN *Told in Hills* 115 This white man . . . could give her a floor of boards and a dinner-pot never empty. **1893** *Voodoo Tales* 202 'To put one's name in the dinner-pot,' is a common form of the 'folk' for 'self-invited to a meal.' — **(9) 1944** *Evanston Rev.* 30 Nov. 80/1 Lost . . . between Hinman and Coronet movie, Dinner Ring, 7 small diamonds.

(10) 1852 *Harper's Mag.* VI. 89 Many readers . . . will perhaps remember hearing Mr. Webster in this city, in that celebrated public dinner-speech [etc.]. **1890** *Harper's Mag.* LXXX. 799/2 The modern dinner speech is a happy blending. — **(11) 1904** O. HENRY *Heart of West* 83 Here's the first dinner-station we've struck where we can get a real good plate of beans. — **(12) 1906** F. LYNDE *Quickening* 128 We'd most luckily escape because there wasn't any dinner-stop on our train.

b. *dinner on the grounds,* at all day religious revivals, the noon meal at which those attending the meetings share at a common table food brought from their homes.

1934 CARMER *Stars Fell* 55 Well, it's time for dinner-on-the-grounds. **1948** *Democrat* 5 Aug. 1/6 Dinner on the grounds with everyone bringing a basket and everyone welcome.

As the last term in **basket, boiled, Clay, corporation, country, field, Hoosier, Jackson, public, secession, shore, stag, Thanksgiving dinner.**

dinner pail. A pail or bucket in which school children, laborers, etc., carry their noon meal.

1856 M. J. HOLMES *Homestead* vi. i, The earthens are each day washed in the little 'tin bucket,' which serves the treble purpose of dinnerpail, washbowl, and drinking cup. **1946** *Chi. D. News* 9 Dec. 6/3 (*caption*), Carrying their dinner pails, coal miners . . . trudge past a string of empty coal cars.

b. dinner pail brigade, workingmen, laborers, who carry dinner pails. *Colloq.*

1890 *The Road* (Denver) 17 May 4/2 Ten cent roulette and keno [are the games] where the boy, the drunkard and the dinner pail brigade drop their dimes. **1938** ASBURY *Sucker's Prog.* 298 Professional gamblers were never admitted into the domain of the Hankinses; they catered exclusively to the 'dinner pail brigade'—amateurs with comparatively small incomes and an incurable passion for the gaming table.

c. full dinner pail, a Republican campaign slogan in 1900, appealing esp. to the laboring classes by stressing the prosperity of McKinley's first term. Also in allusive context.

1900 *Nation* LXXI. 323/2 He [*sc.* Senator Hanna] comes something short of ex-President Harrison's ability to see a 'spiritual significance' in the full dinner-pail. **1904** *Phila. Public Ledger* 26 Aug. 8 Four years ago the 'full dinner-pail' was the battle cry of the national campaign. **1948** *Time* 29 Nov. 23/2 The McKinley program of prosperity and 'the full dinner pail' appealed to farmers and workers as well as employers.

* **dip,** *n.*

1. (See quot. 1908.) Also **dip stick.** Cf. **snuff stick.** *Colloq.*

1853 *Putnam's Mag.* I. 142/2 She . . . will hear ladies inviting ladies to 'come over and take a dip.' **1908** *D.N.* III. 305 Dip. . . . As much snuff as will adhere to a dampened wooden toothbrush [snuff-stick]. **1946** *Atlanta Journal Mag.* 3 March 9/1 A woman might ask for a little grain or smidgin of snuff to go on her dip-stick.

2. Crude turpentine as it is dipped from the "box."

1856 OLMSTED *Slave States* 343 The flow of the first year . . . is of higher value than the ordinary dip. **1862** E. KIRKE *Among Pines* 167 I've four barr'ls of 'dip' and tu of 'hard.' **1896** *Pop. Sci. Mo.* Feb. 473 The *dip* or crude turpentine is emptied.

As the last term in **bayberry, high box, penny, virgin, yellow dip.**

* **dip,** *v.*

1. *S.* and *W. tr.* To take (snuff) usu. by dipping into a box or similar container a small twig the end of which has been frayed so as to form a brush. Also *intr.* or *absol.* Cf. **snuff stick.**

1848 BARTLETT 116 To Dip Snuff, a mode of taking tobacco, practised by women in some parts of the United States, and particularly at the South. **1849** *Knickerb.* XXXIV. 117 The 'gude woman' sat in the corner 'rubbing snuff,' or 'dipping.' **1865** *Nation* I. 335 The woman, going over to the mantel, took down a small circular tin box and began to dip snuff. **1947** *Reader's Digest* Oct. 35/1 They sprawled on the grass, old women dipping snuff, the men chewing midnight plug.

2. To remove (turpentine) from the "box" or receptacle into which it flows from the scarified surface on the tree.

1850 in COMMONS *Doc. Hist.* I. 201 January: 1, finished dipping turpentine. [**1943** *Harper's Mag.* June 87 He'd boxed trees and dipped gum a little, but mostly he'd hunted and fished.]

b. To skim (a milk pail) and remove the cream.

1877 *Vt. Bd. Agric. Rep.* IV. 54 The pails . . . were not dipped as much as they might have been; or, in other words, if we had taken off more cream, we should have made more money.

* **dipper,** *n.*

1. A cup-like receptacle provided with a suitable handle and used chiefly for dipping drinking water from a bucket. Cf. **tin dipper.**

1843 *Knickerb.* XXII. 430 The dipper hangs beside the overflowing water trough. **1898** CANFIELD *Maid of Frontier* 170 Her hand trembled as she raised a dipper of water to her lips. **1948** *Democrat* (Negro Supp.) 1 April 4/2 There are yet too many public drinking dippers and buckets over the county.

2. The buffle duck, *Charitonetta albeola.* Also attrib.

1832 WILLIAMSON *Maine* I. 142 There [are] . . . 5. the river Coot, or ash coloured Duck; 6. the Dipper; 7. the sea Duck. **1847** LANMAN *Summer in Wild.* 73, I killed seven fine looking ducks, which turned out . . . to be unfit to eat, as they were of the dipper species. **1935** *Dept. Agric., Biol. Survey Poster* 31 Aug., Local names [of migratory game birds] . . . Bufflehead.—Butterball, butter duck, dipper, dipper duck.

b. dipper duck, =prec.

1912 in *Birds of Amer.* I. 140 My youthful experience with the Dipper Duck convinced me . . . that it could dive quickly enough to dodge a charge of shot. **1935** [see prec.].

Types of dippers (sense 1)

3. (*cap.*) The seven main stars in Ursa Major, so called because they suggest a dipperlike outline. Also attrib. Cf. ***Ladle,** *n.*

1833 E. H. BURRITT *Geog. Heavens* (1839) 85 Ursa Major. The Great Bear.—This constellation is readily distinguished from all others by means of a remarkable cluster of seven bright stars, forming what is familiarly termed the *Dipper* or *Ladle.* **1922** S. V. BENÉT *Ballad of Wm. Sycamore* (1942) 369 A woman straight as a hunting knife with eyes as bright as the Dipper. **1948** *Pacific Discovery* March–April 28/1 This group will appear to rise higher as the season advances until the Dipper group is above the pole star.

b. Great (or **Big**) **Dipper,** =prec.

1858 THOREAU *Autumn* (1894) 74 [The comet's] tail is at least as long as the whole of the Great Dipper. **1869** MARK TWAIN *Innocents Abroad* 19 They were to . . . search the skies of constellations that never associate with the 'Big Dipper.' **1948** *Atlantic Mo.* Jan. 61/1 Through the night the Big Dipper moves down the slot until its handle rests on the rim where the canyon curves left below camp.

c. Little Dipper, a similar configuration of stars in the constellation of Ursa Minor.

1842 *Lowell Offering* II. 236 The Little Dipper is in Ursa Minor. **1890** C. A. YOUNG *Uranography* § 8 The Pole-Star . . . [is] at the extremity of the handle of the 'Little Dipper.' **1948** *Pacific Discovery* Jan.–Feb. 26/2 It is often called the Seven Sisters, and very frequently mistaken by the inexperienced for the Little Dipper.

4. One who dips snuff. Cf. **snuff dipper.**

1852 *Knickerb.* XL. 93 Fancy yourself . . . married to a 'Dipper!' **1897** *Boston Herald* 26 Sep. 25/4 The dipper . . . would a-dipping go. **1944** CLARK *Pills* 149 Among the hosts of 'dippers' there was a curious folk legend about judging the quality of snuff from the outside of the bottle.

5. One who dips turpentine. Cf. ***dip,** *v.* **2.**

1856 OLMSTED *Slave States* 342 The dippers are constantly employed in emptying the boxes, as they fill with turpentine.

6. In combs. and derivatives: (1) **dipper clam,** the surf or sea clam, *Spisula solidissima,* of the eastern coast; (2) **dredge,** a dredge having a scoop somewhat resembling a huge dipper; (3) **-ful,** the quantity necessary to fill a dipper; (4) **gourd,** a gourd used as a dipper, a plant, *Lagenaria vulgaris,* whose fruit is suitable for use as a dipper, cf. **gourd dipper.**

(1) **1889** *Cent.* 1634/2 [The] dipper-clam . . . attains a large size, is of a subtriangular form, and its valves are sometimes used as dippers or suggest such use. — (2) **1877** *Encycl. Brit.* VII. 465/1 The dipper dredge consists of a barge, with a derrick-crane reaching over the stern, suspending a large wrought-iron bucket which brings up the dredged material. **1879** *Scribner's Mo.* Nov. 55/1 The channel has also been assisted somewhat in its development, by an Osgood dipper dredge. — (3) **1858** *Harper's Mag.* May 729/1 In the midst of a discussion a waggish lad would present a dipperful [of punch] to his excellency the president. **1945** *This Week Mag.* 14 July 16 They [navy beans] are served in their own sweet broth, a dipperful to a bowl. — (4) **1880** ALLAN-OLNEY *New Virginians* I. 199 A bucket of spring-water, with a dipper-gourd in it. **1897** R. M. STUART *Simpkinsville* 146 They ain't nothin' too low down for 'em to mix with . . . f'om a punkin' even down to a dipper-gourd. **1944** DUNCAN *M. Graham* 113 Snow was melted in it, and the children drank from a common dipper-gourd.

As the last term in **candle, mud, Saint Jacob's dipper.**

***dipping,** *n.*

1. *S.* and *W.* The using of snuff by taking it into the mouth, usu. by means of a moistened brush. Also attrib. Cf. **snuff dipping.**

1830 ROYALL *Southern Tour* I. 138 They do not snuff it up the nose, but take it into the mouth—they call it dipping. **1853** *Putnam's Mag.* I. 142/2 Beautiful creatures, with rosy, perfumed mouths, will grow restless at 'dipping time,' and will cautiously desert lover, husband, father, or friend, at the established dipping hour. **1945** WALLACE *Barington* 27 They removed their dipping brushes and spat.

b. dipping stick, a stick used for dipping snuff. Cf. **dip stick, snuff stick.**

1868 *Putnam's Mag.* II. 53 One day, General McNeill happening to get separated from his main escort, an officer of his staff rode up to a house at the fork of the roads, and inquired of the lean, scrawny woman who appeared at the door, vigorously plying the 'dipping-stick,' whether she had recently seen any cavalry. **1869** TOURGEE *Toinette* vi, 'No danger of me,' the woman said, . . . rubbing her dipping-stick about in the box of snuff she held.

2. The process of removing or collecting turpentine from the boxes into which it has drained; the turpentine so collected.

1832 BROWNE *Sylva* 232 The turpentine thus procured is the best, and is called pure dipping. **1862** E. KIRKE *Among Pines* 102 This is the process of 'dipping,' and it is done with a tin or iron vessel constructed to fit the cavity in the tree. **1893** *Outing* Jan. 269/2 His first 'dipping' brought a snug sum of money, for it [turpentine] sold at a high figure then.

dip toast. Also **dipped toast.** Toast over which milk, cream, or drawn butter has been poured.

[**1818** J. PALMER *Jrnl. of Travels* 241 One or two dishes are peculiar to New England, and always on the table, toast dipped in cream and pumpkin pie. **1833** BOARDMAN *America & Americans* 105 Several favourite items [were] peculiar to the American bill of fare. . . . The baptized toast, which I at first mistook for spoiled toast, is the ordinary old-fashioned English buttered toast saturated with milk.] **1855** M. THOMPSON *Doesticks* xxiii. 204 Rest of bill of fare consists of salt ham, . . . dip-toast made with sour milk [etc.]. **1869** HALE *Ingham P.* 17 Good soul, she even made dip-toast for our suppers.

***director,** *n.* The driver of a locomotive, reaper, etc. *Obs.* — **1833** *Niles' Reg.* XLIV. 267/2 It [i.e., anthracite coal] sends forth no sparks to burn or alarm passengers careful of their dresses; and emits no disagreeable or pernicious vapor; and it enables the director to travel without the encumbrance of a tender, as the fuel and the water are both carried on the engine. **1884** WELLS *Pract. Economics* (1885) 237 The director of a mechanical reaper entering the field behind a pair of horses, with gloves on his hands, and an umbrella over his head.

As the last term in **dummy, funeral, school director.**

***directory,** *n.* As the last term in **Congressional, telephone directory.**

***directress,** *n.* A woman who has charge of a school. *Obs.* — **1863** A. D. WHITNEY *F. Gartney* vi, The directress turned toward the throng of faces. **1883** *Student* III. 271 The directresses of these schools ought to endeavor to furnish the primary schools with children well prepared.

***dirt,** *n.*

1. *W.* (See quot. 1857.) Cf. **pay dirt.**

1850 KINGSLEY *Diary* 156 It is slow getting dirt and it is not very rich. **1857** J. D. BORTHWICK *In Calif.* 123 'Dirt' is the word universally used in California to signify the substance dug. . . . The miners talk of rich dirt and poor dirt, and of stripping off so many feet of 'top dirt' before getting to the 'pay dirt.' **1948** JOHNSTON *Gold Rush* 8/2 During the time of the difficulty, hundreds of men jumped into the hole, which was about fifty feet square, and carried away dirt which would pay from fifty to a hundred dollars a sack.

attrib. **1869** S. BOWLES *Our New West* ix. 179 The dirt-washers swept eagerly over the rich surface deposits. *Ib.,* The old and simple dirt washing for gold was resumed. **1871** PINE *Beyond West* 107 The other form of mining, known as gulchmining or dirt washing, is increasing again, and has employed full three hundred men this season.

2. In special combs.: (1) **dirt board,** (see quot.), *obs.;* (2) **car,** a railroad car for hauling dirt; (3) **cart,** a rubbish cart; (4) **cut,** a passage made by excavation, *rare;* (5) **dauber,** *S.* the mud wasp, also attrib.; (6) **eater,** one of a class of poor whites in the South addicted to eating dirt, also transf.; (7) **farmer,** a practical farmer, one who farms his own land, also **dirt farming;** (8) **lodge,** an Indian lodge made of dirt, *obs.;* (9) **road,** an unimproved road [this term may not be of Amer. orig.; it has been found, 1925, in Somerset dial. (see *N. & Q.* (London) 8 Feb., 1941, 99)]; (10) **roof,** a roof made of dirt, also **dirt-roofed;** (11) **scraper,** (see quot. 1874); (12) **seller,** one who sells land, also attrib. in place-names; (13) **track,** (see quot.); (14) **wagon,** a wagon used in hauling dirt.

(1) **1874** KNIGHT 706/2 Dirt-board (carriage), a board for warding off earth from the axle-arm. A cutto-plate. — (2) **1870** EMERSON *Soc. & Solitude* 131 The railroad dirt-cars are good excavators; but there is no porter like Gravitation. **1872** *Harper's Mag.* June 67/2 On all the miles to Ogden, not a spike was driven, not a dirt car was moved. — (3) **1846** *Knickerb.* XXVII. 458 Then, hark! hark! it comes—the dirt-cart! **1888** *Harper's Mag.* Dec. 95/1, I is a man, if I

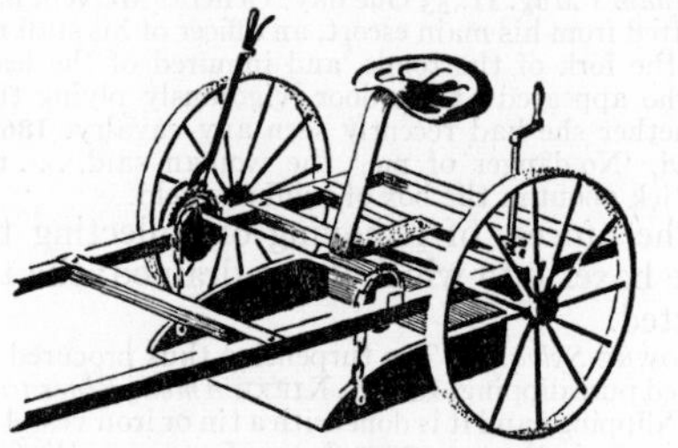

One form of dirt scraper

does drive a dirt cart. — (4) **1873** BEADLE *Undevel. West* 448 It looks more like driving through a dirt cut in some excavation than the streets of a city.

(5) **1838** GOSSE *Letters* 237 The little boys (and boys in these back-woods, as I have before intimated, know a good deal about natural history) informed me that these were the nests of the Dirt-daubers. **1948** *Sat. Ev. Post* 25 Dec. 16/2 So she got her herbs, and dirt-dobber nest, And the other things she needed. — (6) **1844** in CATTERALL *Judicial Cases* II. 392 The defendant drew a receipt for the purchase money . . . in which he stated . . . (they) were dirt eaters. **1913** A. C. COLE *Whig Party in So.* 189 The disunion men [*c.* 1851] . . . tried to discredit the Union movement in the eyes of Democrats by applying to it such epithets as 'Federalists,' 'Feds,' 'Submissionists,' . . . 'Dirt-eaters.' **1940** CUMMINGS *American & His Food* 87. Distinguished from other southerners by hookworm disease were dirt-eaters scattered in sand barrens and pine woods from South Carolina to Mississippi. — (7) **1920** *Boston Ev. Transcript* 2 Oct. IV. 1/1 So Aggie . . . goes on its way, doing its multiple duty of making dirt-farming a fine art; . . . and of making the rural community and home a more livable town and place. **1924** H. CROY *R.F.D. No. 3* 148 I'm going to put up the finest cattle barn in the state—that is, belonging to a real dirt farmer, not to one of them city dudes. **1948** *Sat. Ev. Post* 6 Nov. 6/3 I, being a female, took off the mantle of a teacher and put on the blue jeans of a dirt farmer! — (8) **1823** JAMES *Exped.* I. 181 It [a village] consists of dirt lodges. — (9) **1852** STOWE *Uncle Tom* vii, Lizy'd take de dirt road, bein' it's the least traveled. **1948** *Sierra Club* (So. Calif. Chap.) Sched. 128, 69 Turn right on road leading up Big Rock Creek Canyon for 2.4 miles and 1.1 miles on dirt road to South Fork Big Rock Creek Public Campground.

(10) **1873** BEADLE *Undevel. West* 734 To his joy he came upon a dirt-roofed log-house. **1881** *Rep. Indian Affairs* 121 Agency Buildings at Poplar River are agent's house, . . . carpenter shop, 16 by 24, log, dirt roof. **1910** *Outlook* 2 July 483 A log cabin of two rooms, with a dirt roof. — (11) **1874** KNIGHT 706/2 Dirt-scraper, a grading shovel, a road scraper, an implement drawn by a pair of horses, managed by one man, and used in leveling, banking up, or grading ground. **1891** *Harper's Mag.* Nov. 888/1 He . . . was a busy man, charged with . . . the repairing of all the ironwork of the wagons, cars, and dirt-scrapers. — (12) **1821** *Jrnl. Science* III. 43 One Catecantiskey (the dirt-seller or merchant of earth) was boasting one day. **1883** SMITH *Geol. Survey Ala.* 369 Another similar ridge, called the Dirt-Seller Mountain, . . . is in reality a V-shaped mountain. — (13) **1902** *Encycl. Brit.* XXIX 335/2 Practically all flat racing in the United States is held on 'dirt-tracks,' *i.e.,* courses with soil specially prepared for racing, instead of turf courses. — (14) **1853** *Mich. Agric. Soc. Trans.* 241, I had an ordinary dirt wagon loaded with sand. **1904** *N.Y. Ev. Post* 9 May 2 A team of horses attached to a dirt wagon became unmanageable.

b. In phrases: (1) *To cut dirt,* to run away, to depart in haste, *slang;* (2) *on top of dirt,* above ground, *colloq.;* (3) *to do* (one) *dirt,* to harm (one) in an underhanded manner, *slang.*

(1) **1829** *Negro Song* (B. & L.), He jump up fo' sartin—he cut dirt and run. **1862** LOWELL *Biglow P.* 2 Ser. ii, Why two-thirds o' the Rebbels 'ould cut dirt, Ef they once thought thet Guv'-ment meant to hurt. — (2) **1848** HOOPER *Widow Rugby* (F.), It's no use argufyin' the matter—I'm the ugliest man now on top of dirt. Thar's nary nuther like me. — (3) **1893** *Voodoo Tales* 274 If I tek ter doin' dirt, den Ise willin' ter be jacky-me-lantuhn—an' sarve me right, too! **1947** *Reader's Digest* Oct. 155/2 People had been doing her dirt for 40 years.

As the last term in **blue, chip, color, gold, gopher, old, pay, surface, top dirt.**

* **dirt,** *v.* **1.** *tr.* To cultivate a row crop, esp. corn and cotton, in such a way as to bring dirt around the base of the plants. **2.** To cover with dirt. — (1) **1850** in TURNER *Cotton* (1865) 36, I can dirt easily four acres per horse. **1944** CLARK *Pills* 287 A middle-aged farmer flaunted himself in the face of progress and used a scraper to prepare cotton for chopping, and a twister for 'dirting' corn. — (2) **1903** A. ADAMS *Log Cowboy* 221 It now only remained to sod over and dirt the bridge thoroughly.

* **dis-,** *prefix.* Used in occasional expressions: (1) **discantation,** *n.* descanting, discoursing; (2) **dischargement,** *n.* a discharge; (3) **disconfident,** *n. collect.* those without confidence; (4) **diselect,** *v. tr.* to deprive of the status of having been elected; (5) **disfixment,** the state or condition of not being fixed or settled; (6) **dispensationist,** *n.* one who believes in a particular dispensation; (7) **dispeoplement,** *n.* the process of depopulating; (8) **disquixotted,** *a.* disillusioned; (9) * **disreputable,** *a.* of land, worn out, robbed of fertility; (10) **disreputer,** *n.* one who insists that something is in disrepute; (11) **disretire,** *v. intr.* to advance, fail to retire, *humorous;* (12) **dissatisfactionist,** *n.* one who manifests dissatisfaction; (13) **distemperament,** *n.* disorder, disturbance; (14) **disunwell,** *a.* unwell, ailing; (15) **disvoiced,** *a.* silent, deprived of voice.

(1) **1893** GUNTER *Miss Dividends* 97 This discantation on the absent Oliver, Lawrence enjoys so little . . . that he turns the conversation to his own prospects. — (2) **1638** P. VINCENT in *Mass. H.S. Coll.* 3 Ser. VI. 39 The earth being cast up for their better shelter against the enemy's dischargements. — (3) **1863** *Rio Abajo Press* 17 Feb. 2 We assure the disconfident that, so far as the proprietor of this paper is concerned, they run no risk of losing their subscription money. — (4) **1860** *Cong. Globe* 1 Feb. 651/2 On Friday last, when Mr. Smith . . . was elected Speaker, he was diselected by the withdrawal of certain votes.

(5) **1883** STOCKTON *Rudder Grange* (1890) 77 During one of these intervals of mental disfixment we took a house. — (6) **1856** P. CARTWRIGHT *Autobiog.* 175 If you are one of these old dispensationists, look out for a perfect cure. — (7) **1841** FOOTE *Texas & Texans* I. 14 To mark its dreadful course with the dispeoplement of her infant towns and villages. — (8) **1832** KENNEDY *Swallow Barn* I. 52 He came home the most disquixotted cavalier that ever hung up his shield at the end of a scurvy crusade. — (9) **1857** *Ill. Agric. Soc. Trans.* III. 434 The reason why old land becomes disreputable is the slovenly manner of cultivating it.

(10) **1894** *Voice* (N.Y.) 19 April, The disreputer is confused. — (11) **1866** C. H. SMITH *Bill Arp* 27 More than eighteen months ago you published an edict ordering the boys to retire and be peaceable, but they disretired and went to fighting. — (12) **1893** *Columbus* (O.) *Dispatch* 29 May, The dissatisfactionists became quite noisy. — (13) **1871** *Scribner's Mo.* II. 593 Men were . . . unconscious of the . . . fragilities and distemperaments of their organization. — (14) **1884** SWEET & KNOX *Through Texas* viii. 100, I was disunwell all the time I staid thar.

(15) **1865** LOWELL *Poetical Works* (1896) 345/2 The mighty ones of old sweep by, Disvoiced now and insubstantial things, As noisy once as we.

See also * **disagreeable, discomboberate, disfellowship, disloyalist, dispossess, dispossessory, disrest, disunionism, disunionist.**

* **disagreeable,** *a.* Uneasy, apprehensive. *Colloq.* — **1827** COOPER *Prairie* xii, We are disagreeable about his camping on the prairie, instead of coming in to his own bed. **1844** *P. Parley's Ann.* V. 180 The King felt quite disagreeable. The Russians might drop in upon him very unceremoniously.

disbursing officer. An officer whose duties involve paying out or dispensing funds. — **1831** BENTON *30 Years' View* (1854) I. 196/1 There are two different deposits of public money in the bank; one in the name of the Treasurer of the United States, . . : the other in the name of disbursing officers. **1904** *Indian Laws & Tr.* III. 37 The Commissioner of Indian Affairs . . . is hereby authorized to require any disbursing officer of Indian Department to file a special bond.

discharging scow, *n.* A large flat-bottomed boat used in the process of clearing and deepening rivers, channels, etc. *Obs.* — **1852** in *Whig Almanac 1853* 26/2 For snag-boats, dredge-boats, discharging-scows, &c., to be used on . . . western rivers, . . . $150,000.

∗**Disciples,** *n. pl.* A Christian trinitarian and congregational denomination founded in Pennsylvania in 1810 by Thomas and Alexander Campbell. In full **Disciples of Christ.** Cf. **Campbellites** and **Christians.**

1834 PECK *Gaz. Illinois* 203 A new sect [was] recently organized by a union of 'Reformed Baptists' and 'Christians' who call themselves 'Disciples.' **1835** MARTIN *Description Va.* 76 The precise distinction between the regular Baptists and the Reformers, called the disciples of Christ, not being in all cases drawn, there is no coming to any thing like certain knowledge. **1948** *Newsweek* 22 Nov. 94/2 The Disciples of Christ minister stings complacent and petty-minded Protestants.

∗**discipline,** *v. tr.* (See quot. 1828.)

1828 WEBSTER, Discipline . . . to execute the laws of the church on offenders, with a view to bring them to repentance and reformation of life. **1873** MARK TWAIN & WARNER *Gilded Age* xiv. 133 Fortunately father is already out of the meeting, so they can't discipline him. **1875** BEECHER *Plymouth Pulpit* II. 134 He whose orthodoxy inspires bitterness should be disciplined.

discomboberate dɪskəmˈbɑbəˌret, *v.* Also **discomboborate, discombobulate,** etc. *tr.* To confuse, upset, put out of order. *Slang.*

1834 *Sun* (N.Y.) 21 Mar. 2/3 I'll tell you what, if you'll just throw down them are clubs—and come, one to time, may be some of you don't get *discombobracated.* **1835** *Vade Mecum* (Phila.) 11 Apr. 3/6 If my nerves are discomboberated, who'll treat to settle 'em? **1839** HOFFMAN *Wild Scenes* 171 The lad doesn't love to have his hunting-tools discomboborated. **1948** *Chi. D. News* 24 June 16/3 The introduction of radio to the conventions discombooberated the speech-makers terribly.

∗**discount,** *n.*

1. *Billiards.* (See quot. 1909.)

1857 PHELAN *Game of Billiards* 66 In double and treble discount, twice and thrice the amount of his opponent's gains are deducted from the player's score. **1909** WEBSTER 636/3 Discount, . . . a deduction made from the score of one player for every point made by his opponent.

2. discount day, (see quot. 1891).

1830 *Williams's N.Y. Ann. Reg.* 166 Bills or notes offered for discount, must be inclosed in a letter to the Cashier the day before discount day. **1891** NICHOLS *Business Guide* (ed. 28) 238 Discount Days, the days of the week on which the directors of a bank meet to consider paper offered for discount.

∗**discount,** *v. tr.* (See quot.) Also ∗**discounter,** *n.* — **1857** PHELAN *Game of Billiards* 66 When one player is so much the superior of another that he allows all the counts made by his opponent to be deducted from his own reckoning, he is said to 'discount' his adversary's gains. Thus, if his opponent make a run of ten, ten is added to his count, and ten deducted from the discounter's reckoning.

discovering party. A party sent out to find or locate something or someone. *Obs.* — **1779** *Mass. H.S. Coll.* 2 Ser. II. 469 The Indians attacked a party of our men that were sent out Yesterday as a discoveryng party.

∗**discovery,** *n.*

1. *W.* (See quot. 1881.) Also attrib.

1814 BRACKENRIDGE *Louisiana* 147 What is called a discovery, by those engaged in working the mines, is, when any one happens upon an extensive body of ore. **1881** RAYMOND *Mining Gloss.*, Discovery, the first finding of the mineral deposit in place upon a mining claim. A discovery is necessary before the location can be held by a valid title. The opening in which it is made is called discovery shaft, discovery-tunnel, etc. **1903** *Cin. Enquirer* 19 Jan. 1/3 Pedro Creek, the discovery creek, has not as yet equalled Gold Stream.

transf. **1948** *Time* 19 Jan. 87/2 The discovery well was pouring out 55 barrels a day, the maximum under Texas regulations.

b. discovery claim, (see quots.).

1897 *N.Y. Jrnl.* 30 Aug. 3/2 The expression number so and so above and below means the number of the claim above or below the Discovery claim on that particular creek or gulch. **1902** MCKEE *Land of Nome* 85 There is on every creek a 'discovery' claim, and all the others upon it are known as Nos. 1, 2, 3, etc., 'above' or 'below Discovery,' and are so staked and recorded. **1941** FRITZ *Colorado* 130 The discovery of any new lode or diggings always entitled the discoverer to one claim which he marked as the discovery claim.

2. discovery dance, among Plains Indians, a dance announcing the discovery of game or enemies.

*c*1836 CATLIN *Indians* II. 137 The Beggar's dance, the discovery dance, and the eagle dance, are far more graceful and agreeable. *c*1838 *Ib.* 214 The Discovery Dance . . . was exceedingly droll and picturesque, and acted out with a great deal of pantomimic effect—without music, or any other noise than the patting of their feet.

3. Discovery Day, Oct. 12, usu. known as Columbus Day, in allusion to the discovery of America by Columbus.

1928 M. E. HAZELTINE *Anniversaries and Holidays* 126 Oct. 12 Columbus Day, Discovery of America 1492. Called Discovery Day.

discretionary pool. (See quot. 1900.) — **1900** NELSON *A B C Wall St.* 139 Discretionary pool. At times a powerful pool is formed to depress or advance a stock, and its direction is left to the discretion of one or more members, who work for the benefit of all the members. **1901** *Harper's Wkly.* XLV. 1290/1 Probably the game known as 'discretionary pools' is the most common.

∗**disease,** *n.* As the last term in **caisson, gum, horse, pale, paper-gum, Riggs', snow, snowshoe disease.**

disfellowship dɪsˈfɛləʃɪp, *v. tr.* To exclude (a member) from fellowship in a church or religious group.

1831 *Troy* (N.Y.) *Watchman* 3 Sep. (Th.), They were disfellowshipped by the association. **1881** *Atlantic Mo.* XLVII. 280 We have suffered . . . from the ugly use of the word *fellowship* and even *disfellowship* as verbs. **1942** STEGNER *Mormon C.* 98 One gentleman who rose in the tabernacle a generation ago and asked for an accounting of Church funds was unceremoniously thrown out and disfellowshipped.

∗**dish,** *n.* In combs.: (1) **dish-pan,** a large pan ordinarily used for washing dishes; (2) **rag,** see as a main entry; (3) ∗**water,** (see quots.), also attrib. in the sense of next; (4) **watery,** *a.* weak, insipid.

(1) **1872** *Newton Kansan* 5 Sep. 4/5 Put your corn, while hot, in a dish-pan. **1947** *Collier's* 31 May 26/2 A registered nurse . . . looked up from her dishpan (she was washing dishes because the hospital was short of kitchen help). — (3) **1856** *Town Talk* (S.F.) 22 May 4/2 The dish-water journals of the 'city of corruption' are crying 'peace, peace, let the law (?) take its course!' **1858** O. W. HOLMES *Autocrat* (1883) 224 Flash phraseology . . . is the dish-water from the washings of English dandyism. **1887** *Sanitary Era* (N.Y.) 15 Nov., Rainwater, after all, is nature's dishwater, from washing the great bowl of the atmosphere. — (4) **1890** *Columbus* (O.) *Dispatch* 13 Feb., The review [of a political quarrel] would be in its tenor dishwatery.

As the last term in **birchbark, boil, boiled, chafing, dough, knot, skimming, wash, white man's dish.**

dishrag ˈdɪʃˌræg, *n.*

1. A cloth used in washing dishes, a dishcloth. Also in phrasal use.

The colloq. phrase in quot. 1945, expressive of unwillingness to take second place, is based upon a much earlier one recorded in Ray's *Proverbs* (1678) where *dishclout* is used instead of "dishrag."

1839 *S. Lit. Messenger* V. 320/2 When he landed he lay there as limber as a dish-rag. **1931** *K.C. Times* 31 Oct., The girl who is all at sea about what to do with the dishrag can work wonders with her powder puff in the dark. **1945** *Sat. Review* 27 Jan. 15/1 If I can't be tablecloth, I shore don't aim to be dishrag.

2. The dishcloth gourd. Also attrib.

1890 *Cent.* 5852/3 *Sponge-gourd.* . . . The netted fiber from the interior of the fruit is used for washing and other purposes, hence called *vegetable sponge* or *dish-rag.* **1904** *N.Y. Tribune* 22 May, A novel enterprise, that of raising dishrags, is being exploited by a number of Southern California horticulturists. **1912** I. COBB *Back Home* 289 The Major was . . . a clubman by instinct, yet with no club except . . . the screening of dishrag vines and balsam apples on Priest's front porch.

∗**disk,** *n.* Also ∗**disc.**

1. Short for "disk harrow" or "disk plow" *qq.v.*

1930 *Randolph Enterprise* (Elkins, W.Va.) 30 Oct. 8/2, 1 Deering binder; 1 two-horse disc; 1 manure spreader.

2. *attrib.* Designating agricultural implements having concave steel disks for pulverizing or breaking land, as (1) **disk cultivator,** (2) **drill,** (3) **harrow,** (4) **plow,** (5) **pulverizer.**

(1) **1894** *Irrig. Age* Jan. 34/1, I have found one of the best tools that we have yet used to be the disc cultivator. — (2) **1907** L. H. BAILEY *Cyclo. Amer. Agric.* I. 207 The disc drill is also used very extensively in many sections of the country where the soil is loose. — (3) **1896** *Vt. Agric. Rep.* XV. 101 The tools best suited to orchard use are the plough and wheel or disc harrow. **1949** *Reader's Digest* Feb. 119/1 The disk harrow, the cultivator, the hay rake, the hay loader and scores of other farm tools followed. — (4) **1881** *U.S. Patent* 15 March 9603 Disk plow. **1948** *Pauls Valley* (Okla.) *D. Democrat* 1 July 11/6 Several farmers in the Garvin-Murray soil conservation district plant bermuda roots from a platform built on a moldboard or disk plow. — (5) **1884** *Vt. Agric. Rep.* VIII. 282 Gang plows, disk pulverizers and sulky cultivators.

As the last term in **peyote disk.**

disk dɪsk, *v.* [f. the noun.] *tr.* To break or pulverize (ground) with a disk plow or harrow.

1917 *Nat. Weather & Crop Bul.* March 4/2 Cutting corn-stalks, disking, and plowing have commenced in the central and southern counties [of Nebraska]. **1941** M. L. SMITH *God's Country* 142 We had to disk the ground and then harrow it. **1948** *Calif. Citrograph* March 215/1 Last year the ground was pretty uneven from several seasons of disking in weeds.

b. disking machine, (see quot.).

1884 KNIGHT *Supp.* 261/2 Disking Machine, . . . a steam-cultivating implement to be drawn by an engine over sod or plowed sod, to renew the ground, or to prepare for seeding.

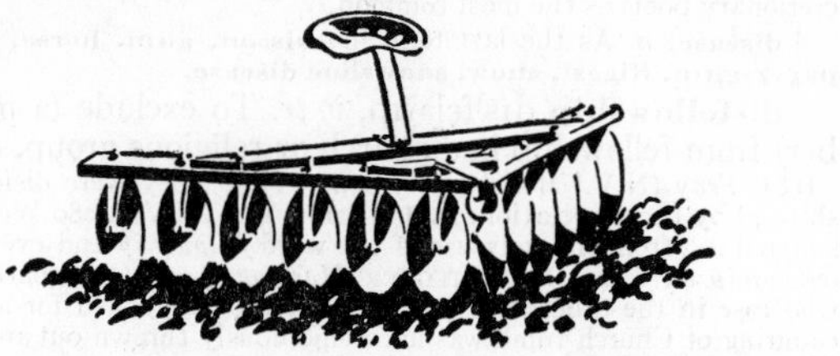

Disk harrow

disloyalist dɪs'lɔɪəlɪst, *n.* During the Civil War (1861–65), one not loyal to the Union. Also transf. *Obs.*

1863 *Boston Sunday Herald* 24 May 1/3. **1886** *Advance* (Chicago) XXI. 99/4 The American Bluebeard [i.e., a Mormon] is quite as dangerous in his character of a disloyalist as that of a polygamist. **1901** CHURCHILL *Crisis* 378 Sixty prominent 'disloyalists' were to be chosen and assessed to make up a sum of ten thousand dollars.

* **dismal,** *a.* and *n.*

1. An especially gloomy, lonely, forbidding swamp. In full **dismal swamp.** Also fig.

*a*1656 BRADFORD *Hist.* 119 They held [an assembly] in a darke and dismale swampe. **1775** *Amer. Husbandry* I. 391 Rice is yet the grand staple production of South Carolina, and that for which the planters neglect the healthy, pleasant back country in order to live in the *Dismals* on the coast, for so the Americans justly call the swamps. **1830** PAULDING *Chron. Gotham* 109 Interrupting the good lady, who was losing herself in a Dismal Swamp of meteors. **1888** J. D. WHITNEY *Names & Places* 211 These swamps are locally known as 'dismals' and also as 'pocosins.'

2. As a place-name, applied especially to the large marshy tract extending from southeastern Virginia well into northwestern North Carolina. Also **Dismal Swamp, Great Dismal Swamp.** Also fig.

1728 BYRD *Dividing Line* (1910) 63 We ordered several men to patrol on the edge of the Dismal. **1763** WASHINGTON *Diaries* I. 192 A small slipe of Land between the said River Peguemen and the Dismal Swamp. **1856** OLMSTED *Slave States* 149 The 'Great Dismal Swamp,' together with the smaller 'Dismals' . . . of the same character, along the North Carolina Coast. *Ib.*, 151 Much of the larger part of the 'Great Dismal' was originally covered by a heavy forest growth. **1944** *Harper's Mag.* March 364/2 For a long time thereafter he was politically in the Dismal Swamp.

Dismalite 'dɪzml,aɪt, *n.* A resident of the Dismal Swamp. *Obs.* — **1775** *N.C. Gazette* (New Berne) 24 Mar. 3/3 Fellow Dismalites and Swampers, are we not the Men whom God hath appointed to curb the Insolence of Britain.

* **dismiss,** *v.* **a.** *intr.* To decamp, go off. *Slang. Rare.* **b.** *tr.* To acquit or discharge (one charged with a crime or misdemeanor). — **(a)** **1845** HOOPER *Taking Census* ii. 175 Bein as my kumpny aint adceptable here, I'll dismiss. — **(b)** **1904** *N.Y. Times* 30 April 9 Judge McCann of the Police Court had received requests from women all over the city asking that Mrs. Wiggs be dismissed.

* **dispatch,** *n.* A telegram. Also **telegraphic dispatch.** Cf. **cipher dispatch.**

1850 *Quincy* (Ill.) *Whig* 12 Nov. 3/1 We learn by a telegraphic despatch . . . that an affray occurred at the Middletown polls on the day of the election. **1863** *N.Y. Tribune* 3 Jan. 1/5 Special Dispatch to The N.Y. Tribune. **1945** *La Junta* (Colo.) *Tribune-Democrat* 15 Feb. 2/1 According to uncensored dispatches now reaching Washington, active guerrilla warfare is flaring up on a mounting scale behind the German lines.

* **dispatcher,** *n.* = **train dispatcher.**

1878 PINKERTON *Strikers* 219 The conductor . . . promptly passed the dreaded word to the dispatcher. **1904** *N.Y. Times* 7 March 5 The destruction of the dispatcher's office caused a suspension of all traffic in the Rome and Watertown division. **1945** *Tracks* June 17 A conductor-pilot, at his field telephone set, tells the dispatcher, 'The gang is clear of the tracks. . . . Let the trains roll!'

* **dispensary,** *n.* A place where liquor is sold under state regulations. Also attrib.

1894 *S.C. Sup. Court Rep.* XLII. 230 The Dispensary Act of 1892 did not, in its title, expressly purport to be a police measure. **1903** HART *Actual Govt.* 504 In South Carolina a system of dispensaries or public salerooms is provided in which pure liquor is sold only in certain quantities and not to be consumed on the premises, and the profits to go into the State treasury. **1926** D. LEIGH COLVIN *Prohibition in the U.S.* 293 Although there had been local dispensaries at Athens, Georgia, and a few other places, the dispensary system as a state measure was put into operation in South Carolina.

dispossess ,dɪspə'zes, *n. attrib.* =next. — **1889** *Cent.* 1680/1 Dispossess proceedings . . . to eject a tenant, as for non-payment of rent. *Ib.*, A dispossess warrant . . . to eject the occupant. (N.Y.) **1931** *New Republic* 22 April 265/1 Finally, she got a dispossess notice.

dispossessory ,dɪspə'zesərɪ, *a.* Pertaining to dispossession. *Rare.* — **1888** *Union Signal* (Chicago) 5 April, The number of distress and dispossessory warrants issued.

* **disputed,** *a.*

1. disputed bounds, (see quot.). *Obs.*

1724 H. JONES *Virginia* 27 North Carolina . . . formerly was the South Part of Virginia. . . . There is a very long List of Land fifteen Miles broad between both Colonies (called the disputed Bounds) in the due Subjection to neither; which is an Asylum for the Runagates of both Countries.

2. disputed territory, (see quot. 1846). *Obs.*

1831 *Boston Transcript* 12 Mar. 2/2 We have . . . a map of the disputed territory, with the lines of the boundaries as claimed by the United States and Great Britain, and the new line as decided by the award of the King of the Netherlands. **1846** MANSFIELD *Winfield Scott* 319 [Scott] learned that hostile movements were on foot on both sides of what was then known as the Disputed territory. This was a territory on the borders of the State of Maine, the boundaries of which the United States and Great Britain had not been able to ascertain.

b. Any territory the possession of which is in dispute.

1839 *N.O. Bee* 6 May The exact terms have not transpired, but the [Seminole] Indians are to keep possession of 'the disputed territory.' **1846** *Quincy* (Ill.) *Whig* 3 Jan. 1/5 In that work the disputed territory [Ore.] is described, as it is everywhere else, as perfectly valueless.

disrest dɪs'rest, *v. tr.* To dislodge or keep (one) from rest. *Obs.*

1675 *Conn. Rec.* II. 353 It is pitty but they should be disrested. **1705** *Boston News-Letter* 26 Feb. 2/2 His Excellency the Governour has at the same time a Cruiser on the Shore of L'acadie to disrest the Enemy there. **1768** in *Pub. Col. Soc.* XXIV. 241 That a great part of the Families are already settled and in some of the Townships the whole number: That it is inconsistent with his Majesty's Interest that the said Grantees should be disrested, That it would be manifest injustice in the Government to suffer it, and that this Government cannot suffer it unless it be done by his Majesty's Orders.

* **dissolve,** *n. Motion pictures.* (See quot. 1918.) — **1918** HOMER CROY *How Motion Pictures are Made* 178 The so-called 'dissolve,' by which the figures of the scene gradually disappear while those of a succeeding scene slowly take their place. **1948** *Time* 2 Aug. 72/2 He took closeups, crosscuts, angle shots and dissolves.

* **dissolver,** *n.* A motion picture apparatus for dissolving a picture. Also attrib. — **1912** F. H. RICHARDSON *Motion Picture Handbook* 377 The stereopticon or dissolver may readily be rigged with home-made color wheels, so that colored lights may be thrown on the stage. *Ib.* 378 Your dissolver lenses must be matched so that they project the same size picture.

* **distance,** *n. To take distance,* to go far away. *Colloq.* See also **long, pigeon distance.** — **1838** *Jefferson* 8 Dec. (Th.), It is hoped that these Mormons will 'take distance,' and leave the haunts of civilized men.

* **distemper,** *n.* As the last term in **Canada, country, Dutch, ear, lame, throat distemper.**

* **distillery,** *n.* (See quot.) *Slang. Obs.* See also **turpentine distillery.** — **1881** *N.Y. Ev. Post* Oct. (Th.), A 'bucket-shop' in New York is a low 'gin-mill,' or 'distillery,' where small quantities of spirits are dispensed in pitchers and pails (buckets).

distributee dɪs,trɪbju'ti, *n.* One who receives a share in the distribution of the estate of an intestate. — **1870** PINKERTON *Guide* 45 Where an Administrator has money belonging to a distributee, whose residence is known, it is his duty to give notice to his readiness to pay it over. **1891** R. LINN in *N. & Q.* 8th Ser. 3 Oct. 269 An Act of Congress was passed for the relief of the distributees of Col. Linn.

* **distributor,** *n.* As the last term in **guano, manure, stamp distributor.**

* **district,** *n.*

1. A subdivision of a city serving as a unit for policing, fire prevention, political representation, etc. Also attrib.

1769 *Phila. Ordinances* 26 No waggon, wain or cart . . . [within] Philadelphia, or within the Northern Liberties thereof, or within the district of Southwark, . . . shall travel . . . on any of the paved parts of the said city. **1894** *Harper's Mag.* LXXXIX. 695/1 The touch of politics is needed to convert a saloon coterie into a district club. **1908** I. N. STEVENS *Liberators* 284 When their district workers could get no information as to how the laboring people were voting; . . . then Tammany Hall became alarmed.

2. The region which later became the state of Kentucky. In full *district of Kentucky*. *Obs.*

1785 in J. M. BROWN *Polit. Beginnings Ky.* 237 This district ought, at some period not far distant, to be separated from the government of Virginia. **1790** *State P.* (1819) I. 17 The district of Kentucky, at present a part of Virginia, . . . is to become a distinct member of the Union. **1835** J. HALL *Sk. of West* II. 93 At the close of the revolution, the state of Virginia rewarded her military officers, by donations of land, in the then *district of Kentucky*.

b. *district of Maine,* the area, formerly a part of Massachusetts, now known as the state of Maine. *Obs.*

1792 *Mass. H.S. Coll.* I. 112 Should therefore the District of Maine be erected into a separate state, it would perhaps be the most convenient place for the seat of government. **1820** *Niles' Reg.* XVIII. 7/1 That part of Massachusetts hitherto known as the district of Maine. **1843** HAYWARD *Gazetteer of Maine* 3 Maine, formerly called the District of Maine, had been connected with Massachusetts in all its political relations, until it became an independent State in 1820.

3. A region or territory whose limits and dimensions are approximately those of a state. *Obs.*

1791 *Ann. 2nd Congress* 201 Such was the apportionment of its members with respect to the unequal districts or States into which this country is divided. **1839** PLUMBE *Sk. Iowa* 12 This District . . . is forever free from the institution of slavery.

4. (See quots.)

1798 MORSE *Gazetteer* 512 South Carolina . . . is divided into 9 districts. **1814** BRACKENRIDGE *Louisiana* 112 The term 'district' corresponds with the county of the states. **1889** *Cent.* 1698/2 In South Carolina, during most of the period from 1768 to 1868, the chief subdivision of the State (except the coast region) was called a *district*, instead of a county as in the other States. **1924** SEITZ *Braxton Bragg* 461 Howell Cobb was given the 'District of Georgia,' which included all the state outside the limits of Hood's operations.

b. *District of Columbia,* the area of about 70 square miles laid out on the northeast bank of the Potomac River as the seat of government of the U.S. Also *District of Columbian*, an inhabitant of this. Cf. **6.** below.

[**1787** *Constitution* I. viii. § 16 The congress shall have power . . . to exercise exclusive legislation . . . over such district, not exceeding ten miles square, as may . . . become the seat of government of the United States.] **1800** *Ann. 6th Congress* 2 Sess. 723 It is with you, gentlemen, to consider whether the local powers over the District of Columbia [etc.]. **1903** *N.Y. Ev. Post* 21 Nov. 10 Not six persons in all the crowd where empowered to vote for any policy whatever. Her audience consisted of District of Columbians.

c. civil, magisterial district, (see quot. 1889).

1858 *Tenn. Tax Laws* (1905) 17 By advertisement at four of the most public places in each civil district, [the collector shall] give twenty days' notice . . . when and where he will attend to receive taxes. **1889** *Cent.* 1698/2 In Virginia and West Virginia the chief subdivision of a county is called a *magisterial district*. . . . In Tennessee it is called a *civil district*. **1906** J. A. FAIRLIE *Local Government* 187 In Virginia . . . they are called magisterial districts, and in Tennessee civil districts.

5. An area, sometimes embracing several square miles, forming a unit in the administration of the public-school system.

1803 *Mass. H.S. Coll.* IX. 129 There are ten districts for schools, and nine school-houses. **1900** *Atlantic Reporter* XLVII. 704 He did not keep the district's money separate from his own, and it is not known what became of the sum unaccounted for. **1948** *Sat. Ev. Post* 14 Aug. 21/2 Families of workers spilled over into the predominantly agricultural Pleasant Hill district, sending their youngsters to the little school.

b. district trustee, = **school trustee.**

1838 *Ind. H. Rep. Jrnls.* 126 Make it the duty of school commissioners to appoint township trustees, and said Trustees to appoint District Trustees.

6. Short for *District of Columbia*. Cf. **4. b.** above.

1817 *Nat. Intelligencer* (Wash., D.C.) 19 Sep., The President concluded . . . by repeating his ardent wishes for the prosperity of the District. **1879** *Chi. Tribune* 17 Feb. 4/6 District-Attorney Riddle . . . treats the General to a . . . nice bit of sarcasm . . . in relation to Butler's threat not to go to Congress if he is not well treated in the District. **1948** *Washington Post* 5 Dec. 23M/2 Sales of electric refrigerators in the District, Prince Georges and Montgomery counties in October totaled 2443 units.

7. In the Methodist Church, an extensive area regarded as a unit in carrying on religious work. Also attrib.

1831 PECK *Guide* 258 There are three districts, the Illinois, the Kaskaskia, and the Wabash districts, over each of which is a presiding Elder. **1889** P. BUTLER *Recoll.* 225 Yearly district meetings were kept up in Northeastern Kansas.

8. (See quot. 1881.) Also attrib.

1852 *N.Y. Wkly. Tribune* 21 Feb. 1/2 The extent of claims being governed by their richness and accessibility, no system of laws can be made applicable in all districts. **1881** RAYMOND *Glossary*, District, in the States and Territories west of the Missouri, a vaguely bounded and temporary division and organization made by the inhabitants of a mining region. A district has one code of mining laws, and one recorder. **1947** CHALFANT *Gold, Guns, & Ghost Towns* 58 The district boundaries took in a hundred square miles, its lines running out across the hills and desert no one knew just where.

9. (See quot.)

1914 *Quart. Jrnl. Economics* Feb. 215 The country is to be divided into not less than eight, nor more than twelve districts, in each of which a Federal Reserve Bank is to be established.

10. In special combs.: (1) **district attorney,** see as a main entry; (2) **bank,** (*a*) one of the branch banks of the second Bank of the U.S., *obs.*, (*b*) a federal reserve bank in a particular federal reserve district; (3) **clerk,** the clerk of a district court; (4) **conference,** (see quot. 1872); (5) **court,** see as a main entry; (6) **heeler,** a party adherent who carries out the instructions of a political boss in a particular district; (7) **judge,** (*a*) a federal judge who presides over a U.S. district court, (*b*) a judge who presides over a state district court; (8) **ranger,** one in charge of the rangers attached to a district station in a national forest or park, also attrib.; (9) **school,** see as a main entry; (10) **superintendent,** see **superintendent;** (11) **system,** (*a*) the system of selecting presidential electors by districts rather than on a general ticket, cf. **elector,** (*b*) the system of selecting representatives to a legislative body by districts.

(2) (*a*) **1816** *Niles' Reg.* X. 17/2 (*caption*), District Banks. **1840** *Niles' Reg.* 11 July 299/1 Mr. Clay, of Alabama, asked that, by consent, the senate would now take up this bill on the District banks. (*b*) **1948** *Time* 23 Aug. 63/1 The Federal Reserve System also moved toward deflation when nine of its twelve district banks raised their rediscount rates. — (**3**) **1823** TUDOR *Otis* p. ii, District Clerk's Office. **1857** BRAMAN *Texas* i. 18 Then resort to the district clerk's office and see that there are no judgments against the owner. — (**4**) **1872** *Gen. Conference Jrnl. M. E. Ch.* 710 Resolved, . . . To organize in each Presiding Elder's district a District Conference, to be composed of all the traveling and local preachers in the district. **1924** *Doctrines of M. E. Ch.* 190.

(**6**) **1890** in *Wks. of Theodore Roosevelt* (1926) XIV. 110 The many forces which combine to produce the ward boss, the district heeler, the boodle alderman. **1935** *Amer. Mercury* Aug. 473 To the court house gang an editor is in the same category as a district heeler. — (**7**) (*a*) **1789** MACLAY *Deb. Senate* 98 We came to the clause which allowed the district judges to sit on the hearing of appeals from themselves. **1911** *U.S. Statutes at Large* XXXVI. i 1087 In each of the districts . . . there shall be a court called a district court, for which there shall be appointed one judge, to be called a district judge. (*b*) **1817** *N.Y. Herald* 2 Aug. 1/4 At York, he was . . . met by a committee of the town, headed by the venerable judge Sewall, . . . first district judge of Maine, who made an extemporaneous address. **1904** *Jud. & Stat. Def. of Words & Phrases* 1 Ser. III. 2138 [It] is not comprehensive enough to authorize any district judge to grant temporary injunctions throughout the state. — (**8**) **1913** *Collier's* 6 Dec. 10/2 Upon the speed and accuracy with which she can sight and locate smoke when it first starts and telephone its location to the district ranger depends the efficiency of the fire-protection system in her district. **1921** *Frontier* Feb. 6 About fifteen miles from the district ranger station lay the heavily timbered Moose Basin country. **1948** *Hungry Horse News* (Columbia Falls, Mont.) 17 Sep. 8/4 Leaving Tuesday for Sequoia national park to fight fire were Glacier national park district rangers, Floyd Henderson and E. M. Hutchinson.

(**11**) (*a*) **1816** *Ann. 14th Congress* 1 Sess. 214 Under the district system, . . . the weight of Pennsylvania, great as she is, dwindled down to a solitary vote. *c***1824** BENTON *30 Years' View* I. 38/1 To give to every portion of the Union its due share in the choice of the Chief Magistrate . . . would be effected by adopting the District System. (*b*) **1823** *Ann. 18th Congress* 1 Sess. 854 The district system is calculated to give to the arts of demagogues an undue ascendency. **1891**

Harper's Mag. June 111/2 Massachusetts, doubtless influenced by the unequal development of the towns of the commonwealth, adopted the district system.

As the last term in **bank, banner, burnt, camp meeting, close, common school, Congressional, Consolidated school, drainage, dry-goods, dumb bell, election, fever and ague, fire gold, grazing, highway, improvement, irrigation, judicial, lamp, land, lighthouse, mining, monkey wrench, oil, patrol, placer, red light, representative, road, school, senate, senatorial, shoestring, timber, turpentine district.**

district 'dɪstrɪkt, *v.* [f. the noun.]

1. *tr.* to divide (a state) into districts for the election of representatives.

1792 *Mass. Acts & Resolves* (1895) 184 Resolve for districting the commonwealth, for the purpose of choosing federal representatives. **1864** WEBSTER 396/2 Legislatures district states for the choice of senators.

2. To divide (a town or city) for various purposes.

1828 WEBSTER, In New England, towns are districted for the purpose of establishing . . . schools. **1881** *Harper's Mag.* LXII. 195/2 In those earlier times—say previous to 1836—the city was not districted.

b. To adjust the limits of school districts.

1941 LEE *Stagecoach North* 74 Time and time again the districting of schools had to be adjusted to suit chore time and family walking habits.

district attorney.

1. In a federal judicial district, the prosecuting officer for the government in suits against violators of federal laws.

1789 *Ann. 1st Congress* I. 86, I also nominate, for District Judges, Attorneys, and Marshals, the persons whose names are below. **1851** FILLMORE in *Pres. Mess. & P.* V. 110, I do further command that the district attorney of the United States . . . cause the foregoing offenders and all such as aided, abetted, or assisted them . . . to be immediately arrested. **1910** *Statutes at Large* XXXVI. 749 For salaries of United States district attorneys and expenses . . . five hundred and forty-five thousand dollars.

2. The prosecuting officer of a judicial district or a county within some states.

1823 COOPER *Pioneers* xxxiii, At length the district attorney called the wood-chopper to the bar. **1883** *Cent. Mag.* July 397 The Ring had received a check through the election of a Democratic mayor and district attorney. **1944** JOHNSON *As I Dare* 202 Cap'n Tom Allen, who seldom wore shoes, and later became Game Warden; and Charlie Weeks, the young lawyer who became Nassau County District Attorney.

b. The office held by such an official.

1898 CANFIELD *Maid of Frontier* 29, I intended to run for District Attorney.

3. (See quots.)

1939 ROLLINS *Gone Haywire* 138 This concoction, a favorite with the puncher, was early known as 'son of a —— stew'; but, after civilization had substituted formal judicial machinery for frontier justice on the cattle range, it oftentimes was ironically termed 'district attorney.' *Ib.* 225 Red's collation . . . included an indifferently cooked 'district attorney' made from a calf supplied by Jim Dooling.

4. district attorneyship, the office of a district attorney.

1881 *Nation* XXXII. 362 They find the Administration giving marshalships, and district-attorneyships. **1898** CANFIELD *Maid of Frontier* 35 The reason given me was Harriott's fear of your election in the coming contest for the District Attorneyship.

district court.

1. The U.S. court for a federal judicial district.

1789 *Statutes at Large* I. 73 And be it further enacted, That there be a court called a District Court. **1886** ALTON *Among Law-Makers* 148 Within each [judicial] district is a Federal court, known as the 'district court,' presided over by a judge known as the 'district judge.' **1943** *Chi. D. News* 12 June 6/1 The Illinois Commerce Commission . . . has issued a firman worthy of a Turk sultan . . . nullifying decrees and orders of the U.S. District Court.

2. A state court of general jurisdiction held in a state judicial district.

1805 *Ky. Court of Appeals Rep.* III. 3 Payton brought a suit in the Danville district court against Lightfoot. **1900** *Texas Sup. Court Rep.* XVIII. 408 The district court is as powerless to pass on amounts below its jurisdiction as justice or county courts to pass on amounts above their jurisdiction. **1948** *Dly. Ardmoreite* (Ardmore, Okla.) 10 Aug. 1/3 A police court case against him was held up while he asked district court for a permanent injunction against the ordinance.

district school. A public elementary school within a particular district, esp. a school district. Also attrib.

1793 FRANCIS ASBURY *Journal* II. (1821) 158, I consulted the minds of our brethren about building a house for conference, preaching, and a district school. **1851** *Knickerb.* XXXVII. 66/1 These lands ought to be let out and pastured and buy district-school libraries. **1946** PARTRIDGE & BETTMAN *As We Were* 19 Only in the backward regions of the country does the district school still survive.

Hence **district schoolhouse.**

1843 *Knickerb.* XXII. 430 Interspersed in every few miles are the district school houses. **1872** HOLMES *Poet* i. 26 Beyond . . . [was] the district school-house, and hard by it Ma'am Hancock's cottage.

disunionism dɪs'junjənɪzəm, *n.* The doctrine favoring the dissolution of the federal Union. *Obs.* **1855** *Boston Post* 24 Aug. 2/1. **1857** J. H. GIHON *Geary and Kansas* 254 Be it resolved . . . that it is the duty of the pro-slavery party, the union-loving men of Kansas Territory, to know but one issue, slavery, and that any party making or attempting to make any other, is and should be held, as an ally of abolitionism and disunionism.

* **disunionist,** *n.* One who favored the dissolution of the American federal Union; esp. a sympathizer with the proposed withdrawal of the southern states. Also attrib. *Obs.* or *hist.*

1832 *Congress. Deb.* 15 June 3572 Those who denounce them . . . are branded as disunionists and nullifiers. **1850** *U.S. Mag.* XXVII. 57 The disunionist party . . . admit the constitutional obligation, but deny its operation when public sentiment . . . is against it. **1888** BRYCE *Amer. Commonwealth* II. III. lvi. 377 The disunionist spirit of the South which led to the war.

* **ditch,** *n.*

1. *W.* (See quot. 1881.) Also attrib.

1855 *N.Y. Herald* 29 Dec. 3/2 Meetings of miners have been held in Nevada county, asking for reduction of water rates by the ditch companies. **1881** RAYMOND *Mining Gloss.*, Ditch, An artificial watercourse, flume, or canal, to convey water for mining. *a***1918** G. STUART *On Frontier* I. 89 We purchased water from a ditch company for our sluices.

2. The Erie Canal. *Humorous* or *derisive.* Cf. **Big Ditch, Clinton's ditch.**

1898 WESTCOTT *D. Harum* xxvi, That old ditch f'm Albany to Buffalo was an almighty big enterprise in them days.

3. *under ditch,* of land: Provided with irrigation ditches. Also *to lay* or *have under (the) ditch,* to provide (land) with irrigation ditches.

1872 TICE *Over Plains* 135 Any one entering land 'under ditch,' . . . that is, that can be irrigated from any completed canal, is required to pay the proprietors of the canal. **1892** *Harper's Mag.* June 93/1 Three-fifths of it [*sc.* the soil] can be laid under the ditch. **1896** *N. Amer. Rev.* CLXIII. 714 They want to have a large quantity of land under ditch.

4. In combs.: (1) **ditch boss,** *W.* one in charge of an irrigation ditch; (2) **grass,** cord or marsh grass, also a slender branching plant, *Ruppia maritima,* with grass-like leaves, which grows along ditches near salt water; (3) **hunter,** during the Civil War, a southern soldier (see next), *humorous, obs.;* (4) **land,** the South, so called because of the Confederates' determination to "fight to the last ditch," *obs.;* (5) **moss,** (see quots.); (6) **rider,** *W.* one who rides along an irrigation ditch and keeps it in repair; (7) **stonecrop,** (see quots.).

(1) **1941** FERGUSSON *Southwest* 251 Every man owed so many days' ditch work under the elected mayordomo, ditch boss, who also doled out the water so the man living up the stream did not rob his downstream neighbor. — (2) **1814** BIGELOW *Florula Bostoniensis* 17 *Spartina glabra,* Ditch grass. . . . A large rank grass, common about muddy shores and in salt water ditches. **1843** TORREY *Flora N.Y.* II. 252 Ditch-grass . . . [is] common in the neighborhood of New-York and on Long Island. **1894** COULTER *Bot. W. Texas* III. 457. — (3) **1862** *N.Y. Tribune* 2 June (Chipman), The roads . . . are thickly strown with the arms and haversacks of General Beauregard's ditch-hunters. *a***1870** CHIPMAN *Notes on Bartlett* (MS) Ditch-hunter. . . . The term originated by allusion to successive retreats from the U.S. armies, of the soldiers of the so-called Confederate States (the leaders of which having boasted and threatened much that rather than yield to the U.S. they would die in the last ditch). — (4) **1864** *N. & Q.* 3 Ser. I. 246/1, I did not know . . . that any such religio-legal enactments had ever been made by the Southern chivalry of the Ditch-land.

(5) **1836** LINCOLN *Botany* App. 146 *Udora . . . canadensis;* stem submersed, dichotomous. Still waters. Ditch moss. Can. to Virg. **1909** *Cent. Supp.* 383 Ditch-moss, . . . the water-weed or water-thyme.

Philotria Canadensis. **1931** CLUTE *Plants* 57 The harmless little ditch-moss (*Elodea canadensis*) found in every aquarium, moved to Europe some time ago and began to fill up the slow-moving streams, whereupon it received the names of American weed and Babington's curse, the latter name for the man who is said to have accidentally introduced it. — (6) **1902** F. NEWELL *Irrigation in the U.S.* 107 The person charged with the management of the canal ... is usually known as the 'watermaster' or 'ditch-rider.' ... It is his business to see that all stockholders or owners receive a fair amount of water. **1945** *Farmington* (N.M.) *T. Hustler* 16 Feb. 3/2 The Farmer's Mutual Ditch Company will receive sealed bids up to and including February 19, 1945, for Ditch Riders. — (7) **1857** GRAY *Botany* 141 Ditch Stone-crop, ... *Penthorum sedoides*, ... [grows in] wet places, everywhere. **1890** *Cent.* 4381/2 *P. sedoides* is the ditch-stonecrop of America. **1947** *Midland Naturalist* July 44 Ditch-stonecrop [is] rare in margins of swamps on flood plain.

As the last term in **Big, Clinton's, irrigating, irrigation, mining, mother, primary ditch.**

***ditch,** *v. tr.* To throw (a train) off the track, to derail.

1875 *Chi. Tribune* 6 Nov. 2/4 Gen. W. T. Sherman, members of his staff, and several ladies, have been ... waiting for the arrival of the passenger-train now lying behind a ditched freight-train. **1891** C. ROBERTS *Adrift America* 74 They had passed over a broken rail which ... had nearly 'ditched the train.'

b. *fig.* To put out of the running, to abandon. *Colloq.*

1911 *Springfield Republican* 31 Aug. 1 Its enactment into law would have ditched them in their present reciprocity campaign. **1924** G. C. HENDERSON *Keys to Crookdom* 104 After they have committed the holdup, they 'ditch' the stolen motor vehicle.

***ditching,** *n.* **1.** Of a train: Derailing, overturning. **2. ditching plow,** (see quot. 1874). **3. ditching shovel,** a shovel esp. designed for use in ditching. *Obs.* See also **grade ditching.**

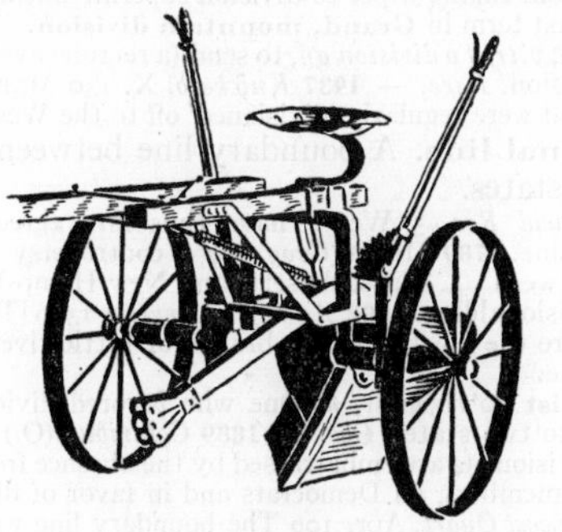

Ditching plow

(1) **1904** *Grand Rapids Ev. Press* 2 June 1 Seven passengers were injured by the ditching of a passenger train near Perry. The train ran into a washout. — (2) **1868** *Mich. Agric. Rep.* VII. 345 F. M. Mattice, Detroit, [for] drain or ditching plow, [won] $5. **1874** KNIGHT 711 Ditching-plow, a plow having a deep, narrow share for cutting drains and trenches, and means for lifting the earth and depositing it at the sides of the excavation. — (3) **1790** *Pa. Packet* 14 April 3/2 William Perkins, Blacksmith, Makes and sells ... banking or ditching shovels, spades, grubbing hoes. **1815** *Niles' Reg.* IX. 94/2 [In Wilmington, Delaware] the following articles of American manufacture were to be had last year. ... Iron and steel shovels (called Devonshire shovels) and ditching shovels.

***dittany,** *n.* Any one of several plants of the mint family, esp. *Cunila origanoides.* See **American dittany.**

1676 GLOVER *Acc. Va.* in *Phil. Trans.* XI. 629 Here is also an herb which some call *Dittany*, others *Pepper-wort;* it is not *Dittany of Candia*, nor *English Dittander*. **1738** BYRD *Dividing Line* (1901) 213 Dittany ... is a Sure Defense against [horseflies]. **1814** PURSH *Flora Amer.* II. 406 The whole herb has an aromatic scent, and is used as tea in severe colds and other complaints, under the name of Dittany. **1947** *Midland Naturalist* July 56 Dittany [is] rare in pine-oak forest; one station in upland oak forest.

ditty box. (See first quot.) — **1883** *Pall Mall Gaz.* 2 June, A 'ditty-box' is an American fisherman's receptacle for all sorts of odds and ends, together with implements of every-day use. **1883** in *Nat. Museum Bul.* No. 27, 177 This was the ditty-box of one of the crew of schooner Grace L. Fears, of Gloucester, Mass.

***dive,** *n.*

1. A place of low resort. *Slang.*

1871 *N.Y. Herald* 6 July 8/2 Being in the vicinity of one of the gayly decorated dives where young ladies of modest proclivities dispense refreshments to thirsty souls with much jeweled hands, Corney dropped in. **1887** F. FRANCIS *Saddle & Moccasin* 227 It occurred to him to drop into a little 'dive' on Jim Street. **1948** *Chi. Tribune* 17 Sep. 8/1 The dives themselves are nuisances, per se, and that is why they have to pay such high license prices.

b. Applied as a proper name to a slum district in Chicago. *Obs.* Cf. **levee 3.**

1892 *Scribner's Mag.* July 6/1 To get to the main floors of these squalid habitations one must climb down many steps; hence the name of the locality, 'The Dive.'

2. dive-keeper, one who runs or operates a dive. *Slang.*

1887 *Chi. Tribune* 4 May 3/1 Consternation has seized the divekeepers. **1913** *Sat. Ev. Post* 1 March 15 These two—the con man and the divekeeper—had never met in their lives before.

***diver,** *n.* As the last term in **dun, hell, Pacific, pigeon diver.**

***divide,** *n.*

1. Mountains or land forming a watershed between two rivers or drainage systems. Cf. **Continental, Great, river divide.**

1806 PIKE *Sources Miss.* (1895) II. 400 Struck & passed the divide between the Grand river and the Verdegris river. **1910** J. HART *Vigilante Girl* 143 We'll be on the divide in half an hour. **1949** *Sierra Club* (So. Calif. Chap.) Sched. 130, 31 The trail leads up Millard Canyon, past Dawn Gold Mine ... to the Millard Canyon-Bear Canyon Divide.

transf. and *fig.* **1879** B. F. TAYLOR *Summer-Savory* ii. 18 His hair parted on the 'divide' of philoprogenitiveness ... and brought up over his ears like two little bundles of oats. **1890** *Railways of Amer.* 100 Among the readers of this volume there will be some who have reached the summit of the 'divide' which separates the spring and summer of life from its autumn and winter.

b. *To go over, cross the divide*, to die. *Colloq.*

1872 TICE *Over Plains* 214 There is no lack of them [=tales] ... of those [hunters] who long since 'have gone over the Divide.' **1912** RAINE *Brand Blotters* 284 Since you've taken his place it will be you that crosses the divide, Mr. Sheriff.

2. A division of gains, spoils, etc. *Colloq.*

1813 *Niles' Reg.* IV. 160/2 They had nearly fell out about the divide, but my old chief the White Racoon, holding me fast, they made the divide and departed to their towns. **1891** *Cong. Rec.* 8 Jan. 1049/1, I am afraid that these gentlemen who own these ships ... will not give a fair 'divide' with the boys who do the work.

***divide,** *v. To divide time*, to share time allotted one to speak with an opponent or fellow speaker. — **1876** in FLEMING *Hist. Reconstruction* II. 408 Appearance at any Republican meeting to 'divide time,' is with a view to impress the blacks with the sense of danger of longer holding out against white rule.

divided land. Land allotted or divided out among colonists. *Obs.* — **1654** *Suffolk Deeds* II. 42 Six Acres of Dyuided Lande & three Acres of meadow lying by pyne Iland Creeke. **1717** *Providence Rec.* XVI 334, I doe ... bequeathe unto ... Joseph Williams ... one third parte of my whole Right ... : both of the Lands devided and undevided.

***dividend,** *n.* Also **divident.** A tract or body of land embraced in a patent or grant; an individual share or allotment of such land. In full **dividend land.** *Obs.* or *hist.*

1621 in *Amer. Sp.* XV. 172/2 His first Generall devident to be augmented and doubled by the said Company. **1643** *Suffolk Deeds* I. 41 Eight Acres of meddowe bounded on the West & south with the Iland that leades to his ffathers farme, on the north with the great dividends. *c***1700** *Md. Gen. Assembly Acts* (1723) 11 The Ascertaining of the Bounds and Limits of the said Town Pasture and Common, and the several lots and Dividends in the same contained. **1882** in E. K. GODFREY *Nantucket* 88 The lands so laid out in divisions were known by the name of 'dividend land.' **1899** GREEN *Va. Word-Book* 118 Dividend, Divident, a body of land contained in one patent or survey.

b. divident line, the line forming the boundary of a dividend; a boundary line. *Obs.*

1644 *Conn. Rec.* I. 105 There shall be a liberty for ether party of 12 inches from the divident lyne. **1803** *Ib.* IV. 445 This Court doth allow of the divident line agreed upon by the inhabitants of Plainfield to be the dividing line of their township.

***dividing,** *a.* In combs.: (1) **dividing bounds,** bounds or limits that divide contiguous areas, *obs.;* (2) **fence,** a fence on the dividing line of adjacent properties; (3) **ground,** a divide or watershed; (4) **hive,** (see quot.); (5) **ridge,** a ridge that forms a divide or watershed.

(1) **1663** *Providence Rec.* I. 50 The place where the first fence stood which fenced in the fild wherein this said Lott Lieth, is the deviding boundes. **1680** *Conn. Rec.* III. 69 They agreed that the divideing

bownds should be at Ashowat to Wongushock. — (2) **1660** *Conn. H.S. Coll.* XIV. 251 To make and mayntaine the halfe of the div[i]eing fence. **1760** WASHINGTON *Diaries* I. 133 Also run Round the Fields in the Lower pasture according as the dividing Fence is to go. **1897** STUART *Simpkinsville* 135 The cordial relations . . . were still indicated by the well worn 'stoop,' set in the dividing-fence between the two gardens. — (3) **1796** in *Amer. Sp.* XV. 172/2 About one mile from the dividing ground that divides the above mentioned branch and the head waters of the North fork of Clinch. **1845** FRÉMONT *Exped.* 211 Between the successive basin, the dividing grounds are usually very slight. — (4) **1870** *Dept. Agric. Rep. 1869* 332 Several patents have been granted on 'dividing-hives,' *i.e.*, hives which may be separated into halves, to each of which a new empty section similar in structure is added, whereby two stocks are produced from one, and swarming, it is claimed, prevented.

(5) **1788** *Steele P.* I. 23 He shall endeavour to obtain from the said Indians an Extension of the Boundary . . . as far as the dividing Ridge between Little River and Tenissee. **1882** C. KING *Rep. Prec. Metals* 108 Some excellent quartz prospects have been found on the dividing ridge at the head of Indian Creek.

* **divinity,** *n.*

1. (See quot. 1851.) *Obs.*

1848 N. AMES *Childe Harvard* 40 One of the young 'Divinities' passed Straight through the College yard. **1851** HALL *College Words* 103 A member of a theological school is often familiarly called a *Divinity*, abbreviated for a Divinity student.

2. A form of soft homemade candy. Also **divinity fudge.**

1913 E. H. GLOVER *'Dame Curtsey's' Book of Candy Making* 34 Divinity Fudge. Three and one-half cups of granulated sugar, one-half cup of 90 per cent corn syrup, two-thirds cup of water [etc.]. **1921** *Wash. Div. Apiculture Rep.* 114 Honey Divinity 2 cups sugar ½ cup milk or water ¼ cup honey 1 egg white [etc.]. **1941** F. M. FARMER *Boston Cook Book* 712 Divinity Fudge 1½ cups light brown sugar . . . 1 egg white. ½ cup chopped nuts *or* coconut [etc.].

As the last term in **New, New Light Divinity.**

* **division,** *n.*

1. A tract of land allotted, or to be allotted, to an individual settler or to settlers. Also attrib. *Obs.*

1639 *Cambridge Prop. Rec.* 68 These Lands in ye Lower Divission. **1657** *Springfield Rec.* I. 256 Ye 3d devission flank & ye brow of ye hill. **1689** *Huntington Rec.* II. 25 It was voatted & ordered that all persons shall bring in to ye Clarke house an account of all their division land, home lotts exsepted. **1882** GODFREY *Nantucket* 89 In 1821 several tracts were laid out and apportioned . . . and these are often spoken of as the 'new divisions.'

2. A part or section of a railroad forming a unit of its operation and management. Also attrib.

1832 *Amer. R.R. Jrnl.* I. 52/3 The city division commences at Pratt street. . . . The second division commences at Ellicotts' Mills. **1865** in FLEMING *Hist. Reconstruction* I. 18 Wood-sheds and water stations and division houses . . . were in complete repair in 1862. **1900** FLYNT *Itinerant Policeman* 238 You wants to look out for 'em when a train pulls into division yards. **1944** *Chi. & N.W. Time Table* 3 Dec. 32 In addition to through trains making a limited number of stops, stations south of Kenosha are most adequately served by frequent suburban service details of which will be found in Milwaukee Division folder.

b. A section of the route or territory covered by a stagecoach line. Also attrib. Now *hist.*

1872 MARK TWAIN *Roughing It.* vi. 54 His beat or jurisdiction of two hundred and fifty miles was called a 'division.' **1890** N. P. LANGFORD *Vigilante Days* (1912) 441 Where his life was passed . . . until he was intrusted with the care of one of the divisions of the Great Overland Stage route in 1859, I have no knowledge. *Ib.* 442 The power he exercised as a division agent was despotic. **1930** BANNING *Six Horses* 399 A division was a line unit of arbitrary length, comprising generally a number of 'drives,' in charge of an agent or a superintendent or both.

3. *Baseball.* A group or classification into which a team is placed on the basis of its performance.

1914 *Sat. Ev. Post* 14 Feb. 8/1, I have since managed another club that wound up in the first division. **1948** *N.Y. Times* 18 April v. 2/4 Every one of our teams has been strengthened, particularly those clubs that finished in the second division last year.

4. In an educational institution, an administrative unit, usu. comprising several related departments.

1910 University Nomenclature, Assoc. Amer. Universities *Proceedings & Addresses of Eleventh Conference* 91 Division is used to indicate any organic portion of a university which is larger or more independent than a department. **1947** *Chi. Maroon* 11 July 1/1 The society, formerly the senior men's honorary group, now embraces the divisions and professional schools of the University.

5. In special combs.: (1) **division bond,** (see quot.); (2) **engineer,** the civil engineer in charge of the tracks and structures of a railway division; (3) **fence,** =**dividing fence;** (4) **line,** a boundary line, cf. **divisional line;** (5) **point,** the place at which two railroad divisions join; (6) **superintendent,** a railroad official having charge of equipment and operations within a division.

(1) **1900** NELSON *A B C Wall St.* 23 In some instances *division bonds* are issued, which, as their name implies, are covered by divisions, and not by the entire railroad. — (2) **1893** A. C. GUNTER *Miss Dividends* 10 This citizen soldier . . . had been one of the division engineers of the Union Pacific Railway. **1940** *Railroad Quiz* [Quest. 250] Under the Engineer of Maintenance of Way are District Engineers and Division Engineers, and under the Division Engineers are Roadmasters. — (3) **1831** PECK *Guide* 185 A half quarter section, with division fences crossing at right angles. **1894** ALLEN *Kentucky Cardinal* xvi, No explanation had ever been made to the mother of that goose of a gate in our division fence. — (4) **1662** *Dedham Rec.* IV. 47 Ensigne Daniell Fisher and Edward Richards were mutually chosin . . . to settle and determine the runinge of the Division line between the 2 parties. **1714** *Duxbury Rec.* 96 We . . . select men for the town of Duxborrough, being met together to settle the bounds and division line between the said towns of Plymouth and Duxborrough. **1900** HANDSAKER in *Pioneer Life* 26 John and George bought the right to a choice tract of land six miles east of Oakland and built their log cabin on the division line.

(5) **1889** *Union Pac. RR. Ore. & Wash.* 207 Grant's Pass is a division point on the Southern Pacific. **1947** *Chi. D. News* 3 Sep. 20/1 The old steam locomotives could operate efficiently for about 200 miles. Division points were spaced approximately that distance apart. — (6) **1878** PINKERTON *Strikers* 375 The master mechanic and division superintendent, with an engine-wiper, boarded a locomotive. **1948** *Chi. D. News* 9 Feb. 14/1 A big railroad says it needs just about everybody from engine wiper to division superintendent.

As the last term in **Grand, mountain division.**

***division,** *v.tr. To division off*, to send (a recruit) away as a member of a division. *Rare.* — **1937** *Knickerb.* X. 130 Many . . . joined the army, and were regularly 'divisioned' off to the West Indies.

divisional line. A boundary line between adjoining regions or states.

1659 *Topsfield Rec.* 5 We . . . have thus fare agreed vpon the deuisionall Line. **1789** MORSE *Geog.* 167 A controversy . . . had long subsisted between . . . Massachusetts and New Hampshire, respecting their divisional line. **1802** *Ann. 7th Congress* 1316 [The boundary runs] to where the most southern branch of Little river crosses the divisional line.

divisionist dəˈvɪʒənɪst, *n.* One who favored dividing Dakota Territory into two states. *Obs.* — **1889** *Columbus* (O.) *Dispatch* 15 Jan., The divisionists are embarrassed by the absence from the house . . . of three members, all Democrats and in favor of division. **1949** *Pacific Northwest Quart.* Apr. 106 The boundary line was extremely objectionable to the Eastern divisionists and anti-divisionists.

divort dɪˈvort, *n.* A divide or watershed. *Obs.* — **1856** ANTISELL in *Rep. Explorations R.R. Route* VII. II. 40 On crossing the divort between the tributary of the Salinas, and the waters of the San Antonio, this bed was found to occupy a large surface and to be the uppermost rock. **1859** BARTLETT 123 *Divort.* This word expresses fully what no word at present does. The word 'divide' is not etymologically applicable, as it does not convey the idea of altitude as the cause of separation; while the word *divort* implies elevation, the cause of the *divortia aquarum*—whence its derivation also.

***Dix,** *n.* A variety of pear. *Obs.* — **1852** *Horticulturist* VII. 54 Some of the worst looking specimens of cracked pears observed anywhere, were on a tree of the Dix. **1868** *Rep. Comm. Agric.* 137 Dix . . . Season, October and November.

Dixianic dɪksɪˈænɪk, *a.* Pertaining to Dixie. *Rare.* — **1862** *N.Y. Tribune* 4 Feb. (Chipman), Unless the blockade is raised very soon, the Dixianic provinces will soon be resolved into . . . Egyptian darkness.

Dixie ˈdɪksɪ, *n.* [See note.]

Many theories have been advanced in vain efforts to account satisfactorily for this term. Those that occur most frequently are: 1. The word preserves the name of a kind slave owner on Manhattan Island, a Mr. Dixy. His rule was so kindly that "Dixy's land" became famed far and wide as an Elysium abounding in material comforts. 2. Ten dollar notes issued by the Citizens Bank of Louisiana before the Civil War bore the French *dix*, ten, on the reverse side and were consequently known as *dixes* or *dixies.* Hence Louisiana and eventually the South in general came to be known as the land of *dixies* or *dixies land.* 3. Dixie is derived somehow from Dixon of Mason and Dixon's line.

1. That portion of the U.S. south of Mason and Dixon's line, the southern states. Also attrib.

1859 EMMETT *Dixie's Land,* Away! away! away down South in Dixie. **1861** *So. Enterprise* (Thomasville, Ga.) 14 Aug. 2/6 The

'Dixie Boys' are coming round In just so wild a storm. **1901** PITTENGER *Great Locomotive Chase* 101 Now I will succeed, or leave my bones in Dixie. **1946** *Negro Digest* Aug. 39/2 They have quietly cut their Southern roots, shaken the dust of Dixie off their feet, and now are pursuing their careers in other, if not more sunny, climes.

b. In full **Dixie('s) land, Dixieland.** Cf. **2. b.** below.

1859 EMMETT *Dixie's Land*, In Dixie Lann whar I was bawn in, Arly on one frosty mawnin. **1863** DICEY *Six Months* II. 31 As the New England regiments passed our train, they shouted to us to tell the people at home that we had seen them in Dixie's Land, and on the way to Richmond. **1948** *Dly. Ardmoreite* (Ardmore, Okla.) 15 July 1/8 The 20-minute-show Dixieland put on for Russell had a hard time getting started, but was more liberally sprinkled with rebel yells.

c. (See quot. 1873.) Also attrib.

1873 BEADLE *Undevel. West* 661 All that part of Mormondom south of the rim of the Great Basin is called Dixie, and extends some distance into Arizona. *Ib.* 660 'Dixie wine,' as the Mormons call it, is rather strong and pungent. **1894** *Irrigation Age* Jan. 38/1 The famous 'Dixie Land,' comprising the counties of Millard, Washington and Beaver, is known as the land of the grape. **1942** STEGNER *Mormon C.* 345 Dixie sleeps peacefully all winter with hardly a Gentile intruder except the transients going up or down on Highway 91.

2. The title of a song, esp. popular in the South, composed in 1859 by Daniel D. Emmett.

1860 *Charleston* (S.C.) *Mercury* 15 Dec. 3/5 At half past eight o'clock away we went, with lightning speed, to the tune of 'Dixie'. **1911** SAUNDERS *Col. Todhunter* 97, I can't keep from hollerin' when I hear *Dixie*, not to save my life. **1948** *Dly. Ardmoreite* (Ardmore, Okla.) 18 July 3/1 The band played 'Dixie' as the nominees came in.

b. Also **Dixie's land.** *Obs.* Cf. **1. b.** above.

1859 [see **1.** above]. **1863** HOPLEY *Life in South* I. 352 With regard to 'Dixie's Land,' a tune as popular in New York as Richmond, some very satirical comments were induced.

Dixieite 'dɪksɪˌaɪt, *n.* A Southerner. *Rare.* — **1869** *Harper's Mag.* Jan. 199/2 The Dixieite held fast by his venerable prejudices.

Dixon's line, *n.* =**Mason and Dixon's line.** *Rare.* — **1827** G. MELLEN *Chronicle of '26* 14 Teach him there is virtue north of Dixon's line.

∗**do,** *v.*

1. *tr.* To report on or "cover" *q.v.* (an event) for a newspaper.

1889 *Cent. Mag.* March 751/1 Society reporters and not dramatic critics are usually assigned to 'do' amateur theatrical performances. **1893** M. PHILIPS *Making Newspaper* 133 A *Herald* correspondent 'doing' the Prince of Wales' travels [etc.].

2. In colloq. expressions: (1) ∗*do as I do*, (see quot.); (2) *to do off*, (*a*) to array, deck out, (*b*) to partition off; (3) ∗*to do* (one) *over*, (*a*) to do or cook (one) brown, to exhaust or wear out, (*b*) to redo or make over; (4) *do tell*, (see quot. 1871); (5) ∗*to do up*, to make a rapid inspection, to "cover"; (6) *to do up right*, to do properly.

(1) **1871** DE VERE 315 *To do as I do* is nearly obsolete. 'Come, gentlemen, *do as I do?*' was once the polite request of one who wished his friends to join him at the bar. — (2) (*a*) **1839** KIRKLAND *New Home* (1840) 227, I . . . reconnoitred the company who were 'done off' (indigenous,) 'in first-rate style,' for this important occasion. (*b*) **1874** *Vt. Bd. Agric. Rep.* II. 514, I have also one small room done off for storing butter in the fall. — (3) (*a*) **1789** W. DUNLAP *Andre* I. i, For while we were watching, like sportsmen for plover, The linen took fire—and did us all over. *Ib.*, We sneak'd into town;—very fairly done over. **1853** P. PAXTON *Yankee in Texas* 96 [The dogs] were completely done over and used up. (*b*) **1908** *Smart Set* Sep. 84/1 If only somebody would 'do over' Browning into English. — (4) [**1815** HUMPHREYS *Yankey* 104 *Du pry tel*, [exclamation probably from] do pray tell.] **1842** BUCKINGHAM *E. & W. States* I. 177 When a person . . . has concluded his narrative, the hearer will reply, 'Oh! *do* tell.' **1871** DE VERE 598 *Do tell*, a cant phrase of New England, which occupies there the ground held in the South by, You don't say so. **1883** WILDER *Sister Ridnour* 138 'Come fur?' 'About eighty miles.' . . . 'Du tell!'

(5) **1869** J. R. BROWNE *Adv. Apache Country* 28 We would feast and hunt and hold pow-wows with the Indians, and do up the whole country even to the Moqui villages. **1872** TICE *Over Plains* 61 After spending the greater part of Saturday in looking over the city, . . . we concluded that we had about 'done up' Denver. — (6) **1864** NORTON *Army Letters* 246 Lieutenant Burrows is a capital hand at carrying out anything of that kind and he determined to do the thing up right.

dobber 'dɑbɚ, *n.* [Du. in same sense.] (See quot. 1848.) Cf. **cork dobber.**

1812 IRVING *Knickerb.* (ed. 2) II. v, He floated on the waves . . . like an angler's dobber. **1844** *Knickerb.* XXIII. 72 Sit all on a rock watching your float, or cork, or dobber, as the Dutch boys call it. **1848** BARTLETT 396 Dobber, a float to a fishing-line. So called in New York.

dobchick, see **dabchick.**

dobie 'dobɪ, *n.* Also **dobe, doby,** etc. *W.* [f. **adobe.**]

1. (See quot. 1872.) Cf. **doughboy 1.**

1838 M. WHITMAN in *Overland to Pacific* VI. (1936) 294 There being no stone near I had walled the cellar with dobies the same as the walls of the house. **1872** MARK TWAIN *Roughing It* iv. 40 (R.), The station buildings were long, low huts, made of sun-dried, mud-coloured bricks, laid up without mortar (Adobes, the Spaniards call these bricks, and Americans shorten it to 'Dobies.) **1897** HOUGH *Story of Cowboy* 22 No heat can penetrate these walls, more than three feet thick, of the sundried native brick or 'dobe.

attrib. **1838** PARKER *Exploring Tour* 347 The buildings generally are in the native style, thatched; many are built with *doba* walls after the spanish manner. **1847** *Calif. Star* (S.F.) 8 May 2/3 With her time-worn, rain-washed 'dobie dwellings, and crumbling mud walls, she looks most primitive I assure you. **1862** HEWITT *Across Plains* (1906) 113 Kearney City, . . . familiarly called 'dobe town,' because it was constructed of sun dried brick, was a small forlorn burg. **1880** NYE *B. Nye & Boomerang* 270, I knocked down a 'dobe cottage, and proceeded to examine it. **1948** *Sat. Ev. Post* 31 July 90/2, I thought of Elijio sitting on his heels against a 'dobe wall with his eyes closed.

b. Short for "adobe soil" *q.v.*

1893 *Outing* July 309/1 Don't hurry, young man; it's raining and you can't ride your horse in the doby. The road here was of a sandy nature, and was excellent for a few miles; then came a miserable stretch of 'doby' into the town of Marysville.

c. A building made of adobes.

1865 in *Annals of Wyoming* VII. (1930) 380 Julesburg. . . . This magnificent city has one log house and two 'dobies.' **1941** FERGUSSON *Southwest* 353 Then follow the caprock till you pass a couple of Texas gates and one cattle-guard. There's a doby there.

2. The Mexican peso or dollar. In full **dobie dollar.**

1906 ADAMS *Cattle Brands* 154 Uncle Sam's strong-box yielded up over a thousand dobes. **1910** *Sat. Ev. Post* 8 Oct. 4/3 They said I had to pay five hundred dobie dollars before I went ahead with the work. **1932** BENTLEY *Sp. Terms* 87 The Mexican silver dollar is sometimes referred to as a *dobie*.

b. (See quot.) *Obs.*

1857 CHANDLESS *Visit Salt Lake* II. i. 146 The fifty dollar California pieces . . . were called 'dobies,' because octagonal.

3. (See quots.) Cf. **dogie,** *n.*

1912 HOUGH *Story of Cowboy* 136 (Bentley), A 'dogy' or 'doby' yearling (a scrubby calf that has not wintered well). **1922** ROLLINS *Cowboy* 217 (Bentley), This . . . provoked much discussion . . . of . . . 'dobes' these last being calves that were scrubby and anaemic.

∗**dobson,** *n.* The hellgrammite or crawler. — **1884** *Stand. Nat. Hist.* II. 156 They [*Corydalus cornutus*] are called by fishermen 'crawlers,' 'dobsons,' and sometimes 'hellgrammites.' **1917** KEPHART *Camping* II. 411 One of the best natural baits for bass, when the water is clear, is that fierce-looking creature called hellgrammite, dobson, or grampus.

doc dɑk, *n.* Colloquial abbreviation for "doctor." Often as an appellative, and sometimes of one who is not a doctor.

1854 in GLISAN *Jrnl. Army Life* 149 Don't you think, Doc, ague makes a fellow powerful weak? **1875** *Cin. Enquirer* 4 July 5/1 'Doc'—which is Chinese for Aaron—Torrence got his baggage all ready and started for California. **1949** *Time* 31 Jan. 49/2 For those who like to sun-bathe, Doc provides benches.

docent 'dosn̩t, *n.* [G. *Dozent* in same sense.] A teacher or lecturer in a college or university. — **1890** *Boston Jrnl.* 9 Sep. 4/9 Dr. Arthur G. Webster of Newton Centre has been appointed Docent in Physics at Clark University. **1915** *Cap & Gown* 26 William Clinton Alden, Ph.D., Docent in Field Geology.

docious 'doʃəs, *a.* (See quot. 1859.) *Obs.* — **1853** P. PAXTON *Yankee in Texas* 120, I can hardly keep my tongue docious now to talk about it. **1859** BARTLETT 123 *Docious*, a corruption of *docile*, as 'a docious young man,' 'a docious horse.'

∗**dock,** *n.*

1. A wharf or pier.

1817 *N.Y. Herald* 20 Aug. 2/2 He left town at 1 o'clock in the morning of the same day, in charge of a friend, who waked him up previous to the packet reaching the dock at Sing-sing. **1896** HASWELL *New York* 90 All the public bulkheads and piers (commonly and erroneously termed docks) and slips were rented for one year for $42,750. **1948** *Democrat* 3 June 1/2 Jordan had 42 gallons of gasoline pumped aboard the boat, and had drifted away from the dock when the explosion occurred.

2. In combs.: (1) **dock fever,** (see quots.), *obs.;* (2) **loafer,** a loafer who frequents docks, *obs.;* (3) **log,** a log suitable for use in making or protecting a dock; (4) **rat,**

= **wharf rat;** (5) **walloper,** one who works about docks and wharves.

(1) **1796** *Gaz. of U.S.* (Phila.) 6 Aug. (Th.), These and such places are visited by the dock fever,—yellow fever if you please. **1799** *Aurora* (Phila.) 2 Aug. (Th.), I presume you have heard of our being again afflicted [in New York] with the Dock, or Yellow Fever. — (2) **1855** *Monterey* (Calif.) *Sentinel* 4 Aug. 1/1 The usual crowd of passengers, newsboys, fruit-venders, cabmen and dock-loafers, was assembled on and about the boat. **1862** *Independent* 6 March 1/6, I have seen . . . emigrants from all countries . . . , dock-loafers, rag-pickers, wandering gypsies [etc.]. — (3) **1817** *Niles' Reg.* XII. 89/1 There are annually made, and transported to the south, . . . dock logs, scantling and other timber to a great amount. **1822** *Mass. Spy* 1 May (Th.), [He] was instantly killed by the fall of a pile of dock-logs, which he was assisting to raft. — (4) **1864** *Harper's Mag.* Feb. 341/1 At our swimming-place we were often much molested by the river-border citizens of the town, variously known as 'dock-rats' and 'townies.' **1872** *Ib.* Oct. 673/2 Our business is with those smaller, but terribly annoying vermin, the 'dock rats,' with the river thieves, and with the junk-shops. — (5) **1838** *N.Y. Advertiser & Exp.* 28 Feb. 3/3 There is not a Dock Wolloper in New York, that would not feel insulted, if told he was no gentleman. **1948** *Time* 21 June 26/3 As a young dock walloper he was the king of Greenpernt's waterfront.

As the last term in **baggage, floating, dry, hydraulic, prairie, sand, screw, stake, steamer dock.**

*** docket,** *n.*

1. A list of cases or of the names of persons having suits depending in court. See also **city, country docket.**

1709 *N.J. Archives* 1 Ser. III. 458 On search of the Docquet of Causes . . . I find a Writ was issued out that bore Test in May term. **1865** *Louisville D. Democrat* 30 Oct. 2/1 The regular term of the County Court commences to-day, when the docket will be called. **1946** *This Week Mag.* 16 Feb. 7/1 Although an all-time, all-world high, that figure is rising. Court dockets are crowded.

attrib. **1844** *Ind. Senate Jrnl.* 219 An act abolishing docket fees.

b. *transf.*

1822 *Ann. 17th Congress* 1 Sess. I. 271 Mr. J. said the docket of congress was never cleared but once.

2. *clear the docket,* see *** clear,** *v.*

3. *fig. On* (or *off*) *the docket,* (see quot. 1864). *Colloq.*

1817 *N.Y. Herald* 21 June 3/2 We conceive this gentleman, though nearly *last* on the docket, in the routine of benefits, not by any means the *least.* **1864** Webster 400/3 On the docket, in hand; under consideration; in process of execution or performance. **1945** *Athol* (Mass.) *D. News* 14 May 4/4 Three games are on the docket for the Minutemen and Coach Erle Witty's boys.

*** docket,** *v. tr.* To place (a case, a suit) on a docket. Also **docketing,** *n.* Also transf.

1844 *Ind. Senate Jrnl.* 178 The clerk of the proper court . . . shall docket the same for this length of time, when the same shall stand for trial and decision. **1898** *McClure's Mag.* X. 246 The world . . . likes to classify its men and things, docket them, and arrange them nicely on its shelves. **1923** Blaisdell *F.T. Com.* 282 The average pendency of cases resulting in cease and desist orders was seven months after docketing.

docking lot. A lot or area conveniently situated for receiving and shipping goods. *Rare.* — **1861** *Chi. Tribune* 26 May 1/8 For Sale . . . Docking Lot, near Hough's Packing House, with a side track from the Alton & St. Louis R.R.

dockmackie ˈdɑkˌmækɪ, *n.* [Prob. Du. f. Delaware Indian *dogekumak,* in same sense.] A shrub, *Viburnum acerifolium,* having white flowers and red berries.

1817–8 Eaton *Botany* (1822) 510 Indians in that vicinity [Columbia County, N.Y.] considered the external application of the leaves of the dockmackie as a sovereign remedy in every kind of inflammatory tumour. **1857** Gray *Botany* 168 Maple-leaved Arrow-wood; Dockmackie. . . . Rocky woods, common: May, June. **1942** Van Dersal *Ornamental Amer. Shrubs* 111 Other names for it are dockmackie, arrowwood, squashberry, and possumhaw.

*** doctor,** *n.*

1. (See quot. 1848.) *Colloq.*

1848 *Western Boatman* May 103 The doctor, or small engine to supply the boilers with water, and work the bilge-water pumps, . . . was first introduced by Captain Shreve on the snag boats. **1907** Stewart *Partners* 115, I guessed they would be fooling with the doctor and maybe blow off the boilers some.

2. (See quot. 1893.) *Colloq.*

1893 *Stand.* 539 Doctor, . . . the cook in a logging-camp. **1909** White *Rules of Game* I. xii, 'Where's the drive, doctor?' asked the lumberman. 'This is the jam camp,' replied the cook.

3. doctor bill, a bill rendered by a physician for professional services. *Colloq.*

[**1830** in Commons *Doc. Hist.* I. 314, I . . . have been so fortunate as to keep clear of the Doctors bills this two years.] **1842** C. M. Kirkland *Forest Life* I. 100 We have no wheat flour this summer, for my old man was so crowded to pay doctor-bills and sich. **1912** Wason *Friar Tuck* 231 All they gave him in return was a little meal and bacon for savin' their souls and doctor-bills.

4. *Doctor of Philosophy,* one of the highest degrees granted by a university. Also one holding such a degree.

The practice of granting this degree was app. taken over from German universities. Cf. G. *Doktor der Philosophie.*

1860 *Yale Coll. Cat.* 1860/61 64 It is required of candidates for the degree of Doctor of Philosophy, that they shall faithfully devote at least two years to a course of study selected from branch pursued in the Department of Philosophy and the Arts. **1896** *Harper's Wkly.* 4 July 654/3 If his hood is edged with blue, he is a doctor of philosophy. **1947** *Woodlawn Booster* (Chicago) 2 July 8/2 Since then he has taken his master and doctor of philosophy degrees.

As the last term in **agency, beauty, business, calomel, company, conjure, faith, foot, government, Indian, play, rifle, root, snake, steam, swamp, trick, vegetable, voodoo, white doctor.**

***doctor,** *v. intr.* To take medicine or undergo medical treatment. Also **doctoring.** *Colloq.* — **1843** Stephens *High Life N.Y.* II. 4, I raly feel as if I must doctor a leetle. **1911** E. Wharton *Ethan Frome* (1919) 193 Not as she's ever given up doctoring, and she's had sick spells right along.

***doctrine,** *n.* As the last term in **Freeport, Monroe, spoils doctrine.**

Dodecatheon ˌdodəˈkæθɪən, *n.* [L. *dodecatheon,* name of an herb.] A genus of herbs of the primrose family; (not *cap.*) a plant of this genus, esp. *D. media,* the shooting star.

1857 Gray *Botany* 272 Dodecatheon, L. American Cowslip. . . . (Name fancifully assumed from δώδεκα, *twelve,* and θεοί, *gods.*) **1903** Austin *Land of Little Rain* 217 At about the nine thousand foot level and in the summer there will be hosts of rosy-winged dodecatheon, called shooting-stars, outlining the crystal runnels in the sod. **1928** Bailey *Cyclo. Horticulture* 1063/2 Dodecatheon is a puzzling genus to systematic botanists. It is found from Maine to Texas and from the Atlantic to the Pacific; and along the Pacific slope, from the islands of Lower Calif. to those of Bering Strait.

*** dodger,** *n.*

1. = **corn dodger.**

1831 Peck *Guide* 152 Dodgers, are masses [of corn meal] like small loaves of bread, prepared in a similar manner [i.e., with water or milk], and baked in the spider or skillet. **1894** *Harper's Mag.* LXXXIX. 628/1 His wife makes it into big rocklike 'dodgers' or pone-cakes with salt and water and 'no rising.' **1946** Nixon *Va. Words.*

2. A small poster or handbill.

1879 *Bernalillo* (N.M.) *Mirror* 8 Mar. 3/1 Circulars, statements, dodgers, tickets, and all kinds of printing done at the *Mirror* office in the best style and at reasonable prices. **1948** *Okla. City Times* 14 June 13/8 The scandal sheet, usually a one-page dodger, devotes a great deal of black ink to besmirching a candidate's character.

As the last term in **corn, lint, pork, tax, vote dodger.**

***dodging,** *n.* (See quot.) *Rare.* — **1790** Maclay *Deb. Senate* 180, I find he is for what the speculators call dodging—selling the land in Europe before he buys it here.

*** doe,** *n.* In combs.: (1) **doe bearskin,** the skin of a female bear, *obs.;* (2) **bird,** the Eskimo curlew, *Phaeopus borealis,* cf. **doughbird;** (3) **face,** see **doughface 2. b.**

(1) **1754** *Va. State P.* I. 249 To 12 Deer Skins—For 9 Doe Bear Skins—3500, Black and White Wampum. — (2) **1844** Giraud *Birds of Long Island* 274 In the vicinity of New York it is known by the name of 'Futes'—in the Eastern States it is called 'Doe Bird.' **1917** *Birds of Amer.* I. 254 Eskimo Curlew. . . . Other names include Dough- or Doe-bird. **1942** [see **doughbird**].

do-funny ˈduˌfʌnɪ, *n.* = **doodad.** *Colloq.* — **1915** *Amer. Mag.* Dec. 87/2 Winifred (from whom a do-funny [for Christmas]) . . . card followed by another do-funny. **1931** *Harper's Mag.* Dec. 78 Many and marvelous . . . were the gadgets and do-funnies offered in the accessory stores.

*** dog,** *n.*

1. = **prairie dog.** Also attrib.

1805 *Balance* (Hudson, N.Y.) 17 Sep. 304 (Th.), How Mr. Lewis . . . came to call the ground-fox squirrel a dog, it is difficult to imagine. **1844** Gregg *Commerce of Prairies* II. 32 But what attracted our attention most were the little dog settlements. **1871** Richardson *Month in Kansas* 414 It is wonderful how one of these ponies will go over all sorts of rough ground, jumping ditches, avoiding dog-holes, if you will only give him his head. **1927** James *Cow Country* 54 The big holes them dogs made looked like a natural place for a horse to put his foot into and turn a flip-flop.

2. a. (*cap.*) *pl.* A division of the Fox Indians. **b.** (See quot.) Both *obs.*

(a) **1819** E. Dana *Geog. Sk.* 268 On the east bank [of the Wisconsin River], is the village of Praira du Chein, deriving its name from a family of Indians, who formerly resided there, known by the appellation of *Dogs.* — (b) **1907** Hodge *Amer. Indians* I. 440/1 Many of the males [of the Etchareottine Indians] are circumcised in infancy; those who are not are called dogs, not opprobriously, but rather affectionately.

3. (See quot.) *Slang. Obs.*

1833 *Sketches D. Crockett* 121, I found out that bonds, or promissory notes, were termed [in the 'Western District'] dogs—and that they were said to be of a good or bad breed, according to the ability and punctuality of the obligor.

4. Contemptible meanness; low-downness. *Slang.*

1848 Hooper *Widow Rugby* 21, I'll whip as much dog out of you as 'll make a full pack of hounds.

5. Show, display, dash, tone, splurge. *Slang.*

1889 Howells *Hazard of Fortunes* I. 267 He's made the thing awfully *chic;* it's jimmy; there's lot's of dog about it. **1902** Lorimer *Lett. Merchant* 233 [He] handed me his new card four times and explained that it was the rawest sort of dog to carry a brace of names in your card holster. **1923** *Nation* 22 Aug. 188/2 Youthful and masculine is Chicago—generous, impulsive, and somewhat sceptical of 'dog.'

b. *To put on (the) dog,* (see quot. 1871). *Slang.* Cf. ***doggy,** *a.*

1871 Bagg *At Yale* 44 *Dog,* style, splurge. To put on dog, is to make a flashy display, to cut a swell. **1923** *L.A. Dly. News* 23 Nov. 20 I'll just put on the dog and not even give her a tumble! **1948** *Savings News* Jan. 7/1 They'd have settled back, bought a big house and put on the dog.

6. In special combs.: (1) **dogfishing,** fishing for dogfish; (2) ***leg,** tobacco of a cheap, inferior grade, in full **dogleg tobacco,** *colloq.;* (3) **nation,** the Cheyenne Indians (see quot. 1907); (4) **pound,** a place where stray dogs are impounded, cf. **dogcatcher** as a main entry; (5) **run,** a dogtrot *q.v.* in **c.** (15) below; (6) **'s age,** a very long time, *colloq.*, cf. **coon's age;** (7) **store,** a store in which dogs are sold; (8) **tussle,** a dogfight, *jocular* and *rare;* (9) **warrior,** a dog soldier *q.v.* as a main entry.

(1) **1857** *Harper's Mag.* Sep. 54/1 At the end of half an hour's dog-fishing . . . you are tempted to think that the entire race of dogs . . . has been duly hooked. **1885** C. F. Holder *Marvels Animal Life* 190 Everybody goes dog-fishing. — (2) **1858** *Nat. Intelligencer* 10 July 3/3 A large quantity of 'dog-leg' tobacco and red pepper is then thrown into the tub. **1891** Ryan *Pagan* 25 Then the black-and-tan man treated himself to a fresh chew of 'dog-leg.' — (3) **1807** Gass *Journal* 254 A great many of the Chien, or Dog nation encamped here. **1907** Hodge *Amer. Indians* I. 251/1 The popular name [Cheyenne] has no connection with the French *chien,* 'dog,' as has sometimes erroneously been supposed. — (4) **1875** Stowe *We & Our Neighbors* 312 Much more judicious use could be made of the city dog-pound in thinning out human brutes. **1947** *Chi. Tribune* 8 June 1. 29/1 It should have been removed to the suburb's dog pound where it could have been reclaimed for a fee.

(5) **1938** Nixon *Forty Acres* opp. p. 15 The dog-run serves as a porch in the cabin of a Georgia tenant farmer. **1938** *Ib.* opp. p. 23 A dog-run house in Alabama, in which a Negro tenant farmer lives. — (6) **1836** *Knickerb.* VII. 17 That blamed line gale has kept me in bilboes such a dog's age. **1947** *Chi. Sun. Tribune* 8 June (Comics) 3 You know darn well you haven't turned on a smile for me in a dog's age! — (7) **1877** Phelps *Story of Avis* 42 Drayton Allen is going to keep a dog-store, and Ben is going to be president of a college. — (8) **1873** Beadle *Undevel. West* 490 They usually have splendid cathedral services in the morning, a dog-tussle about noon, and a cock-fight later in the day. — (9) **1880** *Cong. Rec.* 26 Jan. 522/2 The dog warriors of all these tribes, . . . as soon as they are fed by the United States and armed by traders, . . . mount their horses and join some Indian chief then upon the war-path.

b. In expressions alluding to the use of dogs as draft animals: (1) **dog cariole,** a light sleigh drawn by dogs; (2) **musher,** the driver of a dog team; (3) **pole,** (see quot.), *obs.;* (4) **puncher,** =**dog musher;** (5) **sled,** a sled drawn by dogs, also attrib.; (6) **sledge,** =prec.; (7) **sleigh,** a dog sled, also **dog sleighing;** (8) **team,** a team made up of dogs, also attrib.; (9) **travois,** a travois used on a dog.

(1) **1892** *Harper's Mag.* March 506/2 A dog-cariole of the best pattern—a little suggestive of a burial casket, to be sure. — (2) **1907** Jack London *White Fang* 215 Dog-mushers' cries were heard. . . . They saw, up the trail, two men running with sled and dogs. — (3) **1807** in *D.N.* IV. 378 We . . . passed . . . an old Indian camp, where we found some of their dog-poles, which answer for settling poles. The reason they are called dog-poles is because the Indians fasten their dogs to keep them, and make them draw them from one camp to another loaded with skins and other articles. — (4) **1928** *Publishers' Weekly* 16 June 2461 Walden, Arthur Treadwell [*title*], A dog-puncher on the Yukon.

(5) **1806–8** Pike *Sources Miss.* 85 With my dog-sled [I] arrived at the fort before 10 o'clock. **1935** *Denver Post* 25 Feb. 16/4 There were skating events, . . . a hockey game and a dogsled derby for boys. **1948** *Nat. Hist.* April 178/2 He took a dog sled and sped down to Unalakeet by the sea. — (6) **1856** Hale *If, Yes, & Perhaps* (1868) 150 Lieutenant Pim started with a sledge and seven men, and a dog-sledge. **1894** *Harper's Mag.* LXXXVIII. 472/2 The journey was made with a dog-sledge and a half-breed assistant. — (7) **1855** Oliphant *Minnesota* 101 The more adventurous inhabitants do keep up a communication with Detroit, across Lake Huron, upon the ice, by means of dog-sleighs. **1868** Whymper *Alaska* 119 Our spasmodic conversation would have puzzled a stranger. Now it was dog-sleighing, or reindeer riding; now the policy of the President, or the last opera. — (8) **1855** Oliphant *Minnesota* 282 In winter, the journey is made with dog-

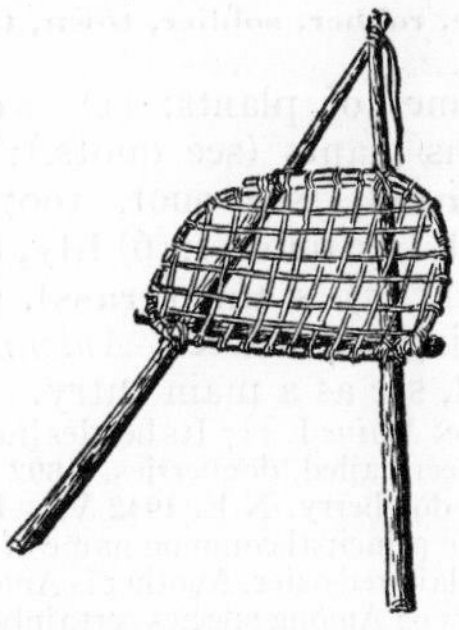

Dog travois

teams and snow-shoes. **1928** *Publishers' Wkly.* 16 June 2461 The author worked as a dog-team freighter in Alaska during the gold-rush. — (9) **1893** *Outing* Oct. 7 (*caption*), The Youngster's Joy—a Dog-Travois. **1942** *Land of Nakoda* 54 The poles on a dog travois were not crossed but came together and bound with wet rawhide which, when dried, held the points strongly together.

c. In combs., often rare or obs., most of the meanings of which are obvious or sufficiently explained in the quots.: (1) **dogbody,** (2) **button,** the seed of nux vomica or a preparation made from this plant, (3) **-eaters,** (4) **farm,** (5) ***fight,** cf. **dog style** below, (6) **hole,** (7) **killer,** (8) **money,** (9) **nap,** (10) **-sburg,** (11) ***-skin,** (12) **style,** (13) ***tail,** (14) **-tail railroad,** (15) **trot.**

(1) **1884** *Nat. Museum Bul.* No. 27, 671 'Dogbody.' . . . This model represents a square stern, decked chebacco boat of about 17 tons; this . . . being the best class of these crafts employed in the fisheries during the early part of the present century. **1926** Gabriel *Pageant of Amer.* III. 301 A larger chebacco, of about seventeen tons and known as the 'dogbody' from its square stern, was used for the longer sail to the Banks. — (2) **1857** S. H. Hammond *Northern Scenes* 77 A dose of 'dog buttons,' or a taste of strychnine, administered with a tempting bit of cold steak, . . . might have aided the operation. **1882** Peck *Sunshine* 80 Six promising pups that had been presented to us . . . had gone the way of all dog flesh, with the distemper and dog buttons. — (3) **1855** Ross *Fur Hunters* (1929) 239 The great Snake nation may be divided into three divisions, namely, the Shirry-dikas, or dog-eaters; the War-are-ree-kas, or fish-eaters; and the Ban-at-ties, or robbers. **1930** Hebard *Washakie* 34 First are the *Shirry-dikas* or 'dog-eaters,' though since they lived by the chase the reason for their name is not evident. — (4) **1872** *Atlantic Mo.* May 553 Some of them also have 'dog-farms' in the country, where they [*sc.* dog-doctors] keep their choicest dogs.

(5) **1923** J. H. Cook *On Old Frontier* 115 Fist-fights, which were engaged in among soldiers of the regular army, freighting outfits, and men following other vocations were called 'dog fights' by the cowboys. — (6) **1859** Bartlett 181 Groggery, a place where spirituous liquors are sold and drank; a grog-shop. In the West, often called a Doggery or Dog-hole. — (7) **1893** Roosevelt *Wilderness Hunter* 163 It is only when a beast is caught while turning that there is a chance to deliver a possibly deadly stab in the flank, with the brow prongs, the 'dog-killers' as they are called in bucks. — (8) **1903** Stiles *Four Years* 63, I am confident every surviving member of our battery who was with us at Leesburg [Va.] will recall the little 'dog money' notes issued by the town, ornamented by a picture of a

majestic Newfoundland dog. — (9) **1860** W. PHILLIPS *Speeches* (1863) 295 That sleepy crier of a New Hampshire court, who was ever dreaming in his dog-naps that the voice of judge or lawyer was a noisy interruption, and always woke shouting 'Silence!'

(10) **1882** STEELE *Frontier Army* (1883) 24 Peralta is the very dogs-burg of a land of squalid towns. — (11) **1845** HOOPER *Taking Census* (1928) 129 Dern my everlastin' dog-skin er I'll stand it! **1850** GARRARD *Wah-To-Yah* xxiv. 298 Feel if you haven't got a hole in your dogskin—I'd hate to be as bad scared as you, by thunder! — (12) **1923** J. H. COOK *On Old Frontier* 115 Fighting 'dog style' was of such rare occurrence among cowboys that in all the time I followed that life I never saw one instance in which men threw down all weapons and engaged in a slugging match. — (13) **1884** CRADDOCK *Where Battle was Fought* 87 The last 'dog-tail,' as the frosted remnant of the cotton is called, still hung on the black and withered stalk. — (14) **1888** J. KIRKLAND *McVeys* 204 It's a 'dog-tail railroad,' as they say around here. A line that starts from a place of no consequence and runs nowhere.

(15) **1933** *Amer. Sp.* Feb. 48 Dogtrot, n. The covered porch or gallery which connects the two parts of a double log cabin. **1946** STUART *Plum Grove Hills* 91 Mom and Pa walk from the kitchen to the dog-trot.

For ***doghouse, robber, soldier, town, train, warp,** see as main entries.

7. In the names of plants: (1) ***dogberry,** used locally for various plants (see quots.); (2) **elder,** (see quot.); (3) ***fennel,** (see quot. 1907); (4) **hobble,** =next; (5) **laurel,** (see quots.); (6) **lily,** the yellow water lily or spatterdock; (7) **'s tail (grass),** (see quots.); (8) **toes,** an everlasting or cudweed, *Antennaria plantaginifolia;* (9) ***wood,** see as a main entry.

(1) **1832** WILLIAMSON *Maine* I. 117 Its berries [i.e., of the poison ash or sumac] . . . have been called 'dogberries.' **1892** *Amer. Folk-Lore* V. 95 *Pyrus arbutifolia*, dog-berry. N.E. **1942** VAN DERSAL *Ornamental Amer. Shrubs* 179 The principal common name of this plant, and the one in widest use, is plain red osier. Another is American dogberry. — (2) **1931** CLUTE *Plants* 94 Among species certainly named for the dog are . . . the dog tansy (*Potentilla anserina*), the dog-elder (*Viburnum Americanum*), and the dog-laurel (*Leocothoe Catesbaei*). — (3) **1907** LYONS *Plant Names* 59 *A[ster] ericoides* L. White Heath-aster, White Rosemary, Dog-fennel. **1944** DUNCAN *M. Graham* 115 But in the hot, dry swelter of August when dog fennel was beginning to bloom, it was religious zeal that boiled up and over, not steamboat talk. — (4) **1922** *Outing* April 292/3, I found it to be a small creek . . . running under laurel and dog-hobble, spraying itself through windfalls, running around slippery logs. **1942** VAN DERSAL *Ornamental Amer. Shrubs* 257 There it is variously known asfetterbush, switch-ivy, dog-hobble, and ivy, no one of which seems to be a particularly apt common name.

(5) **1860** CURTIS *Woody Plants N.C.* 95 Dog Laurel. (*Leucothoe Catesbaei*, Gray.) — Found only in the mountains, where it is also called *Hemlock*, growing on the cool margins of streams. **1931** CLUTE *Plants* 94 Among species certainly named for the dog are . . . the dog tansy (*Potentilla anserina*), the dog-elder (*Viburnum Americanum*), and the dog-laurel (*Leocothoe Catesbaei*). — (6) **1832** WILLIAMSON *Maine* I. 126 We have . . . the yellow water-lily, or dog-lily, or beaver-root. **1892** *Amer. Folk-Lore* V. 91 *Nuphar advena*, cow-lily. Washington Co. Me., dog-lily, New England. — (7) **1857** GRAY *Botany* 554 Dog's-Tail or Wire Grass. **1894** *Amer. Folk-Lore* VII. 104 *Eleusine Indica*, . . . dog's tail-grass, wire-grass. West Va. — (8) **1886** *Cent. Mag.* Sep. 787/1 First it [*sc.* Iowa prairie] is white with 'dog-toes.' **1894** *Amer. Folk-Lore* VII. 91 *Antennaria plantaginifolia*, . . . dog-toes, Concord, Mass.

b. In the names of fishes and other creatures: (1) **-day cicada, harvest fly, locust,** any one of several cicadas of the genus *Tibicen* the shrill note of which is heard during the dog days; (2) ***fish,** a local name for (*a*) the bowfin or mudfish, *Amia calva*, (*b*) the burbot, *Lota maculosa*, and (*c*) (see quot.); (3) **salmon,** a salmon of the genus *Oncorhynchus*, found in the streams of the Northwest; (4) **shark,** (see quot.); (5) **tooth salmon,** **=dog salmon.**

(1) **1854** EMMONS *Agric. N.Y.* V. 152 *Cicada canicularis*. Dogday Harvestfly. **1855** *Trans. Amer. Inst. N.Y.* 210 The seventeen year and the dog-day cicada are . . . familiarly known to us as locusts. *a***1862** THOREAU *Maine Woods* 236, I heard the dog-day locust here. — (2) (*a*) **1848** BARTLETT 198 Lake Lawyer . . . [or] the Western Mud-Fish . . . is found in Lakes Erie and Ontario, where it is known by the name of Dog-fish. **1884** GOODE *Fisheries* I. 659 The Bowfin or Johnny Grindle, *Amia calva*, . . . occurs in the Great Lakes, where it is called 'Dogfish.' (*b*) **1884** *Ib.* 236 The Burbot is known . . . as the Dogfish in Lake Erie. (*c*) **1889** *Cent.* 1719/3 dogfish. . . . A name of the menobranchus or mud-puppy, *Necturus maculatus*, a batrachian reptile. — (3) **1869** *Amer. Naturalist* III. 127 Dog Salmon (*Salmo canis* Suckley). Below the forks of the Spokan, the Indians were catching myriads of this salmon. **1940** SMITH *Puyallup-Nisqually* 238 Smoked salmon was prepared from the dog salmon and from the steelhead when it could be caught in quantity. — (4) **1884** GOODE *Fisheries* I. 676 *Mustelus californicus* Gill. Dog Shark. San Francisco and southward. — (5) **1852** SWAN *Three Years' Residence* (1857) 140 There are several varieties of fall salmon, the most plentiful of which is the hawk-nosed, or hook-billed, or dog-tooth salmon (for it has all those names).

8. In various colloq. or slang phrases, usu. obs.: (1) *To kill one's dog*, to become intoxicated; (2) *what the dog*, what the devil; (3) *dog eat dog*, everyone for himself, tit for tat; (4) *to blow off one's dogs, fig.* to give up an undertaking; (5) *to die dog for*, to be extremely loyal to; (6) *to cut open a dog*, (see quot.); (7) *to put on (the) dog*, see **5. b.** above; (8) *to stay until the last dog is hung*, to remain until the very last; (9) *as stylish as a spotted dog under a red wagon*, quite stylish.

(1) **1737** *Pa. Gazette* 13 Jan. 1/2 He's kill'd his Dog. — (2) **1787** TYLER *Contrast* II. ii, But what the dogs need of all this outlandish lingo? — (3) **1834** CARUTHERS *Kentuckian* I. 22 That's what I call dog eat dog. **1947** *Christian Cent.* 20 Aug. 998/1 Does not the racketeering of the dishonest veterans reflect the climate of opinion produced by a dog-eat-dog society? — (4) **1835** CROCKETT *Van Buren* 42 He determined to *blow off his dogs* and quit the drive.

(5) **1837** BIRD *Nick of Woods* I. 219 I'm the man . . . to die dog for them that pats me. — (6) **1867** B. TAYLOR *Colorado* 60 One who makes a blunder 'cuts open a dog.' — (8) **1902** WHITE *Blazed Trail* 251 They were loyal. It was a point of honor with them to stay 'until the last dog was hung.' — (9) **1939** ROLLINS *Gone Haywire* 95 The mother was soft and pretty as a young calf's ear, stylisher'n a spotted dog under a red wagon.

For *whole team and the dog under the wagon* see **team 1.**

As the last term in **big, bird, black, blue, buffalo, bull, cast-iron, chicken, choke, clay, collar, coon, cow, coyote, devil, feist, fire, French bull, ground, hot, hound, Indian, Jersey blue, medicine, moose, Negro, orange, pack, pelon, plantation, possum, prairie, raccoon, rain, red, republican, rock, sheep killing, sleigh, squirrel, stone, turkey, under, war, water, whiffet, white, yellow dog.**

***dog,** *v.*

1. *tr.* To pin (a log) securely on a carriage in a saw-mill by means of a "dog." Also absol. *Colloq.*

1879 *Lumberman's Gaz.* 15 Oct., We can dog directly into the hardest knot in the heaviest timber and hold the log perfectly safe and true. **1886** G. W. HOTCHKISS in *Encycl. Brit.* XXI. 345/2 When the log reached the carriage it was dogged . . . by the simple movement of a lever.

2. *local.* Of a salmon: To take on the changes of the breeding season

1883 *U.S. Nat. Museum Bul.* No. 27, 419 Before it begins to 'dog' this [*sc.* the gorbushcha, or dog salmon] is an excellent fish, more like a trout than a salmon in flavor.

3. **=bulldog,** *v. Slang.*

1934 *Rocky Mt. News* (Denver) 31 Jan. II. 7/4 A man couldn't come much nearer hell than did the cowmen who 'dogged' the calves and left the owners' indelible marks on their rumps for life.

4. In colloq. and slang phrases: (1) *To dog out*, to rout utterly, to secure by persistence; (2) *to dog at*, to vex, annoy; (3) *to dog it*, to shirk, perform without spirit.

(1) **1843** CARLTON *New Purchase* II. 180 Bust my rifle! we'll dog out the rats now! **1845** S. SMITH *J. Downing's Lett.* 31 'Squire Sharp . . . gets his rents by looking after 'em; he fairly dogs it out of his tenants. — (2) **1896** HARRIS *Sister Jane* 102 'Don't cry, sis,' said the brother. 'The folks in the house'll . . . think I'm doggin' at you.' — (3) **1920** *Collier's* 15 May 62/3 I'm afraid if Roberts gets hurt, early, bein' green, he'll play safe and be satisfied to stall the rest of it and dog it. **1948** *Sat. Ev. Post* 7 Aug. 31/1 They might not be all-city, but they'll play for me, not dog it!

b. Used in mildly profane imprecations.

[**1843** OLIVER *Eight Months* 132 Well, pretty considerable, till of late, when the doctor got a new assistant, who ought to be dogged to death; he killed two men right off.] **1857** *Ill. Agric. Soc. Trans.* II. 232, I did want it, but I'll be dogged if I could use it. **1880** MARK TWAIN *Tramp Abroad* xxxvi. 268 [He said] dog'd if he wanted to risk his neck going over those mountain roads on wheels in the dead of winter.

dogcatcher ˈdɔgˌkætʃɚ, *n.* A town or city employee who impounds stray dogs. Also transf.

1835 *Vade Mecum* (Phila.) 9 May 3/6, I could kill you, George Jake, and cast my future lot with the lot of the dog-ketchers! **1837** J. C. NEAL *Charcoal Sk.* (1838) 47 After ten o'clock, the law is a watchman and a dog ketcher—we're the whole law till breakfast's a'most ready. **1895** G. KING *New Orleans* 38 It was a dog-catcher's work; and dog-catchers performed it. **1947** *Chi. Tribune* 8 June I. 29/2 (*caption*), Miss Bernice White, 21, who is the new dog catcher in Cicero, with her dog, Jackie.

dog dance. (See quot. 1841.) Now *hist.*

1807 PIKE *Sources Miss.* (1810) 84 In the evening we were entertained with the calumet and dog dance. **1841** BUCKINGHAM *America* I. 77 This, however, is exceeded in ferocity by 'the dog dance,' of the same [Sioux] tribe, at which the heart and liver of a dog are taken, raw and bleeding, and, cut into strips, placed on a stand about the height of a man's face from the ground; to this each of the warriors advances in turn, and, biting off a piece of the flesh, utters a yell of exultation. **1946** FOREMAN *Last Trek* 168 Their dog dance was held the first full moon in each year and continued for a week.

***dogger,** *n.* (See quots.) See also **bull dogger.** — **1905** *Forestry Bureau* Bul. 61,11, Dogger, One who attaches the dogs or hooks to a log before it is steam skidded. (S.F.,P.C.F.) **1947** *Reader's Digest* Oct. 113/2 It took Rambo three years to train his two horses—a roper and a dogger.

* **doggery,** *n.* A saloon of a cheap or disreputable sort. *Slang.* Cf. **Dutch doggery.**

1830 ROYALL *Lett. from Ala.* 145 A Doggery is a place where spirituous liquors are sold. **1911** LEWIS *Apaches N.Y.* 13 Tricker stopped for a moment in a little doggery from which came the tump-tump of a piano and the scuffle of a dance. **1944** DUNCAN *M. Graham* 105 John Clary opened what he called a 'grocery' (some termed it 'doggery').

attrib. **1851** *Ore. Statesman* 4 July 1/5 [He] gathered up all the papers he had and sold them for a half pint of rum, to the doggery-keeper, to wrap groceries in. **1856** P. CARTWRIGHT *Autobiog.* 376 There was a general rally from . . . the loose-footed, doggery-haunting, dissipated renegades of the towns.

* **doggy,** *a.* Neat, stylish. *Slang.* Cf. *to put on (the) dog,* *s.v.* * **dog,** *n.* **5. b.**

1915 *D.N.* IV. 233 doggy. Dressy; neat; handsome. [**1919** *Vanity Fair* Dec. 69 The horsey and doggy outdoor girl; the bobbed hair or Greenwich Village sort of child.] **1945** WEBSTER *Town Meeting Country* 180 It was no doggy place with tables.

* **doghouse,** *n.*

1. The mound of earth piled up at the entrance to a prairie-dog burrow. *Rare.*

1847 RUXTON *Adv. Rocky Mts.* (1848) 281, I rolled him [*sc.* a buffalo] over and over in a cloud of dust, leveling to the ground, as he fell, a well-built dog-house.

2. The caboose on a freight train. *Slang.*

1898 HAMBLEN *Gen. Manager's Story* 43 I'll have to drop off a flag, or they'll git our doghouse.

3. In combs.: (1) **doghouse stirrup,** (see quot. 1944); (2) **windows,** (see quot.).

(1) **1927** RUSSELL *Trails* 117 He's sittin' in an old-fashioned lowhorn saddle with 'doghouse' stirrups. **1944** ADAMS *W. Words* 51 *doghouse stirrups:* A slang name for the old, wide wooden stirrups of the early range. It was claimed that they had enough lumber in them to build a dog-house. — (2) **1923** W. NUTTING *Massachusetts* 26 The Cape Cod house is further characterized in its best form by three minute windows on each end in the gable, one on each side under the eaves. . . . These little windows, invariably with four lights of glass, are sometimes called 'dog house windows.'

b. *To be in the doghouse,* to be out of favor. *Slang.*

1944 *Harper's Mag.* March 364/2 It's conceivable that this thought sustains him now, when he is so completely in the doghouse. **1948** *Dly. Ardmoreite* (Ardmore, Okla.) 19 April 4/2 Several big stars are in studio doghouses because of their political affiliations.

dogie ˈdogɪ, *n. W.* [See note.] A motherless calf (see also quot. 1888).

The origin of this term is unknown. Bentley's suggestion that it is probably an adaptation of dobie *q.v.* seems improbable.

1888 *Cent. Mag.* Oct. (F.), A bunch of steers had been seen travelling over the scoria buttes to the head of Elk Creek; they were mostly Texan doughies—a name I have never seen written, it applies to young immigrant cattle—but there were some of the Hash-Knife four-year-olds among them. **1892** *Outing* Feb. 385/2 I remember noticing in a herd of cattle south of Dodge City a queer, pot-bellied little dogy (a calf prematurely weaned by the death of its mother and developed into a runt). **1947** *Trail Riders Bul.* Feb. 20/1 'That's jest the idea,' comes back Sluefoot, with a grin on his puss like a li'l dogey what's foun' a new ma.

attrib. **1911** H. QUICK *Yellowstone N.* v. 124 The Old Man . . . was a one-lunger when this dogie enterprise started. **1924** J. M. FRANKS *Seventy Yrs. in Texas* 81 One of Mr. Austin's best horses . . . had gotten away with a doge loop, a rawhide lariat, about his neck . . . and perished of hunger.

dog robber. (See quots. 1868, 1929.) *Slang.*

1868 *Harper's Mag.* Feb. 300/2 'Dog-robber' was the name by which the soldier designated the cooks and detailed soldiers who were the occupants of the second table of an officers' mess. **1886** *Graphic News* (Chi.) 6 Mar. 10/2 A couple of soldiers, occupying the honorable post of 'strikers' or 'dog robbers,' are setting a long table for supper. **1929** J. PARKER *Old Army* 17 They persecute and call 'dog robber' any soldier who acts as an officer's servant.

dog soldier. Also **Dog Soldier.**

1. (See quots.)

1846 SAGE *Rocky Mt. Life* (1859) 130 While there a dog-soldier [*Note:* This is the title of those selected to superintend the civil affairs of a village.] of the Burnt-thighs received the offer of six horses from an Oglalla brave, for his only daughter. **1870** KEIM *Sheridan's Troopers* (1885) xxvi. 188 It has been asserted that the warriors are composed of out-laws from the other two branches of the parent stock and hence called 'dog soldiers.' **1873** BEADLE *Undevel. West* 505 The murderer simply goes to some other tribe, or becomes a 'dog soldier,' at large in the mountains. **1919** CODY *Buffalo Bill* 267 It was the Fifth Cavalry, hurrying to cut off the Dog Soldiers, as a number of renegade Sioux and Cheyenne were called.

2. (See quot. 1907.) Also attrib.

1851 T. A. CULBERTSON *Smithsonian Rep.* (*Senate Doc.* Spl. Sess., 1851) 143 Cheyenne Nation: The Dog Soldier band, the Yellow Wolf band, the Half Breed band, Principally west of the Black Hills. Originally on the Missouri. **1885** *Rep. Indian Affairs* 79 The 'dog soldiers' are a sort of military organization . . . composed of the most daring, blood-thirsty young men of the tribe. **1907** HODGE *Amer. Indians* I. 862/2 Among the Cheyenne the Hotámitäneo, or Dog Men society ('Dog Soldiers'), acquired such prominence in the frontier wars by virtue of superior number and the bravery of their leadership that the name has frequently been used by writers to designate the whole organization. **1947** *Sat. Ev. Post* 22 Feb. 140/2 Most of them warriors and dog soldiers.

b. Also **Dog-soldier Cheyenne.**

1869 *Harper's Mag.* June 31/1 This one band—the 'Dog-soldier Cheyenne'—has committed two-thirds of the depredations . . . on the Plains.

dog town. Also **dogstown.**

1. a. (See quot.) *Rare.* **b.** (See quot.) *Slang.*

(**a**) **1841** *Spirit of Times* 21 Aug. 299/1 (We.), This is emphatically a Dog Town, a town literally overrun by dogs. — (**b**) **1898** *N.Y. Herald* 4 Oct. 13/5 Washington is becoming quite a 'dog town,' as theatrical people call a city in which they 'try on' plays before bringing them to New York.

2. *W.* An area occupied by a community or colony of prairie dogs. Also attrib.

1843 in *Utah Hist. Quart.* II. (1929) 103 We are now past all the dog towns . . . saw plenty on the South Platte. **1850** *Western Journal* IV. 236 We were traversing a bare dogstown prairie. **1913** CATHER *My Antonia* 33 The dog-town was a long way from any pond or creek. **1942** Nat. Pk. Service *Fading Trails* 255 Now, the huge 'dog towns' of fifty years ago are present only in the memories of grizzled old-timers.

b. dogtown grass, (see quots.).

1913 W. C. BARNES *Western Grazing Grounds* 43 Owing to the presence in many portions of both these desert regions of a grass known as needle or dogtown grass (Aristida) and porcupine grass (Stipa spp.), the sharp awns of each of which work into the wool and finally into the very skin of the animals, sheep cannot be successfully grazed in these lower desert ranges. **1937** *Range Plant Hdbk.* G-20 Red threeawn, also known as dogtown grass, . . . is perhaps the most easily recognized species of the genus.

dog train. A number of dogs harnessed to sleds and traveling in a long line or file.

1825 KEATING *Exped. St. Peter's River* I. 453 In travelling on the snow with dog trains, it is usual for a man to walk a-head of the dogs, with snowshoes, in order to trample down the snow. **1866** *Beadle's Mo.* Mar. 207/2 A third journey to the plains for much-needed buffalo-meat, was undertaken, along with several Indians, with a good dog-train to bring in the meat. **1948** *Sat. Ev. Post* 28 Aug. 76/1 Twelve steamships, 600 mule teams and 500 dog trains kept alive the muckers who were digging, bridging and blasting their way through hundreds of miles of engineering nightmares.

b. (See quot.) *Obs.* Cf. * **train 1.**

1827 T. L. MCKENNEY *Tour to Lakes* 196 The dog train is made of a light frame of wood, and covered round with a dressed skin. . . . Its bottom is of plank.

dog warp. (See 1st quot.) Also as verb.—**1905** *Forestry Bureau Bul.* 61, Dogwarp, n. A rope with a strong hook on the end, which is used in breaking dangerous jams on falls and rapids and in moving logs from other difficult positions. **1905** WIGGIN *Rose* 16, I must be down to the bridge 'fore they start dogwarpin' the side jam. *Ib.* 44 They'd get horses an' dog-warp it off, log by log.

***dogwood,** *n.*

1. The poison sumac.

1850 *N. Eng. Farmer* II. 60 The Dogwood . . . is not to be confounded with the Poison Sumac, usually called Dogwood. **1931** CLUTE *Plants* 94 We must not overlook the poison dog-wood (*Rhus vernix*), which is a species of sumach and one of the very few American plants that are poisonous to the touch.

2. dogwood rain, (see quot.).

1899 *Animal & Plant Lore* 108 There is a rain at the time of the dogwood (*Cornus florida*) blooming, hence called 'dogwood rain.'

3. dogwood winter, (see quots.). *Colloq.*

1907 *Amer. Folk-Lore* 235 'Don't you know what dogwood winter is?' demanded the man from Hickory, N.C. 'There is always a spell of it in May, when the dogwood tree is in bloom. For several days there is cold, disagreeable, cloudy weather, and often a touch of frost.' **1944** *D.N.* Nov. 42 dogwood winter: n. A cool period that sometimes occurs when the dogwoods are blooming. Caldwell Co., N.C.

As the last term in **blue, highland, poison, pond, rock, swamp dogwood.**

doherty wagon, see **Dougherty wagon.**

***doings,** *n. pl.* Usu. **doins.**

1. Food or drink of an indicated kind, as **corn, flour, ham, liquor doings.** *Colloq. Obs.* Cf. **common, dough doings.**

1839 *N.O. Picayune* 25 Jan. 2/2 [He] recommends the printers in that country to set up a shop for retailing the extra 'white-eye' and 'flour doins' sent them for publishing marriage notices. **1843** CARLTON *New Purchase* II. 58 A snug breakfast of chicken fixins, eggs, ham-doins, and corn slap-jacks. **1844** *N.O. Picayune* 241/4, I heerd you'd give us two dollars a day and throw in the 'chicken fixins' and 'corn doins.' **1847** ROBB *Squatter Life* 65, I walked out upon the steam boat 'guard' to cool off from the effects of considerable liquor doin's, participated in during the day. **1862** *Harper's Mag.* Sep. 464/2 How pleasant it was to sit down once more to 'corn doins and chicken fixens.'

2. Lace, trimming, ornaments, etc., of a dress. *Obs.*

a1846 *Quarter Race Ky.* 84 [The girls] came pourin out of the woods . . . fixed out in all sorts of fancy doins, from the broad-striped homespun to the sunflower calico. **1856** *Knickerb.* XLVII. 406 Pretty girl that in the black fixings and white arrangements, with blue doings.

***doll,** *n.* In combs.: (1) **doll baby,** see as a main entry; (2) **buggy,** a doll's carriage, also attrib.; (3) **house,** a doll's house, also attrib.; (4) ***-'s eyes,** (see quot.); (5) **target,** at a circus, fair, etc., an amusement booth where balls are thrown at dolls for prizes.

(2) **1902** *Sears Cat.* (ed. 112) (Index). **1909** CALHOUN *Miss Minerva* 38 Two little girls rolling two doll buggies on which reposed two enormous rag-babies were seen approaching. **1948** *Milwaukee Jrnl.* 18 July 2/6 We were happy to see the youngsters in the parks having doll buggy and coaster parades and free ice cream. — **(3) 1873** PHELPS *Trotty's Wedding* xvii, Pudge . . . didn't care a straw for dolls, or doll-houses. **1948** *Lisle* (Ill.) *Eagle* 21 Oct. 9/3 Children from the first, second and third grades have just finished a cardboard doll-house. — **(4) 1931** CLUTE *Plants* 60 Among other names that seem to be more fanciful than real are . . . doll's eyes for *Actaea alba.*

(5) **1895** *Cent. Mag.* July 323/2 There is also a rifle-range, a merry-go-round, and a doll target at which balls are thrown for prizes.

***dollar,** *n.*

1. The standard unit of value in American money; also the coin or its equivalent in paper money or subsidiary coins. Also attrib.

1785 *Jrnls. Cont. Congress* XXIX. 500 It was Resolved, That the money unit of the United States of America be one dollar . . . [and] That the smallest coin be of copper, of which 200 shall pass for one dollar. **1792** *Ann. 2nd Congress* 1 Sess. 12 Jan. 71 Dollars or units; each to be of the value of a Spanish milled dollar, . . . and to contain three hundred and seventy-one grains and four-sixteenth parts of a grain of pure . . . silver. **1812** *Niles' Reg.* I. 341/2 There were in the pit and boxes 518 dollar tickets. **1948** *Time* 28 June 67/1 Last week set owners could spend hundreds of dollars for extra equipment.

2. In special combs. and derivatives: (1) **dollar-a-day,** designating a cheap boarding house where the rates are only a dollar a day; (2) **-and-cent age,** an age when the acquiring of money is the chief concern; (3) **aristocracy,** the aristocracy composed of those who have only wealth; (4) **-a-year-man,** a man, usu. wealthy, who serves the government in some special capacity for the nominal salary of a dollar a year; (5) **baiting,** struggling to obtain money, *rare;* (6) **ball,** (see quot.), *obs.;* (7) **bill,** a bank note, treasury note, or silver certificate for one dollar; (8) **bug,** *local,* a whirligig beetle; (9) **crazy,** money-mad; (10) **-dee,** (see quot. 1889); (11) **diplomacy,** a nickname for the foreign policy of the U.S. early in the 20th century which was alleged to have for its purpose expanding this country's financial and commercial interests abroad under the pretence of fostering international friendship; (12) **-dom,** a place where getting money is the primary aim of the people, *rare;* (13) **fish,** (see quot.); (14) **hunter,** one who prizes money above everything else; (15) **mark,** (see quot. 1847); (16) **matching,** (see quot.); (17) **note, =dollar bill;** (18) **pitching,** a game in which silver dollars are pitched at small holes in the ground; (19) **sign, =dollar mark;** (20) **store,** a store specializing in articles selling for a dollar or less, also attrib.; (21) **watch,** a watch made to sell for a dollar.

(1) 1902 LORIMER *Lett. Merchant* 59 I'm a little afraid that you're sometimes like the hungry drummer at the dollar-a-day house. — **(2) 1843** *Yale Lit. Mag.* VIII. 406 And this leads me to make some observations on the utter lack of poetic sensibility in this dollar-and-cent age of speculation. — **(3) 1844** in *Amer. Sp.* XVIII. 123/2 The half-British, half-monarchical, dollar aristocracy of the present day. — **(4) 1918** *Lit. Digest* 11 May 11/1 While the 'dollar-a-year men' undoubtedly did good work, the delay and friction in our war-machine became glaringly evident. **1948** *Sat.Ev.Post* 17 July 98/4 There would be no dollar-a-year men flocking to Washington on a temporary basis, many of whom might at times confuse their private interests with their public duty.

(5) 1911 HARRISON *Queed* 107 A man aspires to find some better use for his abilities than dollar-baiting, don't you think? — **(6) 1889** BARRERE & LELAND 220 About fifty years ago in Philadelphia it was usual to speak of balls frequented by factory girls as 'slewers,' and the commoner kind of grisettes as *calico* or dollar balls. — **(7) 1774** in *Jrnl. Nicholas Cresswell* (1925) 21 A considerable sum in Four, Three, Two, One, Two-thirds, One-third and 'One-Ninth' of a Dollar Bills is struck in these Bills of Credit by an Act of the Provincial Assembly. **1944** *Chi. D. News* 8 Aug. 1/7 American dollar bills bring more than 250 francs in Paris. — **(8) 1899** *Animal & Plant Lore* 12 Gyrinidae are called 'lucky bugs,' or 'dollar bugs,' because it is said that if you catch one in the hand you'll find a dollar in it. . . . Eastern Massachusetts. — **(9) 1928** *Sat. Ev. Post* 4 Feb. 96/2 You're just plain dollar crazy.

(10) 1884 GOODE *Fisheries* I. 406 The Blue Sun-fish . . . is known . . . in Kentucky sometimes as the 'Dollardee.' **1889** *Cent.* 1725/1 *Dollardee,* the blue copper-nosed sunfish, *Lepomis pallidis,* . . . is of common occurrence in most parts of the United States. — **(11) 1911** *Amer. Year Bk.* 66 Dollar diplomacy has been severely criticized during the past year. **1946** *New Yorker* 19 Oct. 97 Molotov accused the United States of practicing 'dollar diplomacy' in connection with the Danube question. — **(12) 1852** *Lantern* (N.Y.) I. 109/2 My dear Dollardom, listen to a suggestion of Diogenes. How much better to *disarm* the ignorant burglars, robbers and rowdies of New York, than to *arm* European Patriots! — **(13) 1884** GOODE *Fisheries* I. 333 The 'Butter-fish' of Massachusetts and New York, sometimes known . . in Maine as the 'Dollar-fish,' . . . is common between Cape Cod and Cape Henry. — **(14) 1884** *Cent. Mag.* Aug. 554/1 Old World writers dub the people of the United States a nation of 'dollar-hunters.'

(15) 1847 *Boston Wkly. Mail* 23 Jan. 3/6 The dollar mark in question is only applied, properly, to the United States coin, or currency, of that name; and originally in order to distinguish it as such, it was written with the 'U.S.' affixed; as 'US 100 dollars'; and in process of time the whole became abbreviated to 'US 100,'—and then, by abbreviation, to the two letters in one, the 'S' crossing the 'U'—out of which has grown the '$.' **1857** *Hist. Mag.* I. 186 The earliest use of the dollar-mark that has come to my knowledge, was in 1784, when Jefferson in the memorial which proposed the dollar as the American money-unit, employed the $ sign. **1948** ROLLINSON *Wyo. Cattle Trails* 225 Roberts bought several of the animals, and then branded them with the dollar mark. — **(16) 1943** HICKS *Amer. Dem.* 667 The Smith-Lever Act . . . provided that the United States should match, dollar for dollar, the contributions of . . . states. . . . This measure was followed in 1917 by the Smith Hughes Act, which appropriated funds, again on a dollar-matching basis. — **(17) 1831** *Cong. Deb.* App. 22 Feb. p. cxxxix/2 Taking the issues of one, two, and three dollar notes, in the Eastern States, as a guide. **1898** PAGE *Red Rock* 492 He extracted a dollar note and held it out. — **(18) 1845** HOOPER *Simon Suggs' Adv.* 111 In spite of the excitement of frequent *sorties* upon ox-wagons; of dollar-pitching, and an endless series of games . . . time at last began to hang heavily. — **(19) 1857** [see **dollar mark**]. **1881** *Bradstreet's* 26 Nov. 342/1 There is . . . almost never a dollar sign. **1947** *Time* 1 Dec. 7/1 Let Ratner read the Preamble of the Constitution once more and get the dollar sign out of his eyes if he wants to see the true image of the American People.

(20) **1872** CRAPSEY *Nether Side N.Y.* 72 Gift jewelry, prize candy, 'Milton gold,' gift concerts, dollar stores, . . . and circular swindles of every description, have been only a few of his devices for wheedling people of their money. **1892** QUINN *Fools of Fortune* 402 Another professional sport . . . figured prominently before the public at that time as proprietor of two 'dollar stores,' with back-room attachments where 'bunks' and 'top and bottom' were played. — (21) **1900** *Everybody's Mag.* Nov. 466/2 Even in countries where 50-cent watches are made, the public buys more of the American dollar watches than they do of the home product. **1947** *Trail Riders Bul.* Feb. 20/2 But the trouble wuz, the gratitude wore off plumb quick, like the gol' on a dollah watch.

b. In phrases: (1) *As sound as a dollar*, quite sound and well; (2) *dollar of the daddies, fathers*, a term frequently applied during the silver controversy of 1873–96 to the silver dollar authorized under the original coinage act of 1872, now *obs.* or *hist.;* (3) *it is dollars to doughnuts*, it is practically certain, *slang;* (4) *it is dollars to cobwebs*, =prec., *rare;* (5) *to feel (look) like a million dollars*, to feel or look extremely well, *colloq.*

(1) **1852** CASEY *Two Yrs.* 293 May be ridden or drove by man, woman, or boy—sound as a dollar, or no sale!—as good a horse, gen'lem, as ever wore hair! **1946** *Chi. D. News* 14 Jan. 8/2 The frank physician will not employ euphemisms like 'You're as sound as a dollar.' If he means anemic, let him say so. — (2) **1877** *Phila. Times* 10 Nov. (B. Add.), Of all the unreasoning agitations of recent years, the demand for the dollar of the fathers has been the most unreasoning and absurd. **1878** *Cong. Rec.* 57/2 Shall we continue to disown and disinherit the silver dollar of our fathers, sometimes in latter days facetiously called the 'dollar of our daddies'? **1904** *Phila. Pub. Ledger* 12 July 8 The South has returned to the hard money idea, the 'dollar of our daddies.' — (3) **1904** *Utica Observer* 29 June 6 They talk of fire drills; and that will cause a broad smile along West street, for it is dollars to doughnuts that not an excursion boat in New York harbor ever had one. **1947** *Redbook* Nov. 15/1 Dollars to doughnuts is a pretty even bet today. — (4) **1904** *Boston Herald* 8 Aug. 6 It is dollars to cobwebs that every such person will be disappointed.

(5) **1945** *Good Housekeeping* Dec. 259/1, I get some white paint and make Randy's old ones look like a million dollars. **1947** *Time* 17 Mar. 43 You'll go home feeling like a million dollars, rested and refreshed as never before!

As the last term in **adobe, almighty, Bland, Boston, bottom, buzzard, father's, gold, half hammered, hard, Mexican, one-, paper, sand, silver, silver trade, Siwash, soft, Spanish, Spanish half, Spanish milled, specie, standard, standard gold, standard silver, state, ten, Texas, three, trade, two-dollar.**

doll baby.

1. A small image or representation of the human figure dressed so as to exhibit fashions. *Obs.* Cf. **fashion doll.**

1807 JEFFERSON *Writings* IX. (1898) 83 The dresses of the annual doll-babies from Paris.

2. A doll, a child's toy. Also transf.

1853 BALDWIN *Flush Times Ala.* 292 The little girls, who had been petted by their fathers and mothers like doll-babies. **1897** STUART *Simpkinsville* 59 Every word she'd say would sound clair an' fine same ez if a doll-baby was to commence to talk by machinery. **1913** *Collier's* 13 Dec. 7/2 He was going to buy a doll baby for his little sick girl. **1939** ROLLINS *Gone Haywire* 259 Tumblin' K don't want to hurt any man; but, if all you folks is plum' starvin' for excitement an'll be responsible, th' brute's your doll baby.

3. A pretty but frivolous or silly girl or young woman. Also attrib.

1853 BALDWIN *Flush Times Ala.* 42 She never had more than a thimbleful of brains in her doll-baby head. **1896** *Harper's Mag.* XCII. 808/2, I keep on looking just the same frivolous doll-baby.

4. *W.* A small wooden contrivance used in spinning mecates. *Colloq.*

1930 RAINE & BARNES *Cattle* 314 The little wooden spinners were called 'doll babies' and were whittled out of pieces of hardwood.

***dolly,** *n.* A small platform mounted on a single large roller used as a truck. — **1901** MERWIN & WEBSTER *Calumet K* 104 Gangs of laborers were swarming over the lumber piles, pitching down the planks, and other gangs were carrying them away and piling them on 'dollies,' to be pushed along the plank runways to the hoist. **1948** *Time* 21 June 1/2 With a heavy truck and a tractor pulling, and one of these dollies under each corner, the derrick shown in the picture was moved 3½ miles to a new location.

***Dolly Varden.** [From the name of the little coquette in Dickens' *Barnaby Rudge*, described as wearing a flowered dimity dress.] A char or trout, *Salvelinus malma spectabilis*, found in the streams of the Northwest. It is of an olive-green color and marked with round red or orange spots. Also attrib.

1876 *Yreka* (Calif.) *Union* 3 June, The first spotted trout were caught in McCloud river by white men—Messrs. Josiah Edson of Shasta Valley and Geo. Campbell of Soda Springs, and were given the name of Dolly Vardens by Elda McCloud, a niece of Mr. Campbell. **1879** WILLIAMS *Pacific Tourist* 310/1 The *Dolly Varden* species, with bright red spots on the side, weigh from one pound to twelve pounds. **1884** GOODE *Fisheries* I. 504 The Dolly Varden Trout. . . . In the Sacramento the name 'Dolly Varden' was given to it by the landlady at a hotel, and this name it still retains in that region. **1946** *Trail Riders Bul.* Oct. 5/1 Dr. George Rae . . . landed four Dolly Vardens (14–18 inches, 'tis said!) during a special 'time-out' for the anglers.

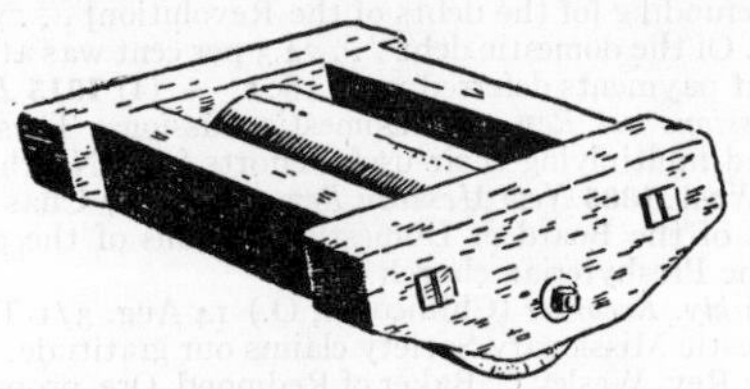

Early type of homemade dolly

b. Designating a spotted horse.

1907 COOK *Border & Buffalo* (1938) 343 Well, Sam, if we don't get him back when we go out after the Quahada again we will get you a Dolly-Varden horse like that buzzard-headed pinto of Cook's that went off with him.

dolly welta, see **dally welta.**

***dom.** A suffix found as the last element in **bachelor-, cheese-, China-, dollar-, Yankee-, Yankee-Doodle-dom.**

***domain,** *n.* As the last term in **eminent, public, sunflower domain.**

***dome,** *n.*

1. (*cap.*) Used in the names of certain mountain peaks in allusion to their rounded tops.

1833 CATLIN *Indians* I. 78 'The Grand Dome' . . . is, perhaps, one of the most grand and beautiful scenes of the kind to be met with in this country. **1864** *Alta California* (S.F.) 16 Jan. 1/4 On the road to Castle Dome, we had passed some fine specimens of that gigantic species of cactus known as the *petahaya.* **1920** *Yosemite* (Nat. Park Service Bul.) 11 Glacier Point commands a magnificent view of . . . Half Domes, mythical seat of an Indian maiden. **1946** *Sierra Club Bul.* Dec. 8 We . . . then built a fire on the highest point in view of the whole valley, to let people know that Half Dome had been conquered!

2. (See quot.)

1874 KNIGHT 718/1 360 Dome, . . . the elevated upper section of a passenger-car projecting above the general level of the roof, forming a space for ventilation, light, and ornament.

***domestic,** *a.* and *n.*

1. *n.* Plain bleached or unbleached cotton cloth, so called orig. to distinguish it from imported cloth. Often *pl.* Cf. **cotton domestic.**

1817 *Austin Papers* (1924) 21 July 317 The Domesticks I expected, have Not arrived they are uncommonly difficult to obtain. **1883** *Rep. Indian Affairs* 193 Supplying . . . a flannel skirt or goods to make the same . . . calico and domestic. **1948** *Sat. Ev. Post* 21 Aug. 47/1 The girls are taught Mexican national dances—not in their ordinary clothes, mind you, but in gay and flashing little costumes made from old sugar sacks or unbleached domestic.

2. A kind of cigar. *Slang.*

1865 SALA *Diary* II. 375 In the cigar trade especially a number of 'bosses,' or masters, have been indignantly denounced for sending to the prisons large orders for the manufacture of those eminently nasty rolls of tobacco called in New York 'domestics.' **1905** F. HOPKINSON SMITH *At Close Range* 74 Sam . . . tilted his domestic at a higher angle, and went out to view the harbor.

3. In special combs.: (1) **domestic coffee,** a beverage made from rye and coffee ground together, *obs.;* (2) **corporation,** a corporation operating within the state under whose laws it was organized; (3) **debt,** the debt to U.S. citizens incurred during the Revolutionary War chiefly by state governments but assumed by the federal government, now *hist.;* (4) **mission,** a home mission; (5) **missionary,** a missionary whose work is carried on in this country, also **Domestic Missionary Society;** (6) **science,** the science dealing with household activities, esp. cooking and sewing, often taught as a school subject; (7) **slavery,** the slavery that existed in the southern states before the Civil War.

(1) **1822** *N. Eng. Farmer* 17 Aug. 19/1 The good people of Boston, and some parts of its vicinity, have lately acquired the practice of using what they call 'Domestic Coffee,' by way of economy. — (2) **1923** *Crowell's Dict. of Business & Finance* 140 Some States treat corporations organized under Federal laws as Domestic Corporations. **1948** *Carthaginian* (Carthage, Miss.) 19 Aug. 2/6 The time of such exemption [is] to commence from the date of charter, if a domestic corporation. — (3) **1789** CUTLER in *Life & Corr.* I. 444 The new Congress will make no other establishment for the payment of the Domestic debt than the western lands. **1913** J. S. BASSETT *Short Hist. U.S.* 260 Refunding [of the debts of the Revolution] . . . was a slow process. . . . Of the domestic debt . . . 24.3 per cent was at 6 per cent with interest payments deferred until 1801. — (4) **1815** *Baptist Bd. Foreign Missions 1st Rep.* 179 Domestic missions. These are still pursuing and multiplying their useful efforts from North to South, and in the West. **1885** *New Mexican Rev.* 5 Feb. 3/7 Chas. Probst vs the trustees of the Board of Domestic Missions of the general assembly of the Presbyterian church.

(5) **1818** *Wkly. Recorder* (Chillicothe, O.) 14 Aug. 3/1 The success of the Domestic Missionary Society claims our gratitude. **1948** *Time* 18 Oct. 76/3 Rev. Wesley C. Baker of Redmond, Ore. proposed a way to handle one energetic brand of domestic missionaries—the Mormons. — (6) **1869** C. E. BEECHER and H. B. STOWE (*title*), The American Woman's Home, or Principles of Domestic Science. **1948** *Chi. D. News* 21 Oct. 13/5 Miss Talbot also taught sanitary science, which became known as domestic science. — (7) **1836** *S. Lit. Messenger* II. 337 Domestic Slavery . . . [is] the basis of all our institutions. *a*1853 in STOWE *Key* 36 Domestic slavery is not, in my judgment, to be set down as an immoral or irreligious relation.

domine ˈdɑmənɪ, *n.* Also **dominie.** [Du. *dominee,* in sense **1.**]

1. A pastor of a Dutch Reformed church.

1669 *N.Y. State Col. Hist.* XII. 466, I perceiue the Little Domine hath played ye Trumpeter to this disorder. **1832** WATSON *Hist. Tales N.Y.* 36 The principal personage in every Dutch village [was] the 'domine' or minister. **1896** EARLE *Col. Days Old N.Y.* 289 This raised a small Dutch tempest, and the new domine soon left that parish. **1949** *Reader's Digest* Jan. 107/2 For a minimum of three hours the frock-coated dominie . . . expatiates on the eternal terror that will be the lot of evildoers.

b. Used as a title.

1680 *New Castle Court Rec.* 390 Ye domeni Teschermarker. **1694** *Mass. H.S. Coll.* 4 Ser. I. 106 Four sermons were preached in it; the 1 and 3d were preached by Domine Dellius, in Dutch.

2. A variety of apple. In full **domine apple,** prob. a translation of Du. *domineesappel.*

1817 W. COXE *Fruit Trees* 115 The Domine was imported from England. **1868** *Mich. Agric. Rep.* VII. 430 Apples [recommended include] . . . Hubbardston Nonsuch, Dominie, Swaar, Green Sweet. **1876** BURROUGHS *Winter Sunshine* vii. 158 If they were the dominie apples . . . he certainly would [hasten his sermon].

dominick, dominicker, see **Dominique.**

* **dominion,** *n.*

1. One of the larger districts organized or established by the Ku-Klux Klan of the Civil War period. Now *hist.*

1868 in *Doc. & Sp. in Amer. Hist.* (1943) III. 79 The Empire shall be divided into four departments . . . the second to be styled the Dominion and to be coterminous with such counties [etc.]. **1880** TOURGEE *Invisible Empire* 413 In order to trace the connection between General Forrest's 'Invisible Empire,' and such inferior 'realms' or 'dominions' [etc.]. **1906** RIDLEY *Battles* 651 At this convention [at Nashville, Tenn., 1867] the territory covered by the Klan was designated as 'The Invisible Empire.' This was subdivided into 'realms,' coterminous with the boundaries of States. The 'realms' were divided into 'dominions,' corresponding to congressional districts.

2. (*cap.*) *attrib.* Of Virginia, Virginian. Cf. **Ancient, Old Dominion.**

1793 *Steele Papers* I. 105 Present [were] . . . the Hon. John Brown of the Senate . . . and Colo. McDowall, with . . . a certain High Priest of the Jews I believe, tho a mighty Dominion man. **1794** W. B. GROVE in *James Sprunt Hist. Mono.* III. 102, I really join you in the opinion that you entertain of the Views and Policy of some of the Dom——n Gentry.

Dominique ˈdɑməˌnɪk, *n.* Also **dominick, dominicker,** etc. [the F. form of *Dominica,* name of an island of the West Indies.] A chicken of an American breed characterized by barred plumage, rose combs, and yellow legs. Also attrib.

1806 LEWIS in *L. & Clark Exped.* IV. (1905) 128 This mixture gives it very much the appearance of that kind of dunghill fowl which the hen-wives of our country call dommanicker. **1849** *N. Eng. Farmer* I. 386 Dominique fowls were exhibited by G. S. Pierce. **1925** BENEFIELD *Chicken-Wagon Family* 19 And what would you teach her—how to smoke a pipe, how to trade a tin pan for a Dominick setting hen? **1943** POWELL *Home Again* 196, I struck at him, and he struck back at me, and we were going at it like two old fighting Dominique roosters.

Don dɑn, *n.* [Sp. title used before the Christian names of men. An Amer. borrowing.] A Spaniard or a person of Spanish descent. Usu. *pl.*

1795 *Pittsburgh Gaz.* 24 Oct. 3/1 They are in hopes that they will now be permitted to give the Dons a *touch,* as they term it, and drive them . . . from the banks of the Missisippi [*sic*]. **1807** *Ann. 10th Congress* 1 Sess. I. 572, I would delight to see Mexico reduced, but I will die in the last ditch before I would yield a foot to the Dons. **1818** *Lynchburg* (Va.) *Press* 7 Aug. 2/5 The poor Dons are so harassed by the 'vile rebels,' the privateers, that even the little coasting trade . . . is cut up. **1930** RAINE & BARNES *Cattle* 219 'What do you want?' the don questioned. **1946** MCWILLIAMS *So. Calif. Country* 79 Such expressions as, 'in the days of the Dons,' and 'in the footsteps of the padres,' had become community colloquialisms in Southern California.

donate ˈdonet, *v.* [Prob. a back formation f. **donation.*] *tr.* To give (something) freely or as a donation.

This term occurs nearly a century earlier here than in British usage. "*Donate* . . . is a word which in Eng. is eschewed by good writers as a pretentious and magniloquent vulgarism. In Am. on the other hand, it has acquired a place in the vocab. of quite reputable terms" (Horwill).

1785 HILTZHEIMER *Diary* (1893) 23 April 72 Went to the State House yard to look at the rows of trees Samuel Vaughan, Esq., donated and is directing the planting of. **1852** *Harper's Mag.* IV. 692/1 In the Senate a bill has been reported . . . to establish a branch mint in the city of New York, on condition that the city donate land for a site. **1947** *Chr. Sci. Monitor* 16 Jan. 12/1 Funds to finance the scholarship program were donated by persons interested in the work of the Association.

absol. **1846** *N.Y. Tribune* 6 Nov. (B.), The friends of the cause in Massachusetts and other places donated liberally. **1904** *Baltimore American* 1 Dec. 14 He donated liberally to the church.

* **donation,** *n.*

1. = **donation party.**

1849 W. BROWN *America* 23 Their preachers have residences, but no stated salaries to live upon; but each member contributes something towards their maintenance. They have also the benefit of a 'Donation.' **1872** M. HOLLEY *My Opinions* (1891) 244 The summer after the Donation and Fare dawned peacefully and fair on Jonesville and the earth. **1919** CADY *Rhymes of Vt.* (1923) 226 It's funny how our ancestors . . . Would gather at the minister's . . . And eat him out of house and home And call it 'A Donation!'

2. A portion of public land in Oregon obtained by a settler under the congressional enactment of 1850. Also attrib. Cf. **Donation Act.**

1850 *Statutes at Large* IX. 498 No one person shall ever receive a patent for more than one donation of land in said territory. *Ib.,* Each person claiming a donation right under this act, shall prove to the satisfaction of the surveyor-general . . . that the settlement . . . had been commenced. **1905** COLE *Early Oregon* 20, I could be located on some unclaimed land which I could take up as a donation.

3. In special combs.: (1) **Donation Act,** (see quot. 1905); (2) **bee,** = **donation party;** (3) **certificate,** (see quot. and cf. next), *obs.;* (4) **claim,** a portion of public land obtained or sought by an owner or prospective owner, also **donation claimant,** also attrib., now *hist.;* (5) **day,** a day on which donations (to a minister) are made, cf. **1.** above; (6) **land,** see as a main entry; (7) **Law,** = **Donation Act;** (8) **lot,** a lot, from public land, which may be obtained by one who complies with certain governmental provisions; (9) **party,** a social gathering of the members of a church, who bring gifts to their minister; (10) **supper,** a public supper the proceeds of which are devoted to some benevolent purpose, *obs.;* (11) **tract,** an area of donation land *q.v.* (sense **1.**), *obs.;* (12) **visit,** = **donation party.**

(1) **1856** BREWERTON *War in Kans.* 211 Neither does the donation act apply to Kansas, but each male of full age, widow or head of

family who has not had a pre-emption under the act of 1841 and does not own 320 acres of land, and who has improved and settled on it—not to sell on speculation, but for his own use and cultivation—is entitled to enter 160 acres, at $1 25 per acre, payable any time before the land sales. **1905** COLE *Early Oregon* 24 Samuel R. Thurston, the first delegate to Congress from Oregon, . . . secured the passage of the donation act which not only allowed the settler a section of land but also to take it in such form as he laid out his claim, so that it was compact. — **(2) 1880** *Scribner's Mo.* Aug. 545/2 A hundred dollars per annum, a bar'l of apples a month, a pair of fowls monthly, donation-bee once a winter. — **(3) 1812** *Ann. 12th Congress* 1 Sess. II. 2352 Citizens . . . whose lands have not been . . . claimed in right of donation or pre-emption certificates . . . [are] confirmed in their respective claims. — **(4) 1804** *Miss. Herald* (Natchez) 10 July 4/1 Those of you who are donation claimants must swear. . . . That you were 21 years of age or the head of a family on or before the 30th day of March, 1798. **1868** *All Year Round* 7 Nov. 521/2 Hailing generally from some border state, early in life, he has settled down on some 'donation' claim. **1944** ROSS *Westward* 22 The feminist Abigail Scott Duniway went so far as to refuse to accept the land to which she had a right lest posterity call her a Donation Claim Bride.

(5) 1865 *Atlantic Mo.* XV. 449 No man in the parish brought a heavier turkey to the parson's larder on donation-days. **1897** *Chi. Record* 3 Mar. 5/1 St. Luke's hospital 'Donation day' occurred yesterday. — **(7) 1882** *Harper's Mag.* Oct. 766/1 In order to make good titles to land taken up when the sovereignty of the region was doubtful, and also to encourage further immigration, Congress passed what is called the 'Donation Law.' — **(8) 1789** CIST *Cincinnati* 205 Twenty-four donation lots. *a***1847** in HOWE *Ohio* 208 Every individual belonging to the party received a donation lot, which he was required to improve, as the condition of obtaining a title. — **(9) 1839** *Dly. Chi. American* 17 Dec. 2/3 Our worthy and talented fellow citizen, the Reverend Mr. Hinton of the Baptist Church, has a *donation party* at his residence, on Thursday evening next. **1944** WILSON *Passing Inst.* 185, I find in my old diary that I contributed a broom to the Methodist preacher when I attended the one donation party of my life.

(10) 1858 *Salem* (Ill.) *Advocate* 14 April 3/1 A donation supper will be given for the benefit of Rev. Wm. Finley, Pastor of the Cumberland Presbyterian Church, on Thursday evening. *Ib.* 26 May 3/2 Donation Suppers seem to have become all 'the go,' during the past winter. — **(11) 1798** *Pittsburgh Gaz.* 23 June 3/3 The subscriber . . . will attend the ensuing summer and fall at his farm on Slippery Rock creek, . . . in order to shew any Donation Tract of Land in any of the said Districts to any person who may apply, for a modest compensation. — **(12) 1860** *Ladies' Repository* XX. 386/2 It was at last settled . . . that they would make Mrs. Brainard, the minister's widow, a genuine old-fashioned donation visit. **1942** RAWSON *N. H. Borns a Town* 155 The most delightful of the prudential ways and means was the Annual Donation Visit, or Party, when the whole parish came bearing gifts of food or wood, clothing, furniture, fancy articles, weavings and spinnings, pies and cakes, to make up in some measure for the salaries which seem to have been often badly delayed. One of these donation visits was unique in delivering $19.00 and a bedquilt.

donation land.

1. Land in northwestern Pennsylvania set aside for allotment to citizens of that state who had served in the colonial army during the Revolutionary War. *Obs.*

1785 *Pa. Archives* 1 Ser. X. 427 By Virtue of the Authority vested in us by the Act of Assembly 'for directing the mode of distributing the Donation Lands, promised to the troops of this Commonwealth.' We have appointed you Agent. **1894** *Pa. Archives* 3 Ser. III. 600 Some of the officers and soldiers of the Pennsylvania Line had not received their donation land.

2. (See quots.)

1845 *Statutes at Large* I. cxi, Donation lands. . . . Donation of Land granted to certain Settlers in Florida. An act granting donations of land to certain actual settlers in the territory of Florida. May 26, 1824. **1893** JAMESON *Dict. U.S. Hist.* (1931) 149 *Donation Lands,* August 4, 1842, Congress passed a donation act for the Territory of East Florida. Persons who could bear arms were allowed one-quarter section of land upon which to settle. September 27, 1850, a donation act was passed for Oregon, granting settlers from 160 to 640 acres.

3. Donation Land Act, Bill, (see quots. and cf. **Donation Act**).

1944 ROSS *Westward* 111 The Donation Land Act of 1850, which gave a man and his wife 640 acres of homestead, 'a mile square of land,' succeeded in booming the female market sky-high. **1949** *Pacific Northwest Quart.* Jan. 3 The donation land bill, the first of its kind enacted by Congress, finally passed in September, 1850.

***done,** *a.* Used colloquially or ignorantly, with adverbial force, in past or perfect tenses to mean "entirely" or "already."

1827 SHERWOOD *Gaz. Georgia* 139 *Done said it,* for has said it. *Done did it,* for has performed, or done it. **1885** JACKSON *Zeph* i, Ef yeow'll step raound ter the front, a piece, I'll let yer in; this gate's done nailed up. **1945** WALLACE *Barington* 18 I don't know what you need with another boy. You done got four.

b. *To be done off,* dressed, fitted out, prepared.

1839 KIRKLAND *New Home* (1840) 243, I took my seat . . . and reconnoitered the company who were 'done off' in first rate style for this important occasion. **1906** FITZGERALD *Sam Steele Adv.* 9 The little room . . . was in one end of the attic of our modest cottage, and the only room 'done off' upstairs.

***donkey,** *n.*

1. (See quot.) *Slang. Obs.*

1851 HALL *College Words* 178 At Washington College, Penn., students of a religious character are called *lap-ears* or *donkeys.*

2. A symbol of the Democratic party. Also, sometimes, the party itself.

A Whig paper, the *Field Piece,* published in Chicago in 1848, several times showed a donkey on what was labeled the "Democratic platform." The earliest occurrence was on July 19, 1848, p. 2, column 4. Nast used this idea in 1870.

[**1870** *Harper's Weekly* XIV. 48/1 (A cartoon by Thomas Nast showing a donkey, labelled 'Copperhead papers,' with caption: 'A live Jackass kicking a Dead Lion.' The dead lion is E. M. Stanton.) **1879** *Ib.* XXIII. 1001 (A cartoon by Nast with a donkey labelled 'Democratic Party,' and an elephant, 'Republican Party.')] **1904** A. B. PAINE *Thomas Nast* 147 The cartoon [of 1870] went to the mark, but is chiefly notable now as being the earliest in which the donkey is used to typify Democratic sentiment. **1948** *Dly. Ardmoreite* (Ardmore, Okla.) 15 July 6/7 If instead the democratic party has purged itself of their movements that have given the donkey such a bad name, it may be all to the good.

3. donkey party, (see quots. 1889, 1901).

1888 *Detroit Free Press* (F.), Mr. Matthews gave a donkey party to the choir of the Lutheran Church on Saturday evening. **1889** FARMER 210/1 *Donkey party,* an amusing parlor pastime. Black-board and chalk are provided, members of the party are blindfolded, and each in turn draws upon the board the representation of a portion of a donkey's anatomy. **1901** *Ladies' Home Jrnl.* Dec. 47/4 Our Donkey Party On Cloth. . . . A sheet having a donkey without a tail printed upon it, and twenty-four cloth tails, furnish the means of playing this amusing game. Each player, blindfolded, endeavors to pin the tail. **1909** O. HENRY *Roads of Destiny* 351 He made the terrors of death seem like an invitation to a donkey-party.

Don Pedro. Some kind of liquor, prob. of inferior quality. *Obs.* Cf. Sp. *Don Pedro,* one who appears to have means but is miserably poor. — **1798** *Mass. Spy* 21 Feb. (Th.), A segar, and fifteen or sixteen glasses of Don Pedro.

don't-care-a-damn-itiveness. The attitude of not caring at all. *Slang. Obs.* Cf. **go-aheadativeness.**

1841 *N.O. Picayune* 24 Feb. 2/3 He . . . had . . . all the nonchalance and dont-care-a-dam-itiveness of De Bar or even Browne himself. **1856** *Spirit of Age* (Sacramento) 7 Mar. 2/2 We assert our prerogatives over the whole continent of America, and the isles of the Pacific, . . . with a species of don't-care-a-damn-ativeness that perfectly paralyzes all opposition. **1879** *Chi. Tribune* 25 Jan. 4/6 The don't-care-a-d——m-ativeness elucidated in its reason for its change of front has at least the merit of brevity.

dodad ˈdudæd, *n.* Also **dodad, dudedad.** [?Fanciful.] Something not readily namable, a "thingumabob"; a fancy ornament. *Colloq.* Cf. **dingus.**

1908 K. MCGAFFEY *Show-Girl* 187 This machine has got a dudedad on it that prevents it from going more than ten. **1929** A. ELLIS *Life* 275, I will make some of those piecrust dodads. **1947** *Dly. Oklahoman* (Okla. City) 5 Nov. 1/5 The Greeks and Romans loved doodads on their armor.

***doodle,** *n.*

1. (*cap.*) During the Civil War, a federal soldier, so called in allusion to Yankee Doodle.

1861 in F. MOORE *Rebellion Rec.* I. III. 64 He'll may-be change his mind, and stay Where the good Doodles do! **1862** *N.Y. Tribune* 13 May (Chipman), Whoop! the Doodles have broken loose Roaring round like the very deuce!

2. =**doodle bug.** Also in phrasal use. *Colloq.*

1887 *Harper's Mag.* July 276/1 She wondered how the nice, fat little round 'doodles' were getting on in their tin can under the house. **1899** *Animal & Plant Lore* 62 *Doodle-bug* or *doodle,* ant-lion. Indiana and Southern States. **1939** *These Are Our Lives* 157 Kate told me of Gloria Paradize, a French girl, . . . and how the women would group around her to get her to talk in her queer language, they not knowing any more than a doodle in the woods what she was saying.

3. *pl.* Figures, often of odd or fantastic shapes, usu. made absent-mindedly. *Colloq.* Cf. ***doodle,** *v.*

1943 *Harper's Mag.* June 85 The young man had picked up a pencil and was leaning over his desk making doodles on a pad of yellow paper. **1946** *New Yorker* 18 May 79/2 His doodles, while not as widely circulated, are every bit as challenging as his movies.

4. doodle-bug, the larva of various insects, esp. the ant lion. Also as a contemptuous epithet.

*c***1866** BAGBY *Old Va. Gentleman* 48 [He must] try to tame a catbird, call doodle-bugs out of their holes. **1908** MULFORD *Orphan* 163 You blamed doodle bug, yu! **1944** *Democrat* 7 Dec. 2/2 Doodlebugs are those little insects which fan out or blow out little conical shaped holes in sandy or dusty places.

b. Any one of various unscientific devices with which it is claimed minerals and oil deposits can be located. *Colloq.*

1924 HENDERSON *Keys to Crookdom* 157 One old fraud who was tried in the Federal court had a 'chemical battery' or 'doodlebug' oil location [*sic*], which he said would spot oil-producing ground at once. **1948** *Chi. Tribune* 5 April I. 13/4 A new device in prospecting ... was a 'doodlebug' which seemed to employ radar in locating likely ground.

Hence **doodlebug artist, doodlebugger, doodlebuggery.**

1944 *Calif. Folklore Quart.* III. 53 There is certainly no justification of or scientific approach to the practice of doodlebuggery; it falls into the limbo of superstition and is in some ways a modern survival of the black arts. *Ib.* 55 In east Texas near the town of Linden a doodlebugger had located an oil field 'that would make Spindle Top look like a rainbow on a slush pile,' as he described it. **1948** *Atlantic Mo.* Sep. 86/1 The ramifications of the cult have led to the use of a general term—'doodlebug artists' or 'doodlebuggers'—for those who use simplified methods of ore location.

c. A gasoline railroad coach or a midget racing car.

1947 BEEBE *Mixed Train Dly.* 330 If you have missed the early morning doodlebug of the Tucson, Cornelia and Gila Bend in the Arizona Desert, you can ride the parlor on the daily freight later on, about noon. **1948** *Time* 16 Aug. 62/3 On the small tracks, the doodlebugs have a ceiling of about 75 m.p.h.

* **doodle,** *v. intr.* To draw doodles during moments of absent-mindedness or enforced idleness. *Colloq.*

1937 *Lit. Digest* 26 June 19/3 'But everybody doodles.' So Gary Cooper, as Longfellow Deeds, in 'Mr. Deeds Goes to Town,' defended himself. He wasn't crazy because he drew squares and circles on scraps of paper—he was just 'doodling.' **1948** *Chi. Tribune* 27 Mar. I. 8/3 A pencil and a pad; I doodle and reveal a skill I never knew I had.

Hence **doodler, doodling.**

1938 *Topeka* (Kans.) *Journal* 29 Oct 3A–2 Howard Hughes is an inveterate doodler with a preference for little inter-locking squares. **1944** *Chi. Tribune* 6 Aug. VII. 3/1 Even the telephone has not escaped a coat of canary yellow and some artistic 'doodling.' **1948** *Time* 19 Jan. 93/1 Now, there's a model doodler for our money!

* **Doolittle,** *n.* A variety of raspberry. *Obs.* — **1862** *Rep. Comm. Patents: Agric.* 169 *Doolittle* has been very highly spoken of by cultivators. Like the wild raspberry, from which it has been produced, it is very productive. **1870** WARNER *Summer in Garden* ii, The raspberries are called Doolittle and Golden Cap.

* **doom,** *v. tr.* (See quot. 1816.) *Obs.*

1809 E. A. KENDALL *Travels* I. 188 A town, neglecting to send a list, is to be '*doomed*,' that is assessed 'at the discretion of the general assembly.' **1816** PICKERING 82 When a person neglects to make a return of his taxable property to the assessors of a town, those officers doom him; that is, judge upon, and fix his tax according to their discretion. **1888** BRYCE *Amer. Commw.* II. II. xliii. 133 *n.*, In New York ... if a person makes no return the assessors are instructed to 'doom' him according to the best of their knowledge and belief.

doomage 'dumɪdʒ, *n.*[* **doom,** *v.*+-*age.*] (See quot. 1792.) *Obs.* — **1792** BELKNAP *New-Hampshire* III. 284 If any person refuse to give an invoice of his rateable estate, it is in the power of the select-men 'to set down to such person as much as they judge equitable, by way of doomage; from which there is no appeal.' **1809** WEBSTER in *Mo. Anthology* Sep. 209, I have indeed introduced into our vocabulary a few words ... such as ... *doomage*, on the authority of Dr. Belknap.

* **door,** *n.* In combs.: (1) **door casing,** a doorcase; (2) **face, =doughface 1,** *colloq.*; (3) **facing, =door casing;** (4) **grass, =doorweed;** (5) **string,** a latchstring; (6) **tender,** a doorkeeper or porter; (7) **-to-door sale,** a sale made by one who stops or calls at the customer's door; (8) **trim,** the framing about a door opening; (9) **weed,** a common weed, *Polygonum aviculare,* also known as knotgrass, goose grass, door grass; (10) **yard,** the yard about the door of a home or dwelling, also attrib.

(1) **1887** MARY E. WILKINS *Humble Romance* 2 He lounged smilingly against the door-casing jingling his scales, and waiting for the woman. — (2) **1939** HARRIS *Purslane* 149 There still were the serenaders to look foward to, and brave threats were made to jerk off the door-faces and see who the serenaders were. **1943** POWELL *Home Again* 70 They would array themselves in grotesque garb, put on one of these comical papier-mâché masks, which we called 'door-faces.' — (3) **1845** SIMMS *Wigwam & Cabin* I Ser. 99, I had been hewing out some door-facings for a new corn-crib and fodder-house. **1877** *Cong. Rec.* 26 Nov. 705/1 This man ... was sitting up in the door with his feet on the door-facing. — (4) **1892** *Amer. Folk-Lore* V. 102 *Polygonum aviculare*, ... door-grass. So. Ind. **1907** LYONS *Plant Names* 369 P[olygonum] aviculare ... Door-grass, Door-weed.

(5) **1876** in GUILD *Old Times* (1878) 395 Pull the door string, and you would the next moment receive a warm, old-fashioned greeting from the host and his wife. — (6) **1886** STAPLETON *Major's Christmas* 18 Looking back he saw the old janitor and door tender coming slowly along. **1917** C. MATHEWSON *Sec. Base Sloan* 286 The door tender took a step towards him. — (7) **1902** *Harper's Mag.* May 1004 When I arrived at the house my son, the editor, had just returned from a door-to-door sale of the *Mosquito*. — (8) **1905** *N.Y. Ev. Post* 30 Dec. 12 (*advt.*), The corridors, floors, stairways, doortrims and walls are of marble. — (9) **1843** TORREY *Flora N.Y.* II 152 *Polygonum aviculare*.... Knot-grass. Door-weed.... About houses, roadsides, gardens, etc. **1857** GRAY *Botany* 373 Door-weed ... [is found in] waste places and gravelly banks. **1937** *Range Plant Hdbk.* W-154 Knotweeds, also known as doorweeds and knotgrasses, compose a fairly large and widely distributed genus.

(10) *c***1764** in WOOLSEY *Hist. Disc. Yale* (1850) 54 The Freshmen ... are forbidden to wear their hats ... in the front door-yard of the President's or Professor's house. **1856** *Harper's Mag.* XII. 858/2 Mrs. Pimperton had 'laid it to heart' for years that her door-yard fence should be whitewashed. **1945** McLEAN *Moment of Time* 16 They left the dooryard through the gate and walked up the road.

b. Also in expressions sufficiently defined in the quots., as (1) **door dung,** (2) **prairie,** (3) **rock,** (4) **spring,** (5) **stop.**

(1) **1790** S. DEANE *N.-Eng. Farmer* 70/2 Door-Dung, a manure taken from the back-yards and doors of dwelling houses. — (2) **1835** *Indiana Quart. Mag. Hist.* IV. 66 You have heard the Door Prairie described. Description gives you no idea of the real splendor of the green. **1837** *S. Lit. Messenger* III. 737 Near La Porte (so called from the 'door prairies' which ... take their name from the fact that they communicate with one another by an opening like a door). — (3) **1877** BARTLETT (ed. 4), Door-rock, the door stone or step. Western. **1942** RAWSON *N.H. Borns a Town* 35 She and her man Isaac camped on the doorrock to rest. — (4) **1874** KNIGHT 721/2 Door-spring, a spring attached to or bearing against a door, so as to automatically close it.

(5) **1874** KNIGHT 721/2 Door-stop. (*Carpentry.*) A knob or block on a skirting-board or floor, against which the door shuts. **1895** WAIT *Car-Builder's Dict.* 43 Door-stop. A peg or block against which a passenger-car door strikes when opened, often provided with a rubber cushion, especially for swinging-doors. *Door-holders,* which both stop the door and retain it, are often called *door-stops.* **1944** *Sears Cat.* Fall and Winter 606 Scotty Door Stop. Black with red painted collar; glass eyes. 8 inches high.

c. (See quots.) *Slang.*

1850 RYAN *Adventures* II. 206–7 You may [in the game of monte], however, be what is termed 'caught in the door;' that is, the colour or suit on which you bet may appear on the top of the pack. In this event, the bettor on that colour gains only half the amount of his stake. **1865** MARK TWAIN *Jumping Frog* (1875) 52 (R.), He'd see in a minute how he'd been imposed on, and how the other dog had him in the door, so to speak.

As the last term in **barn, blind, hoist, puncheon, revolving, scuttle, side, store, storm door.**

* **dopchick,** see **dabchick.**

dope dop, *n.* [Du. *doop,* sauce.]

1. (See quots.)

1807 IRVING *Salmagundi* x, Philo Dripping-pan was remarkable for his predeliction to eating, and his love of what the learned Dutch call *doup.* Our erudite author likewise observes that the citizens are to this day noted for their love of 'a sop in the pan.' **1809** —— *Hist. N.Y.* (1927) III. iii. 138 The tea table was crowned with a huge earthen dish, well stored with slices of fat pork, fried brown, cut up into mouthfuls, and swimming in doup or gravy. **1904** WHITE *Mountains* (1906) 189 The batter is rather thin, is poured into the piping hot greased pan, 'flipped' when brown on one side, and eaten with larrupy dope or brown gravy.

b. Any one of various preparations a more accurate name for which is not immediately available. *Slang.*

1872 *Chi. Tribune* 24 Dec. 4/4 He ... bids us beware of the sugar, for it is full of flour and sand; ... of the milk, for it is compounded of dope. **1901** ADE *40 Modern Fables* 188 Give me some perfumed Dope that will restore a Peaches and Cream Complexion. **1915** E. POOLE *Harbor* 60 Joe's father vaccinated about a score of children that week. The 'dope' he used was mailed to him by a drug firm.

c. (See quot. 1876.)

1876 *Territorial Enterprise* (Va. City, Nev.) 13 Feb., Nothing was known of the mysteries of 'dope'—a preparation of pitch which, being applied to the bottom of the shoes, enables the wearer to glide over snow softened by the warmth of the sun. **1890** *Silverton* (Colo.) *Miner* 1 Mar. 2/3 Great improvements have been made [in skis] and in the lubricating material called 'dope' that makes the rider glide down the mountains with such lightning speed. **1947** PEATTIE *Sierra Nevada* 218 They treated the running surface of the skis with 'dope,' corresponding to our modern downhill wax.

d. An absorbent material, as sawdust, used in making dynamite.

1880 *Amer. Inst. Min. Eng. Trans.* VIII. 417 Hercules powder . . . contains a very large proportion of nitrate of soda, . . . the remainder of the dope being incombustible carbonate of magnesia. **1881** RAYMOND *Mining Gloss.*, Giant-powder, a mixture of nitroglycerin with a dry pulverized mineral or vegetable absorbent or dope.

e. Any preparation, esp. of opium, used to stupefy; an opiate.

1895 J. L. FORD *Lit. Shop* ix. 130 Opium-joints—those mysterious dens in which . . . the fumes of the burning 'dope' cloy the senses. **1947** *Newsweek* 3 March 21/1 He also was the country's leading distributor of dope, and he ran a numbers racket.

f. Short for fly dope *q.v.*

1903 WHITE *Forest* 109 Next in order come the various 'dopes.' . . . From the stickiest, blackest pastes to the silkiest, suavest oils they range. **1948** *Chi. Tribune* 11 July 7/1 Most of these new dopes (developed as a result of war discoveries) are sure to repel denizens of the skeeter and black fly world.

g. (See quots.)

1915 *Printers' Ink* 23 Sep. 46/2 Finally there is the problem with which we are immediately concerned, the propensity of a large proportion of those who regularly drink Coca-Cola to call for their favorite drink as 'dope' or 'coke' or 'koke.' **1931** CALDWELL *Amer. Earth* 21 Everybody likes Coca-Cola. There is nothing better to drink on a hot day, if the dopes are cold.

2. Information or knowledge, esp. of a kind not widely disseminated or easily available. *Slang.*

1901 HOBART *John Henry* 77, I've known Tommy for a long time, so he feels free to read his dope to me. **1945** *Chi. D. News* 22 Sep. 4/3 What does the average layman think, upon getting all this reassuring dope? **1947** *This Week Mag.* 13 Sep. 18/3 Anton, the cabbie, got the dope, and Gard put on the pressure.

3. A person under the influence of, or addicted to the use of, some form of dope or drug. Also transf. *Slang.*

1909 *Sat. Ev. Post* 1 May 5/1 He's an old dope, which he don't look like, or he's on. **1948** *Chi D. News* 11 June 16/4 Cold tea sold to night life dopes for brandy at 75 cents a throw [etc.].

4. In colloq. and slang combs.: (1) **dope book,** a book of information on any subject, also fig.; (2) **bucket,** a bucket containing a lubricant, also fig., *to kick over the dope bucket,* to perform contrary to expectations; (3) **dream,** a dream induced by opium; (4) **fiend,** (see quot. 1896); (5) **figures,** (see quot. and cf. **dope sheet**); (6) **medicine,** a medicine that contains a narcotic; (7) **mill,** a mill in which corn is ground with wheat, cf. **dope, *v.* 2. c;** (8) **peddler,** an illicit vendor of opium; (9) **ring,** a group of those who connive in the illegal marketing of opium; (10) **sheet,** a sheet of information about race horses, their past records, etc.; (11) **toter,** (see quot.).

(1) **1909** *Cent. Supp.* 389/2 dope-book. . . . A miscellaneous collection of racing information. [Racing slang.] **1918** *Amer. Mag.* Aug. 38/2 They are, to wit: . . . the one that invents the dope book on the female race, and the bird that holds a patent on the complete understanding of human nature. **1920** *Collier's* 5 June 10/1 A flash at the dope-book on any sport, profession, trade, gift, art, science, or bad habit will show you what happens then. — (2) **1898** HAMBLEN *Gen. Manager's Story* 14 The first thing he does is to cut down the caboose supplies, till not one conductor out o' three's got a dope bucket. **1944** *Chi. D. News* 4 Oct. 29/8 The Browns further kicked over the dope bucket by blowing 13 out of 22 extra-inning games in '44. — (3) **1908** SINCLAIR *Metropolis* 137 What will people think, . . . seeing you sitting there like a man in a dope dream? — (4) **1896** *N.Y. Sun* Dec., 'A dope fiend.' . . . A victim of the opium habit. **1945** SERVICE *Ploughman* 218 He was also a dope fiend but he was very nice.

(5) **1928** *Liberty* 11 Aug. 52/1 They insisted, so I showed them the dope figures. — (6) **1907** *Collier's* 30 Mar. 13/2 Health Commissioner Darlington has crippled the 'dope' medicines by absolutely forbidding the sale of cocaine nostrums. — (7) **1898** *Cong. Rec.* 22 Feb. (Th. Supp.), The dope mill gets the pure flour price for its product. — (8) **1923** *Jrnl. Amer. Inst. Crim. Law & Criminology* Aug. 292 No other group comes closer to the bootlegger or the dope peddler. **1947** *Chi. Tribune* 22 July 2/7 He was a gambler, but not a gangster and not a dope peddler. — (9) **1943** *Copper Camp* 120 Butte's Chinatown was the hub from which the spokes of the dope ring radiated to every part of the United States. **1947** *Chi. Sun* 25 Nov. 10/4 Her husband was a messenger for a dope ring.

(10) **1903** ADE *People You Know* 111 When he arrived at the Track he gave up for a Badge and a Couple of Perfectos. **1931** SINCLAIR *Wet Parade* 390 The little fellows who read the financial pages and the 'dope-sheet' are nearly all 'bulls,' and this was their market. — (11) **1931** *Illinois Central Mag.* June 30/3 A car oiler gets the title of 'dope toter.'

dope dop, *v.*

1. *tr.* (See quot. 1902.)

1868 *Putnam's Mag.* II. 363 With their snow-shoes thoroughly 'doped,' the crowd resort to some suitable place for the contest, which begins with a grand dash, all participating. **1902** *D.N.* II. 233 *Dope*, v. tr. 1. To smear, or lubricate. **1935** H. L. DAVIS *Honey in the Horn* 12 There was a salad of lettuce whittled into shoestrings, wilted in hot water, and doped with vinegar and bacon grease.

2. To give dope to (a person); to stupefy with a drug; to drug (a liquid). Also fig.

1889 BARRERE & LELAND I. 322 Doping is the stupifying men with tobacco prepared in a peculiar way. . . . Nine out of ten saloons in the slums employ doping as a means to increase their illicit revenue. **1908** H. LORIMER *J. Spurlock* iii. 41, I was so doped with my siren song that I steered straight for the rocks. **1948** *Pauls Valley* (Okla.) *D. Democrat* 2 July 2/5 The first few swallows of the now heavily doped liquid had knocked her off.

b. To "doctor." *Colloq.*

1906 in ASHER & HEAL (1942) *Send No Money* 95 You would like to know just where you are at before you 'dope' that kind of stock with a strange mixture. **1913** *Sunday Times* (Trenton, N.J.) 2 Mar. 1 Alternative offered to the water drinkers of Trenton: Typhoid if the water isn't 'doped' with hypochlorite of lime; an itch if it is. **1931** *K.C. Times* 16 Sep., Chief Getzem of Ore worked late Saturday evening doping his hens with louse powder.

c. To adulterate. Cf. **dopemill.**

1898 *Cong. Rec.* App. 223/1 They will run their flutter mills and mixers, and dope the flour to suit themselves.

3. To find out, to "figure out," to reach a conclusion about something through surmising. Also with *out. Slang.*

1906 O. HENRY *Four Million* 163 All the same, I believe it was the hand of Fate that doped out the way for me to find her. **1916** *Amer. Mag.* May 25/3 This system of 'doping' I have used for twelve years, altering it when errors were revealed of values of positions changed. **1948** *Time* 17 June 78/2 He still thinks he has a chance—if he can dope some angles.

dopester 'dopstɚ, *n.* One who uses "dope" (sense **2.**) in forecasting the results of sporting events, elections, etc. *Slang.* — **1916** *All-Story Wkly.* 25 March 283 The dopesters had looked up those two coast fights, and that ended the betting. **1948** *News-Dispatch* (Michigan City, Ind.) 3 April 9/3 It was a big upset according to ringside dopesters.

dopey 'dopɪ, *a.* [Cf. **dope, *v.* 2.**] Stupid, sluggish, dull as if from a drug, "dumb." *Slang.*

1896 *Cin. Enquirer* 2 Aug. 2/1 There is an impression of truth to the rather 'dopy' proposition that makes it worthy of newspaper space. **1902** *Chi. Record-Herald* 7 Sep. III. 2/5 It must have been very dopy work by Mr. Stock, who could not have reached third base before the ball was caught unless he started the night before. **1948** *Sat. Ev. Post* 14 Aug. 80/4 If he wasn't so dopey he could've got the whole hundred dollars out of Mr. McCallum.

Dorado də'rɑdo, *n.* =**El Dorado.** *Obs.* — **1848** SHERWOOD *California* 33 Ere long, thousands will be flocking to this veritable *Dorado*, so long regarded as a hallucination upon the part of those engaged in the fruitless research. **1859** HENRY VILLARD *The Pikes Peak Gold Fever* (MS) l, Great numbers were yielding to the allurements of the new Dorado.

dor bug. Any one of various beetles, as the June bug, that make a buzzing noise when they fly. *Colloq.* Cf. **dawbug.**

1833 GREENE *Dod. Duckworth* I. 86 It's a dorbug! **1877** *Vt. Bd. Agric. Rep.* IV. 157 A very common beetle is what is known as the dor bug, or June bug. **1890** *Cent.* 3322/3 The species [of *Lachnosterna*] are especially numerous in North America, where they are popularly known as June-bugs, dor-bugs, and May-beetles.

dorg dɔrg, *n.* A humorous variant of "dog." Cf. **purp.**

1860 *Marysville* (Calif.) *Appeal* 31 March 2/2 We saw a female 'dorg' going mournfully up D. street. **1865** *Carson* (Nev.) *Appeal* 5 Nov. 3/2 The 'Dimmercrats' are the worst 'whaled' dorgs in the ring next Tuesday. **1879** *Amer. Punch* Oct. 119/2 No dorg to love, none to caress!

dorm dɔrm, *n.* Short for "dormitory." *Colloq.* — **1929** *Old Oregon* June 8 The original class flag was there to grace the walls of the men's 'dorm' at the alumni luncheon and to give a familiar touch at the reunion dinner. **1948** *Sat. Ev. Post* 14 Aug. 77/2 It was almost dinner-time, and all the other guys were back in the dorms.

dormidera ˌdormɪˈderə, *n.* [Sp., a kind of poppy.] The California poppy, *Eschscholtzia californica*, the state flower of California. — **1898** *Land of Sunshine* Dec. 49 The Dormidera, or wild 'poppy' of California. **1947** *Desert Mag.* July 22 Old-time Spanish-Californians gave it several poetic names, Copa de Oro (Cup of Gold) the most common, Amapola (Poppy), and Dormidera (Sleepy One) because the flowers unfold only in full sunlight.

* **dormitory,** *n.* **a.** (See quot.) **b. dormitory car,** a railroad car in which construction workers live. — **(a) 1850** Browne *Poultry Yard* 83 The dormitory, or roost, should be well ventilated. — **(b) 1884** *Lisbon* (Dak.) *Star* 15 Aug., The dormitory-car in which Bar-

Dormitory car or lodging car (*c*1885)

num's giant Chang was sleeping burned at Jamestown. **1946** Adams *Album Amer. Hist.* III. 392 The men lived in dormitory cars as shown above.

dornick ˈdɔrnɪk, *n.* Also **darnick, dorneck, donoch, donock.** *S. & W.* [Prob. f. Irish *dornōg*, a small round stone.] A stone. *Colloq.*

1840 *Daily Pennant* (St. Louis) 18 June (Th.), Thatar man he tooks up a dornick, and made a heap of cavortins. **1853** P. Paxton *Yankee in Texas* 117 In Arkansas, however, the term *donoch* usurps the place of either rock or stone. **1949** *Time* 7 Mar. 28/3 In the muttering jungle of New York's 771-mile water-front, bollard-necked hoodlums have long kept things regular with gun, knife, cargo hook and dornick.

b. (See quots.)

1903 *D.N.* II. 312 Donnick, or dornick, n. A small mound or tussock [s.e. Mo.]. **1945** *Amer. Sp.* April 157/1 *Life* for May 22, 1944 (p. 110) refers to the 'dornick' gravestone of Cal McCoy and defines 'dornicks' as 'natural slabs of stone which are set up without aid of a professional stone-cutter.'

Dorothy Perkins. A variety of rambler rose introduced by the Jackson & Perkins Nursery, Newark, N.Y., in 1901.

1915 *Country Life* March 49 Dorothy Perkins roses run riot over the rough poled superstructure of the pergola. **1928** *My Okla.* Feb. 7/2 This rose is no other than the beloved Dorothy Perkins. **1948** *Household* Feb. 74/2, I would suggest Dorothy Perkins and American Pillar as quicker to take hold than most of the more refined varieties.

dorp dɔrp, *n.* [Du. in same sense. An Amer. borrowing.] A (Dutch) hamlet or village. *Obs.*

1668 *Doc. Col. Hist.* N.Y. XIII. 419 These are to give notice to all persons concerned in either of the new Dorpses or Villages lately laid out. *Ib.*, We . . . are willing to take o[u]r Dividend of Lotts at the furthest New Dorpe or Village. **1832** J. F. Watson *Hist. Tales N.Y.* 12 To this small *Dorp* or village they gave the stately name of New Amsterdam. **1839** Irving in *Knickerb.* XIII. 319 *n.*, The Saw-Mill River . . . empties itself into the Hudson, at the ancient dorp of Yonkers.

* **Dorr,** *n. attrib.* Of or pertaining to the insurrection led by Thomas Dorr (1805–54). *Obs.* Cf. **Dorr('s) Rebellion.**

1844 *Cong. Globe* 8 March 359/3 Mr. Dorr, aided by worse Dorr-men out of Rhode Island, threw that State into turmoil and confusion. **1858** *Harper's Mag.* Jan. 279/1 During the 'Dorr war' in Rhode Island every one that could shoulder a musket became suddenly valiant. **1941** Mott *Amer. Journalism* 297 The 'Dorr War' in Rhode Island in 1844, the conflict in 'bleeding Kansas' in 1855–56, and the wars against the Mormons . . . were all sensational episodes.

b. Dorrism, the political philosophy of Dorr and his adherents. *Obs.*

1844 *Henry Clay Bugle* (Maysville, Ky.) 2 May 1/2 Let them come out from among them and fight under a leader, that they now in their hearts know to be as much superior to their own as Honor and Order is above Repudiation and Dorrism. **1848** *N.Y. Wkly. Tribune* 5 Feb. 3/1 Let us have Dorrism frankly weighed and measured in the Supreme Court of the Union.

c. Dorrite, a political follower of Thomas Dorr. Also attrib. Cf. **Algerine.**

1844 *Cong. Globe* App. 9 March 269/2 The Dorrites have gained a great deal of sympathy abroad by representing themselves as the exclusive advocates of the democratic doctrine of extended suffrage. **1846** *Nat. Intelligencer* (Wash.) 7 April 1/1 Henry Jackson, the present governor, . . . was sustained by the 'Liberator' (Dorrite) party. **1948** *Nat. Geog. Mag.* Aug. 155/1 Then the Dorrites tried to seize the Providence arsenal, but failed when their museum-piece artillery, captured at the Battle of Saratoga in 1777, failed to fire.

d. Dorr('s) Rebellion, a rebellion or insurrection led by Thomas W. Dorr in Rhode Island in 1842 in an effort to increase the number of those entitled to suffrage.

1844 *Henry Clay Bugle* (Maysville, Ky.) 25 April 4/4 (*heading*), Mr. Clay and the Dorr Rebellion. **1865** *Cong. Globe* 3 Feb. 577/2 Dorr's rebellion arose against the existing government. They had their two legislatures and their two executives, and were ready to enter into a conflict of arms.

* **dory,** *n.*[1] Also **doré.** The wall-eyed pike, *Stizostedion vitreum*. Cf. **hair-finned dory.** — **1884** Goode *Fisheries* I. 419 This fish and the White Bass are the two most important kinds taken at the Green Bay City fisheries, where the former is called 'Dory.' **1947** Dalrymple *Panfish* 217 Though I am not familiar with the origins of such names as Doré, Okow, Jack, I suppose it may be that they have quasi-logical explanations.

dory ˈdorɪ, *n.*[2] [f. *dôri*, *dûri*, native name for a dugout on the Mosquito Coast in Honduras and Nicaragua.] A small flat-bottomed boat with wide flaring sides, noted for its stability.

1709 Lawson *Carolina* 13 The French were very officious in assisting with their small Dories to pass over these Waters. **1832** *Boston Transcript* 10 May 2/1 Witelham, one of the crew of the schr Hero, . . . left that vessel, as usual, with fishermen, in a small 'dorey' to fish, on Wednesday afternoon last. **1947** *Sat. Ev. Post* 8 Mar. 29/3 The big passenger dory started out to pick up personnel and luggage.

attrib. **1889** Munroe *Dorymates* 25 He delighted in being called his father's 'dorymate.'

* **dose,** *n.* In colloq. or slang expressions: (1) *To go through like a dose of salts*, to vanquish utterly, go through rapidly; (2) *to give* (a person) *a dose of his own medicine*, and variants, to treat (a person) as he has treated others.

(1) 1837 *Crockett Almanac* 3 I'll go through the Mexicans like a dose of salts. **1889** K. Munroe *Golden Days* xii. 124 He'd gone through the pockets like a dose of salts. — **(2) 1894** Ford *P. Stirling* 150 'He snubbed me,' . . . explained Miss De Voe, smiling slightly at the thought of treating Peter with a dose of his own medicine. **1927** Siringo *Riata* 107 In killing Bob Ollinger the Kid only gave him a dose of his own kind of medicine.

As the last term in **broken, death dose.**

dossateen ˌdɔsəˈtin, *n.* Also **dorsettee.** (See quot. 1923.) Also attrib. *Obs.*

1776 *N.J. Archives* 2 Ser. I. 28 Stolen. . . . One brown and orange dossateen gown. **1776** *Ib.* 139 Run away . . . an Irish servant man . . . had on . . . a silk handkerchief, felt hat, an old dorsettee jacket. **1923** Van Laer *Minutes of Fort Orange* 224 Dosyntiens, from the French 'draps de douzaine,' a general name for light-weight cloth [with ref. to an unquoted passage of 1659 in the Dutch minutes].

* **dote,** *n.* (See quot. 1905.) — **1874** Knight 564/1 *Clearstuff*, boards free from knots, wane, wind-shakes, ring-hearts, dote, sap. **1905** *Forestry Bureau Bul.* No. 61, 35 *Dote*, the general term used by lumbermen to denote decay or rot in timber.

* **dotted,** *a.* Of fish: Marked with small dots or spots. See also **polka-dotted.**

1819 *Western Rev.* I. 371 Black dotted Perch. . . . The vulgar names of this fish are black perch, widow's perch, dotted bass, [etc.]. **1842** *Nat. Hist. N.Y., Zoology* IV. 141 The Dotted Silverside, *Atherina notata*, . . . is a common species in New York harbor. *Ib.* 167 The Dotted Malthea. *Malthaea notata*. **1884** *Nat. Museum Bul.* No. 27, 438 *Decapterus punctatus*. . . . Dotted Scad. . . . It seems to be rare on our Atlantic coast, but is common at Pensacola, Florida.

* **double,** *a., n.,* and *adv.*

1. *n.* A sharp turn or bend in a mountain. *Colloq.*

1851 *S. Lit. Messenger* XVII. 46/2 The stranger who has been left alone in the doubles of the mountains of Western Virginia has a fair chance of passing the night without supper or bed. **1928** in *Amer. Sp.* XV. 173/1 The ore was mined high up in the double of the mountain.

2. (See quot.)

1863 Randall *Pract. Shepherd* 413 'Old Greasy' was but little wrinkled, having simply the cross on the brisket, the convolution of skin under the chops called by many 'the double,' and a narrow dewlap between them.

3. In baseball, a two-base hit.

1883 *Chi. Tribune* 3 July 6/5 Cassidy's long double to right field sent him home. **1948** *Dly. Ardmoreite* (Ardmore, Okla.) 6 Aug. 8/6 The Ardmore pitcher connected for two doubles and a single in four trips to the plate.

4. In noun and adjective combs.

a. Designating utensils and equipment: (1) **double boiler,** a two-piece cooking utensil in the upper part of which food is cooked without danger of scorching, by boiling water in the lower section; (2) **cinch,** *W.* two cinches or girths on the same saddle; (3) **ender,** (see quot. and cf. **b.** (6) below); (4) **harness,** a harness for horses working in pairs; (5) **moldboard plow,** (see quot. 1874); (6) **plow,** a plow drawn by two draft animals, cf.

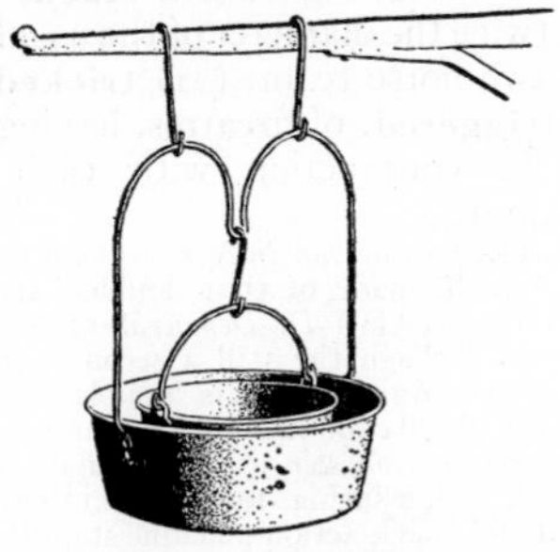

Early type of double boiler

Michigan double plow; (7) **rig(ged) saddle,** *W.* (see quots.); (8) **roller,** a students' device for cheating in recitations and examinations, consisting of two pencils upon which has been rolled a thin sheet of paper containing information on points likely to be asked about, *obs.;* (9) **shooter,** a gun having two barrels, *rare;* (10) **shovel (corn) plow,** a plow having two shovels; (11) **sights,** the front and the rear sights of a gun; (12) **spectacles,** bifocal (*q.v.*) glasses, *obs.;* (13) **tree,** the crosspiece of a wagon or similar vehicle to which the singletrees are attached, also fig.

(1) 1879 Mrs. Whitney *Just How* 260 Or, cut up and boil and mash in their own juice only, in a bain-marie, or double boiler. **1948** *This Week Mag.* 31 Dec. 7/4 Heat a couple of damp washcloths in the top of a double boiler. — **(2) 1907** S. E. White *Arizona Nights* 245 They were good men, addicted to the grass-rope, the double cinch. — **(3) 1889** *Cent.* 1743/2 Double-ender, a cross-cut sawing-machine, with a pair of adjustable circular saws, for equalizing pieces of stuff by sawing both ends at once. — **(4) 1866** *Rep. Indian Affairs* 181 One pair of bay horses, 7 years old; 1 set of double harness; 1 dozen 17-inch mill files. **1936** *Sears Cat.* (ed. 173), *Double Side Straps.* Our best. . . . For double harness.

(5) 1858 C. Flint *Milch Cows* 194 The Michigan or double-mould-board plough leaves the land light. **1874** Knight 727 Double-mold-board plow, . . . a plow having a moldboard on each side of the *sheth,* so as to throw the soil away right and left. **1907** T. F. Hunt *Forage & Fiber Crops* 352 (*Cent. Supp.*) Or by means of a middle 'buster,' which is a double mold-board plow. — **(6) 1856** Davis *Farm Bk.* 24 Run 2 double plows & 7 single in the fresh land. **1883** *Rep. Indian Affairs* 177 We are making for the Indian service . . . 100 sets of double plow harness. — **(7) 1913** W. C. Barnes *Western Grazing Grounds* 381 Double Rig Saddle.—A saddle with two cinches; a 'rim fire' saddle. **1923** J. H. Cook *On Old Frontier* 113 Double-rigged saddles, or those with a front and a back cinch, did not require this.'— **(8) 1871** Bagg *At Yale* 634 At the Sophomore Biennial of '67, one of the sufferers was possessed of a 'double-roller,' upon which was copied the essential part of all the analytics recited by the class. — **(9) 1857** *Harper's Mag.* Aug. 391/2 Fred's piece was a double-shooter, and he stood prepared to let off the other barrel.

(10) 1854 *Pa. Agric. Rep.* 180 There are . . . the Double Shovel Plow, for dressing corn, and the Horse Hay Fork, for unloading hay. **1891** Garland *Main-travelled Roads* (1922) 146 Julia Peterson, . . . was toiling back and forth between the corn-rows, holding the handles of the double-shovel corn-plough. — **(11) 1834** Caruthers *Kentuckian* I. 25 A chap would make a blue fist of takin a dead aim through double sights with the butt end of a psalm in his guzzle. — **(12) 1784** Franklin *Wks.* (1906) IX. 265, I cannot distinguish a Letter even of Large Print; but am happy in the invention of Double Spectacles, which, serving for distant objects as well as near ones, make my Eyes as useful to me as ever they were. — **(13) 1847** Webster 1034/3 (citing Haldeman), A single-tree is fixed upon each end of the double-tree when two horses draw abreast. **1886** *Cong. Rec.* 10 March, I will pull with the gentleman from Kansas and the gentleman from Michigan . . . to keep up my end of the double tree. **1909** Wason *Happy Hawkins* 193 Now, me an' Ches was about as different as they ever get, most ways, an' yet we pulled a level double-tree out in the open. **1948** *Atlantic Mo.* Sep. 19/2 Tugs are not hooked to doubletrees. It is quite impossible . . . for doubletrees have no hooks on them.

b. With reference to railroads, boats or other means of transportation: (1) **double buggy,** a buggy drawn by two horses, and sometimes having two seats; (2) **caboose,** ?a caboose having living quarters in both ends, *rare;* (3) **cut,** see **cut,** *n.* **10. a;** (4) **decked,** see as a main entry; (5) **decker,** see as a main entry; (6) **ender,** a boat whose two ends are similarly rounded, cf. **a.** (3) above; (7) **header,** see as a main entry; (8) **pung,** a pung drawn by two horses, cf. **double buggy;** (9) **railroad,** a double-tracked railroad; (10) **rig,** =**double buggy;** (11) **ripper,** a bobsled (see also quot. 1877 and cf. next); (12) **runner,** two sleds fastened together tandem fashion, a bobsled; (13) **sleigh,** a sleigh drawn by two horses; (14) **sulky,** a sulky designed for two persons; (15) **texas,** ?two sets of cabins on the hurricane deck of a steamer, *rare;* (16) **track,** two parallel lines of railroad track, also attrib.; (17) **trailer,** ?a heavy freight wagon having two smaller vehicles attached behind it, *obs.;* (18) **turnout,** on a railroad, a double-tracked siding.

(1) 1844 *Mass. Statutes* lxxv, [Toll on] double buggy drawn by one horse, 15 cents. **1898** Page *Red Rock* 225 Dr. Still . . . drove over to Birdwood the very next evening in a double buggy. — **(2) 1881** *Rep. Ala. R.R. Comm.* I. 53 The rear car, or double caboose, was thrown from the track.

(6) 1864 *Cong. Globe* 24 Feb. 786/1 The side-wheel gunboats known as double enders. **1905** *N.Y. Ev. Post* 30 Aug. 2 If she wasn't a double-ender the Manhattan [a ferry-boat] would do very well for a yacht. — **(8) 1895** C. C. Coffin *Daughters of Revolution* 87 We pile into a double pung, ride in the moonlight. — **(9) 1858** W. P. Smith *Railway Celebrations* 8 They therefore recommended that measures be taken to construct 'a double railroad' between the city of Baltimore and some suitable point upon the Ohio River.

(10) 1944 Wilson *Passing Inst.* 82 'Drummers' drove 'double rigs' from the livery stables. **1946** ——— *Fidelity* 75 Surries, double rigs from the livery stables; horseback riders, frequently two or more on a horse. — **(11) 1877** Bartlett 188 Double Ripper. Two sleds from six to ten feet apart connected by a plank, upon which boys slide down hill. . . . Also called a Doubler. **1945** *This Week Mag.* 15 Dec. 2/2 We went to town in our double-ripper with the robe tucked around us and soapstones at our feet. — **(12) 1883** *Harper's Mag.* Dec. 146/2 The vehicle was a large two-handed boy's sled—not what you call a double-runner. **1905** *Providence Journal* 23 Feb. 1 A three-sled double runner, with ten youths and girls aboard, crashed into a post of a rail fence, and all were thrown off. — **(13) 1737** Parkman *Diary* 10 Mary Tilestone took a ride with me in a double slay. **1855** M. Cook *Letters* (1946) 7 Mar. 13 Your Pa says to Charley since we came home that they must rig out the double sley and all go. — **(14) 1852** Bristed *Upper Ten Th.* ix. 222 His light gig (of the kind technically called a double-sulky) was painted a dingy yellow ochre.

(15) 1912 I. Cobb *Back Home* 103 [The steamboat] was a regular sidewheeler with a double texas, and rising suns painted on her paddle boxes. — **(16) 1834** *Amer. R.R. Jrnl.* III. 50/3 [There] should be laid a double track railway. **1944** *Chi. and N.W. Time Table* 3 Dec. 48 On a 5½-mile stretch of double track, just outside of Norway, Iowa, Section Foreman Arthur M. (Pal) Holland keeps himself and his crew mighty busy. — **(17) 1906** *Out West* Feb. 99 Freighters still recall with reminiscent regret the . . . huge-wheeled wagons, loaded, 'lead wagon' and 'trail,' with six or eight tons, or more if there were 'double trailers.' — **(18) 1832** *Amer. R.R. Jrnl.* I. 818/2 Counting each double turnout as equal to two . . . there have been 87½.

c. In the names of, or with reference to, games and dancing: (1) **double bagger,** in baseball, a two-base hit; (2) **cross-hop,** a leap in which a dancer repeatedly strikes his heels together or crosses his legs, *obs.;* (3) **header,** see as a main entry; (4) **Pedro,** (see quot.

1938); (5) **play,** in baseball, a play in which two players are put out in immediate succession; (6) **steal,** in baseball, the stealing of bases simultaneously by two base runners; (7) **trouble,** (see quot. 1813), *obs.*

(1) 1879 *Chi. Tribune* 16 May 5/2 Shaffer opened with a single, and was followed by Peters, with a double-bagger. **1886** *Ib.* 14 May 3/3 Three handsome double-baggers were made by Poorman, Radbourn, and Burdock. — **(2) 1835** LONGSTREET *Ga. Scenes* 17 'She'll remember Abram Baldwin,' thought I, 'as soon as she sees the double cross-hop.' It was performed by rising and crossing the legs twice or thrice before lighting, and I used to carry it to the third cross with considerable ease. — **(4) 1899** GEORGE ADE *Fables in Slang* (1911) 48 While in Camp they played Double Pedie, smoked corn-cob Pipes, and cussed the Rations. **1938** ASBURY *Sucker's Prog.* 323 At first the Nevadans used the room principally as a place in which to play Cinch, a variation of All-Fours which was also known as Double Pedro or High Five, but after a few years it was devoted almost entirely to Poker.

(5) 1867 *Ball Players' Chron.* 6 June 2/3 A double play by Willard and Shaw, and the finest fly catch of the match by Shaw on a foul ball, caused the Lowells to retire for a blank score. **1948** *P.C.C. Chronicle* (Pasadena, Calif.) 7 May 4/5 The Muir Club pulled two double plays during the game. — **(6) 1900** *Chi. Times-Herald* 8 May 4/1 Cooley flied to Donahue and Williams was nipped at the plate on the double steal. **1948** *Miami* (Okla.) *D. News-Record* 4 July 4/1 On a double steal try, Hansen's throw to Harris at third deflected off Godla's shoulder and went into leftfield as both Godla and Sanders crossed the plate. — **(7) 1809** IRVING *Knickerb.* VI. iv, [The men from the Winding Bay] did . . . introduce the far-famed step in dancing, called 'double trouble.' **1813** PAULDING *Scottish Fiddle* (1814) 179 The dancing step, called 'double-trouble,' . . . consists in moving both feet without lifting them from the floor, in such a manner as to keep time to the music. **1903** *D.N.* II. 312 Double-trouble, *n.* A negro dancing step.

d. With reference to houses and furniture: (1) **double cabin, =double log cabin;** (2) **deck bed,** a bed with accommodations for two persons, one above the other; (3) **down chair,** ?an especially soft or comfortable chair; (4) **house, log,** see as main entries; (5) **penned cabin, =double log cabin.**

(1) 1837 PECK *New Guide* 124 A double cabin consists of two such buildings [i.e., regular log cabins] with a space of ten or twelve feet between. **1931** WILLISON *Here They Dug Gold* 17 Already thirty or more log houses are built or building to either side of the . . . double cabin. — **(2) 1936** *Sears Cat.* (ed. 173) 538 Two beds in a space ordinarily occupied by one. . . . As a double deck bed: Steel dowels (metal pins) firmly connect the posts of the upper and lower decks making a rigid one-piece unit. — **(3) 1921** *Ladies' Home Jrnl.* May 6/2 'Well,' said the Pleasant Grouch, burrowing his way into the new double-down chair.

(5) 1870 SPARKS *Memoirs of 50 Years* 484 Uncle Ned's tavern was one of those peculiar buildings . . . designated, in some parts of Georgia at that time, as a two-storied house, with both stories on the ground, in other words a double-penned cabin with passage between.

e. In the names of, or with reference to, plants and animals: (1) **double balsam fir,** the Fraser fir, perhaps so called in allusion to its esp. abundant needles; (2) **-crested cormorant,** a common North American species of cormorant, *Phalacrocorax auritus*, found along the northeast coast; (3) **headed snake,** an American snake or snake-like lizard with head and tail very similar in appearance, formerly supposed to have two heads, cf. **two-headed snake;** (4) **spruce,** (see quots.).

(1) 1814 PURSH *Flora* II. 639 Pinus Fraseri. . . . This species, known among the inhabitants by the name of Double-balsam Fir. **1858** WARDER *Hedges & Evergreens* 256 *Picea Fraseri*, the Double Balsam Fir, resembles the preceding [=American silver fir]. — **(2) 1839** PEABODY *Mass. Birds* 397 The Double-crested Cormorant . . . spend the winter on the coast of the eastern states. **1844** *Nat. Hist. N.Y., Zoology* II. 293 The Double-crested Cormorant, *Phalacracorox dilophus*, . . . is peculiar to the shores of America. **1884** *Nat. Museum Bul.* No. 27, 164. — **(3) 1789** *Trans. Philos. Soc.* III. xxiii, The double-headed snake may be a monstrous production; but two specimens of it are found in New-England. **1870** *Amer. Naturalist* IV. 375 Within the last ten years I have had in my possession two specimens of double headed Snakes. . . . Both specimens were the young of our Water Snake, *Regina leberis*. — **(4) 1810** MICHAUX *Arbres* I. 18 *Black* or *Double Spruce*, nom . . . dans les États du nord. **1892** APGAR *Trees Northern U.S.* 179 *Picea nigra*, Link. (Black or Double Spruce.)

f. In miscellaneous combs.: (1) ***double(d) and twisted,** *S.* (see quot. 1932), *colloq.;* (2) **back action,** first-class, superior, *slang;* (3) **beer,** (see quots.); (4) **bit,** a coin having the value of two bit-pieces, *obs.;* (5) **case,** of a watch, a hunting-case; (6) **eagle,** a gold coin of the U.S. having the value of two eagles or twenty dollars; (7) **feature,** a motion picture program that contains two feature attractions; (8) **fisted,** having two capable fists, hence strong, stalwart, *colloq.;* (9) **gown,** a dressing gown of heavy or double material; (10) **header,** see as a main entry; (11) **jaded,** (see quots.), *obs.;* (12) **major course,** in some colleges and universities, a course of study involving twice as much time and credit as a major; (13) **mark,** (see quot. 1851), *obs.;* (14) **minor course,** in some colleges and universities, a course of study involving the same amount of time and credit as two minors or a major; (15) **parker,** one who parks double; (16) **parking,** the action of parking an automobile beside another already parked by the curb; (17) **sawbuck,** a twenty-dollar bill, cf. **sawbuck;** (18) **sighted,** of a gun, provided with a front and a rear sight; (19) **stack,** *S.* a stack of fodder having twice the diameter of the usual single stack; (20) **team,** a two-horse team; (21) **tricked, trickered,** =next; (22) **triggered,** of firearms, having two triggers that operate in conjunction with each other; (23) **worked,** (see quot.).

(1) 1834 CARUTHERS *Kentuckian in N.Y.* 63 Only a breese or so; a few tumblers of punch, made of that doubled and twisted Irish whiskey. **1932** *Durant* (Okla.) *D. Democrat* 12 Nov. 4/6 It [corn whisky] is then run through the still a second time, the 'double-running,' which in mountain jargon, is 'double and twisted.' This . . . drives out of the distillation most of the impurities. — **(2) 1848** *New Negro Forget-me-not Songster* 39, I pick upon de Banjo string, Wid de double back action spring. **1861** NEWELL *Orpheus C. Kerr* I. 316 There was a double back-action machine standing in that chap's front entry. **1908** YESLAH *Tenderfoot S. Calif.* xi. 94 He told me more double-back-action lies in five minutes, than [etc.]. — **(3) 1867** *Terr. Enterprise* (Virginia, Nev.) 17 April 3/2 This beer is about twice as strong as lager and is sometimes called 'double beer.' *Ib.* 4 May 3/1 To-night Sturm & Muller . . . will have on tap the first genuine German 'bock' or double beer ever seen on this side of the mountains. **(4) 1705** *Boston News-Letter* 30 April 2/1 A Proclamation, Prohibiting the Importation of any clipt Money of Bitts or double Bitts. **1731** J. COMER *Diary* (1923) 116 Lodged at Mr. Eyres'. Cost me a double bitt.

(5) 1868 G. G. CHANNING *Recoll. Newport* 240 Small, double-case silver watches, of the most ordinary make, there were. — **(6) 1849** *U.S. Laws Concerning Money* (1910) 508 For all sums whatever, the double eagle shall be a legal tender for twenty dollars. **1948** JOHNSTON *Gold Rush* 41/1 Seizing Kuntz' beard, he yanked it from his collar and a shower of bright double eagles clattered musically to the floor. — **(7) 1932** *Variety* 14 June 5/4 Ratification of the agreement means that double features will be officially ended next fall. **1948** *Dly. Ardmoreite* (Ardmore, Okla.) 9 Aug. 4/2 Double features are on the way out. — **(8) 1853** *Olympia* (Wash.) *Columbian* 2 July (Th. 448), A big double-fisted Hoosier, with a huge pair of yellow whiskers. — **(9) 1850** S. WARNER *Wide, Wide World* xxii, She hurried to finish her dressing, and wrapping her double-gown over all, went down to the kitchen. **1881** JEWETT *Country By-Ways* 153 They got out an old double gown, and let him put it on.

(11) 1835 INGRAHAM *South-West* II. 55 Others mounted on mules . . . with their dames or sweethearts riding 'double-jaded'—as the Yankees term the mode—behind them. **1877** BARTLETT 188 To ride double-jaded is to ride with a pillion. — **(12) 1897–8** *Univ. Chi. Reg.* 169 Double Major Course=a double course for twelve weeks. — **(13) 1804** *Monthly Anthol.* I. 104 They would take particular pains for securing the *double mark* of the English Professor to their poetical compositions. **1851** HALL *College Words* 104 Under the names of those whose themes were of more than ordinary correctness or elegance, *two* lines were drawn, which were called *double marks* — **(14) 1897–8** *Univ. Chi. Reg.* 169 Double Minor Course =a double course (two hours daily) for six weeks.

(15) 1932 *K.C. Star* 5 April 18 Practically all of Commercial street was used by double parkers. — **(16) 1931** *Ib.* 12 Aug., Manhattan and Emporia each has a local ordinance forbidding double-parking of motor cars. **1946** THOMPSON *Amer. Daughter* 242, I had a ticket for double parking, and in a few minutes I would be behind bars. — **(17) 1948** *Time* 17 May 87/1 Any tout or hustler around the track can usually work Eddie for a 'double sawbuck.' — **(18) 1840** COOPER *Pathfinder* vii, One of his notions now, is to prefar [*sic*] a king's piece to a regular double-sighted, long-barrelled rifle. — **(19) 1854** *Florida Plant. Rec.* 92, I have put up 45 double Stacks. I have Fodder Enough to Last a year and a half.

(20) 1846 WHITCHER *Bedott P.* i. 25 A mess o' men in a double team . . . hysted us out. **1855** *N.Y. Herald* 31 Dec. 1/5 Double teams were employed to drag the cars, which even then progressed very slowly. — (21) 1747 in CHALKLEY *Scotch-Irish Settlement Va.* I. 529 They were robbed of . . . women's head cloths, . . . a curb and a snaffle, a rifle gun (double tricked). 1775 ADAIR *Indians* 275 He could not discharge it, as it was double-trickered, contrary to the model of their smooth-bored guns. — (22) 1839 Z. LEONARD *Adventures* (1904) 70 In the hurry, the one that was accustomed to the single trigger, caught up the double triggered gun. — (23) 1851 BARRY *Fruit Garden* 81 When we graft or bud a tree already budded or grafted, we call it 'double-worked.'

5. In verbal expressions: (1) **double-board,** to make or cover (a wall) with two thicknesses of boards; (2) **furrow,** in plowing to throw two furrows together, or cultivate (a row crop) with a furrow on each side, *colloq.;* (3) **head,** of a train, to proceed by means of two engines, or to provide a train of cars with two engines; (4) **out,** to extricate a team, vehicle, etc., from a difficult spot by double-teaming, *colloq.*, cf. **double-team;** (5) **plow,** (see quot.); (6) **quick,** to march or cause to march at double quick time; (7) **team,** see as a main entry; (8) **track,** to provide or equip (a railroad) with two parallel lines of track, also **double-tracked,** *a.*

(1) 1874 *Vt. Bd. Agric. Rep.* II. 512 My plan was to double board and cleat the main body of the barn, having a basement or cellar under the whole barn. — (2) 1938 JESSE STUART *Beyond Dark Hills* 331 This bluff is a new-ground piece of corn. After the brush was burned it was laid off, double-furrowed, and planted. — (3) 1904 *Delineator* Sep. 374 A heavy freight train had double-headed up the mountain, and at the summit the leading engine had been cut off to run down ahead of the train. 1947 BEEBE *Mixed Train Dly.* 195 When more than a dozen cars of freight are to be hauled over the 2.5-percent grade on this stretch the train is double headed. — (4) 1888 J.J. WEBB *Adventures* 48 At Mud Creek . . . we mired down, 'doubled out,' cut grass to bridge and fill, and had the usual experience.

(5) 1851 *De Bow's Review* XI. 50 Occasionally oxen are plowed two to a plow, but only . . . while '*double plowing*,' or breaking up the fallow ground. — (6) 1862 in *Houston* (Tex.) *Tri-Wkly. News* (1863) 7 Jan. 2/3, I ordered the charge, and with a wild defiant shout the command double quicked it, took the battery, etc. 1907 ANDREWS *Recoll.* 196 The ground over which the division had double quicked. — (8) 1867 *Com. & Fin. Chron.* 16 March 343 Double-tracking the entire road. 1887 GEORGE *40 Years on Rail* v. 91 Accidents are reduced to a minimum, owing to good management and to the double-tracked roads. 1912 *Sat. Ev. Post* 20 July 17/3 The Harriman system is double-tracking twenty-five hundred miles of its line.

* **double,** *v.*

1. *tr.* In hauling, to add (another team) or to augment (teams) at a difficult place in the road. Also transf. Cf. **double-team.**

1754 WASHINGTON *Writings* I. 63 Wagons may travel now with 1500 or 1800 weight on them, by doubling the teams at one or two pinches only. 1848 BRYANT *Calif.* (1849) 49 Our wagons were lowered down by ropes, and by doubling teams, they were all finally drawn out of the bed of the stream. 1860 *Cong. Globe* 12 Jan. 423/3, I saw a disposition . . . 'to double teams' on me. *Ib.*, The Senator . . . has no right to say there is any disposition here to 'double teams' on him. 1870 KEIM *Sheridan's Troopers* 91 By doubling teams, however, we made the south side without disaster.

2. *intr.* To marry. Also with *up. Colloq.*

1817 *Niles' Reg.* 12 April 112/1 Jonathan Russell, (to use a yankee phrase) lately 'doubled' with a Miss Smith. 1894 *D.N.* I. 330 Double up: to marry. [N.J.]

3. Of a batter in baseball: To secure a two-base hit.

1904 *St. Louis Globe-Democrat* 2 July 5/1 Jones doubled in the seventh, and Evans doubled, sending him to third. 1948 *Chi. Tribune* 7 Mar. II. 1/4 Walker doubled to right, scoring Jeffcoat.

double-decked ˈdʌblˈdɛkt, *a.*

1. Of a railroad car: Having two decks or floors.

1868 *Ill. Agric. Soc. Trans.* VII. 460 Sheep arrive here from the west in single decked cars, but leave in double decked ones. 1934 LOMAX *Amer. Ballads* 26 'Twas a double-decked stock-car filled with sheep.

2. double-decked engine, a fire engine of a type now obs.

1896 HASWELL *New York* 294 The question of the relative merits of the New York and Philadelphia fire-engines being constantly discussed, the Common Council deputed a committee from its members to proceed to Philadelphia and procure one of its 'gallery' or 'double-decked engines,' which it did, and subsequently a second was obtained. They had much greater capacity, but were too cumbersome for a light company of men.

double decker. A vessel having two decks (see also quot. 1877).

1835 *Western Mo. Review* June 339 The Washington is a splendid double decker, calculated to carry three hundred tons. 1877 WM. WRIGHT *Big Bonanza* 301 The cage [in the shaft of a silver mine] may have but a single floor or platform, or it may have two or three. . . . Those with two platforms are called 'double-deckers,' and those with three platforms are called 'three-deckers.' 1948 *Mazama* Dec. 5/1 Sure enough, the chipperest little green and white boat, a double-decker at that, soon pulled in.

b. Designating a vehicle or railroad car having two floors or levels.

[1856 *N.Y. Herald* 9 Jan. 4/6 We met train after train of these doomed passengers; many of the trains made up of double storied cars, all hogs.] 1867 *Terr. Enterprise* (Virginia, Nev.) 19 July 3/1 Our streets are thronged all day long with vehicles of every description, from a 12-mule double-decker prairie schooner to a Chinaman's wood-donkey. 1944 *Nat. Geog. Mag.* June 676 With 250 spring lambs, each averaging 85 pounds, to each double-decker car, and with the price at 15 cents a pound on the hoof, how much were these seven carloads worth at Ketchum? 1948 *Chi. Sun* 27 Jan. 50/3 There's plenty of heat, which was lacking on the double deckers; also no smoking, which used to suffocate everyone in the double deckers.

c. (See quot.)

1889 *Cent.* 1743/2 double-decker. . . . A tenement-house having two families on one floor: so termed by the police of New York city.

d. double decker collar, an especially high collar. *Colloq.*

1929 *Randolph Enterprise* 28 March 1/2 Austin Woodford as announcer, dressed in his wedding suit, longtailed cutaway coat and white vest with a double-decker collar and string tie, an artificial rosebud in his buttonaire as large as a cabbage head.

e. (See quot. 1945.) *Slang.*

1934 WEBSTER. 1945 COLCORD *Sea Lang.* 64 A large ice-cream cone or a multiple-layer sandwich is a double decker.

f. A bed for two persons to sleep one above the other.

1945 MAXWELL *Folded Leaf* 188 Spud nodded approvingly at the double-decker single beds, each with its cocoon of covers. 1948 *Time* 16 Aug. 29/1 There was a double bed for Alf and Mary, a double-decker for the kids.

double-header ˈdʌblˈhɛdɚ, *n.*

1. A kind of fireworks. *Obs.*

1869 ALDRICH *Bad Boy* 92 Here . . . could be purchased the smaller sort of fireworks, such as pin-wheels, serpents, double-headers, and punk. 1870 *N.Y. Herald* 1 July 4/5 The ordinance against . . . the setting off in the streets of fireworks known as 'snakes,' 'chasers,' 'double-headers,' 'Union or Young America torpedoes,' will be vigorously enforced.

2. A statement or retort of twofold force. *Rare.*

1870 M. HARLAND *For Better, for Worse* 274 Without waiting to witness the effect of this 'double-header,' she shook off his hold and marched out of the room.

3. A long, heavy train drawn by two locomotives; also the locomotives themselves. Also **double-header engine.**

1878 PINKERTON *Strikers* 216 'Double-headers,' or freight trains composed of a larger number of cars than the single train, and drawn by two engines, which economized labor. 1891 *Denver D. News* 20 Dec., A double-header drawing twenty cars of Durango coal from the Porter Mine, will leave Rico at 7 o'clock tomorrow morning. 1947 *Chi. Tribune* 15 June (Grafic Mag.) 14/1 McCann, on the leading double-header engine, was whistling for a signal.

b. (See quot.) *Obs.*

1893 *Outing* July 274/1 Generally two [canal] boats are coupled together, forming what is termed 'a double-header.'

4. In baseball, two games on the same day in immediate succession.

1896 *Cin. Enquirer* 30 July 2/2 In case rain should stop to-day's or to-morrow's games double headers will have to be played the next day, as there is no open time in the Pittsburg series to play off any postponed games. 1944 *Chi. D. News* 4 Aug. 24/1 'Little did I think, when I started to pitch one day in 1942 because my Richmond club had five double-headers in six days, that I would succeed in making a career of it,' the Alabaman drawled.

b. *transf.* and *fig.*

1903 *Cin. Enquirer* 2 Jan. 3/1 The management has decided to make only one price during the season, general admission being 25 cents, . . . a double header, or two games between the four clubs being played every Saturday night for one price of admission. 1911 LEWIS *Apaches* (1912) 220 Double headers, whatever the field of endeavor, are the exception and not the rule of life. 1929 *Cin. Enquirer* 5 Oct. 10/2 Another football double-header today. 1946 *Newsweek* 29 July 66/3 The broadcast was a double-header, marking both the eve of

Bastille Day and the thousandth school in Europe to receive the sponsorship of the federation.

double house. A house having its rooms on each side of a main entrance hall (see also quot. 1923).

1707 *Boston News-Letter* 24 March 2/2 Several other parcels of Land . . . Having thereon a good double House, 4 Rooms on a Floor fit for an Ordinary. **1837** COOPER *Gleanings in Europe* (1928) I. 109 The building she inhabited was one of the ordinary American double-houses, as they are called, with a passage through the centre, the stairs in the passage, and a short corridor, to communicate with the bed-rooms above. **1923** NUTTING *Massachusetts* 22 'Double house,' in the Cape Cod significance, . . . refers to a house with a chimney in the middle and a room on both sides. **1944** BARBOUR *Eden* 35 It is a queer old structure, really a double house.

double log.

1. Short for **double log cabin** or **house.** Also attrib.

1873 BEADLE *Undevel. West* 352 The soil was white or yellow, the timber scrubby, and the few houses of most ancient 'double-log' pattern. *Ib.* xxi. 405 The residence of a 'White Cherokee,' the usual double log with porch between.

2. double log cabin, a log dwelling consisting of two connected cabins or rooms with a hall between them.

1850 LEWIS *La. Swamp Doctor* 147 The house consisted of a double log cabin, of small dimensions, a passage, the full depth of the house, running between the 'pens.' **1853** P. PAXTON *Yankee in Texas* 345 A double log-cabin . . . consists usually of two large rooms, separated by a wide hall, which . . . being generally open at both ends, is not used in inclement days. **1948** STUART *Plum Grove Hills* 41 And right here stood the double-log cabin.

Also **double-logged cabin.** *Rare.*

1834 *Knickerb.* Jan. 32, I pursued my way, until, . . . immediately on the road, appeared a large rude double logged cabin, with a Buck's Horn nailed over the door.

3. double log house, a double house built of logs. Also attrib.

1852 REGAN *Emigrant's Guide* 245 Old Abe's dwelling was what is called a double log-house, consisting of an apartment at each end, with a wide entrance in front, sufficient to run a wagon into. On each side of this *shed* were the smaller entrance-doors of each apartment, right and left. **1873** BEADLE *Undevel. West* 403 We find quarters at the inevitable 'double log-house' hotel with open porch, veranda and multitudinous additions. **1940** WILSON *Wabash* 102 Nor was Ma-con-a-quah allowed to remain because of her double log house, the center of a farm as large and prosperous as any white man's.

***doubler,** *n.* **1.** =**double runner. 2.** (See quot.) Cf. **hard doubler.** — **(1) 1877** [see **double ripper**]. **1905** *Providence Jrnl.* 23 Feb. 1 The doubler comprised three clipper sleds, upon each of which a tall block was fastened, a board nailed to the blocks furnishing the seat. — **(2) 1942** GRAHAM and BEAVEN *Chesapeake Biol. Lab. Pub.* 52, 8 Such paired crabs are known as 'doublers.'

double-team ˈdʌblˈtim, *v.*

1. *intr.* In hauling, to combine two teams into one.

1843 in *Ore. Hist. Quart.* XL. 235 We crawsed . . . a smawl streem. Dubeld teamed & crawsed the hill. **1934** VINES *Green Thicket World* 111 Often they had to double-team.

2. To bring double force to bear *upon* or *on* someone or something. *Colloq.*

1860 *Cong. Globe* 12 Jan. 424/2 In respect to the Senator's allusion to 'double-teaming' upon him . . . I do not exactly agree with my friend from Mississippi. **1865** W. CHESNUT *Diary from Dixie* (1905) 346 (Th. Supp.), Beauregard and Lee were expected, but Grant had double-teamed on Lee. **1904** T. E. WATSON *Bethany* 197 On the next day we double-teamed on one section of his army.

b. *To double-team it,* to act together or in concert.

1884 MARK TWAIN *H. Finn* xix, I reckoned we might double-team it together.

***doubloon,** *n.* As the last term in **Carolus, Cincinnati doubloon.**

***doubtful,** *a.* Designating a state or county likely in an election to favor either or any candidate or party.

1824 *Commentator* (Frankfort, Ky.) 2 Oct. 3/1 New Jersey is one of the most doubtful states. **1887** *Cong. Rec.* App. 20 Jan. 50/1 They may appoint an agent in every doubtful county, in every doubtful State of the Union. **1917** *Ohio Arch. & Hist. Quart.* XXVI. 160 Of the more important states only New York and Ohio were really doubtful. **1948** *Chi. Tribune* 25 June 2/1 It is a doubtful state and will probably lose its state ticket.

***dough,** *n.*

1. The soft, milky stage or state reached by cereal grains just before maturity when the inside of the kernel is of a soft, dough-like consistency. In full **dough stage, state.**

1858 *Texas Almanac 1859* 67 The usual harvesting season extends from the 1st to the last of May. The proper time is when the grain is in the transition from the 'dough' to a hard state. **1869** *Rep. Comm. Agric. 1868* 177 When the heads of the rice are well filled and the last few grains at the bottom are in the *dough,* it is fit to cut. *Ib.* 417 The results . . . are corroborative of the theory, already well established, that wheat should be cut when the grain is in the dough state. **1945** *Democrat* 9 Aug. 2/5 Turn hogs on the field of corn when it has passed the dough stage.

2. Money. Also attrib. *Slang.* Cf. **stage dough.**

1851 *Yale Tomahawk* Feb. (Th.), He thinks he will pick his way out of the Society's embarrassments, provided he can get sufficient dough. **1904** *N.Y. Ev. Post* 7 Nov. 3 This is Tammany's regular annual 'dough day'—that is, the day on which the district leaders come to Tammany Hall for election day funds. **1906** *Ib.* 24 Oct. 4 In the country, election day without some sort of 'dough-bag' is an unheard-of thing. No 'dough-bag' means no votes. **1948** *Pauls Valley* (Okla.) *D. Democrat* 1 July 2/5, I had to pay out my own dough to the winners and take your IOU.

b. *To be in the dough,* to have money. *Slang.*

1944 LAWRENCE *Narrowing Wind* 60 You're in the dough and you kin afford to live there better'n I kin.

3. In special combs.: (1) **dough-ball,** see as a main entry; (2) **bat,** a severe blow, *slang, obs.;* (3) **bird,** the marbled godwit or the doe bird *q.v.;* (4) ***boy,** see as a main entry; (5) **dish,** a dish in which dough, esp. corn-meal dough, is mixed; (6) **doings,** corn bread, *obs.;* (7) **god,** (see quots. 1915, 1947), *slang;* (8) ***head,** a dough-face (sense **2.**), *obs.;* (9) **tray,** a large shallow wooden tray in which dough is kneaded.

(2) 1833 SNELLING *Exposé of Gaming* 26 We expected to see the man get a bounce of the nose, a dough bat, or a bandowzer. — **(3) 1835** AUDUBON *Ornith. Biog.* III. 69 The Esquimaux Curlew . . . are met with on the high sandy heights near the sea-shore, where they feed on the grasshopper and several kinds of berries. On this food they become fat, so as to afford excellent eating, in consequence of which they have probably acquired the name of 'Dough Bird,' which they bear in that district, [Mass.] but which is also applied to several other birds. **1844** *Nat. Hist. N.Y., Zoology* II. 253 It is generally called the Marlin, and less frequently Red Curlew, . . . Dough-bird. **1942** Nat. Pk. Service *Fading Trails* 157 'Dough-birds' or 'doebirds' were names once used for godwits and Eskimo curlews.

(5) 1845 *Lowell Offering* V. 148 Aunt Levi went up to get meal for the 'dough dish.' **1891** WILKINS *N. Eng. Nun* 190 Jane strode after her, the hens' dough-dish in her hand. — **(6) 1845** HOUSTOUN *Texas* 223 Our fare was not bad of its kind, there being 'pork dodgers' and 'dough doings,' (corn bread) chicken fixings and sausage. **1850** ——— *Hesperos* I. 118 As if these dough doings were not sufficiently poisonous in their effects, the benighted people wash it all down with immense quantities of new milk. — **(7) 1899** *Mo. So. Dakotan* I. 176 When the noon hour came and the cattle were turned to their turnips . . . and the hay boy flung himself on the canadensis carpet and ate his dinner of dough-god and bacon with hearty relish. **1915** *D.N.* IV. 244 dough god, *n. phr.* Biscuit. 'I don't care for dough gods.' **1947** *Harper's Mag.* July 81/2 He delighted in baking beans in the ground, fried excellent doughnuts and a somewhat similar product which he called 'dough-gods.' — **(8) 1848** *Albany W. Argus* 19 Aug. 264/1 They squabbled all night, and they squabbled next day. . . . Some for a Northern, or Southern man; But the dough-heads ruled, and the bloodhounds won! — **(9)** *a***1846** *Quarter Race Ky.* 89, I jist grabbed the Dough-tray and split it plumb open over his head! **1891** RYAN *Pagan* 150 'Did Mrs. Riker bring up the bread?' he asked, glancing into an empty dough-tray.

dough-ball ˈdobəl, *n.*

1. A small lump of dough, cooked usu. with vegetables or meat.

1836 THORPE *Life on Lakes* II. 155 The boiling mess was cooked and poured out into a deep tin pan; pork, fish, dough-balls, and no inconsiderable portion of the liquor, called by the men (*dignitate causa,*) soup, all together. **1863** COLES *Louie's Last Term* 168 Dough-balls were her acknowledged passion. **1898** F. H. SMITH *C. West* 56 Dinner was announced, and the Screamer's crew went below to more sizzle and doughballs.

b. dough-ball bait, bait for fishing made of a small quantity of dough.

1948 *Popular Mechanics* June 190/2 This is the trick in taking the wary channel cat with dough-ball baits.

2. (See quots.)

1851 HALL *College Words* 104 *Dough-ball.* At the Anderson Collegiate Institute, Indiana, a name given by the town's people to a student. **1881** FARLOW *Marine Algae* 171 In its typical form *P*[*olysiphonia*] *Olneyi* forms dense soft tufts, sometimes called dough-balls by the sea-shore population.

***doughboy**, *n.*

1. =**dobie 1.** Also attrib. *Obs.*

1856 in *Mont. Hist. Soc. Contrib.* X. (1940) 74 The Carpenters at Work getting the Doughboy tools ready. *Ib.* 75 This evening the men mixed their mud in preparation for making doughboys. *Ib.* 82 The Carpenters made . . . three doughboy moulds.

2. An infantryman in the U.S. Army.

The origin of this nickname is not clear. It may have arisen from **adobe** applied quite early by Spaniards in the Southwest to army personnel. See quot. 1856 *s.v.* **adobe 1.** *transf.* and *fig.*, and note the early conversion of **dobie** (f. **adobe**) into **doughboy** in **1.** above. But cf. also quot. 1887 below.

[**1865** *Harper's Wkly.* 25 Nov. 741/2 The arrival at 'Pit Hole' [a Pa. oil town] was the signal for the inhabitants to enjoy a joke at the expense of the bespattered excursionists. They were designated as 'Bummers,' 'Do-Boys,' 'Raiders,' etc.] **1867** *Beadle's Mo.* May 415/2 To us 'dough-boys' (the origin of the name is one of the inscrutable mysteries of slang,) who wore light blue shoulder-straps and chevrons, and were our own pack-horses, the constant marching off to the flank and skirmishing into positions, only to abandon them and go flanking again, became a wearisome iteration. **1887** CUSTER *Tenting on Plains* xvi. 516 A 'doughboy' is a small, round doughnut served to sailors on shipboard, generally with hash. Early in the Civil War the term was applied to the large globular brass buttons on the infantry uniform, from which it passed, by a natural transition, to the infantrymen themselves. **1948** *Sat. Ev. Post* 7 Aug. 23/2 Today the former doughboy from Kansas . . . is occupying a place of power which destiny reserves for only a few military greats.

attrib. **1898** *Scribner's Mag.* Aug. 133 Horse dealers . . . led their ponies up and down before . . . dough-boy officers. **1899** C. KING *Trooper Galahad* 110 The members of the troop . . . thought to 'run it' on the 'doughboy' captain.

3. *As pat as a doughboy*, quite suitable, appropriate. *Colloq.*

1892 *Amer. Folk-Lore* V. 60 As pat as a dough boy. (An old expression.)

Dougherty wagon. (See quot. 1943.) Cf. **ambulance 1.**

1901 *N. Amer. Rev.* Feb. 228 The Americans had thirteen four-mule army-wagons and one pack train of forty freight mules, besides two or three ambulances and a Dougherty wagon. **1943** WOOD *W. Reed* 92 The doherty wagon, a primitive ancestor of the station wagon, with seats that could be converted into beds at night and canvas sides that rolled down, lurched and bounced behind its four-mule team. *Ib.*, The road had turned out to be so rough that any progress faster than a walk threatened to shake both the ambulance (as the doherty wagon was also called) and its occupants apart.

doughface ˈdoˌfes, *n.*

1. A false face or mask. Cf. **door face.**

1809 *Cong. Deb.* 23 Feb. 1509 Yes, sir, said he [John Randolph], it may bring us to fighting and to disgrace; it is something like dressing ourselves up in a dough-face and winding sheet to frighten others. **1883** MARK TWAIN *Life on the Miss.* liii. 528 (R.), Those giddy young ladies came tiptoeing into the room where she sat reading at midnight by a lamp. The girl at the head of the file wore a shroud and a dough-face; she crept behind the victim, touched her on the shoulder, and she looked up and screamed, and then fell into convulsions. **1908–9** *D.N.* III. 306 *Dough-face*, n. A false-face or mask, especially a comical or ugly one; also a person wearing such a mask, especially in costume as a mummer. . . . Originally *dough-face* was literally a face made of dough.

2. A northern congressman who did not oppose slavery in the South and its extension; a northerner who favored the South during the Civil War period. Now *hist.* Cf. **Northern doughface.**

[**1820** *New Brunswick Times* 13 April (Th.), [John Randolph of Roanoke] said, 'I knew these would give way. They were scared at their dough faces. . . . We had them.'] **1830** *Boston Transcript* 6 Dec. 2/3 To detach Louisiana from the American System party, the protecting duty will be repealed, if the anti-tariff party can get enough dough faces to join them. **1879** *Chi. Tribune* 4 Feb. 4/4 Gen. Bragg, of Wisconsin, a Democrat, who hasn't much the appearance of a dough-face, . . . said he was opposed to the payment of Southern Rebel claims. **1941** BUCKMASTER *Let My People Go* 167 Would the dough-faces, the Northern lovers of the slavocracy, bow—bow and vote as the South told them?

transf. **1949** *Chi. Tribune* 2 Jan. I. 1/1 The modern doughfaces are American men with European principles.

b. Also, app. by confusion, **doeface.** *Obs.*

1848 *R.I. Words* (Bartlett MS), Doeface in allusion to the female deer—which is frightened at her own shadow. **1883** F. H. BRADBURN *Memorial G. Bradburn* 134 Randolph spelled the word D-O-E-face, in allusion to the timid, startled looks of that animal. **1888** *N. & Q.* II. 34 John Randolph is also quoted as having called the 'baser sort of Northern demagogues,' 'doefaces.'

3. dough-faced, *a.* having the characteristics of a dough-face (sense **2.**). *Obs.*

1841 *Loco-Foco* (Chester, Pa.) 17 April 4/1 Those *dough faced* democrats, . . . in their anxiety to please their *southern brethren*, have overthrown the party, and incurred the scorn and contempt of those whom they most desired to please. **1859** MACKAY *Tour* II. 106 But after all, it is not so much the fault of Baltimore or of America as of the dough-faced editors.

Hence **doughfac(e)ism, doughfacing.** *Obs.*

1849 K. C. SNODGRASS *Letter* (B. '59), [If] the people of the free States . . . are firm, the doughfacism of their representatives will be cured. **1855** *N.Y. Herald* 30 Nov. 4/3 Now, a similar rule may be sooner adopted; but unless the game of 'doughfacing' shall be more rife than we believe it to be, no choice will be easily or speedily effected without such a rule. **1879** *Chi. Tribune* 7 Feb. 4/4 His chief competitor in this style of business appears to be Townshend, from Illinois, whose dirty doughfaceism received a fitting rebuke from the Townsend without an 'h' from New York.

***Douglas**, *n.*[1]

1. *attrib.* Designating a follower of, or with reference to, Stephen A. Douglas (1813–61), who, by opposing the admission of Kansas as a slave state, caused a split in the Democratic party of his time.

1855 *N.Y. Wkly. Tribune* 13 Jan. 4/5 The *Council Bluffs Bugle*, a Douglas print, groans dreadfully over the result. **1855** *N.Y. Tribune* 31 Dec. 5/6 Is this the application the Douglas men of Kansas make of the main principle of the Kansas-Nebraska bill?

b. Also **Douglasism, -ite.** *Obs.*

1855 *N.Y. Wkly. Tribune* 27 Jan. 1/6 The State Senate (which contains a Douglasite majority) have several times postponed the election for U.S. Senator. *Ib.*, 17 Feb. 4/6 Douglasism has been already discarded by the Illinois Democracy. **1861** *Charleston* (S.C.) *Mercury* 19 Feb. 1/5 The most rabid Whigs and Douglasites . . . hate the Democrats so fiercely that to triumph over them they would almost be ready to see Virginia sink into the arms of Abolitionism.

2. Douglas Democrat, a Democrat who supported Stephen A. Douglas.

1856 *N.Y. Herald* 8 Jan. 3/5 The Douglas democrats have got rather used up. **1880** TOURGEE *Bricks* 352 His father had been what was termed a 'Douglas Democrat.'

***Douglas**, *n.*[2] [David *Douglas* (1798–1834), a Scottish botanical explorer of the Northwest.] In combs.: (1) **Douglas fir,** the red fir or Oregon pine, also attrib.; (2) **pine,** =prec.; (3) **spirea,** a showy species of spirea, *S. douglasi*, with handsome whitened leaves, growing in the Pacific states; (4) **spruce,** =**Douglas fir;** (5) **squirrel,** a species of ground squirrel, *Otospermophilus grammurus douglasi*, found in the Pacific states.

(1) **1884** SARGENT *Rep. Forests* 209 *Pseudotsuga Douglasii* . . . Red Fir. Yellow Fir. Oregon Pine. Douglass Fir. **1948** *Mt. Morris* (Ill.) *Index* 24 Dec. 1/3 The huge Douglas fir Christmas tree presents a festive appearance. — (2) **1868** WHYMPER *Alaska* 44 Where the Douglas pine, spruce, and hemlock had grown under favourable circumstances, the place resembled a beautiful park. **1945** SERVICE *Ploughman* 156 The shack stood in a clearing, engulfed by Douglas pines three hundred feet high. — (3) **1879** MUIR in *Scribner's Mo.* Jan. 415/2 The white-flowered Douglass spirea and dwarf evergreen oak form graceful fringes along the narrower seams [of the rock]. **1942** VAN DERSAL *Ornamental Amer. Shrubs* 224 Closely allied to the Douglas spiraea is the hardhack spiraea or steeplebush of the East. — (4) **1856** WHIPPLE *Explor. Ry. Route* I. 79 *Douglass spruce*, which is also abundant upon the sides of the mountains, would afford a better material for railroad ties. **1947** PEATTIE *Sierra Nevada* 148 It is called Douglas fir or Douglas spruce indiscriminately.

(5) **1869** MUIR *First Summer in Sierra* (1911) 24 The yellow pine cones . . . are held upside down on the ground by the Douglas squirrel, and turned around gradually until stripped, while he sits usually with his back to a tree, probably for safety. **1947** *Sierra Club Bul.* May 93 We occasionally ran on to Douglas squirrels in the woods—and filled them with frantic terror.

***douse**, *n.* (See quot.) *Obs.* — **1856** OLMSTED *Slave States* 477 In the Carolina mills the product [of rice] is divided into 'prime,' 'middling,' (broken), 'small' or 'chits,' and 'flour' or 'douse.'

***dove**, *n.* In combs.: (1) **dove marble,** (see first quot.); (2) **party,** (see quot.), *rare;* (3) ***tailing,** (see quot. 1848), *obs.*

(1) [**1872** *Vt. Bd. Agric. Rep.* 667 The first [marble] to be mentioned is the 'Dove,' it being of a dove color, which gave it the name.] *Ib.* 675 The first mills at Swanton were wholly employed in the manufacture of grave-stones from the dove-marble. — (2) **1886** *Harper's Mag.*

Dec. 159/2 The 'dove parties,' composed of the wives of cabinet officers and foreign ministers, . . . were exceedingly lively and popular. — **(3) 1848** RUXTON *Adventures* 310 It is unnecessary to say that 'dovetailing' is the process of mutually accommodating each other's legs followed by stage-coach and omnibus passengers. **1864** *Placerville* (Calif.) *D. News* 21 May, General dovetailing process of limbs, a doubling and cramping of feet, damaging corns and soiling the bootblack's polish, doors fastened, whip cracks, bump, swing, juggle, a shake and away we go.

As the last term in **Carolina, common, ground, Inca, mourning, prairie, scaled, turtle, white-winged, wild, Zenaida dove.**

∗ **Dover,** *n.* The trade-mark name of a kitchen utensil for beating eggs of a type orig. (*c*1866) manufactured at Dover, N.H. In full **Dover egg beater.**

1882–3 KNIGHT *Mech. Dict.* 293/1 The Dover egg-beater has two revolving flat loops on different shafts, each passing alternately inside the other, gathering the egg towards the center of the bowl and whirling it in cross currents. **1909** F. M. FARMER *Boston Cook Book* 590 Never put cogs of a Dover Egg-beater in water. **1945** *This Week Mag.* 11 Aug. 13 To the juice of two oranges, add the yolk of one egg and one teaspoon of honey, beat with a Dover.

dowdy ˈdaʊdɪ, *n.* Short for **apple dowdy, pandowdy.** — **1936** LUTES *Country Kitchen* 37 The dowdy would probably reconcile itself to a glass baking dish if it had to.

dower Negro. A Negro slave given to a bride as a dowry or part of a dowry, or owned by her at the time of her marriage. *Obs.* — **1760** WASHINGTON *Diaries* I. 118, 4 negroes lost this Winter; viz. 3 Dower Negroes. **1860** ABBOTT *South & North* 110 To emancipate them [*sc.* the slaves] during her life would . . . be attended with . . . difficulties, on account of their mixture by marriage with the dower negroes.

Dowieism ˈdaʊɪ·ɪzəm, *n.* [John Alexander *Dowie* (1848–1907).] The doctrines of the Christian Catholic Church of Zion City, Ill., in which stress is placed upon communal life, faith-healing, and abstinence. — **1901** *Chi. Tribune* 9 June, Having called in vain for weeks for 'Dr.' John Alexander Dowie to come to her bedside and pray for her, Miss Sarah Sloan, the seventh victim of Dowieism within the last few weeks, died at her rooms in the Zion boarding house. **1903** *N.Y. Times* 17 Oct. 8 Dowieism, wherever it manifests itself, is a direct incitement to breach of the peace, for every one of its peculiar theories and assertions offends any right-thinking man or woman.

Dowieite ˈdaʊɪ·aɪt, *n.* A believer in Dowieism. — **1903** *N.Y. Ev. Post* 14 Oct. 6 The State Court of Appeals has handed down a decision condemning a Dowieite for letting his child die for lack of medical attendance. **1947** *Christian Cent.* 8 Oct. 1210/1 There already *is* a Christian Catholic Church—the 'communistic' sect also known as 'Dowieites' or 'Zionites.' Founded in 1893 or 1896 (my reference sources differ), the group made its headquarters in Chicago until Zion City, Ill., was established.

dowitcher ˈdaʊ·ɪtʃɚ, *n.* [Iroquoian. Cf. Mohawk and Cayuga *tawis,* Onondaga *tawish.*] A long-billed snipe resembling a sand-piper, the *Limnodromus griseus.* Cf. **bastard dowitcher.**

1841 *Spirit of Times* 9 Jan. 529/3 [The music would] rise and rise . . . like the mellow attenuated trill of the soaring dowitcher. **1917** *Birds of Amer.* I. 230 The Dowitcher's regular food includes several species of destructive grasshoppers. **1948** *Atlantic Mo.* Jan. 108/2 Other handles are dowitchers, coots, and curlews, all cleanly cut and convincing.

∗ **down,** *n.* In football, the termination of a period during which a team attempts to advance the ball; the attempt itself or its duration.

1882 in P. H. DAVIS *Football* (1911) 470 They must give up the ball to the other side at the spot where the fourth down was made. **1914** *Collier's* 10 Jan. I. 9/1 In the old game a team had to gain five yards in three downs—one and two-thirds yards to the down. **1948** *Democrat* 4 Nov. 1/4 Frisco City . . . rang up four first downs in succession.

b. (See quot.) *Obs.*

1893 W. CAMP *College Sports* 96 The runner [when he is tackled] must say 'Down,' and the ball is then put on the ground for a scrimmage.

∗ **down,** *a., adv.,* and *prep.* In combs.: (1) **down below,** (see quot. and cf. **outside 1.**); (2) **boat,** a boat on its way downstream; (3) **brakes,** on a railroad train, a signal for brakes to be applied; (4) **cellar,** in or into a cellar; (5) **country,** (see quot. *a*1870); (6) **curve,** (see quot. and cf. **down shoot**); (7) **Down East,** see as a main entry; (8) **freight,** freight or a freight train going in a direction regarded as "down"; (9) **grade,** a downward slope, also fig.; (10) **-hill-of-life,** (see quots.); (11) **log,** the trunk of a tree which has been cut or blown down; (12) **payment,** the initial payment on an instalment purchase; (13) **row,** (see quot. 1886); (14) **shoot,** in baseball, a pitched ball that curves suddenly downward before reaching the batter, a "drop," cf. **down curve;** (15) **south,** in or into the southern states; (16) **state,** that part of a state, esp. a southern part, outside of some dominant large city, also **down-stater;** (17) **timber,** timber that has been blown down; (18) ∗ **town,** see as a main entry.

(1) 1902 McKEE *Land of Nome* 149 It was near this same island that the *Lane,* our transport of last year, struck a reef on her way 'down below' (Nome lingo for Washington, Oregon, or California) a month later. — **(2) 1857** WILLIS *Convalescent* 154 The 'down-boat' touches at the same place to bring us back to Newburgh. — **(3) 1875** *Chi. Tribune* 8 July 2/5 A brakeman . . . was killed at his post, while responding, it is said, to the warning whistle of 'down brakes.' **1904** HARBEN *Georgians* 226 When the engine begun to whistle down-brakes. — **(4) 1805** *Pocumtuc Housewife* (1906) 47 Put it in the soap-grease barrel down cellar. **1947** PAUL *Linden* 131, I rushed down-cellar to get our lantern.

(5) 1823 COOPER *Pioneers* v, To them the road that made the most rapid approaches to the condition of the old, or, as they expressed it, the down countries, was the most pleasant. ***a*1870** CHIPMAN *Notes on Bartlett* 129 *Down-Country.* Used in the interior to denote on or toward the seaboard; occasionally, the seaboard, or the land nearer a river's mouth. — **(6) 1887** *Outing* May 99/2 The ball . . . would be forced downward more rapidly than the force of gravity alone would draw it, resulting in the down curve, or drop ball. — **(8) 1829** in *Williams' N.Y. Ann. Reg. 1830* 121 The whole quantity of down freight . . . that was conveyed on the Erie and Champlain Canals . . . in the year 1829, amounts to seventy-five thousand, five hundred tons. **1864** NICHOLS *Amer. Life* I. 154 Whisky used to make up a large portion of the down freight of the Ohio and Mississippi steamers. **1947** BEEBE *Mixed Train Dly.* 67 The up engine usually remains working freight overnight at Martinsville before powering the down freight the next morning. — **(9) 1858** *Harper's Wkly.* 31 July 483 A train thunders along a down-grade around a curve . . . at the rate of forty miles an hour. **1872** *Newton Kansan* 19 Sep. 4/3 Greeleyism has struck the down grade. **1948** *Chi. Tribune* 25 Jan. 26/2 He could pick up anyone from the dust and raise her to the stars, but for all that he was an old man—on the downgrade.

(10) 1894 *Amer. Folk-Lore* VII. 94 *Lysimachia nummularia* . . . down-hill-of-life, Lincolnton, N.C. **1931** CLUTE *Plants* 134 A species of loosestrife (*Lysimachia nummularia*) is called down-hill-of-life. — **(11) 1928** *Sat. Ev. Post* 10 March 28/2 His rifle was reclining against a down log ten feet away. — **(12) 1930** *San Antonio* (Texas) *Light* 31 Jan. 14/6 Small down payment, balance like rent. — **(13) 1886** P. G. EBBUTT *Emigrant Life* 180 [In corn harvesting] one man takes three rows on one side of the waggon, and another three rows on the other, while a third takes the 'down row,' that is, the row broken down by the waggons, and assists a bit on either side as required. **1946** WILSON *Fidelity* 159 A similar experience came when I took the 'down row' in gathering corn. — **(14) 1885** CHADWICK *Art of Pitching* 14 It is essential to change the direction of the curve . . . from an 'up-shoot' to a 'down-shoot.'

(15) 1834 DAVIS *Lett. J. Downing* 25 Though I tell'd 'em down south my father was an Irishman, . . . I am as clear a Yankee . . . as the Major himself. **1905** A. H. RICE *Sandy* 23, I lived down South, clean off the track of ever'thing. — **(16) 1909** *Dly. Maroon* (Chi.) 2 Oct. 1/4 Others who have already attracted attention . . . are . . . Springer, a husky full-back from down-state; . . . and many others. *Ib.* 12 Oct. 1/1 The down-staters have always supported their men loyally. **1947** *Chi. Tribune* 22 June II. 5/6, I have had a great many letters from downstaters who want to correct the faults, but don't know how to do it. — **(17) 1881** STODDARD *E. Hardery* 263 There was plenty of old 'down timber' to be cut up, and cleared away. **1948** *Sierra Club Bul.* March 111 The next day brought rugged packing—first up interminable slopes of down timber, where the small logs repeatedly broke under the weight of man and pack.

b. In colloq. phrases: (1) *down and out,* utterly used up or done for, one who is in this condition; (2) *down-and-outer,* one who is down and out; (3) *down* (*the*) *river,* see ∗ **river.**

(1) 1904 O. HENRY *Heart of West* 129 Then he delivered the good Saxon knock-out blow . . . and Garcia was down and out. **1917** JEFFERY FARNOL *Definite Object* vi. 49, I don't want 'em to think I'm floatin' around with a down-an'-out from Battyville. **1948** CHAPLIN *Wobbly* 143 The Durst brothers . . . made a practice of advertising extensively for help among the down-and-out in city slums and remote agricultural communities. — **(2) 1909** *Springfield W. Republican* 4 Mar. 2 Compliments from political enemies follow the most distinguished down-and-outer of his day into the seclusion of private life. **1948** *Sat. Review* 17 July 25/1 We were ushered into a hall sprinkled with down-and-outers.

As the last term in **away, back, blow, break, bucking, buckle, call, calling, cash, cave, close, cut, daylight, fall, hands, hoe, knock, lock, look, low, moon, pinch, prairie, put, putting,**

rake-, scamper, set, shake, show, slipper, straight up-and-, sugaring, sun, throw, turn, way, wet down.

* **down,** *v.*

1. *tr.* To swallow. *Colloq.*

1860 HOLMES *Professor* 52 Give a fellah a fo' penny bun in the mornin', an' he downs the whole of it. **1922** MULFORD *Tex* 145 Silently he poured out a drink and downed it mechanically.

2. In football, to bring down or stop (an opponent) by tackling.

1887 *Cent. Mag.* XXXIV. 892/1 [He] endeavors to carry the ball as far as possible into the enemy's territory before he's tackled and 'downed.'

3. *intr.* To die down. *Colloq.*

1924 W. M. RAINE *Troubled Waters* xvii. 180 The rumour would not down that one of the prisoners had turned State's evidence.

Down East. Also **down east.**

1. (See quot. 1945.)

1819–27 J. BERNARD *Retrosp.* 240 He had lately quitted 'Down East,' and was coming South to 'explore' a brother, hid away somewhere among the niggers in Virginny. **1839** *Boston Transcript* 26 Feb. 1/2 As I am always called Squire Smith round in these parts, I want you to direct it to John Smith, Esquire, Smithville, Down East, and it will come to me straight as a hair. **1945** COLCORD *Sea Lang.* 68 *Down East.* A general term for Maine and the Maritime Provinces of Canada. People from these parts 'go up' to Boston and return 'down home.' A 'down-easter' may be either a person or a vessel hailing from that region.

b. Language such as is used Down East. Hence **down-Eastism,** a term characteristic of this speech.

1863 NORTON *Army Letters* 159, I wish I could write their pronunciation of [the word] South; it beats all the down-east you ever heard of. **1868** *Terr. Enterprise* (Virginia, Nev.) 14 April 3/2 Yankee Plummer, disseminator of down-eastisms, . . . will give [a] . . . button-distressing entertainment this evening at the Gold Hill Theatre. **1882** DALY *Our Eng. Friend* (1884) 19, I don't consider them any worse than our own Down-Eastisms. I prefer 'jolly' to scrumptious any time o' day. **1942** RICH *We Took to Woods* (1948) 38 What the guide said he probably lifted from Shirer's book, but translated into Down East, it wouldn't be recognizable.

2. Often used attrib. or as an adj. in the sense: Of or pertaining to, dwelling or being "Down East."

1830 S. SMITH *Major Downing* 1 Hoping that some of the down-east antiquaries and genealogists will favour the world with the information desired. **1900** SMITHWICK *Evolution of a State* 210 He was a genuine down-east Yankee. **1946** *New Yorker* 28 Dec. 1 We're down-east folks, with our own down-east language.

3. Also as an adv.: In the region known as "Down East."

1829 *Mass. Spy* 25 Nov. (Th.), 'Where the deuce is Dennis?' 'Oh, down east.' **1883** in T. HUTCHINSON *Diary & Lett.* II. 438 He went by steamer from Boston down east to the Penobscot River.

b. Also in a mild imprecation.

1891 WILKINS *N. Eng. Nun* 124 I'd see him Down East first.

4. Down-Easter, a native of Down East.

1819–27 J. BERNARD *Retrosp.* 37 This curious class of mammalia, the 'Down-Easter' as it is often called, is divisible into three species—the swapper, the jobber, and the pedler, all agreeing in one grand characteristic—love of prey. **1881** BUEL *Border Outlaws* 167 A Mr. Taylor, of Boston, who had the unmistakable appearance of a 'down easter,' was persecuted. **1945** *Reader's Digest* July 25/1 A down-Easter sat beside me on the grass where I was untangling my fish line.

transf. **1835** INGRAHAM *South-West* I. xv. 161 There were . . . miserable-looking sloops and schooners, compared to which, our 'down easters' are packet ships.

Also **Down Eastern,** *a.*, **Down-Easterner,** *n.*

1851 NORTHALL *Curtain* 165 This magnificent place is built in the eastern style—we don't mean the down-eastern style, but the oriental. **1947** PERRY *Cities of America* 129 None but genuine Down-Easterners would ever have dreamed of offering so little for so much.

downer 'daʊnɚ, *n. W.* A cow that, after a drought or hard winter, is too weak to stand (see also quot. 1913). *Colloq.* See also **low-downer, sun-downer.**

1913 W. C. BARNES *Western Grazing Grounds* 381 Downers.—Cattle and other stock which have been down in the cars during shipment and arrive at the stockyards bruised, dirty and unfit for sale as beef. **1937** HENDRIX *West Texas Today* 7 (Adams), There was an old cowman down in the Brady country a good many years ago, who got all his 'downers' up one frosty morning, and, while they were steadying down, rode over the hill to skin one he felt pretty sure had died during the night.

Downingia daʊ'nɪndʒɪə, *n.* [Named after Andrew Jackson *Downing* (1815–52), a N.Y. pomologist and landscape gardener.] (See quot. 1889.) — **1889** *Cent.* 1751/2 Downingia. . . . A small lobeliaceous genus of Californian plants, consisting of low annuals with showy blue and white flowers. They are occasionally cultivated for ornament. **1928** BAILEY *Cyclo. Horticulture* 1068/1 Downingia . . . Low herbs, much branched, sometimes grown as garden annuals.

* **downtown,** *adv., a.,* and *n.*

1. *n.* The main business section of a town or city.

1851 MELVILLE *Moby Dick* i. 1 [The] extreme down-town of [New York City] is the battery. **1853** J. W. BOND *Minnesota* 139 The central part of the town . . . is not so closely built up as the thickly-settled parts of either 'up town' or 'down town.' **1923** WATTS *L. Nichols* 166 Our 'down-town' is precisely like all the rest of the 'down-towns' in the United States!

b. (See quot.) *Rare.*

1856 GOODRICH *Recoll.* I. 139 [A suburb of a Conn. village] constituted in fact what was called *Down-town,* in distinction from the more eastern and northern section, called *Up-town.*

c. *collect.* Downtowners. *Rare.*

1905 *N.Y. Ev. Post* 4 Mar. 5 One of the diversions of downtown yesterday was watching the sure movements of a steeplejack.

2. *a.* Located in the main business part of a town or city.

1836 HONE *Diary* I. 200 This, at least, is the opinion of the best judges of the value of down-town property. **1883** *Harper's Mag.* Nov. 944/2 In the lobby of a down-town hotel. **1916** S. ANDERSON *Windy McPherson's Son* 254 When he awoke and shaved he went out into the street and to another down-town club. **1944** *Newsweek* 25 Dec. 66/2 Vanderbilt University holds down-town property in Nashville.

b. Of persons: Employed or engaged in business downtown.

1852 *Harper's Mag.* V. 413/2 The down-town men wear an air of *ennui,* and slip uneasily through the brick and mortar labyrinths of Maiden-lane and of John-street. **1909** O. HENRY *Options* 67 He was a down-town broker.

c. Leading to or traversing the main business section of a town or city.

1894 WARNER *Golden House* xxiv, Jack was hurrying to catch the downtown car.

3. *adv.* In or toward the principal business section of a town or city.

1835 *S. Lit. Messenger* IV. 197/1 The Union, Bell, Columbian, and Earley's, are justly quite popular down town. **1898** P. L. FORD *Hon. Peter Stirling* 196 He went down-town and called on an insurance company. **1948** *Chesterton* (Ind.) *Tribune* 28 Oct. 1/7 Charlie formerly had a barber shop down town which he sold because of ill health.

4. downtowner, one who lives in or frequents the downtown part of a city.

1830 WATSON *Philadelphia* 244 They were the Achilles and the Patrocles of the 'downtowners.' **1849** G. G. FOSTER *N.Y in Slices* 67 A regular down-towner surveys the kitchen with his nose as he comes up-stairs. **1887** *Courier-Journal* 8 May 12/5 Jay Gould has set down-towners to eating snails.

5. down-townwards, down-towny, (see quots.). *Rare.*

1871 HOWELLS *Wedding Journey* ii. 47 Up to the time of their getting into one of these phantasmal cars for the return down-townwards they had kept up a show of talk. **1889** FARMER 213/1 *Down-towny,* not good 'form,' or *à la mode*—what in the miserable puny fashionable cant of the day is dubbed as 'vulgar,' by men and women who have yet to learn the ABC of the ethics of the new Democracy.

* **downy,** *a.*

1. *absol.* =**downy woodpecker.**

1884 *Cent. Mag.* Dec. 222 The high-hole appears to drum more promiscuously than does downy. **1946** POUGH *Eastern Land Birds* 46 Downys are commonest in farm country with scattered trees and small wood lots.

2. downy hickory, (see quot.). *Obs.*

1846 J. W. ABERT in Emory *Military Reconn.* 387 Here we noticed the white hickory, or downy hickory.

3. downy woodpecker, a small American woodpecker or sapsucker, *Dryobates pubescens.*

1808 WILSON *Ornithology* I. 153 [The] Downy Woodpecker, *Picus Pubescens,* . . . is the smallest of our Woodpeckers. **1871** BURROUGHS *Wake-Robin* (1886) 129, I climbed up to the nest of the downy woodpecker. **1948** *Pacific Discovery* March–April 18/1 A harsh *spickl* note tells of a downy woodpecker in the neighborhood.

* **drabble,** *n.* A wet mass. *Rare.* — **1893** THANET *Stories Western Town* 3 There was a drabble of dead leaves on the sidewalk.

* **draft,** *n.* Also **draught.**

1. A narrow valley or ravine. *Colloq.*

1655 in *Amer. Sp.* XV. 173/1 Bounding on a draught of Tristrum Nasworthy. **1756** *Lett. to Washington* I. 259 They could only discover their Tracts at the Draughts of the Mountain where the Ground was Soft. **1894** *Harper's Mag.* LXXXIX. 883/1 Now you . . . climb up and down a never-ending succession of ridges and 'drafts,' as the ravines are called. **1928** in *Amer. Sp.* XV. (1940) 173/1 There is a little valley, or low-lying land extending through the Harper and Farror properties to South River. This section was called a 'Draft.'

2. A tributary stream or branch. *Colloq.*

1731 *Md. Hist. Mag.* XIX. 192, I have now ten thousand Acres of Warrant located on the Creeks called Conawago Codoras & their Draughts on Susquehanna. **1742** *Md. Hist. Mag.* XX. 182 When we would Trace the fountain head of a River we follow the Greatest Longest Branches & Drafts. **1807** GASS *Jrnl.* 101 Captain Clarke and his party returned, having found a tolerable good road except where some draughts crossed it.

3. *Baseball.* (See quot. 1947.) Usu. attrib.

1889 *Sporting Life* (Phila.) 24 July 1/6 A. J. Reach, President of the Philadelphia Base Ball Club, endorses A. G. Spalding's proposed draft system. **1910** *Amer. Mag.* Nov. 91/2 Only two players may be taken by draft from some clubs. **1947** *Time* 8 Sep. 2/3 The majors have kept a tight hold on the P[acific] C[oast] L[eague] through the draft law, which forces the clubs to sell their stars or risk having them drafted at season's end for a niggling $10,000. **1948** *Chi. Tribune* 27 Mar. II. 1/5 The Sox are cluttered with raffle, or draft players more than any others and passing them along to farm clubs.

4. draft riots, (see quot. 1888). Now *hist.*

1877 HEDLEY *Sketches of Great Riots* 17 The immediate cause, however, of my taking up the subject, was a request from some of the chief actors in putting down the Draft Riots of 1863, to write a history of them. **1888** M. LANE in *America* 4 Oct. 15 *Draft-Riots.*—These occurred in New York City in 1863. Congress had passed a conscription act, by which all able-bodied citizens between the ages of twenty and forty-five were liable to draft. When the first draft was actually attempted under this law a vigorous howl was made and the rabble resisted the draft, attacked the police. . . . The riots occurred July 14, 1863. **1946** ADAMS *Album Amer. Hist.* III. 152 (*caption*), Destruction of the Provost Marshall's office in New York City during the draft riots of July, 1863.

As the last term in **bank, sight, time draft.**

***draft,** *v.tr.* To force, as it were, (a reluctant or allegedly reluctant person) to accede to the reputed needs of the situation and become a candidate for office. — **1927** *N.Y. Time* 20 May 18/1 If you are drafted by a great party, how can you oppose an imperious general will? **1948** *Chickasha* (Okla.) *D. Express* 4 July 1/1 Nevertheless he could be drafted, if a definite draft movement took place at Philadelphia.

draftee ˌdræfˈti, *n.* One who is drafted or conscripted for military service.

1866 F. KIRKLAND *Bk. Anecdotes* 162 The young draftee appeared a little bewildered. **1930** MARK SULLIVAN *Our Times*, iii, 330 When the Great War combed the South for young men, from 12 to 33 per cent of the draftees were found to have the disease. **1948** *L.A. Times* 30 July 8/2 Each draftee will receive eight weeks basic military training after he has been processed and assigned.

* **drag,** *n.*

1. (See quot.) *Obs.*

1813 *Niles' Reg.* V. Add. A. 11/2 He had invented several ways of conveying wheat . . . to wit, by means of a spiral screw, by a band revolving round pullies or rollers, with blocks fastened on the band, which he called a drag [etc.].

2. *W.* (See quot. 1904.)

*a***1861** WINTHROP *John Brent* viii. 88 Relieved from their drags, the herd frisked away with unwieldy gambolling. **1904** STEEDMAN *Bucking the Sagebrush* 105 The tail end of a herd is called the 'drag.' **1948** ROLLINSON *Wyo. Cattle Trails* 108 Now our former footsore drags were feeling stronger, and since we were away from lava rock, their hoofs became less troublesome.

transf. and *attrib.* **1920** HUNTER *Trail Drivers Texas* I. 211 We cut out four or five of the 'drag yearlings.' **1923** J. H. COOK *On Old Frontier* 117 In all classes of men there were drags—'scrubs'—who managed to ride along by some means on the shoulders of the good ones. **1939** ROLLINS *Gone Haywire* 166 Behind the drag rode still another puncher, the so-called drag man or tail rider.

b. *at drag*, at or beside the drag of a herd.

1942 DALE *Cow Country* 51 In the rear two or three men at 'drag' urged on the lazy, sluggish animals or any that were weak or footsore.

3. Influence, "pull." *Slang.*

1896 G. ADE *Artie* xii. 105 He knows I've got a drag in the precinct.

4. A type of self-propelled dredging machine having its hoisting apparatus on a rotating platform from which there extends a long boom provided with a bucket or scraper. Also **dragline.**

1919 C. F. RAHT *Romance of Davis Mts.* 328 The intake canal was dug with . . . drag lines. **1920** *Outing* Oct. 18/3 Also free were the use of four scoops, two wheel scrapers, . . . two drags, and two plows. **1945** *Dly. Sentinel* (Grand Junction, Colo.) 25 Nov. 14/1 The dragline is being purchased by the directors in anticipation of a more active campaign during the early post-war period for the drainage of Grand valley lands.

5. In special combs.: (1) **drag-driver,** *W.* a cowboy in charge of the drag of a herd; (2) **mill,** (see quot.); (3) ***net,** *transf.* a coördination of efforts to apprehend criminals; (4) **out,** a violent fight, or one who indulges in such a fight, *slang, obs.;* (5) **rope,** *W.* a long rope attached to a horse and allowed to drag behind him; (6) **saw,** (see quot. 1875); (7) **seine,** (see quot. 1890), also **drag-seining.**

(1) **1888** ROOSEVELT in *Cent. Mag.* April 862/1 The rest are in the rear to act as 'drag-drivers' and hurry up the phalanx of reluctant weaklings. **1923** J. H. COOK *On Old Frontier* 123 He did his work well as 'drag driver.' — (2) **1884** KNIGHT *Mech. Dict. Supp.* Drag mill, another name for the arrastra. — (3) **1903** A. H. LEWIS *Boss* 25 Other unfortunates whom the dragnets of the police had brought to these mean shores. **1946** *Chi. D. News* 14 Feb. 3/4 (*headline*), Dragnet Out for G. I. Pair. — (4) *a***1859** *Southern Sketches* (B.), He's a rael stormer, ring clipper, snow belcher, and drag out. **1870** *Nation* 30 June 411/2 We have been forcibly struck with the number of encounters, . . . knock-downs, drag-outs, [etc.] . . . in which the Representative . . . has been engaged.

(5) **1904** O. HENRY *Heart of West* 148 'He bears a drag-rope.' 'Get him and saddle him as quick as you can.' — (6) **1868** *Iowa Agric. Soc. Rep. 1867* 220 Drag-saw, for cutting logs into fire-wood. **1875** KNIGHT 737/2 *Drag-saw*, a cross-cut sawing-machine in which the effective stroke is on the pull motion, not the thrust. **1931** *Randolph Enterprise* (Elkins, W.Va.) 5 March 4/5, 1 Gasoline Engine and drag saw. — (7) **1888** GOODE *Fishes* 179 The method chiefly practiced by the colonists of New England was that of drag-seining. **1890** *Cent.* 5469/3 Drag-seine, a haul-ashore seine.

As the last term in **brush, stone drag.**

* **dragged out.** (See quot. 1848.) *Colloq.*

1831 SMITH *Life & Writings of Downing* 126 (We.), The poor Huntonites seemed to be a most dragged out. **1848** BARTLETT 121 *Dragged out* fatigued; exhausted, worn out with labor. **1872** BRACE *Dangerous Classes N.Y.* 64 A laboring-man . . . returns to his tenement-house after a hard day's work, 'dragged out' and craving excitement.

***dragger,** *n.* A boat used in dragnet fishing. — **1880** *Harper's Mag.* Aug. 340/1 There were in the same way trawlers, draggers, riggers, seiners. **1914** W. D. STEELE *Storm* 29 Dedos . . . was not so heavy by twenty pounds as when the fleet of draggers went out, so nicely slanting.

* **dragon,** *n.* In combs.: (1) * **dragon arum,** (see quots.); (2) * **head,** (see quot. 1931), also * **dragon's head;** (3) * **root,** the jack-in-the-pulpit, *Arisaema triphyllum*, or the green-dragon, *A. dracontium*, also the root of these; (4) * **'s mouth,** (see quot. 1931).

(1) **1850** S. F. COOPER *Rural Hours* 90 We landed and gathered the singular flower of the dragon arum, or Indian turnip, as the country folk call it. **1857** GRAY *Botany* 426 *Arisæma.* Indian Turnip. Dragon-Arum. — (2) **1784** *Mem. Academy* I. 463 *Dracocephalum.* . . . Dragon's Head. . . . By stone walls in Dedham. July. **1931** CLUTE *Plants* 86 There are two dragon-heads (*Dracocephalum parviflorum* and *Prunella vulgaris*)—but of course some dragons are supposed to have two heads—and also a false dragon head (*Physosostegia Virginiana*), a dragon's tail (*Arisaema dracontium*). **1937** PARKS *Valuable Plants Texas* 115 Dragon Head . . . grows in swamps or wet places. — (3) **1784** CUTLER in *Mem. Academy* I. 487 *Arum* . . . Cuckowpint. Dragon-root. Wake-Robin. **1891** *Amer. Folk-Lore* IV. 148 *Arisæma triphyllum* was always Dragon Root, or Lady in a Chaise. New Hampshire. — (4) **1892** *Amer. Folk-Lore* V. 103 *Arethusa bulbosa*, dragon's mouth. Dudley, Mass. **1931** CLUTE *Plants* 86 There are . . . two dragon mouths (*Arethusa bulbosa* and *Antirrhinum majus*).

As the last term in **grand, green dragon.**

dragoness plant. (See quot. 1876.)

1821 *Mass. H.S. Coll.* 2 Ser. IX. 149 Plants, which are indigenous in the township of Middlebury, [Vermont, include] . . . *Dracaena borealis*, Dragoness plant. **1845** LINCOLN *Botany* App. 92/2 *Convallaria borealis*, (wild lily of the valley, dragoness plant). **1876** HOBBS *Bot. Hand-Book* 32 Dragoness plant, Wild lily of the valley, Convallaria borealis.

* **drail,** *n.* A fishhook having a weighted shank for use in trolling, esp. for bluefish.

1634 WOOD *N. Eng. Prospect* (1865) 38 These Macrills are taken with drails which is a long small line, with a lead and hooke at the end of it. **1839** STORER *Mass. Fishes* 58 [The bluefish] is caught from shore by throwing a drail—a hook fixed into a piece of bone or ivory, and sometimes pewter, something in the form of a fish. **1894** *Youth's Companion* 22 Nov. 562/4 A 'bluefish drill' . . . enabled us now to whirl the lines we carried, armed with weighted hooks called 'drails,' skilfully around our heads and then throw them out many fathoms into the ocean.

***drail,** *v. intr.* To fish with a drail. — **1636** *Mass. H.S. Coll.* 4 Ser. VI. 570 Richard Foxwill . . . spake with a boate of ours (draylinge for mackrell). **1887** GOODE *Fisheries* v. I. 300 Capt. James Turner, of Isle au Haut, Maine, . . . assures us that as late as 1815 the fishermen drailed for mackerel.

Hence **drailing,** *n.* — **1873** *U.S. Fish Commissions Rep.* I. 248 The usual method of taking them [*sc.* bluefish] with line is by drailing or trolling. **1888** GOODE *Fishes* 180 It is not known when the custom of drailing for mackerel was first introduced.

***drain,** *n.*

1. A small stream or branch. See also **prairie drain.**

1719 in *Amer. Sp.* XV. 173/2 Down the sd. Meadow side to the great drean thereof then down the said drean to the River. **1770** G. WASHINGTON *Diaries* (1925) I. 442 Till one gets far enough from the River to head the little runs and drains that comes through the Hills. **1836** IRVING *Astoria* II. 154 About noon, the travellers reached the drains and brooks that formed the head-waters of the river.

2. (See quot.)

1888 *Amer. Folk-Lore* I. 78 *Dreen.*—On the island of Mount Desert, the ebb of the tide is spoken of as the *dreen;* the tide is said to *dreen* out, that is, drain out. Dreen for drain was formerly common in Maine and Massachusetts.

3. drainboard, a board or metal plate, usu. grooved, set sloping so as to serve for draining dishes next to a sink, etc.

1905 *Sears Cat.* (ed. 115) 542/2 Nickel plated brass strainer and 24-inch enameled iron drain board with end piece. **1944** LAWRENCE *Narrowing Wind* 9 Resting her hand on the damp wooden drainboard, she stopped and stared into the clean white sink.

***drainage,** *n.* In combs.: (1) **drainage basin,** the area drained by a river and its tributaries; (2) **district,** (see quot. 1914); (3) **system,** an aggregation of means, natural or artificial, whereby an area or city is drained.

(1) **1882** *Nation* 13 July 33/1 The topography of its immediate banks and that of its drainage-basin . . . are fully set forth. **1883** MARK TWAIN *Life on Miss.* i, No other river has so vast a drainage-basin. — (2) **1909** *Indian Laws & Tr.* III. 385 Any such drainage district . . . is hereby authorized to assess the cost of reclaiming the tribal lands of the Omaha and Winnebago Indians. **1914** *Cyclo. Amer. Govt.* III. 242/1 Rural Districts for Other Purposes.—These are sometimes established in particular localities, for carrying out public works which affect several of the regular local districts. Such are drainage districts in Illinois. **1945** *Dly. Sentinel* (Grand Junction, Colo.) 25 Nov. 13/1 Directors of the Grand Valley Drainage district are at this time advertising for bids for the purchase of a dragline machine. — (3) **1865** *Atlantic Mo.* XV. 78 The depurating process . . . lies ready for use in this natural drainage-system. *Ib.* 79 Provided with a totally inadequate drainage-system, operating by a river. **1883** *Cent. Mag.* July 422/2 A proper drainage system shall change all this,—a system which shall include underground sewerage and complete the levee.

***draining,** *n.* **1. draining house,** in sugar refining, a house in which newly-made sugar is allowed to drain or drip. **2. draining loft,** a loft in which newly-made sugar drains or drips. — (1) **1833** SILLIMAN *Man. Sugar Cane* 39 It will be necessary, in the first place, to describe the draining house. — (2) **1833** SILLIMAN *Man. Sugar Cane* 84 A portion of the liquor . . . was conducted into the boilers, through pipes from the draining lofts above.

***dram,** *n.* As the last term in **egg, fog, honey dram.**

***drama,** *n.* As the last term in **comedy, equestrian, Ethiopian, horse, leg, tank drama.**

dramatic agent. A theatrical agent. — **1866** WM. DAVIDGE *Footlight Flashes* 58 Some of my professional brethren . . . in America now . . . will recollect with feelings of respect Ben Smythson, the dramatic agent. **1890** BIFF HALL *Turnover Club* 95 In the shape of a letter received the other day by a dramatic agent here in town.

***draught,** see **draft.**

draw drɔ, *n.*[1] A drawer as in a chest or cabinet. *Colloq.*

This shortened pronunciation of "drawer" may not have originated in this country, but at present there is a lack of British evidence of its use.

1692 *Conn. Probate Rec.* I. 463, I giue to Elizabeth Thomson . . . one table with a draue in it. **1748** *N.H. Probate Rec.* III. 565, I give . . . my Chist of draws to my dafter Lidea. **1829** in MACKENZIE *Van Buren* (1846) 170 My original copy [of a letter] . . . got into that celebrated receptacle of Chancery papers, . . . the draw or bushel basket, (I don't know which,) of his venerable predecessor. **1898** WESTCOTT *D. Harum* 143 They're in the draw there.

attrib. **1850** *Rep. Comm. Patents 1849* 263 The destructive tendencies arising from the unequal expansibility of the metal [are] . . . too slight . . . to endanger the soundness and durability of the . . . curtain pins, draw handles, etc.

***draw,** *n.*[2]

1. A section of a bridge that may be raised up or drawn aside; also the opening or passage made when the draw is raised.

1786 *Md. Journal* 3 Nov. (Th.), A draw is placed over the deepest water, for permitting vessels to pass and repass. **1846** *Sci. Amer.* 17 Oct. 29/4 A special train of cars attempted last week to run over the Neponset Bridge (on the Old Colony Railroad) while the draw was up. **1902** LORIMER *Lett. Merchant* 21 Our schooner was passing out through the draw at Buffalo.

attrib. **1813** *Niles' Reg.* V. 208/2 On Friday night last, the draw house, belonging to the Washington Bridge, . . . was consumed by fire. **1883** *Harper's Mag.* Feb. 357/2 The draw-tender . . . saw repeated visions of his death. **1892** *Cong. Rec.* 14 Jan. 312/2 Said bridge . . . shall contain a drawspan giving a clear opening of not less than 300 feet in length.

2. (See quots.)

1855 DAVIS *Farm Bk.* 180 Set out Spanish potatoes about 1½ acre well watered . . . put 1 pint to 1 quart to each slip or draw. **1909** WEBSTER draw. . . . One of the young spring shoots of the sweet potato.

3. The act of drawing a pistol (or revolver) from its holster, usu. in phrases. Also fig. *Colloq.*

1857 T. H. GLADSTONE *Kansas* v. 54 With my hand upon the pistols . . . he didn't stand out long. But I felt pretty bad . . . till I got the draw on him. **1918** MULFORD *Man from Bar-20* 49 Even now Hopalong could beat him on the draw, but barely. **1947** *Chi. Tribune* 22 June (Comics) 9 That old goat may be more agile than I think, and she might beat me to the draw!

4. =**draw poker.** Cf. **draw bluff.**

1857 *Phoenix* (Sacramento) 20 Sep. 3/2 This mongrel, David, recently lost a sum of money, playing 'draw,' with a party of gentlemen. **1924** MCCONNELL *Frontier Law* 35 Night after night and usually every afternoon, were seated a silent group of persons engaged in a game they called 'draw.' **1945** *New Yorker* 14 April 21 'Dealer's choice,' said Kelly. 'Draw or stud. Fifty-cent ante on draw.'

b. In draw poker, the deal after the discard. Also such a deal in other card games (see quot. 1898).

1857 *Spirit of Times* 28 Feb. 414/1, I went in at 'draw,' and came out with 'nary pair' minus the price of two passages. **1898** W. B. DICK *Amer. Hoyle* (ed. 17) 228 [In the game of cinch] after the draw, the card or cards remaining undealt must be placed, face down, on the table. **1946** MOREHEAD & MOTT-SMITH *Penguin Hoyle* 120 The draw is continued until all other players are satisfied.

5. A natural drain or gully, a coulee, a ravine. Also attrib.

1882 BAILLIE-GROHMAN *Camps in Rockies* Among the rough and steep chains of mountain full of 'draws,' 'pockets,' and gulches, . . . the search is anything but easy. **1913** CATHER *My Antonia* 19 There in the sheltered draw-bottom the wind did not blow very hard. **1949** *Pacific Discovery* Jan.–Feb. 7/1 In mid-day we found them bedded along the rimrocks or in the heads of brushy draws.

6. Plains cattle appropriated or stolen. *Rare.* Cf. ***draw,** *v.* **2.**

1887 F. FRANCIS *Saddle & Moccasin* (B. & L.), I could have raised quite a nice bunch of cattle in a twelvemonth. Half the draw was worth something those times!

7. (See quot.) *Obs.*

1892 *Amer. Folk-Lore* V. 236 Draw.—In Tennessee, at a stated time in the year, the school-teachers assemble for 'the draw,' the receiving of their salary, which is graduated to the number of scholars the teacher has.

As the last term in **five card, over, sand, shoulder draw.**

***draw,** *v.*

1. *tr.* To shape or smooth (clapboards, palings, shingles, etc.) with a drawing knife or similar instrument. Cf. **draw-horse.**

1657 *Essex Inst. Coll.* VII. 39/2 The said John is to . . . drawe the clapboards & shoot [*sic*] their edges. **1854** DAVIS *Farm Bk.* 2 This day rain in abundance very nearly all day hands employed in drawing palings shucking corn & grinding. **1891** SLOAN *Fogy Days* 93 It did not take me long to reach my destination and learn that the old man was already out in the woods, drawing shingles.

Hence **drawed board,** a board that has been drawn.

1730 *Md. Hist. Mag.* VIII. 160 To 1200 drawed boards for the same at 3£ the . . . thousand.

2. (See quot.) *Slang. Obs.* Cf. ***draw,** *n.*[2] **6.**

1847 MCCLELLAN *Mexican War Diary* (1917) 39 Murphy . . . was mounted on the '*crittur*' he had '*drawn*,' i.e. stolen in the bushes.

3. In draw poker, to receive from the dealer (a number of cards corresponding to the number discarded).

1856 *Dem. State Journal* (Sacramento) 14 July 2/5 We was playin' draw poker, and one chap drawed to a pair and got a little full! **1880** *Chi. Tribune* 20 May 4/3 But in 'drawing' they failed to better their hand, and there was nothing left for them but to accept the loss or win by bluff. **1891** QUINN *Fools of Fortune* 216 When a hand is complete so that the holder of it can play without drawing to better it, that is called a 'pat' hand.

fig. **1948** *Dly. Ardmoreite* (Ardmore, Okla.) 29 April 5/2 Henry and June Galoob have a pair to draw to in their two small sons, Henry David, 3, and Maurice, 2.

4. To take off (a coat). *Colloq.*

1872 EGGLESTON *End of World* xxiii. 158 'See yer,' said Bill, trying in vain to draw his coat. **1874** —— *Circuit Rider* xiii. 118 Will you give me time to draw my coat?

5. In combs.: (1) ***drawback,** see as a main entry; (2) **bar,** see as a main entry; (3) **bluff,** the name by which poker was known after the introduction of the "draw" (see ***draw,** *n.*² **4. b)** about 1845; (4) ***boy,** a kind of cotton goods made on a loom requiring a boy (or some mechanism) to pull cords for the figure weaving in the cloth, *obs.;* (5) **day,** in the South just after the Civil War, the day upon which rations were distributed by the government to the destitute, *obs.*, cf. **destitute rations;** (6) ***head,** the end of a drawbar, a coupling; (7) **horse,** a bench-like structure upon which a workman sits in drawing shingles, boards, etc. (see **1.** above and cf. **shaving horse**); (8) **poker,** see as a main entry; (9) **rail,** =**drawbar 1;** (10) **slate,** (see quot. 1929), also attrib.; (11) **stitch,** a kind of stitch in sewing; (12) **tub,** (see quot.).

(3) 1858 *S. Lit. Messenger* XXVII. 353/1 Gi hired a horse-racer and faro-banker . . . to . . . play Draw Bluff with his uncle. **1938** ASBURY *Sucker's Prog.* 27 Apparently this important addition made fairly rapid progress in the affections of Poker players—in 1860 a writer said that 'at the present day, what is termed draw bluff is played more extensively, perhaps, than the old way of playing the game.' — **(4) 1765** *Mass. Gazette* 7 Nov. (Th.), Shalloons, Tammies, Drawboys, &c. **1785** *Md. Journal* 20 May (Th.), [Drawboys are included with check and quilting in an advt.]

(5) 1868 *Harper's Mag.* May 794/2 The first Monday of the month, generally known in the South as 'sale day' on account of its customary public auction, acquired the additional title of 'draw day,' because it was used for the issue of rations. — **(6) 1867** *Rep. Comm. Patents 1865* II. 851 Apparatus for Bending and Punching the Frames of Draw-heads for Railway Cars. **1898** HAMBLEN *Gen'l Manager's Story* 25 When the kicked car fetched up, the drawhead, link and all, were driven clear through his body. — **(7) 1845** JUDD *Margaret* I. xvii. 160 Near Hash stands the draw-horse, on which he smooths and squares his shingles. **1888** *Cent. Mag.* XXXVI 84/1 On entering the barn he was surprised to find Barbara sitting on the 'drawhorse' or shaving-bench. — **(9) 1825** *Catawba Journal* 23 Aug., When they arrived within a short distance, the servant alighted to let down a pair of draw rails.

(10) 1929 *Amer. Sp.* IV. 371 Draw slate—This refers to a layer of slate at the roof of the mine. This layer of slate is dangerous because it is quite loose; hence it must be knocked down by the digger before it falls down unexpectedly. **1931** *Randolph Enterprise* (Elkins, W.Va.) 26 March 1/1 The Laughlin mine-post bill, designed to save the lives of West Virginia miners by placing the control of posting in draw-slate mines in the hands of district inspectors. — **(11) 1893** *Chi. Tribune* 26 April 9/5 Daughters of terror-inspiring Apache Chiefs painting daisies on placques and learning the 'draw stitch.' — **(12) 1874** *Vt. Bd. Agric. Rep.* II. 719 The 'sap-gatherer' or 'draw-tub,' as it is called, is a hogshead containing from one hundred to one hundred and fifty gallons.

6. In colloq. and slang phrases: (1) *To draw the rope,* (see quots.), *obs.;* (2) *to draw in the same yoke,* to get married; (3) *to draw stakes,* to pull up stakes *q.v., s.v.* **stake,** *n.;* (4) *to draw to a shoestring and obtain a tanyard,* ?to venture little and gain much, *obs.*

(1) 1841 G. POWERS *Hist. Sketches of Coos* 107 To prevent this, the men would 'draw the rope,' as they termed it; that is, two men would take a rope, one at each end, and pulling from each other until it was nearly straightened, they would then pass through their wheat fields, and brush off the worms from the stalks. [**1919** WILSON *White Indian* 5 We [in Utah *c*1850] kept the hoppers from settling on this patch by running over and over the field with ropes. We used our bed cords to make a rope long enough.] — **(2) 1850** S. WARNER *Wide, Wide World* xl, We have made up our minds to draw in the same yoke. — **(3) 1856** SIMMS *Charlemont* 19 There needs but few suggestions to persuade the forester to draw stakes, and remove his tents. — **(4) 1882** *Cent. Mag.* XXIII. 884/2 He . . . could draw to a shoe-string, as the saying went, and obtain a tan-yard!

For other phrases in which **draw** occurs, see **color line, sight, straw.**

* **drawback,** *n.*

1. App. some kind of trick or performance. *Obs.*

1806 *Mass. Spy* 27 Aug. (Th.), The whole will conclude with . . . ground tumbling, bottle-breaking, and drawbacks, accompanied with red eye and head ache.

2. An amount paid back to compensate for a loss or for any special favor; a refund.

1829 *Mechanics' Press* (Utica, N.Y.) 12 Dec. 38/2 We understand the distillers from Molasses in different parts of the United States intend to petition congress for the return of the drawback so inconsiderately abolished a long time since. **1848** *Gem of Prairie* (Chi.) 30 Dec. 3/3 Drawback should be allowed on goods exported by the Rio Grande. **1860** *Harper's Mag.* Jan. 280/2 Jones . . . declared himself cheated in the trade, and claimed drawbacks for damages. **1883** *Cent. Mag.* XXVI. 397 A quarter of a million a year in advertising. A considerable portion of this sum was pocketed by the [Phila.] officials themselves in the form of drawbacks from the subsidized newspapers.

b. Esp. a refund, in whole or in part, of an oil company's freight rates. Also a subsidy to an oil company paid by a railroad from the freight charges of competing oil companies.

1872 in *50th Congress 1 Sess.* H.R. Rep. No. 3112, 359 [The Pa. R.R. agrees] to pay and allow to the party hereto of the first part . . . the following rebates, and on all [petroleum] transported for other parties drawbacks of like amounts as the rebates from the gross rates. **1872** in TARBELL *Hist. Standard Oil Co.* I. 306 A rebate is made at the time we pay freight; a drawback is made afterward. **1904** TARBELL *Hist. Standard Oil Co.* 55 The company formed special rebates on its oil, and drawbacks on that of other people.

3. A retraction, the act of taking back something said or written.

1863 RANDALL *Pract. Shepherd* 410, I have to make a sad draw-back on these statements.

drawbar ˈdrɔˌbɑr, *n.*

1. A bar or rail in a fence that may be let down or drawn out to afford passage.

1670 *Groton Rec.* 36 Out of that way . . . a sufficient pair of draw barrs to (be) kept and maintained at the end (of) Natha(niel) Lawrences field. **1836** *S. Lit. Messenger* II. 162 On every side I was met by gates, drawbars, and gaps. **1903** STILES *Four Years* 225 Right there abreast of the wagon was an enticing set of draw-bars.

2. A device for coupling railroad cars. Also transf.

1839 *Franklin Inst. Jrnl.* XXIV. 156 The bumpers or elastic cushions are to be attached . . . to the front and rear drawbar. **1918** *Essex Inst. Coll.* LIV. 213 The cars were shackled together by means of the link and pin, with wrought iron draw bars. **1947** *Chi. D. News* 22 Jan. 14/7, I took the suit back to F st. the next day and showed the man where it had pulled a draw-bar.

* **drawing,** *n.*

1. A portion of tea leaves for steeping.

1846 WHITCHER *Bedott P.* v. 53 She sent to borrer somethin or other—a loaf o' bread—or a drawin' o' tea. **1883** *Harper's Mag.* LXVI. 829/2 To these . . . is given the second drawing of tea.

2. (See quot. 1947.) In full **drawing bee.**

*a*1894 R. E. ROBINSON *Danvis Folks* 222 A good excuse was offered by the drawing bee at Daniel Meeker's. *Ib.* 223, I'm goin' over tu the drawin'. **1947** *Life* 10 Feb. 4/1 A 'drawing bee' was in order whenever an early Vermonter wanted to move his house or barn. Thirty yoke of oxen was a common sight as farmers for miles around came to lend their aid.

3. An amount of money taken in, esp. for amortizing a bond issue.

1900 NELSON *A B C Wall St.* 23 A bond, . . . giving such stipulations as to redemption by drawings and sinking funds.

4. In special combs.: (1) **drawing card,** a person or a thing that attracts a crowd, also **drawing feature,** *colloq.;* (2) **room,** a private compartment in a Pullman car, also **drawing-room car, coach.**

(1) 1887 *Courier-Journal* 4 May 6/2 The Falls City team is the best drawing card here of any in the Association. **1895** *N.Y. Dramatic News* 9 Nov. 12/3 The Boomerang Throwers was the principal drawing feature. **1914** *D.N.* IV. 105 Vocational studies have proved a drawing card in our schools. — **(2) 1867** *Com. & Fin. Chron.* V. 347/2. A new and magnificent sleeping and drawing-room car of the Pullman patent has been . . . placed on the Michigan Central road. **1871** BRYANT *MS Letter* 31 May, I have sent to Chicago for a drawing room in one of Pullman's Palace cars. **1944** *Chi. N.W. Timetable* 3

Dec. 26 Minnesota '400' . . . C. and N.W. Parlor Car with Drawing Room Coaches.

*__drawn,__ *a.* In combs.: (1) **drawn bond,** (see quot.); (2) **butter,** melted butter, usu. blended with hot water and flour, also **drawn butter sauce;** (3) **in,** of mats or rugs, made of small cuttings of material drawn through a burlap foundation, see **hooked rug.**

(1) **1900** S. A. NELSON *A B C Wall St.* 26 Drawn bonds are repayable at any time, and cease to bear interest from the date on which they fall due. — (2) **1826** in COMMONS *Doc. Hist.* I. 299 Cod fish and potatoes, with drawn butter and eggs, . . . have presented themselves to our delightful palates. **1876** M. F. HENDERSON *Cooking* 121 Some persons like drawn-butter sauce slightly acid, in which case add a few drops of vinegar or lemon-juice just before serving. **1941** F. M. FARMER *Boston Cook Book* 226 Drawn Butter Sauce. ⅓ cup butter, 3 tablespoons flour [etc.]. — (3) **1901** *Harper's Mag.* CII. 661/2 Her mother had only drawn-in rugs, which Ellen had watched her make. **1917** FREEMAN & KINGSLEY *Alabaster Box* 130 She's the lady that made that beautiful drawn-in mat you bought at the fair.

draw poker. A kind of poker characterized by a discard after the initial round of betting and a subsequent drawing of other cards to fill out the hands, upon which the betting then proceeds.

"Draw poker was evolved out of straight about the year 1845" (1887 *Courier-Journal* 23 Jan. 15/7).

1849 *N.O. Picayune* 3 June 2/4 Might have been amusing himself at 'seven up,' or a little game of 'draw poker.' **1903** *Cin. Enquirer* 3 Jan. 11/4, I reckon they play what they call draw poker. **1947** *Denver Post* 3 March 19/4 The greatest stride toward honesty in our ancient game of draw poker is not ethics. . . . It is the glass table-top.

*__dray,__ *n.* (See quot. 1905.) See also **Boston, Indian dray.**

1902 WHITE *Blazed Trail* 52 A number of pines had been felled out on the ice, cut in logs, and left in expectation of ice thick enough to bear the travoy 'dray.' **1905** *Forestry Bureau. Bul.* No. 61, 36 *Dray,* a single sled used in dragging logs. One end of the log rests upon the sled. (N[orthern] F[orest].)

b. *To dray-haul,* to haul on such a dray.

1902 WHITE *Blazed Trail* vii. 49 When are you going to dray-haul that Norway across Pine Lake?

c. *To dray in* (see quot.).

1905 *Terms Forestry & Logging* 36 *Dray in, to,* to drag logs from the place where they are cut directly to the skidway or landing.

drayage 'dre·ɪdʒ, *n.* The charge or cost of conveyance by dray.

1791 JEFFERSON in *Harper's Mag.* LXX. 535/2 Pd Wm Forbes freight, storage, drayage of 13 hhds tob[acc]o 42.93. **1872** *Ill. Dept. Agric. Trans.* 11 [For] labor and drayage $9.50.

b. Conveyance by a dray or other vehicle.

1880 *California Sup. Court Rep.* LIV. 242 The removal of coal by any of the ordinary vehicles drawn by horses or steam is, in the legal as well as the usual sense of the term, drayage.

draying 'dre·ɪŋ, *n.* Transportation by means of a dray. Also attrib.

1872 *Newton Kansan* 29 Aug. 2/7 (*advt.*), Draying . . . attended to at all hours of the day. **1906** O. HENRY *4 Million* 248 There was a single gentleman connected with the draying business. **1906** ——— *Rolling Stones* 13 You can get me a bunch of draying contracts.

*__dreadnought,__ *n. attrib.* Designating a person who is afraid of nothing. *Rare.* — **1836** IRVING *Astoria* I. 253 They proved to be three Kentucky hunters, of the true 'dreadnought' stamp.

*__dream,__ *n.* **1. dream book,** a book giving alleged significations of dreams. **2. dream line,** (see quot.). *Rare.* See also **dope dream.**

(1) **1803** WEEMS *Letters* II. 272 To that list you may add. . . . Some dream books, dreaming Dictionaries and above all, some Pilg. Progress. **1938** ASBURY *Sucker's Prog.* 94 The most prolific source of numbers for playing Policy, however, was the dream books, which have always been the real bestsellers of American literature. — (2) **1880** *Harper's Mag.* LXI. 351/2 They represented that if a certain . . . salt strip in the centre of the saltfish, called the 'dream line,' were eaten before going to bed, the girl or the young man one was to marry would be indicated by appearing . . . and handing him or her a glass of water.

*__dreamer,__ *n.* **1.** An Indian member of the dreamer cult. **2. dreamer cult,** an Indian religious cult originated in the Northwest *c*1850 and characterized by trances, visions, and Sunday services imitative of those of the Roman Catholic Church.

(1) **1904** *New International Encycl.* XV. 955 About 1870 the matter came to the notice of the Government from the refusal of the 'Dreamers' to come under reservation restrictions. — (2) **1911** CURTIS *No. Amer. Indians* VII. 77 Among the tribes of the Columbia the so-called dreamer cult was in evidence. *Ib.* VIII. 175 The Wishham still practice a form of the so-called 'dreamer' cult, of which the later religion of Smohalla is a well-known development.

*__dredge,__ *n.* As the last term in **clamshell, dipper, gold mining, placer dredge.**

Dred Scott. [Name of a Negro slave.] Used attrib. with *case* and *decision:* Pertaining to a case (Scott *vs.* Sanford), decided by the Supreme Court (7 March, 1857), by which Dred Scott was denied the status of a citizen of the U.S.

"The opinion of Chief Justice Taney was taken as that of the majority. It dealt with two important points: was a negro a citizen of the United States? and was the Missouri compromise law constitutional?" (1913 Bassett *Short Hist. U.S.* 498).

1857 LINCOLN *Works* (1894) I. 228 But we think the Dred Scott decision is erroneous. We know the court that made it has often overruled its own decisions. **1857** *Dly. Union* (Wash., D.C.) 11 March 4/6 The decision in the Dred Scott case has furnished the closing and clinching confirmation needed. **1941** BUCKMASTER *Let My People Go* 253 The Dred Scott decision and the Lecompton Constitution had provided the Republicans with more syllogisms than they needed. **1948** *Pacific Spectator* Summer 256 The Dred Scott decision, with its concurring and dissenting opinions, occupies 240 pages in the court reports.

b. Dred Scott dictum, the second part of the Dred Scott decision, in which the Missouri Compromise was held unconstitutional under the Fifth Amendment. Also fig.

1857 *Lawrence* (Kansas) *Republican* 4 June 2 Fifthly, the Governor adopts the Dred Scott dictum of the Supreme Court. **1883** *Harper's Mag.* Nov. 955/1 Why should editors be put without the pale of humanity? Has there been some Dred Scott dictum against them?

c. Dred-Scottite, one who approved the Dred Scott decision. *Rare.*

1901 CHURCHILL *Crisis* 152 Every Dred-Scottite carried a torch, and many transparencies, so that the very glory of it had turned night into day.

*__drench,__ *v. Tanning. tr.* To soak (hides) in a solution which begins the process of unliming. Also *__drenching,__ *n.* — **1853** MORFIT *Tanning* 413 The skins are . . . drenched for some days in a fermenting bran-bath. **1885** *Harper's Mag.* Jan. 275/2 The mission of the lime, to preserve the hide and loosen the hair, is accomplished, and this washing in warm water is a preparation for 'drenching,' the first process of unliming.

*__dress,__ *n.*

1. A fertilizing dressing for land. *Rare.*

1872 *Vt. Bd. Agric. Rep.* I. 71 Let the soil be stirred to the depth of a few inches several times during the summer, adding a dress of manure after each heavy crop.

2. In combs.: (1) **dressmaker,** *a.* soft, flowing, exhibiting feminine effects; (2) **parade,** (*a*) a formal military parade in which officers and men wear dress uniforms, (*b*) also fig.; (3) **pattern,** (*a*) a fabric design suitable for, or a quantity of material sufficient for, a dress, (*b*) a guide cut from paper for use in making a dress, also attrib.

(1) **1944** *New Yorker* 7 Oct. 54/2 De Pinna's spectator-sports department has a lot to offer in the way of simple clothes softened with a bit of dressmaker detail. **1948** *Family Circle* June 84/3 Vicky dressed without a shower but with great care, choosing the dressmaker suit that could go anywhere and the hat that made her look like a siren. — (2) (*a*) **1847** *Army Regulations* 91 All company-officers and men will be present at dress-parades, unless especially excused, or on some duty incompatible with such attendance. **1890** CUSTER *Following Guidon* v, The bugle's sharp call summoned him to 'drill' or 'dress parade.' (*b*) **1866** in MOORE *Women of War* 136 Such pride as they [i.e., soldiers in a hospital] felt in them [*sc.* dressing-gowns]! . . . They lay in clean and comfortable rows ready for supper 'on dress parade,' they used to say. **1903** *McClure's Mag.* XXII. 101/1 Wait till evening for your dress-parade; then Jack and I can give you our judgment. — (3) (*a*) **1844** *Lexington Observer* 25 Sep. 1/3 Just received . . . striped Chusans, in dress patterns; . . . and domestic Dry Goods. **1869** MARK TWAIN *Innocents* xiii. 121 Dan . . . thought of buying three or four silk dress patterns for presents. (*b*) **1895** *Chi. Tribune* 6 April 1 An Eton dress pattern for 10 cents is displayed on page 16. **1947** *Time* 16 June 88/2 She was reporting on dress-pattern sales in her department. **1948** CHAPLIN *Wobbly* 224 They discovered a *Ladies' Home Journal* dress

pattern, still in its envelope, which the investigators opened up and spread out on the dining-room table.

As the last term in **high water, hoop, party, rifle, second-day, show, store, war dress.**

***dress,** *v.*

1. *tr.* To search through (a place). *Obs.*

1676 *Conn. Rec.* II. 458 We girt the sd swamp and wth English & Indian souldrs drest it, and within 3 hours slew and tooke prisoners 171. *Ib.* 459 Drest Providence neck; and after that ye same daye drest Warwick neck and slew and tooke captiues 67.

2. a. **dress down*, (see quot. 1861). **b.** *dress-parade*, to engage in dress parades. *Rare.*

(a) 1861 *Harper's Mag.* March 460 The order was given [to] . . . fall to splitting and salting [fish]. This operation which is known as 'dressing down,' is performed on hogshead tubs or boards placed between two barrels. **1889** K. MUNROE *Dorymates* 143 Owing to the delay of the morning, the second catch had to be 'dressed down' by lantern-light. — **(b) 1885** CABLE *Dr. Sevier* liv. 398 They're sort o' dress-paradin' in camp, I reckon.

3. In colloq. and slang phrases: (1) *To dress the lady*, (see quot. 1830–45); (2) *to dress to kill*, to attire (oneself) elaborately, also *dressed to death;* (3) *to dress up drunk*, (see quot.), *obs.*

(1) 1828 *Yankee* April 106/2 One of the favorite diversions of our youth—i.e. a game called dress the lady. **1830–45** FURMAN *Customs* 7 There was another favorite diversion called *Dress the lady*. Each player gave what they liked towards dressing her. When the plate was set spinning, an article of the dress was named, and if the person who gave that particular thing, did not catch the plate before it fell, he or she paid a forfeit. — **(2) 1839** *Spirit of Times* 30 Nov. 459/1 The barber was much at ease, dressed to kill. **1844** *N.O. Picayune* 19 Feb. 1/3 The galls wus dressed to death, and seem'd petickelarly in fine sperits. **1943** HOLT *Carver* 23 By late afternoon George was trudging along the city streets, dressed to kill in his Sabbath suit. — **(3) 1859** BARTLETT 131 In the South, *to dress up drunk* . . . [signifies] to over-dress, dress to excess.

dressage ˈdresɪdʒ, *n.* A dressing gown. *Rare.* — **1896** S. HALE *Letters* 297, I slipped on my red dressage . . . and softly stepped into my own room.

***dresser,** *n.* A bureau. Also attrib.

[**1899** *Boston Transcript* 16 Sep. 1 The combination of wardrobe, chiffonniere and bureau makes what our clever French neighbors call a 'Dresser.'] **1900** STOCKTON *Afield & Afloat* 263 'There,' said he, opening a dresser drawer. **1947** *True* Nov. 32/1 In this crib theres just a few pieces of furniture which consist of a bed—washstand . . . a dresser and maybe two chairs.

b. dresser trunk, =**bureau trunk.**

1905 *Sears Cat.* (ed. 115) 895/4 Our $9.95 Dresser Trunk. **1907** *Ib.* (ed. 117) 991/1 We could offer a cheaper dresser trunk, but you would not want it.

***dressing,** *n.* In combs.: (1) **dressing bureau,** a dresser or bureau; (2) ***case,** *(a)* a dressing table, *(b)* a traveling case somewhat like a suitcase; (3) **comb,** a comb for dressing the hair; (4) **sack, sacque,** a loose jacket worn while making one's toilet; (5) **stand,** a dressing table.

(1) 1841 *Spirit of Times* 10 July 218/1 (We.), Dressing bureaus. **1851** CIST *Cincinnati* 204 Fancy dressing bureaus, . . . corner etagers. **1906** MARK TWAIN *Autob.* (1924) (R.), I. 342 He noticed a bottle on his uncle's dressing bureau. — **(2)** *(a)* **1834** *Amer. R.R. Jrnl.* III. 726/1 Fine specimen of Portable Writing Desk and Dressing Case—a diploma. **1899** CHESNUTT *Wife of His Youth* 49 She went to the maple dressing-case, and opened one of the drawers. *(b)* **1838** COOPER *Home as Found* (1873) xxvi. 443 The dressing-case was complicated and large, having several compartments. **1931** FINLEY *Lady of Godey's* 20 And who is not familiar with Godey's reproductions that depict impossible ladies cavorting in voluminous gowns over wall-papers . . . dressing cases, waste-baskets? — **(3)** [**1790** *Pa. Packet* 19 April 4/2 John Murduck . . . has likewise for Sale . . . Dressing, rake, and tail combs.] **1830** *21st Congress* 1 Sess. H.R. State P. No. 16, 11 [An improvement] in the mode of making or manufacturing dressing combs, of wood [was patented by] Nathaniel Bushnell [of] Middletown, Conn. [on] April 14 [1829]. **1878** *Decorum* 287 The flasks can be carried with dressing-combs and the like in the satchel. — **(4) 1865** A. D. WHITNEY *Gayworthys* xxiii. 217 Aunt Rebecca had on a striped dimity 'short-gown,' old-fashioned for 'dressing-sack.' **1916** DU PUY *Uncle Sam* 105 Sprawled across its floor was the form of a disheveled woman, frowsily blonde, shapely, clad in a dressing sacque.

(5) 1886 *Delineator* Nov. 391 On the dressing-stand there should always be kept a small bottle containing camphor.

As the last term in **French, green, hair, Thousand Island dressing.**

dried pumpkin. Pumpkin dried, often by threading small pieces on a long string, for future use.

1821 J. FOWLER *Journal* 15 Camped near the Indeans from them got some dryed meet corn beens and dryed pumpkins. **1850** GARRARD *Wah-To-Yah* iv. 64 Their mules packed with dried pumpkin, corn, etc. **1853** B. F. TAYLOR *Jan. & June* 252 Festoons of dried pumpkin adorned the ceiling. **1947** DOWNEY *Lusty Forefathers* 188 A New Hampshire woman, lacking the usual ingredients, had made her Thanksgiving mince pies out of bear meat and dried pumpkins, sweetened with maple sugar and with a crust of corn meal.

***drift,** *n.*

1. *W.* The movement of cattle wandering aimlessly before a storm or seeking sustenance. Also attrib.

1907 WHITE *Arizona Nights* 112 There were present probably thirty men from the home ranches round about, and twenty representing owners at a distance, here to pick up the strays inevitable to the season's drift. **1929** DOBIE *Vaquero* ix, This trail of mine will lead into immense boneyards that marked the drifts and die-ups of the open range. **1942** DALE *Cow Country* 194 Since there was no fencing, the cattle of these ranchmen . . . mingled with 'drift cattle' from Kansas.

2. In special combs.: (1) **drift diggings,** *pl. W.* in gold mining, placer workings in which mining is carried on by means of tunnels driven from main shafts; (2) **fence,** *W.* a fence built by ranch owners to prevent cattle from going too far from their home range; (3) **mining,** (see quot. and cf. **drift diggings**); (4) **voter,** ?a voter who "drifts" from one precinct to another, *rare;* (5) ***way,** (see quot. 1884); (6) **whale,** a dead whale that floats ashore, *obs.*

(1) 1876 RAYMOND *8th Rep. Mines* 125 During late years hydraulic mining has been carried on in the outer edges of the old drift-diggings. **1913** GOODWIN *As I Remember Them* 203 In a certain district in Placer county, 'drift diggings' were found. — **(2) 1907** S. E. WHITE *Arizona Nights* II. i. 244 Time and again he and . . . Jed Parker had followed the trail of a stampeded bunch of twenty or thirty . . . to the cut drift fences. **1948** *Pacific Discovery* Jan.–Feb. 11/1 In the valley itself ranching developed, and eventually a seven-mile drift fence to protect ranchers from depredations by the herd further restricted it in the winter. — **(3) 1889** *Cent.* 1770/3 Drift-mining . . . is carried on by following . . . the detrital material in the channel of former rivers. — **(4)** *a***1882** WEED *Autobiog.* 478 The Fredenrichs . . . were to look after the 'drift' voters in the Texas portion of the ninth and tenth wards.

(5) 1884 S. HALE *Christmas in Narragansett* xi. 41 All rode down the driftway together to Rocky Point. . . . 'Drift-way' . . . is . . . a cross-road to the sea by which the sea-weed . . . may be hauled up to their homes. **1939** *L.A.* Map 44. — **(6) 1652** *Plymouth Col. Rec.* XI. 61 Euery towne shall pay one barrell of marchantable oyle for euery drift whale cast or brought on shore. **1690** *Plymouth Laws* 232 Whosoever finds . . . any drift Whale found on the stream a mile from the shore [etc.].

As the last term in **Erie, gopher, out, prairie, sea drift.**

***drift,** *v.*

1. *tr.* and *intr.* To cast a fishing net with the current; to allow (the net) to be borne by the current.

1850 KINGSLEY *Diary* 118 We drifted the seine across the river and floated down with the current. *Ib.* 119 They drifted once more and made up the number of 51 salmon.

2. *intr.* With various adverbs: To come, go, or pass in a casual manner; to wander.

1864 MARK TWAIN *Sketches* (1926) 122 If she . . . will have the goodness to wait a little while, she can calculate on my drifting around in the course of an hour or so. **1876** ——— *T. Sawyer* xxxii, A procession of villagers filed through Judge Thatcher's house, . . . and drifted out raining tears all over the place. **1921** PAINE *Comr. Rolling Ocean* 141, I drifted in for a minute to listen to a nigger with a bully voice. **1944** JOHNSON *As I Dare* 261 Later they would come drifting in, weary and repentant.

3. *W.* Of cattle, to move with a storm.

1874 MCCOY *Cattle* 227 It was impossible to hold them in any given bounds. They were driven before the storm, or, in cattle man's parlance, 'drifted' with the gale. **1920** HUNTER *Trail Drivers Texas* I. 213 Cattle drift before wind-driven rain. **1943** HAMNER *Short Grass & Longhorns* 57 The strays . . . drifted before the wind, a pounding, maddened mass, with cowboys vainly drying to stem the motion.

b. *tr.* To drive stock slowly.

1893 *Stand.* 555/3 *Drift*. . . . (U.S.) *Herding*. To drive cattle slowly, letting them feed as they go. **1903** A. ADAMS *Log Cowboy* iv. 51 We drifted them a free clip towards camp. **1920** HUNTER *Trail Drivers Texas* I. 50 They would drift the horses along with two outfits instead of four. **1926** BRANCH *Cowboy & Interpreters* 74 The herd was 'drifted' with very little pushing, grazing as it went.

*drill, *n.*[1]

1. (See quot. 1884.)

1881 INGERSOLL *Oyster Industry* 244 *Drill.*—A small mollusk. **1884** GOODE *Fisheries* I. 696 Under the name of 'Drill' is included a numerous class of univalve mollusks, which are . . . armed with a tongue-ribbon so shaped and so well supplied with flinty teeth that by means of it they can file a round hole through an enemy's shell. **1948** *Nat. Hist.* Dec. 448/2 This is usually done by dredging up the waste material, consisting of sponges, seaweed, shells, drills, and starfish.

2. (See quot.) *Obs.* Cf. ***drill,** *v.*

1898 HAMBLEN *Gen'l Manager's Story* 26 Simmons . . . I soon found, was the conductor of a 'drill,' a switch engine crew.

3. drill press, an upright metal power drill.

1864 WEBSTER 413/3 *Drill-press,* a machine-tool, embodying one or more drills for making holes in metal. **1870** *Rep. Comm. Patents 1868* II. 550/1 *Drill Press.* . . . The parts are so constructed that the feed and drill may be operated by a continuous circular motion of the lever and pawl in one direction. **1948** *Dly. Ardmoreite* (Ardmore, Okla.) 27 June 6/3 Approximately 308 small lots of useful items will be on display, including fishing kits, tool kits, . . . floor type drill press, . . . office furniture and kitchen equipment.

As the last term in **corn, cornstalk, desk, fire, horse, oil, rock drill.**

***drill,** *n.*[2] (See quot.) *Obs.* — **1813** *Niles' Reg.* V. Add. A.15/2 The Drill. Its use is to move any grain, granulated or pulverized substances, from one place to another; it consists, like the elevator, of an endless strap, rope or chain, &c., with little rakes instead of buckets . . . revolving round two pullies or rollers.

***drill,** *v. tr.* (See quots.) *Colloq.* Cf. ***drill,** *n.*[1] **2.** — **1889** *Cent.* 1771 *Drill,* . . . on American railroads, to shift (cars or locomotives) about, or run them back and forth, at a terminus or station in order to get them into the desired position. **1947** *Sat. Ev. Post* 1 Feb. 53/3 Sometime between six and six-thirty the two cars for 139 are 'drilled' —shifted by two switch engines to the platform where the Washington train to which they are attached is being made up.

***drilling,** *a.* **1. drilling machine,** a machine for boring an oil well. **2. drilling plant, rig,** the aggregate of the equipment for drilling an oil well.

(1) **1865** GESNER *Pract. Treatise Coal, Petrol. & Oils* 34 There are drilling machines which can bore nine feet per hour. — (2) **1913** V. B. LEWES *Oil Fuel* 63 The form of drilling plant or 'rig' as it is generally called. **1948** *Chi. Tribune* 1 Aug. 6/5 Humble Oil . . . built a 2 million dollar steel island, two acres in area, to support the drilling rig [etc.].

***drink,** *n.* A body of water, as an ocean, river, or pond. *Colloq.* Cf. **Big Drink.**

1832 PAULDING *Westward Ho!* I. 121 Sing dumb, or I'll throw you into the drink. **1857** HOLLAND *Bay Path* xii. 137 So you'd better scull your dug-out over the drink again, and go to splittin' oven wood. **1890** B. HALL *Turnover Club* 117 As he reached over to get it, his foot slipped and he slid into the drink again.

As the last term in **black, fire, mixed, square drink.**

drinkery ˈdrɪŋkərɪ, *n.* [**drink, v.* +*-ery.* App. an independent formation, much earlier than, and not connected with, later British use, 1884——.] A grogshop or saloon. *Slang. Obs.*

1840 *N.Y. Mirror* 5 Sep. 87/2 There is scarcely anything among us from a capital down to a drinkery, that has not rendered the name of George Washington immortal. **1845** T. J. GREEN *Texian Exped.* xix. 368 We wended our way up town, and called into the first open 'drinkery.' **1865** *Madison* (Ind.) *D. Ev. Courier* 27 Sep. 4/1 Boys are allowed to lounge around some of the drinkeries, billiard-rooms, tenpin alleys, &c., of the city.

***drinking,** *n.* In combs.: (1) **drinking booth,** a shop or stand where liquor is sold; (2) **gourd,** (see quot. 1918), cf. **dipper gourd, gourd dipper;** (3) **hydrant,** a hydrant from which drinking water is obtained, *obs.;* (4) **joint,** a place where liquor is sold and consumed, *colloq.;* (5) **saloon,** a saloon or barroom; (6) **shop,** a shop in which liquor is sold.

(1) **1796** MORSE *Univ. Geog.* II. 334 The Dutch . . . seem to have borrowed from them [*sc.* the English] the neatness of their drinking-booths. **1867** RICHARDSON *Beyond Miss.* v. 71 Gambling and drinking booths stood upon every corner.—(2) **1851** BURKE *Polly Peablossom* 67 If it a'n't the next place to no whar, you can take my head for er drinkin gourd. **1918** E. WALLER *Illinois* 74 Drinking-gourd, a gourd with a portion grown out like a dipper handle and with one side of it cut away so as to make it like a dipper. One was usually kept at the well. They held from one to three pints and would last a long time. — (3) **1890** *N.Y. City Public Works Rep.* 102, 95 public drinking hydrants were repaired. — (4) **1902** WHITE *Blazed Trail* xxxvii, He opened Camp One, and the Fighting Forty came back from distant drinking joints. **1913** J. B. ELLIS *Lahoma* 52, I reckon a nice clean drinking-joint and a full-stocked bar is about the highest art that can stimulate a man.

(5) **1855** *N.Y. Herald* 12 Nov. 1/4 A row occurred on Saturday night, between a few small fry politicians, at a drinking saloon on Centre street. **1895** ROBINSON *Men Born Equal* 325 Whenever a drinking-saloon was reached men . . . fell out. — (6) **1855** *N.Y. Herald* 6 Nov. 5/3 A multitude of drinking shops have already been closed. **1889** CABLE in *Cent. Mag.* XXXVII. 512/2 The voyagers saw . . . some drinking-shops.

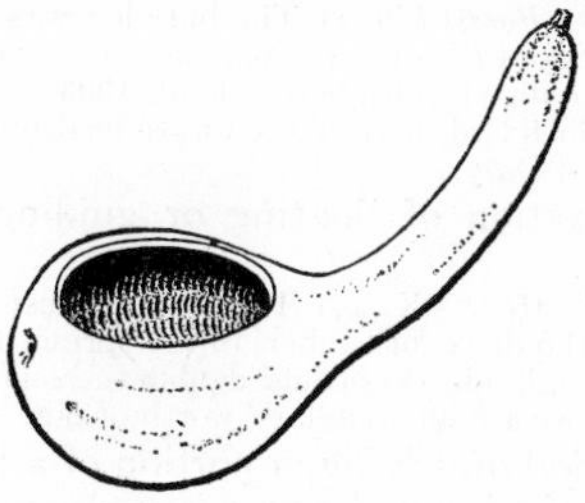

Drinking gourd or gourd dipper

***drip,** *v.*

1. *intr.* Of the weather: To mist, drizzle, rain slowly. *Colloq.*

1730 HEMPSTEAD *Diary* 217 Fair in ye foren[oon] afternoon Dripping at night Rain. **1760** WASHINGTON *Diaries* I. 127 The Morning lowered, and dript as yesterday.

2. *tr.* To prepare (coffee) by allowing boiling water or steam to filter through finely ground coffee beans. Cf. next.

1885 CUSTER *Boots & Saddles* i. 15 And there the never absent 'eureka' coffee-pot was produced and most delicious coffee dripped.

drip coffee. A drink prepared by allowing boiling water to drip through finely ground coffee. Also **dripped coffee.**

1884 F. E. OWENS *Cookbook* 307 Dripped Coffee. . . . Put the amount of ground coffee required in the bottom of the dripper. **1895** SALA *Life* II. 382 In the old French market on Sunday mornings we used to have an irreproachable French *déjeuner à la fourchette,* followed by the renowned 'drip' coffee, which is so strong that it is said to stain the saucer into which it is poured. **1909** O. HENRY *Options* (1916) 50 But if you're ever in the Middle West just mention my name and you'll get foot-warmers and dripped coffee.

b. *attrib.* Designating a receptacle or pot adapted for making coffee of this kind.

1897 *Outing* XXIX. 574/1 He . . . produced a jar of coffee and the drip coffee-pot. **1936–7** *Sears Cat.* Fall & Winter 650 8-Cup Drip Coffee Maker makes coffee by the French drip method, believed by many to produce a superior flavored brew. **1946** *This Week Mag.* 6 April 23/1, I happened to have the bottom of the drip coffee pot in my hand.

***drive,** *n.*

1. The place or run where an organized hunt takes place.

1835 INGRAHAM *South-West* II. 132 We . . . proceeded to the 'drive' . . . as the hunting station is technically termed. *Ib.* 137 An extensive 'drive' or forest frequented by deer. **1836** GILMAN *Recoll.* (1838) 210 Bounce was joined by Diamond, . . . Luna, and Trimbush, who alternately dropped in working the trail of an old buck into the drive. **1858** *Harper's Mag.* Oct. 616/2 The hunters [of deer] having finally reached the 'drive,' a consultation is held as to which stands are most available.

b. A fenced-in, V-shaped run for capturing animals.

1886 ROE *Army Lett.* 342 At one corner of the corral was a small, funnel-shaped 'drive,' the outer opening of which was just large enough to squeeze a sheep through. **1890** *Opelousas* (La.) *Democrat* 29 March 4/7 The rabbit scourge . . . is now threatening parts of California. . . . A drive has been made by stretching fine wire netting about three feet high and seven miles in length, A shaped.

2. The action of rounding up or bringing together cattle from a wide area; the cattle so brought together.

1846 THORPE *Myst. Backwoods* 14 In the excitement of the drive, horses fall, or run headlong over slow-footed cows. **1948** *Great Falls* (Mont.) *Tribune* 18 Sep. 4/4 The first big overland drive of cattle from southern Alberta to Montana in many years swung onto the trail today.

b. The action of driving sheep or cattle from one place to another.

1884 SHEPHERD *Prairie Exp.* 244 Good dogs are of enormous assistance on a drive. **1912** RAINE *Brand Blotters* 121 [Melissy was] to make the drive herself in place of Antonio. There were fifteen hundred sheep in the bunch, and they must be taken care of at once by somebody. **1941** FERGUSSON *Southwest* 34 The first to dare the 'dry drive' across the plains of Texas.

3. A mass of logs floating or to be floated down a watercourse.

1851 SPRINGER *Forest Life* 41 The butt log was so large that the stream did not float it in the spring, and when the drive was taken down we were obliged to leave it behind. **1908** WHITE *Riverman* 54 The drive of which Orde had charge was to be delivered at the booms of Morrison and Daly.

b. The action of floating or guiding logs down a stream.

1860 *Harper's Mag.* XX. 441 The stream must be cleared of obstructions for the drive [of timber] in the spring. **1947** *Sat. Ev. Post* 8 Mar. 54/3 Small mistakes could double the cost of a drive, and a big one could lose a million dollars' worth of pine.

4. A period of driving, a portion of a journey accomplished without a stop for rest (see also quot. 1930).

1860 in *Colo. Mag.* XIV. (1937) 218 Day's drive nearly 12 hours, and not much short of 30 miles; horses nearly worn out. **1866** in *Nebr. Hist. Mag.* XIII. (1932) 147 The first two or three days we made but one drive, getting two meals only. We are now making two drives, yoking about daylight and driving until 9 or 10—getting breakfast, and then yoke up again about 3 and driving until evening. **1926** O. L. SHIPMAN *Taming Big Bend* 44 The scarcity of water and grass . . . frequently made it necessary to divide daily journeys into three drives or camps. **1930** BANNING *Six Horses* 399 A *drive*, which comprised generally a number of stages, was a section of road between the points or stations where drivers, and usually their vehicles, were changed—it was seldom more than 60 miles long.

5. One who drives a tandem or team on a towpath. *Rare.*

1874 B. F. TAYLOR *World on Wheels* I. iii. 27 We took a walk on the 'tow-path' with the 'drive,' who looked like a bundle of old clothes. *Ib.* 28 You confer with the 'drive' as to the chance of passing it [*sc.* a canal-boat] . . . and he gets all the tough pull out of his tandem that there is in it.

6. The selling of goods or stocks at a low price (see also quot. 1900).

1890 *Ann Arbor Reg.* 1 March (*advt.*), Ladies, we are going to give you a Benefit and it will be the drive of the season. **1893** *Chi. Tribune* 2 July 36 A Big Cut in Waists A Big Drive in Corsets. **1900** S. A. NELSON *A B C Wall St.* 139 Drive. An attempt to force prices down. Illustration: 'The bears made a *drive* at the market.'

b. An organized or special effort to gain some end, esp. to raise money.

1928 *Washington Star* 9 Dec., The drive for $100,000 to buy a site for the Lutheran College will get under way tomorrow night at a dinner in the Lee House. **1945** *Springfield* (Mass.) *Union* 13 March 3/6 As soon as the roads are more settled the Service Club will sponsor the scrap paper drive.

attrib. **1945** *Roundup* (Mont.) *R.-Tribune* 15 Feb. 1/7 Personnel of the committees to assist in the drive will be announced by Drive Chairman.

7. A power-transmitting mechanism.

1901 MERWIN-WEBSTER *Calumet K* xiv. 263 He's putting in three drives different from the way they are in the plans. **1903** *Sci. Amer.* LXXXIX. 262/2 The transmission gear is of the planetary type . . . with a direct chain drive from the motor shaft to the rear axle.

8. A forward push made by a team in certain sports, esp. football.

1928 *Collier's* 29 Dec. 17/3 In the Georgia Tech-Vanderbilt game the former started a 60-yard drive, play by play, to Vanderbilt's 10-yard line.

9. Impulse, initiative. *Colloq.*

1929 C. E. MERRIAM *Chicago* 139 The drive toward American assimilation is one of the outstanding characteristics of the immigrant group. **1930** *Sat. Ev. Post* 1 March 40/1 They are wanting in initiative, drive. **1948** *Ib.* 4 Sep. 20/3 In many ways, he typifies the drive and the industrial genius that have made the Giant of the North what it is.

As the last term in **brook, cattle, line, log, ocean, shell, sleigh, spring drive.**

*drive, *v.*

1. *tr.* and *intr.* (See quot. 1803.) *Obs.*

1803 J. DAVIS *Travels in U.S.* 50 *n.*, An Overseer on a Plantation, who preserves subordination among the negroes, is said to *drive well.* **1856** OLMSTED *Slave States* 205 If four men did not harvest more than an acre of wheat a day, they could not have been well *driven.*

2. *tr.* (See quot. 1905.)

1848 THOREAU *Maine Woods* 41 It was easy to see that driving logs must be an exciting as well as arduous and dangerous business. **1905** *Forestry Bureau Bul.* No. 61, *Drive*, to float logs or timbers from the forest to the mill or shipping point. **1948** *Popular Western* June 63/2 How in tarnation d'you figure to drive timber along a dry crick?

b. Used of a stream down which logs are floated. Cf. **4. d.** below.

1882 HUBBARD *Moosehead Lake* 104 The stream, not having been 'driven' of late years, is, higher up, somewhat choked with logs and drift wood.

3. In noun combs.: (1) **drive-in,** designating places into which customers may drive their automobiles and make purchases, attend movies, etc., while seated in their cars, also absol.; (2) **pipe,** a strong pipe used in commencing the process of drilling a well; (3) **way,** see as a main entry; (4) **well,** =**driven well,** also attrib.; (5) **whist,** progressive whist.

(1) 1931 *Randolph Enterprise* (Elkins, W.Va.) 26 Mar. 5/6 [He] applied for a permit to . . . make a drive-in filling station. **1947** *Dly. Ardmoreite* (Ardmore, Okla.) 14 Nov. 6/2 One hundred new drive-in theaters will be built in the U.S. during the next 12 months. **1948** *Chi. Tribune* 3 April 1. 16/3 They drove in his coupe to a drive-in and had hamburgers and coffee. — **(2) 1883** *Cent. Mag.* July 329/2 After the rig is got upon the ground, a drive-pipe is forced down through the earth to the rock. **1942** Sears Roebuck *How to Get Running Water* 7/1 Each length of drive pipe should connect to its neighboring one with a coupling that will provide a water and air-tight joint. — **(4) 1871** *Rep. Comm. Indian Affairs 1870* 522, I had the engineer sink a drive-well 32 feet below the foundation of the mill. **1879** *Bradstreet's* 31 Dec. 5/3 Indiana farmers are annoyed by men who sell them drive-well patents. — **(5) 1888** *San Juan Prospector* (Del Norte, Colo.) 15 May 3/1 Mr. Grover Allen entertained the Young Married Folks at drive whist last Monday evening.

4. In colloq. phrases. **a.** *To drive the center, cross, nail,* to make a perfect shot. Also fig.

1831 AUDUBON *Ornith. Biog.* I. 292 To *drive a nail* is a common feat, not more thought of by the Kentuckians than to cut off a wild turkey's head, at a distance of a hundred yards. *Ib.* 293 Those who drive the nail have a further trial amongst themselves, and the two best shots out of these generally settle the affair. . . . This is technically termed *Driving the Nail.* **1835** LONGSTREET *Ga. Scenes* 276 He was very confident of . . . driving the cross with her [*sc.* a gun]. **1850** *Birmingham Emig. Co. Jrnl.* 4 July, We spent a short time in sellibrating the forth with a shootingmatch, in which I Baird came out best, the senter was drove however several times. **1869** MARK TWAIN *Innocents* ix. 84 They set up the poor criminals at long range, like so many targets, and practiced on them—kept them hopping about and dodging bullets for half an hour before they managed to drive the center.

b. *To drive (away) at,* to work strenuously at (a task).

1835 IRVING in P. M. Irving *Life W. Irving* (1866) III. 82 My cottage is not yet finished, but I shall drive at it as soon as the opening of spring will permit. **1842** GRAY *Letters* (1893) 296, I have been driving away at the 'Flora,' of late, very hard.

c. *To drive team,* short for "to drive a team."

1842 KIRKLAND *Forest Life* I. xiv. 115 And when our friend Dan engaged to 'drive team' for Mr. Margold, he had no idea but that he was to be . . . one of the party. **1913** LONDON *Valley of Moon* I. iv, I'll have to drive team to-morrow with 'em.

d. *To drive the river,* to direct the course of logs down a river.

1860 *Harper's Mag.* March 448/2 How glad I am . . . that you have obtained a substitute to 'drive' the river. **1947** *Sat. Ev. Post* 8 Mar. 20/3 He'd driven the Namakagon, the Totogatic, the Eau Claire and the main river before he'd gone to the Chippewa.

e. *To drive in the pickets,* (see quot.). *Obs.*

1871 GOSS *Soldier's Story* ii. 42 Skirmishing duties [is] a term usually applied to the act of hunting for vermin, a partial hunt being termed driving in the pickets.

f. *To drive in* (a runner), in baseball, to enable a runner to score by securing a hit.

1899 *Sporting Life* (Phila.) 22 May 4/5 Twitchell hit to left . . . and made two bases on it, driving in McKean from second base.

driven well. (See quot. 1874.) Also **drove well.** Cf. **drive well.**

1874 KNIGHT 753/1 *Driven-well*, a well formed of a tube driven into the ground until its perforated end reaches a stratum containing water. **1878** *Ill. Dept. Agric. Trans.* XIV. 146 The east half of our country, with its deep deposits of gravel along the western side of the

Wabash river, enables its occupants to use 'drove wells.' **1923** WATTS *L. Nichols* 5 A driven well . . . went dry in periods of prolonged drought. **1942** Sears, Roebuck *How to Get Running Water* 6/1 A driven well consists of a tightly assembled pipe line driven into the ground and fitted with a well point with a screen at its lower end to permit water to enter and be drawn up for use.

∗ **driver,** *n.*

1. An official authorized to take up and impound swine, cattle, etc., found at large. *Obs.*

1671 *Cambridge Rec.* 189 Driuers of the necke and vewers of the fence Thomas Longhorne and John Stedmon Junior. **1686** *Charlestown Land Rec.* 205 They then Chose . . . drivers of the sd pasture.

2. Before the Civil War, a dependable slave trusted to oversee a group of his fellows. Now *hist.*

1763 GRAINGER *Sugar-Cane* Bk. III. 141 Nor need the driver, Aethiop authriz'd, Thence more inhuman, crack his horrid whip. **1854** *Harper's Mag.* VIII. 453/2 On some plantation there is no 'overseer'; the owner manages his place with the help of a skillful and trustworthy negro, termed the 'driver.' **1947** LUMPKIN *Southerner* 31 He must . . . put the drivers—as slave sub-foremen were generally called—in charge.

3. A lumberman who floats logs downstream, esp. in time of high water. Also attrib. Cf. ∗ **drive,** *v.* **2.**

1848 THOREAU *Maine Woods* 25 Just above McCauslin's, there is a rocky rapid . . . and many 'drivers' are there collected, who frequent his house for supplies. **1902** WHITE *Blazed Trail* 367 You tell Solly to get steam on that tug double quick, and have Dave hustle together his driver crew. **1944** NUTE *Lk. Superior* 211 They would be turned over to professional 'drivers,' who did nothing but guide logs to market down the swollen streams of spring.

4. A horse trained to be driven in harness.

1876 *Vt. Bd. Agric. Rep.* III. 168 Stylish, enduring roadsters, trotters and gentlemen's drivers . . . have not been so successfully produced elsewhere, as in the invigorating climate . . . of Northern New England. **1903** *Cin. Enquirer* 2 May 9/4 The transfers of drivers, draughters and expressers indicate an upward tendency.

5. One who assembles or "rounds up" horses, cattle, etc.

1884 *Harper's Mag.* LXX. 107/2 The horses . . . had grown exceedingly wild. . . . The drivers were, however, familiar with the work before them. **1887** *Scribner's Mag.* II. 512/1, I am not travelled enough to say what the mode is everywhere among the drivers of cattle.

6. *local.* = **dowitcher.**

1889 *Cent.* 1774/1. **1917** *Birds of Amer.* I. 229 Dowitcher. . . . Other names [include] Robin Snipe; Sea Pigeon; Driver; [etc.].

7. driver's seat, *transf.* the place of one in charge. *Colloq.*

1923 *Nation* 18 July 49 He has swung blithely into the driver's seat and cheerfully undertaken to run the nation without knowing how. **1948** *N.Y. Times* 18 April v. 2/1 Leo Durocher, after an involuntary year of exile, is back in the driver's seat.

As the last term in **beef, bull, canal, cow, drag, field, fog, gentleman's, gin, head, herring, horsecar, jitney, log, mule, nail, old, pile, post, river, road, slave, soul, stake, well driver.**

∗ **driveway,** *n.*

1. A way whereby hay, grain, etc., may be hauled into a barn.

1839 *Mass. Agric. Rep. 1838* 80 The building should be so placed that the barn floor could be laid upon the beams, and the drive-way be into the end directly under the roof. **1868** *Rep. Comm. Agric.* 242 Where it is practicable, it is best to have the drive-way for drawing in hay, grain and corn fodder enter the gable end. **1949** *Pacific Spectator* Spring 226 The upper floor, right on a level with the driveway, had a big haymow on the left.

b. (See quots.)

1877 BARTLETT 193 *Driveway*, . . . an unfloored strip of ground covered with a hay-loft used in stage-coach days at hotels, &c. *Ib.* Driveway, . . . a passage overhung with a roof to shelter church-goers alighting at the side door of a church. New England. **1889** WARFIELD *Cattle Breeding* 310 The stalls all open out upon a drive-way formed by a continuation of the roof outward, which is further continued until it forms another row of low stalls.

2. A way, road, or street, a drive.

1870 *Cong. Globe* 2 Feb. 966/3, I doubt as to the policy of allowing this railroad to go along exactly in the track of where we propose to have a public drive-way. **1904** W. H. SMITH *Promoters* 263 There are no driveways in all the world pleasanter to travel over than Nebraska roads. **1945** *Chi. Tribune* 13 May VII. 1/1 Beyond the driveway that runs before her front gate, the greens start popping out of the moist earth.

3. The way or course by which game passes when chased or hunted. Also a station or stand along such a way.

1875 TEMPLE & SHELDON *Hist. Northfield, Mass.* 46 They were wonderfully expert in killing game . . . and in capturing both larger and smaller sorts by means of drive-ways and in rude traps and yank-ups. **1883** ZEIGLER & GROSSCUP *Alleghanies* 156 We four city boys were to occupy drive-ways, and watch for, halt, and slay every deer that passed.

∗ **driving,** *a.* and *n.*

1. *n.* Directing the work of slaves. *Obs.* Cf. ∗ **driver 2.**

1765 J. HABERSHAM *Letters* 39, I have now Hands sufficient to make 700 Barrils Rice annually . . . without Hurry and too much driving. **1839** WELD *Slavery As It Is* 134 The southern newspapers, at the crop season, chronicle carefully the 'cotton brag,' . . . and 'unparalleled driving.' **1856** OLMSTED *Slave States* 206 The same gentleman . . . told me that negroes were very seldom punished . . . ; that the driving of them was generally left to overseers.

2. The action of directing logs down a stream. Cf. ∗ **drive,** *v.* **2.**

1864 *Mich. Gen. Statutes* (1882) I. 1000 Such owner shall be liable to such corporation for the breaking of such jams, and the driving, booming, rafting of said logs, timber and lumber. **1900** BRUNCKEN *N. Amer. Forests* 79 Booms are not the only structures used on the logging rivers to facilitate the 'driving.' **1944** NUTE *Lk. Superior* 211 Small camps often did their own 'driving,' however.

3. *a.* Hurrying, forcing, exacting, energetic. *Colloq.*

1835 INGRAHAM *South-West* II. 92 When they have conquered their prejudices, they become thorough, driving planters. **1856** SIMMS *Charlemont* 371 Without making many allowances for the rough and hilly character of the road, [he] went off at a driving pace. **1941** DANIELS *Tar Heels* 15 Among them are rogues and thieves and rascals, vote stealers and note shavers, driving bosses and stalling workers.

4. In combs.: (1) **driving box,** the journal box of a driving axle; (2) **crew,** a group of men engaged in floating or driving logs down a stream; (3) **park,** an area, field, etc., esp. one with a race track, where horses are exercised, *obs.;* (4) **pike,** a form of pike used in driving and handling logs; (5) **wheel,** a paddle wheel of a steamer.

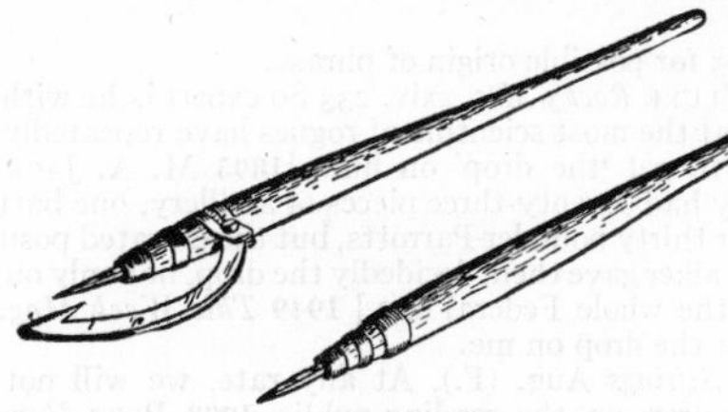

Driving pike and peavey

(1) **1864** WEBSTER 784/1 The frame [of the locomotive-engine] . . . contains the jaws and driving-boxes under the springs. **1898** HAMBLEN *Gen'l Manager's Story* 128 In cleaning the fire a spark had ignited the waste on top of the back driving-box. — (2) **1908** WHITE *Riverman* ii. 11 Members of the driving crew leaped shouting from one log to another. *Ib.* 46 As many of the driving crew as were within distance gathered to watch. — (3) **1879** J. F. HAGEMAN *Hist. Princeton* (ed. 2) II. 33 For little more than a year past a portion of the Castle-Howard farm . . . has been rented and appropriated to the use of a driving park, as such institutions are in these days designated. A good half mile track has been prepared. — (4) **1877** *Lumberman's Gaz.* 8 Dec. 362 Each man . . . carries a 'driving pike,' . . . for the purpose of prying out the logs and releasing them from jams. — (5) **1885** *Harper's Mag.* March 642/2 Never safe from 'snags,' with its driving-wheel gashed and mangled by the floating drift-timber, it [*sc.* the boat] held bravely on its way.

As the last term in **brook, center, log, river, slave driving.**

drizzle-drazzle. A slow, drizzling rain. *Colloq.* — **1855** *Golden Era* (S.F.) 7 Jan. 2/4 The morning brought just what the old deacon wanted, a 'regular old-fashioned drizzle-drazzle.' **1923** *K.C. Star* 23 April, The '*drizzle-drazzle*' is another kind of rain. . . . It is neither a gully-washer nor a sod-soaker. It is more than a mist and yet not a rain.

∗ **droger,** *n.* Also ∗ **drogher.** As the last term in **cotton, hide, lumber, tobacco droger.**

dromedary trunkfish. (See quot.) *Rare.* — **1842** *Nat. Hist. N.Y., Zoology* IV. 341 The Dromedary Trunk-fish. *Lactophrys cameli-*

nus . . . I know nothing of the origin of this species, except that it is said to have been taken on the shore of Long Island.

drool drul, *n.* [? * *drivel.*] **1.** Drivel or spittle. **2.** Stuff, rubbish, nonsense. Both *colloq.*

(1) **1867–9** *Ill. Agric. Soc. Trans.* VII. 179 The drooled matter is filled with air bubbles, and may be described as a 'frothy' drool. **1871** J. H. TRUMBULL in A. J. Ellis *Early Eng. Pron.* (1874) IV. 1220 *Drool* or *dreul.* For 'drivel,' used everywhere by mothers and nurses. The latter is the less polished form. — (2) **1911** HARRISON *Queed* 84 Something loose in his belfry, as ye might have surmised from them damfool tax-drools *i.e.*, articles on taxation. *Ib.* 314 Say, Doc, I been readin' them reformatory drools of yours.

* **drop,** *n.*

1. In various uses (see quots.).

1864 WEBSTER 415/2 *Drop-press* . . . is called also *drop-hammer,* or simply a *drop.* *a***1870** CHIPMAN *Notes on Bartlett* 132 *Drop,* the top-front of pantaloons. **1879** *Postal Laws & Regul.* 427 *Drop,* the opening in a post-office or mail apartment of a [railway postal] car for the mailing of letters . . . by the public.

b. *pl.* (See quot.) *Obs.* Cf. **knockout, pine drops.**

1834 F. LIEBER *Lett. to Gentleman in Germany* 325 Calomel and laudanum . . . are also used unsparingly in families without special advice of the physician. . . . To such an extent is this abuse carried, that laudanum is called simply *drops.* . . . I know a farmer's family in which every child receives regularly some 'drops' before going to bed.

2. *Baseball.* A pitched ball that suddenly drops before reaching the home plate and so confuses the batter. In full **drop ball.**

1867 *Ball Player's Chron.* 5 Sep. 5/1 He pitched slow, 'drop' balls, many of which struck outside of 'the plate,' but were not 'called' by the umpire. **1887** *Courier-Journal* 5 May 6/3 He has a queer drop and out-shoot on which McQuaid failed to give him strikes. **1948** *Dly. Ardmoreite* (Ardmore, Okla.) 1 Aug. 16/1 They can't hit his fast breaking curve, drop and change of pace.

3. An advantage over an opponent. *Colloq.*

1918 MULFORD *Man from Bar-20* 149 Talk's cheap. Th' man with th' drop can find a lot to say, if he's a tin-horn. **1945** *New Yorker* 10 Mar. 66 His motion may be so sudden that raising the rifle to the shoulder and firing a shot in the conventional manner will give the Jap the drop.

b. Esp. *to get* (or *have*) *the drop on,* to cover a person (or have him covered) with a gun before he can draw his own. *Colloq.*

See quot. 1895 for possible origin of phrase.

1869 A. K. MCCLURE *Rocky Mts.* xxiv. 233 So expert is he with his faithful pistol, that the most scientific of rogues have repeatedly attempted in vain to get 'the drop' on him. [**1895** M. A. JACKSON *Memoirs* 618 They had seventy-three pieces of artillery, one battery being siege guns or thirty pounder Parrotts, but the elevated position of McLaws and Walker gave them decidedly the drop, not only on the big guns but on the whole Federal line.] **1949** *This Week Mag.* 12 March 5/1 He got the drop on me.

fig. **1888** *Texas Siftings* Aug. (F.), At any rate, we will not let Arcturus get the drop on the reading public. **1893** POST *Harvard Stories* 108 That is where we . . . Westerners get the drop on the Boston men. **1903** A. H. LEWIS *Boss* 375 The Blackberry president . . . made a play to get the drop on our party.

4. *At the drop of a hat,* at once, immediately. *Colloq.*

1887 M. ROBERTS *Western Avernus* 43 When in a bad temper [he was] ferocious and ready to quarrel 'at the drop of a hat,' as the American saying goes. **1908** WHITE *Riverman* 199 Men eager to fight at the drop of the hat, or sooner. **1948** *Time* 19 July 34/1 He makes a speech at the drop of a hat, at political meetings, church suppers, or almost any other gathering that wants to listen.

As the last term in **back, cold, dew, egg, gum, letter, mint, out, pocketbook, snow, sundrop.** See also **beechdrops.**

* **drop,** *v.*

1. *tr.* To send (a card, line, note) to a person.

Evidently a transf. sense, from dropping a letter into a mailbox.

1777 J. Q. ADAMS *Fam. Lett.* 234, I will drop a line as often as I can. **1865** NORTON *Army Letters* 261, I take the opportunity before we get beyond the reach of mails to drop you a note. **1945** *Bristol* (N.H.) *Enterprise* 15 Feb. 3/4 Just drop a card to your county agent, so that he can send you a regulation score card.

2 To cease to employ (a person).

1845 *Lowell Offering* V. 239 They might 'drop the operative'—they might enter into some other employment. **1895** *Chicago Strike of 1894* 422 It is very easy for the company to drop men and not let the cause of it be known.

b. To dismiss (a student) from college.

1894 *Harper's Mag.* LXXXVIII. 771/1 He must maintain a certain standard of scholarship or he will be 'dropped.' **1944** *Catalogue, U. of Washington, 1944–45* 64 The dean shall decide when the student shall be removed from probation or dropped from college.

3. *intr.* Of lambs: To fall in birth, to be born. *Colloq.*

The corresponding transitive use is old. See *OED.*

1853 T. D. PRICE *MS Diary* 14 March, Lambs dropping, doing tolerably well. **1866** *Maine Agric. Soc. Ret.* 85 Wentworth has his lambs drop in mid-winter in order that his bucks may be ready for service in the fall.

4. In combs.: (1) * **drop box,** a box for the mailing of letters, small packages, etc.; (2) **copy,** of Associated Press dispatches, a duplicate report "dropped" from the wires at any point between the sender and the receiver; (3) **hammer,** a power hammer having a weight that is raised and allowed to drop on the material being worked upon (see quot. 1864); (4) **head,** a device for a desk or table that will permit a typewriter, sewing machine, etc.,

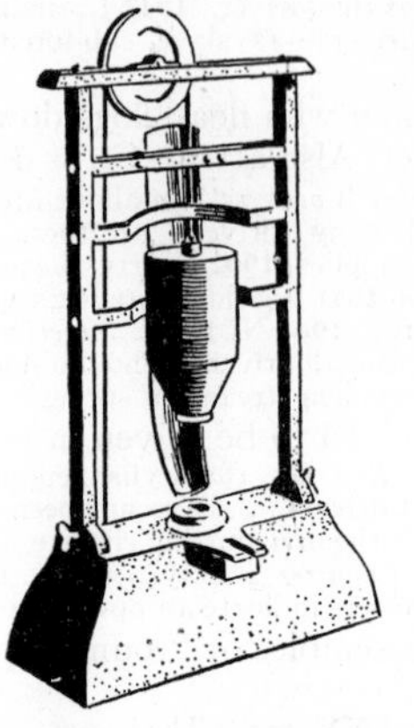

One form of drop hammer

when not in use, to be dropped down so as to leave a flat surface, usu. attrib.; (5) **jaw,** (see quot.); (6) **lamp,** = **drop light;** (7) **letter,** see as a main entry; (8) **light,** a light so fitted that it may be lowered above a desk, table, etc., also a suspended electric light, also attrib.; (9) **line,** a weighted fishing line that is dropped to or near the bottom of a body of water; (10) * **out,** one who drops out, esp. from a school, *rare;* (11) **press,** (see quot. 1864); (12) **shot gang,** a group of little Negroes, *slang;* (13) **worm,** a hangworm that suspends itself by a thread.

(1) **1881** MARSHALL *Thro' America* 11 Windows for the sale of postage stamps and stamped envelopes [in New York] and for the reception of packets too bulky for the drop-boxes. — (2) **1877** *Harper's Mag.* Dec. 57/2 The Pacific coast is served [with Associated Press news] partly from New York, the agent of the California press in Chicago being furnished with 'drop copies' of what is sent from New York so that he may avoid duplication. *Ib.*, Other 'drop copies' of the reports going to California are also taken off the wire at Salt Lake City, Denver, and Cheyenne for the use of local papers. — (3) **1864** WEBSTER 415/2 *Drop-press,* a machine for embossing, punching &c., . . . called also *drop-hammer,* or simply a *drop.* **1866** *Ill. Dept. Agric. Trans.* VI. 79 By means of drop hammers our mouldboards are bent and formed at a single stroke. — (4) **1903** *Sears Cat.* (ed. 113) 420 We recommend the drop head cabinet for the reason that it serves as a protection for the head, and when closed you have in it a handsome stand or table. **1942** ASHER & HEAL *Send No Money* 37 The Sears' $11.25 five-drawer drophead sewing machine sewed, and sewed well, and the cabinet was a good oak cabinet. **1945** *Suburban List* 8 Feb. 19/1 Singer Sewing Machines—will pay cash for drop head treadle or electric machine.

(5) **1900** *Dept. Agric. Yrbk.* (1910) 233 The dumb form of rabies is very common, and many persons know it as 'drop jaw' who have no idea of its true nature. — (6) **1870** H. SPOFFORD in *Harper's Mag.* XLI. 861/2 When dark came we would light the drop-lamp. **1891** *Cent. Mag.* XLI. 940 A long discussion . . . was held . . . between the young people sitting by the drop-lamp. — (8) **1861** *Rep. Comm. Patents 1860* I. 445, I claim . . . the construction of the socket of a drop light joint of a single piece. **1862** *Knickerb.* LIX. 134 The family gathered with books and needles around the drop-light. **1904** LYNDE *Grafters* 387 The judge pressed the button of the drop-light and

waved his visitor to a chair. — **(9) 1847** LANMAN *Summer in Wild.* 158, I have paddled to where the water was fifty feet in depth, and with a drop-line have taken, in twenty minutes, more trout than I could eat in a fortnight. **1855** P. PAXTON *Capt. Priest* 143 Whether the fish be taken by rod and reel, or by drop-line . . . it is about the same thing.

(10) 1930 *Sat. Ev. Post* 1 March 110/2 The drop-outs are usually those with inferior mental capacity. — **(11) 1852** *Rep. Comm. Patents 1851* 285 Improvements in Drop Presses . . . [patented by] Milo Peck. **1864** WEBSTER 415 *Drop-press*, a machine for embossing, punching, &c., consisting of a weight guided vertically, to be raised by a cord and pully worked by the foot, and to drop on an anvil. — **(12)** *c***1870** BAGBY *Old Va. Gentleman* 8 Few days passed that did not witness the 'drop-shot gang' of small Ethiops sweeping up the fallen leaves. — **(13) 1856** *Rep. Comm. Patents: Agric.* 79 The 'drop-worm' . . . generally infests the arbor-vitae, larch, and hemlock-spruce.

b. Designating articles of food in the cooking of which a small amount of dough or batter is dropped or spread on a hot griddle or sheet, as (1) **drop biscuit,** (2) **cake,** (3) **cooky.**

(1) 1853 WEBSTER *Improved Housewife* 119 Virginia Drop Biscuit. — **(2) 1835** *Liberator* (Boston) 5 Dec. 196/5 It seems to me the travellers on whom I bestowed your *drop cakes* at midnight, have leavened this loaf with a blessing. **1941** *America's Cook Book* 593 Marmalade Drop Cakes . . . 1 cup sugar, 2 eggs. . . . Drop from teaspoon on greased baking sheet. — **(3)** *Ib.* 592 Honey Drop Cookies. 3 cups sifted flour. . . . Drop batter from teaspoon on greased baking sheet. **1948** *Household* Feb. 87/1 Drop cookies which I make are thin and spread on the cookie sheet during baking.

c. In phrases: (1) *drop-the-pigeon,* (see quot.), *obs.;* (2) * *to drop on* (*to*), to "get wise to," to become informed about, *slang;* (3) *to drop to,* =prec.; (4) * *to drop out,* (*a*) to drop, fall, (*b*) of a soldier, to leave one's place in ranks.

(1) 1817 *Niles' Reg.* XIII. 79/2 A certain William Kennedy was sentenced to fine and imprisonment for cheating in a game, called in the indictment, '*High cockneyrorum*, or *drop-the-pidgeon!*' — **(2) 1876** *Coso Mining News* (Darwin, Cal.) 3 June 4/6 Drop on yourself Lent, you are out of season. **1892** MARK TWAIN *American Claimant* (R.), xviii. 182 How did you happen to drop on to that idea in this curious fashion? — **(3) 1896** *N.Y. Dramatic News* 18 July 2/2 It is too bad that Mr. Bryan didn't accept the offer before he 'dropped' to his opportunity. **1901** RYAN *Montana* 118, I dropped to the fact that you had some damage done to that left arm. — **(4)** (*a*) **1865** in BOWLES *Across Continent* 434 If the bottom of the Yosemite did 'drop out,' to use a homely but expressive phrase, it was not all done in one piece, or with one movement. (*b*) **1883** MARK TWAIN *Life on Miss.* li. 507, I asked him to hold my musket while I dropped out and got a drink.

drop letter. (See quot. 1843.)

[1718 S. SEWALL *Diary* 23 April, I write to Col. Quinsey to come to town, by a Hingham man that drops the letter [in Braintree as he passes through].] **1843** *28th Congress* 2 Sess. H.R. Doc. No. 2, 688 What are denominated 'drop letters' . . . is a class of letters which are usually sent from one place to another by private conveyance, and are 'dropped' or deposited in the post office for delivery. **1943** *U.S. Postal Guide* July 8 On 'drop letters' and other first-class matter, 2 cents an ounce or fraction thereof when mailed for local delivery at post offices having city or village letter-carrier service.

dropped ball. *Baseball.* (See quot. 1868.) Also **dropped fly.** — **1868** CHADWICK *Base Ball* 40 A ball is called a dropped ball when it is handled by a fielder, but not held long enough to constitute a catch. **1879** *Chi. Tribune* 9 May 6/4 The Whites had but three errors, two of which were dropped flys by Dalrymple.

* **dropper,** *n.*

1. (See quot. 1864.)

1864 WEBSTER 415/2 *Dropper*, . . . (*Mining*), a branch vein which drops off from, or leaves, the main lode. **1878** BEADLE *Western Wilds* 66 At a hundred feet or more in depth . . . there are whims, droppers, feeders.

2. A reaping machine having an attachment for depositing the grain at intervals.

1874 KNIGHT I. 754/2 With the bringing into action of the dropper, a cut-off is brought down to arrest the falling grain. **1886** *Sci. Amer.* LV. 373/3 It causes a Westerner to laugh to see small grain being cut with a 'dropper' or a self-raking reaper.

3. A medicine dropper. Also attrib.

1889 *Internat. Annual, Anthony's Photogr. Bul.* 12 The dropper is filled with alkali solution from the wide-mouthed bottle, a few drops run into the developer. **1944** *Sears Cat.* (ed. 189) 557 *Oleum Percomorphum.* . . . Handy dropper cap included. *Ib.* 558B Sears Approved Nose Drops . . . 1 oz. dropper bottle.

As the last term in **corn, pea, pocketbook dropper.**

* **dropping,** *n.* In combs.: (1) **dropping board,** a board for receiving the droppings of a henroost; (2) **fire,** an irregular, desultory discharge of firearms; (3) **-off-place,** a remote place, the end of the world, *colloq.*, cf. **jumping-off place;** (4) **song,** a song sung by a mocking-bird while dropping and fluttering down from bough to bough; (5) **time,** the time or season when corn and similar crops are planted.

(1) 1871 LEWIS *Poultry Book* 112 Under these dropping boards are the nest-boxes, where the fowls lay. *Ib.*, The dropping boards extended the whole width of the pen. — **(2) 1881–5** MCCLELLAN *Own Story* 325 There had been merely a dropping fire of skirmishers. **1890** *Cent. Mag.* July 447/2 A dropping fire of musketry began. — **(3) 1895** *Cent. Mag.* Sep. 674/2 It's a wild old nest up there, . . . a wild road to nowhere, only the dropping-off place. — **(4) 1885** M. THOMPSON *By-ways & Bird Notes* 10 A mocking-bird . . . sang for me its rarest and the most wonderful combination, called by negroes the 'dropping song.' — **(5) 1845** COOPER *Chainbearer* xix, A man intends to pitch on any partic'lar spot afore next plowin' or droppin' time, as the case may be.

* **droughty, drouthy,** *a.* A term formerly applied to Kansas in allusion to its prohibition laws. *Obs.* — **1869** *Republican Journal* (Lawrence) 5 March, Strangers visiting the State for the first time can scarcely realize that this is '*drouthy Kansas*.' **1878** BEADLE *Western Wilds* 432 'Droughty Kansas' was a standing joke.

* **drover,** *n.*

1. One in charge of a company or group of slaves. *Obs.*

[1776 in *W. & M. Coll. Quart.* XVII. 10 Excessive cold indeed; all my people, tho' well cloathed, playing at hide & seek. As fast as one drover is carried down the hill one way, another comes up on the other side wch Proves they sham because they don't want to be seen when they come in.] **1852** STOWE *Uncle Tom* xii, 'I say, now,' said the drover, touching his elbow, 'there's differences in parsons, an't there?' **1860** OLMSTED *Back Country* 152 In the fall, a great many drovers and slave-dealers passed over the road.

2. A person in charge of, and usu. accompanying, a large number of cattle, hogs, etc., being sent to market by rail. See also **hog, horse, pig drover.**

1855 *N.Y. Herald* 21 Dec. 4/3 There is little doubt but the Erie and Central will have to reduce their rates, or the drovers will effect an arrangement with other lines. **1867** *Com. & Fin. Chron.* 22 June 791 During the year the company constructed 145 box, 40 coal, 4 baggage, 3 drovers' . . . cars. **1944** *Santa Fe Time Table* 12 Nov. 11 Drovers' or caretakers' tickets and Live Stock Contracts will not be honored.

drudge drʌdʒ, *n.* [Origin obscure.] (See quots.) *Obs.* — **1864** WEBSTER 416 *Drudge*, . . . whisky in its raw state, as used in the manufacture of alcohol. **1869** HALDEMAN *Pa. Dutch* (F. & H.), Drudge, another name for raw whiskey, originating in the Eastern States. I doubt whether the word drudge is thirty years old. **1891** *Cent.* 1781/1.

* **drug,** *n.* In combs.: (1) **drug clerk,** a clerk or salesman in a drugstore; (2) **shop,** =**drugstore;** (3) **store,** see as a main entry.

(1) 1849 *Whig Almanac 1850* 25/1 Congress, last session, created, in Minnesota, . . . a drug clerk at $1,000. **1912** *Out West* Mar. 163/1 As to the preparations bought, not even the drug clerk who sold them knew definitely as to their ingredients. — **(2) 1783** FRENEAU *Poems* (1786) 317 Next door to the drug shop of doctor Brownejohn. **1885** *N. Amer. Rev.* CXL. 519 Drug-shops scarcely disguise their liquors behind their soda fountains.

* **druggist,** *n.* **1. druggist shop,** =**drugstore. 2. druggist store,** =**drugstore.** Both *obs.*

(1) 1816 U. BROWN *Journal* I. 346 Dr. Morelands . . . goes back to Town to the Drugist Shop, gets medicine. **1837** W. JENKINS *Ohio Gaz.* 149 It contains . . . 1 druggist shop. — **(2) 1817** S. BROWN *Western Gaz.* 344 Three druggist stores. **1820** *Columbian Centinel* 2 Feb. 3/3 Situation Wanted, By a young Man, in a Druggist Store.

drugstore ˈdrʌgˌstor, *n.* A pharmacy; more recently a store which sells soft drinks, cosmetics, magazines, etc., as well as drugs. Also attrib. See also **cash, corner drugstore.**

1819 M'MURTRIE *Sk. Louisville* 137 There are at this moment, in Louisville, . . . three printing offices, three drug stores. **1884** SWEET & KNOX *Through Texas* xv. 230, I felt a sort of drug-store taste in my mouth. **1900** DIX *Deacon Bradbury* 67 He pictured himself as he had worked eagerly in the little drug-store laboratory. **1948** *Chi. Star* 24 April 3/3 Exempted from the ban would be drug stores, beauty parlors and hairdressing places.

* **drum,** *n.*

1. One of several fishes of the family Sciaenidae, so called because of a drumming noise which they make.

1650 in FORCE *Tracts* III. No. 11, 11 Sturgeon of ten feet, Drummes of sixe in length. **1790** *Pa. Packet* 3 March 3/2 Maxwell, at one haul, took up as many bass, drum, trout, mullet, and whiting, . . . as filled a six oared boat. **1884** GOODE *Fisheries* I. 362 The Drum . . . may be distinguished from all others by the presence of the comparatively short, spiny dorsal fin. **1948** *Chi. Tribune* 25 Jan. II. 2/6 Then we caught some good sized drums, silvery, husky fish that won't give up a fight.

2. (See quots.) Cf. **dumb stove.**

1833 KERCHEVAL *History* 206 Many of the Germans have what they call a drum, through which the stove-pipe passes in their upper rooms. It is made of sheet iron, something in the shape of the military drum. It soon fills with heat from the pipe, by which the rooms become agreeably warm in the coldest weather. **1924** LAMBERT *Pa.-Ger.*, Drumm . . . hollow cylinder for heating a room. d[ialect] G drumm.

3. A cheap or low dive, a "hangout"; also a small and cramped room. *Slang.*

1903 A. H. LEWIS *Boss* 32 He said the Dead Rabbit was a drum for crooks! **1908** MCGAFFEY *Show-Girl* 234 We came to a door which the gee threw open and said, 'This is your stateroom.' Honest, I never saw such a drum. **1925** WITWER *Roughly Speaking* 140 We went down to the Hotel Employment Agency the other day and win ourselves a couple of sweet jobs at the Hotel Egram, the niftiest drum in Loose Angeles!

4. In combs.: (1) **drum corps,** in a military organization, a corps of drummers; (2) **fish,** = ***drum,** *n.* **1,** cf. **black drum;** (3) **fishing,** fishing for drum; (4) **line,** "a stout line used in drum fishing" (Green, *Va. Word-Book*).

(1) **1861** *Chi. Tribune* 19 July 1/2 Commander Dahlgren has also presented each of the drum corps with a rifle-gun of his own invention. **1904** *Brooklyn Standard-Union* 7 June 6 Brooklyn Grand Army Post presenting a flag to an out-of-town drum corps. — (2) **1737** BRICKELL *N. Carolina* 229 The Drum-fish, whereof there are two sorts, viz. the Red and the Black. **1948** *Highway Traveler* Dec. 12/1 The drum-fish is especially fond of oyster meat, and sometimes whole beds are decimated by attacks from drumfish schools. — (3) **1818** in COMMONS *Doc. Hist.* I. 203 Sent the boat a Drum fishing and caught 5 Drum. **1904** *Booklovers Mag.* III. 625/2 Senator Quay . . . was discovered . . . knee-deep in the surf at Atlantic City, drum-fishing. — (4) **1771** *Md. Hist. Mag.* XIII. 172 Send me two knots of Drum-lines. **1803** *Lewis & Clark Exped.* VII. (1905) 233, 4 Groce fishing Hooks assorted. 12 Bunches of Drum Line.

As the last term in **banded, banjo, big, black, fresh-water, Indian, medicine, red, striped drum.**

***drum,** *v.*

1. *intr.* Of ruffed grouse: To make a loud, reverberating sound by the quivering of the wings.

*a***1813** A. WILSON *Foresters* Wks. (1846) 232 Buried in depth of woods. . . . Where pheasants drum. **1831** AUDUBON *Ornith. Biog.* I. 212, I have shot some [Ruffed Grouse] and have heard them *drumming* in such places, when there were no hills nearer than fifteen or twenty miles. **1946** RICHTER *Fields* 168 Back in the woods a cock pheasant must have reckoned it was spring, for he kept drumming.

2. *fig. tr.* To gather up or seek out by soliciting, to rouse. Usu. with *up.*

1830 S. SMITH *Major Downing* 43, I'm going to start . . . on an electioneering cruise. I shall drum 'em up about right. **1851** A. O. HALL *Manhattaner* 168 'Straws' 'drummed' subscribers with his telling and artistic 'Reveille' in St. Louis. **1948** *Chi. Tribune* 1 Feb. (Grafic Mag.) 13/2 Tex Rickard . . . was drumming up additional business for Madison Square garden.

b. *intr.* or *absol.* To canvass.

1839 BRIGGS *H. Franco* I. 90 Augustus . . . had drummed in Arkansas, and collected in the lithograph cities of the west. **1886** *Harper's Mag.* June 107 The commercial drummer . . . comes out fresh as a daisy, and all ready to drum.

3. *To drum logs,* (see quot.).

1905 *Forestry Bureau Bul.* No. 61, 36 *Drum logs, to,* to haul logs by drum and cable out of a hollow or cove (App[alachian Forest]).

***drummer,** *n.* **1.** The squeteague. **2.** One of many species of Pacific Coast sculpin.

(1) **1807** *Mass. H.S. Coll.* 2 Ser. III. 57 The squittee, or drummer, is taken in the Sound, but principally in the harbours and lagunes, in summer. **1892** *Outing* April 54/2 The squeteague or weak-fish [is] . . . known about Cape Cod as the 'drummer,' 'silver fish,' and 'spotted boy.' — (2) **1884** GOODE *Fisheries* I. 259 The Cottidae . . . are represented on the Pacific coast by about eighteen separate species, known by such names as 'Sculpin,' 'Drummer,' 'Salpa,' [etc.]. . . . 'Drummer' comes from the quivering noise made by many species when taken alive out of the water.

As the last term in **cigar, dry-goods, shoe, trap drummer.**

***drumming,** *n.*

1. Soliciting trade, taking orders, etc.

1834 A. GREENE *Perils Pearl Street* ix. 65 None of them [i.e., clerks] could equal Mr. Smirk himself in real acute . . . drumming. **1875** *Chi. Tribune* 5 Oct. 2/3 Tipton . . . and a young man named Weir . . . have been advertised for weeks by monster posters, personal drumming, etc.

2. The peculiar noise made by a prairie chicken or a ruffed grouse. Cf. ***drum,** *v.* **1.** and see ***booming,** *n.*[3]

1893 *Outing* April 40/2 When the females have selected their partners all the drumming, parading, dancing and fighting cease among these feathered knights. **1947** EDMINSTER *Ruffed Grouse* 29 The drumming takes a little time and practice to attain proficiency.

b. drumming grouse, (see quots.).

1897 *Ann. Rep. Comm. Fisheries* 311 *Bonasa umbellus* (Linnaeus). Ruffed Grouse. Popular synonyms: 'Partridge' (in New England); 'Pheasant' (in Southern and Western States); Ruffled Grouse; Drumming Grouse. **1917** *Birds of Amer.* II. 17 Ruffed Grouse. . . . Other names.—Grouse . . . Drumming Grouse.

c. drumming log, a log to which a ruffed grouse resorts for drumming.

1904 CRISSEY *Tattlings* 87 This young reformer was busier than a cock partridge on a drumming log. **1947** BUMP *Ruffed Grouse* 266 But the analogy holds only partially for, although the males establish drumming areas 'staked out' by their drumming logs, there seems to be no recognizable relationship between these and the nesting sites of the females.

***Drummond,** *n.* Used, usu. in the possessive, in names: (1) **Drummond('s) phlox,** an extensively cultivated phlox, native to Texas; (2) **Drummond's snipe,** (see quot.).

(1) **1863** *Horticulturist* XVIII. 127/1 Drummond's Phlox, (*Phlox Drummondii*)—Sow the seed thinly in drills about an inch apart. **1947** *Chr. Sci. Monitor* 21 May 10/3 Drummond phlox makes a delightful accent in the annual border, and enables the gardener who rents his home to have phlox. — (2) **1839** AUDUBON *Ornith. Biog.* V. 319 Drummond's snipe, *Scolopax drummondii*, . . . is common in the Fur Countries up to latitude 65°, and is also found in the recesses of the Rocky Mountains.

***drunkards,** *n. pl. local.* (See quots.)

1890 *Amer. Folk-Lore* III. 64 *Drunkards*, at Hyannis this is the name by which the young, tender leaves of the checkerberry are called. . . . Perhaps the name was given . . . on account of their use as a leading ingredient in the making of home-brewed beer. **1892** *Ib.* V. 100 *Gaultheria procumbens*, young plantlets; drunkards. Barnstable, Mass. **1899** GREEN *Va. Word-Book* 125 Drunkards, small flies that fly about and light in sweetened liquors.

drunkification ˌdrʌŋkəfəˈkeʃən, *n.* A celebration at which people get drunk. *Rare.* — **1887** *Voice* (N.Y.) 11 Aug., The bummers of the city [Louisville, Ky.] have been having a little drunkification over the result down there [i.e., the defeat of prohibition].

drunkist ˈdrʌŋkɪst, *n.* [Irreg. f. ***drunk,** *p.p.* of ***drink.**] One who is drunk. *Rare.* — **1869** *N. Eng. Base-Ballist* 27 Aug. 13/4 An unfortunate individual who was about one-quarter cripple and three-quarters drunkist, fell in Washington street.

***druther,** see **rather.**

***dry,** *n.* A prohibitionist *q.v. Colloq.*

1889 *Cent.* 1784/2 Dry, . . . a member of the Prohibition party. **1896** *Chi. Record* 11 Feb. 6/5 Even though there might be some precincts where the 'wets' outnumbered the 'drys'—yet the whole county would go dry. **1948** *Galveston* (Tex.) *News* 14 June 4/4 The Kansas senator has always been a dry—personally as well as politically.

***dry,** *a.*

1. (See quot.) *Rare.*

1854 HAMMOND *Hills, Lakes* 41 On the eastern shore, tall fir trees of all sizes may be found, many of which are dead, or as the woodmen term it, dry.

2. *Quasi-political.* Opposed to, or free from, the sale of intoxicating liquor.

1870 R. H. DAVIS in *Scribner's Mo.* I. 63 Dry or wet, Mr. Dort? Indifferent, eh? Adolph, a hock-glass. **1948** *Time* 26 April 14/3 In Oasis, Wis., the natives voted 48–47 to keep the town dry.

b. Used quasi-adverbially in phrases *to go dry, to vote dry.*

1888 *Detroit Ev. Jrnl.* 20 Feb. (F.), If a county has voted on local option, and has gone dry [etc.]. **1904** *N.Y. Ev. Post* 3 Oct. 6 If every town and city in Vermont should vote 'dry' at the next election [etc.]. **1946** *Chi. Sun* 25 Dec. 4/5 A proposition that the ward go 'dry' was defeated.

3. In combs.: (1) **dry bellyache,** lead poisoning (see also quot. 1899 and cf. **dry gripes, gripings**); (2) **bone,** (see quots.); (3) **farm,** a farm upon which dry farming is practiced, also transf.; (4) **farmer,** one who dry farms; (5) **farming,** in semiarid regions, a method of farming whereby the rainfall is conserved to the utmost; (6) **goods,** see as a main entry; (7) **gripes, gripings,** = **dry bellyache,** also fig.; (8) **hole,** a well in which no oil is struck as a result of drilling, cf. * **duster 3;** (9) **house,** a building used for drying fruit, fish, etc.; (10) **Dry Ice,** a trade-mark name for carbon dioxide in a solidified state, also (not *cap.*) this cooling agent; (11) * **land,** see as a main entry; (12) **lander,** = **dry farmer;** (13) **murrain,** any one of various diseases among cattle, such as Texas fever; (14) **ranch,** (see quot. 1887); (15) * **skin,** (see quots.); (16) **state,** a state in which the sale of liquor is prohibited; (17) **strawberry,** the barren strawberry; (18) **washing,** *W.* a method of extracting gold from auriferous earth without the use of water, also **dry-wash method;** (19) * **well,** *(a)* a well in which foods, etc., are kept cool, *(b)* = **dry hole.**

(1) **1694** S. Sewall *Diary* I. (1878) 390 Brother tells me Sister fears she shall have the Dry Belly-Ache. **1899** Green *Va. Word-Book* 125 Dry-belly-ache. n. Strong pains in the belly without looseness of the bowels. 'He looks like he had the *dry-belly-ache*.' **1947** *Chi. Tribune* 4 July 6/4 He was also intensely interested in a condition referred to as 'dry bellyache,' which we now call 'lead poisoning.' — (2) **1834** Featherstonhaugh *Slave States* (1844) 76 Wherever the metal runs, this wet red clay accompanies it, ... carrying along with it sometimes nodules of quartz, iron, zinc, and a little galena, a compound to which the miners have given the name *dry bones*. **1857** Dana *Mineralogy* 278 Argillaceous iron, iron pyrites, calamine ('dry bone' of the miners), blende, ... are the most common associated minerals. — (3) **1919** Hough *Sagebrusher* xxxiii, A few scattered dry farms, edging up close to the river in the valley far below, were caught [in the flood] and buried. **1948** *Atlantic Mo.* Jan. 59/2 This is not real tourist country. ... This is a scenic dry-farm, the biggest and almost the last. — (4) **1912** Wason *Friar Tuck* iii. 36 Next came the dry farmer. **1948** Rollinson *Wyo. Cattle Trails* 29 The benchland dry farmer with his plow turned over the 'niggerhead,' or bunch grass, and brought about a state of range ruin in a country which had once been rich in nutritious forage.

(5) **1878** Powell *Lands Arid Region* 78 Bear River 'City' [in Utah] was founded by a company of Danes, [who] ... have obtained a meagre subsistence by dry farming. **1948** *Desert Mag.* July 12/3 Southwestern irrigation farmers have stoutly maintained that profitable dry farming is next to impossible. — (7) **1704** in *Amer. Sp.* XV. 227/2 Lieut. Putnam sick of ye dry gripeings. **1724** Jones *Present State* 50 Besides this, some [in Va.] are troubled with the dry Gripes, proceeding from Colds (I suppose) which take away for a long Time the Use of the Limbs of some, especially hard Drinkers of Rum. **1889** Mark Twain *Conn. Yankee* iv. 53 (R.), Jokes that had given me the dry gripes. — (8) **1883** *Cent. Mag.* July 323/1 New districts are discovered by wasting large sums of money on 'dry holes.' **1948** *Dly. Ardmoreite* (Ardmore, Okla.) 1 Aug. 9/1 A look of despair spread over the stranger's face as he told of drilling three wells that turned out to be 'dry holes.' — (9) [**1776** *N.C. Morav. Rec.* III. (1926) 1101 The dry-house for flax caught fire.] **1867** *Rep. Comm. Patents 1866* II. 1141 *Dry House.* ... The lower part is occupied by the heater ... upon which vessels may be deposited. **1903** G. C. Eggleston *First of Hoosiers* 21 He built a great stone 'dry house,' which I remember very well, though it burned while I was yet a boy.

(10) **1927** *Outlook* 31 Aug. 558/3 Though dry ice costs ten times as much as wet ice, it refrigerates fifteen times as much. **1934** Webster. **1948** *Pacific Discovery* July–Aug. 25/2 He is already, with partial success, causing local rains by scattering dry ice among the clouds. — (12) **1921** *Frontier* Feb. 11 It is good house. He build summer kitchen. None of drylanders have summer kitchen. **1943** Howard *Montana* 37 Neighbors helped themselves to the drylanders' abandoned house. — (13) **1867** *Mo. Bd. Agric. Rep.* II. 16 Wherever they are herding any length of time, our cattle take some disease similar to dry murrain. **1870** *Dept. Agric. Rep. 1869* 39 Diseases locally known as 'murrain,' 'dry murrain,' 'bloody murrain,' and 'staggers,' have prevailed to some extent in different parts of the South. — (14) **1869** Muir *First Summer in Sierra* (1911) 12 We at length discovered a road trending toward Coulterville, which we followed until an hour before sunset, when we reached a dry ranch and camped for the night. **1887** in Lindley *Calif. of South* (1888) 267 The second [tableland], upon which are found the settlements of San Jacinto and Perris, and many so-called dry ranches (because not supplied with water by irrigation ditches), about fifteen hundred feet in altitude.

(15) **1701** Wolley *Journal N.Y.* (1902) 47 The Blubber of the whale will sometimes be half a yard thick or deep, if the Blubber be not fat and free, the whale is call'd a Dry-skin. **1945** Colcord *Sea Lang.* 69 Dry-skin. A whale with scarcely any blubber. Hence in whaling communities, a man who leaves less property than was expected.—

(16) **1931** F. L. Allen *Only Yesterday* 11 After a few dances, Mr. Smith wanders out to the bar (if this is not a dry state). **1947** *Time* 1 Dec. 24/3 He was a wet in a dry state, but he won the election two to one. — (17) **1817–8** Eaton *Botany* (1822) 262 *Dalibarda fragaroides*, dry strawberry. **1869** Fuller *Flower Gatherers* 79 The fruit is dry and hard, on which account it is sometimes called the 'Dry Strawberry.' — (18) **1850** Ryan *Adventures* II. 13 These men were actively pursuing a process that is termed 'dry-washing.' One was shovelling up the sand into a large cloth ... which ... he ... shook until the pebbles and larger particles of stone and dirt came to the surface. **1925** Bryan *Papago Country* 392 There are gold placers near Horseshoe ... which the Papagos still work by dry washing. **1946** McWilliams *So. Calif. Country* 56 The dry-wash method involved the use of the *arrastra*, a crude piece of equipment operated by a water-wheel. — (19) *(a)* **1770** *Md. Hist. Mag.* XII. 354 My dry well, will be compleated by the 20th of next month. **1785** Washington *Diaries* II. 334 Preparing my dry well, and the well in my New Cellar for the reception of Ice. *(b)* **1883** *Cent. Mag.* July 323/2 When a dry well demonstrates that the edge has been reached in one direction, no more are bored so far out. **1901** *Cosmopolitan* July 252/2 His second experiment was in a dry well which had never produced oil.

b. In less frequent combs., often rare or obs.: (1) **dry bridge,** a bridge over a dry ravine; (2) **Mike,** (see quot.); (3) **norther,** esp. in Texas, a sudden strong wind from the north, without rain; (4) **placer machine,** = **dry washing machine;** (5) * **rot,** a disease of cotton; (6) **shower,** ?a blustery storm with little or no rain; (7) **soil farming,** = **dry farming;** (8) **sowing,** a manner of sowing so as to take advantage of all available rainfall; (9) **spiked sedge,** (see quot.); (10) **stuff,** (see quot.); (11) **wash,** (see quot. and cf. **c.** (20) below); (12) **washer,** = next, *obs.;* (13) **washing machine,** in placer mining, a machine for sifting dirt by means of a strong current of air; (14) **weather fly,** (see quot.), *colloq.;* (15) **year,** (see quot.).

(1) **1821** Stansbury *Pedestrian Tour* (1822) 63 A large dry-bridge leads the turnpike over a broad ravine. — (2) **1869** *Overland Mo.* III. 129 When he munched a piece of crust, or any unmoistened provisions, as he sat in his saddle, he was eating his 'dry Mike.' — (3) **1871–3** *Texas Almanac* 97 The people here in Texas divide these winter storms into 'wet northers' and 'dry northers.'— (4) **1878** Hinton *Hdbk. Ariz.* 213 There are two or three of these dry-placer machines in use.

(5) **1855** in Turner *Cotton* (1865) 174 Permit me ... to make known the existence of a disease in our cotton ... called the 'dry rot.' The disease we speak of attacks the top bolls. ... After the disease has taken possession of the whole pod it opens its prongs and presents a thoroughly rotten state in all its parts. — (6) **1853** Simms *Sword & Distaff* 269, I'm as thirsty after work as a bull-frog after a dry-shower. — (7) **1929** J. Parker *Old Army* 124 Which had not been filed upon was capable of cultivation by 'dry soil farming.'— (8) **1874** *Dept. Agric. Rep. 1873* 211 Among others are the settled facts arrived at concerning the dry-sowing of wheat-land—a way having been found whereby to produce a good crop with the smallest possible quantity of moisture from rain-fall [etc.]. — (9) **1843** Torrey *Flora N.Y.* II. 374 *Carex siccata*, ... Dry-spiked Sedge. ... Western part of the State.

(10) **1913** W. C. Barnes *Western Grazing Grounds* 129 After the calves are out of the bunch the 'dry stuff'—steers, dry cows and strays —is taken out and thrown into the 'day herd.' — (11) **1870** Macrae *Americans* I. 253 Even officers had sometimes to content themselves with 'a dry wash,'—that is, taking off their woollen shirts and flapping them against the saddle, to shake the vermin out. — (12) **1885** *Wkly. New Mexican Review* 5 March 3/5 With all the so-called 'dry-washers' and the water supply being limited, it has heretofore cost something like thirty cents per cubic yard. — (13) **1877** H. C. Hodge *Arizona* 63 Dry washing machines have of late been introduced, which ... will ... be the means of working out large tracts of placer mines. — (14) **1897** Terhune *Old-field School* 3 A locust—'a dry-weather fly,' the people there-abouts called it—had perched on the sill on the sunniest window and sang shrilly.

(15) **1894** Robley *Bourbon Co., Kansas* 156 The year 1860 is known as the 'dry year.' The long drouth really commenced in the latter part of 1859.

c. Designating places where there is no water, or streams, lakes, etc., that are dry except in wet weather, as (1) **dry arroyo,** (2) **barren,** (3) **bayou,** (4) **bottom,** (5) **branch,** (6) **camp,** (cf. also **water camp**), (7) **creek,** (8) **diggings,** (9) **gulch,** (10) **gut,** (11) **hollow,** (12) **lake,** (cf. **playa**), (13) **marsh,** (14) **meadow,** (15) **prairie,** (16) **run,** (17) **swamp,** (18) **timberline,** (19) **valley,** (20) **wash,** (cf. also **b.** (11) above).

(1) 1843 Frémont *Exped.* 252 We discovered . . . groves of oak trees on a dry arroyo. **1907** S. E. White *Arizona Nights* 182 Anderson led the way . . . up a dry arroyo. — **(2) 1930** Parker *Amer. Lang. in Indiana* 6 *Dry Barren,* like *dry prairie* and *wet prairie,* seems to have had some cause for its use in designating to settlers and farmers the desirable and undesirable portions of land. — **(3)** [**1841** W. Kennedy *Texas* I. 25 The word *bayou* . . . is rather loosely applied in the topography of Texas and the West. In strictness, I believe it means a deep inlet, which affords a channel for water in time of flood, and remains dry, or nearly so, at other seasons.] **1853** P. Paxton *Yankee in Texas* 29 Poke, so full of the chase that he had not noticed the dry bayou before him, pitched headlong down the precipitous bank.— **(4) 1639** in *Amer. Sp.* XV. 174/2 And att the head of the Swamp wth a dry bottome extending to the head of the dry bottome. **1706** *Ib.,* Begining at the mouth of a Small dry bottom running out of Sacariris Swamp and up the Said bottom to a marked Hickery.

(5) 1661 in *Amer. Sp.* XV. 174/2 To a Corner Oak by a Dry branch. **1824** *Ib.* To a white oak & hickory on the bank of a dry branch. — **(6) 1869** J. R. Browne *Adv. Apache Country* 128 A few hours of night-travel brought us to the Pecacho, a little beyond which we made a dry camp till morning. **1947** *So. Sierran* April 4/2 A dry camp was made at the 2500-foot level two miles further up the canyon. — **(7) 1807** Schultz *Travels* (1810) I. 196 From Blue River you descend a distance of one hundred and twenty miles, without passing either towns or streams, except a few *dry creeks.* **1923** in *Amer. Sp.* XV. 174/2 The waters of a few of the streams on the south slope of Powell Mountain flow in places for miles in a mantle of water-worn boulders, which conspicuously marks the course of the stream, but conceals the water, a fact which gives rise to the popular term 'dry creek.' — **(8) 1848** *Californian* (S.F.) 14 Aug. 2/3 In one part of the mine called the 'dry diggins,' no other implements are necessary than an ordinary sheath knife, to pick the gold from the rocks. **1948** Johnston *Gold Rush* ii/2 Placerville, first known as Old Dry Diggings and then as Hangtown, was settled soon thereafter. — **(9) 1870** in Cramton *Early Hist. Yellowstone Nat. Pk.* 115 We moved in the afternoon at 2.30 p.m., following the course of the valley, crossing several small streams and numerous dry gulches on the way. **1947** *So. Sierran* Jan. 2/3 Again we crossed the creek, went up a dry gulch, and turned to climb a sandy slope.

(10) 1638 in *Amer. Sp.* XV. 174/2 Two hundred and fiftie acres of land . . . butting upon a drye gut or deepe hollow Swamp. — **(11) 1792** in *Amer. Sp.* XV. 174/2 To white oaks and a walnut by a dry Hollow. — **(12) 1849** Hayes *Pioneer Notes* (1929) 42 A large 'dry lake' which had been replenished by winter rains was crossed. **1947** *Sierra Club Bul.* May 19 This haze-filled view down into a dry, baked valley in which swirls of dust rose from the flat, hot bed of a dry lake —could this be any part of the Sierra? — **(13) 1635** in *Amer. Sp.* XV. 174/2 On a long dry marshe along the backside. **1902** *Ib.,* We have two natural wells in this county: one at what is called Dry Marsh, a drain of Opequon, about two miles east of the creek. — **(14) 1651** in *Amer. Sp.* XV 174/2 Very rich Lands, well Timbered and Watered, and large dry Meadows. **1805** Parkinson *Tour* 120 Glades, or wide-extended dry meadows.

(15) 1817 Brown *Western Gazeteer* 23 Dry prairie, bordering all the rivers, lies immediately in the rear of the bottoms, from 30 to 100 feet higher; and from one to ten miles wide, a dry rich soil, and most happily adapted to the purposes of cultivation. **1940** Deam *Flora Indiana* 1127 Oak openings are remnants of dry prairies in northern Indiana where bur oak was the invading tree species. — **(16) 1847** Joel Palmer *Rocky Mts.* (1847) 61 We took up a dry run for one or two miles, thence over a ridge to a running branch. **1893** *Harper's Mag.* April 697/2 Arroyos, or dry runs, . . . collect the storm waters, whose accumulations scour deepening channels in the friable soil. — **(17) 1640** *Conn. Hist. Soc. Coll.* XIV. 223 One parsell . . . of dry swamp. **1684** *Conn. Pub. Records* III. 161 [He was] detaining from them a certaine peice of land lyeing in a place comonly called . . . Weathersfeild dry swampe. — **(18) 1903** *Amer. Geol. Soc. Bul.* XIV. 556 In Southwestern Oregon, Nevada, Southern California, etcetera, where the climate is excessively arid, the dry timber-line is higher than in Idaho, and in certain localities meets the cold timberline, and the mountains are bare of trees from base to summit. **1925** Bryan *Papago Country* 375 The latter type of timber line . . . , called the dry timber line, is well displayed in the Tumacacori Mountains. — **(19) 1645** in *Amer. Sp.* XV. 175/1 Beginning at a dry valley running out of ye White Marsh. **1669** *Ib.,* To a marked white oake at the Head of a Dry valley.

(20) 1872 Bourke *Journal* 25 Nov., There is a dry wash on this road about (3) miles from todays camp. **1944** Johnson *As I Dare* 335 My cabin was separated from the ranch house by a dry wash about forty feet wide.

d. *To be dry behind the ears,* mature, usu. in negative contexts. *Colloq.*

1928 Foy & Harlow *Clowning Thro' Life* 62 We heard mutterings about kids who weren't dry behind the ears yet. **1945** *Chi. D. News* 30 Aug. 22/7 They aren't dry behind the ears, so to speak, but still believe in Santa Claus.

4. In verbal expressions: (1) *to dry farm, W.* to grow crops in a semiarid region without irrigation; (2) *to dry gulch,* to assassinate, *slang;* (3) *to dry wash,* to secure (gold) from auriferous earth by dry washing.

(1) 1917 *U. of Ariz. Agric. Exper. Sta. Ann. Rep. 1916–18* 393 Spring rains . . . contributed to the production of dry-farmed crops. **1927** James *Cow Country* 151 They think they can dry-farm that land but I know better. — **(2) 1930** Raine & Barnes *Cattle* 51 Ben Turner, an ally of the Harrells, was dry-gulched. **1948** Rollinson *Wyo. Cattle Trails* 107 Evidently his new neighbors did not take kindly to his ways of doing business, for he was found 'dry-gulched.' — **(3) 1912** Lumholtz *New Trails* 27 The Papagos also know how to 'dry wash' gold at the placer mines.

* **dry,** *v.* * *To dry up,* to cease talking. *Colloq.*

1853 *S.F. Comm. Advertiser* 9 Dec. 2/4 She defied his Honor and all his officers, . . . and giving assurance of a disposition never to 'dry up,' was carried down below to cool off. **1871** *Harper's Mag.* Oct. 799 Now, Sam, you had better dry up about my Irish blunders, for you Jews have nothing to brag of. **1948** *Chi. Tribune* 27 June (Comics) 3 If my wife starts barking at me, I will tell her to dry up.

* **dry goods.**

1. Clothing.

1851 *Polly Peablossom* 25 A ride over a dusty road is apt to soil a gentleman's dry goods. **1884** Sweet & Knox *Through Texas* xx. 269 They sweat and swear, and are afraid to take off their warm dry-goods.

2. *piece of dry goods,* a girl or woman. *Slang.*

1869 Tourgee *Toinette* xxxv. 362 [The nurse is] the trimmest piece of dry-goods I have seen in many a day.

3. In combs.: (1) **dry-goods box,** a wooden packing case, orig. used for shipping dry goods, also attrib.; (2) **case,** =**dry-goods box;** (3) **clerk,** one who sells dry goods in a store; (4) **district,** the district in a large city where dry goods are sold, usu. a wholesale district; (5) **drummer,** a traveling salesman who sells dry goods; (6) **line,** a supply or stock of dry goods; (7) **palace,** a large dry-goods store; (8) **rack,** a rack for displaying dry goods; (9) **shop,** =**dry-goods store,** now *rare;* (10) **store,** a store which specializes in dry goods, also attrib.

(1) 1845 in *Nebr. Hist. Pub.* XX. 130 Counted 'rising of *thirty large dry goods boxes,* all labeled to different firms in Santa Fe.' **1869** Mark Twain *Innocents* li. 541 They swarmed out of mud bee-hives; out of hovels of dry-goods- box pattern. **1945** Molloy *Pride's Way* 177 That looked like the toy cars the children made out of dry-goods boxes. — **(2) 1852** Hale *If, Yes, & Perhaps* (1868) 36, I wrought my way through a long line of dry-goods cases to a distant counting-room. — **(3) 1848** *Hunt's Merch. Mag.* XVIII. 119 An association of dry-goods clerks should be formed. **1902** Lorimer *Lett. Merchant* 63, I roomed with a dry-goods clerk named Charlie Chase. — **(4) 1884** *Cent. Mag.* Aug. 511/2 The plain fronts that abound, for instance, in the so-called 'dry-goods district' of New York are not beautiful.

(5) 1886 Poore *Reminisc.* I. 316 They are going about the country like dry-goods drummers, exhibiting samples of their wares. — **(6) 1836** W. F. Gray *Diary* (1909) 183 Called . . . to see John Scott, who is doing well here (Mobile) in dry goods line. — **(7) 1860** Mordecai *Virginia* 58 The splendid store of Kent, Pine & Co., the first specimen in Richmond of the Broadway style of dry goods palaces, has risen on the spot. **1882** Howells *Modern Instance* xvi., An old-fashioned hotel, whose site was long ago devoured by a dry-goods palace. — **(8) 1874** *Index to Patents* I. 463 Dry-goods rack [by] C. N. Cadwallader, . . . Philadelphia, Pa. . . . Apr. 1, 1872, [no.] 137,416. — **(9) 1791** in H. M. Brooks *Gleanings* 43 To be let, a Handsome square Shop, . . . suitable either for a Grocery, West India or Dry-Goods Shop. **1894** *Harper's Mag.* LXXXIX. 879/1 A square inch of pure skin is worth more than all the covering in all the dry-goods shops.

(10) 1776 *N.J. Archives* 2 Ser. I. 34 To be sold. . . . Large and convenient house. . . . At one end of said dwelling-house, a good kitchen, and at the other a dry-goods store. **1859** Wilmer *Press Gang* 323 A journalist . . . was assaulted . . . by a dry-goods store-keeper, in an oyster-cellar. **1904** *Forum* Oct. 275 The Baltimore fire originated in a large dry-goods store.

dryki ˈdraɪkɪ, *n.* [Prob. f. *dry-kill,* used by lumberers of standing timber killed by fire.] (See quot. 1901). — **1901** *Everybody's Mag.* June 552/2 The shores are rocky and covered in most parts by fallen timber, called dryki, whose bleached bones shine silvery white against the dark background of everygreens. **1942** Rich *We Took to Woods* (1948) 39 Then Bobcat Bill strolls up from the lake, throws an armful of dry-ki onto the blaze, and a shiver runs around the fire.

* **dry land.**

1. Formerly a name used locally for an area between Bethlehem and Nazareth, Pa.

1788 SCHÖPF *Reise* I. 231 Alles dieses hohe Land, zwischen Bethlehem und Nazareth, und seitwärts gegen Easton, ist unter dem Namen des trockenen Landes, (the dry Land), allgemein bekannt. Und trocken ist es wirklich. 1806 HERRMANN *Deutschen* 160 Der Boden umher [i.e. Nazareth, Penna.] ist, weil er aus Kalk besteht, ungemein trocken, und daher auch nur unter dem Namen des trocknen Landes (*dry land*) bekannt.

2. *attrib.* or as *adj.* Of or pertaining to regions where dry farming or farming by irrigation is practiced.

1893 *Irrigation Age* April 358/2 Nearly or quite every effort that has been made to establish dry-land colonies has ended in failure. 1920 *Harvey's Weekly* 24 July 11/2 Vegetables—'dry-land' and irrigated.

b. dry-land farmer, =**dry farmer.**

1912 BOWER *Flying U* 166 The soil was not fertile enough even for the most optimistic of 'dry land' farmers to locate upon it; and this was before the dry-land farming craze had swept the country, gathering in all public land as claims.

3. dry-land blueberry, a low shrub, *Vaccinium vacillans*, found in dry sandy soil from New Hampshire to Ontario and Michigan and south to Georgia and Kansas.

1924 DEAM *Shrubs of Indiana* 273 It is usually associated with dry-land blueberry and black huckleberry. 1947 *Midland Naturalist* July 54 Dryland Blueberry [is] abundant in pine-oak forest and upland oak forest.

dry-up ˈdraɪˌʌp, *n.* The action of the ground in drying up after a wet spell. *Rare.* — 1873 BEADLE *Undevel. West* 711 The plowman returns to his work without waiting for a 'dry-up.'

Duane's purple. A variety of plum. *Obs.* — 1859 ELLIOTT *Western Fruit Book* 434 *Duane's Purple*. . . . Fruit, large, oblong, oval, one side enlarged, reddish purple in sun, pale red in shade. 1874 *Dept. Agric. Rep. 1873* 443 *Plums.*—Jefferson, Green Gage, Duane's Purple, and Red Gage were all regarded as worthy of cultivation.

***dub,** *n.* One who is inexperienced at anything; any awkward performer. *Colloq.* Cf. **dubster.** — 1887 *Courier-Journal* 20 Jan. 6/4 Dem dubs is goin' to git it in de neck in a minit. 1929 *Randolph Enterprise* (Elkins, W.Va.) 14 March 1/2 People allow some poor dub who is merely looking for a job and a few paltry dollars to wreck and ruin the trees that only God himself can make.

***dubber,** *n.* An instrument used to make pliant, and to remove flesh, hair, etc., from, buffalo skins. Cf. ***flesher.** — 1847 RUXTON *Adv. Rocky Mts.* (1848) 269 Dubbing is the removal of the flesh and fatty particles adhering to the skin, by means of the *dubber*, an instrument made of the stock of an elk's horn. 1850 GARRARD *Wah-To-Yah* iii. 49 A covering of buffalo skin is . . . divested of the hair and rendered pliant by means of the dubber—an adzeshaped piece of iron fitted to an angular section of elk's horn.

dubisary ˈdubəˌserɪ, *n.* ?A due bill *q.v. Rare.* 1836 *Quarter Race Ky.* (1846) 24 My respect for Mr. Wash's dirk-knife . . . induced me to express my entire satisfaction with Mr. Wash's *dubisary*.

dubster ˈdʌbstɚ, *n.* =**dub.** *Slang.* Cf. **dabster.* — 1904 *N.Y. Tribune* 1 May, They seize upon the latest clever dubster and cry him up as a miracle of wit and wisdom.

* **Duchess,** *n.*

1. *Duchesse d'Angoulême*, a variety of large, well-flavored pear.

1843 *Indiana Mag. Hist.* III. 190, I obtained the only specimen of the Duchesse d'Angouleme. 1930 BAILEY *Cyclo. Hort.* 2507/2 Many varieties of pear do well when grafted on the quince root, but the one that is oftenest grown as a dwarf is the Angouleme (Duchesse d'Angouleme).

2. An early-ripening Russian variety of yellowish-red apple grown in the colder parts of the U.S. Also **Duchess apple, Duchess of Oldenburg.**

1859 ELLIOTT *Western Fruit Book* 73 Duchess of Oldenburgh . . . Fruit, medium to large, roundish flattened, light red, striped and splashed on yellow. 1874 *Dept. Agric. Rep. 1873* 434 Fruits . . . which had succeeded best. . . . Apples—Red and White Astrachan, Duchess of Oldenberg. 1948 *News-Palladium* (Benton Harbor, Mich.) 7/1 Duchess apples, No. 1, 2½ inch, moved slowly, between $1.25 and $2.00.

* **duck,** *n.*

1. Ellipt. for "duck shot.'

1687 SEWALL *Letter-Book* I. 64 Six tone of shott, of which three ton Goose, two tone Duck, one pigeon. 1845 SIMMS *Wigwam & Cabin* 334 Draw the loads, Scip, and put in some of the high duck.

2. A chap, person, "guy." *Slang.*

1846 NEAL *Charcoal Sketches* 89 (We.), Isn't he a duck? 1857 *Phoenix* (Sacramento) 11 Oct. 4/1 No such 'duck' as this could *nab* the 'Ubiquitous.' 1948 *Range Riders Western* May 45/2 That Carson's a peculiar duck.

3. *W.* One or two small stones set atop a larger one, placed at intervals to mark an obscure trail. Hence, *v.*, to mark a trail in such a manner.

1921 HALL *Yosemite Nat. Park* 291 In meadows, stakes or ducs are sometimes set along the trail if the trail is not marked where it leaves the meadow. 1948 *So. Sierran* May 6/1 The route was 'ducked' for future climbers.

4. In combs.: (1) **duck-bill(ed) cat,** (see quots.); (2) **bill plow,** a plow the share of which is shaped like a duck's bill, *obs.;* (3) * **egg,** a score of zero in a game, cf. * **goose egg;** (4) **fit,** =**conniption fit,** *slang;* (5) **foot cultivator,** a cultivator provided with triangular-shaped attachments, cf. **walking cultivator;** (6) **grass,** fowl meadow grass, false redtop; (7) * **hawk,** the American peregrine falcon; (8) * **head,** in euchre (see quot.); (9) **oak,** (see quots.); (10) **potato,** (see quot. 1931); (11) **'s bill gar,** (see quot.); (12) * **'s foot,** (see quots.); (13) * **wing,** any breed of domestic fowl with a steel-blue bar on the wings, also attrib.

(1) 1883 *Nat. Museum Bul.* No. 27, 493 Duck-bill Cat. . . . This singular fish grows to a length of 6 feet. 1884 GOODE *Fisheries* I. 660 The 'Paddle-fish' or 'Duck-billed Cat,' *Polyodon spathula*, is one of the most characteristic fishes of the rivers of the Western and Southern States. — (2) 1760 WASHINGTON *Diaries* I. 135 Fitted a two Eyed Plow Instead of a Duck Bill Plow. — (3) 1868 *N. Eng. Base-Ballist* 5 Nov. 54/2 In the 7th inning the Atlantics were neatly disposed of for a duck-egg. — (4) 1900 J. C. HARRIS *On The Wing* 195, I said as much to Horace Greeley, and he and his friends had a good many duck-fits about it. a1906 O. HENRY *Trimmed Lamp* 16 If one was to speak to me, . . . I know I'd have a duck-fit.

(5) 1931 *Walters* (Okla.) *Herald* 20 Aug. 8/2 Preparing a firm seed-bed on fallowed land by means of a duck-foot cultivator. — (6) 1751 J. ELIOT *Cont. Field-Husbandry* 13 The other is Fowl-Meadow, sometimes called Duck-Grass, and sometimes Swamp-wire-Grass. 1875 *Fur, Fin, & Feather* 118 [Along the eastern coast] the duck-grass and wild celery abound. — (7) 1812 WILSON *Ornithology* VI. 85 Few gunners in that quarter [near Cape May] are unacquainted with the Duck Hawk, as it often robs them of their wounded birds before they are able to reach them. 1946 STANWELL-FLETCHER *Driftwood Valley* 247 We've been watching a duck hawk . . . feeding on a large freshly killed snowshoe rabbit out in the middle of the lake. — (8) 1864 DICK *Amer. Hoyle* (1866) 60 Duck-Head.—The card turned up as trump. — (9) 1884 SARGENT *Rep. Forests* 152 *Quercus aquatica*. . . . Water Oak. Duck Oak. 1897 SUDWORTH *Arborescent Flora* 175 Common names [of the water-oak include] . . . Duck Oak, Possum Oak, Punk Oak.

(10) 1931 CLUTE *Plants* 22 The arrow arum was also known as wampee and the name is still applied to the starchy tubers of the arrow leaf (*Sagittaria latifolia*), though they are now more frequently known as duck potatoes, in reference to the wild duck's fondness for them. 1948 *Chi. Tribune* 17 Oct. II. 4/2 The Mississippi river bottoms have excellent stocks of natural food for ducks this year, . . . with long leaf, sago pondweed and duck potato making up the bulk of the waterfowl food supplies. — (11) 1877 BARTLETT 240 At least three species of this fish [*sc.* the gar] are found in our Western rivers: the Duck's-bill Gar, and the Ohio, or common Gar. — (12) 1834 TRAILL *Backwoods* 184 There is a plant in our woods, known by the names of man-drake, may-apple, and duck's-foot: the botanical name of the plant is Podophyllum. 1907 LYONS *Plant Names* 365 P[odophyllum] peltatum . . . Indian Apple, Raccoon-berry, Duck's-foot, Umbrella-plant. — (13) 1871 LEWIS *Poultry Book* 54 The pure Duck-wing Game fowls are the Silver Grays—though there are Yellow or Birchen Duck-wings. *Ib.* 55 The plumage of the Duck-wing Bantams is precisely similar to that of the larger breed.

b. *duck on a* (or *the*) *rock*, a boys' game in which a stone, called a duck is knocked off a rock.

1878 *Harper's Mag.* LVI. 258/1 'Duck on the rock' . . . is far ahead of polo, pallone, lawn tenis [*sic*], or Aunt sally. 1893 POST *Harvard Stories* 234 You will undoubtedly find him playing duck-on-a-rock in a vacant lot back of Holyoke.

As the last term in **army, black, buffle-headed, butter, canvas, canvasback, Carolina, Confederate, cornfield, creek, crow, daub, dead, deaf, dipper, dumpling, dusky, English, fan-crested, fish, fisher, fishing, flock, fool, French, fulvous tree, German, honker, Labrador, lame, mountain, mud, Negro, Oregon, pied, raft, ring-necked, round-crested, ruddy, sand shoal, sea, sharp-tail, sharp-tailed, shoal, shoal water, skunk, spectacle, spirit, sprigtail, squam, Steller's, summer, surf, Sydney, top knot, tufted, velvet, water, western, wheat, wood duck.**

* **duck,** *v. intr.* To get out of sight, esp. surreptitiously; to "back out." *Colloq.*

1855 *N.Y. Herald* 6 Nov. 4/3 Ex-Governor Hunt is said by his Seward enemies to be 'dodging and ducking between wind and water.' 1896 ADE *Artie* ii. 9, I think I'll have to duck on that present. 1948 *Auk* July 348 When the birds saw us they 'ducked' for the bank and swam downstream to the farther shore.

b. *tr.* To avoid, esp. by evasion.

1896 ADE *Artie* vi. 55 Purty soon he ducks 'em and comes over an' touches me for two cases. 1948 *Time* 23 Aug. 54/2 Considering the pressures against them, it was no wonder, he said, that many ducked local controversies and took refuge in faraway topics.

***ducker,** *n.* A duck hunter. Also a gun for shooting ducks.

*a*1835 in AUDUBON *Ornith. Biog.* IV. 8 To give . . . the best promise of success, old duckers recommend that the nearest duck should be in perfect relief above the sight. 1846 *Quincy* (Ill.) *Whig* 12 Feb. 2/2, I put a ball and four slugs into my double barrel, and a half handfull of buckshot into my 'ducker.' 1903 *N.Y. Sun* 8 Nov., The professional ducker goes about his work in an entirely different manner. Killing ducks with these men is a business.

dude dud, *n.* [Origin unknown.]

1. A man whose dress is especially elegant, a dandy. Cf. **seminary dude.**

The origin of this word has been discussed without positive results in *Athenaeum* II. 444, 481, 580, 616.

1883 *Harper's Mag.* Sep. 632/1 The elderly club dude may lament the decay of the good old code of honor—a word of which he has a very ludicrous conception. 1907 G. M. WHITE *Boniface to Burglar* 151, I began to have that feeling which the dude possesses, and . . . I sought a barber-shop. 1944 *Chi. D. News* 20 May 3/1 Where is the dude of the 80's?

b. (See quot.) *Obs.*

1888 *N. & Q.* I. 18 Aug. 184 The supporters of the regular nomination [of James G. Blaine for the Presidency in 1884] affected to believe that these Independents set themselves up as the superiors of their former associates. They were called 'dudes,' 'Pharisees,' etc.

2. *W.* An Easterner or city-bred person, esp. one who vacations on a ranch.

1885 *Weekly New Mexican Review* 28 May 2/5 Dudes and dudesses of Vegas are rehearsing for the opera entitled 'The Doctor of Alcantara.' 1924 CROY *R.F.D. No. 3.* 148 I'm going to put up the finest cattle barn in the state—that is, belonging to a real dirt farmer, not to one of them city dudes. 1946 *Trail Riders* Oct. 5/1 At the end of a day's ride, nothing could revive a wilted dude so fast as the Panther River, which tumbled, clear and cold, past the camp.

attrib. 1884 *Las Vegas* (N.M.) *Optic* 5 Dec. 1/6 C. C. Hale, sometimes familiarly referred to as the 'dude drummer,' went to Watrous this morning. 1898 WISTER *Lin McLean* 57 Mis Molly Wood . . . has been raised too far east, . . . Vermont, or some such dude place. 1921 *Scribner's Mag.* March 343, I am Steve Graydog—dude-puncher. 1941 FERGUSSON *Southwest* 108 His status was implied by the fact that the man set to look after him was called a 'dude-wrangler.'

b. dude ranch, a ranch which provides entertainment in riding, cowpunching, etc., for paying guests. Also **dude rancher.** Cf. **guest ranch.**

1921 *Scribner's Mag.* March 343 'Is this Scott Lawson's dude ranch?' soberly inquired the rider of the pinto. 1941 FERGUSSON *Southwest* 108 Every dude rancher saw his profits disappear underground in pumps, pipes, and septic tanks. 1948 *New World* (Chi.) 2 July 13/1 Horseback riding is the chief interest at the dude ranch.

dude dud, *v. tr.* To dress (oneself) as a dude. Often with *up.* *Colloq.* — 1899 TARKINGTON *Gentleman Ind.* xiii. 240 It was a lady, . . . else why should Cale Parker be wearing a coat, and be otherwise dooded and fixed up beyond any wedding? 1948 *Reader's Digest* Dec. 150/1 All duded up like outlanders were Tildy, Hiram and the Kincaids.

dudedom 'dud·dəm, *n.* The world of the dudes. *Colloq.* — 1893 *Troy* (N.Y.) *D. Times* 30 Sep. 2/2 Van Alen . . . has been more talked about than that once famous monarch of dudedom, Berry Wall. 1894 *Forum* May 345 A bitter attack . . . would relegate its champion to the realms of dudedom and ridicule.

dudeness 'dudnɪs, *n.* The quality or state of being a dude. *Rare.* — 1885 *Boston Jrnl.* 15 June 2/3 The intense dudeness of Lord Beaconsfield in his early days is illustrated by a letter written in 1830.

dudery 'dudərɪ, *n.* Elegant pretentiousness. *Rare.* — 1889 *Voice* (N.Y.) 2 May, The Pharisaical dudery which presumes to deny her [*sc.* woman] a place in the world . . . equal with man.

dudess 'dudɪs, *n.* A female dude. *Colloq.* — 1885 [see **dude,** *n.* 2]. 1889 MARK TWAIN *Conn. Yankee* viii. 101 The remnant [of reverence for title] . . . was restricted to dudes and dudesses.

dudie 'dudɪ, *n.* Diminutive of **dude,** *n.* **1.** *Rare.* — 1889 DALY *Great Unknown* 12 You ought to have seen how miserable he looked. Poor little dudie!

dudine du'din, *n.* (See quots. 1935, 1944.)

1883 *Phila. Times* No. 2892, Not to encourage the development of the dude or dudine. 1935 *Amer. Sp.* April 158 *Dude* and *dudine* are not obsolete, as many think, but in their present-day revival they have changed their meanings and have ceased to be terms of disparagement. In the North and Central West, as in Yellowstone Park slang, they now mean merely 'tourist.' 1944 ADAMS *W. Words* 55 Dudette or dudine. A female dude described by the cowboy as a young lady who comes west to marry a cowboy.

dudish 'dudɪʃ, *a.* Foppish. Also **dudish-looking.** *Colloq.*

1884 *Lisbon* (Dak.) *Star* 20 June, 'Then you was in the war,' put in the dudish-looking bystander. 1887 *Courier-Journal* 23 Jan. 9/7 Every day his face and hands were washed three times and his yellow hair was combed. Now this . . . was dudish in the hardy miner's eyes. 1945 BOTKIN *My Burden* 85, I druv in the carriage with the white folks and was 'bout the most dudish nigger in them parts.

dudishly 'dudɪʃlɪ, *adv.* Like a dude. *Colloq.* — 1890 *Once a Week*, John Ogden Armour, is only twenty-six and good-looking to boot, dresses dudishly and belongs to all the clubs. 1917 CAHAN *Rise David Levinsky* 148 His hair was freshly trimmed and dudishly dressed.

dudism 'dudɪzəm, *n.* The quality or condition of a dude. Also fig. *Colloq.*

1884 MITCHELL *Bound Together* (1907) 256 That pseudo-æstheticism which has had other outcome in Sunflowers, and *Dude-ism*, and crazy quilts. 1887 CUSTER *Tenting on Plains* xii. 354 The tuft on the end, though of little use to intimidate flies, is a marvel of mule-dudism. 1891 EGGLESTON in *Cent. Mag.* Feb. 540 Wearing . . . a coat at dinner is a most disreputable mark of dudism.

dudleyite 'dʌdlɪˌaɪt, *n.* [See quot. 1873] A hydrous mica. — 1873 *Amer. Philos. Soc. Proc.* XIII. 404 Dudleyite (a new species) . . . is named after the locality, Dudleyville, Alabama. 1875 E. S. DANA in *Appendixes to Dana Mineralogy* II. 17 Dudleyite . . . has the form of margarite.

***due,** *a.*

1. On the point of (doing something). With inf. *Colloq.*

1921 R. D. PAINE *Comr. Rolling Ocean* ii. 22 They were about due to find out.

2. due bill, a written acknowledgement of a debt. Also fig.

1792 *Ann. 2nd Congress* 1111 The officers were directed to receive a certificate from the contractor's agent, called a due bill. 1841 COOPER *Deerslayer* vii, There's them about that would look upon you more as a due-bill for the bounty than a human mortal. 1947 LUMPKIN *Southerner* 69 At the end of the year he would redeem in currency any due-bills his laborers had not expended.

duff dʌf, *n.* [f. **duffer* in same sense.] Counterfeit money. *Rare.* — 1895 H. L. WILLIAMS *Love & Lockjaw* 7 Lucky my money won't do him any good. It is duff that I carry for a hold-up.

***duffle, duffel,** *n.* Articles of dress, supplies, and equipment carried on a camping or hunting trip, etc. Also short for next.

1884 G. W. SEARS *Woodcraft* 4 (*Cent.*), Every one has gone to his chosen ground with too much impedimenta, too much duffle. 1925 MULFORD *Cottonwood Gulch* 71 Camp duffle and placer tools lay scattered on the ground. 1946 *Trail Riders Bul.* Oct. 10/1 Duffles are packed and we are all sitting about, getting addresses so that we can exchange notes and pictures. 1948 *Nat. Geog. Mag.* Aug. 216/1 We had to carry and slide our canoes and duffel down the 45 degree grade.

b. duffle bag, a cloth bag for carrying duffle.

1919 LEWIS *Free Air* 103 Claire . . . had enjoyed the sight of their duffle-bags stuck up between the sleek fenders and the hood. 1945 *New Yorker* 17 Mar. 22/2, I ran up to the attic and got out my old duffel-bag.

c. duffle room, (see quot.).

1893 EGGLESTON *Duffels* p. iv, If his camp grows into a house frequented by sportsmen, there will be a duffel room to contain all manner of unclassified things.

***dug,** *a.* In combs.: (1) **dugout,** see as a main entry; (2) **dug road,** a road dug in a cliff, along the bank of a river, etc., also attrib.; (3) **spring,** a well partly filled with water from a subsurface spring; (4) **way,** see as a main entry; (5) **well,** a well made by digging as contrasted with one made by boring.

(2) 1799 in SUMMERS *Ann. S.W. Virginia* (1929) 483 Road established from Humphries Ford to the dug road on the mountain. 1807 ASBURY *Journal* III. 265, I came sliding down a dug-road precipice. — (3) 1873 BEADLE *Undevel. West* 558 In the center was a dug spring, but no running water.

(5) 1934 VINES *Green Thicket World* 32 He would walk to the lot, or go and look down in an old dug well. 1945 BOTKIN *My Burden* 263

The leader of the crowd ride right in the front gate and up to the big dug well.

dugout ˈdʌgˌaʊt, *n.*

1. A canoe made from a hollowed-out tree trunk. In full **dugout canoe.** See also **ferry dugout.**

1722 *Miss. Prov. Arch.* Fr. Dom. III. (1932) 338 List of the things absolutely necessary. . . . A dugout canoe in order to go hunting to procure some fresh food for the sick and workmen. **1819** J. A. Quitman in Claiborne *Life* (1860) I. 42 At Wheeling . . . we purchased a small canoe, called here a 'dug-out,' or 'man-drowner.' **1948** *Sat. Ev. Post* 3 July 19/3 With the conch for a scraper and fire for a helper, they built their dugout canoes.

2. (See quot.) *Obs.*

1854 Bartlett *Personal Narr.* II. xlv. 535 A little futher we came to a 'dug out'—that is, a passage cut or dug across a bar.

3. *W.* A pioneer dwelling, in part at least hollowed out of the ground, often on a hillside.

1860 B. Young in *Journal Disc.* VIII. 293 (Th.), When you have built splendid habitations, be as willing to leave them as you would leave a dug-out. **1886** Ebbutt *Emigrant Life* 94 Their dug-out was a wretched place to live in, as such places usually are. A hole is dug in

One type of dugout (sense 3)

the side of a hill, a few forked posts are put in the corners, poles are laid in the forks, brush and straw as thick as will keep out rain, and with a door in front and a chimney cut in the bank, the house is ready for occupation. **1948** Johnston *Gold Rush* 4/1 Environed in a virgin country, their habitations were of the rudest; brush shelters, dugouts, windowless log cabins, and canvas tents.

attrib. **1872** Roe *Army Lett.* 71 We manage to cool the water a little by keeping it in bottles and canteens down in the dug-out cellar. **1920** Hunter *Trail Drivers Texas* I. 394 He said those dug-out people were different.

4. A low shelter, facing a baseball diamond, where the players' bench is.

1914 *Collier's* 7 Feb. 27/1 The Rube was hissed every step of the way back to the dugout. **1948** *N.Y. Times* 9 May v. 5/8 Vern Stephens threw his grounder into the Boston dugout.

dugway ˈdʌgˌwe, *n.*

1. A dug road.

1718 *Lancaster Rec.* 183 Neer where the path now goes, to witt the parth called the dugway. **1889** *Manti* (Utah) *Home Sentinel* 20 Mar. 4/3, I was delighted to find the county road between those two cities at a place on the dug-way where some few years ago, my life was imperiled from a narrow ill constructed road. **1948** *Sat. Ev. Post* 18 Sep. 167/2 If they don't catch the criminals at Wildcat Fork, up above the shale dugway, . . . why, then will be the time to go down to town and organize a posse.

2. *W.* (See quots.)

1930 Raine & Barnes *Cattle* 88 Huge 'dugways' had to be graded down the steep banks to let cattle and wagons into and out of the stream. **1944** Adams *W. Words* 55 *dugway:* A place on the steep bank of a stream which has been graded down to let cattle and wagons enter or leave a stream.

*** Duke,** *n.*

1. (See quot.) *Rare.*

1800 *Columbian Centinel* 2 July 4/2 Duke—for sale. A Preparation For Punch.

2. Duke's Laws, *hist.* The code of laws adopted for the government of New York, in 1664, after the appointment of Governor Nicolls by the Duke of York.

c1824–38 G. Furman *Antiquites L.I.* 127 The code of laws for the government of the colony of New York, known as the *Duke's Laws,* adopted by the convention of deputies at Hempstead, on Long Island, March 1, 1664, evidently contemplated the establishment of that church [Episcopal Church]. **1943** Hicks *Amer. Dem.* 24 The colony, now renamed New York, exchanged without serious incident that autocratic rule of the Dutch merchants for an almost equally undemocratic system embodied in the 'Duke's laws.'

Duk' o' Darby. [Prob. imitative.] (See quot.) *Obs.* — **1877** Bartlett 195 *Duk' o' Darby.* (Duke of Derby.) The bobolink.

dulce ˈdulsɪ, *n. S.W.* [Sp., sweet, sweetmeat.]

1. A sweetmeat.

1844 Kendall *Santa Fe Exped.* II. 347 At the termination of [the dance] . . . the males are expected to treat their partners to refreshments in the way of dulces. **1890** *Outing* Aug. 355/1 He bought cakes and sticks of *dulce* for the solemn-eyed babies. **1912** Lumholtz *New Trails* 176 It is often used instead of sugar, and a kind of *dulce* is made from it.

2. (See quot. 1912.)

1912 Hough *Story of Cowboy* 212 (Bentley), It [a letter] may be from his 'girl' as he calls it (his dulce, it would be in the South). **1932** D. Coolidge *Fighting Men of West* 275 (Bentley), The next time I visit my dulce I could show her this pistol.

*** dull,** *a.* **1.** Denoting a low grade of tobacco. **2. dull music,** (see quot.). *Obs.*

(1) **1850** *Rep. Comm. Patents: Agric. 1849* 322 There ought, if the quality of a crop will permit, to be four sorts of tobacco, 'Yellow,' 'Bright,' 'Dull,' and 'Second.' *Ib.,* The next person . . . strips off all the bright leaves, . . . and throws the plant to the next, who takes off all the rest, being the 'dull.' — (2) **1848** Bartlett 125 *Dull Music,* a term applied to anything tedious.

dull dʌl, *n.* and *v.* [Irish *dul,* a snare or noose. Cf. *EDD s.v. dull,* sb.] (See quot. 1889.) Also **dulling,** *n.* — **1880** *Forest & Stream* 11 March, I hope that the barbarous practice called dulling has gone out of fashion. **1889** *Cent.* 1795/1 dull. . . . A noose of string or wire used to snare fish; usually, a noose of bright copper wire attached by a short string to a stout pole. . . . To fish with a dull: as, to dull for trout. [Southern U.S.]

Duluthian dəˈluθɪən, *n.* A native of Duluth, Minn. Also the speech of those who live in Duluth. — **1872** *Newton Kansan* 5 Sep. 4/1 On the day before the Fourth, Duluthians wore their overcoats. **1934** *Amer. Sp.* April 78/2, I should agree with the correspondent, but compare Duluthian.

Duluth pack. A large canvas packsack fitted with a head strap in addition to the usual shoulder straps, so called because first made and used in the vicinity of Duluth, Minn.

1920 *Outing* Dec. 113/3 The head strap of the Duluth pack is a relief to use when one's shoulder muscles protest. **1922** *Ib.* Oct. 38/2 Do you recommend the Duluth pack for back-packing or hiking trips? [**1938** *Sears Cat.* (ed. 177) 931 Pack Sack. Duluth. Forest brown duck; water repelling head, and leather shoulder straps.]

dumb dʌm, *n.* =**dumbfish.** *Obs.* — **1825** Cooper *L. Lincoln* xiv. 199 A real dumb is not to be despised, especially when sewed up in a wrapper, and between two coarser fish, to preserve the steam.

dumb dʌm, *a.*[1] Also **dum** and **dumbed.** Used euphemistically for "damned." Also as adv. *Colloq.*

1787 Tyler *Contrast* (1790) II. ii, I must needs say her father is pretty dumb rich. **1845** S. Judd *Margaret* I. xv. 134 He'll have to lose his oxen if it an't paid dum soon. **1870** A. Whitney *We Girls* xci, 'It's a dumb shame!' said Aunt Trixie. **1911** Quick *Yellowstone Nights* 104 A fellow makes a dumb fool of himself such times, neighbor.

Hence **dumbly,** *adv.* Very much. *Rare.*

1854 M. J. Holmes *Tempest & Sunshine* xv. 211, I'm dumbly afeared, Bill, that I acted mighty baby like.

dumb dʌm, *a.*[2] [In **1.** app. f. G. *dumm* or Du. *dom.*]

1. Stupid, dull. *Colloq.*

1823 J. F. Cooper *Pilot* II. iii. 39 'They're a dumb race,' said the cockswain, . . . 'now, there was our sergeant, who ought to know something' [etc.]. **1892** *Harper's Mag.* Feb. 441/1 My, but men are dumb. A woman would have caught on long ago. **1949** *Dly. Oklahoman* (Okla. City) 13 Feb. D. 5/2 My dog is too dumb to learn anything.

2. In combs.: (1) *** dumbbell,** a stupid person, *slang;* (2) **-bell district,** a gerrymandered election district shaped like a dumbbell, *rare;* (3) **Betty,** a name for a household convenience, esp. a washing machine; (4) **bird,** the ruddy duck, so called because of its stupidity when hunted, cf. **dunbird, fool hen;** (5) **bull,** (see quot. 1872), *obs.;* (6) **chill,** (see quots.); (7) **Dumb Democrat,** (see quot.), *rare;* (8) **fish,** =**dunfish,** also the cod that is to be dunned; (9) **flustered, foozled,** greatly dumfounded, *slang, obs.;* (10) **head,** see as a main entry; (11) **Paddy,** (see quot.), *obs.;* (12) **rattlesnake,** the copperhead, so called because it has no rattles; (13) **reading,** (see quot.), *obs.;* (14) **shakes,** a chill accompanied by shaking, cf. **dumb chill;** (15) **stove,** = ∗**drum 2,** *obs.;* (16) ∗**waiter,** a small elevator used to convey food, dishes, etc., from one floor of a building to another; (17) **watches,** the pitcher plant, *Sarracenia purpurea.*

(1) **1920** *Collier's* 3 July 8/1 The gent . . . stands alone as the Crown Prince of dumb-bells. **1948** *Sat. Ev. Post* 4 Sep. 103/2 On the eve of their game for the county title, that dumbbell isn't even with his team! — (2) **1882** *Cong. Rec.* 13 Feb. 1104/2 Mr. McDuffie and Mr. Webster and their cotemporaries would have . . . stood paralyzed with disgust if you had shown them the dumb-bell district of Pennsylvania. *Ib.* 19 July 6222/2 My district in Brooklyn . . . may be called the 'dumb-bell district.' It has been made up . . . more out of all reasonable shape that any other district that has been presented here. — (3) **1766** *Boston Ev. Post* 13 Jan. (Th.), The utility of Tubs, Cags, and Dumb-Bettys. **1814** *Mass. Spy* 14 May (Th.), Jefferson's Dumb Betty, which without the attendance of a servant serves up his chocolate and hot muffins for breakfast. *a***1870** CHIPMAN *Notes on Bartlett* 133 *Dumb Betty.* A washing machine; barrel-shaped, and having a rotary shank with stirrers or vanes.—Mass., in 1820. — (4) **1893** *Stand.* 563/1. **1917** *Birds of Amer.* I. 152 Ruddy duck. . . . Other names [include] . . . Dun-bird; Dumb-bird; Mud-dipper [etc.].

(5) **1843** *Knickerb.* XXI. 46 Another [musical] instrument of peculiar construction, entitled 'dumb-bull,' . . . is prepared to lend dignity to the music. **1872** EGGLESTON *End of World* 294 Bob Short had a dumb-bull, a keg with a strip of raw hide stretched across one end like a drum-head, while the other remained open. — (6) **1859** BARTLETT 133 *Dumb Chill,* or *Dumb Ague.* An expression common in malaria regions to denote that form of intermittent fever which has no well defined 'chill.' **1944** *D.N.* Nov. 8 *dumb chill:* n. A chill accompanied by shaking. Miss., Ala. Lay use. Popular. Reported. (Also Va., N.C.) — (7) **1855** WELD *Vacation Tour* 282 The number of political associations in America is as extraordinary as the strange names which they bear. Here are a few of them. . . . Hook and Ladder Democrats, Dumb Democrats [etc.]. — (8) **1746** *Boston News Letter* 2 Oct. 2/2 Choice good dum fish to be sold. **1792** BELKNAP *New-Hampshire* III. 214 Spring fare . . . produces large thick fish, which after being properly salted and dried, is kept alternately above and under ground, till it becomes so mellow as to be denominated *dumb fish.* **1872** *Atlantic Mo.* Feb. 166 Dumfish, in the old newspapers, were sometimes called 'dumb'd fish.' — (9) *c***1845** W. T. THOMPSON *Chron. Pineville* 172 If I hadn't been completely dumfoozled, I'd never a killed Blaze like I did. **1888** STOCKTON *Dusantes* 70 Don't you see he's so dumbflustered that he hardly knows who he is himself!

(11) **1856** OLMSTED *Slave States* 11 [The Negroes] were much . . . like what our farmers call *dumb Paddies*—that is, Irishmen who do not readily understand the English language, and who are still weak and stiff from the effects of the emigrating voyage. — (12) **1842** *Nat. Hist. N.Y., Zoology* III. 54 The Copper-head . . . has various popular names in different districts; the most common of these are, in this State [N.Y.], Copper-head, Red Adder, and Dumb Rattlesnake. — (13) **1878** DRAKE *Roxbury* 294 The reading of the Bible in the public worship, without exposition, was generally disapproved and stigmatized by the term 'dumb reading.' — (14) **1871** NAPHEYS *Prev. & Cure Dis.* III. ii. 640 The 'dumb shakes' of the Wabash Valley.

(15) **1851** *S.F. Picayune* 30 Sep. 1/6 In the parlor there happened to be an earthen funnel, placed there to admit the passage of a stove pipe from below, which was connected with a 'dumb stove' in the chamber above. — (16) **1847** WEBSTER 372/2 When the kitchen is in the basement, the dumbwaiter is made to rise and fall by means of pulleys and weights. **1945** *New Yorker* 25 Aug. 22 The dumbwaiter ends its creaking trips for garbage. — (17) **1931** CLUTE *Plants* 40 The peculiar shape of the stigma [of *Sarracenia purpurea*] is further emphasized in the name of dumb watches by which this plant is also known.

dumber ˈdʌmɚ, *n.* One who lacks the power of speech. *Rare.* — **1870** EGGLESTON *Queer Stories* 63 Does you need your fingers to tell stories wid, like the dumbers that we heard talk without saying anything?

dumbhead ˈdʌmˌhɛd, *n.* [Cf. **dummkopf,** and see *EDD, dummerhead.*] A blockhead. Also **dumbheadedness.** *Slang.*

1887 FREDERIC *Seth's Brother's Wife* 339 Over in Jay we wouldn't elect sech a dumb-head to be a hog-reeve. **1921** MULFORD *Bar-20 Three* xi. 125 Have I got to do *all* the thinking for this crowd of dumbheads? **1923** *Outing* Feb. 213/3 Their chiefs will come in for some scathing remarks about the 'dumbheadedness' of Forestry officials.

∗**dumbness,** *n.* Dullness, stupidity. — **1858** THOREAU *Autumn* (1894) 94, I see dumb-bells in the minister's study, and some of their dumbness gets into his sermons. **1924** *Chi. Tribune* 26 Oct. (Comics) 6 Whada you say we take a ride so you can tell me how to take some of the dumbness outta the kid?

∗**dumminess,** *n.* A condition of sluggish and defective intelligence in a horse or mule following acute inflammation of the brain. Cf. ∗**dummy 3.** — **1903** *U.S. Dept. Agric., Rep. Diseases Horse* 11 In dumminess, or immobility, the hanging position of the head and the stupid expression are rather characteristic.

dummkopf ˈdumˌkɔpf, *n.* [f. G. *Dummkopf,* or Du. *domkop.*] A dumbhead or blockhead. *Slang.*

1809 IRVING *Hist. N.Y.* (1927) v. ii. 252 We may picture to ourselves this mighty man of Rhodes like a second Ajax, strong in arms, great in the field, but in other respects (meaning no disparagement) as great a dom cop, as if he had been educated among that learned people of Thrace, who Aristotle most slanderously assures us, could not count beyond the number four. **1923** WATTS *L. Nichols* 15 All I got to do is wait on dumkopfs! **1948** *Amer. Sp.* April 108 Mildly derogatory terms are *lausbube* (a bad boy), *dummkopf* (blockhead), and *lump* (a low fellow).

∗**dummy,** *n.* Also **dumby.**

1. A stupid animal or person; a mute. *Slang.*

1823 COOPER *Pioneers* xxxv. 395 'Woa—come hither, Golden,' he cried; 'why, how come you off the end of the bridge, where I left you, dummies?' **1891** FREEMAN *N. Eng. Nun* 172 There, she took that little dumbie out of the poor-house. **1908** *D.N.* III. 308 dummy, n. . . . 2. a dumb person.

2. A locomotive having condensing engines and consequently no noise of escaping steam (see also quot. 1908).

1864 WEBSTER. **1867** *Com. & Fin. Chron.* 2 March 280 Dummies . . . are found to be economical and efficient. **1908** *D.N.* III. 308 dummy, n. 1. A small-sized locomotive engine; also the train pulled by such an engine. 'Are you going to Opelika on the *dummy?*'

attrib. **1872** *Rep. Comm. Patents 1871* II. 656/1 Dummy-Engine.—[patented by] Christian George Spengler. **1884** *Chi. Tribune* 4 May 9/6 Cottage Grove avenue is already obstructed by a dummy track, and an additional double-track as proposed would ruin it entirely. **1891** *Memphis Appeal-Avalanche* 22 April 7 Beginning Monday, April 27, 1891, Free excursions will be run over the Dummy Line to Mount Arlington, East End.

b. =**cable car.** In full **dummy car.**

1873 *S.F. Ev. Bulletin* 1 Aug., It was a platform car, or dummy, loaded with men and boys. **1881** MARSHALL *Through Amer.* (1882) 265 The 'dummy car' is stranger still. Not drawn by horses or mules, nor propelled by any visible machinery, it is worked by an endless-wire underground cable of an inch and a quarter in diameter, by an engine of 500 horse-power. **1946** *Trail & Timberline* May 73/1 The narrow gauge engine calmly adds some standard gauge cars to the train, aided by a dummy car in order to couple-up properly.

3. (See quot.) Cf. ∗**dumminess.**

1901 *Jrnl. Exper. Med.* VI. 66 The duration of the disease [inflammation of the brain] varies from a few hours to a week. . . . Horses which recover are said to become 'dummies'—animals with a permanent cerebral lesion and defective intelligence.

∗**dump,** *n.*

1. A place where the waste and refuse of a city is dumped. See also **log dump.**

1784 HILTZHEIMER *Diary* (1893) 10 April 63 Attended the sale of the street dirt at the dumps. **1891** *Youth's Companion* 9 July 13/1 The emptied cans . . . are thrown by housekeepers into the domestic ash-barrel, and from there are taken to the town or city 'dump.' **1945** *Jefferson Co. Republican* (Golden, Colo.) 21 Nov. 1/6 This dump will serve residents of Lakewood and adjacent territory, including Montair.

b. *transf.* A place (house, town, etc.) that is unattractive or ill-kept. *Slang.*

1903 *Cin. Enquirer* 9 May 13/1 Dump—A house; saloon, hang-out for a gang. **1920** LEWIS *Main Street* 216 One thing I will say for that dump: they had it warm enough. **1945** WILLIAMS *It's a Free Country* 112 You better get used to it. She'll never come back to this—never come back here. To this hole, to this dump.

2. A hay mound. *Rare.*

1898 *Mo. So. Dakotan* I. 87 Fletcher and Watson followed at a slower pace and with forks piled the hay into dumps.

∗**dump,** *v.*

1. *tr.* To unload (the contents of a cart, freight car, etc.), usu. without handling; to throw (something) down.

1784 HILTZHEIMER *Diary* (1893) 16 Mar. 62 The Street Commissioners selected sites to dump the dirt from the streets. **1838** *Knickerb.* XII. 463 The ships . . . may 'dump' their stores at the very doors of the numerous mills. **1931** *K.C. Star* 28 July, Mr. Kennett is the one who dumped a load of wheat on the streets of Bucklin.

2. To sell (goods, stock, etc.) to the disadvantage of the market; to sell (surplus goods) in a foreign market so as not to depress the domestic market.

1868 *Com. & Fin. Chron.* VI. 326/1 New stock secretly issued [was] 'dumped' on the market for what it would fetch. **1884** *Cong. Rec.* 1 May 3663/1 The surplus dumped from foreign pauper markets is the great bane of our industries. **1904** W. H. SMITH *Promoters* 244 We've got to find a place to dump our stuff or we're done up.

b. dump sale, a clearance or bargain sale.

1896 *K.C. Star* 20 July 5/5 (*advt.*), The dump sale advertised for Saturday will be continued this week.

c. To throw away or destroy (part of a commodity) so as to keep up the price of the remainder of it.

1947 *Chi. Sun* 24 Jan. 16/6 The Department of Agriculture announced tonight that it was authorizing farmers to dump all low grade and deteriorating potatoes stored under government price-supporting loans.

3. Used in combs. designating vehicles that may be unloaded by tipping or that have bottoms opening downwards, as (1) **dump car,** (2) **cart,** (3) **truck,** (4) **wagon.**

(1) **1912** *Out West* Feb. 133/1 She stood directly in the narrow track along which the small dump cars were wont to carry the yellow gravel from the cut in Big Butte. — (2) **1868** *Mich. Agric. Rep.* VII. 347 Joram Priest, Detroit, [manufactured the] 2 dump carts. **1948** WESTON *Mother Lode* 94 The large stones were hauled to the location

Dump cart

by mule-drawn makeshift dump-carts. — (3) **1930** *Water Works & Sewerage* Dec. 24/3 Where To Buy . . . Trucks, Dump. **1948** *Calif. Highways* March–April 12/1 The contractors are employing modern excavation equipment consisting of power shovels and dump trucks for the longer hauls. — (4) **1869** *Rep. Comm. Agric. 1868* 357 If it [distance] exceeds five or six rods, wheelbarrows, carts, or dump-wagons will be necessary.

dumpage 'dʌmpɪdʒ, *n.* (See quot.) — **1864** WEBSTER 419 *Dumpage* . . . 1. The privilege of dumping loads from carts, especially loads of refuse matter. 2. A fee paid for such a privilege.

dumper 'dʌmpɚ, *n.* (See quot.) Cf. **gravel dumper.** — **1881** RAYMOND *Mining Glossary, Dumper,* a tilting-car used on dumps.

* **dumping,** *n.*

1. That which has been dumped; the process of dumping something.

1883 HOWELLS *Woman's Reason* xii. The Common, where . . . the monumental dumpings of the icy streets had dismally accumulated. **1886** *Milnor* (Dak.) *Teller* July (*advt.*), Meadow-King Rake . . . is the only rake that does not bind in dumping.

2. In combs.: (1) **dumping cart,** =**dump cart;** (2) **ground,** (*a*) a place where refuse is dumped, (*b*) *transf.*, a country, esp. the U.S., where other countries get rid of surplus goods or persons; (3) **house,** in mining, a house where ore is stored preparatory to milling; (4) **place,** =**dumping ground;** (5) **scow,** a garbage scow; (6) **sled,** (see quot.).

(1) **1863** *Rep. Comm. Agric.* 135 A dumping cart is very useful in handling the cane. **1879** *Scribner's Mo.* Nov. 55/1 Concrete . . . being discharged from the mixer into an iron dumping cart. — (2) (*a*) **1857** *N.Y. Tribune* 18 May (B.), There is much difficulty in getting dumping grounds for the dirt from the streets. **1904** W. H. SMITH *Promoters* 101 The legislatures had . . . repealed the bridge-building laws we got made for 'em, and so the dumping ground was shut off. (*b*) **1837** DEPEW *Orations* (1890) 150 [The United States] cannot afford to become the dumping-ground of the world for its vicious or ignorant. **1888** *Boston Jrnl.* 26 May 2/2 After supplying the neutral markets, the United States will become the dumping-ground for all the manufacturers of England, France and Germany. **1944** *Harper's Mag.* Aug. 218/1 Latin America had been a dumping ground for munitions while factories tooled up for new tasks. — (3) **1873** *Cottonwood Observer* (Alta, Utah) 16 July 2/1 Reaching the dumping-house, a busy scene presented itself. — (4) **1883** *Harper's Mag.* LXVI. 829/1 The blackened old pier is dumping-place for city refuse now.

(5) **1895** *N.Y. Dramatic News* 20 July 2/3 Every Tammany man . . . ought to . . . stay up late sending him bouquets as big as a dumping scow and twice as fragrant. — (6) **1874** KNIGHT 761 *Dumping-sled,* one with an arrangement for sliding back the bed so that it may overbalance and tip out the load.

Dumpler 'dʌmplɚ, *n.* [LG. *dumpelen,* Du. *dompelen,* to immerse.] A Dunker; a "Tumbler."

1778 ANBUREY *Travels* II. 285 Among the numerous sects of religion with which this province abounds, . . . there is a sect . . . called the Dumplers. **1789** MORSE *Geog.* 324 The Tunkers . . . are also called Tumblers, from the manner in which they perform baptism. . . . The Germans sound the letter *t* and *b* like *d* and *p;* hence the words Tunkers and Tumblers have been corruptly written Dunkers and Dumplers. **1801** *Hist. Review & Directory* I. 224 Among the sects which abound in this country, a very distinguished one is that of the Dumplers.

* **dumpling,** *n.* **1.** A term of endearment. *Colloq.* **2. dumpling duck,** a local name for the ruddy duck.

(1) **1847** CORCORAN in *Tall Tales of S.W.* (1930) 193 Yu'se very sick, dumplin, don't take on darlin, if you kin help hit, ducky. — (2) **1889** *Cent.* 1789/1. **1917** *Birds of Amer.* I. 152 *Ruddy Duck.* . . . Other names.—Dumpling Duck; Daub Duck. . . . Dun Diver.

As the last term in **blue, corn, Indian, meal, water dumpling.**

* **dun,** *a.* In combs.: (1) * **dunbird,** [app. so called from the color, but the same bird is known as **dumbbird** because of its stupidity] =**dun diver;** (2) **codfish,** =**dunfish;** (3) * **diver,** *local,* the ruddy duck; (4) **fish,** fish, generally cod, cured by dunning, cf. **dumbfish.**

(1) **1839** PEABODY *Mass. Birds* 391 The Ruddy Duck[s] . . . are sold in Boston, under the name of Dun-birds. **1844** *Nat. Hist. N.Y., Zoology* II. 327 *Fuligula Rubida.* The Dun-bird, Looby or Dun Diver, is rather rare on the coast of this State. **1917** [see **dumbbird**]. — (2) **1818** [see **dunfish**]. **1844** *Knickerb.* XXIV. 471 We agreed there was nothing so delicious as the dun-codfish. — (3) **1844** *Nat. Hist. N.Y., Zoology* II. 327 The Ruddy Duck. *Fuligula rubida.* . . . The Dun-bird, Looby or Dun Diver, is rather rare on the coast of this State [New York]. **1917** *Birds of Amer.* I. 152. — (4) **1818** *Mass. Spy* 23 Dec. (Th.), Dun-fish. . . . The dun or dried cod-fish ought not to be boiled. **1889** *Cent.* 1798/2 *Dunfish,* . . . codfish cured by dunning. . . . The fish are first slack-salted and cured, then taken down cellar and allowed to 'give up,' and then dried again. **1900** KING *When I Lived* (1937) 98 It must be a *dun* fish (whatever that may be) and the proper way to prepare it was to boil it encased in a cloth between two thin fishes.

* **dun,** *v. tr.* To cure fish so as to make them dun-colored. Also * **dunning,** *n.* Cf. **dunfish.**

1818 *Mass. Spy* 23 Dec. (Th.), When cod-fish is dunned, it ought not to be boiled at all. **1828** WEBSTER, *Dunning,* the operation of curing codfish, in such a manner as to give it a particular color and quality. **1873** THAXTER *Isles of Shoals* 83 The process of dunning, which made the Shoals fish so famous a century ago, is almost a lost art, though the chief fisherman at Star still duns a few yearly.

Duncan Phyfe. Used attrib. to designate furniture of a type designed by Duncan Phyfe (1768–1854), a New York cabinet-maker. Also transf.

1926 *Ladies' Home Jrnl.* Nov. 123/3 There were two Chippendale chairs, . . . a Duncan Phyfe mahogany table, and a special French chair upholstered in rose and ivory. **1935** *Montgomery Ward Cat.* (ed. 123) 392 Choice of Duncan Phyfe or 10-leg Heppelwhite Table, One Arm Chair and five Side Chairs. **1948** *Savings News* April 13 This lovely Duncan Phyfe extension table . . . is appropriate as an occasional table, for writing and for card games.

b. Duncan Phyfe log, (see quots.).

1915 *Country Life* April 48/3 Even in the West Indian forests the unlettered natives, who knew no English, had knowledge of his reputed judgment of wood, so that when a particularly fine tree was felled it was called by them a Duncan Phyfe log, was marked 'D.P.,' and put aside for his cargo. **1941** A. TRAIN, JR. *Story Everyday Things* 230 Exporters from Santo Domingo and Cuba would refer to their choicest pieces of timber as 'Duncan Phyfe logs.'

Duncard, see **Dunkard, Dunker.**

dunce block. The block on which dunces in school were compelled to sit. Also attrib. and fig.

1828 A. ROYALL *Black Book* II. 281 They are kept at school—not the dunce-block schools. **1864** NORTON *Army Letters* 219 The 'District of Florida' . . . seems to be a sort of dunce block for the government—a place where they send men good for nothing in any other place. **1876** *Wide Awake* 101/2 This was too serious a matter for the ordinary punishments. Bob and Ike were neither set on the dunce-block, nor made to hold down the nails in the floor.

***dunder-**, *prefix.* **1. dunderfunk,** (see quot. 1900). **2. dunderment,** a state of astonishment or confusion. Both *colloq.*

The source or sources of the first element in these expressions is obscure. In **1,** ***dunder** may be an interesting survival of the *OED* **dunder* (1793, 1795) the lees or dregs of cane-juice. For **dunder* in **2,** cf. such expressions as **dunderhead,* **dunderpate,* **dunderwhelp.*

(1) **1892** DUVAL *Young Explorers* 131 In a little while we sat down to a repast [of] . . . fried bass and perch, flanked by platters of 'dundefunk' highly seasoned with chili pepper. **1900** *Boston Ev. Globe* 15 Oct. 7 Another institution dating from antiquity is 'cracker hash,' or 'hardtack hash.' . . . The addition of molasses before baking makes 'dunderfunk' of this concoction, but molasses, . . . is . . . an expensive article of food,—hence dunderfunk is as rare as plum duff. — (2) **1831** S. SMITH *Major Downing* 76, I was kind of struck with a dunderment. **1835–7** HALIBURTON *Clockmaker* 1 Ser. xvi. 139 You never see'd a fellow in such a dunderment in your life.

***dung,** *n.* As the last term in **chip, door dung.**

dungaree ˌdʌŋgəˈri, *n.* (See quot.) *Obs.* — *a***1870** CHIPMAN *Notes on Bartlett* 134 *Dungaree.* A vessel used for conveying dung, as at N. York.—N.Y. & C[onnecticu]t.

***dunghill,** *n.* A scrub horse. *Obs.*

1841 *Spirit of Times* 17 July 234/3 (We.), The same feeling . . . is excited in us when we hear Virginians pronounce Eclipse 'a dunghill.' *a***1846** *Quarter Race Ky.,* etc. 121 Anybody that has seen a 'quarter-horse' run by a 'dunghill' knows how this was. **1874** *Vt. Bd. Agric. Rep.* II. 398 This horse makes no claim to blood, but calls himself a cold-blooded sprout, or a dung-hill.

dunk dʌŋk, *v.* [See quot. 1924.] *tr.* To dip (bread, doughnuts, etc.) into a liquid before eating. *Colloq.*

[**1867** DIXON *New America* II. 184 They [the Tunkers] profess Baptist tenets; and the word 'tunker' [*sic*] meaning to dip a crumb into gravy, a sop into wine, they are described by those who use it, in a very poor joke, as dippers and sops. **1924** LAMBERT *Pa.-Ger.* 46 *dunke* . . . pp. gedunkt, to dip, immerse. G. tunken.] **1931** *Chi. Sun. Tribune* 1 March 1/5 How could he eat the corn pone with both of the dishes of victuals unless he dunked the corn pone with the potlikker? **1947** *Sat. Ev. Post* 15 March 78/3 Serve Dee-Lite Donuts, piping hot; To dunk them is refined!

transf. **1944** *This Week Mag.* 22 July 2/1 The chow line dunks its mess kits in drums of steaming hot water.

Hence **dunking,** *n.*

1940 *Sat. Ev. Post* 30 March 37/4 You may be interested to know that 'dunking' springs from the same German word ordinarily used to denote baptism by the total immersion. **1946** *Chi. D. News* 19 June 25/6 Dunking is quite all right at a lunch or soda counter.

dunkadoo ˌdʌŋkəˈdu, *n.* (See quots.)

1813 WILSON *Ornithology* VIII. 35 [The] American Bittern, *Ardea Minor.* . . . On the sea coast of New Jersey it is known by the name of *Dunkadoo,* a word probably imitative of its common note. **1889** *Cent.* 1789/1 *Dunkadoo,* the American bittern. (Local, New Eng.) **1946** HAUSMAN *Eastern Birds* 110 American Bittern . . . Bog Bull, Butterbump, Plum Pudd'n, Dunkadoo, Brown Bittern.

Dunkard ˈdʌŋkərd, *n.* = **Dunker.**

1750 WALKER *Journal* 17 March, The Duncards are an odd set of people who make it a matter of Religion not to Shave their Beards. **1878** *N. Amer. Rev.* CXXVI. 255 Near at hand was the meeting-house of a sect of German-Quakers—Tunkers or Dunkards, as they are differently named. **1948** *Sat. Ev. Post* 14 Aug. 27/2 Not a Dunkard lifted his hand or complained.

attrib. **1757** *Lett. to Washington* II. 232 He humbly conceives it would have been prudent to have confin'd the Duncard Doc[to]r till the Return of this Party. **1851** HOWE *Hist. Coll. Great West* 320 A Dunkard preacher was massacred on the road to Chicago. **1903** E. C. WALTZ *Pa Gladden* 268 Melonie Hathaway chose to wear the white serge gown and dove-gray Dunkard bonnet in which her beauty was subdued to a positive loveliness.

Dunker ˈdʌŋkər, *n.* [G. *Tunker,* dipper.] A member of a sect of German-American Baptists. Also (*pl.*) the sect itself.

In 1719 the Dunkers, first organized in Germany, began coming to Pennsylvania, whence the sect has spread to other parts of the country, esp. to Ohio. They believe in the authority of the Bible, triple immersion, nonconformity to the world, esp. in speech and dress; and they condemn war and litigation. There are now five branches of the sect, some more liberal than others.

1744 *Mass. H.S. Coll.* VII. 181 The Governor, the honourable commissioners, and several other gentlemen, went to the Dunker's nunnery. **1880** *Harper's Mag.* July 184/2 The Dunkers . . . are noted in West Virginia as successful farmers and dairymen. **1945** *Amer. Sp.* April 86 The former is employed . . . with other Amish and Plain sectarians (Mennonites, Dunkers, etc.) whose acquaintance has or has not already been made, at meetings, 'singings,' and congregational gatherings.

b. Also **Dunker Baptist, Dunker sect.**

1877 MARK TWAIN *Letters* I. 308 Aunty Cord is a violent Methodist and Lewis an implacable Dunker-Baptist. **1889** *Harper's Mag.* LXXIX. 776 Long-bearded members of the Dunker or German Baptist sect, both speaking Pennsylvania Dutch.

Dunmore's War. *Hist.* A war carried out in 1774 by Lord Dunmore, royal governor of Va., against the Indians, chiefly Shawnee, who were harassing the Virginia frontier. — **1868** BRICE *Hist. Ft. Wayne* 135 This man seems to have been a noted character . . . from Dunmore's war, in 1774, till after the war of 1812. **1941** BRANT *James Madison* 138 This apparently referred to the Virginia Governor's eagerness to bury the difficulties of his administration in the conflict that became known as 'Lord Dunmore's War.'

***Dunstable,** *n.* A straw hat of a type orig. made at Foxboro, Mass. Also **Dunstable straw.** *Obs.*

1830 *Mechanics' Press* (Utica, N.Y.) 24 July 291/2 Foxborough [Mass.], and not Boxford, deserves the credit of the famous Dunstable straws, which stole such a march upon the world of fashion this spring. While supposed to be English bonnets, they sold at $15 and cost but $2 . . . May . . . Foxborough reap a rich reward for the laudable industry of its women. **1849** LONGFELLOW *Kavanagh* 50 A milliner, who sold 'Dunstable and eleven-braid, open-work and colored straws.' **1856** DERBY *Phoenixiana* xxiv. 148 A sweet little thing in a Dunstable, with cherry colored ribbons. **1871** *Scribner's Mo.* II. 210 Straws—Leghorn, Dunstable, Chip, are the novelties of the season.

duplex ˈd(j)uplɛks, *n.* [f. the adj.] A house so divided vertically or horizontally that it may be occupied by two families.

[**1922** *Dly. Ardmoreite* (Ardmore, Okla.) 6 Jan. 9/1 For Rent—6-room duplex bungalow.] **1943** MENEFEE *Assignment* 212 Miners' houses barely large enough for one family are divided into duplexes. **1948** *Savings News* April 7 The old haunted house that nobody would rent is now a duplex.

Dupont ˈd(j)upɑnt, *n.* Gunpowder manufactured by E. I. Du Pont de Nemours and Company, founded in 1802. Also short for this company. — **1844** *Knickerb.* XXIII. 440 Get a cannister of Dupont, and half a dozen pounds of No. 4 shot. **1853** B. F. TAYLOR *Jan. & June* 44 Who talks of arsenals and armories—of Colt's Revolvers and 'Dupont's best'?

***durable,** *a.* Denoting a lease that gives the tenant a permanent interest. Also absol. *Obs.* — **1846** COOPER *Redskins* ii, There are two sorts of 'durable leases' . . . in use among the landlords of New York. Both . . . [are] leases forever, reserving annual rest. *Ib.* xi, We've begun ag'in the Rensselaers, and the durables, and the quarter-sales.

Durand oak. Also **Durand's oak.** (See quot.) — **1897** SUDWORTH *Arborescent Flora* 159 *Quercus breviloba* . . . Durand Oak. Syn. . . . White Oak (Tex.) . . . Basket Oak . . . Durand's Oak (Ala., La., Tex.).

durasnillo ˌdurɑsˈniljo, *n. S.W.* [Sp. *duraznillo,* recorded by Santamaría in sense shown in quot. 1878 given here.] The fruit of *Prunus texana* (see also quot. 1878). — **1878** HINTON *Hdbk. Ariz.* 343 The prickly pear, or durasnillo, grows mostly on highlands. **1942** VAN DERSAL *Ornamental Amer. Shrubs* 157 May plums, they are called in some parts of Texas, or durasnillo (little peach).

***Durham,** *n.*

1. Short for "Bull Durham tobacco," a popular brand of smoking tobacco the trade-mark sign of which is a large Durham bull.

1877 RUEDE *Sod-House Days* 187 After dinner I chopped wood for exercise and then retired to the dugout and smoked all that was left of the Durham that Syd sent me. **1948** *Sat. Review* 28 Aug. 37/1 He pulled a bag of Durham from his breast pocket and quietly rolled one.

2. Durham boat, (see quots. 1915, 1935).

1769 SMITH *Tour* 78 We saw many of those long vessels called Durham Boats so useful to the Upper Parts of the [Delaware] River. **1915** S. DUNBAR *Hist. Travel in Amer.* I. 282 The Durham boat was a keel-boat shaped much like an Indian bark canoe, and it acquired its name from a celebrated eastern builder of river vessels. He was Robert Durham, of Pennsylvania, who began turning out his product about the year 1750 for use on the Delaware River, where the craft became very popular. **1935** DUNAWAY *Hist. Penn.* 290 The first real advance in transportation on the Delaware dates from 1750, when the Durham boats, named from the Durham iron furnace near Easton, began to be constructed.

Duroc ˈd(j)urɑk, *n.* [See quot. 1908.] Short for **Duroc-Jersey.** Also attrib.

1883 in COBURN *Swine Husbandry* (1903) 79 The true Duroc or Jersey Red should be long, quite deep-bodied. **1908** BAILEY *Cyclo. Amer. Agric.* III. 664 The Duroc originated in Saratoga county, New York, and, to put it briefly, resulted from crossing a red boar on the common sows of the district. . . . It is said that the boar was named after a famous stallion, and hence the name of the breed. **1939** *These*

Are Our Lives 214 He propped his elbows on the top rail while he gazed speculatively at the two Duroc hogs in the pen. **1947** *Dly. Oklahoman* (Okla. City) 30 Dec. 2/3 Jess Bazar jr., Chickasha, had the grand champion pen of three barrows, which included the champion Duroc.

b. Duroc-Jersey, a breed of red swine developed from crossing the Duroc with the Jersey Red. Also attrib.

1893 *Nat. Duroc-Jersey Rec.* I. 19 Many breeders . . . assert that the Duroc-Jerseys are the best general purpose hogs in America. **1930** *Lerna* (Ill.) *Wkly. Eagle* 7 Feb. 1/1 (*advt.*), 50 Head Pure Bred, Registered, Duroc Jersey Bred Sows and Gilts.

***dusky,** *a.* In names of birds: (1) **dusky duck,** the black duck, also called black mallard; (2) **flycatcher,** the phoebe; (3) **grouse,** a large grouse found in western U.S.; (4) **poor-will,** (see quot.).

(1) **1804** *Cabinet Nat. Hist.* 49 A New-York dusky Duck . . . *Anas obscura Amer.* Sept. **1944** BARBOUR *Eden* 92 Moreover it was often possible to pick up a few gallinules and the native Florida dusky ducks. — (2) **1917** *Birds of Amer.* II. 198. — (3) **1828** BONAPARTE *Ornithology* III. 34 The Dusky Grouse [*Tetrao obscurus*] is eminently distinguished from all other known species, by having the tail slightly rounded. **1944** *Nat. Geog. Mag.* June 695/1 When the yellow pines give way to the red fir and the Jeffrey pine, you know you are passing from the Transition to the Canadian zone, without having to wait for hermit thrushes, . . . or dusky grouse to tell you so. — (4) **1917** *Birds of Amer.* II. 171 Two closely related subspecies, viz., the Frosted Poor-will . . . and the Dusky, or California, Poor-will (*Philaenoptilus nuttalli californicus*) are recognized by naturalists.

***dust,** *n.*

1. Ellipt. for "gold dust."

1844 GREGG *Commerce of Prairies* I. 307 The gold is mostly *dust*, from the Placer or gold mine near Santa Fé. **1872** *Harper's Mag.* XLVI. 20 Many tourists come to see the gold mines, perhaps longing to pan out some 'dust' for themselves. **1948** *Sat. Ev. Post* 11 Sep. 18/3 With a head start, I can outrun that crowd and get into The Dalles with the dust in four days or less.

2. In combs.: (1) **dust bag,** a bag for gold dust, *obs.;* (2) **blizzard,** a violent dust-laden wind, *rare;* (3) **bowl,** a region, esp. in the western part of the U.S., subject to dust storms and drought, also attrib.; (4) **brand,** (see quot.); (5) **cutter,** a drink of liquor, *slang, obs.;* (6) **flat,** a flat in a desert country, *rare;* (7) **jacket, =jacket 2;** (8) **mulch,** a layer of fine, loose, and dry soil maintained by cultivation, as in dry farming, to prevent evaporation of moisture; (9) **overcoat, ?=duster 2,** *rare;* (10) **pearl,** (see quot.); (11) **pneumonia,** (see quot.), *rare.*

(1) **1889** MUNROE *Golden Days* ix. 101 He weighed it out from the partnership dust bag. — (2) **1887** M. D. WOODWARD in *Checkered Yrs.* (1937) 170 The wind blew hard this morning increasing to a gale until, by noon, there was a dust blizzard in full blast. — (3) **1936** *Durant* (Okla.) *D. Democrat* 26 March 1/7 The panhandle 'dustbowl' was outside the path of the wind. **1948** *Dly. Ardmoreite* (Ardmore, Okla.) 4 April 1/6 The dust storm that struck western Kansas was the worst since the dust bowl days of the 30's. — (4) **1849** *Rep. Comm. Patents: Agric.* 303 The sooty powder on the flowering parts of corn-plants, called smut, chimney-sweepers, and dust brand, is formed of the spores of another uredo.

(5) **1871** *Atlantic Mo.* Nov. 574 Many went to the bar and partook of a 'dust-cutter.' — (6) **1871** *Overland Mo.* VI. 560/2 On the vast dust-flats grew the most beautiful cactus-bushes. — (7) **1947** *Chi. Sun* (Book Week) 6 July 6/4 The publisher's proclamation on the dust jacket designates this book as a novel. **1948** *Sat. Review* 6 Mar. 16/3 Plotwise, it offers little more or little less of what-happens-next interest than may be found in the works of those young writers who are described on dust jackets as 'sensitive' and 'perceptive.' — (8) **1900** *Colo. Agric. Exper. Sta. Bul.* No. 59, 14, I am also convinced that the 'dust mulch' may be just as valuable when covered by a light crust such as is formed by a light rain. — (9) **1902** NORRIS *Pit* v, Jadwin . . . wore . . . a grey 'dust overcoat' with a black velvet collar.

(10) **1897** *Boston Transcript* 13 Nov. 4/2 Pearls are named according to their size. The very large are called paragon pearls; . . . smallest, dust pearls, while badly formed specimens are known as baroques. — (11) **1935** *Durant* (Okla.) *D. Democrat* 2 March 1/5 A form of pneumonia, induced by breathing dust-laden air today claimed a heavy toll of human life and livestock in Eastern Colorado and Western Kansas. . . . Four persons have died from the disease called dust pneumonia for want of a better name in this vicinity.

b. In colloq. phrases: (1) *To have a little dust*, to have a fight or skirmish; (2) *to eat dust*, a variant of "to eat dirt" *q.v.;* (3) *to take the dust of*, to be surpassed in speed by; (4) *to be out for the dust*, to be interested in getting money.

(1) **1806–8** PIKE *Sources Miss.* 203 My men . . . wished to have a little *dust* (as they expressed it) and were likewise fearful of treachery. — (2) **1890** CUSTER *Following Guidon* 32 The bouncer placed his pistol on the table and quietly remarked, 'Any man as calls sop gravy has got to eat dust or 'pologize.' — (3) **1904** O. HENRY *Cabbages & Kings* 50 The rambler—that's her name—don't take the dust of anything afloat. — (4) **1909** —— *Roads of Destiny* 138 I'm out for the dust.

As the last term in **alkali, big, bumblebee, flour, gold, sawdust.**

***dust,** *v.*

1. *intr.* To run, hasten, depart. Also *to dust along, to get up and dust. Colloq.*

1860 *Mesilla* (Ariz.) *Times* 18 Oct. 1/2 The 'gold seekers' thought prudence the better part of valor and 'got up and dusted.' **1874** B. F. TAYLOR *World on Wheels* II. vii. 249 As you dust along the turnpike, you can see [the road]. **1888** *Lit. World* 18 Aug. 261/3 Jonah looked round for his old felt hat and dusted for Nineveh. **1943** *Collier's* 28 Aug. 12/2 'Now you can dust along,' said the tall one.

b. In same sense, with *out.*

1871 HARTE *East & West Poems* 18 Then [Walker] up and dusted out of South Hornitos Across the long Divide. **1945** BOTKIN *My Burden* 40 He just shaking and he dusts out there faster than a wink.

c. With *around.*

1898 WESTCOTT *D. Harum* 333, I dusted around putty lively, an' inside of an hour was back with the nurse.

d. *reflex.* To make haste.

1889 *Boston Jrnl.* 12 Jan. 2/5 Please dust yourselves and oblige a Western girl.

2. *To dust off*, to bring to ruin. *Slang.*

1938 ASBURY *Sucker's Prog.* 385 A considerable part of the fortune that remained to Morrissey after he had been dusted off by Vanderbilt was expended in vain attempts to gratify his own ambition to be known as a gentleman, and that of his wife to be recognized by Society.

***duster,** *n.*

1. *Milling.* A gauze-covered revolving cylinder in which flour is separated from the offal by blowing.

1850 *Western Jrnl.* IV. 279 After the 'offal' is thus ground or severely scoured, it is then passed into the lower bolts, or dusters, when the flour is taken out and sent to the 'cooler.'

2. An overcoat of light material, esp. linen, worn to protect one's clothes from dust. Cf. **linen duster.**

1870 LOWELL *Letters* II. 67 Rose discovered your thin coat, which she called a 'duster.' **1949** *Chi. D. News* 11 Feb. 21/2 Wear your duster for sports, thrown casually open at the neckline, minus the belt and with sleeves rolled smartly back above the elbow.

b. (See quot.)

1902 *Sears Cat.* (ed. 112) 427/3 Our Extra Fine Fancy Drab Color Whipcord Duster or Lap Robe. . . . Linen Whipcord Dusters or Lap Robes.

c. duster-clad, wearing a duster.

1857 *Harper's Mag.* Sep. 558/1 Citizens Brown and Rogers, carpet-bagged and duster-clad, . . . set foot once more . . . on the solid pavement. **1880** *Ib.* March 553/1 [The Commodore] wanted to . . . go where he would not see the perennial and dust-clad tourist, open-eyed and duster-clad.

3. =dry hole. *Colloq.*

1902 U.S. Geol. Survey *Contrib. to Econ. Geol.* 338 Great assistance would have been given in the location of this line of complete saturation had the unsuccessful test wells of the past been divided into two classes, as salt-water wells and dusters, instead of calling them all dry holes, as has generally been done. **1945** *Democrat* 23 Aug. 1/1 Such 'dusters' can be expected as the oil bearing zones are delimited.

4. *S.W.* A dust storm.

1935 *Dly. Oklahoman* 7 April 1/4 (*heading*), New Duster May Blanket State Today. **1948** *Dallas Morning News* 5 Dec. (Book Sec.) 4/1 Another series of 'dusters' may be imminent.

As the last term in **bran, feather, knuckle duster.** See also **Hudson Dusters.**

***dusty,** *a.* Active, energetic. *Rare.* — **1864** MARK TWAIN *Letters* I. iv. 96 Although I am not a very dusty Christian myself, I take an absorbing interest in religious affairs.

***Dutch,** *a.* and *n.*

1. The Northern sympathizers, esp. in Missouri, during the Civil War. Usu. attrib. or as adj.

1865 RICHARDSON *Secret Service* 136 Every steamer at the levee was laden with families, who . . . had hastily packed a few articles of clothing, to flee from the general and bloody conflict supposed to be impending between the Americans and the Dutch, as the Secessionists artfully termed the two parties. *Ib.* 137 A Rebel damsel . . . separated from her Union lover, declaring that no man who favoured the Abolitionists and the 'Dutch hirelings' could be her husband. **1867** J. M. CRAWFORD *Mosby* 115 Mosby moved us some three miles farther into the pines, with the view of surprising a camp of black Dutch cavalry. **1901** CHURCHILL *Crisis* 252, I believe that they are drilling those nasty Dutch hirelings in secret.

2. Temper, "dander." *Colloq.*

1893 LELAND *Memoirs* 320 It woke Colonel John Forney up to the very highest pitch of his fighting 'Injun,' or, as they say in Pennsylvania, his 'Dutch.' **1945** TRYON *Poor Man* 32 Hilda would have stopped me from doing anything rash, but my 'Dutch was up,' as our Pennsylvania neighbors used to say.

3. In special combs.: (1) **Dutch bake-oven,** a Dutch oven; (2) **barn,** =**barrack;** (3) **beer saloon,** a beer shop, *obs.;* (4) **blanket,** a soft woolen blanket made by or for the Dutch of New York, also transf.; (5) **curse,** "the white field daisy, so called from its annoyance to farmers" (B. '77); (6) **distemper,** jail fever, *obs.;* (7) **doggery,** a low grog shop, *obs.;* (8) ***garden,** a German beer garden, *obs.;* (9) **grass,** any one of various now unidentifiable grasses, *obs.*, cf. **Dutch curse;** (10) **grocery,** a poorly kept, greatly disordered grocer's shop, *obs.;* (11) ***man,** see as a main entry; (12) **Methodist,** (see quot.), *obs.;* (13) **pearmain,** a variety of pear, *obs.;* (14) **pike,** (see quot. 1857), *obs.;* (15) **pung,** a pung such as the Dutch used, *obs.;* (16) **quill,** a writing quill hardened and clarified by plunging it into heated sand or passing it rapidly through a flame, *obs.;* (17) **Reformed Church,** an American church, known since 1867 as the Reformed Church in America, having its origin in Holland; (18) **sleigh,** a sleigh of a type used by the Dutch, *obs.;* (19) **stoop,** =**stoop;** (20) **turnpike,** (see quot.), *obs.;* (21) **whip-poor-will,** (see quot.), *obs.*

(1) **1853** BREWERTON *With Kit Carson* (1930) 280 We passed the evening in preparing for our contemplated trip by baking a quantity of biscuit in one of those three-legged contrivances known to the initiated as a 'Dutch bake-oven.' **1880** *Scribner's Mo.* XX. 128 Sometimes the cook used the Dutch bake-oven. — (2) **1772** *N.Y. Gaz.* 16 Nov. 1/1 There is on it a very good Dwelling House . . . , a large Dutch Bar [*sic*], Out Houses, and very good bearing orchard. **1780** *N.J. Archives* 2 Ser. IV. 301 There is on said farm . . . a large Dutch barn of good substantial timbers. — (3) **1887** FREDERIC *Seth's Brother's Wife* 162 You have settled down in a Dutch beer saloon, making associates out of the commonest people in town. — (4) **1757** *Lett. to Washington* II. 120 If any of the Dutch Blankets remain & not wanted for the Indians I have no objection to their being replac'd in the room of those made use of. **1812** *Niles' Reg.* II. 55/1 [The duelist's] jacket was then unbuttoned and . . . a Dutch blanket was discovered in eight folds. **1846** *Knickerb.* XXVII. 185 Fringed snow-flakes ('Dutch blankets' we used to call them,) sailing idly in the soft, yielding atmosphere.

(5) **1895** *D.N.* I. 416 'Dutch cuss' . . . I have always heard . . . used, among farming people, as the specific name of the common, or ox-eyed, daisy. — (6) **1830** WATSON *Philadelphia* 600 It often happened that the servants coming from Germany and Holland, after being purchased, communicated a very malignant fever to whole families and neighbourhoods. . . . It was of such frequent occurrence as to be called in the Gazettes the 'Dutch distemper.' — (7) **1835** D. P. THOMPSON *Adv. T. Peacock* 140 Leaving Timothy in a sort of Dutch doggery, or sailor's hotel, . . . Jenks immediately went in search of the friend. — (8) **1858** *Harper's Mag.* XVII. 854 In a 'Dutch garden,' at the capital, . . . a few young men . . . had been participating rather freely of 'lager.' — (9) **1671** *S.C. Hist. Soc. Coll.* V. 275 Heere in Carolina is as good duch grasse in the sumer & fegg in the winter that Cattoll wilbee broad fed & kept att very easy rates. **1754** ELIOT *Field-Husb.* v. 104 [Blue grass] by many is called Dutch Grass. **1797** I. THOMAS *N.-Eng. Farmer* 276 Quitch Grass, called also Witch grass, Twitch grass, Couch grass, Dutch grass, and Dogs grass.

(10) **1886** JAMES *Bostonians* 185 The establishment was of the kind known to New Yorkers as a Dutch grocery. — (12) **1834** PECK *Gaz. Illinois* 91 In McLean County is a society of United Brethren, or as some call them, Dutch Methodists. — (13) **1817** W. COXE *Fruit Trees* 123 *Golden Pearmain.* Called in New-York and East-Jersey, the Ruckmans, or Dutch Pearmain. — (14) **1856** *Spirit of Times* 20 Sep. 43/2 Kentucky counted up two catfish (dutch pike) one shiner, three half-grown minnows, a dogfish and one gar. **1857** *Porter's Spirit of Times* 3 Jan. 286/1 We reached [Long Lake] in good season for fishing . . . and our only reward was three or four bull-headed cats (dutch pike) and two or three shiners.

(15) **1852** *N.Y. Wkly. Tribune* 24 Jan. 5/2 Every kind of sleigh, from the primeval model of the Dutch pung to the last wrinkle of a modern omnibus, was sported in the streets. — (16) **1733** FRANKLIN *Poor Richard 1734* 23 Sold by the Printer, . . . Dutch Quills. **1865** *Atlantic Mo.* XV. 346 Older boys paid that sum for a single 'Dutch Quill.' — (17) **1823** HOLMES *Account* 387 In Pennsylvania, and . . . New York, there are many Quakers. . . . There are also . . . Dutch Reformed churches. **1871** STOWE *Pink & White Tyranny* 245 Let us thank God for those Dutch-Reformed churches. — (18) **1762** *Boston Ev. Post* 27 Dec. 3/2 A neat Dutch sleigh, with two double seats, upon steel runners. — (19) **1911** MUZZEY *Amer. History* 61 The high Dutch stoops and quaint market places in the villages along the Hudson.

(20) **1818** PALMER *Journal* 124 Where a swampy place occurs, trunks of small trees are laid close together, and continued to the firm ground, this called a 'Dutch turnpike,' from the early Dutch settlers first making them. — (21) **1850–58** O'NEALL-CHAPMAN *Annals* 24 Now and then a solitary 'Chuck-Will's-Widow' commonly called the *Dutch 'Whip-poor-Will,'* enlivened the night.

b. Designating a (1) **lunch,** (2) **party,** (3) **supper,** (4) **treat,** at or in connection with which each person pays his or her own share.

(1) **1904** *Columbus Post-Dispatch* 21 Aug., Dancing was enjoyed by all as was the Dutch lunch which was partaken of at intervals during the evening. **1948** *Dly. Ardmoreite* (Ardmore, Okla.) 12 May 2/5 Carter County Oil Men's association will stage a dutch lunch meeting at Lake Murray state park Thursday night. — (2) **1927** *Observer* 8 May 13/3 Dutch parties are rather more elaborate, in that while the hostess provides the dance floor, music, table, service, and cutlery, her friends bring along the drinks and the viands, raiding their family cellars and larders. — (3) **1904** *Dallas M. News* 10 Sep. 6 Young hopefuls at college . . . need [money] to buy plug-cut and Dutch suppers with. — (4) **1887** *Lippincott's Mag.* Aug. 191 'You'll come along too, won't you?' Lancelot demanded of Ormizon. 'Dutch treat vous savez.' **1949** *Chi. D. News* 8 Jan. 13/2 (*caption*), [They] were part of Dutch treat crowd that took dinner at Fortnightly club.

c. In colloq. phrases: (1) *To beat the Dutch,* said of anyone or anything that is most unusual or surprising; (2) *to take Dutch leave,* to leave one's place in a military organization without permission; (3) *to get in Dutch,* to get into disfavor or disgrace.

(1) **1775** *Revolutionary Song* in *N. Eng. Hist. Reg.* (April, 1857) 191 Our cargoes of meat, drink, and cloaths beat the Dutch. **1906** FREEMAN *By Light of Soul* 277 You women do beat the Dutch. **1940** THOMPSON *Body, Boots* 450 A group from New England who, slightly in the Majority, agreed on a classical name 'to beat the Dutch.' — (2) **1898** HARRIS *Tales Home Folks* 206 You've gone and broke the rules and articles of war. . . . You took Dutch leave. — (3) **1919** STREETER *Same Old Bill* 113 (We.), What the this and that do you mean gettin me in Dutch, you big space filler? **1947** *Newsweek* 11 Aug. 89/1 Anyone might get in Dutch for a dish like Miss Hayward.

As the last term in **Hook and Eye, Jersey, Pennsylvania Dutch.**

***Dutchman,** *n.*

1. (See quots.) *Obs.* Cf. **Pennsylvania Dutchman.**

1857 BORTHWICK *In California* 311 Europeans . . . save French, English, and 'Eyetalians' are in California classed under the general denomination of Dutchmen, or more frequently 'd——d Dutchmen,' merely for the sake of euphony. **1898** WESTCOTT *D. Harum* xxviii, 'Dutchman' was Mr. Harum's generic name for all people native to the Continent of Europe. **1910** G. C. EGGLESTON *Recoll.* 3 To us in the West, at least, all foreigners whose mother tongue was other than English were 'Dutchmen.'

2. In various technical meanings (see quots.).

1859 BARTLETT 134 *Dutchman,* a flaw in a stone or marble slab, filled up by an insertion. **1874** KNIGHT 765/1 *Dutchman* (*Carpentry*), a playful name for a block or wedge of wood driven into a gap to hide the fault in a badly made joint. **1905** *Forestry Bureau Bul.* No. 61, 36 *Dutchman,* a short stick placed transversely between the outer logs of a load to divert the load toward the middle and so keep any logs from falling off. (N[orthern] F[orest].) **1909** *Cent. Dict.* Supp., Dutchman, a layer of suet fastened with skewers into a roast of lean beef or mutton. **1930** *Amer. Sp.* V. 145 *Dutchman,* a ridge in the center of a drill hole causing the steel to stick. **1943** *Copper Camp* 94 A hole was bored and corked tight with a small steel plug known as a 'dutchman.'

3. Used in the possessive in combs.: (1) ***Dutchman's breeches,** a wild herb, *Dicentra cucullaria,* which flowers in spring, also the flower of this; (2) ***pipe,** =**Indian pipe;** (3) **treat,** (see quot. and cf. **Dutch treat**), *rare.*

(1) **1837** DARLINGTON *Flora Cestrica* 398 Hood-like Dielytra. Vulgo —Dutchman's Breeches. **1948** *Life* 5 April 57/1 Here the Dutchmen's

Breeches from the eastern woods grow out near the western meadow grasses. — **(2) 1894** *Amer. Folk-Lore* VII. 93 *Monotropa uniflora*. . . Dutchman's pipe, N.J. — **(3) 1891** *Cent.* 6451/2 *Dutchman's treat, Dutch treat*, a repast or other entertainment in which each person pays for himself. (Slang, U.S.)

Dutchy ˈdʌtʃɪ, *n.* Familiar form of "Dutch." Often used in address.

1835 Hoffman *Winter in West* II. 165 Where's Yankee and Dutchee? the bacon and greens are smoking on the table. **1864** Trowbridge *Cudjo's Cave* 39 See here, Dutchy! ye hain't been foolin' us, have ye? **1941** Seton *Trail of Artist-Naturalist* 329 Dutchy's knowledge of German gave him a great advantage.

Also as *adj.*

1862 A. Gray *Lett.* (1893) 495, I was . . . copying out Grisebach's manuscripts for the printer (for the printer won't touch the Dutchy-looking thing). **1893** J. H. Ross in *King's Business* (New Haven, Conn.) 127 The faces [in Rembrandt's Scripture pictures] are not ideal but Dutchy.

dutied ˈdjutɪd, *a.* Subject to duty or customs. — **1771** Jefferson *Writings* I. (1892) 394 The restrictions will be taken off everything but the dutied articles. **1796** Gallatin *Writings* III. 78 The annual consumption of dutied articles.

Dutton corn. A variety of prolific, early-maturing corn.

1838 Ellsworth *Valley of Wabash* 47 If you send to your son any grains, I wish half a bushel . . . of 'Dutton corn.' **1856** *Rep. Comm. Patents: Agric.* 166 'Dutton Corn' . . . is cultivated in Massachusetts. It has a small yellow kernel and a large cob, weighing 830 grains. **1894** R. E. Robinson *Danvis Folks* 36, I druther hev a peck o' Dutton corn, yis, er Tucket, than a bushel o' their hoss-tooth corn.

* **duty,** *n.* (See quots.)

1890 *Cent. Mag.* XXIX. March 770/2 It becomes necessary to determine the amount of water which is needed to serve an acre of land. This is called the 'duty' of water, and in the United States it varies widely. In some regions of country, where the rainfall is great and the soil favorable, the duty of water is large: a given amount of water will irrigate a broad tract of land. **1891** *Geol. Survey Rep.* XII. 223 The area of land which can be irrigated by a given quantity of water is known for convenience as 'the duty of the water.'

As the last term in **alarm, auction, fire, horse, Mediterranean, settlement, skirmishing duty.**

***duty,** *v. tr.* To place a duty upon (an article). — **1789** *Annals 1st Cong.* I. 210 Now the committee have dutied this article at thirty per cent. upon the prime cost. **1878** A. L. Perry *Elem. Polit. Econ.* 575 These were both dutied in our ports in 1870.

Dwamish ˈdwɑmɪʃ, *n.* [App. f. an Indian term.] (See quot. 1907.)

1854 Stevens in *Ind. Aff. Rep.* (1854) 453. **1866** *Beadle's Mo.* Sep. 191/2 The grand patriarch of all these Indians is Seattle, of the Dewamish tribe. **1885** Jackson *Cent. of Dishonor* 442 The D'Wanish and other allied tribes . . . are generally Christianized. **1907** Hodge *Amer. Indians* I. 407 Dwamish. A small body of Salish near Seattle, Wash., which city was named from a chief of this and the Suquamish tribes.

* **dwelling,** *n.* **1. dwelling plantation,** *S.* a plantation on which the owner has his residence. *Obs.* **2. dwelling room,** a sitting or living room. *Colloq.*

(1) 1695 *Md. Hist. Mag.* I. 8 [Groome's residence was his] dwelling plantation at Gunpowder River. **1752** *Virginia Gaz.* 5 March 3/2 Ran away from the Dwelling-Plantation of the Rev. Mr. Robert Rose . . . Robert McFarlan, a Scotchman. — **(2) 1837** *Knickerb.* X. 432 The coffin was placed in the centre of the largest apartment, in country phrase, the 'dwelling-room.' **1851** Northall *Curtain* 18 He proceeded at once to his dwelling room, which was over the stage door.

As the last term in **cliff, frame, Indian, log dwelling.**

***dwindlings,** *n. pl. local.* (See quot.) — **1911** *Essex Inst. Hist. Coll.* XLVII. 14 The small creeks into which the marsh lots slope are called 'dwindlings.'

* **dye,** *n.* In combs.: (1) **dye-flower,** (see quot.), *colloq.;* (2) **kettle,** a kettle used in dyeing; (3) **pot,** = prec.; (4) **stone ore,** an iron ore found in the Clinton group, and having the property of staining the hands deep red.

(1) 1894 *Amer. Folk-Lore* VII. 92 *Coreopsis*, sp., . . . dye-flowers. Banner Elk, N.C. — **(2) 1704** S. Knight *Jrnl.* 15 The sause was of a deep Purple, w[hi]ch I tho't was boil'd in her dye Kettle. **1894** Wilkins in *Harper's Mag.* LXXXVIII. 499/2 Ichabod Buckley's wife had her dye-kettle out there on forked sticks over a fire. — **(3) 1825** Neal *Bro. Jonathan* I. 148 A family dye-pot . . . is a convenience for ever in the way of those who travel over New England . . . ; the smell is insupportable. **1870** Tomes *Decorum* 112 The wig and dye-pot are . . . going out of fashion. — **(4) 1889** *Cent.* 1808/2 Dyestone ore [is] an ore iron of great economical importance in the United States.

As the last term in **devil's, egg dye.**

* **dyed-in-the-wool,** *a.* In a political or partisan sense: Thoroughgoing, uncompromising.

1830 *Mass. Spy* 10 Feb. (Th.), In half an hour [he can] come out an original democrat, dyed in the wool. **1906** Bell *C. Lee* 225, I am a dyed-in-the-wool Presbyterian, and I've fought, bled, and died for my religion in a family who believe that God created the Church of England. **1948** *Dly. Ardmoreite* (Ardmore, Okla.) 29 April 1/1 The same is true of the ordinary dyed-in-the-wool republican.

dyeing corn. A term used by George Washington for the variety of Indian corn from which the present sweet corn has been developed. *Rare.* Cf. **papoon corn, sweet corn.** — **1789** Washington *Diaries* IV. 45 A Clergyman . . . presented me with an Ear and part of the stalk of the dyeing Corn, and several pieces of Cloth which had been dyed with it.

dyer's cleavers. One of several species of bedstraw, esp. *Galium tinctorium.* — **1814** Bigelow *Florula Bostoniensis* 36 *Galium tinctorium*, Dyers Cleavers. . . . Thickets and low ground. . . . According to Kalm the roots dye a permanent red. **1821** *Mass. H.S. Coll.* 2 Ser. IX. 150 Plants . . . indigenous in the township of Middlebury, [Vermont, include] . . . *Galium asprellum*, Dyer's cleavers.

***dynasty,** *n.* As the last term in **Negro, pipe weed, Virginia dynasty.**

dysentery weed. (See quots. and cf. **stickseed.**) Also **dysentery root.**

1876 Hobbs *Bot. Hand-Book* 33 Dysentery root, dysentery weed, Virginia mouse ear, *Cynoglossum Morrisoni.* **1909** *Cent. Supp.* 405/1 dysentery-root. . . . The stick-seed or beggar's lice, *Lappula Virginiana*, from the supposed medicinal properties of the root. Also called *dysentery-weed.* **1931** Clute *Plants* 123 Familiar examples are asthma-weed (*Lobelia inflata*), dysentery weed (*Lappula Virginica*) . . . etc.

dyspepsia flour. (See quot.) *Obs.* — **1833** J. Boardman *America* 16 It may be requisite to inform my readers, that dyspepsia flour is considered to possess peculiar digestive properties.

E

E,** ***n.

1. Used with various significations as a grade or mark in school (see quots.).

[**1890** in M. L. SMALLWOOD *Exams. & Grading Systems* 53 In each of their courses students are now divided into five groups, called A, B, C, D, E. . . . To graduate a student must have passed in all his courses, and have stood above the group D.] **1896** MOE *Harvard* 45 It is the place where many an unsuspecting Freshman has gone into with lightsome heart, only to emerge with wan cheeks, and eyes that picture despair. For many E's have here been made. **1899** *Western Reserve Univ. Cat.* 67 Students are graded in their studies by letters which have value . . . as follows: E (excellent) [etc.]. **1943** *Lake Forest Cat.* 33 Students' grades are recorded in letters. A signifies excellent scholarship. . . . An E is given for withdrawal from a course without permission.

2. An abbreviation for "error" in baseball.

1880 *Dly. Inter Ocean* (Chi.) 3 June 6/3 The Score: Chicago. AB R BH HR PO A E. **1902** *Chi. Record-Herald* 1 Sep. 10/1 Chicago R. H. P. A. E. **1921** *St. Louis Globe-Dem.* 5 June 14/8 Cleveland . . . AB. H. O. A. E. **1945** *Athol* (Mass.) *D. News* 24 May 4/1.

eagle,** ***n.

1. As a symbol of the U.S.

[**1697** SEWALL *Phænomena quædam Apocalyptica* 8 America is fitly represented by an Eagle, which Royal Bird is very frequent there.] **1798** FESSENDEN *Orig. Poems* (1806) 4 The Eagle of Freedom with rapture behold, Overshadow our land with his plumage of gold! **1853** *Wash. Wkly. Union* 27 Dec. 54/1, 'I think,' said Mr. Smith, 'you will hear the old lion roar about the middle of January.' 'Then,' responded Judge Douglass, 'you will see the eagle flap his wings.' **1885** HOWELLS *S. Lapham* xvi, Our Eagle flapping his wings in approval, at Lincoln's feet, occupied one corner.

b. In slang or colloq. expressions: (1) *To make the eagle scream*, to indulge in high-flown patriotic oratory, cf. **2. b.** below; (2) *to fly the eagle*, =prec.; (3) *flier of the eagle*, an excessively patriotic, bombastic orator.

(1) [**1847** ROBB *Squatter Life* 97 Sich a yell as that would . . . make the United States Eagle scream 'Hail Columby.'] **1904** *N.Y. Ev. Post* 14 Sep. 1 Mr. Fassett was toying with those dear but haggard phrases, . . . and generally making the eagle scream. [**1942** LILLARD *Desert Challenge* 194 He introduced the orator of the day (a Cave City man) and for a while the eagle screamed.] — (2) **1872** MARK TWAIN *Speeches* (1910) 415 You won't mind a body bragging a little about his country on the Fourth of July. It is a fair and legitimate time to fly the eagle. **1906** PITTMAN *Belle of Blue Grass C.* 248 The rostrum, where the politicians were flying the American Eagle, for this was the opening of the campaign season. — (3) **1902** *N. Amer. Rev.* CLXXIV. A crowd of . . . ten thousand proud, untamed democrats, horny-handed sons of toil and of politics, and fliers of the eagle.

2. A gold coin of the U.S. having a value of ten dollars.

This coin was authorized in 1792 and coinage was begun in 1794. The first two quots. are anticipatory.

1786 in *Amer. Museum* (1789) II. 182 There shall be two gold coins; one . . . to be stamped with the impression of the American eagle, and to be called an eagle . . . one . . . to be called a half-eagle. **1792** *Ann. 2nd Congress* 2 April 71 Eagles; each to be of the value of ten dollars or units, and to contain . . . two hundred and seventy grains of standard, gold. **1835–7** HALIBURTON *Clockmaker* 1 Ser. 131 He gave the Eagles such a drive with his fist, he burst his pocket, and sent a whole raft of them a spinnin down his leg to the ground. **1905** DIXON *Clansman* 139 A beggar asked him for a night's lodging, and he tossed him a gold eagle.

b. In phrasal use in allusion to the representation of an eagle used on coins. Cf. **1. b.** (1) above.

1911 SAUNDERS *Col. Todhunter* 44 He squeezes ev'y dollar o' his'n till the eagle screams and flies back into his own pocket, and you know it.

3. (See quots.) Now *hist.*

1810 in *Old-Time N. Eng.* (1928) April 176 Prices of playing cards of a new and superior manufacture, just received for sale by W. Blagrove, No. 61 Cornhill Superfine Eagles. [$]5. **1928** *Old-Time N. Eng.* April 176 The American card makers advertised their cards as 'Columbians' and 'Eagles' and stoutly invited comparison with the 'Moguls,' 'Merry Andrews' and 'Harry the Eighths' of their English competitors.

b. (See quot.)

1944 *Pocket Bk. of Games* 299 In 1938 there appeared a five-suit deck, having the usual 52 cards of the standard deck plus a complete fifth suit. In the United States this fifth suit was green, called Eagles, and marked by an appropriate symbol.

4. (*cap.*) Used in nicknames (see quots.).

1849 *Cong. Globe* App. 16 Feb. 114 [Mr. P. W. Tompkins of Miss.] thought proper . . . to denominate me [Bedinger of Va.] the 'Eagle from Harper's Ferry.' **1893** *Cong. Rec.* 16 Oct. 2561/2 [50 years ago] John Randolph of Roanoke . . . denounced New England and New England Institutions. The grand old man, known as the Bald Eagle of Rhode Island [Tristram Burges] rose to reply.

5. *pl.* (*cap.*) A fraternal order formed in Seattle in 1898. In full **Fraternal Order of Eagles.**

1903 *Cin. Enquirer* 2 Jan. 8/4 The local lodge of Eagles is searching for a suitable site upon which to erect a permanent aerie and clubhouse. **1945** *Chronicle-News* (Trinidad, Colo.) 14 June 1/6 Soon after its founding in 1898 the Fraternal Order of Eagles adopted the eagle as its official fraternal emblem.

6. In golf, a score two strokes below par on any but a par-three hole.

1922 *N.Y. Times* 16 July 22/3 Kneppen . . . halved the hole with Von Elm, who lay in position for an eagle, but missed a putt of nine feet. **1947** *Dly. Oklahoman* (Okla. City) 11 Aug. 13/6 Ben had only two birdies to go with his big eagle.

7. In combs.: (1) ***eagle-back,** a playing card, prob. one having a picture of an eagle on the back, *obs.*, cf. **3.** above; (2) **calumet,** a calumet adorned with eagle feathers; (3) **dance,** an Indian dance performed in honor

Eagle calumet

of the eagle; (4) **scout,** a rank awarded to a first-class boy scout who qualifies for twenty-one merit badges; (5) **tail dance,** (see quot. 1819).

(1) **1880** *Harper's Mag.* Sep. 572/1 A large square table, on which stood . . . two decks of best eagle-backs. — (2) **1833** CATLIN *Indians* I. 111 He took his position in the middle of the room, waving his eagle calumets in each hand. — (3) **c1836** CATLIN *Indians* II. 127 The *Eagle Dance*, a very pretty scene, . . . is got up by their [*sc.* the Choctaws'] young men, in honour of that bird, for which they seem to have a religious regard. **1945** *Pueblo* (Colo.) *Star-Journal* 3 June 8/1 The famous Eagle dance, staged on the huge Thunderdrum of the Koshare Indians, will again highlight the annual ceremonial of this famous group. — (4) **1913** *Boy Scouts' Yearbook* 201 Possibly you will become an Eagle Scout, and thus reach the highest rank in the organization. **1947** *Harper's Mag.* Sep. 248/1 Huck Finn was the cheeriest Eagle Scout you ever heard. — (5) **1765** TIMBERLAKE *Mem.* 85 On the 28th, I was invited to a grand eagle's tail dance, at which about 600 persons of both sexes were assembled. **1819** *Niles' Reg.* XVI. Supp. 101/2 The Eagle-tail dance is still in use among the Cherokees. The design of this dance is to stimulate in the minds of the young growing people the spirit of war.

As the last term in **bald, bald-headed, brown, calumet, Caracara, double, golden, gray, half, king, Mexican, Northern bald, nun's, spread, United States, vulture, war, Washington, white-headed eagle.**

***ear,** *n.*[1] In combs.: (1) **ear biter,** a special agent of the post-office department, so called because about 1845 one of the agents bit off the ear of an opponent in a fight, *obs.;* (2) **distemper,** (see quot.), *obs.;* (3) **fly,** a small gadfly, *Chrysops vittatus,* that attacks horses' ears; (4) **hoop,** a hoop-shaped earring, *obs.;* (5) ***lap(pet), =ear tab;** (6) **lock,** a lock of hair in front of the ear, in former fashions curled and much groomed; (7) **muff,** a covering for the ears to serve as a protection from the cold, usu. *pl.;* (8) ***ring,** *S.* a kind of orchid growing in swamps, *colloq.;* (9) **tab,** a piece of material, usu. a part of a cap, covering the ears as a protection from cold, usu. *pl.,* cf. **ear muff;** (10) **tick,** (see quot.).

(1) 1855 J. HOLBROOK *Among Mail Bags* 27 How much the result of this first investigation, after the restoration of the 'ear-biters' (as they were then sometimes facetiously called,) had to do with the radical change in opinion and action, . . . it may not be advisable . . . to inquire. — **(2) 1836** WESTON *Visit* 119, I this day saw a beef, as the oxen are called, running in an inclosed field at a great rate. . . . It had got what is called the ear-distemper, which is occasioned by a certain insect crawling into the internal ear and depositing its eggs. — **(3) 1806** LEWIS in *L. & Clark Exped.* V. (1905) 87 Found here [are] the butterflies, common house and blowing flies, the horse flies, except the goald coloured ear fly. **1910** *N.J. State Mus. Rep.* 738 These are moderate or large species, popularly known as 'horse-flies,' but locally and referring to special types, also as 'gad-flies,' 'deer-flies,' 'ear-flies,' . . . etc. — **(4) 1808** *Mass. Spy* 18 May (Th.), A large assortment of Earhoops, of different sizes. **1845** JUDD *Margaret* I. x. 64 Many [ladies] wore ear-hoops of pinch-beck, as large as a dollar.
(5) 1863 B. TAYLOR *H. Thurston* 79 Woodbury recognized, projecting between ear-lappets of fur, the curiously-planted nose . . . which belonged to the Rev. Mr. Waldo. **1937** MITCHELL *Horse & Buggy Age* 72 On May Day he changed his heavy winter hat with its earlaps for a large, broad-brimmed, farmer's straw hat. — **(6) 1775** in *Harper's Mag.* LXVII. 736/1 Warren . . . was sufficiently exposed that day to have a musket ball strike the pin out of the hair of his ear-lock. **1867** LOWELL *Poetical Works* (1896) 418/2 His frosted earlocks, striped with foxy brown, Were braided up to hide a desert crown. — **(7) 1859** *Rep. Comm. Patents 1858* II. 572 William P. Ware . . . [patented an] Ear, Cheek, and Chin Muff . . . July 6, 1858. **1947** *Chi. Times* 22 July 2/3 Isn't it about time for the office comic to appear for work in ear muffs? — **(8) 1938** MATSCHAT *Suwannee River* 221 This little one, which covers the low grounds along the riverbanks, is called earrings by the children. — **(9) 1855** *Knickerb.* XLV. 199 In stable-yards, old-looking black boys, in cat-skin caps, with ear-tabs to them, whistle airs from 'Semarimis [*sic*].' **1909** *N.Y. Ev. Post* 28 Jan. (Th.), With the first really cold weather of the winter, there appeared on Broadway the vendors of ear-tabs.
(10) 1918 *Farmers' Bul.* No. 980, 2 Ear Ticks are blood-sucking parasites which infest the ears of cattle, horses, sheep, dogs and other animals. They are prevalent in the semi-arid sections of the south-western part of the United States, where they cause heavy losses among live stock.

b. In colloq. phrases: (1) *To be* (or *get,* etc.) *on one's ear,* to be indignant, to be "on the warpath"; (2) *to hop off on one's ear,* to go off "with a flea in one's ear"; (3) *to spin round on one's ear,* (see quot.); (4) *to hold* (or *keep*) *one's ear to the ground,* to be on the alert about what is going on; (5) *to be wet behind the ears,* to be quite immature, cf. *to be dry behind the ears, s.v.* ***dry,** *a.* **d.**

(1) 1871 *Galveston News* 4 May (De Vere), They . . . said that I was lightning when I got up on my ear. **1882** HOWELLS *Modern Instance* xxix, I can cut your acquaintance fast enough . . . if you're really on your ear! **1907** M. C. HARRIS *Tents of Wickedness* 255, I only hope Paul Fairfax won't read it and get on his ear! — **(2) 1873** *Newton Kansan* 10 April 2/1 The editor has hopped off on his ear. — **(3) 1890** *D.N.* I. 64 'To spin round on one's ear' means to get violently angry. — **(4) 1900** *Cong. Rec.* 29 Jan. 1258/1 He held his ear to the ground, so the newspapers stated. **1909** *Nat. Conservation Cong. Proc.* 9 If these associations are filled with the broad national principles of conservation, then the law makers will hold their ears close to the ground. **1944** ADAMS *W. Words* 93 Long ear. To place a silk neckerchief on hard ground and listen by putting the ear upon it. Old plainsmen often followed this practice, and sounds otherwise inaudible are somehow magnified by this means. From this practice originated the saying, 'Keep your ear to the ground.' meaning to use caution, to go slowly, and listen frequently. — **(5) 1945** WILLIAMS *It's a Free Country* 21 Married! You're still wet behind the ears!

As the last term in **cauliflower, devil's, elephant's, mouse, short, slick, split ear.**

***ear,** *n.*[2]

1. A head of Indian corn; the spike together with its kernels. Cf. **red ear, roasting ear.**

1622 MOURT *Relation* 21 We . . . found a fine great new Basket . . . with some 36. goodly eares of corne, some yellow, and some red, and others mixt with blew. **1781** in PETERS *Hist. Conn.* (1829) 70 To pick an ear of corn growing in a neighbor's garden, shall be deemed theft. **1837** HAWTHORNE in *Democratic Rev.* I. 33 Behind comes a 'sauce-man,' driving a wagon full of new potatoes, green ears of corn, beets, carrots, turnips, and summer squashes. **1944** *Chi. D. News* 4 July 10/2 The old-fashioned corn that we used to feed to Dobbin—four ears or six nubbins a meal—is passe.

b. In Indian parlance, harvest; the length of time from harvest to harvest. *Rare.*

1823 DODDRIDGE *Logan* II. ii, For ten snows and ten ears of corn you have governed our nations.

2. In combs.: (1) **ear corn,** unshelled corn; (2) **worm,** the larva of the moth *Heliothis armigera,* which attacks Indian corn, cotton plants, etc., cf. **boll worm, corn ear worm.**

(1) 1872 EGGLESTON *End of World* 140 Put a bushel of ear-corn in the great washboiler. **1946** *Prairie Farmer* 5 Jan. 4/1 Please tell me how to estimate the amount of ear corn in a crib? **1948** JACOBS *We Chose the Country* 113 It seemed like a wonderful idea . . . to drive out . . . and fill the truck with ear corn for the pig. — **(2) 1802** *Mass. H.S. Coll.* VIII. 190 Five [worms] . . . are very destructive to Indian corn. . . . The fifth is the ear worm; which, after the ear is formed, eats the grains and between them; about an inch long. **1944** *Seed Ann.* 11 Destruction of the remains of each crop after harvesting is essential to check earworms and corn-borers.

b. In phrases: (1) *corn in the ear,* **=ear corn;** (2) *corn on the ear,* (*a*) green corn prepared as food by boiling, (*b*) **=ear corn.**

(1) 1802 ASBURY *Journal* III. We got corn in the ear at a dollar per bushel [in Tennessee]. **1831** PECK *Guide* 166 In autumn they [=oxen] were . . . fed with corn in the ear. [**1854** BARTLETT *Personal Narr.* II. 259 Green corn . . . we had bought for one dollar a hundred, in the ear.] — **(2)** (*a*) **1911** SAUNDERS *Col. Todhunter* 29 The Missouri supper of fried chicken, egg-bread, butterbeans and corn on the ear. (*b*) **1931** *Randolph Enterprise* (Elkins, W.Va.) 26 Nov. 8/5–6 (*advt.*), 600 bushels of Corn on the ear.

***ear,** *v. intr.* Of Indian corn: To produce ears. — **1809** CUMING *Western Tour* 94 Twelve acres of the finest corn I ever saw . . . [was] now twelve feet high, just beginning to ear. **1896** *Vt. Agric. Rep.* XV. 71 Usually it [the Red Cob] does not ear.

Hence ***eared,** *a.* Of Indian corn: In the ear, provided with ears. — **1776** in *W. & M. Coll. Quart.* XVI. 260 Yesterday Phil was catched in the top of my wheat unthreshed, and with him at least a bushel of ear'd corn. **1861** *Ill. Agric. Soc. Trans.* IV. 205 The large yellow being much the heavier growth, best eared and larger ears.

earful ˈɪrˌfʌl, *n. fig.* A great deal of news or gossip. *Slang.* — **1931** *K.C. Star* 13 Aug., White residents in that vicinity . . . are getting an 'earful' from the Lindberghs.

***early,** *a.*

1. early American, used to designate furniture, etc., of the colonial and post-Revolutionary periods.

1922 *Country Life* Sep. 45/1 Furniture from the workshop of Duncan Phyfe holds distinctly a place of its own in the history of early American utilitarian art. **1926** *Ladies' Home Jrnl.* Sep. 98/4 There was first of all a charm created by the primitive simplicity of the antique Early American furniture as seen against nut-brown panelings of old pine. **1931** FINLEY *Lady of Godey's* 20 And who is not familiar with Godey's reproductions that depict impossible ladies cavorting in voluminous gowns over wall-papers, drapery fabrics, lampshades, dressing cases, waste-baskets and what not designed for the decoration of the modern 'early American home?' **1949** *Sat. Ev. Post* 5 Mar. 100/4 Upstairs are an early American bedstead, an old sewing machine and an antique music box.

2. early-morning plank, a political plank advocating the early admission of a territory to statehood.

1910 *Outlook* 25 June 357 The fact that an early morning plank is found in a party platform ought not to weigh for an instant against serious doubt as to the capacity of either Territory to become a part of a self-governing Union.

3. Designating varieties of plants that mature their fruits early, as (1) **early blue,** (2) **bunch grass,** (3) **cabbage, cauliflower,** (4) **comfort bean,** (5) **corn,** (6) **flint,** (7) **harvest,** (8) **muscadine,** (9) **purple potato,** (10) **rose,** (11) **Virginia wheat.** Chiefly *obs.*

(1) **1849** *N. Eng. Farmer* I. 400 Early-Blue is the name of a very old, very early, and excellent variety [of potato] with a rough skin. — (2) **1894** Coulter *Bot. W. Texas* III. 544 *Eatonia obtusata.* (Early bunch-grass.) . . . Moist land. — (3) **1829** *Va. Herald* (Fredericksburg) 7 Feb. 1/2 Real Early York Cabbage, . . . Early Cauliflower. — (4) **1821** *Plough Boy* II. 326/3 The Early Comfort Bush Beans . . . (of) *cool-comfort-garden*, near this City (Charleston) . . . have now taken the name of *early comfort beans*, to distinguish them from all other sorts, both native and imported.

(5) **1788** Schöpf *Reise* I. 456 Sie [i.e., roasting ears] werden gekocht, oder in der Asche gebraten, und mit Salz und Butter genossen; und in den Städten zum Verkauf, warm (hot Corn) ausgeruffen. Man hat aber in diesem Thale eine Gattung Frühkorn (Early Corn), welches zwar kleiner ausfällt aber besser gedeyht. **1944** *Vaughan's Gardening.* 73/2 Extra Early Golden Bantam [Corn]. Matures in about 72 days. [**1948** *Chi. Tribune* 29 Feb. I. 33/1 (*advt.*), New Early Sweet Corn, Biggest, Sweetest Yet.] — (6) **1856** *Rep. Comm. Patents: Agric.* 194 In 1853, I obtained from Baltimore . . . 2 bushels each of 'Australian' and 'Gale's Early-flint.' . . . I harvested 38½ bushels of fine wheat. — (7) **1847** J. M. Ives *N. Eng. Fruit* 34 Early Harvest. This is the earliest apple worthy of cultivation. **1937** Lutes *Home Grown* 132 Dried apples filled in that dismal period between the last of the Baldwins or Russets and the first of the Early Harvests. — (8) **1856** *Rep. Comm. Patents: Agric.* 307, I have several varieties of the grape in my collection, among which is the 'Sweet Water,' or 'Early Muscadine,' and the 'Mammoth Catawba.' — (9) **1849** *N. Eng. Farmer* I. 400 We have a half barrel of Early Purple potatoes.

(10) **1877** *Vt. Bd. Agric. Rep.* IV. 33 Nature can make potato balls, but she couldn't make the Early Rose. **1948** *Hygeia* Jan. 51/1 In America about 1868, when the first Early Rose was first placed on the market, it sold for $66.66 per bushel. — (11) **1846** Bromme *Reisebuch* 94 Der Waizen ist die vornehmste Kornfrucht des Landes. . . . Man baut verschiedene Arten desselben . . . die vorzüglichste aber ist eine frühreise weisse Art, die unter dem Namen 'früher Virginischer Waizen' (*early Virginia-wheat*) bekannt ist.

∗**earn,** *v. Baseball. To earn a base* or *run*, to obtain a base or a run without benefit of errors.

1867 *Ball Players' Chron.* 6 June 2/2 The Harvards went in for some fine batting, Ames leading off and being well followed by McKim, Shaw and Willard, all but McKim earning their bases by their hits. **1886** Chadwick *Art of Batting* 32 In the fifth innings Kelly of the Chicago Nine led off with a safe bounder to left field on which he easily earned his base. **1945** *Athol* (Mass.) *D. News* 14 May 4/1 Athol earned three of its four runs during the day.

Hence **earned base, run.**

[**1867** *Ball Players' Chron.* 6 June 3/3 Pabor caught a foul ball on the fly in style, and Birdsall and Ketcham disposed of Sweezy handsomely at 3d, the innings closing for 4, when 2 runs only were earned.] **1885** Chadwick *Art of Pitching* 93 The hit yields an earned base. **1886** ——*Art of Base Running* 69 No pitcher can be punished by his batting opponents unless his pitching be hit for *earned* runs. **1947** *Chi. Sun* 17 Dec. 42/1 Leading the National League hurlers in effectiveness was Warren Spahn, Braves' southpaw, with an earned run average of 2.33.

∗**earnest,** *n.* (See quot.) *Obs.* — **1877** Bartlett 197 Boys call it playing marbles *in earnest*, when it is understood that the winners shall keep the marbles.

∗**earth,** *n.* In combs.: (1) ∗**earthquake,** a kind of alcoholic drink, *obs.;* (2) **squirrel,** the prairie dog, *rare;* (3) ∗**work,** see as a main entry.

(1) **1869** Mark Twain *Innocents* xv. 149 The uneducated foreigner could not even furnish a Santa Cruz Punch, an Eye-Opener, a Stone-Fence, or an Earthquake. **1888–90** Barrere-Leland I. 342 Earthquake, bottled earthquakes. *Bottled earthquakes* are just as bad as the other kind. Scratch a *bottled earthquake* and you'll find a cocktail. — Chicago Tribune. — (2) **1857** Chandless *Visit Salt Lake* II. x. 311 Little heaps of earth [were] thrown out from the burrowings of the earth-squirrel, who generally sat on the top of the heap, sunning himself.

∗**earthwork,** *n.*

1. A mound made by prehistoric people.

1847 Squier *Monuments of Miss. Valley* Earthworks . . . enclosures, or, as they are familiarly called throughout the West, 'Forts,' constitute a very important and interesting class of remains. **1883** L. Carr *Mounds of the Miss. Valley* It can be shown on undoubted historic authority that these Indians built both mounds and earthworks, which differ in degree but not in kind from similar structures . . . of an extinct people.

2. Work involving the removal or piling up of earth. *Rare.*

1856 Whipple *Explor. Ry. Route* II. 63 In the determination of the earth-work masonry, &c., . . . I would acknowledge the valuable assistance . . . [of the] civil engineer.

b. An embankment on a railroad line.

1869 *Cong. Globe* 6 April 536/1 The road-bed, wherever there is an embankment, is in many places so narrow that the ties overlap the earthwork.

∗**ease,** *v. To ease up*, to move (a thing) gently; to relieve (the mind or a person) from anxiety or pain. *Colloq.*

1870 Mark Twain *Sk., New & Old* 83 You warm the end of your plank . . . and then raise it aloft and ease it up gently against a slumbering chicken's foot. **1898** Westcott *D. Harum* 155 We'd eased up our minds on the subjects of each other's health. **1921** Paine *Comr. Rolling Ocean* 83 The doctor is down there easing up the guys that got the hide burned off 'em.

∗**east,** *n., a.,* and *adv.*

1. (Usu *cap.*) The eastern part of the U.S. Also the people living in that section.

"The East is a relative term as one traverses the American continent. Thus when the California newspapers report that settlers from the East are locating in Glynn county, the far easterner is surprised to read that the reference is to people coming from Dakota" (1907 *Springfield Republican* 28 Feb. 7).

[**1654** Johnson *Wonder-w. Prov.* 16 Indians did abandon those places for feare of death, fleeing more West and by South, observing the East and by northern parts were most smitten with this contagion.] **1782** Freneau *Poems* (1786) 277 The east and the south losing communication, The Yankies will die by the act of starvation. **1876** *Sutter Banner* (Yuba City, Calif.) 3 Aug. 2/2 Only one car-load of immigrants arrived at Sacramento from the East yesterday. **1944** Johnson *As I Dare* 277 The people themselves think of the East as though it were a remote province.

b. *adv.* (see quots.). Cf. **back East, Down East.**

1857 *Lawrence* (Kans.) *Republican* 4 June 3 It has served the very good purpose of exposing the falsity of the cry, raised by a certain class of papers East. **1906** Lynde *Quickening* 209 Money is tighter than a shut fist—up East. **1928** Foy & Harlow *Clowning Thro' Life* 195 It was the high ambition of every Western Variety actor to 'go East.'

2. *N. Eng.* **about east,** completely, in proper form, "O.K." *Colloq.*

*a***1848** in Bartlett 375, I did walk into the beef, and taters, and things, about east. *c***1850** Whitcher *Bedott P.* xxv. 303 If ther's any body that won't knuckle tew her, I tell ye they have to take it about east. **1866** Lowell *Biglow P.* 2 Ser. (Intro.) p. xvii, There was not a Yankee . . . whose problem had not always been to find out what was *about east*, and to shape his course accordingly.

3. In combs.: (1) **eastbound,** (*a*) traveling or headed toward the east, often with reference to freight traffic, (*b*) also absol.; (2) **East India bat,** (see quot.), *obs.;* (3) **Rivers,** (see quot. 1881); (4) **Side,** see as a main entry.

(1) (*a*) **1880** *Bradstreet's* 30 Oct. 4/4 The east-bound freight shipments . . . have undeniably been light. **1898** *Dly. Ardmoreite* (Ardmore, Okla.) 12 July 4/1 He tried to catch a ride on the bumpers of the eastbound local. **1947** *Time* 10 Mar. 21/3 And just east of the now infamous Bennington curve, three cars of an eastbound freight jumped the tracks. (*b*) **1909** Wason *Happy Hawkins* 222 This time the west-bound had to take a sidin' and wait twenty minutes for the east-bound — (2) *c***1728** Catesby *Carolina* I. 8 The Goat-Sucker of Carolina. . . . They are very numerous in Virginia and Carolina, and are called there East-India Bats. — (3) **1854** *Belleview* (Nebr.) *Palladium* 15 Nov. 1/3, I understand that Mr. Chilton, the analytic chemist . . . has been asked to examine into the 'phenomenal condition' of the 'Shrewsburys' and 'East rivers,' and report thereon. **1865** *Harper's Wkly.* 30 Dec. 823/4 Our East River and York River oysters are probably superior to any obtained in European markets. **1881** Ingersoll *Oyster Industry* 244 East Rivers, oysters grown between New Haven, Connecticut, and New York.

As the last term in **back, down, south, Star of the East.**

∗**Easter,** *n.* In combs.: (1) ∗**Easter flower,** any one of various flowers (see quots.); (2) ∗**lily,** any one of various flowers used for decorative purposes at Easter, now usu. *Lilium longiflorum eximium;* (3) **mackerel,** *Pacific Coast*, (see quot.).

(1) **1877** Bartlett 446 Easter flower (*Narcissus pseudo-narcissus*). **1900** Higginson *Outdoor Studies* 62 Beautiful wood-anemones I find, to be sure, trembling on their fragile stems, deserving all their princely names,—Wind-flower, Easter-flower, Pasque-flower, and homoeopathic Pulsatilla. **1907** Lyons *Plant Names* 384 P[ulsatilla] Ludoviciana . . . April-fool, Badger-weed, Easter-flower, Gosling. **1937** *Range Plant Handbook* W159/2 Other appellations as April-fools, Easter-flower, . . . wild-crocus, and windflower have variously designated this species. — (2) **1877** Bartlett 446 The Calla is frequently called Easter Lily. **1945** *Grant Co.* (Wis.) *News* 12 April 1/4 Easter lilies and ivory tapers formed the setting for the nuptial rite. — (3) **1884** Goode *Fisheries* I. 304 The Tinker Mackerel, *S*[*comber*] *pneuma-*

tophorus, is known as 'Mackerel,' 'Easter Mackerel,' . . . and 'Little Mackerel.'

***eastern,** *a.*

1. (*cap.*) Formerly used in Massachusetts with reference to Maine. *Obs.*

1676 SEWALL *Diary* I. 22 And nothing yet lately heard of damage in the Eastern parts. **1719** *Mass. H. Rep. Jrnl.* II. 128 A memorial . . . acknowledging the great Service land [*sic*] Encouragement that the Eastern Settlements have had . . . [and asking for more soldiers] to assist . . . Biddiford and Cape Porpus. **1789** *Ann. 1st Congress* I. 229 In the words that are often used in the Eastern country respecting the inhabitants of Cape Cod, they are too poor to live there, and they are too poor to remove.

2. Pertaining to, originating in, or characteristic of, the eastern part of the U.S., esp. New England.

1776 *Jrnls. Cont. Congress* IV. 347 The Congress took into consideration the report of the committee on the Eastern department. **1876** DODGE *Black Hills* 99 Oak and birch grow in the gorges, and the flora is very 'eastern.' **1930** FERBER *Cimarron* 325 She talked with an Eastern accent, ignored the letter *r*, said eyether and nyether and rh'ally and altogether made herself poisonously unpopular with the girls. **1943** HICKS *Amer. Dem.* 334 Eastern farmers were unable to meet in full the needs of their new industrial centers for foodstuffs.

b. In the superlative with a pejorative implication, imputing affectation and false refinement to the East. *Rare.*

1912 WASON *Friar Tuck* 55 This spring 'at I have in mind, we had as visitor one o' the easternest dudes I was ever tangled up with.

3. (Usu. *cap.*) In special combs.: (1) **Eastern Band,** a division of the Cherokee Indians, *obs.;* (2) **Indians,** (*a*) a collective term applied to the Indian tribes northeast of the Merrimac River, cf. **Eastward Indians,** (*b*) the Indians east of the Mississippi River; (3) **Middle States,** those Middle States that lie farthest east; (4) **money,** bills, credit, etc., originating in the East, as distinguished from the less stable issues of the western states, *obs.;* (5) **Shore,** see as a main entry; (6) **Slope,** (*a*) that part of the Sierra Nevada Mountains extending into Nevada, *obs.*, (*b*) (not *cap.*) that part of the Rocky Mountains the waters of which drain to the east; (7) **standard time,** =**eastern time;** (8) **Star,** see as a main entry; (9) **states,** the states in the eastern part of the U.S., often, esp. in early use, the New England states; (10) **time,** the standard time of the eastern time belt, see **standard time;** (11) **war time,** (see quot. 1944); (12) **waters,** those streams flowing into the Atlantic Ocean, also the country drained by these, *obs.*

(1) 1883 ZEIGLER & GROSSCUP *Alleghanies* 32 The Eastern Band, as those [Cherokees] who remained and purchased farms, and their descendants are known, has been steadily decreasing in numbers. *Ib.* 35 Colonel Thomas became chief of the Eastern Band of the Cherokees. — **(2)** (*a*) **1689** *Mass. H.S. Coll.* 4 Ser. V. 203 Engage a competent number of the friendly Indians to come down . . . to follow and fall upon the eastern Indians. **1731** in *Amer. Sp.* XX. (1945) 271 Six Acts of the Massachusetts Bay, 1731 . . . (iii) for allowing necessary supplies to the Eastern and Western Indians and for regulating trade with them. (*b*) **1947** DEVOTO *Across Wide Missouri* 273 The policy of removing the Eastern Indians to the Western lands reserved to them in perpetuity . . . in December of 1835, got round to the remnants of the once great Cherokee nation. — **(3) 1872** *Harper's Mag.* Dec. 30/1 Strange, though at Georgetown there was no snow, here the road is deep and heavy with it, and the whole scene is one of midwinter in the Eastern Middle States. — **(4) 1837** *N.Y. Herald* 3 Oct. 1/5 Orders received for small notes at 197 Greenwich Street, New York, and those notes redeemed there in silver, small eastern money, or city bank bills. **1840** *N.O. Picayune* 16 Aug. 1/1 James Sharrock Exchange Broker . . . constantly buys and sells Kentucky, Indiana, . . . New York and Eastern Moneys at the most favorable rates.

(6) (*a*) **1865** (*title*), Eastern Slope [Washoe, Nev.]. **1876** POWELL *Nevada* 15 In the summer of 1859, when the silver discovery was made, the population of this part of Utah, then called 'the Eastern Slope,' amounted to a little over a thousand souls. **1947** PEATTIE *Sierra Nevada* 217 Thompson started using skis for utilitarian purposes, and others in the mining towns of the western and eastern slopes of the Sierra did likewise. (*b*) **1945** *Dly. Sentinel* (Grand Jct., Colo.) 25 Nov. 5/1 Mr. Adams . . . formerly lived on the eastern slope. — **(7) 1924** *N.Y. Times* 8 Aug. 27/3 The newly established transcontinental air mail service is operated in both directions daily, leaving Hazelhurst Field (N.Y.) at 11 A.M., Eastern Standard Time. **1945** *Chi. D. News* 14 Sep. 7/1 In 1935 the City Council proposed that Chicago adopt Eastern Standard Time all year round. — **(9) 1776** *Jrnls. Cont. Cong.* VI. 1039 Ordered, That the delegates of the eastern states confer together. **1830** *Amer. Ladies' Mag.* July 316 Last summer I visited the Eastern states, and, of course, passed some time in Boston. **1944** HOLTON *Yankees* 133 With all the rest of the eastern states we shared the great blizzard of '88, a storm which still gets its pictures into the paper at intervals.

(10) 1883 *N.Y. Herald* 18 Nov. 12/3 In the United States the standards will be known as the 'Eastern,' 'Central,' 'Mountain' and 'Pacific' times. **1945** *Chi. D. News* 14 Sep. 7/1 Eastern time would throw Chicago out of tempo with the rest of the country. — **(11) 1944** *World Almanac* 168 By Public Law 403, amending the Act of March 19, 1918, the standard time for each zone in the United States was advanced by one hour, effective Feb. 9, 1942. Following the passage of this law the President issued an order designating the times for the various zones as Eastern War Time (EWT) [etc.]. **1945** *Chi. Sun* 16 Feb. 1/1 The measure will be ignored by cities that operate on eastern war time. — **(12) 1781–82** in *Amer. Sp.* XV. 175/1 We hear of limestone on the Mississippi and Ohio, and in all the mountainous country between the eastern and western waters. **1791** *Ib.*, The further time of twelve months . . . shall be allowed all plats and certificates of surveys on the Eastern Waters.

b. Used in the names of, or with reference to, plants, animals, and trees, as (1) **eastern bluebird,** (2) **Henslow's sparrow,** (3) **meadowlark,** (4) **plane tree,** (5) **smelt,** (6) **snowbird,** (7) **spruce,** (8) **winter wren,** (9) **woodchuck.**

(1) 1874 COUES *Birds N.W.* 13 *Sialia Sialis*, (Linn.) Hald. Eastern Bluebird. . . . Specimens of the Eastern Bluebird are occasionally found with part of the reddish brown of the throat replaced by rich blue. **1949** *Dly. Oklahoman* (Okla. City) 13 Feb. D. 2/1 With wings the color of a summer sky and breast of Oklahoma soil, the eastern bluebird is loved by young and old. — **(2) 1939** *Nat. Geog. Mag.* March 364 Eastern Henslow's sparrows begin to reach the Washington region in spring about April 10. — **(3) 1934** A. A. ALLEN in *Nat. Geog. Mag.* LXVI. 119 The eastern meadowlark ranges northward into southern Canada and westward into Kansas, Iowa, and Texas. — **(4) 1832** WILLIAMSON *Maine* I. 106 Button-wood, or eastern 'plane-tree,' is an unyielding tight-grained wood, as large as a beech.

(5) 1856 *Spirit of Times* 27 Dec. 274/1 The fish taken was not . . . the larger and coarser—though still excellent—Eastern smelt. — **(6) 1874** COUES *Birds N.W.* 141 Eastern Snow-bird . . . breeds from Maine and New Hampshire northward, and in mountains south to the Middle States. **1881** *Amer. Naturalist* XV. 519 Keeping always together, as if by family compact . . . is a pretty domestic feature of our eastern snow-bird. — **(7) 1868** *N.Y. Herald* 1 July 9/2 Eastern spruce was in but little demand. — **(8) 1931** *Check List N.A. Birds* (ed. 4) 242 *Nannus hiemalis hiemalis* . . . Eastern Winter Wren. — **(9) 1917** *Mammals of Amer.* 196 Eastern Woodchuck, *Marmota monax*. Other names are Eastern Marmot; Groundhog.

c. Also as adv. with p.p., as **eastern-bound, eastern-bred.**

1844 GREGG *Commerce of Prairies* II. 14 These men had all been hired by us except three, two of whom were Eastern-bred boys. **1865** *Atlantic Mo.* XV. 405/2 At Buffalo waited the Eastern-bound cars of the New-York Central Railway.

As the last term in **down, southeastern.**

Easterner ˈistənə, *n.* A native or inhabitant of the eastern part of the U.S.

1840 LOWELL *Letters* (1894) I. 59, I am on the best of terms with 'Southerners,' 'Westerners,' and 'Easterners.' **1890** *Voice* 7 Aug., These amounts may seem small to Easterners. **1949** *This Week Mag.* 5 March 28/2 The pinto bean is a stranger on the easterner's table.

***Eastern Shore,** *n.* Also **eastern shore.** The peninsula to the east of Chesapeake Bay, partly in Maryland and partly in Virginia.

1624 in *Amer. Sp.* XV. 175/1 To plant the Secretaries land on the Eastern Shore neere Accomack. **1745** E. KIMBER *Itinerant Observ.* 51 The Inhabitants on the Western Shore are supply'd with prodigious Quantities of Beef, Pork and Grain from this Eastern Shore. **1854** SIMMS *Southward Ho!* 179 In approaching the 'Eastern Shore' of Virginia . . . you find yourself gliding toward . . . scenes of repose, delicacy, and quiet beauty. **1948** *Chi. Tribune* 9 May I. 3/3 Farmers of Maryland's eastern shore found quick produce markets in Wilmington, Del., and Philadelphia.

attrib. **1785** WASHINGTON *Diaries* II. 461 Landed 230 Bushels of Oats to day from an Eastern Shore vessel. **1807** *State. P.* (1819) VI. 46 The day before yesterday he fired many a shot at an Eastern Shore man. **1948** MENCKEN *Supp.* II. 128 It is often difficult to say of a strange Eastern Shoreman, for example, whether he comes from below the Choptank or above.

***Eastern Star.** A benevolent organization, primarily for women but also sometimes including men, affiliated with the Masons, known since 1788 but reorganized in Chicago in 1869. Also attrib. In full **Order of the Eastern Star.**

1887 *Boston Almanac* 118 Order of the Eastern Star. Queen Esther Chapter, No. 16. **1920** LEWIS *Main Street* 258 Ray habitually asked her about . . . the best music for the entertainment at the Eastern Star. **1948** *Lewistown* (Mont.) *D. News* 2 Sep. 8/6 He was a past master of the Masonic lodge and a past patron of the Eastern Star. **1949** *Chi. D. News* 25 March 10/2 (*heading*), Eastern Star Chapter To Hold Fashion Show.

∗ **East Side.** In New York City, the eastern portion of Manhattan borough, esp. below Fourteenth Street, inhabited in the main by the poorer classes. Also attrib.

"In N.Y. one does not speak, as in London, of the *East End* and the *West End*, but of the *East Side* and the *West Side*. Why these parts of the city are called sides and not ends will be clear to any one who glances at a map of Manhattan Island" (Horwill, 286).

1894 WARNER *Golden House* v, She was so full of sympathy with the East-Side work. **1948** CHAPLIN *Wobbly* 376 Their eyes were hard, and their accents unmistakably flavored with the Lower East Side.

b. East Sider, a person born or living on the East Side.

1903 *N.Y. Tribune* 25 Oct., 15,000 East Siders attended the final dedication ceremonies at William H. Seward Park. **1911** O. HENRY *Rolling Stones* (1915) 194 I'd rather see one of the same gang win out before I would an East-Sider, or any of the Flatbush or Hackensack Meadow kind of butt-iners.

c. East Sidese, the language and method of speaking characteristic of the East Side. *Colloq.*

1911 LEWIS *Apaches N.Y.* 22 Gatts is East Sidese for pistols. **1948** *Chi. Sun-Times* 29 Sep. 71/1 Well, it was a nice dog story so I'll translate Sam's clip-clop East Sidese into my own clip-clop English.

∗ **eastward,** *a.* and *n.*

1. *n.* (Usu. *cap.*) Maine, or New England. *Obs.*

1644 *Mass. H.S. Coll.* 4 Ser. VI. 148 There is a great partie for the Kinge to the Eastward. **1725** *N.-Eng. Courant* 1 March 2/1 We have Advice from the Officer that Commands St. George's Fort at the Eastward. **1835** HOFFMAN *Winter in West* I. 187 The settlers, instead of gradually pushing their way together into the depths of the forest, as at the eastward, . . . plant themselves down a day's journey apart.

b. *attrib.* or *adj.* Of, from, belonging to, Maine. *Obs.*

1670 *Harvard Rec.* I. 50 Ordered, that the lost 3 pounds be well repayed to the College stock, out of the Eastward money. **1886** SEWALL *Diary* I. 136 Richard Waldron . . . told me what an Eastward master reported about the coming out of the Rose-Frigot.

2. Eastward Indians, =**Eastern Indians.** *Obs.*

1677 HUBBARD *Indian Wars* (1865) I. 224 Some that belonged to the Eastward Indians. **1726** PENHALLOW *Indian Wars* (1824) 41 Several of our Eastward Indians were confederate with them.

∗ **easy,** *a.*

1. Denoting *money* or *dollars* obtained with little effort. *Colloq.*

1836 WEBSTER *Private Corr.* (1856) II. 21 The deposit and distribution bill has become a law, and money is already getting to be much easier, as the phrase is. **1870** MEDBERY *Men Wall St.* 69 The lender seeks the borrower. Money becomes a drug. Technically it is 'easy' or 'inactive.' **1909** O. HENRY *Roads of Destiny* vi. 88 The boarding houses were corralling the easy dollars of the gamesome lawbreakers. **1941** ASBURY *Gem of Prairie* 61 Attracted by the easy money of a boom town, by the thousands of soldiers on the loose with thousands of dollars from Army payrolls . . . the human scum of a hundred cities swarmed into Chicago.

2. In special colloq. combs.: (1) **easy keep,** (see quot.); (2) **mark,** a person who may be easily imposed upon; (3) **picking,** a person or thing easily mastered, a "pushover"; (4) **street,** an imaginary street symbolizing comfortable circumstances, usu. *on easy street;* (5) **water,** water that is quiet, not disturbed by current.

(1) **1943** *Chi. Sun* 7 Oct. 19 She describes herself as 'easy keep.' It's a term she picked up from a cowboy friend, and on the range it means a horse who feeds on almost anything and thrives on it. — (2) **1899** G. ADE *Fables in Slang* (1902) 2 The Easy Mark collapsed into the Boarding-House Chair and the Man with more Whiskers than Darwin ever saw stood behind Him and ran his Fingers over his Head, Tarantula-Wise. **1947** *Chi. Tribune* 15 June (Grafic Mag.) 11/2 Being a good sport is one thing, being an easy mark is another. — (3) **1912** C. MATHEWSON *Pitching* ii. 25 Why can the Yankees take game after game from Detroit and be easy picking for the Cleveland club in most of their games? **1931** *K.C. Star* 3 Nov., The chickens are so overconfident, after escaping the poor marksmen on the first day, that they make easy picking on the second. — (4) **1902** HOBART *It's Up to You* 31 (We.), A young man who could walk up and down Easy Street. **1948** *Chi. Tribune* 17 Oct. (Grafic Mag.) 20/3 By the time police caught up with her she was on easy street. — (5) **1875** MARK TWAIN *Old Times* iii. 52 Follow along close under the reef—easy water there—not much current. **1884** ——— *H. Finn* vii. 54 He dropped below me with the current, and by and by he came a swinging up shore in the easy water.

b. *To go easy on,* see **go;** *as easy as rolling* (or *falling*) *off a log,* see **log.**

∗ **eat,** *v.*

1. *tr.* To provide (a person) with food. *Colloq.*

1837 *Crockett Almanac* 17 Well, Capting, do you ate us, or do we ate ourselves? **1897** W. E. BARTON *Hero in Homespun* 273 We can eat you all right, but I ain't right sure if we can; hip you. **1928** BENÉT *J. B.'s Body* 367 You ought to be et. We'll eat you up to the house when it's mealin' time.

2. *intr.* (See quot.) *Obs.*

1853 STRICKLAND *Twenty-seven Yrs.* I. 98 The wood eats, which means, that the grain, though straight in the length of the shingle, makes short deep curves, which render it bad to split, and cause holes to appear in the shingles when you come to shave them.

3. *tr.* To concern, disturb, vex (a person). *Slang.*

1893 CRANE *Maggie* (1896) 90 'Well,' he growled, 'what's eatin' yehs?' **1947** *Redbook* Oct. 64/2 'What's eating you?' her boy friend demanded.

4. To go rapidly over (territory, distance). *Colloq.*

1898 CANFIELD *Maid of Frontier* 111 Put my spurs into him an' make him eat up the groun.' **1905** SLOSS *Bk. Automobile* 179 One of the keenest pleasures in possessing a car is being able to annihilate a hill or 'eat it up.'

5. *To eat crow, dirt, dust,* see the nouns.

∗ **eater,** *n.* As the last term in **bean, beaver, bee, biscuit, buffalo, bug, cake, chicken, clay, clover, corn, cotton, crab, dirt, fig, fire, fish, hominy, lunch, man, muscle, pork, rice, root, shad, sheep, snow, worm eater.**

eatery ˈitərɪ, *n.* An eating-house. *Jocular.*

Given as U.S. in the *OED Supp.* but the earliest evidence (as shown here) is from the well-known British humorist.

1923 WODEHOUSE *Inim. Jeeves* i. 11 Why, then, was he lunching the girl at this God-forsaken eatery? **1947** *Dly. Oklahoman* (Okla. City) 21 Sep. D-6/1 The eateries and sleeperies can expand to take care of 50,000,000 summer transients.

∗ **eating,** *n.* In combs.: (1) **eating apron,** an apron worn by a child while eating; (2) **club,** see as a main entry; (3) **palace,** a grandiose term for a restaurant; (4) **saloon,** a restaurant, *obs.;* (5) **station,** a station or stop on a railroad or stagecoach route where food may be obtained; (6) **tobacco,** =**chewing tobacco,** *jocular.*

(1) **1915** CAMPBELL *Proving Virginia* 29 My poor mother . . . led me out bareheaded, with a big eating-apron on. **1933** B. MOSES *Franklin Delano Roosevelt* 53 Ever since he and she wore eating-aprons at Franklin's little table in the Hyde Park nursery where they used to have their bread and milk supper together. — (3) **1902** WISTER *Virginian* xiii. 148, I came upon him one morning in Colonel Cyrus Jones's eating palace. — (4) **1858** VIELÉ *Following Drum* 149 An eating saloon, a bakery and even a 'pharmacie' . . . are found here. **1877** *Rep. Vermont Board Agric.* IV. 199 Grounds are furnished with a . . . floral hall and eating saloon.

(5) **1852** *Harper's Mag.* V. 273/2 Travelers by railroad, who stop at the 'eating stations,' . . . are hurried away . . . before they have begun their repast. **1903** *Cin. Enquirer* 3 Jan. 11/2 We got to an eating station about 10 o'clock in the morning, four hours late. — (6) **1944** *Chi. D. News* 4 Nov. 1/4 (*caption*), Eatin' Tobacco Up 20 Per Cent on Nov. 8. **1949** *Sat. Ev. Post* 2 April 79/3 If things are going well, he presents all hands with gifts of eating tobacco, apples [etc.].

As the last term in **clay, fire eating.**

eating club. A group of people who habitually take their meals together, esp. a club of young men at college who eat together.

"The *eating club* and *eating hall* at an Am. college correspond to the Eng. *dining club* and *dining hall*" (Horwill *Mod. Amer. Usage* 115).

1871 BAGG *At Yale* 238 'Eating clubs,' especially in freshman year, are the approved mediums through which he obtains his food. **1916** H. J. FORD *Woodrow Wilson* 9 His eating club was 'The Alligators,' which he joined in his sophomore year.

eatiphone ˈitəˌfon, *n.* [Of fanciful formation.] =**eatery.** *Rare.* — **1879** *Black Hills News* (Deadwood, Dak. Terr.) 8 July 4/2 The Eatiphone on Lower Main street, gives a good square meal at any hour of the day or night.

Eaton Code. (See quot.) — **1889** *Cent.* 1083/1 *Eaton code,* a collection of laws made by Governor Eaton by authority of the General Court of New Haven Colony, and adopted by it. It was first published in London in 1656, and is largely composed of extracts from the laws of Massachusetts.

*__eats,__ *n. pl.* Things to eat, food. *Slang.* — **1910** *Salt Lake Tribune* 27 Nov. 32/7 The Chief made himself solid with the members because of the toothsome 'eats' he served. **1946** *New Harmony* (Ind.) *Times* 15 Feb. 3/4 Eats will be served and a club membership card is the only ticket required.

*__eave,__ *n.*

1. eave beam, bearer, a particular log (see quot. 1791) in a log house. *Obs.*

1791 in JILLSON *Dark & Bl. Ground* (1930) 109 The eave bearers [of a log cabin] are the end logs which project over to receive the butting poles, against which the lower tier of clapboards rest in forming the roof. **1804** ORDWAY in *Jrnls. of Lewis & O.* 163 We got one line of our huts raised So that we got the Eve Beames on & all of large Timber. **1873** HAYCRAFT *Elizabethtown, Ky.* 70 The first operation was to clear off a spot some thirty feet square in which to erect a round log cabin—puncheon floor and clapboard roof, confined to the house by weight pole, and an eave-bearer, against which the boards rested.

2. With **spout, trough,** designating the apparatus put up along the eaves of a house to carry away rain water.

1852 *Mich. Agric. Soc. Trans.* III. 185 Lightning rod, tin eave troughs, and a permanent cement cistern. **1865** STOWE *House & Home P.* 103 The water barrel . . . stood under the eaves-spout. **1878** *Rep. Indian Affairs* 90 An eave-trough and conductor has also been put on the agent's house. **1889** COOKE *Steadfast* xxxv. 369 A wild November storm . . . shrieked and wailed in the eave-spout.

3. eave(s) swallow, the cliff swallow, *Petrochelidon albifrons;* also the tree swallow, *Iridoprocne bicolor.*

1874 COUES *Birds N.W.* 88 *Petrochelidon lunifrons.* . . . Cliff swallow, eave swallow. **1889** *Cent.* 1826/1 *Eaves-swallow.* . . . This name was first used about 1825, when these birds appeared in settled parts of the eastern United States. **1917** *Birds of Amer.* III. 85 The flocks of Bank, Barn, and Tree Swallows absorb these Eave Swallows, and together they work to clean the air of the island lakes of all the flies and mosquitoes. *Ib.* III. 88 *Tree Swallow.* . . . Other Names.— . . . White-bellied Swallow; Stump Swallow; Eave Swallow.

*__Ebenezer,__ *n.* Also †**ebenezer.**

1. Anger, temper. *Colloq.*

1836 *Phila. Public Ledger* 27 July, That riz Deb's ebenezer. **1849** NASON *Journal* 14 Our steward is under the constant necessity of a checkrein upon his ebenezer.

2. *To set up* (one's) *Ebenezer,* to make up one's mind firmly. *Colloq.*

*c*__1840__ NEAL *Beedle's Sleigh Ride* 26, I took a resolution, and stuck to it firm, for when I once set up my ebenezer I am just like a mountain. **1902** PIDGIN *Quincy A. S.* 71, I sot up by Ebenezer, and I says, 'Silas Putnam, if you gives your property to any one you gives it to me.'

3. Ebenezer Society, a name formerly used for what is now known as the Amana Society *q.v.* Now *hist.*

1908 *Encycl. Religion & Ethics* I. 360 The committee of Inspirationists reached New York City on October 26, 1842. . . . They purchased . . . Seneca Indian Reservation lands in Erie County, New York. . . . Other villages were soon founded, and under the name of 'Ebenezer Society' the Community was formally organized with a written constitution. **1947** *Chi. D. Tribune* 8 June v. 12/5 In 1842 the group moved to New York state to become known as the Ebenezer society.

Ebo, see **Ibo.**

*__ebon,__ *n.* =**ebony 1.** Also attrib. *Obs.* — **1820** *Western Carolinian* 11 July, Many of the free states . . . find the ebon part of their citizens to be, at times, very troublesome. **1895** *Outing* XXVI. 428/2 A little ebon, who had been watching to set open the gates.

*__ebony,__ *n.*

1. A Negro. Also *son of ebony. Obs.*

1852 STOWE *Uncle Tom* vi, Black Sam, as he was commonly called, from his being about three shades blacker than any other son of ebony on the place. **1863** E. KIRKE *Southern Friends* iv. 69 The scented ebony roared. **1877** BARTLETT 782 Ebony, a common term for a Negro.

2. *pl.* The black grips on bicycle handlebars. *Rare.*

1882 *Wheelman* I. 14 How they flew! The wheels appeared but skeleton rims. The others increased speed, . . . now and then letting go the ebonies and clapping their hands.

3. ebony spleenwort, a common North American variety of fern or spleenwort, *Asplenium platyneuron.*

1833 EATON *Botany* (ed. 6) 36 *Asplenium ebeneum,* ebony spleenwort. . . . Rocks and dry places. **1889** *Cent.* 342 Among the more common species [of Asplenium] generally known as spleenwort, are . . . ebony spleenwort (*A. ebeneum*) [etc.].

eboulis ebuˈli, *n.* [Fr. *éboulis,* a landslide.] (See quot.) *Rare.* — **1824** *Commentator* (Frankfort, Ky.) 2 Oct. 2/4 For some days back a number of *eboulis* (sinking of the Levee) have taken place on both banks of the river [at New Orleans].

*__eccentric,__ *n.* (See quot.) *Rare.* — **1871** DE VERE 466 *Eccentric* has in Western parlance obtained a curious meaning, which threatens to spread in spite of its absurdity. 'I want my land down to the *eccentric,*' said an illiterate man in Illinois, objecting to the reservation of mining rights under the purchase.

Echinocactus ɛˌkaɪnəˈkæktəs, *n.* [f. *__echino-__, spiny, +*cactus.*] A genus of spiny cactus, cylindrical or globular, usu. strongly ribbed. Also a cactus of this genus.

1856 WHIPPLE *Explor. Ry. Route* I. 102 There are . . . various kinds of Echino cactus, the most conspicuous being that named Wislizenus, and sometimes called the 'Turk's Head.' **1893** COVILLE *Death Valley Exped.* 110 This small and handsome *Echinocactus* was found in the mountains east of Resting Springs. **1940** BENSON *Cacti of Ariz.* 107 This is the largest barrel cactus in Arizona, although *Echinocactus acanthodes* becomes larger in California.

*__eclectic,__ *n.* (See quot. 1877 and cf. **Thomsonian.**) In full **eclectic physician.** *Obs.* — **1877** BARTLETT 702 [Samuel Thomson's] followers have discarded much that he adopted, and are now known as Eclectic or Botanic physicians. **1905** F. A. MATHEWS *Billy Duane* 161 Marjorie's next move was to send for the three physicians of the place: the homeopathist, the allopathist, and the eclectic.

eclipse wine. (See quot.) *Obs.* — **1834** HONE *Diary* I. 107 This Eclipse wine was imported into Boston in 1806, and arrived at the moment of the great solar eclipse, to which circumstance it owes its name, although it might claim it upon the ground of its eclipsing almost all other wines.

*__Economist.__ *n.* A Harmonist, esp. a member of the communistic colony at Economy, Pennsylvania, founded in 1825. *Obs.* — **1837** PECK *New Guide* 174 The Economists or Harmonists, as they are called, in Indiana, are an industrious, moral and enterprising community, with some peculiarities in their religious notions. **1875** C. NORDHOFF *Communistic Soc. U.S.* 65 [Economy] during many years was a favorite winter as well as summer resort for Pittsburghers, and an important source of income to the Economists.

Economite ɪˈkɑnəmaɪt, iˈkɑnəmaɪt, *n.* =**Economist.**

1864 *Harper's Mag.* Dec. 54/2 The sect . . . were 'Economites' only because they had settled a town called Economy. **1875** C. NORDHOFF *Communistic Soc. U.S.* 63 If you ask the conductor, he will tell you that for some miles here [between Wellsville and Pittsburgh] the land is owned by the 'Economites.' **1909** WEBSTER 984/1 In 1825 it [*sc.* a portion of the Harmonites] founded the settlement of Economy, and its members have since sometimes been known as *Economites.*

Eddyism ˈɛdɪˌɪzəm, *n.* [After Mary Baker *Eddy* (1821–1910), founder of Christian Science.] =**Christian Science.** — **1903** *N.Y. Times* 29 Sep. 8 The description of Eddyism is accurate enough, but we are vastly mistaken if this 'unique product' has not had innumerable predecessors. **1924** *Amer. Mercury* Jan. 104/1 The New Thought was derived originally from the same well of wisdom as Eddyism.

*__edge,__ *n.*

1. *To have the edge on* (a person), and variants, to have an advantage over, to be superior to. *Colloq.*

This expression may have developed from the much older "to have the age" *q.v.* used in poker playing, "age" being erroneously apprehended as the common unschooled pronunciation of "edge."

1896 *Dly. News* 18 Mar. 7/5, I am gone, especially from your own people, who always had an edge on me, and for no reason. **1929** *Publishers' Wkly.* 14 Sep. 1060 Here we have the edge on our rivals, not only because of our superior location, but also because we are reputedly reckless about reducing prices. **1947** *N.Y. Times* 12 Oct. v. 6/4 Penn now has won five straight and holds an edge of ten triumphs to six, with two ties.

b. *To give* (one) *the edge,* to select as a likely winner by a narrow margin. *Colloq.*

1932 *Latimer Co. News-Democrat* (Wilburton, Okla.) 19 Feb. 1/6 Ray Tucker of the Scripps-Howard Newspaper Alliance gives Murray the edge over Roosevelt in the North Dakota primary.

2. edge rail, (see quot. 1874). *Obs.*

1832 *Amer. R.R. Jrnl.* I. 50/1 A form of rail, called the 'Edge Rail' was brought into use. **1849** CHAMBERLAIN *Ind. Gazetteer* 31 With an edge rail of sixty pounds to the yard, it would be about $800,000. **1874** KNIGHT 773/2 *Edge-rail.* (*Railroad.*) *a.* One form of railroad-rail, which bears the rolling stock on its edge. . . . *b.* a rail placed by the side of the main rail at a switch to prevent the train from running off the track when the direction is changed.

As the last term in **feather, ragged, rough, wire, wiry edge.**

*__edging,__ *n.* Waste wood produced in sawing logs into lumber.

1850 JUDD *R. Edney* iv. 51 The Captain . . . flung into the river, like so much edging. **1884** NYE *Baled Hay* 23 The managing editor of the mill lays out the log in his mind, and works it into dimension stuff, shingle bolts, slabs, edgings, two by fours. **1886** STAPLETON *Major's*

Christmas, There, before a feeble open fire of pine edgings and mill refuse, sat a little figure.

Edisonite ˈɛdəsn̩ˌaɪt, *n.* [Thomas A. *Edison* (1847–1931), Amer. inventor.] "Titanic acid occurring in golden-brown orthorhombic crystals" (*OED Supp.*). — **1888** *Amer. Jrnl. Sci.* 3 Ser. XXXVI. 274, I therefore propose for it the name *Edisonite,* after Mr. Thomas Alva Edison.

***edition,** *n.* As the last term in **dime, rush, steamer edition.**

***editor,** *n.* The literary manager of a publishing house.

1930 *Publishers' Wkly.* 5 April 2096 Far more attention might well be given the West's peculiar needs by Eastern editors. **1944** Johnson *As I Dare* 235 An editor who buys a manuscript and fails to publish it within a reasonable time is failing to make full payment and can be forced to return the manuscript to the author. **1948** *Sat. Review* 19 June 4/3 The editor must never cease his search for new writers.

As the last term in **agricultural, art, city, copy, day, field, foreign, managing, news, night, night city, real estate, social, sports, telegraph editor.**

editorial ˌɛdəˈtorɪəl, *n.* An article expressing the views of the editor or publisher, usu. appearing in a department of the publication devoted to such writing.

"*Editorial* [is] . . . an unpleasant Americanism for *leader* or *leading article,* which name is given to the articles in newspapers upon the leading topics of the day" (R. G. White *Words & Their Uses* (1899) 95).

1830 *Collegian* 44 The great green table in the centre groaning under the weight of editorials, and friendly correspondence. **1866** *Beadle's Mo.* Jan. 30/1 The word *editorial* . . . does not appear as a substantive noun in any dictionary, we believe, and yet it is used almost daily by the best scholars and writers as meaning the newspaper or periodical article prepared by the editor. **1883** *Harper's Mag.* March 601/1 The *Daily Proteus* sent Jack twenty dollars . . . for two editorials. **1949** *Chi. D. News* 16 March 22/4 The above quotation was inspired by an editorial from the Chicago *Daily News.*

attrib. **1947** *Dly. Oklahoman* (Okla. City) 5 Nov. 2/3 This editorial cartoonist must be a Republican—he always draws the elephant bigger than the donkey!

b. editorial writer, one who writes the editorials of a periodical.

1877 *Harper's Mag.* Dec. 47/2 The applicant . . . replied, with unconscious impudence, that he expected a chance as 'special correspondent, editorial writer, or something of that sort.' **1905** *Springfield Republican* 1 Sep. 14 Edward Elwell Whiting has lately become an editorial writer on the Boston Advertiser. **1948** *Time* 14 June 57/1 Cartoonists often caricature people in a way no libel-fearing editorial writer would dare.

editorialize ɛdəˈtorɪəlaɪz, *v.*

1. *intr.* To treat a subject in an editorial.

1856 Brewerton *War in Kansas* 75 O, Tempora! O, Moses! as Mrs. Partington feelingly remarked, when Ike tumbled into a barrel of soft soap: 'Isn't it a blessed thing to editorialize for an appreciative public?' **1941** Fergusson *Southwest* 321 After dinner speakers find secession a popular theme; newspapers editorialize about the 'high plains empire' and its right to independence.

2. To write news articles as if they were editorials, incorporating comment and criticisms into the stories.

1917 M. L. Spencer *News Writing* 87 One other caution must be given . . . , that of the necessity of presenting news from an unbiased standpoint, . . . of avoiding 'editorializing.' **1948** *Time* 26 July 52/3 There must be no editorializing or propaganda.

Edmunds Act, Bill. [G. F. *Edmunds* (1828–1919), U.S. Senator from Vermont.] (See quot. 1894.)

1884 *Cent. Mag.* May 122/2 The passage of the Edmunds Bill, in spite of the grave question as to its constitutionality, may have been a wise step. **1894** *Cent. Cyclo. of Names* 352/3 The Edmunds Act [of Congress] of 1882 for the suppression of polygamy in Utah. **1912** Birge *Awakening Desert* 353 The law of 1862, known as the Edmunds Act, declared such cohabitation to be a misdemeanor.

educatable ˌɛdʒəˈketəbl, *a.* Capable of being educated. — **1868** Alcott *Tablets* 105 Not letters but life chiefly educate if we are educatable. **1915** *Harper's Mag.* CXXX. 857/1 Boys unfitted . . . for technical work, although thoroughly educatable along more general lines.

***education,** *n.* In obs. combs.: (1) **education chair,** (see quot.); (2) **convention,** (see quot.); (3) **family,** a missionary family sent out among the Indians by those concerned with the uplift of the Indians; (4) **Education Society,** a society formed in 1815 for preparing young men for the ministry; (5) **table,** app. a kind of abacus, *obs.*

(1) 1865 *Atlantic Mo.* XV. One of those so-called 'education-chairs,' in which poor girls were compelled to sit bolt upright, . . . by-way-of-keeping their shoulders flat and strengthening their spine. — **(2) 1840** *Niles' Reg.* 2 May 131/2 Education convention. The national convention to consider the subject of education in the U. States, is to meet at Washington. — **(3) 1822** Morse *Rep. Indian Affairs* I. 15 An Education Family . . . would have a commanding influence on many populous and powerful Indian Tribes. — **(4) 1823** *Amer. Baptist Mag.* IV. 28 The Executive Committee of the Baptist Education Society of the State of New York, to the Public. **1858** Holland *Titcomb's Lett.* I. 17 The Education Society, and kindred organizations, do much more harm than good. — **(5) 1850** *Rep. Comm. Patents 1849* 247, I make my education tables . . . of two sets or series of grooves, one for the front, the other for the operations of calculation.

b. *Bureau of Education,* see **bureau;** *Board of Education,* see **board.**

As the last term in **common school, Superintendent of Education.**

***Edwardean,** *a.* Derived from, relating or pertaining to, the theological doctrines of Jonathan Edwards. *Obs.* Cf. next. — **1853** M. Blake *Hist. Mendon Assoc.* 30 That scheme [of theology] . . . has been called Edwardean, Hopkinsian, sometimes Emmonsism. . . . It is a system which . . . exalts and honors God as the Sovereign Ruler of His creatures, and abases man.

Edwardsism ˈɛdwədzˌɪzəm, *n.* The doctrines of Jonathan Edwards (1703–58), American theologian and metaphysician. *Obs.* — **1883** *Advance* (Chicago) 21 June, The discussions originating in Edwardsism.

edzactly ɛdˈzæktlɪ, *adv.* Also **adzactly, edxactly, edsac'ly.** Colloq. variant of "exactly."

1832 *Maysville* (Ky.) *Eagle* 2 Feb., 'Edxactly,' giving the lawyer a knowing wink—Captain Rise he gin a treat. *a***1846** *Quarter Race Ky.* 85 Your back looks adzactly like a blaze on a white oak! **1853** Simms *Sword & Distaff* 418 Well, cappin, I doesn't edzactly see that. **1865** Trowbridge *Three Scouts* xxix. 300 That didn't happen edsac'ly's I ca'c'lated! **1885** *Cent. Mag.* April 846/1, I ain't adzactly made up in my mind as to which.

***eel,** *n.*

1. A nickname for a New Englander. *Rare.*

1838 Haliburton *Clockmaker* 2 Ser. xix. 289 People from every state in the Union . . . have all nicknames. There's the hoosiers of Indiana, . . . the wolverines of Michigan, the eels of New England [etc.].

2. In combs.: (1) **eel-back,** (see quot. 1909), in full **eel-back flounder;** (2) **cat,** (see quot. 1909); (3) **creek,** a small stream where eels may be caught, *rare;* (4) **crow,** (see quot.), *rare;* (5) **cut,** a shad that has been partially eaten by eels, *rare;* (6) **grass,** the grass-wrack, *Zostera marina,* or the tape grass, *Valisneria spiralis;* (7) **root,** (see quot.), *rare;* (8) ***skin,** (*a*) paper money, (*b*) a Yankee, (*c*) (see quot.), all *slang* and *obs.;* (9) **snake,** (see quot.), *obs.*

(1) 1884 Goode *Fisheries* I. 183 The Smooth Flounder, or Christmas Flounder, *Pleuronectes glaber,* . . . may be distinguished from the former [the flat-fish] by its smooth skin, which has given to the species, in some localities, the name 'eel-back.' **1909** Webster 700 Eel-back flounder, a small flounder (*Liopsetta putnami*) of the coasts of northern New England and the British Provinces. — **(2) 1898** Jordan & Evermann *Fishes N. & Mid. Amer.* 2789 The eel cat rarely attains a greater weight than 5 pounds. **1909** Webster 700/2 *Eel cat,* a channel catfish (*Ictalurus anguilla*) of the lower Mississippi and Ohio valleys. The name is also applied to *I. punctatus.* — **(3) 1841** C. E. Lester *Glory & Shame England* I. 50 To an American, the Thames seems like a mere eel-creek. — **(4) 1796** Morse *Univ. Geog.* I. 213 Eel crow [given as the popular name of] *Colymbus migratorius.* **(5) 1880** *Harper's Mag.* May 856/1 When the weather becomes warm, the 'eel-cuts' . . . often outnumber the marketable shad. — **(6) 1790** Samuel Deane *N.-Eng. Farmer* (1790) 19/1 The farmer . . . may cart into it (stock yard) . . . marsh-mud, eel-grass, flats, or even sand and loam (for making manure). **1806** *Baltimore Ev. Post* 19 Feb. 3/3 (Th.), A young man at Sullivan (Maine) saw a Fox go down to some eel-grass, and roll himself up in it. **1843** Torrey *Flora N.Y.* II. 265 *Valisneria spiralis.* . . . Tape-grass. Eel-grass. . . . Slow-flowing rivers and shallow bays. . . . It is generally believed that the roots of this plant are the favorite food of the Canvassback Duck. **1919** Cady *Rhymes of Vt.* (1923) 27 The eel grass would have stopped a snake. — **(7) 1790** *Amer. Philos. Soc.* III. 237 They found a plant and dug up the root. . . . The youngest boy took it up, said it was Eel-Root, and he would eat some of it. — **(8)** (*a*) **1834** Caruthers *Kentuckian* I. 98 He gave me an order on the bank for the eel-skins. (*b*) **1836** *Crockett Alman. 1837* 17 (*title*), A Corn Cracker's Account of his Encounter with an Eelskin. (*c*) **1877** Bartlett 199 Eel-Skin, a thin, narrow slip of paper, with the name of a candidate on one side, and coated with mucilage on the other, so as to be quickly and secretly placed over the name of an opponent, on a printed ballot. (New England and New York.) 'Eel-skins,' judiciously distributed, are the most efficient instruments for 'splitting tickets,' and securing the election of some favored nominee on a ticket otherwise in the minority. — **(9) 1709** LAWSON *Carolina* 135 The Eel-Snake, (so call'd, though very improperly, because he is nothing but a Leach, that sucks, and cannot bite, as the Snakes do).

b. In various fig. phrases and proverbs.

*c***1840** NEAL *Beedle's Sleigh Ride* 36 Let every body skin their own eels. *c***1845** W. T. THOMPSON *Chron. Pineville* 27 The clown was doing 'eels in the mud' with such rapid velocity that he looked 'for all the world' like some great spotted snake, writhing and twisting in the wildest contortions. **1852** *Harper's Mag.* V. 849/2 You might as well try to hold a greased eel as a live Yankee!

As the last term in **bullhead, chub, prairie, silver, wolf eel.**

eeling ˈiliŋ, *n.* Catching eels. — **1780** *Naragansett Hist. Reg.* I. 104 Made an eel spear. Went eeling. **1895** *Outing* XXVI. 406/2 It was only when he couldn't go eeling, . . . that we could secure his priceless services.

efficiency expert. One who does things efficiently, esp. one whose profession is to devise more effective, economical methods of doing things.

1922 *Outing* Dec. 133/1 Gently I led him within reach of the net, and the 'Efficiency Expert,' true to form, landed him with a flourish. **1924** SHEPHARD *P. Bunyan* 184 Paul hired a kind of efficiency expert to help him on that, and that fellow, Gerber, used to walk around among the different camps and keep tab on the men and count up how they spent their time, and he certainly could make up some big figgurs, all right. **1948** *Dly. Ardmoreite* (Ardmore, Okla.) 1 April 6/6 Before the war, one efficiency expert figured it cost the government over $100 to answer a letter.

*** egg,** *n.*

1. **=egg coal.** *Colloq.*

1880 *Bradstreet's* 2 Oct. 5/4 The sizes used are 'lump,' 'steamboat,' 'broken,' and 'pea'; while for family use the sizes are 'egg,' 'stove' and 'nut.' **1949** *Black Diamond* 26 Feb. 52/4 Good grades of Central Pennsylvania and Northern West Virginia coals carry prices within the following range: Central Pennsylvania: low volatile: lump and egg, $4.50–$6.50.

2. In combs.: (1) **egg-and-butter money, egg-and-chicken money,** money derived by a farmer's wife from the sale of eggs, butter, and chickens, *colloq.;* (2) **-and-milk (punch),** a beverage similar to eggnog; (3) **beater,** a utensil for beating eggs, whipping cream, etc., also transf., cf. **Dover egg beater;** (4) **bird,** (see quots.); (5) **bread,** corn bread in which eggs are the chief leavening

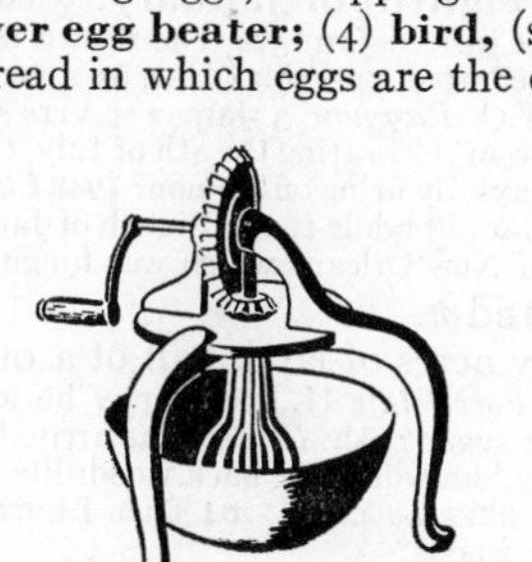

One form of egg-beater

agent [cf. Du. *eierbrood*]; (6) **butter,** (see quot.); (7) **chowder,** (see quots.); (8) **coal,** coal that has been broken into pieces approximately the size of a hen's egg [cf. Du. *eierkolen*]; (9) **dram,** (see quot.), *obs.;* (10) **drop,** a variety of apple, *obs.;* (11) **dye,** (see quot.); (12) **fish,** (see quot.); (13) **fruit,** the fruit of the eggplant; (14) **house,** (see quot.), *rare;* (15) **money,** money derived by a farmer or his wife from the sale of eggs, *colloq.;* (16) **nog,** a drink consisting of beaten eggs, milk, sugar, and usu. rum, wine, or other spirits, also attrib.; (17) **nogging,** the making and drinking of eggnog; (18) **pecking,** the pastime of knocking boiled Easter eggs together to see which contestant can keep his from being broken; (19) **pone,** egg bread made in the form of a pone *q.v.;* (20) **pop,** chiefly *N. Eng.*, a kind of eggnog; (21) ***shell,** a canoe; (22) **snake, =chicken snake;** (23) **supper,** a supper consisting chiefly of eggs, *obs.*

(1) 1896 WILKINS *Madelon* 201 'Guess she's been saving her egg-and-butter money,' Abner said. **1941** *Word Study* XVII. Nov. 8/2 My mother, one who, like myself, hungered and thirsted after knowledge, had bought it before I was born, with carefully hoarded egg-and-chicken money, from a doctor who was temporarily hard up. **1946** STUART *Plum Grove Hills* 71 Mom was helping him all she could with cream money and egg and chicken money. — **(2) 1876** M. F. HENDERSON *Cooking* 326 Egg-and-milk Punch. Stir well a heaping tea-spoonful of sugar, and the yolk of an egg together in a goblet, then add a table-spoonful of best brandy [etc.]. **1896** MOE *Hist. Harvard* 118 Let us all who know him hope that he may long be spared to shake up an egg-'n-milk, Horse's Neck, and all the other famous beverages. — **(3) 1828** E. LESLIE *Receipts* 49 Beat the eggs in a broad shallow pan with a wooden-egg-beater or whisk. **1896** E. HIGGINSON *Land of Snow Pearls* 94 The egg-beater fairly flew round and round. **1948** *C.A. Jrnl.* June 178 One of those strange contraptions known as a helicopter or 'egg-beater' . . . was already there when we landed. — **(4) 1889** *Cent.* 1853/2 *Egg-bird,* . . . a name of sundry . . . sea-birds, as murres, guillemots, etc., . . . whose eggs are of economic or commercial value. **1917** *Birds of Amer.* I. 27 Brunnich's Murre. *Aria lomvia lomvia.* . . . Other Names. . . . Egg-bird. . . . South rarely in winter from Maine to South Carolina.

(5) 1854 M. J. HOLMES *Tempest & Sunshine* 118 Egg-bread, . . . Southern cooks know so well how to make. **1941** J. DANIELS *Tar Heels* 32 It begins . . . with a North Carolina breakfast of shad roe, broiled shad, egg bread, batter cakes, boiled eggs and coffee. — **(6) 1885** *Buckeye Cookery* 250 Egg Butter. Boil a pint of molasses slowly about fifteen or twenty minutes, . . . add three eggs well beaten. — **(7) 1888** OWENS *Cook Book* 67 Egg chowder: Fry the pork, cook onions, potatoes, etc. . . . Just before you take it off, break in as many eggs as there are persons to eat. **1939** WOLCOTT *Yankee Cook Bk.* 19 Egg Chowder . . . ½ cup fat salt pork, diced; 5 large potatoes, sliced; 2 cups milk, scalded; 5 hard boiled eggs, sliced [etc.]. — **(8) 1855** *Santa Barbara* (Calif.) *Gazette* 22 Nov. 1/5 The attempt to make omelets out of 'egg' coal has been abandoned. **1924** A. T. SHURICK *Coal Industry* 144 The broken coal . . . is again screened into egg, stove, and nut coal. — **(9) 1788** SCHÖPF *Reise* II. 346 *Egg-dram, Egg-Toddy*—Eyerdotter mit Zucker und Rum abgerühret, und nach Gefallen mit Wasser verdünnet.

(10) 1876 BURROUGHS *Winter Sunshine* 154 Others are indeed lady apples like the egg-drop and lady-finger. — **(11) 1941** R. S. WALKER *Lookout* 52 Starry coreopsis is one of the most abundant yellow flowers growing on the sides and the summit of the mountain. It begins blooming in June. The mountain people know it by the name of 'egg dye,' because they use its green leaves for coloring eggs. — **(12) 1884** GOODE *Fisheries* I. 170 One species of the bellows-fish family, the common Swell Fish, or Egg Fish, *Tetrodon turgidus,* ranges from Cape Cod to the Gulf of Mexico, being very abundant about the eastern end of Long Island. — **(13) 1817** DARBY *Louisiana* 222 This remark is exemplified in all the solanums, (Irish potatoe, peppers, and egg-fruit,) whose leaves are easily killed by the slightest degree of freezing. **1887** *Harper's Mag.* Jan. 310/1 A dozen well-grown plants will supply a large family with egg-fruit. — **(14) 1824** SINGLETON *Letters* 90 Some few of the plantation-seats, however, are of brick, and accommodated with ample out-buildings. The egg-houses, for the laying and incubation of fowls, are capacious as cots.

(15) 1935 *Amer. Mercury* Aug. 410/2 So that's how you spend my egg money. **1948** JACOBS *We Chose Country* 119 There was plenty of egg money, so she could go shopping in town or choose her luxuries from the brilliant pages of the mail-order catalogues. — **(16)** *c***1775** BOUCHER *Glossary* 1 Fog-drams i' th' morn, or (better still) *egg-nogg,* At night *hot-suppings,* and at mid-day, *grogg.* **1886** POORE *Reminisc.* I. 44 On the Fourth of July, the 22d of February, and other holidays, landlord Brown would concoct foaming egg-nogg in a mammoth punch-bowl once owned by Washington. **1941** F. FARMER *Boston Cook Book* 609 Eggnog Chiffon Pie. . . . Add 3 tablespoons rum. When cold, cover with thin layer of unsweetened whipped cream and sprinkle with nutmeg. — **(17) 1845** *S. Lit. Messenger* XI. 109/1 We are to have a little egg-noggin' at our room . . . ; come down and join us. **1867** LATHAM *Black & White* 27 [On Christmas] everybody calls upon everybody else; and each call is celebrated by a solemn egg-nogging. — **(18) 1835** LONGSTREET *Ga. Scenes* 82 In the meantime Michael was employed in relieving Zeph's stone-house of its provisions; and truly, its contents told well for Zeph's skill in egg-pecking. — **(19) 1898** DUNBAR *Folks from Dixie* 39 They all sat down to the evening meal, of crisp bacon, well-fried potatoes, egg pone, and coffee.

(20) 1776 in *N.J. Hist. Soc. Proc.* 1 Ser. VIII. 122 Many Decanters of Wine suffered shipwreck . . . nor was Egg Pop forgot among our Dainties. **1862** THOREAU *Excursions* 248 Did not the rows of yellowing Willows . . . seem like rows of booths, under which, perhaps, some fluviatile egg-pop equally yellow was effervescing? — **(21) 1817** WILLARD KEYES *Journal* (typewritten copy; original MS at Wis. Hist. Soc.) 10 July 5 Dr. P(eters) arrives . . . we start in a little birch-bark canoe, with a Frenchman, his squaw, 3 children and several hundred-weight of baggage—tis astonishing how much these 'eggshells' will bear up on the water. *a***1862** THOREAU *Maine Woods* 176 Think of our little egg-shell of a canoe tossing across that great lake. — **(22) 1709** LAWSON *Carolina* 134 The Egg or Chicken-Snake is so call'd, because it is frequent about the Hen-Yard, and eats Eggs and Chickens.

1853 BAIRD & GIRARD *Cat. N. Amer. Reptiles* I. 165 Egg Snake (*Ophibolus Sayi*).—(23) 1872 EGGLESTON *End of World* xxiii. 154 There was an egg-supper in the country store at Brayville. *Ib.*, You must know that an egg-supper is a peculiar Western institution.

As the last term in **Creole, goose, lamper, luck, rabbit, ranch, robin's-, rooster, scrambled, shirred egg(s).**

***egg,** *v. tr.* To pelt with eggs. — 1857 *Baltimore Sun* 1 Aug. (B. '59), Bailey, the abolition editor of the Newport (Ky.) News, was egged out of Alexandria. 1883 *Harper's Mag.* Oct. 806/1 An Iowa poet has been egged by the populace.

***egret,** *n.* As the last term in **Peale's, reddish, white egret.**

***Egypt,** *n.* The southern part of Illinois lying between the Ohio and Mississippi rivers.

The name was probably applied because of the name of its principal town, Cairo; later it was alleged to be "with reference to the supposed intellectual darkness of the inhabitants" (Th.).

1843 *Quincy* (Ill.) *Whig* 11 Jan. 2/6 Here was something to stir up the bile of the 'gentleman from Egypt'! What! a 'nigger' in the Senate of Illinois! Monstrous! 1864 BRYANT *MS Lett. to F. Bryant* 2 June, We have had here [in Princeton, Ill.] a clergyman from the south of Illinois, Egypt as it is called. 1947 *Chi. D. News* (News Views) 1 Nov. 9/1 For . . . years the territory covered by 28 counties in the southernmost tip of Illinois has been referred to as "Egypt."

b. *Egypt of the West,* a term used by Lincoln in his message to Congress on Dec. 1, 1862, to refer to the interior region of the U.S. between the Alleghenies and the Rocky Mountains. *Obs.*

1862 *N.Y. Dly. Tribune* 2 Dec. 2/4 They too, and each of them, must have access to this Egypt of the West, without paying toll at the crossing of any national boundary.

***Egyptian,** *a.* and *n.*

1. A native of southern Illinois. Of or pertaining to this section.

1846 *Quincy* (Ill.) *Whig* 12 Feb. 3/2 Is an attack upon him [Stephen A. Douglas] indicative of an assault upon the Egyptian idol, whose shadow has been like that of a rock in the desert to many a renegade Whig. 1857 *Crusader of Freedom* (Doniphan, Kans.) 19 Dec. 1/6 Our modern Egyptians have affections, feelings, passions, senses; if you prick them they will smart; if you strike them they will respond; . . . if you tell them that democracy is the true gospel, and Douglass [*sic*] its apostle, they will swear you're right old hoss. 1947 *Chi. Tribune* 14 June 10/7 If there is anything further you wish to know in connection with wit and humor, just ask one of us Egyptian agriculturists.

2. Egyptian corn, a variety of Indian corn or of millet. *Obs.*

1849 EMMONS *Agric. N.Y.* II. 265 Canada pop-corn, Egyptian corn. . . . There are several varieties . . . used only for popping. 1856 *Porter's Spirit of Times* 18 Oct. 118/1 The *Western Farmers' Journal* speaks of the cultivation of the sugar millet in Warren Co., Ohio, which is used for fattening cattle. . . . It is called there Egyptian Corn. *Ib.* 29 Nov. 214/2 Several persons present, who have grown the sugar millet, (known in Ohio chiefly by the name of 'Egyptian corn') expressed themselves well satisfied that it would be found to be a profitable addition to the present farm crops in the Ohio Valley. 1911 WRIGHT *Winning Barbara Worth* 218 By midsummer many acres of alfalfa, with Egyptian corn and other grains, showed broad fields of living green cut into the dull, dun plain of the Desert and laced with silver threads of water shining in the sun.

b. Egyptian millet, (see quot. 1889).

1829 *Va. Herald* (Fredericksburg) 25 April 2/4 The leaves are of a beautiful green—long, narrow, dagger shaped, not unlike those of the Egyptian millet. 1889 VASEY *Agric. Grasses* 30 *Pennisetum spicatum* . . Pearl Millet, Cat-tail Millet, [or] Egyptian Millet, . . . is best adapted for cultivation in the South.

***eight,** *a.* and *n.*

1. *n.* An honored group at Harvard College (see quot. 1851). *Obs.*

1848 N. AMES *Childe Harvard* 121 'Spring to 't, or you'll be late!' '[I] don't care! 'T was worth "a part" among the "Second Eight."' 1851 HALL *Coll. Words* 109 It was customary [at Harvard] for the first eight scholars in the Junior Class to have 'parts' at the first exhibition, . . . and the third eight at the third exhibition. . . . Although there are now but two exhibitions in the year, twelve performing, . . . yet the students still retain the old phraseology, . . . 'Is he in the first or second *eight?*'

b. (See quot. 1851.) *Obs.*

*a*1851 in HALL *Coll. Words* 109 Numberless the eights he showers Full on my devoted head. 1851 *Ib.* 109 On the scale of merit, at Harvard College, eight is the highest mark which a student can receive for recitation. Students speak of '*getting an eight,*' which is equivalent to saying, that they have made a perfect recitation.

2. In combs.: (1) **eight-day man,** a contemptuous term for one who, during the Civil War, joined the army for only a short period; (2) **rowed,** of Indian corn, having eight rows of kernels on a cob; (3) **Eight Section Act,** (see quot.); (4) **square,** a rifle having an octagonal barrel, in full **eight square rifle.**

(1) 1862 F. MOORE *Rebellion Rec.* V. II. 158 The rebel forces amounted to eighty thousand effective troops, of all grades—volunteers for the war, conscripts, and 'eight-day men.' — (2) 1838 *Mass. Agric. Rep. 1837* 24 The Pickwacket corn, an early eight-rowed variety, . . . has been sound and good in many places. 1888 *Vt. Agric. Rep.* X. 30 He had tried both the 8 and the 12-rowed, and had decided that for him the 12-rowed was the better. 1944 *Burpee's Seeds* 26 If you want the best and sweetest for your table, it's true 8-rowed Golden Bantam. — (3) 1941 FERGUSSON *Southwest* 35 Texas, eager to get its West settled up, encouraged such practices by its Eight Section Act, which allowed a man eight sections of land, which need not be in one piece. — (4) 1897 A. H. LEWIS *Wolfville* 104 Cherokee . . . sends out for Jack Moore's Winchester, which is an eight-squar', latest model. 1907 WHITE *Arizona Nights* 4 He . . . carried across his saddle a heavy 'eight square' rifle.

b. In phrases: (1) *eight by* (or *to*) *seven,* used allusively "with reference to the decision of the Electoral Commission [*q.v.*] in the Hayes-Tilden controversy" (Th.); (2) *to be behind the eight ball,* to be at a disadvantage, in a difficult situation.

(1) 1880 GARFIELD in *Cong. Rec.* 17 March 1639/1 The Supreme Court of the U.S. has decided that the election law is constitutional by a sort of eight-by-seven decision. 1891 *Cong. Rec.* 16 Jan. 1446/1 There was a monotonous 'eight to seven, seven to eight,' . . . from the beginning to the end of the Chapter. — (2) 1944 *N.Y. Herald* (Bk. Review) 24 Sep. 12/4 An attempt to describe what makes the drawings funny lands you behind the eight ball. 1948 *Socialist Call* (N.Y.) 19 Nov. 1/2 That he was able to come out from behind the eight-ball is owing to the fact that conditions in the United States are such that even a Harry Truman can be elected.

Eighteenth Amendment. The so-called "prohibition amendment" to the U.S. Constitution, effective from Jan. 16, 1920, to Dec. 6, 1933. — 1931 F. L. ALLEN *Only Yesterday* 11 Already the ratification of the Eighteenth Amendment had made it certain that prohibition is to be permanent.

Eighth (or **eighth**) **of January.** (See quots.)

1819 *Inquisitor* (Cin.) 26 Jan. 3/4 The return of the noble *eighth of January* was celebrated, on Friday last, by a very handsome Military Ball. 1841 *N.O. Picayune* 3 Jan. 2/4 Vere's the propriety, I should like to know, of celebrating the 4th of July, the 8th of January, and all them 'ere days, by firing off cannon? 1948 *Chi. Tribune* 14 Mar. VII. 1/8 The familiar old fiddle tune, 'Eighth of January,' commemorates the Battle of New Orleans which was fought on Jan. 8, 1815.

***eighty,** *a.* and *n.*

1. *n.* Eighty acres of land, half of a quarter section.

1842 KIRKLAND *Forest Life* II. 207 Happy he whose far reaching 'eighties' enclose a sugar-bush. *Ib.* 230 The arrival in the neighbourhood of the 'eighty,' on which the back woods life was to commence. 1913 STRATTON-PORTER *Laddie* xi. 204 Then I hurried . . . across the west eighty to the woods.

b. eighty acre lot, =prec.

1749 *N.H. Probate Rec.* III. 650, I Give and Bequeath to My Son . . . An Eighty Acre Lott so Called. 1872 *Newton Kansan* 21 Nov. 2/3 Almost every quarter section and some eighty acre lots . . . have neat little residences upon them.

2. eighty-niner, a settler who came into Oklahoma in 1889. Also attrib.

The U.S. Government in 1889 purchased from the Creeks and Seminoles a large tract of land in the Oklahoma Territory. By proclamation, Pres. Harrison opened this land to homestead settlement at 12 o'clock noon, April 22, 1889. At that hour no fewer than 20,000 people raced across the borders seeking choice homesteads.

*c*1902 in DALE & RADER *Okla. Hist.* (1930) 555 Some of the 'eighty-niners of Old Oklahoma' were evidently present. 1909 in THOBURN *Stand. Hist. Okla.* II. 885 In all that legion of '89ers, there was not one Joshua who could have forced the sun to stand still, but every devil of them could force their watches ahead and they did it. 1946 *Dly. Ardmoreite* (Ardmore, Okla.) 6 Dec. 12/2 The old hose-reel cart . . . will be returned to Guthrie for the '89er celebration. 1948 *Dly. Oklahoman* (Okla. City) 25 April D. 2/5 Records show that the First Christian church group got together the first Sunday after the '89er run.

ejido eˈhido, *n. Mex. border.* [Sp. in same sense.] (See quots.) — 1931 CARLETON BEALS *Mexican Maze* 37 (Bentley), Their ejidos (village commons) were again menaced. 1932 BENTLEY *Dict. Sp. Terms* 134 *Ejido*. . . . The land set aside for the common use of a village, generally pasture land for the small herds of goats, pigs, and burros of the villages. Ejido may also signify the entire parcel of land of the township.

El el, *n.* Short for "elevated railroad" or "elevated train." Also attrib. or as adj. *Colloq.* Cf. **L.**

1929 *New Yorker* 17 Aug. 21/2 People said 'the El' . . . , the brevity and humor of the name being another evidence of the metropolitan spirit. **1938** WHITE *One Man's Meat* 2 At that instant an El train joined us and I had to start again and shout. **1946** *Time* 23 Dec. 20/2 Along Third Avenue, blacked out and shaken by the thundering El, Irish bars and French bistros alternate with English and Swedish restaurants.

* **elastic,** *a.* and *n.*

1. *pl.* Garters.

1847 in H. HOWE *Ohio* 48 With the *elastics* supplied by the ladies, for a halter, . . . the young dog passed from the shores of time to yelp no more. **1859** GRATTAN *Civilized Amer.* II. 54 'Corsets,' a word scarcely English, instead of stays, 'elastics' for garters, 'hose' for stocking, and similar conceits, are very general. **1864** *Hist. North-Western Soldiers' Fair* 162 [Donations include] 1 pair of cuffs, 3 pairs of fancy elastics, 1 pair of worsted elastics.

2. elastic clause, (see quot. 1914).

1914 *Cyclo. Amer. Govt.* I. 650 Elastic clause. A name sometimes applied to the clause of the Constitution of the United States [Art. I. Sec. VIII, par. 18.] which provides that Congress shall have power 'to make all laws that are necessary and proper [etc.].' **1943** HICKS *Amer. Dem.* 122 Extremely significant, however, were the new powers, especially those which gave Congress authority . . . 'to make all laws which shall be necessary and proper for carrying into execution the foregoing powers'—the famous 'elastic clause.'

3. elastic pine, prob. the limber pine *q.v. Obs.*

1842 DE SMET *Letters and Sketches* 257 There are several species of the pine: the Norwegian, the resinous, the white, and the elastic, so called because the Indians use it to make bows.

As the last term in **gum elastic.**

***Elberta,** *n.* A popular variety of yellow freestone peach developed *c*1870 by Samuel H. Rumph of Marshallville, Ga., and named by him for his wife. — **1926** ROBERTS *Time of Man* 364 He'll be right glad he took Elbertas when they come to ripen, two or three years from now. **1948** *Dly. Ardmoreite* (Ardmore, Okla.) 29 July 1/2 The young Elberta produced about a peck of peaches this year.

* **elbow,** *n.* In combs.: (1) **elbow bush,** the button bush, so called from its sharply angled branches; (2) **neighbor,** a close or intimate neighbor, *colloq.;* (3) **Elbow Room,** a nickname applied to Gen. Burgoyne in allusion to a boast attributed to him that he would make elbowroom for himself in this country (see also quot. 1776), *obs.*

(1) **1888** *Harper's Mag.* April 743 Tufts of elbow-bushes, and broad reaches of saw-grass. — (2) **1875** MARK TWAIN *Sk., New & Old* 181 We could just sit and talk privately to our elbow-neighbors and have a good sociable time. **1895** *Cong. Rec.* 7 Feb. 1899/1 My objection . . . would have come just as soon if the same suggestion had been made by my elbow neighbor. — (3) **1776** J. LEACOCK *Fall Brit. Tyranny* viii, Dramatis Personæ. . . . Elbow Room, Mr. Howe. [*Note*], It seems to be generally thought, that the expression of *Elbow Room* is to be attributed to General *Howe*, and not to General *Burgoyne*. **1778** *Md. Journal* 20 Jan. (Th.), How much better will the American clergy be employed by Congress, than Mr. Elbow Room was by his master George the Third.

* **elder,** *n.*[1] In combs.: (1) **elder bark tea,** tea made by an infusion of elder bark; (2) * **blow (tea),** tea made by an infusion of elder blossoms; (3) **quill,** (see quot.); (4) **swamp,** a swamp in which elder abounds.

(1) **1834** C. A. DAVIS *Lett. J. Downing* 325 She know'd about the huckleberrys, and about the elder bark tea. *Ib.* 326 My last letter to you tell'd you about the unsartinty of elder bark tea. — (2) **1832** L. M. CHILD *Frugal Housewife* 27 A poultice of elder-blow tea and biscuit is good as a preventive. **1899** A. BROWN *Tiverton Tales* 205 The entire neighborhood knew that Mrs. Pitts . . . was, at the moment, in a dark bedroom at home, helpless under elderblow. **1899** *Animal & Plant Lore* 111 'Elder-blow tea' is used as a febrifuge, laxative, and diuretic. Somewhat general in the United States. — (3) **1881** *Harper's Mag.* April 650/1 Formerly when the Maples were tapped with an auger, an 'elder quill' was inserted in the incision to conduct the sap into the trough below; that is, a small piece of elder wood about three inches long with the pith bored out of it, which formed a tube. — (4) **1838** *Mass. Agric. Rep. 1837* 81 A farmer . . . had the courage to plant himself among these elder-swamps.

As the last term in **black, box, dog, poison, poisonous, red, sweet elder.**

* **elder,** *n.*[2]

1. In some denominations, as in the Baptist Church, a minister or preacher. Cf. **presiding, teaching elder.**

1792 *Mass. H.S. Coll.* II. 30 In the year 1673 settlers came on . . . and employed one Elder Jones as their preacher. **1832** WILLIAMSON *Maine* II. 696 The ministers of the Baptists, called *Elders*, are supported by voluntary contributions. **1925** TILGHMAN *Dugout* 7, I can remember some of the elder's sermon that day, and the text he read.

b. (See quots.) *Colloq.*

1901 *D.N.* II. 139 elder, n. A clergyman of any denomination; common in N.Y. **1921** R. M. JONES *Later Periods Quakerism* I. iv. 120 (*note*), Even now in the rural districts of New England a minister of any denomination is called 'Elder.'

2. *pl.* A division or faction among the Quakers. *Obs.*

1827 *Hallowell* (Me.) *Gaz.* 20 June 2/4 The Philadelphia papers state that the society of Friends, or . . . Quakers, in that city, is divided into two parties, styled the *Elders*, and the *liberal.*

3. Among Mormons, a member of the Melchizedeck priesthood. Cf. **Mormon elder.**

1842 in H. CASWALL *Prophet of the 19th Cent.* 52 Of these the prophet was declared to be 'called and ordained an apostle of Jesus Christ,' and first elder of the new Society. **1878** A. DALY in J. F. Daly *A. Daly* 192 [At Salt Lake City] I attended the tabernacle . . [and] saw the wives and the elders.

* **eldest hand.** Also * **elder hand.** *Poker.* (See quot. 1944.)

1857 *Hoyle's Games* (Amer. ed.) 2 If neither of the players undertake any of the above chances, they say in rotation, beginning with the elder hand, 'Pass,' and there must be another deal. **1864** W. B. DICK *Amer. Hoyle* (1866) 176 *Eldest Hand, or Age.*—The player immediately at the left of the dealer. **1944** *Pocket Bk. of Games* 3 The player at the dealer's left, called the eldest hand or the age (though these terms are rapidly becoming obsolete), has the first right to bet, after which the right to bet passes from player to player in rotation.

* **El Dorado.**

1. The West, or a place in the West, thought to offer fortune to the adventurous immigrant.

1827 COOPER *Prairie* 1, The rugged appearance and careless mien of the sturdy men . . . united to announce a band of emigrants seeking for the El Dorado of the West. **1838** C. NEWELL *Revol. Texas* 181 Though Texas were the Eldorado it has been by some represented [etc.]. **1876** CROFUTT *Trans-continental Tourist* 72 Pioneer-emigrants . . . on their weary way seeking new El Doradoes towards the setting sun. **1930** MCLEOD *Hist. Alturas & Blaine Counties, Ida.* 18 Prospectors, the usual forerunners of civilization in mineralized regions, were still seeking more El Doradoes.

2. Early, and esp. after the discovery of gold there in 1848, applied to California.

1846 BRYANT *California* (1848) 23 Mr. and Mrs. W., although so much advanced in life, appeared to be as resolute as the youngest of the family, and to count with certainty upon seeing the Eldorado of the Pacific. **1850** *Quincy* (Ill.) *Whig* 25 June 3/1 Every thing denotes a high degree of prosperity in El Dorado State. **1907** *Boston Transcript* 9 Nov., El Dorado [is the popular name for] California.

b. Applied specifically to localities where gold had been found, or reputedly found.

[**1830** *Boston Transcript* 24 Sep. 2/4 All ages and conditions are running after the *El Dorado* metal.] **1835** *Vade Mecum* (Phila.) 14 Feb. 3/3 We perceive by the Miner's Journal, that Pottsville—the El Dorado of 1829—has not shared the fate which is usually allotted to such precocious growth. **1897** JAMES *Alaska* 39 The Government itself would be powerless to stay the human tide that is even now swelling toward the wonderful El Dorado in the Klondyke Region. **1948** JOHNSTON *Gold Rush* 2/1 Sailors deserted ships that were anchored in the harbor, and soldiers their garrisons for the new-found El Dorado.

* **election,** *n.* In combs.: (1) **election ball,** a ball held in celebration of an election, *obs.;* (2) **bun,** a bun of a type cooked in celebration of an election, *obs.;* (3) **cake,** a cake, usu. a raised fruit cake, associated with elections (see quot. 1939), also †**elections cake;** (4) **commissioner,** one appointed, usu. as a member of a group, to have charge of an election; (5) **court,** see as a main entry; (6) * **day,** see as a main entry; (7) **district,** (*a*) a division of territory for the administration of an election, (*b*) (see quot.); (8) **pink,** *N. Eng.* the pinkster flower, *Azalea nudiflora;* (9) **posy,** = **painted cup;** (10) **precinct,** (*a*) a precinct created for the administration of an election, cf. **voting precinct,** (*b*) (see quot.); (11) **sermon,** a sermon preached in connection with an election.

(1) **1809** KENDALL *Travels* I. 6 On the evening following that of the election-day, there is an annual ball at Hartford, called the Election Ball. **1885** *Harper's Mag.* Oct. 718/2 The next evening occurred the great 'election ball.' — (2) **1859** HOLMES *Professor* ii. 52 He recol-

lects he had a glazed 'lection bun, and sat eating it, and looking down on the Common. **1891** ——— *Over Teacups* 272 The great days of the year were, Election,—General Election on Wednesday, and Artillery Election on the Monday following, at which time lilacs were in bloom and 'lection buns were in order. — **(3) 1805** *Pocumtuc Housewife* (1906) 30 Elections Cake. **1832** L. M. CHILD *Frugal Housewife* 71 Old-fashioned election cake is made of four pounds of flour [etc.]. **1939** WOLCOTT *Yankee Cook Bk.* 253 Election cake is said to have originated in Hartford, Conn., a century ago and was served to all who voted the straight ticket. **1947** BEROLZHEIMER *Regional Cookbook* 53 Election Cake was always served on Election Day which was also a Muster Day. — **(4) 1899** *K.C. Star* 17 Feb. 1/3 To reporters he said that Julius Wurzberger, an election commissioner of St. Louis, . . . had spent $10 getting him drunk. **1911** *Okla. Session Laws* 3 Legisl. 76 In selecting and commissioning said special election commissioners, the Governor shall assign each said election commissioner to a particular voting precinct.

(7) (*a*) **1799** in *Ann. 7th Congress* 2 Sess. 1411 It was so in every election district in the county. **1902** E. C. MEYER *Nominating Systems* 19 The township or ward, is included in a number of different election districts, each of which has its own convention. (*b*) **1909** WEBSTER 706/3 *Election district*. . . . In some States (Maryland, Montana, and Wyoming), the name is applied to a division of the county for governmental purposes. — **(8) 1891** *Amer. Folk-Lore* IV. 148 *Azalea nudiflora*, called Election Pink, because in bloom at the old-time 'election,' when the governor took his seat in June. **1892** *Ib.* V. 100 *Rhododendron nudiflorum*, election pink. Hillsborough, N.H. — **(9) 1892** *Amer. Folk-Lore* V. 101 *Castilleia coccinea*, . . . election posies. Dudley, Mass. **1907** LYONS *Plant Names* 102 *Castilleja*. . . . Red-Indians, Election-posies, Prairie-fire.

(10) (*a*) **1835** J. HALL *Sk. of West* II. 203 [For] general elections . . . the counties are divided, by the county commissioners, into any convenient number of 'election precincts,' or districts, not more than eight in each county. **1860** S. C. COX *Recoll. Wabash Valley* 18 If men have . . . voted at the same election precinct . . . it is sufficient for them to scrape an acquaintance upon. (*b*) **1909** WEBSTER 706/3 Election precinct. . . . In many States, as Alabama, Colorado, Florida, Illinois, etc. the name is applied to a division of the county for governmental purposes. — **(11) 1644** *Mass. Bay Rec.* II. 71 The printer shall have leave to print the election sermon, with Mr. Mathers consent. **1831** *Boston Transcript* 9 June 3/1 An unsuccessful attempt was made to elect a clergyman to preach the next Election Sermon. **1938** *Amer. Literature* March X. 98 Vail, R. W. G. 'A Check List of New England Election Sermons.' with the listing of copies in over thirty libraries.

As the last term in **artillery, charter, congressional, court of, general, Negro, October, presidential, primary, run-off, school district, special, state election.**

* **electional,** *a.* Pertaining to a political election. *Obs.* — **1808** *Md. Laws* 15 Jan. xxviii, Commissioners [are appointed] . . . to lay off Saint-Mary's county into four separate electional districts.

election court. In New England, esp. in Plymouth and Massachusetts Bay colonies, the general assembly which elected the officers of the colony. Now *hist.* Cf. **court of election.**

"The last Wednesday in Easter tearme yearely, the Governor, Deputy Governor, and Assistant of the said Company, and all other officers of the said Company, shalbe, in the General Court or Assembly, . . . newly chosen for the yeare ensueing" (1629 *Mass. Charter*). This court was attended by all the freemen.

1640 *Plymouth Laws* 69 The Committees of the severall Townes shall see the same so donn the week before the Eleccon Court. **a1656** BRADFORD *Hist.* 229 At ye spring of ye year, about ye time of their Election Court, Oldam came againe amongst them. **1685** SEWALL *Diary* I. 72 They would have had them made a report of next Tuesday, but agreed to be next Election Court.

* **election day.** Inauguration day, esp. in Rhode Island. *Obs.*

Officers of a New England colony were at first usu. installed in office on the same day they were elected by the General Assembly or Court. (See, for example, 1665 *R.I. Col. Rec.* II. 96–8). "Election day" thence remained, esp. in R.I., the name for "Inauguration day" even after the two days were separated.

1860 S. G. ARNOLD *Hist. R.I.* II. 273 Instead of the first Wednesday in May, the third Wednesday in April had become the period of decisive political struggle, while 'election day' . . . ceased to be anything more than the occasion for . . . the inauguration of the new government at Newport. **1869** STOWE *Oldtown Folks* 337 Election day, when the Governor took his seat with pomp and rejoicing, and all the housewives outdid themselves in election cake. **1902** E. FIELD *State of R.I.* I. 392 Newport . . . was compelled to witness the loss of its cherished 'election day' and the removal of its distinction as a state capital [in 1900].

electioneer ɪˌlɛkʃən'ɪr, *n.* [f. the verb.] One who practices electioneering. *Rare.* — **1848** LOWELL *Biglow P.* 1. Ser. vi. 77, I du believe hard coin the stuff Fer 'lectioneers to spout on.

* **electioneered,** *a. College.* Propagandized to join a club or fraternity. *Rare.* — **1851** N.B. *Yale College* 14 June, Information wanted of the 'Sub' who didn't think it an honor to be electioneered.

electioneering ticket. A campaign handbill or poster. *Rare.* — **1829** in *Amer. Sp.* XVIII. 124/1 Our gig was pasted over and over with electioneering tickets and huzzahs.

electioner ɪ'lɛkʃənɚ, *n.* One who believes in predestination. *Rare.* — **1869** STOWE *Oldtown Folks* vi. 72 'Postle Paul an Arminian! He's the biggest 'lectioner of 'em all.

* **elective,** *a.* and *n. Educ.*

1. *n.* A subject of study selected by a student on his own initiative.

1850 *Boston Doc.* No. 38, 45 Making some studies electives and giving to the members of the first class some liberty of choice. **1897** *Scribner's Mag.* XXII. 150/1 Her choice of electives is of more importance to her than her choice of societies. **1947** *Sat. Ev. Post* 6 Sep. 144/2 All students would be required to take specified basic courses, . . . with many fewer electives.

2. *a.* Of a course of study: Selected by free choice, optional.

[**1869** DILKE *Greater Britain* I. 72 The system of elective studies pursued at Michigan is one to which we are year by year tending.] **1871** BAGG *At Yale* 695 'Optional' or 'elective' studies, too, do not always realize the expectations of their advocates. **1890** J. G. FITCH *Notes Amer. Schools* 59 In the high schools and universities the practice of prescribing 'elective' subjects is very common.

b. elective system, a system of education admitting a choice of subjects.

1847 in *Harvard Coll. Ann. Rep. 1883–4* 14 The elective system is now given up in this department. **1911** MONROE *Cyclo. Educ.* II. 65 The curriculum for the University of Virginia, when it was opened in 1825, . . . was the first university curriculum in America to be administered under a virtually complete elective system. **1945** *Harvard Univ. President's Rep.* 9 It is thus not the elective system which is modified by the recent votes of the faculty to which I have just referred.

* **elector,** *n.* A person chosen as a member of the body that elects the President and Vice-President of the U.S. Cf. **District system, presidential elector.**

Electors are usually elected on a general state ticket in which one party gets the whole electoral vote of the state. However, they have, on occasion, been chosen by districts, notably in Maryland and Michigan. As late as 1824, Delaware, Georgia, Louisiana, New York, South Carolina, and Vermont chose electors by their legislatures. South Carolina continued this practice through 1860; Florida, in 1868, and Colorado, in 1876, used the same method. "The electors have no practical power over the election, and have had none since their institution. From the beginning they have stood pledged to vote for the candidates indicated . . . by the public will" (1854 Benton *30 Years' View* I. 37/1).

1787 *Constitution* ii. § 1 Each State shall appoint . . . a number of electors, equal to the whole number of Senators and Representatives to which the State may be entitled in the Congress. **1860** *Harper's Mag.* Dec. 111/2 Missouri, and probably California and Oregon, having 16 electors, vote for Mr. Douglas. **1948** *This Week Mag.* 16 Oct. 5/2 For years some legislatures decided to select the electors themselves without consulting the public.

b. elector-at-large, a presidential elector chosen by a state-wide vote, as differentiated from an elector chosen by a district.

1868 *N.Y. Herald* 7 Aug. 5/2 George A. Merrill was unanimously nominated as elector at large. **1888** *Amer. Almanac* 268 Numerous variations in the Presidential vote [for 1884] are found in the different tables. . . . Some tables take . . . the highest cast for any Elector-at-large.

* **electoral,** *a.*

1. Of or pertaining to the election of the President and Vice-President by means of electors.

1800 *Steele P.* I. 190, [I] could not before give you any satisfactory information relative to the votes for the members to compose the Electoral Assembly. **1886** ALTON *Among Law-Makers* 92 The President of the Senate . . . [gives] the electoral envelopes the 'constitutional rip.' **1916** *N. Amer. Rev.* CCIV. 813 The election has given rise to a great revival of interest, largely hostile, in the electoral system of choosing the President and Vice-President.

2. In special combs.: (1) **electoral college,** (also *cap.*), (*a*) the body of electors of the President and Vice-President (sometimes of a single state, sometimes of the country as a whole), (*b*) also with reference to the president and vice-president of the Southern Confederacy, *obs.;* (2) **commission,** the commission which settled the contested presidential election of 1876 between Hayes and Tilden in favor of Hayes, now *hist.;* (3) **ticket,** a list of party candidates for public office, esp. of candidates seeking election as presidential electors; (4) **vote,** see as a main entry.

(1) (*a*) **1800** *Ann. 6th Congress* 1 Sess. 31 If this body of the Electors of all the States had been directed by the Constitution to assemble in one place, instead . . . of being formed into different Electoral colleges [etc.]. **1868** *N.Y. Herald* 2 July 3/3 Resolved. . . . That the States of Virginia, North Carolina . . . shall not be entitled to representation in the electoral college. **1949** *Pacific Discovery* Jan.–Feb. 3/2 Once we even elected a president of the United States through open and brazen corruption of the electoral college. (*b*) **1861** *Richmond* (Va.) *Examiner* 5 Dec. 3/4 The Electoral College assembled yesterday at 10 o'clock, in the Capitol, and cast the vote of the State for Jefferson Davis and A. H. Stevens for the offices of President and Vice-President. — (2) **1877** *Chi. Tribune* 30 Jan. 1/2 Members of the Electoral Commission were nominated. **1888** M. LANE in *America* 4 Oct. 15 [The] Electoral Commission . . . decided against Tilden on all points by a vote of 8 to 7. **1943** HICKS *Amer. Dem.* 511 The electoral contest thus begun rocked the country, and for a time hope of a peaceful settlement seemed faint. Finally Congress decided to refer the double returns received from the carpet-bag states to an Electoral Commission of fifteen, five each from the Senate, the House, and the Supreme Court. — (3) **1812** *Mass. Spy* 23 Nov. 3/3 The Madisonian ranks at Washington are thrown into utter consternation by the certain information that the Clintonian electoral ticket had prevailed in Ohio, by a majority of 547. **1888** *Amer. Almanac* 268 In Missouri and West Virginia [in 1884], there was a 'fusion' of the Republican and the National Greenback parties, on one Electoral ticket.

electoral vote.

1. The vote of a presidential elector.

1825 in M. BAYARD SMITH *Forty Yrs. Washington Society* (1906) 187 While the electoral votes were counting . . . foreign ministers, strangers of distinction and General Lafayette were present. **1878** *N.Y. Tribune* 12 Nov., The true history of the contest for the electoral votes of Florida in 1876 is told for the first time. **1948** *Herald-Press* (St. Joseph, Mich.) 14 Aug. 3/8 Dixiecrats also want a crack at Texas' 23 electoral votes, the largest bloc in the south.

2. *collect.* The aggregate of electoral votes of a state or of the presidential electors as a whole.

1836 HONE *Diary* I. 237 The electoral vote of good old Massachusetts has been given. **1888** *Amer. Almanac* 269 In 1872, Horace Greeley, Democratic and Liberal-Republican candidate for President . . . died before the Electoral vote was cast. **1916** *N. Amer. Rev.* CCIV. 813 The editor of a metropolitan newspaper reports that his desk has been flooded with letters . . . asking, What is meant by the Electoral Vote?

***electric,** *a.* and *n.*

1. *n. pl.* Electric lights. *Obs.*

1886 *Harper's Mag.* July 314/1 The light of common day . . . is preferable to any manner of . . . alabaster lamps, or even the latest improvement in electrics. **1909** O. HENRY *Roads of Destiny* 296 Eight stories high it stalked up, with new striped awnings, and the electrics had it as light as day.

b. An electric streetcar, train, or automobile.

1890 *Boston Jrnl.* 3 March 1/7 Do the Electrics Travel Too Fast for the Public Safety? **1910** *Sat. Ev. Post* 20 Aug. 36 Westinghouse Motors are found in high grade Electrics only. **1946** T. JONES *Skinny Angel* 123 She . . . got into her veil and duster and then into her electric, and after some angry backing and filling, jolted away down the road.

2. In combs.: (1) **electric automobile,** an automobile propelled by electric motors, the current for which is supplied by storage batteries; (2) **bell,** a bell operated by an electric current; (3) **cab,** an electric automobile used as a taxicab; (4) **car,** (*a*) a trolley car, also attrib., (*b*) =**electric automobile;** (5) **carriage,** a carriage driven by electricity; (6) **chair,** see as a main entry; (7) **clock,** a clock operated by an electric current; (8) **company,** an organization that deals in, and controls a supply of, electricity; (9) **fence,** an electrically charged wire serving as a fence; (10) **fire,** =next, *obs.;* (11) **fluid,** a term formerly used for a supposedly subtle, imponderable, all-pervading fluid which caused electrical phenomena, *obs.;* (12) **iron,** a smoothing iron which is heated by electricity; (13) **light bug,** (see quots.); (14) **locomotive,** a railway locomotive driven by electric power; (15) **railroad,** =next; (16) **railway,** a railway on which cars are moved by electric power; (17) **rod,** a lightning rod, *obs.;* (18) **sign,** a sign illuminated by electricity; (19) **storm,** a storm accompanied by much thunder and lightning; (20) **train,** a train driven by electricity; (21) **wagon,** a wagon driven by electricity.

(1) **1900** *Outing* Oct. 67 Mrs. Clement C. Moore in her Electric Automobile. — (2) **1883** *Harper's Mag.* July 321/1 The electric bell has invaded the hotels. — (3) **1908** PHILLIPS *Old Wives* 306 'I'll never consent to it—never!' she cried, as the electric cab took her toward the Holland. — (4) (*a*) **1888** ROE *Army Lett.* 366, I sometimes ride him, but most of my outings are on the electric cars. **1895** *Chi. Tribune* 6 April 1 Two Italians were fatally injured in an electric car accident at Pittsburg, Pa. **1923** C. J. DUTTON *Shadow on Glass* 11 Then down a hill, crossing the electric car tracks. (*b*) **1947** *Newsweek* 8 Sep. 85/3 Electric cars would do in town, but it took a Model T for mud.

(5) **1901** *Outing* XXVII. 550 The air tires . . . form one of the most formidable terms of expense in the maintenance of the full sized electric carriages. — (7) **1845** *St. Louis Reveille* 22 Jan. 1/6 Mr. Brain has succeeded to admiration in working electric clocks by the current of the earth. **1886** *Mobile* (Ala.) *D. Reg.* 13 April 2/3 (*advt.*), Standard Electric Clock. — (8) **1906** L. BELL *C. Lee* 337 'Who owns the control in the electric company?' asked Judge Lee. — (9) **1945** *Chi. Tribune* 2 Sep. VII. 1/8 We have an electric fence, so we raise white faced cattle.

(10) **1774** HILTZHEIMER *Diary* (1893) 3 May 30 The effigies . . . were hung on a gallows erected near the Coffee House, set on fire by electric fire, and consumed to ashes. **1841** EMERSON *Writings* II. 325 Electric fire dissolves air, but the intellect dissolves fire. — (11) **1753** FRANKLIN *Writings* III. 174 The long wire made use of in the experiment to discover the velocity of the electric fluid [etc.]. **1831** *Boston Transcript* 7 Sep. 2/3 The electric fluid invariably passes, by the shortest possible course, through the best conducting medium communicating with the ground. **1921** *Frontier* Nov. 5 He had a lot of lightning rod material, weather vanes and all the necessary equipment for installing protection from the electric fluid. — (12) **1911** *Sears Cat.* (ed. 122) 755/2 The convenience and comfort of the electric iron as compared with the old fashioned irons is so great that no one who has once used an electric iron would ever go back to the old fashioned method. **1948** *Chesterton* (Ind.) *Tribune* 28 Oct. 4/2 Colette's fellow club members were of a practical turn of mind, and clubbed together to get her an electric iron and ironing board. — (13) **1909** *Cent. Supp.* 172/3 Electric-light bug, either one of two large American water-bugs, *Belostoma Americanum* and *Benacus griseus.* **1940** MENCKEN *Happy Days* 66 When arc-lights began to light the streets, along about 1885, they attracted so many beetles of gigantic size that their glare was actually obscured. These beetles at once acquired the name of electric-light bugs, and it was believed that the arc carbons produced them by a kind of spontaneous generation, and that their bite was as dangerous as that of a tarantula. — (14) **1884** *Pop. Sci. Mo.* XXIV. 745 This motor is connected with the driving-wheels by gearing, belting, [etc.] . . . so that its revolution produces . . . a consequent progressive motion of the electric locomotive. **1904** *Harper's Wkly.* XLVIII. 1837 The new Electric Locomotive of the New York Central . . . had an Official Trial recently at Schenectady, New York.

(15) **1889** *N.J. Laws* 332 Every cable railroad company . . . and every corporation owning, using or operating any cable, electric or horse railroad [etc.]. — (16) **1884** *Pop. Sci. Mo.* XXIV. 747 In mines, in tunnels, and in all places where the smoke of burning coal is objectionable, . . . the electric railway possesses unrivaled advantages. **1904** *Harper's Wkly.* XLVIII. 332/1 The motor almost universally used on electric railways has been a direct current machine. — (17) **1788** BENTLEY *Diary* I. 92 The Meeting house . . . has an handsome appearance, electric rods . . . and a good Bell. **1795** *Ib.* II. 158 Fixed the Electric Rods upon the Steeple, & took away the upper Stages. — (18) **1909** *Sat. Ev. Post* 20 Feb. 8/1 If it were not for the private electric signs the Great White Way would be a Mournful Mauve Way. — (19) **1872** ROE *Army Lett.* 52 There was a terrific rain and electric storm last evening. **1944** G. GRAHAM *Earth & High Heaven* 277 'Must have been a bad electric storm lately,' he remarked.

(20) **1912** *Out West* April 260/2 More than fifty electric trains daily keep Whittier in close touch with the heart of Los Angeles. — (21) **1896** *Cosmopolitan* XX. 422/1 'Electrobat' is the very original name adopted by Messrs. Morris & Salom, of Philadelphia, for the first electric wagon ever constructed in that city.

***electrical,** *a.* In combs.: (1) **electrical chair,** =**electric chair 2;** (2) **execution,** the legal execution of criminals by means of the electric chair, also attrib.; (3) **fire,** =**electric fire,** *obs.;* (4) **fluid,** =**electric fluid,** *obs.;* (5) **storm,** =**electric storm.**

(1) **1947** *True* Nov. 69/1 They would not have interested . . . several hundred citizens facing either the gallows or what in its early days was called the electrical chair. — (2) **1888** *N.Y. Tribune* 5 June 3/2 (*caption*), The Governor Signs the Electrical Execution Bill. **1890** *N.Y. Tribune* 7 Aug. 1/6 To Warden Durston is due much of the

blame for the unfortunate incidents of the first electrical execution. — (3) **1747** FRANKLIN *Lett.* Wks. (1840) V. 182 Draw off the electrical fire. — (4) **1826** *Va. Herald* (Fredericksburg) 27 Sep. 3/3 The electrical fluid ran down a stove pipe, from whence it passed off among the congregation. **1834** *Sun* (N.Y.) 19 May 2/1 The light . . . most probably was a narrow stratum of the electrical fluid, passing at a very high elevation. — (5) **1945** *New Yorker* 31 Mar. 60 (*caption*), Of course, you'd have to take cover during electrical storms. **1946** *Mazama* Dec. 86/1 They had good weather on Washington, but on Jack they ran into a severe electrical storm during the descent.

electric chair.

1. (See quot.) *Obs.*

1872 *Rep. Comm. Patents 1871* II. 735/1 Electric and Vapor Chair, . . . the medical chair . . . for directing electrical currents through the body.

2. A chair suitably equipped for the execution of criminals by means of electricity. Cf. **electrolethe.**

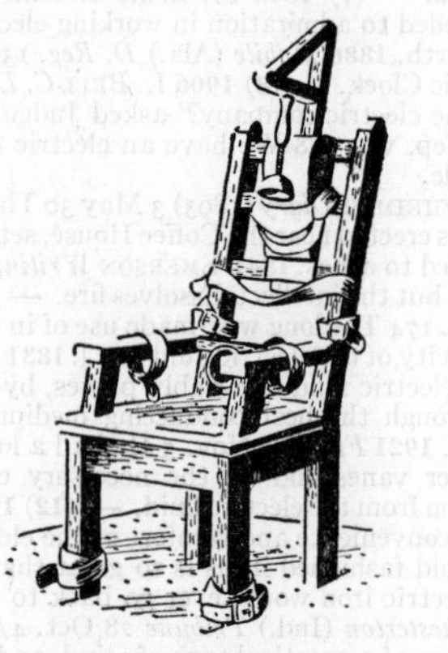

Early type of electric chair

[**1889** *Peel City Guardian* 8 June 6/2 The preparations, which are to consist of taking a seat in an electric chair.] **1890** *N.Y. Herald* 7 Aug. 3/4 The electric chair was taken out of the room. **1919** R. T. BYE *Capital Punishment in U.S.* 1 Within the past twenty-eight years more than three thousand persons have been sent to the scaffold or the electric chair in the United States. **1948** *Chi. D. News* 18 Sep. 3/6 A 24-year-old former convict . . . must die in the electric chair.

electrician ɪˌlɛkˈtrɪʃən, *n.* Originally one who studied and experimented with electricity; now one whose business is to instal and repair electrical equipment.

1751 FRANKLIN in *Phil. Trans.* XLVII. xliv. 291, I have not heard that any of your European electricians have been able to . . . do it. **1806** WEBSTER 99 *Electrician*, . . . one versed in electricity. **1885** *Cent. Mag.* XXX. 581/2 The shop staff commonly includes . . . upholsterers, silversmiths, and an electrician. **1947** *Time* 16 June 33/1 The electrician had to work overtime.

electricide ɪˈlɛktrəˌsaɪd, *n.* =**electrocution.** *Rare.* — **1890** *Saginaw* (Mich.) *Ev. News* 6 July, Dr. Daniel and Dr. Southwick (the father of the system of electricide) believe that Kemmler was dead.

***electrified,** *a.* (See quot.) *Slang. Obs.* — **1891** FARMER *Slang, Electrified* (American), moderately drunk.

electro-chronograph ɪˌlɛktroˈkrɑnəˌgræf, *n.* An instrument for recording short intervals of time automatically by means of electricity. — **1851** CIST *Cincinnati* 302 The invention of the electro-chronograph by Professor Locke of our city, may be properly noticed. **1878** NEWCOMB *Pop. Astron.* II. ii. 157 The electro-chronograph on which his taps are recorded.

electrocute ɪˈlɛktrəˌkjut, *v.* Also †**electricute.** [See note.] *tr.* To put (a criminal, etc.) to death by an electric current.

Irregular f. Gk. *electro-*+L. *-cute;* **electricute,** the proper form, both elements being f. L., never ousted the app. slightly earlier **electrocute.** Similarly **electrocution,** †**electricution.**

1889 *Voice* 1 Aug., Kemmler, the murderer sentenced to be 'electrocuted.' **1890** *Cong. Rec.* 9 Aug. 8375/1 That the gentleman . . . should be 'electrocuted' by the Kemmler process recently adopted in the state of New York. *Ib.* 21 Aug. 8965/1 '[The hogs] were not electricuted, then?' . . . 'No, sir; that highly civilized method had not then been invented.' **1893** F. A. MARCH in *Chautauquan* April 21 (Funk), A Latin word for execute, to go with electric, or a Greek word to go with electro is wanted. The Latin word execute makes electri-execute, which would contract into electricute. **1948** *Dly. Ardmoreite* (Ardmore, Okla.) 13 May 3/1 The Oklahoman frankly admits he is interested in the $100 the state pays for each man electrocuted.

electrocution ɪˌlɛktrəˈkjuʃən, *n.* Also †**electricution.** [See **electrocute.**] Execution by electricity.

[**1889** *N. & Q.* III. 11 May 21 A New Word Wanted.—Correspondents of American Notes and Queries are requested to send suggestions for a word that shall express *execution by electricity.*] **1889** *Cent.* 1868 *Electricution,* the act of electricuting. . . . Recent and colloq. **1890** *N.Y. Herald* 7 Aug. 3/1 The killing of Kemmler to-day marks, I fear, the beginning and end of electrocution. **1948** *Nat. Geog. Mag.* March 395/1 A few whiffs of gas or chloroform are sometimes used, but most ranchers prefer electrocution.

electrolethe ɪˈlɛktrəˌliθɪ, *n.* [f. Gk. *electro-,* electric+*lēthē,* forgetfulness.] A suggested name for an electric chair or similar apparatus. *Rare.* — **1889** E. T. GERRY in *N. Amer. Rev.* CXLIX. 325 What particular kind of current or *electrolethe* . . . is the most efficacious is a question. *Ib.,* To contend that a proper *electrolethe* cannot be constructed . . . is simply to argue an absurdity.

elegant tern. A species of tern, *Thalasseus elegans,* found on the Pacific Coast, so called from the elegance of its appearance. — **1858** BAIRD *Birds Pacific R.R.* 860 The Elegant Tern . . . [is] an inhabitant of the coast of South California. **1891** *Cent.* 6244 *Elegant tern,* . . . a bird of . . . the Pacific Coast of the United States, resembling the Cayenne tern.

***element,** *n.* Spirituous liquor. Also **to be in one's element,* to be drunk. *Slang. Obs.* — **1737** *Penna. Gazette* 13 Jan. 1/3 He's in his Element. **1855** SIMMS *Forayers* 241 At that time [I] hadn't drank a thimbleful of the element.

As the last term in **carpetbag, Free Soil, squatter element.**

***Elementary,** *n.* A colloquial abbreviation for "Webster's Elementary Spelling Book." *Obs.* Cf. ***blueback,** *n.* 3. — **1854** in *PMLA* LVI. 502 There is a great overhauling of old 'Elementaries,' and a wonderful furbishing up of frontispieces, and turning over of clean collars.

***elephant,** *n.*

1. A symbol of the Republican party, used metaphorically for it.

[**1874** *Harper's Wkly.* XVIII. 912 (Cartoon by Thomas Nast in which an elephant is labelled) The Republican Vote.] **1876** *Ib.* 28 Oct. 868 (*caption*), 'The elephant walks around'—and the 'still hunt' is nearly over. **1894** *Cong. Rec.* 15 Jan. 845/1 Pretended fear of 'tariff reform' is now agitating the huge frame of the G.P.O. [G.O.P.] elephant. . . . Old Jumbo was paralyzed in 1892, but by careful nursing he has been kept alive. **1948** *Chi. Tribune* 22 Feb. 1. 20/2 A Republican elephant . . . is complaining, 'And I suppose when I get back on the job, it will be my duty to reduce debts and get blamed for another depression.'

2. ***elephant's ear,** the large-leaved *Colocasia esculenta,* often planted for ornament.

1908 LORIMER *J. Spurlock* 297, I see . . . a bed of elephant's ears on one side of the drive and one of cannas on the other. **1932** W. KELLEY *Inchin' Along* 87 A hot lotion made from the roots of elephant-ear.

3. In colloq. expressions: (1) *To see the elephant, to get a sight of the elephant,* to see the sights, to gain experience of life (see quot. 1844) [cf. *OED, s.v. Lion* 4 *to see the lions,* in same sense]; (2) *to draw the elephant,* to succeed in a most difficult undertaking, *rare;* (3) *to cry up the elephant,* to "talk up" something, *rare.*

(1) [**1835** LONGSTREET *Ga. Scenes* 6 That's sufficient, as Tom Haynes said when he saw the Elephant.] **1844** KENDALL *Santa Fe Exped.* I. 110 When a man is disappointed in anything he undertakes, when he has seen enough, when he gets sick and tired of any job he may have set himself about, he has 'seen the elephant.' **1906** O. HENRY *Four Million* 87 He makes his rounds every evening, while you and I see the elephant once a week. — (2) **1872** *Harper's Mag.* June 70/2 The bill [Pacific Railroad bill] has passed, and we have drawn the elephant. — (3) **1893** LELAND *Memoirs* 210 One thing I set my face against firmly: I never would in any way whatever write up, aid, or advertise the great show or museum, or cry up the elephant.

***elevate,** *v.tr.* To store (grain) in an elevator, also to process and tranship it. — **1860** *Rep. Thos. S. Blackwell, Grand Trunk Railway* 9 The most complete appliances for storing, elevating, and transhipping produce has been provided. **1934** WEBSTER.

***elevated,** *a.* and *n.* [The noun use, f. the adj., is app. of U.S. origin.]

1. *n.* Short for "elevated railroad" or "elevated train" *qq.v.*

1881 MARSHALL *Through Amer.* 24 The effect of the 'elevated'—the 'L,' as New Yorkers generally call it—is, to my mind, anything but beautiful. **1910** O. HENRY *Sixes & Sevens* 49 The elevated crashed raucously. **1947** *Harper's Mag.* May 453/2 A mile to the west the remaining eighty per cent [of the population] cling to the greasy straps of the antiquated, unsanitary, dilapidated, and dangerous Elevated.

2. In combs.: (1) **elevated line,** a line of elevated railway; (2) **railroad,** =next, also attrib.; (3) **railway,** a street railway supported on trestles; (4) **road,** =prec.; (5) **station,** a station on an elevated railroad; (6) **train,** a train that runs on an elevated railroad.

(1) **1945** *Chi. Tribune* 27 Feb. 3/3 A two coach . . . train crashed into the rear of a four car . . . express on the south side elevated line. — (2) **1868** *N.Y. Herald* 1 July 8/6 The elevated railroad through Greenwich street has 'gone up' higher than was contemplated in the charter of the company. **1947** *Life* 13 Jan. 92/2 On a December day in 1867, Charles T. Harvey, dressed in a long frock coat and silk hat, piloted a cable car over the world's first elevated railroad track. — (3) **1868** *N.Y. Tribune* 1 July 8/2 The remarkable work of constructing an elevated railway . . . was again on trial yesterday. **1945** MAXWELL *Folded Leaf* 257 They rode on the elevated railway. — (4) **1868** *Com. & Fin. Chron.* VI. 361/1 Three tiers of roads could be constructed; a basement road . . a surface road . . . and an elevated road. **1906** O. HENRY *Four Million* 8 Standing under a gas-light and looking over the elevated road at the moon, was a man.

(5) **1884** *N.Y. Herald* 27 Oct. 2/2 Commodious First Flat; Rent. $37; Elevated Station 86th st. **1944** *Chi. D. News* 6 Dec. 1/7 I rode in my stepfather's car until I saw an elevated station. — (6) **1881** *Scribner's Mo.* May 159/2 The clatter and roar and groaning wail of the Elevated train. **1948** *Chi. D. News* 3 Jan. 4/3 Workmen are busy restoring an elevated train to the tracks.

* **elevator,** *n.*

1. An apparatus for lifting grain, etc., to an upper floor or level, or into a bin, car, etc. (see quot. 1799).

1787 in *Rep. Comm. Patents 1849* I. 574 One of which [machines], denominated by the said Oliver Evans an elevator, is calculated by its own motion to hoist the wheat or grain from the lower floor . . . to the upper loft of such mill. **1799** WELD *Travels* I. 35 [The meal] is conveyed to the very top of the mill by the elevators, which consist of a number of small buckets of the size of tea-cups, attached to a long band that goes round a wheel at the top, and another at the bottom of the mill. **1869** *Rep. Comm. Agric. 1868* 355 The stone-breaker referred to has elevators connected with it, which carry the stones to a considerable height. **1949** *Time* 12 Sep. 22/2 There was a new $1,500 orchard duster and an elevator that hoisted corn from the wagons into the cribs.

attrib. **1857** *Mich. Agric. Soc. Trans.* VIII. 585 The keeping of water from the quarries while mining . . . is now successfully done by an elevator pump.

2. A cage or car that travels up and down in a shaft in a storied building for conveying passengers or goods from one level to another. Also attrib.

1853 *Harper's Mag.* VII. 130/2 One striking novelty . . . belongs to the New York plan. . . . It is this: the introduction of a steam elevator, by which an indolent, or fatigued, or aristocratic person may deposit himself in a species of dumb waiter at the hall-door, and by whistle, or the jingling of a bell, be borne up . . . to the third, fourth, or fifth floor. **1923** C. J. DUTTON *Shadow on Glass* 83 The elevator door was open, so he took the elevator to the library, which was lighted. **1946** *Sat. Ev. Post* 3 Aug. 86/4 He opened the door, quickly crossed the lobby and saw that the elevator was right there waiting for him.

3. A building specially designed and equipped to elevate, store, and discharge grain, and sometimes to process it. Also transf. Cf. **grain elevator.**

1865 *Wilkes' Spirit of Times* 5 Aug. 363/3 Buffalo really is . . . splendid too, in its monster elevators down by the water, and its palatial residences on Delaware, Main, and several other of the uptown streets. **1882** *Uncle Rufus & Ma* 36 Chicago elevators and grain-handlers must take warning. **1948** *Miami* (Okla.) *D. News-Record* 4 July 3/4 The wheat flood has hit the small country elevators, filling them to their brims.

4. In special combs.: (1) **elevator boy,** a boy who operates a passenger elevator; (2) **building,** a building containing an elevator, *rare;* (3) **cage,** =**elevator 2;** (4) **hall,** a hall giving access to an elevator; (5) **man,** (*a*) a man who operates a passenger or a goods elevator, (*b*) a man who manages a grain elevator; (6) **operator,** one who operates an elevator (sense **2.**); (7) **shaft,** a shaft in a storied building through which an elevator runs; (8) **starter,** one who directs the starting of elevators.

(1) **1879** *Chi. Tribune* 8 May 8/4 As is the custom with elevator-boys—a reprehensible one it is too,—the lad in charge of the elevator started it before closing the door. **1945** MAXWELL *Folded Leaf* 52 The elevator boy delivered them, one at a time, at the fourth floor. — (2) **1884** *Cent. Mag.* Aug. 516/1 The invention of the steam passenger-lift has brought about the invention of what have not improperly been called our 'elevator buildings.' — (3) **1904** LYNDE *Grafters* 300 When the door of the elevator-cage clacked again, Kent was waiting. — (4) **1887** *Courier-Journal* 2 Feb. 8/2 The tenants urged that it was with great difficulty that they could make the entrance and exit of the elevator hall.

(5) (*a*) **1890** *Cong. Rec.* 4 Aug. 8123/2 On this list there are firemen, watchmen, elevator men. **1944** JOHNSON *As I Dare* 125 Even the dignified stenographers and the elevator man, according to O. Henry, were octogenarians, and were surrounded by the *Century* aura. (*b*) **1894** *Cong. Rec.* App. 21 July 1087/2 Sometimes, if the elevator man has a good deal of bad wheat, he gets some of a first-class article and mixes the two in his elevator. **1947** *Newsweek* 7 July 69/1 Among his neighborhood friends and fellow elevator men, his popularity was untarnished by his downfall. — (6) **1945** *Chi. Tribune* 26 Jan. 27/1 (*advt.*), Elevator operator for office building. **1948** *News-Palladium* (Benton Harbor, Mich.) 14 Aug. 2/6 We girls here in the Fidelity have come to know the elevator operator very well and think very highly of her. — (7) **1885** *Cent. Mag.* XXX. 579/1 With staircases and elevator-shafts which must remain open, . . . I see much wisdom in the choice of travelers who seek rooms near the ground. **1947** *Chi. Tribune* 21 June 4/8 The group also discussed the association's proposed amendments to an ordinance passed Dec. 17 compelling hotels to inclose stairways and elevator shafts with fire resistant materials. — (8) **1929** *Publishers' Wkly.* 20 July 252 These may be written by the elevator-starter or the publisher himself. **1946** *Chi. D. News* 14 Nov. 22/5 An elevator starter suffered a fatal heart attack yesterday afternoon.

As the last term in **coal, freight, grain, hod, passenger, rope, steam elevator.**

* **elevener,** *n.* A person accustomed to taking a drink at eleven o'clock in the morning. *Rare.* — **1807** C. JANSON *Stranger in A.* 299 There is a numerous set of people in the Southern States, called *slingers*, and another, styled *eleveners*. *Ib.* 300 A second-rate consumer of distillations from the sugar-cane, the grape, and the juniper-berry, is the *elevener*. . . . These eleveners are generally found strolling about the corners of streets, or other public places, at the eleventh hour, A.M.

eleven-penny bit. A coin, or its equivalent in value, formerly in use in New York and Pennsylvania, and sometimes called a *York shilling;* the Spanish real. *Obs.*

[**1802** *Port Folio* II. 220/1 [There was] a slight fracas between Ned Whiffle and Dick Slang, occasioned by the former refusing to lend the latter eleven pence, to get a glass of gin twist.] **1807** C. W. JANSON *Stranger in Amer.* 186 This description of beggars will also stipulate with you as to the sum they expect to be given them—they will name a quarter of a dollar, a nine-penny or eleven penny bit. **1848** BARTLETT 204 *Levy*, eleven-pence. In the State of Pennsylvania, the eighth part of a dollar, or twelve and a half cents. Sometimes called an elevenpenny bit. **1859** —— 33 Bit. (Span. *pieza.*) The name, in some Southern States, of a silver coin of the value of one eighth of a dollar, the Spanish real (*de plata*). It is called also an *eleven-penny bit* or a *levy*.

elf owl. A small owl, *Micropallas whitneyi*, found in Arizona and California.

1887 RIDGWAY *Manual N.A. Birds* 267 *Hab.* Southwestern United States (southern Arizona and southeastern California . . . Elf Owl). **1903** AUSTIN *Land of Little Rain* 38 The chief witnesses of their presence near the spring are the elf owls. . . . [They] begin a twilight flitting toward the spring, feeding as they go on grasshoppers, lizards and small, swift creatures . . . battling with chipmunks at their own doors. **1945** *Nat. Geog. Mag.* April 477/1 No bigger than a sparrow, the Elf Owl snatches nectar-hunting insects as they are attracted to the yellow blossoms of a century plant.

elft elft, *n.* (See quots.) *Obs.* — **1816** in *N.Y. Hist. Soc. Coll.* II. (1848) 130 The name of the Shad in Dutch is Elft, in German Aloft, and in French Alose, all perhaps from the same root; but being pronounced here *elf*, the number eleven, the number itself possibly came to be considered as the name, and so led to denote others in the same manner. **1913** JAMES tr. Danckaerts *Jrnl.* (1679–80) 53 We tasted here [in New York], for the first time, smoked *twaelft* [twelfth], a fish so called because it is caught in season next after the *elft* [eleventh].

* **Eli,** *n.* [f. *Eli*hu Yale (1648–1721), early benefactor of Yale College.] A Yale man. Also attrib. Also in phr. *children* (or *sons*) *of Eli*, Yale men.

1879 J. S. WOOD *Yale Yarns* 140 They . . . were exceeding glad to get away for the fun,—as we Elis all are. **1899** WELCH & CAMP *Yale* 27 Back of that fence was a stretch of bare ground, trod by the sons of Eli from time immemorial. *Ib.* 30 Even stronger was the sense of its eternal fitness for all the informal occasions when the children of Eli gathered themselves together. **1949** *Time* 14 Mar. 51/1 When James Rowland Angell . . . arrived in New Haven in 1921, he was the first non-Eli since 1766 to have been elected president of Yale.

Elizabeth grape. (See quot.) *Obs.* — **1863** *Horticulturist* XVIII. 33 The Elizabeth grape . . . is a green grape of an oval shape; the bunch and berries are large; the skin is thin, but not tender; the flesh is crisp rather than melting; and it has a perceptible trace of the native aroma.

elk, *n.

1. **=wapiti.**

Some of the quots. prob. refer to the moose, of the same genus as the European elk.

1635 *Md. Relation* iii. 23 In the upper parts of the Countrey there are Bufeloes, Elkes, . . . and Deare there are in great Store. **1709** LAWSON *Carolina* 123 The Elk is a Monster of the Venison sort. **1827** W. BULLOCK *Journey* xxi, A pair of the gigantic elk, or wappetti (nearly the size of horses), ranged through the meadows. **1947** *Steamboat* (Colo.) *Pilot* 2 Jan. 7/2 Mr. Wilson . . . found a band of 200 elk.

2. (*cap.*) A member of the Benevolent and Protective Order of Elks (see quot. 1912). Also, *pl.*, the order itself, or one of its lodges.

1879 *Chi. Tribune* 14 March 5/4 The second annual benefit of Chicago Lodge, No. 4, 'D.,' Protective Order of Elks, was given yesterday afternoon at McVicker's. **1884** JOS. HATTON *H. Irving's Impressions* II. 120 The Irving-Terry reception, by the Elks, Wednesday evening, was a notable social event. **1912** *Hampton Mag.* April 194/1 Originally a theatrical order, the Elks grew out of a colony of English semiprofessional actors who gathered in 1867 at a boarding house on Elm Street, New York. *Ib.*, The Elks now number 400,000 members in nearly 1,300 lodges. **1916** WILSON *Red Gap* 374 They was merchant princes from Sandusky or prominent Elks from Omaha. **1947** *Savings News* Nov. 12/2 My father's an Eagle, an Elk, a Moose and a Lion.

Hence **Elkdom.**

1916 *Lincoln* (Neb.) *State Journal* 4 Dec. 6 Once each year all *Elkdom* bows its head and pays the tribute of a tear to the brothers who nevermore this side of the great river will answer: 'Present.'

3. Used (sense **1.**) in combs., some of which undoubtedly allude to the moose: (1) **elk bark,** the bark of the sweet bay, *Magnolia glauca;* (2) **beef,** the flesh of the elk, *obs.;* (3) **garden,** ?a fertile valley or cover frequented by elk, *obs.;* (4) ***horn,** see as a main entry; (5) **lick,** a salt lick frequented by elk; (6) **nut,** the buffalo nut, *Pyrulia pubera;* (7) **runner,** (see quot.), *rare;* (8) **tallow,** the fat of the elk; (9) **tree,** the sorrel tree or sourwood, *Oxydendrum arboreum,* native to rich woods of Pennsylvania and southward; (10) **wallow,** a depression in the ground made or supposed to have been made by elk, also transf., *obs.;* (11) **wood,** the umbrella tree, *Magnolia tripetala,* also the wood of this tree; (12) **yard,** **=moose yard.**

(1) **1876** HOBBS *Bot. Hand-Book* 34 Elk bark, Magnolia, Magnolia macrophylla. **1889** *Cent.* 451/1 Elk bark . . . [is] also called Indian bark. — **(2)** **1806** LEWIS in *L. & Clark Exped.* III. (1905) 342 A fatiegue of 6 men employed in jerking the Elk beaf. — **(3)** **1787** in *Amer. Sp.* XV. 266/1, 92 acres of land . . . lying in the Elk Garden on the waters of Priests Creek.

(5) **1795** *Ib.* 175/2 Beginning at a hickory and lynn at the Elk lick. — **(6)** **1813** MUHLENBERG *Cat. Plants* 96 Oil nut, or Elk nut. — **(7)** **1847** FIELD *Drama in Pokerville* 109 The Elk Runners [heading] . . . I don't kill elk with my gun, but with my knife. — **(8)** **1805** LEWIS in *Ann. 9th Congress* 2 Sess. 1043 Deer and elk tallow, elk skins dressed and in parchment. **1882** BAILLIE-GROHMAN *Camps in Rockies* 120 And about fifty pounds of fat, or so-called 'elk-tallow.' — **(9)** **1876** HOBBS *Bot. Hand-Book* 34 Elk tree, Sorrel tree, *Andromeda arbores.* **1889–90** *Cent.* 1879/3, 4216/3.

(10) **1786** in *Amer. Sp.* XV. 175/2 To include a Spring Called the Elk Wallow. **1825** *Ib.* To D two chestnuts & a spanish oak in the Big Elk wallow. — **(11)** **1814** PURSH *Flora Amer.* II. 381 *Magnolia tripetala* . . . is generally known by the name of Umbrella-tree; in the mountains they call it Elk-wood. **1880** WEBSTER *Supp., Elkwood,* . . . a name given to the soft spongy wood of the *Magnolia umbrella.* **1901** MOHR *Plant Life Ala.* 506 *Magnolia tripetala.* . . . Elkwood. Umbrella Tree. . . . Carolinian and Louisianian areas. — **(12)** **1868** WOOD *Homes without H.* xxxi. 612 That curious temporary habitation . . . popularly termed an Elk-yard.

Also *elk chip, hunter, meat, range, steak, trail,* etc.

As the last term in **American, black, buck, Rocky Mountain, round-horned, slough, tule elk.**

elk-horn, *n.

1. An antler of a wapiti or red deer; also the substance of which this is made, often used in the handles of implements. Also attrib.

1809 KENDALL *Travels* III. 196 In the same collection are the horns of a red deer, (*cervus elephas*) called, according to an error constantly persisted in by the English colonists in all parts of North America, an *elk's horns.* **1848** PARKMAN in *Knickerb.* XXXI. 191 He had a heavy whip, with a handle of solid elk-horn. **1942** STEGNER *Mormon C.* 54 He may uncover the elkhorn handle of somebody's pocket knife.

2. A variety of cherry tree. *Obs.*

1849 *N. Eng. Farmer* I. 265 Cherry-trees have a great variety of forms. The Black Tartarean, Elkhorn, Richardson, and some others, run up in a high, narrow top.

3. elk-horn cactus, the *Opuntia acanthocarpa* or any one of similar species of spiny, much-branched cacti of this genus.

1941 FERGUSSON *Southwest* 95 The fuzzy nap on the elkhorn cactus turns out to be vicious spines.

ellachick 'elətʃɪk, *n.* [See quot.] A large, edible fresh-water tortoise, *Clemmys marmorata,* of the Pacific Coast. — **1884** GOODE *Fisheries* I. 158 'They are almost constantly for sale in the markets of San Francisco, and make pretty good soups.' . . . The species is called 'El-la-chick' by the Nisquallies.

***elliptic,** *n.* An elliptical spring, or a vehicle having such springs. *Obs.* See **runabout.** — **a1846** *Quarter Race Ky.* 49 The day before, I'd took off the old wooden springs and set the body on elliptics. **1860** in *Amer. Sp.* XXII. 202/2 Sometimes . . . a kind of palanquin is constructed, and a person aged or infirm . . . or a squad of papooses, ride with all the grace and spring of one of our own elliptics.

***elm,** *n.* In combs.: (1) **Elm City,** a nickname of New Haven, Conn.; (2) **goldenrod,** (see quot.); (3) **peeler,** (*a*) a runty variety of swine, *obs.,* (*b*) (see quot.); (4) **tree bug,** the elm-leaf beetle.

(1) [**1854** in SCHMIDT *Briefe* 29 Die herrlichen grossen Ulmen geben der Stadt [New Haven] ein majestätisches Ansehen und haben ihr den Namen 'Ulmenstadt' verliehen.] **1871** DE VERE 664 New Haven in Connecticut, is known . . . as Elm City, from the number and magnificent size of the elm-trees that adorn the public squares. **1887** *Lippincott's Mag.* Aug. 297 Marriages between New Haven girls and [Yale] college men are of rare occurrence. . . . It cannot be that the young ladies of the Elm City are not pretty. — **(2)** **1845** LINCOLN *Botany* App. 170/1 *Solidago ulmifolia* (elm goldenrod). — **(3)** (*a*) **1872** *Ill. Dept. Agric. Trans.* IX. 204 Nearly all farmers strive to raise hogs of the best blood. The old fashioned 'prairie rooter and elm peeler' are banished from the county. **1901** *Munsey's Mag.* XXIV. 494/1 Hogs . . . [and] razorbacks . . . in the Ohio River country . . . were termed elm-peelers. (*b*) **1923** *D.N.* V. 234 *elm-peeler,* n. A poor white who peels elm trees for slippery elm, which he sells. 'He's no count—just an *ellum-peeler.*' — **(4)** **1854** EMMONS *Agric. N.Y.* V. 261 Index, Elmtree bugs, 134. [134. *Galeruca calmariensis* (Lin.) . . . This is a European insect, which has been introduced into this country about Baltimore. It is destructive to the foliage of the elm.]

As the last term in **cedar, cork, European, hickory, Liberty, moose, mucilaginous, red, river, rock, settler's, slippery, swamp, Washington, water, white, winged elm.**

Elmira system. A system of prison management adopted at the reformatory at Elmira, N.Y., in 1876, based upon sentences of indeterminate length with possible commutations.

1891 WINTER *N.Y. State Reformatory* iv, The Elmira system is by no means yet in a perfect or final shape; it is still in course of growth. [**1900** FLYNT *Itinerant Policeman* 92, I visited but one reformatory during my pilgrimage, but it was representative of the latest of these institutions. I refer to the Elmira, N.Y., type.] **1935** FLICK *Hist. State N.Y.* VIII. 295 The Elmira system was unquestionably a real step forward a half century ago.

El Pasoan. A native or inhabitant of El Paso, Texas. — **1941** FERGUSSON *Southwest* 89 An El Pasoan who knew him [Victoriano Huerta] well describes him as 'saddle-colored, with high cheek-bones, aquiline nose, square-shouldered, and baldish.'

Elsanborough grapevine. [f. *Elsanborough,* N.J.] (See quot.) *Obs.* — **1846** BROWNE *Trees Amer.* 135 *Elsanborough Grapevine.* This variety is noted for its sweet, juicy fruit, which is free from pulp, and musky taste.

emancipation, *n.

1. Emancipation Day, among the Negroes, an annual holiday commemorating the freeing of the slaves.

[**1868** ROSE *Great Country* 151, I was in Richmond on 3rd of April, the anniversary of its fall, which the darkies celebrated as the date of their emancipation.] **1884** (*title*), Emancipation Day. **1905** *Hartford Courant* 3 Jan. 10 The 42nd anniversary of Emancipation Day was celebrated last evening by the colored people of this city.

b. The Fourth of July. *Rare.*

1907 C. D. STEWART *Partners* 91 We're all gwine do good dis 'mancipation Day. *Ib.* 119, I told him this was Emancipation Day for white folks and niggers both.

2. Emancipation Proclamation, the proclamation issued by President Lincoln on January 1, 1863, freeing all Negro slaves within certain designated areas; also the anticipated document and the preliminary drafts of the Proclamation.

"As early as July 22, 1862, Lincoln had read to his Cabinet a preliminary draft of an emancipation proclamation. . . . On the 22 of September he read to his Cabinet a second draft of the proclamation. . . . The formal and definite proclamation came January 1, 1863" (COMMAGER, *Documents*, I. 520).

[**1861** NORTON *Army Letters* 29, I am fully satisfied . . . that it [the war] cannot be ended without the emancipation proclamation.] **1863** *Ladies' Repository* XXIII. 128/2 The emancipation Proclamation of President Lincoln makes an era . . . in the history of the war. **1947** *Nat. Geog. Mag.* June 700/1 In the southeast room [of the White House] on the second floor the Emancipation Proclamation was signed.

b. Also **Emancipation Act, Amendment, Message.**

1863 CATE *Two Soldiers* 17 He assumed the position that Confederate acceptance of the Emancipation Act would turn it to our advantage whereas the Lincoln Government was now using it to injure us. **1863** DICEY *Six Months* I. 192 But subsequent conversations with American politicians led me to believe that the Emancipation Message, as it was called at the time, was capable of a far higher and more hopeful construction. **1865** *Harper's Wkly.* 5 Aug. 483/2 New Jersey . . . [is] a state controlled hitherto by the most un-American of parties, and which . . . rejected the Emancipation Amendment, deliberately choosing to chain itself to a corpse.

***Emancipationist,** *n.* One in sympathy with Lincoln's Emancipation Proclamation. *Obs.* — **1863** *N.Y. Tribune* 14 Nov. 6/1 Two Radical Emancipationists were elected on Friday to the United States Senate by the Missouri Legislature.

***Emancipator,** *n.*

1. *pl.* (See quot. 1847.) *Obs.*

1847 L. COLLINS *Kentucky* 111 They [*sc.* certain Baptists urging abolition of slavery] called themselves 'Friends of Humanity,' but are known in the records of those times [*c*1804] by the name of 'Emancipators.' [**1944** DUNCAN *M. Graham* 19 Brush Creek Church and Little Mount Church . . . belonged to an association commonly referred to as 'those emancipation Baptists.']

2. A nickname given President Lincoln because of his Emancipation Proclamation. Also **Great Emancipator.**

1866 F. KIRKLAND *Bk. Anecdotes* 151 The illustrious Emancipator . . . gave to the system its final blow. **1899** CHESNUTT *Wife of His Youth* 159 A national flag was gracefully draped over the platform, and under it hung a lithograph of the Great Emancipator. **1948** *Time* 23 Feb. 25/1 Last week the President . . . paid his respects . . . to the memory of Lincoln by driving to the Lincoln Memorial, watching aides place a wreath at the foot of the Emancipator's statue.

embarcadero ɛmˌbɑrkəˈdɛro, *n. W.* [Sp. in same sense.] A wharf, port, or landing place, freq. one serving an inland city or settlement.

1846 SUTTER *MS Diary* (Soc. Calif. Pioneers Lib.) 13 Jan., Rained, the launcheros did not come so the boat did not leave the embarcadero. **1890** *Outing* Nov. 111/2 In a slough one sometimes finds the decaying hulk of a schooner that once sailed to forgotten towns, and to deserted river landings, or 'embarcaderos,' as they were once called. **1934** *Calif. Hist. Soc. Quart.* Mar. 12 A 'city' had been surveyed at the embarcadero named 'Sacramento.'

***embargo,** *n.*

1. Embargo Act, one of several acts passed by Congress before and during the War of 1812, authorizing the President to restrict or forbid the departure of ships from American ports. Now *hist.* Cf. **O-grab-me.**

1882 COOPER *Amer. Pol.* I. 16 Congress acted promptly, and on the 21st of December passed what is known as the Embargo Act, under the inspiration of the Republican party, which claimed that the only choice of the people lay between the embargo and war, and that there was no other way to obtain redress from England and France. **1943** HICKS *Amer. Dem.* 166 After forbidding British warships the use of American ports and harbors, and demanding reparations from the British government, he laid before Congress as his chief weapon of retaliation an Embargo Act, which ultimately, on December 21, 1807, became law.

b. Also **Embargo laws.**

1809 *Repertory* (Boston) 17 Jan. (Th.), The Embargo laws were called *O grab me* laws.

2. embargo bill, a bill proposing the laying of an embargo.

1807 *Ann. 10th Congress* 1 Sess. 1228 Embargo Bill. **1814** *Niles' Reg.* V. 200/1 A copy of the embargo bill was received at Boston . . . before the injunction of secrecy was removed at Washington.

As the last term in **anti-, ice embargo.**

Embargoroon ɪmˌbɑrgəˈrun, *n.* (See quot. 1912.) *Obs.* — **1808** *Mass. Spy* 28 Sep. (Th.), The wretched dilemmas to which our Embargoroons are reduced in their attempts to prop the falling fabrick of their darling democracy. **1912** THORNTON 289 *Embargoroon*, a nickname for the supporters of the Embargo Act, . . . passed Dec. 22, 1807, and repealed March 1, 1809.

embarras ɪmˈbærəs, *n.* [La. F.] (See quots.) *Obs.*

1727 tr. in McDERMOTT *Glossary* (1941) 72 What we call *embarras* is a mass of floating trees which the river has uprooted and which the current drags onward continually. If these be stopped by a tree that is rooted in the ground, or by a tongue of land, the trees become heaped upon one another, and form enormous piles. **1814** BRACKENRIDGE *Louisiana* 205 At the distance of every mile or two, . . . there are *embarras*, or rafts. **1817** BRADBURY *Travels* 32 The navigation had been very difficult for some days, on account of the frequent occurrence of what is termed by the boatmen *embarras*.

embirch ɪmˈbɜtʃ, *v. intr.* To embark in a birch canoe. *Rare.* — **1853** LOWELL *Fireside Travels* (1885) 147 As we were embirching last evening for our moose-chase, I asked what I was to do with my baggage.

emerald fish. One of several species of goby, esp. *Gobionellus oceanicus.* — **1882** JORDAN & GILBERT *Syn. Fishes N. Amer.* 635 *Gobionellus.* . . . Emerald-fishes. . . . Base of the tongue tuberculate, and shining with bright blue and green reflections, like a precious stone.

***Emergency,** *n.* In the North, the period immediately preceding the battle of Gettysburg when the South was winning the major battles. *Obs.* — **1893** LELAND *Memoirs* 251 And now terrible times came on, followed, for me, by a sad event. The rebels, led by General Lee, had penetrated into Pennsylvania, and Philadelphia was threatened. This period was called the 'Emergency.'

Emersonian ˌɛməˈsonɪən, *a.* and *n.* [Ralph Waldo *Emerson* (1803–82).]

1. *n.* An admirer of the philosophic writings of Emerson. *Obs.*

1881 HAWEIS *Amer. Humorists* 87 Most Emersonians detest Carlyle. **1884** *Cent. Mag.* XXVII. 930/1 It is irritating to Emersonians to be compelled to admit that his strain lacks any essential quality. **1900** *Kans. Gazeteer* 721 The School of Elocution and Physical Culture [is] in charge of an Emersonian from the East.

2. *a.* Of, like, or pertaining to, Emerson, his writings, or his philosophy.

[**1851** *Family Friend* July 120/2 (*title*), Emersonian Treasures.] **1878** *N. Amer. Rev.* CXXVI. 547 If he [Thoreau] had not lived in the woods, and talked the Emersonian dialect. **1884** BURROUGHS in *Cent. Mag.* XXVII. 928/1 Men of the Emersonian and Wordsworthian stamp. **1884** *N. Amer. Rev.* CXXXIX. 166 To be Emersonian is to be American. **1907** *Collier's* 6 April 13/2 An Emersonian paragraph from Boston claimed the prize for Beacon Hill. **1947** *Sat. Review* 30 Aug. 19/1 The Jeffersonian, Emersonian, free-thinking and solitary-thinking democrat is doomed in a world of corrupt organization.

***emery,** *n.*

1. = next. *Rare.*

1864 *Hist. North-Western Soldiers' Fair* 71 [Donations include] 2 soldiers' reticules, 3 pin cushions, 5 emeries, 1 crochet tidy.

2. emery bag, a small bag filled with powdered emery, used for keeping needles clean and bright.

1845 *Lowell Offering* V. 200 The strenuous application, by which I drove the perspiration from every pore of the hand, soon taught me the value of an emery-bag. **1893** MARK TWAIN *P. Wilson* ii., They would smouch provisions, . . . or a brass thimble, . . . or an emery-bag.

b. Also **emery ball, strawberry.**

1864 *Hist. North-Western Soldiers' Fair* 101 [Donations include] 3 bead bracelets, 2 emery balls, 6 scissors cases. **1903** WIGGIN *Rebecca* vi. 69 She polished her needles to nothing, pushing them in and out of the emery strawberry, but they always squeaked.

***emetic,** *n.* **1. emetic holly,** the yaupon, a species of holly native to the southern states. **2. emetic weed,** Indian tobacco, *Lobelia inflata.*

(1) **1846** BROWNE *Trees* 169 *Ilex vomitoria*, The Emetic Holly. **1897** SUDWORTH *Arborescent Flora* 280 *Ilex vomitoria.* Yaupon. Common names include Emetic Holly (S.C.). [Note:] A very fitting local name indicating . . . the medicinal character of the foliage. — (2) **1784** CUTLER in *Mem. Academy* I. 484 Emetic weed. . . . The leaves chewed in the mouth are, at first, insipid, but soon become pungent, occasioning a copious discharge of saliva. **1931** CLUTE *Plants* 124 In addition to other plants mentioned, of undoubted medicinal value, may be included . . . the emetic weed (*Lobelia inflata*).

emigrant ˈɛməgrənt, *n.* [f. L. *emigrans, -antis, pr. part.* of *emigrare*, to emigrate.]

1. One who leaves another country to settle permanently in the U.S. Cf. **immigrant.**

1754 (*title*), A Memorial of the Case of the German Emigrants settled in . . . Pensilvania. **1839** VAN BUREN in *Pres. Mess. & P.* III. 532 Recent information also leads me to hope that the emigrants from Her Majesty's Provinces who have sought refuge within our boundaries are disposed to become peaceable residents and to abstain from all attempts to endanger the peace of that country which has afforded them an asylum. **1945** *Sat. Review* 24 Feb. 17/3 He spends a good deal of introductory writing on the separate careers of his two grandparents, one a German emigrant, the other a Southern planter.

2. One moving from the eastern or more settled part of the U.S. to new lands farther west.

1789 *Ann. 1st Congress* I. 622 [The] situation [of the Western territory] . . . gives the climate a salubrity that accommodates it to the emigrant from both Northern and Southern States. **1862** in F. MOORE *Rebellion Rec.* V. II. 93 Col. E. E. Cross, well known in the West a few years ago as editor, correspondent, etc., and later as an emigrant to Arizona, . . . raged like a lion. *a***1918** G. STUART *On Frontier* I. 39 The storms along the Platte River were . . . accompanied by such fierce gales of wind as often to blow down the tents . . . of the emigrants.

b. An American settler in Texas, esp. one who migrated from the South between 1822 and the admission of Texas into the Union in 1845.

1808 PIKE *Sources Miss.* App. III. 33 The American emigrants [in Texas] are introducing some little spirit of agriculture near to Nacogdoches. **1821** *Austin P.* I. 390 The said Austin (further) agrees to obtain free from all (expenses six hundred) and forty acres of Land for each emigrant. **1841** TYLER in *Pres. Mess. & P.* IV. 79 Settled principally by emigrants from the United States, we have the happiness to know that the great principles of civil liberty are there [in Texas] destined to flourish under wise institutions and wholesome laws.

c. One who left the U.S. to settle in the Oregon country or in Oregon, during the movement commencing in 1842.

1843 FRÉMONT *Exped.* 14 Travelling on the fresh traces of the Oregon emigrants, relieves a little the loneliness of the road. **1851** *Harper's Mag.* Dec. 122/2 From Oregon, we learn that emigrants were coming rapidly.

d. A Mormon settler in the West, esp. one who left Nauvoo, Illinois, in the 1846 migration. Also **Mormon emigrant.**

1846 *Niles' Reg.* 30 May 208/2 The Mormon emigrants leave in companies of four to six and ten wagons. **1858** BUCHANAN in *Pres. Mess. & P.* V. 493 The Territory of Utah was settled by certain emigrants from the States and from foreign countries who have for several years past manifested a spirit of insubordination to the Constitution and laws of the United States.

e. A settler in California, or one who migrated to that region during the gold rush (1848–56).

1847 *Semi-Wkly. News* (Fredericksburg, Va.) 4 Oct. 1/4 The great route for traders and emigrants is by way of Council Grove and Santa Fe. **1916** MONTGOMERY *Student's Amer. Hist.* 392 In the height of the excitement emigrants eagerly paid a thousand dollars for steerage passage with the privilege of sleeping 'in a coil of rope.'

f. One of the settlers who rushed into the territory of Kansas during the struggle to establish Kansas as a pro- or as an anti-slavery state.

1856 SUMNER in *Cong. Globe* App. 19 May 532/3 While opening the Territory to Slavery, the [Kansas-Nebraska] bill also opened it to emigrants from every quarter, who might by their votes redress the wrong. **1877** JOHNSON *Anderson Co., Kansas* 63 During the spring and summer of 1857 several emigrants settled in Garnett, before the Louisville colony arrived. **1914** H. A. TREXLER *Slavery in Mo.* 194 Appeals were now [in 1854] made by the proslavery party for emigrants.

3. A Negro sent to Africa as a colonist by the Colonization Society. *Obs.*

1844 *Niles' Reg.* 10 Feb. 384/2 The Colonization Society is to send off a vessel from New York about the middle of March with emigrants for Africa.

4. In combs. (senses **1.** and **2.**): (1) **emigrant agent,** an agent of a railroad or land company who promotes the settlement of new lands; (2) **Emigrant Aid Company, Society,** see as a main entry; (3) **emigrant car,** a railroad car designed for use in transporting emigrants, cf. **emigrant train;** (4) **Emigrant commission,** a commission appointed to deal with the problems of emigrants; (5) **Emigrant commissioner,** a member of an emigrant commission; (6) **road,** a road made or used by emigrants on their way to the West, cf. **emigration road;** (7) **robber,** one who robbed newly arrived emigrants; (8) **route, =emigrant road;** (9) **runner,** one employed to solicit patronage for hotels, boarding houses, etc., among newly arrived emigrants, cf. **runner;** (10) **sleeping car,** (see quot.); (11) **ticket,** a ticket for transportation sold to an emigrant at a reduced price; (12) **train,** (*a*) a long line of wagons, cattle, etc., on the way to a new settlement, (*b*) a railroad train carrying emigrants (see quot. 1855); (13) **wagon,** a type of large, heavy wagon used by emigrants, a prairie schooner, also attrib.

(1) 1868 *N.Y. Herald* 14 July 6/4 Justice Hogan . . . has recently been appointed emigrant agent of the Erie Railway Company. **1887** *Courier-Journal* 11 Feb. 3/2 He is a land and emigrant agent, and is addicted to spreeing. — **(3) 1843** *Hunt's Merch. Mag.* XVIII. 540 The property of the company consists of . . . 20 eight-wheeled emigrant, 14 eight-wheeled baggage, and 4 eight-wheeled mail and baggage cars. **1902** WILSON *Spenders* 72 Oldaker found a man from New York on the train the other day, up in one of the emigrant cars. **1946** MCWILLIAMS *So. Calif. Country* 127 At one time as many as a hundred special emigrant cars were in use on the Southern Pacific line. — **(4) 1856** MACLEOD *F. Wood* 185 At least a portion of the inmates of the institutions under the control of the Alms-house Governors, who are supported by the city, are properly chargeable to the Emigrant Commission.

(5) 1873 COZZENS *Marvelous Country* 80 'Jim' believed in emigration as firmly as the old emigrant commissioners of Castle Garden believed in it when they made their thirty thousand dollars per annum fees. — **(6) 1845** FRÉMONT *Exped.* 107 Leaving . . . the usual emigrant road [the Oregon Trail] to the mountains, . . . we continued our route. **1918** CONNELLEY *Kansas,* We followed the 'emigrant road' (already broad and well beaten as any turnpike in our country) over a rolling prairie. **1942** SANDOZ *Crazy Horse* 13 Many like that one left their bones for the wolves along the emigrant road. — **(7) 1861** *N.Y. Tribune* 23 Nov. 4/3 Gamblers, ticket swindlers, emigrant robbers, baggage smashers, and all the worst classes of the city, rose into prominence. — **(8) 1947** PEATTIE *Sierra Nevada* 58 Frémont . . . passed over the Sierra Nevada . . . again a year later by the Truckee emigrant route. — **(9) 1856** MACLEOD *F. Wood* 285 Emigrant runners, half-bull-dog and half leech, burst in crowds upon the decks of arriving ships, carried off the poor foreign people, fleeced them, and set them adrift upon the town.

(10) 1895 WAIT *Car-Builder's Dict.* 51 Emigrant sleeping-car. . . . A cheaply finished car without springs or mattresses, but in other respects similar to ordinary sleepers, for the use of emigrants. Now used chiefly on the long runs west of Chicago, and to some extent used for ordinary travel, especially by parties of excursionists. — **(11)** *a***1868** in BRACE *Dangerous Classes N.Y.* 246 On Wednesday evening, with emigrant tickets to Detroit, we started on the *Isaac Newton* for Albany. — **(12)** (*a*) **1854** PIERCE in *Pres. Mess. & P.* V. 282 A piratical resort of outlaws or a camp of savages depredating on emigrant trains or caravans. *a***1918** G. STUART *On Frontier* II. 61 Scarcely an emigrant train passed without being attacked. (*b*) **1855** BESTE *Wabash* I. 112 The invention of what they call 'emigrant trains.' These are cheaper and slower, and perform, for example, in twenty-six hours the three hundred and twenty-eight miles which we, in the express train, were now doing in ten hours. **1946** MCWILLIAMS *So. Calif. Country* 126 Among the devices which the railroads used to attract settlers to Southern California were the excursion party and the emigrant train. — **(13) 1843** FRÉMONT *Exped.* 133 The edge of the wood . . . was dotted with the white covers of emigrant wagons. *Ib.* 136 A huge emigrant wagon, with a large and diversified family, had overtaken us and halted to noon at our encampment. **1908** *Sears Cat.* (ed. 117) 764 White duck emigrant wagon covers. **1912** *Out West* May 289/2 It was then believed that at least seven thousand emigrant wagons would go West, through Independence, that season.

Also *emigrant boarding house, camp, crossing, depot, horse, ship, through-passenger, trail, vessel,* etc.

Emigrant Aid Company, Society. During the struggle over Kansas, any one of various associations formed to help anti-slavery emigrants settle in the West, esp. in Kansas. Now *hist.* Cf. **Blue Lodge, Emigration Society, Northern Emigrant Society.**

"The Kansas struggle, 1854–1858, was a contest between proslavery and anti-slavery settlers, the latter assisted by northern emigrant aid societies, to determine whether Kansas should enter the Union with or without slavery" (*Cyclo. Amer. Govt.* II. 276). "Within six weeks after Congress had repealed the Missouri Compromise the Massachusetts Emigrant Aid company was incorporated with a nominal capital of five million dollars 'for the purpose of assisting emigrants to settle in the west'" (Sparks *Expansion Amer. People,* 356).

1856 W. LAWRENCE *A. Lawrence* 108 Money sent to the New England Emigrant Aid Company will be appropriated as you request. **1860** *Harper's Mag.* March 546/1 Douglas . . . would make it a crime to form conspiracies to invade a State or Territory to control elections, whether such conspiracies took the form of Emigrant Aid

Societies or of Blue Lodges of Missouri. **1910** VILLARD *John Brown* 95 Bands of New Englanders sent out by the Emigrant Aid Societies . . . had intensely inflamed the Missourians. **1945** MARSHALL *Santa Fe* 24 The Emigrant Aid Societies are sending out hundreds of good settlers.

emigrating depot. A depot set up by the government to facilitate the movement or migration of Indians westward. *Obs.* — **1846** MANSFIELD *Winfield Scott* 308 The Indians . . . were escorted to emigrating dépôts as rapidly as was consistent with the collection of their personal effects, their health and comfort.

***emigration,** *n.*

1. The entire body of people who settle in one part of the country.

1816 *Mass. H.S. Coll.* 2 Ser. VII. 115 The inhabitants of Abington, an emigration chiefly from Weymouth, have hitherto pursued . . . similar modes in the improvement of lands. **1848** *Calif. Claims* (Senate Rep. 23 Feb.) 29 The beautiful wheat crop (was) saved from the firebrand, and the large emigration arriving in this country spared the horrors of want. **1857** *Lawrence* (Kans.) *Republican* 11 June 4 The emigration pouring into the territory [=Kansas] is multitudinous.

2. In obs. combs.: (1) **emigration road,** the Oregon Trail, cf. **emigrant road;** (2) **Emigration Society,** (see quot. and cf. **Emigrant Aid Company, Society**); (3) **emigration train,** =**emigrant train** (*b*).

(1) **1852** STANSBURY *Gt. Salt Lake* 15 We followed the 'emigration road,' (already broad and well beaten as any turnpike in our country,) over a rolling prairie, fringed on the south with trees. **1862** R. F. BURTON *City of Saints* 16 Landing in Bleeding Kansas . . . we fell at once into 'Emigration Road,' a great thoroughfare, . . . and undoubtedly the best and the longest natural highway in the world. — (2) **1815** *Niles' Reg.* VIII. 39/1 A 'New England *Emigration* Society' has been established in Boston, 'for the purpose of promoting emigration to the western country.' — (3) *a***1861** WINTHROP *J. Brent* 83 There comes a Salt Lake emigration train.

As the last term in **carpetbag, Mormon emigration.**

***eminent domain.** *Law.* Superior power, authority, or absolute ownership inherent in the federal government or in a state government.

"In Eng. this term is rarely used exc. in connexion with matters of international law. In Am. it is commonly employed to denote the power of expropriation exercised within its own borders by the Federal Government or an individual State" (Horwill 118/2).

1854 in HAMBLETON *H. A. Wise* 23 [In 1787 the U.S. established] the most perfect system of eminent domain, of proprietary titles, and of territorial settlements, which the world had ever beheld to bless the homeless children of men. **1885** INGLE *Local Institutions Va.* 35 An Act of [colonial] Virginia legislators . . . stretched the doctrine of eminent domain to the borders of modern socialism.

b. ***right of eminent domain,** the right of the federal government or of a state government to obtain private property, upon payment of a reasonable compensation, for public use without the owner's consent.

1853 WHARTON *Pa. Digest* 673 § 3 The right of eminent domain, or inherent sovereign power gives the Legislature the control of private property for public use. **1906** *N.Y. Ev. Post* 16 June (resort section) 4 The shores of all these reservoir lakes belong to the State, sufficient land around each for the establishment of a 'flow line' having been given by right of eminent domain.

fig. and *transf.* **1867** HOLMES *Guardian Angel* 234 Clement came into the family circle with the right of eminent domain over the realm of Susan's affections. **1903** E. JOHNSON *Railway Transportation* 307 The state must grant to the corporation 'the right of eminent domain' in order to enable the corporation to secure the real estate required for its roadway and structures.

***Emmanuel,** *n.* **Emmanuel movement,** a movement originated in the Emmanuel Protestant Episcopal Church of Boston, in 1906, by Rev. Elwood Worcester and Rev. Samuel McComb, which aimed, in the case of nervous diseases, to combine mental and moral healing with scientific medical practices.

1908 *Outlook* 90, 704 In yet another direction the Emmanuel Movement has proved of substantial worth—in the direction of emphasizing anew the genuine therapeutic value of faith and prayer.

b. Emmanuelism, the doctrines of those who participated in the Emmanuel movement.

1909 *No. Amer. Rev.* CLXXXIX. 231 When one of the high priests of Emmanuelism, Dr. McComb, is said to have stated in the Trinity Church parish house in Buffalo that ninety per cent. of the people can be hypnotized, it is reasonable to suppose that the reverend gentleman had had experience.

c. Emmanuelist, one who believes in and practices Emmanuelism.

1909 *Springfield W. Republican* 25 Feb. 2 The prompt answer made by the Emmanuelists was an arrangement by which a medical examination was to be made in every case.

Emmonsism 'ɛmənz,ɪzəm, *n.* Also **Emmonism.** The principles or teachings of Nathanael Emmons (1745–1840), a New England divine. *Obs.* — **1853** M. BLAKE *Mendon Assoc.* 30 That scheme [of theology] . . . has been called Edwardean, Hopkinsian, sometimes Emmonsism. It is a system which . . . exalts and honors God as the Sovereign Ruler of His creatures, and abases man. **1882** SCHAFF *Religious Encycl.* I. 721 These eight statements . . . characterize Emmonism as it is grafted upon Hopkinsianism.

***Emory,** *n.* [W. H. *Emory* (1811–87), Amer. soldier and engineer.] **1. Emory('s) oak,** the black oak, *Quercus emoryi*, of the western U.S. **2. Emory's opuntia,** (see quot.).

(1) **1877** *Atlantic Mo.* Oct. 406/2 Here and there is a bunch of the rare western Emory's oak, that, like several other plants, seems to have wandered in from . . . the great Colorado River of Arizona. **1948** *Desert Mag.* Feb. 8/2 Very drouth resistant, the Blackjack or Bellota (everyday names of Emory oak) grows to 250 feet. — (2) **1911** WOOTON *Cacti in N.M.* 32 Emory's Opuntia (named after Colonel E. [*sic*] H. Emory, who had charge of the first Mexican Boundary Survey) has large, fleshy joints 4 or 5 inches long.

***emperor,** *n.*

1. A chief or leader of an Indian tribe. *Obs.* Cf. **Indian emperor.**

1654 in THURLOE *State P.* (1742) 273 Whilst the house was building for the great emperor of Roanoke, he undertook with some of his Indians, to bring some of our men to the emperor of the Tuskarorawes. **1749** *Ga. Col. Rec.* VI. 252 He arrived with three Chiefs from the Creek-Nation (Vizt) Malatchee, whom they call the Emperor and two others. **1820** in MORSE *Rep. Indian Affairs* (1822) II. 33 It appears that he [=the Brachie] is the first Emperor of these tribes.

b. As a title. *Obs.*

1699 *Va. State P.* I. 62 That Indian, commonly known by the name of the Emperour Piscattoway, . . . fled from . . . Maryland.

2. emperor goose, an Alaska goose, *Philacte canagica*, having beautifully colored plumage.

1872 COUES *Key N.A. Birds* 283 Painted Goose. Emperor Goose. Wavy bluish-gray, with lavender or lilac tinting. **1940** GABRIELSON & JEWETT *Birds Ore.* 129 The Emperor Geese usually arrive here as single birds mingling with other species or in small bands of three to six.

***empire,** *n.*

1. (*cap.*) A member of the Empire Club. *Rare.*

1845 *New York W. Tribune* 29 Nov. 5/5 We have not heard of one of the 'Empires' favoring the new party.

2. (*cap.*) =**Invisible Empire.** *Obs.*

*c***1868** in *Cong. Comm. on Southern States* XIII. 36 The Grand Wizard, who is the supreme officer of the empire. **1877** BEARD *K.K.K. Sketches* 74 The Grand Division, or Empire, was subdivided into Realms, Provinces, and Dens. **1880** TOURGEE *Invisible Empire* iv, With the foregoing ideas as to the origin of this formidable 'Empire,' the vast area of territory it controlled [etc.].

3. In combs.: (1) **Empire City,** see as a main entry; (2) **Club,** an auxiliary club of Tammany Hall, esp. influential *c*1844; (3) **plow,** (see quot.), *obs.;* (4) **State,** see as a main entry.

(2) **1844** *New York W. Tribune* 5 Oct. 4/2 The attempt of the Empire Club to pass through that part of Canal-street in which at least 20,000 Whigs were assembled was of itself an act of violence. **1928** ASBURY *Gangs of N.Y.* 43 About 1843 he [*sc.* Captain Rynders] organized the Empire Club, which became the political center of the Sixth Ward and the clearing house of all gangster activities which had to do with politics. — (3) **1850** *Cultivator* VII. 369 The 'Empire' ploughs with wrought steel mould boards, made with bar shares and wrought iron standards, . . . are superseding all other ploughs.

As the last term in **Golden, Grand, Inland, Invisible, Pacific, Southern, Universal Empire.**

Empire City. A nickname for New York City because of its extensive manufacturing and commerce. Also *Empire City of America, of the Western World.*

1838 UNCLE SAM in *Bentley's Misc.* IV. 48 We soon reached the place of debarkation at the bottom of a street so quiet . . . as to afford a curious contrast to the bustle and noise of the empire city. **1861** fn *Jrnl. Ill. State Hist. Soc.* (1948) Sep. 308 There can be no disunionist, there can be no enemy in this Union, in the Empire City of America. **1866** *Wilkes' Spirit of Times* 3 March 13/2 The Empire City of the Western World . . . has long been far behind the age in the erection of Music Halls. **1944** *Newsweek* 24 July 82/3 The Empire City meeting is typical of wartime racing, which, as I have tried to hint, is slightly askew.

Empire State. The state of New York.

"The sobriquet was not, as has been fancied, assumed by its citizens out of State pride or vanity. It was inferentially given to it by General Washington. In his reply to the address of the Common Council of New York City, signed by 'James Duane, Mayor,' and bearing date 'Dec. 2d, 1784,' he says: 'I pray that Heaven bestow its choicest blessings on your city; that a well regulated and beneficial commerce may enrich your citizens, and that your state (at present the seat of Empire) may set [etc.]' " (*Amer. N. & Q.* I. 190).

1834 *Cong. Deb.* 506 We are told, sir, of . . . the empire State of New York. **1885** *Cent. Mag.* April 820 It is no mere figure of speech to call New York the Empire State. **1948** *Ariz. Republic* (Phoenix) 27 Feb. 6/1 The Empire State is 'in the bag' for the GOP.

b. Empire State of the South, a nickname used for (1) Georgia, (2) South Carolina, (3) Texas.

(1) **1855** *N.Y. Herald* 7 Dec. 8/2 The people of the South . . . were rallying to the approved platform of Georgia—the great Empire State of the South. **1948** *Time* 5 July 14/3 They spoke with local pride: Georgia, the empire state of the South . . . the great, free state of Maryland. — (2) **1860** *Charleston* (S.C.) *Mercury* 24 Nov. 4/2 South Carolina is the Empire State of the South—the Captain-General of Resistance. — (3) **1894** *Cong. Rec.* 25 May 5256/2, I live [in] a State which is proud of being called 'the Empire State of the South,' a State which has for its emblem a lone star.

c. Empire State of the West, the state of Illinois. *Rare.*

1862 *Ill. Agric. Soc. Trans.* V. 693 Ours is now the Empire State of the West.

***employ,** *n.* An owner or company of owners of a ship. *Obs.* — **1840** DANA *Two Years* xxxi. 387 High was the reputation of 'the employ' among men and officers, for the character and outfit of their vessels.

***employment,** *n.* In combs.: (1) **employment agency,** =next; (2) **bureau,** an office or agency that facilitates employment by establishing contact between the employee and the employer; (3) **office,** =prec., cf. **public employment office** and see **house of employment.**

(1) **1888** *12th Rep. Ohio Bur. Labor Statistics* 263 'Employment agencies' . . . have very appropriately been characterized as 'a class who trade on the needs of the inexperienced searcher for honest employment.' **1949** *Dly. Oklahoman* (Okla. City) 13 Feb. D. 8/5 Later she established an employment agency. — (2) **1886** *Standard Guide of Washington* 204 Dondore and Morse, Attorneys, prosecute claims before all the departments, also Employment Bureau. **1916** DU PUY *Uncle Sam* 208 The employment bureau immediately supplied her demand. — (3) **1858** *Varieties* (S.F.) 29 May 5/3 M. J. Smith & Co., have opened at 203 Clay street, opposite the Plaza, an employment and general agency office. **1948** *Gainesville* (Tex.) *D. Register* 2 July 5/2 Employers, including farmers, who are needing assistance, are urged to contact the employment office.

***emporium,** *n.* As the last term in **commercial, literary, shine, shoe-shine emporium.**

empresario ˌɛmprəˈsɑrɪo, *n.* [Sp., manager, contractor.] A projector of a colony in Texas when that region belonged to Mexico. Also attrib. Now *hist.*

1821 *Southwestern Hist. Q.* XXXIX. 258 The territory . . . which has usually remained unsettled, begins to be visited by adventurers and empresarios. Some of these take up their residence in the country, pretending that their location has no bearing upon the question of their government's claim or the boundary disputes. **1838** C. NEWELL *Revol. Texas* 185 It may be well to make a few remarks upon Empresario Grants, Texas Land Companies, and their 'Scrip.' **1948** *True* May 123/2 For each hundred families brought in under these terms, Mexico would give to the empresario a grant of 23,040 acres for himself to pay him for his trouble.

emptins ˈɛmptɪnz, *n. pl.* [f. **emptyings.*]

1. Yeast or the yeasty lees of cider, beer, etc. (see quot. 1939). *Colloq.* Cf. **milk emptins, sots.**

1650 in *Essex Antiquarian* VII. 28 Elizabeth Pinion, . . . having come into the house to borrow some emptings, Tobiah took her and threw her. **1839** KIRKLAND *New Home* xviii. 130 Her 'emptins' are the envy of the neighborhood. **1939** *L.A.* Map 290 The term *emptins* (frequently recorded) or *emptin yeast* denotes a kind of liquid leaven formerly much used instead of yeast but now rare. It was often homemade . . . and sometimes carried over from one batch of bread to the next. Emptins were made of potatoes, . . . from the juice of boiled hops, . . . from sour dough, . . . or from a fermentation prepared in bottles set back of the fire place. . . . The term emptins or the preparation so called is regarded as older or old-fashioned, though still in use.

b. *fig.* and *transf.*

1848 LOWELL *Biglow P.* 1 Ser. ix, 131 'Twill take more emptins, a long chalk, than this noo party's gut, To give sech heavy cakes ez them a start. **1848** *Knickerb.* XXXI. 88 They 'laughed consumedly' at the 'empt'in's' of the joke. **1862** LOWELL *Biglow P.* 2 Ser. iii. 109 With ollers room for jes' one more o' your spiled-in-bakin' cusses, Dough 'thout the emptins of a soul, an' yit with means about 'em. **1880** *Scribner's Mo.* Feb. 572/1 Feels as if I could bust into ten thousand emptin's, dey's so agerwatin'.

c. *to run* (*to*) *emptins, emptyings,* (see quot. 1902).

1847 in HAMMOND *Remembrance of Amherst* (1946) 141 (We.), It most plain 'ran emptins' afterward. **1881** *Cong. Rec.* 15 Feb. 1647/1 Mr. Chairman, this bill is nearly played out and is running emptyings. **1895** A. BROWN *Meadow-Grass* 312 The Marden blood run emptin's afore it got to him. **1898** WESTCOTT *D. Harum* 282 Runs a good deal to emptins in his preachin' though, they say. **1902** CLAPIN 173 *To run emptins,* to show signs of not holding out well, as for instance a speech or an enterprise of any kind.

***enabling,** *a.*

1. enabling act, a legislative act making it legal to do something otherwise unlawful. Also an act passed by Congress prescribing the conditions under which a territory may be admitted to the Union as a state.

1856 PIERCE in *Pres. Mess. & P.* V. 358 The States of California, Michigan, and others were self-organized, and as such were admitted into the Union without a previous enabling act of Congress. **1867** *Com. & Fin. Chron.* V. 422/2 A proposed 'enabling act' would permit our city and State bank to withdraw from the National organization, and to bank under State laws. *c***1908** CANTON *Frontier Trails* 234 On June 16, 1906, the Enabling Act was passed, authorizing Oklahoma to become a State. **1947** *Time* 14 July 8/3 Hawaii's enabling act, appropriately dubbed H.R. 49, has been placed on the House calendar for debate.

b. After the Civil War, a similar enactment setting forth the conditions under which a seceding state might return to the Union. *Obs.*

1867 in FLEMING *Hist. Reconstruction* I. 237 Report from Washington says it is probable an enabling act will pass.

2. ***enabling bill,** a bill introduced in Congress prescribing the conditions under which a territory may be admitted into the Union as a state.

1858 *Harper's Mag.* Feb. 400/2 Mr. Douglas . . . submitted an 'enabling bill' authorizing the people of Kansas to form a State Constitution, preparatory to the admission of the Territory into the Union as a State.

***enamel,** *n.* (See quots.) — **1832** *Deb. Congress* 13 Nov. App. 31 The last layer [of the road] which will make up the nine inches, and will constitute its enamel, or wearing surface. **1924** *Publisher's Wkly.* CVI. 390/1 Enamel—Another name for coated paper.

enameled cloth. (See quot.) — **1889** *Cent.* 1056/3 American cloth, a name given in Great Britain to a cotton cloth prepared with a glazed or varnished surface to imitate morocco leather: known in the United States as *enameled cloth.*

Encelia ɛnˈsiliə, *n.* [Said in source of our 1925 quot. to have been so named for C. Encel, a writer on oak galls.] A genus of American plants of the daisy family, characterized by brittle stems, small, crowded leaves, and yellow flowers. Also (not *cap.*) a flower of this genus. Cf. **brittlebush.**

1893 COVILLE *Death Valley Exped.* 50 Of the forty-one shrubs examined, only four, *Aster mohavensis, Atriplex hymenelytra,* and the two *Enceliæ,* have leaves whose surface area exceeds 1 sq. cm. **1912** LUMHOLTZ *New Trails* 313 The larger species was an *encelia.* **1925** W. L. JEPSON *Manual Flowering Plants* 1081 Encèlia. . . . Ours low shrubs or suffrutescent plants. **1946** *Desert Mag.* Mar. 30/2 Encelia began blossoming in late January.

***enchanter,** *n.* (See quot.) *Colloq.* Cf. ***fascinator.** — **1908** *Scribner's Mag.* Feb. 177 A scant worsted 'enchanter' or 'fascinator,' I think she called it, thrown over her head and shoulders.

enchilada ˌɛntʃɪˈlɑdə, *n. S.W.* [Amer. Sp. in same sense.] A tortilla, usu. rolled with meat inside, served with a hot sauce containing chili.

1895 *Amer. Folk-Lore* Jan.–Apr. 62 *Enchiladas* are practically corn fritters allowed to simmer for a moment in chile sauce, and then served hot with a sprinkling of grated cheese and onion. **1912** SAUNDERS *Indian Terraced Houses* 75 What is the difference, then, between the *enchiladas* and the *tamales?* **1948** *L.A. Times* 14 Jan. I. 4/1 We do, of course, have enchiladas at the Farmers Market.

encina ɛnˈsinə, *n. S.W.* [Sp. in same sense.] (See quots.)

[**1772** ULLOA *Noticias Americanas* 102 La hoja es menuda y gruesa al modo de las *Encinas*.] **1910** JEPSON *Silva of Calif.* 226 The Coast Live Oak, or Encina of the Spanish Californians, is distributed in the Coast Range from Sonoma County to Southern and Lower California. **1914** SAUNDERS *With Flowers & Trees* 11 In the language of Spanish-Californians the valley oak, which is deciduous, is called *roble*, and the live oak, *encino* or *encina*. **1938** VAN DERSAL *Native Woody Plants* 334 Encina (*Quercus agrifolia*).

encinal ˌɛnsiˈnɑl, *n. S.W.* [Sp., an oak grove.] An oak grove, a park-like area featured by clusters of *Quercus agrifolia*. Also as a place-name.

1856 *Monterey* (Calif.) *Sentinel* 3 Feb. 1/3 The site . . . was covered with oaks, forming a beautiful park or *encinal*. **1856** *S.F. Bulletin* 13 May 1/2, I wonder why you can't find time to go over to the Eden of California, the Encinal, and take a stroll. **1907** HODGE *Amer. Indians* I. 422 Encinal. . . . Formerly a summer village of the Lagunas, now a permanently occupied pueblo, situated 6 m. n.w. of Laguna, N. Mex. **1933** *Amer. Sp.* Oct. 9/2 This termination 'al' (place where) is often used with words denoting a characteristic growth, as *chaparral*, place of the brush, . . . *encinal*, place of the encinas oak.

attrib. **1943** DICE *Biotic Provinces No. Amer.* 58 The encinal belt covers most of the hills and lower slopes of the mountains. This belt is dominated by oaks of several species.

* **end,** *n.*

1. In football, one of the two players stationed at either end of the scrimmage line. Also the position of such a player.

1892 *Outing* Dec. 50/1 Long gains at the tackles, ends, and around the ends, were common. **1893** STAGG & WILLIAMS *Amer. Football* 43 In defending his territory against these runs the end stands at the most remote part of the field for assistance to help him. **1922** ZUPPKE *Football Technique* 42 As a rule a rangy man is better suited for the position of end than a short man. **1944** *Greeley* (Colo.) *D. Tribune* 24 Sep. 2/1 The Wizards team is well spiked with veterans this year having a veteran backfield, two ends and a letterman tackle.

2. A share, portion, part, side.

1907 in ASHER & HEAL (1942) *Send No Money* 115 After the genial and affable derelicts in the money changing end received the money, the incident was apparently closed, at least no stove has arrived. **1926** J. BLACK *You Can't Win* ix. 105 Didn't him and Smiler bring it [=$200] up here for my end of that chippy gambling house's bank-roll? **1928** *Publishers' Wkly.* 30 June 2598 To talk to such a person about the editorial end of a publishing business means little or nothing.

3. In combs.: (1) **end gate,** a board at the rear end of a wagon body that may be removed to facilitate loading or unloading, a tailboard, also attrib. and fig.; (2) **line,** *football* (see quot.); (3) **man,** in a minstrel show, a man at either end of a row of performers, also transf.; (4) **run,** in football, a run around the end of an opponent's line; (5) **rush, rusher,** in football, a player stationed at or near one end of the line of attack or defense, an end *q.v.;* (6) **-s man,** a paddler at one end of a canoe, *obs.;* (7) **table,** a table suitable for use at the end of a davenport or couch; (8) **town,** a town at the temporary extremity of a line of railroad under construction; (9) **woman,** (see quot.), *obs.;* (10) **zone,** *football* (see quot.).

(1) 1873 *Newton Kansan* 15 May 2/2 An iron end gate rod was thrust easily into the excavation. **1905** *Emporia* (Kans.) *Gaz.* 3 March, Henry kept right on lamming the end gate of the band wagon of reform with a poker. **1911** QUICK *Yellowstone Nights* 316 The end gates were jerked out. — **(2) 1916** BANCROFT *Handbook* 219 End line. Farthest line bounding the end zone, or end of the field of play. — **(3) 1865** SALA *Diary* II. 395 He propounded conundrums to his brother 'end man' who played the banjo. **1884** *Science* IV. 113 A very long series of resolutions, expressing the sentiments of a few endmen on most of the open questions in the broad sphere of modern life, were approved. **1947** PAUL *Linden* 346 The end men crack most of the jokes, using the interlocutor as straight man. — **(4) 1902** *Chi. Record-Herald* 28 Sep. III. 1/4 Perkins made a fifteen-yard end run. **(5) 1887** *Cent. Mag.* XXXIV. 891/2 The two players on the ends of the line, the 'end-rushes,' stand slightly back of the main line. **1893** STAGG & WILLIAMS *Amer. Football* 43 The end-rusher has to meet the runner under most trying circumstances. **1905** *McClure's Mag.* June 121 Brown, . . . end-rush of the football eleven, is having some difficulty in selecting a college. — **(6) 1807** *Mass. H.S. Coll.* 2 Ser. III. 36 After the whale-fishery was introduced, the Indians were employed in that service; and they made excellent oarsmen, and some of them were good endsmen. — **(7) 1851** CIST *Cincinnati* 206 Circular, center, card, and end tables. **1946** *Ft. Collins Coloradoan* 13 June 2/5 Auction Sale . . . floor lamp; 2 rocking chairs; end table. — **(8) 1938** ASBURY *Sucker's Prog.* 339 Cheyenne, probably the most notorious of the 'end towns,' was settled when the Union Pacific Railroad reached there in 1867. — **(9) 1851** HALL *College Words* 111 At Bowdoin College, 'end women,' says a correspondent, 'are the venerable females who officiate as chambermaids in the different entries.' They are so called from the entries being placed at the ends of the buildings. **(10) 1916** BANCROFT *Handbook* 219 End-zone. Ten-yard territory between the end line and the goal line.

b. (*to play*) *both ends against the middle,* (see quots.). *Colloq.* or *slang.*

1938 ASBURY *Sucker's Prog.* 15 Both ends against the middle—A method of trimming cards for dealing a brace game of Faro. A dealer who used such a pack was said to be 'playing both ends against the middle.' *Ib.*, Strippers were cut in various ways, the most popular being hollows, rounds, rakes, wedges, and concave and convex, also known as 'both ends against the middle.'

As the last term in **bone, booster, business, butt, cardboard, daylight, Maryland, south end.**

* **Endeavorer,** *n.* A member of the Young People's Society of Christian Endeavor, an organization which began in 1881. *Colloq.* Cf. **Christian Endeavor.**

1896 *Harper's Wkly.* 22 Aug. 822/2, I found restless Endeavorers still going into and coming out of their state-rooms. **1899** *Chi. Record* 23 Oct. 2/6 Services were also conducted at the jails and hospitals by the Endeavorers. **1922** *Dly. Press* (Ardmore, Okla.) 2 May 3/1 All the Endeavorers and friends are invited to attend this social gathering.

* **ender,** *n.* As the last term in **bitter, butt, double, Point, south, tail ender.**

ending stone. In a flour mill, a stone which removes the ends of the grains of wheat. *Obs.* — **1883** *Harper's Mag.* June 76/1 Now the ending-stones are encountered, which break the germinal point off each grain.

* **endowment,** *n.*

1. In the Mormon Church, a course of instruction concerning ordinances and dispensations, often *pl.* Also attrib.

1843 MARRYAT *Adv. M. Violet* xxxix, In the evening, they met for the endowment. *Ib.*, In 1836, an endowment meeting, or solemn assembly, was called, to be held in the temple at Kirkland. **1881** MARSHALL *Through Amer.* 170 No one, I believe, outside Mormonism is aware of the actual nature of the endowments which a person receives in order . . . [to] be taken into the bosom of the Church. **1892** GUNTER *Miss Dividends* 204 My daughter *shall* take her endowments!

b. endowment house, the house in which the endowment is given (see also quot. 1858).

1858 *Harper's Wkly.* 11 Sep. 605/2 In the next corner of the block stands the Endowment House, in which are conferred the mysterious degrees of Mormon priesthood. **1912** BIRGE *Awakening Desert* 342 In the earlier days of Salt Lake City, this ceremony was performed in a large adobe structure, known as the Endowment House. **1948** *Pacific Spectator* Summer 321 According to the Endowment House Records, they were married on September 11, 1857.

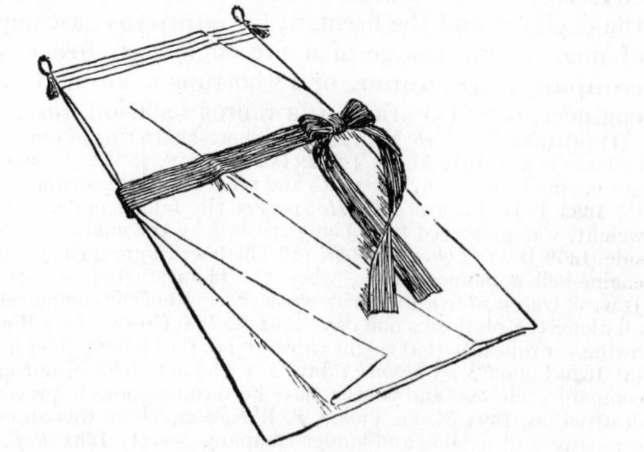

One form of endowment robe

c. endowment robe, an undergarment bestowed upon a Mormon during the endowment rites.

1875 *Chi. Tribune* 8 Dec. 12/4 The couple [bride and bridegroom] . . . are then enjoined never to take off their 'Endowment Robes.' . . . These garments are worn under the nether clothing, and are worn by all orthodox Mormons, even to the day of their death, and then they serve as a shroud. **1883** SCHAFF *Religious Encycl.* 1579/1 An endowment robe; which sacred undergarment is always thereafter to be worn next to the person, carefully shrouding it at the last for its burial.

2. endowment assurance, insurance, a form of life insurance providing for the payment of a fixed sum at a specified time, or a stated amount to designated beneficiaries if the insured dies before the term has expired. Also attrib.

1865 *Nation* I. 157 Endowment Assurance Policies . . . are issued to persons desirous of making provisions for advanced life. **1895** E. CARROLL *Principles Finance* 298 Insurance is divided into Accident and Casualty Insurance, Endowment Insurance, Fire Insurance, Life Insurance, Marine Insurance, etc. **1915** GLOVER *Endowment Insurance* 1 (*caption*), Net Single Premiums per $1000 Endowment Insurance.

b. Also **endowment plan, policy.**

1871 *Harper's Mag.* Aug. 477 Upon rounding a point of rocks, who should I see but Benjamin P. Gunn, seated on the very edge of the crater, explaining the endowment plan to his guide. **1878** CONKLIN *Arizona* 176 She doesn't believe in the endowment policy. **1947** *Coronet* April 21/2 Investigation revealed that the depositor was a large-scale dealer in black-market liquor, who had invested a lot of illicit cash in big endowment policies.

engagé ˌɑngɑˈʒe, *n. N.W.* [Can. F. in same sense.] A canoeman or boatman employed by fur traders and explorers, a voyageur. Now *hist.*

1800 J. MAUDE *Niagara* 176 The *Engagés* (for so the bateau men are called) are always French Canadians. **1836** J. HALL *Statistics of West* xii. 223 Their lading [of the birch canoes] is . . . made up into packages, . . . and these are transported over portages, on the backs of the *engagées*, by means of straps passed over the forehead. **1947** DEVOTO *Across Wide Missouri* 119 At least fifty engagés were always in residence at the fort.

Engelmann spruce. [George *Engelmann* (1809–84), a Missouri botanist.] A Rocky Mountain and northwestern spruce, *Picea engelmanni*, the wood of which is similar to white pine. Also **Engelmann's fir.**

1908 *Bot. Gazette* May 333 The two trees that dominate the society are the Engelmann spruce (*Picea Engelmanni*) and the subalpine fir (*Abies lasiocarpa*). **1912** WOOTON & STANDLEY *Grasses N.M.* 13 Its characteristic trees and shrubs are the Siberian Juniper, . . . Engelmann's Fir, . . . two or three species of Currants, . . . and a low Willow. **1946** *Gunnison* (Colo.) *News-Champion* 2 May 1/1 Minimum price fixed by appraisal is $2.25 per thousand feet board measures for live Engelmann spruce and Douglas fir saw timber.

attrib. **1924** HAWKINS *Trees & Shrubs Yellowstone* 41 Their worst enemy is a careless man and the next worse is the Engelmann spruce beetle.

***engine,** *n.* In combs.: (1) **engine bell,** (*a*) a bell in the engine room of a steamboat to transmit signals from the pilot to the engineer, (*b*) a bell on a railroad locomotive used for giving warning of its approach; (2) **cab,** the covered part of a locomotive that serves as a shelter for the engineer and the fireman; (3) **company,** a company of men having charge of a fire engine, cf. **fire engine company;** (4) **runner,** one who runs a locomotive, an engineer, *rare;* (5) **station,** a railroad station, *rare.*

(1) (*a*) **1845** *Knickerb.* XXV. 59 The short, sharp ring of our engine-bell was heard. **1876** MARK TWAIN *Old Times* iv. 70 We . . . snatched our engine-bells out by the roots and piled on all the steam we had. (*b*) **1883** J. D. FULTON *Sam Hobart* 223 He, falling under the huge weight, was preserved from being crushed by the engine-bell at his side. **1899** JEWETT *Queen's Twin* 108 There was a great ringing of the engine-bell a moment after, when the train started. — (2) **1899** JEWETT *Queen's Twin* 107 There was a cheer out of the engine-cab and all along the platforms one day. **1902** A. MACGOWAN *Last Word* 11 Swing yer rope into that engine cab and jerk that feller out fer me. — (3) **1820** *Columbian Centinel* 1 Jan. 2/4 The activities of our engine companies, citizens and youths, have been conspicuous in preventing destruction. **1894** MARK TWAIN *P. Wilson* xi, There was an engine company and a hook-and-ladder company. — (4) **1881** *Rep. Ala. R.R. Comm.* I. 196 Does your company arrange the night service of engine runners? — (5) **1850** *Hunt's Merch. Mag.* XXII. 286 The company have engines capable of carrying 500 passengers from the engine station in New York to Albany.

b. *To run with the engine,* =*to run with the machine, q.v. s.v.* ***machine.** *Obs.*

1856 *Louisville Democrat* 4 Oct. 2/2 We all run with 1854 engine, and when there is a fire in a 'foreigner's' house, probably we break things *some*.

As the last term in **Consolidated, Corliss, deadhead, freight, helper, hog, mogul, mountain, musical steam, Negro, panhandle, pony, prairie, road, shifting, suction, switch, wild engine.**

***engineer,** *n.* One who runs a locomotive. Also transf.

1832 *Amer. R.R. Jrnl.* I. 356/2 Engineers and attendants on the Engine (ass'd) 7 per diem. **1878** BEADLE *Western Wilds* 53, I took a position as engineer of a six-mule team. **1946** *Chi. D. News* 10 July 11/2 The engineer was killed and several passengers shaken up.

b. Engineer Corps, in the U.S. Army, the Corps of Engineers.

1836 JACKSON in *Pres. Mess. & P.* III. 255 The recommendations of an increase in the Engineer Corps . . . [were] submitted to you in my last annual message. **1898** PAGE *Red Rock* 281, I was in the Engineer Corps under Grant.

As the last term in **chief, county, division, government, locomotive, reclamation, steamboat, switch engineer.**

***engineer,** *v. tr.* To guide, manage, or conduct (an enterprise or individual).

1859 COX *8 Years Congress* (1865) 99 [He] undertakes to engineer a resolution through this House for the expulsion of a brother member. **1883** *American* VI. 117 Politicians just as slippery as any who engineered the great fraud of Mr. Polk's election. **1948** *Time* 6 Sep. 18/2 He had tried to engineer a pool to raise the price of Devoe & Raynolds common stock.

***English,** *a.* and *n.*

1. *n.* (See quot. 1889.) Also transf.

1869 MARK TWAIN *Innocents Abroad* 116 In making a shot you had to allow for the curve or you would infallibly put the 'English' on the wrong side of the ball. **1889** *Cent.* 1932/3 English, . . . in billiards, a twisting or spinning motion imparted by a quick stroke on one side to the cue-ball. . . . The word *English* is generally used only when the ball glances after impact in a direction more or less sharply angular from the object-ball or cushion. **1945** *Democrat* 4 Jan. 1/6 Lee writes that the fox came in to attack him but that he hit it on the head, putting so much English on the stick that he broke it. **1948** *Time* 25 Oct. 88/3 Some 70 years ago, Billiard Fan McConnell reputedly discovered that 'English' could be used on baseballs, then organized a ball team that was undefeated for several seasons before batters caught on.

2. *a.* In the names of, or with reference to, plants: (1) **English bean,** prob. the broad bean, *Vicia faba, obs.;* (2) **corn,** see as a main entry; (3) **grain,** grain of the kinds usu. grown in England; (4) **hawthorn,** a species of European hawthorn, *Crataegus oxyacantha*, used for ornament or hedges; (5) **pea,** see as a main entry; (6) **plantain,** the rib grass or ribwort, *Plantago lanceolata;* (7) **potato,** the Irish potato, *obs.;* (8) **sloe,** the blackthorn, *Prunus spinosa;* (9) **thorn,** =**English hawthorn;** (10) **walnut,** see as a main entry; (11) **wheat,** wheat of a kind commonly grown in England, *obs.*

(1) **1697** SEWALL *Diary* I. 455 Betty gets her Mother a Mess of English Beans. **1790** S. DEANE *N.-Eng. Farmer* 19/1 The English bean, to which the name Windsor is applied. — (3) **1619** *Va. House of Burgesses* 17 Wee bee very desirous to falle to the sowinge of all sorts of our Englishe grain. **1742** *Mass. Pub. Col. Soc.* VI. 24, I . . . oblige myself . . . to give him one half of all the ingles grain I rese [=raise] Evrey year. **1873** BLAKE *Hist. Warwick, Mass.* 111 In many places the soil is so rocky and broken as to render it unfit for cultivation: in other places, tolerable good; not so suitable for English grain as for grass, corn, and potatoes. — (4) **1858** WARDER *Hedges & Evergreens* 24 In the United States, there are many handsome hedges of the English hawthorn, which are entirely effective. **1897** SUDWORTH *Arborescent Flora* 221 English Hawthorn . . . is widely introduced in the United States by cultivation, and in many localities in the Eastern States has escaped and become thoroughly naturalized.

(6) **1843** TORREY *Flora N.Y.* II. 15 *Plantago Lanceolata.* . . . Rib-grass. English Plantain. . . . Fields and upland meadows, very common. . . . This plant is eaten by all kinds of stock. **1894** *Amer. Folk-Lore* VII. 96 *Plantago lanceolata*, . . . buckhorn plantain, ripple, ribwort, English plantain, West Va. — (7) **1750** J. BIRKET *Cursory Remarks* 9 They have . . . abundance of . . . English or whats commonly called Irish Potatoes. **1800** W. TATHAM *Agric. & Commerce* 60 If you plant *Irish* (or English) potatoes (thus distinguished from sweet potatoes), the same year will give you four crops. — (8) **1817–8** EATON *Botany* (1822) 412 *Prunus spinosa*, english sloe. . . . Said to be introduced. **1836** LINCOLN *Botany* App. 129. — (9) **1843** TORREY *Flora N.Y.* I. 221 *Crataegus oxyacantha* . . . Hawthorn. English Thorn. . . . Hedges and fields; a native of Europe, but naturalized in some places. May. **1847** DARLINGTON *Weeds & Plants* 131 Sharp-Thorned Cratægus. Hawthorn, English Thorn.

(11) **1617** *Va. Co. of Lon. Doc. Rec.* III. 71 English wheate, barly, Indyan Corne . . . greate plenty in the ground. **1698** G. THOMAS *Acc. Pa.* 21 They have commonly Two Harvests in the Year; First, of English Wheat, and next of Buck, (or French) Wheat. **1751** MACSPARRAN *Diary* 45 My two Negro's plowing in ye Buckwheat as Manure for English wheat.

b. In similar combs. sufficiently defined in the quots., as (1) **English bluegrass,** (2) **cherry,** (3) **daisy,** (4) **grass,** see as a main entry; (5) **ivy,** (6) *** -man's foot,** (7) **maple,** (8) **mulberry,** (9) **rye grass,** (10) **strawberry,** (11) **thistle,** (12) **watercress.**

(1) **1889** Vasey *Agric. Grasses* 65 *Poa Compressa* (English Blue Grass; Wire Grass). This species has sometimes been confounded with the Kentucky bluegrass.... It thrives well on clay or hard, trodden, and poor soils. **1901** Mohr *Plant Life Ala.* 384 *Poa compressa*, English Blue Grass.... Valuable pasture grass. — (2) **1799** *Poughkeepsie* (N.Y.) *Jrnl.* 31 Dec. 1/2 Also, about 50 large English cherries, and a great variety of other fruit. **1892** Apgar *Trees Northern U.S.* 99 *Prunus ovium.* (Bird-cherry or English Cherry.) ... This is the Cherry tree ... of which there are many named varieties usually cultivated for the fruit. — (3) **1899** Going *Flowers* 347 The little pink-tipped English daisy, so tenderly reared in New-England gardens, is in its own country a troublesome lawn weed. **1944** *Seed Ann.* 38 Bellis (English Daisy). Familiar dwarf hardy perennial with bright double flowers. Excellent for edging spring flower-beds. Stands the winter if given protection.... White, Mixed, Pink.

(5) **1817-8** Eaton *Botany* (1822) 299 *Hedera helix*, english ivy. **1944** *Seed Ann.* 77 *Hedera Helix.* English Ivy. Fine for under trees, on banks or against walls. Good trailing or climb-plant. — (6) **1687** Clayton *Va.* in *Phil. Trans.* XLI. 145 As to our Plantain, or the *Heptapleuron*, they [Virginian Indians] call it the Englishman's-foot. **1876** Hobbs *Bot. Hand-Book* 35 Englishman's foot, Plantain, Plantago major. — (7) **1892** Apgar *Trees Northern U.S.* 87 *Acer campestre.* (English or Cork-bark Maple.) ... A low ... round-headed tree, with the twigs and smaller branches covered with corky bark. — (8) **1743** Catesby *Carolina* App. p. xxi, *Morus fructu nigro.* The English Mulberry-Tree. The common black mulberry produces not so large fruit as they do in England. — (9) **1878** Killebrew *Tennessee Grasses* 98 English Rye Grass, *Lolium perenne*, ... is said to impoverish land rapidly. **1944** *Vaughan's Gardening* 116 English or Perennial Rye Grass (*Lolium perenne*) a lawn grass where quick results are wanted.

(10) **1817-8** Eaton *Botany* (1822) 282 *Fragaria vesca*, english strawberry. E[xotic]. **1847** Darlington *Weeds & Plants* 123 Eatable Fragaria. English Strawberry. Garden Strawberry. — (11) **1894** *Amer. Folk-Lore* VII. 90 *Dipsacus sylvestris*, ... English thistle, water-thistle, West Va. — (12) **1817-8** Eaton *Botany* (1822) 460 *Sisymbrium nasturtium*, english watercress. **1840** Dewey *Mass. Flowering Plants* 36 *Sisymbrium nasturtium*, L. English Water Cress, ... introduced from England.

3. In the names of birds and other animals: (1) **English duck,** (see quots.); (2) **gray,** a variety of chicken, *obs.;* (3) **herring,** the summer herring, *Pomolobus aestivalis;* (4) **-man's fly,** (see quot.), *obs.;* (5) **mockingbird,** (see quot.), *obs.;* (6) **rail,** (see quot.); (7) **robin,** (see quots.); (8) **snipe,** Wilson's snipe, *Capella delicata;* (9) **sparrow,** (see quot. 1917).

(1) **1838** Gosse *Letters* 158 Of these last (*Anas moschata*) there is always a troop of all ages and sizes; it is the only duck *patronised;* the 'English duck,' as our common species is called, being kept only as a curiosity. **1917** *Birds of Amer.* I. 114 Mallard. *Anas platyrhynchos.* ... Other Names.—Common Wild Duck; Stock Duck; English Duck. — (2) **1849** *N. Eng. Farmer* I. 386 [Among chickens] *English Grays* were exhibited by Linus Mantry. — (3) **1817** *N.Y. Herald* 6 Aug. 2/4 Great numbers of Herrings, erroneously called English, have entered the principal rivers in the District of Maine, particularly the Sheepsent and Kennebec. **1884** Goode *Fisheries* I. 582 The *C. æstivalis* is the 'Glut' Herring of the Albemarle and the Chesapeake, and the 'English' Herring of the Ogeechee River — (4) **1778** Anburey *Travels* II. 282 The Indians ... have no word for a bee, and therefore they call them by the name of the Englishman's Fly.

(5) **1810** Wilson *Ornithology* II. 22 The first, or Brown Thrush, from its inferiority of song being called the French, and the other the English mockingbird. A mode of expression probably originating in the prejudices of our forefathers; with whom every thing French was inferior to every thing English. — (6) **1884** *Nat. Hist. N.Y., Zoology* II. 262 The Sora Rail. *Ortygometra carolina.* ... The Sora or Soree, English Rail or Coot of the Southern States. — (7) **1848** S. F. Cooper *Rural Hours* I. 16 The early colonists gave to the gaudy oriole the name of 'English robin,' showing how fondly memory coloured all they had left behind, since one bird is very plain in his plumage, the other remarkably brilliant. **1917** *Wilson Bul.* June 83 *Icterus galbula.*—English robin, Bernardston, Mass. *Passerina ciris.*—English robin, Gloucester, N.C. — (8) **1812** Wilson *Ornithology* VI. 18 Snipe: *Scolopax gallinago:* ... is usually known by the name of the English Snipe, to distinguish it from the Woodcock. **1917** *Birds of Amer.* I. 227 Wilson's Snipe.... Other Names.—Common Snipe; English Snipe; American Snipe. — (9) **1876** *Field & Forest* Oct. 65 The English sparrows lately imported, did good service in some counties in destroying the pests. **1917** *Birds of Amer.* III. 18 The English Sparrow or European House Sparrow was introduced into America in 1850. In the fall of that year eight pairs were brought to Brooklyn, N.Y. and liberated the following spring. **1949** Calif. Acad. Sciences *News Letter* Feb. 2 Who would guess that birds live here—except for park pigeons and English sparrows?

4. In miscellaneous combs.: (1) **English basement,** a basement on the level of the ground or approximately so; (2) **breakfast tea,** congou or a similar kind of black tea; (3) **coal,** cannel coal, *obs.;* (4) **harvest,** the harvest of English corn or the time of such harvest, *obs.;* (5) **house,** a wooden house such as the English colonists in America built, *obs.;* (6) *** Indian,** ?an Indian servant of an English colonist, *obs.;* (7) **monkey,** a preparation of cheese resembling Welsh rarebit; (8) **pasture,** a pasture sown with English grass, *obs.;* (9) **school,** see as a main entry; (10) **wigwam,** (see quot. 1939), now *hist.*

(1) **1861** *Vanity Fair* 9 Feb. 62/1 Freestone front, all modern improvements, English basement, three stories and attic. **1947** *Chi. Tribune* 26 Oct. v. 4/4 Own your own apt. in unusually fine English

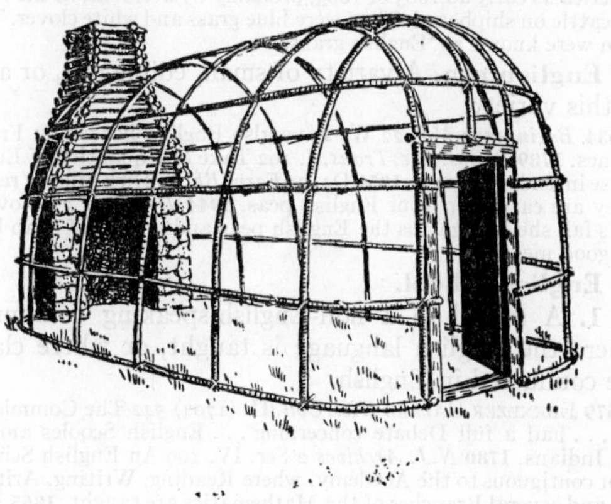

English wigwam

bsmt. 4 apt. bldg. — (2) **1877** Phelps *Story of Avis* 169 Barbara [was] ... capable of bringing the English breakfast-tea in a lotus-leaf. **1943** Farmer *Boston Cook Book* 36 Some familiar black teas are Oolong, Formosa, English Breakfast, etc. — (3) **1847** Collins *Kentucky* 491 The cannel or English coal, of a very superior quality, is also found in great abundance along the banks of these rivers. — (4) **1643** *Mass. Bay Rec.* II. 37 Two bigger Corts are to be kept there, the one between the English and Indian harvest, and the other in the spring. **1761** Niles *Indian Wars* II. 449 He went with his father ... to gather in his English harvest and hay.

(5) [**1624** Smith *Generall Historie* 145 The [Indian] King dwelling but in a Cottage, he [George Thorp] built him a faire house after the English fashion.] **1654** *N.C. Col. Rec.* I. 18, I dispatched ... a carpenter, to build the King an English house. **1809** Kendall *Travels* II. 181 One [an Indian], named Ebenezer Queppe, is master of two yoke of oxen, several cows, a horse, a wooden or *English* house, with barns and other appurtenances. — (6) **1666** *R.I. Col. Rec.* II. 174 Ordered, that noe victualing house ... sell liquors without licence.... And that none sell liquors on the first day to English Indians. — (7) **1934** Webster. **1943** Farmer *Boston Cook Book* 138 English Monkey 1 cup stale bread crumbs ... ½ cup soft, mild cheese, cut in small pieces ... 1 egg [etc.]. — (8) **1688** *Providence Rec.* XVII. 121 Aboute tenn Acres inclosed of English pasture orchad and all medo. **1689** *Plymouth Laws* 218 Meadow and English pasture every acre at ... 5 [shillings].

(10) **1631** in Dow *Every Day Life* 19 Wee have ordered that noe man shall build his chimney with wood nor cover his house with thatch, which was readily assented unto, for that divers houses have been burned since our arrival (the fire always beginning in the wooden chimneys) and some English wigwams which have taken fire in the roofes with thatch or boughs. **1939** Shurtleff *Log Cabin* 35 Thus *wigwam* or *English wigwam* became a common name in New England for a dwelling of saplings, poles, boughs, and mats which would have been called in Old England a booth or arbor.

As the last term in **American, Negro, New, newspaper, Old English.**

*** English,** *v. tr.* In billiards, to cause (a cue-ball) to twist or spin by striking it to the right or left of its center. Also absol. — **1889** *Cent.* 1933/1 He Englished his ball too much. *Ib.*, I Englished just right.

English corn. Any one of various cereals, esp. wheat, in contradistinction to Indian corn or maize. Now *hist.*

1629 *Mass. H.S. Coll.* I. 118 They have tryed our English corne at New Plimmouth plantation. **1696** *First Planters of N. Eng.* 17 Both the English and Indian Corn being at ten shillings a strike . . . we made laws to restrain the selling of Corn to the Indians. **1780** *Warren-Adams Lett.* II. 136 We have lately had fine rains, but they came too late for Hay, and a full Crop of English Corn. **1884** *Cent. Mag.* Jan. 431/1 The device on the seal of East Jersey is wrought of 'English Corn' and 'Indian Corn,'—wheat and maize,—symbols of the soberer expectations at the period of the Scotch and Quaker migrations. **1906** *Old Dartmouth Hist. Sk.* XIII. 14 He sold his homestead for 22 pounds sterling, to be paid in . . . English corn.

English grass. (See quots. 1809, 1937.)

1665 *Dorchester Town Rec.* 129 William Trescots request . . . to have some small parcell of Land . . . for English grass about the Ox pen. **1771** *Md. Hist. Mag.* XIII. 265 Severall small Boys & Girls Have been employed since the Receit of your letters in Picking English grass & white Clover seed. **1809** KENDALL *Travels* I. 228 In all parts, timothy, here called English grass, is the grass cultivated. **1937** LANDON *Everyday Things* 282 English forage plants were introduced into America as early as 1663 or 1665, probably by accident, in the fodder for cattle on shipboard. They were blue grass and white clover. These soon were known as 'English grass.'

English pea. A variety of small, edible pea, or a pea of this variety.

1634 *Beginnings Md.* 22 We have also English Peasen, & French-beanes. **1789** *Philos. Soc. Trans.* I. 292 Take any quantity of English pease intended for seed. **1856** DAVIS *Farm Bk.* 24 Dick killed 3 rabbits They are eating up your English peas. **1944** *Democrat* 23 Nov. 2/2 This fall she brought us the English peas and a mess of snap beans for good measure.

English school.

1. A school in a non-English-speaking community where the English language is taught, or where classes are conducted in English.

1679 EBENEZER HAZARD *Hist. Coll.* II. (1794) 542 The Commissioners . . . had a full Debate concerning . . . English Scooles amongst the Indians. **1780** *N.J. Archives* 2 Ser. IV. 199 An English School is kept contiguous to the Academy, where Reading, Writing, Arithmetic, and several Branches of the Mathematics are taught. **1865** *Wkly. New Mexican* 6 Jan. 2/4 The second term of the Santa Fe English school will open on the ninth.

2. A non-classical school, also **English elementary school.** *Obs.*, except in such names as the "English High School" in Boston.

1780 *N.J. Archives* 2 Ser. IV. 199 An English School is kept contiguous to the Academy, where Reading, Writing, Arithmetic, and several Branches of the Mathematics are taught. **1818** *Niles' Reg.* XIV. 174/2, I am here at a loss to say what is now paid to our English elementary schools. **1836** J. HALL *Statistics of West* xi. 204 A person who teaches a common English school, receives from $2.50 to $3, per quarter for each pupil.

English walnut. An Old World walnut, *Juglans regia*, or its fruit, widely cultivated in the warmer parts of the U.S. Also attrib.

1772 *Md. Hist. Mag.* XIV. 149 It froze Here last Thursday night . . . , it bit the Leaves of the English Walnut tree. **1884** *Cent. Mag.* Jan. 434/2 Neither Lane nor Wiggins . . . succeeded in finding an important agricultural commodity suited to the New England sandy coasts and rocky hillsides; and this, . . . in spite of the licorice, hemp, and indigo tried by [Eliot] . . . and the English walnuts engrafted by Judge Sewall. **1901** GREENOUGH & KITTREDGE *Words & Their Ways* 340 In some parts of America the name *walnut* is given to the 'shagbark,' a kind of hickory nut, and the true walnut is known as the 'English walnut.' **1948** *Aurora* (Ill.) *Beacon-News* 7 Nov. (Supp.) 34/1 The English walnut, for instance, is not English at all.

Englishy ˈɪŋglɪʃɪ, *a.* Resembling that which is English. *Colloq.* — **1873** HOWELLS *Chance Acquaintance* vi. 146 The people, too, had such Englishy faces. **1880** *Scribner's Mo.* XIX. 633/1 'Before the summer ricks are all carted,' 'red haws on the hawthorn and hips on the briar,' etc.—how Englishy such sentences sound!

***enlist,** *v. tr.* To prepare (land) for planting by alternate furrows and ridges; to "list." *Obs.* — **1768** WASHINGTON *Diaries* I. 263 Began to enlist my Corn Ground at the Mill. **1786** *Ib.* III. 30 Nothing but the lateness of the Season could . . . justify my . . . beginning to inlist corn ground.

enna ˈina, *n.* [?Chinook Jargon.] (See quots.) *Obs.* — **1811** in ROSS *First Settlers Ore.* (1849) 95 Of late, since the whites came among them [i.e., Chinooks], the beaver skin called the enna, has been added to the currency. **1838** PARKER *Exploring Tour* 337 Beaver, eena.

***enough,** *a.* and *adv.* Used colloq., usu. with comparatives, to mean amply, sufficiently, very much, esp. **enough sight.** Cf. **'nuf(f) sed.**

1845 JUDD *Margaret* I. xiv. 110 Their music is enough sight better than ours. *c***1848** WHITCHER *Bedott P.* xvi. 163 It's enough ginteeler'n them flambergasted blue and yaller things. **1907** FREEMAN *Light of Soul* 32, I've seen folks enough worse than your mother git well. **1911** LINCOLN *Cap'n Warren's Wards* 251 It was enough sight damper amongst the seats than in those cloth waves.

***enrol,** *v. tr.* To make a smooth copy of (a bill passed by Congress) for the President's examination. *Obs.*

1789 *Ann. 1st Congress* I. 57 When bills are enrolled, they shall be examined by a joint committee of one from the Senate, and two from the House of Representatives, appointed as a standing committee for that purpose, who shall carefully compare the enrolment with the engrossed bills. *Ib.* 672 After a bill shall have passed both Houses, it shall be duly enrolled on parchment by the Clerk of the House of Representatives.

b. Hence **enrolled bill, enrolled resolve,** a copy of a bill or resolve for filing away as a permanent record.

1789 *Ann. 1st Congress* I. 49 The House had appointed a committee . . . for the purpose of examining an enrolled bill imposing duties on tonnage. *Ib.* 73 A message from the House of Representatives, by their Clerk, informed the Senate that the President of the United States had signed an enrolled resolve, for carrying into effect a survey directed by an act of the late Congress. **1839** VAN BUREN in *Pres. Mess. & P.* III. 529 The committee of the Senate . . . were not attended by the Committee on Enrolled Bills of the House. **1906** *Indian Laws & Tr.* III. 263 The words . . . occur in line 40 page 3, of the enrolled bill.

c. Enrolling clerk, a clerk who enrols bills passed by a legislative body.

1838 *Ind. H. Rep. Jrnl.* 6 The House proceeded to the election of Enrolling Clerk. **1886** ALTON *Among Law-Makers* 29 Mr. Sympson, the responsible and still flourishing Enrolling Clerk [in the Senate].

***ensign,** *n.* The lowest-ranking commissioned officer in the U.S. Navy. Also (*cap.*) as a title.

The title was first introduced in 1862, taking the place of "passed midshipman."

1865 *Navy Reg.* 3 Ensigns . . . when at sea [receive an annual salary of $]1,200. **1914** *Ib.* 298 Pay as ensign does not begin until date of qualification and acceptance of commission. **1945** *Chi. Tribune* 8 Mar. 14/2 Ensign Rellis attended Schurz High school and Wright Junior college before entering the navy in April, 1941.

ensilage cutter. (See quot. 1883.) — **1883** KNIGHT *Supp.* 314 *Ensilage Cutter*, a machine for cutting green corn stalks or other green feed, to be stored in pits (silos) for winter feed. **1919** LEWIS *Free Air* 52 Two stores farther on, a bulky farmer hailed, 'Say, Milt, should I get an ensilage cutter yet?'

enswamped ɛnˈswɑmpt, *a.* Hidden in a swamp; converted into a swamp. *Obs.* — **1702** C. MATHER *Magnalia* (1853) I. 183 They were like to make no weapons reach their enswamped adversaries. **1821** NUTTALL *Travels Arkansa* vi. 108, I was now obliged more deeply to wade through the enswamped forests, . . . in consequence of the late rains.

***enter,** *v. tr.* To file a claim on (public land) by recording the required particulars at the general land office, to record pre-emption rights on (public land).

1799 *Columbian Centinel* 1 July 3/1 Real Estates, entered at the Register of Deed's Office. **1818** FLINT *Letters* 92 The lower and richer lands are all entered, (appropriated by individuals). **1901** MCKINLEY in *Okla. Red Book* I. 579 The entryman has resided upon and improved the land entered in good faith for the period of fourteen months. **1944** *News from Belgium* 18 Nov. 344/2 He advised them to take up the rich, unoccupied area on the outskirts of his far-flung parish. . . . Lands were entered in the vicinity of the present Robinsville [Wis.].

***entertainment,** *n.* As the last term in **house of, minstrel, private, public, school, turtle entertainment.**

enthuse ɛnˈθ(j)uz, *v.* [Back formation f. **enthusiasm.*] *tr.* and *intr.* To make or become enthusiastic. Also quasi-adj. in p.p. form.

The earliest quot., 1827, for this term was written by a young Scotsman not long in this country. He may have brought the word with him from Scotland or picked it up in this country.

1827 in *Amer. Sp.* XXII. 286/2 My humble exertions will I trust convey and enthuse, and draw attention to the beautifully varied verdure of N.W. America. **1852** *N.Y. Wkly. Tribune* 24 Jan. 3/2 We were probably not so much 'enthused' as they were. **1859** *Cong. Globe* 16 Feb. 1058/3 They are what they call in the country 'enthused'—run mad on the subject [of Cuba]. **1875** *Chi. Tribune* 16 Oct. 6/3 The people, who are expected to 'enthuse' for one or the other candidate, will have a sufficient stimulus given them. **1948** *Time* 26

April 20/1 An enthused America, speaking through its Government, can make American democracy an article of export.

entire-leaved, *a. Bot.* Having leaves the edges of which are unbroken by indentations or teeth.

1785 MARSHALL *Amer. Grove* 121 *Quercus nigra integrifolia.* Entire-leaved Black Oak. **1821** NUTTALL *Travels Arkansa* vi. 97 Here I found abundance of the *Celtis integrifolia* (entire-leaved nettle tree). **1843** TORREY *Flora N.Y.* I. 271 *Zizia Integerrima.* Entire-leaved Zizia. . . . Rocky woods, hill-sides and banks of rivers. *Ib.* II. 71 *Scutellaria Integrifolia.* . . . Entire leaved-Scullcap. . . . Open woods and borders of moist thickets; near New York, and on Long Island.

entrance way. A way or passage leading into a building. — **1865** *Atlantic Mo.* XV. 143/1 A little table . . . was placed in the entrance-way. **1908** *N.Y. Ev. Post* 9 July 1 A new stoop will be built to the entranceway.

∗**entry,** *n.*

1. The filing of a claim for public land.

1819 COBBETT *Year's Residence* 271 Mr. Birkbeck informs me he has made entry of a large tract of land, lying, part of it, all the way from his residence to the great Wabash. **1881** *Rep. Indian Affairs* 330 His claim is laid upon entries under the Desert land act. **1904** *Indian Laws & Tr.* III. 33 The entryman shall pay the same fees and commissions at the time of commutation or final entry. **1948** *Ariz. Republic* (Phoenix) 2 Mar. 6/3 Upon the reduction or abandonment of military reservations the mineral deposits therein become subject to mineral location and entry.

b. The land sought in this way.

1733 BYRD *Journey to Eden* 287, [I] rode with my Overseer to a new Entry I had made upon Blue Stone Creek about 3 Miles from the Castle. **1792** *Ann. 2nd Congress* 1037 The second reservation covers the following claims: Entries in Sullivan county, amounting to 240,000 acres.

c. A paper, application, or other document recording such action. *Rare.*

1783 W. FLEMING in *Travels Amer. Col.* 662, [I] sent up Archd Woods entry on the Beachfork to Thomas Woods.

2. In combs.: (1) ∗**entry book,** a book in which a record is kept of entries of public land; (2) **clerk,** =**entry-taker,** *obs.;* (3) **man,** one who makes an entry for public land, cf. **homestead entryman;** (4) **money,** the money paid by one making application for public land; (5) **-taker,** an official who receives and takes appropriate action upon entries or applications for public lands, *obs.;* (6) **-way,** =**entrance way,** also attrib.

(1) **1695** *Huntington Rec.* II. 177 [A tract of upland] is to him. . . . Laied out by the towne survairs & entred In our towne Records or entery booke. **1778** *Va. State P.* I. 310 He had constant access to the Entry Books of the Company, which were alike open to him & all other persons. — (2) **1778** *Va. State P.* I. 310 He had acted as Entry Clerk at the request of Henderson. — (3) **1886** *N. Amer. Rev.* Jan. 59 The entryman, under the timber culture act, is not compelled to plant any trees until the third year from date of entry. **1912** *Out West* June 418 His report was heard read with great satisfaction by upwards of a hundred of the entrymen of Los Angeles and vicinity. — (4) **1806** *Balance* (Hudson, N.Y.) 14 Oct. 326/1 In the year 1789, the state of North Carolina . . . ceded to Congress that part of her territory which is now called Tenassee . . . reserving to herself the right of . . . receiving to the use of the state the entry money for the same. (5) **1782** in RAMSEY *Tennessee* (1853) 226 John Adair, Esq., late of Knox county, was the Entry-taker. **1805** *Ann. 8th Congress* 2 Sess. 1142 They . . . [wanted] leave to surrender their lands as an indemnity for the state demands against them in the entrytaker's books. — (6) **1746** *N.H. Probate Rec.* III. 391 It is also agreed by us that the Said Cellar great Doors and the yard the Entryway Stairs . . . all be in Common. **1853** *Knickerb.* XLII. 171 The quaint old building . . . with . . . the 'entry-way.' **1893** M. PHILLIPS *Making of a Newspaper* 96 Patrolman Blucher had finished his nap in the entryway leading to Eckstein's cigar factory.

As the last term in **desert land, form, land, mineral, tomahawk entry.**

enumerated powers. Powers of a governmental kind which are expressed as distinguished from those that are implied.

1791 JAS. MADISON in *Deb. Congress* (1834) 1947 The essential characteristic of the U.S. Government, as composed of limited and enumerated powers. **1819** in *Sp. & Doc. Amer. Hist.* II. (1844) 6 This government is acknowledged by all to be one of enumerated powers. **1895** in *Doc. & Sp. Amer. Hist.* III. (1943) 185 The powers of government are distributed between the State and the nation, and while the latter is properly styled a government of enumerated powers, yet within the limits of such enumeration [etc.].

∗**enunciator,** *n.* See ∗**annunciator.**

∗**envelope,** *n.* As the last term in **freedmen's, pay, penalty, request, special request envelope.**

∗**Ephraim,** *n.* A nickname for the grizzly bear. *Colloq.* Cf. **Caleb, old Ephraim.** — **1859** J. G. WOOD *Nat. Hist.* I. 400 The Grizzly, or 'Ephraim' as the creature is familiarly termed by the hunters. **1908** MULFORD *Orphan* 169, 'I reckon Ephraim may turn around and scratch himself, if you hits him.' 'Why, won't that stop a bear?'

epinette ˌepəˈnɛt, *n.* [F., from voyageur use.]

1. Any one of various North American spruces (see also quot. 1895). Cf. **pinenet.**

1846 LEVINGE *Echoes from Backwoods* 286. **1851** HOWE *Hist. Coll. Great West* 156 All the joints are sewed by long threads made by splitting the roots of a tree, called by the voyageurs *epinette,* and which is probably a spruce. **1895** in MCDERMOTT *Glossary* 73 Epinette of the French voyageurs, the name of the tree we commonly call tamarac or hackmetack, and which the botanists know as black larch, *Larix americana.* [**1907** LYONS *Plant Names* 262 *L[arix] americana* . . . American Larch, Hackmatack, . . . Fr. Épinette rouge.]

2. Canada balsam, a gum obtained from a North American spruce. *Obs.* Cf. **pinenet, prairie epinette.**

1852 J. W. BOND *Minnesota* 283 We . . . paddled down the crooked, muddy river . . . stopping . . . frequently to haul out our leaky, frail canoe, and pitch the bottom with melted epinette, a vegetable gum used for that purpose. *Ib.* 286 Our canoe is so leaky and out of order, that we have frequently to land . . . and gum the bottom with melted epinette.

Episcopal Methodist. A member of the Methodist Episcopal Church.

1819 *Niles' Reg.* XVI. 431/1 The same letter informs us that a large company of episcopal methodists have laid out a city on the Wabash. **1837** JENKINS *Ohio Gaz.* 130 Of this number . . . 725 are episcopal methodists; about 300 are supposed to belong to the ancient order society; 200 to the presbyterians. **1849** CHAMBERLAIN *Ind. Gazetteer* 271 The Episcopal Methodists have five churches, the Wesleyans one.

∗**E Pluribus Unum.** The motto of the U.S.

"It probably originated from the design for the great seal of the United States submitted August, 1776, by Franklin, Jefferson and John Adams" (*Cyclo. Amer. Govt.* I. 672/2).

1782 *Jrnls. Cont. Cong.* XXII. 339 The device for an armorial atchievement and reverse of the great seal for the United States in Congress assembled, is as follows: [Arms] . . . the American eagle . . . and in his beak a scroll inscribed with this motto, '*E Pluribus Unum.*' **1874** *Revised Statutes* Sec. 3517, 697 Upon the coins there shall be the following devices and legends. . . . 'United States of America' and 'E Pluribus Unum.' **1900** *Cong. Rec.* 12 Feb. 1717/1 Upon the reverse side [of the coin] the figure or representation of an eagle with the inscriptions 'United States of America' and 'E Pluribus Unum.'

b. Also as a legend or motto on the seal or flag of certain states.

1850 *Mich. Agric. Soc. Trans.* I. t.-p., [On seal] E pluribus unum. **1881** *Wisconsin Laws* 353 The coat of arms of the state of Wisconsin is hereby declared to be as follows, viz. . . . *motto* (on garter surrounding inescutcheon), 'E Pluribus Unum.' **1911** *North Dakota Laws* cxxxviii. 519 Through the opened beak of the eagle [on the state flag] shall pass a scroll bearing the words '*E Pluribus Unum.*'

Epworth League. A religious organization, originating in 1889 in Cleveland, Ohio, composed of young people of the Methodist Church. Also attrib.

1896 *Cin. Enquirer* 10 July 13/1 The First Vice President of what is known as the Cincinnati Cabinet of the Epworth League, is now in Washington, D.C. **1897** *Chi. Ev. Post* 15 May, The chairman . . . has also asked the roads to signify their wishes in regard to making a one-fare rate for the round trip, plus $2, for the Epworth League convention at Toronto. **1947** COFFIN *Yankee Coast* 247 It is the lust—and it *is* a lust, and what the Middle Ages called lust is an Epworth League virtue beside it—for the standard.

Hence **Epworth Leaguer.**

1896 *Chi. Tribune* 5 July 9/4 Five hundred Epworth Leaguers, from all parts of the city, celebrated the Fourth with an old-fashioned picnic.

∗**equal rights.**

1. Equality of rights, opportunities, privileges, etc., as between men and women. Also attrib.

1867 DIXON *New America* II. 175 Are you a member of the Society of Promoting Equal Rights as between the two sexes? **1870** O. LOGAN *Before Footlights* 295 In these days of battle for 'equal rights,' it seems to me that something ought to be said in behalf of the rights of audiences. **1948** *Dly. Ardmoreite* (Ardmore, Okla.) 31 Mar. 8/3 They want a new amendment to the constitution—an equal rights amendment.

2. (*cap.*) Short for Equal Rights candidate or party. *Rare.*

1888 *Amer. Almanac* 259 In Texas of the scattering votes in 1884, 3508 were cast for St John, Prohibition, . . . and 12 for Mrs. Lockwood, Equal Rights.

3. In combs.: (1) **Equal Rights Association,** an association of persons interested in women's rights; (2) **candidate,** a candidate for President sponsored by the Equal Rights party (sense **2.**); (3) **Democracy,** that faction of the Democratic party made up of Locofocos, *obs.;* (4) **man,** a Locofoco, *q.v., obs.;* (5) **meeting,** a meeting held by those interested in securing equal rights for women; (6) **party,** see as a main entry.

(1) **1867** DIXON *New America* II. 181 The more serious question discussed in the Equal Rights Association is the position of woman in marriage. **1900** *Cong. Rec.* 16 Jan. 849 Mr. Tillman presented a petition of the Equal Rights Association of South Carolina. — (2) **1888** *Amer. Almanac* 268 In Texas, 12 votes were cast for Belva A. Lockwood, Equal Rights candidate. — (3) **1836** in BYRDSALL *Hist. Loco-foco Party* (1842) 56 On the subject of the principles and reforms advocated by the Equal Rights Democracy, your convention has corresponded with the nominees of the Baltimore Convention. — (4) **1854** BUSCH *Wanderungen* II. 343 Ein Triumph der *equal rightsmen* . . . konnte bei der vergleichsweisen Schwäche derselben nicht länger als eine Nacht dauern. **1882** W. G. SUMMER *A. Jackson* 373 The equal rights men maintained impracticable doctrines of civil authority and fantastic dogmas about equality.

(5) **1869** *Washington Star* 6 July, Equal Rights Meeting. . . . A meeting was held last evening . . . for the purpose of forming an Equal Rights Association.

Equal Rights party.

1. A faction of the Democratic party in New York State, 1835–37. Now *hist.* See **Locofoco.**

"After the defeat of the bill to recharter the United States bank, state banks grew up, with special privileges granted them. It was in opposition to these special privileges that the Equal Rights party was formed" (*Cyclo. Amer. Govt.* I. 672/2).

1836 in BYRDSALL *Hist. Loco-foco Party* (1842) 68 [Resolved,] that the name of Equal Rights party be, and the same is hereby adopted, as our political designation. **1842** *Ib.* 162 The prompt approbation of the separation of bank and state given by the Equal Rights Party, comprising over four thousand voters, was of some importance at this juncture. **1848** *N.Y. Wkly. Tribune* 9 Sep. 4/6 The Freeholder counsels the 'Equal Rights' party to keep up a distinct organization, as formerly.

2. (See quot. 1903–5.) Now *hist.*

1884 B. LOCKWOOD in *Columbia Hist. Soc. Rec.* (1935) 200 This campaign of our Equal Rights party will pass into the history of 1884, and become . . . the first practical movement in the history of woman suffrage. **1903–5** *Amer. Encycl.* VI. *s.v.*, Equal Rights Party, in 1884. Belva Lockwood nominated herself for the presidency, on a platform of woman suffrage; and gave her voters this title. **1947** *Pageant* May 99/2 The Equal Rights Party, however, never got on the ballot.

equescurriculum ɪˌkwɛskəˈrɪkjələm, *n.* [f. *equestrian* and *curriculum.* Note quot. 1867.] (See quot. 1888.) *Obs.*

1864 *Washoe* (Nev.) *Herald* 2 July 2/6 Lee & Ryland's Great Equescurriculum And Camel Show. **1867** *Terr. Enterprise* (Virginia, Nev.) 3 (*advt.*), Equuscurriculum, or Horse Opera. **1888** *Boston Transcript* 2 July 5/7 Professor D. M. Bristol's Eques-Curriculum. Humanly Educated Horses, Ponies and Mules.

equestrian drama. A type of play in the action of which one or more horses are featured. *Obs.* Cf. **horse drama.**

1841 *Spirit of Times* 22 May 144/1 (We.), In the equestrian drama, Mr. Creswick did himself much credit. **1844** JOE COWELL *Thirty Yrs. Among Players* 49, I received an offer . . . to undertake the principal character in a magnificent equestrian drama, called 'Gil Blas.' **1880** N. M. LUDLOW *Dramatic Life* 337 This lady had been away on a short 'starring' excursion, but returned . . . to perform in these equestrian dramas.

* **equity,** *n.* The value of property above and beyond the liens and charges against it. — **1904** E. S. MEADE in *Pol. Sci. Quart.* March 50 Its preferred stock is quoted at 18 and its common stock at 5, prices which indicate a general conviction that the equity in the company is worth little. **1932** *Atlantic Mo.* CL. 36 During the heartbreaking years since then, the purchaser, regardless of anything that he might do, has seen his equity extinguished by the decline in price.

equi-vote ˈɛkwɪˌvot, *n.* A tie vote. *Obs.*

1641 *Mass. Liberties* 228 The Governor shall have a casting voice whensoever an Equi vote shall fall out in the Court of Assistants. **1702** C. MATHER *Magnalia* (1853) I. 257 When the matter came to a vote, . . . there was an equi-vote for Mr. Cotton and that other person. **1888** *Advance* (Chicago) 1 March 132/1 In an equi-vote the question shall determine on that side on which the presiding member shall have voted.

* **era,** *n. Era of good feeling(s),* the period from approximately 1817 to 1824 during Monroe's administration when there was little party strife.

1817 *Niles' Reg.* XIII. 166/2 The real or apparent moderation of party spirit, has caused the present to be called 'the era of good-feelings.' **1909** *N.Y. Ev. Post* 1 Nov. (Th.), Monroe's Administration, 'the era of good feeling,' was not a period of complete peace in the politics of New York City. **1948** *Pa. Mag. Hist.* April 113 The period of the 1820's—the so-called but ludicrously named 'Era of Good Feeling'—is one.

transf. **1865** *Republican Banner* (Nashville, Tenn.) 28 Sep. 1/2 For the first time in the history of the Union since the days of Monroe, both parties have met on the platform of the administration as if to enjoy another 'era of good feeling.' **1913** *Chi. D. News* 4 March 1/7 The era of good feeling which attended the transfer of power from the republican to the democratic party was visibly enhanced by the unostentatious but nonetheless handsome courtesies extended by William Howard Taft to his successor in office. **1945** *Ib.* 16 Aug. 10/2 We do not wish to disturb the new 'Era of Good Feeling' in traction, but candor and a clear record require that we point out that the $6,000,000 additional proposed for the security owners does not materialize out of nothing.

As the last term in **carpetbag, gold standard era.**

* **erect,** *v.*

1. *tr.* To establish or found (a colonial plantation or settlement). *Obs.*

1638 UNDERHILL *Newes from America* 14 There are certain plantations, Dedham, Concord, in the Mathethusis Bay, that are newly erected, that do afford large accommodation. **1680** *Conn. Rec.* III. 69 The Deputy . . . propownding to this Court to grant to them liberty to erect a plantation at the north of their bownds.

2. To form or organize (a region or district) into a state, country, or territory of the U.S.

1787 *Constitution* iv. § 3 New States may be admitted by the Congress into the Union; but no new State shall be formed or erected within the jurisdiction of any other State. **1894** ROBLEY *Bourbon Co. Kansas* 4 By act of Congress known as the Missouri Compromise, approved March 6th, 1820, the Territory of Missouri was erected with a view of admission as a State.

ergophile ˈɜgəˌfaɪl, *n.* [Gk. *ergo-*+*-phile.*] (See quot.) *Rare.* — **1931** *Chr. Sci. Mon.* 25 Feb. 1/6 'Ergophile' meaning one who loves his work, was coined yesterday at the closing session of the semi-annual meeting of the National Puzzlers League.

Erie ˈɪrɪ, *n.* [Said to be from an Iroquoian term meaning "people of the panther." The *pl.* is usu. *Eries.*]

1. *pl.* An Iroquoian tribe of Indians formerly living on the shores of Lake Erie.

1761 T. JEFFERYS *Nat. & Civil Hist. French Dominions N. & S. Amer.* I. 103 Much about this time the Iroquois compleated the destruction of the Eries, or Cat Indians. **1800** JEFFERSON *Notes* 99 We also learn that the Erigas, a nation formerly inhabiting on the Ohio, were of the same original stock with the Five Nations, and that they partook also of the Tuscarora language. **1907** HODGE *Amer. Indians* I. 431 Historically little is definitely known of the Erie and their political and social organization, but it may be inferred to have been similar to that of the Hurons. **1940** *Dict. Amer. Hist.* II. 223 Lake Erie . . . was named after the Eries (or Cat Nation).

2. In combs.: (1) **Erie boat,** a boat used on Lake Erie; (2) **Canal,** a barge canal connecting the waters of Lake Erie at Buffalo with the Hudson River at Albany, opened in 1825, see **Clinton's Ditch;** (3) **clique,** a group of manipulators who controlled the Erie Railroad, *obs.;* (4) **drift,** glacial drift in the general region of Lake Erie.

(1) **1887** *Cent. Mag.* XXXIV. 484/2 What we want is an Erie boat. Our canal is the Raritan. — (2) [**1807** in HOSACK *Memoir De Witt Clinton* 300 That improvement which I conceive to be of the greatest importance of any which can be undertaken in the United States [is] . . . a canal from the foot of Lake Erie into the Mohawk River.] **1823** *Niles' Reg.* XXV. 103 The Erie Canal . . . will long serve as a chain to bind together rich and populous territories, far distant from each other. **1943** HICKS *Amer. Dem.* 221 The through traffic that began at once to make use of the Erie Canal was of immense significance in linking the East to the West. — (3) **1870** *Nation* 10 March 157/1 In a Legislature chosen on our plan, Mr. Sweeney, Mr. Tweed, the Erie clique, and the Twenty-third Street gang would all be represented. — (4) **1899** U.S. Geol. Surv. *Water Supp. Paper 21* 33 The blue till of the Erie drift found south from Kendallville is much harder to penetrate than the blue till of the Saginaw drift.

Ermatinger money. Currency issued by the Hudson's Bay Company and circulated on the Pacific Coast about 1842–60, named for Francis Ermatinger, a Hudson's Bay trader. Now *hist.* — **1846** *Oregon Spectator* 17 Sep. (Th.), 82 dolls. and 50 c. in Ermatiger [*sic*] money. **1940** *Oregon Guide* 45 The scarcity of money was a great inconvenience, somewhat mitigated by the issue of what were known as 'Ermatinger money' and 'Abernethy money,' the use of wheat and peltry as mediums of exchange.

erminet ˌɜmɪˈnɛt, *n.* Also **erminetta.** ?A spotted fabric imitating ermine. *Obs.* — **1751** *Boston Ev. Post* 1 July, Fashionable blue & white erminettas. **1754** *S.C. Gazette* 1 Jan. 2/2 Just imported . . . cotton gowns, fine striped hollands, erminets, blue and white printed handkerchiefs.

erolin ˈɜrəlɪn, *n.* [Irreg. f. Gk. *erion*, wool, and L. *linum*, flax.] (See quot.) *Rare.* — **1863** *Rep. Comm. Agric.* 122 Geo. C. Davies . . sends to this department specimens of 'flax wool' or erolin, made from the coarse flax straw of the west.

***errand,** *n.* One who goes on errands. *Rare.* — **1871** *Scribner's Mo.* I. 609 On the register of one night school for girls are recorded the names of fifty as 'errands' for a single large dry goods firm.

***error,** *n.*

1. *Chr. Sci.* (See quots. 1875, 1906.) Also attrib.

1875 Eddy *Science & Health* 22 The absence of Truth, we name error. . . . Error is not an idea, it has neither Principle, nor identity, but is illusion. **1903** C. L. Burnham *Jewel* 260 You get the error man mixed up with the real one. . . . We ride in cable cars and places where we see error people with sorry faces. **1906** Eddy *Science & Health* (final ed.) 287 Error is false, mortal belief; it is illusion, without spiritual identity or foundation, and it has no real existence.

2. In baseball, a faulty play (except wild pitches and passed balls) which permits the batter to remain at bat or allows a runner who should have been put out to advance.

1867 *Ball Players' Chron.* 6 June 2/4 The errors committed by the two nines in the form of missed catches, passed balls, overthrows and missed balls, amounted to a total of 71 in the game. **1880** *S.F. Globe* 12 July 1/5 The outfit took everything that came their way to the extent of seven flys, without an error. **1947** *Dly. Ardmoreite* (Ardmore, Okla.) 11 Aug. 6/8 The All-Stars scored a run in the last of the second on an error and a single.

Hence **errorless(ly),** *a.* and *adv.*

1887 *N.Y. Herald* 5 May 5/6 The home club played an almost errorless game. **1910** *Amer. Mag.* May 3/1, I know that infielders of the National League (pitchers not included) fielded 9,382 ground balls errorlessly during the season of 1909. **1948** *Ada* (Okla.) *Ev. News* 4 July 9/1 For the second straight game, the local team played errorless softball.

3. court of errors, *see **court,** *n.*

erve ɜv, *n.* [f. Du. *erf*, ground, inheritance.] A small parcel of land. *Obs.*

This word is used in South Africa in the sense of a garden plot. **1675** *N.Y. Hist. Soc. Coll.* XLVI. 54, I . . . doe absoulutly bargaine sell & confirme the former sale . . . making over ye said erve or parcell of land. **1675** *New Castle Court Rec.* 63 The houses and Land knowne by the name of the greate house with the blokhouse and kitching with the erves thereto belonging.

Esaw (Indians). The Catawba Indians. — **1709** Lawson *Carolina* 141 The great Nation of the Esaw Indians. **1907** Hodge *Amer. Indians* I. 213 From the earliest period the Catawba have also been known as Esaw, or Issa (Catawba *iswă'*, 'river'), from their residence on the principal stream of the region.

escalator ˈɛskəˌletɚ, *n.* [From "Escalator," a trademark made from *escala*de and eleva*tor*.] A continuous moving stairway by which passengers are carried from one floor to another, usu. in large stores.

1900 *N.Y. Jrnl.* 25 Nov. 59/2 To those who do not know what the escalator is the information is vouchsafed that it is a movable stairway built by the Otis Elevator Company for the use of passengers of the Manhattan Elevated Railway. **1948** *Newsweek* 8 March 44/1 You have probably ridden on an escalator, those so-called 'moving stairways' that carry throngs of shoppers from one floor to another in busy department stores.

fig. **1943** Hicks *Amer. Dem.* 729 Always a dependable regular, he climbed aboard the political escalator in 1899 when he became a councilman. **1948** *Time* 7 June 21/3 Labor leaders have never liked cost-of-living 'escalator' contracts, on the grounds that they tie the worker to a fixed standard of living.

escalin ˌɛskɑˈlæn, *n.* [Sp. or F. See Read, *La.-French*, 140]. (See quots.) — **1883** G. M. Tucker in *Trans. Albany Inst.* X. 336 The 'shilling' of our own State [New York] is the 'levy' of Pennsylvania, the 'bit' of San Francisco, the 'nine-pence' of old New England, and the 'escalan' of New Orleans. **1931** Read *La.-French* 140 *Un escalin* is, then, the equivalent of twelve and one-half cents in Louisiana-French.

***escaloped,** *a. Cookery.* Scalloped, i.e., baked with crumbs, butter, and condiments; baked in a sauce and covered with crumbs.

1832 L. M. Child *Frugal Housewife* 120 Escaloped Oysters.—Put crumbled bread around the sides and bottom of a buttered dish. **1880** Howells *Undisc. Country* 14 A person you might help to escalloped oysters or ice-cream at an evening party. **1883** *Practical Housekeeping* 147 Escaloped Eggs: Moisten bread-crumbs with milk or meat broth; place a layer of this in a well-buttered dish; slice some hard-boiled eggs. *Ib.* 344 Escaloped Tomatoes: Put in a buttered baking-dish a layer of bread or cracker crumbs . . . then a layer of sliced tomatoes.

Eschscholtzia əˈʃoltsɪə, *n.* [f. J. F. v. *Eschscholtz* (1793–1831), a German botanist.] A genus of plants of the poppy family, or (not *cap.*) a plant of this genus. Cf. **California poppy.**

1865 in *So. Calif. Hist. Soc. Pub.* 17, 51 The road hereabouts presented many objects of interest; acres of golden escholtzia. **1878** Jackson *Travel at Home* 153 We had seen fields yellow with the eschscholtzia [in California]. **1947** *Desert Mag.* July 22/1 The watery juice of the *Eschscholtzia* species has mild narcotic properties, similar to opium but without objectionable effects.

escobita ˌɛskəˈbitə, *n. Calif.* [Sp. dim. of *escoba*, broom. Cf. *escobilla* used in Sp. and Amer. Sp. to refer to various plants.] Any one of various California plants of the genus *Orthocarpus.* — **1906** Parsons *Wild Flowers of Calif.* 234 The Spanish-Californians have a pretty name for these blossoms, calling them 'escobitas,' meaning 'little whisk-brooms.' **1937** *Range Plant Handbook* W136 Purple owl-clover (*O. purpurascens*), often called escobita, is another common West Coast species.

Escoces ɛskoˈses, *n. Texas.* [Sp. *escocés*, a Scotsman.] (See quots.) *Obs.* — **1838** C. Newell *Revol. Texas* 8 The Escoces, or Scotch faction, were large proprietors, moderate, and favorable to the establishment of a Royal Government. **1844** Gregg *Commerce of Prairies* II. 103 These bravos, as I was afterwards informed, belonged to the bishop's party, or that of the Escoceses, which was openly at war with the liberalists.

escopeta ɛskoˈpetə, *n. S.W.* Also **escopet, escopette.** [Sp. in same sense. Cf. F. *escopette.*] A short rifle or musket. Now *hist.*

1807 Pike *Sources Miss.* (1810) II. 201 Dragoons and . . . mounted militia of the province, armed in the same manner, viz. Lances, escopates and pistols. **1844** Gregg *Commerce of Prairies* I. 221 A great portion of the militia are obliged to use the clumsy old fashioned escopeta, or firelock of the sixteenth century. **1939** Vestal *Old Santa Fe Trail* 160 Some of these men were able to conceal their own guns and surrender to Cooke the antiquated firelocks and *escopetas* they had just taken from the pueblos.

***escort,** *v. tr.* To keep company, "walk out" with (a woman). *Rare.* — **1890** *Harper's Mag.* Oct. 716/2 A whisper also went the rounds that Dick Jones was escorting Miss Turner.

escortage ɛsˈkɔrtɪdʒ, *n.* The action of escorting a woman. *Obs.* — **1898** Ford *Stirling* 153 She likes my company and finds my escortage very convenient. **1911** Harrison *Queed* 146 At nine, as it chanced, she was to go out under the escortage of Charles Gardiner West.

escribano ɛskriˈbɑno, *n. S.W.* Also **escrivano.** [Sp. in same sense.] A notary public. *Obs.* — **1803** in *Ann. 8th Congress* 2 Sess. 1517 11 They must be presented by the *escribano*, or notary, who is the keeper of the records of the court. **1838** Texian *Mexico v. Texas* 299, I may be killed, and I must make my will. We must have witnesses, and send for an *Escrivano*. *Ib.* 301 The *escrivano* and witnesses having been sent for, the instrument was drawn, signed and sealed.

escrito ɛsˈkrito, *n. Louisiana.* [Sp. in same sense.] A written document. *Obs.* — **1803** in *Ann. 8th Congress* 2 Sess. 1517 Suits are carried on in writings, called *escritos*, which may be drawn up by the parties themselves.

escrod ɛsˈkrɑd, *n.* = **scrod.** *Obs.* — **1844** Webster *Private Corr.* II. 186 A good Boston Breakfast! . . . A glass of Daniel's cider, and that morsel for Monica, an escrod! **1871** De Vere 340 A mysterious term, probably originating in mispronunciation, is the word *scrod*, meaning a small cod broiled; its legitimate form is escrod.

***escrow,** *n. Law. In escrow*, in the custody of a third party, who makes the delivery of deeds, money, etc., when the grantee has fulfilled the conditions agreed upon.

1888 *Boston Jrnl.* 17 Oct. 1/7, $800,000 is held in escrow to pay off unmatured bonds. **1914** Atherton *Perch of Devil* 168 He would execute a deed and place it in escrow. **1948** *Chi. Tribune* 29 Aug. 1. 25/1 The banks refuse to take the gold in escrow because the federal reserve system is opposed to a free gold market.

Escurial ˌɛskɪrɪˈɑl, *n.* [App. f. *Escurial, Escorial*, small towns in Spain.] *attrib.* Used of merino sheep, prob. in allusion to their place of origin. *Obs.* — **1863** Randall *Pract. Shepherd* i. 14 The Escurial breed is supposed to possess the finest wool of all migratory sheep. **1892** *Dept. Agric. Rep.* 180 Escurial Merinos imported into the United States in . . . 1810, shipped by William Jarvis at Lisbon.

*Eskimo, *n.*

1. Eskimo curlew, the now extinct, or nearly extinct, doebird, *Numenius borealis* (Forster); in earlier use, a curlew of a related species.

1813 Wilson *Ornithology* VII. 22 The Esquimaux Curlew . . . is called by our gunners on the sea-coast, the Short-billed Curlew. **1839** Peabody *Mass. Birds* 366 The Esquimaux Curlew, *Numenius Hudsonicus* . . . are shot in Boston Harbor. **1921** *Outing* May 65/1 For that reason the passenger pigeon, the great auk, the heath hen, the Carolina parakeet, the Eskimo curlew are no more.

2. Eskimo Pie, a trade name for a chocolate-covered ice cream bar.

1928 Turnbow & Raffetto *Ice Cream* 57 Chocolate-coated ice cream bars were introduced in 1921 as 'Eskimo Pies.' **1949** *Time* 14 Mar. 31/1 In the '30s he visited the U.S., brought back to Russia the Eskimo Pie.

espagnole (sauce). (See quot. 1909.)

1876 M. F. Henderson *Cooking* 186 Espagnole Sauce. Melt butter the size of an egg; when hot, add to it two or three table-spoonfuls of flour. **1909** Webster 749 *Espagnole sauce,* . . . a brown sauce made by boiling meat, flavoring vegetables and spices, in beef broth to a glaze, thickening with brown roux. **1941** Ward *Encycl. of Food* 190 Espagnole, one of cookery's principal fundamental sauces, and used as a basis for many brown sauces.

Esponshay 'espən,ʃe, *n.* [f. Louis *Espensheid,* a St. Louis wagon-maker, 1851–59.] (See quot.). *Obs.* — **1912** Dawson *Pioneer Tales* 70 The wagon that became the most popular on the Oregon Trail was the Esponshay, as it was pronounced. These wagons were manufactured in St. Louis, Missouri, and were built from thoroughly seasoned woods, light running, but built very strong, having beds four feet deep, weighing from 1700 to 1800 pounds empty. Freighters generally used three or four yokes of oxen on these wagons: hauling three to four tons of freight.

***Espy,** *n.* Prob. a type of ventilator invented by James P. Espy (1785–1860). *Rare.* — **1849** *Western Jrnl.* III. 10 The cars can be well ventilated, night and day, by Espy's at the top.

esquimoot 'eskɪ,mut, *n.* [?Indian.] (See quot.) *Rare.*—**1837** Irving *Bonneville* I. 149 From each side of the saddle hangs an *esquimoot,* a sort of pocket, in which she [*sc.* the Indian wife of a white trapper] bestows the residue of her trinkets and nicknacks, which cannot be crowded on the decoration of her horse or herself.

esquine ɛs'kin, *n.* [F. in same sense.] The American chinaroot, *Smilax pseudo-china. Obs.*

1587 Hakluyt tr. Laudonnière *Notable Historie* 2r There is also there [Fla.] the tree called Esquine which is very good against the Pocks and other cõtagious diseases. [**1758** DuPratz *Histoire de la Louisiane* II. 57 L'Esquine tient de la Liane de la Ronce.] **1763** in *Amer. Sp.* XX. (1945) 46 Besides the sudorific virtue which the *Esquine* possesses in common with the Salsaparilla, it has the property of making the hair grow.

esquipomgole ,ɛskɪ'pɑmgol, *n.* (See quot.) *Obs.* — **1859** Bartlett 137 *Esquipomgole,* another name for Kinnickinnick, or a mixture of tobacco and cornel bark.

esquite ɛs'kite, *n. Texas.* [Amer. Sp. (<Nahuatl) in same sense.] (See quot.) — **1891** *D.N.* I. 190 *Esquite,* pop-corn sweetened.

***essence,** *n.*

1. essence peddler, a peddler of medicinal extracts, cure-alls, etc. Now *hist.*

1838 Hawthorne *Note-Books* I. 119 He was not exclusively an essence-peddler, having a large tin box, which had been filled with dry goods, combs, jewelry, &c., now mostly sold out. **1859** Wilmer *Press Gang* 347 Imagine the fearful risks to which people are exposed when they are dosed by hostlers, farriers, . . . essence-pedlers, and others. **1944** Holton *Yankee* 179 Who later established some of the best known shops in the county; the tin peddler; the essence peddler.

b. *transf.* (See quot. 1871.)

1849 Lowell *Letters* I. 153 There were two of these '*essence pedlers,*' as the Yankees call them. **1871** De Vere 54 With biting irony the animal [*sc.* the skunk] is called by the Yankees an *essence pedlar.* **1890** Custer *Following Guidon* 200 The doctor soon came hurrying back to say that the passage was disputed by a small but well-armed foe, and added that 'as soon as the essence-peddler saw fit to move on, the major-general commanding would issue his order to march.'

2. essence spruce, app. a kind of patent medicine. *Obs.*

1790 *Columbian Centinel* 29 Sep. 19/3 [For sale,] a few barrels pigtail Tobacco, several boxes, containing one doz jars each Essence Spruce, a few barrels fresh Baltimore flour. **1800** *Ib.* 22 Jan. 3/3 He has . . . Goggles, for weak eyes, . . . Rotten Stone; Essence Spruce, by pot or gallon.

***Essex,** *n.* **Essex Junto,** a faction of the Massachusetts Federalists. Also attrib. Now *hist.*

"A name, first used about 1781, which was chiefly applied to a group of extreme Federalist leaders, mostly connected with Essex county, Massachusetts. . . . During the presidency of John Adams they were adherents of Hamilton rather than of the President. Later the name was applied to the Federalists in general" (*Cent.* 3255). "A nickname applied . . . by President John Adams (1797–1801). His exact phrase was 'the Essex Junta' " (Th.).

1801 *Mass. Spy* 16 Sep. (Th.), If such an association existed, and was denominated by its enemies the Essex Junto, it has not retained that name because its members were thought to be confined to [that] county; but the name was extended. **1808** *Ib.* 31 Aug. (Th.), 'Essex Junto Meetings.' This is the title given in the Monitor [Mr. Madison's paper] to the meetings in Newengland for petitioning the President. **1840** in Norton *Reminiscences* 72 With the design and settled purpose to prevent and defeat that re-election, he (Martin Van Buren) had patriotically conspired and associated with the Essex Junto federalists, and the men who subsequently devised and organized the Hartford convention. **1948** *Chi. Tribune* 17 Oct. (Grafic Mag.) 5/4 Few of them were quite so noisy, however, as the members of the Essex Junto, a group of gentlemen farmers and Tories living near Boston, who had plotted secession almost since the government of the United States was formed.

b. Hence **Essex federalist, Essex man.**

1813 Jefferson *Writings* XIII. 210 Anglomany, monarchy, and separation, then, are the principles of the Essex federalists. **1856** C. F. Adams *Life J. Adams* 288 The result [the Mass. Constitution] fell in sufficiently with the views of the Essex men to secure their support.

***establishment,** *n.* As the last term in **dry-goods, forwarding, logging, packing, trading establishment.**

estafiata ɛstɑ'fjɑtə, *n. S.W.* [Amer. Sp. *estafiate* (<Nahuatl) in same sense.] (See quots.) — **1913** Wooton *Trees & Shrubs N.M.* 145 The commoner herbaceous forms [of sagebrush], which are used extensively, go under the Spanish name of *Estafiata* among the Mexican herders. **1931** Dayton *Western Browse Plants* 170 Estafiata (*A[rtemisia] frigida*) is undoubtedly the well-established vernacular name of this species in the Southwest, while pasture sagebrush is probably the name in most general use for the plant toward the North.

estampedo, *v.* See **stampede,** *v.*

estancia ɛs'tɑnsɪə, *n. S.W.* [Sp. in Amer. Sp. sense shown here.] A large cattle ranch.

An earlier borrowing from South American Spanish is recorded in the *OED.*

1839 Briggs *H. Franco* I. 210 If we escaped . . . the Indians, we should find a hearty welcome at any estancia or saladara. **1906** *Nation* 1 March LXXXII. 182/3 The story is constructed out of a series of scenes at different estancias.

estanquillo ,ɛstɑn'kiljo, *n. S.W.* [Sp. in same sense.] (See quots.)

1844 G. W. Kendall *Santa Fe Exped.* II. 161 Entering a estanquillo, or shop licensed to sell cigars, we met two [men]. **1844** Gregg *Commerce of Prairies* I. 156 The tobacco laws are not enforced in New Mexico (there being no *Estanquillo,* or public store-house). **1888** J. J. Webb *Adventures* 95 Near the center [of the plaza in Santa Fe] was the post-office . . . and also the *estanquillo,* where the government sold a limited amount of cigars and tobacco.

estero ɛs'tero, *n. W.* [Sp. in same sense.] An estuary or marshy place. — **1927** Phillips *Hist. Santa Barbara Co., Calif.* 29 Those days the estero, which is now only a swamp, was tidewater. **1929** Rogers *Prehistoric Man Santa Barbara Coast* 368 In the estero grew a rank jungle of tules and rushes.

estopilla ,ɛsto'piljə, *n.* [Sp. in same sense.] Lawn made of the finest hemp or flax. *Rare.* — **1833** *Niles' Reg.* XLIV. 269/1 List of Linens to be admitted . . . [include] lawns: German estopillas: table cloths and napkins.

estray(s) book. A book in which descriptions of estrays are entered. — **1789** *Ky. Gazette* 28 March 1/3 All persons shall have access to the Estray-book, without paying any fee therefor. **1874** *Ill. Revised Statutes* 531 Upon the filing of such certificate, the county clerk shall immediately enter the same at large in a book . . . to be known as the 'estrays book.'

estufa ɛs'tufə, *n. S.W.* [Sp., stove, heated room.]

1. In the various Pueblo Indian villages, an assembly chamber, usu. underground and cylindrical in shape, in which a sacred fire is kept burning. Cf. **kiva, snake estufa.**

1844 Gregg *Commerce of Prairies* I. 271, I have myself descended into the famous *estufas,* or subterranean vaults, of which there were several in the village [of Pecos]. **1875** Parkman in *N. Amer. Rev.* CXX. 45 Each building, if of any considerable size, is provided with one or more estufas, or subterranean chambers, . . . where the men of the community meet for social, deliberative, and religious purposes. **1926** Cather *Death Comes* (1938) 175 And some place in there you may be sure, they keep Popé's *estufa,* but no white man will ever see it. I mean the *estufa* where Popé sealed himself up for four years and never saw the light of day.

2. A stove. *Obs.*

1887 *Scribner's Mag.* II. 509/2 If the weather is cold, you will probably find him [the cowboy] inside, hugging his *estufa* (Sp., stove).

Ethan Allen. ?A Morgan horse. *Rare.* — **1865** *Wilkes' Spirit of Times* 12 Aug. 371/2 Mr. Hamblin, one of our merchant princes, was letting out his splendid pair of Ethan Allens, turning the course under a strong pull at less than a three-minute gait.

etherion əˈθɪrɪən, *n.* [Gk. *aitherion*, ethereal.] (See quots.) — **1898** *Boston Herald* 24 Aug. 5/2 The day was signalized by an announcement in detail of a discovery . . . of a new gas in the atmosphere, that he [C. F. Brush] provisionally calls etherion. **1909** WEBSTER 753/2 *Etherion*, . . . an extremely light gas supposed to be contained in the air. The evidence of its existence is very unsatisfactory.

***etherize,** *v. tr.* **1.** To convert (alcohol, etc.) into ether. **2.** To put (a patient) under ether. Also transf.

(1) **1828** WEBSTER *Etherize* . . . to convert into ether. — (2) **1853** LOWELL *Fireside Trav.* 139 Gradually the mind was etherized to a like dreamy placidity. **1881** *Phila. Telegraph* XXXVI. 2 After the morning bulletin was issued he was etherized. **1887** *Courier-Journal* 17 Feb. 2/6 They etherized him. **1928** BAILEY *Cyclo. Horticulture* 1147/1 Etherized plants come into bloom earlier and may be forced at lower temperature than unetherized plants.

***Ethiopian,** *a.* Pertaining to stage representations of the Negro, esp. of the plantation type popularized by Negro minstrelsy.

1843 in ODELL *Ann. N.Y. Stage* IV. 668 C. D. Jenkins is the highly popular Comic Drollerist, . . . Ethiopian Singer and Extravaganist. **1847** *Chi. Journal* 7 Jan., First appearance of a young gentleman of this city in an Ethiopian Breakdown! **1889** W. DE VERE *De Vere's Negro Sk.* 76 An Ethiopian Dialogue. **1930** WITTKE *Tambo & Bones* 31 These attempts at 'Ethiopian Opera' by Rice were the precursors of the minstrel sketches that became an established feature of minstrel show programs in later years.

b. Ethiopian drama, a brief comic sketch written for performance by Negro impersonators or minstrels. Also collective.

1856 (*title*), Brady's Ethiopian Drama: Oh Hush! **1885** *Gentlemen Coon's Parade* 1 A Complete Descriptive Catalogue of DeWitt's Acting Plays, and DeWitt's Ethiopian and Comic Dramas . . . mailed free and post-paid. **1915** *Scribner's Mag.* LVII. 757/2 There is in print, in a collection of so-called 'Ethiopian Drama,' an amusing sketch entitled the 'Great Mutton Trial.'

c. Ethiopian Serenaders, (see quot. 1919). *Obs.* or *hist.*

1845 *St. Louis Reveille* 8 Jan. 2/3 The *Ethiopian Serenaders* . . . are here, and filling 'Washington Armory' to excess, with the beauty and fashion of the city. **1919** *Lit. Digest* 16 Aug. 28 'The Ethiopian Serenaders' [was a] group of American minstrels and one of the earliest organizations of its kind.

Also *Ethiopian absurdity, burlesque, farce, glee book, joke book, minstrelsy, sketch, stage,* etc.

***ethno-.** A combining form used in the sense of race, people, in such expressions as (1) **ethnobotanical,** of or pertaining to ethnobotany; (2) **botany,** "botany in its relations to the economic uses of plants by different races, especially by aborigines or primitive races" (*Cent. Supp.*); (3) **conchology,** the study of the uses which various peoples make of shells, also **ethnoconchological,** *a.*

(1) **1899** *Smithsonian Rep.* 65 In May, 1899, Dr. Walter Hough was detailed to carry on ethno-botanical researches in Mexico, in connection with certain explorations by the Division of Botany. **1944** ELMORE *Ethnobotany of the Navajo* 13 It is hoped that this will serve as a preliminary study to more extensive ethnobotanical research among the Navajo. — (2) **1890** in *Botanical Gazette* (1896) XXI. 146 (*title*), Purpose of Ethno-botany. **1896** *Amer. Anthro.* Jan. 14, I simply wish to call attention to the interesting field of ethnobotany which the Hopi Indians furnish the ethnologist. **1944** ELMORE (*title*), Ethnobotany of the Navajo. — (3) **1887** *U.S. Nat. Museum Rep.* 297 As we follow the direction of ethno-conchological inquiry over the pathway of dead centuries, we catch glimpses of great events. *Ib.*, (*title*), Ethno-Conchology—a Study of Primitive Money.

Euchee, see **Uchee.**

euchre ˈjukɚ, *n.* [See note.]

Of uncertain origin: "A German game, from whence the highest card or 'Bower' . . . takes its name" (1857 *Hoyle's Games* 285). "Euchre . . . has been traced to the counties of Lancaster, Berks, and Lehigh, in Pennsylvania, where it first made its appearance about forty years since" (1866 Dick *Amer. Hoyle* 57). "Some writers say that Euchre was first played by French settlers in Louisiana, and that both the game and its name are corruptions of the French *Écarté*" (1899 Champlin & Bostwick *Cyclo. Games & Sports* (ed. 2) 300/2).

1. A card game, played usu. by two, three, or four persons with a deck from which all cards lower than seven have been removed, the object of which is for one player (or side) to make three of five tricks or be "euchred," i.e., lose two points.

1841 *S. Lit. Messenger* VII. 54/2 A month ere I embarked I lost at euker. **1846** *Quincy* (Ill.) *Whig* 26 Feb. 3/1 In a short time, Euchre, at the suggestion of the ladies, was changed to Poker. **1945** *Grant Co.* (Wis.) *News* 12 April 7/7 The evening was spent playing euchre.

attrib. **1850** GARRARD *Wah-To-Yah* xx. 243 Jim . . . found himself . . . 'raking' the 'plews' from the less fortunate euchre and poker players. **1869** MARK TWAIN *Innocents* xvii. 160 At night there were gaps in the euchre-parties which could not be satisfactorily filled. **1944** *Pocket Bk. of Games* 181 There are many variants of this family, but the basic Euchre game is for two, three, or four players.

b. A party at which this game is played.

1903 *Cin. Enquirer* 4 Jan. 1/5 Euchres and Club meetings take up so much of the time of their wives that several men have recently been compelled to prepare their own suppers.

c. Used as the second element in names which denote variations of the game. Also attrib.

1845 *Lexington Obs. & Rep.* 29 March 1/2 It may be Crack Loo, Poker, Brag, or back Euchre, but he is not losing anything. **1889** *Cent.* 2022/2 Sometimes an additional card, called the *joker,* which is the highest of all the cards, is used, the game being then known as *railroad euchre.* **1892** DALY *Test Case* I. 21 There's a casino—and we have a progressive euchre club—penny a point. **1898** WESTCOTT *D. Harum* 36 Two-handed euchre! We have played . . . fifteen hundred games, in which he has held both bowers and the ace of trumps . . . fourteen hundred times. **1899** CHAMPLIN & BOSTWICK *Cyclo. Games & Sports* (ed. 2) 299/2 *Set-back Euchre.* . . . At the opening of the game each player's score is credited with five points. *Ib.* 300/2 Back-Handed Euchre. The players hold their cards with the faces toward the table, so that each sees all the hands but his own. **1944** *Pocket Bk. of Games* 183 Three-handed ('Cutthroat') Euchre is similar to the other Euchre games, except that the maker of the trump plays against the other two. *Ib.* 188 Call-Ace Euchre is for three to six players. **1949** *Ill. State Reg.* (Springfield) 1 Feb. 4/4 Members of the Sangamo club met at the clubrooms and participated in a progressive euchre party.

2. The action of the game wherein the player who has made trumps fails to take three tricks.

1876 HARTE *G. Conroy* VI. ii, And where am I now? Echo answers 'where?' and passes for a euchre! **1899** CHAMPLIN & BOSTWICK *Cyclo. Games & Sports* (ed. 2) 299/2 If a euchre is made under these circumstances, the score is four points.

euchre ˈjukɚ, *v.*

1. *intr.* ?To play at euchre. *Rare.*

1841 *S. Lit. Messenger* VII. 54/2 Go down and drink your strong compounded potion, and euker in a warmer atmosphere.

2. *tr.* (See quot. 1944.)

1847 ROBB *Squatter Life* 129 The next hand the stranger ordered the card up and was euchered. **1944** *Pocket Bk. of Games* 182 If he [the player who makes the trump] fails to win three tricks, he is euchred and his adversary scores 2 points.

b. *transf.* To defeat or overcome; to swindle, outwit, outmaneuver. *Slang.*

1855 *Pioneer* (S.F.) Nov. 319 Smith . . . got 'one-eye' Brown to play cards with him, *slipped upon the blind side of him and euchred him!* **1887** *Courier-Journal* 18 Feb. 1/2 A gentleman from Illinois, who was euchred out of his certificate by a technical cavil, also passed. **1905** PHILLIPS *Plum Tree* 144 He . . . worked hard and well for the election of the man who had euchred him out of the nomination. **1949** *Chi. Tribune* 15 Feb. 11/1 The belief that the British have euchred them out of the Marshall plan [has] . . . given the inhabitants of this bomb battered island [Malta] a feeling of having been abandoned by Britain now that they are no longer needed in the war.

eulachon ˈjuləkən, *n.* Also **ulken, ulicon,** etc. [Chinook Jargon *ulâkân*, in same sense.] The candlefish, *Thaleichthys pacificus.* Also attrib.

1807 GASS *Journal* 187 In the afternoon some of the natives came to visit us, and brought some of the small fish, which they call Ulken. **1871** DE VERE 386 *Oulachan* . . . is the native name, often misrepresented as Houlikan, and even Eulachon, of a small salmonoid fish of the Pacific coast. **1880** JACKSON *Alaska* 42 All the early navigators and explorers . . . have spoken of its immense numbers of salmon, cod, herring, halibut, ulicon, etc. **1941** MCCOWAN *Naturalist* 202 The Indians said that sturgeon were never so fat or so good as in oolachon time.

Eureka State. California; a nickname, in allusion to the motto, "Eureka," on the state shield. — **1863** *Humboldt Reg.* (Unionville, Nev.) 2 May 3/5 The climate of the blessed Eureka State is the very perfection of terrestrial and celestial atmospheric and meteorological influences.

∗**European,** *a.*

1. Designating various plants that are native to Europe, but naturalized and cultivated in the U.S., as (1) **European alder,** (2) **ash (tree),** (3) **beech,** (4) **elm,** (5) **filbert,** (6) **goldenrod,** (7) **grape,** (8) **hazelnut,** (9) **holly,** (10) **ivy,** (11) **larch,** (12) **laurel,** (13) **peppergrass,** (14) **silver fir,** (15) **sycamore,** (16) **white birch,** (17) **yew.**

(1) **1897** Sudworth *Arborescent Flora* 144 *Alnus glutinosa,* . . . European Alder. . . . [Note:] This alder . . . has become perfectly naturalized in many localities in the United States. — (2) **1846** Browne *Tree* 384 *Fraxinus excelsior,* The European Ash-tree. **1892** Apgar *Trees Northern U.S.* 124 *Fraxinus excelsior,* European Ash, . . . is common in cultivation. — (3) **1863** Gray *Botany* p. lxxviii, *Fagus sylvatica, European Beech,* . . . —a variety with copper or bronze-colored leaves is planted. **1892** Apgar *Trees Northern U.S.* 161 European Beech. . . . This Beech, with its numerous varieties, is the one usually cultivated. — (4) **1815** *N. Amer. Rev.* II. 59 All the American, but only a single European elm, escaped [destruction]. **1846** Browne *Trees* 479 *Ulmus capestris,* the European or Field Elm.

(5) **1863** Gray *Botany* p. lxxviii, *Corylus Avellana,* European Hazelnut or Filbert. — (6) **1829** Eaton *Botany* (ed. 5) 400 *Solidago virgaurea,* european golden-rod. — (7) **1863** Gray *Botany* p. xli, *Vitis vinifera,* European Grape. Leaves very soon glabrous; flowers all perfect. — (8) **1863** [see **European filbert**]. — (9) **1846** Browne *Trees* 160 The European Holly [*Ilex aquifolium*] is a handsome conical, evergreen tree.

(10) **1837** Lincoln *Botany* 182 European ivy. Hedera. — (11) **1863** Gray *Botany* p. lxxix, *Larix Europaea,* European Larch, is the species commonly planted, a finer tree and of more rapid growth than the American, its leaves longer, and its cones larger, 1½′ long. **1892** Apgar *Trees Northern U.S.* 188 *Larix Europæa* . . . (European Larch). . . . A beautiful tree with horizontal branches and drooping branchlets; abundant in cultivation. — (12) **1846** Browne *Trees* 410 *Laurus nobilis,* the Noble Laurel Tree. . . . European Laurel, Sweet Bay. — (13) **1901** Mohr *Plant Life Ala.* 522 *Lepidium ruderale.* . . . European Peppergrass. . . . Alabama. Coast plain. Waste places. — (14) **1858** Warder *Hedges & Evergreens* 255 *Picea pectinata,* the European Silver Fir, . . . is remarkable for the regularity and symmetry of its form. **1892** Apgar *Trees Northern U.S.* 187 *Abies pectinata.* . . . (European or Common Silver Fir.) . . . Good specimens can be found as far north as Massachusetts, though our climate is not fitted to give them either long life or perfect form.

(15) **1846** Browne *Trees Amer.* 88 *Acer pseudo-platanus.* The European Sycamore-tree. — (16) **1892** Apgar *Trees Northern U.S.* 146 *Betula alba.* (European White Birch.) . . . From Europe, extensively cultivated in this country, under many names. — (17) **1863** Gray *Botany* p. lxxix, *Taxus baccata,* European Yew. . . . Rarely grows well in this country.

Also *European dodder, lime-tree, linden, olive, watercress,* etc.

2. Designating birds and other animals, as (1) **European crossbill,** (2) **goldfinch,** (3) **house sparrow,** (4) **oyster,** (5) **widgeon.**

(1) **1917** *Birds of Amer.* III. 10 European Crossbills have been imported into America, but it is not known if the stock has continued. — (2) **1917** *Birds of Amer.* III. 13 European Goldfinch, *Carduelis carduelis.* . . . Other Names.—Thistle Finch; Thistle Birds. . . . Introduced into the northeastern United States. — (3) **1870** *Amer. Naturalist* III. 635 European House Sparrow. *Passer domestica,* Leach. The few pairs turned loose in the Boston Common a few years since seem to be slowly increasing in numbers, and bid fair to be of great service in checking the ravages of several species of caterpillars that now greatly injure the foliage of the shade trees. **1917** *Birds of Amer.* III. 17. — (4) **1884** *Nat. Museum Bul.* No. 27, 252 *Ostrea edulis* . . . [is known as] European oyster. — (5) **1917** *Birds of Amer.* I. 119 European widgeon. *Mareca penelope.*

3. In special combs., chiefly obs.: (1) **European brigade,** an armed body of men organized among the non-English-speaking residents of New Orleans during the Civil War, cf. **foreign legion;** (2) **goods,** goods made in Europe and imported into the U.S.; (3) **hotel,** a hotel operated on the European plan; (4) **legion,** = **European brigade;** (5) **plan,** the system used in some hotels of charging separately for lodging and for each meal taken in the hotel, also attrib.; (6) **settlement,** a settlement founded by or made up of people who came to America from Europe.

(1) **1862** in F. Moore *Rebellion Rec.* IV. I. 74/1 European brigades are rapidly organizing in New Orleans. — (2) **1715** *Boston News-Letter* 16 May 2/2 (*advt.*), Lately arrived from England . . . new Fashion Looking-Glasses and Chimney-Glasses, and sundry other European Goods. **1811** *Niles' Reg.* I. 45 Strong heavy goods . . . were the most advanced above the European goods of the same kinds. — (3) **1899** Ade *Doc' Horne* 26 It was the Alfalfa European Hotel, Alfalfa, because the name had a pleasing sound; European, because no meals were served in the house. — (4) **1862** in F. Moore *Rebellion Rec.* V. II. 1 The civil authorities [of New Orleans] found it necessary to call for the intervention of an armed body known as the European Legion to preserve public tranquility.

(5) **1834** *Sun* (N.Y.) 26 May 2/1 The hard times did not warrant his taking board on the 'European Plan.' **1847** Briggs *Tom Pepper* I. 201 Her establishment was conducted on the 'European plan,' and silver forks and finger-glasses, were things of course. **1948** *Chi. Tribune* 1 Aug. VII. 18/1 A European plan operation is where there are separate charges for each of these items. — (6) **1789** *Ann. 1st Congress* I. 57 It will be expedient to direct a bill to be brought in for imposing similar restraints upon the trade of the European settlements in America with the United States. **1881** *Harper's Mag.* March 524/1 Albany or Beverwych, is one of the oldest of the permanent European settlements in the United States.

euthenics juˈθɛnɪks, *n.* [f. Gk. *euthēnein,* to thrive, on the pattern of ∗*eugenics.*] (See 1910 quots.)

1910 Richards *Euthenics* vii, The betterment of living conditions, through conscious endeavor, for the purpose of securing efficient human beings, is what the author means by Euthenics. *Ib.* viii, Euthenics precedes eugenics, developing better men now, and thus inevitably creating a better race of men in the future. **1943** *Cat. Vassar Coll.* 93 The purpose of the major field in euthenics is to help the student to group courses which lay stress on acquiring theory and technique in certain fields of knowledge fundamental to the betterment of living.

Hence **euthenist,** *n.*

1912 Goddard *Kallikak Family* 52 It is not possible to convince the euthenists (who hold that environment is the sole factor) that, had the children of Jonathan Edwards and the children of 'Old Max' changed places, the results would not have been such as to show that it was a question of environment and not of heredity.

Evacuation Day. A holiday observed in New York City to commemorate the withdrawal of the British troops at the close of the Revolutionary War (see also quot. 1937).

*c***1824–38** G. Furman *Antiquities L.I.* 269 The Evacuation day, November 25th, the day on which the British army left Brooklyn, on this island, and also the City of New York, in the year 1783, has been observed as a species of holiday on the west end of Long Island. **1898** *N.Y. Tribune* 13 Nov. II. 1/2 The Old Guard will depart from its usual custom this year and celebrate Evacuation Day by a parade in Brooklyn. **1937** *Amer. Bk. of Days* 165 Evacuation Day in Boston: the evacuation of Boston, Mass., by the British on March 17, 1776 is celebrated annually in that city. **1941** Seton *Trail of Artist-Naturalist* 241, I found I had on hand thirteen cents, and ahead of me two blank days—Sunday, and also Monday, which, being Evacuation Day, was a public holiday.

b. Evacuation night, the night following Evacuation Day.

1856 Cozzens *Sparrowgrass P.* vi. 68 One is that of the horse-ghost, who may be seen every Evacuation night.

evalue ɪˈvælju, *v.* [Prob. f. ∗*evaluation,* but cf. F. *évaluer.*] *tr.* To evaluate. — **1904** *Nation* 15 Dec. 487/2 We have but to call the roll of the personal forces he [Arthur Symons] has evalued to apprehend pretty clearly the direction in which the significance of his criticism is to be sought.

∗**evangelical,** *a.*

1. Evangelical Association, (see quot. 1909).

[**1844** Rupp *Relig. Denominations* 209 In Rhode Island, an evangelical association of ministers was formed in 1808. The next year the name was changed to that of the 'Evangelical Consociation,' by which it is now known.] **1883** Schaff *Religious Encycl.* I. 776/1 Several years after his [Jacob Albright's] death (1808) his followers . . . adopted for their organization the name of . . . 'Evangelical Association of North America.' **1909** Webster 758/3 Evangelical Association, a religious body, Methodist in polity and doctrine, founded in 1800 by Jacob Albright in Pennsylvania. . . . Originally, almost entirely composed of German-speaking people.

2. Evangelical Treasury, (see quot.). *Rare.*

1726 *N.-Eng. Courant* 12–19 March 2/1 On Sunday last were read at Seven Meeting Houses in this Place, Proposals for an Evangelical Treasury, to be rais'd by Contribution on publick Fasts and Thanksgivings, and the Money to be drawn out for pious Uses.

∗**evangelist,** *n.* A revivalist.

1847 *Semi-Wkly. News* (Fredericksburg, Va.) 6 Sep. 2/4 'My good woman,' said the evangelist, . . . 'have you got the gospel here?' **1910** O. O. Green *Normal Evangelism* 46 When things begin to drag in church affairs, . . . the first suggestion usually is: 'Let's send for an evangelist.' **1948** CHAPLIN *Wobbly* 302 Billy Sunday, the great Christian evangelist, was reported shouting to his congregations [etc.].

b. Also **evangelism.**

1910 O. O. GREEN *(title)*, Normal Evangelism. **1940** *Dict. Amer. Hist.* II. 230 To a large degree evangelism or revivalism is peculiar to America. . . . Though emotional evangelism has generally been considered as furthered principally by Baptists and Methodists, as a matter of fact, the greatest of all the individual evangelists have been either Presbyterians or Congregationalists.

evaporated milk. Milk concentrated by evaporation to one half or less of its original bulk and canned, without the addition of sugar, for preservation. Cf. **condensed milk.** — **1923** WARD *Encycl. of Food* 146 Condensed and Evaporated Milk. The invention of the first commercially successful process of condensing milk is generally attributed to Gail Borden in the United States in 1856, but some authorities give the credit to Switzerland. **1947** *Atlantic Mo.* June 75/2 It is noticeable that the size of plants, if not the size of corporations, has been shrinking in the ice industry, steam and electric car manufacture, screw-machine products, structural and ornamental metalwork, and condensed and evaporated milk.

***evaporator,** *n.* A shallow rectangular receptacle, usu. with wooden sides and a metal bottom, used on an arch (sense **2.**) in converting sugar cane juice or maple sap into sirup or sugar.

1822 *Farmer's Diary* (1823) (Canandaigua, N.Y.) C3r The evaporators are not removed during the summer, but only turned bottom upwards and exposed to the weather. **1892** *Outing* March 461/2 We draw near the blazing fire and watch the men pour into the great

Evaporator in place on an arch (sense 2)

mysterious evaporators the sap which runs its tortuous course and comes out syrup at the other end. **1948** *Democrat* 5 Aug. 1/4 Galvanized Evaporators for syrup making, sizes 7½, 9 and 10½ ft. lengths.

***Eve,** *n.* In the possessive in the names of plants having a fancied domestic usefulness, as **Eve's cup, Eve's darning needle, Eve's thread,** (see quots.).

1907 LYONS *Plant Names* 415 *S[arracenia] purpurea* . . . Side-saddle Flower, . . . Eve's-cup, . . . Indian-pitcher. — **1892** *Amer. Folk-Lore* V. 104 *Yucca filamentosa*, . . . Eve's darning needle. Fort Worth, Texas. **1931** CLUTE *Plants* 80 Such names as Adam's flannel (*Verbascus thapsus*) and Eve's darning needle (*Yucca filamentosa*) must have been invented after the pair left the garden; at least they apparently had no use for flannel and darning needles earlier. — **1891** *Cent.* 7026/2 From their sharp-pointed leaves with threads hanging from their edges, *Yucca filamentosa* and *Y. aloifolia* are known as *Adam's needle and thread* and as *Eve's thread.* **1894** *Amer. Folk-Lore* VII. 104 *Hemerocallis fulva*, . . . Eve's thread. West Va. **1925** *Univ. Summer Sess. Kansan* (Lawrence, Kans.) 3 July, It [yucca] is also known as 'Soapweed' and 'Adam's needle.' One species is called 'Eve's thread' because of the fine filaments on the ends of the leaves.

***even,** *a.* and *v.*

1. a. *To even up on* or *with*, to make a return or requital to (a person). **b.** *to get even*, to get revenge upon an enemy or opponent, to retaliate.

(a) 1892 GUNTER *Miss Dividends* 88 'You and the Cop has done me a good turn' he says. 'Some day I'll even up on you.' **1912** WASON *Friar Tuck* 107 Now listen; would you be willin' to risk a little money to even up with Eugene? — **(b) 1845** SOL. SMITH *Theatr. Apprent.* 148, I took my seat with the hope of getting even. **1923** VANCE *Baroque* 40 If crooks didn't never get sore on each other and blow the works to get even.

2. *even Stephen*, exactly even, with no advantage to either side. *Colloq.*

1866 C. H. SMITH *Bill Arp* 64 Dick says you allowed the members to exchange two hundred dollars for two hundred dollars of State money, even steven. **1949** *Sat. Ev. Post* 12 Mar. 132/2 It occurred to me irresistibly that it would be only fair if I were to find a woman who could support me in the manner to which I'd become accustomed. Protection for support. Even Stephen.

***evener,** *n.* (See quot. 1874.) See **singletree.** — **1874** KNIGHT 813/2 *Evener*, a double or treble tree to 'even' or divide the work of pulling upon the respective horses. **1919** CADY *Rhymes of Vt.* (1923) 103 You brace your feet and take the reins, The neckyoke bumps, the evener strains.

***evening,** *n.* In combs.: (1) **evening grosbeak,** the sugar bird or American hawfinch, *Hesperiphona vespertina*, found chiefly in the western U.S.; (2) **line,** a boat line with boats scheduled to leave or run in the evening, *obs.*, cf. **day line;** (3) **paper,** a newspaper or an edition of a newspaper designed to go on sale in the afternoon or evening; (4) **Evening Post man,** a political partisan of the N.Y. *Evening Post*, a Federalist party organ founded by Alexander Hamilton, *obs.*, cf. **blue light;** (5) **snow,** a small, white-flowered annual, *Linanthus dichotomus*, found in California.

(1) 1828 BONAPARTE *Ornithology* II. 75 [The] Evening Grosbeak, *Fringilla Vespertina*, . . . appears to have an extensive range in the northern and northwestern parts of this continent. **1949** *Pacific Discovery* Jan.–Feb. 12/2 Evening grosbeaks, acorn woodpeckers, and a galaxy of warblers and flycatchers all added their songs and colors to the sunny mornings. — **(2) 1843** *Hunt's Merch. Mag.* IX. 184 The People's Line consists of the steamboats . . . forming two daily evening lines between New York and Albany. — **(3) 1815** in STEVENS *N.Y. Typographical Soc.* (1913) 63 (We.), If a morning paper, $9 per week; if an evening paper, $8 per week. *a***1946** S. LEWIS *Ghost Patrol* 71 (We.), He purchased an evening paper. — **(4) 1836** in *Amer. Sp.* XVIII 124/1 Während Ihr hier zittertet und zagtet, waren die Blue lights von Connectitut [*sic*], die Evening Post men von Newyork . . . die besten Freunde der Britten. — **(5) 1903** AUSTIN *Land of Little Rain* 146 The white gilias set their pale disks to the westering sun. This is the gilia the children call 'evening snow.'

eventualize ɪˈvɛntʃʊəlˌaɪz, *v. intr.* To come to pass, usually as a result of certain circumstances. — **1908** *Practitioner* Sep. 480 The projected Institute of Medical Sciences might have covered the ground if it had, as the Americans say, 'eventualised.'

eventuate ɪˈvɛntʃʊˌet, *v. intr.* To result, come out, or come to pass.

1789 MORRIS in Sparks *Life G. Morris* I. 313, I am sure it is wrong, and cannot eventuate well. **1836** *S. Lit. Messenger* II. 388/2 Eventuate. The editor of Coleridge's Table Talk very justly denounces this Americanism. **1855** MITCHELL *Fudge Doings* I. 37 He hopes it may 'eventuate' . . . in something practical. **1920** HOWELLS *Vacation of Kelwyns* 156 The help which Parthenope rendered him, eventuated in so large a release of Mrs. Kite [etc.].

b. *tr.* To bring to an issue.

1816 L. DOW *Journal* (1848) 348 The Great Being has a hand to attend, and superintend human affairs to eventuate the same. **1837** HALIBURTON *Clockmaker* 1 Ser. 208 Yes, (to eventuate my story) it did me good.

***ever,** *adv.* Used with a superlative in the sense "ever known." *Colloq.*

1906 O. HENRY *Four Million* vii. (1916) 71 Anna and Maggie worked side by side in the factory, and were the greatest chums ever. **1924** *Westm. Gaz.* 12 Aug., Mr. Coolidge is expected to reach the largest audience ever in his acceptance address as Republican candidate. **1927** B. K. SEYMOUR *Three Wives* I. ix, It *is* the nicest thing—the nicest ever.

everglade ˈɛvəˌgled, *n.* [See note.]

App. f. **ever*+*glade*, but if so the formation is somewhat irregular and the intended etymological sense uncertain, unless *ever* was used loosely in the sense of "interminable."

1. A low, marshy region, usu. under water and overgrown with tall grass, cane, etc. Chiefly *cap.* and *pl.*, with reference to the extensive region of this nature in Florida.

1823 TANNER *Map Florida*, Extensive Inundated Region . . . generally called the Everglades. **1893** *Harper's Mag.* March 508 Many of them [Seminole Indians] have rescued white men who have become lost in the interminable mazes of the grassy and island-cluttered Everglades. **1947** *Nat. Geog. Mag.* Feb. 232/2 Experimental plantings have been made in the Everglades and other points in Florida.

b. Everglades National Park, (see quot.).

1947 *So. Sierran* Aug. 1/1 On June 20, Secretary of Interior Krug signed the order establishing 710 square miles in southern Florida as Everglades National Park.

2. everglade kite, (see quot. 1889).

1889 *Cent.* 2040/2 *Everglade kite, Rostrhamus sociabilis*, having a long, very slender, and much-hooked bill. **1895** *Dept. Agric. Yrbk. 1894* 218 The everglade kite is found within our borders in Florida only, where it is restricted to the middle and southern portions. **1942** Nat. Pks. Service *Fading Trails* 169 In fact, there are only one or two spots in the entire State where, with luck, an Everglade kite may be seen.

* **evergreen,** *a.* In combs.: (1) **evergreen arrowwood,** prob. a species of *Viburnum;* (2) **fetterbush,** (see quot.); (3) **grass,** (see quot. 1889); (4) **millet,** (see quot.); (5) **Evergreen State,** (see quots.).

(1) **1815** D. DRAKE *Cincinnati* ii. 77 [Plants of the Miami region in Ohio include the] Evergreen arrow-wood. — (2) **1901** MOHR *Plant Life Ala.* 122 Evergreen fetterbushes (*Pieris nitida, Leucothöe axillaris*) forming the brushy soil cover. — (3) **1856** *Rep. Comm. Patents: Agric.* 253 The evergreen-grass . . . is very good for pasturing, through the fall and winter. **1889** VASEY *Agricultural Grasses* 52 *Arrhenatherum avenaceum* (Evergreen Grass; Meadow Oat Grass; Fall Oat Grass). — (4) **1889** VASEY *Agric. Grasses* 36 *Sorghum halepense* (Johnson Grass; Mean's Grass). . . . In California it is best known as evergreen millet or Arabian evergreen millet. — (5)**1905** *N. Eng. Mag.* Oct. 113/1 From staid old New England, the cradle of American liberty, to Washington, the Evergreen State, is a far cry even in this day of rapid transit. **1909** WEBSTER 760/1 E[vergreen] State, Washington;—from the abundance of evergreen trees. **1948** *Dly. Ardmoreite* (Ardmore, Okla.) 2 April 7/2 Farmers in the evergreen state are pinning their hopes on the best moisture conditions in several years.

As the last term in **trailing evergreen.**

***everlasting,** *n.* A long-drawn-out card game in which a player turning up a card from his stock that matches another player's exposed card is entitled to all the turned cards beneath it, the game continuing until one player has all the cards. — **1840** DANA *Two Years* xv, The favorite game of 'treinta uno,' a sort of Spanish 'everlasting.' **1873** PHELPS *Trotty's Wedding* v, She played checkers. She played 'everlasting.'

* **everlasting,** *adv.* Very, extremely. *Colloq.*

1832 S. SMITH *Major Downing* 95, I had rather fight forty New Orleans battles than to govern this everlasting great country one year. **1848** LOWELL *Letters* I. 136 It's everlasting hot to-day. **1902** WIGGIN *Rebecca* 262 When she'd clim' as fur as she could in the world, she'd kick the ladder from out under her, everlastin' quick.

b. Also **everlastingly.**

1889 *Cent.* 2040/3 He is everlastingly stingy.

* **every,** *a.* In colloq. expressions: (1) **everydayness,** the state of being prosaic or commonplace; (2) **last,** absolutely all or every one; (3) **time,** on all occasions; (4) **which way,** in every way, in all directions.

(1) **1840** LOWELL *Poetical Works* (1896) 7 The everydayness of this work-day world. **1876** A. D. WHITNEY *Sights & Insights* xxiv, I have not tolerance for this nice, jolly everydayness. — (2) **1888** MARK TWAIN *Meisterschaft* 460 (R.), I know it is with me—every last sentence of it. — (3) **1864** *Ill. Agric Soc. Trans.* (1865) V. 318, I advise every body to plant it, . . . but always charge them to also plant Delaware and Catawba without fail, 'every time.' — (4) **1824** SINGLETON *Letters* 82 They [Virginians] say . . . madam and mistress, instead of our abbreviations. Children learn from the slaves some odd phrases; as, every which way; will you *all* do this? for, will *one* of you do this? **1887** TOURGEE *Button's Inn* 80 You've done . . . more'n any other man would have done, working and contriving every which way. **1949** *Nat. Hist.* April 177/2 The supplejack grows every which way and is the toughest, woodiest, and most luxuriant of the lianas.

***evil,** *n.* As the last term in **foot, milk, snowshoe evil.**

evolute ˈɛvəˌlut, *v.* [Back formation from **evolution.*] *intr.* and *tr.* To develop, to progress by evolution.

1884 *Cambridge* (Mass.) *Tribune* 15 Aug., If those miserable vagrants could only evolute into respectable people there would be converts to evolution at once. **1885** *Rep. Indian Affairs* 33 The changed mode of life . . . will eventually 'evolute' 'Poor Lo' to a higher sphere in the happy hunting grounds. **1893** *Cong. Rec.* 18 Aug. 473/2 While we have been 'evoluting' toward a gold basis.

***evolve,** *v. intr.* To become known, to "turn out." — **1923** UNA L. SILBERRAD *Lett. Jean Armitar* i, However, it evolved in the course of time, chiefly through the agency of Mrs. Clayton, that Jean was remaining here.

* **ex-.** A prefix widely used in terms of obvious meaning, as (1) **ex-boss,** (2) **Confederate,** (3) **congressman,** (4) **governor,** (5) **keelboatman,** (6) **Missourian,** (7) **president,** (8) **reb,** (9) **rebel,** (10) **scissorize,** (11) **senator,** (12) **Union soldier,** (13) **vice-president.**

(1) **1861** WINTHROP *Open Air* 133 'I'm glad to be out of a sinking ship,' said the ex-boss. — (2) **1880** *Harper's Mag.* LXI. 358/2 On the street . . . was the ex-Confederate colonel. *Ib.* 485/1 The conductor was an ex-Confederate captain. **1947** DOWNEY *Lusty Forefathers* 289 Their evil genius, Hastings, died in 1870 in Brazil where he was seeking to found a colony of ex-Confederates. — (3) **1902** MARK TWAIN *Does the Race Love a Lord?* 443 (R.), That is the ex-Congressman: the poor fellow whose life has been ruined by a two-year taste of glory and of fictitious consequence. **1915** BRYAN *Memoirs* (1925) 434 Ex-Congressman John Lentz had been speaking to them. — (4) **1835** *Vade Mecum* (Phila.) 24 Oct. 2/7 Ex-Governor Houston [has] . . . written to Washington to entreat the interference of the National Government in their behalf. **1948** *So. Weekly* 3 Nov. 4/2 To be a governor or an ex-governor of the great State of New York, gives one the inside track in the Presidential derby.

(5) **1883** MARK TWAIN *Life on Miss.* iii. 42 (R.), I remember . . . the ex-keelboatmen and their admiring patronizing successors. — (6) **1867** RICHARDSON *Beyond Miss.* xi. 145 One of my Pro-slavery neighbours, an ex-Missourian, addressed me at the polls. — (7) **1798** F. AMES *Works* (1854) I. 221 On Thursday last, the 22nd, the ex-President's birthday was celebrated in Concert Hall. **1949** *Chi. D. News* 30 Jan. 10/6 Our only living ex-President was given an impolite brushoff in '32. — (8) **1909** O. HENRY *Roads of Destiny* 350 That's why you see me cake-walking with the ex-rebs to the illegitimate tune about 'simmon-seeds and cotton. — (9) **1865** *Nashville* (Tenn.) *D. Union* 13 July 1/6 The writer of the letter is an ex-rebel soldier and is . . . a trifle profane. **1876** *Nevada Tribune* (Carson City) 5 Oct. 3/2 The two candidates are ex-rebels, . . . and the show is said to be as good as a circus.

(10) **1831** *Boston Transcript* 1 April 2/1 The paragraph above quoted, was *ex-scissorized,* some days since, from the New-York Commercial Advertiser. **1846** *Quincy* (Ill.) *Whig* 26 Feb. 3/2 Yes, madam, we exscissorize some, . . . editing a paper. — (11) **1856** MACLEOD *F. Wood* 294 An ex-Senator and a member of the Assembly of the State of New-York, were then introduced. — (12) **1868** in STEVENSON *Ku Klux Klan* (1871) In some districts ex-Union soldiers are persecuted by their more numerous rebel neighbors. **1911** *Okla. Session Laws* 3 Legisl. 217 It shall be lawful for any indigent or disabled ex-Confederate or ex-Union soldier . . . residing in this state . . . to give illustrated lectures. — (13) **1872** *Newton Kansan* 29 Aug. 2/4 There are now five ex-vice presidents living.

Exalted Cyclops, see **Cyclops.**

* **examiner,** *n.*

1. An official in the Patent Office who looks into the advisability of granting particular patents.

1848 *Whig Almanac 1849* 21/2 The Commissioner of Patents . . . is to refer every application for a renewal to the 'Principal Examiner having charge of the class of inventions to which said case belongs.' **1891** *Atlantic Mo.* June 808/1 A colored assistant examiner in the Patent office department has . . . placed at my service a list of some fifty patents taken out by colored people.

2. =**bank examiner.** Cf. **national bank examiner.**

1882 *Cent. Mag.* March 776/2 When the examiner made his visit, the loan was called and credited in New York, but the officers failed to tell him of the fact. **1931** *Blue Valley Farmer* (Okla. City) 10 Sep. 6/2 The examiners, in going to the smaller banks, have criticized and 'blue penciled' farmer paper.

* **excavator,** *n.* A machine for excavating earth, a steam shovel. Cf. **digging machine.**

Patents for such machines began as early as 1820 and by 1873 over one hundred patents had been issued for devices of many kinds called "excavators."

1843 *Niles' Reg.* 25 Nov. 200/1 With this excavator he is levelling hills. **1848** *Rep. Comm. Patents 1847* 72 Two patents have been granted for excavators. **1878** *Pat. Off. Gazette* XIV. 654/2 Excavators [patented by] Anderson W. Terrill. **1910** *Ib.* CLIV. 280/1.

* **excellency,** *n. His Excellency,* a title of honor applied to:

a. A colonial governor in America. *Obs.*

1680 SEWALL *Diary* I. 49 His Excellency, Thomas, Lord Culpeper, Baron of Thorsway, Gov. of Virginia, came to Boston. **1705** *Boston News-Letter* 22–29 Jan. 2/2 By His Excellency's Direction Capt. Tyng and Capt. Stephens with 150 Men with Snow Shoes march'd . . . into the Woods in search of the Enemy. **1780** in *Sp. & Doc. Amer. Hist.* I. (1944) 32 There shall be a supreme executive magistrate, who shall be stiled, The Governor of the Commonwealth of Massachusetts, and whose title shall be His Excellency.

b. The President of the U.S.

1789 *Ann. 1st Congress* I. 33 The question was taken, 'Whether the President of the United States shall be addressed by the title of *His Excellency?*' and it passed in the negative. **1832** FERRALL *Ramble thro' U.S.* 308 The president, is 'his excellency,'—'congress men,' are 'honorables.' **1904** *Providence Jrnl.* 25 Aug. 6 Dr. Swallow makes one curious mistake in addressing his letter to 'His Excellency.' The President of the United States has no such title.

c. A person of note, esp. the governor of a state.

[**1789** FRANKLIN *Letter* 3 Aug. (MS), The word Excellency does not belong to me, and Dr. will be sufficient to distinguish me from my Grandson. **1833** T. HAMILTON *Men & Manners* I. 241 The governor of Massachusetts receives the title of Excellency.] **1857** in JOHNSON *Anderson Co., Kansas* 33 It is ordered by the county commissioners that the following appointments, made by his excellency, John W. Geary, be approved by the court of Anderson county. **1915** *Springfield W. Republican* 20 May 3 In Massachusetts . . . the governor will remain 'his excellency' until the end of the chapter. [**1942** HARRIMAN *Bk. of Etiquette* 449 Although 'Excellency' doesn't officially belong to him, a governor is courteously referred to by that title.]

excelsior ɪkˈsɛlsɪɚ, *a.* and *n.* [L., higher.]

1. *n.* (*cap.*) The motto of New York State. Hence **Excelsior State,** New York.

1778 in *N.Y. Senate 104th Sess.* Doc. No. 61, Plate 1 [facsimile of engraving of state arms], Excelsior. **1871** DE VERE 661 The motto 'excelsior,' upon its coat of arms has made it also known as the Excelsior State. **1948** MENCKEN *Supp.* II. 597 Another obsolete name, *Excelsior State*, was suggested by the fact that *Excelsior* is the motto on the seal of the State.

2. Fine shavings of wood used as a stuffing for cushions and mattresses, and as a packing material.

1868 *Specif. U.S. Patent* No. 75728 A machine for manufacturing that article of commerce technically called 'excelsior' for filling mattresses. **1905** *Outlook* 30 Dec. 1054/1 Nearly five hundred companies obtain their raw material for pulp, wood-acid, excelsior, . . . etc., from the mountain forests of New York State. **1948** *Reader's Digest* May 47/1 Importers of Mexican products have had to send great quantities of excelsior to their Mexican shippers.

3. *a.* Possessing superior qualities. Also absol.

1851 *Cat. Great Exhibition* III. 1467 Excelsior soap [An American Exhibit]. **1862** in F. MOORE *Rebellion Rec.* V. II. 232 Sickles's brigade is composed of the five 'Excelsior regiments.' **1870** *Dept. Agric. Rep. 1867* 253 The Excelsior oats came up promptly, grew vigorously, and produced a stiff, tall straw, with a large yield of heavy oats, which took the highest premium at the county fair. **1894** *Vt. Agric. Rep.* XIV. 379 Sweet corn . . . should be, in case of Potter's excelsior, not less than 8 inches long.

* **exchange,** *n.*

1. A drinking place or saloon. *Colloq. Obs.*

1835 *Vade Mecum* (Phila.) 7 Feb. 3/3 Mr. Coffee is well suited to the post, and will give satisfaction to the frequenters of the Exchange. **1839** *Boston W. Mag.* 1 June 310/3 Another lunch is spread out at 8 o'clock, P.M., at the different drinking places or Exchanges, as they are generally called. **1848** *Gem of Prairie* (Chi.) 25 March 4/1 Walker's celebrated exchange, in Louisville, Kentucky, is the favorite resort of the citizens of that burg. **1882** SALA *Amer. Revisited* II. 13 Here [in New Orleans] the dram shops are called 'exchanges.'

2. A periodical given by one publisher in return for that of another. Also attrib. Cf. **interchange paper, newspaper exchange.**

1798 *Ann. 5th Congress* II. 1318 The report also states that the great number of exchange papers which pass between the printers of newspapers is very troublesome. **1849** *Yale Lit. Mag.* XIV. 380 (Th.), We have space only for a brief notice of our Exchanges. **1948** *Dly. Ardmoreite* (Ardmore, Okla.) 11 July 21/5 If you have no further use for the exchanges that come to you from various small towns, . . . it would help a lot if you'd send a batch or so to me.

b. exchange list, a list of publishers with whom newspapers are exchanged.

1820 *Niles' Reg.* XVII. 385/1 Our exchange list is exceedingly burthensome as well as expensive. **1877** *Harper's Mag.* Dec. 109/1 The Daily Advertiser . . . boasted a circulation in every State and Territory of the Union, secured . . . by a prudent use of the exchange list. **1948** *Trail Riders Bul.* June 10/1 We would appreciate hearing from any such kindred trail organization and adding its name to our exchange list.

3. The central station of a telephone system. Also attrib. Cf. **telephone exchange.**

1887 *Trial H. K. Goodwin* 11 Mr. Swan, . . . became engaged in the telephone business . . . having charge of the Lawrence Exchange and its branches. **1903** *McClure's Mag.* Nov. 73 The exchange girl had come in and asked me what the matter was that I didn't hang up. **1948** *Reader's Digest* Dec. 14/2 Telephone operators remembered Margaret Chase who worked on the Skowhegan exchange in the old days.

4. An association of fruit-growers and marketers such as was first established in California in 1893.

1901 *Resources Santa Barbara Co., Calif.* 99 Marketing . . . is chiefly done through the large packing houses . . . and the Lemon Growers' Exchange. **1910** *Sat. Ev. Post* 16 July 17/3 It was Manager Moore's idea that Grand Valley apples, peaches and pears should be sold in substantially the same way that oranges and lemons are sold by the California Fruit Growers' Exchange. **1946** MCWILLIAMS *So. Calif. Country* 211 Long before the central exchange came into being, however, local packing and marketing associations were established throughout the area.

5. exchange note, a treasury note of the Texas Republic (authorized Dec. 14, 1837) in denominations of one, two, or three dollars, for use in changing notes of larger denominations. *Obs.*

1853 P. PAXTON *Yankee in Texas* 78 The Government had put forth a few exchange notes that were at par.

6. exchange stable, a stable at which horses may be exchanged. *Obs.* Cf. **horse exchange.**

1892 *York Co. Hist. Rev.* 67 Eyster & Wolf, Livery, Sale and Exchange Stables.

As the last term in **cotton, currency, gold, New York Stock, oil, silver, tobacco, Western exchange.**

* **exchequer,** *n.*

1. A currency bill, authorized by the Republic of Texas Jan. 19, 1842, payable on demand and receivable in payment of all public dues. In full **exchequer bill.** *Obs.*

1842 HOUSTON in Gouge *Fiscal Hist. Texas* (1852) 119 The exchequer bills being thus left dependent alone on import duties for their redemption, no other demand existing for them, depreciated. **1843** *Texian & Brazos Farmer* (Washington, Tex.) 22 April 3/1 There are now not more than $20,000 of Exchequers in circulation. **1874** WELLS *Practical Economics* (1885) 15 To the treasury notes succeeded what were termed 'exchequer bills'; but they were comparatively few in number, and never passed to any extent into circulation.

2. (*cap.*) (See quot.) *Obs.*

1877 BEARD *K. K. K. Sketches* 74 The commander of a Den . . . was entitled Grand Cyclops, and under him was an officer known as Exchequer, whose duties . . . applied to the administration of the treasury and recording secretaryship.

Exclusion Act. *Hist.* Any one of several acts passed by Congress to deport undesirable foreigners or prevent them from entering the U.S. — **1894** *Harper's Mag.* LXXXVIII. 480/1 The constitutionality of the Geary Chinese Exclusion Act was sustained by the Supreme Court. **1914** *Cyclo. Amer. Govt.* I. 41 The Anarchist Exclusion Act of March 3, 1903, permits the deportation of immigrants who are advocates of the overthrow of all government, or of the assassination of public officers.

exclusive extra. A vehicle engaged for the exclusive use of an individual or party. *Obs.* — **1836** *Knickerb.* VIII. 347 The 'exclusive extra' performed its locomotive office with wonderful rapidity and effect. **1850** HOUSTOUN *Hesperos* I. 239 We hired a huge coach, here called an 'extra.' . . . The carriage was capable of carrying nine persons in its interior. . . . When a carriage of this description is engaged for a private party, it is dignified by the name of an 'exclusive extra.'

* **excursion,** *n.* As the last term in **colony, land looking excursion.**

excurt ɪkˈskɜt, *v.* Also **excur.** *intr.* To go on an excursion. *Colloq. Obs.*

*c***1850** *Nat. Encycl.* I. 619 [Americanisms:] *Excur*, used as a verb in the sense of to take an excursion. **1870** *Washington Chron.* 17 April (De Vere), President Grant has once more excurted from Washington; he has gone on a visit to Mr. Cameron's home. **1873** *Winfield* (Kans.) *Courier* 5 June 3/1 He'll never be caught again spending two dollars and six bits 'excurting' over the Country.

excusing officer. Also **excuse officer.** A member of the faculty of a college authorized to excuse absences on the part of students. — **1934** BURGESS *Reminiscences* 59 The excusing officer of my class was at that time [1860's] one of the stiffest Puritans in the faculty, that is, one who held all pleasure to be sin. **1943** *Lake Forest Cat.* 32 Requests [for excused absences] from men should be submitted to the Excuse Officer for Men.

* **executive,** *a.* and *n.*

With senses **1.** and **2.** cf. **Chief Executive.**

1. *n.* The governor of a state or of a region that later became a state.

1776 JEFFERSON *Writings* IV. 258 The judicial power ought to be distinct from both the legislature and executive, and independent upon both. **1787** *Constitution* i. § 3 If vacancies [in the Senate] happen . . . during the recess of the Legislature of any State, the Executive thereof may make temporary appointment. **1842** *Diplom. Corr. Texas* III. (1911) 1253 They ought to bear the signature of the present Executive of Texas. **1910** *N.Y. Ev. Post* 21 April (Th.), Mr. Hughes . . . cannot complain now if people draw comparisons between the Executive at Albany and the Executive at Washington.

2. (Usu. *cap.*) The President of the U.S.

[**1774** JOHN ADAMS *Works* IX. 351 We have no council, no house, no legislative, no executive. **1787** RANDOLPH in Elliot *Deb. Constitution* (1836) I. 144 Resolved, That a national executive be instituted, to be chosen by the national legislature.] **1789** MACLAY *Deb. Senate* 79 Treaties formed by the Executive of the United States are to be the laws of the land. **1873** *Newton Kansan* 8 May 4/1 The Executive is bound by his position to enforce the constitution. **1945** *Christian*

Cent. 18 April 484/2 Now the President wants Congress to extend it again, and this time he asks that the executive shall be given power to cut such tariffs as may be involved.

3. Short for **executive department.**

[**1787** JEFFERSON *Writings* (1894) IV. 475, I like the organization of the government into Legislative, Judiciary & Executive.] **1789** *Ann. 1st Congress* I. 43 That six hundred copies of the acts of Congress . . . be printed, and distributed to the executive and judicial, and heads of departments of the Government of the United States, and the executive, legislative, and judicial of the several States. **1885** CRAWFORD *Amer. Politician* 63 We expect that by the mere signature of the head of the executive any man can be turned into an accomplished public officer. **1902** E. C. MEYER *Nominating Systems* 49 The voice of each individual voter . . . finally . . . finds its perfect expression in the legislature, the executive, or the judiciary.

4. The mayor or chief magistrate of a town or city.

1850 *Knickerb.* XXXV. 22 The official honors of the town-executive descended upon one man . . . who was justice of the peace, pathmaster, collector and town clerk. **1905** *Springfield W. Republican* 24 Nov. 3 No doubt the present executive has not pleased everybody. No mayor ever does.

5. An employee or an official of an organization having directive duties.

1902 LORIMER *Lett. Merchant* 22 They will never climb over the railing that separates the clerks from the executives. **1947** *Chi. Tribune* 2 Nov. III. 14/1 Do you want to be a secretary to an executive?

6. *a.* Energetic, competent, qualified to direct and control.

1708 PENN in *Pa. Hist. Soc. Mem.* X. 291 Rouse up, and be vigorous and executive. **1888** BRYCE *Amer. Commw.* II. III. lix. 412 The Americans are, to use their favourite expression, a highly executive people. *Ib.* 413 Long practice, and the fierce competition of the two great parties, have enabled this executive people to surpass itself in the sphere of electioneering politics.

7. Of or pertaining to the governor of a state. See **executive council** in **8.** below, and **Executive Mansion** as a main entry.

1794 *Ann. 4th Congress* 2 Sess. 2838 A separate . . . conduct was expected to be pursued by the Executive Magistrate of Pennsylvania. **1842** *Whig Almanac 1843* 30/2 On the 28th of May, 1834, Mr. Clay introduced resolutions reasserting his often repeated opinions concerning Executive usurpation. **1894** FORD *P. Stirling* 66 He sent in his card to the Governor. . . . he was ushered into the executive chamber.

b. Of or pertaining to the President of the U.S. See also **executive order, patronage** in **8.** below and **Executive Mansion** as a main entry.

1789 *Jrnl. Wm. Maclay* (1927) 107 To what purpose, then, is the executive power lodged with the President. **1829** *Central Watchtower* (Harrodsburg, Ky.) 20 Mar. 2/3 We have had enough of these sort of Executive Messages, and we rejoice to see the new President set out upon a different course. **1884** *N.Y. Herald* 14 Nov. 4/2 Mr. Cleveland takes the Executive chair with his hands free.

8. In special combs.: (1) ***executive committee,** a committee having executive powers in a political party, latterly, a committee which assists the national chairman of a political party; (2) **council,** a council that assists the governor of a state; (3) **department,** see as a main entry; (4) **Executive Mansion,** see as a main entry; (5) ***officer,** an officer ranking immediately below the captain on a U.S. naval vessel; (6) **order,** an order issued by the President, or, with his approval, by the head of a government department, supplementing, elaborating, or applying the provisions of a law passed by Congress; (7) **patronage,** the right or privilege of the President of the U.S. to appoint or nominate persons to offices or positions; (8) **session,** see as a main entry.

(1) **1852** *Dem. Nat. Convention Proc.* 3 In pursuance of the call of the National Democratic Executive Committee, the delegates from the several States of the Union . . . assembled this morning. **1900** *Ib.* 3 The Executive Committee shall be the chief executive power of the National Committee, having authority over all other sub-committees . . . and . . . the duty of carrying out the policies of the whole committee. **1924** *Rep. Campaign Text Book* (cover), Executive Committee, William M. Butler, Chairman (ex officio) Massachusetts; Charles D. Hilles, Vice Chairman [etc.]. — (2) **1778** in *Amer. Sp.* XX. (1945) 271 The same thing is working in Pensilvania, which appears by the address of the President and executive Council (the same as Governor and Council in other States) to the Assembly of Pensilvania. **1898** *K.C. Star* 18 Dec. 4/3 He thinks . . . more efficient men might be chosen by a state convention than by the six men who comprise the executive council.

(5) **1881** *Naval Encycl.* 255/1 The title of 'executive-officer' is of quite recent date, and has been the cause of much discussion, bad temper, and bitter opposition. **1889** *Cent.* 2062/2 [The] executive officer . . . on board a United States man-of-war . . . is next in command to the commanding officer. — (6) **1883** *Cent. Mag.* Aug. 517/1 By an executive order of the President, the little valley in which these Indians took refuge has been set apart for them as a reservation. **1912** TAFT in *Indian Laws & Tr.* 676 It is hereby ordered that Executive orders of August 25, 1887, March 9, 1881, and December 29, 1891, . . . be . . . modified and amended. — (7) **1804** *Ann. 8th Congress* 1 Sess. 1076, I am . . . unwilling to extend Executive patronage beyond the line of irresistible necessity. **1886** *Amer. Hist. Assoc. Papers* I. No. 5, 114 The change of terms from 'the appointing power' of the early period to 'executive patronage' . . . was significant if unconscious.

executive department.

1. In a state government, the department concerned with carrying out the laws.

1776 *Virginia Const.* (1864) 8 Article II. The legislative, executive and judiciary departments shall be separate and distinct, so that neither exercise the powers properly belonging to either of the others. **1855** *La. State Reg.* 29 Concerning the Executive Department . . . the supreme executive power shall be vested in a chief magistrate. **1914** *Mass. Commission on Econ. & Effic.* 43 The Executive Department has some duties relating to elections.

2. A similar department in the federal government at Washington.

1787 *Constitution* ii. § 2 The President . . . may require the Opinion, in writing of the principal Officer in each of the executive Departments, upon any subject [etc.]. **1886** ALTON *Among Law-Makers* 67 Congress has found it advisable to distribute the duties of administration among seven 'established executive departments.' **1948** *Capital-Democrat* (Tishomingo, Okla.) 3 June 6/6 Congress has relinquished all of its duties to the Executive department.

Executive Mansion.

1. The presidential mansion at Washington, D.C.

1838 *Diplom. Corr. Texas* I. (1908) 346, I went to the Executive Mansion and was introduced to the President by him. **1884** *Cent. Mag.* April 803/2 It was determined by Congress that the building should be officially named the 'Executive Mansion'—mansion being then a term of common use for the better-class dwellings of the gentry in Virginia and Maryland. **1945** *Time* 30 April 24 The Executive Mansion's normal order was lost in cheerless confusion and lights that burned late at night.

2. In some states, the residence of the governor.

1846 LYELL *Second Visit* (1849) II. 25 The Governor's lady [in Ga.] called on my wife and took her to her residence, called here the 'Executive Mansion.' **1910** *Okla. Session Laws* 3 Legisl. (1911) 5 The Executive Mansion shall be located in the vicinity of said capital grounds on a site consisting of one-half block, the same to be selected by the Capitol Commission. **1948** *Time* 21 June 22/1 Since he moved to the Executive Mansion, he has become a familiar sight on Harrisburg streets.

executive session. (See quot. 1914.)

1840 *Niles' Reg.* 26 Dec. 269 The senate held a short executive session, and then adjourned. **1868** *N.Y. Herald* 2 July 3/4 After a short executive session the Senate took a recess until half-past seven o'clock. **1914** *Cyclo. Amer. Govt.* I. 688 Executive Sessions. The term is applied to those legislative sessions, usually of the Senate, held to consider confidential business submitted by the executive, especially the confirmation of appointments, and, in the case of the United States Senate, the ratification of treaties.

transf. **1904** *N.Y. Times* 23 Nov. 1 President Orr requested all outsiders to leave the room, saying that the board had decided to discuss the Subway station advertising in 'executive session.' **1926** *Intimate Papers of Col. House* ii. 419 Almost as soon as we arrived, the President and I went into executive session. The President closed his study door so as not to be interrupted.

***exempt,** *n.*

1. A man excused from military duty. *Obs.*

1777 J. JONES *Letters* 1 The enlisting men for the usual bounty is now . . . impracticable, . . . on account of the high bounty given by the militia exempts. **1812** *Niles' Reg.* III. 79/1 In many places companies of exempts are organized. **1868** GREELEY *Autobiog.* 51 He commanded a company of 'exempts,' raised to defend the country in case of British invasion, during the war of 1812.

2. A member of a fire company who has been honorably discharged because of age. Also attrib.

1858 *Calif. Spirit of Times* (S.F.) 7 Aug. 3/1 (*heading*), Exempt Meeting. **1884** CABLE *Dr. Sevier* xlvi, Then came a long line of red-shirted firemen; for he in the hearse had been an 'exempt.'

∗**exercise,** *n.*

1. *pl.* Public proceedings or ceremonies on a special occasion.

[**1766** in B. Peirce *Hist. Harvard Univ.* (1833) 243 Twice in the year . . . some of the scholars, at the direction of the President and Tutors, shall publicly exhibit specimens of their proficiency, by pronouncing orations and delivering dialogues, either in English or in one of the learned languages, or having a forensic disputation, or such other exercise as the President shall direct.] **1841** Buckingham *America* II. 47 The First Reformed Dutch Church, where the 'exercises,' as all proceedings of public meetings are here called, were to take place. **1893** *Harper's Wkly.* 16 Dec. 1211/2 Great bunches of mistletoe were carried to the school-house to deck the barren room for holiday 'exercises.' **1945** *Athol* (Mass.) *D. News* 31 May 8/1 She was home for Memorial Day exercises.

2. A series of paroxysms or convulsions induced by excitement attendant upon revivalistic religious services. Now *hist.*

Cf. **barking, bodily, dancing, falling, jerking, jumping, laughing, rolling, running, singing, whirling exercise.**

1804 in J. Gallaher *Western Sketch-Book* 54 The only thing with us which can be construed into disorder or extravagance, is the motions of the body under the exercise. In most of the cases, when the paroxysm begins to go off, the subject feels the strongest desire for prayer. **1886** Z. F. Smith *Kentucky* 422 In the midst of religious services and enthused exhortation, the exercises of falling prostrate, jerking with nervous motions, and involuntary dancing, would begin. **1948** Dick *Dixie Frontier* 196 These spiritual 'exercises' burst into full flower.

exflunct ɪksˈflʌŋkt, *v. tr.* Also **exflunctícate, exflunctify.** To overcome or beat thoroughly, to "use up" completely. *Slang. Obs.*

1831 *Louisville* (Ky.) *Public Advt.* 17 Oct. 2/3 Clear meat-ax disposition; the best man, if I a'nt, I wish I may be tetotaciously exflunctedǃ **1839** *Chemung* (N.Y.) *Democrat* 30 Nov. (Th.), The mongrel armies are prostrate—used up—exflunctícated. **1840** *Cong. Globe* 21 July 545 [It has been proclaimed abroad] that the Administration is bodaciously used up, tetotaciously exflunctified. **1844** Featherstonhaugh *Excursion* 71 Stranger, if that ar hoss don't go like a screamer, I'll give you leave to ex-flunctify me into no time of day at all.

∗**exhibit,** *v. Educ. tr.* and *intr.* To deliver (a speech or essay) before one's class or as part of an exhibition. *Obs.*

1766 in B. Peirce *Hist. Harvard Univ.* (1833) 243 Twice in the year . . . some of the scholars, at the direction of the President and Tutors, shall publicly exhibit specimens of their proficiency. **1837** *Yale Laws* iv. 29 No Student who shall receive any appointment to exhibit before the class, the College or the Public, shall give any treat . . . on account of those appointments. **1851** Hall *College Words* 115 *Exhibit*, to take part in an exhibition; to speak in public at an exhibition or commencement.

b. Hence ∗**exhibiter,** one who takes part in a school exhibition. *Rare.* Cf. ∗**exhibitioner.**

1820 Tudor *Lett. Eastern States* 291 Every person who has attended a college exhibition, would see . . . more than half the exhibiters speak their parts in such a slovenly, awkward manner, as would not have been tolerated in a village school.

∗**exhibition,** *n. Educ.* A public examination or display of the attainments and abilities of students; an occasion of this. Also attrib. Cf. **school exhibition.**

1784 Freneau *Poems* (1786) 352 Lines, intended for Mr. Peele's Exhibition, Philadelphia, May 10, 1784. **1798** *Harvard Laws* 18 Any scholar, who . . . shall wilfully absent himself at the time of exhibition shall be admonished. **1872** Holmes *Poet* iv. 113 At the end of each term there was what they called an 'exhibition ball,' in which the scholars danced cotillons and country-dances. **1943** Powell *Home Again* 51 At the close of the school next spring, we had the 'Exhibition,' with charades, dialogues, recitations, and so forth.

b. exhibition day, the day upon which a school exhibition is held. *Obs.*

1833 James Boardman *America* 293 We were particularly fortunate in making our visit to Harvard College, on what is termed an exhibition day. **1887** N. Perry *Flock of Girls* 238 On exhibition day the congratulations that poured in on Emily quite turned her head.

As the last term in **cotton, junior exhibition.**

∗**exhibitioner,** *n.* (See quot. 1851 and cf. ∗**exhibiter.**) *Obs.* — **c1663** *Harvard Rec.* III. 318 Such of ye exhibitioners as shall at any solemn examination be found eminently to excell the Rest in ability [etc.]. **1851** Hall *College Words* 118 One who performs a part at an exhibition in American colleges is sometimes called an *exhibitioner.*

exodian ɛkˈsodɪən, *n.* ? =next. *Rare.* — **1880** Tourgee *Bricks* 500 The next morning the light-hearted exodian departed.

exoduster ˈɛksəˌdʌstə, *n.* [In **1.** prob. based on ∗*exodus.* In **2.** the word may be a new formation inspired by ∗*dust.*]

1. A Negro who left the South in the mass migration to the Northwest, esp. to Kansas, *c*1878–80. *Colloq. Obs.*

1880 *Galveston News* 26 March, Thirty-three Ethiopian exodusters passed south today en route from Kansas to their old homes in Grimes country. *Ib.* 31 March, Two caravans of exodusters, containing about a dozen wagons and fifty darkies of assorted sizes each, passed through here to-day en route for Kansas. **1882** *N.Y. Tribune* 21 June, An exoduster was seen a while ago furrowing . . . with a plough drawn by a cow. **1918** Connelley *Kansas* 786 Poor, homeless, trustful, the Exoduster displayed the traits of his race in unfailing cheerfulness and childlike trust in Providence.

2. A refugee from a "dust bowl."

1938 in *Amer. Sp.* XVI. (1941) 318 Most of the exodusters from the Dust Bowl were not 'rooted' anywhere.

∗**expedition,** *n.* As the last term in **filibustering, hunting, logging, Missouri, Santa Fe, trading, trapping expedition.**

∗**experience,** *v. tr. To experience religion*, to become converted. *Colloq.*

1837 *Knickerb.* IX. 356, I have 'experienced religion,' as well as thousands of others, and in the same way. **1878** Stowe *Poganuc People* 102 Hiel had not yet, as he phrased it, experienced religion, nor joined the church. **1903** Wiggin *Rebecca* 198 Young members . . . had 'experienced religion,' and joined the church when nine or ten years old.

experience meeting. A meeting for the telling of one's religious experiences. Also transf.

1868 Beecher *Sermons* (1869) I. 239 He . . . is at last persuaded to go to an 'experience meeting.' **1883** *Cent. Mag.* Sep. 785/1 The great literary symposium on the novel has resolved itself into a general experience-meeting. **1887** *Nation* 5 May 375/3 Just before he [Blaine] went out to the Indian Territory there had been a sort of 'experience meeting' among the editors of the Republican organs of that part of the country.

∗**experiment,** *n.*

1. experiment farm, a farm upon which agricultural experiments are carried on.

1893 Auld *Picturesque Burlington* 128 State Experiment Farm, including farm house, barn, creamery, green-house, apiary, etc. . . . It affords an excellent variety of soils.

2. experiment station, an institution for scientific research, where experiments, esp. agricultural ones, are carried on. Also **experimental station.**

1874 *Conn. Bd. Agric. Rep.* 66 Would it not be an honor . . . to be the pioneer on our Western Continent in the establishment of experiment stations? **1895** *Dept. Agric. Yrbk. 1894* 37 The office of Experiment Stations . . . has during the past year engaged itself almost wholly in preparing for publication works based upon the reports of Agricultural Experiment Stations. **1944** *U. of Wyo. Cat.* 87 It is one of the experimental stations established in each of the forty-eight states according to the provisions of an act passed by Congress in 1887, known as the Hatch Act.

explaterate ɛkˈsplætəˌret, *v.* [App. humorous from ∗*explanation* and ∗*elaborate.*] *intr.* To talk at length, to explain fully. *Slang. Obs.* — **1831** *Boston Transcript* 24 June 2/4 Come gentlemen, let's liquor and then I'll *explaterate* more. **a1889** *Joel Boodler's Campaign* (B. & L.), On this I will explaterate, and all my views profusely state.

∗**Exposition,** *n.* As the last term in **Columbian, Cotton Centennial, World's Exposition.**

∗**express,** *n.*

1. A forwarding system or service for the rapid conveyance and delivery of goods, money, etc. Also attrib.

1839 *Boston Transcript* 21 March 2/2 Harnden's Express, between Boston and New York, has been running since the 4th of March. **1896** Haswell *New York* 330 The nucleus of the now immense railroad and steamboat and steamer expresses appeared in the enterprise of William F. Harnden, who . . . commenced the personal bearing of parcels and executing commissions between this city and Boston. **1947** *Chi. Tribune* 21 June 18/1 Pan American World Airways has announced reductions in international air express rates on its Pacific and Atlantic services.

b. Goods or articles transmitted by this system or service.

1840 *Boston D. Advt.* 7 Feb. 4/3 Mr. Harnden will for the present send his Express via Worcester. **1893** *Harper's Mag.* Jan. 207/1 Rinda came in like a projectile, carrying a large box clasped in her arms. . . . 'Spress!' she exclaimed excitedly. 'Express?' repeated Mrs. Franklin.

2. In special combs.: (1) **express agent,** an agent employed by an express company; (2) **business,** the business engaged in by an express company, the amount of goods transported by express; (3) **car,** a railroad car designed for carrying articles sent by express; (4) **cart,** =**express wagon 1;** (5) **company,** a company engaged in the business of transmitting goods and parcels; (6) **harness,** heavy harness, orig. of a type used on horses that pulled heavy express wagons; (7) **highway,** (see quot. 1931); (8) **line,** (*a*) a public conveyance company operating under one management, (*b*) a system of transportation for forwarding express; (9) **mail,** the system or service by which mail is sent by faster conveyances at a higher postage rate than usual, *obs.;* (10) **man,** see as a main entry; (11) ∗**messenger,** an employee of an express company in charge of goods sent by express; (12) **money order,** (see quots.); (13) **office,** an office or station of an express company; (14) ∗**rider,** one who carried mail for a pony express *q.v.*, now *hist.;* (15) **road,** (*a*) app. a road over which a pony express passed, *obs.*, (*b*) =**express highway;** (16) **seal,** an official seal for an express package, box, etc.; (17) **stamp,** (see quot.); (18) **wagon,** see as a main entry.

(1) 1849 *Hunt's Merch. Mag.* XXI. 683 The [Railroad] company expressly reject any liability for the care of articles in the keeping of Express Agents. **1948** *Dly. Ardmoreite* (Ardmore, Okla.) 18 April 12/1 Think of the lonesome feeling that came over the express agent when he discovered . . . 40,000 bees . . . loose in the little office building. — **(2) 1858** HOMANS *Cyclo. Commerce* 644/1 William F. Harnden, then a conductor upon the Boston and Worcester Railroad, started the express business . . . in the spring of 1839. **1898** *K.C. Star* 18 Dec. 4/3 Padgett adopted that policy himself and reduced his express business very much. — **(3) 1839** *Boston Transcript* 26 Feb. 3/1 (*advt.*), Boston and New York Express Car. **1948** *Sat. Ev. Post* 16 Oct. 31/2 It does an expeditious job of shuttling express cars over 196,000 miles of rail lines on 10,000 daily trains hauling packages to and from its 23,000 offices. — **(4) 1890** *Harper's Mag.* LXXX. 742/1, I saw the express carts this morning. **1905** H. GARLAND *Tyranny of the Dark* 245 Every side-street rang with the clatter of drays and express-carts.

(5) 1854 *Cong. Globe* 7 April 872/2 There are two large express companies, Adams & Co. and Wells, Fargo & Co., which carry mail matter by Nicaragua, charging from twenty-five to fifty cents on a letter. **1948** *Chelsea* (Mass.) *Rec.* 30 Nov. 1/1 Three employees of the express company were arraigned . . . on charges arising from the looting of agency warehouses. — **(6) 1885** *Boston Jrnl.* 20 Dec. (*advt.*), From the best of Stock, made by convict labor, in all grades and descriptions, from the Lightest Carriage to the Heaviest Express and Team Harness, gotten up expressly for New England consumption. **1936** *Sears Cat.* (ed. 173) (Index), Express Harness. — **(7) 1931** *Amer. City* Jan. 152/1 We should call only such streets 'express highways' as will allow maximum speed for automobile traffic absolutely uninterrupted by cross traffic, either vehicular or pedestrian. **1949** *Dly. Ardmoreite* (Ardmore, Okla.) 25 Jan. 1/1 Think of these cars, trucks and buses traveling toward New York City in double rank along two lanes of express highway, loaded to capacity. — **(8)** (*a*) **1826** *Amer. Traveller* 10 March 3/1 The Proprietors of the 'Express Lines' and of the 'Citizens' Coaches' deserve many thanks. (*b*) **1860** GREELEY *Overland Journey* 106 This is the first and only accident that has happened to the express-line, though it has run out some thirty passage wagons from Leavenworth. **1887** CUSTER *Tenting on Plains* xiv. 482 The recommendation he gave the boy . . . was confirmed . . . by the officers of the express line. — **(9) 1813** *Niles' Reg.* IV. 115/2 An express mail is established between Washington and Buffaloe, N.Y. to arrive in 4 days 18 hours. **1874** R. H. COLLINS *Kentucky* I. 42 President's message . . . reaches Maysville by express mail and steamboat.

(11) 1847 ROBB *Squatter Life* 114 He handed his wallet to the express messenger. **1928** BREAKENRIDGE *Helldorado* 236 The express messenger, realizing that it was a hold-up, took what valuables he could, and, as the train slowed up the second time, jumped out of the side door. — **(12) 1903** E. JOHNSON *Railway Transportation* 159 Express companies . . . sell to travelers 'express money-orders,' payable at any of their foreign offices. **1944** *Sears Cat.* (ed. 189) 900 For amounts above $100, you can purchase additional Express Money Orders at same charges as shown above. — **(13) 1840** *Boston D. Advt.* 19 Feb. 4/2 (*advt.*), Harnden's New York Package Express Office. **1948** WESTON *Mother Lode* 86 On one side was . . . Wells Fargo and Company's express office where over fifteen million dollars in gold were weighed within ten years. — **(14) 1847** *Semi-Wkly. News* (Fredericksburg, Va.) 11 Oct. 2/5 The slips for these papers are accordingly taken out of the mail from New Orleans when they reach Mobile and given to the express rider. **1947** *Chi. Tribune* 29 June VII. 6/4 Gold seekers, express riders, railway builders, struggled against the desolation.

(15) (*a*) **1860** GREELEY *Overland Journey* 132 The Missourians' camp, on the express-road, was swept by hurricane. (*b*) **1925** *Lit. Digest* 31 Jan. 46/1 The project for the new kind of express roads . . . has the support of automotive engineers throughout the State and nation. — **(16) 1868** *Putnam's Mag.* I. 34/1 He picked up the parcel; . . . he glanced at the superscription and express seals. — **(17) 1869** J. R. BROWNE *Adv. Apache Country* 315 During my sojourn in Germany I received a letter from California by Pony Express in less than four weeks after it was written; and it was not until I showed the date and express-stamp and carefully explained the whole matter that I was enabled to overcome the incredulity of my Teutonic friends.

Also *express box, boy, carrier, charges, department, matter, package, receipt, robber, route, traffic, trunk,* etc.

As the last term in **ankle, baggage, lightning, limited, Pacific, package, pony, through express.**

∗**express,** *v.*

1. *tr.* To send letters or messages by a special service.

1716 *Mass. H. Rep. Jrnl.* I. 81 Several letters . . . had been expressed to his Honour the Lieut. Governour from the Eastward. *a***1859** *Washington Repub.* (B.), The President's message will be expressed through to Boston, by order of the Postmaster-General.

2. To send (goods, money, etc.) by the medium of an express company.

1864 WEBSTER 483/3 To express a package. **1868** ROSE *Great Country* 107 Candour compels me to admit that I alone was in fault about the luggage, as the system of 'expressing' it, so universally adopted in America, is the best possible. **1917** MCCUTCHEON *Green Fancy* 323 Her trunks are over at the station now, to be expressed to Buffalo. **1948** *Sat. Ev. Post* 23 Oct. 93/2 Dallas, Los Angeles and San Francisco express garments to New York.

Hence **expressing,** *n.*

1948 *Sat. Ev. Post* 18 Sep. 12/2 He had to ask for two dollars to pay the cost of packing and expressing.

expressage ɪk'spresɪdʒ, *n.*

1. The fee charged for transporting goods by express. Also fig.

1857 in *Calif. Hist. Soc. Quart.* IX. (1930) 143 Paid Farley $5 for expressage. **1891** *Memphis Appeal-Avalanche* 22 April 6/5 Parties ordering must pay expressage both ways. **1909** O. HENRY *Roads of Destiny* viii. 133 What'll the expressage be to take me out there with you?

2. The sending of articles by express; articles or goods sent in this way.

1887 GEORGE *40 Years on Rail* ii. 41 He looked on expressage as an intruder and an antagonist. **1905** *N.Y. Ev. Post* 17 May 14 The result is expected to be that Cuba will admit foreign expressage under regulations similar to those in force in the United States.

∗**expresser,** *n.* (See quot.) *Rare.* — **1902** *Bureau of Animal Industry* Bul. 37, 20 Much is heard of English 'light vanners' and 'parcel carters.' These are simply the English forms of what we call expressers, changed somewhat to conform to English requirements—that is, with legs as short as possible. The two names are used for practically the same horse.

expressman ɪk'sprɛsmən, *n.*

1. A man who carries messages, mail, or other communications. *Obs.*

1839 *Knickerb.* XIII. 24 Means for defraying the expenses of expressmen, are furnished by government. **1858** PETERS *Kit Carson* 289 He succeeded in making an exchange of the lieutenant for one of his expressmen.

2. A man who hauls or transmits parcels, packages, trunks, etc., esp. as an employee of an express company. Cf. **baggage expressman, ox expressman, package man.**

1847 THOREAU in *Atlantic Mo.* LXIX 744 Munroe . . . tells the expressman that all is right. **1944** JOHNSON *As I Dare* 306, I . . . was chatting with the expressman in his office. **1948** *Sat. Ev. Post* 16 Oct. 31/1 The versatility of its business, one of the binding family factors that make an expressman always an expressman, is rarely noted by an outsider.

express wagon.

1. A wagon, usu. a large one, for hauling express matter.

1856 *Spirit of Times* 20 Sep. 36/2 As I spoke an immense express wagon—'Harlem, Carmansville, and New York'—came lumbering down upon our frail wagon. **1907** *Collier's* 20 Oct. 12/3 The horseless express wagon and the lumbering auto-truck are now familiar objects in our cities. **1944** JOHNSON *As I Dare* 71 Jackson himself would take my luggage checks, his horse-drawn express wagon lurking just around the corner.

2. A small wagon for the use of children.

1910 *Sat. Ev. Post* 3 Sep. 19/1 A kid taking home a basket of clothes in a little yellow express-wagon had tried to cross in front of me. **1945** MOLLOY *Pride's Way* 148 He could not decide which he wanted the more, an express wagon or a hook-and-ladder truck.

3. (See quot.)

1914 *D.N.* IV. 155 *Express-wagon*, a four-wheeled, one-horse wagon, lighter than a farm-wagon, and usually equipped with two removable seats. [Cape Cod.]

Express wagon (sense 3)

***expunger,** *n.* One who supported the "expunging resolution" *q.v. Obs.* — **1854** BENTON *30 Years' View* I. 731/2 General Jackson . . . gave a grand dinner to the expungers (as they were called) and their wives. *Ib.*, He . . . placed the 'head-expunger' in his chair, and withdrew to his sick chamber.

expunging resolution. *Hist.* A resolution, passed in the U.S. Senate in 1837, directing that a sentence felt to be derogatory to the character of President Jackson be expunged from the Senate Journal of 1834. *Obs.* — **1837** CLAY in Benton *30 Years' View* II. 729 The expunging resolution, which is to blot out or enshroud the four or five lines in which the resolution of 1834 stands recorded. **1852** *Whig Almanac 1853* 11/2 Mr. Webster remained in the Senate till March 4, 1841, and was a leading participator in the discussions growing out of . . . the Expunging Resolution.

* **extension,** *n.*

1. An addition or annex to a building, esp. a dwelling house. Also attrib.

1852 *Cong. Globe* 24 March 854/2 A statement of the materials to be used in the construction . . . of the proposed extension [of the Capitol]. **1867** F. H. LUDLOW *Little Brother* 288 He heard an earnest, boyish voice in the extension-room. **1903** R. HALL *Pine Grove House* 12 The tin roof blew off the extension one windy night.

2. Used in combs. to indicate objects that are or can be extended or expanded: (1) **extension bag,** (2) **chair,** (3) **ladder,** (4) **-leaf dining table,** (5) **table,** (6) **top.**

(1) **1904** *Delineator* Oct. 547 With the genial season arrived every kind of drummer. They came with extension bags filled with samples. — (2) **1882** *Harper's Mag.* Dec. 52/1 A young couple, reclining in extension chairs, were reading a novel. — (3) **1889** BRAYLEY *Boston Fire Dept.* 313 Bangor extension-ladders were supplied to all the ladder companies. **1935** *Mont. Ward Cat.* (ed. 123) 657 Wards Supreme Quality Extension Ladders. — (4) **1900** E. A. DIX *Deacon Bradbury* 10 The three drew up chairs . . . the deacon and his wife at opposite sides of the extension-leaf dining-table.

(5) **1851** CIST *Cincinnati* 202 One of the remarkable articles . . . is an extension table. **1936** *Sears Cat.* (ed. 173) 544 Extension Table: . . . Extends to 52 in; one 10-inch leaf included. — (6) **1884** *N.Y. Herald* 27 Oct. 1/2 Extension Top Phaetons, $100 up. **1887** TOURGEE *Button's Inn* 92 A comfortable extension top might be raised at will to protect the driver from sun or storm. **1888** *Harper's Mag.* June 137/2 They got into Mrs. Wilmington's extension-top carry-all.

***extenuations,** *n. pl.* Thin garments. *Obs.* — **1881** G. W. CABLE in *Scribner's Mo.* May 23 They were clad in silken extenuations from the throat to the feet. **1883** *Pall Mall Gaz.* 12 Sep. 2/2 One side wore . . . extenuations of a . . . green colour.

* **extra,** *n.* and *a.*

1. *n.* An edition or issue of a newspaper brought out in addition to the usual ones. Cf. **sports extra.**

Such an issue was formerly, in both British and U.S. use, called an "Extraordinary," of which the modern "Extra," at first used only in headings (see our first quots.), is app. a shortening.

1793 *Kentucky Gazette Extra.* 23 Mar. **1796** *Herald Extra* 11. 30 Mar. 1. [**1818** *Lynchburg* (Va.) *Press* 25 Dec. 3/4 In order to let our hands partake of Christmas, no paper will appear on Monday next, but if anything of importance, is received by Saturday evening's mail, our subscribers shall receive it in an extra sheet.] **1842** *N.O. Picayune* 11 March 2/4 So great was the anxiety to see our Extra of yesterday, that we found it impossible to strike off numbers sufficient. **1948** *Dly. Ardmoreite* (Ardmore, Okla.) 23 April 8/3 He was working there when the 1918 Armistice was signed and helped to get out the extras telling of that historic event.

2. On a stage line, an additional coach or vehicle for carrying passengers in excess of the usual number; a conveyance specially hired by a party or group. *Obs.* Cf. **exclusive extra,** and see **canal extra.**

1827 MRS. BASIL HALL *Aristocratic Journey* (1931) 106 The journey from here (Pawtucket) to Hartford, our next stopping place, is seventy-two miles. We wished to get an 'Extra' . . . but . . . the Stage Proprietor had the want of conscience to ask thirty-six dollars for an 'Extra.' **1866** A. D. WHITNEY *L. Goldthwaite* vii, Up to this hostelry . . . came . . . such 'extras' as might drive down at any hour of day or night. **1944** KAHN *Cable Car Days* 103 After six hours of waiting an 'extra' arrived and we resumed our journey.

b. (See quot.)

1861 *Remin. Locomotive Engineer* 203 Did George's engine lay up for Sunday at one end of the road, and mine at the other, one of us was sure to go over the road 'extra,' in order that we might be together.

3. An actor hired for a special scene or occasion, as one of a mob or other crowd.

1880 RANOUS *Diary of Daly Deb.* 185 Who should come to call on the Daly young ladies but one of the Philadelphia 'extras' at the theatre. **1921** *Collier's* 11 June 23/1 All I have got to do is battle my ways through between fifteen and forty-seven extras, bust down the door of her dungeon, and rescue her. **1945** *Greeley* (Colo.) *D. Tribune* 13 Mar. 1/7 There were gloomy predictions that some 30,000 people—stars, extras, laborers, craftsmen—would be idle.

4. (See quot.) *Obs.*

1889 FARMER *Americanisms, Extra* (American cadet), an *extra* is a punishment imposed on Saturday and Sunday, when general leave is granted to all except those who are thus doomed to do *extra* sentinel duty.

5. extra base, in baseball, a base reached by a batter beyond that which his hit would ordinarily enable him to reach. Also a hit for more than one base.

1915 *Chi. Tribune* 13 Oct. 13/6 The repporters puts down a single in there book the minute a ball is hit safe in Lewis's field because they know that they aint no body crazy enough to try and take an extra base on this here Lewis. **1917** *Amer. Mag.* July 43/2 He got four [hits] and three of them were for extra bases. **1948** *Chi. D. News* 8 May 15/1 The Dodgers were ahead, compiling their eight runs on only four hits (including just one for extra bases).

Extension table *c*1820

6. extra-fare, of or pertaining to an extra fast passenger train to ride on which an additional fare is charged.

1903 E. JOHNSON *Railway Transportation* 144 The patronage of the 'extra-fare' cars and trains is increasing, and on the main routes of long-distance travel the best trains consist entirely of parlor-, sleeping-, and dining-cars. **1946** *Reader's Digest* Sep. 156/1 That's what man likes about this extra-fare, extra-exclusive commuter special . . . that connects Sunset Boulevard with Wall Street.

7. extra session, a special session of Congress or of a state legislature in addition to the regular sessions, a "special session."

1837 *U.S. Mag.* I. 68 The call of the extra session . . . had served as a theme for that political gossip. **1903** *Nation* LXXVI. Index p. i [Congress] LVIIIth, extra session of Senate: Rebukes of Cannon's censure, Morgan holding up Panama Treaty [etc.].

extraordinary session. =**extra session.** — **1798** *Ann. 5th Congress* I. 482 The bill for allowing a compensation to the Doorkeeper of the Senate and his assistant, for their services during the late extraordinary session of Congress, was read. **1910** *Okla. Session Laws* 3 Legisl. 2 There is hereby appropriated . . . money . . . to pay the per diem and mileage of the contingent expenses of the Extraordinary Session.

*** eye,** *n.* In combs.: (1) **eyebait,** a small herring, *colloq.;* (2) **breaker,** (see quot.), *obs.;* (3) **cap,** (see quot.), *rare;* (4) **cup,** (see quot. 1874); (5) **dag,** (see quots.), *obs.;* (6) **opener,** see as a main entry; (7) **root,** =**goldenseal;** (8) **slip,** a section of sugar-cane stalk on which there is an "eye" or bud, *obs.*

(1) **1884** GOODE *Fisheries* I. 246 The Lant is found in spring or early summer in the open sea, in the neighborhood of banks and shoals remote from land, as is also the sprat in Europe and the 'brit,' 'eyebait,' or small herring in America. — (2) **1857** F. L. OLMSTED *Jour. through Texas* 404 A black gnat, called [in La.] the 'eye-breaker.' . . . They were worse than all manner of musquitoes, flies, and other insects. — (3) **1857** *Mich. Agric. Soc. Trans.* VIII. 170 The orbits of the eye, the eyecap or bone, not too projecting, that it may not form a fatal hindrance in lambing. — (4) **1874** KNIGHT 819/2 Eye-cup. . . . Its lip is held firmly against the open lid, and the eye-wash dashed against the ball. **1918** M. B. OWEN *Typewriting Speed* 134 Fill the eye cup, lower the head until one of the eyes covers the top, then lift the head and throw it backward.

(5) **1806** LEWIS in *L. & Clark Exped.* IV. (1905) 283 The natives . . . wanted an instrument which the Northwest traders call an eye-dag (a sort of war hatchet) which we had not. *Ib.* V. 225 [Indians] were armed with bows and arrows and eyedaggs. — (7) **1876** HOBBS *Bot. Hand-Book* 35 Eye root, Goldenseal, Hydrastis Canadensis. — (8) **1828** in *Amer. Sp.* XVIII. 124/1 The sugar cane planting takes place from August until December, by means of eye-slips.

b. In phrases: (1) *To cut an eye,* to exchange glances with another, to glance at someone, *slang;* (2) *to keep one's eye(s)* (or *eyeteeth*) *skinned,* to keep a sharp lookout, to be on the alert, *slang;* (3) *to keep one's eye peeled,* =prec.; (4) *cut in the eye,* drunk, *slang, obs.;* (5) *eye of America,* (see quot.), *obs.;* (6) *to skin the eyes off someone,* to beat completely, *slang;* (7) *to set one's eyes by,* to love dearly, set great store by, *colloq.;* (8) *to keep an eye out for,* to be on the watch for, *colloq.*

(1) **1827** L. DOW *Journal* (1850) 177/2 (Th. Supp.), Went to New York, took steamboat to New Brunswick, thence Stage No. 7, strangers crossed words and cut eyes. **1898** F. H. SMITH *C. West* 70 'We come purty nigh leavin' everybody on the Ledge las' night,' . . . said Captain Joe, 'cutting' his eye at the skipper as he spoke. — (2) **1833** *Polit. Examiner* (Shelbyville, Ky.) 22 June 4/1, I wish I may be shot if I dont think you had better keep your eyes skinned so that you can look powerful sharp, lest we get rowed up the river this heat. **1868** ROSE *Great Country* 322 As the natives say, 'a man must go about in America with his "eye-teeth" skinned' in order to hold his own. **1936** RAINE *To Ride River* 25 (We.), We'll keep our eyes skinned. — (3) **1853** *St. Louis Morning Herald* 6 Jan. (Th.), Young man! Keep your eye peeled when you are after the women. **1947** *Sports Afield* Dec. 26/3 Jim had told him to keep his eyes peeled for them, they were so rare, nowadays. — (4) **1857** *Quinland* I. 134 You are as *balmy* as a summer evening, as *shiny* as a new boot; you are *sprung* and *cut in the eye;* come, rouse yourself.

(5) **1865** SALA *Diary* II. 34 Boston is quite sensible of its intellectual superiority. . . . It has been called (by scholars who have read Milton) the 'eye' of America. — (6) **1873** *Winfield* (Kans.) *Courier* 15 Feb. 1/4 He has around him a lot who could skin the eyes off the very devil at the game [of poker]. — (7) **1883** WILKINS in *Lippincott's Mag.* XXXI. 502/1 Wall, the cap'n and Mis' Whitlow set their eyes by the child, of course; she was the only one they had. — (8) **1889** MARK TWAIN *Conn. Yankee* ii. 33, I moved away, . . . at the same time keeping an eye out for any chance passenger in his right mind.

As the last term in **bad, bird's, black, brass, buck, buck's, bug, bull's, gander, glass, goggle-, Missouri bird's, moon, ox, peep, pink, pop, red, squinch, thimble, tight, trigger, wall-, white eye.**

eyeleting machine. (See quot. 1874.)

1864 *Rep. Comm. Patents 1863* I. 231 This invention consists in the arrangement . . . of the eyeleting machine [in an improved manner]. **1874** KNIGHT 820/1 *Eyeleting-machine,* a machine for attaching eyelets to garments or other objects. **1885** *Harper's Mag.* LXX. 286/2 1864.—Self-feeding eyeleting machine, foot-power [became an accepted success].

eye-opener.

1. A drink of whisky or wine, esp. one taken early in the morning. Also transf. *Slang.*

1818 FEARON *Sks.* 252 Drinking . . . is effected by individuals taking their solitary 'eye openers,' 'toddy,' and 'phlegm dispensers,' at the bar. **1873** HOWELLS *Chance Acquaintance* (1882) 56 For an eye-opener there is nothing like a glass of milk. **1948** DICK *Dixie Frontier* 189 Ministers regularly took their morning eye-opener and their nightcap in the evening.

2. Something most surprising or enlightening. *Colloq.*

1863 *Rio Abajo Press* (Albuquerque, New Mexico) 3 Feb. 2 Quite a catalogue of similar examples of injustice and meanness . . . might be made . . . , but we merely allude to them as an 'eye-opener' to the public. **1897** *Outing* XXX. 553/2 After this effectual 'eye-opener' we both hurried into our clothes.

3. (See quot.) *Rare.*

1868 *Putnam's Mag.* II. 47 A slight furrow is opened on the 'cotton-bed' with a rude implement which my Irish overseer called an 'eye-opener.'

*** eyes,** *n. pl.* As the last term in **doll's, gold, goo-goo eyes.**

F

*F, *n.* Used as a mark in schools, usu. to indicate failure.

1897 Flandrau *Harvard Episodes* 278 To give him an E—the lowest possible mark . . . always excepting . . . F—would be to bring upon himself Prescott's everlasting anger. **1898** in Smallwood *Exams. & Grading* 52 [Mt. Holyoke] adopted a . . . [modified] plan of marking: A—95–100, . . . F—Failed. **1947** *Jrnl. Crim. Law & Criminology* Nov.-Dec. 315 The school report showed grades of 'A' and 'B' in all subjects for his sophomore year, from 'A' to 'F' (English) in junior year.

Fabian ˈfebɪən, *a.* [L. *Fabianus*, of or pertaining to Fabius. App. 1st used with reference to Washington's delaying tactics in the Revolution.] Inclined to delay, dilatory, in allusion to Q. Fabius Maximus, and his delaying tactics used against Hannibal in the Second Punic War. *Obs.*

1777 in *Pub. Col. Soc.* VIII. 277, I know the comments that some people will make on our Fabian conduct. It will be imputed either to cowardice, or to weakness. **1782** *Ib.* 278 In vain! their Chief superior still Eludes our force with Fabian skill. **1904** [see **Fabius**].

*Fabius, *n.* A nickname for George Washington (see quot. 1904). *Obs.*

[**1775** in *Pub. Col. Soc.* VIII. 276 The inactivity of the two armies is not very agreeable to me. Fabius's *cunctando* was wise and brave.] **1776** *Ib.* 277 America has found her Fabius, before she sought her Cannae. Delay and defence are proved her system. **1779** *Ib.* 278, I resolved to show you that all the eloquence of your fine pen could not tempt our Fabius to do wrong; and, avoiding any representation of my own, I put your letter into his hands, and let it speak for itself. **1904** *Ib.* 277 It is worth remarking, not only that Washington was known to his countrymen, to the Loyalists, and to the British as Fabius, but also that the adjective Fabian possibly made its first appearance in the English language in connection with Washington. His policy by no means won the approval of all, and soon complaints were heard, and the policy was both attacked and defended.

*fabric, *n.* A ship or boat, a vessel. *Obs.*

1823 Cooper *Pioneers* xxiv, The light fabric shot on the gravelly beach for nearly half its length. **1837**—— *Recoll. Europe* I. 27 The boldness of the experiment which launched such massive and complicated fabrics on the ocean. **1869** *Causes Reduct. Tonnage* (1870) 49, I was told that on the Atlantic a wooden vessel cannot stand the action of the propeller. . . . I do not think myself that wooden fabrics would stand the strain.

Fabussa fəˈbʌsɑ, *n.* [Amer. Indian.] (See quot.) *Rare.*—**1898** Cushman *Hist. Indians* 63 The evening before their departure a 'Fabussa' (pole, pro. as Fa-bus-sah) was firmly set up in the ground at the centre point of their encampment, by direction of their chief medicine man . . . to whom . . . the Great Spirit had revealed that the Fabussa would indicate on the following morning, the direction they should march by its leaning.

*face, *n.* In combs.: (1) **face brick**, a brick of superior finish, used esp. in the fronts of buildings; (2) **-lifting**, (see quot. 1922), also transf.; (3) **log**, (see quot.); (4) **raising**, =**face-lifting**, (5) **wall**, (see quots.).

(1) **1807** *Independent Chronicle* 21 Sep. 3/2 The Subscriber has been at considerable expense for several years past in the improvement of Face Bricks . . . superior to the Philadelphia Bricks, both for appearance and for turning water. **1909** *Cent. Supp.* 457/3 In a brick wall, the face-work may be of what are called face-brick, and laid with thinner points. — (2) **1922** Courtenay *Physical Beauty* 57 One of the greatest actual triumphs of plastic surgery is the 'face-raising' or 'face-lifting' process, which does away with wrinkles, mouth and eyelines, and sagging cheeks. **1947** *Time* 21 July 1/1 Those are electric irons going through acid, being plated with nickel and made ready for their last 'face-lifting' of chrome for a permanently bright and shiny look. — (3) **1905** *Forestry Bureau Bul.* No. 61, 39 *Head log.* . . . The front bottom log on a skidway. (N[orthern] F[orest].) Syn.: face log. — (4) **1922** [see **face-lifting**]. — (5) **1874** Knight 822/2 *Face-wall.* (Building,) the front wall. **1887** Wilkins *Humble Romance* 37 The house itself . . . was raised from the street-level the height of a face-wall. **1909** *Cent. Supp.* 457/3 *Face-wall*, . . . a wall built to sustain the face of an excavation.

b. In colloq. and slang phrases: (1) *To run one's face*, to depend altogether on one's looks for favors or credit; (2) *to travel on* (or *upon*) *one's face*, =prec.; (3) *to open one's face*, to speak, *slang;* (4) *to shut one's face*, to cease speaking.

(1) **1840** *N.O. Picayune* 6 Aug. 2/1 Jim has taken the temperance pledge . . . , but never could keep it more than an hour at a time, so long as he could run his face or make a raise of a picayune. **1870** W. W. Fowler *Ten Yrs. Wall St.* 237, I had to get the hack-man to trust me, and 'ran my face' for a dinner that day. — (2) **1856** *Knickerb.* XLVIII. 504, I must travel on my face after this. **1859** *Yale Lit. Mag.* 60 (Th.), If you have not a ready tongue, and cannot travel upon your face, you had better [etc.]. — (3) **1896** Ade *Artie* iii. 26 If you open your face to this lady again tonight I'll separate you from your breath. — (4) **1917** Sinclair *King Coal* 200 The marshal bade him 'shut his face,' and emphasised the command by a twist at his coat-collar.

As the last term in **all, bald, black, bull, cat, dead, doe, dough, full, leather, moose, pale, poker, smut, tomahawk, white face.**

*faced, *a.* As the last term in **dough, hickory, leather, pale, poker-faced.**

*facial, *n.* A face massage. Also transf. — **1914** G. Atherton *Perch of Devil* i. 84 I've got fourteen heads to dress . . . and most of them want a facial, too. **1932** *K.C. Times* 26 April 16 The Cass County Democrat reports that the north side of the courthouse clock is peeling. . . . The newspaper suggests a facial.

*facility, *n.* (See 1st quot. 1856.) In full **facility note.** *Obs.*

1818 *Niles' Reg.* XIV. 39/2 Others . . . have issued a species of paper called *facility notes*, purporting to be payable in neither money, country produce, or any thing else that has body or shape. **1856** Goodrich *Recoll.* I. 493 The chief circulation [during the war of 1812] consisted of bills of suspended banks, or what were called 'facilities'; that is, bank-notes, authorized by the legislature of Connecticut, redeemable in three years after the war. These were at fifteen to twenty-five per cent. discount compared with specie. *Ib.* 494 You remember I was only entitled to a facility and not to a specie bill?

facing slip. In post offices, a slip or a strip of paper bearing direction particulars, etc., affixed to a package of mail.

1873 *Postal Laws* 288. **1874** *Postmaster Gen. Rep.* 209 A facing or label slip bearing the address of the package, the office or route upon which it was made up, with the name of the clerk making the distribution. **1893** Cushing *Story of P.O.* 101 The 'facing slips,' of which about 600,000 are printed yearly.

*fact, *n.* *that's a fact*, an assertive expression used for emphasis. For **cold fact, fixed fact,** see the adjectives.

1834 *Boston Post* 5 Aug. 7/2 To this statement of facts he replied—'I was groggy, I *know;* but what I *did*, I *don't* know, that's a fact.' **1851** *Harper's Mag.* Dec. 88/1 As our neighbors in America would put it, 'that's a fact.' **1909** Parrish *My Lady of South* 21, I just don't know, Joe, that's a fact. *Ib.* 22 Ye see, he never done treated dis nigger ver' nice, dat's a fact, fer shore.

factional ˈfækʃənḷ, *n.* A member of a faction. *Rare.* — **1904** *N.Y. Ev. Post* 5 July 5 At his left sat the Harrison factionals of Chicago.

factionalism ˈfækʃənḷˌɪzəm, *n.* A tendency to factional differences. — **1904** *Nation* 31 March 244/1 Under our system of party government, the natural remedy for such arrogance, such corruption, such fierce factionalism as the Republicans are now displaying in office, is to turn them out. **1905** *Springfield W. Republican* 31 March 2 Factionalism within the republican party in Wisconsin.

*factor, *n.*

1. An agent stationed among Indians as a representative of the federal government or of a fur company.

1822 Morse *Rep. Indian Affairs* I. 42 Col. B. recommends, . . . that sub-factors, or agents, should be planted in suitable stations to accommodate the Indians, and to sell them, in their own villages, goods at prices fixed by the government Factor. **1888** Perrin *Ky. Pioneer Press* 33 President Monroe appointed him Indian agent, or, as then called, factor, among the Cherokee Indians in Arkansas. **1946** Stan-

WELL-FLETCHER *Driftwood Valley* 125 Reports of these dogs were written up during the last century by . . . various factors of the Hudson's Bay Company, and others.

2. *local.* A garnishee. Cf. ∗**factorize,** *v.*

1878 DRAKE *Suits by Attachment* (ed. 5) 361 In Vermont and Connecticut, he [=the garnishee] is sometimes called a *factor,* and the process [of garnishing], *factorizing process.*

As the last term in **book, candle, cotton, Indian, turpentine factor.**

∗**factorize,** *v. Vt.* and *Conn.*

1. *tr.* To make a (third party) a garnishee by the serving of a writ. Used esp. in **factorizing process.**

1859 *Conn. Sup. Ct. Rep.* XXVIII. 103 This action was commenced by a writ of attachment, with a factorizing process, and the sheriff was factorized upon it as the agent, trustee and debtor of Boggs & Co. **1922** *Corpus Juris* XXVIII. 15/2 In some few jurisdictions the proceeding [of garnishment] is called 'trustee process,' or it is designated by the statute or usage as 'factorizing process,' or 'attachment execution.'

2. (See quot.)

1864 WEBSTER 490/3 *Factorize,* . . . to give warning to: said of a person in whose hands the effects of another are attached, the warning being to the effect that he shall . . . appear and answer the suit of the plaintiff. . . . To attach the effects of a debtor in the hands of a third person; to garnish.

∗**factory,** *n.*

1. An Indian agency, or the trading establishment connected with it, maintained by the federal government. Now *hist.*

1797 *Ann. 5th Congress* I. 43 Byers [is] one of the agents in the public factory at Tellico Blockhouse. **1813** STUART *Narratives* 238 There is a United States Factory here for all tribes who chuse to come for the purposes of trade. **1846** M'KENNEY *Memoirs* I. 19 Not a drop of brandy, rum, or whiskey being permitted to pass through the factories [to the Indians].

2. (See quots.) In full **factory cotton.**

1859 BARTLETT 140 *Factory cotton,* unbleached cotton goods, of domestic manufacture. **1906** *Out West* Jan. 50 The wagon waited under the maple trees by the door, its stout cover of unbleached 'factory' bulging over the high hickory bows. **1907** *D.N.* III. 230 Domestic . . . is a plain, smooth, bleached or unbleached cotton cloth, without any woven or printed design. Also called *factory.* [n.w. Ark.]

3. In combs.: (1) **factory store,** a store or trading post at an Indian agency, *obs.;* (2) **thread,** thread made at a factory as distinguished from that spun at home, which was too coarse for use in sewing machines; (3) **village,** a village whose economic life centers about a factory or factories, also attrib.

(1) **1812** *Niles' Reg.* III. 155/1 The neighboring Indians . . . came in . . . to receive the goods in the factory store. — (2) **1865** *Nation* I. 339 The attraction was a quantity of factory thread, stowed away in the government stores, which they wanted as warp for their looms. **1898** HARRIS *Tales* 367 She had gone to town with butter and eggs to exchange for some factory thread—'spun truck' Mrs. Pruet called it. — (3) **1832** *Boston Transcript* 24 Mar. 1/2 In the Chickopee Factory Village, Springfield, Mass., and also in the town of New Market, N.H. we also learn that schools are provided. **1868** BEECHER *Norwood* 218 Who is Jacquin, Brett? One of your factory-villagemen? **1905** *World's Work* IX. 5752/1 Ludlow, Mass., . . . shows what a factory village may be made by intelligent effort.

b. Designating products made in a factory as distinguished from those made at home, as **factory bag, butter, cheese, cloth, homespun, thread,** (see **3.** (2) above), **wagon.**

1887 ALDEN *Little Fishers* xxii, The factory bag . . . she had made for the money. — **1888** *Vt. Agric. Rep.* X. 14 Factory butter secures an average higher price than its patrons could secure if they made it at home. — **1870** *Rep. Comm. Agric.* 533 The improvement in the quality of Ohio factory cheese has fully kept pace with that in New York. — **1872** M. HOLLEY *My Opinions* (1891) 205 Paul didn't have to buy . . . 50 yards of merrymac calico and factory cloth. **1914** APPLEGATE *Recollections Boyhood* (1934) 159 After a time a heavy unbleached muslin, commonly called 'factory cloth,' could be gotten at Oregon City. — *c***1845** *Big Bear Ark.,* etc. 94 One could see the eend of my factry homespun shurt! — **1883** *Cent. Mag.* Nov. 43/2 Factory wagons protrude their shafts from the mouths of low, broad archways.

As the last term in **ax, bell, butter, cabinet, candy, cheese, clock, cracker, fish canning, gin, gun, hemp, maverick, nail, oil, saleratus, salt, tobacco, wagon factory.**

facultized ˈfækḷˌtaɪzd, *a.* Also **faculized.** *local.* [f. ∗*faculty.*] Practical, having executive ability.

1816 D. THOMAS *Travels Western Country* (1819) 118 This expression is a good match for that of 'a well *faculized* person,' so common in the eastern part of New-York state. **1871** STOWE *Sam Lawson* 53 She was one o' these 'ere facultised persons who has a gift for most any thing. **1882** GIBBONS *Pa. Dutch* 51 New England women will not be willing to admit that they do not understand housework, and are not eminently 'faculized.'

∗**faculty,** *n.* A body of persons responsible for the governing and the teaching in an educational institution, consisting usu. of the president or principal, certain other administrative officers, and the teaching staff. Also attrib. Cf. **college faculty.**

1767 in J. MACLEAN *Hist. College N. Jersey* (1877) I. 292 They find those gentlemen . . . still heartily desirous of concurring with the Trustees of this College in the establishment and support of a Faculty. **1839** HENRY CASWALL *America* 200 [The professors] form a body denominated the Faculty, and conduct the government of the institution by regulations and laws established by themselves in 'Faculty meetings' from time to time. **1911** H. S. HARRISON *Queed* 218 The president sat up late . . . going over and over his faculty list. **1945** *Life* 16 July 72/1 On these pages are pictured members of Chicago's faculty, one of the most awesome collections of brains ever set before the camera.

b. faculty adviser, a member of the faculty of a school, one of whose duties is to advise students, a counselor.

1942 *Hiram Coll. Cat.* 33 All freshman students are assigned to specific faculty advisers.

∗**fade,** *n.* In moving pictures, the action or act of fading. Used esp. in **fade-in** and **fade-out.** Also attrib. and transf.

1918 CROY *How Motion Pictures Are Made* 175/6 It was in such experiments that the principle of fade was discovered, by means of which a scene could be made gradually to grow plainer until the full details were before the audience. This in photographic parlance came to be known as the fade-in. . . . The reverse of this—the gradual elimination of the scene came to be known as fade-out. *Ib.,* The second means of accomplishing a fade picture is by means of the dissolving shutter. **1924** A. J. SMALL *Frozen Gold* i. 39 It isn't natural for a whole tribe of stick-at-nothings to be able to do a fade-out like that. **1946** *Trail Riders Bul.* May 11/2 Hoss opry stars never stoop to such vulgar behavior as going into a clinch with the one and only at the fadeout. **1948** MENJOU & MUSSELMAN *It Took 9 Tailors* 45 Griffith is credited also with using the close-up to give additional punch to his scenes and the 'fade' as a method of lowering the curtain at the conclusion of a sequence.

∗**fade,** *v.*

1. *tr.* In moving pictures, to cause (a picture) to change in degree of distinctness, esp. **fade in, fade out.** Also transf.

1918 CROY *How Motion Pictures Are Made* 177 The fourth method of fading a picture is by means of a chemical process. *Ib.,* This shutter device for fading out a picture. **1918** V. O. FREEBURG *Photoplay Making* 122 Then the scene shifts downward to a chaotic mass of broken rocks at the foot of the cliff, and the caption 'The Depths of Shame' is faded in.

2. (See quots.)

1934 WEBSTER. **1946** MOREHEAD & MOTT-SMITH *Penguin Hoyle* 217 Any other player or players may *fade* such portions of the bet as they wish, by placing that amount in the center with the shooter's bet. **1947** DEVOTO *Across Wide Missouri* 98 The whites played it as individuals, making it a variation of craps with elaborate fadings and parlays.

3. fade-away, a. The act of disappearing. **b.** (See quot. 1916.)

(a) **1911** HARRISON *Queed* v. 56 She had only pretended to die in order to make a fade-away with the gate receipts. **1932** *K.C. Times* 25 Feb. 20 For instance, you can put a peck in a pan, add a few drops of water and set it on a hot stove and it immediately begins to do the fade-away. — (b) **1909** *Amer. Mag.* May 31/1 Matty dropped his famous 'fade away' over the plate, and Tinker drove a long, high, line fly to left center. **1916** BANCROFT *Handbook* 79 Fadeaway. A method of pitching a 'drop ball' invented by Mathewson, whereby the ball goes with speed almost to the plate, and then slows up and drops with a rapid curve, deceiving the batter as to the height at which it should be hit.

∗**fag,** *n. To stand* (one) *a fag,* to stand a chance (with one). *Colloq.* — **1801** *Sp. Farmer's Mus.* 97 In boxing, no Yankee can stand me a fag. **1840** THOMPSON *Green Mt. Boys* I. 138 If they come on, Ethan Allen, Warrington, and Member Baker, with all they can raise, will stand no fag at all with a regular York army.

faggot bones. ?In certain fish, a group of small bones attached together at one end but spreading out into a fan shape at the other,

Rare. — **1805** LEWIS in *L. & Clark Exped.* II. (1904) 369 We hawled and caught a large number of fine trout and a kind of mullet about 16 inches long, which I had not seen before, . . . it has the faggot bones, from which I have supposed it to be of the mullet kind.

* **fail,** *v. N. Eng. To fail up,* to become bankrupt, to fail. *Colloq.*

1890 JEWETT *Strangers* 144 He'd failed up and got into trouble. **1893** WIGGIN *Polly Oliver* v. 57 If compartment two . . . had only met its rightful obligations, compartment three needn't have 'failed up' as they say in New England; but as it is, poor compartment four is entirely bankrupt. **1901** WILKINS *Understudies* 203 The bank he kept it in has failed up.

* **failure,** *n.* In schools, the fact of failing in a course, an examination, or exercise; the grade given for failing work.

1854 in SMALLWOOD *Exams. & Grading* 73 An absence from a weekly exercise shall count one—a failure three [demerit marks]. **1895–6** *Nebraska Univ. Cat.* 34 A 'condition' must be made up within a year or it becomes a 'failure.' **1944** *Eng. High School Cat.* 12 D denotes *failure*, and entitles a pupil to no credit. E denotes bad *failure*.

fainting spell. A fainting fit; a period marked by an inclination to faint. — **1891** WILKINS *N. Eng. Nun* 73 She had a fainting-spell. **1947** *1st Conf. Problems Early Infancy* 25 The surgeons did not encounter shock reactions; fainting spells were never seen.

* **fair,** *n.*[1]

1. A periodic or occasional joint exhibition, freq. competitive, of agricultural, industrial, or other products, usu. accompanied by amusements of various kinds. See **county, state, territorial, world's fair.**

The modern American fair developed from the older type of fair, a periodical market. "Near the opening of the new century (1801) a suggestion was made . . . that fairs should be regularly held in May and October on Cambridge Common and bounties given for certain articles. This plan included not only the exhibition of agricultural products, but also stated open markets for their sale. No action was taken" (1895 *Yearbook Dept. Agric. 1894* 83). "American Fairs date from the year 1815" (1879 *People's Cyclo.* I. 693/2).

1805 *Nat. Intelligencer* 24 April 3/2 Washington Fairs. It will be perceived . . . that . . . the premiums offered, may be an inducement to graziers and farmers to bring their cattle and other effects to the city. **1829** A. ROYALL *Pennsylvania* I. 155 The Germans in Pennsylvania have . . . a Fair, which they hold twice a year. These are distinct from the fairs for selling wares and cattle, and are something like the Thanksgiving in New England, that is, a kind of merry-making. **1938** WHITE *One Man's Meat* 13 It was a fine clear day for the Fair this year, and I went up early to see how the Ferris wheel was doing and to take a ride.

attrib. **1872** HOLMES *Poet* xii. 404 A great pumpkin, the wonder of a village, seemed to lose at least a third of its dimensions between the field where it grew and the cattle-show fair-table. **1893** HOWELLS *Coast of Bohemia* 4 A number of these embittered women brokenly fringed the piazza of the fair-house. **1905** RICE *Sandy* 154 The frivolous-minded of Clayton were bent upon the festivities of fair week.

b. Fair Association, an organization for promoting a fair.

1871 *Ill. Dept. Agric. Trans.* IX. 13 The Union Fair Association will enter into good and sufficient bonds to meet the requirements of the State Board. **1882** *Nation* 2 Nov. 370/2 The Board of Directors of the Garfield Monument Fair Association at Washington . . . is in daily receipt of donations and exhibits from all parts of the country.

c. * **fairground(s),** the grounds, usu. with equipment for exhibitions and entertainment, on which a fair is held.

Fairgrounds vary in size from those of the town and county fairs, which usually have a grandstand, a race track, and temporary buildings or tents, to those of the state, or interstate fairs, provided with permanent buildings for exhibits, lecture halls, side shows, etc. The grounds of a world's fair are always elaborately constructed, with an appearance of permanence, but usually of a temporary nature.

1851 QUENTIN *Reisebilder* II. 89 Dem Strome von Menschen und Fuhrwerk nachfolgend, gelangte ich bald zu den 'Fair-Grounds,' einer Miniatür-Copie des 'Albany-Fair.' **1855** in *Ill. Agric. Soc. Trans.* II. 25 In case you choose a spot of ground . . . south of this city for fair grounds. **1864** *Ohio Agric. Rep.* XVIII. 101 With the imperfect appliances on a Fair Ground, . . . the probabilities would be against the most successful operator. **1946** *Pueblo* (Colo.) *Chieftain* 27 June 1/2 An on-the-spot investigation was nullified yesterday when Stewart went to the fairgrounds as the last of the purported stored cars were being removed.

2. A special sale of fancywork, homemade foods, etc., to raise funds for a charity, a church, etc., usu. sponsored by women. Cf. **church fair.**

1827 in M. BAYARD SMITH *Forty Yrs. Washington Soc.* (1906) 209 Next week there is to be a Fair, for the benefit of the Orphan Asylum. **1863** CUMMING *Hospital Life* (1866) 58/2, I have been to a fair, given for the benefit of the Protestant orphans. **1947** PAUL *Linden* 350 Usually, the Fair netted the church about twenty-five dollars a night, when all expenses were paid.

As the last term in **citrus, corn, county, gift, good, Indian, ladies', Sanitary, state, territorial, town, whore, World's fair.**

fair fɛr, *n.*[2] *Football.* (See quots. 1893, 1911.) *Obs.*

1882 in P. H. DAVIS *Football* (1911) 470 If on three consecutive fairs and downs a team shall not have advanced the ball five yards or lost ten, they must give up the ball. **1893** CAMP *College Sports* 109 In a 'fair,' or putting the ball in from the touch . . . , the same general formation prevails as in the ordinary scrimmage. **1911** P. H. DAVIS *Football* 470 A 'fair' was the technical name of putting the ball in play from the side line when out of bounds.

* **fair,** *a.*

1. Designating a grade of cotton.

1847 *Semi-Wkly. News* (Fredericksburg, Va.) 19 July 3/2 Our latest quotations are for Upland and Mobile 7 3/8; fair Orleans 7 5/8 per lb. **1891** *Appeal-Avalanche* (Memphis) 7 May 6/1 Cotton Exchange Quotations . . . Middling Fair. Nom. Fair. Nom.

2. *Baseball.*

The use of "fair" in baseball is technical and subject to variation. Only quite general definitions are here attempted.

a. Of a pitched ball: Meeting conditions prescribed for a "strike." Cf. **fair ball 2.**

1856 *Spirit of Times* 22 Nov. 197/2 At most, every three fair pitched balls should be considered as one strike. **1887** *Courier-Journal* 30 Jan. 10/3 Any ball that goes over the plate between lines drawn at the batsman's knees and shoulders is fair.

b. fair ball, see as a main entry.

c. fair foul, app. a batted ball that lands in foul territory but rolls or bounces into "fair ground." *Obs.*

1870 *Cin. Commercial* 13 May 5/1 Harry Wright earned his third on a huge 'fair foul' hit to right. **1909** *Collier's* 15 May 14/3 He tried to master the fair foul, and one day he rolled off from the bat a short, weak tap which died in front of the pitcher's box.

d. fair ground, the territory bounded by the foul lines.

1878 *De Witt's Baseball Guide* 12 To strike a 'fair foul' he should stand as close to the front line and as near the 'fair' ground as possible. **1917** MATHEWSON *Sec. Base Sloan* 240 Wayne realized that had a runner been on fair ground he would probably have been hit by the ball.

e. fair hit, (see quot.).

1910 *Spalding's Baseball Guide* 343 A fair hit is also any legally batted ball that first falls on fair territory beyond first base or third base.

f. fair strike, =**fair ball 2.**

1867 *Ball Players' Chron.* 15 Aug. 1/4 As the error was a palpable one the umpire was fully justified in reversing his decision, and promptly correcting his error by calling out 'fair strike.'

3. Of leather: (See quot.). Cf. **fair-top(ped) boots.**

1875 KNIGHT 1274/2 Fair leather is finished . . . in the natural color imparted by the bark, and not specifically colored.

4. In special combs.: (1) **fair catch,** (see quot. 1909 and cf. **fair,** *n.*[2]); (2) **hack,** a fair chance, *colloq.;* (3) * **-haired boy,** a favorite, *colloq.;* (4) **lick,** (see quot. 1851), *obs.;* (5) * **maid,** (*a*) a variety of sour apple, cultivated esp. in Pennsylvania, *obs.,* (*b*) *Va.,* the porgy or scup, *Stenotomus versicolor;* (6) **shake,** a fair chance or bargain, *slang;* (7) **-top(ped) boots,** boots with tops of light leather, also **fair tops;** (8) * **trader,** (see quot.), *obs.*

(1) **1867** *Ball Players' Chron.* 14 Nov. 9/2 If the ball be kicked from out of *touch*, or from behind *goal-line*, a fair catch cannot be made. **1909** WEBSTER 784/2 *Fair catch,* . . . a catch made by a player on side who makes a prescribed signal that he will not attempt to advance the ball when caught. **1948** *Minneapolis Morn. Tribune* 28 Sep. 16/1 Leahy ordered his athletes to signal for a fair catch on the kickoff. — (2) **1880** TOURGEE *Bricks* 344 Jordan Jackson . . . knew what he wanted—it was light, liberty, education, and a 'fair hack' for all men. *Ib.* 349 It was right and fair to free the niggers and let them have a fair show and a white man's chance—votin' and all. That's what I call a fair hack. — (3) **1909** *Sat. Ev. Post* 24 April 26/2 The old crowd of Fair-haired Correspondent Boys who hung to the ear of President Roosevelt with viselike grip dissolved, but a new one formed immediately which included the men who had been with Taft in his campaign. **1949** *Time* 14 Mar. 30/1 Vishinsky was Stalin's newest fair-haired boy. — (4) **1837** *Harvardiana* IV. 22 *'Fair lick!'* he cried, and rais'd his dreadful foot. **1851** HALL *Coll. Words* 121 In the game of

football, when the ball is fairly caught or kicked beyond the bounds, the cry usually heard, is *Fair lick! Fair lick!*

(5) (*a*) **1867** WARDER *Pomology* 718 Fair maid.... Penn. (*b*) **1884** GOODE *Fisheries* I. 387 On the Virginia coast the Southern Scup is known as the 'Fair Maid.' — (**6**) **1830** *Central Watchtower* (Harrodsburg, Ky.) 22 May, Says I . . . any way that will be a fair shake. **1948** *Antioch Rev.* Autumn 160, I figure that's a fair shake. — (**7**) **1799** in CIST *Cincinnati* (1841) 159 As an illustration of fashions . . . fair-top boots. **1805** in *Commons Doc. Hist.* III. 368 Back Strap Boots, fair tops, 4 Dol[lar]s. **1884** *Cent. Mag.* Oct. 959/1 Dem dar boots! . . . nine dollar and sebenty-four cent' for dem fa'-topped boots. — (**8**) **1888** M. LANE in *America* 4 Oct. 15 Fair-Traders.—Semi-protectionists who endeavor to occupy a halfway position between free trade and protection. A man who advocates a 'tariff for revenue, with incidental protection,' is a fair sample of the class.

fair ball.

1. In baseball, a batted ball that is not a foul.

1856 *Spirit of Times* 6 Dec. 229/1 A player must make his first base after striking a fair ball. **1868** CHADWICK *Base Ball* 40 Fair Balls.—A fair ball is one sent from the bat and striking the ground *forward* of the lines of the bases. **1919** *Amer. Mag.* Aug. 66 The ball was curving fifteen feet foul, and Ryan did not run until Hurst yelled: 'Fair ball! Fair ball!'

2. A ball delivered by the pitcher to the batter in such a way as to conform to current rules for a "strike."

1865 in CHADWICK *Base Ball Player* (1866) 13 Sec. 6. Should the pitcher repeatedly fail to deliver to the striker fair balls, for the apparent purpose of delaying the game, or for any cause, the umpire, after warning him, shall call one ball, and if the pitcher persists in such action, two and three balls. **1886** CHADWICK *Art of Pitching* 60 A Fair-ball is a ball delivered by the Pitcher while standing wholly within the lines of his position, and facing the batsman, the ball, so delivered, to pass over the home base, and at the height called for by the batsman. **1887** *Lippincott's Mag.* May. 836 The batsman was only privileged to let three fair balls pass him without being struck at before he became amenable to the penalty of being declared out on strikes.

fair ground, *v. W. tr.* (See quot.) — **1920** HUNTER *Trail Drivers Texas* 298 To '*fair ground*' is to rope an animal by the head, throw the rope over the back while still running and then throw the animal violently to the ground.

* **fairy,** *n.* In attrib. uses, chiefly local, in plant names (see quots.).

1891 *Cent.* 7033/1 *Z[ephyranthes] Atamasco*, found from Mexico to Pennsylvania, with rose-colored flowers, is cultivated under the name of *fairy lily*, or *atamasco-lily*. **1892** *Amer. Folk-Lore* V. 103 *Juniperus communis*, fairy circle. **1893** *Ib.* VI. 142 *Mitella diphylla*, false sanicle; fringe cup; fairy cup. N.Y. **1907** LYONS *Plant Names* 17 *A[dlumia] fungosa*.... Climbing Fumitory, . . . Alleghany-vine, Canary-vine, Cypress-vine, Fairy-creeper. **1925** JEPSON *Flowering Plants Calif.* 674 *C[larkia] breweri*.... Fairy Fans. *Ib.* 237 *C[alochortus] pulchellus*.... Golden Lantern . . . [is] also called Golden Lily Bell and Fairy Lantern. **1941** R. S. WALKER *Lookout* 55 The staminate plants of fairywand is an exquisite floral creation blooming in April and May on the sides of the mountain. **1943** PEATTIE *Great Smokies* 196 There was . . . a brilliant lilac-purple display from that splendid orchid, the fairyfringe.

* **faith,** *n.* In combs.: (1) **faith cure,** a cure of bodily ailment by means of faith, esp. by "the prayer of faith" (Jas. 5:15), also attrib.; (2) **curer,** one who believes in or practices faith cure; (3) **curist,** =prec.; (4) **doctor,** (*a*) (see quot.), *rare*, (*b*) one who practices healing by faith cure; (5) **healer,** =**faith curer.**

(1) **1885** *Cent. Mag.* XXXI. 274 A faith-cure is a cure wrought by God in answer to prayer, without any other means. *Ib.* 276/2 The singular use of language which faith-cure folk permit themselves to employ. **1897** *Chi. Tribune* 4 July 4/4 She gave me a clipping from a faith cure magazine. **1944** JOHNSON *As I Dare* 328 Christian Scientists have reared the whole structure of their religion upon faith cure, and have their own scripture and ritual. — (**2**) **1888** *Pop. Science* XXXII. 507 The miracles claimed by the faith-curers are in the same line of argument. **1888** *Forum* V. 692 Among these . . . 'faith-curers' there are some more or less intelligent people. — (**3**) **1883** *Homiletic Mo.* Aug. 661 An exaggerated report of my conquest by the faith curist. **1893** *N. Amer. Rev.* March 292 The Faith Curists . . . declare their power to be objective. — (**4**) (*a*) **1828** J. HALL *Lett. from West* 340 Your *faith doctor* is one who practices without diploma. (*b*) **1891** EGGLESTON *Faith Doctor* 210 Phillida's work as a faith-doctor had begun. — (**5**) **1885** *Cent. Mag.* XXXI. 276/1 Of these cases the faith-healers give no detailed account. **1948** *Time* 2 Feb. 30/1 Avak, dark-bearded faith healer . . . arrived in Florida from California and quickly endeared himself to the Chamber of Commerce.

faithist ˈfeθɪst, *n.* One of a communistic religious sect whose faith is based on angelic communications.

1885 *Santa Fe W. New Mexican* 23 July 4/4 Tanner has joined the new community or sect of faithists near Las Cruces, N.M. **1892** *Voice* (New York) 30 June, The Faithists, who have started a Communistic colony in New Mexico for the education of children in their ideas, are just now making great efforts in Boston. They . . . hold weekly meetings where they discuss 'Ospree' and their 'New Bible.'

* **fake,** *n.*

1. *Theater.* A person or thing that has passed its time of usefulness.

1886 *Wkly. Republican* (Waterbury, Conn.) 15 Oct. (*Cent.*) To call such social lepers actors is . . . illogical and unfair.... Professionally considered your fake is as unworthy as he is socially. **1889** *Cent.* 2123/2 Fake, . . . *Theat.*, any unused or worn-out and worthless piece of property. **1926** *Amer. Mercury* Feb. 239/2 This quack-clapping of the fakes who infest the musical auditorium must enrage all.

2. One who fakes, a swindler or trickster.

1888 *N.Y. Mercury* (F.), Both ladies then came to the conclusion that the fortune-teller was a fake, and they decided to notify the police. **1944** STAFFORD *Boston Adven.* 281 She isn't southern at all. . . . She's just a terrible fake.

fake fek, *a.* [f. the noun.] False, pretended, counterfeit. *Colloq.*

1890 *Stock Grower & Farmer* 15 March 7/1 The Rio Grande C. & I. company . . . still continues the farce of surveying for their fake ditch. **1902** MCKEE *Land of Nome* 40 It was a common belief that no gold had been discovered there, and that it was a mere real-estate boom and a fake excitement. **1916** SANDBURG *Chicago Poems* 61 He never made any fake passes and everything he said went.

fakery ˈfekərɪ, *n.* The practice or product of faking. *Colloq.* — **1925** M. R. WERNER *Brigham Young* 31 It is impossible to determine exactly whether the golden plates of the Book of Mormon . . . were a piece of conscious fakery. **1947** *Atlantic Mo.* Nov. 81/2 Luce proved that magazines could win millions of readers without resorting to sentimentality, fakery, or evasion.

fakir ˈfekɚ, *n.* [App. erron. for **faker*, in a somewhat similar sense.] A peddler of cheap, worthless goods, esp. in the street or at fairs.

1882 in POE *Buckboard Days* (1936) 99 Notice: To Thieves, Thugs, Fakirs and Bunkco-Steerers.... If Found within the Limits of this City after Ten O'Clock P.M. this Night, you will be Invited to attend a Grand Neck-tie Party. **1891** QUINN *Fools of Fortune* 42 Here it was opened in the presence of a large crowd of 'fakirs' who had been drawn to Columbia by the fair then in progress. **1932** WILSON *Amer. Jitters* 95 (Horwill), They find the patent-medicine fakir on his motor-truck still holding a considerable crowd.

* **falcon,** *n.* As the last term in **Peale's, pigeon, prairie, rough-legged, rusty-crowned falcon.**

falda ˈfaldə, *n. W.* [Sp. in same sense.] The part of a mountain or range that slopes into the plain. Cf. **valda.**

1852 CAZNEAU *Eagle Pass* 123 Our shepherds have their camp in a sweet, secluded *falda* . . . that slopes down to the water's edge in a thick carpet of mezquit grass. **1876** HARTE *G. Conroy* III. viii, On the slope of the falda. **1891** ——— *Sappho of Green Springs* 150 The range of Major Randolph lay on a rich *falda* of the Coast Range. **1893** ——— *Susy* 159 The falda of the second terrace.

* **fall,** *n.*

1. =**fallfish.** *Colloq.*

1850 *Knickerb.* XXXVI. 105 He will squat under a big, projecting rock the live-long day; now soberly hauling up an eel, now a 'catty,' or a 'fall,' or a 'parch.'

2. In combs.: (1) **fall clip,** a growth of wool shorn in the fall, also attrib. and transf.; (2) **feed,** feed or pasturage for stock in the autumn; (3) **feeding,** (*a*) (see quot. 1856), (*b*) the feeding of stock during the autumn; (4) **fever,** (see quot. 1889); (5) **goods,** a stock of goods, usu. imported or bought in a trade center, serving the fall trade; (6) **grain,** grain that is sown in the fall, cf. **fall wheat;** (7) **growth,** the growth of various grasses after the first crop has been cut or otherwise disposed of; (8) **hunt,** a hunt made in the autumn, also **fall hunting;** (9) **Indians,** "a loosely defined Shahaptian group living formerly on and about Deschutes r., Oreg." (Hodge); (10) **plowing,** plowing done in the autumn; (11) **race,** a racing event that takes place in the fall; (12) **Falls City,** a nickname for Louisville, Ky.; (13) **season,** the autumn; (14) **session,** a meeting of a court or legislative body during the autumn; (15) **sown,** *a.* planted in the autumn; (16) **term,** see as a main entry; (17) **trade,** trade, beginning during the summer, in commodities for fall and winter sale or consumption; (18) **wheat,** wheat that is planted in the fall, winter wheat.

(1) **1885** *Santa Fe W. New Mex.* 1 Oct. 2 A Las Vegas schemer . . . made written contracts with the flock owners to deliver their fall clip at Lamy junction. **1904** O. HENRY *Heart of West* 237 It took a third of the fall clip to buy it. **1909** ——— *Options* 190 But, anyhow, Myra was a nine-pound, full-merino, fall-clip fleece, sacked and loaded on a four-horse team for San Antone. — (2) **1813** *Essex Inst. Coll.* XLIV. 336, I am to have the fall feed and Corn Stalks. **1861–2** *Ill. Agric. Soc. Trans.* V. 196 The scattered grain at once springs up and gives him a good supply of the best fall feed for his stock. — (3) (*a*) **1856** *Mass. Bd. Agric. Rep.* I. 209 Fall Feeding . . . is the term applied to feeding off the aftermath of mowing lands. **1868** *Rep. Comm. Agric.* 240 Probably one half [of the fences] is for convenience in 'fall feeding' mowing lands, which is poor economy. (*b*) **1868** *Iowa Agric. Soc. Rep. 1867* 95 Hogs [are] . . . in good condition for receiving their fall-feeding of corn. — (4) **1774** FITHIAN *Journal* I. 191 With us in Jersey wet Weather about this time . . . is . . . a forerunner of Agues, Fall-Fevers, Fluxes, & our Horse-Distempers. **1831** PECK *Guide* 295 It will be more exposed to fall fevers than an elevated and airy situation. **1889** *Cent.* 2194/3 *Fall fever,* (a) Typhoid fever. (b) Remittent fever.

(5) **1770** T. HUTCHINSON *Diary & Lett.* I. 24 The merchants . . . wrote for their goods, and by this means procured a large supply of fall goods. **1902** LORIMER *Lett. Merchant* ix. 122 Mose Greenebaum, who happened to be going up to town for his fall goods, got into the parlor car with him. — (6) **1790** MACLAY *Deb. Senate* 182 The snows, which fall regularly at their proper season in winter, insure a plentiful harvest of the fall grain. **1867** *Iowa Agric. Soc. Rep. 1867* 132 An excellent plan is to have some kind of fall grain to turn calves into. — (7) **1844** *Knickerb.* XXIV. 588 She had . . . [been] cropping the fall-growth of timothy and clover. **1845** FRÉMONT *Exped.* 171 This is the fall or second growth, the dried grass having been burnt off by the Indians. — (8) **1820** in ANDREAS *Hist. Kansas* (1883) 62 On this they feast, with the dried meat saved in summer, till September, when what remains is cashed, and they set out on the fall hunt, from which they return about Christmas. **1873** ABBOTT *C. Carson* 133 The trappers . . . were elated with their extraordinary prosperity. There is the spring hunting and the fall hunting. But there is a period in midsummer when the fur is valueless or cannot easily be taken. **1916** EASTMAN *From Deep Woods* 32 It seemed to me more like one of our regular fall hunts than like going to school. — (9) **1842** PARKER *Tour* 137 Above the Falls there is a large island, on the south side of which is a commodious bay, near which and upon the river De Shutes, which here unites with the Columbia, there is a village of the Fall Indians of about thirty lodges. **1845** DUNN *Ore. Terr.* 57 Bloodshed, rapine, and unbridled lust, are the characteristics of the fierce hordes of Assiniboines, Piegans, Blackfeet, Circees, Fall, and Blood Indians. **1920** DRUMM *Jrnl. Fur-Trading Exped.* 102 The Grosventres of the Prairie, or Fall Indians, as they were generally called, were the most relentlessly hostile tribe ever encountered by the whites in any part of the West, if not in any part of America. The trapper always understood that to meet with one of these Indians meant an instant and deadly fight.

(10) **1816** *Niles' Reg.* X. 33/2 The process consists, simply, in three successive fall plowings, . . . as follows: The first fall plowing to be succeeded by a crop of Indian corn [etc.]. **1932** W. KELLEY *Inchin' Along* 35 He says he is going to start his Fall plowing right away. — (11) **1840** *Dly. Picayune* 15 Oct. 2/2 Nashville Fall Races . . . over the Nashville (Tenn.) Course commenced on Monday, 28th ult. **1891** RYAN *Told in Hills* 12 Has your three-year-old come in last in the fall race? — (12) **1859** *Ladies' Repository* XIX. 51/1 Louisville, Kentucky, is the 'Falls City,' from its situation at the falls of the Ohio River. **1944** CLARK *Pills* 28 When prominent Confederate soldiers died, store doors in the Falls City were closed out of respect. — (13) **1786** in RAMSEY *Tennessee* (1853) 379 It appears impracticable to proceed on that business before the fall season. **1881** *Scribner's Mo.* XXII. 858/2 As the fall season approaches, he [the bear] climbs after the wild grape. — (14) **1715** *Mass. H. Rep. Jrnl.* I. 57 Summon them to attend this court on the second Wednesday of the next Fall-Session. **1722** in BUCKINGHAM *Newspaper Lit.* I. 339 Franklin [is to] give Security before the Justices of the Superior Court . . . to be of the good Behaviour to the End of the next Fall Sessions of this Court.

(15) **1868** *Mich. Agric. Rep.* VII. 161 The fall-sown wheat is well rooted, and in good condition to go into the winter. **1917** *Farmer's Bul.* No. 786, 4 Only the hardier fall-sown grains, winter wheat and rye, survive there [western Md., Va., and W.Va.] with certainty. — (17) **1851** *Hunt's Merch. Mag.* XXV. 202 It is but midsummer, and yet the *fall* trade has commenced in earnest. . . . The 'elder heads' among us can remember when the terms *spring* and *fall* trade represented almost literally the duration of the two seasons of business. **1923** WATTS *L. Nichols* 295 She herself was now hurrying and worrying over preparations for the fall trade and her opening-day. — (18) **1800** TATHAM *Agric. & Commerce* 56 The Americans . . . are possessed of many kinds of wheat . . . which they distinguish by the general epithets, *fall* wheat, *winter* wheat, *spring* wheat, &c. **1914** J. H. KEATE *Destruction Mephisto's Web* 94 Mr. Joyce was busily engaged in superintending the planting of his fall wheat.

b. In similar but less frequent combs., often rare or obs.: (1) **fall backset,** in plowing, a restoration, made in the fall, of the ridges of plowed prairie land to their original position, *colloq.;* (2) **burning,** (see quot.); (3) **butter,** butter made in the fall, cf. **d.** (3) below; (4) **clipping,** = **fall clip;** (5) **company,** a company of persons who emigrated west in the fall of the year; (6) **credit,** credit extended to an Indian in the fall by one interested in the furs he may secure during the winter; (7) **range,** a range for cattle, sheep, etc., used in the fall; (8) **supplies,** formerly supplies furnished Indians in the fall; (9) **trader,** a trader who during the fall supplies trappers, woodsmen, etc., with goods for the winter; (10) **trot,** a trotting match that takes place in the fall; (11) **way,** (see quot.).

(1) **1884** M. D. WOODWARD in *Checkered Yrs.* (1937) 41 People mentioned the autumn as the usual time to backset. That was called the 'fall backset.' — (2) **1863** *Ladies' Repository* XXIII. 700/1 Prairie land, when kept from the annual Fall burning formerly practised by the Indians, rapidly produces a growth of trees. — (3) **1858** C. FLINT *Milch Cows* 238 The fall butter should be packed separately in tubs. — (4) **1885** *Santa Fe W. New Mexican* 1 Oct. 2/7 The fall clipping will not fall short of 150,000 pounds.

(5) **1844** GREGG *Commerce of Prairies* I. 306 The caravans . . . have also crossed occasionally in the spring. . . . Even the 'fall companies,' in fact, are small when compared with the outward-bound caravans. — (6) **1837** CATLIN *Indians* II. 177 Pardon me a little, while I . . . attend to some Indians who are in my store, trading, and taking their fall credits. — (7) **1905** *Forestry Bureau Bul.* No. 62, 28 In some of the States there is an area along the lower slopes of the mountains which is called spring and fall range. — (8) **1823** *Amer. State P.: Indian Affairs* II. 421 The fall supplies, intended for the Indian trade, did arrive . . . late. — (9) **1842** *S. Lit. Messenger* VIII. 146/1 The feather-bed legs of yours will shrink up with the cold, younker, if we do not meet the fall traders, and increase our stock of Spanish blankets.

(10) **1905** RICE *Sandy* 215 Nelson wants the fellow to drive for him at the fall trots. — (11) **1859** BARTLETT 140 *Fall-Way,* the opening or well through which goods are raised and lowered by a fall. It is often merely a succession of openings through the several floors of the building.

c. In the names of fish, insects, etc.: (1) **fall army worm,** (see quots.); (2) **cankerworm,** (see quot.); (3) **fish,** see as a main entry; (4) **herring,** (see quot. 1889); (5) **mackerel,** (see quot. 1890); (6) **salmon,** the dog salmon, *Oncorhynchus keta,* abundant in the streams of the Pacific Coast; (7) **shad,** (see quot.); (8) **snipe,** the red-backed sandpiper or American dunlin; (9) **web-worm,** the larva of the arctiid moth *Hyphantria cunea.*

(1) **1881** *Ill. Entomologist Rep.* No. 10, 138 *Laphygma frugiperda,* Guen. The Fall Army-worm. . . . Appears in the Fall and feeds on both Wheat and Corn. **1892** KELLOGG *Kansas Insects* 39 Fall army-worm (*Laphygma frugiperda*). . . . A naked, pale-brown to dirty-green caterpillar, about one to one and a half inches long, eating grass, corn, rye, wheat, and various succulent plants in the autumn. — (2) **1890** *Vt. Agric. Rep.* 242 The Fall Canker Worm, *Anisopteryx pometaria,* Harr., is found, not only in the fall, but throughout the season in one form or another. — (4) **1814** MITCHILL *Fishes N.Y.* 451 Long-Island Herring. *Clupea mattowacca.* Called also the autumnal or fall herring. **1889** *Cent.* 2809/3 Fall herring, *Clupea mediocris,* . . . rather common along the Atlantic coast of the United States from Florida to the Bay of Fundy, and of little economic value.

(5) **1824** *Shipping & Comm. List* 31 July (Pettigrew P.), Fall mackerel. **1842** *Nat. Hist. N.Y., Zoology* IV. 103 The Fall Mackerel. *Scomber grex.* . . . In the autumnal months, the species appears in great numbers on our coast. **1890** *Cent.* 3561/3 Fall mackerel are simply tinkers, about 10 inches long, of wandering or irregular habits. — (6) **1850** HINES *Voyage* 331 In this country they are generally distinguished by the names of spring-salmon and fall-salmon. **1940** SMITH *Puyallup-Nisqually* 235 The fall salmon, however, cannot be taken in quantity in the rivers until their flesh has deteriorated. — (7) **1814** MITCHILL *Fishes N.Y.* 452 Long-Island Herring. *Clupea mattowacca.* . . . Some call this fish the *shad herring,* and some the *fall shad.* — (8) **1888** G. TRUMBULL *Names & Portraits of Birds* 182 At Pine Point, Me., Seaford, L.I., and Pleasantville (Atlantic Co.), N.J., [the Dunlin is called] *Fall Snipe.* **1917** *Birds of Amer.* I. 237 Red-backed Sandpiper. . . . Other Names.—American Dunlin; . . . Fall Snipe. — (9) **1862** *Ill. Agric. Soc. Trans.* V. (1865) 755 The *Hyphantria textor,* or fall web-worm is a gregarious caterpillar. **1892** KELLOGG *Kansas Insects* 83 Fall web-worm (*Hyphantria textor*), . . .

attacking the apple; . . . feeding in swarms within large webs, occasionally outside of the webs, in late summer and early autumn.

d. Designating plants or fruit that bloom or mature in the fall, as (1) **fall apple,** (2) **bird's nest,** (3) **butter (pear),** (cf. **b.** (3) above), (4) **dandelion,** (5) **fescue,** (6) **grape,** (7) **hoodwort,** (8) **pippin.**

(1) **1849** *N. Eng. Farmer* I. 25 The Hubbardston Nonsuch is one of our best late fall apples. **1872** *Vt. Bd. Agric. Rep.* I. 99 The Astrachans are still early fall apples. — (2) **1869** FULLER *Flower Gatherers* 190 The other flower he mentioned was the 'Albany Beech-drops,' or 'Fall-Bird's Nest.' — (3) **1843** *Ind. Q. Mag. Hist.* III. 191 The St. Michael (or fall butter, as it is called here) thrives and bears excellently well. **1847** *Cultivator* ns. V. 87 A valuable tree of Fall Butter pears was much affected in 1846. — (4) **1847** DARLINGTON *Weeds & Plants* 202 Hawkbit. Fall Dandelion. . . . This introduced plant is especially abundant in New England. **1892** TORREY *Foot-Path Way* 60 The names of these hardy adventurers [as] . . . fall dandelion.

(5) **1863** *Ill. Agric. Soc. Trans.* V. 865 *Festuca elatior*, Meadow Fescue or Fall Fescue, is a valuable grass. — (6) **1815** DRAKE *Cincinnati* 77 The botanical resources of this . . . Forest of the Miami country [include] . . . *Vitis labrusca*, Fall grape. **1827** DRAKE & MANSFIELD *Cincinnati* iii. 33 Among the domestic fruits, may be enumerated . . . fall, winter, and fox grapes. — (7) **1784** CUTLER in *Mem. Academy* I. 463 *Scutellaria*. . . . Fall Hoodwort. Blossoms pale blue. — (8) **1817** W. COXE *Fruit Trees* 109 Fall, or Holland Pippin. This is one of the finest, and most beautiful apples of the season. **1863** MITCHELL *My Farm* 143 A few trees of various old-fashioned sorts, such as the Fall-Pippin.

e. Designating or pertaining to clothing worn in the fall, as (1) **fall costume,** (2) **style,** (3) **suit,** (4) **weight.**

(1) **1883** *Cent. Mag.* XXV. 587/2 Beautiful women . . . rustling by in rich fall costumes. — (2) **1900** MUNN *Uncle Terry* 250 John Nason's store was filled with new fall styles. — (3) **1898** C. A. BATES *Clothing Book* No. 1276 If you haven't bought your fall suit yet. — (4) **1898** C. A. BATES *Clothing Book* No. 2580, A Fall-weight overcoat is an absolute necessity.

f. *To take* (or *get*) *a fall out of,* to get the best of. *Colloq.*

1889 DALY *Great Unknown* 29 But I really have been hard at work, Cousin Neddie—and I've stowed a lot. You just see me take a fall out of my 'Universal History.' **1913** LONDON *Valley of Moon* III. 2 I'll get a fall outa whatever it is.

As the last term in **dead, deer, timber, water, windfall.**

***fall,** *v.*

1. *intr.* To wither or wilt.

1850 *Rep. Comm. Patents: Agric. 1849* 320 Let it [tobacco] lay on the ground for a short time to 'fall' or wilt.

2. To drop to the ground in an ecstasy of religious fervor. *Obs.* Cf. ***exercise,** *n.* **2.**

1850 J. GALLAHER *Western Sk.-Book* 34 The language employed at that time [1800], by the plain western people, in describing the results of these [religious] meetings, was, that so many 'fell.' At one meeting, 'fifty fell' [etc.].

3. *tr.* Of a horse, to unseat or throw (the rider). *Rare.*

*a***1851** COLTON *Ship & Shore* viii. 139 The servant-boy . . . by way of apology . . . told how an animal [=a horse] had falled him three times.

4. In combs.: (1) **fallback,** (*a*) a chaise having a hood or top that may be folded back, in full **fallback chaise,** *obs.*, (*b*) designating a top that may be folded back on such a vehicle, *obs.;* (2) **down,** that part of a trap that falls when tripped; (3) **guy,** one who is the "goat" in a situation, one left in the lurch, *slang;* (4) **leaf,** the drop leaf of certain makes of tables, also attrib. with *table;* (5) **line,** the boundary between the older Appalachian uplands and the younger sea plain, also attrib.; (6) **money,** (see quots.).

(1) (*a*) **1760** *Boston Gaz.* 21 April 3/3 Smith wants a good handsome Fall back chaise. *Ib.* 28 April 4/1, 2 second-hand chaises, one a fall-back, the other a landright. **1832** *N.H. Hist. Soc. Coll.* III. 37 He was the proprietor of a fall back chaise, which went to decay and was never replaced. (*b*) **1840** *Boston Transcript* 19 June 3/1 Fall back top, elliptic springs, wheel guards. — (2) **1853** F. W. THOMAS *J. Randolph* 106 There stood the trap with the fall-down about ten feet from us. — (3) **1908** *Sat. Ev. Post* 5 Dec. 18/1 They had the nerve to try to ring me in for the fall guy on a green-goods play, baited up with a stage farmer from One Hundred and Sixtieth Street. **1949** *Time* 4 April 25/3 Browder, who stands ready to testify for the defense, was the fall guy of the Communist policy shift dictated by Moscow. — (4) **1853** B. F. TAYLOR *Jan. & June* 204 It was the old table with the fall leaves. **1870** *Rep. Comm. Patents 1868* II. 21/2 Fall Leaf Table. . . . The leaf is hinged to a piece which slides beneath the top. **1882** WAITE *Adv. Far West* 189 [A] fall-leaf table, chairs painted oak.

(5) **1882** *Nation* 13 July 33/1 It is here, at the 'fall line,' that the most available water-powers are to be found. *Ib.*, Above the 'fall line' the currents of the streams are much more rapid. **1949** *N.Y. Times* (Book Review) 6 March 8/2 The fall-line zone is where rivers begin to fall on their way to the sea. In the South, the line runs through Virginia down to Georgia, then swings toward the Mississippi in a big arc. — (6) **1900** FLYNT *Itinerant Policeman* 68 Practically all successful [pickpocket] mobs have 'fall money' (an expense fund for paying lawyers, etc., when they get arrested). **1901** ——— *World of Graft* 219 *Fall money*, funds saved by criminals to pay lawyers, secure cash bail, and to bribe officials.

5. In colloq. phrases: (1) *To fall down* (*on*), to fail, to prove deficient in (something), to "break down," esp. *to fall down on the job;* (2) *to fall for* (something), to be captivated or allured by (something), hence, to be deceived or "taken in," also *to fall,* ellipt. for whole phrase, *slang;* (3) *to fall over oneself* (*one another, each other*), to exert (oneself) excessively, to engage in vigorous rivalry, *colloq.;* (4) *to fall a snake,* see ***snake;** (5) *as easy as falling off a log,* see ***log.**

(1) **1873** BEADLE *Undevel. West* 704 We'll reach Sioux City by 5 o'clock, if we don't fall down. **1898** *Scribner's Mag.* XXIX. 689/1 All I'll have to do . . . is to fall down on this assignment . . . and I'll be allowed to resign. **1921** PAINE *Comr. Rolling Ocean* xviii. 312 His Chinese joss fell down on the job. **1928** *Publishers' Wkly.* 26 May 2175 We know of many cases where we fell down on buying books written by authors that had had successful books before.

(2) **1903** MCCARDELL *Conversations Chorus Girl* 28 (We.), The mayor fell for it. **1908** MCGAFFEY *Show-Girl* 83, I am learning how to skate. Yes, I fell for it. *Ib.* 92 Every time the Johns would fall, except in Milwaukee. **1944** *Evanston Review* 12 Oct. 3/3 But for the republicans who fall for their line, it is the exact opposite of smart.

(3) **1904** *Brooklyn Standard Union* 2 Aug. 6 The bonafide independent element is not falling over itself to come to Parker's assistance. **1904** *N.Y. Ev. Post* 8 Nov. 7 The party of the President . . . fall over one another in their anxiety to advertise said promise of immunity. **1904** W. H. SMITH *Promoters* 144 Capitalists are getting ready to fall over each other in availing themselves of the opportunity of utilizing the situation. **1921** PAINE *Comr. Rolling Ocean* 130 The thirsty outlaws fall over themselves to hand you ten or twelve dollars a quart for it.

Fallawater ˈfɔlə͵wɔtɚ *n.* [See quot. 1854. For variant forms see esp. quot. 1905.] (See quots.)

1854 ELLIOTT *Fruit Book* 79 *Fallenwalder* . . . American. Originated in Berks Co., Penn. 'It sprung up in the woods, and was left standing after the other trees were cut down; hence the name Fallenwalder, or apple of the cut-down woods.' **1857** E. J. HOOPER *Western Fruit Book* 35 Fallowater, or Fallenwalder, or Apple of the Fallen Timber, called, also, Tulpehocken, from the creek of that name. **1867** WARDER *Pomology* 405 *Fallawater*. . . . A native of Pennsylvania, where it is a great favorite; extensively cultivated through the West. . . . This is essentially a market apple, having little to recommend it but its size, appearance and productiveness. **1905** W. H. RAGAN *Nomenclature of Apple* 106 Fallawater. . . . Syn[onym]s. . . . Dutch Codlin (erroneously), Falder, Fallawalder, Fall de Walldes, Fallenwalder, Falwalder, Frenwalder, Green Mountain Pippin [etc.]. **1928** BAILEY *Cyclo. Horticulture* 321/2 Varieties of apples recommended. . . . *Winter*—Tompkins King, . . . American Golden Russet, Fallawater.

***fallen,** *a.*

1. fallen hide, (see quot.). *Obs.*

1929 DOBIE *Vaquero* 23 In the first place, the custom of the country was that any man could take a 'fallen hide' (a hide off a dead cow) when he found it, no matter what brand the animal bore.

2. fallen timber, (see quot. 1824).

1824 DODDRIDGE *Indian Wars* 85 Blackberries grew in abundance in those places where shortly before the settlement of the country, the timber had been blown by hurricanes. Those places we called the 'fallen timber.' **1870** in CRAMTON *Early Hist. Yellowstone Nat. Pk.* 133 Passing thence westward we became entangled in fallen timbers of the worst description on steep hillsides, and among impassable ravines. **1948** *Trail Riders Bul.* Dec. 6/1 Even fallen timbers failed to daunt the noble animals and the ride progressed smoothly and without incident.

b. *Battle of Fallen Timbers,* a battle on Aug. 20, 1794, in which General Anthony Wayne won a decisive and significant victory over a force of some eight hundred Indians at the rapids of the Maumee River in northwestern Ohio in a region called Fallen Timbers.

1894 in *Ohio Arch. & Hist. Soc. Pub.* (1901) IX. 222 The day before the battle of 'Fallen Timber' a council of war was called and a plan of march and battle submitted by Lieutenant William Henry Harrison was adopted. **1948** *N.W. Ohio Quart.* Jan. 37 He was one of the actors on that bloody field at the battle of Fallen Timbers.

fallfish ˈfɔlˌfɪʃ, *n.* (See quots.) Cf. **red fallfish.**

*a***1811** HENRY *Camp. Quebec* 32 Several of our company angled successfully for trout, and a delicious chub, which we call a fall-fish. **1820** RAFINESQUE in *Western Rev.* II. 241 Baiting Fallfish. *Rutilus compressus* . . . a small fish from two to four inches long, called Fallfish, Bait-fish, Minny, &c. It is found in the Alleghany Mountains. . . . The name of Fall-fish arises from its being often found near falls and ripples. **1884** GOODE *Fisheries* I. 617 The Fall-fish—*Semotilus bullaris.* The 'Fall-fish,' 'Chub,' 'Roach,' or 'Dace' is abundant in the streams of the Eastern and Middle States east of the Alleghanies. **1947** DALRYMPLE *Panfish* 321 The Fallfish, *Semotilus corporalis,* though much smaller, stands in about the same relationship to the Trout, in waters east of the Alleghanies.

***falling,** *a.* and *n.*

1. *n.* =**falling exercise.** Also **falling down.** Cf. ***exercise,** *n.* **2.** *Obs.*

1824 R. H. BISHOP *Hist. Church Ky.* 353 The first bodily exercise, which appeared in our worshipping assemblies, was *falling.* **1850** GALLAHER *Western Sketch-Book* 32 The Falling Down. This was one of the forms of that *bodily exercise,* as it was then called, which accompanied this remarkable work.

2. In combs.: (1) **falling ax,** see as a main entry; (2) **bank,** (see quot. 1807), also **falling-in bank,** *obs.;* (3) **collar,** a collar that turns down and lies flat about the neck, *rare;* (4) **creek,** ?a creek with a rapid current, *obs.;* (5) **exercise,** a condition in which one is overcome by excessive concern over religion and falls to the ground in uncontrollable nervous paroxysms, now *hist.,* cf. ***exercise,** *n.* **2;** (6) **spring,** ?a spring on the side of a declivity or hill, *obs.;* (7) **top,** a buggy top that folds back, *obs.,* cf. **fallback;** (8) **trap,** a deadfall, *obs.*

(2) 1807 C. SCHULTZ *Travels* II. 31 *Falling Banks* are so called from their being undermined by the current, in such a manner, that small portions are continually falling. It very often happens, that masses of an acre in extent, disappear in an instant. **1823** JAMES *Exped.* I. 109 Willow islands, moving sand-bars, and *falling-in* banks, are as frequent [in the Kansas R.] as in the Missouri. **1836** H. HALL *Statistics of West* ii. 44 The crews of the boats are employed in cutting away the overhanging timber from the *falling in banks,*—that is from such banks as are gradually becoming undermined by the action of the current. — **(3) 1861** *Army Regulations* 478 A sack coat . . . made loose, without sleeve or body lining, falling collar, inside pocket on the left side. — **(4) 1646** in *Amer. Sp.* XV. 176/2 North with a falling creek.

(5) 1807 R. M'NEMAR *Ky. Revival* 26 The various operations and exercises . . . were indescribable. The falling exercise was the most noted. **1847** R. DAVIDSON *Presbyterian Ch. in Ky.* 137 The spectacle of persons falling down in a paroxysm of feeling, first exhibited at Gasper river Church, in August, 1799, became now [1801] so common as to receive a distinct title, and to be known as the *Falling Exercise.* **1948** DICK *Dixie Frontier* 196 The 'falling exercise' appeared at the McGee meeting mentioned above. — **(6) 1745** in *Amer. Sp.* XV. 176/2 Beginning at two white Oaks and a Hiccory on a Point by the falling Spring run. **1781** *Ib.* 177/1, 280 Acres on the west side of the falling springs. — **(7) 1854** *Pa. Agric. Rep.* 208 Two Buggies, with patent Falling Tops. — **(8) 1643** R. WILLIAMS *Key* (1866) 191 Upon this the Indian makes a falling trap called Gunnúckkig, (with a great weight of stones) and so sometimes knocks the Wolfe on the head. **1806** LEWIS in *L. & Clark Exped.* V. (1905) 4 In the creek near our encampment I observed a falling trap constructed on the same plan with those frequent seen in the atlantic states for catching the fish descending the stream.

falling ax. (See quot. 1905.)

1678 *New Castle Court Rec.* 362, 3 falling axses. **1787** ELLICOTT in *Life & Lett.* 64 We immediately set out . . . with no other implements than three falling axes, two or three Tomahawks and a Chisel. **1805** PIKE *Sources Miss.* 35 This, considering we had only two falling-axes and three hatchets, was pretty good work. **1905** *Forestry Bureau Bul.* No. 61, 37 *Falling ax,* an ax with a long helve, and a long, narrow bit, designed especially for felling trees.

fallish ˈfɔlɪʃ, *a.* Like fall. *Colloq.* — **1885** JEWETT *Marsh Island* ii. 13 The old place never looks so well as it does in one of these yaller, fallish sundowns. **1899** ——— *Queen's Twin* 206 There was one o' them late crickets got into the room an' begun to chirp, an' it sounded kind o' fallish.

***fallow,** *n.*

1. (See quot. 1819.) Also attrib. *Obs.*

1819 C. B. JOHNSON *Lett. from Pa.* 56 When the timber is cut down, ready for burning, it is called a fallow. **1845** *Knickerb.* XXV. 388 Our western sky, . . . be-dimmed with the pervading smoke of fallow-fires. **1852** MOODIE *Roughing It* 24, I found Moodie and Monaghan employed in piling up heaps of bush near the house, which they intended to burn off by hand previous to firing the rest of the fallow, to prevent any risk to the building from fire.

2. fallow-plow, *v. tr.* (See quot.) *Rare.*

1804 J. ROBERTS *Pa. Farmer* 24, I fallow-ploughed it [*sc.* a field], that is, . . . I ploughed in the stubble and laid it up in one bout ridges, and let it lie in that rough state, till the following spring.

***falls,** *n.* As the last term in **fishing, French falls.**

fall term.

1. A session of a court held in the fall.

1833 *Ind. Mag. Hist.* XV. 242 The fall term of court . . . commenced . . . on the 14th of September. **1876** *Fur, Fin, & Feather* Sep. 133 After the conclusion of the fall term of the District Court Dr. Boyce . . . concluded to make an expedition to the 'Ojos Calientes.'

2. A school term which begins in the fall.

1871 BAGG *At Yale* 421 At the opening of the fall term of 1870, it was announced that the time of holding presentation Day had been changed. **1904** WALLER *Wood-Carver* 307 She had obtained the position of principal's assistant at the Academy for the next fall term.

***false,** *a.*

1. Designating various plants which resemble other well-known plants, as (1) **false beech-drops,** (2) **buckwheat,** (3) **buffalo grass,** (4) **cohosh,** (5) **pennyroyal,** (6) **sunflower,** (7) **violet,** (8) **wintergreen.**

Many additional combinations are listed in botanies and other technical works.

(1) 1857 GRAY *Botany* 262 *Monotropa Hypopitys.* Pine-sap. False Beech-drops. . . . Oak and pine woods; common. **1892** COULTER *Bot. W. Texas* II. 254 False beech-drops [are] somewhat pubescent or downy, tawny, whitish, or reddish, commonly fragrant plants. — **(2)** *a***1862** THOREAU *Maine Woods* 315 *Polygonum cilinode* (fringe-jointed false buckwheat). **1876** JACKSON *Travel at Home* 186 Solid knitted and knotted banks of vines on either hand, . . . woodbine, groundnut vine, wild or 'false' buckwheat. **1909** WEBSTER 787/2 F[alse] buckwheat, an American climbing polygonaceous herb (*Polygonum scandens*), having large triangular seeds resembling buckwheat. — **(3) 1894** *Amer. Folk-Lore* VII. 104 *Munroa squarrosa,* . . . false buffalo-grass. — **(4) 1840** DEWEY *Mass. Flowering Plants* 41 *Leontice thalictroides,* Poppoose Root, and False Cohosh, . . . blossoms in April and May.

(5) 1817–8 EATON *Botany* (1822) 320 *Isanthus caeruleus,* blue gentian, false pennyroyal. Along the Hudson. . . . Odour resembles the spikenard. **1901** MOHR *Plant Life Ala.* 707 *Isanthus.* . . . False Pennyroyal. One species, Eastern North America. *Isanthus brachiatus.* . . . False Pennyroyal. — **(6) 1817–8** EATON *Botany* (1822) 301 *Helenium autumnale,* false sunflower. . . . At Hudson it grows in the mud of South Bay. **1890** *Cent.* 2774/3 The best-known species [of *Helenium*], . . . sneezeweed, . . . is also called false sunflower. — **(7) 1821** *Mass. H.S. Coll.* 2 Ser. IX. 149 Plants, which are indigenous in the township of Middlebury, [Vermont, include]. . . . *Dalibarda violaoides,* False violet. — **(8) 1871** BURROUGHS *Wake-Robin* (1886) 75 Here and there in the bordering a spire of the false wintergreen strung with faint pink flowers.

2. In special combs.: (1) **false burying,** (see quot.); (2) **caterpillar,** the larva of a sawfly; (3) **chinch bug,** (see quot.); (4) **counter,** an election official who reports the count of an election return falsely; (5) **front,** see as a main entry; (6) **pound,** (see quots.); (7) **quahaug,** the black quahog, *Cyprina islandica.*

(1) 1836 GILMAN *Recol.* (1838) 81 When a funeral occurs at too great a distance from the city to procure tea, coffee etc., . . . the body is interred, and the friends afterward celebrate . . . a 'false burying,' where religious ceremonies are performed, and refreshments provided. — **(2) 1884** *Rep. Comm. Agric.* 326 False-caterpillars, of which the Imported Currant worm is a familiar type. — **(3) 1884** *Rep. Comm. Agric.* 316 In the False Chinch-bug we have . . . a very injurious insect. — **(4) 1879** *Cong. Rec.* 24 April 805/2 Let repeaters, false-counters, and ruffians no longer be employed to carry elections. **1883** *Cent. Mag.* July 399/1 The work of the committee has terrorized the whole gang of ballot-box stuffers, personators, repeaters, and false counters.

(6) 1844 GREGG *Commerce of Prairies* I. 23 Frequently led astray by the deceptive glimmer of the mirage, or false ponds, as those treacherous oases of the desert are called. *Ib.* 98 The most perplexing phenomenon, occasioned by optical deception, is the *mirage* or, as familiarly called upon the Prairies, the 'false ponds.' **1943** DEVOTO *Yr. of Decis.* 289 Twenty-five miles out from Bent's Fort Susan Magoffin, just alive, saw no blade of grass but 'with anxious eyes and heart to gain first the long wished luxury' saw her first 'false ponds' or mirages. — **(7) 1883** *Nat. Museum Bul.* No. 27, 232 *Cyprina islandica* . . . is the 'sea-clam' or 'false quahaug.' It is found in deep water, from Black Island to the Arctic.

false front.

1. (See quot. 1889.)

1889 *Cent.* 2388/3 A sort of half-wig worn by women with a cap or bonnet, to cover only the front part of the head: distinctively called a *false front.* **1899** A. BROWN *Tiverton Tales* 71 An' there's cousin Hattie's cashmere shawl, an' Obed's spe'tacles. An if there ain't old Mis' Eaton's false front!

2. The front of a building so built as to extend above or beyond the building proper.

1889 HOWELLS *Hazard of Fortunes* I. 106 A lot of stores and doggeries strung along with false fronts a story higher than the back. **1948** JOHNSTON *Gold Rush* 28/2 The old bank still stands, the painted letters visible on its false front.

transf. **1948–9** *Antioch Review* Winter 408 The oil plunderers, and the various false fronts behind which they are at work, are overlooking no chances to get Congress to give away the nation's birthright.

fame flower. (See quot. 1891.) — **1891** *Cent.* 6169/2 *T[alinum] teretifolium,* a native of the United States from Pennsylvania to Colorado and southward, . . . has been called fame-flower from the transitoriness of its elegant purple petals. **1941** R. S. WALKER *Lookout* 47 It appears on the sandstones at Rock City at the north end of the mountains and travels all the way to the southern extremity, reaching the pockets filled with leaf mold at Noccalula Falls. This is fameflower.

Fameuse fəˈmjuz, *n.* [F., famous.] A fall variety of apple.

1847 IVES *N. Eng. Fruit* 40 *Fameuse.* Fruit middle size; of a flat form; skin light yellow and green. **1863** *Horticulturist* XVIII. 262 Of Apples, we may mention . . . Fameuse, Gravenstein [etc.]. **1928** BAILEY *Cyclo. Horticulture* 319/1 Here the leading varieties in the older orchards are Baldwin, Rhode Island Greening, . . . Fameuse, Tolman, . . . and Wealthy.

*** family,** *n.*

1. An organized unit of Shakers or Friends.

*a*1772 WOOLMAN *Journal* (1882) 153 We visited Joseph White's family, he being in England. *Ib.* 184, I accompanied some Friends in a visit to the families of Friends in Mount Holly. **1832** WILLIAMSON *Maine* II. 699 The Shakers live in families, having a community of goods, or all things common. **1920** HOWELLS *Kelwyns* 209 The Family will have to take them at the referees' valuation.

2. In combs.: (1) *** family boat,** see as a main entry; (2) *** circle,** the upper gallery in a theater; (3) **company,** company consisting of relatives; (4) **council,** (see quot.); (5) **entrance,** a side entrance to a saloon for those not wishing to go directly to the public bar; (6) **fort,** (see quot.), *obs.;* (7) **grant,** a grant of public land made to a family, *obs.;* (8) **grocery,** a grocery store that caters to the needs of an entire family; (9) **horse,** a horse so gentle as to be used by all members of a family; (10) **lot,** a cemetery lot in which members of a family are buried; (11) **mansion,** an elegant or pretentious ancestral home; (12) *** meeting,** =**family council;** (13) **pie,** (see quots.), *obs.;* (14) **porterhouse,** a porterhouse steak large enough for a family; (15) **record,** the pages of a family Bible designed for use in keeping a record of the births, deaths, and marriages in a family, also the record itself; (16) **remedy,** a patent medicine; (17) **room,** a living room or sitting room; (18) **sitting,** a gathering of members of the Society of Friends for worship, *obs.;* (19) **sleigh,** a sleigh large enough for a family; (20) **style,** designating a boardinghouse where the food is placed on the table in serving dishes so that each may help himself; (21) **wagon,** a wagon suitable for the use of a family; (22) **wash,** the laundry belonging to a family, also **family washing.**

(2) **1868** *Chi. Times* 29 Nov., The upper gallery [in the Dearborn Theater] is to be called the family circle. **1896** BIRKMIRE *Amer. Theatres* 5 Above the two box-tiers [in the Metropolitan Opera House] come the dress-circle, the balcony, and the family circle, in the order named. — (3) **1889** *Cent. Mag.* April 845/1 What we in the South call 'family company.' — (4) **1889** *Cent.* 2134/1 *Family council, family meeting,* in civil law, as in Louisiana and Quebec, a council of the relatives or friends of a person for whose sake a judicial proceeding, as the appointment of a guardian, is to be taken, called and presided over by a judicial officer, and held under legal forms.

(5) **1881** MARSHALL *Through Amer.* (1882) 41 A good many of them have their back or 'family' entrances, as they are called, the doors of which are left unfastened while the front ones are locked. **1947** PAUL *Linden* 55 Unescorted women, theoretically, were not admitted through the 'Family Entrance.' — (6) **1837** BIRD *Nick of Woods* I 183 A fortified private dwelling, a favorable specimen, perhaps, of the family-forts of the day. — (7) **1738** W. STEPHENS *Proc. Georgia* 238 He succeeded so far as to get a Family Grant, which being numerous in Children and Servants, . . . came to thirteen hundred Acres. — (8) **1834** *Sun* (N.Y.) 17 May 2/1 Corner of Morton street—Scott's Family Grocery, roof partially burnt. — (9) **1843** CARLTON *New Purchase* I. 118 Dick was bought as a family horse. **1899** *Chi. Record* 4 Jan. 11/3 I will pay $18 per month for the board of my family and road horse 'Judson' until my return from abroad.

(10) **1902** MCFAUL *Ike Glidden* 15 Joe Glidden was laid at rest in the family lot. — (11) **1848** IRVING *Knickerb.* (rev. ed.) IV. i, Such are my feelings when I revisit the family mansion of the Knickerbockers. **1900** STOCKTON *Afield & Afloat* 360 Is this one of the old family mansions of Landover? — (12) **1856** BOUVIER *Law. Dict.* (ed. 6). **1889** [see **family council**]. — (13) **1818** *Boston Centinel* Sep. (Th.), *Family pye* is, in the New England dialect, nearly synonymous with mammoth pye. **1818** *Mass. Spy* 7 Oct. (Th.), Where each . . . carves for himself from the broad earthen platter A slice of the sweet yellow family pie. — (14) **1913** LONDON *Valley of Moon* II. xvii, Here's family porterhouse, a dollar and a half.

(15) **1801** WEEMS *Letters* II. 210 Some of the Bibles have no family record! **1852** MITCHELL *Dream Life* 105 Those prettily bordered pages, which lie between the Testaments, and which hold the Family Record. — (16) **1924** CROY *R.F.D. No. 3* 162 In earlier days itinerant peddlers had driven from house to house in the country districts of this section, selling so-called 'family remedies.' — (17) **1853** *Harper's Mag.* VI. 443 The first night of my arrival I was honored with a spare family room. **1931** FINLEY *Lady of Godey's* 34 Whether her description of the 'family room' in her first novel, 'Northwood,' published in 1827, is a picture of her own parlor one cannot be sure. — (18) *a*1772 WOOLMAN *Journal* (1882) 153 We had also a family-sitting at the house of an elder who bore us company. — (19) **1861** E. COWELL *Diary* 241 The cosy family sleigh . . . is built to hold 7 or 8.

(20) **1932** *K.C. Star* 2 May 18 The worst luck that can happen to a family-style boarding house patron . . . is to be called to the telephone just as the meal starts. — (21) **1790** *Pa. Packet* 22 April 2/1 For Sale, A neat, new, high, finished Coache, or Family Waggon. **1890** C. KING *Sunset Pass* 10 Captain Gwynne . . . had two fine horses and a capital family wagon, covered. — (22) **1870** FERN *Ginger-Snaps* 68 Nursery-labor must often make up the deficiencies involved in the terrible 'family-wash.' **1884** *N.Y. Herald* 27 Oct. 7/4 Respectable Woman to do ladies' or family washing. **1931** *Blue Valley Farmer* (Okla. City) 12 Nov. 5/2 His wife was hanging out the family wash.

b. * *man of family,* (see quot. 1794). *Colloq.*

1794 HODGKINSON *Lett. on Emigration* 74, I could not help smiling at the American definition of *a man of family*—With them it signifies one who has got a wife and five or six children. **1859** BARTLETT 141 *Family.* This word is often used to denote a man's wife and children, especially the latter. Hence the phrases, 'a man of family,' [etc.].

As the last term in **bonanza, bourbon, butter, education, first, happy, mission, official, president's, scuppernong, secession, Shaker, shanty, Uchean family.**

*** family boat.** A boat used in pioneer times by a family in emigrating down rivers, esp. the Ohio and the Mississippi. Cf. *** ark,** *n.* **1.**

1806 T. ASHE *Travels* V. 37 In autumn and spring it [the river] is generally covered with what are here called trading and family boats. **1818** J. FLINT *Lett. from Amer.* 73 The craft, called family boats, are square arks, nine or ten feet wide, and varying in length as occasion may require. They are roofed all over, except a small portion of the fore part, where two persons row. **1886** *Cent. Mag.* Nov. 12/1 Early in the year 1870 three hundred 'large family boats' arrived at the Falls of the Ohio.

*** fan,** *n.*[1]

1. A branch or bough of the palmetto palm or of the balsam tree. Also attrib. Cf. **turkey feather fan.**

1893 *Harper's Mag.* May 894/2 Expanses . . . carpeted with flowers and ferns and the fans of the dwarf-palmetto. **1903** WHITE *Forest* 43 Fell a good thrifty young balsam, and set to work pulling off the fans. *Ib.,* Now thatch the rest on top of this, thrusting the butt ends underneath the layer already placed in such a manner as to leave the fan ends curving up and down.

2. In combs.: (1) **fan blower,** "a blower in which a series of vanes fixed on a rotating shaft creates a blast of air . . . or a current" (Knight); (2) **crested duck,** the hooded merganser or fanhead, *Lophodytes cucullatus;* (3) **head,** =prec.; (4) **leaf palm,** a palm, *Washingtonia filifera,* with fan-shaped leaves; (5) *** light,** a skylight, also attrib.; (6) **mussel,** the sea fan, a species of *Gorgonia;* (7) **plant,** a variety of palmetto; (8) *** tail,** the overhang at the stern of a steamboat or yacht, also attrib.

(1) **1847** *Rep. Comm. Patents 1846* 84 The fan blowers now used in steamboats for blowing the fires in the furnaces, are generally made from two to three feet in diameter. **1876** RAYMOND *8th Rep. Mines* 349 A small furnace with a fan-blower. — (2) **1799** BARTON *Fragm. Nat. Hist. Penna.* 2 *Mergus cucullatus*, Fan-crested-Duck. **1917** *Birds of Amer.* I. 112 Hooded Merganser, *Lophodytes cucullatus*. . . . Other names.— . . . Round-crested Duck; Fan-crested Duck; Tree Duck. — (3) **1897** *Outing* XXX. 58/1 The hooded merganser [*Lophodytes cucullatus*], generally termed 'fan-head' owing to its beautiful crest, is a fish duck and worthless for the table, but the drakes are lovely in their bravery of velvet-black and snow-white, and make handsome specimens if properly mounted. — (4) **1884** SARGENT *Rep. Forests* 217 *Washingtonia filifera*. . . . Fanleaf Palm. **1897** SUDWORTH *Arborescent Flora* 105 *Neowashingtonia filamentosa*. (Wend.) . . . Fanleaf Palm (Cal.).

(5) **1904** *N.Y. Times* 27 July 1 Entrance to the store was gained through a fanlight on the roof. **1939** LYLE SAXON *Fabulous New Orleans* 325 There are three large fan-light windows, open to the warm air of the afternoon. — (6) **1870** *Amer. Naturalist* III. 284 In Florida are numerous specimens of the Fan Mussels (Pinna); . . . these submarine weavers spin a byssus, or beard, by which they attach themselves to the bottom of the sea. — (7) **1844** MRS. HOUSTOUN *Texas* II. 11 The monotonous brown of the earth's covering was, however, varied by frequent tufts of the fan-plant; as it is here called. This graceful plant shoots up its broad fan-like leaves, of the most vivid green, and its peculiar shape and hue are calculated to give an appearance of tropical vegetation to the scenery. — (8) **1882** *Harper's Mag.* LXIV. 174/2 The stalactites of ice that at the start lent the wheel and 'fan-tail' a novel beauty fall off or melt away. **1883** *Ib.* LXVII. 449/2 A fan-tail overhang, which ends in a moulded arch-board [of a yacht]. **1948** *Chi. D. News* 17 Nov. 2/1 At night the fantail of a ship is a dark, lonesome place.

As the last term in **alluvial, Big, palmetto, palm leaf fan.**

fan fæn, *n.*[2] [Usu. derived from **fanatic*, but poss. f. **fancy*, collect. for those who frequent prize fights.] An enthusiastic devotee or follower of a sport, hobby, etc., esp. baseball; an admirer of a writer, actor, etc. *Colloq.*

1896 ADE *Artie* xvii. 158, I'm goin' to be the worst fan in the whole bunch. **1903** *Cin. Enquirer* 1 Jan. 4/2 Within a fortnight the work on the new stands in the Land of Bleach at League Park and all other improvements adjacent to the Palace of the Fans are expected to be under way. **1948** *Capital-Democrat* (Tishomingo, Okla.) 3 June 7/1 Local fans will get their first home glimpse of league action Sunday afternoon when the locals meet the Durant juniors.

b. fan mail, mail received by a celebrity from fans. Also **fan letter.**

1925 WITWER *Roughly Speaking* 228 [He] stopped . . . to leave me the morning paper and my fan mail. **1947** *Parade* 23 Feb. 21/1 Long before she could read, she was receiving 15,000 fan letters per week. **1948** *Time* 10 May 85/1 The place was snowed under with fan mail.

c. fanfest, see **fest,** *n.*

***fan,** *v.*

1. *intr.* (See quot. 1859.) Also *to fan out. Slang. Obs.*

1834 in *Military & Naval Mag. U.S.* III. 25 My first appearance before the Blackboard . . . that delight of him who hopes to 'fan.' **1859** BARTLETT 141 *To Fan out*, to make a show at an examination. . . . The term originated at the United States Military Academy at West Point, where for years it was local; but it is now gradually finding its way through the country.

b. **To fan out*, to whip or overcome. *Colloq.*

1879 TOURGEE *Fool's Errand* xxxvii. 261 When . . . we met them in battle, there was always one satisfaction, whoever got 'fanned out,'— it was always our own folks that did it. **1895** HARRIS *Mr. Rabbit at Home* 187 He had met the great Brindle Dog . . . and had fanned him out in a fair fight.

2. *tr.* (See quot. and cf. **Big Fan.**) *Obs.*

1852 GUNNISON *Mormons* 114 It was when these men were leaving that the Danite band was formed to *fan* them, and keep their mouths closed, and others from deserting,—they were the fruits of peace and prosperity.

3. Of a pitcher in baseball: To cause (a batter) to strike out.

1909 WEBSTER *Fan*. . . . To strike (the batter) out. *Slang.* **1912** C. MATHEWSON *Pitching* v. 101 He fanned the next two men. **1948** *Green Bay* (Wis.) *Press-Gazette* 12 July 15/3 Brown fanned nine and walked eight.

b. *intr.* Of a batter: To strike out.

1886 *Outing* July 477/2 The man who . . . 'fans out' or 'pops one up.' **1903** *Cin. Enquirer* 1 May 3/1 Peltz cast anchor at second, and after Sutthoff had fanned in a vain attempt to advance him, Heiny pulled his throttle wide open, and shot for third. **1945** *This Week Mag.* 21 April 10 He always did that at the ball bark when he fanned in a pinch and the opposition booed.

4. *W. tr.* and *intr.* (See quots. 1901 and 1929.) Cf. ***fanning,** *n.*, and see ***thumb,** *v.*

1901 NORRIS *Octopus* 258 He 'fanned' his revolver, spinning it about his index finger by the trigger-guard with incredible swiftness. **1929** DOBIE *Vaquero* 268 To 'fan' a gun the person gripped it in his left hand and with rapid passes of his right hand knocked back and released the hammer. The gun used in 'fanning' had, of course, no trigger. A man might 'fan' for pastime, but seldom for his life. **1948** *Popular Western* June 32/1 Degrew was fanning his triggerless Colt with the heel of his other hand.

b. To flourish (a knife) in a threatening manner. *Slang.*

1907 MULFORD *Bar-20* viii. 86 Then I wants a drink an' he goes an' fans a knife at me.

c. *to fan off*, to shoot off by fanning. *Rare.*

1910 W. R. RAINE *B. O'Connor* 39, I recognized York Neil by him being shy that trigger finger I fanned off down at Tombstone.

d. To file or adjust (the "dog" or catch, or trigger of a revolver) so that the weapon may be more easily "fanned."

1931 *Red Book Mag.* Dec. 26 But that part of their attire which belonged most definitely to the past was the guns at their belts; guns the triggers of which had been 'fanned' when swift shooting was the only medicine for adding years to a man's life. [**1945** M. JAMES *Cherokee Strip* 32 The gun was a cedar-handled, single-action, long-barreled Colt .45, with the 'dog' filed for fanning the hammer.]

5. (See quot.) *Colloq.*

1901 H. W. WILSON *With Flag to Pretoria* II. 472 It was our . . . task to 'fan' this [*sc.* a wooded valley], as an American officer would say, by scattering a ceaseless shower of bullets throughout its length.

6. To move smartly, clear out. *Slang.*

1902 O. WISTER *Virginian* xv. 168 This hyeh train? . . . Why, it's been fanning it a right smart little while. **1905** REX BEACH *Pardners* v. (1912) 120 He saw I was drunk, and fanned out, me shootin' at him with every jump. **1927** JAMES *Cow Country* 230 Todd, seeing that no timbers was left to knock him off the saddle, stuck to his seat and fanned his pony on out to the open.

***fancy,** *n.*

1. In the names of homes or estates with the owners' names prefixed. *Obs.*

1671 *Md. Hist. Mag.* XXI. 344 Davids fancy, 100 acr[es] Sur[veyed] the 22 June 1671 for David Williams. *Ib.* 350 Knighton fancy, 100 acr[es] Sur[veyed] the 2 Sep[tembe]r 1671 for Thomas Knighton. **1682** *Ib.* 352 Philipes fancy, 69 acr[es] Sur[veyed] the 1st Aprill 1682 for William Cromwell. **1695** *Ib.* 285 Hectors Fancy 100 acr[es] Sur[veyed] the 20 Feb[rua]ry 1695 for Hector Marklan.

2. *pl.* **=fancy stocks.**

1841 *Week in Wall St.* 82 A very large portion of the stocks termed 'fancies,' are entirely worthless in themselves. **1882** *Cent. Mag.* XXIV. 538 Even the 'fancies' . . . Record a sharp advance.

***fancy,** *a.*

1. (See quots.)

1881 WORCESTER 1860/2 *Fancy*, in the United States, a term applied to the grade of flour made of a mixture of red winter and spring wheat, bolted clean. **1883** *Harper's Mag.* June 78/1 'Fancy' flour differs from the ordinary superfine in that the middlings are ground through smooth rollers.

2. In special combs.: (1) **fancy fixings,** household supplies or conveniences of a somewhat superior kind, *colloq.*; (2) **grass,** a variety of varicolored or striped grass, *obs.*; (3) **horse,** a stallion, *colloq.*; (4) **stocks,** *pl.* (see quots.); (5) **store,** a variety store.

(1) **1853** KANE *Grinnell Exped.* 154 They had to rough it: to use a Western phrase, they had no fancy fixings. **1887** *Harper's Mag.* April 666 The countryman . . . took back his year's supply of . . . whiskey, wearing apparel, and 'fancy fixin's' for the goddess of his household. — (2) **1784** WASHINGTON *Diaries* II. 307 A grass, not much unlike what is called fancy grass, without the varigated colours of it. **1794** ——— *Writings* XIII. 10 If cattle or horses will eat the fancy grass in the green state, or made into hay, it certainly must be very valuable. — (3) **1870** NOWLAND *Indianapolis* 38 A Kentucky lawyer . . . did keep a 'fancy horse.' *Ib.* 137 The writer of these sketches won a fancy horse on that occasion. — (4) **1841** *Week in Wall St.* 85 The brokers are less to blame than those who support them; and, if left to themselves, their trade in fancy-stocks would soon cease. **1871** DE VERE 469 Fancy-stocks are such as exist only on paper. **1900** NELSON *A B C Wall St.* 141 *Fancy stocks*, new stocks quoted at high figures; highly speculative stocks that are notorious for manipulation. — (5) **1829** A. ROYALL *Pennsylvania* I. 9 Stepping into a fancy store . . . I was not only gratified, but astonished, at the richness and brilliancy of the wares. **1894** WARNER *Golden House* iv, Vicky was seventeen, and had been in a fancy store.

∗**fandango,** *n.* In various transferred senses (see quots.). *Obs.*

1797 BENTLEY *Diary* II. 237 [At Bunker's Hill] a Fandango is erected, which was invented at Haverhill. On two ropes a chain slides down hill to a place accommodated to receive it, with the person who dismounts below. **1871** DE VERE 133 In the Eastern States . . . any very boisterous assembly, even a row, is familiarly called a *fandango*. **1890** J. JEFFERSON *Autobiog.* 59 He kept a bar-room in conjunction with a fandango, a keno-table, and a faro-bank. *Ib.*, 287 A 'fandango' . . . [is] a place where Spanish girls sing and dance, and play the guitars and castanets. The company is kinder mixed, and it's a little dangerous sometimes.

fandango fæn'dæŋgo, *v.* **1.** *tr.* To honor (a person) with a fandango. **2.** *transf.* To arrange or fix. Both *obs.* — **(1) 1845** GREEN *Texian Exped.* 41 They had a favourable opportunity of taking shelter under the protection of the Texian general by feasting and fandangoing him. — **(2) 1858** *Santa Fe Gaz.* 22 May 1/4, I regarded them as being . . . the result of a packed meeting, fandangoed up by one of the importers and a few individuals.

fandom 'fændəm, *n.* The world of sport enthusiasts. Cf. **fan,** *n.*² — **1903** *Cin. Enquirer* 2 Jan. 3/1 Fandom Puzzled Over Johnsonian Statements. **1928** *Publishers' Wkly.* 30 June, Ty Cobb, the idol of baseball fandom.

fanega fə'nɛgə, *n. S.W.* [Sp. in same sense. An Amer. borrowing.] A dry measure usu. equivalent to a little more than two and one-half bushels.

1808 SHALER *Journal* (1935) 63 Its production the first year were 1500 fanegos of wheat, and 500 of corn. **1856** WHIPPLE *Explor. Ry. Route* I. 41 Thousands of bushels of this year's growth [of corn] were to be purchased at two dollars per fanega. **1901** L. P. POWELL *Historic Towns* 454 (Bentley), The Indians paid an annual tribute of a vara of cotton cloth and a fanega of corn per family.

b. (See quots.)

1844 GREGG *Commerce of Prairies* I. 152 Husbandmen rate their fields by the amount of wheat necessary to sow them; and thus speak of a *fanega* of land. **1891** *D.N.* I. 190 *Fanega*, a dry measure, about two and a half bushels. By extension as much land as may be sowed with a *fanega* of seed. [Texas.]

∗**fanner,** *n.* One who fans a gun. See ∗**fan,** *v.* **4,** and cf. **gun fanner,** ∗**thumb,** *v.*, and **thumber.**

1902 *Out West* 308 Wm. Martin, Esq., walked into the only ball of six he could find at a six-foot range; took it in good part and a short rib, and dispassionately cracked the 'fanner's' skull with his fist. **1928** *Lariat Mag.* Jan. 'Texas', Dogie drawled and appeared to resent this questioning, 'I have the reputation for being the only fanner in Montana!' **1932** *K.C. Star* 17 May, Two Schools of Old-Time Gunmen—the 'Fanners' and the 'Thumbers.'

∗**fanning,** *n.* (See quots.) *Slang.* Cf. **gun fanning.** — **1898** *Science Siftings* XV. 79/1 The destructive area of the gun can . . . be greatly increased by moving it gently from side to side while it is being fired. . . . This process is known as fanning. **1907** MULFORD *Bar-20* i. 11 'Fanning' is the name of a certain style of gun play and was universal among the bad men of the West.

∗**Fanny Wright.** [Mme. Frances (*Fanny*) *Wright* d'Arusmont (1795–1852), Scottish-American reformer, writer, and lecturer.] Used attrib. with *doctrine, man,* etc., in allusion to Miss Wright's attacks on religion, marriage, and other social institutions, and her championship of equal rights for women. *Obs.*

1830 *Mechanics' Press* (Utica, N.Y.) 19 June 262/1 It has been generally believed, that the workingmen of this city, were agrarians . . . and Fanny Wright men. **1834** *Vt. Free Press* 20 Dec. (Th.), They have elected an avowed infidel, a trustee of the Fanny Wright fund. **1836** *Knickerb.* VII. 43, I care not whether the Fanny Wright doctrines or Agrarianism prevails. **1838** in BUCKINGHAM *America* (1841) I. 176 In a city of 300,000 inhabitants, 2,000 radicals, agrarians, Fanny Wright men, and Locofocos can be found. **1840** *Cong. Globe* App. 14 Feb. 179/2 He regretted to see . . . [the] disorganizing and levelling doctrines . . . of the Fanny Wright school of politicians. **1844** *Ib.* April 510/1 The Fanny-Wright party . . . is, in the anger of debate, [a name] sometimes applied to the democratic party.

b. Fanny Wrightism, advocacy or practice of the ideas or teachings of Fanny Wright. *Obs.*

1830 *Mechanics' Press* (Utica, N.Y.) 19 June 254/2 What a precious compound of almost all that is unprincipled, is here presented:—Agrarianism, Owenism, Fanny Wrightism, Scidmoreism, Antimasonry and Infidelity. **1838** *N.Y. Advertiser & Exp.* 17 Jan. 2/1 Loco Focoism, make the best of it, is Agrarianism, Fanny Wrightism, Equality of all races, colors, breeds, and tribes. **1844** *Cong. Globe* 29 March 464/1 Was the gentleman afraid that there was not enough Fanny-Wrightism in Indiana? *Ib.* App. April 510/2 This charge of Fanny Wrightism, as applied to the democratic party, has no foundation in truth.

∗**Fantasticals,** *n. pl.* (See quot. 1838.) *Obs.* — **1838** UNCLE SAM in *Bentley's Misc.* IV. 295 An American of a particular kind; one who is neither in the army nor the 'military,' and was not even one of the 'Fantasticals,' or Colonel Pluck's dragoons. [*Note:*] Some militiamen who parade in fantastic dresses to ridicule the 'military,' (volunteers,) who sport very splendid uniforms. **1842** in THOMPSON *M. Jones* (1872) 40 'Shaw, no, Majer,' ses she, 'its only the Fantastikils!'

∗**Fantastics,** *n. pl.* (See quots.) *Obs.* — **1851** HALL *Coll. Words* 121 *Fantastics*. At Princeton College, an exhibition on Commencement evening, of a number of students on horseback, fantastically dressed in masks, &c. **1900** HARRIS *On the Wing* 82 He dressed himself up after the style of the 'Fantastics,' as modern mummers were called in the South just prior to the war.

∗**far,** *a.*

1. far East, the eastern part of the U.S., jocular from **Far West.** *Rare.*

1846 *Ore. Spectator* 28 May 2/1 Quite a number of the *sovereigns* of Clackamas county met in Oregon City, . . . such was their curiosity to witness, in this '*sun-down*' land, scenes with which they had once been familiar in the *far east*.

Hence **far easterner.** *Rare.*

1907 *Springfield Republican* 28 Feb. 7 The East is a relative term as one traverses the American continent. Thus when the California newspapers report that settlers from the East are locating in Glynn county, the far easterner is surprised to read that the reference is to people coming from Dakota.

2. far North, the northernmost part of the U.S.

1903 FOX *Little Shepherd* xix. In the far North, as in the Far South, men had but to drift with the tide. [**1917** *Birds of Amer.* I. 163/1 Emperor Goose . . . 'is the least known and the most beautiful' of all the wild geese which make their summer home in the Far North.]

3. far South, =**deep South.**

1835 *Vade Mecum* (Phila.) 14 Feb. 3/2, I witnessed a terrible scene a few days since, which will give you some idea of the customs of the 'far South.' **1898** PAGE *Red Rock* 5 Old Peggy, Steve's 'Momma,' . . . had come from the far South with him. **1948** MENCKEN *Supp.* II. 7 Save, in fact, for a few oddities in vocabulary, it was perfectly possible to understand any man encountered along the road, even in the Far South or beyond the Alleghanies.

4. far West, a term for regions farther and farther west of earlier settled areas, now (*cap.*) used for the Rocky Mountain and Pacific states region.

1830 *Cong. Deb.* 8 May 920/2 [The] general importance [of the protective system] to the whole country, and particularly to the West, even the 'far, far West,' to use the terms of the gentleman [Mr. Cambreleng] from New York. **1892** DUVAL *Young Explorers* 116 The 'far west' gits further and further off every day—and ef it's a fact, as some say, that the world is round, I s'pose arter a while the nighest way to git to it will be to travel east. **1948** *N.Y. Star* 30 June 18/1 Naturally these voters are in all parts of the country, but mainly in the cities of the Midwest, Far West and East.

b. (*cap.*) The name of a Mormon settlement in Caldwell County, Mo.

1838 *Test* (Rushville, Ill.) 12 Dec. 3/4 The Strollings' store in Gallatin, Daviess county, was pillaged and burnt and the contents carried to Far West. **1905** *Out West* Sep. 245 It was at Far West, Caldwell county, Missouri, that the law of tithing was instituted. **1948** *Amer. Folk-Lore* Jan.–Mar. 29 The cornerstone of the Far West, Missouri, temple is said to have fallen from heaven.

c. far wester, far westerner, (also *cap.*), an inhabitant of the Far West.

1843 CARLTON *New Purchase* I. 135 An uproar none but true honest-hearted far westers . . . ever did, or can make. **1909** *Boston Transcript* 24 Dec. II. 5/5 The Far Westerner's glorification and magnification of the things that are his occasions our admiration. **1948** *Pacific Discovery* May–June 15/1 During June and July—in fact, often throughout the year—the cloud that Far Westerners near the coast see most frequently is the *advection fog*.

d. far western, *a.*, of or pertaining to the far West.

1845 *Knickerb.* XXVI. 283 A county in one of our far-western states . . . numbers just four whigs. **1874** B. F. TAYLOR *World on Wheels* vi. 50 Such touches of border-life give a Far Western train a character of its own. **1948** *Chi. Tribune* 29 Sep. 21/1 Far western voters want to know which candidates, if elected, can be most confidently relied upon to obtain federal appropriation of the billions of dollars that will be necessary to divert rivers to provide drinking water for fast growing cities.

Farallon(e) 'færə,lon, *n.* [f. *Farallone* Islands.] **Farallon(e) bird, cormorant, rail,** (see quots.).

1917 *Birds of Amer.* I. 26 California Murre, *Uria triolle californica*. . . . Other Names.—California Guillemot; California Egg-bird; Farallon Bird. — **1887** RIDGEWAY *Manual N.A. Birds* 138 Farallone Cormorant. **1917** *Birds of Amer.* I. 97 There are several subspecies of the Double-crested Cormorant. . . . [One of these is] the Farallon Cormorant (*Phalacrocorax auritus albociliatus*) of the coast and inland lakes of the Pacific slope. **1940** GABRIELSON & JEWETT *Birds Ore.* 95 Just prior to the breeding season, the Farallon Cormorants sometimes develop white head plumes that are very ephemeral. — **1884** *Nat. Museum Bul.* No. 27, 155 *Porzana jamaicensis coturniculus* Baird. Farallone Rail. Farallone Islands, coast of California. **1940** GABRIELSON & JEWETT *Birds Ore.* 234 The admission of the Farallon Rail to the Oregon lists rests solely on Bendire's records.

farce-comedy. *n.* A light comedy approaching farce in absurdity, improbability, etc. (see quot. 1902).

1887 *Courier-Journal* 2 Feb. 3/1 In these degenerate days of dime museums and 'farce-comedies,' its services are frequently needed. **1895** *N.Y. Dramatic News* 9 Nov. 3/4 The farce comedy called Crazy Patch . . . is to be revived with Kittie Mitchell as the star. **1902** CLAPIN 178 *Farce-comedy*, a play in which the characters are taken by variety-show 'artists,' who introduce their specialties, generally in the form of songs, dances, etc.

attrib. **1901** CLARA MORRIS *Life on Stage* 193 He was one of the most versatile of actors . . . crying old men or broad farce-comedy old men.

Fardown ˈfɑrˌdaʊn, *n.* (See quot. a1837). *Obs.* — **1834** [see **Corkonian**]. *a*1837 R. J. BRECKINRIDGE *Memoranda* I. 29 This city [Cork] gives name to one of those bloody factions, which under the appellations of *Corkonians* and *Fardowns* divide the lowest classes of Irish Catholics in that distant land [U.S.]. **1943** Mont. Writers' Proj. *Copper Camp* 6 The 'Far-Downs,' as North-of-Ireland Protestants were known, shoveled and blessed themselves with their left hand.

* **fare,** *n.*

1. The load or catch of fish taken by a boat engaged in fishing; a cargo of fish.

1707 *Essex Inst. Coll.* XLII. 165 Loosing their last faires of fish. **1807** *Ann. 10th Congress* 1 Sess. I. 1218 Such ship or vessel . . . shall return with her fishing fare to some port or place within the United States. **1904** *N.Y. Ev. Post* 18 June, The prices brought by the 'fares,' which are . . . cargoes of fresh or salted fish.

2. farebox, a box for deposit of passengers' fares.

1874 KNIGHT 826/2 [The] Fare-box . . . has a receiving aperture, windows at which the money or ticket may be seen by the passenger inside and the driver outside the car. **1948** *Neb. Hist. Mag.* March 21 When once upon the platform the passenger was expected to drop his nickel or celluloid 'check' into the fare box.

As the last term in **accommodation, five-cent, half, Shaker, thorough, through, wayfare.**

* **farewell,** *n.*

1. * **farewell-(to-)summer,** any one of various late-blooming asters, as the calico aster, *Aster lateriflorus.*

1894 *Amer. Folk-Lore* VII. 91 *Aster diffusus*, farewell-summer, nail-rod, West Va. **1940** STUART *Trees of Heaven* 49 Farewell-to-summer is blooming on the cliffs in purple and white masses.

2. farewell-to-spring, a showy-flowered annual, *Godetia amoena.*

1902 *Out West* May 512, I love the parted lips Of that weird flower folk call 'farewell-to-spring.' **1948** *Nat. Hist.* June 260/2 Here was . . . a Joseph's coat of golden poppies, blue lupines, white primroses, and mauve godetia, those tissue-petaled Farewells to Spring.

* **fare-you-well,** *n. to (a) fare-you-well*, abundantly, completely, to perfection. *Colloq.*

[1775 S. HAWS in *Mil. Jrnls.* (1855) 80 It was a very rainy day and we went to chidses and had a fudg fairyouwell my friends.] **1885** CABLE *Dr. Sevier* liv. 400 And then it means a house . . . , and milk, anyhow, till you can't rest, and buttermilk to fare-you-well. **1910** RAINE *B. O'Connor* 77 The little cuss has got me bluffed to a fare-you-well. **1943** LEWIS *G. Planish* 132 (Wentworth), You can lambast Brother Rood to a fare-you-well.

Also **fare-thee-well.**

1940 *Sat. Ev. Post* 3 Feb. 53 (Wentworth), Can she play the piano? To a fare-thee-well. **1944** HALSEY *Best Friends* 64 Even Mrs. S. wouldn't have said what she did if she hadn't been snubbed to a fare-thee-well by a merchant seaman.

* **farina,** *n.* (See quot. 1857.)

1849 G. G. FOSTER *N.Y. in Slices* 126 Farina and Wheaten Grits . . . have already become extensively popular, being the most wholesome and nourishing forms in which the staff of life has ever been prepared. **1857** YOUMANS *Domestic Science* 237 *Farina.*—A wheaten preparation under this name has come recently into general use, the same formerly known as 'pearled wheat.' It consists of the inner portion of the kernel of the finest wheat, freed from bran and crushed into grains, (*granulated,*) the fine floury dust and smaller particles being all removed. **1866** MOORE *Women of War* 203 She . . . replenishes the fire, gets the bag of farina from the ambulance, as also the sugar, . . . and flavoring extracts. **1948** *Consumer Reports* May 216/2 Sixteen brands of farina are listed in order of increasing cost per serving.

b. farina boiler, kettle, (see quot. 1889).

1857 YOUMANS *Household Science* 45 Hacker's farina kettle . . . is a culinary contrivance of this kind. **1889** *Cent.* 2143/1 Farina-boiler, . . . a saucepan or kettle used for cooking farinaceous articles, or any delicate food likely to scorch.

farkleberry ˈfɑrklˌbɛrɪ, *n.* Also †**fartleberry.** [Origin obscure. Poss. related to **sparkleberry.**] A shrub or small tree, *Vaccinium arboreum*, of the southern states, bearing a small, globose, many-seeded black berry. Also called **tree huckleberry.**

1765 J. BARTRAM *Diary* 11 July, Trees which naturally grows there is . . . very fine long-leaved pine pitch pine yapon fartle berry chinkapin. **1829** EATON *Botany* (ed. 5) 434 *Vaccinum arboreum*, farkleberry. **1901** MOHR *Plant Life Ala.* 89 Farkleberry, and the poison laurel . . . shade the rocky banks of the swift mountain streams. **1942** TEHON *Native Ill. Shrubs* 232 The Farkleberry ranges in dry sandy soils in open woods from Virginia to Florida and westward into Texas.

* **farm,** *n.*

1. (See quot.)

1915 POOLE *Harbor* 322 There are many 'farms' on the waterfront of N.Y. Harbor, for a 'farm' is simply the open shore space in front of a dock.

2. A baseball club or minor league owned by, or affiliated with, a major league in such a manner that outstanding players in the former graduate into the latter organization. (See also quot. 1948.) Also attrib.

1930 *Dixon* (Ill.) *Ev. Telegraph* 26 Sep. 6/1 The Cardinals, he said, must take him back or send him to a team not connected with the club's 'farm' system. **1946** *Dly. Ardmoreite* (Ardmore, Okla.) 6 Dec. 8/2 Baseball's independents claim the farms started the whole business of paying oversized bonuses and ignoring salary limits and the others have to keep up or give up. **1948** *Downers Grove* (Ill.) *Reporter* 21 Oct. 1/1 Major league hockey teams have adopted farm systems similar to those employed by big time baseball and football. **1949** *Newsweek* 18 April 82/3 He had only to look at Cleveland's San Diego farm.

3. In special combs.: (1) **farm agent,** =**county agent;** (2) **barn,** a barn on a farm; (3) **bloc,** a bloc in Congress formed in 1921 by members from agricultural states seeking to obtain legislation favorable to farmers, also attrib.; (4) **bridge,** a railroad bridge on a farm, providing a safe crossing for livestock, *obs.;* (5) **bureau,** a local association of farmers, constituting a unit in a national federation, seeking to better farming conditions, also attrib.; (6) **credit union,** an organization of farmers through which they obtain credit on unusually favorable terms; (7) **crossing,** a place where a railroad crosses the boundary of a farm; (8) **demonstrator,** =**county agent;** (9) **help,** those employed on a farm; (10) **home,** the residence of a farmer's family; (11) **horn,** a dinner horn; (12) **landing,** a landing place for boats on a farm situated on a stream; (13) **lane,** a lane on a farm or bordering a farm; (14) **line,** the boundary line of a farm; (15) **lobby,** a lobby working for agricultural interests; (16) **lot,** a lot or tract of land suitable or used for a farm, *obs.;* (17) **market,** a market among the farming population; (18) **pen,** (see quot. 1899); (19) **relief,** government aid to agricultural interests, also attrib.; (20) **report,** a report on the state or operations of a farm or farms; (21) **road,** (*a*) a road on a farm or one made to serve the needs of a farm, (*b*) also *farm to market highway* or *road;* (22) **village,** a village in a farming area, a farming center; (23) **wife,** the wife of a farmer.

(1) **1938** DANIELS *Southerner* 258 We can have enough Neegro farm agents to teach the Neegroes how to make more so thay could have more and the planters more, too. **1948** *Dly. Ardmoreite* (Ardmore, Okla.) 10 May 1/2 The Grady county farm agent . . . said the rain came at the right time to benefit all crops. — (2) **1920** *3rd Nat. Country Life Conf. Proc.* 157 You see the red roofs of the unmistakable farm barns. — (3) **1922** *Commoner* Feb. 11 Bryan . . . launched into a glowing tribute of the farm bloc in congress. **1948** *Time* 10 May 18/3 Farm-bloc Congressmen fought for U.S. cows as though the margarine-makers were going to throw them all into giant hamburger machines. **1949** *Chi. Tribune* 25 Feb. I. 5/4 A strong farm bloc in congress is demanding repeal of the Aiken law. — (4) **1839** *Amer.*

R.R. Jrnl. IX. 167 Some turn-outs, farm bridges &c. [were] not constructed.

(5) **1920** *3rd Nat. Country Life Conf. Proc.* 205 Existing organizations such as the farm bureau . . . might become the agencies through which the program is initiated and controlled. **1945** *Democrat* 30 Aug. 2/2 We are supposed to feature . . . Farm Bureau meetings, all-day singings and decorations. — **(6) 1921** *Rural Organization* 115 The other social urge in rural areas that is beginning to be manifest is farm credit unions. — **(7) 1839** *Amer. R.R. Jrnl.* IX. 218, 1 road bridge, road and farm crossings. **1875** *Mich. Gen. Statutes* I. (1882) 866 Such railroad shall erect and maintain . . . convenient farm crossings, and gates or bars therefor. — **(8) 1921** *Rural Organization* 46 Among this number there are only six negro farm-demonstrators. — **(9) 1884** M. TWAIN *Letters* (1917) II. xxix 304 (R.), Everybody on the farm flocked to the arbor . . . farm-help, the colored servants. **1917** *Wis. Agric. Exper. Sta. Bul.* No. 284, 26 Farm help. Both speed and efficiency come with experience.

(10) 1872 *Newton Kansan* 17 Oct. 2/3 Also dinnered with Dr. T.S. Floyd . . . at his farm home near town. **1925** BRYAN *Memoirs* 17 One of the first things to stay in my memory is our removal to our farm home. — **(11) 1867** *Atlantic Mo.* Feb. 159/1 The cheery sound of a farm-horn breaking the silence. **1882** LATHROP *Echo of Passion* iv, We'll have the farm horn tooted. — **(12) 1887** JACKSON *Between Whiles* iv. 226 She looked more like a craft for festive sailing than for cruising about from one farm-landing to another. — **(13) 1869** TOURGEE *Toinette* xvi. 175, I . . . just turned an' run . . . along the farm-lane, to the Lodge. **1876** WHITMAN *Specimen Days* 83 A real farm-lane fenced by old chestnut-rails. — **(14) 1685** *Manchester Rec.* 23 A Litel black oak tree . . . standin in the farm line. **1898** FORD *Tattle-Tales* 120 What a pity it is you and I don't have the settling of that farmline!

(15) 1943 MENEFEE *Assignment* 237 Congress has done its best to wreck the FSA program, largely because the farm lobby opposes anything which would deplete the supply of cheap farm labor. — **(16) 1641** *Suffolk Deeds* I. 23, I . . . appointe . . . my trew & lawfull Atornyes . . . to dispose of . . . a farme lott of 80: acres. **1742** *Ga. Col. Rec.* VI. 46 The Farm Lotts or Lands . . . should also . . . be laid out. — **(17) 1930** *Publishers' Wkly.* 12 July 175 In many states the bulk of the population, if towns of under 5,000 population are included, is predominantly rural. It is known as the farm market. — **(18) 1786** WASHINGTON *Diaries* III. 134, I rid to the Plantations at the Ferry, Dogue run, and Muddy hole, making a farm pen at the latter. **1836** *S. Lit. Messenger* II. 160 The cattle are gathered to the farm-pen, to ruminate over a rasping shuck or a marrowless cornstalk. **1899** GREEN *Va. Word-Book* 136 *Farm-pen*, pen in which stock is shut up and fed. — **(19) 1928** *Collier's* 3 Nov. 35/2 A Protestant and dry Democrat might have carried the State if he had a farm relief program to offer. **1943** HOLT *Carver* 81 When he [Henry C. Wallace] became Secretary of Agriculture in Harding's cabinet, [he] launched the phrase 'Farm Relief.'

(20) 1838 *Mass. Agric. Survey 1st Rep.* 6 The commissioner . . . distributed extensively . . . a blank form of a Farm Report. **1852** *Mich. Agric. Soc. Trans.* III. 129 Premium . . . for best farm report. *Ib.* 187 The space usually allotted to farm reports. — **(21)** (*a*) **1883** ALLEN *New Farm Book* 319 Farm Roads. Good roads in the interior of a farm . . . are indispensable. **1887** J. C. HARRIS in *Cent. Mag.* XXXIV. 884 Dey wuz layin' close by a little farm road. (*b*) **1945** *Ault* (Colo.) *Progress* 7 June 1/5 He pointed out this would be for use on farm-to-market roads, not federal-aid highways. **1947** *Dly. Oklahoman* (Okla. City) 11 Aug. 11/5 A meeting will be held soon . . . for the purpose of discussing Seminole county farm to market road projects. — **(22) 1879** *Scribner's Mo.* XIX. 135/2 The farm village,—an expedient by which the farmer secures all the benefits of society. **1888** CABLE in *Cent. Mag.* XXXVI. 501/1 [In] a New England farm village . . . there is no distinct 'mass' to elevate. — **(23) 1880** HOWELLS *Undiscovered Country* 261 Ford had nothing to do but to note the growth of the bargaining passion in the wary farm-wives. **1919** LEWIS *Free Air* 68 Over and over there were the same manipulations: . . . waving to a lonely farmwife in her small, baked dooryard.

As the last term in **agency, back, bonanza, Brook, chicken, clam, college, cotton, county, creek, dog, dry, experiment, fox, frog, fruit, hill, horse, ice, Indian, indigo, maple sugar, market, mission, Morgan horse, muscle, poor, prairie, river, school, state, state experimental, sugar, timber, tobacco, truck, tule, turpentine farm.**

∗ **farmer**, *n.*

1. *local.* (See quot. 1800.) Cf. ∗ **planter**, *n.* **1.**

1799 WELD *Travels* 89 [In Va.] those who raise tobacco and Indian corn are called planters, and those who cultivate small grain, farmers. **1800** TATHAM *Agric. & Commerce* 46 The cultivator who follows the ancient track of his ancestors, is called a *planter:* he who sows wheat, and waters meadows, is a *farmer.* **1805** PARKINSON *Tour* 424 Washington, who formerly had been a planter, but lately a farmer, had no land left that would bring a crop of tobacco.

2. (See quot. 1902.) *Colloq.*

1902 GREENOUGH & KITTREDGE *Words* 285 In this country . . . 'farmer' is sometimes jocosely applied to a greenhorn, or to a person who has made himself ridiculous, particularly by awkwardness or stupidity. **1903** A. H. LEWIS *Boss* 263 Me fadder aint such a farmer as to go leavin' his address wit' no one.

3. Used in the possessive, usu. pl., in combs.: (1) **Farmers' Alliance,** see as a main entry; (2) **institute,** an occasion when farmers assemble to hear discussions about improved methods in farming, etc.; (3) **League,** (see quots.); (4) **farmers' satin,** "a durable material of wool, or cotton and wool, having a satin-like appearance" (*Cent.* 5348/3); (5) **union,** one or other of various associations of farmers for promoting mutual interests.

(2) 1902 CLAPIN 240 Institute. A convention, a meeting. Farmers' institutes, lasting two or three days, with lectures and discussions, are especially very common at the West. **1948** *Chesterton* (Ind.) *Tribune* 28 Oct. 1/7 Porter County Farmers' Institute dates have been set for this season as follows. — **(3)** *a***1890** in H. R. CHAMBERLAIN *Farmers' Alliance* 72 The Farmers' League is a non-secret, independent, nonpartisan organization, in harmony with the Alliance, Wheel, Farmers' Union, Grange, and kindred associations. **1914** *Cyclo. Amer. Govt.* I. 711/2 The National Farmers' League was organized in 1890, with purposes mainly political. — **(4) 1893** *Harper's Mag.* April 668/2 The milliners' work made of Canton flannel and farmer's satin, is often as stylish as if it was seen on Broadway. **1901** NORRIS *Octopus* 236 She was dressed in what had been Mrs. Hooven's wedding gown, a cheap affair of 'farmer's satin.' — **(5) 1873** *Winfield* (Kans.) *Courier* 5 June 1/5 The movement in favor of farmers' unions throughout the country is becoming quite formidable. Unions, or 'Granges,' are being formed in every neighborhood throughout the agricultural districts of the west. **1891** DUNNING *Farmer's Alliance Hist.* 218 One of the four agricultural organizations that formed what is known as the National Farmers' Alliance and Industrial Union, was the Farmers' Co-operative Union of Louisiana.

As the last term in **agency, back, bonanza, book, cotton, dirt, dry, dry land, fisherman, fruit, guess, Indian, paper, pilot, river, small, sucker, truck, turpentine, Wall Street, western farmer.**

farmerette ˌfɑrməˈrɛt, *n.* A woman who works on a farm. — **1918** *Independent* 14 Sep., The farmerettes are producing food which creates the bodies and minds of mankind and sustains them. **1945** *Chi. D. News* 2 Aug. 3/4 (*caption*), Farmerettes Stick It Out, Heat and All.

farmerine ˌfɑrməˈrin, *n.* A farmer's wife. *Rare.* — **1888** *Voice* (N.Y.) 8 March, Then the average farmerine will be as near the millennium as she is ever likely to get.

Farmers' Alliance. Any one of several associations of farmers for mutual benefit, sometimes acting as a distinct political party. Also attrib.

At first local associations, farmers' alliances were subsequently combined into state and regional organizations, most important of which were the National Farmers Alliance of the Northwest and the Farmers' Alliance and Industrial Union of the South.

1880 in DUNNING *Farmers' Alliance Hist.* 28 We as the Farmers' Alliance . . . should set forth our declaration of intentions. **1893** THANET *Stories* 52 Nelson . . . had been an Abolitionist, a Fourierist, a Socialist, a Greenbacker, a Farmers' Alliance man. **1904** in *Kansas Hist. Soc.* IX. 1 The first Farmer's Alliance originated in Lampassas county, Texas, in 1874 or 1875, and was organized for the purpose of protecting the farmers from the encroachments of the wealthy cattlemen, who sought to prevent the settlement of farmers in that section and to keep the lands in pasture for the use of their ranch herds. **1943** HICKS *Amer. Dem.* 561 The National Farmers' Alliance representing the Northwest, and the Farmers' Alliance and Industrial Union representing the South.

∗ **farming**, *n.* As the last term in **bonanza, book, chicken, dry, dry soil, mixed, small, truck farming.**

∗ **fascinator**, *n.* A knitted or crocheted scarf worn as a kerchief. *Colloq.* Cf. ∗ **enchanter.**

1878 WIGGIN in N. A. SMITH *K. D. Wiggin* 35 Mother crocheting a fascinator—Phil reading the 'Pilot.' **1903** FOX *Little Shepherd* xviii. Margaret caught up some flimsy garment and wound it about her pretty round throat—they call it a 'fascinator' in the South. **1948** *Sky Line Trail* June 13/1 A hankie on the head for one of your years might be permissible . . . even 'fascinators' would be more suitable.

∗ **fascine**, *v. tr.* To protect or strengthen (a levee) with fascines. *Obs.* — **1829** *La. Acts 1828–29* 78 Every new levee . . . shall be fascined on the side of the river, either with palmetto or otherwise with picquets. **1870** in A. A. HUMPHREYS *Physics & Hydraulics of Miss. R.* 163 All new or old levees on the unsettled and uncultivated lands, situated on the river or on the bayous running to and from the same, or other waters connected therewith, shall be constantly fascined or palisaded.

* **fashion,** *n.* **1. fashion doll, =doll baby; 2. fashion letter,** one of a series of newspaper articles on current fashions, appearing at regular intervals. Both *obs.*

(1) **1899** VANDERBILT *Flatbush* 145 We have a vivid remembrance of the old age of one of these fashion-dolls which had been sent from Paris to a fashionable mantua-maker in New York. When the dress had changed as to style, the dressmaker sold the doll to one of her customers, and 'Miss Nancy Dawson' passed into the obscurity of humbler dollies who had never been sent as ministers plenipotentiary from the court of fashion. — (2) **1894** SHUMAN *Steps Into Journalism* 154 *n.*, Jennie June, . . . who is known all over the country for her syndicate fashion letters.

As the last term in **Boston, California, cob, coon, Indian, Kentuck, man, papoose, spider, spoon, squaw, wheelbarrow, wickiup, worm fashion.**

Fashion doll or doll baby (sense 1)

fasola 'faso,la, *n. S. Music.* [A term made up of *fa, sol,* and *la,* the fourth, fifth, and sixth tones of a diatonic scale.] Usu. attrib. in expressions referring to singing in which buckwheat notes *q.v.* are used and to those who sing by these notes. *Colloq.*

1933 JACKSON (*title*), White Spirituals The Story of the Fasola Folk. *Ib.* 3 The word 'Fasola' is not of my making. . . . But ask almost any real country person of mature years anywhere in the wide stretches of the southern states . . . if he knows anything about fasola singers, and he will very likely be able to direct you to one of them. **1933** *Musical Quart.* Oct. 397 The 'Fasola Folk,' those who still apply the Elizabethan names to the notes of songs made in pre-Revolutionary America and sing them with the help of the 132-year-old 'patent notes,' still number from about 30,000 to 50,000 souls. **1943** POWELL *Home Again* 72 We called it 'do-ra-me' or 'fa-so-la' singing.

* **fast,** *a.*

1. Of water, frozen solid. *Colloq.*

1706 *Boston News-Letter* 21 Jan. 2/2 New-York Jan. 7th. . . . Hudsons River was froze over and continued fast several days. **1761** DRINKER *Journal* 18 H. D. informs me that ye River is fast. **1796** *Ib.* 296 The river fast to day.

2. In combs.: (1) **fast freight,** (*a*) freight that is handled or expedited more rapidly than ordinary freight, *ellipt.*, a freight train conveying freight of this class, (*b*) **fast freight line,** (see quot. 1895); (2) * **land,** land not subject to overflow or flooding; (3) **quarter-horse,** (see quot.); (4) **time,** (*a*) (see quot.), (*b*) daylight-saving time.

(1) (*a*) **1875** *Chi. Tribune* 11 Sep. 3/4 'Through freight' . . . was transferred and retransferred, and 'fast freight' did not exist. **1904** *N.Y. Times* 11 May 3 He saw the fast freight approach at high speed. (*b*) **1881** *Chi. Times* 12 March, The initiative in this competitive cutting of tariffs was taken by the Commercial Express Fast-Freight line. **1895** *Johnson's Univ. Cyclo.* III. 296/1 *Fast Freight Line:* an organization for prompt delivery of through freight.— (2) **1681** *New Castle Court Rec.* 504, 724 acres of fast Land. **1862** *Cong. Globe* 11 July 3264/2 By 'fast land' . . . I mean to refer to land originally above the ebb and flow of the tide. **1893** *D.N.* I. 330 *Fast land,* upland near coast (South Jersey). — (3) **1938** ASBURY *Sucker's Prog.* 146 The peripatetic gambler who toured the country with a fast quarter-horse (fn. That is, a horse trained to run very fast for a quarter of a mile). — (4) (*a*) **1931** *Amer. Sp.* Aug. 466 Central time is spoken of as 'fast time,' and mountain time as 'slow time.' Some sandhillers prefer to regulate their timepieces by 'half time,' meaning half an hour slower than 'fast time' and half an hour faster than 'slow time.' (*b*) **1942** *Amer. Sp.* April 113/2 The official terms (Eastern Standard and Daylight Saving) were, however, quite rare, especially in the country; they were frequently replaced by 'old time' and 'new time,' but most commonly by 'slow time' and 'fast time.' **1946** *Birmingham* (Ala.) *News-Age-Herald* 28 April 1-A/7 States which will observe 'fast time' are New Jersey, Massachusetts, New Hampshire, Rhode Island, Vermont and Connecticut. **1949** *Chesterton* (Ind.) *Tribune* 28 April 5/4 Yes, we are trying to fool the Lord going on fast time. But a lot of us will not get there even at that.

* **fast,** *adv.* Of freezing: Firmly, solidly. *Colloq.*

1708 *Boston News-Letter* 2–9 Feb. 2/2 Our River is froze fast against Philadelphia that people pass continually over the Ice. **1777** in SPARKS *Corr. Amer. Rev.* I. 548, I have seen the Mohawk River fast frozen on the 10th of November.

b. *to set fast,* to freeze. *Rare.*

1849 M'LEAN *Notes* I. 142 The Bonne Chere river is very rapid in the upper part, and does not 'set fast' until late in the season, unless the cold be very intense.

* **fast day.** A day in the spring of the year appointed in some of the New England states for appropriate religious observances. Also attrib.

1788 J. MAY *Jrnl. & Lett.* 18 After breakfast [April 17] met numbers of people going to meeting, in their old clothes, it being fast-day. **1866** LOWELL *Poetical Works* (1896) 431/1 As near to the present occasions of men As a Fast Day discourse of the year eighteen ten. **1910** *Springfield Republican* 17 March 1 Old-fashioned Fast day still obtains in Connecticut, and Gov. Weeks has appointed it for the 25th.

***fasten,** *v. intr.* To freeze over. *Rare.* — **1784** E. DRINKER *Journal* 151 Ye River fastened last night—H. D. walked over it.

* **fat,** *a.* and *n.*

1. *n.* (See quot.) *Obs.*

1883 BEADLE *Western Wilds* 584 Here and there . . . are sometimes found little accretions of pure silver, which miners speak of as 'the fat of the vein.'

2. *a.* Of wood: Containing much resin, resinous. See also **fat pine.**

1705 BEVERLEY *Virginia* III. iii. 12 [The Indians] generally burn Pine, or Lightwood, (that is, the fat Knots of dead Pine). **1808** *Mass. Spy* 9 Nov. (Th.), A pine post, fat with pitch, had taken fire. **1889** *Harper's Mag.* LXXVIII. 243/2 A negro woman . . . was hastily lighting a fire on the broad hearth with fat lightwood.

3. In special combs.: (1) **fat back,** see as a main entry; (2) * **bird,** *local* (see quots.); (3) * **cow,** meat from a buffalo cow, *rare;* (4) **fleece, =dépouille,** *rare;* (5) **gourd,** *S.* a gourd used as a receptacle for fat or lard; (6) * **head,** (*a*) *Calif.*, the redfish, *Pimelometopon pulcher,* (*b*) *Miss. Valley,* the black-head minnow, *Pimephales promelas;* (7) **pine,** see as a main entry; (8) **toad lizard, =chuckwalla,** *obs.*

(2) **1844** *Nat. Hist. N.Y., Zoology* II. 242 [*Tringa pectoralis*] passes under the various names of Meadow Snipe, Jack Snipe, Short-neck, and according to Mr. Giraud it is called Fat-bird on the coast of New-Jersey. **1917** *Birds of Amer.* I. 233 Pectoral Sandpiper, *Pisobia maculata.* . . . Other names.—. . . Triddler; Hay-bird; Fat-bird; Short-neck etc. — (3) **1848** RUXTON in *Blackw. Mag.* LXIV. 296 All night long he grumbled his horror at seeing 'fat cow spiled in that fashion.' — (4) **1848** RUXTON in *Blackw. Mag.* LXIV. 23 They moved along hungry and sulky, the theme of conversation being the well remembered merits of good buffalo meat,—of 'fat fleece,' . . . and 'tender loin.'

(5) **1835** LONGSTREET *Ga. Scenes* 22 The best man . . . that ever stole cracklins out of his mammy's fat gourd. **1908** *D.N.* III. 309 Fat-gourd, a receptacle for grease, meat drippings, etc., originally a large gourd used for this purpose [e. Ark.]. — (6) (*a*) **1884** GOODE *Fisheries* I. 275 The Red-fish, of California. . . . The name 'Fat-head' is occasionally used. (*b*) **1883** *Nat. Museum Bul.* No. 27, 481 Fat-head; Black-head minnow. Ohio Valley westward to the Upper Missouri. — (8) **1869** CRONISE *Natural Wealth Calif.* 481 The 'Fat Toad Lizard' . . . is a large heavy blackish species nearly a foot long, found near the Mexican boundary.

As the last term in **back, bear, black, cow, hog, marrow, possum, raccoon, rattlesnake, seal, skunk, soap, winter fat.**

fat back.

1. A species of mullet. Also the menhaden, *Brevoortia tyrannus.*

1709 LAWSON *Carolina* 157 Fat-Backs are a small Fish, like Mullets, but the fattest ever known. **1878** *Nat. Museum Proc.* I. 384 *Brevoortia tyrannus.*—Fat Back; Yellow Tail; Bug Fish. Very abundant. **1884** GOODE *Fisheries* 449 The name 'Fat-back' is also in use, but whether this name is used for Mullets in general, or simply for those in particularly good condition, I have been unable to learn. *Ib.* 569 In

North Carolina occurs the name 'Fat-back,' which prevails as far south as Florida, and refers to the oiliness of the flesh [of the menhaden].

2. *S.* The top half of a side of pork which remains after the shoulder, ham, loin, and belly have been removed.

1903 *Sears Cat.* (ed. 113) 18/1 Clear Back Pork. This pork is made from the fat backs of prime hogs, is free from lean and bone. **1948** *Sat. Ev. Post* 16 Oct. 116/4 Many of them cry for corn bread, fatback and molasses.

* **fate,** *n.* **1.** A person whom one is fated to marry. *Jocular.* **2. fate-tree,** (see quot.). *Obs.*

(1) **1856** STOWE *Dred* I. 25 Well, she is my fate. **1899** CHESNUTT *Wife of His Youth* 99 It had become fashionable . . . to go traveling, ostensibly for pleasure, but with the serious hope that they might meet their fate away from home. — (2) **1892** APGAR *Trees Northern U.S.* 129 *Clerodendron trichotomum,* Thumb. (Fate-tree) . . . A small tree from Japan; hardy at Washington and south.

* **father,** *n.*

1. *pl.* The early, or first, colonists of New England, esp. of the Plymouth colony. Often *cap.* Cf. **Pilgrim Fathers, first fathers.**

1676 I. MATHER *King Philip* (1862) 38 That . . .was the professed, pious, and a main design of the Fathers of this Colony. **1774** G. HITCHCOCK *Sermon* (1775) 35 With respect to the fathers of New England, . . . I . . . [am] persuaded, that their religion was derived from the fountain of truth. **1802** *Columbian Centinel* 22 Dec. 2/3 The 'Sons of the Pilgrims' Will this day celebrate the 181st anniversary of the landing of The Fathers at Plymouth. **1899** in *Cong. Rec.* 15 Jan. (1900) 824/2 The people are the rightful source of all power. One of those early fathers wrote [etc.].

b. *pl.* The framers of the Constitution, freq. *Fathers of the Republic.* Cf. *dollar of the fathers.*

1854 SIMMS *Southward Ho!* 246 My grandmother has papered her kitchen with the 'I. O. U.' S' of our fathers of Independence. **1859** BUCHANAN in *Pres. Mess. & P.* V. 555 Our history proves that the fathers of the Republic . . . condemned the African slave trade. **1886** LOGAN *Great Conspiracy* 667 This State government . . . is a Republican form of government, in the American sense—in the sense contemplated by the Fathers. **1902** LORIMER *Lett. Merchant* 11 [He] couldn't place a set of the Library of the Fathers of the Republic, though they were offered on little easy payments.

2. Used by or to Indians in referring to their allies or friends, esp. to those in authority among the whites. Cf. **Great Father, Great White Father.**

See quot. 1904 (cf. quot. 1727) for an indication of the origin and spread of this use.

[**1727** in *Pub. Col. Soc.* VIII. 282 When the Governor of Canada speaks to us of the Chain, he calls us *Children,* and saith, *I am your Father you must hold fast the Chain, and I will do the same. I will protect you as a Father doth his Children.*] **1751** *N.J. Archives* 1 Ser. VII. 598 The Susquehannah Indians only want leave from the Mohawks whom they call their Fathers in order to their accepting of a missionary. **1754** *Mass. H.S. Coll.* 3 Ser. V. 30, I have invited you here by the command of the great King, our common Father, to receive a present from him. **1867** DIXON *New Amer.* I. 55 The red-men of these Prairies have been taking counsel . . . as to the policy of allowing the white men, headed by their Big Father in Washington, to open a new road. **1904** *Pub. Col. Soc.* VIII. 283 Thus, as these extracts show, the expression was transferred from the French Governor of Canada to the King of France, from the King of France to the King of Great Britain, and from the King of Great Britain to the President of the United States.

3. Often used of George Washington, esp. in the expression * *The Father of his Country.*

This title was app. first used in Pa. as early as 1778. Francis Baily, who had served under Washington, got out a *Nord Americanische Kalender* for 1779 at Lancaster, Pa., on the cover of which was a flying Fame with a medallion of Washington. Sounding from her trumpet were the words "Des Landes Vater." See Adams, *Dict. Amer. Hist.* II. 254/2.

1787 in WASHINGTON *Writings* XI. 123 *n.*, The glorious republican epithet, The Father of your Country. **1789** *Pa. Packet* 9 July 2/3 An independent Legislature, at the head of which we this day celebrate The Father of his Country. **1799** TRUMBULL in *Autobiog.* 382, I hope to have the happiness of . . . saluting you, . . . not merely as the father of the United States, but of the united empires of America. **1849** TAYLOR in *Pres. Mess. & P.* V. 5, I shall always defer with reverence . . . to his example who was by so many titles 'the Father of his Country.' **1905** TRENT *Southern Writers* 28 The student may be reminded that the Father of his Country was born [etc.].

b. Applied also to Gov. John Winthrop of the Massachusetts colony. *Rare.*

1764 T. HUTCHINSON *Hist. Mass.* (1765) I. 151 In the beginning of 1649 (March) died Mr. Winthrop, the father of the country.

4. In combs.: (1) * **Father Abraham,** a nickname for Abraham Lincoln; (2) **Father Mississippi,** =*Father of Waters;* (3) **Father's Day,** a day appointed for honoring fatherhood, cf. **Mother's Day;** (4) **fathers' dollar,** = *dollar of the fathers, obs.,* Cf. **1. b.** above.

(1) **1861** *Southern Enterprise* (Thomasville, Ga.) 1 May 2/2 Father Abraham would doubtless be surprised to learn that he has become the 'defendant' in a law suit in Thomas County, 'away down here in Georgia,' but it is true nevertheless. **1940** *Sat. Ev. Post* 17 Feb. 15/2 In fact, it was a Friend who wrote We are Coming, Father Abraham. — (2) **1842** in *Amer. Sp.* XVIII. 124 No true American slights Father Mississippi. **1949** *N.O. Times-Picayune* (Mag.) 20 Feb. 2/2 For a layman, he is well acquainted with Father Mississippi. — (3) **1943** *Greeley* (Colo.) *D. Tribune* 5 June 5/5 By executive order, Governor Vivian proclaimed Sunday, June 30, as Father's Day. **1948** *Kankakee* (Ill.) *D. Jrnl.* 5 June 12/4 Special Father's Day cards also for 'Husband,' 'Grandfather,' 'One Who Has Been Like a Father,' etc. — (4) **1878** *Nation* 21 Feb. 126/1 The facts . . . , if known, would make the theory of 'the fathers' dollar' as ridiculous as the theory that the Coinage Act [of 1873] was passed secretly.

b. In phrases: (1) *Father of Waters* (or *Floods, Rivers*), the Mississippi River; (2) *Father of the House, Senate,* (see quot. 1864), also transf.; (3) *Father of the Constitution,* James Madison (1751–1836).

(1) **1763** in *Amer. Sp.* XXI. (1946) 117/2 By some savages of the North it is called *Meact-Chassipi,* which literally denotes, *the ancient Father of Rivers,* of which the *French* have, by corruption, formed *Mississipi.* **1809** T. ASHE *Travels* 280 Throughout this great water, the Father of Floods, as the Indians call it, in some places islands are seen sinking into annihilation. **1813** *Niles' Reg.* V. (Supp.) 176/2 The Mississippi is the Nile of America. The aborigines who resided on its banks, called it Mechaseba, or Father of waters. **1949** *N.O. Times-Picayune* (Mag.) 27 Mar. 7 With summer approaching, the unique craft will start slipping down Father of Waters looking for thrills.

(2) **1854** BENTON *30 Years' View* I. 7/2 Mr. Lewis Williams . . . entered the House young, and remained long enough to be called its 'Father.' **1864** WEBSTER 499/2 *Father of the house,* the member of a legislative body who has served longest. **1867** *Atlantic Mo.* Feb. 251/1 His [a senior boarder] usual title is Father of the House. **1886** ALTON *Among Law-Makers* 31 Senator Anthony . . . was called the 'Father of the Senate.' . . . In 1872 the 'Father of the House' was Representative Dawes.

(3) **1831** *Niles' Reg.* 26 Nov. 236/1 When *James Madison,* the father of the constitution, took his oath of office as president of the United States, in 1809, he was also clothed in the products of American labor. **1948** *Time* 15 March 110/3 The Father of the Constitution was once described as a man who never said or did an indiscreet thing.

As the last term in **big, city, first, fore, Great, Pilgrim, Plymouth, Puritan, Seminole, white father(s).**

fathom fish. *local.* (See quot.) — **1849** A. ROSS *Adv. Oregon River* vi. 109 To prepare them [*sc.* the eulachons] for a distant market, they are laid side by side, head and tail alternately, and then a thread run through both extremities links them together, in which state they are dried, smoked, and sold by the fathom, hence they have obtained the name of fathom-fish.

* **fatigues,** *n. pl.* Fatigue uniforms. *Colloq.* — **1836** HILDRETH *Campaigns Rocky Mts.* I. 51 We have not yet received our uniforms, . . . but even in our 'fatigues,' we make an imposing appearance when mounted. **1947** *Mazama* Oct. 7/2 We climbed in 'fatigues' and field jackets and combat boots.

fat pine.

1. = * **lightwood.** Also attrib.

1674 JOSSELYN *Two Voyages* 66 The knots of this Tree [fir] and fat-pine are used by the *English* instead of Candles. **1791** BARTRAM *Travels* 470 Some take with them little fascines of fat Pine splinters. **1881** PIERSON *In the Brush* 286 That long procession, with their flaming fat-pine torches. **1948** *Reader's Digest* January 70/1 Anywhere in America has its particular hearth perfume— . . . fat pine in Carolina.

2. A resinous pine tree, esp. the long-leaved or Georgia pine, *Pinus palustris.*

1849 LANMAN *Alleghany Mts.* xi. 92 A couple of torches made of a fat pine. **1898** *Forestry Bureau Bul.* No. 17, 19 *Pinus palustris.* . . . Names in use. . . . Fat Pine (Southern States).

fatty bread. *S.* (See quot. 1903.) *Colloq.* — **1884** J. C. HARRIS *Mingo* 44 She was a fair representative of that portion of the race that has poisoned whole generations by improving the frying-pan and perpetuating 'fatty bread.' **1903** *D.N.* 313 Fatty-bread, *n.* A kind of shortened corn-bread. 'Fine as fatty-bread.' A common expression meaning, 'in fine condition' [s.e. Mo.].

faubourg ˈfobʊr, -bʊrg, *n. La.* [F. in same sense. An Amer. borrowing.] A subdivision or a suburb built outside the original walls or limits of a town or city. *Obs.* or *hist.*
1826 FLINT *Recoll.* 302 The greater number of the houses in this fauxbourg [in New Orleans] are of brick, and built in the American style. **1883** CABLE in *Cent. Mag.* June 220/2 Large areas of the batture [in New Orleans] were reclaimed in front of the faubourg, and the Americans covered them with store buildings. **1922** J. S. KENDALL *Hist. New Orleans* II. 674 A noted land speculator of the '40s ... laid out a 'faubourg' behind the 'vieux carré.'

Fauntleroy ˈfɔntləˌrɔɪ, *v. intr.* To commit forgery, in allusion to Henry Fauntleroy (1785–1824), a British forger whose trial and execution aroused widespread interest. *Obs.* — **1825** *Catawba Journal* 1 March, Fauntleroying.—A young man who had been Fauntleroying, or committing forgery in Chester county, made his escape.

* **favorite,** *n.* and *a.*

1. Favorite son, a commendatory title given to George Washington. Freq. in **Columbia's favorite son.** *Obs.*

For further information, see essay by Albert Matthews on "The Sobriquet Favorite Son" in *Mass. Col. Soc. Pub.* (1910–11) pp. 100–109, and Thornton.

[1777 in *Pub. Col. Soc.* XIII. 105 Hail! Patriot hail! Grave Columbean, Heaven's Favorite, Freedom's fairest Son.] **1789** *N.Y. Daily Gaz.* 1 May 426/1 Washington, the favourite son of liberty, and deliverer of his countrv. **1789** *Mass. Centinel* 8 July (Th.), The friend of Liberty,—Columbia's favourite son. **1800** *Columbian Centinel* 19 Feb. 4/1 We mourn 'Columbia's fav'rite son.' He's gone.... The worthy, virtuous Washington.

b. A man who has endeared himself to a particular country or state, used esp. of a candidate for high office favored by the constituency or political leaders of the state from which he comes.

1806 in C. L. LEWIS *Romantic Decatur* (1937) 85 That country welcomes your return to her bosom. She hails you as one of her favorite sons. **1825** in GARLAND *Life of Randolph* II. 240 [John Randolph] thought himself unkindly treated by his native State. He will now, I trust, see in himself her favorite son. **1858** *Salem* (Ill.) *Advocate* 1 Jan. 2/2 In this glorious battle the favorite son of Illinois will be victorious. **1948** *Chi. D. News* 1 May 6/1 It means empowering the 'favorite son' to barter convention votes.

fawn lily. A Californian dogtooth violet having creamy white or somewhat yellowish flowers. — **1895** BURROUGHS *Riverby* (1904) 29 'Fawn lily' would be better than 'adder's-tongue.' **1942** *Stand. Plant Names* 215 Erythronium ... Fawnlily. Members of this genus are also known as Adderstongue, Dogtooth Violet and Troutlily.

* **fay,** *v.* **1.** *intr. To fay in,* to fit nicely into place. **2.** *tr.* To fill in (a gap).

(1) **1848** D. P. THOMPSON *L. Amsden* 138, I have no notion of spoiling sense to make it fay in with book rules. **1906** P. LOWELL *Mars & Its Canals* 347 The explanation ... fays in with the former.— (2) **1865** LOWELL *Biglow P.* 2 Ser. x. 219 Ther' gaps our lives can't never fay in.

F.B.I., FBI. Abbrev. for "Federal Bureau of Investigation," so named in 1935. Also attrib. Cf. **G-Man.**
1936 *Lit. Digest* 21 Nov. 36 The outlaws shot their way out killing one FBI man while 'Little Mel' traded shots with 'Baby Face' Nelson. **1947** *Denver Post* 8 June (Mag.) 2/1 The FBI showed the 'students' how the bureau's great laboratory in Washington, D.C., may be used to best advantage. **1948** *Woman's Day* March 9/1 The F.B.I. and all the other investigators get on the scene to search for subversive causes.

***feast,** *n.* As the last term in **corn, fish, husking, love, scalp, virgin, war feast.**

* **Feast of Shells.** A festival to commemorate the founding of the Massachusetts colony, held on the anniversary of the landing of the first colonists at Plymouth.
This feast originated in Boston shortly before the end of the eighteenth century and died out about 1806 for political reasons. Two suggestions have been made as to why it was so called: (1) in honor of the early settlers "who were fed with clams and other bounties of the sea" and (2) for the Feast of Shells mentioned in Macpherson's *Ossian*. Records show that a pantomime taken from the Ossianic poems was given on March 14, 1796 at the Boston theater; part of this pantomime is laid in the Hall of Fingal at the Feast of Shells. See *Mass. Col. Soc. Pub.* XVII. 327 ff., 347.
1798 in *Mass. Col. Soc. Pub.* XVII. 323 Dined Concert Hall. Feast of Shells. **1798** *Independent Chron.* 31 Dec. 2 The publisher of the toasts given at the Feast of Shells, says that justice is done to our first and later worthies. **1800** *Ib.* 29 Dec. 2 The Feast of Shells was introduced some years ago by a number of men, who wished to perpetuate the honor of the first American emigrants. **1806** *Ib.* 2 Jan., Hamilton ... died in the field of murder, in a duel, yet his party, the party at the late feast of shells, celebrate his character.

* **feather,** *n.* In combs.: (1) **feather-bedding,** the practice on the part of unions of forcing employers to hire more men than are needed for a particular job, *slang;* (2) **bone,** (see quot. 1889); (3) **dance,** a form of Indian dance, *obs.;* (4) * **duster,** an Indian, *rare;* (5) * **edge,** see as a main entry; (6) **renovator,** (see quot.); (7) **tick,** a bed tick filled with feathers.
(1) **1943** in *Amer. Sp.* Dec. (1944) 305/2 For the unions, featherbedding has become an established business procedure; it makes more jobs for more members who pay more dues. **1947** *Chi. Sun* 14 Oct. 21/1 It's to your interest to know about this proposed *feather-bedding!* — (2) **1887** *Advance* (Chicago) 17 Feb. 112 *'Featherbone,'* prepared from the quills of geese and turkeys, is largely taking the place of whalebone in the manufacture of whips [etc.]. **1889** *Cent.* 2164/2 *Featherbone,* ... a substitute for whalebone, made from the quills of domestic fowls. The quills are slit into strips, which are twisted, and the resulting cords are wrapped together and pressed. — (3) **1751** GIST *Journals* 53 The Crier ... came by the King's Order and invited Us to the long House to see the Warriors Feather Dance — (4) **1907** MULFORD *Bar-20* 103, I had a little argument with some feather dusters. **1911** —— *Bar-20 Days* 82 We'll see if two infant feather-dusters can lick the Bar-20.
(6) **1874** KNIGHT 828/2 *Feather-renovator,* a machine in which old feathers may be scalded, purified, and dried, so as to remove effete matter from them. — (7) **1903** ADE *People You Know* 218 Chub slept on a Feather Tick up in a Room where they had the Seed Corn hung on the Rafters.

b. In the names of plants: (1) * **feather bed,** (see quots.); (2) * **flower,** poss. the feather cockscomb, *Celosia argentea, obs.;* (3) **geranium,** (see quots.); (4) * **grass,** (*a*) velvet grass, *Holcus lanatus,* (*b*) a grass found in the South, *Leptochloa filiformis;* (5) **weed,** the balsam-weed, *Gnaphalium polycephalum.*
(1) **1817–8** EATON *Botany* (1822) 234 *Chara vulgaris,* feather-beds. ... Odour disagreeable. Ponds and ditches mostly stagnant. **1847** WOOD *Botany* 637 *C[hara] vulgaris.* Feather-beds.... It appears in dense tufts, like a soft bed, undulating with the motion of the water. — (2) **1869** TOURGEE *Toinette* xxv. 259 The feather-flower, with its white plumes drooping. — (3) **1857** GRAY *Botany* 364 *C[henopodium] Botrys.* (Jerusalem Oak. Feather Geranium.) **1894** COULTER *Bot. W. Texas* III. 368 *Chenopodium botrys.* (Jerusalem oak. Feather geranium.) — (4) (*a*) **1847** DARLINGTON *Weeds & Plants* 396 *H. lanatus....* Velvet-grass. Feather-grass. White Timothy. **1894** *Amer. Folk-Lore* VII. 104 *Holcus lanatus* ... old white top, feather-grass, velvet-grass. West Va. (*b*) **1854** *S. Lit. Messenger* XX. 618/1 Sprigs of feather-grass, red-top, and ox-eye. **1901** MOHR *Plant Life Ala.* 376 *Leptochloa mucronata....* Feather Grass.... Alabama. From the Coast plain to the Central Pine belt. Sandy fields. — (5) **1892** *Amer. Folk-Lore* V. 98 *Gnaphalium polycephalum,* ... feather-weed. No. New York.

c. In phrases: (1) *To rise at a feather,* to get angry on slight provocation; (2) *to make the feathers fly,* to trounce an opponent, cf. * **fur, b.**
(1) **1794** JEFFERSON *Writings* IX. 296 Being so patient of the kicks and scoffs of our enemies, and rising at a feather against our friends. — (2) **1825** J. NEAL *Bro. Jonathan* I. 94 If my New York master only had hold o' him; he'd make the feathers fly.
As the last term in **full, gay, water feather.** Also **Montana feathers, Old Fuss and Feathers, tar and feathers.**

* **feather,** *v.*

1. *intr.* (See quot. 1816.)
1816 PICKERING 201 *To Feather....* This colloquial word ... is used in some parts of New England, to denote the appearance of curdled cream; when it rises upon the surface of a cup of tea or coffee, in the form of little flakes, somewhat resembling feathers. We say—The cream feathers. **1890** *Critic* 21 June 314/1 To keep cream from feathering in hot weather.

2. feather-embroider, to embroider with feather-stitches.
1873 PHELPS *Trotty's Wedding* xviii, I have set my heart on feather-embroidering all my old plaited waists.

3. *to feather out,* to become covered with, or as with, feathers.
1889 *Cent.* 2164/2 The chickens, or the willows, are beginning to feather out.

* **featheredge,** *n.*

1. Excessive spirit, extreme mettlesomeness or fieriness; *not to put a featheredge on it,* to speak plainly. *Colloq.* or *slang.*

1891 *Harper's Mag.* July 210/1 Let the pony have a little fun. . . . This takes the feather-edge off him. 1903 A. H. LEWIS *Boss* 59 Not to put a feather-edge on it, I thought I'd run you over, an' see if they'd been fixin' you.

2. a. featheredge file, (see quot.). **b. featheredge haircut,** a haircut in which the hair on the back of the neck is closely clipped but not shaved off.

(a) 1874 KNIGHT 828/1 *Feather-edge File.* A file with an acute edge; the cross-section of the file being an isosceles triangle with a short base. A *knife*-file. — (b) 1944 CLARK *Pills* 221 It was not until the First World War that the 'feather edge' haircut done with clippers came into popular style.

***feature,** *n.* **1. feature article,** in a periodical, an important or distinctive article. **2. feature story,** =prec. — (1) 1932 *DAB* VIII. 485 Hearn soon gave this up to do feature articles for the Sunday *Cincinnati Enquirer* (1873). — (2) 1928 *Publishers' Wkly.* 16 June 2440 A single Sunday newspaper sometimes has three or four feature stories about authors.

***feature,** *v. tr.* (See quot. 1889.)

1888 *St. Louis Globe-Democrat* 29 April (Farmer), The biggest thing I saw at the wedding was a lot of glassware and block tin knives and forks, which were featured in one of the rooms. 1889 FARMER *Americanisms, Featured, to be,* to be displayed; to be set out to the best advantage, literally to be made a feature. 1928 *Publishers' Wkly.* 12 May 1932 You will know then why so many booksellers feature Macaulay books. *Ib.* 9 June 2352 All three [books] will be featured in a lavish and spectacular joint display.

Fed fɛd, *n.* Also **fed.**

1. Short for **Federalist,** *n.* **1.**

1788 *Mass. Centinel* 31 Dec., Antis, and Feds, usurp the glory, So long enjoy'd by Whig and Tory. 1848 *Campaign Flag* (Maysville, Ky.) 24 Mar. 1/1 The feds have got to polling the passengers on steamboats again. 1947 *West. Pa. Hist. Mag.* March–June 22 There were few marriageable men left in the narrow confines to which the aristocratic 'Feds' had limited themselves.

attrib. 1806 FESSENDEN *Democracy Unveiled* I. 115 The fed-wit serv'd the scoundrel fry.

2. Short for **Federal,** *n.* **2.** *Obs.*

1866 F. KIRKLAND *Book Anecdotes* 115 Our army was allers whipping the Feds. *Ib.* 315 He found half a dozen Feds in full possession. 1895 *N.Y. Dramatic News* 23 Nov. 3/3 What became of that comedy of yours which I produced under the title of Feds and Confeds?

b. = **G-Man.** *Colloq.* or *slang.*

1935 F. H. VIZETELLY in *Lit. Digest* 22 June 38 'G Men' have also been called 'feds.' 1949 *N.O. Times-Picayune* (Mag.) 13 Feb. 6/1 In this raid the feds captured a '49 car, which was 'loaded.'

***fed,** *a.* As the last term in **corn, grass, still fed.**

Federal 'fɛdərəl, *n.*

1. One who favored the adoption of the federal Constitution; a member of the Federal party.

1806 WEBSTER 115 *Federal, Federalist,* . . . a friend to the Constitution of the U. States. 1816 J. PICKERING 91 *Federal,* as a noun . . . is never heard except in the mouths of the most illiterate people; and it has always been considered as a corruption of Federalist. 1894 S. LEAVITT *Our Money Wars* 31 The First Bank of the United States, under the Constitution, . . . chartered Feb. 25, 1791, . . . was the work of the Federals, who hated and wished to avoid Treasury notes.

2. During the Civil War, a soldier in the Federal army. Now *hist.*

1861 *Dly. Dispatch* (Richmond, Va.) 24 July 3/5 The federals advanced gradually among the masked batteries. 1885 *Cent. Mag.* XXX. 452/2 Knapsacks, cartridge-boxes, clothing, rifles by the thousand were thrown away by the Federals. 1948 *Ill. State Hist. Soc. Jrnl.* Dec. 367 Lincoln had been disturbed by the ease with which the defeated Confederates had marched away while the victorious Federals were unable to follow.

***federal,** *a.*

1. Owned by, pertaining to, or representing the U.S. Government.

1786 *Jrnls. Cont. Cong.* 8 Aug. 504 One [of the copper coins shall be] equal to the one hundredth part of the federal dollar, to be called a *cent.* 1861 *Charleston* (S.C.) *Mercury* 15 Jan. 3/6 Some Southern men here are now canvassing the propriety of the Convention of the seceding States at Montgomery adopting the form of the present Federal Government as a whole. 1913 LAFOLLETTE *Autobiog.* 328 Of course . . . with Spooner and Babcock strongly influential with their 'federal crowd,' there was small chance for us. 1948 *Dly. Ardmoreite* (Ardmore, Okla.) 26 May 6/1 These critical individuals insist that the stamps are acquired by persons who propose to sell liquor—as a sort of occupational tax paid to Uncle Sam for the right to dispense booze and be free of possible interference by federal agents.

b. Pertaining to, or situated in the Federal City, or Washington, D.C. *Obs.*

1790 FRENEAU *Poems* (1795) 420 Have we not toil'd through cold and heat, To make the Federal Pile [the Capitol] complete? 1834 *S. Lit. Messenger* I. 75, I dreaded to drive through the interminable streets of the federal metropolis. 1873 *Republic* I. 5 Congress met in the Federal capital Monday, December 2, 1872.

c. Designating a *road* or *highway* built or maintained by the federal government.

1824 HODGSON *Letters* I. 126 The road [from Fort Mitchell in Ga. to Mobile], which is called the Federal Road, though tolerable for horses, would with us be considered impassable for wheels. 1945 MCATEE *Pheasant* 97 Ditches along state and federal highways are kept cleanest.

2. Favorable to, or endorsing the principles of, the Federalists (sense **1.**).

1788 HILTZHEIMER *Diary* (1893) 4 July 146 The Federal procession of to-day was in honor of the ratification of the Constitution of the United States. 1802 JEFFERSON *Writings* X. 321 New Hampshire . . . wanted a few hundreds only of turning out their federal Governor. 1847 *Semi-Wkly. News* (Fredericksburg, Va.) 22 July 3/1 Federal Massachusetts was the earliest and loudest to denounce British Tyranny. 1947 *West. Pa. Hist. Mag.* March–June 22 The Federal ladies refused to visit any newcomers, however desirable, unless they were proved to be true-blue Federalists.

b. Applied to factions, parties, etc., believing in principles apparently similar to those of Federalism.

1842 *Whig Almanac 1843* 16/1 It is the cardinal conviction of those known as Whigs, ('Democratic' or 'federal' Whigs, as you please,) [etc.]. 1855 in HAMBLETON *H. A. Wise* 152 The Federal Know-Nothings put one of their own men at the head of the distributing department. 1856 *Ib.* 42 Mr. Wise . . . vindicated John Tyler against the charges of . . . Arnoldism . . . , and the thousand and one coarse . . . epithets which have been heaped upon him by Federal Whiggery.

3. Of or pertaining to the Mexican government in Texas. *Obs.*

1838 C. NEWELL *Revol. Texas* 16 The rights of the Colonists consisted in security of person and property, guaranteed to them . . . by the Federal Law and Constitution of 1824. 1840 *Diplom. Corr. Texas* I. (1908) 448 The barbarous murder of Col. Johnson and party on his return from the Federal Camp, I shall immediately communicate.

4. During the Civil War, pertaining or belonging to the Federal army. Now *hist.*

1861 *Charleston* (S.C.) *Mercury* 8 Jan. 3/3 He will regard any attempt of the Federal troops to pass across Virginia for the purpose of coercing any Southern State, as an act of invasion which is to be repelled. 1895 M. A. JACKSON *Gen. Jackson* 551 The plank road was swept by the fire of the Federal cannon at Fairview. 1947 *N.Y. Herald-Tribune* 14 Dec. v. 11/2 Thousands of Federal officer prisoners were held in the gloomy closeness of Libby Prison, which had been converted from a warehouse.

5. Designating certain government agencies, as (1) **Federal Bureau of Investigation,** (2) **Emergency Relief Administration,** (3) **Housing Administration,** (4) **Radio Commission,** (5) **Trade Commission.**

(1) 1943 HICKS *Amer. Dem.* 762 The Investigation Division of the Federal Department of Justice, headed by J. Edgar Hoover and known later as the Federal Bureau of Investigation. — (2) *Ib.* 791 Through a Federal Emergency Relief Administration, created May 22, 1933, unreturnable contributions instead of RFC loans were made available to states for relief purposes. — (3) *Ib.* 804 Another agency, the Federal Housing Administration, established in 1934, undertook to insure home mortgages of which it approved up to eighty (later ninety) per cent of the appraised value of the property involved. — (4) *Ib.* 752 The resulting confusion led Congress to establish next year a Federal Radio Commission of five members with the right to license broadcasting stations, and to determine the power, wave-lengths, and hours of operation to be allotted to each. — (5) 1914 in COMMAGER *Documents* II. 278 *Be it enacted,* That a commission is hereby created and established, to be known as the Federal Trade Commission . . . , which shall be composed of five commissioners, who shall be appointed by the President, by and with the advice and consent of the Senate. 1948 *News-Palladium* (Benton Harbor, Mich.) 14 Aug. 2/3 The Federal Trade Commission . . . hits down some small businesses to the advantage of big business in the matter of the basing point.

6. In special combs. (often *cap.*): (1) **Federal army,** the U.S. Army, esp. with reference to the Civil War; (2) **blue,** blue cloth of a kind formerly worn by Federal troops, so named during the Civil War, also a uniform made of this; (3) **City,** Washington, D.C., now *hist.;* (4) **constitution,** (*a*) the Articles of Confederation, *rare,* (*b*) the U.S. Constitution, framed in 1787; (5) **con-**

vention, =**constitutional convention,** also a suggested convention of delegates from the several states to amend the present Constitution; (6) **court,** see as a main entry; (7) **executive,** the President of the U.S.; (8) **government,** the national government of the U.S.; (9) **judiciary,** the system of courts of justice composing one branch of the federal government, also the judges who officiate in that system; (10) **land bank,** any one of twelve regional banks, established in accordance with the Federal Farm Loan Act of 1916, designed to provide farmers with long-term loans secured by first mortgages on their farms, also attrib.; (11) **offense,** an offense punishable under federal law; (12) **officer,** (*a*) an officer of the U.S. Government, (*b*) an officer in the Federal army in the Civil War period; (13) **party,** see as a main entry; (14) **population,** before the adoption of the Fourteenth Amendment (July 23, 1868), an estimated or computed population for determining the representation allowed a state in Congress, now *hist.;* (15) **republican,** (*a*) a member of the Federal party, now *hist.,* (*b*) (see quot.), now *hist.;* (16) **Reserve,** see as a main entry; (17) **Union,** the union of the states under the Articles of Confederation and under the Constitution.

(1) **1842** *Cong. Globe* App. 24 May 418/1 There are higher considerations than a mere admiration of the glories of the Federal army. **1861** HOLMES *Pages from Old Vol. Life* 2 A sad disaster to the Federal army was told the other day. *a***1918** G. STUART *On Frontier* I. 189 He was going to enlist in the Federal Army. — (2) **1867** LOCKE *Swingin' Round* 288 We patched up the confedrit gray with Federal blue. **1877** ROE *Army Lett.* 155, I have always thought that he [Jefferson Davis] was deeply moved by once again seeing the Federal Blue under such friendly circumstances. **1884** *Cent. Mag.* Nov. 107 The Federal blue had not yet been issued, and the troops wore either the uniforms of their militia organizations or those furnished by the several States. — (3) **1792** IMLAY *Western Territory* 148 The removal of obstructions in Cheat river will render passage from Alexandria, or the federal city to the Ohio, both cheap and easy. **1847** *Knickerb.* XXIX. 536 She ... last winter travelled with her uncle as far as the 'Federal City.' **1947** PERRY *Cities of America* 268 Meanwhile Washington's existence as 'the Federal City' had become imperiled. — (4) (*a*) **1786** in ELLIOT *Debates* (1836) I. 132 The house ... proceeded, by joint ballot with the Senate, to the appointment of seven deputies, from this commonwealth [Virginia], to a Convention proposed to be held in the city of Philadelphia, in May next, for the purpose of revising the Federal Constitution. (*b*) **1787** CUTLER in *Life & Corr.* I. 254 Members of the Continental Convention, now convened in this city for the purpose of forming a Federal Constitution. **1884** BLAINE *20 Years of Congress* I. 266 It was numbered as the thirteenth amendment to the Federal Constitution. **1949** *Lisle* (Ill.) *Eagle* 10 Mar. 6/5 It does not spring from any defect in the federal constitution.

(5) **1787** BARLOW *Oration 4 July* 11 Much is expected from the Federal Convention now sitting at Philadelphia. **1788** JEFFERSON *Writings* VII. 236 Friends of the new government will oppose ... amendment [of the Constitution] by a federal convention. **1857** BENTON *Exam. Dred Scott Case* 38 The two bodies sat at the same time—the Continental Congress at New York, the Federal Convention in Philadelphia. — (7) **1854** HAMBLETON *H. A. Wise* 61 All the unconstitutional laws ... were once placed at the mercy of a Federal executive. **1865** *Amer. Ann. Cyclo.* V. 14/2 We should accept the freeing of the slaves by the act of the Federal Executive and the bayonet. — (8) **1788** *Ann. 1st Congress* I. 31 Sir: We, the Senate of the United States, ... congratulate you on the complete organization of the Federal Government. **1925** BRYAN *Memoirs* 218 The Grange with its demand for the issuance of greenbacks by the Federal Government. — (9) **1784** in *S. Lit. Messenger* XXVIII. 35/2, I have read the Bill for establishing the Federal Judiciary with attention. **1822** *Ann. 17th Congress* 1 Sess. 81 A disposition widely different in the revival of State laws ... proves the strong bias of the Federal judiciary in support of federal power. **1870** *Nation* 13 Jan 22/2 Then and now a member of the Federal judiciary.

(10) **1916** *Statutes at Large* XXXIX. I. 362 The Federal Farm Loan Board shall establish in each Federal land bank district a Federal land bank. **1917** *Fed. Land Bank of Baltimore Circular No. 1* 1 National Farm Loan Associations are ... organized to obtain through Federal Land Banks mortgage loans on lands. — (11) **1943** *Sat. Ev. Post* 1 May 13/1 You're insane, and it's a Federal offense. — (12) (*a*) **1787** MADISON in *Sp. & Doc. Amer. Hist.* (1944) I. 67 That the Executives ... ought to appoint all federal officers not otherwise provided for. (*b*) **1870** *Cong. Globe* 29 Jan. 881/1 A Federal officer bearing himself gallantly through the entire war. **1898** PAGE *Red Rock* 520 Leech ... found himself in the presence of a Federal officer. — (14) **1842** *Whig Almanac 1843* 37/1 Each of the States composing the Union is entitled to two members of the Senate, and of the House as many as its Federal Population shall entitle it to choose.

(15) **1806** *Balance* 6 May 143/1 The proceedings of the Federal Republicans of New-York [were] read ... and unanimously adopted. **1812** MELISH *Travels* I. 63 They equally lay claim to the title of *republicans,* and are often styled *federal republicans* and *democratic republicans.* **1914** *Cyclo. Amer. Govt.* I. 717/2 *Federal Republicans,* a name adopted by the followers of George Clinton in New York, who organized, in 1787, to oppose the adoption of the Constitution and in 1789 supported Clinton against Adams for Vice-President. — (17) [**1778** in SERLE *Journal* 307 Taxation shd. be entirely given up, but that the Parliament shd. have Authority to bind in all other Cases; and this wd. lay the Foundation of (what he called) a 'Foederal Union.'] **1786** in MARSHALL *Kentucky* (1812) 265 Provided ... that the proposed state shall ... be admitted into the Federal Union. **1948** *Chi. Tribune* 10 Oct. (Grafic Mag.) 5/1 Twice, after his country elected him to the Vice Presidency, he led movements aimed at the dissolution of the federal Union.

b. In similar, usu. less frequent, combs., now obsolete: (1) **Federal American,** (see quot.); (2) **basis,** =**Federal number;** (3) **currency,** the currency of the U.S.; (4) **Hill,** =**Capitol Hill,** cf. **hill,** *n.* **1;** (5) **house,** a house or home for the President of the U.S.; (6) **language,** a proposed or suggested language, other than English, for use in the U.S.; (7) **man,** =**Federalist,** *n.* **1;** (8) **money,** money issued by the U.S. Government as opposed to state and foreign money; (9) **number,** a number arrived at (see quot. 1842) as a basis for determining the number of representatives a state should have in Congress; (10) **rib,** coarse cloth having a ribbed surface; (11) **senator,** a member of the U.S. Senate; (12) **town,** a projected town to serve as the seat of government of the U.S.

(1) **1786** T. JEFFERSON *Writings* V. 420 You have properly observed that we can no longer be called Anglo-Americans. That appellation now describes only the inhabitants of Nova Scotia, Canada, &c. I had applied that of Federal Americans to our citizens. — (2) **1830** *Va. Lit. Museum* 574/2 Mr. Doddridge proposed ... that ... there should be ... a new apportionment of representation on the white basis in the House of Delegates and the 'federal basis' in the senate. — (3) **1848** BARTLETT 133 *Federal currency,* the legal currency of the United States. **1865** *Atlantic Mo.* XV. 731 The national debt of England amounted in Federal currency to $4,305,000,000. — (4) **1827** *Spirit of Seventy-Six* (Frankfort, Ky.) 3 May 1/5 You may elevate the tenant of another *Federal Hill* to senatorial dignity.

(5) **1790** HILTZHEIMER *Diary* (1893) 26 Aug. 163 Met Messrs. Powell, Coxe, Fisher, Latimer, and Dunlap, a committee of the City Corporation, to consult about raising funds to erect the Federal House. — (6) **1877** *Galaxy* XXIV. 682 In the procession on occasion of the adoption of the federal Constitution, an association of young men, of which the writer was one, called the Philological Society, carried through the streets of New York a book inscribed *'Federal Language.'* — (7) **1788** *Mass. Spy* 3 April 2/4 We had great rejoicing here yesterday, by the Federal Men, on account of the Ratification of the New Constitution by the State of Massachusetts. **1857** BENTON *Exam. Dred Scott Case* 56 It would escape the notice of the eminent Federal men in Congress, no friends to the acquisition of Louisiana. — (8) **1806** *Balance* (Hudson) 20 May 159/1 Mr. Randolph said ... that we, meaning the Government, had long been living upon the good old federal money. **1831** W. SLOCOMB *Amer. Calculator* 28 Federal money is the coin of the United States, established by Congress in 1786. **1839** BUEL *Farmers' Companion* 296 Various Foreign Coins, &c., with their value in Federal Money, as established by an act of Congress. — (9) **1830** *Va. Lit. Museum* 571/1 Mr. Doddridge moved to amend the amendment, by substituting for the federal number, the mixed basis of white population and taxation combined. **1842** *Whig Almanac 1843* 37/1 To the whole number of its Free White inhabitants is added three-fifths of all other persons, excluding Indians not taxed. The amount obtained by adding these together is termed the Federal Numbers of the State.

(10) **1788** *Maryland Jrnl.* 15 July (Th.), A spinning machine of 80 spindles, drawing cotton suitable for fine jeans or federal rib. — (11) **1840** *Ill. State Reg.* (Springfield) 14 Feb. 2/1 The object of all this *secret* manœuvreing is to carry the Legislature and elect a Federal Senator to Congress. **1846** *Dollar Newspaper* (Phila.) 18 Mar. 2/2 Federal Senators, in the debate upon the Oregon question, are talking about concession and compromise, implying that they are willing to make them. — (12) **1783** *Warren-Adams Lett.* II. 234 How do you approve the Resolve for establishing Two Federal Towns, Trentown and George Town on the Potomock. **1789** *Ann. 1st Congress* I. 898 Mr. Fitzsimons inquired ... what part of the State of Maryland, lying on the Susquehanna, ... was fit for a Federal town?

Also *federal authority, building, debt, officeholder,* etc.

federal court. A U.S. court as distinguished from a state court. Also **federal district court.**

1789 *Ann. 1st Congress* I. 783 Mr. Tucker was . . . against dividing the United States into districts, for the purpose of instituting inferior Federal courts. **1873** *Harper's Mag.* March 571/1 The construction given by State courts to State laws will, as a general rule, be accepted by the Federal courts. **1948** *Time* 22 March 23/3 But when his hand was called in Washington's Federal District Court, he folded.

b. (See quot.) *Obs.*

1861 *Texas Secession Convention Jrnl.* (1912) 194 It is the sense of this Convention that the jurisdiction of the federal courts of the Confederate States shall be so defined and restricted by law as to avoid a repetition of such abuses.

* **federalism,** *n.* The political principles of the early Federalists. *Obs.*

1789 MACLAY *Deb. Senate* 87 Federalism was general, but there was a general abhorrence of the pomp and splendid expense of Government. **1797** *Ann. 5th Congress* I. 91 When the Federal Constitution was submitted to the people, to approve it, and endeavor to procure its ratification, it was federalism.

b. The political principles of the post-Constitution Federalists or of those favoring a strong centralized government.

[**1788** *Mass. Centinel* 14 June 103/2 On the 4th day of July next, will be sold, *for the benefit of the Antifederalists*, the Old Articles of Confederation . . . Union & Federalism, Auctioniers.] **1833** S. SMITH *Major Downing* 145 Now about this republicanism and federalism, I've minded that it always keeps changing and always has. **1905** *Forum* April 488 The federal authority is everywhere paramount; and federalism, against which our forefathers fought most strenuously, is now almost a national hobby. **1948** *Wm. & Mary Quart.* Oct. 476 Fisher Ames, the bellwether of Massachusetts Federalism, wrote in January, 1800 [etc.].

c. (*cap.*) =**Federal party.** *Obs.*

1814 *Ann. 13th Congress* 2 Sess. 1620 That proposition must have indeed been an anomaly in politics, which united in opposition to it the Federalism of Massachusetts and the Democracy of Tennessee. **1856** GOODRICH *Recoll.* I. 484 *Blue Lights*, meaning treason on the part of Connecticut federalism during the war [of 1812], is a standard word in the flash dictionary of low democracy.

Federalist ˈfɛdərəlɪst, *n.*

1. A member of the party that led the fight for the adoption of the Constitution. In later use, one who accepted the principles of this party. Now *hist.*

There is some continuity in the history of the early and late Federalists, for most of the post-Constitution Federalists had been pre-Constitution Federalists as well. However, many an early Federalist who favored the Constitution rejected the principle of a strong centralized government.

1787 MADISON *Federalist* x. According to the degree of pleasure and pride we feel in being republicans, ought to be our zeal in cherishing the spirit and supporting the character of Federalists. **1790** CUTLER in *Life & Corr.* I. 461 Gerry . . . has certainly done himself much credit in the view of the Federalists. **1849** A. MACKAY *Western World* I. 225 'Federalists' is a term of reproach given . . . by the Democrats to their antagonists, who only recognise for themselves the style and title of 'Whigs.' **1948** *Gainesville* (Tex.) *D. Register* 2 July 4/2 The first twenty years, under Washington and the Federalists, were very conservative.

2. *The Federalist*, a series of political essays written by Hamilton, Madison, and Jay, in 1787–88, to explain the provisions of the Federal Constitution and to urge its ratification by the states. Also attrib.

1787 WASHINGTON *Writings* XI. 189 An as antidote to these opinions, and in order to investigate the grounds of objections to the constitution which is submitted, the *Federalist* . . . is written. **1854** BENTON *30 Years' View* I. 84/2 Without the crowning work of the 'Essays' in behalf of the constitution which have been embodied under the name of 'Federalist.' **1943** HICKS *Amer. Dem.* 126 A series . . . signed *The Federalist* attracted much attention. These documents, collected to form a book, still constitute the best commentary on the Constitution. **1949** *New Yorker* 22 Jan. 64/2 'The people,' said a *Federalist* paper of uncertain authorship, 'can never err more than in supposing that by multiplying their representatives beyond a certain limit, they strengthen the barrier against government of the few.'

3. A Union soldier during the Civil War.

1861 *Dly. Dispatch* (Richmond, Va.) 19 June 3/2 Eight car loads of provisions were destroyed to prevent their falling into the hands of the Federalists. **1884** *Harper's Mag.* April 752/1 'Federalists,' . . . uniformed in blue and white.

As the last term in **anti-, Essex, high-minded Federalist.**

* **Federalist,** *a.* Of or pertaining to federalism or to the Federalists.

1837 MARTINEAU *Soc. Amer.* III. 289 The federalist merchants and lawyers consider the clergy so little fit for common affairs as to call them a set of people between men and women. **1902** E. C. MEYER *Nominating Systems* 12 The congressional caucus developed out of semi-official meetings held by the Federalist members of Congress. **1913** A. C. COLE *Whig Party in So.* 66 There were many reasons why they [whig leaders of the South], even when of state rights antecedents and inclinations, should not drop their connection with the 'federalist' Whigs of the North.

b. Federalist party, =**Federal party.** Now *hist.*

1876 *N. Amer. Rev.* July 130 The Federalist party was a very remarkable political organization. **1948** *Chi. Tribune* 11 April I. 24/3 The conflict between the almost royalist Federalist party of John Adams and the new republican party of Jefferson was dangerously impassioned.

Federal party. The political party that took the lead in securing the ratification by the states of the Constitution and after its adoption continued to stand for a strong central government. *Obs.* Cf. **Federalist,** *n.* **1.**

1788 MADISON in R. King *Corr.* I. (1894) 330 The federal party are apparently in the best spirits. **1813** S. MORSE in *N. Amer. Rev.* July (1912) 123 They know nothing of the Federal or Democratic parties. **1847** *Semi-Wkly. News* (Fredericksburg, Va.) 22 July 3/1 There are not a few, who are at this moment fully impressed with the belief that the old Federal party, if not identical with, was at least cousin german to the Tories of the Revolution. **1888** BRYCE *Amer. Commw.* II. III. liii. 332 The disappearance of the Federal party between 1815 and 1820 left the Republicans masters of the field.

b. = * **Democratic party.** *Obs.*

1838 *Quincy* (Ill.) *Argus* 1 Dec. 2/2 The last hope of the Federal party is placed on the supposition that they may possibly be able to carry the presidential election in 1840 into the house of representatives. **1841** *Chi. Morn. Democrat* 26 Feb. 2/1 We certainly hope that the federal Judiciary may all be sent into federal circuits where the federal party can see a fair specimen of *our Judiciary as it was*. **1848** *Campaign* (Wash., D.C.) 7 June 24/1 The federal party is the party of privilege.

Federal Reserve. Designating a system of banking established in 1913 to consolidate the country's banking resources and provide an elastic currency.

1919 *New Intern. Year Book* 84 The great strength and value of the Federal Reserve System, only five years old on Nov. 16, 1919, were more apparent than ever before. **1945** *New Yorker* 10 Feb. 29/2 Marriner S. Eccles, head of the Federal Reserve System, was generally held responsible and was believed to be poking fun at Wall Street.

b. Federal Reserve Bank, one of the twelve mutually independent "bankers' banks" that operate within the Federal Reserve System of banking.

1914 *Quart. Jrnl. Economics* Feb. 213 Banks of a new class, to be known as Federal Reserve Banks, are to be established, and upon these banks is to rest the heavy responsibility of supporting the structure of credit in periods of financial stress. **1949** *This Week Mag.* 5 March 19/3 According to the Atlanta Federal Reserve Bank, pennies are legal tender.

Also **Federal Reserve Board, note.**

1913 *Quart. Jrnl. Economics* Aug. 743 Its administration was placed under the control and direction of the Federal Reserve Board. **1914** *Ib.* Feb. 237 (*heading*), Federal Reserve Notes and National Bank Notes. **1943** HICKS *Amer. Dem.* 664 The law also provided for a new type of currency, Federal Reserve notes, which would vary in quantity according to the needs of business. **1948** *St. Paul* (Minn.) *Dispatch* 17 Sep. 31/5 The Federal reserve board asked for an increase in bank reserves.

* **federation,** *n.*

1. federation pike, (see quots.).

1842 *Nat. Hist. N.Y., Zoology* IV. 225 The Federation Pike. *Esox tredecem-radiatus*. . . . The flesh is savory and fine. **1890** *Cent.* 4484/2 federation pike, a pickerel, *Esox americanus:* so called in allusion to the bands with which its body is crossed and rays being often thirteen in number.

2. federation squirrel, (see quots.).

1891 *Cent.* 5882/3 *Federation squirrel*, the thirteen-lined spermophile, or striped gopher: so called in allusion to the thirteen stripes of the flag of the original States of the American Union. **1947** CAHALANE *Mammals* 349 The 'thirteen-lined ground squirrel' is supposed to have thirteen stars and stripes. For this reason it is sometimes called the federation squirrel. The scientific name also means 'thirteen lines,' but the animal may have a few more or a few less.

federo- ˈfɛdəro, *prefix.* In now obs. expressions: **1. federo-American,** =**Federal American. 2. federo-republicanism,** a system of political philosophy characterized by federal and republican features. — (1) **1786** JEFFERSON *Writings* V. 402, I had applied that appellation of Federo Americans to our citizens. — (2) **1804** JEFFERSON *Writings* XI. 24 A bastard system of federo-republicanism will rise on the ruins of the true principles of our revolution.

fedora fɪˈdorə, *n.* [See note.] A soft hat, usu. for men, with a low crown creased lengthwise; formerly one with the brim rolled high on the sides. In full **fedora hat.**

In 1882 the French playwright Victorien Sardou produced a tragedy, *Fédora*, named from its heroine, Fédora Romanoff, a Russian princess. In 1883 this play became quite popular in this country with Fanny Davenport as the leading lady. It was app. the name of the Russian princess in the play that inspired the use of "fedora" here shown.

1899 ADE *Doc' Horne* 59, I had on a new white Fedora hat, cost me three-fifty. **1910** *N.Y. Ev. Post* 21 April, Then one forgot the coffee-

Fedora, Stetson, and derby hats

stained coat and the fedora dented at wrong angles. **1948** *Dly. Ardmoreite* (Ardmore, Okla.) 29 April 1/2 These new creations will soon replace the old fedora.

Also *transf.*

1946 *Newsweek* 14 Jan. 87/1 The caption, 'Under the Hat,' was decorated by a cut of the famous ten-gallon Fiorello fedora.

***fee,** *n.* As the last term in **admission, donation, grass, initiation, tobacco fee.**

fee bill. A bill listing the fees charged by a lawyer. — **1825** *Austin P.* (1924) II. 1123 In the Fee bill published by him 20th May. **1878** BEADLE *Western Wilds* 172 The weary way of contending claimants lay across a desert of fruitless litigation, diversified only by mountains of fee-bills.

***feed,** *n.*

1. Food for human beings. *Colloq.* Cf. **feed joint, shack, station,** in **2.** below.

1818 FEARON *Sketches* 194, I guess whiskey is all the feed we have on sale. *Ib.* 224 The small farmer . . . raises a sufficient 'feed' for his family. **1835** *Knickerb.* V. 304 A John Smith lives next door, to whom half my choice rounds and sirloins, selected personally in the market, —for I love good feed,—are sent without distinction. **1898** WESTCOTT *D. Harum* 283 You want a change o' feed once in a while, or you may git the colic.

2. In combs.: (1) **feed bag,** a nose bag; (2) **basket,** a basket used for carrying feed to livestock; (3) **bin,** a trough for holding feed for livestock; (4) **box,** see as a main entry; (5) **bunk, =feed bin;** (6) **chopper, =feed cutter;** (7) **corral,** a corral in which cattle are fed; (8) **crusher,** a machine for crushing feed for livestock; (9) **cutter,** a machine for cutting or chopping up cornstalks, etc., into feed, cf. **corn cutter;** (10) **floor,** a snug, tight floor upon which hogs, etc., can be fed with a minimum of waste; (11) **grinder,** a machine for grinding feed for stock; (12) **joint,** an eating place, *slang;* (13) **lot,** an inclosure in which livestock are fed, also transf.; (14) **mill,** a mill for grinding feed for livestock; (15) **roll,** (see quot. 1889); (16) **room,** a room in a barn, store, etc., where feed for stock is kept, also attrib.; (17) **shack,** a shack or shanty serving as a restaurant, *slang;* (18) **stable,** a stable where horses, etc., are fed and cared for; (19) **station, =feed joint,** *slang;* (20) **store,** a store where hay, grain, etc., are sold; (21) **stuff,** anything used as food; (22) ***trough,** a trough in which the feed for domestic animals is placed; (23) **wagon,** a wagon for carrying feed for stock, esp. in a caravan; (24) **yard,** (*a*) a place where livestock is fed, (*b*) a place where feed, grain, etc., are sold.

(1) **1840** C. MATHEWS *Politicians* I. i, You prefer to be mystified more after the manner of a cert in cartman's horse, with his head in a feed-bag. **1924** *Scribner's Mag.* Dec. 645/1 Mac spat at a mouse that ran out of a feedbag. — (2) **1910** C. HARRIS *Eve's Husband* 293 On one side of her was a feed basket full of the quinces. **1936** *Sears Cat.* 921 Has many other uses about the home or farm—as pick-up basket, vegetable or feed basket, etc. — (3) **1898** DELAND *Old Chester Tales* 250 She . . . advised him as to which end of the open space between the stalls and the feed-bins should be the stage. **1946** *Jefferson Co. Republican* (Golden, Colo.) 20 Feb. 2/6 We Can Furnish Wood Form Sections for Concrete Forms, Frame Homes, Barns, Sheds, Feed Bins, . . . and for Many Other Purposes.

(5) **1931** *K.C. Star* 19 Oct., George said that he had just repaired the feed bunk. **1944** *Sears Cat.* (ed. 189) 876Y Farm-Master Feed Bunks . . . Outside of bunk is creosoted to resist decay. — (6) **1903** *Cin. Enquirer* 9 May 14/1 He got a motor for the corn sheller and feed chopper. **1916** WILSON *Somewhere* vii. 304 Rex II didn't get in till next day and looked like he'd come through a feed chopper. — (7) **1894** *S.F. Midwinter Appeal* 19 May 5/4 Last Saturday the Revenue Marine Steamer Corwin came into the port like a locoed horse striking a feed corral. **1928** BREAKENRIDGE *Helldorado* 47 He went there and opened a large feed corral. **1947** PRICE *Trails I Rode* 97 They talked so long that John decided he could not make it back to the feed corral. — (8) **1883** KNIGHT *Supp.* 327/2 *Feed Crusher*, a mill for flattening grain to render it more easily masticated. **1930** *Randolph Enterprise* (Elkins, W.Va.) 30 Oct. 8/2, 1 windmill; 1 corn sheller; 1 feed crusher and belt. — (9) **1863** *Rep. Comm. Patents 1861* I. 476 Improvement in Feed-Cutters. **1942** ASHER & HEAL *Send No Money* 37 The $6.98 feed cutter chopped up feed for the stock with quick efficiency.

(10) **1867** *Rep. Iowa Agric. Soc.* (1868) 104 Put them [*sc.* hogs] in small yards with . . . a good plank feed-floor. — (11) **1871** *U.S Patent Rep.* **1944** *Democrat* 10 Feb. 1/6 War Food Administration has removed pressure cookers and feed grinders from rationing. — (12) **1909** WASON *Happy Hawkins* 304 We sidled into a feed-joint. — (13) **1889** *Las Cruces* (N.M.) *News* 16 Nov., [The new lower rate] allows Kansas feeders to ship from this territory or Arizona to their feed lots, fatten them and ship on to market. **1949** *Dly. Oklahoman* (Okla. City) 13 Feb. D. 6/1 In the old Colbert feed lots, the co-operative acted as hotel keeper to over 40,000 head of cattle. — (14) **1872** *Rep. Comm. Patents 1871* II. 847/2 The arrangement, in a feed-mill, of a hopper [etc.]. **1947** *Pageant* May 79/1 You can feed the birds quail or pheasant mash—sold by feed mills—or turkey mash.

(15) **1889** *Cent.* 2169/3 *Feed-roll*, . . . in a typewriter, a roll covered with india-rubber or other elastic material, which moves the paper as required, line by line. **1918** M. B. OWEN *Typewriting Speed* 17 Holding the paper . . . , let it fall between the paper rest and the feed rolls of the typewriter. — (16) **1887** TOURGEE *Button's Inn* 142 A great towel . . . hung inside the feed room door. **1944** CLARK *Pills* 41 In a corner of these cases, . . . were plain little cardboard boxes which contained the iniquitous devices of contraception which were called for in private conference behind the closed doors of the feed rooms. — (17) **1903** *Cin. Enquirer* 9 May 12/2 He was grinning broadly as he stepped into the feed shack and addressed me. — (18) **1877** HODGE *Arizona* 154 Tucson has . . . one news depot, . . . four feed and livery stables. **1924** MCCONNELL *Frontier Law* 170 He continued, however, to reside in Boisé, as proprietor of a saloon and feed stable. — (19) **1910** RAINE *B. O'Connor* 106 Jay Hardman's place, a tumble-down feed-station on the edge of town.

(20) **1829** B. HALL *Travels in N.A.* I. 18, I amused myself one morning by noting down a few of the signs over the shop doors. . . . Flour and feed store—Cheap Store—Clothing Store [etc.]. **1947** *Nat. Geog. Mag.* Dec. 836 From the Feed Store, Now a Fashion Emporium, Comes Sackcloth for Colorful Dresses. — (21) **1856** *Porter's Spirit of Times* 4 Oct. 74/3 But a few years since our whole supplies of bread and feed-stuffs [in Calif.] were drawn from abroad. **1925** TILGHMAN *Dugout* 91 She was able to sell all of her crop of feedstuff to a cattle man, with a small profit. — (22) **1845** in *Ind. Mag. Hist.* XXIII. 212 He then wrote to Crouch . . . to come with their wagons, and grain, and hay, and feed troughs and watering buckets. **1904** *Pat. Off. Gazette* CVIII. 103/2 A feed-trough having upwardly-extended ends, and a shield pivotally connected to said . . . ends. — (23) **1850** LEANDER V. LOOMIS in *Journal* (1928) 26 Having an old feed-wagon . . . we took the exeltree out of it and before sundown had it riged in the other wagon and ready to rool on in the morning. — (24) (*a*) **1879** *Chi. Tribune* 14 May 7/4 The feed-yards in Chicago are extensive. **1911** H. QUICK *Yellowstone N.* iv. 109 One, two, three farmsteads we passed, with its white house hidden in trees, low hog-houses, its feed yards. (*b*) **1884** *Cent. Mag.* April 832/2 He has filled some places under the Maryland and Baltimore political governments, and now keeps a coal, wood, and feed yard in North Baltimore.

As the last term in **chicken, chop, cut, deer, fall, mixed, square, still, tall feed.**

***feed,** *v. tr.* To give or supply (corn, hay, oats, etc.) to domestic animals.

1852 *Mich. Agric. Soc. Trans.* III. 145, I feed almost every thing hay, oats, straw, . . . etc. **1894** *Vt. Agric. Rep.* XIV. 56, I have made it a rule to buy a carload of cotton-seed meal and feed as much as I dared. **1944** *Sears Cat.* (ed. 189) 876Y Feed Bunks. Good for feeding all kinds of rations, minerals, etc.

transf. **1904** *Grand Rapids Ev. Press* 2 June 3 The professor . . . fed snake sandwiches to his college class at a party. *a***1935** in HORWILL 128 If mince pie makes the Mount Holyoke girls drowsy after luncheon it ought to be fed them at night.

b. *To feed out,* to give or supply (corn, hay, etc.) as feed to animals. Also to feed (animals) until they are in a marketable condition.

1818 in *Ill. Hist. Soc. Trans.* (1910) 158 They either have to feed out their corn or their cattle get very poor. **1868** *Iowa Agric. Soc. Rep. 1867* 148 Corn is husked and cribbed and fed out to stock. **1946** *Harper's Mag.* Oct. 311/1 Now and then my father would have to borrow money to 'feed-out' the steers.

c. *To feed on soft corn,* see **soft corn.**

feedbox ˈfid͵bɑks, *n.* A box used in feeding stock, esp. one from which horses eat.

1836 ELIZABETH L. WILLSON *Journal* (1929) 21 May, We ferried the Susquehanna. I . . . stood behind the wagon and held to the feed box. **1846** FARNHAM *Prairie Land* 329 He . . . harnesses his four horses before it [a wagon], hands his 'bucket' beneath and his 'feed-box' behind [etc.]. **1890** D'OYLE *Notches* 128 Then he looked to the wants of his horse, and putting a feed into the 'feed-box' of hers too, went back to the house. **1947** *Time* 3 Feb. 20/3 Each tried to butt the other out of the feedbox.

b. A box from which or in which fowls are fed.

1871 LEWIS *Poultry Book* 136 (*caption*), Feed Box for Ducks. **1876** *Field & Forest* II. 58, I carried the Grouse home and put it in a large feed-box, which was standing in the open air.

c. In transf. and attrib. uses (see quots.).

1860 *Harper's Mag.* July 149/1 The [canal] boats are constructed in two parts, for convenience in going over the planes. . . . Midships, or where the two parts are connected, a portion of each is floored over, and on this space the feed-boxes are kept. **1882** *Cent. Mag.* Jan. 477/1 A comparatively new machine [for ginning cotton] . . . consists of a suction fan, a 'whipper-wheel,' or light paddle . . . and a suitable feed-box or hopper. **1932** *Blue Valley Farmer* (Okla. City) 10 March 1/3 A wabbling 'business administration' backed by a coalition congress and a system of feedbox publications, are . . . badly frightened.

***feeder,** *n.*

1. A root. In full **feeder root.**

1874 *Vt. Bd. Agric. Rep.* II. 214 You will observe by mulching your fruit trees that these feeders will grow higher and higher every year. **1911** J. F. WILSON *Land Claimers* 40 The roar [of the wind] . . . ripping long feeder roots out of their hold in the soil.

2. A container for feed from which hogs, poultry, etc., may secure it at any time with a minimum of waste.

1877 *Harper's Mag.* Jan 267/2 Upon the other side of the store stood sturdily rakes and hoes, shellers and feeders, even the more costly implements of agriculture. **1944** *Sears Cat.* (ed. 189) 877G A strongly built, big capacity feeder for flocks up to 50 birds. Holds 1 bushel of feed; 22 to 26 birds can eat at one time.

3. An animal, designed for slaughter, sold to one who makes a business of fattening such animals and selling them to meat packers. Usu. *pl.*

1880 *Bradstreet's* 16 Oct. 2/2 The exception is the present scarcity of what are termed 'feeders.' **1905** *Forestry Bureau Bul.* No. 62, 19 Cattle from the ranges of Arizona supply Phoenix with feeders. **1948** *News-Palladium* (Benton Harbor, Mich.) 14 Aug. 10/1 You should have some feeders this fall, so be sure to attend.

attrib. **1931** *Chi. D. News* 9 Jan. 40/12 Cattle Prices follow. . . . Feeder and stocker steers [etc.]. **1945** *Prairie Farmer* 22 Dec. 4/2 Shipments of feeder lambs to the feeding areas of the Corn Belt were the second largest on record. **1948** *Capital-Democrat* (Tishomingo, Okla.) 17 June 1/3 Some 150 persons arrived at the Frank Gillespie ranch Friday afternoon after a look at Leon Daube's feeder cattle.

b. The men who feed these cattle.

1889 [see **feed lot**]. **1946** *Chi. D. News* 23 March 3/1 Under a special rule, 'feeders' can purchase live animals, feed them for 30 days, slaughter them and collect the government subsidy.

4. feeder dam, the dam of a feeder stream.

1838 *Ind. H. Rep. Jrnl.* 10 By 1843 . . . the Central Canal from Evansville to the feeder dam on White River . . . will all be completed. **1851** CIST *Cincinnati* 142 The great flood in the Whitewater river . . . swept away the feeder-dam.

As the last term in **cattle, self-, sheep, snake feeder.**

***feeding,** *n.* Used in combs.: (1) **feeding bag,** =**feed bag;** (2) **lot,** =**feed lot;** (3) **right,** the right to graze cattle; (4) **station,** (*a*) a station or stopping place where soldiers or reservation Indians are supplied with food, *obs.;* (*b*) a place where birds are fed; (5) **trough,** =**feed trough.**

(1) **1812** *Niles' Reg.* II. 131/1 The purveyor of public supplies advertises for . . . 3000 nose or feeding bags. — (2) **1870** *Rep. Comm. Agric.* 372 The stock . . . consists of stock cattle, ready . . . for turning into 'feeding lots' for 'full feeding' for spring market. **1948** *Great Falls* (Mont.) *Tribune* 18 Sep. 4/4 American buyers are moving close to 1,000 head of choice stock to United States feeding lots and packing plants. — (3) **1882** GODFREY *Nantucket* 92 Every fractional part of a common or privilege was noted. . . . These fractions existed as well in the 'general field' as in the 'feeding rights.' — (4) (*a*) **1865** *Atlantic Mo.* XV. 242/2 Where the distance from the battle-field to the base of supplies is great, what are called feeding-stations are established every few miles. **1871** *Rep. Indian Affairs* (1872) 68 No reports have been received at this office from feeding stations. (*b*) **1934** *Nat. Geog. Mag.* LXVI. 129 A few winters ago a northern shrike, attracted by the many birds at the feeding station, took up his abode in my garden. **1948** *Chi. Tribune* 20 Nov. 8/5 Chunks of suet, hunks of

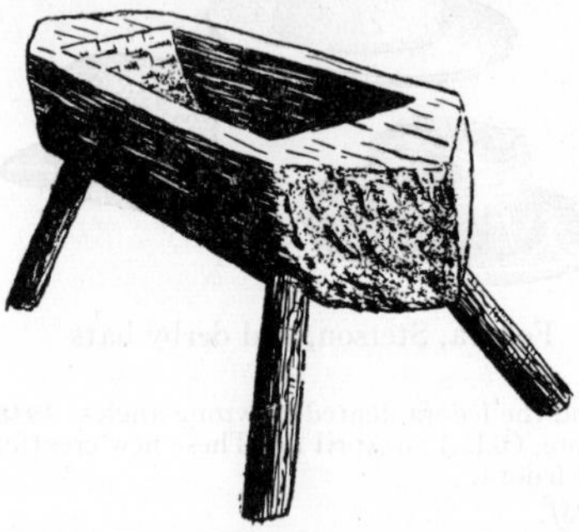

Feed trough

fat pork, seeds and other foods bring the downy to a feeding station. — (5) **1839** *Spirit of Times* 9 Nov. 423/2 (We.), A feeding trof is just the caper. **1919** *Sears Cat.* (ed. 138) 1049 Galvanized Feeding Trough. Prevents waste and keeps fowls from tramping . . . their food.

As the last term in **fall feeding.**

***feel,** *v.*

1. *To feel like,* to have a desire or inclination for (doing something). *Colloq.*

1829 *Va. Lit. Museum* 30 Dec. 458 *Like* . . . is also used, as follows, in the south: 'I do not feel like eating.' *Vulgarism.* **1855** B. YOUNG in *Jrnl. Discourses* II. 257 (Th.), Brethren, I have not apostatized yet, and don't feel like doing so. **1867** in CUSTER *Tenting on Plains* (1887) xix. 575 After your letter came, I felt like a ride.

2. *To feel one's oats,* see ***oat 3.**

3. **To feel to,* to feel inclined or disposed to (do something). *Colloq.* or *dial.*

"An expression commonly used by some clergymen" (B. '59). The seven examples (1852–57) in Thornton are from the *Journal of Discourses.*

1837 *Knickerb.* X. 429 She could not any way feel to it. **1852** B. YOUNG in *Jrnl. Discourses* I. 362 (Th.), It makes me feel to loathe such hypocritical show. **1922** A. BROWN *Old Crow* 81, I didn't go ag'in. I didn't feel to.

4. *To feel good,* see ***good 3.**

5. *To feel pale,* (see quots.). *Colloq.*

1877 BARTLETT 782 *To feel pale* is a humorous way of saying that one is sick. **1889** FARMER 236/1 *To feel pale,* to experience fright, or sudden shock. Familiarly colloquial.

***feeling,** *n.* As the last term in **race, secession, State rights feeling.**

***feet,** *n.*

1. Used facetiously for a foot, twelve inches. *Colloq.*

"There are people who consider it witty to use this plural instead of its singular" (B. '59). "This piece of attempted wit is fortunately obsolete" (Th., who gives seven quotations, 1842–57).

1842 *Spirit of Times* (Phila.) 11 Oct. (Th.), His tail hung down a feet. **1870** W. M. STEWART *Western States* 96 'You must have had a borrowed love-letter sent ye lately.' . . . 'You'd better stop; you're a gettin into me a feet.'

2. Feet-washing Baptists, Primitive or Hard-Shell Baptists. *Colloq.*

1856 FERGUSSON *America* 231 Another who call themselves 'the Church of God,' commonly known as 'Weinbrennarians,' or 'Feet-washing Baptists.' [**1947** *Amer. Sp.* Feb. 73/1 Another unusual practice is the 'feet-washing' which concludes the communion service, observing the New Testament injunction.]

As the last term in **Black, cold, moccasin feet.**

Feginny fəˈdʒɪnɪ, *n.* ?Alteration of *Virginia.* Also attrib. *Obs.* — **1830** ROYALL *Lett. from Ala.* 21, I will try to beguile the time in amusing myself with 'my host' and hostess who I dare say expect to make their Jack out of me—'old Feginny begging!' *Ib.* 23 Finding a stranger in the house, she frisked back, and began to adjust her Feginny cloth dress.

Feijoa feˈhoə, *n.* [J. de Silva *Feijo*, director Nat. Hist. Museum, San Sebastian, Spain.] The subtropical strawberry guava, *Psidium cattleyanum.*

1929 BAILEY *Cyclo. Horticulture* 1204/2 The feijoa does not seem to thrive under strictly tropical conditions, preferring a climate such as that of southern California or the Riviera. **1935** MCMINN & MAINO *Pacific Coast Trees* 318 Feijoa . . . [is] cultivated in the warmer parts of California for its edible fruits and ornamental flowers and foliage. **1949** *L.A. Times* (Home Mag.) 17 April 33/2 Tall growing shrubs include arbutus, or strawberry shrub, cotoneasters, . . . Feijoa.

feist faɪst, *n.* Also **fice, fist.** Chiefly *S.* [See note.] A small dog, sometimes with a derogatory implication.

Cf. in *OED fysting curre* (1529), *fisting hound* (1576), *foisting hound* (1611), *fisting dog* (1688), etc.

[**1770** WASHINGTON *Diaries* I. 371 A small foist looking yellow cur.] **1805** DOW *Journal* (1814) 265 Bob Sample, one of the most popular A-double-L-part [predestinarian] preachers in the country, . . . like a little fice (or cur dog) would rail behind my back. **1850** GARRARD *Wah-To-Yah* iv. 60 In our lodge were three huge curs and four cross feists. **1917** MATHEWSON *Sec. Base Sloan* 34 In Missouri or Mississippi he would have been labelled 'fice,' which is equivalent to saying that he was a terrier-like dog of no particular breed. **1949** *Democrat* 17 March 7/2 Good squirrel and o'possum dog for sale. Small feist 3½ years old.

attrib. and *transf.* **1857** *Spirit of Times* 20 June 247/1 Mr. Talley . . . has a small dog of the fice species, that follows a milch cow of his to the pasture every morning, . . . and at night drives her home. **1945** *Amer. Sp.* April 157 Some feists, mongrels and cheap politicians have been yapping around over this country that your judge drinks.

b. Also **fice dog.**

1843 *Missouri Reporter* (St. Louis) 29 June (Th.), Did you ever see a pack composed of five or six little fice dogs, barking furiously? **1944** CLARK *Pills* 158 A farmer without meat, without corn, with his patch of cotton mortgaged to the guano man, five mangy fice dogs at home, . . . he was indeed a picture to behold.

Hence **fice-dogged.** *Rare.*

1842 *Cong. Globe* 4 May 478/1 Private individuals were bull-dogged —or fice-dogged, if the gentleman pleases.

feisty ˈfaɪstɪ, *a.* [f. prec.] Fidgety, belligerent. *Colloq.*

1913 KEPHART *So. Highlanders* 94 Feisty means when a feller's allers wigglin' about, wantin' ever'body to see him, like a kid when the preacher comes. **1926** ROBERTS *Time of Man* 152 That-there feisty bay mare jumped straight upwards and broke the tongue outen the plow. **1947** *Sat. Review* 27 Sep. 12/3 It signifies nothing, and is washed away in mirth and song, dust of road, clamor of county fair, folk-talk unspoiled with learning, part Bible, part Elizabethan, 'feisty and fractious,' as Samantha says.

* **fellow,** *n.*

1. In certain colleges, one of the corporation or governing body, a trustee.

1650 *Harvard Charter* in *Harvard Cat.* (1940) ix, It is therefore ordered and enacted. . . . That for the furthering of so good a worke . . . that the said Colledge . . . shalbe a Corporation Consisting of seauen persons (to wit) a President fiue Fellowes and a Treasurer or Burser. **1866** *Yale Sheffield Sci. School Rep.* I. 15 On learning of your acceptance of this trust, and of the assent of the President and Fellows of Yale College. . . . I shall be prepared to pay over to you the sum I have named. **1925** *Pub. Col. Soc.* XV. cxxxiii, In this [the 1650 charter] the word Fellow was used in a new, specific, and hitherto (either in England or at Harvard) unknown sense—namely, as designating one of the five persons who, in addition to the President and the Treasurer, made up the Corporation.

b. In full **fellow of the corporation,** (see also quot. 1940).

1716 in *Pub. Col. Soc.* XVI. 435 The Corporation for the Managmt of the Affairs of the sd College had made choice of the Revd Mr Ioseph Stevens to be one of the Fellows of the sd Corporation. **1846** C. SUMNER *Scholar* 53 He [Channing] was a son of the University, and for many years connected with its government as . . . a Fellow of the Corporation. **1940** *Harvard Cat.* x-xi, Until 1692, every teacher in the College was also a Fellow of the Corporation.

2. fellow countrywoman, a woman associated with others as a citizen of a common country. *Rare.*

1898 HARPER *S. B. Anthony* I. 253 Many noble men . . . for years past . . . have appealed . . . for an enlargement of the legal and civil status of their fellow-countrywomen.

As the last term in **cotton, gophering, Kentucky, resident, secesh fellow.**

***Fellowship,** *n.* In place-names. *Obs.* — **1696** *Md. Hist. Mag.* XXI. 354 Fellowshipe. **1698** *Ib.* XIX. 367 Battsons Fellowship.

* **female,** *n.*

1. female suffrage, suffrage for women. Also attrib.

1867 in *Kans. Hist. Quart.* VIII. 212 We consider the subject of female suffrage before the people of Kansas in so grave a shape as to warrant the candid consideration of what may be said, pro or con. **1893** *Harper's Mag.* April 707/2 Prohibition, female suffrage, fiat money, free silver, every incoherent and fantastic dream of social improvement.

b. female suffragist, a woman who advocates women's suffrage.

1871 *Billings' Farmer's Allminax* II. Q.—Who iz the coming man? A.–The female suffragist. **1872** *Chi. Ev. Jrnl.* 30 Nov., The aim of the author has been to burlesque the female suffragists.

2. female tom, (see quot. and cf. **tom**). *Obs.*

1851 *True Standard* (S.F.) 6 Mar. 2/4 The miners near Placerville . . . now haul their earth a distance of two or three miles to be washed, using a tom of new construction called a female tom. It works on the same principle as the long tom's of olden time, but the dimensions are greatly increased. Instead of being a foot in width, the modern tom is two or three feet wide.

* **fence,** *n.*

1. In baseball, the backstop. *Obs.*

1878 *De Witt's Baseball Guide* 24 The umpire . . . should note whether the catcher's *fence* is at the proper distance from the home base.

2. In politics, a position favoring neither party or side. *Colloq.*

1843 *Knickerb.* XXII. 233 The fence, sir, the fence is our only and our tee-total safety on these p'ints. **1865** HOLLAND *Plain Talk* iv. 134 But in time of disturbance, when opinions are clashing and a great moral conflict is in progress, the fence is his invariable resort. **1947** *Time* 21 July 18/1 Western Republicans were already warning California's Governor Earl Warren that unless he got off the fence soon, western delegates would swing to Dewey.

b. Chiefly attrib. in expressions of obvious meaning, often with reference to those unwilling to take a positive stand for fear of being on the losing side, as (1) **fence man,** cf. **3.** (10) below, (2) **politician,** (3) **rider,** cf. **3.** (14) below, (4) **riding,** cf. **3.** (15) below; (5) **sitting,** (6) **straddler.**

(1) **1829** ORNE *Letters of Columbus* 19 Fence-man. **1830** *Boston Transcript* 15 Sep. 2/4 The Centinel suggests a doubt whether the Palladium is in favour of *Henry Clay*, or *a luke warm fence man.* **1884** *Boston Jrnl.* Aug., 'The President does not create the policy of his party, but the party creates it for him and he is guided by it.' This assertion is a good one for the fence-men to study. — (2) **1843** STEPHENS *High Life N.Y.* I. 202 She looked sort a like a nice harnsome chap, and sort a like a gal, kinder half and half, like a fence politician. **1851** in CLAIBORNE *Life Quitman* II. 141 It would have the happiest effect on every fence politician in the state. — (3) **1834** J. DOWNING *A. Jackson* 91 The fence riders now took courage and jumpt clean off. — (4) *a*1859 *N.Y. Mirror* (B.), The South will not vote for a Northern candidate who is nominated as such, nor the North for a Southern man who is nominated on exclusive Southern principles. In this matter there can be no neutral ground. The dividing line is narrow, but distinct; it admits of no fence-riding. **1868** *Cong. Globe* 17 July (De Vere), This question is one of clear right and wrong, and there can be no fence-riding, when the rights of four millions of men are at stake. (5) **1944** *Chi. D. News* 21 Oct. 5/3 The degree of Wisconsin's isolationism is attracting Democratic attention . . . because of Senator LaFollette's fence-sitting. — (6) **1948** *Time* 12 April 24/2 His critics say he is a confirmed fence-straddler who rides the donkey and the elephant at the same time.

c. Also in phrases: (1) *To be on the fence,* (2) *to ride the fence,* see ***ride,** *v.* **4.** (1).

(1) **1828** *Niles' Reg.* XXXIII. 374/2 Two members, one in each house, are said to be on the fence. **1944** *Chi. D. News* 21 Oct. 5/4 With LaFollette on the fence nationally, the Democrat fear is that Sauthoff will draw liberal New Deal votes.

3. In special combs.: (1) **fence breaker,** =**fence cutter,** *obs.*; (2) **building,** looking after one's political interests; (3) **corner,** the angle made where a fence turns or meets another, one of the nooks or angles in a zigzag rail fence, also attrib.; (4) **cutter,** *W.* during the fence war *q.v.*, one who engaged in cutting the wire fences around fenced grazing lands; (5) **jack,** (see quot.), *obs.;* (6) **jamb,** = **fence corner;** (7) **law,** a law concerning the erection and maintenance of fences; (8) **lizard,** (see quot. 1898); (9) **log,** one of the logs used in making a log fence *q.v., obs.;* (10) **man,** = **fence viewer,** *obs.,* cf. **2. b.** (1) above; (11) **mending,** keeping up one's political interests, *colloq.;* (12) **mouse,** (see quot.); (13) **rail,** one of the wooden bars, usu. about ten feet long and four or five inches in diameter, of which a rail fence is made; (14) **rider,** *W.* on a cattle ranch, a man whose job it is to ride along the fences, looking for breaks and making repairs, cf. **line rider,** and see **2. b.** (3) above; (15) **riding,** *W.* designating a job as a fence rider on a ranch, cf. **2. b.** (4) above; (16) **row,** a strip of land at the edge of a field, immediately adjoining a fence; (17) **stake,** a stake used in a staked and ridered fence; (18) **tag,** a variety of the game of tag; (19) **viewer,** see as a main entry; (20) **war,** *W.* a feud among cattlemen who protested the action of certain ranch owners in fencing off parts of what had been formerly open cattle range, also **fence cutting war,** cf. **fence cutter;** (21) **worm,** (see quots. and cf. **b.** (5) below).

(1) **1888** *Austin* (Tex.) *Statesman* 1 Nov. 6/2 If the fence breakers had been promptly dealt with at first the evil would never have assumed the magnitude it has. — (2) **1895** *Amer. Federationist* Nov. 166/2 It will be well to keep a close watch on congress,—watch the 'pipe-laying,' 'wire-pulling,' and 'fence-building.' — (3) **1832** KENNEDY *Swallow Barn* I. 153 He slowly went to the fence corner and untied his horse. **1901** WHITE *Claim Jumpers* (1916) 64 It was such a diminutive beast, . . . quite smaller than our own fence-corner chipmunks of the East. **1947** LUMPKIN *Southerner* 24 In any event, fence corners should be cleaned, ditches opened, . . . and the poor work animals . . . be put at rail-hauling. — (4) **1883** *Albany* (Tex.) *Echo* 12 Dec., Build a Chinese wall around Coleman County, put all the fence-cutters inside it, furnish them with wire fence and nippers, and tell them to wade in. **1890** *Stock Grower & Farmer* 23 Aug. 3/4 The fence cutters are on the wrong track. . . . The course they are pursuing will put them beyond the pale of friendship.

(5) **1874** KNIGHT 836/1 *Fence-jack*, a lever jack adapted for lifting the corner or lock of a worm-fence in order to lay in a new bottom-rail, a fence-chunk, or a stone. — (6) **1865** TURNER *Cotton* 89 All decaying vegetable matter about the plantation, such as weeds, grass, &c., that grow and collect in the fence jams, in low wet places, in the ditches, &c., should be carefully raked up, and at a convenient time hauled into the stock lots. **1939** MCILWAINE *Poor-White* 211 He 'threw her off like a nigger's shoe in a fence-jamb.' — (7) **1858** WARDER *Hedges & Evergreens* 143 The courtesy of its [the Cincinnati Law Library's] Directors has enabled me to gather the material for this exposition of the fence-laws of our country. **1944** CLARK *Pills* 59 Few issues were so hotly debated as that of fence laws. — (8) **1869** *Amer. Naturalist* III. 478 A large Fence Lizard (Sceloporus magister?), eight inches long, began to frequent the trees March 20th. **1898** *Smithsonian Rep.* 373 The *Sceloporus undulatus*, or 'Fence lizard,' as it is commonly called, is abundant in dry and wild regions in the Alleghenian and Carolinian districts of the Eastern region. It is usually seen running on fences, logs, or trunks of trees with great activity. — (9) **1756** PATTEN *Diary* 25 Had Jerret rowans and Benjn Smiths oxen helping me in the afternoon to hall fence logs at the Little Meadow. **1775** *Ib.* 337 Jamey and Bob cut fence loggs for Mr. Shed it was a frolick.

(10) **1699** *Groton Rec.* 118 For fence men Joseph Laken and Joseph Cade. — (11) **1944** CLARK *Pills* 87 A local politician in one of the outlying beats hastened a note off to the storekeeper to come at once and help do some fence mending at the polls. — (12) **1859** *Rep. Comm. Patents: Agric. 1857* 75 In Northern Illinois, I have heard the German farmers very generally call it [the striped prairie squirrel] 'Fence Mouse,' which name they also apply to the *Tamias striatus.* — (13) **1733** BYRD *Journey to Eden* (1901) 301 We found the Land uneaven, but tolerably good, tho very thin of Trees, and those that were standing fit for little but fewel and Fence-Rails. **1893** *Harper's Mag.* LXXXVIII. 24/1 Young man, in my country we make fence rails of walnut. **1945** *Reader's Digest* Jan. 53/2 He hewed out 300 fence rails, ten feet long. — (14) **1885** *Wkly. New Mexican Rev.* 12 Feb. 4/3 When one or more of the wires [about the ranch] are broken the ringing bells in the house signal the break, locating the same, thus saving the expense of the fence rider. **1944** JOHNSON *As I Dare* 281 It was on the western slopes of the Sangre de Cristo, and not an over-night tourist cabin, since it had been built for a fence rider on a ranch which handles live stock rather than tourists.

(15) **1909** R. A. WASON *Happy Hawkins* 211, I couldn't make up my mind what to do, an' I wanted that fence-ridin' job more than ever. — (16) **1842** *Amer. Pioneer* I. 43, I was alone, clearing out a fence row, about a quarter of a mile from the house. **1948** *Country Gentleman* May 175/2 He had cut the fence rows from the board fence around the shack, barn and garden. — (17) **1835** AUDUBON *Ornith. Biog.* III. 566 The mocking birds on the fence-stakes. **1857** HAMMOND *Northern Scenes* 44 The meadow lark perched upon his fence stake. — (18) **1891** *Amer. Folk-Lore* IV. 222 Tag is sometimes varied by increasing the difficulties of the pursuit, as in Fence Tag. Bounds are chosen along a fence.

(20) **1884** *Nation* 24 Jan. 65/2 It is evident that the blue devils . . . are endeavoring to give the fence war the air of a struggle between poverty and banded wealth. **1942** DALE *Cow Country* 83 'Fence cutting wars' broke out, and bill after bill was introduced in the Texas legislature forbidding the use of barbed wire for fencing. — (21) **1918** E. WALLER *Illinois* 75 Fence-worm, the first rail of each panel of a rail fence. They were built zig-zag to enable them to cross the rails at the ends. It was not an easy job to lay a fence-worm. **1946** *Atlanta Jrnl. Mag.* 3 March 8/2 Neighbors usually help each other lay the worm for a new fence. A fence worm is the first rails forming the pattern of a fence.

b. In colloq. phrases: (1) *To be under fence*, to be fenced, also *to put under fence*, to fence, cf. **fork fence,** quot. 1796; (2) *to be on* (one's) *side of the fence*, to agree with one; (3) *to keep* (one) *on his side of the fence*, to keep one in his place; (4) *to be on the other* (or *same*) *side of the fence*, to be opposed to (or in agreement with) someone or something; (5) *to lay fence-worm,* (see quot.); (6) *to look after* (or *mend*, etc.) *one's fences*, to look after one's political interests (see quot. 1927).

(1) **1760** *N.J. Archives* XX. 431 The Premises under pretty good Fence. **1841** in JILLSON *Dark & Bloody Ground* 86 We cleared & put under fence about 30 acres of land. **1927** JAMES *Cow Country* 167 Picturing the whole of the range counties to be all under fence and plowed and irrigated, as they had, didn't give 'em much ambition to be on the move. — (2) **1852** STOWE *Uncle Tom's Cabin* vi. 86 It's allers best to stand missis's side the fence, now I tell yer. — (3) **1905** PHILLIPS *Social Secretary* 121 When she heard his study door close 'ma' said to me in a complacent voice: 'There's nothing like keeping a a man always to his side of the fence.' — (4) **1865** TROWBRIDGE *Three Scouts* i. 15, I judge your sympathies are more on t'other side of the secession fence than on ours. **1888** *Texas Siftings* 7 July (F.), Journals on the other side of the fence will represent him to be a weak, feeble old man. **1946** *Reader's Digest* Jan. 83 One year you might be competing ruthlessly with him, the next you'd both be on the same side of the fence.

(5) **1872** MORRELL *Flowers & Fruits* 304 As I approached the house of my old friend Morrell, . . . the horse . . . commenced 'pitching,' or, as the old Texans sometimes said, 'laying fence-worm.' — (6) **1888** *Cong. Rec.* 16 Aug. 7646/1, I presume they [the absent members] are at home seeking renomination or looking after their fences. **1906** *Forum* April 444 An early adjournment of the session is deemed essential in order that the members may go home to mend their fences, as the saying is. **1927** PEASE *United States* 527 When visiting the State in 1879, ostensibly to look after his farms, he [Sen. John Sherman of Ohio] had protested that he came only to 'repair my fences,' a term to which the newspapers promptly gave its present political meaning. **1947** *Newsweek* 7 July 31/3 Henry Wallace already was more concerned with building his own fences than with helping the new President.

As the last term in **back, board, brush, bush, close, crooked, dividing, division, drift, electric, five rail, fork, fork-and-rail, forked, four rail, fyke, general, hell, hog, Indian, iron, land, limestone, line, live, log, mud, old field, panel, partition, partitional, partnership, picket, pine, plank, pole, political, rail, rock, root, shad, shad belly, Shanghai, six-rail, snake, snow, sod, spite, stock, stone, stump, ten rail, three rail, Virginia, Virginian, water, willow, wood, worm, zigzag fence.**

fence viewer. Chiefly *N. Eng.* [Poss. f. Du. *heining schouwer*, in same sense.] An official having charge of the location, erection, and inspection of fences in a particular district.

[**1657** in *Records E.-Hampton* I. 113 It is farther ordered yt Tho Chatfeild is chosen to vew the fences yt they be kept sufisient according to law.] **1661** *Dorchester Rec.* 109 Fence viewers: for the necke of land, Richard Withington [etc.]. **1771** *Copley-Pelham Lett.* 125 She will apply to the Fence viewers to have the Fences made up. **1858** WARDER *Hedges & Evergreens* 162 Fence-viewers [are] to assign the portions to each occupant when they cannot agree. **1944** *Amer. N. & Q.* Nov. 120/1 Non-New Englanders often regard appointments to these seemingly antiquated posts as amusing; yet fence viewers officiated only very recently in Portsmouth, New Hampshire.

*__fencing,__ *n.*

1. The materials from which fences are made, usu. = **fencing wire.**

1889 *Cent.* 2180/1 fencing. . . . Material used in making fences. **1936** *Sears Cat.* (ed. 173) 950 All Sears fencing is made from full-gauge, true copper-bearing steel wire, containing not less than .20% pure copper. **1946** *Athol* (Mass.) *D. News* 6 July 8/1 (*advt.*), Fencing, Fence Posts, Plywood Panels [etc.].

2. In combs.: (1) **fencing rail,** = **fence rail;** (2) **stuff,** material for use in making fence; (3) **wire,** wire used in fencing.

(1) **1780** *N.H. Hist. Soc. Coll.* IX. 210 The officer of the police . . . will be answerable that no fencing raels or Inclosures whatever about the Camp are destroyed. **1802** DRAYTON *S. Carolina* 80 Loblolly pine. (*Pinus palustris.*) Grows in low places, in the lower country; is appropriated to common plantation uses, and for fencing rails. — (2) **1644** *Dedham Rec.* 103 The towne shall se cause to desire a fence. . . . Michael is to prouide ye fencing stuffe. **1779** E. PARKMAN *Diary* 106, I walked to Mr. Thad. Warrin's to hire him to get out Fencing stuff, posts and Rails. **1892** TORREY *Foot-Path Way* 72 No wonder such fields do not pay for fencing-stuff. — (3) **1878** *Rep. Indian Affairs* 35, I suggested that fencing-wire be supplied as an annuity. **1920** HUNTER *Trail Drivers Texas* I. 173 Fencing wire had not been invented.

As the last term in **board, plank, worm fencing.**

*__fender,__ *n.*

1. A cowcatcher or similar contrivance on a locomotive or streetcar.

1858 W. P. SMITH *Railway Celebrations* 225 The train . . . was brought to a stand-still . . . by the breakage of a massive cross-bar sustaining the cow-catcher or 'fender,' in front of the engine. **1910** O. HENRY *Strictly Business* 26 The street cars bewildered him, and the fender of one upset him against a pushcart laden with oranges.

One type of fender (sense 2) or fire screen (*a*)

b. The guard over the wheel of an automobile or other motor vehicle.

1919 LEWIS *Free Air* 103 Claire . . . had enjoyed the sight of their duffle-bags stuck up between the sleek fenders and the hood. **1948** *New Yorker* 25 Sep. 23/1 We may yet be able to buy special mail-order fenders that permit a car to be parked without the help of radar.

2. (See quot. 1874.)

1874 KNIGHT 836 *Fender,* . . . a structure in front of a fire or fire-place, to keep children or lunatics from burning themselves. In the example shown, the fender is secured by hooks to the grate-bars. In lunatic asylums the fender is a large cage. [**1904** *Pat. Off. Gazette* CXI. 2265/1 Grate-Fender. . . . A fender having a pair of elongated engaging fingers.]

*__Fenian,__ *n.* A member of a secret organization of Irish-Americans, established *c*1858, which advocated the forcible separation of Ireland from England, and in June, 1866, made an abortive attempt to invade Canada (see also quot. 1900). Also attrib. or as adj.

1863 *N.Y. Wkly. Tribune* 13 Nov. 4/3 For several years a new political organization has been forming among the Irish population of the United States, calling itself the Fenian Brotherhood, and having for its avowed object the liberation of Ireland from British rule. **1866** *N.Y. Tribune* 6 June 1/4 Gen. Meade received a dispatch this afternoon stating that a column of Fenians, estimated 1,000 strong, commenced a movement from Highgate, Vt., toward Canada this forenoon. **1900** *Chi. Times-Herald* 4 May 1/6 (*heading*), Fear of a Fenian Invasion Canadian Troops Ordered to Be Ready to March Immediately. **1943** HICKS *Amer. Dem.* 441 At that time the Fenian Brotherhood, an organization of Irish-Americans whose ultimate goal was freedom for Ireland, not only planned an invasion of Canada from American soil, but in June, 1866, actually crossed the border in some force and fought a battle with Canadian volunteers.

Hence **Fenianism.** *Obs.*

1865 *Harper's Wkly.* 28 Oct. 673/4 We find in this indifference no excuse for Fenianism. **1866** *Wilkes' Spirit of Times* 21 April 120/1 The sudden lull in the great political topics of the country . . . has again given a temporary prominence to Fenianism.

*__fennel,__ *n.* As the last term in **dog, hog, prairie fennel.**

feria ˈferɪə, *n. S.W.* [Sp. in same sense.] (See quot. 1892.) — **1844** GREGG *Commerce of Prairies* III. 85 At certain seasons of the year, there are held regular *ferias,* at which people assemble in great numbers, as well of sellers as of purchasers. **1892** *D.N.* I. 247 Feria: a fair, often synonymous with *fiesta.* (Texas.)

*__fern,__ *n.* As the last term in **Boston, Christmas, cinnamon, climbing, kidney, New York, New York Shield, rattlesnake, resurrection, rock, sensitive, sweet, walking, walnut fern.**

fern snakeroot. A fernlike plant, or its root, formerly used as a cure for snake bites. Also **fern rattlesnake root.** *Obs.* Cf. **snakeroot.**

1743 CLAYTON *Flora Virginica* 196 Fern-Rattle-Snake-root. **1775** ADAIR *Indians* 235 Everyone carries in his shot-pouch, a piece of the best snake-root, such as the Seneeka, or fern-snake-root—or the wild hore-hound, . . . [which] will effect a thorough and speedy cure if timely applied. **1791** *Amer. Philos. Soc. Trans.* III. 115 *Osmunda virginiana* (Virginian Osmunda, Fern-Rattle-Snake-root).

Ferris wheel. [G. W. G. *Ferris,* Amer. engineer, who designed the first such wheel for the World's Columbian Exposition in Chicago in 1893.] A large, vertical, power-driven wheel revolving on a stationary axis and having passenger cars suspended around its rim, used as an amusement device.

*c*__1894__ IVES *Dream City* n. p., The Ferris Wheel.—The chief wonder of the Fair of 1893 was the work of George Washington Gale Ferris. . . . At a Saturday afternoon club dinner, in a city chop-house, while the Fair was building, Mr. Ferris conceived the idea of the wheel. **1938** WHITE *One Man's Meat* 13 It was a fine clear day for the Fair this year, and I went up early to see how the Ferris wheel was doing and to take a ride. **1948** *Reader's Digest* Dec. 150/2 But she loved the Ferris wheel.

*__ferruginous,__ *a.* Designating various American birds of a brown or reddish color, as (1) **ferruginous buzzard,** (2) **finch,** (3) **roughleg,** (4) **thrush,** (see quots.).

(1) **1874** COUES *Birds N.W.* 363 *Archibuteo Ferrugineus,* . . . Ferrugineous Buzzard, or California Squirrel Hawk. — (2) **1917** *Birds of Amer.* III. 55 Fox sparrow (*Passerella iliaca*). . . . Ferruginous Finch. — (3) **1895** *Dept. Agric. Yrbk. 1894* 219 The rough-legged hawk, and the ferruginous roughleg, or squirrel hawk, . . . are among our largest and at the same time the most beneficial hawks. — (4) **1810** WILSON *Ornithology* II. 83 Ferruginous Thrush, *Turdus Rufus,* . . . is the Brown Thrush, or Thrasher of the middle and eastern states. **1871** BURROUGHS *Wake-Robin* (1886) 162 The ferruginous thrush (when it builds its nest) . . . collects together a mass of material that would fill a half-bushel measure.

*__ferry,__ *n.* In combs.: (1) **ferry bridge,** (see quots.); (2) **dugout,** a dugout canoe or boat used for ferrying purposes, *rare;* (3) **flat,** a large flatboat or scow used at a ferry for transporting wagons, horses, etc.; (4) **float,** a floating platform supporting one end of a ferry bridge, *rare;* (5) **land,** land immediately adjoining a ferry, *obs.;* (6) **lot,** a lot or area of land at a ferry, *obs.;* (7) **master,** one who has charge of a ferry; (8) **railway,** (see quot.), *obs.;* (9) **scow,** a scow used for ferrying purposes; (10) **slip,** an opening between two wharves or piers used as a landing place for a ferry boat; (11) **steamer,** a steamboat used for ferry purposes.

(1) **1874** KNIGHT 837/2 *Ferry-bridge,* a form of ferry-boat in which the railway-train moves on to the elevated deck, is transported across the water and then lands upon the other side. **1909** WEBSTER 806/3 Ferry bridge, . . . a floating or hanging structure hinged or movably fastened to a wharf to facilitate passing on or off a ferry-boat. — (2) **1856** *Porter's Spirit of Times* 22 Nov. 195/3 Dan Tucker . . . being stabled on the opposite side of the river, could not cross it in the ferry 'dugout,' on account of the weather. — (3) **1819** SCHOOLCRAFT *Journal* 84, [I] was conveyed over in a ferry-flat, or scow. **1884** *Harper's Mag.* June LXIX. 124 Of smaller vessels there were 'covered sleds,' 'ferry flats,' and 'Alleghany skiffs'; 'pirogues' made from two

tree trunks, or 'dug-outs' consisting of one. — (4) **1879** *Scribner's Mo.* May 38/2 We lately found $3,700 worth of velvets and silks on such a ferry-float in Jersey City.

(5) **1683** *Derby Rec.* 134 Have entertained Henry Hilt upon ye ffery land. **1714** *Providence Rec.* XI. 173 The high way should be laid out . . . to go to the Carrs or Gate at the fferey land. — (6) **1678** *Derby* (Conn.) *Rec.* 82 Bounded on the South with the ferry lott so called. **1693** *Ib.* 167 Bounded on the South with the fery lot So called. — (7) **1862** *N.Y. Tribune* 29 May 8/4 The passage at the ferry-master's window was jammed . . . with women asking . . . when the soldiers would be over. **1881** *Harper's Mag.* Jan. 205/1 Mr. Forester got the ferry-master to promise to keep the boat in the slip. — (8) **1874** Knight 837/2 *Ferry-railway*, one whose track is on the bottom of the water-course and whose carriage has an elevated deck which supports the train. — (9) **1835** Hoffman *Winter in West* II. 144 The ferry-scow had been carried away by a recent freshet.

(10) **1856** *N.Y. Herald* 21 Jan. 1/4 Ice is everywhere . . . pendant from the eaves of the houses . . . around the ferry slips, floating in the rivers. **1943** Forbes *J. Tremain* 227, I was down by the ferry slip and saw a British major coming over from Charlestown. — (11) **1863** G. Hamilton *Gala-Days* 106 A ferry-steamer will be here directly. **1886** Logan *Great Conspiracy* 212 General Benjamin F. Butler . . . seized a large ferry steamer, embarked his men on her, steamed down . . . to Annapolis [etc.].

As the last term in **car, flatboat, ocean, opposition, rope, steam, swing, wire ferry.**

***fertilizer,** *n.* **1. fertilizer distributor,** a farm implement for distributing commercial fertilizer. **2. fertilizer spreader,** an apparatus for spreading barnyard manure over land.

(1) **1934** Webster. **1947** *Democrat* 27 Feb. 6/2 For Sale—One Marvel Fertilizer and Seed Distributor. — (2) **1929** *Sears Cat.* Spring 889 Endgate Lime and Fertilizer Spreaders. **1949** *Chi. D News* 1 April 3/2, I work the combine, disc, hay baler and fertilizer spreader.

fess fɛs, *v. West Point.* [Origin unknown.] *intr.* (See quots.) *Slang.*

1834 in *Military and Naval Mag. of U.S.* III. 25 Mar., My first appearance before the Blackboard—that terror to all 'fifth-section men;' that abomination of him who has to ''fess'—that delight of him who hopes to 'fan.' **1862** Strong *Cadet Life West Point* 85 They sent me to the board to discuss the subject of cubic equations. I *fessed* cold, and was thereby thrown to the foot of the second section. **1937** Banning *West Point Today* 295 Cadet Lingo. . . . Fes, *v.* To fail completely in a recitation.

fest fɛst, *n.* [G., festival.] Used as the second element in miscellaneous expressions denoting spirited gatherings of an indicated kind, as **bund-, fun-, saenger-, schuetzen-, volksfest.** *Colloq.*

More established combinations of this kind are **gabfest, talkfest, turnerfest,** *qq.v.*

1865 *Harper's Wkly.* 5 Aug. 490/2 Arrangements were made for the Saengerfest, which will be celebrated at Philadelphia in 1867. **1870** *N.Y. Tribune* 15 June 5/5 Second Day of the Schuetzen Fest. **1880** *Dly. Inter-Ocean* (Chi.) 1 June 7/6 The bundesvost was located at St. Louis for the next two years, and the same city was chosen for the bundesfest next year. **1893** *Chi. Tribune* 10 July 4/1 A volksfest was given yesterday for the benefit of the German Old People's Home. **1948** *Lawton* (Okla.) *Constitution* 30 June 2/1 Lawton Rotarians and their Rotary Anns turned the annual installation of officers into a funfest last night.

b. In expressions relating to baseball, as **fanfest, slugfest, swatfest.** *Colloq.*

1904 *N.Y. Ev. Amer.* 27 July, There was a regular fanfest over the rumors of difficulties among the Giants. **1904** *St. Louis Globe-Democrat* 5 July 7/1 Schlei took advantage of the swatfest to get a single. **1930** *Dixon* (Ill.) *Ev. Telegraph* 24 Sep. 7/1 The slugfest . . . produced 26 hits for the winners and 16 for the defeated Phillies.

***festival,** *n.* An entertainment, usu. for charitable purposes, at which food is sold. Cf. ***fair,** *n.*[1] **2.**

1869 Mark Twain *Innocents Abroad* lv. 602 (R.), I have heard shameless people say they were glad to get away from Ladies' Festivals where they were importuned to buy by bevies of lovely young ladies. **1944** *Greeley* (Colo.) *D. Tribune* 21 Sep. 3/3 Sum of $600 was collected at the annual mission festival, conducted by the Zion Evangelical Lutheran church Sunday.

b. (See quot.) *Rare.*

1891 Thanet *Otto the Knight* 73 A festival in the Arkansas rural districts has not its Northern associations with piety, strawberries, and weak lemonade. It is a winter entertainment of a private character. The Negroes combine sociability and business, inviting all their friends to their houses, and selling them cake and candy.

As the last term in **corn, fish, ice cream, strawberry festival.**

festoon pine. Any one of various creeping evergreen plants of the clubmoss family.

1817–8 Eaton *Botany* (1822) 344 *Lycopodium rupestre*, festoon pine. . . . Rocks and gravelly banks. **1832** Traill *Backwoods* 93 The Americans ornament their chimney-glasses with garlands of this plant, mixed with the dried blossoms of the life-everlasting (the pretty white and yellow flowers we call love-everlasting): this plant is also called festoon-pine. **1938** Small *Ferns of Southeastern States* 418 *Lycopodium* . . . has received many popular names, such as, Trailing Christmas-green, Festoon pine, Crowfoot, Hagbed, and Creeping-jennie.

***fetch,** *v.*

1. *tr.* To kill or "lay out" (a person). *Colloq.*

1873 Beadle *Undevel. West* 369 [He] killed him right in front of this car. Shot at him twice afore. Fetched him dead that time. **1877** Harte *Story of Mine* 357, I got in another shot and fetched him.

b. To overcome (a person) with argument. Also *to fetch around.*

1860 Holland *Miss Gilbert* xxvii. 470, I thought you'd fetched me once but somehow it didn't stick. **1885** Cooke *Deacon's Week* 19 It was seein' one honest Christian man fetched me round to 't. **1896** Harris *Sister Jane* 24, I lay that would fetch her.

c. To get the better of, remove.

1876 Mark Twain *Tom Sawyer* vi, That'll fetch any wart.

2. *intr.* To reach a similar conclusion or agree *with* a person. *Rare.*

1888 *Detroit Free Press* 15 Sep. (F.), Men, take a good look at him! You'll all fetch with me that if any man in these yere hills ever considers to chitter him ([i.e.,] stops to question his right) that ere man has got to die!

***fetched,** *a.* Euphemism for **damned. Colloq.* Cf. ***dad.** — **1854** M. J. Holmes *Tempest & Sunshine* 203, I've got such fetched big corns on my feet, that I ain't goin' to be cramped with none of your toggery. **1860** ——— *Maude* xii. 155 I'se not gwine to spile what little beauty I've got with that fetched complaint.

fetch up. The sudden stop at the end of a fall. *Colloq.* — **1866** A. D. Whitney *L. Goldthwaite* x, It isn't the fall that hurts,—it's the fetch-up. **1897** *Outing* XXX. 558/2 Then [there was] a final lightning race down a precipice, with a dismembering 'fetch-up' at the bottom.

feterita fetəˈritə, *n.* [Origin obscure. Prob. f. Arabic.] A variety of sorghum resembling durra grown extensively in the Southwest. — **1933** Small *Southeastern Flora* 47 *H[olcus] Sorghum* . . . has been cultivated from prehistoric times in many varieties for food and forage—Sorgo, . . . Broom-corn, Egyptian-corn, Chicken-corn, Jerusalem-corn, Feterita—and for its sweet juice which is made into sirup. **1943** Van Dersal *Amer. Land* 43 These include names in familiar use—kafir corn, durra, milo, shallu, kaoliang, feterita, hegari—but all these are grain sorghums.

fetterbush ˈfɛtəˌbʊʃ, *n.* A plant belonging to any one of several genera of ericaceous shrubs, as *Neopieris nitida*, of the southern states. Cf. **evergreen fetterbush.**

1857 Gray *Botany* 254 *A[ndromeda] nitida*, . . . the Fetterbush, . . . may grow in S. Virginia. **1860** Curtis *Woody Plants N.C.* 95 *Fetter-Bush* (*Andromeda nitida.*) Found only in the Lower District in low Pine barrens. **1942** Van Dersal *Ornamental Amer. Shrubs* 257 *Leucothoe catesbaei* . . . is variously known as fetterbush, switch-ivy, doghobble, and ivy.

fetticus ˈfɛtəkəs, *n.* Also **fattikows, vettekost, vettikost.** [Du. *vettekous*, literally "fat stocking." Cf. G. *Fettkausch.*] Corn salad, any one of several half-succulent herbs, esp. *Valerianella locusta.*

1848 Bartlett 136 *Fetticus, Vettikost*, Vulg. *Fattikows*. . . . Corn-salad, or lamb's-lettuce. A word used in New York. **1867** De Voe *Market Ass't* 330 Corn salad, lamb's lettuce, or fetticus. **1889** *N. & Q* IV. 22 The plant called corn-salad, or lamb-lettuce, is called *fetticus*, or *vettekost*, by gardeners. **1891** *Cent. Dict.* 6688/2 *V[alerianella] olitoria* . . . is now often cultivated under glass as an early salad under the name of fetticus.

feudist ˈfjudɪst, *n.* One engaged in a feud. — **1901** *Munsey's Mag.* XXV. 614/1 To speak of his feud to a feudist is a serious breach of the mountain etiquette. **1948** *Sat. Ev. Post* 16 Oct. 38/1 This literature tells of Indian fighters, trail drivers, fence cutters, feudists, monumental liars.

feudsman ˈfjudzmən, *n.* =**feudist.** — **1898** J. Fox *Kentuckians* 52 By-the-way, can't you make use of a trusty for a day or two in the garden? I'll send you a feudsman, if you are getting interested in mountaineers.

***fever,** *n.*

1. A current fad or enthusiasm for a designated thing or person.

1806 *Balance* V. 2/2 False philosophy and seventy-six fever still predominate. **1850** *N. Eng. Farmer* II. 223 If the present hen fever should rage long, . . . [millet] may become an important crop for feeding young chickens. **1948** *Fargo* (N.D.) *Forum* 28 Sep. 6/1 They had the fever bad, just like the 49'ers of California.

2. =**yellow fever.**

1822 in *Memoirs of Charles Mathews* III. (1839) 328 Here we are—confidence restored — fever gone. . . . I firmly believe you know nothing of the horrors of the yellow fever by newspaper report. **1886** ALCOTT *Jo's Boys* x. 195 No one guessed that he had caught the fever. **1947** *Coronet* July 40/2 Five mosquitoes which had recently gorged themselves on the blood of fever-ridden patients were let into the enclosure with the human guinea pig.

3. =**Texas fever.**

1885 *Wkly. New Mexican Rev.* 15 Jan. 1/3 If they [Texas cattle] come over early in the season they may not bring the fever with them. **1906** ADAMS *Cattle Brands* 44 We haven't had a case of fever on our range for years, nor a winter in five years that would kill an old cow.

4. In combs.: (1) **fever and ague,** see as a main entry; (2) **belt,** (see quot.); (3) **bush,** any one of several shrubs, esp. the spicebush and winterberry, which have been used as remedies for fever; (4) **line,** a line defining the northern limits of the area where Texas fever prevails; (5) **plant,** the evening primrose; (6) **root,** see as a main entry; (7) **tree,** (*a*) (see quot. 1868), (*b*) the eucalyptus or blue gum tree; (8) * **weed,** an American foxglove (see also quots. 1892, 1899); (9) **worm,** =**fever and ague b;** (10) * **wort,** =**feverroot.**

(2) **1893** G. W. CURTIS *Horses* 162 In the Southern States—comprising what is known as the 'fever belt'—they [*sc.* Durhams] have not proved easy to acclimate. — **(3) 1778** CARVER *Travels* 510 The Fever Bush grows about five or six feet high; . . . and it bears a reddish berry of a spicy flavour. **1847** DARLINGTON *Weeds & Plants* 286 *B[enzoin] odoriferum.* . . . Spice-wood. Wild All-spice, Fever-bush. . . . An infusion of the brittle spicy twigs . . . is now chiefly prescribed as a diet-drink for sickly cows, in the spring of the year. **1949** *Amer. Photography* Feb. 115/2 Probably the commonest of these are the two winterberries: the Virginia winterberry (*Ilex verticillata*), sometimes called black alder or feverbush, and the smooth winterberry (*Ilex laevigata*).—**(4) 1890** *Stock Grower & Farmer* Fig. Feb. 16/2 The 'fever line' has been changed, being now located a considerable distance to the south and west of where it has heretofore been drawn. *Ib.* 22 Feb. 4/3 The government has decided to establish the fever line nearly a hundred miles further north, and by it places under the ban all of the Indian Territory and Texas except that portion of the panhandle lying north of the thirty-fourth parallel.

(5) 1893 *Amer. Folk-Lore* VI. 142 *Oenothera biennis,* . . . fever-plant; coffee-plant. Eastern States. — **(7)** (*a*) **1868** GRAY *Field Botany* 176 Georgia Bark or Fevertree, . . . *Pinckneya pubens,* . . . is a rather downy small tree or shrub, in wet pine barrens, S. Car. to Georgia. **1897** SUDWORTH *Arborescent Flora* 337 *Pinckneya pubens.* . . . Common Names . . . Fevertree (Ala.) (*b*) **1876** *Forest & Stream* 13 July 375/3 The large tribe of the Eucalyptus (honey or fever trees). — **(8) 1842** BUCKINGHAM *E. & W. States* I. 162 The fireweed, fever-weed, foxglove, . . . [are] carefully collected and prepared for medicinal purposes. **1892** *Amer. Folk-Lore* V. 102 *Verbena stricta,* fever-weed. Peoria, Ill. **1899** *Animal & Plant Lore* 116 A common vervain (*Verbena stricta*) is popularly known as 'fever-weed' from its supposed efficacy as a remedy for fever and ague. Central Illinois. — **(9) 1899** *Animal & Plant Lore* 17 Tawny and brown caterpillars are called [in Louisville, Ky.] 'fever-worms.' One must spit on meeting one of these to keep off fever.

(10) 1814 BIGELOW *Florula Bostoniensis* 56 *Triosteum perfoliatum.* Feverwort. . . . Not very common. . . . Flowers in June.

As the last term in **Arizona, breakbone, broken bone, buck, buffalo, bull, cabin, California, cape, cattle, Chicago, chill-and-, clipper, coast, congestive, country, dengue, dock, fall, Florida, Genesee, gold, grape, James River, lake, land, Ohio, oil, Oklahoma, Oregon, Orleans, Palatine, Panama, Pike's Peak (gold), rabbit, railroad, residential, river, rose, Russian breakbone, sheep, Shrewsbury, southern, Spanish, spindle, splenic, spring, stranger's, swamp, Texas, war, Washoe, western, winter, yellow fever.**

fever and ague. A form of malarial fever in which fever alternates with chills.

[**1658** JOHN HULL *Diary Occurr.* June 184 Much sickness in the southern colonies,—fevers and agues, of which many died.] **1671** in ALVORD & BIDGOOD *Trans-Allegheny Region* 187 Percente being taken very sick of a fever and ague every afternoon . . . we resolved to leave our horses. **1709** *N.H. Hist. Soc. Coll.* III. 44 He had been ten weeks weakened with the fever and ague. **1876** *Bedrock Democrat* (Baker, Ore.) 23 Aug. 4/1 A Cincinnati fiend advertised for men with fever and ague to shake carpets. **1904** CAPT. R. E. LEE *Recollections and Letters of Gen. Robert E. Lee* 346 To keep him free from fever-and-ague, my brother dosed him freely with cholagogue.

attrib. **1823** COOPER *Pioneers* xxi, My face was as pale as one of your fever-and-ague visages. **1847** PARKMAN in *Knickerb.* XXX. 130 Among the emigrants there was an over-grown boy . . . with a head as round and about as large as a pumpkin, and fever-and-ague fits had dyed his face of a corresponding color.

b. (See quot.) *Obs.*

1824 SINGLETON *Letters* 106 In the fields, a kind of foxtail grass here [in Ky.] becomes timothy; and our black-and-yellow caterpillar is named fever-and-ague.

2. In special combs., now obs.: (1) **fever and ague blossom,** (see quot. 1807); (2) **root,** =?**feverroot;** (3) **seed,** (see quot. 1807).

(1) [**1807** C. SCHULTZ *Travels* I. 25 The lake [Oneida, N.Y.] was in blossom. . . . The lake is, in a great measure, bordered with swamps and low grounds, which produce innumerable swarms of small butterflies. . . . These insects cannot fly any great distance without resting, and a very light breeze off shore will prevent their regaining the land . . . in consequence of which, they soon fall with outspread wings and cover the lake so completely as fully to justify the expression of its being 'in blossom.'] **1826** FLINT *Recoll.* 316, I judge it to be vegetable matter, brought in by the Bayou, by which the lake communicates with the Mississippi, and like that singular appearance on the northern lakes, called 'fever and ague blossoms.' — **(2) 1676** GLOVER *Acc. Va.* in *Phil. Trans.* XI. 630 Here groweth a Plant about a foot and a half or two foot in height. . . . The English call it the Fever and Ague-root. — **(3) 1807** C. SCHULTZ *Travels* I. 25 [For a period of about six weeks] the water of the lake [L. Oneida, N.Y.] . . . will be found to be full of small particles, which the boatmen call *fever and ague seeds;* but, in reality, are the eggs of certain insects. **1823** COOPER *Pioneers* xii, I've drunk the Onondaga water a hundred times, while I've been watching the deer-licks, when the fever-an-agy seeds was to be seen in it as plain and as plenty as you can see the rattlesnakes on old Crumhorn.

b. Designating areas where fever and ague prevails, as (1) **fever and ague bottom,** (2) **district,** (3) **plain.**

(1) **1827** COOPER *Prairie* (1836) II. 224, I will engage to get the brats acclimated to a fever-an-agy bottom in a week. **1836** HOLLEY *Texas* iii. 45 His soil . . . presents . . . no necessity for acclimation to a 'fever and ague bottom.' — **(2) 1859** *Harper's Mag.* Sep. 574/1 Morgan County—a noted fever-and-ague district [in Indiana]. — **(3) 1856** *S. Lit. Messenger* XXII. 178/2 They . . . [were] rejoicing in their escape from the rich fever and ague plains of Illinois.

c. Also in derisive use.

1839 *N.O. Picayune* 31 Mar. 2/4 A Yankee preacher . . . has recently settled in one of the Western fever-and-ague towns. **1850** *Calif. Courier* (S.F.) 2 Oct. 2/4 Upon this mongrel, bilious, fever-and-ague ticket, there are, as I have said, nine Locofocos and three Whigs.

feverroot ˈfivɚˌrut, *n.* Any one of various plants, esp. horse gentian *q.v.*, the roots of which are regarded as efficacious in cases of fever.

1743 CLAYTON *Flora Virginica* 23 *Lonicera* . . . Feverroot & Cinque. **1790** *Amer. Philos. Soc. Trans.* III. 234, I have heard this poisonous herb, called by the names of Wild-Carrot, Wild Parsnep, Fever-Root, and Mock-Eel-Root. **1832** WILLIAMSON *Maine* I. 123 The Fever-root, or wild Ipecac, occurs in limestone soils. . . . It may be used for an emetic or cathartic. **1901** MOHR *Plant Life Ala.* 744 Triosteum perfoliatum . . . Tinker's Root. Fever Root.

F.F. A member of a First Family *q.v.* Also attrib. and transf. *Colloq.*

1818 WEEMS *Drunkard's Looking Glass* 10 With hearts full charged with F. F. Slings, they came upon the ground, and there *swelled,* and *strutted,* and *crowed.* **1850** LEWIS *La. Swamp Doctor* 178 Major Smith . . . [was] the first one of the race [of Virginians] to acknowledge that he was not an F. F. **1917** *Birds of Amer.* III. 64/2 Better yet, he [the cardinal] is an FF of America.

b. F.F.T., (see quot. 1947).

1865 *Cin. D. Gazette* 3 Aug. 1/3 An F.F.T. was charged by two dusky women as being the father of two children to whom they had recently given birth. **1947** *Sports Afield* Dec. 56/2 Bimpo was . . . member of the F.F.T., or first families of Tennessee.

c. F.F.V., abbreviation for *First Families of* (or *in*) *Virginia,* a member or descendant of such a family.

1847 *Knickerb.* XXIX. 495 The old things we could make out among the unknown writing were a set of letters that looked like a disorderly F. F. V. **1861** *N.Y. Tribune* 2 Aug. (Chipman), The famous initials F.F.V. have had their significance changed by some of our [Maryland] boys in the late campaign, in consequence of their constant alacrity in running, to Fast Footed Virginians. **1947** COFFIN *Yankee Coast* 229 Others drifted up and down the coast, some on down to Jamestown, to become F. F. V.'s; but maybe, too, some remained on the coast here, to become the F. F. M.'s [i.e., First Families of Maine] of our history.

attrib. and *transf.* **1909** O. HENRY *Options* 10 What Federal prison did Moore escape from, or what's the name of the F. F. V. family that he carries as a handicap? **1948** *Chi. Sun-Times* 20 April 21/4 The F.F.V. (Fast Flying Virginian) pulled in to the green valley below the Greenbriar and the duchess stepped down to be welcomed by her host, Mr. Young.

fiat ˈfaɪət, *a.* [f. **fiat*, *n.*] Established or made valid by government fiat or legislative enactment.

1879 *Cong. Rec.* 17 May 1438/1 You now have the 'fiat dollar' . . ; redeemable in pulp. **1879** *Harper's Mag.* Dec. 30/1 Atlanta is a 'fiat' town, and was put where she is by act of Legislature. **1885** Wells *Practical Economics* 53 Gold and silver are . . . not a *fiat* currency. **1887** *New Princeton Rev.* IV. 176 The verdict of approval, however, has usually taken a form which implies a certain fiat power in the Convention.

b. fiat money, paper currency issued by the government but not representing specie, and containing no promise of redemption by the government but made legal tender by government fiat. Also **fiat paper money.** Cf. **greenback.**

1874 Wells *Practical Economics* 17 The generations of Texans who had had this experience of 'fiat paper money' never again looked with favor upon any other currency than specie. **1885** *Ib.* 42 Neither gold or silver can be made *fiat* money as to future transactions. **1949** *Chi. Tribune* 7 Feb. 18/3 The national government, unable to check the dizzy whirl, is trying at least to slow it down with the printing of fiat money.

fiat ˈfaɪət, *v. tr.* To effect by a "fiat." *Rare.* — **1879** *Cong. Rec.* 17 May 1438/1 You can 'fiat' eighty-five cents to be worth a hundred cents.

fiatism ˈfaɪətˌɪzəm, *n.* The principle that by a fiat a government can make paper money legal tender. — **1896** *N. Amer. Rev.* Dec. 698 [The introduction of] the theory of fiatism as applied to our currency issues . . . [has resulted in] injury instead of benefit.

fiatist ˈfaɪətɪst, *n.* One who advocates fiatism. — **1896** *N. Amer. Rev.* Dec. 701 The Republican party . . . has profited by the efforts of those . . . who . . . repudiated the doctrines of the fiatist, the Populist and the Socialist. **1904** J. G. Cannon in *N.Y. Times* 23 June 2 When the first battle was fought against greenback or fiat money, whatever they were on the Atlantic Coast, they were fiatists in the West.

fiber-faced paper. (See quot.) — **1884** Knight *Dict. Mech.* (Supp.), *Fiber-faced Paper*, a means of security against the restoration of the surface of check or draft-paper after it has been tampered with. It consists in imbedding in the pulp . . . a layer of fibers, the outer ends of which are then raised in the form of a nap [etc.].

fibrillia faɪˈbrɪlɪə, *n.* [f. **fibril.*] (See quots.)

1861 *Illustr. Lond. News* 18 May 476/2 Fibrilia is a generic term given in the United States to fibres obtained from a large number of plants. *Ib.*, A paper . . . was read at a recent meeting of the French Academy when tissue made from fibrilia were shown. **1862** *Rep. Comm. Patents: Agric.* 93 A few years ago the public attention was called to a process, patented both in this country and in Europe, by Claussen, for making from unrotted flax a substance resembling cotton, and which he called 'flax-cotton,' and since, by some American manufacturers, called '*fibrillia.*'

fice, *n.* See **feist.**

* **fiddle,** *n.*

1. (See quot.) *Obs.*

1874 *Slang Dict.*, *Fiddle.* . . . In America, a swindle or an imposture.

2. fiddleneck, the young frond of a cinnamon fern. Also attrib.

1902 Parsons *According to Season* 44 *Botrychium* is not a true fern, and consequently its young frond does not curl up in conventional 'fiddle-neck' fashion, but folds over the fertile part, which is also 'doubled-up' in the bud. **1945** Damon *Sense of H.* 114 But hadn't I heard that 'fiddle-necks' are good to eat, and hadn't these things before they were boiled looked like 'fiddle-necks'? *Ib.* Nowadays even New Yorkers can have fiddle-neck greens (without the fun of gathering them), for they are being canned in Maine.

b. Either of two western plants, *Amsinckia intermedia*, or *Phacelia tanacetifolia*, so called from the shape of the flower racemes.

1911 Richter *Honey Plants* 978 Next of importance are the deciduous fruits, . . . followed by the orange, . . . filaree, burr clover, fiddle neck, tarweed and other spring flowers. **1925** Jepson *Flowering Plants Calif.* 822 P[hacelia] tanacetifolia . . . Fiddle-neck. **1947** *So. Sierran* May 4/2 There were also . . . Desert Calico, . . . Tidy-tips, Buckwheat, and Fiddle-neck.

As the last term in **bull, cornstalk, gourd, horse, Lord's, straw fiddle.**

* **fiddler,** *n.*

1. A small burrowing sand crab of the genus *Uca*, common along the Atlantic Coast. In full **fiddler crab.** Cf. **sand fiddler.**

1709 Lawson *Carolina* 162 Fiddlars are a sort of small Crabs, that lie in Holes in the Marshes. The Raccoons eat them very much. **1843** *Nat. Hist. N.Y.*, *Zoology* vi. 14 The movable finger is curved, and extends beyond the tip of the other, which is almost straight; from this results a figure somewhat resembling the bow of a violin, and has probably suggested its popular name of Fidler Crab. **1865** *Wilkes' Spirit of Times* 26 Aug. 413/1 There is an abundance of game in the neighborhood, consisting principally of swallows, who 'homeward fly,' and a species of crab called 'fiddlers.' **1948** *N.Y. Times* 23 May v. 5/6 If you want to fish from a bridge or a rowboat you may collect a can of fiddler crabs and take a bushel of sheepshead.

2. (See quots.) Also **fiddler catfish.**

1940 Wilson *Wabash* 186 Fried chicken such as can be found nowhere else, . . . fiddler catfish . . . hickory barbecue . . . roasting ears. **1947** Dalrymple *Panfish* 291 That excellent little gent, the Channel-Cat proper, *Ictalurus punctatus*, or, as many net fishermen along the Mississippi call him, the Fiddler, . . . is the Beau Brummell of the tribe.

3. In phrases: (1) *To pay the fiddler*, to suffer the consequences of one's actions; (2) *drunk as a fiddler*, extremely intoxicated.

(1) 1867 Edwards *Shelby* xv. 250 Those who dance must pay the fiddler, says an adage. **1931** *K.C. Times* 23 Oct., The world has danced for the last ten or more years. . . . Now it can't pay the fiddler. — **(2) 1848** Hammond *Remembrance of Amherst* (1946) 217 (We.), In Jenk's room tonight met Wood, 'drunk as a fiddler.' **1884** Mark Twain *H. Finn* 31 Toward daylight he crawled out again, drunk as a fiddler.

fid hook. (See quot. 1905.) — **1851** Springer *Forest Life* 108 He examines . . . the 'fid-hook' and the 'dog-hook,' the former that it does not work out, the latter that it loose not its grappling hold upon the tree. **1905** *Forestry Bureau. Bul.* No. 61, 37 Fid hook, a slender, flat hook used to keep another hook from slipping on a chain. (N[orth] W[oods] L[ake] S[tates Forest].)

fie-for-shames. Trousers. *Rare.* — **1847** *Knickerb.* XXIX. 386 Following the general practice I usually, in pulling off my 'fie-for-shames,' hung them up to the ceiling of the state-room opposite the door.

* **field,** *n.*

1. The ground or area upon which baseball is played; the outfield; the area covered by the side not at bat.

1856 *Spirit of Times* 4 Oct. 85/2 The playing on both sides was excellent, the Newark being a little better in the field, but the Columbia leading in the batting. **1880** N. Brooks *Fairport Nine* ii. 30 The Fairport Nine . . . always thought it an advantage to go first to the field. **1884** *Dly. Ardmoreite* (Ardmore, Okla.) 28 April 8/1 Smith had the guts . . . to go out on the field and put himself on the spot by playing.

b. (See quot.) *Obs.*

1857 *Spirit of Times* 28 Feb. 420/3 In playing all matches, nine players from each club shall constitute a full field.

2. (See quot. 1894.) Also short for **oil field.**

[**1872** Holmes *Poet* i. 25 Beyond the garden was 'the field,' a vast domain of four acres or thereabout, by the measurement of after years.] **1894** *D.N.* I. 330 Field, deserted farm overgrown with pine, scrub oak, and brambles. Some of these fields—the term is equivalent to plantation—are from a century to a century and a half old [New Jersey]. **1948** *Dly. Ardmoreite* (Ardmore, Okla.) 4 May 1/3 The well is in northeastern Lea county, 18 miles north and 25 miles east of the Caprock field.

3. In combs.: (1) **field agent,** one who travels around in his work for another person, institution, etc.; (2) * **bed,** (see quot. 1845), *obs.;* (3) **couch,** a pallet on the floor in front of the fire, *rare;* (4) **cured,** of corn forage, cured in the field; (5) * **day,** see as a main entry; (6) **deputy,** *local*, an assistant deputy whose duties extend over a prescribed territory; (7) **dinner,** a picnic dinner in the open; (8) **driver,** "a civil officer, whose duty it is to take up and impound swine, cattle, sheep, horses, etc., going at large in the public highways, or on common and unimproved land, and not under the charge of a keeper. New England" (B. '59), cf. **driver;** (9) **editor,** (see quot.); (10) * **fire,** = **firing 1;** (11) **goal,** (*a*) in football, a goal from the field, (*b*) in basketball, a goal scored while the ball is in play; (12) **house,** a building on or near an athletic field containing dressing rooms, etc., for the use of athletes; (13) **ice,** (see quot. 1840); (14) * **land,** land under, or suitable for, cultivation; (15) **manager,** the woods boss employed by a lumber company, *rare;* (16) **nine,** in baseball, the team that is in the field as distinguished from that at bat; (17) **notes,** see as a main entry; (18) **school,** =**old field school,** *obs.;* (19) **secretary,** (see quot. 1935); (20) ***service,** of Negro slaves, labor in the field, *obs.;* (21) **study,** a study based on data gathered over an extensive area; (22) **survey,** a survey made over a wide area; (23) **umpire,** (see quot.).

(1) 1945 MENCKEN *Supp.* I. 409 The field agents of *American Speech* report *disappearingest, actorest* [etc.]. — **(2) 1828** *Yankee* Sep. 288 As for their delightful good old fashioned wheel-barrow kisses I think they are all of a piece with red-ear kisses, field-beds and bundling. **1845** *St. Louis Reveille* 6 Feb. 2/1 One bed four feet wide, will, on occasion, flank one whole side of the house, and is called a field-bed, and large parties will range themselves on opposite sides of the house as economically as candles in a box. — **(3) 1851** *Polly Peablossom* 189 The mammy made up a field couch upon the floor in front of the fire. — **(4) 1888** *Vt. Agric. Rep.* X. 29 If the field-cured corn fodder is cut up in small pieces . . . it will slightly heat in the course of forty-eight hours. **1894** *Ib.* XIV. 40 A record of five years of field corn, raised for both grain and stover, . . . averaged a little over three tons per acre of field-cured crop.

(6) 1911 *Okla. Session Laws* 3 Legisl. 28 In counties of over ten thousand . . . population and less than thirty thousand . . . population, the sheriff may appoint one field deputy. — **(7) 1857** E. STONE *Life of Howland* xii. 282 A field dinner and Rhode Island clam bake . . . was announced to follow the services on the heights. *Ib.* 284 A company of fifty or more [e]merged from the orchard, in which they had partaken of their 'field dinner.' — **(8) 1694** *Manchester Rec.* I. 56 John Elathorp & William Allen sen[ior] weare chosen hawards or feld Drivers. **1826** CUSHING *Newburyport* 119 Field Drivers, Moses Somerby, Charles Toppan. **1944** *Amer. N. & Q.* Nov. 120/1 Some of these offices, however, have lost their active status through changing conditions—the pound keeper, field drivers (drovers), hog reeves, and possibly fence viewers are in this class. — **(9) 1923** H. M. SWETLAND *Industrial Publishing* 54 On a paper covering a wide territory there may be an assistant editor (sometimes called field editor) stationed at each important center.

(10) 1881 *10th Census Agric.: Tobacco* 173 The Yellow Pryor [tobacco] will stand on the hill longer, resisting field-fire. — **(11)** *(a)* **1902** *Chi. Record-Herald* 28 Sep. 2/3 A try for a field goal was made, but . . . the kick was easily blocked. **1947** *Redbook* Oct. 56/3 No man with a bum leg could kick a field goal from the 37-yard line with the wind against him. *(b)* **1907** REACH *Basket Ball Guide* 11 Kinney scored the most field goals, and Flint the most foul goals. **1948** *Dly. Ardmoreite* (Ardmore, Okla.) 23 Jan. 6/4 Hankins has rimmed 149 field goals and 59 free throws for 357 points through games of Jan. 17. — **(12) 1895** WILLIAMS *Princeton Stories* 189 They moaned, and stamped their heels into the frosty ground, and gazed out sadly toward the dear, frowzy head of the man who was being carried to the field-house. **1948** *Chi. Star* 1 May 6/1 Horseshoes thud softly into the stakepits over behind the Union Park fieldhouse. — **(13) 1796** MORSE *Amer. Geog.* II. 13 The field-ice is of two or three fathoms thickness. **1840** DANA *Two Years* xxxi. 384 At sundown of this day, a man at the mast-head saw large fields of floating ice, called 'field-ice,' at the southeast. **1887** SCHLEY *Greeley Relief Exped.* 44/a *(caption)*, Field Ice Near Littleton Island. — **(14) 1851** HALL *Manhattaner* 120, I have seen a million dollars worth of property . . . plantations; field lands; sugar-houses.

(15) 1904 STRATTON-PORTER *Freckles* 10, I am the field manager of a big lumber company. We have just leased two thousand acres of the Limberlost. — **(16) 1878** *De Witt's Base-Ball Guide* 77 The captain of the field nine . . . can place his men in the field as he chooses. — **(18) 1858** *Texas Almanac 1859* 120 Washington College had been removed to Lexington, and a 'Field school' was kept in the ruined old edifice. — **(19) 1909** *Advocate of Peace* June 131 The labors of the Field Secretary during the year have been put forth in increasing the membership of the Society. **1935** HORWILL 129 A *field secretary* is an officer of a society whose sphere lies in the country—in visiting branches, in general propaganda, and so on. He is thus a sort of organizing or travelling secretary, in distinction from the *desk secretary*, whose duties lie in the office.

(20) 1835 INGRAHAM *South-West* I. 82 An old crippled *gouvernante*, who, being past 'field service,' was thus promoted. **1865** *Nation* I. 291 An odium attaches to field service among the blacks. — **(21) 1930** HUNT *An Audit of Amer.* 8 (Horwill), We have as yet no method for summing up individual incomes into a family income, exc. that of direct field studies. — **(22) 1932** BREARLEY *Homicide in U.S.* 10 (Horwill), There is need of a thorough field survey to determine how accurate are the homicide reports now being made to state and federal bureaus of vital statistics. — **(23) 1910** *Spalding's Base Ball Guide* 375 The Field Umpire shall take such positions on the playing field as in his judgment are best suited for the rendering of base decisions.

b. In the names of, or with reference to, plants and animals: (1) **field corn,** any one of several varieties of Indian corn especially suitable for feeding stock or for marketing; (2) **martin,** *S.* the kingbird or bee martin; (3) **plover,** *(a)* an American sandpiper, *Bartramia longicauda*, resembling a plover, *(b)* the golden plover; (4) ***sparrow,** =**bush sparrow.**

(1) 1856 *Rep. Comm. Patents: Agric. 1855* 177 All who reside in this vicinity say that it ripens at least two weeks earlier than other field corn. **1948** *Nat. Geog. Mag.* Aug. 235/2 Nubbins of field corn featured our dinner. — **(2) 1810** WILSON *Ornithology* II. 66 [The] Tyrant Fly-catcher, or King-Bird, *Muscicapa Tyrannus*, . . . is the *Field Martin* of Maryland and some of the southern states, and the *King-bird* of Pennsylvania and several of the northern districts. **1917** *Birds of Amer.* II. 192. — **(3)** *(a)* **1844** *Nat. Hist. N.Y., Zoology* II. 247 The Grey Plover . . . is known under the various names of . . . Grass Plover, Upland Plover, and Field Plover. **1917** *Birds of Amer.* I. 247 Upland Plover, *Bartramia longicauda*. . . . Other Names.—Bartramian Sandpiper; . . . Field Plover; Highland Plover. *(b) Ib.* 257 Golden Plover, *Charadrius dominicus dominicus*. . . . Other Names.—American Golden Plover; . . . Field Plover; Greenback. — **(4) 1810** WILSON *Ornithology* II. 121 Field Sparrow, *Fringilla Pusilla*. **1948** *Green Bay* (Wis.) *Press-Gazette* 13 July 11/4 Birds that sang in the afternoon were the song, vesper and field sparrows.

c. In combs., now obs. or hist., designating those performing agricultural work in the field, as (1) **field boy,** (2) **darky,** (3) **gang,** (4) **guard,** (5) **hand,** (6) **Indian,** (7) **Negro,** (8) **overseer,** (9) **slave.**

(1) 1836 GILMAN *Recoll.* (1838) 126 One day, as a field-boy was scrubbing the entry leading to the street door, I heard his voice. — **(2) 1854** THORPE *Master's House* 139 Some indiwiduals don't suppose that field darkies can learn to open and shut a gate at de same time. — **(3) 1880** CABLE *Grandissimes* xlii. 331 The others were here and there, some in the Grandissime households or field-gangs. — **(4) 1859** *Harper's Mag.* Feb. 423/1 It was rice harvest, and Steve, the field guard, suggested . . . the advantage to my larder of a few loads of powder and lead intrusted to him.

(5) 1826 *Cong. Deb.* 25 June (1832) 3758/2*n.*, The price of labor, fields [*sic*] hands, from eighty to one hundred and twenty dollars per annum and found. **1948** *Sat. Ev. Post* 23 Oct. 66/2 The first Irish came before the Civil War to work as coachmen, field hands and serving girls — **(6) 1848** E. BRYANT *California* xxi. 268 The laboring or field Indians about the fort are fed upon the offal of slaughtered animals. — **(7) 1772** *Political Reg.* XI. 76 The field Negro [in West Indies] . . . has a house which contains himself, wife and children, and sometimes a pig, and a few fowls are raised in an adjoining crowl, or enclosure. **1781** *Va. State P.* I. 613 List of fourteen 'Field negroes' and two 'House negroes,' entered and recorded by Nicholas Eveleigh. **1870** *Nation* 10 March 148/2 The field negro, being at liberty, goes down to Charleston, and not to Beaufort and the Sea Islands. — **(8) 1862** E. KIRKE *Among Pines* 152 Drivers. [Footnote:] The negro-whippers and field overseers. — **(9) 1782** *Royal Gazette* (Charleston, S.C.) 13 July 4/1 On the most reasonable terms will be hired, a gang of about twenty-five or thirty good Field Slaves. **1839** in STOWE *Key* 91/1 Our plantation was three miles from this family mansion. There all the field-slaves lived and worked.

As the last term in **back, ball, baseball, beaver, berry, broken, bush, by, camass, cane, center, corn, cotton, cranberry, fodder, forty-acre, gas, general, gold, hickory, Indian, Indian corn, left, line, mowing, oil, old, old Indian, out, outer, placer, planting, pocket, poison, poisoned, right, sand, second, sedge, short, slip, stalk, tobacco, training, wood field.**

***field day.**

1. (See quot. 1889.)

1887 *Cent. Mag.* XXXIV. 728/2 The 'Field Day' has become an institution with the amateur societies [for photographers]. **1889** *Cent.* 2203/3 *Field-day*, . . . a day when explorations, scientific investigations, etc., as of a society, are carried on in the field. **1948** *Fargo* (N.D.) *Forum* 19 Sep. 23/2 North Dakota's four hybrid corn field trials will be sites for farm field days with dates to be announced when farmers in each area are notified.

2. In schools and colleges, a day devoted to open-air sports and athletic competitions or drill.

1888 *Pleiad* (Albion, Mich.) April, This scheme of holding but one Field Day each year for all the colleges will take less of the time of those who participate. **1918** *Dly. Maroon* (Univ. of Chi.) 7 June 3/1 Field day is now to be an annual event.

***fielder,** *n.* As the last term in **center, left, out, short fielder.**

fielder's choice. In baseball, an attempt by a fielder to put out a base-runner other than the batter, who might be retired by a play to first base. Also attrib.

1902 *Chi. Record-Herald* 1 Sep. 10/1 For Baltimore, a fielder's choice, a double and an error, gave them their first run in the eighth. **1948** *Dly. Ardmoreite* (Ardmore, Okla.) 10 May 6/1 A fielder's choice gave the Giants their ninth run. **1948** *McAlester* (Okla.) *News-*

Capital 3 July 6/3 Shreveport uncorked a four-run rally on two singles, three walks and a couple of fielder's choice plays.

field notes.

1. Notes made by a surveyor describing the lines he runs in such detail as to assist those who come later in finding them.

1786 WASHINGTON *Diaries* III. 55 Not having Hough's field Notes, and no Corner trees being noted in His Plat, I did not attempt to look for lines. [**1849** W. S. DARLING *Sketches of Canadian Life* 41 When that was put a stop to, the land speculators in York and thereabouts used to get hold of the surveyors' field-notes, I believe they call them, and choose all the best lots for which they got the deeds.] **1909** *Instructions for Survey of Mineral Lands U.S.* (Gen. Land Office) 6 Field notes and other reports must be written in a clear and legible hand. **1948** DICK *Dixie Frontier* 8 Daniel Boone in his field notes of July 9, 1776 states [etc.].

2. Notes jotted down by a naturalist in the field. Also transf.

1867 *Amer. Naturalist* I. 282 The following pages are prepared mainly from field-notes taken by the writer during his residence in the Territory [Arizona]. **1944** *Mass. Audubon Soc. Bul.* Dec. 249 The photograph of a party of observers on Mt. Greylock, used with the 'Field Notes' in the October Bulletin, should have been credited to Miss Frances Burnett of Manchester.

* **fiend,** *n.* One especially devoted or addicted to some practice or subject. *Colloq.* Cf. **dope fiend.**

"*Fiend* (a characteristic American hyperbole) has already produced a great many [new words], e.g., *movie-fiend, drug-fiend, bridge-fiend, golf-fiend, coke-fiend, kissing-fiend*" (1921 Mencken 194).

1886 *Calif. Maverick* (S.F.) 13 Feb. 1/3 To him I related the famous fiend's new invention—this 'phone that could talk in foreign languages. **1904** *Phila. Ev. Telegraph* 25 July 6 The camera fiend is after him, hot foot. **1947** *Mazama* Oct. 2/1 Due to the impracticability of heating open windowed dormitories, the fresh air fiends will hold sway topside.

* **fierce,** *a.* Outrageous. Also as adv., violently. *Slang.* — *a***1906** O. HENRY *Trimmed Lamp* 6 How can you wear a waist like that, Lou? . . . It shows fierce taste. *Ib.* 210 But it's fierce, now, how cynical I am, ain't it? **1927** *Atlantic Mo.* Mar. 338, I broke a finger on my right hand. It ached fierce.

fierro ˈfjɛro, *n. S.W.* [Sp. in Amer. Sp. sense shown here.] (See quots.) — **1844** GREGG *Commerce of Prairies* I. 186 No matter how many proprietors a horse or mule may have had, every one marks him with a huge hieroglyphic brand, which is called the *fierro*, and again, upon selling him, with his *venta*, or sale-brand. **1856** DAVIS *El Gringo* (1857) 206 Each person has his own brand, with which he marks all his mules, horses, and other animals as soon as they come into his possession. . . . This is called the *fierro*, or buying brand.

* **fiery,** *a.* In combs.: (1) **fiery azalea,** = **flame azalea;** (2) * **cross,** a large cross set up and usu. fired by Ku-Klux Klanners to intimidate persons whom they wish to drive out of a community; (3) **-crowned wren,** = **golden-crowned wren;** (4) **thorn,** the fire thorn, *Pyracantha coccinea*, a member of the rose family.

(1) *c*1792 WM. BARTRAM in W. R. Van Dersal *Ornamental Amer. Shrubs* (1942) 79 The epithet fiery, I annex to this most celebrated species of azalea, as being expressive of the appearance of its flowers. . . . This is certainly the most gay and brilliant flowering shrub yet known. — (2) **1926** *New Masses* July 7/2 Three hundred klansmen are burning a fiery cross on a hillside to the east, and are marching on the prison. **1948** *Chi. Tribune* 2 July 1/7 A 10 foot fiery cross was set ablaze in his front yard last night. — (3) **1839** PEABODY *Mass. Birds* 314 The Fiery-crowned Wren, *Regulus tricolor*, . . . rears its young in Labrador, and is seen here on its return in October, when it collects its food, consisting of the larvae and eggs of insects. **1917** *Birds of Amer.* III. 220 Fiery-crowned Wren . . . [is found] along Allegheny Mountains to western North Carolina (in spruce belt). — (4) **1858** J. A. WARDER *Hedges & Evergreens* II. 276 Fiery Thorn is an evergreen with dark foliage and bright-red berries. **1930** BAILEY *Cyclo. Horticulture* 2863/2 [Pyracantha] coccinea . . . Firethorn. Fiery Thorn. Everlasting Thorn.

fiesta fɪˈɛstə, *n.* [Sp. in same sense.] A festivity or celebration. Now used loosely to designate any party where Spanish food, decorations, or costumes are featured.

1844 GREGG *Commerce of Prairies* I. 208 These *carretas* . . . [are] the 'pleasure-carriages' of the rancheros, whose families are conveyed in them to the towns, whether to market, or the *fiestas*, or on other joyful occasions. **1882** SWEET & KNOX *Texas Siftings* 91 The Mexicans have received considerable assistance from the Americans in properly celebrating the fiestas. **1948** *Sat. Ev. Post* 31 July 16/2 Reckon you came here to see our big fiesta, huh?

* **Fife,** *n.* [See quot. 1920.] The name of a group of spring-wheat varieties. Freq. with distinguishing adjectives. In full **Fife wheat.**

1882 *Rep. Comm. Agric. 1881–2* 560 The Improved Fife commends itself to everyone who has seen and raised it. . . . It is an improvement on the old Saxon Fife. **1899** *Dept. Agric. Yrbk. 1898* 262 The principal varieties found to be the most resistant to orange leaf rust . . . are . . . the spring wheats, Haynes Blue Stem and Saskatchewan Fife. **1920** *Dept. Agric. Bul.* No. 878, 4 The original Red Fife Wheat is supposed to have come from Russia by way of Germany and Scotland. About 75 years ago a Mr. David Fife, of Otonabee, Ontario, Canada, . . . sowed the wheat [received from abroad] in the spring, but it proved to be a winter wheat. However, a plant of spring wheat developed, . . . and this was saved and increased. This wheat became widely grown in Canada and known as Red Fife.

* **fifteen,** *a.* In combs.: (1) **fifteen cent house,** (see quot.), *obs.;* (2) **gallon law,** a prohibition law passed in Massachusetts prohibiting the sale of less than fifteen gallons of whisky at a time, thus paving the way for the first "blind pigs" where liquor was sold by the drink, *obs.;* (3) **shooter,** a repeating rifle that shoots fifteen times without reloading.

(1) **1882** G. A. SALA *Amer. Revisited* I. 92 On the lower rungs of the social ladder are the so called 'fifteen cent houses,' where for sevenpence half penny you may be served with a cut from a hot joint, etc. — (2) **1839** *Boston Transcript* 11 June 2/3 The informers and spies under the Massachusetts 15 gallon law, have received the *soubriquet* of 'striped hog reeves.' **1880** *Harper's Mag.* Jan. 191/1 In April, 1838, Massachusetts had passed its famous Fifteen-gallon Law—far more stringent than that of Mississippi (1839), which forbade the selling of liquor in quantities of less than a gallon. In 1840 the Massachusetts statute was repealed. — (3) **1845** *Quincy* (Ill.) *Whig* 2 Dec. 2/4 One fifteen shooter (rifle) stood in the corner to protect the persons of the Twelve.

Fifteenth Amendment. The amendment to the Constitution, ratified in 1870, which declares that the right to vote shall not be denied to citizens of the U.S. "on account of race, color, or previous condition of servitude."

1870 GRANT in *Pres. Mess. & P.* VII. 55 The adoption of the fifteenth amendment to the Constitution . . . constitutes the most important event that has occurred since the nation came into life. **1948** *Sat. Ev. Post* 23 Oct 32/2 The Negro in the United States is making clear-cut strides toward the full citizenship and full opportunity promised so long ago in the Thirteenth, Fourteenth and Fifteenth Amendments to the Constitution. **1949** D. O. MCGOVNEY *Amer. Suffrage* 5 The defect of the Fifteenth and Twentieth Amendments is that they do not affirmatively grant to every adult citizen the right to vote regardless of sex or race.

* **fifth,** *a.* In combs.: (1) **Fifth Avenue,** one of the principal streets of New York City, frequently used as a symbol of wealth, elegance, fashion, etc., also attrib. and transf.; (2) **chain,** (see quot. 1874), *obs.;* (3) **quarter,** (see quots.), now *hist.*

(1) [**1857** *S.F. Call* 15 Mar. 1/2 Speaking of the *décolleté* style of dress in vogue in public assemblies in New York, he . . . [terms the Upper Tendom] the class of the '*fifth Avenuedity!*'] **1858** *Spirit of Times* 27 Feb. 409/3 The Fifth Avenue does not drive out or walk out on Sunday. They do not consider it to be in good taste. **1869** J. H. BROWNE *Great Metropolis* 520 A charming Fifth avenue belle is soon to be led to the altar by a prominent member of the stock board. **1946** *Coronet* Oct. 129/1 Thousands of New Yorkers . . . satisfy Fifth Avenue tastes on a five-and-ten budget. — (2) **1853** *La Crosse Democrat* 10 May 3/3 Hay Forks, Scythes, Snathes Ox Chains, Fifth and Trace Chains. **1874** KNIGHT *Dict. Mech.* I. 839/2 *Fifth chain*, the chain by which the single lead horse in a team of five is hitched to the end of the tongue. — (3) **1801** in C. CIST *Cincinnati* (1841) 188 To kill beef cattle, the butcher to receive for his share the 'fifth quarter.' **1918** E. WALLER *Illinois* 75 Fifth Quarter, the hide and tallow of a beef. It was sometimes given to an expert rifleman at a shooting match in order to appease him for being ruled out of the game. **1948** DICK *Dixie Frontier* 144 The 'fifth quarter' consisted of hide and tallow.

* **fifty,** *n.*

1. *Southampton, L.I.* A plot of land the estimated worth of which was fifty pounds. *Obs.*

1665 *Southampton Rec.* II. 237 Hee is to have . . . a fifty pound lot, and hee is to pay in all rates for a fifty. **1679** *Ib.* II. 80 In exchange Henry Pierson gives a piece of land laid out to the north sea people instead of what they should have had in the oxpasture, five 50s he bouth of Iohn Beswick. **1735** *Ib.* III. 4 Voted that David Burnet shall have his fifty of land in ye last division.

2. A fifty-dollar bill. *Colloq.*

1838 *Hennepin* (Ill.) *Jrnl.* 3 March 1/4 The counterfeits are 10's on the State Bank of Indiana; . . . and 50's on the Mechanics' Bank of New York. **1867** *Harper's Wkly.* 7 Sep. 576/3, $100.00 in Greenbacks Packed in this Brand Daily. $100 U.S. Note on Mondays; 2 Fifties on Tuesdays. **1910** *Sat. Ev. Post* 8 Oct. 16/2 Say, did that guy pass you a bad fifty?

3. In combs.: (1) **fifty-cent piece,** a half dollar; (2) **-four forty,** see as a main entry; (3) **-fifty,** equally, equally divided, *slang;* (4) **-niner,** one taking part in the Pike's Peak gold rush of 1859; (5) **spot,** a fifty-dollar bill.

(1) **1836** *Niles' Reg.* 19 Nov. 192/2 The U.S. mint is about to issue fifty cent pieces of a new and beautiful coinage. **1943** HALE *Between Dark and Daylight* 231 And you put a fifty-cent piece in a bowl of flour and try to get it out with your teeth. — (3) **1913** *Sat. Ev. Post* 1 Nov. 27/1 Cato Sells, Indian commissioner, . . . splits his cognomen fifty-fifty between a Roman emperor and the title of a circus. **1931** *K.C. Star* 31 Oct. 12 Coeds have been interviewed at various universities and without exception disapproved of any fifty-fifty business. — (4) **1870** *Colo. Gazeteer* 156 The pioneer miners and prospectors who are still in the mining district, are known as "59ers,' and are proud of the title. **1928** BREAKENRIDGE *Helldorado* xviii, The young muleskinner Billy Breakenridge was not a fifty-niner. — (5) **1868** *Ballou's Mag.* Nov. 398/1 He pulled out a fifty spot, the largest bill he had, and offered to bet that on the game.

fifty-four forty. The 54°40′ parallel of latitude proposed as a boundary between the U.S. and British possessions from the Rocky Mountains to Puget Sound. Also attrib.

[**1846** *Cong. Globe* 5 Feb. 290/1 The popularity of the President . . . depended not on his 54°40′, but upon his moderation and wisdom. *Ib.* 453/1, I know that it [such language] is nothing but—54°40′.] **1846** *Quincy* (Ill.) *Whig* 24 Mar. 3/2 How came he, the friend of Mr. Calhoun and negotiation and compromise, to be so intimate with Mr. Polk, a professed 54 40 man! **1847** *Santa Fe Republican* 23 Oct. 2/3 Mr. Polk and his cabinet will . . . require more energy to meet the emergency than they have exhibited either on the 54 40 business or in the war with Mexico.

b. One who advocated this parallel as a boundary. *Obs.*

1846 *N.Y. Tribune* 17 June 1/1 The Oregon Question Settled! The 54 40s Extinguished! **1884** BLAINE *20 Years of Congress* I. 50 The treaty . . . would have seriously interfered with the success of Mr. Polk's candidacy by destroying the prestige of the 'Fifty-four forties.'

c. *Fifty-four forty or fight,* a popular rallying cry used by the Democrats in the presidential campaign of 1844. Now *hist.*

1846 *Dollar Newspaper* (Phila.) 8 April 3/3 Definitions . . . P.P.P.P. Phifty-Phour Phorty or Phight. **1852** *Amer. Whig Review* XVI. July 3/2 Previous to the election of 1844, both Mr. Polk and the Convention which nominated him were committed . . . to the policy of '*fifty-four forty, or fight.*' **1948** *Pac. Northwest Quart.* April 101 President Polk's battle-cry of the 1844 election, 'fifty-four-forty or fight,' served its purpose well.

* **fig,** *n.* In combs.: (1) **fig bitters,** a tonic beverage made from figs, *obs.;* (2) * **eater,** *S.* a beetle, *Cotinis nitida,* that harms figs; (3) **Newton,** a trade-mark name for a cooky bar containing pressed figs; (4) **tobacco,** ?tobacco in small pieces, *obs.*

(1) *a*1881 in MARSHALL *Through Amer.* 336 Announcements that we noticed [in n. Calif. included] . . . 'Try Fig Bitters,' 'Fig Bitters for Indigestion.' — (2) **1869** *Rep. Comm. Agric. 1868* 90 In some of the southern States [these beetles] are so very destructive to ripe figs as to have acquired the local name of fig-eaters. **1889** *Cent.* 2207/2 *Fig-eater,* . . . a scarabæoid beetle, *Allorhina nitida.* (Southern U.S.) — (3) **1944** STAFFORD *Boston Adv.* 44, I had not come home at lunch time but instead had eaten an apple and a fig-Newton given to me by the Hendersons. **1948** *Time* 1 Nov. 82/2 He was so broke that for a time he lived on Fig Newtons. — (4) [**1837–40** HALIBURTON *Clockmaker* (1862) 187 How are you off for tobacco? said Mr. Slick. Grand, said he, got half a fig left yet.] **1837** HAWTHORNE *Twice-told Tales* (1879) I. 118 The pedler . . . sold him many a bunch of long nines, and a great deal of pigtail, lady's twist, and fig tobacco.

b. *fig and gum drops,* ?a kind of confection. *Obs.*

1865 SALA *Diary* I. 104 Intelligent youths passed to and fro in the cars offering for sale 'fig and gum drops.' *Ib.* 214 The boys who sell 'fig and gum drops' in the cars, the infernal hotel gong, the hardness of the times, . . . anything, in fine, you please to mention—anything but this.

As the last term in **devil's, Indian, tangle fig.**

* **fight,** *n.* As the last term in **booze, bush, chicken, courthouse, dog, finish, free, gun, piny woods, rock, spelling fight.**

* **fight,** *v.*

1. *To fight fire,* to endeavor to put out a fire.

[**1824** OWEN *Diary* 83 Then they fight it [fire], as it is termed, endeavoring to overcome it by striking it with clapboards, which are about 2 or 2½ feet long and are used to cover log houses.] **1835** ABBOTT *New England* 21 For days and nights together, all the physical force of the village has been arrayed in 'fighting the fire.' **1944** *Paul Bunyan's Quiz* [Quest.] 96 How many men are needed each year to fight fires? Over 61,000 men are constantly ready to respond to the call of forest rangers and forest wardens in state, county, private, and federal organizations.

2. To strive with (an animal) for mastery. *Slang.*

1908 MULFORD *Orphan* I. 13 He mounted and fought the animal for a few minutes, just as he always had to fight it. **1920** HUNTER *Trail Drivers Texas* 231, I 'fought' cattle for nine years almost night and day.

3. In phrases: (1) *To fight it out on this line,* "a famous phrase used by General Grant . . . in his dispatch to Secretary Seward, after the battle of Spottsylvania, May 11, 1864" (Th.), also transf.; (2) *to fight the stranger,* to drink deep and often, *slang, obs.* See also *to fight the tiger, s.v.* * **tiger.**

(1) **1864** *Cong. Globe* 2 June 2672/2 (Th.), According to the modest but electric words of General Grant, he is to 'fight it out on this line if it takes all summer.' **1880** *Dly. Inter-Ocean* (Chi.) 3 June 1/7 The friends of General Grant have become inspired with the spirit of their candidate, and they propose 'to fight it out on this line if it takes all summer.' **1910** *N.Y. Ev. Post* 9 May (Th.), Arguing in favor of leaving the proposed income tax amendment as it stands and fighting it out on that line, the Springfield *Republican* says [etc.]. — (2) *c*1845 *Big Bear Ark.* 121 They'd been fightin' the stranger mightily comin' up, and war perfectly wolfish arter some har of the dog.

* **fighter,** *n.* As the last term in **booze, bush, chicken, free, gun, horse, Indian, squaw fighter.**

* **fighting,** *n.* and *a.* In combs.: (1) **fighting chance,** a possible chance, *colloq.;* (2) **clip,** a style of haircut preferred by pugilists, also ellipt. for *fighting clip style;* (3) **Quaker,** (see quots.).

(1) **1894** *Cong. Rec.* 1 Feb. 1786 [The manufacturer] can not be beaten out of hand. He will have a fighting chance. **1894** *Outing* XXIV. 295/1 The captain decided to . . . land the sailor so as to give him a fighting chance for his life in the hospital — (2) **1881** HOWELL *Doctor Breen's Practice* 49 'Do you admire such a *very* fighting-clip as Mr. Libby has on?' asked Mrs. Scott. 'It must be nice for summer.' *Ib.*, I wish *I* could go in the fighting-clip. One doesn't know what to do with one's hair at the sea-side; it's always in the way. — (3) **1788** SCHÖPF *Reise* I. 89 Ihre Anzahl ist nicht gross; und man unterscheidet sie durch den Zunamen der fechtenden Quäker, (fighting Quakers). **1803** *Monthly Mag.* XVI. 123 They are a very peaceable quiet people, although numbers of them are of that class called *fighting Quakers,* because they do not object to take up arms. **1868** ROSE *Great Country* 107 One Quakers' meeting-house is remarkable as having been built by those anomalous individuals, 'The Fighting Quakers,' who figured in the War of Independence. **1904** *Old Dartmouth Hist. Sketches* VIII. 18/1.

As the last term in **bush, fire, gun, rooster fighting.**

fightingest 'faitiŋist, *a.* Most given to fighting. *Colloq.* — **1871** STOWE *Sam Lawson* 209 There was old Dick, Ike's bell-wether, was the fightin'est old crittur that ever yer see. **1878** BEADLE *Western Wilds* 183 When it come to 'lectin a constable, I reckon the fightinest man stood in with the boys.

* **figure,** *n.*

1. figure 4 (or **four**), a trap set with triggers which, when in place, resemble the figure 4; the triggers used with this. Also attrib.

1785 THOMAS B. HAZARD *Nailer Tom's Diary* (1930) 76/2, I made and Sott a trap with a figger 4 for quails. **1843** OLIVER *Eight Months* 82 Prairie hens (pinnated grouse) and quails come about the fences in hundreds, and with a very primitive trap, made of split sticks, with a figure 4 trigger, we caught numbers of both within view of the door of the house. **1861** *Ill. Agric. Soc. Trans.* V. 734 [White-breasted nuthatches] are especially fond of pumpkin seeds. Boys take the advantage of this to capture them by means of a 'figure four' trap baited with these seeds. **1943** *This Week Mag.* 31 July 2/3 We were masters of the art of trapping rabbits in cracker boxes half-opened by a figure 4.

Also **figure of four, figure-y 4, figgery four.**

1831 AUDUBON *Ornith. Biog.* I. 216 Many of them [Ruffed grouse] are taken alive in trap boxes during winter, although the more common method of catching or rather destroying them is by setting dead falls with a figure-of-four trigger. **1837** *N.Y. Mirror* 18 Nov. 165/1 The poor quail has to contend with . . . the figure-y 4 box-traps of vagabond hen-roost pilferers. **1872** Holmes *Poet* i. 8 Rabbits are entrapped in 'figgery fours.'

transf. **1837** Neal *Charcoal Sk.* (1838) 12, I often have the most beautiful notions . . . but they're all lost for the want of a trap; an intellectual figgery four. *c***1853** Lowell *Poetical Works* (1896) 159/2 So bait your moral figure-of-fours to catch the Orson public.

2. big figure, (see quot.).

1864 W. B. Dick *Amer. Hoyle* (1866) 202 Explanation of the Lay-Out.—The King, Queen, and Jack are called 'the Big Figure'—the ace, deuce, and trois, 'the Little Figure.'

b. *To go the big figure,* and variants, to make quite a display, to "cut a dash." *Colloq.* or *slang.*

1831 *Boston Transcript* 28 Oct. 2/2 The opponents of the existing militia system, who are not enlisted in the corps of *exempts*, are 'going it' at New York 'on the big figure.' **1836** Crockett *Exploits* 52 When a man sets about going the big figure, halfway measures won't answer no how. **1848** *Glance at N.Y.* 16 A foo-foo, or an outsider, is a chap that can't come the big figure. . . . The big figure here, is three cents for a glass of grog and a nights' lodging.

One form of figure-four trap

3. In other colloq. phrases: (1) *To miss a figure,* (see quots.); (2) *to go the whole figure,* to do a thing thoroughly.

(1) 1819 in Barnes *Memoir of T. Weed* (1884) 12 (We.), But they have missed a figure. **1839** Marryat *Diary in A.* II. 235 When a person had made a mistake, or is out in his calculation, they say, 'You missed a figure that time.' **1877** Bartlett 396 *To miss a Figure* is to commit a vital error. — **(2) 1834** *Sun* (N.Y.) 25 Mar. 2/3 (*heading*), Going the whole figure. **1839** *Havana* (N.Y.) *Republican* 21 Aug. (Th.), I was determined to go the hull figure, and see all. **1914** James *Ivory Tower* 309 The . . . momentous season, or scene, . . . in which she goes the whole 'figure.'

As the last term in **seven, six figure.**

***figure,** *v.*

1. *To figure on, upon,* to think about, consider, count on. *Colloq.*

1837 *Cong. Globe* App. 247/1, I . . . cannot understand the Secretary's report. I figured upon its data until I threw down my slate in despair. **1877** Bartlett 215 'Figure on that' means to consider it; to think it over. Western. **1933** T. Williamson *Woods Colt* 4 Well, that laid me up, an' I *figgered* on stayin' mighty close to the shanty till the corn got ripe.

2. *To figure out,* to ascertain or find out as if by a calculation. *Colloq.*

1834 C. A. Davis *Lett. J. Downing* 41 As I said before, I'm stump'd about that Bank of U.S., and I want you to help me figure it out. **1923** Vance *Baroque* 173 She figures it out . . . you'll put up one terrible holler. **1946** *Democrat* 8 Aug. 2/2 Kenneth stood there trying to figure it all out.

3. *To figure for,* to lay plans for. *Colloq.*

*a***1889** *Burlington Free Press* (F.), The next evening we came to a drove of small pigs and began to figure for one.

fike, see **fyke.**

filaree ˌfɪlə'ri, *n.* =**alfilaria.**

1889 Vasey *Agric. Grasses* 102 *Erodium cicutarium* (*alfilaria*) . . . is known as storksbill, pin clover, pin grass, and filaree. It is neither a grass nor a clover, but belongs to the geranium family. **1914** Brininstool *Trail Dust* 141 They'll liven up and no mistake, When they hev browsed on filaree! **1946** Linsdale *Calif. Ground Squirrel* 457 Among the plants observed to be prominent as squirrel food on the Reservation are oats, acorns, windmill pink, filaree, and poor man's weather glass.

***file,** *n.*[1] As the last term in **featheredge, Indian, nail file.**

file faɪl, *n.*[2] *local.* [Du. dial. and LG. *feil,* in sense shown here.] (See quots.) Also attrib.

1850 S. Warner *Wide, Wide World* xlvi, 'You never touch your fingers to a file nowadays,—do you?' 'A file!' . . . 'Margery calls it a dishcloth, or a floorcloth, or something else.' **1859** Bartlett 147 *File,* cloth used for wiping a floor after scrubbing. *Ib., File-Pail,* or *Filing-Pail,* a wash-pail. **1889** *Cent.* 2212/3 *File* . . . [is called] also *file-cloth.*

filé fi'le, *n.* (See quots. and cf. **gumbo filé.**)

1806 Pike *Sources Miss.* (1810) 61 My men had an excellent room furnished them, and were presented with potatoes and fille. **1885** *La Cuisine Creole* 18 Take the large bones from the pot, and add okra or a preparation of dried and pounded sassafras leaves, called filee. **1931** Read *La.-French* 122 This powder [of sassafras leaves] goes by the name of *filé,* the past participle of French *filer,* 'to twist.' **1946** Tallant *Voodoo in N.O.* 101 One of her favorite *gris-gris* to break up such an affair was a mixture of gunpowder, mud from a wasp nest, flaxseed, cayenne pepper, BB shots, filé, bluestone and dragon's blood.

***file,** *v.*[1] *intr.* To make or submit an application or claim for possession of a particular area or tract of public land. Usu. *to file on, upon.*

1871 *Scribner's Mo.* II. 254 The half-breed who had 'filed on' the claim alongside Lindsley's. **1879** *Ib.* XIX. 132/1 There are liberal intervals [of Kansas prairie] not yet 'filed upon' or 'opened up.' **1911** J. F. Wilson *Land Claimers* 2 The relinquishment has been made in Portland where you filed. **1948** *Popular Western* June 12/1 Henchley has filed on a section of land which adjoined Grant's Box G up the river.

b. To make application for (a mining claim). Cf. ***filer.**

1948 *Sat. Ev. Post* 4 Dec. 70/2 He had made a lot of test borings and had assays made and was on the way to file his claim, but I got him drunk and filed myself.

file faɪl, *v.*[2] *local.* [f. **file,** *n.*[2]] *tr.* (See quot. 1896.)

1750 S. Warner *Wide, Wide World* XVI, I've seen you file off tables down yonder a few times, ha'n't I? **1896** *D.N.* I. 417 *File,* . . . to scrub with a file (hand-mop). . . . Albany Co., St. Lawrence Co., N.Y., Tannersville, Pa.

b. Also **filing pail,** "a wash-pail" (B. '59). *Obs.*

file-closer. A military officer stationed in the rear of a file, or in the flank of a column to keep the file in order.

1836 Hildreth *Campaigns Rocky Mts.* I. 48 The adjutant . . . 'told off' the batallion by equal troops, the subalterns taking their stations in the rank of file-closers. **1861** *Army Regulations* 55 The reviewing officer . . . passes along the front of the battalion, and proceeds round the left flank, and along the rear of the file-closers, to the right. **1888** Sheridan *Memoirs* I. 12 In giving me the order he was prompted by the duty of his position as a file closer.

***filer,** *n.* One who files a mining claim. — **1869** *New No. West* (Deer Lodge, Mont.) 15 Oct. 2/3 [I] am well acquainted with the party who struck the camp, and also with all of the '. . . hog-ers' and 'filers' from Lemki; (as the Boise men call us).

filibuster 'fɪləˌbʌstə, *n.* [Sp. *filibustero,* in sense similar to that in **1.** shown here. An Amer. borrowing.]

1. One of the American or Texan citizens who engaged in fomenting insurrection in certain Latin American areas.

The filibusters who joined Narcisso Lopez against Cuba in 1850–51, and those who were led by William Walker against Sonora, Mexico, in 1853–54, and against Nicaragua in 1855–58, were the best-known organized groups.

1851 *Boston Advertiser* 27 Aug. 2/1 'The Flibustiers' rejects 'Fillibustiers.' **1857** *Lawrence* (Kans.) *Republican* 4 June 2 Walker, the fillibuster, has been forced to capitulate. **1912** R. H. Davis in *Scribner's Mag.* Aug. 140/2 No longer was David of a mind to sue the filibusters if they did not put him ashore. **1948** *Time* 15 Nov. 38/3 Since the days of famed Filibusterer [*sic*] William Walker, who tried to take over Nicaragua in the 1850s, the dry season has been the shooting season.

attrib. **1853** Baldwin *Flush Times Ala.* 84 There were no Mexican wars and filibuster expeditions in those days. **1858** Vielé *Following Drum* 108 [Brownsville's] population has not . . . increased, owing to the unsettled state of the frontier, from the Indians and filibuster warfare. *Ib.* 172 General Harney . . . hearing rumors of numerous filibuster and Indian troubles, had come down. **1889** Bancroft *Hist. Ariz. & N. Mex.* 502 In 1856–7 Henry A. Crabb of California had attempted a filibuster conquest of Sonora under the guise of colonization. **1948** *Chi. Tribune* 10 Oct. (Grafic Mag.) 17/3 At best, Burr intended to lead a filibuster expedition into Mexico in order to drive out the Spaniards and make himself ruler of the country.

b. *transf.* Applied to other persons whose tactics were similar to those of the American filibusters.

1857 Henningsen in *Knowledge* (1887) 113/2 (Th.), What were the Normans . . . but filibusters? What the Pilgrim Fathers but filibusters? **1863–5** Browne *A. Ward His Travels* 124 The savages owned the country, and Columbus was a fillibuster. **1867** L. M. Child *Rom. Republic* xxi. 358 That unprincipled filibuster called William the Conqueror.

2. A vessel engaged in filibustering. Also attrib.

1855 *Wkly. Oregonian* 15 Sep. (Th.), Judge Gayle had decided that the filibuster bark 'Magnolia,' as well as the arms on board, were not forfeited to the U.S. **1896** *Boston Journal* 29 Dec. 2/2 The report [was] cabled from New York that the filibuster Three Friends had been fired upon by a Spanish cruiser. **1912** R. H. Davis in *Scribner's Mag.* Aug. 140/1 *'The Three Friends!'* shrieked David. 'She's a filibuster! She's a pirate!'

3. A member of a minority in a legislative body who employs dilatory tactics and stratagems to impede action by the majority. Also attrib.

1853 *Oregonian* (Portland) 5 Feb. 2/4 Filibustero principles do not appear to meet with much consideration from the southern members of congress. **1889** *Boston Journal* 14 Jan. 2/2 The surrender of legislative functions by the majority of the House and the carrying on of business . . . only by a humiliating 'treaty' with a single determined filibuster is something entirely anomalous in a country . . . governed by majority action. **1915** *N.Y. Times* 31 Jan. III. 2/3 The Senate sits . . . and the overwearied filibusters simply cannot talk.

4. An instance of obstructing legislation by dilatory parliamentary tactics, such as speaking merely to consume time.

1890 *Cong. Rec.* 11 Feb. 1217/2 A filibuster was indulged in which lasted . . . for nine continuous calendar days. **1948** *Chi. D. News* 9 Feb. 14/3 The price is a filibuster. It might prove the filibuster to end filibusters.

filibuster ˈfɪləˌbʌstɚ, *v. intr.* and *tr.* To engage in a legislative filibuster; to prevent the passage of (a bill) by a filibuster.

1853 *Cong. Globe* 4 Jan. 194/1, I saw my friend . . . filibustering, as I thought, against the United States. **1915** *N.Y. Times* 16 Feb. 11/2 The Republicans will filibuster . . . against the cloture rule. **1945** *Nation* CLX. 28 April (Back Cover), 'Southern senators already are preparing to filibuster to death the bill that would make permanent the Fair Employment Practice Committee.' **1947** *Chi. Times* 22 July 18/1 You're filibustering against the wrong bill, Senator—the resolution before the Senate is for adjournment.

b. To get possession of or obtain (land) by the methods of a freebooter. *Obs.*

1857 in *Knowledge* (1887) 113/2 (Th.), What State, what territory in this Union has not been filibustered from the Indians, or purchased from those who had filibustered it?

c. To succeed in forcing by the methods of filibusters. *Rare.*

1862 Taylor *At Home & Abroad* 2 Ser. ii. 67 When the inmates of a prison have enjoyed a satisfactory period of rest and seclusion, they join in companies, and filibuster their way out.

filibustering ˈfɪləˌbʌstərɪŋ, *n.*

1. The practice of engaging in expeditions against parts of Latin America. *Obs.*

1853 Longfellow in S. Longfellow *H. W. Longfellow* II. 247 Intelligent youths, but rather inclined to filibustering in Cuba. **1886** Z. F. Smith *Kentucky* 430 The love of adventure and conquest . . . is not all gone yet; but in these modern days, we entitle it 'filibustering.' *transf.* **1919** C. G. Raht *Romance of Davis Mts.* 172 Filibustering or an avoidance of customs duty. **1948** *Time* 15 Nov. 39/1 The stability-loving U.S. State Department wants no filibustering [i.e., revolts] in the Caribbean.

b. filibustering expedition, (see quot. 1888).

1853 *Harper's Mag.* Jan. 269 Every Filibustering expedition from Mississippi or New Orleans is a justification of an abolition rescue at Boston or Syracuse. **1888** Lane *Pol. Catch-Words* 4 Oct. 16 Such expeditions [as that of the followers of Lopez to Cuba] became known as filibustering expeditions, and were considered as merely harrassing and annoying rather than revolutionary. **1891** *Scribner's Mag.* X. 84 Aside from the early filibustering expeditions, Mexico has no ground of complaint.

2. The using of dilatory tactics to prevent legislative action. Also attrib. or as adj.

1858 *Cong. Globe* 21 May 2293/2 Gentlemen on the other side of the House consumed the day by filibustering. **1886** Alton *Among Law-Makers* 166 These dilatory tactics are known in the technical language (or rather 'slang') of parliamentary procedure as 'filibustering.' **1949** *Chi. D. News* 12 March 8/1 Cain's filibustering tactics are motivated by a personal antipathy.

filibusterism ˌfɪləˈbʌstəˌrɪzəm, *n.* The practice of filibustering. — **1852** *Lantern* (N.Y.) I. 161/2 We have had nothing superior to the above *programme* of *Fillabusterism!* **1892** *Nation* 22 Dec. 467/2 [When] Democratic policy was identified with slavery and involved the constant threat of . . . filibusterism, . . . it distinctly repelled and alarmed South American sentiment.

* **fill,** *n.*

1. An embankment or filled-in portion of a railway roadbed across a ravine or low ground.

1850 *Cong. Globe* App. 4 April 531/1 It was like . . . making deep cuts and large fills with a view to construct a railroad. **1909** *Outing* LIV. 6/2 The amount of his excavation should very nearly balance the amount of embankment 'fill.' **1948** *Calif. Highways* March–April 12/1 A blanket of river bed sand and gravel is being laid as a base for the fills.

2. The act of filling one's hand in poker. Cf. * **fill,** *v.* **3.**

1866 *Wilkes' Spirit of Times* 10 March 28/3 In a game of draw-poker on the draw or fill, a party, on betting his hand, discovers that he has only four cards, and claims the right to contend with this number of cards for the pot. **1887** *N.Y. Clipper Annual* 43/2 The frequent, speculative, fateful 'draw,' The 'fill,' or not—too often not; the 'age.'

Fill or filling on a railroad

* **fill,** *v.*

1. *tr.* Of dentists: To treat (teeth) by putting in fillings. Cf. * **filling,** *n.* **2.**

1848 *Literary Amer.* 29 July 64/2 Teeth filled with gold (if preferred), extracted and cleaned. **1923** *Sunset* Mar. 6/1 You get these two hollow teeth filled. **1945** Baker *Party Line* 92 Dick not only filled and pulled teeth, but he went modern and practiced orthodontia.

2. To comply with (an order) by supplying the goods requested.

1860 *Richmond Enquirer* 2 Nov. 1/7 The Executive of the State is making the most strenuous efforts to fill the orders for arms that come to him from all parts of the State. **1932** Grayson *Leaders* 362 By 1888, in spite of much popular prejudice which had to be overcome the Westinghouse Electric Company was booking more orders for the new type of equipment than it could conveniently fill.

b. To prepare or compound (a prescription).

1891 Tuckley *Under the Queen* 25 The individual who fills their prescriptions. **1923** *Ohio State U. Bul. College of Pharmacy* XXVII. No. 27, 10 The College of Pharmacy maintains a dispensary where prescriptions of the University physician are filled at a nominal cost.

3. (See quot. 1909.)

1903 *Out West* Feb. 726 Give me the top one. If I do fill, look out for yourselves. **1909** *Cent. Supp.* 472/3 fill. . . . In poker, to draw cards which improve the hand: usually restricted to filling four-card flushes or straights. **1928** *Amer. Mercury* Oct. 136/2 I'd made maybe a straight flush, [h]a[ve] filled somehow anyway, and cleaned him.

4. In phrases: (1) *To fill the bill,* to come up to requirements or expectations (see also quot. 1891), *colloq.;* (2) * *to fill up,* to cram (a person) with erroneous information, *colloq.;* (3) *to fill out* (blanks, orders, etc.), to write the required information on (blanks, etc.); (4) *to fill an engagement,* to keep an appointment, usu. one of a public nature.

(1) **1860** *Ill. Agric. Soc. Trans.* IV. 471 Shaker's Seedling [strawberry] Dr. W. hopes well from because of its great vigor, but doubts if it fills the bill. **1891** Farmer *Slang Dict., Fill the bill,* to excel in conspicuousness: as a star actor whose name is 'billed' to the exclusion of the rest of the company. **1943** Menefee *Assignment* 252 Partisans in Congress will be primarily responsible if this policy fails to fill the bill. — (2) **1880** Mark Twain *Tramp Abroad* xxv. 256 It is a plain case: they simply took your measure, and concluded to fill you up. **1903** *N.Y. Ev. Post* 23 Sep. 6 Filling up Mr. Jerome with tales about dissatisfaction in the Citizens' Union. — (3) **1903** W. E.

CURTIS *True Abraham Lincoln* 59 Mr. Lanman forwarded to him a blank to be filled out with facts and dates. **1944** *Sears Cat.* (ed. 189) 578c If you are a farmer and need any of those farm supplies for the operation of your farm, it is important that you fill out one of the certificates below, sign it and attach it to your order. — (4) [**1870** O. LOGAN *Before Footlights* 205 Therefore, when it was urged that I had better relinquish all idea of filling my nights in Nashville, I received the proposition with coldness and disdain.] **1926** COLVIN *Prohibition in U.S.* 171 During the campaign he filled one hundred and twenty-five speaking engagements.

b. *To fill the bases, sacks,* in baseball, to cause all the bases to be occupied by base-runners.

1902 *Chi. Record-Herald* 3 Sep. 8/2 Frazer filled the sacks by giving Menefee a base on balls. **1904** *St. Louis Globe-Democrat* 4 July 12/3 Twice during the game the Browns had the bases filled but each time the hit which would have counted tallies failed to come.

filled cheese. A food product made from whole or skimmed milk and various added fatty materials. Also attrib.

1896 *Cong. Rec.* 10 April 3847/2 The so-called . . . 'filled-cheese' bill . . . is of the greatest importance. *Ib.* 23 May 5605/1 Filled cheese is made by manufacturing establishments who take the milk and skim off all . . . [the] cream . . . and then . . . insert lard, cooked more or less, and various forms of oil to take the place of the natural cream. *Ib.* 5605/2 We heard the manufacturers . . . of the filled-cheese interest.

fillee fɪˈli, *n.* [F. *filet,* in Can. F. sense shown here.] A drink of whisky, orig. and usu. a ration of liquor allowed voyageurs. Now *hist.*

1851 HOWE *Hist. Coll. Great West* 256 The steersman's horn called them to their morning 'fillee' and their toil. **1852** BENNETT *Mike Fink* 28/2 Shall we go below and take an extra fillee, and a game o' cards? **1941** BALDWIN *Keelboat Age* 87 A drink of whiskey, or a 'fillee,' as it was called, was the reward of the crew after each arduous struggle with the current.

* **filling,** *n.*

1. = **fill,** *n.* **1.**

1861 *Charleston* (S.C.) *Mercury* 2 Feb. 2/2 The filling at 'Hampton's' and 'Beaver Dam' has been continued, and at the latter is very nearly finished. **1874** KNIGHT 844/1 *Filling,* an embankment of stone, gravel, earth, etc., to make a raised bed for a road, railroad track, or canal. An artificial, elevated way.

2. The material used in filling a cavity in a tooth. Cf. * **fill,** *v.* **3.**

1848 *Literary Amer.* 29 July 64/2 Indestructible Filling for the Teeth. **1925** *Jrnl. Amer. Dental Association* June 702/2 We do not favor the so-called 'prophylactic cement fillings.'

3. filling station, a station where gasoline and oil are retailed.

1921 *Outing* May 66/2 He should not attempt the trip without a small reserve can of gasoline and one of oil, enough to carry him to a filling station in case of leakage. **1948** *Life* 5 April 117/2 A disappointed few will be taken aside and quietly advised to forget the whole thing and get a job in a filling station.

fillipeener(er), see **philopena.**

Fillmoreite ˈfɪlmorˌaɪt, *n.* A political supporter of Millard Fillmore (1800–1874). Also **Fillmourner,** in jocular allusion to Fillmore's defeat for the presidency by James Buchanan in 1856. *Obs.* — **1856** *Dollar Times* (Cin.) 18 Sep. 2/8 Some Old Liners here, but few Fremont men, Fillmoreites plenty, and more sassy. **1856** *Louisville Courier* 8 Nov. 3/2 The Fillmourners pull at the cord like a colt with the first halter.

* **fin,** *n.* As the last term in **ballast, black, blue, bow, red, silver, yellow fin.**

* **fin,** *v.* **1.** *tr.* Of fish: To traverse (water or a way) by means of fins, also *to fin it.* **2.** To wound with fins.

(1) **1807** BARLOW *Columbiad* VIII. 285 Renascent swarms by nature's care supplied, Repeople still the shoals and fin the fruitful tide. *a***1861** WINTHROP *Canoe & Saddle* 134 In midsummer salmon fin it along the reaches of Whulge. **1894** *Outing* XXIV. 140/1 For this [stump] the rascal [trout] steers, as fast as he can fin his way. — (2) **1889** *Columbus* (O.) *Dispatch* 15 Feb., He had never been bitten by a dog, but . . . had been finned by fish.

* **final,** *a.* and *n.*

1. An interest-bearing certificate issued by the Continental Congress in 1780 to redeem continental money at its depreciated value. Also **Final Settlements,** the certificates so issued. *Obs.*

1788 *Md. Journal* 26 Feb. (Th.), Wanted at said office, Finals, Depreciation Certificates, and every other kind of Paper retaining any kind of value. *Ib.* 27 May (Th.), Finals given for Loan Office certificates, at a moderate allowance. **1794** *Statutes at L.* I. 353 All claims for the renewal of certificates of the unsubscribed debt of the United States, of the descriptions commonly called 'Loan Office Certificates,' or 'Final Settlements,' which may have been accidentally destroyed, shall be forever barred [etc.].

2. final proof, the final step in "proving up" a claim for a tract of government land.

1884 *Milnor* (Dak.) *Teller* 5 Sep., A. Wells, the . . . land and loan agent of Forman, . . . makes final proofs and attends to all business of that kind.

Finality Men. (See quot.) — **1914** *Cyclo. Amer. Govt.* I. 732 Finality Men. A name applied by the Free-Soilers, 1850–1854, to those who attempted to hush the slavery agitation and who considered that the Compromise of 1850 . . . had forever settled the slavery controversy.

finback calf. *Pacific Coast.* The sharp-headed finner, *Balaenoptera davidsoni.* — **1889** *Cent.* 2219/2 *Finback-calf* . . . [is] a whaler's name . . . [on the] Pacific coast, U.S.

* **finch,** *n.* As the last term in **Arkansas, canyon, ferruginous, fox-colored, house, Gambel, gold, grass, indigo, lark, lazuli, Lincoln's, Nelson's (sharp-tailed), Oregon snow, painted, pine, prairie, purple, rose-breasted, savanna, seaside, sharp tail, sharp-tailed, Southern pine, summer, swamp, Tom's finch.**

finch creeper. The parula warbler, *Compsothlypis americana.* — *c***1730** CATESBY *Carolina* I. 64 *Parus Fringillaris.* The Finch-Creeper. . . . These birds . . . feed on insects, which they gather from the crevices of the bark. They remain the winter in Carolina. **1917** *Birds of Amer.* III. 122 Parula Warbler, *Compsothlypis americana americana.* . . . Other Names.—Blue yellow-backed Warbler; . . . Finch Creeper; Southern Parula Warbler.

* **find,** *n.* A person whose genius, talents, abilities, etc., go unrecognized until someone discovers them. *Colloq.* — **1890** *Sporting Life* (Phila.) 8 Jan. 7/1 As to Secretary Rogers' two 'finds,' Day and Anderson, little can be said in their favor. **1914** GRAU *Theatre of Science* 139 Miss Snow, however, must be set down as a Thanhouser 'find.'

* **finder,** *n.* (See quot.) *Obs.* Cf. **money, path, water finder.** — **1839** MARRYAT *Diary in A.* II. 129 This occasioned a new class of people to spring up in this speculative country [near the Wisconsin R.], namely, *finders,* who would search all over the country for what they called a good *prospect,* that is, every appearance on the surface of a good vein of metal.

* **findings,** *n. pl.* Supplies, trimmings, tools, etc., used by shoemakers, dressmakers, etc. (see quot. 1847). Also attrib. Cf. **shoe findings.**

1833 *Boston Directory* 13 (*advt.*), Findings and trimmings, . . . lasts, boot trees, . . . shoe horns, [etc.]. **1847** WORCESTER 453/1 *Findings,* . . . the tools together with thread and wax, which a journeyman shoemaker is to furnish in his employment. **1862** ASHCROFT *Railway Directory* 22 (*advt.*), Railroad and car findings. **1896** *Godey's Mag.* Feb. 222/2 The cost of findings for a waist, . . . silk, . . . binding [etc.], . . . $2.09.

attrib. in *sing.* **1885** *Harper's Mag.* Jan. 280/1 The houses which sell these different component parts of a shoe are known as leather, stock, or finding dealers.

finding store. (See quot. 1858.) — **1827** *Boston Directory* (*advt.*), General Finding Store for boot and shoe makers . . . keeps all kinds of tools and other articles used by shoe makers. **1858** SIMMONDS *Dict. Trade Products, Finding-stores,* an American name for what are termed in England grindery-warehouses; shops where shoemakers' tools, etc. are vended.

* **fine,** *a.*

1. (See quots.)

The quots. in this sense are from British travelers in this country.

1819 FAUX *Memorable Days* 30 Fine man,—smart man or woman, seems the highest praise amongst the commonalty. **1837** H. MARTINEAU *Society* III. 83 When they [the Americans] speak of a fine woman, they refer to mental or moral, not at all to physical superiority. The effect was strange, after being told, here and there, that I was about to see a very fine woman, to meet in such cases almost the only plain women I saw in the country. **1863** C. C. HOPLEY *Life in South* II. 196 'Such a very fine man,' my friends informed me; 'fine' being a quality referring only to mental not personal perfections, and used in the same signification as 'estimable' in England.

2. Denoting a certain grade of cotton or flour.

1792 BRISSOT *Reise* 76 Es waren drei Gänge darin [the mill]. Auf dem einen ward das Mehl zum Handel (*fine flower* [*sic*]) gemahlen. **1847** *Semi-Wkly. News* (Fredericksburg, Va.) 23 Sep. 3/1 Cotton.—Bowed Georgia, ordinary to fine, 6 1–8@8d.

3. In combs., sometimes with adverbial force: (1) **fine-appearing,** good-looking, *colloq.;* (2) **blooded,** of excellent stock; (3) **chance,** see * **chance;** (4) * **cut,** tobacco cut into fine shreds, in full **fine-cut chewing tobacco;** (5) * **gold,** placer gold occurring in minute particles as contrasted with coarse gold *q.v.;* (6) * **haired,** overcultivated, too refined, *colloq.;* (7) **-scaled sucker,** the common sucker; (8) **-tooth(ed) comb,** a comb having slender teeth set close together, also in fig. and allusive contexts; (9) **top,** redtop, a valuable pasture grass, *Agrostis stolonifera major,* common in the eastern states.

(1) **1879** HOWELLS *Lady of Aroostook* xviii. 215 'She is very fine-appearing,' said Lydia. Staniford smiled at the countrified phrase. **1887** *Harper's Mag.* May 990/2 A fine-appearing gentleman came in. — (2) **1927** SIRINGO *Riata* 92 Mr. Beals presented me with a fine-blooded colt, which I afterwards sold for two hundred dollars. — (4) **1837** *Knickerb.* IX. 268 He ejected a quid from his mouth, that would have shamed in size the largest paper of Lorillard's fine-cut chewing tobacco. **1844** *Ib.* XXIII. 288, I thrust a ball of 'Mrs. Miller's fine cut,' . . . between the sub-maxillary bone and its carnal casement. **1909** O. HENRY *Roads of Destiny* xxi. 355 Haven't got a chew of fine-cut on you, have you?

(5) **1848** FOLSOM in Bryant *California* App. 473 The coarse gold, from its massiveness and great specific gravity, was not removed from the mountain sides, whereas the fine gold was swept off to the plains below. **1850** *S.F. Picayune* 31 Aug. 2/1 The Company are taking out considerable quantities of gold mixed with quartz, besides the fine gold in the forms usually found on bars. **1948** WESTON *Mother Lode* 18 The medium of exchange was gold—gold in every form—fine gold, coarse gold, quartz gold, and nuggets. — (6) **1873** MILLER *Amongst Modocs* 38 You high-toned, fine-haired gamblers don't play me—not much, you don't! *Ib.* 162 He was, as an expression of the time went, a little too 'fine-haired.' He spoke too properly; he never 'got on any glorious benders,' with the western men. **1933** T. WILLIAMSON *Woods Colt* 56 Purty fine-haired them Starbucks is a-gittin', 'pears to me. I hear they got screens on their winders. — (7) **1883** *Nat. Museum Bul.* No. 27, 478 *Catostomus commersonii.* . . . Brook Sucker; Fine-scaled Sucker. . . . This is not a good fish, and yet it is sold in large quantities.— (8) **1843** in *Amer. Sp.* (1948) Feb. 44/2 How eagerly she gazed, as it drew the surface in the process of biting off, like the transit of a fine-tooth comb. **1850** *Rep. Comm. Patents 1849* 267 Improvement in making Ivory fine-tooth Combs. **1948** *Land o' Lakes News* Feb. 4/2 They went over the Grocery Bill Item by Item with a Fine-Toothed Comb. — (9) **1856** *Mass. Bd. Agric. Rep.* I. 26 Redtop, Finetop, Burdin's Grass, Dew Grass, Herds Grass of Pennsylvania and Southern States. **1889** VASEY *Agric. Grasses* 46 *Agrostis vulgaris* (Redtop, Finetop, Herds Grass, Bent Grass, etc.)

* **finger,** *n.*

1. A portion of liquor that fills a glass to a depth equal to the width of one finger.

1856 *Porter's Spirit of Times* 4 Oct. 73/1 We each took a first mate's drink—i.e. three fingers. **1905** N. DAVIS *Northerner* 284 'You've been drinking,' he said coldly. 'Only a finger as I came by town, sir.'

2. In combs.: (1) **finger bar,** the cutter bar of a reaper or mower; (2) **beam,** ?=prec., *obs.;* (3) * **berry,** (see quot.); (4) * **board,** a board indicating the way to a place, a sign board, also fig.; (5) **fish,** (see quot. 1796); (6) **grass,** [cf. Du. *vingergras*], any one of several species of crab grass; (7) **Indian grass,** bluestem, *Andropogon furcatus;* (8) **lake,** (see quot. 1909), also attrib.; (9) **spiked wood grass,** =**finger Indian grass.**

(1) **1865** *Ill. Agric. Soc. Trans.* VI. 52 Patent Cold Rolled Reaper and Mower Finger Bars. **1870** *Iowa Agric. Soc. Rep. 1867* VII. 312 The greatest objections to a joint in the finger-bar of a mower. — (2) **1852** *Mich. Agric. Soc. Trans.* III. 158 Lapping the finger beam above or below. — (3) **1893** *Amer. Folk-Lore* VI. 141 *Rubus villosus* . . . finger berry; thimble berry. N.Y. — (4) **1804** *Fredericktown* (Md.) *Herald* 11 Feb. 3/1 Holding the finger board in a wrong direction for Carter's Mountain. **1886** *Chautauqua Assembly Annual* (Long Beach, Calif.) 10 The humble village pastor saw . . . no finger-boards along life's highways to point the people thither [to knowledge]. **1894** MARK TWAIN *Defence of H. Shelley* 245 (R.), A literary swamp which has so many misleading finger-boards as this book is furnished with.

(5) **1796** MORSE *Amer. Geog.* I. 228 Star Fish or Finger Fish. — (6) **1821** *Mass. H.S. Coll.* 2 Ser. IX. 149 Plants, which are indigenous in the township of Middlebury, [Vermont, include]. . . . Finger grass. **1943** PEATTIE *Great Smokies* 168 In the first year after abandonment there is a one-year stage when horseweed and finger grass predominate. — (7) **1863** *Ill. Agric. Soc. Trans.* V. 867 Beard-grass . . . [and] Finger Indian-grass are given as specimens of very worthless native grasses. — (8) **1909** *Cent. Supp.* 473/3 finger-lake. . . . In *geog.*, one of a group of lakes which diverge somewhat like the fingers of an open hand: such a group occurs in central New York. **1949** *Sat. Ev. Post* 2 April 49/1 Father and mother, on their honeymoon, had walked for two weeks, up and down glens and chasms, past orchards and vineyards in the Finger Lake district. — (9) **1843** TORREY *Flora N.Y.* II. 478 *Andropogon furcatus.* . . . Finger-spiked Wood-grass. . . . Rocky banks and hill-sides. **1856** *Mass. Bd. Agric. Rep.* I. 88 Finger-Spiked Wood Grass. . . . Of this genus about sixty species are known to botanists.

* **fingerling,** *n.* Any small fish of approximately a finger's length. Also attrib. — **1888** GOODE *Amer. Fishes* 38 Fingerlings . . . swarm in great schools upon the bars of the river above and below the tide-waters of the Delaware. **1931** *Randolph Enterprise* (Elkins, W.Va.) 28 May 1/1 About fifteen thousand fry and fingerling bass were taken. . . . Trout fingerlings and legal size were distributed.

finish fight. A fight to the finish. *Colloq.* — **1909** R. A. WASON *Happy Hawkins* 143 The' ain't nothin' ever satisfies a civilized human except a finish fight. **1947** *Chi. D. News* 15 Oct. 1/6 In the finish fight, the mob is opposed by James D. Crowley.

fink fɪŋk, *n.* [Poss. f. * *finger*, in the slang sense of an informer.] A strikebreaker. Also transf. *Slang.*

1926 *Amer. Mercury* Jan. 63/1 Dating from the famous Homestead strike of 1892 is the odious *fink.* [It] according to one version was originally *Pink*, a contraction of Pinkerton, and referred to the army of strikebreakers recruited by the detective agency. **1935** *Voice of Youth* (S.F.) 21 Nov. 3/4 'They must be finks,' he said at last. **1948** WADE MILLER *Fatal Step* 174 This gag was made up by a cheap fink.

fip fɪp, *n.* =next. *Obs.* Cf. **Quaker, silver fip.** — **1822** *Phila. Freeman's Jrnl.* 5 Sep. (Th.), A dispute now commenced between two persons respecting some cents and a 'fip,' which had fallen from his pocket. **1891** WELCH *Recoll. 1830–40* 169 It was common, particularly in New England, to call a sixpence or a half dime, a *fip.*

fip(p)enny bit. The half real, a Spanish silver coin, formerly passing current in the U.S. with a value of about six cents. Also attrib. and fig. Cf. * **fourpence, picayune,** * **sixpence.**

In New England this coin was known as a *fourpence ha'penny,* or *fourpence;* in New York as a *sixpence;* in Louisiana as a *picayune;* in Pennsylvania and some of the adjacent states as a *fippenny bit* or *fip.*

1802 *Port Folio* 27 Feb. 62/2 For ourselves we are positive that in these fortunate revolutionary times, we shall gather *fipenny-bits* from every parsley bed. **1848** BARTLETT 139 *Fippenny Bit,* or contracted *Fip.* Fivepence. In the State of Pennsylvania, the vulgar name for the Spanish half-real. **1856** STOWE *Dred* I. 235 What do we want to send our girls there, to get fipenny-bit ideas?

* **fir,** *n.* As the last term in **alpine, balsam, Douglas, European silver, Gilead, golden, Nootka, Oregon white, red, Shasta, silver, white, yellow fir.**

fir balsam, *n.* =**balsam fir.**

1810 MICHAUX *Arbres* I. 18 Sylvir fir, . . . Fir balsam, . . . [ou] Balsam of Gilead tree. **1848** THOREAU *Maine Woods* 9 Delicate and beautiful specimens of the larch, arbor-vitae, ball-spruce, and fir-balsam . . . lined [the sides of the road]. **1899** JEWETT *Queen's Twin* 16 Now, you see them little peakéd-topped spruces an' fir balsams comin' up over the hill all green an' hearty. **1908** *Suburban Life* Aug. 84/2 We were content to take an empty mattress tick and filled it with fir balsam when we reached camp.

* **fire,** *n.*

1. In the speech of Indians or in imitation of this: **a.** A household, family, or nation.

The *OED* lists "fire" meaning a household, with quots. 1630, 1653. The use shown here is prob. an independent development.

1775 ADAIR *Indians* 329, I charged them with . . . the continuance of a fair open trade with a free people, who by treaty were become *allies* of Great Britain; not *subjects,* . . . people of one fire. **1804** CLARK in *Lewis & C. Exped.* I. (1904) 47 [The Missouri Indians] once the most noumerous [*sic*] nation in this part of the Continent now reduced to about 30 fires. **1821** NUTTALL *Travels Arkansa* 62 [The Arkansas Indians] informed me, . . . that their company was about five or six families or fires. **1939** CLEAVES *Old Tippecanoe* 226 The Seventeen Fires, though usually peaceable, were able and willing to fight.

b. One of the states of the Union. Cf. **thirteen fires.** *Obs.*

1801 HAWKINS *Letters* 377 No sooner did our new father, Thomas Jefferson, find himself at the head of all the white people and sixteen fires than he turned his thoughts towards his red children.

2. (See quot.) *Colloq.*

1891 *Amer. Folk-Lore* IV. 237 Fire is a game in which the new boy is made a fireman, who is sent in search of a fire; and when he cries out, as he has been instructed, 'Fire! fire! fire!' the others coming running from their engine-house, and salute him with a shower of stones.

3. In combs. designating persons or organizations concerned with fire control: (1) **fire boss,** (see quots.); (2) **chief,** the officer in charge of a fire department; (3) * **club,** a voluntary organization of the citizens of any community for the purpose of collective fire-fighting, *obs.,* cf. **Fire Society;** (4) **commissioner,** in a town or city, an official having duties pertaining to fire prevention and control; (5) **company,** a company or group of men organized to extinguish fires, cf. **7.** (4) below and see **volunteer fire company;** (6) **department,** a municipal or city department that protects the public against fire, cf. **paid, volunteer fire department;** (7) * **dog,** ?one experienced in fire-fighting, *obs.;* (8) **engine company,** a group of firemen in charge of a fire engine; (9) **guard,** see as a main entry; (10) **laddie,** an affectionate term for a fire-fighter, *colloq.;* (11) * **man,** see as a main entry; (12) **marshal,** the head of the fire department of a municipality or city, charged with enforcing fire ordinances; (13) **patrol,** a squad of firemen, esp. a group of men employed by an insurance company to protect property against damage from fire; (14) **police,** ?police having special duties in cases of fire, *obs.;* (15) **ranger,** one who is employed in a forest preserve to prevent or extinguish forest fires; (16) **Society,** =**fire club;** (17) **ward,** an officer authorized to take or order precautions against fires, and to direct the extinguishing of them; (18) **warden,** =prec.

(1) 1883 GREELEY *Glossary Coal Mining, Fire-bosses* (U.S.A.), underground officials who examine the mine for gas, and inspect every safety-lamp taken into the colliery. **1917** SINCLAIR *King Coal* 30 The 'fire-boss' was supposed to make his rounds in the early morning, and the law specified that no one should go to work till he had certified that all was safe. — **(2) 1902** *Harper's Mag.* Feb. 427 Even the fire-chief recognized that the business of rescue was in good hands. **1948** *Chelsea* (Mass.) *Record* 30 Nov. 8/8 The ordinance was referred to the committee of the whole with the fire chief . . . to be present. — **(3)** *c***1744** *Essex Inst. Coll.* XXXIX. 5 We, the subscribers, members of the Old Fire Club, . . . do agree to the following articles. **1870** EMERSON *Soc. & Solitude* i. 8 The moral union is for comparatively low and external purposes, like the co-operation of ships company or of a fire-club. — **(4) 1840** *Hunt's Merch. Mag.* II. 255 We append a table, compiled from the Fire Commissioners' Report in the City of New York. **1868** *N.Y. Herald* 2 July 6/1 The Board of Fire Commissioners yesterday dropped Patrick W. Hand from the roll of engineers.

(5) 1744 in *Amer. Sp.* XXI. (1946) 117/2 The Union Fire-Company of Philadelphia, do hereby offer a Reward of Five Pounds. **1862** CUMMING *Hospital Life* 37/1 The company [of soldiers] . . . was composed of the members of a fire company. **1915** *Cincinnati Ann. Rep. 1914* 343 Temporary quarters have been provided for Fire Company No. 54. — **(6) 1825** *Mass. Laws* X. 91 The Fire Department of the City of Boston shall hereafter consist of one Chief Engineer, and as many other Engineers, Fire-wardens, Firemen, Hosemen, and Hook and Ladder men, as shall . . . be elected and appointed by the Mayor and Aldermen. **1948** *Chi. D. News* 9 Jan. 14/1 The . . . fire department has invented a short cut to solve the cat problem which Chicago's smoke eaters may find useful. — **(7) 1840** *Boston Transcript* 11 Feb. 2/2 Col Amory, Capt Barnicoat, and three or four other old fire-dogs are to examine the machine when ready for trial. — **(8) 1835** *N.Y. City Ordinances* III. 284 The Mayor, Aldermen and Commonalty of the city of New York . . . do Ordain. . . . That two persons be appointed to each Fire Engine and Hose Company. **1915** *Cincinnati Ann. Rep. 1914* 354 The department is comprised of thirty-two steam fire engine companies.

(10) 1887 *Harper's Mag.* Jan. 317/2 The fire laddie was always a popular hero in New York. **1948** *Dly. Ardmoreite* (Ardmore, Okla.) 27 June 9/1 The fire laddies will don their work clothes the third week to receive drill evolution on ladders, hose, fire stream, protective breathing devices, and driving and pumping operations. — **(12) 1861** in M. WILLSON DISHER *Cowells in Amer.* (1934) 277 All the newspapers agree in 'thinking the fire to be the work of an incendiary.' The Fire-marshal is already making investigations. **1949** *Sat. Ev. Post* 5 Mar. 19/1 The job of chief fire marshal of New York City is a twenty-four-hour-a-day responsibility. — **(13) 1889** BRAYLEY *Boston Fire Dept.* 291 The establishment of a fire patrol in each district by detail from the department. **1909** *Worcester City Docs. 1907–08* No. 63, 972 The Fire Patrol continues to work in harmony with the Fire Department. — **(14) 1889** BRAYLEY *Boston Fire Dept.* 292 The estabishment of a body of fire police, in accordance with the prayer of the petitioners.

(15) 1920 *Outing* June 137/2 If you discover a fire, put it out if possible. If you cannot, get word to the nearest U.S. Fire Ranger or State Fire Warden. — **(16) 1825** in BRAYLEY *Boston Fire Dept.* 155 Formerly, one could not open the front door of the highest or the finest citizen without having his eye greeted with at least two buckets, containing fire-bags and a bed key, all duly labelled, indicating to which fire society he belonged. — **(17) 1711** *Mass. Acts & Resolves* I. 677 Prudent persons of known fidelity, not exceeding ten . . . who shall be denominated and called firewards . . . to command and require assistance for the extinguishing and putting out the fire. **1810** *Columbian Centinel* 20 Jan. 3/4 The Firewards recommend to their fellow-Citizens, during the severity of the winter, to pay attention to their Pumps. **1889** BRAYLEY *Boston Fire Dept.* 31 On the 31st the town was divided into fire districts, under the management of firewards. — **(18) 1724** *N.-Eng. Courant* 10–17 Aug. 2/2, [I propose] that no Person, either Male or Female, be allow'd to rejoice openly at the Progress of the Fires, . . . without leave first obtain'd from the Firewardens. **1875** *Chi. Tribune* 2 July 3/4 The seven Fire Wardens were also abolished by reason of the Council failing to make any appropriation for their salaries. **1945** WEBSTER *Town Meeting Country* 207 The fire warden says five words, and J. Irving is left deflated.

4. With reference to devices, measures, etc., used in the control or fighting of fire: (1) **fire bag,** see as a main entry; (2) * **boat,** a boat equipped to extinguish fires; (3) **break,** a strip of plowed or cleared land made to check the spread of a forest or prairie fire; (4) **curtain,** in theaters, etc., a fireproof curtain; (5) **district,** an area in a city forming a unit in a fire-control system; (6) * **drill,** a practice drill in the use of fire-fighting equipment, or in the proper manner of leaving a building in case of fire; (7) **duty,** duty in connection with extinguishing or controlling fires; (8) **finder,** a device for determining the location of forest fires; (9) **guard,** see as a main entry; (10) **hat,** a strong helmet worn by a fireman as a protection against falling embers, etc.; (11) **horn,** a horn used by firemen in clearing a way to a fire, *obs.;* (12) **hydrant,** =**hydrant;** (13) **land,** =**firebreak,** cf. **7.** (9) below; (14) **limit,** a boundary line inclosing an area in a city in which only certain fireproof types of building may be erected, usu. *pl.,* also attrib.; (15) **line,** see as a main entry; (16) **prairie,** ?an area of prairie land plowed as a protection against prairie fire, *rare;* (17) **sail,** app. a large piece of canvas formerly used by firemen, *obs.;* (18) **shoot,** a fire escape which operates as a chute, *rare;* (19) **tower,** a tower from which a watch is kept for forest fires; (20) **trail,** a trail or road enabling men and equipment to reach quickly the scene of a forest fire; (21) **wall,** a fireproof wall constructed to prevent the spread of a fire in a building; (22) **water,** see as a main entry.

(2) 1849 *Western Boatman* June 396 (*title*), The Protection of Boats in Port by a Fire-Boat. **1948** *Sat. Ev. Post* 26 June 25/1 Tugs whistled, big ships brayed and fire-boats sprayed curtains of water high in the air. — **(3) 1885** *Boston Jrnl.* 26 Sep. 4/1 Fears are entertained of the safety of the town [Dickinson, Dak.], and teams are out plowing fire-breaks around it. **1947** *Time* 13 Jan. 10/3 It is time to get out the bulldozers and dig down for a system of real firebreaks. — **(4) 1912** P. MCKEON *Fire Prevention* 153 In order to make this wall a solid fire stop, all these openings have special protection against fire. The doorways have duplicate fire-doors. . . . The proscenium arch has a fire curtain.

(5) 1851 ROSS *In New York* 31 The city is divided into eight fire-districts. **1914** *Pittsfield* (Mass.) *Municipal Reg.* 179 In the first fire district all concealed work must be . . . installed in conduit or flexible steel cable. — **(6) 1893** *Standard Dict.* 683/3 fire-drill. . . . Drilling, as of pupils in a school, to accustom them to proper action in case of fire. **1948** *Hungry Horse News* (Columbia Falls, Mont.) 24 Sep. 4/3 Fire drills have been successfully carried out once a week according to the Montana school law. — **(7) 1837** *S. Lit. Messenger* III. 644 The same free person of color enjoys an exemption from militia, from patrol, from fire and jury duty. **1881** *Harper's Mag.* Jan. 205/2 An assistant engineer of the New York Fire Department went to Fortress Monroe . . . and staid there performing 'fire duty.' — **(8) 1926** *Sunset* July 46/3 As the lookout . . . spots the first thin spiral of smoke indicating danger, he immediately locates it by means of the Fire Finder, and should within two minutes be able to make his first telephone report to the nearest fire-warden or platting agent's station.

(10) 1851 CIST *Cincinnati* 213 George E. Minister . . . makes . . . fire hats. **1889** BRAYLEY *Boston Fire Dept.* 72 By this order the first badge and fire-hat were adopted. — **(11) 1876** INGRAM *Centennial Exp.* 662 Banners, torches, silver-plated fire-horns, and the entire paraphernalia of the Fire Department, all made up a picture of novelty. — **(12) 1912** *Out West* April 259/2 The city has an excellent fire department, with 112 fire hydrants and high water pressure. **1947** *Chi. D. News* 3 Jan. 1/5 She answered the charge of parking her car in front of a fire hydrant. — **(13) 1869** *Republican D. Jrnl.* (Lawrence, Kans.) 13 Nov., Any farmer who does not have a broad fire-land plowed around his premises is in constant danger of having his fences destroyed. — **(14) 1848** *Hunt's Merch. Mag.* XIX. 505 Wooden buildings are not permitted to be built, under present regulations, within what are denominated the fire limits. **1914** *Cyclo. Amer. Govt.* II. 18/2 A fire limit ordinance may be defined as a 'law passed by a city council defining the boundaries of territory . . . in which only certain kinds of buildings may be constructed.'

(16) 1808 in ANDREAS *Hist. Kansas* (1883) 61 The United States, being anxious to promote peace, friendship, and intercourse with the Osage tribes, . . . have thought proper to build a fort on the right bank of the Missouri, a few miles above the fire prairie. — **(17) 1806** in *Mass. Laws 1805–06* 98 The enginemen . . . shall . . . attend fires . . . with axes, firehooks, fire-sails and ladders. **1829** *Ib.* XI. 238 A Company of Hook and Ladder-men . . . shall . . . attend fires . . . with fire-hooks, fire sails and ladders. — **(18) 1859** *Rep. Comm. Patents 1858* I. 707 The nature of this invention consists in combining a fire 'shoot' with a pair of folding ladders, and a yielding bed or bottom. — **(19) 1931** *Randolph Enterprise* (Elkins, W.Va.) 4 June 1/1 The state has hardly enough men to man the fire towers which it has erected. **1947** *Democrat* 16 Oct. 1/5 Two, and possibly three, more fire towers are to be erected in Clarke County.

(20) 1946 *Reader's Digest* July 87/1 A map disclosed that fire trails, which wind among the mountain trees, were numbered. — **(21)** [**1759** in *Morav. Hist. Soc. Trans.* XI. (1936) 163 Every House is to be built with Stone. . . . The Wall is to be two or three foot in the Ground & two Foot thick. The Chimneys & Fire-Walls shall be made strictly according to the Draft.] **1851** CIST *Cincinnati* 230 Three smoke-houses . . . are separated by twelve inch walls, slushed, with fire-walls on the roof. **1912** MCKEON *Fire Prevention* 162 Two fire walls . . . could have been made by placing fireproof doors at the brick walls which separated the rotunda from the front and rear vestibules.

b. In similar combs. sufficiently explained in the quots.: (1) **fire alarm telegraph,** (2) **hall,** (3) **house,** (4) **lane,** (5) **ride,** (6) **stop, stopping.**

(1) 1858 *Rep. Comm. Patents 1857* II. 78 Improvement in Fire-Alarm Telegraph.—Patent dated May 19, 1857. **1874** KNIGHT 849/2 Fire-alarm Telegraph. The name applied to the system of telegraphy usually adopted in this country for giving notice of fires. **1887** *Cent. Mag.* Aug. 493/2 The forward flag-pole carried away the fire-alarm telegraph wire and started half the bells in Trenton ringing. — **(2) 1906** *D.N.* III. 136 *Fire-hall, Fire-house,* public building containing apparatus for extinguishing fires. 'We've got a fire-house, but no engine.' [n.w. Ark.] — **(3) 1906** [see **fire hall**]. **1945** *Sat. Review* 7 July 21/1 Sometimes it's as elevated as the conversation in back of the firehouse in Salem, Ohio. — **(4) 1905** [see (as a main entry) **fire line 2**].

(5) 1900 BRUNCKEN *N. Amer. Forests* 186 In the first place, every forest is penetrated, in addition to the main roads, by a network of open lanes, so-called 'fire-rides.' These are kept bare, not merely of trees and underbrush, but also, as far as possible, of the ranker vegetation of grass and herbage. — **(6) 1897** F. C. MOORE *How to Build a Home* 7 The ceiling should be plastered on metallic lathing. This will be an effectual fire-stop in case of fire started in the cellar. *Ib.* 18 It is therefore only necessary to cut off all of these upright air-spaces, . . . so that there will be a fire-stop at every floor. **1909** WEBSTER 820/1 *Fire stop,* any incombustible member or material used to fill or close open parts of a structure, to prevent the passage of fire. **1916** A. HUTSON *Fire Prevention & Protection* 349 The firestopping shall be arranged to cut off all concealed draft openings.

5. In the names of, or with reference to, plants and animals: (1) **fire beetle,** an insect injurious to sugar cane, *obs.;* (2) ∗**bird,** see as a main entry; (3) **bug,** a firefly, cf. **7.** (3) below; (4) ∗**grass,** =∗**fireweed;** (5) **horse,** a horse that draws a fire engine or wagon, cf. **7.** (7) below; (6) **weed,** see as a main entry.

(1) 1855 BÜCHELE *Land* 32 Bemerken wir zunächst den Feuerkäfer (*fire beetle*), 1 Zoll lang, in Louisiana und Texas, von lebhaftem Glanze, der besonders dem Zuckerrohr viel Schaden thut. — **(3) 1789** MORSE *Amer. Geog.* 62 Of the astonishing variety of Insects found in America, we will mention . . . Fire Fly or Bug. **1877** J. M. BAILEY *Folks in Danbury* 46 (Th.), [The lamp] don't give more light than a fire-bug. — **(4)** *a***1817** DWIGHT *Travels* IV. 61 Immediately after the fires, a species of grass springs up, sometimes called fire grass, because it usually succeeds a conflagration. — **(5) 1899** *Decatur* (Ill.) *Herald* 18 Oct. 2/4 The crowds were so dense that the fire horses could not make good time. **1946** T. JONES *Skinny Angel* 81 She heard the fire company gong clanging behind her, and the thunder of the fire horses' hoofs.

b. In similar combs. of obvious meaning or sufficiently explained in the quots.: (1) **fireball,** (2) **bob,** (3) **cherry,** (4) **-cracker flower,** etc., see **firecracker** as a main entry, (5) **hangbird,** see as a main entry; (6) **pink,** (7) **thorn,** (8) **top,** (9) **worm.**

(1) 1889 *Cent.* 2228/2. **1892** *Amer. Folk-Lore* V. 93 *Lychnis chalcedonica,* sweetwilliam. . . . Fire balls. Mansfield, O. — **(2) 1825** J. PICKERING *Inquiries Emigrant* (1831) 27, I amused myself by observing the motions of the numerous 'fire bobs' (flies) flashing in the air like candles. — **(3) 1897** SUDWORTH *Arborescent Flora* 240 *Prunus pennsylvanica,* Wild Red Cherry. . . . [Also called] Fire Cherry (N.Y.). **1943** PEATTIE *Great Smokies* 162 When it is clean-cut or burned off, it is replaced by fire cherry, a worthless little weed of a tree under which the seeds of its noble predecessors do not readily germinate.

(6) 1857 GRAY *Botany* 56 *Silene Virginica,* Fire Pink, Catchfly. . . . Open woods, W. New York to Illinois and southward. June–Aug. **1901** MOHR *Plant Life Ala.* 497 *Silene Virginica.* . . . Fire Pink. Catchfly. . . . Mountain region to Upper division of Coast Pine belt. Open woods. **1943** PEATTIE *Great Smokies* 196 Nature plunged boldly ahead with her efforts to mingle vermilion with lilac, by adding everywhere the shooting stars of the fire pink, which is about as 'pink' as the dress uniforms at Buckingham Palace. — **(7) 1909** *Cent. Supp.* 475/2 firethorn. . . . The pyracanth or evergreen thorn, *Cotoneaster Pyracantha.* **1948** *Times-Picayune Mag.* (N.O.) 5 Dec. 2/2 It's a shrub of the rose family [and] . . . it's sometimes called firethorn. **1948** *L.A. Times* (Home Mag.) 19 Dec. 27/1 This fire-thorn shrub lends itself to formal as well as informal treatment. — **(8) 1893** *Amer. Folk-Lore* VI. 142 *Epilobium angustifolium,* fire-top; burnt weed. Penobscot River, Me. (lumbermen). — **(9) 1884** *Rep. Comm. Agric.* 395 This insect, the Fire-Worm, which had in previous seasons done so much damage, has this year been kept pretty well under control. **1909** WEBSTER 820/1 *Fireworm.* . . . The larva of a small tortricid moth which eats the leaves of the cranberry, so that the vines look as if burned.

6. Designating processes, operations, etc., in which fire or heat plays a prominent part: (1) **fire assay,** an assay in which a material is subjected to heat; (2) **cured,** of tobacco, cured by exposure to artificial heat, also **fire curing;** (3) **dance,** among Indians, a dance in which lighted bundles of reeds play a conspicuous part; (4) **drying,** (see quot.); (5) **fishing,** see as a main entry; (6) **hunt,** (see quots. 1843, 1859, and cf. **fire-hunting 2**); (7) **hunting,** see as a main entry; (8) **lighting,** =**fire-hunting 2,** *obs.;* (9) **painting,** in pottery-making, unusual effects of coloring produced by a special kind of firing; (10) **shooting,** shooting game at night by the aid of a torch, *obs.;* (11) **silver,** (see quot.), *obs.;* (12) **test,** a test devised to judge the contents or quality of something by subjecting it to fire or heat.

(1) 1869 BRACE *New West* 167 Mills charge 20 per cent. less for working, and guarantee 75 per cent. returns on the fire assay. **1872** MARK TWAIN *Roughing It* xxxvi. 255 From our bricks a little corner was chipped off for the 'fire assay'—a method used to determine the proportions of gold, silver, and base metals in the mass. — **(2) 1848** *Rep. Comm. Patents 1847* 170 The following experiment respecting the curing of tobacco . . . shows that fire-curing is not necessary. **1881** *10th Census Agric.: Tobacco* 18 Fire-cured fillers of the heavy tobacco districts . . . are employed in making a coarse, strong chewing-tobacco. **1948** *Chi. D. News* 17 Nov. 26/1 A government bulletin . . . proclaimed marketing quotas for the 1949 crop of fire-cured and dark air-cured tobacco. — **(3) 1901** *Land of Sunshine* Mar. 217 It is notorious that no two of the 'Fire-dances' are precisely alike. **1944** JOHNSON *As I Dare* 321 That series of dances . . . included the fire dance. . . . Each man started slapping the man ahead of him with these burning torches and the man ahead would pretend to writhe in discomfort and leap high. — **(4) 1843** TALBOT *Journals* 34 Shanties were accordingly built out of slender willows, the meat cut in thin strips and hung upon them, fires kindled and the process 'fire drying,' duly commenced.

(6) 1788 M. DEWEES *Journal* (MS) 17v Had several Gentlemen to dine on board the Arke expecting a fire hunt of some deer. **1843** F. L. HAWKS *D. Boone* 21/22 Two people are always necessary for a fire-hunt. One goes before, carrying a blazing torch of pitch-pine wood . . . , while the other follows behind with his rifle. **1859** BARTLETT 149 *Fire-Hunt,* a hunt for game in the night with the aid of a long-handled pan containing light wood or pitch-pine knots ignited. This is carried on the shoulder of the hunter until he sees the eyes of the animal of which he is in pursuit. — **(8) 1849** LANMAN *Alleghany Mts.* vi. 48 In killing wild animals he pursues but two methods, called 'fire-lighting' and 'still-hunting.' — **(9) 1901** E. A. BARBER *Pottery & Porcelain of U.S.* 494 (*Cent. Supp.*), If returned to the special kiln once more the Fire-Painting will again be restored in all its prismatic brilliancy.

(10) 1857 *Spirit of Times* 25 July 323/1 Mike, what kind of a night would this be for fire-shooting? **1876** HABBERTON *Jericho Road* x. 95 He had done 'fire-shooting' near springs elsewhere. — **(11) 1849** F. ROBINSON *Calif. & Gold Regions* 31 The Indians . . . crush the ore between rocks, and then melt it in rude mud furnaces, producing what is called fire silver, an article inferior to the mercury silver. — **(12) 1865** *Atlantic Mo.* XV. 397 'You don't use the fire test [for testing the contents of oils being refined] in this building . . . ?' 'Indade, no,

Ma'am. There's niver a light nor yet a lanthern allowed here.' **1893** E. A. Barber *Pottery & Porcelain in U.S.* 127 (*Cent. Supp.*), Indeed, fire-tests . . . show that the Tucker porcelain will stand a higher degree of heat.

b. Designating foods and drinks: (1) **fire cake,** a small cake made before an open fire, *obs.;* (2) **drink,** a drink of firewater or whisky; (3) **liquid,** =next, *obs.;* (4) **water,** see as a main entry.

(1) **1777** in *Pa. Mag. Hist.* XXI. 310 But why do I talk of hunger & hard usage, when so many in the World have not even fire Cake & Water to eat. **1805** *Pocumtuc Housewife* (1906) 22 Fire Cakes. . . . When they are brown one side, slip and turn to brown the other. — (2) **1840** *Niles' Reg.* 29 Aug. 414/3 A young Indian named Micke-noch, . . . having indulged too freely in the use of fire drinks, . . . stabbed . . . a son of one of the chiefs. — (3) **1849** *Pres. Mess. Congress* II. 1147 Each male member, rehearsing his own experience while under the influence of fire-liquid, and showing the nature, tendency, and consequence of intemperance.

7. In miscellaneous combs.: (1) **fire auction,** an auction of goods damaged by fire, usu. attrib., cf. **fire sale;** (2) **bag,** see as a main entry; (3) **bug,** a pyromaniac, an incendiary, also transf., *colloq.*, cf. **5.** (3) above, and see **forest firebug;** (4) **company,** a fire insurance company, *obs.*, cf. **3.** (5) above; (5) **cracker,** see as a main entry; (6) **eater,** a violent and uncompromising partisan, used esp. of Southerners during the Civil War period, also **fire-eating,** *a.;* (7) **horse,** a locomotive, cf. **5.** (5) above; (8) **hunter,** one who fire-hunts; (9) **lands,** (see quot. 1812), cf. **4.** (13) above; (10) * **maker,** among certain Indians, one who starts the ceremonial fires for his tribe, *obs.*, cf. * **fireman 1;** (11) * **pan,** a pan or shallow container for fire, attached to a pole and used as the source of light in fire-hunting; (12) * **place,** see as a main entry; (13) **proof,** a place that is fireproof, *obs.;* (14) **room,** see as a main entry; (15) **sale,** a special sale of goods allegedly damaged by fire, sometimes the occasion of fraud as suggested in fig. quot. 1902; (16) * **screen,** (*a*) =**fender 2,** (*b*) a household device, usu. ornamental, for screening or hiding from view a fireplace in summer; (17) **-side chat,** see as a main entry; (18) * **stick,** see as a main entry; (19) **tool,** an instrument for making or dealing with a fire, also attrib.; (20) * **works,** (*a*) the implements or means for producing fire, (*b*) a gun or guns, *rare*, cf. **Fourth of July fireworks;** (21) **Zouave,** during the Civil War, a Federal soldier of one of the volunteer companies made up of former firemen of New York City who adopted the dress and drill of the Zouaves, also **fire zou-zou,** also, in the *pl.*, the company itself, now *hist.*, cf. **Zu-Zu.**

(1) **1904** Mark Twain *Autobiography* (1924) I. 196 (R.), Some fire-auction carpets which blaspheme the standards of color and art. — (3) **1872** Holmes *Poet* i, Those chaps that are setting folks on to burn us all in our beds. Political fire-bugs we call 'em up our way. **1881** Mark Twain in *Cent. Mag.* Nov. 46/2 Wicklow . . . coldly described him as a counterfeiter, nigger-trader, horse-thief, and fire-bug from the most notorious rascal-nest in Galveston. **1949** *Chi. D. News* 9 March 1/5 Police began a search for two known firebugs. — (4) **1792** *Fayetteville* (N.C.) *Gaz.* 16 Oct., Proposals from the Maryland Insurance Fire-company. **1821** in W. B. Wood *Personal Recoll.* (1855) 254 We, the subscribers, members of the Fire Companies, in the city of Philadelphia, have accurately examined the New Theatre, and are of opinion [etc.].

(6) **1846** *Quincy* (Ill.) *Whig* 10 Jan. 2/3 Let Mr. Polk, father Richie, Judge Douglass, little Walker, and the other fire-eaters, be obliged to do their share of the fighting, and who does not *know* that the matter would be more likely to be amicably arranged without an appeal to arms. **1863** Hawthorne *Our Old Home* 46 My fire-eating friend has had ample opportunities to banquet on his favorite diet. **1937** Mitchell *Horse & Buggy Age* 147 Chief Eaton was a veteran of the Civil War, a fire-eater if there ever was one. — (7) **1835** *Knickerb.* V. 53 See the fire-horse, with long trains, of cars careering through the air. **1872** Tice *Over Plains* 53 A prairie wolf . . . was seen trying his 'level best' to get out of the way of the 'fire horse.' — (8) **1833** *Amer. Turf Reg.* Feb. 305 Here we took our first drive; but were unsuccessful in it, as a '*fire hunter*' had anticipated us the previous night. **1876** Habberton *Jericho Road* 96 He puzzled his brain to know who the men might be. Fire-hunters? That *would* be a shame. — (9) **1812** Melish *Travels* II. 272 In 1793 the [Conn.] legislature granted 500,000 acres of the western part of it [the Western Reserve in Ohio] to indemnify the sufferers by fire during the war, and this tract is called the *Fire lands.* **1940** Hatcher *Buckeye Country* 29 Huron County in the Firelands tract, Ottawa County just east of Toledo . . . and Pontiac, now thought of as a motor car, was, in earlier days, the name of an Ottawa chief, one of the greatest Indian leaders.

(10) **1772** Taitt in *Travels Amer. Col.* 538 The made Dog of this Town is very bussie preparing Physick and causing the people to dance every night on purpose to bring back to life their fire maker who was killed six months ago. **1800** Hawkins *Sk. Creek Country* 75 The fire-maker makes the fire as early in the morning as he can, by friction. — (11) **1826** Flint *Recoll.* 339 Two or three black boys carry over their shoulders fire-pans, being a grating of iron hoops. **1927** J. D. Freeman *When West Was Young* 70 The firepan was made of a steel basket fastened to a long, light piece of timber. — (13) **1804** in *Harper's Mag.* XLIV. 492/2 The projection of the arches for the fire-proof [is] annexed to section B. **1857** *Knickerb.* XLIX. 42 Sam opened the fire-proof, and bringing out a bottle, and two tumblers, and a china mug, invited us to draw what water we required for our brandy.

(15) **1891** Wyckoff *Workers the West* (1898) 24 Whole fronts of some buildings are fairly covered with temporary signs . . . 'bankrupt,' and 'fire sales.' **1902** Lorimer *Lett. Merchant* 148 There was no give in Doc; no compromises with creditors; no fire sales. **1945** O. Lewis *Uncertain Journey* 27 Where's the fire sale? — (16) (*a*) **1874** Knight 871/1 *Fire-screen*, . . . a fire-guard or fender. (*b*) **1882** *Cent. Mag.* Feb. 634/2 Another and very useful form . . . enables any one wishing to decorate . . . a wall, a fire-screen, panel, . . . to apply the decoration without the aid of a paper-hanger. **1944** Wilson *Passing Inst.* 4 In summer, after the season for fires was over, the fireplace was hidden by a fire-screen. — (19) **1843** *Amer. Pioneer* II. 82 He carries the 'fire tools,' the steel, flint and spunk, and strikes up the fires at each encampment. **1912** Ilgen *Forge Work* 4 Fire Tools. A, poker; B, rake; C, shovel; D, dipper; E, sprinkler. **1936** *Sears Cat.* (ed. 173) 1001, 5-piece Fire Tool Set: Consists of tongs, brush, poker, shovel, and stand.

(20) (*a*) **1824** Marshall *Kentucky* I. 135 Nor had their ignited arrows the desired effect, owing, no doubt, to their imperfect skill in fire-works. (*b*) **1853** Paxton *Yankee in Texas* 128 The old woman said Charley didn't take his fire-works. — (21) **1861** in F. Moore *Rebellion Rec.* I. III. 95 A number of the Fire Zouaves, who are encamped in the neighborhood of the Insane Asylum, took a stroll some distance into St. George's county. **1864** *Alta California* (S.F.) 13 Jan. 1/2 James Robinson . . . bears a most striking resemblance to Ben Cotton, when gotten up as a fire zou-zou. **1940** Limpus *Hist. N.Y. Fire Dept.* 230 The Fire Zouaves were very proud of the fact that they were the first volunteer regiment to be mustered into service, and when the Union forces prepared to occupy Alexandria, Virginia, Ellsworth insisted that they deserved the place of honor at the head of the column.

b. In similar but less frequent combs., now obs.: (1) **fire-bed iron,** iron that has not gone through a rolling mill; (2) * **hole,** in Yellowstone National Park, a hole filled with hot water; (3) **hood,** ?a screen for a fireplace; (4) **money,** a fine imposed upon some Long Island Indians in payment for houses wilfully burned; (5) **plug hat,** =**plug hat** (and prob. the original form of that expression); (6) **rowdy,** a rowdy who frequents fires; (7) **safe,** a fireproof safe; (8) **slash,** a tract of fallen and partially burned timber resulting from a fire; (9) **sloop,** ?a type of fireship; (10) **study,** in a students' hall or dormitory, a private room or study in which there is a fireplace.

(1) **1851** Cist *Cincinnati* 213 One thousand tons fire-bed and sheet-iron. — (2) **1872** McClellan *Golden State* 628 The new road . . . follows the valley of the Yellowstone river, with its fertility, sterility, forests, deserts, lakes, water-falls, fire-holes. — (3) **1776** *Jrnls. Cont. Congress* VI. 971 To John Bates, for two fire hoods, shovel, tongs, &c. for the use of the treasury office, 16 36/90 dollars. — (4) **1667** *South. Rec.* I. 167 Know all men by these presents that I Iohn Ogden of Elisebeth Towne in New Iersey have truly and duly owing unto me the full and just sum of fourty pounds from Shinecock Indians as in remaine of what became due to mee from them vpon the tax of fire money (as it hath been commonly called).

(5) **1856** *Spirit of Age* (Sacramento) 25 Nov. 3/2 A Digger gentleman of fashion, . . . *sans* everything else, sported a fire plug hat, under the impression that he was a leader of fashion and the Beau Brummel of his tribe. — (6) **1851** Hall *Manhattaner* 87 The genus loafer is almost unknown in the natural history of New Orleans; and cigar smoking juvenile-pittites, fire-rowdies and brave insulters of woman, are only heard of now and then. — (7) **1845** Cist *Cincinnati Misc.* 268 The late fire at Pittsburgh had demonstrated that . . . there are many Fire Safes absolutely worthless and unsafe. — (8) **1872** Richardson *Wonders of Yellowstone* 131 Passing northward through

dense woods and almost impenetrable fire-slashes, the next noteworthy region arrived at is the valley of Bridge Creek. — (9) **1776** in JOHNSON *N. Hale* 146 The Genl. has been pleased to reward their bravery with forty Dollars each, except the last man that quitted the fire-sloop who had fifty.

(10) *a***1640** *Harvard Rec.* I. 19 The two fire studyes in the old house valued alike at 5s. by the quarter.

c. In similar combs. of obvious meaning or sufficiently explained in the quots., as (1) * **fire and brimstone,** (2) **frame,** see as a main entry; (3) * **jack,** (4) **scald,** (5) **stand,** (6) **stink.**

(1) **1805** CUTLER in *Life & Corr.* II. 182 John Randolph made his *fire and brimstone* speech on the Georgia Land business. — (3) **1933** T. WILLIAMSON *Woods Colt* 222 What makes the fire is in the middle o' the skift, pine knots burnin' in a *fire jack*, a kind of a iron basket on the end of a iron rod that sets down into the boat an' fastens there. The glare from the pine knots makes enough light for ye to see the fish, then down you jab with your gig pole. — (4) **1895** CRADDOCK *Myst. Witch-Face Mt.* i. 2 A stretch of burnt, broken timber that goes by the name of 'fire-scald.'

(5) **1944** FOOTNER *Rivers of East. Shore* 105 These fire stands are still used at camp meetings. Little platforms are erected on a stand of tall posts, and thickly heaped with mud or sand. On such beds fires are kept burning to give light to the proceedings at night. — (6) **1881** RAYMOND *Mining Gloss., Fire-stink*, . . . the stench from decomposing iron pyrites, caused by the formation of sulphuretted hydrogen. **1883** GRESLEY *Gloss. Coal Mining, Fire-stink*, smell indicating spontaneous combustion in a coal pit.

8. In verbal expressions: (1) **fireguard,** to protect an area by means of a fireguard (sense **2.**), *rare;* (2) **fire-hunt,** to hunt animals at night by the aid of a light; (3) **stop,** to make (a partition or wall) into a firestop, *rare.*

(1) **1874** J. G. MCCOY *Hist. Sk. Cattle Trade* 217 A large adjacent tract of land, embracing many thousands of acres, will be 'fire-guarded,' in order to secure a winter range from the ravages of prairie fires. . . . Two or more plow furrows, about four rods apart, are run around the tract of land desired to be 'fire-guarded,' and then . . . the intervening strip is set fire and . . . consumed. — (2) **1814** *Sporting Mag.* XLIV. 62 The method of approaching . . . the red deer . . . by means of fire-hunting them. **1942** RAWLINGS *C. Creek* 158 Now you know the law says you can't fire-hunt deer at night. — (3) **1916** A. HUTSON *Fire Prevention & Protection* 349 All partitions which rest directly over each other, shall be completely fire-stopped with brick work.

As the last term in **back, branding, brush, bush, camp, center, cook, corncob, council, devil, dropping, electric, fallow, field, forest, fox, ground, head, hell, lightwood, liquid, lodge, mesquite, mosquito, prairie, railroad, range, rim, ring, sacred, sleeper, smoke, sugar, sure, top, wood fire.** Also (*pl.*) **Seven Council, thirteen fires.**

* **fire,** *v.*

1. *tr.* To eject or throw (a person) bodily from a place, to put out by forcible means. *Colloq.*

1871 *Overland Mo.* March 285 (De Vere), The thought that I was fired by some stranger, who wasn't a-takin' no hand . . . is not a good thought to die on. **1887** *Courier-Journal* 8 May 11/5 Two drunken men . . . were fired from the train by Conductor Webb. **1893** *Harper's Mag.* Dec. 127/1 We are all Seniors, or last-year men, for those who don't graduate will be fired.

b. To dismiss or discharge (a person). Also absol.

1885 *Canon City* (Colo.) *Gate City* Nov. 4/4 In China when a bank suspends on the Shackamaxon principle they immediately suspend the cashier and fire the directors. **1911** HARRISON *Queed* 44 'Colonel Cowles is the man who hires and fires,' he explained. **1948** *Chi. D. News* 18 Sep. 6/3 Can you fire a guy for the same quality which makes him simultaneously a genius and a flop?

c. To reject (a picture sent for an exhibition). *Rare.*

1892 *Nation* 15 Dec. 447/2 Artists of genuine ability have found their canvasses fired.

d. *To fire out*, to dismiss, eject forcibly.

1882 SWEET & KNOX *Texas Siftings* 42 If Gould fires you out, the only railroad in Texas that will employ you will be some street railroad. **1889** *Cent. Mag.* April 888/1 He was warned . . . that he was to be 'fired out.'

2. *To fire down*, to allow a furnace fire to become low. *Rare.*

1874 RAYMOND *6th Rep. Mines* 400 Then the furnace is gradually 'fired down,' the condensers are cleaned of accumulated soot, and all necessary repairs are made to the brick-work.

3. In slang and colloq. phrases: (1) *Fire away Flanagan*, keep it up, go on, continue, *obs.;* (2) *to fire into the wrong flock*, (see quot. 1848).

(1) **1783** FRENEAU *Poems* (1786) 321 Scarce a broadside was ended 'till another began again—By Jove! it was nothing but *Fire away Flannagan!* **1839** *N.O. Picayune* 10 Feb. 2/3 Fire away, Flanagan. I'll be as grave as a jackass; or a justice of the peace when he wants his dinner. — (2) **1835** CROCKETT *Tour* 81, I said, when he [Pres. Jackson] cocked his gun and began his war upon the senate, he would find he had fired into the wrong flock. **1848** BARTLETT 139 To fire into the wrong flock, is a metaphorical expression used at the West, denoting that one had mistaken his object, as when a sportsman fires at a different flock from what he intended. **1858** *N.Y. Herald* 9 Nov. (De Vere), When Mr. Salusbury rose and called the Speaker's attention to the alleged blunder in the Secretary's report, his own friends jumped up in great excitement and pulled him down; he soon found out that he had fired into the wrong flock.

fire bag.

1. A bag used by firemen to carry things from a burning building. *Obs.*

1769 *Mass. Gazette* 2 Feb. (Th.), Some silk, 'lately found in a *fire bag*.' **1825** in BRAYLEY *Boston Fire Dept.* 155 Formerly, one could not open the front door of the highest or the richest citizen without having his eye greeted with at least two buckets, containing fire-bags and a bed key, all duly labelled, indicating to which fire society he belonged.

2. A bag for carrying materials used in starting a fire. *Obs.*

[**1844** *Jrnl. Bishop of Montreal* (1845) 103 The powder-horn and the fire-bag, in which the shot is carried loose, are flung upon belts crossing each other upon the breast.] **1862** in *Harper's Mag.* LXXXIV. 496/1 The men appeared in gaudy array, with beaded fire-bag, gay sash, blue or scarlet leggings. **1892** *Ib.* 497/1 The Sioux . . . each carried a fire-bag, a quiver, and a brightly painted shield, giving up the quiver and shield when guns came into use.

* **firebird,** *n.* Any one of various small birds of bright red or orange plumage, esp. the Baltimore oriole *q.v.* Cf. **fire hangbird.**

1778 ANBUREY *Travels* II. 198 The most remarkable are the Fire-bird, Hanging-bird, Blue-bird and Humming-bird. **1808** WILSON *Ornithology* I. 23 Baltimore Oriole, *Oriolus Baltimore*, . . . is generally known, and as usual honored with a variety of names, such as Hang-nest, Hanging-bird, Golden Robin, Fire-Bird (from the bright orange seen through the green leaves resembling a flash of fire). **1824** IRVING *Traveller* II. 357 The fire-bird streamed by them with his deep-red plumage. **1844** *Nat. Hist. N.Y., Zoology* II. 176 The Black-winged Red-bird [*Pyranga rubra*], or Fire-bird and Tanager, as it is often called in this State, . . . is a shy solitary bird, breeding in this State. **1917** *Birds of Amer.* II. 258 Baltimore Oriole. *Icterus galbula*. . . . Other names.—Golden Robin; . . . Fire-bird; Pea-bird.

firecracker ˈfaɪrˌkrækɚ, *n.*

1. A paper cylinder containing a fuse and a small amount of explosive. Also attrib. and transf.

1829 *N.Y. Journal of Commerce* 4 July 4/2 (*heading*), Fire Crackers. **1852** STOWE *Uncle Tom* xxiii, The boy is . . . a perfect firecracker when excited. **1872** *Rep. Comm. Patents 1870* II. 681/1 Fire-cracker Holder. . . . A fire-cracker pistol, having a swinging breech-piece. **1948** *Okla. City Times* 14 June 2/2 The firecracker sizzled but nothing else happened.

2. Designating a California *flower* or *plant* of the genus *Brodiaea* (see also quot. 1942).

1907 LYONS *Plant Names* 510 Brodiaea coccinea. . . . Firecracker Flower. **1925** JEPSON *Flowering Plants Calif.* 229 B[rodiaea] ida-maia. . . . Fire-cracker Plant. **1942** VAN DERSAL *Ornamental Amer. Shrubs* 191 The red buckeye, *Aesculus pavia* . . . has bright red clusters of small flowers that appear in March or April in the South and as late as June in the North. . . . It is also known as scarlet buckeye and firecracker plant.

* **fired,** *a.* **1. fired corn,** baked bread, a pone or ash cake. **2. fired up,** intoxicated. Both *rare.* — (1) *a***1861** T. WINTHROP *Canoe & Saddle* iii. 30 Take also hard tack at discretion,—'pire sapolel,' or fired corn, as ye [Clallam Indians] name it. — (2) **1847** FIELD *Drama in Pokerville* 50 Another whirl on the road announced Dr. Slunk, and that gentleman, tolerably 'fired up' and in an evident ill humour, 'paraded himself.'

fire-fishing ˈfaɪrˌfɪʃɪŋ, *n.* (See quots.)

1841 BONNYCASTLE *Canadas* II. 6 We went to see two of the *voyageurs* launch the canoe for the purpose of fire-fishing. This sport is pursued by placing over the bow a bundle of bark, pine-knots full of turpentine, or other combustible wood, and then paddling slowly over the water. **1870** NOWLAND *Indianapolis* 97 He had several ways of fishing, but his favorite was fire-fishing. He would build a platform on the bow of his canoe; on this he would build a fire, the reflection of which would show him the fish at the bottom of the deepest water. **1889** *Cent.* 2229/3 *Fire-fishing*, . . . fishing by fire-light, as when blazing torches are used to attract fish to a boat or to the side of a stream so that they may be caught or speared. Also called *torch fishing*.

fire frame. (See quot. 1897.) *Obs.* Cf. ∗**fireplace 2.** and see **Franklin stove, Pennsylvania fireplace.**

1854 O. OPTIC *In Doors & Out* (1876) 132 The young husband, quietly crossing his legs over the top of the fire frame. **1891** WELCH *Recoll. 1830–40* 420 A few heroic experimenters had their deep, wide fire-places walled up, and 'fire frames' adjusted in front. **1897** *Essex Antiq.* I. 187 Early in this century iron fire-frames, as they were called, being a sort of fireplace with sides and top, but no back or front, were in use in some houses. They were made to be set against the chimney, so that the chimney would form the back of the frame, an aperture being in the chimney at the upper part of the frame. It stood on a hearth of brick, on which the fire was built, the wood being raised above the hearth by andirons. . . . These fire-frames were often quite ornamental; and may yet be seen in old houses in Essex county.

∗**fireguard,** *n.*

1. One whose duties are to prevent or to extinguish fires.

1833 *Niles' Reg.* XLIV. 259/2 There were twenty-three engine and hose companies, . . . and four divisions of fire guards. **1851** CIST *Cincinnati* 168 There are beside, two hook and ladder companies, and one company of fire guards, to render appropriate services, as they may be required. **1947** *Coronet* July 25/2 Simultaneously an alarm went to the fireguards stationed in the park and to a crew of jumpers at Seeley Lake, Montana, 225 miles away.

b. The guarding against the danger of fire.

1874 *Harper's Wkly.* 28 Feb. 192/4 'All men on fire-guard!' is the order, which is speedily obeyed.

2. A firebreak *q.v.*, *s.v.* ∗**fire,** *n.* **4.** (3).

1874 J. G. MCCOY *Hist. Sk. Cattle Trade* 217 An impassable barrier would be created between the unburned grass within the encircled tract, and that upon the outside of the 'fire-guard.' **1947** *Sky Line Trail* Feb. 4/1 We are hoping to go by bus . . . along the fire-guard road south of the Bow River to the ford over Red Earth Creek.

fire hangbird. The Baltimore oriole.

1844 *Nat. Hist. N.Y., Zoology* II. 139 The Oriole, Hang-bird, Fire Hang-bird, or Golden Robin . . . is well known under all these names. **1867** HOLMES *Guardian Angel* 32 It was natural enough that Cyprian Eveleth should have called her the fire-hang-bird, and her little chamber the fire-hang-bird's nest,—using the country boy's synonyme for the Baltimore oriole. **1891** COOKE *Huckleberries* (1896) 179 More pernickity 'n a fire-hang-bird. **1946** HAUSMAN *Eastern Birds* 556 The Fire Hang-birds' long purse-like, gray, pendent nests are familiar objects dangling from long drooping elm branches along our roadways.

fire-hunting ˈfaɪrˌhʌntɪŋ, *n.*

1. The action of forcing animals from a wooded area by setting fire to the trees and brush; hence, the slaughter of the animals as they attempt to escape from the fire. *Obs.* Cf. **circle hunt.**

1705 BEVERLEY *Virginia* II. 39 They had a better Way of killing the Elks, Buffaloes, Deer and greater Game, by a method which we call Fire-Hunting. **1743** CATESBY *Carolina* App. p. xi, [The Carolina Indians'] annual custom of fire-hunting is usually in October. At this sport associate some hundreds of Indians, who, spreading themselves in length through a great extent of country, set the woods on fire. **1801** *Hist. Review* II. 193 It is inconceivable what immense quantities of the finest and most valuable timber have been destroyed by the practice of fire hunting, which the Europeans borrowed from the Indians.

2. The hunting of animals at night by shining their eyes with a torch or other light. Also attrib.

1826 T. FLINT *Recoll.* 339 Their most interesting hunts [in Louisiana] are practised by night, and are called fire-huntings. **1876** HABBERTON *Jericho Road* x. 97 Two, or three men at most, were as many as ever composed a fire-hunting party. **1948** DICK *Dixie Frontier* 35 Another method was fire hunting, which was most effective on a dark night.

fireless cooker. A well-insulated apparatus for cooking by means of the stored-up heat from an initial heating. Also, sometimes, in colloq. use, a pressure cooker.

1908 E. A. HUNTINGTON (*title*), The Fireless Cooker. [**1912** *Out West* Jan. 96/1 The appliance is designed to burn the waste by means of a very powerful gas fire in a stove that is insulated as thoroughly as a first rate fireless cook stove.] **1945** MOLLOY *Pride's Way* 291, I believe Mrs. Wilson approves of a fireless cooker.

fire line.

1. (See quot. 1909.)

1903 *N.Y. Ev. Post* 19 Sep. 1 During the fire a Columbus Avenue open car became stalled in the fire lines. **1909** WEBSTER 819/3 *Fire line*, . . . Usually in *pl.* Police barriers or lines about burning buildings.

2. (See quot. 1905.)

1905 *Forestry Bureau Bul.* No. 61, 10 *Fire line*, a strip kept clear of inflammable material as a protection against the spread of forest fire, . . . [also called] fire lane, fire trace. **1911** PLUMMER *Chaparral* 40 Usually the fire line is cleared along the ridges, while roads and trails follow gradients on the sidehills. **1925** BRYAN *Papago Country* 382 The Forestry Service also provides fire guards, cuts fire lines, and builds roads and trails through the forest.

3. The front line of an advancing forest fire.

1920 *Outing* April 26/3 The fire line's about fifty yards ahead and it's traveling about three miles an hour. **1947** *Mazama* Aug. 3/1 Have you battled on the fireline night and day?

∗**fireman,** *n.*

1. (See quots.) Now *hist.* Cf. ∗**fire maker,** *s.v.* ∗**fire,** *n.* **7.** (10).

1843 *Amer. Pioneer* II. 82 Amongst the Caddoes, and some other tribes of Indians, one man of the hunting party is the fire-man, who is also the 'medicine-man,' priest or conjurer. It is his business to provide fire for the party. He carries the 'fire tools,' the steel, flint and spunk. **1928** LONG LANCE *Long Lance* 16 We had a professional 'fire-man' with the tribe, a man whose business it was to carry fire with him from camp to camp and sell it to members of the tribe when they got ready to make their fires.

2. firemen's anniversary, an annual celebration given in honor of firemen.

1842 *N.O. Picayune* 4 March 2/2 Firemen's anniversary. . . . The orator of the day is a gentleman highly esteemed. **1862** CUMMING *Hospital Life* (1866) 11/1, [I] reminded him of that day, one year ago, when he participated in one of the finest displays of which the city of Mobile boasts—the Fireman's Anniversary.

3. firemen's ball, a ball given by, or for the benefit of, firemen.

1842 *N.O. Picayune* 23 Jan. 2/3 The firemen's ball, at the Planters' Hotel, St. Louis, . . . was the most brilliant ball ever given in that city. . . . An addition of more than one thousand dollars was made to the firemen's fund. **1937** MITCHELL *Horse & Buggy Age* 123 The Firemen's Ball was always held the night of Washington's Birthday and was usually broken up by some practical joker turning in a false alarm.

4. firemen's fund, a fund raised for the benefit of the members or former members of a fire company. Also attrib.

1841 *N.O. Picayune* 25 May 2/5 There has been an extensive turn out in St. Louis for a 'Firemen's Fund Benefit.' **1842** [see **fireman's ball**].

As the last term in **independent, steamer fireman.**

∗**fireplace,** *n.*

1. *L.I.* (See quot. 1939.) Now *hist.*

1655 in *E.-Hampton Rec.* 84 It is also Ordered by the Maior part that Jeremiah Mecham & Richard Brookes shall have all yt medow allong by the beach Calld the ffire place that is undevidad from William Mulfords lott to be Equally Devided between them as ther full pportion and share of all the medow vndevided. **1666** *Ib.* I. 249, I Benjamine Price . . . have sould unto Alice Stanberough . . . all my meadow at Accabonock being three Divisions one at the landing place one at the humock & one at the fire place. **1939** W. O. STEVENS *Discovering L.I.* 90 The nearest land lay three and a half miles to the west of the Manor, at a spot still called 'Fireplace' on our road map. On this strip of beach it was the custom to make a great fire of dried seaweed whenever anyone wanted a boat to come over from the island. On seeing the smoke, a boatman would row over for the visitor.

2. =**fire frame.** Now *hist.* Also **Pennsylvania fireplace.**

1741 *Pa. Gazette* 3 Dec. 4/1 To be sold at the post office, Philadelphia, the new invented iron fire-places. **1744** FRANKLIN *Writings* II. 256 To avoid the several Inconveniences, and at the same time retain all the Advantages of other Fire-places, was contrived the Pennsylvania Fire-Place. *Ib.* 267 This Fire-place cures most smoaky chimneys, and thereby preserves both the Eyes and Furniture. **1747** in DOW *Every Day Life* 132 On the 11th Instant, early in the Morning, a Fire broke out at *Mr. Pierpont's* House near the Fortification, occasioned by the Heat of the Iron Hearth of one of the newly invented Fireplaces, whereby the Floor was set on Fire; the People being in Bed, perceived a great Smoke, got up, and happily discover'd and timely distinguished [*sic*] the Fire. **1931** *Old-Time New Eng.* Oct. 71/1 The first departure in America from the open fireplace, . . . was the castiron fireplace invented by Benjamin Franklin in 1742.

As the last term in **stick-and-clay, stick-and-dirt fireplace.**

fireroom ˈfaɪrˌrum, *n.*

1. A room containing a fireplace.

1708 *Boston News-Letter* 5 Jan. 2/2 There is a good Dwelling House, three Fire Rooms on a Floor . . . to be Lett. **1899** WILKINS *Colonial Times* II. 31 All the drawbacks to her delight was that Grandma should have the southwest fire-room.

2. A furnace room, esp. on a ship.

1836 *S. Lit. Messenger* II. 734, I went on board, and passing the fire-room, . . . I stopped with unfeigned horror. a1904 WHITE *Blazed Trail Stories* 70 Factory owners . . . raised up their voices in bitterness over flooded fire-rooms.

fireside chat. A more or less informal talk of national interest over a radio network; specifically, and for about twelve years exclusively, such a talk by President F. D. Roosevelt. — **1935** *Amer. Mercury* July 325/2 Now and again, of course, one may find a half-hearted Hoosier who turns from the lamp to listen to a 'Fireside Chat.' **1947** *Newsweek* 16 June 31/3 He addressed the 309th annual dinner of the Ancient and Honorable Artillery and gave his weekly fireside chat.

* **firestick,** *n.* **1.** A poker, or (in *pl.*) tongs for arranging a fire. **2.** A stick of wood suitable for a campfire.

(1) **1637** R. WILLIAMS *Letters* (1874) 80 She of all natives in Boston is the worse used: is beaten with fire-sticks. **1896** HARRIS *Sister Jane* 100 Sister Jane, armed with the fire-stick (a heavy piece of metal weighing four or five pounds), and as red in the face as Mandy was white, was waving her weapon. **1902** *Nat. Museum Rep. 1900* 180 In the same plate are included a pair of wooden fire sticks or tongs [of the Tulare Indians]. — (2) **1853** *Harper's Mag.* VIII. 35/1 'There now!' said he, 'some of you smart gentlemen may chop that fellow into fire-sticks and carry them to the camp.'

firewater ˈfaɪrˌwɔtɚ, *n.* [See note.]

In the earliest examples of the use of this term it is ascribed to Indians. It is prob. a translation of some Indian expression. Cf. Algonquin *scoutiouabou*, firewater.

1. Any strong or hard liquor, whisky.

1817 BRADBURY *Travels* 156 He informed me that they [the Indian chiefs] called the whiskey fire water. **1868** WHYMPER *Alaska* 37 The importation of 'fire-water' is not the only evil. **1947** COFFIN *Yankee Coast* 230 We stole the Abenakis' hunting grounds, cut their tall pines, ruined their sons with firewater.

fig. **1846** CHILD *Fact & Fiction* 169 They too learn that love is the glowing wine, the exhilarating 'fire-water' of the soul.

2. Water to be used for extinguishing fires. *Rare.*

1887 *Courier-Journal* 11 Feb. 3/5 Fire Extinguishers and Fire Water.

* **fireweed,** *n.* Any one of various weeds that spring up in areas that have been burned over. Also used of plants that in some way suggest fire (see also quot. 1913).

1784 CUTLER in *Mem. Academy* I. 477 *Carlina* . . . Fire-Weed. Blossoms White. It abounds in new plantations where the ground has been burnt over. **1817–8** EATON *Botany* (1822) 457 *Senecio hieracifolius*, fire weed, . . . is very strong scented, and is said to be useful in hemorhagy. **1913** BARNES *Western Grazing Grounds* 236 In the southwest and on some of the ranges in the northern regions . . . (Guttierrezia) known locally as snakeweed, fireweed, turpentine weed, and possibly by other names. . . . The flowers bear little white seeds that seem to be filled with a resinous substance which makes it burn like tinder. Hence the name fire or turpentine weed. **1942** *Nat. Geog. Mag.* May 594 Eager to gather the blue lupines, pink roses, and magenta fireweed along the trail, Jo was not careful where she walked.

* **firing,** *n.*

1. A disease of tobacco (see quot. 1688).

1688 CLAYTON *Acc. Va. in Phil. Trans.* XVII. 947 What they call Firing is this: When Plants are of small Substance, as when there has been a very wet and cold season, and very hot Weather suddenly ensues, the Leaves [of tobacco] turn brown, and dry to dust. **1800** TATHAM *Tobacco* 22 During very rainy seasons, and in some kinds of unfavourable soil, the plant is subject to a malady called *firing.*

2. The appearance of something resembling fire. *Rare.*

1880 *Harper's Mag.* Sep. 511/2 The schools [of fish] worked nearer the top at night, and their presence was betrayed by a phosphorescent 'firing' in the water.

3. Discharging an employee. Cf. * **fire,** *v.* **1. b.**

1947 *Chi. Sun* 4 Nov. 6/5 (*heading*), Oak Park Firings Laid to Patronage. The meeting of the village trustees . . . was attended by 200 persons who protested the firings. **1948** *Spokesman-Review* (Spokane, Wash.) 23 Sep. 4/7 The firings will not bother the politically-pegged swivel boys in the Washington office.

4. a. firing business, the activity connected with the discharging of an employee. *Rare.* **b.** * **firing place,** (see quot.).

(a) **1887** *Courier-Journal* 18 Jan. 2/2 The Senate will follow by firing Republicans, and in every case with proper justification. . . . You may, therefore, expect the firing business to be lively the rest of the week. — (b) **1902** CLAPIN 185 *Firing-place*, in New Jersey, a common name applied to a spot suitable for charcoal burning.

As the last term in **back, bush, word firing.**

firm name. The name of a commercial house or company. — **1869** TOURGEE *Toinette* xlvi. 459 There is the firm name of my New York factors. **1876** INGRAM *Centennial Exp.* xi. 377 All the needles manufactured by this firm . . . have, in addition to the firm-name, the name of Mr. Thornton on them, as a guarantee of their genuineness.

* **first,** *a.*

1. Designating a district, church, bank, etc., organized, incorporated, or named as the first of its kind in a given community.

a. Of an election district, ward, precinct, etc.

1792 *Mass. Acts & Resolves* (1895) 185 The first district shall consist of the counties of Suffolk Essex & Middlesex & shall be entitled to choose four representatives. **1812** *Ann. 12th Congress* 1 Sess. II. 1436 The proceedings of a public meeting of Republican citizens of the First Congressional district of Pennsylvania. **1897** *R.I. Secy. State Manual* 225 First Judicial District. (County of Newport.) **1945** *Evanston Review* 12 April 56/1 First Precinct, embracing that part of the District north and west of the Sanitary District Drainage Canal.

b. Of a church. Cf. **5.** (6) below.

The ellipt. expression "First Church" is often used for the fuller title, such as "First Baptist Church," whenever the denomination is otherwise implied.

[**1827** R. KNIGHT *Six Principle Baptists* 244 The first church in Newport, was formed in 1644.] **1839** HAGUE *Hist. Discourse* 7 The First Baptist Church . . . of the city of Providence . . . voted unanimously, that the thanks of this Committee be returned to the Rev. William Hague. **1848** LOWELL *Biglow P.* 1 Ser. 6 Of 'Rev. Homer Wilbur, A.M., Pastor of the First Church in Jaalam,' we have small care to speak here. **1948** *Life* 16 Feb. 96/2 Dodds is a lay preacher . . . in the First Brethren Church, a Protestant denomination found principally in the Middle West.

c. Of banks.

1873 *R.I. Secy. State Manual* 132 First National Bank of Hopkinton. **1948** *Dly. Ardmoreite* (Ardmore, Okla.) 18 May 6/5 In 1892 he helped organize the First National bank of Vinita.

2. Designating the best or most able group, athletic team, etc.

1846 *Spirit of Times* 9 May 126/3 The defeat of the Philadelphia Club, in both games [of cricket]—the 'first Eleven' being beaten badly in a single innings, and the 'second Eleven' by 15 runs only. **1856** *Spirit of Times* 6 Dec. 229/2 The other members of the 'first nine' are Messrs. Davis, Conover and Kissam, who play in the field. **1895** WILLIAMS *Princeton Stories* 43 It is better to have First Group than the Glee Club. **1901** *Denver Republican* 26 Aug. 6/1 Denver pushed into the first division yesterday after months spent among the despond of the second division. **1948** *Dly. Ardmoreite* (Ardmore, Okla.) 30 Mar. 6/1 Detroit hasn't a first-division ball club.

3. the first, so much as one, even a single. *Colloq.*

1849 *N.Y. Tribune* 23 May 2/2 My knees, which I couldn't move the first inch. **1857** *Cong. Globe* 27 Feb. 926/1, I am not aware of committing the first act, or doing the first thing, which should call upon me the displeasure of this House.

4. *absol.* **a.** The first time.

1862 NORTON *Army Letters* 95 Yesterday was the first that we could write at all. **1916** *Outing* April 98/1 [One is] pretty sure of landing a respectable number of fair-sized ones [i.e., fish], even on the 'first.'

b. *Baseball.* =**first base.**

1867 *Ball Players' Chron.* 6 June 2/2 Hunniwell led off on the Harvard side, and by a muff of Sumner's made his first. **1885** *Santa Fe W. New Mexican* 10 Sep. 4 Dallas . . . by a quick throw to Cavanaugh at first doubled up Walton who was attempting to go second base. **1948** *Green Bay* (Wis.) *Press-Gazette* 30 June 11/1 Kurtz, the third baseman, threw wild to first and Ackermann scored.

5. In special combs.: (1) **first balcony,** the lowest balcony in a theater, also **first balcony circle;** (2) **base,** see as a main entry; (3) **best,** foremost, first in distinction, *colloq.;* (4) **board,** see **board,** *n.* **4. b;** (5) **bottom,** see **bottom,** *n.* **2;** (6) **First Church of Christ, Scientist,** the organization or the building itself of the Christian Science Church at Boston, or the Christian Science church first organized in a community; (7) * **class,** see as a main entry; (8) **cost,** the initial cost; (9) **-day school,** Sunday school, used chiefly by Quakers; (10) **degree,** see **degree;** (11) **family,** see as a main entry; (12) * **grade,** see as a main entry; (13) **lady,** the wife of the President of the U.S., also **first lady of (in) the land;** (14) **magistrate,** (*a*) the governor of a state, (*b*) the President of the U.S., cf. **chief magistrate;** (15) * **members,** particular members of the Mother Church of the First Church of Christ, Scientist, who had administrative functions from 1892 to 1901 and continued to function until 1903; (16) **money,** first prize, also *fig.;* (17) **name,** a Christian name; (18) **papers,** the first documents of record in the naturalization of a foreigner; (19) **presidency,** see **presidency;** (20) ***rate,** see as a main entry; (21) ***reader,** the member of a Christian Science church or society elected to conduct the principal part of its services; (22) **reader class,** the school class using the first reader; (23) **settler,** one who takes up land and settles first or early in a given region; (24) ***story,** the ground floor of a building, also attrib.

(1) 1871 *Chi. Ev. Jrnl.* 26 Aug., Passing by the easy graded stairway to the first balcony circle, a lobby [etc.]. *Ib.*, Above the first balcony is the second balcony. **1872** *Chi. Tribune* 6 Oct., The dress circle and first balcony are seated with chairs of the latest style. — **(3) 1862** LOWELL *Biglow P.* 2 Ser. iii. 94 Where every fem'ly is fus'-best an' nary white man works. **1891** *Scribner's Mag.* X. 771 He has come out first best in the costly contest with those who would have revised nature.

(6) 1893 *Christian Science Jrnl.* Sep. 272 The Annual Meeting of 'The First Church of Christ, Scientist,' in Boston, Mass., will be held . . . Oct. 3, 1893. **1945** *Evanston Review* 12 April 82/3 She was a member of the . . . First Church of Christ, Scientist. — **(8) 1773** FRANKLIN *Writings* V. 456 At least a Million of Americans drink Tea twice a Day, which, at the first Cost here, can scarce be reckoned at less than half a Guinea a Head *per Annum.* **1857** *Ill. Agric. Soc. Trans.* II. 20 Corn, oats, bran and meal will be furnished, at first cost, on the grounds. — **(9) 1842** *Amer. Pioneer* I. 166 The fifty-first anniversary of the First Day, or Sunday School Society, was held at 146 Chesnut street. **1923** *Orthodox Friends' Yearly Meeting* (Phila.) *Minutes* 99 We would that our members might be more fully alive to the opportunities afforded by First-day schools and Bible classes.

(13) 1863 RUSSELL *Diary* II. 393 The gentleman who furnished fashionable paragraphs for the Washington paper has some charming little pieces of gossip about 'the first Lady in the Land.' **1886** POORE *Reminisc.* II. 353 'The first lady of the land' discarded the vulgar extravagances which had become common at Washington. **1948** *Chi. Tribune* 26 June I. 1/4 Mrs. Thomas E. Dewey disclosed today what kind of first lady she will be. — **(14)** *(a)* **1789** in F. CHASE *Hist. Dartmouth Coll.* (1891) I. 609 The board of trustees [have] the highest confidence of the influence of the first Magistrate of the State [i.e., the governor of N.H.] in favor of the interests of the College. *(b)* **1789** *N.Y. Dly. Gazette* 1 May 426/1 Yesterday the Great and illustrious Washington . . . entered upon execution of the office of First Magistrate of the United States of America. **1801** HAMILTON *Works* VII. 219 It must be a matter of profound regret that a proposal which could give rise to it should have come from the First Magistrate of the United States.

(15) 1895 EDDY *Church Manual* (ed. 1) i. § 1 Only the First Members of the church are required to vote on admitting candidates, and attend to the transaction of any church business that may properly come before the meeting. **1901** *Ib.* (ed. 20) vi, The business of The Mother Church hitherto transacted by the First Members shall be done by its Christian Science Board of Directors. **1903** *Ib.* (ed. 29) v. § 1 The members known as First Members prior to March 17, 1903, . . . shall bear the title and be known as Executive Members. — **(16) 1894** *Vt. Agric. Rep.* XIV. 96 He trotted in seventeen races this year; won nine first moneys. **1898** WESTCOTT *D. Harum* xxix, 'It took fust money, that did,' said Mr. Harum. — **(17) 1839** BRIGGS *H. Franco* I. 74 'My first name is Harry,' I said. **1949** *Chi. D. News* 23 March 26/3 The indiscriminate use of first names blurs all these distinctions and cheapens the favor of conferring friendship. — **(18) 1912** J. HART *Vigilante Girl* 388 Before securing naturalization a man must take out his first papers, under the law, and then remain in the country for five years. **1947** PAUL *Linden* 216 He had his first papers, and knew the answers which would win him his second papers.

(21) 1896 EDDY *Misc. Writings* 314 The First Reader . . . shall read all the selections from Science and Health referred to in the Sunday Lessons. **1920** *N.Y. Times* 8 June 10/7 John Randall Dunn of St. Louis was elected first reader, and Miss Margaret Glenn of New York . . . was elected second reader, each for a term of three years. — **(22) 1894** *Harper's Mag.* March 643/1 His education . . . had not carried him beyond the First Reader class in the local district school. **1904** M. KELLY *Little Citizens* 203 The First Reader Class filed down the yard for recess. — **(23) 1654** *Boston Rec.* 51 The first lot . . . is bounded by the lines or highway which divides the land of the first goers or first settlers of Woodstock and the stayers, or other inhabitants of Roxbury. **1854** BENTON *30 Years' View* I. 12/2 [The relief plan for purchasers of public lands failed to allow] a pre-emptive right to all first settlers. **1948** DICK *Dixie Frontier* 11 In western Georgia, Alabama, and parts of Mississippi were to be found . . . first settlers. — **(24) 1881** *Harper's Mag.* Jan 193/2, I was knocked flat . . . by the falling mass of brick, and was forced . . . through the first-story floor, into the cellar. **1897** F. C. MOORE *How to Build a Home* 39 The ceilings of summer houses should be not less than eleven feet for the first story and ten feet for bedroom stories.

b. In less frequent, usu. obs., combs.: (1) **first ball hitter,** (see quot.); (2) **breath of spring,** (see quot.); (3) **comer,** an early settler, one of the forefathers, cf. **old charter bill;** (4) **courser, -course student,** in medical schools, a student in his first year of study; (5) **cut,** the best, *slang;* (6) **fathers,** early emigrants to America; (7) **goer,** one who goes into a community first; (8) **growth,** (see quot.); (9) **low ground,** =**first bottom;** (10) **magistracy,** the office of the first magistrate; (11) ***page,** designating news of great interest, *colloq.;* (12) **shot,** strong whisky; (13) **swathe,** first-rate; (14) **teller,** (see quot.); (15) **termer,** a congressman serving his first term.

(1) 1912 MATHEWSON *Pitching* 128 Murray and Devore are what are known in baseball as 'first-ball hitters.' That is, they invariably hit at the first one delivered. — **(2) 1931** CLUTE *Plants* 139 In the shrubberies, the fragrant honeysuckle (*Lonicera fragrantissima*) sends forth a perfume that may well make the name of first-breath-of-spring a tangible thing. — **(3)** *a***1861** T. WINTHROP *Canoe & Saddle* xiii. 293 There was the sutler's shop near the shore, and, grouped about it, tents of the first-comers of the overland emigration. **1894** *Cent. Mag.* April 850/1 No doubt many of the first-comers said 'year' for 'ear,' as many of their descendants do today. — **(4) 1850** LEWIS *La. Swamp Doctor* 121 John Smith suffers, and always appears in the police reports, when the first course student is put in the watch-house. *Ib.* 122, [I] had followed after the manner of *first coursers,* and would have been a fac simile of the candidate, or second course student, had it not been for my habitual laziness.

(5) 1843 STEPHENS *High Life N.Y.* I. 115 But jest as I lifted up my head, and drew up my foot, arter making of my fust cut bows, she stood jest afore me. — **(6) 1670** I. MATHER *Life R. Mather* 55 Posterity may thereby see what were the swaying Motives which prevailed with the First-fathers of N[ew] E[ngland] to venture upon that unparallell'd Undertaking. — **(7) 1654** [see **first settler**]. — **(8) 1905** *Forestry Bureau Bul.* No. 61, 10 *First growth.* 1. Natural forest in which no cuttings have been made. . . . 2. Trees grown before lumbering or severe fire entered the forest; belonging to the original stand. — **(9) 1771** in *Amer. Sp.* XV. 177/2 It is all first and second low Grounds, very level, and will produce any Thing usually cultivated in this Colony.

(10) 1796 in S. K. PADOVER *Jefferson* (1942) 245 But tho' at that date your election to the first magistracy seems not to have been known as a fact. — **(11) 1928** *Publishers' Wkly.* 30 June 2603 Anything that he may say or discuss in London is first page news in the American press. — **(12) 1840** *N.O. Picayune* 30 Aug. 2/4, O, it's illigant, Mrs. Mahoney, and as strong as fust shot. — **(13) 1841–2** MATHEWS *Puffer Hopkins* (B. '48), Nothing'll serve you but a first-swathe mug, about twenty-three years old. *a***1871** in DE VERE 602 She was a first-swathe gal, if ever there was one in our village, and the way she made the money fly, when she came to town to shop! — **(14) 1895** E. CARROLL *Principles Finance* 118 *Paying Teller.* The paying teller is often called the 'first teller.'

(15) 1888 *Cong. Rec.* 25 May 4634/2 He was going upon the idea . . . that a first-termer has not much standing in this House.

c. In phrases: (1) *first Tuesday after the first Monday,* general election day in the month of November in election years; (2) *first, last, and all the time,* permanent, unwavering, *colloq.;* (3) *first of the year,* (see quot. 1935).

(1) [**1872** *Statutes at Large* 2 Feb. 28 The Tuesday next after the first Monday in November . . . is hereby fixed . . . for the election of Representatives and Delegates to the forty-fifth Congress.] **1919** *World Almanac 1920* 30 Election Day (1st Tuesday after the 1st Monday in November, all over Union, except Dist. of Col.). — **(2) 1904** *N.Y. Tribune* 3 June 8 The supporters of other Presidential candidates have not usually been so wary about pledging a 'first, last and all the time' support to their chosen favorites. **1935** HORWILL 133 *First, last, and all the time* is originally a formula used by the spokesman of a State delegation at a national party convention in putting forward a candidate for the Presidential nomination. It pledges (or seems to pledge) these delegates not to 'trade' their vote to any other candidate while the struggle for the nomination is in process. — **(3) 1928** *Publishers' Wkly.* 25 Feb. 782 It is reasonable to expect a request for the exchange of a Christmas gift to be made within a couple of weeks after the first of the year. **1935** HORWILL 132 In Eng. one may speak of *the first* of the month meaning the first day of it. In Am. one may speak also of *the first* of the year, or of the week; not, however, meaning the first day of this period but the first part of it.

first base. *Baseball.*

1. The base that must be touched first by a runner.

1845 in *Wilkes' Spirit of Times* (1864) 17 Dec. 244/2 A ball knocked outside the range of the first or third base is foul. **1891** N. CRANE *Baseball* iv. 31 He must drop his bat and run at once for first base.

1948 *Dly. Ardmoreite* (Ardmore, Okla.) 19 April 6/1 He failed to touch first base after poling the ball over the leftfield fence in the seventh. *attrib.* 1946 *Birmingham News-Age-Her.* 14 July 1B/1 Pesky scored as Bobby Doerr bunted safely down the first base line.

b. *To reach (get to) first base, fig.* to be at least moderately successful, usu. in negative contexts. *Slang.*

1931 *Variety* 29 Dec. 21/1 Vaudeville in its entirety failed to reach first base at any time during 1931. 1948 *Chi. Tribune* 18 Mar. I. 4/5, I discovered he lived in my neighborhood but I couldn't get to first base with him.

2. =next. Also **first base player.**

1856 *Spirit of Times* 8 Nov. 165/2 *Runs:* T. S. Darkin (pitcher) 3; ... J. E. Davidson, jr. (first base), 1. 1867 *Ball Players' Chron.* 27 June 1/4 The Mutuals were minus the services of Bierman only, their first base player. 1880 N. Brooks *Fairport Nine* ii. 24 Eph Weeks was the catcher of the White Bears, and Joe Patchen was the first base.

3. first baseman, the player who is stationed at first base.

1857 *Spirit of Times* 7 Nov. 148/2 It is claimed by his friends that he is the best first base man in any club. 1886 *Outing* June 365/2 The Pittsburgh club ... releases Scott, its first baseman, who has signed with the Baltimore club. 1948 *Green Bay* (Wis.) *Press-Gazette* 30 June 11/1 The first-baseman threw wild to the plate.

* **first class.** *n.* and *a.*

1. *n.* **a.** The class in which beginning pupils are enrolled. Also attrib. **b.** The class in which finishing students are enrolled. Also attrib. Cf. **first classman.**

a. 1750 Franklin *Writings* III. 22 First or Lowest Class. Let the first class learn the English Grammar Rules. 1821 in Cubberley *Pub. Educ. in U.S.* 304 No one in the first class shall be recommended [for promotion] ... unless he or she can spell correctly. 1854 E. Sargent (*title*), The First-Class Standard Reader.

b. 1845 in *Boston School Rep. 1841–1850* 153 It is believed that the average age of the first class in all the [writing] schools is about twelve or thirteen years. 1858 *Boston School Comm. Rep. 1857* 26 A disposition was manifested on the part of the teachers to present the performances of the first class. 1948 *Atlantic Mo.* March 39/2 Then, in first class year, he reaches the ultimate. He is allowed to show initiative, to do the leading.

2. *a.* Of mail: Comprising, in general, all matter sealed or otherwise closed against ready inspection, as well as written matter sealed or unsealed.

"Mailable matter shall be divided into three classes, namely: first, letters; second, regular printed matter; third, miscellaneous matter. ... The first class embraces all correspondence, wholly or partly in writing, except that mentioned in the third class" (1863 *Statutes at Large* XII. 705).

1878 *Rep. Postmaster-Gen.* 33 The efficiency and security of the registry system of first-class mail matter suggested the propriety of extending its provisions to valuable matter of the third class. 1887 *Postal Laws* 138 A 'drop letter' ... is first-class matter and should be returned to the writer, if unclaimed. 1948 *Chi. Sun-Times* 11 July 24/1 The only profitable classes of mail under existing rates are first class mail and foreign 'surface' mail.

3. In special combs.: (1) * **first-class clerk,** a clerk in the lowest salary bracket; (2) * **man,** at Annapolis and West Point, a fourth-year man; (3) **postage,** postage for first-class mail.

(1) 1865 *Atlantic Mo.* XV. 327 Worthy young men ... refused to entertain the idea of marriage with girls whose mere personal outfit cost a sum equal to the year's salary of a first-class clerk. — (2) 1886 Dorsey *Midshipman Bob* 127 When Lanman, a sturdy, well-built first-classman, stepped into the ring, the building rang with applause. 1948 *Atlantic Mo.* March 39/2 There were trying times in my case, when four years seemed a long while, when the first classmen were particularly exacting. — (3) 1879 *Postal Laws* 72 The Postmaster-General may prescribe ... the manner of wrapping ... all packages of matter not charged with first-class postage. 1924 H. A. Blackman *Business Mail* 15 In this connection it is well to remember that first-class postage is never an odd number of cents.

First Family. Also **first family.**

1. One of the first or earliest families to settle in a new community; hence freq. a family of social rank or pretensions. Often used derisively.

1844 *S. Lit. Messenger* X. 485/2 He sprang from one of those numerous 'first families,' which have so plentifully peopled the southwest in these latter years. 1878 Stowe *Poganuc People* xxxviii. 354 All this talk ... of 'first families' and their ways and laws and opinions ... amuses me. 1900 Ade *More Fables* 51 All the First Families in the State were related to him.

attrib. and *transf.* 1856 Phillips *Kansas* 235 He went with an easy swagger, and from the tip of his slouched hat to the point of his toes he looked an unmistakable member of the 'first family' of ruffians. 1874 Aldrich *P. Palfrey* xi, There isn't any 'first-family' nonsense about him. 1948 *Reader's Digest* January 52/1 No Boston First Family party is complete without some discussion of genealogy.

b. Esp. *First Families of* (or *in*) *Virginia.* Also attrib. Cf. **F.F.V.**

1847 *Knickerb.* XXIX. 495 A Virginia scion insisted that they were an abbreviation he had seen used in the navy to represent 'First Family in Virginia.' 1850 *Cong. Globe* App. 6 March 337 They were 'as mute as a mouse in a cheese'—yes, sir, as a first family Virginia mouse in an English cheese. 1947 *Chi. Sun* (Bk. Week) 29 June 2/2 A girl, member of one of the fabled First Families of Virginia ... accepts an offer to teach.

first grade.

1. The foremost quality or distinction. Also attrib.

1818 Fearon *Sketches* 30 Neither trades are (to use an Americanism) of the first grade. 1904 *Newark Ev. News* 8 Aug. 1 A first grade chanceman of the First Precinct was suspended.

2. The beginning class in an elementary school. Also attrib.

1835 *S. Lit. Messenger* I. 275 In the first and second grades boys and girls are schooled together. 1894 M. H. Page *Graded Schools U.S.* 39 Elementary fractions are taught in the first grade. 1918 *Bureau Educ. Bul.* No. 15, 127 Many influences work together to deter the progress of first-grade children. 1944 *Athol* (Mass.) *Town Report* 66 Assignment changes.... First and second grade teacher at the Ellen Bigelow School to grade two.

b. first-grader, a pupil in such a class.

1945 MacDonald *Egg & I* 229, I thought what a long day eight o'clock to four-thirty must be for six-year-old first graders.

* **first-rate,** *a.* and *adv.* In colloq. uses.

1. In excellent health, very well.

1840 A. M. Maxwell *Run through U.S.* I. 82 The old one saying to the young one—'Well, my fine chap, how d'ye find yourself?' and the laconic reply of 'First-rate!' 1880 Howells *Undiscovered Country* iv. 79, I want to go away to-morrow feeling first-rate.

2. Excellently, very well.

1842 Allen *Ten Years in Ore.* (1848) 154 Esquire Crocker wishes me to say that he likes sleeping out of doors on a single blanket, very well; and feeding on fat buffalo meat alone, first rate. 1890 Jewett *Strangers* 9, I liked Tobin first-rate.

b. first-rate bad, very bad indeed. *Rare.*

1829 Barnum *Struggles & Triumphs* 259 We stopped at the Washington House, which at that time was 'first-rate bad.' It was filthy.

c. first-rate and a half, an intensified form of **first-rate,** most excellent.

1834 *Amer. R.R. Jrnl.* III. 304/3, I sort o' think that's first rate and a half. 1898 Cahan *Imported Bridegroom* 168, I do like it, first-rate and a half.

fir tree, *n.* As the last term in **New Jersey, Pennsylvania fir tree.**

fiscal fɪsˈkəl, *n. S.W.* [Sp. in same sense.] An attorney-general, one who acts for the government. *Obs.* — 1871 *Rep. Indian Affairs* (1872) 392 The officers consist of a governor, lieutenant governor, casique, fiscal, superintendent of acequias. 1881 Morgan *Contrib. to Amer. Ethnology* 148 The six fiscals are a kind of town police.

fiscal year. A financial year; in commerce, the year between one annual settlement or balancing of accounts and another.

1843 Tyler in *Pres. Mess. & P.* 264 By the act of 1842 a new arrangement of the fiscal year was made, so that it should commence on the 1st day of July in each year. 1871 Raymond *3rd Rep. Mines* 99 The above figures represent the condition of the company at the close of the fiscal year ending June 30. 1948 *Lawton* (Okla.) *Constitution* 30 June 1/1 The effective date of the ordinance is July 1, coinciding with the first day of the new fiscal year.

* **fish,** *n.*

1. (See quot.) *Obs.* Cf. * **fish,** *v.* **2,** * **fisher 2,** * **fishing 1.**

1851 Hall *College Words* 129 *Fish, Fisher,* one who attempts to ingratiate himself with his instructor, thereby to obtain favor or advantage; one who curries favor.

2. (See quot. 1944.)

1903 A. Adams *Log Cowboy* iv. 47, I ... flaunted my 'fish' in their [=cattle's] faces. 1944 Adams *W. Words* 59 Fish: The yellow oilskin slicker that all oldtime cowboys kept neatly rolled and tied behind the cantles of their saddles took this name from the picture of its trademark, a fish.

3. In the names of devices, organizations, etc., concerned with the catching of fish: (1) * **fish basket,** a basket for catching fish; (2) **car,** a watertight box in which fish are kept alive, also a car for fish; (3) **company,** a company organized to catch and market fish; (4) **coop,** a box which covers and shadows a fisherman in fishing through ice, thus enabling him to lure and spear fish; (5) **dam,** (see quot. 1784); (6) **gorge,** (see quot. 1907); (7) **pole,** a light pole or rod for use in fishing; (8) * **pot,** (see quot. 1775); (9) **pound,** (see quot. *a*1870); (10) **slide,** (see quot.); (11) **trap,** a trap for catching fish, esp. a fish pot, also, *transf.*, a person's mouth, *slang;* (12) **worm,** an angleworm, also attrib. with *oil.*

(1) **1814** BRACKENRIDGE *Louisiana* 179 They unite, and thus form a semicircle like a fish basket. **1844** in DE VERE 351 Various species are abundantly caught . . . in fish-baskets, made of lathwork, with diverging walls of stone. **1867** *Pa. Game Laws* in *Fur, Fin, & Feather* (1872) 100 It shall not be lawful to take, catch, or kill . . . any fish, by means of any fishbasket. — (2) **1818** THOMAS B. HAZARD *Nailer Tom's Diary* (1930) 512/2 Son Benja[min] and Joseph M Taylor Carried the Lobster Potts and Fish Carr to the Pier and brought home a lode of Eal Grass. **1867** DE VOE *Market Ass't* 21 His early visit gave him the desired opportunity to select . . . and *catch* the lively, jumping fish, which, ten minutes before, were swimming in the fish-cars. — (3) **1882** *Uncle Rufus & Ma* 33 Two fish companies caught 2,646,384 pounds of fish, valued at $132,319. — (4) **1889** *Cent.* 2236/2 [The] fish-coop . . . is used on lakes in western New York.

(5) **1784** ZEISBERGER *Diary* I. (1885) 190 Our Indians made fish-dams in different places; they stopped up the creek so that the fish could not go down. **1844** FRÉMONT *Exped.* 220 There were Indian lodges and fish-dams on the stream. — (6) **1883** *Cent. Mag.* April 900/2 Among the many implements discovered are fish-gorges made of bronze-wire. [**1907** HODGE *Amer. Indians* I. 463/1 Another ingenious device employed along the n. Pacific coast for catching fish consisted of a straight pin, sharp at both ends and fastened to a line by the middle; this pin was run through a dead minnow, and, being gorged by another fish, a jerk of the string caused the points to pierce the mouth of the fish.] — (7) **1834** *Visit to Texas* ix. 88 We touched [a flame] to a few of the tall canes, at this season as dry as fishpoles. **1886** *Leslie's Mo.* Feb. 150/1 Who'd a-thought I'd-a-lived to own a bamboo Chinee fishpole. — (8) **1775** CRESSWELL *Journal* 69 [In Va.] these fish pots are made by throwing up the small stones and gravel something like a mill weir, beginning at the side of the River and proceeding in a diagonal line, till they meet in the middle of the stream, where they fix a thing like the body of a cart, contracted where the water flows in just to admit the fish, but so contrived as to prevent their return or escape. **1874** R. H. COLLINS *Kentucky* I. 544 Requiring overseers . . . to 'work it' [the stream] with hands from the neighborhood—*i.e.* to remove all fish-pots. — (9) **1859** *Huntington Rec.* III. 447 Application of William Spriggs and Charles S. Hartt to put down fish pounds in Northport harbor for the purpose of catching fish. *a***1870** CHIPMAN *Notes on Bartlett* 151 *Fish-pound*, a net attached to stakes and used for entrapping and catching fish; a weare.—Conn. **1874** *Rep. Comm. Agric. 1873* 289 This decrease is attributable to the combined effect of the fish-pounds or weirs.

(10) **1884** *Nat. Museum Bul.* No. 27, 1017 Fish-slide or trap. . . . A series of wooden slats set in a sloping frame. . . . 'A slide of this kind is set in the current of a shallow stream, its upper surface raised from the bottom at an angle of 25 to 30 degrees, the lower edge, which comes in contact with the water, facing up stream, and the top edge reaching above the water.' — (11) **1813** in *East Tenn. Hist. Soc. Pub.* XII. 124 We wase Cuting of a large pine tree on the Side of the Creeck I Stood by . . . ther was the apearance of a old fich trap that might have bin built fifty yeares agoo. **1853** SIMMS *Sword & Distaff* 59 'Shut up your fish-trap, you ——, . . . or I'll tear out your tongue.' **1934** VINES *Green Thicket World* 12 They completely worked the territory around a torn-up fish trap. — (12) **1870** EMERSON *Soc. & Solitude* 163 The savant is often an amateur. His performance is a memoir to the Academy on fish-worms, tadpoles, or spiders' legs. **1910** MCCUTCHEON *Rose in Ring* 61 Say, are you goin' to learn the business? If you are, I got some fishworm oil that's jest the thing to limber up yer joints. **1945** *Athol* (Mass.) *D. News* 31 May 7/3 (*advt.*), For Sale . . . Fish Worms.

b. In the names of, or with reference to, measures, devices, or organizations whose purpose is the culture and protection of fish: (1) **fish commission,** a commission established to protect the fish in streams, lakes, etc., or to regulate fishing practices; (2) **commissioner,** a member of a fish commission; (3) **cultural,** *a.* pertaining to fish culture; (4) **culturist,** one engaged in fish culture; (5) **hatchery,** a place where fish are artificially hatched and raised; (6) **ladder,** a series of steps over a dam or falls to enable fish to pass upstream; (7) **preserve,** an area set aside for the raising of fish; (8) **ward, warden,** an officer authorized to look after the fishing interests of a community; (9) **wheel,** a large wheel placed in a stream and provided with devices for lifting fish over a dam or falls.

(1) **1875** *Fisheries Bureau Rep.* III. p. xv, The work of the United States Fish Commission in multiplying useful food-fishes was commenced in 1872. **1902** W. HULBERT *Forest Neighbors* (1903) 63 [The fish] was not a native of the stream, but of one of the hatcheries of the Michigan Fish Commission. — (2) **1866** *Vt. Laws* 70 The Governor of the State is . . . empowered to appoint two persons, to be styled fish commissioners, whose duties shall be to confer with the fish commissioners of the New England States and Canada. **1897** *Cong. Rec.* 8 July 2464/1 The Fish Commissioner has already promised me to make a recommendation as to the waters in North Carolina. — (3) **1880** (*title*), Transactions of the American Fish-cultural Association. **1909** *Rep. Comm. Fisheries 1907* 5 Fish-cultural work varies little from year to year. — (4) **1872** (*title*), Proceedings of the American Fish Culturists' Association. **1883** in *Nat. Museum Bul.* No. 27, 56 In 1880 the Grand Prize of the International Fisheries Exhibition at Berlin was awarded to Professor Baird as 'the first fish-culturist in the world.'

(5) **1885** *Laramie* (Wyo.) *Boomerang* 21 Oct. 1/7 Manager Slocum, of the Wyoming fish hatchery, came into town this morning. **1947** *Steamboat* (Colo.) *Pilot* 2 Jan. 2/2 S. E. Land, superintendent of the Steamboat fish hatchery, went to Denver to get 200,000 rainbow trout eggs to hatch here. — (6) **1865** *Mich. Gen. Statutes* I. (1882) 574 There shall be erected and maintained in each dam now existing or which may hereafter be constructed across any (stream or) river in this state sufficient and permanent shutes or fish ladders to admit of the free and uninterrupted passage of fish over such dam or dams. **1948** *Pacific Discovery* July–Aug. 27/1 The fish ladder is at the south end away from the main stream flow. — (7) **1892** *Vt. Agric. Rep.* XII. 159 Many of our abandoned farms can be turned into fish and game preserves. — (8) **1790** *Mass. Acts & Laws* (1894) V. 498 Every town in this Common-wealth bordering on Merrimack river . . . shall at their annual meeting . . . choose by ballot, at least four suitable and fit persons, as fish wardens. *a***1867** *N.H. Gen. Statutes 1867* 508 All nets, seines, fishing tackle, spears, or other implements used in catching or taking fish . . . may be seized by any fishward, constable, or selectman. — (9) **1893** *Outing* XXII. 135/1 A fish-wheel with nets which extend to the falls of the river.

c. In the names of foods and of social functions at which fish is eaten: (1) **fish ball,** a fried cake made of shredded fish (usu. salted codfish) and mashed potato, usu. *pl.*, cf. **codfish ball,** and see **5.** (1) below; (2) **cake,** =prec.; (3) **chowder,** a chowder the chief ingredients of which are fish, potatoes, and onions; (4) **feast,** a feast consisting chiefly of fish; (5) **festival,** among Indians of the Northwest, a time of celebration and feasting on fish; (6) **fry,** a picnic or party where fish are fried and eaten; (7) **muddle,** (see quot. and cf. **muddle**).

(1) [**1832** L. M. CHILD *Amer. Frugal Housewife* 60 There is no way of preparing salt fish for breakfast, so nice as to roll it up in little balls, after it is mixed with mashed potatoes.] **1854** SHILLABER *Mrs. Partington* 100 The breakfast was waiting for him, the fishballs were getting cold. **1944** JOHNSON *As I Dare* 7 Only in parts of New England do beans and brown bread come always for Saturday supper, and fish balls for Sunday breakfast. — (2) **1883** *Fisheries Exhib. Cat.* 316 Fishcakes in Curry. **1948** *Sat. Ev. Post* 4 Dec. 123/3 She'd had one fish cake at the Automat for supper. — (3) **1838** E. C. WINES *Trip to Boston* 79 We had 'clam chowder' and 'fish chowder.' **1947** COFFIN *Yankee Coast* 297 A fish-chowder that is right starts with pork scraps fried in an iron kettle. — (4) **1774** FITHIAN *Journal* I. 242, I was invited this morning by Captain Fibbs to a Barbecue: this differs but little from the Fish Feasts, instead of Fish the Dinner is roasted Pig. **1837** IRVING *Bonneville* II. 186 It was now the season of the annual fish-feast, with which the Indians in these parts celebrate the first appearance of the salmon in this river [i.e., the Columbia].

(5) **1845** DE SMET *Oregon Missions* (1847) 119, I arrived among the *Arcs-a-plats* in time to witness the grand fish festival, which is yearly celebrated. — (6) **1824** SINGLETON *Letters* 66 Fish-fries are held about once in a fortnight, during the fish season; when twenty or thirty men collect, to regale on whiskey, and fresh fish, and soft crabs just out of their sloughs. **1948** *Galveston* (Tex.) *News* 14 June 1/6 The group will go to Stewart Beach for a fish fry at 7 p.m. — (7) **1941** DANIELS *Tar Heels* 257 Fish Muddle is a name for fish stew, the ingredients of which vary with what you have got. *Ib.* 258 But the barbecues and the fish muddles (both are the name for the gatherings as well as the dishes), in the eastern part of the State . . . are occasions for both eating and drinking.

d. Designating fertilizers made from or of fish: (1) **fish flour,** (2) **guano,** (3) **manure,** (4) **scrap.**

(1) **1889** *Cent.* 2237/1 *Fish-flour*, . . . a dry inodorous fertilizer made from fishes, used for manure. — (2) **1856** *Maine Bd. Agric. Rep.* 81 The manufacture of 'fish guano,' as recently attempted, seems to indicate something of the kind, as both practicable and possibly, not

very far distant. **1884** *Rep. Comm. Fisheries 1881* 663 In the fall of 1879 the inquiry, 'Is fish guano in any of its forms used by your farmers?' was addressed to every postmaster in the United States. **1890** [see **fish scrap**]. — **(3) 1788** WASHINGTON *Diaries* III. 330 The effect of the fish Manure w[hi]ch was put into the Corn hills in May last was visible with the Wheat. **1868** *Mass. Bd. Agric. Rep.* I. 105 Fish manures, the product of the oil-fisheries on our coast, . . . sell at about forty-five dollars per ton. — **(4) 1889** *Cent.* 2238/1 Fish-scrap, in either a crude or a dried state, is of great commercial importance as a fertilizer. **1890** *Ib.* 4611/3 Fish-scrap . . . is dried by exposure to the sun and ground up into fish-guano.

4. In the names of plants: (1) **fish begonia,** (see quot.); (2) **blossom,** (see quots.); (3) **geranium,** (see quots.); (4) **head,** (see quot.); (5) **-hook cactus,** any of several cacti having recurved spines; (6) **poison,** any one of various plants used, or allegedly used, in stupefying and catching fish; (7) **wood,** (see quot. 1860).

(1) 1892 *Amer. Folk-Lore* V. 96 *Begonia maculata*, trout begonia. Bedford, Mass. fish begonia. Cambridge, Mass. — **(2) 1816** THOMAS *Travels Western Country* (1819) 67 *Cercis canadensis* fish blossom, or Judas tree. **1940** CLUTE *Amer. Plant Names* (ed. 3) 255 *Cercis Canadensis.* Fish blossoms, red Judas-tree. — **(3) 1865** *Ill. Agric. Soc. Trans.* V. 581, I remarked to her, on viewing some fish geraniums in the window, how much their scent was like that emitted from the scales of a fresh fish. **1909** WEBSTER 821 *Fish geranium*, . . . with velvety leaves and scarlet flowers. It is an ancestor of the garden geranium. — **(4) 1784** CUTLER in *Mem. Academy* I. 464 *Chelone* . . . Chelone. Fish-head. Snake-head. Blossoms in spikes; white. Common by fences and amongst bushes in moist land. August.

(5) 1846 *30th Congress* 1 Sess. H.R. Ex. Doc. No. 41, 612 The fish-hook cactus is found here [in s. California]. **1875** *Amer. Naturalist* IX. 20 'The fish-hook cactus,' is found as a rarity in rocky clefts, at this season adorned with its bright red fruit. **1947** *So. Sierran* May 4/2 And last, rare and very beautiful, the Mohave Fishhook or Pineapple Cactus, *Echinocactus Polyancistrus*, with clustered iridescent magenta-pink blossoms, seen in considerable number to our delight on this trip. — **(6) 1802** DRAYTON *S. Carolina* 67 Fish poison, horse chesnut, or buck's eye. (*Æsculus Pavia.*) Grows in high land. Its root, is used as soap, for washing woollens; and if thrown into water, it has a property of stupifying the fish, so that they will lay on the top of the water, and may be taken with the hand; the Indians in this manner use it for catching fish. **1806** SHECUT *Flora Carolinæensis* I. 105 Scarlet flowering Horse chesnut, Fish Poison, or Buck Eye, an indigenious perennial plant. **1889** *Cent.* 2238/1 *Fish-poison.* . . . *Lepidium Piscidium;* the mullen, *Verbascum Thapsus;* and the red buckeye, *Aesculus Pavia.* — **(7) 1860** CURTIS *Woody Plants N.C.* 102 Strawberry Bush. . . . A shrub 2 to 5 feet high, . . . and known by the names of Burning Bush, Fish-wood, and Bursting Heart, besides the one first given. **1889** *Cent.* 2238/2.

b. In the names of birds: (1) **fish brant,** (2) **crow,** (3) **duck,** (4) **-tail hawk,** (see quots.).

(1) 1874 LONG *Wild-Fowl* 243 The snow-geese are all called fish-brant. — **(2) 1812** WILSON *Ornithology* V. 27 Fish-crow: *Corvus ossifragus* . . . is another roving inhabitant on our sea-coasts, ponds, and river shores. **1934** *Nat. Geog. Mag.* LXV. 610 Was this, I wondered, a clever move to mislead such devourers of its eggs as the bear, raccoon, skunk, and fish crows? — **(3) 1858** BAIRD *Birds Pacific R.R.* 813 *Mergus americanus.* Goosander; Sheldrake; Fish Duck. **1917** *Birds of Amer.* I. 111 Red-breasted Merganser. . . . Other Names. . . . Fishing Duck; Fish Duck; Red-breasted Sheldrake. — **(4) 1873** *Amer. Naturalist* VII. 202 Numbers of exquisitely graceful swallow-tailed kites or 'snake hawks' (*Nauclerus forficatus*, also locally known as 'fish-tail hawk') were seen sailing about in every direction.

5. In miscellaneous combs.: (1) **fish ball,** (see quot.), *obs.*, cf. **c.** (1) above; (2) **bar,** (see quot. 1874); (3) **cannery,** a place where fish are canned; (4) **canning factory,** =prec.; (5) **dance,** a form of Indian dance, *obs.;* (6) **eater,** any one of various western Indians whose chief food is fish; (7) **flake,** a frame on which fish are dried; (8) **horn,** a horn originally used by itinerant fish peddlers, later merely as a noise-making device, also transf.; (9) ***market,** *collect.* the entire group of markets which supply fish to a community, also the trade or economic conditions under which fish are bought and sold; (10) **rack,** =**fish flake;** (11) **store,** a store where fish are sold; (12) **story,** an exaggerated story, a cock-and-bull story, *colloq.;* (13) **torpedo,** a self-propelled torpedo somewhat resembling a fish; (14) **warehouse,** a building in which fish are stored.

(1) 1912 MATHEWSON *Pitching* x. 222 Out of the South . . . drift tales each spring of the 'fish' ball and the new 'hook' jump and the 'stop' ball and many more eccentric curves. — **(2) 1872** HUNTINGTON *Road-Master's Ass't* 27 Expansion . . . is supposed to have been provided for at the rolling-mill, by elongating the bold-hole both in the rail and fish-bar. **1874** KNIGHT 872/1 *Fish-bar*, the splice bar which breaks the joints of two meeting objects, as of railroad rails or scarfed timber. — **(3) 1919** J. COBB *Canning Fishery Products* 4 The raw material for fish canneries would come over the fish dock. — **(4) 1886** STAPLETON *Major's Christmas* 271, I can get you a place in the fish-canning factory to-morrow.

(5) 1849 M. EASTMAN *Dahcotah* 97 Preparations were immediately made to celebrate the Fish dance, in order to ward off any danger of which the dream might have been the omen. — **(6) 1776** in *Catholic Church in Utah* (tr.) (1909) 182 The Indians of whom we have spoken, live in the neighborhood, and subsist upon the abundant fish of the lake, for which reason the Yutas and Sabueganas called them the

Fish racks or flakes

Fish-eaters. **1873** MILLER *Amongst Modocs* ix. 111 The sea-coast Indians are 'fish-eaters.' — **(7) 1767** *Boston Gazette* 26 Jan. (Th.), Several Fish Houses, and Fish Flakes now fit for Curing Fish. **1838** HALIBURTON *Clockmaker* 2 Ser. v. 65 The Endgians . . . used to make a sort o' fish flakes, and catch herrin' and tom cods, and such sort o' fish, and put 'em on the flakes, and then crawl onder themselves. **1902** CLAPIN 185 *Fish-flake.* In New England, a kind of fagot-hurdle used for drying fish. — **(8) 1856** COZZENS *Sparrowgrass P.* iii. 38 Mrs. Sparrowgrass asked me who that was 'blowing a fish-horn.' **1877** PHELPS *Story of Avis* 106, I suppose I must make a fish-horn of my fingers. *Ib.*, The tin fish-horns that we find in galleries to see the pictures through. **1914** NORRIS *Bandover* 293 There were about twenty college men on top . . . and they were blowing fish-horns. — **(9) 1802** J. SANSOM *Lett. from Europe* II. 447 The Fish Market of New York is probably the finest in the World, whether for cheapness, excellence, or variety. **1808** *Ann. 10th Congress* 2 Sess. 121 It would be a great object with Old England utterly to destroy the New England fish market. **1885** *Rep. Indian Affairs* 147 Chinamen monopolize Mud Lake and at times overstock the fish-market to the detriment of the Indians fishing on Pyramid Lake.

(10) 1900 MUNN *Uncle Terry* 198 She's a poor old soul who lives alone and works on the fish racks. **1922** CURWOOD *Country Beyond* 149 Foreboding of evil was oppressing him when he came upon the fish-racks of the Indians. — **(11) 1944** *Democrat* 14 Sep. 2/1 Three boys are reported to have gathered enough sea food to net them $68.00 at a nearby fish store. — **(12) 1819** *St. Louis Enquirer* 8 Dec. (Th.), A fish story! . . . In consequence of the shoals of white-fish which . . . choaked the channel . . . the steamboat could not pass. **1948** *Dly. Ardmoreite* (Ardmore, Okla.) 5 May 5/1 As yet he is too young to tell very big fish stories; besides, his daddy is a preacher. — **(13) 1876** INGRAM *Centennial Exp.* v. 140 Next to this was the 'fish' torpedo, the power of propulsion of which is thirty atmospheres. **1891** *Cent.* 6392/1 The Whitehead torpedo, or fish-torpedo, may be described as a cigar-shaped vessel [etc.]. — **(14) 1701** *N.H. Probate Rec.* I. 473, I will & bequeath . . . the fish-warehouse (so called) & the wharf thereto belonging.

As the last term in **alligator, bar, barrel, basket, battle, bayonet, bellows, bill, black, blanket, blind, blue, bone, bony, brook, buffalo, bug, bur, candle, cat, cigar, cotton, creek, crow, date, devil, devil-jack-diamond, dog, dollar, drum, dumb, dun, dun cod, egg, emerald, fall, fathom, finger, Florida pipe, fly, fool, freshwater sun, frost, gar, gold, goose, green, harvest, hat, head, hog, horse, jack, Jamaica, king, lake white, log, market, May, Menominee white, merit, Michigan, moccasin, moon, mud, mud cat, mutton, Negro, New York black, New York flat, onion, oyster, paddle, pan, pappy, peel, pig, pilot, pin, pirate, pond, pork, purse net, rabbit, rainbow, rain water, rat, red, rock, rose, sail, sailor, scabbard, school, senorita, sergeant, shell, shovel, singing, soap, spatula, spear, spoon, spot, squirrel, star, suck, sun, surf, surgeon, swell, thimble, tile, toad, tree, weak, wheat, wind, yellow fish.**

*** fish**, *v.*

1. *tr.* To fertilize (ground) with fish or parts of fish. *Obs.*

"A new formation on the sb." *OED.*

1634 WOOD *N. Eng. Prospect* (1865) 48 Upon this necke where the most of the houses stand is very bad and sandie ground, yet for seaven yeares together it hath brought forth exceeding good corne, by being fished but every third yeare. **1894** EGGLESTON in *Cent. Mag.* April 851 In New England the peculiar mode of fertilizing learned from the Indians introduced a new verb; the first-comers 'fished' their corn ground.

2. *intr.* (See quot. 1851.) *College slang. Obs.* Cf. *** fish,** *n.* **1.**

1774 HUTCHINSON *Diary* I. 261 He courts me a good deal, and fishes. **1819** A. PIERCE *Rebelliad* 33 Did I not promise those who fish'd And pimp'd most, any part they wish'd. **1851** HALL *College Words* 128 *Fish.* At Harvard College, to seek or gain the good-will of an instructor by flattery, caresses, kindness, or officious civilities; to curry favor.

3. *To fish or cut bait,* to decide one way or the other. *Colloq.*

1876 *Cong. Rec.* 5 Aug. 5226/1 Now I want you gentlemen on the other side of the House to 'fish or cut bait.' **1904** *N.Y. Ev. Post* 15 Jan. 6 A visitor said the other day that it was to be wished that Senator Hanna would either 'fish or cut bait.' But the shrewd Ohio man will probably maintain for a time his ambigious position. **1948** *Green Bay* (Wis.) *Press-Gazette* 30 June 8/4 Our duly appointed delegates at the Philadelphia convention must have realized that they had to either fish or cut bait.

*** fisher**, *n.*

1. A North American animal, *Martes pennantis*, of the weasel family. Cf. **black cat, fox marten, pekan.**

1685 T. BUDD *Pa. & N.J.* 38 The Commodities fit to send to England . . . are the Skins of the several Wild Beasts that are in the Country, as . . . Fisher, Bear [etc.]. **1806** CLARK in *Lewis & C. Exped.* IV. (1905) 88 The black Fox or as they are more frequently called by the N West Trader Fisher is found in the woody country on this coast. **1945** *Boulder* (Colo.) *D. Camera* 1 Nov. 10/4 There is no open season on beaver, fisher, martin and otter. **1947** V. H. CAHALANE *Mammals* 175 Who named the fisher? It does not fish! It will eat fish if somebody else will catch it.

b. The flesh of this as food.

1877 W. WRIGHT *Big Bonanza* 93 The Captain said fisher warn't good till it had first been parboiled.

2. = *** fish,** *n.* **1.** *College slang. Obs.*

1804 *Monthly Anthology* I. 153 You besought me to respect my teachers, and to be attentive to my studies, though it shall procure me the odious title of a '*fisher.*' **1851** HALL *College Words* 129 *Fishing*, the act performed by a fisher.

3. A fishing boat.

1864 THOREAU *Cape Cod* ix. 211 Now we saw countless sails of mackerel fishers abroad on the deep.

4. In combs.: (1) **fisher bean,** (see quot.), *obs.;* (2) **cat,** = **fisher 1;** (3) **duck,** a merganser; (4) *** man,** see as a main entry; (5) **raccoon,** = **raccoon,** *obs.;* (6) **weasel,** = *** fisher 1.**

(1) **1821** *Plough Boy* II. 358/3 An opinion prevails here [Columbus, Ohio] that our soil is *too rich* for the profitable culture of the *bush bean*, (called, I believe, at the eastward, the *fisher bean*). — (2) **1868** *Amer. Naturalist* I. 655 Fisher, or Fisher-Cat (*Mustela Pennantii*). The Fisher is much like the sable, but larger, weighing . . . say from eight to ten pounds. **1900** HIGGINSON *Outdoor Studies* 254 The hedgehog is in winter the chief food of the 'fisher-cat.' — (3) **1813** WILSON *Ornithology* VIII. 126 The Smew, or White Nun. . . . This is another of those Mergansers commonly known in this country by the appellation of Fishermen, Fisher Ducks, or Divers.

(5) **1850** E. S. SEYMOUR *Sketches of Minnesota* 240 The wolf, the fox, the wolverine, the fisher raccoon, musk-rat, mink. — (6) **1838** *Mass. Zool. Survey Rep.* 24 *Mustela Canadensis*, Pekan Weasel or Fisher Weasel. . . . Very troublesome on sable lines by robbing the traps of the sable.

As the last term in **arrow, blue, gill, sun fisher.**

*** fisherman**, *n.*

1. = **fisher duck.** *Obs.*

1737 BRICKELL *N. Carolina* 208 The Fishermen, so called, from their Dexterity in Fishing, . . . are like a Duck, only they have narrow bills with sets of Teeth. They feed on small Fish and Fry, which they catch as they swim. **1813** [see **fisher duck**].

2. fisherman farmer, (see quot. 1877). *Obs.*

1877 BARTLETT 220 *Fisherman Farmer.* Said of such persons as alternate farming and fishing at different periods, expecially such as customarily farm in one, and fish in another part of each year. Seacoast of Massachusetts. **1897** *Outing* XXX. 58/2 Then we paddled ashore below a small farm-house wherein dwelt a fisherman-farmer whom I knew well.

*** fishery**, *n.* As the last term in **rock, shore fishery.**

*** fishing**, *n.* and *a.*

1. The action of currying favor; "rushing." *College slang. Obs.*

1795 C. PRENTISS *Fugitive Essays* (1797) 89 To those, who've parts at exhibition, Obtain'd by long, unwearied fishing. **1851** HALL *College Words* 129 At Dartmouth College, the electioneering for members of the secret societies was formerly called *fishing.* **1852** C. C. FELTON *Mem. J. S. Popkin* p. xxvii, If he did not appear to despise the esteem and approbation of his instructors, . . . he was suspected of fishing.

2. In combs.: (1) **fishing bounty,** a bounty allowed by act of Congress in 1792 to persons engaged in cod-fishing, *obs.;* (2) **cane,** a fishing rod made of a cane or reed; (3) **duck,** = **fisher duck;** (4) **float,** (see quot.); (5) **frolic,** a fishing excursion; (6) **light,** a light used in fishing at night, see **fire-fishing;** (7) **party,** (*a*) a group of people on a fishing trip, (*b*) a social gathering at which fishing is the chief form of entertainment, a fish fry; (8) **plummet,** a stone or pebble fashioned by Indians, app. for use as a sinker in fishing; (9) **pole,** = **fish pole;** (10) *** rod,** a cane or reed of a kind often used as a fishing pole; (11) **root,** a plant resembling angelica, *rare;* (12) **schooner,** a schooner used in fishing; (13) **time,** *N. Eng.* the time when a town's chief attention is turned to the task of fishing; (14) **tool,** in oil-well-drilling, a tool used to grasp and hoist broken apparatus from a well; (15) **warden,** = **fish warden.**

(1) **1840** *Niles' Reg.* 18 April 107/1 Mr. Benton, from a select committee, made a report on the origin and character of the fishing bounties and allowances. **1860** in LOGAN *Great Conspiracy* 221 The first [of these evils] was the Fishing Bounties, paid mostly to the sailors of New England. — (2) **1767** J. ROWE *Diary* 135, I got no harm only broke my fishing Cane. **1902** HARBEN *A. Daniel* 124 At the bars he met Abner Daniel with a fishing cane in his hands. — (3) **1805** LEWIS in *L. & Clark Exped.* II. (1904) 179, I have seen for the first time on the Missouri at these falls, a species of fishing ducks with white wings, brown and white body and the head and part of the neck adjoining a brick red. **1917** *Birds of Amer.* I. 110, 111. — (4) **1893** *Standard Dict. Fishing-float,* a scow used in seine-fishing, from which an apron is let down to the bed of the river for the more convenient handling of the seine.

(5) **1881** TOURGEE *'Zouri's Christmas* iii, Not unfrequently 'Marse Ben' had joined his employé in a 'fishing frolic.' — (6) **1845** KIRKLAND *Western Clearings* 120 Nobody broke his windows or pulled the shingles off his roof to make fishing-lights or quail-traps. — (7) (*a*) **1775** in JOHNSON *N. Hale* 167, 200 men had been draughted out that morning for a fishing party. **1919** HOUGH *Sagebrusher* ix, Onct in a while a woman would come out with some fishing party in a automobile. (*b*) **1836** GILMAN *Recoll.* (1838) 176 Fishing parties, and the chase soon occupied his leisure moments. **1906** BELL *C. Lee* 326 Mrs. Gordon Fitzhugh . . . advised a fishing-party and picnic, rather an oddity in November. — (8) **1872** *Amer. Naturalist* VI. 225 Girdled, globular or oval pebbles, which have been designated 'fishing-plummets,' are very abundant. — (9) **1791** THOMAS B. HAZARD *Nailer Tom's Diary* (1930) 127/1, I broke my Fishing Pole Cought 4 Pickrel 3 Eeels and 6 Trout. **1949** *Time* 18 April 70/2 He used to sit in school daydreaming, and I always suspected he had his fishing pole hidden out back somewheres.

(10) **1834** *Visit to Texas* xx. 192 There are tracts of land . . . overgrown with the long reeds which we know in the Northern States as fishing rods. **1836** EDWARD *Hist. Texas* 67 These canes . . . are known in the Northern States as *fishing rods.* — (11) **1687** CLAYTON *Va.* in *Phil. Trans.* XLI. 157 You have gotten some of the Fishing-root, The Fishing-root! replied F; pray why do you give it that Name? Because, said he, when we were boys, we used to get some of it to lay with our Baits to invite the Fish to bite. — (12) **1761** NILES *Indian Wars* II. 427 Five fishing-schooners being in Tennent's Harbor, . . . 17 of the men went on shore to get bait. **1875** HOWELLS *Lady of Aroostook* iv, Here and there a small fishing schooner came lagging slowly in, as belated. — (13) **1633** *Mass. Bay Rec.* I. 104 It is ordered, that if any swine shall, in fishing time, come within a quarter of a myle of the stage att Marble Harb[ou]r, that they shalbe forfected to the owners of the said stadge. **1696** SCOTTOW *Massachusetts* 11 Also divers Merchants of Bristol have yearly for these eight years . . . sent Ships hither at the fishing times to Trade for Bever. — (14) **1886** *Cent. Mag.* July 330/1 In connection with the 'outfit' . . . must be mentioned the 'sucker-rods,' long sticks of ash coupled together and used in pumping, and the 'fishing tools,' which come into important service when the drilling apparatus or the rope breaks in the well. **1922** *Dly. Ardmoreite* (Ardmore, Okla.) 10 Jan. 6/2 A string of fishing tools were dropped when the line broke.

(15) **1868** *N.H. Laws 1867–71* 132 Any town in this state . . . may . . . choose one or more fishing-wardens.

b. Also designating places where fishing is carried on, or structures of various kinds erected in connection with fishing, as (1) **fishing camp,** (2) **fall,** (3) **flake,** (4) **hole,** (5) **hut,** (6) **lot,** (7) **place,** see as a main entry, (8) **roost,** (9) **shack,** (10) **shanty,** (11) **shore,** (12) **stage,** see as a main entry, (13) **stand,** (14) **station.**

(1) **1806** LEWIS in *L. & Clark Exped.* IV. (1905) 200 We arrived at a Cathlahmah fishing cam[p] of one lodge; here we found 3 men [etc.] . . . who from appearances had remained here some time for the purpose of taking sturgeon. **1946** *Birmingham News-Age-Herald* 7 April 1-B/8 Fishing camps where boats may be obtained are fairly well distributed about the fishing waters. — (2) **1837** IRVING *Bonneville* II. 45 These [falls of the Snake R. in Idaho] are called by some the Fishing falls; as the salmon are taken here in immense quantities. — (3) **1861** L. L. NOBLE *After Icebergs* 20 We are glad to jump ashore at Mrs. Bridget Kennedy's fishing-flake. — (4) **1796** in *Amer. Sp.* XV. 177/2 On the bank of sd. river a little below the great Fishing hole. **1898** PAGE *Red Rock* 56 The bridges were gone, and the fishing-holes were dammed with fallen trees.

(5) *a***1841** HAWES *Sporting Scenes* I. 24 This discourse hath brought us in front of the fishing-hut of Raynor Rock, near the lighthouse on the beach. **1883** *Wheelman* I. 353/1 The fishing huts are moved hurriedly to the store; or . . . are abandoned. — (6) **1636** *Essex Inst. Coll.* IV. 94/1 [They] may haue one fishing lot on the neck. *Ib.* IX. 33 William Hackford Received for an Inhabitant & may also haue a ffishing Lott. **1639** *Ib.* V. 168/1 Granted to Willm. Moore an half acre of land for a fishing lott. — (8) **1876** *Fur, Fin, & Feather* Sep. 144 Nashawena Island . . . is a splendid fishing-roost. — (9) **1912** *Out West* Jan. 52/1 Given a bunch of fishing shacks with boats on the beach and you have a picture that in lines and color expresses the sense of rest that all find beside the Ocean.

(10) **1883** *Wheelman* I. 352/2 These fishing shanties are . . . tall enough so that a fourteen-foot fish-spear can be wielded on the inside. **1893** *Outing* June 224/1 A rough little fishing-shanty furnished temporary shelter for our weary horse. — (11) **1786** WASHINGTON *Diaries* III. 62 In the Afternoon a John Halley . . . applied to rent a fishing shore of me at Sheridin's point. — (13) **1806** LEWIS in *L. & Clark Exped.* V. (1905) 46 Fishing stand . . . is a small stage or warf constructed of sticks and projecting about 10 feet into the river and about 3 feet above the surface of the water. On the extremity of this the fisherman stands with his scooping net. — (14) **1828** SHERBURNE *Memoirs* ii. 54 Those benches are to be found wherever you find a fishing station in Newfoundland. **1879** *Harper's Mag.* June 70/1 Upon the upper waters of the Chesapeake . . . are numerous fishing stations.

As the last term in **blue, brook, cape, dog, drum, fire, jug, pan, sun, trap, weak fishing.**

fishing place. A place where the fishing is good, a fishing lot (see also quot. 1889).

1622 MOURT *Relation* 82 Master Carver with fiue other went to the great Ponds, which seeme to be excellent fishing-places. **1704** *Derby Rec.* 230 Entered a caution ag[ains]t any highway being recorded through ye long lott or fishing place. **1804** *Steele P.* I. 429 As to the fishing place, it appeared to him, to be the property of the Young Man on whose shore the Sein landed. **1889** *Cent.* 2237/2 *Fishing place,* . . . 2. A prescribed length of shore in shore-fishing to which the sweep of a seine is limited.

fishing stage. (See quot. 1857.)

*a*1676 JOHN WINTHROP in *Phil. Trans.* No. 142 (1678) 1066 The *English* have learned the like Husbandry, . . . they are near the Fishing-stages; having there the Heads and Garbage of Cod-fish in abundance, at no charge but the fetching. **1765** ROGERS *Acc. N. America* 6 [The French] laid siege to, and demolished the town of St. John's, with all the fishing stages, &c. but could not reduce the fort. **1857** WILLIS *Convalescent* 255 Along on the beach, at certain distances, are rows of huts, for the shelter of the islanders in rough weather, called 'fishing-stages.'

***fishy,** *a.* Inebriated. *Slang. Obs.* — **1737** *Pa. Gazette* 13 Jan. 1/3 He's Fishy.

fissure vein. (See quot. 1881.)

1870 W. W. FOWLER *Ten Yrs. in Wall St.* 299 Their talk was in mining slang, and 'pockets,' 'fissure veins,' 'faults' . . . ran all through their vocabulary. **1881** RAYMOND *Mining Glossary, Fissure vein,* a fissure in the earth's crust filled with mineral. **1901** WHITE *Westerners* 208 He showed them leads, fissure veins, red quartz.

***fist,** *n.*[1] *fist and skull,* designating, or with reference to, a fight in which no weapons are used. *Colloq.* See also **sling fist.**

1833 HALL *Legend of West* 51 They never come out boldly into the open field, and take a fair fight, fist and skull, as Christians do. **1904** TOM WATSON *Bethany* (1920) 51 Upon his return he would tell us about it . . . giving us an account of some 'fist and skull' fight which had taken place. **1944** CLARK *Pills* 66 Often these discussions were comedies of rare flavor in civil affairs, but at other times they led to vicious 'fist and skull' fighting on the wagon grounds.

fist, *n.*[2] See **feist.**

***fit,** *n.*[1]

1. fit root, =**Indian pipe.**

1876 HOBBS *Bot. Hand-Book* 38 Fit root plant, Ice plant, Monotropa uniflora. **1931** CLUTE *Plants* 123 Fit-root (*Monotropa uniflora*).

2. In colloquial phrases: (1) *To give* (a person) *fits,* to scold violently; (2) *to have forty fits,* to have a "conniption fit."

(1) **1844** KENDALL *Santa Fe Exped.* (De Vere), The man ran after the thievish Indian, and the corporal cried out to him to give him fits if he caught him. **1907** STEWART *Partners* 307 The Professor started right in and give us fits about them [the giant & the tattooed man].— (2) **1877** JEWETT *Deephaven* iii. 53, I should have forty fits, if I undertook it.

As the last term in **cat, chicken, conniption, death, duck fit.**

***fit,** *n.*[2] A training or education that fits one for college. Cf. ***fit,** *v. Obs.* — **1871** BAGG *At Yale* 687 No boy should enter Yale until he is eighteen years old. . . . He should get his 'fit,' too, at one of the large preparatory schools. **1883** *N. Eng. Jrnl. Educ.* XVII. 133 Phillips Academy . . . has for many years given an excellent fit for college.

***fit,** *v. intr.* To prepare (for college). *Colloq.*

1835 *Harvardiana* I. 322, I was sent to an Academy . . . to 'fit' for College. **1856** STOWE *Dred* I. 23, I'm really much like the minister in our town where we fitted for college. **1876** TRIPP *Student-Life* 34 Why, he fitted for college in two years. **1904** *N.Y. Ev. Post* 13 May 7 Groton School, where her eldest son is fitting for college.

fitch tippet. A tippet made of the fur of a polecat. *Obs.* — **1891** WILKINS *N. Eng. Nun* 91, I had a fitch tippet an' muff that cost twenty-five dollars. **1895** A. BROWN *Meadow-Grass* 89 The Widder Poll, clad not only in the Tycoon rep, but her best palm-leaf shawl, her fitch tippet, and pumpkin hood.

fitified 'fɪtɪfaɪd, *a.* Chiefly *S.* Epileptic.

1822 in PHILLIPS *Life & Labor in Old South* (1939) 275 The fellow you bought of Tutt is fitified or subject to convulsions. **1853** J. G. BALDWIN *Flush Times Ala.* 171 Miss Julia Pritcher, a *girl* of about thirty-five, . . . was lank . . . and, the boys said, fitified. **1943** PEATTIE *Great Smokies* 87 The once beautiful woman got poorly, and ugly, and turned fitified.

***fitting,** *n.*

1. Preparation for college. Cf. ***fit,** *n.*[2]

1884 H. S. CUMMINGS *Dartmouth Class 1862* 103, [I] take rather pardonable pride in the style and manner of 'fitting' which I gave several young men for college.

b. fitting school, a school preparing students for college, a "prep school." Also transf.

1871 BAGG *At Yale* 73 An anxiety for their successors prompts them to dispatch messengers to the large fitting-schools. **1901** *Forum* May 289 In fitting-school and in college he had gone deeply into sports. **1907** *Springfield W. Republican* 18 April 16 The New York state library school at Albany is regarded as one of the most exacting fitting schools for librarians in the country.

***five,** *a.*

1. *absol.* A five-dollar bill. *Colloq.*

1821 *Olive Branch* (Danville, Ky.) 23 June 3/1 The sums are in notes of small denominations; say, ones, fives and tens. **1893** B. MATTHEWS in *Harper's Mag.* Dec. 33/2 You can give me a five, if you like, or a ten. **1949** *Amer. Mercury* July 97/2 Cashiers had specimen ones, fives, tens and twenties of real money under glass near their cash registers.

2. In special combs.: (1) **five card draw,** in draw poker, a draw in which a full new hand is taken; (2) **cattle team,** (see quot.), *obs.;* (3) **Five Civilized Tribes,** see as a main entry; (4) **fingered ivy,** =**Virginia creeper;** (5) **foot,** used with reference to a notable collection of classics selected by Charles W. Eliot, usu. **five foot shelf;** (6) ***gallon,** used to designate a very large hat or sombrero, cf. **ten gallon hat;** (7) ***hundred,** a variety of euchre in which a joker is added to the deck, and players bid for the privilege of naming the trump, five hundred points making a game, cf. **c.** (1) below; (8) **leaved Jack,** (see quot.); (9) **minute rule,** a rule of Congress adopted in 1847 and modified in 1850, which limits debate in committees of the whole house (see quot. 1914); (10) ***Five Nations,** see as a main entry; (11) **plate stove,** (see quot. and cf. **German stove, jamb stove, six plate stove**); (12) **Five Pointer,** one of a band of

New York rowdies from the once notorious Five Points district, *obs.;* (13) ***points,** see as a main entry; (14) **rail fence,** see **rail fence;** (15) **shooter,** *W.* a revolver that shoots five times without reloading, *obs.;* (16) **shooting rifle,** a repeating rifle having a cylinder like a revolver which contains five chambers for charges, *obs.*, cf. ***repeater;** (17) **spotted sphinx,** (see quot. 1876).

(1) **1913** LONDON *Valley of Moon* III. x, The winner . . . on the day following might be riding his luck to royal flushes on five-card draws. — (2) **1929** SHELTON *Salt-box House* viii. 56 His slaves might be hired by the day, as might also his 'five-cattle team' (two yokes of oxen and a horse). — (4) **1893** *Amer. Folk-Lore* VI. 139 *Ampelopsis quinquefolia*, five-fingered ivy; American joy. N.Y.

(5) **1910** *Outlook* 30 April 969/2 There is no such thing as *the* hundred best books, or *the* best five-foot library. **1921** *Outing* May 66/1 Someone found a mine of fiction and fact piled along the roadside at the petrified forest in Arizona, and someone else received the remainder of our 'five-foot shelf' over near the Grand Canyon. **1949** *Sat. Ev. Post* 19 Mar. 99/2, I will personally make you eat the Harvard Five Foot Shelf of Classics. — (6) **1930** FERBER *Cimarron* 132 They wore their pink and purple shirts, their five-gallon hats, their gayest neckerchiefs, their most ornate high-heeled boots. *Ib.* 152 The collection was taken up, in two five-gallon sombreros. **1948** *Sat. Ev. Post* 31 July 59/1 There were big, five-gallon hats very much in evidence, gaudy neckware, mustaches, whiskers and an occasional full beard. — (7) **1920** LEWIS *Main Street* 195 What do you say we go down to Jack Elder's and have a game of five hundred this afternoon? **1946** MOREHEAD & MOTT-SMITH *Penguin Hoyle* 29 Five Hundred . . . is one of the few games that are entirely American, having been invented and developed in this country. — (8) **1869** FULLER *Flower Gatherers* 74 There is still another species of Arum found in the South, called *Five-leaved Jack.* — (9) **1886** ALTON *Among Law-Makers* 54 The 'five-minute rule' . . . restricts debate upon any question to five minutes. **1914** *Cyclo. Amer. Govt.* II. 25 The five minute rule . . . provides that when general debate is closed by order of the house, any member shall be allowed five minutes to explain any amendment he may offer, after which the member who shall first obtain the floor shall be allowed to speak five minutes in opposition to it.

(11) **1931** *Old-Time New Eng.* Oct. 71/2 They were called 'Five-Plate' or 'Jamb Stoves,' and were made up of two sides, a back, a bottom, and top, the whole bolted together. Three sizes were made, the largest weighing about 450 pounds and selling at about 5 each. These stoves were built into the wall of the brick or stone house or placed against the back of the fireplace in the chimney. — (12) **1836** HONE *Diary* I. 209 The public . . . must acquiesce, . . . or engage in a disgraceful contest with the loafers and Five-pointers. **1878** B. F. TAYLOR *Between Gates* 88 [A hoodlum] is neither the rowdy, the Five-Pointer, the wharf rat, the Bowery boy or the bummer.

(15) **1848** *Gem of Prairie* (Chi.) 30 Sep. 6/2 These desperadoes are . . . well armed with the formidable 'five-shooter,' which they know so well how to wield. **1853** *S.F. Commercial Advt.* 8 Dec. 2/3 He drew a 'five-shooter' but fortunately his arm was knocked down at the instant he pulled the trigger, and the ball missed his intended victim. *c***1900** R. L. HALE *Log of Forty-Niner* 92, I had seen in his belt a bowie, and a five shooter. — (16) **1857** *So. Illinoisian* (Shawneetown) 1 May 1/1 We have the self-loading twenty-four repeating rifle, the Minie rifle, Browning revolving five-shooting rifle, Colt's rifle and pistol, and a revolving cannon. — (17) **1876** *Vt. Bd. Agric. Rep.* III. 567 Another insect that sometimes does some damage to the potato crop is the five spotted sphinx (*Macrosila quinque maculata*), the larva of which is the common large potato or tomato worm. **1891** *Cent.* 6372/1 The common five-spotted sphinx . . . feeds on the foliage of the tomato-plant in the United States.

b. In the names of coins or currency, or with reference to money and bonds: (1) **five case note,** =**fiver,** *slang;* (2) **cent,** see as a main entry; (3) **dollar (bank) bill,** a piece of paper currency having the face value of five dollars; (4) **dollar (gold) piece,** =**half eagle;** (5) ***pence,** the half dime, *obs.;* (6) **penny bit,** =**fippenny bit,** *obs.;* (7) **spot,** =**fiver,** *slang;* (8) **twenty,** see as a main entry.

(1) **1929** [see **fiver**]. — (3) **1778** PATTEN *Diary* 384, I gave Samuell Kennedy a Summons for Evidences in his case with George Addison and for that advice I gave hem he made a present of a five Dollar bill to me. **1794** *Balt. D. Intelligencer* 15 Sep. 3/2 They are of the denomination five and ten dollar bills. **1799** *Steele P.* I. 172 Do me the honor of paying Mr. Wm. Cobbett five dollars out of it and remitting the balance in five dollar bank bills. **1940** WHITE *One Man's Meat* 133 I'll make my government a proposition: for a five-dollar bill (and costs) I *will* state it plainly. — (4) **1859** M. W. DICKINSON *Amer. Numismatical Manual* 222 Five dollar piece, since 1834. 'North Carolina Gold.' . . . $4.89 to $4.93. A safe estimate of five dollar pieces as they come would be $4.84. **1894** B. MATTHEWS in *Harper's Mag.* Aug. 461/2 She took out a five-dollar gold piece. **1915** KIRKPATRICK *Use of Money* 12 My grandmother had given me a five-dollar gold piece as a present.

(5) **1849** *Knickerb.* XXXIV. 11 We gave the urchin a bran new five-pence. — (6) **1799** in *Ann. 7th Congress* 2 Sess. 1410 A five-penny-bit each [was] paid freely for a copy. **1805** *Theatrical Censor* (Phila.) Dec. 35 Let him sink the *five-penny bit*, in the name of common sense! [footnote:] An uncouth expression, used by citizens, for *shortness*, instead of *six* cents. — (7) **1929** [see **fiver**]. **1945** *Good Housekeeping* Dec. 260/2, If you want to be a cheapskate, just give me back that five spot I paid you for that darned thing and we'll call it a deal.

c. In phrases: (1) *like five hundred*, at a great rate, cf. **2.** (7) above; (2) *five and ten (cent store)*, a store in which orig. all articles sold for five or ten cents, also, *colloq.*, *five and dime store*, cf. **five-cent store;** (3) *to talk around a five-cornered stump*, (see quot. 1889), *obs.;* (4) *block of five*, a group of five voters or floaters, also attrib., *obs.*

(1) **1854** M. J. HOLMES *Tempest & Sunshine* ii. 25 We seen a bright light, and . . . heard the niggers larfin like five hundred. — (2) **1880** in *Sat. Ev. Post* (1940) 10 Feb. 23/3 Woolworth Bros. 5 & 10 Cent Store. **1907** O. HENRY *Trimmed Lamp* 115 Did you ever notice me . . . peering in the window of the five-and-ten? **1948** *Time* 7 June 80/2 They could have bought them much cheaper at a five-&-dime store. — (3) **1888** *Chicago Inter-Ocean* 8 March (F.), Mr. Sargent can talk around a five cornered stump when he wishes, and considerable winnowing was necessary to separate the grains of wheat from Mr. Sargent's chaff. **1889** FARMER 242/1 To talk round a five cornered stump is a simile for loquacious talk, more or less of an exaggerated character. — (4) **1892** *Cong. Rec.* 25 Feb. 1455/1 It was expensive to divide the floaters into blocks of five. *Ib.* 1455/2 The author of the blocks-of-five letter was known.

As the last term in **forty, high, short five.**

five cent. In combs.: (1) **five-cent bill,** a bill of exchange worth five cents, *obs.*, cf. **five-cent note;** (2) **cigar,** a cigar that retails for five cents, also, *colloq.*, **five-center;** (3) **fare,** a charge of five cents for riding on a streetcar, subway, train, etc.; (4) **hour,** a certain time each day during which the fare on the elevated railways in New York was five cents; (5) **nickel,** a nickel coin worth five cents; (6) **note,** =**five-cent bill,** *obs.;* (7) **piece,** a coin of the U.S. worth five cents, also, *colloq.*, **five-center piece** ["Half-dismes—each to be of the value of one-twentieth of a dollar" were authorized by Congress April 2, 1792. These were silver coins, and were not minted after 1873. The first five-cent piece made of copper and nickel was of 1866.]; (8) **store,** a store in which all articles sold at five cents each, the forerunner of the *five and ten (cent store)*, *q.v.*

(1) **1864** WHITMAN *Spec. Days* 57, I provide myself with a quantity of bright new ten-cent and five-cent bills. **1867** LATHAM *Black & White* 12 F—— received a Five-cent bill yesterday in change. — (2) **1867** *Harper's Wkly.* 25 May 330/2 Leaving Smith smoking one of my five-cent cigars, which he always gets for nothing when he meets me, I turned my footsteps toward the studio. **1940** MENCKEN *Happy Days* 228 When Kilroy himself blew up the five-center went with him, and Sam became Baltimore agent for a cigar factory in Philadelphia. **1948** *Sat. Ev. Post* 10 July 71/1 Tom Marshall, of Indiana, was . . . destined to win immortality with a sentence: 'What this country needs is a good five-cent cigar.' — (3) **1884** *Boston Journal* 6 Sep., The Governor's veto of the Five-cent Fare bill. **1921** *Lit. Digest* 19 Nov. 12 The voters of New York, completely deceived as to a five-cent fare, with every other issue thrust far into the background . . . [reëlected] Mr. Hylan. — (4) **1882** MCCABE *N.Y. by Sunlight & Gaslight* 188 The over-crowded [elevated] trains which run so frequently during the five-cent, or 'commission' hours, are exceedingly liable to accident.

(5) **1875** *Chi. Tribune* 6 Nov. 5/6 He went to the bottom of his pockets, turned them inside out, but he could find nothing but a 5-cent nickel. **1910** *N.Y. Post* 8 Dec. 8 Until recently the 'five-cent nickle' has for all practical purposes been the lowest unit of legal tender [in the West]. — (6) **1867** *Atlantic Mo.* Jan 121/2 You may safely bet the nation's collective income-tax against a five-cent note, that your grandchildren will do the same. **1880** *Bradstreet's* 25 Aug. 3/2 The 5-cent notes were all issued in 1862, 1863, and 1864. — (7) **1829** *Central Watchtower* (Harrodsburg, Ky.) 13 June 2/4 A Kentucky farmer offers a premium of $100 to the first student . . . who will determine . . . in how many different ways it is possible to pay $100, without using any other money than pieces of silver, each 3, 5, and 7 cents, and likewise if paid in 3, 5, 7 and 10 cent pieces. **1884** MARK TWAIN *H. Finn* ii. 10 Jim always kept that five-center piece round his neck with a string. **1935** MITCHELL *America* 21 A five cent piece, usually bearing a buffalo on one side and lo the poor Indian on the other, is called a nickel. — (8) **1879** WOOLWORTH in *Sat. Ev. Post*

(1940) 10 Feb. 22/2 No one knew there was a 5¢ store in this city until Friday night, and we managed to sell yesterday in one day $127.65.

Five Civilized Tribes. "A term used both officially and unofficially in modern times to designate collectively the Cherokee, Chickasaw, Choctaw, Creek, and Seminole tribes in Indian Ter., applied on account of the advance made by these tribes toward civilized life and customs" (Hodge).

Under the government of the former "Indian Territory" their institutions combined tribal features with features of American state governments. Their own government, however, is now largely superseded by the government of Oklahoma.

1876 *Rep. Indian Affairs* 61 The Cherokees occupy and own perhaps the best reservation among the five civilized tribes. **1900** *Cong. Rec.* 3 Jan. 627/2 An agreement concluded by the Commission to the Five Civilized Tribes, on behalf of the Government of the United States, with a commission representing the Choctaw and Chickasaw nations on September 5, 1899. **1948** *Dly. Ardmoreite* (Ardmore, Okla.) 11 May 10/4 The president has approved senate joint resolution 189 to provide for the issuance of a special stamp in honor of the Five Civilized Tribes in Oklahoma.

Five Nations. Also **Five Indian Nations.** The confederacy of Iroquoian tribes: the Cayugas, Mohawks, Oneidas, Onondagas, and Senecas. Cf. **Iroquois** and **Six Nations.**

"The date of the formation of this confederation (probably not the first, but the last of a series of attempts to unite the several tribes in a federal union) was not earlier than about the year 1570, which is some 30 years anterior to that of the Huron tribes" (Hodge I. 618).

1688 *Pa. Archives* I. 104 The five Nations or Cantons of Indians. **1694** *Pa. Col. Rec.* I. 459 The five Indian nations . . . wer now debauched to the french interest. **1754** *Mass. H.S. Coll.* 3 Ser. V. 9 A General Convention of Commissioners . . . is appointed to be held at the city of Albany in the month of June next, for holding an interview with the Indians of the Five Nations. **1852** REYNOLDS *Hist. Illinois* 35 The bitter hostility of the Iroquois or Five Nations to the French, prevented . . . the explorers of the Mississippi from visiting the Ohio Valley. **1949** *Chi. D. News* 25 March 45/4 The Iroquois Confederacy . . . was also known as the Five Nations and later as the Six Nations. According to tradition the Confederacy was formed by Hiawatha about the beginning of the 15th century.

***five points.**

1. A five-pointed star, used as a symbol in various patriotic designs of the U.S. *Obs.*

1846 COOPER *Redskins* vii, Spread-eagles, five-points, American flags, huzzas for Polk! . . . were scattered up and down.

2. (*cap.*) A district in the lower part of New York City formerly noted for its crime and poverty.

"In N.Y. the spot where Worth, Baxter, and Park Streets intersect is popularly called *Five Points*. The number is five, not six, because originally Worth Street only met the other two streets and did not run across them. At one time the Five Points district was proverbial for rowdyism and vice" (Horwill, 133).

1832 *Boston Transcript* 5 Jan. 2/3 The stern censors of New York have decreed in council, that the *Five Points* shall be no more; that interesting triangle is to be hurled from the height of fame, and buried in the bosom of a public *square*. **1904** *N.Y. Ev. Post* 14 Oct. 12 'Where were you brought up, at Five Points?' The New York mother of a generation ago would say when her child forgot to say 'Thank you.' **1946** PARTRIDGE & BETTMANN *As We Were* 122 The slum district around the Five Points was described as exceeding in degradation, criminality, and horror any like area in the world.

b. Ellipt. for some such expression as "Five Points crowd." Cf. **Five Pointer.**

1857 *Semi-Weekly Times* (N.Y.) 7 July 1/1 The 'Bowery Crowd' were finally forced to retreat, and the 'Five Points,' *alias* 'Dead Rabbits,' *alias* 'Roach Guard,' then retired. **1911** LEWIS *Apaches N.Y.* 16 True, there was a coolness between himself and Kelly, albeit, both being of the Five Points, they were of the same tribe.

***fiver,** *n.* A five-dollar bill.

1883 *Harper's Mag.* Oct. 784/1, I'll bet a pony to a fiver they've got him. **1929** *Amer. Sp.* IV. 358 A five-dollar bill is a *fiver*, a *five-spot*, or a *five-case note*. **1948** *Sat. Ev. Post* 7 Aug. 10/3, I had never been in business then; if I had, I couldn't have won the fiver.

five-twenty ˈfaɪvˌtwentɪ, *a.* Denoting a six-per-cent U.S. bond issued during the Civil War period, redeemable after five years and payable in full in twenty years. Also **five-twenties,** *n. pl.*

1865 *U.S. Laws Concerning Money* (1910) 189 Any bonds known as five-twenties, issued under the act of [25 Feb., 1862], . . . remaining unsold to an amount not exceeding four millions of dollars, may be disposed of by the Secretary of the Treasury. **1867** *Nation* Oct. 296/1 The Ten-Forty bonds have stood in the market at almost precisely the same figure as the Five-Twenty bonds. **1913** WATKINS *Hist. Nebr.* III. 38/2 The *Herald* approved 'Pendleton's doctrine' of paying the 5–20 bonds in greenbacks. **1946** PARTRIDGE & BETTMANN *As We Were* 57 Jay Cooke, the Philadelphia banker, was made sole agent for the 'Five-Twenties' authorized in February 1862.

fix fɪks, *n.*

1. A condition, situation, state, etc.; now a situation from which it is difficult to escape, a predicament. *Colloq.*

1809 WEEMS *Marion* (1833) 121 They are in a mighty good fix. **1834** CARUTHERS *Kentuckian* I. 96 You see he has the rogues in the city like a coon when he's treed; an old dog's better than a young one in such a fix. **1841** *Knickerb.* XVII. 527, I'm in a *fix*, and no mistake! **1931** *K.C. Times* 7 Dec. 16 What a fix this old world might have been in if our boys had not made it safe for democracy.

b. Of horses, physical condition, fettle.

1839 *Spirit of Times* 27 April 90/3 (We.), The filly is a keener, but looked out of fix. **1868** WOODRUFF *Trotting Horse* xi. 113 In getting a whole stable of horses into fix to trot races, there will seldom be two whose treatment during their preparation ought to be the same. **1898** CANFIELD *Maid of Frontier* 36 His horses are in good fix.

c. out of fix, not in good repair, out of condition or order.

1839 [see prec.]. **1842** W. T. THOMPSON *Maj. Jones's Courtship* (1872) 76 The axeltree of the world wanted greasin or somethin or other was out of fix, for it didn't seem to turn round half so fast as it used to do. **1892** *D.N.* I. 230 [In Kentucky] 'out of fix' = out of health, out of humor, out of almost any normal condition of body or mind. (Also known in Michigan.) **1895** *Outing* XXVI. 356/1 George's rod is splintered and the Kid's reel out of fix.

2. A specified arrangement or position.

1834 CARUTHERS *Kentuckian* I. 29, I couldn't get my hands in no sort of a comfortable fix. **1836** P. H. NICKLIN *Pleasant Peregrination* 50 (Th.), Tables and settees are put into a sleeping fix in the twinkling of a bedpost.

3. A costume, dress, wardrobe. Cf. **wedding fix.**

1843 STEPHENS *High Life N.Y.* I. 148 He kinder grinned a little when he see . . . that I hadn't got my fix on yet. **1908** *Collier's* 21 Nov. 15 Why don't Amy Horton teach school and earn enough money to get her fix and furnish her house?

4. The material used to line a puddling furnace.

1871 *Amer. Inst. Mining Eng. Trans.* I. 327 In puddling 30 per cent. less 'fix' was required. **1881** RAYMOND *Mining Glossary*, Fix, to fettle or line with a fix or fettling . . . the hearth of a puddling furnace.

***fix,** *v.*

1. *tr.* To determine the action of (a jury, legislature, etc.) by bribery or "pull"; to "bring around" by bribery. *Slang.* Cf. ***fixed 2,** ***fixer.**

1790 in *Jrnl. Wm. Maclay* (1927) 248 We expected something political would be proposed by Fitzsimons, and out it came: 'Gentlemen, it is expected of us that we should fix the Governor of Pennsylvania.' **1882** *Nation* 28 Sep. 256/1 The decision of the question, who should be the Republican candidate for the Governorship, . . . was in the hands of the politicians who 'fix' and 'run' primaries. **1944** *Chi. D. News* 24 July 1/1 Two deputy sheriffs were adjudged in contempt of court today in an attempt to 'fix' the jury. **1947** CHALFANT *Gold, Guns, & Ghost Towns* 80 Litigants were rather less concerned with owning judges than with 'fixing' the sheriff to reach the jury.

b. To tamper with (anything) for purposes of dishonesty.

1865 *Cin. D. Commercial* 4 July 1/6 These cards are not in the same condition as cards which are usually used in the game of faro; they are sandpapered, as it is termed, or fixed for cheating. **1945** *Greeley* (Colo.) *D. Tribune* 4 Aug. 2/6 Law enforcement is being hampered by 'too much fixing of traffic tickets.' **1948** *Chi. Tribune* 8 Aug. 1/6 The doping of racing animals and the fixing of races are adult practices.

2. To put (a person) out of the running, to put (one) in an awkward position, to get even with. *Colloq.*

1800 *Aurora* 8 April (Th.), Have fix'd Randolph,—wish the other house would fix Mason. **1865** NORTON *Army Letters* 278 The way I punish an unruly teamster is to make him dig a big hole and then fill it up, dig it and fill it up the second time, and that is enough for any man. It fixes them. **1914** D. W. ROBERTS *Rangers & Sovereignty* 48 In my eagerness to 'fix' him I did fire and missed him.

3. With adverbs in colloq. phrases: (1) *to fix down*, to settle down, to "locate" in a certain place; (2) **to fix off*, to get started on one's way; (3) *fix out*, (*a*) to fit out, to make provision for, also absol., (*b*) *transf.*, as an understatement, to kill; (4) **to fix up*, to concoct or arrange (a plan, match, etc.), sometimes by conspiracy, to "patch up," make up.

(1) **1787** CUTLER *Life & Corr.* I. 292 What could induce Mechard to fix down in this awful, gloomy, lonely, miserable spot, is beyond my power to conceive. **1797** HAWKINS *Letters* 98 The troops have arrived from the northward and are fixed and fixing down to keep peace on these frontiers. — (2) *c***1783** in *Ohio Arch. and Hist. Quart.* XVI. 358 We fixed off, traveled hard and in the evening arrived at Englishe's Station, the first in the Kentucky settlement. **1866** H. D. BROWN *Two College Girls* 5 We'll have tea in the neighborhood of five, so that you can fix off early and get well home before dark. — (3) (*a*) *Lancaster* (Mass.) *Early Rec.* 237, I fixed the men out with the stores. **1871** STOWE *Sam Lawson* 39 He was a fixin' out for the voyage. **1917** MATHEWSON *Sec. Base Sloan* 279 Tell him to show that to the man at the ticket office and he will fix him out. (*b*) **1869** BARNUM *Struggles & Triumphs* 531 'Yes,' replied Adams, 'that will fix me out. It had nearly healed.' — (4) **1861** *Cong. Globe* App. 20 Feb. 226/1 Too many . . . are over-anxious, in the quaint . . . language of the day, to 'fix up' something to save the Union. **1871** EGGLESTON *Hoosier Schoolm.* xxxiv. 225 Bud . . . said as how him and Martha had fixed it all up. **1928** *Sat. Ev. Post* 12 May 119/1 'All right,' said the sergeant, 'it's all fixed up.'

b. In other colloq. phrases: (1) *To fix a horse,* (*a*) to shoe a horse, *rare,* (*b*) to tamper with a horse to prevent its winning a race; (2) *to fix it,* to arrange or adjust matters generally, freq. *any way* (or *nohow*) *you can fix it;* (3) *to fix one's mutton,* to settle, dispose of (one), *rare;* (4) *to fix a cause,* to arrange for the trial of a case in court.

(1) (*a*) **1737** E. PARKMAN *Diary* 16, I rode to Mr. Cook's [the blacksmith's] to fix my Horse. (*b*) **1881** *Standard* 7 Sep. 5/2 It is true that they talk of 'fixing' a horse, but they also use 'nobbling' in the same sense. — (2) **1836** CROCKETT *Exploits* 125 If he had stolen the pennies . . . in Louisiana, the people in Texas would have nothing to do with that affair, nohow they could fix it. **1860** HOLMES *Professor* (1902) 21 But if you can't fix it so as to be born here [Boston], you can come and live here. **1901** HARRIGAN *Mulligans* 24 'We can't marry at the ball, Tommy,' said Kitty. 'Well,' replied Tom, in a low voice, 'I mean I'll fix it.' — (3) *a***1846** *Quarter Race Ky.* 190 Now tho', he thought, the time had come for him to walk into one on 'em [bears] at laast, and fix his mutton for him right. — (4) **1851** A. O. HALL *Manhattaner* 80 This is Saturday morning, and they [lawyers] are fixing their causes. . . . All the suits which are at issue, will be called by the clerk this morning.

4. In colloq. noun combs., usu. obs.: (1) **fix-out,** (see quot.); (2) **fix-up,** (*a*) an unusual article of dress or one that makes the wearer conspicuous, (*b*) a situation that appears by chance or by prearrangement, (*c*) a reconciliation of differences, (*d*) a kind of mixed drink.

(1) *a***1870** CHIPMAN *Notes on Bartlett* 152 *Fix-out, n.* Adornment, arrangement, 'out-fit.' — (2) (*a*) **1832** *Polit. Examiner.* (Shelbyville, Ky.) 8 Dec. 4/1 She says Mr. Bunker sit down, well I thought I would whilst she was getting her fixups off. **1873** MILLER *Amongst Modocs* 126 The lady who has the least amount of natural hair, has invariably the largest amount of artificial fix-ups on her head. (*b*) **1855** *Knickerb.* XLVI. 84 The old gentleman . . . drawled out: 'Well, if this isn't one uf the curiousest fix-ups ever I did see!' (*c*) **1861** *N.Y. Tribune* 27 Nov. (Chipman), The 'Albany Argus,' still hoping for some sort of a compromise or fix-up with the rebels, says [etc.]. (*d*) **1867** DIXON *New Amer.* I. 191 In this absence of public solicitation to sip either claret-cobbler, . . . eye-opener, fix-ups, or any other Yankee deception in the shape of liquor, the city is certainly very much unlike Leavenworth.

* **fixed,** *a.*

1. Armed, well prepared, "heeled." *Colloq.* Cf. **well fixed.**

1870 MARK TWAIN *Sk., New & Old* 277 My grandfather knew him well, and he says Franklin was always fixed—always ready. **1872** —— *Roughing It* vi. 57 He always went 'fixed' to make things go along smoothly. **1914** JAMES *Ivory Tower* 204 What are you but just 'fixed' to marry.

2. Of a juryman, etc.: Bribed to act in a certain way. *Slang.* Cf. * **fix,** *v.* **1.**

*a***1889** *S.F. News Letter* (F.), His friends on the grand jury, . . . acted precisely as fixed jurors had been known to act. **1902** E. C. MEYER *Nominating Systems* 57 Three classes of delegates may be distinguished in conventions: The 'fixed' delegates who represent the 'machine-controlled' primaries [etc.].

b. Of races, games, etc.: Having an outcome decided upon before the performance, "set."

1901 *Denver Republican* 26 Aug. 3/4 It is well known that in many of the police protected gambling houses of Denver there are 'fixed' roulette wheels, 'squeeze' faro boxes, loaded dice and marked cards. **1931** *Autobiog. L. Steffens* 37 Being in with the stables, I soon began to hear about 'fixed races.' *Ib.*, Since they, the jockeys, grooms, trainers, and owners, were all betters, they could make 'big killings' when they were 'in on the know' of a fixed race.

3. In special combs.: (1) **fixed ammunition,** (see quot. 1874), *obs.;* (2) * **charge,** a charge that does not vary in the accounts of a business, or that cannot be escaped or shifted; (3) **fact,** a well-established fact.

(1) **1805** LEWIS in *L. & Clark Exped.* (1904) II. 188 The articles to be deposited in the cash consisting of . . . 2 blunderbushes, 1/2 a keg of fixed ammunition and some other small articles belonging to the party. **1874** KNIGHT I. 874/2 *Fixed ammunition,* a charge of powder and shot inclosed together in a wrapper or case, ready for loading. **1877** *Rep. Indian Affairs* 46 The Indians have had only to go off their reserve to obtain all the arms and ammunition, both 'loose' and 'fixed,' which they desire. — (2) **1895** T. F. WOODLOCK *Anatomy of R.R. Report* 20 A '*Profit and Loss*' account may also be arranged so as to exhibit the payments for expenses, fixed charges, and dividends. **1909** WEBSTER 824/1 Under the head of *fixed charges,* in railroad reports, are reckoned interest on funded debt, interest on floating debt, rentals, taxes, and sinking funds. — (3) **1842** *Cong. Globe* 29 Dec. 97/1 Have you gained anything in warring against the veto—this fixed fact in the Constitution? **1890** *Cong. Rec.* 23 June 6392/2 The Long Bridge [at Washington] is there as a fixed fact, and was there long before the tracks of this railroad were laid.

* **fixer,** *n.* One who fixes (an election board, etc.); an adjuster of matters generally. *Colloq.* Cf. **jury fixer.**

1889 *Amer. Mission.* Dec. 363 Where the 'boss' and the fixer of elections are unknown. **1912** COBB *Back Home* 140, I'm the fixer for this show—the legal adjuster, see? **1938** ASBURY *Sucker's Prog.* 306 Johnny Fix-'Em Condon was one of Mike McDonald's protégés, and first appeared in Chicago as handy man and fixer for the McDonald-Varnell-Hankins syndicate.

* **fixing,** *n.*

1. *pl.* Equipment and appurtenances of various kinds, freq. something fancy or extra, as tools, camping equipment, clothing, foods, etc. *Colloq.*

Cf. **chicken, cider, fancy, party, wheat, York fixings.**

1820 J. HALL *Lett. from West* 304 (Th.), These little fixens [*sc.* knife, flint, and steel] make a man feel right peart, when he is three or four hundred miles from any body or any place. **1825** *N.H. Patriot* 23 May (Th.), The veteran [Missouri] trapper was furnished with such other appliances, or fixens, as he would term them, as put him in plight again to take the field. **1828** *Western Souv. 1829* 147, I feel powerful weak; but I don't like the fixens [i.e., food] here, no how. **1857** *Mag. of Travel* I. 179 Mebby you think, boys, that this ere old gun wont shoot, cause she haint got any shiny fixens and fancy flumiddles on her. **1948** *Democrat* 2 Dec. 1/2 Wild turkey with all the fixings was served for dinner.

b. Any objects to which the fancy may apply the name.

1840 *Ky. Rifle* Oct. 31 110/2 Let every man that can play a fiddle or blow a horn, bring his fixins along and make music. **1889** *Cent. Mag.* April 905/1 The player addressed looked at his hand [of cards] carefully and quietly rejoined, 'You might scare me, pard, but you can't scare de fixin's I'se got yere.'

c. Special attentions, frills, "trimmings."

1847 ROBB *Squatter Life* 31 Throw yourself wide on the literary fixins and poetry, for the galls. **1862** LOWELL *Biglow P.* 2 Ser. i. 21 We don't make no charge for the ride an' all the other fixins. **1944** *Sat. Review* 2 Sep. 23 Court-room tale, complete with all the fixin's, including romance and a thrilling finish.

2. Anything that is built or fixed up.

1851 CIST *Cincinnati* 102 To this 'drag,' by aid of a yoke, or wooden collar, he geared his *bull*, and with this *fixin'* the water was furnished. **1861** G. F. BERKELEY *Eng. Sportsman* 211 The place at once showed me that whoever built that 'fixing' had defence from Indians in his mind, as well as the mere confinement of his beasts.

As the last term in **jury, wedding fixing.**

* **fixture,** *n.* An attachment or article that serves a special function.

1761 *N.J. Archives* XX. 547 The furniture . . . consists . . . of several genteel beds, looking-glasses, wallnut and mahogany leather bottom'd chairs, tables, chests of drawers, fixtures, &c. **1823** *Niles' Reg.* 15 Nov. 176/2 Capt. Joseph Edwards . . . lately removed the asylum house, in Carpenter street [Salem], with the chimneys, furniture and fixtures, over *thirty feet*, by means of a slide. **1854** BARTLETT *Mex. Boundary* I. 12 The blacksmiths . . . were employed in making many small fixtures to the wagons. **1944** *Sears Cat.* (ed. 189) 756c Porcelain Fixtures for bath, kitchen. These smart looking, matching, built-in fixtures harmonize with any style bathroom.

b. Anything used as an accessory, such as clothing, traveling equipment.

1845 in *Tall Tales of S.W.* (1930) 26 The idea of pulling off my boots before the girl was death. And as to doffing my other fixtures, I would sooner have my leg taken off. **1856** CARTWRIGHT *Autobiog.* 330, I carried all my traveling fixtures over [the creek] perfectly dry. **1874** COUES *Field Ornith.* I. 41 When travelling your fixtures must ordinarily be limited to a collecting-chest.

* **fizzle,** *n.* One who fails or peters out. *Colloq.*

1849 *Gallinipper* 6 Dec., Not a wail was heard, or a 'fizzles' mild sigh, As his corps o'er the pavement we hurried. **1896** W. A. WHITE in *Emporia Gaz.* 15 Aug., Put the lazy greasy fizzle who can't pay his debts on an altar. **1910** C. HARRIS *Eve's Husband* 49, I am by nature a sort of fizzle.

* **fizzle,** *v.*

1. *intr.* (See quot. 1849.) Also *to fizzle through,* to get through a recitation badly. *College slang. Obs.*

1847 *Yale Banger* 22 Oct., My dignity is outraged at beholding those who *fizzle* and flunk in my presence tower above me. **1849** *Yale Lit. Mag.* XIV. 144 *Fizzle,* to rise with modest reluctance, to hesitate often, to decline finally; generally, to misunderstand the question. **1854** *Songs of Yale* (1860) 63, I 'skinned,' and 'fizzled' through.

b. To fail. *Slang.*

1869 J. R. BROWNE *Adv. Apache Country* 385 Likely as not they'll fizzle. **1948** *Time* 13 Dec. 51/1 *Variety* bluntly headlined that Met Otello Preem Fizzles, and grumbled that it was a mediocre affair.

2. *tr.* (See quot. 1851.) *Slang. Obs.*

1848 *Yale Lit. Mag.* XIII. 321 Fizzle him tenderly, Bore him with care. **1851** HALL *College Words* 131 *Fizzle,* . . . to cause one to fail in reciting. Said of an instructor.

3. *To fizzle out.*

a. *intr.* To prove a failure, peter out. *Colloq.*

*a***1848** *Cincinnati Gaz.* (B.), It cannot be possible, after all that has been said and done about a 'splendid hotel,' that our enterprising business men will let it fizzle out. **1854** *Olympia* (Wash.) *Pioneer* 15 April (Th.), The Steilacoom gold excitement has entirely fizzled out. **1897** *Chi. Tribune* 21 Aug. 11/1 (*caption*), Meeting fizzled out. Manufacturers of strawboard talked, but did not combine.

b. *tr.* To cause (a person) to fail. *Obs.*

1855 HALIBURTON *Nat. & Hum. Nat.* II. 156 Oh, she was a most a beautiful cook, but she was fizzled out by bad cookery at de last.

Hence **fizzle-out,** *n.* A fiasco. *Rare.*

1861 NORTON *Army Letters* 23 The Erie Regiment is one grand fizzle out.

fizzy 'fɪzɪ, *n.* [Origin unknown.] (See quot. 1888.) — **1888** TRUMBULL *Names of Birds* 107 The female (and young) [of the American scoter (*Oidemia americana*) are] . . . known at Salem [Mass.] as Smutty Coot, at Chatham, same state, as Fizzy, and at Bellport and Moriches, L.I., as Broad-billed Coot. **1917** *Birds of Amer.* I. 148.

* **flag,** *n.*[1] In combs.: (1) **flag bottom,** = **flag chair,** *obs.;* (2) **canoe,** a canoe made of flags or rushes, *obs.;* (3) **chair,** a chair having a seat made of flags or rushes; (4) **collar,** a kind of cheap horse-collar made, often in prisons, of flags and rushes, cf. **shuck collar;** (5) **grass,** any one of various grasses having coarse ensiform leaves, found usu. in moist places; (6) **lily,** = **blue flag;** (7) **root,** a sweet flag, *Acorus calamus,* also its root.

(1) **1856** M. J. HOLMES *Homestead* VII.ii, Six yellow chairs . . . gave up their long-standing right to flag-bottoms of a more moderate date. — (2) **1828** in MAURICE S. SULLIVAN *Travels of Jedediah Smith* (1934) 57, I crossed over the river at an indian village of 50 lodges they made a flag canoe to assist me in crossing. — (3) **1694** in SINGLETON *Furniture of Our Forefathers* I. 47 Nine old flag and wooden chairs [are appraised at eighteen shillings]. **1775** *Essex Inst. Coll.* XIII. 187, 1 Couch, 1 armed, 1 Fudling, 1 low leather & 1 flag Chair. **1861** *Chi. Tribune* 19 July 1/9 Genteel furniture, Crockery Ware, Flag Chairs. Piano Forte. &c. — (4) **1681** in *D.N.* VI. (1936) 521 A flagg Collor for a horse [in R.I.]. **1682** *Providence Rec.* (1894) VI. 81 A flagg collor for a horse, traces, swingletree & chaine 00–04–00. **1936** *D.N.* VI. 521 Mr. Forgie states that he remembers having seen flag collars as recently as 1920; but he doubts that they are being manufactured today.

(5) **1846** EMORY *Military Reconn.* 92 [The island] was overgrown with willow, cane, Gila grass, flag grass, &c. **1857** HAMMOND *Northern Scenes* 145 [A moose] was feeding upon the lily pads and flag grass. — (6) **1884** CRADDOCK *Tenn. Mts.* 18 Among their roots flag-lilies . . . and devil-in-the-bush mingled in a floral mosaic. **1892** *Amer. Folk-Lore* V. 103 *Iris versicolor,* poison flag, flag-lily. — (7) **1851** THOREAU *Autumn* 77 Flagroot . . . looks like a cock's tail or a peacock's feather in form. **1881** McLEAN *Cape Cod Folks* v. 107 Grandma fed him with bits of unsweetened flag-root.

* **flag,** *n.*[2] In combs.: (1) **flag bed quilt,** ?a quilt the top of which resembles a flag, *obs.;* (2) **Flag Day,** a day (June 14) commemorating the adoption by Congress in 1777 of the Stars and Stripes as the national flag, also attrib.; (3) **guard,** a squad of soldiers detailed to guard the colors, a color guard, *rare;* (4) **handkerchief,** a handkerchief which in coloring, design, etc., resembles a flag, *obs.;* (5) * **man,** see as a main entry; (6) * **officer,** formerly in the U.S. Navy, an officer next above a captain in rank and commanding a squadron, also as a title; (7) **-pole sitter,** one who perches on a flagpole as long as he is able in an effort to obtain cheap notoriety; (8) **raising,** see as a main entry; (9) **rush,** a contest between two college classes for possession of a flag; (10) **station,** a railroad station at which trains stop only when flagged or signaled.

(1) **1861** in RICHARDS *Village Life* (1912) 141 The girls in our society say that if any of the members do send a soldier to the war they shall have a flag bed quilt, made by the society, and have the girls' names on the stars. — (2) **1894** *Chi. Tribune* 17 June 1/7 American Flag day has come to stay. *Ib.,* Le Roy Van Horn . . . will be long and affectionately remembered . . . for being the founder of the American Flag Day Association. **1948** *Houston* (Tex.) *Post* 14 June 10/3 La Vallita chapter will emphasize Flag day with a radio talk at 4:15 p.m. over a local radio station. — (3) **1781** in RAMSEY *Tennessee* (1853) 267 To give him time to meet them with a flag-guard, on Holston River, at the boundary line. — (4) **1817** *Cape-Fear Recorder* 5 April, 2 bales Silk Bandano and Flag Handkerchiefs. **1823** in McKENNEY *Memoirs* I. 297 Some of them [the goods] were not high; the flag handkerchiefs, for instance. **1827** *Hallowell* (Me.) *Gaz.* 20 June 3/5 Canton Crepes, and every description of Silks; fancy, Flag and Bandanna Handkerchiefs, some very nice.

(6) **1861** McCLELLAN in *Own Story* 206 Should the flag-officer require any assistance in seizing or holding the debouches of the canal [etc.]. **1895** G. KING *New Orleans* 305 When flag-officer Farragut reported to General Butler the tearing down of the United States flag [etc.]. — (7) **1931** *K.C. Star* 18 Sep., There can't be much doubt as to the fact that a man who would do that would do most anything, even to being a flagpole sitter. — (9) **1903** *N.Y. Ev. Post* 25 Sep. 2 The annual flag rush of the sophomore and freshmen classes of Columbia University was held this morning in South Field.

(10) **1849** *Mass. R.R. Rep.* 21 Whole number of way stations, nineteen, Whole number of flag stations, fifteen. **1943** POWELL *Home Again* 251–2 A Negro woman got on with tickets to Williamsburg (a flag station in a Negro settlement seven miles beyond Arlington).

As the last term in **battle, Bear, blue, bucktail, Confederate, garrison, God's, Henry Clay, Lone Star, Louisiana, Minute Man, National, palmetto, Pelican, pine-tree, rattlesnake, secesh, secession, Spanish, State rights, store, storm, union flag.**

* **flag,** *v.*

1. *tr.* To decoy (an antelope) within range by waving or exhibiting an object like a flag to attract its attention.

1884 *Harper's Mag.* LXIX. Aug. 367/2, I will give you a point or two on flagging antelope. **1885** ROOSEVELT *Hunting Trip* 181 One method of hunting them [antelopes] is to . . . flag them up to the hunters by waving a red handkerchief . . . to and fro in the air.

2. To stop (a train) by signaling with a flag, or with something used as a flag.

1856 *N.Y. Herald* 12 Jan. 1/3, I flagged the Albany express train about one hundred rods, with my white flag. **1902** *Out West* Jan. 55 A man had been sent ahead to flag the up freight so it would not run into our wreck. **1944** *Harper's Mag.* June 17/1 To flag an approaching train, the flagman is required by railroad rules to walk for a quarter-mile or so to the rear of the stalled train to give a warning, and the fireman must similarly walk to the front.

b. To stop (a passing vehicle or person) by signaling or hailing. Also absol.

1871 J. G. HOLLAND in *Scribner's Mo.* II. 433 Perhaps you know old Tom, who flagged at the Cherry street crossing. **1899** QUINN *Pa. Stories* 168 At Broad Street the outfit was flagged by a Sergeant. **1909** O. HENRY *Options* 144 A white cloud of dust began to rise. . . . It was the mailwagon. . . . Goodloe flagged it.

Also *to flag down.*

1932 *K.C. Times* 18 Feb. 22 That's the kind of subscribers we like to meet—those fellows who flag a newspaper man down in order to get a chance to pay a subscription. **1946** *Fort Collins Coloradoan* 13 June 1/5 F. H. Davison of Houston, Tex., vacation-bound for Los Angeles, was flagged down by sheriff's deputies here.

* **flagman,** *n.*

1. An assistant to a surveyor.

1837 PECK *New Guide* 135 Deputy-surveyors are employed to do the work . . . [and they] employ chain-bearers, an axe and flag man [etc.]. **1847** in HOWE *Hist. Coll. Ohio* 477 In making the traverse of the lake shore, Mr. Stow acted as flag-man.

2. (See quot. 1909.)

1856 *N.Y. Herald* 11 Jan. 1/3, I am a flagman on the Hudson Railroad. **1909** *Forward* 25 Dec. 423 The flagman is the rear brakeman on a train. He runs back with the flag when the train is stopped for any reasons between stations, and when there is heavy traffic he aids in collecting the tickets and fares. **1948** *Sat. Ev. Post* 25 Dec. 22/1 To the crew of a freight train—conductor, brakeman, flagman—home is where the caboose is.

flag raising.

1. The raising of the U.S. flag or the ceremony attendant upon this. Also attrib.

1863 *National Almanac* 543/1 Flag-raising over almost every large building and many private edifices of the North became at this time [May, 1861] a complete furor, as also the wearing of tri-colored rosettes and other insignia of loyalty to the Union. **1865** BOUDRYE *Fifth N.Y. Cavalry* 189 We witnessed the ceremony of a flag raising. **1945** *Chi. D. News* 9 June 3/2 This is the new . . . stamp featuring Joe Rosenthal's famed Iwo Jima flag-raising picture.

2. (See quots.) *Obs.*

1864 SALA in *Daily Tel.* 18 Nov., Flag-raising consists in stretching a big banner . . . across a street, and this banner contains a colossal transcription of the particular 'ticket' which the flag-raisers support. **1888** *Boston Journal* 5 Oct. 2/5 Flag Raising at Winchester. . . . The Republicans unfurled this afternoon a large and handsome flag bearing the names and portraits of Harrison and Morton.

∗**flake,** *n.*

1. flake room, ?a room in which fish are dried. *Obs.* Cf. next.

1707 *N.H. Probate Rec.* I. 593, I give and bequeath unto . . . [the] sons of my son in law . . . all my House, warehouses, stage & flake-rooms. **1718** *Ib.* II. 9, I order that all my estate . . . as dwelling houses stage flak rooms, . . . be equally divided among my children.

2. flake yard, (see quot. 1889). Cf. **fish flake.**

1856 J. REYNOLDS *Peter Gott* (B.), The owners of vessels [in fishing districts] have a flake-yard in the vicinity of the landing-places, to which the fish are carried on being landed. **1889** *Cent.* 2250/1 *Flake-yard*, . . . an inclosure in which flakes for drying salted fish are built, and in which fish are dried. **1896** *N. Eng. Mag.* Feb. 682 'Flake yard,' store and fish-houses of a typical fish-curing establishment.

As the last term in **fish, upland flake.** Also **corn flakes, soap flakes.**

flambeau flæm'bo, *n.* Chiefly *La.* [F., used in La. in the sense shown here.] One of the kettles, esp. the fourth, in a series, usu. of five, in which sugar-cane juice is treated in sugar-making. *Obs.* Cf. **prop,** *n.*[1], ∗**battery,** *n.*[2] **2.**

1833 SILLIMAN *Man. Sugar Cane* 33 The different kettles are as follows: the largest is called the *grande*, the next the *flambeau*. **1887** *Cent. Mag.* Nov. 116/1 In the course of boiling [the sirup] is ladled successively into the others, called, in order, 'the prop' or 'proy,' 'the flambeau,' the 'sirop,' and 'the battery.' *Ib.*, The 'flambeau' [is so called] because the flames of the furnace strike it with most force.

flamdoodle 'flæm,dudl, *n.* [Var. of ∗*flapdoodle*.] Nonsense, excessive or showy finery. Also attrib. *Colloq.* — **1888** *N.Y. Sun* (F.), [We] planted Uncle George in ship-shape and proper manner. We wasn't goin' to have any highfalutin' flamdoodle business over him. **1902** HARBEN *Abner Daniel* 82 Durned ef I don't like 'er better without a hat on than with all the fluffy flamdoodle that gals put on when they go out.

flame azalea. An ornamental plant, *Azalea lutea*, having showy orange-colored flowers. Also **flame-colored azalea.**

1847 WOOD *Botany* 376 *R[hododendron] calendulaceum*. . . . Flame Azalea. . . . A splendid flowering shrub, in mountains and woods, Penn. to Ohio. **1857** GRAY *Botany* 257 *A. calendulacea*. Flame-colored Azalea . . . [is a] shrub . . . covered when the leaves appear with a profusion of large orange blossoms, usually turning to flame-color. **1947** *Nat. Geog. Mag.* July 65/1 Both of these, the Catawba Rhododendron and Flame Azalea, belong to the same group of plants, the Ericaceae or Heath Family.

flaming pinxter. =prec. — **1869** FULLER *Flower-Gatherers* 60 The flowers are a reddish yellow, so bright it is often called the *Flaming pinxter*.

∗**flanger,** *n.* (See quots.) — **1893** *Stand. Dict.* 690/2 Flanger . . . *R.R.* A vertical iron or steel bar for scraping snow and ice from the insides of rail-heads to make room for the wheel-flanges. **1910** *Sat. Ev. Post* 23 July 40/1 By eight o'clock he had ordered the flangers (plows) on all his regular road engines.

∗**flank,** *v.*

1. *tr.* To dodge, evade, escape (see also quot. 1871). Also absol. *Obs.*

1865 *Diary of Alex. H. Stephens* (1880) 103 (Th.), I asked the Captain if he had Mr. Toombs. 'No,' he replied, 'Mr. Toombs flanked us.' **1867** GOSS *Soldier's Story* x. 184 Those who had means bribed; those who had none 'flanked.' **1871** DE VERE 286 To *flank*, . . . from the strategy of the generals, descended in the mouth of privates to very lowly and not always honorable meanings. When the men wished to escape the attention of pickets and guards by slipping past them, they said they *flanked* them; drill and detail and every irksome duty was *flanked*, when it could be avoided by some cunning trick. Soon, however, honesty itself was thus treated, and the poor farmer was *flanked* out of his pig and his poultry, and not unfrequently even the comrade out of his pipe and tobacco, if not his rations. **1879** *Southern Hist. Soc. P.* VII. 394 (Th.), The Government never made anything by employing these 'rebels,' as they invariably 'flanked' more than they received as pay.

b. *To flank out,* (see quot.). *Obs.*

1888 GRIGSBY *Smoked Yank* xiii. (1891) 102 When a prisoner could manage to get out with those who were selected to carry wood without being specially detailed from any division, it was called 'flanking out.'

2. *tr.* To remove the flank cut from (pork).

1867 *Ill. Agric. Soc. Trans.* VI. 639 Mess Pork.—Shall be packed from sides of well fatted hogs, cut into strips . . . , and flanked according to diagram.

3. *W.* (See quot.)

1920 HUNTER *Trail Drivers Texas* 297 'Flanking' consists in seizing the animal by the skin of the flank opposite the cowboy. . . . When the animal jumps with all four feet off the ground the cowboy by a jerk throws it on its side.

∗**flanker,** *n.*

1. (See quot. 1867.) *Obs.* Cf. ∗**flank,** *v.* **1.**

1867 GOSS *Soldier's Story* v. 81 We arrived on the spot just in season to save the pail from the hands of the ruthless 'flankers'—another term for thieves used among us. **1888** GRIGSBY *Smoked Yank* xiii. (1891) 102 The flanker kept for himself all that he could carry in.

2. *W.* One who flanks calves.

1920 HUNTER *Trail Drivers Texas* I. 297 The flankers and assistants . . . call out 'hot iron.' **1944** ADAMS *W. Words* 60 Usually flankers work in pairs.

3. flanker seat, (see quot. 1858). *Obs.*

1702 *Suffield Doc. Hist.* 142 It was agreed, & voted: to estimate, or account ye four flanker seats equivalent to, or equal with the second seats in the body of seats. **1858** in CHIPMAN *Notes on Bartlett* 154 *Flanker seats*, seats on the side (flank) of a church and which, therefore, face the side (flank) of the pulpit.

∗**flannel,** *n.*

1. flannel bush, a Californian and Mexican shrub (see quots.), the coverings of the lower leaf surfaces of which suggest flannel.

1910 JEPSON *Silva of Calif.* 40 Flannel bush . . . is a diffuse tall shrub of the Sierra Nevada. **1942** VAN DERSAL *Ornamental Amer. Shrubs* 239 Known locally as flannelbush, or California slippery elm (!), but officially as California fremontia, *F. californica* has a rather large range in California.

2. flannel-mouth, (see quot.).

1884 GOODE *Fisheries* I. 398 The grunts or pig-fishes . . . are distinguished by the brilliant red color of the inside of the mouth and throat, from which they have sometimes been called Red Mouths, or Flannel Mouths.

b. *transf.* Used contemptously of persons. Also attrib.

1870 MCCLOSKEY *Across Continent* 74 (We.), You Irish flannel-mouth mick. **1912** DREISER *Financier* 8 You do, and I'll kick your head off, you flannel mouth. **1929** A. ELLIS *Life* 202 George starts to complain that it was run by a bunch of 'flannel mouths.'

c. flannel-mouth(ed) cat, (see quots.).

1884 GOODE *Fisheries* I. 628 The Great Lake Catfish; Flannel-mouth Cat (the young)—*Ictalurus nigricans*. **1889** *Cent.* 2253/2 The flannel-mouthed cat . . . [inhabits] the great North American lakes.

d. flannel-mouthed porgy, (see quot.).

1884 GOODE *Fisheries* I. 398 The Red-mouth Grunt, *Diabasis aurolineatus*, is probably the Flannel-mouthed Porgy.

As the last term in **butternut, red, Shaker flannel.**

∗**flap,** *n.*

1. A breechclout *q.v.* or similar piece of clothing worn by an Indian.

[**1701** WOLLEY *Journal N.Y.* (1860) 20 A piece of Cloth about a yard and a half long, put between their groins, tied with a snake's Skin about their middle, and hanging down with a flap before.] **1707** *Boston News-Letter* 22 Sep. 2/2 About 20 or 30 all naked save their flaps with most dismal roaring and hideous exclamation fell on those that were behind. **1795** *Pittsburgh Gazette* 19 Dec. 3/3 The baggage consisted of their blankets and cloathing (except their flaps). **1870** KEIM *Sheridan's Troopers* xxvii. 197 The Kiowa women wear an ornamented flap, attached to the top and rear part of the liggins, which trails at the heels. **1919** C. G. Raht *Romance of Davis Mts.* 54 The clothing . . . consisted usually of leggings . . . the breech clout, or 'flap.'

2. In combs.: (1) **flapboard,** the back of a chuck wagon, hinged at the bottom, which can be let down to serve as a table; (2) **cake,** a flapjack or griddle cake; (3) ***jack,** a somersault or flip-flop, cf. **Indian flapjack.**

(1) **1926** Branch *Cowboy* 75 The flap-board on the chuck-wagon had been let down, and a cold lunch was ready for the trail-drivers. — (2) **1835** P. Shirreff *Tour* 221 Into one of these pans some small loaves were placed . . . and in the other, batter-cakes, called flap-cakes, were prepared. — (3) **1835** Cooper *Monikins* viii, He threw three summersets, or flapjacks. *Ib.* xii, He knew that he should break his neck the very first flap-jack.

***flash,** *n.*

1. A brief news report, usu. received by telegraph or teletype. Cf. **news flash.**

1857 *Richmond* (Va.) *D. Whig* 31 Aug. 3/1 The first flash came across the ocean by the Submarine Telegraph at noon to-day. **1900** *Everybody's Mag.* Nov. 226/1 Another device for beating time is the 'flash.' **1946** *This Week Mag.* 21 April 2/4 Flash. Here's a newspaper story we heard the other day.

2. In combs.: (1) **flashback,** in motion pictures, a cutback; (2) ***light,** a small electric torch operated on a battery or batteries, also the light of this.

(1) **1918** V. O. Freeburg *Photoplay Making* 19 The devices of leaders, cut-ins, close-ups, flash-backs, visions, dissolving views, fade-outs, fade-ins, double-exposures, dual rôles, etc., have a strong appeal of novelty. **1948** *Chi. Tribune* 20 April 1. 22/5 Flashbacks depict the relationship of the two men, which goes back to childhood. — (2) **1901** *Field & Stream* Jan. 774/2 The Comet Baby Flash Light. **1946** *Mazama* Dec. 18/2 After some very unpleasant and awkward rock climbing with our heavy packs by flashlight, we finally . . . compromised on a little shelf at least 500 feet short of our goal. **1949** *Chi. D. News* 18 Feb. 1/7 Using flashlights, they permitted no house lights to be turned on.

***flasher,** *n.* (See quots.) — **1856** Gill in *Smithsonian Inst. Rep.* 260 *Lobotes surinamensis.* . . . I saw a single specimen of this species in Fulton market last year. . . . It did not seem to be known. The owner called it 'flasher'; why it was so named, I was unable to learn. **1888** Goode *Amer. Fishes* 148 The 'Flasher' or 'Triple-tail' of New York, *Labotes surinamensis*, . . . is spoken of by various authors as the 'Black Triple-tail.'

***flat,** *n.*

1. A tract or extent of elevated level land. Cf. **German flats.**

1733 *Ga. Col. Rec.* III. 380 The banks [of the river at Savannah] are about Forty Feet high, and on the Top a Flat, which they call a Bluff. **1791** W. Sargent *Diary* (1851) 24 A rich bottom of three hundred yards, upon a high extreme fine Flat of open woods. **1891** Ryan *Pagan* 287 Don . . . was walking alone on one of the 'flats.' high up above the forge ravine.

2. =**flathead 1.** *Obs.*

1791 Bartram *Travels* 517 The Chactaws are called by the traders flats, or flat heads.

3. A woman's straw hat having a broad brim and a low crown.

1821 *Mass. Spy* 17 Oct. (Th.), An entire flat of Leghorn is extended over a small body like the shade of a spreading oak over a mushroom. **1901** Ryan *Montana* 92 The hat was a civilized affair . . . and was a wide, pretty 'flat' of brown straw.

4. (See quot.) *Slang. Obs.* Cf. ***flat,** *v.* **2.**

1859 Bartlett 155 *Flat,* . . . a rejection, dismissal. *Ib.*, 'Miss Deborah gave Ike the flat.' 'He's got the flat.'

5. =**flat car.** *Colloq.*

1864 Webster 519/1 *Flat.* . . . A car without a roof; a platform car. **1910** *Sat. Ev. Post* 23 July 8/2 There are more of these extra parts—axles and wheels and four-wheel trucks—on a 'flat' that is fastened to the tool-car.

As the last term in **alkali, beech, camass, canyon, coal, dust, ferry, French, grass, grease(wood), horse, Kentucky, leghorn, mesquite, oak, Parisian, pin, pine, poker, post oak, river, row, sagebrush, salt, soap, steam, white oak, wood flat.**

***flat,** *a.* and *adv.*

1. (See quots.)

1841 *N.Y. Standard* Jan. (Th.), *Flat,* without interest, in brokers' slang. **1870** Medbery *Men Wall St.* 61 Stock can almost always be obtained by borrowers, either *flat,* i.e., with no interest on either side, or with interest at market rates. **1885** *Harper's Mag.* Nov. 843/2 To lend 'flat' means without interest.

2. Financially destitute, penniless. In full **flat broke.** *Colloq.*

1833 [see ***case,** *n.*[1] **2.**] **1846** *Quincy* (Ill.) *Whig* 6 Jan. 1/4 Why I used to go to Galena clean—no I'll take that word back—plum flat broke, with a *daub of ochre on my hat*, and every merchant I met was ready to 'ford f'cilities. **1930** *Times Lit. Supp.* 4 Sep. 698/2 Satisfying his desires freely when he can, starving when he is 'flat.' **1949** *This Week Mag.* 26 March 16/4, I was flat broke.

3. (See quot. 1909.)

1909 Webster 827/3 Without excess; exactly; due;—used chiefly of numbers or quantities; as, to run a hundred yards in ten seconds *flat.* **1945** *Sat. Review* 4 Aug. 22 This one, for instance, . . . all you fiendishly clever people will solve in no time flat.

4. In special combs.: (1) ***flatboat,** a large shoe, *jocular;* (2) **Flatbow,** an Indian of the Kutenai group inhabiting the northwestern U.S. and British Columbia; (3) ***bread,** [cf. Norwegian *fladbröd*], bread that is flat, esp. an unleavened Norwegian bread baked on top of a stove and resembling hardtack (see quot. 1897); (4) **car,** a platform railroad car; (5) ***foot,** (*a*) (see quot.), *obs.*, (*b*) a policeman or detective, *slang;* (6) **furrow plow,** a plow that cuts a furrow that is flat on the bottom, *obs.;* (7) ***head,** see as a main entry; (8) **house,** a house at a ferry where a flat is operated; (9) **jack,** a flapjack, *obs.;* (10) **load,** as much as a flatboat will carry; (11) **root,** some now unidentifiable plant, *rare;* (12) **-side dogs,** an Athapascan tribe of Indians in the Northwest, so called because their Indian name, Thlingchadinne, is said to mean "dog-flank people"; (13) **silver,** silver tableware that is flat, as knives, forks, spoons, etc.; (14) **swamp,** a flat area so poorly drained as to form a swamp, *rare;* (15) **tire,** a dull or uninteresting person, *slang;* (16) **ware,** tableware that is flat, as knives, forks, spoons, etc. (see also quot. 1889); (17) **woods,** low-lying level areas of timberland, usu. having poor natural drainage, also attrib.

(1) **1903** *Cin. Enquirer* 10 May IV. 3/7 Don't you know a switchman oughtn't t' put his feet in flatboats? Don't you know you'll get your foot stuck in a tongue or a guard? — (2) **1845** De Smet *Oregon Missions* (1847) 122 The *Flat-bows* and *Koetenays* now form one tribe. **1907** Hodge *Amer. Indians* I. 776 From the time of their earliest contact with the whites they have been called Flatbows, for what reason is not known, but they are now generally called Lower Kootenay. — (3) **1876** Warner *Gold of Chickaree* 37 Porridge and flat-brod and cheese . . . were set on the table. **1897** E. L. Wakeman in *Columbus Dispatch* 2 Jan., The great and universal staple, however, is 'fladbrod' or flatbread. . . . It is simply a dough of barley and oatmeal, unfermented and containing a little salt, rolled to the thinness of wafers of great circumference and baked upon an iron plate like a large griddle over a 'slow' fire. **1929** *Randolph Enterprise* (Elkins, W.Va.) 14 Nov. 1/3 Housewives made a specialty of 'flat bread,' designed to keep fresh and good for a week. — (4) **1862** in F. Moore *Rebellion Rec.* V. II. 147 The enemy had heard of his movements, and had a train of box-cars and flat cars, with flying artillery and five thousand infantry, running up and down the road to prevent him from reaching it. **1948** *Nat. Geog. Mag.* March 289/2 Every year millions of people watch . . . the big wagons rolled off the flatcars in the railroad yards.

(5) (*a*) **1887** R. A. Proctor 'Americanism" in *Knowledge* 1 June 184/1 An American 'flatfoot' is a man who stands firmly for his party. (*b*) **1922** J. A. Dunn *Man Trap* xiv. 203 Royce hasn't the sense of a flatfoot in the gas district. **1948** *Dly. Ardmoreite* (Ardmore, Okla.) 17 Aug. 8 Ridding the world of the great flatfoot will be the sensation of 1948. — (6) **1853** *Mich. Agric. Soc. Trans.* (1854) 53 Farm Implements 1 flat-furrow plow. — (8) **1698** Sewall *Diary* 9 Mar. (1878) I. 472 Word is brought us that our Horses are broke out of themselves, or else taken out of the stable; . . . Sent presently to their flat-house, but hear nothing of them. **1706** *Ib.* 25 Mar. (1879) II. 157 Din'd at Barker's; surpris'd the Sheriff and his Men at the Flat-house. **1904** E. W. Pringle *Rice Planter* 116 The last sheaf was put in the flat and . . . could be poled up the river and put safely in the flat-house. — (9) **1846** Howland *N.E. Econ. Housekeeper* 25 Common Flat-Jacks, No. 1. Indian Flat-Jacks, No. 2. 26 Indian Griddle Cakes, or Flat-Jacks, No. 3. Rice Flat-Jacks, No. 4.

(10) **1847** Robb *Squatter Life* 134, I wur agoin to start to Lusiane next day, with a flat load of tobaccer and other groceries. **1904** Pringle *Rice Planter* 67, I had had three flatloads of mud cut and put on the bank, and everything was at hand. — (11) **1763** in *Amer. Sp.* XX. (1945) 48 The *Flat-Root* receives its name from the form of its root, which is thin, flat, and pretty often indented. — (12) **1845** De Smet *Oregon Missions* (1847) 164 Within the limits . . . are found the Black-Feet, . . . Flat-side Dogs, Slaves, and Deer-Skins. — (13) **1928** Emily Post *Etiquette* 626 The most complete list of flat silver

possible. **1948** *Dly. Ardmoreite* (Ardmore, Okla.) 24 May 5/3 Money was voted to purchase of flat silver for the community building. — **(14) 1735** in *Amer. Sp.* XV. 179/1 Then . . . to a Gum by the Side of the Flat Swamp aforesaid.

(15) 1929 *Cent. Mag.* Autumn 64 'Bonehead,' 'nickel-nurser,' and 'flat-tire' are original tokens of his esteem for humanity. **1945** *New Yorker* 9 June 16/2 Only a back number or a flat tire would need to be told that a Wolf License is a small fibreboard badge. — **(16) 1889** *Cent.* 2259/2 *flat-ware.* . . . In *ceram.*, plates, dishes, saucers, and the like, collectively, as distinguished from hollow-ware. **1948** *Democrat* 2 Dec. 8/5 International Sterling Silver Flatware, one piece or a full set. — **(17) 1841** in *Amer. Sp.* XV. 179/1 Running up under the foot of the ridge to a large span oak tree and a forked sugar standing in a flat woods. **1866** C. H. SMITH *Bill Arp* 122 Your currency bill has put them down to one hundred and fifty, and it won't buy the hide and tallow of a flatwoods heifer. **1946** WILSON *Fidelity* 95 We got to see funny people from up the creek and out in the Flatwoods.

b. In similar combs., usu. of obvious meaning or sufficiently explained in the quots., as (1) **flatback,** (2) **bar track,** cf. **strap rail,** (3) **boat ferry,** (4) **boatman,** (5) ***footed,** see as a main entry, (6) **gig,** see **gig,** (7) **joint,** (8) **map,** (9) **nose,** (10) **prairie,** (11) **razor clam,** see **razor clam,** (12) **side,** (13) **top.**

(1) 1856 *Spirit of Times* 27 Dec. 270/3 We have, in this region [Va.], the pike, perch, chub, mullet, and 'flat-back,' or *sucker.* **1877** BAGBY *Old Va. Gentleman* 130 The 'flatback,' you know, is called 'sucker' in some parts of the country, and, with its broad, mottled, green back, its large fins and black eyes, makes as pretty a fish as any that swim in our waters. — **(2) 1851** WATKIN *Trip* 124 Thus, with the exception of a few of the New England lines, the older railways were at first unballasted, and laid as 'flat bar track'; that is, with a thin, flat bar of iron nailed on to longitudinal sleepers. The cars cannot run fast on this road; and 'snake heads,' the starting up of the bar under the wheels, cause frequent accidents. — **(3) 1869** *Rep. Comm. Agric. 1868* 351 Many of the unfordable streams are still crossed by flat-boat ferries. **1885** *Cent. Mag.* Jan. 454 The lake, . . . is outside the reservation, and is only accessible by the way of Baptiste's flat-boat ferry. — **(4) 1832** TROLLOPE *Domestic Manners* I. 21 The deck, as is usual, was occupied by the Kentucky flat-boat men, returning from New Orleans. **1946** WILSON *Fidelity* 112 We imagined ourselves raftsmen or flatboatmen.

(7) 1912 I. COBB *Back Home* 147 The highpitch man and his brother of the flat joint were at work. **1937** MENCKEN *Amer. Lang.* 584 A gambling concession is a *flat-joint*, and the man operating it is a *thief.* — **(8) 1936** *Dly. Oklahoman* 2 Sep. 1/2 Tuesday night's weather capers emerged from what Walgren called a 'flat map,' a general low pressure area covering most of the middle west and centering over Missouri. — **(9) 1816** THOMAS *Travels Western Country* (1819) 211 The *shovel fish* or *flat nose* is another species of sturgeon.

(10) 1845 *Cultivator* ns. II. 124 In some of the fields on flat prairie, the crop was not worth gathering. **1849** CHAMBERLAIN *Ind. Gazetteer* 433 Grass grows well in the flat prairies where there is less sand mixed with the soil. — **(12) 1857** *Spirit of Times* 4 April 70/2 There is the roach, or flat-side, or sun-fish, as he is variously called, . . . which seem to me to be the identical chaps we used to catch in the sunny pond-holes, in the Mississippi bottoms. **1947** CARPENTER & SEIGLER *Fishes N.H.* 68 Pumpkinseed (Flatside, Kivver, Kibbee, Sunfish) *Lepomis gibbosus* (Linnaeus). — **(13) 1817–8** EATON *Botany* (1822) 508 *Vernonia noveboracensis*, flat top. **1859** BARTLETT 218 Iron Weed . . . called in the North-eastern States Flat Top, almost the only tall weed found in the beautiful 'woods pastures' of Kentucky and Tennessee. Western. **1889** *Cent.* 2259/1 *Flattop*, . . . an American perennial herb, *Vernonia Noveboracensis*. Also called ironweed.

***flat,** *v.*

1. *tr.* To transport or haul (stone, etc.) on a flat or flatboat.

1753 *N.J. Archives* XIX. 237 William Richardson was employ'd by James Baldwin to flat some wood to Philadelphia on the 25th of December last. **1770** WASHINGTON *Diaries* I. 380 Began to flat Stone round, as also to carry wood round for burning Lyme. **1845** in COMMONS *Doc. Hist.* I. 166 Having to cross two rivers, & a canal in flatting the crop from it.

2. (See quot.) *Obs.* Cf. ***flat,** *n.* **4.**

1859 BARTLETT 155 *To Flat*, to reject a lover. . . . 'She flatted him.' Western.

3. *To flat off*, to become level gradually. *Rare.*

*a***1862** THOREAU *Cape Cod.* ix. 166 The bank flatted off for the last ten miles.

4. *To flat out*, to fail, collapse, come to naught (see quot. 1887).

1839 KIRKLAND *New Home* xxxi. 221 The bank never would have 'flatted out,' if he had had a finger in the pie. **1865** HOLLAND *Plain Talk* 129 Generally, disappointed and broken down men are those who have failed in trade . . . or to use an expressive Yankee phrase, have 'flatted out' in a calling or profession. **1887** *Knowledge* 1 June 184/1 *To flat out*, to diminish in value—a Western phrase suggested by the diminished productiveness of metallic layers as they grow thinner.

Also as a noun.

*a***1870** CHIPMAN *Notes on Bartlett* 156 *To Flat Out*. . . . It is heard also as a noun. 'It was a complete flat-out.' 'He made a flat-out.'—N[ew] E[ngland]. **1886** *Cent. Mag.* March 727/1, I didn't know't was goin' to be s'ch a perfect flat-out.

b. To relax, lose vigor. *Colloq.*

1863 G. HAMILTON *Gala-Days* 89 Before twelve o'clock we flatted out and made jests.

flatboat ˈflæt,bot, *v. tr.* and *intr.* To transport in a flatboat. Also **flatboating,** *n.*

1858 WILKIE *Davenport* 194 Capt. May commenced flat-boating on the Ohio in 1822. **1858** *Nat. Intelligencer* 29 July 3/4 His first enterprise . . . was a trading excursion to New Orleans with fruit, which he flat-boated from Wheeling to that point, when the time occupied in making the voyage was six weeks. **1861** NEWELL *Orpheus C. Kerr* I. 32 [Abraham Lincoln,] when he took to flat-boating, . . . was so tall and straight, that a fellow once took him for a smoke-stack on a steamboat. **1870** O. OPTIC *Field & Forest* 279, I took to the river for a livin'. I worked a choppin', a flat boatin' and firin' on a steamboat.

***flat-footed,** *a.* and *adv.* Also **flat-footedly.**

1. Plain, positive, forthright. *Colloq.*

1828 ROYALL *Black Book* II. 114 He was one of your right down flat-footed ox-drivers. **1854** *Knickerb.* XLIII. 439 A 'Flat-Footed Candidate' for Justice of the Peace . . . comes out . . . with following address. **1938** DANIELS *Southerner* 280 It was headed: 'Tennessee Coal, Iron and Railroad Company Endorses Soil Conservations.' And that's flat-footed, I said to myself.

b. Also *to come out* (or *catch*) *flatfooted* (or *flatfootedly*).

1846 *N.Y. Herald* 30 June (B.), Mr. Pickens has come out flat-footed for the Administration, a real red-hot Democrat, dyed in the wool. **1886** LOGAN *Great Conspiracy* 660 The old Rebel leaders . . . came out flat-footedly again with the 'demand that all Custom-house taxation shall be only for revenue.' **1945** *New Yorker* 25 Aug. 15 Caught flat-footed, like everybody else.

c. (See quot.)

1853 P. PAXTON *Yankee in Texas* 204 The horse is his last resource. . . . When lost, the quondam owner is said to be flat broke or flat footed.

2. flatfooted boys, a nickname for the ignorant, vicious element of butcher-knife-wearing frontiersmen and backwoodsmen in the early settlement of Illinois, *c*1800. *Obs.*

1847 T. FORD *Hist. Illinois* 88 Since the butcher knife has been disused as an article of dress, the fashion has been, to call this class of people 'the bare-footed boys,' 'the flat-footed boys,' and 'the huge-pawed boys,' names with which they seem to be greatly tickled and pleased, and their influence is yet considerable in all elections.

***flathead,** *n.*

1. (*cap.*) *pl.* Any one of various tribes of North American Indians who practiced, or were thought to practice, head-flattening.

1709 LAWSON *Carolina* 33 These [Carolina] Indians are of an extraordinary Stature, and call'd by their Neighbours flat Heads, which seems a very suitable Name for them. **1888** ROOSEVELT in *Cent. Mag.* June 205/2 The Indians, . . . said to be Flatheads or their kin, on a visit from the coast region,—had set fire to the woods. **1944** Ross *Westward* 24 The Indians had signified their readiness for the gospel, as far back as 1831, by sending a delegation of Flatheads and Nez Percés to St. Louis.

b. *sing.* An Indian of one of these tribes (cf. **Nez Percé**). Also, *contemptuous*, a greenhorn, simpleton, fool.

*a***1861** T. WINTHROP *Canoe & Saddle* iii. 32 'Lo the flat-head.' Among them a tight-strapped cushion controls the elastic skull of childhood. **1884** MARK TWAIN *H. Finn* xxiii. 229 Greenhorns, flatheads! **1909** WASON *Happy Hawkins* 306, [I] chased a flat-head clear into the Palace Hotel for throwin' a pear at me.

2. Often used attrib., as **Flathead nation, reservation, tribal council, tribe.**

1807 GASS *Journal* 165 We suppose them to be a band of the Flathead nation, as all their heads are compressed into the same form. **1841** WILLIAMS *Tour to Ore.* (1921) 45 Here the Flat Heads met the Catholic priest, who, with his little company, left us, and turned to the right to go to the Flat Head tribes, where he had a mission. **1882** *Cent. Mag.* XXIV. 864 The Flathead reservation contains about 1,500,000 acres of land, and is inhabited by less than twelve hundred Indians and half-breeds. **1947** *Harper's Mag.* March 235/2 Into the record went a resolution of the Flathead Tribal Council charging that Montana Power had been 'a corrupting, blackmailing, and unscrupulous influence' on the reservation.

b. Esp. **Flathead Indian,** or, with reference to the tribes, **Flathead Indians.**

1715 *Boston News-Letter* 11 July 2/1 Some of our Indians were gone to War against the Flatt Head Indians near Carolina. **1856** DERBY *Phoenixiana* ii. 34 The same insufficiency of adjectives exist in all except that [language] of the Flathead Indians of Puget Sound. **1890** *Boston Journal* 28 Oct. 1/6 Two of the four Flathead Indians . . . have been on trial. *a***1918** G. STUART *On Frontier* I. 134 Just below us on the creek were camped eight lodges of Flathead Indians.

Also *Flathead child, country, horse, man, squaw, woman,* etc.

3. (See quots.)

1838 *Knickerb. Mag.* XL. 518 Often have the flat heads of the gate-posts served as a platform to the branches. **1891** *Scribner's Mag.* Sep. 311/1 Contemplate, for instance, the flat-head houses of Brooklyn—two stories high in front and three in the rear.

4. =**hognose snake.** In full **flathead adder.**

1875 *Amer. Naturalist* IX. 10, I have known the Flat-head Adder or Blowing Viper, *Heterodon platyrhinos,* to eat the heads of the common eel. **1888** *Pop. Sci. Mo.* XXXIII. 660 The blow-snake of Illinois is variously known in other localities as hog-nose, flat-head, viper, and puff-adder.

5. flathead (catfish), the mud cat, *Opladelus olivaris.*

1947 *Watonga* (Okla.) *Republican* 31 July 1/4 Monday he was showing a live Flathead catfish in his back yard that he claims is the largest to be brought in. **1948** *Capital-Democrat* (Tishomingo, Okla.) 24 June 3/5 He took also 8 flatheads weighing 13, 16, 14, 22, 18, 19, 20 and 8½ lbs. on trotline baited with cut carp.

flathead ˈflætˌhɛd, *v. tr.* To elongate or flatten the head (of an Indian papoose). *Rare.* — *a***1861** WINTHROP *Canoe & Saddle* x. 204 One infant, evidently malcontent, was being flat-headed.

***flatter,** *n.* A flatboatman. *Slang.* — **1933** BLAIR & MEINE *Mike Fink* 106 Come on, you flatters, you bargers, you milk-white mechanics, an' see how tough I am to chaw! **1941** BALDWIN *Keelboat Age* 97 The eyes she was makin' . . . might fetch a greenhorn or a flatter.

***flaunt,** *v. tr.* To flout, to treat with contempt. — **1933** *DAB* X. 472 (Horwill), Though a temperate discussion of the desirability of birth control . . . the treatise, flaunting many accepted conceptions and values of the period, did not escape court action. **1934** M. A. ELLIOTT & F. E. MERRILL *Social Disorg.* 573 When self-support appears easy, the temptation to flaunt family control is very great.

***flax,** *n.* In combs.: (1) ***flax bird,** (see quots.); (2) **cotton,** flax that has been cottonized, *obs.;* (3) **pulling,** a social gathering or bee for pulling up flax, *obs.;* (4) ***seed,** (see quots.); (5) **snapdragon,** (see quots.).

(1) **1822** LATHAM *Hist. Birds* VI. 120 American Gold Finch . . . feeds on the seeds of flax, alder, &c., and is called in the back parts of Carolina, the Flax Bird. **1931** *Randolph Enterprise* (Elkins, W.Va.) 24 Sep. 5/4 We used to wonder why old folks of early days called the wild canary the 'beet bird' until this summer they eat our beet tops. They also called them flax birds. — (2) **1851** LOWELL *Letters* I. 192 The flax-cotton is a great thing. **1863** *Rep. Comm. Agric. 1862* 406 Flax fibre can, by mechanical, chemical, or other means, be converted into flax-cotton of a suitable quality for use as a substitute for cotton in the cotton-mills of our country. — (3) **1852** REYNOLDS *Hist. Illinois* 167 The girls frequently attended these flax pullings. — (4) **1862** *Ill. Agric. Soc. Trans.* V. 485 Mr. Frick . . . was kind enough to take me to a wheat stubble, full of Hessian flies in the 'flax seed' or pupa state. **1886** *Times* (London) 18 Aug. 10/6 Pupae . . . resembling small and rather elongated flax seeds . . . are called 'flax seeds' in America. **1888** *Riverside Nat. Hist.* II. 410 The larvæ [of the Hessian fly] assume the pupa state, called the flaxseed stage. — (5) **1817–8** EATON *Botany* (1822) 176 *Antirrhinum canadense,* flax snap dragon . . . flowers small. **1840** DEWEY *Mass. Flowering Plants* 158 Flax Snap-Dragon, or Toad-flax, scarcely deserves a notice here; small, mere weeds, . . . July. **1845** LINCOLN *Botany* App. 74/2.

As the last term in **Missouri, mountain flax.**

***flax,** *v.*

1. *To flax out,* to beat or thrash severely. Also fig. *Colloq.*

1839 *N.O. Picayune* 8 Mar. 2/4 Now, it's my opinion, that if they du cum to hard blows the Maine boys 'll flax out them are Brunswickers like sixty. *c***1849** PAIGE *Dow's Sermons* I. 54 When you commence a pugilistic encounter, . . . you are ready to do mischief—to either flax out your opponent, or give nature special fits in the undertaking. **1900** in HANDSAKER *Pioneer Life* 43 Yes you look like a votin for him again dont you when you and all the rest was flaxt outen your shoes when you voted for him before.

b. To give out, become exhausted or overweary.

1891 WILKINS *N. Eng. Nun* 180 These dretful smart, handsome folks are just the ones that flax out sometimes. **1903** *D.N.* II. 351 *Flax out,* To wear out; be weary, 'I'm all flaxed out,' O[hio].

2. *To flax (a)round,* to be busy, bustle about. *Colloq.*

1841 *N.O. Picayune* 24 Mar. 2/2, I wish you'd flax round and git supper as fast as you can, 'cause I'm allfired hungry and tired tu. **1896** W. A. WHITE *Real Issue* 96 She . . . done all her own work, flaxed around and fixed up the house. **1902** PIDGIN *S. Holton* 237 You've flaxed around like a house afire. What do you want? Some money?

***flea,** *n.* **1. flea breeder,** (see quot.). *Slang. Obs.* **2. flea bug,** a flea beetle. **3. flea circus,** an exhibition of trained fleas.

(1) **1852** *Mich. Agric. Soc. Trans.* III. 332 We have among our grubs and in our puddles about 10,000 things which Wolverine audacity have denominated swine—variously known as narragansetts, alligators, land sharks and flea breeders. — (2) **1877** *Vt. Bd. Agric. Rep.* IV. 158 [The insect] is very lively in its movements, and is sometimes called flea-bug. Its scientific name is *Corimelaena publicaria.* **1883** SMITH *Geol. Survey Ala.* 547 Cotton is injured by lice, flea-bugs, boll-worms, caterpillars, shedding and rust. — (3) **1932** *Screenland* April 89/1 Shooting galleries, the flea circus, and ending the spree by having their pictures made. **1948** *Sat. Ev. Post* 4 Sep. 99/2 The men of Room 301 were jammed around her, open-mouthed, like old geezers who don't believe what they see at a flea circus.

As the last term in **beach, snow flea.**

***fleece,** *n.*

1. The pure fat obtained from a bear, esp. that from the omentum. *Obs.* Cf. **fat fleece.**

1805 LEWIS in *L. & Clark Exped.* II. (1904) 34 The bear being old the flesh was indifferent, they therefore only took the skin and fleece, the latter made us several gallons of oil. **1844** FEATHERSTONHAUGH *Excursion* 111 As to what is called bear's meat, it is literally nothing but the fat of the omentum. The fleshy part is all given to the dogs. Of this fat, which the hunters call *the fleece,* they are ravenously fond.

2. (See later quots.) Now *hist.* Cf. **dépouille.**

1806 CLARK in *Lewis & C. Exped* V. (1904) 352 The Chyenne Chief . . . had a robe and a fleece of fat Buffalow meat brought and gave me. **1834** A. PIKE *Sketches* 96 The sala, or long hall . . . was garnished with vast quantities of buffalo meat, in thin, dry fleeces. **1891** *Army & Navy Jrnl.* 5 Sep. 30/1 The fleece [of a buffalo] is the meat lying on each side of the hump ribs and resting on the outside of the side ribs. **1945** *La Junta* (Colo.) *Tribune-Democrat* 12 June 2/7 In butchering them the hide was cut from the hump back to the tail and the 'fleece' extending along either side of the backbone taken out.

b. *transf.* (See quot.) *Rare.*

1848 RUXTON *Adventures* 221 Half an hour after I killed a large black-tail deer, and, as it was also in miserable condition, I took merely the fleeces (as the meat on the back and ribs is called), leaving four fifths of the animal untouched.

***fleet,** *n.* As the last term in **dandelion, gulf, rum, stone, tobacco fleet.**

***flesher,** *n.* A tool used in tanneries to remove flesh from hides. Also one who uses this. Cf. ***dubber.**

1883 KNIGHT *Supp.* 346 *Flesher,* . . . a long, two-handled and somewhat blunt-edged knife . . . used to scrape off the hair, scarf-skin, loose flesh [of hides]. **1891** *Nat. Museum Rep. 1889* 554 The extraneous flesh [is] taken off with a flesher, an instrument like a drawing knife, sharp on one edge and dull and smooth on the other. **1891** CHASE & CLOW *Industry* II. 68 Here they are in the beam-house among the 'hairers' and 'fleshers.'

Fletcherism ˈflɛtʃərɪzəm, *n.* The dietary principles of Horace Fletcher (1849–1919), who advocated eating only when hungry and taking only very small quantities of food thoroughly masticated. — **1906** *Suburban Life* Aug. 101/1 It is really an account of his investigation of what has been known as Fletcherism. **1913** *Ladies' Home Jrnl.* March 69 A woman . . . who weighed more than two hundred pounds has also undertaken Fletcherism and is getting good results.

Fletcherite ˈflɛtʃəraɪt, *n.* [See prec.] One who practices Fletcherism. — **1904** *London Dly. Chronicle* 31 Oct. 4/7 The Fletcherites preach the gospel of chewing. **1914** FLETCHER in *Ladies' Home Jrnl.* May 80 To the practised 'Fletcherite' . . . those disorders do not happen at all. *Ib.* 81 If wine and tea experts 'Fletcherized' their food as they do the 'goods' they are expert upon they would be ideal 'Fletcherites.'

Fletcherize ˈflɛtʃəraɪz, *v.* [See **Fletcherism.**] *tr.* To chew thoroughly. Also fig.

1903 *Lit. Digest* 28 Nov. 739/1 Owing to a recent crusade in its favor by Horace Fletcher . . . it is now proposed to speak of the 'Fletcherizing' of food that is thoroughly chewed. **1910** O. HENRY *Strictly Business* xvii. 203 Annette Fletcherized large numbers of romantic novels. **1926** J. BLACK *You Can't Win* xviii. 273, I heard of Fletcher and his system of Fletcherizing food.

flicker ˈflɪkɚ, *n.* [Prob. imitative.] The yellow-hammer or golden-winged woodpecker, *Colaptes auratus.* Cf. **red-shafted, western flicker.** — **1808** WILSON *Ornithology* I. 53 It has numerous provincial appellations . . . , such as 'High-hole,' . . . 'Piut,' 'Flicker,' by which last it is usually known in Pennsylvania. **1916** SETON *Woodcraft Man.* 312 *Flicker or Highhole* (*Colaptes auratus*). This large and beautiful woodpecker is twelve inches long. . . . Its beautiful plumage and loud splendid 'clucker' cry make it a joy in every woodland.

flickertail ˈflɪkəˌtel, *n.* One of the numerous small ground squirrels, *Citellus richardsoni,* of the western prairie region. Also **Flickertail State,** (see quot. 1890).

1890 *Brighton* (Colo.) *Reg.* 11 Jan. 4/1 The nickname of North Dakota is the 'flickertail state.' **1943** CAHALANE *Meeting Mammals* 69 If the squirrels observe any signs of danger they run to their homes, and with a last twitch of the tail disappear. This final gesture has given them another nickname—'flickertail.' **1946** THOMPSON *Amer. Daughter* 36 As the wild rose was the official state flower, so was the gopher, commonly called the flickertail, its namesake.

transf. **1946** McWILLIAMS *So. Calif. Country* 172 North Dakotans are 'flicker tails.'

***flier,** see ***flyer.**

***flight,** *n.* **1.** A herd of buffalo. *Rare.* **2. flight goose,** (see quots.).

(1) **1827** COOPER *Prairie* I. v, A rushing sound was heard, similar to that which might be expected to precede the passage of a flight of buffaloes. — (2) **1835** AUDUBON *Ornith. Biog.* III. 17 That species [of Canada Goose] is distinguished there [in Maine] by the name of *Flight Goose,* and is said to be entirely migratory. **1839** PEABODY *Mass. Birds* 385 Hutchins' Goose, *Anser Hutchinsii.* . . . [Audubon and Nuttall] call it the Flight, or Winter Goose.

flimflammer ˈflɪmˌflæmə, *n.* [f. **flimflam, v.* to humbug.] One who is given to flimflamming, cheating, trickery. *Colloq.*

1894 *Columbus* (Ohio) *Dispatch* 31 Jan., The New York flim-flammers . . . are still out of the clutches of the United States Secret Service. **1909** WASON *Happy Hawkins* 169 That rascally real-estate owner wasn't nothing but a flim-flammer. **1946** PARTRIDGE & BETTMANN *As We Were* 164 Their places were hangouts for pickpockets, confidence men, and flimflammers of various sorts.

***flint,** *n.*

1. A variety of Indian corn having unusually hard kernels. In full **flint corn.** Also attrib. Cf. **white, yellow flint corn.**

1705 BEVERLEY *Virginia* II. 29 One looks as smooth, and as full as the early ripe Corn, and this they call *Flint-Corn.* **1802** DRAYTON *S. Carolina* 137 The flint is more hard and nourishing, and grinds more into grist. **1833** *Boston Mercantile Jrnl.* 5 Feb. 3/3 A few barrels of Prime Flint Corn Grits for making Homony, for sale. **1947** *Annals Mo. Bot. Garden* Feb. 17 There is as yet little exact evidence as to how completely the gene combinations introduced from the northern flints have been broken up in modern dent corns.

2. Attrib. with **knob, ridge,** to indicate terrain abounding in flint.

1814 BRACKENRIDGE *Views* 62 This is the natural consequence of the difference of habit, arising from the prairies, and flint knobs, which of course give birth to distinct tribes in the vegetable kingdom. **1831** PECK *Guide* 14 The remainder is made up of abrupt hills, flint and limestone ridges, bluffs, and ravines.

3. In special combs.: (1) **flinthead,** a local name for the wood ibis, *Mycteria americana;* (2) **-ware,** stoneware (see quot. 1889).

(1) **1938** MATSCHAT *Suwannee River* 97 With a loud whosh-whosh of wings, a large flock of wood ibis swept slowly by and came to rest a little way from the punt. . . . 'Flintheads,' he breathed.— (2) **1744** *Pa. Gazette* 15 Nov. 3/2 Just imported and to be sold by John Ord, . . . flint ware by the crate, and sundry other shop goods at retail. **1889** *Cent.* 2271/3 flintware. . . . In *ceram.:* (*a*) Pottery distinguished by the use of ground flints mixed with the clay. (*b*) Pottery having a slip in which ground flints enter for a considerable part of its volume.

As the last term in **blue, early, gun, horn, white flint.**

***flint,** *v. intr.* (See quot.) *Obs.* — **1877** BARTLETT 782 *To flint in,* to begin doing something, as to work or to eat, energetically and without ceremony.

***flip,** *v.*

1. *To flip up,* to toss a coin to decide a chance. *Colloq.*

1879 *N.Y. Tribune* 4 Oct. (*Cent.*), The two great men could flip up to see which should have the second place. **1889** C. L. MARSH *Opening the Oyster* 169 'Let's flip up!' proposed Ned, taking a coin from his pocket. 'Heads means style, and tails economy; here goes!'

2. ***flipflap, a.** a kind of tea cake, *obs.* **b.** (see quots.).

(a) **1876** BESANT & RICE *Golden Butterfly* xviii, As we sat over her doughnuts and flipflaps. — (b) **1889** *Cent.* 2272/1 *Flipflap,* . . . the dobson or hellgrammite. (Virginia.) **1948** *Field & Stream* July 42/2 Various stages of the dobson are known as . . . bogarts, hell-devils, flip-flaps, snake doctors and hell-divers.

3. flip-flop, a handspring or somersault, a "*flip-flap." *Colloq.*

1902 LORIMER *Lett. Merchant* 245 And when a fellow's turning flip-flops up among the clouds, he's naturally going to have the farmers gaping at him. **1946** *Gunnison* (Colo.) *News-Champion* 2 May 1/2 The convertible Ford coupe of Becker's which he was driving, missed a narrow bridge near Elkhorn, . . . turned a flip-flop in the air and came to a stop right side up in waist-deep waters of the Gunnison river.

transf. **1948** *Time* 6 Dec. 21/3 As Murray's attacks mounted in fervency, some old party-liners did some curious flip-flops.

Hence **flip-flopping,** a sharp flopping sound. Also, *slang,* becoming erratic in performance, failing.

1897 *Outing* (U.S.) XXX. 176/1, I could hear a vigorous flip-flopping going on beyond the weeds, and I knew the captive was a trout. **1947** *Chi. Tribune* 11 July 21/5 By way of avoiding suspense for the rabid Brooklyn customers, the Cubs started flip-flopping early in the first game.

flip-iron. An iron for heating flip. — **1869** MRS. STOWE *Oldtown Folks* xxxvii. 480 Draw the flip-iron from the fire and stir the foaming bowl. **1947** DOWNEY *Lusty Forefathers* 7 Shaking flip-irons in each other's face, as the saying went, 'at loggerheads.'

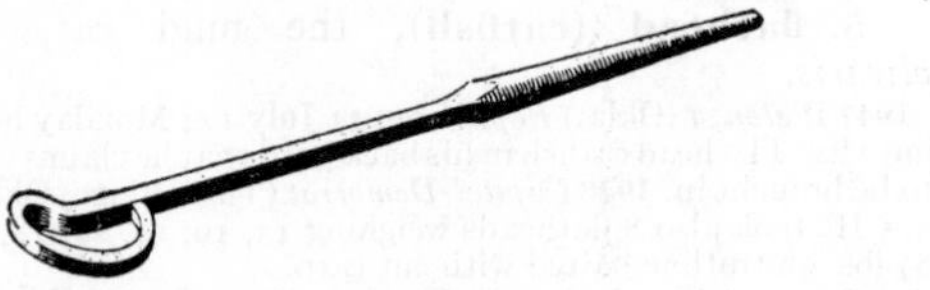

Flip-iron (*c*1850)

***flipper,** *n.* A flapjack, pancake, also **corn flipper, flour flipper.** *Colloq. Obs.*

1850 KINGSLEY *Diary* 114 We arrived at the bar in time to . . . get supper &c which consisted of flippers & fried pork. **1856** PHILLIPS *Kansas* 367 It was almost worth a dinner, and better than the dinner they thus prepared, to see them manufacturing corn and flour flippers. **1882** HUBBARD *Moosehead Lake* 26 Flippers, or 'flap-jacks,' are mixed like bread, except that a little more baking powder is used, and a good deal more water.

flivver ˈflɪvə, *n.* [Origin unknown.]

1. A fizzle, a failure, *Slang.*

1915 H. L. WILSON *Ruggles of Red Gap* xiii. (1917) 230 He's the human flivver. Put him in a car of dressed beef and he'd freeze it between here and Spokane.

2. A small, cheap car, esp. a Ford. *Colloq.*

*c***1914** in SULLIVAN *Our Times* (1932) 71 There was a fat man of Fall River, Who said as he drove his Ford 'flivver' [etc.]. **1949** *Mazama* Feb. 3/2 Just crank up that old flivver.

b. *attrib.* Designating things small of their kind (see quots.).

1918 in C. A. SMITH *New Words* 72 He commanded a flivver, which is the service name for the smaller class of destroyers, the 750-ton ones. In our navy there are plenty of your officers who tell you that they never built destroyers which keep the sea better than that same little flivver class. **1929** *Forum* March 160/2 For example, after flying to a city, it will be possible to land outside its limits and then use the plane as an automobile. Fundamentally this is the flivver air plane which I visualize. **1944** *Chi. D. News* 14 July 10/2 Despite the tremendous technological advances incidental to the war, the public must not expect revolutionary new automobiles, houses, . . . television sets or flivver helicopters in the immediate future.

flivver ˈflɪvə, *v.* **1.** *intr.* To fail. **2.** To travel in a flivver. Both *colloq.*

(1) **1912** L. J. VANCE *Destroying Angel* vi. 74 If the production flivvers, I'll need that thirty cents. **1948** *Sat. Ev. Post* 20 Nov. 42/1 Plan for Liverwurstless Day flivvered. . . . [It] would cross up Department's plan to get Americans to eat more rye bread. — (2) **1927** EUBANK *Horse & Buggy Days* 30 With the women voting and the girls cavorting and the boys flivvering [etc.]. **1947** *Time* 10 Mar. 43/1 About 10,000 of them flivvered down to Juniper Grove to get in on the 3,000-lb. beef barbecue.

***float,** *n.*

1. A certificate given an Indian entitling him to a specified amount of public land selected by him anywhere within a prescribed region. Also, *pl.,* the region itself. *Obs.* Cf. **floating claim, Indian float.**

Such certificates were issued by the federal government upon the acquisition of Indian lands in exchange for others more remote. The holder of such a certificate was at liberty to dispose of it, and many of the floats passed into the hands of unscrupulous speculators for mere trifles.

1835 in BASSETT *South. Plant.* 46, I intended to have Requested you (to) ascertain if you could how the Lands belonging to the Chickasaw Indians To Wit (the Reserves and Floats, as they are called) will be disposed of There are a great many persons among the Indians buying their Reserves and Floats. **1852** *S. Lit. Messenger* XVIII. 753/2 The land, left subject to entry, if the 'Floats' had been good, was not worth entering.

b. With the names of Indian tribes: **Choctaw, Wyandot floats.**

1852 *S. Lit. Messenger* XVIII. 753/2 Tom Edmundson . . . invested the balance, on private information kindly given him, in 'Choctaw Floats;' a most lucrative investment. **1856** PHILLIPS *Kansas* 28 Several Wyandot 'floats' were located on the site, the city being laid out two miles square. These Wyandot floats are transferable rights, by which each of the Wyandot Indians could locate a section of land, six hundred and forty acres, on any unoccupied public land, and hold it in fee simple. **1906** *Kansas Hist. Soc.* IX. 82 These sections of land . . . could be located anywhere west of the Mississippi on Indian land not already occupied. They were known as Wyandot 'floats.'

c. A government certificate entitling the holder to an indicated acreage of unoccupied or unpaid-for public land which might be selected by the grantee anywhere within a prescribed area. Now *hist.* Cf. ∗**float,** *v.* **3.**

The purpose of these certificates was to protect settlers whose pre-emption claims overlapped, but they were often issued on flimsy pretexts and were productive of much fraud.

1837 H. MARTINEAU *Society* II. 92 Large companies . . . procure affidavits of improvements to be made, get the warrants issued upon them, and whenever a good tract of land is ready for sale, cover it over with their *floats*, (warrants of the required habitation,) and thus put down competition. **1857** *Lawrence* (Kans.) *Republican* 11 June 3 We learn of Gov. Robinson that he has not withdrawn his float from the south part of Lawrence. **1948** DICK *Dixie Frontier* 74 Quantities of affidavits were printed and distributed to paid agents, who with the co-operation of ignorant or corrupt justices of the peace secured floats wholesale for speculators.

2. *local.* (See quot.)

1846 THORPE *Myst. Backwoods* 36 In late spring . . . the fish come near the surface of the water and expose their mouths to the air, keeping up, at the same time, a constant motion with it, called 'piping.' Fish thus exposed are in groups, and are called a 'float.'

3. (See quot. 1874.)

1852 *Statutes at Large* X. 62 Every such vessel carrying passengers, shall also be provided with a good life-preserver, . . . or float well adapted to the purpose, for each and every passenger, which life-preservers and floats shall always be kept in . . . readiness. **1874** KNIGHT 883/2 float . . . an inflated bag or pillow to sustain a person in the water.

4. = **floater 1.**

1865 RICHARDSON *Secret Service* xii. 167 In firm and determined men, the two parties were about equally divided, but there were a good many 'floats' who held the balance of power. **1885** *Pall Mall Gaz.* 6 Nov. 2 We know that seven-eighths of the negroes in northern cities never vote without getting paid for it, and that something like one-twelfth of the remaining voters are 'floats'—that is, men who are looking for money.

5. A wave or crowd. *Obs.*

1873 J. H. BEADLE *Undevel. West* xviii. 329 Their mode of life engenders a love of gaming, and following close upon them . . . is a 'float' of gamblers, strikers [etc.].

6. A dessert made of custard and whipped cream or beaten egg whites. Cf. **float pudding.**

1876 in GUILD *Old Times* (1878) 396 And then came the fourth and final course, of fruit, wines, float, sillabub, and pickles. **1889** *Harper's Mag.* June 124/2 'Drusy' in housewifely discomfiture . . . without the red cloth on the table, or time to beat up a bowl of float.

7. The amount of money covered by checks which are in the process of collection. *Colloq.*

1924 W. O. SCROGGS *Century Banking Progress* 273 The amount of these checks continually in transit, the 'float,' was estimated at about $300,000,000.

As the last term in **cotton, ferry, fishing, sculling, wood float.**

∗**float,** *v.*

1. *intr.* To hunt *for* deer by approaching them at night in a boat. Cf. ∗**floating,** *n.* **1.**

1871 BURROUGHS *Wake-Robin* (1886) 100 Our guide proposed to conduct us to a lake . . . where we could float for deer. **1885** *Outing* VII. 80/2 'Kill any deers over there?' 'No,' said Carl; 'we floated two nights, but it was terrible foggy.'

2. *Mining.* Of gold: To flow away or escape during the mining process. Cf. **float gold 1.**

1873 RAYMOND *Silver & Gold* 17 This shows that $5.85 per ton [of gold] 'floats,' which probably is at least 20 per cent. of the yield.

3. *tr.* To transfer the location of (a claim to or a grant of) public land by surreptitious means. Cf. ∗**float,** *n.* **1.**

1874 RAYMOND *6th Rep. Mines* 513 How difficult it is for any searcher of records to find out whether any given claim was ever really made where it purports to have been located, or whether it was floated, *i.e.*, fraudulently transported from another portion of the district. **1879** HINTON *Hand-Book Ariz.* 193 The property has been claimed as belonging to a Spanish land grant, floated over the region. **1948** WESTON *Mother Lode* 3 Fremont's forty-four-thousand-acre Mexican land grant [was] originally purchased in the San Joaquin Valley but 'floated' to the foothills after the discovery of gold, merely by shifting the boundary lines.

4. To file (the teeth of a horse). *Colloq.*

1886 *N.Y. Wkly. Tribune* 28 Dec. (*Cent.*), Many an old horse will renew its life if its teeth are floated, as the process is called.

5. In combs.: (1) **float gold,** see as a main entry; (2) **pole,** = **floatstick;** (3) **pudding,** a sweetened, flavored dessert in which ice cream is floated; (4) **road,** (see quot. 1905); (5) **stick,** (see quot. 1848).

(2) **1856** BONNER *Life J. P. Beckwourth* (1931) 92 We searched diligently along the river and the bank for a considerable distance, but the trap was among the missing. The float-pole also was gone—a pole ten or twelve feet long and four inches thick. — (3) **1881** MARSHALL *Through Amer.* 109 Dessert . . . [includes] Float Pudding. Fruit. Strawberries. — (4) **1901** MONTGOMERY *Reminiscences* 115 Next morning I determined to follow an old float road in which we found ourselves. **1905** *Forestry Bureau. Bul. 61* Float road. A channel cleared in a swamp and used to float cypress logs from the woods to the boom at the river or mill. — (5) **1848** RUXTON *Adventures* 235 A 'float-stick' is made fast to the trap by a cord a few feet long, which, if the animal carry away the trap, floats on the water and points out its position. **1947** DE VOTO *Across Wide Missouri* 157 The pole or a separate 'float stick' that had been attached would show where the carcass was.

∗**floatables,** *n. pl.* That which floats or can be floated. *Obs.* — **1864** *Mich. Laws* 23 The business of running, driving, booming, and rafting logs, timber, lumber, and other floatables on any of the streams within this State. **1869** *Mich. Gen. Statutes* I. (1882) 985 Such company shall have a lien upon all logs, rafts, timber, or lumber, or other floatables driven, rafted, or run through such stream or waters upon which toll shall be due.

∗**floatage,** *n.* The using of a stream to float boats, logs, etc., or that which floats or is floated on such a stream. *Obs.*

1853 *Mich. Sup. Ct. Rep.* II. 524 It is of the first importance that the rights of the public be recognized, to the free use of all streams susceptible of any valuable floatage. **1855** *Mich. Gen. Statutes* I. (1882) 994 No such rollway, boom, pier, or other construction, shall interrupt or hinder the free use, navigation, or floatage upon such streams or waters. *Ib.* 995 If any person or persons shall . . . obstruct the floatage or navigation, . . . it shall be lawful for such company to cause such rollways or jams to be broken.

∗**floater,** *n.*

1. One who makes a practice of selling his vote.

1847 *Knickerb.* April 329 Early the next morning the 'floaters' were marched in single file, with votes in hand, to the ballot box. **1888** *Cong. Rec.* App. 12 Dec. 8/1 [President Jackson, in his farewell address,] seems to have had in contemplation the Dudley scheme of purchasing floaters in 'blocks of five' in the doubtful State of Indiana. **1948** *New Yorker* 235 Sep. 26/1 Floaters are retainers of political organizations, and it's still common practice to 'colonize' doubtful districts with them.

2. A dead body found floating in water.

1852 A. T. JACKSON *Forty-niner* (1920) 185, I was working on the mine Thursday afternoon . . . when I saw a floater come bobbing down the river. **1932** *N.Y. World Telegram* 21 June, What's a Floater. . . . We were uncertain whether it meant a drowned person or some sort of fish.

b. A log floating down a stream.

1873 BEADLE *Undevel. West* 718 We generally knew of a coming 'drive' a day or two beforehand, by the increase of 'floaters.'

3. A member of a state legislature or convention who represents an irregular constituency, such as one made up of the population of two or more sparsely settled counties.

1853 *Texas State Gaz.* 16 July (F.), A candidate for floater in the district composed of the counties of Fayette, Bastrop, and Travis. **1891** CRADDOCK in *Harper's Mag.* Jan. 203/2 He 'lows ez he's jes kem hyar along o' Leonard Rhodes ez be a-'lectioneerin' fur floater fur the Legislatur'.

4. One who has no fixed abode or employment.

1858 in WOODWARD *Reminiscences* (1939) 49 He was a floater, under the treaty, but . . . he located him a tract in the fork of Coosa and Tallapoosa. **1899** *Boston Herald* 8 Sep. 6/2 Army 'floaters' without regular employment at home. **1947** *Coronet* April 38/2 Many of them live like floaters, without a home, without furniture, without any possession more substantial than a compact and a snapshot of a man in uniform.

5. *Baseball.* A pitched ball that appears to float rather than spin on its way to the batter.

1902 *Chi. Record-Herald* 3 Sep. 8/2 Iberg's floaters were the cause of Chicago's undoing in the first game.

6. (See quot.)

1903 *Sci. Amer. Supp.* 22, 911/2 Occasionally some of the land is torn away and becomes an island. Such islands are known as *flottants* or floaters, by the Creoles, and are among the most picturesque sights of these Louisiana lakes.

7. A release from jail granted a prisoner on condition that he leave town at once. *Slang.*

1934 LOMAX *Amer. Ballads* 25 The John had a 'bindle'—a workers' plea—So they gave him a floater and set him free. **1943** *Copper Camp* 177 A Butte police judge handed him a 'floater,' which meant twenty-four hours to leave town.

float gold.

1. Gold that escapes during refining.

1873 RAYMOND *Silver & Gold* 17 We have a yearly loss in 'float gold' alone . . . of $84,960 from two single mills!

2. Gold brought down from a vein or lode by the action of water. Also **floated gold.**

1873 MILLER *Amongst Modocs* 204 They had found only a few bars with float gold. **1883** ERNEST INGERSOLL *Knocking Round Rockies* 85 Therefore placer-gold is sometimes known as 'floated' gold. **1931** WILLISON *Here They Dug Gold* 55 At the mouth of the gulch soon to take his name, Gregory stops to dig for 'float' gold washed down from veins on the mountains above. [**1947** CHALFANT *Gold, Guns, & Ghost Towns* 142 I've picked up some of the richest float [ore] over there that has ever been seen in these parts.]

∗ **floating,** *n.* and *a.*

1. *n.* Hunting deer or moose at night by approaching them in a boat.

1859 *Harper's Mag.* July 175/1 The usual method of hunting the deer in midsummer is by 'floating.' **1894** *Cent. Mag.* Jan. 354/1 'Jacking,' or 'floating,' for moose is seldom practised, from the difficulty found in getting near enough to flash the light on the game.

3. In combs.: (1) ∗ **floating bridge,** a raft or accumulation of debris on the surface of a river, now *hist.;* cf. **floodwood, wooden island;** (2) **candidate,** a candidate-at-large, *obs.;* (3) **claim,** a float (*q.v.*) for a portion of public land, *obs.;* (4) **dry dock,** a structure that can be submerged to allow a vessel to enter it, and then floated again to raise the vessel high and dry; (5) **gang,** a section gang, *obs.;* (6) **grist mill,** = **floating mill,** *obs.;* (7) ∗ **island,** (*a*) a detached mass of floating trees, logs, and accumulated debris formerly found in western rivers, cf. **floating bridge, wooden island,** (*b*) *transf.* a river steamer and its tow of barges, *rare;* (8) **mill,** a mill for grinding Indian corn and wheat anchored in a stream and operated by its current, now *hist.;* (9) **outfit,** *W.* (see quot. 1944); (10) **palace,** a laudatory expression used with reference to pretentious steamboats, now *hist.;* (11) **policy,** an insurance policy that does not specify precisely the subject (or its worth) covered by it; (12) **population,** an unsettled, migratory population; (13) **prairie,** (see quot.); (14) **residence,** a temporary residence, *rare;* (15) **store,** a store on a river boat or houseboat; (16) **town,** a hell-on-wheels *q.v.* (sense **2.**) type of town built along an advancing railroad and moving as construction advances; (17) **vote,** *collect.* the vote cast by floaters, cf. ∗ **floater,** *n.* **1;** (18) **voter,** = ∗ **floater,** *n.* **1.**

(1) **1802** ELLICOTT *Journal* 124 This surprising floating bridge, or raft, is constantly augmented by the trees and rubbish, which the Chafalia draws out of the Mississippi. **1948** DICK *Dixie Frontier* 114 In time ligneous material covered the wood, and often willow trees, many of them ten inches in diameter, grew up from these 'floating bridges,' as they were called. — (2) **1840** *Boston Transcript* 14 Mar. 2/3 Gentlemen, I am the floating candidate for the superfluous district, and I only want to make a few remarks at this time. — (3) **1817** *Annals 14th Cong.* 2 Sess. 771 Inquire into the expediency of prohibiting, by law, the location of any floating claim in the Territory of Missouri, on any lands, the right, title, or claim to which has been at any time heretofore given notice of, or filed with either of the boards of commissioners in said Territory, or with the recorder of land titles, acting as such under any law of Congress for the adjustment of land titles in said Territory. **1837** VAN BUREN in *Pres. Mess. & P.* III. 389 Under no circumstances is it considered expedient to authorize floating claims in any shape. — (4) **1838** FLAGG *Far West* I. 135 Upon the river-bank . . . stands the 'Floating Dry Dock,' . . . the invention of a gentleman of St. Louis. **1849** *Whig Almanac 1850* 25/1 Stone and Floating Dry Docks, $1,140,000.

(5) **1861** *Charleston* (S.C.) *Mercury* 2 Feb. 2/2 It is proposed to curtail the Road Police to a 'hand to the mile,' now that there is but little necessity for keeping up the 'floating and assistant gangs.' — (6) **1823** *N. Eng. Farmer* II. 86 Floating Grist Mills.—This kind of mill is used in abundance on the river Ohio. — (7) (*a*) **1807** C. SCHULTZ *Travels* II. 32 *Floating Islands* are the same as the above [i.e., Wooden Islands], being indifferently known by both names. **1849** LYELL *Second Visit to U.S.* II. 143 There is a floating island in it, well wooded. (*b*) **1865** *Atlantic Mo.* XV. 81/2 The traveller new to Hudson River scenery will be startled, any summer day . . . , by the apparition . . . of floating islands, settled by a large commercial population. *Ib.*, These floating islands are but little drops of vital blood from the great heart of the West. — (8) **1796** ELLICOTT in Mathews *Life A. Ellicott* 138 These floating mills are erected upon two, or more, large canoes or boats, and anchored out in a strong current. **1810** F. CUMING *Western Tour* 116 At six we were . . . abreast of . . . a floating mill owned by an Irishman named Pickets. **1948** DICK *Dixie Frontier* 250 Some of the first water-power mills were 'floating mills.' These were built on two large dugout canoes. An undershot wheel was placed between them. — (9) **1890** *Stock Grower & Farmer* (Las Vegas, N. Mex.) 8 Feb. 6/2 Stock doing well. . . . The winter floating outfits have cattle pushed pretty well north. *Ib.* 22 Feb. 7/1 The 'floating outfit' is an organized outfit of men in the employ of the association, who ride the range during the winter months to prevent the cattle of the members of association from drifting. *Ib.* 22 March 3/3 Over 50 per cent of the cattle in that neighborhood that have been driven this winter by the floating outfit will starve to death. **1944** ADAMS *W. Words* 61 Floating outfit: Five or six men and a cook kept by the larger ranches riding the range in the winter months to brand late calves and ones which had escaped the roundup.

(10) **1819** P. WAKEFIELD *Excursions in North Amer.* 25 There is one of these boats, which without exaggeration, may be denominated a floating palace. **1886** POORE *Reminiscences* I. 482 Mrs. Tayloe . . . in traveling on one of those floating palaces, the day-boats on the Hudson River . . . was struck with the business energy and desire to please everybody manifested by the steward. **1947** CRANE *Sins of N.Y.* 83 On the *Providence*, the following day, luxurious floating 'palace' of the Narragansett Line, . . . Grant had become the guest of the Prince of Erie himself. — (11) **1839** *S. Lit. Messenger* V. 7/1 The packets, by their 'floating policies of insurance' offer another inducement to shippers. **1895** E. CARROLL, JR. *Principles Finance* 300 *Floating Policies.* (Fire Insurance) Policies on goods in undesignated buildings, or in two or more named buildings, where the amount of goods in each . . . is not specified. — (12) **1839** *N.O. Picayune* 9 Feb. 2/1 There is a large *floating* population in this city about these days. **1945** MARSHALL *Santa Fe* 70 Dodge always claimed a large floating population and could have floated it on hard liquor without trouble. — (13) **1944** HARNETT T. KANE *Deep Delta Country* 14 'Floating prairie,' a growth out of a matted base suspended over water or liquid mud. — (14) **1857** *Kansas Hist. Coll.* (1890) IV. 682 No man should be permitted to vote upon a floating residence.

(15) **1845** F. N. MOORE *Diary* (1946) 71 We passed today a very little steamer called the Lawrence, a floating store. **1944** *Reader's Digest* July 109 These floating stores are stocked with candy, razors, overalls—anything to strike the shantyman's fancy. — (16) **1892** LUMMIS *Tramp Across Continent* 26 Kit Carson, which I reached that night, was a good example of the 'floating towns' of early Colorado. — (17) **1847** *Knickerb.* April 328 Such [uninformed and unprincipled citizens] constitute what in common parlance is called the 'floating vote.' **1892** *Courier-Journal* 3 Oct. 1/7 It is well known that the floating vote in both Indiana and New York was bought in 1888. — (18) **1905** D. G. PHILLIPS *Plum Tree* 14 Those . . . 'floating voters' . . . had been bought up by a rich candidate of the opposition.

b. In the names of plants, as **floating foxtail, heart, meadow grass,** (see quots.).

1856 *Mass. Board Agric. Rep.* I. 22 Floating Foxtail, (*Alopecurus geniculatus*). *Ib.* 50 The Floating Meadow Grass, or Common Manna Grass. **1857** GRAY *Botany* 348 Floating Heart, . . . *Limnanthemum lacunosum.* . . . Shallow ponds, from Maine and N. New York to Virginia and southward. **1934** *Nat. Geog. Mag.* LXV. 598 The small purple blossoms of watershield project above the wide-spread masses of its rounded, floating leaves, and the dainty white display of floating-heart nods over its own reflection in the water.

Flobert ˈflobɚt, *n.* Also **flobert.** [f. M. *Flobert* (1819–94), a French arms-maker who invented this type of gun *c*1850.] A cheap, light rifle of small caliber for target practice and small game. In full **Flobert rifle.** Now *hist.* — **1901** S. E. WHITE *Westerners* XVI. 129

'This rifle's a flobert,' he observed. **1905** *Sears Cat.* 314 We do not recommend or guarantee Flobert rifles. Buy a good rifle. It will pay in the end.

flock duck. (See quots.) — **1889** *Cent.* 2276/2 The black-heads or scaup ducks, *Aithyia marila* and *A. affinis* . . . [are] called raft-duck, flock-duck, and troop-fowl. **1917** *Birds of Amer.* I. 135 Scaup Duck. *Marila marila*. . . . Other Names.—Mussel Duck; . . . Flock Duck; Shuffler.

flocking fowl. *local.* =prec. — **1835** AUDUBON *Ornith. Biog.* III. 226 In a few weeks these flocks are joined by others, for which reason the species is named in Kentucky the 'Flocking Fowl.' **1889** *Cent.* 2276/2 *Flocking-fowl*, . . . a gunners' name in the United States of the blackheads or scaup ducks, *Aithyia marila* and *A. affinis*, from their flocking.

* **flood,** *n.* In combs.: (1) **flood control,** the practice of attempting to prevent or lessen damage caused by floods, also attrib.; (2) **dam,** (see quot. 1905); (3) **gull,** (see quots.); (4) * **wood,** (*a*) =**floating bridge,** (*b*) in transf. senses (see quots.), *obs.*

(1) **1928** *Publishers' Wkly.* 16 June 2459 Library of Congress. Division of bibliography. Bibliography on flood control. **1948** *Capital-Democrat* (Tishomingo, Okla.) 24 June 7/3 The Washita Flood Control work on upper Mill Creek will start this week. — (2) **1879** *Lumberman's Gaz.* Dec. 14 A drive on the Chippewa, the result of rains and flood dams, has let down 25,000,000 feet of logs. **1905** *Forestry Bureau. Bul.* No. 61, 49 *Splash dam*, a dam built to store a head of water for driving logs. . . . [Also called] flood dam. — (3) **1844** *Nat. Hist. N.Y., Zoology* II. 217 The American oyster-catcher, *Haematopus palliotus*, . . . is better known among our gunners by the name of Flood Gull. *Ib.* 297 The . . . Razor-bill, Cutwater, Flood Gull, . . . for it [*sc.* the black skimmer, *Rhynchops nigra*] is known under all these names, reaches our coast from Tropical America in May. — (4) (*a*) **1822** *Mass. Spy* 6 Feb. (Th.), There are two short carrying places in this distance, occasioned by flood-wood. **1854** HAMMOND *Hills, Lakes* 177 Further down the river still, is what is known as the 'flood-wood,' a Red river raft in miniature. (*b*) **1839** MARRYAT *Diary in A.* I. 229 But the major part of the men were what they call here *flood-wood*, that is, of all sizes and heights—a term suggested by the pieces of wood borne down by the freshets of the river. **1851** *Knickerb.* XXXVIII. 463 The owner was regarding the 'flood-wood' of his fortunes with a sad and wistful eye.

flooding spring. ?A spring that periodically overflows. *Rare.* **1847** H. HOWE *Ohio* 157 The source of Coal creek, is a beautiful and curious flooding spring, rising from a level prairie at the village.

* **floor,** *n.* In combs.: (1) **floor leader,** one chosen by the representatives of his political party or faction to take the lead in advancing its program in an assembly or convention; (2) **man,** (*a*) an assistant to a blacksmith, *rare*, (*b*) ?one who trades on the floor of an exchange for another or for others; (3) **manager,** (*a*) the master of ceremonies at a dance, (*b*) the manager of an aisle, section, or department in a department store; (4) **show,** an entertainment consisting of music, singing, dancing, given in a hotel, night club, etc.; (5) **sweeper,** =**carpet sweeper,** *obs.*; (6) **walker,** one who walks about as an overseer or supervisor in a retail store.

(1) **1899** *Cong. Rec.* 11 Feb. 1764/2 Congress has witnessed very few more successful floor leaders than Mr. Dingley. **1945** *Reader's Digest* Oct. 32/1 Governor Gene Talmadge thought well enough of this record to make him his floor leader. — (2) (*a*) **1887** *Courier-Journal* 20 Feb. 3/6 Wanted—Horse-Shoer—A good Floor Man. (*b*) **1912** DREISER *Financier* 63 How would you like to try your hand at being a floor-man for me? — (3) (*a*) **1887** *Harper's Mag.* May 967/1 Jerry, as one of the floor-managers, was gorgeous. **1913** LONDON *Valley of Moon* III. xiii, An' here's you makin' roughhouse at a dance, an' I'm the floor manager, an' I gotta put you out. (*b*) **1892** *Harper's Mag.* Feb. 439/1 Like the floor-walkers in the stores, they're all floor or aisle managers now. **1949** *This Week Mag.* 26 March 10/4 Miss Hyde recalled one applicant for a job as a floor-manager. — (4) **1929** *Liberty* 30 Nov. 45/1 Like the floor show? **1945** *Chi. Maroon* 8 Jun. 3/4 (*advt.*), Marine Dining Room. . . . Floor Show Twice Nightly except Mondays. . . . Edgewater Beach Hotel.
(5) **1859** *Rep. Comm. Patents 1858* II. 444 Carpet or floor sweepers in which a revolving brush . . . is made to take up and deposit the sweepings in a case covering the brush. — (6) **1876** *Scribner's Mo.* Feb. 509/2 When I entered I approached the 'floorwalker.' **1948** *Chi. D. News* 3 March 20/1 The father of three sets of twins is a floor-walker.

b. In phrases pertaining to parliamentary procedure: (1) *To get the floor*, to obtain the privilege of speaking, also (2) *to have, hold, obtain, occupy, take the floor.*

(1) **1816** PICKERING 93 *Floor.* Used in Congress, in this expression—to get the floor; that is, to obtain an opportunity of taking a part in a debate. — (2) **1837** *U.S. Mag.* I. 75 The floor at that time was forever occupied. **1842** *Niles' Reg.* 4 June 220/3 Mr. Cushing obtained the floor, and moved that the committee rise. **1846** POLK *Diary* (1929) 138 Senator Davis of Massachusetts took the floor and spoke until the time had expired, so as to defeat action on it. **1848** COOPER *Oak Openings* II. iii, In parliamentary language, each may be said to have had floor at the same time. **1923** H. M. ROBERT *Parliamentary Law* 183 In the U.S. Senate, senators have held the floor until physically exhausted. **1947** *Chi. D. News* 21 June 1/8 Hours later Morse still had the floor.

As the last term in **board, feed, forest, ground, puncheon, second floor.**

* **flop,** *n.*

1. (See quot.) *Slang. Obs.*

1851 HALL *College Words*, Any 'cute' performance by which a man is sold [deceived] is a good flop.

2. A turn-around, a sudden change of policy or party. *Slang.*

1904 *Springfield* (Mass.) *W. Republican* 7 Oct. 2 That a flop by the most militant of the unionists is under contemplation has been denied. **1911** H. S. HARRISON *Queed* xviii, 230 So ran the editorial, which was offensively headed 'West's Fatal Flop.' **1929** *Collier's* 5 Jan. 41/1 It was basically a 'flop.'

3. Short for **flophouse.** Also a place to sleep, a bed. *Slang.*

1916 *Amer. Mag.* May 14/1 She said to tell you this ain't no hobos' flop, neither. **1925** *Lit. Digest* 11 July 50/1 You better go around to one of the missions. There's a couple of 'em will give you a flop for nothing—if they ain't too full. *Ib.* 52/3 Dere's one flop here might do something for me if it was open.

4. A person or thing that fails to come up to expectations. *Slang.*

1920 *Collier's* 20 March 39/1, I hear the Bermuda joint's a flop, anyways. **1946** *Casper* (Wyo.) *Tribune-Herald* 29 Mar. 9/4 A fellow with a 10-year batting average of .324 and who hit .311 last season doesn't slip from a hero to a flop in one year.

As the last term in **belly, cow, flip flop.**

* **flop,** *v.*

1. *tr.* (See quots.) *Slang. Obs.*

1851 HALL *College Words s.v.*, 'A man writes cards during examination to feeze the profs . . . and he flops the examination if he gets a good mark by the means.' One usually flops his marks by feigning sickness. **1856** *Ib.* (ed. 2) 204 At the University of Vermont, to *flop a twenty* is to make a perfect recitation, twenty being the maximum mark for scholarship.

2. *intr.* To change suddenly in conduct or political allegiance. Sometimes with *over.* Also *tr.*

1889 *Cent.* 2278/2 *To flop over*, . . . to go over suddenly to another side or party; make a sudden change of association or allegiance. (Slang.) **1894** *Dly. Ardmoreite* (Ardmore, Okla.) 18 Jan. 1/4 The purported change was, as we have always surmised, a fake to enable that canine barnacle, Soule, to flop his politics. **1926** COOPER *Oklahoma* 123 Hurriedly lawmakers who had been opposed to it 'flopped' to the other side, so suddenly in fact that the final passage was not in the form of a bill at all, but merely a 'rider' on an appropriations measure.

3. To spend the night. *Slang.* Cf. **flophouse.**

1927 *Amer. Mercury* Oct. 147/2, I went to flop at a little hotel.

flophouse 'flɑpˌhaʊs, *n.* A cheap, low-class lodging house. *Slang.* — **1923** *Jrnl. Amer. Inst. Crim. Law & Criminology* Aug. 310 These are called 'flop' houses or 'scratch' houses and boys frequently find their way into them. **1948** *So. Bend* (Ind.) *Tribune* 5 Aug. 1. 8/5 He roamed saloons and flophouses, working only enough to satisfy his craving for alcohol.

flopped hat. A jocose term for a Quaker. *Rare.* — **1755** in *Amer. Antiq. Soc. Proc.* n.s. XLI. (1931) 123 After dinner went in company with Mr. Franklin (of Philadelphia) to the State house, waited some before there was Floped Hatts Enough to go on Business . . . in the afternoon (of the next day) . . . Mr Fox with the grave smiles of Quaker waited on me.

* **flopper,** *n.* **1.** A paddle for a boat or canoe. *Rare.* **2.** One who has deserted his political party for another.

(1) **1837** BIRD *Nick of Woods* I. 219 Ax'd me out a flopper with my tom-axe in no time, . . . jumped in . . . and came down the falls like a cob in a corn-van. — (2) **1884** *Lisbon* (Dak.) *Star* 15 Aug., The kept organ refers to the great masses of the people . . . who conscientiously oppose Mr. Stevens' election to the legislature, as a 'little body of floppers and kickers.' **1905** *N.Y. Ev. Post* 28 Dec. 1 Assemblyman Rogers is a flopper because he withdrew from the speakership race and re-entered it.

floral hall. A large hall in which plants are exhibited. Also attrib. *Obs.*

1863 *Ohio Agric. Rep.* XVIII. 119 Next to the Floral Hall, the Fine Arts Hall was the most complete feature of the Fair. *Ib.* 134 The

Floral Hall department, on account of the continued rain and the lateness of the season, was but poorly represented [at the fair of the Carroll Co. Agric. Soc.]. **1872** *Ill. Dept. Agric. Trans.* 162 We own . . . a large floral hall, composed of a center 40×40 feet (octagon), with three (3) wings.

Flora's paintbrush. *local.* The orange hawkweed. — **1894** *Amer. Folk-Lore* VII. 92 *Hieracium aurantiacum*, . . . Flora's paint brush, Oxford Co. and Penobscot Co., Me.

Florida ˈflɔrədə, *n.* [Sp., the name given the region in 1512 by Ponce de Leon.]

1. *pl.* A collective term for East Florida and West Florida, the two divisions made by England, in 1763, of the region previously known as Florida. Now *hist.*

1779 in *Amer. Sp.* XX. (1945) 271 If we are reinforced from England, some small expeditions to Chesapeak; Georgia only kept as a frontier, which is done as easily as the Floridas, for that effectually guards the Floridas. **1818** *W. Recorder* (Chillicothe, O.) 14 Aug. 8/1 The President, no doubt, sees . . . the great advantages the United States would derive from the entire possession of the Floridas. **1889** DELAND *Florida Days* 158 The kiss . . . carries the same meaning in the Floridas as upon the banks of the Mediterranean.

b. The Florida Indians. *Obs.*

1741 *S.C. Hist. Soc. Coll.* IV. 21 [Gen. Oglethorpe] had advice that Tonahowi with 200 men had gone against the Floridas.

c. Varieties of cotton grown in Florida. *Obs.*

1860 *Charleston* (S.C.) *Mercury* 24 Nov. 3/1 The enquiry is quite light, and confined to Floridas only.

d. Short for "Florida oranges."

1892 D. HALE *Letters* 270 Oranges are delicious. . . . I think they must be Floridas. **1923** WARD *Encycl. of Food* (1941) 360 The best Louisiana oranges are upheld by many as of equal rank with the Floridas.

2. In special combs.: (1) **Florida cracker,** a cracker (*q.v.*) living in Florida; (2) **fever,** (see quot.), *obs.;* (3) **Indian,** an Indian living in Florida; (4) **orange,** an orange grown in Florida, usu. as distinguished from a California orange; (5) **war,** the war carried on (1835–42) by the U.S. with the Seminole Indians in Florida, *obs.;* (6) **water,** a proprietary name for a particular kind of toilet water; (7) **wrapper,** the leaf of a tobacco raised in Florida and used on the outside of cigars.

(1) **1856** *Spirit of Times* 1 Nov. 149/3 William Crooked Legs [a Seminole chief], . . . joined with the Florida Crackers, has cost Uncle Sam many a dollar. **1944** ROBSJOHN-GIBBINGS *Goodbye* 40 Down under the palm trees Florida crackers had the surprise of their lives coming to them. — (2) **1879** BISHOP *4 Months in Sneak-Box* 255 Some settlers, beguiled to this desolate region by the sentimental idea of pioneer life in a fine climate, known as 'Florida Fever,' were starving on a fish diet. — (3) **1739** W. STEPHENS *Proc. Georgia* 327 Divers of them in Concert with others of the Creek Nation, making preparation to attack the Florida Indians. **1743** in *Doc. Col. Hist. N.Y.* VI. 243 He . . . together with four other persons . . ., being on shore at Florida Keys, were taken by the Florida Indians. **1904–5** *Encycl. Amer.* XVI. s.v. *Zamia*, The Florida Indians call the last [species of *Zamia*] 'coontie.' — (4) **1863** *Rep. Comm. Agric. 1862* 61 The Florida orange is larger and more aromatic than the Cuban. **1923** WARD *Encycl. of Food* (1941) 360 The Florida orange is typically sweeter and less 'sprightly' than the California.

(5) **1837** *S. Lit. Messenger* III. 651 The Florida war has sprung entirely from want of such freedom. **1843** *Quincy* (Ill.) *Herald* 3 Aug. 2/5 The expenditures of Mr. Van Buren's administration in 1840, exclusive of the Florida war was only about seventeen millions of dollars. — (6) **1840** *N.O. Picayune* 28 July 4/1 [Merchandise includes] lavender and Florida waters; perfumed toilet and pearl powders. **1927** BENÉT *J. B.'s Body* 79 The . . . congressmen, Come out to see the gladiator's show Like Iliad gods, wrapped in the sacred cloud of Florida-water. — (7) **1849** *Rep. Comm. Patents: Agric.* (1850) 456 The object in cultivating 'Florida wrappers' is to produce an article that will command the highest price per pound.

b. In the names of, or with reference to, plants: (1) **Florida arrowroot,** see ***arrowroot;** (2) **clover,** a plant, *Richardsonia scabra*, found in tropical America and often grown for forage; (3) **coffee,** =**coffee weed;** (4) **jasmine,** =**yellow jasmine;** (5) **moss,** =**Spanish moss;** (6) **vanilla,** (see quot.); (7) **yew,** =**stinking cedar.**

(2) **1883** SMITH *Geol. Survey Ala.* 521 The Florida clover, or 'poor man's trouble,' is the greatest pest in the way of a weed. **1889** VASEY *Agric. Grasses* 103 *Richardsonia scabra* (Mexican Clover; Spanish Clover; Florida Clover; Water Parsley, [etc.]). — (3) **1838** GOSSE *Letters* 212 There is a plant now abundantly in blossom, which grows in neglected fields and such-like places. . . . From its local name, Florida Coffee, I infer that these seeds are roasted. **1849** *Cin. Commercial* 10 Dec. 2/1 She ate some of the seeds and buds of what is called Florida coffee, the consequence of which was death. — (4) **1835** AUDUBON *Ornith. Biog.* I. 114 The Florida jessamine. Gelseminum Nitidum.

(5) **1888** G. TRUMBULL *Bird Names* 75 A large bunch of 'Florida moss.' — (6) **1891** *N. & Q.* VI. 225 The *Liatris odoratissima*, deer's tongue, is also used for this purpose. Its leaves are gathered and sold as *Florida Vanilla*, but this name is objectionable, since Florida has a species of true vanilla. — (7) **1901** MOHR *Plant Life Ala.* 34 The Florida yew (*Taxus floridana*) of the valley of the Apalachicola River in western Florida . . . present similar striking instances of a strange localization.

Also *Florida buttonwood, guava, lily, pepper, star anise*, etc.

c. In the names of birds and other animals: (1) **Florida cormorant,** a cormorant belonging to any one of four sub-species of the double-crested cormorant; (2) **gallinule,** an American bird of the family Rallidae; (3) **grackle,** (see quots.); (4) **jay,** a jay, *Aphelocoma coerulescens*, found in Florida, also **Florida blue jay;** (5) **screech owl,** (see quot.); (6) **water rat,** the round-tailed muskrat, *Neofiber alleni;* (7) **white-tailed deer,** (see quot.); (8) **wren,** a species of wren very similar to the Carolina wren.

(1) **1835** AUDUBON *Ornith. Biog.* III. 387 The Florida Cormorant, *P. Floridanus*, is a constant resident in the southern parts of the country from which it derives its name. **1883** *Nat. Museum Bul.* No. 27, 165 *Phalacrocorax dilophus floridanus*. Florida Cormorant. . . . Eastern North America, breeding southward. — (2) **1833** BONAPARTE *Ornithology* IV. 132 The Florida Gallinule, or Water Hen, . . . is common in Florida and Jamaica on the streams and pools. **1917** *Birds of Amer.* I. 213 Florida Gallinules possess a wonderful repertoire in the matter of calls. — (3) **1895** *Dept. Agric. Yrbk. 1894* 233 The common purple grackle (*Quiscalus Quiscula*) . . . [has] two subspecies, the bronzed grackle (*Quiscalus q. æneus*) and the Florida grackle (*Quiscalus q. aglœus*). **1945** *Nat. Geog. Mag.* June 739 Along the central Atlantic coast is found its relative, the Purple Grackle; and in Florida, the Florida Grackle. — (4) **1828** BONAPARTE *Ornithology* II. 60 The Florida Jay . . . is not confined to Florida, where it was first noticed by Bartram, being found also in Louisiana, and in the West extends northward to Kentucky. **1894** B. TORREY *Fla. Sketch-Book* 62 The Florida blue jay (a smaller and less conspicuously crested duplicate of our common Northern bird), to which it bearslittle resemblance either in personal appearance or in voice. **1917** *Birds of Amer.* II. 221 *Aphelocoma cyanea*. . . . The Florida Jay is . . . one of the few American birds whose range is restricted to a comparatively small area—in this instance, the peninsula of Florida.

(5) **1889** *Rep. Secy. Agric.* 376 The Florida Screech Owl (*Megascops asio floridanus*) inhabits the Gulf States from Louisiana to Florida, and extends north to South Carolina. — (6) **1934** *Nat. Geog. Mag.* LXV. 619 The discovery of the Florida water rat in 1884 was a noteworthy event in the annals of American mammalogy, for the animal represents a distinct genus as well as species. It might be looked upon as a muskrat in miniature, with a rounded instead of a compressed tail. **1938** MATSCHAT *Suwannee River* 34 Maiden cane grows in dense green masses three or four feet high, and there rice rats and Florida water rats . . . make their nests. — (7) **1917** *Mammals of Amer.* 8/2 Florida White-tailed Deer.—*Odocoileus osceola*. . . . Size of Texas Deer, but much darker. — (8) **1887** RIDGWAY *Manual N.A. Birds* 550 Larger, and darker colored [than the Carolina Wren]. . . . *Thryothorus ludovicanus miamensis*. Florida Wren. **1917** *Birds of Amer.* III. 191 The Florida Wren . . . is found only in the peninsula of Florida, south of the Suwanee River.

Also *Florida cooter* (see **cooter b.**), *gray fox, manatee, pipefish, raccoon*, etc.

Floridan ˈflɔrədən, *a.* and *n.*

1. *n. pl.* The Florida Indians. Also **Floridan Indians, women.**

1763 W. ROBERTS *Nat. Hist. Florida* 3 The size, firmness, . . . and longevity of the Floridan Indians. *Ib.* 101 The Floridans are a manly well-shaped race. **1778** CARVER *Travels* 199, I must exclude the stories he has introduced of the Huron and Floridan women. **1791** W. BARTRAM *Travels* 208 The Creeks subdued the remnant tribes of the ancient Floridans.

b. An inhabitant of Florida. Cf. **Cape Floridan, West Floridan.**

1856 PHILLIPS *Kansas* 320 Shortly after the sack of Lawrence, Colonel Titus, the Floridan, offered three hundred dollars for his head. **1904–5** *Encycl. Amer.* VII. *s.v. Florida*, Another cold wave in 1899 . . . [gave] native Floridans the unprecedented sight of several inches of snow.

2. Floridan holly, the American holly, *Ilex opaca. Rare.*

1775 ROMANS *Nat. Hist. Florida* 26 Floridan holly, with indented leaves and red berries.

Floridian flə'rɪdɪən, *a.* and *n.*

1. *n. pl.* The Florida Indians. *Obs.*

1777 in JENKINS *B. Gwinnett* 218 The southern Frontiers of this State are frequently alarmed by the inroads & depredations of the Floridians.

2. A native or inhabitant of Florida. Cf. **West Floridian.**

1827 WILLIAMS *West Florida* 26 The barking, yelping, and howling of a congregation of half starved whelps, is music to the ear of a native Floridian. **1883** *Cent. Mag.* July 383/1 The Floridians . . . use a long rod or pole for still-fishing, skittering, and bobbing. **1948** *Chi. Sun-Times* 18 Mar. 53/2 Floridians feel sorry for us—don't blame them.

3. *a.* Of or pertaining to Florida.

1819 *Western Rev.* I. 307 In the basin of the St. Lawrence or even in the Floridian waters, a total difference of [fish] inhabitants may be detected. **1901** STILLMAN *Autobiog. Journalist* I. 287 It is worthy to note here, in justice to the old days of the Floridian society, . . . that the kindliness to the slaves was universal on the St. John's River. **1945** MCATEE *John & Joe* 14 There are in fact no fewer than 10 species and sub-species of birds in the Floridian region.

* **flossy,** *a.* "Smooth" or slick; fancy or showy. *Slang.*

1889 *The Road* (Denver, Colo.) 28 Dec. 4/3 Phil, we have got it in for you if you don't quit being so flossy. **1914** BRININSTOOL *Trail Dust* 238 She had ol' Sagebrush locoed by the flossy talk she slung. **1947** *Time* 21 July 10/3 In Muncie, Ind., the Chamber of Commerce called a halt to its flossy preparations for a Muncie Centennial when one Dorothea Bump gave the boys a quiet nudge: the city is still only 93 years old.

* **flounder,** *n.* As the last term in **belly, deep sea, diamond, four-spotted, long-toothed, rusty, sand, starry, summer, water, winter flounder.**

* **flour,** *n.*

1. (See quots.)

1856 OLMSTED *Slave States* 477 In the Carolina mills the product [of rice] is divided into 'prime,' 'middling' (broken), 'small' or 'chits,' and 'flour' or 'douse.' **1905** PRINGLE *Rice Planter* 142 The cows and pigs are fed on the flour, a gray substance that comes from the grain as the chaff is removed in the pounding mill.

2. In combs.: (1) **flour and feed store,** a flour store in which various kinds of stock feed are also sold; (2) **barrel,** a barrel designed to hold 196 pounds of flour; (3) **broker,** a broker who deals in flour; (4) **certificate,** a certificate of stock in a flour company; (5) **Flour City,** (see quot. 1859); (6) **corn,** (see quot. 1917 and cf. **flour maize**); (7) **doings,** see **doings;** (8) **dust,** (see quot. and cf. **flour gold**); (9) **flipper,** see **flipper;** (10) **gold,** gold occurring in very small flakes or particles; (11) **inspector,** one appointed to inspect flour; (12) **maize,** (see quot. and cf. **flour corn**), *obs.;* (13) **potato,** (see quot.), *obs.;* (14) **riot,** a riot in New York City *c*1836–37 in which wheat and flour were thrown from stores where they were being held for high prices; (15) **store,** a store in which flour is sold.

(1) **1844** J. R. GODLEY *Letters from Amer.* II. 43, I see one advertising for sale 'Johnny cakes,' . . . another 'flour and feed-store, relishes at all hours.' — (2) **1777** *Jrnls. Cont. Congress* IX. 977 Resolved, That the commissary general of issues be directed to preserve the flour barrels of the army. **1877** *Harper's Mag.* Jan. 249/2 Suppose we sit on these two water pails and eat our lunch off the flour barrel. **1940** MENCKEN *Happy Days* 220 The beer was usually Anheuser-Busch from St. Louis, and it came in flour-barrels holding 96 bottles, packed in straw. — (3) **1881** *Harper's Mag.* Sep. 581/2 Loring . . . was a retired flour-broker. — (4) **1898** *McClure's Mag.* X. 499/1 Mr. Ward . . . set forth the safety of an investment in flour certificates, which his position as clerk of the Exchange gave him special insight into.

(5) [**1836** *Niles' Reg.* 29 Oct. 144/3 The town of Rochester, N.Y. is probably the greatest flour manufactory in the world.] **1859** *Ladies' Repository* XIX. 51/1 Rochester, New York, is called the 'Flour City,' owing to the number of its flour-mills, some of which are said to be the largest in the world. **1943** MENEFEE *Assignment* 100 And since the flour city is also a city of churches he became well known. — (6) **1917** WILL & HYDE *Corn Among Indians* 117 This green corn which was picked while in the milk and still soft . . . was the common species of soft field-corn, known as flour corn. **1942** CASTETTER & BELL *Pima & Papago Agric.* 80 This flour corn of early times was of three distinct colors—white, yellow and blue—the white most common, yellow next. — (8) **1871** RAYMOND *3rd Rep. Mines* 200 The extreme fineness of the particles [of gold], however, it being what is denominated 'flour dust,' prevented these diggings being worked at that day.

(10) **1875** *Chi. Tribune* 16 Nov. 7/6 They prospected and found fine flour gold. **1904** E. ROBINS *Magn. North* 148 A few flakes of flour gold . . . but no real 'pay.' — (11) **1795** *Baltimore Town Rec.* 98 For the Purpose of appointing a flour Inspector for the year ensuing. **1850** *Rep. Comm. Patents 1849: Agric.* 257 This grader was to be sworn, as flour inspectors and other agents are, to discharge the duties . . . faithfully. — (12) **1763** tr. DUPRATZ *Hist. Louisiana* II. 3 Louisiana produces several kinds of *maiz*, namely *flour-maiz*, which is white, with a flat and shrivelled surface. — (13) **1797** I. THOMAS *N. Eng. Farmer* 269 A large white potato, a great bearer, known by the name of the flour potato. — (14) **1896** HASWELL *New York* 326 They proceeded to the store of S. H. Herrick & Co., 5 Coenties Slip, where they in like manner broke in and commenced destruction. . . . This was known as the Flour Riot.

(15) **1898** CAHAN *Imported Bridegroom* 9 What with his flour store, two bakeries, and some real estate, he had been too busy to live.

As the last term in **acorn, Atlantic, barrel, buckwheat, coal, cold, corn, dyspepsia, fine, fish, Genesee, graham, Indian corn, Ohio, parched-corn, patent, Philadelphia, self-rising, straight flour.**

* **flour,** *v. tr.* To grind or convert (wheat) into flour.

1806 WEBSTER 120 *Flour*, . . . to grind and bolt. **1828** —— *s.v.*, Great quantities of it [wheat] are floured in the interior countries. **1844** *Cong. Globe* App. 7 May 440/1 A farmer raises his crop of wheat and sells it at the market price; it is floured, taken to New York [etc.]. **1873** *Newton Kansan* 2 Jan. 2/3 We cannot flour it at home.

flouring 'flaʊərɪŋ, *n.*

1. The grinding of grain into flour. Also attrib.

1797 *Southampton Rec.* III. 353 John Jermain [shall] have privilege . . . of erecting a grist mill . . . for flouring or for packing. **1837** PECK *Gaz. Illinois* 30 Steam mills for flouring . . . are profitable. **1880** FARRAR *Five Years Minn.* 52 Ten miles higher up the stream the great 'lumbering and flouring' city of Minneapolis . . . possesses in the picturesque Falls of St. Anthony the largest water-power in the North-west.

2. flouring mill, a mill in which wheat is ground into flour.

1797 *N.Y. State Soc. Arts* I. 375 Possessing some flouring mills, I was naturally led to converse at times with my millers . . . on the economy of water in grinding. **1831** PECK *Guide* 149 Flouring mills begin to be erected, which will create a demand for this article. **1928** BRECKENRIDGE *Helldorado* 91 He had met in Tucson a man named Lee, who had some means, was the owner of a flouring mill, etc.

b. flouring millstones, millstones used in grinding wheat into flour.

1842 *Amer. Pioneer* I. 204 In the city and its vicinity are twenty-five pairs of flouring mill-stones.

* **flow,** *n.* **1.** The irrigating of rice fields. Cf. **harvest, point, sprout flow. 2.** *In full flow*, of a cow: Capable of giving normal quantities of milk. — (1) **1856** OLMSTED *Slave States* 473 The 'long flow' and the 'lay-by flow' are sometimes united, the water being gradually raised, as the [rice] plant increases in hight. — (2) **1882** *Maine Bd. Agric. Rep.* XXVI. 21 While it is well adapted to the keeping of cows that are in full flow it may not always pay in the case of dry cows or young growing stock.

flowage 'flo·ɪdʒ, *n.* The flooding or overflowing of lands. Also attrib. and the proper name of a place overflowed.

1830 *Mass. Spy* 3 Feb. (Th.), The flowage, which would be occasioned by a dam to turn the water into the Feeder. **1860** *Mass. Bd. Agric. Rep.* I. 243 The subject of the flowage of low lands . . . was referred to a committee of three. **1884** *Harper's Mag.* Sep. 621/1 Flowage line [of a reservoir]. **1948** *Wis. Fishing Regulations* 2 A closed season is established for the taking, catching, or killing fish of any variety or fishing for fish from December 1 to the following April 30, both dates inclusive, on all waters commonly known as the Chippewa Flowage.

flowed land. Land subject to being overflowed. *Rare.* — **1892** *Vt. Agric. Rep.* XII. 114 The areas of interval, or flowed lands, of the Otter Creek and some of its tributaries are very extensive.

* **flower,** *n.* In combs.: (1) **Flower City,** (see quot.); (2) **flower-of-an-hour,** the bladder ketmie, *Hibiscus trionum;* (3) **-pot judge,** (see quot.), *obs.;* (4) **shut,** the time just before night when flowers close, *rare;* (5) **store,** a florist's shop.

(1) **1871** DE VERE 664 Rochester, in New York, rejoices in the double name of Flour City and Flower City, being as famous for her love of flowers and unrivalled nursery-trade, as for the peculiarly fine flour made in her numerous mills. — (2) **1817–8** EATON *Botany* (1822) 306 Bladder ketmia, flower of an hour. **1939** *Nat. Geog. Mag.* Aug. 229/2 The dainty little flower-of-an-hour . . . clothes waysides,

roadsides, ditches, and waste places. — (3) **1856** *Knickerb.* XLVIII. 287 (Th.), Mr. Stowder was a Pennsylvania judge, one of that description known in Vermont and other places as 'Flower-pot Judges,' as associate judges are there called to distinguish them from law judges. — (4) **1849** WILLIS *Rural Lett.* 17 Between five in the morning and 'flower-shut,' I feel as if four walls and a ceiling would stop my breath. — (5) **1905** PHILLIPS *Social Secretary* 112 In the afternoon I was in a flower store in Pennsylvania Avenue, and Nadeshda joined me.

As the last term in **bay, bee, bell, black, breeches, bubby, bunch, burr, button, calico, California side-saddle, cardinal, carrion, chigger, chocolate, compass, day, Easter, fame, feather, frost, Georgia, ghost, grass, June, lace, leather, may, Mexican, mist, moccasin, moon, moose, Mormon, Ohio wall, pickerel, prairie, shad, side saddle, spider, star, state, sun, thimble, twin, yellow flower.**

* **flowering,** *a.* In the names of plants: (1) **flowering currant,** the golden currant, *Ribes aureum;* (2) **nettle,** (*a*) a plant of the genus *Galeopsis* having foliage like that of a nettle, (*b*) bedstraw, a plant of the genus *Galium;* (3) **poplar,** the tulip tree, *Liriodendron tulipifera;* (4) **wintergreen,** a small herb, *Polygala paucifolia,* having leaves resembling those of wintergreen.

(1) **1842** KIRKLAND *Forest Life* II. 142 The flowering currant, a climbing shrub, [is] already strung with golden, clove-scented wreaths. **1908** GALE *Friendship Village* 219 Boughs of my Flowering-currant filled my little hall and curved about the line of sight at table. — (2) (*a*) **1817–8** EATON *Botany* (1822) 285 *Galeopsis tetrahit,* flowering nettle. **1898** BRITTON & BROWN *Illust. Flora Northern U.S.* III. 575/2 Nettle, Flowering [=hemp nettle, *Galeopsis tetrahit*]. (*b*) **1821** *Mass. H.S. Coll.* 2 Ser. IX. 150 Plants . . . of Middlebury, [Vermont, include] . . . *Galium trifidum,* Flowering nettle. — (3) **1775** BURNABY *Travels* 12 They are likewise adorned and beautified with . . . scarlet-flowering chestnuts, fringe-trees, flowering poplars. **1888** EGGLESTON in *Cent. Mag.* XXXVI. 265/2 He came out and stood in the fresh air, on the 'butt-cut' of a tulip-tree, or 'flowering poplar.' — (4) **1817–8** EATON *Botany* (1822) 398 *Polygala paucifolia,* flowering wintergreen. **1898** CREEVEY *Flowers of Field, Hill, & Swamp* 314 Fringed Polygala. Flowering Wintergreen.

flub flʌb, *v. tr.* To make a botch of. *Colloq.* — **1931** *Durant* (Okla.) *D. Democrat* 2 Feb. 6/4 A team . . . flubbed its major assignments horribly.

flubdub ˈflʌbˌdʌb, *n.* [Fanciful.] Useless talk, "bunk," "hot air." *Slang.*

1888 *Detroit Free Press* Aug. (Farmer), By swiping out the flub-dub and guff, I guess we'll have room to put in the points. **1910** *Sat. Ev. Post* 23 July 19/1 They nominated him and everybody else Mr. Penrose picked out for them in about ninety minutes by the clock, including speeches and other such flub-dub as the case seemed to require. **1947** CRANE *Sins of N.Y.* 259 He had, by intently listening to lawyers, . . . acquired an astonishing hash of legalistic flubdub.

b. Showy clothing, finery.

1915 D. R. CAMPBELL *Proving Virginia* 241 Thanks to Henrietta, you have plenty of pretty gowns and flub-dubs.

flugens ˈfludʒɪnz, *n.* [Fanciful.] An expression having the force of "deuce take it," "the dickens," etc. *Colloq.*

1830 *N. J. Chronicle* (Mt. Holly) 20 Aug. 2/2 'Oh dad,' says he, 'I'm making money like flugens.' **1849** J. B. JONES *Wild West Scenes* vi. 86 You're a nice chap to run like flugins from a dead man that you killed yourself! **1898** HARRIS *Tales* 129 It's colder 'n Flujens.

* **fluke,** *n.*

1. A barb on a harpoon.

1847 *Rep. Comm. Patents 1846* 338 What we claim as our joint invention, . . . is the construction of the fluke or barb of the harpoon in two parts. **1884** *Nat. Museum Bul.* No. 27, 277 Innovations have been made by hinging or pivoting one or two additional barbs or 'flukes' in the rear of the heads of both types [of harpoon].

2. (See quot.) *Obs.*

1890 *N. & Q.* IV. 22 March 250 *Flukes,* for the implements called hoeharrows in some localities, cultivators in others.

3. In combs.: (1) **fluke chain,** a chain passed around the flukes of a whale in order to fasten or hold it; (2) **plow,** *S.* poss. a sweep *q.v.* (sense **1.**) in allusion to its flat, fluke-shaped wings, also attrib., *obs.*

(1) **1851** MELVILLE *Moby Dick* lxxxii. 399 The whale . . . was strongly secured there by the stiffest fluke-chains. **1883** *Nat. Museum Bul.* No. 27, 335 *Fluker.* . . . An implement used on a whaling-vessel for passing a rope attached to one end of the fluke-chain [etc.]. — (2) **1722** *Md. Hist. Mag.* XVIII. 206 To a Sett fluke plow Irons 17 lb. weight 9*d.*, £0-12-9. **1800** W. TATHAM *Agric. & Commerce* 55 Now one of these boys and one little horse are generally sufficient for the *flook* plough; which is almost universally in use among those called *Virginia planters.* **1848** *Rep. Comm. Patents 1847* 543 This I think is at last attained by a recent improvement in the fluke plough.

* **fluke,** *v. intr.* To plow with a fluke plow. Also *fluke out. Obs.*— **1856** *Magnolia Place Jrnl.* 24 Oct. (N.C. Univ. MS), Began . . . to Cross Plow the Cane Ground in the upper Field with the Plows that were marking and Flukeing. *Ib.* 22 Oct., 2 Plows Fluking out and 3 Plows Covering Cane.

* **flume,** *n.*

1. A narrow channel for water maintained to provide power, float logs, convey water to a placer mine, etc.

1748 *Duxbury Rec.* 292 Isaac Partridge being obliged to make and maintain a good floom for term of Twenty years next coming, for the stream to pass through. **1821** *Mass. H.S. Coll.* 2 Ser. IX. 128 Water, in sufficient quantity to carry all the stones, and other machinery, flows into a floom, . . . fortified by solid rock. **1852** *Calif. Express* (Marysville) 25 Aug. 2/2 The miners have for the most part been constructing their *dams* for the purpose of turning water into their *flumes.* **1948** JOHNSTON *Gold Rush* 24/1 Water was conveyed, often for great distances, through flumes and ditches to a reservoir high above the ground that was to be mined.

transf. **1881** *Harper's Mag.* April 650/2 If the grove is on a hill and the sugar-house is in a hollow, the sap as it is gathered is emptied into a 'flume.'

b. Attrib. with **box, car, company, route, washing.**

1851 *S.F. Picayune* 14 Oct. 2/4 A few words in relation to . . . flume washing . . . may not be deemed out of place. **1876** RAYMOND *8th Rep. Mines* 265 There are two flume companies in the upper and one in the lower district. **1883** KNIGHT *Supp.* 350/1 *Flume Car.* A car to travel in a flume; wheels rest on the sides of the flume, and the water runs a paddle wheel. **1903** *Electrical World* 16 May 837/2 The soil along the proposed flume route is of a peculiar nature. *a***1918** G. STUART *On Frontier* I. 207 Then we set our flume boxes ready to begin washing.

2. A narrow defile or ravine worn or cut out by a stream. Also (*cap.*) as a proper name.

1784 BELKNAP *Tour White Mts.* (1876) 17 One of them [*sc.* streams] is so narrow as exactly to resemble a flume, and goes by that name. **1889** J. D. WHITNEY *United States* 222 A purely American name for something which is not of uncommon occurrence in mountain regions is the word 'flume', which as applied in the United States, and chiefly in the White Mountains means a narrow passage or defile between nearly perpendicular rocks, through which runs a stream, and usually with a succession of cascades. **1948** *Sat. Review* 3 July 28/2 There are, to be sure, plenty of New Hampshire sights like the Flume, Old Man of the Mountain, and Lost River, being altogether no less original than Niagara Falls.

3. *To go* (or *be*) *up the flume,* to come to grief, to be done for. *Slang.* (Cf. Eng. slang *up the flue.*)

1865 *Eastern Slope* (Washoe, Nev.) 23 Dec. 3/1 The great Stockholder . . . has in the classic language of the mines, 'gone up the flume.' **1889** K. MONROE *Golden Days* xii. 124 And, pard, he has moseyed with the map, and we're up a flume. **1890** *Denver Republican* 4 May 24/3 You frequently hear people say when a firm fails or great loss by fire is experienced, 'Well, they're gone up the flume.'

As the last term in **boom, lumber, tail, washing flume.**

* **flume,** *v. tr.* (See quots.)

1861 STONE *Pacific Song Book* 16, I remember, when we flumed American river. **1876** *Encycl. Brit.* IV. 701 [In California] the rivers . . . were 'flumed'—that is, the water was taken out of the natural channel by means of wooden flumes. **1905** *Forestry Bureau Bul.* No. 61, 37 *Flume,* to transport logs or timbers by a flume.

* **fluming,** *n.* The using or making of a flume. Also attrib.

1851 *S.F. Picayune* 23 Sep. 2/5 There is another fluming company just below, that will commence operations this week. **1889** J. D. WHITNEY *United States* 310 The rivers themselves were . . . entirely carried to one side of their natural channels by 'fluming,' or building artificial channels of timber. **1903** *Electrical World* 16 May 837/1 The original scheme was to develop the Coquitlam by fluming along the steep hillside a distance of about seven miles.

flummerdiddle ˈflʌmɚˌdɪdl, *n.* Also **fumadiddle, flummadiddle,** etc. [Prob. fanciful f. **flummery* and **diddle.*]

1. Nonsense, trifles, useless frills and frippery. Also attrib. *Colloq.* Cf. **fofarrow.**

1854 M. J. HOLMES *Tempest & Sunshine* iv, What does she want of any more flummerdiddle notions? **1868** BRACKETT *Farm Talk* 70 What's the use of so much 'flummy-diddle'? Plain common sense is enough for any farmer's paper. **1882** *Cent. Mag.* Oct. 837 Well, see all that flumer-diddle he got off about it. **1941** O. R. COHEN in *Sat. Ev. Post* 25 Oct. 35/3 An' does you try any fumadiddles, you is right away gwine happen to a catastrophe.

b. (See quot. 1944.)

1882 *Advance* 21 Sep., Directions for . . . crocheting all sorts of flummediddles. **1944** ADAMS *W. Words* 63 Fumadiddle. A western term for fancy dress. Faradiddle and fofaraw are also used in this sense. **1948** *Popular Western* June 104/2, I know a California vaquero feels positively naked if he don't have some fumadiddle about his get-up.

2. (See quot.)

1857 *Harper's Mag. Sep.* 538/2 Flummadiddle is a compound mixture . . . the component parts of which are stale bread, pork fat, molasses, water, cinnamon, allspice, and cloves. It is a kind of *mush*, baked in the oven.

flunk flʌŋk, *n.* [See note.]

The origin of this term and the corresponding verb is discussed without positive results in *Amer. Sp.* Feb. 1946 pp. 16–18,

A complete failure in a course, examination, etc., or a grade indicative of this. Also transf. *Slang.*

1846 *Yale Banger* 10 Nov., This . . . meant a perfect *flunk.* **1888** *Missouri Repub.* 11 Feb. (F.), Riddleberger forced the presidential possibilities of the senate to a complete flunk. **1904** *N.Y. Ev. Post* 6 Jan. 5 A sprinter and football player has received a flunk in one study and a condition in another. **1925** *Lit. Digest* 14 March 64/2 A 'flunk' is a man who has failed to pass an exam. **1948** *Time* 16 Feb. 94/3 This time there were twice as many flunks.

flunk flʌŋk, *v.* [See the noun.]

1. *intr.* To fail at anything, to give up, back down. Also with *out* and *under. Slang.*

1823 *Crayon* 3 To joke in earnest, gentlemen, we must have, at least, as many subscribers as there are students in College, or 'flunk out.' **1834** in *Mil. & Naval Mag. of U.S.* IV. (Nov.) 206 'Why, it wont do, you see, Tremaine,' replied Purnly, 'for me to appear to flunk, nor I won't, that's flat!' **1859** STOWE *Minister's Wooing* xvii, You a man, and not stan' by your color, and flunk under to mean white ways! **1910** J. HART *Vigilante Girl* 294, I don't mean that he's flunking, for he's no coward.

b. Esp. to fail in a course, examination, or school career. *Slang.* Cf. **flunk,** *n.*, and see **4.** below.

1847 in HAMMOND *Remembrance of Amherst* (1946) 66 (We.), I fear I should have flunked. **1898** *Scribner's Mag.* XXIV. 55/2 And so she did not worry, Nor sit up late to cram, . . . And she flunked in her exam. **1947** *This Week Mag.* 8 March 15/3 There's no excuse these days for flunking out.

2. *tr.* (See second quot.) *Slang. Obs.* Cf. **flunky 1.**

1841 JACKSON *Week in Wall-St.* ix, He will not deny, that, in the expressive language of Wall-street, he has himself been 'flunked.' *Ib.* 112 What does Swartwout mean by being flunked? . . . That's a Wall-street word, and means that he has been outwitted, in tryin to make up the money he was behind.

3. To give (a student) a grade below passing on a recitation or examination, or in a course. *Slang.*

1843 *Yale Lit. Mag.* IX. 61 That day poor Fullman was *flunked*, and was never again reinstated in the good graces of our officer. **1910** *N.Y. Ev. Post* 29 Nov. 8 Examining boards may 'flunk' an officer in his first examination. **1948** *Dly. Ardmoreite* (Ardmore, Okla.) 30 April 1/4 Four teen-agers were accused today of blasting a pretty young high school teacher's home with gunfire after a telephoned death threat warning her not to flunk anybody in mathematics.

4. To shirk (a duty or obligation); to fail (a subject or course). *Slang.*

1871 G. R. CUTTING *Student Life at Amherst College* 22 We might incidentally add that the fine for 'flunking' an appointment at a 'special meeting' was two dollars, and for leaving the room while it was in progress, fifty cents. **1915** WILSON *Ruggles* xv. 263 He flunked a meeting of the Onwards and Upwards Society. **1941** *Harper's Mag.* Oct. 490/1 It's from Junior at Harvard. He says he's flunked Southwestern History again.

flunker ˈflʌŋkɚ, *n.* A teacher or a professor with a reputation for failing students. Also a student who flunks. *Slang.* — **1910** O. JOHNSON *Varmint* i. 14 'What had he done to you?' said Jimmy, winking at Mr. Hopkins, . . . master of the Latin line and distinguished flunker of boys. **1948** *Chi. D. News* 2 Nov. 10/5 Regarding . . . [the] article about college flunkers, an omission seems to have been made.

flunkology ˌflʌŋkˈɑlədʒɪ, *n.* (See quot. 1856.) *Slang. Obs.* — **1852–3** *Burlesque Catalogue* (Yale) 28 The scholarship, is awarded to the student in each Freshman Class who passes the poorest examination in Flunkology. **1856** HALL *College Words* (ed. 2) 206 *Flunkology*, a farcical word, designed to express the science of *flunking*.

flunky ˈflʌŋkɪ, *n.* [See **flunk,** *v.*] **1.** (See quot. 1841.) **2.** One who fails in schoolwork. Both *slang* and *obs.*

(1) **1841** *Week in Wall St.* 81 Deceived by appearances, [this class] come into market without any knowledge of it, and generally lose what they invest. These are called *flunkies.* **1893** *N.Y. Tribune* 2 March 4 The lambs that we have in the Street these days were called flunkeys . . . forty-five or fifty years ago. — (2) **1854** *Yale Lit Mag.* XX. 76 (Th.), I am a college pony (*i.e.* a 'crib'). . . . I bore him safe through Horace, Saved him from the flunkey's doom. **1856** HALL *College Words* (ed. 2) 206 *Flunkey.* In college parlance, one who makes a complete failure at recitation; one who *flunks.*

fluoroscope ˈflʊrəˌskop, *n.* [*∗fluorescence*+-*(o)scope.*] An instrument used for observing fluorescence, or, with X rays, in diagnostic medical examinations.

1896 *Lancaster* (Pa.) *D. New Era* 2 April 2 [Edison] calls his instrument the fluoroscope. **1898** *Pop. Science Mo.* LII. 569 Any variation in the size or position of the heart are [*sic*] readily made out by the use of the fluoroscope. **1948** *Sat. Ev. Post* 13 Nov. 121/2, I wonder if you realize how much more can be accomplished in the laboratory; the uses of the fluoroscope, the spectrograph, and other equipment.

Also as a verb.

1948 MENJOU & MUSSELMAN *It Took 9 Tailors* 172 A couple of eminent specialists poked, stethoscoped, X-rayed, and fluoroscoped me but failed to diagnose or cure my pains.

∗ **flurry,** *n.* A sudden gust, shower, or downpour as of wind, rain, hail, or snow.

1686 SEWALL *Diary* I. 132 High wind, and flurries of Hail. **1772** *Md. Hist. Mag.* XIV. 364 We had a flurry of Wind & Rain this morning. **1833** HOFFMAN *Winter in West* I. 38 We had two flurries [of snow] on successive days. **1893** B. MATTHEWS in *Harper's Mag.* May 863/1 A sudden flurry of rain forced them all to button their collars.

transf. **1868** LOWELL *Poetical Works* (1896) 350/2 The sudden flurries of snow-birds, Like brown leaves whirling by. **1898** WARMAN *Story of Railroad* 204 What they call the 'flurry'—the local hurricane produced by the passing of a snowslide.

b. In the stock exchange, sudden and short-lived activity and excitement in the market.

1876 *Fur, Fin, & Feather* Sep. 129 The prospect of a flurry in stocks . . . is sure to strip the island of visitors. **1907** FIELD *Six-Cylinder Courtship* 80 A column . . . sandwiched in between The Latest Armenian Atrocities and the Unprecedented Flurry in Chewing Gum.

∗ **flurry,** *v. intr.* To flutter or settle down like flakes of snow. — **1883** *Harper's Mag.* Nov. 947/2 The music seemed . . . to flurry like snow-flakes, from the ceiling. **1884** ROE *Nature's Story* vii, The petals of the cherry were flurrying down like snow in every passing breeze.

∗ **flush,** *n.* and *a.*

1. flush tank, a tank for water forming part of a sewerage system.

1879 *Harper's Mag.* June 133/2 At the upper end of each main sewer there is placed a Field's flush tank. **1910** GERHARD *Water Supply of Modern City Buildings* 403 Flush tanks shall be constructed of hard burned brick laid in cement mortar and built perfectly water-tight.

2. flush times, *pl.*, a period of unusual prosperity.

[**1840** W. IRVING *Life & Lett.* (1866) III. 153 If times ever again come smooth and flush with me.] **1852** *S. Lit. Messenger* XVIII. 435/1 Such a spendthrift never made a track even in the flush times of 1836. **1949** *Chi. Sun. Tribune* (Book Sec.) 20 Feb. 4/1 In flush times there is great emphasis on novelty and quick turnover.

As the last term in **bobtail, bob-tailed, royal, straight flush.**

∗ **flush,** *v. tr.* (See quots.) Also **flush plow.** Hence **flushing,** *n. Obs.*

1787 WASHINGTON *Diaries* III. 181 The land next to this was untouched having been flush plowed in the fall. **1805** PARKINSON *Tour* II. 326 To prepare land for Indian corn, is in the fall to plough it, what is termed flushing it. **1849** *Rep. Comm. Patents: Agric.* (1850) 313, I strive to break up the land with two-horse ploughs—what I term flushing, that is, breaking up 30 to 50 feet beds.

flusterer ˈflʌstərɚ, *n.* The American coot or mud hen, *Fulica americana.*

1709 LAWSON *Carolina* 149 Black Flusterers; some call these Old Wives. They are as black as Ink. The Cocks have white Faces. **1813** WILSON *Ornithology* IX. 62 In Carolina they [coots] are called *Flusterers*, from the noise they make in flying along the surface of the water. **1917** *Birds of Amer.* I. 214 Coot, *Fulica americana.* . . . Other names. —American Coot; . . . Flusterer; Blue Peter.

flusticated ˈflʌstəˌketɪd, *a.* [App. f. ∗*fluster, v.*, and ∗*intoxicated.*] Flustered or fuddled, as with drink. *Slang. Obs.* — **1835** KENNEDY *Horse Shoe Robinson* I. 78 [The English] listed you . . . when you was flusticated with liquor. **c1845** *Big Bear Ark.* 98 Being sorter flusticated like, . . . I didn't notis perticlar where I sot.

fluted scale. =**cushion scale.** — **1889** *Rep. Secy. Agric.* 334 The Fluted or White Scale is practically no longer a factor to be considered in the cultivation of oranges and lemons in California.

∗ **flutter,** *n.* and *v.* In combs.: (1) **flutter bird,** a gay, frivolous person, *colloq., obs.;* (2) **mill,** a small water wheel placed in a stream and serving as a child's plaything, also transf., cf. **flutter wheel 2;** (3) **pigeon, stick,** (see quot.), *obs.;* (4) **wheel,** see as a main entry.

(1) **1894** FORD *P. Stirling* 327 To him we are nothing but dancing, dressing, prattling flutter-birds. *Ib.* 332 Do you think I'm nothing but a foolish society flutter-bird? — (2) **1866** C. H. SMITH *Bill Arp* 85 The Choctaw children built their flutter mills and toyed with frogs and tadpoles whilst these majestic streams were but little spring branches. **1898** *Cong. Rec.* App. 22 Feb. 223/1 (Th. S.), They will run their flutter-mills and mixers, and dope the flour to suit themselves. **1900** J. C. HARRIS *On The Wing* 176 When I git to talkin' my tongue runs like a flutter-mill. — (3) **1794** J. DRAYTON *Letter* 74 They then place under the sweep of the net, but upon the ground, the flutter pidgeons; (so called from being fixed to a flutter stick, which by reason of a string communicating to the skreen, they raise up and down, when the pidgeons are flying over) and have the flier pidgeon ready on a roost, tied to the skreen by a long string.

flutter wheel.

1. (See quot. 1860.) Also (*cap.*) in a place-name.

1818 *15th Congress* 1 Sess. H.R. Doc. No. 48, 10 [An invention for] letting water on the flutter wheel [was patented July 1, 1817, by] Jarvis Smith. **1860** *Harper's Mag.* April 609/2 The elevation of many rich mines has given rise to a variety of ingenious inventions for raising and supplying them with water. Among these is the 'flutter-wheel.' . . . It consists of a wheel, sometimes thirty feet in diameter, the paddles of which are furnished with large buckets made to catch themselves full of water at each revolution, and to discharge into a trough which it flows to the tom, or sluice. **1895** GRAHAM *Stories of Foot-Hills* 40 Lysander was at work in the cañon some distance below the new tunnel, 'ditching' the water of Flutterwheel Spring to Mrs. Withrow's land.

2. =**flutter mill.**

1870 EGGLESTON *Queer Stories* i. 99 All the boys made little water-mills to be run by the force of the stream. We call them 'flutter-wheels.'

fly flaɪ, *n.*[1] [Du. dial. *vlei*, dim. of *vallei*, valley.]

1. A swamp or marsh; also a creek. Cf. **vly.**

1645 in *Amer. Sp.* V. (1930) 161 The word is old; Kieft's Patent 1645 to the town of Gravesend 'at ye head of a fly or marsh.' **1675** *Hempstead Rec.* I. 301 One part frunting on the lott of John Ellisons which lys in the fly. **1735** *Brookhaven Rec.* 139 The feftene aker lots . . . which run from a place called Squasacx pinte, to the littel fly.

2. (*cap.*) A market in New York City (see quot. 1896). In full **Fly Market.** Now *hist.*

1775 HONYMAN *Journal* 26 Last night went to a Public house in Fly market, the first that occurred. **1896** HASWELL *New York* 27 The markets were the Fly (Vlie or Vly, an abbreviation of valley), located at the foot of Maiden Lane, which was this year [i.e., 1816] ordered to be removed. **1944** BROOKS *World of Wash. Irving* 33 New Yorkers could remember him, in the days when he [Lindley Murray] lived near Peck-slip, returning from the Fly-market, basket in hand.

attrib. **1809** *Knickerb. Hist.* v. ii. 184 They were the first institutors of that honorable order of knighthood called Fly-market shirks. **1854** BUSCH *Wanderungen* I. 349 Freilich war Alfred Allen, der jetzige Kapitän derselben, einst Anführer der verrufenen *Flymarket-Boys* gewesen.

* **fly**, *n.*[2]

1. In baseball, a ball batted so as to fly through the air. Cf. **fly ball.**

1867 *Ball Players' Chron.* 20 June 2/2 Their fielding was good, Osborne taking four splendid flys and Tompkins putting out twelve of his opponents on fly tips and foul bounds. **1896** *Cin. Enquirer* 30 July 2/3 It is no wonder that he was not able to judge that high fly that was hit 'right into the sun.' **1948** *Dly. Ardmoreite* (Ardmore, Okla.) 26 May 10/4 She ran into her team's shortstop as they each wanted to catch the same fly.

b. * *On the fly*, (see quot. 1868). Also transf.

1856 *Spirit of Times* 8 Nov. 165/1 An important improvement in the fielding of this match, was shown by several fine catches being made on the fly, instead of the child's play, 'from the bound.' **1868** CHADWICK *Base Ball* 15 If the ball he hits should be caught by any one of the fielders before touching the ground—or 'on the fly,' as it is called —he is out. **1886** HARTE *Snow-bound* 13 You see you can't prove anything agin them unless you take them 'on the fly.' **1902** *Chi. Record-Herald* 7 Sep. III. 2/3 The latter bunting for a sacrifice hit a weak fly that O'Hagan ran in fifteen feet for and took on the fly.

2. In politics, an addition to an act. *Rare.*

1870 *Cong. Globe* 1 July 5062/1 This was put in as a 'fly' in the act of March 18, 1869.

3. In combs. in which "fly" is from various sources: (1) **fly ball,** =**fly,** *n.*[2] **1;** (2) **brush,** a brush for driving away flies; (3) **catch,** (*a*) the winter wren, *Nannus hiemalis hiemalis, rare,* (*b*) (see quot. 1916); (4) **catcher,** see as a main entry; (5) **catch grass,** (see quot.); (6) **catching,** (see quot.); (7) **cop,** (see quot. 1859 and cf. British slang **fly*, a policeman), *slang;* (8) **dope,** (see quots. 1916, 1947), *colloq.;* (9) **fish,** (see quot.); (10) * **flapper,** ?a headdress worn by women, *obs.;* (11) **game,** a baseball game in which only "fly catches" are counted, *obs.;* (12) * **net,** (*a*) a net for taking fish, (*b*) a covering of meshes or a fringe of leather strips to protect a horse from flies; (13) **out,** in baseball, an "out" resulting from the catching of a fly ball; (14) **poison,** see as a main entry; (15) **proof,** not susceptible to injury by flies, proof against flies; (16) **snapper,** (see quot. 1917); (17) **stone,** ground cobalt, used as the principal ingredient in poisons for flies, worms, etc.; (18) **swatter,** a device for killing flies, usu. of wire netting, rubber, or straw, with a handle attached; (19) * **time,** see as a main entry; (20) * **tip,** in baseball, a pitched ball grazed or slightly fouled by the batter; (21) * **trap,** see as a main entry; (22) **way,** (*a*) the usual route through the air followed by migrating birds, (*b*) (see quot.); (23) **weevil,** (see quot. 1889).

(1) **1865** *Wilkes' Spirit of Times* 25 March 54/3 Connorton led at the bat, W. Murtha taking seven flyballs in fine style. **1947** *Chi. Tribune* 29 June 1. 20/6 Is baseball so important that it should be purchased at the price of forcing mothers to wheel their buggies out of the park for fear of being hit with a fly ball? — (2) **1833** CATLIN *Indians* I. 113 The Indian's fly brush was made of the buffalo's tail. **1944** WILSON *Passing Inst.* 16 Screens are fine things, but they have cheated the younger generation out of an acquaintance with the fly brush or broom. — (3) (*a*) **1806** LEWIS in *L. & Clark Exped.* IV. (1905) 133 There are two species of the flycatch, a small redish brown species with a short tail. . . . This is the same with that which remains all winter in Virginia where it is sometimes called the wren. (*b*) **1867** *S.F. Dramatic Chronicle* 1 July 2/1 The world wags on, and we expect before long to hear of the 'King of the Cannibal Islands,' making a clean home run on the best fly catch. **1916** BANCROFT *Handbook* 80 Fly catch. The catching of a fly ball.

(5) **1857** GRAY *Botany* 540 *Leersia lenticularis*, Flycatch grass, . . . grows in low grounds, Virginia, Illinois, and southward. — (6) **1868** CHADWICK *Base Ball* 40 *Fly Catching* . . . a ball so falling can be stopped without pain and held firmly, by . . . allowing the hands to check its progress gradually instead of abruptly. — (7) **1859** MATSELL *Vocabulum* 34 Fly-Cop. Sharp officer; an officer that is well posted; one who understands his business. **1922** PARRISH *Case & Girl* 234 You are not a 'fly-cop,' only a measly busy-body sticking your nose into some one else's business. — (8) **1897** *Outing* XXX. 377/1 One thing must not be forgotten, which is the 'fly dope,' or preventative against the attacks of insects. **1916** KEPHART *Camping & Woodcraft* II. 243 Everybody has some kind or other of 'fly-dope,' by which elegant name we mean any preparation which, being rubbed over the exposed parts of one's skin, is supposed to discourage insects from repeating their attacks. **1947** DALRYMPLE *Panfish* 161 Take this little bottle of fly dope, which is really only a mixture of paraffin dissolved in energine, and waterproof your fly with it. — (9) **1884** GOODE *Fisheries* I. 264 *Sebastichthys rhodochloris*. . . . The inexplicable name of 'Fly-fish' is given to this species by the fishermen at Monterey. . . . It is known only from very deep water about Monterey and the Farallones.

(10) **1798** *Mass. Spy* 5 Sep. (Th.), Their pretty faces are either obscured by a black or white fly-flapper, or wholly hidden by their poking bonnets. **1872** S. HALE *Letters* 113 Can you live to hear that there was a fly-flapper embroidered out of the Bazaar? — (11) **1864** *Wilkes' Spirit of Times* 17 Dec. 244/3 The shortest fly-game occupied but fifty-eight minutes to play the nine innings. **1868** *N.E. Base-Ballist* 6 Aug. 1/3 This game is also of importance inasmuch as it was the first 'fly game' played in Boston as previous to this, the bound catch was allowed in all games. — (12) (*a*) **1819** *Mass. Laws* 230 [No person] shall draw or drag any seine, drag net, or fly net . . . in any of the said rivers or streams. **1871** *N.Y. Laws* 1681 Nothing in chapter five hundred and sixty-seven . . . shall apply to or affect the setting or using of any pound, weir, set or fly-net. (*b*) **1858** *Texas Almanac* (*advt.*), Hughes' Saddle, Harness and Trunk Manufactory. . . . Saddle and horse Blankets, Fly Netts. **1902** *Sears Cat.* 423 Cotton and leather fly nets. — (13) **1887** *Courier-Journal* 26 May 2/6 When Collins was on second base, he attempted to reach third on Wolf's fly out, but Terry cut him off by a splendid throw to Pinckney. **1947** *Dly. Oklahoman* (Okla. City) 11 Aug. 13/1 Welch's flyout to left and Frank Kellert's single ran it to 6–0 in the second.

(15) **1817** *Niles' Reg.* XII. 284/1, I found several of the other kinds of wheat . . . growing on some farms in the same field with the fly-proof or Lawler wheat. *a***1918** G. STUART *On Frontier* I. 240, I tried to fix the meat-house so it would be fly proof. — (16) **1895** C. C. ABBOTT *Birds About Us* II. 75 Well . . . did the flysnapper only make believe to launch out after insects? **1917** *Birds of Amer.* III. 97 *Phainopepla.* Other Names.—Silky Flycatcher; Shining Crested Flycatcher; Shining Fly-snapper; Black-crested Flycatcher. — (17) **1805** PARKINSON *Tour* 364 Small black flies are so numerous, that it

is usual to have some kind of poison to destroy them. For which purpose a substance, called fly-stone, mixed with sugar and water, is spread on a plate. **1870** *Rep. Comm. Agric. 1869* 296 He then mixed an ounce of 'fly-stone,' or cobalt, with water, making the compound very sweet with honey. — **(18) 1931** *K.C. Times* 28 Aug., Can you remember when you saw your first fly swatter? **1941** *Yankee* Dec. 39/2 They list shuck dolls at 25 cents and 50 cents; colored splint fly swatters are 30 cents.

(20) 1865 *Sun. Mercury* (Phila.) 20 Aug. 3/5 Kleinfelder distinguished himself by catching eleven 'fly-tips.' **1903** *Cin. Enquirer* 23 May 11/5 In those days, if you remember, a fly tip caught off the bat meant out. — **(22)** *(a)* **1930** PHILLIPS & LINCOLN *Amer. Waterfowl* 57 The principal flyways of the North American continent are, from east to west, the Atlantic, the Mississippi Valley, the Great Plains, the Rocky Mountains, and the Pacific. **1947** *Time* 17 Nov. 16/2 The smallest contingent, about 15%, usually heads down the Atlantic flyway bound for Chesapeake Bay and the Carolina swamps. *(b)* **1948** *Conservation* in *Action* V. 8/1 The term 'flyway' denotes a vast geographic region that is occupied by definite bird populations and contains both breeding and wintering grounds, connected by a more or less complex system of migration routes. — **(23) 1768** *Amer. Philos. Soc.* I. 274 The Fly-Weevil . . . destroys the wheat. **1790** *Pa. Packet* 30 March 1/4 Information . . . for preventing damage to crops by insects; especially the Hessian-fly, the wheat-fly, or fly-weevil, the pea-bug, and the corn chinch bug. **1889** *Cent.* 2296/2 *Fly-weevil*, the common grain-moth, *Gelechia cerealella*. (Southern U.S.)

As the last term in **bar, bee, black, blowing, bluetail, buck, buffalo, burning, caribou, carpet, cattle, chin, cow, deer, dog day harvest, drove, dry weather, ear, Englishman's, fair, foul, green, harvest, heel, Hessian, horn, horse, human, jar, Mexican fruit, moose, Mormon, mountain, mow, pea, plantation, pop, potato, prairie, salt marsh, screw, screw worm, shad, shoo, spittle, stable, swamp, sweat, tail, tobacco, Webster, wheat, white man's fly.**

* **fly**, *v.* [In **1.** prob. a new formation based on the noun.]

1. *Baseball. intr.* To hit a fly ball. Also with *out.*

1893 *Chi. Tribune* 3 July 7/3 Kittridge flied out to Brodie. **1904** *St. Louis Globe-Democrat* 4 July 12/3 Wallace flew to Lush for the third out. **1948** *Durant* (Okla.) *D. Democrat* 2 July 4/4 Baker then flied to center and neither runner was able to advance.

2. Used colloq. with adverbs: **a.** *fly around*, to bustle about, be busy. **b.** *fly in*, to fall to, "pitch in."

(a) 1831 SMITH *Life & Writings of Downing* 151 (We.), I flew round and washed my face and hands. **1898** CANFIELD *Maid of Frontier* 31 Lordy, Anne, fly 'roun' an' git th' Cap'n a cheer. — **(b) 1895** REMINGTON *Pony Tracks* 114 William . . . put the 'grub,' on a pack-saddle blanket and said, 'Now, gemmen, fly in.'

3. In colloq. and slang phrases: *to fly off one's jib*, (see quot.); *to fly one's own kite*, to look out for one's own interests; *to fly all to pieces at*, to become enraged at.

1848 J. MITCHELL *Nantucketisms* 40 'Hanks flying off his jib.' Getting old, or in poor health. — **1865** A. D. WHITNEY *Gayworthys* viii. 85 They had their own kite to fly, now; and there was nothing to remind them that they had ever helped to tie a bob to the tail of anybody's else. — **1868** *Cong. Globe* 20 Feb. 1294/3, I saw Mr. Callaway, who flew all to pieces at me.

For to *fly off the handle, to fly the eagle, to fly the track*, see the nouns. For **fly-up-the-creek**, see as a main entry.

flyaway grass. The hair grass, *Agrostis hiemalis.* — **1857** *Mass. Bd. Agric. Rep. 1856* I. 29 Hair Grass, or Fly Away Grass, Tickle Grass, (*agrostis scabra*,) is another species.

* **flycatcher**, *n.*

1. Any one of various American passerine birds that catch flies. Also attrib.

1796 WANSEY *Excursion U.S.* 105 [In New Jersey] the birds in greatest plenty were partridge, . . . Fly-catchers, and wood-peckers. **1862** *N.H. Laws* 2609 If any person shall . . . take, kill or destroy any of the birds called . . . linnets, fly-catchers or warblers; . . . he shall forfeit . . . the sum of one dollar. **1948** *Green Bay* (Wis.) *Press-Gazette* 30 June 4/1 In summer they eat insects too, which they catch flycatcher fashion, that is, perched in one spot and darting out at them when they come near.

2. = **Venus('s) fly-trap.**

1803 DAVIS *Travels* 96 In bogs, and marshy situations, is found the singular plant called the fly-catcher by the natives, and, I believe, *dionæ muscipula* by botanists.

As the last term in **Acadian, Arkansas, Bonaparte's, brown, Canada, Canadian, chattering, crested, dusky, Lawrence's, least, Mexican, olive-sided, pewee, pewit, red-eyed, scissor-tail(ed), short-legged, small-headed, swallow-tailed, Townsend, Traill's, white-eyed, yellow-bellied flycatcher.**

* **flyer**, *n.* Also **flier.**

1. A venture or investment, esp. in stocks, involving considerable financial risk. *Colloq.*

1846 *Spirit of Times* 11 July 229/3 Lend me a quarter—*one* quarter —just for a flyer. **1885** *Harper's Mag.* Nov. 841/1 He . . . takes 'a flier,' or small side venture, that does not employ his entire capital. **1949** *Highway Traveler* Feb. 9/1 A Montreal lawyer . . . went ski-minded and 'took a flyer' in building a magnificent resort 'just for fun.'

transf. **1865** MARK TWAIN *Sketches* (1926) 170 My refusal of the position [a pastorate] at $7,000 a year was not precisely meant to be final, but was intended for what the ungodly term a 'flyer'—the object being to bring about an increase of the amount. **1883** BEADLE *Western Wilds* 589 An expert . . . condemned the mine as a flyer—that is, a mere freak of nature, without sign of permanence. **1946** T. JONES *Skinny Angel* 21 He took a flyer into the future, predicting that chickens would be raised scientifically for meat or eggs.

2. (See quot.)

1884 GOODE *Fisheries* I. 183 In Penobscot Bay they [flounders] are taken in traps, or 'fliers,' as the fishermen call them shaped something like lobster-traps and baited.

3. (See quots.)

1889 *Lit. World* 21 Dec. 485/2 The device of inserting gaily-colored advertising fliers in the body of the magazine. **1942** ASHER & HEAL *Send No Money* 46 Publications took on the appearance of a Sears, Roebuck & Company flyer, the small supplementary catalogue issued by the firm in between big catalogues.

4. A trapeze.

1898 DELAND *Old Chester Tales* 240, I saw the rope giving, and I jumped to catch a flyer; and I missed it. But I wasn't killed.

5. (See quot.)

1899 *Dept. Agric. Yrbk.* 435 Flyers, the first two bottom leaves [of tobacco]; . . . are overripe and very trashy.

6. flyer pigeon, a decoy pigeon (see quot.). *Obs.*

1867 DE VOE *Market Ass't* 173 A 'flyer-pigeon' (and sometimes two or three), are also blinded, and their legs tied to a fishing-line, sixty or one hundred feet long.

As the last term in **Baltimore, panhandle flyer.**

* **flying**, *a.*

1. With reference to cattle brands: Wavy or flowing in appearance.

1887 *Scribner's Mag.* II. 508/2 Words used in connection with . . . life on the plains: . . . *flying-brand; lazy-brand* [etc.]. **1894** *McClure's Mag.* III. 100/2 An open flying A looked all too like a running W. *Ib.* 111/2 There is, first and simplest, the mere addition . . . of flourishes to a plain letter to make a flying letter of it. **1947** *Southern Sierran* April 4/3 At least one Jersey is headed for the barbecue pit when the Sierra Club visits the Flying H Ranch during Easter week.

2. In special combs.: (1) **flying-barked hickory,** = **scaly-bark hickory,** *obs.;* (2) **calamary,** (see quot.); (3) * **squirrel,** any one of various small squirrels having on each side of their bodies between the fore and hind legs a fold of skin which enables them to glide through the air, esp. such a squirrel of the genus *Glaucomys;* (4) **store,** (see quot.), *obs.;* (5) **switch,** (see quot.).

(1) 1709 LAWSON *Carolina* 99 The third is call'd the Flying-bark'd Hiccory, from its brittle and scaly Bark. — **(2) 1883** *Nat. Museum Bul.* No. 27, 189 *Ommastrephes illecebrosa*, . . . the most common squid north of Cape Cod, . . . is known as the . . . 'flying calamary.' — **(3) c1613** SPELMAN in Smith *Works* (1884) I. p. cvi, Ther be in this country [Virginia] Lions, Beares, woulues, foxes, muske catts, Hares, fleinge squirells [etc.]. **1843** OLIVER *Eight Months* 142 Of squirrels there are, in the West, the fox, grey, flying and ground squirrel or chip-munk. **1943** BENÉT *Western Star* 50 A flying-squirrel leapt from a swaying branch. — **(4) 1791** in IMLAY *Western Territory* (ed. 3) 467 It is the constant practice in America, for small traders to establish what is called flying stores, for the sale of goods wherever new settlements are made. — **(5) 1884** *Harper's Mag.* July 273/1 The dispatcher . . . gives it a flying switch . . . the locomotive is uncoupled from the cars, and they are thrown on one track, while it is thrown over to another.

fly poison. A lily-like plant, *Amianthium muscaetoxicum*, of the bunchflower family, decoctions of which are used as insecticides.

1773–4 W. BARTRAM *Georgia & Fla.* I. 7 Took notice of a pretty species of Asphodelus called here [Ga.] by the Inhabitants Fly poison, having a long loose spike of white Flowers. **1857** GRAY *Botany* 477 Amianthium muscætoxicum, Fly-Poison, . . . [grows in] open woods, New Jersey and Pennsylvania to Kentucky and southward. **1943** PEATTIE *Great Smokies* 196 The curious big flypoison lit up the sward with flecks of white.

b. The Jimson weed.

1941 R. S. Walker *Lookout* 52 In some of the oldest gardens on Lookout Mountain is still found a plant that for more than two centuries has followed the old settlers and filled an important niche in their economic lives. This is fly-poison plant, or the Apple-of-Peru.

fly time. Used fig. in phrasal comparisons (see quots.). *Colloq.*

1819 *Ky. Alman. 1820* (Lexington) 29 [He] has no more chance for the worth of his dollar, than a stump tail bull in fly time. **1831** *Working-man's Gazette* (Woodstock, Vt.) 19 Jan. 129/2 The wags often fastened upon him with their jokes, and often made him feel as uncomfortable as a short-tailed horse in fly-time. *c*1849 Paige *Dow's Sermons* I. 99 Human law is no more of a barrier in their way, than a brush fence is to a mad bull in fly-time. **1853** Simms *Sword & Distaff* 234 We both sweated like an overseer's horse in fly-time. **1898** Ford *Tattle-Tales* 12 My Major [was] suffering worse than a docked horse in fly-time.

* **flytrap,** *n.*

1. a. App. a contemptuous term for some contrivance used by an incompetent surveyor. *Obs.* **b.** A wretched hovel or office. *Contemptuous.*

(a) **1816** U. Brown *Journal* II. 231 He could take a reference & fall into the Right Course (he carrying a flie-trap slung on his Back to assist him on such Occasions). — (b) **1909** O. Henry *Options* (1916) 62 Old Jerome was lingering long after breakfast . . before setting forth to his down town fly-trap.

2. = **pitcherplant.** Also attrib. Cf. **Venus('s) flytrap.**

1860 *Charleston* (S.C.) *Mercury* 25 Dec. 1/8 Amair's Sarracenia or Fly Trap Bitters, The Great Southern remedy for Dyspepsia. **1876** Hobbs *Bot. Hand-Book* 39 Fly trap, Sidesaddle plant, Sarracenia purpurea. **1907** Lyons *Plant Names* 415 S[arracenia] purpurea. . . . Pitcher-plant, Side-saddle Flower, Fly-trap.

fly-up-the-creek.

1. A small American heron, as the green heron.

1840 *Spirit of Times* 25 Jan. 559/1 (We.), He saw nothing but a bird, vulgarly called 'a fly-up-the-creek,' perched on a dead tree. **1893** *Advance* 3 Aug., One of the . . . finds of the day was the nest of a green heron, often called fly-up-the-creek. **1946** Hausman *Eastern Birds* 107 Other Names—Green Bittern, Little Green Heron, Fly-up-the-Creek.

b. (See quot.) *Colloq.*

1889 *Cent.* 2296/2 *Fly-up-the-creek*, a giddy, capricious person.

2. (*cap.*) (See quots.)

1845 *St. Louis Reveille* 14 May 2/4 The inhabitants of . . . Florida [are called] Fly-up-the-Creeks. *c*1888 Whitman *November Boughs* 406 Those from . . . Florida . . . [were call'd] Fly up the Creeks. **1946** McWilliams *So. Calif. Country* 172 Florida is the 'fly-up-the-creek state.'

F.M. ?A first man of a community. *Rare.* — **1840** *N.O. Picayune* 21 Aug. 2/1 We yesterday dropped into Recorder Bertus' court, and saw several of our F.M. around and about the bench.

f.m.c. (See quots. 1865, 1882.) Cf. **f.w.c.** Now *hist.*

1840 *N.O. Picayune* 16 Aug. 2/2 Bazile Croker, *f.m.c.* sworn, Witness is owner of a slave named Nelson. *Ib.* 25 Aug. 2/1 True bills for counterfeiting were found against J. Kernigan, . . . and Lewis Dango, *f. m. c.* **1865** Richardson *Secret Service* iv. 64 They would sometimes record briefly the killing of a master by his negroes . . . ; C—f. m. c. (free man of color)—for violating one of the many laws. **1882** *Cent. Mag.* Feb. 605/2 The following relates to the sad and silent 'f. m. c.' ('free man of color'). **1929** *Amer. Mercury* Mar. 284/1 They found what they were after, his great-great-grandfather's name, and following it like an overweighted tail to a tugging kite, the letters f.m.c. **1936** Asbury *French Quarter* 88 These free men and women of color—after the American occupation they were commonly designated, in the newspapers and in many legal documents, simply by the initials 'f.m.c.' and 'f.w.c.'—never formed more than a small proportion of the population.

* **foal,** *v. absol.* Of a ewe, to yean. *Rare.* — **1883** *Harper's Mag.* April 652/2 The ewes are . . . kept until they have foaled.

foamflower 'fom,flaʊɚ, *n.* A small, white-flowered herbaceous perennial of the saxifrage family, native to the eastern U.S. — **1908** *Suburban Life* July 20/2 The foam flower, the clintonia, the exquisitely sweet maianthemum make a carpet in a certain bit of woods. **1933** Small *Southeastern Flora* 594 Tiarella L. . . . False-Mitreworts. Coolworts. Foam-flowers.

* **fob,** *n.*[1] *To come the fob on* (someone), to deceive, trick. *Slang. Obs.* — **1848** Judson *Mysteries N.Y.* 62 He come ze fob on some of ze *nobilitie.*

* **fob,** *n.*[2]

1. = **fob chain.**

1885 Custer *Boots & Saddles* xxiii. 219 He wore his grandfather's fob and seal. **1889** McHatton-Ripley *From Flag to Flag* xxiv. 211 The tempting fob . . . hung from his pocket. **1902** *Sears Cat.* (ed. 112) 69 These fobs are of the finest silk web. . . . The fob is one of the most beautiful and practical gentleman's chains for Sunday and dress wear. . . . Be in line. Everybody is wearing a fob.

b. A seal or ornament, esp. one worn on a watch chain. Cf. **watch fob.**

1936 *Sears Cat.* (ed. 173) 759 Your initial is also on the blue enameled metal fob with leather strap. **1944** *Chi. D. News* 16 June 25/7 The newest accent for your summer suit is a leather fob decorated with an enormous jeweled center in dramatic shades of shocking pink or gold.

2. fob chain, a short chain or ribbon, freq. with seals or ornaments, worn on a watch carried in the fob pocket.

1845 J. W. Norris *Chi. Directory* 122 Clocks, Jewelry, Gold Safety Chains, Gold Fob Chains. **1891** S. M. Welch *Recoll. 1930–40* 180 The watch was carried in the fob of the trousers from which a heavy 'fob chain' depended.

3. fob-tailed mouse, (see quot.).

1857 *Rep. Comm. Patents 1856: Agric.* 96 This animal is known as the 'Long-tailed Deer Mouse,' 'Fob-tailed Mouse,' 'Kangaroo Mouse,' . . . 'Wood Mouse,' and other names, common also to the Mus leucopus.

* **fodder,** *n.*

1. The Indian corn plant, cured and used as food for cattle.

*a*1676 John Winthrop in *Philos. Trans.* No. 142 (1678) 1067 The Stalks of this Corn, cut up before too much dryed, and so laid up, are good Winter-fodder for Cattle. But they usually leave them on the Ground for the Cattle to feed on. **1847** *Rep. Comm. Patents 1846* 220 What we do claim as our invention . . . is the arrangement of the hopper . . . for cutting and grinding fodder. **1907** *Farmers' Bul.* No. 313, 9 [In the corn belt] the term 'fodder' is applied to the entire plants as ordinarily cut and shocked.

b. Esp. in the South, the leaves or blades of the plant stripped from the stalk and used as cattle and horse feed. Cf. **blade fodder.**

1688 Clayton *Account Va.* in *Phil. Trans.* XVII. 947 Much of their Indian Corn-blades, which they gather for their fodder. **1724** Jones *Virginia* 41 The Blades and Tops [of Indian corn] are excellent Fodder, when well cured, which is commonly used though many raise good clover and Oats. **1799** Weld *Travels* 105 They feed their cattle upon fodder, that is, the leaves of the Indian corn plant. **1893** *Outing* Jan. 274/1 That afternoon [Zeke was] . . . busy with his fodder (the blades of Indian corn which are stripped from the stalks, tied in small bundles, and later, when cured, into larger ones). **1944** Fast *F. Road* 155 The yellow ears of corn were stacked in the temporary cribs that had been built; a rough shed housed their fodder and stock.

2. In combs.: (1) **fodder blade,** a blade of corn used for fodder, *colloq.*; (2) **corn,** [app. a new formation and

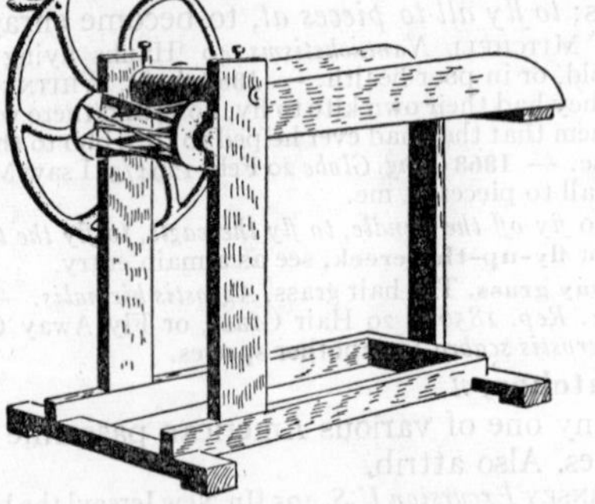

Fodder cutter (*c*1848)

not a continuation of the use indicated by *OED*'s 1655 quot.], corn grown for fodder rather than grain; (3) **cutter,** (see quot. 1883); (4) **field,** a cornfield from which the fodder (sense **1. b.**) is being harvested; (5) **house,** a house or structure, usu. temporary, for storing fodder, cf. **Virginia fodder house;** (6) **hut,** =prec., *obs.*; (7) * **loft,** a loft for the fodder stripped from corn; (8) **pea,** a pea raised for forage, *obs.*; (9) **pulling,** the stripping of the fodder (leaves) from the corn plant; (10) * **stack,** *S.* a cylindrical stack made up of bundles of the blades of Indian corn placed in a circle about a stack pole *q.v.*, also attrib.

(1) **1877** BAGBY *Old Va. Gentleman* 127 The corn has been topped and stripped of its broad fodder blades. — (2) **1856** DAVIS *Farm Bk.* 82 Hauled up two loads wood & 1 of fodder corn. **1888** *Vt. Agric. Rep.* X. 18 E. R. Towle spoke in favor of raising fodder corn. **1947** *Reader's Digest* Jan. 59/2 Barns and stable-loft bulging with hay, grain and fodder corn. — (3) **1868** *Mass. Bd. Agric. Rep. 1867* I. 297 Hay and fodder cutters have become quite indispensable in the barn and the stable. **1883** KNIGHT *Supp.* 352/1 *Fodder Cutter*, a machine for cutting corn stalks for feed. — (4) **1939** HARRIS *Purslane* 74 Letha . . . called Calvin from the fodder field.

(5) **1786** WASHINGTON *Diaries* III. 42 This spot contained 16 A., 1R., 24P., including the fodder Ho. **1895** HOWELLS *Recollections* 148 The fodder-house was commonly made ten feet high, and as long as was necessary, and it was used up through the winter by feeding the fodder to the cattle, beginning at the back, which would be temporarily closed by a few bundles of the top. — (6) **1754** in FRIES *N.C. Morav. Rec.* I. (1922) 106 We thatched the fodder huts built in the 1st field yesterday. — (7) **1882** *Cent. Mag.* XXIV. 873 These bundles are . . . thrown into the fodder-loft. — (8) **1850** in COMMONS *Doc. Hist.* I. 201 April . . . 9, planted fodder peas. — (9) **1868** *Harper's Mag.* Sep. 486/1 The fodder pulling had stripped the enormous corn-fields to bare stalks. **1948** DICK *Dixie Frontier* 173 Many schools ran for only a few weeks in the winter or for a short period in the summer after corn was 'laid by' and before 'fodder-pulling.'

(10) **1788** WASHINGTON *Diaries* III. 424 At Dogue Run, the Cart was drawing Rails for a fodder Stack. **1866** C. H. SMITH *Bill Arp* 54 The Governor . . . is constrained to get on a fodder-stack pole. **1939** HARRIS *Purslane* 92 Plump ears of corn nestled against dry stalks in corn fields, and the wind rattled tan fodder stacks.

b. *To cut one's own fodder*, ?to attend to one's own business, *obs.*; *to stand up to the* (or *one's*) *rack, fodder or no fodder*, see ∗**rack,** *n.*

1838 in BARNES *Memoir of T. Weed* (1884) 69 (We.), When he had no practical talent to cut his own fodder . . . his desertion would never be regarded as a loss to any cause or party. **1843** STEPHENS *High Life N.Y.* I. 32 It's my notion that in a free country every feller ought to cut his own fodder.

As the last term in **blade, cane, corn, cornstalk, cow fodder.**

fofarraw ˈfofəˌrɔ, *n.* Orig. *W.* [Sp. *fanfarrón*, braggart, also, as an adj., cheap and showy. Cf. F. *fanfaron*, braggart, blusterer.]

1. Gaudy wearing apparel. *Obs.*

1848 RUXTON *Far West* 128 Thus equipped, with both his better halves attired in all the glory of fofarraw, he went his way rejoicing. *Ib.* 250 Indian squaws . . . strut about in all the pride of beads and fofarraw. **1850** GARRARD *Wah-To-Yah* 105 You've got so much 'fofarraw' stuck 'bout you, this child didn't savvy at fust!

b. Also as an adj. or adv., haughty, proudly.

1848 RUXTON *Far West* 19 Them white gals are too much like picture, and a deal too 'fofarraw' (fanfaron). **1941** BALDWIN *Keelboat Age* 97 She had no business acting so fofarrow for she was jist a yaller gal.

2. Lightness, gaiety, ostentation.

1945 CLARENCE M. WEBSTER *Town Meeting Country* 42 Our ancestors are supposed to have all been sober men who downed their rum dourly and foreswore the froofraw of life. **1949** *Sat. Ev. Post* 12 Mar. 6/4 The refreshing thing about it is the lack of drumbeating and foo-foo-rah.

∗**fog,** *n.* [In sense **1.** the origin is obscure; perhaps not the same word as in **2.**]

1. *S.* Currency issued by a state bank. In full **fog note.** *Obs.* Cf. **paper fog.**

1816 *Niles' Reg.* X. 216 The secretary of the treasury . . . permits the debtors in the middle and southern states to discharge theirs in paper '*fog*,' which is depreciated 10 per cent below treasury notes. *Ib.* As these [bank notes] were probably southern *fog notes*, the charge cannot lay against these preachers.

2. In combs.: (1) **fog bell,** a bell to warn seamen away from rocks, etc., in time of fog; (2) **fruit,** one or other species of the genus *Lippia;* (3) **whistle,** a whistle placed on a coast and blown as a guide or warning to ships in a fog.

(1) **1832** *Boston Transcript* 8 June 2/2 A fog bell, for the Western Seal Island, weighing 1050 lbs, has arrived in the brig Woodman. **1913** EATON *Barn Doors & Byways* 105 When the deafening vibration of her whistle has grown fainter, you hear on your own starboard bow the mournful fog-bell off St. George. — (2) **1817–8** EATON *Botany* (1822) 519 *Zapania nodiflora*, fog-fruit. **1898** CREEVEY *Flowers of Field, Hill & Swamp* 20 Fog-fruit. *Lippia lanceolata*. . . . A creeping plant, with range from Pennsylvania southward and westward. **1931** DAYTON *Western Browse Plants* 140 In addition there are about four western species of the herbaceous fog-fruit genus (*Phyla* spp.), which some authors merge in Lippia. — (3) **1859** *First Impressions of New World* 3 We had a good deal of fog when off Newfoundland, which obliged us to use the fog-whistle frequently. **1880** *Harper's Mag.* Sep. 502/1 If it should be found, Middleton wished it might be by the plucky fellow in charge of the steam fog-whistle on Menana.

b. Used to designate various stimulating drinks or cocktails: (1) **fog breaker,** (2) **clearer,** (3) **cutter,** (4) **dram,** (5) **driver.** All *obs.*

(1) **1845** JUDD *Margaret* III. 441 The old man is still mercurial; but . . . cold-water is his only fog-breaker. — (2) **1844** UNCLE SAM *Peculiarities* I. 161 The farmers up here wouldn't take her ginger-vengeance airly in the morning instead of eye-openers and fog-clearers. — (3) **1833** *Sketches D. Crockett* 157 They then take a fog-cutter, eat breakfast, and Slim returns to the charge. **1835** D. P. THOMPSON *Adv. T. Peacock* 150 He encountered Van Stetter . . . telling him that the internal application of a double fog-cutter, would prove a much more pleasant and effective medicine. — (4) **1800** BOUCHER *Glossary* p. l, *Fog-drams; drams* resorted to on the pretence of their protecting from the danger of fogs. — (5) **1806** *Balance* (Hudson, N.Y.) 13 May 146, I have heard of a *jorum*, of *phlegm-cutter* and *fog-driver*.

∗**fog,** *v.* Also ∗**fag.** *W. tr.* and *intr.* To attack, shoot, belabor; to go at top speed. *Slang.*

1914 D. W. ROBERTS *Rangers & Sovereignty* 10 The Rangers kept 'fogging' them until they all quit their horses. **1920** HUNTER *Trail Drivers Texas* I. 300 Moving fast is '*foggin*.' **1927** JAMES *Cow Country* 57 Being I didn't want to lose the cattle, I fogged in on them and kept 'em headed straight for the cutting-grounds. **1939** ROLLINS *Gone Haywire* 119 With that the man, 'thout speakin' to me or givin' me a chance to thank 'im, climbs on 'is bronc an' fogs it.

b. Esp. with reference to drawing a gun and going into action.

1930 RAINE & BARNES *Cattle* 133 When in doubt they played trumps; that is to say, 'came a-foggin',' not waiting for the other party to get into action. **1948** *Popular Western* June 20/2, I told you to get out of town once, or fog your guns the next time our trails crossed.

fogmatic fɔgˈmætɪk, *n.* and *a.* [Cf. ∗**fog,** *n.* **2. b.**] **1.** *n.* =**antifogmatic. 2.** *a.* Intoxicated, inebriated. Both *slang* and *obs.* — (1) **1828** COOPER *Red Rover* viii, The cordial was then very generally taken, in the British provinces, under the various names of 'bitters' 'juleps,' 'morning drams,' 'fogmatics,' etc. — (2) *a***1856** in HALL *College Words* (ed. 2) 461 A few of the various words and phrases which have been in use . . . to signify some stage of inebriation: Over the bay, . . . fogmatic, blue-eyed.

∗**fogy,** *n.* Also **fogey.** (See quots.) Also attrib. *Slang.* — **1879** *Cong. Rec.* 25 April 907 The meaning of it, then, is that the officer is to have pay allowed him computing all the time of service while in the Army . . . , in addition to what is called the fogy ration, or longevity ration? **1902** HANNOCK *Life at West Point* 215 Any officer of grade between second lieutenant and colonel receives what are known as 'fogeys.' These are ten-per-cent. increases of pay for each five years of service, and an officer who had served twenty years is entitled to four 'fogeys' of ten per cent. each.

∗**fold,** *v. intr. To fold up*, to fail, to go out of existence. *Colloq.* or *slang.* — **1939** GILBERT *Forty Yrs.* 142 The result is that young people are getting scarce along the country back roads. And the little country schools where we used to find them are folding up. **1945** *Suburban List* 8 Feb. 10/1 From the bad financial statement, it would look as though the St. J. & L.C. would have to fold up.

∗**folder,** *n.*

1. An instrument or machine that folds. Cf. **bill, paper folder.**

1846 WORCESTER 286/2 Folder . . . an instrument for folding paper, etc. **1851** MELVILLE *Moby Dick* xxxii. 155 However this one-sided horn may really be used by the Narwhale . . . it would certainly be very convenient to him for a folder in reading pamphlets. **1886** *N.Y. Herald* 27 Oct. 6/3 The press is a new Hoe perfecting machine, with a folder attached.

2. (See quot.)

1874 KNIGHT 899/1 *Folder*, . . . a form of spectacles in which the lenses fold together for the pocket, and grasp the nose by a spring bow or stiff joint when in use.

3. A sheet, pamphlet, map, etc., that folds up, freq. to pocket size. Also attrib.

1887 *Congregationalist* 14 July (*Cent.*), The Fitchburg Railroad has just issued a local folder corrected to July 5, . . . containing well-arranged time-tables, a good map, and much local information. **1908** YESLAH *Tenderfoot S. Calif.* iv. 45 That ain't no printed folder talk either. **1923** *Sears Cat.* (ed. 146) 555 A double flap slip in folder, especially designed to meet the needs of the amateur photographer.

4. A large filing envelope or cover for holding loose papers.

1911 HARRISON *Queed* 329 West went to a filing cabinet in the corner of the room, pulled out a large folder marked, Reformatory. **1918**

Sears Cat. (ed. 137) 1101 Four-Drawer Filing Cabinet. . . . Guides and folders are shown . . . at right.

∗**folding,** *a.* In combs.: (1) **folding boat,** a boat having a collapsible frame; (2) **machine,** (*a*) a machine for folding newly woven fabrics, (*b*) (see quots.); (3) **money,** paper money, *jocular.*

(1) **1872** *Pat. Off. Gazette* II. 70/2 Folding-Boat. . . . A pontoon-boat having certain fastening devices in connection with its hinged sections. **1884** *Nat. Museum Bul.* No. 27, 702 Osgood's portable folding canvas boat. — (2) (*a*) **1848** *Hunt's Merch. Mag.* XIX. 68 The end of one of the pieces of cloth . . . is put into a folding machine. (*b*) **1874** KNIGHT 899/2 *Folding-machine* . . . (Metal.) One which bends pans and tin-ware to form. **1883** ——— *Supp.* 353/2 *Folding Machine.* (Sheet Metal Working.) A machine for folding the edges of blanks preparatory to seaming . . . (Printing.) A folder attached to a perfecting printing machine. (Bookbinding.) A machine for folding sheets, signatures, or quires. — (3) **1946** *Science Digest* Aug. 23/2 The late head of a chain of drug stores got such a kick out of folding money that he sometimes carried $50,000 to $60,000 in his coat pocket. **1948** *Savings News* Nov. 13 Daddy says the airplane ride takes a lot of folding money.

foliated angler. (See quot.) *Obs.* — **1814** MITCHILL *Fishes N.Y.* 467 Foliated Angler. *Lophius foliatus.* With a leafy expansion on his dorsal rays.

folk house. A community house. *Rare.* — **1824** JEFFERSON *Writings* XVI. 46 Each ward should . . . give in at their folk-house, their votes for all functionaries reserved to their election.

folksy ˈfoksɪ, *a.* Sociable, given to associating with common people. *Colloq.* Cf. **poor folksy, poor white folksy.** — **1868** A. D WHITNEY *P. Strong's Outings* 178 So pleasant and folksy. **1948** *Chi., Aurora & Elgin Ry. Time Table* 14 June 7 Breathe clean pure air. . . . Enjoy sunshine, 'folksie' neighbors.

folle avoine. *local* [F. wild oats.] (See quot. 1871 and cf. **wild rice.**) Occas. *pl.*

1817 S. BROWN *Western Gaz.* 157 Water fowl . . . resort here to harvest the folle avoine, profusely sown by nature's hand. *Ib.* 159 [The Huron River] winds its way two or three miles through a vast meadow of *folle avoine*, in which the water is from five to seven feet deep. **1871** DE VERE 409 The Wild Rice (*Zizania aquatica*) also, although a water-plant, resembles the grasses, and especially oats, so that the early French settlers used to call it, after their home-fashion, *folles avoines.* **1945** *Nature Mag.* Nov. 465 Menomin, the good berry, is none other than wild rice, or the *folle avoine*—wild oats—of the early French explorers.

b. (*cap.*) (See quots.)

1823 BELTRAMI *Pilgrimage* (1828) II. 173, I met there some of the Menomenis, whom the French distinguish by the name of *Folle Avoine;* because, with more prudence than most other savages, they collect in summer a quantity of wild oats, which grow in great abundance upon lake Hinlin. **1941** MCDERMOTT *Glossary* 77 *Folles avoines* was also the French name for the Menominee Indians.

∗**follow,** *v.* **1. follow-me-lad(s),** (see quot. 1902). *Obs.* **2. follow-my-master,** the game of follow-my-leader.

(1) **1902** GREENOUGH & KITTREDGE *Words & Their Ways* 190 Kiss-me-quick, hug-me-tight, follow-me-lads,—names for articles of feminine attire. **1928** K. H. BROWN *Father* i, Miss Evelina Amberley, in all her frills and laces and follow-me-lads, as scalloped and frilled and fluted as her name. *Ib.* ix, The knife sawed through Aunt Euphemia's follow-me-lad, slashed out a thick chunk of somber plush. — (2) **1880** *Harper's Mag.* July 293/1 It was discovered . . . that when the girl came to spend a Saturday with her cousins, she was available for 'follow-my-master,' and even for leap-frog.

∗**folly,** *n.*

1. A term applied by Augustin Daly to a rather formless theatrical piece having many local scenes. *Obs.*

1872 *N.Y. Tribune* 25 Nov. 7/6 Augustin Daly's new local sensation 'folly,' *Round the Clock*, a grand dramatic and picturesque panorama of the realities and the fascinations of city life. **1872** *N.Y. Herald* 26 Nov. 5/3 The New 'Folly' at the Grand Opera House. . . . The word 'folly' describes the character of the piece ['Round the Clock' and] . . . is a full description of its intent and purpose. The aim of the piece is . . . to show what is the thing that we are apt to call 'life' in this city.

2. (*cap.*) *pl.* A term used as the title of a revue, esp. **Ziegfeld Follies.** (Cf. *Folies-Bergère.*)

1908 *Theatre Mag.* Aug. 201/1 In novelty of ideas, variety, talent of performers and general smartness of production, 'Follies of 1908' is fully up to the standard of the best this enterprising . . . young manager [*sc.* Ziegfeld] has yet attempted. **1916** *Chi. Tribune* 2 Oct. 19/1 It is curious to see the cameo faced Lillian Gish capering about as a dancer of the follies. **1945** *Chronicle-News* (Trinidad, Colo.) 20 Oct. 2/4 The island of Bali is just one big Ziegfeld Follies—without the box office.

∗**Folsom,** *n.* [*Folsom*, N. Mex.]

1. Folsom man, a Stone Age man thought to have lived in North America about 15,000 B.C.

1933 HARRINGTON *Gypsum Cave, Nev.* 190 [The] Late Pleistocene, 15,000 to 13,000 B.C., . . . was the day of 'Folsom man.' **1947** BROWN *Outdoors Unlimited* 183 They're still searching for the mysterious Folsom man whose distinctive weapons and other artifacts were found in New Mexico.

2. Folsom point, a flint point, probably for a javelin, thought to have been used by Folsom man.

1933 HARRINGTON *Gypsum Cave, Nev.* 176 The Texas specimens, although suggesting the Folsom points in chipping and general form,

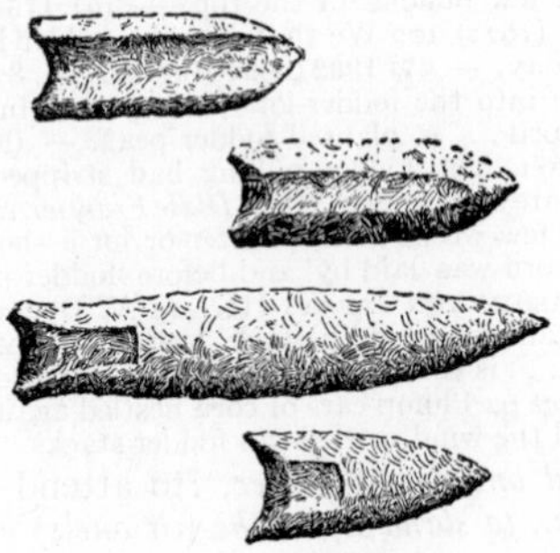

Types of Folsom points

lack this groove. **1947** *Chr. Sci. Monitor* 3 Dec. I. 4/6 Many sites are listed in Arizona, Alaska, California, Colorado, Kentucky, and New Mexico, all containing artifacts of the so-called exquisite Yuma points or Folsom points.

fonda ˈfondə, *n. S.W.* [Sp. in same sense. Also borrowed by British in S. America. See *OED.*] A hotel, restaurant or inn.

1844 GREGG *Commerce of Prairies* II. 98 Fondas, however, are mere restaurants, and consequently without accommodations for lodging. **1880** *Harper's Mag.* April 678/2 He sits on the porch of the excellent *fonda*, or lounges in one of the great arm-chairs that the editor of the *Sentinel* provides for his visitors. **1948** *Sat. Ev. Post* 18 Sep. 134/3 In that former *fonda* the mountain men and the teamsters celebrated in heroic fashion their return to civilization after months in the wilderness.

∗**food,** *n.* In combs.: (1) **food faker,** one who misrepresents foods that he makes or sells; (2) **inspection,** the inspection of food for impurities of any sort; (3) **inspector,** one who inspects food; (4) **producing,** *a.* that or who produces food; (5) **store,** a store in which food of various sorts is sold.

(1) **1915** *Lit. Digest* 21 Aug. 340/2 Fake foods for fighters. . . . The food-faker is of no particular race—his aspect is truly international. — (2) **1894** FORD *P. Stirling* 108 Then you think my views on license, and food-inspection, and tenement-house regulation are 'Deformities'? — (3) **1911** PERSONS *Mass. Labor Laws* 231 Kansas and Washington have separate inspectors of hotels, West Virginia a state fire marshal, Minnesota a food inspector, all of whom enforce laws which protect employees as well as the general public. — (4) **1870** BRYANT *Iliad* II. xiv. 59 Lay one hand Upon the food-producing earth. **1873** *Newton Kansan* 5 June 1/5 We claim to be a great food-producing people. **1892** *Vt. Agric. Rep.* XII. 142 [Washington County] is almost wholly an agricultural County, and one of the best food producing regions in the country. — (5) **1944** *Chi. D. News* 10 Jan. 9/4 A proposal to ask Chicago housewives to volunteer as saleswomen in Chicago food stores because of the labor shortage will be considered. **1948** *Ice Cream Trade Jrnl.* Sep. 22 Our whole program on ice cream originated from an address entitled 'Food Store Opportunities for Ice Cream.'

As the last term in **angel('s), breakfast, devil's, health, long, pure food.**

foo-foo ˈfuˌfu, *n.* [Origin unknown.] (See quot. 1877.)

1848 *Glance at N.Y.* 16 A foo-foo, or an outsider, is a chap that can't come the big figure. . . . The big figure here, is three cents for a glass of grog and a night's lodging. **1877** BARTLETT 229 *Foo Foo.* In New York a term of contempt, nearly equivalent to 'small potatoes,' a man not worth notice. **1881** MARK TWAIN *Prince & Pauper* xvii, A tinker shrieked out a suggestion: 'Foo-foo the First, king of the Mooncalves!'

*fool, *n.* and *a.* In combs.: (1) **fool bird,** (see quot.); (2) ***catcher,** *local* (see quot.), *slang;* (3) **duck,** the ruddy duck; (4) **fish,** see as a main entry; (5) **hay,** (see quot.); (6) **hen,** see as a main entry; (7) **killer,** (*a*) an imaginary character whose business it is to exterminate fools, *jocular,* (*b*) (see quot.), *colloq.;* (8) **proof,** *a.* designating that which is so simple and easy of operation as to be proof against stupidity and carelessness, safeguarded against accident; (9) **quail,** Mearns's quail, found in the Southwest; (10) **'s gold,** an ore resembling gold, esp. iron pyrite, also fig.; (11) **'s hill,** a fool's paradise, an adolescent, know-it-all period, esp. in *to climb over fool's hill,* also fig.; (12) **('s) water,** =**firewater 1.**

(1) **1895** *Outing* XXVII. 218/1 The spruce partridge.... The Indians call them 'fool birds,' so easily are they caught. — (2) **1920** THOMAS *Ky. Super.* 224 Do not buy tobacco of pawpaw color (motley color); it is called 'fool-catcher.' — (3) **1888** G. TRUMBULL *Names & Portraits of Birds* 111 Others at Detroit, and the 'punters' of St. Clair Flats, refer to the species [the ruddy duck] still as Fool-Duck, Deaf-Duck, and Shot-Pouch. **1917** *Birds of Amer.* I. 152 Ruddy Duck. *Erismatura jamaicensis....* Other Names.—Dumpling Duck; ... Fool Duck; Sleepy Duck.

(5) **1890** *N. & Q.* V. 101 Certain kinds of grass ... in the far West produce such light hay (in proportion to its great bulk) that their product is called fool hay by the ranchmen, because they are fooled or deceived in estimating its weight. — (7) (*a*) **1853** P. KENNEDY *Blackwater Chron.* iv. 44 What a fool-killer he would make! **1948** *Ga. Review* Spring 91 Yet by evening, the greatest Fool Killer Known in the State let his zeal subside. (*b*) **1947** *Harper's Mag.* July 80/1 A fool-killer, equally dangerous, was a live tree bent over by a fallen one so that when an unwary chopper drove an axe into it the tremendous tension, suddenly released, sent the tree splitting and charging up to catch him under the chin. — (8) **1902** A. C. HARMSWORTH *Motors & Motor-driving* 309 The car ... is comparatively 'fool-proof.' **1947** *Coronet* July 37/2 Meanwhile, our troops in Europe were having trouble with a supposedly foolproof signaling device. — (9) **1936** *Univ. Ariz. Gen. Bul.* No. 3, 85 Its black and white clownlike face might be thought responsible for its designation as the 'fool quail,' but in reality this term comes from its complete faith in the efficacy of its hiding.

(10) **1872** *Harper's Mag.* Dec. 23/1 A lump of the glittering yellow 'fool's-gold' is often called quartz by unlearned miners, while the same name is commonly applied to the pay rock, heavy with the cubic pyrites, by those who should know better. **1945** BAKER *Party Line* 200, I think she divined intuitively that there was more than fool's gold to the glitter of Claudia Bilberry. **1948** *Life* 2 Feb. 49/1 Prospectors waited to discover whether they had hit pay dirt or 'fool's gold,' the shiny but worthless iron pyrites. — (11) **1882** *Cong. Rec.* 12 April 2825/2 Wise statesmen ... led her [England] down from 'fool's hill.' **1923** J. H. COOK *On Old Frontier* 137, I had climbed almost over Fool's Hill, after groping in ignorance for quite a period in my earlier years. — (12) **1837** WETMORE *Gaz. Missouri* 290 The disturber, ... by the Indians appropriately named 'fire-water,' and more emphatically 'fool-water,' was happily beyond their reach. **1846** SAGE *Scenes Rocky Mts.* (1859) xv. 172 Alcohol has received from the Crows, the appellation of 'Fool's Water,' a term at once attesting their nice moral discernment and good sense.

b. *A fool for luck,* one regarded as exceptionally lucky. *Colloq.*

1875 *Chi. Tribune* 8 Dec. 1/4 (*headline*), A Fool for Luck.

***fool,** *v.* In phrases: (1) *to fool along,* to proceed or move aimlessly; (2) *to fool (a)round,* (*a*) to hang around or near (a girl), (*b*) to hang around idly or aimlessly, to waste time *with;* (3) *to fool around the stump,* to beat around the bush.

(1) **1866** C. H. SMITH *Bill Arp* 44 You get a government contract for a few thousand pounds and you fool along with it, selling what you make to these drug men at a bigger price. **1934** VINES *Green Thicket World* 20 They fooled along and did not much try to reach the ferryman's house. — (2) (*a*) **1887** A. GREENE *Glance at N.Y.* (F.), He mustn't come foolin' round my gal, or I'll give him fits. **1896** WILKINS *Madelon* 102 He used to fool 'round her ... afore he went courtin' the parson's gal. (*b*) **1870** MARK TWAIN in *Galaxy* May 726/2 Nell, what did Abel come fooling around there for? **1921** PAINE *Comr. Rolling Ocean* 129, I fooled around with Bert Maddigan after declaring myself in favor of using violence on him. **1942** WARNICK *Dialect Garrett Co., Md.* 7 Fooling around, v. phr., wasting time. — (3) **1880** *Scribner's Mo.* XIX. 428/2 Thar aint no use in foolin' round the stump! ... I might jest as well come out with it, plain an' squar!

Fooley Ann. A kind of card game. *Obs.* — **1897** S. HALE *Letters* 307, I was sitting in my red bear, playing Fooley Ann. *Ib.* 314 As in Fooley Ann, you wonder what card near the bottom of the thirteen it will be to come to the rescue and win the game.

foolfish ˈfulˌfɪʃ, *n.*

1. Any one of various filefish.

1842 *Nat. Hist. N.Y., Zoology* IV. 335 The Long-finned File-fish. *Monocanthus broccus....* Our fishermen apply to it the whimsical name of Fool-fish, in allusion to what they consider its absurd mode of swimming. **1878** *Nat. Museum Proc.* I. 367 *Alutera cuspicauda....* Fool-fish. Rather common in Beaufort Harbor. Numerous specimens obtained. **1884** GOODE *Fisheries* I. 171 The Orange File Fish, *Alutera Schoepfii,* also called 'Barnacle-eater' and 'Fool Fish,' ... is rather common in Southern New England.

2. The winter flounder, *Pleuronectes glaber.*

1884 GOODE *Fisheries* I. 183 At Salem ... they [smooth flounders] are also called 'Fool Fish,' because, in their anxiety for food, they will bite at any kind of bait, even at a rag. **1885** KINGSLEY *Riverside Nat. Hist.* III. 279 The *Pleuronectes glaber* ... is called fool-fish at Salem, because they are easily decoyed and bite even at a rag.

fool hen. Any one of various grouse or quail which are remarkably unsuspicious and hence easily killed.

[**1838** PARKER *Exploring Tour* 116, I saw ... a new species of pheasant.... It is remarkably tame, as if unacquainted with enemies; and when assailed with stones by the Indians, appeared to be amazed, and made scarcely any effort to escape.] **1877** STANLEY *Rambles in Wonderland* 144 They will often sit or run by the roadside and the driver slays them with his whip, or knocks them over with a club. From this remarkable trait they are frequently known as 'fool-hens'—a suggestive title. **1912** WHEELER *Selkirk Mts.* 176 Immediately below is the habitat of Franklin's Grouse (*Dendrogapus franklinii*), the 'fool-hen' of the prospector and so called because it sits complacently on a branch until killed by a stick or a stone. **1945** MATHEWS *Talking* 112 Immature quail ... are ... like the dusky grouse in the Rockies called by the natives 'fool hens.'

attrib. **1880** *Rep. Supt. Yellowstone Nat. Pk.* (1881) 43 The fool-hen variety of the grouse is numerous around the margins of hot springs.

***foot,** *n.*

1. The bottom of, or the lowest place in, a class, section, division, etc. Cf. **4.** (4) below, and see **going foot,** *s.v.* ***going,** and ***head,** *n.* **6.**

1833 in *PMLA* LVI. (June, 1941) 499 You, Miss, must lose a day or two, and then find yourself at the foot with those blockhead boys who always abide there. **1862** G. C. STRONG *Cadet Life at West Point* 85 They sent me to the board to discuss the subject of cubic equations. I *fessed* cold, and was thereby thrown to the foot of the second section. **1946** *Chi. D. News* 28 March 10/5 Our son is in the third grade and is neither at the head nor the foot of his class.

2. *W.* In mining, twelve inches in length on the lode, regardless of its width, and extending its entire depth toward the center of the earth.

1860 *No. Californian* (Arcata) 30 May 2/3 The claims that I owned are not worth a straw, although parties in them sold ground adjoining for fifty dollars a foot. **1913** GOODWIN *As I Remember Them* 234 'Sandy' Bowers, an illiterate and uncouth man in many ways, a rough miner, also owned twenty feet of the Gold Hill ground. **1947** CHALFANT *Gold, Guns, & Ghost Towns* 61 Mines in those days were held in terms of feet rather than shares.

fig. **1878** *Cherry Creek* (Nev.) *Independent* 24 Feb. 1/1 Tommy, the bootblack ... got feet in the Sweet By-and-By and sold for twenty thousand.

3. In combs.: (1) ***footboard,** (*a*) a board set across the lower end of a door opening, *rare;* (*b*) (see quot. 1864); (2) **box,** a box on which one sets the foot for the cleaning or polishing of one's shoes; (3) **cavalry,** in the Civil War, a term applied to the infantry command of "Stonewall" Jackson, because of its extraordinary rapidity of movement in the Shenandoah campaign of 1862; (4) **evil,** a disease affecting the feet of cattle, horses, etc.; (5) ***gin,** a form of cotton gin operated by foot power, *obs.;* (6) **hill,** a hill at the foot of a mountain or mountain range, usu. *pl.,* also attrib.; (7) ***hold,** (see quot. 1889); (8) **log,** a log across a stream, ravine, etc., used as a foot bridge, also fig.; (9) **muff,** (see quot. 1847); (10) **scraper,** a metal device for scraping dirt and mud from the feet before entering a house, freq. attached to a step [the *OED* records *scraper* in this sense 1792——]; (11) **screw,** (see quot. 1889); (12) **trail,** a trail formed and used by persons on foot; (13) ***washing,** an occasion upon which Primitive Baptists wash each other's feet as a religious memorial; (14) **washing Baptist,** a member of any one of several sects of Baptists who practice foot washing; (15) **wear,** wearing apparel for the feet, esp. shoes, rubbers, boots, etc., *colloq.;* (16) **wheel,** (*a*) a form of spinning wheel operated by a treadle, (*b*) a wheel at the front end of a harrow, etc., which regulates the depth of the cultivation, see **wheel cultivator.**

(1) (*a*) **1850** *Knickerb.* XXXVI. 73 The door opened. A high foot-board was nailed against its lower part, as if to keep toddling babies in. (*b*) **1864** WEBSTER 530 *Foot-board.* . . . The platform on which the driver and fireman of a locomotive stand; a foot-plate. **1883** FULTON *Sam Hobart* 83 The Brotherhood of Locomotive Engineers . . . had 13,000 . . . was formed in the city of Detroit in August, 1863, as the Brotherhood of the Footboard. **1898** *McClure's Mag.* X. 362, I set the cans upon the footboard. — (2) **1861** *Vanity Fair* 23 March 133/1 A newly built fire roaring in a stove, . . . not far from the size of an exaggerated foot-box, . . . emboldened him to believe that other forms of civilization must be near by. **1887** *Cent. Mag.* XXXIV. 724/1 An English detective is described as having disguised himself as a bootblack and hidden a camera in a foot-box. — (3) **1877** BAGBY *Old Va. Gentleman* 106 He joined the army, became one of

Common type of foot scraper

Jackson's 'foot cavalry,' was in the great campaign of the Valley. **1917** MORGAN *Recollections* 84, I found him flushed with victory, having just returned from the marvelous Shenandoah Valley campaign in which Jackson had fought so many battles in so few weeks, and he seemed very proud to belong to Jackson's 'foot cavalry.' — (4) **1845** FRÉMONT *Exped.* 259 Many animals are destroyed . . . by a disease called the foot evil. **1868** *Ill. Agric. Soc. Trans.* VII. 144 The disease known to stock-growers as foot evil, or foules, to which our native cattle are occasionally liable.

(5) **1802** J. DRAYTON *S. Carolina* 133 Foot gins are worked with cranks, by a foot board, or treadle, almost resembling a turner's lathe. . . . A negro will gin from twenty to twenty five pounds of clean black seed cotton in a day. **1862** *N.Y. Tribune* 19 Feb. 6/5 The ginning . . . is done either by gins operated by steam or by the well-known foot gins. — (6) **1850** *Western Star* (Milwaukie, Ore.) 21 Nov. 3/2 The most productive portions, the past season, have been in the foot-hills. **1912** *Out West* April 274/1 In the beginning of the development of the state the peculiar attractiveness and richness of the slopes near the foot of the mountains, 'the foothill country,' became known and grew in appreciation. **1948** *Pacific Discovery* March–April 10/2, I went to Cabezon . . . , then up Millard Creek Canyon into the foot-hills of the San Bernardino Mountains to the north. — (7) **1889** *Cent.* 2311/2 *foothold.* . . . A kind of light india-rubber overshoe, leaving the heel unprotected; a sandal. Sometimes called *tip.* **1914** *Sears Cat.* (ed. 129) 377 Profile. First Quality. Women's Foothold. — (8) *c***1845** *Big Bear Ark.* 130, I husseled off to the hossin-gum and Jem to the foot log. **1902** HARBEN *A. Daniel* 73 Alan . . . don't have to walk any particular kind o' foot-log to do his work. **1945** BOTKIN *My Burden* 252 Go to the mill and cross on a foot log. — (9) **1847** WEBSTER *Foot-muff,* a receptacle for the feet, lined with fur, &c. **1856** KANE *Arctic Explor.* I. 183 [The fox] was coiled up, with his nose buried in his bushy tail, like a fancy foot-muff. **1876** S. & A. WARNER *Gold of Chickaree* 211 Then she ran down the steps after her old friend, and gave little finishing touches to his comfort in the shape of a foot-muff.

(10) **1872** FLAGG *Good Investment* xii. 547/2 Foot-scrapers and mats were doubled at all the approaches. **1902** *Sears Cat.* (ed. 112) 738 Extra Heavy Unbreakable Foot Scraper. The best and strongest foot scraper we have ever seen. — (11) **1856** WHIPPLE *Explor. Ry. Route* I. 54 Upon three foot-screws rests a circular base, to which are attached, by movable screws, the vertical uprights forming the Y's [of the transit]. **1889** *Cent.* 2313/1 *Foot-screw,* . . . an adjusting-screw fitted to the leg of a table or bench, to bring the surface of the table to a perfectly horizontal position. — (12) **1848** BRYANT *California* xvii. 219 We crossed an Indian foot-trail. **1903** AUSTIN *Land of Little Rain* 41 The immemorial foot trail goes up from Saline Flat toward Black Mountain. — (13) **1943** *Nat. Geog. Mag.* Dec. 768/1 One of the most interesting services is the 'foot washin' ' of the Primitive Baptists. This ceremony takes place once a year. **1946** WILSON *Fidelity* 101 We kept up attendance rather well, unless the young people wanted to go in a farm wagon up the creek to a foot-washing at a Primitive Baptist church. — (14) **1872** *Cong. Globe* App. 30 May 478/3, I belong now to the Foot-washing Baptists—the simplest form of the Christian faith. **1888** J. WALLACE *Carpetbag Rule in Fla.* 226 The freedmen prior to the emancipation knew nothing of any other churches than the Missionary Baptist, Primitive or foot-washing Baptists, and the Methodist Episcopal.

(15) **1881** *Chi. Times* 11 June, If values were based upon present quotations of leather, an advance would be necessary upon several descriptions of foot-wear. **1910** W. BORSODI *Footwear Advertising* 9 The men and women wishing footwear of the most correct and dressy character will appreciate Wanamaker $5 shoes. — (16) (*a*) **1783** E. PARKMAN *Diary* 299 One large wheel 2/8 two foot wheels 6/. **1841** *Knickerb.* XVIII. 216 He will find . . . the grandame . . . turning the footwheel, less for gain than as a thrifty pastime. (*b*) **1839** BUEL *Farmer's Companion* 206 The foot-wheel [on a harrow] is to regulate the depth of the work.

b. In less frequent or rare combs.: (1) **foot bound,** the lower boundary of a tract or area; (2) **breeches,** ?trousers that fit snugly below the knee; (3) **burner,** one who tortures another by burning the bottoms of his feet; (4) **casing,** a footwall; (5) **causey,** a paved footpath; (6) **curtain,** a curtain for the foot of a bed; (7) **doctor,** a chiropodist; (8) **front,** =**front foot;** (9) **grating,** a grating that can be walked upon; (10) **-hills yellow pine,** (see quot.); (11) **Indians,** (see quot.); (12) **ladder,** ?a stationary ladder with flat steps; (13) **organ,** a key-board instrument played with the feet to supply the bass to a pianoforte; (14) **people,** people who travel on foot; (15) **washer,** =**foot washing Baptist.**

(1) **1679** *Plymouth Rec.* 161 The brook being the foote bounds of the said-land. — (2) **1917** KEPHART *Camping* I. 144 To wear with leggings the 'foot breeches' of our infantry . . . fit better than trousers that must be lapped over. — (3) **1896** O. READ *Jucklins* 27 A lot of foot-burners come to my house one night durin' the war and took me out and told me that if I didn't give them my money they would roast my shanks. — (4) **1873** MARK TWAIN & WARNER *Gilded Age* lxii. 561 Where coal is, limestone with these fossils in it is pretty certain to lie against its foot-casing.

(5) **1649** *Conn. H.S. Coll.* VI. 89 There shall bee a foot Causy made from ye Dwelling howse of George Steele along in the highway to the great Bridge. — (6) **1886** *Cent. Mag.* Feb. 583/2 High feather beds, with blue and white checked foot-curtains concealing the unpainted pine posts of the bedsteads. — (7) **1870** TOMES *Decorum* 70 The employment of a skillful and judicious shoemaker . . . will prevent all occasion for consulting the *pedicure,* or foot-doctor. — (8) **1818** *Niles' Reg.* XIV. 152/1 It cost $1000 a foot front, being already covered with fine buildings. — (9) **1847** *Knickerb.* XXX. 456 He has been inspired by looking down through the iron foot-grating of a great lake-steamer.

(10) **1897** SUDWORTH *Arborescent Flora* 20 *Pinus ponderosa,* Bull Pine. . . . Common Names. . . . Foothills Yellow Pine (*P. Benthamiana*). — (11) **1879** WILLIAMS *Pacific Tourist* 88/1 'Foot Indians,' those which inhabit the plains, and are peaceable, most invariably bury their dead in the ground. — (12) **1838** *Yale Lit. Mag.* III. 7 A loft of second story . . . was gained by a foot ladder. — (13) **1802** CUTLER in *Life & Corr.* II. 60 The foot organ is a prodigious addition to Forte-Pianoes. — (14) **1806** PIKE *Sources Miss.* (1810) 114 My Indians and foot people were yet in the rear. **1850** JUDD *R. Edney* i. 14 Wagons are driven faster, and foot-people increase their momentum.

(15) **1934** CARMER *Stars Fell* 63 Each of the footwashers was unlacing the left shoe of the person he faced.

c. Also in combs. to designate shackles for the feet, as **foot bolt, cuff, hobble, irons, lock.**

*a***1811** HENRY *Camp Quebec* 162 It became his lot to have an immense foot-bolt fastened to his leg. — **1856** KANE *Arctic Explor.* II. 111, I placed a pair of foot-cuffs on Metch's sledge. — *a***1811** HENRY *Camp. Quebec* 162 Long and weighty irons; such as bilboes, foot-hobbles and hand-cuffs. — **1835** COOPER *Monikins* viii, It was self-evident a man would jump farther without being in foot-irons. — **1763** *Essex Inst. Coll.* XLIX. 140 [The escaped prisoner] had on when he went away, Part of a Chain and Foot Lock.

4. In colloq. phrases: (1) *To be at foot-ball,* to be equals or on an equal footing, *obs.;* (2) *on foot,* of cattle, on the hoof; (3) *to get one's foot in,* to get a start in; (4) *to begin foot, to go (to the) foot,* to begin at, to go to, the bottom or foot of a class; (5) *to have foot for,* of horses, to be adaptable to.

(1) **1711** SEWALL *Diary* II. 303 Mr. Bridgham declining to sign, saying it was not fit for him to sign with persons so much above him; I said pleasantly, We are at Foot-ball now; and then he presently Sign'd. **1711** *N.C. Col. Rec.* I. 770 [These people in N.C.] think there is no difference between a Gentleman and a labourer all fellows at Foot Ball. — (2) **1794** *Ky. Gazette* VIII. 25 Oct. 3/3, I will enter into contracts for Beef-Cattle or Pork, On Foot, delivered at Fort Washington or this place. **1846** MCKENNEY *Memoirs* I. 217 Beef could be purchased in Missouri and Illinois, on foot, at from one dollar to one dollar and fifty cents per hundred pounds. — (3) **1815** HUMPHREYS *Yankey in Eng.* 49 Let's try now to tune my pipes and kick up a dust, to git my foot in. — (4) **1843** *Amer. Pioneer* II. 456 Having missed the evening's spelling I always began foot, but that did not annoy me, nor prevent me from ending head, when the mile must again be run over to dinner, and I to my work. **1903** G. C. EGGLESTON *First of Hoosiers* 45 At the close of the exercise the scholar who stood at the head of the class was assigned to the foot of it for the next day, and a record was kept of the number of times that each had 'gone foot.' **1946** *Chi. D. News* 18 March 8/3 Go to the foot of the class, Mr. Principal. — (5) **1852** BRISTED *Upper Ten Th.* i. 26 His nag has less foot for a brush than the pacer.

As the last term in **acre, athlete's, bare, black, board, bull's, cat, cat's, claw, deer, duck's, Englishman's, flat, front, fumble, horse, hot, lion's, mule, pay, pussy, rabbit, single, slew, sling, tangle, under, wash, web, white man's foot.**

* **footage,** *n.*

1. In moving pictures, the length in linear feet of film used in photographing a scene, subject, etc. Also attrib.

1916 B. M. BOWER *Phantom Herd* ii. 22 He visualized a stampede and the probable amount of footage it would require. **1918** H. CROY *How Motion Pictures are Made* v. 128 Directors . . . craftily working to keep the production expense as low as possible, do not altogether forget the footage possibilities of an exterior love scene. *Ib.* vi. 150 The amounts are added up and a footage rate determined.

2. The aggregate of board feet in a given amount of timber or lumber.

1927 KNIGHT & WULPI *Veneers and Plywood* 189 The customary way of measuring is to turn two sheets at a time and measure with tape from edge to edge, later computing the total footage. **1948** *Sat. Ev. Post* 24 Jan. 44/3 These teams . . . are paid by the footage they fall.

***footed,** *a.* As the last term in **claw, flat, mule, pussy-, single footed.**

***footer,** *n.* As the last term in **cold, pussy, single, ten footer.**

***foozle,** *v. intr.* To fool *around with* a girl. *Slang. Rare.* — **1861** STOWE *Pearl Orr's Isl.* II. xii. 106 Sally Kittridge may think he's goin' to have her because he's been foozling round with her all summer.

* **forage,** *n.* **1. forage bag,** a bag in which forage may be collected and carried. *Obs.* **2. forage poisoning,** staggers, a disease of animals caused by spoiled fodder.

(1) **1779** *N.J. Archives* 2 Ser. III. 408 Others now in the service, have in their possession waggons, horses, tents, waggon covers, forrage bags, etc. **1823** JAMES *Exped.* II. 114 Our outfit comprised . . . forage-bags, canteens, bullet-pouches [etc.]. — (2) **1942** RAWLINGS *C. Creek* 338 The veterinarian identified the trouble as forage poisoning. . . . The poison is like the rust on wheat or corn and grows sometimes on the marsh grass in puffy black balls. . . . Its substance is ergot.

* **force,** *n.*

1. Any group of workers engaged in a common task, esp. (*S.*) the body of Negro slaves in the service of an estate or plantation. *Obs.*

1807 JANSON *Stranger in Amer.* 309 Force, is here applied when speaking of the number of slaves employed in field labour on each plantation. **1837** MARTINEAU *Society* I. 344 All the 'force' that could be collected on a hasty summons,—that is, almost every able-bodied man in the city and neighbourhood, was sent out with axes to build us a bridge. **1899** *Mo. So. Dakotan* I. 138 A high wind . . . showered down hundreds of bushels of apples, [and] one is confronted by the alternative of sending for the 'force' to pick them up on Sunday or letting the sun scald and ruin them.

fig. **1881** *Nation* 16 June 415/2 'Taking the command of his forces' means hiring a bedroom in a hotel and sallying out from it to ask members of the Legislature for their votes.

2. (See quot. 1881.)

1864 W. B. DICK *Amer. Hoyle* (1866) 414 Too many beginners, in their haste to play like adepts, disdain the practice of these strokes and jump at once to twisting shots, forces, jumps, and even massés. **1881** COLLENDER *Mod. Billiards* 23 *Draw, or Force.*—Striking the cue ball one-half or more below its centre, causing it, if played full at the object-ball, to recoil or return toward the player.

3. force bill, a name popularly applied to several bills passed by, or introduced in, Congress:

a. A bill (made law March 2, 1833) empowering President Jackson to use the Army and the Navy for enforcing tariff laws in South Carolina. See **Bloody Bill.**

1833 *Cong. Deb.* 27 Feb. 1818 He was pledged to meet this force bill fairly and openly, and he should do it. **1872** *Cong. Globe* 2 April 2110/1 [Henry Clay] proposed in the tariff bill to hold out the olive branch of peace to South Carolina, and in the 'force bill' to hold out the sword. **1913** A. C. COLE *Whig Party in So.* 22 Jackson . . . had requested further provision for carrying out the principles laid down in his proclamation, out of which grew the force bill or 'bloody bill.'

b. One of the various bills of the Reconstruction period intended to enforce the Fourteenth and Fifteenth amendments, stop the activities of the Ku-Klux Klan, etc.

1871 *Nation* 20 April XII. 268/1 The Force Bill. . . . In passing the statute popularly known as the Ku-klux Bill, Congress has confessedly entered upon a new field of legislation. **1903–4** *Encycl. Amer.* VII. *s.v.*, *Force Bill*, a popular name in the United States for four different congressional bills, used at the time of their passage; all aimed at the South, and intended to suppress by national force direct or indirect nullification of national laws.

c. One of various election bills purporting to keep order at the polls.

1890 *Cong. Rec.* 23 Aug. 9092/2 What relief do you propose to give the negro? You propose to give him the force bill. **1948** *Time* 11 Oct. 24/3 These were the 'fo'ce bills' which he denounced.

As the last term in **day, detective, hoe, office, section force.** Also **liquor forces.**

* **force,** *v.*

1. *Baseball. tr.* To put out (a base-runner) who is compelled to leave his base by an advancing runner, in full *to force out* (see quot. 1867).

[**1867** CHADWICK *Base Ball Reference* 138 You are forced to leave a base either when all are occupied, and you stand on any one of the bases when the striker hits a fair ball, or when you are on the first base and a fair ball is struck.] **1870** *N.Y. Herald* 5 July 8/3 Pike reached first, but was forced out at second by McDonald. **1900** *Chi. Times-Herald* 5 May 10/1 When Garvin forced Tim at second Clingman came home. **1902** *Chi. Record-Herald* 2 Sep. 8/5 Strang was then forced out by Jones. **1948** *Green Bay* (Wis.) *Press-Gazette* 30 June 11/1 Pantos was forced at third by Jack Tree's ground ball to that base.

b. Of a pitcher: To compel a runner to score by walking or hitting a batter when the bases are full.

1904 *St. Louis Globe-Democrat* 4 July 12/3 Rhoades was kind enough to force the only run the Browns got over the plate by hitting Padden.

2. (See quot. 1870.)

1870 MEDBERY *Men Wall St.* 135 Forcing Quotations, is where brokers wish to keep up the price of stock, and to prevent its falling out of sight. This is generally accomplished by a small sale, or by 'washing.' **1900** NELSON *A B C Wall St.* 142.

3. *Baseball.* In noun combs.: (1) **force-off,** =**force play;** (2) **out,** a play in which a runner is put out during a force play, in full **force-out play;** (3) **play,** also **forced play,** a play in which a runner, forced off his base, may be put out in his attempt to reach the next base, also transf.

(1) **1885** CHADWICK *Art of Pitching* 72 Should there be runners on first as well as second base when such a ball is hit, however, the pitcher should . . . throw the ball to the third baseman so as to insure the 'force off.' **1886** —— *Art of Batting* 28 In the case of a chance for a catch, purposely missed in order to secure a chance for a double play from a 'force off,' no error should be charged. — (2) **1896** CHADWICK *Spalding's Base B. Guide* 76 The result being a force-out play to second, if not a double play. **1926** *N.Y. Times* 11 Oct. 24/1 His grounder to Bell was turned into a forceout of Ruth at second while Combs dashed on to third. — (3) **1897** A. H. LEWIS *Wolfville* 91 It's a forced play, I tells you. . . . Them Injuns has us treed. It's a case of fight or give up. **1912** MATHEWSON *Pitching* 136 Doyle, thinking that they were trying for a force play, increased his efforts to reach second.

* **forced,** *a.* In combs.: (1) **forced play,** see * **force,** *v.* **3.** (3); (2) **run,** (see quot.); (3) **sale,** (see quot. 1891); (4) **trade,** (see quot.).

(2) **1916** BANCROFT *Handbook* 80 Forced run. The forcing of a runner who is waiting on first, second, or third bases, to go forward to the next base by the coming to his base of another runner, it being against the rules for more than one runner to be on a base at once. — (3) **1848** *Hunt's Merch. Mag.* XX. (1849) 223 Forced sales in foreign markets . . . cannot be taken as the true market value of such goods.

1891 *Cent.* 5311/1 *Forced sale,* a sale compelled by a creditor or other claimant, without regard to the interest of the owner to be favored with delay in order to secure a full price. — (4) **1851** CIST *Cincinnati* 320 The forced trade, that is, the portion which comes not upon order, but is the unsold stock of the manufactures, to be forced without limit—goes to the most noted sale point.

forceps-tail. The scorpion fly. *Rare.* — **1867** *Amer. Naturalist* I. 279 The Forceps-tail, or Panorpa, *P. rufescens,* . . . is found in bushy fields and shrubbery.

* **forcing house.** *fig.* A house where ideas or literary talent may be nurtured. *Obs.*

1866 LOWELL *My Study Windows* 210 There is hardly enough fervor of political life there [in England] at present to ripen anything but the fruits of the literary forcing-houses, so fair outwardly and so flavorless. **1867** LACKLAND *Homespun* II. 173 The wits of Charles the Second's time . . . were wont to make of the tavern their council chamber; and at length it became a forcing-house for all the sayings . . . that delighted the town or provoked to reading. **1884** LOWELL *On Democracy* 13 Perhaps the best forcing-house of robust individuality would be where public opinion is inclined to be most overbearing.

ford way. A road or way across a ford.

1672 *Groton Rec.* 169 Above the foord way upward on the east sid of the brook to the pond. **1721** in TEMPLE & SHELDON *Hist. Northfield, Mass.* 223 On Dry brook, between Deerfield and Northfield, beginning 20 rods west of the fordway. **1858** REDFIELD *Law Railways* (1869) I. 231 Where a ford-way was destroyed by the erection of a dam across a river . . . it was held the owner of the ford-way could recover no compensation from the state.

* **fore,** *a.* and *adv.* In combs.: (1) **fore alley,** a passage in front of the pulpit in a meeting house, *obs.;* (2) * **-and-aft,** see as a main entry; (3) * **-and-after,** see as a main entry; (4) **beam,** (see quot.); (5) **closable,** *a.* subject to foreclosure, *colloq.;* (6) * **father,** see as a main entry; (7) **gad,** see **gad;** (8) * **gate,** the wagon gate in the front end of a wagon body, *rare,* cf. **tail gate;** (9) * **goer,** the lead dog in a dog team, *rare;* (10) * **gone,** a forefather, *rare;* (11) **handedly,** *adv.* with forehandedness; (12) **handedness,** the quality of being forehanded; (13) **hopple,** (see quot.); (14) **lady,** a forewoman; (15) **log,** = **forestick;** (16) **pay,** one who pays in advance, *colloq.;* (17) * **runner,** (see quot.); (18) **starling,** (see quot.); (19) **stick,** the log in the front part of a hearth fire; (20) * **top,** the driver's seat on top of a vehicle, *obs.*

(1) 1716 SEWALL *Diary* III. 102 Lord's Day. . . . William Brown and Elizabeth his wife . . . stood in the Fore-Ally and were admitted, confessing their Sin of Fornication. — **(4) 1874** KNIGHT 904/2 *Fore-beam,* (Weaving,) the breast-beam of a loom.

(5) 1890 *Harper's Mag.* June 154/2 A highly foreclosable mortgage in stock. **1892** *Nation* 1 Dec. 407/2 We in the United States continue to regard railroad bonds as foreclosable. — **(8) 1845** HOOPER *Taking Census* (1928) 119 The quizzical face of our old friend, projecting over the fore-gate of his wagon. — **(9) 1892** *Harper's Mag.* March 505/1 The leader, or foregoer, is always the best of the team. The dog next to him is called the steady dog.

(10) 1863 *Ill. Agric. Soc. Trans.* V. 866 The toils of pioneer life of our foregones. — **(11) 1930** MARK SULLIVAN *Our Times* iii. 12 An engineer in charge forehandedly took a coffin to the Isthmus with him. — **(12) 1840** DANA *Two Years* xxxvii. 478 Regular habits, forehandedness (if I may use the word) in worldly affairs, and hours reclaimed from indolence and vice . . . follow in the wake of the converted man. **1905** *Springfield W. Republican* 8 Dec. 1 The attempt that is being made to persuade people to do their Christmas shopping early appears to be making headway. Such forehandedness is in the interest of the buyers as well as the clerks. — **(13) 1844** GREGG *Commerce of Prairies* I. 63 The 'fore-hopple' (a leather strap or rope manacle upon the fore legs) . . . was more frequently used. — **(14) 1889** FARMER 250/2. **1891** *Boston Journal* 13 Aug. 2/3 A Buffalo newspaper speaks politely of the 'forelady' of a factory. **1923** WATTS *L. Nichols* 191 She had advanced . . . grade by grade of unflinching attention to . . . the position of forewoman—again, pardon!—of forelady at Stein and Merkel's.

(15) 1868 BEECHER *Norwood* 143 Barton was looking at the coals under the fore-log. **1883** E. H. ROLLINS *N. Eng. Bygones* 68 [The backlogs] were buried in embers and then supplemented with fore-logs. — **(16) 1859** BARTLETT 159 *Fore Pay.* 'There are two bad paymasters, no pay and fore pay.' This proverbial expression is frequently heard in the West. — **(17) 1884** GOODE *Fisheries* I. 608 [The hickory shad, *Clupea mediocris*] is in some rivers called a 'Forerunner,' from the fact that it makes its appearance shortly before the Shad. — **(18) 1874** KNIGHT 905/1 *Fore-starling,* an ice-breaker in advance of the starling of a bridge. — **(19) 1793** *Mass. Spy* 7 March 3/2 He found his companion lying in a large body of live coals, her head on the backlog and knees on the forestick. **1888** J. Q. BITTINGER *Hist. Haverhill* (N.H.) 356 The large stick back was called the 'back-log,' . . . On this was placed a 'top-stick,' and in front the 'fore-stick.'

(20) 1850 TAYLOR *Eldorado* xliii, One has to face the cold from the foretop of a diligence. **1869** MARK TWAIN *Innocents* xii. 106 It was worth a lifetime of city toiling and moiling, to perch in the foretop with the driver and see the six mustangs scamper.

* **fore-and-aft,** *a.*

1. *transf.* Placed or running lengthwise.

1868 MARK TWAIN *Sk., New & Old* 289 The last grand charge . . . had broken the fore-and-aft shaft of the driving-wheel [of the locomotive]! **1880** ——— *Tramp Abroad* xxxi. 329 It was the fore-and-aft gear that was broken—the thing that leads aft from the forward part of the horse and is made fast to the thing that pulls the wagon. **1883** *Harper's Mag.* Oct. 726/2 The fore and aft rake of his cap.

2. In special combs.: (1) **fore-and-aft road,** (see quot.); (2) **schooner,** a schooner having fore-and-aft sails; (3) **tree,** (see quot.); (4) **wagon,** a prairie schooner (cf. quot. 1887 *s.v.* * **fore-and-after 1**).

(1) 1905 *Forestry Bureau Bul.* No. 61, 37 *Fore-and-aft road,* a skid road made of logs placed parallel to its direction, making the road resemble a chute. (P[acific] C[oast] F[orest].) — **(2) 1856** *Farmer's Mag.* Nov. 26 The Dean Richmond [from U.S.A. at Liverpool] is a fore-and-aft schooner. **1904–5** *Encycl Amer.* XIV. *s.v. Ship building,* The fore-and-aft schooner has always been a favorite type of ship in the American merchant trade, whether coasting or deep-sea. — **(3) 1917** KEPHART *Camping* II. 66 All trees that stand directly on the line of survey have two chops or notches cut on each side of them, without any other marks whatever. These are called 'sight trees' or 'line trees' (sometimes 'fore and aft trees'). — **(4) 1877** *So. Atlantic* (Wilmington, N.C.) I. 61 James Farley, whose whiskey, put up in his own mountain-made barrels and casks, and stamped with his brand, often crossed the mountains in the immense 'fore-and-aft' wagons of the period.

* **fore-and-after,** *n.*

1. = **fore-and-aft schooner.**

1823 COOPER *Pioneer* xv, I went a few trips in a fore-and-after. **1887** CUSTER *Tenting on Plains* 352 The great army wagons called prairie schooners . . . were well named, as the two ends of the wagon inclined upward, like the bow and stern of a fore-and-after. **1891** *Scribner's Mag.* X. 781 The big 'fore-and-after' now showing a torch-light, rushed at almost ten-knot speed across the bows of the propeller.

2. A kind of dance. *Obs.*

1841 *S. Lit. Messenger* VII. 762/2 The fiddler would be sawing away for life and death, and two or three couple in the floor—men and women—dancing fore and after. *Ib.* 768/2, I was one of six sailors and women in a regular fore and after. **1848** JUDSON *Mysteries N.Y.* I. 60 Cotillions, fore-and-afters, reels, and waltzes were danced.

* **forefather,** *n.*

1. (*cap.*) *pl.* The original settlers of Plymouth colony (see also quot. 1849). Cf. **Pilgrim forefathers.**

1736 PRINCE *Chron. Hist. N.-Eng.* A4v May You ever keep in View the Principal and Noble Ends of these [New England] Religious Settlements So will you be with your Dear Forefathers, an eternal excellence. **1849** in *Pub. Col. Soc.* XVII. 363 By all the historians of New England these later pilgrims [those who came on the Anne and the Little James] are reckoned with those who came in the Mayflower and Fortune, as the Old Comers or Forefathers. **1900** DIX *Deacon Bradbury* 32 All the old, stern, passionate fire of devotion . . . would flame out on his countenance, as it had flamed on those of his Puritan forefathers.

2. Forefather(s') Day, (see note and quots.).

"Forefathers' Day was first celebrated at Plymouth in 1769 and in Boston in 1797 or 1798" (1914 A. Matthews in *Mass. Col. Soc. Pub.* XVII. 295). "On account of a mistake in reckoning the change from Old Style to New Style, it has generally been celebrated on the 22d" (1909 Webster 849/2).

1826 J. DAVIS (ed.) Morton *New Englands Memoriall* 48*n*, The 22d of December . . . has long been observed at Plymouth, and occasionally at Boston, in commemoration of the landing of the Fathers. . . . At Plymouth it has universally the familiar and endearing appellation of Forefather-Day. **1832** THACHER *Hist. Plymouth* 25 If, therefore, it be desirable to celebrate the precise portion of time corresponding with their date, . . . the twenty-first and not the twenty-second of December should be commemorated as Forefathers Day. **1855** *N.Y. Wkly. Tribune* 20 Jan. 3/5 Forefathers' Day was celebrated yesterday by the New-Englanders in high style. **1937** DOUGLAS *Amer. Bk. of Days* 621 Forefathers' Day. New England Societies thruout the nation celebrate December 22 as the anniversary of the landing of the Pilgrim Fathers at Plymouth, Mass., in 1620.

attrib. **1882** *Nation* 24 Aug. 157/2 Judge Davis . . . was a Forefathers' Day orator and ode-maker. **1903** *Boston Transcript* 22 Dec. 10 We shall not be surprised if the Forefathers's Day addresses this year hark back to Pilgrim and Puritan ideals.

3. forefathers'-pitcher, the pitcher plant, *Sarracenia purpurea.* Also **forefathers'-cup.**

1818 *Mass. H. S. Coll.* 2 Ser. VIII. 171 Among the plants in the neighbouring towns, . . . [are] the purple sarracenia, or, as it is here called, meadow cups and forefathers' pitcher, and the beautiful larch. **1832** WILLIAMSON *Maine* I. 126 Meadow-cup, called forefathers' pitcher, or Whippoorwill's shoes. **1876** HOBBS *Bot. Hand-Book* 39 Forefathers' cup, Side saddle plant, Sarracenia purpurea.

* **foreign,** *a.*

1. Containing a population born outside the U.S. *Rare.*

1884 *Cent. Mag.* Sep. 766 New York . . . is not the most foreign State.

2. In combs.: (1) **foreign car,** (see quot.); (2) **corporation,** an out-of-state corporation; (3) **editor,** an editor of a periodical who deals with foreign news; (4) **Indian,** an Indian not a native of a particular place or district, *obs.;* (5) * **Legion,** = **European Brigade,** *obs.*

(1) **1903** E. JOHNSON *Railway Transportation* 124 Every road uses 'foreign' cars (those belonging to other companies as well as its own). — (2) **1948** *Carthaginian* (Carthage, Miss.) 19 Aug. 2/6 The time of such exemption [is] to commence from the date of charter, if a domestic corporation and if a foreign corporation, from the date of such corporation's qualification to do business in Mississippi. — (3) **1877** *Harper's Mag.* Dec. 53/2 [He puts] foreign correspondence in the hands of a foreign editor. — (4) **1632** *Mass. Bay Rec.* I. 96 Euery planter inhabiting within this pattent shall pay to the Court . . . xijd for euery pound of beavr that hee shall trade for . . . with any forraine Indean. **1713** *Va. State P.* I. 168 The next matter, I shall recommend to you, is the providing more effectually for the Security of your Frontiers against foreign Indians. **1715** in J. W. LYDEKKER *Faithful Mohawks* (1938) 47 Indeed I live here in a great deal of danger, what of Foreign Indians that are coming here and of such of our own that are not so good as they should be. — (5) **1884** CABLE *Dr. Sevier* 368 The Confederate Guards were having their daily dress parade in Coliseum Place, and only they and the Foreign Legion remained.

foreignership ˈfɔrɪnəʳˌʃɪp, *n.* The quality or condition of a foreigner. *Obs.* — **1881** *Harper's Mag.* Oct. 695/2 A kind of chivalry extended to his foreignership exempted him as in the case of all Americans, from the wood and soap fetching. **1891** *Voice* 5 March, Their inability to handle the American vernacular . . . will cause the aroma of foreignership to cling to them always.

* **foreignism,** *n.* **1.** Opposition to the principles of the Know-Nothing party. **2.** A foreign word or idiom. Both *obs.*

(1) **1855** in HAMBLETON *H. A. Wise* 336 We are agitating in the South against foreignism as an evil. **1856** *Western Citizen* (Paris, Ky.) 18 Jan. 3/1 They have gone, avowing themselves confident and determined to conquer this commonwealth for their piebald party, and array it under the banner of *foreignism.* — (2) **1877** *Congregationalist* 15 Aug. (*Cent.*), That he [Miles Coverdale] left in his Bible some few foreignisms . . . is not surprising. **1887** *Scribner's Mag.* II. 509/1 Many of these foreignisms have crept into the common speech of the Rocky Mountain States.

forensic fəˈrɛnsɪk, *n.* [f. the adj.] In schools, a written speech defending one side or the other of a debatable question. *Obs.*

1814 *Harvard Laws* App. 1 On the first Thursday of the first Term, half the Class read Forensics, P.M., and on the second Thursday . . . the whole Class present Themes. **1851** HALL *College Words* 133 In Harvard College, the two senior classes are required to write forensics. **1884** *Harvard Coll. Rep. 1883–4* 84 The number of forensics heretofore required has been four in each of the last two years.

forepole ˈforˌpol, *v.* Also **forepale.** *tr.* To keep the working face of a mine closely timbered to prevent rocks, debris, etc., from falling. Hence **forepoling,** *n.* — **1871** *Amer. Inst. Mining Eng. Trans.* I. 352 After driving fifty yards through heavy rock-tumbles, where every foot had to be forepaled. **1881** RAYMOND *Mining Gloss.*, Fore-poling, a method of securing drifts in progress through quicksand by driving ahead poles, lath, boards, slabs, etc., to prevent the inflow of the quicksand on the sides and top, the face being protected by breast-boards.

* **forest,** *n.* In combs.: (1) **forest ball,** a country ball or party, *obs.;* (2) **belt,** a stretch of forest timber extending from one point to another; (3) **City,** see as a main entry; (4) **commissioner,** an official whose duty it is to protect the forests; (5) **fire,** a fire that breaks out in a forest; (6) **firebug,** one who sets forest fires, *rare;* (7) **Indian,** an Indian living in the forest in distinction from one living on the plains, *obs.*, cf. **Boisbrûlé;** (8) **light,** the torch or light used in fire-hunting, *obs.;* (9) **preserve,** = **forest reserve** (*a*), also **forest preservation;** (10) * **ranger,** in forestry work, an officer whose duty it is to patrol and guard a forest preserve; (11) **reservation,** = **forest reserve** (*a*); (12) **reserve,** (*a*) an area of forest set aside by the government as a reserve, also attrib., (*b*) one who assists in patrolling and preserving this; (13) **service,** that branch of the government service having to do with protecting forest preserves; (14) **station,** a place serving as the headquarters of a group of forest rangers; (15) **tent caterpillar,** the larva of a lasiocampid moth, *Malacosoma disstrium.*

(1) *c***1775** BOUCHER *Glossary* p. l, Last *forest-ball*, I felt like one forlorn, Though Ebo-Nan was play'd, and then *Parch'd Corn.* — (2) **1889** *Rep. Secy. Agric.* 276 Successful reclamation of these broad acres and effectual checking of the destructive winds by means of systematic planting of forest belts can only be attained by co-operation, *i.e.*, by government management, be it national, State, or county. **1910** *Boston Ev. Transcript* 11 June III. 3/5 The steam sawmills of the northern forest belt from Minnesota to Oregon are in considerable part Indian-manned. — (4) **1896** *Vt. Agric. Rep.* XV. 81 Maine two years ago appointed a Forest Commissioner at a salary sufficient to secure a trained business man. **1907** ANDREWS *Recoll.* 13 [He served] the State year after year— . . . as Forestry Commissioner or as secretary of the board of forest commissioners.

(5) [**1779** in FRIES *N.C. Morav. Rec.* III. (1926) 1318 After a rather long dry spell . . . the air . . . became very heavy from the smoke of forest fires.] **1878** HOUGH *Rep. Forestry* I. 158 The frequent occurrence of forest-fires along railroad-lines . . . leads us to consider the measures available for their prevention. **1948** *Reader's Digest* May 22/2 The forest fire, sweeping down out of the Maine hills . . . , had leveled every building for almost a mile. — (6) **1922** *Lit. Digest.* 18 Mar. 25 (*caption*), Tracking Forest Firebugs. — (7) **1847** RUXTON *Adv. Rocky Mts.* (1848) 238 The 'Forest Indian' . . . is as distinct in character and appearance from him of the 'plains' as a bear from a bluebottle. — (8) **1831** AUDUBON *Ornith. Biog.* I. 337 The mode of destroying deer by *fire-light*, or, as it is named in some parts of the country, *forest-light*, never fails to produce a very singular feeling in him who witnesses it for the first time. — (9) **1883** *Nation* 6 Sep. 201/1 A National Forest Preserve. The importance of forest preservation as a national measure has been widely discussed in the public press. **1948** *Highway Traveler* Aug.–Sep. 35/1 Black Lake, Twin and Carp Lakes are within the forest preserve.

(10) **1904** WHITE *Mountains* 6 Occasionally, from some hunter or forest-ranger, we gained little items of information. **1947** *Democrat* 20 Feb. 1/5 Forest Ranger, H. Y. Reynolds . . . and the Patrolmen are putting forth every effort to prevent the numerous fires. — (11) **1890** *Statutes at Large* XXVI. 650 An act to set apart certain tracts of land in the State of California as forest reservations. **1897** *Statutes at Large* XXX. 35 For the purpose of preserving the living and growing timber and promoting the younger growth on forest reservations, the Secretary of the Interior . . . , may sell the same for not less than the appraised value.—(12) (*a*) **1882** *N. Amer. Rev.* Oct. 400 The practicability . . . of preserving certain portions of them [*sc.* forests] as Government forest reserves, is worthy of the most careful consideration. **1945** *Craig* (Colo.) *Empire-Courier* 25 July 2/4 Yep, there's forest reserve country up there that's just waiting for you. (*b*) **1946** *Mazama* Dec. 61/1 Others served their country as Forest Reserves—served their nation, protecting our forest resources.—(13) **1910** *Out West* Feb. 186, I believe in the Forest Service and in the men who have created it from small and fragmentary beginnings. **1947** *Coronet* July 25/1 Today, smoke-jumping is a well-organized, venturesome, super-active part of the Forest Service, employing 225 trained men who work out of four primary bases. — (14) **1935** MITCHELL *America* 235 There is a forest station at Halsey, quite a unique affair.

(15) **1854** EMMONS *Agric. N.Y.* V. 240 The direct means for destroying the forest tent caterpillar are . . . destruction of the webs and their contents.

b. In combs. of obvious meaning or sufficiently explained in the quots., as (1) **forest cover,** (2) **floor,** (3) **management,** (4) **-master.**

(1) **1841** COOPER *Deerslayer* i, Broad belts of the virgin wilderness, . . . affording forest covers to the noiseless moccasin of the native warrior. **1905** *Forest Bureau Bul.* No. 61, 11 *Forest cover*, all trees and other plants in a forest. — (2) **1854** LOWELL in *Putnam's Mo. Mag.* April 380/2 A gray, soft moss of ashes [on the burned logs] . . . [mocked] the poor wood with a pale travesty of that green and gradual decay on forest-floors, its natural end. **1898** S. B. GREEN *Forestry in Minn.* 295 *Forest floor*, the decayed leaves and twigs which cover the soil in forests. **1905** *Forestry Bureau Bul.* No. 61, 11 A ground fire is one which burns in the forest floor and does not appear above the ground. — (3) **1896** *Vt. Agric. Rep.* XV. 86 It can only be done by working out the best course of forest management. **1905** *Forestry Bureau Bul.* No. 61, 11 *Forest management*, the practical application

of the principles of forestry to a forest area. *Ib.*, Three great systems of forest management are distinguished: The seed system, the sprout system, and the composite system. — (4) **1896** BRACE *New West* vii. 86 By a wise selection he has been appointed by the State Commission, which has charge of the Yosemite, Forest-master, to take care of the wonderful trees.

As the last term in **all-aged, back, cactus, index, maple, mesquite, mixed, national, petrified, protection, seed, son of the, state, underground forest.**

Forest City. A nickname that has been applied to Cleveland, O., Portland, Me., and Savannah, Ga.

1858 *Spirit of Times* 13 Feb. 378/1 We are off for an expedition to the Forest City (Portland), within a few days. **1859** *Ladies' Repository* XIX. 51/1 Cleveland, Ohio, is the 'Forest City,' from the original forest trees still standing in the parks and public squares, and from the strikingly-rural aspect of many of its streets and private grounds. **1860** *So. Enterprise* (Thomasville, Ga.) 2 May 2/1 A visit here will explain why Savannah is called the Forest City. **1948** *Ohio St. Arch. Quart.* Jan. 68 Every journal in the large cities of the nation carried several columns upon the reception in the 'Forest City.'

forestation ˌfɔrɪsˈteʃən, *n.* A forest growth, or the planting and maintaining of such a growth. — **1898** *Engineering Mag.* Feb. 807 (*caption*), The Relation of Forestation to Water-Supply. **1912** *Forest Service Bul.* No. 121, 8 There is no real obstacle to forestation except fire.

***forester,** *n.* The official at the head of the forest service of the federal government or of a state. — **1902** *Statutes at Large* XXXII. 295 Bureau of Forestry, salaries: One forester, who shall be Chief of Bureau, three thousand five hundred dollars. **1914** *Cyclo. Amer. Govt.* II. 38/2 The Forest Service is a division of the Department of Agriculture . . . under the charge of the Forester. . . . He first took charge of the national forests . . . on February 1, 1905.

***forestry,** *n.* In combs.: (1) **forestry cloth,** (see quot.); (2) **commissioner,** =**forest commissioner;** (3) **preserve,** =**forest reserve** (*a*).

(1) **1922** *Outing* Feb. 226/1 Forestry cloth, a dark brownish green, is becoming to everyone, shows soil as little as anything and comes in three weights—heavy and light serge, and flannel. It is tough and closely woven and catches on stubs and twigs less easily than any other fabric. — (2) **1907** ANDREWS *Recoll.* 13 [He served] as Forestry Commissioner or as secretary of the board of forest commissioners. — (3) **1942** *Gen. Cat. U. of Wis.* 415 The University Arboretum, Wild Life Refuge, and Forestry Preserve is a tract of 1137 acres of land on the shore of Lake Wingra, on the outskirts of Madison.

***forget,** *v.*

1. In colloq. or slang phrases: **a.** *don't you forget it,* be sure to bear it in mind. **b.** *forget it,* take no more notice of it, "skip it."

(a) **1888** *Boston W. Globe* 29 Feb. (F.), If the public demand dirt the newspapers will furnish dirt—and don't you forget it. **1908** E. C. HALL *Aunt Jane of Ky.* ii. 32, I'd like to 'a' seen anybody callin' Parson Page 'Lem Page.' He was the Rev. Lemuel Page, and don't you forgit it. — (b) **1903** MCCARDELL *Conversations Chorus Girl* 91 (We.), I gave him the laugh, and said, 'Forget it!' **1921** MENCKEN *Amer. Language* 16 [A writer in the London *Daily News*] protested bitterly against the intrusion of such commonplace Americanisms as *firewater, daffy, forget it,* and *boot-legger.* **1943** BROWNE *See What I Mean* 138 (We.), Forget it!

2. ***forget-me-not, a.** The bluet, *Houstonia caerulea.* **b.** (See quot.)

(a) **1829** EATON *Botany* (ed. 5) 246 *Houstonia cærulea*, venus' pride, forget-me-not. **1892** *Amer. Folk-Lore* V. 97 *Houstonia cœrulea*, forget-me-not. Kentucky. — (b) **1833** S. J. HALE *Flora* 65 Forget-me-not. *Viola cucula.* A species of the Violet common to America. Color blue.

forgettery fəˈgetərɪ, *n.* The faculty or power of forgetting. *Colloq.* — **1862** *Harper's Mag.* June 133/2 Her memory being rather a forgettery, all she could say . . . was weighed in the balance an' come up missin'. **1863** *Ib.* July 279/1 He had a bad memory and first-rate forgettery.

***fork,** *n.*

1. The point of juncture of two or more streams. Also the area about such a place. Often *pl.*

1645 *Mass. H.S. Coll.* 4 Ser. VI. 376, 2 of our Towne going downe the Riuer . . . were cast away, eather a litle before they came to the forks or at the first enterance. **1735** *New Voyage to Georgia* 55 We reached the Forks, as they call it, that same night, where the river divides into two very beautiful branches. **1771** MEASE *Narrative* 68 Went early this morning to a Place near what are called the Forcks of the Iberville. **1817** S. BROWN *Western Gaz.* 8 The Tallapoose is boatable to the great falls, thirty or forty miles above the fork. **1890** M. TOWNSEND *U.S. Index* 139 Where the union of the streams takes place is known as the fork.

transf. **1658** in *Amer. Sp.* XV. 263/1 Beginning upon the south side of a main Swamp and at a marked Oak near the fork of the said Swamp. **1747** *Ib.*, A white oake Standing in the fork of a Swamp which makes out of Yeococomico River.

b. *in the fork(s),* situated, lying, or being immediately above the juncture of two streams and between them.

1674 in *Amer. Sp.* XV. 262/2 Beginning at a small marked ash in the forke of a branch Issueing out of Lawnes Creek. **1692** *Md. Hist. Mag.* I. 11 Being in the forks of Gunpowder River by the side of the said River. **1787** WASHINGTON *Diaries* III. 196 The ground in the fork . . . was sown both with Oats and the mixture of Clover Orchd. grass. **1885** *Cent. Mag.* April 844/1 Nobody ever had any doubt as to the pride that Mr. Kittrell had in . . . his fine plantation so snug in the fork. **1949** *Lubbock* (Tex.) *Morn. Avalanche* 23 Feb. II. 9/5 The boys in the forks of the creek are doing their share in proportion to their ability to pay.

c. Either or any one of the streams that come together; a tributary of a main stream. Also in proper names.

1697 *R.I. Col. Rec.* III. 323 The north side of Pawtuxet river, so far as it extends itself westward to that branch or fork which issueth out of Penhongansett Pond. **1793** *Mass. H.S. Coll.* 3 Ser. V. 170 And then he goes on to describe . . . the country between the two forks. **1851** *S.F. Picayune* 19 Sep. 2/5 A party of five from Nevada, while prospecting upon the South Fork of the North Fork of the Yuba river, struck upon a quartz lead. **1948** *Sierra Club Bul.* Mar. 18 This area is the winter range of many animals inhabiting the park drainage of the north fork of the Flathead River.

d. A settlement located at the fork of a river, also freq. in place-names, as Grand Forks, N.D.

1873 M. TWAIN *Gilded Age* i. 21 (R.), He's come back to the Forks.

2. A forked cut in an animal's ear to denote ownership. Cf. **swallow fork.**

1669 *Portsmouth Rec.* 279 The Eare-marke . . . a forke on the left eare. **1773** in SUMMERS *Ann. S.W. Va.* 596 It is ordered that his Mark be Recorded a small fork in the Right ear and under keel in the left ear. **1845** *Portsmouth Rec.* 387 The Ear Mark of the Creatures of Soloman Hedly is a fork or Swallows tail on the Right Ear.

3. A branching of a road or path; a road that branches off from another; the point of juncture of two or more roads or paths.

1779 ANBUREY *Travels* II. 338 You'll come to a road that has three forks, (which is their manner of describing the partings in the roads) [in Va.]. **1797** BAILY *Tour* 354 We arrived at what is called the Forks of the Path; for here one branch extends into the Chactaw nation, and the other . . . into the Chickasaw nation. **1806** CLARK in *Lewis & C. Exped.* V. (1905) 13 At the distance of 2 miles we passd. a lodge of 2 fires on a fork of the road which leads to the right. **1948** *Pacific Discovery* March–April 26/1 The right fork climbs across about thirty miles of rocky lava mesas of the Sierra Giganta to Comundú.

4. In combs.: (1) **fork-and-rail fence,** =**fork fence,** *obs.;* (2) **chickweed,** =**forked chickweed;** (3) **fence,** a form of rail fence in which the rails are supported at the ends by posts made of forked saplings, *obs.;* (4) **-leaf blackjack,** see **blackjack 1. b;** (5) **people,** people who live in the "forks" of a river, *rare;* (6) **spike,** =**forked spike;** (7) **tail,** the fork-tailed kite, in full **fork-tail hawk,** cf. **forked-tail hawk.**

(1) **1792** POPE *Tour S. & W.* 63 Their Inclosure are Fork and Rail Fences. — (2) **1845** LINCOLN *Botany* App. 74/2 *Anychia dichotoma*, fork chickweed. — (3) **1796** HAWKINS *Letters* 39, I went down the river on the left bank, passing 5 separate Indian settlements, under fork fences, good against cattle only. **1797** *Ib.* 64 The river forms two sides and a small fork fence with stakes and three rails, the other of the fields.

(5) **1757** *Lett. to Washington* II. 186 Before my arrival here with ye Troops, there was not a Soule Between ye north R[ive]r & Vauses, but since most of the fork people has Returned. — (6) **1839** in *Mich. Agric. Soc. Trans.* VII. 400 *Andropogon furcatus.* Fork-spike. — (7) **1808** T. ASHE *Travels* xvii. 159 Between ninety and an hundred American birds have been described by Catesby . . . as follows: fork-tail hawk. **1844** *Nat. Hist. N.Y., Zoology* II. 12 The Swallow-tailed Hawk, or Fork Tail, is a southern species.

As the last term in **hay, pie, sluice, spading, swallow fork.**

***fork,** *v.*

1. *W. tr.* To mount and ride (a horse). *Colloq.*

1903 A. ADAMS *Log Cowboy* xix. 295 So fork that swimming horse of yours and wet your big toe again in the North Platte. **1947** *Trail Riders Bul.* Feb. 20/2 We forked our cayuses over tuh Rimrock.

2. With adverbs in colloq. expressions:

a. *To fork into,* to get possession of. *Rare.*

1839 MARRYAT *Diary* II. 231, I heard a young man, a farmer in Vermont, say, when talking about another having gained the heart of a pretty girl, 'Well, how he contrived to fork *into* her young affections, I can't tell.'

b. *to fork on,* (see quot.). *Obs.*

1851 HALL *College Words* 134 At Hamilton College, *to fork on,* to appropriate to one's self.

c. *to fork over,* to hand over, pay, "cough up."

1835 *New Yorker* 2 May 3/3 After a significantly pathetic and pompous appeal in behalf of their 'undertake-in' the publishers close with the parting injunction—'Reader fork over!' **1948** *Sat. Ev. Post* 24 April 171/1 If she passes the surveyor, I have to accept her and fork over the final payment of a quarter of a million dollars.

d. ∗*to fork up,* (*a*) =prec., (*b*) to set up as with a prop, *rare.*

(*a*) **1836** *Franklin Repository* (Chambersburg, Pa.) 29 Mar. 1/2 'Fork up, and that instantly, or take the contents of this,' he added fiercely, as he thrust the cold barrel of the pistol against the supplicant's cheek. **1947** *Time* 20 Jan. 38/2 Though . . . a good unionist, forking up 30¢ a day for dues and the benefit fund, and never failing to consult his delegate on all important matters, he is no Communist. (*b*) **1843** CARLTON *New Purchase* I. 195 She would take the very coverlet and fork it up for a curtain!

∗**forked,** *a.*

1. Remarkable, alarming. *Rare.*

1851 *Polly Peablossom* 72 The way they hustle her about mongst the straw and shucks was forked!

2. In combs.; (1) **forked beard grass,** =**forked spike;** (2) **chickweed,** a small-branched weed, *Anychia canadensis,* cf. **fork chickweed;** (3) **fence,** =**fork fence,** *obs.;* (4) **horned antelope,** a pronghorn antelope, *rare;* (5) **-leaf blackjack, -leaved blackjack,** see **blackjack 1. b;** (6) **post,** a post made of a sapling that has a suitable fork; (7) **spike,** the bluestem, *Andropogon furcatus,* cf. **fork spike;** (8) **-tail hawk,** =**fork tail;** (9) **tongue,** used, in imitation of Indian speech, to mean a lying tongue, a false tongue.

(1) **1840** DEWEY *Mass. Flowering Plants* 238 *Andropogon furcatum.* Forked Spike. Forked Beard-Grass. . . . In sandy soil, along hedges, and in alluvial meadows. — (2) **1839** in *Mich. Agric. Soc. Trans.* VII. 417 *Queria canadensis.* Forked Chickweed. **1840** DEWEY *Mass. Flowering Plants* 95 Forked Chickweed . . . blossoms in July; dry soil, in fields. **1901** MOHR *Plant Life Ala.* 502 *Anychia.* . . . Forked Chickweed. Two species, Atlantic America. — (3) **1800** HAWKINS *Sk. Creek Country* 59 [The Creek Indians] appear to be industrious, have forked fences. — (4) *c***1810** *Rees's Cyclo.* (Phila.) *s.v. Antelope,* The forked-horned, or Missouri Antelope, so called by captain Lewis. (6) **1775** ADAIR *Indians* 183 Those bone-houses are scaffolds raised on durable pitch-pine forked posts, in the form of a house covered a-top, but open at both ends. **1823** JAMES *Exped.* I. 113 Bedsteads are formed in the simplest manner of numerous sticks, or slender pieces of wood resting at their ends on cross pieces, which are supported by short notched or forked posts. — (7) **1833** EATON *Botany* (ed. 6) 18 *Andropogon furcatus,* forked spike. **1847** WOOD *Botany* 621 *A*[*ndropogon*] *furcatus* 'Forked Spike.' — (8) **1849** *Rep. U.S. Comm. Patents* (1850) 621 Only two other birds he knew perform such a feat, the forked-tail hawk and the swift or chimney swallow. — (9) **1836** IRVING *Astoria* II. 55 Mr. Hunt . . . now changed his tone with the Indians, charged them with . . . talking with a 'forked tongue,' or, in other words, with lying. **1867** *Wkly. New Mexican* (Santa Fe) 6 April 2/1 The Great Father, as they [the Navahos] are wont to style the Government speaks with a forked tongue. **1923** J. H. COOK *On Old Frontier* 214 Indian traders and agency employees . . . might . . . repeat as facts incidents of his early life told them by forked tongues.

forlornity fəˈlɔrnɪtɪ, *n.* **1.** (See quot. 1870.) *Rare.* **2.** A person who is forlorn. *Colloq.*

(1) **1870** CHIPMAN *Notes on Bartlett* 160 *Forlornity,* forlorn condition. Word in a S[unday] School Book, by Mrs. ——. — (2) **1897** HOWELLS *Open-eyed Conspiracy* iv, Saratoga is reeking with just such forlornities the whole summer long. **1917** COMSTOCK *The Man* 320 Thomas explained and apologized for the admittance of the two 'forlornities,' as he called them.

∗**form,** *n.*

1. A cotton bud or square.

1833 J. STUART *Three Years N.A.* II. 124 On the cups of the flower balls or cocoombs, or, as they are here called, forms, grow three or four elliptical seeds, three or four times as large as a wheat kernel, and of an oily consistency. **1896** *54th Congress* 2 Sess. H.R. Doc. No. 267, 263 Forms on May 24 made open bolls August 9.

2. a. form letter, a letter so phrased that it may be sent to many different people. **b. form square,** (see quot.).

(a) **1909** *Sat. Ev. Post* 13 Feb. 8/1 The credit man . . . had a perfect passion for form letters. **1946** FAIR *Crows Can't Count* 53 Bertha is always sending out those damn form letters which she insists must be individually typed. — (b) **1895** REMINGTON *Pony Tracks* 203 Another movement is the 'form square,' which is an adaptation of the 'Indian circle,' it being a movement from a centre to a circle, and useful when escorting wagons or when surprised.

3. In library cataloguing, used with reference to classifications based upon the form or type of literature involved, as (1) **form catalogue,** (2) **entry,** (3) **heading, list.**

(1) **1876** C. A. CUTTER *Rules Dict. Cat.* (Contents), Form catalogue. **1913** J. H. QUINN *Library Cat.* 30 Form-Catalogue is one in which the entries are arranged according to the forms of literature and the languages in which the books are written, either alphabetically or according to the relations of the forms to one another. — (2) **1876** C. A. CUTTER *Rules Dict. Cat.* 14 *Form-entry,* registry under the name of the kind of literature to which the book belongs. *Ib.* 49 In the catalogues of libraries consisting chiefly of English books, if it is thought most convenient to make form-entries under the headings Poetry, Drama, Fiction, it may be done. — (3) **1876** C. A. CUTTER *Rules Dict. Cat.* 49 There is no reason but want of room why only collections should be entered under form-headings. *Ib.,* In the case of English fiction a form-list is of such constant use that nearly all libraries have separate fiction catalogues.

4. ∗*out of form,* in baseball, not in a good position for batting. *Colloq.*

1885 CHADWICK *Art of Pitching* 58 A quick delivery will catch him [the batter] 'out of form' and get a strike called or a poor hit.

∗**form,** *v. intr.* Of cotton: To produce forms. — **1829** in COMMONS *Doc. Hist.* I. 241 Cotton very fine; knee high & well branched & formed. **1865** TURNER *Cotton* 25 In a wet one, it may be profitably delayed, until it has begun to form, or later even.

∗**former,** *a.* Designating one who formerly held an indicated office or position.

1885 *Santa Fe Wkly. New Mexican* 10 Sep. 4/7 Dougher & Skidmore . . . leased the Las Cruces smelter and ousted Roney, the former superintendent. **1904** *St. Louis Globe-Democrat* 1 July 7/4 Former Senator Marion Butler of North Carolina, chairman of the Populist committee, has tendered his resignation. **1905** *N.Y. Herald* 5 Feb. 47 Former President Cleveland is among the arrivals of the week at the Lakewood Hotel. **1919** MENCKEN *Amer. Lang.* 118 Such clumsy quasi-titles as ex-United States Senator, . . . and former Chief of the Fire Department. **1948** *Minneapolis Morn. Tribune* 28 Sep. 1/6 Sen. George Wilson, threatened by Democratic former Sen. Guy M. Gillette, was frankly warned by Dewey's advisers to intensify his campaign.

∗**Forster,** *n.* [Johann Reinhold *Forster* (1729–89), German traveler and author.] **1. Forster's shrew,** (see quot.). **2. Forster's tern,** (see quot. 1858).

(1) **1842** *Nat. Hist. N.Y., Zoology* I. 20 Forster's Shrew. *Sorex forsteri.* . . . This hardly little animal is found as far north as the sixty-seventh degree of latitude. — (2) **1858** BAIRD *Birds Pacific R.R.* 862 *Sterna Forsteri.* . . . Forster's tern. . . . Louisiana to Florida; New York, fur countries, and California. **1948** *Chi. Tribune* 29 Sep. 1. 1/4 Forster's and Caspian terns also were stopping on Chicago's lakes before heading for the southern coasts for the winter.

Forsythe cotton. A brownish-yellow cotton; nankeen. *Obs.* — **1838** *S. Lit. Messenger* IV. 638/2 The aforesaid breeches . . . were made . . . of what is now called 'par excellence'—*the Forsythe cotton. Ib.,* The Forsythe cotton, . . . then as common as any other kind under the title of '*nankeen cotton.*'

Forsythia fəˈsɪθɪə, *n.* [f. Wm. *Forsyth* (1737–1804), who brought it from China.] A genus of ornamental oleaceous spring-flowering shrubs having bright-yellow bell-shaped flowers, also (not *cap.*) a plant of this genus.

1814 O. O. RICH *Amer. Plants* 57 *Decumaria.* . . . Forsythia. . . . Calyx urceolate, 8–10 toothed, superior; Corol 8–10-petalled. **1893** *Harper's Mag.* April 677/1 The jasmine and the forsythia began to burst into blossom. **1945** MACDONALD *Egg & I* 104, I had read of beauty-starved farm wives standing for an hour on their back stoops absorbing the glory of a sun-drenched branch of forsythia.

∗**fort,** *n.*

1. A trading post, orig. fortified. *Obs.*

1776 SMITH *Wealth of Nations* (1869) II. 328 The whole number of people whom they [the Hudson's Bay Company] maintain in their different settlements and habitations, which they have honoured with the name of forts, is said not to exceed a hundred and twenty persons. **1836** IRVING *Astoria* II. 16 The Snakes were to return to Fort Henry, as the new trading post was called, and take charge of the horses.

2. An Indian mound or earthwork.

1806 CRAMER *Navigator* 22 On the point of the upper bank, are the remains of an old fort, within which, and a considerable distance below the surface, are yet to be found human bones of a very large size.

1847 SQUIER & DAVIS *Monuments of Miss. Valley* 8 Earthworks, . . . Enclosures, or, as they are familiarly called throughout the West, 'Forts,' constitute a very important and interesting class of remains. **1949** *Pacific Discovery* Jan.–Feb. 12/2 A 'council ring' of heavy stones, a masonry 'fort,' rocks inscribed with primitive hieroglyphics, and accumulated potsherds marked the spot as an important center of activity.

3. (See quot.) *College slang. Obs.*

1851 HALL *College Words* 134 At Jefferson and at Washington Colleges in Pennsylvania, the boarding-houses for the students are called *forts*.

4. *W.* A military post in the Indian country (see quot. 1868).

1857 CHANDLESS *Visit Salt Lake* I. 62 It has no fortifications, but every post in Indian country is termed 'fort.' **1868** W. E. WATERS *Life among Mormons* 9 The term 'Forts,' as applied to military posts on the frontier, has caused a very general misconception of their real character. . . . Fort Kearney . . . consists simply of a number of two story frame buildings, arranged in the usual way around a parade ground. **1874** GLISAN *Jrnl. Army Life* 452 But, at forts in the center of the wild Indian Country there are few if any ladies.

5. fort house, a. a blockhouse. **b.** a house within a fort. Both *obs.*

(a) 1676 *Conn. Rec.* II. 468 The fort house . . . is near finisht. — **(b) 1846** SAGE *Scenes Rocky Mts.* viii, Our visitors crowded the Fort houses in quest of articles of plunder.

As the last term in **block, Indian, log, picket, rock, snow, stock, stockade, trading fort.**

∗**fort,** *v.*

1. *tr.* To protect (a person) with a fortification, to establish in a fortified position. Also with *in, up.*

1707 *Va. State P.* I. 110, I will forthwith fort myself in, being a frontier . . . have many of my neighbours to take shelter under my fort. **1757** WASHINGTON *Writings* I. 508 The few families that are forted on the Branch. **1853** RAMSEY *Tennessee* 79 The survivors then forted themselves and maintained a protracted war. **1905** COLE *Early Oregon* iv. 53 We started on and arriving at Grave creek, found the people 'forted up.'

fig. **1797** ASBURY *Journal* II. 348, I think Satan forts himself in my melancholy, unemployed, unsocial, and inactive hours.

b. To convert (a residence) into a fort. *Obs.*

1704 in *T. Dwight's Trav.* (1821) I. 348 (Th.), She was in a fortified house, or, as then vulgarly called, a house which was forted.

2. *intr.* To build fortifications; to seek refuge in a fort. Also with *in.*

1723 in SHELDON *Hist. Deerfield, Mass.* I. 396 These towns can't stand the strain upon them to watch and ward, scout and fort without pay. *c***1836** HITCHCOCK *Diary* 106 Next day before noon we reached the town of Helena, where the people were greatly alarmed and busily engaged 'forting-in' as it was called. They had cut logs twenty feet long and were setting them up in a stockade around the town, leaving loopholes to fire through. **1878** BEADLE *Western Wilds* 186 They lit on the Yorker and his friends and druv 'em back into Miller's store, when they forted and held their own. **1948** DICK *Dixie Frontier* 267 Castleman warned the pioneers to 'fort.'

forthputting, *n.* Forwardness, obstrusive behavior. *Colloq.* — **1856** STOWE *Dred* I. 153 Nina was as much annoyed at Clayton's silence, and his quiet, observant reserve, as with Carson's forthputting. **1862** LOWELL *Biglow P.* 2 Ser. i. 3, I say . . . this . . . the further to secure myself against any imputation of unseemly forth putting.

fortino fɔr'taɪno, *adv.* Also **forzino, fortiner,** etc. (See quots.) *Colloq. Obs.*

1815 HUMPHREYS *Yankey* 105 *Fortino, fortizno*, for aught I know. *Forzino*, far as I know. **1848** BARTLETT 149 *Fortiner.* (For-aught-I know.) This remarkable specimen of clipping and condensing a phrase, approaches the Indian method of forming words. The word is very common through New England, Long Island, and the rest of New York. *a***1870** CHIPMAN *Notes on Bartlett* 160 *Forzino.* So far as I know.—Occasional in N[ew] E[ng.].

∗**fortune,** *n.* **1. fortune stew,** (see quot.). *Obs.* **2. fortune wheel,** a game of chance played with a wheel of fortune. — **(1) 1881** McLEAN *Cape Cod Folks* ii. 37 Fortune stew was a dish of small, round blue potatoes served perfectly whole in milk gravy. — **(2) 1852** A. T. JACKSON *Forty-Niner* (1920) 159 'Twenty-one,' 'Rondo,' and 'Fortune Wheels' are the banking games, and they play poker and 'Brag' for big stakes.

∗**forty,** *a.* and *n.*

1. A forty-acre piece of land, one-sixteenth of a section.

1845 KIRKLAND *Western Clearings* 70 He'll want as much as one forty cleared right off. **1900** BRUNCKEN *N. Amer. Forests* 191 Even now, a party buying timber-lands buys so many 'forties.' **1949** *Pacific Discovery* Jan.–Feb. 5/1 This was *wilderness*, as distinct from the *back forty*.

2. In combs.: (1) **forty-acre,** designating a field, lot, or piece of land embracing forty acres; (2) **-days maize,** (see quot.), *obs.;* (3) ∗**-eight,** (see quots.); (4) ∗**-five,** a .45 caliber pistol, also used allusively, cf. **frontier Colt;** (5) ∗**-four,** a .44 caliber pistol, also attrib.; (6) **-gallon Baptist,** (see quot. 1871), also attrib.; (7) ∗**-knot,** a prostrate herb, *Achyranthes repens;* (8) **-'leven,** a fictitious, extremely large but indefinite number or degree, also **forty-eleventh,** *colloq.;* (9) ∗**nine,** (*a*) *pl.* those who urged that the 49th parallel of latitude be agreed upon as a compromise in the Oregon boundary dispute with Great Britain, *obs.*, cf. **forty-niner** (*a*), (*b*) used allusively with reference to 1849 as the year of the California gold rush, *colloq.;* (10) **-niner,** (*a*) one who favored the 49th parallel of latitude as a compromise Oregon boundary line, *obs.*, (*b*) one who went to California in 1849 during the gold rush, also transf.; (11) **rod,** see as a main entry.

(1) 1742 *N.H. Probate Rec.* III. 94, I give to my Grand Son . . . one Forty Acre Lot. **1873** *Newton Kansan* 3 July 3/2 [A] forty acre piece of school land. **1943** CROW *Amer. Customer* 185 There was no reason why a farmer could not plant a whole forty-acre field in wheat. — **(2) 1855** BROWNE in *Amer. Inst. N.Y. Trans.* 593 Forty-days maize, (*Mais quarantain*,) a dwarf variety from the south of Spain. . . . The object of introducing this grain into the United States, was on account of its quick growth, early maturity, and sweet flavor in the green state, as well as the delicacy of bread made from its meal. — **(3) 1885** TODD *Notes* 16 Many tavern keepers have bowling alley *ten* pins, because *nine* pins are illegal. A Faro-table keeper profitting by this hint, called it *forty-eight.* **1938** ASBURY *Sucker's Prog.* 216 The gamblers attempted to evade the law by removing the sevens from the deck and calling the game 'Forty-eight', but the Tennessee courts held that it was the same game within the meaning of the statute.— **(4) 1881** ROMSPERT *Western Echo* 285 We now used the six-shooters,—known as forty-fives,—and which were also deadly weapons. **1947** *Coronet* July 150/2 She said she felt like a young colt, but she looked more like an old .45.

(5) 1884 *Cent. Mag.* Nov. 55 His hand resting easily on the handle of his forty-four. **1885** *Harper's Mag.* May 830/1 My heart fluttered disagreeably as I pulled and cocked a large 44 Colt's revolver. **1922** SANDBURG *Slabs of Sunburnt West* 10 Or a 44-gat cracks and lets the skylight Into one more bank messenger. — **(6) 1871** EGGLESTON *Hoosier Schoolm.* xii. 102 The 'Hardshell Baptists' or, as they are otherwise called, the 'whiskey Baptists' and the 'Forty-gallon Baptists,' exist in all the old Western and South-western States. **1885** *Cent. Mag.* March 678 He kin preach all round any o' yer Meth'dist bible-bangers 'at ever I see, don't keer ef ye do call 'im a Hardshell an' a Forty-gallon, an' a' Iron-Jacket Baptus. **1940** STUART *Trees of Heaven* 292 He was kicked out'n the Forty-Gallon Baptist Church. — **(7) 1889** *Cent.* 2346/1 *Forty-knot* . . . is said to have diuretic properties. — **(8) 1860** HOLMES *Professor* vii. 208 On asking him what was the number of his room, he answered, that it was forty-'leven, skyparlour floor. **1871** DE VERE 313 A forty-eleventh cousin, for instance, expresses an infinitesimal degree of relationship, one too small to be stated accurately. **1948** *Time* 5 July 18/3, I have said forty-eleven times that I do not want him nominated. — **(9)** (*a*) **1846** *Nat. Intelligencer* (Wash.) 4 April 1/1 The overwhelming strength given to the party of the *forty-nines* by the great names of Jefferson, Madison and Monroe, put any serious opposition out of the question. (*b*) **1859** J. W. PALMER *New & Old* 89 (*Cent.*), In the rough winter of Forty-nine and Fifty the poor Kanakas of San Francisco . . . died under filthy sheds of hide. **1890** LANGFORD *Vigilante Days* (1912) 534 An old California refrain entitled, 'The Days of Forty-Nine.' **1948** JOHNSTON *Gold Rush*, There was seldom or never any difficulty, because of a universal spirit of fair play that actuated the miners of 'fortynine.

(10) (*a*) **1846** *Dollar Newspaper* (Phila.) 8 April 3/4 General Cass, Mr. B. said, by relying on Mr. Greenhow's book, instead of going to the authentic documents, had constituted himself a prisoner in the hands of the Forty-niners—doomed to dwell at 49. (*b*) **1853** *Mt. Echo* (Downieville, Calif.) 12 Feb. 1/1 Speeches were made by some of the worthy old forty-nin-ers, who spoke in glowing eloquence of the prosperous and peaceful times when their brother miners were the sole legislators, judges and executors of the law. **1873** BEADLE *Undevel. West* 268 The 'voyage of Jason and the Argonauts' is no doubt a poetic account of the '49-ers' of Greece. **1948** *Life* 2 Feb. 44/2 By the spring of the next year thousands of emigrants who called themselves forty-niners were headed west.

b. In colloq. phrases: (1) *as, by, like forty,* used as an intensive; (2) *with a forty foot pole,* used in negative expressions to denote the utmost of means, cf. **ten foot**

pole, *s.v.* **ten;** (3) *forty acres and a mule*, used in allusion to a promise made by rascally politicians to newly freed slaves after the Civil War that each of them was to receive a present of forty acres of land and a mule, now *hist.;* (4) *to have forty fits*, see ***fit.**

(1) **1829** *Western M. Rev.* II. 643 Such is Mr. Owen's romance of the social system . . . ; as loving as the Vermonter said, as *forty.* **1831** *Boston Transcript* 10 May 1/1 'There! by forty,' said the captain, 'now see if you can keep straight.' **1843** Oliver *Eight Months* 176 But if it hadn't been that I was the worse for liquor and he got me down, the way in which I would have walked into him would have been a caution. I'd have whipped him like forty. **1944** *Speleological Soc. Bul.* July 58/2 This stream is about 15′ wide with an average depth of 1½–2′, and goes like forty. — (2) **1838** *Lexington Observer* 2 June, I can't touch her with a forty foot pole. **1873** *Newton Kansan* 26 June 1/5 Their owner cannot touch them [*sc.* bonds in a bank vault] with a forty-foot pole. — (3) **1871** *Cong. Globe* 1 April 398/1 The slaves only appreciated the advantages of fighting for freedom when this privilege was accompanied with a present bounty or future prospect of 'forty acres and a mule.' **1947** Lumpkin *Southerner* 59 When we were children we used to ridicule the slogan 'forty acres and a mule' as a stupid deception used by the Yankees to get black men to vote for the Republicans.

As the last term in **fifty-four, home, ten, two forty.** See also **Roaring Forties.**

***forty rod.**

1. A name given facetiously to cheap, strong whisky. *Slang.*

[**1856** Brewerton *War in Kans.* 254 The title is nothing more nor less than 'rot-gut whisky,' with an addenda about its 'killing forty rods around a corner.' **1858** in *Amer. Sp.* XII. 115/1 *liquor* . . . warranted to kill at *forty rods.*] **1863** Russell *Diary* II. 11 Their cries for water were incessant to allay the internal fires caused by '40 rod' and '60 rod,' as whiskey is called, which is supposed to kill people at those distances. **1948** *Dly. Oklahoman* (Okla. City) 7 June 8/1 The mere possession of a few gills of forty rod is not counted as an ample offset to planned assassination.

2. *attrib.* Designating various kinds of "mean" liquor. *Slang.*

1872 *Newton Kansan* 29 Aug. 4/5 The chief ingredient was forty-rod rum. **1888** *Walla Walla* (Wash.) *Union* 16 June 3/4 Close to the road . . . was lying a dirty siwash whose skin was filled up with benzine of the most approved forty-rod variety. **1897** F. Norris *Third Circle* (1909) 108 And a mouthful of cold water, which the same we will thicken with forty-rod rye. **1931** Willison *Here They Dug Gold* 235 The Odeon especially is notorious for its 'forty-rod vitriol.'

transf. **1896** M. Twain in *Harper's Mag.* Sep. 524 (R.), Then he busted out and had another one of them forty-rod laughs of his'n.

***forward,** *a.* and *adv.*

1. forward of, in front of.

1838 Hawthorne *Notebooks* (1932) 29 Forward of the ward-room, adjoining it . . . is the midshipmen's room. **1891** Wilkins *Humble Romance* 165 Two little thin dancing curls . . . just forward of her cap.

2. forward pass, in football, a pass toward the opponents' goal.

1906 *Collier's* 22 Dec. 18/1 One would hardly risk a forward pass when he had the old five-yard rule. **1908** in P. H. Davis *Football* (1911) 498 Of the players of the side making a forward pass only the player who first legally touched the ball shall be entitled to touch or recover the ball until it has been touched by an opponent. **1948** *Newsweek* 15 Nov. 78/3 Of the 24 forward passes . . . sixteen were completed.

b. Also as a verb. Hence **forward passer.**

1913 *Collier's* 13 Dec. 26/3 Notre Dame forward-passed her way to five touchdowns and ran up 35 points against 13. *Ib.* 20 Dec. 3/2 Dorais, as quarterback, [is] an excellent forward-passer.

3. forward two, a dance step. *Obs.*

1847 Robb *Squatter Life* 90 A pair of boots now commenced a very fair *forward-two* to a boot-jack which was busily engaged in executing a *chassez.* **1870** O. Logan *Before Footlights* 250 He sprang to his feet and executed a 'forward two' in true Parisian style.

***forwarding,** *a.* Used to designate businesses, people, etc., connected with the forwarding or expediting of goods and passengers, esp. immigrants: (1) **forwarding agency,** (2) **business,** (3) **establishment,** (4) **house,** (5) **merchant,** (6) **note,** (7) **office.**

(1) **1897** *Outing* XXX. 197/2 The tourist should look after his own mount. . . . and he should not send it by an independent forwarding agency. — (2) **1837** Peck *Gaz. Illinois* 153 [Beardstown] has thirteen stores, four of which do commission and forwarding business. **1887** Tourgee *Button's Inn* 93 He was already contemplating . . . engaging in a new kind of forwarding business. — (3) **1847** Howe *Hist. Coll. Ohio* 43 The harbor of Ashtabula . . . has several forwarding establishments. **1851** Quentin *Reisebilder* I. 48 Dies sind Personen, welche sich bemühen, so viele Auswanderer, als möglich, denjenigen Transport-Geschäftshäusern (Forwarding Establishments) zuzuführen. — (4) **1837** W. Jenkins *Ohio Gaz.* 126 It has . . . ten heavy forwarding houses, connected with lake and canal transportation. **1864** Nichols *Amer. Life* I. 133 Canallers . . . mingled with some of the wilder young clerks from the forwarding houses.

(5) **1839** Story *Bailments* (Index), Forwarding merchant. **1889** *Cent.* 2347/1 Forwarding merchant, a merchant whose business is to receive and forward goods for others. — (6) **1882** *Encyclopædic Dict., Forwarding note*, . . . a note in which is entered a description of goods or parcels, with the names and addresses of the consignor and consignee, to be sent along with goods, &c., conveyed by a carrier (American). — (7) **1852** Fleischmann *Wegweiser* 56 Mit einem sogenannten Beförderungs-Bureau (*forwarding office*) und anderen Zwischenhändlern dürfen sie sich nicht einlassen, ohne nicht voerst von dessen Rechtlichkeit unterrichtet zu sein.

***forwardly,** *adv.* Toward the front, in front. *Obs.* — **1876** A. D. Whitney *Sights & Insights* vi, We did not come upon it forwardly . . . we moved alongside it. **1884** *Harper's Mag.* Jan. 263/1 The . . . hands were stretched out forwardly, as though feeling the way.

forzino, see **fortino.**

foskey fɔskɪ, *n.* [Amer. Ind.] = **black drink.** *Obs.* — **1868** C. C. Jones *Tomo-chi-chi* 118 Oglethorpe . . . partook of the *Foskey*, or black-medicine drink, and smoked with them the . . . hallowed pipe of peace. [*Note:*] Foskey . . . is prepared with much formality, and, being considered a sacred beverage, none but the chiefs, war captains, and priests or beloved men partake of it; and these only upon special occasions.

***Fothergilla,** *n.* [John *Fothergill*, Eng. doctor.] (See quots.) — **1785** Marshall *Amer. Grove* 47 *Fothergilla Gardeni.* Carolinian Fothergilla. This small, but beautiful flowering shrub grows naturally in Carolina, on the borders of savannahs. *Ib.* 48 Carolinian Fothergilla . . . has been called Youngsonia, in honour of William Young, Botanist, of Pennsylvania; but by Dr. Linnæus, Fothergilla in honour of the late Dr. Fothergill of London. **1909** Webster 857/3 Fothergilla. . . . A genus of hamamelidaceous shrubs containing two species, natives of the southern United States.

***foul,** *a.* and *n.*

1. *n.* = **foul ball.** Cf. **fair foul, tip foul.**

1867 *Chi. Republican* 6 July 3/1 Wheeler out on a foul by Stearns. **1906** *Spalding's Base Ball Guide* 116 If the attempt to bunt result in a foul not legally caught, a strike shall be called by the umpire. **1947** *Chi. Tribune* 22 June (Grafic Mag.) 18/5 A moment or so later a line drive foul plunked the vendor on the head while he was selling a sack of his goods.

b. Formerly in baseball, a pitched ball that is not a strike. *Obs.*

1866 *Wilkes' Spirit of Times* 9 June 230/2 He is a very unsteady pitcher, and despite the numerous cautionary commands of both Charley Smith and the umpire, sent in 'fouls' without number.

c. *Basketball.* (See quot. 1905.)

1905 Fisher *Basketball Guide* 83 A foul is a violation of a rule for which a free trial for goal is allowed. **1948** *Chi. Sun* 27 Jan. 23/5 Illinois players were charged with 77 fouls, the opposition with 90 fouls.

2. *a. Baseball.* Of a hit ball: Batted outside the foul lines. Also denoting *ground* or *territory* outside the foul lines.

1845 in *Appletons' Ann. Cyclo.* XXV. 77/2 A ball knocked outside the range of the first or third base is foul. **1857** *Spirit of Times* 28 Feb. 420/3 If the ball from a stroke of the bat is caught behind the range of home and the first base or home and the third base, without having touched the ground, or first touches the ground behind those bases, it shall be termed foul. **1878** *De Witt's Baseball Guide* 12 *All* balls which strike the ground *fair*, but which rebound to the foul ground before passing in front of the first or third bases, are to be called foul balls. **1917** Mathewson *Sec. Base Sloan* 240 By keeping on foul territory he was safe.

3. In combs. relating to baseball: (1) **foul balk,** an illegal delivery by the pitcher, *obs.;* (2) **ball,** a hit ball that is not fair, also attrib.; (3) **bound,** a batted ball which strikes fair but bounds into foul territory, *obs.*, cf. quot. 1878 under **2.** above; (4) **fly,** a fly ball which is foul, also attrib.; (5) **line,** either of two straight lines that run to the boundary of the field from the back corner of home plate across (now the outer edge of) first and third bases respectively; (6) **post,** one of the posts placed on the foul lines at the boundary of the field; (7) **strike,** (see quots. 1909, 1916); (8) **tip,** (see quot. 1916).

(1) **1878** *De Witt's Baseball Guide* 80 Should the pitcher deliver the ball by an overhand throw, a 'foul balk' shall be declared. — (2) **1860**

in *Ball Players' Chron.* (1867) 12 Dec. 2/4 H. Worth played very prettily behind, making some excellent catches on foul balls. **1867** *Ball Players' Chron.* 4 July 5/1 There must be chalk lines to mark the foul ball lines. **1948** *Ponca City* (Okla.) *News* 4 July 13/3 He added a sparkling catch of a foul ball in the eighth to his performance. — (3) **1867** *Ball Players' Chron.* 6 June 2/1 Willard was second out on a finely-taken foul-bound by Wilder. **1870** *N.Y. Herald* 5 July 8/3 Wood was missed on a foul bound by Smith, after which he slipped a cutter out to left field. — (4) **1867** *Ball Players' Chron.* 27 June 1/2 Before he could get home Mills captured two victims on foul flys. **1868** CHADWICK *Base Ball* 98 A fine foul fly catch by Fox then closed the innings for the two runs scored. **1880** N. BROOKS *Fairport Nine* xiv. 184 Billy Hetherington followed with a foul fly which he sent straight into the catcher's hands.

(5) **1878** *De Witt's Baseball Guide* 84 The foul lines shall be unlimited in length, and shall run from the right and left hand corners of the home base through the centre of the first and third bases to the foul posts. **1948** *Miami* (Okla.) *News-Record* 2 July 4/2 Harris' dribble down the first base foul line counted Reaugh. — (6) **1878** *De Witt's Baseball Guide* 84 The foul posts . . . shall be located at the boundary of the field and within the range of home and first base, and home and third base. — (7) **1845** in *Wilkes' Spirit of Times* (1864) 17 Dec. 244/2 No ace or base can be made on a foul strike. **1909** WEBSTER 858/1 F[oul] strike, . . . a foul counted as a strike. **1916** BANCROFT *Handbook* 80 Foul strike. A hit by the batter made with one or both feet outside the space called the batter's box. — (8) **1870** *Cin. Commercial* 13 May 5/1 Allison out on foul tip at his brother's hands. **1916** BANCROFT *Handbook* 80 Foul tip. A misplay by the batsman in which the ball merely touches the tip of the bat without changing direction. This counts as a foul strike.

b. (1) **foul hand,** (see quot. 1864); (2) **foul-in-the-foot,** (see quots.).

(1) **1864** W. B. DICK *Amer. Hoyle* (1866) 176 *Foul Hand.*—A hand composed of more or less than five cards. **1887** KELLER *Draw Poker* 10. — (2) **1858** FLINT *Milch Cows* 284 Cows and other stock, when fed in low, wet pastures, will often suffer from ulcers or sores, generally appearing first between the claws. This is commonly called foul in the foot, and is analogous to foot-rot. **1884** *Rep. Comm. Agric.* 229 The disease known as foul-in-the-foot, and often called foot-rot, has its origin in the skin.

***foul,** *v.*

1. *Baseball. tr.* To hit a ball so that a foul results.

1889 *Cent.* 2350/3 *Foul*, . . . to strike a foul ball. **1948** *Dly. Ardmoreite* (Ardmore, Okla.) 15 July 12/1 Raschi had two strikes on him and continued to foul balls until he got the one he wanted.

b. *To foul out,* (see quot. 1889).

1870 *N.Y. Herald* 5 July 8/3 Start fouled out. **1889** *Cent.* 2350/3 To foul out, . . . to be retired from the bat through the catching of a foul ball by one of the opposite nine. **1948** *Dly. Ardmoreite* (Ardmore, Okla.) 28 April 8/1 He made a couple of errors, struck out twice, singled, fouled out to the catcher.

2. *intr.* In basketball, to transgress a rule of the game. Also *to foul out,* to be declared out of the game because of personal fouls.

1948 *Dly. Ardmoreite* (Ardmore, Okla.) 21 Jan. 8/1 The taller Duncan quintet succeeded in getting Joe Smith and Jim Wagoner to foul out before the second quarter ended. *Ib.* 22 Jan. 10/2 This seems to prove that skilled operatives can play basketball without fouling. **1948** *Chi. Sun* 27 Jan. 23/4 Twenty-five players on the invading teams fouled out as compared to 15 on the home team.

***found,** *a. and found,* with food and lodging in addition to wages. *Colloq.*

1830 S. SMITH *Major Downing* 13, I get 12 dollars a month and found, and now and then some old clothes, which is better than keeping school at five dollars. **1853** B. F. TAYLOR *Jan. & June* (1871) 273 A story . . . he wouldn't have whispered for twelve dollars a month 'and found.' **1923** B. M. BOWER *Parowan Bonanza* iv. 48, I got him cheap for yuh. Three dollars and found.

***foundation,** *n.*

1. An established fund or endowment for students, a scholarship fund. Also attrib.

1724 *Md. Hist. Mag.* VI. 3 [The scholars appointed by the visitors were known as] foundation scholars. **1851** HALL *College Words* 134 *Foundation.* . . . In America it is also applied to a donation or legacy appropriated especially to maintain poor and deserving, or other students at a college. **1943** *U. of Chi. Cat.* 27 The La Verne Noyes Foundation . . . provides part tuition fees for students who [etc.].

2. The blood or lineage of a horse. Also attrib.

1883 *Harper's Mag.* Oct. 724/2 Many consider two trotting crosses upon a thorough-bred foundation the nearest to perfection that has been reached. **1893** G. W. CURTIS *Horses, Cattle* 58 The association recognizes as 'foundation stock' . . . the following individual sources of saddle blood.

3. (See quot. 1888.) *Obs.*

1887 *Cent. Mag.* (F.), The two foundations so near together were evidence of a dispute about the title to the little strip of meadow land, on which the occupants perhaps expected to find gold. **1888** *Ib.* Jan. 411/2 A 'foundation' in Montana means four logs laid across each other so as to form a square, and is a legal notification of intent to build a cabin and take up a claim.

founding fathers. The statesmen of the Revolutionary period, esp. the members of the Convention of 1787. — **1941** K. B. UMBRIET (*title*), Founding Fathers: Men Who Shaped Our Tradition. **1947** *Chr. Sci. Monitor* 21 May 12/4 The founding fathers determined that there should be free exercise of religion and wrote it into the Bill of Rights. **1949** *Chi. D. News* 12 March 8/1 The founding fathers wisely provided a government of checks and balances.

***fountain,** *n.*

1. = **soda fountain.** Also attrib.

1843 CARLTON *New Purchase* I. 52, I shall make no attempt to record their . . . puns—good things of the sort, like soda-water, had better be taken at the fountain. **1874** KNIGHT 910/2 *Fountain,* . . . a box B

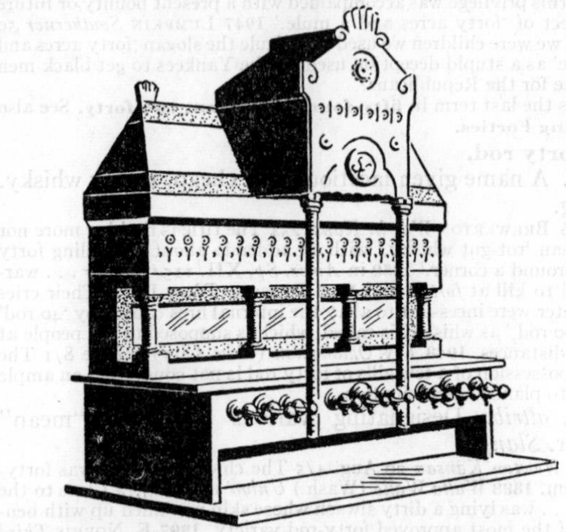

Early (*c*1880) type of fountain or soda fountain

containing ice and a coil through which aërated water, known as 'soda-water,' is conducted to the nozzle, when it is drawn into glasses. **1948** *Life* 31 May 85 Get your fountain drinks where they use clean, safe Dixie cups.

2. In combs.: (1) **Fountain City,** a nickname for Fond du Lac, Wisconsin; (2) **cock,** a cock on a soda fountain; (3) **ink eraser,** an ink eraser with a reservoir of chemical fluid; (4) **plant,** a garden amaranth, *Amaranthus tricolor angustior.*

(1) **1859** *Ladies' Repository* XIX. 308/2 Fond Du Lac, Wisconsin—'the Fountain City'—from the multiplicity of its fountains; as good, pure water can be obtained only by boring. — (2) **1851** CIST *Cincinnati* 174 Fountain cocks and generator work. — (3) **1892** *Voice* 8 Dec. (*advt.*), Wanted—Salesmen . . . to sell . . . our famous Fountain Ink Eraser. — (4) *Amer. Folk-Lore* VII. 97 *Amarantus salicifolius,* . . . fountain-plant. Boston florists' catalogue.

***four,** *a.*

1. In noun combs.: (1) **four flush,** (*a*) in stud poker, four cards of the same suit, (*b*) designating a bluffer or someone or something pretentious, *colloq.;* (2) **flusher,** one who four-flushes, also **four-card flusher,** *slang;* (3) ***fold,** "a quadruple assessment for neglect to make return of taxable estate" (W. 1806), *obs.;* (4) **Four-H,** (usu. **4-H**), designating a club or unit in a national system of education in home economics and agriculture, esp. for children of rural areas, so called because of its fourfold aim in improving the head, heart, hands, and health; (5) **hundred,** a name applied to the exclusive set of a community, esp. New York, cf. **four million;** (6) **-in-hand drag,** a heavy coach with seats on top, drawn by four horses; (7) **million,** the common people, *slang;* (8) ***-pence,** *N. Eng.* = next, *obs.*, cf. **fip(p)enny bit, picayune, sixpence;** (9) ***pence halfpenny,** a silver coin, the Spanish half real, with a value of about five or six cents, *obs.;* (10) **rail fence,** see **rail fence;** (11) **shift system,** a system of farming land by dividing it into four parts, one part of which is cowpenned each year; (12) **spanner,** a wagon together with the four pairs of horses that draw it, *colloq.;* (13) **straight,** in poker, a hand with a sequence of four cards in two or more suits; (14) **up,** some kind of gambling game; (15) ***winged,** *a.* a designation applied to the snowdrop tree, *Halesia carolina.*

(1) (*a*) **1887** [see **four straight**]. **1946** MOREHEAD & MOTT-SMITH *Penguin Hoyle* 123 In Stud Poker, it is occasionally ruled that a four-flush beats a pair. (*b*) **1899** GEORGE ADE *Fables in Slang* (1911) 12 But she always saw the same old line of Four-Flush Drummers from Chicago and St. Louis. **1904** *N.Y. Ev. Post* 20 Feb. 10 Mayor Harrison's assertion that the Sunday closing law is a 'four-flush' law—one that was meant to deceive and not meant for actual enforcement. — (2) **1910** *Outlook* 25 June 376 Though he was just home from Los Angeles with flying prizes won there, many doubted his intention, and one newspaper called him a 'four-flusher' and advised its readers that no start would be attempted. **1911** R. D. SAUNDERS *Col. Todhunter* vii. 98 You know it, you little fo'-card flusher, you. **1948** *Pacific Spectator* Spring 131 They are fourflushers, heels, or stuffed shirts. — (3) **1779** *Vermont State P.* (1823) 296 The listers shall add the sum total of such additions and four-folds, to the sum total before mentioned. **c1796** *Conn. Laws in Force* 276 The Sum Total thereof, shall by the Listers in each Town, be returned (with the Additions and Fourfolds) to the General Assembly in May. — (4) **1927** *Ardmore* (Okla.) *Statesman* 6 Jan. 3/2 'Helpfulness' is the single word used by President Coolidge in his New Years greeting to all 4-H clubs, Boy Scouts and Lone Scouts, to express the principles and purposes of those organizations. **1949** *Democrat* 31 March 4/3 They are being taught through the 4-H Clubs.

(5) **1888** *N.Y. Tribune* 8 April 5/1 Not all of 'the 400' have yet returned from the South, although many of them are now on their way back. **1948** *Coronet* Aug. 36/1 To social strivers she is Queen of the 400. — (6) **1886** *Outing* April 63/1 The upright position, almost standing against the sloping cushion of a four-in-hand drag or mail phaeton, . . . is a mistake [made by many drivers]. **1898** *Ib.* April 58/2 It was like taking the brake off from a four-in-hand drag on a steep grade. — (7) **1906** O. HENRY *Four Million* (Foreword), Not very long ago some one invented the assertion that there were only 'Four Hundred' people in New York City who were really worth noticing. But a wiser man has arisen—the census taker—and his larger estimate of human interest has been preferred in marking out the field of these little stories of the 'Four Million.' — (8) [**1759** *Essex Inst. Coll.* XLIX. 3 A Salor coming from a vessel in the Harbour was a nigh as a four pence to a groat of being drowned.] **1829** *Yankee* April 120/1 The man, who will give but a four-pence to save his soul, will give twenty-five cents for relief from sickness—and a dollar to have his own will. **1869** BARNUM *Struggles & Triumphs* 26 Before I was five years of age, I began to accumulate pennies and 'four-pences.' — (9) **1834** C. A. DAVIS *Lett. J. Downing* 35 When they say they can hit a dollar, tell 'em you can hit a fourpencehappeny. **1856** GOODRICH *Recoll.* I. 285 She spent a large part of her life in cheating her husband out of *fourpence-ha'pennies.* [*Note:*] This word was formerly the shibboleth of the Yankees—every one being set down as a New Englander who said *fourpence-ha'penny.* **1880** N. BROOKS *Fairport Nine* x. 125 Abel Grindel . . . found about two thousand pieces, but many of them were small, scarcely as large as the fourpence ha'penny, or six-and-a-quarter-cents coin, which circulated then.

(11) **1814** J. TAYLOR *Arator* 126 Those tied by habit to . . . the three shift system, object to the inclosing and four shift system, 'that having labor adequate to the tilling one third of their arable land, a portion of it would be unemployed, by restricting this labor to the cultivation of a fourth only.' **1839** BUEL *Farmer's Companion* 75 Cattle fed with turnips are computed to make double the manure that those do which are fed upon dry fodder. . . . By this mode of management, ample means may be provided for keeping up the fertility of the soil, when put under the four-shift system. — (12) **1896** *Advance* 26 March 450/2, I drove a four-spanner [or wagon] six, seven months, off'n on. — (13) **1887** J. W. KELLER *Draw Poker* 35 If in opening a pot a player finds in his hand a pair and a four flush, or four straight, he may break his pair and draw to the straight or the flush. — (14) **1931** BRADFORD *John Henry* 42 Four-up, coon-can, skin, or dice. Hit's all one and de same to me, and I plays you even.

(15) **1785** MARSHALL *Amer. Grove* 57 *Halesia tetraptera.* Four-winged fruited Halesia. . . . The flowers . . . are succeeded by sharp-pointed fruit having four wings. **1897** SUDWORTH *Arborescent Flora* 323 *Halesia Carolina.* . . . Four-winged Halesia (Ala.).

b. In similar combs. of obvious meaning or sufficiently explained in the quots.: (1) **four and four,** (2) **balls,** (3) **bits,** see **bit,** *n.* **2. b,** (4) **-cornered cat,** (5) **corners,** (6) **-day meeting,** (7) **gallon act,** cf. **fifteen gallon law,** (8) **-handed reel,** (9) **-lined ground squirrel,** (10) **minute men,** (11) **mule team,** (12) **Nations,** (13) **patch,** (14) **paws,** (15) **-spot beetle,** (16) **-spotted flounder.**

(1) **1929** SHELTON *Salt-box House* xii. 89 The every-day dress was simple; short gowns and petticoats were of home-made woolens, and striped or 'checked' linens, 'four and four' (thread to the check) or linsey-woolsey. — (2) **1910** *Spalding's Base Ball Guide* 369 The batsman becomes a base runner . . . instantly after 'Four Balls' have been called by the umpire. — (4) **1888** *Cosmopolitan* Oct. 443 'One-cornered cat' . . . was, therefore, forced to give way to a further development called 'three-cornered cat,' which in turn was followed by a 'four-cornered cat,' and from this finally was developed the primitive 'base-ball.'

(5) **1857** *Spirit of Times* 13 June 226/3 Off the two cronies put for the 'Four Corners,' distant perhaps four miles. **1889** *Cent.* 1269/3 *Four-corners.* . . . A place where two main highways intersect each other at right angles: sometimes used in names of places in the United States: as, Chatham Four Corners in Columbia county, New York. — (6) **1835** GRIFFITHS *Two Years* 175 The common name of these [religious] Meetings in Ohio, is 'Four-day Meetings,' because, under ordinary circumstances, they are held four days. — (7) **1865** *Harper's Mag.* Sep. 544/1 A few years since the Legislature of Michigan passed what was termed the 'Four Gallon Act,' which prohibited the sale of ale or malt liquors in less quantities than four gallons. — (8) **1852** REYNOLDS *Hist. Illinois* 266 In those days, they danced jiggs, and four-handed reels, as they were called. — (9) **1820** JAMES *Exped.* II. 234 Among the animals taken here was the four-lined squirrel, . . . a very small and very handsome species. **1857** *Rep. Comm. Patents 1856: Agric.* 73, I learn from Dr. Hoy that the four-lined ground squirrel (*Tamias quadrivittatus,* of Say) is found in Northern Wisconsin.

(10) **1917** *N.Y. Times* 30 Sep. II. 4/5 Reports are being circulated that the Four Minute Men are paid for the work they are doing. *Ib.* 19 Nov. 4/2 President Wilson . . . expresses his appreciation of the patriotic work being done by the Four-Minute Men, a Government agency who present wartime messages of the Administration to theatre audiences throughout the country. — (11) **1880** *Rep. Supt. Yellowstone Nat. Pk. 1879* 3 The purchase of an excellent four-mule team . . . enabled me to speedily construct a rough log building upon the McCartney Creek. **1936** MCKENNA *Black Range* 270 When I last saw you in '78 you were hiring a four-mule team hitched to a Government wagon to go down there. — (12) **1797** in *Ga. Hist. Soc. Coll.* III. i, I have not yet determined to set up in that capacity in either of the Four Nations. **1907** HODGE *Amer. Indians* I. 472/1 Four Nations. Mentioned with the Kawita and Kasihta as having a conference with the English near the mouth of Apalachicola r., Fla., in 1814. . . . Probably the Oakfuskee, with their 3 villages on the Chattahoochee, were meant. — (13) **1898** E. C. HALL *Aunt Jane* 57 There seemed to be every pattern of quilt that the ingenuity of woman could devise and the industry of woman put together,—'four-patches,' 'nine-patches,' . . . 'rising suns.' — (14) **1905** *Forestry Bureau Bul.* No. 61, 35 Two coupling grabs joined by a short cable, used for fastening logs together, . . . [are called in the Pacific Coast Forest] four paws.

(15) **1854** EMMONS *Agric. N.Y.* V. 271 *Tetraopes,* or Fourspot-beetle: Foureyed Tetraope. . . . *Tetraopes tetrophthalma.* — (16) **1883** *Nat. Museum Bul.* No. 27, 496 *Paralichthys oblongus.* . . . Four-spotted Flounder. **1884** GOODE *Fisheries* I. 181 The common Four-spotted Flounder, *Paralichthys oblongus,* . . . occasionally finds its way to market in company with the Plaice, and is doubtless sold under the same name. . . . It may be readily distinguished by the presence upon the back of four large, dark spots.

c. *To hit a four-bagger,* to do something remarkably well, in allusion to knocking a home run in baseball. *Colloq.*

1925 WITWER *Roughly Speaking* 296 Hazel Killian hit a four-bagger as a prophet on that last remark.

2. In verb combs.: (1) **four-flush,** in poker, to bluff with a four flush hand, also, transf., to bluff by making false claims of any kind, usu. **four-flushing,** *slang;* (2) ***fold,** (*a*) (see quots. and cf. **four-fold,** *n.*), *obs.;* (*b*) in ellipt. context, to quadruple the cables on (a capstan), *obs.*

(1) **1901** J. FLYNT *World of Graft* 46 They make a pinch o' some second-class old thief. . . . That's what I call four-flushin'. **1904** *Sat. Ev. Post* 6 Feb. 2/1 There is a good, plain, honest virtue in the word 'four-flushing' . . . it draws its name from the poker table. **1920** OSTRANDER *How Many Cards?* 245, I've an idea that Waverly is four-flushing financially . . . and is in on a percentage of Cutler's games. **1942** STEGNER *Mormon C.* 286 So, perhaps, was a four-flushing holdup man named Gunplay Maxwell.

(2) (*a*) **c1796** *Conn. Laws in Force* 275 The said Listers . . . shall . . . add Fourfold for all the rateable Estate they shall find left out of the List, . . . giving Notice thereof to the Persons fourfolded. **a1817**

DWIGHT *Travels* IV. 285 If the proprietor gives in a false list, he is punished by having the falsified article increased in the list fourfold. . . . We therefore, style this punishment *Four-folding.* (*b*) **1815** *Niles' Reg.* IX. 201/2 In order to move the arch sideways, . . . we four-folded all the capstans, except one.

As the last term in **big, figgery, figure, forty, two-by-four.**

Fourteenth Amendment. An amendment to the Constitution, proposed just after the Civil War and ratified by 1868, granting citizenship to the former slaves and embodying various other principles of reconstruction.

1868 *Nation* 23 July 61/1 The Fourteenth Constitutional Amendment has been so long before the people that the average reader has very likely forgotten just what it is. . . . On Tuesday, Congress passed a concurrent resolution declaring the amendment part of the Constitution. **1891** *Atlantic Mo.* June 810/1 It is one good result of the Fourteenth Amendment that no distinction is made in law between property owned by white and that owned by blacks. **1949** D. O. MCGOVNEY *Amer. Suffrage* 4 The Fourteenth Amendment, adopted in 1868, directs Congress to reduce the number of representatives in Congress from any state that disfranchises any adult male citizen.

* **fourth,** *a.* and *n.*

1. (Usu. *cap.*) Short for **Fourth of July,** freq. **glorious fourth.**

1827 LONGFELLOW in S. Longfellow *H. W. Longfellow* I. 121 We did not celebrate the 'glorious Fourth' here. **1829** GARRISON in W. P. & F. J. Garrison *W. L. Garrison* I. 125 My address, for the Fourth, is almost completed. **1948** *Miami* (Okla.) *D. News-Record* 4 July 1/5 Where are Miami's glorious fourths of yesteryear?

2. In combs.: (1) **fourth class,** see as a main entry; (2) **house,** (see quot. and cf. **third house** (*b*)); (3) **of July,** see as a main entry; (4) **proof,** (*a*) of spirits, four times refined, highly refined, also as a noun, (*b*) also fig.

(2) **1888** M. LANE in *America* 4 Oct. 16 *Fourth House.*—A name given in Congress, and, in conventions, to the reporters' gallery in consequence of the influence that their reports and criticisms are supposed to have upon intended action or legislation. — (4) (*a*) **1828** SHERBURNE *Memoirs* i. 24 My share was about one ton of sugar, from thirty to forty gallons of fourth proof Jamaica rum. **1845** SIMMS *Wigwam & Cabin* 423 [He] concluded with a glowing eulogy upon the quality of his 'powerful, fine, gennywine, fourt' proof', the best in Holland's establishment. (*b*) **1836** *Quarter Race Ky.* (1846) 17 They used fourth-proof oaths with a volubility that would bother a congressional reporter. **1886** MARK TWAIN *Speeches* (1923) 137 Tons of A No. 1, fourth-proof, hard-boiled, hide-bound grammar.

fourth class.

1. The freshman class, esp. in the Naval and Military academies. Also attrib.

1862 STRONG *Cadet Life W. Point* 116 We were evidently appearing too comfortable to suit a second or third classman's ideas of fourth-class propriety. **1905** LINCOLN *Partners* 70 At the end of the year he was 'promoted'—that is, he was no longer a member of the fourth class, but instead proudly left his seat when the third was called. **1908** *D.N.* III. 312 *Fourth* class, freshman class. Also *fourth* classman, etc. [e. Ala.]

2. One of the classifications for mail, domestic parcel post exceeding eight ounces in weight and including, chiefly, merchandise, farm and factory products, and printed matter. Also attrib.

1879 *Statutes at Large* XX. 360 All matter of the fourth class shall be subject to examination. **1901** RYAN *Montana* 87 The mail came every two weeks, and its magnitude was of the fourth-class order. **1948** *Chi. Sun-Times* 11 July 24/5 Fourth class, parcel post over eight ounces, earns 15 per cent of total revenue and costs 18.2 per cent of total expenses.

Fourth of July.

1. The day in 1776 when American independence was declared, or the anniversary of this day. Sometimes preceded by "glorious." Cf. * **fourth, 1.**

[**1777** *Jrnls. Cont. Congress* VIII. 625 There is due . . . a bill for materials, workmanship, &c. furnished for the fireworks on the 4 July, the sum of 102 69/90 dollars.] **1779** *N.H. Hist. Soc. Coll.* VI. 317 Toasts were drank, to wit: . . . The Fourth of July, '76: The memorable era of American Independence. **1852** *Harper's Mag.* V. 264/2, The bare thought that our glorious old Fourth of July could never more be celebrated in its true spirit . . . is enough to check the wildest faction. **1948** *Popular Western* June 27/2 Monday was the Fourth of July and Caprock's false fronts were festooned with gay bunting.

transf. and *fig.* **1835** *Vade Mecum* (Phila.) 31 Jan. 4/6, I had ya hea I'd come up da and knock boff ya eyes into next forf' o' July, ya young scoundal. **1867** DEVENS *Pictorial Bk.* 120 He 'felt his Fourth of July [i.e., patriotic ardor] rising too fast.' **1870** *Terr. Enterprise* (Virginia, Nev.) 18 Mar. 3/2 Yesterday was St. Patrick's Day—the Hibernian Fourth of July—the city was free from broils as usual. **1897** HOWELLS *Open-eyed Conspiracy* iii, Why, it's *all* gaiety, in one way. Saratoga is a perpetual Fourth of July, we think.

2. A celebration held on the Fourth of July.

1872 EGGLESTON *End of World* xvi. 110, I kin rattle off . . . big words picked up at Fourth-of-Julys. **1923** *D.N.* V. 207 We're aimin' on havin' a Fourth o' July down on the creek. [In Ozark Mts.]

3. Often attrib., esp. to designate celebrations and events taking place on July 4, as **Fourth of July celebration, dinner, idea, oration, orator, oratory.**

1807 WEEMS *Letters* II. 369 From these reflections . . . we may collect some good fourth-of-July ideas. **1807** IRVING *Salmagundi* xiv. 388 He thunders with peculiar emphasis and pompous enunciation, in the true style of a Fourth of July orator. **1816** U. BROWN *Journal* I. 353 The 4th of July's Celebration was the cause of this Disappointment. **1817** PAULDING *Lett. from South* I. 249 The mass of Fourth of July orations . . . come forth 'hissing hot,' in which the glories of the revolution are obscured by the manner of celebrating them. **1860** *Ladies' Repository* XX. 28/2 At a political mass meeting, at even a Fourth of July dinner. **1948** *Gainesville* (Tex.) *D. Reg.* 3 July 2/1 Fourth of July oratory is not what it used to be.

b. Fourth of July fireworks, fireworks set off to celebrate the Fourth. Also fig. and attrib.

1861 NEWELL *Orpheus C. Kerr* I. 19 All of a suddint somethin' knocked Fourth-o'-July fireworks out of my eyes, and I went to grass with my heels up. **1870** MARK TWAIN *Sk., New & Old* 26 All the falling stars and Fourth-of-July fireworks of a generation . . . would not have any advantage of the pyrotechnic display [etc.]. **1894** *Harper's Mag.* July 301 In the evening we'll have a genuine Fourth of July fireworks show.

c. Fourth-of-Julyism, a jingoistic declaration or remark.

1853 *S. Lit. Messenger* XIX. 473/1 Fourth-of-Julyisms fled to the stump or the national anniversary barbecues. **1874** B. F. TAYLOR *World on Wheels* 183 A Fourth-of-Julyism has somehow become an object of contempt. People tell us, . . . that speeches are idle, because they have heard that silence is golden.

* **fowl,** *n.*

1. fowl grass, =next.

1751 ELIOT *Field-Husb.* iii. 57 Of these Two sorts of Natural Grass, the Fowl Grass is much the best.

2. fowl meadow (grass), false redtop, *Poa palustris,* also meadow spear grass, *Glyceria striata.*

1748 ELIOT *Field-Husb.* 6, I then proceeded to sow Grass-Seed, such as red Clover, foul Meadow Grass, English Spear Grass, and Herd Grass. **1751** *Ib.* iii. 57 There are [in New England] Two sorts of Grass . . . which I would Recommend; these are Herd-Grass . . . and Fowl-Meadow, sometimes called Duck-Grass, and sometimes Swampwire-Grass. **1874** *Vt. Bd. Agric. Rep.* II. 207 Sows foul meadow also on upland, and finds it stands very well. **1889** VASEY *Agric. Grasses* 67 *Poa serotina* (Fowl Meadow Grass). . . . This species is most common in the Northern States, particularly in New England, New York, and westward to Wisconsin.

As the last term in **dominique, flocking, Japan, moor, mountain, prairie, raft, sage, troop fowl.**

* **fox,** *n.*

1. (*cap.*) *pl.* A tribe of Algonquian Indians formerly resident about Green Bay, Wisconsin, but now in Oklahoma, Iowa, and Kansas.

1737 *N.Y. State Col. Hist.* VI. 104 Young People . . . [have promised] the French to Joyn them in a Warlike Expedition against the Foxes. **1820** *Niles' Reg.* XVIII. 257/1 The presence of the Sacks and Foxes has restrained them [the Winnebagos] hitherto. **1868** *N.Y. Herald* 31 July 5/4 The Senate . . . ratified treaties with the Potawatamies Sacs and Foxes, of Kansas.

b. Also (*sing.*) attrib.

1765 ROBERT ROGERS *North Amer.* (London ed.) 163 Into the north end of it [Green Bay] flows a large river . . . called the river of Foxes, on which live a nation of Indians, called the Fox Indians. **1819** in *Wis. State H.S. Coll.* VIII. 288 About ninety miles from Prairie du Chien, and seven miles from the west side of the river, is a lead mine which is worked by the Fox Indians. **1839** *N.O. Picayune* 26 Feb. 2/4 *Iowa,* in the language of the Fox tribe of Indians, signifies 'This is the Land.' **1948** *New World* (Chi.) 2 July 13/3 The Sauk and Fox Indians . . . gathered on Watch Tower hill overlooking Rock River for their feasts, competitive games and tribal pow-wows.

2. A variety of potato. *Rare.*

1844 *Knickerb.* XXIII. 32 Are they kidneys, blue-noses, or fox?—and will they bu'st open white and mealy?

3. (*cap.*) A nickname for an inhabitant of Maine. *Obs.*

1845 *St. Louis Reveille* 14 May 2/4 The inhabitants of Maine, are called Foxes. **1889** *N. & Q.* IV. 16 Nov. 33 Foxes.—The 'Imperial

Dictionary' informs us that the people of Maine are called 'foxes' in the United States. I once lived in that State, yet I never have heard the nickname applied as indicated. **1949** *Amer. Sp.* Feb. 29 *Fox* for a Maine man seems to embalm an early impression that the citizens of the state were smart fellows.

4. A freshman. *Obs.* [Cf. G. *Fuchs,* in the same sense, and see **assassin collar.**]

1847 *Yale Lit. Mag.* XII. 116 'Hallo there, Herdman, fox!,' yelled another lusty tippler.

5. In special combs.: (1) **fox breeding,** the breeding of foxes for their pelts; (2) **farm,** a farm where foxes are bred for the commercial value of their pelts, also **fox farming;** (3) ***fire,** in fig. and transf. uses (see quots.); (4) **ranch,** =**fox farm;** (5) ***skin,** a cap made of a fox skin, in full **fox skin cap;** (6) **tail saw,** (see quot.); (7) **trot,** see as a main entry; (8) **walk,** =**fox trot 1.**

(1) **1900** *Scientific Amer.* 21 April 242/3 Fox breeding for their pelts is assuming proportions of considerable magnitude on the Alaskan Islands. — (2) **1906** *Country Life* Jan. 294/2 The best working out of fox farming as a paying commercial enterprise that I have seen is at Dover, Me. **1913** *Outing* Dec. 321/1 A typical fox farm is made up of an inner group of small breeding-pens surrounded by an outer fence. — (3) **1853** *S. Lit. Messenger* XIX. 473/2 After the first bustle of their coming with the fox-fire of their old reputation sticking to their gowns, it was generally found, . . . that the new importation would not suit the market. **1890** *Voice* 26 June, About time sensible people quit frightening themselves with the fox-fire of a lot of office-thirsty politicians. **1920** HUNTER *Trail Drivers Texas* I. 149 [In a storm] you could see phosphorescence (fox fire) on our horses' ears. — (4) **1900** *Scientific Amer.* 21 April 242/3 There are no less than thirty-five [Alaskan] islands occupied by proprietors of fox ranges.

(5) **1823** COOPER *Pioneers* v. Nothing could have wrought a greater transformation than the single act of removing the rough fox-skin cap. **1853** F. W. THOMAS *J. Randolph* 129 Ladies, don't be frightened, said old Kentuck, . . . taking off his fox-skin. **1880** *Harper's Mag.* May 907/2 We encountered a heavily bearded man wearing a fox skin cap. — (6) **1874** KNIGHT 912 Fox-tail Saw. A dovetail saw. — (8) **1879** TOURGEE *Fool's Errand* xxxvi. 249 The horse fell into the swinging fox-walk . . . whenever the character of the road or the mood of his rider demanded.

b. In the names of birds and other animals: (1) **fox-colored finch,** =**fox sparrow;** (2) **colored sparrow,** =**fox sparrow;** (3) **colored thrush,** the brown thrasher, *Toxostoma rufum;* (4) **marten,** =**fisher 1;** (5) **snake,** a harmless snake of a reddish color, *Elaphe vulpina;* (6) **sparrow,** a large sparrow of the species *Passerella iliaca;* (7) **squirrel,** any one of three varieties of arboreal squirrel—*Sciurus niger rufiventer,* of the Mississippi Valley, *S. n. neglectus,* of the eastern states, or *S. n. niger,* of the South, also a squirrel belonging to one of these varieties, cf. **gray, ground fox squirrel.**

(1) **1839** AUDUBON *Birds of Amer.* III. 142 The Fox-coloured Finch is found abundantly on the Columbia river. — (2) **1811** WILSON *Ornithology* III. 53 The Fox-Colored Sparrow, *Fringilla Rufa,* . . . frequents low sheltered thickets; . . . scraping the ground, and rustling among the fallen leaves. **1858** BAIRD *Birds Pacific R.R.* 488 Fox-colored sparrow. . . . Eastern United States to the Mississippi.— (3) **c1729** CATESBY *Carolina* I. 28 *Turdus ruffus.* The Fox coloured Thrush. . . . This Bird is called in Virginia the French Mock-bird. It remains all the year in Carolina and Virginia. **1917** *Birds of Amer.* III. 179. — (4) **1818** *Jrnl. Science* I. 83, I have, therefore, given to it the name of *Mustela vulpina,* or Fox Marten, owing to its head and tail being somewhat similar to that of a fox.

(5) **1857** *Rep. Comm. Patents 1856: Agric.* 88 [Meadow-mice] are also found in the stomachs of the milk-snake, and of the large fox-snake (*Scotophis vulpinus*). **1892** *Smithsonian Rep.* 832 The fox snake appears to be moderately common in some localities. — (6) **1865** BURROUGHS in *Atlantic Mo.* May 521/2, I have met here many of the rarer species, such as the . . . Blue-Winged Swamp-Warbler, . . . the Worm-Eating Warbler, the Fox-Sparrow, etc. **1948** *Pacific Discovery* March–April 18/1 The fox sparrow breaks the purple skin of the persimmon fruits with its stout bill, and eats greedily of the orange pulp. — (7) **1682** ASH *Carolina* 22 There are . . . the Red, the Grey, the Fox and Black Squirrels. **1737** BRICKELL *N. Carolina* 127 The Fox-Squirrel, so call'd, from its being the largest, and smelling like a Fox. **1834** PECK *Gaz. Illinois* 37 The gray and fox squirrels often do mischief in the corn fields and the hunting of them makes fine sport for the boys. **1948** *Sierra Club Bul.* Mar. 12 The opossum, fox squirrel, and bullfrog have fitted fairly well into our faunal community.

c. In the names of plants: (1) **foxberry,** (*a*) the bearberry, *Arctostaphylos uva-ursi,* also attrib., (*b*) (see quots.); (2) **grape,** see as a main entry; (3) ***grass** the salt grass, *Spartina patens;* (4) **sedge,** (see quot.); (5) **-tail pine,** see as a main entry; (6) **wood,** (see quot. 1889).

(1) (*a*) **1784** CUTLER in *Mem. Academy* I. 444 *Arbutus.* . . . Foxberry. Checkerberry. **1873** PHELPS *Trotty's Wedding* xx, The ruins of little foxberry blossoms . . . turned wax-white at sight of her. (*b*) **1876** HOBBS *Bot. Hand-Book* 39 Fox berry, Frost grape, Vitis vulpina. **1931** DAYTON *Western Browse Plants* 136 Mountain cranberry, . . . frequently called foxberry, . . . is of some value as winter browse for reindeer and caribou in Alaska. — (3) **1838** *Mass. Agric. Survey 1st Rep.* 18 The next grass is the Red grass or Fox grass, a very fine reedy grass, abundant and excellent. — (4) **1843** TORREY *Flora N.Y.* II. 376 *Carex vulpinoidea.* . . . Fox Sedge. . . . Low grounds: common.

(6) **1775** in DEANE *Corr.* 333 He always depended on fox-wood, which gives light in the dark, to fix on the points of the needle of his compass, and in his barometer. **1889** *Cent.* 2356/2 *Fox-wood* . . . decayed wood, especially such as emits a phosphorescent light (U.S.).

As the last term in **black, blacktail, coast, cross, desert gray, Florida gray, grass, gray, grizzly, kit, plain, prairie, raccoon, red, royal, sierra red, silver, silver gray, swamp, swift fox.**

***fox,** *v. tr.* To disguise or confuse (a trail). *Obs.* — **1873** MILLER *Amongst Modocs* 184, I saw that Klamat kept an eye constantly on his rifle when not foxing the trail and eyeing the pursuers.

fox grape, *n.* Either of two species of wild grapes: the northern fox grape, *Vitis labrusca,* and the southern fox grape, *V. rotundifolia;* also the fruit or a plant of these species.

The northern fox grape is the source of Isabella, Concord, and other cultivated varieties; the southern is the source of the scuppernong.

1638 in *Md. Hist. Soc. Pub.* No. 28 (1899) 208, I haue not seene as yett any white grape excepting the foxgrape which hath some stayne of white. **1640** PARKINSON *Theater of Plants* 1556 The Foxe Grape . . . hath more rugged barke, a very broad leafe, without any division almost but dented, and the Grape is white, but smelleth and tasteth like unto a Foxe. **1737** BRICKELL *Nat. Hist. N.C.* (1911) 92 The Vines that are Spontaneous and produce Grapes in Carolina, are of six Kinds, and are as follows. The *Fox-grape,* whereof there are four sorts, Two of which are call'd the *Summer-Fox-grape,* because they are ripe in July. **1913** CATHER *O Pioneers!* 29 Stout as she was, she roamed the scrubby banks of Norway Creek looking for fox grapes and goose plums, like a wild creature in search of prey. **1942** TEHON *Native Ill. Shrubs* 186 The Fox Grape, which prefers woods along streams and bodies of water, ranges from New England to Illinois and south to Georgia.

attrib. **1942** WEYGANDT *Plenty of Penna.* 176 She was proud of her elderberry wine and her fox grape jelly.

b. The winter or frost grape.

1893 *Amer. Folk-Lore* VI. 139 *Vitis Cordifolia,* fox grapes. Ferrisburgh, Vt.

***foxing,** *n.* **1.** The action of confusing or obliterating a trail. **2.** Hunting fox. Both *rare.* — (1) **1855** SIMMS *Forayers* 478 They're quite too old at foxing to go right across, making but one step from the old track into the new one. — (2) **1877** HALLOCK *Sportsman's Gaz.* 17 With us of the North, foxing is by some followed during . . . winter.

foxtail pine. (See quot. 1909.)

1884 SARGENT *Rep. Forests* 191 *Pinus Balfouriana.* . . . Foxtail Pine. Hickory Pine. **1909** WEBSTER 860/2 *F[oxtail] pine,* any of several American pines, so called from their densely leafy branches, esp. *P. balfouriana* and *P. aristata* of the Pacific coast and *P. tæda* of the eastern states. **1948** *Pacific Discovery* Nov.–Dec. 20/2 At 10,000 feet elevation, where snow always lingers, may be found the foxtail pine.

fox trot.

1. A smooth and easy trotting gait of a horse.

1872 ROE *Army Lett.* 70 He has a fox trot, which is wonderfully easy. **1911** WRIGHT *Winning Barbara Worth* 386 They went on . . . without pause or check save the occasional change in gait from the swinging lope to the shuffling fox-trot. **1945** MATHEWS *Talking* 178 He does not need to be urged to strike a foxtrot down the backbone of the ridge.

2. A ballroom dance in four-four time. Also the music for this.

1915 *Victor Record Cat.* May, Dance Records. . . . Fox Trots. **1920** E. SCOTT *All about Latest Dances* 68 The true basis of the American Fox-Trot is an alternation of four slow and four or eight quick movements, depending on the step chosen. **1946** STANWELL-FLETCHER *Driftwood Valley* 127 They played mostly fox trots and we occasionally recognized the familiar strain of a modern tune.

fox-trot ˈfɑksˌtrɑt, *v. intr.* To dance a fox trot. Also **fox-trotting,** *a.*

1921 PAINE *Comr. Rolling Ocean* 75 A dozen couples . . . fox-trotted in a clear space of the forward deck. **1931** F. L. ALLEN *Only Yesterday*

11 There are a good many military uniforms among the fox-trotting dancers. **1948** *Chi. Tribune* 24 Mar. 1. 16/3 I'll be happy to teach you to fox trot.

*** fraction,** *n.* A piece of land smaller than the standard unit of measurement, esp. a fractional township or section.

"*Fractions*, are parts of quarter sections intersected by streams, or confirmed claims" (1838 Colton *Ind. Delineated* 66).

1789 in CIST *Cincinnati* (1841) 209 The whole of the township and fraction to be surveyed. **1847** in H. HOWE *Hist. Coll. Ohio* 206 Matthias Denman . . . had purchased the fraction of land on the bank of the Ohio, and the entire section adjoining it on the north. **1901** WHITE *Westerners* 156 Thar is a lode . . . over on the J. G. fraction that's shore th' purtiest bit of quartz leed you ever see.

b. **To a fraction, fig.* to a nicety, perfectly. *Colloq.*

1811 IRVING in P. M. Irving *Life & Lett. W. Irving* (1869) I. 201 This place would suit you to a fraction. **1858** D. K. BENNETT *Chronology N.C.* 24 They both lived to a very old age, truthful, faithful, obedient and honest to a fraction.

*** fractional,** *a.* In combs.: (1) **fractional bill,** a bill for less than a dollar, *obs.;* (2) **currency,** paper money in small denominations first issued in 1863 and recalled in 1876, also transf., cf. **shinplaster;** (3) **money,** =prec., *obs.;* (4) **note,** a paper note or bill for less than one dollar issued by the U.S. Government, a shinplaster, *obs.;* (5) **scrip,** a note of fractional currency, *obs.;* (6) **section,** a piece of surveyed land with less, rarely more, than 640 acres, irregularly defined because of topographical obstacles, also one of the sections on the north and west sides of a township slightly reduced in size to correct for the convergence of meridians, cf. **fraction;** (7) **township,** an area comprising less, or more, than thirty-six sections, irregularly defined because of topographical obstacles, cf. **fraction.**

(1) **1853** *Hunt's Merch. Mag.* XXVIII. 211 Fractional bills have been issued by individuals and firms. — (2) **1862** S. P. CHASE *Rep. Secy. Treas. June 30, 1862* (1863) 9 Congress, upon the recommendation of the Secretary, authorized the use of postage and revenue stamps as a fractional currency. **1892** LUMMIS *Tramp Across Continent* 145 The trader had been besieged by a crowd of women, bearing under their arms the fractional currency of the pueblo—the sheepskin, worth ten or fifteen cents according to weight. **1946** ADAMS *Album Amer. Hist.* III. 135 Later (July, 1862) Congress legalized small change notes by providing for the issuance of fractional currency in denominations of 3, 5, 10, 15, 25 and 50 cents. — (3) **1930** NEIL CAROTHERS (*title*), Fractional Money, A History of the small coins and Fractional Paper Currency of the United States. — (4) **1863** *Statutes at Large* XII. 711 In lieu of postage and revenue stamps for fractional currency, and of fractional notes, commonly called postage currency, issued or to be issued, the Secretary of the Treasury may issue fractional notes of like amounts in such form as he may deem expedient. **1903** STILES *Four Years* 63 In the South during the war banks, municipalities, companies, and, even in some cases, individuals issued fractional notes or shin plasters which passed as currency supplementary to the Treasury notes issued by the Confederate Government.

(5) **1891** in HEATH *Labor & Finance Revol.* p. xxiv, Mr. Heath . . . was convinced that the necessity which forced the green back dollar and fractional scrip into general use, . . . had demonstrated the utility and practicability of a pure paper currency based upon the wealth and credit of the nation. — (6) **1815** DRAKE *Cincinnati* 129 Cincinnati is built upon one entire and two fractional sections. **1831** PECK *Guide* 294 This town is laid out on fractional sections thirteen and fourteen, in township 5 north. **1837** —— *Gaz. Illinois* 56 The canal . . . enters the Illinois river, in the corner of fractional section 21, in township 33. — (7) **1797** *Statutes at Large* I. 466 There shall be no reservations, except for salt springs, in fractional townships. **1839** PLUMBE *Sk. Iowa* 65 At the opening of the Land Office in the Burlington land district, twenty-five townships or fractional townships of land were proclaimed to be sold. **1924** *Chi. D. News Almanac 1925* 912/2 Cook County Township High Schools. . . . Thornton Frac[tional Township High School].—Otis W. Glamore [principal], Calumet City.

fraktur fræk'tur, *n.* [G.]

1. (See quots.)

1904 T. L. DEVINNE *Mod. Book Composition* 253 (*Cent.*), Though black and forbidding, fraktur is a thin character. The small letters are about one fifth narrower than roman letters of same size of body. **1909** *Cent. Supp.* 495/2 fraktur. . . . In *printing*, the form of pointed letter used in ordinary German books and newspapers.

2. *attrib.* Of or pertaining to the Pennsylvania Dutch art of lettering and painting, esp. on birth and marriage certificates.

[**1924** LAMBERT *Pa. Ger.* 57/2 fraktura . . . pl. Gothic letters or figures. G. Frakturen.] **1938** HARK *Hex Marks Spot* 25 In fractur painting—that Pennsylvania Dutch survival of medieval illumination—they were extremely prevalent, together with additional forms and figures, such as roses, peacocks, angels. **1944** ADAMS *Album Amer. Hist.* I. 338 Among the Pennsylvania Germans the art of penmanship was highly developed, and certificates were decorated with what is known as the fraktur method.

*** frame,** *n.*

1. An unfattened beef animal.

1880 *Bradstreet's* 29 Sep. 3/4 The north British farmers are finding it profitable to import what the American dealers graphically call 'frames' to feed for market.

2. In combs.

In some of these combs. the first element is verbal, but the terms are grouped together for convenience of reference. The status of the "frame" terms for buildings is uncertain. The lack or lateness of British evidence in the *OED* may or may not be indicative of Amer. origin. At any rate, such combs. have been and still are widely current in U.S. use.

Designating structures and buildings made completely or almost entirely of wood, the supporting framework consisting of timbers nailed or mortised together, as (1) **frame addition,** (2) **barn,** (3) **building,** (4) **church,** (5) **cottage,** (6) **dwelling (house),** (7) **house,** (8) **land office,** (9) **laundry,** (10) **shack,** (11) **shanty,** (12) **shop,** (13) **store,** (14) **tenement.**

(1) **1901** DUNCAN & SCOTT *Allen & Woodson Co., Kansas* 74 The first house . . . was a log house which disappeared several years ago but the frame addition to which yet stands. — (2) **1753** in *N.J. Archives* 1 Ser. XIX. 248 To be Sold. . . . Plantation . . . there is on it . . . a large frame barn, and stables. **1884** *Cent. Mag.* Feb. 518/1 His little herd of sheep . . . were sheltered from the chill of winter nights in a frame barn bigger than their master's log house. — (3) **1791** BARTRAM *Travels* 92 The trunks of these trees . . . afford excellent shingles, boards, and other timber, adapted to every purpose in frame buildings. **1898** *Mo. So. Dakotan* I. 52 They had dreamed of the time when a white frame building with green blinds should take the place of the old sod house. — (4) **1862** MCCLELLAN in *Own Story* 355 My camp is at an old frame church in a grove.

(5) **1881** CABLE *Mme. Delphine* iv. 18 His dwelling was a little frame cottage, standing on high pillars just inside a tall, close fence. **1923** WYATT *Invisible Gods* 109 Her permanent abiding place was a small frame cottage. — (6) **1760** in *N.J. Archives* 1 Ser. XX. 425 To be sold, a certain Tract of Land . . . with three good frame Dwelling-houses. **1818** *Niles' Reg.* XV. 139/2 There were three frame dwellings and a blockmaker's and ship joiner's shop burnt to the ground. **1913** LONDON *Valley of Moon* III. xiv, He had just begun work on a small frame dwelling. — (7) **1735** in *N.J. Archives* 1 Ser. XI. 416 To be Sold, a Tract of Land . . . with a large Frame House on it. **1945** MAXWELL *Folded Leaf* 11 It was all right for him to think about . . . the tall, roomy, old-fashioned white frame house. — (8) **1930** HENRY *Conquer. Plains* 47 Later my brother's small frame land office . . . sprang into existence just to the north of our house. — (9) **1881** *Rep. Indian Affairs* 106 The Pottawattomie school buildings consist of a commodious and convenient school-building . . . frame laundry with cellar [etc.].

(10) **1924** MULFORD *Rustlers' Valley* 38 The street was a busy one in front of a line of lighted buildings, frame, one-story shacks all. **1942** STEGNER *Mormon C.* 265 The flimsy frame shacks went up like kindling. — (11) **1860** in *Amer. Sp.* XXII. 202/2, I found a single frame shanty erected. **1948** *Pacific Discovery* July–Aug. 9/2 It is a little frame shanty, perhaps twelve feet square. — (12) **1775** in *N.J. Archives* 1 Ser. XXXI. 224 To be sold . . . plantation . . . whereon is a frame house and shop, a barn and cow house, and other out houses. **1893** MARK TWAIN *P. Wilson* i, In each block two or three brick stores . . . towered above interjected bunches of little frame shops. — (13) **1835** HOFFMAN *Winter in West* I. 180 An enterprising young gentleman . . . is creating a flourishing establishment around him; a frame store and several log cabins. **1872** MCCLELLAN *Golden State* 126 A rude shell of a frame store or cotton tent rented for fabulous prices. — (14) **1799** *Aurora* 13 Aug. (Th.), Frame tenement at Auction.

As the last term in **balloon, cold, fire, hand, hog, house, lodge, mosquito, ox, papoose, spreading frame.**

*** frame,** *v.*

1. *tr.* To concoct a false charge or accusation against, to make (one) the victim of a "frame-up." *Slang.*

1922 TITUS *Timber* xxvi. 234 So they were after Bryant were they? They were framing him? **1948** *Range Riders Western* July 100/1 Ain't I told you we wuz framed?

2. *To frame up,* to arrange (an event, undertaking, etc.) secretly, usu. for a sinister purpose. *Colloq.* and *slang.*

[**1909** S. E. WHITE *Rules of Game* II. i. 110 Fresno . . . is a nice, well-built city. . . . But it is not framed up for tourists.] **1910** WALCOTT *Open Door* 86 'An' then he frames up dis job on me,' said Jimmy bitterly. **1921** R. D. PAINE *Comr. Rolling Ocean* vii. 121 All I need is a little work with your catcher, to frame up signals and so on.

Hence **frame-up,** *n.*

1907 REX BEACH *Barrier* vii. (1908) 100 You go about it queer. . . . Your frame-up may work double. **1932** *Blue Valley Farmer* (Okla. City) 4 Feb. 1/4 All the relatives . . . swear . . . there is a 'frame-up,' or something else.

Franciscan fræn'sɪskən, *n.* An inhabitant of San Francisco. *Rare.* Cf. **San Franciscan.** — **1857** *Ladies' Repository* XVII. 105/2 The Franciscans talked of dollars as men elsewhere speak of dimes.

* **Franco-.** In combs.: (1) **Franco-American,** an American of French ancestry, also attrib.; (2) **Canadian,** a Canadian of French ancestry; (3) **Mexican,** a Mexican of French ancestry.

(1) **1859** GREELEY *Overland Journey* 158 Some of them are Frenchmen, or Franco-Americans, who have been trapping. **1880** CABLE *Grandissimes* liii. 402 It is not certain that they entered deeper . . . than a comparison of . . . Anglo-American and Franco-American conventionalities. **1943** J. DUCHARME *Shadows of Trees* 231 This habit of translating or adopting names is not peculiar to Franco-Americans. — (2) **1845** *Knickerb.* XXV. 59 The ever-noisy sailors, with their strange Franco-Canadian *patois,* 'made the air vocal with sweet sounds.' **1846** SAGE *Scenes Rocky Mts.* xvii, An old Franco-Canadian, of our crew, here favored us with, perhaps, a little the biggest fish story of any told at the present day. — (3) **1879** *Scribner's Mo.* Aug. 615/2 We crossed the street to the quiet restaurant, kept by a Franco-Mexican family.

Frank fræŋk, *n.* A nickname for an inhabitant of the temporary state of Franklin, or Frankland, *qq.v. Obs.* — **1883** ZEIGLER & GROSSCUP *Alleghanies* 221 On the day of trial [*c*1780], two of the 'Franks,' as they were called . . . rode up before the court-house.

frankfurter 'fræŋkfətɚ, *n.* Also **frankfurt, frankfort.** [G. *frankfurter,* pertaining to *Frankfurt,* Frankfort, Ger.] A smoked, highly-seasoned link sausage composed chiefly of pork and beef. Also a small roll of bread made into a sandwich with a piece of this garnished to taste.

1894 *S.F. Midwinter Appeal* 17 Feb. 2/1 Four bits for a Frankfurter seems rather steep. **1901** *Cosmopolitan* Sep. 537/1 In the 'Alt Nurnberg' . . . the American girl gathers in force for dinner and nibbles imported frankfurters at forty-five cents each. **1948** *Parents' Mag.* March 161/2 Is outdoor cooking confined to frankfurters and marshmallows or will he learn to prepare a complete meal or cook on a rock? *attrib.* **1899** *Chi. D. News* 16 May 5/4 Agar Bros.' Frankfurt Sausage, per lb. 7c. **1904** *Brooklyn Eagle* 9 June 4 People swelter and puff to get near a merry-go-round or a frankfurter stand. **1905** *Nation* 19 Jan. 42/2 The messenger boys, cab drivers, and frankfurter-peddlers of Broad Street [N.Y.].

b. frankfurt roll, a long raised roll which may be split to hold a frankfurter.

1941 *L.A.* Map 283. **1945** *Athol* (Mass.) *D. News* 5 July 3/6 (*advt.*), Frankfort or Dinner Rolls 13¢.

frankincense pine. The loblolly pine, *Pinus taeda,* of the southern U.S. — **1785** MARSHALL *Amer. Grove* 102 Virginian Swamp, or Frankincence Pine. This grows to a pretty large size. **1897** SUDWORTH *Arborescent Flora* 26 *Pinus tæda,* Loblolly Pine. . . . Common names [include] . . . Longshucks (Md., Va.), Black Slash Pine (S.C.), Frankincense Pine (lit.).

Frankland 'fræŋklənd, *n.* **1.** = **Franklin 1. 2.** (See quot.) Both *obs.*

(1) **1786** FRANKLIN *Writings* IX. 534, I had never before been acquainted that the name of your new State had any relation with my name, having understood that it was called *Frankland.* **1838** *Boston Wkly. Mag.* 24 Nov. 89/1 The sparklings of that lost pleiad of American States—the little republic of *Frankland,* that scintillated a moment on that ridgy horizon, and then was extinguished forever—are worthy to be chronicled. — (2) **1841** A. JOHNSON in *Nashville Whig* 10 Dec., *Resolved* by the General Assembly of the State of Tennessee that . . . the eastern portion of the State (commonly called East Tennessee) . . . [be] formed into a sovereign and independent State to be called the State of Frankland.

* **Franklin,** *n.* [Benjamin *Franklin* (1706–90).]

1. A temporary state (1784–88) formed of the western land ceded by North Carolina to the general government in 1784, now a part of eastern Tennessee.

1784 in S. C. WILLIAMS *Hist. Lost State of Franklin* (1924) 42 Declaration of the State of Franklin. **1898** *Cong. Rec.* 30 June 6523/2 My own native State of Tennessee, first organized as the 'State of Franklin,' but which afterwards became Tennessee. **1939** *Nat. Geog. Soc.* May 555/2 Even in Franklin there was a strong faction opposed to the new State. After nearly four years of struggle, the State of Franklin passed from the scene. **1948** DICK *Dixie Frontier* 331 Sevier actually wrote offering to place the state of Franklin under the protection of Spain. This action was aimed at North Carolina rather than the United States.

2. A lightning rod or conductor. *Obs.*

1818 PALMER *Journal* 104 Franklins, or conductors, are a certain safe-guard, and generally used. **1830** S. BRECK in *Recollections* (1877) ii. 71 Our professor of natural philosophy was desirous to erect on the old lofty tower . . . a lightning-rod, very properly called at that time a 'Franklin.'

3. = **Franklin stove.** Now *hist.* Cf. **pipe Franklin.**

1818 PALMER *Journal* 15 In the best room some have an iron fireplace (on the hearth plan) called a Franklin; these look very neat, and will much sooner heat a room than the open fire-place. **1879** B. F. TAYLOR *Summer-Savory* x. 95 Within the wide door was the bar-room, with a great hospitable Franklin. [**1931** *Old-Time New Eng.* Oct. 71 Later, this type of fireplace was set out into the room and by means of a funnel was connected with the smoke flue on the chimney. The portable fireplace then became a stove.]

transf. **1876** *Atlantic Mo.* Dec. 682 The fourth [side of the cabin] is a high bowlder, which slants away at just the right angle to make a fireplace. The stone is of a soft, friable kind, and the fire has slowly eaten its way in, now and then cracking off a huge slice, until there is quite a fine 'open Franklin' for the cabin.

4. In combs. in which the first element refers to Benjamin Franklin: (1) **Franklin-back chimney, app.** a chimney having a Franklin stove connected with it, *rare;* (2) **cent,** = **fugio,** *obs.* or *hist.,* (3) **Community,** (see quot.), *obs.;* (4) **furnace,** = **Franklin stove,** *obs.;* (5)

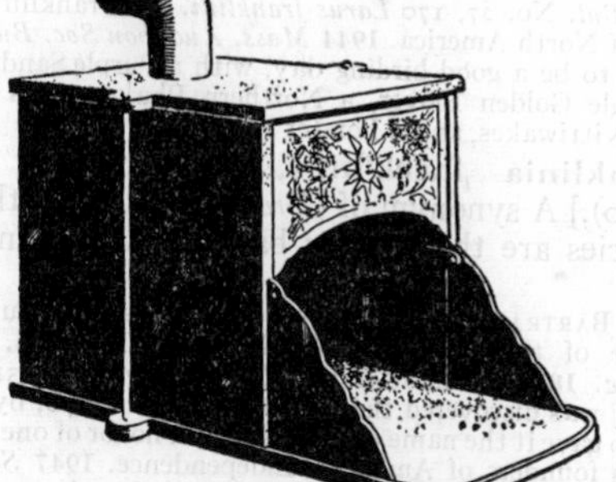

Franklin furnace or stove (*c*1780)

heater, = **Franklin stove;** (6) **rod,** = **Franklin 2,** *obs.;* (7) **spectacles,** (see quot. and cf. **bifocal**), *obs.;* (8) **stove,** a kind of iron fireplace invented by Benjamin Franklin which stands well out in a room and connects with the chimney by a funnel or pipe, later applied to open stoves of various types, cf. **fireplace** (*b*), **Franklin 3, Franklin furnace, Franklin heater, pipe Franklin;** (9) **tree,** an ornamental tree or shrub, *Gordonia alatamaha,* having showy white flowers, cf. **Franklinia.**

(1) **1945** BOTKIN *My Burden* 79 He even had one of them Franklin-back chimneys. — (2) **1859** E. COGAN *Sale Cat. Coins of C. B. Foote* 6, 1788 Franklin Cent. fine. **1880** *Sale Cat. Coins of W. L. Jenks* 22 Fugio, or Franklin Cents; varieties. 4 pieces. **1928** *Bur. of Mint Cat. Coins U.S.* 4 This terse expression of practical sense, being so much in the spirit of Poor Richard, has won the coin the name of 'Franklin Cent.' — (3) **1826** *Va. Herald* (Fredericksburg) 11 Oct. 2/3 A community recently established at Haverstraw, in this state [N.Y.] . . . is denominated the 'Franklin Community,' [and] bears a striking resemblance to Mr. Owen's establishment, and is openly opposed to revealed religion. — (4) *a*1846 *Quarter Race Ky.* 75 The reverend gentleman . . . has been officiating, with his back in close proximity to a hot fire in a Franklin furnace.

(5) **1939** *These Are Our Lives* 253 A Franklin heater, in which a fire was roaring filled the room with suffocating heat. — (6) **1817** HARRIS *Remarks* 13 At each pier a Franklin rod, as a precaution against lightning. [**1824** SINGLETON *Letters* 139 Our ship has the martial Maid

of Orleans, Joan la Pucelle, on her prow, and, up her shrouds, spiring above the topmast, and pointing its guardian fingers to the clouds, one of Franklin's rods.] — **(7) 1883** KNIGHT *New Mechanical Dict.* 356 Franklin Spectacles. The lens in each bow is divided on its major axis; the upper section for *far*, and the lower for *near* observation; for distance and for reading. — **(8) 1787** *Mass. Centinel* 3 Nov. 3/3 An assortment of Franklin stoves. **1871** L. H. BAGG *At Yale* 293 Open grates, though in the minority, are not uncommon; and large Franklin stoves, with open wood-fires, are sometimes discovered in the rooms of the luxurious. **1949** *L.A. Times* 3 April (Home Mag.) 20/2 In the living room, an old Franklin stove substitutes for a fireplace. — **(9) 1787** CUTLER in *Life & Corr.* I. 273 The Franklin tree is very curious. It is found only on one particular spot in Georgia. **1795** WINTERBOTHAM *Hist. View* III. 392 Flowering Trees. Shrubs, &c. . . . Franklin tree. **1942** *Amer. Philos. Soc. Trans.* XXXIII. 66/2 A sand-hill bog . . . about 1.7 miles northwest of Cox is believed to be the type locality of the famous Franklin tree (*Franklinia alatamaha*) which the Bartrams discovered here, apparently in association wth the Georgia bark.

b. In combs. in which the allusion is to Sir John Franklin (1786–1847), an English explorer: (1) **Franklin ground squirrel,** (see quot.); (2) **'s grouse,** a grouse, *Canachites franklini*, found in the spruce regions of the Northwest, also **Franklin's spruce grouse;** (3) **'s gull,** a small white gull, *Larus franklini*, having a dark, slate-colored head and breeding in the marshes of the prairie regions of the Dakotas, Iowa, etc., also **Franklin's rosy gull.**

(1) 1941 SETON *Trail of Artist-Naturalist* 189 The gray or Franklin ground squirrel [is] notable for its loud, ringing, musical call-note. — **(2) 1858** BAIRD *Birds Pacific R.R.* 623 *Tetrao Franklinii.* . . . Franklin's Grouse. **1874** COUES *Birds N.W.* 394 *Tetrao Canadensis* var. *Franklini.* . . . Franklin's Spruce Grouse. **1946** STANWELL-FLETCHER *Driftwood Valley* 181 The other day, in the pine grove near the cabin, I met a Franklin's grouse. — **(3) 1858** BAIRD *Birds Pacific R.R.* 75 *Chroicocephalus Franklinii.* . . . Franklin's Rosy Gull. **1883** *Nat. Museum Bul.* No. 27, 170 *Larus franklini.* . . . Franklin's Gull. . . . Interior of North America. **1944** *Mass. Audubon Soc. Bul.* Dec. 261 It proved to be a good birding day, with a Purple Sandpiper found . . . a single Golden Plover, a Northern Phalarope, a Franklin's Gull, six Kittiwakes, and a Forster's Tern.

Franklinia ˌfræŋkˈlɪnɪə, *n.* [Benjamin *Franklin*, (1706–90).] A synonym of *Gordonia*, of which the American species are the loblolly bay and the Franklin tree, *qq.v.*

1791 W. BARTRAM *Travels* (1792) 465 *n.*, We have honoured [it] with the name of the illustrious Dr. Benjamin Franklin. *Franklinia Alatamaha.* **1859** HILLHOUSE tr. Michaux *Sylva* II. 31 [*Gordonia pubescens*] was discovered there [in Georgia], in 1770, by John Bartram, who gave it the name of Franklinia, in honor of one of the most illustrious founders of American Independence. **1947** *Sports Afield* Dec. 20/2 In this swamp William Bartram found a new tree, the Franklinia, which today grows in cultivation.

Franklinian ˌfræŋkˈlɪnɪən, *a.* Of or pertaining to Benjamin Franklin. *Obs.*

1767 PRIESTLEY in Franklin *Works* (1887) II. 65 To form a just idea of the great and deserved reputation of Dr. Franklin, we must read the foreign publications on the subject of electricity; in many of which the terms *Franklinism, Franklinist*, and the *Franklinian system*, occur in almost every page. **a1811** HENRY *Camp. Quebec* 145 The Jennerian discovery tends to save the lives of millions, the Franklinian of hundreds. **1814** J. ADAMS *Works* X. 90 In politics, Rittenhouse was . . . Franklinian, democrat, totally ignorant of the world.

Franklinism ˈfræŋklɪnˌɪzəm, *n.* [See above.] A pithy proverb after the pattern of those by Benjamin Franklin. *Obs.* — [**1767** see **Franklinian.**] **1795** *Tablet* 21 My acquaintance . . . requests me to compose an essay in his [Noah Webster's] laconic style. No, I replied, he has exhausted *Franklinisms*, he has commented upon almost every common saying in the popular mouth.

Franklinist ˈfræŋklɪnˌɪst, *n.* [See ∗**Franklin 2.**] (See quot.) *Rare.* — **1772** FRANKLIN *Writings* V. 415 Abbé Nollet . . . has but one of his sect now remaining in the Academy. All the rest, who have in any degree acquainted themselves with electricity, are as he calls them *Franklinists*.

Franklinite ˈfræŋklɪnˌaɪt, *n.* [*Franklin* (N.J.) + *-ite.*] A valuable oxide of iron, zinc, and manganese. Also attrib.

1820 *Amer. Jrnl. Science* II. 323 The black zinciferous mineral, the Franklinite. **1876** RAYMOND *8th Rep. Mines* 422 The employment of any material that will last equal to chilled or Franklinite iron. **1889** *Cent.* 2363/1 *Franklinite* . . . is found in New Jersey near the village of Franklin or Franklin Furnace (whence the name), associated with the zinc oxid zincite [etc.]. **1894** *Harper's Mag.* March 590/1 The Franklinite ore of New Jersey yields excellent manganese compounds, and is therefore of great value.

frappé fræˈpe, *n.* [See next.] A flavored water-ice or semi-frozen mixture served in a glass (see 1st quot.), often of a designated kind.

1903 *Harper's Bazaar* Feb. 175/1 Café frappé is strong coffee, well sweetened, and with a good deal of cream, which is frozen to the consistency of wet snow. **1909** F. FARMER *Boston Cook Book* 434 If a larger proportion of salt is used, mixture will freeze in shorter time and be of granular consistency, which is desirable only for frappé. **1922** *Glasgow Herald* 13 May 6 Besides untold recipes for cobblers, coolers, highballs, frappés, daisies, sangarees. **1945** *This Week Mag.* 11 Aug. 13 *Fruit Frappé* is but fruit juice and cracked ice, shaken mightily together for a five-carat sparkle.

frappé fræˈpe, *a.* [F., artificially chilled.] Iced, cooled.

1848 LONGFELLOW in *Life* (1891) II. 121 A warm morning; *frappé* at noon with an east wind. **1870** LOWELL *Study Windows, Good Word for Winter*, The air you drink is frappé.

b. Hence as a verb, to cool or chill (a person), also fig. *Colloq. Obs.*

1890 BIFF HALL *Turnover Club* 230 After . . . the guests had rubbed the luckless Agent against the ice-box until he was thoroughly frapped, the Proprietor resumed. **1897** *Outing* July 325/1 Even the resourceful New York Central could hardly be expected to *frappé* passengers to order in their berths. **1907** O. HENRY *Trimmed Lamp* 160 Your old man is too frappéd and slow to ever give you a punch.

frat fræt, *n.* Short for ∗**fraternity.**

1895 GORE *Student Slang* (We.), Frat (n.) A fraternity; a member of a fraternity. **1913** *Ladies' Home Jrnl.* Nov. 19/1 In the 'co-ed' 'varsities the 'frats' and sororities pair off just as brothers and sisters do in a large family. **1947** *Chi. Tribune* 2 July 19 Too bad he couldn't go to college. He doesn't know what proms and frats an' trig an' hot dates are all about.

attrib. **1902** *Chi. Record-Herald* 7 Sep. 1. 1/3 Alfalfa Eta Fraternity Frat House. **1916** *Amer. Mag.* Aug. 8/2, I got a frat pin offen a pawnbroker in Detroit. **1946** THOMPSON *Amer. Daughter* 164 Frat brothers and sorority sisters loudly acclaimed old students, and Big Sister representatives came to the rescue of bewildered freshmen.

b. Hence **fratdom.** *Rare.*

1896 *Columbus* (Ohio) *Dispatch* 18 March 6/4 Eight new members were ushered into law fratdom.

∗**fraternal,** *a.* **1. Fraternal Day,** (see quot.). **2. fraternal order,** a brotherhood or friendly society. — **(1) 1937** DOUGLAS *Amer. Bk. of Days* 503 In 1915, however, the act making Columbus Day a holiday was repealed and in its place an act was passed setting apart the second Tuesday in October . . . as Fraternal Day. — **(2) 1905** B. G. PHILLIPS *Plum Tree* 267 Local machine leaders of Scarborough's party, with corruptible labor and fraternal order leaders.

∗**fraternity,** *n.* A national or local society or organization among students, usu. of a college, for promoting social and academic interests. Cf. **college, Greek-letter fraternity.**

Fraternities are usu. (cf. **b.** below) for men only and have names made up of Greek letters. Many honorary fraternities such as Phi Beta Kappa and Delta Sigma Rho have members of both sexes. There are occasional high school fraternities.

1777 in F. W. SHEPARDSON *Phi Beta Kappa* (1915) 9 [At the January meeting of 1777 . . . a mode of initiation was reported.] 'I, A.B. do swear . . . to prove true, just, and deeply attached to this our growing fraternity.' **1871** BAGG *At Yale* 110 Though there are other important chaptered fraternities existing in American colleges, the three represented at Yale are undoubtedly the leading and most extensive ones. **1895** W. M. SLOANE in *Four Amer. Universities* 145 There are no Greek-letter fraternities to gather in and crystallize social sets. **1947** *Nat. Geog. Mag.* July 110/1 Incidentally, Union cradled the country's oldest college social-fraternities. **1949** *Newsweek* 2 May 56/2 His 'Atom Bomb and Peace' series in 1946 earned him a citation from Sigma Delta Chi, the journalistic fraternity.

attrib. **1899** QUINN *Pa. Stories* 59 He could not help seeing that the Fraternity men were in general the best dressed. **1902** CORBIN *American at Oxford* 269 The fraternity houses so widely diffused in America offer almost a counterpart of the halls of the golden age in the mediaeval university. **1905** RICE *Sandy* 125 Annette counted her fraternity pins and tried to look severe. **1923** HERRICK *Lilla* 135 Lee Smith, a young 'fraternity brother' of Gordon, . . . had come to Chicago to sell text-books. **1948** *Our Dumb Animals* May 3 The pledges had been told to bring a freshly-killed dog to the fraternity house; one that had not been poisoned, because they were going to have to eat it.

b. A sorority.

1879 BAIRD *Amer. College Fraternities* 144 Delta Chi Alpha. A fraternity founded at Ohio Wesleyan University, in May, 1879, by Misses M. Conklin, L. Milward [etc.]. **1905** *D.N.* II. 80 The University girls have two fraternities.

c. fraternity rushing, the entertaining of students by a fraternity with a view toward pledging new members from among them.

1931 *K.C. Star* 10 Oct., Fraternity rushing is entirely over and the freshmen have been told their place in life.

* **fraud,** *n.* As the last term in **great, marrow fat, whisky fraud.**

fraud order. (See quots.) — **1905** E. E. Calkins & R. Holden *Art of Modern Advertising* 258 It is often impossible to prosecute the advertisers, and the most the post-office department can do is to issue what is known as a fraud order. Such an order peremptorily and without redress stops the mail of the advertiser. **1931** C. Kelly *U.S. Postal Policy* 150 Under a 'fraud order' all mail directed to such persons or company is stamped 'Fraudulent' on the outside and returned to the sender.

frazil frəˈzɪl, *n.* [Prob. Can. F. *frasil* (f. *fraisil,* cinders), snow floating in the water.] Ice formed at the bottom of a stream, ground ice. Cf. **anchor ice.** — **1888** *Montreal Gaz.* 17 Mar. (*Cent.*), It has been suggested that it may be due to the accumulation of frazil or anchor-ice. **1893** *Youth's Companion* 9 Feb. 71/4 The greater the surface of the swift open water, the greater the quantity of frazil made in a minute, hour, or day. Every open rapid is, in 'zero weather,' a frazil-factory.

* **frazzle,** *n.* [See note.]

This form app. arose from Brit. dial. *fazle* (*q.v.* in *OED* and *EDD*) in the same sense. It is not likely that the form with [r] occurred first in the U.S.

A frayed end or loose fiber, used in colloq. phrases indicative of complete or utter discomfiture, exhaustion, etc.

1872 *Cong. Globe* App. 30 May 578/2 They . . . got great big long brushes . . . and they whipped them all into frassels. **1905** *Washington Star* 24 Nov. 22 The Beckham machine whipped Blackburn to a frazzle. **1910** J. Hart *Vigilante Girl* 294, I reckon his nerves are all of a frazzle. **1928** *Sat. Ev. Post* 121/3 'Licked to a frazzle,' was his mental observation.

* **frazzled,** *a.* Tired out, exhausted, "used up." Also **frazzled out.** *Colloq.*

1883 *Amer. Philol. Assoc. Trans.* XIV. 48 We have also in the South the expression *all frazled out,* figuratively used, about equivalent to 'used up.' **1892** Duval *Young Explorers* 202 We arrived at camp a little after sun set completely 'frazzled out' with our tramp of twenty miles. **1911** Ferber *Dawn O'Hara* 15 No woman not even a frazzled-out newspaper woman—could receive the love and care that they gave me.

Frede frid, *n.* =**Fredonian 1.** *Rare.* — **1803** *Med. Repository* 450 Thereby the time will be noted carefully, when a native of this land, on being asked who he is, and whence he came, began to answer, in one word, that he was a Frede, instead of using the tedious circumlocution, that he was 'a citizen of the United States of America.' **1816** [see **Fredonia 1**].

* **Frederick,** *n.* (See quots.) *Obs.* Cf. **Little Frederick.** — **1784** J. Smyth *Tour U.S.* II. 129 There are seven different kinds of tobacco, particularly adapted to the different qualities of the soil on which they are cultivated, and each varying from the other. They are named Hudson, Frederick [etc.]. **1788** Schöpf *Reise* II. 115 Zum Kanaster soll sich der Toback besonders ausnehmen, welcher um little Frederick gezogen und Frederick genannt wird.

Fredish ˈfridɪʃ, *a.* (See quot. and cf. **Fredon, Fredonia.**) *Rare* and *obs.* — **1803** *Med. Repository* 449 The events of Fredish history will be more minutely known and better understood than those of Russian, Turkish or Arabic. *Ib.*, Fredish, an adjective to denote the relations and concerns of the United States. **1816** [see **Fredonia 1**].

Fredon ˈfridon, *n.* (See quot. and cf. next.) *Obs.* — **1803** *Med. Repository* 448 Fredon is probably better supplied with the materials of her own history than Britain, France, or any other country of the old world. *Ib.* 449 Fredon, the aggregate noun for the whole territory of the United States.

Fredonia friˈdonɪə, *n.* [See note.]

1. (See quots.) Now *hist.*

This term and **Frede, Fredish, Fredon, Fredonian,** were invented by Dr. Samuel Latham Mitchill (1764–1831), whose inspiration for them was based on **free* or **freedom.*

1803 *Med. Repository* 449 Fredon, the aggregate noun for the whole territory of the United States. Fredonia, a noun of the same import, for *rhetorical* and *poetical* use. **1806** Fessenden *Democracy Unveiled* I. 121*n.*, Fredonia is a cant phrase, which certain small poets or prosaic scribblers . . . would have us adopt as an appellative to designate the United States of America. **1816** Pickering 94 *Fredonia, Fredonian, Frede, Fredish,* &c. &c. These extraordinary words which have been deservedly ridiculed here as well as in England, were proposed some-time ago, and countenanced by two or three individuals, as names for the territory and people of the United States. . . . The words . . . are never now used in the United States, except by way of ridicule. **1831** *Naval Songster* 43 The trident of Neptune, long by Britain wielded, At length to Fredonia reluctantly is yielded. **1947** *St. Louis Globe-Democrat* 14 Sep., The one that appealed most widely, next to Columbia, was Fredonia. That name was suggested shortly before 1800 by Dr. Samuel Latham Mitchell of New York City. . . . He was never able to decide whether it meant a 'free gift,' or the land where things are 'freely done.'

2. (See quots.) Now *hist.*

1827 *Spirit of Seventy-Six* (Frankfort, Ky.) 8 Mar. 1/3 This new Republic has been christened the '*Republic of Fredonia,*' and . . . their Flag . . . consisted of a stripe of red and white, being emblematic of union between Red and White men. **1827** Dewees *Lett. from Texas* 72 Last year, an attempt was made by a body of adventurers and speculators, to erect Texas into a Republic under the name of Fredonia. **1948** *True* May 121 Just west of the twilight of Louisiana and a bit east of the dawn of Texas there once existed the Republic of Fredonia.

Fredonian friˈdonɪən, *n.* [See above.]

1. An inhabitant of Fredonia (sense **1.**). *Obs.* or *hist.*

1803 *Med. Repository* 449 The attention of the Fredonians was much sooner directed, after their settlement, to the collection and preservation of their facts and records, than that of the Dutch and Irish. **1809** Fessenden *Pills* 125 Suspicious crowds to fight with phantoms vain, With Federal chains Fredonians wont to bind. **1816** [see **Fredonia 1**].

2. One of a group of adventurers who attempted in 1827 to erect a Texan republic under the name of Fredonia. Now *hist.* Cf. **Fredonia 2.**

1827 *Spirit of Seventy-Six* (Frankfort, Ky.) 8 Mar. 1/4 If the Fredonians . . . should get to San Antonio, before they have time to recruit from the adjacent posts, (and the nearest of which is 300 miles,) they may take San Antonia [*sic*]. **1841** Foote *Texas & Texans* I. 257 An angry quarrel [broke] out among the Fredonians. **1948** *True* May 133/2 The document was signed by Edwards and Mayo for the Fredonians and Hunter and Field for the Indians.

b. Also attrib. or as adj. Now *hist.*

1841 Foote *Texas & Texans* I. 234 [He] is about to become the Leader in the Fredonian war. **1948** *True* May 135/1 He had signed the Fredonian Declaration of Independence.

* **free,** *a.* In combs.: (1) **free bank,** a bank operating under the free banking system, also attrib., *obs.;* (2) **Baptist,** a Freewill Baptist, *obs.;* (3) **bottom,** a ship sailing during wartime under the flag of a neutral country, also attrib., *obs.;* (4) * **chapel,** a chapel in which contributions are entirely voluntary, also attrib., *obs.;* (5) * **church,** a church in which the pews are not rented or leased, *obs.;* (6) **dealer,** a married woman engaged in business on her own account, a feme sole; (7) **Democratic party,** a national political organization (1852–54) made up of the more radical anti-slavery members of the former Free Soil party, *obs.;* (8) **fight,** a riotous fight in which a number of people join promiscuously, *colloq.;* (9) **fighter,** (see quot. *a*1870), *obs.;* (10) **grass,** *W.* free pasturage on public land, also attrib., cf. **free range;** (11) **-issue Negro,** app. a Negro born free just after the Civil War, *obs.;* (12) **love,** the doctrine of free choice in sexual relations without the restraints of marriage or other legal obligations; (13) **lover,** one who advocates free love; (14) **milling,** (see quot. 1881); (15) **papers,** documents given to a freed slave attesting his new status, *obs.;* (16) **range,** =**free grass;** (17) **speech,** the privilege accorded by the U.S. Government to anyone to speak and write without governmental interference; (18) **territory,** territory of the U.S. in which slavery was prohibited, *obs.;* (19) **throw,** in basketball, a throw for a basket from a designated spot, granted because of a foul made by the other team and executed without interference from the opposing team, also attrib.; (20) **white,** a white person not under bondage of any kind, also attrib., *obs.*

(1) **1840** *Niles' Reg.* 16 May 164/3 On the 1st of January 1837, the circulation of the incorporated banks exceeded $24,000,000. No free banks were then in existence. **1850** *Western Journal* IV. 217 The chartered banks, many of them, have surrendered their charters for the purpose of adopting the free bank system. — (2) **1867** Dixon *New Amer.* II. 308 In a very short time this [Baptist] body was divided into Old School Baptists, . . . Tunkers, Free-Will Baptist, with their sub-section of Free Baptists [etc.]. **1895** Wiggin *Village Watch-Tower* 107 She had good Orthodox beaux, Free and Close Baptists, Millerites and Adventists. — (3) **1797** *Ann. 5th Congress* I. 141 During the armed neutrality, the United States had owned that free bottoms should make free goods. **1842** *S. Lit. Messenger* VIII. 413/1 Our com-

mander . . . stuck for the 'free bottom' principle where the government and its servants were concerned. — (4) **1842** *Lowell Offering* II. 119 The 'Free Chapel Enterprise' is a phase unintelligible to many of our operatives. *Ib.* 122 There are now three Free Chapels in Boston, and as many 'Ministers at Large.'

(5) **1835** J. MARTIN *Descr. Virginia* 126 Contains several dwelling houses—one free church—one common school. **1860** *Mass. Acts and Resolves* clxxxi, An act to incorporate the trustees of the free church of Saint Mary, for sailors. — (6) **1853–4** *Alabama House Jrnl.* 124 Mr Judge presented the petition of Eliza Jeffcoat and others to make Mrs. Martha Ann Greene a free dealer. **1859–60** *Alabama Senate Jrnl.* 521 [A bill] To make Hannah Fuguson, of winston county, a free dealer as to property hereafter to be acquired by her. — (7) **1853** *National Era* 6 Jan., The next four years will be decisive as to the existence of the Free Democratic party as such. **1895** T. C. SMITH *Free Soil Party in Wis.* 135 The Wisconsin Free Democratic party [in 1852] . . . had developed into something materially different from the 'Barnburners' of 1848, and far more like the Liberty Party. — (8) **1856** *S. Lit. Messenger* 258/2 There is what we would call in Kentucky a free fight. **1882** McCABE *New York* 329 The fun . . . sometimes degenerates into a free fight. — (9) **1862** *N.Y. Tribune* May (Chipman), We publish the recent act of [the Confederate] Congress, authorizing the raising and bringing into service of partisan rangers. Now is the time for free fighters, the men of dash and daring. *a***1870** CHIPMAN *Notes on Bartlett, Free-Fighter*, a partisan ranger; a guerilla soldier.

(10) **1888** ROOSEVELT in *Cent. Mag.* Feb. 510/1 In our northern country we have free grass: that is, the stockmen rarely own more than small portions of the land over which their cattle range. **1924** BECHDOLT *Tales* 94 He was . . . a rider of the wide free-grass lands. **1948** *Dallas Morning News* 5 Dec. (Book Sec.) 8/1 The two brothers had established a ranch—on free grass—south of the Nueces River. — (11) **1893** T. N. PAGE *Ole Virginia* 40 Dem heah free-issue niggers don' know what Christmas is. **1893** *Harper's Mag.* May 975/1, I ain't no free issue nigger nor preacher. — (12) **1856** in *Amer. Sp.* XII. 115/2 Felt a 'passional attraction,' As the *'Free-love'* people have it: Which means—every girl have husbands, Ten or twenty if she needs them. **1870** J. H. NOYES *Hist. Amer. Socialism* 638 They [i.e., Bible Communists] invented the term *Free Love* to designate the social state of the Kingdom of Heaven as defined in *Bible Communism*. **1948** *Social Forces* Dec. 212 'Free love' is a mockery; with love altogether 'free,' how many fathers would be 'around' when the children they had begotten arrive? — (13) **1858** *Baltimore Sun* 28 June (Bartlett), Abolitionists, spiritualists, and free lovers. **1900** ESTLAKE *Oneida Community* 81 The communists did not in later days call themselves 'free lovers'; the people of Central New York had been accustomed to the name, and they fastened it on to the Oneida Community without stopping to consider the fitness of the term. — (14) **1881** RAYMOND *Mining Gloss.*, Free-milling, applied to ores which contain free gold or silver, and can be reduced by crushing and amalgamation, without roasting or other chemical treatment. **1893** *Harper's Mag.* May 944/1 Much of the Colorado ore is of the free-milling variety not treated at the smelteries.

(15) **1838** in BUCKINGHAM *Amer., N. States* I. 282 Henry has relations . . . some of them free, and likely he has free papers. **1881** *Cent. Mag.* Nov. 126/1 It was the custom in the state of Maryland to require the free colored people to have what were called free papers. — (16) **1912** MULFORD *Buck P.* 186 Outlying free range had been thoroughly combed. **1947** *Steamboat* (Colo.) *Pilot* 13 Feb. 8/4 Then sheep commenced to come for a share of the free range. — (17) **1848** *N.Y. Wkly. Tribune* 15 July 3/4 Resolved, That this meeting, through their Chairman, request John Van Buren and Benjamin F Butler, Esqs. to address the citizens of Berkshire upon the subject of *Free Soil* and *Free Speech*. **1898** HARPER *S. B. Anthony* I. 147, I do not desire to interfere with your 'free speech.' — (18) **1854** BENTON *30 Years' View* I. 18/1 There was not a ripple of discontent visible on the surface of the public mind at this mighty transfer of slave into free territory. **1865** RICHARDSON *Secret Service* v. 88 They fear . . . that the border will gradually become Abolitionized, and extend free territory to the Gulf itself. — (19) **1916** BANCROFT *Handbook* 114 Free throw lane; Foul lane. A space marked in front of each goal within which no player may enter while an opponent is making a free throw for goal. **1948** *Chesterton* (Ind.) *Tribune* 28 Oct. 1/1 He also hit 55 free throws out of 92 for a .599 average.

(20) **1817** S. BROWN *Western Gaz.* 16 Free white inhabitants. **1835** MARTIN *Descr. Virginia* 68 In the same period [1800–1830], the free whites increased 180,020, or 35 per cent. **1886** LOGAN *Great Conspiracy* 461 Individuals greedily ambitious of power . . . advocated Free-Trade as a means of degrading Free White labor to the level of Black Slave labor.

b. Also in less frequent, now obs., combs.: (1) **Free Democrat,** a member of the Free Democratic party; (2) **Democratic,** *a.* of or pertaining to the Free Democratic party; (3) **dirter,** =**Free Soiler;** (4) **Inquirer,** one who accepted the social philosophy of Robert Dale Owen and Frances Wright; (5) **Methodism,** the principles and practices of the Free Methodists; (6) **Quakers,** a sect of Quakers originating during the Revolutionary War who favored joining the patriots; (7) **squatter,** one who took part as a Free Soiler in the struggle in Kansas over slavery, cf. **free state man.**

(1) **1857** BUNGAY *Off-Hand* 316 We have the 'Silver Greys' and the 'Hunkers,' . . . the 'Free Democrats,' which of course implies there are Democrats that are not free [etc.]. — (2) **1854** *N.Y. Tribune* 27 Sep. 4/2 The Free Democratic Convention . . . passed resolves strongly condemning the Fugitive Slave law. . . . A Free Democratic ticket was nominated. — (3) **1855** *Herald of Freedom* 11 Aug. 2/8 We have . . . three printing offices, (Free Dirters). — (4) **1829** B. ALCOTT *Journals* 21 Passed the evening with Dr. Winship, who is anxious that I should engage as an instructor of the children of the Free Inquirers of Boston.

(5) **1870** *Free Meth. Ch. Minutes Ann. Sess. 1870–79* 12 The warm and earnest acknowledgments of the members . . . of this Conference are due to the members of the Free Methodist Churches and congregations of New York . . . for their . . . generous invitation to all who feel any interest in Free Methodism. — (6) **1792** BRISSOT *Reise* 227 Im letzten Kriege bildete sich eine andere Sekte, die sich *Free-Quakers*, Frei-Quäker, nannte. Sie bestand anfänglich aus Personen, die schon vor dem Kriege wegen schlechter Aufführung waren exkommunicirt worden. — (7) **1859** W. P. THOMLINSON *Kansas in 1858* 294 Go where you may among the free-squatters of Southern Kansas, you will find . . . that a *man had better hold his peace* than say aught derogatory to the character of James Montgomery.

For **free banking, coinage, delivery, -for-all, labor, *list, lunch, *man, Methodist, press, *school, silver, soil, -Soiler, -Soilism, state, *stone, trader, trapper, *-willer,** see as main entries.

free banking. Banking carried on with little or no state or federal supervision or regulation. Usu. attrib.

This system of banking superseded that under the safety fund (*q.v.*) system.

1841 *Hunt's Merch. Mag.* March 250 The system . . . is substantially the same with that introduced by the late free-banking act. **1850** *Western Journal* IV. 221 In advocating an amendment of the Constitution, however, we would not open the door for joint stock companies or Free Banking, without providing for the safety of the billholder. **1892** BROCKETT *Our Country's Wealth* 600/2 The law of April, 1838, called the 'free banking law.' **1936** G. W. DOWRIE *Money and Banking* 188 The Free Banking System. This system derives its name from the fact that it obviated the need for a special act of the legislature whenever a bank was chartered.

free coinage. Coinage without charge, at a government mint, esp. of silver bullion for a private individual.

1890 *Cong. Rec.* 15 Jan. 818 Under free coinage, so long as silver is in the slightest degree below par as compared with gold, the entire demand for money for payment of debts will fall upon silver. **1890** *Public Opinion* 7 Dec. 210 We have a set of people in this country who . . . raise their eyes in holy horror and shout 'bonanza kings' the moment we broach the subject of free coinage. **1914** *Cyclo. Amer. Govt.* I. 313 Until 1873 there was free coinage of both gold and silver. . . . Since 1873 there has been free coinage only of gold. The term 'free coinage' came into popular use during the long struggle, 1875–1896, to restore silver to full privileges at the mint, and, as so used, always relates to silver.

attrib. **1897** *Chi. Tribune* 3 July 12/2 The purchasing power of the free coinage dollar would be less than that of the gold dollar.

b. Esp. *free coinage of silver.*

1890 *Nation* 29 May 424/1 Nobody will believe in free coinage of silver any more. **1900** *Cong. Rec.* 4 Jan. 652 The persistent antagonism of the friends of the free coinage of silver and the advocates of a silver standard to all sound monetary principles.

free delivery. The delivery of mail matter without charge. Also attrib. Cf. **rural free delivery.**

1871 BAGG *At Yale* 213 A branch post-office was connected with the Bookstore. . . . There was no 'general delivery' in connection with it. . . . New Haven has a 'free delivery.' **1919** CUNNINGHAM *Chronicle* 145 A few hours after the free delivery man left, old Thad come a foamin'. **1924** *Frontier* Nov. 23 It is true that the automobile, the free delivery, the telephone, and radio are all useful and wonderful.

freedery ˈfridərɪ, *n.* Freedom, unconstrainedness. *Slang. Obs.* — **1837** NEAL *Charcoal Sk.* (1838) 217 [The world] treats me with despise and unbecoming freedery. **1893** *Columbus* (Ohio) *Dispatch* 13 April, Between all these odd folk and the London actors of the dramatic stage, there is endless emulation mingled with tantalizing attempts at 'freedery' and airiness on the one side, and a fadeless dread and contempt on the other.

***freedman,** *n. Hist.* Used in the possessive in the names of organizations, funds, and banks for assisting Negroes recently freed from slavery at the close of the Civil War. Usu. *pl. Obs.*

1863 KETTELL *Hist. Rebellion* II. 616 The majority of those persons went under the auspices of the 'National Freedmen's Relief Association.' **1864** (*title*), Annual Report of the Executive Committee of the Barnard Freedmen's Aid Society of Dorchester. **1865** in FLEMING *Hist. Reconstruction* I. 285 A fund to be called the Freedmen's Pauper Fund. *Ib.* 352 Abandoned lands . . . under the control of the Bureau of Refugees, Freedmen and abandoned Lands . . . shall be set apart for the use of loyal refugees and freedmen. **1870** *Ib.* 372 The political operations were carried on . . . by the American Missionary Society, and the Freedmen's Savings Bank. **1894** S. LEAVITT *Our Money Wars* 129 Another act of March 3, 1865, established the Freedmen's Bank, authorizing loans to be made upon Government bonds only.

b. Freedmen's Bureau, the popular designation of the Bureau of Refugees, Freedmen, and Abandoned Lands. Also attrib.

This bureau was established by Congress on March 3, 1865, to issue supplies to destitute freedmen and to rent to them abandoned or confiscated land. The bureau was discontinued in 1872.

[**1865** *Statutes at Large* XIII. 507 An Act to establish a Bureau for the Relief of Freedmen and Refugees.] **1865** *Nation* I. 169 The Assistant Commissioners of the Freedmen's Bureau are furnishing, and will continue to furnish, the knowledge which is so desirable. **1870** *Cong. Globe* 6 April 2461/2 He is one of a ring known as the 'Freedmen's Bureau ring,' . . . whose position has been to devote the official authority and power of the bureau to personal and political profit. **1948** *Time* 24 May 106/2 His recital of his postwar experiences in the Freedmen's Bureau in Greenville, S.C. is compounded of vivid scenes and well-remembered dialogue.

c. Freedman's school, a school for the instruction and benefit of the recently freed slaves at the close of the Civil War. *Obs.*

1865 in FLEMING *Hist. Reconstruction* II. 174 The negro adult or child, before he enters the Freedman's school, has been at a very bad preparatory school. **1887** *Courier-Journal* 20 Feb. 10/3 In 1866 Mr. Marshall opened a Freedman's school at Hardinsburg.

d. freedmen's envelope, (see quot.). *Obs.*

1870 MACRAE *Americans* II. 72 Envelopes of a deep crimson dye were in vogue amongst them [Negroes] when I was there. 'Freedmen's envelopes,' they were called.

***freedom,** *n. attrib.* Designating *clothing*, a *treat*, or a *party* formerly given to a boy upon the completion of his apprenticeship, to assist him in beginning the practice of his trade or profession. *Obs.*

1694 *Col. Rec. N. Carolina* I. 407 Ye sd cloth he received upon the account of his ffredome cloths. **1842** *Boston Transcript* 14 Dec. 2/4 We well remember the '*Freedom treat*,' given at the hospitable mansion of his master, '*Major Ben*,' who, by his urbanity and hilarity, gave a tone and zest to the entertainment. **1845** C. M. KIRKLAND *Western Clearings* 48 George, arrayed in the 'freedom suit'—solemn black, of course, as became his profession—made the agreeable to his male guests. *Ib.* 49 The next day, it became too evident that the freedom-party had cost Mr. George Burnet a violent fever.

As the last term in **academic, bird of, son of (fair) freedom.**

free-for-all.

1. A horse race in which the horses of all comers may compete. Also attrib.

1881 *Chi. Times* 11 June, The grand free-for-all horse race, open to the world. **1892** *Courier-Journal* 1 Oct. 4/3 Walter F. disposed of the next three heats in better average time than that shown in the free-for-all. **1907** MULFORD *Bar-20* 70 The Virginia reel was a marvel of supple, exaggerated grace, and the quadrille looked like a free-for-all for unbroken colts.

transf. **1884** PECK *Peck's Boss Book* (1892) 216 (We.), There is some free-for-all, go-as-you-please party or reception.

2. =**free fight.** Also transf. and attrib.

1902 WHITE *Blazed Trail* 175 In a free-for-all knock-down-and-drag-out, kicking, gouging, and biting are all legitimate. **1918** MULFORD *Man from Bar-20* 56 More squealing came from the corral and grew in volume as other horses joined in it. From the noise it appeared to be turning into a free-for-all. **1932** *Blue Valley Farmer* (Okla. City) 7 Jan. 5/5, I hurried back to guard my rights, got back for the free for all fights.

free labor. Labor performed by a freeman or by freemen as distinguished from that of slaves; free laborers. Also attrib.

1820 *Ann. 16th Congress* 1 Sess. I. 1213 Free labor and slave labor cannot be employed together. **1856** WHITTIER *Panorama* 476 Then shall Free Labor's hardy children stand The equal sovereigns of a slaveless land. **1863** *Ladies' Repository* XXIII. 700/1 All that remains necessary is to settle it with a free labor population. **1867** *Atlantic Mo.* March 372/2 The habits of life and modes of thinking characteristic of free-labor society. **1943** DEVOTO *Yr. of Decision* 478 'Freesoil,' their slogan said, 'free speech, free labor, and free men.'

***free list.**

1. A list or a register of articles that may be brought into a country without payment of duty.

1833 *Cong. Deb.* 20 Feb. 1749 The free list of imports. **1845** *Treasury Rep.* V. 6 An adequate revenue will still be produced, and permit the addition to the free list of salt and guano. **1913** LA FOLLETTE *Autobiog.* 102 Gear, of Iowa, and I made the chief fight to put sugar on the free list.

2. (See quot. 1870.)

1870 MEDBERY *Men Wall St.* 20 The securities dealt in by the Board [of the N.Y. Stock Exchange] are divided into two classes, known respectively as the Regular and the Free List. . . . The Regular List must be called in sequence by the Vice-President in the chair: the Free List may or may not be called at the option of members. **1882** MCCABE *New York* 337 The order of proceedings is the same on both occasions. Two lists of stocks, the Regular and the Free List, being called each time.

free lunch. Food given without charge, esp. in a saloon to encourage the purchase of drinks. Also attrib.

1854 *Wide West* (S.F.) 26 Nov. 2/3 The excitement during the week on the subject of the 'free lunches' has been of the most intense character. **1880** *Amer. Punch* May 71/2 Nothing . . . would make the average tramp so mad as to squander five cents for beer where a free lunch counter is in full blast, . . . but finds that the hungry customers before him have eaten all the lunch. **1948** *Green Bay* (Wis.) *Press-Gazette* 12 July 6/4 Adam piled the free lunch counter high with frankfurters, pig's knuckles, cheese and salads.

Hence **free-luncher.**

1876 *Ventura Free Press* (San Buenaventura, Calif.) 8 Jan. 1/6 A healthy free luncher . . . walked unostentatiously up to a plate, and commenced operations with a sandwich. **1893** *Chicago Record* 7 July 3/6 The hardened free-luncher accepted it and said 'Thank you.'

***freeman,** *n.*

1. In colonial days, one possessing full rights as a citizen, such status depending upon church membership, property, and the like. Now *hist.*

The requirements for this station differed from time to time and from place to place. See quot. 1720. Early town records contain many lists of men who had qualified and taken the proper oath.

[**1629** *Mass. Charter* (1853) 10 There shalbe one Governor . . . and eighteen Assistants of the same Company, to be from tyme to tyme constituted, elected, and chosen out of the freemen of the saide Company.] **1641** *R.I. Col. Rec.* I. 112 It is in the Powre of the Body of Freemen orderly assembled . . . to make or constitute Just Lawes. **1690** *Boston Rec.* 202 Voted that the freemen proceed to choose seaven Comissionrs for ye tryall of small Cases. **1720** NEAL *Hist. of N. Eng.* II, Freemen. All *Englishmen*, Members of Churches found in Faith, regular in Life, Freeholders, rateable at 10s. being twenty-four Years old, may be made free. . . . The County Court administers the Oath of a Freeman, to any admitted by the General Court. **1775** *Md. Hist. Mag.* X. 302 At a meeting of the Freemen of the middle district of Frederick County . . . the following Gentlemen were chosen a Committee of Observation for said district. **1948** CHAPLIN *Wobbly* 420 Hugh Chaplin became a Freeman, which previous to 1664 meant that they were members of the same Congregational Church, had taken the Freeman's oath and were thereby entitled to vote.

2. (See quots.) *Obs.* Cf. **free trapper.**

1828 MCLOUGHLIN *Letters* (1941) I. 66 Mr. A. McLeod starts with the Willamette Freemen, on a Trapping Expedition South of the Willamette. **1836** IRVING *Astoria* I. 126 Brugiere was of a class of beaver trappers and hunters technically called freemen, in the language of the traders. They are generally Canadians by birth, and of French descent, who have been employed for a term of years by some fur company, but, their term being expired, continue to hunt and trap on their own account, trading with the company like the Indians. **1852** STANSBURY *Gt. Salt Lake* 239 Mr. Henry Frappe had a party of what, in the language of the country, are called 'free men'—that is, independent traders.

Free Methodist. A branch of the Methodist movement organized in 1860 with the avowed purpose of returning to Wesleyan simplicity. Also attrib.

1862 (*title*), Synopsis of the Minutes of the First General Conference of the Free Methodist Church. **1891** *Chi. D. News Almanac* 302 Strength of the Churches. . . . Free Methodists . . . 952 [churches,] 513 [ministers,] 19,998 [communicants]. **1904** *Ib.* 329 Religious denominations in the United States [include] . . . Free Methodist, Independent Methodist, Evangelist Missionary [etc.].

Freeport Doctrine. [*Freeport*, Ill.] A doctrine that the people of a U.S. territory, prior to the formation of a state constitution, could in practice make the territory slave or free by local police regulations. Expounded by Stephen A. Douglas at Freeport, on Aug. 27, 1858, during the Lincoln-Douglas debates. Also **Freeport heresy.** Now *hist.*

1893 J. F. RHODES *Hist. U.S.* II. 327 Lincoln likewise asked Douglas four questions. In the answer to one, Douglas enunciated what is known as the Freeport doctrine. **1901** CHURCHILL *Crisis* 159 Judge Douglas, uneasy will you lie to-night, for you have uttered the Freeport Heresy. **1910** H. P. WILLIS *Stephen A. Douglas* 298 Brown of Mississippi . . . [took] issue with Douglas's 'Freeport doctrine' . . . [Jefferson] Davis plainly said . . . he [Douglas] was now 'as full of heresy as he once was of adherence to the doctrine of popular sovereignty.'

free press. A press not censored or controlled by the government.

[**1792** in SCHUYLER *Liberty of Press in Amer. Colonies* (1905) 77 The press shall be free to every citizen who undertakes to examine the official conduct of men acting in a public capacity.] **1829** CHANNING *Works* (1886) 633/1 Through a free press, all public measures should be brought before the tribunal of the people. **1920** F. P. ADAMS in Lippmann *Liberty & the News* 6 There is much pettiness . . . in the so-called free press; but it is the pettiness . . . common to the so-called human race.

* **free school.** A school maintained by the government, usu. of a state, for the children of a particular district, who attend it without charge. Cf. **Indian free school.**

1670 *Boston Rec.* 57 Mr. Cheuers . . . [should] treate with them concerninge the free schoole. **1741** *Manchester Rec.* II. 34 That the Assessers shall Assess the town for the seaporte of a free school £75. **1892** J. E. COOKE *B. Hallam* 103 Is it possible that you could for a moment be in favor of such a doctrine as you stated, that the men of property should put their hands into their pockets to take out money for people they know nothing of, to support free schools? **1944** WILSON *Passing Inst.* 105 As the 'free schools,' those supported by the state, were taught in the fall, spring was the time for subscription schools.

attrib. **1818** FLINT *Lett. from Amer.* 30 The other institutions [include] . . . thirteen charitable institutions, eight free school societies [etc.]. **1826** J. G. CARTER *Essays upon Pop. Educ.* 49 A very important part of the free school system. **1886** Z. F. SMITH *Kentucky* 712 This was a step in advance of the State on the free-school question.

free silver. The free coinage of silver bullion at government mints. Also the political views or philosophy of those favoring this. Also transf. Cf. **free coinage.**

[**1890** *Nation* 1 May 346/1 The latest bill agreed upon provides for . . . the purchase by the Treasury of 4,500,000 ounces of 'free silver' per month. What is meant by free silver we do not know. . . . We conclude that it means pure silver as distinguished from standard silver nine-tenths fine.] **1895** *Chi. Tribune* 6 April 1 Free Silver or Ruin, Hinrichsen will force his Fiat Money campaign. **1898** *K.C. Star* 20 Dec. 10/2 They are the passport to our affection—made of free silver, but redeemable in the pure gold of patriotic admiration. **1942** LILLARD *Desert Challenge* 50 Free silver was the symbol in a nation-wide struggle of poor man against rich man, of the agricultural West and South against the financial East.

attrib. **1896** *Cin. Enquirer* 30 July 1/3 What about the free silver sentiment among the Republicans of your state? **1903** *Ib.* 3 Jan. 4/2 The Democrats had no patent on the free-silver resolution of a problem that has since been solved by the works of nature. **1948** *Chi. Tribune* 11 July (Grafic Mag.) 5/5 It was doubtful that the free silver crowd could maneuver its way into control of the convention.

Hence **free-silverism, free-silverite.**

1896 *Chi. Tribune* 12 Aug. 6/5 'If he calls you a liar hit him!' vociferates an angry free silverite. **1901** *World's Work* July 911/1 Tillmanism and Free-Silverism have now had their period, and the newer Democratic doctrine of anti-expansion has been set at rest by the Supreme Court.

free soil.

1. An area or region where slavery is not permitted. Also attrib. Now *hist.* Cf. **Northern Free Soil.**

1848 *Free Soil Platform*, We inscribe on our banner, 'Free Soil, Free Speech, Free Labor, and Free Men.' **1848** *N.Y. Wkly. Tribune* 1 July 3/1 The bulk of the Free States can be carried against both Taylor and Cass on a Free Soil issue. **1872** *Newton Kansan* 26 Sep. 2/3 [He] was a candidate . . . on the free soil ticket. **1948** *Pacific Spectator* Spring 151 They had translated their moral repudiation of slavery into the doctrine of 'free soil.'

b. Used in the predicate to designate a person entertaining free-soil principles. Cf. **Free-Soiler.**

1848 S. HALE *Letters* 3 She is very enthusiastic about the election, and furious against Charles Sumner for being Free-Soil. **1856** *Harper's Mag.* XII. 404/1 The trouble originated . . . between a man named Colemand and one Charles W. Dow—the former being pro-slavery and the latter free-soil.

Also **Free-Soilish,** *a. Obs.*

1861 *N.Y. Tribune* 10 Aug. (Chipman), Mr. Clingman was a Douglas Democrat but little more than a year ago, and his proclivities had, not very far back, been considered decidedly Free-Soilish.

2. Free-Soil party, a political party (1848–54) composed of those who were opposed to slavery in the territories of the U.S. and to the admission of slave states into the Union. Also attrib. Now *hist.*

1848 *N.Y. Wkly. Tribune* 29 July 3/3 Hon. James H. Cravens, Ex-Member of Congress from the Lawrenceburg District, has joined the Free Soil party in Indiana. **1884** HURLBERT in *19th Cent.* XVI. 1007 Ex-President Van Buren and Mr. Charles Francis Adams . . . [were] candidates of a new third party which took the name of the 'Free Soil' party. **1907** ANDREWS *Recoll.* 51 The ship of the Free-soil party has had a lie flying from its masts. **1949** *Pacific Spectator* Winter 26 Here was news beside which the front-page items of Free-Soil party meetings and General Taylor's grand fancy ball paled to insignificance.

b. Also (1) **Free-Soil border ruffian,** (2) **candidate,** (3) **democracy,** (4) **democrat,** (5) **element,** (6) **governor,** (7) **movement,** (8) **settler,** (9) **ticket.**

(1) **1860** *Richmond Enquirer* 4 Dec. 1/7 (Th.), Abe Lincoln . . . is the beau ideal of a relentless Free-Soil border ruffian.—(2) **1848** *N.Y. Wkly. Tribune* 1 July 3/1 Only let the issue be placed between Taylor and a Free Soil candidate, and we stand with the latter. — (3) **1848** *N.Y. Wkly. Tribune* 24 June 4/6 The first-named was chosen a delegate to the State Convention of the Free Soil Democracy. **1880** *Dly. Inter-Ocean* (Chi.) 3 June 9/4 The Free-soil Democracy held a national convention on the 11th of August, 1852. — (4) **1867** *Harper's Wkly.* 7 Dec. 770/1 In 1852 the Whig party disappeared, and . . . the mass of it united with the Free-Soil Democrats in forming the Republican party.

(5) **1881–5** McCLELLAN *Own Story* 149 Although the Free-Soil element was strong in the North, the Abolitionists proper were weak. — (6) **1855** in HAMBLETON *H. A. Wise* 320 Kansas . . . has shown that an overwhelming majority of her people are in favor of slavery, notwithstanding the Executive influence of the Freesoil Governor. — (7) **1846** in COMMONS *Doc. Hist.* VII. 343 We are now unitedly for the Free Soil movement. — (8) **1886** LOGAN *Great Conspiracy* 43 The Free-Soil settlers of Kansas, in Mass Convention at Big Springs, utterly repudiated the bogus Legislature and all its acts. — (9) **1884** BLAINE *20 Years of Congress* I. 82 They argued . . . that the Free-soil ticket would draw more largely from the Whigs than from the Democrats.

3. Free-Soil Whig, a member of the Whig party who joined the Free-Soil party. *Obs.*

1848 *Whig Almanac 1849* 58/2 Free Soil Whig. **1855** in HAMBLETON *H. A. Wise* 36 The abolitionized state of Massachusetts, where Democrats were odious, and even Free Soil Whigs were wanting in rankness. **1913** A. C. COLE *Whig Party in South* 228 In the North there was the division into free-soil Whigs and 'silver-grey' or national Whigs.

Free-Soiler. A member of the Free-Soil party, or one in sympathy with its principles. Now *hist.*

1849 *Whig Almanac 1850* 3 Whigs in *Italics;* Locos in Roman; Freesoilers in SMALL CAPS. **1927** BENÉT *J. B.'s Body* 116 But Pop hadn't wanted to join with the Free-Soilers. **1948** *Chi. Tribune* 8 Aug. 7/2 Gov. Andrew was a Free Soiler, and one of the pillars of his party.

b. (See quot.) *Obs.*

1856 *Spirit of Times* 29 Nov. 204/3 The fluke and flounder are called [in R.I.] 'free-soilers,' because they incline to the bottom with such pertinacity.

Free-Soilism. The principles of the Free-Soil party.

1849 *Cong. Globe* 13 Dec. 24/2 We do not charge him with Abolitionism or Free-Soilism, but with duplicity. **1875** *N. Amer. Rev.* CXX. 73 Atchison . . . openly advised the people of Missouri to go and vote in Kansas. General Stringfellow told them to take their bowie-knives and exterminate every scoundrel who was tainted with Free-Soilism or Abolitionism. **1941** BUCKMASTER *Let My People Go* 162 Quincy wrote . . . that Free Soilism 'has carried off multitudes of our abolitionists.'

* **free state.**

1. Before the Civil War, a state in which slavery was prohibited. Now *hist.* Cf. **border free state.**

1819 FLINT *Lett. from Amer.* 135, I would not live in a free state, where one white man cleans the boots of another. **1865** *Nation* I. 108 Ohio and Pennsylvania, and the rest of the old 'free States,' shall purge themselves. **1894** MARK TWAIN *P. Wilson* xviii, He says that her coming here instead of flying to a free state looks bad for me.

b. (See quot.) *Obs.*

1861 *Alexandria* (Va.) *Gaz.* 27 April 3/2 Amherst [Co., Va.] has long borne the sobriquet of the 'free State.'

c. Used as a nickname for, or in allusion to, Maryland.

1923 in MENCKEN *Supp.* II. 603 It caught on quickly, and the *Maryland Free State* is now heard of almost as often as Maryland. **1949** *Sat. Ev. Post* 5 Mar. 93/2 This isn't Russia. It's Annapolis, in the free state of Maryland.

2. *attrib.* Designating persons, organizations, etc., that advocated or supported the view that in new states admitted into the Union, slavery should not be permitted. Now *hist.*

1855 *34th Congress* 1 Sess. Sen. Rep. No. 34, 29 Fellow-soldiers in the free-State army. **1857** *Lawrence* (Kans.) *Republican* 28 May 1 None are more devoted to our Union and Constitution than the free-state citizens of Kansas. **1860** GREELEY *Overland Journey* 36 All those people of Kansas who care to do so may consider my notions of 'Free-State Democracy' and 'Squatter Sovereignty.' *a***1877** in JOHNSON *Anderson Co., Kansas* 55 It became at times a serious question with the Free State settlers how to supply our wants. **1907** ANDREWS *Recoll.* 96 Border warfare became more serious and the free-state people took up arms as the pro-slavery men had done some months before. **1945** MARSHALL *Santa Fe* 28 The Missourians were driven out and Free State troops held the border.

b. Esp. **free state man,** one who opposed slavery in Kansas.

1856 *Harper's Mag.* XII. 404/2 Missourians were told that a large band of free-state men had rescued from the Sheriff of Douglass County a person accused of murdering a pro-slavery man. **1901** DUNCAN & SCOTT *Allen & Woodson Co., Kansas* 64 The early settlers of Allen county were very largely Free State men and therefore Republicans. **1948** DICK *Dixie Frontier* 292 The Kansas freestate men . . . carried their papers safely through that hostile slave state openly in a jug.

c. Also in derivatives: **Free Stateism, free stater** (cf. **Kansas free stater**).

1856 *N.Y. Herald* 21 Jan. 1/1 This latter ticket . . . will, we fancy, be elected, even if Free Stateism should be obliged to lower her uprightness to a fusion with 'moderate pro-slavery.' **1859** *Lawrence* (Kans.) *Republican* 4 Aug. 2/2 These recreants to the history of Free-Stateism in Kansas will be compelled to do the bidding of their stern masters. **1948** *Chi. Tribune* 11 July (Grafic Mag.) 2/3 This was the first act of violence on the part of the free staters.

* **freestone,** *n.*

1. Freestone State, a nickname for Connecticut, in allusion to its freestone quarries.

1846 *Warrock's Alman. 1847* (Richmond, Va.) 22 Connecticut, Freestone [State]. **1886** *Chi. Wkly. News* 29 April 4/3 Connecticut is the Nutmeg state, and its people are Nutmegs from their success in selling wooden for genuine nutmegs, it is also called the Freestone state.

2. freestone water, water in which there is little or no dissolved substance such as calcium, magnesium, etc.

1805 LEWIS in *L. & Clark Exped.* II. (1904) 269 We passed a number of . . . springs which burst out underneath the Lar[boar]d clifts near the edge of the water; they wer[e] very cold and freestone water. **1849** *Rep. Comm. Patents 1849: Agric.* 135 Our free-stone water [i.e., in Cumberland County, Va.] is not well suited to irrigation. **1934** VINES *Green Thicket World* 70 And the men . . . drank mellow whiskey and good freestone water.

free trader. An independent trader among the Indians.

1837 IRVING *Bonneville* I. 71 [Gros Ventres of the Prairie were] waylaying and dogging the caravans of the free traders, and murdering the solitary trapper. **1902** WHITE *Conjurors' House* 39 Brooding on his imprisonment the Free Trader forgot his surroundings. **1945** SERVICE *Ploughman* 429 McTosh is a free trader . . . and hates the Company.

free trapper. (See quot. 1941.) Cf. ***freeman 2.**

1832 R. COX *Adv. Columbia R.* xxix. 311 He declared . . . he should send her to her father (who was a free trapper). **1845** DUNN *Ore. Terr.* 44 These men were often employed for a stated time by the Company as trappers and canoe-men, . . . but generally in the end they became *free trappers.* **1941** FRITZ *Colorado* 87 The 'free' trapper sought the prized fur-bearing animals, trapped them, collected his furs and sold them to whomever he pleased.

* **free-willer,** *n.*

1. (See quot. 1889.) *Obs.*

1770 W. EDDIS *Lett. from Amer.* 71 The situation of the free-willer is, in almost every instance, more to be lamented than either that of the convict or the indented servant. **1889** *Cent.* 2370/3 *Free-willer*, in Maryland, during the colonial period, an immigrant who had voluntarily sold his labor under contract for a certain number of years.

2. A member of the Freewill Baptist Church. *Colloq.*

*a***1817** DWIGHT *Travels* IV. 161 Various other parts of the neighboring country [in New Hampshire], are principally inhabited by Baptists, of the class vulgarly called *Free Willers.* **1880** *Lib. Universal Knowl.* II. 200 They wished to be known simply as Baptists, but their opponents called them 'free-willers,' and both names having been combined, the denomination has adopted 'Free-will Baptists' as their distinctive appellation. **1946** STUART *Plum Grove Hills* 157 If you're a Free-Willer you're a son of Satan among the Mountain Baptists.

* **freeze,** *v.*

1. *intr.* To desire ardently, to long *for* something. *Slang. Obs.*

1848 RUXTON *Far West* (B.), This child felt like going West for many a month, being half froze for buffalo meat and mountain doins. **1884** MARK TWAIN *H. Finn.* xx. 194 I'm jist a-freezin' for something fresh, anyway. **1889** FARMER *Americanisms s.v.*, Another meaning is to become possessed of an intense longing for anything; as I freeze to go back, would be the expression of one thoroughly home-sick.

2. To remain motionless or stock-still. *Colloq.*

1865 *Detroit Tribune* 6 Oct. 3/1 The raiders remained in the back room some minutes without making any demonstration, and Smith in the meantime 'froze' to the door latch. **1908** WHITE *Riverman* 27 Orde, a thick slice of bread halfway to his lips, had frozen in an attitude of attentive listening. **1949** *Pacific Discovery* Jan.–Feb. 11/2 The adults were expert at distracting attention while the chicks scattered and 'froze' in the grass.

3. *fig. tr.* To intimidate (one) by unfriendly behavior. *Colloq.*

1876 HARTE *Two Men of Sandy Bar* 93 Why, the first day I came here on business, the old man froze me so that I couldn't thaw a deposit out of my pocket.

4. To fix or establish a price or assessment at a certain figure. *Colloq.* or *slang.*

1937 *Harper's Mag.* July 192/1 With the excessive costs freezing taxes on poverty. **1948** *Milwaukee Jrnl.* 18 July 12/7 Freezing of property assessments until the city completes its revaluation program was asked Friday in a resolution filed with the common council.

5. In various colloq. and slang phrases: (1) *To freeze down*, to stick closely, to settle or become established; (2) *to freeze in*, to fall to, "pitch in"; (3) *to freeze on(to)*, (*a*) =prec., (*b*) to seize firmly, hold tenaciously; (4) **to freeze out*, (*a*) to drive out or exclude (a person) from society, business, etc., by cool treatment, stratagems, etc., (*b*) to become so cold as to have to get out of bed to keep warm, (*c*) of plants, to die or suffer injury from cold; (5) *to freeze to*, =*to freeze on(to)* (*b*).

(1) **1840** HALIBURTON *Clockmaker* 3 Ser. iii, This is the way, freeze down solid to it, square up to it, as if you was a-goin' to have an all out-door fight of it. **1862** LOWELL *Biglow P.* 2 Ser. i. 26, I friz down right where I wus, merried the Widder Shennon.

(2) **1876** HABBERTON *Jericho Road* 8 Freeze in, and show them snails how to travel.

(3) (*a*) **1847** *Yale Lit. Mag.* XII. 111 'Now, boys,' said Bob, '*freeze on*,' and at it they went. (*b*) **1867** CRAWFORD *Mosby* 241 Before the match was applied to the wagons containing the officers' baggage, our men froze on the valises, and brought them away. **1882** *Cent. Mag.* 541 We bought at seventy. . . . It now is seventy-two. O fortunate young man! freeze onto it, And you will reap a bigger profit yet. **1918** in *Liberty* 11 Aug. (1928) 8/1 By freezing on to them, Supply Company often got a day's vacation.

(4) (*a*) **1861** G. K. WILDER *Diary* (MS) 20 July, We finally froze him out. **1911** SAUNDERS *Col. Todhunter* 43 You've been frozen out of the state committee chairmanship because that bunch ain't got no more use for you'n a hossthief's got for a square sheriff. **1936** MCKENNA *Black Range* 278 We lost our interest, being froze out by some law that was passed by the state legislature, and in stock gambling. (*b*) **1862** NORTON *Army Lett.* 62 J. and the Rabbi froze out at midnight and got up and made a big fire and snoozed by that the rest of the night. **1895** REMINGTON *Pony Tracks* 27 This freezing out of your blankets four or five times every night [etc.]. (*c*) **1868** *Iowa Agric. Soc. 1867* 196 What [grapevines] do not freeze out in Winter, will blight out in Summer. **1872** *Vt. Bd. Agric. Rep.* I. 128 Alsike luxuriates in damp soils, and will not freeze out as red clover.

(5) **1851** HALL *College Words* 135 We *freeze* to apples in the orchards, to fellows whom we electioneer for in our secret societies, and alas! some even go so far as to *freeze* to the ladies. **1907** MULFORD *Bar-20* 105 So in a month he'd sneak in an' freeze to a chair by th' door.

freeze-out ˈfriz͵aut, *n.*

1. A variety of poker in which each player, as soon as his capital is exhausted, drops out of the game, all the stakes going to the last player left in.

[**1855** *Quincy* (Calif.) *Prospector* 7 April 2/3 Bill held a flush, to Ned's threes, out; And cried, 'hurrah my Ned, its freezeout.'] **1856** *Butte Record* (Oroville, Calif.) 25 Oct. 1/6 He was at the Mountain House playing 'freeze-out' for the whiskey. **1908** LORIMER *J. Spurlock* 288 We started a friendly game of freeze-out. **1945** SERVICE *Ploughman* 214 Say, Pard, if you like I'll play you for one of them there geese. Stud poker or freeze out.

b. (See quots. and cf. ∗**freeze,** *v.* **5.** (4) (*b*).)

1886 *Kansas Hist. Coll.* III. 405 The *Sod House* is doing duty in snug quarters on the Cimarron, in Ford county—playing a game of 'freeze-out,' as it were. **1894** *Harper's Mag.* Feb. 356/1 Getting up in the night to poke the fire and thaw the stiffening out of one's legs is called by the boys 'playing freeze-out.'

One type of freezer or ice cream freezer

c. (See quots.)

1903 *Cin. Enquirer* 3 Jan. 13/4 He helped himself to chips and cards, declared a ten-dollar freeze-out. **1944** *Pocket Bk. of Games* 21 Freeze-Out. This is merely a method of fixing minimum stakes.

2. An act of excluding or freezing out, in full **freeze-out game.** *Slang.* Cf. ∗**freeze,** *v.* **5.** (4) (*a*).

1863 *Washoe* (Nev.) *Times* 11 July 2/5 We never before exactly understood the villainous process of the 'freeze-out game.' **1875** *Scribner's Mo.* X. 277/1 [At San Francisco] 'clean out,' 'freeze out,' are synonyms for rascally operations in business. **1904** LYNDE *Grafters* 190 Enough of the stock will have changed hands on the 'wreck' price to put the Plantagould people safely in the saddle, and the freeze-out will be a fact accomplished. **1947** CHALFANT *Gold, Guns, & Ghost Towns* 141 It was just a freeze-out game, and I let my stock go without paying the assessment.

∗**freezer,** *n.* =**ice cream freezer.** Cf. **cream freezer.**

1847 in *Mo. Hist. Rev.* XXXVI. 121 As preliminary to its manufacture [i.e., of ice cream], there will be needed an article called a 'Freezer,' which consists of a cylindrical jar, made of block tin, and fitted with a close cover. **1870** E. PRENTISS *Life & Letters* 350 Papa bought a new fashioned freezer, that professed to freeze in two minutes. **1948** *Reader's Digest* Dec. 154/2, [I] got six water-melons and a freezer of ice cream.

freeze-up ˈfriz,ʌp, *n.* The freezing fast of lakes, rivers, and streams. Also transf.

1876 *The Dalles* (Ore.) *Tribune* 29 Jan. 3/2 We hope to see the day when . . . all the inhabitants east of the Cascades will not be detrimentally affected by any freeze-up which may occur. **1882** *Golden* (N.M.) *Retort* 28 July 3/2 He says a freeze-up occurred from insufficient fluxing, but thinks the smelter will start up again soon. **1904** J. LYNCH *3 Yrs. Klondike* 129 A couple of steam-engines had been . . . brought to Dawson last October just before the freeze-up.

∗**freezing out.**

1. Exposure to severe cold. Also attrib.

1864 *Ohio Agric. Rep.* XVIII. 131 The principal cause of injury to the wheat was 'freezing out.' **1868** WOODRUFF *Trotting Horse* 92 [The plan is] often adopted of turning the horse out into a field, to endure the bitter blasts and intensely cold nights of a severe winter, with nothing but a hovel for shelter, and sometimes not that. . . . A horse turned loose to undergo this 'freezing out,' as it is called, is apt to be neglected. *Ib.*, I can see no advantage to be gained by the 'freezing-out plan.'

2. The elimination or exclusion of rivals, etc. Also attrib. *Colloq.*

1877 HARTE *Story of Mine* 35 That ingenuous American pastime which my countrymen dismiss in their epigrammatic way as the 'freezing-out process.' **1884** CRADDOCK *Where Battle Was Fought* 48 By a dexterous use of the system known as 'freezing out,' the two had become exclusive owners of a certain silver mine in Colorado.

∗**freight,** *n.*

1. Goods or merchandise transported overland by wagons, railroads, etc.

1813 *Boston Gaz.* 21 June (Th.), [I] will take Freight [from Boston to Philadelphia] on reasonable terms. **1863** *Washoe* (Nev.) *Times* 11 July 1/5 Here we discharged some government freight, and, having wooded, started off again. **1946** *Fortune* May 135 Passenger airlines that have established cargo departments carry freight of twenty-five pounds or more on a common-carrier basis.

2. A charge made for transporting goods by land.

1840 *Niles' Reg.* 4 April 80/2 Freight of flour. . . . The proprietors of the principal transportation lines have resolved to give the shipper or owner the full advantage of the reduction of twenty cents per barrel, in the toll of flour, from Pittsburg to Philadelphia. **1888** *Harper's Mag.* 718/2 It is very likely that Columbus may in time surpass both Cleveland and Cincinnati . . . as a railroad centre. Fuel is cheap, freights are extremely low. **1948** *Chi. D. News* 4 May 12/3 The absorption of freight in the delivered price is a practice in many an industry.

3. =**freight train 1.**

1861 *Remin. Locomotive Engineer* 123 He was running the Night Express, a fast run, while I was running the through freight. **1900** FLYNT *Itinerant Policeman* 174 We had an hour at our disposal until the next 'freight' was due. **1948** *Chi. Sun* 27 Jan. 22/4 'What would you do?' 'Blow town on the next freight.'

b. =**freight engine.**

1883 FULTON *Sam Hobart* 222 His locomotive was a large freight.

4. In combs.: (1) **freight blockade,** a temporary congestion in the handling of freight, *rare;* (2) **depot,** a building or part of a building in which a railroad company stores freight; (3) **elevator,** a large elevator for the raising and lowering of heavy goods; (4) **engine,** (see quot. 1864); (5) **house,** =**freight depot;** (6) **line,** (*a*) a system operating as a common carrier for the transportation of goods sent as freight, a railway that performs this function, (*b*) a line of wagons engaged in hauling freight, *rare;* (7) **outfit,** a wagon train engaged in hauling goods across the plains, cf. **freighter,** *n.* **2. c;** (8) **railway,** a railroad for hauling freight; (9) **rate,** a rate or charge established by a freight company, also attrib.; (10) **room,** a room where freight is temporarily stored; (11) **shed,** a storage shed for railroad freight; (12) **team,** a team used in hauling freight in wagons, cf. **freighter,** *n.* **2. c;** (13) **train,** see as a main entry; (14) **traffic,** that part of the business of a railroad which is concerned with the carrying of goods, also attrib.; (15) **yard,** an area in or near a city provided with tracks, warehouses, offices, etc., serving as the local center of a particular railroad.

(1) **1882** *Belleville* (Ill.) *Advocate* 9 June 4/6 Heretofore all branches of business have suffered on account of freight blockades at East St. Louis. — (2) **1841** *Spirit of Times* 25 Sep. 354/1 (We.), Freight Depot. **1849** *Hunt's Merch. Mag.* XX. 342 A spacious freight and passenger depot . . . has been completed in the lower part of Detroit. **1906** *Springfield W. Republican* 4 Oct. 7 What the English call a 'railway goods station,' . . . we call a freight depot. — (3) **1903** ADE *In Babel* 18 He had patented certain devices which were used by all makers of passenger and freight elevators. **1948** *Life* 5 April 69 Using freight elevator, a student unlocks controls with elevator key given to paraplegics so they can get from class to class without assistance. — (4) **1864** WEBSTER 542/3 *Freight-engine,* a locomotive for hauling freight-cars. **1909** O. HENRY *Roads of Destiny* 147 Two hours later an Iron Mountain freight engine pulled out of the railroad yards, Texas bound.

(5) **1848** *Hunt's Merch. Mag.* XVIII. 383 The Worcester Railroad . . . has a freight-house in Boston. **1948** *Dly. Ardmoreite* (Ardmore, Okla.) 28 July 13/2 The car was shunted to a siding near the freight house yesterday afternoon. — (6) (*a*) **1859** *Harper's Mag.* Aug. 425/2 The freight lines represented in New York employ a small army of freight solicitors, or . . . 'contracting agents.' **1918** RIDEOUT *Key of Fields* 270 The rails and ties of a disused freight line crossed the levee in this depression. (*b*) **1896** SHINN *Story of Mine* 116 The freight lines opened to let the stages through. — (7) **1899** *Mo. So. Dakotan* I. 196 About noon we met Volin's freight outfit eating dinner at Pena Springs. *a*1918 G. STUART *On Frontier* I. 253, I advised him to go over to the mines, where he could get work and later return across the plains with some freight outfit. — (8) **1846** *Hunt's Merch. Mag.* XIV. 383 A substantial freight railway, to connect New York with the Connecticut Valley. — (9) **1848** *Hunt's Merch. Mag.* XVIII. 101 Freight rates.—Iron, 25 cents per 100 pounds. **1881** *Chi. Times* 12 March, A freight-rate war between the eastern lines of railroads is regarded . . . as unavoidable. **1944** *Sears Cat.* (ed. 189) 900 On freight orders of 100 pounds or less, made up of several articles taking different freight rates, the highest rate applies to the entire shipment.

(10) **1899** TARKINGTON *Gentleman from Indiana* xix. 354 The doors of the freight-room were thrown open, and a big bundle of colored stuffs was dragged out and hastily unfolded. — (11) **1881** *Chi. Times* 17 June, The building is located between the gas-works and the

freight-sheds of the Chicago and Northwestern railway. **1917** MATHEWSON *Sec. Base Sloan* 19 A man at the freight shed directed us. — **(12) 1860** in *Colo. Mag.* XIV. (1937) 207 Met a freight team here (near the Platte bluffs), returning from Denver with oxen. **1923** E. G. WADE *Early Days at Paonia* (MS) 3 Samuel Wade hired freight teams.

(14) 1881 *Chi. Times* 17 June, [The] freight-traffic manager of the Chicago and Northwestern railway, officially announces the following appointments. **1903** E. JOHNSON *Railway Transportation* 56 The railroads in this group have the heaviest freight traffic of any roads in the country. — **(15) 1881** *Chi. Times* 14 May, Twelve days ago the railroad switchmen in all but one of the freight-yards in this city struck for a slight increase of their wages. **1948** *Houston* (Tex.) *Post* 14 June 6/5 Every capitalist is your enemy and every workingman is your friend, Eugene Debs told freight-yard audiences.

b. Designating vehicles for transporting freight, as (1) **freight boat,** (2) **car,** cf. **burden car,** (3) **plane,** (4) **scow,** (5) **wagon.**

(1) **1825** in *Amer. Sp.* XXI. (1946) 306/1 When the Canals are as much occupied by freight boats, . . . they must be abandoned by all travellers, except those of mere curiosity. **1946** STANWELL-FLETCHER *Driftwood Valley* 202 It was arranged that . . . J. should catch the

One type of freight wagon

weekly freight boat. — **(2) 1833** *Amer. R.R. Jrnl.* II. 325/2 [There are] 10 freight cars. **1947** *Chi. D. News* 17 Jan. 4/2 A freight car and caboose were destroyed by fire. — **(3) 1946** STANWELL-FLETCHER *Driftwood Valley* 161 Riding in a small heavily loaded freight plane through wild uncharted mountain ranges is very different from sitting at ease in a passenger plane over gently rolling cultivated country. — **(4) 1946** STANWELL-FLETCHER *Driftwood Valley* 22 We've cooled our heels here at Takla waiting for the long overdue freight scow.

(5) *(a)* **1832** *Amer. R.R. Jrnl.* I. 85/3 The snow has not prevented the running of carriages or freight waggons. *(b)* **1855** BARNUM *Life* 69 My father . . . ran a freight wagon to Norwalk. **1880** INGHAM *Digging Gold* xiii. 307 In this Black Hills forwarding business there are regularly employed one thousand four hundred large freight wagons. **1945** MATHEWS *Talking* 2 The occasional freight wagons stopped in the area only to let the horses blow after the climb or the driver take a shot at the floating white tails of a deer.

c. Denoting persons: (1) **freight agent,** a representative of a company that transports freight, cf. **general freight agent;** (2) **brakeman,** a man employed to operate brakes on a freight train, cf. **brakeman;** (3) **conductor,** a railway employee on a freight train in charge of freight; (4) **driver,** =**freighter 2;** (5) **handler,** one who handles freight; (6) **wrangler,** one who moves heavy freight.

(1) **1843** *Rep. Western R.R.* 17 Freight-agent. **1853** *Hunt's Merch. Mag.* XXVIII. 477 The statements of the canal collector and freight agent of the M. S. R. R. were appealed to. **1944** *Sears Cat.* (ed. 189) 900 If there is a freight agent at your station, you pay freight charges when shipment is received. — **(2) 1901** *Munsey's Mag.* Aug. 740/2 When he was a freight brakeman, no one knew him except as Freckles. — **(3) 1849** *Hunt's Merch. Mag.* XXI. 580 Freight conductors receive from $40 to $45 per month. **1857** *Spirit of Times* 9 May. 157/1 The freight conductors on the Baltimore and Ohio Railroad struck for wages last week. — **(4) 1912** DAWSON *Pioneer Tales* 74 The pay of freight drivers ranged from $40 to $75 per month.

(5) **1882** *Nation* 6 July 6/3 Strikes like that of the freight-handlers have occurred before. **1903** *N.Y. Times* 1 Sep., A committee representing 3,000 telegraph operators and a like number of freight handlers employed by the Pennsylvania Railroad Co. — **(6) 1923** WATTS *L. Nichols* 43 Yes, Sir, he's one good freight wrangler, Mac is.

d. In phrases: (1) *by freight,* on a freight train, occas. by truck; (2) *to pull one's freight,* to depart speedily or at once, *slang;* (3) *to haul freight,* =prec.

(1) **1889** *Cent.* 2371/2 Shall it be sent by freight or by express? **1944** *Sears Cat.* (ed. 189) 898 If necessary to return goods by freight or express . . . write us first for instructions. — **(2) 1895** REMINGTON *Pony Tracks* 252 The wily old fellow . . . concluded that we were not a cow outfit, whereat he had discreetly 'pulled his freight.' **1922** *Dly. Ardmoreite* (Ardmore, Okla.) 26 March (Comics) 4 Tell him t' pull his freight! — **(3) 1944** *Chi. D. News* 28 Dec. 11/2 'About then I hauled freight,' Porky admitted.

Also *freight association, bill, bureau, business, charge, claim, crew, hand, hire, law, loader, money, office, party, route, schedule, station, truck, warehouse,* etc.

As the last term in **down, fast, local, through, up, way freight.**

***freight,** *v.*

1. *tr.* To load (a train) with freight. Also transf.

1874 B. F. TAYLOR *World on Wheels* 144 No matter how carefully you freight a train, there is always something gets on board that never appears on the bill of lading. **1875** *Amer. Naturalist* IX. 153 [Prairie gophers] stow away the provender in their pouches. . . . When duly freighted they make for their holes.

2. To convey or transport (goods) overland.

1881 HAYES *New Colorado* 85 When he lit out, it took a four-mule team to freight his trunks. **1913** LONDON *Valley of Moon* III. ix, I guess they just about quit tryin' to use this road in the winter. . . . I can just see 'm freightin' that marble out over it I don't think. **1948** *Popular Western* June 36/2 Amos Chaffin ordered $500 worth more of whisky freighted in and congratulated himself on his business acumen.

transf. **1898** *McClure's Mag.* X. 208 It is a common thing to see a waiter freighting your breakfast . . . a half block in a pouring rain.

b. *absol.* To engage in the business of transporting freight.

1855 *N.Y. Wkly. Tribune* 6 Jan. 1/2 Generally, the Ohio Railroads are freighting heavily, in spite of short crops and hard times. **1920** HUNTER *Trail Drivers Texas* I. 163 My father sold them several yoke of old oxen which he had freighted to Mexico with. **1931** *Randolph Enterprise* (Elkins, W.Va.) 8 Jan. 4/5 He lived at Brownsville, Nebraska, and freighted from there to Fort Riley.

3. With adverbs. (1) *To freight out,* =**freight,** *v.* **2;** (2) *to freight up,* to take in a large supply, *colloq.*

(1) **1841** *St. Louis Republican* 28 Sep., Only one or two of the old [Santa Fé] traders have returned, the majority of the party being composed of those who freighted out goods in the spring. **1941** FERGUSSON *Southwest* 157 Most Southwestern families boast of the first grand piano freighted out across the plains. — **(2) 1889** MARK TWAIN *Conn. Yankee* xiii. 153 Those Britons . . . [knew] how to freight up against probable fasts before starting.

***freightage,** *n.* The transportation of goods by land. — **1872** MARK TWAIN *Roughing It* xvii. 137 The high prices charged for trifles were eloquent of high freights and bewildering distances of freightage. **1886** *Harper's Mag.* Jan. 217/2 All travel and freightage [in Persia] are still, as of old, conducted by means of horses, asses, camels, and mules.

***freighter,** *n.*

1. A vessel engaged in carrying goods.

1839 *S. Lit. Messenger* V. 5/2 The Great Britain is now sailing as a mere freighter, and larger vessels are sailing as packets. **1910** J. C. MILLS *Our Inland Seas* 224 The great freighter *Delaware*, . . . of three thousand, nine hundred tons' register, was added [to the Anchor Line]. **1947** *Beaver* June 18/1 The third canoe, a new eighteen-foot freighter, and the rest of the supplies, accompanied us on the S.S. *Kenora*.

2. One engaged in transporting goods in wagons across the plains of the West. Now *hist.*

1852 *Knickerb.* March 224 The freighters were as impatient of delay as those Æneas saw crowding the shores of Styx. **1884** W. SHEPHERD *Prairie Exper.* 200 The freighters are a special class, who have much to tell of the glories of the road in the days gone by. **1947** *True* Nov. 107/1 Old Est snapped a hasty shot at the nosy freighter which caught him over the heart and knocked him over his load of lumber.

b. =**freight engine.**

1861 *Charleston* (S.C.) *Mercury* 2 Feb. 2/2 It will be seen that none of the Locomotives reported in service on the 31st of December, 1859, have been condemned, and that we have added during the year two Passengers and two Freighters.

c. A freight wagon. Now *hist.* Cf. **Conestoga 2.**

1885 *Cent. Mag.* Nov. 65/1 Heavily loaded freighters were lurching in. **1929** *Randolph Enterprise* (Elkins, W.Va.) 14 Nov. 1/3 The Conestoga Wagon, known as the freighter, hauled travelers, too.

As the last term in **silver, wagon freighter.**

***freighting,** *n.* The transporting of goods overland, esp. by wagons and wagon trains in the West. Also attrib. or as adj. Cf. **green freighting.**

1873 *Newton Kansan* 15 May 2/2 Their road will hereafter deserve and obtain all of the Government freighting for the southwest. **1891** O'BEIRNE *Leaders Ind. Territory* 231/2 Mr. Talley devoted his first few years to the business of freighting, . . . and was employed by the U.S. government carrying goods from Caddo, Indian Territory, to the Indian Reservation at Fort Sill. **1923** J. H. COOK *On Old Frontier* 115 Fist-fights . . . were engaged in among soldiers of the regular army, freighting outfits, and men following other vocations. **1944** DUNCAN *M. Graham* 235 Many settlers turned to freighting as a livelihood.

freight train.

1. A railroad train that carries freight. Also attrib. Cf. **double-header 3, way freight train.**

1847 *Hunt's Merch. Mag.* XVII. 303 The total number of miles run by passenger, freight, and other trains, during the year 1846, amounted to 48,910. **1898** *McClure's Mag.* X. 395 The poor fellows on freight . . . must not exceed the regular schedule of freight-train speed. **1948** *Newsweek* 19 April 68/2 Watch a freight train pounding past and you'll see a miracle in the making.

2. A wagon train engaged in hauling freight.

1869 J. R. BROWNE *Adv. Apache Country* 450 Freight trains were drawn up in front of the tavern, the teams tied to the wagon-poles. **1900** DRANNAN *Plains & Mts.* 386 The second day's travel after crossing the summit of this mountain we met a freight train on its return to Salt Lake City.

***Fremont,** *n.* [John C. *Frémont* (1813–90), Amer. explorer.] Used attrib. and in the possessive in the names of western trees, shrubs, and animals: (1) **Fremont cottonwood,** (see quot. 1897); (2) **mahonia,** the Fremont hollygrape, *Mahonia fremonti;* (3) **phacelia,** a lavender-flowered herb, *Phacelia fremonti,* found in desert areas in the Southwest; (4) **(-'s) chickaree, =Fremont's (pine) squirrel;** (5) **-'s nut pine,** a single-leaved piñon, *Pinus cembroides monophylla;* (6) **-'s (pine) squirrel,** (see quot. 1931).

(1) 1897 SUDWORTH *Arborescent Flora* 135 *Populus fremontii,* . . . Fremont Cottonwood. **1921** HALL *Yosemite Nat. Park* 125 From the train one sees along the Merced River bottom numerous Fremont cottonwoods and valley oaks. — **(2) 1942** VAN DERSAL *Ornamental Amer. Shrubs* 173 Closely resembling the Fremont mahonia, but with blood-red berries instead of blue, is *Mahonia haematocarpa,* the red mahonia. — **(3) 1947** *Desert Mag.* Mar. 28/3 Lupine, long tube primrose, groundsel, Fremont phacelia and Eriophyllum were found in bloom on January 8 in El Dorado canyon. — **(4) 1878** HINTON *Ariz.* 336 Squirrels are well represented, . . . and include the tuft-eared, the Arizona gray, Fremont's chickaree. **1928** SETON *Lives Game Animals* IV. 163 A more exact map with full details would give to the Fremont Chickaree all of the fir and spruce forests on the mountains between the pine belt and timberline, from the extreme southeast of Arizona to and into the extreme southwest of Wyoming.

(5) 1897 SUDWORTH *Arborescent Flora* 18 *Pinus monophylla,* . . . Fremont's Nut Pine. — **(6) 1931** BAILEY *Mammals N.M.* 74 Sciurus fremonti fremonti Audubon and Bachman. Fremont's Pine Squirrel; Gray Chickaree. . . . A small, short-eared squirrel of the chickaree group, with dark olive-gray back and light gray belly in the winter but in summer more of a brownish gray above with a black line along each side, and with whitish lower parts. **1936** *Univ. Ariz. Gen. Bul.* No. 3, 76 Smallest and most vociferous of these are the Frémont's squirrels or chickarees.

Fremontia frəˈmɑntɪə, *n.* [See prec.]

1. The black greasewood (see quots. 1850, 1893).

1844 FRÉMONT *Exped.* 214 The country otherwise is a perfect barren, without a blade of grass, the only plants being some dwarf Fremontias. **1846** in EMORY *Military Reconn.* 612 The vegetation on the jornada is the creosote bush, the mesquite, the Fremontia [etc.]. **1850** TORREY *Obs. on Batis Maritima* 7 The Batis (?) vermicularis of Hooker is my former Fremontia, a Chenopodiaceous plant, which I described several years ago as a new genus, without being aware at the time that it had shortly before been published by Nees, under the name of Sarcobatus. **1893** COVILLE *Death Valley Exped.* 74 The generic name *Fremontia* was first applied by Torrey to the plant now known as *Sarcobatus vermiculatus,* but the name *Sarcobatus* had already been given to this genus by Nees von Esenbeck, and *Fremontia* became a synonym.

2. The plant genus to which the flannelbush of California belongs. Also (not *cap.*) the flannelbush. Cf. **slippery elm 2.**

1850 TORREY *Plantæ Fremontianæ* 7 In my memoir on Batis . . . I have given the reason for relinquishing the former genus Fremontia, and my intention of bestowing the name on a new plant from California, first detected by the distinguished traveller himself, whose valuable services to North American Botany it is thus intended to commemorate. **1889** *Cent.* 2372/1 *Fremontia,* . . . a genus of plants, of a single species, *F. Californica,* a common shrub upon the dry hills of California, known as *California slippery-elm.* **1942** VAN DERSAL *Ornamental Amer. Shrubs* 239 This species goes by the name of San Diego fremontia, a reflection of the fact that it is found in the United States only in San Diego County, California.

Fremontism ˈfrimɑntɪzəm, *n.* [See **Fremont.**] The political principles of the Republican party as embodied in John C. Frémont, the party's first presidential candidate in 1856. *Rare.* — **1856** *Dollar Times* (Cin.) 27 Nov. 4/6 He advised all Americans to do the same, and thus defeat their greatest enemy—Fremontism.

***French,** *n.*

1. =**frenching,** *n.* **1.** *Rare.*

1856 *Rep. Comm. Patents 1855: Agric.* 231 Indian corn, however, is subject to 'French'; and, in this case, the disease has been attributed to some imperfection of the soil.

2. In combs.: (1) **French boot,** a light shoe for dress wear imported from France or made in a French style, *obs.,* cf. **French fall shoes;** (2) ***bulldog,** (see quot.), *obs.;* (3) **Canadian,** see as a main entry; (4) **church,** a church of French Protestants or Huguenots, *obs.;* (5) **clover,** crimson clover, or the globe amaranth; (6) **Creole,** a Creole *q.v.* of French extraction, also attrib.; (7) **dressing,** a salad dressing made of oil, vinegar, salt, pepper, and other seasoning; (8) **falls,** see as a main entry; (9) **flat,** see as a main entry; (10) **Grant,** (see quot.), *obs.;* (11) **harp,** a harmonica; (12) **Indian,** see as a main entry; (13) **land,** land which fails to produce a crop because of frenching *q.v., obs.;* (14) ***man,** (see quots.), cf. **Canadian Frenchman;** (15) **monte,** see as a main entry; (16) **Neutral,** an Acadian, esp. one of those who, in 1755, were deported to the British colonies, *obs.;* (17) **party,** (see quot.), *obs.;* (18) **philopena,** see **philopena;** (19) **pony,** a small, wiry horse of the type used and developed by the early French settlers in the Illinois country, *obs.;* (20) **quarter,** that part of New Orleans occupied by the French or their descendants; (21) **rust,** a disease of cotton esp. prevalent on blackjack soils and bottom lands, *obs.;* (22) **toast,** (see quot.).

(1) 1850 LEWIS *La. Swamp Doctor* 138 A veritable 'Swamp Doctor,' to whom French boots and broadcloth must be obsolete ideas. **1891** WELCH *Recoll. 1830–40* 179 At balls or parties, pumps were worn, sometimes light French boots. — **(2) 1875** *Chi. Tribune* 26 Nov. 5/2 The weapon is one of the kind generally known as the French bull-dog. . . . It is a seven-shooter, self-cocker, and is a 32 calibre. — **(4) 1699** SEWALL *Diary* I. 491 This day I spake with Mr. Newman about his partaking with the French Church on the 25. December on account of its being Christmas-day, as they abusively call it. **1740** in *Mass. Hist. Soc. Proc.* V. 110 There are nine Independent meeting-houses, one Anabaptist meeting, one Quakers' meeting, and one French Church. **1883** SCHAFF *Religious Encycl.* II. 1036/2 The French church in Charleston alone survives to the present day, and uses an excellent liturgy.

(5) 1826 *New Mo. Mag.* XVII. II. 252 In one part of the country, you find the English walnut, and the French walnut; . . . in another, the English clover, and the French clover. **1889** VASEY *Agric. Grasses* 82 *Trifolium incarnatum* (French clover) . . . has been introduced and tried to some extent for cultivation. **1892** *Amer. Folk-Lore* V. 102 *Gomphrena globosa,* French clover. No. Ohio. — **(6) 1836** IRVING *Astoria* I. 211 [The two Arikaras] were accompanied by an interpreter; a French creole; one of those haphazard wights of Gallic origin, who abound upon our frontier, living among the Indians like one of their own race. **1868** ROSE *Great Country* 195 The French Creole ladies, descended from the earliest settlers, are many of them beautiful, and dressed in good Parisian style. — **(7)** [**1884** F. E. OWENS *Cook Book* 119 French Salad Dressing, for any vegetable salad, one tablespoon vinegar, 3 tablespoons salad oil [etc.].] **1945** *La Junta* (Colo.) *Tribune-Democrat* 15 Feb. 2/6 Country Club Tavern . . . Featuring Broiled Maine Live Lobster . . . French Fried Onions Chef's Salad with French Dressing.

(10) 1847 HOWE *Hist. Coll. Ohio* 456 The 'French Grant,' a tract of 24,000 acres is situated in the southeastern part of this [Scioto] county. It was granted by Congress in March, 1795, to a number of French families who lost their lands at Gallipolis, by invalid titles. — **(11) 1883** RILEY *Old Swimmin'-Hole* 25 A slice of warter-melon's like a French-harp in their hands. **1946** WILSON *Fidelity* 196 She would play the organ for me, and I would play my French harp. — **(13) 1856** [see **French,** *v.* **1**]. — **(14) 1688** JOHN CLAYTON in *Phil. Trans.* XVII. 948 *French-men* they [Virginians] call those Plants, whose Leaves do not spread and grow large, but rather spire upwards, and grow tall; these Plants they do not tend, being not worthy their Labour. **1896** P. A. BRUCE *Econ. Hist. Va.* I. 439 For this reason they were always referred to as 'Frenchmen,' a people who were associated in the Virginian mind with tallness and attenuation in form. **1944** *D.N.* Nov. 66 Frenchman; Frenchmen: n. Stalk(s) with short, erect small leaves and worthless as to quality. E. Va.

(**16**) **1755** in *Md. Hist. Mag.* III. 10 Sunday last (Nov. 30) arrived here the two last of the vessels from Nova-Scotia, with French Neutrals for this Place. **1832** WILLIAMSON *Maine* II. 264 The energetic exertions of its government to bring the Acadians or French Neutrals, into obedience, were circumstances indicative of its rising strength. — (**17**) **1898** CUSHMAN *Hist. Indians* 473 The French retained many friends among the Choctaws, who were now called 'the French party.' — (**19**) **1835** HOFFMAN *Winter in West* I. 206 The southern horse won the race; but I was told that, in nine cases out of ten, the nags from his part of the country, could not stand against a French pony. **1857** *Ill. Agric. Soc. Trans.* II. 354 Their horses, known as 'French ponies,' were numerous, and of excellent pedigree.

(**20**) **1865** RICHARDSON *Secret Service* iii. 47 On the lower side of it [Canal Street in New Orleans] is the 'French Quarter,' more un-American even than the famous German portion of Cincinnati known as 'Over the Rhine.' **1947** *Chi. Tribune* 1 Nov. 14/8 Tourists wandering about the French quarter buy them in cute cotton bale packages and send them out by dozens to their friends 'up north.' — (**21**) **1843** in TURNER *Cotton* (1865) 169 In this section of country, we have two species of rust—the red or common rust, and the brown or French. I cannot give you the derivation of the latter term, but it is of general prevalence in this neighborhood. — (**22**) **1882** F. E. OWENS *Cook Book* 128 French Toast. Make a batter of two eggs, one-half cup of milk, pinch of salt, and teaspoon of cornstarch. Dip thin slices of bread in and fry brown in a well-buttered frying pan.

b. Denoting foods, esp. potatoes, prepared by frying in deep fat, as (1) **French fried potatoes,** (also **French frieds, French fries**), (2) **French fried shrimp.**

(**1**) **1908** DAVENPORT *Butte Beneath X-Ray* 59 When I look over this vast assortment of Ox-Tail-Soup, . . . Boston Baked Beans and French Fried Potatoes . . . I send up a wireless telegram . . . to my Maker thanking Him that I am here to-night. **1944** *This Week Mag.* 18 March 12/2 Sirloin steak I get them, with French frieds and mushrooms, salad and honeydew melons, ice cream and cake. **1947** *Chi. D. News* 22 Oct. 47 I'll have steak, French fries, corn-on-the-cob. — (**2**) **1941** *Dly. Oklahoman* (Okla. City) 28 Oct., A heated plate of French fried shrimp is nice for buffet tables.

c. In the names of birds: (1) **French blackbird,** (see quot.); (2) **duck,** (see quot 1889); (3) **mocker,** (see quot.); (4) **mocking bird,** the brown thrasher, *Toxostoma rufum*, also, *obs.*, **French mockbird;** (5) * **woodpecker,** =**California woodpecker.**

(**1**) **1826** FLINT *Recoll.* 243, I saw early in the spring a flock of those merry and chattering birds, that we call bob-a-link, or French blackbird. — (**2**) **1820** in MORSE *Rep. Indian Affairs* (1822) II. 32 Throughout this north-western country, are . . . several kinds of ducks, as the black, French (resembling the tame) wood duck, etc. . . . , and the gull. **1889** *Cent.* 1789/1 *French duck*, the mallard. (Louisiana.) — (**3**) **1908** *D.N.* III. 313 *French mocker*, the butcher bird. — (**4**) *c***1729** CATESBY *Carolina* I. 28 The Fox coloured Thrush . . . is called in Virginia the French Mockbird. . . . It sings with some variety of Notes. **1797** in LATROBE *Journal* 111 We stopped, and saw two of the birds, called the French mocking bird. **1877** BARTLETT 70 Brown thrasher (*Turdus rufus*). . . . In Maryland, it is called the French Mocking-bird. **1917** *Birds of Amer.* III. 179. — (**5**) **1851** WOODS *Gold Diggings* 83, I have seen but few birds among the mountains of California. The large French woodpecker is the most common. It feeds upon the acorn, of which it lays up immense supplies after they have fallen from the trees.

As the last term in **Canadian, Creole, Gumbo French.**

* **french,** *v.* Also * **French.**

1. *intr.* Of corn, tobacco, etc.: To suffer from the disease known as frenching *q.v. Obs.*

1852 *Fla. Plant. Rec.* 67 My Corn Crop Looks better than it did Last year this time. it have Frenched a Little I see in Places but it will Come out as soon as it gets a good rain on it. **1856** *Rep. Comm. Patents 1855: Agric.* 231 When corn is thus Frenched on what are termed 'French lands,' it grows light colored sometimes almost white, or striped, and bears no crop.

2. (See quot.)

1889 *N. & Q.* III. 285 In North Carolina, land which suddenly and unaccountably fails to produce crops is said to *french*; such land is *frenchy*.

3. *tr.* (See quot.)

1892 *Stand.* 723/2 *French*. 1. To prepare, as a chop, by partially cutting the meat from the shank and leaving bare the bone in such a manner as to fit it for convenient handling. 2. In general, to prepare or cook in the style or manner of the French.

4. *intr.* To take French leave. *Slang.*

1907 *N.Y. Times* 14 Sep. 18 The midshipman recently recommended for dismissal from the Naval Academy for 'frenching' from his ship during the late summer cruise.

French Canadian, *n.* and *a.*

1. *n.* A French settler in Canada or a Canadian of French ancestry.

1775 ADAIR *Indians* 153 The French Canadians are highly censurable . . . for debauching our peaceable northern Indians, with their infernal catechism. **1800** J. MAUDE *Niagara* 176 The *Engagés* (for so the bateau men are called) are always French Canadians. **1867** in PERSONS *Mass. Labor Laws* (1911) 93 Our whole factory population is . . . composed mainly of English, Irish and French Canadians. **1947** *Chi. Tribune* 1 Nov. 3/3 For three generations my parents were French Canadians.

2. *a.* Of or pertaining to French Canadians.

1775 ADAIR *Indians* 164 Unless the black tribe, the French Canadian priests, corrupted their [French Indians'] traditions, they would think such actions defiling. **1858** *Spirit of Times* 30 Jan. 346/3 Immunity from disease of the legs and feet, under the most unfavorable circumstances, when ill-groomed, ill-shod, and subject to every trial and hardship, appears to be the distinguishing marks of the French Canadian Horse. **1892** *Outing* Jan. 282/1 There burst out into the clear space a saddled French-Canadian black stallion. **1947** *Chi. Tribune* 1 Nov. 3/3 It was a piece about the common civilization of North America, reviewing all the cultures on the continent from the French Canadian point of view.

b. Also in the predicate.

1853 STRICKLAND *Twenty-seven Yrs.* I. 39 One pair of our horses were French Canadian. Generally speaking, they are rough-looking beasts, with shaggy manes and tails, but strong, active, and stout for their size.

Frenched land. =**French land.** *Obs.* — **1856** *Rep. Comm. Patents 1855: Agric.* 231 Until this Frenched land has been thoroughly . . . analysed, it would be useless to say anything more.

Frencher ˈfrentʃɚ, *n.* A Frenchman. *Colloq.* — **1826** COOPER *Mohicans* xix, Your Frenchers, when they have done a clever thing, like to get back and have a dance or a merry-making with the women over their success. **1845** *Jonathan Sharp* I. 13 These Frenchers, and even the English, . . . are always loaded with trunks and linen.

French falls. Shoes of a type associated in some way with French style. In full **French fall shoes.** *Obs.*

1677 *Conn. Public Rec.* II. 325 Noe shoemaker shall take aboue fiue pence halfe penny a size for all playne and wooden heeld shoes, for all sizes aboue the men's seuens, three soled shoes well made and wrought, nor aboue seven pence halfe penny a size for well wrought French falls. **1705** *Boston News-Letter* 10 Dec. 4/2 (*advt.*), Ran-away from his Master William Pepperil Esqr. at Kittery, . . . a Negro Man-Slave named Peter . . . has on a mixt gray home-spun Coat, white home spun Jacket and Breeches, French fall Shoes. **1714** *Ib.* 7–14 June 2/2 [A runaway] has on a close-bodied Coat, . . . and French fall Shoes, the heels goes much back.

French flat. (See quot. 1938.) Now *hist.*

1879 F. R. STOCKTON *Rudder Grange* vi. 58 He . . . was now keeping house in a French flat in the upper part of the city. **1882** MCCABE *New York* 250 Above 34th street the upper floors of the buildings are laid off in French flats. **1938** HART *New Yorkers* 176 Many of the reasonably well to do of the city lived in Greenwich Village, in apartments then known as 'French Flats' which were separately sublet floors of what previously had been private houses. There was, at first, only one door bell for the entire house; callers rang one or more times according to the floor on which their hosts dwelt. Upstairs residents had to come to the street floor to let them in. A system of wires was then invented by which the downstairs door unlocked by pulling a lever.

French Indian. **1.** An Indian friendly to the French or under French influence. **2.** The language used between the French and the Indians. Both *obs.*

(**1**) **1696** *Doc. Hist. N.Y. State* (1849) I. 323 All the ffrench Indians & Ottawawaes are together. **1750** CROGHAN *Journal* 54 It will be dangerous for the [English] Traders to travel the Roads for fear of being surprised by some of the French and French Indians. **1847** PARKMAN in *Knickerb.* XXX. 289 This system of contemptible trickery did not tend to remove the prejudice which the emigrants entertained against the French Indians. — (**2**) **1759** *Va. Gazette* 30 Nov. 3/2 There is a Person now in Gaol, who says he speaks French-Indian well.

frenching ˈfrentʃɪŋ, *n.*

1. A plant disease characterized by the thickening, curling, and narrowing of plant leaves, found esp. in tobacco and cotton.

1856 *Rep. Comm. Patents 1855: Agric.* 231 In certain portions of the plantations, in many parts of Florida, individual [cotton] plants grow with white or variegated leaves. This peculiarity is termed 'Frenching.' **1888** *Cong. Rec.* 12 May 4069/2 [The cotton plant] begins to blight; then comes frenching and the shedding of squares and forms

1940 *Newsweek* 12 Aug. 47 If seedlings of Turkish tobacco are grown in fluids containing the drug [sulfanilamide], the result is a condition similar to 'frenching,' a disease which has baffled plant experts for 250 years.

2. *Fla.* A disease of citrous plants characterized by yellowing leaves and stunted growth.

1895 *Dept. Agric. Yrbk. 1894* 198 On Florida orange lands . . . 'frenching,' a disease, or probably more properly a symptom of disease [of orange trees], . . . is not uncommon.

French monte. A form of the gambling game known usu. as monte. *Obs.*

1851 KINGSLEY *Diary* 176 All kinds of gameing is going on from Faro & Monte to French Monte & Thimble-rig. **1872** EGGLESTON *End of World* 200 Like the cards in French-Monte, a-turnin' up suddenly in mighty onexpected places.

attrib. **1850** *Jrnl. Birmingham Emig. Co.* 15 Aug., You might see the Famous French-Monty Dealer, sitting cross legged on a plank, throwing out his cards in such a loose manner, that by one not acquainted with the game, it would look like a verry easy matter to pick up the winning card. **1851** *Pacific News* (S.F.) 27 Feb. 2/5 A fight occurred over a French monte table, between . . . Fred. J. Roe and a miner. **1855** *Golden Era* (S.F.) 14 Jan. 1/4 Thimble riggers and French monte sharps were then getting into bad odor.

* **frenchy,** *a.* (See quot.) — **1889** *N. & Q.* III. 285 In North Carolina, land which suddenly and unaccountably fails to produce crops is said to *french;* such land is *frenchy.*

* **fresh,** *n.*

1. Short for "freshman." Also collect. and attrib. *Slang.* Cf. * **fresh,** *a.* **2.** (8), **freshy, frosh.**

1827 *Harvard Reg.* Oct. 251 The college clock struck twelve—that awful hour When Sophs meet Fresh, power met opposing power. *a***1860** *Songs of Yale* 38 Bright the sky is beaming o'er us, Fresh and Soph'more years are o'er. **1899** QUINN *Pa. Stories* 72 Come right in. Here, Fresh, one of you take his suit case upstairs.

2. Short for "fresh meat" or "fresh water." *Colloq.*

1849 KINGSLEY *Diary* 39 [We] had half of a beef sent aboard which as a fresh was quite a treat. **1883** S. BONNER *Dialect Tales* 83 Never did she sit you down to her table unless she had 'fresh,' an' maybe a couple o' chickens besides. **1892** DUVAL *Young Explorers* 193 Take a cheer and I'll send to the spring for a bucket of fresh.

* **fresh,** *a.*

1. Forward, impudent. *Slang.* Cf. **freshness, freshy 2.**

This sense may reflect the influence of G. *frech,* saucy, impudent.

1848 BARTLETT 399, *Fresh.* Forward; as, 'don't make yourself too fresh here'; that is to say, not quite so much at home. *a* **1906** O. HENRY *Trimmed Lamp* 98, I can tell in a minute if a fellow is one who is likely to get fresh. **1921** PAINE *Comr. Rolling Ocean* 41 When a man gets too fresh in my town, somebody is liable to push his face for him.

2. In combs.: (1) * **fresh air,** see as a main entry; (2) **creek,** =**fresh-water creek,** *obs.;* (3) **ground,** =next; (4) **land,** land newly cleared or prepared for cultivation; (5) * **man,** see as a main entry; (6) **meadow,** low-lying grassland moist with, or subject to overflow by, fresh water; (7) **river,** =**fresh-water river,** also as a proper name, now *hist.;* (8) **-sophomore,** =**freshman-sophomore,** *obs.;* (9) * **-water,** see as a main entry.

(2) **1646** in *Amer. Sp.* XV. 264/1 West upon the fresh Creeke. — (3) **1766** *Ib.* XV 264/2 There is fresh ground cleared sufficient to work ten hands. — (4) **1752** *Ib.*, I have near 30,000 Acres of extraordinary good fresh Land, in Fairfax and Prince William. **1805** PARKINSON *Tour* II. 300 What is termed fresh land is the best for Indian corn. **1856** DAVIS *Farm Bk.* 24 Run 2 double plows & 7 single in the fresh land.

(6) **1635** *Cambridge Prop. Rec.* 36 All the right title and Intrest w[hi]ch he hath in the ffresh Meaddows and the Ox pastuer. **1769** *Mass. Col. Soc. Pub.* VI. 30 [We] took a Lease of Said Drowne for the fresh meadows. — (7) **1637** *R.I. Col. Rec.* I. 18 Ye lands and meadowes upon the two fresh rivers. **1653** JOHNSON *Wonder-w. Prov.* 110 A faire fresh River, whose Rivulets are filled with fresh Marsh, and her streames with Fish. **1909** in *Pub. Col. Soc.* XII. 366 The Connecticut River was named the Fresh River by the Dutch, and continued to be so called by them long after the adoption by the English of the name Connecticut. — (8) **1847** *Yale Lit. Mag.* XII. 114, I was a Fresh-Sophomore then, and a waiter in the commons' hall.

* **fresh-air.** *attrib.* Designating charitable movements, funds, societies, etc., concerned with giving underprivileged city children country outings.

1882 *N.Y. Tribune* 2 July 7/1 The work of the Fresh Air Fund . . . [is] sending children for a week or two from poor homes in unhealthy quarters of the city to healthful villages and farms. **1891** *Scribner's Mag.* April 515/1 It was only after months of earnest thought . . . that the Fresh-Air project was launched. *Ib.* 524/2 This Fresh-Air movement all began in a small hamlet in northeastern Pennsylvania. **1948** *Sat. Ev. Post* 4 Sep. 75/1 He holds office in such diverse organizations as the Boy Scouts, . . . Navy League, a fresh-air camp and twenty-two others.

Hence **fresh-air children.**

1909 *Outing* Aug. 538/1 A gray-haired gateman . . . stood watching a group of Fresh Air children as they filed past him toward a train.

freshhood ˈfreʃhud, *n.* The state of being a freshman. *Rare.* — **1836** *Harvardiana* III. 98 When to the college I came, in the first dear day of my fresh-hood, Like to the school we had left I imagined the new situation.

freshie, see **freshy.**

* **freshman,** *n.*

1. Used with designating terms indicating a first-year college student having particular status or duties, as **butler's, college, parietal, president's, proctor's, regent's, tutor's freshman.** All *obs.*

1816 *Harvard Laws* 47 When any student shall return to town, after such leave, or after any vacation, he shall apply to the Regent's freshman, at his room, to enter the time of his return. **1851** HALL *College Words* 136 *Freshman, butler's,* at Harvard and Yale Colleges, a Freshman, formerly hired by the Butler, to perform certain duties pertaining to his office, was called by this name. *Ib.*, The College Freshman . . . was commonly called the bookkeeper. The duties of this office are now performed by one of the Proctors. *Ib.* 137 In Harvard College, the member of the Freshman Class who gives notice to those whom the chairman of the Parietal Committee wishes to see, is known by the name of the Parietal Freshman. For his services he receives about forty dollars per annum, and the rent of his room. *Ib.*, *Freshman, president's,* a member of the Freshman Class who performs the official errands of the President. *Ib.* 145 *Freshman, tutor's,* in Harvard College, the Freshman who occupies a room under a Tutor. He is required to do the errands of the Tutor which relate to College, and in return has a high choice of rooms in his Sophomore year. The same remarks . . . apply to the Proctor's Freshman. **1876** TRIPP *Student-Life* 15 If you can manage to be tutor's or proctor's Freshman, you have a first-rate room.

2. A first-year student in a high school.

1902 G. M. MARTIN *Emmy Lou* 227 A freshman in the high school is a mere abecedarian part of an ever-moving line, which toils, weighted with pounds of text-books. **1945** *Roundup* (Mont.) *R. Tribune* 22 Feb. 4/2 She is a freshman in the high school here.

3. In combs.: (1) **freshman class,** a class in high school or college composed of first-year students, also attrib.; (2) **English,** an English course, chiefly in composition, usu. required of all college freshmen; (3) **nine,** a baseball team composed of freshmen; (4) **-'s Bible,** (see quot.), *obs.;* (5) **sophomore,** (see quot.), *obs.;* (6) **year,** the first year of college, high school, or junior college.

(1) *c*1764 in WOOLSEY *Hist. Disc. Yale* (1850) 54 The whole Freshman class, or any particular member of it. **1887** *Lippincott's Mag.* Oct. 573 This is caused by an attempt to break up the first Freshman class-sing, which action is made a point of honor by the Sophomores. **1945** *Mt. Holyoke Cat.* 158 Six competitive scholarships for one year's tuition are awarded annually to members of the freshman class. — (2) **1944** JOHNSON *As I Dare* 183 Practically every student in each American college takes Freshman English, and uses as a textbook a bulky and expensive anthology of current literature. **1946** THOMPSON *Amer. Daughter* 172, I was crossing the campus to Freshman English when I ran into Gwyn. — (3) **1868** *N.Y. Herald* 24 July 4/5 A base ball match between the Freshman nines of Yale and Harvard University clubs resulted . . . in a victory for the Harvards. **1888** *Harper's Mag.* June 139/2 Her son is one of the Freshman Nine. — (4) **1851** HALL *College Words* 138 Freshman's Bible. This is the name given by the students to the laws of a college.

(5) **1851** HALL *College Words* 145 *Freshman-sophomore,* one who enters college in the Sophomore year, having passed the time of the Freshman year elsewhere. — (6) **1851** [see **freshman-sophomore**]. **1855** *Harvard Mag.* I. 413 [The] many-sidedness of college life struck us with peculiar force in the Freshman year. **1945** *Mt. Holyoke Cat.* 33 In the freshman year a student is required to elect English Language and Literature 101–102 and Physical Education 101–102.

b. Designating times of the college year, preceding the beginning of classes, devoted to the orientation of new students, as **freshman days, period, week.**

1942 *Hiram Coll. Cat.* 33 The adviser has his first conference with his freshman advisees during Freshman Days. **1942** *U. of Wis. Cat.* 21 Freshman Period: All freshmen are required to be present at the University on the Monday preceding the beginning of instruction and to remain throughout the week. **1942** *Cat. Vanderbilt Univ.* 66 Freshman Week: During the several days before classes begin in September, the College offers an orientation program for freshmen. **1945** *Mt. Holyoke Cat.* 146 Freshman week is designated to help new students become acquainted with the College, its traditions and equipment.

freshmanic frɛʃ'mænɪk, *a.* Of or pertaining to a freshman. *Obs.* — **1837** *Harvardiana* III. 316 The Junior Class . . . asserted with that peculiar dignity which should at all times excite terror and awe in the Freshmanic breast, that they would countenance no such proceedings. **1876** TRIPP *Student-Life* 154 They . . . backed up their crew with an enthusiasm that was quite Freshmanic.

*****freshness,** *n.* Forwardness, pertness. *Colloq.* Cf. ***fresh,** *a.* **1, freshy 2.** — **1882** MCCABE *N.Y. by Sunlight & Gaslight* 192 The ubiquitous small boy . . . was projected into our midst [on an elevated train] from the Houston street station, at which he flung a parting comment on some one's freshness. **1928** J. C. LINCOLN *Silas Bradford's Boy* 13 The captain's dignity was slightly ruffled by what he considered freshness on the part of his nephew.

*** fresh-water,** *a.* In combs.: (1) **fresh-water clam,** a fresh-water mussel; (2) **college,** a small or little-known college, a third-rate college; (3) **cord grass,** a kind of coarse grass (see quots.); (4) **creek,** a creek the water of which is fresh, *obs.*, cf. **fresh creek;** (5) **marsh,** a marsh or swamp containing fresh as opposed to salt water; (6) **marsh hen,** the king rail, *Rallus elegans*, or the Virginia rail, *Rallus virginianus;* (7) **marsh wren,** the short-billed marsh wren; (8) **river,** a river the water of which is fresh; (9) **sunfish,** any one of various perchlike fishes of the family Centrarchidae found in the streams of the northern and the eastern states; (10) **tailor,** =**fall herring;** (11) **terrapin,** the wood terrapin or wood tortoise, *Clemmys insculpta.*

(1) **1849** DANA *Geology* 27 The fresh-water clam (*Unionidae*). **1903** AUSTIN *Land of Little Rain* 163 Seyavi and the boy lay up in the caverns of the Black Rock and ate tule roots and fresh-water clams.— (2) **1860** HOLMES *E. Venner* vii, He was acquainted with a Sophomore from one of the fresh-water colleges. **1946** HOWE *We Happy Few* 83 He had appeared on the Harvard scene from some small fresh-water college, and after a few years he would return to another. — (3) **1857** *Mass. Bd. Agric. Rep.* IV. I. 38 Fresh Water Cord Grass, (*spartina cynosuroides*). This is found on the banks of streams and lakes. **1895** *Dept. Agric. Yrbk. 1894* 436 Fresh-water cord grass (*Spartina cynosuroides*) grows abundantly along the Missouri and other rivers of the interior, and especially along sloughs in the prairie regions, where it is best known as slough grass. *Ib.*, The stouter fresh-water cord grass . . . grows . . . also along the margins of fresh-water lakes and rivers. — (4) **1741** in *Amer. Sp.* XV. 264/1 On the said Banks & fresh water Creek.

(5) **1754** *Ga. Col. Rec.* VI. 427 He prayed for three hundred and forty Acres . . . situated on a fresh Water Marsh. **1890** *Cent.* 3689/2 In the United States, however, *swamp* is often used in the restricted sense of 'fresh-water marsh.' — (6) **1835** AUDUBON *Ornith. Biog.* III. 27 The Fresh-water Marsh-Hen is abundant in South Carolina. **1917** *Birds of Amer.* I. 203 King Rail. . . . [Also called] Fresh-water Marsh Hen. *Ib.* 205 Virginia Rail. . . . [Also called] Fresh-water Marsh Hen; Long-billed Rail. — (7) **1839** PEABODY *Mass. Birds* 315 The Fresh-water Marsh Wren, *Troglodytes brevirostris*, . . . is known to boys by its song, *chip-a-day-day*, which is so often heard in the meadow. — (8) **1645** *Providence Rec.* IV. 160 All that Land . . . [lies] upon the south side of the great fresh Water River. **1895** [see **fresh-water cord grass**]. — (9) **1814** MITCHILL *Fishes N.Y.* 403 Fresh-water Sunfish, or Pond Perch (*Labrus auritus*). . . . Lives in fresh water altogether, and is taken both by the hook and seine, for pastime and food. **1839** STORER *Mass. Fishes* 11 *Pomotis vulgaris*, Fresh water Sun Fish. . . . This very common species in the numerous ponds of our State is . . . generally known by the vulgar name of Bream.

(10) **1884** GOODE *Fisheries* I. 608 In the Potomac the species [*Clupea mediocris*] is called the 'Tailor Shad,' or the 'Fresh-water Tailor.' — (11) **1842** *Nat. Hist. N.Y., Zoology* III. 15 The Wood Terrapin, *Emys insculpta*, . . . is also called the Fresh-water Terrapin. **1884** GOODE *Fisheries* I. 152 The marsh and river Tortoises constitute a large group, well represented in North America. It includes . . . the Fresh-water Terrapins.

freshy 'frɛʃɪ, *n.* Also **freshie. 1.** A freshman. **2.** A "fresh" person. Both *slang.* Cf. ***fresh,** *a.* **1, freshness,** *n.*

(1) **1847** in HAMMOND *Remembrance of Amherst* (1946) 179 (We.), In which the freshies were tremendously beat. **1871** BAGG *At Yale* 64 Then up he flies into the air again, amid admiring shrieks of 'Go it, Freshie!' **1931** *K.C. Times* 10 Sep., And fall into line once more with a thousand other freshies at the portals of the registrar's office. — (2) **1909** O. HENRY *Options* 41 But he's easy-spoken and not a freshy.

fresno 'frɛzno, *n.* A buck scrape or buck scraper *qq.v.*, so called from the Fresno Agricultural Works, Fresno, Calif., which began making such scrapers about 1882. Orig. **Fresno scraper.**

1893 *Irrigation Age* April 359/1 This work was done by four-horse Fresno scrapers. **1911** WRIGHT *Winning Barbara Worth* 322 Teamsters left their teams and Fresnos on the Company works, ranchers left their crops and cattle, newly located settlers forsook their ditching and leveling, zanjeros deserted their water gates and levees. **1944** *Greeley* (Colo.) *D. Tribune* 30 Sep. 2/5 Public Auction . . . McCormick mower, good shape; 2-horse fresno; walking plow.

*** friar,** *n.* (See quot. 1889.)

1883 *Nat. Museum Bul.* No. 27, 440 *Menidia dentex.* . . . Friar; Silversides. Atlantic coast of the Southern United States, entering streams. **1884** GOODE *Fisheries* I. 456 The most important species [of sand smelt] on the Atlantic side is the Green Smelt of the Connecticut coast, *Menidia notata*, also called in some parts of New England the 'Friar.' **1889** *Cent.* 2376/3 *Friar*, . . . a fish of the family *Atherinidæ*.

frib frɪb, *n.* [Origin obscure. Cf. ****fribble***, also *EDD* ****frip***, "anything worthless or trifling."] A small, dirty lock of wool. — **1850** *Rep. Comm. Patents 1849: Agric.* 251 The manufacturers . . . are [not] yet prepared to pay a sufficient advance beyond the present prices, to justify the growers of wool in removing all of the fribs, belly locks, and skirts from the fleece. **1863** RANDALL *Pract. Shepherd* xvi. 172 The catcher . . . next should go back, pick up every 'frib,' and sweep the place so that it will be ready for another sheep.

*** friction,** *n.*

1. friction match, a match that ignites by friction. Also attrib. Cf. *** card,** *n.*[2] **3.**

1839 HOFFMAN *Wild Scenes* 42 Our friction matches would not ignite. **1848** THOREAU *Maine Woods* 3 Think how stood the white-pine tree on the shore of Chesuncook, . . . sold, perchance, to the New England Friction-Match Company. **1891** WELCH *Recoll. 1830–40* 76 There was no friction or locofoco matches in those days. **1949** *Friends* April 16/2 It was Thomas Sanford who invented the friction match.

2. friction primer, (see quot.). *Obs.*

1874 KNIGHT 916/2 *Friction-primer*, a small brass tube filled with gunpowder, and having a smaller tube containing friction composition inserted at right angles near the top.

*** fried,** *a.* In combs.: (1) **fried cake,** a cruller or doughnut; (2) **chicken,** chicken cooked by frying [cf. *EDD fried chickens*, "chicken broth with eggs dropped into it, orig. friar's chickens"]; (3) **hominy,** hominy or hominy grits sautéed; (4) **mush,** cold mush sliced and sautéed; (5) **pudding,** =prec.; (6) **shirt,** a boiled shirt *q.v., slang.*

(1) **1857** *Quinland* I. 36 The 'nut-cakes' are an institution of the country. Some call 'em 'dough-nuts,' and some 'fried cakes.' **1902** C. MORRIS *Stage Confidences* 113 The old woman . . . drew forth two long, twisted, fried cakes. **1944** ROSS *Westward* 26 Narcissa herself dropped hints in her journal . . . of the attentions of certain fur company leaders, in particular a Mr. McLeod, who made the ladies fried cakes as a treat. — (2) **1710** BYRD *Secret Diary* (1941) 242, I dined here and ate fried chicken. **1884** HILL *Colo. Pioneers* 133 Being from the South myself, Jim often came in to talk about the old home, the fried chicken, sweet potatoes, and the many good things to us then 'non-come-at-able.' **1948** *Newsweek* 27 Sep. 18/1 After peeling off his coat and eating heartily of fried chicken and apple pie, President Truman reboarded the Ferdinand Magellan and headed for the Pacific. — (3) **1777** SALLY WISTER *Journal* (1902) 107 How good turkey hash and fry'd hominy is. **1892** DUVAL *Young Explorers* 49 In a little while a pot of hot coffee, a couple of fat, juicy steaks . . . and a dish of fried hominy were smoking on the table. **1947** BEROLZHEIMER *Regional Cookbook* 119 Popovers [are] a Favorite for Breakfast With Fresh Mackerel or Fried Hominy. — (4) **1847** GEORGE B. MCCLELLAN *Mexican War Diary* (1917) 32 For our Christmas dinner we had a beefsteak and some fried mush. **1940** WILSON *Wabash* 73 Hot fried mush and sorghum molasses appear on the breakfast table again.

(5) **1805** *Pocumtuc Housewife* (1906) 6 In summer fried pudding is too heating. [**1939** WOLCOTT *Yankee Cook Book* 165 Any [hasty] pudding that was not eaten was turned into a bread pan, sliced and fried for breakfast.] — (6) **1925** O. P. WHITE *Them Was the Days* 147 Wearing a fried shirt, a boiled collar, . . . patent leather shoes . . . and a cane.

*** friend,** *n.*

1. (*cap.*) *pl.* (See quot. and cf. *** wide-awake 1.**) *Obs.*

1890 C. MARTYN *W. Phillips, Agitator* 122 A circle of wide-awakes meeting at irregular intervals under the names of 'The Friends.'

2. In combs.: (1) **friend Indian,** an Indian friendly to the white colonists or settlers, *obs.;* (2) **pipe,** among American Indians, a peace pipe or calumet, *rare*, cf. **eagle calumet.**

(1) **1649** *Md. Archives* I. 250 Anyone whosoever that shall take, entice . . . sell or dispose of any freind Indian or Indians . . . shall suffer Death. **1744** *Boston News Letter* 8 Nov. 2/1, I do hereby strictly forbid the said Friend-Indians, or any of them, as they tender their own Safety, to move into the Districts of the said *St. John's* and *Cape Sables;* or *Nova-Scotia* Indians. — (2) **1775** ADAIR *Indians* 167 They first smoke out of the friend-pipe, and eat together; then they drink of the Cusseena.

b. *Friends of America, Friends of Government,* during the Revolution, those who favored the colonists and Great Britain respectively. *Obs.*

1775 in *Amer. Sp.* XX. (1945) 271 Depositions and information dated 7 June against Joseph Habersham and others. 'The Friends of America in Georgia' for ordering Messrs Tongue, Law, White and Gumersall to quit the province in seven days. **1775** J. ADAMS in *Hist. MSS Comm.* 9th Rep. App. III. II. (1910) 7 To have arrested every friend of Government on the continent. **1776** in *Life and Letters of Charles Inglis* 157 The King's Troops totally abandoning this Province, reduced the Friends of Government here to a most disagreeable & dangerous Situation.

As the last term in **boy, gentleman, girl, Hicksite friend.**

**frier,* see **fryer.*

frigerator ˈfrɪdʒəˌretɚ, *n.* [f. **refrigerator.*] An icebox for storing food. *Colloq.* — **1886** STAPLETON *Major's Christmas* 81 An ironing board, which was everything from a step-ladder to a 'frigerator. **1909** STRATTON-PORTER *Girl of Limberlost* 462 'There is plenty in the frigerator,' suggested Alice.

frijol friˈhol, *n. S.W.* [Sp. in same sense. An Amer. borrowing.] Any bean of the genus *Phaseolus,* esp. the kidney bean, *P. vulgaris.*

1759 tr. VENEGAS *Nat. Hist. Calif.* I. 45 Father Francisco Maria Picolo . . . relates, that they have . . . the red frixoles, or kidney beans. **1831** BEECHEY *Voyage to Pacific* II. 50 Having served them with what he termed the *viatico,* consisting of a plentiful supply of cold fricole beans, bread, and eggs, he led the party to their sleeping apartment. **1949** *This Week Mag.* 5 March 28/2 That's the bean called pink, called frijole, called the Mexican strawberry.

b. A poker chip. *Rare.*

1903 *Cin. Enquirer* 2 May 12/2 Do these 18 blue frijoles that I hold go for Hogan?

* **frill,** *n. fig.* An affectation in manner; superfluity or extravagance. Usu. *pl. Colloq.*

1865 MARK TWAIN *Sketches of Sixties* (1926) 189 You put on as many frills, and make as much fuss about your obscure 'kingdom' [a true woman's heart] as if it were . . . a first class power among nations. **1870** in DE VERE 603, I can't bear his talk, it's all frills. **1919** L. F. CODY *Buffalo Bill* 21 There were no frills about Will Cody's story as he told it to me.

* **fringe,** *n.* In combs.: (1) **fringe bush,** =**fringe tree;** (2) **pod,** any one of several species of lacepod, esp. *Thysanocarpus curvipes,* found in California and the Northwest; (3) **tree,** a shrub or small tree of the southern states, *Chionanthus virginica,* bearing clusters of white flowers, also attrib., cf. **mountain fringe.**

(1) **1909** *Cent. Supp.* 498/1 fringe-bush. . . . Same as *fringe-tree.* **1943** PEATTIE *Great Smokies* 166 The sourwood, the fringe bush, and the mountain laurel, are understory trees. — (2) **1889** *Cent.* 2382/3 Fringepod . . . [has] flattened, orbicular, winged pods, the margin of which is frequently lobed or fringed. **1925** JEPSON *Flowering Plants Calif.* 447 Fringe-pod . . . [is] frequent in the open hill country of Cal., 100 to 5000 ft., n. to B.C. and Ida. — (3) *c*1730 CATESBY *Carolina* I. 68 *Amelanchior Virginiana.* . . . The Fringe Tree. On the banks of rivulets and running streams this Shrub is most commonly found. **1854** EMMONS *Agric. N.Y.* V. 218 *Sphinx chionanthi.* Fringe-tree Moth. The moth has three yellowish round spots on each side of the abdomen. **1948** *Household* March 49/1 America is blessed with . . . wild crabs, plums, . . . sourwood, silverbells, and fringe trees.

fringed gentian, *n.* A fall-flowering wild flower of the genus *Gentiana* having blue flowers with fringed lobes.

1814 BIGELOW *Florula Bostoniensis* 64 *Gentiana crinita.* Fringed Gentian. . . . This gentian is exceeded by few native plants in the delicacy and beauty of its flowers. **1913** EATON *Barn Doors & Byways* 37 The fringed gentians bloom in the wheel-ruts. **1948** *Prairie Club Bul.* Sep. 18 Parry's primrose and several kinds of gentians, including big patches of fringed gentians, were other treasures.

Frisco ˈfrɪsko, *n.* A nickname for San Francisco, California. Also attrib. *Colloq.* Cf. **Frisky.**

1854 *Placer Times* (S.F.) 14 Jan. 4/6 You come down to 'Frisco' with a 'pile,' didn't you? **1913** LONDON *Valley of Moon* II. vii. You'll hear that every Frisco carpenter is union an' gettin' full union wages. **1945** *Estes Park* (Colo.) *Trail* 9 Nov. 2/2 Having the grandest time—we made Frisco over with our daughter and son-in-law.

b. Hence **Friscoite.**

1909 R. A. WASON *Happy Hawkins* 304 Take the real native-son brand of Friscoite, an' he'll tell you [etc.].

Frisky ˈfrɪskɪ, *n.* =**Frisco.** *Obs.*

1850 *S.F. Picayune* 18 Sep. 4/1 The row wos okkashund by the announsement that the steemers 'Noo Wurld' & 'Hartford' were going too run to Frisky at from 3 to 5 dolls a tikket. **1851** *S.F. Sunday Clarion* 27 April 2/2 If some of the hombres of our city . . . but knew the rich sights their doings afford . . . they would sell themselves cheap to the Digger Indians up country, and be seen no more in Frisky. **1851** *Ore. Statesman* 9 Sep. 1/2 We'll rest content with quiet lot, In spite of lots in 'Frisky.'

***fritter,** *n.* As the last term in **clam, corn, molasses, oyster fritter.**

***frizen, frizin,** *n.* [Cf. *EDD frizzens,* "plow irons."] The frizzle of a flintlock gun; the pan cover or plate struck by the flint. *Colloq.* — **1850** LEWIS *La. Swamp Doctor* 173, I primed old 'bar death' fresh, and rubbed the frizin, for it war no time for rifle to get to snappin'. **1853** P. PAXTON *Yankee in Texas* 175 Down I sat, shook out my priming, wiped the frizen, then up again, and taking a long, deliberate aim, touched the hair trigger.

***frizzle,** *n.* A barnyard or domestic fowl of a variety having curled feathers. *Obs.* — **1854** *Pa. Agric. Rep.* 163 The immediate progeny of foreign importations, comprising, in the tribe of barn-yard fowls, . . . the Frizzle; the Creely and the Creepy.

***frock,** *n. frock and pants,* a term used contemptuously for the Bloomer costume. See also **hunting frock, rifle frock.** — **1851** *Washington Telegraph* in *Illustr. London News* 19 July 86/1 Garments as graceful and becoming as are the 'frock and pants.'

frockee ˌfrɑkˈi, *n.* [**frock*+*-ee.*] (See quot.) *Obs.* — **1818** *Lancaster* (Pa.) *Jrnl.* 5 Aug. (Th.), A little great coat; commonly called a frockee.

***frocking,** *n.* Coarse, serviceable cloth, as jean. — **1853** LOWELL *Fireside Trav.* 112 Enormous cowhide boots, over which large blue trousers of frocking strove in vain to crowd themselves. **1866** *Maine Agric. Soc. Returns 1865* 26 Ornamental articles . . . have given place to home made cloths for men's and women's wear, such as . . . frocking, shirting, linen, etc.

* **frog,** *n.*

1. In railroading, a heavy, channeled iron plate or similar device for guiding car and engine wheels where tracks cross or diverge.

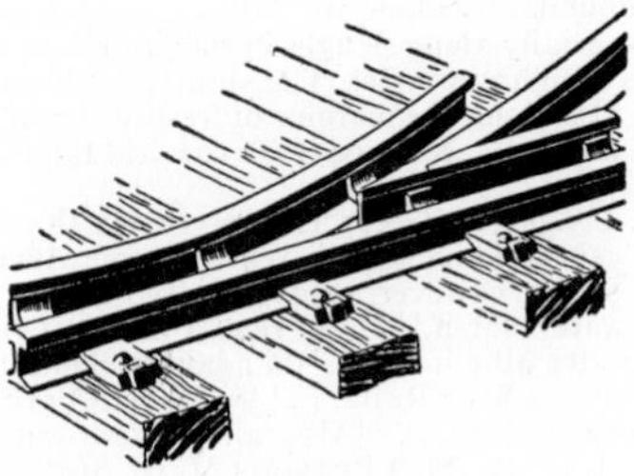

Frog (sense 1)

1847 *Rep. Comm. Patents 1846* 95 Frogs are used having guards or grinders on their outsides, and double inclined planes up and down, by which the wheels are guided to the right track. **1898** HAMBLEN *Gen'l Manager's Story* 186, I jolted those cars into the siding fully as fast as it is safe to back over a frog.

b. (See quot.)

1905 *Forestry Bureau Bul.* No. 61, 37 *Frog.* 1. The junction of two branches of a flume (P[acific] C[oast] F[orest]). 2. A timber placed at the mouth of a slide to direct the discharge of the logs.

2. The muscular lump that appears on the flexed upper arm. *Colloq.*

1858 *S. Lit. Messenger* XXVI. 121/2, I warnt afeard that somebody was goin to hert me, for I has bonier nuckles than most men and you know the size uv the frog in my arm.

3. In combs.: (1) **frog bit,** an American water plant, *Limnobius spongia,* having large, roundish leaves and white flowers, also **frog's bit;** (2) **catcher,** any one of various birds, as the night heron, that catch frogs; (3) **concert,** the noise made by frogs, *obs.;* (4) **farm,** a place where frogs are bred for the market; (5) **house,** (see quot. 1908), *colloq.;* (6) **lily,** spatterdock, dog lily; (7) **plant,** the orpine; (8) **-pondian,** ?a frog, an inhabitant of a frog pond, also a contemptuous expression used by Edgar

Allan Poe for Bostonians, *obs.;* (9) **skin,** (see quot. 1922), *slang;* (10) **sticker,** (see quot. 1908), *colloq.* [cf. *EDD stick-frog,* for a blunt, clumsy-looking knife].

(1) **1857** GRAY *Botany* 440 *Limnobium.* . . . American Frog's-bit. **1866** *Treas. Bot. s.v.,* Frog-bit, American, *Limnobium.* **1894** COULTER *Bot. W. Texas* III. 422 *Limnobium* (American Frog's-bit). — (2) **1791** W. BARTRAM *Travels* (1793, ed. 3) 291 A[rdea] clamator, corpore subcæruleo; the quaw bird, or frogcatcher. **1832** WILLIAMSON *Maine* I. 150 There are several others, the genus of which is not known; as the *Frog-catcher,* also the Hagdel, of a dark brown colour, about as large as a Murr, though its feathers are longer. — (3) **1794** WM. PRIEST *Travels* (1802) 49 Prepared as I was to hear something extraordinary from these animals, I confess the first frog *concert* I heard in America was so much beyond any thing I could conceive of the *powers* of these *musicians,* that I was truly astonished. **1833** J. FINCH *Travels* 39 Near the city of New York I first heard the noise of the frogs, or what is usually called a frog concert; they were distant a quarter of a mile, but I heard their notes very distinctly. — (4) **1901** *Westm. Gaz.* 2 Aug. 10/1 There are extensive frog farms in Indiana and Illinois.

(5) **1877** BAGBY *Old Va. Gentleman* 48 [He must] make frog-houses over his feet in the wet sand, and find woodpecker nests. **1908** *D.N.* III. 313 frog-house, *n.* A small cave or hollow mound made in dampened sand by children, usually by heaping the sand about the bare foot. Toads often appropriate these 'houses' as hiding places. — (6) **1869** FULLER *Flower Gatherers* 204 It flourishes best in dull, stagnant pools, and is often called the *Frog-lily.* **1931** CLUTE *Plants* 111 The frog lily (*Nymphaea advena*) is better named, for frogs delight to rest on its round floating leaves. — (7) **1892** *Amer. Folk-Lore* V. 96 *Sedum Telephium* . . . frog-plant. N.H. — (8) **1855** SIMMS *Forayers* 512 Thus it was that the rustic poet of the partisans, gave forth extempore an embodiment of the music of the frogpondians. **1880** *Harper's Mag.* Oct. 788/1 Boston said that he was drunk. Poe retorted that the poem was good enough for the Frogpondians. — (9) **1902** *D.N.* II. 274 One gentleman, only remotely interested in our Society, has recently offered two not hitherto reported [words], 'frog-skins' used in Virginia for paper money or 'greenbacks,' and *stiver for,* a verbal phrase used in Maine for quick and eager action. **1922** *Ib.* V. 163 frog-skin, n. A greenback or piece of paper money. Virginia.

(10) **1836** SIMMS *Mellichampe* xliii. 357 Wait a bit, till I . . . find my frog-sticker, which has somehow tumbled out of the belt. **1908** *D.N.* III. 313 *frog-sticker,* n. A pocket-knife; often used humorously as a term of derogation. 'Lend me your *frog-sticker,*' i.e., 'lend me that sorry old knife of yours.' **1945** *Chi. Tribune* (Comics) 14 Oct., Step soft now, Sheriff, or out comes yer liver on th' end of this frogsticker!

As the last term in **bell, bull, gopher, green, Hoosier, horn, horned, leopard, marsh, pickerel, pond, rain, savanna, shad, shad leopard, squirrel, spotted, spring, tiger, Virginia, wood frog.**

* **frolic,** *n.* =**bee,** *n.*[2] **1.** *Obs.*

1775 PATTEN *Diary* 337 Jamey and Bob cut fence loggs for Mr. Shed it was a frolick. **1781** *View of N.A.* 92 Every particular piece of work is done by what they call a *frolick,* which is the gathering of a number of the neighbours together, and doing it off at once. **1837** H. MARTINEAU *Society* II. 99 Every one has heard of the 'frolic' or 'bee,' by means of which the clearing of lots, the raising of houses, the harvesting of crops is achieved. **1845** *Lowell Offering* V. 87 My mind involuntarily reverted to the merry-making scenes, the tea parties, the quilting matches, the apple-cut frolics, and kindred associations.

As the last term in **boiling, cartridge, chopping, cider, courting, fishing, grubbing, guessing, husking, knitting, picking, plantation, quilting, reaping, rifle, rolling, sewing, sleigh, sleighing, spinning, stone, sugar, waffle, wood, working frolic.**

* **front,** *n.*

1. A building having a front of a specified kind.

[**1839** MARRYAT *Diary in Amer.* I. 65 Many of the shops, or stores, as they are here called . . . have already been fitted up with large plate-glass fronts, similar to those in London.] **1868** *Putnam's Mag.* Oct. 415/2 A little 'fancy store' in a modest wooden house nestled shyly between two pretentious 'marble-fronts.' **1872** TICE *Over Plains* 80 The town now contains about 350 buildings, from board shanties to brick fronts. **1884** *N.Y. Herald* 27 Oct. 2/1 To Let. . . . A four story iron front building.

2. A person or a thing that serves as a cover for illicit or illegal activities. *Colloq.* Cf. **front man.**

1905 *McClure's Mag.* XXIV. 346 For Brayton was the front, not the head of the System. **1926** J. BLACK *You Can't Win* iv. 27, I further learned that the store was but a 'front' or blind for a poker game and dice games in the back room, and that I was a part of the 'front.' **1945** *Chronicle-News* (Trinidad, Colo.) 16 Oct. 7, I thought he was a prosperous cigar dealer, but later I learned his cigar store was a front for a speakeasy.

3. In combs.: (1) **front brick,** *collect.* brick used for the front of a house; (2) * **foot,** a foot measured along the front of a lot or other piece of land (see quot. 1923), also attrib.; (3) **lot,** an allotment of ground in what is considered the front of a parcel of land, a lot in front of another lot; (4) **man,** =**front 2;** (5) **matter,** (see quot. 1909); (6) **office,** the head or main office, the office of the president or the one in authority, also attrib.; (7) **page,** the first page of a newspaper, esp. as an adj. to denote something important or striking; (8) **woods,** in pioneer country, the region most remote from the backwoods, *rare;* (9) **yard,** the open space or grounds in front of a dwelling, also transf. and attrib.

(1) **1865** *Ill. Agric. Soc. Trans.* VI. 39 Best Brick Machine for making fine Front Brick. **1874** KNIGHT 823/1 *Facing-brick,* (Building,) Front or pressed brick. — (2) **1812** *Ann. 12th Congress* 1 Sess. II. 2288 [The city of Washington] shall have power to cause [street improvements] to be done at any expense not exceeding two dollars and fifty cents per front foot. **1923** E. FISHER *Principles Real Estate Practice* 125 The writ value [of land] in most places is the 'front foot,' by which is meant a strip a foot wide running the depth of the usual lot in the city at right angles to the street. **1925** B. SNYDER *Real Estate Handbook* 341 The land value map is designed to show the value of the land per front foot. . . . These front-foot values are called unit values. — (3) **1657** *Hempstead Town Rec.* I. 16 It is ordered by the Townesmen that all the fences of the front lottes that rune into the filld shall bee suffishantly and substanshally fensed. **1905** A. H. RICE *Sandy* 73 'For mercy sake! what is that in the front lot?' exclaimed Mrs. Hollis. — (4) **1938** ASBURY *Sucker's Prog.* 345 Their agent and front man was the Chief of Police. **1948** *Newsweek* 8 Nov. 23/3 He insinuated that Thomas E. Dewey was a 'front man' for powerful forces.

(5) **1909** *Cent. Supp.* 498/3 Front matter, in *printing,* all the typework before the text of a book. Title-page, dedication, table of contents, preface, etc. are rated as front matter. **1930** *Publishers' Wkly.* 4 Oct. 1660/2 We have cast-off your manuscript and estimate it will make 8 pages of front matter and 248 pages of text. — (6) **1900** FLYNT *Itinerant Policeman* 73 The capture dwindles down to a request on the part of the chief or his officer that the man shall go to the 'front office,' which he does, wondering all the while who it was that 'beefed' on him. **1948** *Dly. Ardmoreite* (Ardmore, Okla.) 16 July 8/1 Another fan was a little plainer on his criticism of the way the front office ran the club. **1949** *Sat. Ev. Post* 2 April 118/4 Campaigns are matters of front-office policy and are handed out by the publisher or executive editor. — (7) **1902** *Out West* Jan. 39 His paper jumped, in a day, to modern journalism, bearing on its front page a picture of the murderer, and the 'story.' **1930** FERBER *Cimarron* 338 They were of more absorbing interest to Oklahomans than front-page stories of war, romance, intrigue, royalty, crime. **1946** *Gunnison* (Colo.) *News-Champion* 2 May 1/1 Salida Mail has a big front page story about a secret water diversion meeting pulled off there recently. — (8) **1894** *Advance* 23 Aug., The Windham Church, organized in Connecticut Congregational, after twelve months in the frontwoods [in Ohio] became Presbyterian. — (9) **1767** J. BROWNE *Diary* 122 My pump in the front yard froze. **1822** A. GREEN *Discourses* 276 A professor's house was added to the establishment . . . on the East side of the front yard of the college [at Princeton]. **1848** THOREAU *Maine Woods* 9 More perfect specimens than any front-yard plot can show, grew there to grace the passage of the Houlton teams. **1947** *Nat. Geog. Mag.* Sep. 337/1 The sand ruts . . . took me through the front yards . . . of Duck, North Carolina.

b. In colloq. phrases: (1) *front of,* in front of; (2) *to take a front seat,* to occupy a position of importance, *colloq.;* (3) *to get in front of oneself,* to become confused or mixed up.

(1) **1843** CARLTON *New Purchase* I. 110 Front of the fire-place was the parlour. **1871** STOWE *Sam Lawson* 45 Wal, she was a standin' front o' this. — (2) **1866** F. KIRKLAND *Book Anecdotes* 65 We are determined that those who took front seats in this little show shall keep them throughout. **1878** *Ill. Dept. Agric. Trans.* XIV. 241 We must take front seats or become second class breeders. — (3) **1907** *Dly. Chron.* 21 Oct. 6/4 There is a common American phrase, which expresses better than anything else the curious effect of this policy of 'hustle' upon the national temperament. They say that a man gets 'in front of himself.'

As the last term in **beach, brownstone, false, foot, moccasin, store, swell, water front.**

* **frontier,** *n.*

1. A region in what is now the U.S., newly or sparsely settled and immediately adjoining the wilderness or unoccupied territory. See also **back, Indian, western frontier.**

[**1671** *N.J. Archives* 1 Ser. I. 76 If a good Worke were throwne about Matinicock House, and that strengthened with a considerable Guard, It would be an admirable Frontier.] **1676** in *Amer. Sp.* XV. 265/1 Calling downe our Forces from the defence of the Frontiers, and most weake Exposed Places. **1756** WASHINGTON *Writings* I. 360 Last night I returned from a very long and troublesome jaunt on the Frontiers. **1870** EMERSON *Soc. & Solitude* ii. 17 'Tis wonderful how soon a piano gets into a log-hut on the frontier. **1946** *Reader's Digest* Jan. 110/1 The recipient would return full value by pushing back the frontier and increasing the national wealth.

b. With a designating term.

1707 *Boston News-Letter* 17 Nov. 2/2 A Company of men . . . will range the Woods of the Eastern Frontiers in quest of the Indian Enemy. **1832** *Polit. Examiner.* (Shelbyville, Ky.) 9 June 3/2 Fifteen individuals have been massacred by the Indians on the Illinois frontiers. **1832** *Boston Transcript* 12 July 2/2 Custom House officers should be stationed along the Connecticut frontier to stop the importation of oak and cabbage leaf cigars. **1910** F. L. PAXSON *Last American Frontier* 386 The last frontier, the same that Long had described as the American Desert in 1820, had been won [by 1889]. **1948** *Atlantic Mo.* Feb. 61/1 Protestantism was the religion of the common man in the days of the American frontier.

Also *Indian, Mexican, Missouri, northern, north-western, Texas frontier.*

c. (See quot. 1893.)

The term in this sense is said to have been first used in 1874 by census officials.

1893 TURNER *Signif. of Frontier in Amer. Hist.* 3 What is the frontier? It is not the European frontier—a fortified boundary line running through dense populations. . . . In the census reports it is treated as the margin of that settlement which has a density of two or more to the square mile. **1935** HORWILL *Amer. Usage* 142/2 In Eng. *frontier* means a boundary between two countries, or the territory adjacent to the boundary line on either side, in Am. it is used to denote the limit of settlement within the U.S., as defined by a certain density of population.

2. *pl.* The inhabitants of the frontier. *Obs.*

1677 W. HUBBARD *Narrative of Troubles* I. 144 But the Frontiers discerning Indians in the Edg of the Swamp, fired immediately upon them. **1697** SEWALL *Letter-Book* I. 186, [I] ordered his 127 of Indian and 36½ of Rye to the Fronteers there, who are in great want. **1726** PENHALLOW *Indian Wars* 99 The frontiers being thus alarmed, two companies of volunteers went from New-Hampshire on the bounty act.

3. =**frontier Colt.** *Rare.*

1918 MULFORD *Man from Bar-20* v. 50 He . . . did not care to call attention to his wooden-handled, flare-butt Frontiers.

4. In combs.: (1) **frontier Colt,** a Colt revolver of a type popular on the frontier, also **frontier model Colt;** (2) **Frontier Day,** (see quot. 1937).

(1) **1918** MULFORD *Man from Bar-20* viii. 78 A plain Frontier Colt peeked coyly from his hip at the surprised and chagrined gentleman across the street. **1945** BAKER *Party Line* 31 He had two bone-handled Frontier Model Colts, which were kept carefully oiled and reposed on the mantel. — (2) **1912** R. A. WASON *Friar Tuck* xvii. 123 She had took part in a couple o' frontier day exhibitions. **1937** DOUGLAS *Amer. Bk. of Days* 395 Beginning in 1897, Cheyenne, the capital of Wyoming arranged an annual Frontier Day celebration to keep alive the sports and customs of the early days of the State.

b. Designating persons or places associated with, or situated on, the frontier, as (1) **frontier county,** (2) **-man,** (3) **people,** (4) **place,** (5) **plantation,** (6) **post,** (7) **settlement,** (8) **-sman,** (9) **town,** (10) **village.**

(1) **1687** *Doc. Hist. N.Y. State* (1849) I. 179 Mr. Pretty is Sheriff of that County and having a great deal of other concerns upon his hands, . . . that being a frontier County to Canada. **1847** PARKMAN in *Knickerb.* Sep. 232 [The emigrants] came from one of the least barbarous of the frontier counties. **1944** *Reader's Digest* Oct. 56/1 He was tax collector of that frontier county. — (2) **1782** CRÈVECOEUR *Letters* 270 (*caption*), Distresses of a Frontier Man. **1884** W. SHEPHERD *Prairie Exper.* 27 The Indian mounts his pony, and burdened with nothing but his gun, will travel any distance. . . . The experienced frontier-man can very nearly rival this. — (3) **1655** R. WILLIAMS *Letters* (1874) 296 Our dangers (being a frontier people to the barbarians) are greater than those of other colonies. **1795** *Ann. 3d Congress* 1259 What use was there for expending millions every year in defence of the frontier people, if they were to be at liberty to cross the Indian line as often as they pleased? **1879** *Scribner's Mo.* Nov. 134/1 [Corn] is a crop that also has special favor with frontier people. — (4) **1671** *N.Y. State Col. Hist.* XII. 487 The like Resolucon proposed as to Matinicock, It being a ffrontier Place, it is also allowed and approved of. **1705** *R.I. Col. Rec.* III. 526 We have been necessitated to raise men for the security of our frontier places in our Collany.

(5) **1680** *Md. Hist. Mag.* XV. 111 The late league [was] made with them [the Senecas] in order to prevent their makeing any incursions upon the ffrontier Plantations that lye in their roade. **1700** *Va. State P.* I. 70, I have Raised 12 men, & have sent every way to search our ffrontears & back fforrist Plantations. — (6) **1690** *Mass. H. S. Coll.* 4 Ser. V. 232 The unexpected surprisal of Schenectady by the French and their Indian confederates has so alarmed the frontier post of Albany . . . , that it is thought a work necessary . . . how to secure that place. **1898** PAGE *Red Rock* 181 When Middleton arrived at the court-house, . . . he found an order transferring his company to a frontier post in the far Northwest. — (7) **1789** WASHINGTON in *Ann. 1st Congress* I. 67 The distance of the Choctaws and Chickasaws from the frontier settlements seems to have prevented those tribes from being involved in similar difficulties with the Cherokees. **1870** KEIM *Sheridan's Troopers* i. 13 Frontier settlements have sprung up around in the fertile vallies of the Caw. — (8) **1814** BRACKENRIDGE *Louisiana* 116 There seems to prevail a rage amongst the frontiers-men, for emigration to that quarter. **1923** J. H. COOK *On Old Frontier* 7 Soon after my arrival in San Antonio I was fortunate enough to meet one of the most noted frontiersmen of Texas. **1948** DICK *Dixie Frontier* 65 The fighting frontiersmen felt that there was no good Indian but a dead one. — (9) **1654** JOHNSON *Wonder-W. Prov.* 61 The frontire Towns of *Charles Towne,* and *Boston* were [not safe] for the habitation of such as the Lord had prepared to Governe this Pilgrim People. **1941** ASBURY *Gem of Prairie* 37 As in other American frontier towns, the gamblers were followed by the prostitutes and their pimps.

(10) **1841** *Spirit of Times* 9 Jan. 534/3 (We.), Industry and perseverance have erected . . . all the other apparatus, of a smart frontier village. **1880** *Harper's Mag* Dec. 45/1 Fisheries . . . now formed the only business of the once thriving frontier village.

Also *frontier affair, cabin, coat, colonel, custom, district, farmhouse, fort, garrison, girl, Indian, inhabitant, law, life, lot, male, militia, punishment, scouting, settler, station, woman,* etc.

frontierism frʌnˈtɪrɪzəm, *n.* A mode of expression or a practice frequent on the frontier; the crude manner of living associated with the frontier.

1887 F. FRANCIS JR. *Saddle & Moccasin* 124 It has always been a marvel to me to see the ease with which such men shed, like an old coat, all such frontierisms when they return to more cultured society. **1890** *Harper's Mag.* Aug. 383/1 Reno came quickly to a shallow 'cooley' (frontierism for gully) that led down through the bluff to the stream. **1900** *Kans. Hist. Coll.* VI. 211 The inevitable political contest in Kansas between refined enlightenment and frontierism (to put it crudely) came off in 1864.

***fronting,** *n.* Of land, frontage, extent of front. *Obs.* — **1665** *Hempstead Town Rec.* I. 161 Every man that hath any ffrontting upon the ffeeld shall sofichantly mand itt vp. **1723** *N.H. Probate Rec.* I. 615 He is to have Fronting on the Highway Leading from the old Meeting House.

frosh frɑʃ, *n.* Colloq. for "freshman," "freshmen." Also attrib.

1915 in *Sooner Mag.* (1947) Nov. 14/1 The 'frosh' started a 'back to nature movement.' **1944** *Chi. D. News* 29 Nov. 3/1 Dr. Snyder followed her dutifully, after donning the frosh cap she had brought for him. **1949** *Ib.* 5 March 15/6 (*heading*), Frosh-Soph Hold Meet At Wheaton.

***frost,** *n.*

1. *pl.* App. shoes provided with calks or frost nails to prevent slipping on ice. *Obs.* Cf. **calk, creepers.**

1718 SEWALL *Diary* III. 161, Jany. 19. Great Rain, and very Slippery: was fain to wear Frosts. *Ib.* 165 Had like to have fallen grievously, by reason of my Frosts, on the Steps in the night: but recover'd.

2. In combs.: (1) **frost aster,** =**frost flower;** (2) **bird,** (see quots.); (3) **blow,** =**frost flower;** (4) **fish,** see as a main entry; (5) **flower,** any one of various species of aster, the flower of one of these plants, also fig., cf. **farewell summer;** (6) **grape,** see as a main entry; (7) **grass,** a small grass (see quot.) native to Texas and California; (8) **line,** the line marking the limits of frost; (9) **plant,** =**frostweed 2;** (10) **weed,** see as a main entry; (11) **wort,** (see quot. 1848).

(1) **1941** R. S. WALKER *Lookout* 53 Frost aster which grows on the side and the top of the mountain is one of most exquisite species of the Aster genus. — (2) **1844** *Nat. Hist. N.Y., Zoology* II. 213 The Golden Plover. *Charadrius Virginiacus.* . . . As they appear in the greatest numbers after a sharp frost, they are popularly known under the name of Frost-bird. **1946** L. A. HAUSMAN *Field Book of Eastern Birds* 257 Golden Plover. . . . Other Names—Some thirty or more local names, among them: Blackbreast, Fieldbird, Pasture Bird, Frostbird. — (3) **1845** LYELL *Second Visit* (1849) I. 53 There were also golden rods, everlastings, and asters in profusion; one of the asters being called 'frost blow,' because flowering after the first frost.

(5) **1831** *Amer. Jrnl. Geol. & Nat. Science* I. 23. **1860** HOLMES *Professor* iii. 82 Old men's first children—frost flowers of the early winter season. **1937** COFFIN *Kennebec* 278 The white everlasting roses crowd up to my pasture bars, frost-flowers climb up the ledges to the pines that are centuries old. — (7) **1940** JAEGER *Calif. Deserts* 165 After spring rains the little frost grass (*Triodia pulchella*) comes up in

enormous quantities and, true to its common name, makes the desert where it grows appear as if covered with frost. — **(8) 1865** WHITTIER *Poetical Works* (1895) 401/1 While the red logs before us beat The frost-line back with tropic heat. **1886** I. D. HARDY *Oranges & Alligators* 63 And proved . . . that there is no such thing as a 'frost line' here [Florida]. — **(9) 1817-8** EATON *Botany* (1822) 238 *Cistus canadensis*, rock rose, frost plant. . . . At the foot of the Pine-rock, New Haven, the barren plains produce great quantities of this plant.

(11) 1843 TORREY *Flora N.Y.* I. 77 Frost-weed. Frost wort. Dry sandy woods and hillsides. . . . Sometimes employed as an astringent and tonic. **1848** BARTLETT 150 Frostwort. (*Cistus Canadensis.*) A medical plant prepared by the Shakers and used for its astringent and tonic properties.

frosted poorwill. (See quots.) — **1887** RIDGWAY *Manual N.A. Birds* 588 *P[halaenoptilus] nuttalli nitidus.* Frosted Poor-will. **1917** *Birds of Amer.* II. 171 Two closely related subspecies [of the poor-will], viz., the Frosted Poor-will . . . and the Dusky, or California, Poor-will . . . are recognized by naturalists.

frostfish ˈfrɔst͵fɪʃ, *n.* [See quot. 1884 in **1.**]

1. The tomcod, abundant along the New-England coast in winter.

1634 WOOD *N. Eng. Prospect* (1865) 36 Th' Frost fish and the Smelt. **1795** J. SULLIVAN *Hist. Maine* 21 The people have tom cod, or what they call frost fish, smelts, and also alewives in great plenty. **1884** GOODE *Fisheries* I. 223 The Atlantic Tom Cod, *Microgadus tomcod*, . . . is ordinarily known as the Tom Cod, but in the Bay of Fundy, and in various places south of Cape Cod, it is known as the Frost Fish, owing to the fact that it becomes most abundant in the early part of the winter. **1918** *Essex Inst. Coll.* LIV. 290 Frost fish were very abundant in its waters [i.e., those of Porter's River, Salem, Mass.].

attrib. **1638** in *Essex Inst. Coll.* IV. 119/1 The little brooke called the frost fishe brooke. **1884** *Nat. Museum Bul.* No. 27, 867 Frostfish spear. A row of twelve sail-needles set in flat pieces of wood on Southern New England coast for the capture of frostfish.

2. The common American smelt.

1871 *Amer. Naturalist* IV. 717 Professor George H. Cook, State Geologist, sent to the author of this paper a number of 'frost-fish' or 'smelt' (*Osmerus mordax*). **1883** *Nat. Museum Bul.* No. 27, 472 *Osmerus mordax*. . . . Smelt; Frost-fish. . . . This is a food-fish of great excellence.

frost grape. The chicken grape, *Vitis cordifolia*, or its fruit (see also quot. 1862).

1789 *Amer. Philos. Soc. Trans.* I. 261 The frost or winter grape is known to every body, both the bunches and berries are small, and yield but little juice. **1862** *Rep. Comm. Patents 1861: Agric.* 481 The common names given to this species [*Vitis labrusca*] and *æstivalis* and *V. cordifolia* are not uniformly constant. All three are called in different sections 'Frost grape' and 'Fox grape,' and both æstivalis and cordifolia are often named 'Frost grape' and 'Chicken grape' in the middle States. . . . The Frost grape has long, compound racemes, with a smaller thinner skin, and fruit more acid. **1875** BURROUGHS *Winter Sunshine* ii. 48 If the weather is cold, he eats the frost grapes and the persimmons. **1942** TEHON *Native Ill. Shrubs* 191 The Frost Grape ranges, in woods and thickets, from New York to Nebraska, and south to Florida and Texas.

frostweed ˈfrɔst͵wid, *n.* Any one of various American plants, as (1) (see quot.), (2) the rock rose, *Helianthemum canadense*, (3) any one of various asters.

(1) 1828 RAFINESQUE *Medical Flora* I. 162 *Erigeron philadelphicum*. . . . Vulgar Names—Skevish, Scabish, . . . Frostwood, Fieldweed, Squawweed, &c. — **(2) 1837** DARLINGTON *Flora Cestrica* 313-14 Rock Rose. Frost weed. . . . Prof. *Eaton* and Dr. *Bigelow* have noticed the formation, in freezing weather, of curiously curved ice-chrystals near the root of *H. canadense*. **1891** COULTER *Bot. W. Texas* I. 24 *Helianthemum canadense*, . . . the common 'frost-weed' of the Atlantic States, occurs in eastern Texas and may be found within our eastern limit. — **(3) 1926** ROBERTS *Time of Man* 144 Ellen bought a fresh ribbon for her dress and a bit of lace for her throat and blossomed anew with the frostweeds and the last of the chicory that lingered far into October.

frowchey ˈfraʊtʃɪ, *n.* [See quot. 1902.] (See quots.) *Obs.* — **1848** BARTLETT, *Frowchey*, . . . a furbelowed old woman. Local in New York and its vicinity. **1902** CLAPIN 198 Frowchey (Dutch *vrouwtje*). In city of New York and vicinity, a term applied to an old woman, with bent shoulders, and deep-wrinkled, furbelowed face. A wellnigh desperate attempt to render, into English, the staid old greeting 'Vrouwtje,' so much in use amongst the good burgher's [*sic*] wives in Knickerbocker times.

frow horse. A brake, sometimes utilizing a forked portion of a tree trunk, for securing bolts that are being rived. Cf. **shaving horse, shingle horse.** — **1925** *Old-Time New Eng.* April 176 Having placed a block (red oak in Penna.) about eighteen inches long and squared, or quartered from the log, to the required five-inch width, the worker, holding the handle vertically in the left hand, sets the heavy, wide-backed blade of the instrument [frow], on the top of the block placed vertically in the tree fork 'Frow Horse,' shown in Fig. 14.

∗**frozen,** *a.*

1. Of facts or truth: Hard, actual, real. *Colloq.*

1883 MARK TWAIN *Life on Miss.* 374 What these gentlemen want for a book is the frozen truth. **1884** *Boston Herald* 25 Sep., 'Frozen Facts' is a purely American expression, and one, too, of recent origin. **1884** *Boston Journal* 22 Oct. 2/2 We were simply stating the frozen truth, with the utmost calmness.

One form of frow horse

2. frozen-sap blight, a disease of pear trees caused by the unseasonable occurrence of severe cold.

1867 *Ill. Agric. Soc. Trans.* VII. 503 Frozen Sap Blight is also confined to comparatively young branches. **1872** *Vt. Bd. Agric. Rep.* I. 117 More trees are lost from frozen sap blight, than from any or all other causes.

∗**fruit,** *n.*

1. The boll of the cotton plant.

1854 *Fla. Plant. Rec.* 89 Still they [=there] is a good deal of grown and half grown fruit on the cotton. *Ib.* 98 He did not get the fruit to stick on his cotton as I did.

2. In combs.: (1) **fruit belt,** a section of the country where fruit is raised on a large scale; (2) **can,** a tin container or a glass jar in which fruit is canned; (3) **car,** (see quot. 1889); (4) **cocktail,** a mixture of fruits and fruit juices served as an appetizer; (5) **cup,** =prec.; (6) **farm,** a farm where special or exclusive attention is given to raising fruit; (7) **gatherer,** a mechanical contrivance for use in gathering fruit; (8) **growers' association,** an organization of fruit-growers, esp. a coöperative group formed to standardize practices and to engage in collective buying and selling; (9) **jar,** a glass jar in which fruit,

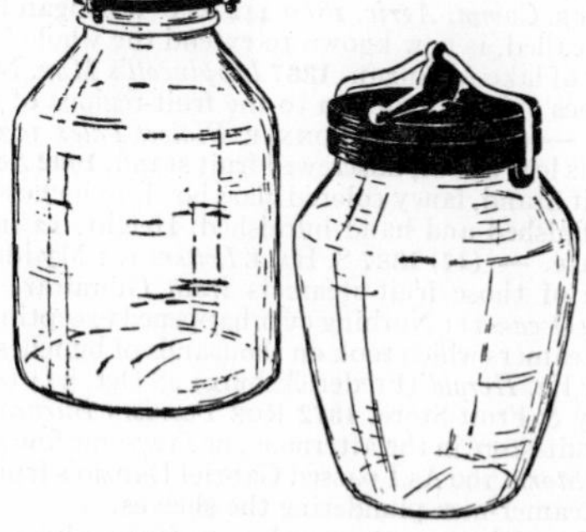

Fruit jars of early types

vegetables, etc., are canned, also attrib.; (10) **orchard,** a large inclosure in which fruit is grown; (11) **peddler,** one who hawks or peddles fruit; (12) **pie,** a pie made of fruit; (13) **raising,** the growing of fruit; (14) **ranch,** *W.* =**fruit farm;** (15) **region,** a region particularly suited for growing fruit; (16) ∗**stand,** a supported receptacle or container for fruit; (17) **steamer,** a steamship engaged in transporting fruit; (18) **store,** a store in which fruit is sold.

(1) **1874** *Rep. Comm. Agric. 1873* 428 A wide field for the operations of such an organization is afforded by the almost unsurpassed fruit-belt of a fair portion of the Michigan peninsula. **1947** *Want Ad News* (Chi.) 25 Oct. 2/5 You . . . will be able to live in the heart of Michigan's great 'fruit belt,' where the climate is always 'just right.' — (2) **1868** *Mich. Agric. Rep.* VII. 348 S. B. Rowley, Philadelphia, Pa., [exhibited] 1 lot fruit cans (glass). **1903** O. HENRY *Heart of West* 250 In the grass lay an empty fruit can. — (3) **1858** *So. Cultivator* XVI. 288/1 (*headline*), Fruit Cars Wanted. **1889** *Cent.* 2394 *Fruit-car*, . . . a railroad-car of special design for the carriage of fruit and other perishable products requiring ventilation and provision against the effects of undue heat or cold. *Car-builder's Dict.* — (4) **1928** *Sat. Ev. Post* 12 May 107/1 Mr. Montgomery had taken a morsel of fruit cocktail. **1949** *Canning Trade* 28 Mar. 20/1 The past week has been marked by quite a general lowering of prices on fruit cocktail.

(5) **1930** *Good Housekeeping* Mar. 297/2 A fruit cup or salad without too great cost—without opening a number of cans of fruit or shopping for too many different products. **1944** *Chi. D. News* 13 July 21/2 Fruit cup is always a favorite for the appetizer course. — (6) **1872** *Ill. Dept Agric. Trans.* IX. 65 The first consideration in the establishment of a fruit farm is accessibility to market. **1909** *Amer. Homes & Gardens* Oct. Supp. 4 (*caption*), Florida Fruit Farm. — (7) **1847** *Rep. Comm. Patents 1846* 19 A fruit-gatherer, of very ingenious and simple construction, has been patented. **1902** *Sears Cat.* (ed. 112) 585 It will be observed that the Acme Fruit Gatherer is remarkably simple in construction. — (8) **1897** *Boston Journal* 11 March 7/6 The third annual meeting of the Massachusetts Fruit-Growers' Association was held in Horticultural Hall today. **1911** *Dept. Agric. Yrbk. 1910* 396 Several factors have contributed to the downfall of fruit-growers' associations. — (9) **1865** *Chi. Tribune* 15 April 1 Kerosene Lamps, Lanterns, Looking Glasses, Fruit Jars, Flasks [for sale]. **1946** *Democrat* 31 Jan. 2/5 But this particular 'possum had a fruit jar rubber around its neck.

(10) **1829** CUMINGS *Western Pilot* 5 The country . . . is celebrated for its . . . fruit-orchards. **1896** *Vt. Agric. Rep.* XV. 87, I have yet to meet the man who has practiced this method [of reforesting] and pronounced its profitable except with maple and fruit orchards and with shade trees. — (11) **1880** MARK TWAIN *Tramp Abroad* 328 Indeed, from Lucerne to Interlaken we had the spectacle, among other scenery, of an unbroken procession of fruit-peddlers and tourist carriages. **1881** STODDARD *E. Hardery* 32 He's not in any condition to come out in the character of a fruit peddler. — (12) **1782** CRÈVECOEUR *Lett.* 11 [Mr. F. B.] lived upon nothing but fruit-pies. **1852** *Harper's Mag.* June 133/1 Sonnet On a Youth Who Died of Excessive Fruit-Pie. **1904** A. DALE *Wanted, a Cook* 153 It was a cozy little dinner of . . . a tender chicken, ably accompanied with parsley sauce; vegetables, and a fruit pie. — (13) **1869** DANA *Two Years* (new ed.) 452 The vast grants of the Castro and Soto families, where farming and fruit-raising are done on so large a scale. **1894** WARNER *Golden House* iii, The fad is to be American, with . . . a large continental kind of attitude, begotten of hearing much about Western roughing it, of Alaska, of horse-breeding and fruit-raising on the Pacific, of the Colorado River Cañon. — (14) **1893** SANBORN *So. Calif.* 125 'Lagunita Rancho' is the name of an immense fruit ranch in Vacaville. **1948** JACOBS *We Chose the Country* 12 The western fruit ranch was a parallel to it—doing something for which others would reap the profit.

(15) **1870** *Rep. Comm. Agric. 1860* 442 The 'Michigan fruit region,' popularly so called, is now known to extend the whole length of the eastern shore of lake Michigan. **1887** *Lippincott's Mag.* Nov. 737 Our friend . . . [goes on] an excursion to the fruit-regions of Sunderland, and a drive. — (16) **1883** S. BONNER *Dialect Tales* 103 Uncle Ned tottered on his legs like an unscrewed fruit stand. **1902** *Sears Cat.* (ed. 112) 110 Fruit Stand, fancy colored glass bowl, 10 inches in diameter, frame satin finished and hand burnished. Height, 12 inches; width 5 inches at base. — (17) **1887** S. HALE *Letters* 181 My idea is to come home in one of those fruit-steamers from Gibraltar. **1921** PAINE *Comr. Rolling Ocean* 111 Nothing ever happened excepting the arrival of the fruit steamers which took on thousands of bunches of bananas. — (18) **1826** *Va. Herald* (Fredericksburg) 28 Oct. 3/4 (*advt.*), Goodwin's Grocery & Fruit Store. **1872** ROE *Barriers Burned Away* xxvi, Going by a fruit-store in the afternoon, he saw some fine strawberries. **1914** STEELE *Storm* 196 As I passed Gabriel Danzio's fruit store I saw a crowd of steamer-men plundering the shelves.

b. In less frequent combs., often obs.: (1) **fruit cannery,** a building where fruit is canned commercially; (2) **cave,** a kind of fruit cellar; (3) **farmer,** one who owns or operates a fruit farm; (4) **panoche,** a panoche *q.v.* containing fruit; (5) **patch,** a patch in which fruit is grown; (6) **pitter,** an implement for removing the pits from fruit; (7) **safe,** a place for storing fruit; (8) **schooner,** a schooner engaged in the fruit trade; (9) **train,** a special train for transporting fruit.

(1) **1887** *Harper's Mag.* Nov. 818 Attempts have frequently been made to establish a fruit cannery. — (2) **1862** *Ill. Agric. Soc. Trans.* V. 207 A Fruit Cave.—Mr. Coe had just completed a fruit cellar or cave, a description of which will be of interest to fruit growers. — (3) **1872** *Ill. Dept. Agric. Trans.* IX. 66 The fruit farmer can raise cheap pork in his apple and peach orchards. — (4) **1923** H. G. WILSON *Early Transportation Arizona* (Bentley), On these creaky, wobbly carretas, fruit panoche, and zarapes were brought from Mexico.

(5) **1926** *Chi. Drovers' Jrnl.* 27 April 3/3 The ground . . . is now used as a chicken yard and fruit patch combined. — (6) **1877** in KNIGHT *Supp.* 359/1 Fruit pitter. — (7) **1868** *Mich. Agric. Rep.* VII. 440 The 'Field's Fruit-safe' for peaches was next presented by Mr. Sairdge. — (8) **1845** *Knickerb.* XXVI. 433 The captain of a West Indian fruit-schooner was pacing up and down his deck. — (9) **1877** in MARTIN *Hist. Great Riots* 172 Several extra trains for the east have been placed on the road, including fast fruit trains for the accommodation of shippers.

As the last term in **bread, citrus, egg, fog, grape, hen, Shaker, small fruit.**

* **fruiterer,** *n.* A vessel carrying a cargo of fruit. — **1835** INGRAHAM *South-West* I. 51 The remaining vessels . . . were fast dispersing over the sea—this Yankee 'fruiterer' being the only one sailing within a league of us. **1882** *Harper's Mag.* Aug. 359/1 [The ship] was both a fruiterer and an oyster-boat, prosecuting these callings at different seasons.

* **fry,** *n.* An outdoor social gathering at which food, usu. fish, is fried and eaten. Cf. **bacon, clam, fish, steak fry.**

1833 *Amer. Turf Reg.* Aug. 643, I had almost forgotten to say a day is fixed for another fry, *early in the action*, and a bill of fare is inclosed. **1853** *S. Lit. Messenger* XIX. 367/1 The ancient pond . . . had slept thus from the times of Powhatan, perchance, and dusky warriors had, perhaps, drawn fish from it, and had their barbarous 'fries' upon its banks. **1946** *Democrat* 27 June 1/7 This fry was supposed to have been given.

* **fry,** *v.* *To fry out fat, to fry the fat out of,* to obtain money by extortionary or high pressure means. *Slang.*

1890 *Cong. Rec.* 10 July 7088/1 That process which in the U.S. is called the 'frying of fat' out of people. *Ib.* 16 July 7790/1, I did not suppose there had been any authority of law for 'frying the fat' out of the manufacturers in the last presidential campaign. **1904** *Nation* 28 April 321 His main qualification is admitted to be that of a good collector of funds. No one could, in the historic phrase, fry out more fat.

* **fryer,** *n.* Also **frier.** A young chicken of suitable size for frying. — **1923** *D.N.* V. 207 Frier, n. A chicken of frying size. [McDonald Co., Mo.] **1948** *Democrat* 4 Nov. 1/2 We may be able to get in some flocks of broilers and fryers.

* **frying,** *n.*

1. frying chicken, = * **fryer.**

1897 THANET *Missionary Sheriff* 171 Therefore she bought her eggs and her 'frying chickens' of George Washington, a worthy colored man. **1905** MILES *Spirit of Mts.* 29 A frying chicken (the creature called a 'broiler' in northern and eastern communities), camping on Baby's trail of crumbs, chirps querulously.

2. frying size, used with reference to young chickens of the proper size for frying. Also absol. Also **frying-sized chicken.**

1904 HARBEN *Georgians* 119 They was the best fryin' size I ever raised. **1926** ROBERTS *Time of Man* 141 Say you had twenty hens to start, you could raise two hundred or three hundred frying-sizes in no time. **1946** WILSON *Fidelity* 80 You recall certain homely foods, foods associated with the old-fashioned country home, with its well-stocked smokehouse and with plenty of frying-sized chickens running around.

transf. **1884** C. H. SMITH *Peace Papers* 314 When I wer a fryin size chicken the biggest thing out was a trip to Augusty. **1904** HARBEN *Georgians* 99 He had a wife, some little fryin'-size children, an' a beautiful young daughter. **1943** POWELL *Home Again* 99 He . . . was much annoyed by a bunch of 'frying-sized' girls who kept going in and out of the church with the obvious purpose of showing off their new Sunday frocks. **1948** *N.O. Times-Picayune Mag.* 24 Oct. 7/3 Figuring that it takes two to four years for them to sprout again, these six- to eight-inch diameter trees are from 95 to 97 years old. Why, they're just frying size!

fry-pan ˈfraɪˌpæn, *n.* A frying pan. *Colloq.*

*a*1862 THOREAU *Maine Woods* 323 The following will be a good outfit for one who wishes to make an excursion of *twelve* days into the Maine woods in July . . . two tin dippers, three tin plates, a fry-pan. **1885** *Harper's Mag.* Jan 217/2 Whar's yer fry-pan, yer bake-pan, yer biling-water kittle, yer dipper? **1946** STANWELL-FLETCHER *Driftwood Valley* 103 To watch the pot and frypan I had to kneel on the snow-bank and lean above the fire, receiving directly in the face clouds of sparks and smoke made wherever snow touched the logs.

* **fudge,** *n.* (See quot. 1900.) Also attrib. Cf. **chocolate, divinity, walnut fudge.** — **1900** WEBSTER *Supp.* 81/3 *Fudge*, . . . a kind of soft candy composed of sugar, milk, butter, chocolate, or the like, boiled and stirred to a proper consistency. **1948** *Democrat* 19 Aug. 6/6

Homemade fudge may be shipped successfully, if it is poured while warm.

***fudge,** *v. intr.* (See quot. 1921.) *Colloq.* Cf. **fulk* in *OED* in same sense.

1849 *N.O. Picayune* 5 May 2/1 It reminds us of boys playing marbles; one cries, 'Vence roundance; nuckle down; no fudging; if you fudge it shan't count.' 'It should count; you fudged.' 'Well,' says the other, 'didn't you fudge last?' **1921** *D.N.* V. 116 *Fudge*.... With the hillsman it means to cheat, or 'poke up,' in marbles. [Ky.] **1932** *K.C. Times* 9 April 28 Knuckle down, screwbonny tight. Quit fudging. That's the language of the . . . boys . . . competing for the right to represent Jefferson City in a state wide marble tournament soon.

fugio 'fjudʒɪo, *n.* [L., *I fly*, no doubt in allusion to *tempus fugit.*] A copper coin, inscribed with the word "fugio" and with the picture of a sundial surmounted by the sun, designed by Benjamin Franklin and issued in 1787 by the authority of Congress. In full **fugio cent.** Also attrib. Cf. **Franklin cent.**

The fugio was coined at the New Haven mint. A somewhat similar coin is said to have been struck in 1776. (See HICKCOX, *Amer. Coinage*, 75–76).

[**1787** *Jrnls. Continental Cong.* 6 July 303 Resolved that the board of Treasury direct the contractor for the copper coinage, to stamp . . . on the opposite side . . . a meridian sun above; on one side of which, is to be the word 'fugio.'] **1862** *Sale Cat. Coins of W. A. Lilliendahl 26–8 May* (Bangs, Merwin & Co.) 48 [No.] 1126. Fugio Cent, 1787; known as the Franklin Cent; rev. 'United States,' original, extremely fine. Scarce. **1883** J. S. DYE *Dye's Coin Encycl.* 247 The Fugios were the first coinage made by authority of the United States. There is but little on record concerning this series of coppers. *Ib.* 252 The Fugio Pattern Pieces. With the regular authorized Fugio currency of the United States, have been found a number of coins of like general character. **1945** *Chi. Tribune* 16 Sep. (Book Sec.) 12/2 Here is the first United States coin, the 'Fugio Cent,' with the blunt motto, 'Mind your business.'

***fugitive slave.** In combs.: (1) **fugitive slave act,** (*a*) an act passed by a state legislature or by Congress relating to the recovery of escaped Negro slaves, (*b*) (*cap.*) =**Fugitive Slave Law;** (2) **Bill,** the bill embodying the Fugitive Slave Law, cf. **Missouri Compromise;** (3) **Law,** a law passed by Congress in 1850 strengthening the legal provisions for the return to their owners of fugitive slaves, now *hist.*

(1) (*a*) **1857** BENTON *Exam. Dred Scott Case* 28 It is an organic provision, barren of execution until a law should be passed under it to give it effect—which was done in the fugitive slave and criminal act of 1793. **1865** *Atlantic Mo.* Jan. 120/1 The fugitive-slave acts that disfigured our statute-book were blotted out, and fugitive-slave-stealer acts filled their vacant places. (*b*) **1857** *Lawrence* (Kans.) *Republican* 25 June 1 The court thought the Fugitive Slave act of 1850 unauthorized by the federal constitution. **1886** LOGAN *Great Conspiracy* 40 The Slave Trade in the District of Columbia was abolished; and a more effectual Fugitive Slave Act passed. — **(2)** **1851** B. ALCOTT *Journals* 243 Elliott . . . deserved insult from every right-minded citizen for his late vote on the Fugitive Slave bill. **1882** THAYER *From Log-Cabin* xx. 302 He had been a great admirer of Daniel Webster, but his advocacy of the fugitive slave bill awakened his contempt. — **(3)** **1850** *Harper's Mag.* Dec. 122/1 The Fugitive Slave Law contained many unjust provisions. **1882** COOPER *Amer. Pol.* I. 11 With a view to better protect their rights to slave property, they then advocated and succeeded in passing the first fugitive slave law. This was approved February 12, 1793. **1946** *Chi. D. News* 4 Sep. 14/1 On the basis of American experience with an unenforceable fugitive slave law, we do not hesitate to advise Premier Attlee.

fuik, fuik net, see **fyke.**

***full,** *a.* and *adv.*

1. *absol.* =**full hand 2.** *Colloq.*

1844 J. COWELL *Thirty Years* 94 Three aces, for example, or three kings, with any two of the other cards, or four queens, or Jacks or tens, is called a full. **1899** CHAMPLIN & BOSTWICK *Cyclo. Games & Sports* (ed. 2) 268/1 *A Full House, Full Hand,* or *Full.* Triplets and a Pair together.

2. Said of the bases in baseball when there are runners on first, second, and third. *Colloq.*

1944 *Chi. D. News* 4 Oct. 29/7 A home run with the bases full by Stan Benjamin . . . kept the Orioles in the running.

3. In combs.: (1) **full blast,** fully, at maximum capacity, usu. in the phrase *in full blast, colloq.;* (2) ***blood,** see as a main entry; (3) ***blooded,** see as a main entry; (4) **box,** (see quot.), *rare;* (5) **bred,** *a.* thoroughbred, also **full breed,** a thoroughbred, *colloq.;* (6) **chisel,** *adv.* at headlong speed, impetuously, *colloq.;* (7) **-cream cheese,** a cheese made from whole or unskimmed milk, also **full cream store cheese;** (8) **deck,** *a.* designating a variety of poker played with a full deck, *obs.;* (9) **dinner pail,** see **dinner pail c;** (10) ***face,** used with reference to type of the ordinary plain face but with thick lines that print black or bold; (11) ***hand,** see as a main entry; (12) ***house,** =***full hand 2;** (13) **-milk cheese,** =**full-cream cheese;** (14) **professor,** one who has the highest professorial rank in a college or university; (15) **stock,** (see quot. 1848); (16) **team,** (see quot.), *colloq., obs.*

(1) **1839** MARRYAT *Diary in Amer.* II. 36 In *full blast*—something in the extreme. 'When she came to meeting, with her yellow hat and feathers, was'n't she in *full blast?*' **1863** *Seattle Gazette* 10 Dec. 3/2 The 'irrepressible conflict' proceeds here in full blast between the Governor and Secretary Evans. **1948** *P.C.C. Chronicle* (Pasadena, Calif.) 7 May 4/1 Intra-mural basketball seems to be going full blast.—**(4)** **1885** *Cent. Mag.* Aug. 642/2 The second [shell] ranged . . . through the ward-room and steerage and out upon the birth-deck, killing every one of the 'full-boxes'—that is, the cooks and ward-room boys, who were the powder passers from the after magazine.

(5) **1816** U. BROWN *Journal* I. 346 This Henry is a full Bred Land Jobber a native of the West. **1841** NICOLLET *Report* 49 For many years they were only in small numbers, . . . in consequence of outrages committed upon them by the full breeds. — **(6)** **1835** S. SMITH *Major Downing* 125 We are coming on full chisel. . . . When we've been on the road I couldn't catch my breath . . . we kept flying so fast. **1878** STOWE *Poganuc People* ix. 76 The only way to get that fellow to heaven would be to set out to drive him to hell; then he'd turn and run up the narrow way full chisel. — **(7)** **1881** *Chi. Times* 16 April, The full-cream cheese [is] manufactured in the states of Wisconsin and Illinois. **1894** *Vt. Agric. Rep.* XIV. 25 A full cream store cheese is run through a grinder. — **(8)** **1887** *Courier-Journal* 23 Jan. 15/7 Then came full-deck straight poker, and that was rather a slow game.

(10) **1854** *L.A. Star* 24 June 4/2 *Compositor:* 'Do you want a "full face" head to "Jenny Lind's Family"?' **1898** *Nation* 17 Feb. 131/3 The full-face captions of divisions and subdivisions have of course been set by hand. — **(12)** **1903** *Cin. Enquirer* 2 May 13/4 We hadn't played more than 20 minutes before the first struggle came between a flush and a full house. **1949** *Lubbock* (Tex.) *Morn. Avalanche* 23 Feb. I. 8/7 His faith in betting a beaten hand into a pat full-house borders on eccentricity. — **(13)** **1858** FLINT *Milch Cows* 269 A full-milk cheese differs but little from pure milk, except in the absence of sugar. — **(14)** **1934** BURGESS *Reminiscences* 42 The faculty of the college was at that time a strong body of teachers, most of them being full professors of long experience and high standing.

(15) **1848** W. ARMSTRONG *Stocks* 5 The par value is most commonly $100 or $50. The first is called 'full stock,' and the latter 'half stock.' **1900** NELSON *A B C Wall St.* 21 The custom is to buy 200 shares of a 'half' stock, which would be equivalent to the usual 100 shares of 'full' or $100 a share stocks. — **(16)** *a***1870** CHIPMAN *Notes on Bartlett* 164 *Full Team.* A powerful man; a man of consequence.

full blood.

1. An Indian of unmixed racial ancestry, a full-blooded Indian.

1846 SAGE *Scenes Rocky Mts.* xx, [The half-breed children] were more beautiful, interesting, and intelligent than the same number of full-bloods,—either of whites or Indians. **1898** CUSHMAN *Hist. Indians* 172 The young half-breeds mingle with the whites ninety per cent more than the full-bloods. **1949** *Dly. Oklahoman* (Okla. City) 13 Feb. D. 14/5 The notice listed more than 150 Cherokee Indians, mostly full-bloods, as owners.

2. An animal of an unmixed or pure breed.

1863 RANDALL *Pract. Shepherd* xi. 102 The full blood, or pure blood, or thorough-bred animal . . . can inherit from its parents . . . only the same family characteristics. **1884** *Cent. Mag.* Feb. 517/2 Almost every Vermont farmer was a shepherd, and had his half hundred or hundreds or thousands of grade sheep or full bloods dotting the ferny pastures of the hill country. **1894** *Vt. Agric. Rep.* XIV. 104 The terms 'thoroughbred,' 'full-blood,' and 'pure-bred,' are generally used in this country as practically synonymous.

***full-blood,** *a.*

1. Of animals: Full-blooded, unmixed in breed.

1812 *Niles' Reg.* II. 408/1 Forty dollars . . . to his excellency Ed. Lloyd of Wye, Talbot county, . . . for his full blood merino ram lamb. **1850** *Rep. Comm. Patents 1848: Agric.* 88 Vermont once numbered nearly one and a half million of sheep, which have dwindled down, probably to about half a million, . . . ranging in quality from half to full-blood merino.

2. Of Indians: Uncontaminated, of pure Indian descent.

1844 Gregg *Commerce of Prairies* II. 270 There is a post-nuptial custom peculiar to the full-blood Indian of the Choctaws, which deserves particular notice. **1893** *Columbus* (Ohio) *Dispatch* 2 Oct., His mother [was] a full-blood Potawatomie squaw. **1923** J. H. Cook *On Old Frontier* 225 His mother, by the way, was a full-blood Sioux and his father a Frenchman.

full-blooded, *a.* Of pure or unmixed descent, uncontaminated; thoroughgoing, vigorous.

1774 Fithian *Journal* I. 89 Balantine, either to shew himself a true full-blooded Buck, or out of mere wantonness . . . turned the Bones . . . into many improper and indecent postures. **1801** *Steele P.* I. 218 The present Secy. altho' a full blooded Yankee, as we call him in these parts, knows the importance of this place. **1812** *Niles' Reg.* II. 408/1 Premium . . . [goes] to gen. John Mason, of Annslostan Island, District of Columbia, for his full blooded merino ram lamb. **1870** R. H. Davis *Scribner's Mo.* I. 60 The sense of beauty . . . had reached this full-blooded dogmatic young fellow through the girl, for the first time in his life. **1949** Murray *This Our Land* 94 Only two horses were entered this time—a full-blooded sorrel filly, and 'Medusa,' a breeding mare.

b. Of Indians.

1831 *American* (Harrodsburg, Ky.) 11 Mar. 1/1 Many of the old and full blooded Indians are dissatisfied. **1894** *Pop. Science Mo.* June 163 The 'chief' . . . is a full-blooded Indian. **1948** *Dly. Ardmoreite* (Ardmore, Okla.) 18 April 3/5 He is a full-blooded Apache and a grandson of Geronimo.

c. Of Negroes.

1859 Grattan *Civilized Amer.* II. 441 Its operation only warrants the enslaving of the absolute, or what the Americans designate 'the full-blooded' negro, the manifest black. **1894** *Harper's Mag.* June 160/2 He was a full-blooded negro, as black as the absence of light.

* **full hand.**

1. One who is capable of performing as much labor as a full-grown, able-bodied man.

1850 *Hunt's Merch. Mag.* XXIII. 107 No. of full hands in the field. **1865** *S. Carolina Statutes at Large* 38 After the words 'servant in husbandry' may be inserted . . . the words 'to be rated as (full hand, three-fourths hand, half hand, or one-fourth hand'). **1872** Flagg *Good Investment* iv. 224/1 His wages were fixed at one dollar and a quarter a day, being only a quarter of a dollar less than was paid to 'full hands,' as empty-handed poor folk are sometimes called.

2. (See quots.)

1850 Bohn *Handbook Games* 382 *Full Hand*, consists of three of equal value, and one single pair. **1944** *Pocket Bk. of Games* 4 Full house, or full hand. Three of a kind and a pair; for example, three sevens and two fours.

fulvous tree duck. *n.* A species of long-legged, long-necked duck, *Dendrocygna bicolor.* — **1883** *Nat. Museum Bul.* No. 27, 159 *Dendrocygna fulva.* Fulvous Tree Duck. . . . Middle America, north to Louisiana, Texas, Nevada, and California. **1887** Ridgway *Manual N.A. Birds* 119.

fumadiddle, see **flummerdiddle.**

fumble foot. ?A disease that affects cabbage. *Rare.* — **1790** Deane *N.-Eng. Farmer* 35/1 The principal things which prevent the growth of cabbage, are the fumble foot, so called, grubs, and lice.

fumigator ˈfjuməˌgetɚ, *n.* One who or that which fumigates.

1854 Simms *Southward Ho!* 320 You may see him, any day, in a fog of his own making, . . . with his nose half buried in a fumigator of turpentine. **1869** Mark Twain *Innocents* xxi. 209 We feel no malice toward these fumigators. **1888** *Scientific Amer.* ns. LIX. 177 A corps of physicians and fumigators . . . thoroughly disinfected and fumigated the room.

* **functional,** *a.* Of or pertaining to a system of specializing and dividing the functions of managers, workers, etc., in a factory or other business. — **1903** F. W. Taylor *Shop Management* § 234 'Functional management' consists in so dividing the work of management that each man from the assistant superintendent down shall have as few functions as possible to perform. *Ib.* § 240 The four functional bosses who are a part of the planning department. **1930** M. Clark *Home Trade* 198 Foremen are of the type termed 'functional.'

functionalize ˈfʌŋkʃənlˌaɪz, *v. tr.* In business management, to distribute or assign (work) with due regard to the special function of the individual worker. Hence **functionalization,** *n.*

1923 R. H. Lansburgh *Indust. Management* 55 Functionalization has brought with it basic changes in the structure of industrial organizations. *Ib.* 60 These functionalized foremen. *Ib.* 63 Functionalized departments working through one foreman. **1925** W. H. Leffingwell *Office Management* 108 As business grows ever larger and becomes increasingly functionalized and specialized. *Ib.* 118 The functionalization of all industrial departments.

* **fund,** *n.* In the Massachusetts colony, a bank, sum of money, or land, serving as the basis of financial security and credit for facilitating business transactions. *Obs.*

1682 *Mass. Bay Currency Tracts* 5 A proposal for erecting a Fund of Land; by Authority, or private Persons, in the nature of a Money-Bank. **1714** *Ib.* 70 There being no other Expedient in our view for the Reviving and Encouraging of Trade, . . . but by Establishing a Fund or Bank of Credit upon Land Security, which may give the Bills Issued there-from a General Currency amongst us. **1714** *Ib.* 71 We will from time to time . . . give Credit to the Bills Emitted from this Fund or Bank, equal to what is given to the Bills of Credit on the Province of the Massachusetts-Bay. **1719** *Ib.* 218 The Fund or Security for Province Bills, is the Duties of Impost and Excise, and also the Tax to be levied on Polls, and Estates both Real and Personal.

As the last term in **bounty, campaign, conscience, firemen's, grasshopper, highway, lobby, Mediterranean, revolving, safety, saline, school, slush, treaty, university fund.**

fundamentalism ˌfʌndəˈmɛntḷˌɪzəm, *n.* A religious movement which became active among some American Protestant bodies after World War I, re-affirming as fundamental to Christianity strict adherence to traditional orthodox tenets, such as belief in the literal inerrancy of the scriptures, the virgin birth, physical resurrection of Christ, etc. — **1923** *Cent. Mag.* May 158/1, I have sought in vain for one redeeming feature in either the purpose or the plea of the religious fundamentalism. **1946** Mencken *The Gods* 281 In Fundamentalism it reaches the nadir of theology.

fundamentalist ˌfʌndəˈmɛntḷɪst, *n.* (See quot. 1931.) Also transf.

1922 *N.Y. Times* 2 July III. 4/5 It is not only upon beliefs like the Virgin birth, the miracles, the resurrection of the body and the atonement that the Fundamentalists insist. **1931** F. L. Allen *Only Yesterday* 199 Those who believed in the letter of the Bible and refused to accept any teaching, even of science, which seemed to conflict with it, began in 1921 to call themselves Fundamentalists. **1947** *Christian Cent.* 24 Dec. 1597/2 A one-man 50-year fight in Minnesota against religious 'liberalism' ended with the death on Dec. 5 of William B. Riley, widely known Baptist fundamentalist.

attrib. **1929** Paul Douglas *Church Comity* 149 They make selective appeals; one, for example, to fundamentalist constituents, another to people of advanced theological position. **1948** Chaplin *Wobbly* 369 Isn't it strange that a state as beautiful as Tennessee should produce such simple, unquestioning fundamentalist faith?

Fundamental Orders. *Hist.* A document drawn up in Connecticut in 1639 (see quots.). — **1914** *Cyclo. Amer. Govt.* I. 232 The 'Fundamental Orders' of Connecticut in 1639, provided: 'It is ordered and decreed, that the deputyes thus chosen shall haue power and liberty to appoynt a tyme and a place of meeting togather before any Generall Courte to aduise and consult of all such things as may appear to legalize the publike.' **1935** *Col. of Conn.* 1 In their adoption in 1639 of the famous Fundamental Orders inspired by Thomas Hooker, in which its authors declared that the foundation of authority lay in the free consent of the people [etc.].

funder ˈfʌndɚ, *n.* One who favors funding a debt (see esp. quot 1889). Hence **Funder Democrat.**

1870 *Nation* 14 April 231/2 In this way the credit of the Congressional 'funders' would be saved in the eyes of innocent people, and it would seem as if they were really putting off bonds in the market, as they said they were going to do, at four per cent. interest. **1881** *Nation* 23 June 379/2 A fusion of the Readjusters with the Republicans seems necessary to defeat the Funder Democrats. **1889** *Cent.* 2409/2 *Funder*, . . . in U.S. politics, from about 1878 onward, a Virginian who was in favor of funding and paying the entire debt of the State (less the quota properly falling upon West Virginia), in distinction from a so-called re-adjuster, who advocated the repudiation of a part of the debt.

fundor ˈfʌndɚ, *n.* One having credit in the fund *q.v.* created by the Massachusetts Bay colony. *Rare.* — **1682** *Mass. Bay Currency Tracts* 11 If one Fundor passeth Credit to another, it ought to be by a Pass-bill.

fundum ˌfʌndəm, *n.* [L.] (See quot. *a*1870.) *Obs.*

*a***1861** Winthrop *Canoe & Saddle* 24 Chesapeakes and the like do very well for oyster 'fundums.' **1861** *N.Y. Tribune* 20 Dec. (Chipman), The great Virginia Fundum. Re-opening of the Oyster Trade. *a***1870** Chipman *Notes on Bartlett, Fundum*, . . . a sea-bottom. This term, used first by Governor Wise of Virginia, in a message to the Legislature, is occasionally heard derisively.

* **funeral,** *n.*

1. funeral director, one who prepares the dead for interment and conducts burials, an undertaker. Cf. **mortician.**

1886 *Standard Guide of Washington* 178 Charles E. Carter, Jr., General Furnishing Undertaker and Funeral Director. **1945** *Ledger-News* (Antonito, Colo.) 19 July 1/2 Morticians and Funeral Directors must also adjust the sales tax charges to comply with the present law and regulations thereto.

2. funeral home, a building or rooms in a building which may be rented for funeral services, an undertaker's parlors.

1936 MENCKEN *Amer. Lang.* 287 A *mortician* never handles a *corpse;* he *prepares* a *body* or *patient.* This business is carried on in a *preparation-room* or *operating-room,* and when it is achieved the patient is put into a *casket* and stored in the *reposing-room* or *slumber-room* of a *funeral-home.* **1948** *Capital-Democrat* (Tishomingo, Okla.) 10 June 11/2 The Chapman Funeral Home, established by Russell's father, has been operating under the same name for 50 years.

3. In various colloq. phrases (see quots.), to denote that a matter is (or is not) the concern or worry of the person indicated.

1854 *Oregon W. Times* 25 Nov. (Th.), A boy said to an outsider who was making a great ado during some impressive mortuary ceremonies, 'What are you crying about? It's none of your funeral.' **1916** BOWER *Phantom Herd* 200 She's none of my funeral; I don't know her from Adam. **1948** *Sat. Ev. Post* 26 June 82/4 I assured LaGuardia that it was 'his funeral, and not mine.'

As the last term in **Jackson, rope funeral.**

funeralist ˈfjunərəlˌɪst, *n.* One who attends a funeral. *Rare.* — **1888** *Advance* 2 Aug., [In New England,] gin, brandy and rum were the funeral liquors that always sat in the long hall, awaiting the funeralists.

***funeralize,** *v. tr.* and *intr.* (See quot. 1859.) — **1859** BARTLETT 164 *To Funeralize,* to perform the clerical duties preparatory to a funeral. Southern. **1948** *Time* 13 Dec. 29/1 Four days after his death, in the shed-like white church at the edge of a rutted white-clay road, his children, grandchildren and great-grandchildren gathered to funeralize Uncle Row.

fungo ˈfʌŋgo, *n.* [Origin unknown. The manufacturers of fungo bats (see **c.** below) are unable to account for the name.] (See quots.)

1867 CHADWICK *Base Ball Reference* 138 Fungoes.—A preliminary practice game in which one player takes the bat and tossing the ball up hits it as it falls, and if the ball is caught in the field on the fly, the player catching it takes the bat. It is useless as practice in batting, but good for taking fly balls. **1891** *Amer. Folk-Lore* IV. 232 Fungo. The game is played on a vacant lot, or in the middle of a wide street. One boy is chosen for batsman, and the others stand around at some distance from him. A base ball is used, and the batsman throws it in the air, and then bats it out to the fielders, who endeavor to catch the ball 'on the fly.' The one who first catches the ball, a certain number of times that has been agreed upon, takes the batsman's place for another game.

b. A ball knocked out in this game. Also attrib.

1910 *Amer. Mag.* Jan. 383/2 Wagner gave him a fearful pounding, making that marvelous slow 'knuckle ball' look as if it were a lobbed ball for 'fungo' hitting. **1915** *Sat. Ev. Post* 31 July 16/1 Then him and Carey was together in left field catching fungoes. **1948** *Chi. Star* 1 May 6/1 Behind his back three lads are knocking out fungoes.

c. fungo bat, a light bat, often with an enlarged end, for knocking out fungoes or flies.

1938 *Chi. Times* 9 Nov., Cap. Trebmal . . . sends a diagram of the lettering on his own fungo bat, now twenty-five years old.

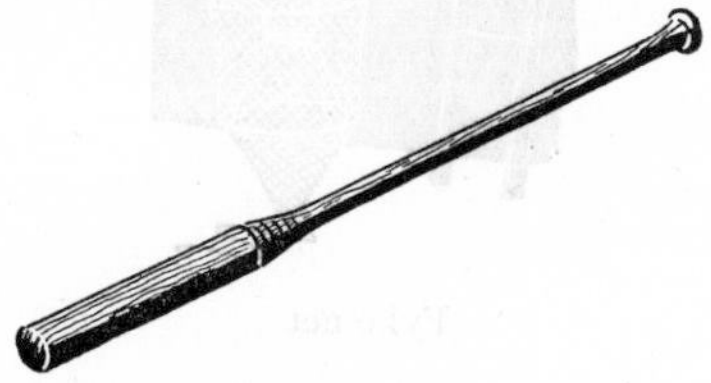

Fungo bat

Funk fʌŋk, *n.* =**Peter Funk.** *Colloq.*

1845 *Quincy* (Ill.) *Whig* 4 Nov. 2/4 He threw down his money on the counter and walked off, leaving the Funks in utter amazement, for the lot was worth at least eighty-five dollars. **1853** *Mt. Echo* (Downieville, Calif.) 30 April 1/5 The Vermonter examined the watch carefully, and the bidding among the outside Funks assumed an aspect of profound interest. **1858** *N.Y. Tribune* 30 July 7/6 A stranger named Jacob Gable complained to the Mayor on Thursday afternoon that he had invested $8 in a make-believe watch at No. 2 Park row. Jackman, the Funk, was made by Officer Place to refund the money.

attrib. **1857** *S.F. Call.* 5 Feb. 2/3 Queer things were brought to light by the fire. A 'Funk' shop, that appeared to have plenty of goods, was found to be well stocked with bundles of straw representing packages of shirts, etc.

Hence **Funker,** in the same sense. *Obs.*

1852 *Lantern* (N.Y.) I. 239/1 Petronius Funk, Fictitious Auctioneer. Wylie, Bonnett, Associate Funkers.

***funnel,** *n.* A sink or sinkhole. *Obs.*

1791 W. BARTRAM *Travels* 246 The ground . . . [presented] to view, those funnels, sinks and wells in groups of rocks. **1814** BRACKENRIDGE *Louisiana* 106 A strange appearance is also given by the number of funnels, or sink holes, formed by the washing of the earth into fissures of the limestone rock. [**1823** LONG *Exped.* I. 54 They [sinkholes] are in the form of vast funnels.]

***funny,** *a.* and *n.*

1. *n. pl.* Orig. jokes, witticisms, cartoons, etc., in a newspaper; later comic strips, or the section of a newspaper devoted to these. Cf. **comic strip.**

1852 *Lantern* (N.Y.) II. 114/1 It is our desire . . . to give full reports of the Market, keeping our dear public advised of all operations in the 'Funnies.' The past week has been very dull, very; Puns have gone down when a good article was offered, but Jokes are flat. **1920** C. SANDBURG *Smoke & Steel* 33 About the funnies in the papers. **1948** *Dly. Ardmoreite* (Ardmore, Okla.) 27 May 5/1 There are more than 40 million copies a year in circulation of these funnies, most of which are far from funny.

2. *a.* Denoting portions of a newspaper devoted to or made up of cartoons, jokes, comics, witty paragraphs, etc. See also **funny paper.**

1860 HANCOCK *Five Years* 93 A glance at the 'funny' column of any American journal will testify, and bear the impress of the national taste and temperament. **1880** MARK TWAIN *Tramp Abroad* 626 [German newspapers] contain no 'editorials' whatever; no 'personal' . . . ; no funny-paragraph column. **1931** *K.C. Times* 31 Aug., A Kansas congress member says that if one will confide in him as to which of the 'funny strips' one most enjoys he will promptly indicate what sort of a chap one is.

3. In special combs.: (1) **funny business,** deceitful or treacherous conduct, also, rarely, **funny dope,** *slang;* (2) **man,** a professional humorist; (3) **paper,** a paper largely or entirely devoted to fun or humor; (4) **pictures,** pictures such as appear in the funny papers.

(1) **1883** NYE *Baled Hay* 38 There was no funny business in his nature. **1915** FOREST & DILNOT *Crime Club* xii, Especially if you try to put any of the funny dope over on me. **1931** *K.C. Times* 28 Aug., Funny Business in Rock Port. — (2) **1852** *Lantern* (N.Y.) I. 111/1 Listen to the modern Funnyman of the world, the Democritus of New York. **1877** *Amer. Union* (S.F.) 30 Aug. 1/3 Both were employed on the Enterprise—Dan as the 'rock sharp' and Mark as the 'funny man.' **1948** *Ariz. Republic* (Phoenix) 2 Mar. 8/1 A funnyman named Henny Youngman is currently entertaining at the Copacabana.— (3) **1874** HEARN *Amer. Miscellany* (1924) I. 20 The public cannot comprehend or appreciate so lofty an order of humor . . . , therefore strenuous effords shall be made to convince the said public that the said *Giglampz* is not a funny paper. **1947** *Redbook* July 24/1 Up to then, gossip had been just something to laugh about, something 'corny' out of the funny papers. — (4) **1857** *Spirit of Times* 7 Mar. 6/3 Full many funny pictures I've bought and owned since then. **1910** *Bookman* May 288/2 Ask the maker of funny pictures how or where he secures his ideas, . . . and he will probably confess that he does not know.

***fur,** *n.* In combs.: (1) **fur brigade,** =**brigade 2;** (2) **country,** a region where fur-bearing animals abound; (3) **dealer,** one who engages in the buying and selling of furs; (4) **hunter,** one who hunts fur-bearing animals to secure their fur or pelts; (5) **trader,** one engaged in the fur trade; (6) **trading,** *a.* relating to trade in furs.

(1) **1948** *Chi. Tribune* 25 April 1. 24/3 Trappers for the fur brigades . . . led the way over mountain and desert trails. — (2) **1839** AUDUBON *Ornith. Biog.* V. 38 Arctic Blue Bird . . . [is] a summer visitor to the Fur Countries. *Ib.* 474 [The] Blue Jay . . . visits the Fur Countries, in summer up to the 56th parallel. **1874** COUES *Birds N.W.* 355, I have never heard of it [the red-shouldered buzzard] from the fur countries. — (3) **1819** *Niles' Reg.* XVI. 405/2 Whatsoever has a tendency to settle them [i.e., the Indians] down to a state of quietness and plenty, derivable from the cultivation of the earth, is in enmity to the fur dealer. **1920** *Lit. Digest* 28 Feb. 42/1 American fur dealers say this country has become the center of the fur industry. — (4) **1836** RUSCHENBERGER *Narrative* (1838) II. 410 While at Monte-rey, the ship was visited by several trappers or fur hunters of the 'far west.' **1894** in *So. Dak. Hist. Coll.* I. 275 It was during this year that three experienced fur hunters . . . formed a partnership for the Indian trade.

(5) **1819** *Niles' Reg.* XVI. 406/1 You must have been particularly struck with . . . the 4th division of the essay, entitled—'the protection of the Missouri fur traders.' **1946** STANWELL-FLETCHER *Driftwood Valley* 7 Apparently their only contacts with white civilization have come from business with fur traders. — **(6)** *c***1834** CATLIN *Indians* II. 29 St. Louis . . . is the great depot of all the Fur Trading Companies to the Upper Missouri and Rocky Mountains. **1880** *Harper's Mag.* Dec. 31 There was scarcely a family on the island that did not cherish its tradition of the merry fur-trading times when 'grandfather' was a factor, a superintendent. **1911** *N. Amer. Rev.* March 390 One man in America grasped the possibilities of . . . a company that would form a line of fur-trading posts along the southern border of the Great Lakes.

b. *To make the fur fly, fig.* to thrash soundly, create a commotion, precipitate a brawl, etc. *Colloq.*

1814 *Niles' Reg.* VI. 67/2 Smugglers look out, or you will soon see 'the fur fly.' **1896** *N.Y. Dramatic News* 4 July 7/1 Al Hayman is going to make the fur fly when he gets back from Europe. **1932** *Screenland* April 100/1 But, baby, does the fur fly if she has a crying scene to do.

As the last term in **musquash, raccoon fur.**

furlough ˈfɜlo, *v. tr.* To give (a soldier) leave of absence, also transf.

1781 *Va. State P.* I. 589 He has thought it proper to furlough all the drafted men, until their bounties are paid them according to law. **1881** BUEL *Border Outlaws* 100 Meeting . . . furloughed militia, it was an inflexible rule to kill them. **1931** *Randolph Enterprise* (Elkins, W.Va.) 5 March 4/4 He got furloughed at the Sabraton shops last summer.

* **furnace,** *n.* As the last term in **agricultural, cooking, Franklin, log, salt, shaft furnace.**

furnishing store. A store in which supplies, furnishings, or wearing apparel may be purchased. — **1848** BRYANT *California* i. 14 Messrs. Wilson & Clarke . . . keep a general furnishing store for these expeditions. **1898** *Scribner's Mag.* XXIII. 455/2 He went back into the business portion of the city, sought a cheap furnishing-store, and bought a modest suit of clothing.

* **furniture,** *n.* In combs.: (1) **furniture check,** cloth of a check or checkered pattern for use in covering furniture, *obs.;* (2) **store,** a store in which furniture is sold; (3) **wagon,** (see quot. 1948); (4) **wareroom,** a display room for furniture, a furniture store, *obs.*

Furniture wagon

(1) 1762 *Boston News Letter* 25 March 4/3 To be sold by Nathaniel Williams . . . the following Goods . . . furniture Check, Cambricks [etc.]. **1843** *Amer. Pioneer* II. 446 The [bed] curtains were, very likely, partly, if not wholly, of good old furniture check, which, with many other relics of times gone by, were treasured by the family. — **(2) 1877** JOHNSON *Anderson Co., Kansas* 176 F. G. Burns opened a furniture store on the corner of Sixth avenue and Cedar street in 1857. **1948** *Kankakee* (Ill.) *D. Jrnl.* 5 June 1/1 As the flames died this morning, broken walls were all that was left of the brick furniture store building. — **(3) 1844** *Lexington Observer* 25 Sep. 4/6 Having provided himself with a Furniture Wagon, all articles bought of him will be delivered. **1894** ALLEN *Ky. Cardinal* vii., Sylvia was invited to sit with a bevy of girls in a large furniture wagon covered with flags. **1948** RITTENHOUSE *Vehicles* 90 Furniture Wagon. A spring wagon especially designed for hauling furniture. Design of the sides permitted ease in lashing loads, and the use of three springs at both front and rear cushioned the load on cobblestone streets. — **(4) 1844** *Lexington Observer* 20 July 4/4 (*advt.*), Furniture Ware-Room, Immediately Opposite Brennan's Hotel, Main St. **1873** PHELPS *Trotty's Wedding* vii, H. Jasper kept furniture warerooms.

As the last term in **cabinet, mission, saloon, store furniture.**

* **furrow,** *n. To draw a straight furrow,* or variant (see quot. 1848). *Colloq. Obs.* — **1847** LOWELL *Biglow P.* 1 Ser. iii. 34 Guverner B. is a sensible man; He stays to his home an' looks arter his folks, He draws his furrer ez straight ez he can, An' into nobody's tater-patch pokes. **1848** *Ib.* (Glossary) 144/2 Metaphorically, to draw a straight furrow is to live uprightly or decorously.

As the last term in **back, dead, disk, double furrow.**

* **furrowing,** *n.* (See quot.) *Obs.* — **1790** DEANE *N.-Eng. Farmer* 110/2 Furrowing in this country is understood to mean marking ground into little squares with a horse-plough, in order to plant Indian-corn.

* **Fury,** *n.* An officer of a certain rank and position in the Ku-Klux Klan. — **1867** *Prescript of the* ** [*Ku-Klux Klan*] 5 He shall have power to appoint his Furies; also to appoint a Grand Scribe and a Grand Exchequer for his department. **1924** *Amer. Mercury* Feb. 207/1, I think that my friend Chill Burton is an Exalted Cyclops, although he may be only a Fury, or a lesser Titan.

fusion ticket. A ticket agreed upon as a result of a fusion. Also **fusion electoral ticket.**

1855 *Chi. Times* 3 Feb. 2/1 Think of the minister . . . thundering forth the anathemas of the 'church' against all men who will not vote the 'fusion' ticket. **1876** *N.Y. Tribune* Oct. (B), Some steps are being taken to secure after the State election a union of the Greenbackers and the Democrats on a fusion electoral ticket. **1896** *Daily News* (London) 27 July 7/5 Great difficulties are inevitable in making a fusion ticket in the various States.

* **fuss,** *n.*

1. = **fuss-budget.** *Colloq.*

1875 HOWELLS *Foregone Conclusion* 75, I am a fuss, and I don't deny it. **1880** ALDRICH *Stillwater Tragedy* ix. 98 I hope you are not a fidget. A what? A fuss then,—a person who always wants everything some other way.

2. fuss-budget, one who makes much ado about trifles. *Colloq.*

1904 *D.N.* II. 397 fuss-budget. . . . A nervous, fidgety person. **1948** MATHEWS *Southernisms* 2 Cartoons representing them as funny old fuss-budgets without much practical sense.

3. Fuss and Feathers, (see quots.). Cf. **Old Fuss and Feathers.**

1852 *Fredericksburg News* 12 July 2/6 'Fuss and Feathers.'—This epithet is used in derision by all of our adversaries. . . . The Covington (Ky.) Journal says: 'The epithet, "Fuss and Feathers," was first applied to Scott at Lundy's Lane, by the British.' **1892** W. S. WALSH *Literary Curiosities* 402 Fuss and Feathers, a nickname given to General Winfield Scott by his detractors, intimating that he was 'fussy,' vain, and self-important.

Fyke net

* **fuss,** *v. tr.* and *intr. To fuss up,* to "dike" or "doll" up, to make neat or pretty. *Colloq.* — **1873** PHELPS *Trotty's Wedding* xvi, I wonder why girls fuss up and boys don't? **1875** STOWE *We & Neighbors* vi. 69, I told her the way she is beginning—of petting Mary, and fussing up her room with carpet and pictures . . . —wouldn't work.

fuste ˈfustɪ, *n. W.* [Sp. in Amer. Sp. sense similar to that shown here.] A Mexican saddle or saddle-tree of wooden construction. — **1844** GREGG *Commerce of Prairies* 212 (Bentley), A cover of embossed leather embroidered with fancy silk and tinsel, with ornaments of silver, is thrown loose over the cushion and fuste or saddle-tree. **1932** BENTLEY *Dict. Spanish Terms* 138 The *fuste* is rarely used by the American cowboy or rider and is becoming less popular with the Mexican vaqueros who are adopting the American cowboy saddle.

fute fjut, *n. local.* [Prob. f. the obs. verb. **fute,* to whistle.] The Eskimo curlew. — **1844** J. P. GIRAUD *Birds of Long Island* 274 In the vicinity of New York it is known by the name of 'Futes'—in the Eastern States it is called 'Doe Bird.' **1917** *Birds of Amer.* I. 254.

Future State. (See quot.) *Obs.* — **1846** LYELL *Second Visit* (1849) II. 16 New York is called the Empire State, . . . and Vermont, when the question of its separation from New Hampshire was long under discussion 'the Future State.'

***futurity,** *n.* A race held long after the competitors are nominated or entered for the contest. Also attrib. Cf. **Kentucky Futurity.**

1886 *Outing* Mar. 722/2 The Futurity—a produce stake for two-year olds, to be run at Sheepshead Bay in 1888—attracted 758 entries, the largest entry ever made to any one stake. **1902** *Encycl. Brit.* XXIX. 336/2 The Futurity Stakes, the richest event of the year . . . is for two-year-olds, and is run at Sheepshead Bay. **1947** *Dly. Racing Form* (Chi.) 6 Nov. 36/1 Pimlico will stage its Futurity on Saturday with the Exterminator Handicap the secondary feature. When the entries closed for the Futurity in December of 1944, no less than 601 were nominated for the race.

f.w.c. Abbreviation of "free woman of color." *Obs.* Cf. **f.m.c.** — **1840** *N.O. Picayune* 16 Aug. 2/2 Widow Louis Dupré, *f.w.c.* sworn. **1936** [see **f.m.c.**].

fyke faɪk, *n.* [Du. *fuik*, a bow net.]

1. =**fyke net.** Cf. **shad fyke.**

1832 in DE VOE *Market Ass't* (1867) 197 While some men were rowing up Newtown Creek, day before yesterday, they discovered a sea-dog stealing bass from a fuik of a bass-net. **1871** *N.Y. Laws 1685* The meshes . . . of fykes set in any of the waters surrounding Long Island, Fire Island, Staten Island . . . [shall be] not less than four and one-half inches in size. **1903** *N.Y. Ev. Post* 20 Oct. 3 He stopped up the stream with the exception of one narrow outlet, in which he placed his fyke. **1942** WEYGANDT *Plenty of Penna.* 45 They snig many an eel from the little ponds and they set fykes for the up-stream run of suckers in March.

2. In combs.: (1) **fyke fence,** (see quot.); (2) **fisherman,** (see quot.); (3) **net,** a hoop net for taking fish.

(1) **1858** *Harper's Wkly.* 24 April 267/1 To the uninitiated I would describe a fyke fence as a string of twigs, of a heavy growth, made like the panels of a fence and fastened to poles driven into the mud. An opening is left in the centre of this contrivance, to which a circular net is affixed, so that all fish coming with the tide, finding a barrier before their further progress up or down the river, turn aside, and pass into this inevitable net. — (2) **1889** *Cent.* 2422/2 *Fyke-fisherman*, . . . one who fishes with a fyke. — (3) **1842** *Nat. Hist. N.Y., Zoology* I. 54 Mr. Everson . . . has taken them [*sc.* common seals or sea dogs], almost every year, in the River Passaic, in the fyke-nets. **1908** BAILEY *Harmful & Beneficial Mammals* 13 This is practically the fyke net used for catching fish.

G

*G, see *grand 1.

gabfest ˈgæbˌfɛst, *n.* (See quot. 1919.) *Colloq.* Cf. **fest.**

1897 *Boston Transcript* 7 Jan. 15/7 A Chicago paper speaks of the speechmaking on Andrew Jackson's day as 'the Democratic gabfest.' **1919** *Editor & Publisher* 25 Dec. 30 (Mencken '36), McCullagh coined the word while writing a comment upon an unusually prolonged and empty debate in Congress.... As a great percentage of the readers of the *Globe-Democrat* throughout the Central West were of German birth or origin, *gabfest* was seized upon with hearty zest, and it is to-day very generally applied to any protracted and particularly loquacious gathering. **1949** *Ev. Northwestern* (Chi.) 11 April 2/4 Plans are made for a combination food-fest and gab-fest.

Gabrieleño ˌgebrɪəˈlino, *n. S.W.* [Sp., "one from (the mission of San) Gabriel," near Los Angeles.] A division of Shoshonean Indians formerly occupying chiefly all of Los Angeles County, Calif.; also an Indian of this division.

1883 JACKSON *Ramona* 310 An old woman, a Gabrieleno, who came over into Temecula, told me she saw that. **1930** CAREW *Hist. Pasadena* I. 73 The customs of the Juaneño were very similar to those of Gabrieliño. **1946** MCWILLIAMS *So. Calif. Country* 26 The Gabrieleno and the Chumash had shell fish hooks distinctly Micronesian in form. *attrib.* **1949** *L.A. Times* 25 April II. 1/3 The native Indian name is believed to be the Chumash pronunciation of the Gabrieleno word Haras-nga.

gachupin ˌgɑtʃuˈpin, *n. S.W.* [See note.] A Spaniard.

This term passed into American English from the Spanish of the Southwest. Santamaría favors deriving the Sp. *gachupín* from a Nahuatl expression meaning "a man with prickers," a term the natives may well have applied to Spanish horsemen in allusion to their wearing spurs.

1811 tr. HUMBOLDT *Political Essay* I. 153 Whites born in Europe... bear the name of *Chapetones* or *Gachupines*. **1842** *Texas Times* (Galveston) 7 Dec. 1/3, I do not like to oblige the *gachupins;* they never pay me. **1886** H. H. MCLANE *Irene Viesca* 79 (Bentley), They took a large caballada of horses and mules belonging to the Gauchipins. **1931** M. AUSTIN *Starry Adventure* 100 He was a gauchapin, whatever that meant.

* **gad,** *n. local.* A mark or cut made in the ears of cattle to indicate ownership, usu. **fore** or **hind(er) gad.** *Obs.*

1666 *Portsmouth Rec.* 265 Gadd one...[entry mutilated].... Cattle a gadd one... [entry mutilated]. **1667** *Ib.* 269 A fore gadd one the r[ight ear] The eare marke... is two hinder gads. The eare marke... is a hinder gadd. **1845** *Ib.* 390 The Ear mark of the Creatures of Edward Anthony is a hind Gad on the left ear.

* **Gadsden,** *n. Hist.* Used attrib., esp. with **purchase,** with reference to the purchase from Mexico in 1853 of the territory now forming the southern parts of New Mexico and Arizona bordering on Mexico, James Gadsden (1788–1858) being then U.S. minister to Mexico.

1856 *Western Citizen* (Paris, Ky.) 26 Dec. 2/4 A want of water, a scarcity of soil, an excess of gravel, a superfluity of serpents, and paucity of population, are the distinguishing characteristics of that part of the Gadsden Purchase proposed to be erected into a Territory now, and into a State soon, under the name of Arezonia. **1857** BENTON *Exam. Dred Scott Case* 193, I speak of the Gadsden negotiation, and of the fifty millions he was authorized to give for a broad side of Mexico, with a port on the Gulf of California. **1861** in M. WILLSON DISHER *Cowells in Amer.* (1934) 286 Arizona is 'the Gadsden country, the territory acquired by the Gadsden treaty, and for which the U.S. paid ten millions of dollars to Mexico.' **1941** FERGUSSON *Southwest* 64 The United States honorably ended the discussion by the Gadsden Purchase, which gave us 45,535 square miles of territory for ten million dollars and the cancellation of certain Mexican debts. **1949** *Iowa Jrnl. Hist.* Jan. 14 Like the northern railroad promoters who used their influence in Congress against the Gadsden purchase, Davis considered sectional advantages to be of paramount importance.

* **gaff,** *n.* In phrases: *To get, give, stand, take the gaff,* to get, give, etc., the severest kind of treatment, criticism, etc. *Slang.* See also **chicken gaff.**

1896 ADE *Artie* xii. 111 If he gets the gaff [fails to be elected as alderman], he'll be flat on his back. **1899** A. THOMAS *Arizona* 124 All we care about now is, will they [hired men] stand the gaff? Will they set sixty hours in the saddle, holdin' a herd that's tryin' to stampede all the time? **1903** STEFFENS in *McClure's Mag.* Oct. 563 'Good,' they cheer, when you find fault; 'give us the gaff. We deserve it and it does us good.' **1913** LA FOLLETTE *Autobiog.* 435 Bob has been taking the gaff all these years, and isn't going to take it alone any longer. **1921** PAINE *Comr. Rolling Ocean* 66 It was dead white of you to stand the gaff and keep your mouth shut.

* **gaff,** *v. tr.* To equip (a fighting cock) with gaffs.

1837 *S. Lit. Messenger* III. 218 In gaffing a cock, I became supreme. **1886** PAGE in *Harper's Mag.* Dec. 38/2 He could gaff a chicken as well as Drinkwater Torm. **1908** LORIMER *J. Spurlock* 151 If one cock won't fight, we must gaff another.

* **gag,** *n.*[1]

1. In a legislative body, a law or ruling designed to restrict or prevent discussion on a particular subject. Also transf. Cf. **Atherton gag.**

The so-called "gag" tactics have been resorted to chiefly in Congress with reference to the restriction of the freedom of the press in 1798 and the suppression of the discussion of slavery from 1836 to 1844.

1840 J. Q. ADAMS *Memoirs* X. 273 Then came Atherton, of New Hampshire, the man of the mongrel gag. **1882** MORSE *J. Q. Adams* (1892) 252 Regularly in each new Congress when the adoption of rules came up, Mr. Adams moved to rescind the 'gag.' **1947** *Newsweek* 29 Dec. 19/3 Leader Alben W. Barkley, although denouncing the Taft measure as 'utterly inadequate and incomplete,' could not cry 'gag' as Democratic leaders in the House had done.

b. Attrib. with (1) **act,** (2) **bill,** (3) **law,** (4) **rule,** (5) **system.**

(1) **1803** B. AUSTIN *Constitutional Republicanism* xxxix. 159 If Mr. Jefferson should pursue them [the Federalists] in the same manner as was formerly practised, their personal cowardice would be sufficient 'gag-act' to check their insolence. — (2) **1798** *Aurora* (Phila.) 1 Aug. (Th.), Have the Cherokees any gag-bill? — (3) **1799** *Ann. 5th Congress* III. 2698 Who knows but... that it may be desirable they [the French] may come here... for preventing the British party from keeping up a system of alarm; in order to induce the people to believe... that the gag-law is a blessing? **1875** J. F. CLARKE in *N. Amer. Rev.* Jan. 62 It took ten years to accomplish the actual repeal of these gag-laws. — (4) **1810** *Mass. Spy* 7 Feb. (Th.), It is to be hoped the majority in Congress will extend the Gag Rule to fiddles, and the whole tribe of musical instruments. **1944** *Reader's Digest* August 28 It cannot understand how the membership stands for the dictatorial methods by which the leaders carry on, and the gag rules that bar criticisms of the officials in power. — (5) **1841** *Cong. Globe* 215/1 He had resorted to the gag system to prevent discussion.

2. One who is the object of ridicule or jest. *Rare.*

1840 HALIBURTON *Clockmaker* 3 Ser. ii, Sam, says he, they tell me you broke down the other day in the house of representatives, and made a proper gag of yourself.

3. gag man, one who makes up jokes for plays or actors. *Slang.*

1928 *Sunday Express* 15 Jan. 4 'Gag men' have long flourished in America. One of them thought of making the villain sit on a red-hot stove. **1928** *Collier's* 29 Dec. 28/3 'What you need is a smart gag man,' I say.

4. gagroot, (see quot.).

1889 *Cent.* 2429/2 *Gagroot,* ... The *Lobelia inflata,* so called from its emetic properties: more usually known as *Indian tobacco.*

gag gæg, *n.*[2] [Origin obscure, poss. same word as preceding.] A common name for the grouper, *Trisotropis microlepis,* or a fish of an allied species, found on the southern coast of the U.S.

1884 GOODE *Fisheries* I. 413 There appear to be... at Key West, as well as in Bermuda, various local forms closely related to this [the rockfish], one of which is known by the name 'Gag.' **1896** JORDAN &

EVERMANN *Fishes Amer.* 1177 *Mycteroperca Microlepsis* (Gag). . . . South Atlantic and Gulf Coast of the United States. . . . Along the coast of Florida it is generally abundant on the banks and reefs.

Gageite ˈgedʒart, *n.* A British soldier serving in this country in the army of Gen. Thomas Gage (1721–87). *Obs.* — **1775** PAUL LUNT *Diary* 7 The Gageites fired upon our troops at Roxbury, hove a number of carcasses and bombs, but did no damage. **1775** in JOHNSTON *N. Hale* 165 The number of those Slain in the Battle between Putnam and the Gagites is uncertain.

Gaillardia geˈlɑrdɪə, *n.* [f. *Gaillard* de Marentonneau, a French botanist.] A genus of showy composite plants, family Carduaceae, native from Texas to Alberta, and popular as garden flowers. Also (not *cap.*) a plant of this genus.

1910 WARD *Canadian Born* 206 Anderson had brought her to a wild garden of incredible beauty . . . harebell, speedwell, golden-brown gaillardias. **1929** BAILEY *Cyclo. Horticulture* 1307/1 The gaillardias are conspicuous for profusion and duration of flowers. **1937** PARKS *Valuable Plants Texas* 150 [This is] a peculiar Gaillardia found in all parts of the state with the exception of piney woods and Gulf Coast. **1948** *Dly. Ardmoreite* (Ardmore, Okla.) 11 July 21/4 Dixie and I enjoyed the fields of coreopsis and gaillardias.

gain gen, *n.*[1] [Origin unknown.] (See quot. 1883.)

1838 ELLSWORTH *Valley of Wabash* v. 55 A cylindrical saw excavates a small 'gain,' eight feet from the bottom of the studs. **1874** KNIGHT 935/1 *Gaining-machine.* . . . Two circular saws are placed at a distance apart equal to the width of the desired gain. **1883** — *Supp.* 366/1 *Gain,* a notch, as made in the side or edge of a piece of timber to receive another bar of the frame.

* **gain,** *n.*[2]

1. *W.* An amount (of gold) gained or obtained in mining. *Obs.*

1849 *Lady's Western Mag.* June 174/1 One of them showed us a gain of gold since that is the agreed term for it, of the size of an orange.

2. *On the gain,* getting better. *Colloq.*

1850 MITCHELL *Lorgnette* iii. 57 The town is certainly on the gain in these matters. **1850** KINGSLEY *Diary* 101 The sick are on the gain. **1894** R. E. ROBINSON *Danvis Folks* 4 Their mother . . . had been ill for weeks with an intermittent fever, but was now 'on the gain.'

Gairdner's woodpecker. [Meredith *Gairdner* (d. 1837), Scottish naturalist.] A variety of downy woodpecker found along the Pacific Coast.

1839 AUDUBON *Ornith. Biog.* V. 317 Gairdner's Woodpecker. *Picus Gairdnerii.* **1917** *Birds of Amer.* II. 142/2 There are five other varieties of the Downy [Woodpecker] scattered over temperate North America: . . . Gairdner's Woodpecker (*Dryobates pubescens gairdneri*) along the Pacific coast from southern British Columbia to northern California [etc.]. **1940** GABRIELSON & JEWETT *Birds of Oregon* 385 Audubon (1839) described Gairdner's Woodpecker . . . from specimens collected at Fort Vancouver, Oregon.

* **gait,** *n.* Trade, occupation, way of livelihood. *Slang.*

1859 MATSELL *Vocabulum* 35, 'I say, Tim, what's your gait now?' 'Why, you see, I'm on the crack,' (burglary). **1865** MARK TWAIN *Sk., New & Old* 74 Preachin' was his nateral gait, but he warn't a man to lay back . . . because there didn't happen to be nothin' doin' in his own especial line. **1889** FARMER 257/1 In the patter of the criminal classes, one's *gait* does not so much refer to style or pace in walking, as, by a curious transition, to one's 'walk in life'; calling; trade; profession—in short, the manner of making a living is one's *gait.*

* **gaiter,** *n.* A shoe having uppers wholly or partially of cloth, a Congress boot. In full **gaiter boot, shoe.** Cf. **Congress gaiter.**

1793 T. COXE *View U.S.* 121 Not less than eight millions of pair of shoes, boots, half boots, gueters, . . . and goloshoes, are annually consumed in or exported from the United States. **1840** *N.O. Picayune* 30 July 2/4 Many of the ladies of Philadelphia . . . now wear . . . gaiter boots, with little straps of black leather. **1849** WILLIS *Rural Lett.* 230 Dandies . . . stealing an occasional look at their loose *demi-saison* pantaloons and gaiter-shoes. **1889** RILEY *Pipes o' Pan* 66 He heard . . . the quick italicized patter of determined gaiters down the hall. **1908** *D.N.* III. 313.

Galax ˈgelæks, *n.* [App. based on Gk. *gala,* milk, in allusion to its white flowers.] (See quot. 1889.)

1753 C. LINNAEUS *Species Plantarum* (1762) I. 289 Galax. 1. Galax. . . . *Habitat in* Virginia. **1850** TORREY *Plantae Fremontianae* 19 The genus Galax . . . was first referred to Ericaceae by Michaux, and afterwards to a separate tribe of Pyrolaceae by De Candolle. **1889** *Cent.* 2432/3 *Galax,* . . . a genus of plants, referred to the natural order *Diapensiaceæ,* of a single species, *G. aphylla,* found in open woods from Virginia to Georgia. **1901** MOHR *Plant Life Ala.* 661 *Diapensiaceæ.* Diapensia Family. *Galax.* . . . One species, Atlantic America. *Galax aphylla.* . . . Galax.

b. (not *cap.*) A plant of this genus. Also attrib.

1922 M. B. HOUSTON *Witch-man* xi, The darkly polished galax leaves. **1941** R. S. WALKER *Lookout* 53 Galax . . . is one of the plants that is more highly prized for is round heart-shaped evergreen leaf than for its long spikelike raceme of white flowers. **1943** PEATTIE *Great Smokies* 337 In the woods across the road from the parking place are great clumps of galax.

gal boy. *local.* (See quots.) — **1848** BARTLETT 153 *Gal-boy.* In New England, a romping girl; called also a *tom-boy.* **1881** TOURGEE *'Zouri's Christmas* vi, [The boy's father] was afraid he was going to grow up a 'milksop sort of gal-boy, anyhow.'

* **gale,** *n. fig.* A state of pleasant excitement or hilarity. See also **line gale.**

1838 *S. Lit. Messenger* IV. 65/2 On the way Wirt was in 'a great gale'; his spirits high, his hopes buoyant, his gaiety of heart overflowing. **1885** HOWELLS *S. Lapham* ix, And we had such a laugh! We got into a regular gale. **1948** *Reader's Digest* Sep. 70 The congregation went into gales of laughter, and the minister promptly closed the service.

* **Galena,** *n.* [In **2,** and poss. in **1.** also, in allusion to *Galena,* Ill., noted for its lead mines.] **1.** (See quot.) **2. Galena (blue) pill,** (see quot. 1846 and cf. **blue pill**). Both *obs.*

(1) 1856 *Rep. Comm. Patents 1855: Agric.* 220 Potatoes, in this section [Allegheny Co., Pa.], are one of our most profitable crops. Several varieties are cultivated. The 'Mercer,' the 'Pinkeye,' the 'Galena,' and the 'Long Reds,' are the principal. — **(2) 1846** *Hancock Eagle* (Nauvoo, Ill.) 10 April 3/1 'Galena blue pills' is another name for bullets in this region. **1849** *Lady's Western Mag.* April 98/1 Crack!—aha my old fellow! But no!—he turns away and shakes his head as much as to say, 'One Galena pill is no dose for me—come on with a whole lead mine!'

* **gall,** *n.*

1. Short for **gallberry.** *Rare.*

1860 CURTIS *Woody Plants N.C.* 60 *Gallberry.* (*I[lex] glabra,* Gray.)—This and the next species are evergreen shrubs, indiscriminately called by the above name, sometimes *Galls,* more rarely *Inkberries,* names apparently derived from their black bitter berries.

2. *fig.* Brazen impudence, effrontery. *Slang.*

1882 *Denver Republican* 23 Jan. 4/1 There is only one word which thoroughly expresses the quality of Dr. Anderson's communication. That word is the strong expression, 'gall.' **1921** MULFORD *Bar-20 Three* 195 You got plenty of gall, comin' down here an' throwin' a gun on me, for that! **1947** *Chi. Herald-Amer.* 7 Feb. 3/1 The gall of this inveterate crook . . . is as fascinating as any other phase of his revolting character.

3. In combs.: (1) **gallberry,** = **inkberry,** also attrib., cf. **tall gallberry;** (2) **bitters,** *W.* a beverage or tonic made of buffalo gall diluted in water, *obs.;* (3) **breaker,** (see quot.), *obs.;* (4) **bug,** (see quot.), *obs.;* (5) **bush,** a gallberry bush; (6) **nut,** (see quot.).

(1) 1709 LAWSON *Carolina* 90 Gall-Berry-Tree, bearing a black Berry, with which the Women dye their Cloaths and Yarn black; 'tis a pretty Ever-green, and very plentiful. **1859** G. W. PERRY *Turpentine Farming* 9 After this, the land needs no cultivation, but every kind of turf should be turned over, such as low bush huckleberry, gallberry, percosan bush. **1947** *Sports Afield* Dec. 20/3 The sand road twisted into a thicket of pine and gallberry for 15 miles to Jones Island landing. — **(2) 1846** SAGE *Scenes Rocky Mts.* xvi. 133 Were those labouring under . . . this disease [dyspepsia] to drink gall-bitters . . . [thousands] would be restored to perfect soundness. — **(3) 1810** J. LAMBERT *Travels U.S.* III. 82 A gall-breaker, is about half a pint of ardent spirits. — **(4) 1837** WILLIAMS *Florida* 69 Gall Bug.—chermes. An insect similar in appearance to the puceron, but the chermes enter the twig, or leaf, and raise an excrescence about it which we call gall-nut.

(5) 1728 in *N.C. Col. Rec.* II. (1886) 802 They measured . . . 16 chains and 70 links to a Gall Bush. **1853** SIMMS *Sword & Distaff* 81 The gall-bushes which are apt to associate with it [the 'hurrah-bush'], mass themselves together with a luxuriance of top which effectually closes every aperture of sight. — **(6) 1837** [see **gall bug**].

b. * *gall of the earth,* the lion's foot, *Prenanthes serpentaria,* a species of sow thistle.

1804 MICHAUX *Voyage à l'Ouest* 160 Au milieu de ces graminées, croît une grande variété de plantes, parmi lesquelles dominoient alors: la *Gerardia flava, gall of the earth.* **1840** DEWEY *Mass. Flowering Plants* 120 At the South, . . . S[*onchus*] *Floridanus,* is used as a remedy for the poison of the rattlesnake, and is called *Gall of the Earth.* **1933** SMALL *Southeastern Flora* 1490 Nabalus. . . . Rattlesnake-roots. White-lettuces. Lion's-foot. Gall-of-the-earth.

As the last term in **bay, buffalo, clay, cypress, tomato gall.**

∗ **gallery**, *n.*

1. The studio of a photographer.

1866 *Harper's Mag.* Oct. 677/2 There came along a photographer and his wife.... In furnishing the 'gallery' the happy couple got into some dispute. **1903** *Cin. Enquirer* 3 May 5 We will reopen our new Improved and Modern Gallery, now under the management of a New York Photographer, and with a French Modelist and Draper in attendance. *c***1918** G. Stuart *On Frontier* II. 23 Mr. A. M. Smith arrived in Virginia City with a camera and photographic supplies and opened a gallery. **1949** *Sun. World-Herald Mag.* (Omaha) 22 May 5/2 He wired a coil bedspring to the ceiling of the gallery and then hung the wagon cover background to the bedsprings.

2. (See quot.) *Obs.*

1896 Haswell *New York* 294 The question of the relative merits of the New York and Philadelphia fire-engines being constantly discussed, the Common Council [*c*1834–5] deputed a committee from its members to proceed to Philadelphia and procure one of its 'gallery' or 'double-decked engines,' which it did, and subsequently a second was obtained. They had much greater capacity, but were too cumbersome for a light company of men.

As the last term in **colored, first, Negro, peanut, photograph, photographic, pistol, rogues', singing, store gallery.**

galleta gɑˈjetə, *n. S.W.* [Sp., "hardtack."] Either of two grasses of the genus *Hilaria* used for hay and grazing in the southwestern states. In full **galleta grass.**

1856 *Wide West* (S.F.) Oct. 4/6. **1872** *Overland Mo.* Aug. 146/1 The coarse, dry bunch-grass or *gaieta*, never abundant on this route [in southern Ariz.], was unusually scarce that summer. **1919** J. S. Chase *Calif. Desert Trails* 196 (Bentley), About ten o'clock I found a few scraps of blue-stem (galleta grass) and burro-weed... and we stopped to rest and lunch. **1940** Jaeger *Calif. Deserts* 165 A chance to see good stands of galleta grass is offered the traveler in West Cronese Valley.

galley-west, *adv.* [Var. of Eng. dial. *colly-west, -weston*, see *EDD.*] *To knock galley-west*, to knock into smithereens. *Colloq.* — **1875** Mark Twain *Letters* I. xv. 250 Your verdict... has knocked what little [critical penetration] I did have galley-west! **1928** Foy & Harlow *Clowning Thro' Life* 26 Another came at him, and Jimmy likewise knocked him galley-west.

gallinipper ˈgæləˌnɪpɚ, *n.* Also †**galknipper, gadnipper, gallon-nipper.** [See note. Poss. variant of **gurnipper.**]

The origin of this word is obscure. Webster derives it from *galley+nipper*, and suggests that it might have at first been applied to insects that infest ships. The variants shown here, and the much earlier gurnipper *q.v.* make this explanation doubtful.

A large mosquito or other insect capable of inflicting an exceptionally painful sting or bite. Cf. **Georgia piercer.**

1709 in *Protestant Episc. Hist. Soc. Coll.* I. 64 Poor brother Jenkins was baited to death with musquitoes, and blood thirsty Gal-Knippers, which would not let him rest night nor day. **1801** *Port Folio* (Phila.) I. 40 (Th.), These Gallinippers are a noble breed Sent down on earth to buz and feed, With monstrous paunches, and with wings of lace. **1829** J. Mactaggart *Three Years* I. 186 The *gadnipper*, a large species of gadfly, is also common, but not so troublesome as those above described. **1831** *Boston Transcript* 13 Aug. 2/2, I have been pricked by a stiletto—by the gallon-nipper, by the blood-sucker, and the hornet. **1897** *Outing* XXX. 73/2 Others were swarming in through the open window, the fiercest, most bloodthirsty gallinippers that the Potomac flats could raise.

b. *transf.* (See quots.)

1944 Duncan *M. Graham* 126 Many a rural gallinipper hove in, a 'dominacker' rooster under his arm to put up to fight for drinks. **1945** *Sky Line Trail* June 20/2 Censorship long hid the fact that our Yoho Gallinippers were shipped overseas. Fitted with machine guns... and renamed *Spitfires*, they served valiantly during the Battle of Britain.

∗**gallinule**, *n.* As the last term in **Florida, purple gallinule.**

gallito gɑˈjito, *n. S.W.* [Sp., little rooster.] Any one of various long-spurred violets. Cf. ∗**rooster.** — **1906** Parsons *Wild Flowers Calif.* 124 The Spanish-Californian children knew them as 'gallitos.' **1920** Rice *Calif. Wild Flowers* 57 They are seen but to be loved, and they may be called Violets, Pansies, Johnny-Jump-Ups, or by the Spanish children's name of Gallitos.

Gallo-American. One of combined French and American character. Also as adj. *Obs.* — **1797** Jefferson *Writings* (1830) III. 358 Indeed its future fortunes will be in the air, if war is made on us by France, and if Louisiana becomes a Gallo-American colony. **1810** *Raleigh* (N.C.) *Reg.* 5 July 2/3 Those few who had been [to Oxford], had called themselves in the matriculation book, *Anglo Americans*—and those from French settlements in America, *Gallo Americans.*

gallon law. A law formerly in force in Mississippi prohibiting the sale of less than a gallon of intoxicating liquor at a time. *Obs.* — **1839** *N.O. Picayune* 23 April 2/1 The coffee-house loafers in Mississippi are said to suffer unaccountably since the 'gallon law' went into effect. **1842** in Buckingham *Slave States* I. 420 From and after Tuesday next, the 'gallon law' will be in full force and effect; and the worst wish we have for its opposers is, that they may live to see the day when the morals of the people shall become vastly improved, . . . through the instrumentality of this same gallon law.

∗**gallows**, *n.* (See quots.) *Colloq.*

[**1835** Griffiths *Two Years* 63 Indian corn is cut in October, when from sixty to seventy hills of corn are set together in what is called a hock, or stack, four hills being bent down to one another, and twisted for the purpose of supporting the hock, which is tied round the top with a pumpkin-vine to keep it together.] **1862** *Ill. Agric. Soc. Trans.* V. 160, I selected the gallows stalks or breaks of my shocks [of sorghum]. **1874** Knight 936/2 *Gallows*, . . . the central core of four corn-stalks interlaced diagonally, and bound at the intersection, forming a *stool* or support for cut corn, which is bound around it to form a *shock.* **1938** *Reader's Digest* Aug. 124/2 First you find the four central hills in an area 14 hills square, bend down the tops, and tie them all together. The 'gallus' thus formed, which is not to be cut until the fodder is hauled in, is the core of the shock, and provides something against which to lean the first armfuls of fodder.

galvanized Yank, Yankee. A term used in the South during the Civil War for a Southerner who was sympathetic towards the Union. Also attrib. Now *hist.*

1864 Grigsby *Smoked Yank* xxi. 182 There were some more galvanized Yanks turned in to-day. **1866** *Rep. Joint Comm. Reconstruction* III. 11 [The people of Alabama] manifest the most perfect contempt for a man who is known to be an unequivocal Union man; call him a 'galvanized Yankee,' and apply other terms and epithets to him. **1929** Parker *Old Army* 120 An officer of a 'Galvanized Yankee' regiment in 1865.

Also **galvanized man.**

1912 Crumpton *Two Boys* 123 He had been with Jeff Thompson, the Confederate Cavalry General, but had been caught and made to take the oath of allegiance. Such men, I afterwards discovered, were called 'galvanized' men.

gam gæm, *n.*[1] [Poss. a dial. var. of ∗*game*, or f. some Scandinavian equivalent.] (See quots.) Cf. ∗**jam,** *n.* **2.**

1846 J. R. Browne *Whaling Voyage* 76 When two whalers meet on any of the whaling grounds, it is usual to have a 'gam,' or mutual visit. **1850** Cheever *Whaleman's Adv.* xiii. 184 Gam is the word by which they [whalemen] designate the meeting, exchanging visits, and keeping company of two or more whale ships, or a sociable family of whales. **1902** Clapin 200 Gam. A sea-faring term, often used, on the Atlantic coast, in the sense of a social visit, and especially of a long and merry chat among acquaintances. Originally applied to occasions when meeting friends or countrymen in a strange land, or where few opportunities exist for social intercourse. **1948** *Sat. Ev. Post* 9 Oct. 138/3 The chair was used to lower her to a waiting whaleboat, so that she could pay a visit—in whaling circles, a gam—to another ship met somewhere on the lonely ocean.

gam gæm, *n.*[2] Short for gambler, usu. *pl. Slang.* — **1875** *Chi. Tribune* 10 Dec. 2/4 A Hard Place for Gams.... The Mayor has all the gambling-houses closed to-night. **1903** A. H. Lewis *Boss* 291 He came... padded with th' long green... an' them gams took it off him so fast he caught cold.

gam gæm, *v.* [?f. **gam,** *n.*[1]] *intr.* To take part in a "gam," to gossip or visit. *Colloq.*

1849 Cooper *Sea Lions* viii, I see no reason why we should not be neighborly and 'gam' it a little, when we've nothing better to do. **1906** *Harper's Mag.* May 841 The skipper came over with a boat's crew and gammed with us.

Hence **gamming chair.**

1948 *Sat. Ev. Post* 9 Oct. 138/3 One of the oddest sights is the massive gamming chair.

b. *To go gamming*, to go on a gossiping visit.

1849 Cooper *Sea Lions* viii, After many passages of nautical compliments, by means of signals and the trumpet, Roswell Gardiner... lowered a boat into the water, and went a 'gamming,' as it is termed, on board the other schooner. **1890** *Cent. Mag.* Aug. 510/2 If the door [of the post-office] still refuses to yield [you] are informed [in Nantucket, Mass.] that probably the postmistress has... gone 'gamming.'

gama grass. A tall, stout, productive, drought-resisting grass, *Tripsacum dactyloides*, valued for forage. Cf. **grama.** — **1833** *Amer. R.R. Jrnl.* II. 526/2, I promised to send you some account and description of the Gama Grass. **1894** Coulter *Bot. W. Texas* III. 491 *Tripsacum dactyloides.* (Gama grass.)... Low land, eastern Texas and eastward.

∗ **Gambel**, *n.* [Wm. *Gambel* (1821–49), Amer. ornithologist.] Used attrib. or in the possessive to designate various western species of American animals, chiefly birds, as

Gambel's finch, goose, partridge, quail, sparrow, woodmouse.

1860 BAIRD in *Ives's Rep.* V. 6 *Zonotrichia gambelii*, Gambel, Gambel's finch. Above Fort Yuma. — **1868** *Proc. Calif. Acad. Sci.* IV. 8 Mr. Lorquin has a specimen which appears to be a hybrid of the Snow Goose with Gambel's Goose. — **1851** *Proc. Acad. Nat. Sci.* V. 222 Gambel's Quail, or Partridge, . . . is much disposed to seek the farms, if any be within reach, and to cultivate the acquaintance of man. **1948** *Arizona Highways* April 11 The Gambel Quail is one of the proudest and most beautiful of the desert birds. — **1901** GRINNELL *Gold Hunting in Alaska* 15 Every morning I hear the plaintive song of the Gambel's sparrows from the bushy thickets on the hillsides. **1940** JAEGER *Calif. Deserts* 97 Like a glad harbinger of the glorious, sunny, winter days to come, the Gambel white-crowned sparrows appear from the north early in November. — **1869** *Amer. Naturalist* III. 476 Other mammals which I had obtained were Gambel's Woodmouse, before mentioned [etc.].

b. Gambel oak, a small white oak, *Quercus gambelli*, growing at high elevations from Montana to northern Mexico.

1937 *Range Plant Hdbk.* B-121 Gambel oak is best known throughout its range in its autumnal aspect, when its gorgeous leaves color the foothills and mountain slopes.

***Gambia,** *n. attrib.* Designating slaves brought from Gambia, Africa. *Obs.* — **1754** *S.C. Gazette* 15–22 Jan. 2/3 Run away, . . . 4 Gambia new negro men. **1810** LAMBERT *Travels thro' U.S.* II. 443 All the papers are well stocked with advertisements, among which, prime Congo, Gambia, and Angola slaves for sale at Gadsden's wharf, were very conspicuous.

***gamble,** *n. On a gamble*, at a venture. *Colloq.* — **1924** MULFORD *Rustlers' Valley* vi. 68 On a gamble he raised his sombrero.

***gambler,** *n.* As the last term in **river, rough, train gambler.**

***gambling,** *n.* Used with (1) **alley,** (2) **joint,** (3) **saloon,** to designate a shabby locality or place where gambling is indulged in. See also **pool gambling.**

(1) **1848** *Knickerb.* XVIII. 521 He was busy about the village, penetrating every grog-hole and gambling-alley. — (2) **1901** S. E. WHITE *Westerners* xiii. 94 Bunco men can clean him out in a gambling joint. **1949** *Chi. D. News* 26 March 3/1 Cicero's gambling joints are running wide-open. — (3) **1861** A. S. BILLINGSLEY *Diary* 1 (MS), Music in the gambling saloons. **1896** HARRIS *Sister Jane* 262, I could have picked up a fair living in the gambling-saloons.

***gambrel,** *n.*

1. Short for next.

1848 BARTLETT 153 *Gambrel*, a hipped roof to a house. **1873** T. W. HIGGINSON *Oldport Days* 45 Buildings, . . . sometimes with the long, sloping roof of Massachusetts, oftener with the quaint gambrel of Rhode Island.

2. gambrel roof, a roof having on each side two parts of unequal slope. Also †**gambering roof,** †**gambrel-roofed,** †**gamble roof.**

1737 in *Old-Time New Eng.* (1926) July 21 Gambering Roof. . . . One Tenement two Stories upright, with a Gambering Roof, three Rooms on a Floor, a good Yard and Garden, being sixty foot on the Street and sixty feet Rear, & about fifty-four feet deep. **1765** *Mass. Gazette* 19 Dec. (Th.), To be sold, a large building with two upright Stories and a Gambrel Roof. **1779** *Mass. H. S. Coll.* 2 Ser. II. 466 The [Indian] Queens Pallace was a gambril ruft house. **1855** MITCHELL *Fudge Doings* I. 129 There are . . . houses with gamble-roofs, and mossy, mouldy-looking, dormer-windows. **1928** KIMBALL *Architecture* 59 The gambrel roof, rare in most of the provinces of Holland, was taken up in New York as in the other English Colonies, but assumed a special form with a lower angle.

gambusino ˌgæmbəˈsino, *n. S.W.* [See note.]

A Spanish dialect term used in Amer. Sp. in the sense of a prospector, gold hunter. The suggestion by Santamaría that the word originated from the efforts of Mexican miners to pronounce the English "gamble-business" is interesting but app. quite without value.

A prospector, petty miner; an ore thief.

1844 GREGG *Commerce of Prairies* I. 173 The [New Mexican] gold regions are, for the most part, a kind of common property, and have been wrought chiefly by an indigent class of people, known familiarly as *gambucinos*, a name applied to petty miners who work 'on their own hook.' **1864** MOWRY *Ariz. & Sonora* 44 It still yields a good profit to the '*Gambussino*,' a sort of mining filibuster, who works regardless of the future of the mine. **1932** D. COOLIDGE *Fighting Men of West* 147 He made such an impression that he was invited to join the gambusinos.

***game,** *n.* In combs.: (1) ***gamecock,** (often *cap.*), (*a*) as a nickname for persons (see quots.), (*b*) with reference to places and states (see quots.); (2) **hog,** one who kills game out of season or in excess of legal limits; (3) **park,** (see quot.), *rare;* (4) **trace, trail,** a trace or trail made by game in the forest.

(1) (*a*) **1840** *Niles' Reg.* 9 May 154/3 In the revolutionary war, . . . Captain Caldwell had a company recruited from Kent and Sussex [in Delaware] called by the rest 'Caldwell's game cocks.' **1900** *Cong. Rec.* 29 Jan. 1262/2 Marion, the 'Swamp Fox,' and Sumter, the 'Gamecock,' and the other men who fought and continued to fight [in the Revolutionary War] were hiding out. (*b*) **1840** *Maysville* (Ky.) *Eagle* 25 March 2/6 How is the Sparta, the game cock of the Confederacy, going to vote? **1860** *Charleston* (S.C.) *Mercury* 27 Dec. 1/8 All honor and glory to [S.C.] the game cock of the South. **1862** *N. Y. Times* 12 May 4/5 At the battle of Williamsburgh, on the [Virginian] peninsula, last Monday, there were no less than eight regiments of South Carolina troops engaged . . . some of which are the 'crack' regiments of the 'Gamecock' State. — (2) **1900** *Cong. Rec.* 30 April 4872/1 The 'game hog' formerly had himself photographed surrounded by the fruits of a day's 'sport,' and regarded the photograph as imperfect unless he had a hundred dead ducks, grouse, or geese around him. **1948** *Democrat* 7 Oct. 4/1 The majority and better element of hunters have . . . contempt for game hogs. — (3) **1897** ALLEN *Choir Invisible* xiii, The backwoodsmen of the Blue Ridge and the Alleghanies . . . had entered and conquered the great neutral game-park of the Northern and the Southern Indians [Kentucky]. — (4) **1885** *Cent. Mag.* June 222/1 The third, . . . a very powerful fellow, followed a well-beaten game trail leading through the bushy point. **1897** ALLEN *Choir Invisible* xv, This immemorial game-trace had become a warpath. **1946** *Mazama* Dec. 21/2 When we reached the trees, we dropped into a low saddle to the right and lo, there was the game trail that had eluded us earlier in the day!

b. *Game of the arrow,* (see quot.). *Obs.*

1833 CATLIN *Indians* I. 141 In a favourite amusement which they call the 'game of the arrow,' . . . the young men who are the most distinguished in this exercise, assemble on the prairie [and] . . . step forward in turn, shooting their arrows into the air, endeavoring to see who can get the greatest number flying in the air at one time, thrown from the same bow.

As the last term in **anybody's, badger, ball, banking, big, brace, bunko, Choctaw ball, cinch, clock, con, cow, crap, dominique, fall, fly, grab, gum, hand, hogging, home, Massachusetts, match, moccasin, national, old army, panel, pitcher's, Polk, practice, Salmon Pile, scrub, shell, short, skin, soap, square, stick dice, strap, summer, tie game.**

***gamester,** *n.* One who hunts wild game. *Rare.* — **1866** *Ill. Agric. Soc. Trans.* VI. 406 [A report on birds] was gotten up to please the gamesters in the cities.

gamutize ˈgæmətaɪz, *v.* [f. **gamut, n.*] *tr.* (See quot.) *Obs.* — **1859** BRYANT in Durfee *Hist. Williams Coll.* (1860) 107 It had been the practice for the members of the Sophomore Class, in the first term of their year, to seize upon the persons of some of the Freshmen, bring them before an assembly of Sophomores, and compel them to go through a series of burlesque ceremonies, and receive certain mock injunctions with regard to their future behavior. This was called *gamutizing* the Freshmen.

***gamy,** *a.* Consisting of game. *Rare.* — **1878** BEADLE *Western Wilds* 189 Every wooded cañon invited the hunter to rest and a gamy feast.

***gander,** *n.* In colloq. combs.: (1) **gander eye,** an eye resembling that of a gander, a gray eye; (2) **legged,** *a.* having long, straight legs like those of a gander; (3) **party,** (see quot. 1867); (4) **plucked,** *a.* (see quot.), *rare;* (5) **pull,** = **gander pulling;** (6) **puller,** one who takes part in gander pullings; (7) **pulling,** (see quot. 1818, cf. **goose-riding* and Du. *ganstrekken*), also attrib.

(1) **1830** ROYALL *Southern Tour* I. 168 Gander eyes is always a bad sign. — (2) **1844** in THOMPSON *M. Jones* (1872) 186 They say he's a monstrous grate, long, gander-legged feller, and he may be 'bomination ugly for all I know. — (3) **1867** LOWELL *Biglow P.* 2 Ser. p. lviii, A few phrases not in Mr. Bartlett's book which I have heard [include] . . . *Gander-party:* a social gathering of men only. **1900** MUNN *Uncle Terry* 154 If you and I have any outing on the yacht, we must make up a gander party. — (4) **1841** PLAYFAIR *Papers* I. 37 It was said formerly every second man in Kentucky had an eye gouged out, and every third a nose or ear gander-plucked—that is, bitten off.

(5) **1894** *Harper's Mag.* Sep. 629/2, I wish there was room for descriptions of their [i.e., the West Virginians'] dances, . . . and of that queerest of all sports, the gander-pull. — (6) **1835** *S. Lit. Messenger* I. 645 Of the most conspicuous '*minora sidera*' the Kentuckian horse drover, the horse jockey, the gander puller might be mentioned. — (7) **1818** FEARON *Sketches* 247 They have also another practice . . . called 'gander pulling.' This diversion consists in tying a live gander to a tree or pole, greasing its neck, riding past it at full gallop, and he who succeeds in pulling off the head of the victim, receives the laurel crown. **1835** LONGSTREET *Ga. Scenes* 121 He laid off his gander-pulling ground, on the nearest suitable unappropriated spot, to the centre point between Springfield and Harrisburg. **1944** DUNCAN *M.*

Graham 75 The worst that ever happened on Brush Creek was gander pullings.

b. *To see how the gander hops*, a fanciful variant of "to see how the cat jumps." *Rare.*

c1845 *Big Bear Ark.* 96 Seein' how the gander hopped, I jumped up and hollered, Git out, Tromp, you old raskel!

As the last term in **gone gander.** For *to take a gander*, see next.

gander, *v. intr.* (See quot. 1903.) Also *to take a gander*, to take a look. *Slang.*

1903 *Cin. Enquirer* 9 May 13/1 Gander—To stretch or rubber your neck. **1947** BASKINS *Dr. Has Baby* 32 Thought I'd take a gander at the offspring. **1948** *Sat. Ev. Post* 17 July 47/2 'Take another gander, Bill,' he suggested dryly.

∗**gang,** *n.*

1. A herd or flock of animals or birds of the same kind.

1657 *Md. Hist. Mag.* VIII. 33 Great complaint of many [was made against Deere] for common frequenting the wild gang, killing cattle, and marking of calves. **1709** LAWSON *Carolina* 55 We were got about half way, (meeting great Gangs of Turkies) when we saw . . . 30 loaded Horses. **1882** *Standard* 10 Feb. 5/3 It might puzzle . . . to . . . tell what is the precise difference in the vocabulary of the hunter between a 'herd' and a 'gang' of elk. **1930** VINES *River Goes with Heaven* 65 My old daddy allus kept a gang [of sheep].

2. A derisive or belittling designation for a political group. *Colloq.*

1833 J. Q. ADAMS *Diary* (1928) 434 Duff Green and his *Telegraph* were set up here against my Administration, and for its overthrow, by . . . the united gang of Calhoun and Jackson conspirators against me. **1901** *McClure's Mag.* Dec. 152 Bill Jones . . . was defeated for a place in the county convention by the John Smith gang, has finally got Tom Brown on his side. **1945** *Somerset News* 29 March 3/3 As we see it optimists should preface all their remarks with: 'After we get rid of the gang around the White House.'

3. (See quots. 1872, 1883.)

1857 *Spirit of Times* 20 June 246/2 We were fully equipped with rods, reels, flies, trolling gangs, spoons, gaffs, and landing nets. **1872** *Rep. Comm. Fish* I. 257 In the southern half of Lake Michigan the fishermen use a large boat, with five and six gangs to the boat; each gang having from twenty-five to thirty-six nets, and employing five men to the boat. **1876** *Fur, Fin, & Feather* Sep. 143 He has taken bass with the fly, spoon, gang, live minnow, and belly of yellow perch. **1883** EGGLESTON *Hoosier School-Boy* xvii. 109 They got a 'gang' or, as they called it, a 'trotline' to lay down in the river for catfish, perch etc.

4. In combs.: (1) **gang boss,** one in charge of a gang of workmen; (2) **edger,** (see quot. 1875); (3) **hook,** two or three fishhooks having their shanks joined; (4) **land,** a region infested by gangsters, also attrib.; (5) **mill,** a sawmill in which gang saws are used, also **gang saw mill;** (6) **plank,** a narrow, bridgelike, movable structure affording a passageway for persons or animals going aboard or leaving a vessel, a gangboard; (7) **plow,** a plow having

Early type of gang plow

two or more shares that operate as a unit; (8) **saw,** (see quot. 1877), also attrib.; (9) **sawed,** *a.* sawed or cut up with a gang saw.

(1) **1887** GEORGE *40 Years on Rail* ix. 193, I was in charge of a construction train, being engineer, conductor and gang-boss combined. — (2) **1875** KNIGHT I. 940/1 Gang-edger. A machine in which a movable and a stationary circular saw are mounted on one arbor for the purpose of dressing boards to uniform width, as they come from the log. **1880** *Northwest. Lumberman* 24 Jan., The mill will be equipped throughout with . . . gang edgers. — (3) **1633** *N.H. Doc. & Rec.* I. 79 Gang hooks for cott, 11. **1943** *Waynesville Mountaineer* 15 April, All trout under seven inches in length must be returned to the water. Treble or gang hooks are prohibited. — (4) **1911** LEWIS *Apaches N.Y.* 15 The first lesson of Gangland is never to inform nor give evidence. **1931** *Dly. Express* (London) 28 April 2/1 All crimes attributable either to the gangland chief or his henchmen. **1948** *Chi. Tribune* 24 Aug. 18/4 There are fist fights, gun fights, . . . two gangland ambushes, and some automobile chases.

(5) **1848** *Sci. Amer.* 30 Sep. 10/3 In this Village, Mr. G. Reynale has introduced it in his large Gang Saw mill for cutting ship plank and sawing stone. **1871** *Winnebago Co. Press* (Neenah Wis.) 1 July, There are eight gang mills with a capacity ranging from 80,000 to 150,000 feet of lumber per day each. **1879** *Lumberman's Gaz.* 15 Oct., David Fox of Bay City . . . put in the first gang-mill upon the Saginaw river. — (6) **1846** *Knickerb.* XXVII. 469 The last bell rang; the gang-plank was drawn inboard; the hawsers were cast off. **1948** *This Week Mag.* 10 July 9/1 My legs gave way as I started down the gangplank. — (7) **1850** *Cultivator* ns. VII. 369 We stand much in need of . . . gang plows. **1945** *Nat. Geog. Mag.* May 520 The damming lister is a sort of gang plow which opens up narrow trenches 20 inches apart and from 6 inches to a foot deep. — (8) **1848** [see **gang mill**]. **1853** *Frontier Journal* (Calais, Me.) 28 June 2/1 The facility with which our 'gang saws' '*chew up*' a spruce log, would astonish any one unaccustomed to the business. **1877** BARTLETT 782 *Gang-Saw*, a collection of large saws hung together in a frame or sash, and set at fixed distances apart corresponding with the thickness of the log to be cut. **1894** WARNER *Golden House* ix, You might as well try to stand in with a combination of gang-saws, or to make friends with the Department of the Interior. — (9) **1861** *Chi. Tribune* 26 May 1/9, 10,000,000 Feet of Gang-Sawed Lumber, For Sale on Contract.

As the last term in **alchy, chain, construction, field, grading, house, live, lumber, lumbering, minny, plow, press, road, saw, scow, section, shanty, slabber, trash, wrecking gang.**

∗**gang,** *v.* **1.** *tr.* To arrange (implements) in gangs. **2.** To overcome or attack (a person) in or by means of a gang. *Colloq.*

(1) **1900** *U.S. Dept. Agric. Yearbook* 540 The plows are usually ganged, two to one frame. — (2) **1931** *K.C. Times* 17 Aug., Flapper girls gang the men. **1940** MENCKEN *Happy Days* 274 Jim, a decent widower, had been ganged and undone by the massed yallah gals of three alleys.

gangster ˈgæŋstɚ, *n.* A member of a gang of roughs, criminals, etc. Hence **gangsterdom, gangsterism.**

1896 *Columbus* (O.) *Dispatch* 10 April 4/2 The gangster may play all sorts of pranks with the ballot box, but in its own good time the latter will get even by kicking the gangster into the gutter. **1923** *Nation* 26 Dec. 743/1 'Haunch Paunch and Jowl' is the autobiography of one who has come up in the world from sneak-thiefery and gangsterdom. **1927** *New Masses* March 19/4 Gangsterism reigned supreme, both in and out of the convention hall. **1947** *Chi. Sun* 30 June 8/1 Before I left Kentucky for my first visit to Chicago my mother warned me facetiously 'to be careful about the Chicago gangsters.'

∗**gap,** *n.*

1. A place in a fence where drawbars serve as a gate.

1636 *Boston Rec.* 12 [They] shall raynge theire payle upon each of their grounds streight from the corner of William Wilkes his house, or from the upper poast of his garding gap. **1698** *Providence Rec.* VI. 199 The Gapp or barrs where we did use to goe into the orchard. **1836** *S. Lit. Messenger* II. 162 On every side I was met by gates, drawbars, and *gaps*—the necessary appendages in the economy of Virginian idleness.

2. (See quots.)

1851 *Knickerb.* XXXVII. 393 He then took a seat at one of the windows, here [Fla.] very properly called 'gaps,' as they were only square holes, with rough pine-shutters. **1875** KNIGHT 942/1 Gap-window. . . . A long and narrow window.

As the last term in **canyon, cattle, river, stock, Virginia, water, wind gap.**

Gape and Stare, see ∗**Bolingbroke.**

G.A.R. Abbrev. of *Grand Army of the Republic.* Also attrib. — **1867** *Dept. of R.I. G.A.R. Proc.* I. 10 Headquarters, Provisional Department of Rhode Island, G.A.R., Providence, August 1, 1867. **1948** *Reader's Digest* May 22/1 His long-visored GAR cap was gripped in his left hand.

gar gar, *n.* [f. ∗*garfish.*]

1. Short for ∗**garfish.**

1765 J. BARTRAM in W. Stork *Acct. E. Fla.* (1766) 10 'Tis full of large fish, as cats, garr, mullets, and several other kinds. **1835** *Vade Mecum* (Phila.) 3 Jan. 4/2 An enormous gar made his appearance where I was fishing. **1948** *Milwaukee Jrnl.* 18 July 6/3 Gars are rejected as food by most anglers.

2. In combs.: (1) **garbroth,** *S.* broth or soup made of the garfish, also *as mean as a garbroth*, also attrib., *colloq.*; (2) ∗**fish,** any one of various long-nosed, scaly, fresh-water fish of the family Lepisosteidae.

(1) **1832** PAULDING *Westward Ho!* II. 100 If I hadn't sooner eat garbroth with a real nigger, may I never see a tree. **1832** PAULDING

Westward Ho! I. 185 The Garbroth people are cluttering up the country. **1893** M. A. OWEN *Voodoo Tales* 32 One time dey wuz er man dat wuz meaner'n gyar-broth. **1898** HARRIS *Tales of Home Folks* 106 Some of 'em was good people, but one—old Mr. Watkins—was mean as garbroth. — **(2) 1772** ROMANS in Phillips *Notes* 124 There is also a fish Called the Gar Fish or Allegator Fish from the Shape of its head and teeth, by the french Called poisson armé, and not ill described by their Writers. **1884** GOODE *Amer. Fishes* 459 The peculiar green color of the bones is said to prejudice many people against them. I have myself tasted the American Gar-fish and found it exceedingly palatable; and I cannot doubt that at some future time they will be highly prized by our people, as they richly deserve to be. **1949** *Chi. Tribune* 16 Feb. II. 2/1 It also may save some motorist from joining the garfish and snakes in a muddy canal.

As the last term in **alligator, bony, duck's bill, long-nosed, short-nosed, soft gar.**

garambullo ˌgarəmˈbujo, *n.* [Sp., applied in Amer. Sp. to various plants in the Southwest.] Any one of various shrubs of the genus *Lycium* native to the Southwest.

The plant referred to in quot. 1902 may be a cactus (*Cereus garambullo*).

1902 *Out West* April 404, I did not see a single tree, . . . but only now and then a cactus, and a rare garumbullo. **1904** WOOTON *Native Ornamental Plants N.M.* 28 Garrambullo . . . [has] small scarlet tomato-like berries which the Mexican children seem to relish. **1913** ——— *Trees & Shrubs N.M.* 134 The Garrambullo (*Lycium torreyi*) is a shrub 3 to 5 feet high, common in the valleys of the southern end of the State. **1931** DAYTON *Western Browse Plants* 142 These bushes are common and characteristic and a wealth of vernacular names has been bestowed upon them, including boxthorn, buckbrush, . . . garambullo, rabbit thorn.

garañon ˌgarəˈŋon, *n. S.W.* [Sp. *garañón,* in same sense, obs. except in Amer. Sp.] A stallion. — **1874** HITTELL *Resources Calif.* 288 The garañon . . . guards his manada with . . . jealous care. **1898** *Land of Sunshine* March 184 The sultan garañon keeps a jealous eye over his harem.

garapata ˌgarəˈpatə, *n.* [Sp. *garrapata,* a tick.] **a.** A tick. **b. garapata bean,** (see quot.).

(a) 1836 C. J. LATROBE *Rambler in Mexico* 35 (Bentley), Every leaf, every spray holds its myriads of *garapatos,* a species of wood bug. **1846** *Dollar Newspaper* (Phila.) 10 June 4/3 They may meet with a few bloody-minded mosquitoes, an occasional *garapata,* or a wild Mexican in the chapparels. **1934** MORRIS *Digging In Southwest* 19 There are more *garapatas* than ever. — **(b) 1912** FREEMAN *Southwestern Beans* 578 Garaypata or Mexican Tick bean . . . takes its name from the flecked markings of the seed coat, which somewhat resembles those on castor beans and on certain varieties of ticks which occur in Mexico.

***garbage,** *n.* In combs.: (1) **garbage box,** a box in which garbage is placed for disposal, *obs.;* (2) **can,** a large, cylindrical metal container for garbage, also transf.; (3) **collector,** =next; (4) **man,** a man who collects garbage.

(1) 1867 *Rep. Comm. Patents 1866* II. 899 The garbage box, with its top constructed so as to form a part of the sidewalk of the street. **1882** MCCABE *New York* 586 These same hands have just been turning over the filthy scraps from the garbage-boxes and the gutters. — **(2) 1906** *N.Y. Ev. Post* 23 Aug. 2 The landlords are not providing the tenants with garbage and ash cans. **1948** *Sat. Review* 15 May 9/3 He had already had a widely varied and full life, ranging from the Federal Immigration Service . . . , the odorous garbage can of Manhattan politics, to the no less odorous pits of Capitol Hill. — **(3) 1924** *Collier's* 19 Jan. 19/3 They determine whether the garbage collector or the street cleaner is responsible for the removal of dead cats from blind alleys. **1926** *Good Housekeeping* June 246/3 The garbage container put out for the garbage collector should be adapted to the instructions given out by the department. **1949** *Time* 30 May 21/3 Eighty percent of us get less money than a garbage collector. — **(4) 1888** *Harper's Mag.* Dec. 95/1 The very garbage man, looking as if he himself had been fished out of the garbage of humanity for the office, grumbled. **1945** MENCKEN *Supp.* I. 579 The lowly garbage-man and ash-man . . . have begun to disappear from the American fauna: they are now becoming *sanitary officers.*

garbanzo garˈbanso, *n. S.W.* [Sp. in same sense.] The chick pea.

1759 tr. VENEGAS *Nat. Hist. Calif.* I. 45 The same success attended the experiments made with . . . garvanzo, or a kind of pease, and all sorts of esculents. **1844** KENDALL *Santa Fe Exped.* II. 225 The lower cup was generally filled with mutton broth, having a piece of the meat left within it, and also a quantity of garbanzos, or large Spanish peas. **1942** CASTETTER & BELL *Pima & Papago Agric.* 196 It has been reported that *garbanzos* will endure a temperature of 13° F. without being injured.

***Garcia,** *n.* [*García* Íñiguez (?1836–98), Cuban general.] *To carry a message to Garcia,* to accomplish a task, fulfill an assignment, in allusion to the well-known prose piece *A Message to Garcia,* written by Elbert Hubbard in 1899 (see 1st quot.).

1899 HUBBARD in *Philistine* March 116 The world cries out for such; he is needed and needed badly—the man who can 'Carry a Message to Garcia.' **1910** *Fra* April 24/1 In all the talk about carrying a message to Garcia, this point is to be observed. **1924** *Amer. Mercury* July 352/2 What you have to do, young man, is to carry a message to Garcia. That's your task. You go back to the Research Laboratory and do it! **1948** *Rotarian* April 11/2 He and even his children know that to 'carry the message to Garcia' means doing the job you are assigned to do.

***garden,** *n.*

1. (See quot.) *Obs.*

1882 MCCABE *New York* 253 They do not hesitate to accost men, and too often succeed in inducing them to accompany them to one of the dance-houses, or 'gardens.'

2. *Baseball.* The outfield. *Slang.*

1911 *Chi. D. News* 4 April 6/1 Bodie, Brinker, Chouinard and Johnston . . . are conceded a chance to land in the outer garden.

3. In combs.: (1) **garden catalogue,** a catalogue advertising seeds and plants suitable for a garden; (2) **lot,** a piece of ground used or suitable for a garden, *obs.;* (3) **patch,** =prec.; (4) **sauce,** vegetables grown in a garden; (5) **spot,** (*a*) a garden or a place suitable for a garden, (*b*) a region regarded as possessing superior excellences in the way of fertility, climate, etc.; (6) **truck, =garden sauce;** (7) **week,** a week during which people are encouraged to devote especial attention to gardening.

(1) 1943 *Sat. Ev. Post* 1 May 30/3, I leaf through Peter Henderson, his Garden Catalogue. — **(2) 1636** *Essex Inst. Coll.* IX. 27 A howse lott & a garden lott or ground for the placing of their flakes. **1737** W. STEPHENS *Proc. Georgia* I. 60 Mr. Bradley had employed some of them in working at a Garden-Lot of his Son's. **1741** *Ib.* II. 207 They were injured in their little Plantations and Garden-Lots near the Town. — **(3) 1832** KENNEDY *Swallow Barn* II. 224 Little garden-patches . . . where cymblings, cucumbers, . . . flourished. **1924** R. CUMMINS *Sky-High Corral* 17 The fat cook puffed in from the garden patch dragging a sack with half a dozen potatoes in it. — **(4) 1791** *Amer. Museum* X. 179 For want of garden sauce, they (Somnose and family) eat more flesh than is consistent with their health or his purse. **1816** R. B. THOMAS *Farmer's Almanack* 21 April, Garden sauce saves much meat—beside, meat is food for tigers, vegetables for lambs. **1948** *Sat. Ev. Post* 24 July 24/2 We cooked up some garden sass to feed the kids with.

(5) (*a*) **1687** *Plymouth Rec.* 190 From thence we are bounded by goodman Watson's garden spot. **1794** *Mass. H.S. Coll.* III. 250 The dwelling houses in Boston have an advantage above most of the large towns on the continent with respect to garden spots. **1896** JEWETT *Pointed Firs* 147 We all three regarded with deep interest . . . the barns and garden-spots and poultry. (*b*) **1813** *Niles' Reg.* IV. 317/2 The Rapids of the Miami may justly be termed the 'garden spot' of the territory. **1808** PAGE *Red Rock* 298 It's the garden spot of the world—the money's jest layin' round to waste on the ground. — **(6) 1807** GASS *Journal* 51 The Rees . . . had left . . . some garden truck, such as squashes. **1923** WATTS *L. Nichols* 292 He might have come in from Deer-creek with a wagon-load of garden-truck. — **(7) 1928** *Publishers' Wkly.* 30 June 2616 The editor will be Ellen Wangner. . . . One of her outstanding editorial achievements was the starting of National Garden Week from which seven hundred new garden clubs resulted.

b. (*cap.*) Used in nicknames: (1) **Garden City,** (see quots.); (2) **County,** a county regarded as exceptionally beautiful, fertile, etc.; (3) **of America,** (see quot.); (4) **of the Gods,** (*a*) a region of great natural beauty and picturesqueness near Colorado Springs, Colorado, (*b*) also transf.; (5) **of the West,** (see quots.); (6) **of Virginia,** (see quot.); (7) **State,** see as a main entry.

(1) 1848 *Gem of Prairie* (Chi.) 25 Nov. 3/3 In my rambles round the Garden city for some time past, I have found many things that might be mended. **1871** DE VERE 665 Savannah, in Georgia, is the third city claiming the name of Garden City, in virtue of the numerous and beautiful parks with which it is adorned. **1880** *Dly. Inter-Ocean* (Chi.) 3 June 2/3 The universal expression of the Garden City's guests was that, as a watering place and summer resort, Chicago was simply immense. — **(2) 1872** *Newton Kansan* 21 Nov. 2/3 This bids fair to be the favored spot in the garden county. **1892** *Vt. Agric. Rep.* XII. 113 This is often called the Garden County of Vermont. — **(3) 1803** *Steele P.* I. 374 He speaks of the Lands found in the neighborhood of the Walnut Hills [site of present Vicksburg, Miss.], as being the

Garden of America. — (4) (*a*) **1866** *Beadle's Mo.* June 495/2 Near Colorado City they culminate in an immense gateway of solid rock, known as the entrance to the Garden of the Gods. **1940** *Life* 7 Oct. 66/1 In the Garden of the Gods students from the art center hold their classes in landscape painting. (*b*) **1876** *Pacific Star* (S.F.) 24 Aug. 2/5, I leave you . . . after three day's communion with . . . the solemn grandeur of the spirit that pervades the Yosemite—the 'Garden of the Gods.' **1943** *Waynesville Mountaineer* 27 May, He created the mountain region of North Carolina. . . . It was a veritable Garden of the Gods; a land of indescribable and inimitable grandeur.
(5) **1834** Audubon *Ornith. Biog.* II. 491, I thought that the Barrens must have been the parts from which Kentucky derived her name of the 'Garden of the West.' **1875** *Chambers' Journal* 13 March 171/2 Kansas is another Garden of the West, but . . . is occupied by Jayhawkers. *Ib.*, Illinois rejoices in three names: . . . Garden of the West, Sucker State, and Prairie State. **1886** *Chi. W. News* 29 April 4/3 Kansas is the Garden of the West and its people are Jayhawkers, a name the people got in the troublesome times preceding its admission as a state. — (6) **1871** Cooke *R. E. Lee* 154 General Lee and his army passed the brilliant days of autumn in the beautiful valley of the Shenandoah. . . . The region, in fact, is known as the 'Garden of Virginia.'

As the last term in **beer, Dutch, elk, German, ice cream, lager beer, palm, rock, roof, sale, squaw, summer, truck garden.**

Gardenia gɑrˈdinɪə, *n.* [Dr. Alexander *Garden* (1730–91), Amer. botanist.] A genus of tropical shrubs and trees cultivated, esp. in the South, for its fragrant white or yellow flowers. Also (usu. not *cap.*) the flower of a plant of this genus.

1757 in *Scientific Mo.* (1948) July 18/2 Mr. Miller has called it Basteria. But if you will please to follow my advice, I would call it Gardenia, from our worthy friend Dr. Alexander Garden of S. Carolina. **1758** Linnaeus in *Scientific Mo.* (1948) July 19/1 If Dr. Garden will send me a new genus, I shall be truly happy to name it after him, Gardenia. **1817** *N.Y. Herald* 29 March 3/5 William Price has for sale . . . a few hundred very flourishing plants of the Gardenia Florida or Cape Jasmine. **1941** Daniels *Tar Heels* 95 A grammar grade school-teacher, from the tiny town of LaGrange, came, with a gardenia against her brown curls. **1947** *Nat. Geog. Mag.* July 17/1 At Otranto, Alexander Garden, physician and plantsman, was carrying on a correspondence with Linnaeus, the great Swedish botanist. The *Gardenia* was named for him.
attrib. **1949** *Chesterton* (Ind.) *Tribune* 7 April 8/5 The bride's mother also wore a gardenia corsage.

gardening, n.* As the last term in **kitchen, truck gardening.

Garden State. A nickname applied to various states, as Illinois, Kansas, New Jersey.

1865 *Dly. Morning Chronicle* (Wash., D.C.) 29 Sep. 2/3 Verily, Illinois is justly called 'The Garden State.' **1871** De Vere 659 Kansas is often called the Garden State, from the beautiful appearance of rolling prairies and vast cultivated fields which abound in that fertile region. **1883** Beadle *Western Wilds* 612 Through the glades blows the cool and stimulating air, and over all is the soft blue sky of the Garden State. **1948** *Sat. Ev. Post* 20 Nov. 57/2 When the first nip of frost chills the New Jersey air, cooks in the Garden State revive this recipe for heartening Shepherd's Pie.

***garget,** *n.* =**pokeweed.** — **1778** Carver *Travels* 517 Gargit or Skoke is a large kind of weed, the leaves of which are about six inches long. **1894** Coulter *Bot. W. Texas* III. 372 *Phytolacca decandra.* (Common poke or scoke. Garget. Pigeon berry.)

***garibaldi,** *n.* A red market fish of the family Pomacentridae, found in California. — **1884** Goode *Fisheries* I. 276 On the California coast occurs a species, *Pomacentrus rubicundus*, conspicuous by reason of its uniformly deep crimson or orange coloration, which is usually known as the 'Garibaldi' among the Italians. **1885** Kingsley *Riverside Nat. Hist.* III. 237 A species occurring along the southern Californian coast, and known as the goldfish, red perch, and Garibaldi—the *Hypsypops rubicundus.*

Garlandite ˈgɑrləndaɪt, *n.* A political supporter of Augustus Hill Garland (1832–99), elected governor of Ark. in 1874 upon the overthrow of the carpetbag regime in that state. *Obs.* — **1875** *Cong. Rec.* 2 March 2114/1 The Dorrites of that day, like the Garlandites of this day, were not without their supporters.

***garment,** *n.* As the last term in **custom, union garment.**

* **Garrison,** *n.*[1] *attrib.*

1. Of or pertaining to William Lloyd Garrison (1805–79), a prominent American abolitionist. Now *hist.*

1834 Garrison in W. P. & F. J. Garrison *W. L. Garrison* I. 461 Are . . . not all [abolitionists] tauntingly stigmatized as *'Garrison-men'*? **1851** J. F. W. Johnston *Notes N. Amer.* II. 482 During my stay in Boston, I have attended two separate meetings in Faneuil Hall on the subject of slavery—one called by the Free-soil party, the other by the extreme Abolitionist or Garrison party. *c***1903** Howes *Boston* 260 The day of the 'Garrison mob'—to call the riot by its historic name—has left one of the darkest spots in the whole calendar of Boston history.

2. Garrison finish, (see quot. 1943).

1943 *Copper Camp* 232 Montana was the horse that came from behind in the 1892 Suburban Handicap with Snapper Garrison up, to pass a top-notch field in a driving finish. . . . Since that race, in any line of sport when a competitor comes from behind to win, it is known by the tag line—a Garrison finish. **1948** *Dallas Morn. News* 5 Dec. II. 1/1 SMU's garrison finish failed to reach the climax as the Texas Tech Red Raiders basketball team downed the Mustangs, 60 to 58, Saturday night.

* **garrison,** *n.*[2]

1. garrison flag, (see quot.).

1889 *Cent.* 2247/1 *Garrison flag*, a large flag furnished to the principal military posts in the United States, to be displayed on occasions of national importance.

2. garrison house, in frontier times, a strongly fortified log house serving as a refuge for settlers during Indian uprisings. *Obs.*

1676 Sewall *Diary* I. 12 The said Town burned, Garrison houses except. **1722** *N.-Eng. Courant* 10–17 Sep. 2/2 The Indian Rebels, to the Number of 7 or 800, did on Monday last burn all the Houses at

Garrison house

Arrowsick, except the 3 Garrison-Houses and 2 others. **1857** E. Stone *Life of Howland* i. 23 On this lot there then stood the old garrison house. **1927** *Old-Time New Eng.* Oct. 63/2 When all is summed up, it appears that the oldest log structures now standing in the United States are in New England, of which the McIntire 'garrison house' near York, Me., may be the earliest.

Garrisonian gærəˈsonɪən, *n.* and *a.* [Cf. * **Garrison 1.**] A follower of W. L. Garrison; of or pertaining to him. Now *hist.*

1844 *Liberator* (Boston) 12 Jan. 5/1 Another of our articles, exposing the unprincipled position of Garrisonian abolitionism, has appeared in the 'Refuge of Oppression' since the publication of our last paper. *Ib.* 15 Nov. 181/2 The Greenfield Gazette has a wonderful sympathy for Garrisonians. **1898** Siebert *Underground Railroad* 100 These persons belonged to the Quakers, or to the Garrisonian abolitionists. **1941** Buckmaster *Let My People Go* 79 The pyrotechnics must be pushed off onto the Garrisonians.

Garrisonism ˈgærəsn̩ˌɪzəm, *n.* [Cf. * **Garrison 1.**] The political views or teachings of W. L. Garrison. Now *hist.*

1843 *Liberator* (Boston) 26 May 83/1 The editor of the Emancipator rejoices at 'the assurance that we shall have no Garrisonism at the Convention!' **1878** *N. Amer. Rev.* CXXVII. 98 The wires of Calhounism and Garrisonism were joined and the war began. **1941** Buckmaster *Let My People Go* 82 They were willing for the sake of Garrisonism to sink their delicacy into the task of being 'female itinerants.'

Garrisonite ˈgærəsn̩ˌaɪt, *n.* [Cf. * **Garrison 1.**] A Garrisonian. *Rare.* — **1834** Garrison in W. P. & F. J. Garrison *W. L. Garrison* I. 461 As soon as any man becomes . . . friendly to abolition, is he not . . . stamped by the enemy as a *Garrisonite?*

***garrupa,** *n.* (See quot. 1884.) — **1884** Goode *Fisheries* I. 263 Speckled Garrupa (*Sebastichthys nebulosus* . . .) . . . is known as 'Garrupa' and 'Rock Cod.' It ranges from Monterey to Puget Sound. *Ib.* 265 Green Garrupa (*Sebastichthys atrovirens*). . . . [Also called] 'Green Rock-fish.' **1897** *Outing* XXIX. 231/2 The grouper, or 'groper,' or 'garoupha' . . . is large and logy, but fine fun with moderate light tackle.

*garter, *n.*

1. Short for next. Cf. **slough, swamp garter.**

1880 *New Virginians* I. 132 This rockery . . . will be a regular snake nursery! The garter and the copperhead will think you put it up on purpose for them. **1884** MARK TWAIN *H. Finn* xxxix. 396 [We] grabbed a couple of dozen garters and house-snakes.

2. garter snake, any one of various small, brightly-colored snakes of the genus *Thamnophis.*

1769 SMITH *Tour* 41 We saw Two Garter Snakes and one of our savages snapt his Gun at 4 Wolves. **1884** MARK TWAIN *H. Finn* xxxviii. 392 We can get you some garter-snakes. **1949** *Scientific Mo.* Jan. 57/2 He maintains these are not 'nasty' like the garter snake and other kinds.

*gas, *n.*[1]

1. *fig.* Pretentious or empty talk. *Slang.*

Orig. in allusion to the gas used to inflate a balloon.

[**1793** CUTLER in *Life & Corr.* II. 279 [E. C. Genêt's] gas is now pretty well expended, and he has descended into universal contempt.] **1856** FERGUSSON *America* 319 'Dat all gas, massa,' was Sam's cool reply,—'gas' in Yankee, being equivalent to our 'moonshine.' **1889** *Amer. Folk-Lore* II. 64 Gas, . . . in the United States . . . is much used in the sense of idle talk, windy eloquence.

2. In combs.: (1) ***gas bag,** an empty talker, a windbag; (2) **field,** (see quot. 1889); (3) **heater,** a heater that burns gas; (4) **log,** a hollow perforated fixture, somewhat resembling a log of wood, used as a gas burner in a fireplace; (5) **machine,** a machine for making illuminating gas; (6) ***man,** a man who lights gas lamps on the street (see also quot. 1889); (7) **range,** (see quot. 1883); (8) **refrigerator,** a refrigerator operated by illuminating gas; (9) **spring,** a spring the water of which contains gas, cf. **burning spring;** (10) **well,** a well which produces natural gas, also attrib.

(1) **1873** *Newton Kansan* 2 Jan. 2/3 Gas bags were never known to do more than make a noise. **1918** LINCOLN *Shavings* 16, I judge I'm the 'this' you and that gas bag have been talkin' about. — (2) **1889** *Cent.* 2462/1 *Gas-field,* a region or area of territory from which natural gas is obtained in sufficient quantity to be of economical importance. **1947** *Dly. Oklahoman* (Okla. City) 30 Dec. (Year-End Rev.) 1/6 In the 11 1/2 months of this year there were completed 783 wildcat wells, resulting in 107 new oil fields, 20 gas fields and nine distillate fields. — (3) **1866** *Rep. Comm. Patents 1864* I. 1012 Drum Gas Heater.—December 27, 1864. . . . It is designed to suspend the drum . . . over a gas burner. **1922** *N.Y. Times* 1 Nov. 18/1 Gas heaters should be connected with a chimney. — (4) **1885** *Cent. Mag.* Jan. 467 Some grates have the andirons and clay gas logs, in imitation of a wood fire. **1922** *N.Y. Times* 1 Nov. 18/1 Important improvements have been made in recent years on the old-fashioned 'gas log.'

(5) **1870** *Rep. Comm. Patents 1868* II. 501/1 Gas Machine. . . . This invention relates to machines in which the atmospheric air is carbureted by passing it through the more volatile hydrocarbon oils. **1897** F. C. MOORE *How To Build a Home* 57 A good gas-machine . . . is safer than ordinary kerosene lamps. — (6) **1854** CUMMINS *Lamplighter* 520 Just then, the gasman came quickly up the street, lit, as by an electric touch, the bright burners. **1863** MASSETT *Drifting About* 50 The narrow and gloomy passage slightly illuminated by one or two jets of gas, which 'Tom the Gasman' (quite a character in those days, and one of the 'institutions') had a few moments before lighted. **1889** *Cent.* 2462/3 *Gas-man,* . . . in coal-mining, an employee who examines the underground workings for the purpose of ascertaining whether fire-damp is present in dangerous quantity, and who also has supervision of the ventilation. — (7) **1883** KNIGHT *Supp.* 391 *Gas-range,* a form of cooking-stove heated by gas-jets. **1947** *Mazama* Oct. 2/1 A new gas range is yet to be installed, on delivery, in the small kitchen. — (8) **1945** *Chi. Tribune* 5 April 17 (*advt.*), Plan to buy a beautiful Servel Gas Refrigerator when appliances are again available.

(9) **1837** W. JENKINS *Ohio Gaz.* 297 There are three gas springs situated within a short distance of each other. **1843** *Nat. Hist. N.Y., Geology* IV. 308 In this district the only mineral springs of interest are the salines, the sulphur springs, the inflammable gas springs, and the springs of Conoga, yielding nitrogen. — (10) **1847** *Amer. Philos. Soc. Proc.* IV. 366 An account of the inflammable Gas-wells on the banks of the Kanawha river. **1899** *U.S. Geol. Surv. Water Supp. Paper* 21, 24 Another gas-well boring in that city was carried to a depth of 239 feet into the Trenton [formation]. **1913** *Bureau of Mines Rep.* No. 45, 32 Gas was escaping from a large gas well in sec. 13.

gas gæs, *n.*[2] Short for **gasoline.** Also attrib.

1905 REX BEACH *Pardners* v. (1912) 125 We passed a hawser to the *Detroit,* and I turned the gas into the tug, blowin' for the Wells Street Bridge. **1925** *Frontier* Mar. 20 On the opposite side of town one finds . . . an occasional garage or gas-filling station. **1949** *This Week Mag.* 23 April 2/2 The reader . . . stopped at a gas station and there was the hog-caller.

b. *To step* (or *tramp*) *on the gas,* to press down on the accelerator of an automobile and so increase its speed. Also fig. *Slang.*

1916 H. L. WILSON *Somewhere in Red Gap* vii. 289 Once she'd tramped on the gas of a ninety-horsepower racer. **1921** *Collier's* 1 Jan. 8/3 He nods understandingly, steps on the gas, and with a cheerful grin, says: 'Ex-actly.' **1948** *Sat. Review* 29 May 4/1 Many of the improvements in equipment and service stem from C. & O.'s persistent gadfly, Robert Young, but his competitors are beginning to step on the gas themselves.

c. *To give her the gas,* to speed the motor of an automobile. *Slang.*

1942 RICH *We Took to Woods* (1948) 66, I remember shoving for dear life while Ralph gave her the gas.

*gas, *v. intr.* To engage in idle talk, to brag or boast. *Slang.*

1853 *Wkly. Chi. Democrat* 1 Jan., We were about to gas a little upon our newspaper establishment. **1896** WHITE *Real Issue* 91 Well, what are you kids gassing about? **1948** *Time* 21 June 22/1 He has become a familiar sight on Harrisburg streets—window-shopping, . . . gassing with the cop on the corner.

gasoline ˌgæsəˈlin, *n.* [f. *gas + *-ol + *-ine.] A volatile, highly inflammable liquid usu. obtained by refining petroleum.

1865 *Appleton Ann. Cyclo. for 1864* 669/2 The lightest naphtha . . . to this the name gasolene has been given. **1871** SOMERS *Southern States since War* 264 Among the novelties of manufacture, one of the two gas companies of the town [*sc.* Memphis] supplies gasoline made by vaporisation from the mineral oil of Pennsylvania. **1922** CATHER *One of Ours* 11 Occasionally a motor dashed along the road toward town, and a cloud of dust and a smell of gasoline blew in over the creek bottom. **1949** *N.O. Times-Picayune Mag.* 22 May 5/3 Black oil, yellow sulphur and crystal gasoline flow . . . through the massive gates along with other treasures, bound for the far places of the world.

attrib. **1881** *Harper's Mag.* May 815/1 The street hawkers, with gasoline torches, are crying their wares. **1927** JAMES *Cow Country* 171 There was stores along that highway too, and gasoline stations, school houses, and high elevators for the farmers' grain. **1949** *Desplaines Valley News* (Summit, Ill.) 8 April 1/3 Funds from the gasoline tax will be utilized to purchase and maintain 15 street light standards of the latest type.

*gasometer, *n.* A windbag, a blowhard. *Slang. Obs.* — **1853** *S.F. Commercial Advt.* 9 Dec. 2/4 The members of the late No. 2 are composed of working men, who are . . . not like 'IXL,' mere gasometers. **1856** *Wide West* (S.F.) 16 Mar. 1/3 The Gasometer called the meeting to order, and after the usual opening business, he called on a young fellow named Adams for a story.

gaspergou ˈgæspərˌgu, *n.* [f. La. F. *casse-burgau* (<*casser,* to break + *burgau,* a species of shellfish, with reference to its feeding habits.) See W. A. Read in *Amer. Sp.* Dec. 1945, p. 277 ff.] The fresh-water drum, or the common sheepshead.

1809 CUMING *Western Tour* 302 Marsolis gave us a tolerably good supper . . . of coffee, bread and butter, sliced bacon, and a fine dish of gaspar-goo, the best fish I had yet tasted of the produce of the Mississippi. **1884** GOODE *Fisheries* I. 370 The Fresh-Water Drum—*Haploidonotus Grunniens* . . . , southwestward, in Louisiana, Texas, and Arkansas, . . . is always known as the 'Gaspergou.' **1947** DALRYMPLE *Panfish* 344 For years they've been catching Sheepshead and Gaspergou.

b. (See quot.)

1885 *Outing* Feb. 336/2 Gaspergoo [is] an Indian word meaning 'fish,' and applied to anything fishy, from the delicate sheep's-head to the nasty mud-suckers of the Mississippi.

*gasser, *n.* A well, esp. an oil well, that yields gas.

1910 *Sat. Ev. Post* 2 July 44/2 One day a gasser was struck within a mile of Petroleum, blowing the derrick to pieces and injuring a couple of workmen. **1922** *Dly. Ardmoreite* (Ardmore, Okla.) 6 Jan. 6/1 Kirk No. 1, . . . an old gasser being drilled deeper, has reached a depth of 1770 feet. **1948** *Duncan* (Okla.) *D. Banner* 1 July 1/6 Helmerich & Payne have added a small gasser in the Doyle area to Stephens county production.

*gassy, *a.* Given to empty, inconsequential talk. *Colloq.* — **1857** C. ROBINSON *Kansas Conflict* (1892) 360, I suppose . . . ten . . . men (not gassy) . . . could bring it about in the course of eight or ten days. **1875** WHITNEY *Life & Growth of Lang.* 17 We call an empty and sophistical but ready talker *gassy.*

gat gæt, *n.* [f. ***Gatling b.**] A revolver or pistol. *Slang.* Cf. **forty-four gat.**

1911 LEWIS *Apaches N.Y.* 22 Gatts is East Sidese for pistols. 1913 *D.N.* IV. 26 gat, *n.* An automatic revolver. 1949 *Boston Globe* 15 May (Fiction Mag.) 2/5 I'm figgered handy with a gat.

***gate,** *n.*

1. A frame in which a saw or set of saws is fixed to prevent buckling. Cf. **gate saw.**

1815 DRAKE *Cincinnati* iii. 145 The engine drives four saws in separate *gates*, acting at the rate of 80 times in a minute. 1876 KNIGHT 2030/2 A mill-saw strained in a *gate*, or *sash*, as it is sometimes called.

2. A faucet. Cf. **molasses gate.**

1861 *Ill. Agric. Soc. Trans.* V. 165 It was drawn through a faucet, or gate, into the evaporator.

3. (*cap.*) Short for **Golden Gate.**

1869 DANA *Two Years* (new ed.) 440 The Presidio . . . has a noble situation, and I saw from it a clipper ship of the very largest class, coming through the Gate, under her fore-and-aft sails. 1948 *Sat. Ev. Post* 23 Oct. 20/2 A day or two later the Coast Guard would pick him up thirty miles downbay, bumping the pilings somewhere along the Frisco water front as the ebb swept him toward the Gate.

4. In combs.: (1) **Gate City,** see as a main entry; (2) **crasher,** (see quot. 1927), also **gate crashing;** (3) **lifting,** (see quot.), *obs.;* (4) **saw,** (see quot. 1875); (5) ***way,** see as a main entry.

(2) 1927 *Dly. News* (London) 28 June 5/3 'One-eyed Connolly,' the champion American 'gate crasher' (one who gains admittance to big sporting events without payment). 1948 *Chi. D. News* 28 April 35/1 Gate-crashing efforts reach their peak in Louisville on Derby Day. 1949 *Ib.* 7 March 12/1 He is a gate-crasher and a go-getter. — (3) 1871 BAGG *At Yale* 263 Another disreputable practice of the Freshmen . . . was known as 'gate-lifting.' . . . Crowds of Freshmen were wont to range about the city, unshipping the gates of the citizens, carrying them off [etc.]. — (4) 1875 KNIGHT 959/1 *Gate-saw*, a mill-saw which is strained in a *gate* or *sash* to prevent *buckling*. 1879 *Lumberman's Gazette* 15 Oct., This was an improvement over the gate saw, almost as great as was the gate.

b. In colloq. phrases: (1) *between you and me and the gatepost*, confidentially; (2) *to get the gate*, to be discharged, also *to give one the gate*, to dismiss or reject as a suitor.

(1) 1884 CRADDOCK *Where Battle was Fought* 152 Between you and me and the gate-post, old Walter Percy is a fool about everything in this world except money. — (2) 1921 *Collier's* 27 Aug. 20/2 He got the gate there too for holding out bets gave him to place by women and come-ons. 1924 P. MARKS *Plastic Age* 273, I guess his girl has given him the gate. 1928 L. NORTH *Parasites* 62 Anyhow, it would stop me from submitting the same ideas he got the gate for.

As the last term in **big, end, fore, Golden, hand, head, molasses, ox, picket, plantation, stock, tail, wagon gate.**

Gate City.

1. A nickname for various cities thought of as being situated at the entrance to a region or section of the country.

1859 *Ladies' Repository* XIX. 51/2 Keokuk, Iowa, is the 'Gate City,' —a translation, I believe, of its Indian name. 1866 E. A. POLLARD *Southern Hist. War* II. 382 The Battles of Atlanta—The Fall of 'The Gate City.' 1887 *Courier-Journal* 8 May 9/16 The traveler who starts Southward . . . will not have commenced his mission properly unless he enters the new South through the gate city. Louisville is to the South what Chicago is to the Northwest.

2. *The Gate City of the West* (or *South*), designations for Pittsburgh, Pa., and Atlanta, Ga., respectively.

1865 *Atlanta D. Intelligencer* 1 Oct. 2/1 What this journal has been . . . to Atlanta, the 'Gate City' of the South—our readers, doubtless, justly appreciate. 1882 *Harper's Mag.* Jan. 164/1 Pittsburgh, aptly termed the 'Gate City of the West.' 1904 O. HENRY *Roads of Destiny* 348 In the Gate City of the South the Confederate Veterans were reuniting.

***gateway,** *n.* A place serving as the entrance *of* or *to* a specified region.

1884 *Harper's Mag.* May 878/2 Snoqualmie Pass . . . is the lowest gateway of the Cascade Range. 1888 SHERIDAN *Memoirs* I. 272 The enemy had meanwhile concentrated most of his forces at Chattanooga for the two-fold purpose of holding this gateway of the Cumberland Mountains [etc.]. 1948 *Highway Traveler* Aug.-Sep. 35/1 Gateway to this almost primitive country is Rogers City, county seat of Presque Isle County.

b. *Gateway to the West,* (see quot. and cf. **Gate City 2**).

1906 *N.Y. Ev. Post* 10 March, When an outsider hears the name of Pittsburgh, he thinks of . . . the 'Gateway to the West.'

***gather,** *v.*

1. *tr.* To organize (a church). *Obs.*

1639 *New Haven Col. Rec.* 12 A chur[ch] nott being then gathered, but was deferred till a chur[ch] might be gathered according to God. 1676 *Conn. Rec.* II. 446, I am the 1 man & onely left of those that gathered the Chvrch that is now in Dorchester.

2. *tr.* and *intr.* To associate with or join a religious sect or group, to receive (a person) into such a group.

1855 B. YOUNG *Jrnl. Discourses* II. 257 (Th.), 'Why don't you gather with the Saints?' 'O, I am poor now; but I would very much like to gather with them.' 1880 HOWELLS *Undiscovered Country* 192, I first saw this place in a vision. It was when I was a young man, and several years before I was gathered in from the world outside.

3. *To gather up*, to catch, arrest, lead away. *Colloq.*

1843 W. T. THOMPSON *Chron. Pineville* 182 'Gather him up, boys,' said the judge, 'the sentence of the law must be executed!' 1907 WHITE *Arizona Nights* 76 My hosses acted some surprised at being gathered up again, but I couldn't help that.

***gatherer,** *n.* As the last term in **boom, cranberry, fruit, news, sap gatherer.**

***Gatling,** *n. Mil.* A light, rapid-fire gun of a type perfected about 1862 by an American inventor, R. J. Gatling (1818–1903). In full **Gatling gun.** Also **Gatling battery.** Cf. **hopper mine, Union gun.**

1867 in C. B. NORTON & W. J. VALENTINE *Rep. Munitions* 96 The large bore Gatling gun . . . is said to make a good target up to 2,000 yards. 1867 *Ib.* 95 The only field gun in the American Section [at the

Early type of Gatling gun

Paris Universal Exhibition, 1867] is the 'Gatling Battery,' exhibited by Mr. R. J. Gatling, of Indianapolis, Indiana. 1880 *Harper's Mag.* May 917/1 The artillery is almost entirely the old brass Napoleon, no breech-loading field-pieces being in the hands of the National Guards, and but few Gatlings. 1947 *Westerner's Brand Book* 29 He not only refused five troops of the Second Cavalry but also Gatling guns; they would slow down his march.

b. **=gat.** *Slang.*

1880 *Amer. Punch* April 56/1 Is this yer a goll durned Republic where every sole kin kerry a gatlin under his cote tale an' vote as often as he pleezes? 1867 A. H. LEWIS *Wolfville* 99 The victim . . . brings his gatlin' into play surprisin'.

gator ˈgetɚ, *n.* Short for ******alligator.* *Colloq.* See also **bull gator.**

1844 *Knickerb.* XXIII. 407 The 'gator isn't what you may call a han'some critter. 1946 *Democrat* 6 June 2/3 The 'gator wasn't near any sizeable stream or body of water.

attrib. 1886 *Outing* VIII. 60/2 The natives often feed their dogs and hogs boiled 'gator meat. 1930 *Scientific Mo.* XXXI. 60 The gator-holes . . . are miniature lakes in the prairies and elsewhere, varying from perhaps one to ten rods in diameter and generally not more than four or five feet deep. . . . Generally two or more gator-roads lead from each gator-hole out into the surrounding prairie. 1948 *Good Housekeeping* Jan. 105/1 You oughta get out of 'gator huntin' into something with a future in it.

***gauge,** *n.* As the last term in **broad, narrow, salt gauge.**

gaunt gɔnt, *v.tr.* To deprive (an animal) of rations, to make (an animal) gaunt. — 1887 *Outing* X. 115/2 Jim, do you want to gaunt Peg-leg for a race, or will you give him hisration? 1890 SHIELDS *Big Game N. Amer.* 476 A gorged Wolf is not fast, . . . but when properly 'gaunted,' few horses can catch a Gray Wolf.

***gavel,** *n.* [Eng. dial. var. of ******gable*, see *EDD s.v. Tympany.*] A hammer or setting-maul one end of which has a gable or V shape. Also a small wooden hammer or mallet used by a presiding officer.

1805 T. S. WEBB *Freemason's Monitor* (1812) 35 The common gavel is an instrument made use of by operative masons, to break off the corners of rough stones, the better to fit them for the builder's use; but we, as free and accepted masons, are taught to make use of it for the more noble and glorious purpose of divesting our minds and consciences of all the vices. 1860 WORCESTER 608/3 *Gavel.* . . . A small mallet used by presiding officers to attract attention & preserve order; an emblem of authority. *Shepard.* 1948 *Minneapolis Star* 17

Sep. 27/1 A gavel made from wood grown at Mount Vernon, home of George Washington, . . . is now in possession of the Minneapolis Board of Realtors.

Hence **gavel,** *v. tr.* and *intr.* (See quots.) *Colloq.*

1948 *Chi. Tribune* 23 June 1. 1/7 Gov. Green gaveled for attention at 10:22 a.m. **1948** *Time* 2 Aug. 12/3 The rules were gaveled through by Convention Chairman Albert Fitzgerald, president of the United Electric Workers.

* **gay,** *a.* In combs.: (1) **gay cat,** a young or amateur tramp, *slang;* (2) **feather,** (see quot. 1881); (3) **lady's slipper,** = **showy lady's slipper;** (4) **Nineties,** the 1890's, so called from the fashions and manners of the time; (5) **quaker,** (see quot.), *obs.;* (6) **Gayway,** the midway of the San Francisco Exposition; (7) **wings,** the Indian pink, *Polygala paucifolia.*

(1) **1897** J. Flynt in *Forum* Feb. 741 Nothing arouses his [*sc.* the hobo's] scorn more than the dilettante, or 'gay-cat,' as he calls him, who gives up waiting and buys a regulation ticket. **1926** J. Black *You Can't Win* x. 129 When a bum's 'convention' is to be held, the jungle is first cleared of all outsiders such as 'gay cats,' 'dingbats' [etc.]. — (2) **1817–8** Eaton *Botany* (1822) 336 *Liatris spicata,* gay feather, button snakeroot. . . . Diuretic and tonic. **1881** *Lib. Universal Knowledge* VI. 493 *Gay-feather,* the common name for the *Liatris scariosa* and *L. spicata.* — (3) **1817–8** Eaton *Botany* (1822) 261 *Cypripedium spectabile,* gay ladies' slipper. . . . Stem leafy. . . . Woods. **1836** Lincoln *Botany* App. 92 *Cypripedium spectabile,* (gay ladies' slipper, . . .) stem leafy; lobe of the style ovalcordate. — (4) **1937** Mitchell *Horse & Buggy Age* 81 Such a street was Washington Street in Hartford during the elegant Eighties and gay Nineties. **1949** *Chi. D. News* 8 Jan. 13/5 Princes and potentates, . . . couples in gay nineties attire . . . were part of the costume parade.

(5) **1793** *Aurora* (Phila.) 6 Nov. (Th.), Her dress was pretty nearly that marked as 'gay quakers'; she wore a white gown, white gloves, green petticoat, and drab cloak. — (6) **1939** *News Letter and Wasp* (S.F.) 24 Feb. 5 Not all the concessions on the Gayway at the Exposition are devoted to fun and frolic. — (7) **1850** S. F. Cooper *Rural Hours* 86 As for the May-wings, or 'gay-wings,' they are in truth one of the gayest little blossoms we have. **1893** *Amer. Folk-Lore* VI. 140 *Polygala paucifolia,* gay wings. Ferrisburgh, Vt.; N.Y. **1900** Higginson *Outdoor Studies* 36 Some early plants . . . are still found near Worcester in the greatest abundance,—as the larger Yellow Violet, the Red Trillium, . . . and the pretty fringed Polygala, which Miss Cooper christened 'Gay-Wings.'

b. *To get gay,* to take undue liberties. *Slang.*

1899 G. Ade *Fables in Slang* (1900) 109 The Cooper, perceiving that he had come very near getting Gay with our First Families, apologized for Cutting In. **1911** J. F. Wilson *Land Claimers* vi. 80 And I wouldn't get gay round her.

gazabo gəˈzebo, *n.* [Sp. *gazapo,* a shrewd fellow.] A gawky fellow, a guy (see also quot. 1903). *Slang.*

1896 G. Ade *Artie* v. 44 Who does I meet comin' out o' the house but a cheap gazabo. **1903** *Cin. Enquirer* 9 May 13/1 Gazabo—A prowler; rounder or proprietor. **1947** Paul *Linden* 124 Would that have anything to do with *dementia praecox,* or whatever the old gazabo from Malden said she had?

G.B., see **grand bounce.** Also **g.b.**

* **gee,** *interj.* and *n.* [See note.]

In **1. gee** is app. a minced form of * *Jesus.* In **2.** it is the old term used in driving horses, etc. In **3.** the appropriateness of the first element is not clear.

1. Used in various expressions, as **gee buck, gee whillikin(s), gee whitaker, gee whiz,** denoting surprise or strong feeling. *Colloq.*

1895 *D.N.* I. 376 Gee buck! See all them bees drownded in the honey! — **1851** *Polly Peablossom* 52 Jewhilliken, how he could whip er nigger! **1857** *Knickerb.* Nov. 435 And great Gewhilikins! wasn't the snow peppering down! — **1856** *Town Talk* (S.F.) 20 July 1/1 Gee-whitaker! what a kurchy she made, and bowed so low that I nearly fell outer my dickey onto the floor. **1902** L. Richards *Mrs. Tree* 221 But Squashnose he sung out 'Gee whittakers!' and raised up his head. — **1885** Gray *Bad Boy at Home* 8 (We.), Gee wiz. **1948** *Redbook Mag.* April 73/1 'Gee whiz!' he exclaimed.

2. gee pole, the pole by which a dog sled is guided.

1904 S. E. White *Silent Places* xvii. 180 The girl took charge of the gee-pole with which the sledge would be guided. **1913** *Outing* Feb. 525/1 Following me came the dogs driven by the man at the 'gee-pole,' who also wore snowshoes.

3. gee string, a breechclout or breech-cloth. Also **G-string.**

1878 Beadle *Western Wilds* 249 Around each boy's waist is the tight 'geestring,' from which a single strip of cloth runs between the limbs from front to back. **1891** *Harper's Mag.* Dec. 36/2 Some of the boys wore only 'G-strings' (as, for some reason, the breech-clout is commonly called on the prairie). **1948** *Time* 5 April 12/3 The American Airlines' lost & found department was looking interestedly for whatever party had lost a case of beer, an automatic back-scratcher, three burlesque-type G-strings, a strait jacket.

* **gem,** *n.*

1. A form of muffin made of coarse flour. Also attrib. Cf. **graham gem, hominy gem.**

1875 *Carson Valley News* 20 Feb., Take, for example, the gem pans, which must be good tools to work with. **1882** Owens *Cook Book* 132 Heat gem irons quite hot. **1885** *Buckeye Cookery* 44 [Recipe for] Wheaten Gems. **1920** Howells *Vacation of Kelwyns* 102 She smoothly reappeared with a plate of gems in her hand.

2. gem tomato, = ?**cherry tomato.** *Rare.*

1882 Lathrop *Echo of Passion* iv, The lawyer was gradually led away from his theme by a diversion to small fruits and gem tomatoes.

3. (*cap.*) In nicknames (see quots.). *Obs.*

1860 Hancock *Five Years* 196 My ultimate destination being Cold Spring . . . a spot which has been well christened the 'Gem of the Hudson.' **1881** Marshall *Through Amer.* (1882) 135 Soon we reach Laramie, called the 'Gem City of the Mountains.'

b. Esp. **Gem State, Gem of the Mountains,** nicknames for Idaho, in allusion to the alleged meaning of the Indian word "Idaho" (see quot. 1885).

[**1885** Onderdonk *Idaho* 10 Idaho in English signifies 'the Gem of the Mountains.'] **1914** *Sunset* April 772 The 'Gem State' holds no greater treasure than the emerald of its fields and water-courses. **1948** *Distribution Age* April 8 Come to Idaho, Gem of the Mountains.

Hence **Gem Stater,** an Idahoan.

1947 *Chr. Sci. Mon.* 20 Dec. 11/2 With virtually a new squad, the Gem Staters are an unknown quantity this season.

gemma grass. = **gama grass.** *Rare.* — **1890** Gunter *Miss Nobody* iv. (1891) 47 The mesa is bare of everything for five hundred yards but gemma grasses.

* **general,** *a.* and *n.*

1. *n. N. Eng.* (See quot. 1889.)

1763 in *Pub. Col. Soc.* XIX. 383 From this Sum . . . deduct the great General, which is Salt, Bait, Candles, Ballast, Boots etc. . . . From the Crew's 5/8 . . . is to be deducted the small General so called, being for Wood and Provisions of all Sorts, paid for by the Crew. **1889** *Cent.* 2482/3 *Great generals,* the general charges furnished by the owner of a fishing-vessel, including wood, water, lights, knives, salt, bait, etc. . . . *Small generals,* the general charges furnished by the crew of a fishing-vessel, as the provisions, lines, hooks, etc.

2. A complimentary title conferred informally by popular usage. *Colloq.*

1805 Parkinson *Tour* I. 272 Of the company then present, there will not be one out of ten who is not either Esquire, General, Colonel [etc.]. **1884** Shepherd *Prairie Exper.* 95 Along the road he saluted several acquaintances as General, or Judge. **1907** London *Road* 148 'General' Kelly, with an army of two thousand hoboes, lay in camp at Chautauqua Park.

3. One of the two leaders of rival groups at a corn husking. *Obs.*

1882 *Cent. Mag.* XXIV. 874 Two 'gin'r'ls' are chosen from among the most famous corn-shuckers on the ground, and these proceed to divide the shuckers into two parties.

4. *a.* In combs.: (1) **general assembly,** the legislature of a colony or state; (2) **association,** (*a*) an association of the American colonies to resist Great Britain, also **general continental association,** *obs.,* (*b*) an association of Baptist churches for coöperative effort; (3) **conference,** a conference or congress of representatives of the Methodist Episcopal Church, constituting its highest legislative and judicial authority; (4) **court,** see as a main entry; (5) **delivery,** the department of a post office having charge of mail to be delivered to those who call for it, also attrib.; (6) **election,** see as a main entry; (7) **freight agent,** a railroad official having general supervision over freight; (8) **government,** the federal government of the U.S.; (9) **land office,** a bureau of the federal government or of a state government which has charge of the surveying and sale of public lands, consideration of land claims, etc.; (10) * **manager,** a city manager who has supervision over all aspects of municipal administration (see also quot. 1905), also attrib.; (11) **merchant,** the owner of a general store; (12) **partner,** in a business firm, a partner whose liability is unlimited; (13) **pas-**

senger agent, a railroad executive who has general supervision over passenger traffic; (14) **railway mail superintendent,** a railway executive who has general supervision of the carrying of the mail by the railroad; (15) **store,** a store having a varied assortment of goods; (16) **superintendent,** an executive official of a railroad, also a clergyman who supervises many churches within a denomination; (17) **ticket,** see as a main entry; (18) **treat,** (see quots. 1848, 1881).

(1) **1619** *Va. House of Burgesses* 16 It is fully agreed att this Generall Assembly [etc.]. **1800** JEFFERSON *Notes* 115 They on the 24th of July 1621, by charter under their common seal, declared that from thenceforward there should be two supreme councils in Virginia, the one to be called the council of state . . . the other to be called the general assembly to be convened by the governor once yearly or oftener, which was to consist of the council of state, and two burgesses out of every town, hundred, or plantation, to be respectively chosen by the inhabitants. **1949** *Chi. D. News* 9 March 1/7 The General Assembly Wednesday ordered an investigation of Communist 'and other subversive activities' at the University of Chicago and Roosevelt College in Chicago. — (2) (*a*) **1775** in *Amer. Sp.* XX. (1945) 271 Georgia has joined the General Association and appointed delegates to the Continental Congress. **1775** *Jrnls. Cont. Congress* II. 251 The convention of that Colony [=Ga.] agreed to enter into the general continental association. (*b*) **1849** CHAMBERLAIN *Ind. Gazetteer* 72 [The Baptists] have a 'General Association' for Domestic Missionary purposes. — (3) **1792** RICHARD WHATCOAT *MS Jrnl.* 1 Nov., Began our general Conference. **1829** A. SHERWOOD *Gaz. Georgia* (ed. 2) 248 It is difficult for them to realize the *one hundred dollars* allowed them by the General Conference. **1924** *M. E. General Conference Jrnl.* 180 The Commission makes its formal report to this General Conference.

(5) **1846** *Hunt's Merch. Mag.* XIV. 130 The polite and faithful attendants in the general delivery department belong to his gang. **1902** *U.S. Post. Laws & Reg.* § 636 Letters having as a part of their address the words 'Transient,' 'To be called for': . . . must be placed in the general delivery. — (7) **1880** *Bradstreet's* 17 Nov. 3/3 [It] resulted from a misapprehension on the part of the general freight agent. — (8) **1788** in W. LITTELL *Polit. Trans. Kentucky* (1926) 97 Declared independent of Virginia, to whom is she [Kentucky] to look up for succour! . . . She may call on the present general government, but whatever may be the wish of congress, they can give them no relief. **1898** *Boston Herald* 3 June 10/3 The general government imposed upon the railroads the duty of equipping their freight cars with automatic drawbars. — (9) **1790** HAMILTON *Works* VII. 48 It seems requisite that the general land-office should be established at the seat of government. **1949** *Time* 3 Jan. 52/2 The underwater lands are one of the juiciest holdings of the Texas General Land Office, which uses the proceeds to help finance the state's schools.

(10) **1905** *McClure's Mag.* 337 The head of this committee is Senator Nelson W. Aldrich, who has been described as 'the boss of the United States,' 'the power behind the throne,' 'the general manager of the United States.' **1910** *Harper's Wkly.* 21 May LIV. 14/3 We are now doing all our work under the direction and supervision of the General Manager, where we formerly did the same work by contract. . . . The general-manager plan can be applied to large cities as well as to smaller ones. — (11) **1877** JOHNSON *Anderson Co., Kansas* 177 G. W. Iler and W. J. Bayles . . . opened a store as general merchants. **1891** O'BEIRNE *Leaders Ind. Territory* 35/2 John R. Davis . . . had the tie contract in the Choctaw Nation and was a general merchant at Durant. — (12) **1887** *Courier-Journal* 5 Feb. 5/6 J. T. Williams, J. S. Calloway are general partners, and said C. C. Mengel, Jr. is special partner. — (13) **1873** *Newton Kansan* 3 July 3/2 A. E. Touzalin, general passenger agent and manager of the land department of the A.T. & S. railroad, is one of the directors of the Harvey county Savings Bank. **1895** *N.Y. Dramatic News* 14 Dec. 2/2 This general scheme of making business so good for theatrical companies . . . is the invention of General Passenger Agent Charlton. — (14) **1890** *Railways of Amer.* 317 Subsequently, Colonel Armstrong became the first General Railway Mail Superintendent, and held this office until ill-health compelled him to resign, in 1871.

(15) **1835** MARTIN *Descr. Va.* 134 A neat village with considerable trade, and containing 16 dwelling houses, 3 general stores, 2 groceries. **1948** *Bangor* (Me.) *D. News* 28 July 1 Stopping at the general store here to replenish his food supply, Shaffer . . . said he expected to be at Mt. Katahdin, Aug. 4. — (16) **1897** T. C. CLARKE *Amer. Railway* 154 The general manager is assisted by general or division superintendents in charge of roadway, motive power, and trains of one or more separate divisions. **1924** *M. E. General Conference Jrnl.* 159 The General Superintendents wish to express their appreciation of the generous bearing maintained toward them both by the ministry and the laity. — (18) *a***1848** HOFFMAN in Bartlett 155, I nearly got myself into a difficulty with my new acquaintances by handing the landlord a share of the reckoning, for having presumed to pay a part of a general treat while laboring under the disqualification of being a stranger. **1848** BARTLETT 155 A general treat is a treat of a glass of liquor given by a person in a tavern to the whole company present. **1881** PIERSON *In the Brush* 169 'A general treat' is where the whisky is purchased by a 'general collection' taken in this way, and put into a water-bucket or larger vessel, and all parties come forward and help themselves with a gourd dipper.

b. In less frequent or rare combs., now obs.: (1) **general assistant,** a colonial town official; (2) **camp meeting,** (see quot.); (3) **fence,** in colonial times, a fence around a general field; (4) **field,** in colonial times, a field owned or used in common by a group of colonists; (5) **land agency,** a business establishment dealing in all kinds of real estate; (6) **land agent,** a broker or agent engaged in buying and selling land; (7) **line,** ?the boundary line of a colony; (8) **Lynch,** a personification of the leader of a lawless mob, cf. **lynch,** *v.;* (9) * **officer,** (see quot.); (10) **recorder,** in colonial Rhode Island, a public official having custody of the records of the colony; (11) **sergeant,** an official in Rhode Island in colonial times having duties corresponding in general to those of a sheriff; (12) **treasurer,** in colonial times in Rhode Island, the title of the treasurer of the colony.

(1) **1648** *Providence Rec.* XV. 15 If ye sd. prsidt. shall dye then ye Genr. Assistt. of That Towne wher the Presidt. was Chosen shall supply [etc.]. **1685** *Ib.* XVII. 62 To Captaine Arthur fennor mr. Joseph Jenckes And mr. Richard Arnold generall Assistants in providence. — (2) **1847** R. DAVIDSON *Presbyterian Ch. in Ky.* 136 Although each denomination sometimes operated apart, the customary method was to hold their meetings conjointly, under the name of General camp-meetings. — (3) **1638** *R.I. Col. Rec.* I. 53 It is also ordered that a General Fence be made. **1662** *Conn. Rec.* I. 381 There is great neglect in veiwinge Generall fences. — (4) **1676** in *E.-Hampton Rec.* I. 386 Which is to be vnderstood yt noe Cattell shalbe kept or bayted within the Generall feild & yt uppon the penaltie of five shillinges for every beast soe bayted kept or turned with the said Common feild Contrarie to this order. **1697** *Providence Rec.* XI. 29 All the Generall ffields about & belonging to this Towne of Providence.

(5) **1853** *S. Lit. Messenger* XIX. 334/2 Beechim . . . had some two or three years before 'located' in the country, and was doing a general land-agency and collecting business, surveying lands, &c. — (6) **1845** J. W. NORRIS *Chi. Directory* 84 Henry W. Clarke. . . . Conveyancer and General Land Agent. — (7) **1684** *E.-Hampton Rec.* II. 148 All horses or horse kind that shall bee found in ye streete or by the Generall line without ffetters shall be liable to be pounded. — (8) **1832** *Polit. Examiner* (Shelbyville, Ky.) 26 May 2/3 One or two of their most respectable citizens acted as *General Lynch* gave the war whoop, and proceeded to tear down several houses, . . . breaking and destroying the furniture as they went along. — (9) **1641** *Mass. Liberties* 227 By Generall officers we meane, our Governor, Deputy Governor, Assistants, Treasurer, Generall of our warres.

(10) **1647** *R.I. Col. Rec.* I. 195 The General Recorder's Office shall be in the generall, to keep a Coppie of all the Records or Acts of the Generall Assemblie, Generall and Particular Courts of Judicature [etc.]. **1685** *Providence Rec.* XVII. 65 John Sanford of Portsmouth Gennerall Recorder of this Colloney of Rhode Island. —(11) **1647** *R.I. Col. Rec.* I. 197 He that is chosen Generall Sargant shall be an able man of Estate, for so ought a Sheriff to be, whose place he supplies; whose office shall be to attend all Colony Courts of Tryall, and to serve . . . all Writts originall or judiciall. **1670** *Providence Rec.* III. 150 James Rogers Genrl: Serjant Coming into this present meeting. — (12) **1654** *Providence Rec.* II. 76 John Sayles [is chosen] Genll. Treasurer. **1690** *Portsmouth Rec.* 244 Return thereof to be made to the Generall Treasurer of this Colony.

As the last term in **big, Captain-, clothier, corn, lieutenant, paymaster, physician, political, president, solicitor, state surveyor, surveyor general.**

general court.

1. (*cap.*) *N. Eng.* A legislative assembly, esp. the legislature of Massachusetts or New Hampshire.

In early times such a body exercised judicial as well as legislative functions, hence the name. See John Noble, *Records of the Courts of Assistants of the Colony of the Massachusetts Bay 1630–1692.*

1629 *Mass. Charter,* The last Wednesday in Easter tearme, . . . [all] officers of the said Company shalbe, in the General Court or Assembly, . . . newly chosen for the yeare ensueing. **1649** *R.I. Court Rec.* I. 6 Cace . . . refferred untill the next General Court to be houlden at Portsmouth. **1721** *Jrnls. H. Rep. Mass.* III. 70 His Excellency . . . was pleased to Adjourn the General Court unto Monday the 10th Corrant. **1891** (*title*), The New Hampshire Manual for the General Court. **1933** *Pub. Col. Soc.* XXIX. xxii–xxiii, The possession of these various judicial powers plainly made the General Court much more than the legislative body it is today. Like the assemblies in other colonies, in many respects it was really a court. **1949** *N. Eng. Quart.* Mar. 11 This was an annual gathering of the ministers of the province at the time of the May General Court.

b. *Great and General Court,* (see quots.).

1629 *Mass. Charter,* There shall or maie be held . . . upon every last Wednesday in Hillary, Easter, Trinity, and Michas termes . . . one greate, generall, and solemne Assemblie, which foure Generall Assemblies shalbe stiled and called the Foure Greate and Generall Courts of the saide Company. **1872** Holmes *Poet* ii. 56 The House of Representatives, otherwise called the Great and General Court of the State of Massachusetts. **1919** *Pub. Col. Soc.* XXI. 421 In Massachusetts, by the law of 1634, the towns were to send two or three deputies to the Great and General Court.

c. Also used of a state legislature outside of New England (see quots.).

1765 R. Rogers *Acct. N. Amer.* 134 At which three places their [=N.C.] general court of assembly for enacting laws sit alternately. **1948** *Chi. Tribune* 11 June 1. 24/3 The tax proposals, if adopted, would permit the general court [in Illinois] . . . to impose an electric energy tax.

2. A trial court of general jurisdiction. *Obs.*

[**1675** Andros in Easton *Indian War* 106 There was at the City Hall an Order of the last Gen[er]all Court of Assizes the 12th Instant.] **1705** Beverley *Virginia* IV. 21 The General Court, is a Court held by the Governour and Council . . . who by Custom are the Judges of it, in all Civil Disputes. . . . This court . . . take cognizance of all Causes, Criminal, Penal, Ecclesiastical and Civil. . . . This Court is held twice a year, beginning on the 15th of April, and on the 15th of October. **1783** Stokes *View* 95 The superior Court of common law, which was formerly called [in Maryland] the Provincial Court, is now called 'the General Court,' and has three Judges, who are appointed by the same authority. **1874** *Southampton* (N.Y.) *Rec.* I. iv, All affairs of any consequence to the town in general were decided at the Quarter Courts, and in almost every case where the General Court is referred to, the Quarter Courts are meant. These are composed of the freemen of the town.

general election.

1. (*cap.*) In the Massachusetts Bay colony after 1691, the annual election by the House of Representatives of its own officers together with the election by the General Court of members of the Council. Cf. **election court.**

1716 *Mass. H. Rep. Jrnl.* I. 80 Nothing but the General Election prevents me from doing my Duty to my Country in Visiting the Frontiers. **1725** *N.-Eng. Courant* 24–31 May 2/1 Wednesday last being our General Election, the [Mass.] House of Representatives chose William Dudley Esq; for their Speaker, and John Wainwright Esq; Clerk.

b. general election court, =election court. *Obs.*

*c***1680** J. Hull *Diary* 202, 22d of 3d [=March] was our general election court.

2. An election, occurring on a date set by law, in which every constituency in a given community or state selects a representative for its legislature.

1789 *Phila. Ordinances* (1812) 64 The general election next preceding every election to be held in pursuance of this act. **1911** *Okla. Session Laws* 3 Legisl. 266 The first of the said legislative periods shall begin within the 16th day after the general election in November.

general ticket.

1. *Polit.* A ticket having on it the names of candidates to be voted on throughout a state as a whole rather than within a district of the state. Also attrib.

1800 Jefferson *Writings* X. 134 On the subject of an election by a general ticket or by districts, most persons here [in Phila.] seem to have made up their minds. *c***1824** Benton *30 Years' View* I. 38/1 The general ticket system now existing in ten States was . . . adopted by the leading men of those States, to enable them to consolidate the vote of the State. **1902** Meyer *Nominating Systems* 14 The advantage offered by the general ticket,—the maintenance of the sovereign individuality of the State and of the supremacy of the party, could only be secured on condition that a single list of candidates for electors, was regularly put into shape somewhere on behalf of the people who were to vote for it.

2. general ticket agent, on a railroad, an official in charge of ticket sales.

1857 in W. P. Smith *Railway Celebrations* II. 36 Endorsed S. M. Cole, General Ticket Agent, B. and Ohio Railroad. **1907** *Railroad Gazette* 19 July 81/2 F. M. Howell . . . has been appointed General Passenger and Ticket Agent, succeeding to the duties of James D. Whittington, General Ticket Agent.

Genesee ˌdʒɛnəˈsi, *n.* [*Genesee* Co., N.Y.] In combs. now obs.: (1) **Genesee fever,** (see quot.); (2) **flour,** flour made from Genesee wheat; (3) **oil,** (see quots.); (4) **wheat,** wheat of superior quality grown in the Genesee region of western N.Y.

(1) **1800** J. Maude *Niagara* 92 The insalubrity of the Genesee was however proverbial, and the intermittent fever, or in common parlance, the fever and ague, was, when speaking of this district called the Genesee fever. — (2) [**1826** *Va. Herald* (Fredericksburg) 18 Oct. 3/1 The last sales of Genessee brought 103 cents, and an advance on the latter is now required.] **1867** *N.Y. Tribune* 27 Nov. 4/1 Forty years ago, 'Genesee Flour' was known and prized in foreign markets. — (3) **1813** *N.Y. State Soc. Arts* III. 28 Amber has been found in New Jersey, and Petroleum, under the name of Genessee or Seneka oil, is obtained in the western district of this state. **1857** Dana *Mineralogy* 96 Petroleum is . . . commonly called *Genesee* or *Seneca oil,* under which name it is sold in market. — (4) **1850** Howard *Travels* 26, I fancy that quotations of the price of Gennessee wheat are familiar to the frequenters of our corn market.

***Genie,** *n.* One of ten assistants of the Grand Wizard of the Ku-Klux Klan. *Obs.* — **1867** in Lester & Wilson *Ku Klux Klan* 136 The officers . . . shall consist of a Grand Wizard of the Empire and his ten Genii [etc.].

gente ˈhɛntə, *n. S.W.* [Sp.] The intelligentsia. In full **gente de razon.** *Colloq.*

1831 Beechey *Voyage to Pacific* II. 47 They style themselves *Gente de Razon,* to distinguish themselves from the Indians, whose intellectual qualities are frequent subjects of animadversion amongst these enlightened communities. **1852** *L.A. Star* 3 April 2/3 He staked all the cash he had (the proceeds of many a pile and blister), his horse, and then his cloak, and the last we saw him, he was bantering the *gente* to stake his hat upon the mare. **1872** *Overland Mo.* Aug. 164/1 An incident is related, which is about as worthy of credence as the majority of ghost stories related by the *gente de razon.* **1946** McWilliams *So. Calif. Country* 51 It must be emphasized that the number of families constituting this Spanish upper crust—the *gente de razon* of the province—was never large.

***gentian,** *n.* As the last term in **closed, fringed, horse, soap, soapwort gentian.**

***gentile,** *n.*

1. Among the Mormons, a non-Mormon. Usu. *cap.*

1838 *Test* (Rushville, Ill.) 12 Dec. 3/3 It was intimated from the Head Quarters of the Mormons, they ought not to pay their debts—that the 'gentiles were bound to support the chosen people of God.' **1843** H. Caswall *Prophet of the 19th Cent.* 157 If any one of them found a brother Danite in difficulty with a Gentile, they must rescue him, whether right or wrong. **1904** *N.Y. Ev. Post* 12 March 5 Representative Gentiles of Salt Lake City have taken preliminary steps toward the organization of a non-Mormon party. **1947** *Time* 21 July 18/3 Salt Lake City is probably the one city in the world where a Jew is a Gentile too.

attrib. **1846** *Ill. State Reg.* (Springfield) 20 Oct. 2/6 The Mormons, in their palmy days, . . . [were] formidable to their 'gentile' neighbors. **1899** Catherwood *Mackinac Stories* 98 Is it true that a Gentile sailboat was sunk in Lake Galilee and kept hidden there until inquiry ceased, and then was raised, repainted, and launched again, a good Mormon boat?

2. Among Shakers, one who is not a Shaker. Also attrib. *Obs.*

1857 *Harper's Mag.* July 167/2 Opposite my lodgings was the house for public worship. . . . Soon the seats between the entrance doors, called the 'lobby,' were filled by 'the Gentiles.' **1867** Dixon *New Amer.* (1869) 272 The [Shaker] store, at which pretty trumperies are sold to the Gentile belles.

***gentleman,** *n.*

1. *The gentleman from,* in a legislative body, as the House of Representatives, the usual method of referring to a fellow member.

1787 J. Madison in *Sp. & Doc. Amer. Hist.* I. 59 Mr. Wilson was in favour of the motion. It had been opposed by the gentleman from Virga. [Mr Randolph] but the arguments used had not convinced him. **1860** *36th Congress* 1 Sess. H. R. Rep. No. 249, 111 The question before the committee is the point of order raised by the gentleman from Arkansas. **1905** T. Dixon *Clansman* 138 The presiding officer recognised the young Democrat and responded: 'The gentleman from New York.'

transf. **1856** *Western Citizen* (Paris, Ky.) 14 Mar. 1/5 My feelings are much like those of the gentleman from Bourbon.

2. (See quot.) *Colloq.*

1902 *D.N.* II. 235 *Gentlemen.* Used in exclamation denoting astonishment, or when anything extraordinary is beyond description. 'George don't git mad very often, but when he does git mad—*Gentlemen!!!*'

3. In combs.: (1) **gentleman friend,** a masculine friend or beau; (2) **tailor,** a man who is a tailor, *obs.;* (3)

tory, a tory *q.v.* of the rank of "gentleman," *obs.;* (4) **turkey,** (see quot.—prob. *jocose*), *obs.*

(1) **1829** M. B. SMITH *Forty Yrs. Washington Society* (1906) 307 We have at least 6 or 7 young gentlemen friends, who are frequently with us. **1886** JAMES *Bostonians* 203 She had been indebted for this service to a 'gentleman-friend,' who wrote her everything that happened in Boston, and what every one had every day for dinner. **1909** C. FORT *Outcast Manufacturers* 15, I have a gentleman friend. — (2) **1838** BELL *Men & Things* 232 Very differently paid from the poor 'tailoresses' are the 'gentlemen tailors.' **1855** BESTE *Wabash* II. 140 He put his spectacles on his nose, and read to me what purported to be a writ at the suit of D. Hartsock (such was the name of the 'gentleman' tailor). — (3) **1775** in *Boston Ev. Transcript* 26 April III. 12/7 They take all Gentlemen Toreys that come from Boston. — (4) **1859** BARTLETT, Gentleman Turkey. A turkey cock. The mock modesty of Western States requires that a male turkey should be so called.

b. In the possessive: (1) **gentleman's** (or **gentlemen's**) **agreement, bargain,** an agreement not legally binding, but the keeping of which is a matter of honor; (2) **cane,** the prince's feather, *Persicaria orientalis;* (3) **driver,** (see quot.), *obs.;* (4) **pea,** (see quot.), *obs.;* (5) **sorrel,** field sorrel, *Rumex acetosella.*

(1) **1886** in WINKLER *Morgan the Magnificent* (1930) 107 [In 1886 . . . was the first of a series of memorable dinner-table conferences. At them were formulated so-called] gentlemen's agreements. **1930** *News-Chron.* 5 Dec. 9/1 The arrangement respecting the cinemas was a 'gentleman's bargain.' **1949** *Time* 14 Mar. 82/3 The three partners met again . . . and came to a gentleman's agreement. — (2) **1894** *Amer. Folk-Lore* VII. 97 *Polygonum orientale,* . . . gentleman's cane. Mansfield, O. — (3) **1892** *Vt. Agric. Rep.* XII. 152 The horse that I believe is in the best demand to-day . . . is the so-called gentleman's driver or light carriage horse. — (4) **1788** WASHINGTON *Diaries* III. 346 Counted the number of the following articles which are contained in a pint: viz. of The small round pease commonly called Gentleman's Pease. — (5) **1892** *Amer. Folk-Lore* V. 102 *Rumex acetosella,* gentlemen's sorrel. Cambridge, Mass.

As the last term in **buckra, gift, southern, sporting gentleman.**

***gentry,** *n.* As the last term in **carpetbag, dominion, patent, silk-stocking gentry.**

geoduck ˈguɪˌdʌk, *n.* [See note.] A large, edible clam, *Panope generosa,* found on the Pacific Coast.

No doubt from a Nisqualli Indian term meaning "dig deep." See Webster *s.v. gweduc.* In *Natural History,* April 1948, 190, the name is said to be based on that of a certain John F. Gowey. The pronunciation given here is the one said to be correct on p. 163 of the magazine cited, but *Cent. Supp., s.v. goeduk,* has [ˈgoidʌk].

1883 *Nat. Museum Bul.* No. 27, 239 *Glycimeris generosa* . . . is a Pacific coast species, known as the 'Geoduck' or 'Giant Clam.' *Ib.* 263 Geoduck or Giant Clam . . . [is found on] Pacific coast, in rivers and estuaries, from Puget Sound to San Diego. **1903** *Sci. Amer. Supp.* 11 April 22, 805 In Alaskan waters is found a monster clam, the 'geoduck,' one of which would afford a meal for several persons. **1948** *Nat. Hist.* April 165/3 The shovel was laid aside, and two skillful hands reached into the ooze to lift the great geoduck gently from its home.

Hence **geoducker, geoducking.**

1948 *Nat. Hist.* April 162/1 All this was before we went gooeyducking. *Ib.* 190/2 It would not only be poor sportsmanship but also illegal to jab a fishhook into a bivalve's projecting part and let the wounded animal draw down with it into the mud a cord or stick for the geoducker to follow in his digging.

geographic tortoise. (See quots.) — **1842** *Nat. Hist. N.Y., Zoology* III. 18 The Geographic Tortoise. *Emys geographica.* . . . They are exceedingly active and vigorous. **1884** GOODE *Fisheries* 156 The other two species [of the genus *Malacoclemmys*] the Geographic Tortoises, *M. geographica* and *M. Lesueuri,* are of comparatively rare occurrence, and are not used for food to any considerable extent.

geological survey. The preparation of topographic and geologic maps and similar data.

For an account of the history of the state and federal surveys, see *Bulletin of the National Research Council,* no. 88 (1932).

1835 *N.J. Acts 1834–5* 90 The Governor . . . is hereby empowered to employ some suitable and scientific person or persons to make a Geological and Mineralogical survey of the state. **1895** *N. Dakota Laws* 97 The geological survey shall be carried on with a view to a complete account of the mineral kingdom, as represented in the State.

b. (*cap.*) A bureau that gathers and publishes such data.

1867 (*title*), Annual Report of the United States Geological and Geographical Survey of the Territories. **1903** *Dept. Agric. Yrbk. 1902* 735 The Department of the Interior, through the Hydrographic Division of the Geological Survey, deals with questions relating to the water supply. **1947** *Mazama* Sep. 1/2 On June 30 he retired from the United States Geological Survey where he has served for many years.

***geometer,** *n.* A surveyor. *Obs.* — **1773** in *Amer. Sp.* XX. (1945) 271 Is informed that his geometer Joseph Purcell has secretly taken copies of his surveys since his absence from America. **1802** in A. ELLICOTT *Jrnl.* (1803) 51 The geometer, and other officers that are to be employed, are already on their way from New Orleans.

***George,** *n.*

1. *Let George do it,* let someone (or something) else do the work or take the responsibility. *Colloq.* or *slang.*

1910 *Bookman* May 293/2 George McManus is holding something in store for those who liked 'The Newlyweds,' and his later creation, 'Let George do It.' What's going to happen when Lovey asks papa to hold Snookums and that hitherto devoted parent replies, 'Let George do it.' **1912** F. H. RICHARDSON *Motion Picture Handbook* 366 The objection to the motor-drive is the temptation for the operator to 'let George to it,' the motor representing 'George.' **1948** *Chi. Tribune* 10 Oct. (Grafic Mag.) 8/1 Producers have a way of saying 'Let George do it' whenever a particularly difficult villain role turns up.

2. George's cod, fish, (see quots.).

1884 GOODE *Fisheries* I. 201 In the markets the Cod from George's Bank are usually classed as 'George's fish,' and are considered to be of superior value. . . . The name is becoming a commercial term to describe Codfish of the finest quality. *Ib.,* 'Bank Cod' and 'Shore Cod' are commercial names, used in the same manner as the name 'George's Cod.'

***Georgia,** *n.* [Name of a southern state.] In combs., chiefly southern: (1) **Georgia bark,** a southern tree, *Pinckneya pubens,* the bark of which is used for medicinal purposes; (2) **butternut,** a brown color or shade such as that obtained by using butternut bark (*q.v.*) in dyeing, *obs.;* (3) **button,** (see quots.), *colloq.;* (4) **cracker,** a cracker (*q.v.*) living in Georgia; (5) **currency,** currency issued by Georgia, *obs.;* (6) **flower,** (see quot.); (7) **hamster,** (see quot. 1889), *obs.;* (8) **major,** a Georgian who has the honorary title of "Major," *jocose;* (9) **man,** (*a*) a citizen of Georgia, (*b*) (see quot.), *obs.;* (10) **pen,** a log prison formerly associated particularly with Georgia, *obs.;* (11) **piercer,** (see quot.), *rare;* (12) **(pitch) pine,** the longleaf pine, *Pinus palustris,* of the southern states, or its wood, also attrib.; (13) **ranger,** a ranger serving in or recruited from Georgia, *obs.;* (14) **stock,** see as a main entry; (15) **vocabulary,** a backwoods vocabulary thought of as characteristic of Georgians, *rare,* cf. **Georgiaism;** (16) **yellow pine,** = **Georgia (pitch) pine,** also attrib.

(1) **1810** MICHAUX *Arbres* I. 30 Georgia bark (*Pinckneya pubens*). . . . Georgia bark tree (Quinquina de la Georgia), nom donné par moi. **1813** MUHLENBERG *Cat. Plants* 23 Georgia bark, or Downy Pinkneya. **1942** *Amer. Philos. Soc. Trans.* XXXIII. 66/2 A sand-hill bog . . . about 1.7 miles northwest of Cox is believed to be the type locality of the famous Franklin tree (*Franklinia alatamaha*) which the Bartrams discovered here, apparently in association with the Georgia bark. — (2) **1889** *Cent. Mag.* Jan. 462/2 In time we appeared in every shade from Melton gray to Georgia butternut. — (3) [**1888** *Cent. Mag.* XXXVI. 769/2 The whites of the Confederacy were content with them, while the slaves skewered their 'galluses' to their trousers with wooden pins or the thorns of the locust.] **1933** *Montgomery Advt.* 6 Aug., 'Skewers,' in the South known as 'Georgia buttons,' are just crude forms of moles [*sic*] and the bone and shell pins of primitive peoples served the same purpose. — (4) **1830** *Boston Transcript* 1 Sep. 3/1 They are 'pernickety' now—to speak in the elegant language of the Georgia Cracker Dictionary. **1947** PERRY *Cities of Amer.* 198 She has some nine hundred factories of varied size and importance, which manufacture everything from gingham for Georgia peaches to cheese for Georgia crackers.

(5) **1831** W. SLOCOMB *Amer. Calculator* 86 The dollar is reckoned in . . . S. Carolina and Georgia 4s. 8d. = 7/30 Georgia currency. **1865** TROWBRIDGE *Three Scouts* xv. 158, I'll give ye a thousand dollars for that nigger, Georgia currency. — (6) **1942** RAWLINGS *C. Creek* 21 She had always 'porch plants' about, grown from slips, of geranium and aspidistra; fuchsia, 'the Georgia flower' [etc.]. — (7) [**1822** *Amer. Jrnl. Science* IV. 185 The Hamster of Georgia, called by some the *Gopper* [*sic*], which was described to me in 1804.] **1889** *Cent.* 2699/1 *Georgia hamster,* Rafinesque's name of the gopher of the southern United States, *Geomys tuza.* — (8) **1843** in THOMPSON *M. Jones* (1872) 163 It is now '*vexata questio*' (as the Lawyers say) with gentlemen of the 'Sword and Plume' whether you intend to extend your prohibition to 'Georgia Majors' and their subalterns—whether there are to be any exceptions to universal smooth faces. **1854** *Wide West* (S.F.) 27 Aug. 2/5 Digger Indians . . . are seen in the streets here;

the gentlemen in attire bordering on the summer costume of the Georgia major. — (9) (a) 1741 W. STEPHENS *Proc. Georgia* II. 80 A *Georgia* Man . . . was hardly to expect common Justice, or even common Civilty [in Charleston, S.C.]. (b) 1853 F. W. THOMAS *J. Randolph* 85 There I thought . . . that some Georgia man, as the negroes then called the slave-dealers—for to Georgia many of the negroes were then sold . . . would leap upon me from the woods.

(10) 1853 STOWE *Key* 160/1 The brothers were handcuffed, and, with their sisters, . . . put into a prison called a Georgia Pen. 1865 KELLOGG *Rebel Prisons* 353 I'd like to know if my girl has gone and married another, while I've been down in our Georgia pen. — (11) 1862 *Harper's Mag.* Nov. 737/1 The *Stomoxys georgina*—'Georgia Piercer,' or 'Gallinipper'— . . . if curses could annihilate it, would soon be driven from off the earth. — (12) 1796 *Ann. 4th Congress* 2 Sess. 2789 No. of feet of Georgia pine planks for decks, 85,930. 1810 MICHAUX *Arbres* I. 17 *Southern pine*, . . . [ou] *Georgia Pitch Pine*, dans les colonies des Indes occidentales et en Angleterre. 1842 BUCKINGHAM *Slave States* I. 177 The Georgia pitch pine is abundant, and it is a highly valuable tree. This is called by a great variety of names, such as the southern, the red, the brown, the yellow, and the long-leaved pine; but they all indicate the same kind of tree. 1919 CADY *Rhymes of Vt.* (1923) 57 Paid, Georgia pine for culvert beams; He'd better bought some chocolate creams. — (13) 1740 *S.C. Hist. Soc. Coll.* IV. 60 Capt. Palmer, with his own and the Georgia Rangers . . . , made Excursions everyday.

(15) 1835 LONGSTREET *Ga. Scenes* 53 Two men who were admitted on all hands to be the very *best men* in the country — which in the Georgia vocabulary, means they could flog any other two men in the country. — (16) 1814 *Ann. 13th Congress* 1 Sess. I. 668 Six cargoes, amounting to twenty-six hundred tons, of Georgia yellow pine timber . . . have been purchased on favorable terms. 1897 F. C. MOORE *How to Build a Home* 21 Georgia yellow pine is the best material for beams, but either spruce or hemlock makes fairly good floor-beams.

Georgiaism ˈdʒɔrdʒəˌɪzəm, *n.* An expression thought to be typical of the speech of Georgians. *Rare.* — 1851 *Polly Peablossom* 45 This Cole, though a limb of the law, was, to use a Georgiaism, a 'peert gambler.'

***Georgian,** *a.* and *n.*

1. *n.* A native or inhabitant of the colony or state of Georgia. Cf. **piny woods Georgian.**

1714 *S.C. Hist. Soc. Coll.* IV. 22 To assist him towards the Siege of St. Augustine [the General needed]. . . . Pay and the like allowance of Provisions for 200 Georgians. 1867 MUIR *Thousand-Mile Walk* (1916) 83 In particular, Georgians, even the commonest, have a most charmingly cordial way of saying to strangers, as they proceed on their journey, 'I wish you well, sir.' 1947 *Time* 27 Jan. 21/3 To Georgians it looked only like the end of Act Two of the breathless melodrama. 1949 D. O. MCGOVNEY *Amer. Suffrage* 120 The determination of Georgians to discriminate against whites of low economic status became obvious.

2. *a.* Of or pertaining to Georgia.

1762 WESLEY *Journal* (1827) III. 91 We had another Georgian day. 1866 F. KIRKLAND *Bk. Anecdotes* 496/1 The taunting Georgian girls on the porch clapped their dainty, tiny hands. 1948 *Ga. Review Spring* 99 The Georgian language is still spoken and there is a rustic air about the place.

b. Esp. with reference to a variety of cotton.

1797 F. BAILY *Tour* (1856) 285 There is a great deal of cotton raised in this district, which is sent down the river to New Orleans: it is of the nature of Georgian cotton. 1856 *Rep. Comm. Patents 1855: Agric.* 319 The different varieties of cotton cultivated in the United States are believed to belong to one species; that is, that the 'Georgian,' or 'Short-staple,' is the Sea Island, carried into the interior.

Georgia stock. A light plowstock, usu. of wood, formerly popular in Georgia and elsewhere in the South. Also **Georgia scooter stock.**

1891 *Memphis Appeal-Avalanche* 25 April 5/6 Headquarters for Single and Double Georgia Stocks, Wood and Iron Double Shovels, Eye and Handled Planter's Hoes. 1902 *Sears Cat.* 478/2 Our Steel Beam Georgia Stocks combine lightness and strength. 1944 CLARK *Pills* 110 They were selling the very same implements . . . Georgia scooter stocks, side harrows [etc.]. *Ib.* 281 Piled high around the foot of the counters among the nail and horseshoe kegs were the so-called 'plow irons' or the detachable shares which went with the homemade or shop-designed iron 'Georgia' stocks.

***geranium,** *n.* As the last term **in apple, balm, feather, fish, Martha Washington geranium.**

Gerardia dʒəˈrɑrdɪə, *n.* [John *Gerard* (1545–1612), Eng. botanist.] A genus of tropical American plants of the family Acanthaceae having yellow or rosy-purple flowers. Also (not *cap.*) a plant of this genus, often preceded by a distinguishing adjective.

1804 [see **gall of the earth*]. 1851 THOREAU *Autumn* (1894) 70 Still, purplish asters, late golden-rods . . . purple gerardia, etc. 1875 *Amer. Naturalist* IX. 388 On lower ground and in more moist soil, are several species of gerardia with rose-purple flowers. 1892 TORREY *Foot-Path Way* 81 The dainty rose gerardia, just now coming into bloom. 1939 *Nat. Geog. Mag.* Aug. 240/1 This pink gerardia . . . is a lovely shade of rose with a pale-yellow throat.

gerga ˈhɛrgə, *n. S.W.* [Sp. *jerga*, coarse cloth.] (See quot. 1844.) *Obs.* Cf. **xerga.** — 1844 GREGG *Commerce of Prairies* I. 209 Besides blankets, the New Mexicans manufacture a kind of coarse twilled woollen stuff, called *gerga*, which is checkered with black and white, and is used for carpets, and also by the peasantry for clothing. 1867 MELINE *Santa Fe & Back* 254 When the Mexicans speak of a man who has risen to a sufficiently prosperous condition to dress as Americans do, they say, 'Why, only a few years ago, he wore gerga!'

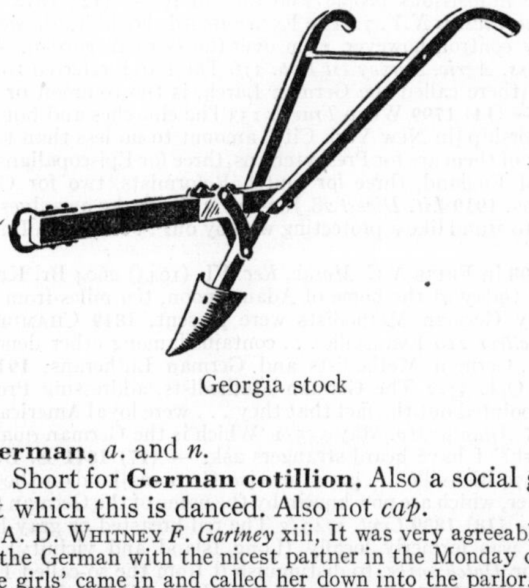

Georgia stock

***German,** *a.* and *n.*

1. Short for **German cotillion.** Also a social gathering at which this is danced. Also not *cap.*

1863 A. D. WHITNEY *F. Gartney* xiii, It was very agreeable . . . to dance the German with the nicest partner in the Monday class. *Ib.* x, 'The girls' came in and called her down into the parlor,—about pretty looks, and becoming dresses, and who danced with who at the 'German' last night. 1908 O. HENRY *Options* 189 He had a vocabulary of about three hundred and fifty words that he made stretch over four germans a week. 1947 SESSIONS *Cities of Amer.* 53 It is at this club's germans that the daughters of Baltimore's bon ton make their debut.

2. In combs.: (1) **German-American,** see as a main entry; (2) **aster,** a China aster; (3) **Baptists,** (see quot. 1904); (4) **club,** a social club at the meetings of which the german is danced; (5) **Coast,** see as a main entry; (6) **corn,** (see quot.), *obs.;* (7) **cotillion,** a round dance characterized by various involved steps and figures; (8) **cotton rose,** herb impious; (9) **Day,** a day upon which Germans in this country manifest their interest in or loyalty to Germany; (10) ***duck,** (see quot. 1889); (11) **Flats,** a region in Herkimer County, N.Y., near Utica, occupied as early as 1723 by German colonists, *obs.;* (12) **garden,** =**beer garden;** (13) **larch,** (see quot.); (14) **Lutheran,** a member of a Lutheran church established by Germans or German-Americans, the religious denomination composed of these, also attrib.; (15) **Methodist,** an American Methodist of German birth or extraction; (16) **quarter,** a part of a city occupied chiefly by Germans; (17) **Settlements,** (see quot. and cf. **German Coast**), *obs.;* (18) **snipe,** (see quot.); (19) **sock,** (see quots.); (20) **stove,** (see quot. and cf. **five-plate stove**), *obs.;* (21) **town,** see as a main entry.

(2) 1863 *Horticulturist* XVIII. 127/2 German Asters. . . . There are numerous varieties of the Aster, growing from four inches to two feet high. — (3) 1844 in RUPP *Relig. Denominations* 92 The German Baptists, or Brethren, are a denomination of Christians who emigrated to this country from Germany between the years 1718 and 1730. 1904 *Buffalo Commercial* 26 May 8 The National Conference of the religious sect known as 'the Dunkards' has voted to change its name to 'German Baptists.' — (4) 1884 *Cent. Mag.* March 657/1 But those who think society exists only for dancing have ample opportunities for their amusement in the constant number of balls given by the different german clubs in public halls. 1908 O. HENRY *Options* 188 Willie and I belonged to the same german club and athletic association.

(6) 1741 *Georgia Col. Rec.* IV. 680 A Woman having two Years ago picked out of *Indian* Corn, bought at *Purysburgh*, no more than three Grains of Rye (called here *German* Corn). — (7) 1839 M. PENCIL

White Sulphur P. 85 Tonight for the first time, we had the German cotillion. **1860** MOTLEY *Netherlands* (1868) I.ii.36 If I am ever caught dancing the German cotillon. — **(8) 1868** GRAY *Field Botany* 189 *F. Germanica*, German Cotton-rose. . . . Old dry fields from New York S. — **(9) 1943** MENEFEE *Assignment* 103 As many as 2000 Sheboygan people could be found celebrating German Day in the local park with the swastika flying overhead.

(10) 1844 *Nat. Hist. N.Y., Zoology* II. 343 In New Jersey, it [the gray duck] is called the Welsh or German Duck. **1889** *Cent.* 1789/1 German duck, the gadwall. Also called *Welsh drake.* — **(11) 1765** R. ROGERS *Concise Acct.* 67 [The Mohawk River] has adjacent to it many fine inter-vales, particularly that called the German Flats, being settled with Germans. **1839** H. CASWALL *America* 15 We then passed through a highly cultivated region, denominated the 'German Flats,' from the industrious people who inhabit it. — **(12) 1872** BRACE *Dangerous Classes N.Y.* 72 The Excise Board should be allowed very summary control, however, even over the German garden. — **(13) 1838** *Mass. Agric. Survey 1st Rep.* 116 The Larch referred to in the text and there called the German Larch, is the common or White Larch. — **(14) 1799** WELD *Travels* 153 The churches and houses for public worship [in New York City] amount to no less than twenty-two; four of them are for Presbyterians, three for Episcopalians of the church of England, three for Dutch Reformists, two for German Lutherans. **1919** *Lit. Digest* 28 June 34/1 We make ourselves ready in order to stand like a protecting wall by our . . . German Lutheran service.

(15) 1798 in FRIES *N.C. Morav. Rec.* VI. (1943) 2604 Br. Kramsch preached today at the home of Adam Spoon, ten miles from Hope. . . . Many German Methodists were present. **1849** CHAMBERLAIN *Ind. Gazetteer* 219 Evansville . . . contains [among other denominations] . . . German Methodists and German Lutherans. **1919** *Lit. Digest* 4 Oct. 34/2 The German Methodists, addressing President Wilson, pointed out the fact that they . . . were loyal Americans. — **(16) 1867** *Atlantic Mo.* May 555/1 'Which is the German quarter of New York?' I have heard strangers ask. — **(17) 1841** E. BUNNER *Hist. La.* 70 Bienville . . . gave them [*sc.* Germans] land on the banks of the river, which are now known by the name of the German Settlements. — **(18) 1889** *Cent.* 1749/2 The red-breasted or gray-backed snipe . . . was formerly locally (Long Island and vicinity) called *German* or *Dutch snipe*, to distinguish it from the so-called English snipe. — **(19) 1917** KEPHART *Camping* I. 161 Dress the feet with soft woolen socks, and over these draw a pair of long, thick 'German socks' that strap at the top. **1920** LEWIS *Main Street* 179 Kennicott drew from the injured leg the thick red 'German sock.'

(20) 1744 FRANKLIN *Acct. Fire-Places* 12 The German Stove is like a Box, one Side wanting. 'Tis composed of Five Iron Plates, scru'd together, and fix'd so as that you may put the fuel into it from another Room, or from the Outside of the House. 'Tis a kind of Oven revers'd, its Mouth being without, and Body within the Room that is to be warm'd by it.

As the last term in **Pennsylvania German.**

German-American. An American of German ancestry.

1824 CANDLER *Summary View of Amer.* 333 He said that he was in earnest, for that natives of Germany all told the German Americans of their bad language, and that mine corresponded with that of the native Germans much more than his. **1920** *Lit. Digest* 18 Sep. 11/2 The opposition of German-Americans to the League of Nations is not in the interest of Germany. **1948** *Time* 31 May 17/1 In other words, American Jews are in the same position as Irish-Americans, German-Americans, etc.

attrib. or as *adj.* **1880** *Harper's Mag.* Sep. 567 A German-American School . . . is kept over a disreputable little grog-shop. **1896** *Godey's Mag.* Feb. 161/2 The despair of that early time is still so potent in the memory of the German-American citizen that he can scarce repress his tears as he recalls it. **1920** *Lit. Digest* 18 Sep. 12/1 This movement to mobilize the German-American vote is gaining headway in Greater New York.

b. German-Americanism, loyalty of German-Americans to the U.S.

1915 *N.Y. Staats Ztg.* 21 Jan. 3/6 There is no stain upon the shield of German-Americanism.

German Coast. (See quot. 1904.)

1803 in *Concord Soc. Bul.* No. 9, 15 What is called here the 'German Coast' is the most industrious (la plus industrieuse), the most populous (la plus peuplée), . . . part of the inhabitants of this colony. **1854** GAYARRÉ *Hist. La.* I. 354 These German families . . . were prevailed upon to settle at a distance of about thirty miles from New Orleans, on a section of the banks of the river, which . . . drew the appellation of the *German Coast.* **1904** A. FORTIER *Hist. La.* I. 70 About two hundred and fifty Germans who had been sent to Law's concession in Arkansas were reduced to great distress, and in 1723 received grants of land on the coast of the Mississippi and founded the German Coast, now St. Charles and St. John Parishes. **1948** MENCKEN *Supp.* II. 155 This is some distance above the so-called German Coast of Louisiana.

Germantown ˈdʒɜmən͵taʊn, *n.*

1. (See quot. 1909.) Also **Germantown carriage.** *Obs.* Cf. **rockaway 1.**

1860 *Charleston* (S.C.) *Mercury* 6 Nov. 1/7 (*advt.*), Chaises, Carriages, Rockaways, Germantowns, Top Buggies, No Top Buggies, and Concord Wagons. **1874** *Cong. Rec.* 25 April 3377/2 The business of the Department . . . could not be done in an ordinary wagon, but had to be done in a fine Germantown carriage. **1884** H. C. MCCOOK *Tenants Old Farm* 322 Farmers came in their buggies, germantowns and farm-waggons. **1909** *Cent. Supp.* 521/3 *germantown.* . . . A carryall with a standing top, first built at Germantown, Pennsylvania, in 1816: the first vehicle of the class known as a *rockaway.*

2. A strong, lightly twisted yarn.

1903 HOLLISTER *Navajo & His Blanket* 121 The red is bayeta; the white and black, native wool; and the green and yellow, Germantown. **1936** REICHARD *Navajo Shepherd & Weaver* 23 In the face of the exaggeration, especially of value, which is put on bayeta by collectors, it should not be forgotten that the contemporary Germantowns and Saxonys were yarns quite worthy of combination with the much lauded bayeta.

Gerrymander ˈgɛrɪ͵mændɚ, *n.* Also **gerrymander.** [Elbridge *Gerry* (1744–1814) and sala*mander*.]

1. A caricature, or the imaginary dragonlike creature this supposedly represents, based upon the irregular outlines of an election district devised for party purposes in northeastern Massachusetts in 1812, during the governorship of Elbridge Gerry. Also attrib. *Obs.*

1812 BENTLEY *Diary* 2 April 92 The division of this County [Essex, Mass.] into districts has given an opportunity for a Caracatura stamped at Boston and freely circulated here called the Gerrymander. **1833** *Columbian Centinel* 31 March 2/2 The *Salem Gazette* of yesterday gave another full-length Portrait of this 'Gerrymander Beast,' begotten last year, on the district of Essex. **1871** *Boston Advertiser* 6 Dec. (F. and H.), Gerrimander was the name printed under a picture of a pretended monster, whose shape was modified from the distorted geography which Mr. Gerry's friends inflicted on part of the State for the sake of economizing majorities.

2. The action of prescribing the limits of an election district in such a way as to favor a political party or faction. Also attrib.

1812 *Columbian Centinel* 23 May 2/3 (Ernst), The sensibility of the good people of Massachusetts is at present too much awakened to this 'Gerrymander' to require [etc.]. **1812** *Boston Gaz.* 23 Nov. (Th.), Some returns from democratic towns are not made conformable to the Gerrymander law of last February. **1899** TARKINGTON *Gentleman from Ind.* i, By grace of the last gerrymander, the nomination carried with it the certainty of election. **1946** *Chi. D. News* 13 June 12/2 The U.S. Supreme Court has refused to interfere with the infamous gerrymander that makes representative government in this state a mockery.

b. A representative elected by gerrymandering. Also attrib. *Obs.*

1812 *Mass. Spy* 4 Nov. (Th.), [The same paper prints a short article from the Repertory entitled] Gerrymander Senate. **1813** *Ib.* 12 May (Th.), An official statement of the returns of voters for senators give[s] twenty nine friends of peace, and eleven gerrymanders. **1814** *Col. Centinel* 2 April 2/2 Do you believe the *Gerrymanders* are made moderate, more honest, less selfish than they were? What has converted them? Has any miracle changed their Ethiopian skin?

c. (See quots.) *Obs.*

1814 *Mass. Manual* 6 (Ernst), Feb. 8, 1812, The bill nicknamed the 'Gerrymander' for districting the Commonwealth of Massachusetts, for the choice of State Senators, passed in the House of Representatives. **1816** *Ann. 14th Congress* 2 Sess. 354 They [the senatorial districts of Mass.] were called Gerrymanders, from the name of the gentleman who was then at the head of the faction which produced the shapeless brood.

Gerrymander ˈgɛrɪ͵mændɚ, *v.* Also **gerrymander.** [f. the noun.] *tr.* To subject (a state or district) to a gerrymander.

1812 *N.Y. Post* 28 Dec. 3/1 They attempted also to *Gerrymander* the State [N.H.] for the choice of Representatives to Congress. **1850** *Quincy* (Ill.) *Whig* 12 Nov. 2/3 Col. Singleton is the first Whig Representative ever sent to the Legislature since the district was Gerrymandered for party purposes. **1925** BRYAN *Memoirs* 253 The district [in Nebraska] had been gerrymandered and was more hopelessly Republican than ever.

transf. **1813** *Boston Gazette* 8 April (Th.), The term Gerry-mander is now used throughout the U.S. as synonimous with deception. As, when a man has been swindled out of his rights by a villain, he says he has been Gerrymandered. *a***1861** T. WINTHROP *E. Brothertoft* 111 All around was a great scope of fertile plain, gerrymandered into farms. **1947** *Chi. D. News* 25 Sep. 16 (*heading*), Gerrymandering Votes on North Side.

gerrymanderer ˈgerɪˌmændərɚ, *n.* One who gerrymanders a state or district. — **1890** *Cin. Commercial Gaz.* 28 June, If it should . . . kill them both, the gerrymanderers would smile. **1892** *Nation* 10 Nov. 363/2 This last achievement shows how a gerrymander may serve to confound the gerrymanderers.

gerrymandering ˈgerɪˌmændərɪŋ, *n.* Redistricting; manipulating by, or in the manner of, a gerrymander.

1812 *Salem Gaz.* 22 Dec. 2/4 So much (says the N.Y. Gaz.) for *War* and *Gerrymandering.* **1875** G. P. BURNHAM *Three Years* 270 The gerry-manderings in many of the Courts of New York are such. **1949** *Time* 21 Feb. 32/2 The Catholic party bitterly resented such gerry-mandering.

∗ **Gertrude,** *n.* A long, loose slip of cotton or flannel for an infant. Also **Gertrude skirt.**

1926 *Mont. Ward Cat.* (ed. 105) 84 A long Gertrude Skirt of high quality white flannelette with white shell crochet stitching around neck, armholes and bottom. **1940** EASTMAN *Expectant Motherhood* 99 [Layette:] 4 *Gertrudes.* Depending on the season, flanelette, cotton and wool, silk and wool, and nainsook are the materials most commonly employed. **1947** *Infants' & Children's Review* Nov. 144/1 (*advt.*), Cotton Gertrudes, Embroidered Top & Bottom.

Gesundheit gəˈzʊntˌhaɪt, *n.* [G.] An ejaculatory good wish addressed to one who has sneezed. — **1909** *Cent. Supp.* 522/3 *gesundheit. . . .* Zur gesundheit, 'to your health,' a good wish addressed by Germans to one who has just sneezed. **1948** *Time* 6 Dec. 26/2 'C-c-comrade Stalin,' he stammered, 'it was I who s-s-s-sneezed.' 'Ah,' said the dictator genially: '*Gesundheit!*' and the meeting went on.

∗ **get,** *v.*

1. *tr.* To kill (a person or animal). *Slang.*

1853 P. PAXTON *Yankee in Texas* 118 [A Texan] does not kill his game, he *saves* or *gets it*, or *makes it come.* **1887** F. FRANCIS JR. *Saddle & Mocassin* viii. 138 They'll get you one of these days, Colonel, when you are driving around in your wagon. **1947** *Chi. Tribune* 28 June 4/3 The anonymous caller, a man, said 'Tell your husband we're out to get him and we'll do it.'

2. *intr.* Short for *get up, q.v.*, or "*get out,*" usu. in the imperative in the form "git." *Colloq.*

1864 *Harper's Mag.* Oct. 565/2 George, after belaboring the mules till he was tired, and telling them to 'git' till he was hoarse, would lean back in his seat and think. **1884** *Graceville* (Minn.) *Transcript* 25 Aug., He presented a cocked revolver and told them to get, and they got. **1917** *D.N.* IV. 393 git, *v. i.* There is a tendency to specialize this form. People who would ordinarily use *get* might say, 'You *git!*'

3. *Polit. tr.* To have the right to recommend (a person) for appointment to office.

1882 *Nation* 17 Aug. 121/2 Senator Don Cameron 'gets' eighteen clerks, Senator Logan seven, Representative White, from Kentucky, as many as twenty-one.

4. To succeed in making. *Colloq.*

1891 *Outing* Dec. 246/2 Rum had so far 'got him dead.' **1897** MARK TWAIN *Following Equator* lii. 504 He got me so nervous that I couldn't look at the view. **1927** *Atlantic Mo.* Feb. 148, I love to work, but this God-forsaken country gets me discouraged.

5. To comprehend or understand (a person or an idea). *Slang.*

1892 MARK TWAIN *Amer. Claim.* xiv. 149 (R.), I don't know that I quite get the bearings of your position. **1928** F. N. HART *Bellamy Trial* v. 166, I have a first-class opportunity . . . if you get what I mean.

6. Used colloq., esp. with adverbs and prepositions.

a. ∗ *To get after*, to attack, ask, importune.

1869 MARK TWAIN *Innocents Abroad* v. 51 (R.), A little fort. . . . If we were ever to get after it with one of our turreted monitors they would have to move it out in the country. **1877** RUEDE *Sod-House Days* 32 After the Hoots had left they got after me to sing, and I favored them with T.82 and a couple of others, and then went to bed.

b. ∗ *To get along*, to manage, fare, succeed.

1830 S. SMITH *Major Downing* 34, I wish you'd write me . . . whether you think I could get along with the business. **1892** MARK TWAIN *Amer. Claim.* xii. 126 (R.), A young journeyman tinner . . . was getting along all right till he fell sick and lost his job.

c. *To get around*, to circumvent, evade.

1848 RUXTON *Far West* 89 One from the Land of Cakes . . . sought to 'get around' (in trade) a right 'smart' Yankee, but couldn't 'shine.' **1894** MARK TWAIN *Those Extra. Twins* iv. 362 (R.), There is no getting around proof like that.

d. ∗ *To get behind*, to support, indorse.

1903 *N.Y. Tribune* 20 Sep., Irrespective of party, good citizens should get behind candidates who are clean and honest.

e. *To get busy*, to bestir oneself.

1904 *Courier-Journal* 27 Sep. 3 It was necessary to call upon the sergeant-at-arms to escort them out. When that functionary got busy there came near being a riot. **1906** O. HENRY *Four Million* 121 'Ikey,' said he, . . . 'get busy with your ear. It's drugs for me if you've got the line I need.'

f. *To get by*, to escape or evade (something), to succeed, get along.

1904 S. E. WHITE *Blazed Trail Stories* II. v. 199 How he had gotten by the office boy Brown could not conceive. **1923** *Nation* 5 Dec. 624 Lesser men than he have 'got by.' **1931** *Atlantic Mo.* Feb. 235 Some have thought it clever to 'get by' [at college] without work.

g. *To get even*, to retaliate.

1845 SOL. SMITH *Theatr. Apprent.* 148, I took my seat with the hope of getting even. **1923** VANCE *Baroque* 40 If crooks didn't never get sore on each other and blow the works to get even.

h. *To get going*, to begin acting in a characteristic manner.

1898 E. N. WESTCOTT *D. Harum* 391 David is not only living, but appears almost no older than when we first knew him, and is still just as likely to 'git goin' ' on occasion.

i. *To get into:* (1) To find out about.

1788 JEFFERSON *Writings* VI. 454, I endeavored to get, as well as I could, into the state of national credit there.

(2) To get control or hold of.

1876 MARK TWAIN *Tom Sawyer* iii. 37 All through supper his spirits were so high that his aunt wondered 'what had got into the child.' **1925** FOSTER *Adv. Trop. Tramp* 107, I don't know what's gotten into our girls these days. No pride, no self-respect whatsoever!

j. *To get off:* (1) To issue, put out.

1834 C. A. DAVIS *Lett. J. Downing* 82 The natur of paper-money makers is always to git off as much as they can. **1853** *Yale Lit. Mag.* XIX. 156 When we pitched into the editorial business, we thought it was a very small matter to 'get off' a magazine.

(2) To say or express (a joke or witticism).

1849 *Yale Lit. Mag.* XIV. 187 (Th.), There is the writing of one who tried to 'get off,' as the boys said, something comic on every occasion. **1911** HARRISON *Queed* 15, I heard a feller get it off at the shop the other day.

(3) To deliver (a speech).

1877 BARTLETT 783 He got off a great speech in Congress.

(4) To alight from (a train).

1890 *Cent. Mag.* July 349/1 When I got off the train, I found myself on a moss-grown platform. **1926** *Ladies' Home Jrnl.* Jan. 3/3, I got off the train at the little village in Maine.

k. ∗ *To get out*, to become known.

1884 MARK TWAIN *H. Finn* 368 (R.), It ain't right and it ain't moral, and I wouldn't like it to get out. **1891** *Boston* (Mass.) *Jrnl.* 28 Nov. 2/3 The fact that this step was to be taken did not get out till the charges were safe in the hands of the Governor.

l. *To get outside*, see ∗ **outside.**

m. ∗ *To get over*, to succeed with, "put across."

1932 TARBELL *O. D. Young* 246 He gives time, if he has it, rather delights I judge in taking pains with what he wants to get over.

n. ∗ *To get round*, to attend to all one's duties.

1885 JACKSON *Zeph* iv, With this new absorbing interest added to her other duties, she appeared to somehow lose time out of each day, and never, as she phrased it, 'get round.'

o. *To get there*, to succeed, also *to get there with both feet*, to succeed exceptionally well. Cf. **8.** (4).

1883 NYE *Baled Hay* 49 They were high-toned, and they got there. **1887** F. FRANCIS JR. *Saddle & Mocassin* viii. 144 He 'got there with both feet' at starting. **1894** *Cong. Rec.* 17 April 3804/2 He told the Democratic candidate for county clerk that, if he would agree to appoint him deputy, he would hustle for him, and he thought [he] would 'get there.'

p. *To get through*, to secure favorable action upon.

1873 MARK TWAIN & WARNER *Gilded Age* xx. 190 The Senator . . . favored the appropriation and he gave the Colonel . . . to understand that he would endeavor to get it through. **1900** *Cong. Rec.* 6 Feb. 1556/2 No such disfranchising scheme as this could ever be gotten through a Democratic caucus or a Democratic legislature.

q. ∗ *To get together*, to agree, work in harmony. Cf. **8.** (5).

1889 *Judge* 10 Aug. 282/1 Five Men . . . are to be hanged on the same day. In other words, they will follow Mr. Dana's advice and get together. **1932** GRAYSON *Leaders* 394 Able men . . . after years of competition in their field, eventually got together on a basis of business understanding which constituted a monopoly of the meat trade.

r. ∗ *To get up*, to "go on," used as a command to a horse. Cf. **7. q.** and **r.** and ∗ **get-up,** *n.* **1.**

1849 CHITTICK *Ring-Tailed Roarers* (1941) 248 (We.), Git up, you lazy Injun! **1887** F. FRANCIS JR. *Saddle & Mocassin* vii. 123 Get up!—get up . . . he says . . . and once more the horses resume their gait. **1902** LORIMER *Lett. Merchant* 158 These young fellows . . . lazy along trying to turn in at every gate where there seems to be a little shade, and sulking and balking whenever you say 'get-ap' to them.

7. In colloq. and slang phrases.

a. *To get a line* (or *line-up*) *on,* to get an idea or information about.

1903 *N.Y. Sun* 18 Nov. 4 These dressmakers . . . cannot get a line on the styles except at the Horse Show. **1931** *K.C. Times* 18 Nov. 20 We'd rather get a line-up on a credit prospect from a girl collector than we would from the prospect's banker. **1947** *Chi. Tribune* 22 July 1/5 If we can find any one who saw her at a dance after 10:30 p.m. we may be able to get a line on whom she was dancing with and whose company she was in when she left.

b. *To get a move on,* to hurry, hasten.

1893 *Columbus Dispatch* 7 July, Now is the time for the mover of dead animals 'to get a move on himself.' **1923** WATTS *L. Nichols* 83 [Mr. Schulte ordered] him to hunt up Nichols, with a further recommendation to get a move on!

c. *To get away with:* (1) To make away with, get the advantage of.

1878 BEADLE *Western Wilds* 41 More'n once the robbers would tackle some gritty man that was handy with his 'barkers,' an' he'd get away with two or three of 'em. **1908** *D.N.* III. 314 You can't get away with me.

(2) To succeed in taking or doing something and getting off safely. Cf. ***baggage,** *n.* **b.**

1886 *Boston Journal* 18 Dec. 2/4 They got away with the pennant three successive seasons. **1925** *Motion Picture* Oct. 93/1 The effect was marvelous but not a person in the world save Gloria could have gotten away with it! **1946** *Reader's Digest* Sep. 37/1 To look at the man is to understand something of how he got away with it.

(3) To dispose of, eat.

1888 *Battle Creek Moon* 17 March, 'You seem to be hungry?' . . . 'I am, or I wouldn't be able to get away with much of this pie.' **1888** *Milnor* (Dak.) *Teller* 18 May 6/5 Praise the cake and get away with one more biscuit than you want.

d. *To get back at,* to repay in kind, retaliate.

1888 *Chi. Inter-Ocean* (F.), The open letter writers in the newspapers are getting back at Sam for his fondness for tobacco. **1911** FERBER *Dawn O'Hara* 99 Some day we'll have money enough to get back at some of the people we know.

e. *To get broke in,* to become accustomed to a situation.

1846 FARNHAM *Prairie Land* 42, I reckon I'll want to see them and the young ones a little, till I get broke in. **1923** H. COOK *On Old Frontier* 5 The best place to 'get broke in,' they said was either in Sedgwick or Sumner County, Kansas.

f. *To get down on,* to develop a dislike for.

1875 LEWIS *Quad's Odds* 381 (We.), The adult male population . . . got down on [him]. **1898** WESTCOTT *D. Harum* 105 Dave got down on him fer some little thing or other, an' he's got his walkin' papers.

g. *To get down sick,* to become ill.

1852 *Knickerb.* XXXIX. 480 In summer these [amusements] are varied by getting out manure, hoeing corn, acting as scare-crows, and 'getting down sick,' eating green apples.

h. *To get in bad* (or *good*), to get into the ill (or good) graces of one.

1928 *Observer* 19 Feb. 16/2 Young Woodley . . . prefers poetry to cricket. That, of course, 'gets him in bad' with his house master. **1931** *K.C. Star* 7 Nov., The husband, jumping at a chance 'to get in good' came home from work the next day with a bundle of books. **1945** BOTKIN *My Burden* 48 All before that I is heard it gits you in bad.

i. *To get next* (*to*): (1) To get wise (to), find out about.

1903 *Cin. Enquirer* 9 May 12/5 Be dead certain not to let anybody, even pikers, get next, so that none of the fellows in the ring will get hit with that 30 to 1 chalked up. **1908** K. MCGAFFEY *Show-Girl* 72 You had better drop in your penny and get next to yourselves. **1922** *Sunset* Dec. 11/2 The guy who was smart enough to pull that stuff on you was smart enough to get next to your mark and duplicate it.

(2) To take or appropriate.

1908 K. MCGAFFEY *Show-Girl* 28 Some hussy got next to all my toothpicks and I had to use a hairpin for a liner.

j. *To get* (something) *on* (someone), to have an advantage over one, to have incriminating information about one.

1919 *Detective Story Mag.* 25 Nov. 129 He gave me the slip. . . . Maybe it's just as well since I haven't got anything on him yet. **1926** *Ladies' Home Jrnl.* Nov. 129 There was no competition except the scenery. After all, almost any woman's got it on a mountain. **1946** T. JONES *Skinny Angel* 85 Those fellows are trying to get something on someone.

k. **To get onto,* to become wise to, come to understand.

1880 *Chi. Inter-Ocean* 2 June 6/3 Providence registered her second defeat for the Buckeye blue-legs this afternoon, the visitors taking kindly to Ward's curves, Dunlap and McCormick especially getting on to him in fine style. **1915** *Everybody's Mag.* Oct. 451/1 'But these other Indians will get on to me,' said he. **1925** *Red Book Mag.* Oct. 114/3, I was now getting on to the game and knew how to talk.

l. *To get out from under,* to avoid impending danger or risk.

1875 *Scribner's Mo.* Nov. 124/2 The system is rotten, root and branch, and, if the nation cares for its life, the quicker it gets 'out from under' the better. **1925** *Amer. Mercury* Aug. 401 You traveled Like the devil to get out from under.

m. *To get out the vote,* to see that voters come out and vote.

1938 ASBURY *Sucker's Prog.* 279 In getting out the vote and manipulating a nominating convention he is said to have been one of the most skillful men of his time. **1949** *Time* 30 May 19/1 Communist Party workers got out the vote, all right, but the vote was heavily anti-Communist.

n. *To get over the footlights,* to succeed as a playwright or actor.

1915 *Munsey's Mag.* Aug. 515/1 Shaw was generally considered altogether too wild to stand a chance of getting over the footlights.

o. *To get religion,* to become converted.

1772 in FITHIAN *Jrnl.* I. 22 We have had a considerable stir of religion in college since you went away, Lewis Willson is thought to have got religion. **1832** J. HALL *Legends of West* 46 Tom got religion at a camp-meeting, and for a while was quite a reformed man. **1948** *Annals Iowa* July 385 They were 'blood and thunder' affairs, where men and women 'got religion' at the mourners' bench.

p. *To get that way,* to think or feel in a certain way.

1922 C. SANDBURG *Slabs of Sunburnt West* 6 How do you get that way?

q. *To get up and get,* to make all possible haste.

1864 COTTON *Songster* 10 Poor Mexico's in trouble, but the time will come, 'you bet,' When Monsieur will be invited to just 'get up and get.' **1903** FOX *Little Shepherd* xxii, A voice bellowed from the rear, . . . 'Git up and git, boys!' That was the order for the charge.

r. *To get up and hump,* =prec. Cf. ***hump,** *v.*

1894 MARK TWAIN *H. Finn* xi. 96 Git up and hump yourself, Jim!

s. *To get what's coming to one,* to get one's deserts.

1929 *Randolph Enterprise* 7 March 1/5 The darkey got what was coming to him anyhow. **1944** JOHNSON *As I Dare* 219, I was at that affair the other night and Ellis Butler certainly got what was coming to him.

For *to get down to* **brass tacks,** *to get one's* **goat,** *to get* **left,** *to get it in the* **neck,** *to get* **rough,** *to get* **sore,** see the words in boldface.

8. In colloq. noun and attrib. formations, usu. with adverbs: (1) **get-a-long-ability,** the ability to get along or prosper, *rare,* cf. **6. b.** above; (2) ***away,** see as a main entry; (3) **-rich-quick,** used attrib. to designate activities, plans, etc., that promise quick and lucrative returns but involve risky, questionable, or illegitimate means; (4) **there,** energy, ambition, cf. **6. o.** above; (5) **together,** an assembly, a coming-together, cf. **6. q.** above; (6) **up,** see as a main entry.

(1) 1838 DRAKE *Tales & Sketches* 80 To good classical attainments, he united shrewdness, enterprise and that get-a-long-ability, which are common to his countrymen. — **(3)** [**1902** WISTER *Virginian* xxxi, Well, that does not change him any, for it seems he's disturbed over getting rich quick and being a big man in the Territory.] **1910** *Sat. Ev. Post* 30 July 40/1 The project of raising poultry goes to the feminine head more dizzily than any other get-rich-quick scheme. **1932** HAMBLEY *Hold Your Money* 84 There are about twenty get-rich-quick investment houses running full blast in the financial district by men who have prison records for similar racketeering. — **(4) 1898** WESTCOTT *D. Harum* xix. 169 Charley's a likely 'nough boy some ways, but he hain't got much 'git there' in his make-up, not more'n enough fer one anyhow, I reckon.

(5) 1911 *Springfield W. Republican* 9 Feb. 12 It was the biggest get-together the organization has ever held. **1948** *Pauls Valley* (Okla.) *D. Democrat* 1 July 1/6 Squeaking wagons clattered down Main street to Riverview park where the big 'get-together' was held each year.

***getaway,** *n.* In racing slang: **1. getaway day,** the last day of a series of races when competing owners leave. **2. getaway money, purse,** money raced for on getaway day to enable the winning owners to get on to another racing event.

(1) **1891** *Memphis Appeal-Avalanche* 25 April 5/1 (*heading*), Track Talk. Get-away-day. — (2) **1895** *Chi. Times-Herald* 6 Nov. 10/1 (*heading*), Last Day at Morris. Get-Away Purses are Divided. **1923** VAN LOAN *Old Man Curry* 137 All the burglars at the track will be levelling for the get-away money.

***get-up,** *n.*

1. A command to urge a horse on. *Colloq.* Cf. ***get,** *v.* **6. r.**

1843 R. CARLTON *New Purchase* xix. 162 All cherrups and get-ups and even old-rascals-you . . . all, all were in vain!

2. Initiative, energy, aptitude, ambition. *Colloq.*

*c***1849** PAIGE *Dow's Sermons* I. 260 It flats right down, and stays there, like a junk of dough—no get up to it. **1863** *Ladies' Repository* Aug. 477/1 In vain I tried to convince him that there was some 'get-up' in the animal. **1947** *Chi. D. News* 2 Aug. 13/6 Therein lies the answer to any charge that he hasn't any 'git-up' to him.

b. Also *get-up-and-get, get-up-and-hustle. Colloq.*

1884 PECK *Peck's Boss Book* (1892) 183 (We.), The adjutant . . . felt that his position demanded a horse that had some git-up-and-git. **1910** W. M. RAINE *B. O'Connor* 223 When it comes to the get-up-and-hustle, she's there. **1949** *Time* 7 Mar. 63/1 There was plenty of farm news if someone only had the get-up-and-git to go after it.

***G'hal,** *n.* The girl friend of a Bowery tough or rowdy. *Slang. Obs.* — **1849** G. G. FOSTER *N.Y. in Slices* 45 If you would see the B'hoy . . . at the top of his career—in the *ne plus ultra* of his mundane state—you must see him taking a drive with his G'hal on the avenues. **1888** M. LANE in *America* 20 Sep. 15 The B'hoys were well matched with the G'hals, and between the two they managed in the olden days to make a good deal of noise and confusion upon the New York streets.

***ghost,** *n.*

1. *W. attrib.* Designating a habitation, town, etc., that is deserted, as (1) **ghost cabin,** (2) **city,** (3) **(mining) camp,** (4) **(mining) town.**

(1) **1927** RUSSELL *Trails* 38 McCartyville consists of a graveyard an' one or two ghost cabins now, but then it's a construction camp for the Great Northern. — (2) **1915** *Sat. Ev. Post* 31 July 3/1 Nevada is the land of ghost cities. **1945** *Life* 20 Nov. 11/2, I happened to be in Dawson, Yukon territory, the ghost city of the great Klondike gold stampede. — (3) **1920** *Cosmopolitan* Sep. 26/1 Yellow Jack is a ghost mining-camp that me and Uncle Jimmy put on the map along in the summer of '82. **1947** CHALFANT *Gold, Guns, & Ghost Towns* 87 Among the many scores of ghost camps which are or were on the Nevada map, not many have been so completely forgotten as Hamilton. — (4) [**1875** *Cin. Enquirer* 2 July 5/1 We . . . sped down into the Valley of the Stanislaus, and up to Sonora; through the deserted mining towns, like the ghosts of their departed prosperity.] **1931** WILLISON *Here They Dug Gold* 71 Today all lie ghost towns smelling of the long slow processes of ruin and decay. **1949** *Sat. Ev. Post* 5 Mar. 27/1 It has an outstanding library—something no ghost mining town ever boasted.

2. In miscellaneous combs.: (1) **ghost crab,** a sand crab; (2) **dance,** (see quot. 1946), also attrib.; (3) **dancer,** a participant in an Indian ghost dance; (4) **dancing,** the dancing of the ghost dance; (5) **flower,** the Indian pipe, *Monotropa uniflora;* (6) **moccasin,** =prec., *rare;* (7) **racket,** "any event or narrative into which the spiritual or ghostly element enters" (Barrère & Leland), *obs.;* (8) **shirt,** a shirt worn by a ghost dancer; (9) **writer,** (*a*) (see quot. and cf. **ghostwrite,** *v.*), (*b*) one who writes for an ostensible author who has employed him to do such work, cf. ***ghost,** *v.*, **ghostwrite,** *v.*

(1) **1908** *Suburban Life* Sep. 132/1 Among the most interesting creatures to be found on the sandy beaches along the Atlantic coast is the Ghost Crab, which ranges in size from three to seven inches. **1944** HARNETT T. KANE *Bayous of La.* 80 Small crabs, the color of the beach . . . 'ghost crabs,' say the islanders. — (2) **1890** *Boston Journal* 21 Nov. 1/9 The ghost dances, under the lead of Little Wound, Six Feathers and other chiefs, are still going on. **1946** FOREMAN *Last Trek* 245 The Ghost dance was a ceremonial religious dance connected with the Messiah doctrine which originated among the Paviotso in Nevada in 1888 and spread rapidly among other tribes until it numbered among its adherents nearly all the Indians of the interior basin from the Missouri River or to beyond the Rockies. **1948** *Sat. Ev. Post* 10 July 117/2 He was at Fort Sill, Oklahoma, getting information on the famous Ghost Dance uprising. — (3) **1890** *Boston Journal* 29 Nov. 2/3 The sudden metamorphosis of a great number of the ghost-dancers . . . into cattle-stealers. **1946** ADAMS *Album Amer. Hist.* III. 415 The 'ghost dancers' on Wounded Knee Creek in the Pine Ridge Agency . . . were being disarmed. — (4) **1901** S. E. WHITE *Westerners* xxxvi. 328, Sitting Bull joined Buffalo Bill's show, where he had a good time until he began ghost-dancing and was killed in the Wounded Knee campaign. **1923** J. H. COOK *On Old Frontier* 234 All trouble could have been averted had there been the right kind of official in charge of affairs at the agency when the ghost dancing began.

(5) **1892** *Amer. Folk-Lore* V. 100 *Monotropa uniflora*, ghost-flower. **1899** GOING *Flowers* 260 In July pine-roots give a home and a maintenance to some curious parasitic plants—'pine-drops,' 'pine-sap,' and 'Indian-pipe' or 'ghost-flower.' **1938** THOMPSON *High Trails* 86 (*caption*), Indian pipes or ghost flower. — (6) **1840** HOFFMAN *Greyslaer* I. 61 Old roots, rotten leaves, and sich things . . . go to make up a soil only fit to raise toadstools, ghost moccasins [etc.]. — (7) *a***1889** *Chi. Tribune* (B. & L.), The most novel ghost-racket on record has just been worked by a Jersey detective. *a***1889** *Washington* (Pa.) *Eagle* (B. & L.), We have had the tallest ghost-racket here in our town that you ever did audit. — (8) **1895** REMINGTON *Pony Tracks* 53 One young warrior . . . had seen that the medicine was bad, and his faith in the ghost shirt had vanished. **1946** ADAMS *Album Amer. Hist.* III. 415 Wrapped in 'ghost shirts,' . . . the Indians indulged in wild dances which created a state of excitement judged by the reservation superintendents to be dangerous. — (9) (*a*) **1900** J. FLYNT *Tramping* 393 *ghost-writer*, any statement or report that is not true. (*b*)**1941** *Decision* March 42, I was to be a ghostwriter. **1947** *Time* 3 Feb. 81/1 Scorning ghostwriters, he writes all his own magazine articles.

***ghost,** *v. tr.* Short for next. — **1934** WEBSTER. **1945** *Sat. Review* 5 May 13/3 The title page carries somebody else's name. I ghosted the book. I'm a ghost writer.

ghostwrite, *v. tr.* and *intr.* To write (something) for an employer who is the ostensible author; to write as a ghost writer for another. Also **ghostwriting, ghostwritten.** *Colloq.*

1928 *Forum* LXXIX. 27 Take for instance the rapid development of the phenomenon known to the trade as 'ghost writing.' **1932** *New Republic* 10 Feb. 347 He even reaches a point of enthusiasm where he is able to say of the autobiographical boloney ghost-written by Samuel Crowther for Ford that 'it might well be the Bible, as Ford is the prophet, of business.' **1947** *True* Nov. 8 We can assure that this story is not ghost-written. **1949** *Time* 30 May 64/3 Huie later ghost-wrote an attack on the 'obsolete' Navy for an Air Force general.

b. To write (a supposedly factual account) entirely from imagination.

1931 *K.C. Times* 17 July, Farm board, to the reporter, suggested Chairman Legge, and the hot weather suggested staying in off the dusty roads, and so he 'ghost-wrote' the interview which turned out to be an exhortation on legs.

***Ghouls,** *n. pl.* (See quot.) *Obs.* — **1868** in *Doc. & Sp. Amer. Hist.* (1943) III. 79 The body politic of the Order [i.e., the Ku-Klux Klan] shall be known and designated as 'Ghouls.'

***giant,** *n.* and *a.*

1. A machine capable of delivering a powerful jet of water for use in hydraulic mining.

1876 RAYMOND *8th Rep. Mines* 97 These giants under the former pressure with seven-inch nozzle will throw 1,000 inches of water. **1882** *47th Congress* 1 Sess. H.R. Ex. Doc. No. 216, 627 From the distributor the streams are piped to the 'monitors,' or 'giants.' These are the discharge-pipes which concentrate the stream and enable its projection upon a desirable point. **1949** *Nat. Geog. Mag.* Oct. 507 They had turned their 'giants' or nozzles, on an exposed embankment, and powerful streams of water bit into the permanently frozen ground.

2. In combs.: (1) **giant cactus,** =**saguaro;** (2) **cedar,** the giant arborvitae, *Thuja plicata;* (3) **cracker,** a large firecracker; (4) **powder,** a form of dynamite; (5) **swing,** a gymnastic feat consisting of a complete swing of the body at arm's length around a horizontal bar.

(1) **1861** NEWBERRY *Geol. Rep.* 21 The higher portion is occupied by beds of gravel deeply cut by washes and covered with the giant cactus. **1949** *Nat. Hist.* Feb. 64/1 In a few localities the ospreys nest in the crotches formed by the branching arms of the giant cactus. — (2) **1866** GRAY *First Lessons Bot.* 152 Over twelve hundred layers have actually been counted on the stump of an aged tree, such as the Giant Cedar or Redwood of California. — (3) **1877** *Harper's Mag.* Jan. 298/2 Tom explained how the colt had been frightened . . . at a giant cracker. — (4) **1871** RAYMOND *3rd Rep. Mines* 189 Mr. Cassell . . . has introduced Giant powder and the single-hand drill. **1896** SHINN *Story of Mine* 235 Some miners . . . wished to 'thaw out' their frozen giant powder. — (5) **1873** MARK TWAIN *Gilded Age* xii. 117 He could do the giant swing in the gymnasium.

As the last term in **grand, Little Giant.**

gibbous chub sucker. An American fresh-water fish of the Catostomidae family. — **1842** *Nat. Hist. N.Y., Zoology* IV. 194 The Gibbous Chubsucker. *Labeo gibbosus*. . . . I have seen . . . in the Mohawk, and have reason to believe it to be common in many other fresh-water streams in this State.

gibbsite ˈgɪbzaɪt, *n.* [f. George *Gibbs* (1776–1833), Amer. mineralogist.] (See quot. 1889.) — **1827** COMSTOCK *Minerology* 70

Gibbsite . . . This is a new mineral. *Local. U. S.* Richmond, *Mass.* in a neglected mine of brown haematite, where it was discovered by Dr. Emmons. **1889** *Cent.* 2508/3 gibbsite. . . . A hydrate of aluminium, a whitish mineral, found in Massachusetts in irregular stalactitic masses, presenting an aggregation of elongated tuberous branches, parallel and united.

Gibson girl. The type of American girl of the 1890's portrayed by Charles Dana Gibson, chiefly in his illustrations of novels. Also attrib.

1901 *Cosmopolitan* June 120/1 It is a saying among artists that nine out of ten models who come . . . seeking employment say they are the original 'Gibson girl' or the 'Diana of the Garden.' **1936** *Sears Cat.* (ed. 173) 401 In great demand for Gibson-Girl Petticoats, blouses, rustling evening dresses and wraps. **1948** *Pacific Discovery* July–Aug. 10/1 The latest book of Gibson Girl drawings had just been issued for the holiday trade.

* **Gideon,** *n.* [f. *Gideon,* the Israelitish hero told of in Judges 6:11 ff.] A member of a Christian organization of American commercial travelers, founded in 1899. Usu. *pl.* with reference to the organization.

1906 *Springfield W. Republican* 13 Sep. 11 The religiously-minded commercial travelers, known as Gideons, have four prosperous camps in cities of New York state. **1920** *Atlantic Mo.* July 88 He replied in words that may still be read, thanks to the Gideons, in any hotel room. **1948** *Time* 10 May 25/2 The Gideons added a realistic touch to 2,000 Bibles which they presented to Chicago's Stevens Hotel—the cover of each book was alcohol-proof.

b. Gideon Bible, a Bible purchased by this organization and placed in a hotel room, Pullman car, etc.

1922 *Bookman* Feb. 552/2 He has stolen, to date, fifty-eight Gideon Bibles, twenty-seven from the Hotel Astor alone, and presented them to friends. **1949** *Chi. D. News* 18 May 28/1 The distribution of Gideon Bibles to children . . . has been protested by two Roman Catholic priests.

* **Gideonites,** *n. pl.* An order in the early Mormon Church. *Obs.* — **1838** *Peoria* (Ill.) *Reg.* 24 Nov. 1/5 Among many other things, they had assembed them into three different societies, called Danites, Gideonites, and the Destroying Angels.

* **gift,** *n.*

1. *attrib.* Used in expressions designed to cloak what are in reality illegal lottery enterprises, as (1) **gift bookstore,** (2) **concert,** (3) **enterprise,** (4) **fair,** (5) **lottery,** (6) **store.**

From early times lotteries flourished here, but by the early 19th century public sentiment was aroused and laws were passed against them. See A. R. Spofford in *Ann. Rep. Amer. Hist. Assoc.* for 1892, pp. 173–195.

(1) **1873** W. Mathews *Getting On in World* vii. 100 To-day some shrewd Yankee starts a 'gift' bookstore, and immediately all the newspapers in the land are flooded with advertisements of gift enterprises. — (2) **1867** *Atlantic Mo.* Feb. 202/2 George Fiske went into the gift-concert business. **1873** W. Mathews *Getting On in World* xix. 310 Whether they steal a railway or a man's money by gift concerts. — (3) **1855** J. Holbrook *Among Mail Bags* 262 The scheme certainly had as fair an appearance as any 'Gift Enterprise.' [**1866** *Dly. Richmond Enquirer* 16 Feb. 1/2 The great original gift book enterprise, the only one in existence!] **1898** Westcott *D. Harum* 8 This ain't no gift enterprise, an' I guess we ain't goin' to trade. **1949** *N.Y. Times* 4 June 16/3 A Circuit Judge, denouncing the gift of automobiles to spectators from the St. Louis Cardinals, today accused Cardinal owner Fred Saigh of tying the club 'to the tail of a gift enterprise lottery.' — (4) **1868** *N.Y. Herald* 2 July 5/1 Dis Chile has tried lots of gift fairs and tings for a prize, but nebber could draw anything at all. — (5) **1855** *Chi. Times* 24 Jan. 3/1 These are the implements of a swindling scheme yclept 'gift lottery.' **1884** Cable *Dr. Sevier* xlix, Pennons, cock-feathers, clattering steeds, pealing salvos, banners, columns, ladies' favors, balls, concerts, toasts, the Free Gift Lottery—don't you recollect? — (6) **1872** Talmadge *Abominations Mod. Society* 177 In this class of gambler makers I also put the 'gift stores.'

2. In other combs., usu. rare or obs.: (1) **gift deed,** a deed of gift; (2) **free,** (see quot.); (3) **gentleman,** a man active in some kind of gift enterprise; (4) **shop,** a shop dealing in articles suitable for gifts; (5) **tree,** a Christmas tree.

(1) **1855** Barnum *Life* 10 My delighted ancestor . . . handed to my mother a gift deed in my behalf. — (2) **1848** Ruxton in *Blackw. Mag.* LXIV. 306 Two excellent Indian horses were . . . presented to them 'on the prairie' or 'gift-free,' by the kind-hearted stranger. — (3) **1855** Holbrook *Among Mail Bags* 344 That was the last thing that the 'Gift' gentleman could think of doing. — (4) **1918** Carolyn Wells *Vicky Van* i. 10 Little faddly prize bags of gift-shop novelties are her stakes. **1948** *Sat. Review* 17 July 5/1 We are a gift shop and do not handle books. — (5) **1898** Canfield *Maid of Frontier* 117 He had gone to the little church where the gift-tree festivities were in progress.

As the last term in **Christmas, Indian, king's, white gift(s).**

* **gig,** *n.*

1. A combination of numbers, usu. three, selected to appear among those drawn from a policy wheel. Also **flat gig.**

1847 C. White *Policy Players* (1874) 5, I make it 4, 11, and 44; and a very good gig it is, too. **1872** Crapsey *Nether Side N.Y.* 106 A 'flat gig' is three numbers played for all three to be drawn, and gets its name, I presume, from the fact that it is played by nobody but fools, who are known in the dialect of detectives and thieves as 'flats.' **1890** *Cong. Rec.* 16 Aug. 8713/2 The 'washerwoman's gig'—4-11-14—[is] the chance that these three, or any other three numbers, will, in any order, be the first three numbers out of the thirteen taken from the wheel. **1910** Wilson *Chi. Cess-pools of Infamy* 158 Three numbers make a 'gig' and win $150 to $225.

2. gig and saddle, (see quot. and cf. **cross gig and saddle**).

1890 *Cong. Rec.* 16 Aug. 8713/2 [In the Louisiana lottery] by paying an extra 25 cents on a ticket, you can put what is called a 'gig and saddle' on it, and then in the event that two of the numbers on your ticket correspond to any two of the thirteen numbers drawn from the wheel, a prize of $2.45 is paid.

gig gɪg, *v.* [In **1.** f. * *gig, n.;* the origin of the word in **2.** is not clear.]

1. *tr.* To spear (fish) with a gig. Also transf. Cf. **gigging.**

1803 Lewis in *Jrnls. of L. & Ordway* 36 We fixed some spears after the indian method but have had too much to attend to of more importance than gigging fish. **1902** Gordon *Recoll. Lynchburg* 100 On either side of which stands a man 'gigging' buffalo fish as the current hurries them through the break. **1934** Vines *Green Thicket World* 17 Men often tried to get Lat Lisper to gig the Fork Shoals with them.

2. *To gig backwards,* to bring (the carriage of a sawmill) back to its starting-place. Also transf.

1815 *Niles' Reg.* IX. 36/1 The carriages run upon cast racks, are propelled by the improved short hand and gigged backwards by bevel wheels, in the manner of the best mills. **1900** Garland *Eagle's Heart* 297 The broncho-busting contest Mose declined. 'How's that?' inquired Haney, who hated to see his favorite 'gig back' at a point where his courage could be tested.

gigantic pine. The sugar pine of California and Oregon. — **1858** Warder *Hedges & Evergreens* 252 *Pinus Lambertiana,* Lambert's or Gigantic Pine, is found in the north-west coast of North America. **1897** Sudworth *Arborescent Flora* 15 *Pinus lambertiana.* . . . Common Names . . . Gigantic Pine (Cal. lit.).

gigging 'gɪgɪŋ, *n.* (See quots.)

1852 *S. Lit. Messenger* XVIII. 358/1 Smoke-embrowned rafters . . . support . . . numerous three-pronged spears for night-fishing—'gigging,' as they called the sport at the time [1680]. **1871** De Vere 339 Gigging, in the sense of catching fish with a gig, is in Virginia still used to denote night-fishing with a three-pronged spear, as it was done in the days of Captain John Smith. **1934** Vines *Green Thicket World* 8 He had to go on home . . . and hurry back for the gigging that night.

gig wagon. A gig. *Obs.* — **1835** A. A. Parker *Trip to West* 164 Baggage wagons are quite numerous, but I found only one pleasure carriage in the whole province, and that was a gig-wagon. *Ib.* 76 One of them was in a light gig-wagon.

Gila 'hilə, *n.* [*Gila* River in Arizona.] In combs.: (1) **Gila bat,** prob. the California little brown bat, *Vespertilio californicus;* (2) **chipmunk,** (see quot.); (3) **grass,** an unidentifiable species of grass found in the Southwest, *rare;* (4) **monster,** a poisonous lizard of the genus *Heloderma* found in the Southwest, sometimes attaining a length of two feet; (5) **trout,** a cyprinoid fish found in the Colorado basin; (6) **woodpecker,** the saguaro woodpecker of the Southwest.

(1) **1868** *Calif. Acad. Sci. Proc.* IV. 6 Vespertilo Yumanensis Allen—Gila Bat. — (2) **1867** *Amer. Naturalist* I. 358 Of the Striped Ground Squirrels, or 'Chipmunks,' composing the genus *Tamias,* only one species is common, which is the Gila Chipmunk (*T. dorsalis*). **1878** Hinton *Ariz.* 336 Squirrels are well represented, both in number and variety, and include the tuft-eared, . . . the four-striped and the pale four-striped squirrels; also the Gila chipmunk, which may be a variety of one of the preceding. — (3) **1846** Emory *Military Reconn.* 92 It [*sc.* the island] was overgrown with willow, cane, Gila grass, flag grass, &c. — (4) **1877** H. C. Hodge *Arizona* 226 There are many varieties of the surian lizard species. . . . There is one variety, however, peculiar to Arizona, found principally in the Gila River valley, and

locally known as the Gila monster. **1948** *Calif. Acad. Sciences News Letter* Oct. 2 The villain of the piece [is] a Gila monster, only venomous lizard in the United States.

(5) **1854** BARTLETT *Personal Narrative* 192 A number of the fish called by Major Emory the 'Gila trout' were caught near our camp. **1900** *Land of Sunshine* Dec. 436 It is popularly known as Bony-Tail, Gila Trout and Round-Tail. — (6) **1858** BAIRD *Birds Pacific R.R.* 111 Gila Woodpecker. *Centurus uropygialis*. . . . Lower Colorado river of the West. **1917** *Birds of Amer.* II. 162/1 The peculiarity of the Gila Woodpecker is its apparent preference for the stem of the giant cactus as a homesite. **1948** *Desert Mag.* Feb. 27/3 It would not come to our camp as the Gila woodpecker did.

Gilbert's relief grass. Southern canary grass, *Phalaris caroliniana*, found in the southern states. — **1889** VASEY *Agric. Grasses* 39 *Phalaris intermedia* (Southern Reed Canary Grass; Gilbert's Relief Grass; Stewart's Canary Grass; California Timothy Grass) . . . grows in South Carolina and the Gulf States, extending to Texas. **1896** BEAL *Grasses No. Amer.* II. 182 *P[halaris] intermedia*. . . Canary-grass. Gilbert's Relief-grass. . . . Some consider it a good grass for winter pasture.

Gilead fir. (See quot.) — **1859** BARTLETT 20 Balsam Fir . . . is also called Canada Balsam and Gilead Fir.

gilia ˈdʒɪlɪə, *n.* [Felipe Luis *Gil*, Sp. botanist of the latter half of the 18th cent.] A plant of the genus *Gilia* of the phlox family, found chiefly from Texas to California, having handsome flowers of a tubular or salver form. Cf. **cypress, scarlet gilia.**

[**1843** TORREY in Frémont *Exped.* (1845) 174 Along the Sweet Water, many interesting plants were collected, as . . . *thermopsis montana*, Nutt.; *gilia pulchella*, Dougl.] **1869** MUIR *First Summer in Sierra* (1911) 43 Back from the bank most of the sunshine reaches the ground, calling up the grasses and flowers in glorious array, tall bromus waving like bamboos, . . . lupines, gilias, violets, glad children of light. **1947** *Sierra Club Bul.* May 17 There were only four woody plants—two pines, an alpine currant, and a granite gilia.

* **gill,** *n.* In combs.: (1) **gill-fisher,** a fisherman who uses gill nets; (2) **net,** a net designed to catch fish by their gills as they attempt to swim through it; (3) **netting,** netting of which gill nets are made; (4) **seine,** a seine for catching fish by their gills.

(1) **1879** *Harper's Mag.* June 73/2 The gill-fishers set out their nets also. — (2) **1796** MORSE *Univ. Geog.* I. 369 The fishermen turn the course of the river . . . or compress it into a narrow channel, where they fix their gill nets. **1935** LINCOLN *Cape Cod Yesterdays* 150 He had a string of gill-nets set in the outer bay. — (3) **1884** *Nat. Museum Bul.* No. 27, 1005 Series of samples of gill-netting, One piece, 300 yards long, . . . colored red. — (4) **1871** *Delaware Laws* XIV. I. 86 It shall be unlawful for any person to lay out, float, or set any gill-seine or net . . . nearer than one mile from the shore.

As the last term in **blue, green gill.**

giller ˈgɪlɚ, *n.* (See quot.) — **1880** *Harper's Mag.* May 854/2 The head of Chesapeake Bay is the centre of a large fleet of drift-net fishing-boats, or 'gillers,' which is the comprehensive local term.

gilling ˈgɪlɪŋ, *n. attrib.* **1. gilling ground,** the part of a fishing ground where gill nets are set. **2. gilling twine,** strong twine used in making gill nets. — (1) **1880** *Harper's Mag.* May 854/2 The 'gilling ground' extends from Havre de Grace, Maryland, eastward and southward to the mouth of the Chester River. — (2) **1878** *Rep. Indian Affairs* 361 Class 7. Notions. . . . Gilling-twine.

Gillite ˈgɪlaɪt, *n.* (See quot.) *Obs.* — **1823** FAUX *Memorable Days* 119 Sunday, August 1st. I heard the Rev. Dr. Allison, a judicious Gillite. [Note:] Calvinists are here [in the district of Columbia] called Gillites, or disciples of the late Dr. Gill.

gilsonite ˈgɪlsənaɪt, *n.* Uintaite, a kind of asphalt found in abundance in Utah, and first brought into prominence as an article of utility by S. H. Gilson, of Salt Lake City. Also attrib.

1890 *N. & Q.* V. (28 June) 101 Gilsonite is a mineral wax found in Utah, and mined to some extent. It was named from its discoverer, a Mr. Gilson. There is a Gilsonite Company in Salt Lake City, which handles the commercial product. **1903** *Indian Laws & Tr.* III. 18 In the lands within the former Uncompahgre Indian Reservation, in the state of Utah, containing gilsonite, asphaltum, elaterite. **1947** *Steamboat* (Colo.) *Pilot* 16 Jan. 3/3 Buckley M. Harrison, Uintah county horseman and ranch hand, was found dead at the old Rainbow gilsonite mine.

gimbal-jawed, see **jimberjawed.**

gimmick ˈgɪmɪk, *n.* [?f. **gimcrack*.] Any small device, esp. one used secretly or in a tricky manner. Also transf. — **1928** *Amer. Sp.* June 414 *Gimmick*—The brake, tip-up, or other device used on games of chance to make them crooked or unfair to the towner who plays them. **1949** *Chi. D. News* 26 March 6/7 The gimmick the White House advisers are most fearful of is the amendment tacked on in the House.

* **gin,** *n.*[1]

1. Formerly on Long Island, an inclosure into which the stock of the colonists was driven when it was desired to move, inspect, or drive the cattle from field to field or to town in wintertime. Also attrib. *Obs.* Cf. * **gin,** *v.*[1] **1.**

1654 *Southampton Rec.* I. 91 An Indian . . . may keep the plaines instead or the ginfence. **1663** *Ib.* II. 39 There lyeth a little goar of comon land against half an acre in ye . . . little plains, of Joseph Raynor, and between that said half acre, and his gin acre. **1665** *East-Hampton Rec.* I. 229 There is damage done upon the plaine by the neglect of those that keepe the gin. **1684** *Ib.* II. 145 Tis Agreed with the Indean Called Jephery; & his Squaw that the[y] are to keepe ginn at the East End of the playns. **1698** *Ib.* 399 Richard Shaw should be viewer of the Easte Gennerall Lyne of fence and agreed with We homp to keep the East Ginn for 20 in Caish. **1826** (in a letter to the editor) This term was also used as late as a hundred years ago, for in the Trustees' Records for . . . July 10, 1826, they agreed to employ Elisha Parsons again to make a fence by the 'gin.'

b. Also **gin keeper, gin man, gin wigwam.** *Obs.*

1665 *Southampton Rec.* II. 237 The vacant land . . . shall not bee disposed to any in particular, but reserved to accommodate the gin keeper. **1681** *East-Hampton Rec.* II. 110 To Stephen Hedges for a peece of Land & plowing it for y Ginman. **1688** *Ib.* 220 Carting the Gin wigwam . . . 3 [shillings].

c. As the name of a place where such an inclosure was located. [Cf. modern "Gin Beach" at Montauk and "Gin Lane" in Southampton.]

1661 *Southampton Rec.* II. 214 Whether they [*sc.* swine] come at the place called the gin, or wheresoever else, the owners of the said swine shall pay to them that impound them 6 pence a peece. **1695** *East-Hampton Rec.* II. 329 Also one piec of land within fence Lying at a Place commonly called the ginn.

2. A machine for removing the seed from cotton (see also quot. 1835). Cf. **cotton gin.**

[**1740** W. STEPHENS *Proc. Georgia* 541 Cotton cannot be cleansed by the ordinary Way of Gin.] **1835** INGRAHAM *South-West* II. 288 Gin, in the common acceptation, signifies the house and all the machinery required to separate the lint from the seed. **1947** *Democrat* 18 Dec. 1/2

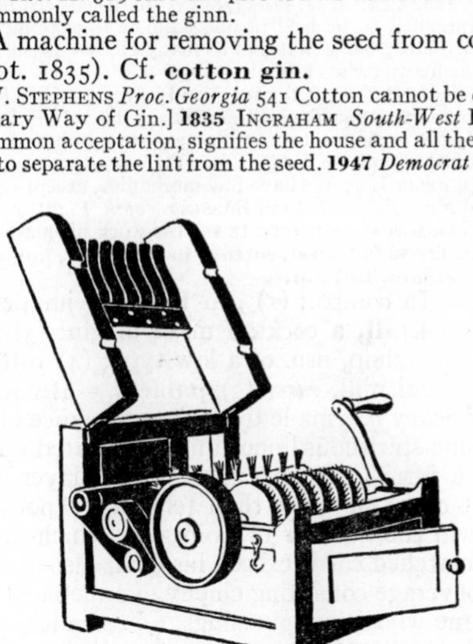

Early type of gin (sense 2) or cotton gin

Clarke County Gin Declares Dividend. **1948** DICK *Dixie Frontier* 252 The gin (a corruption of the word 'engine') was run by horsepower.

attrib. **1934** VINES *Green Thicket World* 33 By the time they came in sight of . . . the gin and the gin lot . . . they heard Lat's voice. **1946** *Democrat* 22 Aug. 4/1 Wearing bell with gin belt collar. Should have calf by side. **1948** DICK *Dixie Frontier* 84 Surrounding the 'mansion' were barns, a smokehouse . . . a gin house where the gin and press were operated.

b. A form of roller gin for sea-island cotton.

1779 in ANBUREY *Travels* II. 425 The seeds which are naturally mixed with the cotton are cleaned by means of a machine called a gen, which is made of two smooth rollers placed close and parallel to each other in a frame. **1858** *Texas Almanac 1850* 191 Seeing lately a Sea Island Gin made with rollers eighteen inches long, and 4 in diameter.

3. In special combs. relating to a cotton gin: (1) **gin band,** a band or belt that passes over and turns the main cylinder and brush of a gin; (2) **brush,** a gin-roller provided with brushes that sweep cotton on to or, more usu., away from the saws; (3) **driver,** formerly one who drove the horse or horses used to operate a gin, *obs.;* (4) **factory,** a place where gins are made; (5) **hopper,** the receptacle for cotton that is being ginned; (6) * **house,** the main building at a place where cotton is ginned; (7) **roller,** a cylinder provided with saws or brushes used in a gin; (8) **saw,** a small circular saw used in a gin, also attrib.; (9) **screw,** a large screw, orig. of wood, used in packing ginned cotton into bags or bales; (10) **stand,** the stand and frame that support and contain the saws and brushes of a cotton gin; (11) **wright,** a mechanic who instals and repairs cotton gins.

(1) **1843** in BASSETT *South. Plant.* 171, I wan a jinban (gin band) very bad indeed for I cant get long well with this. — (2) **1859** *Rep. Comm. Patents 1858* I. 595, I claim the lower carding-brush . . . in combination with the gin-brush and comb-brush, as set forth. — (3) **1850** LEWIS *La. Swamp Doctor* 35, I was a student of medicine, and had been almost a printer, a cotton-picker, plough-boy, gin-driver. — (4) **1846** *De Bow's Review* II. 153 In connection with the gin factory, I have a saw, grist, and flouring mill.

(5) **1854** *Harper's Mag.* VIII. 456/1 The 'packing-room' is the loft of the gin-house, and is over the gin-stand. By this arrangement the cotton is conveniently shoved down a causeway into the 'gin-hopper.' — (6) **1827** SHERWOOD *Gaz. Georgia* 116 At three or four gin-houses much of the cotton raised in the vicinity, and in Burke, was cleaned. **1948** DICK *Dixie Frontier* 84 Surrounding the 'mansion' were barns, a smoke-house, where the pork was cured, a gin house where the gin and press were operated. — (7) **1875** KNIGHT 969/2 Another [gin] has a roller-knife acting in combination with a gin-roller. — (8) **1849** *Hunt's Merch. Mag.* XXI. 635 The Legislature of Tennessee also agreed to pay twenty-seven and a half cents for each gin saw used in the State. **1882** *Cent. Mag.* Jan. 478/1 A small self-feeding gin-saw sharpener, intended to be held in one hand, was examined. — (9) **1896** HARRIS *Sister Jane* 221 It had as many elbows as the Baptizin' Creek, and as many twists as a gin-screw.

(10) **1825** *Austin P.* II. (1924) 1055 Also I have agreed to furnish all irons Gin stand etc. **1860** *Texas Almanac* 303 These Gin-Stands . . . are especially distinguished for combining great ginning speed with a much improved sample of cotton. — (11) **1823** QUITMAN in Claiborne *Life Quitman* I. 77 We have few mechanics, except carpenters, masons, and gin-wrights. **1840** in BASSETT *South. Plant.* 140, I got a ginwright to look at the ginstand to see the work hit needed.

As the last term in **barrel, cotton, hand-roller, horse, Negro, roller, saw, steam, toll gin.**

* **gin,** *n.*[2] In combs.: (1) **gin berry,** a juniper berry, *rare;* (2) **cocktail,** a cocktail made of gin; (3) **mill,** a saloon or grog shop, usu. of a low type; (4) **miller,** the keeper of a gin mill, *rare;* (5) **palace,** = **gin mill;** (6) **rickey,** a rickey *q.v.* made by adding the juice of a fresh lime to some spirituous liquor and carbonated water; (7) **rummy,** a form of rummy in which a player who has cards that count no more than ten may "knock" in an effort to win the number of points by which his opponent's unmatched cards exceed his own, also attrib.; (8) **sling,** a beverage consisting chiefly of sweetened gin; (9) **slinger,** one who mixes gin slings, a bartender.

(1) **1839** Z. LEONARD *Adventures* (1904) 170 Here we passed the night without any thing to eat except these gin berries. — (2) *c*1845 PAULDING *Madmen All* 194 We drink . . . gin-cocktails pretty considerable. **1872** *Newton Kansan* 7 Nov. 4/5 Moreover, our idea of bitters was totally irreconcilable with 'gin-cocktails,' 'brandy-smashes.' — (3) **1865** *Phila. Sun. Mercury* 3 Sep. 4/2 Ruby Nose Peg then came forward and said that she was the proprietor of an unlicensed gin mill. **1948** *Reader's Digest* Nov. 117/1 Chicago's invisible police, . . . to be discovered mainly in gin mills and horse parlors. — (4) **1888** *Voice* 9 Aug., The Barney Rourke Association, a social organization named after that gin-miller and Republican 'boss' in the 8th Assembly District.

(5) **1846** *Californian* (Monterey) 17 Oct. 1/2 To supply one '*gin palace*' . . . nine horses, drawing three large wagons loaded with the baneful poison, are seen at regular periods progressing in a sort of procession. — (6) **1895** *Voice* (N.Y.) 4 July 41/4 Spittoons, gin rickies, Manhattan cocktails, and dirty 'bums' before the bar. **1947** *N. & Q.* Sep. 90. An amusing account of the origin of the gin rickey appears in George R. Brown's 'not too serious history'—*Washington* (Baltimore, 1930). — (7) **1944** *Sat. Ev. Post* 18 March 45/2, I happen to know a grandmother of seventy-five who cheats at gin rummy. **1949** *Newsweek* 23 May 79/1, I find that there are two main types of gin-rummy players. — (8) **1800** *Mass. Spy* 9 July (Th.), [They] were sitting in a cellar kitchen in Grubbstreet, regaling themselves in drinking gin sling and smoking segars. **1946** *St. Louis Globe-Democrat* 20 Oct., Long before 1849, the river boatmen along Loutre Slough had such names as Slingtown, from the 'ginslings' that were among their favorite drinks. — (9) **1887** *Voice* (Extra) 1 Sep., Saloon-keepers and white-aproned gin-slingers stood in the doors of the saloons. **1894** *S.F. Midwinter Appeal* 17 Feb. 4/1 Last Saturday the wife of Mayor Bogg sloped with a gin-slinger at the El Dorado saloon.

* **gin,** *v.*[1]

1. *intr.* To keep watch at a gin (see * **gin,** *n.*[1] **1.** above). Hence **ginning,** *n. Obs.*

1685 *East-Hampton Rec.* II. 165 Tis Agreed with the Indian called Quasequeg and his Sqa; that they are to Gin at the East End of the playne. **1698** *E.-Hampton Rec.* II. 392 To Wehomp as part of pay for Ginning [£]1. **1698** *Ib.* 396 To Weomp for jinning in the year 1698 [£]1.

2. In colloq. expressions: (1) *To gin around,* to cause (cattle) to run or move about uneasily; (2) *to gin her up,* to make things hum; (3) *to gin up,* to use up, kill.

(1) **1884** ALDRIDGE *Life on Ranch* 88 The boss of the range has appointed two of his men to help to hold the herd, and also to prevent everybody from rushing in, as soon as the cattle are rounded up, and 'ginning them around.' — (2) **1887** F. FRANCIS *Saddle & Moccasin* vii. 124 The Apaches were out to beat hell. . . . And they were ginning her up, and making things a bit lively. — (3) **1907** J. R. COOK *Border & Buffalo* 336 Captain Lee . . . complimented us . . . for the manner in which we had 'ginned them up.'

gin dʒɪn, *v.*[2] *To gin up,* to indulge in gin. Hence *ginned up. Slang.*

1894 *S.F. Midwinter Appeal* 17 Feb. 4/5 As for jags, he held that he can gin up when he likes. **1900** DRANNAN *Plains & Mts.* 121 The third day we arrived at the place spoken of, this man Shewman got pretty well ginned up. **1928** *Sat. Ev. Post* 4 Feb. 105/2 The man who wrote that was all ginned up.

* **ginger,** *n.*

1. Spirit, temper. *Slang.*

1843 HALIBURTON *Attaché* 1 Ser. xv, Curb him [a horse] up, talk Yankee to him, and get his ginger up. **1888** *World* (N.Y.) 13 May (F.), Your spinal column is requiring a hinge, and . . . considerable ginger is departing from your resolution to bear up and enjoy yourself. **1942** WARNICK *Dialect Garrett Co., Md.* 7 Ginger, n., temper. 'She's got her ginger up this morning.'

b. (*By*) *ginger!* a euphemistic expletive. *Colloq.*

1865 LOWELL *Letters* I. 348 There, by ginger! I meant to give the merest hint of a sentiment, and I have gone splash into a moral. **1891** COOKE *Huckleberries* (1896) 41 Ginger! this here's sport, ain't it? **1916** E. PORTER *David* 309 'Well, by ginger!' exclaimed the man again.

2. In combs.: (1) **ginger champagne,** app. a non-alcoholic beverage flavored with ginger, also attrib., *obs.;* (2) **cooky,** a ginger cake or gingersnap; (3) **Jake,** a local name for a concoction (see quot. and cf. **jake,** *n.*[2]) sometimes indulged in during the prohibition period (1920–33); (4) **pine,** the Oregon cedar, *Chamaecyparis lawsoniana;* (5) **tea,** a medicinal preparation made by steeping ginger in boiling water.

(1) **1842** UNCLE SAM *Peculiarities* I. 42 The military are for a minute obstructed by six gaudily-painted covered carts filled with merchandise, which their owners, the 'western merchants,' are carrying home; . . . an 'American ginger champaign' waggon. *Ib.* 43 On the outside . . . is printed the following thirsty announcement: . . . Congress Water, Sarsaparilla Soda, Ginger Champaign. — (2) **1880** *Harper's Mag.* March 576/1 Aunty'll give you ginger-cookey this very minute! **1945** *Chi. Tribune* 26 Aug. VII. 1/2 We were ready for . . . the plates of ginger cookies. — (3) **1944** *Reader's Digest* August 19 If they aren't concerned with something as dramatic as 'Ginger Jake'—a beverage made with a varnish thickener (for ginger flavor!) which inflicted some 30,000 people with a form of paralysis [etc.]. — (4) **1884** SARGENT *Rep. Forests* 179 *Chamaecyparis Lawsoniana.* . . . Port Orford Cedar. Oregon Cedar. White Cedar. Lawson's Cypress. Ginger Pine. **1897** SUDWORTH *Arborescent Flora* 82 *Chamaecyparis lawsonia.* . . . Common names [include] . . . Ginger Pine.

(5) **1857** ERASTUS BEADLE *To Nebraska in '57* (1923) 31 Getting somewhat wet being out so long in the snow and my throat sore I took some ginger tea and doctored up to take an early start. **1906** PRINGLE *Rice Planter* 362, I immediately went out to the kitchen and made a cup of hot ginger tea which I forced her to drink.

* **gingerbread,** *n.* As the last term in **Lafayette, molasses gingerbread.**

gingerette ˌdʒɪndʒəˈret, *n.* A beverage flavored with ginger. *Rare.* — **1895** *Advance* 31 Oct. 362/1 The ladies fanned themselves and lemonade and gingerette were passed.

gink gɪŋk, *n.* [Origin obscure. Cf. *EDD ginkie,* a term of reproach for a woman.] An odd or eccentric fellow. *Slang.* — **1910** *Sat. Ev. Post* 22 Oct. 12/3, I don't believe that all these ginks have got coin enough to support one good game, anyhow. **1947** *Mazama* Mar. 4/2 Oh what a funny gink is man, he climbs the dizzy summit, to place his name within a can and gets real pleasure from it.

ginned cotton. Cotton that has been ginned, lint cotton.

1829 SHERWOOD *Gaz. Georgia* (ed. 2) 259 A Tariff Cotton Gin, which should give every man as much ginned cotton as he delivered in the seed. **1856** *Rep. Comm. Patents 1855: Agric.* 322 The mean quantity over all is estimated at 125 pounds of ginned cotton . . . to an acre. **1862** *Ill. Agric. Soc. Trans.* V. 518 Two hundred and fifty pounds of ginned cotton to the acre is a good yield with us.

ginner ˈdʒɪnə, *n.* One who operates a cotton gin.

1858 *Texas Almanac* (*advt.*), The liability of injury to the ginner while tending the gin is entirely obviated. **1893** *Columbus* (O.) *Dispatch* 18 Sep., Several ginners disregarded the notices and opened their establishments for business. **1949** *Lubbock* (Tex.) *Morn. Avalanche* 23 Feb. II. 8/1 Attention Farmers & Ginners. We have moved to the Rogers Cotton Building.

ginnery ˈdʒɪnərɪ, *n.* A place where cotton is ginned. — **1887** *Harper's Mag.* Aug. 432/1 Colonel Macquard drove them, . . showing them . . . the ginneries where cotton-seed oil was made. **1904** *Boston Transcript* 9 Feb. 3/5 There were 30,171 active ginneries in operation.

* **giraffe,** *n.*

1. (See quot. 1896.) *Obs.*

1877 W. WRIGHT *Big Bonanza* 172 The engines for driving the huge reel, and thus hoisting this iron car or 'giraffe,' with its load of ore and the 25,000 pounds of cable, are two in number and of 200-horse power each. **1896** SHINN *Story of Mine* 225 The car used for hoisting through an incline is a 'giraffe,' absurdly called so 'because the hind wheels are very large and the front ones low, so as to keep the car level.'

2. In phrases (see quots.) relating to cheating or getting the better of someone. *Slang. Obs.*

1844 *N.O. Picayune* 14 Oct. 273 'No you don't,' said the watchman, 'you don't come the giraffe over me that a way.' **1844** M. C. HOUSTOUN *Texas* (1845) 76 The latter, with the eternal quid in the corner of his mouth, is clearly looking out 'for the giraffe.' *c*1845 *Big Bear Ark.* 60 But our animal know'd how to come the giraffe over *him.*

giraffe dʒəˈræf, *v. tr.* To humbug or cheat. *Obs.* — **1840** *Kentucky Rifle* 31 Oct., We can never be humbugged or Giraffed long.

* **girdle,** *n.* A ring or gash cut around the trunk of a tree to kill it. — **1825** LORAIN *Pract. Husb.* 63 All of them eventually die, provided the girdle be carefully cut through the sap into the heart-wood of the tree. **1896** P. A. BRUCE *Econ. Hist. Virginia* I. 150 The method employed by the Indians for the removal of the forest . . . consists in running a girdle around the trunks of the largest trees by cutting away the bark with a rude stone instrument, the object of this being to intercept the flow of the sap.

* **girdle,** *v. tr.* To kill (a tree) by cutting a circular ring around its trunk. Cf. * **belt,** *v.* **1.**

Quot. 1650 suggests that this custom may have been taken over from the Indians.

[**1650** in FORCE *Tracts* III. No. 11, 48 If he but unbarke the Trees one foot round after the Indian mode to prevent the shade occasioned by the leaves, which such unbarking quite destroyes, the Corne (set betwixt those Trees) will thrive and prosper exceedingly.] **1659** *Jamaica* (L.I.) *Rec.* I. 6 Whosoever hath or doth possesse hold or enjoy a home Lot within ye Town shall ffell or girdle all such trees . . . prejudiciall to their Neighbors. **1788** JOHN PENN *Journal* 293 Several trees, before I arrived at the Susquehanna-ferry, had been girdled, as it is termed, that is cut all around thro' the bark, so as to prevent their continuing alive. **1833** J. STUART *Three Years No. Amer.* I. 134 When the bark is cut in the manner described, the trees are said to be girdled. **1946** STANWELL-FLETCHER *Driftwood Valley* 195 If they girdle trees to kill for firewood they choose those with a fairly large diameter.

transf. **1899** *Nation* 16 Nov. LXIX. 380/1 That repeal [of the Missouri Compromise] gave birth to the determined purpose of the free States to 'girdle' the system of slavery, by declaring that there should be no more slave States. **1948** BOYCE *Forest Pathology* 239 In northern Idaho, *Phomopsis boycei* Hahn causes cankers on saplings and poles of lowland white fir that girdle and kill many branches during some seasons.

b. Used with reference to the injuring of trees by rodents or fire.

1852 *Mich. Agric. Soc. Trans.* III. 185 Eight apple trees were girdled by mice. **1883** SHIELDS *S. S. Prentiss* 63 The undergrowth was cindered to ashes, the heavy timber girdled to death [by fire]. **1948** *Chi. Tribune* 14 Mar. III. 10/3 During very severe weather, rabbits may girdle young fruit trees.

* **girdled,** *a.* Of trees: Killed by girdling.

1685 *E.-Hampton Rec.* II. 176 Granted unto Mr John Mulford all that land that is by his land that is known by the name of the girdled tres. **1809** CUMING *Western Tour* 42 The stumps or girdled trees [were] still standing. **1933** T. WILLIAMSON *Woods Colt* 66 You might keep up for a little while, same's a *girdled tree* in a corn patch, but it wouldn't be for long.

* **girdling,** *n.* The cutting of girdles or rings about trees to kill them.

1779 *Mass. H. S. Coll.* 2 Ser. II. 473 Those flatts from Tioga to Wyoming have all ben improved and clear'd by girdling. **1851** HOWE *Hist. Coll. Great West* 284 By degrees, the surrounding trees are killed by *girdling.* **1898** N. E. JONES *Squirrel Hunters of Ohio* 26 The usual plan for their removal was by 'girdling,' or cutting a circle around the trunk of each sufficiently deep to kill the tree.

b. (See quot.) *Obs.*

1859 BARTLETT 170 The place so cleared is thence called a girdling.

* **girl,** *n.*

1. girl friend, a female companion or sweetheart. *Colloq.*

1945 *Democrat* 24 May 4/3 We used to visit our girl friends back in the states. **1947** *Science Illust.* July 92/3 The steering wheel is a nuisance when one is parked with the girl friend observing the scenery on a moonlit Saturday night.

2. girl scout, a member of the Girl Scouts, an organization (known orig. as Girl Guides) formed in 1912 at Savannah, Ga. Often (*cap.*), in the *pl.*, the organization itself. Also attrib.

1920 *Ladies' Home Jrnl.* June 145/1 In 1912 Mrs. Juliette Low, now president emeritus of the Girl Scouts in America, started the first troop in Savannah, Georgia. *Ib.* 146/4 In Philadelphia the Girl Scout troops compete in a monthly banner contest, points for which are won almost entirely for 'homekeeping.' **1945** *Somerset News* 19 April 2/1 Girl Scouts will give out pamphlets and receive donations. **1949** *Lisle* (Ill.) *Eagle* 10 Mar. 2/3 This is the first verse of a Girl Scout song written about the Chalet.

Hence **Girl Scouting.**

1949 *Lisle* (Ill.) *Eagle* 10 Mar. 2/3 Each year, March 12, is a red letter day in Girl Scouting.

As the last term in **bachelor, bathing, best, Bowery, bus, business, casket, chumpa, college, cow, Gibson, good time, hello, hired, house, Kodak, mustang, news, old, parlor, sales, second, sewing machine, table, tall, telephone, trading, type, typewriter, waiter, yellow girl.**

* **girth,** *n.* A horizontal beam or girder.

1821 COOPER *Spy* xxxiii, A heavy piece of timber lay across the girths of the barn. **1889** *Cent.* 252/1 *Girth,* . . . in car-building, a long horizontal bracing-timber on the inside of the frame of a box-car. **1929** SHELTON *Salt-box House* ix, At the corners square beams stood upright, these being held by the line of 'girths' at the next story.

* **give,** *v.*

1. *tr.* To offer, propose, insinuate. *Colloq.*

1883 HAY *Bread-Winners* xviii. 275 'Why, what are you givin' me now?' 'I'm a-givin' you truth and friendship.' **1889** MARK TWAIN *Conn. Yankee* i. 22 What are you giving me? . . . Get along back to your circus, or I'll report you.

2. To connect (one speaking over the telephone) with a desired subscriber or number.

1887 *Trial H. K. Goodwin* 26, I heard him call, 'Give me police station.' **1914** *Bell Telephone News* March 19/1 Subscriber: 'Give me 1000.' Operator: 'What office, please?'

3. * *To give away,* to betray (a secret), esp. unintentionally, to expose (a person). *Colloq.* Cf. **giveaway** (*b*).

1862 in *Southern Hist. Soc. P.* (1884) XII. 272 Remarking, 'Boys, your game is up—Busy Bill gave it away,' [the sergeant] walked up. **1890** *Boston Journal* 21 Nov. 2/3 A Cincinnati teamster . . . gave away his brother-in-law, who was a deserter from the regular army, and thereby scooped in $30 in cash.

4. In noun combs.: (1) **giveaway,** (*a*) designating games in which the object is to lose points, to force one's opponent to make captures, etc., (*b*) a betrayal, esp. an unintentional one, *slang,* cf. **dead giveaway;** (2) **give-out,** a state of being weary or exhausted, *rare.*

(1) (*a*) **1872** *Newton Kansan* 19 Dec. 2/2 We are decidedly opposed to the give-away game. **1899** CHAMPLIN & BOSTWICK *Cyclo. Games & Sports* (ed. 2) 181 *Give-away* Chess. . . . The Give-away game differs from the ordinary one. (*b*) **1897** FLANDRAU *Harvard Episodes* 224, I gave my own name, but Dilly didn't; he had one all ready that went with the initials on his underclothes, so it wouldn't be a give-away. **1948** *Time* 29 Nov. 65/1 How fast will the XF7U-1 go? It is no secret (and the shape itself would be a giveaway) that it was designed to fly considerably faster than Mach 1. — (2) **1853** *Knickerb.* XLIII. 53 There was no give-out about that little boy; he was always ready for his work.

* **giver,** *n. Baseball.* The pitcher. *Obs.*

1857 *Spirit of Times* 23 May 180/3 During this game, J. B. Atherton, on the part of the Bay State men, was giver, with Charles H. Hopkins as catcher. For the Olympic Club, H. Furbush was giver, with H. F. Gill as catcher. **1868** *N. Eng. Base-Ballist* 6 Aug. 1/1 Five [men], would suffice for a game, with one at the bat, a catcher out, giver and a chaser or two, the fun would continue for hours. **1909** *Collier's* 8 May 12/3 The pitcher—known as the 'thrower' or 'giver'—stood midway of the polygon.

As the last term in **Indian giver.**

* **gizzard,** *n.* Any one of several American fishes of the genus *Dorosoma* having strong, muscular stomachs resembling gizzards. In full **gizzard shad.**

1820 RAFINESQUE in *Western Rev.* II. 172 Spotted Gizzard. *Dorosoma notata.* . . . I found it below the falls of the Ohio in August . . . Vulgar names Gizzard, Hickory Shad, White Shad, &c. **1857** *Harper's Mag.* March 442/1 The refuse fish commonly taken are sturgeon; . . . perch, mullet, gar, gizzard-shad or ale-wife. **1884** GOODE *Fisheries* I. 610 The names 'Gizzard Shad' or 'Hickory Shad' refer to the peculiar muscular stomach [of the mud shad]. **1947** DALRYMPLE *Panfish* 243 They go chopping their way through a school of small Gizzard Shad, or Minnows, like ruthless invaders on the offensive.

* **glad,** *a.* and *n.*

1. *pl.* One's finest or best clothes. Also **glad rags.** *Slang.*

1903 *Cin. Enquirer* 10 May IV. 3/1 In the Evening you can put on your Glads and drink $47 worth of Vintage Wines and take in two or three Theaters. **1904** *Dly. Chron.* 6 Oct. 8/2 Donning an elaborate evening frock—the slangy American girl calls it 'gettin' into her glad rags.' **1948** *Dly. Ardmoreite* (Ardmore, Okla.) 23 July 6 Hi, Buck! Why the glad rags?

Also **glad clothes.**

1905 *Dly. Chron.* 11 Jan. 4/5 Only when starvation stares him in the face will he relinquish his 'glad clothes,' as the cowboys call them.

2. glad hand, the hand extended in cordial greeting, usu. fig. Also attrib. Also **glad hander.** *Colloq.* or *slang.*

1896 G. ADE *Artie* i. 4 She meets me at the door, puts out the glad hand an' says [etc.]. **1904** CRISSEY *Tattlings* 273 Put not your trust in the Gladhand Brigade. **1929** MERRIAM *Chicago* 275 One type is the good fellow, the mixer, the 'joiner,' the glad hander, whose chief reliance is the cultivation of the personal friendship of individuals and the acquaintance with all sorts of groups and societies. **1947** *Steamboat* (Colo.) *Pilot* 13 Feb. 2/1 He is not a 'glad-hander' nor a 'back slapper.'

Gladdenite ˈglædnˌaɪt, *n.* A follower of Gladden Bishop, who was one of the aspirants to leadership in the Mormon Church after the death of Joseph Smith. Hence **Gladdenism.** *Obs.*

1853 B. YOUNG in T. B. H. Stenhouse *Rocky Mt. Saints* (1873) 306 Now, you Gladdenites, keep your tongues still, lest sudden destruction come upon you. . . . Now, you nasty apostates, clear out. **1870** BEADLE *Utah* 124 Most of the other aspirants took off various sects, known in the Brighamite church as 'Gladdenites,' 'Strangites,' 'Brewsterites,' 'Gatherers,' etc. **1902** W. A. LINN *Story of Mormons* 436 On Sunday, March 20, 1853, a meeting . . . which the Gladdenites were holding . . . was dispersed by the city marshal. . . . This was the practical end of Gladdenism.

* **glade,** *n.*

1. A marshy tract of low ground covered with grass (see quot. 1859).

1644 in *Amer. Sp.* XV. 266/1 Thence . . . unto a Small White oake and a Pocickerry that Stands in the Glade and then paralell to the Glade or white Marsh. **1731** *Ib.* 266/2 Four hundred and ninety Six acres . . . bounded near the head of a Small Glade or Marsh issuing into a Little Creek. **1806** CLARK in *Lewis & C. Exped.* V. (1905) 251 Through small glades on either side of the branch the glades at some places 1/2 a mile wide with several small streams falling on either side up which there is small glades to the narrows. **1859** BARTLETT 170 Glades. Everglades; tracts of land at the South covered with water and grass. So called in Maryland, where they are divided into wet and dry *glades.* **1948** *Good Housekeeping* Jan. 107/1 She had gotten out on the last truck to leave the 'Glades.

b. Used as the name of a particular area of this sort.

1724 *Md. Hist. Mag.* XVIII. 16 Christopher Gist . . . is ordered to clear the Old Indian Road . . . to go by the head of the Western Glade. **1784** WASHINGTON *Diaries* II. 281 There are two Glades which go under the denomination of the Great Glades—one, on the Waters of the Yohiogany, the other on those of Cheat River; and distinguished by the name of the Sandy Creek Glades. **1816** U. BROWN *Journal* II. 359 We would take the road to the Great Glades & Surround the 1900 Acres & come in on it from the Maryland or East side of it. **1945** *Md. Conservationist* 13/1 At another time while on the way to the Yough glade, 'level as the surface of a lake,' he writes [etc.].

2. (See quots.)

1698 SEWALL *Diary* I. 472 A considerable quantity of Ice went away last night: so that now there is a glade of water along by Governor's Island about as far as Bird Island. **1828** WEBSTER, *Glade,* . . . in New England, an opening in the ice of rivers or lakes, or a place left unfrozen. **1864** NICHOLS *Amer. Life* I. 18, I used to skate miles up and down the Connecticut river, and when thirsty, creep carefully to the edges of the air-holes, or 'glades,' in the ice, and drink.

3. (See quots.)

[**1788** SCHÖPF *Reise* I. 358 Hier ist man am Eingange der Glades, oder Glade-Settlements. So nennet man vorzugsweise das grosse und breite Bergthal, welches zwischen dem Alleghany und dem nächstfolgenden Laurelhill liegt, und hier zwischen 10–12 Meilen Breite hat.] **1832** BROWNE *Sylva* 214 [The crab apple] abounds above all, in the glades, which is the name of a tract of land fifteen or eighteen miles, on the summit of the Alleghanies. **1868** H. M. FLINT *Railroads* 12 'The Glades' are the mountain meadows, a region on the high table land at the summit of the Alleghany mountains.

b. (See quots.)

1815 *Mass. H. S. Coll.* 2 Ser. IV. 223 Every tide, however, . . . flows far into Scituate southerly, over Extensive marshes, leaving east of it an high ridge, termed the 'Glades,' in Scituate.

4. *N. Eng.* A long, narrow tract or way covered with ice.

1806 *Mass. Spy* 27 Aug. (Th.), The glade of hail in [Vermont] . . . was about one mile wide. **1889** *Cent.* 2525/3 The path was a glade of ice. (New Eng[land].)

5. In combs.: (1) **glade butter,** ?butter from cows that range in glades, *obs.;* (2) **land,** level land well situated for farming but of only moderate fertility; (3) **lily,** a red-flowered lily found in the eastern states; (4) **mallow,** an American plant, *Napaea dioica,* having small white flowers; (5) **road,** a road passing through a glade; (6) **run,** a small stream flowing into or out of a glade, *obs.*

(1) **1841** ELIZA A. STEELE *Summer Journey in West* 267 These grassy hills are famous for the 'glade butter.' — (2) **1834** BAIRD *Valley Miss.* 109 The soil of the southern counties is generally good excepting some which are called glade lands. **1848** *S. Lit. Messenger* XIV. 222/2 Some salt springs [are] in the mixed glade lands near Cheat River. — (3) **1894** *Amer. Folk-Lore* VII. 102 *Lillium Philadelphicum* . . . tiger-lily, N.J. glade-lily, West Va. — (4) **1857** GRAY *Botany* 67 *Napaea.* Glade Mallow. . . . Limestone valleys, Penn. and southward to the Valley of Virginia, west to Ohio and Illinois; rare. **1884** *Amer. Naturalist* XVIII. 724 The glade mallow is a diœcious plant.

(5) **1810** M. DWIGHT *Journey to Ohio* 47 We are on the old Pennsylvania road—the Glade road is said to be ten times worse than this. **1891** RYAN *Pagan* 123 They had parted from the others and were riding out over the 'glade' road. — (6) **1785** in *Amer. Sp.* XV. 266/2 To a cherry tree on a Glade Run corner to Levy Beatty.

As the last term in **cedar, moon, post oak glade.**

glance glæns, *v.* [?Du. *glanzen.*] *tr.* To planish, to make smooth or plane. — **1894** *Times* 16 Aug. 6/3 Sheet steel, polished, planished, or glanced, . . . one and three-fourth cents per pound.

g'lang glaŋ, *v. intr.* Short for "go along," often used as a command to a horse; also to say "go along," hence **g'langing,** *n.* — **1852** BRISTED *Upper Ten Th.* i. 28 G'lang, old fellow. **1887** WILKINS *Humble Romance* 139 Wa'al, Israel g'langed to the horse, an' put the whip over her, but she jest jagged right along. *Ib.*, The horse was dreadful lazy, an' it was nothin' but g'langin' an' slappin' an' whippin' all the way.

glare glɛr, *n.* [Cf. Eng. dial. *glaur,* slippery ice.]

1. A shining ice surface.

1854 CUMMINGS *Lamplighter* xiii, You noticed how everything was covered with ice, this morning. . . . The side-walks were . . . a perfect glare. **1878** BEADLE *Western Wilds* 457 In ten minutes the road was a glare of ice, our wrappings stiff as armor.

2. glare ice, ice having a smooth, glassy surface.

1832 WILLIAMSON *Maine* I. 100 The rain sometimes freezes as it falls; covers the face of the earth with a glare ice, and adorns the trees with glistening pendants. **1869** STOWE *Oldtown Folks* vi. 73 We was clear down in a well fifty feet deep, and the sides all round nothin' but glare ice. **1890** W. P. LETT in Shields *Big Game No. Amer.*, It [the Caribou] then suddenly squats upon its haunches, and slides along the glare-ice. **1949** *Sat. Ev. Post* 16 April 178/3 There were times when sudden thaws turned the highway to glare ice.

* **glass,** *n.* In combs.: (1) * **glass eye,** short for next; (2) **-eyed pike,** the wall-eyed pike or perch; (3) **snake,** a snakelike lizard, *Ophisaurus ventralis,* of the southern states, so called from its fragility, its long tail breaking readily into small pieces.

(1) **1818** MITCHILL in *Amer. Mo. Mag.* II. 247 Glass-Eye—*Perca vitrea,* with the pupils of the eyes appearing like the semi-globes of glass in the decks of vessels. . . . Found in the Cayuga Lake. **1947** DALRYMPLE *Panfish* 217 The names which allude to Old Bleary's odd-looking eyes are certainly logical enough: i.e., Glass-Eye, White-

Eye, and of course his most common names, Walleye, or Wall-Eyed Pike. — (2) **1865** *Wilkes' Spirit of Times* 23 Sep. 54/1 In Canandaigua lake, trolling for pickerel, glass-eyed pike, and an occasional trout, is persisted in by many novices. **1872** *Fur, Fin, & Feather: Game Laws* 131 The Mohawk River is stocked with black and Oswego bass and the Ohio salmon, or glass-eyed pike. — (3) **1709** LAWSON *Carolina* 134 They might as well have call'd it a Glass-Snake, for it is as brittle as a Tobacco-Pipe, so that if you give it the least Touch of a small Twigg, it immediately breaks into several Pieces. **1842** BUCKINGHAM *Slave States* I. 535 Some of the harmless snakes of the country were seen on the rails or zig-zag fences of the road, one of which, called the glass-snake, appeared to be of peculiar brightness. **1949** *Scientific Mo.* Jan. 55/1 The traditional American glass snake is not, however, a true snake but rather the legless lizard *Ophisaurus ventralis*.

As the last term in **Boston window, cylinder, ogling, road, Sandwich, Steigel glass.**

glass glæs, *v. tr.* In tanning, to dress (a hide) with a glassing stick. Also with *out*. Cf. **glassing jack.** — **1885** *Harper's Mag.* Jan. 278/1 To obtain the finish, the hides are blacked on the flesh side with a preparation of soap and lamp-black, spread with a stout brush, and again 'glassed.' **1897** C. T. DAVIS *Manuf. Leather* (ed. 2) 268 For the morocco or lining finisher it [a machine] will glaze, roll, pebble and glass out.

glassichord ˈglæsəˌkɔrd, *n.* A musical instrument in which the notes are produced by means of graduated glasses or tubes of glass. Also transf. *Obs.*

1835 INGRAHAM *South-West* I. 24 The musical rippling of the eddies—like a glassichord, rapidly run over by light fingers. **1838** ——— *Burton* II. 25 The words were tremulously uttered, like the broken notes of a glassichord rudely swept with the fingers. **1886** *Harper's Mag.* July 286/1 Turning upon his perch, he [the meadow grasshopper] brings to view his 'glassichord,' or shrilling organ.

glassing jack. (See quots. and cf. **glass,** *v.*) — **1883** KNIGHT *Supp.* 404/2 *Glassing Jack*, . . . a machine in which is fitted a plate glass slicker for polishing and smoothing leather. **1885** *Harper's Mag.* Jan. 278/1 To further prepare the surface [of the hides] each one is held under a 'glassing-jack'—a kind of bar or arm moving swiftly to and fro above a solid bed.

∗**glaucous,** *a.*

1. glaucous willow, the American pussy willow, *Salix discolor.*

1843 TORREY *Flora N.Y.* II. 206 *Salix discolor*. . . . Glaucous Willow. Swamps and borders of rivers; frequent. **1884** SARGENT *Rep. Forests* 169 *Salix discolor*. . . . Glaucous Willow. **1897** SUDWORTH *Arborescent Flora* 124 *Salix discolor*. . . . Glaucus Willow (R.I., N.Y., Pa., Miss., Mich., Minn., Ont.).

2. glaucous-winged gull, a gull, *Larus glaucescens,* found along the Pacific Coast.

1858 BAIRD *Birds Pacific R.R.* 842 The Glaucus-winged Gull. . . . Northwest coast of North America. **1874** COUES *Birds N.W.* 622 [The] glaucus-winged Gull . . . [inhabits the] Pacific coast of North America. **1908** *Pacific Mo.* Feb. 127/2 The Glaucous-winged Gull . . . is the bird which throngs our harbors in the Winter season.

∗**glaze,** *n.* **1.** A coating of smooth ice, an area covered with such a coating. Also attrib. **2.** The condition of fully-matured seed with a glazed or sheeny outer surface. *Rare.*

(1) **1853** KANE *Grinnell Exped.* 229 Old seasoned hummock, covered with a slippery glaze. **1896** *N.Y. Wkly. Witness* 22 Dec. 4/1 Much of the ice was glaze-ice. — (2) **1863** *Maine Bd. Agric. Rep.* 11, I think the crop would be required to be cut before the seed was in full glaze.

∗**glaze,** *v. intr.* Of seed: To take on, in maturing, a glazed or sheeny appearance. — **1868** BRACKETT *Farm Talk* 15 There was a fair yield, but it was very backward, and many fields [of corn] were frost-bitten before the kernel was fairly 'glazed.' **1896** *Vt. Agric. Rep.* XV. 72 You should cut your corn just as the ears are beginning to glaze.

∗**gleaner,** *n.* =**brown creeper.** *Obs.* — **1839** AUDUBON *Ornith. Biog.* V. 159 The name of 'Gleaner,' applied to this bird, is, in my opinion, very inappropriate.

glebe lot. A lot assigned to a minister as part of his benefice. *Obs.* — **1730** *Md. Hist. Mag.* VIII. 157 Mr. John Humphreys . . . hath Liberty from this Vestry to remove the house he built on the Glebe Lot in the City of Annapolis. **1794** S. WILLIAMS *Hist. Vermont* 338 Any incumbent to have the care of the glebe lots.

glen fish. (See quot.) *Rare.* — **1772** ROMANS in Phillips *Notes on B. Romans* (1924) 123 It Abounds here in fish of all kinds, . . . the Hog Fish, the Croaker, the Glen Fish, not unlike the Trout in Europe, and of the same Outward Appearance and so Called here.

∗**globe,** *n.* In combs.: (1) **globe cactus,** a large globular or cylindrical spiny cactus, *Echinocactus horizonthalonius,* found in the Southwest; (2) **sight,** a type of sight for a rifle, see **California sight;** (3) **sighted,** *a.* of a rifle, equipped with a globe sight; (4) **tulip,** any one of various herbs of the genus *Calochortus* found in the West.

(1) **1856** REID *Desert Home* 90 They were dark-green masses, of different sizes—the largest of them about the size of a beecap. They looked like a number of huge hedge-hogs rolled up, and presenting on all sides their thorny spikes. . . . I knew they were the *globe cacti*. — (2) **1884** *Harper's Mag.* Aug. 367/1 At this short distance you don't care for the peep and globe sights. **1936** *Sears Cat.* 817 Globe target front sight with 8 inserts. — (3) **1852** CASEY *Two Yrs.* 125 His equipment was a treat to see; his rifle (a telescope and globe-sighted one), revolvers, &c., being of the highest finish, and most improved principles. **1899** WYETH *Forrest* 411 With fatal precision, scarcely excelled by the sharp-shooter with his Whitworth, globe-sighted rifle, Captain John W. Morton, . . . with clear eye and steady heart was sending his shells with deadly purpose right to the spot. — (4) **1901** *Land of Sunshine* Nov. 334, I once found in Eaton's Cañon a fine specimen of the globe tulip, Calochortus albus, with four petals and four sepals, instead of the customary three.

As the last term in **Congressional Globe.**

∗**glorious,** *a.* In combs.: (1) ∗**glorious day,** the Fourth of July; (2) **Eighth (of January),** the eighth of January, celebrated in commemoration of General Andrew Jackson's defeat of the British at New Orleans, Jan. 8, 1815; (3) **Fourth,** see ∗**fourth.**

(1) **1890** *Detroit Free Press* 3 July, Is this decoration for the Fourth? . . . Whoop! I can't wait! I'm ready to bust to-day! What you going to do on the glorious day? — (2) **1839** *Jamestown* (N.Y.) *Jrnl.* 23 Jan. 3/2 A change has come over the spirit of Tammany and not a single rocket welcomes the glorious Eighth. **1870** *N.Y. Herald* 10 Jan. 4/3 'The Glorious Eighth of January' . . . has almost died out as a democratic day of jubilee.

∗**glory hole.** An open pit produced by surface mining.

1909 WEBSTER. **1943** *Copper Camp* 29 Parks' 'gloryhole' became the Parrot, Number One, and eventually turned out over a million dollars' worth of high grade copper.

Hence **glory hole,** *v.*, to carry on surface mining.

1927 BURNS *Tombstone* 381 In this tunnel beneath the town the Grand Central mine 'gloryholed,' taking out $840,000. **1948** *Nev. Highways* July–Aug. 30/1 Caving of waste material into the hole also added to the difficulty. As a result 'glory holing' as it was called eventually ceased altogether.

∗**Gloucester,** *n.* The name of a county in Virginia, used attrib. in the names of fruits, as **Gloucester bean, hickory nut, nut, walnut, white (apple).** *Obs.*

1764 WASHINGTON *Diaries* I. 200 Grafted also in the 7 Row 43 Gloucester white apple. **1786** *Ib.* III. 54 In my Botanical Garden . . . I put Gloucester hiccory Nuts. **1788** *Ib.* 311 In the other half of the 6th. land and the 7th. were a bushel of the Gloucester Beans from Mr. Peachy. **1814** PURSH *Flora Amer.* II. 637 *Juglans sulcata* . . . is called Thick Shellbark Hickory, Springfield or Glocester Nut. **1817** W. COXE *Fruit Trees* 114 Gloucester White. This apple is of a middling size. **1832** BROWNE *Sylva* 176 [The thick shellbark hickory] is also found in the county of Gloucester in Virginia, under the name of Gloucester Walnut.

b. gloucester swing, ?a hammock, in allusion to those used on fishing boats out of Gloucester, Mass.

1920 H. K. WEBSTER *Mary Wollaston* 257 Her habit on warm nights was to sleep on the gloucester swing in the screened verandah.

∗**glover,** *n.* (See quot.) *Slang. Obs.* — **1854** *Cong. Globe* 17 Jan. App. 1220, I have always found (President Franklin Pierce) a very kind and agreeable man—what the 'rounders' in New York would term a 'glover.'

∗**gloves,** *n. pl.* As the last term in **hoskin, Lafayette gloves.**

gluten meal. A branless meal which is a by-product of the manufacture of glucose from corn.

1896 *Vt. Agric. Rep.* XV. 59 Corn should be supplemented by . . . a combination of waste products, such as gluten or linseed meals. *Ib.* 74 Gluten meal is made from corn meal, and is a by-product of the glucose factories. **1904–5** *Encycl. Amer.* VII. *s.v. Gluten,* Corn oil cake and gluten-meal are exported extensively.

glut herring. The summer herring, *Pomolobus aestivalis,* of the Atlantic Coast. — **1884** GOODE *Fisheries* I. 582 The *C[lupea] aestivalis* is the 'Glut' Herring of the Albemarle and the Chesapeake.

∗**glycine,** *n.* The groundnut or wild bean, *Apios tuberosa,* of the Atlantic states; also (*cap.*) an obsolete synonym for *Apios.*

1814 BIGELOW *Florula Bostoniensis* 178 *Glycine apios*. Tuberous Glycine. Ground nut. . . . Not unfrequent in moist woods and thickets. **1850** S. F. COOPER *Rural Hours* 170 But the glycine, or ground-nut, is not uncommon in our thickets. **1882** *Harper's Mag.* May 859/2 The dull red blossoms of the glycine tell of sweet tubers beneath the ground.

glyptorama ˌglɪptəˈræmə, *n.* [Gk. *glypt-*, carved, +*horama*, that which is seen.] (See quots.) *Rare.* — **1895** *N.Y. Dramatic News* 7 Dec. 12/1 At Koster and Bial's last night, Glyptorama, the most pretentious reproduction of famous paintings ever shown, was exhibited for the first time on any stage. *Ib.* 14 Dec. 12/1 The only defect in the production of Glyptorama, at Koster and Bial's, was the impossibility of moving the background and floats at a uniform speed.

G-man. (See quot. 1935.)

1935 F. H. VIZETELLY in *Lit. Digest* 22 June 38 'G Men'—a name, which originated in the underworld within the last two or three years, for Special Agents of the Department of Justice, Division of Investigation, meaning 'Government Men'; later, the name was picked up and used in the movies and the newspapers. 'G Men' have also been called 'Feds,' 'Dee Jays,' and 'Whiskers' (*Uncle Sam's* Agents). **1947** *Denver Post* 8 June (Mag.) 2/2 The 'G-men' have been organized since 1908, although many persons first heard of them when John Dillinger was menacing the nation behind a sawed-off shotgun.

***gnat,** *n.* As the last term in **buffalo, tule, turkey gnat.**

gnatcatcher ˈnætˌkætʃɚ, *n.* Any one of various small singing birds of the genus *Polioptila.*

1869 *Amer. Naturalist* III. 474 Not found westward of this [i.e., the Colorado] valley . . . [was] the lead-colored gnat-catcher. **1883** *Cent. Mag.* Sep. 685/1 The nest of the humming bird and the little gray gnat-catcher. **1934** *Nat. Geog. Mag.* LXV. 596 Gnatcatchers as a group are active and vivacious little birds that move rapidly through the branches.

***go,** *n.*

1. A prize fight. *Colloq.*

1896 ADE *Artie* 3 Get a couple o' handy boys and put on a six-round go for a finish. **1903** *Cin. Enquirer* 1 Jan. 4/5 The old year went out to-night at the Empire Theater with an advertised ten-round go between Patsy Hogan . . . and Louisville Tommy West.

2. a. *from the word go,* from the very first, from the start. **b.** *it's a go,* it's a bargain. Both *colloq.*

(a) 1834 CROCKETT *Life* 59, I was plaguy well pleased with her from the word go. **1921** *Sat. Ev. Post* 7 May 66, I saw that he was a cool, quick little man, bald of head, unsympathetic of eye, business from the word go. — **(b) 1878** HARTE *Tales of Argonauts* 329 'Then it's a go!' . . . 'It's a go.' **1914** ATHERTON *Perch of Devil* 195 'It's a go. . . . Shake.' And she gave his hand a hearty grasp.

***go,** *v.* In colloq. and dial. uses.

1. *tr.* To yield or produce (a certain amount).

1816 U. BROWN *Journal* I. 369 None [of the wheat fields] that I saw will go 15 Bushels to the Acre. **1869** MARK TWAIN *Innocents* 57 An altar with facings of solid silver—at least they call it so and I think myself it would go a couple of hundred to the ton (to speak after the fashion of the silver miners).

2. To master (a certain pronunciation). *Rare.*

1830 ROYALL *Southern Tour* I. 43 These low Virginians cannot go the letter *r.*

b. To support or vote for (someone or something); to accept, stomach, put up with.

1830 *Illinois Mo.* Nov. 74, 'I can't go it, sir!' replied the dandy, strutting up and down. **1835–7** HALIBURTON *Clockmaker* 1 Ser. iv, I love the Quakers, I hope they'll go the Webster ticket yet. **1946** *Longmont* (Colo.) *Times-Call* 15 June 1/1, I can drink milk, coffee and pop, but I can't go tea.

c. To stand, afford, go to the extent of.

1866 DAVIDGE *Footlight Flashes* 210 As he quaintly expresses it, 'The governor wouldn't go that, not at no price, he's sure!' **1877** RUEDE *Sod-House Days* 45, I drove a yoke of oxen this evening awhile. It goes rather slow, but I like it. We will have to wait till next spring for a yoke, for we can't go it yet. **1926** *Ladies' Home Jrnl.* Nov. 10 All the same, if you ever feel like sending me a little something to go a bust with, old girl, don't deprive yourself of the pleasure.

3. To wager (someone) a specified amount.

1831 *Boston Transcript* 16 Dec. 2/2 Well, said the 'Cotton man,' what will you go now? 'Go,' said the farmer, . . . 'I'll go the whole hog.' *a***1889** *Spirit of Times* (F.), 'I goes you five dollars, this time,' says Jim.

b. To accept the offer of (someone).

1902 WHITE *Blazed Trail* 161 'Surely you won't refuse to be my guest here!' . . . 'Wallace,' said Thorpe, 'I'll go you.' **1908** O. HENRY *Options* (1916) 38 'Believe I'll go you,' he said, brightening. . . . 'I'll accept the invitation gladly.'

4. To be acceptable.

1891 *Harper's Mag.* Dec. 104/2 Any other night goes, but not this night. **1914** ATHERTON *Perch of Devil* 194 'May I call her Ora to you?' 'Ora goes.'

b. To carry authority, to be done without any question or quibble.

1901 MERWIN & WEBSTER *Calumet 'K'* 62 My only order was, 'Clear the road,—and be damn quick about it.' What I said went. **1908** MULFORD *Orphan* 137 'Since it's your last wish, why, it goes,' replied the Sheriff. **1929** H. L. GATES *Lipstick* 277, I told you I didn't want to dance in this mob, and that goes.

5. In colloq. and slang combs., esp. with adverbs and prepositions: (1) ***to go back,** in bridge, to redouble, *obs.;* (2) **big,** =*to go over big,* see **6. m.** below; (3) ***blind,** to bet (something) on a hand without looking at the cards, cf. **6. f.** below; (4) ***down,** to decline in health; (5) **for,** =*to go in for,* see **6. d.** below; (6) ***forward,** to go to the front in a church as a sign of conversion, *obs.,* cf. ***going** (4); (7) **glimmering,** to pass out or fade out; (8) ***in,** (*a*) in poker, to make good the ante (and the straddles or raises, if any) in order to draw and play for the pool, cf. **6. d.** below, (*b*) to return to an older, more settled region, *rare;* (9) ***on,** (*a*) to sign (a bond, etc.) as a co-surety, (*b*) to care for or concern oneself about, usu. in negative contexts; (10) ***out,** (*a*) in baseball, to strike out or be put out, (*b*) of a dam or bridge, to collapse under the pressure of water, to wash out; (11) ***over,** (*a*) of a motion, resolution, bill, etc., to be postponed for consideration until a later time, (*b*) in bridge, to double, *obs.;* (12) **through,** see **b.** below; (13) ***together,** to keep steady company as lovers; (14) ***under,** (*a*) to die, (*b*) of a person or firm, to fail financially; (15) ***up,** (*a*) to be hanged, *rare,* cf. **6. o.** below and ***gone,** *a.* **3. c,** (*b*) to become bankrupt.

(1) 1907 R. F. FOSTER *Bridge* 16 If either the eldest hand or the pone doubles, it is the privilege of the player who named the trump to double him again, the usual expression being: 'I go back.' — **(2) 1930** *Publishers' Circular* 22 Feb. 186 We have reason to believe that *The Miracle of Peille* . . . will go big. — **(3) 1859** *Harper's Mag.* Sep. 572/2 He riffled the kurds, and Mike went blind. **1876** *Ventura Free Press* (San Buenaventura, Calif.) 8 Jan. 4/1 He'd play you draw, he'd ante a slug, And go a hatful blind. — **(4) 1892** WILKINS *Jane Field* 10 Well, I hope Lois ain't goin' down. I heard she looked dreadful. **1910** J. W. TOMPKINS *Mothers & Fathers* 276 Mr. Rix rallied as suddenly as he had gone down.

(5) 1947 *Newsweek* 1 Sep. 19/3 He gives serious speeches. The rednecks don't go for that. — **(6) 1848** *Ladies' Repository* Sep. 270/2, I cannot be at church to night; do you go, and go forward to the altar. — **(7) 1891** *Appeal-Avalanche* (Memphis) 8 May 4/1 The union depot project appears to have gone glimmering down the vale of things that were. **1945** *La Junta* (Colo.) *Tribune-Democrat* 1 June 1/8 Plans for a new building and remodeling at the La Junta nursery school went glimmering today as School District 11 was turned down on its application for Lanham [Act] funds for this purpose. — **(8)** (*a*) **1823** LONG *Hoyle's Games* 161 Each player, in rotation, having examined his hand, decides whether he will *go in.* **1835** *Vade Mecum* (Phila.) 23 May 4/4 If he does not *go in,* he throws up his cards, unexposed, and waits for the next deal. **1887** *Courier-Journal* 24 Jan. 2/4 Each man had gone in with two pairs, and each had fitted. (*b*) **1844** *Filson Club Quarterly* IX. (1935) 238 The last year that we lived at the station, fall, I suppose, of 1783, my father went in to get my grandfather's legacy. — **(9)** (*a*) **1869** J. H. BROWNE *Great Metropolis* 208 [She] would have been wealthy still, if poor, dear Mr. Dobbs hadn't gone on the paper of his friends, and lost his entire fortune. **1884** *N. Mex. Terr. Rep. 1882–3* 81 The Hillsboro gentleman was going on 'Topy' Johnson's bond. (*b*) **1882** HARTE *Flip* ii, We don't go much on that kind of cattle here. **1910** RAINE *B. O'Connor* 15 We don't go much on heroes out here.

(10) (*a*) **1886** *Outing* Nov. 181/1 Ward, then pitcher of the Providences, accomplished this feat . . . when the Buffalos went out in one, two and three order. (*b*) **1902** WHITE *Blazed Trail* xlix. 344 The dam's gone out. **1906** *N.Y. Ev. Post* 26 March 1 The middle span of the big railroad bridge went out as the result of floods. — **(11)** (*a*) **1894** MARK TWAIN *P. Wilson* xi, According to the by-laws it must go over to the next regular meeting for action. **1900** *Cong. Rec.* 3 Jan. 632/2, I ask that it may go over until to-morrow, so that we can have an opportunity to see it. . . . The resolution goes over under the rule. (*b*) **1902** J. B. ELWELL *Bridge* 111 *Going over.* . . . The effect of 'over,' 'over,' etc., is that the value of each trick point is doubled, quadrupled, etc. **1920** R. F. FOSTER *Auction Made Easy* 111 Going over, *obsolete* for doubling. — **(13) 1899** WILKINS *Jamesons* 77 People began to say that Harry Liscom and the eldest Jameson girl were going together. **1929** E. W. HOWE *Plain People* 69 Libby's sister seemed to approve of our 'going together.' — **(14)** (*a*) RUXTON in *Blackw. Mag.* LXIII. 730 'Whar's Bill Williams?' 'Gone under they say: the Diggers took his hair.' **1910** MULFORD *Hopalong Cassidy* 87, I'll fight until th' last man goes under! (*b*) **1860** D. RICE *Original*

Effusions 77 (We.), My impression is that he will go under. **1896** *Typographical Jrnl.* IX. 447 The Shreveport Standard . . . has long since 'went under.'

(15) (*a*) **1825** NEAL *Bro. Jonathan* III. 233 Whose narrow escape, when his brother spy 'went up,' he said, was quite a 'muricle.' (*b*) **1864** *Index* (London) 2 June 343/1 Soon after the blockade many thought that we [Confederates] should 'go up' on the salt question—couldn't salt our meat, and should be starved into subjection. **1892** STEVENSON & OSBOURNE *Wrecker* xvi. 248 We've rather bad news for you. . . . Your firm's gone up.

b. Esp. * *to go through* (1) to search and rob (a person); (2) (see quots.); (3) (see quot.); (4) to get official or final sanction.

(1) **1861** *Calif. Police Gaz.* (S.F.) 31 Mar. 2/4 Upon 'going through him,' over $2,000 was found upon his person. **1945** SERVICE *Ploughman* 194 When the time was ripe, they would draw the curtains of the box, and go through him. . . . The girls were 'going through' a drunken sailor. — (2) **1871** *Baltimore Sun* April (De Vere), It was a grand sight to see Farnsworth go through him; he did not leave him a single leg to stand upon. **1871** DE VERE 605 *To go through* a man is new; it means . . . to expose his political treachery, or any other weakness of which he may be guilty. **1873** *Winfield* (Kans.) *Courier* 15 Feb. 1/4 Of course everybody wanted to know who had been able to 'go through' so distinguished a manipulator as the Hon. John.— (3) **1877** BARTLETT 256 We say, Does this train 'go through to Portland?' An Englishmen would simply say '*go* to Portland.' Our expression would indicate a tunnel to him. — (4) **1895** *Boston Journal* 14 Jan. 7/7 Confirmation of Secretary Francis considered, but does not go through.

For combs. used as nouns or adjectives, as **go-ahead, go back, go-devil, go-down, go-easy, go-getter, go-getting, go-round, go-to-meeting,** see as main entries. For *go above, ahead, by,* see the second elements.

6. In colloq. and slang phrases.

a. *To go back of,* to go behind, investigate.

1890 *Science* 14 Feb. 104/2 The public . . . ought not to be compelled to go back of academic titles to find out what they mean. **1891** *N.Y. Tribune* 14 Nov. 6/3 They cannot go back of the returns. It is their business simply officially to announce the result.

b. *To go back on,* to fail (one), to break (one's word).

1868 *Putnam's Mag.* Jan. 21 Are those Dobbs' Ferry villagers A going back on Dobbs! 'Twould n't be more anom'lous If Rome went back on Rom'lus. **1917** S. MERWIN *Temperamental Henry* 271 We can't go back on our word, my dear. **1923** TARKINGTON *Harlequin & Columbine* 172 Old Tinker . . . inquired: 'Gone back on it?'

c. *To go easy on,* to touch upon lightly.

1900 WINCHESTER *W. Castle* vii. 143 You will have to go easy on that subject.

d. *To go in for,* to favor, approve, practice, cf. **5.** (5) above.

1835 LONGSTREET *Ga. Scenes* 119 [The city of Springfield] would . . . 'go in' for Augusta, live or die, hit or miss, right or wrong. **1922** LEWIS *Babbitt* 308 Ted was 'going in for' everything but books.

e. *To go it alone,* to act alone, play a lone hand.

1855 *Knickerb.* April 335 A ball through his frontal bone Laid him flat on his back on the hard-fought ground, And left Captain Davis to go it alone. **1897** *Boston Ev. Globe* 17 April 3/7 This year the Massachusetts interclub decided to go it alone. **1947** *Time* 17 Mar. 21/1 But now, said Hilldring, 'we are forced to go it alone.'

f. *To go it blind,* to proceed without sufficient information. Cf. **5.** (3) above.

1856 *Sacramento Spirit of Age* 13 March 2/1 The Council, probably, intend we should 'go it blind.'

g. *To go it on the loud,* to succeed, go ahead prosperously. *Rare.*

1844 *Lee Co. Democrat* (Ft. Madison, Ia.) 19 Oct. 2/3 Millerism is again going it on the loud in Louisville, a large number of proslytes [*sic*] were recently added to their number.

h. *To go it strong on,* to favor zealously.

1869 BROWNE *Adv. Apache Country* 379, I am disposed to go it strong, therefore, on the many-ledge theory.

i. *To go it with a looseness, rush,* (see quot. 1859), *obs.*

1841 *N.O. Picayune* 10 Dec. 2/2 The horses will travel round to the old brushing ground where they 'go it with a rush.' **1859** BARTLETT 172 *To go it with a looseness,* is to act in an unrestrained, rash, headstrong manner. . . . So also 'to go it with a *rush.*'

j. *To go nuts,* to go crazy.

1931 *K.C. Times* 28 Oct., Then there was the linotype operator who took an empty basket to the Sunday school picnic . . . so he wouldn't go nuts setting that line 'All brought well-filled baskets.'

k. *To go on with the procession,* (see quot.).

1902 CLAPIN 206 *Go on with the procession.* To continue; to allow no break in the continuity of any act. A simile drawn from processions being quite a feature in American public life.

l. *To go out for,* =*to go in for.*

1920 LEWIS *Main Street,* Don't you think that there's a lot of these women that go out for all these movements and so on that sacrifice [etc.].

m. *To go over big,* to become a pronounced success. Cf. **5.** (2) above.

1927 *Amer. Sp.* Oct. 21 A comedy that 'goes over big' and is very funny is often referred to as a 'wow.' **1932** *Blue Valley Farmer* (Okla. City) 10 March 6/5 That ought to go over big.

n. *To go to it,* to go ahead, do it yourself.

1918 M. B. COOKE *Threshold* 98 Go to it, Pat. I wish I could help you. **1924** C. WELLS *Prillilgirl* 317 Go to it yourself.

o. *To go up a tree,* (see quot. and cf. **5.** (15) above, * **gone,** *a.* **3. c.**).

1867 [see **gone,** *a.* **3. c.**]. **1902** CLAPIN 210 *Go up a tree,* to be in difficulties, like an opossum going up a tree when hunted.

p. *To go up in the air,* to become angry or greatly excited.

1906 *N.Y. Ev. Post* 13 Jan. 4 Representatives . . . have . . . 'gone up in the air' because they could not 'land' their men. **1912** BOWER *Flying U* 88 He'd go straight up in the air.

q. *To go West,* to seek one's fortune in the West. Cf. * **going** (9).

1890 *Ann Arbor Review* 20 Feb., Among them being several well-dressed and respectable-appearing fellows who had gone West to grow up with the country. **1947** *Denver Post* 28 Feb. 19/1 The general superintendent of Portland, Ore., public schools left New England Friday with about sixty contracts in his briefcase signed by dissatisfied teachers who've decided to heed Horace Greeley's 'go west' advice.

r. *To go with the party,* to support the party.

1829 D. WEBSTER *Private Corr.* (1857) I. 467 He will either go with the party, as they say in New York, or go the whole hog, as it is phrased elsewhere. **1848** *Whig Almanac 1849* 6/1 When the just expectations . . . were blasted by the Oregon Treaty, . . . many thousands who had hitherto 'gone with the party' were repelled and alienated.

s. *As Maine goes, so goes the nation* (or *union*), an adage reflecting the view that the political party which wins in Maine will be successful in the country at large. (See also quot. 1848.)

1848 *N.Y. Wkly. Tribune* 5 Feb. 4/5 As goes Dutchess County, so goes the State, and as New York goes, so goes the Union. **1880** *S.F. Globe* 17 Sep. 2/2 'As goes Maine, so goes the Union,' and the Pine Tree State has most certainly repudiated the Republican Party. **1948** *Newsweek* 27 Sep. 19/3 Would the adage, 'As Maine goes, so goes the nation,' hold true?

For other "go" phrases see * **death,** * **figure,** * **grass,** * **hash, haywire,** * **record.**

goad stick. An oxgoad. Also, *jocose,* **goard stick.** *Obs.*

1825 NEAL *Bro. Jonathan* I. 159 (Th.), I fetches it a rap with my goard stick. **1839** *Knickerb.* XIII. 298 A small man, . . . holding a goad-stick in his hand, . . . entered the room. **1869** MARK TWAIN *Innocents* vi. 58 And they banged the donkeys with their goad-sticks.

go-ahead, *a.* and *n.*

1. *n.* The action of going forward; ambition, spirit, authority to proceed. *Colloq.*

1840 HOFFMAN *Greyslaer* I. 32 Sarting! he does make a clean go ahead of it. But when did he come up here to mix in our doings? **1844** KENDALL *Santa Fe Exped.* II. 362 There is a little 'go-ahead' in a spirited, showy, well-trained Mexican horse. **1885** HOWELLS *Silas Lapham* xi, In the army . . . some of the fellows that had the most go-ahead were fellows that hadn't ever had much more to do than girls before the war broke out. **1948** *Sierra Club Bul.* May 2/2 However, it must receive Congressional approval, not that of the FPC, for its go-ahead on construction.

2. *a.* Disposed to push ahead, "up and coming." *Colloq.*

1834 *Sun* (N.Y.) 20 Mar. 2/2 [The 'frail sisters'] were next called up to the bar, accompanied (as a kind of counsel, we suppose) by the 'man wot sings Zip Coon, on the *go-ahead* principle.' **1856** *Knickerb.* March 271 Hiram Twine was a good specimen of a go-ahead, yet honest, Yankee. **1898** FREDERIC *Deserter* 103 Asa had made a good exchange in getting such an industrious and go-ahead chap as Job Parshall in Mose's place.

b. Also **go-ahead bell, signal.**

1883 MARK TWAIN *Life on Miss.* xxiv. 264 'This,' putting his hand on a go-ahead bell, 'is to call the texas-tender.' **1943** *Gunnison* (Colo.) *News-Champion* 23 Sep. 1/3 When the emergency is over it will be ready for the 'go-ahead' signal.

3. In colloq. and now obs. derivatives: (1) **go-aheadative,** progressive; (2) **go-aheadativeness,** the spirit or disposition to keep on pushing forward, progressiveness; (3) **go-aheadedness, -ishness, -ism, -ity, -ivity, -ness,** =prec.

(1) **1872** *Ill. Dept. Agric. Trans.* 173 This is one among the most interprising and go-aheadative villages in the county. — (2) **1842** *Greene Co. Torchlight* (Xenia, O.) 6 Jan. 2/2 This sentiment does not seem to be a favourite in these latter days of *Go-a-headativeness.* **1900** *Cong. Rec.* 6 Feb. 1570/1 The brown man in the Orient can be imbued with . . . the industry, progressiveness, and goaheadativeness of white men in the Occident. — (3) **1839** *Spirit of Times* 15 June 175/2 (We.), Indeed, the go-aheadedness of Kentucky no one ever doubted. — **1882** M. E. BRADDON *Mt. Royal* I. 136 The young ladies of the present day have a certain Yankee go-a-headishness which very much lightens the chaperon's responsibility. — **1838** COOPER *Home as Found* ii, But there were a delay and a finish in this arrangement that suited neither Aristabulus's go-a-head-ism, nor his organ of acquisitiveness. **1855** M. THOMPSON *Doesticks* xxxiii. 293 A very baby of a city, . . . without energy enough to cry when it is hurt, or go-aheadism sufficient to keep its nose clean. — **1839** *N.O. Picayune* 23 April 2/4 The voyage, like unto all voyages upon flat boats in these days of steam and go-aheadity, was necessarily tedious. **1844** KENDALL *Santa Fe Exped* I. 214 The indefatigable *go-a-headity* which characterizes the Anglo-Saxon race. — **1844** *Knickerb.* XXIV. 73 Our state of society in America with . . . its helter-skelterism and go-aheadivity. — **1857** STACEY *Journal* 43 What are these camels the representation of? Not a high civilization exactly, but of the 'go-aheadness' of the American character. **1898** *Chi. Times-Herald* 2 Apr. 11/3 The secret of Miss Johnson's goaheadness is that she was born near Chicago.

* **goat,** *n.*

1. The pronghorn, *Antilocapra americana*, or the Rocky Mountain goat, *Oreamnos montanus.*

1759 in DARLINGTON *Memorials J. Bartram & H. Marshall* (1849) 217, I have lately been reading Hennepin's *Travels.* . . . He often mentions they were sustained by killing *goats.* **1855** ROSS *Fur Hunters* 193 The mountain sheep, and goat white as snow, browsed on the rocks and ridges. **1917** *Mammals of Amer.* 56 Erroneously called 'goat,' this animal is in reality an Antelope closely related to the Himalayan Serow. **1948** *Hungry Horse News* (Columbia Falls, Mont.) 24 Sep. 7/2 Grizzly season also opens October 1, and goats can be hunted for five days from that date.

2. =**goatee.** *Obs.*

1856 GOODRICH *Recoll.* I. 210 His special admirers saw great merit in . . . his long shaggy *goat.* **1876** INGRAM *Centennial Exp.* v. 151 The little, puckered-mouth, pug-nosed, Esquimaux, with his slight sprinkling of a moustache and 'goat,' was also exhibited.

3. In combs.: (1) * **goat antelope,** the Rocky Mountain goat; (2) **bush,** a bitter-barked shrub, *Castela texana*, found in the Southwest; (3) **knot,** a goatee, *rare;* (4) **lock,** chin whiskers suggestive of a goat's beard; (5) **nut,** =**jojoba;** (6) **ranch,** a ranch upon which goats are raised; (7) **'s-head porgy,** (see quot.); (8) * **'s-rue,** a fabaceous plant, *Tephrosia virginiana*, also known as catgut.

(1) **1868** *Rep. Comm. Agric.* 218 *Aplocerus montanus*, known as the Rocky mountain goat, . . . is not a goat at all, but a goat-antelope, one of two species existing in North America. — (2) **1885** HAVARD *Flora W. & S. Texas* 515 *Castela erecta*, Turpin. (Goat Bush; the Amargoso of the Mexicans.) . . . Common on the gravelly bluffs of the Lower Rio Grande from Eagle Pass downward. — (3) **1843** in THOMPSON *M. Jones* (1872) 152 The way my last letter has cradled off the soap-locks and imperials, and goat-knots and mustyshows is truly alarmin to the vermin what usually inhabits them regions, as the geografy ses. — (4) **c1845** *Big Bear Ark.* 171 Henry had a big pair of goat locks under his chin.

(5) **1859** *Proc. Calif. Acad. Sci.* II. (1863) 21 Simmondsia. . . . Goat Nut. **1940** JAEGER *Calif. Deserts* 171 Along the clayey banks of washes at low elevations one is quite likely to see the goat-nut. — (6) **1902** *Everybody's Mag.* June 619/1 I'm a-goin' to take it up fer a goat ranch. **1941** FERGUSSON *Southwest* 109 Goat ranches in the hill country provide cabins and horses to give Houston, Galveston, and San Antonio people a chance to escape their steaming summers. — (7) **1884** GOODE *Fisheries* I. 393 A species closely related to the Scup is the 'Goat's head Porgy' of the Gulf of Mexico, *Stenotomus caprinus.* — (8) **1791** MUHLENBERG *Index Florae* 175. **1901** MOHR *Plant Life Ala.* 822 In the region of the Lower division of the Coast Pine belt or the rolling pine hills . . . many species of the pea family—tick trefoils . . . ; goat's rue (*Cracca smallii, C. hispidula, C. virginiana*)—blazing star [etc.] . . . give character to the flora.

b. In colloq. phrases: (1) *To be the goat,* to be the scapegoat, to bear the blame for others; (2) *to ride the goat,* to be initiated; (3) *to get* (one's) *goat,* to chagrin, tease, or torment (one), as by ribbing, joking, etc.

(1) **1894** *Outing* XXIV. 373/1, I was in for no less a scheme than actually smuggling a cargo into New York! . . . for no other reason than 'to be the goat' (as Jim Stern had it) to prove a theory. **1948** *Dly. Ardmoreite* (Ardmore, Okla.) 28 April 8/1 But like in all ball games there is sometimes a goat for the fans to hop on and they chose their target as Smith. — (2) **1904** *N.Y. Times* 8 March 2 Congressman Harrison 'rode the goat' last night at the monthly meeting of the Tammany Society. Two other new members were initiated. — (3) **1912** LONDON *Smoke Bellew* 184 Just keep a-coming and don't look down. That's what got my goat. **1948** *Capital-Democrat* (Tishomingo, Okla.) 17 June 2/2 We'll bet it got her goat.

As the last term in **mountain, Rocky Mountain, white goat.**

goatee goˈti, *n.* Chin whiskers trimmed in the form of a tuft like the beard of a he-goat.

[**1842** in THOMPSON *M. Jones* (1872) 65 One chap's jest come from the north, rigged out like a show monkey, with a little tag of hair hangin down under his chin jest like our old billy goat, that's a leetle

Man with goatee

too smart for this latitude, I think.] **1844** LEE & FROST *Oregon* viii. 102 A few individuals . . . leave what is called, by some of their politer neighbors, a 'goaty' under the chin. **1949** *N.Y. Times Book Review* 13 March 25/2 His zeal . . . has led him to smear that clay well up toward Bill's famous goatee.

goateed goˈtid, *a.* Having a goatee. — **1847** HOLLINGSWORTH *Jrnl.* 20 Jan., Sufficient time elapsed to have the attention of the passers-by, drawn to . . . the air of timidity, half screened from detection by his martial whiskers, of our goateed staff. **1949** *Time* 4 April 53/1 McClure gave his goateed managing editor a jolt straight from the shoulder.

* **gob,** *n.* [See note.] (See quot. 1919.)

The reason for this application of the word is not clear. It may be a new formation from *gobby* (itself of unknown origin), coastguardsman, given in *OED Supp.* 1890——.

1919 *N.Y. Tribune* 28 Jan., A 'gob' is a new sailor: a seaman in the navy is a 'bluejacket.' . . . The term 'gob' was never heard in the United States navy until about six years ago. **1944** *Chi. D. News* 10 Feb. 10/7 This gob took a print of the famous trio at Teheran, and dubbed in a picture of himself.

go-back ˈgoˌbæk, *n.* In colloq. uses.

1. One who returns to the East after making a poor go of it in the West.

1859 *Rocky Mt. News* (Cherry Creek, Kans. Terr.) 18 June (Th.), Farewell to the 'gobacks'; they have had their day, and soon will be forgotten. **1884** HILL *Colo. Pioneers* 29 The army of 'go-backs' grew greater than the advancing host, and they did many a tale unfold, declaring there was not a thimbleful of gold in the country. **1933** HAFEN *Colorado* 116 Converts to the theory of a 'Pike's Peak Humbug' swelled the ranks of the 'go backs.'

2. *pl.* A condition among children of being undersized or underweight.

1863 *Young Parson* 154 [The child] only had the op-nemma, that's the go backs. **1892** *Amer. Folk-Lore* V. 108 [When] the gap between the growth which the mother wants and that which baby yields seems to widen, . . . some wiser dame whispers the dreaded words: 'It has the Go-backs.'

3. (See quot. 1904.) Also **go-back land,** land once in cultivation but no longer so.

1904 *N.Y. Ev. Post* 30 July 3 Vagrant grass, called by the natives [in the West] 'go-back,' because it has gone back from the breaking-up process that was given by the settlers years ago. **1915** *Lit. Digest* 10 April 830/3 The grass generally is ranker on goback land than on prairie sod.

4. go-back road, (see quot.).

1905 *Forestry Bureau Bul.* No. 61, 38 *Go-back road*, a road upon which unloaded logging sleds can return to the skidways for reloading, without meeting the loaded sleds en route to the landing. (N[orthern] F[orest].)

* **gobble,** *v. tr.* To put *on* (clothes) hurriedly; to seize upon greedily or graspingly, to snatch. *Slang.*

1825 NEAL *Bro. Jonathan* III. 144 Then, he . . . sprang up; gobbled on the clothes, half military, half civil, as they were. **1898** *McClure's Mag.* Jan 280/2 A twelve-pound cannon . . . was 'gobbled,' and, with the gun carriage, shipped to the same destination. **1931** *K.C. Times* 23 Oct., His oldest son . . . was captured by a school ma'am. No sooner was his second son of marriageable age than a school ma'am gobbled him.

b. Also with *up.*

1826 JEFFERSON *Writings* XVII. 463 My request is, only to be permitted to sell my own property freely to pay my own debts. To sell it, I say, and not to sacrifice it, not to have it gobbled up by speculators to make fortunes for themselves. **1898** CUSHMAN *Hist. Indians* 483 So it arrayed one tribe against another, then gobbled up all. **1900** *Cong. Rec.* 16 Feb. 1880/1 The people from Maryland might come here and gobble up all the offices.

* **goblin,** *n.* **1.** (*cap.*) An officer of the Ku-Klux Klan. *Obs.* Cf. **Grand Goblin. 2.** (See quot.) — **(1) 1867** in LESTER & WILSON *Ku Klux Klan* 136 The officers . . . shall consist of . . . a Grand Giant of the Province and his four Goblins. — **(2) 1884** GOODE *Fisheries* I. 259 In the lakes and streams of the Northern States are numerous species of *Uranidea* and allied genera, known in some localities . . . [as] 'Bull-heads,' 'Goblins,' 'Blobs,' and 'Muffle-jaws.'

* **God,** *n.*

1. *pl.* (See quot.) *Rare.*

1882 WAITE *Adv. Far West* 250 Brigham Young and his two counselors form the first Presidency, under the title of the Gods, or Grand Archees.

2. God-awful, impressively large, frightful, terrible. *Slang.*

1883 BEADLE *Western Wilds* 615 Put thirty acres . . . into wheat and went to work with a hurrah in 1874 to make a God-awful crop. **1945** *Reader's Digest* June 42/1 They said there was the most god-awful crash when the car plunged off the track and turned over.

3. * **godlike,** *a.* an epithet applied to Daniel Webster. *Obs.*

1838 *Columbian Reg.* (New Haven, Conn.) 26 June, Having done this, he dismounts, and with great magnanimity permits his rival . . . to scour the country, make speeches, and reap all the glory left behind by the 'godlike man.' **1915** DODD *Expansion & Conflict* 180 Although he was again the follower of Clay, he was henceforth 'the God-like Webster' to northern conservatives.

Hence (usu. cap.) as a nickname for Webster. *Obs.*

1846 *Cong. Globe* 12 May 807/2 A sermon was preached in favor of the godlike; of the positon he has taken; and against the party that is opposed to him. *Ib.* App. 13 May 558/2 We have thrown up our Caps and shouted glory to 'the God-like.' **1850** *Quincy* (Ill.) *Whig* 12 Nov. 3/2 Black Dan, alias the Godlike, as he has been cognomened by his especial admirers, is a sort of intellectual hippopotamus. **1871** *Harper's Mag.* Nov. 949/1 An anecdote of Ezekial Webster, brother of the 'godlike,' may be aptly quoted.

4. Used in the possessive in various colloq. expressions, as (1) *God's country,* (2) *flag,* (3) *Great Out-of-Doors,* (4) *green earth,* (5) *plenty,* (6) *for God's sake,* (7) *time,* (in allusion to daylight-saving time), (8) *weather,* (see quots.).

(1) 1865 R. H. KELLOGG *Rebel Prisons* 118, I was willing to work hard, if I could only get out of that horrible den, into God's country once more. **1946** THOMPSON *Amer. Daughter* 10 We worked hard and got this home, but we can work for another one, a real home this time, out in God's country! — **(2) 1867** GOSS *Soldier's Story* 171 In referring to the North, as distinguished from the South, it was often spoken of as 'God's country,' and the old old flag as 'God's flag.' — **(3) 1912** *Out West* June 395 It is my purpose to present . . . an article dealing with God's Great-Out-of-Doors in the West from a personal ethical standpoint. — **(4) 1900** *Cong. Rec.* 5 Feb. 1507/2 No better people live anywhere on God's green earth than some of them. **(5) 1945** *Nation* CLX. II. 17 March 314/2 The way it was handled by camera men and cutters was merely right, which is a rarity and somewhere near a God's plenty. — **(6) 1877** BARTLETT 230 *For God's Sake,* thoroughly. 'They used to build for God's sake in those days.' 'That was nailed for God's sake.' — **(7) 1919** *Scientific Mo.* Nov. 391 Many letters were written by farmers and farmers' wives to local papers protesting against the unholy interference with God's time. — **(8) 1839** HOFFMAN *Wild Scenes* 137 God's weather! had you seen those horrible faces glowering upon you from out the fire, you would have cowered.

5. In phrases: (1) *In God we trust,* a legend used on some American coins; (2) *God and Morality Party,* (see quots.); (3) *by guess and by God,* at random, haphazard. *Slang.*

(1) 1865 *U.S. Laws concerning Money* (1910) 525 It shall be lawful for the Director of the Mint, with the approval of the Secretary of the Treasury, to cause the motto 'In God we trust' to be placed upon such coins hereafter to be issued as shall admit of such legend thereon. **1892** WALSH *Literary Curiosities* 420 A two-cent bronze piece was authorized to be coined by Congress, April 22, 1864, upon which was first stamped the motto 'In God we trust,' in lieu of the long standing 'E Pluribus Unum.' — **(2) 1875** *Cin. Enquirer* 1 July 1/5 The Democratic party is the whisky party. The Republican party is the God and morality party; therefore you had all better leave the former and join with us. **1906** in *Kansas Hist. Soc.* IX. 392 The party of Lincoln, which had been named 'The God and Morality Party' by its Democratic opponents, was to be its champion. — **(3) 1943** *Reader's Digest* Oct. 79 No more job training 'by guess and by God.'

As the last term in **buckra, dough, good, Lord God.**

Godbeite ˈgɑdbɪˌaɪt, *n.* [See quot. 1912.] A member of a Mormon sect that protested the church's control of civil and business matters. Also attrib.

1870 BEADLE *Utah* 506 It was on this principle of business management by the priesthood, that the Godbeites first took their stand. **1890** *N. & Q.* V. 184/2 The main body of Mormons are sometimes called *Twelveites,* probably as being followers of the Twelve Apostles. . . . There also is, or was, a sect of *Godbeites.* **1912** BIRGE *Awakening Desert* 355 Much of the merchandise . . . was consigned to William S. Godbe, who was at the head of the so-called Godbeite movement.

go-devil ˈgoˌdɛvl, *n.*

1. (See quot.) *Obs.*

1835 *Knickerb.* April 273 [The figures drawn on the slate] would be led on by what they call in school-sports, a go-devil, prancing about in high horns, and a spear on the end of his tail.

2. As the name of various contrivances.

a. Any one of various farm implements (see quots.). Also attrib.

1852 FLEISCHMANN *Wegweiser* 173 In Indiana und Illinois bedient man sich zum Zudecken der Maiskörner einer Art Hacke, welche unter dem Namen *Goe-Devil* bekannt ist. Dieselbe wird durch ein Pferd gezogen, ist leicht und kann mit einer Hand geführt werden. **1885** *Harper's Mag.* June 14/2 And the graceful 'go-devil' rake, travelling idly over the hay fields and gathering up the hay with all the ease of a lady's carpet-sweeper. **1945** *D.N.* 10 go-devil. . . . A farm implement used in cultivating very young corn in a field that has been listed (deeply furrowed). It resembles a high sled with a seat on it. At the back of the sled is a disk on each side which throws a little dirt in to the corn.

b. Any one of various contrivances (see quots.) used in connection with drilling for oil.

1886 *St. Nicholas* Nov. 48/1 A queer-looking, pointed piece of iron, called the 'go-devil,' is dropped down the well, and [strikes] . . . a cap on the top of the torpedo. **1896** B. REDWOOD *Petroleum* I. 275 To explode the charge, an iron weight, known as a *go-devil,* was dropped into the well, and, striking the disc, exploded the cap and fired the torpedo. Now, however, a miniature torpedo, known as a *go-devil squib,* holding about a quart of nitroglycerine, . . . is almost invariably employed. **1936** *Dly. Oklahoman* (Okla. City) 30 Aug. 8-B/1 The drift indicator can either be lowered into the hole on a steel line or can be dropped in a 'go-devil,' a steel-protective case with 'feelers' attached to slow the rapid movement of the instrument through the drill pipe to the bottom of the hole.

c. (See quots.)

1896 B. REDWOOD *Petroleum* II. 473 To remove obstructions in the pipes . . . an automatic rotary scraper is forced through. . . . The scraper is known as a 'go-devil.' **1901** in *D.N.* II. 341 go-devil. . . . A conical brush of steel wire furnished at the base, or rear end, with a leather valve in four sections and with steel wire guides. The 'go-devil' is pumped thro' [the pipe-line] with the oil, and travels at about 3 miles an hour. **1916** A. B. THOMPSON *Oil-Field Development* 548 The 'go-devil' is a tool with cutters that rotate when impelled forward to the pump after insertion in the pipe line.

d. (See quot.)

1889 *Cent.* 2562/2 *Go-devil,* . . . a rough sled used for holding one end of a log in hauling it out of the woods, etc., the other end dragging.

e. (See quot.)

1918 *D.N.* V. 25 *Go-devil,* a hand-car. General in northern Idaho, where the steep railroad grades make hand-car speeding good sport.

f. A heavy, sled-like drag used in clearing roads of snow.

1931 *Randolph Enterprise* (Elkins, W.Va.) 1 Jan. 1/1 We had to do that [open the roads] ourselves with big sleds, bob-sleds and then sleighs, 'Yankee Jumpers' and 'Go Devils.' **1948** *Salt Lake Tribune* 19 Jan. 13/1 This Hungry Behemoth Clears Snow. . . . It's a far cry from 'go-devils' and snow shovels.

g. A crude platform suspended from, and traveling on, a cable stretched across a stream.

1931 *Country Gentleman* April 24/1 Involuntarily the Westerner ejaculated, 'How'd you get acrost that river?' . . . Sal answered more loudly, 'In the go-devil pa and Mr. Damson hev put in above the old ford.'

h. An ax-like tool having a wedge on one end and a head suitable for driving on the other.

1937 LUTES *Home G.* 64 Old Man Covell came over to borrow a go-devil with which to split a stubborn log, and he and my father

Go-devil (sense **2d**)

spent some time at the barn—a longer time than my father was wont to spend with his shiftless, borrowing neighbor, whose ways he so thoroughly disliked. **1944** *D.N.* Nov. 43 *go-devil: n.* A heavy ax used to split logs. 'You won't [stay at home], less'n it's rainin' *go-devils*.'—Negro woman, 50. Charlotte Co., Va. Also, reported from other parts of Va. Generally used by Negroes.

* **Godfrey,** *n.* Euphemistic extension of *God*, used as an exclamation. Also *by guess and by Godfrey. Slang.*

1906 W. CHURCHILL *Coniston* 274 'Godfrey!' exclaimed Ephraim, 'they told me he was hard to talk to. Why, he's as simple as a child.' **1909** J. C. LINCOLN *Keziah Coffin* vii. 104 If ever a craft was steered by guess and by godfrey, 'twas that old hooker of Zach's t'other night. **1930** HENRY *Conquer. Plains* 136 And there are the Government troops at Riley and Harker—by Godfrey!—if it comes to that. **1935** LINCOLN *Cape Cod Yesterdays* 69 'Godfrey's mighty!' he sighed fervently

***go-down,** *n. W.* (See quot.) *Colloq.* — **1881** in *N. & Q.* 6 Ser. V. (1882) 65 *Go down.*—A cutting in the bank of a stream for enabling animals to cross or to get to water.

***godwit,** *n.* As the last term in **Hudsonian, telltale godwit.**

go-easy ˈgoˌizɪ, *a.* Easy-going. *Colloq.* — **1877** *Vt. Dairymen's Assoc. Rep.* VIII. 22 The many serious drawbacks which the 'go easy' dairymen of Vermont are compelled to encounter.

***goer,** *n.* As the last term in **first, fore, thorough goer.**

go-getter ˈgoˈgɛtɚ, *n.* An active, enterprising person, a hustler. *Slang.* — **1922** P. B. KYNE (*title*), The Go-Getter. A story that tells you how to be one. **1947** *Time* 6 Jan. 17/3 Wherry, a go-getter and vehement anti-New Dealer, will serve as party whip.

go-getting ˈgoˈgɛtɪŋ, *n.* Enterprise, aggressiveness. Also as adj. *Slang.*

1924 R. CUMMINS *Sky-High Corral* 25 He was one of them flyin' son-of-a-guns an' they say he was a go-gettin' fool. **1931** F. F. BOND *Mr. Miller of 'The Times'* 170 The students herded to hear breezy young instructors exhale the new gospel of 'go-getting.' **1948** *Chi. Tribune* 18 Aug. II. 11/2 If you are the practical, common-sense, go-getting type of engineer, we need you.

* **goggle-eye,** *n.* Any one of various fish having large, prominent eyes.

1840 *Spirit of Times* 426/1 (We.), *Goggle-eye* lights upon a red worm. **1890** *Geol. Survey Tex. Rep.* 487 The goggle-eye, yellow perch, . . . and red-eye are some of the species I have seen. **1948** *Democrat* 15 July 1/5 Those who went about the business seriously brought in fine strings of bass, bream and goggle eye.

attrib. **1884** GOODE *Fisheries* I. 406 The Calico Bass—*Pomoxys sparoides*. . . . In the South, like *Ambloplites rupestris*, it becomes a 'Goggle-eye' or 'Goggle-eyed Perch.' **1948** *Life* 5 April 58/2 Fishing Farm Boy stands under a willow tree and tries to catch goggle-eye bass. **1948** *Capital-Democrat* (Tishomingo, Okla.) 10 June 4/2 Vernon . . . caught 30 goggle eye perch fly fishing on Pennington Saturday.

* **going,** *n.* and *a.* In colloq. combs.: (1) * **going ahead,** prospering, daring, enterprising; (2) **-away clothes,** best or Sunday clothes; (3) **foot,** the action on the part of a student of taking a position at the foot of a class; (4) * **forward,** the action of publicly confessing one's sins by going to the altar in a church service, cf. *to go forward;* (5) **off,** a start, outset; (6) * **over,** (*a*) a passage over a stream, *obs.*, (*b*) a taking to task, a talking to, (*c*) an overhauling; (7) **price,** the current price, *obs.;* (8) * **up,** the action of fish in going from the open sea into streams to spawn, *obs.;* (9) **West,** the action of migrating to the western part of the U.S., cf. *to go West.*

(1) **1836** R. WESTON *Visit* 59 'Going ahead' is used for our term 'succeeding in business.' **1840** *Cong. Globe* App. 20 Feb. 186/1 Ours are a going-ahead sort of people, always in a gallop, and have at all times more things upon their hands than forty times their number could execute. — (2) **1941** LYON *Hills* 219 But he had on his going-away clothes and shoes, and he wouldn't get all muddy and Spanish-needly going through the woods,—not, by George, if he sat there all day! — (3) **1944** CLARK *Pills* 182 Sometimes humiliation at 'going foot' was insufficient punishment and the master's flail fell heavily as a reminder that spelling was one of man's major achievements. — (4) **1901** STILLMAN *Autobiog. Journalist* I. 38 A sense of having made one's self ridiculous . . . was, in my own and many other cases in my knowledge, a powerful influence adverse to the going forward at the meetings.

(5) **1845** KIRKLAND *Western Clearings* 14 You'd better tell 'em at the first goin' off that you a'n't land hunters.—(6) (*a*) **1662** *Providence Rec.* III. 17 The high way which leadeth from the goeing over att the River. *c*1750 *Smithtown Rec.* 87 We also assert and lay out another high way from the going over at the River westward to Platt Smiths upper gate four poles wide. (*b*) **1872** *Chi. Tribune* 23 Oct. 4/2 The Cincinnati *Commercial* gives these male Mrs. Grundys a 'going over' in an article well worth reading. **1947** *Chi. Sun* 14 Oct. 3/5 After giving Sullivan a 'going over' for permitting the bookies to operate, Prendergast mentioned the '19th hole' incident. (*c*) **1931** *K.C. Star* 18 July, She knew the lawn mower could profit by a complete 'going over' so she proceeded to administer the same. — (7) **1828** SHERBURNE *Memoirs* vii. 154 It was about thirty-three dollars, and belonged to John Hooper, who agreed to let me have it at the 'going price.' **1846** *Knickerb.* XXVII. 125, I want you to sell my oats at the going price. — (8) **1673** *Plymouth Rec.* 131 The ffish Called the alewives be not hindered . . . in theire goeing up. **1682** *Ib.* 171 That the alewives or herrings soe called shall not be stoped in their goeing up. — (9) **1877** *Harper's Mag.* Jan. 318/2 Some years ago, when 'going West' was more of an undertaking than at present, a young man was leaving his home in Vermont for Illinois.

* **gold,** *n.* and *a.*

1. In combs. relating to the use of gold as money: (1) **goldback,** a legal-tender note of the U.S. Government redeemable in gold and having the devices on the back printed in a golden color, cf. **greenback, yellowback;** (2) **bank,** =**gold note bank,** *obs.;* (3) * **bearing,** designating a bond calling for the payment of the principal and interest in gold; (4) **certificate,** a certificate of a type first authorized in 1863, issued by the Secretary of the Treasury, certifying that gold coin or bullion to the amount stated on the face of the certificate has been deposited for redeeming it, also attrib.; (5) **check,** (see quot. 1865), *obs.;* (6) **dollar,** a coin containing 25.8 grains of gold nine-tenths fine, coined from 1849 to 1890, also the intrinsic value in gold of this coin as a monetary unit; (7) * **dust,** see as a main entry; (8) **exchange,** an association or body of brokers who deal in the exchange of gold, the building in which such a group carries on its business, also attrib.; (9) **note,** (*a*) a circulating note issued by a national bank and redeemable only in gold, (*b*) a note issued to a federal reserve bank by the Secretary of the Treasury and redeemable only in gold (see quot.); (10) **note bank,** a national bank, organized under a law of 1870, authorized to issue gold notes, now *hist.;* (11) **paying bond,** a bond the interest upon which is paid in gold; (12) **pit,** =**gold exchange,** *obs.;* (13) **reserve,** (*a*) a quantity of gold held in reserve by a bank, (*b*) a quantity of gold held in reserve by the federal government to protect the issue of treasury notes; (14) **standard,** see as a main entry.

(1) **1873** *Chi. Tribune* 2 Jan. 3/2 I'm the man to deal in cold facts, For ten thousand—green or gold-backs. **1948** *Ib.* 29 Aug. 25/1 Reminiscent of the old goldbacks, the warehouse gold receipts may be transmitted freely thruout the United States. — (2) **1872** *Banker's Mag.* Aug. 139 Only three national gold banks are at present in operation under the law creating that class of financial institutions, two of which are in California, . . . the third in Boston. **1900** J. J.

KNOX *Hist. Banking* 112 Gold banks were [in 1872] gradually making way in California. — **(3) 1869** *Kansas Pacific Ry. Gold Loan* 5 Dabney, Morgan & Co. [etc.] . . . have accepted the Agency of the Kansas Pacific Railway Company for the sake of its new Seven Per Cent. Gold-bearing Railroad and Land-Grant Sinking Fund Bonds. — **(4) 1864** *Santa Fe W. New Mexican* 27 May 2/3 The boys in New York have . . . join[ed] in the procession of gold certificate buyers. **1907** *U.S. Laws concerning Money* (1910) 456 The Secretary of the Treasury is hereby authorized . . . to issue gold certificates therefor in denominations of not less than ten dollars.

(5) 1865 *N.Y. Herald* 16 Aug. 1/2 Gold checks . . . are simply certified checks of the Bank of New York, supposed to stand in the place of that precious metal stored by the parties obtaining the certificates in the capacious vaults of that establishment. **1891** THANET *Otto the Knight* 105 Atherton went on to tell René about the gold checks: how his clerks were instructed to offer the other checks first, and only give gold checks when they were demanded. — **(6) 1846** *Dollar Newspaper* (Phila.) 1 April 2/7 Gold dollar.—A Committee of the House of Representatives has reported against the coining any gold coin of the value of one dollar. **1900** *Cong. Rec.* ii Jan. 774/1 The outstanding obligations of the Government are payable in gold dollars containing 25 8/10 grains of standard gold. **1948** *Minneapolis Morn. Tribune* 28 Sep. 6/5 It was a Democratic president, FDR, who boosted our standard gold dollar 70 per cent. — **(8) 1867** *Harper's Wkly.* 23 Feb. 114/2 Said half past ten is the busiest hour of the day in the Gold Exchange. **1900** NELSON *A B C Wall St.* 38 The experience of the members of this Exchange in clearing is generally limited to the gold clearing of the New York Gold Exchange Board.—**(9)** *(a)* **1870** *Statutes at Large* XVI. 252 Every national banking association . . . shall receive at par in the payment of debts the gold notes of every other such banking association. *(b)* **1913** *Statutes at Large* XXXVIII. I. 269 Upon application of any Federal reserve bank, approved by the Federal Reserve Board, the Secretary of the Treasury may issue, in exchange for United States two per centum gold bonds bearing the circulation privilege, but against which no circulation is outstanding, one-year gold notes of the United States without the circulation privilege, to an amount not to exceed one-half of the two per centum bonds so tendered.

(10) 1872 *Banker's Mag.* July 66 There are now two gold note banks in operation in San Francisco, each with a capital of a million dollars. — **(11) 1867** *Central Pacific R.R.* (Fisk & Hatch) 20 The City of San Francisco has donated . . . four hundred thousand dollars, in city seven per cent. thirty year gold paying bonds. — **(12) 1869** *New No. West* (Deer Lodge, Mont.) 15 Oct. 1/1 Up from the Gold Pit's nether hell . . . loud and higher the bidding rose. — **(13)** *(a)* **1870** *N.Y. Herald* 8 July 4/3 [The national banks'] interests . . . lie in a paper circulation only, and in not being compelled to hold a gold reserve. *(b)* **1900** *Cong. Rec.* 31 Jan. 1336/2 The Secretary of the Treasury may issue as many bonds as, in his judgment, he may deem proper in order to maintain the gold reserve.

2. In the names of animals, esp. birds and fishes: (1) **gold chub,** (see quot.); (2) **eyes,** (see quot. 1819); (3) ***finch,** any one of various small finches of the genus *Spinus*, cf. **American, European, Lawrence's, willow goldfinch;** (4) ***fish,** (see quot.); (5) **herring,** a local name for the golden shiner, *obs.*, cf. **Ohio gold herring;** (6) ***ring,** (see quot.); (7) **robin,** =**Baltimore oriole;** (8) **shad,** (see quot. and cf. **Ohio gold shad**); (9) ***smith,** a large, bright-yellow beetle, *Cotalpa lanigera*, of the family Scarabaeidae, in full **goldsmith beetle;** (10) **tit,** (see quot.); (11) **winged woodpecker,** =**flicker,** cf. **golden-winged woodpecker.**

(1) 1820 *Western Rev.* II. 238 Goldhead Shiner. *Luxilus chrysocephalus*. . . . Vulgar names, Gold Chub, Shiner, Goldhead, &c. . . . It is found in the Kentucky, Ohio, Cumberland, Green river, &c. — **(2) 1819** *Western Rev.* I. 370 Golden-eye Perch. *Perca chrysops*. . . . Vulgar names Rock Fish, Rock bass, Rock perch, Gold eyes, Striped bass, &c. **1943** *Sat. Ev. Post* 1 May 25/1 Do the gold-eyes still bite the way they used to? — **(3)** [**1737** BRICKNELL *N. Carolina* 196 The Goldfinches. There are a sort of Birds like these to be met with here, variegated with Orange and Yellow Feathers.] **1872** *Md. Laws* 664 It shall be unlawful . . . to shoot or trap . . . any of the following named birds: . . . wren, pewit, goldfinch, sapsucker [etc.]. **1948** *Chi. Tribune* 18 Aug. I. 1/5 Today the goldfinches are active—a lovely splash of color aganst the purple thistles. — **(4) 1884** GOODE *Fisheries* I. 276 On the California coast occurs. . . . *Pomacentrus rubicundus*, . . . which is usually known as the 'Garibaldi' among the Italians. The names 'Gold-fish' and 'Red Perch' are also used.

(5) 1820 *Western Rev.* II. 173 Ohio Gold Herring *Notemigonus auratus*. . . . Not uncommon in Ohio, Kentucky, Miami, &c. The vulgar names are Gold Herring and Yellow Herring. — **(6) 1820** *Western Rev.* II. 53 *Pomoxis annularis*. . . . Vulgar names Gold-ring and Silver-perch. . . . Found in August at the falls [of the Ohio River]; probably permanent. — **(7) 1839** PEABODY *Mass. Birds* 280 The Baltimore Oriole, *Icterus Baltimore*, . . . is known by various names; children call it the gold-robin; it is often called the hang-bird. **1872** WHITTIER *Poetical Works* (1895) 109/2 The gold-robin cried, A-swing upon his elm. — **(8) 1820** *Western Rev.* II. 171 Ohio Goldshad. *Pomolobus chrysochloris*. . . . It seldom goes as far as Pittsburgh, and does not run up the creeks. . . . Its vulgar names are Ohio Shad, Gold Shad, Green Herring. — **(9) 1854** EMMONS *Agric. N.Y.* V. 65 The common horn beetle . . . [and] the goldsmith beetle . . . fly about in the evening in the months of June and July. **1862** *Rep. Comm. Patents 1841: Agric.* 601 *Gymnetis nitida* . . . [is] commonly called in this locality [Lancaster, Pa.] the 'Goldsmith.' **1868** *Amer. Naturalist* June 189, I have never found the Goldsmith in the fall. **1877** *Vt. Bd. Agric. Rep.* IV. 158 This beetle, *Cotalpa Lanigera*, or goldsmith beetle, is not common enough to do much damage with us.

(10) 1917 *Birds of Amer.* III. 216 Verdin. *Auriparus flaviceps flaviceps*; . . . [also called] Gold-Tit; Yellow-headed Bush-Tit.—**(11)** *c***1728** CATESBY *Carolina* I. 18 The Gold-winged Wood-pecker . . . weighs five ounces. . . . The beams of all the wing feathers are of a bright gold-color. **1823** in JAMES *Exped.* I. 265 *Picus auratus*—Gold-winged woodpecker. **1828** BONAPARTE *Synopsis* 44.

b. In the names of plants: (1) **gold-and-silver plant,** (see quot.); (2) **-cup oak,** the canyon live oak of California; (3) **fern,** any one of various ferns that have the under surface of the fronds covered with a yellow- or golden-colored powder; (4) **fields,** any one of various yellow-flowered California herbs of the genus *Baeria;* (5) ***seed (rice),** a variety of rice, *obs.;* (6) ***thread,** (see quot. 1855); (7) ***watch,** (see quot.).

(1) 1893 *Amer. Folk-Lore* VI. 138 *Lunaria biennis*, gold-and-silver-plant. N.J. — **(2) 1869** MUIR *First Summer in Sierra* (1911) 345 Here is about the upper limit of the dwarf form of goldcup oak,—eight thousand feet above sea-level. — **(3) 1883** JACKSON *Ramona* 146 The next morning she had found, lying at the chapel door, a pile of such ferns as she had never before seen; tall ones, like ostrich-plumes, . . . the feathery maiden-hair, and the gold fern. **1925** JEPSON *Flowering Plants Calif.* 26 G[ymnogramme] triangularis Kaulf. Gold Fern. — **(4) 1915** *Nat. & Science Pac. Coast* 149 *Baeria chrysostoma* grows in such abundance that it is known as gold-fields. **1947** *Desert Mag.* April 12/3 April possibilities: staghorn cholla, hedgehog cactus, prickly pear, brittle bush, . . . scorpion weed, gold fields, fiddleneck and crownbeard.

(5) 1848 *Rep. Comm. Patents 1847* 173 Among the varieties of rice is the gold seed rice. **1854** *New Orleans Delta* 28 May, It resembles the white husk upland variety of South Carolina, . . . but is not so highly esteemed in commerce as the 'Gold Seed.' — **(6) 1778** CARVER *Travels* 513 Gold thread. This is a plant of the small vine kind, which grows in swampy places, and lies on the ground. The roots . . . resemble a large entangled skain of thread of a fine bright gold colour; and I am persuaded would yield a beautiful and permanent yellow dye. **1855** *Harvard Mag.* I. 236 A pretty and delicate little plant is the Goldthread, *Coptis trifolia*, so called from the bright golden color of its roots. **1913** EATON *Barn Doors & Byways* 276 The tiny jewels of gold-thread are the foreground for a vista of falling brook and emerald vale to the blue dome of the Taconics. — **(7) 1893** *Amer. Folk-Lore* VI. 136 *Nuphar advena*, gold watch, Mauch Chunk, Pa. (name perhaps not general there).

3. In combs. (chiefly obs.) designating tools, contrivances, etc., used in gold-mining or in connection with gold, as (1) ***gold beater,** (2) **borer,** (3) **canoe,** (4)

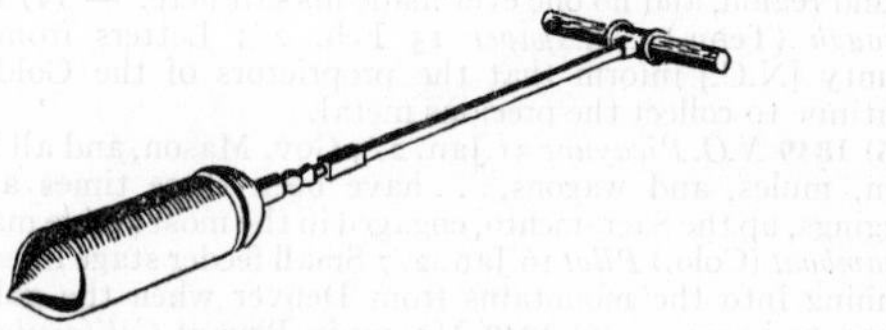

Gold borer (*c*1850)

collector, (5) **(mining) dredge,** (6) **monkey,** (see **goldometer**), (7) **pan,** (8) **rocker,** see as a main entry, (9) **separator,** (10) **sluice,** (11) **washer,** see as a main entry, (12) **washing pan,** (13) **weight.**

(1) 1853 *Rep. Comm. Patents 1852* 127 Improved Mechanical Gold-beater. — **(2) 1850** RYAN *Adventures* II. 17 The second machine, in importance, is the gold-borer. It is particularly useful in examining the bottom of streams, and consists of a short conical cylinder at the end of a long handle. . . . This instrument is used in the same manner as an augur. — **(3) 1849** J. T. BROOKS *Gold-Finders Calif.* 69 Building our cradles, or 'gold canoes.' — **(4) 1855** *Rep. Comm. Patents 1854* I. 729 Improvement in Gold-Collectors. . . . [For] collecting the matter containing gold in the beds of rivers.

(5) **1945** *Jefferson Co. Republican* (Golden, Colo.) 31 Oct. 2/1 On Sunday afternoon, the troops visited a large gold mining dredge and saw it in operation. **1948** JOHNSTON *Gold Rush* 25/1 Thus land that has once been mined by a gold dredge is utterly ruined for all time. — (6) **1931** DOBIE *Coronado's C.* 107 They possessed a 'gold monkey'—a mineral rod—and this instrument they took to the fort; it oscillated towards the west and made two locations. — (7) **1873** MILLER *Amongst Modocs* 57 [The miners] . . . washed their hands and faces in the gold-pan that stood by the door. **1948** *Gary* (Ind.) *Post-Tribune* 1 July 7/3 Prospectors roaming Alaska's wilds have discarded their gold pans and sluice boxes. — (9) **1853** *Hunt's Merch. Mag.* XXVIII. 124 An application for a patent for a Gold Separator . . . was rejected.

(10) **1869** BRACE *New West* 127 The ancient gold-sluices, in which water was brought from distant mountains, are now used as irrigating canals. — (12) **1944** LANKS *Alaska* 4 Here the prospector and miner can buy complete equipment, from a simple gold-washing pan to intricate mining machinery. — (13) **1850** *Calif. Courier* (S.F.) 6 Sep. 2/5 We were presented, yesterday, with a splendid set of gold weights, from 81¼ oz. (equal to $500,) down to 12½ cents.

Prospector using a gold pan

4. Designating places or areas where gold is found or mined, as (1) **gold belt,** (2) **claim,** (3) **country,** (4) **creek,** (5) **diggings,** (6) **district,** (7) **gulch,** (8) **land,** (9) **ledge,** (10) **placer,** (11) **range,** (12) **region,** (13) **washings.**

(1) **1879** *Harper's Mag.* Sep. 508/2 The 'gold belt' . . . consists of a strip of land running . . due northeast and southwest across the northern end of the State [of Georgia]. **1947** PEATTIE *Sierra Nevada* 27 Wide-open, rip-roaring mining towns sprang up along the Mother Lode, the gold belt which extends for 120 miles through the foothills. — (2) **1897** *Chautauquan* Oct. 55/1 Who ever heard before of a considerable colony of gold-claim owners none of whom drew a blank? — (3) **1821** *Amer. Jrnl. Science* III. 3 The Gold country lies in Cabarras County, North Carolina, where the gold is found in small pieces, from the size of half a pea to mere dust, in the beds of little rills emptying into the waters of Rocky River. **1865** A. D. WHITNEY *Gayworthys* xxxii, 'Where would you go, Gabriel?' . . . 'To the gold country.' **1948** *Pacific Discovery* July–Aug. 10/1 This is not gold country, this lava-bound region, and no one ever made his salt here. — (4) **1804** *Jonesborough* (Tenn.) *Newspaper* 15 Feb. 2/3 Letters from Cabarrus county [N.C.] inform that the proprietors of the Gold creek . . . continue to collect the precious metal.

(5) **1849** *N.O. Picayune* 31 Jan. 2/3 Gov. Mason, and all his officers, men, mules, and wagons, . . . have been three times at the gold diggings, up the Sacramento, engaged in the most active manner. **1947** *Steamboat* (Colo.) *Pilot* 16 Jan. 2/7 Small feeder stage lines soon were running into the mountains from Denver when the gold diggings began to boom. — (6) **1848** MASON in Bryant *California*. App. 461 The entire gold district, with some very few exceptions . . . is on land belonging to the United States. **1848** POLK in *Pres. Mess. & P.* IV. 636 Nearly the whole of the male population of the country have gone to the gold districts. — (7) **1870** BEADLE *Utah* 271 He has traveled hundreds of miles among the mines and cañons, digging into drift, wash dirt, gravel, quartz, and gold gulch. [**1936** MCKENNA *Black Range* 283 The prospectors went in there, but as the gold-bearin' gulches were on the Indian reservation, they were driven off by the Government troops.] — (8) **1855** *Pioneer* (S.F.) June 362 We did not dream then that we should meet in the wild glens of the Gold Land. **1856** *Ill. State Reg.* (Springfield) 26 June 4/1 He got there and grabbed up a tract of gold land worth millions of dollars. — (9) **1869** BROWNE *Adv. Apache Country* 234 We took a ride over the intervening hills to see a gold ledge, called the 'Tenaja,' or 'Tank,' of which I made a sketch.

(10) **1846** *Ore. Spectator* 26 Nov. 4/2 In the rear of Pueblo de Los Angelos there exists a gold 'Placer' or washing, said to be eighteen leagues square. **1943** HOWARD *Montana* 38 Bannack's thin gold placers were already worked out, and it was destined to become a ghost town in another couple of years. — (11) **1869** BRACE *New West* 163 These are the richest lands for tillage in the undulant country of the gold ranges. — (12) **1832** *Cherokee Phenix* (New Echota, Ga.) 21 April 3/1 The gold region is to be laid off into lots of forty acres. **1948** JOHNSTON *Gold Rush* 32/1 Instances of failures in the gold region, however, are overshadowed by fabulous tales of success. — (13) **1832** OUSELEY *Remarks* 170 In this state [N.C.], the counties of Burke and Rutherford contains the best *gold washings*, as they are called; that is, the gold there is found in small and *pure* particles mixed with the sand. [**1869** BRACE *New West* 161 It is a sad pity to see the beautiful rivers of California so spoiled by the gold-washings from above.]

5. In miscellaneous combs.: (1) **gold Bible,** =**golden plates,** *obs.;* (2) **blossom,** *W. mining*, prob. pieces of blossom rock, i.e., pieces of rock which have been detached from a vein, but not transported, that contain traces of gold; (3) **brick, bug, coast,** see as main entries; (4) **cure,** =**gold treatment;** (5) **Democrat,** a Democrat who, during the money crisis in the 1890's, favored a single monetary standard based on gold; (6) **digger,** see as a main entry; (7) **digging,** (*a*) digging for gold, (*b*) the action of a girl or woman who is a gold digger (sense **2.**), *slang;* (8) **hunter,** (*a*) one who seeks gold, a prospector, (*b*) (*cap.*) (see quots.); (9) ***leaf,** used attrib. in the sense of fine, excellent, precise, *slang;* (10) **man,** =**gold-bug 2;** (11) **plank,** a plank in a party platform expressing the stand taken by the party on gold or on questions relating to gold; (12) ***plates,** =**golden plates,** *obs.;* (13) **quartz,** used attrib. to designate either a formation in which quartz containing gold is found or machinery for extracting this gold; (14) **Republican,** a Republican who, during the money crisis in the 1890's, favored a single monetary standard based on gold; (15) **room,** see as a main entry; (16) **shell,** (*a*) (see quot.), (*b*) (see quot. 1889); (17) **spike,** a railroad spike made of gold and used in ceremonies connected with the completion of transcontinental railroads, now *hist.;* (18) **Star,** designating a parent who lost a son or daughter in World War I or II; (19) **story,** a "tall story" about gold or events in the gold fields, *obs.*, cf. **fish story;** (20) **treatment,** a treatment for drunkenness in which a preparation containing gold is used or is allegedly used.

(1) **1833** in J. C. BENNETT *Hist. of Saints* (1842) 74 The Gold Bible business, so called, was the topic of conversation. . . . The plates . . . were but an introduction to the Gold Bible. **1844** HUNT *Hist. Mormon War* 75 If the reader will turn to the revelation given by Smith to O. Cowdery, in Harmony, Pennsylvania, April, 1829, while translating the Gold Bible, . . . he will perceive that Oliver's faith had begun to fail. — (2) **1846** SAGE *Scenes Rocky Mts.* (1859) 334 The surface affords large quantities of 'gold blossom.' — (4) **1897** CHRISTISON *Crime & Criminals* 25 He does not believe in the 'gold cure' and so has not tried it. **1912** *Out West* Jan. 79/1, I went home and got on clean clothes and she prayed for me and fed me up and sent me to the 'Gold Cure.'

(5) **1896** *St. Louis Globe-Democrat* 29 June 1/4 The gold Democrats who would vote with the Republicans . . . would not be sufficiently numerous to help keep the State [Washington] from going for free silver. **1914** *Cyclo. Amer. Govt.* II. 85/1 With the passage of the gold standard act of March 14, 1900, the activity of the gold Democrats terminated. [**1947** *Chi. Herald-Amer.* 7 Feb. 20/4 In September, 1896, a convention of sound-money Democrats, so-called, the Gold Democratic convention met in Indianapolis.] — (7) (*a*) **1831** *Boston Transcript* 27 May 2/3 There is every reason to fear that Gold digging, combined with slave holding, may always keep those states a whole century behind their neighbors who are *apparently less highly favored.* **1948** WESTON *Mother Lode* 46 Martial law was proclaimed to prevent vandals from seizing the burned lots for gold digging. (*b*) **1927** *Cleveland Press* 29 Jan., The charge of gold-digging is one of the major counts in Browning's case. [Divorce action against his wife.] **1947** *Redbook* Nov. 44/1 She was financially embarrassed. So you can't blame her for doing a little gold-digging. — (8) (*a*) **1825** *Amer. Jrnl. Science* IX. 6 This locality [in N. Carolina] was discovered only two years since by a 'gold-hunter.' **1897** LEONARD *Gold Fields Klondike* 34, I could not help contrasting them with the crowd of gold hunters I took with me on the last trip up. **1908** *Pacific Mo.* Jan 2/2 By this time he was detested and set out with the swarming troop of gold-hunters for Idaho. (*b*) **1872** *Harper's Mag.* Jan. 317/2 Nicknames given to the States and people of this republic [include] . . . California, Gold-Hunters. **1886** *Chi. W. News* 29 April 4/3 California is

the Golden state and its people are Gold-Hunters. — **(9) 1873** TWAIN & WARNER *Gilded Age* iv. 48 If it's Wash Hastings—well, what he don't know about the river ain't worth knowing—a regular gold-leaf, kid-glove, diamond-breastpin pilot Wash Hastings is. **1884** MARK TWAIN *H. Finn* xxxv. 363, I couldn't see no advantage in my representing a prisoner if I got to set down and chaw over a lot of gold-leaf distinctions like that.

(10) 1896 *Harper's Wkly.* 4 July 650/3 In 1892 the money plank was intended to catch the votes of both gold and silver men. **1900** *Cong. Rec.* 19 Jan. 985/1 The gold men in this bill are trying to seize upon silver dollars and silver certificates and wash them over with gold. — **(11) 1913** BASSETT *Short Hist. U.S.* 760 Before the convention assembled he [McKinley] accepted a gold plank suggested by a group of Western business men. — **(12) 1833** in J. C. BENNETT *Hist. of Saints* (1842) 75, I would not give credit to the report he [Joseph Smith] made about the gold plates. — **(13) 1850** *Calif. Courier* (S.F.) 18 July 2/3 If gold quartz rock comes in, in this way, we will begin to believe that Mr. Wright is right, and we are wrong. **1882** C. KING *Rep. Prec. Metals* 290 A large gold-quartz ledge has also recently been discovered. **1891** *Cent. Mag.* Feb. 533 The most notable improvements . . . in gold-quartz machinery. — **(14) 1908** *Pacific Mo.* April 481/1 The present junior Senator from Oregon, Mr. Bourne, is accused of having defeated Senator Dolph, a Gold Republican, in 1895.

(16) *(a)* **1875** KNIGHT 995/1 *Gold-shell*, powdered gold or gold-leaf ground up with gum-water and spread on shells. Used by artists. *(b)* **1881** INGERSOLL *Oyster Industry* 244 *Gold Shell.*—Species of *Anomia.* **1889** *Cent.* 2567/2 *Gold-shell*, . . . *Anomia ephippium*, a bivalve mollusk, so called from one of its varieties having a golden luster. — **(17)** [**1869** *Harper's Wkly.* 29 May 341/3 By a connection of the telegraph with the last spike (a gold one, from California), the last blow given announced to the world the completion of the grand enterprise.] **1889** *Union Pac. R.R. Ore. & Wash.* 234 Even railroad schemes could not inflate her real property into an unsafe investment, nor the explosion and collapse that followed the driving of the last gold spike, halt her steady and substantial progress. **1949** *Nat. Geog. Mag.* May 593/1 The gold spike driven at Promontory Point in Utah, when east and west sections met, is being exhibited. — **(18) 1923** ADAMS *Pioneer Hist.* 650 Mathias Housel was a Civil War veteran, and Mr. and Mrs. Robert Wright are 'Gold Star' Parents. **1949** *Downers Grove* (Ill.) *Reporter* 31 Mar. 1/4 He is a Gold Star father; his only son was lost in the Normandy invasion. — **(19) 1849** *Alta California* (S.F.) 12 July 2/1 Gold Story. . . . The boys play at taw with huge diamonds instead of marbles. **1850** *Calif. Courier* (S.F.) 23 July 2/4 We copy the following gold story, to show how big a lie the Pacific News *can* tell.

(20) 1895 *N.Y. Dramatic News* 6 July 8/2 If it were possible to secure complete statistics regarding the effect of the Keeley gold treatment upon [dipsomaniacal] followers of the stage calling, an interesting state of affairs would certainly be revealed.

b. In combs., sometimes occasional, of obvious meaning, as (1) **gold camp,** (2) **dirt,** (3) **discovery,** (4) **excitement,** (5) **fever,** (also **gold feverish**), see also **Pike's Peak gold fever** and cf. **yellow fever,** (6) **hunt,** (7) **hunting,** (8) **mania,** (9) **nugget,** (10) **panning,** (11) **pencil,** (12) **rock,** (13) **rush,** (also **gold rusher**), (14) **seeker,** (15) **smitten,** (16) **strike.**

(1) 1894 *Harper's Wkly.* 30 June 619/2 One of the greatest gold camps in America has received a wound which will take some time to heal. **1946** *Trail & Timberline* May 74/2 Cripple Creek, only recently discovered, was a gold camp and continued to thrive. — **(2) 1880** *Scribner's Mo.* July 454/1 He climbed the hill . . . where he believed the wash or gold-dirt would naturally come from. — **(3) 1849** *Placer Times* (Sacramento) 28 April, *The Gold discoveries—intense excitement.* **1947** *Denver & Colo. Hotel Greeters Guide* 31 Jan. 22/1 In 1910 the dome was completely covered with gold leaf as a tribute to the pioneer prospectors whose gold and silver discoveries made the Colorado Rockies the treasure chest of the nation. — **(4) 1848** FOLSOM in Bryant *California* App. 468, I proceed to give you a hasty account of California as it is seen under the influence of the gold excitement now prevailing throughout the country. **1948** JOHNSTON *Gold Rush* 2/2 Every community between Kansas and the Atlantic seaboard felt the effects of gold excitement.

(5) 1847 *Californian* (S.F.) 22 May 4/1 After the gold fever was over, these ships were very successful in taking oil in the bay. **1858** *San Joaquin Republican* (Stockton, Calif.) 19 May, There was quite an excitement in Stockton when the advent of this material proof was made known, and several gentlemen became suddenly decidedly Frazer River gold feverish. **1948** WESTON *Mother Lode* 18 In 1850 Louis Trabuco, smitten with gold fever, . . . joined a wagon train headed for the California gold fields. — **(6) 1850** COLTON *Three Years Calif.* xxi. 285 My companions, who have been out on a gold-hunt for several hours, have just returned. **1882** H. PATTERSON *New Golden Age* 105 Thus began the gold-hunt . . . —tens of thousands of adventurers rushing and racing to get first to the Golden Land [California]. — **(7) 1830** *Boston Transcript* 15 Dec. 2/3 Numerous individuals . . . are described as having got through very long and marked attacks of the *gold-hunting fever,* and survived the crises with little left but life. **1848** FOSTER *Guide* v, The crowds who, tempted by the glorious promises of gold-hunting, will go there, will at once establish a large and wealthy market. **1947** *Watonga* (Okla.) *Republican* 31 July 1/5 The gold hunting tour . . . came to an abrupt end. — **(8) 1849** *N.Y. Herald* 30 June, For the purpose of answering them, and keeping our readers informed of the progress of the gold mania, we annex a table. — **(9) 1854** *L.A. Star* 21 Sep. 2/3 A gold nugget, weighing 5 lbs. 4½ ounces, was found last week near Columbia. **1948** *Popular Western* June 14/1 A gold nugget watch chain dropped in twin nodes across his bed-of-flowers waistcoat.

(10) 1945 *Jefferson Co. Republican* (Golden, Colo.) 31 Oct. 2/1 Rev. Hillhouse engaged the services of 'George,' an old prospector to give a demonstration of gold panning. — **(11) 1848** *Santa Fe Republican* 11 March 1/4 The prize conundrum which took the gold pencil at a concert of the Sable Harmonists, recently given in Cincinnati was this: [etc.]. — **(12) 1851** *L.A. Star* 17 May 2/2 In this ravine and running nearly parallel with it is a vein of gold rock, dipping slightly to the west. — **(13) 1876** W. M. FISHER *Californians* 35 Go back to 'the flush times,' to the year of 'the gold rush,' to 1849. **1902** LONDON *Daughter of Snows* 15 More than one gold-rusher . . . affirmed Del Bishop's judgment. **1948** *Pacific Discovery* May–June 3/1 Even in the rude Gold Rush days of 1853 there were, among San Francisco's 50,000, seven men of sufficient intellectual and scientific curiosity to meet together and form 'The California Academy of Natural Sciences.' — **(14) 1848** *Calif. Star* (S.F.) 10 June 2/1 We have . . . returns of enthusiastic gold seekers. **1948** JOHNSTON *Gold Rush* iv/2 Gold-seekers en route to California overland from Oregon were responsible for the discovery and original settlement of the Trinity Mines.

(15) 1850 *Deseret News* (Salt Lake City) 2 Nov. 145/3, I have said nothing of . . . the lonely wastes, with no trace of any green thing, except, perhaps, a few gold-smitten immigrants. — **(16) 1897** MARK TWAIN *Following Equator* 231 (R.), The first great gold-strike made in Australia. **1947** *Time* 21 July 20/2 When the Mormons heard the news of the gold strike at Sutter's Mill, he cried: 'Gold is for paving streets,' and rallied the faithful to their toil.

As the last term in **black, British, California, coarse, cob, coyote, fine, float, flour, fool's, gulch, placer, river, rusty, shot, wash, wire gold.**

goldarn ˌgɑlˈdɑrn, *a.*, *adv.*, *v.*, *interj.* A minced form of "God damn" used as a mild oath. *Slang.* Cf. next.

1832 BUCKINGHAM in *N. Eng. Mag.* III. 380 We have . . . *'Gaul darn you'* for G—— d—— you . . . and other like creations of the union of wrath and principle. **1885** *Harper's Mag.* Aug. 397/2 Hannah-Maria-Jemimy! goldarn an' blue blazes! *Ib.* 400/2 You're a goldarn liar, Balaam, and blast your old buttons, you kin walk home by yourself. **1892** *Cent. Mag.* June 263/2 Law suits, Mr. Huntley, is gold darn uncertain. **1928** *Liberty* 11 Aug. 29/2 But still—gol*darn* it, he was getting the wrong kind of muscle!

goldarned ˌgɑlˈdɑrnd, *a.* Darned, doggoned. *Slang.*

1849 *N.O. Picayune* 6 May 2/6 I'll be gaul-durned ef I deu. **1893** WISTER in *Harper's Mag.* Dec. 57/2, I'll be gol-darned if I'll have Lin McLean make any more of a fool of me to-night. **1903** FREEMAN *Six Trees* 181 It'll have to be pooty goll durned bad to be any worse. **1948** *Reader's Digest* March 128 'Oh, Lord!' groaned Colonel John. 'Another great story ruined by a goldurned eyewitness.'

goldasted ˌgɑlˈdæstɪd, *a.* =prec. — **1888** *Cin. Enquirer* (F.), That goldasted St. Louis mugwump has made suckers of us again.

gold brick.

1. Gold in the form of a brick or bar.

1853 *S.F. Sun* 7 June 2/2 (*heading*), Gold Brick. **1876** RAYMOND *8th Rep. Mines* 354 Individuals are constantly carrying out bags of gold and gold bricks and some silver bricks. **1899** *Mo. So. Dakotan* I. 196 [He] commenced looking around and found in a water hole a gunny sack in which was a gold brick.

2. A valueless brick that appears to be made of gold; hence, anything that appears to have value, but really has none. Usu. attrib. and in the phrase *to sell* (one) *a gold brick*, to swindle, cheat.

1887 *Courier-Journal* 29 Jan. 5/3 Gilmore swindled Patrick Burke, a citizen of St. Louis, out of $3,700 by the gold-brick trick. **1900** ADE *More Fables* 180 He began to think that in making any Outlay for Lutie's Vocal Training he had bought a Gold Brick. **1901** WHITE *Westerners* 94 Bunco men can clean him out in a gambling joint, but who ever heard of their selling him a gold brick? **1947** *Chi. D. News* 16 May 18/5 It used to be the city slicker who sold gold bricks to the hick from the country.

3. (See quots.)

1914 *D.N.* IV. 107 Gold-brick, n. Applied to army lieutenants appointed from civil life. 'The gold-bricks are overbearing.' **1943** *Reader's Digest* Oct. 97 The wise guy always complains when there is work to do. Sometimes [in the army] he is called a Gold Brick.

gold brick, *v.*

1. *tr.* To swindle. *Slang.*

1902 H. L. WILSON *Spenders* xxviii. 328 He'll be gold-bricked if he wears 'em [*sc.* his whiskers] scrambled that way around this place. **1908** *Sat. Ev. Post* 5 Dec. 18/1 They always have coin. . . . They get it gold-bricking New Yorkers.

2. *intr.* To shirk. Hence **gold-bricking, gold-bricker.** *Slang.*

1932 *Blue Valley Farmer* (Okla. City) 4 Feb. 8/4 No country worth fighting for was ever built on slackers' devotion or gold-bricker's patriotism. **1944** *New Yorker* 7 Oct. 14/3 You're not sick, Burrows, you're gold-bricking. **1945** *Newsweek* 26 Nov. 15 A boy of 18 is very impressionable, and usually will pick up such habits, as swearing, drinking, gambling, 'gold-bricking' in a very short time. **1948** *Sat. Ev. Post* 11 Sep. 138/3 He had difficulty with a captain who thought his wish to take part in the army show, Stars and Gripes, was a gold-bricking attempt.

goldbug ˈgoldˌbʌg, *n.*

1. Any one of various beetles having a golden luster. Also "The Gold Bug," the title of a well-known story by Edgar A. Poe.

1843 POE (*title*), The Gold Bug. **1895** *Standard Dict.* 776/2. **1909** *N.J. State Museum Rep.* 355 It is one of the the 'gold-bugs,' the larvae of which are known as 'peddlers.'

2. An advocate of the gold standard. Also a badge or emblem worn by one of these. Also attrib. *Colloq.* or *slang.* Cf. **gold Democrat, gold Republican.**

1878 *Nation* 21 Feb. 126/1 [Our forefathers] carried on business in gold. . . . In short, they were 'goldites,' 'gold-bugs,' and 'gold-sharps.' **1893** *Ores & Metals* (Denver) 23 Aug. 396/2 There is not a goldbug paper in the whole Territory of New Mexico. **1896** *Cin. Enquirer* 30 July 1/7, I had a gold bug on my coat. A farmer came up to me and took hold of my coat collar and held the gold button up to view. 'That's the bug that got into our wheat,' he said, 'and reduced it 50 per cent.' **1942** LILLARD *Desert Challenge* 52 Bryan's inspired campaign, . . . the testimonials of Wall Street's 'goldbug' economists, the tension, the hysteria, and the final narrow victory for McKinley . . . is a chapter in the history of America.

Hence **gold-bugism.**

1895 *Voice* 11 July 4 We believe in the demonetization of both metals. If that is gold-bugism, tell it not in Wall Street.

∗**gold coast.** (Usu. *cap.*)

1. Designating or pertaining to Negro slaves brought from the region so named in West Africa. *Obs.*

1726 *Boston News-Letter* 11–17 Nov. 2/2 Several choice Gold Coast Negroes lately Arrived, To be Sold at Mr. Bulfinch's. **1838** COOPER *Homeward B.* xxiv, His color . . . was about half-way between that of a Gold Coast importation, and a rice-plantation overseer.

2. = **Golden Coast** (*a*).

1854 C. GAYARRÉ *Hist. La.* I. 355 The *German Coast* . . . became in time the producer and the receptacle of such wealth, that, a century after, it was called the *Gold Coast*, or *Côte d'or.* **1925** H. E. CHAMBERS *Hist. La.* I. 144 The industry and frugality of these peoples [German settlers in early 18th cent.], brought them not only competence, but in time such wealth that *Coté des Allemandes* soon came to be known as *Coté d'Or*—the Gold Coast.

3. A coastal area of northern California and southern Oregon. *Obs.*

1853 *S.F. Commercial Advt.* 9 Dec. 2/2 The topic of the gold coast survives and agitates the mind and eyes of our people longer than humbugs and fictions are wont to do in this country. **1876** RAYMOND *8th Rep. Mines* 66 The gold-coast of Klamath and Del Norte.

4. A group of luxurious and privately owned dormitories at Harvard. Also attrib.

1902 *Record* (Harvard) 18 March, Out of the 'Yard'—How the Harvard students have gone to the 'Gold Coast.' **1913** *Boston Post* 13 Feb., Harvard must secure control of the Gold Coast structures, according to Dean LeBaron Russell Briggs.

5. A popular name for an exclusive residential section occupied by wealthy people.

1920 R. SHACKLETON *Book of Chicago* 328 In that region there is so much of wealth . . . that the name of the Gold Coast has been aptly given to it. **1948** *Chi. Tribune* 1 Aug. 1. 12/3 The families of Russian personnel at the United Nations have converted a bourgeois chateau on the Long Island gold coast into a proletarian warren.

gold digger.

1. One who mines gold, esp. a placer miner. Cf. **Oregon gold digger.**

1830 *Cherokee Phenix* (New Echota, Ga.) 24 Mar. 3/3 There are tippling shops on every hill where these gold diggers are collected, and . . . intemperance, of course, may here be witnessed in its aggravated form. **1889** MUNROE *Golden Days* i. 3 He was better fitted to be a gold-digger than anything else. **1948** WESTON *Mother Lode* 28 Savage and his party of Indian gold diggers encamped under a big oak, the largest on the Mother Lode.

2. A girl or woman whose paramount object is to obtain money from the men with whom she associates. *Slang.*

1925 WITWER *Roughly Speaking* 308 My beautiful chum was a candid gold-digger who would have made the Forty-Niners gnash their teeth with envy. **1948** *Duncan* (Okla.) *D. Banner* 1 July 16/6 Some gold-diggers are moved by a display of money, but . . . most girls are not.

∗**gold dust.**

1. A yellow perennial, *Alyssum saxatile.*

1944 *Burpee's Seed Cat.* 97 *Alyssum:* Rock Madwort, Gold Dust. . . . Charming, attractive dwarf early blooming plants for rock gardens and borders.

2. a. gold dust exchange, the exchanging of gold dust for money or its equivalent. **b. gold dust scales,** scales used for weighing gold dust.

(a) **1889** *Union Pac. R.R. Ore. & Wash.* 207 Grant's Pass is the supply point for the richest gold mining region on the Pacific Coast, the gold dust exchange often reaching as high as $800,000 per annum. — (b) **1942** LILLARD *Desert Challenge* 293 W. Parker Lyon . . . acquired hundreds of thousands of relics for his Pony Express Museum: gold-dust scales, Wells, Fargo, ledgers, . . . barbers chairs, and so on.

∗**golden,** *a.*

1. In the names of birds: (1) **goldenback,** (see quot.); (2) **crested wren,** = **golden-crown(ed) wren;** (3) **crowned kinglet,** = **golden-crown(ed) wren;** (4) **crowned sparrow,** (see quot.); (5) **crown(ed) thrush,** an ovenbird, *Seiurus aurocapillus*; (6) **crown(ed) wren,** the kinglet, *Regulus satrapa;* (7) ∗**eagle,** see as a main entry; (8) **oriole,** (see quot. 1844); (9) **robin,** (see quot. 1808); (10) **shafted woodpecker,** a local name for the flicker; (11) **warbler,** (see quot.); (12) **wing,** the golden-winged warbler or the flicker; (13) **winged warbler,** a North American warbler, *Vermivora chrysoptera*, having yellow wings; (14) **winged woodpecker,** = **flicker.**

(1) **1889** *Cent.* 2566/2 *Goldenback*, the American golden plover. — (2) **1921** *Outing* March 257/3 Far overhead, up among the gale, the golden-crested wren was buzzing about . . . among the battling twigs, looking for insects that mere human beings couldn't see. — (3) **1871** BURROUGHS *Wake-Robin* (1886) 178 A golden-crowned kinglet [was near Washington, D.C.]. **1948** *Pacific Discovery* March–April 18/1 More rarely a golden-crowned kinglet forages outside the window. — (4) **1858** BAIRD *Birds Pacific R.R.* 461 *Zonotrichia Coronata.* . . . Golden-crowned Sparrow.

(5) **1796** MORSE *Univ. Geog.* I. 209 Least Golden Crown Thrush. *Turdus minimus, vertice aurio.* **1810** WILSON *Ornithology* II. 88 The Golden-Crowned Thrush, *Turdus Aurocapillus*, . . . is also a migratory species, arriving in Pennsylvania late in April. **1900** HIGGINSON *Outdoor Studies* 142 Some [nests], indeed, are very elaborately concealed, as of the Golden-crowned Thrush. — (6) **1743** CATESBY *Carolina* II. p. xxxvi, European Land-Birds inhabiting America: . . . The golden Crown Wren. **1865** BURROUGHS in *Atlantic Mo.* May 514/2 Presently I likewise perceive a troop of . . . Golden and Ruby-Crowned Wrens, flashing through the Chestnut-branches. — (8) **1844** *Nat. Hist. N.Y., Zoology* II. 139 The Golden Oriole. *Icterus Baltimore.* . . . The Oriole, Hang-bird, Fire Hang-bird, or Golden Robin, for it is known under all these names, is found in the summer season throughout the State. **1881** NASH *Two Yrs. Ore.* 99 Among them is sometimes seen the golden oriole, . . . with his orange jacket and black cap. — (9) **1808** WILSON *Ornithology* I. 23 [The Baltimore oriole is] honored with a variety of names, such as Hang-nest, Hang-ing-bird, Golden Robin, Fire-bird, . . . but more generally the Baltimore bird. **1899** JEWETT *Queen's Twin* 167 It was a bright cool evening in June, the golden robins sang in the elms.

(10) **1877** BURROUGHS *Birds & Poets* 118 Another marked April note . . . is the call of the high-hole, or golden-shafted wood-pecker. — (11) **1874** COUES *Birds N.W.* 54 *Dendrœca Aestiva.* . . . Blue-eyed Yellow Warbler; Golden Warbler; Summer Warbler. — (12) **1865** BURROUGHS in *Atlantic Mo.* May 518/1 The Golden-Wing prefers the fields and the borders of the forest to the deeper seclusion of the woods. **1895** *Atlantic Mo.* July 61/1, I had a call from a family of flickers, or goldenwings. — (13) **1810** WILSON *Ornithology* II. 113 [The] Golden-Winged Warbler, *Sylvia Chrysoptera*, . . . is another spring passenger thro the United States to the North. **1917** *Birds of Amer.* III. 118 Golden-winged Warbler. . . . [Also called] Golden-winged Flycatcher; Golden-winged Swamp Warbler; Blue Golden-winged Warbler. — (14) **1806** LANGSDORFF *Voyages* (1817) 441 The finest ornament for the head consists of the two middle tail-feathers

of the golden-winged wood-pecker, *picus auratus*, the shafts of which are by nature of a very bright vermilion colour. **1917** *Birds of Amer.* II. 163 Flicker. *Colaptes auratus auratus.* . . . [Also called] Yellow-shafted Woodpecker; Golden-winged Woodpecker; Clape [etc.].

b. In the obs. names of breeds of domestic fowls, as **golden (spangled) Hamburgh, Sebright, spangled Poland.**

1850 BROWNE *Poultry Yard* 52 The fleshy rose comb of the golden Hamburgh . . . is well described. *Ib.* 58 The Spangled Hamburgh Fowl, Golden Spangled Hamburgh, Silver Spangled Hamburgh Fowl, of the English and Anglo-Americans. — **1871** LEWIS *Poultry Book* 68 The plumage of the Golden Sebright is of golden color, and the Silver Sebright of a silver white. — *Ib.* 50 Golden Spangled Poland. — This variety varies in the color of its plumage from a light to a dark golden yellow.

c. In the names of fishes: (1) **golden eyes perch,** (see quot.), *obs.;* (2) **mullet,** (see quot.); (3) **trout,** any one of various beautifully colored trout found in California.

(1) **1819** *Western Rev.* I. 370 Golden-eyes Perch. *Perca chrysops.* Perche oeil-d'or. . . . Its usual size is about one foot. It is very good to eat. — (2) **1842** *Nat. Hist. N.Y., Zoology* IV. 201 The Mullet Sucker, *Catostomus aureolus*, at Buffalo passes under the various names of Mullet, Golden Mullet, and Red Horse. — (3) **1883** in *Sierra Club Bul.* (May, 1947) 82 We pushed on to Whitney Creek . . . and we went farther up and stopped to fish. *Golden trout*—lovelier than gold fish, with red splashes on their sides—hundreds of them. **1947** *Sierra Club Bul.* May 77 Dr. Barton Warren Evermann . . . was in the Kern River region investigating the golden trout.

2. In the names of plants: (1) **golden aster,** a plant of the genus *Chrysopsis* having yellow rays; (2) **bell,** a shrub of the genus *Forsythia;* (3) **club,** an aquatic plant having a yellow, club-shaped spadix; (4) **-cup oak,** =**goldcup oak;** (5) **currant,** a shrub, *Ribes aureum*, found in the West, having fragrant yellow flowers; (6) **fir,** (see quot.); (7) **glow,** (see quot. 1939); (8) **-leaf chinquapin,** the *Castanopsis chrysophylla*, found in California and Oregon; (9) **oak,** see as a main entry; (10) **prairie flower,** (see quot.); (11) ∗**seal,** a perennial herb, *Hydrastis canadensis*, the dried rhizome and roots of which are sometimes used as a tonic; (12) ∗**thread,** =∗**goldthread;** (13) **top,** (see quot.).

(1) **1907** LYONS *Plant Names* 119 Chrysopsis, Nutt. 1818. Golden Aster. **1924** HAWKINS *Trees & Shrubs Yellowstone* 91 Golden asters, like street gamins, look quite uninteresting till one learns to like them. — (2) **1929** BAILEY *Cyclo. Horticulture* 1268/1 The golden-bells are highly ornamental free-flowering shrubs, with simple or ternate leaves and showy yellow flowers, borne in great profusion along the slender branches in early spring before the leaves. **1948** *No. & So. Dak. Horticulture* July–Aug. 101/1 This season forsythias, or goldenbells, were showy as the rich yellow flowers adorned the shrubs to their tips. — (3) **1837** DARLINGTON *Flora Cestrica* 226 Aquatic Orontium. *Vulgo*—Golden Club, Never wet. **1902** *Amer. Folk-Lore* 261 Tawkee. A name formerly much in use in New Jersey and parts of Pennsylvania for the 'golden club' (*Orontium aquaticum*). — (4) **1897** SUDWORTH *Arborescent Flora* 164 *Quercus chrysolepis*, . . . Golden-cup Oak (Cal.). **1948** *Desert Mag.* Feb. 8/1 The desert oak that I know best is the Canyon oak, Golden-Cup oak or Maul oak.

(5) **1904** WOOTON *Native Ornamental Plants N.M.* 28 The Golden Currant . . . grows wild in our mountains and along some of the streams. **1913** ——— *Trees & Shrubs N.M.* 73 It is already well known in cultivation, generally going under the name of Golden Currant or the Missouri Currant. — (6) **1897** SUDWORTH *Arborescent Flora* 58 *Abies magnifica.* . . . Shasta Fir. . . . Common Names. . . . Golden Fir (Cal.lit.). — (7) **1902** LESTER *So. N.M. Flower Garden* 25 Rudbeckia, (Golden Glow). This comparatively new flower has done exceedingly well with the author. **1939** *Nat. Geog. Mag.* Aug. 260/2 The tall coneflower (*R. laciniata*) . . . is deservedly popular under the name of 'golden glow.' Autumn glory and autumn sun are varieties of still another species. **1942** LILLARD *Desert Challenge* 235 In the gardens are apple and pear trees, sunflowers, golden glows, and bachelor's-buttons. — (8) **1897** SUDWORTH *Arborescent Flora* 149 Goldenleaf Chinquapin. . . . Common names [include] Chinquapin (Cal., Oreg.), . . . Western Chinquapin.

(10) **1863** *Rep. Comm. Agric. 1862* 159 The Yellow Acacia is known as 'Golden Prairie Flower' in Arkansas. — (11) **1839** in *Mich. Agric. Soc. Trans.* VII. 409 *Hydrastis canadensis.* Golden seal. Yellow-root. **1947** *Chi. Tribune* 8 June VII. 9/3 The talk then turned to the greens, then in their prime, for food or medicinal use . . . mustard, deer tongue, wild onions, bloodroot, and golden seal. — (12) **1784** CUTLER in *Mem. Academy* I. 457 *Nigella.* . . . Goldenthread. Mouth Root. The roots are astringent, and of a bitterish taste. Chewed in the mouth they cure apthas and cankerous sores. It is frequently an ingredient in gargles for sore throats. **1832** WILLIAMSON *Maine* I. 124 Goldenthread derives its name from its roots, which are of a bright yellow colour, running in all directions like silken cords; . . . a tincture made of the root, digested in rectified spirits of wine, is a good tonic bitter, promotive of digestion and strengthening to the stomach. — (13) **1909** *Cent. Supp. Goldentop*, an ornamental grass, *Achyrodes aureum*, . . . introduced from the Mediterranean region into southern California. **1925** JEPSON *Flora Calif.* 96 L[amarckia] aurea Moench. Golden-top.

b. In the names (chiefly obs.) of varieties of apples, as **golden Ball, pearmain, sweet, sweeting, wilding.**

1817 W. COXE *Fruit Trees* 123 Golden Pearmain. Called in New-York and East-Jersey, the Ruckmans, or Dutch Pearmain; and in other places the Red Russet. **1847** J. M. IVES *N. Eng. Fruit* 49 *Golden Ball*—This fruit was also brought forward by Mr. Cole. . . . It is a fine apple for cooking, as well as for the table. **1863** *Rep. Comm. Agric. 1862* 167 The Golden Sweeting is extremely valuable as a baking apple. **1870** *Ib. 1869* 191 Golden Wilding [apple]. Originated near Fayetteville, North Carolina. **1878** STOWE *Poganuc People* xvi. 176 The apples of every name and race harvested in autumn from the family orchard: Permains, . . .Golden Sweets, and other forgotten kinds. **1943** DAMON *Sense of H.* 231 Before the Astrachans were all gone, the long-stemmed small Golden Sweets began to turn from pale green to pale yellow.

c. In the names (chiefly obs.) of varieties of corn for table use, as **Golden Bantam, chaff, corn, Sioux (corn).**

1909 *Suburban Life* May 251/1 For the earliest plant Peep o' Day; for second-early Golden Bantam, Early Fordhook or Extra-early Adams. **1947** *This Week Mag.* 18 July 20/3 Yet she's as busy and as happy as a corn borer in an ear of Golden Bantam. — **1854** DAVIS *Farm Bk.* 34 Put in 4 rows of the Heard rare ripe & two of the Monk rare ripe. . . . We planted the Golden chaff seed in all the fresh land. — **1828** COBBETT *Treatise on Corn* § 26 The white corn is, in America, generally called flint-corn, and the yellow is called golden-corn. — **1848** C. L. FLEISCHMANN *Nordamerikanische Landwirth* 113 Golden Sioux, oder Northern Yellow Flint-Corn. **1849** EMMONS *Agric. N.Y.* II. 264 *Golden Sioux corn*, . . . The meal is as rich as that of either of the preceding kinds, providing it has ripened well.

3. In miscellaneous combs.: (1) **Golden beaver,** a beaver, *Castor canadensis subauratus*, native to California, having a sepia or cinnamon-brown coat; (2) **Bible,** see as a main entry; (3) **buck,** Welsh rarebit with a poached egg on it, *slang, obs.;* (4) **Circle,** (see quot. 1902); (5) ∗**eagle,** see as a main entry; (6) **mines,** (see quot.), *obs.;* (7) ∗**plates,** see as a main entry; (8) **spike,** =**gold spike,** now *hist.;* (9) ∗**star,** a representation of a star symbolizing California's admission to the Union, *rare.*

(1) **1921** HALL *Yosemite Nat. Park* 127 A day put in at a representative point, such as Snelling, would show the presence there of Mockingbirds, Texas Nighthawks, . . . Fresno Pocket Gophers, Merced Kangaroo Rats, Golden Beavers, and other exclusively warm-belt types of animals. **1939** HAMILTON *Amer. Mammals* 298 Contrariwise, it is the lack of water which limits the spread of the Golden Beaver. — (3) **1898** MARK TWAIN *Appetite Cure* 157 (R.), Luncheon: cold tongue . . . pickled pig's feet, grilled bones, golden buck. — (4) **1865** *Nation* I. 66 The particular aversion of the Golden Circle was radicalism of every sort, and hence no lodges were erected in South Carolina or Massachusetts. **1902** CLAPIN 207 *Golden Circle.* An organization formed among 'Copperheads' during the Civil War, to aid in the rescue of confederate prisoners. Also one of the alleged names of the 'Klu-Klux-Klan' [*sic*].

(6) **1763** in *S.C. Hist. Coll.* II. 468 A swamp is any low, watery place, that is covered with tree or canes; there are three kinds of them, cypress, river, and cane swamps: they are called the golden mines of Carolina; from them all our rice is produced, consequently they are the source of infinite wealth. — (8) **1869** *N.Y. Herald* 11 May 6/5 The golden spike . . . closes the final link of the Pacific Railroad. **1883** *Harper's Wkly.* 22 Sep. 594/3 Driving the Golden Spike. The excursion and ceremonies in commemoration of the completion of the Northern Pacific Railroad were evidently most imposing. **1949** *Sat. Ev. Post* 28 May 112/2 This followed the historic driving of the 'golden spike.' — (9) **1852** in *Pioneer* (S.F.) (1855) July 23 For lo! from 'midst our flag's brave blue, leaps out a *golden* star.

b. (*cap.*) In names and nicknames: (1) **Golden Bear State,** =**Golden State;** (2) **Belt,** (see quot.), *obs.;* (3) **City,** (see quot. 1871); (4) **Coast,** (*a*) a variant name for the Gold Coast of Louisiana on the banks of the Mississippi about thirty miles above New Orleans, (*b*) the coast of California; (5) **Country,** a name formerly used for California; (6) **Empire,** (see quot.), *obs.;* (7) **Gate,** the strait at the entrance of San Francisco Bay, Calif., also attrib., cf. ∗**gate 3;** (8) **Land,** California, or the western slope region, *obs.;* (9) **State,** California.

(1) 1942 LILLARD *Desert Challenge* 74 Any Nevadan on his vacation heads, more than likely, for the Golden Bear State. — **(2) 1879** WHITMAN *Spec. Days* 142 For a long distance we follow the line of the Kansas river, ... a stretch of very rich, dark soil, famed for its wheat, and call'd the Golden Belt. — **(3)** [**1860** *Alta California* (S.F.) 28 May 1/1 A city near the Chrysopolæ would properly be named Chrysopolis, or Golden City; and hence Chrysopolis ... is a suitable name for a seaport.] **1871** DE VERE 665 San Francisco ... finds compensation for the curt way in which it is treated by Western men, who call it simply Frisco, in the high-sounding name, Golden City, under which it is elsewhere known. **1891** QUINN *Fools of Fortune* 447 The chief operations were carried on in the Golden City where two mining boards were arranged. — **(4)** *(a)* **1847** LONGFELLOW *Poetical Works* (1893) 86/1 The region where reigns perpetual summer, Where through the Golden Coast, ... Sweeps ... the river away to the eastward. **1894** CHOPIN *Bayou Folk* 67 Monsieur Alphonse Laballière; an aristocrat from the 'golden coast.' *(b)* **1943** HOWARD *Montana* 39 On the golden coast, however, it had been speedily modified by the influx of northerners who followed the southern pioneers to the new diggings.

(5) 1850 *Calif. Courier* (S.F.) 1 July 1/4 In view of the countless thousands who are here and on their way to the Golden Country, I deem it a fit opportunity, to place before the readers of your valuable paper some few facts with regard to Oregon. — **(6) 1854** *S. Lit. Messenger* XX. 551 All of the available force of the nation could ... be concentrated in California in ten days.... [This] would give us an absolute security in the possession of that Golden Empire. — **(7) 1848** *30th Congress* 1 Sess. Sen. Misc. Doc. No. 148 (map of Frémont's expeditions), Chrysopylae or Golden Gate. **1947** *Sierra Club Bul.* May 109 The relative intelligence of mules and men is easily demonstrated: men voluntarily jump off the Golden Gate Bridge into the dark tidal waters far below. No mule jumps off the Golden Gate Bridge; you cannot by any possibility even push a mule off that long span across the Golden Gate. — **(8) 1849** *Alta California* (S.F.) 1 May, It has been [hailed] with joy by millions as opening a speedy and safe communication with the 'Golden land' to which all eyes are constantly turned. **1854** *Pioneer* (S.F.) Feb. 77 He thinks of those on board of that homeward bound steamer, who ... are now gaily looking for the last time upon the Golden Land. — **(9) 1847** *Cong. Rec.* 7 May App. 246/2 From the hills of the Golden State we will send ... cattle of every breed. **1946** *New Yorker* 10 Aug. 13/1 You know how things are in the Golden State.

c. In phrases (see quots.).

1883 in WARE *Passing English* 79/2 Edward's Folly Dramatic Company is reported as having climbed the golden stairs. **1909** WARE *Passing English* 79/2 *Climb the Golden Staircase, To* (*Amer.*). One of the U.S.A. equivalents to the Latin 'join the majority.' — **1890** *Amer. Hist. Mag.* July XXIV. 1 The expression or term 'The Golden Age of Colonial New York' has been generally understood to refer to a period about the middle of the eighteenth century.

Golden Bible. The *Book of Mormon,* allegedly translated from an original engraved on thin golden plates. *Obs.* See also ∗**golden plates.**

1830 *Wheeling* (W.Va.) *Gazette* 24 April 4/4 A work has recently been published in the western part of New-York, entitled *Book of Mormon,* or the Golden Bible. **1835** *Sentinel & Star in West* (Philomath, Ind.) 27 June 26/2 The notorious impostor, Jo. Smith, of golden Bible memory, reached 'the promised land' in Ohio, with his deluded followers. *a***1847** in HOWE *Hist. Coll. Ohio* 286 Some months ago I borrowed the Golden Bible.... Since that, I have more fully examined the said Golden Bible, and have no hesitation in saying that the historical part of it is principally, if not wholly taken from the 'Manuscript Found' [of Solomon Spalding]. [**1853** *Harper's Mag.* April 606/2 It was confirmatory of a legend long known to money-diggers in Canada that a golden Bible was somewhere buried.]

∗**golden eagle.**

1. The representation of an eagle worn as a badge. Cf. ∗**eagle 1.**

1789 DUNLAP *Father* II. i, Why didst thou not live past Princeton's glorious day, to have worn with me the golden eagle and the honest scar?

2. = ∗**eagle 2.**

1808 *Ann. 10th Congress* 1 Sess. I. 335 A golden eagle will bribe but one man. **1857** *Quinland* II. 73 'Excellent; and here is a bird for you,' Morley said, carelessly dropping a golden eagle into his red horny hand.

3. (See quot. 1916.)

1839 PEABODY *Mass. Birds* 262 The Golden Eagle, *Falco fulvus,* ... loves the wildness of desert and mountainous regions, where it neither seeks nor fears the presence of man. **1916** SETON *Woodcraft Man.* 305 The only other eagle found in the United States (beside the Bald Eagle) is the *Golden or War Eagle* (*Aquila chrysaetos*). This is a little larger ... the two species may always be distinguished by the legs. The War Eagle wears leggings—his legs are feathered to the toes.... The Bald Eagle has the legs bald, or bare on the lower half. **1947** CAHALANE *Mammals* 174 Trappers believe that the golden eagle is an important enemy [of the fisher].

golden oak.

1. (See quots. 1909, 1916.)

1909 *Cent. Supp.* 739/2 *Cañon live-oak, Quercus chrysolepis,* an evergreen oak of the Pacific coast.... Also called golden oak, maul-oak, and Valparaiso oak. **1916** SETON *Woodcraft Man.* 283 Black Oak, Golden Oak, or Quercitron (*Quercus velutina*) Seventy to 80 or even 150 feet high. The outer bark is very rough, bumpy, and blackish; inner bark yellow. This yields a yellow dye called *quercitron.* **1921** HALL *Yosemite Nat. Park* 127 The Transition Zone ... is characterized by the yellow pine, Douglas spruce, golden oak, black oak, and incense cedar.

2. Oak finished in a light golden color; also furniture made of this. Usu. attrib.

1899 *Chi. D. News* 30 May 14/3 Solid golden oak finish handsome dressers—one lot only, ... 5.49. **1902** *Sears Cat.* (ed. 112) 608/2 Made of best selected and well seasoned rock elm; finished in golden oak. **1928** F. N. HART *Bellamy Trail* i. 2 Nine rows of the golden-oak seats packed with grimly triumphant humanity. **1949** *Sat. Ev. Post* 15 Jan. 88/4 We traverse the years of the stereopticon, the mandolin, golden oak, wall telephone ... down to the overstuffed-sofa, cloche-hat, early-radio, Maxfield Parrish '20's.

∗**golden plates.** Plates, allegedly of gold and covered with ancient writing, said to have been found by Joseph Smith (1805–44), who translated from them the *Book of Mormon.* Cf. **Golden Bible.**

1833 in J. C. BENNETT *Hist. of Saints* (1842) 74 They told me that the report that Joseph, Jr., had found golden plates, was true. **1844** J. H. HUNT *Mormonism* 6 Here [in Ontario County, New York, in 1827] the golden plates were found, containing the important facts upon which the salvation of a world depends. **1925** M. R. WERNER *Brigham Young* 31 It is impossible to determine exactly whether the golden plates of the Book of Mormon ... were a piece of conscious fakery. **1947** *Time* 21 July 19/2 An angel named Moroni had told him where to unearth some golden plates covered with mystic symbols.

goldite ˈgoldaɪt, *n.* One who advocates the gold standard. Also attrib. *Obs.* Cf. **goldbug 2.**

1878 [see **goldbug 2.**] **1896** *Nation* LXII. 130/2 It is generally assumed that there is a 'goldite' majority in the House. **1900** *Cong. Rec.* 12 Feb. 1723/1, I challenge any Goldite ... to point to one instance in the world where one dollar has ever failed to be at a parity with any other dollar.

goldometer golˈdɑmətɚ, *n.* A device allegedly useful in locating gold or gold deposits. *Obs.* Cf. **gold monkey.** — **1850** *Calif. Courier* (S.F.) 9 Sep. 2/5 Some soft heads in the southern diggings are mightily taken with what is called a 'Goldometer.' It is asserted that, by the aid of this instrument, a miner can tell where to dig for gold. **1909** *Collier's Mag.* 22 May 14/1 Magic needles—rods, goldometers, chronometers, etc., for treasure-seekers.

gold rocker. = ∗**cradle,** *n.* **1.**

1852 *Mt. Echo* (Downieville, Calif.) 17 July 1/4 A new gold rocker has been recently perfected by Col. Butler of Trinidad. **1880** BURNETT *Old Pioneer* 255, I took plank in the bottoms of my wagons, with which I constructed a gold-rocker. **1949** *Sun. World-Herald Mag.* (Omaha) 3 April 18/3 Such items as gold washers, gold rockers, long toms, English and American iron, ... were all available at St. Louis prices.

gold room. 1. In the New York Exchange, a room in which transactions involving gold were carried on. Now *hist.* **2.** (See quot.)

(1) 1867 *Alpine Miner* (Monitor, Calif.) 2 Mar. 2/1, I had almost said that the gold room regulates all the prices in the United States. **1946** ADAMS *Album Amer. Hist.* III. 242 (*caption*), Black Friday in the Gold Room of the New York Stock Exchange. — **(2) 1911** HOVEY *Morgan* 29 The favorite place to watch this terrifying upward movement was the 'gold room.' This peculiar institution was a private enterprise, kept by a man named Gallagher in a building at the corner of William Street and Exchange Place. Anyone could deal in the gold room after paying a fee of twenty-five dollars a year. It was open all day, whereas the Stock Exhange, which then held two sessions, closed its morning session at twelve.

gold standard.

1. The legal weight and fineness of gold that, actually or theoretically, went into American gold coins. *Obs.*

1831 *Cong. Deb.* App. 22 Feb. p. cl, The present rate (of our gold Standard) was the result of information clearly incorrect. **1876** *44th Congress* 2 Sess. H.R. Ex. Doc. No. 3 p. liii, The act of June 28, 1834, which reduced the gold standard about six and one-fourth per cent; practically demonetized the silver coinage.

2. The standard of monetary value solely in terms of gold, the single standard. Cf. **limping gold standard.**

Virtually on the gold standard since 1834, the U.S. adopted it legally in 1900 and abandoned it in 1933.

1857 *Alta California* (S.F.) 6 Sep. 1/6 In our view, the present forced export [of Calif. gold] will continue, more or less, until India adopts a gold standard, or at least until some grand catastrophe occurs in France. **1914** CONWAY & PATTERSON *Operation New Banking Act* 195 Gold Standard Reaffirmed . . . by the Act of March 14, 1900. **1948** *Chi. Tribune* 11 July (Grafic Mag.) 5/1 He won the enmity of J. Sterling Morton, boss of the Nebraska Democrats and a firm believer in the gold standard for the nation's money.

b. Attrib. with **act, candidate, contractionist, Democrat, era, plank, platform.**

1887 *Courier-Journal* 3 Feb. 4/2 [Certain newspapers] only say what has resulted from a price-depreciation, which they state as beginning in the first year of the gold-standard era. **1892** *Cong. Rec.* 30 June 5658/1 Senators . . . can defeat the will of the people and serve the gold-standard contractionists; they can serve Lombard and Wall streets by being absent. **1896** *St. Louis Globe-Democrat* 19 June 1/3 Senator Teller offered a free coinage substitute for the gold standard plank. **1896** *Harper's Wkly.* 8 Aug. 770/3 Mr. McKinley is . . . the only gold-standard candidate for the Presidency who has any chance of success. **1900** *Cong. Rec.* 8 Feb. 1644/2 The votes and support of the gold-standard Democrats in the Presidential election, has forced upon the Republican party a total abandonment of bimetallism. *Ib.* 14 Feb. 1776/2 The Times-Herald is authority in Republican circles. The proprietor of it claims to have been the author of the gold-standard platform at St. Louis. **1914** *Cyclo. Amer. Govt.* II. 85/1 With the passage of the gold standard act of March 14, 1900, the activity of the gold Democrats terminated.

gold washer. 1. = * **cradle,** *n.* **1. 2.** One who mines gold by washing auriferous earth.

(1) 1831 *21st Congress.* 2 Sess. H.R. Doc. No. 49, 51 King, Roswell . . . [inventor of] Gold washer, vertical cylindrical, Oct. 1 [1830]. **1853** *Calif. Express* (Marysville) 12 Mar. 3/4 The gold washer at Ousley's which operates by steam is not yet successful. **1949** [see **gold rocker**]. — **(2) 1948** WESTON *Mother Lode* 56 First came the gold washers, armed with pick, pan, and shovel.

golet ˈgolɪt, *n.* [Origin unknown.] (See quot. 1889.) — **1889** *Cent.* 2568/1 *Golet.* . . . A California trout: same as *Dolly Varden.* **1896** JORDAN *No. Amer. Fishes* 293.

golfire ˈgalˈfaɪr, *v.* [App. f. "God" and "hell fire."] = **goldarn,** *v.* Also **golfired,** *a. Slang. Obs.* — **1861** NEWELL *Orpheus C. Kerr* I. 266 [He] mumbled, in extreme agitation: 'Golfire your cursed abolition soul!' *Ib.* 21 There's a couple of golfired fools somewheres in this country. **1864** *Harper's Mag.* Oct. 684/2 We didn't git much honey, but we broke up their gol-fired haunt.

goloid ˌgolɔɪd, *n.* [f. *gold*+*-oid,* (like or resembling gold) as in *alkaloid, asteroid,* etc.] A mixture of gold and alloys. Also attrib. *Obs.* Cf. **oroide,** *n.*

1879 *Cong. Rec.* 8 May 1171/1 The Greeks and Romans descended to plated coin, and . . . tried at length the 'goloid,' the very mixture which the distinguished gentleman from Georgia, the chairman of the Committee on Coinage, Weights, and Measures, now admires and recommends. **1881** *Chi. Times* 30 April, Dr. Hubbell . . . calls himself the 'inventor' of a certain mixture of gold, silver, and copper to which he has given the pretty name of goloid. *Ib.*, He also describes his goloid dollar, which consists mostly of silver.

gombo, see **gumbo.**

gomee ˈgamɪ, *n.* [Origin unknown.] A variety of green tea. *Obs.* — **1816** *Ann. 14th Congress* 1 Sess. 1863 Duty on tea from China . . . gomee . . . fifty cents per pound.

* **gondola,** *n.* Also **gundalow.** [In sense **1.** cf. Du. *gondel,* a rowboat.]

1. *N. Eng.* A large, flat-bottomed river boat or lighter, formerly sometimes used as a gunboat.

1694 *New Hampshire Prov. Papers* (1868) II. 147 Ordered, . . . that the said W. Furber keep attendance and a sufficient boat or gundaloe. **1723** *N.-Eng. Courant* 20–7 May 2/1 One Indian has likewise been lately kill'd by the English, who fir'd upon him from a Gondola going up a River at N. Yarmouth. **1809** KENDALL *Travels* III. 31 But vessels of the burden above described are floated down to the sea, by means of flat boats or lighters, here [in N. Eng.] called *gondolas,* and elsewhere *scows.* **1886** *Harper's Mag.* July 241/1 The 'gondola'—pronounced by the natives gundolo, with accent on the first syllable—is an unwieldy sloop-rigged vessel still in use in the shallow waters of the New England coast. **1948** *Chi. Tribune* 10 Oct. (Grafic Mag.) 18/2 The powder was taken away, loaded on gundalows, shipped to Durham, N.H., and later removed to Madbury.

b. (See quot.)

1886 POORE *Reminisc.* I. 51 Another source of trade was the Potomac River, which was navigable above Georgetown as far as Cumberland in long, flat-bottomed boats, sharp at both ends, called 'gondolas.'

2. A flatcar with low side-planks, usu. fixed but sometimes hinged and in some cases removable. In full **gondola car.**

1871 DE VERE 480 *Gondola,* . . . the use of the word for a peculiarly shaped railroad-car is not unknown in England. **1884** JOSEPH HATTON *Henry Irving's Impressions of Amer.* II. 265 And one huge gondola-car, which was made to carry all the flat scenery. **1887** *Courier-Journal* 17 Jan. 2/3 [The strikers] marched directly to the float bridges, where brakemen were engaged in placing a train of forty-eight gondola coal cars upon transfer barges. **1949** *Sat. Ev. Post* 28 May 106/2 Johnny . . . stopped on the way home from school to play around a string of empty gondola cars standing in a railroad yard.

3. *W.* (See quot.)

1931 *Amer. Sp.* Oct. 79 The *gondola* is a long wagon, deep in the middle, and sloping up towards the ends. It is used for hauling where the roads permit. Where deep ruts have formed its use has to be given up, for the middle is only a foot and half from the ground.

Gondola car

* **gone,** *a.*

1. In slang and usu. obs. combs. in the sense of hopeless, done for, used up, as (1) **gone beaver,** see * **beaver,** *n.* **4.** (5), (2) **case,** (3) **chick(en),** (4) **coon,** (5) **fawn-skin,** (6) **gander,** (7) **goose,** (8) **gosling,** (9) **horse,** (10) **Negro,** (11) **sucker.**

(2) **1735** EDWARDS *Works* VII. (1809) 466 When it is come to that [i.e., when backsliders no longer care about their convictions], it is commonly a gone case with persons as to those convictions. **1899** C. KING *Trooper Galahad* 17 Ought I not to make poor Lawrence understand that it's a gone case? He is legally out already. — **(3) 1834** SIMMS *Guy Rivers* 171 Yes, I thought myself a gone chick under that spur. **1835** *Vade Mecum* (Phila.) 28 Feb. 3/5, I really believe I'm assassinated—I'm a gone chicken! **1948** *Sat. Ev. Post* 11 Sep. 19/1 If they pick up your tracks you're a gone chicken. — **(4) 1839** MARRYAT *Diary in A.* II. 232 In the Western States. . . . 'I'm a *gone 'coon'* implies 'I am distressed—or ruined—or lost.' **1898** FREDERIC *Deserter* 119 If he hadn't come just as he did I'd been a gone coon. **(5) 1833** *Polit. Examiner* (Shelbyville, Ky.) 22 June 4/2 You know that if they drop me, I'm a gone fawn skin. — **(6) 1848** BARTLETT 160 In New York it is said 'He's a *gone gander,*' i.e. a lost man. — **(7) 1830** *Salida* (N.Y.) *Herald* 19 May 2/1 'You're a gone goose, friend,' said another, with an ominous shake of the head. **1845** S. SMITH *J. Downing's Letters* 86, I'll go for the doctor. . . . It may be he can do something for her, though she looks to me as though it was a gone goose with her. **1949** *Sat. Ev. Post* 19 Mar. 108/3 Two minutes more of her and I'm a gone goose. — **(8) 1934** VINES *Green Thicket World* 143 Then we're gone goslings. **1941** STUART *Men of Mts.* 95 If he'd a-been ten yards closter to me I'd a-been a gone-goslin. — **(9) 1840** KENNEDY *Quodlibet* 91 Nim Porter ses . . . that you are a gone horse. **(10) 1840** BIRD *Robin Day* 68 It's only a gone nigger. **1945** BOTKIN *My Burden* 21, I knows I's a gone nigger. — **(11) 1832** PAULDING *Westward Ho!* I. 80, I wouldn't risk a huckleberry to a persimmon that we don't every soul get treed and sink to the bottom like gone suckers. **1853** F. W. THOMAS *J. Randolph* 288 Well, thinks I, if I am a gone coon — I never was a coon — I'm a gone sucker.

2. * **gone in,** exhausted; **gone off,** fallen off in fashion or popularity. *Colloq.*

1876 *Scribner's Mo.* April 820/1 [Etagères] are a little gone off in these days, serving no real use but only to put futile bits of glass and china on for the housemaid to break. **c1895** NORRIS *Vandover* (1914) 276 Put me to bed, will you, Bandy? I feel all gone in.

3. * **gone up,** of a crop: Parched by drought, worthless.

1864 *Ill. Agric. Soc. Trans.* V. 318 Wheat here is mixed, some fields good, others 'gone up,' others fair.

b. Hopeless, desperate, finished.

1865 KELLOGG *Rebel Prisons* 98 We heard nothing from Richmond, although one of the guards told one of our boys, at this time, that it was 'a gone-up case.' **1867** GOSS *Soldier's Story* vi. 123, I thought we were 'gone up'; but he merely stirred his fire. **1875** *Chi.*

Tribune 3 Nov. 1/7 The Huck men were hopeful, but the Hesingites felt themselves toward night clean gone-up.

c. (See quots.) Cf. ∗**go,** *v.* **5.** (15), **6. o.**

1867 DIXON *New Amer.* I. 132 Gone up, in the slang of Denver, means gone up a tree. . . . In plain English, the man is said to have been *hung*. **1888** SHERIDAN *Memoirs* I. 86 In reply to Meek's question, I stated that I had not seen Spencer's family, when he remarked, 'Well, I fear that they are gone up,' a phrase used in that country in early days to mean that they had been killed.

goneness 'gɔnnɪs, *n.* A state of great weariness or exhaustion. *Colloq.*

1848 *R.I. Words* (Bartlett MS), *Goneness*, a peculiar feeling in the stomach. **1879** R. G. WHITE in *Atlantic Mo.* XLIII. 90 *Goneness*, indeed, has some humor and suggestiveness, and might be accepted as good slang if it were in sufficiently common use. It is described as being a 'woman's word'; but I have heard it from men. **1891** COOKE *Huckleberries* (1896) 342, I feel a goneness that I never had ketch hold o' me before.

∗**gong,** *n.*

1. gong bell, a bell that produces the sound of a gong when struck.

1882 HOWELLS *Modern Instance* iv, She answered the door when Bartley turned the crank that snapped the gong-bell in its center. **1887** MARK TWAIN *Conn. Yankee* xv. 182 Konductr'll strike the gong-bell two minutes before train leaves.

2. gong punch, (see quot. 1877). Cf. **bell punch.**

*a*1877 *Providence Press* (B.), The royalty paid for use of gong-punches . . . would be quite adequate [etc.]. **1877** BARTLETT 253 *Gong-Punch.* An instrument used by conductors and those who receive the fare in horse-railroad cars and omnibuses, by means of which a complete record is kept of the number of passengers who pay their fare; a bell-punch.

gonus 'gɔnəs, *n.* [See note.] (See quots.) *Obs.*

Perhaps a collegiate Latinizing of *gawney*, a simpleton, a "yawny" person. *EDD* lists among the variant forms *goney, gonny,* and *gooney.* This may well be the source of the recently popular *goon.* See *Amer. Sp.* XVIII. 68, XIX. 235.

1842 *Dartmouth* IV. 116 A stupid fellow, a dolt, a boot-jack, an ignoramus is called here a *gonus*. **1848** *Amherst Indicator* I. 76 Future gonuses will swear by his name, and quote him in their daily maledictions of the appointment system.

goo gu, *n.* [Poss. f. ∗*burgoo.*] A thick, viscid liquid or semifluid substance. *Slang.* Cf. **gooey,** *a.* — **1911** E. FERBER *Dawn O'Hara* iii. 31 You mean to tell me that you woke me . . . to make me drink that goo? . . . I'll bet it's another egg-nogg. **1943** POWELL *Home Again* 91 'Goo' sounds just the way goo feels when it gets into your clothing, your hair, your eyebrows, all over your skin.

goober 'gubɚ, *n.* Also **gouber.** *S.* [Kongo *nguba*, kidney, peanut.]

1. =**peanut.** *Colloq.*

1834 *Cherokee Phenix* (New Echota, Ga.) 24 May 3/4 But he so seam I frade of he, I guess he steal my goober. **1866** C. H. SMITH *Bill Arp* 81 It makes no difference whether it is goobers or grindstones, sugar or salt. **1902** *Everybody's Mag.* Jan. 71/2 They stand about in picturesque groups, chewing tobacco, cracking 'gubbers.' **1948** *Dly. Ardmoreite* (Ardmore, Okla.) 21 Jan. 10/1 North Carolina's peanut harvest brings in about $38,500,000 worth of the goobers.

attrib. **1880** HARRIS *U. Remus* (1884) 100 Dar wuz one season . . . w'en Brer Fox say to hisse'f dat he speck he better whirl in en plant a goober-patch.

b. (*cap.*) A nickname for a North Carolinian. *Obs.*

1863 BOUDRYE *Fifth N.Y. Cavalry* (1868) 339 Conscripts by the dozen. . . . Some from Mississippi state and 'Goobers' from Tar river. **1871** DE VERE 57 During the late Civil War a conscript from the so-called 'piney woods' of that State [N.C.] was apt to be nick-named a Goober.

c. (See quot.)

1890 *N. & Q.* V. 248 Besides the ordinary goober, or pinder (*Arachis hypogæa*), there is a wild plant, not uncommon in the North as well as the South, the *Amphicarpæa monoica*, which is locally known as the goober in some districts of the Southern States.

2. In special combs.: (1) **goober grabber, grabbler, grubber,** (see quots.); (2) **pea,** =**peanut;** (3) **State,** a nickname for Georgia.

(1) **1867** *Ball Players' Chron.* 27 June 6/2 As to playing for the 'championship bat of Georgia,' with a club outside of the State, we most respectfully decline—as that belongs to the so-called 'goober grabbers' alone. **1869** *Overland Mo.* III. 129 A Georgian is popularly known in the South as a 'Gouber-grabbler.' **1880** *Harper's Mag.* Feb. 388/2 'What are gruber-grubbers?' 'Why, pea-nut diggers—worst lot you ever saw.' **1946** MCWILLIAMS *So. Calif. Country* 172 Georgians are 'crackers' and 'gauber grubbers.' — (2) **1833** *Louisville Pub. Advt.* 7 Nov., A few bags Gouber Pea, or Ground Pea [for sale]. **1912** CRUMPTON *Two Boys* 163 Chatting with my mess-mates wholly at my ease Good gracious! how delicious; eating Gooberpeas. **1946** NIXON *Va. Words* 23. — (3) **1877** BEARD *K.K.K. Sketches* 147 In brief, Uncle Jack had been the proud proprietor of the largest and best known pack of 'nigger dogs' in the 'Goober State.'

b. *To hull the goobers for,* to vanquish, defeat. *Colloq. Obs.*

1867 *Ball Players' Chron.* 27 June 6/1 The Gate City boys think they can 'hull the goobers' for all comers.

∗**good,** *a.* and *adv.*

1. Designating grades of ginned cotton, as **good fair, middling, ordinary.** Cf. **middling.**

1848 *De Bow's Review* VI. 447 The quality ranging from Middling Fair to Good Fair . . . 6½ *a* 7½ cents for Middling to Good Middling. **1851** in BASSETT *Plantation Overseer* 229 A few days ago we received the first shipment of your crop of cotton pr steamer 'Monroe,' being 75 bales of which 56 bales are in quality a high order of 'middling' to 'good middling.' **1887** *Courier-Journal* 17 Jan. 7/6 Cotton market was dull middling 9 1/16 c; low middling 8¾ c; good ordinary 8 5/16 c. **1948** *Okla. Cotton Grower* 15 June 2/4 Premiums and Discounts for all Grades of 1948 American Upland Cotton . . . Good Ordinary . . . Good Middling.

2. In combs.: (1) ∗**good and,** as an intensive; (2) **-bye summer,** any one of various southern asters having purple flowers; (3) **christian,** a variety of pear, *rare;* (4) **fellow,** (see quot.), *slang, obs.;* (5) **god,** (*a*) a colloq. name for the pileated woodpecker, (*b*) (see quot.); (6) **gravy,** see **gravy;** (7) **Indian,** see as a main entry; (8) **land,** see **land;** (9) **lick(s),** an exclamation expressive of satisfaction or earnestness [cf. ∗*good lack!*]; (10) **looker,** one who is handsome, esp. a girl or woman, *slang;* (11) ∗**man,** *S.W.* an arbitrator [tr. of Sp. *hombre bueno* in the same sense], *rare;* (12) **mixer,** see **mixer;** (13) **-morning-spring,** (see quots.); (14) ∗**roads,** used attrib. to designate organizations that support the policy of building good roads; (15) **scout,** see ∗**scout;** (16) **sport,** see ∗**sport;** (17) **squaw,** see **squaw;** (18) **Templars,** *pl.* a temperance society organized at Utica, N.Y., in 1851, also **Good Templary;** (19) ∗**time,** the time by which a prisoner is allowed to reduce his sentence by good behavior, *rare;* (20) **time girl,** a girl whose chief object in life is pleasure, *rare.*

(1) **1834** C. A. DAVIS *Lett. J. Downing* 6 Don't forgit my face, and the Gineral's face; and let the likenesses be good and natural. **1894** WISTER in *Harper's Mag.* Jan. 296/1 You'd claim Indians object to killing a white man when they run onto him good and far from human help? **1919** LEWIS *Free Air* 33 He made a good and plenty lot out of pulling out tourists. — (2) **1894** *Amer. Folk-Lore* VII. 91 Asters (a purple species), Good-by Summer. Lincolntown, N.C. — (3) **1817–8** *Botany* (1822) 417 *Pyrus communis*, pear. . . . Var. *pompeiana* (good christian). — (4) **1856** HALL *College Words* (ed. 2) 230 *Good fellow.* At the University of Vermont, this term is used with a signification directly opposite to that which it usually has. It there indicates a soft-brained boy; one who is lacking in intellect, or, . . . 'an epithetical fool.'

(5) (*a*) **1906** *D.N.* III. 138 good god. . . . A large variety of woodpecker. Logan Co. [Ark.] **1946** *Democrat* 12 Sep. 2/3 Yes, it's true that Kenneth killed a 'good god' for a squirrel. (*b*) **1945** MCATEE *Nomina Abitera* 47 I heard the name Good God applied to the redhead duck in Arkansas, but fear that somewhere along the line there had been confusion with the pileated wood-pecker in the cypress swamps of that country. — (9) **1854** *Harper's Mag.* Dec. 135/1 'We might as well have it [a drink] up here.' 'Good lick; but how are we to call for it?' **1876** MARK TWAIN *Tom Sawyer* 272 No! Oh good-licks, are you in real deadwood earnest, Tom?

(10) **1894** *Harper's Mag.* March 498/2 'What sort of a girl is she?' . . . 'She's a good-looker, . . . although they say she's gone off a little lately.' **1920** LEWIS *Main Street* 33, I bet she iss Doc Kennicott's new bride, good-looker, nice legs, but she wore a hell of a plain suit. — (11) **1836** EDWARD *Hist. Texas* 160 When the amount of the demand exceeds ten dollars and less than one hundred, each of the interested parties will nominate a *good-man.* — (13) **1892** *Amer. Folk-Lore* V. 93 *Claytonia Virginica*, good-morning-spring . . . wild potatoes. Union Co., Pa. **1931** CLUTE *Plants* 139 Close in its wake come the spring beauties (*Claytonia Virginica*), just in time to make the name of good-morning-spring applicable. — (14) **1897** *Outing* Aug. 492/2 [The Long Island Wheelmen] have been unusually enthusiastic in carrying on and furthering the work of the Good Roads Association. **1899** *N.Y. Journal* 10 June 1/1 Cyclers and Good Roads Clubs want it. **1914** *Cyclo. Amer. Govt.* II. 123/1 The state highway commissioner is a necessary part of the good roads movement.

(18) **1859** (*title*), Constitutions of the Grand and Subordinate Lodges of the I.O. of Good Templars, of Massachusetts. **1887** *Voice* 15 Dec., He had . . . the only complete collection . . . of books and journals pertaining to Good Templary. **1942** *Encycl. Americana* 56/2 Good Templars. . . . The order maintains the Washingtonian Home for Inebriates at Chicago, Ill., and an orphans' home at Vallejo, Cal. — (19) **1872** *Ill. Laws 1871–2* 295 For more than four offenses, the warden shall have power to deprive him [a convict], at his discretion, of any portion or all of the good time that the convict may have earned.

(20) **1928** *Publishers' Wkly.* 9 June 2393 Gerry Harris was a 'good time girl,' who sought men only as playmates.

3. In colloq. phrases.

a. *To feel good*, to feel well or elated.

[**1823** in *Memoirs of Charles Mathews* III. 387 'How's Miss Sabrina?'—'She's quite *good* (well)—She's a *foine girl*.'] **1839** MARRYAT *Diary* II. 224 And as bad is tantamount to *not good*, I have heard a lady say, 'I don't feel *at all good*, this morning.' **1854** *Jrnl. Discourses* II. 224 (Th.), You will see how good we will make the transient residents feel. **1904** *N.Y. Ev. Post* 23 June 3 The captain himself said, 'I feel good,' but he did not look well. **1924** *Collier's* 26 Jan. 8/4, I began to feel pretty good.

b. *A good enough Morgan*, a political expression used with reference to any device, scheme, etc., which can be used temporarily to influence voters, in allusion to the charge brought against the Masons of having made away with Wm. Morgan, who disappeared Sep. 12, 1826, on the eve of the publication of his book revealing secrets of Masonry. *Obs.*

1827 in T. WEED *Autobiog.* (1883) I. 319 'After we have proven that the body found at Oak Orchard is that of Timothy Monroe, what will you do for a Morgan?' . . . 'That is a good enough Morgan for us until you bring back the one you carried off.' **1880** *Dly. Inter-Ocean* (Chi.) 3 June 10/3 The third-term twaddle is a 'good enough Morgan' until after the convention. **1920** *Collier's* 14 Feb. 18/2 'Anyway, it's a good-enough Morgan until after the election,' remarked Thurlow Weed, who was one of the party's early leaders.

c. *Good for you! good for him!*, etc., expressions of approval.

1861 in M. WILLSON DISHER *Cowells in Amer.* (1934) 297 Sam's share $43.33.—Good for him! **1904** *N.Y. Ev. Post* 8 Sep. 1 During his speech there were many shouts of 'Good for you' and similar expressions of approbation.

d. *To be good for*, to be capable of producing, valid for.

1873 BEADLE *Undevel. West* 337 From thirty to forty tons of ore . . . [were] good for an average profit of a hundred and fifty dollars per ton. **1903** *N.Y. Tribune* 20 Sep., A 50-cent combination ticket good for every amusement on the island. **1927** CATHER *Death Comes* 1 The sun was still good for an hour of supreme splendor.

e. *To make good:* (1) (See quots.) (2) To prosper, succeed, fulfill a promise or obligation.

(1) **1882** C. WELSH *Poker: How to Play It* 8 When all who wish to play have gone in, the person putting up the ante . . . can play like the others who have gone in, by 'making good,'—that is putting up in addition to the ante as much more as will make him equal in stake to the rest. **1904** R. F. FOSTER *Pract. Poker* 232 *Make good.*—Adding enough to the blind or straddle to make it equal to the ante. — (2) **1901** MERWIN & WEBSTER *Calumet 'K'* 20 It'll play the devil with us if we can't make good. **1946** THOMPSON *Amer. Daughter* 225 You go on and make good.

f. *Be good!*, a jocular exhortation at parting, "take care of yourself."

1908 WHITE *Riverman* 29 Well, good-bye, boys. . . . Be good!

g. *To look* (or *listen*) *good*, to appear (or sound) attractive or promising.

1911 SAUNDERS *Col. Todhunter* 43 It looks good to me, suh. **1916** WILSON *Somewhere* 252 That listens good to her till she finds she has to give fifty-two dollars for the deck first. **1932** *K.C. Times* 1 March, It listened good.

good Indian.

1. An Indian not troublesome to the whites, a friendly Indian. See also ∗**listen,** *v.*

[**1745** *Itinerant Observ.* 14 The good Indians regaled us, and for greens, boiled us the Tops of China-Briars, which eat almost as well as Asparagus.] **1852** KELLY *Across Rocky Mts.* 102 Before leaving, the chief asked, and got from me, a written acknowledgment that he was a 'good Indian,' and 'treated us kindly,' which he would show to the commandant at Fort Kearney, to propitiate his good opinion. **1893** *Chi. Record* 5 July 9/4 He was a good Indian, . . . the white man's friend. **1947** *Amer. Sp.* April 93/2 The variant, *honest Indian*, shown below, is not necessarily an affectation; since it may be influenced by concurrent use of the term in the sense of 'good Indian.'

transf. **1900** *Cong. Rec.* 14 Feb. 1782/2, I want to put a question now to the distinguished Senator from Rhode Island . . . and ask him to answer it as an honest man and 'good Indian.' **1949** *Sat. Ev. Post* 12 March 58/4, I changed my line of attack, and soon we had him [a ram] on the run, and he became a good Indian for as long as we had him.

2. *W.* A dead Indian. *Jocular.*

1868 *Cong. Globe* 28 May 2638/3, I like an Indian better dead than living. I have never in my life seen a good Indian (and I have seen thousands) except when I have seen a dead Indian. **1884** W. SHEPHERD *Prairie Exper.* 62 On the frontier a good Indian means a 'dead Indian.' **1930** BANNING *Six Horses* 149 He was apt to pay with at least two 'good Indians' shot from his dusty ranks. **1948** DICK *Dixie Frontier* 65 The fighting frontiersmen felt that there was no good Indian but a dead one.

∗**goods,** *n. pl.*

1. (See quot. 1859.)

[**1812** *Norfolk* (Va.) *Herald* 29 May 314 (Th.), Federalists call the troops now raising 'a standing army.' They are mistaken in the goods.] **1859** BARTLETT 175 *Goods.* This word is used by Western shopkeepers as a singular noun for a piece of goods; as 'that *goods*,' speaking of cloth or linen. **1909** STRATTON-PORTER *Girl of Limberlost* 252 The moth struck full against it and clung to the goods.

fig. **1905** WIGGIN *Rose* 41 He never worked with me much, but he wa'n't cut off the same piece o' goods.

2. The qualities necessary to do or qualify for something, a performance that comes up to expectations. *Colloq.*

1899 ADE *Fables in Slang* (1902) 4 Reverence—well, when it comes to Reverence, you're certainly There with the Goods! **1912** MATHEWSON *Pitching* 33 Now O'Toole is all right if he has the pitching goods. **1917** SINCLAIR *King Coal* 110 Mind you—I want the goods. I've got other fellows working, and I'm comparing 'em.

3. In sing. sense: A person who possesses the qualities or competence expected of him. *Slang.*

1902 LORIMER *Lett. Merchant* 304 A girl can usually catch a whisper to the effect that she's the showiest goods on the shelf. **1927** *Hutchinson's Mystery Story Mag.* Feb. 117 If there were ever any doubt in his mind about our being 'the goods,' it disappeared.

4. Stolen articles found on a thief, fig. in context. *Slang.* Cf. *to catch with the goods, to have the goods on* (one) in **6.** below.

1911 *N.Y. Ev. Post* 15 June (Th.), 'We've got you . . . now, and you're going to yield the stolen goods.' The goods in question were the office of Commissioner of Jurors [etc.].

5. goods box, a large wooden box, usu. of soft white pine, in which merchandise is shipped. Also transf.

1850 LEANDER V. LOOMIS *Journal* (1928) 131 As we . . . made our way to the center [of Sacramento], we would see an old pork barrell, or an old goods box. **1880** MARK TWAIN *Tramp Abroad* xix. 173 A strapping, ruddy girl was beating flax or some such stuff in a little bit of a goods-box of a barn. **1943** HOLT *Carver* 65 Merchants cheerfully gave him goods boxes.

b. goods trader, a trader among the Indians. *Rare.*

1846 SAGE *Scenes Rocky Mts.* ix, Because the goods-trader happened to be in the lodge of one of the weaker party, they attacked him.

6. In slang phrases: (1) ∗*To deliver the goods*, to fulfill a contract, to supply what has been promised, do what is expected; (2) *to catch with the goods*, to catch red-handed; (3) *to have the goods on* (one), to have indubitable evidence of one's guilt.

(1) **1879** *Cong. Rec.* 4 April 236/1 There are men in the North who walk around . . . saying, '. . . I will take you to victory.' They cannot deliver the goods. **1917** MATHEWSON *Sec. Base Sloan* xiv. 186 But he delivered the goods didn' he? — (2) **1919** *Detective Story Mag.* XXVIII. Nov. 50 Detective Craddock had informed Thubway Tham that, sooner or later, he was going to 'catch him with the goods.' **1921** R. D. PAINE *Comr. Rolling Ocean* xiv. 245 You have caught me with the goods, Wyman. **1924** *Collier's* 12 Jan. 30/3 'What does this mean, Joe?' he asked harshly. Well, I'm caught with the goods! — (3) **1916** WILSON *Somewhere* 177 No one ought to talk that way about any one if they ain't got the goods on 'em. **1924** W. M. RAINE *Troubled Waters* xxii. 233 They had the goods on us. We were going to hang—every one of us.

As the last term in **annuity, dry, English, fall, government, green, Indian, penny, shelf, sporting, store, straight, trade, wet goods.**

Goodwood ˈgʊdˌwʊd, *n.* An annual celebration at Columbia College, 1863–78, on the occasion of the selection of the most popular man in the junior class, and the presentation to him of a carved wooden cup. Also attrib. *Obs.* — **1938** *Columbia Alumni News* 16 Dec. 7 Subsequent classes continued the idea and every Spring staged an elaborate dance, which they called the Goodwood. *Ib.*, The next to last available Goodwood Cup came into the Columbiana office recently to put another piece of University history under glass for future generations. *Ib.*, There was never mere bad weather on Goodwood Day.

* **goody,** *n.*[1] At Harvard, a woman who takes care of students' rooms.

1819 PIERCE *Rebelliad* 11 Because 'Old Goody' is a name Applied to ev'ry College dame. **1884** R. GRANT *Average Man* 28 Enthusiastic audiences . . . even extend their patronage to the college 'goodies' which is the still more aged title of the venerable dames who have charge of rooms. **1902** CORBIN *American at Oxford* 12 The scout is in effect a porter, 'goody,' and eating-club waiter rolled into one.

goody ˈgʊdɪ, *n.*[2] [f. the adj.]

1. (See quot. *a*1870.) Also **goody-goody.**

*a***1870** CHIPMAN *Notes on Bartlett* 175 *Goody.* . . . A well-disposed, but small minded person; sometimes said of males. **1878** J. COOK *Conscience* 49 [The] man of weak will, . . . although he may be a good man,—and especially if he is a goody, a very different thing,—will quail. **1919** CADY *Rhymes of Vt.* (1923) 124 If any stranger thinks Vermont A place that goody-goodies haunt.

2. a. (See quot.) **b.** (See quot.)

(a) 1884 GOODE *Fisheries* I. 370 The Lafayette, or 'Spot,' *Liostomus xanthurus*, is known . . . on the coast of New Jersey as the 'Goody' and sometimes as the 'Cape May Goody.' — **(b) 1871** DE VERE 459 *Cracklings*, a favorite toothsome dish of the Southern States, consisting of pieces of the rind of pork roasted, which are baked into the bread of negroes, and make one of their greatest luxuries, known as *goody-bread*.

gooey ˈguɪ, *a.* [f. **goo,** *n.*] Viscid, sticky. *Colloq.* — **1923** H. L. FOSTER *Beachcomber in Orient* i. 9 She . . . extracted a gooey substance from a tube of tinfoil and smeared it with a stick upon the bowls. **1949** MURRAY *This Our Land* 189 Negroes would . . . dig the mud from the creek banks, and row the heavy, gooey mass home.

goofer ˈgufɚ, *n. S.* [Of African origin.]

1. A witch doctor; a curse, spell, or conjuration.

1899 in BENTLEY 260/2 *Negro* Aun' Peggy tuk de goopher off'n her.

2. goofer dust, a powder useful in conjuration. Also attrib. Cf. **gopher dirt.**

1943 *Copper Camp* 269 Nigger Riley . . . is hauled away to sleep off his 'goofer dust' jag in the Hotel de Clink. **1946** TALLANT *Voodoo in N.O.* 167 Then he started messin' around in the place too much, digging up dirt and taking dust from the tops of tombs to sell as goofer dust. **1947** DEVOTO *Across Wide Missouri* 139 Their ceremonies were without end: . . . private magic at the dictates of private medicines, individual quests for game or vision or feathers or goopher dust that required the co-operation of neighbors.

google ˈgugl̩, *n.* [Prob. a variant of **guzzle*, throat.] (See quots.) Cf. **goose guzzle.** — **1859** TALIAFERRO *Fisher's R.* 29 Two things he was particularly fond of, and upon which he flourished whenever he could get them—turnip greens and 'hog's gullicks,' the 'Adam's apple' of a hog's haslet, or the 'google,' as it is commonly called. **1897** *Boston Globe* 18 July 27/8 The word is 'google,' meaning Adam's apple, and is a Missouri provincialism.

* **goose,** *n.*

1. Used allusively with reference to the phrase *to be right* (or *sound*) *on the goose* (*q.v.* under **4.** below), or to the struggle over slavery in Kansas. *Rare.* Cf. **goose question.**

1856 *Three Years on Kansas Border* 42 Could the 'goose' speak, it would say: O, all ye faithful in 'gooseology,' take George [W. Bayliss] for an example—his faith must be sound whose conduct's in the right. O, ye adepts in gooseology, beware of that vilest of all heresies, Solifidianism—'faith without works is dead.'

2. = **keno goose.**

1871 *Cin. Commercial* 1 Sep. 8/1 The 'goose,' the cards, pegs, buttons and register were also taken to the station house.

3. In combs.: (1) **goose bump,** goose flesh; (2) **creek,** a term of depreciation for a small stream, also as a proper name; (3) * **egg, grease,** see as main entries; (4) **guzzle,** a fife, *rare,* cf. **google;** (5) * **neck,** a crooked way or path, *rare;* (6) **poke,** = **goose yoke** ["poke" here may have arisen from construing the written *y* in "yoke" as a *þ*]; (7) **pulling,** = **gander pulling;** (8) **question,** the slavery issue, any issue of great importance, *obs.,* cf. **4. a.** below; (9) * **trap,** a swindle, *rare;* (10) **yoke,** a light wooden fork or bow placed on the neck of a goose to prevent its going through a fence or hedge.

(1) 1867 SCOTT *Partisan Life* 407 And they all looked at Dr. Gog and laughed, he standing there forlorn and covered with goose-bumps. **1928** *Liberty* 11 Aug. 13/1 Uncork that batch of rye and gin and chase these goose bumps from my skin. — **(2)** *c***1715** in *Records E.-Hampton* I. 460 His part . . . is bounded . . . by land that Joseph Stretton pretends right to, and Common land, and Goose Creeck toward the Northeast. **1878** *Cong. Rec.* 23 April 2747/1 Farther inland [than Texas] . . . you find little 'goose creeks,' trout streams, and almost waterless rivers. — **(4) 1834** CARUTHERS *Kentuckian* I. 221 There's the squeakin of the wheels, that would go for them goose guzzles them fellers are pipin on.

(5) 1912 WASON *Friar Tuck* 45 They lay in wait for him one night as he was comin' up the goose neck. — **(6) 1869** W. MURRAY *Adventures* 116 If I stumbled and fell, the confounded things would come like a goose-poke athwart my neck, pinning me down. **1878** STOWE *Poganuc People* xv. 160 Tim was whittling a goose-poke. — **(7) 1947** *Time* 17 Mar. 25/1 A fortnight ago, sportsmen at South Carolina's Branchdale Jockey Club revived the ancient sport of goose pulling. — **(8) 1855** C. ROBINSON *Kansas Conflict* (1892) 112 O! K! on the Goose Question. All Hail! Pro-slavery Party Victorious! ! . . . Kansas has proved herself to be S. G. Q. **1862** *N.Y. Tribune* 16 Jan. 8/2 The coast survey, the Government contracts, or whatever else may happen to be the particular 'goose question' of the hour—he (Vallandigham) begged pardon, but was that not known as a classic phrase? **1866** C. H. SMITH *Bill Arp* 47 Me and you are about even on the goose question. — **(9) 1799** *Aurora* (Phila.) 31 Jan. (Th.), The gulls and goose-traps that have been sported for some time past all come from the shop in which the Washington Lottery wheels remain undrawn, and where a new goosetrap, the Amuskeag canal, was some time since hammered out.

(10) [**1841** BONNYCASTLE *Canadas* II. 118 Here [near Quebec] I saw, for the first time, a couple of tame outardes. . . . The female had a wooden yoke on her neck, to prevent her straying through fences.] **1896** HARRIS *Sister Jane* 43 Go show your grandmother how to make a goose-yoke.

b. In combs., often colloq. and rare, of obvious meaning or sufficiently explained in the quots., as (1) **goose drownder,** (2) **hair,** (3) **moon,** (4) **-neck hoe,** (5) **nest land,** (6) **pasture,** (7) **pen,** (8) **pimple,** (9) **plucking,** (10) **yard.**

(1) 1933 T. WILLIAMSON *Woods Colt* 73 A regular old goose-drowneder of a rain, this un is. **1944** *Democrat* 20 July 2/2 A superb rainstorm after a long drought becomes a goose-drownder. — **(2) 1897** A. H. LEWIS *Wolfville* 117 Cherokee, risin' up a little, while Faro Nell puts another, goose-ha'r piller onder him. — **(3) 1850** BROWNE *Poultry Yard* 238 [The Canada geese's] arrival in the fur countries, from the south, is impatiently expected; it is the harbinger of spring, and the month is named by the Indians the 'goose moon.' — **(4) 1908** *D.N.* III. 316 *Goose-neck* (*hoe*), n. A hoe with the connecting piece between the blade and the handle in the shape of a goose's neck. Distinguished from *Scovill* . . . [e. Ala.].

(5) 1905 JOHNSON *Highways* 148 Sink-holes. . . . Their form and frequency has given the name of 'Goose-nest land' to that part of Kentucky. — **(6) 1863** NORTON *Army Lett.* 139 Some of the Virginia farms remind me of . . . a house in the middle of a goose pasture. — **(7) 1905** *Forestry Bureau Bul.* No. 61, 38 *Goosepen*, a large hole burned in a standing tree. P[acific] C[oast] F[orest]. — **(8) 1914** *D.N.* IV. 155 goose-pimples, n. Goose-flesh. ('Goose-flesh' is never used.) 'Don't stay in bathing so long that you're all *goose-pimples* when you come out.' [Cape Cod.] **1947** *N.Y. Times Mag.* 2 Feb. 18/4 The way it scraped in this maneuver makes goose-pimples on my spine even now. — **(9) 1872** *Harper's Mag.* Sep. 508/1 There was to be a goose-plucking, at which all the gay society of the fork would be gathered.

(10) 1768 WASHINGTON *Diaries* I. 254 Carpenters all . . . went to Sawing Pailing for a Goose yard.

c. In the names of trees and plants: (1) **goosefoot maple,** the striped maple; (2) **grass,** any one of various American grasses, as the silverweed, Texas millet; (3) **plum,** an American wild plum.

(1) 1884 SARGENT *Rep. Forests* 46 *Acer Pennsylvanicum.* . . . Striped Maple. Moose Wood. Goosefoot Maple. Whistle Wood — **(2) 1847** WOOD *Botany* 252 Silver-weed. Goose-grass. **1878** KILLEBREW *Tenn. Grasses* 161 Goose Grass, *Poa annua,* . . . is a valuable grazing grass and sows itself. **1889** VASEY *Agric. Grasses* 25 *Panicum Texanum* (Texas Millet). . . . In some localities it is known as river grass; in others as goose grass, from its being supposed to have been introduced by wild geese. **1945** MATHEWS *Talking* 51 The goose grass is like a green velvet ceremonial rug. — **(3) 1913** CATHER *O Pioneers!* 29 Stout as she was, she roamed the scrubby banks of Norway Creek looking for fox grapes and goose plums, like a wild creature in search of prey.

d. In the names of birds and fish: (1) **goose bird,** (see quot. 1917); (2) **brant,** app. the black brant, *Branta nigricans;* (3) **fish,** the marine fish, angler, *Lophius piscatorius.*

(1) **1844** *Nat. Hist. N.Y., Zoology* II. 254 The Ring-Tailed Marlin, *Limosa Hudsonica*, . . . is not as common along our coast as the Marlin. In Boston it is called the *Goose-bird*. **1917** *Birds of Amer.* I. 240 Hudsonian Godwit. *Limosa hoemastica*. . . . [Also called] Field Marlin; Goose-bird; Black-tailed Godwit. — (2) **1857** *Lawrence* (Kans.) *Republican* 2 July 1 Water fowl of every variety, the swan, goose brant, ducks, marmots, the armadillo. — (3) **1807** *Mass. H. S. Coll.* 2 Ser. III. 55 The sting-ray, the skaite, and the goose fish, or monk, or fishing frog, are common. **1883** *Cent. Mag.* Sep. 733/2 It was no mean triumph, for instance, to have reared those young flounders and goose-fish from eggs scooped up in the open sea. **1914** STEELE *Storm* 50, I was as gloomy and dull as any goose-fish.

4. In colloq. phrases.

a. *To be right* (or *sound*) *on the goose*, an expression of unexplained origin first used during the struggle over slavery in Kansas with reference to those favoring slavery.

1855 *Olympia* (Wash.) *Pioneer* 29 (Th.), The democracy of the other counties may rest assured that Thurston [County] is 'right on the goose,' and that 'Sam' is winked out beautifully in this latitude. **1856** *Sacramento Age* 21 Sep. 4/1 He preaches electioneering sermons . . . and makes his people take a vote on the Presidential question every Sabbath, to see that they are all 'sound on the goose.' **1859** BARTLETT 175 'To be *sound on the goose*' or '*all right on the goose*,' is a South-western phrase, meaning to be orthodox on the slavery question, i.e. pro-slavery. Although it only got into general use during the recent Kansas troubles, I am not able to give its origin. **1900** CONNELLEY *Kansas Territorial Governors* 67 They crowded around Governor Geary, wherever he might chance to be, eager to ask questions, volunteer advice, and ascertain satisfactorily, whether, in their own chaste phrase, he was 'sound on the goose.'

Also transf. and allusive.

1856 PHILLIPS *Kansas* 302 Said reflection was responded to in a manner calculated to strike terror into unbelievers, and such who could not prove unmistakably their soundness on the Goose. **1860** *Charleston* (S.C.) *Mercury* 15 Nov. 2/7 That fulsome language—'Sound on the Goose,' being gone, she must replace it by something good—probably obedience would do. **1904** *Boston Herald* 12 Oct. 6/6 Chairman Tom Taggart once more vouches for Mr. Bryan's soundness on the goose. And who's vouching for the voucher?

b. *The goose hangs high*, prospects are bright, things look encouraging. *Colloq.*

No satisfactory explanation of the origin of this expression has yet appeared. The theory that it was originally *the goose honks high*, with reference to the fact that in fine weather geese fly at greater heights than usual, is unsubstantiated by any early evidence.

1863 CONVERSE *Old Cremona Songster* 26 Oh! you bet, your bogus dollars, Oh! you bet, the goose hangs high. **1894** *Cong. Rec.* 14 Feb. 2185/2 If you believe there is a plethora of money, if you believe everything is lovely and the goose hangs high, go down to the soup houses in the city of New York. **1943** *Sat. Review* 4 Sep. 14/2 Inquiry about the origin of the expression 'the goose hangs high' has brought forth a bewildering variety of explanations.

transf. **1866** *Wilkes' Spirit of Times* 27 Jan. 339/3 Then, my dear Wilkes, as you know, the public goose does 'hang high' enough, and beats turkey all to nothing, at thirty-five cents a pound, wholesale price.

As the last term in **blue, cravat, Emperor, flight, gone, Hutchins', keno, mackerel, marsh, mud, painted, sea, secesh, snow, tin, wild goose.**

***goose,** *v. tr.* (See quot.) *Obs.* — **1848** BARTLETT 399 *To goose boots*, to repair them by putting on a new front half way up, and a new bottom.

***gooseberry,** *n.* As the last term in **Indian, mountain wild, prickly, swamp gooseberry.**

* **goose egg.** A score of zero in a game. Also transf. and attrib.

1866 *Wilkes' Spirit of Times* 14 July 304/2 At this stage of the game our opponents had fourteen runs—we had five large 'goose eggs' as our share. **1867** *Ball Players' Chron.* 20 June 4/3 In Chicago a nine is 'busted' when they retire at the end of an innings with a blank score, and . . . in Philadelphia it is 'a goose egg.' **1949** *Chi. D. News* 29 March 10/7 It is called the 'Goose-Egg Record of the "No-Can-Do" Congress.'

Also as a verb, *tr.*

1875 *Chi. Tribune* 22 Aug. 9/2 During the last three innings the Bronens were goose-egged. **1948** *Sat. Ev. Post* 28 Feb. 133/1, I now had twenty-two consecutive World Series innings in which I goose-egged the National League.

* **goose grease.** In allusive and humorous contexts, a very slippery or slimy substance. *Colloq.*

1836 HOWARD *Stewart* 66 He was as slick on the tongue as goose-grease. **1892** *Harper's Mag.* Dec. 117, I don't believe he knows gingham from goose-grease. **1894** C. H. HOYT *Texas Steer* (1925) 39, I do not object to your dashing out the spoonful of goose grease that has for years served you for brains. **1948** *Popular Western* June 99/2 Then he adds smooth as goose grease, 'That is, unless yuh pull yore freight quick and sudden.'

gooseology gusˈɑlədʒɪ, *n.* The political philosophy of those who were "sound on the goose" in the struggle over slavery in Kansas. *Rare.* — **1856** [see **goose 1.**]

G.O.P. Abbreviation of "Grand Old Party," i.e., the Republican party.

1887 *Courier-Journal* 5 May 4/2 (*caption*), The G.O.P. On a Still Hunt For a National Leader For the Battle. **1890** HAY in W. R. Thayer *J. Hay* II. 81 The G.O.P. went to wreck over McKinley's Bill. **1949** *Chi. D. News* 26 March 6/4 Revolt of the Young Republican organization against the 'old guard' domination of the Illinois G.O.P. is reported gathering momentum.

attrib. **1947** *Chi. D. News* 21 June 1/8 The G.O.P. leaders plan to keep going until midnight.

gopher ˈgofɚ, *n.* [See note.]

In sense **2.** prob. f. F. *gaufre*, honeycomb, in allusion to the creatures' honeycombing the earth, but in sense **1.** app. a shortening of **magofer.**

1. The hard-shell land tortoise, *Gopherus polyphemus*, of the southern coastal region.

1791 W. BARTRAM *Travels* 182 Observed . . . the dens of the great land tortoise, called gopher. **1828** *Western Mo. Rev.* I. 591 In the pine barrens of Florida, Alabama and Mississippi, is found an animal, apparently of the tortoise class, commonly called the *gouffre*. **1944** *Democrat* 23 March 1/3 Mandolin Made From Shell Of A Gopher.

attrib. **1858** *S. Lit. Messenger* XXVI. 230/1 [To astronomy] we had introduced a class of sand hill boys and gopher trapping girls, ranging in age from fourteen to twenty years. [S. Ga.].

b. (See quot.) *Obs.*

1923 ADAMS *Pioneer Hist.* 615 The Jones children in those days took their sleigh rides in a 'gopher,' or what is better known as a 'pung,' a home-made sleigh where roots or limbs of trees with the right bend were used for runners.

2. *W.* and *S.* Any one of certain burrowing rodents or ground squirrels of various genera, as *Geomys, Thomomys, Citellus.*

1814 BRACKENRIDGE *Louisiana* 58 The gopher . . . lives underground, in the prairies, and is also found east of the Mississippi. **1875** *Amer. Naturalist* IX. 148 Naturalists . . . have no English name for these animals. . . . But by the people who live among them they are universally called 'gophers'; and as this name will certainly stick in the vernacular for all time, we may as well accept it. **1946** *Science News Letter* 9 March 149 Two albino gophers were captured by a student.

attrib. **1836** J. HALL *Statistics of West* v. 78 The inhabitants call them gopher hills, under the belief that they are raised by a small quadruped of that name. I never saw a gopher [in the prairies]. **1872** *Newton Kansan* 22 Aug. 2/1 A State full of no newspaper towns would not be as respectable as a desert of gopher colonies. *Ib.* 20 Feb. 4/1 The bounty of 15 cents on gopher scalps is said to have cost Nebraska $25,000 in two years. **1903** A. ADAMS *Log Cowboy* iv. 42 Officer's horse suddenly struck a Gopher burrow with his front feet.

b. (*cap.*) As a nickname (see quots.).

In quot. 1869 the allusion is to the land tortoise (sense **1.** above), though of course the "skin" of such a creature was never used as money.

1845 *St. Louis Reveille* 14 May 2/4 The inhabitants of . . . Arkansas [are called] Gophers. **1866** SHANKS *Recollections* 47 As a singular fact, showing the impression made on the minds of the men by the changed tactics which this campaign [Sherman's march to the sea] rendered necessary, I may mention that the soldiers called each other 'gophers' and 'beavers.' **1869** *Overland Mo.* Aug. 129/1 On account of the great number of gophers in that State, and the former use of their skins for money, a Floridian is called a 'Gopher.' **1872** *Harper's Mag.* Jan. 317/2 Below will be found a careful compilation of the various nicknames given to the States and people of this republic. . . . Minnesota, Gophers.

c. Gopher State, (see quot. 1880).

1880 FARRAR *Five Years Minn.* 166 Gophers are here such a pest to the farmer that Minnesota has been called the 'Gopher State.' [**1907** *Boston Transcript* 9 Nov., A list of the popular names of the States: . . . Gopher—Minnesota.]

3. = **gopher plow.**

1854 *Spirit of Times* 4 Nov. 447/3, I hitched him onto the gopher, and away we went. **1868** *Rep. Comm. Agric. 1867* 424 Then there is the 'scraper,' the 'half-shovel,' 'gopher,' and other peculiar forms of implements. **1894** *Cong. Rec.* 15 March 2995/1 The gopher is an iron plow.

4. In special combs.: (1) **gopher dirt,** app. dirt brought up by the southern land tortoise in making his hole, but cf. **goofer dust,** *colloq.;* (2) **drift,** (see quot.); (3) **frog,** a frog, *Rana aesopus*, often found in the holes of the southern burrowing land tortoise; (4) **hole,** see as a main entry; (5) **-like,** *a.* very slow, in allusion to the gait of the southern land tortoise, *colloq.;* (6) **man,** (see quots.), *slang;* (7) **plow,** *S.* some form of iron plow (see quot. 1894 under **3.** above), *obs.;* (8) **politician,** ?an entrenched politician, *rare;* (9) **snake,** see as a main entry; (10) **tortoise,** (see quot.); (11) **trader,** one who catches and sells southern land tortoises, *rare;* (12) **trap,** a trap for gophers (sense **2.**); (13) **turtle,** =**gopher,** *n.* **1.**

(1) **1893** M. A. OWEN *Voodoo Tales* 149 Gopheh-duht [dirt] mighty good ef yo' got de misery in de stummick. — (2) **1881** RAYMOND *Mining Glossary, Gopher* or *Gopher-drift,* an irregular prospecting-drift, following or seeking the ore without regard to maintenance of a regular grade or section. — (3) **1907** M. C. DICKERSON *Frog Book* 193 The Gopher Frog, *Rana aesopus,* . . . is reported from Florida only. **1938** MATSCHAT *Suwannee River* 76 Many of these are only temporary guests, but a few others, such as the gopher frog, apparently move in permanently.

(5) **1865** in STERLING *Belle* (1904) 235 He . . . is 'inching' upon Richmond surely and methodically in a way that seems as gopher-like as it is certain. — (6) **1901** FLYNT *World of Graft* 220 *Gopher-men,* safe-blowers. **1926** J. BLACK *You Can't Win* ii. 12 Famous 'gopher men' who tunneled under banks like gophers and carried away their plunder after months of dangerous endeavor. — (7) **1854** *Spirit of Times* (N.Y.) 4 Nov. 447/3, I shouldered the gopher plow, an' tuck hole ove the bridil. — (8) **1888** *S.F. News Letter* 4 Feb. (F.), The last Presidential election illustrated these truths. When the machine had nominated Blaine and connubiated with Tammany and waved the shirt, every gopher politician in the band actually believed that every factor in the case had been accounted for.

(10) **1884** GOODE *Fisheries* I. 158 *n.,* The three Gopher Tortoises of the South and West [are] the Florida 'Gopher,' *Xerobates polyphemus* . . . ; Agassiz's Gopher, *X. Agassizi,* . . . found in Southern California and Arizona; and Berlandier's Tortoise, *X. Berlandieri,* . . . Southern Texas. — (11) **1886** *Cent. Mag.* Feb. 586/1, I went down inter the piny woods of Alabama an' j'ined the gopher traders, but it wasn't a payin' business. — (12) **1871** *Rep. Comm. Patents 1869* II. 617/1 A gopher-trap consisting of the tube A, lever C, slides D E [etc.]. **1902** *Sears Cat.* (ed. 112) 753/1 Out o' Sight Gopher Trap . . . is a perfect trap and better suited for the purpose intended than all other makes. — (13) **1934** *Nat. Geog. Mag.* LXV. 612 In the dry pine barrens along the eastern border of the swamp the gopher turtle constructs its burrows and becomes host to numerous animal guests. **1944** BARBOUR *Eden* 91, I picked up some gopher turtles.

b. In the names of plants, as **gopher plum, root, weed.** Cf. **gopher wood** as a main entry.

1884 SARGENT *Rep. Forests* 91 *Nyssa capitata.* . . . Ogeechee Lime. Sour Tupelo. Gopher Plum. **1889** *Cent.* 2577/1 Gopher-root, . . . a low rosaceous shrub, *Chrysobalanus oblongifolius,* with extensively creeping underground stems, found in the sandy pine-barrens of Florida, Georgia, and Alabama. **1893** *Amer. Folk-Lore* VI. 140 *Baptisia lanceolata,* gopher-weed. Ga.

As the last term in **pocket, prairie, striped gopher.**

gopher ˈgofɚ, *v.*

1. *intr.* (See quot. 1889.) *Colloq.*

1889 *Cent.* 2577/1 *Gopher.* . . . To begin or carry on mining operations at haphazard, or on a small scale; mine without any reference to the possibility of future permanent development. Such mine-openings are frequently called *gopher-holes* and *coyote-holes.* (Pacific States.) **1910** *Sat. Ev. Post* 13 Aug. 4/1 Promising mines did 'gophering' or development work by contract at the same liberal rate. **1927** RUSSELL *Trails* 129 This old boy is a prospector and goes gopherin' 'round the hills, hopin' he'll find something.

b. To burrow like a gopher. *Colloq.*

1893 *Scribner's Mag.* April 473/2 At first were those who . . . gophered under the mighty walls of the temple.

2. gophering fellow, (see quot.). *Obs.*

1870 *Amer. Naturalist* III. 457 In California, a man who practices deception, or acts in an underhanded manner, is sometimes called a 'gophering fellow.'

gopher hole.

1. A hole or burrow made by a gopher.

1837 WILLIAMS *Florida* 67 The pine woods are so frequently burnt over that most of the reptile tribes are . . . destroyed; some few get into the gopher holes and shelter themselves from the flames. **1875** *Amer. Naturalist* IX. 148 Throughout a vast stretch of country in the northwest, gopher-holes and buffalo-chips are the most noticeable points about the landscape. **1920** MULFORD *J. Nelson* 126 There ain't no sense in totin' it by th' glass to a crowd of blotters. They'll hold more liquor than a gopher hole. **1948** *Democrat* 2 Dec. 1/6 One of the dogs bayed an o'possum in a gopher hole. The boys twisted it out and came leading it to the house with a rope.

b. gopher-hole cricket, ?a cricket often found in gopher holes. *Rare.*

1934 *Nat. Geog. Mag.* LXV. 612 Of invertebrates, the gopher-hole cricket is perhaps the most characteristic and abundant inhabitant.

2. A hole or trench in which soldiers and others seek to protect themselves.

1846 *Spirit of Times* 6 June 176/2 Almost every man has a 'gopher' hole dug to jump into to escape the explosion of the shells. **1866** SHANKS *Recollections* 47, I may mention that the soldiers called each other 'gophers' and 'beavers'; and 'gopher-holes' were more common in the armies' track than were camp-fires. **1906** RIDLEY *Battles* 483 The old gopher holes in the railroad embankment where citizens had taken shelter during the storming of Atlanta, remained.

3. *W.* A dugout. *Obs.*

1880 FARRAR *Five Years Minn.* 51 There still exist in the State houses, nearly underground, covered with a roof of thatch, the whole not appearing more than a foot or two above the surface of the earth, and known as 'Gopher-holes,' which were the habitations of the earliest pioneers of settlement.

gopher snake. A large harmless snake, *Drymarchon corias couperi,* of the southern states, which when pursued often takes refuge in a gopher (sense **1.**) hole. Also the bull snake *q.v.* Cf. **indigo snake.**

1837 WILLIAMS *Florida* 68 The Bull Snake . . . is sometimes called the Gopher snake. **1889** *Cent.* 2577/1 Gopher, . . . a snake, *Spilotes couperi.* **1948** *Atlantic Mo.* Feb. 88/1 We acquired the hog-nosed viper and the gopher snake and the ringneck, and a dozen or more assorted reptiles.

∗**gopher wood.** The southern yellowwood, *Cladrastis lutea.* — **1884** SARGENT *Rep. Forests* 57 *Cladrastis tinctoria.* . . . Yellow Wood. Yellow Ash. Gopher Wood. **1931** MATTOON *Forest Trees Okla.* 82 The yellow wood, also called gopher wood, is one of the rarest and most beautiful trees of the American forest.

Gore breed. [f. Christopher *Gore* (1758–1827).] A breed of long-horned cattle once popular in Massachusetts. *Obs.* — **1865** *Maine Bd. Agric. Rep.* X. 196 This animal [born in 1792] was the progenitor of the cattle which became so much talked of for years, in Massachusetts, as 'the Gore breed.'

∗**gorge,** *n.* Short for **ice gorge.** See also **fish gorge.** — **1852** *Knickerb.* XL. 154 The Licking added *her* tribute very modestly to the total, which, not now estopped . . . by the 'gorge' on the bar, went booming by. **1887** *Courier-Journal* 20 Jan. 3/5 There is very little ice in the river owing to the gorge above at Grassy Flats.

∗ **gorge,** *v. intr.* Of floating ice, or of a river with floating ice in it: To form into an ice gorge, to become blocked by ice. Also **gorged,** *a.*

EDD records ∗*goor, v.* "Of streams: to become choked with masses of ice and snow in a thaw."

1852 *Knickerb.* XL. 153 Accumulated waters and ice of incredible thickness, . . . finding no outlet below, and eddied up stream by the gorged water, dashed across the river. *Ib.,* 157 After an hour's plunging through the ice, which had accumulated in such masses as almost to 'gorge,' we came to where it lay. **1873** BEADLE *Undevel. West* 738 The ice . . . gorged against a bluff bank in a short bend of the stream, and dammed the water. **1887** *Courier-Journal* 20 Jan. 3/5 The river has gorged at Wolf's creek below here.

gorilla gəˈrɪlə, *n.* [App. an African name. See note.]

This word, the name given by Hanno's African interpreters to the wild, hairy creatures found by the Carthaginian admiral in the Sierra Leone region of West Africa about 500 B.C., is preserved in the accusative plural form *gorillas* in the Greek translation of Hanno's account of his voyage. It is not clear what the creatures found by Hanno were.

1. The largest of the manlike apes, found chiefly in forest regions of West Africa from the Cameroons to the Congo River.

1847 T. S. SAVAGE in *Boston Jrnl. Nat. Hist.* V. 419 The specific name, *gorilla,* has been adopted, a term used by Hanno, in describing the 'wild men' found on the coast of Africa, probably one of the species of the Orang. **1849** *Amer. Jrnl. Science* 2 Ser. VIII. 141 For the first recognition of gorilla (Engé-ena of the natives of Gaboon) as a new species, the scientific world is indebted to Dr. Thomas S. Savage. **1867** *Amer. Naturalist* I. 177 The Gorilla. . . . New England has the honor of having discovered this celebrated ape. The first specimen was brought to Boston by Dr. Savage. It was discovered by Professor Jeffries Wyman, and named by him after the wild men (*gorillae*) which Hanno mentions. **1949** *Reader's Digest* April 65/2 The supreme animal thinkers unquestionably are the three Great Apes—the orangutan, chimpanzee and gorilla.

2. (*cap.*) *transf.* A vituperative nickname applied to Abraham Lincoln during the Civil War. *Obs.* Cf. **Illinois gorilla.**

1861 *Richmond* (Va.) *Dispatch* 13 Nov. 3/3 He was long detained in Washington, having interviews with Abe, the Gorilla; Seward, the

Raven; and Feathers Scott. **1881–5** McClellan *Own Story* 152 The extreme virulence with which he abused the President, the administration, and the Republican party. . . . [Stanton] never spoke of the President in any other way than as the 'original gorilla.'

b. As a general term of contempt for a person; in modern use, a highwayman or thug. *Slang.*

1869 Mark Twain *Innocents* iii. 36 Who is that spider-legged gorilla yonder with the sanctimonious countenance? **1910** *N. Eng. Mag.* July 587/1 The 'gorilla,' the strong-arm highwayman, . . . holds up people on the roadside and relieves them of their valuables. **1947** *Chi. Tribune* 2 Nov. (Comics) 11 When the plane rolled to a stop 'The Head's' gorillas hid it under some bushes and took Jack into custody.

go-round, *n.*

1. A merry-go-round. Also attrib.

1886 *Harper's Mag.* July 172/2 The rink and the go-round opposite the hotel were in full tilt. *Ib.* 174/1 The rink band opposite kept up a lively competition, grinding out its go-round music.

2. The action of going around; a fistic bout or quarrel. *Colloq.*

1891 Wilkins *N. Eng. Nun* 382 All this go-round [to find a lost person]. **1898** Westcott *D. Harum* xvi, 'Me an' him had a little go-round to-day.' 'You hain't had no words, hev ye?'

Gortonian gɔrˈtonɪən, *n.* A member of a short-lived sect founded by Samuel Gorton (*c*1600–1677). *Obs.*

1674 Josselyn *Two Voyages* 259 Samuel Gorton of Warwick-shire, . . . the Author of the Sects of Gortinians [*sic*], banish'd Plimouth plantation [in 1638]. **1773** *Hist. Brit. Dominions N. Amer.* II. 275 The Muggletonians are extinct. . . . The Gortonians of Warwick in Rhode Island were of short duration. **1883** Schaff *Religious Encycl.* II. 891/1 The 'Gortonians' . . . 'contemned a clergy and all outward forms, held that by union with Christ believers partook of the perfection of God, that Christ is both human and divine, and that heaven and hell have no existence save in the mind.'

Gortonist ˈgɔrtn̩ɪst, *n.* = prec. *Obs.*

*a***1649** Winthrop *Hist.* II. 340 The Gortonists of Shaomett. . . began to consider how they might make their peace with us. **1654** Johnson *Wonder-w. Prov.* 8 The Gortonists, . . . deny the Humanity of Christ, and most blasphemously and proudly professe themselves to be personally Christ. **1767** Hutchinson *Hist. Mass.* II. 3 Baptists, quakers, Gortonists, &c. preferred complaints against the [Mass.] colony. **1771** E. Stiles in *R.I. Hist. Soc. Coll.* II. 19 Mr. John Angell . . . is not a Quaker, nor Baptist, nor Presbyterian, but a Gortonist.

* **gosh,** *interj.* Euphemistic for *God*, used in various phrases and combs. *Colloq.*

For additional combs. and phrases of this kind see *D.N.* V.

1832 *Boston Transcript* 15 Feb. 1/1 Oh, gosh-a-mighty! trike a poor black fellow on de shin! **1857** *Lawrence* (Kans.) *Republican* 2 July 4 'Gosh all Potomac!' exclaimed our Yankee. **1865** Trowbridge *Three Scouts* xii. 126 Gosh all hemlock! . . . won't ye never stop twittin' a feller? **1917** McCutcheon *Green Fancy* 19, I want to get a good square peep at a man who . . . is boob enough to come to this gosh-awful place. **1921** Hebert *40 Yrs. Prospecting* 11 Fred Dorrington, you are a gosh burned son of a gun! **1947** *N.Y. Times Mag.* 2 Feb. 18/4 We would get the most gosh-awful jerk this side of a Salem witch hanging.

b. *By guess and by gosh*, a mild form of *by guess and by God q. v., s. v.* * **God 5.** (3). *Colloq.*

1947 *Nat. Geog. Mag.* Sep. 326/2 The long sand trail needs one who can drive by guess and by gosh and feel cheerful in the midst of seeming chaos. **1948** *Savings News* Jan. 6/1 Corn farming, 400 years after the Indians had revealed it was still a by-guess and by-gosh gamble.

* **Goshen,** *n.* Used to designate (1) **butter** and (2) **cheese** produced at Goshen, N.Y. *Obs.*

(1) **1814** *Niles' Reg.* VI. 67/2 Ten waggon loads of *Goshen butter* arrived at Charleston, S.C. **1867** *Harper's Wkly.* 4 May 277/4 The agricultural productions, trade, etc., are ridiculously disproportionate to its area, the former comprising principally ice-bergs and snow-drifts, and the latter amounting annually to considerably less than the 'Goshen butter' or 'Queens County milk' trade. — (2) **1818** J. Palmer *Travels U.S.* 443 Philadelphia General Price Current. . . . Cheese, Goshen. **1840** *N.O. Picayune* 9 Oct. 2/6 Landing from ships Orleans and Gor. Troup: . . . 80 kegs Goshen Butter . . . 40 boxes Goshen cheese.

Gosiute ˈgoʃut, *n.* Usu. *pl.* (See quot. 1919.)

1864 *Virginia* (Nev.) *Bul.* 29 April 3/2 The hostile Goshute lay concealed behind rocks, waiting with rifle in hand, to slay the driver of the coach and passengers. **1919** Wilson *White Indian* 220 Gosiutes. . . . Name given to scattered bands of Indians living in the deserts of western Utah and eastern Nevada. 'Go' in this Indian dialect is said to mean desert or waste place; hence *Gosiutes* would mean desert Utes. **1947** DeVoto *Across Wide Missouri* 432 Ethnologists lump most of the others together (and loosely) as Gosiutes (in Utah) and Paiutes (in Nevada).

attrib. **1948** *Sat. Ev. Post* 23 Oct. 25/3 Word came one day that the Indians on the Goshute Reservation had been ordered to register for the draft.

goslet ˈgɑzlɪt, *n.* [Dim. of **goose.*] A pygmy goose, genus *Nettapus*, having certain attributes of a duck. *Obs.* — **1885** Kingsley *Riverside Nat. Hist.* IV. 142 A few diminutive species of geese, the so-called goslets (*Nettepus*).

* **gosling,** *n.*

1. *Stock exchange.* A person unable to pay his obligations. *Slang.*

1870 Medbery *Men Wall St.* 136 *Gosling*, a Lame Goose. **1885** *Harper's Mag.* Nov. 842/2 In that event [being caught by worthless securities] he [the broker] runs the risk of classification as a 'gosling,' or a 'lame duck,' who cannot meet his engagements, or a 'dead duck,' who is absolutely bankrupt.

2. The American pasqueflower, *Anemone ludoviciana.*

1893 *Amer. Folk-Lore* VI. 136 *Anemone patens*, gosling. **1937** *Range Plant Handbook* W159/2 The large downy-hairy buds suggest baby fowl to children who often call them goslings.

* **gospel,** *n.* In combs.: (1) **gospel army,** the body of Christian believers, *colloq.;* (2) **bishop,** a clergyman, *obs.;* (3) **grinder,** a preacher who regularly grinds out a sermon, *rare;* (4) **hunt,** a camp-meeting, *rare;* (5) **lot,** (see quot.), *obs.;* (6) **magistrate,** in the Massachusetts Bay colony, a magistrate opposed to the antinomianism of Anne Hutchinson (*c*1590–1643); (7) **mill,** a jocular or slang term for a church; (8) **preaching,** an evangelistic type of preaching; (9) **shark,** a preacher, *slang;* (10) **sharp,** = prec.; (11) **song,** a church song characterized by its fervor or evangelistic message; (12) **train,** *fig.* the train on which are all those bound for heaven; (13) **wagon,** a wagon used by an itinerant preacher.

(1) **1898** Dunbar *Folks from Dixie* Cries of 'Bless de Lawd, one mo' recruit fu de Gospel ahmy.' — (2) **1788** *Independent Chron.* (Boston) 6 Nov. 1/3 The Rev. Ezra Conant, on the 20th ult. was ordained a Gospel Bishop, and received the pastoral charge of the Church of Christ, in Winchester. — (3) **1876** Besant & Rice *Golden Butterfly* I. 150 The high tides and the low tides keep us fresh. Else we should be as stagnant as a Connecticut gospel-grinder in his village location. — (4) **1857** Underhill & Thompson *Elephant Club* 133 The presiding officers of the gospel-hunt were to be of a sable complexion.

(5) **1859** Bartlett 176 *Gospel Lot*, a lot set apart in new townships for a church, on the same principle as a school lot. New York. — (6) **1720** D. Neal *Hist. N.-Eng.* I. 167 There was such an Interest made against the next Election of Magistrates for the Massachuset Colony, to get in *Gospel-Magistrates*, as they call them, that they were forced to adjourn the Court to New-Town, for Fear of a Riot. — (7) **1872** Mark Twain *Roughing It* xlvii. 331 'Are you the duck that runs the gospel-mill next door?' — (8) **1868** M. H. Smith *Sunshine & Shadow* 142 But for 'gospel preaching' as it is called, one sermon a day is as much as our people care to hear, and more than they inwardly digest. — (9) **1897** *Scribner's Mag.* Dec. 723/1 Gospel sharks we know, and camp cooks, and honest Jew pedlers. **1920** Hunter *Trail Drivers Texas* I. 257 Fightin' Parson Potter, a reformed gambler, . . . [is] now a regular *gospel shark.*

(10) **1872** M. Twain *Roughing It* xlvii. 333 'What we want is a gospel-sharp. See?' 'A what?' 'Gospel-sharp. Parson.' **1897** A. H. Lewis *Wolfville* 50, I've took the trouble to bring a gospel-sharp over from Tucson to do the marryin'. **1902** C. Morris *Stage Confidences* 224 The driver with the . . . unlimited assurance of the Western hack-man remarked genially: 'Madame Elize, there's another gospel-sharp out on the edge of town.' — (11) **1905** *Methodist Rev.* LXXXVII. 704 The attitude to take toward the sort of tune . . . variously denominated, 'gospel song,' 'spiritual song,' 'pennyroyal,' has cost the Commission a good deal of vexation of spirit. — (12) **1943** Benét *Western Star* 5 So, when the gospel train pulls out And God calls 'All aboard!' Will you be there with the Lord, brother? . . . — (13) **1929** E. W. Howe *Plain People* 290 The other day I encountered a man preaching from a Gospel Wagon.

gospelizing peddler. (See quot.) *Rare.* — *a***1870** Chipman *Notes on Bartlett* 176 *Gospelizing Pedler.*—An itinerant, or other, preacher of the gospel. An Idler at a tavern, having vainly sought to lead a clergyman to avow his being such, said at last: 'But, anyhow, aint you one of these gospelizing pedlers?' The occurrence was early in 1842 and at Greenwich, Mass.

gospo ˈgɑspo, *n.* [Poss. based on **Gossypium*, the genus to which cotton belongs.] A compound of lard and cottonseed oil. *Obs.* — **1894** *Cong. Rec.* App. 21 July 1085/1 Honest dealing was to be enforced and the people permitted to buy pure gospo, instead of an alleged 'impure mixture injurious to health and fraudulently branded.'

goss gɔs, *n.*[1] [?Var. of ∗*Cos.*] The Cos lettuce. Also **goss cabbage.** *Obs.* — **1774** *Boston Ev. Post* 4 April (Th.), [Susannah Renken sells garden seeds including] white goss, early green goss, large green goss, bloody goss, Aleppo goss. *Ib.* 11 April (Th.), Green and white goss Cabbage [seeds].

goss gɔs, *n.*[2] [See note.]

Of obscure, but prob. not Amer., origin. *OED* records *gos* as an obs. form of *goose*, and *EDD* has "*to get goose*, to get a good scolding." Also *EDD* VI. *s.v. goss* has the phrase *as tough as goss*, very tough indeed.

Used in phrases (see quots.) in the sense of a severe scolding or other harsh treatment. *Colloq.*

1840 *N.O. Picayune* 29 July 2/4 Six victims to report this morning—nothing important—offences trivial—loafing and drunkenness. Some of them got *gos*, and some got nothing. **1844** Cist *Cincinnati Misc.* 13, I incurred . . . the displeasure of the proprietors of that house, and was informed . . . that I should catch goss, on the first suitable opportunity. **1859** *No. Californian* (Union) 2 Mar. 1/2 Ef I don't the old man (the Judge) will give me goss. **1914** Applegate *Recollections Boyhood* (1934) 60 The joke was on Andy, and 'Give her goss, Andy,' was a favorite joke among the boys long after.

∗ **gossamer,** *n.* A thin waterproof coat or cloak. *Obs.*

1882 Rittenhouse *Maud* 94 Will and I got to the hill and there, in gossamer, shawl, and under umbrella we sat till my feet were soaked. **1894** *Outing* Feb. 381/1 *n.*, Be sure to have a mackintosh or gossamer with you, for health depends a good deal upon keeping dry. **1902** Clapin 209 *Gossamer.* In the East, a waterproof cloak.

gossip mill. A newspaper or place by or from which gossip is disseminated. *Colloq.* — **1875** Stowe *We & Neighbors* 292 Here are four or five big dailies running the general gossip-mill for these great United States. **1887** Custer *Tenting on Plains* v. 178 Not being with those who daily congregated at the sutler's store, the real 'gossip-mill' of the garrison, he heard but little of what was going on.

gostration gɑˈstreʃən, *n.* The action of putting on airs. *Obs.* — **1840** *Cong. Globe* 20 July 545/2 Why have we witnessed sundry manifestations of what must here, I suppose, be called chivalry, but which, in the hoosier State, the boys would call *gostration? Ib.* 11 April 1556/1 With the blustering gostration of the cock [he] would scare the enemy to death without a fight and save his powder.

∗ **Gotham,** *n.* A nickname for New York City.

Usu. accredited to the authors of *Salmagundi*, who used it in allusion to certain inhabitants of New York who were regarded as wiseacres.

[**1806** *Lancaster* (Pa.) *Intelligencer* 6 May (Th.), The Man of Gotham, who prints the Freeman's Journal [published in Philadelphia], won't credit the Appointment.] **1807** Irving *Salmagundi* xvii. 456 They all capered toward the devoted city of Gotham. **1883** *Pall Mall Gaz.* 9 July, John Jacob [Astor] has become, chiefly by the appreciation of the values of the property purchased by his father and grandfather, one of the three phenomenally rich men of Gotham. **1946** *Chi. Sun Book Week* 2 June 3/4 The lights of the city gleamed with impersonal brilliance on the good folk of Gotham hurrying home to their firesides and air-conditioned penthouses for the night.

Gothamic gɑˈθæmɪk, *a.* Of or pertaining to New York City. *Obs.* — **1851** A. O. Hall *Manhattaner* 39 The layers of mud are ten times worse in pedestrial effect than Gothamic or Bostonian deposits of snow and ice.

∗ **Gothamite,** *n.* An inhabitant of New York City.

1807 Irving *Salmagundi* xvii. 460 Whereat the Gothamites . . . marvelled exceedinglie. **1852** *Lantern* (N.Y.) I. 111/1 On behalf of the Gothamites Diogenes returns thanks for the compliment he has paid them of making this city his . . . *head* quarters. **1944** *Chi. D. News* 10 July 8/1 Hizzoner 'Butch' La Guardia . . . delivered a broadcast to his fellow Gothamites.

Gothamitis ˌgɑθəmˈaɪtɪs, *n.* Excessive fondness for New York City. *Obs.* — **1925** O. P. White *Them Was Days* 144 The disease soon became known as 'Gothamitis.'

∗ **gothic,** *n.* *Printing.* (See quots.)

1889 *Cent.* 2582/3 What is called simply *gothic* in America is known in England as *grotesque*, and lighter faces known in England as *sans-serif* are in America called *gothic condensed, light-face gothic*, etc. **1937** *Manual of Style* 213 *Gothic* is perfectly plain, with lines of uniform thickness and without serifs. It is sometimes known as *block letter.* **1949** *Ib.* 270 *Gothic* or *sans serif* is perfectly plain, with lines of uniform thickness and without serifs.

go-to-meeting, *a.* and *n.*

1. *n.* A garment suitable for wearing to church on Sunday. *Colloq.* Cf. **Sunday-go-to-meeting.**

1841 *Chi. Morn. Democrat* 26 Feb. 2/1 Their Servant's a regular 'Miss Nancy with her go-to-meetings on.' **1878** Cooke *Happy Dodd* 70 Why, Miss Rice she didn't never have more'n one caliker gown to her name, an' an old alipacky for a go-to-meeting. **1881** ——— *Somebody's Neighbors* 265 He had gone and his shirts an' go-to-meetin's too.

2. *a.* Suitable for use on Sunday or other special occasions. *Colloq.* Cf. **Sunday-go-to-meeting.**

1787 Tyler *Contrast* (1790) III. i, All my tunes [are] go to meeting tunes. **1800** Fessenden *Orig. Poems* (1806) 115 Each scrapes, huzzas, and kicks and bounces, Waves high her go-to-meeting cap. **1848** Durivage & Burnham *Stray Subjects* 77 [The devil] suggested to them the idea of having a ride in the 'go-to-meetin' ' sleigh. **1870** F. Fern *Ginger-Snaps* 59, I should keep my best bonnet in a bandbox under my desk, for any sudden dress emergency, as do editors their go-to-meetin' hats. *Ib.* 303 What an all-over consciousness of 'go-to-meetin' ' fixins, in every lineament and limb! **1937** Wilson *Aroostook* 41 Housewives learned the expedience of potato starch—how to grate raw potatoes, leave the pulp standing in cold water, drain the water for use as a final rinsing for Sunday shirts and go-to-meeting dresses.

b. Of persons: Church-going.

1853 *Harper's Mag.* VII. 562/2 As a matter of course, he was looked up to with emulation, if not astonishment, by the 'go-to-meeting' young folk of the town. **1868** G. G. Channing *Recoll. Newport* 83, I was quite a go-to-meeting lad.

go-to-mill bag. A bag used for taking corn to the mill to be ground. *Obs.* Cf. **meal bag.** — **1829** Royall *Pennsylvania* I. 96 She had no baggage but a bag about the size of our old go-to-mill bags.

∗ **gouge,** *n.*

1. The action of gouging out an opponent's eye in a fight. *Obs.* Cf. ∗ **gouge,** *v.* **1.**

1787 Attmore *Jrnl.* 43 Womble, one of the disputants declared 'I cannot fight without a Gouge.' One of the company supported his declaration saying 'Ay! A Gouge all weathers.' **1843** Poe *Works* IV. 117 'Oh my golly!' . . . roared the terrified Jupiter, placing his hand upon his right organ of vision, . . . as if in immediate dread of his master's attempt at a gouge.

2. A place that appears to have been gouged out; a corner, the eroded bank of a river bend. *Colloq.*

1804 Clark in *Lewis & C. Exped.* I. (1904) 159 At Daylight proceeded on to the Gouge of this Great bend [of the Missouri R. near Ft. Thompson]. **1853** P. Kennedy *Blackwater Chron.* viii. 103 About half a mile up we halted by the little Elk-lick—a deep and wood-embosomed *gouge*—as the hunters called it. **1873** Phelps *Trotty's Wedding* xii, It was so dark in the *gouge* where the bed stood. **1913** London *Valley of the Moon* III xxii, It's a gouge into his land, for he owns everything on three sides of it.

b. *Mining.* (See quot. 1881.)

1876 Raymond *8th Rep. Mines* 107 It is incased in well-defined walls of metamorphic slate, with a few inches of gouge between the walls and quartz. **1881** ——— *Mining Glossary, Gouge*, a layer of soft material along the wall of a vein, favoring the miner, by enabling him after 'gouging' it out with a pick, to attack the solid vein from the side.

3. A stamping tool.

1843 Carlton *New Purchase* II. 32 [The blacksmith] even made the steel gouges for stamping names on his own work. **1875** Knight 997/1.

4. The action of stealing; hence a fraud, robbery, trick. *Colloq.*

1845 *N.Y. Tribune* 10 Dec. (B.), R—— and H—— will probably receive from Mr. Polk's administration $100,000 more than respectable printers would have done the work for. This is a clean plain gouge of this sum out of the people's strong box. **1887** *American* XIV. 344 Another 'gouge' was to charge the women a nominally cost price per spool for the thread furnished them.

b. A person who gouges, a cheat, impostor. *Slang.*

1877 Burdette *Rise of Mustache* 298 Billinger says he knew he would get the law on the old gouge if he held on long enough.

∗ **gouge,** *v.*

1. *tr.* In fighting, orig. to force (an opponent's eye) from its socket with the thumb, now to thrust the thumb in an opponent's eye. Also absol.

1779 Anburey *Travels* (1789) II. 347, I was shewn a gentleman of the town . . . who had the misfortune to have one of his eyes gouged out. **1797** *Mass. Spy* 12 July (Th.), [The Georgians] can keep Negro slaves, race horses, gouge out eyes . . . and be honored in the land. **1903** Fox *Little Shepherd* ii, 'He don't fight fair,' said Chad, panting, and rubbing his right eye, which his enemy had tried to 'gouge.' **1948** *Sat. Ev. Post* 26 June 81/1 He gouges, bites and scratches, and sometimes even hits in the clinches.

b. With a person as direct object.

a **1793** Freneau *Poems* (1809) II. 98 The Gougers: On seeing a traveller gouged, and otherwise ill treated by some citizens of Logtown, near a pine barren. **1848** Durivage & Burnham *Stray Subjects* 73 He was gouged and bit to death In a fight in Illinois.

c. *intr.* To make a quick, sharp movement as if to gouge.

1863 *Cong. Globe* 28 Feb. 1373/1 If, like a pen of ill-managed cattle, one gouges one way, and one another, how are we to come together?

2. To spur a horse. *Rare.* Cf. ∗**gouging,** *n.* **2.**

1843 *Knickerb.* III. 32 He gouged his old horse, who wriggled, shot forward, and curled it so rapidly, that all which remained visible of him was a dark streak.

3. To cheat or defraud. *Colloq.*

1842 UNCLE SAM *Peculiarities* I. 118 The receiver of goods gouged by domestic helps from their bosses. **1904** LORIMER *Old Gorgon Graham* 120 We stood to lose a little over a million apiece right there, and no knowing what the crowd that was under the market would gouge us for in the end. **1948** *Calif. Citrograph* April 177/3 The canners gouged the growers pretty badly.

gouger ˈgaʊdʒɚ, *n.*

1. One who gouges out an opponent's eyes in fighting. *Obs.* Cf. **Carolina, Virginia gouger.**

*a*1793 [see **gouge,** *v.* **1. b.**]. **1812** PAULDING *J. Bull & Bro. Jon.* xviii. 93 When the trader got home, he . . . would tell terrible stories of the Southlanders being gougers. **1843** CARLTON *New Purchase* II. 158 Rowdy Bill, be it known, was famous as a gouger.

2. One who gouges another for his money, a shyster, a "fixer." *Slang.*

1819 QUITMAN in Claiborne *Life Quitman* 42, I have joined a society, composed chiefly of young lawyers (here called 'Gougers'). **1900** ADE *More Fables* 12 Perceiving that the Race-Track was in the hands of Gougers, Uncle Brewster walked back to the Hotel. **1917** *Nation* 1 Oct., The price boosters, the gougers who are making fortunes on war prices, are forcing the predicted famine.

3. (See quots.)

1889 *Cent.* 2583/2 Gouger . . . the bow oar of a flatboat. (Mississippi river and tributaries.) **1903** *Sci. Amer.* 3 Jan. 8 Then came the heavier device known as the 'gouger'—a strongly built box car with an immense flat scraper at its head, set sufficiently low to enable it to run under and into the snow like a wedge, and supplemented by wings set upon hinges and designed to assist in widening the opening made by the prow.

∗**gouging,** *n.*

1. In a fight, the action of forcing an opponent's eye from its socket with the thumb. Also attrib.

1774 FITHIAN *Journal* I. 243 Every diabolical Stratagem for Mastery is allowed. . . . Scratching, . . . Biting, Butting, . . . Gouging. **1832** FERRALL *Ramble* 169 One of the gentlemen demanded of another if there had not been a 'gouging scrape' at the 'Colonel's Tavern' the evening before. **1902** WHITE *Blazed Trail* 186 In a free-for-all knock-down-and-drag-out, kicking, gouging, and biting are all legitimate. Anything to injure the other man, provided always you do not knife him. **1947** *Sat. Ev. Post* 8 March 20/3 Saloon doors snapped open, men tumbled out, locked and gouging or whaling away, and no one looked.

b. Taking unfair advantage, as in a business deal.

1851 *Ore. Statesman* 30 Sep. 2/5 They charge the government officers three and five hundred per cent more for work they do for them, thus gouging both ways. **1946** *Pueblo* (Colo.) *Chieftain* 3 July 1/1 Rents were climbing in many sections—there were reports of rent gouging in some cases.

2. Spurring a horse. *Rare.* Cf. ∗**gouge,** *v.* **2.**

1875 *Chi. Tribune* 22 July 5/3 [The horse races] were conducted, as was evident to those to whom the 'pulling' and gouging of the day before had rendered watchful, entirely upon the square.

3. *Mining.* The action of taking out small quantities of ore, as with a gouge.

1876 RAYMOND *8th Rep. Mines* 314 Excepting a little 'gouging' done by lessees, the Home Stake . . . has been idle during the year.

4. (See quot. 1902.)

1886 DORSEY *Midshipman Bob* 241 Of all academic vices, 'gouging' is the most despised and most severely punished. **1902** CLAPIN 210 *Gouging,* at the Naval Academy of Annapolis, dishonesty in work, as for instance the copying as one's own of a theme written by another.

∗**gouging,** *a.* Who squeezes or presses out an opponent's eye. *Obs.* — **1796** *Gazette of U. S.* (N.Y.) 10 May (Th.), Brave Abraham, despising railleries, In presence of the House and galleries, Dar'd tell them all, in valiant trim, That gouging Gunn had challenged him. **1825** PAULDING *J. Bull. in Amer.* i. 2, I also fully believed that the people were a bundling, gouging, drinking, spitting, impious race.

goujon ˈgudʒən, *n.* [La. F. in same sense.] (See quots.)

1883 *Nat. Museum Bul.* No. 27, 491 *Leptops olivaris*. . . . Mud Cat; . . . Goujon. Ohio and Mississippi Valleys. . . . It is much used as food. **1884** GOODE *Fisheries* I. 628 The 'Mud Cat,' 'Yellow Cat,' 'Goujon,' or 'Bashaw' is found in all the large rivers of the West and South. **1947** DALRYMPLE *Panfish* 290 Many are the colloquial names for it—Yellow Cat, Mud-Cat, Morgan Cat, Shovelhead Cat, Flatbelly, Nigger-belly, Goujon.

∗**gourd,** *n.* In combs.: (1) **gourd corn,** a variety of corn, *obs.*, cf. (6) below; (2) **dipper,** a water dipper made of a gourd, also, rarely, **gourd-shell dipper,** cf. **dipper, drinking gourd;** (3) **fiddle,** a crude fiddle made of a gourd, *colloq.;* (4) **head,** (see quots.); (5) **sawyer,** one who snores or "saws gourds," *colloq.;* (6) **seed,** see as a main entry; (7) **-seed sucker,** the black horse or Missouri sucker, *Cycleptus elongatus;* (8) **vine,** the plant that bears gourds.

(1) **1802** DRAYTON *S. Carolina* 137 It consists of several varieties, of which the gourd and flint corn, are principally planted. The difference betwixt these kinds of corn, are, that the *gourd* is flowery, and wastes much in the grinding; whereas the *flint* is more hard and nourishing, and grinds more into grist. — (2) **1850** JUDD *R. Edney* xli. 406 The gourd-dipper,—how often had he dipped water with it, and held it by both hands to drink! **1868** *Harper's Mag.* Mar. 542/1 [We] asked for a drink of water. We were plentifully supplied from a gourd-shell dipper. **1948** *Popular Western* June 76/1 There were a dozen tables, a bar, an *olla* of fresh water with a gourd dipper, and strings of peppers everywhere. — (3) **1858** D. K. BENNETT *Chron. N.C.* 102 'Gourd fiddles' were then in vogue, 'puncheon floors,' and 'corn-stalk bows!' **1945** BOTKIN *My Burden* 114 Some nigger women go back to the quarters and git the gourd fiddles and the clapping bones made outen beef ribs. — (4) **1909** WEBSTER 935 *Gourdhead,* or *gourdhead buffalo.* The buffalo fish *Ictiobus cyprinella. Louisiana.* **1917** *Birds of Amer.* I. 178 Wood Ibis. *Mycteria americana*. . . . [Also called] Goard, or Gourd, Head.

(5) **1892** DUVAL *Young Explorers* 204 Many's the night I've got up at taverns and other places where I've been stoppin' and gone and slept under a tree, fur no reason in the 'vasal world but because they had put one of these gourd sawyers in the room with me. — (7) **1884** GOODE *Fisheries* I. 615 [The] 'Gourd-seed Sucker' . . . is found chiefly in the river channels of the Ohio and Mississippi. — (8) **1856** *Rep. Comm. Patents 1855: Agric.* 66 Mr. George Sunday next tried the bloom of the gourd-vine with better success. **1892** *Harper's Mag.* LXXXIV. 936/2 A boot-shaped bottle of 'hair-ile' . . . for potency of perfume put both gourd-vine and jimson-weed to shame.

b. *gourd of hog's lard,* a derisive name for a fat person. *Rare.*

1835 LONGSTREET *Ga. Scenes* 127 If he'd o' been in his place, it would o' flung Bostwick right where that gourd o' hog's lard was.

c. In phrases of obvious meaning. *Colloq.* See also *to saw gourds, s.v.* ∗**saw,** *v.*

1851 *Polly Peablossom* 31 They'll never make gourds out o' me [i.e., swindle me]. **1902** HARBEN *A. Daniel* 87, I'm as green as a gourd in business matters.

As the last term in **darning, dipper, fat, martin, powder, prairie, punger, salt, soap gourd.**

gourde gurd, *n.* [See note.] (See quot. 1931.)

Prob. F. *gourde* (f. *piastre gourde*), a coin. The story in Read *La.-French,* p. 41 (based on an account by John W. Vandercook) is interesting but unaccompanied by substantiating evidence.

1858 in SIMMONDS *Dict. Trade.* **1880** CABLE *Grandissimes* xxviii. 227 Bras-Coupé . . . in six months was the most valuable man ever bought for gourde dollars. **1931** READ *La.-French* 41 Gourde. . . . In South Louisiana *gourde,* 'gourd,' is used with the value of 'dollar.'

∗**gourdseed,** *n.* A variety of corn. In full **gourdseed corn.** Cf. **Virginia gourdseed.**

1780 DUNBAR *Life* 73 Planted white Corn & goard Seed Corn. **1819** THOMAS *Travels* 101 The gourd seed corn is generally cultivated. . . . The ears of this kind of corn are thick; and the grains so crowded as to be elongated like the seed of the gourd or calabash. **1870** *Rep. Comm. Agric.* 271 In the last made furrows the corn—a gourd-seed, red cob variety— . . . was drilled in, at distances of ten inches. **1947** *Ann. Mo. Botanical Garden* Feb. 15 The commonest name for these soft dents was 'Gourdseed,' since the flat kernels with a collapsed and more or less pointed tip resembled a pumpkin seed or gourd seed.

∗**government,** *n.*

1. Formerly at Harvard, the faculty or the college faculty. *Obs.* Cf. ∗**faculty.**

1787 in HALL *College Words* (1851) 149 The Government of college met. And Willard ruled the stern debate. **1812** in R. T. PAINE *Works* p. xxix, Paine was graduated with the esteem of the government and the regard of his contemporaries. **1861** in *Pub. Col. Soc.* XXVII. 67 The Government wishing to put an end to all such convivial meetings, and having effected their purpose with the present sophomores, forbade the class from joining in the said supper.

2. (See quot.) *Rare.*

1809 KENDALL *Travels* III. 253 Mr. attorney, for the government, (and of whom his adversaries spoke by the name of *the government,*) insisted that enough was before the honourable court to justify a commitment.

3. *pl.* Government securities.

1865 *Balt. D. Commercial* 4 Oct. 1/1 Governments were steady, as were also City 6's and railroad bonds. **1870** *N.Y. Herald* 12 July 9/2 The home market for governments was lower but firm. **1948** *Green Bay* (Wis.) *Press-Gazette* 12 July 22/1 U.S. governments held steady.

4. In combs.: (1) **government account,** used with *on* in the sense of "on behalf of the government," *rare;* (2) **bank,** a bank conducted under government auspices as distinguished from a private bank, *rare;* (3) **bond,** (*a*) a bond issued by the republic of Texas, *obs.*, (*b*) a bond issued by the U.S. Government, also attrib.; (4) **crib,** *fig.* the treasury of the federal government, *colloq.;* (5) * **house,** see as a main entry; (6) **note,** a note or bond issued by the federal government; (7) **price,** a price set by Congress, esp. with reference to government land, since 1820, $1.25 an acre, cash; (8) **road,** a road built or maintained by the government, cf. **federal road;** (9) **sixes,** (see quot.); (10) **survey,** (*a*) a field study made under federal auspices, (*b*) a survey or record of survey of public lands made by the U.S. Government; (11) **train,** *W.* a caravan of wagons in the service of the federal government.

(1) **1809** A. HENRY *Travels* 58 Here . . . was kept a small garrison, commanded by an officer . . . who managed the Indian trade here, on government account. — (2) **1841** in MACLEOD *F. Wood* 87 We need not a Government bank to regulate exchanges. — (3) (*a*) **1836** *Diplom. Corr. Texas* I. (1908) 80 B. T. Archer will leave tomorrow for Virginia, for the purpose of trying to negotiate the Government Bonds. (*b*) **1872** *Atlantic Mo.* April 516 The discussion about paying the government bonds in currency was another incident of the keen legal scent of the American politician. **1948** *Newsweek* 27 Sep. 66/2 The support of the government bond market . . . is today the principal inflationary factor in our economy. — (4) **1900** GOODLANDER *Fort Scott* 19 This I turned over to Colonel Campbell to pay for my board, so the first money I earned in Kansas was from the government crib.

(6) **1790** *Ann. 1st Congress* I. 1160, I mentioned also the case of a bond, and supposed that we were bound to the punctual payment of government notes. — (7) **1838** ELLSWORTH *Valley of Wabash* v. 51 It is found, in general, that the first two crops will pay for land at government prices. **1847** *Ind. Hist. Soc. Pub.* III. 440 In many of the townships in the poorer counties . . . the school section would not sell for the government price. — (8) **1884** *Harper's Mag.* June 105/2 [In comparison with] the government road . . . the roughest 'corduroy' would appear a brilliant . . . innovation. — (9) **1852** BRISTED *Upper Ten Th.* i. 21 He is thinking of what a good hit he made in government sixes [six per cent bonds] last week, and how comfortable the sleigh is.

(10) (*a*) **1870** *Rep. Comm. Agric. 1869* 16 Recent government surveys are also adding constantly to this accumulating stock [of plants]. (*b*) **1877** JOHNSON *Anderson Co., Kansas* 59 In the fall of 1855 and winter and spring of 1856 the government survey of the public lands was made. **1883** *Harper's Mag.* June 132/2 We do not call our hills the names they have in maps and government surveys. — (11) **1848** PARKMAN in *Knickerb.* Oct. 312 He told Coates, the master-wagoner, that the commissary at the fort had given him an order for sick-rations, directed to the master of any government train. **1852** *Harper's Mag.* Dec. 121 The government train had arrived at Fort Laramie with the goods intended for annuities to the Indians. **1860** G. T. CLARK *MS Diary* 6 Met two government trains.

b. Designating things or institutions conducted or owned by the U.S. Government, as (1) **government agency,** (2) **armory,** (3) **corral,** (4) **goods,** (5) **land,** (6) **mule,** (7) **reservation,** (8) **wagon.**

(1) **1837** IRVING *Bonneville* II. 172 [The voyagers] stopped . . . at a government agency for an Indian tribe. — (2) **1848** POLK in *Pres. Mess. & P.* IV. 581 The invention for the construction of these arms being patented, the United States can not manufacture them at the Government armories without a previous purchase of the right so to do. — (3) **1871** ROE *Army Lett.* 15 They made a wonderful turn and took us safely to the government corral. — (4) **1873** BEADLE *Undevel. West* 586 They now receive regular annuities of Government goods.

(5) **1839** MARRYAT *Diary in Amer.* I. 59 Government lands, which could only be paid for in specie, were eagerly sought after. **1939** MATSCHAT *Suwannee River* 65 But no poachin' on gov'ment land. . . . We-uns be a law-abidin' lot. — (6) **1865** in *Kans. Hist. Quart.* VII. 45 One teamster arrested for firing on road and another for stealing and selling a government mule. **1949** *Chi. Tribune* 15 Feb. 2/3 Roads which at times could hardly be negotiated by a government mule. — (7) **1923** HERRICK *Lilla* 17 She had left the wire down thoughtlessly in the upper pasture, letting the brood mares escape into the government reservation. — (8) **1848** PARKMAN in *Knickerb.* Oct. 312 Just after leaving the government wagons . . . we heard Tête Rouge's voice behind us. **1888** *Cent. Mag.* Nov. 136/1 The burning of two schooners laden with forage, and fourteen Government wagons, . . . were the precise results of this expedition.

c. Designating individuals or groups in the service of the government, as **government agent, broker, doctor, engineer, gauger, scout, surveyor, troops.**

1836 *Diplom. Corr. Texas* I. (1908) 58 Such ratification is published by the Government Agent in this city. **1851** GREEN *Twelve Days* 73 The charge against me was, that I had obtained the two hundred and fifty dollars, and the few pieces of dry goods before mentioned, by representing that I was a government agent. — **1870** MEDBERY *Men Wall St.* 35 In these chairs the Government Brokers sit. — **1916** EASTMAN *From Deep Woods* 88 No Government doctor has ever gone freely among them before. — **1883** *Harper's Mag.* July 304 The Secretary inclines . . . to place the work [the erection of a shaft] in charge of a government engineer. *Ib.* 261 [I took] notes about high wines, government gaugers [of beer], the maltsters at work [etc.]. — **1868** *N.Y. Herald* 11 July 5/5, I have just seen Lieutenant Beecher of the Third Infantry, chief of government scouts. — **1877** JOHNSON *Anderson Co., Kansas* 59 He jumped the claim made by one Card, a government surveyor. — **1866** F. KIRKLAND *Book Anecdotes* 80 The Virginia militiamen having driven Brown and his gang into the engine house, awaited anxiously the arrival of government troops.

As the last term in **bay, carpetbag, commission, federal, general, immediate, national, Negro, provisional, representative, skin, slave, state, territorial, wheelbarrow, white man's government.**

governmental ˌgʌvənˈmɛntl], *a.* Of or pertaining to the government.

1744 *Ga. Hist. Soc. Coll.* I. 96 The governmental view . . . was, with numbers of free white people, well settled to strengthen the southern part of the English settlements. **1809** *Monthly Anthology* VII. 263 *Congressional, Presidential* and *Departmental* are barbarisms, in common use, we allow; but one of the same class, *governmental*, which is equally worthless, is omitted [from Webster's Dictionary]. **1893** *Harper's Mag.* Jan. 314/2 If we could get rid of the tremendous way and governmental machinery, life would be sort of picnic.

* **government house.**

1. In New York City, a mansion erected in 1790 and intended for the residence of the Presidents of the U.S. *Obs.*

1799 in WILLIS *Convalescent* 454 The procession will move . . . through Beaver street to the Bowling-Green; round the Bowling-Green, in front of the Government House; up Broadway to St. Paul's Church.

2. In areas formerly Spanish, a building serving as the seat of government. *Obs.*

1802 ELLICOTT *Journal* 114 The [Spanish] Governor offered them the use of government house [in Natchez, Miss.]. **1808** PIKE *Sources Miss.* 212 The public square is in the centre of the town [Santa Fe] on the north side of which is situated the palace . . . or government house. **1843** MARRYAT *M. Violet* v, In the centre, the presidio, or government-house; on one side the graceful spire of a church, on the other the massive walls of a convent.

3. The official residence of a state governor. *Obs.*

1809 CUMING *Western Tour* 170 The publick buildings here [Frankfort, Ky.], are a state-house, a court-house, . . . and a government house occupied by Mr. Greenup, who now holds that office. **1837** A. SHERWOOD *Gaz. Georgia* (ed. 3) 201 The house called the *Governor*, is more properly the *Government* house. A new one is now in a state of forwardness.

* **governor,** *n.*

1. The chief of an Indian tribe or pueblo.

1705 in *Amer. Sp.* (1948) April 118/2 having some little encouragement from one of ye Sachems or Governors, I bought some Biscake in order to go up into ye Country & to settle my kinsman among them. **1808** PIKE *Sources Miss.* 219 Captain D'Almansa was waited on by the governor [of Santo Domingo, N.M.]. **1864** *Santa Fe W. New Mexican* 27 May 2/1 The party executing the order of the casiques and governors of the pueblos invariably carrying one [of the staffs] as the emblem of his authority. **1891** O'BEIRNE *Leaders Ind. Territory* 43/2 She is highly connected both on her father's and mother's side; her nephew, William Byrd, being Governor of the Chickasaw Nation.

2. The executive head of a state government.

1778 *Jrnls. Cont. Congress* X. 37 That a copy of said letter and resolutions be also transmitted to his Excellency the Governor of Virginia. **1859** *Ohio Rev. Statutes* (1860) I. 549 It shall be the duty of the governor, auditor and secretary of state, to canvass the votes cast at the annual election. **1948** *Time* 8 March 20/2 [He] easily defeated Sam Houston Jones in the Democratic runoff primary for governor.

3. The civil executive head of a territory of the U.S. or of an area under the control of the U.S.

1787 *Northwest Ordinance,* There shall be appointed, from time to time, by Congress, a governor, whose commission shall continue in force for the term of three years. **1847** *Santa Fe Republican* 11 Dec. 2/3 The Governor's Message . . . would be no discredit to one of our State governors. **1900** *Civil Code of Alaska* I. 1. 2 There shall be appointed for the district a governor.

4. In combs.: (1) **governor-elect,** a state governor who has been elected but who has not yet taken office; (2) **-'s council,** (see quot. 1889); (3) **-'s guard,** a body of soldiers serving as the escort of a governor, also **governor's foot guards;** (4) **-'s mansion,** the official residence of the governor of a state; (5) **-'s message,** a message relative to needed legislation addressed by a state governor to the legislature; (6) **Winthrop,** designating a type of combination desk and bookcase, app. in allusion to John Winthrop (1588–1649), governor of the Massachusetts colony.

(1) **1849** in STOWE *Key* 58 My term of office will expire soon, and the governor elect, Gen. William Trousdale, will take my place. **1946** *Democrat* 6 June 1/6 James E. Folsom becomes Alabama's 46th governor-elect. — (2) **1889** *Cent.* 1299/2 Governor's council, in some of the United States, a body of men designated to advise the governor, as in Massachusetts and Maine. **1922** F. A. OGG & P. O. RAY *Intro. Amer. Govt.* 636 In some states he [the lieutenant-governor] has the right . . . to serve *ex-officio* as a member of the governor's council. —(3) **1771** *Conn. Rec.* 545 Resolved by this Assembly, that . . . hereby [is] constituted a distinct military company by the name of the Governor's Guard, consisting of sixty-four in number, rank and file, to attend upon and guard the Governor and General Assembly annually on the election days and at all other times as occasion require. **1837** HAWTHORNE *Twice-told Tales* (1879) I. 14 Sir Edmund Andros and his favorite councillors . . . assembled the red-coats of the Governor's Guard, and made their appearance in the streets of Boston. **1896** *Conn. Quarterly* II. 352 Connecticut at the Atlanta Exposition: [picture with the title:] Connecticut Day: Governor's Foot Guards. — (4) **1892** M. A. JACKSON *Gen. Jackson* 473 We were . . . driven through the most retired streets to the governor's mansion. **1948** *Chickasaw* (Okla.) *D. Express* 30 June 2/7 He is at the governor's mansion recovering from a wrenched back received last weekend.

(5) **1775** in *Amer. Sp.* XX. (1945) 271 Governor's Message to the Assembly. **1838** D. D. BARNARD *Sp. in Assembly of N.Y.* p. ix, Made a report to the House on that part of the Governor's message which relates to Public Instruction. — (6) **1926** *Ladies' Home Jrnl.* Nov. 18/3 The Governor Winthrop desk helps to fit this living-dining room of the past for real use. **1944** STAFFORD *Boston Adv.* 164 The outer wall was taken up by two long casements between which stood a Governor Winthrop secretary. **1949** *Sat. Ev. Post* 5 Mar. 122/4 You'll find their card in your Governor Winthrop desk.

As the last term in **deputy, ex-, Free Soil, lieutenant, military, presidential, provisional, war governor.**

* **governorship,** *n.* The office of a state governor.

1873 *Newton Kansan* 9 Jan. 2/3 Now he . . . will step into the governorship. **1912** NICHOLSON *Hoosier Chron.* 96 'The next steps are obvious,' suggested Harwood, encouragingly—'the governorship, the United States Senate—ever onward and upward.' **1948** *Time* 30 Aug. 18/3 Last year Earl—who had been patiently raising cattle in Winn Parish and mending his fences—set boldly out to get the governorship again.

gowdy ˈgaʊdɪ, *n. To give gowdy,* an expression of uncertain origin and meaning. *Obs.* — **1856** HALL *College Words* (ed. 2) 204 The discomfited individual declares that they 'are all on a side,' and gives up, or 'rolls over' by giving his opponent 'gowdy.' **1865** *Atlantic Mo.* Nov. 521 Do you feel . . . an incipient earthquake fit, Accompanied with awful raps? But give 'em gowdy, give 'em gowdy, And it'll soon clear away.

goy-blamed ˈgɔɪˈblemd, *a.* [f. dial. * *goy,* "God"+ * *blamed.*] Goldarned, dad-blamed. *Slang. Obs.*

1832 PAULDING *Westward Ho!* I. 184 I'll be goy blamed if you would. **1838** *Knickerb.* XII. 202 But I'll try this new way before I'm a month older. 'I'm [*sic*] be goy-blamed if I don't!' **1844** *Ib.* XXIII. 296, 'I'll be goy-blamed if I do!' **1851** *Harper's Mag.* III. 572/1 Goy-blamed ef I don't think he's friz to death.

* **grab,** *n.* In combs.: (1) **grab bag,** see as a main entry; (2) **barrel,** a barrel containing small articles of varying or trifling worth, *rare;* (3) **box,** a box serving as a grab bag; (4) **game,** see as a main entry; (5) **hooking,** (see quot.); (6) **law,** prob. a slang expression used in reference to the law of attachments (*Revised Laws of N.H.,* chapter 388, sec. 1), *obs.;* (7) **loo,** a kind of grab-bag game conducted for some charitable purpose, *obs.;* (8) **mortgage,** a mortgage enabling its holder to "grab" or take possession of that which is called for in it, *obs.;* (9) **racket,** a grab game.

(2) **1905** VALENTINE *H. Sandwith* 148 Archy . . . answered ironically, surreptitiously thrusting his hand into the 'grab-barrel' of rank half-Spanish cigars. — (3) **1864** *Yale Lit. Mag.* XXIX. 208 (Th.), In one corner [of the Fair] was a fish-pond, a kind of old-fashioned grab-box. **1867** *Territorial Enterprise* (Virginia, Nev.) 16 Jan. 3/1 All who feel an interest in the Festival . . . are requested to donate articles for the fancy and refreshment tables, grab-box, etc.

(5) **1902** *Rep. Comm. Fisheries* XXVII. 276 Some of them were caught by what we call grab-hooking, which is to tie a number of hooks to a line and drag it through the water. — (6) **1854** O. OPTIC *In Doors & Out* (1876) 114 It was in the state of New Hampshire; and at the time of which I write, the 'grab law' was in force, and is still, for aught I know. One morning, as Mr. Burton returned from a journey to a neighboring town, he found his stock attached on the claim of Farmer Waxwell. **1880** *Bradstreet's* 28 Feb. 2/3 The law is practically preference-operating, resembling the 'grab law' of New Hampshire. — (7) **1851** GREEN *Twelve Days* 157 The late game of '*Grab Loo*' . . . is one of the small order of games. . . . The 'grab loo' is generally managed by one of the most impudent of the committee. — (8) **1869** S. BOWLES *Our New West* iv. 89 National banks emit their greenbacks and will 'do' your little note most graciously at from one to two per cent a month and 'a grab mortgage.' — (9) **1892** STEVENSON & OSBOURNE *Wrecker* (ed. 2) 219 Now boss! . . . is this to be run shipshape? or is it a Dutch grab-racket?

b. In colloq. phrases: (1) *To be on the grab,* to be on the alert for surreptitious gain; (2) *by grab(s),* a mild imprecation.

(1) **1887** STOCKTON *Hundredth Man* xxix, The pie-man is on the grab for it. **1909** WASON *Happy Hawkins* 34 Bill he thought I was still on the grab. — (2) **1887** *Scribner's Mag.* (F.), 'Dadgum ye!' cried Jeff irritably, 'Whut—by grabs, hit's a human critter!' **1930** HENRY *Conquer. Plains* 74 The wind began to blow, an' rain began to fall; An' it looked, by grab, like we was goin' ter lose 'em all.

As the last term in **land, nail, penny, pension, salary grab.**

* **grab,** *v. intr. To grab for,* to make a grab at (something). *Colloq.* — **1876** MARK TWAIN *Tom Sawyer* v. 56 Tom's hands itched to grab for it [a bug]. **1885** *N.Y. Weekly Sun* 13 May 5/1 He made a jump for the knife and Short grabs for it at the same time.

grab bag. At fairs or amusement places, a bag or receptacle of small articles from which one may, usu. for a small charge, make a drawing, sight unseen.

1855 M. THOMPSON *Doesticks* 135 Young woman wanted me to invest in the 'grab bag'; gave half a dollar, and fished in; got, in three times trying, a tin whistle, half a stick of candy, and a peanut done up in tissue paper. **1889** *Azusa* (Calif.) *News* 16 Nov. 3/2 The church of the future will have no grab-bag, no lotteries, no gambling and no liquor selling at its fairs. **1948** *Dly. Ardmoreite* (Ardmore, Okla.) 29 April 4/4 A full attendance was reported, and a grab bag was the main feature of the program.

transf. and *attrib.* **1879** *N.Y. Tribune* 23 Sep. 2/1 It is a grab-bag from which every disappointed politician hopes to draw a prize. **1886** *Harper's Mag.* Jan. 237 The woodman's axe now resounded with the busy notes of preparation for a dive into nature's great grab-bag. **1919** *World's Work* Feb. 370/1 The outworn, discredited grab-bag diplomacy that caused this war. **1945** *Chi. D. News* 29 May 6/3 The New York Times has taken a whack at the grab-bag boys for this, and its editorial concludes: 'Is this Congress responsible?'

* **grabber,** *n.* As the last term in **goober, land, pension, salary grabber.**

grab game. (See quot. 1859.)

1846 SAGE *Scenes Rocky Mts.* xxxii. 282 'Just as you like,' responded his two companions; 'that is, provided you wont attempt the *grab* game on us.' **1859** BARTLETT 177 *Grab Game.* A mode of swindling, or rather stealing, practised by sharpers in our large cities. Bets are made in which considerable sums of money are involved, when a dispute is purposely planned, in the midst of which one of the confederates seizes or 'grabs' the money at stake and runs off. The term is also used in a more general sense to signify stealing, and making off with the booty. **1917** FREEMAN & KINGSLEY *Alabaster Box* 278, I ain't a-going to stand for no grab-game.

fig. **1870** *Nation* 21 April 247/1 It is neither more nor less than a 'grab game,' in which each man gets all he can out of the pockets of the people. **1894** CABLE *J. March* xvii, Religion is not a grab game—if you'll forgive so coarse a word.

grace hoop.

1. (See quot. 1899.)

The *OED* records "the graces" as the name of this game as early as 1842.

1854 TROWBRIDGE *M. Merrivale* 367 We will go into the large drawing-room, and play ball or grace-hoop, if he likes. **1899** CHAMPLIN &

BOSTWICK *Cyclo. Games & Sports* (ed. 2) 376/2 *Grace Hoops*, or *Graces*, a game played by any number of persons (each of whom has two sticks about four feet long) with wooden rings or hoops from 12 to 18 inches in diameter. A player, holding a stick firmly in each hand, places the hoop over them, crosses them, and draws them quickly apart, thus sending the hoop into the air toward another player, who catches it on his sticks; and the sport thus goes on.

b. Also **grace sticks.**

1887 *Nation* 14 April 316/3 The result is . . . a wild scene of confusion in the school-rooms, girls scrambling over desks and crawling under benches in a frantic game of 'hide and seek,' besides various small side shows in the way of 'jump-rope,' 'grace-sticks,' and 'class-ball.'

2. A hoop used in this game.

1856 M. J. HOLMES *L. Rivers* x. 133 Gradually the sound of their voices increased, and as 'Lena's clear, musical laugh rang out above the rest, Mrs. Graham and Carrie looked out just in time to see Durward holding the struggling girl, while John Jr. claimed the reward of his having thrown the 'grace hoop' upon her head. **1899** CHAMPLIN & BOSTWICK *Cyclo. Games & Sports* (ed. 2) 377/1 The Grace Hoops sold at toy stores are usually covered with velvet or colored cloth.

Grace's warbler. A warbler, *Dendroica graciae*, discovered in 1864 by Elliott Coues and named for his sister.

1872 COUES *Key to No. Amer. Birds* 103 *Grace's Warbler*. . . . Chin, throat and breast rich yellow. **1887** RIDGWAY *Manual No. Amer. Birds* 506 *D[endroica] graciæ*. . . . Grace's Warbler. **1917** *Birds of Amer.* III. 140/1 Grace's Warbler was discovered in 1864 by the great naturalist, Dr. Elliott Coues, who gave the bird his sister's name.

* **grackle,** *n.* Also †**grakle.**

1. Any one of various American blackbirds of the family Icteridae. Cf. **purple grackle.**

1806 WEBSTER 31/1 *Blackbird*, in England a singing bird, in America the grackle. **1850** COOPER *Rural Hours* 49 A flock of the rusty blackbird or grakles about the village. **1945** *Mass. Audubon Soc. Bul.* March 63 Dr. John B. May started the new year right by having two Bluebirds at Cohasset on New Year's day. Two Grackles stayed through December and January about the premises of E. C. Staples, Amherst.

2. A type of artificial fly used in fishing.

1894 *Outing* XXIV. 227/1 Bass flies of proved merit include grackle, all the palmers [etc.].

As the last term in **boat-tailed, bronzed, Florida, purple, rusty grackle.**

grad græd, *n.* Short for "graduate." *Colloq.* Cf. **old grad.** — **1893** POST *Harvard Stories* p. ix, Reverend grads., from the tales I have heard ye tell, I opine that the undergraduate is still the same. **1947** *Democrat* 26 June 1/3 Grads Given Chance To Continue Studies.

* **gradation,** *n.* The reduction of a road to a uniform level or permissible gradients. — **1808** *Ann. 10th Congress* 1 Sess. II. 2746 They have completed the location, gradation, and marking of the route, from Cumberland to . . . the Monongahela river. **1867** *Harper's Mag.* June 2/2 The engineer and his locating party have . . . left their stakes marked ready for the gradation of the road.

* **grade,** *n.*

1. In a road or railroad, the amount or degree of slope or variation from a level.

1808 *Ann. 10th Congress* 1 Sess. II. 2746 The Commissioners . . . have completed the . . . marking of the route [of the Cumberland Road], . . . agreeably to a plot of the courses, distances, and grades. **1849** CHAMBERLAIN *Ind. Gazetteer* 33 This is the only point in the State from which the interior can be reached at such moderate grades. **1945** *Tracks* June 32/2 They know how much better the roadbeds are and how much easier the grades and curves.

attrib. **1867** *Harper's Mag.* June 4/1 The railroad constructed . . . on slight embankments to elevate the grade-line above the water.

b. A graded ascending or descending portion of a road.

1811 *Ann. 12th Congress* 1 Sess. II. 2171 Each grade of the [Cumberland] road to be perfectly levelled, brought to the proper degree, and approved. **1863** *Amador Ledger* (Jackson, Calif.) 19 Sep. 1/4 The work on this grade was done under the superintendence of John Horsley, and I shall here take the liberty of christening the grade on the west side of the Summit the 'Horsley Grade.' **1949** *Boston Globe Mag.* 29 May 7/4 The road left the valley and climbed some sharp grades.

c. An improved road, esp. one in a hilly or mountainous region.

1867 RICHARDSON *Beyond Miss.* 26 On the hill above, where 'the Grade' was being cut fifteen or twenty feet deep, through abrupt bluffs. **1876** RAYMOND *8th Rep. Mines* 278 The surface works of the mine are situated about 300 feet above the 'grade,' or stage-road. **1894** ROBLEY *Bourbon Co., Kansas* 14 The military road from Fort Leavenworth was completed about 1843. The pike, or grade, like a railroad grade, was constructed across all river and creek bottoms.

d. *at, over,* or *under grade*, at, over, or under the level of a road or railroad where it is crossed by another.

1849 *Mass. Acts & Resolves* 126 Number of public ways crossed at grade, Number of railroads crossed at grade. **1881** *Rep. Ala. R.R. Comm.* I. 193 What rail roads cross your road over or under grade in this State? **1907** *Springfield W. Republican* 17 Oct. 1 Vermont has taken hold of the important matter of the abolition of railroad crossings at grade.

2. One of the divisions or parts of the elementary school course usually requiring a year for its completion. Also the pupils included in such a division.

1835 *S. Lit. Messenger* I. 275 In the first and second grades boys and girls are schooled together; in the higher grades, male and female schools, are separate. **1857** *Boston School Comm. Rep.* 25 In visiting the grades above the primary, I generally made a cursory inspection [etc.]. **1890** *Ib.* 136 Our primary classes are now, for the most part, arranged in three grades. **1945** *Roundup* (Mont.) *R. Tribune* 22 Feb. 4/2 The children of each grade plan these parties and serve the lunch.

b. Often attrib. as **grade room, school, teacher.**

1902 W. J. GHENT *Our Benevolent Feudalism* 61 This company has established kindergartens, libraries, and, in remote places, grade schools for the children of its employees. **1906** *Springfield W. Republican* 12 April 6 The grade teachers . . . [set] the class to sing music already familiar. **1909** STRATTON-PORTER *Girl of Limberlost* 63 The Bird Woman says the grade rooms want leaves, grasses, birds' nests, and cocoons. **1949** *Time* 7 Feb. 43/2 Professional fields where recruits are still badly needed: medicine, dentistry, nursing and grade-school teaching.

3. An animal of a type produced by crossbreeding.

[**1796** MORSE *Univ. Geog.* I. 196 The other sort is . . . the Ranging Bear, and seems to be a grade between the preceding and the wolf.] **1850** JOHNSTON *Notes* I. 164 In the New England States and in New York the Devon blood prevails. Most of the stock are *grades*, as they are called, or crosses of the pure Devon bull with the older stock of the country, which is originally of mixed English and Dutch of various kinds. **1900** GARLAND *Eagle's Heart* 152 His pony, a vicious and powerful roan 'grade,' was on its haunches half the time. **1945** *N. Eng. Homestead* 13 Oct. 9/2 I'm glad to have you say that the longer you've had those purebreds the better you like them. . . . If you mess around with breedin' purebreds a while longer you'll be so much in love that you'll never go back t' keepin' grades.

b. Often attrib. as **grade animal, breeder, hen, Jersey, mare, sheep.** Cf. **grade horse** in **5.** below.

1852 *Mich. Agric. Soc. Trans.* III. 142 A few full blood Saxons; the rest are a grade sheep. **1857** *Ill. Agric. Soc. Trans.* III. 463 Our best roadsters are produced from a cross of the thoroughbred or Morgan stallions with grade mares. **1882** *Maine Bd. Agric. Rep.* XXVI. 190 Now these grade Jerseys do not produce as large veal calves. **1889** WARFIELD *Cattle-Breeding* 212 What the grade-breeder needs, then, is to use improved bulls, and from only one breed. **1894** *Vt. Bd. Agric. Rep.* XIV. 167 The farmer . . . will realize more dollars . . . by keeping grade hens and using always a pure bred male. **1947** *Hygeia* Oct. 806/3 The disease is most prevalent, other things being equal, in those herds of hogs and cattle which are highly bred and much more valuable than grade animals.

4. A mark given a pupil as an estimate of his achievement in a course.

1889 *Harvard Faculty Rec.* 15 Oct., Any member of the graduating class who has attained Grade C or a higher grade in eighteen courses [etc.]. **1949** *Lubbock* (Tex.) *Morn. Avalanche* 23 Feb. I. 1/2 When his grades started to slip near the danger mark . . . he gave up his part time job and tried baby sitting as an experiment.

b. The relative rank of an academic degree obtained by a student.

1886 *Ann. Rep. Pres. Harvard 1885–6* 72 The marks received by a student in the several studies of his college course have until now been combined to determine the grade of his degree. *c***1886** in THAYER *Hist. Sk. Harvard* (1890) 25/2 For the various grades of the degree, honors, honorable mention, etc., similar regulations are made.

5. In special combs.: (1) **grade A,** first-class; (2) **book,** (see quot.); (3) **crossing,** a railroad crossing at grade; (4) **curve,** a curve or graph sometimes used in schools to show the pattern usu. followed by the grades of the students; (5) **ditching,** ditching to a prescribed grade, *rare;* (6) **horse,** (see quot.); (7) **separation,** on an improved highway, a place where, by means of an underpass or an overpass, a railroad or another highway is crossed otherwise than at grade, cf. **1. d.** above. (8)

stake, a stake put down by a road engineer to indicate the grade desired at a particular place.

(1) **1920** *Collier's* 20 March 35/3 All you could see was her little peaches and grade A cream face stickin' out over the top. **1949** *Dly. Oklahoman* (Okla. City) 13 Feb. D. 5/5 The Ada city council has adopted an amendment to the city's milk ordinance strengthening its provisions for safeguarding Grade A requirements for milk sold within the city. — (2) **1940** RIESENBERG *Golden Gate* 220 The seaman's objection to the grade book, in which was listed his sea service record, was that it could be, and was, used to blacklist him. — (3) **1890** *Boston Journal* 26 Aug. 4/2 (*caption*), Want a Grade Crossing. **1946** *Pueblo* (Colo.) *Star-Journal* 30 June 8/1 We want them to show their appreciation in a fair and practical manner in this problem of grade crossing elimination. — (4) **1922** *Grey Towers* 50 The 'Grade Curve' had settled all that. . . . It was a scale—so many A's and B's and C's in a class. **1946** *Sat. Ev. Post* 3 Aug. 59/3 The dean believed in something called a Normal Grade Curve. He said Feathers gave too many A's and F's; he ought to give more B's, C's and D's.

(5) **1865** TURNER *Cotton* 73 All your manure and manure-making, with your grade-ditching and horizontaling, and your rotations, &c, &c, are conditions actually essential to the improvement of our agriculture. — (6) **1891** *Harper's Mag.* Nov. 888/1 He had the keeping of all the 'grade-horses' so called—those which draw the stone and dirt carts and the little dump cars. — (7) **1931** *Amer. City* Jan. 86/1 Upon completion of grade separation, around which traffic is now detoured, this objectionable 'bottle-neck' will have been eliminated. **1943** MENEFEE *Assignment* 98 And a forty-seven million dollar project to extend into the city center and along the riverfront the main highways from the southwest, west and northwest, with grade separations at all intersections. — (8) **1872** HUNTINGTON *Road-Master's Ass't* 15 It is the practice of some engineers to set grade-stakes 20 feet apart for laying ties.

b. In phrases: (1) *To go over the grade, W.* of a vehicle, to capsize; (2) *to make the grade,* to come up to the required standard.

(1) **1869** BROWNE *Adv. Apache Country* 312 Last summer a few stages went over the grade, but nobody was hurt bad. — (2) **1922** *Collier's* 7 Oct. 5/1, I don't think he can make the grade. **1948** *Great Falls* (Mont.) *Tribune* 27 Sep. 1/4 Many thousands of veterans can continue to find new opportunities and make the grade in businesses of their own.

As the last term in **down, first, high, railroad, side, turnpike, up, water grade.**

* **grade,** *v.*

1. *tr.* To reduce or bring (a road, railroad, etc.) to a practicable level.

1825 *Cong. Deb.* App. 21 Nov. 20 Nearly the whole extent of [the Cumberland Road] . . . has been cleared, cut, graded, and shaped, so as to be ready for receiving the first course, of metal. **1879** WILLIAMS *Pacific Tourist* 13/2 The ground had already been graded and ties placed in position. **1949** *Pacific Discovery* Jan.–Feb. 5/1 The narrow, rocky road of eleven years back was graded and ditched.

b. *To grade down,* to wear down or reduce (a bank, road, etc.) in steepness or height.

*c***1836** CATLIN *Indians* II. 95, I at length . . . came to an old buffalo ford, where the banks were graded down. **1865** BOUDRYE *Fifth N. Y. Cavalry* 109 The road was graded down about four feet with perpendicular banks supported by cedar boughs interlaced.

c. To smooth up or level (a lawn, bank, etc.).

1838 COOPER *Home as Found* xxii, The lookers-on . . . had already begun to calculate the cost of what they termed grading the lawns, it being with them as much a matter of course to bring pleasure grounds down to a mathematical surface, as to bring a railroad route down to the proper level. **1862** GAIL HAMILTON *Country Living* 21, I suggested . . . that the gravel-heap . . . be graded and turfed. **1948** *Democrat* 15 Jan. 1/1 He first plowed the field and has since disked and graded it.

2. To systematize (a school) by grouping the pupils into grades; to place (a pupil) in the grade for which his previous study has prepared him.

1865 *Nation* I. 779/1 [The State Superintendent of Educ. in S.C.] at once proceeded to grade the schools in the city [of Charleston]. **1916** E. PORTER *David* 252 The teacher set to work to grade her new pupil.

b. To read and mark a student's paper.

1932 *Atlantic Mo.* CXLIX. 626 A large proportion of the graduate students of Harvard University, 56 per cent, to-day are merely part-time students—that is, having received a poor education in high school and college, they are now teaching or assisting or grading papers. **1948** *Chr. Sci. Mon.* 22 April 4/3 The robot prof. is a machine that automatically grades homework and examination papers, at the rate of 10 a minute.

3. To improve (stock) by crossbreeding. Also with *up.*

1873–4 *Vt. Bd. Agric. Rep.* II. 92 He . . . thought he should improve the color of his butter by grading his herd with Jersey blood. **1887** F. FRANCIS *Saddle & Moccasin* ix. 161 The expense of turning in good bulls and grading up your stock. **1949** *Southwestern Hist. Quart.* April 437 The process of 'grading up' the native cattle continued until some 25,000 Shorthorns and 25,000 Hereford cows roamed the ranges of the King Ranch.

4. *intr.* To be of a good or specified quality, to measure *up* to a standard or expectation.

1891 *N.Y. Tribune* 30 Oct. 7/3 They have had no frost and the wheat is grading nearly all No. 1 hard. **1902** NORRIS *Pit* (1922) x, Two-thirds of that wheat won't grade, and Europe will take nearly all of it. **1922** MULFORD *Black Buttes* 227 Strikes me funny, though, the way they [*sc.* the new cattle] grade up.

5. *To grade up with,* to be equal to in rank or capabilities. *Colloq.*

1904 O. HENRY *Heart of West* i. 5 When a man marries a queen he ought to grade up with her. **1909** ——— *Roads of Destiny* ix. 155, I never yet see anything on the hoof that he exactly grades up with.

* **graded,** *a.*

1. Of roads and railroads: Made level or reduced to practicable gradients.

1835 in *S. Lit. Messenger* IV. 303/1 Several vehicles . . . were dashing along the well graded road. **1882** *Harper's Mag.* Dec. 60/2 A half mile of graded road-bed alone remains.

2. Of animals: Improved by careful crossbreeding.

1879 WILLIAMS *Pacific Tourist* 185/2 The immense range fenced in at this point is occupied by a select herd of graded stock. **1891** *Fur, Fin, & Feather* March 150 'Buffalo' Jones . . . has a very large ranch at Garden City, on which he has some two hundred full-blooded and graded bisons. **1948** *Chi. Tribune* 11 July 11/2 His herd is not registered, altho all his stock is graded.

3. graded school, an elementary school in which the pupils are grouped into grades according to their advancement.

1852 *Ind. Hist. Soc. Pub.* II. 615 Union, or graded schools, for the terms are synonymous, are simply the schools of a given township, village or city, classified and arranged according to the attainments of the pupils. **1889** *Union Pac. R.R., Ore. & Wash.* 42 Among the schools worthy of mention is one first-class graded school, costing $20,000. **1945** *Democrat* 30 Aug. 3/3 The Grove Hill Graded School will also open on the above named date.

grader ˈgredɚ, *n.*

1. One engaged in grading a railroad.

1832 *Polit. Examiner* (Shelbyville, Ky.) 23 June 2/5 The Contractors on the Lexington Rail Road pay the highest wages to Stone Masons, Stone Cutters, Stone Breakers, Graders, and Laboring Hands of all descriptions. **1897** *Kansas Hist. Coll.* (1900) VI. 35 In 1867 the Union Pacific railroad was built as far west as Fort Hays, and . . . the graders were constantly being attacked by Indians. **1911** WRIGHT *Winning Barbara Worth* 474 The waiting trains loaded with ties and steel began to move and the construction gangs followed close on the heels of the graders.

b. A machine or implement for grading a road or railroad. Cf. **railroad grader, road grader.**

1869 *Rep. Comm. Agric. 1868* 361 The side tracks [should be] kept in order by the use of the grader. **1948** *Ada* (Okla.) *Ev. News* 4 July 12/5 Three graders . . . required between $500 or $600 to repair for usable condition.

2. One who classifies commodities according to their quality.

1849 *Rep. Comm. Patents: Agric.* 257 This grader was to be sworn . . . to discharge the duties of his station faithfully and impartially. **1889** *Columbus* (O.) *Dispatch* 22 Nov., Clerks and graders whose business is to classify cotton for English markets. **1949** *Dly. Oklahoman* (Okla. City) 13 Feb. D. 6/1 It also acted as grader, storage agent and sales agency for 198,000 pounds of grease wool.

b. (See quot.)

1901 *World's Work* May 720/2 When the fruit is ready to market it is taken to Mr. Russell's packing-house, and there 'sorted' by an ingenious machine grader into three or four grades or sizes.

c. One who reads and assigns grades or marks to papers written by students.

1948 *Time* 16 Feb. 94/3 Graders had marked the papers as tolerantly as they could.

3. A pupil of a designated level in a grade school. Cf. **first grader.**

1934 WEBSTER. **1949** *Lisle* (Ill.) *Eagle* 10 Mar. 5/2 Last week the second graders were busy working on the lunch-room blackboard, decorating it with pictures for the month of March.

* **grading,** *n.*

1. The action of reducing (a roadbed, uneven surface, etc.) to a practicable or desired gradient. Cf. **railway grading.**

1835 *Franklin Institute Jrnl.* XV. 233 The amount of labour in grading, fixing rails, and forming all other parts of the road. **1908** in THOBURN *Stand. Hist. Okla.* (1916) I. 436 The grading was done by various contracting parties. **1949** *Democrat* 24 Feb. 1/1 The work of grading and landscaping has already begun.

Attrib. with **plow, purposes, scraper** (see **scraper**), **team.**

1875 KNIGHT 1000/1 *Grading-plow.* One used for breaking up soil or plowing down banks, in order to fit the earth for being scooped up by the earth-scraper, and thereby deported. — **1853** *Mich. Agric. Soc. Trans.* IV. 86 Self-loading dumping cart, a very useful and convenient article for heavy grading purposes. — **1875** KNIGHT 1000/1 *Grading-scraper.* A large two-handled shovel drawn by a pair of horses and used as an earth-scoop for raising and removing loosened earth. It is used in road-making [etc.]. — **1913** LONDON *Valley of Moon* II. xii, Billy got a job driving a grading team for the contractors of the big bridge then building at Niles.

b. Esp. (1) **grading camp,** the headquarters of workmen who are grading; (2) **gang,** a group of workmen who are grading.

(1) **1901** *Land of Sunshine* June 519 About four miles below this point . . . a grading camp has been established and graders are now at work. **1926** COOPER *Oklahoma* 232 Mort Sturdevant rode often to the grading camp, once work swung into full activity. — (2) **1911** WRIGHT *Winning Barbara Worth* 29 Mr. Worth, permit me to introduce Mr. Patrick Mooney whom I have known for years as the best boss of a grading gang in the West. **1912** *Out West* Feb. 133/1 Down the track the grading gang dug and scraped and carried on in the hot sun like ants on some queerly elongated ant hill.

2. The process of separating into grades indicative of quality.

1852 *Mich. Agric. Soc. Trans.* III. 150 Compare the grading of my clip . . . with that of Joseph Barnard. **1883** *Harper's Mag.* June 76/2 The first operation . . . is the grading of the middlings.

b. The grouping of children in school according to their advancement.

1903 A. B. HART *Actual Government* 543 The number of children is great enough to allow complete grading.

3. (See quot.)

1889 W. WARFIELD *Cattle-Breeding* 202 This breeding of one animal of an improved breed with another of an unimproved or native stock is usually spoken of as grading or grading up.

gradualism ˈgrædʒʊəlˌɪzəm, *n.* The abolition of slavery gradually rather than at once. *Obs.* — **1835** *Liberator* V. 144 *Immediatism* . . . is the opposite of *gradualism,* another new coinage. **1865** LOWELL in *N. Amer. Rev.* April 559 We have purposely avoided any discussion on gradualism as an element in emancipation, because we consider its evil results to have been demonstrated in the British West Indies.

gradualist ˈgrædʒʊəlɪst, *n.* A supporter of the policy of gradual emancipation of slaves. *Obs.*

1835 *Liberator* V. 744 The Colonization Society . . . are gradualists. **1880** *Lib. Universal Knowl.* IX. 235 Mr. Lundy, like most of the antislavery men of that day was a gradualist, fearing . . . that a sudden emancipation would be dangerous to the public welfare.

b. One who believes in proceeding gradually in granting Negroes full rights as citizens.

1945 *Chi. D. News* 4 Oct. 12/7 On a higher level of thought, we've labeled ourselves 'gradualists'; and stilled any uneasy twinge of conscience by assuming that everything will wash out in the fullness of time.

* **graduate,** *n.*

1. One who has finished at a school of lower rank than a college.

1773 J. ADAMS *Diary* Works II. 321 Their academy [in Phila.] emits from nine to fourteen graduates annually. **1852** *Boston City Doc.* No. 32, 19 Graduates from the City Schools. *Ib.* App. 4 The proposed Normal School will prepare from eighty to one hundred graduates every year. **1945** *Chi. D. News* 28 June 8/5 School bells of 45 years ago rang again last night in the memories of the living graduates of the 1900 class at the Burr Elementary School.

2. In combs.: (1) **graduate chapter,** (see quot.); (2) **course,** in a college or university, an advanced course, open, usu., to graduate students only; (3) **department,** a department in a college or university concerned entirely with advanced or graduate work; (4) **school,** a school, or a department in a college or university, in which only graduate work is given; (5) **studies,** studies or courses of study in a graduate department; (6) **work,** work in a graduate course or department.

(1) **1871** BAGG *At Yale* 112 Delta Phi has also four alumni associations, or 'graduate chapters.' — (2) **1880** *Harvard Cat.* 190 Any Graduate course which is taken by less than three students may be withdrawn at the option of the Instructor. — (3) **1880** *Harvard Cat.* 190 (*heading*), Graduate department. — (4) **1895–6** *Univ. Nebraska Calendar* 37 The Graduate School provides for advanced University work on the basis of completed undergraduate studies.

(5) **1947** *This Week Mag.* 17 May 7/2, I gave up tournament golf the day I began my graduate studies. — (6) **1944** *New Yorker* 7 Oct. 63/1, I was an undergraduate at a little place in the Middle West that you never heard of, but then I went to business school at Harvard. Graduate work, of course. **1948** *Chi. D. News* 29 Jan. 27/2 He . . . later did graduate work at Harvard and the University of Chicago.

As the last term in **post, resident, sub graduate.**

* **graduate,** *v.*

1. *tr.* To reduce (a road or street) to a more gradual slope, to make more nearly level. *Obs.*

1789 MORSE *Amer. Geog.* 363 The laborious part of the business is entirely accomplished, by removing the obstacles and graduating the descent. **1815** DRAKE *Cincinnati* ii. 62 The streets shall be graduated from the Hill to the river shore. **1833** *Niles' Reg.* XLIV. 192/2 In the construction of the graduated road aforesaid, . . . payments of the $266,000 shall be made monthly.

2. *intr.* To complete an elementary or high school course.

1882 RITTENHOUSE *Maud* 77 The very minute that she found out she was too far behind the class to graduate she stopped school. **1945** *Chi. D. News* 27 June 12/4 The American Legion for the last several years has been awarding Certificates of Honor to the most outstanding boy and girl graduating from the elementary schools and the high schools.

graduating class. A class whose members are finishing the last year of a college or high-school course.

1803 in *W. & M. Coll. Quart.* 1 Ser. VIII. 218 We [at Yale] then celebrate commencement . . . orations, disputes, &c., composed and performed by a part of the graduating class. **1850** *Knickerb.* XXXVI. 526 The speeches of the graduating class were delivered. **1909** STRATTON-PORTER *Girl of Limberlost* 190 It was the custom for each graduating class to give a great entertainment.

* **graduation,** *n.*

1. (See quot. 1840.) *Obs.*

1832 *22d Congress* 2 Sess. H.R. Doc. No. 101, 171 The graduation and masonry of the Baltimore and Ohio railroad have been completed as far as to Frederick city. **1840** TANNER *Canals & Rail Roads U.S.* 163 *Graduation,* the act of modifying or adjusting a roadway into a particular line. In rail-road making, it signifies the process by which a required grade is obtained. **1864** *Pa. R.R. 18th Rep.* 95 Graduation and railway superstructure.

2. *attrib.* Of or pertaining to various bills, one of which became law in 1854, providing for a gradual reduction in price of unsold public lands. *Obs.*

1844 *Cong. Rec.* 19 Dec. 50/3 The graduation bill . . . is one intended for the benefit of the great agricultural interests of the country. **1854** *Ib.* 2 Aug. 2202/2 The House . . . [has passed] two great measures in respect to the disposition of public lands. One is the homestead bill; the other is the graduation bill. *Ib.* 3 Aug. 2203/1 The Senate resumed the consideration of the graduation bill. **1884** T. DONALDSON *Public Domain* 291 Lands [were] sold at graduation prices . . . after the repeal of the graduation law, June 2, 1862. **1948** DICK *Dixie Frontier* 76–7 Now and then settlers urged Congress to pass a graduation act. . . . It provided that after land had been offered for sale a number of years . . . the price should be reduced automatically . . . until . . . low enough to attract buyers.

* **graft,** *n.*

1. (See quot. 1901.) *Slang.* Cf. * **graft,** *v.* **2.**

1865 *Police Gazette* (N.Y.) 8 July 1/3 'Twas handy that we were so related, as, when about a 'graft,' or 'doing stur,' both sisters could keep each other company. **1901** FLYNT *World of Graft* 4 In regard to the word 'graft' which is used freely in the text, I desire to state that it is a generic slang term for all kinds of theft and illegal practices generally. **1945** *College English* May 469/2 How they preserved their deep integrity . . . makes a story which will be a boon to many readers of graft and greed in fiction.

2. One's calling, employment, or way of securing money. *Slang.*

"Graft" in the sense of work, esp. hard work, is recorded by the *OED* as early as 1890.

1896 *Typographical Jrnl.* IX. 317 Fargo boasted of having a printers' ball nine worthy of a better 'graft' than sticking type at thirty-five cents per thousand. **1900** FLYNT *Itinerant Policeman* iii, Their main 'graft,' or business, is pocket-picking, but in a well equipped 'mob' there are also burglars, sneak-thieves, and professional gamblers. **1911** WRIGHT *Winning Barbara Worth* 213 It looks shameful, all right, . . . the way these four-flushers come in here and attempt to work their graft right under our eyes.

* **graft,** *v.*

1. *tr.* To mend (stockings) by knitting in new material in place of that worn out or ruined (see also quot. 1859). *Obs.*

1749 in SINGLETON *Social N.Y.* 248 Elizabeth Boyd . . . follows as usual new grafting and footing all sorts of stockings. **1770** *Pa. Chron.* 10–17 Sep. 138/1 They also scour, stove, foot, mend and graft all sorts of silk stockings in the neatest and best manner. **1859** BARTLETT 178 To 'graft boots' is to repair them by adding new soles, and surrounding the feet with new leather. So called in Connecticut.

2. *intr.* To obtain money by shady or dishonest means, also *to graft onto. Slang.*

1859 *Nat. Police Gaz.* (N.Y.) 14 May 3/4 Liz Thompson and her husband . . . do not intend going out to 'graft' until the summer season sets in, when they are going to Newport, Saratoga, and other fashionable watering resorts, at which game she made out so good last season. **1865** *Sun. Mercury* (Phila.) 3 Sep. 4/2 The granting of licenses (payable monthly) to 'graft' on the City Railways is a great accommodation. **1903** A. ADAMS *Log Cowboy* xiii. 84 He had a card or two up his sleeve by which he expected to graft on to some of the coin of the realm. **1910** in H. ASBURY *Gem of Prairie* 267 Hell, they all graft. There is not a policeman around here that doesn't hold us girls up.

b. *To graft upon,* to prey upon. *Slang.*

1905 *McClure's Mag.* 352 In Pawtucket, the worst elements in both parties combine to graft upon the city.

graftdom ˈgræfdəm, *n.* The realm in which graft and grafting prevails. *Slang.* — **1901** FLYNT *World of Graft* 9 The opinions of Chicago as a city of graftdom are many and varied, according to the individual experience of the man who happens to be expressing himself. **1903** H. HAPGOOD *Autobiog. of Thief* 54 She had lived in Graftdom ever since she was a tid-bit.

* **grafter,** *n.* One who profits by illicit means, esp. a corrupt official. Also transf. *Slang.* Cf. **vice grafter.**

1896 *Columbus* (O.) *Dispatch* 20 April 3/8 Most of the 'grafters' have left the town and not many of them will remain here. **1905** *McClure's Mag.* 338 The 'grafters' who batten on us say so. **1920** ALSAKER *Maintaining Health* 356 Children who are waited upon must become selfish. They soon become grafters, expecting and taking everything and giving nothing.

* **grafting,** *n.* Obtaining money, office, etc., by dishonest means. Also as adj.

1901 FLYNT *World of Graft* 78 They make their living, such as it is, by grafting. **1905** *McClure's Mag.* 42 He organized the Democratic party into a grafting machine. **1917** SINCLAIR *King Coal* 275 He proceeded to draw out Little Jerry on other aspects of coal-mining: on short weights and long hours, grafting bosses and camp-marshals.

graght grɑkt, *n. local.* [Du. *gracht.*] A ditch or moat, usu. in place-names. *Obs.* — **1673** *N.Y. Hist. Soc. Col.* XLVI. 4 In this Citty to the east of the moate or Ditch, commonly called the prince Graght. *Ib.*, On the west the said moate or Graght. *Ib.* 13 A Lott of ground . . . to the North of Bevers graght.

graham ˈgreəm, *n.* Orig. **Graham.** [Sylvester *Graham* (1794–1851), Amer. physician.]

1. Short for **graham flour.**

1874 *Vt. Bd. Agric. Rep.* II. 509 The cook room . . should be one of great convenience, large enough to hold the flour, the meal, the rye, the graham, butter. **1918** *Nation* 7 Feb. 130/1 Rye, oats, corn, and graham ought to be cheaper.

2. In names for various articles of food made of graham flour, as (1) **graham biscuit,** (2) **bread,** (3) **cracker,** (4) **crust,** (5) **gem.**

(1) **1873** BEADLE *Undevel. West* 532 The first meal I was delighted to see our Indian servant bring in what I recognized as an old Yankee acquaintance—'Graham biscuits.' **1888** HARGIS *Graded Cook Book* 226 Graham biscuits . . . cut with a common biscuit cutter. — (2) **1834** *Sun* (N.Y.) 20 Aug. 2/3 The employer . . . observed with astonishment that the mason had built about two feet of the wall with loaves of *Graham bread.* **1947** *Atlantic Mo.* Dec. 112/2 Gone too, with these luscious homemade loaves are other substantial and tasty favorites: . . . french loaves . . . ; sweet graham bread made with molasses and raisins. — (3) **1882** M. HARLAND *Eve's Daughters* 443 Eat lightly—dry bread or biscuit, Graham crackers—anything that is easy of digestion. **1946** *Mazama* Dec. 56/1 Still half asleep, I forced some chocolate-flavored mud down my throat and ate a few soggy graham crackers. — (4) **1873** PHELPS *Trotty's Wedding* v, He had to go without his molasses gingerbread, and live on Graham crusts that his mother left before she went. — (5) **1882** PECK *Sunshine* 82 His head is about as big as a graham gem.

b. Also (1) **Graham boarding house,** a boarding house catering to Grahamites, now *hist.;* (2) **fever,** fervid enthusiasm for Grahamism, *obs.;* (3) **flour,** whole-wheat flour; (4) **grits,** grits from the whole grains of various cereals, esp. corn; (5) **system,** a system of diet prescribed by Sylvester Graham, *obs.*

(1) **1852** *Knickerb.* XXXIX. 278 A Pair of Missives From a 'Grahamite' and a 'Gourmet.' . . . The first dates from a 'Graham Boarding-House.' **1947** DOWNEY *Lusty Forefathers* 297 Graham boarding-houses sprang up in the larger cities. — (2) **1834** *Boston Post* 31 July 2/2 Some of the Portland Tavern Keepers seem to have taken the *Graham fever* the natural way. . . . Job's biles were a mere trifle to waiting two hours for a breakfast with a *salt water appetite,* and sitting down at last to dish-water and scraps. — (3) **1834** GARRISON in W. P. & F. J. Garrison *W. L. Garrison* I. 428 If they are Grahamites, we have a fine spring of water in our cellar, and plenty of Graham flour upstairs. **1938** DAMON *Grandma* 103, 5 lbs. graham flour 4 cans condensed milk. — (4) **1885** E. W. HOWE *Mystery of Locks* 71 There's oatmeal, and graham grits, and such like—they are healthy. — (5) **1842** J. STURGE *Visit to U.S.* 107 The 'Graham system,' as it is called numbers many adherents in America, who are decided in its praise.

c. *To out-Graham Graham,* to exceed Dr. Sylvester Graham in dieting. *Rare.*

1834 *Boston Ev. Transcript.* 11 Aug. 2/3 A married woman is exhibiting herself at Montreal, who for abstemiousness outGrahams Graham 'all the world to nothing.' She has subsisted for two years past on nothing—saving milk or tea.

Grahamism ˈgreəmˌɪzəm, *n.* The principles regarding diet advocated by Sylvester Graham (1794–1851). Now *hist.*

1837 GREENE *Glance at N.Y.* 191 This system, . . . commonly called *Grahamism,* from the Rev. Sylvester Graham, who first taught it here, five or six years ago—is now, we believe, very much fallen into disfavor. **1845** LOWELL *Letters* I. 87, I am becoming more and more inclined to Grahamism every day. **1870** *N.Y. Med. Jrnl.* XI. 567 (*Cent.*), Grahamism was advocated and practised by many. **1947** DOWNEY *Lusty Forefathers* 299 Grahamism could concentrate on other much-needed reforms.

Grahamite ˈgreəmaɪt, *n.*[1] A believer in the dietetic system of Sylvester Graham. Now *hist.*

1834 *Sun* (N.Y.) 20 Aug. 2/3 A good Joke for the Grahamites. **1846** *Sci. Amer.* 21 Nov. 69/1 Butter has hitherto been supposed to be animal matter, and as such has been rejected by some of the Grahamites. **1947** DOWNEY *Lusty Forefathers* 296 Receipts to the amount of $2,278.98 were added to the society's relief fund, which sum, opined the Grahamites, probably would fail to go very far.

attrib. **1839** *N.O. Picayune* 3 Feb. 2/2 It would be no more than justice to subject this Grahamite professor to the fate of Nebuchadnezzar. **1947** DOWNEY *Lusty Forefathers* 297 Resort dining-rooms were forced to install Grahamite tables.

Grahamite ˈgreəmaɪt, *n.*[2] [J. A. and J. L. *Graham,* in whose mine in W. Va. this was first found.] A bituminous mineral similar to asphalt. — **1866** *Amer. Jrnl. Science* XCII. 420 Wurtz has proposed the name Grahamite for the pitch-black Albertite-like mineral of Virginia. **1880** *Lib. Universal Knowl.* VIII. 139 Grahamite is black, and has a variable luster; is fusible under pressure.

Grahamitish ˈgreəmˌaɪtɪʃ, *n.* Of or pertaining to Grahamism. *Obs.* — **1837** *S. Lit. Messenger* III. 105 My desire to devour this *light* food was entirely Grahamitish. **1839** *Knickerb.* XIII . 233 'What wonder,' exclaims a grahamitish friend of mine, who . . . lets out his spleen against all vile narcotics.

* **grain,** *n.* In combs.: (1) **grain belt,** a region where grain is the chief agricultural product; (2) **corner,** a corner *q.v.* brought about by the buying up of the whole or available supply of grain; (3) **elevator,** =**elevator 3;** (4) **lot,** a plot of land on which grain is grown; (5) **man,** one who buys and sells grain as corn or wheat; (6) **ranch,** *W.* a ranch upon which grain is grown, also **grain rancher;** (7) **state,** a state in which grain is the chief agricultural product; (8) **store,** a store in which grain is sold; (9) **scalping,** (see quot.)

(1) **1886** *Cent. Mag.* May 47/1 With the remarkably productive new grain-belt of the Pacific slope as a reserve . . . , the Minneapolis millers need fear no check to their vast industry. — (2) **1882** *Nation* 21 Dec. 519/3 The Committee of the Legislature . . . is trying to find out whether there is anything wrong in 'grain corners.' — (3) **1858** *Rep. Comm. Patents 1857* II. 210 Improvement in Clearing-Guard of Grain Elevators. **1913** CATHER *O Pioneers!* 3 The main street . . . ran from the squat red railway station and the grain 'elevator' at the north end of the town to the lumber yard and the horse pond at the

south end. **1949** *Highway Traveler* April 15/1 In 1842 Joseph Dart astounded the world with his mechanical grain elevator. — (4) **1880** DEMING *Adirondack Stories* 7 Standing by the house, they could see . . . the level stubble of the grain-lot.

(5) **1867** *Atlantic Mo.* March 331/2 Those little slips of paper, changing hands on 'Change, constitute the business of the 'grain men' of Chicago. **1887** *Courier-Journal* 3 May 4/2 [The committee] contains two grain men and two flour merchants. — (6) **1888** LINDLEY *Calif. of South* 240 There are a few great grain-ranches in the valley. **1912** *Out West* Mar. 213/2 The grain rancher found it profitable in some seasons, but no man would have called it a garden spot. **1922** *Outing* April 299/1 All of us do not know the gold and purple of the prairies at twilight, . . . the magic beauty of the vast grain ranches, each neat farm-house nesting in its dark green grove. **1949** *L.A. Times* 7 May 1. 11/3 Grain ranchers . . . have completed an extensive war against ground squirrels. — (7) **1822** *Ann. 17th Congress* 1 Sess. I. 245 The farmers in the grain states would find a profitable market for their

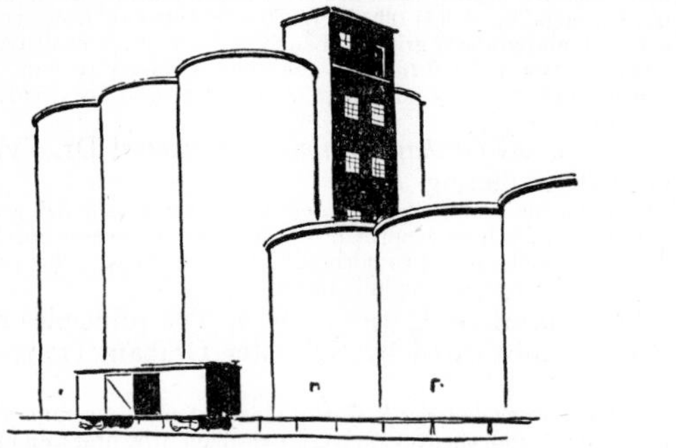

Grain elevators

rye and corn. — (8) **1877** JOHNSON *Anderson Co., Kansas* 182 This was the first grain store in the town. **1891** C. ROBERTS *Adrift America* 201 A man came out of a grain store and asked me if I wanted work. — (9) **1923** BLAISDELL *F. T. Comm.* 133 Another practice was grain 'scalping.' This is selling and reselling grain before its final disposal.

As the last term in **bread, English, fall, small, sod grain.**

* **grain,** *v.*

1. *tr.* To graze or abrade (the skin). *Colloq.*

1845 HOOPER *Daddy Biggs' Scrape* 197 It took raal nice judgment to keep the infernal hook outen my meat; it grained the skin several times, as 'twas. **1857** HAMMOND *Northern Scenes* 330 Spalding's bullet had grazed its belly, raking off the hair and graining the skin. **1923** *D.N.* V. 209 *Grain,* . . . to abraid slightly, as the skin in shaving, [McDonald Co., Mo.].

2. To feed (stock) on grain.

Cf. Du. *granen* in same sense.

1874 *Vt. Bd. Agric. Rep.* II. 406 Older sheep should be grained the first of the season, after which they may do without till the first of March. **1883** A. E. BOYD *MS Letter,* When our horses are not doing any kind of work, we do not grain them, but merely give them hay. **1892** F. P. HUMPHREY *N. Eng. Cactus* 185 After the horses were put up an' grained. **1923** *D.N.* V. 209, I ain't a-grainin' my cows now. [McDonald Co., Mo.] **1949** *Sat. Ev. Post* 9 April 132/4 We throwed our drive into a pole-fence pasture, grained Blaze and Blackie's *grullo,* then went up to the main house.

grama ˈgræmə, *n.* Also **gramma.** *W.* [Sp. *grama,* grass.] A common name for any one of various native low grasses of the genus *Bouteloua* of the western plains. In full **grama grass.**

1828 in *Overland to Pacific* II. (1933) 194 Our mules have been recently much benefitted by the gramme grass, the best pasturage between the Atlantic and Pacific ocean. **1844** GREGG *Commerce of Prairies* I. 160 The high prairies of all Northern Mexico . . . are mostly clothed with different species of a highly nutritious grass called *grama,* which is of a very short and curly quality. **1922** CATHER *One of Ours* 66 Now he was trading a pleasant old farm that didn't bring in anything for a grama-grass ranch in Colorado. **1937** *Range Plant Handbook* G25 The Spanish conquistadores, finding extensive areas of *Bouteloua* species in the tablelands of central Mexico, called them grama (literally grass), probably because the flaglike spikes reminded them of the familiar related grama of Spain (what we call Bermuda grass). **1949** *Pacific Discovery* Jan.–Feb. 4/1 The ungrazed mat of grama grass held back both soil and water, and from this sponge the springs were fed throughout the year.

b. With a descriptive term.

1872 BOURKE *Journal* Dec. 15 Hills today well grassed with blue and white gramma. **1937** *Range Plant Handbook* G27 Side-oats grama, also called tall grama, derives its common and specific names from the peculiar arrangement of the many spikes, commonly from 20 to 60, which hang pendent on one side of the stem. *Ib.* G26 Sprucetop grama, esteemed as a very valuable grass wherever it occurs, is an erect mostly tufted perennial.

* **grammar school.** (See quot. 1860.) Also attrib.

1823 *System of Education in Boston* 9 The object of the primary schools is to qualify children for entering the English Grammar Schools. **1860** WORCESTER 634/2 *Grammar-school,* . . . a school next in rank above a primary school and below a high school. (U.S.) **1911** PERSONS *Mass. Labor Laws* 197 There are in Boston 66 grammar schools from which children may go to work. **1945** *Athol* (Mass.) *D. News* 14 May 4/5 (*caption*), Reds Take Browns 12–2 In Grammar School League.

Gramophone ˈgræməˌfon, *n.* Also **gramophone.** [See note.] The trade-mark name of a type of sound-recording and reproducing machine. Also attrib.

"App. formed by inversion of *Phonogram.* The spelling *grammo-* (not the inventor's) is an attempt to make the word look more like a correct formation" (*OED*).

1887 *Pat. Off. Gazette* 8 Nov. 620/2 Gramophone [patented by] Emile Berliner, Washington, D.C. **1895** BERLINER in *Franklin Inst. Jrnl.* Dec. 434 The most difficult part of the gramophone work consisted in giving to the recording sound box [etc.]. **1948** *Time* 26 Jan. 19/1 The commercial 'gramophones' which followed (colloquially called screech boxes) were not much better.

* **grampus,** *n.* (See quot.) See also **mottled grampus, water grampus.** — **1917** KEPHART *Camping* II. 411 One of the best natural baits for bass, when the water is clear, is that fierce-looking creature called hellgrammite, dobson, or grampus. This is the larva of a large winged insect, the horned corydalis.

granary weevil. A small beetle, *Sitophilus granarius,* injurious to stored grain.

1850 *Rep. Comm. Patents 1849: Agric.* 335 The other species of corn-weevil alluded to, . . . the granary weevil, is more common in this country. **1895** *Dep. Agric. Yrbk. 1894* 279 The granary weevil is the 'curculio' and 'weevil' of early writings. **1949** *Prairie Farmer* 4 June 6/3 Rice and granary weevils do the most damage.

granatoid ˈgrænəˌtɔɪd, *n.* (See quot.) *Obs.* — **1929** *K.C. Times* 3 April, The first cement used to replace board and bricks for the use of pedestrians was popularly called 'granatoid.' These walks were the pride of the town, but now they are the only kind to be found anywhere.

* **grand,** *a.* and *n.*

1. *n.* A thousand dollars. *Slang.*

1921 *Collier's* 27 Aug. 4/3 *'I lose twenty-five thousand dollars!'* Sweet Spirits of Niter, Baby—twenty-five grand! **1948** *Pauls Valley* (Okla.) *D. Democrat* 1 July 2/4 That would be a lot for you to give up for just ten grand.

Also **G.**

1947 *Chi. D. News* 10 Jan. 11/1 (*heading*), As Lawyer, He Wants His Rights or 50 Gs.

2. *a.* Denoting a trunk canal or railroad.

[**1825** *N.Y. Advertiser* 29 Oct. (*heading*), Grand Canal Celebration by the City of New York.] **1832** *Amer. R.R. Jrnl.* I. 177/2 There should then be constructed from the Grand Canal to this *Grand Rail-road,* lateral Rail-roads and Canals. **1868** *Comm. & Fin. Chron.* VI. 196/1 The prospect that the whole grand line to the Pacific will be Completed in 1870 was never better.

3. (*cap.*) In the titles of officers in the Ku-Klux Klan, as **Grand Dragon, Ensign, Exchequer, Giant, Goblin, Klokard, Kludd, Magi, Monk, Scribe, Sentinel, Titan, Turk, Wizard.** *Obs.* or *hist.*

For **Grand Cyclops** see **cyclops.**

1867 *41st Congress* 2 Sess. H.R. Misc. Doc. No. 53, 315 The officers of the Ku-Klux Klan . . . shall consist of a Grand Wizard of the Empire . . . ; a Grand Dragon of the Realm . . . ; a Grand Titan of the Dominion . . . ; a Grand Giant of the Province . . . a Grand Magi, a Grand Monk, a Grand Exchequer, a Grand Turk, a Grand Scribe, a Grand Sentinel, and a Grand Ensign. **1867** *Prescript of the* ** [*Ku-Klux Klan*] 2 It shall be the duty of the Grand Wizard, who is the Supreme Officer of the Empire, to communicate with and receive reports from the Grand Dragons of Realms, as to the condition, strength, efficiency and progress of the *s within their respective Realms. **1926** *N.Y. Times* 1 Aug. 2/8 At 8 o'clock children of the order were christened by the Rev. J. J. Messler of the Wesley M.E. Church of Pleasantville, Grand Kludd of the order. . . . Addresses on Americanism and the Ku Klux Klan were then delivered by the Rev. A. M. Young, Grand Klokard [etc.]. **1931** F. L. ALLEN *Only Yesterday* 66 The country was divided into Realms headed by King Kleagles, and the Realms into Domains headed by Grand Goblins. **1946** *Coronet* Oct. 6/1 The entire South was organized as an Invisible Empire under a Grand Wizard, the ex-Confederate cavalry hero, N. B. Forrest.

4. In special combs. (freq. *cap.*): (1) **Grand Archee,** see **Archee;** (2) **Basin,** =**Great Basin;** (3) **Division, Empire,** (see quots.), *obs.;* (4) **harmonicon, harmonicum,** see **harmonicon;** (5) **junctioner,** ?a director of a "Grand Junction" railroad, *rare;* (6) **Krout,** (see quot.), *rare;* (7) **march,** a formal march or promenade at the opening of a ball, also transf.; (8) **medicine,** (see quots. and cf. ∗**medicine**), *obs.;* (9) **mystery,** (see quot.); (10) **Prairie,** a name formerly given to an extensive prairie in northern Indiana and Illinois; (11) **Sachem,** see **sachem;** (12) ∗**stand,** used attrib. to designate anything spectacular or done for show, *slang;* (13) **stander,** one given to showing off, also **grandstanding,** *a. slang.*

(2) **1848** RUXTON in *Blackw. Mag.* LXIX. 308 In the 'Grand Basin,' it is reported, neither human nor animal life can be supported. — (3) **1862** E. KIRKE *Among Pines* 42 Thanking the worthy gentleman for the caution, I followed him up stairs, and soon lost, in a sweet oblivion, all thoughts of Abolitionists, niggers, and the Grand Empire. **1877** BEARD *K.K.K. Sketches* 74 The Grand Division, or Empire, was subdivided into Realms, Provinces, and Dens.

(5) **1860** EMERSON *Cond. Life* (1861) iii. 58 Railroad presidents, copper-miners, grand-junctioners [etc.]. — (6) **1896** HASWELL *New York* 62 Also the Krout Club, which later was presided over by a Grand Krout, who once in a year was declared to have nodded, thereby indicating his assent to a meeting. — (7) **1899** *Caddo* (Okla.) *Herald* 21 April 3/2 The ball was . . . opened with a grand march. **1943** HALE *Between Dark & Daylight* 165 At the end of each dancing-class we formed for the Grand March, and paraded two by two around the room. **1947** LUMPKIN *Southerner* 104 Who would now lead the grand march at the Assembly Ball? — (8) **1826** FLINT *Recoll.* 163 After four days of unavailable siege, the Indians gave a yell, exclaimed, that the house was a 'grand medecine,' meaning, that it was charmed and impregnable, and went away. **1847** LANMAN *Summer in Wild.* 105 White men and Indians who have never been initiated into the mysteries of the Grand Medicine, are not allowed to be present. **1916** EASTMAN *From Deep Woods* 169 The 'Grand Medicine Dance,' invoked the protection and blessing of the 'Grand Mystery.' — (9) **1916** [see **grand medicine**].

(10) **1818** J. C. PACKARD in *R. I. Hist.* I. 89 A great many have taken lands on the Grand Prairie over the Illinois. **1855** *Amer. Inst. N.Y., Trans.* 405, I lived on the Grand Prairie of Indiana. — (12) **1893** POST *Harvard Stories* 308 They all hold on to something or clasp their knees tightly—to faint or fall over would be a grand-stand play. **1912** RAINE *Brand Blotters* 162 There wasn't any way for it but that grand-stand escape of Mr. Boone's. **1948** *Chi. Sun-Times* 14 Oct. 42/3 Truman has been accused of trying to make a grandstand play for political effect. — (13) **1913** BLYTHE *Fakers* 163 That old grand-stander, Rollins, is making a good deal of a row over the franchise matter. **1944** GARDNER *Black-Eyed Blonde* 180 He's a fourflushing, grandstanding, hypocritical, selfish, conceited jackass. **1948** *Sat. Ev. Post* 24 July 21/1 Editorial blasts . . . have described the general in many unflattering terms—namely: a blunderer; a grandstander; a bull in a china shop; a trouble causer.

For **Grand Army, grand bounce, Grand Canyon,** ∗**grand committee, Grand Council,** ∗**granddaddy,** ∗**grandfather,** ∗**grandmother, Grand Old Party, Grand Pawnee,** see as main entries.

Grand Army.

1. The Union army organized at Washington in 1861–62 to operate against Richmond. Also *Grand Army of the Potomac.*

1861 NEWELL *Orpheus C. Kerr* I. 63 While the Grand Army is making its preparations for an advance upon the Southern Confederacy. **1863** HOPLEY *Life in South* II. 158 The Southern army had held their ground, and kept back the 'grand army of the Potomac.' **1866** POLLARD *So. Hist.* I. 89 General Johnston had penetrated the designs of the enemy, which were to hold him in check, while 'the Grand Army' under McDowell was to bear down upon General Beauregard at Manassas.

2. =next. Also attrib.

1874 *G. A. R.* (Mass.) *Ann. Encampment Proc.* 9 The Grand Army in this State was never more flourishing than now. **1913** LONDON *Valley of Moon* III. iv, He was an old man, and reminded Saxon of the sort she had been used to see in Grand Army processions on Decoration Day. **1944** HOLTON *Yankees* 43 Yet, since the Grand Army was a thoroughly democratic organization, every man who had actually or theoretically given his blood for his country was eligible to hold office.

3. *Grand Army of the Republic,* an organization composed of those who served on the Union side during the Civil War. Cf. **G.A.R.**

1866 (*title*), Proceedings of enlistment . . . of the Grand army of the republic. **1925** *G. A. R. 59th Nat. Encampment Jrnl.* 47 Any member of the Grand Army of the Republic . . . has the privilege to sit in the gallery. **1949** *Chi. D. News* 6 April 37/3 The founding of the Grand Army of the Republic in 1866 will be commemorated . . . April 9.

grand bounce. (See quots.) Also **G.B., g.b.** *Slang.*

1877 BARTLETT 777 To get the *grand bounce* is to be dismissed from service; particularly from an office under government. **1880** *Cimarron News & Press* 23 Dec. 1/7 'Well, I've got the g.b.' 'The geebee, Thomas! What in the nation is that?' . . . 'I've got the grand bounce —g.b. grand bounce. . . . I've been fired!' **1909** S. E. WHITE *Rules of Game* (1916) iii. 19 'I'm mighty sorry, old man,' he whispered, furtively. 'Did you get the G.B.?'

Grand Canyon, Cañon. The main or most scenically spectacular canyon in any system, used esp. of those on the Colorado, Yellowstone, Snake, and Arkansas rivers.

[**1861** NEWBERRY *Geol. Rep.* 45 The Great Cañon of the Colorado would be considered a vast fissure or rent in the earth's crust.] **1878** HINTON *Ariz.* 55 This group constitutes the most conspicuous feature of the Grand Cañon of the Colorado and its tributary gorges. **1879** WILLIAMS *Pacific Tourist* 344/2 A short distance above the mouth of Tower Creek, is the lower end of the 'Grand Canon' of the Yellowstone. **1906** ADAMS *Cattle Brands* 242 The climax of this night's run was the Grand Cañon of the Arkansas. **1948** *Dly. Ardmoreite* (Ardmore, Okla.) 22 July 2/8 Idaho's Grand Canyon of the Snake river is the deepest gorge in North America.

attrib. **1876** *Rep. Geol. Eastern Portion Uinta Mts.* 70 The Grand Cañon Group rests unconformably upon the crystalline schists. . . . Fossils have been found at the base of the Grand Canon series. . . . Red Creek Quartzite and Grand Cañon schists . . . are believed to be Eozoic. **1948** *Sierra Club Bul.* Dec. 4/2 The construction of the Bridge Canyon Dam . . . would flood eighteen miles along one boundary of the western portion of Grand Canyon National Park.

∗**grand committee.**

1. (See quot.)

1841 BUCKINGHAM *America* II. 419 Without the agreement of the majority of both houses no act can become law [in R.I.]; but sometimes both houses meet in grand committee, as it is called—that is, they unite their numbers, and sit together as one assembly—when the majority of the whole united number decides the questions in debate.

2. (See quot. 1914.)

1891 J. SCHOULER *Hist. U.S.* V. 172 Foote of Mississippi . . . proposed a grand committee in February. **1914** *Cyclo. Amer. Govt.* II. 94 Grand Committee. This name has commonly been applied to committees of one from each state, and dates from the Federal Convention where such a committee was formed to adjust the controversies over representation. . . . Since that time [i.e., 1860] the states have been too numerous to make such a committee practicable.

Grand Council.

1. An executive council having exceptionally wide or important duties in assisting a governor or chief executive. *Obs.*

1694 *N. C. Col. Rec.* I. 431 Philpot . . . giving good security to render ye same or an acct thereof to ye Grand Councell whensoever he shall be thereunto required. **1754** *Mass. H. S. Coll.* 3 Ser. V. 70 [It is proposed] that the said general government be administered by a President-General, . . . and a Grand Council, to be chosen by the representatives of the people of the several colonies met in their respective Assemblies. **1784** *Mass. Centinel* 31 March 2/1 The shafts of his virulence and abuse were aimed directly at the breasts of the Grand Council of America.

2. The governing body of the Know-Nothing party. *Obs.*

1854 in HAMBLETON *H. A. Wise* 47 The Grand Council shall be composed of thirteen delegates, from each state, to be chosen by the State Councils. . . . In all sessions of the Grand Council, thirty-two delegates . . . shall constitute a quorum.

3. Among American Indians, a council having supreme or superior authority.

1864 *Ladies' Repository* XXIV. 200/2 The Grand Council had enacted very stringent laws for the protection of missionaries. **1865** PIKE *Scout & Ranger* (1932) 14 At Boggy Depot we saw a great many Choctaws and Chickasaws assembled to hold a grand council, and, like all political meetings it was a mixed crowd.

∗**granddaddy,** *n.* Also ∗**grandaddy.**

1. granddaddy graybeard, (*a*) =**granddaddy longlegs,** (*b*) =**grandfather graybeard.**

(*a*) **1899** *Animal & Plant Lore* 38 A grand-daddy gray-beard (daddy-long-legs) running over clothes means that you will soon have a new garment. Boxford Mass., and Cazenovia, N.Y. — (*b*) **1945** *Democrat* 29 March 2/1 Being out turkey hunting some spring afternoon with the air heavy with the scent of wild honey suckle and sweet shrubs, and with the white of the grandaddy graybeards and the dogwoods peeping out from the delicate green of the beeches.

2. granddaddy longlegs, a daddy-longlegs.

1875 Mark Twain *Sk., New & Old* 130 The learned and aged Lord Grand-Daddy-Longlegs . . . had been sitting, in deep study, with his slender limbs crossed. **1890** Howells *Boy's Town* 201 You must not kill a granddaddy-long-legs, or a lady-bug, it was bad luck.

3. granddaddy clause, =**grandfather clause.** *Colloq.*

1928 Bradford *Ol' Man Adam* 261 Hit's a primary law and hit's a granddaddy-clause law, and de niggers don't do much votin'.

grande grɑnd, *n.* [F.] (See quots.)

1833 Silliman *Man. Sugar Cane* 33 The names apropriated [*sic*] to the different kettles are as follows: the largest is called the *grande.* **1859** *Rep. Comm. Patents 1858* I. 697 Setting the kettles known as the 'battery' and the 'flambeau' over separate furnaces, . . . both communicating with the 'grande,' or first kettle of the series. **1875** Knight 1009/1 *Grande.* (*Sugar Manufacture.*) The largest evaporating-pan of a battery.

grande écaille. [La. F. "big scale."] The tarpon, *Tarpon atlanticus,* common on the coast of Florida and in the Gulf of Mexico.

1844 Moore *Texas* 36 Among these are red fish, grundiquoit, mullet, sea perch, sea trout, &c. **1932** *Sea Fishes & Sea Fishing Bul.* No. 21, 55 The Tarpon, Silver king or Grande Ecaille (Tarpon atlanticus) is the sportsman's supreme prize. **1946** *N.O. Times-Picayune* 24 Mar. II. 2/1 The grand-ecoy seems to be a fish, and a misspelled fish at that.

* **grandfather,** *n.*

1. grandfather clause, a clause in the constitutions of some southern states designed to disfranchise Negro voters by means of an educational qualification from which only those are exempt whose fathers, grandfathers, etc., voted before 1867.

1900 *Cong. Rec.* 22 Jan. 1033/1 The grandfather clause will not avail those citizens who . . . are unable to pay their poll tax. **1948** *Ga. Hist. Quart.* March 1 In 1898, Louisiana wrote the notorious 'Grandfather Clause' into its constitution.

2. grandfather graybeard, the southern fringe tree. Also **gransy graybeard.**

[**1910–12** *Trans. Tex. Acad. Sci.* (1913) 87 *Chionanthus Virginiana* L. (Grandfather's Beard).] **1931** Clute *Plants* 88 Old man's whiskers . . . may merely suggest an elderly gentleman, especially as *Chionanthus Virginica* is also known as grandfather graybeard. **1946** *Democrat* 13 June 2/3 Every street in Grove Hill should be lined with gransy graybeards (fringe trees), redbuds, crape myrtles and mimosas.

* **grandmother,** *n.*

1. Used in exclamations. *Slang.*

1870 in *Screamers* (1871) 50 'Shake the tree—' 'Shake your grandmother! Turnips don't grow on trees!' **1883** Mark Twain *Life on Mississippi* 60 'Yes, sir, it's as true as the world.' 'Oh, your grandmother!' **1883** *Harper's Mag.* 889/2 Well, this does beat my grandmother, I must say.

2. grandmother story, (see quot.).

1946 Foreman *Last Trek* 221 The Absentee Shawnee cherished a prophetic tradition generally known as the 'grandmother story' as told by a Shawnee woman, having reference to certain present and eternal judgments that would be visited upon the unfortunate head of any Indian who laid aside the blanket to adopt the white man's dress.

Grand Old Party.

1. The Democratic party. *Obs.*

Used without capitals and prob. not specific.

1879 Hill of Ga. in *Cong. Rec.* 11 June 1913/1 We are for national parties now. We come back to the grand old party of the North that never went off after secession, that never went after the Baals of consolidation. If there are any men on the earth for whom I have a higher regard than others, they are the democrats of the North. **1888** Lane of Ill. *Ib.* 10 May 3981/1 The Republican party is responsible for all this misrule, but a brighter day is about to dawn. . . . I am glad that I am a member of that grand old party that assures a better trade to our people, larger wages to labor, better times to the farmer, and greater glory to the American name at home and abroad.

2. The Republican party. Cf. **G.O.P.**

1888 *Cong. Rec.* 1 May 3598/1 [A proposed protection tax] is the doings of the G.O.P.—the grand old party—the Republican party. **1948** *Chi. D. News* 24 Aug. 18/6 The Grand Old Party will suffer, in November, its worst defeat since the Alf Landon debacle.

Grand Pawnee. The Chaui, an Indian tribe of the Pawnee confederacy. Also attrib.

1810 Pike *Sources Miss.* 143 *n.*, [Lt. Malgares] was met by the chiefs and warriors of the Grand Pawnees. **1856** Bonner *Life J. P. Beckwourth* (1931) 13 This is a band of the Pawnee tribe of Indians, which is thus divided: The Grand Pawnee Band, The Republican Pawnee Band [etc.]. **1946** Foreman *Last Trek* 182 This treaty was signed by representatives of the . . . Grand Pawnee.

* **Grange,** *n.* Also **grange.** A coöperative association of farmers known as "Patrons of Husbandry," organized primarily to bring producers and consumers into direct and friendly relations; a local unit or lodge of this association. See **National, state grange.**

1868 in Commons *Doc. Hist.* X. 79 Every Grange is in intimate relation with its neighboring Granges, and these with the State Grange, and the State Granges are in unity with the National Grange. **1882** Cooper *Amer. Pol.* I. 218 So early as 1867 a secret society had been formed first in Washington, known as the Patrons of Husbandry, and it soon succeeded in forming subordinate lodges or granges in Illinois, Wisconsin, and other States. **1920** *3d Nat. Country Life Conf. Proc.* 2 In fact, the grange is a family of families.

attrib. **1873** *Winfield* (Kans.) *Courier* 22 May 2/2 The 'Grange' organizations and 'paper farmer's club' are good enough in their way, but you cannot grow rich by simply belonging to a farmers club. **1941** *Yankee* Dec. 25/1 Gossip and Apple Pie are only a small part of a Grange meeting. **1946** Holbrook *Lost Men* 215 Traveling often on something less than a shoestring, Kelley swept through the Middle West, dispensing charters for local granges to pay his expenses.

* **Granger,** *n.* Also * **granger.**

1. A member of a farmer's grange, usu. *pl.* as a name for the organization.

1873 *Winfield* (Kans.) *Courier* 14 Aug. 1/5 The grangers consider that our home merchants, dealers and mechanics are their friends. **1885** *Mag. Amer. Hist.* Feb. 201/1 *Grangers.*—'The Patrons of Husbandry.' A secret society, nominally non-political, but really taking a hand in politics when occasion offers to favor agricultural interests. It is numerically strong and extends throughout the United states. **1947** *Atlantic Mo.* June 73/1 In the nineties the revolt begun by Grangers, Knights of Labor, and Populists was focused in the fiery oratory of Bryan, who threw a brief scare into the big men in 1896.

b. Attrib. with **agitation, legislature, movement, party.**

1913 La Follette *Autobiog.* 20 They asserted that the panic of 1873 was caused by the Granger agitation and that capital was being driven from the state by popular clamor. — **1907** *N.Y. Ev. Post* (s.-w. ed.) 11 Feb. 4 No Granger Legislature ever passed a law which, had the railroads observed it in good faith, would have caused them to be run at a loss. — **1875** *N. Amer. Rev.* CXX. 395 That Granger movement, . . . during the last four years, has played a most prominent part in the politics of certain of the North-western States. — **1888** Bryce *Amer. Commw.* II. II. xlvi. 202 A Granger party . . . secured drastic legislation against the railroad companies.

2. *pl.* Shares or stocks in railroads carrying principally farm products grown by grangers.

1880 *Dly. Inter-Ocean* (Chi.) 3 June 7/1 Stocks strong, . . . the grangers being prominent in the improvement. **1885** *Atlantic Mo.* April 449/1 There arises to the mind a congeries of difficult questions dealing with Western 'grangers.' **1900** Nelson *A B C Wall St.* 17 Railroad stocks . . . are divided in distinctive groups, including the Trunk Lines, Coalers, Grangers, Southerns.

b. Also **Granger laws, lines, shares.**

1898 *Mo. So. Dakotan* I. 9 The courts in the early seventies held under the 'Granger laws' that railways were subject to the control and regulation of the states granting them the privilege and protection of the laws of the state. **1907** *Collier's* 30 Mar. 25/2 The 'Granger laws' in the Western states attempted to subject the roads to some sort of public control. — **1903** E. Johnson *Railway Transportation* 58 West of the sections occupied by the granger and Southwestern lines lies the territory occupied by the transcontinental or Pacific roads. — **1880** *Dly. Inter-Ocean* (Chi.) 2 June 6/4 Speculation was weak and uncertain, Erie, Western Union, Lake Shore, and granger shares being the most prominent in the downward movement. **1881** *Chi. Times* 12 March, The chief speculative interest centered in the high-priced granger shares.

grangerism ˈgrendʒɚˌɪzəm, *n.* The principles of the farmers'-grange movement. *Obs.* — **1875** *Chi. Tribune* 9 Nov. 4/4 Last fall the election was a Congressional one and did not involve the element of Grangerism to any material extent.

* **granite,** *n.*

1. (See quots.)

1869 Mark Twain *Innocents Abroad* 232 Hundreds and hundreds of people [were] at small tables, smoking and taking *granite* (a first cousin to ice-cream). **1887** *N.Y. Tribune* 7 April 2/2 Granites . . . are a rough kind of sorbets. They are sometimes called rock punch and rock ice-cream, and are made of fruit juice, sugar and water.

2. In combs.: (1) **Granite Boy,** a nickname for a native or citizen of New Hampshire; (2) **college,** a prison, *slang, obs.;* (3) **-man,** = **Granite Boy,** *obs.;* (4) **State,** a nickname for New Hampshire, cf. **Old Granite State.**

(1) **1845** *St. Louis Reveille* 14 May 2/4 The inhabitants of . . . New Hampshire [are called] Granite Boys. **1888** WHITMAN *November Boughs* 406 Those from . . . New Hampshire [were called] Granite Boys. — (2) **1831** *Boston Transcript* 10 Mar. 2/1 If we can discover the gentle light-finger, we shall certainly cause him to be indited, and sent to the Granite College until he has finished his education. — (3) **1842** COOPER *Wing-and-Wing* II. 135 Our hero found Ithuel sleeping in the boat, in perfect security. The graniteman thoroughly understood his situation. — (4) **1830** *Mass. Spy* 20 Oct. (Th.), [Daniel Webster is] a genuine son of the 'Granite State,' and a plain farmer's boy. **1948** *Chi. Tribune* 10 Oct. (Grafic Mag.) 18/2 New Hampshire, famous Granite State of New England, has provided The Chicago Tribune with a piece of granite rock.

As the last term in **coffee, mourning, strawberry granite.**

granjeno grɑnˈheno, *n. S.W.* [Amer. Sp. in same sense.] A hackberry, *Celtis pallida,* having edible berries.

1895 *Amer. Folk-Lore* Jan.–Apr. 47 The *Granjeno* is a parasitic bush. **1937** PARKS *Valuable Plants Texas* 25 *Celtis pallida* Torr. Granjeno. **1949** *Chi. Tribune* 20 Feb. 30/3 Cedar and mesquite alone are costing Texas ranchers 115 million dollars a year. Add the sage and cactus, . . . persimmon, huisache, granjeno . . . and prickly pear and the toll is terrific.

grannified ˈgrænɪˌfaɪd, *a.* Like an old woman or granny. *Rare.* — **1862** *Constitution* (Middletown, Conn.) 7 May (B.), That querulous and grannified manner peculiar to old people who have outlived their usefulness.

***granny,** *n.*

1. A midwife or nurse.

1794 WASHINGTON *Writings* XIII. 18 An applicaton was made to me by Kate at Muddy hole (through her husband, Will) to serve the negro women (as a Grany) on my estate. **1824** WEEMS *Marion* (1833) II. 20 Among the Mohawks of Sparta, it was a constant practice on the birth of a male infant, to set a military granny to examine him, as a butcher would a veal for the market. **1923** *D. N.* V. 209 *granny,* n. A midwife, a senile man or woman. [Mo.]

2. Used in exclamations of surprise or emphasis. *Colloq.*

1863 *Ladies' Repository* XXIII. 482/2 'Repose, your granny,' answered Addie, who, when vexed never stopped for elegant phrases. **1876** MARK TWAIN *Tom Sawyer* xxv. 193 'Do they hop?' 'Hop—your granny! No.' **1894** ——— *Those Twins* i, Sick your granny; what's to make him sick? **1917** MCCUTCHEON *Green Fancy* 256 'Secret granny!' almost shouted O'Dowd.

granny ˈgrænɪ, *v. tr.* To serve (a mother) as a midwife. Also *intr. Colloq.*

1897 STUART *Simpkinsville* 85 She grannied yore mother when you was born. **1923** *D. N.* V. 209 granny . . . v. To perform the duties of a midwife. [Mo.] **1948** *Sat. Ev. Post* 25 Dec. 16/2 She got her herbs. . . . And grannied for Poor Little Jesus!

granodiorite ˌgrænəˈdaɪəraɪt, *n.* [f. ***granite** and *diorite.*] (See quot. 1911.) — **1893** *Amer. Jrnl. Sci.* 3 Ser. XLVI. 203 The granodiorite is later than the quartzitic slates of Signal Peak or Red Mountain north of Cisco. . . . At Meadow Lake several interesting facies of the granodiorite occur. **1911** *Encycl. Brit.* XXVII. 1/1 Granodiorite . . . has been very generally adopted in America for rocks which are intermediate in character between the granites and the diorites.

***grant,** *n.*[1]

1. A tract or area of land granted to an individual, state, etc. See also **Hampshire, New Hampshire grants.**

1636 *Watertown Rec.* I. II. 149 A grant of Plowlands at Beaverbrook Plaines divided and lotted out by ye freemen to all the Townsmen. **1721** *Mass. H. Rep. Jrnl.* III. 12 Voted, That the said 3700 Acres of Land, be added to their former grant of 7000 Acres, . . . Provided it do not intrench upon any former grant. **1872** TICE *Over Plains* 18 The railroad has a grant of land of every alternate section for ten miles on each side of the road. **1943** DALE *Cow Country* 70 It, too, soon made large grants to railroads, usually in alternate sections, and other large areas were set aside for the use of the public schools.

b. In full **grant land.** *Obs.*

1714 *Suffield Doc. Hist.* 188 We computed Feather Street Common, and computed ye whole of ye first grant Land in ye Town. **1873** BEADLE *Undevel. West* 177 Many got 'grant land' and got too much, and are bothered to pay for it.

c. (See quots.)

1836 M. A. HOLLEY *Texas* 222 The Empresarios' contracts, by an inadvertency, . . . have been called grants. **1881** INGERSOLL *Oyster Industry* 244 *Grant.*—Stipulated area 'granted' by the state for oyster culture. (Massachusetts.)

2. (*cap.*) *pl.* Short for **New Hampshire grants.**

1777 A. HAMILTON *Wks.* (1886) VII. 514 They may be obliged to increase their attention to this matter by keeping a body of men somewhere about the Grants. **1798** I. ALLEN *Hist. of Vermont* 31 Mr. J. Munroe . . . had rendered himself obnoxious by his partiality for New York, and persecution of the settlers of the grants. **1898** in *Pub. Col. Soc.* V. 272 In the Grants he came across Ethan Allen, who married his step-daughter Frances. **1942** CANNON *Mountain* 60 Well, I ain't never been up into the Grants.

b. Those living in the Grants. *Rare.*

1782 *Essex Inst. Coll.* XXXV. 238 Large quantitys of salt, rum, &c, [had been sent] for the use of the grants.

3. grant ring, a group or clique that secured through fraud extensive land grants in the West. *Obs.*

1883 *Gringo & Greaser* 1 Sep. 2/2 Col. Webb of Golden, the dashing hot-shot artillerist of the Retort Battery—the man who is so disagreeable to grant rings and land thieves generally—called on us.

As the last term in **bounty, canal, confirmation, family, French, homestead, land, Ohio, railroad, Spanish, swamp grant.**

***Grant,** *n.*[2] [f. Ulysses S. *Grant* (1822–85), Amer. general and 18th President.]

1. The name of one of the largest of the giant redwoods in California and of a national park created primarily to preserve it (see quot. 1946).

1901 J. MUIR *Our National Parks* 298 A short distance south of this forest lies a beautiful grove, now mostly included in the General Grant National Park. . . . One of the shake-makers directed me to an 'old snag biggeren Grant.' **1938** *World Almanac* 361/1 The National Parks. . . . General Grant, 1890, Middle Eastern California. . . . Created to preserve the celebrated General Grant Tree and grove of Big Trees. **1946** *Sierra Club Bul.* Dec. 133 What was once General Grant National Park has become the General Grant Grove of Kings Canyon National Park.

2. Grant Ranger, (see quot.). *Obs.*

1904 FLEMING *Documents rel. Reconstruction* No. 3, 5 The dislike of the whites to the Union League was so great that the local bodies began to assume other names: 'Red Strings' and 'Heroes of America' in North and South Carolina, 'Grant Rangers' in Georgia, 'Alcorn Clubs' in Mississippi, 'National Guards' in Alabama, etc.

Grantism ˈgræntɪzəm, *n.* [See prec.] The political philosophy and practices of President Grant and his followers. *Obs.*

1876 *Moving Ball* (Marlin, Tex.) 23 Mar. 2/1 To nominate him for President is to nominate Grantism. **1876** *Harper's Wkly.* 7 Oct. 806/4 That is their meaning of the term 'Grantism.' **1877** *Nation* 15 Mar. 156/1 The great fear [has been] . . . that we should thus be treated to four more years of the regime known as 'Grantism.'

granza ˈgrænzə, *n. S. W.* [Sp., usu. in *pl. granzas,* siftings, refuse.] (See quots.) — **1873** *Mining & Sci. Press* 21 Mar., The next lower or ordinary grade of [quicksilver] ore is called 'granza.' **1889** *Cent.* 2600/1 Granza. . . . In the quicksilver-mines of California, the second-class ore obtained in small lumps, and inferior in yield to the grueso.

***grape,** *n.*

1. = ***grapevine 2.** *Slang. Obs.*

1864 in HUNDLEY *Prison Echoes* 104 The prison is greatly agitated tonight with a fearful 'grape' from Atlanta. **1865** in *Southern Hist. Soc. P.* III. 56 Plenty of 'grape,' *i.e.,* rumors afloat of a speedy general exchange.

2. In combs.: (1) **grape arbor,** an arbor or bower overgrown with grapevines; (2) **belt,** (see quot.); (3) **box,** a box used for grapes, also designating a type of hat suggestive of this, *rare;* (4) **concentrate,** (see quot. 1931), *obs.;* (5) **fever,** unusual enthusiasm for grape culture; (6) **fruit,** a large, roundish citrus fruit widely grown in subtropical regions, also attrib.; (7) **hoe,** a hoe, esp. one drawn by a single horse, for cultivating between rows of grapevines; (8) **ranch,** a ranch or large farm upon which grape-growing is the chief activity; (9) ***shot,** designating a type of revolver (see quot.), *rare;* (10) **soda,** (see quot.); (11) **stake,** a stake for a grapevine; (12) **swamp,** a swamp where wild grapes grow; (13) ***vine,** see as a main entry; (14) **whisky,** whisky made from grapes, *rare.*

(1) **1809** CUMING *Western Tour* 167 He has opened a little publick garden behind his house, which he calls Vaux-hall. It has a most luxuriant grape arbour, and two or three summer houses! **1939** WHITE *One Man's Meat* 82 Under the porte-cochère stands the reconditioned station wagon; under the grape arbor sit the puppies for sale. — (2) **1897** BAILEY *Prin. Fruit-growing* 41 The famous Chautauqua grape-

belt is confined to a strip about two or three miles wide lying upon Lake Erie. — **(3) 1865** [Patent No. 48,192, 12 June.] **1900** GARLAND *Eagle's Heart* 188 Now, you mustn't wear that broad hat; you wear a grape-box straw hat while you're here. — **(4) 1931** *Durant* (Okla.) *D. Democrat* 30 July 4/5 Sales of grape concentrates, a by-product of California wine grapes sold for making 'grape beverages' in the home, are increasing tremendously. **1932** *Blue Valley Farmer* (Okla. City) 14 Jan. 6/4 Nor is the prohibition issue available, with the government spending millions in support of the California grape concentrate racket and other millions to prosecute those who mishandle the fruit of the vine.

(5) 1864 *Ohio Agric. Rep.* XVIII. 151 We have not had, it is true, 'the grape fever,' which has visited some other sections of our state, but that there is growing interest in the culture of the grape is a gratifying fact. — **(6)** [**1859** BARTLETT 179 *Grape Fruit*, a variety of *Citrus racemosus*. Barbadoes.] **1896** *N.Y. Herald* 2 April 10/1 Grape fruit varies in price, according to size, bringing from ten cents to forty cents each. **1947** *Chi. Tribune* 2 Nov. (Grafic Mag.) 7/5 He cooked himself some lima beans and ham, after wetting his whistle with a big slug of Florida grapefruit juice. — **(7) 1862** *Rep. Comm. Patents 1861: Agric.* 514 In the spring before the eyes burst out, the ground around the vine is dug up with the grape-hoe from four to six inches deep. — **(8) 1898** ATHERTON *Californians* 312 Caro was engaged to marry an Englishman who had bought a grape-ranch some twenty miles from Menlo. — **(9) 1917** MORGAN *Recollections* 94 Soon there arrived a Frenchman, a Colonel Le Mat, the inventor of the 'grapeshot revolver,' a horrible contraption, the cylinder of which revolved around a section of the gun barrel. The cylinder contained ten bullets, and the grapeshot barrel was loaded with buckshot which, when fired, would almost tear the arm off a man with its recoil.

(10) 1892 *York County Hist. Rev.* 18 Various kinds of carbonated beverages, such as . . . ginger ale, grape soda, sarsaparilla, and soft drinks. — **(11) 1907** *Collier's* 19 Oct. 19/1 He intended, when the summer demand for grape stakes was over, to put his crew to cutting stove wood. **1947** *Sierra Club Bul.* Nov. iii, We see all-but-ageless Big Tree stands blasted down for fence-posts and grape stakes (the fragments being hardly good for anything else). — **(12) 1685** *Derby Rec.* 138 Also they have sold to him: 2 acres of grape Swomp: . . . att ye North End of yt Swomp. — **(14) 1834** A. PIKE *Sketches* 112 A cuartillo of aguardiente, or grape whiskey, was . . . placed upon the table.

b. In the names of various insects and diseases injurious to grapes, as **grape beetle, -berry moth, borer, codling, -leaf gall louse, louse, moth, rot, worm.**

1863 *Horticulturist* Sep. 287/2 Grape Rot and Mildew. **1868** *Rep. Comm. Agric. 1867* 72 Specimens of the root of the grapevine destroyed by the grape-borer (*Aegeria polistoformis*) have been received. *Ib.* A grape-leaf-gall-louse, *Dactylosphæra vitifoliæ* . . . causes green, fleshy excrescences, about the size of a pea, on the lower surface of the leaf. **1869** *Rep. Comm. Agric. 1868* 217 New York: The grape beetle, thrips, rose-bug, and caterpillar appear. **1871** *Ill. Agric. Soc. Trans.* VIII. 158 The *Penthina Vitivorana*, or Grape-berry moth, [is] called also Grape-codling, for the reason that its destructive work in the vineyard is . . . similar to that of the Apple-codling in the orchard. **1873** *Maine Bd. Agric. Rep.* 126 The grape worm is apt to trouble them [*sc.* onions], but they are very easily killed. **1889** *Cent.* 2600/3 *Grape-louse*, . . . the vine-pest or phylloxera. **1890** WEBSTER 645/2 *Grape moth*, . . . a small moth (*Eudemis botrana*), which in the larval state eats the interior of grapes, and often binds them together with silk.

As the last term in **arroyo, beach, bull, bullet, California, cape, Catawba, chicken, coon, Diana, Elizabeth, European, fall, fox, frost, hill, Isabella, island, jack, June, mission, Missouri, mountain, mustang, Oregon, pine wood(s), post oak, raccoon, red, river, Roanoke, rock, sand, scuppernong, seaside, skunk, sugar, summer, summer fox, sweet mountain, wine, winter grape.**

* **grapevine,** *n.*

1. = **grapevine swing.**

1845 KIRKLAND *Western Clearings* 105 Ruth was swinging in a grapevine which had been slung so conveniently by the freakish hand of nature.

2. A rumor, report, or news obtained by way of a grapevine telegraph; the system of conveying such news. Also attrib. Cf. **grapevine telegraph.**

1863 in *Atlantic Mo.* XXXV. 336/1 It's all a nightmare, all a humbug and a bore; Just another foolish *grapevine*. **1868** *Alta California* (S.F.) 30 April 7/6 Major-General Thomas is no sensationalist; he is not given to grape-vine despatches. **1920** *Pacific Review* June 30 Many papers habitually 'raise dates' on 'grapevine' news . . . trying to give the impression that the story was written yesterday and came by wire when it did not. **1947** *Mazama* Sep. 2/1 We have advance information via the Mazama grapevine this is one trip you must not miss.

3. In special combs.: (1) **grapevine bridge,** a grapevine serving as a bridge, also transf.; (2) **bridle,** a piece of grapevine used as a bridle, *colloq.;* (3) **cigar,** a piece of grapevine used by boys as a make-believe cigar; (4) **cradle,** a local name for a now undefinable kind of grain cradle, *obs.;* (5) **daily,** (see quot.); (6) **land,** (see quot.); (7) **mesquite,** (see quot.); (8) **road,** a poor road which is especially crooked, *colloq.;* (9) **swing,** the vine of a wild grape used as a swing; (10) **telegraph,** any surreptitious means of transmitting information, *colloq.* [allegedly first used of a telegraph line constructed in 1859 between Placerville and Virginia City, see C. H. Shinn, *The Story of the Mine*, p. 72]; (11) **whisky,** (see quot.), *obs.*

(1) 1890 Goss *Recollections* 48 The 'Grapevine' bridge . . . had been built of logs over the swampy bottom, and . . . was sustained in place by ropes tied to stumps on the upstream side. **1903** *Critic* XLIII. 305 Along the ridge, . . . a cat may cross on the grapevine bridge. — **(2) 1809** WEEMS *Marion* (1833) 47 [You could see] the fences all strung along with starved tackies, in grape-vine bridles. — **(3) 1896** WHITE *Real Issue* 63 Piggy Pennington did not take to the enchantment of corn silk cigarettes and rattan and grape vine cigars. — **(4) 1884** *Canon City* (Colo.) *Mercury* 22 Aug. 1/5 'Grapevine' and 'Turky wing' cradles are the ones that cut most of the Hawes' grain. [**1923** ADAMS *Pioneer Hist.* 319 Until I was seven years old the sickle cut all the grain in the neighborhood; then the turkey-wing cradle, the grape-vine, the mully, [etc.].]

(5) 1912 NICHOLSON *Hoosier Chron.* 171 Harwood . . . had little patience with what he called the 'grapevine dailies,' with their scrappy local news, patent insides, and servile partisan opinions. — **(6) 1871** DE VERE 407 The comparatively poor land, on which grapevines grow wild, and which is hence called Grapevine land. — **(7) 1937** *Range Plant Handbook* G92 Vine-mesquite is unusual among western range grasses in that it produces creeping stems or stolons, which sometimes are 10 feet long. It is also known, especially in Texas, as grapevine-mesquite. — **(8) 1862** in F. MOORE *Rebellion Rec.* V. II. 89 The old 'Grape Vine' road, which had gone into disuse these many years, had been reöpened. — **(9) 1853** SIMMS *Poems* 'The Grape-Vine Swing.' **1944** DUNCAN *M. Graham* 33 A grapevine swing dangled above the creek, offering the thrill of traveling from bank to bank over the falls by the weavery.

(10) 1865 *Flag's Dispatch* (S.F.) 12 April 2/2 (*headline*), By Grape-vine Telegraph—Three Miles East of Julesburg. **1943** *Chr. Century* 22 Dec. 1504/1 Dispatches report that the 'grapevine telegraph' told every American soldier the news within twenty-four hours. — **(11) 1875** *Chi. Tribune* 21 Nov. 4/2 In St. Louis the revenue officers kept with religious fidelity two reports,—one of every gallon of straight whisky produced and sold . . . and second, as faithful an account of every gallon of crooked or grape-vine whisky.

b. In the names of insects esp. injurious to grapevines, as **grapevine beetle, borer, sphinx.**

1862 *Rep. Comm. Patents 1861: Agric.* 602 Figure 39 is *Anomala lucicola*, the 'Anomalous grape-vine beetle.' **1868** *Iowa Agric. Soc. Rep. 1867* 189 The grape-vine beetle, (*Pelidnota Punctata*), has not been seen. — **1868** *Rep. Comm. Agric. 1867* 72 The Scuppernong grape alone is said to be exempt from the attacks of the grapevine borer. — **1886** *Harper's Mag.* June 45/2 Leaf-rollers, the grape-vine sphinx, and caterpillars . . . must be caught by hand.

Graphophone (*c*1900)

graphophone ˈgræfəˌfon, *n.* [See note.]

Prob. f. Gk. *grapho-*, writing + *phone*, voice, sound, but if so, of slightly unusual formation. Poss. an inversion of the considerably earlier **phonograph*, *q.v.* Cf. **Gramophone.**

An instrument for recording and reproducing sounds, esp. one bearing the trade-mark name of Graphophone.

1886 *Boston Herald* 16 July, The 'graphaphone' or improved phonograph. **1891** *Appleton's Ann. Cyclo. 1890* 709/1 In 1886, J. S. Taintor, working along the lines followed by Mr. Edison, produced a talking machine, which was called the *graphophone*, or *phonograph-grapho-*

phone. **1944** CLARK *Pills* 92 A customer wished to buy a sewing machine or a graphophone on the installment plan.

attrib. **1902** *Sears Cat.* (ed. 112) 261 While these songs are being sung by the graphophone and sung in such a manner as possibly was never heard before from a graphophone record, beautiful colored slides from life posings are thrown on the screen.

b. A disk or cylinder that could be folded and sent through the mail and used on such a machine. *Obs.*

1890 *Boston Transcript* 3 Feb. 2/5 'Drop me a graphophone,' instead of 'drop me a line,' will soon be the good-bye word at railway partings.

Hence **graphophonic,** *a. Rare.*

1901 *N. Amer. Review* Feb. 216 It executes with a marvellous mechanism the orders it receives; it transmits with a graphophonic accuracy the communications made to it.

***grapple,** *n.* (See quot. 1883.) — **1872** *Maine Spl. Laws* 77 No person shall be allowed to take or catch any pickerel with spears, hooks or grapples, from Worthly pond. **1883** KNIGHT *Supp.* 421/1 *Grapple,* . . . a tool with spring jaws which are closed by striking the fish.

***grasper,** *n.* An insect of a family (Mantidae) characterized by forelegs peculiarly suited for grasping prey. — **1854** EMMONS *Agric. N.Y.* V. 142 *Mantidae.* This family . . . consists of insects technically called *Raptores* or graspers. **1879** *Scribner's Mo.* Aug. 499/1 The graspers (*Orthoptera raptoria*), such as the mantis.

***grass,** *n.*

1. In combs.: (1) **grass-bellied,** (see quot. 1944), *colloq.;* (2) ***butter,** butter made in the spring from the milk of cows that feed upon fresh grass [poss. a translation of Du. *grasboter*], *obs.;* (3) **dance,** see as a main entry; (4) ***fed,** (*a*) rural, countrified, *colloq.,* (*b*) (see quot.), *obs.;* (5) **fee,** *W.* a fee for grazing privileges, esp. money paid to Indians for grazing rights on their land; (6) **linen,** a fine light cloth resembling linen, woven from the fibers of the inner bark of China grass [cf. Du. *graslinnen*]; (7) **lodge,** an Indian lodge made of grass; (8) **lodge dance,** =**grass dance;** (9) **lot,** a lot or area producing grass; (10) **question,** *W.* the question or problem of grazing rights or privileges; (11) ***roots,** see as a main entry;

Grass lodge of Plains Indians

(12) **rope,** see as a main entry; (13) **trail,** *W.* a cattle trail along which grass is available for the herds, *obs.;* (14) **water,** the everglades.

(1) **1898** WISTER *Lin McLean* 113 I'm grass-bellied with spot-cash. **1902** MOORE *Songs & Stories* 186 Their rule, es fur es I was able to see, was to hump up themselves on their grass-bellied ponies an' git up an' git. **1944** ADAMS *W. Words* 67 grass-bellied Pot-gutted. grass-bellied with spot cash Rich, to have plenty. — (2) **1820** *Cin. Advertiser* 27 June 3/3 Fine *grass* butter has been sold in the Philadelphia market this season at 6¼ cents per lb. and milk at 3 cents per quart. **1850** COOPER *Rural Hours* 41 Fresh grass butter from the farm today. **1852** *Knickerb.* XXXIX. 563 Where would be the yellowness of 'spring' (usually denominated 'grass') butter? — (4) (*a*) **1831** in MACKENZIE *Van Buren* (1846) 228 The intelligence of the Senate has been beaten by the ignorant-wise, grass-fed members who compose a large majority of the Legislature. **1906** O. HENRY *Heart of West* 86 Not for the grass-fed man of the pampas! (*b*) **1857** BATES *Incidents Pacific Coast* 151 There is a kind of grass in the valleys the Indians eat, that is pleasant to the taste and nutritious. . . . The children all go naked. This grass has a tendency to increase their ordinary dimensions; and you will often hear it remarked as one makes his appearance, 'There comes a little grass-fed.'

(5) **1920** HUNTER *Trail Drivers Texas* I. 168 The Indians were there to count us up for a grass fee. — (6) **1866** MRS. WHITNEY *L. Goldthwaite* viii. (1867) 175 A strip of sheer, delicate grass-linen, which needle and thread . . . were turning into a cobweb border. **1884** *S.-F. Pioneer-Press* Sep., Maguey is . . . a feature of this country. . . . The fiber of the leaf, beaten and spun, forms a fine and beautiful thread called pita, glossy as silk in texture, which much resembles 'grass' linen when woven into fabric. — (7) **1881** *Rep. Indian Affairs* 78 Seldom, if at all, would be seen the grass lodge. — (8) **1881** *Rep. Indian Affairs* 29 The 'Grass Lodge' dance is still practiced among the Indians. — (9) **1660** *Conn. Hist. Soc. Coll.* XIV. 426 To make keep & mayntayne for euer a Sufficient fence between my grass lott & Thomas Watts his thre acre lott by ye wolfe pownd. **1847** DARLINGTON *Weeds & Plants* 284 Broad-leaved Dock [grows in] grass lots; gardens, meadows, &c.

(10) **1883** *Rep. Indian Affairs* 71 The grass question seems to be the most difficult thing I have to contend with. — (13) **1920** HUNTER *Trail Drivers Texas* I. 153 From the early days of the grass trails . . . he has been an active participant. — (14) **1840** *Niles' Reg.* 7 March 3/2 He intends operating by light canoes built in South Carolina . . . and the dogs will be available in scenting among the islands which are said to be in the grass-water. **1891** *Harper's Mag.* Sep. 594/2 Hunters following their game just within the borders of the 'grass water' have seen smoke rising above the tops of the tall oaks and palmettoes far within. **1942** KENNEDY *Palmetto Country* 17 The Tamiami Trail affords motorists an awe-inspiring panorama of Grass-Water, beside which the road and canal seem insignificant.

b. In similar combs., often rare or obs., of obvious meaning or sufficiently explained in the quots., as (1) **grass-burning stove,** (2) **cattle,** (3) **cow,** (4) **harvester,** (5) **man,** (6) **shaver,** (7) **staggers.**

(1) **1883** KNIGHT *Supp.* 421/2 *Grass-burning Stove,* a stove for burning prairie grass where coal and wood are scarce. — (2) **1884** *Harper's Mag.* July 297/1 Into the former [department] come the choice corn-fed animals . . . as well as the best 'grass' cattle which have had the run of the summer ranges. **1903** *Cin. Enquirer* 2 May 9/4 Traders look for this betterment right along until the 'grass' cattle begin arriving. — (3) **1869** *Ill. Agric. Soc. Trans.* VII. 422 Grass cows were in plentiful, and indeed excessive supply. — (4) **1850** *Rep. Comm. Patents 1849* 458 Of the above mentioned twelve grain and grass harvesters, two are designed for collecting clover heads.

(5) **1844** LEE & FROST *Oregon* xii. 132 Mr. Nuttall, the 'Grass Man,' as the Indians term a botanist, visited the settlement and spent some time at the mission about midsummer. **1859** A. GRAY *Letters* (1893) 450, I asked Thurber the name of a couple of Grasses. Let the Grass-man speak. — (6) **1908** MULFORD *Orphan* 12 He was exceedingly weary of having to guard herds of bleating grass-shavers which so often passed across his domain. — (7) **1887** *Science* IX. 32/1 A curious affection exists among the horses of north-western Texas known as 'grass-staggers.' It is caused by their eating the 'loco-weed,' and the affected animals are said to be 'locoed.' At first they lose flesh, and then become weak and staggering, and finally crazy.

2. In the names of plants and animals: (1) **grass bass,** =**calico bass;** (2) ***bird,** any one of various small American birds usu. found in grassy places, cf. **hill, red grassbird;** (3) **caterpillar,** a caterpillar that feeds upon grass [cf. Du. *grasrups*]; (4) **finch,** (see quot. 1917); (5) **flower,** the blue-eyed grass, or the spring beauty; (6) **fox,** (see quot.); (7) **hopper,** see as a main entry; (8) **nut,** the sweet tuberous root of various grasses, a peanut; (9) **pike,** ?the green pike; (10) **pink,** any one of various orchids, esp. of the genus *Calopogon;* (11) **porgy,** (see quot.); (12) **rockfish,** (see quot.); (13) ***snake,** either of two bright-green, harmless North American snakes; (14) **snipe,** the pectoral sandpiper; (15) **sponge,** an inferior commercial sponge found off the coast of Florida; (16) ***worm,** the larva of a moth, *Laphygma frugiperda,* injurious to grass and grain.

(1) **1883** *Cent. Mag.* July 276/2 [Black bass] have received names somewhat descriptive of their habitat, as . . . moss, grass, and Oswego bass. **1911** *Rep. Fisheries 1908* 308 In Lake Erie and in Ohio generally it is called 'strawberry bass' or 'grass bass.' — (2) **1785** [see **grass finch**]. **1844** *Nat. Hist. N.Y., Zoology* II. 151 The Bay-winged Sparrow, *Fringilla graminea,* . . . [is] known in many parts of this State as the Grass-bird and Grey Grass-bird. **1917** *Birds of Amer.* I. 233/1 Pectoral Sandpiper. *Pisobia maculata.* . . . [Also called] Jack Snipe; Grass-bird; Meadow Snipe. — (3) **1852** *Fla. Plant Rec.* 75, I Notice that the grass Caterpiller is Eating all the grass up. **1856** *Rep. Comm.*

Patents 1855: Agric. 78 The grass-caterpillars, when in confinement, very often kill and devour each other. — **(4) 1785** PENNANT *Arctic Zool.* (1792) II. 65 Grass Finch. . . . Inhabits New York. . . . Called the Grey Grass-Bird. **1917** *Birds of Amer.* III. 23/1 Vesper Sparrow. *Poœcetes gramineus gramineus.* . . . [Also called] Bay-winged Bunting; Grass Finch; Gray Bird.

(5) 1894 *Amer. Folk-Lore* VII. 101 *Sisyrinchium angustifolium*, . . . blue-grass, grass-flower, star-eyed grass, Concord, Mass. **1932** WILDER *Little House* 113 Buttercups and violets, thimble flowers and tiny starry grassflowers were everywhere. — **(6) 1842** *Nat. Hist. N.Y., Zoology* I. 46 This species [i.e., the gray fox] is more common in the southern counties than farther north. On Long Island it is very abundant, and is there frequently known under the name of the *Plain* or *Grass Fox*. — **(8) 1806** CLARK in *Lewis & C. Exped.* V. (1905) 73 One [squirrel] which I examined had in his mouth two small bulbs of a species of grass, which resembles very much what is sometimes called Grass Nut. **1835** LONGSTREET *Ga. Scenes* 201 He was born in Nocatchey, and was raised upon nothing but grass-nuts and sweet potatoes. **1900** SMITHWICK *Evolution of State* 179 California Indians gathered . . . grass nuts which constituted their staple food. — **(9) 1876** *Fur, Fin, & Feather* Sep. 143 Black bass, grass pike . . . are abundant. **1947** BROWN *Outdoors Unlimited* 164 His dwarf kinsman that rarely exceeds a foot in length is known as the grass pike.

(10) 1817–8 EATON *Botany* (1882) 258 *Cymbidium pulchellum*, grass pink. **1901** MOHR *Plant Life Ala.* 459 *Limodorum tuberosum.* . . . Grass-pink. — **(11) 1888** GOODE *Amer. Fishes* 100 *C[alamus] arctifrons*, the 'Shad Porgy' or 'Grass Porgy' of Key West. — **(12) 1884** GOODE *Fisheries* I. 264 Grass Rock-fish (*Sebastichthys rastrelliger*). . . At San Francisco it is often called 'Grass Rock-fish,' perhaps from its color. — **(13) 1842** *Nat. Hist. N.Y., Zoology* III. 40 The Grass Snake is found from Massachusetts to Pennsylvania. **1884–5** *Riverside Nat. Hist.* (1888) III. 370 With the common people it [*Tropidonotus natrix*] is known as the ringed or grass-snake, and is often tamed. **1949** *Scientific Mo.* Jan. 57/2 Our smooth green, or grass, snake (*Opheodrys vernalis*) is remarkably gentle and inoffensive. — **(14) 1874** COUES *Birds N.W.* 468 *Tringa Maculata.* . . . Grass Snipe; Jack Snipe. **1948** *Sat. Ev. Post* 16 Oct. 54/4 He is an expert on the feeding habits of the pectoral sandpiper, or grass snipe.

(15) 1875 in GOODE *Fisheries* I. 848 [*Spongia graminea*] is one of the Grass Sponges of Commerce. . . . This species occurs in Key West, Florida. **1883** *Nat. Museum Bul.* No. 27, 124 The American species and subspecies [of sponges] are as follows: . . . *S[pongia] equina*, subsp. *cerebriformis*—Grass Sponge [etc.]. — **(16) 1815** *Lit. & Phil. Soc. N.Y. Trans.* I. 65 The ravages of the . . . canker worm, palmer worm, grass worm, and rose bug, are incalculably injurious. **1882** *Rep. Comm. Agric. 1881–2* 138 The injuries of the Grass worm to rice need never be feared.

3. In combs. (usu. occasional or obs.) designating places or areas overgrown by grass, as (1) **grass flat,** (2) **hole,** (3) **island,** (4) **plain,** (5) **pond,** (6) **prairie,** (7) **range,** (8) **swamp.**

(1) 1840 CUMINGS *Western Pilot* 49 About a mile and half below . . . is grass flats, channel at either side. — **(2) 1809** KENDALL *Travels* II. 39 There are in the town sixty-eight of these ponds that supply fish, and that are consequently permanent bodies of water; besides many others, that being filled only in the wet seasons, and affording grass in the dry, are denominated *grass-holes*. — **(3) 1842** *Amer. Pioneer* I. 284 By extraordinary efforts he made one of the grass islands, where he rested, got out of the skiff, and towed it up the river as far as he could wade. — **(4) 1826** FLINT *Recoll.* 372 Then commence the vast prairies, or grass plains, that reach to the Passo del Norte. **1900** BRUNCKEN *N. Amer. Forests* 5 The immense areas lying between these subdivisions are occupied by the grass plains of the eastern slope and the alkali and sage-brush deserts of the interior.

(5) 1837 WILLIAMS *Florida* 13 The back country presents a singular alternation of savannas, hammocks, lagoons and grass ponds, called altogether the Everglades. — **(6) 1826** FLINT *Recoll.* 110 A little beyond the town, there is considerable smooth grass prairie. **1851** M. REID *Scalp-Hunters* i. 11 This is the grass prairie, the boundless pasture of the bison. — **(7) 1864** *Harper's Mag.* Nov. 701/2 Mr. Woolsey . . . was returning from the grass range with his loaded wagon. **1890** LANGFORD *Vigilante Days* (1912) 227 My horse was immediately put in charge of a rancher . . . who . . . would send it with a herd to a convenient grass range. — **(8) 1718** *N.H. Probate Rec.* II. 4, I give & bequeath unto my sone John Green a lot of land lying by the grass swamp.

4. In colloq. phrases.

a. *To go to grass* (*and eat mullen*), to go to the dickens.

1807 *Balance* (Hudson, N.Y.) 17 Feb. 51 (Th.), Now he will have to go to grass, as the saying is. **1833** S. SMITH *Major Downing* 108 As for going to South Carolina to fight such chaps as these, I'd sooner let nullification go to grass and eat mullen. **1857** STROTHER *Virginia* 32 'Look here, gentlemen,' said he, triumphantly, 'you may now go to grass with your shed. I wouldn't change places with the man in the middle.'

b. *To be in the grass*, etc. (see quot. 1945).

1838 in BASSETT *Plantation Overseer* 111 He is somewhat in the grass, but promises with fair weather, which we now have, to be out in two weeks. **1944** CLARK *Pills* 88 Behind him at home was a cotton crop which had been rained out or that had been caught hopelessly in the grass. **1945** *N. & Q.* Nov. 117/1 He could easily remember the lengths to which an overseer or a Negro would go to avoid 'getting in the grass' (i.e., letting grass get a headstart in a cotton field).

c. *Between grass and hay* (or *between hay and grass*): (1) (See quot. 1871.) (2) (See quots.)

(1) 1848 J. MITCHELL *Nantucketisms* 40 *Betwixt hay & grass*, between Boyhood & Manhood. **1871** DE VERE 208 The peculiar phrase in which the youth, who is no longer a boy, and not yet a man, is picturesquely said to be *between grass and hay*. — **(2) 1886** HOWELLS *Minister's Charge* 188 On the way up he had time to explain that the clerk, who usually ran the elevator when they had no elevator-boy, had kicked, and they were just between hay and grass, as you might say. **1891** BUNNER *Zadoc Pine* 17 He . . . got a couple of eggs cooked for his private supper. . . . The eggs were, as he told Mr. Bryan, 'kinder 'twixt grass and hay.' **1943** DEVOTO *Yr. of Decis.* 91 The season was significantly known on the prairies as 'between hay and grass.'

d. *As long as grass grows and water runs*, forever.

1871 *Rep. Indian Affairs* (1872) 180 It had been solemnly pledged by all Departments of the government for the exclusive homes of the Indians as long as 'grass grows and water runs.' **1907** *Collier's* 30 Nov. 11/2 The invaders pleaded for Statehood, and Statehood forever laid aside the promise to the red man that he should have freedom 'as long as grass grows and water runs.'

e. *More rain more rest* (or *grass*), (see quot.).

1891 SLOAN *Fogy Days* 39 And Sambo said, more rain more ress; What, sir? 'I sez more rain more grass.'

As the last term in **ague, alkali, alkaline, Andes, aparejo, arrow, barn, beach, bear, Bermuda, bird, black, blue, blue-eyed, bonnet, bottle, branch, broom, buffalo, bunch, burden, candy, cane, canvasback, carpet, catchfly, chop, Colorado, cow, crab, creek, crop, Cuba, deer, devil, ditch, dog's tail, dog-town, door, duck, Dutch, early bunch, eel, English, English blue, English ray, English rye, English spire, evergreen, false buffalo, fancy, feather, finger, finger Indian, fire, flyaway, fly catch, forked beard, foul meadow, fox, free, freshwater cord, galleta, gama, gemma, Gila, Gilbert's relief, goose, grama, Guatemala, Guinea, hen, herd, high, hopper, Hungarian, Indian, Johnson, joint, June, king, knot-root, lawn, leafy meadow, Lewis, long, Louisiana, marsh, Means, mesquite, needle, old witch, orange, pigeon, pin, plume, porcupine, poverty, prairie, rattlesnake, red, redtop, rescue, resin, river, sage, Salem, salt, sand, sand beach, savanna(h), saw, scratch, scud, sedge, Seneca, sesame, short, short hair, sickle, silk, silky, silver, silver beard, skunktail, slough, smart, smut, soda, Spanish needle, spear, spider bent, spike, spiked, spiked gama, squaw, squirrel, stagger, stink, strong, sunken, swamp, swamp wire, switch, tall, tape, thatch, thin, tickle, timothy, toothache, turnip, vanilla, velvet, vomit, wampum, whip, white, white bent, white man's foot, wild, wild oat, winter, wire, witch, wood hair, wool, yard, yellow-eyed grass.**

grass dance. *W.* A dance by Indian warriors who have bunches of grass, orig. symbolical of scalps, suspended from their breechclouts. Now *hist.*

1885 *Rep. Indian Affairs* 59 Many of the old heathen customs and practices are kept up by them, such as the 'grass-dance.' **1892** in *So. Dak. Hist. Coll.* I. 53 [The Sioux's] war dance had ceased, and the grass dance soon must go. **1947** *Primitive Men* July 42 It was then that the Gros Ventres had their first Grass dance alone.

grasser ˈgræsɚ, *n. W.* A beef animal fattened on grass.

1881 *Chi. Times* 1 June, Several droves of Texas 'grassers' were among the fresh arrivals. **1911** QUICK *Yellowstone Nights* 143 Top grassers, they was at last, in weight an' price. **1948** *St. Paul* (Minn.) *Dispatch* 17 Sep. 42/1 Medium grade short fed steers and heifers were taken at $27 @ 29, with grassers at $22 @ 26.

grasset ˈgræsɪt, *n.* [F., adj., plump.] (See quots.) Cf. **joree,** *n.*

1831 AUDUBON *Ornith. Biog.* I. 151 It is a plump bird, and becomes very fat in winter, in consequence of which it is named *Grasset* in Louisiana, where many are shot for the table by the French planters. **1844** *Nat. Hist. N.Y., Zoology* II. 172 The Chewink, or Ground Robin, *Pipilio Erythrophthalmus*, . . . in Louisiana . . . is called, from its plumpness, Grasset, and is esteemed by epicures. **1931** READ *La.-French* 43 *Grasset, m.*, or its synonym *Grasset, m.*, 'fatty.' The Towhee or Chewink (*Pipilo erythrophthalmus erythrophthalmus* L.), which in winter becomes so fat that it was formerly shot for the table.

* **grasshopper,** *n.*

1. (See quot. 1829.) *Obs.*

1776 *Remembrancer* (1777) III. 193 Lieutenant Dunbar, who arrived the night before, was ordered to take post on the right of the 62d regiment, . . . with two grasshoppers. **1794** in *N. J. Hist. Soc. Proc.*

1 Ser. III. 179 Marched from Carlisle in the following order . . . 1st, an advance guard of horse . . . 3d, the artillery, consisting of seventeen pieces of six pounds, two mortars, and some grasshoppers. **1829** COOPER *Wish-ton-Wish* v, A small cannon, of a kind once known and much used under the name of grasshoppers, had been raised to the place.

2. *W.* Orig. a plow that could be drawn, though often only by fits and starts, through tough prairie sod by the inadequate, poorly-trained teams then available (see also quot. 1948). In full **grasshopper plow.**

1877 RUEDE *Sod-House Days* 229 Such a time as we had, learning to get the grasshopper to go into the sod and remain there I hope never to have again. **1927** SANDBURG *Songbag* 129 With a Texas pony and a grasshopper plow. **1948** *Amer. Sp.* Feb. 73/1 Later, in my childhood, *grasshopper plow* meant a light riding plow with either breaker or backset bottom, synonymous with *buggy plow,* if the latter was set very shallow.

3. In special combs., usu. rare or obs.: (1) **grasshopper battle,** a battle between Delaware and Shawnee Indians alleged to have grown out of a quarrel among children over the possession of a grasshopper; (2) **fruit cake,** a jocose term for a breadlike preparation of service berries crushed and mixed with pulverized grasshoppers, much enjoyed by certain western Indians; (3) **fund,** (see quot.); (4) **hawk,** the American sparrow hawk; (5) **Indians,** the Ute Indians; (6) **mouse,** any one of various short-tailed, partially insectivorous mice of the genus *Onychomys,* found in the western states; (7) **party,** (see quot.); (8) **pie,** a jocular term for a preparation of grasshoppers; (9) **plague,** a plague or infestation of grasshoppers; (10) **region,** a region where grasshoppers abound; (11) **season,** a season during which grasshoppers are destructive to crops; (12) **sparrow,** any one of various American sparrows of the genus *Ammodramus;* (13) **state,** a nickname for Kansas; (14) **year,** a year when grasshoppers are destructive to crops.

(1) **1873** WRIGHT *Sks.* 56 The evacuation of the Shawnees is based upon the consequence of their defeat by the Delawares in the memorable Grasshopper battle. — (2) **1848** BRYANT *California* xi. 162 The prejudice against the grasshopper 'fruit-cake' was strong at first, but it soon wore off. — (3) **1886** EBBUTT *Emigrant Life* 144 There was much distress all over the State [of Kansas], and a fund was organised, called the 'Grasshopper Fund,' to relieve the destitute people. Contributions were sent in great numbers and from every State in the Union. — (4) **1917** *Birds of Amer.* II. 90/1 Sparrow Hawk. *Falco sparverius sparverius.* . . . [Also called] Rusty-crowned Falcon; Grasshopper Hawk; Mouse Hawk.

(5) **1831** PATTIE *Personal Narr.* 100 The Grasshopper Indians . . . derive their name from gathering grasshoppers, drying them, and pulverizing them. — (6) **1908** *U. S. Dept. Agric. Farmers' Bul.* 335, 13 The grasshopper mouse is common throughout the sagebrush valleys of the Great Basin Country. **1947** *So. Sierran* March 3/3 The Grasshopper Mouse . . . is noteworthy because its favorite food consists of grasshoppers, scorpions and the like. — (7) **1873** *Northern Vindicator* (Estherville, Ia.) 6 Dec., 'Grasshopper parties' are being held in some portions of Iowa to raise money for the destitute Osceola county homesteaders. — (8) **a1861** WINTHROP *J. Brent* xvi. 183 Now they may sleep till they dry and turn to grass hopper pie, for me. **1872** MCCLELLAN *Golden State* 44 The red man alone was supreme in his animal life, hunting the deer and making his acorn and grasshopper pie. — (9) **1898** *Mo. So. Dakotan* I. 42 The Indians had only corn for their subsistance, and its destruction by the grasshopper plague reduced them almost to the verge of starvation.

(10) **1875** *Chi. Tribune* 12 July 4/7 There is no barrier to obstruct his progress as far as Omaha and the grasshopper region. — (11) **1881** HAYES *New Colorado* i. 21 There was hardly any farming in the early times; there were terrible grasshopper seasons before 1876. — (12) **1883** *Encycl. Brit.* (ed. 9) *Amer. Supp.* I. 350/1 The leading forms [of small spotted and streaked sparrows of N. Amer.] are: . . . the grass sparrows (*Poœcetes gramineus*); the grasshopper sparrows (*Coturniculus passerinus, C. henslowi, C. lecontii*) [etc.]. **1949** *Nat. Hist.* April 160 The nest of the grasshopper sparrow is rarely found, because it is cleverly concealed under a covering of grass. — (13) **1890** *Stock Grower & Farmer* (Las Vegas, N.M.) 21 June 3/2 The fever of speculation has seized upon our friends of the grasshopper state. — (14) **1880** *Scribner's Mo.* July 458/1 Then came 1875 and 1876, which were 'grasshopper years,' when no crops of consequence were raised in the whole state. **1906** in *Kansas Hist. Soc.* IX. 504 The drought and grasshopper year of 1874 is famous in the annals of Kansas. **1949** *Chi. Tribune* 5 June 1/3 He predicted it will be the worst grasshopper year since 1936.

b. *Knee-high to a grasshopper,* see ***knee-high.**

As the last term in **horse, lubber, red-legged, Rocky Mountain, traveling grasshopper.**

grasshopper ˈgræsˌhɑpɚ, *v. intr.* To move a boat *over* a shoal or other obstacle by pushing on both sides with poles. *Obs.* — **1873** BEADLE *Undevel. West* 704 When they spar thus on both sides, they are said to 'grasshopper over.'

***grass-roots,** *n. pl.*

1. *Mining.* The soil immediately below the surface of the ground. Also attrib.

1876 DODGE *Black Hills* 104 Gold is found almost everywhere, in the bars, in the gravel and sand of the beds, even in the 'grass roots.' **1906** *Out West* Feb. 85 Yet this era of 'grass-root bonanzas' was enough to turn the brains of the wildest dreamers. **1926** *Amer. Mercury* Feb. 149/2 Struck hard rock below the grass roots, 'n' had ter use chisels. **1948** WESTON *Mother Lode* 160 Discovered in 1848, 'grass-root gold' and a rich strike in 1850 were responsible for Grass Valley growing into a large and important gold camp.

b. Also *to get down to grass-roots,* to get down to basic facts.

1945 MENCKEN *Supp.* I. 297 (*note*), The late Dr. Frank H. Vizetelly told me in 1935 that he had been informed that *grass-roots,* in the verb-phrase, *to get down to grass-roots,* was in use in Ohio *c.* 1885, but he could never track down a printed record of it, and neither could I.

Hence **grass rooter.**

1947 *Chi. Times* 28 June 13/4 Other straw polls in other states indicate that Republican 'Grass rooters' quite generally feel the same way.

2. *attrib.* Basic, fundamental, rustic. *Colloq.*

1932 *Durant* (Okla.) *D. Democrat* 24 Feb. 1/2 Oklahoma's picturesque governor, W. H. (Alfalfa Bill) Murray, put his grass roots candidacy for the Democratic president nomination before the citizens of Indiana here today. **1947** *Time* 20 Jan. 76/2 Most of them have found real satisfaction in the Friends' experiment in grassroots international relations. **1949** *This Week Mag.* 9 Jan. 5/2 Occasionally grassroots justices do double duty.

grass rope. *S.* Any fiber rope other than one of cotton, orig. one made from bear grass, whence the name, but now usually made from sisal or manila hemp.

[**1830** J. F. WATSON *Philadelphia* 444 The Indians made their ropes, bridles, and twine for nets, out of a wild weed, growing abundantly in old corn fields, commonly called Indian hemp—(i.e. Linum Virginianum). The Swedes used to buy fourteen yards of the rope for a loaf of bread, and deemed them more lasting in the water than that made of true hemp]. **1841** GURNEY *Journey* 69 A species of aloe is cultivated here, called the Bear's grass, the long spiked leaves of which consist of tough fibres. From these the Americans manufacture the 'grass rope,' which is quite as strong as that made of hemp. **1916** BOWER *Phantom Herd* 26 The rope was a good 'grass' rope worn smooth and hard with much use.

grassy hole. *N. Eng.* A low-lying area overgrown with grass; also as a place-name. *Obs.* Cf. **grass hole.** — **1683** *Derby Rec.* 99 One parcell of low land that lies in the little grassy hole that lies per Woodbery old path. **1705** *Ib.* 371 A certain parsell of low land lying in grasey hole so called.

***grater,** *n.* (See quot.) *Obs.* — **1878** STOWE *Poganuc People* xix. 217 'You can find some of them sweet-flag "graters" if you want.' This was the blossom-bud of the sweet flag, which when young and tender was reckoned a delicacy among omnivorous children.

***grave,** *n.* In combs., usu. rare and obs.: (1) **grave-board,** (*a*) one of the boards placed immediately above, and serving as a covering for, a coffin in interment, (*b*) a board, suitably inscribed, marking the head of a grave; (2) **chill,** ?a temporary chilly sensation caused, according to a folk-saying, by a rabbit's running over one's destined grave; (3) **house,** (see quot.); (4) **lot,** a lot or plot set aside for burial purposes; (5) **post,** a post, inscribed with symbolic figures, placed over the grave of an Indian; (6) **rock,** a gravestone; (7) **room,** room or space for burial; (8) **stick,** (see quot. and cf. (5) above); (9) ***yard,** see as a main entry.

(1) (*a*) **1844** in THOMPSON *M. Jones* (1872) 183, I could almost hear the rumblin of the fust shovelful of yeath on the grave boards of my little boy. (*b*) **1851** SCHOOLCRAFT *Indian Tribes* I. 356 At the head of the grave a tabular piece of cedar, or other wood, called the adjedatig, is set. This graveboard contains the symbolic or representative figures which record, if it be a warrior, his totem. — (2) **1840** C. F. HOFFMAN *Greyslaer* I. ix. 106 He shivered as with a grave-chill; and . . . he essayed in prayer to beseech a pardon and recall his words. — (3) **1948** DICK *Dixie Frontier* 223 A grave house was constructed over the grave to protect it from the elements and the grave robber. — (4) **1883** E. W. HOWE *Country Town* (1926) 3 As if the ghosts from the

grave lot had crawled up there. **1949** *Desplaines Valley News* (Summit, Ill.) 8 April 12/1 For Sale—6 grave lot in Archer Woods cemetery.

(5) 1840 *S. Lit. Messenger* VI. 191/1 When an Indian dies, it is his family or surname, that is put on his grave-post, or *adjedatigwan.* **1881** MORGAN *Houses Amer. Aborigines* 257 We have here the Copan cemetery, and . . . these idols are the grave-posts . . . of Copan chiefs. — **(6) 1901** HARBEN *Westerfelt* xx. 279, I'm goin' back to put a grave-rock over Jasper's remains. — **(7) 1890** M. E. RYAN *Told in Hills* 235 Captain Holt [was] a man who had no use for an Indian . . . and whose only idea of settling the vexed question of their rights was total extermination and grave-room. — **(8) 1840** *S. Lit. Messenger* VI. 191/2 This friend [an Indian] puts the deceased's *totem* or family name in hieroglyphics, on the *grave-stick,* as the original word imports.

As the last term in **Indian, land, Wet Grave.**

* **gravel,** *n.*

1. (See quot.) *Obs.*

1868 LOSSING *Hudson* 280 Many vessels are employed in carrying away lime, limestone, and 'gravel' (pulverized limestone, not fit for the kiln).

2. In combs.: (1) **gravel bar,** a bar (in a stream) covered with or composed of gravel, often containing gold deposits; (2) **car,** (see quot. 1895); (3) **claim,** a mining claim or area in a gravelly formation; (4) **day,** (see quot. 1847), *obs.;* (5) **diggings,** a gravelly formation in which gold occurs; (6) **dumper,** a type of gravel car; (7) **mill,** a mill for crushing gravel; (8) **mine,** a mine in a gravelly formation; (9) **mineral,** (see quot.); (10) **ore,** (see quot.); (11) **plant,** (see quot.); (12) **range,** a deposit of valuable ore occurring in a gravelly formation, cf. * **range,** *n.;* (13) **root,** (see quot.); (14) **train,** a train that hauls gravel; (15) **weed,** the bush honeysuckle.

(1) 1821 NUTTALL *Travels Arkansa* 97 Four miles above Dardennes', commences the first gravel-bar, accompanied by very rapid water. **1875** *Chi. Tribune* 20 Aug. 1/7 In localities in the valleys of the streams [in Black Hills], gravel bars . . . contain gold in quantities. **1947** *Field & Stream* June 30/3 Quite a few men are to be found going over gravel bars that were turned over many, many times by placer miners in years gone by. — **(2) 1847** *Seab. & Roanoke R.R. Rep.* 7 (Ernst). **1895** WAIT *Car-Builder's Dict.* 63 Gravel-car. A car for carrying gravel; usually either a tip-car or a flat-car, the latter most used. — **(3) 1881** *47th Congress* 1 Sess. H.R. Ex. Doc. No. 216, 12 It is still an open question as to what will be the best method for . . . the development of the gravel claims. **1948** JOHNSTON *Gold Rush* 30/1 Miners from the gravel claims came to gaze in wonder at that small piece of gold-flecked stone. — **(4) 1847** WELLS & DAVIS *Sk. Williams College* 78 On the second Monday of the first term in the year, if the weather be at all favorable, it has been customary . . . to petition the president for 'Gravel Day.' We did so this morning. The day was granted, and recitations being dispensed with, the students turned out en masse to re-gravel the college walks. **1854** *Boston Ev. Traveller* 12 July (Hale), Nearly every college has its own peculiar customs. . . . Among ours [at Williams] are 'gravel day,' 'chip day,' and 'mountain day,' occurring one in each of the three terms.

(5) 1876 RAYMOND *8th Rep. Mines* 35 There are about forty acres on this claim, all rich gravel-diggings. **1877** W. WRIGHT *Big Bonanza* 53 John Bishop . . . bought Old Virginia's interest in the sluices, gravel-diggings and water. — **(6) 1856** *Mich. Agric. Soc. Trans.* VII. 334 There are on the road . . . 20 gravel dumpers. — **(7) 1881** *47th Congress* 1 Sess. H.R. Ex. Doc. No. 216, 624 The gravel must then be crushed in a gravel mill. — **(8) 1876** W. WRIGHT *Big Bonanza* 42 [They] had no idea of there being a rich vein of gold and silver-bearing quartz underlying the whole region upon which they were staking off their gravel-mines. **1881** *47th Congress* 1 Sess. H.R. Ex Doc. No. 216, 650 Two of the principal gravel mines in the State of California . . . now appear for the first time for years among those that levied assessments. — **(9) 1857** DANA *Mineralogy* 278 Fragments of lead ('gravel mineral') [occur in the soil in Wisconsin].

(10) 1814 BRACKENRIDGE *Louisiana* 148 There is also, what is called gravel ore, from being found in small pieces in gravel. — **(11) 1907** LYONS *Plant Names* 178 E[pigaea] repens. . . . Trailing Arbutus, Gravel-plant, May-flower. — **(12) 1873** RAYMOND *Silver & Gold* 103 Next west of Kelly's is a gravel-range, upon which an opening has been made, known in former days as Bell's Diggings. — **(13) 1899** *Animal & Plant Lore* 112 *Eupatorium purpureum,* the Joe-pye-weed, is called 'gravel-root,' and is evidently thought to be a remedy for calculi [W.Va.]. — **(14) 1847** *Boston Ev. Traveller* 14 April 1/4 A collision took place this morning . . . between a gravel train and a locomotive. **1902** GORDON *Recoll. Lynchburg* 43 It's bad 'nough to come from a gravel train to a place like this.

(15) 1907 LYONS *Plant Names* 164 Diervilla. . . . Bush Honeysuckle, Gravel-weed, Life-of-man. **1943** PEATTIE *Great Smokies* 274 For me these white and pinkish waxy blooms, as delightful in their fragrance as they are humble in their growth ('gravelweed,' the mountain people call the plant), always serve to mark a significant period in the chronicle of the year.

b. *To scratch gravel,* see * **scratch,** *v.*

As the last term in **blue, pay gravel.**

* **graveyard,** *n.*

1. (See quots.) *Colloq.*

1843 *Quincy* (Ill.) *Whig* 7 Jan. 2/6 The iron steamer Valley Forge has been sunk at the 'Grave Yard' below St. Louis. **1847** LANMAN *Summer in Wild.* On your left [is] an array of sand bars and islands, where lie imbedded the wrecks of some fifty steamboats. . . . This is the spot which has been rightly named the Grave Yard. **1853** KANE *Grinnell Exp.* xlii. (1856) 389, I remember . . . coming to a little graveyard of ice-tablets. **1947** *Chi. Tribune* 9 Nov. 1. 11/4 A little coast guard cutter raced 150 miles . . . to snatch a disabled frater and her crew of 28 to safety from the treacherous reefs of Lake Michigan's 'graveyard of ships' near here [Ludington, Mich.].

2. In combs.: (1) **graveyard cough,** a churchyard cough, one symptomatic of approaching death, *colloq.;* (2) **digging,** an occasion upon which neighbors assemble to clean up and care for a graveyard; (3) **heart,** a sad heart, *rare;* (4) **issue,** an issue that is dead and buried; (5) **luncheon,** ?a luncheon partaken of in a graveyard, *rare;* (6) **rabbit,** a rabbit that lives in a graveyard and accordingly, in folk belief, possesses various magical endowments, *colloq.;* (7) **rate,** an estimate of taxes for the upkeep of a graveyard; (8) **shift,** (see quots. 1907, 1908); (9) **weed,** cypress spurge.

(1) 1873 BEADLE *Undevel. West* 33, I was shaken by an ominous graveyard cough. — **(2) 1945** *New Yorker* 10 Mar. 44 The occasion was what was called 'a graveyard digging.' All the families that had kinfolks buried there went to the digging. They brought their dinners in baskets, tubs, or buckets, and everyone carried hoes, rakes, spades, shovels, or wire stretchers. — **(3) 1909** STRATTON-PORTER *Girl of Limberlost* 430 When I think of walking off and leaving Freckles . . . , it gives me a graveyard heart. — **(4) 1888** *N.Y. World* 14 Feb. (Farmer), Sherman . . . is not up to the demands of the period. His campaign would be one of graveyard issues. The war, the South and tissue ballots are dead.

(5) 1874 B. F. TAYLOR *World on Wheels* I. xvi. 118 Something is written elsewhere of the grave-yard luncheons they took in the Sunday noonings. — **(6) 1892** HARRIS *U. Remus & Friends* 33 You er one er deze yer graveyard rabbits, dat w'at you is. **1903** BROWN *How to Beat Game* 33 If, for instance, the player uses, as a mascotte, a graveyard rabbit's foot, or a St. Joseph, reach over, and under pretense of a desire to examine, pick it up and playfully decline to return it. — **(7) 1772** PATTEN *Diary* 291 We finished makeing the Province County Ministers and Grave yard Rates. — **(8) 1907** *Collier's* 26 Jan. 14/1 From the saloons came the clink of the chips. For it was the 'graveyard gamblers' shift. . . . The small hours of the morning, when the carelessly speculative world is asleep, are theirs. **1908** *Sat. Ev. Post* 7 Nov. 27/2 A month later he and his fellows went on 'graveyard' shift. 'Graveyard' is the interval between twelve, midnight, and eight in the morning. **1945** *Jefferson Co. Republican* (Golden, Colo.) 25 July 2/2 Bill Jarrett had been working for six weeks on graveyard shift. — **(9) 1894** *Amer. Folk-Lore* VII. 98 *Euphorbia Cyparissias* . . . graveyard-weed, West Va. **1931** CLUTE *Plants* 133.

b. (See quots.) *Colloq.*

1882 MARK TWAIN *Innocents At Home* iii. 278 A desperado . . . who 'kept his private graveyard,' as the phrase went. **1888–90** BARRERE-LELAND I. 427 Graveyard (American), a 'private graveyard,' men who affect great ferocity, or who assume to be desperadoes, sometimes boast in America that they keep graveyards of their own in which to bury their victims.

* **gravy,** *n.*

1. Used, esp. in dial., with various significations (see quots.).

1845 HOOPER *Simon Sugg's Adv.* iii. 33 They call sop, *gravy.* **1848** BARTLETT 163 *Gravy.* Used in New England instead of *juice* as the *gravy* of a pie. **1870** NOWLAND *Indianapolis* 301 He said he had gone to Greensburg, Decatur County, and that the tavern-keeper called sop gravy, and he thought that he was far enough from home, for he did not know what they would call it by the time he reached 'Sinsinnatty.' **1895** *D.N.* I. 374 sop: gravy. 'We like bread and *sop.*' [Tenn. mts.] **1946** PEASE *Sequestered Vales* 3 His youth, passed largely in New Orleans and in Georgia, had left in him two notable survivals, the use of the phrases 'I reckon'—instead of the Yankee 'I guess'—and 'dip' instead of 'gravy.'

2. *By* (or *good*) *gravy,* "by jingo," "by golly," an exclamation. *Colloq.*

1831 *Working-man's Gazette* (Woodstock, Vt.) 19 Jan. 130/1 By gravy! I'll get up early to-morrow morning! *a*1855 KELLEY *Humors*

357 Good gravy, but don't they? **1906** LYNDE *Quickening* 168 By gravy! I tell Brother Silas on you, Tom-Jeff?

3. Something obtained without effort; graft, esp. illegal gains through political connivance. *Slang.*

1910 *Sat. Ev. Post* 30 July 13/1 Stick him for all you can. You're a hard worker, and you mustn't let somebody else git the gravy. **1943** OTTLEY *New World* 211 Tammany Hall attracted men of a similar stripe, whose sole purpose in politics was the gravy.

b. gravy boat, train, a situation, position, business, etc., which is easy and profitable. *Slang.*

1945 BOTKIN *My Burden* 82 They is on the gravy train and don't know it, but they is headed straight for 'struction and perdition. **1948** MENJOU & MUSSELMAN *It Took 9 Tailors* 141 Once you get on the Hollywood gravy boat, it is no trick to make money; the trick is to keep it.

As the last term in **good, milk, political, red gravy.**

* **gray,** *a.* and *n.* Also * **grey.**

1. Short for **cadet gray.** *Obs.*

1848 in WOOD *West Point Scrap Book* (1871 ed.) 76 But with right stout hearts we'll play our parts, When we change the Grey for the Blue.

2. The uniform worn by Confederate soldiers. Now *hist.* Cf. **Jeff Davis Grays.**

1862 in F. MOORE *Rebellion Rec.* V. II. 72 An Irishman of the Seventeenth New-York came up to the General, . . . driving three prisoners in gray before him. **1879** TOURGEE *Fool's Errand* xxii. 134, I have no . . . ill-will, towards any one who wore the gray. **1948** *Realty & Bldg.* 15 May 11/2 Colonel John was a Johnny Reb who delighted in telling of the exploits of the boys in gray.

3. A wolf. *Rare.*

1886 *Outing* Nov. 102/1 'See what a lot of coyotes, back there by the forest edge!' 'They don't like ter interrupt the grays at their feast.'

4. In the names of birds: (1) **gray bird,** =**sage thrasher;** (2) **cheek,** =next; (3) **cheeked thrush,** an American thrush, *Hylocichla minima aliciae;* (4) **crowned,** *a.* designating a variety of finch; (5) **eagle,** the immature bald eagle, once regarded as a distinct species, also (*cap.*) as a nickname (see quot. 1949); (6) **kingbird,** a tyrant flycatcher, *Tyrannus dominicensis;* (7) **snipe,** the dowitcher, *Limnodromus griseus,* in winter plumage.

(1) **1837** J. K. TOWNSEND in *Jrnl. Acad. Nat. Sci.* (Phila.) 7 (2) 187–92. **1872** *Amer. Naturalist* July VI. 396 The mountain mockingbird, familiarly known to the settlers as the 'gray bird,' is said to have similarly increased. — (2) **1892** TORREY *Foot-Path Way* 97 Just after leaving the house it was possible to hear three kinds of thrushes singing at once,—gray-cheeks, olive-backs, and hermits. **1945** *Mass. Audubon Soc. Bul.* March 43 Two Thrushes of annual interest to students are the migrant Olive-back and the Gray-cheek. — (3) **1858** BAIRD *Birds Pacific R.R.* 217 *Turdus Aliciae.* . . . Gray-cheeked Thrush . . . Mississippi region to the Missouri. **1939** LINCOLN *Migration* 176 The gray-cheeked Thrush and the Olive-backed Thrush so closely resemble each other. — (4) **1852** BAIRD in Stansbury *Gt. Salt Lake* 317 *Leucosticte Tephrocotis.* . . . Gray-crowned Finch. **1876** *Field & Forest* II. 31, I published a 'Monograph of the Genus Leucosticte, or Gray-crowned Purple Finches.' **1917** *Birds of Amer.* III. 10 Gray-crowned Rosy Finch. *Leucosticte tephrocotis tephrocotis.*

(5) **1778** CARVER *Travels* 466 There are only two sorts of eagles in these parts, the bald and the grey. **1874** COUES *Birds N.W.* 370 From the circumstance that several years . . . are required for the gaining of the perfect plumage [in the bald eagle], when the head and tail are entirely white, it follows that 'Gray Eagles' and 'Birds of Washington' are much the more frequently met with. **1917** *Birds of Amer.* II. 80. **1949** *Sat. Ev. Post* 23 April 144/3 You'll find yourself with a quarrel on your hands if you suggest to the old Gray Eagle [Tris Speaker] that baseball is a white man's game and that people like Doby have no place in it. — (6) **1858** BAIRD *Birds Pacific R.R.* 172 *Tyrannus Dominicensis.* . . . Gray King-bird . . . South Carolina coast, accidental; Florida Keys and West Indies. **1917** *Birds of Amer.* II. 194/2 The Gray Kingbirds reach Florida early in April. — (7) **1870** *Pa. Laws* 50 No person shall kill, capture, [or] take . . . any gray snipe. **1874** COUES *Birds N.W.* 476 *Macrorhamphus Griseus.* . . . Gray Snipe. . . . This species has a very extensive distribution in the Western Hemisphere.

b. In the names of other animals: (1) * **graybeard,** (see quot. and cf. **5.** (2) below); (2) **fox,** see as a main entry; (3) **grub,** (see quot.); (4) **moose,** a name used locally for the common moose because of its color; (5) **perch,** (see quot.); (6) **rabbit,** the common cottontail; (7) **rattlesnake,** prob. the western massasauga, *Sistrurus catenatus tergeminus;* (8) **snapper,** a basslike marine food fish, *Lutianus griseus,* found along the coast of Florida; (9) **squirrel,** a large squirrel, *Sciurus carolinensis,* having a bushy tail, and found south of Lake Ontario and east of the plains region, cf. **cat squirrel;** (10) **trout,** a weakfish, *Cynoscion regalis,* found on the Atlantic Coast; (11) **whale,** a large whale found off the coast of California, also **California gray whale;** (12) **wolf,** the timber wolf, *Canis occidentalis,* also transf.; (13) **worm,** ?the cutworm, *obs.*

(1) **1881** E. INGERSOLL *Oyster Industry* 245 Gray Beard—The common hydroid of northern oyster beds, *Sertularia argentea.* — (3) **1875** *Vt. Bd. Agric. Rep.* III. 567 The larva of this moth [*Agrotis tessellata*] is sometimes called the gray grub. — (4) **1743** CATESBY *Carolina* II. xxviii, *Cervus Major Americanus.* The Stag of America. . . . In New England it is known by the name of the grey Moose, to distinguish it from the preceding beast, which they call the black Moose. **1917** *Mammals of Amer.* 23 The gray moose was the first to recover himself.

(5) **1884** GOODE *Fisheries* I. 370 In the Ohio River it [the fresh-water drum] is usually called 'White Perch' or 'Gray Perch.' — (6) **1842** *Nat. Hist. N.Y., Zoology* I. 93 The American Grey Rabbit, *Lepus nanus,* . . . changes but little with the season. **1917** *Mammals of Amer.* 289/1 The Cottontail or Gray Rabbit, is a smaller animal than the Hare. — (7) **1846** in EMORY *Military Reconn.* 396 A grey snake, marked with a row of blackish spots along the back . . . is called the grey rattlesnake. — (8) **1775** ROMANS *Nat. Hist. Fla.* App. 52 The fish caught here . . . are such as . . . red, grey and black snappers. **1884** GOODE *Fisheries* I. 397 The Gray Snapper—*Lutjanus caxis* . . . is most abundant in South Florida. — (9) [**1624** SMITH *Gen. Hist. Va.* II. 27 Their Squirrels some are neare as great as our smallest sort of wilde Rabbets, some blackish or blacke and white, but the most are gray.] **1674** JOSSELYN *Two Voyages* 86 There are three sorts, the mouse squirril, the gray squirril, and the flying-squirril. **1893** *Harper's Mag.* Feb. 355/2 What with the child, and the dogs, and Rip Van Winkle, the cat, and a tame gray squirrel who hunts our pockets for nuts, we contrive to get through the short dark days. **1945** MATHEWS *Talking* 156 The gray squirrels cling high in the tall, white sycamores and redoaks.

(10) **1870** O. OPTIC *Field & Forest* 254, I dreamed that I went a fishing with her, and that a big gray trout pulled her into the water. — (11) **1884** *Nat. Museum Bul.* No. 27, 634 The Gray Whale, *Rhachianectes glaucus,* . . . in the last thirty years . . . has diminished in abundance in an alarming degree. **1888** *Amer. Naturalist* XXII. 509 The California Gray Whale, (*Rhacheanectes glaucus* Cope,) . . . is the most interesting of all the species of whale known to inhabit the great seas. **1949** *Nat. Hist.* June 249 The Gray Whale reaches a length of 40 to 50 feet and a weight of 20 tons. — (12) **1814** LEWIS & CLARK *Trav. Missouri* (1815) I. 206 We caught in a trap a large gray wolf. **1904** *Grand Rapids Ev. Press* 8 June 4 In plain words, a gray wolf, in Chicago phraseology, is a professional grafter. **1923** J. H. COOK *On Old Frontier* 221 Indian spirits, in form of coyotes or big gray wolves, may sing serenades about his bones for years to come. — (13) **1802** *Mass. H.S. Coll.* VIII. 190 The *gray worm;* . . . descends into the ground in the day, rises in the night, and devours the blade [of corn]. **1803** *Ib.* IX. 203 But this worm is by no means so great a plague as the *gray worm,* perhaps the *palmer worm,* which visited this town [Compton, R.I.] about thirty-three years ago.

5. In the names of, or with reference to, plants: (1) **gray ash,** see **6.** (1) (*a*) below; (2) **beard moss,** =**Spanish moss,** see also **granddaddy, grandfather graybeard,** and cf. **4. b.** (1) above; (3) **birch,** either of two species of American birch, esp. *Betula populifolia;* (4) **crowder,** see **crowder;** (5) **house,** a variety of apple, or cider made from such apples, *obs.;* (6) **lock,** (see quot.), *obs.;* (7) **oak,** any one of several species of oak, esp. the scarlet oak, *Quercus coccinea,* or red oak, *Q. borealis;* (8) **pine,** any one of various American pines, esp. the grayleaf pine, *Pinus sabiniana,* or the jack pine, *P. banksiana;* (9) **willow,** the silky willow, *Salix sericea.*

(2) **1858** *Harper's Mag.* Dec. 12/2 The tender green of the budding cypress contrasted strikingly with the graybeard moss that hung from every bough. [**1883** MARK TWAIN *Life on the Miss.* 293 Shade trees hung with venerable gray-beards of Spanish moss.] — (3) **1851** SPRINGER *Forest Life* 23 Of the Birch family there are several varieties, called the Black, Yellow, Red, Canoe, the Gray, and the Dwarf. **1905** *Forestry Bureau Bul.* No. 63, 18 The burning over of the lumbered area favors a thick growth of gray birch. **1945** PEARSON *Country Flavor* 52 The gray birch is a humble, unpretentious sort of tree.

(5) **1817** W. COXE *Fruit Trees* 154 The Greyhouse, is thought to be the finest cider brought to the Philadelphia market. **1834** *N. Eng. Farmer* 5 March 267/3 The *Grey House* . . . holds the same rank as a cider apple. — (6) **1849** *N. Eng. Farmer* I. 231 We are indebted to

Hon. A. Foote, of Williamstown, Mass., for a barrel of his new variety of potato, called the *Greylock*. — (7) **1697** *Boston Rec.* 8 By Braintry road a heap of stones, . . . from thence to another wallnut tree and so straight to a gray oak. **1832** WILLIAMSON *Hist. Maine* I. 109 There is also another variety, called the 'Gray Oak.' **1885** HAVARD *Flora W. & S. Texas* 504 *Quercus grisea.* Gray Oak. The most abundant, . . . the characteristic, Oak of Western Texas. Found west of the Pecos in all mountain cañons. — (8) **1810** MICHAUX *Arbres* I. 7 Dans le District du Maine et à la Nouvelle-Écosse, y est connue sous le nom de *Scrub Pine*, Pin chétif; et dans le Bas-Canada, sous celui de *grey Pine*, Pin gris. **1917** KEPHART *Camping* I. 239 The gray (Labrador) pine or jack pine is considered good fuel in the far North. **1945** DARLINGTON *Higher Plants Mich.* 13 Areas of gray pine or so-called Jack pine (*Pinus Banksiana*) occur in the interior. — (9) **1813** MUHLENBERG *Cat. Plants* 91. **1860** CURTIS *Woody Plants N.C.* 75 Gray Willow. (*S[alix] tristis*, Ait.)—A shrub 1 to 2 feet high. . . . I have met with this insignificant plant only in the mountain counties. **1892** APGAR *Trees Northern U.S.* 167 *Salix cinerea.* (Gray or Ash-colored Willow.)

6. In miscellaneous combs.: (1) **gray ash,** (*a*) a variety of ash, *obs.*, (*b*) a variety of coal; (2) ***back,** see as a main entry; (3) ***coat,** (*a*) =**grayback 1,** *rare*, (*b*) =**grayback 2,** *obs.*; (4) ***hound,** (*a*) (see quot.), *obs.*, (*b*) a fast ocean steamer, *colloq.*; (5) **jacket,** (*a*) a gray squirrel, *rare*, (*b*) (see quot. and cf. **2.** above).

(1) (*a*) **1813** MUHLENBERG *Cat. Plants* 96. **1843** TORREY *Flora N.Y.* II. 126 *Fraxinus pubescens.* . . . Gray Ash. . . . Margin of rivulets, and in situations that are often overflowed. (*b*) **1857** *Harper's Mag.* Sep. 460/2 The veins of the first, second, and third axes are of the white-ash variety: overlying these is a transition group, called gray or pink ash, and upon these in turn occur the red-ash series. — (3) (*a*) **1829** ROYALL *Pennsylvania* I. 152 The sole and all-weighing cause of my partiality for the Germans, is their aversion to the gray coats, or, as they are called in Pennsylvania, *blue stockings*. (*b*) **1866** J. E. COOKE *Surry* 302 The Federal cavalry were charged by a detachment of gray-coats. **1884** CABLE *Dr. Sevier* lvi, The gray-coats stood guard in the wavering fire-light. — (4) (*a*) **1872** POWERS *Afoot & Alone* 118 Ox-driving Eastern Texas furnished to the Confederacy several infantry regiments who were worth more than all the mustang cavalry together . . . and who . . . earned from the Union troops the complimentary equivoque of 'Greyhounds.' (*b*) **1886** *Harper's Mag.* Aug. 383/2 Captain James Price . . . has commanded all the crack 'greyhounds' of the company. **1948** *American Fabrics* No. 6, 65/1 Her clipper fleet was developed and the greyhounds of the sea visited every Asiatic port in the quest for silk.

(5) (*a*) **1835** SIMMS *Partisan* 86 See what thou gettest for thy stupidity. Think you gray-jacket knew not all you were saying? He did: not a word escaped him. (*b*) **1876** in *Southern Hist. Soc. P.* II. 131 A short waisted, single breasted jacket usurped the place of the long tail coat. . . . The enemy noticed this peculiarity, and called the Confederates gray jackets, which name was immediately transferred to those lively creatures, which were the constant admirers and inseparable companions of the Boys in Gray and Blue.

b. In phrases: (1) ****In the gray,*** (see quot.); (2) *Gray-Eyed Man of Destiny*, an expression used of William Walker (1824–60), an American adventurer and filibuster.

(1) **1838** GOSSE *Letters* 266 Deer-hunting has now commenced. . . . The animal is now said to be 'in the grey,' as in the summer he is 'in the red.' — (2) **1863** RUSSELL *Diary* I. 95 But this gentleman was a professed buccaneer, a friend of Walker, the grey-eyed man of destiny. **1947** *Chi. D. News* 31 Jan. 14/7 Strange how that project fascinated brilliant, but warped, minds from Aaron Burr to Joaquin Miller's 'Grey-Eyed Man of Destiny,' William Walker.

As the last term in **blue, cadet, Confederate, English, rebel, sheep's, Silver, Vermont gray.**

***grayback,** *n.*

1. (See quot.) *Rare.*

1829 ROYALL *Pennsylvania* I. 152 [Professed Christians] have a number of names here, as in other States, 'Grey-backs, Round-heads, &c.'

2. A Confederate soldier. Now *hist.* Cf. ***gray 2, gray coat** (*b*), **gray jacket** (*b*).

1864 *Dly. Telegraph* (London) 7 July 3/4 The last thing he [Lee] is likely to attempt is to send a solitary grayback or an army of graybacks beyond the mountains on the Rapidan. **1898** *McClure's Mag.* X. 352 The gray-backs came through with a rush, and soon the musket balls and the cannon shot began to reach the place where we stood. **1917** MORGAN *Recollections* 214 The Union soldiers craved tobacco of which the Southerners had an abundance and the 'grayback' longed for coffee or sugar.

3. A treasury note issued by the Confederate government. *Obs.*

1875 *Chi. Tribune* 29 July 4/3 We printed a partial history of the issue, decline, and fall of the grayback. **1897** *Cent. Mag.* Aug. 593/2 The depreciation in the purchasing power of 'graybacks,' as we call the rebel treasury notes, is so rapid.

4. (See quot. and cf. **gray whale.**)

1884 J. S. KINGSLEY *Riverside Nat. Hist.* V. 186 The gray whale has received many curious titles, such as 'hard-head,' 'mussel-digger,' 'devil-fish,' and 'gray-back.'

5. A page or messenger boy. *Rare.*

1885 *Harper's Mag.* Nov. 846/2 The employés . . . include about fifty pages, called 'graybacks,' from the color of their uniforms.

6. An old-timer, one wise from experience. *Rare.*

1889 MARK TWAIN *Conn. Yankee* xxxi. 401 He thinks he's a Sheol of a farmer; thinks he's old Grayback from Wayback.

gray fox.

1. The common grayish-colored fox, *Urocyon cinereoargenteus*, of North America. Also the pelt of such a fox. Also attrib. Cf. **desert, Florida, wood gray fox.**

1678–9 WOLLEY *Journal* (1701) 30 The price of Indian Commodities as sold by the Christian Merchants is as followeth Bevers—00—10—3 a Pound. . . . Minks—00—05—0 Grey Foxes—00—03—0. **1738** CATESBY *Carolina* II. 78 *Vulpis cinereus Americanus.* The Grey Fox. . . . They are equally mischievous with those [foxes] in Europe, destroying poultry, &c. **1819** *Western Rev.* I. 235 The common grey fox of the United States is different by having the tip of the ears and a spot near them black. **1917** *Mammals of Amer.* 80 Gray Fox. *Urocyon cinereoargenteus.* . . . The eastern Gray Fox is of medium size with moderately long hair and long bushy tail. **1949** *Amer. Photography* June 351/2 We surprised a sleek gray fox on a grassy hillside.

2. **gray fox squirrel,** a gray or light-reddish eastern variety of fox squirrel.

1738 CATESBY *Carolina* II. 73 These [black squirrels], with the grey Fox-Squirrel, are very numerous and destructive to corn in the fields. **1789** MORSE *Amer. Geog.* 54 Beasts common to North America: grey fox squirrel.

***grazier,** *n.* A grazing animal. *Obs.* — [**1851** C. CIST *Cincinnati* 279 The hogs raised for this market, are generally a cross of Irish Grazier, Byfield, . . . and China.] **1852** *Trans. Mich. Agric. Soc.* III. 138 They [*sc.* Durham heifers] are good graziers and winter well.

***grazing,** *n.* Used attrib. with **district, lease, park, range, service, tax.**

1817 S. BROWN *Western Gaz.* 92 The grazing parks have a peculiar neatness. **1881** *Rep. Indian Affairs* 95, I have purchased for them, from money collected as a grazing tax, 10 stirring plows. **1885** *Ib.* 6 In so far as I can learn there is no way of extirpating the 'Canada' thistles on the grazing ranges. **1905** *Forestry Bureau Bul.* No. 62, 9 Your Commission recommends that suitable authority be given to the President to set aside, by proclamation, certain grazing districts or reserves. **1945** *Roundup* (Mont.) *R. Tribune* 22 Feb. 4/3 A grazing lease for a period of one year was entered into with the Pole Creek Grazing District. **1948** *Sierra Club Bul.* Feb. 15/1 The Grazing Service issued grazing permits to livestock owners much in the manner of the Forest Service.

***grease,** *n.*

1. **greasebush,** =**greasewood.** Cf. **buffalo greasebush.**

1846 *30th Congress* 1 Sess. H.R. Ex. Doc. No. 41, 434 As there was no wood fit to burn, we were forced to use the grease bush; so the voyageurs call it on account of its burning with such a brilliant light. **1881** *Amer. Naturalist* XV. 24 Although the grease bushes, contrary to the rule of desert growths, are leafy, their abundant foliage is of precisely the same dull whitish color as the clay in which they grow.

2. **greaseroot, greaseweed,** =next.

1853 SITGREAVES *Exped. Zuni & Colo. Rivers* 34 From El Paso, passing up the Rio Grande, along which stream the vegetation alters but little, the timber being principally . . . the creosote plant, (*Larrea Mexicana*,) grease-weed, (*Obione canescens*,) . . . and various specimens of artemisia and yucca. **1890** CUSTER *Following Guidon* 71 The dull sagebush, or grease-root, or the sparse buffalo-grass, were all that the sun spared from its scorching rays.

3. **greasewood,** a name widely applied to any one of various resinous plants and shrubs common to western desert regions.

1838 in *Frontier* XI. (1931) 285/2 Most of the country we have traveled since leaving Ft. Williams has been a sandy desert, bearing little but sedge and wormwood, flowers and grease wood. **1942** STEGNER *Mormon C.* 122 There were dyeing vats for the coloring of cotton and wool cloth with home-made dyes like . . . greasewood. **1948** *Sat. Ev. Post* 25 Dec. 12/3 It was a fairly large thicket of greasewood.

attrib. **1853** in *Frontier* VIII. (1928) 126 Came to a flat sage and grease wood plain. **1863** in *Mont. Hist. Soc. Contrib.* I. (1876) 178 Soil seems too sandy here for farming, and where it is not sand it is greasewood flats. a1918 G. STUART *On Frontier* II. 103 Greasewood bottoms and bluffs on north side of river runs [*sic*] in close to the river. **1927** CATHER *Death Comes* 240 Soon they left the wagon road and took a trail running straight south, through an empty greasewood country.

As the last term in **axle, goose, rattlesnake, soap, wagon grease.**

* **greaser,** *n.*

1. A derogatory nickname for a Mexican or Spanish American. *Slang.* See also **gun greaser, skid greaser.**

1836 G. A. MCCALL *Lett. from Frontiers* (1868) 298 The terrific yells and shouts of the maddened Texans carried fear to the hearts of their enemy; and the pervading sentiment among the defeated and disorganized '*Greasers*' was, '*sauve qui peut.*' **1874** MCCOY *Cattle* 375 The 'Greasers' are the result of Spanish, Indian and negro miscegenation, and as a class are unenterprising, energyless and decidedly at a standstill so far as progress, enlightenment, civilization, education, or religion is concerned. **1948** JOHNSTON *Gold Rush* 11/1 In many cases. the viler elements of the several camps perpetrated egregious atrocities upon the 'greasers,' as the Mexicans were contemptuously called.

attrib. **1854** *Wide West* (S.F.) 23 July 1/2 We have gallantly drunk the health of the greaser girls, and they must now return the compliment by drinking ours. **1887** *Denver Graphic* 29 Jan. 1/5, I saw a greaser shepherd on the Puente Hills. **1920** MULFORD *J. Nelson* 184 See many Texas an' Greaser cattle up there?

b. Spanish such as "greasers" speak. *Rare.*

1907 COOK *Border & Buffalo* (1938) 297, I could now talk a little 'Greaser' and make understandable signs.

c. Greaserdom, used derisively for New Mexico. *Rare.*

1873 BEADLE *Undevel. West* 29 (*heading*), 'Greaserdom.'

2. (See quots.)

1870 CHIPMAN *Notes on Bartlett* 179 *Greaser* . . . 2. An assistant to the fireman of a steam-boat; one who oils the machinery.—N.Y. 3. A producer of oil.—Petroleum region of Pa.—Phila. *Press*, 8 Jan., 1870. **1905** *Forestry Bureau Bul.* No. 61, 45 *Road monkey.* One whose duty is to keep a logging road in proper condition. (N[orth] W[oods], L[ake] S[tates] F[orest].) . . . [Also called] blue jay, greaser. (P[acific] C[oast] F[orest].)

greasy cutworm. The black cutworm, *Agrotis ypsilon.* — **1868** *Mo. Entomologist 1st. Rep.* 80 The Greasy Cut-Worm. . . . In the *Prairie Farmer* for June 22, 1867, I described a large cut-worm under the name of the 'Black cut-worm.' I have since . . . concluded to give it the above appellation. **1884** *Rep. Comm. Agric.* 294.

* **great,** *a.* and *n.*

1. *n.* Short for "great deal," "great amount." *Colloq.*

1724 *Essex Inst. Coll.* XXXVI. 337 Mackey's Sloop Sunk at Boston, & Spoild a great of our English Goods. **1884** JEWETT *Country Doctor* ii. 12 There's only one little bough that bears any great. **1891** HOLMES *Over Teacups* 221 Our folks in them days didn't care no great abaout Lord Percy and Sir William Haowe.

2. *No great of*, no outstanding example, specimen, or model of. *Colloq.*

1865 A. D. WHITNEY *Gayworthys* i, She made 'no great of a match.' **1877** JEWETT *Deephaven* iii. 48 She never was no great of a mouser. **1896** ——— *Pointed Firs* 106 'T was never called no great of a fishin'-ground before. **1901** ——— in *Harper's Mag.* Dec. 47/1 They've got a story up our way that poor Mis' Dennett ain't no gre't of a housekeeper.

3. *a.* Fine, splendid, excellent. *Colloq.*

1839 MARRYAT *Diary* II. 225 The word great is oddly used for fine, splendid. 'She's the *greatest* gal in the whole Union.' **1873** *Harper's Mag.* XLVI. 276 She was great in the management and pacification of children. **1911** FERBER *Dawn O'Hara* 18 It doesn't look restful, but he says it's great.

4. (Often *cap.*) In miscellaneous combs.: (1) **Great Awakening,** see as a main entry; (2) **Father,** (*a*) (see quots. and cf. * **father,** *n.* **2, 3,** and see (14) below), (*b*) the Mississippi River, *rare;* (3) **Fraud,** an opprobrious term applied to the election of Rutherford B. Hayes as President in the contested election of 1876, *obs.;* (4r * **house,** the main or chief residence on an estate o) plantation, cf. **big house** (*a*); (5) **knife,** =**big knife,** *obs.;* (6) **medicine,** in, or after the manner of, Indian speech, anything regarded as particularly efficacious or awe inspiring, cf. * **medicine,** now *hist.;* (7) **Medicine Road,** (see quot.); (8) **Pawnee,** =**Grand Pawnee,** *obs.;* (9) **Rebellion,** see as a main entry; (10) **Republic,** the U.S.; (11) **Revival,** see as a main entry; (12) **Spirit,** the manito of the Indians, also **Great Spirit Father;** (13) **western,** *a.* of or pertaining to the Great West; (14) **White Father,** in Indian speech, the President of the U.S., also transf.; (15) **White Way,** that part of Broadway immediately adjacent to Times Square in New York City, so called from its being brilliantly illuminated at night; (16) **White Plague,** tuberculosis, esp. of the lungs, cf. **white plague.**

(2) (*a*) **1808** PIKE *Sources Miss.* 5, I spoke to them [*sc.* Indians] to the following purport: 'That their great father, the president of the United States, [etc.].' **1877** *Nation* 15 Mar. 154/1 The President has no right, under our system of government, to play the part of 'Great Father' to the Southern negroes as long as they are American citizens. **1948** *Chi. Tribune* 18 April 1. 24/2 Italy's cut in the Marshall fund depends on Italian votes for the western block and the Great Father in Washington. (*b*) **1898** CUSHMAN *Hist. Indians* 64 This is surely the Great Father the true source of all waters. — (3) **1877** *N. Amer. Rev.* July 6 [Louisiana] was the principal theater of the 'Great Fraud.' *Ib.* 10 The story of four thousand murders is part of the *Great Fraud.* *Ib.* 34 If the friends of free government shall ever again have such a contest, let them take care how they leave the decision of it to a tribunal like that which betrayed the nation by enthroning the *Great Fraud* of 1876. — (4) **1633** *New-Hampshire Doc. & Rec.* I. 77 In the Great House [are] 3 ruggs and 2 pentodoes. **1849** *S. Lit. Messenger* XV. 71/2, I can get one of the children to carry them up to the great house. **1939** *These Are Our Lives* 29 De Yankees broke in de smokehouse, brought big middlin's o' meat in de great-house, and throwed 'em on de fire whole.

(5) **1791** J. LONG *Voyages* 151 Our great Father has sent me this way to take the skins and furs that are in the Dog's Field . . . least the Great Knives (meaning the Americans) should plunder them. **1799** J. SMITH *Acct. Remarkable Occurrences* (1870) 101 The chiefs . . . said they were anxious to see what the Great Knife (as they called the Virginian) could do. — (6) **1804** CLARK in *Lewis & C. Exped.* (1904) I. 209 We . . . entertained Several of the Curious Chiefs whome, wished to see the Boat which was verry curious to them viewing it as great medison, (*whatever is mysterious or unintelligible is called great medicine*). **1888** *Scribner's Mag.* Jan. 29/2 The oil was known to be 'great medicine' and good for rheumatism, sores, and troubled souls. — (7) **1929** A. J. DICKSON *Across Plains* 52 The indian road that was to become the trail to the west for the white man, and to be known as the Oregon Trail, which the Indians in time called 'the Great Medicine Road of the Whites.' — (8) **1814** LEWIS & CLARK *Travels* (1817) I. opp. p. 1 (*map*), Great Pawnee & Republican Vill. 4000 Souls. **1843** MARRYAT *M. Violet* xviii, Many among them [the Blackfeet] had taken scalps of the Osages . . . and even of the great Pawnees.

(10) **1846** T. H. JAMES *Rambles U.S.* 1 All the books . . . are quite inadequate to give the reader anything more than a very vague and faint idea of the Great Republic, as the natives delight to call it. **1900** *Cong. Rec.* 23 Jan. 1101/2 There was a possibility of this great Republic of the West crumbling to pieces. — (12) **1790** MACLAY *Deb. Senate* 170 Ames delivered a long string of studied sentences . . . [referring to] public credit, honor, and, above all, justice, as often over as an Indian would the Great Spirit. **1923** J. H. COOK *On Old Frontier* 211 Are you afraid of the Indians when they pray to their Great Spirit Father to help and protect them from those who have taken their country and food from them? **1947** *Beaver* June 14/1 They were more than astonished, and said that he must certainly be a favorite of the Great Spirit. — (13) **1805** CLARK in *Lewis & C. Exped.* III. (1905) 262 [It] is now 24 days since we arrived in sight of the Great Western Ocian, I cant say Pasific. **1806** *Ann. 9th Congress* 1 Sess. 619 Wagoners [are] constantly employed in hauling merchandise . . . on the great Western road to Pittsburg. — (14) **1916** WILSON *Red Gap* 332 Old Pete . . . calls out: 'You tell the Great White Father at Washington to go to hell.' **1949** *Reader's Digest* April 25/2 It is devouring the substance of self-supporting people to render them self-supporting no longer and to establish a condition of universal reliance upon the biased paternalism of a Great White Father.

(15) **1909** *Sat. Ev. Post* 20 Feb. 8/1 Start at Fifty-ninth Street and walk down what the Manhattanese call The Great White Way. **1948** *Sat. Review* 17 July 22/3 To many Americans Broadway is synonymous with the 'Great White Way.' — (16) **1908** *Sat. Ev. Post* 19 Sep. 3/1 Still another stirring phrase of inestimable value in rousing us from our torpor was that coined by the brilliant and lovable physician-philosopher, Oliver Wendell Holmes, 'The Great White Plague of the North.' **1913** *Collier's* 6 Dec. 11/2 The 'movie' . . . depicts a family . . . rescued and saved by the agencies which teach the cure of the Great White Plague through fresh air and careful living.

b. In more occasional, now obs., combs.: (1) **Great Belly Indians,** the Gros Ventres, *obs.*, cf. **Big Belly;** (2) **bug,** (see quot.); (3) **captain,** in Indian speech, one in supreme command; (4) * **coat,** ?a long, close-fitting jacket worn by women; (5) **eclipse,** (see quot.); (6)

Mother, (see quot.); (7) **warrior,** the leader of an Indian war party.

(1) **1791** *Mass. H.S. Coll.* I Ser. III. 24 The tribes of Indians . . . were called the . . . Great Belly Indians, Beaver Indians [etc.]. — (2) **1840** BIRD *Robin Day* 31 [He] was a 'great bug,' that is, a great personage. — (3) **1866** *Rep. Indian Affairs* 112 We need no urging from the great captain of the whites to turn our feet towards the mountains. — (4) **1782** *Jrnl. of Young Lady of Va.* (1871) 33 Shall I tell you our dresses? I hear you say 'Yes.' Mrs. P. wears a brocade; Cousin M. her pink Great-Coat, and I my pink.

(5) **1837** *Yale Lit. Mag.* II. 66 The eclipse of 1806 is the one familiarly spoken of in New England as the '*great* eclipse.' — (6) **1845** POLK *Diary* I. 23 In their talk they [*sc.* the Indians] addressed the President as their Great Father, and Mrs. Polk as their Great Mother. — (7) **1800** HAWKINS *Sk. Creek Country* 72 The Great Warrior, when he marches, gives notice where he shall encamp.

For other terms in which **great* is used see ***dipper, Grand Cyclops, hominy, national road, quarter court, raft, Sachem, trading path.** For *Great and General Court* see **general court, 1. b.**

5. In geographical designations: (1) **Great American Desert,** =**American Desert;** (2) **American Plains,** =**Great Plains;** (3) **Barrens,** (see quot.), *obs.;* (4) **Basin,** an extensive area surrounded by higher lands (see quot. 1843), also **Great Interior Basin;** (5) **Bay,** Cape Cod Bay, *obs.;* (6) **belt,** (see quot.), *obs.;* (7) **Desert,** = **American Desert,** *rare;* (8) **lake,** see as a main entry; (9) **Open Spaces,** a region of ample extent, esp. the West; (10) **Plains,** the prairie lands of the West; (11) **prairie,** =prec.; (12) ***River,** in Indian speech, the Mississippi River; (13) **Swamp,** the Dismal Swamp *q.v.;* (14) **water,** in Indian speech, the Atlantic Ocean, also (*cap.*), in *pl.*, the Mississippi River, *obs.;* (15) **West,** the western portion of the U.S.

(1) **1834** PIKE *Sketches* 10 It is into this great American desert that I wish to conduct my readers. **1875** *Cin. Enquirer* 2 July 2/2 We found a new empire in the West almost unknown to us, and our idea of the great American Desert has been moved back some four hundred miles. **1945** *Nat. Geog. Mag.* May 513 Geographies described Nebraska, then a six-year-old Territory, as 'an uninhabitable portion of the Great American Desert.' **1949** *Pacific Northwest Quart.* April 93 The myth of the 'Great American Desert' . . . discouraged settlement of this region. — (2) **1930** HENRY *Conquer. Plains* 3 About forty years ago, or the year 1890, I happened to be riding in a buggy in the eastern central part of the former Great American Plains. — (3) **1809** T. ASHE *Travels in Amer.* 220 To the S.E. lie the Great Barrens —several millions of acres, of no utility to man or beast, being entirely destitute of water. To the west, a considerable way, flow the two great rivers called Cumberland and Tennessee. — (4) **1843** FRÉMONT *Exped.* 175 Great Basin—a term which I apply to the intermediate region between the Rocky Mountains and the next range, containing many lakes. **1869** BOWLES *New West* xiv. 277 These alkaline valleys of the Great Interior Basin. **1949** *Kans. Hist. Quart.* Feb. 39 Across the plains the great trend of migration had swept to Oregon, California and the Great Basin.

(5) **1634** WOOD *N. Eng. Prospect* Map, The great Baye [=Cape Cod Bay]. **1664** *Brookhaven Rec.* 11 The Grate baye. — (6) **1880** G. INGHAM *Digging Gold* ix. 253 The oldest and best-known mines are situated on what is termed 'the Great Belt,' a mammoth lode of several miles in length . . . extending from . . . Central City . . . to Lead City. — (7) **1784** SMYTH *Tour* II. 239 This place is also called the *Great Desert*, on account of its being destitute of human inhabitants. — (9) [**1924** *Frontier* March 24, I have found a freedom here that I believe is unknown to the 'great spaces of the west'.] **1945** SERVICE *Ploughman* 371 As one attuned to the Great Open Spaces I professed a proper contempt for civilization.

(10) **1806** *Ann. 9th Congress* 2 Sess. 1140 The great plains reach far beyond the Red river to the south, and northward over the Arkansas river, and among the numerous branches of the Missouri. **1948** *Bul. Atomic Scientists* May 135/1 Our tastes in art, literature, and philosophy . . . have differences as great as those that mark the Great Plains from the crags of the Tetons. — (11) **1805** *Ann. 9th Congress* 2 Sess. 1104 After getting into the Great Prairie, the season being dry, they were forced to turn back for want of water. **1859** BARTLETT 10 *Apishamore*, a saddle-blanket, made of buffalo-calf skins, used on the great prairies. — (12) **1872** *Amer. Naturalist* VI. 82 It was here, too, that the missionaries heard of the Great River, and here, for the first time in history, appear those two Algonquin words, *Messi-Sepe.* **1898** CUSHMAN *Hist. Indians* 396, I know very well that the smoke of our council fires you have never seen, as we live on the other side of the Great River. — (13) **1802** *Guardian of Freedom* (Frankfort, Ky.) 7 July 3/2 They have embodied in large companies, armed, in the Great Swamp, near the Virginia line. — (14) **1808** BARKER *Indian Princess* II. i, They have risen, in monstrous canoes, through the great water, to spoil and ravish from us our fruitful inheritance. **1812** *Niles' Reg.* II. 81/2 We have been told that the king over the great water has greatly injured our white brethren of the great council fires. **1837** PECK *Gaz. Illinois* 13 The aboriginal name [of the Mississippi River] is said to signify '*Father of Waters*,' or '*Great Waters.*'

(15) **1832** *Boston Transcript* 6 April 2/1 Queen Elizabeth was personated by a dashing beauty from the 'great west.' **1916** WILSON *Somewhere* 353 He joined this bunch of noble redmen to advertise the vanishing romance of the Great West. **1948** *Utah Humanities Rev.* Jan. 20 Hearing of Fremont's description of the 'Great West' and the Mormon exodus, he was stirred to penetrate the romantic regions of the West.

For **Great Divide,** see as a main entry. For **Great Dismal Swamp,** see ***dismal.**

6. In the names of, or with reference to, plants and animals: (1) **great American shrike,** the butcherbird; (2) **bindweed,** (see quot.); (3) **blue heron,** the blue crane, *Ardea herodias;* (4) **corn,** (see quot.), *obs.;* (5) **-footed hawk,** (see quot. 1917); (6) **head,** the American goldeneye duck; (7) **laurel,** the rhododendron; (8) **marbled godwit,** the marbled godwit; (9) **northern pike,** =**muskellunge;** (10) **palmetto,** the cabbage palmetto, *rare;* (11) **tree,** the sequoia.

(1) **1823** JAMES *Exped.* I. 263 *Lanius borealis*, Vieil.—Great American shrike, Wilson. **1839** PEABODY *Mass. Birds* 291 The great American shrike, *Lanius septentrionalis*, . . . [has a] curious habit of impaling on thorns the insects it has caught and there leaving them to decay. — (2) **1840** DEWEY *Mass. Flowering Plants* 150 *Convolvulus sepium.* Wild Morning Glory . . . often called Great Bindweed; . . . grows on low grounds, running over shrubs. — (3) **1835** AUDUBON *Ornith. Biog.* III. 87 When wounded, the great Blue Heron immediately prepares for defence. **1946** *So. Sierran* Oct. 4/1 Occasionally a great blue heron slowly winged his way alongside our craft. — (4) **1750** J. BIRKET *Some Cursory Remarks* 36 Here they produce wheat, Rye, Hops & abundance of Maze or Great corn which they Ship of at Newhaven.

(5) **1813** WILSON *Ornithology* IX. 120 Great-footed Hawk . . . was described as darting with the rapidity of an arrow on the ducks when on the wing, and striking them down. **1917** *Birds of Amer.* II. 87 Duck Hawk, *Falco peregrinus anatum.* . . . [Also called] Great-footed Hawk. — (6) **1844** *Nat. Hist. N.Y., Zoology* II. 330 *Fuligula clangula*, the Brass-eye, Whistler or Greathead, . . . is another northern species. **1888** G. TRUMBULL *Game Birds* xxiii. 79 *Glaucionetta clangula americana.* American Golden-eye. . . . At Seaford (Hempstead), L.I., Great-head. — (7) **1784** *Mem. Academy* I. 442 Great Laurel. Winter-green. . . . The roots [are sometimes employed by people] in making small dishes, spoons, and other utensils. **1893** DANA *Wild Flowers* 60 American Rhododendron. Great Laurel.— (8) **1813** WILSON *Ornithology* VII. 30 Great Marbled Godwit: *Scolopax fedoa;* . . . is another transient visitant of our sea coasts in spring and autumn. **1874** COUES *Birds N.W.* 492 Great Marbled Godwit. *Scolopax fedoa.* . . . Entire temperate North America. **1917** *Birds of Amer.* I. 241. — (9) **1856** *Spirit of Times* 29 Nov. 209/2 In the great northern pike, the lower jaw is nearly straight. **1948** *Sat. Ev. Post* 31 July 72/2 It is all pike water, full of wall-eyed and great northern pike.

(10) **1802** ELLICOTT *Journal* 286 Great palmetto, or cabbage tree. — (11) **1855** *Amer. Inst. N.Y. Trans.* 191 The great tree of California has attracted the attention of the American Journal of Science and Art.

For *great* **American aloe, blue crane, Carolina wren, crested flycatcher, laurel magnolia, magnolia,** see the terms in boldface.

7. In nicknames: (1) **Great American Mudhole,** (see quot.), *rare;* (2) ***Commoner,** see as a main entry; (3) **Expounder (of the Constitution),** (see quot. 1893); (4) **Magician,** (see quot. 1844); (5) **Metropolis,** (see quot.), *rare;* (6) **Monster,** (see quot.), *obs.;* (7) **Pacificator,** (see quot. 1843); (8) ***unwashed,** Democrats or the Democratic party, *obs.*

(1) **1938** ASBURY *Sucker's Prog.* 134 Houses exclusively for gambling appeared sometime between 1815 and 1820, when Washington had begun to outgrow its early nicknames of 'The Capital of Miserable Huts,' and 'The Great American Mudhole.' — (3) **1831** *Boston Transcript* 5 July 2/2 *The town of Salisbury, N.H.*—remarkable as the birth place of the great expounder of the constitution. **1893** *Cong. Rec.* 24 Feb. 2138/1 In the district which I had the honor to represent . . . lie buried the mortal remains of Daniel Webster, the great expounder and defender of the Constitution. — (4) **1832** *Polit. Examiner* (Shelbyville, Ky.) 11 Aug. 2/3 As the President was 'born to command,' and as Mr. Van Buren is *his choice*, we presume the 'true republican party,' will not have the hardihood to vote against the 'great magician.' **1844** *Henry Clay Bugle* (Maysville, Ky.) 11 April 1/2 During the Presidential canvass, which preceded the first election of Gen. Jackson. . . . Martin Van Buren obtained by his agency in it, the soubriquet of the 'Great Magician.'

(5) **1846** T. H. JAMES *Rambles U.S.* 36 New York is everywhere called the Great Metropolis. — (6) **1838** BELL *Men & Things* 110 In this he was earnestly opposed by several; and one man in particular railed most intemperately against the 'great monster,'—meaning the United States Bank. — (7) **1843** JUNIUS *Life of Henry Clay* 8 Mr. Clay had scarcely been at the seat of Government over a month [in 1821], . . . [when] the whole country hailed him as 'the Great Pacificator.' **1861** HAYES *Pioneer Notes* (1929) 253 Their respective partizans [are] apparently hugging the delusion that each will fall heir to the envied title of honor which History has assigned alone to the Great Pacificator. — (8) **1856** BREWERTON *War in Kans.* 136 He [the governor of Kansas Territory] was sitting upon a white horse, *a la* General Taylor—or as the 'great unwashed' delight to call him, 'Old Rough and Ready.' **1901** *Cong. Rec.* 23 June 1345/2 The Democratic party . . . have been long known as the 'great unwashed.'

For **Great Compromiser, Emancipator, Nullifier,** see the nouns.

8. In phrases: (1) *Great and General Court,* see **general court, 1. b;** (2) *that's a great spoon,* (see quot.), *obs.;* (3) *by the great horn(ed) spoon,* a euphemistic oath, often humorous, also *by the sacred horn spoon;* (4) *great jumping Judas!,* an exclamation of astonishment; (5) *to be no great shakes,* see ✱**shake.**

(2) **1848** J. MITCHELL *Nantucketisms* 42 'That's a great spoon.' Good, promising. — (3) **1842** *Amer. Nat. Song Bk.* II. 222 He vow'd by the great horn spoon, . . . He'd give them a licking, and that pretty soon. **1857** UNDERHILL & THOMPSON *Elephant Club* 72 You do solemnly swear, by the sacred horn spoon. **1943** in *Amer. Sp.* XIX. (1944) 117 'Do this or get out!' and by the *Great Horned Spoon,* he doeth it or getteth out. **1948** *Time* 22 Nov. 25/1 Operators had sworn by the Great Horn Spoon that they would not negotiate with Harry ('The Nose') Bridges. — (4) **1917** FREEMAN & KINGSLEY *Alabaster Box* 56 'Gr-reat jumping Judas!' cried the irrepressible Lute, whose other name was Parsons.

b. Also **great snakes!** as an ejaculatory expression. *Colloq.*

1916 E. PORTER *David* 233 'Great snakes!' muttered Perry Larson, reaching out his hand and gingerly picking up one of the gold-pieces.

Great Awakening. A religious revival which began in the American colonies, esp. New England, about 1734. Cf. **Great Revival.**

1736 EDWARDS *Faithful Narr.* 23 A Minister . . . told me of a very great awakening of many in a Place called the Mountains. **1890** *N. Eng. Mag.* April 171 The Great Awakening was hardly over, when the muttering against Mr. Edwards in his own parish began to grow stronger. **1949** *N. Eng. Quart.* Mar. 61 Edwards recoiled from the Billy Sunday type of sweaty-shirt oratory and dramatic shouting of his colleagues in the Great Awakening.

✱ **Great Commoner.** Applied as a nickname to various prominent American political leaders, as Henry Clay, Thaddeus Stevens, W. J. Bryan, and Thomas Jefferson.

1843 JUNIUS *Tracts* Sep. 56 In Kentucky, Mr. Clay had early acquired the name of *'the Great Commoner,'* the people's man. **1844** E. SARGENT *H. Clay* 6/2 Mr. Clay . . . was soon regarded as the leading spirit of the opposition party; and it was about this time that the title of 'The Great Commoner' was bestowed upon him. — **1868** *Cong. Globe* 17 Dec. 131/1 With his own supporters . . . 'Old Thad' was a phrase of endearment; while even his foes spoke of him with pride as the 'great Commoner.' — **1906** *Rev. of Reviews* XXXIV. 259/1 Most of these anti-Bryan leaders have fallen into line and are loudly proclaiming their allegiance to the 'Great Commoner.' **1947** *Newsweek* 8 Sep. 22/2 The Great Commoner [W. J. Bryan] once had planked two statues in front of the driveway to his farm home. — **1910** *Sat. Ev. Post* 8 Oct. 49/3 If Thomas Jefferson, the Great Commoner, were alive today, and if his sound sense, keen insight and shrewd judgment turned to the important and practical matter of shoes, it's a pretty safe guess that he would favor an American-made shoe.

Great Divide. =**Continental Divide.** Also **Great Continental Divide.**

1861 NEWBERRY *Geol. Rep.* 44 Basin-shaped depressions on this mesa contain fresh-water Tertiary strata, both east and west of the great 'divide.' **1868** W. J. PALMER *Surveys across Continent* 171 The great Continental Divide at Arkansas Pass. **1945** *This Week Mag.* 19 May 20/2 The train picked up speed across the flatlands, across the Great Divide, into the Rockies.

transf. **1868** *Cong. Globe* 14 July 4068/1 The doctrine of political equality forms the great 'divide' between parties now as heretofore. **1880** *Cong. Rec.* 27 May 3854/1 A vast number of public building provisions were grouped together on what is called the log-rolling principle and I think the wags called it 'the little divide,' to distinguish it from the river and harbor bill, . . . which goes by the very appropriate title of 'the great divide,' . . . [being] a method of apportioning out the public money into where there is not any water or anything else—into private hands.

b. *To cross the Great Divide,* to die. *Colloq.*

1915 YOUNG *Hard Knocks* 242, I am still residing in Portland, Oregon, . . . where I hope to remain until I cross the Great Divide. **1943** DALE *Cow Country* 63 The little mound . . . marked the last resting place of a cow hand who in the line of duty had crossed the Great Divide 'to that new range which never fails.'

great lake.

1. *(cap.) pl.* The five large, connected lakes, Superior, Michigan, Huron, Erie, and Ontario, which, with the exception of Lake Michigan, border Canada and the U.S. Also attrib.

1683 PENN *Works* (1726) II. 700 The Reason of this *Cold* is given, from the *Great Lakes* that are fed by the *Fountains of Canada.* **1722** COXE *Descr. Carolana* (Pref.), A short Description . . . of the Lands to the Northwards, as far as, and among the Five Great Lakes. **1909** *Boston Herald* 17 Dec. 4/4 A through route from Boston by way of the great lakes to the west and northwest. **1946** *Reader's Digest* Nov. 38/2 The sands of the Great Lakes dunes are ideal for artist Nature's purpose. **1949** *Nat. Hist.* April 180/2 Probably it lies in long-term changes in the weather over the Great Lakes region as a whole.

b. Great Lake catfish, (see quot.).

1842 *Nat. Hist. N.Y., Zoology* IV. 180 The Great Lake Catfish, *Pimelodus nigricans,* . . . is held in very little estimation as an article of food.

2. The Atlantic Ocean. *Obs.*

1684 *Doc. Hist. N.Y. State* I. 402 Wee have put ourselves under the Great Sachim Charles that lives over the Great Lake. **1772** in SPARKS *Life G. Morris* I. 19, I know others that never saw the east side of the great lake.

Great Rebellion. The Civil War. Also transf.

1862 in HEADLEY *Great Rebellion* I. (1863) 7 Unexampled success . . . has attended our Agents in canvassing for the 'Great Rebellion.' **1890** LANGFORD *Vigilante Days* (1912) 514 Just before the great rebellion I was married to one I dearly loved. **1945** *Chi. Sun Bk. Week* 30 Sep. 7/3 Blackford nevertheless was sufficiently discerning and literate to produce one of the best of all personal memoirs of the Great Rebellion.

Great Revival. A religious revival which began in Tennessee and Kentucky about 1800. Cf. **Great Awakening.**

[**1800** N. BANGS *History of Methodism* II. 108 Last year [1799] was celebrated for the commencement of those Great Revivals of Religion in the Western Country, which induced the practice of holding camp-meetings.] **1804** L. DOW *Journal* (1814) 197 It appears that many have undervalued the great revival, and attempted to account for it altogether on natural principles. **1854** J. B. FINLEY *Sketches of Western Methodism* 74 The great revival commenced and spread throughout all the western country; so that at the end of the conference year 1802, we had doubled our numbers from that of 1795. **1948** DICK *Dixie Frontier* 195 The Great Revival of 1800 and its attendant institution, the camp-meeting, were pure products of the frontier of the Old Southwest.

✱**grebe,** *n.* As the last term in **Clark's, horned, pied-billed, Saint Domingo grebe.**

✱ **Grecian,** *a.*

1. Grecian bend, (see quot. 1841). Now *hist.*

1841 *N.O. Picayune* 12 Feb. 2/3 Some ingenious chap in Philadelphia . . . has invented and taken out a patent for a new *bustle* for the ladies, to which he gives the classical name of the 'Grecian Bend.' **1870** M. H. SMITH *20 Yrs. Wall St.* 274 They wear in their office, hats, heavy chignons, grecian bends, and talmas. **1948** *Utah Humanities Rev.* Jan. 47 'The Grecian Bend,' with its yards of waste material, offended Brigham Young's sense of economy.

Hence **Grecian-bender,** *n.,* one who follows this style. *Obs.*

1876 PHILLIPS *Lett. From Calif.* (1877) 131 These shoes . . . are very low at the heel, and the soles so sloped off at each end as to leave a *very high heel* in the middle of the sole, some of them almost as high as the heels of the Grecian-benders of a few years ago at Saratoga.

b. A revolver. *Jocular* and *rare.*

1880 NYE *B. Nye & Boomerang* 252 Dangerous Davis caressed his brass-mounted Grecian bend.

c. An early name for caisson disease or bends *q.v. Obs.*

1881 WOODWARD *St. Louis Bridge* 247 A workman walking about with difficult step and a slight stoop was at first regarded as a fit object for jokes, and cases of paralysis and cramp soon became popularly known by the name of 'Grecian bend.'

2. Grecian Lady, (see quot.). *Obs.*

1838 AUDUBON *Ornith. Biog.* IV. 138 In the southern parts of Florida, it [i.e., the snakebird *q.v.*] is called the 'Grecian Lady.'

***Greek,** *n.*

1. a. *pl.* (See quot.) *Obs.* **b.** A member of a Greek-letter fraternity in college. Also as adj.

(a) **1860** S. C. COX *Recollections of Wabash Valley* 145 After he got beyond danger from the 'Greeks,' as the Hoosiers in those days [*c*1830] called the Irish. — (b) **1949** *Time* 21 Mar. 47/2 Non-fraternity men, who outnumber the Greeks two to one, held a mass meeting. **1949** Univ. Okla. *News of Mo.* April 7/1 More than 85 percent of O.U.'s population is non-'Greek.'

2. ***Greek-letter,** designating a student **fraternity, society,** or **sorority** the name of which is made up of letters of the Greek alphabet.

1871 BAGG *At Yale* 52 Those [organizations] of the three lower classes resemble Phi Beta Kappa in being 'Greek-letter societies.' **1879** W. R. BAIRD *Amer. College Fraternities* 145 Kappa Alpha Theta was the first of the ladies' societies organized [1870] with principles and methods akin to those of the Greek-Letter fraternities. **1945** *Chi. Tribune* 27 Dec. 8/8 Invited as special guests are Mrs. Edgar Withrow of Wilmette, national first vice president of the Greek letter sorority. **1947** *Chi. Maroon* 4 Nov. 2/3 Alpha Delta Phi is the oldest Greek letter fraternity now active in the U.S.

***Greeley,** *n. attrib.* Of or pertaining to Horace Greeley (1811–72), prominent American editor and politician. *Obs.*

1872 *Cin. Times & Chronicle* 1 July 2/1 The Greeley Liberal party would no doubt support him 'as one man.' **1872** *Dly. Chronicle* (Wash., D.C.) 9 July 1/2 About one hundred Greeleyites got together and sang a Greeley song to the tune of 'John Brown.' **1872** *Nation* 18 July 29/2 [Delegates were] fanning themselves with the 'Greeley fan'—a repulsive, ghastly, flesh-colored thing, a portrait head of the candidate fastened to a stick and fringed with wool to represent white hair and whiskers. **1872** *Newton Kansan* 22 Aug. 3/3 A larger and enthusiastic Greeley meeting was held in Newton, at the Carmichael hall. *Ib.* 5 Sep. 4/1 The political bummers . . . are rallying everywhere around the Greeley standard. **1874** in FLEMING *Hist. Reconstruction* II. 160 Mr. Brooks . . . in 1872 . . . deserted his party and ran on the Greeley or reform ticket for governor. **1908** *Sat. Ev. Post* 31 Oct. 3/2 Do you remember the 'Tanners,' with their oil-skin capes, the flaming torches, the Greeley hats, the maniacal shrieks, . . . the gesticulating swarms of hot-eyed men outside of each polling place?

Hence **Greeleyism, Greeleyite.** Also **Greeleyized,** *a. Obs.*

1872 *Nation* 27 June 416/2 The answer came from a Maine Greeleyite Democrat, Mr. Pillsbury. **1872** *Cin. Times & Chron.* 1 July 2/1 The Volksfreund, which at first saluted Greeley's nomination with a contemptuous 'Pfui, pfui,' is gradually but surely 'declining' to the level of Greeleyism. **1872** *Ib.* 2 July 2/1 Schell, of Tammany fame, is the favorite of the Greeleyized Democrats for Belmont's place. *Ib.* 8 July 2/1 Nearly every Greeleyite but the officers of the meeting was affected that way at the grand Dolly Varden ratification.

***green,** *a.* In combs.: (1) **greenback,** see as a main entry; (2) **branch,** ?a branch the borders of which are esp. green with vegetation, *obs.;* (3) **cropping,** (see quot. 1855), *obs.;* (4) **dressing,** (see quots.), *obs.;* (5) **freighting,** (see quot.), *obs.;* (6) **goods,** see as a main entry; (7) **lands,** (see quot. and cf. **green swamp**), *obs.;* (8) **Mountain,** see as a main entry; (9) **ribbon,** see **ribbon;** (10) **River,** see as a main entry; (11) **scalp,** a fresh or undried human scalp, *obs.;* (12) **sea,** (see quot.), *obs.;* (13) **swamp,** a swamp in which the vegetation consists largely of evergreens, *obs.,* cf. **laurel swamp;** (14) **tar,** tar obtained from green, as distinguished from that obtained from dead, wood, *obs.,* cf. **dead tar;** (15) **waterproof,** (see quot.).

(2) **1654** in *Amer. Sp.* XV. 267/1 Running to the head of the green branch. **1700** *Ib.,* A red oake Corner tree Standing in the side of the green branch or Glead. — (3) **1848** *Rep. Comm. Patents 1847* 157 It would not be good hay, but would be, . . . fine for green food, and for green cropping and liming. **1855** BARNUM *Life* 369 The system of 'green cropping,'—that is sowing crops and ploughing them in while green . . . is now, I believe, generally acknowledged an excellent substitute for other manures. — (4) **1790** DEANE *N.-Eng. Farmer* 116/1 Green-dressing, turning a crop of green plants into the ground in summer, to enrich the soil. **1804** J. ROBERTS *Pa. Farmer* 35 Clover ploughed in, is a good green dressing.

(5) **1911** *Essex Hist. Coll.* XLVII. 16 This side of marsh work [gathering marsh hay at low water in flat hay boats] was the most dangerous of all and was called 'green freighting' from the fact that the thatch was gathered green and cured on shore. — (7) **1869** *Mich. Agric. Rep.* VII. 483 Swamp lands in regard to which a conflict has arisen between the United States and the State of Michigan, commonly known as 'Green Lands.'

(11) **1758** *Captivity of R. Eastburn* (Phila.) 11 An Indian . . . had a large Bunch of green Scalps, taken off our Men's Heads. **1780** J. DODGE *Narrative* 18 They murdered them, and delivered their green scalps in a few hours after to those British Barbarians. — (12) **1835** MARTIN *Descr. Va.* 41 Toward the south, there is a very large tract covered with reeds, without any trees, which being constantly green and waving in the wind, is called the green sea. — (13) **1639** in *Amer. Sp.* XV. 267/1 Bounded upon the Westerly side wth a little ridge of hills and at the head wth a greene swampe or valley. **1688** *Ib.,* On a poynt in the forke of a small branch which Issueth into the Greene Swampe. — (14) **1788** SCHÖPF *Reise* II. 222 Der davon bereitete Ther wird todter Ther (dead Tar) genannt, zum Unterschied vom grünen Ther (green Tar) welcher aus frischgefällten Bäumen, die man vorher einige Jahre auf Terpentin benuzt hatte, erhalten wird.

(15) **1917** KEPHART *Camping* I. 71 What is known in this country as 'green waterproof' has gone through the cupro-ammonium process and then is lightly waxed besides, making it quite waterproof but more pliable and slower burning than plain waxed stuff.

b. In the names of animals: (1) **green bass,** a black bass; (2) **-blue swallow,** the white-bellied swallow, *Iridoprocne bicolor;* (3) **crested flycatcher,** (see quot. 1917); (4) **crested pewee,** =prec.; (5) ***fish,** (see quot.); (6) ***fly,** the bluebottle or blowfly; (7) **frog,** the common frog, *Rana clamitans,* found in the eastern part of the U.S.; (8) **garrupa,** see ***garrupa;** (9) **gill, gilled oyster,** an oyster having gills or other parts of a green color from having fed on green vegetable organisms; (10) **head,** see as a main entry; (11) **heron,** a small American heron of the genus *Butorides,* esp. *B. virescens;* (12) **lizard,** a popular name, chiefly in the South, for any one of various small American lizards of the genus *Anolis;* (13) **smelt,** (see quots.); (14) **snake,** either of two small, green-colored American snakes, *Liopeltis vernalis* and *Opheodrys aestivus;* (15) **-striped maple worm,** (see quot.).

(1) **1820** RAFINESQUE in *Western Rev.* II. 54 Ohio Red-eye. *Aplocentrus calliops.* . . . It lives in the lower parts of the Ohio, in Green river, &c. Vulgar names Red-eyes, Bride pearch, Batchelor's pearch, Green bass. **1897** *Outing* Aug. 438/1 [To] the boys . . . large and small-mouth black bass were known as 'green' bass. — (2) **1812** WILSON *Ornithology* V. 44 Green-Blue, or White-Bellied Swallow: *Hirundo viridis* . . . is the species hitherto supposed by Europeans to be the same with their common Martin. **1828** BONAPARTE *Synopsis* 65 The Green-blue Swallow . . . inhabits the United States during summer.—(3) **1810** WILSON *Ornithology* II. 77 [The] Small, Green, Crested Flycatcher, *Muscicapa Querula,* . . . arrives from the south about the middle of May. **1839** AUDUBON *Ornith. Biog.* V. 427 [The] Small green Crested Flycatcher . . . does not appear to inhabit the Fur Countries. **1917** *Birds of Amer.* II. 207 Acadian Flycatcher. *Empidonax virescens.* . . . [Also called] Green-crested Flycatcher. — (4) **1871** BURROUGHS *Wake-Robin* (1886) 162 The green-crested pewee builds its nest . . . of the blossoms of the white-oak.

(5) **1884** GOODE *Fisheries* I. 433 The Bluefish—*Pomatomus saltatrix* . . . is said to be called the 'Green-fish' [in North Carolina, Virginia, and Maryland]. — (6) **1805** LEWIS in *L. & Clark Exped.* II. (1904) 319 The eye knats have disappeared. The green or blowing flies are still in swarms. **1851** *S. Lit. Messenger* XVII. 351/2 Indians carried wallet of beef on one side, canteen of water on 'tother; green flies follow 'em 'bout in great swarms. **1945** MATHEWS *Talking* 195 Green flies buzzed about the place where I had dressed some quail. — (7) **1709** LAWSON *Carolina* 132 The small green Frogs get upon Trees, and make a Noise. **1907** M. C. DICKERSON *Frog Book* 198 The Green Frog, *Rana clamitans,* . . . [is] very common throughout eastern North America. — (9) **1881** E. INGERSOLL *Oyster Industry* 245 Green Gill.—In Richmond, and Petersberg, and on the York river in Virginia, are to be found in the markets what are called 'green-gilled oysters.'

(11) **1855** *Knickerb.* XLVI. 222 Night-herons, snowy-herons, green-herons, and little-herons construct their nests so closely together that four or five hundred of them may be counted upon twenty or thirty cedars. **1883** *Cent. Mag.* 653 Among the most common birds are the green herons. — (12) **1709** LAWSON *Carolina* 131 Green Lizards are very harmless and beautiful, having a little Bladder under their Throat, which they fill with Wind, and evacuate the same at Pleasure. **1738** CATESBY *Carolina* II. 65 *Lacertus viridis Caroliniensis.* The Green-Lizard of Carolina. . . . They frequent houses, are familiar and harmless, and are suffered with impunity to sport and catch flies on tables and windows. **1917** COMSTOCK *The Man* 128 Go in there, now, you green lizard; turn about an' get on yer belly like the crawlin' thing yo' are! — (13) **1884** GOODE *Fisheries* I. 543 The 'green' Smelts, as they are called, or those which have never been frozen, are

much the more highly esteemed. *Ib.* 456 In general appearance they [*Atherinidae*] resemble the smelt, and at various places are called 'Sand Smelts' and 'Green Smelts.' — **(14) 1709** LAWSON *Carolina* 132 Green-Snakes are very small, tho' pretty. **1778** CARVER *Travels* 486 The Green Snake is about a foot and a half long, and in colour so near to grass and herbs, that it cannot be discovered as it lies on the ground. **1885** *Amer. Naturalist* Sep. 922 A second species of green snake, the slender green snake, *Cyclophis aestivus*, an austroriparian species, collected by Colonel N. S. Goss, at Neosho falls.

(15) 1892 KELLOGG *Kansas Insects* 101 Green-striped Maple-Worm. (*Anisota rubicunda* Fabr.; Order, Lepidoptera.)

c. In the names of plants: (1) **green ash,** the red ash, *Fraxinus pennsylvanica;* (2) **beans,** (see quot.); (3) **brier,** any one of various plants of the genus *Smilax*, esp. *S. rotundifolia* of the eastern states, also attrib.; (4) **corn,** see as a main entry; (5) ***dragon,** an American herb, *Arisaema dracontium*, related to the jack-in-the-pulpit; (6) ***hellebore, =American hellebore;** (7) **-land sandwort,** the mountain sandwort; (8) **maple,** (see quot.); (9) **milkweed,** a plant of the genus *Acerates* found in the eastern states; (10) **pepper,** the sweet pepper plant, *Capsicum grossum*, or its fruit, esp. in its immature stage; (11) **seed,** a variety of upland cotton having green seeds, also **green-seeded cotton;** (12) **sweet,** a variety of apple, *obs.*

(1) 1810 MICHAUX *Arbres* I. 34 Green ash (*Fraxinus viridis*), . . . nom donné par moi. **1885** HAVARD *Flora W. & S. Texas* 509 Texas Green Ash [is] the most common Ash of Southern and Western Texas. **1901** MOHR *Plant Life Ala.* 667 *Fraxinus lanceolata*. . . . Green Ash. — **(2) 1942** RAWLINGS *C. Creek* 214 Even string beans, which here [in Fla.] we call green beans or wax beans according to color, now seem insipid to me. — **(3)** *c***1785** S. PEARS *Narrative* (MS) 4 We had not anything to live on . . . except . . . greenbrier berreys. **1892** TORREY *Foot-Path Way* 80 Another novelty was the pale greenbrier, *Smilax glauca*. **1943** SHIMER *Plant Names* 19 The same plant is called Cat briar for its sharp stout prickles, and Green briar because of its bright green bark.

(5) 1817–8 EATON *Botany* (1822) 182 *Arum dracontium*, green dragon. **1939** *Nat. Geog. Mag.* Aug. 220/1 Color in this charming ground cover is provided by blue and yellow violets . . . Jacob's-ladder, the mottled jack-in-the-pulpit and green dragon. — **(6) 1874** GARROD *Materia Med.* (1880) 382 *Veratri Viridis Radix*. Green Hellebore Root. The dried rhizome of *Veratrum viride;* American or Green Hellebore. — **(7) 1892** TORREY *Foot-Path Way* 103 The whole summit . . . was sprinkled with the modest and beautiful Greenland Sandwort, springing up in every little patch of thin soil where nothing else would flourish. — **(8) 1844** LEE & FROST *Oregon* vii. 81 The whole of the north-west coast is exceedingly mountainous and rugged, with dense forests of fir, hemlock, spruce, . . . and a species of maple, called green-maple, or 'devil wood,' remarkable for its toughness. — **(9) 1829** EATON *Botany* (ed. 5) 90 *Acerates viridiflora*, green milkweed. **1892** COULTER *Bot. W. Texas* II. 267. **1931** CLUTE *Plants* 11/6.

(10) 1834 A. PIKE *Sketches* 96 The salad . . . was garnished with . . . huge strings . . . of red and green pepper. **1945** *Chi. D. News* 29 May 9/2 Combine . . . one teaspoon finely chopped green pepper . . . and one-fourth teaspoon prepared mustard. — **(11) 1775** ROMANS *Nat. Hist. Fla.* 140 The sort we must cultivate here is . . . also known by the name of green seeded cotton. **1796** B. HAWKINS *Lett.* 30, I advised him, . . . as from his information the black seed cotton will not do here, to plant only the green seed. **1882** *Cent. Mag.* Feb. 573/1 It has not been supposed that any roller gin existed which could be applied to the green seed or common cotton of commerce in an economic way. — **(12) 1847** J. M. IVES *N. Eng. Fruit* 45 *Green Sweet*. This apple is of small size, round, and rather flat.

greenback ˈgrinˌbæk, *n.* [See quot. 1890.]

1. A legal-tender, non-interest-bearing note of a kind first issued by the federal government during the Civil War, and originally not redeemable in silver or gold. Now used loosely for any paper bill. See also **treasury greenback,** and cf. **fiat money.**

1862 *N.Y. Tribune* 14 June 4/2 The green-backs are popular; the People have had a fresh taste of a paper currency which will pay debts and buy goods alike in New York and Nebraska. **1890** *Harper's Mag.* Oct. 704/2 Secretary Chase decided that the backs of the legal-tender notes should be printed with this patented green ink, giving to such notes literally green backs. The soldiers . . . gave them the name of 'greenbacks.' **1946** *Coronet* Dec. 155/2, I was told the old lady left a fortune hidden in the papers, one greenback for each day of the last 50 years of her life.

attrib. **1865** KELLOGG *Rebel Prisons* 41 For a small piece of pie I gave the last 'greenback' dollar I had in the world. **1870** MEDBERY *Men Wall St.* 8 Large emissions of greenback currency took the place of gold. **1927** SIRINGO *Riata* 20 On leaving Galveston, Uncle Nick slipped some greenback money into my pocket.

2. a. The golden plover. **b.** An American warbler of the family Sylviidae.

(a) 1844 *Nat. Hist. N.Y., Zoology* II. 213 The Golden Plover. *Charadrius Virginiacus*. . . . They are frequently also called Greenbacks. **1917** *Birds of Amer.* I. 257. — **(b) 1869** BURROUGHS in *Galaxy* Aug. 170 The finest songster among the Sylvia . . . is the black-throated greenback.

3. Short for **Greenback party.** *Obs.*

1876 *Tribune Almanac 1877* 119/2 In 1st District in 1876, there were 40 votes for Benj. G. Chace, 'Greenback'; . . . 47 for John M. Bailey, 'Greenback.'

attrib. **1868** *N.Y. Herald* 4 July 4/2 Kansas Delegation is enthusiastic in favor of the greenback candidate. **1876** *N.Y. Tribune* 18 May 5/4 The National Greenback Convention at 10 o'clock this morning [May 17]. **1876** *Tribune Almanac 1877* 64/2 'Greenback' ticket 289 votes. *Ib.* 66/1 In 1876, Greenback vote on President was 774. **1880** *Harper's Mag.* Dec. 156 The New Hampshire Greenback State convention met at Manchester, September 29, and nominated for Governor Warren S. Brown.

4. Greenback-Labor, short for next. Also **Greenback and Labor.**

1879 *Tribune Almanac 1880* 21/1 Party Platforms, 1879. . . . New-York Greenback-Labor. (Adopted August 29.) **1884** *Boston Journal* Aug., There are now several regularly nominated tickets in the field. They are . . . National Christian, Anti-Monopoly, and Greenback-Labor. . . . General Butler . . . says that he will accept the Greenback and Labor nomination.

5. Greenback-Labor party, the name adopted by the Greenback party *q.v.* after the joining with it in 1878 of those primarily interested in problems of labor and capital. *Obs.* Cf. prec.

1879 *Bradstreet's* 10 Dec. 4/1 What is known as the greenback-labor party went before the country. **1894** LEAVITT *Our Money Wars* 224 The most remarkable occurrence in 1878 was the extraordinary growth of the Greenback-Labor party.

6. Greenback party, a political party made up of those who favored the preservation and increase of greenback currency and opposed the substitution for it of the notes of the national banks. Now *hist.* Cf. **3.** above.

1876 *N.Y. Tribune* 18 May 1/1 Two National and five State Conventions were held yesterday, namely: Those of the National Greenback and Prohibition parties [etc.]. **1890** *Harper's Mag.* Oct. 705/2 Together they organized a political party called the Greenback party. **1948** *Dly. Ardmoreite* (Ardmore, Okla.) 23 July 6/6 The Greenback party of the 1870s was built around bankrupt farmers who wanted monetary relief.

Also **Greenbacker,** a member of this party. Also attrib.

1876 *Chi. Tribune* 4 Aug. 2/1 The declaration of the Cincinnati platform in favor of honest money . . . left the inflationist greenbackers in an unhappy frame of mind. **1948** *Ib.* 4 Jan. I. 4/4 Scattering votes received by Benjamin F. Butler, Greenbacker candidate, and John P. St. John, Prohibitionist, were enough to keep James G. Blaine, a Republican, from the White House in 1884.

Greenbackism ˈgrinbækˌɪzəm, *n.* The economic philosophy of the Greenback party. Now *hist.*

1876 *Chi. Tribune* 4 Aug. 2/2 The Democratic managers, for this year at least, are solicitous to suppress the greenbackism that would array Democrats in hostility practically to Tilden. **1882** *Nation* 4 Sep. 231/2 The Mississippi alliance with Greenbackism is as disgraceful as the Virginia alliance with repudiation. **1932** GRAYSON *Leaders* 279 For a time greenbackism was a real menace to the welfare of our country. **1949** *Social Studies* May 216/1 Many of its members embraced greenbackism.

***green corn.**

1. Indian corn, esp. the ears in the milky stage, prepared as food by roasting or boiling; roasting ears.

1645 *Springfield Rec.* I. 181 Divers that keepe teames on the other side of ye River . . . have much damnified other men by theyr Cattell, in eating the greene corne. **1697** *Md. Hist. Mag.* XV. 116 [An Indian] comes on the Back of his [*sc.* a settler's] Plantation, gathers his Green Corn, cutts up his Corn stalks [etc.]. **1716** CHURCH *Philip's War* 51 This [salt] season'd his Cow-beaf so that with it and the dry'd green-corn . . . he made a very hearty Supper. **1745** MACSPARRAN *Diary* 35 Molly Browne went home in the afternoon, after eating some green Corn. **1894** ALLEN *Kentucky Cardinal* xvi. When you send your servants over for green corn, you can let them come through that little gate. **1946** NEWTON *P. Bunyan* 173 We plucked and ate roasted ears of green corn right off the stalk.

b. *attrib.* Of or pertaining to an annual celebration among some of the southern Indians at the season of green corn, which was eaten during this ceremonial meeting, as **green corn ceremony, feast, festival.** Cf. next.

1800 ASBURY *Journal* II. 467 The gentry had made a dinner at a small distance from the town—a kind of green-corn feast, with a roasted animal. **1835** SIMMS *Yemassee* I. 40 The green corn festival! I must be there, Sanutee, and you must not deny me. **1907** HODGE *Amer. Indians* I. 460/2 New fire was made in the Green-corn ceremony of the Creeks. **1946** FOREMAN *Last Trek* 345 As late as 1882 they still danced around a fire to drive away sickness and held their yearly green-corn feast.

2. green corn dance, =busk.

1725 in *Travels Amer. Col.* 134, I have given Orders to them to meet me at the Great dance here (called the Green Corn dance). **1821** *Jrnl. Science* III. 43, I now return to the Cherokees, and their green corn dance. **1898** CUSHMAN *Hist. Indians* 20 Mordecai . . . asserted that in their Green Corn Dances he had often heard them utter Yavayaha! Yavayaha!

transf. **1941** DANIELS *Tar Heels* 245 Methodists and Baptists move in the Green Corn Dance still at harvest time in appreciation to gods whose dance they remember even if their names are forgotten by some of the dancers.

green goods.

1. *attrib.* Of or pertaining to fresh vegetables. *Rare.*

1888 *Boston Transcript* (F.), Get a good melon, and if you can't tell for yourself by that intuition which is the best guide in such matters, then trust to your green goods grocer's judgment.

2. Counterfeit greenback money. Also attrib. *Slang.*

1889 *Cong. Rec.* 29 Jan. 1308/1 James T. Holland . . . [was] decoyed to New York to buy 'green goods.' *Ib.* 1307/2 The 'green-goods' dealer drops him [the small investor] from the list [of 'suckers']. **1903** A. H. LEWIS *Boss* 167 The gamblers can run; an' I don't find any fault with even th' green-goods people. **1908** LORIMER *J. Spurlock* viii. 174 Wouldn't the come-on take the package of green goods?

fig. **1902** LORIMER *Lett. Merchant* 117, I want you to understand that the girl who marries you for my money is getting a package of green goods in more ways than one.

b. green goods man, a counterfeiter or one who deals in counterfeit money.

1888 *Troy D. Times* 3 Feb. (F.), The green-goodsman escaped, for the only proof against him was that he sold a quantity of paper cut in the shape of bills and done up in packages of that size. **1912** N. WOODROW *Sally Salt* 101 He's one of the best-known green-goods men in the country.

***greenhead,** *n.*

1. (See quots.) Cf. **creeping greenhead.**

1815 *Lit. & Phil. Soc. N.Y. Trans.* I. 503 The largest rock-fish, that is, those that weigh from twenty-five pounds to sixty pounds, are called green heads. **1884** GOODE *Fisheries* I. 425 The Striped Bass [*Roccus lineatus*] . . . [is] sometimes known in New England by the names 'Greenhead' and 'Squid-hound.'

2. Any one of various horseflies having compound eyes that are green. In full **greenhead fly.**

1837 WETMORE *Gaz. Missouri* 65 In the early settlement of the country, the value of the prairies was underrated by a knowledge of the mischievous power vested in the greenheads, or prairie fly. **1920** LINCOLN *Mr. Pratt* 96 As for the live stock, that was seven thousand hop-toads . . . and green-heads and mosquitoes forever and ever, amen. **1946** FOREMAN *Last Trek* 250 The weather was exceedingly hot, and the teams terribly annoyed and bitten by 'greenhead' flies.

3. (See quots.)

1852 in STANSBURY *Gt. Salt Lake* 322 *Anas Boschas.*—Mallard; Greenhead. Found throughout the United States, California, Oregon, and fur countries. **1917** *Birds of Amer.* I. 114 Mallard. *Anas platyrhynchos.* . . . [Also called] Green-head (male); Gray Duck (female). *Ib.* 135 Scaup Duck. Marila marila. . . . [Also called] Green-head.

4. (See quots.)

1877 BARTLETT 777 *Bottle-Head.* . . . The black-bellied plover; also called 'beetle-head' and 'green head.' **1917** *Birds of Amer.* I. 257 Golden Plover. *Charadrius dominicus dominicus.* . . . [Also called] Brass-back; Greenhead; Pale-breast.

5. (See quot.)

1899 *Animal & Plant Lore* 61 Folk-names of Animals [include] . . . Green-heads, large frogs, *Rana clamata.*

***greening,** *n.* As the last term in **Jersey, Rhode Island greening.**

greenlet 'grinlɪt, *n.* A vireo. Cf. **Philadelphia, red-eyed greenlet.** — **1831** J. RICHARDSON *Fauna Boreali-Americana* II. 233 *Vireo olivaceus* (Bonaparte), Red-eyed Greenlet. **1917** *Birds of Amer.* III. 102 Vireos are sometimes called Greenlets; the Latin word *Vireo* means 'I am green.'

Green Mountain.

1. A variety of potato.

1914 *Country Life* Jan. 84/3, I started the three sections of the field containing Early Rose, Green Mountain, and Irish Cobblers respectively. **1945** PEARSON *Country Flavor* 29 The democrat was strong enough to carry a barrel of Baldwins or Northern Spies and a couple of sacks of Green Mountains to Uncle Barzoola and Aunt Hezekiah.

2. *attrib.* Of or pertaining to the Green Mountains or to Vermont.

1778 HUTCHINSON *Diary & Lett.* II. 230 Col Stewart bro't a copy of a letter wrote by Mr Ethan Allen, in behalf of the Green Mountain Men, who refuse to acknowledge the Congress. **1869** *Overland Mo.* III. 126, I met a man, with a pinched face and a yellow beard, who was mounted on a clay-bank horse as lank as a Green Mountain pad when it has been about a month in the Horse Latitudes. **1902** WISTER *Virginian* viii, She could have been enrolled in the Boston Tea Party, the Ethan Allen Ticonderogas, the Green Mountain Daughters, the Saratoga Sacred Circle, and the Confederated Colonial Chatelaines.

3. Green Mountain boy, a Vermonter; orig. a member of an informal militia organized *c*1771 to protect the settlers occupying the New Hampshire grants from claimants holding New York grants.

1772 *Vt. Hist. Soc. Coll.* I. 6 Captain Warner's company of Green Mountain Boys . . . fired three volleys of small arms. **1811** *Niles' Reg.* I. 133/2 Three or four thousand 'Green mountain boys' employed to look towards Canada. **1942** PEATTIE *Friendly Mts.* 67 They have an ironic sense of humor, a trait which was in the Green Mountain Boys perhaps more volatile than it is now.

4. Green Mountain State, a nickname for Vermont.

1838 *N.Y. Advertiser & Exp.* 7 Feb. 3/4 A Mr. Fletcher of Vermont, the only Administration member from the Green Mountain States [*sic*], appeared in the Hall looking like the ghost of Hamlet's father. **1906** *Springfield W. Republican* 12 July 2 The Green Mountain State stands in great need of a political shaking up. **1948** *Vt. Quart.* July 74 It is of much historic interest to the Green Mountain State.

b. Green Mountain City, (see quot.).

1859 *Ladies' Repository* XIX. 51/2 Montpelier, Vermont, is the 'Green Mountain City,' being the capital of the Green Mountain state.

Green Mountaineer. A Vermonter. — **1829** *Western Mo. Rev.* II. 592 We could see the brawny Green mountaineer quaffing the bosom-warming cheer, and handing to his rosy Charmer. **1872** *Newton Kansan* 12 Sep. 2/1 The 'Green' Mountaineers turned their faces toward the rising sun.

***Greenough,** *n.* Used in the possessive in the name of an illuminating oil. *Obs.* — **1843** *Amer. Pioneer* II. 453 In Carolina we had the real fat light-wood, not merely pine knots, but the fat straight pine. This, from the brilliancy of our parlor, of winter evenings, might be supposed to put, not only candles, lamps, camphine, Greenough's chemical oil, but even gas itself to the blush.

Green River.

1. Green River claim, plum, tumbler, (see quots.). *Obs.*

1792 IMLAY *Western Territory* 210 Green-river plumb. **1801–3** J. LYLE *Diary* (MS) 45 Mr. Rice . . . said long meetings night watching &c. would produce religious insanity &c. like the Shakers Green river tumblers &c. **1836** J. HALL *Statistics of West* 208 In Kentucky, the lands south of Green river, were sold by the state, to her citizens, upon credit. . . . Every year brought the purchasers of land before the legislature, as petitioners, for extension of the time of payment; and although thirty years have elapsed since the sales commenced, the same process is annually continued. . . . The 'Green river claim,' has become a standing theme.

2. *Up to Green River,* (see quots.). *Obs.*

1848 RUXTON *Life Far West* viii. 294 The knives used by the hunters and trappers are manufactured at the 'Green River' works, and have that name stamped upon the blade. Hence the mountain term for doing anything effectual is 'up to Green River.' **1850** GARRARD *Wah-To-Yah* xiii. 168, I follers thar trail, an' at night, . . . socks my big knife up to the Green River, first dig.

b. *To send* (or *go*) *up Green River,* to kill, to die. *Colloq.*

1871 DE VERE 200 The mountaineers in the wilder parts of the Southwest . . . say they send a man *up Green River,* when they have killed him. **1945** *Tracks* June 30/1 Four early expressions for conductor—*superintendent, pilot, captain,* and *master of the cars*—have gone up Green River.

***greens,** *n. pl.* As the last term in **beet, dandelion, poke greens.**

***grid,** *n.* **=gridiron 2.** Also attrib. *Colloq.*

1928 *Chi. Tribune* 13 Dec. 25/8 (*headline*), Law . . . to lead Irish on Grid in 1929. **1946** *Democrat* 12 Sep. 1/3 (*caption*), Thirty-Four Out For Grid Practice. **1948** *Shelby* (Mont.) *Promoter* 16 Sep. 1/8

Local grid fans will be able to see all the home games of the Coyotes and still save 25 cents.

gridder ˈgrɪdɚ, *n.* A football player. *Colloq.* — **1929** *Randolph Enterprise* (Elkins, W.Va.) 7 Nov. 4/2 The University is expecting to play host to about 2,000 gridders Saturday. **1948** *Fargo* (N.D.) *Forum* 28 Sep. 12/1 He had quite a few changes in mind for this week in an attempt to stir the Deacon gridders from their lethargy.

∗ **griddle,** *n.* Short for "griddle cake." *Obs.*

1842 KIRKLAND *Forest Life* II. 106 My woman wants to set some griddles and she took a notion she must have risin' to put in 'em. **1859** *Harper's Mag.* March 486/2 Do take some more of the griddles, will thee? **1871** DE VERE 482 Griddles are not only the utensils for baking cakes, but also the cakes themselves.

b. griddle-spade, a flat-bladed implement for turning cakes on a griddle.

1879 MRS. WHITNEY *Just How* 28 Keep a knife or griddle-spade in your hand, and raise the cake occasionally.

∗ **gridiron,** *n.*

1. A nickname for the Stars and Stripes, the flag of the U.S. Also **gridiron flag.**

1812 *Niles' Reg.* 12 Sep. III. 31/2 The masts from which they flew, went over the side, while Hull's four *'gridirons'* floated in the air triumphant. **1866** in E. A. POLLARD *So Hist. War* II. 103 It was . . . the identical 'gridiron' carried from Fort Sumter in 1861. **1901** *Munsey's Mag.* XXV. 648/2 The gridiron flag . . . became the sole legal cover for ships in the slave trade.

2. The field upon which football is played. Also attrib.

1897 *N.Y. Journal* 5 Sep. 41/4 Captain Garret Cochran will marshal a small army of gridiron warriors on the 'varsity athletic ground.' **1913** *Collier's* 20 Dec. 27/2 He is one of the best handlers of the ball on the gridiron. **1949** *Sat. Ev. Post* 19 Mar. 99/2, I can assure you . . . that you will not be able to bull your way through this course as you do through the opposition on the gridiron.

3. gridiron bridge, a corduroy bridge. *Obs.*

1835 ABBOTT *N. Eng.* 225 He must . . . run the risk of having his bones dislocated by rattling over *gridiron bridges.*

griffe grɪf, *n.* [See note.] (See quots. 1859 and 1931.)

The *Dictionnaire de Trévoux* (1771 ed.), under *griffe,* says that this word was applied in Santo Domingo to the offspring of a Negro and a native, and adds, "Ce sont les Espagnols qui leur ont donné ce nom, à cause de leur laideur ordinaire." The word may be f. Sp. *grifo,* "kinky," "frizzled," which Santamaría records in Puerto Rico and Cuba in the sense of a Negro.

[**1724** HAUTERIVE in *Histoire de l'Académie des Sciences* 17 (Buffon), Les enfants d'un mulâtre et d'une noire, ou d'un noir et d'une mulâtresse, qu'on appelle *griffes,* sont d'un jaune plus noir, et ont les cheveux noirs; de sorte qu'il semble qu'une nation originairement formée de noirs et de mulâtres retourneroit au noir parfait. **17—** BUFFON *Variétés dans l'Espèce humaine* (Addition) (1827) 409 Il paroit, par cette notice donnée à l'Académie par M. de Hauterive, que . . . les griffes nés d'un père nègre et d'une mulâtresse ont aussi des cheveux, et point de laine, ce dont je doute.] **1840** *N.O. Picayune* 2 Aug. 2/6 $25 Reward will be given for the slave Harry, . . . a dark griffe, heavy built [etc.]. *Ib.* 23 Sep. 2/6 $10 Reward will be given for the apprehension and delivery to the undersigned of the girl Lucy who ran away. . . . Lucy is a *griffane.* **1859** BARTLETT 180 Griffin, Griffe. This word, like the French *griffone,* is constantly used in Louisiana, both in conversation and in print, for a mulatto, particularly the woman. **1931** READ *La.-French* 44 Griffe, *f.* The offspring of a negro and a mulatress, of obscure origin; perhaps a backformation from Fr. *griffon,* 'griffin.'

attrib. **1889** *Amer. Folk-Lore* II. 229 A certain man is described as having a 'griff complexion.'

∗ **grill,** *n.* (See quot. 1896.)

1886 TIFFANY *Postage Stamps U.S.A.* 170 All these values were issued with a grille, of which there are several sizes. **1896** *N. Eng. Mag.* Jan. 656/1 Some persons discovered that cancelled stamps could easily be cleaned and used again. It was to prevent this that the government, in 1868, adopted what is called a grill—the stamp being embossed, with small, square points in the form of a rectangle, which broke the fibre, allowing the cancellation ink to penetrate the paper. **1935** *Scott's Postage Stamp Cat.* 4/3 On the issued stamps the grill breaks through the paper and forms tiny crosses within squares.

Hence **grilling,** *n.*

1896 *N. Eng. Mag.* Jan. 566/1 The grilling of the stamps was continued until 1872, when a new ink was used that could not be removed from the paper without injuring the stamps.

grill grɪl, *v. tr.* To subject (a person) to severe questioning. — **1928** A. G. HAYS *Let Freedom Ring* 289 The three men were grilled about their movements on the day of the attempted hold-up. **1948** *Chi. Tribune* 15 Jan. 15 *Grill* him! Beat it out of him! Make him tell you where he's hidden that bloody poker!

Grimes Golden (Pippin). [Thomas P. *Grimes.*] A variety of late golden-yellow apple; also the tree producing such apples.

1857 E. J. HOOPER *Western Fruit Book* 42 Grimes's Golden Pippin. Remarks.—'A good seedling from Virginia.' **1881** *Amer. Naturalist* XV. 529 The apple trees are Grimes's Golden, and the quince, Angers. **1921** FOLGER & THOMSON *Com. Apple Industry* 404 Grimes Golden. Originating in West Virginia, and mentioned as a commercial variety as early as 1800, the Grimes Golden has rather wide distribution.

∗ **grind,** *n.* **1.** A student who works slavishly at his lessons, a drudge. **2.** (See quot.) *Obs.*

(1) **1893** W. K. POST *Harvard Stories* 11 Come now, old grind, do take a day off. **1947** *Chi. D. News* 22 Sep. 1/1 He is always the 'straight A' grind from Taft school, Yale college, and Harvard law school. — (2) **1896** *Peterson Mag.* ns. VI. 302/2 Dramatic companies at Wellesley . . . usually play original or adapted comedies, plentifully sprinkled with 'grinds,' which is the college vernacular for local hits.

∗ **grind,** *v. tr.* To press (sugar cane) between rollers to extract its juice. — **1875** MARK TWAIN *Old Times on Miss.* iv. 73 When they have finished grinding the cane, they form the refuse of the stalks into great piles and set fire to them.

Grindelia ˌgrɪnˈdiljə, *n.* [f. David Hieronymus *Grindel* (1776–1836), Russian botanist.] (See quot. 1889.) Also (not *cap.*) a plant of this genus. Cf. **gum plant.**

1882 *Cent. Mag.* June 223/1 Here [in Calif.] were bahia, madia, . . . corethrogyne, grindelia, etc., growing in close social congregations of various shades of yellow. **1889** *Cent.* 2625/2 Grindelia. . . . A genus of asteroid composites, coarse herbs or sometimes shrubby, with rather large radiate terminal heads of yellow flowers, and with the foliage usually covered with a viscid balsamic secretion. **1937** *Range Plant Handbook* w-86 Curlycup gumweed is one of the several species of Grindelia employed in the treatment of poison-oak and poison-ivy inflammation.

∗ **grinder,** *n.* As the last term in **corn, feed, gospel, sausage grinder.**

∗ **grinding,** *n.*

1. Extracting juice from sugar cane. Also attrib.

1833 SILLIMAN *Man. Sugar Cane* 16 It might be possible to complete the grinding . . . without exposure to an accident. **1856** *Porter's Spirit of Times* 15 Nov. 172/3 It was towards the close of the grinding season . . . at the sugar-house. **1887** *Cent. Mag.* Nov. 104/1 It is true that cane planting and grinding require a stricter and more systematic labor organization than raising cotton or rice.

2. ∗ **grinding mill,** = **cane mill.**

1829 SHERWOOD *Gaz. Georgia* (ed. 2) 253 A grinding mill, for breaking the canes and extracting the juice, may be of a very simple construction, having three upright rollers. **1868** *Putnam's Mag.* I. 594/2 *Bogasse* (all that is left of the cane after it has passed between the immense rollers of the grinding-mill).

grindle ˈgrɪndl, *n.* [Prob. a variant of ∗ *grundel.*] The bowfin. See also **John A. Grindle, Johnny Grindle.**

1709 LAWSON *Carolina* 160 Grindals are a long scaled fish with small eyes; and frequent Ponds, Lakes, and slow-running Creeks and Swamps. **1902** GORDON *Recoll. Lynchburg* 117 How full were the holes of craw-fish, turtles, sun-perch, grindles, and of daring, voracious pike. **1947** DALRYMPLE *Panfish* 359 He is the Dogfish, Bowfin, or Grindle, depending upon where you cross purposes with him—*Amia calva,* only existing species of an ancient and once great and abundant race.

gringo ˈgrɪŋgo, *n.* [Sp. in Amer. Sp. sense shown here. See Bentley, 141 f.] A term used contemptuously by Spanish Americans for a person from the U.S.

1849 AUDUBON *Western Journal* (1906) 13 June 100 We were hooted and shouted at as we passed through, and called 'Gringoes.' **1863** *Rio Abajo Press* 14 July 4/1 The principal part of his patronage is derived from Americans, Germans, Irish, Scotch,—to all of whom the natives apply the generic term 'Gringo,' and whom they consider Americans. **1948** *Chi. D. News* 11 June 16/7 Us native Peruvians never cease to marvel at the ingenuity of the gringo.

attrib. **1871** *Republican Rev.* 14 Jan. 2/2 Three Mexicans from Socorro . . . calling her a *gringo* bitch, finally threw her on the body of her husband. **1897** *Outing* XXIX. 596/1 Tender bits of *gringo* ears being sent to our several friends with the grewsome admonition that the rest of the consignment would follow if sundry fat ransoms were not instantly forthcoming. **1947** *Time* 20 Jan. 75/2 Such invitations from gringo-distrusting, Catholic Mexico are high testimony to the special approach of the Quakers.

∗ **grip,** *n.*

1. = **grip car.** Also attrib.

1883 *Pall Mall Gaz.* 11 Dec. 2/2 'Will you take the grip?' is equivalent [in U.S.] to 'Will you take the cable tramway?' **1888** *Harper's Mag.* Aug. 430/1 The traveller . . . visit[s] the suburbs, climbing, into them, out of the smoke and grime, by steam 'inclines' and grip railways. **1894** HOWELLS *Trav. from Altruria* 218 Under the streets . . . [there was] a tangle of gas-pipes, steam-pipes, . . . electric motor-wires and grip-cables.

b. The device by which a grip car grasps the cable which draws it. Cf. **cable grip.**

[**1881** MARSHALL *Through Amer.* (1882) 267 The driver . . . controls the progress of his car, and the one behind it, by means of a 'gripping clamp' or large lever, which grapples the cable underground.] **1882** *Chi. Tribune* 23 Jan. 8/2 The grip of the first car was then closed on the cable, and the four horses started off at a slow pace, dragging the heavy iron wire through the channel. **1944** KAHN *Cable Car Days* 118 Mr. Hallidie's grip consisted of an upper and lower plate to be clamped to the cable by a large screw.

2. A scene-shifter in a theater.

1888 *Scribner's Mag.* IV. 444/2 Meanwhile the 'grips' . . . have hold of the side scenes ready to shove them on. **1947** *Harper's Mag.* Oct. 384/1 For two and a half hours we sat in those canvas-and-wood directors' chairs, our view obstructed by lights, baffles, technicians, 'grips,' and the enormous technicolor camera.

3. =**gripsack.** Also attrib. Cf. **alligator grip, hand grip.**

1879 *Chi. Tribune* 7 March 9/5 At Cherokee I stepped from the train, took my 'grip,' and began in earnest the life of a pilgrim. **1890** *The Road* (Denver) 24 May 5/1 [The song] was composed by an old time drummer, John de Witt, well and favorably known to many 'grip luggers.' **1946** *This Week Mag.* 12 Jan. 7/1, I bought a small grip which could pass for a doctor's valise.

4. The grippe or influenza. Also attrib.

1890 *Ann Arbor Review* Feb. 6 One of our city druggists says that sales of quinine increased 5-fold during the grip season. **1895** WILLIAMS *Princeton Stories* 143 One of the second basses had the grip and another a dead grandmother. **1905** LINCOLN *Partners* 232 In August Miss Prissy threw the household into consternation by coming down with the grip.

5. grip car, a streetcar provided with a device for gripping or clutching an endless cable driven by a stationary engine; a cable car. Also **grip coach.** Now *obs.* or *hist.* Cf. **cable car.**

1882 *Chi. Tribune* 23 Jan. 8/2 A force of men then ran it [*sc.* a cable] down under the car track to the manhole at Twentieth street, and there it remained until the grip-cars were brought out at night. **1888** *Chi. Inter-Ocean* 14 Feb. 8/3 The first trial of the North Side grip system was made last night. . . . The first car, a combination grip-coach, left the Diversey avenue barn shortly after midnight. **1889** in SALMONS *Burlington Strike* 279 The engineer who used to jangle a bell on a State street grip car was hastily informed that he was not wanted. **1900** *Chi. Record* 8 May 5/2 Grip Car hits an ice wagon.

b. grip man, the operator of a grip car.

1886 *Science* VIII. 275/2 The driver, or gripman, then opened the valve admitting air to the engine. **1891** *Boston Jrnl.* 21 Feb. 2/3 A gripman on the cable road at San Diego, Cal., stands 7 feet 2 inches in hight [*sic*]. **1947** PEATTIE *Sierra Nevada* 217 His control lay in the skillful use of a long pole, astride of which he could ride, pulling back on the upward end with all the energy (but not all the comfort!) of a San Francisco cable-car gripman putting on the brakes when he wants to stop.

c. grip road, a road upon which a grip car operates. *Obs.*

1882 *Ideographic* (S.F.) 25 July 2/3 The cable- or 'grip' road, as they term it in Cincinnati, seems to have made an unenviable reputation in that city, having caused the death of several persons during its short existence.

6. gripsack, a handbag or valise. Also transf.

1877 BURDETTE *Rise of Mustache* 59 If I was going to Europe, I would just rush into the house, put on a clean shirt, grab up my gripsack, and fly. **1889** *Cent. Mag.* April 905/2 Pipes were filled, smoked, and returned to that cavalryman's gripsack, the boot-leg. **1946** FORD *Honolulu Story* 16 Even the men waiting with duffel bags and blue and khaki canvas gripsacks at the elevator brightened up and looked as long as she was alone.

b. *attrib.* Of or pertaining to carpetbaggers in the South during Reconstruction. *Obs.*

1881 *Cong. Rec.* 30 March 124/1 These gentlemen . . . treat with contempt the charges of the grip-sack republicans. *Ib.* 14 April 290/2 They mean to swap off their republican allies in Virginia, their 'grip-sack' friends, . . . for the readjuster party. *Ib.*, The republican party in the United States have found at last that their attempt to govern the Southern States through 'the grip-sack party,' . . . or the carpet-bag party, . . . is a failure.

7. In colloq. phrases: (1) *To lose one's grip,* to lose one's effectiveness or enthusiasm; (2) *to hold one's grip,* to maintain one's position, to keep up one's courage.

(1) **1876** MILLER *First Families* 246 Lost my 'grip' as they say, didn't have any 'snap' any more. **1894** MARK TWAIN *Pudd'nhead Wilson* xx, Come, cheer up, old man; there's no use in losing your grip. — (2) **1892** MARK TWAIN *Switzerland* (1917) 206 (R.), You got a wrong start, that's the whole trouble. But you hold your grip, and we'll see what can be done. **1894** —— *Pudd'nhead Wilson* 234 (R.), Now hold your grip, hold your grip, I tell you, and I'll land him sure.

gris-gris ˈgrigri, *n. La.* [f. La. F. See note.] (See quots.)

"As *gris-gris* is commonly associated with voodoo rites, it is generally believed to be of African origin. In Senegal, indeed, the word designates any kind of amulet. . . . In Spain, where the word is also found, it is the name of a relic containing the names of certain saints and worn as a talisman by the Moors. Thus the word traveled to Louisiana not only from Africa, doubtless by the way of the Spanish West Indies, but also directly from Spain. The ultimate source of *gris-gris* is Arabic *hirz acihr*, 'amulet of enchantment' " (Read, pp. 122 f).

1763 in *Amer. Sp.* XX. (1945) 48 They [the Negroes] are very superstitious, and are much attached to their prejudices, and little toys which they call *gris, gris.* **1883** *Cent. Mag.* Nov. 45/2 The male dancers fastened bits of tinkling metal or tin rattles about their ankles, like those strings of copper gris-gris worn by the negroes of the Soudan. **1931** READ *La.-French* 122 Gris-gris, *m.* An object worn as a protective charm against evil, or used, on the other hand, for the purpose of inflicting injury. . . . Among the *gris-gris* that protect against evil or bring good luck a favorite was, and is, a dime with a hole in it, which is often worn about the ankle. **1947** TALLANT *Voodoo in N.O.* 16 They wore all kinds of *gris-gris* tied on their bodies—dolls made out of feathers and hair, skins of snakes and pieces of human bone.

attrib. and *transf.* **1882** BUEL *Metropolitan Life Unveiled* 532 We shall make a grigri charm to hold him fast. **1883** *Harper's Wkly.* 17 Jan. 43/4 There are mothers who still teach their children the old songs—heirlooms of melody resonant with fetich words—threads of tune strung with *grigris* from the Ivory Coast.

***grisly,** see ***grizzly.**

***grist,** *n.* A large amount, number, or quantity. *Colloq.*

1833 PAULDING *Banks of Ohio* 133 There has been a mighty grist of rain lately up above. **1881** MCLEAN *Cape Cod Folks* 295 'Grists on 'em, this year!' he said. 'Heaps!' Aunt Patty responded, readily. **1906** *Springfield W. Republican* 8 Feb. 9 A good-sized grist of matters was presented in the House last week under suspension of the rules.

***grist mill.** As the last term in **floating, screw auger, water grist mill.**

***grit,** *n.*[1]

1. *pl.* Coarsely ground grain, esp. corn; hominy grits. Cf. **corn, graham grits.**

1800 B. HAWKINS *Sk. Creek Country* 78 He eats two or three spoonfuls of boiled grits. **1883** *Harper's Mag.* Aug. 462/1 All the fancy grits and groats in the market did not meet his demand. **1948** DICK *Dixie Frontier* 249 By means of a crude homemade sifter the coarse material, called grits, was separated from the fine and then boiled for hominy.

2. a. Coined or metallic currency. *Rare.* **b.** A malic precipitate that is cast down in making maple sirup.

(**a**) **1834** CROCKETT *Narrative* iii. 23 So I sold my part of the beef for five dollars in the real grit, for I believe that was before bank-notes was invented. — (**b**) **1882** *Vt. Bd. Agric. Rep.* VII. 64 In speaking of malate of lime or what is known as 'grit,' said he has known a sample to contain nearly one-half in weight of this substance.

3. *To cut grit, to hit the grit,* to make off, depart. *Slang.*

1859 *Harper's Mag.* Dec. 139/1 As soon as I cut grit they all started too, and let loose two big bull-dogs they had chained. **1911** WRIGHT *Winning Barbara Worth* 268 We'll hit the grit good and hard now for we must be in the sand hills by morning. **1949** *Exciting Western* May 16/1 Let's hit the grit, pardner!

***grit,** *n.*[2] Obstinate, unflinching physical courage or determination, often **clear, pure grit.** *Slang.* Cf. **true, Yankee grit.**

1808 D. HITCHCOCK *Poet. Dict.* 53 The prude doats on beauty, the bully on *grit.* **1825** NEAL *Bro. Jonathan* II. 14 A chap, who was clear grit for a tussle, any time—any where. **1836** HOWARD *Stewart* 63 My mother was of the pure grit; she learned me and all her children to steal as soon as we could walk. **1941** BALDWIN *Keelboat Age* 97 He was heap brave with plenty of grit and wasn't a bit skeered.

attrib. **1833** *Polit. Examiner* (Shelbyville, Ky.) 22 June 4/1 He told me that he was printing a clare grit democratic newspaper.

***grit,** *v.*

1. *tr.* To grind (the teeth) in rage or determination.

1797 JEFFERSON *Writings* I. 416 Mr. Adams, . . . gritting his teeth said, . . . 'you see that an elective government will not do.' **1887**

STOCKTON *Borrowed Month* 27, I gritted my teeth as I thought what a despicable thing it would be. **1949** *Time* 11 July 27/1 U.S. occupation officers on the spot cursed and gritted their teeth over the 'inefficiency' of the Japanese authorities.

b. *To grit up*, to summon one's grit or courage. *Slang. Rare.*

1890 *Harper's Mag.* April 714/2, I see I must jest grit up for I'd got a big job o' work.

2. *absol.* To grate immature corn into a coarse meal. *Obs.*

1897 W. E. BARTON *Trouble at Roundstone* 79 We've ben grittin' ever sence roastin' years got good. But they kin grind now, I reckon.

* **gritted,** *a.* **1.** Of teeth: Ground in determination. **2. gritted bread,** corn bread made of gritted meal. **3. gritted corn pone,** corn pone made of gritted meal.

(1) **1897** *Outing* XXX. 422/1 The gritted teeth, and the tension of the body, show what power this player has put into his shot. — (2) **1886** *Harper's Mag.* June 59/2 Over this [punched] tin the ears are rubbed, producing a coarse meal, of which 'gritted bread' is made. — (3) **1897** W. E. BARTON *Trouble at Roundstone* 15 To eat bread with a crust less hard and a texture less coarsely grained than gritted corn pone.

gritter ˈgrɪtɚ, *n.* (See quot. 1888.) — *a*1877 in BARTLETT 265 Some carried the gritter in their haversacks, others had it slung to their belts. **1888** *Cong. Rec.* 1 May 3587/2 The 'gritter' is a piece of cast-away tin or sheet-iron, through which holes have been punched with a nail, so as to throw out the surface on one side and make it rough. In its use it is what we would call a grater. It is used by good Kentucky women.

* **gritting,** *n.* **1.** The action of grinding (the teeth). **2.** The grating of immature corn into coarse meal.

(1) **1823** *Mass. Spy* 30 April (Th.), The harmony arising from the filing of a saw, or the gritting of teeth. **1849** POE *Works* VI. 222, I could have sworn that it was the gritting of this vagabond's teeth. — (2) **1848** ROBINSON *Santa Fe Exped.* 28 It is a very quick method of grinding, and I think quite preferable to gritting, which is frequently practiced in the west. **1948** DICK *Dixie Frontier* 289 When the kernels grew more mature and hard, the ears were rubbed over the rough side of a piece of tin studded with nail holes. This was called 'gritting' (grating) and made the sweetest corn meal imaginable.

gritty ˈgrɪtɪ, *a.* Angry; full of grit or courage. *Slang.*

1843 STEPHENS *High Life N.Y.* II. 2 Darn her! it makes me gritty only jest to think on it. **1878** BEADLE *Western Wilds* 41 More 'n once the robbers would tackle some gritty man that was handy with his 'barkers.' **1912** MATHEWSON *Pitching* 303 He deeply regretted letting the gritty, little shortstop . . . leave the club.

* **grizzly,** *a.* and *n.*

1. Short for **grizzly bear.** Cf. **cinnamon, mountain, silver tip grizzly.**

1851 *Polly Peablossom* iii, I saw comin' my gray mule, . . . and a few yards behind her was a grizzly. **1908** PHILLIPS *Old Wives* 93 Charley here missed a cornered grizzly and it closed in on him. **1949** *Mazama* Feb. 2/2 He has made frequent trips to Canada for grizzly and moose.

attrib. and *fig.* **1828** in SULLIVAN *Travels Jedediah Smith* (1934) 122 Bears said to be numerous of the Grizzly Kind. **1876** *Santa Cruz* (Calif.) *Local Item* 28 July 2/3 The *Chronicle*, a regular old Durham, has raised a set of claws, and is a grizzly of the worst type. **1946** STANWELL-FLETCHER *Driftwood Valley* 6 The trail goes through the worst grizzly country (grizzlies are apparently the species of animal most universally feared and respected). **1948** *Hungry Horse News* (Columbia Falls, Mont.) 24 Sep. 1/7 The grizzly open season conforms to that of elk.

b. Also * **grisly.**

1808 PIKE *Sources Miss.* III. App. 7 North Mexico produces elk, deer, buffalo, cabrie, the gresley, black bear, and wild horses. **1892** LUMMIS *Tramp Across Continent* 82 One day I wounded an old she grisly, breaking her fore paw, but didn't get her. **1893** ROOSEVELT *Wilderness Hunter* 265 They insist on many species; not merely the black and the grisly, but the brown, the cinnamon, the gray [etc.].

2. *W.* A kind of drink. Also **grizzly lager.** *Slang. Obs.*

1857 *Santa Barbara* (Calif.) *Gazette* 29 Jan. 4/3 The drinks ain't no good here—there ain't no variety in them, neither; no . . . grisly, talabogus, switched fly, gum-ticklers, phlegm-cutters, juleps, skate-cutters, cast steel cocktails. **1858** *Calif. Spirit of Times* (S.F.) 7 Aug. 3/2 The way champagne flowed was a caution; why grizzly lager was nowhere.

3. *Mining.* A screening device made of iron bars.

1876 RAYMOND *8th Rep. Mines* 56 The *débris* . . . is again caught up, the bowlders precipitated over a 'grizzly' into the cañon below. **1896** SHINN *Story of Mine* 218 A grizzly is a screen of parallel iron bars three inches apart . . . set sloping, and loose at one end. **1949** *Black Diamond* 26 Feb. 20/1 Coal is delivered to the receiving building . . . and is dumped from the cars through 'grizzlies' into the hoppers below the floor.

4. grizzly bear, a large, ferocious bear, *Ursus horribilis*, found in the Rocky Mountain region.

The name is prob. derived from * *grizzly*, gray, in allusion to the color of some specimens, but * *grisly* (see **1. b.** above and **b.** below) suggests that terror or horror (cf. the scientific **name**) was early associated with the animal.

1791 J. LONG *Voyages* 95 The large white bear, commonly called the grizly bear, is a very dangerous animal. **1842** *S. Lit. Messenger* VIII. 584/1 Those pioneers . . . seek their pleasure in the hunt of . . . a grizzly bear or a buffalo. **1947** CAHALANE *Mammals* 144 The grizzly bear is the largest carnivore on the earth.

attrib. and *transf.* *a*1842 O. RUSSELL *Journal* (1921) 69 Our camp keeper had prepared an excellent supper of grizzly bear meat and mutton. **1893** *Harper's Mag.* April 787/2 He invited these officers to Sonoma to witness a grizzly-bear hunt. **1948** *Sat. Ev. Post* 4 Sep. 20/2 Sir William Van Horne, the bluff grizzly bear who bulled the ribbons of steel across the continent, was the great builder. **1949** *Sat. Ev. Post* 5 Mar. 68/4 The lake of riches lay behind them, untouched until 1862, when John W. Searles, a grizzly-bear hunter and prospector, visited it.

b. Also **grisly bear.**

1839 *Knickerb.* XIV. 288 He saw one of the largest of those most ferocious of animals, the grisly bear, making toward him. **1850** GARRARD *Wah-To-Yah* x. 135 An object, which was immediately pronounced a grisly bear.

c. A kind of dance in which the walk and hug of a grizzly bear are somewhat imitated. *Slang.*

1912 *Lit. Digest* 30 March 656/2 George came whirling and spinning . . . across the field, . . . developing steps that would have ruled him off any cotillion floor in New York in these days of the ban on the grizzly-bear and kindred dances. **1947** *Chi. Herald-Amer.* 11 Jan. (Home Mag.) 7/2 At any rate, along about 1910, the Grizzly Bear became the Big Thing with the Snooty Ones at Newport and the next year, the craze swung over to the Turkey Trot.

d. grizzly bear cactus, opuntia, *S.W.* a prickly pear, *Opuntia erinacea.*

1929 BAILEY *Cyclo. Horticulture* 2363/1 [Opuntia] ursina, Web. Grizzly-Bear Opuntia. **1947** *Desert Mag.* May 28/3 Visitors in May and June will find a good display of . . . beavertail and grizzly bear cactus.

5. grizzly fox, (see quot.). *Obs.*

1819 *Western Rev.* I. 230 Black-tail Fox. . . . This fox is found in Ohio, Indiana and Kentucky. It is sometimes called grey fox or grizzly-fox, being hardly distinguished from the common grey fox . . . which is however very different.

6. grizzly king, queen, an artificial fly for fishing having a green body, dark-gray hackle, scarlet tail, and spotted wings.

1866 *Wilkes' Spirit of Times* 16 June 246/3 Besides these imitations of natural flies, there are hosts of others. . . . such as 'grizzly king,' 'biles,' etc., which experts in the 'gentle art' will find more than ornamental. **1894** *Outing* XXIV. 227/1 Bass flies of proved merit include the bob white, grizzly queen, grizzly king.

* **grocer,** *n.* A liquor-seller. *Obs.* — **1818** [see **grocery store** (*b*)]. **1839** *Ind. H. Rep. Jrnl.* 334 Mr. Eggleston presented the petition of sundry citizens of Dearborn county, praying a change in the law granting license to grocers.

* **grocery,** *n.*

1. = **grocery store** (*a*).

[**1659** *Pa. Archives* 2 Ser. V. 387 The best wares (shirts, hats, shoes, etc.) are disbursed for provisions . . . many of which were sold . . . for Wampum . . . in small quantities, so that the store might well be called a grocery.] **1791** in H. M. BROOKS *Gleanings* 43 To be let, a Handsome square Shop . . . suitable either for a Grocery, West India or Dry-Goods Shop. **1859** GRATTAN *Civilized Amer.* I. 265 No woman does any of that essential business beyond giving an order at the 'Grocery,' or the 'Provision store.' **1947** *Reader's Digest* Oct. 97/1 Of course he can open a grocery, a filling station or the like.

2. = **grocery store** (*b*). Now *hist.*

1806 *Balance* 28 Jan. 31 (Th.), A writer in the *Albany Gazette* states that there are 174 licensed groceries in the city of Albany. **1847** *Protestant Monitor* (Greenville, Ill.) 5 March 2/2 Selling liquor *at the groceries* is the devil and all of a business. **1946** FOREMAN *Last Trek* 201 A majority of them were living within fifteen miles of the Missouri state line, all along which were placed the so-called 'groceries,' which were nothing more than grog-shops.

attrib. **1839** *Ind. H. Rep. Jrnl.* 321 The committee . . . to whom the petition of certain females of Clark county on the subject of grocery licenses was referred.

3. In special combs: (1) **grocery shop,** (*a*) = **grocery store** (*a*), (*b*) = **grocery store** (*b*); (2) **store,** (*a*) a store in which groceries or articles of food are sold, also fig., (*b*) a whisky shop or tavern, *obs.*

(1) (*a*) **1815** *Mass. H.S. Coll.* 2 Ser. IV. 191 Mr. Hastings . . . removed thence to Boston, where he kept a grocery shop. **1894** *Harper's Mag.* March 650/1 Doctor S—— was passing a small grocery shop on L—— Street when he saw some ripe peaches. (*b*) **1835** TODD *Notes* 37 The good city of New York; wherein are 1,600 spirit or *grocery* shops. — (2) (*a*) **1774** *Pa. Packet* 19 Sep. 1/3 Cheshire Cheese, to be Sold by Henry Dougherty, At his Grocery Store on Cuthbert's wharf. **1896** *Harper's Mag.* XCIII. 158/1, I found Mr. Bush seated on the counter in Shanks's grocery store. **1901** *World's Work* July 1011/1 The canal . . . would bring Chicago, 'the grocery store and meat shop of the world,' 900 miles nearer to Liverpool on the through trip than it is now. **1948** *Chi. D. News* 4 May 12/4 One look at the prices in the grocery stores . . . should be sufficient. (*b*) **1818** FEARON *Sketches* 28 Both wholesale and retail wine and spirit sellers are grocers: their establishments are called grocery stores. **1825** J. PICKERING *Inquiries Emigrant* (1831) 31 Almost all the roads leading to a town in America are full of houses on their sides, called 'taverns,' or 'liquor,' 'beer and cake,' or 'grocery,' stores.

b. In combs. (sense **1.**) of obvious meaning, as (1) **grocery chain,** (2) **clerk,** (3) **counter,** (4) **keeper,** (5) **man,** (6) **order.**

(1) **1914** *Printers Ink* 8 Oct. 37/2 There is all the difference in the world, in many respects, between the high-grade stores . . . and the popular low-priced grocery chains. — (2) **1918** LINCOLN *Shavings* 36 As a grocery clerk Jed was not a success. — (3) **1902** WISTER *Virginian* ii, He stood against the grocery counter, contemplating the Virginian. — (4) **1839** *Ind. H.R. Jrnl.* 274 Mr. Field presented two petitions from sundry citizens of Clark county, praying for an act to be passed repealing the present law granting license to grocery keepers. **1888** BRYCE *Amer. Commw.* II. II. xliii. 134 *n.*, License taxes or occupation taxes may be imposed . . . [on] grocery keepers, liquor dealers, insurance, vendors of patents [etc.].

(5) **1879** STOCKTON *Rudder Grange* vii, Euphemia went over to call on the groceryman's wife until I returned. **1931** *K.C. Times* 14 Aug., He told the groceryman that he was looking for work. — (6) **1844** UNCLE SAM *Peculiarities* I. 81, I have considerable of *grocery orders*—memoranda of credit on various stores.

As the last term in **corner, crossroads, Dutch, liquor, log-house, village grocery.**

groceteria ˌgrosəˈtɪrɪə, *n.* [f. **grocery*, after **cafeteria.**] (See quot. 1925.)

1916 *Illus. World* (Chi.) Jan. 655/1 In Pomona, California, a small grocery store has suddenly sprung into prominence and popularity by adopting the 'wait-on-yourself' plan of cafeteria. A 'Grocerteria' if you please. **1919** *Polk St. Journal* (S.F.) 2 May 5/1 Harry Holt of the H. & H. Groceteria sailed for Honolulu Wednesday. **1925** *Amer. Sp.* I. 38 *Grocerteria, groceteria, groceryteria*, a place where groceries are temptingly displayed on tables and counters, and one helps himself to those he wants and pays for them as he passes out.

* **grog,** *n.* In combs.: (1) **grog boss,** at a bee one who supplies liquid refreshments to those working, *rare;* (2) **hole,** a low grogshop, *obs.;* (3) **shanty,** =prec., *rare.*

(1) **1853** STRICKLAND *Twenty-seven Yrs.* I. 34 A man with a pail of spring water with a wooden cup floating on the surface in one hand, and a bottle of whiskey and glass in the other, now approached. . . . This man is the most important personage at the 'Bee,' and is known by the appellation of the 'Grog-bos.' — (2) **1848** *Knickerb.* XVIII. 521 He was busy about the village, penetrating every grog-hole and gambling-alley. **1871** *Scribner's Mo.* I. 537 Grog-holes, billiard saloons . . . were well patronized. — (3) **1888** WARNER *On Horseback* 47 The woods were full of grog-shanties, where the inflaming fluid was sold as 'native brandy.'

groggery ˈgrɑgərɪ, *n.*

1. A low tavern or grogshop. Cf. **corner groggery.**

1822 QUITMAN in Claiborne *Life Quitman* I. 71 [Natchez is] a straggling town . . . , consisting of warehouses, low taverns, groggeries, dens of prostitution, and gaming-houses. **1884** ROE *Nature's Story* 287 Lumley had to pass more than one groggery on his way to the mountains.

2. groggery-keeper, one who keeps a groggery. Now *obs.* or *hist.*

1863 E. KIRKE *Southern Friends* 68 A young man . . . should be 'bout better business than gittin' inter brawls with low groggery keepers. **1892** A. E. LEE *Hist. Columbus, O.* II. 127 A groggery keeper . . . was implicated with Price.

groggy ˈgrɑgɪ, *n.* An anti-prohibitionist, one who sells grog or supports the grog-sellers. *Rare.* — **1893** *Voice* 16 Nov., We said . . . that the 'groggies' of Iowa were bigger fools than we ever knew them to be.

* **groom,** *v. tr.* To provide (a political candidate or prospective candidate) with such duties, favorable publicity, etc., as to promote his candidacy for public office.

1887 *Courier-Journal* 3 May 4/5, I learn that Sam Hill, of Hartford, is being groomed for the temporary chairmanship of the Convention. **1903** J. HAWTHORNE *Hawthorne & Circle* 264 Grover Cleveland was being groomed for his first Presidential term. **1945** *Newsweek* 11 June 27/2 Next move will be to bring him [i.e., Ed Pauley] back to the U.S. for another high position, thus grooming him for the nomination with Truman in 1948.

* **grosbeak,** *n.* As the last term in **black-headed, blue, cardinal, evening, pine, rose-breasted grosbeak.**

gros-corne. [F.] =**big-horn.** *Obs.* — **1820** GILLELAND *Ohio & Miss. Pilot* 138 The gross-corne, or sheep of the rocky mountains, . . . is a species of fine wooled goat. **1831** PATTIE *Personal Narr.* 55 The French call them the gros cornes, from the size of their horns which curl around their ears like our domestic sheep.

Gros Ventre. An Indian belonging to a detached band of the Arapaho, also known as Gros Ventres of the Prairie, or one belonging to the Hidatsa tribe of the Sioux. Usu. *pl.*, as a designation for one of these two distinct tribes. Cf. **Big Belly, Great Belly Indians.**

1804 CLARK in *Lewis & C. Exped.* I. (1904) 210 We Sent the Chiefs of the Gross Vantres to Smoke a pipe with the Grand Chef of the Mandans in his Village. **1834** F. A. CHARDON *Fort Clark Jrnl.* (1932) 3 Battle with the Yanctons and Mandans, 1 Sioux—1 Mandan—1 Gros Ventre Killed—5 Mandans wounded. **1920** DRUMM *Jrnl. of Fur-Trading Exped.* 102 The Grosventres of the Prairie, or Fall Indians, as they were generally called, were the most relentlessly hostile tribe ever encountered by the whites in any part of the West, if not in any part of America. The trapper always understood that to meet with one of these Indians meant an instant and deadly fight. **1947** *Primitive Man* July 41 The Gros Ventres were camped on the Milk River.

attrib. **1893** *Outing* Sep. 472/2 A *gros-ventre* buck offered me five for Spy once.

Also as adj. in the predicate.

1949 *No. Dak. Hist.* Jan. 38 The four communities that border the western segment are predominantly Gros Ventre.

grouch graʊtʃ, *n.* [App. a var. of **grutch*, but cf. **grout, grouty.**]

1. A grumbling, sulky mood. Also attrib. *Colloq.*

1900 FLYNT *Notes Itinerant Policeman* 160 They began to get a grouch on against the gay-cats that kep' comin' to their camps. **1908** K. MCGAFFEY *Show-Girl* 152, I have met gentlemen who threw the lid of their grouch bag in the gutter and didn't care if they ever found it again. **1914** S. H. ADAMS *Clarion* 335 'Something's biting the old geezer,' he informed Hal and Ellis. 'Seems to have a grouch.'

2. One who is usu. in such a mood, a grumbler. *Colloq.*

1919 H. L. WILSON *Ma Pettengill* ii. 61 In the section across from us was a fifty-five-year-old-male grouch . . . who had been snarling at everyone that came near him ever since the train left New York. **1920** W. H. PORTER *Eating to Live Long* 146 We pity poor old Carlyle, a crabbed, grumbling grouch all his life long.

grouch graʊtʃ, *v.* [?f. the noun.] *intr.* To grumble. *Colloq.* — **1925** H. L. FOSTER *Trop. Tramp Tourists* 137 The tourists . . . all came back to the train at a painfully slow walk, . . . and grouched all the way home. **1926** J. BLACK *You Can't Win* viii. 90 'Oh, sure,' he grouched, 'Everything's all right—just like Denmark.'

grouched graʊtʃt, *a.* =**grouchy.** *Rare.* — **1913** LONDON *Valley of Moon* I. ii, They're grouched because they got to dance together.

grouchy ˈgraʊtʃɪ, *a.* Ill-humored, peevish. *Colloq.*

1902 *Dly. Chron.* 25 Jan. 7/2 Thus we may learn which of them, in the opinion of his fellows, is . . . the slouchiest, the biggest fusser, the 'grouchiest.' **1931** *K.C. Star* 28 July, Garden City . . . is grouchy because children shouted so loudly at a municipal band concert . . . that the music was drowned out.

Hence **grouchily,** *adv.*, **grouchiness,** *n.*

1907 MULFORD *Bar-20* xxiii. 221 His definition, grouchily expressed. **1925** ——— *Cottonwood Gulch* vi. 87 He . . . departed to speak confidentially with the second bar-tender, whose grouchiness was due to lack of proper sleep.

* **ground,** *n.*

1. *pl.* A region occupied by Indians. *Rare.*

*c***1830** HITCHCOCK *Diary* 74 Before the evening set in Colonel Taylor ordered the prisoners released and the whole are now on their way to their 'grounds.'

2. In combs.: (1) **ground ball,** =**ground hit;** (2) **blizzard,** see **blizzard, 2. b;** (3) **bridge,** (see quot.), *obs.;* (4) **chimney,** ?a large chimney having its foundations on the ground, *obs.;* (5) **fire,** (see quot. 1905); (6) * **floor,** see as a main entry; (7) **gripper,** a shoe the sole of which is provided with spikes to give the wearer especially firm footing, worn by runners; (8) **hit,** in baseball, a batted ball that rolls or bounds along the ground; (9) **itch,** an infectious itching condition, usu. on the feet, caused by the larvae of the hook-worm; (10) *keeper, one employed to keep a baseball field in condition for play; (11) **rule,** see as a main entry; (12) **scuffle,** a rough-and-tumble fight, also fig.; (13) **sled,** (see quots.), *colloq.;* (14) **sluicer,** one who in mining washes down earth by means of sluices; (15) **sluicing,** the use of ground sluices in mining; (16) **tumbler,** an acrobat who performs feats of tumbling, cf. **d.** below.

(1) 1857 *Spirit of Times* 7 Nov. 148/1 The batting was not heavy, with the exception of several ground balls, which were struck during the latter portion of the game. **1948** *P.C.C. Chronicle* (Pasadena, Calif.) 7 May 4/5 Salter hit a hard ground ball to shortstop Bill Davis. — **(3) 1859** BARTLETT 181 *Ground Bridge,* the well-known corduroy road of the South, laid on the bed of a creek or other body of water, to render it fordable. — **(4) 1712-3** in *Old-Time N. Eng.* (1926) July 21 Ground Chimneys. A double house 'with three Ground Chimneys, two Chamber Chimneys,' advertised for sale by Capt. Nathaniel Hall of Hingham.

(5) 1900 E. BRUNCKEN *N. Amer. Forests* 109 There is something horrible in the slow, steady approach of a top fire. . . . You can fight a ground fire, by trying to beat it out with brush, or throwing earth upon it. You cannot fight a fire that seizes tree top after tree top, far above your reach. **1905** *Forestry Bureau Bul.* 61 A ground fire is one which burns in the forest floor and does not appear above the ground. — **(7) 1927** *Sat. Ev. Post* 24 Dec. 24/3 Then they would discard the leather ground-grippers and skip around barefoot. — **(8) 1868** CHADWICK *Base Ball* 101 Studley came to the rescue with a good ground hit, on which he made his second. **1910** *Spalding's Base Ball Guide* 343 A ground hit that first strikes fair territory and rolls outside of the foul line between first and home, or third and home, is a foul hit. — **(9) 1823** J. THACHER *Military Jrnl.* 177 A considerable number of men . . . were infected with the *ground itch,* generated by laying on the ground. **1857** E. STONE *Life J. Howland* 81 My first effort at improvement was to eradicate the last stages of the Scotch distemper, the ground itch.

(10) 1903 *Cin. Enquirer* 10 May IV. 3/9 A methodical ground-keeper was whitening up the base lines and sowing sawdust around in the damp spots around the home plate. — **(12) 1834** CARUTHERS *Kentuckian* I. 95 He'd find it rather a different business at an honest ground-scuffle. **1880** TOURGEE *Bricks* 451 A man who comes here must pitch in and count for all he's worth. It's a regular ground-scuffle, open to all. — **(13) 1913** O. A. ROTHERT *Hist. Muhlenberg Co.* (Ky.) 113 In the early days, and even until comparatively recent times, some of the farmers used a ground-sled or a 'landslide' for short hauls. It was built on the principle of a sled, and so used during all seasons. **1948** DICK *Dixie Frontier* 308 When horses were available much hauling was done with a ground sled known as a 'landslide.' Built like a sled, it was used at all seasons, even as a family vehicle. — **(14) 1860** *Harper's Mag.* April 612/2 At Gold Hill . . . one of our party . . . bought an interest in a company of ground sluicers, by which he cleared three ounces of gold dust.

(15) 1857 *Hutchings Mag.* July 8/1 Among the more important operations connected with gold mining upon an extensive scale, is 'ground sluicing.' **1884** [see **grub wages**]. — **(16) 1874** B. F. TAYLOR *World on Wheels* 64 Once he was the Champion ground-tumbler of the West.

b. In the names of, or with reference to, animals: (1) **ground beaver,** =**bank beaver,** *obs.;* (2) **bird,** the field sparrow, *Spizella pusilla;* (3) **builder,** a bird that nests on the ground; (4) **cuckoo,** =**chaparral cock;** (5) **dog,** =**ground puppy;** (6) **dove,** any one of various small American doves of the genus *Columbigallina;* (7) **fox squirrel,** =?**ground squirrel,** *rare;* (8) **hog,** see as a main entry; (9) **mocking-bird,** the brown thrush or thrasher; (10) **mole,** any one of various common moles of the genus *Scalopus;* (11) **mouse,** a meadow mouse; (12) **owl,** =**burrowing owl;** (13) **perch,** (see quot.), *obs.;* (14) **pike,** =**sauger;** (15) **puppy,** =**hellbender;** (16) **rat,** (see quot. 1804), *obs.;* (17) **rattler,** =next; (18) **rattlesnake,** the massasauga or pygmy rattlesnake, *Sistrurus miliarius,* of the southern states; (19) **robin,** (*a*) the towhee, (*b*) (see quot.); (20) **sparrow,** any one of various sparrows that nest on the ground; (21) **squirrel,** any one of various burrowing rodents, esp. the chipmunk, belonging to the squirrel family.

(1) 1765 R. ROGERS *Acc't N. Amer.* 257 The *Ground-Beaver,* as they are called, conduct their affairs in a different manner; all the care they take is, to make a kind of covered-way to the water.—**(2) 1799** in BANCROFT *N.W. Amer.* (1888) I. 714 In the woods are woodpeckers, robins, . . . long-tailed thrush, ground-birds, tomtits. **1884** ROE *Nature's Story* 189 One of these little sober-coated creatures that Thoreau well calls a 'ground-bird' would fly to the top of a plum-tree and trill out a song. **1917** *Birds of Amer.* III. 43. — **(3) 1859** *Amer. Cyclo.* III. 282/1 The hawks are platform-builders, ground-builders, occupants of hollow trees &c. **1875** BURROUGHS *Winter Sunshine* iii. 82 The birds, especially the ground-builders, suffer in like manner. — **(4) 1869** *Amer. Naturalist* III. 477, I obtained . . . a ground Cuckoo (*Geococcyx Californianus*). **1936** McKENNA *Black Range* 225 The roadrunner, or chaparral cock . . . is known . . . [as] the 'ground cuckoo,' because he cannot fly high or far.

(5) 1899 *Animal & Plant Lore* 62 Ground-dog or ground-puppy or puppy, salamander, *Necturus maculatus.* [Chestertown, Md.] — **(6) c1729** CATESBY *Carolina* I. 26 The Ground-Dove. . . . They sometimes approach so far North as Carolina, and visit the lower parts of the country near the Sea. **1812** WILSON *Ornithology* VI. 15 The Ground Dove is a native of North and South Carolina, Georgia, the new state of Louisiana, Florida, and the islands of the west Indies. **1944** *Nat. Geog. Mag.* June 302 Pl. VI, Florida Ground Doves are not much larger than Sparrows; yet, with their mincing steps, small heads, and chunky bodies, they are typical doves. — **(7) 1805** *Balance* (Hudson, N.Y.) 17 Sep. 304 (Th.), How Mr. Lewis . . . came to call the ground-fox squirrel a dog, it is difficult to imagine. — **(9) 1709** LAWSON *Carolina* 143 There is another sort call'd the Ground-Mocking-Bird. She is the same bigness, and of a Cinnamon-Colour. **1848** BARTLETT 50 Brown Thrasher, (*Ferruginous thrush* . . .). The popular name of the brown thrush. It is also called the ground mocking-bird.

(10) 1819 THOMAS *Travels* 212 The *Ground Mole* of this country is nearly as large as the common rat. It is very injurious in gardens. It moves along at the depth of two or three inches under ground, raising a considerable ridge. **1918** LINCOLN *Shavings* 173 'Twas a-a mouse, or a ground mole, wasn't it? — **(11) 1839** BUEL *Farmer's Companion* 99 Moles or ground mice cannot penetrate and find a shelter. **1883** *Harper's Mag.* Aug. 462/2 A storm of expletives that must have startled the ground-mice and the birds. — **(12) 1911** WRIGHT *Winning Barbara Worth* 138 Always there were the same deep nights, with the lonely stars so far away in the velvet purple darkness; . . . the weird, quavering call of the ground owl; or the wild coyote chorus. **1948** *Chi. Tribune* 30 May (Roto.) 14 The ground owl burrows into the earth to make its home. — **(13) c1733** CATESBY *Carolina* II. 8 The Fresh-Water Pearch . . . they are called by some Ground Pearch, from their burrowing into, and covering themselves, in the mud or sand. — **(14) 1884** GOODE *Fisheries* I. 424 The 'Sauger,' known also as the Gray Pike, Sand Pike, Ground Pike [etc.], . . . has its habitat . . . in the Saint Lawrence River, Great Lake region [etc.].

(15) 1825 *Amer. Jrnl. Science* XI. 278 Hell-bender. Mud-devil. Ground-puppy. Tweeg. Young Alligator. Vulgo. **1899** [see **ground dog**]. — **(16) 1791** W. BARTRAM *Travels* 7 There is a large ground-rat, more than twice the size of the common Norway rat. In the night time, it throws out the earth, forming little mounds, or hillocks. **1804** CLARK in *Lewis & C. Exped.* I. (1904) 142 Killed a Dark rattle Snake near with a Ground rat (*or prairie dog*) in him. — **(17) 1938** MATSCHAT *Suwannee River* 27 Six are deadly poisonous . . . the small ground rattler; the cottonmouth or water moccasin, much more numerous than all the rattlesnakes and even more dangerous. **1946** *Democrat* 11 April 1/4 It must have been a ground rattler. — **(18) 1827** WILLIAMS *West Florida* 28 There is a little ground rattlesnake, that escapes the fires in his burrow, he is very diminutive . . . but his bite is very poisonous. **1837** ——— *Florida* 67 The Ground Rattlesnake is about 12 inches long. **1866** *Beadle's Mo.* June 569/2 There is a smaller variety, called the ground-rattlesnake. — **(19)** (*a*) **1794** *Philos. Soc. Trans.* IV. 110 This bird was the chewink, or ground-robin. **1867** *Ohio Laws* 101 It shall be unlawful for any person . . . to catch, kill or injure . . . [any] chewing [*sic*] or ground robin. **1917** *Birds of Amer.* III. 58. (*b*) **1808** WILSON *Ornithology* I. 29 Wood Thrush, *Turdus Melodus,* . . . is called by some the Wood Robin, by others the Ground Robin.

(20) 1858 *Atlantic Mo.* Oct. 594/2 In several localities, these two species [the song sparrow and vesper bird] are distinguished by the names of Bush-Sparrow and Ground-Sparrow, from their supposed different habits of placing their nests, one in a bush and the other on the ground. **1946** STUART *Plum Grove Hills* 65 A ground sparrow fed its young by a stump among the weeds. — **(21) 1688** in FORCE *Tracts* III No. 12, 36 The third is the Ground-Squirrel, I never saw any of this sort. **1784** J. SMYTH *Tour U.S.* I. 6 The most beautiful of the whole species is the ground squirrel, which is small and most delicately striped. **1949** *Reader's Digest* Jan. 134/2 They have learned to dig up ground squirrels.

c. In the names of, or with reference to, plants: (1) **ground apple,** the edible tuberous root of *Psoralea esculenta,* found from the Saskatchewan to Texas, cf. **breadroot;** (2) **bean,** =?**groundnut 1,** *obs.;* (3) **berry,** the partridge berry, also the checkerberry; (4) **cedar,** any one of various club mosses; (5) **cherry,** any one of various plants of the genus *Physalis* or the fruit of such a plant; (6) **hemlock,** (see quot. 1931); (7) **laurel,** the trailing arbutus; (8) **leaf,** a leaf of a tobacco plant growing at or near the ground; (9) ∗**nut,** see as a main entry; (10) **pea,** (*a*) the peanut or goober, (*b*) =**groundnut 1;** (11) ∗**pine,** see as a main entry; (12) **plum,** any one of various plants of the genus *Geoprumnon;* (13) **violet,** a violet the leaves of which lie close to the ground.

(1) **1823** LONG *Exped.* I. 187 They often bear a heavy staff of wood, sharpened to a broad edge for the purpose of digging up the Nugare, or ground apple, called by the French *Pomme blanche.* **1841** W. KENNEDY *Texas* I. 107 Primroses, violets, and the delicate flower of the ground-apple, are common embellishments of the soil. — (2) **1648** *Mass. H.S. Coll.* 4 Ser. I. 203 Ground nuts, ground beans, not gathered till, warmth doth the earth release. **1682** *Captivity of M. Rawlinson* (Cambridge) 61 They eat also . . . ground beans. — (3) **1867** DE VOE *Market Ass't* 392 Tallow-berries, or ground-berries. . . . These small red berries are found growing on a small, tender vine resting on the ground, in the cleared woods; and when eaten, they have a sort of sweetish, tallowy taste, but rather pleasant. **1891** *Cent.* 6944/2 *Wintergreen.* . . . Other names are *deerberry, groundberry, hillberry, spiceberry.* — (4) [**1836** C. P. TRAILL *Backwoods Canada* 120 A trailing plant bearing a near resemblance to the cedar, which . . . has . . . a claim to the name of ground or creeping cedar.] **1854** HAMMOND *Hills, Lakes* 39 A fawn . . . had been hid away by its dam beneath the ground-cedar.

(5) **1807** J. SCOTT *Md. & Del.* 26 Common and white plantain, thorowax, . . . ground cherries, persley and yams. **1913** CATHER *O Pioneers!* 29 She made a yellow jam of the insipid ground-cherries that grew on the prairie. **1947** *Desert Mag.* May 28/3 Until the middle of June visitors will find . . . desert aster and ground cherry in the Valley of Fire and other rocky areas. — (6) **1832** WILLIAMSON *Maine* I. 116 Low or Ground hemlock is a shrub which branches upon the ground. . . . The Indians use a tea made of its boughs steeped, as a sovereign remedy for rheumatism. **1931** CLUTE *Plants* 69 In northern forests, the ground is often covered with the dark spreading evergreen branches of the yew (*Taxus canadensis*). This we usually call ground hemlock after a more noticeable evergreen, being unfamiliar with the European yew-tree. — (7) **1814** BIGELOW *Florula Bostoniensis* 101 Ground laurel . . . grows in woods. **1898** C. A. CREEVEY *Flowers of Field* 332 Trailing Arbutus. Ground Laurel. Mayflower. . . . A universal favorite and a candidate for honorable mention as our national flower. **1931** CLUTE *Plants* 64 Even the trailing arbutus is occasionally called ground laurel. — (8) **1640** *Md. Archives* 98 Bad Tobacco shall be judged ground leafes [etc.]. **1784** J. SMYTH *Tour U.S.* II. 136 In stripping they are careful to throw away all the ground leaves, and faulty tobacco. **1850** *Rep. Comm. Patents 1849: Agric.* 459 Do not mistake the scorched and dried up 'ground leaves,' for ripe and mature tobacco.

(10) (*a*) **1769** WATSON in *Phil. Trans.* LIX. 379 They . . . are the produce of a plant . . . much cultivated, in the Southern colonies, and in our American sugar islands, where they are called ground nuts, or ground pease. **1854** *Fla. Plant. Rec.* 115, I have picked 80 bushels of ground peas. **1946** NIXON *Va. Words.* (*b*) **1823** JAMES *Exped.* I. 200 The squaws . . . are often necessitated to dig the pomme de terre . . . and to scratch the groundpea. **1893** *Amer. Folk-Lore* VI. 140 *Apios tuberosa,* ground-pea. N.E. — (12) **1857** GRAY *Botany* 97 *A*[*stragalus*] *caryocarpus.* (Ground Plum.) . . . On the Mississippi River, at the junction of the St. Peter's. **1871** *Amer. Naturalist* V. 213 These [pods] . . . assume a fine purple tinge, which gives them the appearance of grapes or plums; hence the plant is commonly called Ground Plum. — (13) **1817–8** EATON *Botany* (1822) 514 *Viola rotundifolia,* ground violet. . . . The leaves lie very close to the ground. **1840** DEWEY *Mass. Flowering Plants* 79 *Viola rotundifolia.* Ground Violet. . . . An early species, blooms in April.

d. In phrases: (1) *ground and lofty tumbling,* acrobatic feats, as somersaults, handsprings, etc., performed on the ground and on the trapeze, parallel bars, tightrope, etc., also transf. and attrib., hence *ground and lofty tumbler;* (2) *ground and lofty,* "fine and dandy," *colloq., obs.*

(1) **1843** T. WEED *Letters* (1866) 108 A strolling company of ground and lofty tumblers. **1850** *Knickerb.* XXXVI. 191 His style of writing . . . is still admired by some who have ceased to relish any thing else pertaining to this uncouth, disjointed, and ground-and-lofty-tumbling author. **1907** M. C. HARRIS *Tents of Wickedness* 260 He has resigned his parish, left the ministry and bought a seat on the Stock Exchange. Isn't that ground and lofty tumbling? — (2) **1879** STOCKTON *Rudder Grange* xiii, The bull stuck to him like a burr, and they was havin' it, ground and lofty. **1916** WILSON *Somewhere* 118 We done some ground-and-lofty skidding before we got there.

As the last term in **ball, banking, bear, bed, bedding, beech, bloody, booming, bottom, buffalo, burning, camass, camp, camp meeting, cattle, chicken, cornstalk, cotton, cowpen, cutting, dance, Dark and Bloody, dividing, dumping, fair, fresh, gilling, herd, hickory, hiring, hunting, medicine, middle, moose, mowing, neutral, new, old, old field, palmetto, parade, payment, placer, pleasure, preaching, rodeo, roosting, second low, sedge, sod, stamping, thatch, tobacco, tobacco new, trapping, treaty, under, waste, water, wildcat, wintering ground.**

∗**ground floor.**

1. The most advantageous position or relationship in, or with reference to, a business matter or "deal." Also attrib. *Colloq.*

1868 R. B. KIMBALL *H. Powers* 157 (Th. Supp.), There must always be some one to stand between the seller and the company, else there could be no 'ground floor.' **1909** E. BARNETT *Dragnet* 12 To take advantage of this ground floor proposition Alexander and Company will have to give up its identity, and be a branch.

2. In phrases having reference to entering a business or transaction under especially favorable circumstances.

1872 TALMAGE *Abominations* 118 A select number go in on the 'ground floor.' **1901** MERWIN & WEBSTER *Calumet 'K'* 211 Well then, we'll have to let you in on the ground floor. **1904** O. HENRY *Cabbages & Kings* 206 He's heard of the boom along this coast, and wants to get in on the ground floor. **1946** *Chi. D. News* 29 April 8/3 I'm darn grateful he's letting me in on the ground floor of this fabulous offer. **1949** *Nat. Hist.* June 244/2 He got in on the ground floor and was one of the privileged few that had a wide choice in selection.

ground hog. [Bense may be correct in his surmise that this term was "formed after the word *aard-vark* from Du. *aard-varken.*"]

1. The woodchuck, *Marmota monax.* Also attrib.

[**1656** VAN DER DONCK in *N.Y. Hist. Soc. Coll.* 2 Ser. I. (1841) 171 Ground hogs, English skunks, drummers, and several other kinds of animals . . . are known and found in the country.] **1784** FILSON *Kentucke* 28 Nor are the animals common to other parts wanting, such as foxes, . . . racoons, ground-hogs, pole-cats, and oppossums. **1807** GASS *Journal* 126, I saw one [Indian robe] made of ground hog skins. **1890** *N. & Q.* IV. 189 The ground-hog is very numerous in Lancaster county, and in some of our rural districts is a positive pest, playing havoc with the young clover crop, and in the proper season it is a common thing for our 'crack shots' to bag a score of them in a single day. **1947** *Collier's* 29 Mar. 93/2 Our ground hogs aren't hogs at all, but rodents, and even their correct name of 'woodchucks' is a corruption of an Indian name.

transf. **1893** *Chi. Tribune* 26 April 6/4 It looks as though that political groundhog, the Hon. Bill Springer, had seen his own shadow about March 4, and had gone back into his hole to stay for four years. **1903** *D.N.* II. 135 *Ground-hog,* . . . a small thrashing-machine without separator. Formerly very commonly used.

2. In special combs.: (1) **ground-hog case,** a desperate case or plight, one in which there is no alternative but great effort, *colloq.;* (2) **day,** (see quot. 1871).

(1) **1885** SIRINGO *Texas Cow Boy* 125 Dangerous to cross. But the wagons being over made it a ground hog case. **1926** *Amer. Sp.* II. 52 Groundhog case—'An extreme case.' — (2) **1871** DE VERE 369 Candlemas is known as Ground-hog Day, for on that day the ground-hog comes annually out of his hole, after a long winter nap, to look for his shadow. If he perceives it, he retires again to his burrow, which he does not leave for six weeks—weeks necessarily of stormy weather. But if he does not see his shadow, for lack of sunshine, he stays out of his hole till he can, and the weather is sure to become mild and pleasant. **1948** *Time* 9 Feb. 21/3 Amateur weather prophets, amid much labored clowning, generally agreed that ground hogs saw their shadows on Ground-Hog Day (Feb. 2)—and that meant six more weeks of winter.

∗**groundnut,** *n.*

1. The wild bean, *Apios tuberosa,* or its edible tuberous root.

1602 JOHN BRERETON *Virginia* 7 Also . . . great store of Ground nuts, fortie together on a string, some of them as bigge as hennes egges; they grow not two inches under ground. **1854** THOREAU *Walden* 257 Digging one day for fishworms I discovered the ground-nut . . . on its string, the potato of the aborigines. **1949** *Amer. Photography* April 247/3 There are few country boys, I am sure, who do not know the groundnut (*Apios tuberosa*).

2. The peanut. Also attrib.

1769 [see **ground pea** (*a*)]. **1811** *Agric. Museum* I. 233 From the kernel of the ground nut I have obtained an oil perfectly sweet. **1945** MOLLOY *Pride's Way* 135 Here comes the old groundnut cake woman. Get me a nickel's worth of groundnut cakes. . . . Sarah appeared a moment later with tough discs of molasses taffy and peanuts, each resting on a circular piece of butcher's paper.

∗**ground pine.** Any one of various American plants, as the orange grass, *Sarothra gentianoides,* or a club moss, often used for Christmas decorations.

1743 CLAYTON *Flora Virginica* 29 Ground-pine. **1792** IMLAY *Western Territory* 208 Of herbs, &c. we have of the wild sort . . . colewort, ground-pine, tooth-wort. **1850** Cooper *Rural Hours* 433 We contributed a basket-full of ground-pine, both the erect and running kinds, with some glittering club-moss. **1920** Howells *Vacation of Kelwyns* 115 The place was garlanded with ground-pine caught up with knots and branches of the pink and white laurel. **1949** *Amer. Photography* Feb. 114/3 This is particularly true of the ground pine (*Lycopodium obscurum*).

ground rule. In baseball, any special rule modifying the play within a given ball park where local conditions require special regulations.

[**1857** *Spirit of Times* 28 Feb. 420/3 Clubs may adopt such rules respecting balls knocked beyond or outside the bounds of the fields, as circumstances of the ground may demand.] **1890** H. Palmer *Stories of Base Ball Field* 70 In the olden days there was a ground rule which only allowed two bases for a hit over this fence. **1910** *Spalding's Base Ball Guide* 353 To obviate the necessity for ground rules, the shortest distance from a fence or stand on fair territory to the home base should be 235 feet.

attrib. **1948** *Herald-Press* (St. Joseph, Mich.) 14 Aug. 7/2 It was ruled a ground rule double.

***grounds,** *n. pl.* As the last term in **annuity, hitching, store grounds.**

***groundsel,** *n.* A North American shrub belonging to any one of various species of the genus *Baccharis.* In full **groundsel tree.**

1741 *Complete Fam.-Piece* II. 412 You have also the black Hellebore now in Flower, with the Spurge Laurel, Virginian Groundsel Tree. **1892** Apgar *Trees Northern U.S.* 115 Groundsel-Tree. . . . Wild on sea-beaches, Massachusetts and south. **1901** Mohr *Plant Life Ala.* 45 Bosquets of groundsels . . . dot here and there the salt marshes of the seashore. **1931** Dayton *West. Browse Plants* 158 Seepwillow (*B[accharis] glutinosa*), locally named false, Gila, or water willow, groundsel tree, water motie, and water-wally, . . . has an enormous distribution from western Texas to Colorado and southern California and south . . . to Chile.

ground-sluice ˈgraʊndˌslus, *v. intr.* In mining, to wash down earth by means of sluices. Also *tr.* and transf. Cf. **ground sluicer, sluicing.**

1875 *Measure for Measure* (Battle Mt., Nev.) 28 Aug. 3/2 In the spring they dig in the banks along the ravines, and ground-sluice, as they learned to in California. **1882** *47th Cong.* 1 Sess H.R. Ex. Doc. No. 218, 104 Cherry Creek is owned by four companies who ground sluice during the winter. **1902** Wilson *Spenders* 292 That party that ground-sluiced us . . . met a party in Spokane the other day that seen her in Paris last spring.

***grouse,** *n.* As the last term in **blue, Canada, drumming, dusky, Franklin's, mountain, Oregon, Oregon ruffed, pine, pinnated, pin-tailed, prairie, ruffed, ruffled, sage, sharp-tailed, sierra, spike-tailed, sprigtail, spruce, timber, tyee, white-tailed, willow, wood grouse.**

***grout,** *v.* [Prob. the same word as **grout*, to root, as swine.] *intr.* To grumble, sulk. *Rare.* — **1848** Lowell *Biglow P.* II. iii, Ez long 'z the people git their rattle, Wut is there fer 'm to grout about.

***grouty,** *a.* Sulky, ill-tempered. Hence **groutiness,** *n. Colloq.*

Though not so regarded by the *OED*, prob. the same word as dial. **grouty*, muddy, dirty, thundery; and the sense shown here may not have originated in the U.S.

1836 Lowell *Lett.* (1894) I. i. 11 Been quite 'grouty' all the vacation; 'black as Erebus.' **1894** *Chi. Record* 15 July 2/1 It was in the ninth that Mullane got grouty. **1895** *Columbus Dispatch* 23 May 9/4 He can take a passenger's groutiness for what it is worth.

***grove,** *n.* As the last term in **buckeye, mammoth, maple sugar, mesquite, orange, papaw, persimmon, redwood, sap sugar, sugar grove.**

grove meeting. A meeting held in a grove, esp. one of a religious nature. *Obs.* — **1851** Springer *Forest Life* 15 The Methodist denomination may not claim originality in holding grove or camp-meetings. **1882** Thayer *From Log-Cabin* 304 During the month of June, the entire school went in carriages to their annual grove-meeting, at Randolph.

***growler,** *n.*

1. Any one of various fish of the genus *Haemulon.*

1835 Audubon *Ornith. Biog.* III. 199 The usual length of this fish, which on the Ohio is called the White Perch, and in the State of New York the Growler, is from fifteen to twenty inches. **1880** *Lib. Univ. Knowl.* II. 281 The growler . . . is the white salmon of the southern states. **1889** *Cent.* 2643/1 *Grunt*, . . . a fish of the family *Hæmulonidæ*, as those of the genera *Hæmulon* and *Orthopristis:* so called from the noise they make when hauled out of the water. Also called *pig-fish* and *growler* for the same reason.

2. A can or mug for beer. *Slang.*

1890 H. Palmer *Stories Base Ball Field* 70 President Thorner . . . was one of the first to help put down his share of the growler's contents. **1903** O. Kildare *My Mamie Rose* 24 At these visits the most frequently used utensil was the 'can' or 'growler.' **1943** *Copper Camp* 9 One crew from the Moonlight Mine daily climbed two hundred and fitfy feet to surface in the dark up a rickety ladder so as to have a fresh 'growler' for the lunch period.

b. *To rush the growler*, to carry a growler to a saloon for beer; to guzzle beer. *Slang.*

1888 *N.Y. Herald* 29 July 15/1 The employment by hands . . . of boys and girls . . . to fetch beer for them, or in other words to 'rush the growler.' **1920** Lewis *Main St.* 391 He made for her a picture of his work in a large tailor shop in Minneapolis: the steam and heat, . . . men who 'rushed growlers of beer.' **1932** *K.C. Times* 3 May 18 Others would prefer the time honored custom of 'rushing the growler.'

***growth,** *n.* As the last term in **black, fall, first, old field, short, soft growth.**

***grub,** *n.*

1. (See quot. 1905.) *Colloq.* Cf. **grub prairie, puller.**

1788 Washington *Diaries* III. 336 The Women . . . were employed in taking up the Persinnow grubs in No. 7. **1852** *Mich. Agric. Soc. Trans.* III. 332 We have among our grubs . . . about 10,000 things which Wolverine audacity have [*sic*] denominated swine. **1905** *D.N.* III. 82 grub, *n.* Root, sprout. 'I've been getting *grubs* out of this field all day long.' Common. [N.W. Ark.] **1924** J. M. Franks *Seventy Yrs. in Texas* 43 Any person can have plenty of wood by digging it. In the sand the grubs grow larger.

2. A grind *q.v.* sense **1.** *Slang. Obs.*

1847 Wells & Davis *Sk. Williams College* 76 A man must not be ashamed to be called a 'grub' in college, if he would shine in the world. **1887** *Lippincott's Mag.* Oct. 575 The reputation of a 'grub' is hardly a desirable one at the present day.

3. (See quot. and cf. **grub plank.**) *Colloq.*

1895 Burroughs *Pepacton* 27 Some parts of the framework of the raft they call 'grubs'; much depends upon these grubs.

4. In combs.: (1) **grub cache,** a store of provisions for future use; (2) **hole,** (see quot.), *obs.;* (3) **liner,** *W.* an unemployed cowboy who rides from one ranch to another taking advantage of traditional hospitality, also *to ride the grub line*, cf. **chuck,** *n.*[1] **2. b;** (4) **pile,** see as a main entry; (5) **plank,** "refuse plank used in fastening together the parts of a lumber-raft" (*Cent.*); (6) **prairie,** an area, once forested, that through successive annual fires has become a grassland; (7) **puller,** a mechanical

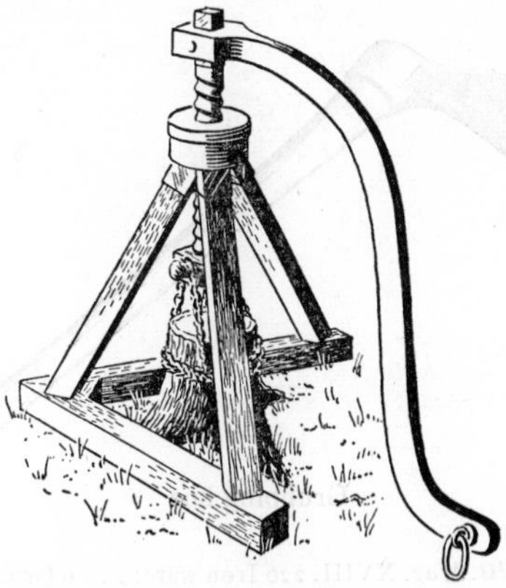

Early (*c*1848) type of grub puller or stump puller

contrivance for pulling out grubs, stumps, etc.; (8) **ranch,** *W.* a place where food is obtained, *rare;* (9) **rider,** =**grub liner;** (10) **root,** (see quot.); (11) **stake, staker,** see as main entries; (12) **tent,** (see quot.), *rare;* (13) **wages,** wages merely sufficient to keep one in food; (14) **wagon,** a wagon carrying the food supplies for cowboys, freighters, construction workers, etc.

(1) **1925** Heming *Living Forest* 123 Also to form enough water below the winter's ice to allow swimmin' to the grub cache. — (2) **1853** Strickland *Twenty-seven Yrs.* 282 In squaring the butt-end [of a stick of timber], a large mortice—or grub-hole as it is termed—must be left to pass the chain through to draw the mast. — (3) **1912** Raine *Brand Blotters* 27 He was no booze-fighting grubliner. **1941** A. Train, Jr. *Story Everyday Things* 303 Cowboys hired for the season

saddle up and 'ride the grub line' from ranch to ranch, looking for another job.

(5) **1844** in *Pa. Mag. Hist.* LI. 73 After examining it [lodged raft], found that by cutting the grub plank in two we might get it off. — (6) **1882** F. B. HOUGH *Elements of Forestry* 52 In grub-prairies in the Northwestern states, the soil is full of the roots of trees and bushes, often of the jack-oak, hazel, etc., that have been killed . . . by annual fires. — (7) **1868** *Mich. Agric. Rep.* VII. 347 N. Pierce, Chelsea, [manufactured a] stump and grub puller, 'Little Giant.' **1888** *Sci. Amer.* 21 April 247 The John Cornelius Grub and Stump Puller. — (8) **1889** MUNROE *Golden Days* 60 Let's pack our traps up to the grub ranch. — (9) **1920** *Outing* July–August 201/1 All 'Grub riders' (cowpunchers out of a job) have always been sure of a meal and a place to sleep at his ranch or any of his camps.

(10) **1876** J. BURROUGHS *Winter Sunshine* I. 29 Bloodroot they [*sc.* Negro women] generally call 'grubroot.' — (12) **1891** *Harper's Mag.* Nov. 890/1 The fact suggests a mention of the principal building in the camp—the mess hall, or 'grub tent.' — (13) **1884** HARTE *On Frontier* 233 He proposed to us white men to settle down to plain ground sluicing, making 'grub' wages just like any chinaman. **1910** HART *Vigilante Girl* xiv. 185 You will see white-haired miners working over the debris of today's diggings—merely for 'grub wages,' just enough to sustain life. — (14) **1891** *Fur, Fin, & Feather* March 150 They take with them a grub wagon and ten saddle horses, and expect to be absent four months. **1920** HUNTER *Trail Drivers Texas* I. 69 We were two miles from the grub wagon.

b. grub-in-the-head, (see quot.). *Rare.*

1877 *Vt. Dairym. Assoc. Rep.* VIII. 105 Grub-in-the-head is a botworm, from an egg deposited by a fly, a cousin to the bots in horses, which passes into the head from the nose.

As the last term in **cattle, corn, gray, hickory, oak, persimmon, saw, saw cut, store, white grub.**

* **grubbing,** *n.*

1. =next. *Obs.*

1859 TALIAFERRO *Fisher's R.* 114 There were endless ways of getting the 'young folks' together. In the spring there would be 'grubbings' and 'log-rollings.'

2. grubbing frolic, a social occasion when neighbors assemble to assist another at grubbing. *Obs.*

1753 in CHALKLEY *Scotch-Irish Settlement Va.* III. 94 Cash paid for liquor at a grubbing frolick, 6 quarts at 9 per quart, £0. 5. 6. **1829** *Mechanics' Press* (Utica, N.Y.) 12 Dec. 38/2 Several young men of this neighborhood . . . were returning from a *grubbing frolic.*

3. grubbing hoe, a heavy, narrow hoe used as a mattock in grubbing.

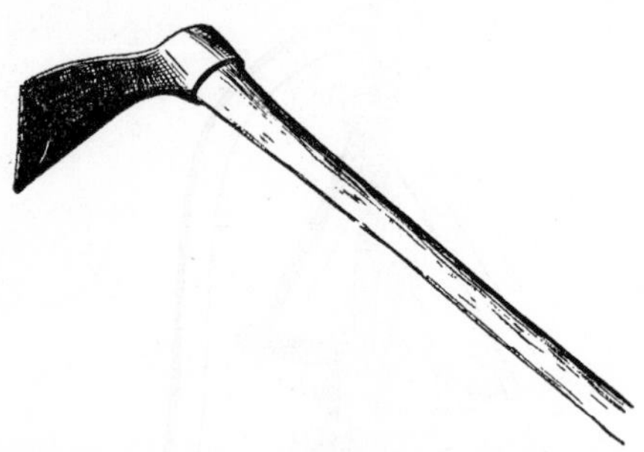

Grubbing hoe

1727 *Md. Hist. Mag.* XVIII. 226 Iron ware: . . . 6 Grubbing hoes, 6 weeding hoes. **1838** GOSSE *Letters* 87 The scanty underbrush of scattered shrubs and slender saplings is torn up with an instrument called a grubbing hoe. **1897** *Scribner's Mag.* XXII. 731/2 Supplied each with an axe, a cant-hook, and a grubbing-hoe, we began the work of cutting through the brush-wood. **1948** DICK *Dixie Frontier* 99 The shrubs and brush were dug out with a heavy grubbing hoe.

grub pile. *W.* A store of provisions. Also eating-time, or a call to eat. *Colloq.*

1863 in *Mont. Hist. Soc. Contrib.* III. (1900) 133 Bill asks 'If we can get some coffee?' I go to the grub pile. Sugar and coffee all gone. **1884** SHEPHERD *Prairie Exp.* 221 The word is given, 'Grub pile'; every man washes his face and hands, and seizing his *couvert*, he helps himself and eats. **1924** MULFORD *Rustler's Valley* 69 By th' way, what time is grub-pile 'round here? **1949** *Sat. Ev. Post* 9 April 132/4 'Grub pile, Blackie!' somebody laughed.

grubstake ˈgrʌbˌstek, *n. W.* The supplies needed by a prospector, supplied him by a patron who shares in his findings. Also attrib. *Colloq.*

1863 in *Mont. Hist. Soc. Contrib.* III. (1900) 138 'A grub stake is what we are after' was our watchword all day, and it is one hundred and fifty dollars in good dust. **1897** JAMES *Alaska* 36 'Grub-stake' miners are men employed by others for a consideration to prospect or work and then make a division of their finds. **1897** LEONARD *Gold Fields Klondike* 22 In spite of the rich prospects on the surface it was generally regarded as a 'grub-stake' strike on which one might succeed in getting a winter outfit. **1947** *Reader's Digest* Oct. 165/2 Some years they barely made their grubstake.

b. One who has secured a grubstake. *Colloq.*

1885 *Cent. Mag.* Nov. 65/1 Beside his loaded donkey trudged the humble 'grub-stake.'

grubstake ˈgrʌbˌstek, *v. tr.* To supply with a grubstake. Also transf.

1879 *Chi. Tribune* 15 May 9/6 Judge Pendery, a former Congressman, politician, and lawyer, has been grub-staking a party of miners who were digging a shaft down near the base of the hill. **1902** LONDON *Daughter of Snows* 59 Men drifted into the land. . . . He encouraged them, grub-staked them, carried them on the books of the company. **1947** *Chi. D. News* 15 Sep. 1/3 America lent vast sums to 'grubstake' other countries.

grubstaker ˈgrʌbˌstekɚ, *n. W.* One who gives, or one who receives, a grubstake. *Colloq.*

1881 HAYES *New Colorado* 107 Here does the whilom grub-staker and present millionaire purchase his corner lot. **1901** GRINNELL *Gold Hunting in Alaska* 45 We may have to foot it home just like . . . prodigal sons who have wasted their substance and that of our grubstakers in 'riotous living.' **1942** LILLARD *Desert Challenge* 175 By now, if not before, he was ready to try to induce a grubstaker to finance him in sinking a shaft a hundred feet or more. **1949** WYNN *Desert Bonanza* 262 The grubstaker usually receives half of anything found or developed.

grueso gruˈeso, *n. W.* [Sp. *a.* and *n.*, coarse, bulky; bulk, main part.] (See quots.) — **1873** *Mining & Sci. Press* 21 Mar., In explanation of the table, it may be stated that the 'grueso' or first class [quicksilver] ore is composed of the largest and richest pieces. [New Almaden Mine, Calif.] **1889** *Cent.* 2641/3 grueso. . . . In the quicksilver-mines of California, the best or first-class ore in large lumps, generally several inches in diameter.

grullo ˈgrujo, *n.* and *a. S.W.* [In **1.** f. Sp. *grulla*, crane. In **2.** f. Amer. Sp. in the sense shown here.]

1. *n.* (See quots.)

1846 ABERT *Exam. N.M.* 45 We noticed some large 'grullas,' blue cranes, in the low grounds. **1864** *Harper's Mag.* Oct. 567/1 The wild croaking of the groojas, or sand-hill cranes, falls mournfully on the ear.

2. *a.* (See quot. 1949.)

1866 *Wilkes' Spirit of Times* 21 April 130/3 We had little pot-gutted duns, with manes like buffalo; 'gruyays,' or crane color [etc.]. **1903** O. HENRY *Heart of West* 147 (Bentley), The Mexicans, who have a hundred names for the colors of a horse, called him *gruyo.* **1931** *Lariat* April 4 (Bentley), He had never roped much of anything except catclaw bushes and the . . . tail of his gruya mule. **1949** *Sat. Ev. Post* 9 April 43/1 The horse he was on was a dull gray-brown color that I couldn't put a name to then, but which I later learned to call *grullo.*

grunion grunˈjon, *n.* [App. f. Sp. *gruñón*, grunter.] A silversides, *Leuresthes tenuis*, great numbers of which, at certain high tides, come in on the California coast and may be caught (legally) only with the hands and feet. Also attrib.

1932 MILLER *I Cover Waterfront* 112 The spring tides, which accompany the full and the dark of the moon, are the time-tables by which the grunion runs can be predicted. **1940** *N.Y. Times Mag.* 28 July 17/1 California law forbids the catching of grunion with anything but human hands and feet. **1949** *L.A. Times* 17 May IV. 4/2 Numerous calls have come in daily to your Gossiper lately as to whether grunion are running.

* **grunter,** *n.* As the last term in **speckled, toad grunter.**

G-string, see **gee string.**

G.T.T. (See quots.) Now *hist.*

1840 HALIBURTON *Clockmaker* 3 Ser. viii, I believe I must hang out the G. T. T. sign.—Why, what the plague is that? says I—Gone to Texas, said he. **1864** NICHOLS *Amer. Life* I. 210 Whenever, at one period, a smart Yankee failed in his business or expectations, he made himself scarce in his ancient locality, leaving behind him only the mystical letters 'G. T. T.' **1944** *Chi. D. News* 2 Feb. 8/1 In former times justices of the peace throughout Kentucky, Tennessee, Missouri, and the 'border' generally, had a habit of closing certain dockets with the initials 'G.T.T.,' an abbreviation for 'Gone to Texas.' **1949** *Sat. Ev. Post* 4 June 30/2 In its place there now remains only that famous old initialed forwarding address: 'G.T.T.' Spelled out, it means 'Gone to Texas.'

guaco ˈgwako, *n.* [Amer. Sp., but the senses here shown are not given in Santamaría. An Amer. borrowing.]

The Rocky Mountain bee plant, *Cleome serrulata;* an extract from this used as a standard black pigment in decorating Pueblo pottery. Also attrib.

1844 GREGG *Commerce of Prairies* I. 278 This kind of crockery . . . is often fancifully painted with colored earths and the juice of a plant called *guaco*, which brightens by burning. [**1904** *Bur. Amer. Ethnol.* 23rd Ann. Rep. 374 Water from boiled Cleome serrulata (Mexican name waco) is mixed with black pigment (a manganiferons [*sic*] clay containing organic matter) in decorating pottery.] **1936** KIDDER *Pottery of Pecos* II. 415 After guaco paint is fired, a coat of powdery ash, which is easily brushed off, usually covers the surface. *Ib.* 421 Some modern Pueblo potters add *guaco* to their ore which gives it a good spreading quality and also binds it when dry.

Guadalupe ˌgwɑdəˈlup, *n.* [Sp. place-name.] **1.** A breed of sheep. **2.** *attrib.* (see quot.). — **(1) 1863** RANDALL *Pract. Shepherd* 14 The Guadeloupe . . . are likewise celebrated for the quantity and quality of their wool. — **(2) 1897** SUDWORTH *Arborescent Flora* 76 *Cupressus guadalupensis.* . . . Arizona Cypress. . . . [Also called] Guadalupe Cypress.

guage ˈgwɑhe, *n.* Also **guaje.** *S.W.* [Amer. Sp. *guaje* (<Nahuatl), in same sense.] A calabash. *Obs.*

1834 A. PIKE *Sketches* 103 His guaje, or little gourd, was always filled by her, with the best punche. **1844** GREGG *Commerce of Prairies* I. 188 The *guage* is a kind of gourd, of which there are some beautiful specimens with two bulbs. **1848** RUXTON *Far West* viii, During a lull, guages filled with whisky go the rounds.

* **guano,** *n.*

1. Fertilizer made from the residue of fish, etc. Cf. **fish guano, Pacific guano.**

1844 EMERSON *Nature; Add. & Lect.* (1849) 369 Agricultural chemistry . . . offering, by means of a tea-spoonful of artificial guano, to turn a sand-bank into corn. **1884** *Nat. Mus. Bul.* No. 27, 1049 From fish-oil refuse there is also made a good guano.

2. Attrib. with **bag, distributor, mixer, sower, spreader.**

1854 *Pa. Agric. Rep.* 396 Best Guano Spreader. **1856** *Porter's Spirit of Times* 4 Oct. 81/3 The State Inspector of Guano in Maryland . . . [urges] farmers to destroy or erase the marks on guano bags after emptying them. **1869** *Rep. Comm. Patents 1868* 804/2 *Guano Distributor.* . . . An improvement in machines for sowing fertilizers. **1875** KNIGHT 1027/2 The guano-sower . . . [has] devices to keep the stuff stirred up and prevent its becoming aggregated in lumps. **1884** *Nat. Museum Bul.* No. 27, 1091 Guano Mixer. . . . This mixer is employed in the fish-guano works for the purpose of thoroughly mixing the fish scrap with the mineral phosphates and sulphuric acid.

* **guard,** *n.*

1. The part of a boat's deck extended beyond the hull, built esp. on the sidewheel type of steamboat so as to curve out over the paddle wheels.

1829 T. FLINT *G. Mason* 140 Madam Mason was this evening sitting on the guards of the boat. **1894** MARK TWAIN *P. Wilson* xvi, The boat bore Roxy away from St. Louis . . . and she stood on the lower guard abaft the paddle-box.

b. *Loaded to the guards*, heavily loaded. Also transf.

1876 HEARN *Amer. Miscellany* (1924) I. 151 Yonder goes the Wildwood, She's loaded to the guards. **1902** A. MACGOWAN *Last Word* 149, I come to Washington in the interest of the Western sheep fellows, just loaded down to the guards with authority. **1947** CHALFANT *Gold, Guns, & Ghost Towns* 8 General Bidwell had packed out from there a mule 'loaded to the guards' with clean gold dust, the proceeds of a few months' work.

2. **=cowcatcher.** *Obs.*

1832 *Amer. R.R. Jrnl.* I. 401/2 The *guard*—an apparatus for removing obstructions. **1838** D. STEVENSON *Sk. Civil Engin. N. Amer.* 260 [To] render railway travelling more safe, an apparatus called a 'guard' has been very generally introduced.

3. **=horse guard 1.**

1836 *Knickerb.* VIII. 689, I have frequently seen horses come running from the barrens, like furies, . . . to seek the spots frequented by the 'guards'—a species of hornet, which catches the flies and protects beasts of all kinds from pain, and doubtless even from death.

4. **=firebreak.**

1884 ALDRIDGE *Life on Ranch* 14 After the plowing and mowing were done, we proceeded to burn the guard.

5. In football, one of two linemen who play on either side of the center; in basketball, one of two players whose chief duty is to guard their team's goal.

1893 WILLIAMS *Princeton Stories* 180 The other 'varsity guard and the centre, who were not light, had thrown themselves upon these. **1922** E. J. MATHER & E. D. MITCHELL *Basket Ball* 39 The two guards should have plenty of practice in meeting the situation wherein three opponents are pitted against them. **1947** *Chi. D. News* 20 Nov. 40/4 (*caption*), Co-Captains Dunlap and Ganey, guards who weigh 175 and 180, respectively, are all but dwarfed by Lagoni.

6. In combs.: (1) * **guardhouse,** a jail or lockup; (2) **line,** the limits of a prison camp, *obs.;* (3) **lock,** (*a*) a lock for guarding a canal from excessive water, (*b*) (see quot.); (4) * **rail,** (*a*) a cast-iron railroad rail strengthened by a wrought-iron rod embedded laterally in it, *obs.,* (*b*) (see quot. 1875); (5) **seat,** in some N. Eng. meeting houses in colonial times, a seat reserved for one delegated to keep order, esp. among children, *obs.;* (6) **tent,** one of the tents occupied by the guard when the command is in the field or in camp, a jail tent, *obs.*

(1) [**1660** in *Doc. Rel. to Col. Hist. New-York* XII. (1877) 308 When I had directed him to return the horse, his wife came and made a great noise . . . whereupon I threatened to imprison her in the guardhouse.] **1741** *Ga. H.S. Coll.* II. 103 This deponent sent James Shepherd to the guardhouse, for abusing this deponent and Mr. John Caldwell, third bailiff, in the execution of their office. **1870** O. LOGAN *Before Footlights* 42 The struggling children . . . fancied it was the guardhouse, in which colored persons are liable to be confined if they are found in the streets after a certain hour without a 'pass.' — **(2) 1865** KELLOGG *Rebel Prisons* 297 She immediately went to an ambulance which stood near the guard line. **1867** Goss *Soldier's Story* 191 Some few [people of Charleston] came with food to sell, but were not allowed to trade over the guard line with prisoners. — **(3)** (*a*) **1815–6** *Niles' Reg.* IX. (Supp.) 164 [At Montague on the Conn. R.] is a guard lock which is used only at the times of freshets . . . for the preservation of the canal. **1897** *Outing* XXX. 357/1 When the guard-lock at Port Colbourne was passed, the sides of the Ontario boats were for the first time lapped by the blue waters of treacherous Lake Erie. (*b*) **1875** KNIGHT 1028/1 *Guard-lock* (Hydraulic Engineering.) A tide-lock, forming a communication between a basin and tide-water. — **(4)** (*a*) **1833** *Amer. R.R. Jrnl.* II. 8/2 (*caption*), New York Patent Guard Rail. *Ib.* 210 The Guard Rail is constructed on an entirely new principle. (*b*) **1872** HUNTINGTON *Road-Master's Ass't* 48 It is an old rule, still adhered to by many, to place the guard rail just the width of the [spiking] hammer. **1875** KNIGHT 1028/1 *Guard-rail*, . . . a short rail placed on the inside of a main rail, so as to keep a wheel on the track.

(5) 1666 *First Cent. Hist. Springfield, Mass.* (1898) I. 344 The Seate wch was made by ye Towne as a Common Towne Charge (formerly called the Guard Seate) is now appointed by the Selectmen. **1669** *Ib.* 376 Anthony Dorchester is to sit on ye Guard Seate for ye like end [i.e., keeping the boys in order]. — **(6) 1848** BRYANT *California* iv. 52 They were greatly alarmed when brought to the guard-tent, expecting immediate punishment. **1865** TROWBRIDGE *Three Scouts* 169 He was immediately taken to the guard-tent and confined.

As the last term in **advance, cabin, cattle, cow, day, field, fire, flag, governor's-, herd, home, horse, ice, life, log, Mississippi, mosquito, mule, National, old, palmetto, provost, state, stock, Stonewall, wagon, water, wheel guard.**

* **guard,** *v.* **1.** *tr.* (See quot.) *Obs.* **2.** *To guard a hill*, (see quot.). — **(1) 1851** HALL *College Words* 154 'The custom of *guarding Freshmen*,' says a correspondent from Dartmouth College, 'is comparatively a late one. Persons masked would go into another's room at night, and oblige him to do anything they commanded him.' — **(2) 1905** *Forestry Bureau Bul.* No. 61, 38 *Guard a hill, to.* To keep a logging road on a steep incline in condition for use.

* **Guardian,** *n.* An officer of a local unit of the Ku-Klux Klan. *Obs.* — **1877** J. M. BEARD *K.K.K. Sketches* 75 Each thoroughly organized Den had its Conductors and Guardians, who were local.

guardo ˈgɑrdo, *n.* [?f. * *guard*+-*o*.] (See quot. 1909.) — *a***1846** J. A. GARDNER *Recoll.* (1906) 116 A droll old guardo midshipman. **1909** *Cent. Supp.* 552/3 guardo. . . . A receiving-ship or -vessel on which enlisted men are temporarily quartered until drafted to seagoing vessels. [Naval sailors' slang.] guardo-move . . . a trick played upon a landsman on a receiving-ship.

guatamote, see **batamote.**

Guatemala grass. (See quots.) — **1896** W. J. BEAL *Grasses N. Amer.* II. 14 Teosinte. Guatemala grass. *E. Mexicana* . . . considerably resembles Indian corn, sometimes attaining the height of 4–5 m., branching freely near the ground. **1901** MOHR *Plant Life Ala.* 135 To which, near the coast, can be added the Guatemala grass or teosinte (*Euchlaena mexicana*), the genuine Guinea grass (*Panicum jumentorum*), and Para grass (*Panicum molle*).

guayacan ˌgwɑjəˈkɑn *n.* [Amer. Sp. *guayacán*, in same sense.] A tree, *Porlieria angustifolia*, of western Texas. — **1891** COULTER *Bot. W. Texas* I. 49 *Guiacum angustifolium.* . . . A straggling shrub (on bluffs) or a small tree (in valleys) with very smooth branches and leaves. . . . Called 'guayacan,' and of considerable repute in various diseases.

guayave gwɑˈjɑvə, *n. S.W.* [Amer. Sp. name of a group of Sobaipuri Indians or something belonging or pertaining to them.]

1. Bread made from corn or some species of agave (see quots.).

1844 GREGG *Commerce of Prairies* I. 280 [Pueblo Indians] make another singular kind of bread, if we may so style it, called *guayave*, a roll of which so much resembles a 'hornets' nest,' that by strangers it is often designated by this title. **1849** *31st Congress* 1 Sess. Sen. Ex. Doc. No. 64, 62 At the house of the governor [of Santo Domingo], I noticed a woman . . . going through the process of baking a very thin species of corn cake, called . . . *guayave*. **1892** LUMMIS *Tramp Across Continent* 109 This batter is then spread on flat rocks over the fire, and then baked into *guayaves*.

2. *transf.* A roll of money, in allusion to the shape of such bread.

1870 *Republican Rev.* 23 April 2/3 Messrs. A. & L. Zechendorf are selling out prior to leaving for Tucson, those who have got the *guayaves* have now a chance to invest.

guayule gwɑˈjule, *n.* [Amer. Sp. (<Nahuatl) in same sense.] A shrubby rubber-yielding herb, *Parthenium argentatum*, found in the Southwest. Also attrib.

1906 *Bul. Imper. Inst.* IV. 114 The Guayule rubber of Mexico. **1911** *Nat. Geog. Mag.* May 495/2 Two-thirds is obtained from the rubber trees of the hot country and one-third from the shrub 'guayule' which flourishes upon the desert plains. **1918** VISHER *So. Dakota* 69 Two decades ago, for example, it was not anticipated that the guayule shrub would give to desert lands a value of as much as $20 per acre which it now does because it became profitable to extract the rubber which it was found to contain. **1947** *Greeley* (Colo.) *D. Tribune* 14 Sep. 1/7 Dr. William G. McGinnies, for the last two years in charge of research and land selection for the guayule rubber project at Salinas, Calif., was named today by the forest service as director of the Rocky Mountain forest and range experiment station.

gubernatorial ˌgubərnəˈtorɪəl, *a.* [f. L. *gubernator*, governor.] Of or pertaining to the governor of an American colony or state.

1734 *N.J. Archives* XI. 368, I thought it very unlikely that the Governor in his gubernatorial Capacity, should refuse His essential Assent. **1824** *Green River Correspondent* (Bowling Green, Ky.) 25 Sep. 1/3 Nothing can be more fallacious, on this question, than the Gubernatorial election. **1948** *Time* 17 May 25/2 He won his gubernatorial primary handily.

b. gubernatorial chair, the office of the governor of a state.

1809 IRVING *Hist. N.Y.* IV. i. 177 Wilhelmus Kieft . . . in 1634 ascended the Gubernatorial chair, (to borrow a favourite, though clumsy appellation of modern phraseologists). **1859** GRATTAN *Civilized Amer.* I. 139 His proper sphere was the Presidency of the neighbouring college, rather than the 'Gubernatorial chair' (as the phrase goes) or a seat in Congress.

Guelder(land) ˈgɛldər(ˌlænd), *n.* [See quot. 1871.] A breed of chickens. — **1849** *N.-Eng. Farmer* I. 309 The Guelderlands are a noble, quiet race, but rather tender, so that the chickens are hard to raise. **1871** LEWIS *Poultry Book* 65 The Guelders . . . were first found in Holland and Belgium, and are known in those countries as Guelderlands, being so called after a province in Holland, lying south of the Zuyder-Zee.

* **guerrilla,** *n.* (See quots.) *Obs.*

1859 MATSELL *Vocabulum* 39 *Guerrillas*. This name is applied by gamblers to fellows who skin suckers when and where they can, who do not like the professional gamblers, but try to beat them, sometimes inform on them, and tell the suckers that they have been cheated. **1885** *Harper's Mag.* Nov. 839/1 The guerrillas are a sub-class of the scalpers, few in number, and by making specialty of dealing in inactive stocks have formerly fixed the unsavory appellations of 'Hell's Kitchen' and 'Robber's Roost' upon certain localities of the floor.

guerrillero ˌgɛrɪlˈjɛro, *n. S.W.* [Sp. in same sense.] A guerrilla, a bushwhacker. *Obs.* — **1865** *Atlantic Mo.* XV. 764 Trial of John Y. Beall, as a Spy and Guerrillero, by Military commission. **1910** J. HART *Vigilante Girl* 179 Clodomiro Chavez, an old guerillero of the Mexican War for Independence, excelled in planning raids.

* **guess,** *n.* *To miss one's guess*, to be wrong in one's surmise. *Colloq.* — **1911** J. C. LINCOLN *Cap'n Warren's Wards* xxi. 336 He declared . . . that they would have some good times aboard her or he missed his guess. **1930** N. W. STEPHENSON *Nelson W. Aldrich* 308 He was confident that the President had missed his guess, that at the pinch the Democrats would not hold together.

For *by guess and by* **God, Godfrey, Gosh,** see the terms in boldface.

* **guess,** *v.*

1. a. guess cake, a cake to be given as a prize in a guessing contest. **b. guess farmer,** (see quot.). Both *rare.*

(a) 1929 *Randolph Enterprise* (Elkins, W. Va.) 14 Nov. 5/4 Ice Cream and Cake, Guess Cake and numerous features of pleasure. Everybody invited. — **(b) 1868** BRACKETT *Farm Talk* 10 Ninety-nine [farmers] keep all their accounts 'in their head,' as it is termed, and consequently are properly called *guess farmers*, for they never *know* anything, only *guess* it is so and so.

2. In phrases: (1) *To guess* (one) *up a tree*, (see quot.), *rare*; (2) *to guess off*, *W.* (see quot.); (3) *to keep one guessing*, to keep one in suspense.

(1) 1825 in *Memoirs of Charles Mathews* (1839) III. 521 Or, as they have it in their country, when they have outwitted a very cautious traveller, that he had 'guessed you up a tree.' — **(2) 1874** McCOY *Cattle* 69 If there are no facilities for weighing provided by Government, it is usual for the contractor and Indian agent to estimate the weight, or 'guess off' the herd or lot of cattle about being turned over. — **(3) 1905** *Springfield W. Republican* 24 Nov. 1 The governor seems determined to keep us guessing. **1930** H. ZINK *City Bosses of U.S.* 23 Murphy proceeded with considerable caution, sometimes withdrawing from a position, sometimes forcing it, and altogether keeping his opponents guessing what he would do next.

* **guesser,** *n.* One who habitually says, "I guess"; a Yankee. *Colloq. Obs.* — **1825** NEAL *Bro. Jonathan* I. 3 He was permitted every 'Sabbath' afternoon to pass through the crowd by the 'meeting-house'. or to wander among the graves . . . without being pestered or plagued with a single 'guesser.' **1857** B. YOUNG in *Jrnl. Discourses* V. 77 (Th.), I am a Yankee guesser; and I guess that James Buchanan has ordered this expedition to appease the wrath of the angry hounds who are howling around him.

* **guessing,** *n. attrib.* Denoting a *frolic* or *party* at which those present, for a small fee, make bets about the weight of a pig which is awarded as a prize to the who one makes the best guess. *Obs.* Cf. **hog guessing.** — **1837** WILKIE *Sketches* 180 It is denominated 'a guessing frolic.' **1844** UNCLE SAM *Peculiarities* I. 167 What may a guessing party be? Why, it war for a pig. Him as guessed nearest the weight of the critter had it for his dollar and a round of stone-fence.

guest ranch. Euphemistic for dude ranch *q.v.* — **1932** *Ariz. Agric. Exp. Sta.* Bul. 141, 2 Unclassified. Land owned and operated by the State or a public agency, guest ranches, private estates, forest products. **1948** *Spokesman-Review* (Spokane, Wash.) 23 Sep. 12/7 For Sale—Wyoming Ranch. Beautifully located combination cattle and guest ranch.

* **guff,** *n.* Nonsense, windy talk. *Slang.*

1888 *Scribner's Mag.* Aug. 219/1, I tell you all this talk is guff, and it just comes down to the money. **1916** H. L. WILSON *Somewhere* viii. 332 Why can't he be nice and submit to the decencies of civilization—and so on—a lot of guff like that. **1948** *Dly. Ardmoreite* (Ardmore, Okla.) 29 July 6/3 Save that guff for your wife, baldy.

guia ˈgiə, *n. S.W.* [Sp. in same sense.] A writing which certifies that merchandise being transported has been cleared through a customhouse; a permit, passport or certificate of safe conduct. *Obs.*

1834 *Visit to Texas* (1834) 256 The trader was seized . . . on the charge of having no *guia*, which is tantamount to a passport. **1844** GREGG *Commerce of Prairies* II. 66 Before setting out, the entire bill of merchandise has to be translated into Spanish; then, duplicates of the translation being presented to the custom-house, one is retained, while the other, accompanied by the *guia* (a sort of clearance or mercantile passport), is carried along with the cargo by the conductor. **1888** J. J. WEBB *Adventures* 229 All trains passing from one state to the other were compelled to present their *guias*, or manifests for inspection.

Guiana plum. The Florida plum, *Drypetes lateriflora*. — **1884** SARGENT *Rep. Forests* 121 *Drypetes cocea*. . . . Guiana Plum. White Wood. **1897** SUDWORTH *Arborescent Flora* 271.

* **guide,** *n.*

1. A spirit believed to guide or control the utterances of a medium. *Obs.* See also **Indian guide, post guide.**

1885 *Cent. Mag.* XXX. 381/2, I can't seem to do anything in these days, now that I no longer have a Guide, you know. **1887** *Courier-Journal* 18 Jan. 1/7 As a spirit medium he is as greatly in need of a 'guide' as the fellow in 'The Ratcatcher.'

2. In combs.: (1) **guide-bird,** *W.* a now unidentifiable bird, *obs.*; (2) **board,** see as a main entry; (3) **line,** in surveying, an accurately measured line upon which other measurements are based; (4) **meridian,** (see quot.).

(1) 1872 RICHARDSON *Wonders of Yellowstone* 111 Mention is also made of the guide-bird, whose habits correspond with its name. It resembles the blackbird, but is larger. — **(3) 1785** ELLICOTT in Mathews *Life A. Ellicott* 44 My Brother Joseph at Present runs the guide Line for the Choppers. **1798** ——— in *Ann. 10th Congress* 1 Sess. II. 2740, I shall . . . proceed to the Pearl river, where the guide line will be corrected. **1802** ——— *Journal* 186 We were employed in laying off the correction, and making the necessary arrangements for carrying on a guide line to the Mobile. — **(4) 1890** *Manual Surveying Instructions* (Gen. Land Office) 36 Guide meridians shall be extended north and south from the base line, at intervals of every 24 miles east and west from the principal meridian.

***guide,** *v.* **1.** *intr.* To act as a guide. **2.** Of a horse, to be guided. Both *rare.* (1) **1891** BUNNER *Zadoc Pine* 3 He had 'guided' for parties of New York men, and he had learned enough to make himself sure that New York was too large for him. — (2) **1891** *Harper's Mag.* Aug. 364/2 A horse is nowadays not even permitted to guide by the neck.

guideboard ˈgaɪdˌbord, *n.* A board posted beside a road giving information as to the way. Also fig. Cf. **mile board.**

1829 *Yankee* April 120/2 Saw a guide-board ahead—conjectured I had arrived at another town. **1870** MARK TWAIN *New & Old* 245 He was missing the guide-boards I had set up to warn him the whole thing was a fraud. **1880** *Cong. Rec.* 22 Jan. 481/1 We have undertaken to make an open pathway, and with guideboards to point the youngest member of Congress. **1897** *Outing* XXX. 290/2 The near proximity of the railroad, and occasionally a guideboard, enable the touring novice to find his way without difficulty.

guilder ˈgɪldɚ, *n.* [See note.]

The occurrence of this term only in those areas settled by or in close contact with the Dutch suggests that its use here was an American borrowing and not a continuation of earlier British usage. For **2.** see *WNT,* 1257.

1. A Dutch coin formerly in use in regions of Dutch influence in America. Also **guilder piece.** *Obs.*

1649 *Conn. Rec.* I. 192 For his bond at the Dutch being 400 Gilders. **1675** *N.Y. State Col. Hist. Doc.* XII. 527 His debt 521 guilders. **1741** *N.J. Archives* 1 Ser. VI. 118 Three gilder pieces of Holland twenty penny weight and seven grains, five shillings and two pence one farthing.

2. Carol guilder, a rendering of Du. *Carolus-gulden,* or *Caroli gulden,* a guilder so named from the celebrity whose image it bore. *Obs.*

1657 *Hempstead Rec.* I. 18 Whosoever shall refues to gather aney towne rate or rates being ordered by the townesmen shall pay for his refusing it six Carrot [*sic*] guilder for the first refuesall thereof. **1659** *Ib.* 106 I . . . doe hereby . . . sell and delliver vnto William Smith of Hemsteede aforesaid, . . . the meadow-land w'th the appurtenances there vnto belongeing for and in concideration of six hundred carol guilders.

Guilford (red). A variety of apple. *Obs.* — **1870** *Rep. Comm. Agric. 1869* 197 Apples for the southern states. Guilford Red. **1905** W. A. RAGAN *Nomenclature of Apple* 133 *Guilford Red.* . . . Syn [onym] of Guilford.

***guillotine,** *n. fig.* An imaginary knife or ax wielded to cut a person out of his job.

1850 HAWTHORNE *Scarlet Letter* 56 Keeping up the metaphor of the political guillotine, the whole may be considered as the Posthumous Papers of a Decapitated Surveyor. **1883** DE VERE in *Encyl. Brit.* Amer. Supp. I. 200/1 The *axe*, or rather the *guillotine*, is made to represent the dismissal of Government officials upon the coming in of a new President, or in case of some grave complication, and the victims are said to be beheaded. **1893** *Boston Journal* 20 March 1/2 (*caption*), The Post Office Guillotine Working Rapidly.

***guillemot,** *n.* As the last term in **pigeon, thick-billed guillemot.**

***Guinea,** *n.*

1. A Negro newly brought from the Guinea coast, or from Africa. In full **Guinea Negro.** Now *hist.*

1789 S. LOW *Politician Outwitted* III. i, He talks as crooked as a Guinea niger. **1823** COOPER *Pioneers* xxx, He was one of them Guineas down in the kitchen there. **1861** LOWELL *Bigelow P.* 2 Ser. i. 25 'Taint quite hendy to pass off one o' your six-foot Guineas. **1896** J. G. WILLIAMS *Ole Plantation* (Pref.), I remember hearing the old plantation negroes before the war speak of one as a 'Gullah nigger' and another as a 'Guinea nigger.' **1947** *Amer. Sp.* April 85 It should also be noted that . . . 'guinea Negro' used to be applied to any newly arrived Negro slave.

attrib. **1835** *Vade Mecum* (Phila.) 31 Jan. 4/6 A negro of real Guinea stamp . . . sat under a hill fishing.

2. A fellow or "guy," usu. applied to an immigrant from southern Europe, as an Italian or Spaniard. *Slang.*

1910 *Sat. Ev. Post* 3 Sep. 18/1 Almost every Ginny . . . or Dutchman who lands in New York has in his 'kick,' or wallet, the written address of some boarding-house or cheap hotel. **1911** L. J. VANCE *Cynthia* 183, I guess it's only what was comin' to me for trustin' a ginny like Perez. **1948** *Dly. Ardmoreite* (Ardmore, Okla.) 30 July 6/6 There are stresses and strains in the home, . . . and the Hunkeys, the Spicks, the Guineas and the Ginks are down on the rest of the family.

3. Guinea corn, a species of millet or grain sorghum.

1671 *S.C. Hist. Soc. Coll.* V. 333 Guiney Corne growes very well here. **1743** CATESBY *Carolina* App. p. xviii, *Milium Indicum.* Bunched Guinea Corn. But little of this grain is propagated, and that chiefly by negroes, who make bread of it, and boil it in like manner of firmety. Its chief use is for feeding fowls. . . . It was at first introduced from Africa by the negroes. **1857** *Rep. Comm. Patents 1856: Agric.* 125 Seeds of different kinds, rice, grass, and Guinea-corn are their [the blue grosbeaks'] usual food. **1949** MURRAY *This Our Land* 86 A writer who failed to sign his name wrote on Guinea corn.

b. (See quot.)

1892 *Amer. Folk-Lore* V. 105 *Zea mays,* a species of pop-corn, with variegated ears; guinea-corn. Mansfield, O. . . . [*Note:*] Because speckled like a guinea-fowl.

4. *Guinea grass, (see quots.). Cf. **Alabama guinea grass.**

1889 VASEY *Agric. Grasses* 36 *Sorghum halepense* (Johnson Grass; Mean's Grass) . . . has been called Egyptian Grass . . . [and] Alabama Guinea Grass. **1896** BEAL *Grasses N. Amer.* I. 172 It [i.e., Johnson grass] has sometimes been called *Guinea grass,* though this name has more generally been applied to another, *Panicum jumentorum.* **1935** HITCHCOCK *Grasses U.S.* 2 Two grasses, important in the Tropics but in the United States grown only in southern Florida and southern Texas, are Guinea grass . . . and Para grass.

5. Guinea keet, =**keet.**

1859 [see **keet**]. **1894** *Outing* Jan. 276/1 The Guinea keets, warned by strange instinct, have left their haunts in the box wood. **1924** *Farmers' Bul.* No. 1377 9 In some markets guineas are called 'keets' or 'guinea keets.'

guisado giˈsɑdo, *n. S.W.* [Sp. in same sense.] A stew of meat, vegetables, etc. *Obs.* — **1826** FLINT *F. Berrian* I. 134 We were then seated to chocolate, a supper, a gisado [*sic*], and confectionary. **1878** *Harper's Mag.* Jan. 272/2 Of these the guisado of the country would be made, which answers to the *pot au feu* of the French, only more warmly flavored with this pepper.

gulch gʌltʃ, *n.* [Origin obscure. Cf. Eng. dial. *gulch, gulsh,* of land: to sink in.]

1. A ravine, canyon, or gully; the deep and narrow bed of a torrent or intermittent stream. Cf. **box gulch, gold gulch.**

1835 WIX *Newfoundland Missionary's Jrnl.* 19 (De Vere), In Fortune Bay, . . . in winter, it might be necessary to make a circuit of fifteen miles, to get round the deep precipitous chasms or 'gulshes' and ravines. *a***1842** O. RUSSELL *Journal* (1921) 55 We came to a deep, narrow gulch, made by the water running from the hills [near Yellowstone] in the spring season. **1873** BEADLE *Undevel. West.* 658 The town site is irrigated from a considerable creek running out of a narrow gulch. **1945** STEINBECK *C. Row* 72 On one side of the gulch was a fine old adobe and on the other the house of the doctor.

attrib. **1890** RYAN *Told in Hills* 288, I started for the gulch trail, and couldn't make it with snow on the ground.

2. *W.* Esp. such a place where gold is prospected for or mined. Also in proper names.

1850 TYSON *Diary in Calif.* 61 Three . . . deserts . . . happened on one of these rich '*gulches.*' **1885** *Graceville* (Minn.) *Transcript* 11 April 2/2 The ambitious candidates . . . are coming in from the outlying camps and surrounding gulches in scores. *a***1918** G. STUART *On Frontier* II. 83 A party of Piegans appeared at Confederate gulch, drove off all the horses and fired a parting shot at some miners working in a gulch just below town. **1948** JOHNSTON *Gold Rush* 46/1 The gulches in surrounding hills teemed with miners who wielded picks, pans, long toms, and built long and efficient sluices.

b. In combs. of obvious meaning, as (1) **gulch claim,** (2) **diggings,** (3) **gold,** (4) **man,** (5) **mine,** (6) **miner,** (7) **mining,** (8) **washings.**

(1) **1865** in *Frontier* VIII. (1928) 131 A Gulch Claim [in Elk Creek district, Deer Lodge Co., Mont.] shall be two hundred feet in length and shall extend three hundred feet on each side of the gulch. **1941** FRITZ *Colorado* 128 The size of a gulch claim was usually one hundred feet up and down the gulch and extending from bank to bank. — (2) **1859** *S.F. Bulletin* 5 May 1/2 The gulch diggings are also paying well for the labor expended. **1882** *47th Congress* 1 Sess. H.R. Ex. Doc. No. 216, 328 As many of those engaged in the gulch diggings . . . were Mexicans, a considerable portion of [gold] . . . found its way into old Mexico. — (3) **1876** RAYMOND *8th Rep. Mines* 297 The production of gulch-gold on and below Spanish Bar has amounted, as nearly as can be ascertained, to $80,000. — (4) **1869** A. K. MCCLURE *Rocky Mts.* 210 The unfortunate politician is 'corraled' by the mountaineers, the gulchmen, or the settlers.

(5) **1866** *Beadle's Mo.* Oct. 279/1 The diggings yielded very richly . . . but, like most gulch mines, were soon exhausted. **1876** RAYMOND *8th Rep. Mines* 313 Gold from the gulch-mines and Printer Boy Mine, $95,940. — (6) **1867** MELINE *Santa Fe & Back* 63 The gulch miner has been here in all his pristine strength and glory. **1870** *Colo. Gazetteer* 43 The first settlers of the county were gulch miners, who worked in the valley along Clear creek only. — (7) **1867** *Harper's Mag.* June 11/2 We . . . passed over a creek which had been brought by an artificial ditch for gulch-mining purposes. **1883** RITCH *Illust. N. Mex.* 75 In addition to gulch mining, much work has been done on

lodes. — (8) **1876** RAYMOND *8th Rep. Mines* 186 The gold comes from the gulch-washings in Indian district near the Eagle Mine.

gulch gʌltʃ, *v.* [f. the noun.]

1. *tr.* To drag (wood) down a gulch. *Rare.*

1876 RAYMOND *8th Rep. Mines* 98 Cost of 1 cord of wood at furnace: Cutting cord of wood, $2.50, Gulching it to wagon-road, 1.00. **1877** ——— *Statist. Mines & Mining* 28 Cutting and gulching 50 cords of wood, at $2.50 per cord.

2. *intr.* To dig for gold or silver in a gulch. *Obs.*

1879 H. DRUMMOND in *Life* (1899) 157 A hundred prospectors gulching for gold and silver. **1879** VIVIAN *Wanderings Western Lands* 331 We saw plenty of signs of gold-mining, . . . at first chiefly of the so-called 'hydraulic mining, but afterwards of the older 'placer working,' or 'gulching.'

3. *tr.* To trap (an animal) in a gulch.

1906 *Harper's Mag.* Oct. 760 An accident had occurred by the sheep being gulched.

gulchy ˈgʌltʃɪ, *a.* Abounding in gulches. *Colloq.* — **1861** *Harper's Mag.* June 8/2 If the day's travel happens to be unusually rough, he calls the trail 'a little gulchy,' but promises that it will be 'all easy work to-morrow.'

* **gulf,** *n.*[1]

1. (*cap.*) Short for "Gulf of Mexico," used allusively for the southern boundary of the U.S.

1861 *Chi. Tribune* 26 May 1/5 Our great chieftain . . . might yet . . . have the joy of seeing that flag re-established, and waving in its beauty and glory at every point, from the Lakes to the Gulf, and from Eastern shore to the Western. **1865** RICHARDSON *Secret Service* 88 They fear . . . that the border will gradually become Abolitionized, and extend free territory to the Gulf itself.

b. *pl.* Short for "Gulf of Mexico oysters." *Colloq.*

1910 *Sat. Ev. Post* 8 Oct. 29/3 Gulfs are grown exclusively in the waters of the Gulf of Mexico.

2. Short for **Gulf Stream.**

1873 *Harper's Mag.* XLVI. 711 Going to England, mariners keep in the 'Gulf.'

3. In combs. (usu. *cap.*): (1) **Gulf City,** (see quot.); (2) **Coast,** the southern portion of the U.S. along the Gulf of Mexico; (3) **Confederacy,** a confederacy of those states adjacent to the Gulf of Mexico, *obs.;* (4) **department,** a military district which included the Gulf States, *obs.;* (5) **fleet,** during the Civil War, that part of the federal fleet which operated in the Gulf of Mexico, *obs.;* (6) **state,** (*a*) a state which borders on the Gulf of Mexico, (*b*) (*cap.*) a nickname for Florida; (7) **Stream,** see as a main entry.

(1) **1889** FARMER 280/1 *Gulf City,* New Orleans. — (2) **1889** HAGERTY *State No. Dakota* 54 Down on the Gulf coast 30° above zero is more penetrating and chilly than zero in North Dakota. **1947** *Chi. D. News* 22 Sep. 1/8 Ugly, poisonous water moccasins today crawled over the beaches along the Gulf Coast. **1948** *Chi. Tribune* 4 April VI. 2/4 The Mississippi gulf coast . . . is all dolled up for the Spring tourist season. — (3) **1862** in LOGAN *Great Conspiracy* 419 This cunningly-devised plan for securing a Gulf-Confederacy, commanding the mouths of the great Western rivers, the Gulf of Mexico, and the Southern Atlantic ocean . . . succeeded too well. — (4) **1865** CUMMING *Hospital Life* (1866) 191/2 Some were from Lee's army, going south, others from the Mississippi and Gulf department, going north.

(5) **1862** in F. MOORE *Rebellion Rec.* V. II. 119 Perhaps the Commander-in-Chief is waiting for the Gulf-fleet to occupy Memphis. — (6) (*a*) **1837** *Knickerb.* X. 381 Any one may single out the Georgian and the inhabitants of any of the Gulf-states. **1948** *Houston* (Tex.) *Post* 14 June 14/4 Some of our giant live oaks in the Gulf states are over 35 feet in trunk circumference. (*b*) **1871** DE VERE 659 Florida is the Gulf State. **1885** *Harper's Mag.* Jan. 221/2 On the southern end of the Gulf State there may be seen on the map a stretch called the Ten Thousand Islands.

b. Chiefly obs. in the names of, or with reference to, birds and other animals: (1) **Gulf bird,** (see quot.); (2) **cattle,** cattle of the region adjacent to the Gulf of Mexico; (3) **cotton,** cotton particularly suited to the soil and climate of the Gulf Coast region of the southern states; (4) **menhaden,** a species of menhaden, *Brevoortia patronus,* closely allied to that of the Atlantic Coast; (5) **seed,** the seed of Gulf cotton; (6) **worm,** a shipworm.

(1) **1917** *Birds of Amer.* I. 217/1 [The] Red Phalarope . . . [or] Gulf-bird . . . migrates along both coasts of United States. — (2) **1867–9** *Ill. Agric. Soc. Trans.* VII. 141 The Gulf cattle are much worse than those from Northern Texas. — (3) **1847** *De Bow's Review* III. 6 But there is no *'gulf cotton.'* — (4) **1883** *Nat. Museum Bul.* No. 27, 454 [The] Gulf Menhaden . . . has no economic importance.

(5) **1847** *De Bow's Review* III. 6 A fresh supply of *'Gulf seed'* is necessary. — (6) **1837** WILLIAMS *Florida* 84 Cabbage Palm. . . . The timber resists the Gulf worm, so destructive to vessels.

Gulf Stream. [App. brought into currency by B. Franklin; see quot. 1939.] A great warm ocean current issuing from the Gulf of Mexico and running parallel to the Atlantic Coast as far as Newfoundland, where it turns in the direction of Europe.

1769 FRANKLIN *Wks.* V. (1906) 232 The Whales are found generally near the Edges of the *Gulph Stream,* a strong Current so called, which comes out of the Gulph of Florida. **1873** *Harper's Mag.* XLVI. 711 The Gulf Stream guides, or rules to a large extent, the course of ships crossing the Atlantic. [**1939** *Reader's Digest* April 65 Dr. Franklin put his scientific mind to work, talked with an experienced Nantucket whaler captain and learned enough to chart the stream, giving it the name is still bears.] **1949** *N.Y. Times Bk. Review* 10 April 2/2 The clear aquamarine of the Gulf Stream [etc.].

b. (See quot. 1938.)

1938 ALBION *Square-Riggers* 5 During the packet period, the whole current, from Florida to Ireland, was called the Gulf Stream. More recently, that name has been restricted to the coastal section and the ocean portion is often designated as the 'Gulf Stream drift.' **1949** *Nat. Hist.* June 272/3 It is here that the cold southward-flowing Labrador Stream meets the warm subtropical waters of the Gulf Stream as it flows to the northeast.

* **gull,** *n.* As the last term in **Bonaparte's, flood, Franklin's, glaucous-winged, Heermann's, ice, mackerel, ring-billed, sheepshead, western gull.**

Gullah ˈgʌlə, *n.* [See note.]

The origin of this term is not clear. It is poss. f. *Gola,* a tribe and language of Liberia, or f. *Ngola,* the name of a tribe in the Hamba Basin of Angola.

1. One of a group of Negroes living on the Sea Islands and the tidewater coastal strip bordering South Carolina and Georgia. Usu. attrib.

1822 in SMITH *Gullah* (1926) 7 [In an entry of the Charleston City Council, under the year 1822, reference is made to] 'Gullah Jack' [and his company of] 'Gullah or Angola Negroes.' **1881** HARRIS *Uncle Remus,* (introd.), It is the negro dialect in its most primitive state—the 'Gullah' talk of some of the negroes on the Sea islands [etc.]. **1922** A. E. GONZALES (*title*), The Black Border, Gullah Stories of the Carolina Coast. **1947** BEROLZHEIMER *Regional Cookbook* 163 The cooking varies, even between North Carolina and the 'Gullahs' of the South Carolina low country.

2. The dialect spoken by these Negroes.

1896 J. G. WILLIAMS *Old Plantation* p. v, The older ones of that set of negroes . . . speak as pure Gullah as their grandfathers. . . . They seem to have been scarcely affected in their low-country Gullah speech [etc.]. **1909** *So. Atlantic Quart.* 43 There are in Gullah many words properly pronounced. **1945** MOLLOY *Pride's Way* 286, 'I does like fuh to dream 'bout 'em, he said in his richest Gullah.

gull house. A structure for trapping gulls. *Obs.* — **1793** *Mass. H.S. Coll.* III. 120 The method of killing gulls, in the gull house, is no doubt an Indian invention. *Ib.,* The gull house is built with crotches fixed in the ground on the beach, and covered with poles, the sides being covered with stakes and sea-weed, the poles on the top covered with lean whale.

gully ˈgʌlɪ, *v.* [f. the noun.] *tr.* To erode (land) so as to form gullies; to hollow out (holes in the soil). Usu. **gullied,** *a.*

1754 *Remembrancer* (1778) V. 490/1 The lands between these, hilly, gullied all the way. **1805** PARKINSON *Tour* 45 The land at Mount Vernon . . . was (as it is termed in America) *gullied.* . . . This effect is produced by the winter's frost and summer's rain, which cut the land into cavities of from ten feet wide and ten feet deep (and upwards) in many places. **1897** *Outing* XXX. 164/1 The current had gullied out deep holes around the big bowlders. **1945** *Jefferson Co. Republican* (Golden, Colo.) 2 May 1/1 Check dams of brush or other materials may be used effectively in checking the movement of silt and permit the gullied area to heal.

gully keeper. "Probably a local pron. of the children's game still called in Missouri *goal-keeper* or *goalie-keeper,* a variation of prisoner's base" (Ramsay). — **1876** MARK TWAIN *Tom Sawyer* xxix. 217 (R.), They had an exhausting time playing 'hi-spy' and 'gully-keeper.' **1948** *Parade* 11 July 24/4 Tom and Huck of 1848 played 'hi-spy,' 'gulley keeper,' 'pirates,' and 'Robin Hood.'

gullywasher ˈgʌlɪˌwɑʃɚ, *n.* A tremendous rain. Also transf. *Colloq.*

1923 *K.C.* (Mo.) *Star* 23 April, He meant to say that what Kansas needs now is a regular 'gully-washer'; a rain that will fill all the small streams bank full, start the water to running in the pasture creeks, and cause the springs at the head of the draws to flowing. **1945** *Reader's Digest* March 84/2 If a man's terraces break when the gully-washers come . . . then he might as well have no terraces at all. **1948** *Capital-Democrat* (Tishomingo, Okla.) 17 June 1/7 The drouth of senatorial candidates in Johnston county will be broken with a 'gulley washer' here this week.

***gum,** *n.*

1. Short for **gum tree.**

1700 *Md. Hist. Mag.* XIX. 347 Timber Proof, 200 acres Sur. the 22d of decembr 1672 for George Wells in delph Creek at a marked gum. **1841** W. KENNEDY *Texas* I. 100 There are also ash, cypress, red cedar, cotton tree, china tree, cherry, elm, gum, hackberry [etc.]. **1921** DEAM *Trees Indiana* 261 The greater amount of gum is used as rough stuff.

2. A section of a hollow gum tree suitable for use as a barrel, beehive, etc.

1767 in WOODWARD *Ploughs* (1931) 297 They [potatoes] are kept over in Gums or boxes putt in the Chimney corner packed in Dry Sand. **1815** *Niles' Reg.* VIII. 135/1 The inhabitants sunk (hollow) gums into the sand and gravel at that place [a salt lick]. *c*1866 BAGBY *Old Va. Gentleman* 48 [He must] set gums for 'Mollie-cotton-tales,' mash-traps and deadfalls for minks. **1948** DICK *Dixie Frontier* 30 A gum was a container made of a hollowed-out section of a log, set upright and fitted with a bottom and a lid.

Gums (sense 2)

3. Short for **chewing gum.**

1842 *Spirit of Times* (Phila.) 11 April (Th.), [She] asked me if I didn't want a piece of gum to chaw. **1909** STRATTON-PORTER *Girl of Limberlost* 144 He took us to the show, and he got us gum. **1944** *Newsweek* 15 May 62 Wrigley's new gum will be sold under the name 'Orbit.'

4. Short for **gum boot, gumshoe.**

1855 *Mass. Acts & Resolves* 495 Manufactories for preparation of gums. **1892** *Harper's Mag.* Jan. 272/1 Amanda put on her overshoes, which she, like the rest of Penniville, called 'gums.' **1899** MUIRHEAD *Baedeker's U.S.* p. xxx, *Gums*, overshoes.

5. In combs.: (1) **gum chewer,** one who chews gum; (2) **chewing,** the action of chewing gum, also attrib.; (3) **disease,** a disease affecting the bark of orange trees; (4) **drop, game,** see as main entries; (5) **habit,** the habit of chewing gum; (6) **rocker,** *W. mining* (see quot.), *obs.;* (7) **social,** ?a jocular term for a gathering or party at which the chewing of gum is indulged in, *rare;* (8) **sucking,** see as a main entry; (9) **swamp,** a swamp in which gum trees predominate; (10) **tea,** a tea made of some species of gum, *rare;* (11) **turpentine,** (see quot.); (12) ***water,** rain water that collects in the box cut in a pine as a receptacle for turpentine, *rare;* (13) **woods,** a woods in which there are many gum trees.

(1) **1850** JUDD *R. Edney* 158 There are the Gum-chewers,—all backlotters; and vulgar. **1944** *N. & Q.* IV. 56 Since the beginning of the war we have had here [Lancashire, England] representatives of every nation, and yet among all the service men I have met or observed, the Americans appear to be the only gum-chewers. — (2) **1889** *Pueblo* (Colo.) *Opinion* 14 July 4/5 The careful observer can not fail to note the growing prevalency of gum chewing. **1944** *Chi. D. News* 21 Oct. 4/1 To attract what we once called the gum-chewing trade. — (3) **1896** *U.S. Dept. Agric., Div. Veg. Physiol. & Pathol.* Bul. 8, 30 Psorosis, a disease known in Florida as 'tears' or 'gum disease,' is often confounded with foot rot, but is unquestionably quite distinct. . . . Psorosis does not kill the bark entirely.

(5) **1889** THANET in *Harper's Bazaar* 4 May 330/1 An extraordinary abandonment to 'the gum habit' is a feature of Hot Springs. — (6) **1879** *Harper's Mag.* Sep. 508 The gravel [was washed] . . . by running it through sluice-boxes and splint baskets into a 'gum-rocker' which was nothing but a split and hollowed out log a dozen or so feet in length. — (7) **1889** *Pueblo* (Colo.) *Opinion* 14 July 4/3 Lawn-tennis is steadily and surely usurping the place of gum socials and riding parties. — (9) **1743** in *Amer. Sp.* XV. 268/2 Lying upon the Cypres Swamp runing up the gum swamp. **1834** *Sun* (N.Y.) 29 Aug. 4/1 The woods, including a portion of the Gum Swamp, was scoured to an extent of from ten to fifteen miles by the whole neighborhood.

(10) **1841** *S. Lit. Messenger* VII. 44/1 Our piney-wood's Esculapius . . . enjoins perfect quiet, with the rigorous enaction of gum-tea. — (11) **1894** SARGENT *Rep. Forests* 517 The following grades of turpentine are recognized in the trade: 'Virgin dip,' or 'Soft white gum turpentine'—the product the first year the trees are worked [etc.]. — (12) **1872** POWERS *Afoot & Alone* 21 Let us dip our drinking-cups into this deft little pocket chopped in the pine, and quaff some gum-water. — (13) **1850** *Knickerb.* XXXV. 22 My father's mill was close upon a 'gumwoods,' and one Sunday, . . . I went with a lot of boys 'gumming.'

b. Designating things made wholly or in part of rubber, as (1) **gum ball,** (2) **blanket,** (3) **boot,** (4) **(cloth) coat,** (5) **ring.** See also **gumshoe,** as a main entry.

(1) **1903** O. HENRY *Heart of West* 94 McGuire, . . . all-round sport, and manipulator of the gum balls and walnut shells, looked up. — (2) **1864** NORTON *Army Lett.* 229, I curled myself up in my gum blanket. **1888** *Cent. Mag.* XXXVI. 738/1 He would have been very glad to please her had they only thought to bring along a gum-blanket. — (3) **1850** in *One Man's Gold* (1930) 119, I put on my long gum boots and waded through the water. **1948** *Hoosier Folklore* March 12, Shoes, slippers, old gum boots. — (4) **1862** *N.Y. Tribune* 24 Jan. (Chipman), A gum-coat concealed his uniform. **1885** *Cent. Mag.* XXX. 448/2 He was under the shelter of his gum-cloth coat. — (5) **1856** COZZENS *Sparrowgrass P.* 138 [The baby] sat up rigidly in its mother's lap, . . . cutting its teeth without a gum-ring.

c. In the names of, or with reference to, plants: (1) **gum berry,** the fruit of the black gum; (2) **-berry tree,** the black gum; (3) ***elastic,** (see quots.); (4) ***elemi,** (*a*) (see quot.), *rare,* (*b*) =**gumbo limbo;** (5) **lemon shrub,** =***gum elemi** (*a*), *rare;* (6) **plant,** any one of several plants of the genus *Grindelia* having a gummy coating on the leaves; (7) **tree,** see as a main entry; (8) **weed,** (see quot.).

(1) **1709** LAWSON *Carolina* 116 Neither is it [the flesh of the bear] good, when he feeds on Gum-berries. **1913** EATON *Barn Doors & Byways* 198 Many bears are killed in the swamp, . . . when the leaves are off the trees and the little blue gum-berries, which the bears love, are ripe. — (2) **1894** *Harper's Mag.* Aug. 339/2 The quiet waterways have the peculiar Southern color, which some attribute . . . to contact with the roots of the gumberry-trees. — (3) **1884** SARGENT *Rep. Forests* 102 *Bumelia lanuginosa*. . . Gum Elastic . . . Shittim Wood. **1892** COULTER *Bot. W. Texas* II. 257 Extending from the Gulf States and Lower Mississippi Valley States to the Rio Grande . . . [is found] 'gum elastic.'—(4) (*a*) **1806** SHECUT *Flora Carolinaensis* I. 146 *Amyris elmifera*. Gum Elemi, or Gum Lemon Shrub. . . . [It] is a native of Carolina. . . . It grows to the height of about six feet. (*b*) **1837** [see **gumbo limbo**]. **1884** SARGENT *Rep. Forests* 33 *Bursera gummifera* . . . Gum Elemi. Gumbo Limbo. West Indian Birch. **1933** SMALL *Southeastern Flora* 764 E[laphrium] Simaruba . . . West-Indian birch. Gumbo-limbo. Gum-elemi.

(5) **1806** [see **gum elemi** (*a*)]. — (6) **1885** HAVARD *Flora W. & S. Texas* 522 *Grindelia squarrosa*, Dunal. (Gum Plant.) Common on prairies west of the Pecos, and . . . useful in bronchial affections and as a topical application in (Ivy) poisoning. — (8) **1933** CHELEY *Camping Out* 513 Fluid extract of California tarweed or gumweed (*Grindelia robusta*) is said to be beneficial in treating this poison.

Also *gum knot, land, log, plank, wood,* etc.

d. *To come the gum over*, to hoodwink, deceive. *Slang. Obs.* Cf. **gum game,** as a main entry.

1884 J. MITCHELL *Nantucketisms* 40 'He tried to cum the gum over him, but, By Golla! Lijah was up & dressed.' Ready—not to be taken in.

As the last term in **ash, bee, canoe, chawing, chewing, chicle, cotton, honey, pine, red, rifle, sour, spruce, spruce chewing, star-leaved, swamp, sweet, tupelo, white gum.**

***gum,** *v.*[1]

1. *intr.* **a.** *To gum up*, (see quot.). *Obs.* **b.** *To go gumming*, to gather or collect gum. *Colloq.*

(a) **1832** WILLIAMSON *Maine* I. 133 Before it retires in November, it [the bear] *gums* up, as the hunters call it, by taking into its stomach a quantity of gum and turpentine as large as a man's fist. — (b) **1850** *Knickerb.* XXXV. 22 My father's mill was close upon a 'gumwoods,' and one Sunday, . . . I went with a lot of boys 'gumming.' **1864** *Wilkes' Spirit of Times* 17 Dec. 242/1 In the afternoon several of the younger members went 'gumming,' as they term collecting the gum of the spruce-tree, so universally chewed down East.

2. *tr.* To impose upon, take in, humbug (a person). *Slang.*

1840 *Spirit of Times* 5 Sep. 324/3 (We.), You are attempting to gum us with these pretended expenses. **1876** HABBERTON *Jericho Road* 106 That'll bring out the truth, if he's tryin' to gum us.

3. To impair or clog as if with gum. Often with *up. Slang.*

1901 *Yale Fun* 27 (We.), The plot that was gummed. **1931** *K.C. Star* 26 Nov. 20 A lot of watchful wives gummed up the plans. **1945** *Chi. D. News* 11 Aug. 4/1 Uncle Sam . . . has a right to demand that his hired hands guard their tongues in order not to gum up the boss' business.

* **gum,** *v.*[2]

1. *tr.* To enlarge and deepen the spaces between the teeth (of a worn saw).

1777 DUNBAR *Life* 41 Begun to gum one of our old saws, having unfortunately broke one of the new ones by the fall of a Log. **1851** CIST *Cincinnati* 237 Circular saws . . . gummed and hammered . . . restored as good as new. **1887** *Scientific Amer.* 26 Feb. 130 The operation of gumming saws with an emery wheel.

2. To bite with the gums.

1893 *Columbus* (Ohio) *Dispatch* 26 Sep., There are rattles, rings and what-not, and a rubber she can 'gum.' **1931** *K.C. Times* 31 July, More recently his grinders gave way, probably due to chewing the rag too much, at any rate he is now gumming it, living off of soup as so many have been doing during the past months of Hoover prosperity.

gumbo ˈgʌmbo, *n.* and *a.* Also **gombo.** [f. a native name for okra in the Bantu of central or northern Angola, Africa.]

1. The okra plant or its pods. Also short for **gumbo soup.**

1805 in *Amer. Pioneer* II. 233 Shrimps are much eaten here [in New Orleans]; also a dish called *gumbo*. This last is made of every eatable substance, and especially of those shrimps which can be caught at any time. **1845** *Bangor Mercury* (Th.), At St. Peter's [Ill.] there is a large commerce carried on between the whites and redskins, for beads and whiskey, in exchange for skins and gumbo. **1905** W. R. BEATTIE *Okra* 5 Okra, or gumbo, as it is commonly called, . . . is a tropical annual belonging to the order Malvaceæ. **1947** *Chi. D. News* 30 Oct. 33/1 Gumbos are New Orleans specialties, and there's a curious lack of uniformity about the ingredients which distinguish the various styles.

2. One of mixed (chiefly French and Indian) blood; a Negro. Also attrib.

The word in this and the following senses may be from Kongo *nkombo*, runaway slave, hence (in **3.**) the language of slaves.

1835 HOFFMAN *Winter in West* II. 11 The seats, rising like the pit of a theatre, were so adjusted as to separate the audience into three divisions: . . . 'gumboes,' Indians, and a negro servant or two made up the third. **1839** ——— *Wild Scenes* II. 113, I saw at once it was an old gumbo hunter, and knowing what a guileless set they are I felt instantly at ease. **1858** *N.Y. Tribune* 13 April 3/3 Gumbo [a Negro] was considerably astonished. **1947** *Sat. Ev. Post* 17 May 103/2 She saw the old gumbo Negro in his ragged overalls.

3. (See quots. 1882, 1931.) Also attrib. Cf. **gumbo French.**

1880 CABLE *Grandissimes* 227 Bras-Coupé . . . mastered the 'Gumbo' dialect in a few weeks. **1882** SALA *Amer. Revisited* (1885) 325 The coloured people [in New Orleans] . . . gabble a wondrous salmagundi of a patois, made up of French, Spanish, and indigenous African, which is known as 'Gumbo.' **1931** READ *La.-French* 122 *Gombo* is also applied to a heavy, sticky soil and to the negro-French patois.

4. Applied, esp. in the western states, to any one of various types of soil suggestive in some way of mucilaginous gumbo soup (see quots. and cf. **prairie gumbo**).

1881 *Chi. Times* 16 April, Such a thing as hard-pan, bed rock near the surface or gumbo is not found here [in Nebraska]. **1894** *Cent. Mag.* Jan. 453/1 Gumbo is . . . the clay of Northern Wyoming. When wet, it is the blackest, stickiest . . . mud that exists on earth. **1898** CY WARMAN *Story of the R.R.* 206 It is on the slope of the Selkirks that the 'gumbo' is found. This is a sandy loam quicksand, which oozes out of the sides of the cuts and covers the tracks. **1948** *Time* 13 Dec. 78/1 Rain turned Tanforan's racing strip into thick, black gumbo.

b. Used attrib. or as adj. with reference to such soils.

1883 *Rep. Indian Affairs* 21 The buildings stand upon about as unfertile a piece of 'gumbo' land as can be found along the river. **1888** ROOSEVELT in *Cent. Mag.* March 659/1 Isolated peaks of sandstone, marl, or 'gumbo' clay, which rain turns into slippery glue. **1895** *Neb. Agric. Exper. Sta. Bul.* No. 43, 107 The effect of subsoiling land having a 'gumbo' subsoil has not been ascertained. **1897** *Boston Transcript* 13 Nov. 12/3 A big gumbo-burning plant at Brubaker, Ill., is now in operation. Gumbo is a sort of clay found in that and other sections of the country, the burning of which produces, in the estimation of railroad people, the best ballasting material possible. **1905** *Bureau of Forestry Bul.* No. 62, 60 Eastern Washington was once covered by a sheet of lava. The rock formed by this lava . . . has weathered into a stiff, dark, claylike or 'gumbo' soil, constituting the famous wheat lands of that region. **1947** PRICE *Trails I Rode* 36 They couldn't go ahead or turn around and go back, and it was raining hard on that gumbo mud.

5. In special combs.: (1) **gumbo ball,** (see quots.), *obs.;* (2) **box,** [cf. Kongo *nkumbi*, a drum] (see quot.), *obs.;* (3) **filé,** see as a main entry; (4) **French,** a French patois used by Negroes and Creoles in Louisiana; (5) **grass,** bluestem, *Andropogon furcatus;* (6) **limbo,** [cf. *ulimbo*, birdlime, in the Bantu speech of Nyasaland, Africa], a small tree of the West Indies, *Bursera simaruba*, also a similar tree, *Simaruba glauca*, found in Florida, also attrib.; (7) **okra,** okra, *rare;* (8) **soup,** any one of various thick, palatable soups in which okra pods are used, sometimes with the addition of powdered sassafras leaves; (9) **town,** a contemptuous term for a small town, *obs.*

(1) **1819** R. L. MASON *Narrative* (1915) 13 Nov. 54 The inhabitants of this part of the country [near Cahokia, Ill.] . . . hold their Gumbo balls twice a week. **1835** HOFFMAN *Winter in West* II. 14 Here [at Prairie du Chien] the officers sometimes amuse themselves in getting up what is called a gumbo ball, which, from the descriptions I have had of them, must be a kind of harlequinade. — (2) **1861** H. JACOBS *Life Slave Girl* 180 A box, covered with sheepskin, is called the gumbo box. — (4) **1838** FLAGG *Far West* II. 36 A spirited colloquy ensued in the patois of these old hamlets—a species of gumbo-French. **1939** LYLE SAXON *Fabulous New Orleans* 271 Then, too, there is the 'gumbo' French . . . —a sort of patois.

(5) **1892** LUMMIS *Tramp Across Continent* 22 Coming back through a patch of thick, tall, gumbo grass . . . a sharp sk-r-r-r-! under my very feet, sent me about a yard into the air. — (6) **1837** J. L. WILLIAMS *Territory of Fla.* 26 (Th.), [The Indians] make bird-lime from the juice of the Gum Elemi, which they call gumbo-limbo. *Ib.* 98 Gum Elemi, called by the inhabitants gumbo-limbo, is a large spreading tree, with a smooth brown bark, which has the appearance of having been varnished. **1890** H. M. FIELD *Bright Skies* 70 Perhaps some old savage, . . . has been punished for his cruelty by being turned into that gumbo-limbo tree. **1948** *Highway Traveler* Dec. 8/1 The gumbo-limbo is so full of life that it is said that fence posts cut from such a tree will grow. — (7) **1855** *Amer. Inst. N.Y. Trans.* 401 They have machinery with which that excellent *gumbo-ochra* is rapidly cut up in thin slices. — (8) **1813** *Cramer's Alman. 1814* (Pittsburgh) 55 Beyond our usual dinner [we had] . . . squashes, stewed tomatoes, boiled corn, and gumbo soup. **1905** W. R. BEATTIE *Okra* 5 The principal use of okra is in soups and various culinary preparations in which meats form an important factor, as in the so-called gumbo soups. — (9) **1832** *Illinois Mo.* May 373, I am on business of importance—more depends on it, than your paltry gumbo town is worth—so, stir yourself, or I'll be shot if I don't make a fuss.

As the last term in **chicken, crab, oyster, prairie, shrimp gumbo.**

gumbo filé. (See quot. 1931.) Cf. **filé,** *n.*

1823 G. A. MCCALL *Lett. from Frontiers* (1868) 121 In a few minutes the door opened, and black François entered with a tureen of *gombo file*, a special favorite in the South. **1880** HEARN *Creole Sketches* (1924) 103 Gombo Filé . . . is made exactly like the other, but with pulverized okra instead of fresh green okra. **1931** READ *La.-French* 122 Gombo . . . now applied . . . to other kinds of gumbo thickened with a powder prepared from sassafras leaves. This powder goes by the name of *filé*, the past participle of French *filer*, 'to twist'; hence *gombo filé* signifies properly 'ropy or stringy gumbo.' **1942** HARLOW *Trees Eastern U.S.* 191 The Choctaw Indians of Louisiana powdered the leaves (then called 'gumbo filet,' 'gombo file,' or 'gumbo zab') and used them for flavoring and giving a ropy consistency to soup.

gumbotil ˈgʌmbɑtl, *n.* [**gumbo 4.** + **till*, glacial drift, so named by G. F. Key of the Iowa Geological Survey.] A slick, dark-colored clay. — **1931** *Nature* 3 Jan. 7 Gumbotils and the Pleistocene Succession.

gumdrop ˈgʌmˌdrɑp, *n.* A small, roundish candy, usu. made of corn sirup to which gelatin or gum arabic has been added. Also attrib. and fig.

1860 *North-West* (Port Townsend, Wash.) 5 July 3/3 Candies, Gum Drops, Mottoes. **1870** O. LOGAN *Before Footlights* 262 How those poor little wretches get a livelihood is a mystery to me; certainly it is not through the activity of their business in the gum-drop line. **1902**

WILSON *Spenders* 344 Think of a husky, two-fisted boy like him lettin' himself be called by a measly little gum-drop name like Percival. **1944** HOLTON *Yankees* 182 No matter how earnestly he might look at a dime added to the price of a pair of pants, he thought nothing of spending two dimes on gumdrops.

gum game. An attempt at deception, a trick, usu. in the phrase *to come the gum game over. Slang.*

1840 in *Amer. Sp.* XVI. (1941) 299 I've come the gum game over you. **1859** BARTLETT 185 Opossums and raccoons, when pursued, will fly for refuge to the Sweet Gum tree, in preference to any other. . . . This is called 'coming the *gum game*' over the hunter. **1885** *Lisbon* (Dak.) *Star* 18 Sep., They tried the gum-game on me down in Pennsylvania . . . but I came out ahead.

gummation gʌˈmeʃən, *n.* [A fanciful formation.] (See quot. 1851.) *Obs.* — **1832** *Tour through College* 13 We soon found ourselves subject to all manner of sly tricks and '*gummations*.' **1851** HALL *College Words* 155 *Gummation*, a trick; raillery.

gummer ˈgʌmɚ, *n.* [in **1.** f. ∗**gum,** *v.*²; in **2.** f. ∗**gum,** *v.*¹] **1.** A machine for gumming saws; also one who gums saws. Cf. **saw gummer. 2.** An apparatus for putting gum on envelopes. *Rare.*

(1) 1859 BARTLETT 185 *To Gum a Saw*, to punch out and give the set to the teeth of a saw, by means of a machine called a *gummer*. **1907** *Springfield W. Republican* 3 Oct. 3 The Maine 'gummer' puts in about two months in the woods in the fall. — **(2) 1876** INGRAM *Centennial Exp.* 165 Over this plate was the gummer, a die on a revolving shaft, the shaft working on two supports, with a vertical motion.

gumming card. (See quot.) *Obs.* — **1851** HALL *College Words* 122 A man writes cards during examinations to '*freeze* the profs'; said cards are 'gumming cards.'

gummy ˈgʌmɪ, *interj.* [Jocular f. "by gum!"] A euphemistic oath. *Colloq.*

1845 JUDD *Margaret* I. xvi. 139 'Gummy!' retorted the woman. 'He has been a talkin' about me.' **1904** PORTER *Freckles* 57, I'll be having a book about all the birds. . . . Yes, by gummy! **1928** *Sat. Ev. Post* 12 May 27/2 Gummy, you 'n' me better go out and spy around some.

∗**gumption,** *n.* (See quot.) *Colloq. Obs.* — **1881** in M. R. WARNER *P. T. Barnum* (1923) 13 Everybody [in 1810] had barrels of cider in their cellars and cider-spirits called 'gumption.'

gumshoe ˈgʌmˌʃu, *n.*

1. *pl.* Shoes, usu. with canvas uppers, having rubber soles; also rubber overshoes.

1863 *Young Parson* 12 A little boy who wore his father's gum shoes in dry weather. **1881** *American* IV. 186 [The] invention of Goodyear, who gave us the gum-shoes. **1931** *Randolph Enterprise* (Elkins, W.Va.) 12 Feb. 8 (*advt.*), Boys' Gum Shoes . . . $2.39.

2. *transf.* and *fig.* A symbol of something that goes about quietly; a detective; **gumshoe campaign,** a political campaign carried on quietly.

1904 *Omaha Bee* 24 Oct. 4 No gumshoe democratic campaign in Nebraska. **1906** QUICK *Double Trouble* 230 No noise for ours, anyhow. The gum-shoe is our emblem, and we don't let our right hand know what our left wing is driving at. **1920** I. OSTRANDER *How Many Cards?* 8 Maybe my old friend Inspector Druet . . . could happen along up here before the gumshoes from the bushes have a chance to ball the game. **1948** CHAPLIN *Wobbly* 214 We were already being shadowed night and day by federal and city 'gumshoes.'

gumshoe ˈgʌmˌʃu, *v. intr.* To go about noiselessly, to sneak about. *Colloq.* — **1912** NICHOLSON *Hoosier Chron.* 463, I always knew you didn't belong in that bunch of lobbyists that was always gumshoeing through the marble halls of the State House. **1948** *Sat. Ev. Post* 14 Aug. 101/2 I'm satisfied that old A.B. Carr is up there gumshoeing around for no particular good.

gumshoer ˈgʌmˌʃuɚ, *n.* One who goes about without noise, a sneak. *Colloq.* — **1910** O. HENRY *Strictly Business* 59 You're a funny kind of sleuth. You must be one of the Central Office gumshoers.

gum sucking. (See quots.) *Slang. Obs.*

1871 DE VERE 420 The resinous gum exuding from these trees [*sc.* the Black Gum and Sour Gum] and the Juniper is much used for chewing in North Carolina, Virginia, and the Western States, where *gumsuckings* are quite a festive occasion for the votaries of that amusement. *c***1873** ——— *MS Notes* 420 *Gumsucking* =kiss[in]g in Ky. and Tenn.; coupled with *neck-sawing*. **1877** BARTLETT 271 *Gum-Sucking*, a disgusting word, applied to the tendency of lovers, young ones especially, to carry their innocent endearments to an excess that displeases a third party. A friend informs me that he first heard it at Princeton College, in 1854, and thinks it may be a Jersey word.

gum tickler. (See quot. 1810.) *Slang. Obs.*

1810 J. LAMBERT *Travels* (1813) II. 299 A *gum-tickler* is a gill of spirits, generally rum, taken fasting. **1840** HALIBURTON *Clockmaker* 3 Ser. xi, Name your drink, my man, and let's have a gum tickler, for old acquaintance. **1862** MACDERMOTT *Guide to Int. Exhib.* 185 Visiters may indulge in 'juleps,' 'cocktails,' 'cobblers,' 'rattlesnakes,' 'gum-ticklers,' 'eye-openers,' . . . and a variety of similar beverages.

gum tree. A black gum or sweet gum.

1676 T. GLOVER in *Phil. Trans.* XI. 628 There is likewise black Walnut, . . . Gum-tree, Locust, . . . with several others. **1737** WESLEY *Journal* I. 402 [In Ga.] the soil is a blackish sand, producing . . . sumach-trees, gum-trees (a sort of sycamore), dog-trees. **1894** ALLEN *Kentucky Cardinal* ii, The gum-tree . . . stands a pillar of red twilight fire in the dark November woods.

attrib. **1856** STOWE *Dred* I. 287 The gum-tree cradle trough took precedence of all other articles.

b. (See quot.)

1914 *Bul. Dep. Hist. Queens Univ.* No. 12, 13 He then selected what was known as a gumtree, being a tree with a hollow trunk from which could be cut a section known as a gum.

∗**gun,** *n.*

1. A revolver or pistol. Cf. **gun battle, carrying, fight,** etc., in **3.**

1744 A. HAMILTON *Itin.* (1907) 150 'Then surely you had needs ride with guns' (meaning my pistols). **1851** GLISAN *Jrnl. Army Life* 80 He might . . . not fire unless his gun has a revolving chamber with more than one load. **1914** BOWER *Flying U Ranch* 208 Now you keep your hand away from that gun—that you ain't honest enough to carry where folks can see it, but 've got it cached in your pocket! **1948** *This Week Mag.* 9 Oct. 22/2 Police believe that if more people carried guns, murders and suicides would zoom.

2. A militiaman armed with a gun. *Rare.*

1837 BIRD *Nick of Woods* I. 38 'What force do you tote down to the Falls tomorrow?' 'Twenty-seven guns in all; but several quite too young to face an enemy.' *Ib.* 94 If your men will fight, . . . march your guns after me.

b. A thief or pickpocket; a gunman or thug. *Slang.*

1865 *Police Gazette* (N.Y.) 8 July 4/1, I leave my readers to guess how they made things pay during the season, and the 'guns' who go there do so likewise—leastwise the bulk of them do. **1910** *N. Eng. Mag.* July 587/1 'A gun' is a thief who does not use force, somewhat of a paradox. **1916** *Amer. Mag.* May 15/1 'You're no burglar—you're a bungler.' 'Well, . . . Nobody ever showed me. I'm a self made gun, I am.'

3. In combs.: (1) ∗**gun carrying,** going about armed with a revolver; (2) ∗**flint,** see as a main entry; (3) **house,** formerly in New England a house in which the guns of the militia were kept, *obs.*; (4) **moll,** a girl or woman who associates with gangsters, *slang;* (5) **opera,** a western movie, *slang;* (6) **play,** a shooting affray; (7) **sling,** a strap attached to a gun to suspend it from the shoulders; (8) **-sman,** see as a main entry; (9) **store,** a store in which guns are sold; (10) **tow,** gun cotton, *rare.*

(1) 1927 *Cleveland Press* 29 Jan., The present *gun-carrying* evil in the country. — **(3) 1725–6** *Boston Selectmen* 148 The Select men then Lett to mr Joseph Russell the use of the Gun House in the Common. **1776** *Essex Inst. Coll.* XLII. 205 We took our Departure from the Gun House in the Training field. **1825** NEAL *Bro. Jonathan* III. 54 The large doors of a gun-house, flew open. — **(4) 1910** *N. Eng. Mag.* July 587/2 A woman thief is called a 'gun-moll.' **1932** *Fort Worth Star-Telegram* 21 Feb. 1/3 The gun molls of greater gangland are going into the big time. **1949** *L.A. Times* 7 April 23/1 Teen-age gun molls—more vicious than their male companions—are reported operating in Brooklyn.

(5) 1921 *Collier's* 11 June 23/1, I am fed up on makin' these gun-opera serials. — **(6) 1881** in BEEBE *Mixed Train Dly.* (1947) 124 He has been the hero of several 'gun plays' recently and has been reported wounded and killed several times. **1947** *Loyola News* (Chi.) 6 Nov. 10/4 From then on the plot is as usual. Gunplay, threats, and Dr. Christian to the rescue—exercising those phenomenal faculties of analysis and crime-detection that led him to the practice of medicine. — **(7) 1812** *Niles' Reg.* II. 131/1 The purveyor of public supplies advertises for . . . 2500 gun slings. **1861** *Army Regulations* 405 Implements, Equipments for Small Arms: . . . Gun slings. Waist belts, blackleather [etc.]. — **(9) 1866** F. KIRKLAND *Book Anecdotes* 161 A matronly lady, accompanied by her son, . . . entered a gun-store on Broadway, New York, and purchased a full outfit for him.

(10) 1850 *Rep. Comm. Patents 1849: Agric.* 506 Gun-tow or cotton, . . . seems more promising than gunpowder.

b. In combs. alluding esp. to the West: (1) **gun battle,** =**gun fight;** (2) **fanner,** one who carries or "fans" a revolver, also **gun fanning,** cf. ∗**fan,** *v.* **4.** (3) ∗**fight,** a fight with pistols or revolvers, a shooting scrape; (4) **fighter,** one accustomed to engage in gun fights; (5) **fighting,** fighting with revolvers as weapons, also as adj.; (6) **hand,** the hand used in firing a pistol or revolver, *rare;* (7) **handler,** a gun fighter, *rare;* (8)

∗ **man,** a desperado or gangster; (9) **pulling,** drawing a revolver from its holster.

(1) **1945** *Everybody's Digest* Aug. 89 A gun battle used to bring a puncher out 'a-smokin.'' — (2) **1903** *Cin. Enquirer* 2 May 12/2 [Gambling houses] took it as a regular thing and they were glad to chip in to that extent for the night gun fanner [i.e., night marshal]. *Ib.* 30 May 12/1, I ain't goin't' let no gun-fannin' ombrey in this camp stick me up and poke lead into my frame. — (3) **1898** CRANE in *McClure's Mag.* Feb. 380 You don't mean there is going to be a gun-fight? **1948** JOHNSTON *Gold Rush* 19/2 In the doorway leading to that barroom from the street, bullet holes bear witness to a gunfight. — (4) **1894** *S.F. Midwinter Appeal* 27 Jan. 2/3 The gun-fighters rushed up with cocked revolvers and ordered him to halt. **1938** ASBURY *Sucker's Prog.* 345 Their agent and front man was the Chief of Police, James Marshall, a gambler and gun-fighter known as Three-Fingered Jim.

(5) **1924** R. CUMMINS *Sky-High Corral* 34, I hear the Forest lads have got a gun-fighting bad man coming up to run him out. **1947** *True* Nov. 29/1 To most people gun fighting means something that was done a long time ago. — (6) **1907** MULFORD *Bar-20* 4 He . . . worked the hammer with the thumb of the 'gun hand.' — (7) **1928** FOY & HARLOW *Clowning Thro' Life* 111 Such men rather eagerly welcomed the chance when some noted gun-handler gave them an excuse to shoot. — (8) **1903** *N.Y. Sun* 23 Nov. 1 A notorious outlaw and one of the most expert gun men of the West. **1949** *Chi. D. News* 18 Feb. 1/7 Three of the gunmen located the safe. — (9) *a*1909 O. HENRY *Roads of Destiny* xvi. 271 The bystanders asserted that it was met by the most beautiful exhibition of lightning gun-pulling ever witnessed in the Southwest.

c. In combs., often occasional and obs., of obvious meaning or sufficiently explained in the quots., as (1) ∗ **gunboat,** (see also **cotton, tinclad gunboat** and cf. **gum boot**), (2) **car,** (3) **closet,** (4) **dance,** (5) **factory,** (6) **greaser,** (7) **shop,** (8) **toter,** (9) **toting.**

(1) **1870** MACRAE *Americans* I. 68 Most of the people wear rubbers over their boots—gunboats as they sometimes call them from their size. — (2) **1895** WAIT *Car-Builder's Dict.* 64 Gun-car or cannon-car. A specially heavy car for transporting ordnance, often having sixteen wheels. — (3) **1927** SIRINGO *Riata* 105 In his hands was the shotgun. This he had secured by kicking open the door to the gun-closet. — (4) **1800** B. HAWKINS *Sk. Creek Country* 76 This day, about ten o'clock, the women dance Its-ho-bun-gau, (gun dance).

(5) **1780** *Va. State P.* I. 372, I received your favour . . . with the warrant for Six thousand pounds on account of the Gun Factory. **1912** *New Chapter in Old Story* (Remington Co.) 20 At this time [1816] there were no real gun-factories in America, although gunsmiths were located in most of the larger towns. — (6) **1875** *Fur, Fin, & Feather* 826 The smaller species of loon I have heard variously called the spike-bill, . . . the gun-greaser [etc.]. — (7) **1865** *Atlantic Mo.* XV. 717 The better class of workmen had gone to Springfield or to private gun-shops in the North. **1902** CLAPIN 218 *Gun-shop,* a gun-smith's shop. — (8) **1925** O. P. WHITE *Them Was Days* 120 This opened up the field for the renegade white man . . . the gun-toter [etc.]. **1948** *Sat. Review* 28 Aug. 37/1 His steps were the measured pace of a gun toter. — (9) **1912** I. COBB *Back Home* 293, I reckon none of you young fellows . . . can remember when this wasn't a gun-toting country down here? **1949** *Sat. Ev. Post* 28 May 158/3 There a gun-toting sheriff openly charged us with car stealing.

As the last term in **alligator, ball, BB, bear, bird, black, blow, buffalo, cap, Christmas, hinge, Indian, mackinaw, Napoleon, northwest, northwestern, Parrott, potato, Rodman, saddle, sausage, scatter, secesh, set, shot, six, Springfield, squirrel, squirt, steamboat, trade, two, union, Washington, whaling gun.**

∗ **gun,** *v.*

1. *intr.* To hunt for, or shoot at, game with a gun.

1698 SEWALL *Diary* I. 432 Purchase Capen had been Gunning, or shot a fowl by the by as was at work. **1809** *Mass. Spy* 22 Nov. (Th.), Mr. Joseph Bagley and Mr. Obed Rice went down the river, gunning. **1910** *N.Y. Ev. Post* 9 Dec. 1 He had been out gunning for ducks.

b. To fight with guns. *Obs.*

1835 *Knickerb.* V. 145 The inference instantly transpired over town, that we had 'gone gunning at each other,'—or in other words, to fight a duel. **1865** GRANT in *Cent. Mag.* XVII. 146/2 The whole captures since the army started out gunning will amount to not less than twelve thousand men and probably fifty pieces of artillery.

c. *fig.* To seek out with the intention of settling a dispute or quarrel or with the purpose of getting support or favor. With *after* or *for. Slang.*

1882 *Cong. Rec.* 9 Feb. 1012/1 The Senator from Kentucky (Mr. Beck) went gunning after the Senator from Vermont (Mr. Morrill) on account of some unguarded declarations he made. **1894** *Harper's Mag.* May 972/2 The people saw that they must unload or lose their money, so they sent the Mayor East to gun for capitalists. **1908** SINCLAIR *Metropolis* 153 Mrs. Vivie wished to go home, and asked him to find her escort, . . . for whom her husband was gunning. **1948** *Range Riders Western* May 21/1 If Min dies, I'll be gunnin' for you.

2. *tr.* (*a*) To shoot (game), *obs.,* (*b*) to shoot (a person), *slang.*

(*a*) **1790** *Mass. Centinel* 1 May, The frequency of persons gunning or shooting birds, at various parts of the town, in direct violation of the law. (*b*) **1898** CANFIELD *Maid of Frontier* 83, I'll gun you if you do that again. **1916** WILSON *Somewhere* 35 Wilfred went pasty, indeed, thinking his host was going to gun him.

3. (See quots.)

1870 MEDBERY *Men Wall St.* 136 Gunning a stock, is to use every art to produce a 'break,' when it is known that a certain house is heavily supplied, and would be unable to resist an attack. **1905** *Forestry Bureau Bul.* No. 61, 39 *Gun,* to aim a tree in felling it. In the case of very large, brittle trees, such as redwood, a sighting device (gunning stick) is used. P[acific] C[oast] F[orest].

gundalow, see **gondola.**

∗ **gunflint,** *n.*

1. (See quot. 1814.) *Obs.*

1814 MITCHELL in *Mineral. Jrnl.* I. 3 Black flint or gun flint . . . abounds at Blackrock and in the Seneka prairies, imbedded in limestone. **1819** SCHOOLCRAFT *Mo. Lead Mines* 180 Pervading the chalk, are found . . . occasionally nodules of pure black gun flint.

2. (*cap.*) (See quots.) *Obs.*

1845 *St. Louis Reveille* 14 May 2/4 The inhabitants of . . . Rhode Island are called] Gun Flints. **1949** *Amer. Sp.* Feb. 27 To this list may be added . . . *Gunflint* for a Rhode Islander.

3. *By gunflints!* a mild imprecation. *Colloq.*

1847 ROBB *Squatter Life* 62 The young ones at the table would . . . look at my straps . . . till at last the old man seed 'em. 'Well, by gun flints,' said he, 'ef you ain't makin' a josey.'

As the last term in **horn gunflint.**

gunja ˈgʌndʒə, *n. S.* [App. African f. Hansa *kanja, ganja,* ginger. Cf. Gullah *kanja, kanjabread,* a kind of molasses bread.] A form of sponge cake sweetened with molasses (see quot. 1939). *Colloq.*

1836 SIMMS *Mellichampe* 393 Take piece of gunja—he berry good, Mass Booram—My wife make 'em. **1852** *As Good as a Comedy* 50 (Th.), [The damsels are] spreading their baskets of cakes, gunjas, as they call them, and boiling huge vessels of coffee. **1939** HARRIS *Purslane* 3 The supper dishes washed, the milk set to clabber, a pan of gungers [footnote: Molasses cookies] made for tomorrow, Dele slipped into the shed room.

gunsman ˈgʌnzmən, *n.*

1. (See quot.) *Obs.*

1766 in W. SMITH *Bouquet's Exped.* (1868) 156 In this list their warriors or gunsmen are 1180, and their inhabitants about 6000.

2. A marksman. *Obs.*

1775 ADAIR *Indians* 281 The outmost boundaries of the colony, where commonly the best gunsmen reside. **1818** *Nashville* (Tenn.) *Clarion* 17 Nov. 2/1 The Americans are unquestionably the most excellent guns-men in the world.

3. A hunter. *Rare.*

1906 LYNDE *Quickening* 371 There were bones with meat on them to be had without following a gunsman who never shot anything, miles on end on the mountain side.

∗ **Gunter,** *n.* [Edmund *Gunter* (1581–1626), English mathematician.]

1. *Gauging by Gunter,* gauging by the most exact methods. *Obs.*

1751 *R.I. Acts & Resolves* 22 No Rum, Molasses, Wine, Cyder, Beer, Brandy, or any other Liquid whatsoever, usually sold by Measure in Casks, shall be gagued [*sic*] in any other Way or Method, but according to the most approved and exact mathematical Rule, commonly called, Gauging by *Gunter.* **1923** *R.I. Gen. Laws* 871 All casks which shall be gauged in this state shall be gauged by the method or rule commonly called 'gauging by Gunter.'

2. *According to Gunter,* in the proper manner, correctly. *Obs.*

1843 STEPHENS *High Life N.Y.* I. 145 If I don't du everything according to gunter, he'll be turning red and fussing about like an old hen. *a*1859 *N.Y. Tribune* (B.), Mr. K. . . . has published a letter entirely exonerating General Cass from the charge of having defrauded his association in the land speculations. He was positive that all was done according to Gunter.

∗ **gurnard,** *n.* Any one of various spiny-finned fishes of the genus *Merlinus* or *Prionotus.* Cf. **banded gurney, sea robin.**

1778 J. ADAMS *Diary* Wks. III. 116 This forenoon a fisherman came alongside, with hakes, skates, and gurnards. **1814** MITCHILL *Fishes*

N.Y. 430 Gurnard, or Sea Robin. *Trigla Lineata.* **1911** *Rep. Fisheries 1908* 315/2 Sea robin (*Prionotus carolinus*). . . . They are also called 'gurnards,' 'wing-fish,' 'sea bat,' etc.

gurnipper 'gɜ͵nɪpɚ, *n.* [Origin obscure.] = **gallinipper.** *Obs.* — **1634** Wood *N. Eng. Prospect* I. xi. 46 The third [fly] is Gurnipper which is a small blacke fly no bigger than a flea; her biting causeth an itching upon the hands or face, which provoketh scratching. **1674** Josselyn *Two Voyages* 122 There is another sort of fly called a Gurnipper that are like our horse-flyes, and will bite desperately.

gurry 'gɜɪ, *n.* [Origin obscure.]

1. The offal of fish, fish oil (see quots.).

1776 *R.I. Col. Rec.* (1862) VII. 493 They have a sloop with a large quantity of oil and gurry, at Gaspee, in the province of Canada. **1838** *Mass. Agric. Survey 1st Rep.* 101 Animal Manures. Fish. Fish oil. Gurry and blubber. **1850** Cheever *Whale & Captors* 204 *Gurry* is the term by which they call the combined water, oil, and dirt that 'cutting in' a whale leaves on deck and below. **1939** Colby *Guide to Alaska* xl, *gurry n.* (A.) the offal from a fish cannery.

2. gurry shark, (see quot.).

1884 Goode *Fisheries* I. 675 The 'Gurry' or Ground Shark . . . on our coast ranges south to Cape Cod.

***gush,** *n.* A large quantity, an abundance. *Colloq.* See **ice gush.** — **1849** *Knickerb.* XXXIV. 407/2 Shese a powerfull big boat, and kin tote a gush of pork. **1859** Bartlett 186 *Gush,* a great abundance. A Texan would say, 'We have got a gush of peaches in our neck of the woods.'

***gusher,** *n.* An oil well with a profuse natural flow.

1886 *Pall Mall Gaz.* 13 Oct. 6/1 Tagieff's 'gusher' beats out and out every previous record in the oil regions of the two hemispheres. **1903** *Out West* Feb. 148 There are scores of 'gushers' among the several thousand oil wells of California. **1945** *Elk Mt. Pilot* (Crested Butte, Colo.) 19 July 4/6 'Gushers' are no longer permitted to perform except for the comparatively short interval required for the drilling crew to control the flow induced by high gas pressure.

***guttersnipe,** *n.*

1. "A Wall Street term for brokers who do business chiefly on the sidewalk or in the street, and who are not members of the Stock Exchange" (Bartlett '77).

1856 in *Amer. Sp.* XII. 115/2 He belongs to a class of beings in New York . . . known by the ornithological appellation of '*gutter-snipes.*' **1885** *Harper's Mag.* Nov. 842/2 Quoting the vernacular of the Board Room: 'The gutter snipe carries his office in his hat.'

2. (See quots.)

1871 L. Ringwalt *Amer. Encycl. Printing* 193/1 *Gutter-Snipe,* a small and narrow bill or poster, which is usually pasted on curbstones. **1874** R. Ridgway *Birds Ill.* in *Annals Lyceum N.Y.* X. 383 *G[allinago] gallinaria* . . . var. *Wilsonii.* . . . Common Snipe; Gutter Snipe; English Snipe.

***guy,** *n.*[1] A male person, a fellow. *Slang.* Cf. **fall guy, wise guy.** — **1896** Ade *Artie* 3 You guys must think I'm a quitter. **1948** *Chi. Tribune* 16 May (Comics) 6 I'll take on guys my size, any old time.

guy gaɪ, *n.*[2] [f. **guy, v.* to ridicule.] A joke. *Slang.* — **1887** *Cong. Rec.* 1022/1 He was a democrat, as he says, for a 'guy.' **1911** J. C. Lincoln *Cap'n Warren's Wards* iii, 37, I was only joking. . . . It's a standing guy, you know.

guy gaɪ, *interj.* An exclamation, app. orig. **guyhang it!** *Obs.*

*c*1815 Paulding *Bucktails* (1847) III. 46 But don't you know, guyhang it, if there be two of anything, one can swear for the other. **1838** *Knickerb.* XII. 297 'Guy!' said he, in a tone which seemed hardly to realize the truth, 'I b'lieve I'm upsot!' *c*1845 Paulding *Noble Exile* 140 Guy, he's as careful as a city mosquito in the autumn.

***guy,** *v.*

1. *tr.* To trifle with (a theatrical part), to distort or make absurd. *Obs.*

1890 J. Jefferson *Autobiog.* 219 With all this at stake, some wanton actor deliberately 'guys' his part and overturns the patient care of his comrade. **1891** *N.Y. Herald* 31 May 12/4 (F. and H.), I would remind them that they are apt to 'guy' their cause by making guys of themselves, and that the best way of making women a power in the land is by encouraging them to be womanly women.

2. *To guy the life out of* (someone), to joke or tease (one) unmercifully. *Colloq.*

1880 Ranous *Diary of Daly Débutante* 200, I am glad Harry Lacy and John Drew are not here. . . . They would 'guy' the life out of us. **1902** L. Bell *Hope Loring* 120 I'd have had the life guyed out of me if I'd let a girl wear such a looking thing.

guyanosa ͵gaɪə'nosə, *n.* Also **gyanousa.** [A fanciful formation.] = next. *Obs.* — **1846** *Knickerb.* XXVIII. 37 The Gyanousa, from the disputed territory of Penobscot; a monster of gigantic proportions. He vegetates on the tops of trees, and gets his living on the tallest branches of the poplar. *Ib.* 38 Ladies and gentlemen! leave the house immediately! Save yourselves! The Gya nousa am loose! **1853** *Harper's Mag.* Oct. 709/1 The lecturer dwelt at some length upon . . . the ravenous nature of the *Guyanosa,* and his enormous strength.

guyascutus ͵gaɪəs'kʌtəs, *n.* Also **guyasticutus,** etc. [A fanciful formation.]

1. An imaginary animal of an extremely ferocious, terriifying kind. Also transf.

The story of the *guyanosa* or *guyascutus* (see *Knickerbocker Mag.* XXVIII. 36–38 and *Harper's Mag.* VII. 708–709) tells of some sharpers who sold tickets to the public to see this strange and savage animal. When the time came to reveal the much advertised monster, the sharpers set up a great din behind the scenes and then excitedly shouted to the audience to flee for their lives, that "the guyanosa am loose." For a discussion of this term and others of a similar nature see Mencken, *Supp.* I. 245 ff.

1846 in *Amer. Sp.* XXI. (1946) 117/2 The Guiaskiutus is not only remarkable for his ferocious appearance, but for the terrible tones of his voice. **1869** *Overland Mo.* III. 130 When one of the fellows is a 'guyascutus,' and the other is a 'kiamuck,' you may look for some rare sport. **1911** Saunders *Col. Todhunter* 132 Blamed if you wouldn't ha' thought I was the original roarin' ring-tailed guyasticutus of Calveras County. **1948** Mencken *Supp.* II. 627 His labors lifted the bird at one stroke to the level of the guyascutus, . . . the wiffle-poofle and other such fauna of the Great Plains.

2. A homemade device for producing noise. Also attrib. *Obs.*

1854 H. H. Riley *Puddleford* 94 (Th.), The 'gyastacutus' was a nailkeg, with a raw hide strained over it, like a drum-head, and inside of the keg, attached to the center of this drum-head, a string hung, with which the instrument was worked. **1855** in Blair *Amer. Humor* (1937) 395 This glorious composition was produced . . . by a very full orchestra . . . and a chorus composed of the entire 'Sauer Kraut-Verein,' the 'Wee Gates Association,' and choice selections from the 'Gyascutus' and 'Pikeharmonic' societies.

guyer 'gaɪɚ, *n.* One who guys or pokes fun at (others) in a good-natured manner. *Colloq.* — **1879** Ranous *Diary of Daly Débutante* 23 I don't think even Mr. Daly has discovered what an inveterate 'guyer' he [John Drew] is. **1902** Clara Morris *Life on Stage* 30, I had not been more than two or three days in the theatre when I discovered that its people seemed to be divided into two distinct parties —the guyers and the guyed—those who laughed and those who were laughed at.

***gym,** *n.* A school course in athletic exercise. *Colloq.* — **1897** *Scribner's Mag.* XXII. 154/2 Very few college women live in golf clothes or sweaters; . . . most of them detest 'gym,' and evade its practice whenever they can.

gyp dʒɪp, n.[1] [Poss. f. *Gypsy* or *Gyp,* used as a proper name for a bitch.] A bitch.

1890 J. Cooke in G. O. Shields *Big Game N. Amer.* 48 Old Tige had filled up on the first Deer's inwards. He looked like a gyp, and near her time. **1895** A. Hunter in *Outing* XXVII. 75/2 One of the pack— a long-limbed gyp named Queen . . . covered with black pitch-like mud. **1927** Birney *King of Mesa* 19, I see a little fox-terrier gyp one time lick the living daylights outa a bull-dog.

gyp dʒɪp, *n.*[2] *W.* [App. f. **gypsum.*]

1. Water that is alkaline or otherwise brackish and unusable. In full **gyp water.** *Colloq.*

1904 D. H. Biggers *From Cattle Range to Cotton Patch* (1944) 30 The water in the Clear Fork . . . was 'gyp' and wholly unfit to drink. **1909** *Pioneer Days Southwest* 314 We all started up the river to the water and when we got there it was alkali or jip. **1948** *Neb. Hist.* June 101 'Gyp water' was a sore trial to many a family, while livestock often died from the effects of drinking 'alkali water.'

b. Also **gyp well.**

1942 Philips *Big Spring* 187 The dry creek on the road to the Spring had several gyp wells of shallow water. When this water was first drawn, it was extremely cold and had no taste at all, but the result was the same as Epsom salts.

2. gyprock, ?gypsum.

1943 L. V. Hamner *Short Grass* 7 Walls were whitewashed by baking 'gyprock,' crushing it, and mixing it with water to form a plaster.

gypsy weed. A local name for the common speedwell. — **1894** *Amer. Folk-Lore* VII. 96 Veronica officinalis, . . . gypsy-weed, West Va.

H

∗**H,** *n.* **1.** (See quot.) **2. H rail,** a railroad rail a cross section of which had the shape of the letter H. Both *obs.*

(1) **1661** G. Bishop *N. Eng. Judged* (1703) 204 H. Norton was . . . burnt in the Hand with the Letter (H) for Heresie. — (2) **1848** *Hunt's Merch. Mag.* XVIII. 94 The H rail is used. **1857** *Spirit of Times* 20 June 244/1 The 'T' rail . . . has since given place, in a measure, to a still heavier one, the 'H' rail, also his [Robert L. Stevens] invention.

∗**haberdasher,** *n.* A dealer in men's wear.

1887 (*title*), The Haberdasher. **1917** McCutcheon *Green Fancy* 78 The names of the haberdasher, the hat dealer and the book maker had been as effectually destroyed. **1949** *Time* 13 June 17/3 The one-time haberdasher whipped off his four-in-hand, skillfully knotted the bow tie without looking in a mirror.

habitant ˈhæbətənt, *n.* Also **habitan.** [F., an Amer. borrowing.] A French farmer or his descendant in Louisiana or Canada.

[**1719** in Pierre Margry *Découvertes* VI. (1888) 250 Nous fismes rencontre d'une pirogue, appartenant au nommé Beaulieu, habitant des Natchitoches, lequel descendoit à la Nouvelle-Orleans chargé de mahis, d'huile d'ours et de tabac.] **1814** in Cox *Adv. Columbia R.* 131 Then what a glorious winter in Montreal, with captured Jonathans, triumphant Britons, astonished Indians, gaping *habitans* [etc.]. **1901** *Harper's Wkly.* XLV. 312 He did it simply as part of his duty; if he didn't, some other habitant would. **1948** *Time* 4 Oct. 35/3 The sons of the *habitants* wanted to know about engineering and business.

attrib. **1948** *Amer. Folk-Lore* April–June 119 He spoke habitant French, and was quite a character.

hacendado ˌɑsɛnˈdɑdo, *n. S.W.* [Sp. in same sense.] The owner of a ranch or farm.

1840 David Turnbull *Travels in West* 98 (Bentley), In the unexpected case of the confiscation of the rural property of a Hacendado, the civil judge of the district . . . is directed to proceed to the spot. **1910** *Sat. Ev. Post* 3 Sep. 20/2 The vast estates of the old *hidalgo hacendado* would still stretch for many thousands of acres with never a fence. **1948** *Pacific Spectator* Winter 101 The martyred death of Francisco I. Madero, and the agrarian movement of Francisco Villa, . . . have all been commented upon, . . . as have been also . . . the less glamorous but no less dramatic actions of this or that particular hacendado.

hacienda ˌɑsɪˈɛndə, *n. W.* and *S.W.* [Sp. in sense **2.** An Amer. borrowing.]

1. The principal dwelling on a ranch or estate.

1808 Pike *Sources Miss.* 256 The Hacienda of Pattos was a square enclosure of about three hundred feet, the building being one story high. **1904** *McClure's Mag.* Feb. 358 Rumor painted occasional black doings at the hacienda. **1947** *Nat. Geog. Mag.* Feb. 137/2 Our good friend Don Vicente Rubiera guided us to the beautiful hacienda.

2. The estate or ranch itself.

1825 *Austin P.* (1924) II. 1016 He sends you the Notes of my Hacienda and the notes of Gates Tract. **1875** Bourke *Journal* 5 April, The rich haciendas of Short, Wilson, Stoneman and others lined the way and prepared us in some measure for the bright little city of the Angels. **1948** *N.M. Hist. Rev.* July 170 The post office was originally located in a small room at the Celso Baca y Baca hacienda.

attrib. **1944** *Harper's Mag.* Aug. 201/2 The Rio Blanco textile works set up in Mexico . . . were designed to produce cloth for sale at hacienda stores to sweated peons.

∗**hack,** *n.* [The uses here shown involve "hacks" of different sources brought together for ease of reference.]

1. a. A chance, a "try," a "whack." *Colloq.* **b.** (See quot.) *Rare.*

(a) **1836** Crockett *Adventures* 79 Better take a hack by way of trying your luck at guessing. **1898** Deland *Old Chester Tales* 244, I get more men in a saloon, . . . and when the show's done, I get a hack at 'em. — (b) **1887** *Forest & Stream* XXVIII. 179/2 Curt and I went into the woods . . . to cut a hack (a blazed line) as a guide in hunting.

2. In combs.: (1) **hackback,** (see quot.), *rare*, cf. **hock-hack;** (2) ∗**berry,** see as a main entry; (3) **line,** a route over which hacks travel on regular schedules; (4) **man,** a hack driver; (5) **road,** a road suitable for hacks, *rare;* (6) **sleigh,** (see quot.); (7) **tree,** a local term for a hackberry tree.

(1) **1824** *Mass. Spy* 3 March (Th.), Hackback is properly a gourd; but since [the Indians] have seen glass bottles and decanters, they call them by the same name. — (3) **1882** *Golden* (N.M.) *Retort* 28 July 3/3 We now have a tri-weekly hack line to Albuquerque, under the management of Mr. L. D. Coffer of that place. **1901** Harben *Westerfelt* 42 The hack-line will pay with the mail it carries an' the passenger travel twixt heer an' Darley. — (4) **1796** *Boston Directory* 238 Culmer, Daniel, hackman, Wing's lane. **1899** Chesnutt *Wife of His Youth* 228 He at length reached the door, beyond which . . . stood a number of hackmen, vociferously soliciting patronage.

(5) **1862** in F. Moore *Rebellion Rec.* V. II. 271 Townshend came in contact with the enemy's pickets near Easel's house, on the 'Hack road,' leading from Purdy to Corinth. — (6) **1937** Mitchell *Horse & Buggy Age* 86 The hack sleighs—hacks with their wheels removed and runners substituted—were apt to be top-heavy. — (7) **1897** Sudworth *Arborescent Flora* 185 *Celtis occidentalis* . . . [is also called] Hack Tree (Minn.).

b. In colloq. phrases: (1) *To bring to a hack,* to show one up, to cause one to renege [cf. Du. *Iemand op den hak nemen,* to make a fool of one, see *WNT,* 1536]; (2) *to be under hack,* (see quot.).

(1) **1835** Longstreet *Ga. Scenes* 27 You cut such high shines, that I thought I'd like to back you out; and I've done it. Gentlemen, you see I've brought him to a hack. — (2) **1899** Green *Va. Word-Book* 173 A person is said to be 'under hack' when he is controlled and ordered by another.

As the last term in **booby, Concord, fair, hard hack.**

∗**hack,** *v.*[1] *intr.* To ride in a hack. *Rare.* — **1879** *Phila. Times* 8 May (*Cent.*), Are we more content to depend on street cars and walking, with the accustomed alternative of hacking at six times the money?

∗**hack,** *v.*[2] *tr.* To embarrass or chagrin. *Colloq.* — **1892** Harris *U. Remus & Friends* 349 When you once git 'em hacked dey er hacked fer good; dey des give right up en roll der eyes. **1917** *D.N.* IV. 413 hack, *v. t.* To annoy; nettle. 'That joke *hacks* Steve to this day.' Ky.

hackamore ˈhækəˌmor, *n. W.* [Sp. *jáquima,* headstall.] (See quot. 1944.)

1850 Ryan *Adventures* I. 100 A leathern blind is attached to the *hackamore* placed ready for that purpose on his forehead, and a strap fastened loosely round his body. **1944** Adams *W. Words* 71 hackamore. . . . It is usually an ordinary halter having reins instead of a leading rope. More commonly it consists of a headpiece something like a bridle with a bosal in place of a bit, and a brow-band about three inches wide that can be slid down the cheeks to cover the horse's eyes, but it has no throat-latch.

Also **hackamore rope.**

1926 Branch *Cowboy* 39 But having the 'hackimore' rope fastened to my belt I held to him until help arrived. **1947** Price *Trails I Rode* 136, I held onto the hackamore rope but he was kicking and bucking around, and on top of me.

∗**hackberry,** *n.*

1. Any one of several varieties of trees or shrubs of the genus *Celtis,* having elmlike leaves and bearing small fruit; also a single tree of one of these species.

1785 V. B. Howard *Heroes* (1932) 144 North . . . to a hackberry marked WIGSIF. **1836** Hildreth *Dragoon Campaigns* I. 95 The sassafras and hackberry send forth their delicious fragrance. **1877** Bartlett 36 The Hoop-ash (*Celtis occidentalis*), or Hackberry, is also called Beaver-wood. **1947** *Democrat* 25 Sep. 4/2 Here it is for what it's worth: pine, oak, . . . hackberry, cedar, pecan.

attrib. **1805** Clark in *Lewis & C. Exped.* (1905) III. 111 No timber of any kind, a few Hackberry bushes & willows excepted.

b. Also **hackberry tree.**

1780 in L. Summers *Hist. S.W. Va.* 700 Marking a Poplar and two Hackberry trees with initials of our names. **1834** A. Pike *Sketches* 53 We found two or three hackberry trees, and several of us delayed, picking the berries. **1949** *Amer. Photography* June 351/2 One of the cubs emerged from the other hole and sat at the base of a hackberry tree.

2. The fruit of the hackberry tree.

1854 GLISAN *Jrnl. Army Life* 132 For nearly a fortnight subsequent to her escape she subsisted upon hackberries. **1870** KEIM *Sheridan's Troopers* 108 The turkey particularly had a richness about it derived from the hackberry upon which it feeds. **1949** *Dly. Oklahoman* (Okla. City) 13 Feb. D. 2/1 During the winter bluebirds feed largely on wild berries, such as cedar, sumach, wild grape, hackberry, greenbrier, mistletoe.

hackee ˈhækɪ, *n.* [Prob. f. its note.] A chipmunk or ground squirrel.

1849 AUDUBON *Quadrupeds N. Amer.* I. 75 The *Tamias striatus* differs ... widely from our American Chipping Squirrel or Hackee. **1863** WOOD *Illust. Nat. Hist.* I. 599 The Hackee ... is one of the most familiar of North American quadrupeds. **1947** CAHALANE *Mammals* 379 Other names applied rarely are 'hackie,' chipping squirrel, striped ground squirrel, and just ground squirrel.

* **hacker,** *n.* One who hacks or cuts turpentine boxes in pines. Cf. **score hacker.** — **1856** OLMSTED *Slave States* 342 The hackers are wholly employed in scarifying the trees. A task, of a certain number of trees, is given to each [Negro], which he is required to go over, hacking each tree, once in seven or eight days.

hackmatack ˈhækməˌtæk, *n.* [f. Algonquian name.] Any one of various species of coniferous trees, such as the larch, juniper, tamarack, or pine. Also a tree of one of these species, or the wood of such a tree.

1792 BELKNAP *Hist. New Hampshire* III. 33 On some mountains we find a shrubbery of hemlock and spruce, whose branches are knit together so as to be impenetrable.... These are called by the Indians, Hakmantaks. **1806** FESSENDEN *Orig. Poems* 131 Miss Tabitha Towzer is fair, ... Like a hakmatak slender and spare. **1848** *N. Eng. Farmer* I. 5 Your hackmatack ... combines strength with durability.... The alder, black ash, and cedar are its neighbors. **1947** *N.Y. Times Mag.* 2 Feb. 47/2 This came at the precise place where ... the hackmatacks began.

attrib. **1834** AUDUBON *Ornith. Biog.* II. 438 The larch forests, which are there [in Maine] called 'Hackmetack Woods,' are as difficult to traverse as the most tangled swamps of Labrador. **1855** HALIBURTON *Nat. & Hum. Nat.* I. 100 'Is he [a horse] sound?' 'Sound as a new hackmetack trenail.'

b. hackmatack knee, a hard, hollow outgrowth from the roots of a hackmatack tree. Cf. * **knee.**

1889 *Cent. Mag.* Feb. 576/1 The posts being fitted with hackmatack knees.

hagdel ˈhægdl̩, *n.* [Var. of **hagden*, **hagdown*, the greater shearwater.] An American shearwater or fulmar. *Obs.*

Quot. 1813 app. involves an error, as the oyster-catcher was never more than a rare straggler to Mass. in historical times.

1813 WILSON *Ornithology* VIII. 17 Some time ago I received a stuffed specimen of the Oyster-catcher from a gentleman of Boston. ... He informed me that two very old men to whom it was shewn called it a *Hagdel*. **1832** WILLIAMSON *Maine.* I. 150 The *Hagdel* [is] of a dark brown colour, about as large as a Murr, though its feathers are longer.

Haida ˈhaɪdɑ, *n.* [f. a native word meaning "people."] (See quot. 1907.) Also **Haida people.**

1882 *Harper's Mag.* Aug. 404/1 The permanent villages of the Haidas are invariably situated at the sea-shore. **1903** JAMES *Indian Basketry* 51 The Haida people live on Dall and the Prince of Wales Islands, or Alaska. **1907** HODGE *Amer. Indians* I. 520/1 Haida.... The native and popular name for the Indians of the Queen Charlotte ids., Brit. Col., and the s. end of Prince of Wales id., Alaska, comprising the Skittagetan family. **1943** HOWARD *Montana* 324 Sarcees of the plains and Montagnais of the snowy peaks, the mysterious Haidas of the north Pacific coast, the Navajos and bloody Apaches of the southwest—all these are Athapaskans. **1949** *Nat. Hist.* May 201/1 The Haidas found their 'slate' carvings excellent items for barter with the mainland tribes.

* **hail,** *n.* **1.** * **hailstone,** some kind of drink, cf. next. **2.** * **hailstorm,** a mint julep. Both *slang* and *obs.*

(1) 1774 in *Pliny Moore P.* (1929) IV. 10 Saterday June the 11th I Drank Sum ... More Sour Punch Do with Mr. *Keep* & *Bemant* and Mr. *Fellows* Made with Hail Stones. **1835** LATROBE *Rambler* II. 61 It was agreed by the majority ... to go on drinking and stimulating with mint-julep, mint-sling, bitters, hailstone. — **(2) 1832** *Polit. Examiner* (Shelbyville, Ky.) 16 June 3/3 In order to moderate the intense heat of mid-day and early afternoon, recourse ought to be had to his Hail-Storms, which infallibly overcome the most sultry drought. **1857** *Santa Barbara* (Calif.) *Gaz.* 29 Jan. 4/3 The drinks ain't no good here—there ain't no variety in them, neither: no white-nose, apple-jack, ... railroad, hailstorm.

Hail Columbia. The title of a patriotic song written in 1798 by Joseph Hopkinson (1770–1842). Also allusively as a name for the U.S. or as an expression of intense national pride.

1804 *Guardian of Liberty* (Frankfort, Ky.) 14 July 2/2 The toasts were succeeded with Hail Columbia, &c. **1847** ROBB *Squatter Life* 97 Sich a yell as that would ... make the United States Eagle scream 'Hail Columby.' **1848** LOWELL *Biglow P.* 1 Ser. ix. 124 Hail Columby's happy land is goin' thru a crisis. **1913** *Collier's* 27 Dec. 6/2 Yuh oughtta hear 'em, though, Play '*Hail Columbi-a.*'

b. As a euphemism for "hell," esp. in phrases, as *to give* (or *get, raise,*) *Hail Columbia.*

1854 *Oregon W. Times* 9 Sep. (Th.), The note in which he says we gave him Hail Columby. **1861** LOWELL *Biglow P.* 2 Ser. i. 18 People's impulsiver down here than wut our folks to home be, An' kin' o' go it 'ith a resh in raisin' Hail Columby. **1910** *D.N.* III. 442 You'll get Hail Columbia when your mother comes. **1946** *New Yorker* 25 May 25/3, I got Hail Columbia from Father for that escapade.

haiqua, see **hiaqua.**

* **hair,** *n.*

1. A scalp. *Slang.* Cf. * **hair buyer, lifter** in **3.**

1848 RUXTON in *Blackw. Mag.* LXIV. 20 Sufficing for a hundred wigs is the 'hair' each hunter has 'lifted' from Indians' scalps. **1852** WATSON *Nights in Block-House* 18 The red varmints want his hair bad.

b. Esp. in phrases.

1848 RUXTON *Life Far West* 16, I've raised the hair of more than one Apach. **1852** WATSON *Nights in Block-House* 46 Owen Little, Lonas Wiley, Michael O'Byrne, and the Kentuckian, Hurlbut, hurried out to 'lift the hair,' as they termed scalping. **1854** *Harper's Mag.* April 579/2 Our mountaineers '*allowed* that a greaser wanted to raise my *har*'; which, being translated into plain English, signifies that I had that day served as a target for some prowling Mexicans. **1948** *Popular Western* June 89/1 See the savages haven't lifted your hair yet, amigo!

2. (See quot.)

1939 GILBERT *Forty Yrs.* 36 This meant that the sap was boiled down enough for syrup, but if the drip came off the dipper and made a long 'hair,' it was done well enough for granulated sugar.

3. In combs.: (1) **hair album,** an album containing mounted locks of hair, together with sentiments contributed by their donors, cf. **hair wreath,** *obs.;* (2) **buyer,** a purchaser of scalps, also **hair-buying,** *obs.;* (3) **cinch,** a cinch or saddle girth made of hair; (4) **do,** a way of dressing the hair; (5) * **dressing,** see as a main entry; (6) **jewelry,** ornaments made of hair, *obs.,* cf. **hair wreath;** (7) **lariat,** a lariat made of hair, usu. that plucked from the tails of horses; (8) **lifter,** an Indian, *jocose;* (9) * **pin,** (see quot. 1892), cf. **Sherman's hairpin;** (10) **pipe,** a kind of pipe mentioned several times in the Lewis and Clark journals and app. used as a present to, or in traffic with, the Indians, *obs.;* (11) **raiser,** something which causes one's hair to rise in excitement, a thriller, *colloq.;* (12) **riata,** a riata made of hair; (13) **spinner,** *W.* app. a tarrabee *q.v.;* (14) **spring,** (see quot.), *obs.;* (15) **straightener,** a substance for straightening kinky hair, as that of Negroes; (16) * **trigger,** see as a main entry; (17) **wreath,** a wreath made of human hair fashioned into artificial flowers and suitably mounted and framed to hang on the wall as an ornament.

(1) 1888 *Lewis Co. Bee* (Chehalis, Wash.) 13 Jan. 1/2 The latest craze among the girls is a hair album, made up of locks from the heads of their gentleman friends. — **(2) 1779** *Va. State P.* I. 315 A Late Menuvr of the Famous Hair Buyer General, Henry Hamilton Esqr Lieut: Governor of De Troit, hath allarmed us much. **1852** J. REYNOLDS *Hist. Illinois* 84 Clark ... had captured the General of the hair-buying Government. — **(3) 1873** MILLER *Amongst Modocs* 177 At length the leader set his spurs in the broad hair-sinch, ... and rode down to the water's edge. — **(4)** [**1917** *Ladies' Home Jrnl.* May 100/2, I had Madame Lily come out and do my hair.] **1943** *Reader's Digest* Oct. 42/1 A woman can change her hair-do. **1948** *Dly. Ardmoreite* (Ardmore, Okla.) 19 Jan. 2/2 Mrs. Fisher wore a fur-trimmed coat and had an upsweep hair-do.

(6) 1868 *Mich. Agric. Rep.* VII. 356 R. C. Wilson, Detroit, [displayed] hair jewelry. — **(7) 1844** KENDALL *Santa Fe Exped.* I. 93 It is said that they [*sc.* rattlesnakes] will never cross a hair lariat. **1920** MULFORD *J. Nelson* 328 A braided hair lariat was coiled at the pommel. — **(8) 1876** *Cong. Rec.* 25 Jan. 628/2 Agents of the Government are penetrating ... wherever ... the best specimens of the American hair-lifter can be found. — **(9) 1879** R. GRANT *Little Tin Gods* 8 He won't be snared again, not by a jugfull! That is the kind of a hairpin that he is! **1892** WALSH *Literary Curiosities* 438 *Hair-pin,* humorous American for a man, used only in the phrase 'That's the sort of a hair-pin I am.' **1910** RAINE *B.O'Connor* 214 Collins ain't that kind of a hairpin.

(10) 1804 CLARK in *Lewis & C. Exped.* (1904) VI. 271, 1 Hairpipe. **[1910** HODGE *Amer. Indians* II. 258/2 Elaborate ornaments for the [pipe] stems have been said to be made by the women with beads, porcupine quills, feathers, hair, etc., but it is probable that they were put on by the men.] — **(11) 1902** LONDON *Daughter of Snows* 142 'Then tell us a canoe story,' the baron begged. 'A good one! A—what you Yankees call—a *hair-raiser!*' — **(12) 1869** BROWNE *Adv. Apache Country* 272 A band of four or five Apaches came one night and attempted to cut through the wall by sawing a gap in it with their hair riatas. — **(13) 1913** W. C. BARNES *Western Grazing Grounds* 119 Let there come an odd afternoon when the outfit is not working and out from some one's bed roll comes a set of hair spinners.—**(14)** *c***1830** FURMAN in *N.Y. Hist. Soc. Bul.* (1939) Jan. 4/5 Their long hair was combed back, and secured just below the neck with a steel clasp, some six inches long (called a hair spring), thence falling in rich waves, it floated below the waist.

(15) 1918 *Chi. Defender* 6 April 10/5 A delightfully perfumed pomade and perfect hair straightener. **1934** CARMER *Stars Fell* 144 When he returned he brought a carload of bottles containing a dark liquid—the first of the long line of hair straighteners for kinky heads. **1944** CLARK *Pills* 241 One of the quickest ways to make a small fortune in the South after the Civil War was to manufacture and distribute a reasonable satisfactory hair straightener. — **(17) 1854** *Pa. Agric. Rep.* 98 A very handsome and ingeniously contrived hair wreath. **1943** *Democrat* 3 June 2/4 Hair Wreaths. . . . A lovely wreath of flowers fashioned and woven by hand, from locks of hair contributed by her loved ones, in 1892, adorns the living room wall of Mrs. Many Chapman Wilson's home near Grove Hill, Ala.

4. In the names of, or with reference to, plants and animals: (1) **hair bird,** the chipping sparrow (see quot. 1917); (2) **-cap moss,** a moss of the genus *Polytrichum;* (3) **-finned dory,** a name formerly given to the young of the look-down or moonfish under the misapprehension that they represented a kind of dory, *obs.;* (4) **snake,** (see quot.), *colloq.;* (5) **sparrow, =hair bird.**

(1) 1853 THOREAU *Summer: Jrnl. Thoreau* (1898) 227 If I wish for a horse-hair for my compass sights, I must go to the stable; but the hair-bird, with her sharp eyes, goes to the road. **1917** *Birds of Amer.* III. 41 Another popular name, 'Hair-bird,' refers to the bird's fondness for horse-hairs as material for its nest. — **(2) 1817–8** EATON *Botany* (1822) 403 *Polytrichum juniperinum*, hair-cap moss. . . . In dry woods. **1889** *Cent.* 492/2 The hair-cap moss, a species of *Polytrichum* which grows in broad, soft mats. Also called *bearmoss.* — **(3) 1814** MITCHILL *Fishes N.Y.* 383 Hair-finned Dory. *Zeus capillaris.* . . . A rhomboidal, ill-shaped fish, four inches and a half long. **1855** BAIRD in *Smithsonian Rep.* 337 The Hair-finned Dory. *Argyreiosus capillaris.* . . . One specimen was taken in August while hauling the seine in the surf. — **(4) 1890** HOWELLS *Boy's Town* 201 No one had ever seen it happen, but everyone knew that if you put long horse-hairs into a puddle of water and let them stay, they would turn into hair-snakes. — **(5) 1917** *Birds of Amer.* I. 93 Chipping Sparrow. . . . Other names.—Chip-bird; Chippy; Hair-bird; Social Sparrow; Hair Sparrow.

5. In phrases: (1) *To dress in the hair*, to dress (skins) with the hair on; (2) *to make the hair fly*, (ellipt. in context), to create a rumpus or fracas; (3) *to have* (someone) *in one's hair*, to be persistently annoyed by someone; (4) *to have* (one, etc.) *where the hair is short*, to have mastery or control over, *colloq.* [cf. *OED Supp.* "to get by the short hairs," in same sense].

For other phrases see **1. b.** above.

(1) 1806 LEWIS in *L.& Clark Exped.* IV. (1905) 185 At other times the skin is dressed in the hair and woarn without any further preparation. —**(2) 1855** S. SMITH *My 30 Yrs.* 437 The money would have to be planked right down on the nail, or the hair would fly somewhere. — **(3) 1851** *Ore. Statesman* 30 Sep. 1/2, I shall depend on your honor . . . that you won't tell on me, cause if you did, I should have Hetty Gawkins in my hair in no time. **1948** *Savings News* May 17/1 'That's three fellows we won't have in our hair for quite a few years,' one of the detectives said. — **(4) 1880** MARK TWAIN *Tramp Abroad* xx. 193 (R.), I've got it [the German language] where the hair's short, I think. **1927** *Amer. Sp.* II. 356/2 *Have where the hair is short* (verb phrase), to be in a position in which one can be dictated to. 'You certainly have him where the hair is short.'

As the last term in **frog's, goose, horse, long, moose, possum, short hair.**

∗**hair,** *v. tr.* To adjust the lock of a gun so that the slightest touch on the trigger will cause it to act. *Rare.* — *a***1850** in H. GARLAND *Life of Randolph* (1850) II. 260 Tattnall insisted on hairing the trigger.

∗**hair dressing.** *attrib.* Designating a *parlor, room,* or *saloon* to which patrons resort to have their hair dressed.

1856 FERGUSSON *America* 67, I determined to indulge in the whole process in all its luxury, and resigned myself into the hands of one of the assistants in 'Phalon's Hair-dressing Saloon.' **1876** INGRAM *Centennial Exp.* 701 It contained . . . ladies' hair-dressing rooms, lavatories, etc. **1892** *York Co. Hist. Rev.* 60 William Schreiber's Fashionable Shaving and Hair-Dressing Parlors. *a***1918** G. STUART *On Frontier* II. 23 There was also a 'hair dressing parlor' opened by Thomas White, where one could not only have his hair cut and combed, but could also have it colored.

∗**hair trigger.**

1. A revolver or pistol having a delicately adjusted trigger.

1832 *Polit. Examiner* (Shelbyville, Ky.) 19 May 2/5 His pistol, which was a hair trigger, stopped at half cock. **1882** *Cent. Mag.* April 884/2 He traveled with a dusky valet, a silver-headed cane, two ruffled shirts, and a case of hair-triggers. **1887** *Courier-Journal* 2 Jan. 11/3 As the young man commenced to examine the pistol, Kean exclaimed: 'Be careful, young fellow, that is a hair-trigger.'

attrib. **1948** *Colo. Mag.* March 48 The gun is a very early hair-trigger type, breaking in the middle.

2. *attrib.* Designating a person or thing that is quick-acting or easily moved to action. Also as a predicate adj. *Colloq.*

1841 *Cong. Globe* App. 4 Aug. 499 When the bill is reported to the House, some hair-trigger gentleman of your party will spring to the floor, move the 'previous question' [etc.]. **1911** HARRISON *Queed* 87 Queed found himself drinking a foaming, tingling, hair-trigger concoction under orders to put it all down at a gulp. **1945** *Newsweek* 1 Jan. 69/1 President William B. Hatcher who has a reputation for being hair-trigger on occasions, called the tract a distasteful exhortation to 'free love.'

∗**hairy,** *a.* In combs.: (1) **hairy back,** a gizzard shad or thread herring; (2) **head,** (see quots.); (3) **honeysuckle,** any one of various American shrubs of the genus *Lonicera,* also **hairy fly-honeysuckle;** (4) **huckleberry,** a species of huckleberry found in some of the southern states; (5) **mesquite,** side oats, *Bouteloua curtipendula,* valued as a forage grass; (6) **woodpecker,** any one of various North American woodpeckers, esp. *Dryobates villosus* of the eastern states.

(1) 1884 GOODE *Fisheries* 610 The 'Mud-Shad' . . . is known . . . in North Carolina as the 'Hairy-back' or the 'Thread Herring.' — **(2) 1813** WILSON *Ornithology* VIII. 79 Hooded Merganser. *Mergus cucullatus;* . . . on the sea coast is usually called the Hairy head. **1917** *Birds of Amer.* I. 112 Hooded Merganser. . . . Other names [are] . . . Hairy-head; . . . Tow-head [etc.].—**(3) 1843** TORREY *Flora N.Y.* I. 298 *Lonicera hirsuta.* . . . Hairy Honeysuckle. . . . Rocky banks of rivers, and on mountains; not rare. June. *Ib.* 299 *Lonicera caerulea.* . . Hairy Fly-Honeysuckle. . . . Woods, and on the sides of mountains. Poughkeepsie, Highlands of Putnam County. **1850** COOPER *Rural Hours* 343 Found many vines along the bank in that direction; bitter-sweet, with its red berries; hairy honeysuckle; green-briars. — **(4) 1901** MOHR *Plant Life Ala.* 657 *Gaylussacia hirtella,* . . . Hairy Huckleberry, . . . [is a] shrub 2 to 3 feet high.

(5) 1878 KILLEBREW *Tenn. Grasses* 160 Hairy Musket, Mezquite, Mesquit, . . . is the grass of the Northern and western prairies, and is very nutritious. — **(6)** *c***1728** CATESBY *Carolina* I. 19 *Picus medius, quasi villosus.* The Hairy Wood-pecker, weighs two ounces. **1808** WILSON *Ornithology* I. 150 [The] Hairy Woodpecker . . . is another of our resident birds, . . . a haunter of orchards, and borer of apple trees, an eager hunter of insects. **1945** *Nat. Geog. Mag.* June 731 Larger double of the downy is the hairy woodpecker.

∗**hake,** *n.* The kingfish, *Menticirrhus saxatilis.* Cf. **silver hake, squirrel hake.** — **1884** GOODE *Fisheries* I. 375 The King-fish, also known as the 'Hake' on the coast of New Jersey and Delaware, . . . ranges from Cape Ann south at least as far as the mouth of the Saint John's River, Florida.

haker ˈhekɚ, *n.* (See quots.) — **1880** *Harper's Mag.* Aug. 340/1 The man who fished for hake, and also his boat, was a 'haker.' *Ib.* Sep. 498/1 Lying off it [=the Rock] at night; with only a solitary haker for a consort.

Halesia həˈliʒɪə, *n.* [f. Stephen *Hales*, Br. botanist.] A genus of small trees of the storax family found in the southeastern states, also (not *cap.*) a plant of this genus.

1760 J. ELLIS in *Phil. Trans.* LI. (1761) 929 Of the plants Halesia and Gardenia . . . which you have introduced into your garden from North America. **1785** MARSHALL *Amer. Grove* 57 *Halesia tetraptera.* Four-winged fruited Halesia. **1865** PARKMAN *Pioneers of Fr.* iv, Here [in Florida] the halesia hangs out its silvery bells. **1948** *Scientific Mo.* July 18/1 Together Ellis and Garden named the genus *Halesia* in honor of the man whose name Garden had used when first addressing himself to Ellis.

* **half,** *n.* and *a.*

1. *n.* Short for **half dollar.**

1859 *Valley Tan* (Salt Lake City) 12 April 4/1 Well, the ante was two bits, and Lem Hanks bet a half on his little 'par.' **1882** in S. LEAVITT *Our Money Wars* (1894) 93 In 1853 Congress demonetized all silver halves, quarters and dimes in sums over $5.

2. *a.* Denoting one whose authority is shared or limited by a co-worker or a superior. *Obs.*

1753 WASHINGTON *Diaries* I. 45 The Half-king was out at his hunting Cabbin on little *Beaver* Creek. **1824** J. Q. ADAMS *Diary* 313 Gates [is] the half-editor of the National Intelligencer. **1844** CIST *Cincinnati Misc.* 137 There were also some sub or half Chiefs; among those of the latter rank, Benjamin F. Warner, a white or half-breed.

3. In noun and adj. combs.: (1) **half alligator,** boisterous, rambunctious, ferocious, *slang, obs.*, cf. **half horse (and) half alligator,** as a main entry; (2) **clipper,** designating a vessel of a design suggestive of a clipper, *obs.;* (3) **cracked,** partially demented, half-witted, *colloq.;* (4) **dugout,** (see quot. and cf. **dugout**); (5) **fare,** in a system of public transportation, a fare consisting of only half the amount usu. charged, also attrib.; (6) **man,** (see quots. and cf. **half horse (and) half alligator** as a main entry), *obs.;* (7) * **shaved,** half-drunk, *obs.;* (8) **shot,** =prec., *slang;* (9) **staff,** of a flag, half-mast.

(1) **1849** *Knickerb.* XXXIII. 301 A young tree or two, blown down and lying across the road, was considered no impediment by our invincible half-alligator driver. **1882** SWEET & KNOX *Texas Siftings* 105 His is half alligator, half human.—(2) **1853** *Alta California* (S.F.) 23 Feb., The half clipper ship Queen of the Pacific was also at last accounts receiving an equal amount of ice for this company. **1885** *Outing* Aug. 551 Some twenty years later [*c*1840] the first of what were known as 'half-clipper' schooners were built, and their advent was viewed with great mistrust by all. — (3) **1877** WHITMAN *Spec. Days* 104 Some good people may think it a feeble or half-cracked way of spending one's time and thinking. **1918** SANDBURG *Cornhuskers* 142 Three times ten million men thirsting the blood Of a half-cracked one-armed child of the German kings? — (4) **1943** L. V. HAMNER *Short Grass* 6 Later half dugouts were made, several feet in the ground, several feet built above.

(5) **1857** *Ill. Agric. Soc. Trans.* II. 24 [The] president of the Rock Island road . . . offered the free use of that line for animals and articles on exhibition, and half-fare tickets to our visitors. **1947** *N. & Q.* July 59/1 Some account of the development of the custom of allowing children to travel at half fare on public conveyances appears in Clyde H. Freed's *The Story of Railroad Passenger Fares* (Washington, D.C., 1942). — (6) **1809** [see **half horse (and) half alligator 1**]. **1853** SIMMS *Sword & Distaff* 448 Hafe man, hafe horse, and two parts alligator, I reckin. — (7) **1818** WEEMS *Letters* III. 225 One night, getting half shaved, he was easily over-persuaded, (a common curse of whiskey) to try his luck at All Fours! *c***1851** WHITCHER *Bedott P.* xxviii. 354, I've seen that man half shaved on cider afore breakfast in the mornin'. — (8) **1837** NEAL *Charcoal Sk.* (1838) 13 Moseying is only to be done when a gemman's half shot. *a***1918** G. STUART *On Frontier* I. 174 Charlie 'half-shot' came along and begun to issue orders. — (9) **1849** R. JONES in *Pres. Mess. & P.* V. 9 The national flag will be displayed at half-staff. **1949** *Chi. D. News* 9 April 6/5 Easter vacation tourists here for the first time are impressed by the flag's always being at half staff at Arlington cemetery.

b. In less frequent combs. of this kind: (1) **half bank,** of a river, a stage when the water is halfway to the top of the banks; (2) * **century,** a fifty-dollar bill, *slang,* cf. * **century;** (3) **cut,** rude, uncultured, *colloq., obs.;* (4) **-high wall,** (see quot.); (5) **human,** (see quot.); (6) **shave,** (see quot.), *obs.;* (7) * **shells,** app. a political faction or group thought of as being somewhat between the Hard-Shells and the Soft-Shells, *obs.;* (8) **stock,** (see quot.); (9) **white,** a mulatto, *rare.*

(1) **1906** MARK TWAIN *Autobiog.* (1924) I. 299 (R.), Drifting straight along like a river at half-bank with no reefs in it. — (2) **1908** *Sat. Ev. Post* 5 Dec. 17/2 No, none of these twenties are from the new batch, . . . but this half-century is one that we're all proud of. — (3) **1843** R. CARLTON *New Purchase* lviii. 254 Horse-pistols were sought and fixed . . . since there were half-cut backwoodsmen enough, and some degenerate natives to use them. — (4) **1897** *Essex Antiq.* I. 27 When neither stones nor timbers were plenty the half-high wall, surmounted by a rail resting on crossed stakes driven into the ground . . . was early used, and is still common.

(5) **1943** HAMNER *Short Grass & Longhorns* 57 A big dugout was made, a 'half-human,' as the type was called. Part was dug back into the wall, but the front was of pickets, daubed with mud, with a dirt floor and a dirt roof. — (6) **1871** W. L. GOSS *Soldier's Story* v. 101 A thief, for instance, was termed a 'flanker,' or a 'half shave,' the latter term originating in a wholesome custom, which prevailed in prison of shaving the heads of those who were caught pilfering, on one side, and leaving the other untouched. — (7) **1855** *N.Y. Herald* 8 Dec. 1/6 They would, therefore, record that the attention of the democratic party—irrespective of factions and the absurd and puerile affectation of unmeaning distinctions, as hard shells, soft shells, half shells, and the like—be earnestly called to the platform of this association. *Ib.* 10 Dec. 4/6 The half shells are determined to go on and hold their primary elections. — (8) *a***1918** G. STUART *On Frontier* I. 33 A half stock rifle was one in which the wood only extended along the barrel about one-third of the way to the muzzle, and from its end to the muzzle, on the under side of the barrel was a slender piece of iron called a rib, on which was soldered from two to four small pieces of iron or brass tubing called thimbles, in which the ramrod of tough hickory was carried. — (9) **1897** MARK TWAIN *Following Equator* 63 (R.), I asked after 'Billy' Ragsdale, interpreter in the Parliament in my time—a half-white.

Half-high wall or rock fence

c. In combs. denoting coins: (1) **half bit,** see * **bit,** *n.* **2. c;** (2) **case,** (see quot.), *slang, obs.;* (3) **cent,** a coin minted from 1793 to 1857, worth half a cent; (4) **copper,** =prec., *obs.;* (5) **dime, dollar, eagle, joe,** see as main entries; (6) **johannes,** the Portuguese Johannes, a gold coin, valued at approximately $8.00, which formerly circulated in the U.S., cf. **half joe.**

(2) **1878** PINKERTON *Strikers* 55 These careless fellows will hang about the printing offices, hide about for printers in luck to borrow a 'half-case' (a half dollar) from them. — (3) **1786** *Jrnls. Cont. Congress* XXXI. 504 The two copper coins shall be as follows: One equal to the one hundredth part of the federal dollar, to be called *a cent:* And one equal to the two-hundredth part of the federal dollar to be called *A half cent.* **1857** *Statutes at Large* XI. (1863) 163 The coinage of the half cent shall cease. **1948** *Numismatic Gallery Mo.* May 3/2, 1835 Half Cent, uncirculated $2.00. — (4) **1825** NEAL *Bro. Jonathan* II. 137 It amounted to one dollar and a quarter, 'hard money'; or ten shillings 'York currency'—or two hundred and fifty half coppers.

(6) **1761** in MRS. C. V. R. BONNEY *Legacy of Hist. Gleanings* (1875) I. 34, I . . . paid him yesterday in half Johanneses & Dolls. **1792** BRACKENRIDGE *Mod. Chivalry* (1937) 59 It is probable you may bring him up to a half Joannes more, by holding out a little.

For **half (a) pistareen,** see **pistareen.**

d. In combs. relating to animals: (1) **half-bison,** =**catalo,** *obs.;* (2) **blood, breed,** see as main entries; (3) * **deck,** any one of various marine shells of the genus *Crepidula;* (4) **hill worm,** a cutworm, *obs.;* (5) **-looper moth,** a grain moth, *Phytometra zea.*

(1) **1867** DE VOE *Market Ass't* 38 Half-bison (or buffalo) heifer.—An animal of the half-breed, or cross of the bison bull and Durham cow. — (3) **1807** *Mass. H.S. Coll.* 2 Ser. III. 59 There are beside these testaceous worms, the sweet meat, or half-deck, and several others. **1881** E. INGERSOLL *Oyster Industry* 245 *Half Deck,* the slipper limpet, *Crepidula fornicata.* — (4) **1802** *Mass. H.S. Coll.* VIII. 190 The half-hill worm . . . first appears the 20th of June; draws the blade [of Indian corn] under ground, and there devours it. — (5) **1861** *Harper's Mag.* Aug. 323/1 The 'Half-looper Moth of the Corn' . . . is found throughout the country wherever Indian corn grows.

For * **half-and-half, half-faced,** *a.*, **half hand, half horse (and) half alligator,** * **half-moon,** * **half-penny, half section, half shire,** see as main entries.

4. In phrases: (1) *Half wages and leave to school,* (see quot.), *obs.;* (2) *to go off half cocked,* to speak or act impulsively or without due deliberation, *colloq.;* (3) *to let on* *halves,* to rent land for one half of what is made on it; (4) *on the half shell,* of oysters, served with the upper shell removed, also attrib. and transf.; (5) *like a half sled on ice,* etc., said of anything that does not proceed evenly or harmoniously.

(1) **1826** *Monthly Mag.* I. 8 Every farmer's boy, if unable to purchase an acre of land for himself when he is free, begins the world by working out for somebody else, for what are called 'half wages, with leave to school,'—that is with leave to go to school at one of the petty schools which are paid for out of the public treasury. — (2) **1833** *Cong. Deb.* 31 Jan. 1521 The gentleman from Maryland has gone off half cocked. **1920** Lewis *Main St.* 349 Well—I don't suppose I ought to have gone off half-cocked, and not jollied him along. — (3) **1850** Johnston *Notes* I. 174 Farmers do not like to be tenants; and when land falls into the hands of mortgagees, and must be let, it is usually let on shares, sometimes on halves, as it is called. — (4) **1860** in *Amer. Sp.* XXII. 203/1 Honest Abe Taking Them on the Half Shell. . . . Democrats fried, stewed, roasted, or on the half shell. **1861** *Vanity Fair* 30 March 148/1 Hard Shell, Soft Shell, and on the Half Shell Bapt-*ists*, Secession-*ists*, . . . and all other *ists*—you can all be citizens in Minnesota. **1893** B. Matthews in *Harper's Mag.* Dec. 33/1 'Blue Points on the half-shell, of course,' he began, adding to the waiter, 'be sure that they are on the deep shell.'

(5) **1873** Beadle *Undevel. West* 743 First one side getting ahead and then the other . . . as we used to say on the Wabash, 'like a half sled on ice.' **1893** M. A. Owen *Voodoo Tales* 272 Granny told them candidly that they were 'kyarin' on lak er half-sled in er snow-stawm.'

As the last term in **diamond, scrub, shelter half.**

* **half-and-half,** *n.*

1. = **half-breed 1.** Also attrib. *Obs.*

1827 Cooper *Prairie* iii, The half-and-halfs that one meets in these distant districts are altogether more barbarous than the real savage. **1840** Kennedy *Quodlibet* 144 We shall get the custom of the . . . half-and-halfs. **1854** Hammond *Hills, Lakes* 73 He's a half-breed, and his wife's a half-breed. . . . Whatever he has about him, is half-and-half. **1865** Trowbridge *Three Scouts* 42 Durn these half-and-half men.

2. (See quot.) *Obs.*

1835 Featherstonhaugh *Canoe Voyage* I. 63 That class of thirsty wayfarers . . . never passes their alluring thresholds without refreshing the burning palate with a cool half-pint of 'half-and-half.' [footnote:] 'Half whisky, half cider-brandy, and no *mistake*,' a word which in the preparation of this libation represents water.

* **half-blood,** *n.*

1. Of sheep and cattle: An animal which is the product of a cross between an inferior and a superior breed of stock. Also attrib.

1915 *Niles' Reg.* VIII. 320/2 Yeaned from 28 common ewes, . . . *forty-three lambs,* (half bloods) forty-one of which are now living and growing well. **1874** *Vt. Bd. Agric. Rep.* II. 365 Mr. Chester Lamberton sold a pair of half-blood steers in July.

2. Of persons: One who is the offspring of parents of different races, esp. of the white and Indian or white and Negro races.

1824 Blaine *Excursion U.S.* 408 As the white men occasionally form a very intimate acquaintance with the Squaws, a race of what the Americans call half-bloods is the consequence. **1899** H. B. Cushman *Hist. Indians* 268 In conversation with a Chickasaw (half-blood), he answered my inquiries concerning the chastity of Comanche women.

attrib. **1835** Hoffman *Winter in West* I. 215 The driver was also accompanied on the box by a well made young half-blood Chippeway. *Ib.* II. 25, I found two . . . young girls of sixteen or eighteen, whose raven locks and eyes of jet alone proclaimed their half-blood origin. **1878** Beadle *Western Wilds* 207 She was a bright, half-blood Cherokee. **1923** J. H. Cook *On Old Frontier* 194 Baptiste Garnier, a half-blood Sioux Indian whose father was of French descent.

half-breed ˈhæfˌbrid, *n.* and *a.*

1. *n.* A half-blood, esp. the offspring of a white father and an Indian mother.

1760 *Newport Mercury* 22 April 2/1 On the 18th a Half-Breed, who is a Leader and Head Warrior . . . came . . . to Fort Augusta. **1876** *Cong. Rec.* 20 May 3236/1 The great body of the Indians and half-breeds are utterly unfit by reason of their ignorance to exercise intelligently the rights and privileges of citizens. **1948** Dick *Dixie Frontier* 11 Some were honorable men who married Indian women and . . . reared respectable half-breeds.

transf. **1846** *Quincy* (Ill.) *Whig* 27 Jan. 2/4 It seems that all the Jacks in the county, consisting of T. H. Owen, John Harper, Backenstos, Bedell, and a few 'half breeds,' were to assemble at Carthage on the day the Democratic County Convention was to be held. **1899** Mark Twain *My First Lie* 164 (R.), I happened to tell him a lie—a modified one, of course; a half-breed, a mulatto.

2. (*cap.*) One of the Republicans in New York State who opposed the nomination of Grant for a third term and supported President Garfield in his controversies with the Stalwarts *q.v.*

1881 *Chi. Tribune* 5 June 4/7 The two parties at Albany—The Half-Breeds and the Half-Bred: or the Homoousians and the Homoiousians. **1884** *Ib.* 5 May 4/2 All the 'Half-Breeds' and most of the 'Stalwarts' are for the Plumed Knight. **1926** T. Roosevelt *Wks.* XIV. xvi, And with the feud between the 'Stalwarts' and the 'half-breeds' of the Empire State culminating in a positive split.

3. *a.* Having parents of different races; having one parent of good and another of inferior stock.

1761 S. Niles *Indian Wars* II. 538 One Molton, a half-breed fellow, . . . seized the fellow that wounded Mr. Atkins. **1857** *Spirit of Times* 16 May 163/3 Off we started for Arkansas, with nothing in the universal world but that old rifle, two half-breed dogs, and five dollars in silver. **1892** Duval *Young Explorers* 117, I only laughed at his warnings, and told him all the Indians in the Comanche nation couldn't catch me on 'Gitout,' as I called the half-breed horse I have now. **1923** J. R. Cook *On Old Frontier* 191 The services of many Indian and half-breed scouts . . . proved extremely valuable. **1947** *True* Nov. 90/1 The wolfers were mostly of Yankee extraction with a smattering of the half-breed sons of the early trappers.

b. Of or pertaining to a member of a faction in the Republican party (see quots. and cf. **2.** above). *Obs.*

1881 *Washington Republican* 24 June (Th.), N. K. McClure, the Half-Breed editor of the Phila. Times, is the father-confessor of Atty.-Genl. Wayne Mac Veagh, the Half-Breed pol'tician of Pennsylvania. **1888** Bryce *Amer. Commw.* II. II. xlvi. 203 The 'Stalwart' and 'Half-breed' sections of the Republican party in the same State [New York] . . . a few years ago, were mere factions . . . without distinctive principles.

4. In special combs. now obs.: (1) **half-breed buffalo,** a catalo, *rare;* (2) **lands,** any one of several tracts of land reserved for half-breed Indians in accordance with treaties made between the U.S. Government and various Indian tribes; (3) **scrip,** a certificate issued to any half-breed Indian who ceded land to the U.S. Government and entitling him to an equivalent measure of land elsewhere; (4) **tract,** an area of half-breed lands.

(1) **1880** *Cimarron News & Press* 30 Sep. 2/4 We do know that half-breed buffalos do not become non-productive like the mule, but will produce as often as desired. — (2) **1839** in *Iowa Sup. Court Rep.* I. 618 The several commissioners appointed . . . [may] commence actions before the District Court of Lee county, for their several accounts against the owners of the said half-breed lands. **1849** *31st Congress* 1 Sess. H.R. Ex. Doc. No. 5 II. 1068, I would next call your attention to the necessity of some speedy action in reference to the half breed lands near the mouth of the Kanzas river. **1855** in *34th Congress* 1 Sess. Sen. Rep. No. 33, 18 In consequence of your (Governor Reeder's) purchase of half-breed lands [etc.]. — (3) **1870** McClung *Minnesota* 174 The lands are also sometimes purchased in advance of coming into market or being surveyed, with half-breed scrip. **1884** *Cong. Rec.* 10 June 4994/2 [The lumbermen] have long been in the habit of getting it [pineland] under different forms of scrip, under the soldiers' additional scrip, under the Sioux half-breed scrip [etc.]. — (4) **1846** *Iowa Rep.* I. 627 This cession includes the half-breed tract, and shows that the parties to these treaties did not understand that tract to have been ceded by the treaty of 1824. **1894** *Hist. Lectures upon Leaders in Professions in Iowa* 88 The famous 'half breed tract' was in litigation for years, exercising the ability of eminent attorneys.

half dime. A silver coin worth five cents, the coining of which ceased in 1873. Also attrib.

1792 *Ann. 2nd Congress* 71 [Coins to be minted include] half dimes; each to be of the value of one-twentieth of a dollar. **1820** *Niles' Reg.* XVIII. 274/2 It is ardently to be wished that they [certain Spanish coins] should be superceded by our dismes and half dismes. **1901** Jameson & Buel *Encycl. Dict. Amer. Ref.* I. 257 Some silver half-dimes were the first coins struck by the U.S. Mint in 1792. **1947** *Denver Post* 23 Feb. A. 7/2 The half-dime novel fell into evil ways in 1889 when a speaker used a dime novel as the theme of a commencement address at Harvard.

half dollar. A silver coin worth fifty cents, first coined in 1794. Also **half-a-dollar.**

The 1st quot. below has reference to the Spanish peso.

[**1756** in *Lett. to Washington* I. 370 After giving him half a Dollar for Expences.] **1786** *Jrnls. Cont. Congress* XXXI. 504 The silver coins shall be as follows: One coin containing one hundred and eighty-seven grains and eighty-two hundredths of a grain of fine silver, to be called *A half dollar.* **1844** *St. Louis Reveille* 15 Dec. 2/3, I borrowed half a dollar and went into the pit. **1948** *Chi. D. News* 4 May 12/1

Issuance of the new Benjamin Franklin half dollars at this particular time is . . . a fortunate coincidence.

attrib. **1857** HAMMOND *Northern Scenes* 259 The frog was a little animal, certainly, not larger than a half-dollar piece. **1868** *Figaro* (S.F.) 27 April 1/2 Just hear Mrs. Toodles' description of her visit to the Opposition Half-Dollar Store. **1883** MARK TWAIN *Life on Miss.* xxxiv, A plain gill of half-a-dollar brandy.

half eagle. A U.S. gold coin worth five dollars.

1786 *Amer. Museum* (1787) II. 182/2 There shall be two gold coins; one containing one hundred and twenty-three grains, and one hundred and thirty-four thousanths of a grain of fine gold, equal to five dollars, to be stamped in like manner, and to be called a half-eagle. **1890** LANGFORD *Vigilante Days* (1913) 431 He then picked up five half-eagles, and placed them in the palm of his hand. **1948** Numismatic Gallery *U.S. Gold Coins* 13 It is probably unique and takes its place alongside the 1822 half eagle.

half-faced ˈhæfˈfest, *a.*

1. half-faced cabin, a frontiersman's shelter or hunter's cabin which is built open on one side.

1824 DODDRIDGE *Notes* 124 A hunting camp, or what was called a half faced cabin was of the following form; the back-part of it was sometimes a large log [etc.]. **1886** Z. F. SMITH *Kentucky* 4 The hunter's camp was so much a part of the earliest back woodsman's life, that we must not omit to describe it here. It was called a 'half-faced cabin.'

2. half-faced camp, a temporary shelter inclosed on three sides and covered. Also **half-face camp.**

1837 *Knickerb.* X. 409 Here the emigrants landed and pitched their half-face camp. **1886** *Cent. Mag.* Nov. 18/1 Thomas Lincoln . . . built a temporary shelter of the sort called in the frontier language 'a half-faced camp,' merely a shed of poles, which defended the inmates on three sides from the foul weather, but left them open to its inclemency in front. **1948** DICK *Dixie Frontier* 26 Another type of shelter was the half-faced camp. It could be made in several ways.

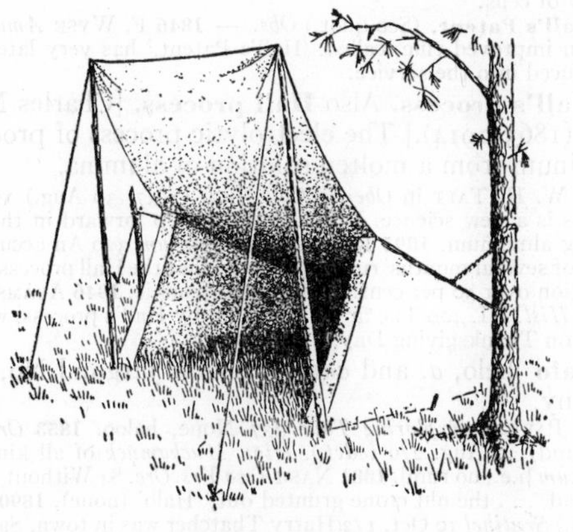

Half-faced camp

3. half-faced shanty, = **half-faced cabin.**

1850 *Ind. Quart. Mag. Hist.* XII. 233, I . . . continued at my father's half-faced shanty until near the middle of June.

half hand.

1. A laborer who performs half as much work as a "full hand."

1856 OLMSTED *Slave States* 433 The children beginning as 'quarter-hands,' advancing to 'half-hands,' and then to 'three-quarter hands' and, finally, . . . to 'full hands.' **1873** MILLER *Amongst Modocs* 203 The Doctor unsaddled his mule, gathered up wood, and was a full half-hand at supper. [**1927** SIRINGO *Riata* 3 During the harvest I made a half a hand binding and shocking wheat.]

2. half-hand kerchief, some now undefinable article of personal dress.

1847 FIELD *Drama in Pokerville* 87 As for Cynthy, she received more dresses, and shoes, and half-hand kerchiefs, and half dollars, than she knew what to do with.

b. half-hand mittens, mittens that cover half the hand.

1897 ALLEN *Choir Invisible* 3 On her hands she had drawn white half-hand mittens of home-knit.

half horse (and) half alligator.

1. An appellation used by or about boasting frontiersmen and boatmen in the West. Also attrib. Now *hist.*

1809 IRVING *Hist. N.Y.* VI. ii. 85 It is for similar reasons, and probably with equal truth, that the back-wood-men of Kentucky are styled half man, half horse, and half alligator by the settlers on the Mississippi, and held accordingly in great respect and abhorrence. **1812** *Salem Gaz.* 12 June (Th.), 'Half horse half alligator' has hitherto been the boast of our up-country boatmen, when quarreling. **1831** *Boston Transcript* 20 July 2/3 Our traveller was a half horse-and-half-alligator man, and boasted that he could thrash his weight in wild cats. **1860** *Oregon Argus* 13 Oct. (Th.), These half horse and half alligator sort of politicians are becoming a stench in the nostrils of the American people. **1948** DICK *Dixie Frontier* 241 An Englishman was astonished to find that more than once a 'half-horse and half-alligator' possessed accurate information on politics and government.

2. Also with various fanciful embellishments (see quots.). *Obs.*

1832 PAULDING *Westward Ho!* I. 130 Whereas before he was accustomed to designate himself as 'half horse, half alligator, and a little of the steamboat,' he ever afterwards added 'a small sprinkling of an earthquake' to the former ingredients. **1833** *Sketches D. Crockett* 164, I'm that same David Crockett, fresh from the backwoods, half-horse, half-alligator, a little touched with the snapping turtle. **1835** H. C. TODD *Notes* 50 The manners of Kentucky boatmen . . . are so proverbially rough, that they are described as 'half horse and half alligator, with a cross of the wild cat.' **1841** H. PLAYFAIR *Papers* I. 32 'Half-horse, half-alligator,' with a 'streak of the snap-turtle,' is the usual appellation of those amphibious men who spend their lives on the banks, and as boatmen on the waters of the Mississippi.

half joe. = **half johannes.** Now *hist.*

1772 CHASE *Hist. Dartmouth Coll.* (1891) I. 262 *n.*, Let Mr. Ripley have a guinea, half a jo and 9 coppers. **1865** PHILLIPS *Amer. Paper Curr.* II. 72 A half Joe sells for between £ 15 & £ 20. **1882** BROCKETT *Our Country's Wealth* 611/1 Guineas, joes, and half joes, doubloons, and pistoles of various origin constituted the gold currency [in colonial times]. **1945** ADAMS *Album Amer. Hist.* II. 30 The Brazilian half-Joannes, commonly known as half-joes, were worth about $8.00.

* **half-moon,** *n.* **1.** A kind of dance. *Obs.* **2.** A marine food fish, *Medialuna californiensis.* **3.** (See quot.)

(1) 1847 in H. HOWE *Ohio* 121 It is doubtful if the anniversary of American independence was ever celebrated in Cleveland by a more joyful and harmonious company, than those who danced the scamper-down, double-shuffle, western-swing and half-moon, forty-six years ago in the log cabin of Major Carter. — **(2) 1884** GOODE *Fisheries* I, 394 'The "Half-Moon" . . . takes the hook readily, is an excellent food-fish, and, in the Los Angeles market, is second only to the barracuda in importance.' — **(3) 1942** RAWLINGS *C. Creek* 101 The mark was a half-moon in one ear and a bit in the other.

* **half-penny,** *n.* An earmark of identification for hogs, sheep, cattle, etc.

1658 *E.-Hampton Rec.* I. 151 John Woodroff marked a horse colt with a hapenny under the left eare. **1666** *Portsmouth Rec.* 266 A hinde and a halfpenny from the Route one ye hinder side of ye Eare. **1773** in L. SUMMERS *Ann. S.W. Va.* 602 It is ordered that his mark be recorded a Crop and a half Penny out behind in the Left ear and two Slits in the right ear. **1845** *Portsmouth Rec.* 387 The Ear Mark of the creatures of David Baker is two half pennys before the near or left ear.

half section. A tract of land embracing half of one square mile or 320 acres. Also attrib.

1806 *Ann. 9th Congress* 2 Sess. 1032 The public lands are now sold in sections, half sections, and quarter sections. **1872** *Newton Kansan* 12 Dec. 2/1 All settlers . . . may enter a half section of land under the homestead law. **1910** *Okla. Session Laws* 3 Legisl. 5 The permanent capitol of the state shall be erected on the following described lands: Fifteen acres of land surrounding a point on the half-section line.

half shire. *N. Eng.*

1. One of two subdivisions of a county. *Obs.*

1798 I. ALLEN *Hist. Vermont* 22 The new county was divided into half shires.

2. half-shire town, the seat or capital of a half shire. *Obs.*

1789 MORSE *Amer. Geog.* 218 Courts are also held in Haddam, which is the best half shire town of Middlesex county in Connecticut. **1797** —— *Gazetteer* 71/1 *Cambridge*, the half shire town of Middlesex co. Massachusetts, is one of the largest and most respectable townships of the county. *a***1817** DWIGHT *Travels* II. 101 Charlestown, as I have heretofore observed, is a half-shire town.

halfway covenant. An obsolete form of membership in the Congregational Church of New England which allowed only part of the privilege of full membership; the covenant that created this form of membership. Now *hist.*

1769 *Mass. Gaz.* 9 March 2/3 This Day Published, And sold by Kneeland & Adams in Milk-Street; (Price Six Coppers.) The Half-way Covenant. A Dialogue. By Joseph Bellamy, D.D. **1787** *Columbian Mag.* 445/1 He stands in half-way cov'nant sure; Full five long years or more, One foot in church's pale secure, The other out of door. **1856** LAWRENCE *N.H. Churches* 95 The giving out of the Tokens and the Halfway Covenant . . . were both continued into Dr. Dana's ministry [1822 to 1826]. **1892** WALSH *Lit. Curiosities* 440 In consequence of the preaching of Whitefield, the 'Half-Way Covenant' was practically abandoned.

* **halibut,** *n.* As the last term in **bank, bastard, Monterey halibut.**

halitosis ˌhælə'tosɪs, *n.* [f. L. *halit*us, breath, +*-osis.*] The condition of having offensive breath.

1885 BUCK *Handbook Med. Sci.* I. 695/2 Toxic halitosis. **1926** *Chi. Tribune* 22 Sep. 27/3 How many people actually have halitosis? **1948** *Time* 1 Mar. 96/3, 150 coal miners walked off the job when a pit pony developed halitosis, reconsidered when the management offered to mix fragrant musk in its feed.

* **hall,** *n.*

1. =**college 1.** Usu. preceded by a designating term. *Obs.*

1699 in *Pub. Col. Soc.* XV. cxxix, William Stoughton—'proves that he Loves our Nation, by Building us another Edifice for the Supply of all our Synagogues, and Stoughton-Hall outshines Harvard-Colledge.' **1831** in *D.N.* II. 101 With respect to Stoughton Hall, I was at College at the time of the earthquake. **1900** A. MATTHEWS in *D.N.* II. 104 It has been shown that the word Hall was introduced at Harvard in 1720, and that by 1780 it had won the day officially and had driven College entirely from the field.

b. (See quot.) *Obs.*

1888 *Cent. Mag.* Sep. 751/1 Twin literary societies, or 'halls,' generally secret, . . . have been institutions at every leading college in the land.

2. (See quots.)

1853 *Harper's Mag.* VI. 448/1 Sometimes what is termed a *hall,* that is to say, a cavity large enough to hold a keg of powder, is formed behind a great mass of rock which it is desired to remove. **1907** LONDON *Road* 87 A 'hall' is not a corridor. . . . A cube and encompassing building constituted a 'hall' in the Erie County Penitentiary.

3. A billiard hall. *Obs.*

1869 *Boyd's Business Directory* 19 Billiards! Billiards! Latimere Hall Billiard Saloon. **1890** McCLEERY *Method of Billiard Playing* 14 America's First Hall.—The first large billiard room opened in this country was by E. D. Bassford in 1832 [in New York City].

4. In combs.: (1) **hall bedroom,** a small bedroom partitioned off at one end of a hall; (2) **bedroomer,** one who occupies a hall bedroom, *rare;* (3) **boy,** a porter or call boy in attendance at a hotel, apartment house, public building, etc.; (4) **man,** see as a main entry; (5) **room,** =**hall bedroom,** also attrib.; (6) **tree,** =**hat tree;** (7) **way,** a narrow passageway or entrance hall.

(1) **1738** *N.H. Probate Rec.* II. 280 Samuel Brewster shall Have . . . ye Hall Bed Room. **1886** JAMES *Bostonians* 186 One of his rooms was directly above the street-door of the house; such a dormitory, when it is so exiguous, is called in the nomenclature of New York a 'hall bedroom.' **1947** *True* Nov. 68/1 For years the photographs were standard items of decoration in pool parlors, political clubs, and hall bedrooms throughout the country. — (2) **1899** J. L. WILLIAMS *Stolen Story* 230 Like many an other lonely hall-bed roomer. — (3) **1884** *N.Y. Herald* 27 Oct. 2/2 Janitors and hall boys in attendance. **1908** PHILLIPS *Old Wives* 354 And when . . . the hall boy knocked to tell him Murdock had come he was able to say: 'Take down the bag.'

(5) **1859** *Ladies' Repository* XIX. 466/2 The little hall-room is just large enough for the boys to sleep in. **1948** *Pacific Spectator* Spring 196 Some of the hallroom adolescents were growing up into a keener appreciation of literary values. — (6) **1875** STOWE *We & Neighbors* 87 She snatched from the hall-tree a shawl. **1891** *Harper's Mag.* June 79/1 One could distinguish . . . the hall tree, whereon Rhodes's hat swung in its place.— (7) **1876** HABBERTON *Jericho Road* 173 It passed through the narrow hallway which separated the cell from the jailor's apartments. **1916** WILSON *Somewhere* 33 She found Alonzo in the hallway telling Beryl Mae how flowerlike her beauty was.

b. *Halls of (the) Montezuma(s),* halls or palaces once occupied by Montezuma, in allusion to the Marine Corps hymn beginning "From the halls of Montezuma to the shores of Tripoli."

1847 *Santa Fe Republican* 4 Dec. 2/4 Even now the blind goddess is dispensing justice in the palacios of tyrants, and the 'Halls of the Montezumas' are become the garrisons of republican soldiers. **1880** *Harper's Mag.* LX. 196/1 A little narrow-gauge railroad . . . destined . . . to establish its ultimate terminal station in one of those 'halls of Montezumas' of which we so often hear. **1948** *Newsweek* 5 Jan. 68/3 A onetime servant girl . . . looks better and better as time lags on the road to the halls of Montezuma.

c. Hall of Fame, an institution established in 1900 by New York University as a permanent memorial for famous Americans.

1901 *Land of Sunshine* Jan. 61 The Columbia College 'Hall of Fame' includes various more or less useful Americans and excludes Edgar Allan Poe. **1913** EATON *Barn Doors & Byways* 122 Only a year or two ago a red fox was seen in New York City, . . . on the wooded hillside sloping toward the Harlem River at University Heights near the Hall of Fame.

transf. **1927** *My Okla.* June 14/1 In the Hall of Fame of the aboriginals there is no name like that of Sequoyah. **1946** *New Yorker* 18 May 30/3 They gathered together ten or twelve of us old fellows—Henry Ford, Frank Duryea, Ranny Olds, Charlie Nash, and a few others—and elected us to a doodad they call the Automotive Hall of Fame. **1947** *Time* 3 Feb. 54/3 Baseball's Hall of Fame exists mostly in the minds of sportswriters.

As the last term in **bachelor's, beer, boarding, city, dance, floral, Liberty, lodging, lyceum, pool, representative, sewing, social, state, Tammany Hall.**

* **hallman,** *n.*

1. =**hall boy.**

1884 *N.Y. Herald* 27 Oct. 2/2 Desirable Apartments, . . . janitor and hallman in attendance. **1916** DU PUY *Uncle Sam* 205 On that floor the hallman said that the white-haired gentleman had run down the steps to the second. **1919** T. K. HOLMES *Man from Tall Timber* 3 'Shucks! why didn't you say H. Harvey Stafford?' interrupted the hall-man.

2. A prison trusty.

1907 LONDON *Road* 91 My pal . . . had been promptly appointed a trusty of the kind technically known as 'hall-man.' *Ib.*, There were thirteen hall-men in that hall. Ten of them had charge each of a gallery of cells.

Hall's Patent. (See quot.) *Obs.* — **1846** F. WYSE *America* II. 102 An improved rifle, called, 'Hall's Patent,' has very lately been introduced into the service.

Hall's process. Also **Hall process.** [Charles Martin *Hall* (1863–1914).] The electrolytic process of producing aluminum from a molten solution of alumina.

1893 W. H. TAFT in *Oberlin Coll. Bul.* (1937, 30 Aug.) 17 Hall's process is a new science. It is a decided step forward in the art of making aluminum. **1895** RICHARDS *Aluminium* 329 An accurate account of several months' running showed that the Hall process obtains a fraction over 50 per cent. of the metal from it. **1946** ADAMS *Album Amer. Hist.* III. 400 The first aluminum, by Hall's process, was produced on Thanksgiving Day, 1888.

halo 'helo, *a.* and *adv.* [Chinook Jargon.] No, none, not any.

1838 PARKER *Exploring Tour* 337 None, haloo. **1853** *Oregonian* (Portland) 20 Aug. 2/6 (*advt.*), *Hiou Muckamuck* of all kinds, but *Halo Lum* [i.e., no rum]. **1881** NASH *Two Yrs. Ore.* 84 Without turning her head, . . . the old crone grunted out, 'Halo' (none). **1890** *Asotin* (Wash.) *Sentinel* 10 Oct. 1/2 Harry Thatcher was in town, Saturday, in the interest of Frank Brothers, but halo mules.

* **halt,** *n. To call a halt,* to demand that a course of action cease; to come to a complete stop.

1875 *Cong. Rec.* 4 Feb. 982/2 It ought to be enough to 'call a halt' that entire States, once proud and majestic commonwealths, are in ruins. **1888** *Ib.* 7 May 3793/1 Is it not high time to call a halt, and stop this reckless expenditure? **1900** *Ib.* 31 Jan. 1344/1 But can we not call a halt on it? Can we not stop where we are?

halter-break, *v. tr.* To accustom (a colt, calf, etc.) to being led by a halter. Also transf. Hence **halter-breaking,** *n.*

1837 *N.Y. Mirror* 28 Oct. 140/3 The moose has been frequently tamed, and unlike the common deer, can be halter-broken as easily as a horse. **1860** HOLLAND *Miss Gilbert* 350 You want to halter-break 'em when they're little and get 'em kind o' wonted to the feel of the harness. **1947** *Trail Riders Bul.* Feb. 7/1 Halter breaking is slow tedious work, as you must go back to pulling him around from side to side every few minutes.

b. Also (*transf.*) **halter-broke,** *a.*

1910 *Sat. Ev. Post* 27 Aug. 50/1 The law-abiding then term him an outlaw, and he in turn describes the law-abiding as 'halter-broke'—a mutual misjudging based upon insufficient premises.

halving system. A system of farming in which the landlord and the renter share equally in the crop. *Rare.* — **1831** J. FOWLER *Tour New York* 76 The *share,* or *halving system,* as it is called, is not very extensively practiced.

* **ham,** *n.*

1. An inferior boxer or fighter. *Slang.*

1888 *Missouri Repub.* 27 March (F.), He is a good fighter but will allow the veriest ham to whip him. **1929** *Sat. Ev. Post* 14 Dec. 144/3 They want me to slug with this big ham.

2. Short for **ham actor** or **hamfatter.** *Slang.*

1902 CLAPIN 220 *Ham.* . . . In theatrical parlance, a tenth-rate actor or variety performer. **1948** *Good Housekeeping* Jan. 162/1 Suddenly I realized that this girl was potentially as big a ham as I was.

3. An amateur radio operator. *Slang.*

1928 *Collier's* 22 Sep. 26 The amateur radio 'hams' have the ends of the earth for neighbors. **1947** *Chr. Sci. Mon.* 15 Jan. 9/1 You will understand what I mean if you come with me and visit the amateur transmitting station of a 'ham' named Al.

b. (See quot.) *Slang.*

1929 *Amer. Sp.* IV. 288 At either end of a wire an unskillful operator is a 'lid,' 'ham,' 'bum' or 'plug.'

4. In combs.: (1) **ham actor,** =**hamfatter,** *slang;* (2) **-and-egg stake,** a grubstake *q.v.*, *rare;* (3) **doings,** see **doings;** (4) **fatter,** (see quot. 1889); (5) * **meat,** (see quot. 1927), *colloq.;* (6) **radio,** radio operated by "hams" who build their own sets; (7) **stub,** ?the small end of a ham, *rare.*

(1) **1925** WITWER *Roughly Speaking* 223 Ham actors get a extra split week at a picture house if their fearful monologs put the ladies on the broiler. **1949** *Chi. D. News* 22 April 20/3 Dickens was pompous, stuffy, insensitive, quarrelsome, and an incredible ham actor. — (2) **1936** MCKENNA *Black Range* 295 Many a time since I have turned to Ed for a ham-and-egg stake, and he's never failed me yet. — (4) **1882** G. A. SALA *Amer. Revisited* I. 66 Every American who does not wish to be thought 'small potatoes' or a 'ham-fatter' or a 'corner loafer.' **1889** *Cent.* 2696/2 *Hamfatter*, a term of contempt for an actor of a low grade, as a negro minstrel, Said to be derived from an old-style negro song called 'The Ham-fat Man.' **1948** MENCKEN *Supp.* II. 689/2 The Lexicon of Trade Argot prefers to derive it from the fact that actors formerly used ham-fat instead of cold cream to remove their make-up, and this is supported by a variant form, *ham-fatter.*

(5) **1927** *D.N.* V. 469 *ham-meat*, n. Bacon [Appalachian Mts.]. **1933** T. WILLIAMSON *Woods Colt* 218 No trackin' *ham-meat*, no linin' a bee tree, no nothin'. — (6) **1941** *Harper's Mag.* Oct. 541/2 Train and hotel accommodations are often reserved by ham radio. — (7) **1919** CADY *Rhymes of Vt.* (1923) 62 The ham stubs, knuckles, bacon rinds, . . . Perhaps some headcheese, turning strong.

b. In the names of dishes of which ham is an ingredient. Also *ham-and-egg(s) pension*, a derisive term for an impracticably generous old age pension.

1784 J. F. D. SMYTH *Tour U.S.* I. 42 A ham and greens or cabbage, is always a standing dish. **1837** in *So. Hist. Assoc. Pub.* VI. 473 They gave me fryed ham and eggs and biscuit, bread & Coffee. **1938** *Sat. Ev. Post* 5 Nov. 77/2 Doctor Townsend attacked the Ham-an-Eggs pension program as an alluring rainbow which could not succeed because merchants and bankers would not accept the scrip. **1947** *So. Sierran* Feb. 2/2 One may chuckle at the account of our most famous evangelist, our ham-and-egg pension men, the swamis and hundreds of mystic cults.

c. *No ham and all hominy*, a slang phrase equivalent to "no pay and all work." *Rare.*

1846 CORCORAN *Pickings* 47 How *all*-fired easy it is to make money in it, but it's no 'ham' and all 'hominy,' I reckon.

As the last term in **bacon, basswood, bear, California, canvas, mutton, picnic, pork, Smithfield, sugar, Virginia, wooden ham.**

hamamelis ˌhæmɪˈmilɪs, *n.* [Gk., a service tree or medlar.] A tree or genus of trees of which the witch hazel is typical. Also attrib.

1766 J. BARTRAM *Journal* 3 Feb. 59 The land . . . produces . . . palmetto, hamamelis, and cedar. **1794** S. WILLIAMS *Hist. Vermont* 71 The Witch Hazel (*hamamelis*) is endowed with the singular property of putting forth its blossoms, after the frost has destroyed its leaves. **1885** *Harper's Mag.* May 910/2 The Hamamelis bark is one of her annual crops. **1947** *Woodlawn Booster* (Chi.) 3 Sep. 4/2 Witch hazel comes from the hamamelis shrub.

Hambletonian ˌhæmbl̩ˈtonɪən, *n.* Also **Hamiltonian.** [See def.] A horse or strain of horses descended from a stallion named Hambletonian.

1856 *Spirit of Times* 6 Dec. 228/1 There was 'Americans,' 'Black Hawks,' 'Hambletonians,' 'Bullocks,' 'Normans' and 'Rattlers'—all gathered to the show, and their owners claimed them all as trotters. **1894** *Vt. Agric. Rep.* XIV. 94 The horses of Vermont are somewhat similar in blood, tracing back in common with the various families of Hambletonians to a common ancestry. [**1947** *Chi. Sun Bk. Week* 14 Sep. 4/2 The great founding sire of the breed, for example, Hambletonian, was bought from his employer by a New York State farmhand for $125—with the colt's crippled mother thrown in.]

attrib. **1856** *Rep. Comm. Patents 1855: Agric.* 40 A Hamiltonian Morgan, five years old, a very fine animal, is owned in this town, which, at three years old, took the first premium at the Horse Fair at Springfield, Massachusetts, in 1854. **1866** *Wilkes' Spirit of Times* 5 May 150/3 This is an entire *Hambletonian* stable. **1873** *Harper's Mag.* Sep. 605/1 As so much money is invested in Hambletonian stock, the fever for this class of horses must continue to rage for some time to come.

b. A race for three-year-old trotters, named in honor of Hambletonian, because of his fame as a sire of trotting horses. Also attrib.

1926 *N.Y. Times* 1 Aug. IX. 7/6 A secondary feature of the race and a fact that brings another Hambletonian possibility to the front was the showing of the filly Ella Trabue, in the stable of Charley Valentine. **1948** *Time* 23 Aug. 34/1 No amateur had ever won the famed Hambletonian, trotting's Kentucky Derby.

hamburg ˈhæmbɝg, *n.* Also **Hamburg.** [App. f. *Hamburg*, Ger.] Beef finely ground or chopped. In full **Hamburg steak.**

1884 *Boston Journal* 16 Feb. 2/2 We take a chicken and boil it. When it is cold we cut it up as they do meat to make Hamburg steak. **1903** A. BOSS *Meat on Farm* 34 Lean beaf from the round makes the choicest Hamburg. **1945** *Progressive* 7 May In the East, culinary tradition records that 'hamburg' was first heard of about the turn of the century, and I can remember 'going to the store' for it about that time.

b. hamburg joint, a place where hamburgers are sold.

1942 BRANSON *Pricking Thumb* 19 There were . . . neon lights indicating a filling station, a hamburg joint, two or three beer gardens, and the hotel.

hamburger ˈhæmbɝgɚ, *n.*

1. Hamburg steak; a sandwich, usu. on a bun, containing a grilled cake of this.

1912 I. COBB *Back Home* 147 A vender . . . sold to the same customers . . . odorous hamburger and flat slabs . . . of striped ice-cream. **1924** W. H. BLACK & E. W. MCCOMAS *Beef on Farm* 29 Making hamburger.—Grind lean beef, such as the round, neck, flank, and trimmings, and a little fat in a sausage grinder. **1948** *Nat. Geog. Mag.* Aug. 214/1 Vernon and I made hamburgers—three parts top ground round and one part onion.

transf. **1928** BRADFORD *Ol' Man Adam* 177 I'm gonter make hamburgers outer yo' measly army.

2. Attrib. with **bun, house, joint, sandwich, stand, steak.**

1889 *Walla Walla* (Wash.) *Union* 5 Jan. 2/4 You are asked if you will have 'porkchopbeefsteakhamandegghamburgersteakorliverandbacon.' **1932** *K.C. Star* 11 Feb. 18 The Gazette says an Augusta husband has quit taking his wife to a hamburger stand for a meal in order to save money. **1935** MITCHELL *America* 117 You are in a country where you can . . . be understood when you ask for a hamburger sandwich or pie *à la mode.* **1941** DANIELS *Tar Heels* 225 Too often around the fences and the views are the cheap souvenir stands, the hamburger house, the trained bear that will drink the soda pop the pop stand owner will be glad to sell. **1947** *Chi. Tribune* 22 July 20 Yeah—I snapped this bird's picture in a hamburger joint on Second Avenue. **1949** *L.A. Times* (Home Mag.) 19 June 15/2 Split toasted English muffins make excellent hamburger buns.

* **hame,** *n.* **1. hame bells,** bells used as ornaments on the hames of wagon horses. *Obs.* **2. hame string,** a strong string or rope by which the lower ends of a pair of hames are fastened together. — (1) **1930** OMWAKE *Conestoga Teams* 45 Whenever one wagoner helped another in distress on those rough or slippery roads, he received as a reward the hame bells of the hapless one. — (2) **1856** DAVIS *Farm Bk.* 66 Bring in 11 plow lines single & 1 hame string.

Hamiltonian ˌhæml̩ˈtonɪən, *n.* A follower of, or a believer in the political doctrines of, Alexander Hamilton (1757–1804).

1797 JEFFERSON *Writings* IX. 382 These machinations will proceed from the Hamiltonians by whom he [President Adams] is surrounded, and who are only a little less hostile to him than to me. **1906** *Cin. Enquirer* 14 April 1/6 The people of the United States are becoming Hamiltonians very rapidly. **1946** *Newsweek* 17 June 106/2 His book can be read by Jeffersonians, Jacksonians, and Hamiltonians alike without shock.

b. Also as an adj.

1843 in HAMBLETON *Biog. Sk.* (1856) 43 You would see no little dipping and doging [*sic*] in the crowd, among the old Hamiltonian National Republican Federalists. **1861** *Richmond* (Va.) *Examiner* 7 Dec. 2/2 The old Hamiltonian maxim of a *government debt, a public blessing* . . . is the philosophy of the first thoroughly Yankee administration that has acceded to power. **1896** *N. Eng. Mag.* ns. XIV. 703/1 It is not necessary, however, in perceiving the failure of the Hamiltonian scheme . . . to overlook the fact that there are features of the plan which will be suggestive and useful.

***hamlet,** *n.* (See quot. 1888.) Also attrib. *Obs.* — **1879** *Ohio Gen. & Local Laws* LXXVI. 116 The inhabitants of any territory laid off into village or hamlet lots . . . may obtain the organization of a village or hamlet, in the manner provided in this title. **1888** BRYCE *Amer. Commw.* II. II. xlviii. 247 Ohio . . . divides her municipal corporations into (*a*) cities . . . ; (*b*) villages . . . ; and (*c*) hamlets, incorporated places with less than 200 inhabitants.

hamletize 'hæmlɪtˌaɪz, *v. tr.* To incorporate a community as a "hamlet." Hence **hamletization,** *n.* Both *rare.* Cf. ***hamlet,** *n.*, quot. 1888. — **1893** *Columbus* (Ohio) *Dispatch* 9 Feb., Relating to the controversy concerning the hamletizing of Bullitt Park, the undersigned [etc.]. *Ib.* (*caption*), A Farmer in the Territory Wants It to Remain as It Is, But, at the Proper Time, Says Annexation, Not Hamletization, Should Occur.

***hammer,** *n.*

1. One who beats down the price of stock. *Slang. Rare.* Cf. **hammer,** *v.* **1.**

1846 *Knickerb.* XXVIII. 124, I had my 'hammers' to knock down a stock, or my 'bulls' to cry it up.

2. In combs.: (1) **hammer bug,** (see quot.); (2) ***head, -head sucker,** (see quots.), *colloq.*; (3) **oil,** (see quot.), *obs.*

(1) **1862** *Rep. Comm. Patents 1861: Agric.* 608 The *Elateridæ* . . . to which has been applied the names of '*spring beetle*,' '*hammer bug*,' &c., from the well-known faculty they have of throwing themselves upwards or on their feet again when they are laid on their backs, by a quick jerk of the head and thorax. — (2) **1884** GOODE *Fisheries* I. 615 The Stone-roller or Hammer-head Sucker, *Catostomus nigricans*, abounds in most waters from the Great Lakes southward. **1889** *Cent.* 2698/1 *Hammerhead*, . . . a catostomine fish, *Hypentelium nigricans*. . . . It abounds in the fresh waters of the United States, from New York to Kansas and Alabama. **1944** ADAMS *W. Words* 72 hammerhead An unintelligent horse. — (3) **1792** BENTLEY *Diary* I. 362 An Abraham Solis, advertised mountebank fashion in the Gazette, the Haerlaemer Oil, vulgarly called Hammer Oil.

b. *Dead as a hammer*, quite dead. *Colloq.*

1822 *N.J. Almanac 1823*, I soon shall be dead as a hammer. **1891** THANET *Otto the Knight* 219 Feller keeled over dead's a hammer. Never seen a purtier shoot.

As the last term in **ax, bush, drop, jack, sheriff's, trip, yellow-hammer.**

***hammer,** *v.* **1.** *tr.* To beat down the price of (a stock). **2.** (See quot.) *Slang.*

(1) **1846** *Knickerb.* XXVIII. 119 Our conversation I found took a uniform turn to stocks . . . with some peculiarity of terms as to . . . 'hammering down' another stock. **1875** *Chi. Tribune* 15 Aug. 8/4 The low prices, however, are attracting buyers for some of the stocks known to be unduly 'hammered.' — (2) **1900** *Everybody's Mag.* II. 585/2 To criticise adversely. (Synonymous with 'to hammer.')

hammered dollar. (See quots.) *Obs.* — **1852** GOUGE *Fiscal Hist. Texas* 228 A great part of the currency [of Texas] consisted of 'hammered dollars,' that is, of old Spanish dollars, from which the royal effigy had been effaced by the Mexicans, as a testimony of their indignation towards their ancient rulers. *Ib.*, The 'hammered dollars' . . . were valued at only ninety cents. *Ib.*, At Brownsville, and other towns on the Rio Grande, there is much of this 'hammered money' still in use.

hammock 'hæmək, *n.* [Var. of **hummock.**]

1. =**hummock 1.**

The quots. show that this term is used with varying significations in different localities.

1637 in *Amer. Sp.* XV. 269/2 Being in severall parcels of Hamocks of land between said Neck, the baye & hogshead quarter. **1683** *Huntington Rec.* I. 371, I, Capt. Oposum . . . have bargained, sold, alienated and in present Possession Delivered . . . the Hammock or Broken Meadow . . . unto Adam Wright. **1731** *Southampton Rec.* III. 2 Ye hamack of upland . . . is granted to John Hanes for his Right of meadow. **1838** GOSSE *Letters* 266 The ground which a southern hunter best likes is that which is designated by the name of 'hammocks'; undulating hills, covered with oak, hickory, and magnolia, threaded by a good number of roads and cattle-paths. Of such land there is a good deal in this neighbourhood [*sc.* Dallas Co., Ala.]. **1893** *Harper's Mag.* March 507 Hammock, as it is used in Florida, serves to characterize fertile soil, not by reference to the dirt itself, but to what grows in it. . . . Wherever there is a dense forest, swamp, or jungle growth, the place is called a hammock. **1943** GABRIELSON *W. Refuges* 116 Incidentally, the lily pads are 'bonnets,' while a 'hammock' is an area covered by a dense growth of broad-leaved trees.

attrib. **1775** ROMANS *Nat. Hist. Florida* 17 The true hammock soil is a mixture of clay and a blackish sand, and in some spots a kind of ochre. **1837** WILLIAMS *Florida* 37 Some [of the keys] are covered with . . . hammock trees.

b. hammock land, (see quots.). Also **hammocky land.**

1766 J. BARTRAM *Journal* 69 That which is called hammocky land is generally full of large evergreen and water-oaks, mixed with red-bay and magnolia. **1775** ROMANS *Nat. Hist. Florida* 17 The hammock land [is] so called from its appearing in tufts among the lofty pines. **1826** FLINT *Recoll.* 24 Beyond them [the bluffs and bottoms] there is generally a considerable tract of country, in the south, denominated 'hammock-land,' and in Ohio 'second bottom.' **1901** MOHR *Plant Life Ala.* 468 American beech. . . . Common on the hammock lands of the coast.

2. A mudbank in a stream.

1835 in *Amer. Sp.* XV. 270/1 It was formerly navigable for batteaux for two or three miles to a manufacturing mill, but its bed has now become so obstructed by hammocks, as to impede their progress. **1901** *Ib.* 270/2 To keep the channel of the river clear of snags and hammocks.

As the last term in **cabbage, cedar, oak, sand, shell hammock.**

***Hampshire,** *n.* **1. Hampshire grants,** =**New Hampshire grants. 2. Hampshire old tenor,** a form of paper currency once used in what is now New Hampshire. See **old tenor.** *Obs.* or *hist.*

(1) **1898** in *Pub. Col. Soc.* 272 In 1771 he removed to the 'Hampshire Grants,' where he held some 50,000 acres, and in the controversies between the settlers of the Grants and New York he took an active part and was a strong partisan of New York. **1944** JOHNSON *As I Dare* 58 Behind them marched or straggled men of Massachusetts, Rhode Island and Connecticut, and the less godly Hampshire Grants and the Maine coast. — (2) **1770** PATTEN *Diary* 246, I settled with Whitefield Gillmor on my Note and I owe him yet of prinsaple and Interest 1–17–7 Hampshire old Tenor.

***Hampton,** *n.* [f. proper names.]

1. *attrib.* Of or pertaining to the preëminently practical type of education provided for Negroes in Hampton Institute at Hampton, Va.

1881 *Harper's Mag.* April 675/2 Education . . . first for the heart, then for the health, and last for the mind . . . is the Hampton idea of education.

2. Hampton boat, (see quot. 1880).

1834 AUDUBON *Ornith. Biog.* II. 522 For every couple of these hardy tars, a Hampton boat is provided. **1880** *Harper's Mag.* Aug. 350/1 Between times he runs out to sea for a day or two in his cat-boat, his 'Hampton boat,' or his jigger. . . . The Hampton boat, a modified pink-stern, with shoulder of mutton sails on its mast, was the 'abler,' that is to say, better qualified to stand the exigencies of all sorts of weather. **1947** COFFIN *Yankee Coast* 163 It is the Hampton boat, the reach-boat, the backbone of the profession of lobstering, which is the boat that now most means Maine.

Hancockorian ˌhænkɑk'orɪən, *a.* Of or pertaining to John Hancock (1737–93), Governor of Massachusetts. *Rare.* — **1789** J. MAY *Jrnl. & Lett.* (1873) 143 Hope . . . the rest of the wards have got officers of the same kidney—which may truly be called Hancockorian.

hancockite 'hænkɑkˌaɪt, *n.* [E. H. *Hancock* of Burlington, N.J.] An epidote mineral containing strontium and lead, found in N J. — **1900** *Jrnl. Chem. Soc.* LXXVIII. II. 88 Hancockite. This occurs as brownish-red, cellular masses of minute, lath-shaped crystals, which are monoclinic.

***hand,** *n.*

1. Short for hand game, *q.v.* as a main entry.

1837 IRVING *Bonneville* II. 185 The choral chant, in fact, which had thus acted as a charm, was a kind of wild accompaniment to the favorite Indian game of 'Hand.' **1846** SAGE *Scenes Rocky Mts.* x, Several Indians had betted largely upon a 'game of hand.' *a***1918** G. STUART *On Frontier* I. 128 Much of the time during these long winter nights and short winter days, was taken up by playing the Indian gambling game 'Hands.'

2. *Baseball.* A turn or chance at batting, a player having such a turn. *Obs.*

1845 in *Appleton's Ann. Cyclo.* (1886) X. 77/2 Three hands out, all out. **1868** CHADWICK *Base Ball* 41 Hands Lost.—This is the old way of recording the outs in a match. Whenever a player is put out, a 'hand is lost,' and an 'out' is recorded in the score books.

3. A unit of measure for wampum, poss. a string a handbreadth in length, or as many strings as can be grasped in the hand. *Obs.* Cf. next.

1723 in G. SHELDON *Hist. Deerfield, Mass.* I. 402 The Cagnawagos have sent seven hands of wampum that yy [=they] will come in the Spring to treat . . . about theire friendship. [**1910** HODGE *Amer. Indians* II. 907/1 For use in public affairs and in official communications, in ritualistic and fiducial transactions, wampum was wrought into two well-known products—strings, often tied into bundles or sheaves of strings, and belts or scarfs or sashes.]

4. A small bundle of tobacco leaves, i.e., as many as can be grasped conveniently in one hand.

1784 SMYTH *Tour* II. 136 Every night the negroes are sent to the tobacco house to strip, that is to pull off the leaves from the stalk, and tie them up in hands or bundles. **1851** *Polly Peablossom* 114 They steals a dozen or so 'hands' every night, and next mornin' ef you notice, you'll see all the tops of the pinoaks around the plantation kivered with them a-dryin'. **1948** *Amer. Sp.* XXIII. 309/2 Hand (handful) of tobacco as it is taken from the stalk is laid in a box lined with heavy Tobacco Wrapping Paper.

b. (See quots.)

1882 *Cent. Mag.* Oct. 873/1 The first work toward gathering the corn crop in Georgia is . . . the laborer stripping the blades from stalk after stalk until he gets his hands full, and then tying them together with a few blades of the same; and this constitutes a 'hand.' **1908** *D.N.* III. 318 hand, *n.* . . . A handful, especially a handful of fodder. . . . 'Five to eight *hands* make a bundle.'

5. In combs.: (1) **hand board,** a support for reading or writing materials, a lectern, cf. * **stand,** *n.* **4;** (2) * **book,** see as a main entry; (3) **camerist,** one who uses a hand camera, *rare;* (4) **carter,** see * **handcart,** as a main entry; (5) **cheese,** ?a cheese in the form of a small lump fashioned by hand, *rare;* (6) **game,** see as a main entry; (7) * **money,** (see quot.); (8) **organist,** see **hand organ,** as a main entry; (9) **out,** see as a main entry; (10) **piece,** see as a main entry; (11) **-roomance,** room for one's hands, "elbow room," *colloq.;* (12) **round,** (see quots.), *obs.*, cf. **6.** (1) below; (13) **slap,** applause by the clapping of hands, *rare;* (14) * **-s up,** a command to surrender; (15) **tobacco,** ?leaf tobacco in the form of "hands," *rare*, cf. **4.** above; (16) **violet,** (see quot. 1840); (17) **vote,** a vote in which preferences are indicated by a show of hands, *obs.*

(1) **1734** *Ga. Col. Rec.* III. 130 [Received] Part of the Twenty one Pieces of Mahogany, Ash, Sycamore, Ilex and Red Bay Timber the Growth of Georgia used in the Experiments for making Hand Boards &c. **1856** P. CARTWRIGHT *Autobiog.* 203 They drove a stake down, and nailed a board to it, . . . and this was my hand-board. — (3) **1892** *Photog. Ann.* II. 52 It is this ungentlemanly abuse of the hand camera which brings the whole class of hand camerists into disrepute.

(5) **1890** *Harper's Mag.* July 231/1 Her balls of hand-cheese, strewed with caraway seeds, are white and appetizing. — (7) **1891** NICHOLS *Business Guide* (ed. 28) 240 *Hand-money.*—Money paid by the purchaser at the closing of a contract or sale.

(11) **1868** *Jasper* (Texas) *News-Boy* 11 Jan. 4 'Hand-roomance!' shouts the boy at his game of marbles. **1892** HARRIS *U. Remus & Friends* 306, I got ter have all de han' roomance what I kin git. — (12) **1868** *Putnam's Mag.* Dec. 674/1 We do dance, of course; but a hand-round, out here, is where we don't set a table, but hand round the vittles. **1902** CLAPIN 220 *Hand-round*, a Western term for a social gathering or entertainment, where refreshments, instead of being served at a table, are simply handed round. — (13) **1930** *Randolph Enterprise* (Elkins, W.Va.) 16 Oct. 4/5 When he came in he got a good hand slap. — (14) **1873** MILLER *Amongst Modocs* 193 Hands up, gentlemen! hands up! Don't trouble yourselves to move! **1946** *Trail & Timberline* June 84/2 Sergeant Casperson, in English, said 'Hands up!'

(15) **1865** *Nation* I. 77 One, addressed as 'Captain,' urged the other to buy of him fifty pounds of hand tobacco. — (16) **1817–8** EATON *Botany* (1822) 512 *Viola palmata*, hand violet. **1840** DEWEY *Mass. Flowering Plants* 78 Hand Violet. Receives its name from the leaves being lobed and cut to resemble the shape of a hand. — (17) **1713** *Boston Rec.* 99 Voted. That the Town will Choose Seven Overseers of the Poor and that they be Chosen by a hand Vote. **1734** *Ib.* 69 Voted, That the Affair . . . shall be determined by a Hand-vote.

b. Designating or pertaining to vehicles, tools, etc., operated by hand or carried in the hand: (1) **hand car,** a small, light car so provided with levers and gearing that it may be operated on a railway by those riding on it; (2) * **cart,** see as a main entry; (3) **cornplanter,** =**hand planter;** (4) **frame,** a kind of hand-barrow used in iron furnaces; (5) **gate,** an ordinary gate in a fence as distinguished from drawbars, *obs.;* (6) **grip,** an ordinary grip or suitcase such as is carried in the hand; (7) **husker,** any one of various devices used as aids in husking corn; (8) **laundry,** a laundry in which the work is done by hand rather than with machinery; (9) **organ,** see as a main entry; (10) **planter,** a hand-operated implement used for planting corn, *obs.;* (11) **raker,** a reaping machine which requires that raking be done by hand, *obs.;* (12) **rocker,** a hand-operated rocker used in washing gold from gravel, sand, etc., *obs.*, cf. * **cradle,** *n.* **1;** (13) **roller gin,** a roller gin *q.v.* operated by hand, *obs.;* (14) **sheller,** a form of corn-sheller operated by hand, see * **sheller;** (15) **sled,** a light sled which may be pulled by hand; (16) **sledge,** see as a main entry; (17) **sleigh,** =**hand sled;** (18) **stamp,** a stamp operated by hand; (19) **strap,** (see quots.); (20) **trunk,** see as a main entry; (21) **valise,** a small bag or case usu. carried in the hand.

(1) **1846** in LYELL *Second Visit* (1849) II. 22, I left the hand-car and entered a railway-train. **1948** *Dly. Oklahoman* (Okla. City) 4 June 11/5 A 30 car-cattle train was due at the place of accident an hour after the handcar left the rails. — (3) **1863** *Rep. Comm. Patents 1861* I. 313 Improvement in Hand Corn-Planters. . . . The attachment to hand corn or seed planters of a tube [etc.]. — (4) **1879** *N.Y. Tribune* 2 Dec., A monster cup supported on an iron hand-frame.

(5) **1666** *Boston Town Rec.* VII. 32 Euery man . . . is to make hand gates for more conueniensy, for to pass thorow & not to haue onely railes to drawe. — (6) **1947** *Chi. Sun* 25 Nov. 10/3 The huge narcotic supply . . . was found in an unlocked hand grip. — (7) **1870** *Rep. Comm. Agric. 1869* 329 These hand-huskers are not of much importance, as their main object is to save the hand of the operator. — (8) *a***1906** O. HENRY *Trimmed Lamp* 3 Lou is a piece-work ironer in a hand laundry.

(10) **1855** *Chi. W. Times* 18 Oct. 1/7 There are at least half a dozen different varieties of hand-planters, some planting two hills, and some only one hill at a time. **1868** *Iowa Agric. Soc. Rep. 1867* 140 The common process of cultivation is deep spring plowing, . . . planting with hand-planters. — (11) **1857** *Ill. Agric. Soc. Trans.* II. 120 A self raker, and even a binder, may be just as simple in its structure as some *hand raker*, considering what it does. **1868** *Mich. Agric. Rep.* VII. 285 Some of the self-rakers performed better in the various circumstances in which they were tried, than any of the hand-rakers. — (12) **1847** *Rep. Comm. Patents 1846* 44 In the hand rocker and semi-circular, . . . the quantity of sand and gravel which these machines can work is small. — (13) **1846** *De Bow's Review* I. April 306 The cotton was either prepared by hand-roller gins . . . or it was sent in the seed to Philadelphia. — (14) **1946** *Harper's Mag.* Oct. 307/1, I used to shell corn with a hand-sheller.

(15) **1746** *N.H. Hist. Soc. Coll.* IX. 141, [I] went to mill with a hand sled. **1794** A. BRADMAN *Sufferings R. Forbes* 4 They undertook to haul [it] on . . . hand sleds. **1922** CADY *Rhymes* (1926) 35 Old handsleds, hoops and phosphate bags.—(17) **1836** TRAILL *Backwoods* 110 We were overtaken on our return by S——with a handsleigh, which is a sort of wheelbarrow, such as porters use, without sides, and instead of a wheel, is fixed on wooden runners, which you can drag over the snow and ice with the greatest ease, if ever so heavily laden. **1923** *Outing* Jan. 152/3 Farther along, the land takes the form of a hog's-back, an ideal place for the toboggan and the hand sleigh. — (18) **1882** *Postal Guide for Jan.* 719 Matter produced by the hand-stamp, the typewriter, or the copy-press. **1886** *Delineator* XXVIII. 402 We are prepared to furnish Rubber Hand-Stamps and Daters. — (19) [**1856** *Knickerb.* XLVII. 278 Now the aisle [of a streetcar] is full, and short men are hanging upon the leather straps.] **1895** WAIT *Car-Builder's Dict.* 65 Hand-straps (street and suburban cars). Straps attached to the inside hand-rail for passengers to hold on by. Generally made in the form of a double loop. — (21) **1882** LATHROP *Echo of Passion* viii, He seemed to consider, and went to his hand-valise. **1891** ELLIS *Check No. 2134* 228 Isaac Garrity, carrying a small hand valise, entered the first car after the smoker.

6. In colloq. and slang phrases: (1) *hands round, hands-all-round*, one of the "calls" in square dancing, also transf., cf. **5.** (12) above; (2) *(to be) on hand*, (*a*) to be present, (*b*) of money, in hand; (3) *to get a (good) hand*, to receive applause; (4) *to tip one's hand*, to reveal one's intentions, *slang;* (5) *to play a lone hand*, to carry out one's plans without assistance; (6) *to call one's hand*, see * **call,** *v.* **5.** (9).

(1) **1835** LONGSTREET *Ga. Scenes* (1843) 127 'Music!' said Crouch. 'Hands round!' said the fiddler; and the whole band struck into something like 'The Dead March.' **1864** *Rio Abajo Press* 5 April 3/1 The *Arizona Miner* . . . and the Press will go 'Hands-all-round' for anything that may be for the mutual interest of both Territories. — (2) (*a*) **1835** *Knickerb.* V. 200 We who are now 'on hand' are no better discriminators than those who have gone before us. **1925** *Chattanooga* (Tenn.) *Times* 15 Nov. 31/3 The debutantes and collegians, men and women are on hand for the Yuletide holidays. (*b*) **1917** MERWIN *Temperamental Henry* 45 Cash on hand—$0.10. **1926** *Sat. Ev. Post* 30 Jan. 58/1 Just how much money have you on hand? — (3) **1890** in H. PALMER *Stories Base Ball Field* 66 Browning was sure to be recognized and given a 'hand' every time he came to the bat. **1922**

SANDBURG *Slabs of Sunburnt West* 39 It's a good act—we got a good hand. — **(4) 1927** RUSSELL *Trails* 35 The country's rough, an' by holdin' the coulees they're within a hundred yards before they're noticed. It's an old bull that tips their hand; this old boy kinks his tail and jumps stiff-legged. — **(5) 1932** *Blue Valley Farmer* (Okla. City) 3 March 6/7 Any statesman who becomes so radical must 'play a lone hand,' according to the publicity organs of the unpunished criminals of Wall Street.

b. *To hand weed*, to clean (a crop) by removing the weeds with the hands.

1786 WASHINGTON *Diaries* III. 12, I began to hand weed the drilled Wheat from the Cape. **1873** *Maine Bd. Agric. Rep.* 126 The rows should be run straight, as this will give an opportunity to hoe close, and thereby save a good deal of hand-weeding. **1887** *Courier-Journal* 31 Jan. 6/5 The rows require hand-weeding and thinning out to the proper distances.

As the last term in **big, Black, blind, boat, brush, coarse, cotton, cow, dead man's, deck, elder, foul, glad, field, full, gun, half, hired, hoe, off, over, pat, plow, razor, section, shore, task, three quarter, top hand.**

* **hand,** *v.*

1. *tr.* To give, grant, concede, also with *out. Slang.*

1901 MERWIN-WEBSTER *Calumet K.* ii. 21, I told him he ought to give it to somebody else, and he handed me a lot of stuff about my experience. **1929** *Randolph Enterprise* (Elkins, W.Va.) 18 April 1/6 Mayor Maxwell looked them over and handed out various fines.

b. *To hand it to*, to give, concede begrudgingly. *Slang.*

1909 O. HENRY *Options* 28 I've had it handed to me in the neck, too. **1923** H. L. FOSTER *Beachcomber in Orient* xiv. 377, I do not like John [Chinaman]. . . . But, to use the vernacular, you have to hand it to him.

c. *To hand one the can*, to discharge, to "can." *Slang.*

1919 *Detective Story Mag.* 23 Nov. 49 Yesterday—was it yesterday? —the manager handed me the can.

* **handbook,** *n.* A book in which bets, usu. on horse races, are recorded, or a place where such bets are made. Also attrib.

1894 *Voice* 20 Sep., In every saloon which boasts a ticker are to be found men who will register a bet to any amount. These 'handbook' men are all [etc.]. **1914** *Sunset* Feb. 82/1 I've known 'em to go as low as four a week for protecting a hand-book. **1938** ASBURY *Sucker's Prog.* 306 Until the election of Fred Busse as Mayor in 1907 gambling was largely confined to betting on the races, and naturally Chicago became the biggest handbook and poolroom town in the country. **1946** *Chi. D. News* 26 June 14/2 The mob was . . . operating handbooks with full knowledge of your police department.

b. Also **handbooking,** *n. attrib.*

1904 *N.Y. Times* 15 June 1 The handbooking possibilities on the Derby are the bone of contention.

* **handcart,** *n.*

1. *attrib.* Of or pertaining to those who emigrated to the Far West in handcarts, esp. to those Mormons who went on foot with handcarts to Utah in 1856.

[**1855** *N.Y. Herald* 4 Dec. 4/3 The *Mormon* . . . is out with a long article illustrating to the enterprising Saints bound for the Great Salt Lake, who cannot raise the means for horses, mules or oxen, the feasibility of using handcarts for the transportation of their small children and baggage . . . over the great plains and desert defiles.] **1878** BEADLE *Western Wilds* 300 She had embraced Mormonism at the age of twenty, and come at once to Utah (sixteen years before) in the first hand-cart company. *Ib.* 333 Two divisions of the hand-cart emigrants were on the plains, and in danger of starvation. **1942** STENGER *Mormon C.* 79 The first three handcart companies which came through in 1856 had no more severe a time than almost any company crossing the plains. **1949** *Sun. World-Herald Mag.* (Omaha) 22 May 17/3 Strangest caravans to cross Nebraska in pre-railroad days were the Mormon handcart expeditions of 1856–60.

2. handcarter, one who went West with his supplies and possessions in a handcart, esp. during the Colorado gold rush of 1859.

1859 H. VILLARD *Pike's Peak Gold Fever* (MS) 21 Quite a number of 'hand carters' were brought in by the stage. **1860** ——— *Pike's Peak Gold Regions* 23 One came up almost hourly with hand-carters and footmen that slowly journeyed over the sandy undulations of the Plains. **1931** WILLISON *Here They Dug Gold* 46 These poor handcarters and footmen, wantonly deceived by guidebooks and editors, were soon 'hungry, in rags, shoeless, with sore and swollen feet and without shelter from the rains, snows and chilling winds.'

hand game. *W.* An Indian gambling game wherein one player guesses in which hand another has concealed a stone or other small object. Also transf. Now *hist.*

1740 *S. Car. Hist. Soc. Coll.* IV. 92 We will play a Hand Game upon them, and do not Doubt to restrain the Spanish Garrison, keeping them in and till the Craft is Safe. **1910** MOORHEAD *Stone Age N. Amer.* I. 437 The native game called 'hand-game' or 'guessing-game' was played. **1947** DEVOTO *Across Wide Missouri* 101 Cards, the hand game, drinking, brawling, an attempt at lynching, . . . engaged the interest of Edward Warren, Stewart's surrogate, in the first days of this rendezvous.

* **handkerchief,** *n.* As the last term in **bear's, flag, head handkerchief.**

* **handle,** *n.*

1. In colloq. phrases: **a.** *To be* (*go, slip*) *off the handle*, to become overexcited, lose self control; to die.

1825 NEAL *Bro. Jonathan* I. 107 How they pulled foot, when they seed us commin', most off the handle, some o' the tribe, I guess. **1843** STEPHENS *High Life N.Y.* II. 10 Sartinly you must [go]—the old woman would go off the handle if I should come back without you. **1843** HALIBURTON *Attaché* 1 Ser. xxviii, If Old Cran. was to slip off the handle, I think I should make up to . . . [his daughter], for she is . . . most a heavenly splice. **1872** HOLMES *Poet* x. 331 My old gentleman means to be Mayor or Governor or President or something or other before he goes off the handle.

Articles used in the hand game, Indian poker or stick dice

b. *To* (or *up to*) *the handle*, quite fully, wholeheartedly.

1833 *Louisville Public Advt.* 9 May, He is determined to carry on the contest 'to the handle.' **1835** LONGSTREET *Ga. Scenes* 234 We'll all go in for you here up to the handle. **1884** *Milnor* (Dak.) *Teller* 19 Sep., A band of fifty-two pretty American girls are . . . doing the Old World 'up to the handle.'

c. *To fly off the handle* (or *helve*), to lose one's composure or self control, esp. through anger.

1820 in *Amer. Sp.* XXI. (1946) 117/2 Mr. Clay . . . is almost headlong in his eloquence. To use a *back-woods* similie, he seems as tho' he would *'fly off the helve,'* during the paroxisms of declamation. **1869** MARK TWAIN *Innocents* iv. 45 George's voice was just 'turning,' and when he was singing . . . it was apt to fly off the handle and startle every body. **1948** *Dly. Ardmoreite* (Ardmore, Okla.) 15 July 6/1 You can't fly off the handle when people goad you too far.

d. *Like the handle of a jug*, (see quot.).

1836 CROCKETT *Adventures* 24 Such judges I should take it are like the handle of a jug, all on one side.

2. handlebar mustache, a flowing mustache suggestive in shape of the handlebars of a bicycle. *Colloq.*

1933 JACKSON *White Spirituals* 65 An elderly man with handle-bar moustache was leading in the most approved manner, holding his book in the left hand and beating time. **1948** *Houston* (Tex.) *Post* 14 June 2/2 The Handlebar moustache and the high button shoe have long since made their exit.

As the last term in **jug, panhandle.**

* **handle,** *v.*

1. *To handle without gloves* (or *with gloves off*), to deal with harshly or with exceptional plainness or frankness.

1827 A. SHERWOOD *Gaz. Georgia* 94 Marion County has been handled without gloves. **1828** *Richmond Enquirer* 20 May 3/4 (Th.), The Baltimore Republican handles Mr. Clay with gloves off. **1892** *Nation* 5 May 345/2 The prophets and practitioners of the naturalistic school . . . are here handled without gloves.

2. *tr.* **a.** To master (an opponent), esp. at wrestling. **b.** (See quot.) Both *colloq.*

(a) **1848** Bartlett 169. **1858** Thoreau *Maine Woods* 137 The most interesting question entertained at the lumberers' camp was, which man could 'handle' any other on the carry. — (b) **1895** *Pop. Science Mo.* July 377 Each counsel is interested in selecting twelve men he can influence to his view of the case, or, in the court language, 'men he can handle readily.'

3. To transport or deal in (commodities).

1876 Raymond *8th Rep. Mines* 461 It should be stated that the Central Pacific Railroad handled much of their own coal, bringing it from the Lincoln Mine, California. **1903** *Booklovers Mag.* Oct. 403 All stores handle post-cards as side lines.

4. To proceed against (a person) at law. *Colloq.*

1902 Harben *A. Daniel* 231 I'll agree to use my influence with Alan Bishop not to handle you by law. **1902** ——— *Georgians* 267 Ef you come inside my yard an' tetch a thing I'll handle you for trespass.

handler ˈhændlɚ, *n.* [Du. *handelaar*, trader.] One engaged in trade, esp. among the Indians. *Obs.* Cf. also **freight, gun, pan-handler.** — **1697** in Munsell *Ann. Albany* III. 22 Ordered the sheriffe to goe throw the handlers, and require them to rebuild the house. **1754** *Mass. H.S. Coll.* 3 Ser. V. 25 We, the traders (or handlers) to Oswego, most humbly beg leave to remonstrate to your Honor the many hazards and difficulties we are subject to.

* **handling,** *n.* The care given to cotton in harvesting and marketing. *Obs.* — **1833** *Niles' Reg.* XLIV. 178/2 It [the cotton] was selected from his crop, and in point of color, cleanliness, staple and *handling*, (as it is termed by growers), is equal to any we remember to have seen.

hand-me-downer. A dealer who handles hand-me-down clothing. *Rare.* — **1884** *Boston Journal* 23 Aug., 'You remember the second hand overcoat I bought here for $8 yesterday?' 'Never dakes pack anythings ven once solt, my frent,' said the hand-me-downer.

hand organ. A portable organ played mechanically by turning a crank with the hand. Also attrib.

[**1796** Morse *Univ. Geog.* II. 334 Not to mention their hand-organs [i.e., of the Dutch], and other musical inventions.] **1837** Hawthorne in *U.S. Mag.* I. 34 Here a Frenchman, with a hand-organ on his shoulder; and there an itinerant Swiss jeweller. **1858** Holmes *Autocrat* viii. 210, I am but a hand-organ man,—say rather, a hand-organ. **1891** *Atlantic Mo.* June 809/2 In New Orleans, I was astounded at the strange phenomenon of a colored hand-organ grinder. **1944** Holton *Yankees* 52 For instance, she was as excited as I over the hand-organ monkeys and the cinnamon bears.

Also **hand-organist,** one who operates a hand organ.

1896 Howells *Impressions & Experiences, Tribulations Cheerful Giver* iv. 162 Ought one to give money to a hand-organist, who is manifestly making himself a nuisance before the door of some one else?

hand out.

1. *Baseball.* (See quots. and cf. * **hand,** *n.* **2.**) *Obs.*

1845 in *Appleton's Ann. Cyclo.* (1886) X. 77/2 A ball being struck or tipped, and caught . . . is a hand out. **1856** *Porter's Spirit of Times* 6 Dec. 229/1 A player who shall intentionally prevent an adversary from catching or getting a ball, is a hand out. *Ib.*, A ball being struck at and tipped, and caught, either flying or on the first bound, is a hand out.

2. Someting to eat, as a sandwich, handed to a tramp. Also attrib. and transf. *Slang.*

1882 Sweet & Knox *Texas Siftings* 195 If I can't get a 'hand-out' for it I can at least expatiate on its merits. **1910** *Salt Lake Tribune* 27 Nov. 32/7 On the first floor 'hand-out' luncheons were served. **1949** *Va. Quart. Review* Winter 49 His vote . . . had been based on the assumption that ERP would be another UNRRA, a relief measure, a handout.

3. The process of dealing or drawing cards. *Rare.*

1904 White *Blazed Trail Stories* II. iv. 193 I'll turn you fer it. First man that gits a jack in th' hand-out stays.

hand piece.

1. *pl.* (See quots.)

1840 *Spirit of Times* 31 Oct. 414/2 (We.), By 'hand pieces' our readers will understand that we refer to loops buckling on to the reins which gives one a better hold. **1897** *Outing* XXX. 111/1 The hand-pieces of four-in-hand reins should be about an inch or inch and an eighth wide and of moderate thickness.

2. (See quot.)

1887 *Postal Laws* 413 Registered packages which are to pass to postal clerks by hand-to-hand receipts, known as 'hand' pieces.

hand sledge. (See quot. 1848 and cf. **hand sled.**)

1848 Ballantyne *Hudson Bay* (1890) 83 The hand-sledge is a thin flat slip or plank of wood, from five to six feet long by one foot broad, and is turned up at one end. It is extremely light and Indians invariably use it when visiting their traps, for the purpose of dragging home the animals or game they may have caught. **1856** Kane *Arct. Exped.* II. xxv. 249 They have given us hand sledges for our baggage. **1932** *Old-Time N. Eng.* Jan . 136/1 We hear of Leftenant Law coming again to Sharon . . . bringing with him, this time, a brass kettle on a hand sledge.

* **handsome,** *a.* [See note.]

"The Americans use the word 'handsome' much more extensively than we do: saying that Webster made a handsome speech in the Senate: that a lady talks handsomely, (eloquently:) that a book sells handsomely. A gentleman asked me on the Catskill Mountain, whether I thought the sun handsomer there than at New York" (1837 Martineau *Society*, III. 83).

1. Of any aspect of a landscape: Satisfying to the eye, of pleasing appearance. *Obs.*

1751 *N.J. Archives* XIX. 103 The said lot makes a handsome corner between two roads, the one leading to Trenton and the other to Brunswick. **1804** Clark in *Lewis & C. Exped.* I. (1904) 82 He saw Som handsom Countrey. **1860** C. Durfee *Hist. Williams College* 164 He had been free . . . of his opinion that the College could never flourish in the valley of the Hoosac, one of the handsomest valleys in the world.

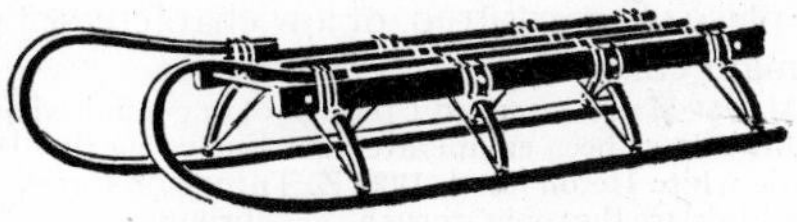

Hand sledge or Indian sleigh

2. *To do something handsome, to do the handsome thing,* (see quot. 1877).

1796 Washington *Writings* XIII. 268 The proprietors of the federal city have talked of doing something handsome towards it like wise. **1853** Haliburton *Wise Saws* iii, When a feller has just given me a snug travellin' job onasked, and done the handsome thing, it ain't any great return to make arter all to let him put his oar in sometimes. **1877** Bartlett 274 To do the handsome thing is to be generous, particularly in returning a favor; to be very polite.

3. handsome Harry, deer grass.

1893 *Amer. Folk-Lore* VI. 142 *Rhexia Virginica*, handsome Harry. Hanover, Mass.

hand trunk. A small trunk that may be carried in the hand.

1641 *Conn. Probate Rec.* I. 39 Goods, belonging to Joyce Ward, wydow, . . . one boxe, with a little hand Trunke. **1863** M. Harland *Husks* 225 She was dressed in black, wore a crape veil, and carried a small hand-trunk. **1879** B. F. Taylor *Summer-Savory* 74 A little hand-trunk, about the size of a large woodchuck, is brought out, girt with a little leather strap.

* **handy,** *a.* **1. handy cake,** (see quot.), *obs.* **2. handy vote,** =**hand vote,** *obs.* **3.** *handy as a pocket in a shirt*, (see quot.), *colloq.*

(1) **1799** *Monthly Mag.* VIII. 873 The cake under consideration is called *pot-ash cake*, because pot-ash is one of the articles which enter into the composition of it. They call it likewise *handy-cake*, because it can be made so *handily*. — (2) **1713** Sewall *Diary* II. 398 Took the Churches Handy vote; Church sat in the Gallery. **1742** *Boston Rec.* 305 He was Chose by a Handy Vote. — (3) **1942** Warnick *Dialect Garrett Co., Md.* 8 Handy as a pocket in a shirt, adj. phr., very convenient.

* **hang,** *n.*

1. A hanging. *Rare.*

1846 Farnham *Prairie Land* 105, I reckon you never see a real hang, did you?

2. In colloq. phrases: (1) *To get, get into, acquire the hang of*, to understand the meaning, operation, or significance of something; (2) *to lose the hang of*, to get out of touch with, *rare;* (3) *not to give* (or *care*) *a hang*, not to care, or attach any significance to.

(1) **1839** *N.O. Picayune* 8 Mar. 2/4 I'm jealous I've got the hang of the way they du things in that cold section about as well as the general run of folks. **1845** N. S. Prime *Hist. L.I.* 82 If you must have an indifferent teacher for your children, let it be after they . . . have acquired 'the hang of the tools' for themselves. **1852** Regan *Emigrant's Guide* 85 It's an all-sufficient piece o' nonsense that grammar—I never could git into the *hang* of it. **1944** *Evanston Review* 12 Oct. 20/3 Before long I got the hang of that, too. — (2) **1857** T. S. Woodward *Reminisc.* (1939) 6 There are but few of that detachment of Georgians now living. . . . If there are any more of them it is very few, and I have lost the hang of them. — (3) **1910** *Collier's* 26 Feb. 11/2 Our friend up the river . . . don't care a hang. **1945** *Nation* 17 March 289/2 The Minister of War had gone over his head in the Montiero case, and he no longer gave a hang what the press did.

***hang**, *v.*

1. *tr.* To hitch or secure (a horse) to a gatepost, tree, etc. *Colloq. Obs.*

1835 *S. Lit. Messenger* I. 581 Having arrived at Blank, we *hung* our horses, as Virginians always do after riding them. *c***1845** W. T. THOMPSON *Chron. Pineville* 110 I hung him hard and fast.

2. *intr.* and *tr.* To fail, or cause (a jury) to fail, to reach a verdict, usu. **hung,** *a.* as **hung jury.**

1846 BRYANT *California* xxvi. 291 The jury, after the case was referred to them, were what is called 'hung'; they could not agree. **1850** J. WEIR *Lonz Powers* I. 142 [These men] either caused their acquittal or hung the panel, . . . by opposing or refusing to agree to any verdict, saving that of 'Not Guilty.' **1930** *Randolph Enterprise* (Elkins, W.Va.) 13 Feb. 1/6 She had been tried once before for the crime and the result was a hung jury.

3. In substantival combs.: (1) **hangbird,** (see quot. 1917 and cf. **fire hangbird**); (2) ***nest,** (see quots. and cf. **Baltimore, chestnut, orchard hangnest**); (3) ***out,** a place of resort, freq. of low characters; (4) **over,** see as a main entry.

(1) **1789** MORSE *Amer. Geog.* 59 Upwards of one hundred and thirty American Birds have been enumerated . . . [including the] Hangbird, Heron, Little white Heron [etc.]. **1824** Z. THOMPSON *Gazetteer Vt.* 18 The singing birds are the robin, thrush, . . . springbird, goldfinch, and hangbird. **1917** *Birds of Amer.* II. 258 Baltimore Oriole. . . . Other Names.—Golden Robin; English Robin; Hang-bird; Hang-nest. — (2) [**1730** BAILEY *Dict.*, Xochaitotl, a bird in America . . . called the Hang Nest or Hang Bird.] **1796** MORSE *Univ. Geog.* II. 209 Baltimore bird, or hang nest, *Oriolus Baltimore.* **1917** *Birds of Amer.* II. 258.— (3) **1895** *Harper's Mag.* April 712/1 He [the tramp] . . . calls his clubhouse a hang-out. **1947** *True* Nov. 93/1 At a hangout there . . . the harried leaders of the outlaws had rendezvous'd.

b. In verbal combs.: (1) *To hang around,* (see quot. 1848); (2) *to hang round,* =prec.; (3) **to hang up,* (*a*) to stop, suspend effort, (*b*) in logging, to discontinue a drive, also of logs and lumber, to be held up by lack of water, (*c*) of a jury, to fail to reach a decision, cf. **2.** above.

(1) **1848** BARTLETT 170 *To hang around,* to loiter about. **1937** SUTHERLAND *Professional Thief* 23 In all cases the severance of legitimate connections is followed by . . . hanging around places frequented by thieves. — (2) **1830** *Corrector* (Sag Harbor, N.Y.) 26 June 1/3 What a number of young gentlemen you have in this city—hanging round the corners—standing in hotel doors. **1910** MCCUTCHEON *Rose in Ring* 297 Dick had said that Braddock was 'hanging 'round' with his brother. — (3) (*a*) **1854** *Cong. Globe* App. 24 Jan. 108/2 When I came to that point I 'was befogged, and hung up for the night.' **1895** *D.N.* I. 372 A mower, when rain was comin on: 'I reckon we'll have to hang up for all day.' (*b*) **1878** *Lumberman's Gaz.* 18 Dec. 476 Others . . . find . . . their logs 'hung up' for want of water to float them. **1908** WHITE *Riverman* 14 We can't afford to hang up the drive. (*c*) **1931** *Randolph Enterprise* (Elkins, W.Va.) 29 Oct. 1/1 The jury hung up on it and had to be discharged.

c. In colloq. phrases: (1) *To hang up one's fiddle,* to give up, quit; (2) *to hang to the ropes,* to persevere in one's efforts; (3) *to hang the landlady,* (see quot.); (4) *to hang one on,* to deal (one) a blow; (5) *to hang and rattle,* (see quot.).

(1) **1830** SMITH *Life & Writings of Downing* 90 (We.), You'll have to hang up your fiddle till another year. *a***1848** in BARTLETT 170 When a man loses his temper and ain't cool, he might as well hang up his fiddle. — (2) *a***1872** in W. MATHEWS *Getting On in World* 314 He was unstable in mind, and although his friends advised him to 'hang to the ropes,' he was not getting rich fast enough. — (3) **1902** CLAPIN 220 *Hang the landlady,* to decamp without payment, a phrase applied to 'moonshining' practices of all descriptions. — (4) **1908** MCGAFFEY *Show-Girl* 200 Hauling off wifey hangs one on Alla's map. — (5) **1936** BARNARD *Rider* 113, I was buffaloed and was riding like a Cheyenne squaw, when the boys yelled, 'Stay with him, Parson. Hang and rattle.'

***hanger,** *n.*

1. A building in which tobacco is cured. *Obs.*

1763 in *Amer. Sp.* XX. (1945) 46 You must take care to have ready a *hanger* (or *tobacco-house*) . . . making thus the form of a house of an oblong square . . . and cover . . . with cypress-bark, or palmetto-leaves. **1797** IMLAY *Western Territory* (ed. 3) 246 Care must be taken to have ready a hanger (or tobacco-house) . . . [built in] the form of a house of an oblong square . . . , and covered with cypress bark or palmetto leaves.

2. (See quots. 1899, 1905.)

1897 CLOVER *Paul Travers' Adv.* 97 The bottles were neatly arranged in pyramids around the octagonal counter, while attractive hangers and flaring dodgers proclaimed the virtues of the lotion in the most effective manner. **1899** *Boston Herald* 19 Jan. 8/4 Will you please send me a hanger of the United States; I believe you call it the commercial map of the United States. **1905** CALKINS & HOLDEN *Modern Advertising* 352 Hangers are printed or lithographed cards of various shapes and sizes, to be hung up in a store.

***hanging,** *n.* and *a.* In combs.: (1) **hanging bee,** a public execution by hanging, a lynching, *facetious;* (2) **bird,** =**hangbird;** (3) **bridge,** a suspension bridge, *obs.;* (4) **day,** Friday, as the day upon which executions by hanging usu. take place; (5) **ears,** the Kalispel, a Salishan tribe of Indians formerly found in n. Idaho and n.e. Washington; (6) **match,** =**hanging bee,** *rare;* (7) **moss,** =**Spanish moss;** (8) **rock,** an overhanging rock, one which appears to be without support; (9) **shelf,** a shelf which is suspended from an overhead support.

(1) **1836** R. WESTON *Visit* 96 The chief topic of discourse seemed to be the 'hanging-bee' at Trenton. **1943** HICKS *Amer. Dem.* 498 These unfortunates paid the full penalty for their crime at a great hanging-bee, held at Mankato, Minnesota, the day after Christmas, 1862. — (2) **1789** ANBUREY *Travels* II. 198 The most remarkable are the Fire-bird, Hanging-bird, Blue-bird and Humming-bird. **1872** *Md. Laws* 664 It shall be unlawful . . . to shoot . . . any of the following named birds . . . viz: Robin, blue-bird, thrush, . . . hanging bird and woodpecker. — (3) **1815** *Niles' Reg.* IX. 92/1 The main post-road . . . crosses the Brandywine on a hanging bridge. **1841** *Knickerb.* XVII. 234 Models of hanging bridges . . . and a thousand other half-completed plans, all prepared for patents, were mingled in inextricable confusion. — (4) **1806** *Balance* (Th.), 11 Nov. 355 Next Friday [the newspaper] promises to make its debut. Friday—that's hanging day—but no matter. **1846** *Dollar Newspaper* (Phila.) 25 Nov. 3/5 Friday last was 'hanging day' with us.

(5) **1837** IRVING *Bonneville* I. xii. 127 The Nez Percés, the Flatheads, and the Hanging-ears, pride themselves upon the number of their horses. — (6) **1833** *Niles' Reg.* XLIV. 282/2 Even a hanging-match has brought 20 or 30,000 of them together. — (7) **1853** P. PAXTON *Yankee in Texas* 59 'Hanging moss,' . . . feeds, and thrives only upon malaria and vapor of the most deadly kind. **1900** *Cent. Mag.* Feb. 510/1 Though you should pass yet farther to the south, . . . until you reached the land of hanging moss, you still might see . . . the sphinx face of the old West. — (8) **1809** in *Amer. Sp.* XV. 270/2 At the hanging rock on the north side Gap of Coopers Mountain. **1923** *Ib.*, The sharp turning up, and in most cases overturning, of the massive sandstones of the Lee and Pennington make 'hanging rocks' where streams cross this belt of intense folding. — (9) **1825** NEAL *Bro. Jonathan* I. 188 A wide board which ran below the ceiling, . . . from one side of the room to the other; a hanging shelf such as may be found in every New Englander's farmhouse, to this day; loaded with cheeses, ropes of onions [etc.]. **1881** MCLEAN *Cape Cod Folks* ii. 31 In one dark recess I came into forcible contact with a hanging-shelf of pies.

hang-over ˈhæŋˌovɚ, *n.*

1. One who remains or is left over.

1894 *Outing* XXIV. 67/2 Then there are a few 'hangovers' who have tried before, and two or three green candidates. **1932** LEWINSON *Race* 272 One candidate was branded as a hangover from the corrupt aldermanic machine.

transf. **1947** *Redbook* Oct. 100/3 Maybe it was a hangover from the day when dreaming mammas thought *Fauntleroy* was the beau ideal for little lads.

2. The aftereffect of alcoholic dissipation. *Slang.*

1912 W. IRWIN *Red Button* 93 This was the first time in his life that Tommy North had ever admitted a 'hangover.' **1947** *Chi. Tribune* 22 July 2/7 I've got a hangover from a party that lasted until five o'clock this morning.

Hannahills ˈhænəˌhɪlz, *n. pl.* Also **hannahills.** (See quots.)

1814 MITCHILL *Fishes N.Y.* 416 Black harry, hannahills, and blue-fish, are some of the names by which he [=sea bass] is known. **1842** *Nat. Hist. N.Y., Zoology* IV. 25 Sea Bass . . . is sometimes called Blue-fish, Black Harry, Hannahills, and Black Bass. **1884** GOODE *Fisheries* I. 407 In the Middle States the Sea Bass is called . . . 'Hannahills.'

***happen,** *v.*

1. *To happen at,* to be present at a particular place by chance. *Colloq.*

1800 WEEMS *Washington* i. 5 Some young American happening at Toulon. **1891** F. CHASE *Hist. Dartmouth Coll.* I. 478 [Ira Allen] providentially happened at said Convention.

2. *To happen in, into,* to drop in or come in casually or by chance. *Colloq.*

1749 G. O. SEILHAMER *Hist. Amer. Theatre* I. 29 Joseph Morris and I happened in at Peacock Bigger's and drank tea there. **1845** SOL. SMITH *Theatr. Apprent.* ii. 26 One day I happened in at Mr. Hall's bakehouse. **1904** A. FRENCH *Barrier* 174 Mather, . . . happening into the store while she was there, had told her that the increase of his business was forcing him to employ more stenographers.

b. Also *to happen down by, over at, round at.*

1860 HOLMES *E. Vener* xxiv, I jest happened daown by the mansion-haouse last night. **1871** EGGLESTON *Hoosier Schoolm.* xxxii. 222 Miss Nancy just happened over at Mrs. Thomson's humble home. **1901** CHURCHILL *Crisis* 366, I happened round at Colonel Carvel's this afternoon.

***happenstance** ˈhæpənˌstæns, *n.* [f. **happen, v.*+*-stance.* Cf. **circumstance.*] An occurrence or happening, an accident. *Colloq.* — **1897** *Outing* XXX. 557/1, I guess it was just a 'happenstance.' **1948** *Minneapolis Morn. Tribune* 28 Sep. 6/2 A sad happenstance occurred the other day when a mildewed French tavern named Emile's was condemned, to make way for modern city development.

* **happy,** *a.*

1. (See quot. 1923.) *Colloq.*

1851 *Polly Peablossom* 84 He munched a bunch of grass and looked on as quietly as if his master was *happy* at a camp-meeting. **1923** *D.N.* V. 209 happy, adj. Overcome with religious excitement to the extent of hysteria. [Mo.]

2. Happy Family, a collection of birds and animals which P. T. Barnum purchased in Coventry, England, for $2,500 and exhibited in his museum. Also transf.

1861 *Cin. Commercial* 2 April 1/5 The Happy Families—Black Spirits and 'Yaller' Spirits. . . . Here we have vipers, serpents, rattlesnakes and skunks, all in the same bed. **1863** GAIL HAMILTON *Gala-Days* 345, I remembered Barnum's Happy Family, and went out to the hen pen, and brought in a little auburn chicken. **1947** *Redbook* Aug. 90/3 He suggested a pony ride to distract her from showing him any more happy families, but she shook her head.

3. happy hunting ground, a region abounding in game, thought of by the Indians as the paradise to which the souls of warriors and hunters passed after death. Often pl. and transf.

1837 IRVING *Bonneville* 260 Then we killed at his grave fifteen of our best and strongest horses, to serve him when he should arrive at the happy hunting grounds. **1876** COZZENS *Ariz.& New Mex.* 424 Animals were hunted in the 'happy hunting-grounds' for amusement only, but were never killed. **1948** Calif. Acad. Sciences *News Letter* Oct. 4 Marin County—naturalists' happy hunting ground—supplied the thirty nature subjects now displayed in the Mineral Hall corridor of North American Hall.

* **harbor,** *n.*

1. A river, or the mouth of a creek, serving as a place of safety for ships. *Obs.*

1646 *New Haven Col. Rec.* 199 On the east side of the great river or harbour. **1710** *Providence Rec.* XI. 146 Ye west side of ye Salt River or harbour lieing against the southerne End of Providence Twone. **1846** POLK in *Pres. Mess. & P.* IV. 464 And for the mouths of creeks, denominated harbors.

2. In combs.: (1) * **harbor master,** (see quot.); (2) **police,** (see quots.), *obs.;* (3) **porpoise,** a cetacean, *Phocaena phocaena,* found on the north Atlantic and Pacific coasts; (4) **seal,** a small seal found along the north Atlantic Coast of the U.S.

(1) **1935** *N.Y. Hist. Soc. Bul.* July XIX. 28 During the night an enormous section of ice, locally known as a 'harbor-master,' broke off and floated down the Hudson River. — (2) *a*1870 CHIPMAN *Notes on Bartlett* 188 *Harbor Police,* police whose special duty is to prevent roguery in or near the shipping.—N.Y. city. **1882** McCABE *New York* 375 Special detachments . . . watch over the neighboring waters as a 'Harbor Police.' — (3) **1884** GOODE *Fisheries* I. 14 On the Atlantic coast occurs most abundantly the little Harbor Porpoise *Phocaena brachycion* Cope known to the fishermen as 'Puffer,' 'Snuffer' [etc.]. **1911** *Rep. Fisheries 1908* 314. — (4) **1884** *Nat. Museum Bul.* No. 27. 643 *Phoca vitulina,* Linné. Harbor Seal. North Atlantic, from New Jersey . . . northward. **1884** GOODE *Fisheries* I. 55 The Harbor Seal appears to have formerly been much more numerous on portions of our eastern coast than it is at present.

* **hard,** *n.*

1. One who advocated the use of metallic money as the national currency. Often **Hards,** the political faction favoring hard money. Now *hist.*

For the use of this word as a political term see *Amer. Sp.* V. 408–13.

1844 *Lexington Observer* 14 Aug. 3/2 The locofocos, . . . are divided in that State [Missouri], and are known by the distinctive appellations of the '*Hards*' and '*Softs*,' in consequence of their views upon the currency question. **1847** *Cong. Globe* 17 Feb. 442/1 [Mr. Sawyer] was known as a disorganizer in Ohio; as a 'soft.' . . . Since he came here, he has occupied the position of what is termed a 'hard.' **1876** *Chi. Tribune* 3 Aug. 1/5 The Hards stand on the platform because they desire resumption, and the repeal of the Resumption act is necessary to have it. **1946** *St. Louis Globe-Democrat* 18 Aug., In 1840 he fought one of his greatest battles, leading the wing of the party known as the 'Hards' to victory over the 'Softs.'

2. (*cap.*) *pl.* The conservative faction of the Democratic party in New York about 1852–60. Cf. * **Hard-Shell,** *n.* **2.**

1853 *N.Y. Tribune* 2 April (B.), The *Hards* embrace the Cass Hunkers of 1848, of the National school of politics. **1859** *Harper's Mag.* Nov. 833/1 The main subject of difference between the two parties in the Convention referred to the manner of choosing the delegates to Charleston—the 'Softs' wishing them appointed by the State Convention, the 'Hards' desiring them to be chosen by the people in the several congressional districts. **1914** *Cyclo. Amer. Govt.* I. 111 The 'hards' were New York Democrats, the name 'hard' being applied to the regulars by the opposing faction. . . . The factions, 'hards' and 'softs' . . . continued up to the Civil War.

* **hard,** *a.*

1. Of a person or place: Tough, indomitable, given to, or characterized by, violence or outlawry. *Colloq.* or *slang.*

1818 WEEMS *Drunkard's Looking Glass* 17 Hurra, for me! a hard horse I am gentlemen, a proper hard horse, depend! **1834** *Sun* (N.Y.) 14 April 2/2 The prisoner was what some people would call a 'hard colt.' **1873** BEADLE *Undevel. West* 304 If one has read a description of the 'hard quarter' of one city, he knows enough about all. **1893** JAMES *Cow-Boy Life* 12 The thieves, cut-throats, thugs and hard characters of every State in the Union had swooped down upon Texas. **1945** *Reader's Digest* June 92/2 One hard character called Dutch Kate held up a California stage to recoup a gambling loss of $2000.

b. hard case, a hardened criminal or outlaw.

1836 *Quarter Race Ky.* (1854) 38 (We.), A 'hard case' called Emanuel Allen. **1900** GARLAND *Eagle's Heart* 64, I like you and I don't want you to think I'm a hard case. **1947** *Atlantic Mo.* Oct. 60/1, I was taken over to Cell Block 9 which is the solitary block where they keep all the hard cases.

c. Hard-cases, (see quots.). Also **Hard-case State.**

1845 *St. Louis Reveille* 14 May 2/4 The inhabitants of . . . Oregon [are called] Hard Cases. **1875** *Chamber's Journal* 13 March 171/2 The inhabitants of . . . Oregon [are called] Hard-cases or Web-feet. **1948** MENCKEN *Supp.* II. 638 *Hard-case State* . . . had reference to the large number of evil characters who flocked into the Oregon country in the early days.

d. hard lot, a ne'er-do-well, or good-for-nothing. *Colloq.*

1876 MARK TWAIN *Tom Sawyer* xxx. 228, I'm a kind of a hard lot—least everybody says so. **1884** —— *H. Finn* xi. 88 She told . . . all about pop and what a hard lot he was.

e. hard ticket, (see quot.).

1877 BARTLETT 703 A 'hard ticket,' a man whom other people had better let alone; an unscrupulous man to deal with.

2. (*cap.*) Of or pertaining to the Hard-Shell or Hunker faction of the Democratic party in N.Y. *Obs.*

1853 *Knickerb.* XLII. 653 What and who entered into the contest? 'Hard' men a plenty—'Softs' not a few. **1872** *Harper's Mag.* May 847/2 Having called a meeting of their followers to indorse the Hard State nominations at Tammany Hall [etc.].

b. Of or pertaining to those who advocated metallic money. *Obs.* Cf. * **hard,** *n.* **1.**

1844 *N.O. Picayune* 26 Aug. 221/3 We don't know whether he runs on the *hard* or *soft* ticket; but we think . . . he will give his opponents a *hard* run of it.

3. In miscellaneous combs.: (1) **hard bake,** hard upper soil, hardpan, *rare;* (2) * **cider,** see as a main entry; (3) **copy,** (see quot.); (4) **land,** (see quot.); (5) **luck story,** a story of one's ill fortune, *colloq.;* (6) **metal,** ?designating plates or dishes made of tin or iron, *obs.;* (7) * **pan,** see as a main entry; (8) * **rock,** denoting a miner accustomed to underground work in hard massive formations, also **hard rocker;** (9) **scrabble,** see as a main entry; (10) **shell,** see as a main entry; (11) **sledding,** see **sledding;** (12) **spot,** (see quot.); (13) **surface,** denoting an improved road having a hard top, also **hard surfacing,** cf. **hard surfaced;** (14) * **times,** * **ware,** see as main entries.

(1) **1885** BAYLOR *On Both Sides* 318 You can't mine in hard-bake with a pewter spoon. — (3) **1890** *Railways of Amer.* 182 To facilitate taking copies they are printed with an ink which will give several impressions on strong, thin tissue-paper, forming 'soft copies,' while

the 'hard copy,' or original, goes with the freight to be checked against it when the car is unloaded. — **(4) 1827** MRS. HALL *Letters* 106 The country which we passed through to-day is of the same character as the rest of the New England States that we have seen, 'hard land,' as some people call it, I suppose in ridicule, as it is neither more nor less than good, honest rocks and stones.

(5) 1909 O. HENRY *Roads of Destiny* 62 [What she] said when the prince fitted that 3½ A on her foot was a hard-luck story compared to the things I told myself. **1947** DOWNEY *Lusty Forefathers* 322 The Road agent . . . spared anyone with a plausible hard luck story. — **(6) 1758** in SHELTON *Salt-Box House* (1900) 297, 1 Doz. Large Hardmettle Ditto [i.e., plates]. **1762** *Essex Hist. Coll.* XLIX. 276 To Be Sold . . . best Hardmetal Plates and Dishes. — **(8) 1923** B. M. BOWER *Caravan Bonanza* iv. 48 Tommy's an old, hard-rock man. **1943** HOWARD *Montana* 41 These officials were mostly easterners, pilgrims and tenderfeet; the 'hill rats' and 'hardrockers' didn't take to them, and the feeling was mutual. **1949** *Chi. D. News* 9 April 1/6 A machinist drilling with a crew of hardrock miners 75 feet below the surface of the vacant lot where Kathy fell . . . said the pipe had not been completely opened.

(12) 1900 S. A. NELSON *A B C Wall St.* 144 Hard spot. A strong feature of the market indicating that a certain stock or group of stocks holds up unusually well, despite a weak or heavy market in respect to the remainder of the list. — **(13) 1926** *K.C. Times* 11 May, Just one-half mile south of Turner, Kansas, on hard-surface road. **1926** *Hutchinson* (Kans.) *News* 8 May, Where the county commissioners have allowed a petition for hard surfacing a road over a definite route, they cannot . . . make a substantial change in the route.

b. In the names of, or with reference to, plants and animals: (1) ***hard-bargain,** (see quot.); (2) **hard-bark hickory, =mockernut hickory;** (3) **clam,** (see quot. 1883); (4) **doubler,** a mating crab with a hard shell, *colloq.;* (5) **hack,** any one of several American shrubs, esp. *Spiraea tomentosa* and the shrubby cinquefoil, *Potentilla fruticosa,* also attrib.; (6) ***head,** see as a main entry; (7) **maple,** the sugar maple, *Acer saccharum,* also one of several other species of maple; (8) **pine,** any one of various pines the wood of which is somewhat hard, as the longleaf pine, *Pinus palustris;* (9) **tail,** (*a*) a jurel, *Paratractus crysos,* or either one of two cyprinoid fishes, *Gila elegans* and *G. robusta,* of the Colorado basin, (*b*) a mule, *slang;* (10) ***wood,** see as a main entry.

(1) 1894 *Chi. Record* 1 May 13/2 So far as learned by fishermen here [N.Y.], not one has been caught thus far in either the Connecticut or Thames river, although 'hard-bargains,' (alewives) have been here some time. — **(2) 1897** SUDWORTH *Arborescent Flora* 114 Hicoria alba . . . Mockernut (Hickory). . . . Common Names. . . . Hardbark Hickory (Ill.) — **(3) 1846** COOPER *Redskins* i, Softclams . . . are not made for gentlemen to eat. Of course I mean the hard clam. **1883** *Nat. Museum Bul.* No. 27, 233 *Venus mercenaria* . . . is the 'quahaug,' or 'round clam,' sometimes known as the 'hard clam.' **1943** CARSON *Food From Sea* 67 The hard clam, on the other hand, is much more abundant south of the Cape, and occurs all the way to Texas. — **(4) 1942** DAVIS *Chesapeake Biol. Lab. Pub.* 53, 13 Last stage immature female peelers ('hard doublers').

(5) 1814 BIGELOW *Florula Bostoniensis* 120 *Spiræa tomentosa.* Downy Spiræa. Hardhack. . . . A very common shrub in pastures and low grounds. **1894** R. E. ROBINSON *Danvis Folks* 224 [He] resumed his way toward the bee, still carrying the hardhack sapling. **1947** *Sat. Review* 31 May 15/2 The hill pastures . . . are in season apt to be full of spiraea tomentosa, alias hardhack, alias steeple bush. — **(7) [1778** CARVER *Travels* 496 The Maple. Of this tree there are two sorts, the hard and the soft.] **1810** MICHAUX *Arbres* I. 28 Sugar maple. . . . Rock maple . . . [ou] Hard maple, . . . secondairement en usage. **1832** BROWNE *Sylva* 108 This species, the most interesting of American maples, is called Rock Maple, Hard Maple and Sugar Maple. **1916** SETON *Woodcraft Man.* 290 Sugar Maple, Rock Maple, or Hard Maple (*Acer saccharum*). A large, splendid forest tree, 80 to 120 feet high; red in autumn . . . Bird's-eye and curled Maple are freaks of the grain. . . . Its sap produces the famous maple sugar. — **(8) 1884** SARGENT *Rep. Forests* 202 *Pinus palustris.* . . . Long-leaved Pine. Southern Pine. Georgia Pine. Yellow Pine. Hard Pine. **1890** *Boston Journal* 3 Nov. (*advt.*), A valuable tract of hard-pine timber-land. **1916** SETON *Woodcraft Man.* 267 Long-leaved Pine, Georgia Pine, Southern Pine, Yellow Pine, or Hard Pine (*Pinus palustris*). A fine tree, up to 100 feet high; evergreen; found in great forests in the Southern states; it supplies much of our lumber now; and most of our turpentine, tar, and rosin. — **(9)** (*a*) **1884** GOODE *Fisheries* I. 325 The Hard-tail is a most voracious fish, waging active war upon the schools of small fish. **1911** *Rep. Fisheries 1908* 311. (*b*) **1932** W. KELLEY *Inchin' Along* 243 'Hit de grit, hardtails,' Big Shine roared. **1938** NIXON *Forty Acres* 41 The barn thus becomes a sort of club, sometimes a harmonious inter-racial club, for gossip about the weather, crops, personalities, and mules, which may be referred to by proper names or as 'jar-heads' or 'hard-tails.'

c. In terms relating to money or currency: (1) **hard currency,** metallic as distinguished from paper currency, *obs.;* (2) **dollar,** orig. the Spanish or Spanish American peso, called in Sp. *peso duro,* later a coined metallic dollar, or money in general; (3) **Jackson,** metallic currency as distinguished from paper notes, *obs.;* (4) ***money,** see as a main entry.

(1) 1851 GREEN *Twelve Days* 33 The politicians were fiercely discussing the 'hard' and 'soft' currency question. —**(2) 1780** *N.J. Gaz.* 22 Nov. (Th.), 'Three hard Dollars Reward' for the recovery of a black mare. **1842** *S. Lit. Messenger* VIII. 406/1 After receiving a quantum of hard dollars . . . we bade adieu to the lively town. **1909** O. HENRY *Roads of Destiny* 156 I'd blow de express car and make hard dollars where you guys gets wind. — **(3) 1844** UNCLE SAM *Peculiarities* I. 217 Whoever prefers a small quantity of hard Jackson, as they call it, to a pocketful of shin-plasters, as they call 'em, is a goney.

For *To have a hard row to hoe,* see ***row,** *n.*

***hard,** *adv.*

1. Very much, extremely, with severity. *Colloq.*

1850 KINGSLEY *Diary* 97 Mr. Hopkins is hard sick. **1907** O. HENRY *Trimmed Lamp* 13 He isn't a millionaire so hard that you could notice it, anyhow.

2. In combs.: (1) **hard-backed cooter,** see **cooter;** (2) **boiled,** see as a main entry; (3) **burned, burnt,** rendered exceptionally hard by severe burning in a kiln; (4) **looking,** denoting one who is a hard case *q.v.;* (5) **shelled,** see as a main entry; (6) **surfaced,** of a road, having a surface that is hard.

(3) 1851 C. CIST *Cincinnati* 214 Walls of hard-burnt brick. **1868** *Rep. U.S. Comm. Agric.* (1869) 360 Hard-burned terra cotta pipes. **1893** KATE SANBORN *Truthful Woman* 45 Half-cylindrical plates of hard-burnt clay. — **(4) 1862** *So. Confederacy* (Atlanta) 3 May (Th.), The other prisoners are all sharp, intelligent-looking men, no hard-looking cases like Yankee prisoners . . . usually are. **1890** *Harper's Mag.* May 894/1 The hardest-looking case I had ever seen came to the door.

(6) 1929 *Randolph Enterprise* (Elkins, W.Va.) 26 Sep. 2/1 A corps of men . . . have been surveying . . . the piece of hard-surfaced road.

3. In phrases: (1) *To be hard run,* to be in straitened circumstances, cf. next; (2) *to have it hard, to be hard up against it,* to be beset by hardships and difficulties. Both *colloq.*

(1) 1791 in *Jrnl. Wm. Maclay* (1927) 354 He is your enemy. He said you will be hard run, and mentioned Smilie as being your competitor. **1834** *Cong. Deb.* 10 March 848 Men, I say, who, . . . are 'hard run' to make ends meet, . . . when they receive the magic touch of the 'pressure,' they burst, like a bombshell. **1845** SOL. SMITH *Theatr. Apprent.* 65, I am not the only actor who has been 'hard run' at Pittsburgh. — **(2) 1890** JEWETT *Strangers* 56 She's real good feelin', but she's had it very hard and gits discouraged. **1895** ——— *Nancy* 29 Nancy has had it hard. **1903** ADE *People You Know* 41 Florine was up against it ever so Hard.

***hard-boiled,** *a.* **1.** Rigid, narrow, pedantic. **2.** Denoting stiff articles of clothing, esp. a derby hat. Cf. **boiled shirt. 3.** Hard-headed, callous, shrewd.

(1) 1886 MARK TWAIN *Speeches* 137 (R.), Hard-boiled, hide-bound grammar. — **(2) 1903** A. ADAMS *Log Cowboy* ix. 58 That fellow in front of the drug store over there with the hard-boiled hat on. **1907** S. E. WHITE *Arizona Nights* 321 He sifted in wearin' one of these hard-boiled hats. **1919** LEWIS *Free Air* 86 To Claire, traveling men were merely commercial persons in hard-boiled suits. — **(3) 1919** in F. A. POTTLE *Stretchers* (1930) 354 We are too hardboiled to make much of a demonstration. *Ib.* 358 Two hardboiled Irish sergeants are terrorizing the barrack. **1945** *Craig* (Colo.) *Empire-Courier* 25 July 2/4 Those guys are not a bit hardboiled, the taxpayers pay their salaries and they'd be happy to do what the majority want.

***hard cider.**

1. hard cider campaign, the presidential campaign of Gen. William Henry Harrison in 1840, in which his supporters used hard cider and log cabins as symbols of the frontier hardihood and democratic simplicity of their candidate. Cf. **log cabin 1. b.**

1857 *Spirit of Times* 3 Jan. 281/1 It was not infrequent, as late as the hard-cider campaign of 1840, (in which I took an active part for Martin, *le Renard,*) that I heard some old farmer remark . . . 'Stop a little, and let's hear what the *boy* has to say.' **1890** HOWELLS *Boy's Town* 4 The wild hard-cider campaign roared by my boy's little life without leaving a trace in it.

2. In expressions alluding to this campaign or to the

supporters of Harrison, as **hard cider congress, democrat, quilting.** Also **Hard Ciderism, -ite.** *Obs.*

1840 *Spirit of Times* 20 June 187/3 (We.), Hard cider democrat; Hard cider quiltins. **1840** *Rough Hewer* (Albany, N.Y.) 13 Aug. 207/1 The hard ciderites, it would seem, have joined in a league with the Prince of Darkness himself, to decry and ridicule even the holy rites of religion. **1841** *Kendall's Expositor* (Wash., D.C.) 17 Feb. 19/2 A political rhymester in Ohio has the following touch at Hard Ciderism. **1842** F. Wood in *Cong. Globe* App. 20 May 413/1 The people . . . thought best to substitute a *hard cider* Congress.

***hardhead,** *n.*

1. Any one of various American fishes, esp. the alewife or the menhaden. Also **hardhead shad.**

1812 Bentley *Diary* IV. 124 The true Herring . . . [is] very distinct from the species common on our coast, called Alewive & Hardhead. **1884** Goode *Fisheries* I. 474 This species [of salmon] is everywhere known as the 'Steel-head.' The name 'Hard-Head' is sometimes applied to it. *Ib.* 569 About Cape Ann, 'Pogy' [as a name for the menhaden] is partially replaced by 'Hard-head,' or 'Hard-head Shad.' **1947** *Times-Herald* (Wash., D.C.) 9 May D-3/1 While there are thousands upon thousands of hardheads in the Chesapeake Bay country at present it's just not the proper time for the anglers.

2. (See quots.)

1821 *Jrnl. Science* III. 57 The ore bed . . . is covered by a stratum of sand, about two inches thick, containing innumerable round, quartzose stones of various sizes, called by the inhabitants of the town [Bennington, Vt.], *hard-heads.* **1884** Goode *Fisheries* I. 31 The California Gray Whale . . . [is] called by whalemen 'Devil-fish,' 'Hard Head,' 'Gray Back' [etc.]. *Ib.* 845 [American commercial sponges include] Glove Sponge . . . and Yellow and Hard Head, both under the name of (*Spongia agaricina*), subspecies *corlosia.*

***hard money.**

1. Ready money, cash. *Colloq.*

1842 Kirkland *Forest Life* II. 161, I could readily have exchanged the wool for yarn at the store, . . . or I could have sold it for 'hard money.' **1872** Powers *Afoot & Alone* 199 Your true American miner has no opinion which is not worth hard money.

2. *attrib.* Of or pertaining to those who favored metallic currency.

1831 in Benton *30 Yrs. View* I. (1854) 187/2 If I was going to establish a working man's party, it should be on the basis of hard money:—a hard money party, against a paper party. **1838** Nancy N. Scott *Memoir of H. L. White* 231 For myself, I now am, and ever have been a hard money man. **1875** *Chi. Tribune* 12 July 4/7 A hard-money Democrat such as Gov. Tilden. *Ib.* 13 Sep. 4/2 Success followed the hard-money platforms of the Democratic party in New Jersey and New York. **1877** Hale *G. T. T.* 47 He is the same man that beat Allen on the hard money question last year. **1947** *Time* 10 Mar. 19/3 Lew Douglas was an internationalist first, a 'hard-money' man second.

b. Also **hard money government, law.** *Obs.*

1834 *Cong. Deb.* 17 Jan. 264 The restoration of the Government to what it was intended by the framers of the constitution to be, a hard-money Government. **1852** Gouge *Fiscal Hist. Texas* 235 The bank then proves too powerful for the State, with all its hard-money laws, and its hard-money constitution.

***hardpan,** *n. fig.* The lowest, most basic part of anything. Also attrib. *Colloq.*

1852 W. B. Pike in *N. Hawthorne & Wife* (1885) I. 444 You are the only one who breaks through the hard-pan. **1883** *Boston Journal* 11 Nov., The City Council is making rapid progress toward the hard pan of disgrace when a first-class hotel keeper refuses to trust its members. **1896** Frederick *Damnation of T. Ware* 53 He's all wool an' a yard wide when it comes to right-down hard-pan religion.

b. Also in phrases.

1873 Aldrich *Marjorie Daw* 168 He's a realist,—believes in coming down to what he calls 'the hard pan.' **1883** *Cent. Mag.* June 285/2 [The book] didn't appear to get down to hard-pan or to take a firm grip on life. **1908** *Springfield W. Republican* 13 Feb. 3 It will be well for Springfield to get down to hard pan.

hard scrabble.

1. A place thought of as the acme of barrenness where a livelihood may be obtained only with great difficulty. Also attrib. Often as a proper name. Also *colloq.*

1804 *Lewis & Clark Exped.* VII. (1905) 38 Got on our way at hard Scrable Perarie. **1888** *Cong. Rec.* 1 May 3589/1 For the farmer, in those days, there was mighty bad sledding on the road to Hard Scrabble. **1904** *Pittsburgh Gazette* 7 July 4 In the early days of my ministry . . . I was sent to take charge of a little hard-scrabble circuit. **1946** Partridge & Bettmann *As We Were* 173 Many a farmer who had barely been able to eke a living from a hard-scrabble hillside came into a prosperous business of 'taking in' summer boarders. **1949** *Sat. Ev. Post* 30 April 22/3 She was the daughter of a hard-scrabble rancher over on Butter Creek.

Hence **hard scrabbler.**

1948 *Sat. Ev. Post* 31 July 96/2 Capt. John Smith's hard scrabblers could see for themselves that if they didn't get the timber cleared from the land there would be no place to plant corn, and if the corn wasn't planted nobody would eat.

2. A vigorous effort made under great stress. *Colloq.*

1812 *Salem Gazette* 29 May 2/3 Presidential Hard Scrabble! **1854** S. Hale *Letters* 7 By a well-organised hard-scrabble, Luc. and I get the breakfast things washed by nine o'clock.

***Hard-Shell,** *n.* Also ***hard-shell.**

1. (*cap.*) =**Hard-Shell Baptist.**

1845 *Knickerb.* XXVI. 285 A 'Hard-Shell' recently turned a 'Soft-Shell' out of church. **1896** *Sunday School World* Oct. 340/1 The Hard-shells have a church six miles from here on the top of the Blue Ridge. **1934** Carmer *Stars Fell* 58 What I don't like about hardshells, they think everybody but them is goin' t' hell—even the little dead babies.

attrib. **1848** in Thompson *M. Jones* (1872) 260 Ther was . . . a old hardshell preacher, as they call 'em in Georgia. **1866** F. Kirkland *Bk. Anecdotes* 67 [He stopped] to surround the Hard-shell church, at which his miseries had all been so augmented. **1943** Holt *Carver* 27 Jim would oblige with the 'Hard-Shell Sermon.'

b. *transf.* A severe or strait-laced person. Also attrib.

1858 *So. Cultivator* XVI. 187/2 We have, however, one or two specimens in our eye of the genus, *hard shell*, who still do as their *daddies* did. **1901** *World's Work* June 798/1 Now the schoolmaster and the manufacturer are fast getting the better of these 'hard-shell' types of men. **1948** *Time* 9 Feb. 17/2 Almost everybody except hardshell pacifists agreed that the U.S. must be stronger than before World War II.

2. A member of the more conservative of the two factions of the New York Democratic party between 1852 and 1860. In full **hard-shell democrat.** Now *hist.*

1853 *N.Y. Tribune* 2 April (B.), The difference between a *Hardshell* and a *Softshell* is this: one favors the execution of the Fugitive Slave Law and goes for a distribution of the offices among the Nationals, while the other is a loud stickler for Union and Harmony. **1859** Bartlett 190 *'Hardshell democrats,'* also called 'Hardshells,' and again abbreviated into Hards . . . The Hards embrace the Cass Hunkers of 1848, of the National school of politics; while the softs are composed of the remnants of the Van Buren and Adams party of 1848. **1896** Haswell *New York* 416 Later they were termed 'soft shells,' and the other faction 'old hunkers,' or 'hard shells.'

b. Also **hard-shell democracy.** *Obs.*

1867 *Harper's Wkly.* 23 Mar. 178/3 They are the tool of the only aristocracy that ever existed in the country, and are therefore the 'real grit hard-shell' Democracy.

3. Hard-Shell Baptist, a member of the Primitive Baptist Church, an Old-School or Antimissionary Baptist.

1845 *Knickerb.* XXVI. 285 They have singular denominational distinctions in the west, among which the *'Hard and Soft Shell Baptists'* are most remarkable. **1900** *Cong. Rec.* 31 Jan. 1363/2 One of the best old preachers that ever I knew . . . was a Hardshell Baptist. **1945** *Amer. Sp.* April 81 One is a 'Primitive Baptist,' a 'Fundamental Baptist,' or just a plain 'Hardshell Baptist.'

attrib. **1853** in Glisan *Jrnl. Army Life* (1874) 123 His first two sermons sounded very much like good old hard shell baptist harangues. **1853** Baldwin *Flush Times Ala.* 122 His grandfather . . . was a noted divine of the Anti-Missionary or Hardshell Baptist persuasion in Georgia.

b. Hard-Shell Baptist church, a church of this denomination.

1905 Rice *Sandy* 82 Mr. Meech was the pastor of the Hard-Shell Baptist Church in Clayton. **1944** Duncan *M. Graham* 23 Jeremiah, who had been churched for mild drinking by the strict rule of the Hard-Shell Baptist church, found spiritual food at the courthouse.

c. Hard-Shell Baptist preacher, a minister of this faith.

1838 in *S.W. Hist. Quart.* XVII. 54 Was introduced to Daddy Spraggins, a Hardshell Baptist preacher. **1858** *Salem* (Ill.) *Advocate* 27 Jan. 1/2, I am an unlearnt Hard shell Baptist preacher. **1932** W. Kelley *Inchin' Along* 158 He had been a hard-shell Baptist Preacher.

4. hard-shell clam, =**hard clam.**

1818 *Amer. Mo. Mag.* II. 296 The hard shell clam . . . is cooked by roasting, or is made into soup. **1855** *Knickerb.* XLVI. 222 In the sounds, 'hard-shell' clam-catchers, fishermen, and oyster-men steadily ply their different callings. **1876** *Marin Co. Jrnl.* (San Rafael, Calif.) 27 July 3/3 Hard and soft shell clams are abundant and easily gathered.

∗hard-shelled, a.

1. *fig.* Thick-skinned, stubborn, not easily changed. *Colloq.*

1861 *N.Y. Tribune* 2 Dec. (Chipman), Hard-shelled but honest-hearted Democrat. **1873** W. MATHEWS *Getting On in World* 153 There is no man so 'hard-shelled' that his soul cannot be reached by kindness. **1894** *Chi. Record* 2 May 1/7 He can perceive no change in what he calls the 'hard-shelled' attitude of congress toward his measures. **1938** *Rocky Mt. News* (Denver) 30 April 8/4 There is a real chance to get some worthwhile decisions from our Supreme Court since our President UN-packed that old hard-shelled outfit.

2. In combs.: (1) **Hard-shelled Baptist,** =**Hard-Shell Baptist;** (2) **clam,** =**hard clam;** (3) **hickory,** the shagbark or scaly-bark hickory.

(1) **1842** BUCKINGHAM *Slave States* I. 238 In this quarter there are two descriptions of Baptists: the orthodox, or evangelical, who are practically as well as theoretically pious, and disposed to assist in all benevolent undertakings; and the Antinomians, or, as they are here called, 'hard shelled' Baptists. **1941** STUART *Men of Mts.* 331 If you could see all of us Republicans, Democrats, Methodists, Forty-Gallon Baptists, Hard-shelled Baptists, . . . shaking hands and asking the other how he is after the long night o' sleep. — (2) **1839** BRIGGS *H. Franco* II. 2 Close by, was a negro opening hard-shelled clams. **1883** *Nat. Museum Bul.* No. 27, 240 *Taper staminea* . . . known as the 'Carpet-Shell,' 'Little-Neck Clam,' and 'Hard-Shelled Clam,' is abundant on the whole Californian coast. **1889** *Pall Mall Gaz.* 30 Nov. 7/1 There are two distinct varieties of clam in America, hard and soft shelled. The latter are never eaten raw. — (3) **1796** B. HAWKINS *Letters* 17 After entering the savanna 1/4 of a mile, enter a grove of dwarf hard shelled hickory trees. **1800** ——— *Sk. Creek Country* 28 The whole of this flat . . . is covered with oak and the small hard shelled hickory.

∗hard times.

1. (See quot. 1891.) Also attrib. *Obs.*

1844 in *Amer. Sp.* XXII. 203/1 At Conference, he [Bishop Morris] appeared in character, with 'hard-times' coat and striped blanket, looking quite as much like a missionary as any of us. **1891** WELCH *Recoll. 1830–40* 354 A kind of goods were manufactured . . . for men's clothing, adapted for and called 'Hard Times,' a mixed cloth, of black and white or grey and black, spun and woven of coarse, loose thread, presenting the appearance of heavy wool mixtures, which was really nothing but a sort of cotton shoddy, and sold for twenty-five cents per yard. **1894** R. E. ROBINSON *Danvis Folks* 102 The shelves bore the same rolls of calicoes, ginghams, jeans, hard-times, and cotton.

2. hard-times party, social, =**tacky party.** *Colloq.*

1923 *Outing* April 6/3 Well, Sparks, you might just as well hang up the rest of that shirt somewhere; it's draped over your shoulders like a costume for a hard-times social. **1948** *Aurora* (Ill.) *Beacon-News* 7 Nov. 21/6 This yearly dance has the aura of hard times parties as the guests come attired in blue jeans, slacks and sweaters.

∗hardware, n.

1. Hard liquor, whisky. *Obs.*

1839 *Spirit of Times* 1 June 153/3 (We.), He prepared to swallow his fifth invoice of 'hardware.' **1852** *Knickerb.* XXXIX. 105 He was reckless and 'extravagant'; that is, he spent all his money for 'hardware.'

2. *Collect.* Weapons, esp. pistols. *Slang.*

1865 BOUDRYE *Fifth N.Y. Cavalry* (1868) 38 Capt. Hammond . . . charged upon the rebels in his front, crying as he flew forward, 'give them your hardware, boys!' **1946** *Cong. Rec.* App. A 4019/1 A delegation of thin-lipped citizens, toting impressive-looking hardware, called.

3. In combs.: (1) **hardware house,** a place where hardware is sold; (2) **paper,** (see quot.), *obs.;* (3) **store,** a store in which hardware is sold; (4) **wheat,** a now unidentifiable variety of wheat, *rare.*

(1) **1848** *Ladies' Repository* VIII. 281 They . . . roll them out into long bars, such as you see on sale at hardware houses. [**1851** WATKIN *Trip* 11 Here [in New York City], was a quarter of a mile of 'hardware' warehouses.] — (2) **1886** *Harper's Mag.* June 48/1 Wrapping the stem [of the peach tree] . . . with strong hardware or sheathing paper. — (3) **1789** *Boston Directory* 196 Richards, Samuel, hard-ware store, south-corner of Ann-street. **1817** S. BROWN *Western Gaz.* 236 Six new dry goods stores, one hardware store. **1945** WALLACE *Barington* 72 A notable thing about the hardware store was that drummers who sold dry goods and groceries spent much time there after they had made the rounds of their own firms. — (4) **1848** *Hunt's Merch. Mag.* XIX. 481 He terms [it] 'Hardware wheat.'

∗hardwood, n.

1. *attrib.* Designating *land* or a *ridge* where hardwood is the prevailing growth.

*a***1817** DWIGHT *Travels* II. 165 The land in this township is that, which is here called *hardwood land;* or land, producing oak and other kinds of wood . . . which are called hard. **1859** HILLHOUSE (tr.) Michaux *Sylva* I. 154 They grow on level grounds or on gentle declivities, and form what are denominated *Hard-wood lands.* **1867–8** *Ill. Agric. Soc. Trans.* VII. 578 Some elevated ridges—called technically, hard wood ridges—escaped wholly, or in part the effects of the fire. **1881** *Harper's Mag.* Oct. 687/1 A hard-wood ridge, . . . supplied us with the best of firewood.

2. hardwood timber, timber consisting of hardwood.

1850 E. S. SEYMOUR *Sk. Minnesota* 170 The country is covered with a dense forest of hardwood timber. **1946** *Democrat* 25 July 4/3 For Sale—200 acres Hardwood timber and land.

∗hare, n.

1. hare fly, prob. any one of various large, usu. dark-colored botflies. *Obs.*

1805 LEWIS in *L. & Clark Exped.* (1904) II. 319 The large biteing or hare fly as they [are] sometimes called are very troublesome to us. I observe two Kinds of them a large black species and a small brown species with a green head.

2. hare-lip sucker, a sucker, *Lagochila lacera*, of the Mississippi Valley. Cf. **cutlips** (*b*).

1877 *Phila. Acad. Nat. Sci. Proc.* 281 The commonest and most valued species of sucker found in [Ga.] . . . is everywhere known by the name of 'hare-lip Sucker.' **1896** D. S. JORDAN *Check List of Fishes* 243 *Lagochila lacera* . . . [is called] Hare-lip Sucker; Cut-lips; Split-mouth Sucker; May Sucker [etc.].

As the last term in **black-tailed, California, changeable, little chief, prairie, red, Rocky Mountain, sage, Sierra, snow-shoe, swamp hare.**

hark from the tomb. Something in the extreme, as a beating, scolding. *Colloq.* — **1884** MARK TWAIN *Huck. Finn* 246 (R.), Then Susan she waltzed in, and if you'll believe me, she did give Hare-lip hark from the tomb! **1900** ——— *Autobiog.* 179 (R.), You will write him a letter and give him Hark from the Tomb?

∗Harlan, n. [Dr. Richard *Harlan* (1796–1843), a Philadelphia naturalist.] Used in the possessive to designate a *buzzard* or *hawk*, *Buteo harlani*, sometimes considered a form of the red-tailed hawk but perhaps better treated as a distinct species.

1857 *Rep. Comm. Patents 1856: Agric.* 112 Harlan's buzzard was added to the fauna of the United States by Mr. Audubon about the year 1830, and by him called after Dr. Richard Harlan, of Philadelphia. **1872** *Amer. Naturalist* VII. 172 Prof. Baird . . . expressed a desire to see the specimens designated in my 'Catalogue of the Birds of Kansas' as 'Harlan's Hawk' and the 'Florida Cormorant.' **1874** COUES *Birds N.W.* 352 *Buteo harlani*. . . . Harlan's Buzzard; Black Warrior. . . . I regard the claims of this species to validity as not yet established. **1917** *Birds of Amer.* II. 72 Harlan's Hawk (*Buteo borealis harlani*) is nearly uniform black; its tail is much mottled with grayish, rufous and white, and has a subterminal band of black.

Harlemite ˈharləmˌaɪt, *n.* A native or inhabitant of Harlem in New York City.

1896 *N.Y. Dramatic News* 4 July 6/3 With music nightly the place will be of great benefit to Harlemites. **1897** *Outing* XXX. 488/1 As a contrast to the scope and aim of the Harlemites, . . . the Riverside Wheelmen, of New York, may be quoted. **1938** *Newsweek* 10 Jan. 28/3 Fight fans, Harlemites, and the unduly curious will be entertained by Joe Louis' awkward debut as a screen actor.

∗harlequin, n.

1. The bead snake *q.v.*, or a snake of similar appearance. In full **harlequin snake.** Cf. **∗coral snake.**

1831 AUDUBON *Ornith. Biog.* I. 276 The beautiful little snake . . . is commonly called the *Harlequin Snake*, and is, I believe, quite harmless. **1885** C. F. HOLDER *Marvels Anim. Life* 131 The coloring of the harlequin . . . is exceedingly rich. **1921** *Outing* Aug. 219/2 The coral snake (known also as the harlequin snake) ranges from South Carolina southwestward to Texas.

2. harlequin (cabbage) bug, a hemipterous insect, *Murgantia histrionica*, injurious to cabbage and other garden vegetables. Cf. **calicoback.**

1870 *Rep. Comm. Agric.* (1871) 90 The harlequin cabbage-bug . . . has been much complained of during the past year as doing great damage to the cabbage in North Carolina and elsewhere. **1884** *Ib.* 309 The Harlequin Cabbage-bug derives its name from the gay, theatrical, harlequin-like manner in which the black and orange-yellow colors are arranged upon its body. **1946** *Progress* March 11/2 It is quick and certain death to leaf hoppers, Lygus bugs, chinch bugs, squash bugs cabbage caterpillars, the harlequin bug, the fireworm (on cranberries), and cattle lice.

∗**harmless,** *a.* (Often *cap.*) Used of religious groups, esp. Dunkers, to emphasize their innocence, meekness, etc. *Obs.*

1796 MORSE *Univ. Geog.* I. 282 They appear to be humble, well-meaning Christians, and have acquired the character of the *harmless* Tunkers. *Ib.* 283 They [Mennonists] call themselves the Harmless Christians, Revengeless Christians, and Weaponless Christians. **1867** DIXON *New Amer.* II. 184 The name by which they [Tunkers] are known in the neighbourhood of their villages in Pennsylvania, Ohio, and Indiana, is that of the Harmless People. **1872** C. LANMAN *Japanese in Amer.* 277 The Tunkers or Harmless People . . . profess to be animated in their religion by fraternal love.

Harmonian hɑr'moniən, *n.* =**Harmonist.** *Obs.* — **1825** in DUNN *Indiana* (1919) II. 1099 This is a specimen of the means resorted to, in order to injure the reputation of the Harmonians. **1826** *Va. Herald* (Fredericksburg) 11 Nov. 3/1 The Harmonians lately established at Economy, sixteen miles below Pittsburgh, are progressing most rapidly in some of the most important manufactories.

harmonica hɑr'mɑnɪkə, *n.* [L., fem. of *harmonicus*, harmonic.]

1. A musical instrument, invented by Benjamin Franklin, consisting essentially of tuned or musical glasses so arranged as to be conveniently played upon, orig. by rubbing their edges with the moistened finger. *Obs.* Cf. **armonica, harmonicon.**

*c*1765 *Lett. to Franklin* (1859) 24 Now for the room we call yours: there is in it your desk, the harmonica made like a desk, a large chest [etc.]. **1786** JEFFERSON *Writings* VII. 21, I am much pleased with your project on the Harmonica, and the prospect of your succeeding

Harmonica (*c*1820)

in the application of keys to it. **1861** J. S. ADAMS *5000 Musical Terms*, Harmonica, a musical instrument, the tones of which are produced from globular glasses.

2. A small reed musical instrument played by blowing; a mouth organ. Cf. **harmonicon b.**

1873 BAILEY *Life in Danbury* 237 A Danbury boy of ten winters . . . stole a harmonica Friday evening to serenade his girl with. **1908** *Sears Cat.* (ed. 118) 351 The Hohner Chromatic Harmonica is the result of many years of thought and experimenting and is the first and only practical instrument of its kind. **1949** *Sat. Ev. Post* 9 April 80/4 As children, she and her harmonica-playing brother, Danny, danced for the family and neighbors and in school entertainments.

harmonicon hɑr'mɑnəˌkɑn, *n.* [Gk. *harmonikon*, neuter sing. of *harmonikos*, harmonic.] =**armonica.** Also **grand harmonicon, harmonicum.** *Obs.* Cf. **steam harmonicon.**

1826 *19th Congress* 1 Sess. H. R. Doc. No. 22, 9 Musical Glasses, called the Grand Harmonicum . . . April 7, 1825, Francis H. Smith—Northampton, Virginia. **1827** *Md. Hist. Mag.* XVII. 265 The ladies of the family went in the evening to hear Mr. Smith play on the grand harmonicon, an instrument of his own invention. **1876** in ODELL *Annals N.Y. Stage* X. 37 Sallie Adams, the Musical Queen, will give selections from her Artistic Solos upon the Violin, . . . Piano, Harmonicon, and Banjo.

b. flute harmonicon, a wind instrument somewhat like the harmonica (sense **2.**). *Obs.*

1880 JAMES *Amateur Negro Minstrel's Guide* 35/1 Flute harmonicons, or musical sardine boxes. Each $3.

Harmonist 'hɑrmənɪst, *n.* [f. *Harmony*, Pa., see def.] A member of a communistic celibate religious group whose best-known settlement was made in 1803 at Harmony, Pa. Cf. **Economist, Economite, Rappist.**

1814 *Niles' Reg.* 28 May 208/2 *Harmony*, Butler county, has several valuable manufactories. It was settled in 1803–4, by about 160 families of *Harmonists* from Germany. **1866** WILLIAMS *Harmony Society* 82 The Harmonists have never been a litigious people. **1903** *Encycl. Americana* VIII. *s.v.*, *Harmonists*, also called Rappists and Economists, . . . emigrated to America, settling in the Connoquenessing Valley, where the Harmony Society was established. **1949** *Chi. Tribune* 9 Jan. 17/1 He is the last living member of the religious sect known as Harmonists.

Harmonite 'hɑrmənˌaɪt, *n.* =prec.

1817 BIRKBECK *Journey in Amer.* (1818) 137 The Harmonites . . . set a good example of neatness and industry. **1866** WILLIAMS *Harmony Society* 32 The twaddle of the writer about the silly weakness of the Harmonite women at the sight of a child, is also a gross caricature. **1949** *Chi. Tribune* 26 Feb. 7/1 Owen and Maclure invested $100,000 each to buy 30,000 acres on which were located the houses, mills and factories of the Harmonites.

∗**harmonium,** *n.* A wind instrument consisting of three (or four) harmonicas (sense **2.**) mounted on one central spindle. *Obs.* — **1880** JAMES *Amateur Negro Minstrel's Guide* 35/2 Three-sided Harmoniums, $2.25. Four-sided Harmoniums, $4.00.

∗**Harmony,** *n.* A religious settlement in Pennsylvania made by the Harmonists or Rappists. Usu. attrib. with reference to this group or a similar one at New Harmony, Indiana.

1826 *Va. Herald* (Fredericksburg) 16 Aug. 2/4 The oracle of Harmony spoke in a blaze of illumination. **1901** *World's Work* Oct. 1256/2 The Harmony Society, with almost the same experience—early struggles, hard-won success, and then agitation for division—has so far staved off dissolution. **1948** *Indiana Mag. Hist.* March 24 The original Harmonie Community was planted by the followers of George Rapp. **1949** *Chi. Tribune* 9 Jan. 17/2 The Harmony Society which founded New Harmony 'made a wonderful success of it.'

∗**harness,** *n.* In combs.: (1) **harness bull,** a uniformed policeman, *slang;* (2) **cop,** =prec.; (3) ∗**horse,** (*a*) a piece of equipment used in weaving, *obs.*, (*b*) =**harness racer;** (4) **horse racing,** =**harness racing;** (5) **racer,** a horse trained to race in harness; (6) **racing,** the racing of horses harnessed to light vehicles.

(1) **1903** A. H. LEWIS *Boss* 262 [The] Captain sends along a couple of his harness bulls from Mulberry Street. **1948** *Sat. Ev. Post* 17 July 18/1 To harness bulls anywhere, Monday is usually a quiet night. — (2) **1926** J. BLACK *You Can't Win* iv. 31 The 'harness cop' who had been at the front door went back to his beat. — (3) (*a*) **1881** *Rep. Indian Affairs* 93 The articles manufactured by the carpenter . . . were . . . two brick molds, fourteen beetles, one harness-horse and forty ax-handles. (*b*) **1947** *Reader's Digest* March 97/1 In the early 1900's a crooked-legged mahogany bay harness horse—a pacer—grossed an estimated million dollars for his owner. — (4) **1909** *World Almanac* 213 Harness horse racing.
(5) **1946** *Chi. D. News* 6 June 33 (*caption*), The rhythmic hoof beat of the harness racer accompanied by the click of the mutuel machines will make its debut to the Chicago sports fans tonight. — (6) **1901** *World Almanac* 266 Harness racing. **1947** *Newsweek* 8 Sep. 71/1 Harness racing is doing very well in keeping up with the flashy bankrolls of the times.

b. In colloq. phrases: (1) *To trot in double harness*, to live as man and wife; (2) *to work in harness*, to get along well together.

(1) **1838** *Lexington Observer & Rep.* 2 June, We soon hitch'd traces to trot in double harness. — (2) **1873** MARK TWAIN *Gilded Age* 373 (R.), He and I are sworn brothers on that measure; we work in harness.

As the last term in **buggy, double, express, lead, swinging harness.**

∗**harp,** *n.* (Also *cap.*) An Irishman. *Slang.* See also **French, mouth, Sacred Harp.**—**1926** T. BEER *Mauve Decade* iv. 162, I sewed up his head for a young Italamerican who had been trying to impress the haughty Harps on his street. **1944** HALSEY *Best Friends* 83 The wops and the sheenies and the harps, the Polacks and the Hunkies on the casualty lists.

harpen 'hɑrpən, *v.* [Of obscure origin.] *Naut. To harpen in*, to tighten (rigging), to draw taut. *Rare.* — **1827** COOPER *Red Rover* II. 210 Her lower rigging is harpened in, like the waist of Nell Dell, after she has had a fresh pull upon her stay-lanyards.

∗**harrier,** *n.* The marsh hawk, *Circus hudsonius.* — **1860** BAIRD *Birds of N. Amer.* 38 *Circus hudsonius*, . . . The Harrier—The Marsh Hawk. . . . Well known as one of the most common hawks inhabiting the States of the Atlantic, . . . equally abundant on the coasts of the

Pacific. **1917** *Birds of Amer.* II. 65 Slowly and steadily . . . the Harrier quarters back and forth across the fields.

* **Harris,** *n.* [Edward *Harris* (1799–1863), companion of Audubon on the Missouri River trip in 1843.] Used in the possessive in the names of various birds (see quots.).

1839 AUDUBON *Ornith. Biog.* V. 191 Harris's Woodpecker. *Picus Harrisük.* It is to Dr. Townsend that we are indebted for the discovery of this singularly marked species. **1928** *Condor* Sep.–Oct. 281 A companion . . . whom Audubon, in naming Harris' Sparrow (*Zonotrichia querula*) characterized as 'one of the best friends I have in the world.' **1939** LINCOLN *Migration* 173 One of these is the migration of Harris' Sparrow.

For **Harris' buzzard** see **buzzard,** *n.* **4.**

Harrisonian ˌhærəˈsonɪən, *n.* A political supporter of Wm. Henry Harrison (1773–1841). Also **Harrisonite.** *Obs.*

1839 *Ky. Observer* (Lexington) 25 Sep. 2/3 We are neither a *Clayite* nor a *Harrisonite.* **1840** *Ill. State Reg.* (Springfield) 4 Feb. 2/5 The Whigs are in doubt what name they should assume; whether that of Harrison-men, Harrisonites, Tippecanoe-men, or Tippecanoers. **1843** *S. Lit. Messenger* IX. 651/1 They made a Harrisonian of me in about a quarter of an hour.

* **harrow,** *n.* As the last term in **A, chain, cutaway, disk, hoe, iron tooth, side harrow.**

Harry of the West. A nickname for Henry Clay (1777–1852). *Obs.* or *hist.*

1839 *Ky. Observer* (Lexington) 24 July 3/3 'Harry of the West' came early, and General Scott later in August. **1844** *Republican Sentinel* (Richmond, Va.) 27 April 3/3 He is to be invested with a 'fine, old fashioned cocked hat,' as being the kind to which Harry of the West has been most accustomed. **1887** SCHURZ *Life Henry Clay* I. 327 With proud admiration his followers called him 'the gallant Harry of the West.'

Hartford ˈhɑrtfɚd, *n.* [*Hartford,* Conn.]

1. *attrib.* Designating a variety of grape. *Obs.*

1862 *Rep. Comm. Patents 1861: Agric.* 500 There are several species of the grape indigenous to America. . . . Of these varieties the most familiar are the Catawba, Isabella, Diana, Concord, Hartford Prolific, &c.

2. Hartford climbing fern, a delicate fern, *Lygodium palmatum,* valued esp. as an ornament.

1899 GOING *Flowers* 262 The Hartford climbing-fern, the common sensitive-fern and a few others.

3. Hartford Convention, a convention of New England Federalists which met at Hartford, Conn., in December, 1814, to consider the grievances of the New England states arising out of the War of 1812.

1814 *Niles' Reg.* 24 Dec. 269/2 Hartford convention met on the 15th, as proposed, in the council chamber of the state-house. **1854** BENTON *30 Years' View* I. 138/2 [Mr. Hayne] made allusions . . . to the assemblage known as the Hartford convention, . . . to which designs unfriendly to the Union had been attributed. **1948** *Chi. Tribune* 10 Oct. (Grafic Mag.) 17/3 The conspirators . . . again made the attempt with their infamous Hartford convention.

attrib. and *transf.* **1833** S. SMITH *Major Downing* 153 Daniel is a federalist, a Hartford Convention federalist. **1864** NICHOLS *Amer. Life* I. 49 The party that opposed it [war]—the Peace party, the Hartford Convention federalists—have never recovered from the odium of alleged British sympathies. **a1882** T. WEED *Autobiog.* 37 One of his purposes was to attend a sort of Hartford Convention at Albany.

b. Hence **Hartford conventionalist, Hartford conventionism, Hartford conventionist.** All *obs.*

1818 FEARON *Sketches* 145 It is an unholy league between apostates . . . on one part, and on the other . . . the Hartford conventionalists, the blue-light men, the embargo-breakers. **1835** H. C. TODD *Notes* 34 The names of their political parties are *Patent Democrats, Old Schoolmen, Hartford Conventionalists,* and *Blue-light Men.* — **1830** S. SMITH *Major Downing* 31 The rest of the papers . . . talk about politics, and patriotism, . . . Jacksonism, and Hartford Conventionism. — **1815** *Niles' Reg.* VIII. 56/2 Hartford Conventionists. . . . Reports have reached us . . . that the state(s) of Massachusetts, Connecticut, New Hampshire, Rhode-Island, and Vermont, have absolved all ties by which they were bound to the former federal government. **1827** *Cin. Enquirer* 7 April 2/3 They hoped thereby to drive Mr. Madison from office, and elevate Hartford conventionists in his stead.

* **Harvard,** *n.* A student at, or a graduate of, Harvard (see also quot. 1871). *Obs.*

1722 FRANKLIN *Dogood Papers* Wks. (1905) II. 24 Having mixed all these Ingredients well, put them into the empty Scull of some young Harvard. **1871** BAGG *At Yale* 386 At Worcester the Cambridge crew are almost always spoken of as 'the Harvards'; but 'the Yales' is a term less often employed to designate their antagonists. **1948** *Sat. Ev. Post* 13 Nov. 158/3, I know a man in Boston and we'll lay a bob or two upon the Harvards.

Harvardian hɑrˈvɑrdɪən, *n.* One who has studied at, or graduated from, Harvard. — **1702** C. MATHER *Magnalia* (1853) II. 27 Not a few of these 'Harvardians' have by their published writings been useful unto the world. **1912** NICHOLSON *Hoosier Chron.* 83 They combined against a lone Harvardian, who bitterly resented Harwood's habit of smoking a cob pipe.

Harvardine ˈhɑrvɚˌdin, *a.* Of or pertaining to Harvard College. *Obs.* — **1676** B. THOMPSON *Poet. Works* 63 What meanes this silence of Harvardine quils? **1722** *N.-Eng. Courant* 6 Aug. 1/1 Thou only canst express with fluent Quill, The mighty Product of *Harvardine* Skill.

* **harvest,** *n.* In combs.: (1) **harvest fish,** a marine fish, *Peprilus paru,* found along the Atlantic Coast, esp. in harvest time, also any one of various allied fish, as the dollarfish *q.v.;* (2) **flow,** (see quot.) *obs.;* (3) **fly,** any one of various insects or species of insects of the family Cicadidae whose note is heard about harvest time; (4) **mite,** an American mite or species of mite, *Trombicula irritans,* especially troublesome at harvest time, cf. **chigger;** (5) **root,** (see quot.); (6) **water,** (see quot. and cf. **harvest flow**).

(1) **1814** MITCHILL *Fishes N.Y.* 366 Harvest fish. *Stromateus longipinnis.* . . . So called by some of the fishermen, because he visits the coast about the season of harvest. **1884** GOODE *Fisheries* I. 333 The 'Butter-fish' of Massachusetts and New York, sometimes known in New Jersey as the 'Harvest-fish,' in Maine as the 'Dollar-fish,' . . . is common between Cape Cod and Cape Henry. **1897** *N.Y. Forest, Fish, & Game Comm.* 2d Rep. 239 *Rhombus triacanthus* . . . Harvard-Fish . . . is found in Gravesend Bay from April to November. — (2) **1859** MACKAY *Tour* I. 325 The rice is submitted to three several floodings before it is fit to be harvested. . . . The last [is called] 'the harvest flow.' — (3) **1753** CHAMBERS *Cyclo. Supp., Harvest-fly, Cicada* . . . the name of a large fly, remarkable for the noise which it makes in the summer-months, and particularly about the time of harvest. **1881** *Harper's Mag.* Dec. 75/1 Even the cicada, or drumming harvest-fly, . . . is his [the sand-hornet's] very common victim. **1910** DOUGLAS (ed.) Parkman *Oregon Trail* 351 *Locust.* In the United States the harvest-fly is improperly called a locust. — (4) **1873** *Amer. Naturalist* VII. 17 The American Harvest mite . . . is barely visible with the naked eye, moves readily and is found more frequently upon children than upon adults. **1915** *Farmer's Bul.* No. 671, 2 Soon after the harvest mite burrows under the human skin a small red spot appears.

(5) **1830** *Huntingdon* (Pa.) *Courier* 15 Sep. 4/5 Harvest Root or Butterfly Wort, (Asclepias Tuberosa.) — (6) **1867** *Harper's Wkly.* 5 Jan. 6/1 This flooding is kept up with the changes of the tide—being careful not to stretch the rice too much—till the time arrives for harvest-water, which is the last flooding.

As the last term in **bee, cotton, early, English, Indian corn harvest.**

* **harvester,** *n.* A machine used in harvesting a crop.

1850 *Rep. Comm. Patents 1849* I. 209, [I have] thus described the construction and operation of my improved harvester. **1887** M. D. WOODWARD in *Checkered Yrs.* (1937) 182 Walter bought a new harvester, and the experts are here to set it up and overhaul the five old ones. **1945** *N. Eng. Homestead* 22 Sep. 20/3 The hay baler and Fox Field Harvester play a big part.

attrib. **1859** *Rep. Comm. Patents 1858: Agric.* I. 414 Improvement in Harvester Fingers. **1913** *Commoner* 10 Jan. 7/2 The harvester trust is spending that million in order that it may get back more millions from the farmer.

As the last term in **cornstalk, cotton, grass, hemp, ice, maize, marsh harvester.**

harvesting machine. =prec. — **1836** *U.S. Patents* 28 June, Harvesting machine. **1850** *Rep. Comm. Patents 1849: Agric.* 258 Having thus described the construction and operation of our improved harvesting machine, what we claim [etc.]. **1875** KNIGHT 1069/2.

* **Harvey,** *n. attrib.*

1. Designating a variety of apple and a kind of sauce. *Obs.*

1709 LAWSON *Carolina* 108 Harvey-Apple; that which we call so, is esteem'd very good to make cider of. **1844** in *Amer. Sp.* XVIII. 125/1 Friend Whitely delighted himself over the remains of 'Harvey sauce' which we, since our departure from New Orleans . . . had used as a condiment for our mutton and lamb.

2. Of or pertaining to a system of superior restaurants begun in the West and Southwest by Fred Harvey (b. 1835) in the 1870's.

1895 in MARSHALL *Santa Fe* 101 We all couldn't eat without 'em but the slickest things about 'em, Is the Harvey skirts that hustle up the feeds. **1906** *Ib.* 108 Oh, the pretty Harvey Girl beside my chair, A fairer maiden I shall never see. **1912** *Out West* Feb. 114/1 Navajo blankets of the finest weave and design are offered for sale . . . in the hotels of the Fred Harvey system. **1921** *Outing* Jan. 178/1, I hate to admit it, but my experience with the Harvey restaurants is only a few months old. **1928** STARR *One Hundred Yrs. Amer. Railroading* opp. 284 Contrast the luxury and comfort of this Fred Harvey Diner with conditions of even fifty years ago. **1941** FERGUSSON *Southwest* 198 One snowy, blustery day a friend and I arrived at a Harvey House, and the Southwest offers no more grateful refuge after a hard trip.

Harveyized ˈhɑrvɪˌaɪzd, *a.* Denoting steel that has its surface hardened by a process invented by H. A. Harvey (1824–93), an American inventor. — **1906** *Amer. Illust. Mag.* Jan. 331/2 Her slim body was as hard as Harveyized steel.

Also **Harveyizing process.** — **1898** *Chi. Times-Herald* 10 April 17/6 In the Harveyizing process the surface of the plate is carbonized to a depth of three or four inches by spreading silica sand, salt and a clay mixture over the plate and subjecting it to an intense heat, from which it is allowed to cool gradually in the furnace.

* **has been. 1.** *attrib.* Former, outmoded. *Colloq.* **2. has-beens,** old times. *Rare.* — (1) **1896** *N.Y. Dramatic News* 4 July 2/4 The Phoenix club is composed largely of gouty old persons of the 'has been' type. — (2) **1904** W. H. SMITH *Promoters* v. 91, I met old Bishop Slosher . . . and just for has-beens I took him to lunch with me.

* **hash,** *n.*

1. A meal or meals Also attrib. *Colloq.*

1868 *Terr. Enterprise* (Virginia, Nev.) 25 Mar. 3/2 Yesterday we dropped in at a popular restaurant . . . for our regular 'hash.' **1891** ROBERTS *Adrift Amer.* 205, I just sleep till the hash bell goes, and then I go in and eat. **1946** WILSON *Fidelity* 82 It is better form, to keep your social standing among your fellow cynics, to call it 'grub' or 'hash.'

b. (See quot.)

1871 O. E. WOOD *West Point Scrap Book* 338 Expressions and phrases used in the corps of cadets. . . . Hash.—Supper cooked in room after taps.

2. In special combs.: (1) **hash house,** a cheap eating house, also attrib.; (2) **mark,** (see quot. 1907), also transf.; (3) **pile,** (see quot. and cf. **grub pile**), *slang;* (4) **slinger,** a waiter or waitress in a restaurant, *slang.*

(1) **1869** *Terr. Enterprise* (Virginia, Nev.) 21 Sep. 3/1 The Mayor proposes to double the tax on all 'hash houses.' **1903** LEWIS *Boss* 273 His is this deadfall on Barclay Street, with that hash-house keeper to give him th' dough for his checks. **1947** CHALFANT *Gold, Guns, & Ghost Towns* 60 The company boardinghouses were of better grade than the general run of 'hash houses.' — (2) **1907** *N.Y. Ev. Post* 8 Aug. 1 'Hash-marks' are the stripes showing the number of enlistments a man has served. **1945** *Gunnison* (Colo.) *Courier* 26 July 1/4 He has been overseas more than two years and wears the accordant number of hash marks. **1947** DEVOTO *Across Wide Missouri* 124 Crow marriage might be described as a serial taking and putting-away: a veteran husband might wear hashmarks on his shirt signifying that he had made briefly happy as many as eighteen wives. — (3) **1891** C. ROBERTS *Adrift Amer.* 63 In the morning we were all roused out before daylight by somebody beating a kerosine tin, and shouting 'hash-pile!' which my bed-fellow informed me was the signal that breakfast was ready. — (4) **1868** *Gold Hill* (Nevada) *News* 6 May, The nice young man of Washoe may or may not be some kind of a clerk, a hash-slinger, or a check-guerrilla. **1949** *Chi. Tribune* 22 Feb. I. 14/7 She was a hash slinger, but missed her calling.

b. In phrases: (1) *To go back on* (or *upon*) *one's hash,* to find fault with one's food (see quot. 1902); (2) *to fix one's hash,* to do for one, do one in, *slang.*

(1) **1888** *Cornhill Mag.* Oct. 374 In the Far West, . . . the tenderfoot must not go back upon his hash, and must gulp down pumpkin pie as if he liked it. **1902** CLAPIN 206 *Go back on one's hash.* In the racy vernacular of the West, to weaken in face of unexpected difficulties or hardships; having put one's hand to the plough, to turn back. — (2) **1907** C. D. STEWART *Partners* 102 I've seen the mate and if you eat along them hogways he'll fix your hash.

hash hæʃ, *v. tr.* To supply (one) with meals. *Slang. Rare.* —**1883** *Gringo & Greaser* 1 Sep. 2/1 If we can find some other philanthropist who will kindly hash, beer and sleep us, we'll be there.

hashery ˈhæʃərɪ, *n.* A hash house. *Slang.* — **1870** *Alaska Times* (Sitka) 8 Jan. 1/3 Having lately opened a hashery, I send you this, my rules and regulations. **1912** *Sat. Ev. Post* 13 July 3/1 They sure don't call 'em hasheries when they cost you eight bones a day up!

Hassayampa ˈhæsəˌjæmpə, *n.* Also **Hassayamper.** [See note.] (See quot. 1906.) Also attrib.

Orig. "Assamp" or "Haviamp" in mining days, later embellished. Based on an Indian term of doubtful significance. See W. C. Barnes, *Arizona Place Names,* pp. 200 f. The Hassayampa River was the scene of an early gold rush, whence a legend arose that whoever drinks of this river can never again tell the truth.

1901 *Land of Sunshine* July 55 Even Bancroft 'had fun' with these Hassayamper myths. **1906** *Out West* Feb. 73 It is not the stranger who has made Arizona what she is today, but the 'Hassayamper'—the man who came in his youth and lost none of his faith and enthusiasm with the graying of his hair. [**1935** W. C. BARNES *Arizona Place Names* 200 You've heard about the wondrous stream They call the Hassayamp. They say it turns a truthful guy into a lying scamp.]

* **hasty pudding.**

1. Corn-meal mush.

[*c***1691** JOUTEL in *La. Hist. Coll.* I. (1846) 173 Whilst we stayed for our hunters (Indians), we prepared some sagamite, or their sort of hasty-pudding.] **1743** D. BRAINERD *Diary* (1902) 105 Most of my diet consists of boiled corn, hasty-pudding, etc. **1897** C. A. DANA *Recoll. Civil War* 197 The earth . . . had been trampled by the fighting of the thousands of men until it was soft, like thin hasty pudding. **1948** *Newsweek* 5 Jan. 66/1 Corn meal, nutmeg, ginger, eggs, water, milk, molasses, and butter. Cook in an iron pot; turn out on a dish and the result: hasty pudding.

attrib. **1867** GOSS *Soldier's Story* 108 Hasty-pudding dealers and sour beer sellers . . . sat on the ground.

2. Hasty Pudding Club, a literary society formed by students at Harvard University in Sep., 1795.

1837 LOWELL *Lett.* I. 13 Since I wrote to you I was chosen into the Hasty Pudding Club. **1889** *Cent. Mag.* March 753/2 Amateur performances . . . given . . . by the Harvard Hasty Pudding Club. **1911** J. C. SAVERY *The Crystal Gazer* (t. p.), A comedy in Two Acts. . . . Presented by the Hasty Pudding Club of Harvard University, 1911, Hasty Pudding Club Theatre. [**1948** *Newsweek* 5 Jan. 66/2 This year's Hasty Pudding show, 'Here's the Pitch,' is no exception. It is the 100th production of the Harvard club.]

* **hat,** *n.* In combs.: (1) **hat ball,** see as a main entry; (2) **boy,** a boy who checks hats and coats at a hotel, restaurant, etc.; (3) **fish,** a local name for a now unidentifiable fish, *obs.;* (4) **Indian,** (see quot. and cf. **blanket Indian**), *obs.;* (5) **law,** a Yale College law or rule, passed in 1775, prohibiting freshmen from wearing hats in the college yard until after May vacation, *obs.;* (6) **store,** a store or shop in which hats are sold; (7) **tree,** an upright stand having hooks or projections upon which hats may be hung.

(2) **1887** *Courier-Journal* 5 Feb. 4/6 He went to the Gayoso House four years ago as hat boy. **1916** WILSON *Somewhere* 142 A hat-boy had actually tried to reason with him. — (3) **1803** *Mass. H. S. Coll.* IX. 202 The fishes which are taken in the ponds [at Compton, Rhode Island], and among the rocks along the sea-shore are called the sheeps head, sea-bass . . . hat-fish, frost-fish or smelts, and eels. — (4) **1898** *Cong. Rec.* Jan. 1048/1 Even among Indians there are two parties. There is the 'hat' Indian and the 'blanket' Indian. The Indian who believes in progress, who wears the hat, who wears boots instead of moccasins, is called a 'hat' Indian.

(5) **1775** in ZUNDER *Early Days of Joel Barlow* (1934) 34 The freshmen got the hatlaw repealed in part. — (6) **1796** *Boston Directory* 251 Green, John B., hat store, Ann street. **1850** *Knickerb.* XXXV. 461 It was in the long-room of a good big buildin', over . . . a hat-store. **1941** LEE *Stagecoach North* 12 There were dry goods stores, hat stores, bookstores. — (7) **1819** *Mass. Res.* 18 June, p.m. 87 (Ernst), Bryant, Nathaniel, for two hat trees. **1883** *Cent. Mag.* Sep. 644/1 [Men of Cape Cod] who hang Calcutta hats upon their hat-trees; whose parlors give out a sandal-wood perfume from the islands of the Pacific.

b. In colloq. phrases: (1) *To have on one's little hat,* to be intoxicated, *obs.;* (2) *to bet one's hat,* to stake one's all; (3) *to hang one's hat on,* to rely upon; (4) *to hang one's hat inside,* to be at home in; (5) *to pass* (*around*) *the hat,* to take up a collection; (6) *to talk through one's hat,* to make foolish or nonsensical remarks; (7) (*to be*) *under one's hat,* to be secret or confidential.

(1) **1737** *Pa. Gazette* 13 Jan. 3/1 He's Got on his little Hat. — (2) **1879** R. GRANT *Little Tin Gods* 6 Ne'er will be caught again, Not if we know ourselves, you bet your hat on it! — (3) **1881** HAYES *New Colorado* 118 Why that's *my* preacher. I hang my hat on him every time. — (4) **1904** *N.Y. American* 18 July 2 If the Tammany leader expects to hang his hat inside Judge Parker's political headquarters, he must come here voluntarily.

(5) **1882** MCCABE *New York* 256 They stop to pass around the hat. **1945** MENCKEN *Supp.* I. 235 Reformers of a thousand varieties swarmed the land, whooping up their new arcana and passing the hat. — (6) **1888** *N.Y. World* 13 May, Dis is only a bluff dey're makin'—see! Dey're talkin' tru deir hats. **1944** *Chi. D. News* 9 Dec. 4/3 But when Mr. Wallace says that . . . he is talking through his hat. — (7) **1908** MCGAFFEY *Show-Girl* 127 He expects to shake down enough to start us housekeeping, but, of course, that is strictly under

your hat, and I pray you do not mention it. **1928** *Sat. Ev. Post* 4 Feb. 100/3 I'm not telling anyone else—so, under your hat.

For *to have one's hat chalked,* see **chalk,** *v.* **1;** *at the drop of a hat,* see **drop,** *n.; to have a brick in one's hat,* see **brick,** *n.*

As the last term in **balloon, bathing, beaverette, bloomer, brush, California, Campeachy, chalked, cockup, cowboy, daisy, derby, fire, five-gallon, flopped, high, Jim Crow, low pressure, palmetto, palm leaf, Palo Alto, plug, pole, roram, rowdy, shade, sheet iron, shuck, skimmer, soft, sombrero, Stetson, stovepipe, ten-gallon, Texas, willow, Wolfe, wool hat.**

hat ball. A boys' ball game in which the player into whose hat the ball is dropped has the privilege of throwing it at any other player. (See also quot. 1946.)

1832 KENNEDY *Swallow Barn* I. 37 It [a boy's skull-cap] finds hard service at hat-ball where . . . it is popular for its pliability. **1883** EGGLESTON *Hoosier School-Boy* vii. 49, I am going to show the boys how to play hat-ball. **1946** WILSON *Fidelity* 145 In Hat Ball we 'nailed to the cross' the loser, that is, the one who got the most forfeits or 'pigs.' . . . The boy, often a little fellow like me who could not throw well and had thus acquired many pigs, was stood against a sapling while all the boys took turns at throwing a ball at him.

***hatchet,** *n.*

1. (See quot.) *Obs.*

1877 BARTLETT 279 *Hatchet,* . . . a consideration or bribe received by the customs officers in New York for permitting imported dutiable goods to remain on the wharf, when they ought to go to the general storehouse.

2. hatchetman, a pioneer or axman serving in a military unit. *Obs.*

1755 WASHINGTON *Writings* I. 299, I think it will be advisable to detain both mulattoes and negroes in your company, and employ them as Pioneers or Hatchetmen. **1758** *Lett. to Washington* II. 335 Two Batmen are Allowed to Each Company, two hatchet & two Camp Colour men clear of all Camp Duty.

b. In some cities, a member of an organized band of Chinese criminals who commit murder for pay. Also transf.

1889 *Boston Jrnl.* 3 May 1/3 Chinese 'Freemasonry' in this country, and the work of the hatchetmen among the enemies of the organization, will be described in *The Sunday Globe.* **1940** RIESENBERG *Golden Gate* 165 When the Hoodlums, a gang of roughs inspired by the vituperation of newspapers, invaded Chinatown to attack venerable men and defile places of worship, San Francisco learned of the dread 'hatchetmen,' salaried slayers of the tongs. **1949** *So. Wkly.* 23 Mar. 1/1 Truman's hatchetman . . . announces that he is sending organizing teams into the South to work for the defeat of Congressmen and Senators who oppose the Truman-CIO legislative program.

3. hatchet pipe, = **tomahawk pipe.** *Obs.*

1907 HODGE *Amer. Indians* I. 536/1 According to some authors the hatchet pipe was a formidable weapon in war, but in the forms known to-day it is too light and fragile to have taken the place of the stone ax or the iron hatchet.

Hatchet pipes

4. In phrases with reference to the hatchet as a symbol of war among and with Indians.

a. *To bury the hatchet,* to cease hostilities, to make peace. *Obs.*

[**1680** SEWALL in *N. Eng. Hist. Reg.* XXIV. 121 Meeting with the Sachem the[y] came to an agreement and buried two Axes in the Ground; . . . which ceremony to them is more significant and binding than all Articles of Peace the Hatchet being a principal weapon.] **1754** *Mass. H.S. Coll.* 3 Ser. V. 10 We have ordered . . . our Governor of New York to hold an interview with them [*sc.* the Six Nations] for delivering those presents [and] for burying the hatchet. **1840** COOPER *Pathfinder* II. ii, I'm as ready to bury the hatchet with the Mingos as with the French.

In transf. uses.

1807 *Ann. 10th Congress* 1 Sess. I. 617, I had long been persecuted by the General, but wished to bury the hatchet. **1882** *Ill. Republican* (Taylorville) 15 Nov. 1/5 Now that the election is over, let us all, republicans, democrats and bolters, bury the hatchet, handle and all. [**1948** *Chi. Tribune* 15 Jan. 2/3 Would it not be a picturesque and timely gesture if the city of Boston or the commonwealth of Massachusetts should now demonstrate how deeply the hatchet—or tomahawk—is buried by sending a cargo of tea to England?]

b. *To take up the hatchet,* to go to war, to begin hostilities. *Obs.*

1694 *State P.* Colonial Ser. XIV. 402 The governor replied that he had put the axe into the hand of all his people. The Praying Indians, however, did not wish to take up the hatchet. **1705** *Mass. Prov. Laws* VIII. 101 To take up the hatchet against the French. **1870** KEIM *Sheridan's Troopers* 34 But two tribes, the Cheyennes and Arrapahoes were known to have taken up hatchets.

c. In other phrasal and allusive expressions of obvious meaning.

1724 in G. SHELDON *Hist. Deerfield* I. 415 They in ye name and in behalf of ye four tribes aforesaid, have Laid down the hatchet of war against New England. **1745** *Pa. Rec.* V. 18 If we should so suddenly lift up the Hatchet without acquainting our Allies, it would perhaps disoblige them. **1766** R. ROGERS *Ponteach* II. ii, To raise the Hatchet from its short Repose, and stain it deep with Blood. **1812** *Boston Gaz.* 17 Dec., What has provoked them of late to dig up the hatchet they had so long buried? **1826** COOPER *Last of Mohicans* x, Did Magua say that the hatchet was out of the ground, and that his hand had dug it up? **1894** WINSOR *Cartier to Frontenac* 169 With much parade the emblematic belts were hung up and counted, and the hatchet was thrown away.

As the last term in **Indian, pocket hatchet.**

***hatchet,** *v. tr.* To kill with a hatchet, to tomahawk. *Rare.* — **1764** FRANKLIN *Writings* IV. 292 These poor defenceless creatures [*sc.* Indians] were . . . stabbed, and hatcheted to Death!

***hate,** *v. To hate out,* to drive (a person) out by hating. Now *hist.*

1824 DODDRIDGE *Notes* 168 The punishment for idleness, lying, dishonesty, and ill fame generally, was that of 'Hating the offender out,' as they expressed it. *Ib.* 168 He was hated out as a coward. **1872** DE VERE 190 If a man did not do his share of the public service, he was hated out as a coward. **1948** DICK *Dixie Frontier* 263 So hot did public disapproval wax that he felt it more comfortable to leave the country. In such a case he was said to have been 'hated out.'

***haul,** *n.* The distance and route over which something is hauled, usu. **long haul, short haul.** Also attrib. Cf. **cross, sleigh, water haul.**

1877 in TARBELL *Hist. Standard Oil Co.* I. 372 We will endeavor to deliver the oil to you at points from which you will have short hauls. **1909** H. N. CASSON *Life C. H. McCormick* 213 Today it is not the long haul of wheat, but the short haul, that is more expensive. **1947** BEEBE *Mixed Train Dly.* 3 The happy hunting ground of the ultimately sophisticated connoisseur of short-haul railroading is in Colorado, Nevada and California.

***haul,** *v.*

1. *Railroad. tr.* To draw or pull a train of cars.

1882 *Rep. Ala. R.R. Comm.* II. 19 A passenger car . . . can be hauled back, empty. **1910** *Springfield W. Republican* 8 Dec. 16 A second of the four [engines] was at once set hauling trains east-bound through the tunnel.

2. In colloq. verbal expressions: (1) ***haul off,** to draw back one's fist, arm, etc., preparatory to delivering a blow; (2) **haul out,** to set out, to depart; (3) ***haul up,** to stop, come to rest.

(1) 1870 MARK TWAIN *Curious Republic* 45 Suppose he should take deliberate aim and 'haul off' and fetch me with the butt-end of the gun? **1908** K. MCGAFFEY *Show-Girl* 200 And hauling off wifey hangs one on Alla's map. — **(2) 1866** in *Neb. Hist. Mag.* XIII. 156 Hauled out before sunrise and corralled at the Springs by 9'o'clock. **1902** A. D. MCFAUL *Ike Glidden* xxx. 282 The train hauled out while the officer was taking him into custody. — **(3) 1845** SIMMS *Wigwam & Cabin* 2 Ser. 90 They had hauled up, and were seemingly awaiting my approach. **1899** JEWETT *Queen's Twin* 180 They hauled up out front o' the house, and mother an' I went right out.

b. In substantival combs.: (1) **haulabout,** a barge-like vessel used for coaling ships; (2) **haulback,** (see quot.); (3) **haul-mealer,** (see quot. and cf. **hauled mealer**), *obs.;* (4) **haulover,** a portage or place over which commodities have to be hauled or carried; (5) **haul up,** (see quot.).

(1) **1904** *Sci. Amer.* 23 July 63/2 Another type of coaling device which has proved highly successful is what is known as the 'haul-about.' — (2) **1905** *Forestry Bureau Bul.* 61 B, *Haul back*, a small wire rope, travelling between the donkey engine and a pulley set near the logs to be dragged, used to return the cable. — (3) **1887** A. A. HAYES *Jesuit's Ring* 52 A *haul-mealer* is a being . . . who is hauled to his or her refectory on a buck-board. — (4) **1837** WILLIAMS *Florida* 52 Its [*sc.* the river's] course, to the haulover, is about S.E. **1882** GODFREY *Nantucket* 27 An appropriation of money to 'improve Nantucket Harbor,' the petition having again in view the project of cutting through the 'Haulover.' *Ib.* 84 The 'Haulover' divides the harbor from the ocean and is very narrow. — (5) **1905** *Forestry Bureau Bul.* 61 B, *Haul up*, a light chain and hook by which a horse may be hitched to a cable in order to move it where desired.

hauled mealer. = **haul-mealer.** *Obs.* — **1880** *Harper's Mag.* Sep. 620/1 Payson . . . thought of her as classed under the generic name of 'hauled mealer.' **1883** M. F. SWEETSER *Summer Days* 126 (Ernst), The buckboard . . . finds practical use in transporting that class of the community known as 'hauled mealers.'

* **hauling,** *n.* Conveying in a wagon, cart, etc. Also attrib.

1714 *N.H. Probate Rec.* I. 738, I giue to my sons . . . all Materialls of Iron and Wood for hauling plowing & such Like. **1878** *Vt. Bd. Agric. Rep.* 109 The hauling tubs and store tubs should be made of cedar, bound with iron and well painted. **1898** PAGE *Red Rock* 302 He . . . had come to see if they 'mightn't like to have a little hauling done when their furniture came.' **1946** *Democrat* 9 May 4/4 We solicit your hauling and are prepared to give you prompt, efficient service.

b. hauling plow, (see quot.). *Obs.*

1868 *Rep. Comm. Agric. 1867* 255 The hauling plough, so called because the engine that operates the plough is placed upon one side of the field, and moves along a headland.

havalena, see **javalina.**

Havasupai ˌhɑvəˈsupaɪ, *n.* [f. Yuma *aha*, water; *vasu*, blue; *apa*, man—blue or green water people.] "A small isolated tribe of the Yuman stock . . . who occupy Cataract canyon of the Rio Colorado in N.W. Arizona" (Hodge). Also an Indian of this tribe.

1882 *Atlantic Mo.* Sep. 374/1 The first Ha-va-sup-pai I saw may be taken as a type of his race. **1908** CURTIS *N. Amer. Indians* II. 98 The home of the Havasupai is almost a subtropical spot that produces luxuriant vegetation with fruits of several kinds. **1948** *Nat. Geog. Mag.* May 655/1 After the beautiful stream that flows merrily through their canyon home they are called Havasupai (People of the Blue-green Water).

attrib. **1880** *Dly. Inter-Ocean* (Chi.) 2 June 12/7 From Pine Spring the party directed their course for the Ava Supai village. **1905** *Out West* Oct. 305 Of them all none so nearly approaches the mighty parent of the Cataract, or Cañon of the Havasu, the deep, wild, little-known home of the Havasupai Indians, the People of the Blue Water. **1948** *Pacific Discovery* May–June 11/1 Those who have visited the region have found the canyon scenery so enchanting and the Havasupai Indians so interesting they have neglected to comment on the spectacle here described.

b. The language of these Indians.

1882 *Atlantic Mo.* Oct. 547/1 One of them asked me to write the sentence, 'Give it to me,' in English, Ha-va-su-paí, and Zuñi.

* **have,** *v.*

1. *tr.* To accept in marriage. *Colloq.*

1839 *Lexington Observer & Rep.* 10 April, Sal will you have me? **1898** HARRIS *Tales* 227, I couldn't take two steps away from the house but what he'd jump out of the bushes an' ast me to have 'im. An' a whole passel of people up an' tol' me I'd better marry 'im. **1948** DICK *Dixie Frontier* 133 A backwoodsman with whom he talked said he would ask the lady the first time he went to see her if she would have him.

2. To represent as doing something.

1928 *Amer. Sp.* 379 William DeMorgan, in *Alice for Short*, has the 'toffs' say *daw* and *flaw* for 'door' and 'floor.'

3. In colloq. phrases: (1) *To have it on* (or *all over*), to have the advantage of, to be superior to; (2) *to have nothing on*, to have no incriminating evidence against, not to be superior to; (3) *to have it coming to one*, to deserve something; (4) *to have it in one*, to be inherently capable of something.

(1) **1909** S. E. WHITE *Rules of Game* v. xxiv, They believe that we did actually colonize the lands. In other words they think they have it on us straight enough. **1917** S. MERWIN *Temperamental Henry* 31 He had it all over the banjo-strumming Thomas P. of the unpleasantly rasping voice. — (2) **1912** MATHEWSON *Pitching* 7 'Hans' Wagner, of Pittsburg, has always been a hard man for me, but in that I have had nothing on a lot of other pitchers. **1927** *Hutchinson's Mystery Story Mag.* Feb. 104 The man offered me his car to search for the woman, but I had nothing on her, and did not accept the offer. **1930** *Publishers' Wkly.* 5 July 27 The antique hussies of history in spite of their hot reputations have nothing on her. — (3) **1921** PAINE *Comr. Rolling Ocean* 44 You had it coming to you. — (4) **1928** FOY & HARLOW *Clowning Thro' Life* 297, I didn't believe he had it in him.

* **Havelock,** *n.* [Gen. Henry *Havelock*, British officer during the Sepoy Mutiny of 1857.] (See quot. 1888.) Also attrib. *Obs.*

1861 JACKSON in M. A. Jackson *Gen. Jackson* 163, I regret to see our ladies making those things they call 'Havelocks.' **1880** *Harper's Mag.* Aug. 399 A poncho and havelock cap comprise the rubber clothing outfit. **1888** BILLINGS *Hardtack* 276 One of the first supposed-to-be useful, if not ornamental stupidities, . . . was the *Havelock*. . . . It was a simple covering of white linen for the cap, with a cape depending for the protection of the neck from the sun.

* **haw,** *n.* As the last term in **apple, black, May, parsley, pear, purple, red, scarlet, Shawnee, summer haw.**

hawey ˈhɔ·ɪ, *n.* [Origin obscure.] (See quot.) *Rare.* — **1837** WILLIAMS *Florida* 32 The hawey, a minute fig, is first seen on these islands [*sc.* the Oyster Islands].

* **hawk,** *n.* As the last term in **bird, black, blue, broad-winged, brown, bullet, chicken, desert sparrow, duck, fishtail, fork-tail, forked-tail, grasshopper, great-footed, hen, herring, jay, marsh, meat, mosquito, mouse, night, partridge, prairie, rabbit, red, red-tailed, red-tailed black, rough-legged, sharp-shinned, slate-colored, snail, snake, squealing, squirrel, Swainson's, swamp, tarantula, tom, venison, war, wet, white-breasted (chicken), white-tailed, winter hawk.**

* **hawkeye,** *n.*

1. (*cap.*) A nickname for a native or an inhabitant of Iowa, allegedly from the name of an Indian chief.

1839 (*title*), Hawk-eye and Iowa Patriot [founded at Burlington, 5 Sep.]. **1845** *St. Louis Reveille* 14 May 2/4 The inhabitants of . . . Iowa [are called] Hawk-eyes. **1878** BEADLE *Western Wilds* 36 We was as much skeered of each other as we was of the Hawkeyes. **1888** WHITMAN *Nov. Boughs* 406 Those from . . . Iowa . . . [were called] Hawkeyes. **1949** *Amer. Sp.* Feb. 26 Almost every American has heard . . . *Hawkeye* for an Iowan.

b. Hawkeye State, a nickname for Iowa.

1859 *Harper's Mag.* June 140/2 The Solons of the Hawk-eye State . . . were not all in the Legislature of 1851. **1894** *Chi. Record* 1 May 1/7 The large store . . . was filled with persons who wanted a near view of the little man who is raising such a commotion in the Hawk-eye state. **1948** *Chi. Tribune* 29 Aug. 23/3 To residents of the Hawk-eye state Pike's Peak is a 500 foot bluff of the Mississippi near here [*sc.* McGregor, Iowa].

2. One of the sobriquets of Natty Bumppo, the central character in Cooper's *Leatherstocking Tales.*

1839 TOWNSEND *Narrative* xiv. 337, I can sit for hours and hear old Maniquon relate the particulars of his numerous campaigns . . . and his 'scrimmages,' as old Hawk-eye would say.

* **Hawkins,** *n.* Also **Hawken.** [See quot. 1921.] A muzzle-loading rifle, so called from the name of its maker. Usu. **Hawkins gun, Hawkins rifle.** Now *hist.*

1850 GARRARD *Wah-To-Yah* ix. (1927) 120 Out in the pinyon, that morning, with his big Saint Loui' gun, a Jake Hawkins gun, she was. **1855** in *Mont. Hist. Soc. Contrib.* X. (1940) 141 Hawkins sickened him & three rounds from Colts put him past fighting. [**1921** *Outing* July 174/3 The father of Jacob and Samuel Hawken was Henry Hawkins, an 18th century gunmaker of Lancaster, Pa., who later was employed in the Harper's Ferry Armory, and about 1808 moved to St. Louis and continued to make rifles there. . . . The name was then spelled Hawkins, but pronounced Hawken, and . . . the sons adopted the latter spelling.] **1947** DEVOTO *Across Wide Missouri* 430 A Hawken rifle was accurate well beyond a hundred yards when new and kept in condition and when aimed by a man in no hurry.

Hawkins' whetstone. [J. H. W. *Hawkins* (1797–1858).] (See quot.) *Obs.* — **1866** LOWELL *Biglow P.* 2 Ser. p. lviii, Hawkins's whetstone: rum; in derision of one Hawkins, a well-known temperance-lecturer.

* **hawk's-eye,** *n.* A local name for the golden plover, *Pluvialis dominica.* — **1813** WILSON *Ornithology* VII. 42 It is said, that at Hudson's Bay it [*sc.* the black-bellied plover] is called the Hawk's-eye on account of its brilliancy. **1917** *Birds of Amer.* I. 257/1 Golden Plover. . . . Other Names.—American Golden Plover; . . . Toad-Head; Hawk's eye.

* **hay,** *n.* In combs.: (1) **haybag,** a derisive term for a fat old woman; (2) **bale,** a bale or compact bundle of hay, also attrib.; (3) **burner,** see as a main entry; (4) **camp,** *W.* an encampment of those engaged in cutting plains grass for hay; (5) **chaff,** hay cut up fine as food for cattle; (6) **cold,** hay fever, *facetious;* (7) * **fever,** (see quot.); (8) * **maker,** see as a main entry; (9) **rancher,** *W.* one

interested in securing hay from an extensive area of native grass; (10) **ride,** see as a main entry; (11) ***seed,** see as a main entry; (12) **weigher,** a town official having supervision of the weighing of hay offered for sale, *obs.*

(1) **1939** Abbott-Smith *We Pointed* 143 A woman they called Big Ox, who was one of those haybags that used to follow the buffalo camps. — (2) **1851** A. O. Hall *Manhattaner* 5 It was a modest commercial plain . . . with . . . bits of machinery, and ploughs, and oat bags, and hay bales. **1947** *Time* 21 July 17/1 Polishing up his grass-roots tactics, he stopped to admire a local farmer's hay bale loader. — (4) **1867** *Wkly. New Mexican Rev.* 6 April 1/3 Major Brooks . . . ordered the guard at the hay-camp to fire upon any Indian stock found grazing at that camp. **1935** Sandoz *Old Jules* 126 He had spent the night at the Hippach hay camp with half a dozen hay waddies.

(5) **1945** *Bristol* (N.H.) *Enterprise* 15 Feb. 3/3, I have a request for hay chaff. Where can I get several bags? — (6) **1875** *Chi. Tribune* 26 July 3/2 Mr. Beecher cannot travel or lecture in September on account of the 'hay cold.' — (7) **1931** Clute *Plants* 125 A few plants have been named for the diseases they cause or are reputed to cause. Most famous of these is the hay-fever (*Ambrosia artemisaefolia*). — (9) **1869** *Harper's Mag.* Sep. 470/1 The little valley that satisfies the 'hay rancher.'

(12) **1770** *Boston Selectmen* 10 Jan. 53 The Hay-weighers to be chosen shall pay for hire of the Engine. **1800** *Columbian Centinel* 25 Jan. 1/1 It is recommended to the Inhabitants of this town not to purchase any load of Hay brought in to this market that has not been weighed by the Hayweigher of said town.

b. Denoting machines, tools, etc., used in handling hay: (1) **hay-baler,** an apparatus or machine for baling hay; (2) **barge,** a barge for transporting hay; (3) **barrack,** see as a main entry; (4) **boat,** a boat for transporting hay; (5) **cap,** a covering for a stack or pile of hay; (6) **car,** (see quot.); (7) **chopper,** an instrument for chopping up hay; (8) ***fork,** a horse-operated device for loading and unloading hay; (9) **loader,** "a device attached to a wagon to collect or raise the hay from the swath, windrow, or cock, and deposit it on the wagon" (Knight); (10) **press,** a machine for pressing hay into bales or bundles, a hay-baler; (11) ***rack,** see as a main entry; (12) **rig, rigging,** (see quot. 1896 and cf. **hay-rack**); (13) **scales,** large scales for weighing hay, cattle scales, cf. **patent hay scales;** (14) **spreader,** a machine for spreading hay to cure it; (15) **stacker,** (see quot. 1875); (16) **tedder,** =**hay spreader,** cf. **tedder;** (17) **wire,** see as a main entry.

(1) **1895** M. Graham *Stories of Foot-Hills* 209 The song of the hay-balers and the whir of the threshing machine had died out of the valley. **1949** *Chi. D. News* 1 April 3/2, I work the combine, disc, hay baler and fertiliser spreader. — (2) **1872** Brace *Dangerous Classes N.Y.* 97 To sleep . . . under stairways, or in hay-barges on the coldest winter-nights, for a mere child, was hard enough. — (4) **1703** *N.H. Probate Rec.* I. 504 [I give] all my Implements of Husbandry, & Hay boate. **1885** Jewett *Marsh Island* 80 The stupid-looking square hay-boat floated lightly. **1943** *Copper Camp* 157 Hundreds of them journeyed to there each summer and drove the rakes, mowers and hay boats of the Big Hole cattlemen.

(5) **1855** *Chi. W. Times* 19 July 4/6 This loss may be saved by simply being provided with a supply of hay caps. These can be made by pieces of common sheeting. **1874** *Vt. Bd. Agric. Rep.* II. 187 He cures his grass . . . the day it is cut, and puts it up in medium-sized cocks for the night, covering each with a 'hay-cap.' — (6) **1895** Wait *Car-Builder's Dict.* 65 Hay-car. A box-car for carrying baled hay; usually made with larger bodies and doors than ordinary box freight cars. — (7) **1904** Mackaye *Panchronicon* 17 Ef a feller'll jest take a grip on the North Pole an' go whirlin' round it, he'll be cuttin' meridians as fast as a hay-chopper. — (8) **1854** *Pa. Agric. Rep.* 81 The same gentleman also exhibited a horse power hay fork. **1875** Knight 1081/2 *Hay-fork,* . . . a fork elevated by a rope and horse, in unloading hay from a wagon to a mow, or *vice versa.* **1947** *Chi. Tribune* 22 July 5/2 A few smart old timers used a buckrake mounted on the front of their tractors to pick up big piles of hay on the field and transport it to the hay fork at the barn. — (9) **1864** *Maine Agric. Soc. Returns* 116 Attach Bentley's Hayloader to [the cart]. **1949** *Reader's Digest* Feb. 119/1 The hay rake, the hay loader and scores of other farm tools followed.

(10) **1829** *20th Congress* 2 Sess. State P. No. 59, 3 [Improvement] in the hay press [patented Jan.] 26 [1828 by] Moses B. Bliss. **1946** *Democrat* 22 Aug. 4/3 Wanted—To buy hay press. — (12) **1852** *Mich. Agric. Soc. Trans.* III. 30 Best hay rigging. **1865** A. D. Whitney *Gayworthys* vi, Gabriel . . . stood high up on the loaded hay-rigging. **1896** *Advance* 19 March 414/1 Two great farm wagons, provided with those wide projecting frames, technically known as hay-rigs. —

(13) **1773** *Boston Selectmen* 7 Dec. 204 The Ground on which the Hay Scales stands. **1919** Cady *Rhymes of Vt.* (1923) 85 Whene'er an auction bill I see On barn or hayscales, bridge or tree. — (14) **1864** *Maine Agric. Rep.* 115 The hay tedder or spreader . . . tosses the hay about, opening it to the sun. **1944** *Chi. D. News* 1 May 1/3 He also stated that the firm handled hay spreaders, corn and cotton planters and other kinds of farm equipment.

(15) **1875** Knight 1083/2 Hay-stacker . . . A portable derrick for the suspension of tackle in the use of the horse hay-fork in stacking. **1885** *Laramie* (Wyo.) *Boomerang* 21 Oct. 1/6 (*advt.*), Champion Hay-stacker. — (16) **1864** [see **hay spreader**]. **1888** *Vt. Agric. Rep.* X. 42 Six implements have been invented which reduce the cost of farm operating 50 per cent. . . . The hay tedder [is one].

c. In combs., chiefly obs., denoting places and areas where hay is produced: (1) **hay cow lot,** in colonial times, an area allotted a colonist from which to secure hay for a cow; (2) **creek,** a creek along which native grass may be secured as hay; (3) **lot,** in colonial times, a lot from which to secure hay; (4) **ranch,** *W.* a ranch upon which a great deal of hay is produced, cf. **hay rancher;** (5) **slough,** a slough where wild grass may be obtained as hay; (6) **swamp,** a swamp where wild grass may be obtained as hay.

(1) **1641** *Charlestown Land Rec.* 122, I doe sell . . . four Hay Cowe Lotts of salt marsh meadow. — (2) **1704** *N.H. Probate Rec.* I. 516, I do also give him . . . all the hay creek marsh on this side of the hay creek. — (3) **1638** *Charlestown Land Rec.* 56, 3 of those hay lotts are sould to Peeter Tuft. **1671** *Ib.* 166 William Stetson . . . sold . . . ffive hay lotts . . . According to the usuall Custome of hay lotts in Charlstowne. — (4) **1869** Browne *Adv. Apache Country* 396 Several fine valleys, now used as hay and cattle ranches, lie between Aurora and Bodie. **1948** Johnston *Gold Rush* 32/1 In less than twenty-four hours the whole hay ranch was staked out in claims fifty feet square, and as history shows, the ravaged owners failed to acquire a single claim.

(5) **1911** H. Quick *Yellowstone N.* v. 129 On the hay-slews we had to prime the rake with old hay 'fore we could make a windrow. — (6) **1898** *McClure's Mag.* X. 445 There are over 300 good hay swamps . . . where feed for horses can be found in abundance.

d. In colloq. and slang phrases: (1) *To beat the hay,* to sleep; (2) *to hit the hay,* to retire, go to bed; (3) *between hay and grass,* see ***grass.**

(1) **1908** K. McGaffey *Show-Girl* 118 The next morning while she was yet beating the hay, I . . . took it on the run away from there. — (2) **1924** *Frontier* May 22 Tom suggested that we should be 'hitting the hay,' an agricultural term which he explained to me meant 'to retire.' **1949** *Chi. Sun-Times* 24 Mar. 63, I think we both ought to hit the hay early!

As the last term in **cut, fool, pea vine, prairie, redtop, salt marsh, slough, stock, tame, timothy, wild hay.**

hay barrack. (See quot. 1848 and cf. **barrack.**)

1767 Hiltzheimer *Diary* (1893) 6 Jan. 13 Thomas Shoemaker and I measured the hay barrack, below the house. **1807** Vancouver *Agric. Devon* (1813) 129 This contrivance is called a hay-barrack, in Pennsylvania, where they are equally used for the protection of hay as well as of corn. **1848** Bartlett 173 *Hay barrack* (Dutch, *hooi-berg,* a hay-rick), a straw-thatched roof supported by four posts, capable of being raised or lowered at pleasure, under which hay is kept. A term peculiar to New York State. **1949** *Amer. Photography* Feb. 116 They are found beneath loose boards and shingles, and the crannies in the hay barracks beneath the conical roof are a favorite haunt for their hibernations.

hay-burner ˈheˌbɝnɚ, *n.* (See quots.) *Colloq.* and *slang.*

1921 *D.N.* V. 114 hay-burner, *n.* 1. A horse. 2. A smoking-pipe. 3. A cheap automobile. Rural slang, occasionally elsewhere. [Calif.] **1945** *Chi. D. News* 12 July 12/2 On the basis of the old World War I formula of 40 hommes, eight chevaux, one hay burner [i.e., horse] was equivalent to five soldiers. **1948** Wilson Tucker *Dove* 35 'What is a hay-burner?' Elizabeth interrupted. 'A horse opera,' Horne provided. 'An oater, a Western.' **1948** *Neb. Hist.* June 96 In some parts of Nebraska, Kansas, western Oklahoma, and other prairie states, a stove was sometimes fitted out as a 'hayburner.'

* **haymaker,** *n.*

1. (See quot. 1833.) Now *hist.*

1833 J. E. Alexander *Transatlantic Sk.* II. 64 Thus a General from the Eastward, in passing up the Mississippi, made use of a silver fork to eat his meals with—('haymakers,' or two-pronged forks, are as yet only used there, and both these and the knives are set in carved buckhorn handles). **1948** Dick *Dixie Frontier* 328 At that time two-pronged forks with buckhorn handles, called 'hay-makers,' were the only kind in use in that region.

2. A violent blow in fighting. Also **hay-making,** *a.*

1912 C. MATHEWSON *Pitching* 150 If a prizefighter is supposed to have a haymaking punch in his left hand [etc.]. **1918** *Amer. Mag.* April 113/3 'Gitteloutahere,' panted Slough, aiming a haymaker at Doug. **1947** *Life* 13 Oct. 66 The defender is allowed to follow this tactic with a haymaker but cannot follow up his advantage.

* **hayrack,** *n.* (See quot. 1875), also a wagon equipped with a structure of this kind.

1875 KNIGHT 1082/2 Hay-rack. . . . A frame mounted on the running gears of a wagon, and used in hauling hay, straw, sheaves, etc. **1946** *Reader's Digest* Jan. 141/1 They hoisted the boat up, backed a hayrack under it and took it down beneath the barn. **1949** *Chesterton* (Ind.) *Tribune* 7 April 12/6 One hammer mill; one rubber tire wagon with hay rack.

Hay on a hayrack

b. hayrack ride, =**hayride.**

1938 *Dly. Ardmoreite* (Ardmore, Okla.) 13 April 4/1 Si Ci Ci members. . . . Tuesday afternoon made plans for a hay rack ride and picnic to be held April 29 at Lake Murray. **1948** *Lisle* (Ill.) *Eagle* 21 Oct. 2/3 There will be a Hay-rack Ride Friday, Oct. 22, for the safety patrol and auxiliary, sponsored by the P.T.A.

hayride ˈheˌraɪd, *n.* A ride taken by a pleasure party in a large wagon partially filled with hay. Also attrib.

[**1856** *Spirit of Times* 8 Nov. 154/2 The invitations he had at first received to join pic-nics, boating excursions on the river, and hay-wagon rides, after a while became intermittent, and towards the end of the summer were dropped altogether.] **1896** *Advance* 19 March 414/2 Everybody being as comfortable as hay-ride etiquette permitted, the word was given, and away they went. **1949** *Ev. Northwestern* (Chi.) 11 April 4/1 Phi Gams weren't daunted recently when hayride plans were flooded out.

Hence **hayrider.**

1947 *Chi. D. News* 15 Nov. 1/1, 20 Hayriders In Auto Mishap.

* **hayseed,** *n.* A rustic, a countryman. Also attrib.

1889 *Boston Jrnl.* 29 April 2/2 To send a glimmer of returning reason through the mind of the frontier hayseed. **1897** *Chi. Tribune* 15 Aug. 29/2 Unlike the majority of 'hayseed shows,' as they are known in the profession, there is no caricaturing of the country types of character. **1947** *Time* 6 Jan. 57/1 Marlowe does a couple of good wide turns as an overgrown hayseed.

Hence **hayseeder.**

1891 WELCH *Recoll. 1830–40* 368 These young swells scorned the waiting for the afterpiece, or farce, as vulgar; only the thing for 'hayseeders' or common people to do.

haywire ˈheˌwaɪr, *n.*

1. Smooth wire used in baling hay.

1921 *Outing* Dec. 101/1 You can't run a logging camp without snuff and hay wire. **1941** WHITE *One Man's Meat* 240 So into the village in the truck, after wiring the tailboard up with a piece of haywire, to prevent wholesale loss of life.

2. haywire outfit (or **rig**), (see quots. 1905, 1942). *Slang.*

1905 *Forestry Bureau Bul.* 61 B, hay wire outfit. A contemptuous term for loggers with poor logging equipment. **1942** RICH *We Took to Woods* (1948) 254 Anything that is held together with haywire is a haywire rig. Broadening the scope of the term, so is any makeshift expedient whatever. If you run out of corn starch and have to thicken a chocolate pudding with flour, that's a haywire rig. **1944** BINNS *Timber Beast* 269 Roberts is dead, and Larry Jones is starting over again with a haywire outfit over on the Peninsula.

3. *To go haywire*, to get out of order, to become confused or unreasonable. *Slang.*

1929 *N.Y. Times* 13 Oct., When some element in the recording system becomes defective it is said to have gone haywire. **1948** *Ice Cream Trade Jrnl.* Sep. 22 Some of them have gone completely haywire on their retail prices.

* **haze,** *v.*

1. *Educ. tr.* To subject (a fellow student, esp. a freshman) to humiliating or embarrassing treatment. Also absol.

1850 in HALL *College Words* (1856) 251 'Tis the Sophomores rushing the Freshmen to haze. **1864** in W. S. TYLER *Hist. Amherst College* (1873) 611 That in our opinion any student who shall be convicted of the vicious habit of 'hazing Freshmen' should be cut off from all aid from the Charity Fund. **1916** EATON *Idyl of Twin Fires* 157 They used ter what yer call haze in them days, an' the soph'mores, they come into the young Jedge's room to smoke him out.

b. To embarrass, humiliate, annoy, tease, or vex (someone).

1852 BRISTED *Upper Ten Th.* 205 So here have I been five days . . . hazing—what you call slanging—upholsterers. **1906** *Springfield W. Republican* 13 Dec. 8 The slap-dash way of doing things which has characterized the Roosevelt administration has given the Senate a welcome chance to haze the executive.

2. *W.* To urge, compel, drive (an animal) in a specified way or direction.

1890 D'OYLE *Notches* 68 Bill 'hazed' 'em again, and they ran up and stood about opposite to me, and I got two. **1912** BOWER *Flying U* 55 You go haze in the team, Happy. **1947** *Trail Riders Bul.* Feb. 20/1 A squarer fella never hazed broncs.

* **hazel,** *n.* In combs.: (1) **hazelbrush,** shrubs, bushes, etc., of some variety of American hazel, also attrib.; (2) **rough,** a hazel copse; (3) **splitter,** a hog of an unimproved ranging breed, *colloq., obs.;* (4) **wizard,** one who proposes to locate bodies of water in the ground by means of a hazel wand, *rare.*

(1) **1856** *Rep. Comm. Patents 1855: Agric.* 194 Only about 7 acres were harvested, the remainder being 'hazel-brush' land, which was choked down by weeds. **1897** W. E. BARTON *Daughter-in-Law* 24 If she could smell oats once again, instead of living the year round on hazel brush and faith. — (2) **1893** *Advance* 23 Nov., Among the hazel-roughs are still a few chewinks. — (3) **1865–6** *Ill. Agric. Soc. Trans.* VI. 334 They belong to a class . . . who prefer the active, energetic 'hazel splitters' to the lazy Berkshire. **1878** *Ill. Dept. Agric. Trans.* XIV. 146 When the old hazel-splitters were the entire stock there was no cholera. — (4) **1843** CARLTON *New Purchase* LII. 206 We had ceased from digging a well, after finding no water at twenty-five feet; although we had employed a great hazel-wizzard.

hazer ˈhezɚ, *n.* **1.** One who hazes freshmen in college. (Cf. * **haze,** *v.* **1.**) **2.** *W.* (See quot. and cf. * **haze,** *v.* **2.**)

(1) **1876** *Harper's Wkly.* 25 Nov. 958/1 'Hazers' at the United States Naval Academy at Annapolis are in trouble. **1890** *Columbus* (O.) *Dispatch* 15 March, The board [of trustees] adopted resolutions reprimanding the hazers. — (2) **1897** HOUGH *Story of Cowboy* 90 Two other men, sometimes known in these days of modern ranching as 'hazers,' now mount and ride up with their quirts in hand ready to drive on the horse that is to be broken.

* **hazing,** *n.* Subjecting a student, esp. a freshman, to humiliation, physical chastisement, etc.

1854–5 *Harvard Mag.* I. 413 (B.), The absurd and barbarous custom of hazing . . . has long prevailed in the college. **1907** *N.Y. Ev. Post* (semi-weekly ed.) 27 May 4 Hazing . . . is described as 'any act that injures, frightens, degrades, or disgraces, or tends to injure, frighten, degrade, or disgrace any fellow-student or person attending such institution.' **1948** *Atlantic Mo.* March 37/1 These critics imply that hazing is the sum and substance of plebe year. As a matter of fact, physical hazing is no part of the official system of discipline and military training through which a plebe must pass.

* **he,** *pron.* Used as a prefix: (1) **he-balsam,** the black spruce, *Picea mariana*, as distinguished from the she-balsam *q.v.;* (2) **-biddy,** a rooster or cock, also transf., in jocular allusion to American squeamishness regarding "cock"; (3) **-man,** an exceptionally strong, virile man, also attrib.

(1) **1883** P. M. HALE *Woods N. Carolina* 48 And it is, I believe, what is most commonly and absurdly called *He Balsam.* **1943** PEATTIE *Great Smokies* 161 They named this the 'she-balsam.' Thinking perhaps that it needed a mate, and finding the spruce tree, which is devoid of 'milk,' commonly accompanying it, they named it the 'he-balsam'! — (2) **1835** *Vade Mecum* (Phila.) 10 Jan. 3/3 It is little better than an insult to style a 'he-biddy,' as the Yankee young ladies say, when speaking of the masculine gender, by a word so undignified as man. **1871** DE VERE 380 There is little harm, perhaps in calling a hen a *biddy* . . . ; but to make from it a *hebiddy* for the cock, . . . is a somewhat violent proceeding. — (3) **1832** PAULDING *Westward Ho!* I. 101 A young fellow who could . . . tree a rackoon with any he man that ever breathed in all out of doors. **1925** *Sat. Ev. Post* 4 July 42/3

He did not bother with what he called formality stuff, but went after the customers in two-fisted, he-man fashion. **1948** *Herald-Press* (St. Joseph, Mich.) 14 Aug. 5/2 She thinks Clark Gable packs terrific he-man glamor.

* **head,** *n.*

1. The extreme limit or furthermost part of a town or frontier. *Obs.*

1704 *Boston News-Letter* 7 Aug. 2/1 The Enemy was beaten off with loss, but are yet hovering on the head of those Towns. **1706** *Ib.* 28 Jan. 2/2 Capt. Brown . . . and Capt. Stevens . . . are . . . to Scout from Connecticut River to Sacho River, Forty Miles above the Heads of the Fronteers, to discover any Stragling Indians.

2. *heads of department(s),* the administrative officers in charge of departments of the U.S. Government and, by virtue of their positions, members of the President's Cabinet.

1789 HAMILTON *Works* VII. 45 The heads of departments will, of course, have this privilege. **1842** *Cong. Globe* 4 May 478/1 Heads of Departments, Senators, Members of the House, and private individuals were bull-dogged. **1886** ALTON *Among Law-Makers* 67 These . . . 'Heads of Department' . . . form the 'Cabinet,' or body of 'confidential advisers' of the President.

b. *head of a department,* a professor who administers the affairs of a college or university department.

1899 in T. W. GOODSPEED *Hist. Univ. Chicago* (1916) 151 The idea of a head of a department. **1940** *Univ. Ill. Bul.* 12 Arthur Byron Coble . . . Professor of Mathematics and Head of the Department.

3. (See quot.) *Obs.*

1833 *Louisville Public Advt.* 19 June, He raised his piece gradually until the head (that being the name given by the Kentuckians to the sight) of the barrel was brought to a line with the spot which he intended to hit.

4. *head of steam,* the pressure, per unit area, of a confined body of steam. Also transf.

1835 *Vade Mecum* (Phila.) 16 May 3/2 He then put on the whole head of accumulated steam, and the car started like the wind. **1846** *Spirit of Times* (N.Y.) 16 May 133/2 We were shooting down the Ohio, under a head of steam 'chock up' to 54 40! **1949** *Sat. Ev. Post* 9 April 128/3 By this time festivities at the Air Force camp were in full swing and all the intrepid birdmen had a good head of steam up.

b. Also *head of water.*

1948 WESTON *Mother Lode* 154 They had a good head of water, with great pressure down from the hills.

5. The butt end of a "hand" or small bundle of tobacco leaves. *Obs.*

1839 BRIGGS *H. Franco* I. 254 The boatswain . . . bet his silver call, chain and all, against a head of tobacco. **1863** *Ill. Agric. Soc. Trans.* V. 668 Others . . . tie them in bands of six or eight leaves . . . so as to form a head of one and a half to two inches in length.

6. *Educ.* In a class, the place occupied by the pupil who excels, the position furthest from the foot *q.v.* Cf. **headmark** (*b*).

1843 *Amer. Pioneer* II. 456 Having missed the evening's spelling I always began foot, but that did not annoy me, nor prevent me from ending head. **1883** *Cent. Mag.* Sep. 790/1 There is no reward or punishment, no head or foot of the class. **1948** *Sat. Ev. Post* 24 Jan. 29/3 Angus ultimately graduated at the head of his class.

b. A place of preëminence, as *head of navigation, head of the ticket.* Cf. **head town** in **7.** below.

1850 HOUSTOUN *Hesperos* I. 81 This is owing in a great measure to its being nearer the 'head of navigation,' and this, I am told, is considered a great advantage in the commercial position of all American cities. **1929** *Liberty* 30 Nov. 4/2 Joe . . . took the nomination for vice president, campaigned for the head of the ticket, and went down with his colors flying.

7. In combs.: (1) **head betony,** the lousewort, *Pedicularis canadensis;* (2) **branch,** the main branch or one of the main branches of a stream; (3) **breaker,** an Indian war club, *rare;* (4) * **center,** the place of most importance at which an action begins, also transf.; (5) **cheese,** [cf. Du. *hoofdkaas* in same sense], meat from the head or head and feet of hogs, pressed into a cheeselike mass after suitable seasoning and boiling; (6) **fire,** an advancing forest or prairie fire, cf. **backfire;** (7) **fish,** (see quot. 1889); (8) **flaw,** a gust of contrary wind, *fig.* in quots., *obs.;* (9) **hoop,** a hoop for or from the head of a barrel; (10) **lamp,** = **headlight 1;** (11) * **land,** public land granted the head of a family to encourage settlement in a particular area, *obs.;* (12) **liner,** an actor or entertainer who is the chief attraction in a theatrical performance, also transf., cf. * **headline 2;** (13) **lining,** (see quot.), *obs.;* (14) * **mark,** (*a*) a mark or object having some bearing on the head or bow of a river steamboat in piloting, (*b*) a token or credit given a student for being at the head of a class, cf. **6.** above; (15) **on,** *a.* and *adv.* (*a*) with the head or end pointed full at something, (*b*) straight ahead, *rare;* (16) **salad,** any one of several varieties of lettuce having tight, firm heads, *obs.;* (17) **souse,** = **headcheese;** (18) **start,** a considerable lead or advantage, as in a race; (19) **town,** the principal town in a county or region; (20) **tree,** (see quot. 1905); (21) * **way,** (see quot. 1893).

(1) 1795 WINTERBOTHAM *Hist. View* III. 398 Among the native and uncultivated plants of New-England, the following have been employed for medical purposes: . . . Head Betony, . . . Horsemint, spearmint [etc.]. — **(2) 1643** in *Amer. Sp.* XV. 271/2 Twoe hundred acres of land . . . lying upon the head branch of a branch called the Clarks Creeke. **1737** *Ib.*, Several Trees marked EE on the head branches of the North ffork of James River. **1837** W. JENKINS *Ohio Gaz.* 120 Claridon, a post township of Geauga county, . . . situated on the two head branches of the Cuyahoga [River]. — **(3) 1707** in SEWALL *Diary* II. 60 The Salvages . . . employ'd a Head-breaker on the Child. — **(4) 1873** PHELPS *Trotty's Wedding* xiv, I shall strike out from Cousin Madge as a head-centre. **1892** *Vt. Agric. Rep.* XII. 142 Here is the head center of the granite works, employing several thousand men.

(5) 1841 *S. Lit. Messenger* VII. 39/2 The animal . . . may be traced in the stewed chine and souse, the head-cheese and sausages. **1948** *Sat. Ev. Post* 14 Aug. 94/4 They see nothing wrong with calling something 'head cheese' or 'hog maw,' and any outlander who can overcome a slight shuddering repugnance to taste them will wonder why he never even heard of such dishes before. — **(6) 1898** *Mo. So. Dakotan* Dec. 130 A scorching headfire broke through the marsh with flame and smoke. **1946** THOMPSON *Amer. Daughter* 48 Jumping the firebreak, the headfire went within half a mile of our hayfield. — **(7) 1842** *Nat. Hist. N.Y., Zoology* IV. 331 The Great Sun-fish, or Head-fish, is not unfrequently captured along the coast. **1843** *Amer. Philos. Soc. Proc.* IV. 11 A fish found upon Squam Beach, N.J., [is] called by the fishermen, the Head-fish. **1889** *Cent.* 2750/3 *Head-fish,* . . . a sunfish of the family *Molidæ.* — **(8) 1803** WEEMS *Lett.* II. 280 A head flaw . . . has taken me all aback again. **1834** S. SMITH *Lett. Major Jack Downing* 90 A good many head flaws and worriments. — **(9) 1859** G. W. PERRY *Turpentine Farming* 157 Head hoops should be got six feet long, and in making fourteen inches lap should be allowed.

(10) 1898 *McClure's Mag.* X. 218/2 As it was daylight, there was not even the glare of a head-lamp to give us the fraction of a second's warning. *Ib.* 393/1 The stack and head-lamp were both tied fast on the back of the tender. — **(11)** *a***1752** WM. DOUGLASS *Brit. Settlements* II. 274 The head-lands were to settlers in any place exceeding ten miles from the sea, eighty acres per head, and to those who settle nearer, sixty acres. — **(12) 1896** *N.Y. Dramatic News* 4 July 10/3 That clever pair, Stinson and Merton, were the headliners at Proctor's last week. **1925** *Scribner's Mag.* Sep. 38 Lardner . . . is by all odds the headliner among American humorists. **1947** *Amer. Wkly.* 2 Nov. 17/1 Talent was so scarce that third- and fourth-raters became headliners. — **(13) 1864** WEBSTER, Head-lining, the lining of the head or hood of a carriage; the oil-cloth or other textile lining of the roof of a railway car. — **(14)** (*a*) **1875** MARK TWAIN *Life on Miss.* (1883) 109 That pilot can . . . give you such a lot of head-marks, stern-marks, and side-marks to guide you. (*b*) **1904** DARROW *Farmington* 47 In their efforts to make us study, they resorted to every sort of means—head-marks, presents, praise. **1946** WILSON *Fidelity* 136 We also had headmarks, that is, the one standing at the head at the end of the lesson was given a mark of merit.

(15) (*a*) **1840** DANA *Two Years* ii. 15 The two vessels stood 'head on,' bowing and curveting at each other. **1931** *K.C. Star* 3 Nov., A head-on collision ensued. (*b*) **1870** KEIM *Sheridan's Troopers* 39 To fire 'head on' would be but a waste of ammunition. — **(16) 1847** DARLINGTON *Weeds & Plants* 205 Those forms [of lettuce] known as Curled and Head Salad, formerly considered as distinct species, are now believed to be mere varieties of [*Lactuca scariola*]. — **(17) 1704** S. KNIGHT *Journal* 35 My guide said it smelt strong of head sause. — **(18) 1908** GALE *Friendship Village* 141 [The fire's] got such a head-start the whol' thing'll go like a shell. **1932** *K.C. Times* 25 Jan. 16 The Abilene Reflector believes Eddie Cantor had too much head start. — **(19) 1701** *Conn. Rec.* IV. 349 To be deposited in the head townes of each countie. **1775** ADAIR *Indians* 410 The Choktah so highly esteem this vegetable, that they call one of their head-towns, by its name.

(20) 1905 *Forestry Bureau Bul.* 61 B, *Head tree,* in steam skidding the tree to which the cable upon which the traveller runs is attached. (S.F.) *c***1945** HOPKINS *Okefenokee* 41 A defective link in a chain holding a block at the top of a 'head-tree' or spar at a skidder caused one [accident]. — (21) **1893** *Stand.* 828/1 *Headway* . . . The interval of time or the distance between two consecutive railway-trains, street-cars, or the like, on the same line and going in the same direction; as, trains running on ten-minute *headway*. **1898** *Engineering Mag.* XVI. 67 If it takes, say, thirty minutes to switch a train and put it in shape for a return trip, that is the average headway on which trains can be run.

For ***headache, head block, head gate, headlight, *headline, *head money, headright, *headwork,** see as main entries. For **head pistareen,** see **pistareen.**

b. Denoting persons occupying positions of rank or leadership: (1) **head boss,** the principal boss; (2) **chief,** the ranking one among Indian chiefs; (3) **coach,** a coach in charge of the coaching activities in a school's athletic program; (4) **driver,** (*a*) one having immediate supervision, usu. under an overseer or owner, of the work of slaves, *obs.*, (*b*) (see quot.); (5) ***man,** =**head driver** (*a*), *obs.*; (6) **marshal,** in some colonies the chief officer executing judicial orders, *obs.*, cf. **marshal general;** (7) **professor,** a professor of the highest rank, *rare;* (8) **push,** (see quot.); (9) **quill,** one in authority in a newspaper office, *slang, rare;* (10) **warrior,** an Indian warrior occupying a place of leadership in his tribe.

(1) **1882** *Nation* 7 Sep. 194/2 A permanent President . . . who in Washington, as the fountain of the patronage, would play the part of a head boss. — (2) **1806** ORDWAY in *Jrnls. Lewis & O.* 355 The head chief . . . informd us that the most of our horses and pack Saddles were Safe. *a***1918** G. STUART *On Frontier* I. 96 The head chief proposed to meet the interpreter unarmed and talk with him. **1946** FOREMAN *Last Trek* 23 In this the treaty-makers were described as 'head chiefs and warriors of the Kaskaskia Tribe of Indians.' — (3) **1897** *N.Y. Jrnl.* 5 Sep. 41/4 Princeton will have no head coach. **1898** *Outing* April 10/2 The crew this year has been placed under the tutelage of Justus A. B. Cowles, '81, as head coach. **1949** *Register* (Denver) 5 June 6/8 George Deklotz . . . accepted the post of head basketball coach at his alma mater, the University of South Dakota. — (4) (*a*)**1839** F. A. KEMBLE *Journal* 43 Their remedy lies in reporting the unmanageable individual either to the head driver or the overseer. (*b*) **1905** *Forestry Bureau Bul.* 61 B, Head driver. An expert river driver who, during the drive is stationed at a point where a jam is feared. Head drivers usually work in pairs (N.F.).

(5) **1828** MRS. HALL *Letters* 219 At the door of the house we were met by the head man, or driver as he is called, a black man of the name of Solomon. **1839** F. A. KEMBLE *Journal* 43 To return to our head driver, or, as he is familiarly called, head man, Frank. — (6) **1652** *Plymouth Col. Rec.* III. 11 [He] shall safely keepe, as head marshall, all such persons as shallbee committed to his custedie. **1679** *N.H. Prov. P.* XIX. 661 John Roberts of Dover is chosen head marshall of this province. — (7) **1891** *Univ. Chi. Official Bul.* No. 1, 11 Lecturers and Teachers . . . shall be classified as follows: (1) The Head-Professor. — (8) **1905** *Forestry Bureau Bul.* 61 B, Head push. . . . A sub-foreman in a logging camp (N.W.L.S.). — (9) **1873** BEADLE *Undevel. West* 35 The Head Quill of the Indianapolis Journal briefly declined.

(10) **1725** *Travels Amer. Col.* 113 The head Warriour got up and told the People what I had said. **1844** *Knickerb.* XXIV. 241 The sachems . . . were sustained by twelve head-warriors, or generals.

c. Denoting articles used or worn on the head: (1) **head-band,** (see quot. and cf. **tumpline**); (2) **handkerchief,** a handkerchief, as a bandana, suitable for wearing on the head; (3) **light,** see **headlight** (as a main entry) **3;** (4) **net,** a net worn over the head as a protection against mosquitoes, bees, etc.; (5) **protector,** a piece of football equipment designed to protect the player's head; (6) ***stall,** (see quot.), *obs.*; (7) **strap,** a strap passing across the forehead used in carrying a burden, a tumpline; (8) **tie,** a scarf or kerchief for tying over the head.

(1) **1917** KEPHART *Camping* II. 121 The tump or head-band is a good addition not only to a pack harness but to almost any other kind of pack used for carrying heavy weights. . . . When fording a swift stream, crossing on a foot-log or fallen tree, going over windfalls . . . the shoulder straps may be dropped. — (2) **1852** EASTMAN *Aunt Phillis's Cabin* 252 She has on a head-handkerchief and apron white as snow. **1898** HARRIS *Tales* 409 On her face there was a frown, and her 'head-han' k'cher,' which usually sat straight back from her forehead, had an upward tilt that gave her a warlike appearance. — (4) **1886** H. P. WELLS *Salmon-Fisherman* 84 Head-nets, to go over the hat and tuck in under the shirt-collar, are to me almost as intolerable as the insects themselves.

(5) **1903** in P. H. DAVIS *Football* (1911) 493 If head protectors are worn, no sole-leather, papier-maché, or other hard or unyielding material shall be used in their construction. — (6) **1877** BARTLETT 281 Headstall. A knitted worsted cap, covering all the head but the face, worn by boys in winter. — (7) **1849** M. EASTMAN *Dahcotah* 48 The head-strap is made of buffalo skin. It is from eight to ten, or sometimes twenty-four feet long. The [Indian] women fasten their heavy burdens to this strap, which goes around the forehead. — (8) **1857** M. GRIFFITH *Autobiog. Female Slave* 17 One gave a yard of ribbon, another a half-paper of pins, a third presented a painted cotton head-tie. **1900** WILKINS in *Harper's Bazaar* 17 Feb. 132, I put on my shawl and head-tie.

d. In phrases (see also **2.** and **4.** above): (1) *To be in head,* of grain, to be in the stage of heading out; (2) *to shut one's head,* to shut up, cease speaking, usu. imperative, *slang;* (3) *to put a head on,* to give a severe beating, *slang;* (4) *to open one's head,* to talk, speak, *slang;* (5) *head and footer,* (see quot. 1901).

(1) **1836** LUNDY WILSON *N.J. to Ohio & Return* (1929) 20 Here [western Penna.] we find some good grain; one field of wheat is in head. — (2) **1856** M. J. HOLMES *L. Rivers* xxxv. 382 'Shut up your head,' roared John. **1894** WISTER in *Harper's Mag.* Sep. 511/2 Specimen Jones told them all to shut their heads. — (3) **1868** WHYMPER *Alaska* 283 One calls the other a 'regular dead beat!' at which he, in return, threatens to 'put a head on him!' **1921** HEBERT *40 Yrs. Prospecting* 34 If you open your mouth again about that book I will put a head on you. — (4) **1885** H. H. JACKSON *Zeph* 44 He never opens his head to nobody. **1898** DELAND *Old Chester Tales* 307 Jones said, afterwards, that he hardly opened his head for the whole twenty-one miles.

(5) **1891** *Amer. Folk-Lore* IV. 227 One boy will squat down, and cry, 'First down for Head and Footer.' **1901** *D.N.* II. 141 head-and-footer, *n.* The name of a game somewhat like leap-frog. Ithaca.

As the last term in **arrow, beef, beetle, big, bitter, black, blue, bone, bonnet, boom, bottle, buffle, bulk, bull, bullet, bust, butt, calf's, cat, chuckle, chunk, copperhead, cotton, crow, curly, dead, deck, double, dragon('s), draw, duck, dumb, fan, fat, fish, flat, flint, gourd, great, green, hairy, hard, hog, hogs, horny, horse, Indian, iron, jar, jewel, jug, leather, level, lint, mast, moor, Morocco, moss, mud, mullet, mush, Negro, owl, patch, pin, pumpkin, putty, ram's, red, rough, round, Sagamore('s), shaved, sheep('s), shovel, skunk, sluice, snake('s), sore, steel, swell, swelled, toad, tough, Turk's, turtle, white, wool, woolly head.**

***head,** *v.*

1. *tr.* To go round the head of (a stream, lake, or other natural barrier).

*a***1656** BRADFORD *Hist.* 98 [They] followed their [Indians'] tracte till they had headed a great creake. **1711** *Boston News-Letter* 26 Feb. 2/2 Ice . . . cut their Cannoo's to pieces, made them Travel the rest of the way by Land through a horrid desert place, being forced to head Rivers, Lakes. **1788** WASHINGTON *Diaries* III. 457 The Carriage . . . was obliged to head Occoquam on account of the Ice which had impeded the passage. **1886** MARY CONE *Life Rufus Putnam* (Cleveland) 136 Such [streams] as were of any size they were obliged to 'head,' as it is called in backwoods phrase, or travel up on the lower side until they approached so near to the head as to be able to ford them without getting very deep in the water.

2. *intr.* Of a stream: To rise or have its source.

1755 L. EVANS *Middle Brit. Colonies* 10, I have no other Information of it, than that it heads with the Cayuga Branch of Susquehanna. **1805** CLARK in *Lewis & C. Exped.* (1904) I. 349 Those runs head at a fiew miles in the hills and discharge but little water. **1900** DRANNAN *Plains & Mts.* 110 Battle Creek heads in the Pike's Peak range of mountains.

3. *tr.* To place (something) on the head to carry it. *Rare.*

1852 *Knickerb.* XL. 217 A procession of darkies shoulder or head your baggage.

4. In colloq. expressions: (1) *To head for,* to make for, direct one's way toward; (2) *to head north* (or *south,* etc.), to go north (or south, etc.); (3) **to head off, fig.* to anticipate or forestall; (4) *to head on to,* to come into an indicated state or condition, *rare;* (5) *to head out,* to leave; (6) *to head up,* (*a*) =**2.** above, (*b*) to direct one's course *alongside* or *to,* (*c*) to take form, shape up.

(1) **1835** WILLIS *Pencillings* I. 167 We head for Venice. **1926** J. BLACK *You Can't Win* v. 51 Nothing would do but we must head for home. **1949** *Time* 13 June 23/1 The sheriff jumped into his car and headed for the tin-roofed Negro juke joint four miles away. — (2) **1907** S. E. WHITE *Arizona Nights* iv. 76 One day . . . we ran smack on this Texas outfit again, headed north. **1910** W. M. RAINE *B. O'Connor* 26 We're headed south, tell him. — (3) **1857** *Harper's Mag.* Feb. 399/1 The bridal party had been . . . offered a free ticket, in view of . . . 'heading off' any newspaper complaints. **1922** A. BROWN *Old Crow* 217 When you had a meddler in the family, you never knew where you'd have to head her off. — (4) **1888** JEWETT *King of Folly Island* 11 They [i.e., sick people] was headin' on to be dangerous.

(5) **1913** LONDON *Valley of Moon* III. xiv, You made me pull up stakes an' head out. — (6) (*a*) **1763** WASHINGTON *Diaries* I. 193 Several small Creeks, making out of South Rivr., head up in the Dismal. **1770** *Ib.* 419 Muddy Creek . . . heads up against, and with, some of the waters of Monongahela. (*b*) **1847** ROBB *Squatter Life* 106, I headed up alongside of Molly, and shyed a few soft things at her. **1876** MILLER *First Families* 128 A true Californian of Sierras . . . heads straight up to the bar. (*c*) **1906** *Springfield W. Republican* 29 Nov. 3 A period when important questions are heading up as never before in Springfield's history.

* **headache,** *n.*

1. *attrib.* (See quot.) *Obs.*

1819 PEIRCE *Rebelliad* 12 A box . . . was fill'd with vulgar stuff, Call'd maccaboy, or headache snuff.

b. Designating plants regarded as useful in cases of headache (see quots.).

1875 *Amer. Naturalist* IX. 145 [In southern Utah] is a plant . . . , probably a Pectis, . . . its foliage so strongly charged with an aromatic oil that it is extracted by a rough process of distilling for domestic use, the plant receiving the popular name of 'head-ache weed.' **1893** *Amer. Folk-Lore* VI. 136 *Anemone patens*, var. *Nuttalliana*, headache plant. **1931** CLUTE *Plants* 124 Familiar examples are . . . headache-plant (*Anemone pulsatilla*).

2. A thing, situation, etc., which is the cause of great bother, vexation, etc. *Slang.*

1939 GILBERT *Forty Yrs.* 77 The new rectory was both beautiful and expensive, but it proved to be a great headache. **1949** *Amer. Gas Jrnl.* Jan. 26/3 This is, of course, one of the headaches we are confronted with in the South in trying to handle peak loads.

head block.

1. A heavy block serving as a support in a structure. *Rare.*

1813 *Niles' Reg.* III. 323/1 The three ribs, extending across the river, . . . are set in cast iron head blocks.

2. (See quot. 1875.)

1853 *Mich. Agric. Soc. Trans.* IV. 35 G. S. Snyder, Lancaster O. improved head block for setting logs on saw mills. **1875** KNIGHT 1084 *Head-block.* 1. (*Saw-mill.*) *a.* The block on which the head—or forward end—of a log rests in the ordinary saw-mill; the other end is the tail-block. **1878** *Scientific Amer.* XXXVIII. 291 An improved head block . . . for saw mills.

* **headed,** *a.* As the last term in **blue, bone, butt, copper, high, level, low, lunk, mealy, mullet, pin, snake, tow, up-headed.**

* **header,** *n.*

1. A reaping machine that cuts the heads off standing grain.

1862 *Ill. Agric. Soc. Trans.* V. 234 We are aware of the claim . . . that grain may be cut by the Header and safely stacked after it. **1913** CATHER *O Pioneers!* 251 He bought a new header, you know, because all the wheat's so short this year. **1926** *K.C.* (Mo.) *Times* 15 June, Headers and binders started cutting wheat in the southwest part of the state this week.

attrib. **1875** PHILLIPS *Letters from Calif.* (1877) 41 Wheat, in all these valleys, is usually cut by the 'header' machines. **1881** NASH *Two Yrs. Ore.* 65 As soon as the header-wagon is filled it is drawn to the thrasher, whirling away in the center of the field, and an empty one takes its place **1926** *K.C.* (Mo.) *Star* 11 June, They are the harvesters who plan to be in the heart of the wheat belt when the first header barge and the first binder take the field to harvest the huge crop.

2. A top layer. *Rare.*

1865–6 *Ill. Agric. Soc. Trans.* VI. 641 Prime Pork—Shall be packed with a header of side cuts, the regular width, three half heads.

head gate. (See quot. 1875.)

1839 C. M. KIRKLAND *New Home* xxix. 205 The tired fire-fighters raced, one and all, to the dam, where they found the water pouring through a hole near the head-gate. **1875** KNIGHT 1085/1 *Head-gate.* (*Hydraulic Engineering.*) a. One of the upper pair of gates of a canal lock. . . . b. A crown-gate, flood-gate, water-gate, by which water is admitted to a race, run, sluice, etc

b. The main gate in an irrigation system.

1903 AUSTIN *Land of Little Rain* 226 Perhaps to get into the mood of the waterways . . . one needs to have seen old Amos Judson asquat on the headgate with his gun, guarding his water right toward the end of a dry summer. **1942** *Neb. Dept. Rds. & Irrig. Rep.* II. 67 It is further shown that the bureau of irrigation closed the headgate of this district for one day and then permitted it to reopen.

* **heading,** *n.*

1. *S.* (See quots.) *Colloq.*

1853 in *Amer. Sp.* XIX. 44 A bed was prepared . . . of blankets and counterpanes, with anything and everything stuck under the end for 'heading.' **1875** N. H. BISHOP *Voy. Paper Canoe* 236 A roll of homespun for a pillow, which the women called 'heading.' **1927** *D.N.* V. 474 heading, n. Pillow. 'Corncobs is all right in their place, but they shore make a mighty sorry *headin*'. [Ozarks.]

2. *pl.* (See quot. 1892.) *Obs.*

1878 ROE *Army Lett.* 189 The whole dress . . . was made of the headings of [the *N.Y. Herald*]. **1892** WALSH *Lit. Curiosities* 454 *Headings, Newspaper*, or *Head-Lines*, an American journalistic invention, which arrests the attention of the reader and whets his appetite by startling titular lines, . . . condensing and epigrammatizing the news in the body of the article. They are generally supposed to be of recent date, and to have originated during the Civil War. But as far back as the Revolution an original has been found.

b. headings editor, a newspaper editor who has charge of headlines. *Obs.*

1882 G. A. SALA *Amer. Revisited* II. 123 (*footnote*), One Chicago paper pays its 'Headings Editor' (he does nothing else) a salary of a thousand dollars a year.

headlight 'hɛd,laɪt, *n.*

1. A powerful light on the front of a locomotive to light up the track at night.

1861 *Remin. Life Locomotive Engineer* 124, I saw the glimmer of his head-light when he first turned the curve and entered upon the straight track. **1892** GUNTER *Miss Dividends* 63 The train . . . passes with illuminated Pullmans and flashing headlight into the night of the plains. **1944** *Chi. D. News* 14 July 10/8 His vision travels like a locomotive headlight far down the aisles of time, illuminating the lives even of the unborn.

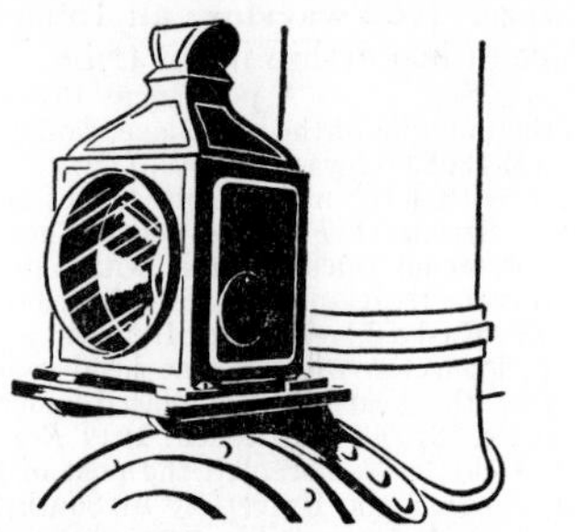

Headlight or head lamp for locomotive

2. A light on an automobile, bicycle, or motorcycle.

1939 *These Are Our Lives* 37 The headlights of the automobile pick up the bush of red roses lush and beautiful under the artificial glare. **1944** *Vogue* 1 Oct. 188 The powerful beam of a motorcycle's mud-flecked headlight pinned him in an inappropriate glare. **1947** *Nat. Geog. Mag.* Sep. 349/1 The beams of my headlight seemed to be absorbed into the sand.

3. A light for use on the head as a miner's lamp.

1944 *Speleological Soc. Bul.* July 35/2 If a head light is not desired, nothing is lost; whereas it is exceedingly difficult later to add a light bracket to a hat that did not originally have one.

* **headline,** *n.*

1. A reference line in a survey, a boundary line. *Obs.*

1656 *N.H. Doc. & Rec.* I. 221 From the said head lyne we measured for the length . . . 6 miles & a halfe. **1687** *Conn. Rec.* III. 232 That tree which allso hath been granted to Fayrefeild by the Court to be theire west line or head lyne. **1704** *N.H. Probate Rec.* I. 514, I give and bequeath . . . all my land . . . viz as far as, to butt against Andrews head line.

2. A caption in large letters in a newspaper. Also attrib. Cf. **headliner.**

1867 D. R. LOCKE *Swingin' Round* 14 [He] glanced at the head lines. **1948** *Chi. D. News* 13 Dec. 16/3 Mr. Truman is right when he says that members of Congress are headline hunters.

Hence as a verb, *tr.* To provide (a news item, story, etc.) with headlines.

1912 *Out West* April 237/2 Mechanically, excitedly, he was running through the other sections of the paper when a big headlined, illustrated, human interest story, the pride of some reporter's heart, stared at him. **1919** SALTUS *Palser Case* 1 The murder of Monty Palser, headlined that morning in the papers, shook the metropolis at breakfast. **1948** *Time* 12 Jan. 75/1 Newspapers headlined the scoreboard of production like bulletins from the front.

3. A line used to fasten the head of a vessel.

1876 MARK TWAIN *Tom Sawyer* ii. 29 Get out that head-line! Lively now! come out with your spring-line. **1876** HABBERTON *Jericho Road* 9 The head-line was cast off as the pilot's bell rang.

∗**head-money. 1.** Money paid as a bounty for prisoners or for the scalps of enemies. *Obs.* **2.** A tax levied upon immigrants for the support of those of their number who might become sick, needy, or destitute in this country. Also attrib.

(1) **1814** *Niles' Reg.* VI. 36/2 The prince regent has agreed to the claims of the indian warriors, in regard to head money, for prisoners of war brought in by them. **1841** Cooper *Deerslayer* vi, There's bounty enough sleeping round that fire to make a heavy division of head-money. — (2) **1872** *Chi. Tribune* 17 Oct. 4/2 Boston submitted a proposition to abolish all taxes or head-money on immigrants. **1882** *Nation* 3 Aug. 84/1 The Emigrant, or 'Head-Money,' Bill was passed without opposition. **1889** *Cent.* 2752/1 *Head-money cases,* three cases decided by the United States Supreme Court in 1884 (112 U.S., 580), which held that an act of Congress (August 3d, 1882) imposing upon owners of vessels a duty for immigrants entering the United States was valid.

headright ˈhɛdˌraɪt, *n.*

1. A right to a portion of public land granted by the government to the head of a family settling upon it; also the land so granted. *Obs.* or *hist.*

1799 in Rothert *Muhlenberg Co.* 45 Colonel William Campbell's headright on Caney adjoining the lands of the heirs of William Russell. **1832** Clay *Speeches* (1842) 221 [Kentucky] was tempted to offer her waste lands to settlers . . . under the name of head-rights or pre-emptions. **1909** O. Henry *Roads of Destiny* 93 [He] refused his head-right and veteran donation certificates.

b. (See quot.) *Obs.*

1896 P. A. Bruce *Econ. Hist. Va.* I. 512 The third ground on which a patent was granted was the head right. The head right was in operation in 1618. . . . Every shareholder who transported an emigrant, whether free or bound, to the Colony, acquired thereby a claim to fifty acres if the person remained in Virginia for a period of three years.

2. A similar provision, or the land held by virtue of it, in Texas.

1828 *Laws of Texas* Nov. (B. '59), So much of the vacant lands . . . shall be surveyed and sectionized . . . as will be sufficient to satisfy all claims for scrip sold, soldier's claims, and head-rights. **1873** Cozzens *Marvellous Country* 48 Thirty Americans . . . had gone there to 'spekelate' in 'head rights' that had been issued by the State of Texas to such persons as had served in her wars. **1941** Rascoe *Belle Starr* 297 Under former laws of Texas, a headright was the inheritable right given to certain immigrating heads of families to grants of free land.

attrib. **1857** Braman *Texas* 152 Every head of a family, where the family resided in the country, was entitled to a head-right certificate of one league and labor of land.

3. The right or claim of an Indian to a share of the property accruing to his or her tribe.

1871 *Rep. Indian Affairs* (1872) 587 Very often the Indians are obliged to sell their head-rights to clothe their nakedness. **1894** Robley *Bourbon Co., Kans.* 155 In several instances the settlers on the Neutral Land Married Cherokee women, thereby becoming 'squawmen'—legally Cherokees—and entitled to a 'headright,' and thus securing their claims. **1948** *Dly. Oklahoman* (Okla. City) 7 June 9/7 The regular quarterly payment to shareholders of Osage Indian headrights will be made June 15.

∗**headwork,** *n.*

1. The practice of carrying loads on the head. *Rare.*

1840 R. H. Dana *Two Years* xiv, We soon found that . . . 'head-work' was the only system for California.

2. *pl.* A structure for controlling the flow of water in a river, canal, or irrigation system.

1891 *Scribner's Mag.* X. 468 The river flowing between firm banks, could be permanently controlled by headworks of masonry. **1903** *Sci. Amer. Supp.* 10 Jan. 22597 (*Cent. Supp.*), Headworks can be placed more easily along the banks of smaller streams, or dams built across their beds, raising or controlling the waters. **1906** *Out West* Jan. 10 Great chances were taken in omitting headworks from these intakes.

3. *pl.* (See quot.)

1905 *Terms Forestry & Logging* 40 *Headworks,* a platform or raft, with windlass or capstan, which is attached to the front of a log raft or boom of logs, for warping, kedging, or winding it through lakes and still water, by hand or horse power.

∗**healer,** *n.* (See quot. 1909.) Cf. **faith, metaphysical healer.** — **1907** Mark Twain *Christian Science* 74 (R.), A healer has to have the Annex and the Scriptures, or he is not allowed to work the game. . . . The exactions of the ordinary C. S. 'healer' are not exorbitant. **1909** Webster, healer. . . . A Christian Science practitioner; a Scientist;—not so called by the Christian Scientists themselves.

∗**health,** *n.* In combs.: (1) **health board,** a board of health; (2) **department,** a division of a state or municipal government that deals with matters of public health, also attrib.; (3) **food,** food regarded as being especially conducive to health, also attrib.; (4) **law,** a law pertaining to public health, usu. *pl.;* (5) **lift,** (see last quot.), *obs.;* (6) **officer,** an officer charged with enforcing the laws relating to public health and sanitation; (7) **seeker,** one who goes from place to place in the interest of his health; (8) **underwear,** underwear of a kind regarded as conducive to health.

(1) **1888** A. K. Green *Behind Closed Doors* iii, He is on the Health Board. **1894** Ford *P. Stirling* 72 What is the Health Board about, that poison for children can be sold in the public streets? — (2) **1868** *Boston City Council Doc.* I. No. 7, 15 The Health Department abate nuisances upon private property. **1922** *Fall River City Doc.* No. 75, 612 Householders are urged to co-operate with the Health Department. **1949** *Amer. Jrnl. Pub. Health* May 613/2 Diabetes, one of the chronic diseases which have long been neglected, should have a place in a local health department program. — (3) **1882** Howells *Modern Instance* xxviii, I put the camp on a health-food basis. **1912** Irwin *Red Button* 2 Professor Noll was a diet delusionist, the assistant editor of a health-food magazine. *Ib.* 178 Professor Noll intended to read a paper at the Health Food Conference. — (4) **1801** *Steele P.* I. 230 The amount [was] expended in purchasing of Land & erecting wharves & buildings under the act respecting quarantine & health laws. **1911** Persons *Mass. Labor Laws* 262 The new studies . . . reveal the intricate relation between health laws and 'hour, age, and safety' laws.

(5) **1875** *Chi. Tribune* 22 Aug. 16/1 Feeling in his hip-pocket for $20 with which to take lessons on the health lift. **1875** Knight 1306/1 *Lifting-machine.* An exercising-machine belonging to the furnishing of a gymnasium, in which a weight is so disposed with handles or straps for the hands, hips, or shoulders, that a person may conveniently try his strength, and improve by persistent trying at gradually increasing weights. . . . Fig. 2939 shows Butler's standard health-lift. — (6) **1755** *Pa. Col. Rec.* VI. 346 The Governor . . . shall Commissionate and appoint one of such Two Persons so to be recommended to him from Time to Time to be the Health Officer. **1879** *Mich. Gen. Statutes* I. (1882) 472 It shall be the duty of the health officer of each village and city . . . to give notice [of any neglect to comply with the health laws] to the prosecuting attorney of his county. **1914** S. H. Adams *Clarion* 325 From all I can learn, Merritt has got the goods as a health officer. — (7) **1885** *Wkly. New Mexican Rev.* 23 April 2/5 It behooves Santa Fe to look to her laurels, else less fortunate competitors . . . deprive her even of a fair share of the patronage of the tourists and health-seekers. **1894** *Voice* 30 Aug., Colorado was peopled first by mad seekers after gold . . . to which has been added later the ever-increasing horde of healthseekers and the genus tourist. — (8) **1899** Ade *Doc' Horne* 166 She made him wear a kind of health underwear that gave him the hives.

b. *For one's health,* used in negative contexts to emphasize that the person referred to is acting in his own interest. *Slang.*

1900 *Cong. Rec.* 5 Feb. 1520/2, I am not making this speech for fun, nor for my health, nor as an oratorical exercise. **1911** *Toledo Blade* Aug. (Th.), I'm not in politics for my health.

∗**healthy,** *a. fig.* or *ironical.* Wholesome, conducive to health, vigorous, alive.

1831 Smith *Life & Writings of Downing* 149 (We.), Major Eaton, it won't be healthy for you to come on to these steps to-night. **1856** Brewerton *War in Kans.* 255 Here we halted, for it would not have been 'healthy,' in the then excited state of party feeling, for Major Clarke to have entered the place. **1945** R. Wright *Black Boy* 177 (We.), Keep your eyes where they belong if you want to be healthy!

∗**heap,** *n., a.,* and *adv.*

1. In Indian speech or in imitation of this: Very, a great deal. *Colloq.*

1848 Ruxton in *Blackw. Mag.* LXIII. 719 An Indian is always a 'heap' hungry or thirsty—loves a 'heap'—is a 'heap' brave—in fact, 'heap' is tantamount to very much. **1860** *Mountaineer* (Salt Lake City) 21 July 190/6 The Indians, however, always retire, crying out that they wanted 'heap fight.' **1947** *Steamboat* (Colo.) *Pilot* 9 Jan. 7/4 He said the Utes were 'heap scared.' His 'heap scared' was a favorite expression.

b. heap sight, much, a whole lot. *Colloq.*

1874 Eggleston *Circuit Rider* i. 14 He 'low'd there was a heap sight more corn. **1911** Saunders *Col. Todhunter* 152 You're a heapsight smarter man than I gave you credit for bein'.

2. heap row, *agric.* a row along which heaps or piles of corn, fertilizer, etc., are made.

1865 Turner *Cotton* 89 In the commencement, a row is selected, fifteen feet from the fence or beginning. This is the heap row. Fifteen feet from the end of this row, the first heap, or half the load is deposited; it is raked out by removing the hind gate of the body.

As the last term in **brush, cradle, junk, log, potato, rack, wreck heap.**

∗ **heaping,** *a.* In expressions of measure: Heaped. Also fig.

1838 *Cong. Globe* App. 24 May 470/1 Here is a fair contract, (dictated by Ross himself,) founded on *a high and heaping price.* **1872** *Vt. Bd. Agric. Rep.* I. 57 Mix a heaping table-spoonful of the powder with two gallons of water. **1908** *Smart Set* June 25/1 Aunt Natica waddled off . . . to fetch Thorndyke a heaping portion of the *dulce.*

∗ **hear,** *v.*

1. *tr.* To give assent, agree, listen *to,* usu. in negative expressions. *Colloq.*

1833 *Md. Hist. Mag.* XIII. 379, I made a move to depart—but they would not hear to that. **1869** Stowe *Oldtown Folks* xx. 243 She has her own ways and doings, and she won't hear to reason. **1915** Poole *Harbor* 202 When I tried at last to turn our talk to our affairs at home, at first she would not hear to it.

2. (See quot.)

1900 Nelson *A B C Wall St.* 145 Wall Street tipsters . . . never say 'I *know* that such and such a thing will happen,' but preface their tips, points and advice with 'I hear,' or 'I understand.' The qualification gives them a loophole for escape.

∗ **heart,** *n.* In combs.: (1) **heart bag,** ?a heart-shaped tobacco pouch, *rare;* (2) **bird,** (see quots.); (3) **leaf,** floating heart, also any one of various American species of *Asarum;* (4) **leaved,** *a.* see as a main entry; (5) **lesson,** (see quot.), *colloq.;* (6) **motto,** motto candy, *obs.;* (7) **nut,** (see quot.), *obs.;* (8) **-of-palm,** the heart of the cabbage palmetto, also attrib.; (9) ∗**-'s-ease,** a name given locally to various American plants, esp. the common persicary and the pansy; (10) **seed,** the balloon vine; (11) **snakeroot,** an American perennial herb, *Asarum canadense;* (12) **spot knotweed,** (see quot.); (13) **-to-heart,** *a.* utterly frank, sincere, without reserve, also absol.; (14) **weed,** (see quot.); (15) **worm,** a bud worm which attacks young corn, *rare.*

(1) **1923** J. H. Cook *On Old Frontier* 242 He produced a 'heart bag,' filled it with tobacco and the inner bark of the dogwood, and we 'made a little smoke.' — (2) [**1808–14** Wilson *Ornithology* IV. 76 In this country the Magpie was first taken notice of at the factories or trading houses, on Hudson's bay, where the Indians used sometimes to bring it in, and gave it the name of Heart-bird, for what reason is uncertain.] **1844** *Nat. Hist. N.Y., Zoology* II. 216 [The Turnstone] is known among our *gunners* . . . under the name of Brant-bird, Heart-bird, Horse-foot Snipe and Beach bird. — (3) **1854** Thoreau *Walden* 194 Of noticeable plants [in Walden Pond there are] . . . only a few small heart-leaves and potamogetons. **1894** *Amer. Folk-Lore* VII. 97 *Asarum arifolium,* . . . heart-leaves Ga. *Asarum Virginicum* . . . heart-leaves, Banner Elk, N.C.

(5) **1932** Randolph *Ozark Mt.* 24 Thar was some as would make reg'lar speeches, too—we called them kind o' speeches heart-lessons. — (6) **1923** J. H. Cook *On Old Frontier* 178 The candies which did not suit their tastes, such as those known as 'heart mottoes,' they discarded. — (7) **1899** Vanderbilt *Flatbush* 295 There was a nut-tree which grew on a line with, and directly north of, what is now the Almshouse. It bore nuts which were highly valued; they were thin-shelled, and were a superior species of hickory-nut. They were called heart-nuts from their shape. — (8) **1938** Matschat *Suwannee River* 211 The most common palm in Florida is the cabbage palm. . . . This is the salad served today as 'hearts of palm.' **1942** Kennedy *Palmetto Country* 4 They also gather the buds for sale at three cents each and the buds are canned and shipped to appear on America's ultra-swank menus as 'Heart-of-Palm Salad,' usually at a dollar a plate. — (9) **1778** Carver *Travels* 520 Heart's Ease, Lilies red and yellow. **1832** W. D. Williamson *Hist. Maine* I. 124 *Heart's-ease* resembles arsmart in appearance, except that it has a large reddish heart-formed spot on its leaf. **1938** Damon *Grandma* 81 There was love-in-a-mist, bleeding heart, and heart's-ease.

(10) **1847** Wood *Botany* 215 Heart-seed. Balloon-vine. . . . Native on the Missouri and its branches. **1891** Coulter *Bot. W. Texas* I. 65 *Cardiospermum.* Heart seed, Balloon-vine. — (11) **1736** Catesby *Carolina* II. 41 The Indians . . . have likewise some Roots, which they pretend will effect the Cure [of a rattlesnake bite], particularly a kind of *Assarum,* commonly called Heart-Snake-root. **1791** *Amer. Philos. Soc.* III. 114 *Asarum—virginicum?* (Heart Snake-roots). — (12) **1817** Eaton *Botany* (1822) 338 *Polygonum persicaria,* ladies' thumb, heart-spot knotweed. — (13) **1894** *Advance* 11 Oct., A kind of public religious 'orphanage,' where no true heart-to-heart 'mothering' . . . was possible. **1910** White *Rules of Game* 444 Let's have a heart-to-heart, and find out how we stand. **1931** *K.C. Star* 31 Dec. 12 The first step would be to have a heart-to-heart talk with Marion. — (14) **1931** Clute *Plants* 127 The heartweed (*Polygonum persicaria*), which has heart-shaped markings on the leaves.

(15) **1855** Davis *Farm Bk.* 184 The ants the grasshoppers and the heart or bud worm have all done mischief to the stand [of corn].

b. *To declare to one's heart,* to declare or state most emphatically. *Colloq.*

1881 Jewett *Country By-Ways* 227, I declare to my heart if you are n't Mahaly Robinson!

As the last term in **bleeding, bursting, floating, graveyard, lion's, ox, Purple, ring heart.**

∗ **heart-leaved,** *a.*

1. Having leaves of a heart-shaped form.

1814 Bigelow *Florula Bostoniensis* 202 *Aster cordifolius.* Heart leaved Aster. **1832** Browne *Sylva* 254 Heart-Leaved Balsam Poplar, *Populus candicans* . . . is commonly seen growing before the houses [in R.I., Mass., and N.H.]. **1843** Torrey *Flora N.Y.* II. 15 *Plantago cordata,* . . . Heart-leaved Plantain. . . . Borders of creeks, wet meadows, etc. **1892** Apgar *Trees Northern U.S.* 148 *Alnus cordifolia,* (Heart-leaved Alder.) . . . A large and very handsome Alder.

2. heart-leaved cucumber tree, a magnolia, *Magnolia cordata,* of the southern states.

1832 Browne *Sylva* 208 From the cordiform shape of its leaves we have adopted the name of Heart-Leaved Cucumber Tree. **1860** Curtis *Woody Plants N.C.* 68 Heart-leaved cucumber tree . . . is equally desirable in private grounds as well for its symmetrical form as for the beauty of its flowers and its luxuriant foliage.

3. heart-leaved willow, an American willow having large heart-shaped leaves.

1813 Muhlenberg *Cat. Plants* 91 *Salix cordata,* heart-leaved willow. **1892** Apgar *Trees Northern U.S.* 165 (Heart-leaved Willow.) . . . Shrub or small tree, 8 to 20 ft. high, very common in low or wet places.

∗ **heat,** *n.*

1. heat lightning, vivid flashes of electric light seen near the horizon, esp. after hot days, resembling ordinary lightning, but not accompanied by thunder. Also transf.

1834 C. A. Davis *Lett. J. Downing* 17 You may just as well try to paint a flash of heat-lightning in dog-days. **1853** Lowell *Fireside Trav.* 106 We saw heat-lightnings of unsuccessful matches. **1884** Mark Twain *H. Finn* xx. 191 The heat-lightning was squirting around low down in the sky. **1949** *Time* 14 Mar. 21/1 For an instant, like heat lightning, an announcement dimly outlined a far horizon. There had been a shake-up in Russia's high command.

2. heat register, a contrivance fitted into the floor or wall of a room for admitting hot air from a furnace.

1902 C. Morris *Life on Stage* 373 Old heat-registers and things carry voices.

heated term. The hot season of the year.

1855 *N.Y. Herald* 26 Dec. 3/4 Our 'heated terms' are over, and we now begin to look out for the approach of the 'northers.' **1873** Beadle *Undevel. West* 793 The average of the 'heated term,' one day with another, is there recorded at eighty-four degrees. **1876** *Placer Argus* (Auburn, Calif.) 17 June 3/2 (*heading*), The Heated Term. **1949** *Chi. Tribune* 11 Sep. I. 43/5 What a month ago appeared to be a trivial item of conversation during the heated term has become a raging topic among scientists.

∗ **heater,** *n.* As the last term in **Franklin, gas, self-heater.**

∗ **heathen,** *n.*

1. *collect.* The American Indians. *Obs.*

1645 Williams *Christenings* (1881) 4 Men stand upon their tearmes of high opposition between . . . the Christian and the Heathen, that is the naked American. **1689** *Mass. H.S. Coll.* 4 Ser. V. 203 The present distressed state and condition of the eastern parts, by the barbarous murders and outrages committed by the heathen upon the inhabitants there. **1711** *Boston News-Letter* 31 Dec. 2/2 They write from North-Carolina, that they are distressed there with Intestine Broils, the Fury of the Heathen, and a Mortal Distemper.

2. heathen Chinee, a jocose term for a Chinese, after a character in Bret Harte's poem "Plain Language from Truthful James." Also attrib.

1870 Harte *Plain Language* line 5 The heathen Chinee is peculiar. **1890** *Cong. Rec.* 7 June 5791/2 [It seems to me that this bill] has something of a Heathen Chinee flavor about it. **1949** *Wis. Mag. Hist.* Mar. 322 Remember how the 'heathen Chinee' of the dim past discovered roast pork—and thereafter burned down his house every time he wanted some.

∗ **heath hen.**

1. A grouse, *Tympanuchus cupido,* related to the prairie chicken, formerly found chiefly in the midland and southern New England states but now extinct (see quot. 1946).

1644 in *N.Y. Hist. Soc. Coll.* 2 Ser. III. (1857) 150 In the forests here there are also many partridges, heath-hens and pigeons. **1781** PETERS *Hist. Conn.* 255 The feathered tribe in Connecticut are . . . heath-hens, blackbirds. **1832** *Boston Transcript* 6 April 2/1 They have passed an act to prevent the destruction of the *heath-hen.* **1946** McATEE *Wildlife Conservation* (MS) 9 The heath hen, once common in scrub oak barrens of New Jersey and Long Island, was long ago extirpated there; restricted for many years to Martha's Vineyard, the last bird perished in 1930. **1949** *Amer. Photography* June 382/1 The latest member of our wild bird life to disappear is the heath hen, a member of the grouse family.

b. heath-hen plum, (see quot.).

1810 in WILSON *Ornithology* III. 109 A favourite article of their diet is the *heath-hen plum,* or partridge-berry.

2. The prairie chicken.

1807 GASS *Journal* 151 In the plains are a great many hares and a number of fowls, between the size of a pheasant and turkey, called heath hens or grous.

* **heave,** *n.*

1. *pl.* A disease, chiefly of horses, in which the lungs become inelastic and breathing becomes difficult.

1793 *Mass. Spy* 8 Aug. 1/1 If an old maiden chances to have the heaves, 'tis . . . dignified with a polypus upon the heart. **1885** PHELPS *Old Maids* II. 41 Some Boston acquaintances said their horses always had the heaves. **1945** TRYON *Poor Man* 16 Our poor old steed, Dolly, while able enough along the level, used to get the heaves at the slightest hill.

b. heave powder, a powder given to horses that have heaves.

1856 *Porter's Spirit of Times* 18 Oct. 115/2, I tried all sorts of heave powders on my patient, with no effect whatever. **1898** FREDERIC *Deserter* 160 [Lafe] had to work, . . . now stripping willows for the basket-factory, now packing 'heave-powders' for the local horse-doctor.

2. A free drink or "handout." *Slang. Obs.*

1840 *S. Lit. Messenger* VI. 511/2 Joe took to drinking . . . and was always to be found hanging about where there was a chance of getting a heave.

* **heave,** *v. intr.* and *tr.* Of plants: To rise or to be raised out of the ground, esp. by alternate thawings and freezings. Hence * **heaving,** *n.*

1747 FRANKLIN *Lett.* Wks. (1887) II. 81 The rye-grass seed failed, and the red clover heaves out much for want of being thicker. **1788** WASHINGTON *Diaries* III. 406 Land was also sowed with Buck Wheat, for the experiment of . . . laying on the Wht. during the Winter keeping it warm and from being hove out of the gr[oun]d. **1856** *Mich. Agric. Soc. Trans.* VII. 199 Much wheat is annually lost by being 'heaved' up by the frost. **1948** BOYCE *Forest Pathology* 72 Young seedlings suffer from heaving caused by repeated freezing and thawing of the upper soil layers with the accompanying expansion and contraction.

b. *intr.* Used of rocks.

1873 *Vt. Bd. Agric. Rep.* 664 Mr. Halbert replied that stones were troublesome on account of heaving to the surface. **1874** *Ib.* 219 Ridged wet clay land will heave so badly that good grass will not succeed.

c. To lose (a baseball game) by conniving. *Obs.* Cf. * **throw,** *v.* **2.**

1865 *Wilkes' Spirit of Times* 11 Nov. 166/1 We are going to 'heave' this game and we will give you $300 if you like to stand in with us.

* **heaven,** *n.* As the last term in **horse, huckleberry, Negro, patent heaven.**

* **heavy,** *a.*

1. Wealthy, principal, most important. *Colloq.*

1842 BUCKINGHAM *E. & W. States* I. 181 The congregation is not numerous, but it is said to contain some 'very heavy men,' by which is meant wealthy [Maine]. **1883** *N.Y. Tribune* 9 Jan. 1/2 Truman B. Handy . . . has associated with him several heavy New-York capitalists.

2. Of timber: Large and abundant. Cf. **heavy timber.**

1849 NASON *Journal* 69 The timber is very heavy, and the country nearly level.

3. Important, consequential, requiring superior talents. *Contemptuous.* Cf. **heavy swell, heavy weight.**

1874 *Vt. Bd. Agric. Rep.* II. 654 If not honest workers, they should not be allowed to do the 'heavy laying round' at the public expense. **1931** *K.C. Times* 8 Aug., Dean Frank Martin . . . is supposed to do the 'heavy work' which President Williams formerly did.

4. *Baseball.* Hard, frequent, successful. *Colloq.*

1875 *Chi. Tribune* 23 Oct. 10/7 In the seventh they clinched it, getting 7 runs on some free, heavy batting, though they earned only one. **1885** CHADWICK *Art of Pitching* 30 With the heavy hitting class, it is a pretty safe game to play. **1896** ——— *Spalding's Base B. Guide* 19 'If we had their pitchers,' 'or if we had their heavy batters,' etc., etc., 'we would have won the pennant.'

5. Of ores: Rich in some particular element or substance.

1876 RAYMOND *8th Rep. Mines* 25 Dry ores . . . are left standing in the mines for future workings and attention is turned to following the heavy ores which answer for smelting. *Ib.* 382 The ores rich in sulphur are called heavy ores.

6. In special combs.: (1) **heavy leaf,** a variety of tobacco, *obs.;* (2) **swell,** one of fancied importance, a "big shot," also attrib., *slang;* (3) **timber,** a dense forest of large trees; (4) **timbered,** *a.* overgrown by many large trees, made of heavy timber or logs; (5) * **weight,** (see quot. 1889), *colloq.;* (6) **wooded pine,** (see quots.).

(1) **1852** *Hunt's Merch. Mag.* XXVII. 555 The 'heavy leaf' is grown on the Kentucky River. — (2) **1901** RYAN *Montana* vi. 95 Guess he must be a heavy swell where he comes from, and where all the fandangoes are got up in gilt-edged style. **1917** J. F. DALY *Life A. Daly* 355 Lewis . . . was afraid of his part, which he thought was to be played in the 'heavy swell' manner. — (3) **1843** *Yale Lit. Mag.* VIII. 406, I fear there are multitudes of people . . . who can discern in this patch of 'heavy timber,' not a single vestige of the huge abbey. *c***1908** CANTON *Frontier Trails* 114 We made a camp in the hills where there was heavy timber and water. — (4) **1831** PECK *Guide* 40 In the southern and middle regions of this [Mississippi] valley the wide, level, and heavy timbered alluvions, are . . . unhealthy. **1902** WHITE *Conjuror's House* 39 The fort itself [was] a medley of heavy-timbered stockades and square blockhouses.

(5) **1879** B. F. TAYLOR *Summer-Savory* xviii. 146 He is a heavy-weight wherever he is. **1889** *Cent.* 2764/3 *Heavy-weight,* . . . A person of weight or importance; one of much influence. — (6) **1858** WARDER *Hedges & Evergreens* 250 *Pinus ponderosa,* or Heavy-wooded Pine, has leaves from nine inches to a foot long. **1897** SUDWORTH *Arborescent Flora* 20 *Pinus ponderosa.* . . . Common Names. . . . Heavy-wooded Pine (Eng.). Western Pitch Pine.

* **hedge,** *n.* **1. hedge cactus,** a cactus grown as a hedge plant. **2. hedge clause,** a safeguarding clause in a contract. — (1) **1883** J. H. BEADLE *Western Wilds* xxxvi. 593 There is . . . the hedge cactus, with which Mexicans fence their fields. — (2) **1928** *Sat. Ev. Post* 10 March 185/2 In the Wall Street language these are called hedge clauses. They signify that if the representations turn out to be wrong the banker shall not be held accountable.

As the last term in **Cherokee, live, Osage, Osage orange, shelter hedge.**

* **hedgehog,** *n.*

1. Any one of various American animals of the family Erethizontidae, having stiff, detachable spines in their hair; the American porcupine.

1605 ROSIER *Virginia* (1887) 159 Beasts: Reine-Deere, Stagges, Fallow-Deere, Beares, Wolues, Beauer, Otter, Hare, Cony, Hedge-Hoggs. **1736** J. GYLES *Mem. Captivity* 26 Our Hedge Hog . . . is about the bigness of a Hog of six months old. **1832** WILLIAMSON *Maine* I. 138 The Porcupine, or Hedgehog, or more scientifically, the Urchin, is a quadruped, slow in motion, of a gray colour. **1947** CAHALANE *Mammals* 571 Because the North American porcupine has quills something like those of the Old World hedgehog, it is frequently called a hedgehog.

fig. **1869** S. WARNER *Daisy in Field* (1876) xiv. 173 That hedgehog of thoughts began to stir and unfold and come to life.

2. In combs.: (1) **hedgehog cactus,** (see quot. 1889); (2) **club rush,** a North American sedge, *Cyperus ovularis,* or *C. globulosus;* (3) **holly,** (see quot.); (4) **ray,** (see quot.); (5) * **-'s quills,** (see quot.), *obs.*

(1) **1876** HOBBS *Bot. Hand-Book* 52 Hedge hog cactus, Echinocactus Texensis. **1889** *Cent.* 2768/2 hedgehog cactus. . . . A cactus of the genus *Echinocactus,* of which about 200 species are known and a large number cultivated. They are all natives of Texas, Mexico, and South America. **1947** *So. Sierran* May 4/2 The yellow Encelia, the apricot Mallow and magenta Hedgehog cactus also captured our interest. — (2) **1833** EATON *Botany* (ed. 6) 220 *Mariscus echinatus,* hedgehog club rush. — (3) **1785** MARSHALL *Amer. Grove* 64 *Ilex canadensis.* Canadian, or Hedgehog Holly. — (4) **1842** *Nat. Hist. N.Y., Zoology* IV. 372 The Hedge-hog Ray, *Raia erinaceus* . . . was taken off the coast of New Jersey, in seven fathoms of water. — (5) **1830** *Zion's Advocate* (Portland, Me.) 26 Aug. 4/5 We [have] . . . just heard a person call on a trader for a quantity of *'hedge hog's quills'* meaning cider brandy.

hediondilla ˌhedionˈdijə, *n. S.W.* [f. Sp. *hediondo,* stinking, in the Amer. Sp. sense shown here. Note the spellings, the earliest being without the dim. ending.] The creosote bush. Cf. * **creosote,** *n.*

[1846 EMORY *Military Reconn.* 52 The iodeodonda is a new plant, very offensive to the smell, and, when crushed resembling creosote.] 1853 SITGREAVES *Exped. Zuni & Colo. Rivers* 39 Ascending a sandy aroyo, there was to be seen occasionally a ... hediondea, or stinking weed of the Mexicans. 1878 HINTON *Arizona* 347 The hedeundilla is the bush or shrub which covers the as yet dry valleys and high mesas of Arizona to such an extent as to be met with at every step. 1904 WOOTON *Native Ornamental Plants N.M.* 32 Hediondilla (*Covillea tridentata*) ... is an evergreen shrub of the mesas which would make an excellent low hedge plant. 1912 LUMHOLTZ *New Trails* 223 The Mexicans for the same reason call it by the unpleasant name *hediondia*. 1932 *Ariz. Agric. Exp. Sta.* Bul. 141 24 These include creosote bush or hediondillo, gray thorn or desert buckthorn, ... and mimosas.

* **heel,** *n.* In combs.: (1) **heel fly,** any one of various dipterous flies that lay eggs on the feet and legs of cattle and cause warbles; (2) **kicking,** a dance, *obs.;* (3) **nail,** ?a nail used in bootheels, *rare;* (4) **path,** a path along the side of a canal opposite the towing path, so used in jocular allusion to **towpath* (as if *toepath*), also attrib., cf. **berm;** (5) **tap,** a winged and threaded tap or nut used on a bolt that secures a plowshare to the foot of the stock, *colloq.*

(1) 1878 RUEDE *Sod-House Days* 224 The 'heel flies' troubled the cattle very much the last few days, and they tore loose and ran off; today I greased their heels, which seemed to relieve them. 1949 *10 Story Western* May 37/1 I'd just as soon have a bunch of heel flies around a herd. — (2) 1788 WEBSTER in Ford *Notes on N. Webster* I. 225 January 15. At a heelkicking at Mr. Huletts Public. — (3) 1775 in ZUNDER *Early days of Joel Barlow* (1934) 34 Cook goes to the Blacksmith about his heelnails, calling to mind the fate of Achilles who was wounded in the heel. — (4) 1853 *Oregonian* (Portland) 12 Mar. 1/5 A *snubber,* may it please the court, ... snubs the boat when she heaves to on the heel-path shore, and unships the whiffle-trees in passing a lock. 1891 WELCH *Recoll. 1830–40* 27 The sand was deposited in heaps beyond the heel-path on the eastern side. — (5) 1854 DAVIS *Farm Bk.* 1 Worked in the B. S. Shop made heel bolts & Taps.

As the last term in **coon, crosscut, raw, rosin, spring, Tar-heel.**

* **heel,** *v.*

1. *W. reflexive.* To arm or provide (oneself) with a weapon. *Slang.*

1873 MILLER *Amongst Modocs* 301 This was his signal to 'heel' himself and come upon the ground. 1877 W. WRIGHT *Big Bonanza* 363 His man had gone off to 'heel himself,' and there would soon be trouble. 1947 CHALFANT *Gold, Guns, & Ghost Towns* 72 Vance posed as one of the original bad men, and abused Carberry until the latter told him to wait until he could 'heel himself.'

2. *W.* (See quots.)

1887 *Scribner's Mag.* II. 508/2 The common [cowboy] terms are ... *heel,* to lariat an animal by the hind leg; *hondou* [etc.]. 1944 ADAMS *W. Words* 74 heel To rope an animal by the hind feet. Never used on horses.

3. To heel in, to cover temporarily the roots (of a plant) with soil. Hence **heeling in.**

1857 *Rep. Comm. Patents 1856: Agric.* 93 In nurseries, fruit-trees are often taken up and 'heeled in'; that is, laid down close together, with the roots placed in a trench, and then covered. 1908 BAKER *Timber of Iowa* 17 When seedlings can not be planted at once, they should be removed from the packing case and 'heeled in' in some shaded situation. 1949 *L.A. Times* 9 Jan. (Home Mag.) 20/3 Lean trees against the sloping sides of your ditch and keep tops near the ground. This is called 'heeling in.'

* **heeled,** *a.*

1. Armed. *Slang.*

1867 *Terr. Enterprise* (Virginia, Nev.) 15 Mar. 3/1 Let those in the habit of going 'heeled' take heed. 1926 J. BLACK *You Can't Win* iii. 24 I assured him that I was well heeled, having two pistols. 1948 *Popular Western* June 47/2 You're not heeled for trouble.

transf. 1880 MARK TWAIN *Tramp Abroad* xxxii. 341 Her stripling brought an armful of aged sheet-music from their room—for this bride went 'heeled' as you might say. 1883 HARRIS *Nights* (1911) 167, I let you know dey'd fine out terreckly dat de ole nigger heel'd wid rabbit foot.

2. Provided with money. *Slang.*

1880 *Pacific Metropolis* (S.F.) 12 June 8/4 His friends want him to go 'heeled' and so they've got up the biggest sort of a bill for Dashaway Hall next Wednesday night. 1897 E. W. BRODHEAD *Bound in Shallows* 153, I ain't so well-heeled right now. 1948 *Range Riders Western* May 80/2 Railroad coming through here will make all those farmers well heeled.

b. heeled bet, (see quot.).

1938 ASBURY *Sucker's Prog.* 15 Heeled bets—Wagers which played one card to win and another to lose.

* **heeler,** *n.* A servile political party follower whose allegiance is dependent upon his prospects of personal gain. Cf. **district, Tammany, ward heeler.**

a1877 *N.Y. Herald* (B.), Wirt Sykes the politician ... has been a heeler about the capital. 1903 A. B. HART *Actual Government* 99 The local man, often called a 'heeler,' has his body of adherents. 1938 ASBURY *Sucker's Prog.* 428 It was small wonder that political heelers retired with fortunes, and that poorly paid policemen owned yachts and country estates.

Heermann's gull. [A. L. *Heermann* (1818–65), Amer. naturalist.] The white-headed gull, *Larus heermanni,* of the Pacific Coast. — 1883 *Nat. Museum Bul.* No. 27, 169 Heermann's Gull. ... Pacific coast of North America, from British Columbia to Panama. ... Santa Barbara, California. 1917 *Birds of Amer.* I. 48 Heermann's Gulls ... are inveterate loafers.

* **heft,** *n.* The main portion or part. *Colloq.*

1816 PICKERING 104 A part of the crop of corn was good, but the heft of it was bad. 1852 *Ore. Statesman* 11 May 1/5 I'll kiver that and go the heft of my pile over that. 1926 *Ladies' Home Jrnl.* Dec. 5 If she turns out to be no good—which is the way the heft of her kind turn out—you get rid of her.

* **hefty,** *a.* **1.** Easy or convenient to handle. *Rare.* **2.** Violent, impetuous [cf. G. *heftig*]. Also as adv. *Colloq.*

(1) 1885 *American* IX. 232 A book ... should be hefty, light and of a form that can be easily held in the hand. — (2) 1886 BURNETT *Fauntleroy* xi, A hefty un she was—a regular tiger-cat. 1903 W. FREEMAN *Six Trees* 183, I come down pooty hefty, I guess.

* **heifer,** *n.*

1. A young female buffalo. *Obs.*

1775 *Jrnl. Nicholas Cresswell* (1925) 78 Surrounded 30 Buffaloes as they were crossing the River, shot two young Heifers and caught two calves alive. 1846 THORPE *Myst. Backwoods* 105, I kept close at the heels of 'Breeches,' who soon brought a fine young heifer bellowing to the ground.

2. A girl or woman. *Colloq.*

1835 LONGSTREET *Ga. Scenes* 143 He rushed into the Kitchen in a fury. 'You infernal heifer!' said he to Aunt Clory. 1902 LORIMER *Lett. Merchant* 261 The woman looked like a good, safe, reliable old heifer.

* **height,** *n.*

1. (*cap.*) *pl.* =**Negro heaven.** *Obs.*

1863 HOOLEY *Opera House Songster* 25 Ward Beecher took me by the arm, And spoke in gentle tones, To condescend and please the 'Heights,' With a solo on the bones.

2. height of land, a ridge of high land serving as a divide.

1725 in SHELDON *Hist. Deerfield* I. 559 Therefore they told us they w[oul]d travel to the hight of land by black river. 1848 *N. Eng. Farmer* I. 6 We are located on what is frequently termed the 'height of land,' situated about midway between the Penobscot and Kennebeck Rivers. 1948 *C. A. Jrnl.* June 134 On the 27th they arrived at the height of land dividing it from the Beaverfoot River.

Helderberg ˈhɛldɚˌbɝg, *n.* [f. *Helderbergs,* a range of hills in N.Y. State.]

1. *Geol.* A subdivision in the eastern part of the U.S. of the lower Devonian. Also attrib. and **Helderbergian,** *a.*

1851 FOSTER & WHITNEY *Geol. Lake Superior* 162 The upper Helderberg series rests directly on the Onondaga salt group. 1906 CHAMBERLAIN & SALISBURY *Geol.* II. 454 From this intermediate or transitional assemblage the Helderberg fauna seems to have taken its origin. *Ib.* 455 The capulid shells which abound at some localities in the Helderbergian ... faunas. 1915 *Geol. Survey Ohio* 4 Ser. Bul. 8, 41 The Lower Helderberg, or Waterlime, forms the rock floor of much of Western Ohio.

2. Helderberg War, (see quot. 1841). *Obs.*

1841 LYELL *Travels N. Amer.* (1845) I. 68 This being the third year of the 'Helderberg war,' or a successful resistance by an armed tenantry to the legal demands of their landlord, Mr. Van Renssalaer. 1844 *Quincy* (Ill.) *Herald* 11 Oct. 2/2 The Helderberg war, it seems, is not yet ended. 1871 DE VERE 167 The *Helderberg War* ... could be quelled only by the presence of a large armed force.

* **hell,** *n.*

1. (See quots.) *Colloq.*

1883 ZEIGLER & GROSSCUP *Alleghanies* 139 Nature has ... planted in vast tracts [in N.C.] impenetrable tangles of the rhododendron and palmia. These tangles are locally called 'Hells,' with a proper noun possessive in remembrance of poor unfortunates lost in their mazes. 1917 KEPHART *Camping* II. 24 Those great tracts of rhododendron ... cover mile after mile of steep mountainside where few men have ever been. The natives call such wastes 'laurel slicks,' 'woolly heads,' 'lettuce beds,' 'yaller patches,' and 'hells.' 1947 COFFIN *Yankee Coast*

199 We had walked one whole day and part of a night, through bogs and gullies, through junipers and blackberry hells.

2. In combs.: (1) **hell bag,** the venom bag or gland of a poisonous snake, *rare;* (2) **bender, bent, diver,** see as main entries; (3) **fence,** a fence extremely difficult to get over or through, *obs.;* (4) * **fire,** whisky of an especially fiery, cheap grade, *colloq.;* (5) **night,** the night when college students are initiated into fraternities and sororities; (6) **-'s delight,** (see quot.), *obs.;* (7) **-'s half acre,** (*a*) a low dive or groggery, *obs.,* (*b*) (see quot. 1882); (8) **-'s Kitchen,** see as a main entry; (9) **vine,** the trumpet creeper; (10) **week,** the week during which those selected as new members of a college fraternity or sorority are "hazed" before being admitted into the organization.

(1) **1825** JOHN NEAL *Bro. Jonathan* III. 257 Reptiles . . . attracted by the sharp odour of his deviltry . . . creeping there, to feed upon his heart . . . to replenish their exhausted hell-bags. — (3) **1886** S. W. MITCHELL *R. Blake* 21 'A hell-fence?' . . . 'That's what they call 'em here,—pig-tight, ox-proof, hoss-high, stumps upside down. *Ib.*, Blake then . . . with some little trouble got through the hell-fence. — (4) **1863** E. KIRKE *Southern Friends* iv. 61 'Taint right to give even nigs such hell-fire as they sell round har. **1909** WASON *Happy Hawkins* 163 Get me a drink of hell-fire!

(5) **1947** *Woodlawn Booster* (Chi.) 20 Aug. 6/1 Last Wednesday, August 13, was 'Hell' night for the girls at the 55th Street beach. — (6) **1876** MILLER *First Families* xv. 126 All of the following popular drinks, that is, Old Tiger, . . . Hell's Delight, . . . were all made from the same decoction of bad rum, worse tobasco, and first-class cayenne pepper. — (7) (*a*) **1874** McCOY *Cattle* 141 The keepers of those 'hell's half acres' find some pretext arising from 'business jealousies' or other causes, to suddenly become belligerent. (*b*) **1882** WYLIE *Yellowstone Nat. Pk.* 29 This locality is perhaps better known as *Devil's* or *Hell's Half Acre*, although the much preferable, though not more appropriate, name of Middle Geyser Basin has been given it by the Superintendent of the Park. **1945** *Jefferson Co. Republican* (Golden, Colo.) 25 July 2/2 He planned to leave the following week for a trip to Devil's Play Ground in Hell's Half Acre. — (9) **1924** DEAM *Shrubs Indiana* 289 This vine in the Wabash bottoms where it is a menace to the farmers, is known as 'hell-vine' and 'shoe-strings.'

(10) **1930** *Randolph Enterprise* (Elkins, W. Va.) 18 Dec. 1/6 They were strongly in favor of eliminating 'Hell Week' from fraternity procedure entirely. **1948** *Time* 9 Feb. 76/2 Nine Theta Chis were jailed for breaking into a grocery store on a Hell Week scavenger hunt.

b. Used in epithets and expressions referring to or designating one hated or held in contempt, as **hell-face, -kicking, -pup, -raiser, -rotter.** *Slang.*

1796 *Gazette of U.S.* 28 Oct. (Th.), [May we never have] a Jefferson nor any other hell-kicking treaty member to domineer over a free people. **1871** WHITMAN *Democratic Vistas* 30, I have mark'd the brazen hell-faces of secession and slavery gazing defiantly from all the windows and doorways. **1903** FOX *Little Shepherd* xxi, I've got one word to say to you, you hell-pup. **1910** MCCUTCHEON *Rose in Ring* 266 That's what he did, the hell-rotter that he is. **1914** *Emporia* (Kans.) *Gaz.* 13 Jan., He is a four-flusher, a ring-tailed, rip-snorting hell-raiser, and a grandstander.

c. Used in slang expressions denoting strong, vehement feeling, as **hell's bells, hell's blazes, hell's mint, hell sweat.**

1832 O'FERRALL *Ramble* 298 'Liberty!—why hell sweat'—here I—slipped out at the side door. **1853** SIMMS *Sword & Distaff* 462 In h–ll's blazes, didn't you, and warn't you mighty glad to think so? **1873** MARK TWAIN *Gilded Age* 21 (R.), He's come back to the Forks with jist a hell's-mint o' whoop-jamboree notions. **1920** LEWIS *Main Street* 352 Hell's bells, Harry, no harm in being polite.

d. In slang phrases (and their variants) of obvious meaning, as (1) *quicker than hell could scorch a feather,* (2) *to be hell on,* (3) *to give one hell,* (4) *hell-to-split,* (5) *hell west and crooked,* (6) *hell and high water,* (7) *hell for breakfast.*

(1) **1840** *Crockett Almanac* 11 I'll be in his hair quicker than hell could scorch a feather. — (2) **1850** *Cong. Globe* 31 Jan. App. 91 Mammy has always been hell on dignity! — (3) **1851** *Harper's Mag.* III. 461/1 At daybreak old Riley shouted, 'Forward and give them h–ll!' **1883** SWEET & KNOX *Through Texas* iv. 49 It won't help us much, except to the extent that it will give Galveston hell. — (4) **1867** *Terr. Enterprise* (Virginia, Nev.) 1 Jan. 1/4 The firemen in . . . returning to house their hose carts came 'hellety split.' **1871** HAY *Little Breeches* iii, Hell-to-split over the prairie Went team, Little Breeches and all. **1912** RAINE *Brand Blotters* 160 Jim Little saw her cutting across country from the head-gates hell-to-split.

(5) **1898** CANFIELD *Maid of Frontier* 100 Break 'em with a snaffle, an' they bolt hell-western crooked. **1906** *McClure's Mag.* XXXVI. 419 Now all this knocked me h—— west and crooked. — (6) **1915** *Everybody's Mag.* June 69/2 He'll be one of us in spite of hell and high water. **1949** *Sat. Ev. Post* 4 June 144/4 [He is] a character who wants his own way and gets it, come hell or high water, and not a stupid trapper on a spree. — (7) **1940** THOMPSON *Body, Boots & Britches* 499 All the way from hell to breakfast; or, hell to Harlem. **1943** *Reader's Digest* 115/2 She and the cans went snorting out, hell-for-breakfast after the sub.

e. Hell-(up)on-wheels, (1) (see quot.), *rare;* (2) of towns, wild, lawless, also as a name given in succession to the towns at the end of construction of the Union Pacific Railroad, cf. **end town;** (3) of a horse or mule, vicious, incorrigible, also as a name for such an animal.

(1) **1843** *Quincy* (Ill.) *Herald* 10 March 1/4 *Hell-upon-Wheels!* now if that ain't the most appropriate name for that craft [i.e., a steamboat named *Heliopolis*], you may blow me. — (2) **1868** BOWLES *Colorado* (1869) 21 It is a most aggravated specimen of the border town of America, not inaptly called 'Hell on Wheels.' **1923** *El Palacio* (Santa Fe) 15 Mar. 88/1 The railhead towns were 'hell on wheels,' and the vigilantes were at work hanging men for murder. **1947** PERRY *Cities of Amer.* 109 You can slip up on Detroit in the dead of night, consider it from any standpoint, and it's still: hell on wheels. — (3) **1908** *Sat. Ev. Post* 24 Oct. 10/1 On the edge of the band stood a . . . mule . . . [whose] name was Hell-on-wheels. **1927** JAMES *Cow Country* 119 He ain't in your string, and besides, he's sure hell on wheels when it comes to bucking.

* **hell,** *v. intr.* To pursue a reckless, dissipated way of life. *Slang.*

1898 WISTER *Lin McLean* 60 A man was liable to go sporting and helling around till he waked up. **1902** —— *Virginian* xxiii. 272, I was fooling around the earth, jumping from job to job, and helling all over town between whiles. **1928** J. P. McEVOY *Show Girl* 166 You were in the show business and throwing your best years away helling around.

hellbender ˈhɛlˌbɛndɚ, *n.* [Origin obscure.]

1. (See quot. 1933.) Cf. **land pike.**

1812 B. S. BARTON (*title*), Memoir concerning an Animal . . . which is known by the name of Alligator or Hell-bender. **1933** *Amer. Sp.* Feb. 81 Hellbender. A species of mud puppy found only in the Allegheny River and its tributaries. The scientific name is Cryptobranchus Alleghenensis. **1948** *Sat. Ev. Post* 4 Dec. 10/2 It was like a gigantic hellbender.

2. Anything regarded as a superior specimen of its kind. *Slang.*

1867 SCOTT *Partisan Life* 197 Give us, then, 'Billy in the Low Grounds,' or 'Sugar in the Gourd,' or 'The Arkansas Traveler,' or some hellbender of your own! **1877** BARTLETT 283 *Hell-Bender.* . . . Often as qualitative noun. 'Jack has been on a perfect hell-bender of a spree.' **1948** *Popular Western* June 48/1 That hellbender Kinsey.

hell-bent ˈhɛlˈbɛnt, *a.* Recklessly determined, dogged, usu. with *for. Slang.*

1835 *Knickerb.* VI. 12 He discovered that he was in the midst of a large encampment of savages, hideously painted, and 'hell-bent' on carnage. **1856** *Spirit of Age* (Sacramento, Calif.) 24 April, Our [Mormon] husband's bound by law to support us and take equal care of us —and then we are so *hell-bent* for Heaven! **1945** *Dly. Sentinel* (Grand Junction, Colo.) 26 Nov. 1/7 Cordell Hull declared today that the Japanese were 'hell-bent' for war in November, 1941.

b. *hell-bent for breakfast,* (see quot.). *Slang.*

1931 DOBIE *Coronado's C.* 104, I was going lickety-split, hell-bent for breakfast, trying to head off a gotch-eared brown stallion and his bunch when all of a sudden I ran into a lot of human bones.

hell-diver ˈhɛlˌdaɪvɚ, *n.* (See quots.)

1839 IRVING in *Knickerb.* Oct. 344 He could live under water like that notable species of wild duck, commonly called the Hell-diver. **1917** *Birds of Amer.* I. 7 Pied-billed Grebe. . . . Other names [include] Hell-diver; Devil-diver; Water-witch; Dabchick [etc.]. **1941** SETON *Trail of Artist-Naturalist* 89, I traced them to the pied-bill grebe, or little helldiver.

hellgrammite ˈhɛlgrəˌmaɪt, *n.* [Origin obscure.] (See quot. 1917.)

1866 *Wilkes' Spirit of Times* 14 July 315/3 There is another bait for bass called *kill devil*—a sort of indescribable Barnum-what-is-it thing, about three inches in length. An old friend of mine denominated them hell gramites. **1917** KEPHART *Camping* II. 411 One of the best natural baits for bass, when the water is clear, is that fierce-looking creature called hellgrammite, dobson, or grampus. This is the larva of a large winged insect, the horned corydalis. **1947** *Mazama* Dec. 20/2 A crow would pick a helgramite from the side of the log.

hello girl. A girl who operates a telephone switchboard. — **1889** MARK TWAIN *Conn. Yankee* xv. 177 The humblest hello-girl . . .

could teach . . . manners; to the highest duchess in Arthur's land. **1948** *Chi. D. News* 27 Aug. 10/6 (*heading*), Hello Girls Seek HCL Raise Here.

Hell's Kitchen. A place regarded as extremely disreputable. *Slang.*

1838 HAWTHORNE *Notebooks* (1932) 15 He talked with Bridge about the boundary question, and swore fervently in favor of driving the British 'into Hell's kitchen' by main force. **1885** *Harper's Mag.* Nov. 839/1 The guerrillas . . . have formerly fixed the unsavory appellations of 'Hell's Kitchen' and 'Robber's Roost' upon certain localities of the floor. **1941** SKINNER *Soap Behind Ears* 168 She asked me a few routine questions . . . in the manner of someone questioning a welfare worker concerning life in Hell's Kitchen.

b. Esp. in New York City, a district on Manhattan Island around lower Tenth Avenue, once regarded as the home of thieves and gunmen.

1905 *N.Y. Ev. Post* 27 Sep. 14 McGinley had a beat in 'Hell's Kitchen' when that unsavory district was at its worst. **1949** *Sat. Ev. Post* 15 Jan. 39/1 It stands between a greasy garage and a tawdry row of brownstone tenements on the edge of Hell's Kitchen, west of Eighth Avenue on 49th Street.

helmet quail. Any one of several American partridges constituting the genus *Lophortyx.* — **1884** COUES *Key to N. Amer. Birds* (ed. 2) 591 *Lophortyx* . . . Helmet Quail. . . . Two elegant species in the U.S. **1917** *Birds of Amer.* II. 8 Helmet Quail . . . is one of the liveliest of all American game birds.

* **help,** *n.*

1. Hired labor, those hired to perform the labor about a farm, household, etc. Cf. **hired, white help.**

1630 *Mass. Bay Rec.* I. 77 For help to washe, brewe, & bake, xx s. **1711** in F. L. HAWKS *Hist. N.C.* II. 215 Help is not to be had at any rate, every one having business of his own. **1817** BRADBURY *Travels* 318 A great number of farmers have more land enclosed in fence than they can well manage: ask one of them the reason, he replies, 'I want help.' **1917** MCCUTCHEON *Green Fancy* 50 Though under sentence to eat at six with the rest of the 'help,' [they]were quite sanguine that old man Jones wouldn't mind if they ate again at seven.

2. Chiefly *N. Eng.* A hired laborer or domestic servant. Also *collect.*

1645 *Mass. Bay Rec.* II. 139 James Penn shall have 20 s, to be disposed among such of his servants & helps [etc.] **1819** in THWAITES *Early Western Travels* X. 94 No curses or oaths toward their servants, or helps as they choose to call themselves. **1837** F. GRUND *Americans* II. 66 The inhabitants of New England are quite as willing to call their servants 'helps' or 'domestics,' as the latter repudiate the title of 'masters' in their employers. **1908** WHITE *Riverman* 70 He and Grandpa and Grandma Orde dwelt . . . alone, save for the one girl who called herself the 'help.' **1948** DICK *Dixie Frontier* 332 In Indiana and Illinois, where white servants were employed, they would not tolerate being called servants. They were known as 'the help.'

* **helper,** *n.*

1. = * **help 2.**

1817 BRADBURY *Travels* 319 Even his employer was probably the helper to some one formerly. **1916** *Ladies' Home Jrnl.* Sep. 54 The great mistake of the domestic helper is in her notion of what constitutes success. If success in her eyes means 'to get out of the kitchen' . . . the chances are that she will never make a success.

2. = **helper engine.**

1947 BEEBE *Mixed Train Dly.* 143 A leased engine from the D. & R.G.W. leads . . . with a helper cut into the middle of the train a few cars back. **1949** *L.A. Times* 1 May 22/2 W. R. Williams, fireman of the helper, and John McGawn, brakeman who was left with the helper locomotive after uncoupling it, were not relieved of duty.

3. In combs.: (1) **helper engine,** an engine that helps another; (2) **horse,** a horse that helps draw a horsecar up a grade, *obs.;* (3) **ring,** (see quot.), *obs.*

(1) 1889 *Western Liberal* (Lordsburg, N.M.) 8 Mar. 3/3 It is often necessary to send a helper engine to Stein's Pass with a heavy train. **1945** MARSHALL *Santa Fe* 280 At San Bernardino a helper engine was coupled on for the run up Cajon Pass. — **(2) 1883** [see **helper ring**]. — **(3) 1883** KNIGHT *Dict. Mech. Supp.* 456/1 Helper Ring. A ring on the edge of a street-car platform for the attachment of the hook of the singletree of the *helper* horse during the ascent of a grade.

hemdurgan hɛm'dɜgən, *n.* [Origin obscure.] (See quots.) — **1839** STORER *Mass. Fishes* 26 *Sebastes Norvegicus.* The Norway Haddock. . . . By our fishermen it is known by the names of 'Rosefish,' 'Hemdurgan,' and Snapper. **1884** GOODE *Fisheries* I. 260 The Rosefish, *Sebastes marinus,* is . . . also known as . . . 'Hemdurgan.'

* **hemlock,** *n.*

1. Any one of various American evergreen trees of the genus *Tsuga,* as *T. canadensis,* the Canadian or eastern hemlock. Also attrib.

1662 EVELYN *Silva* (1729) 119 The Hemlock-tree (as they call it in New-England) is a kind of Spruce. **1728** *Boston Rec.* 222 We are of opinion that no Popler, Chesnut, Pine, Henlock [*sic*], Sassifax, Black ash, Basswood, or Ceder shall be corded up. **1807** GASS *Journal* 195 [Mr. M'Kenzie] states that of the inner rind of the hemlock . . . [the western Indians] make a kind of cakes. **1879** B. F. TAYLOR *Summer-Savory* x. 81 [The name] the House of Hanover, which glitters with coronets and crowns and magnificent possibilities, may designate a hemlock tavern in the West. **1948** *Sierra Club Bul.* Mar. 25 We were under the Minarets now, camped in a scattered grove of hemlocks above Lake Ediza.

b. (See quot. 1860.)

1860 CURTIS *Woody Plants N.C.* 95 *Dog Laurel.* (*Leucothoe Catesbaei,* Gray.)—Found only in the mountains, where it is also called *Hemlock,* growing on the cool margins of streams. **1894** *Amer. Folk-Lore* VII. 93.

2. In special combs.: (1) **hemlock balsam,** (see quot.), *obs.;* (2) **broom,** (see quot. 1935); (3) **land,** land upon which hemlock is the native growth; (4) **monacid,** a kind of leather tanned with hemlock bark, *obs.;* (5) **pine,** any one of several varieties of spruce pine; (6) **sole,** short for "hemlock sole leather," i.e., sole leather in the tanning of which hemlock bark is used; (7) **spruce,** = **hemlock 1,** also attrib.; (8) **swamp,** a swamp in which hemlock trees are numerous; (9) **tanned,** *a.* of leather, tanned with hemlock bark; (10) **tea,** tea made from hemlock, *obs.;* (11) **warbler,** a small, brilliantly colored warbler, *Dendroica fusca,* found in the eastern part of the U.S.

(1) 1832 BROWNE *Sylva Amer.* 98 The bark contains a small quantity of resin, commonly called Hemlock Balsam. — **(2) 1825** NEAL *Bro. Jonathan* I. 11 [She traced] patterns and flowers . . . upon the white sanded floor, with a great hemlock broom. **1935** *Col. of Conn.* 11 Hemlock brooms: . . . . A bunch of close-growing, full-foliaged hemlock branches was tied tightly together. . . . These were wound with hempen twine. . . . A sharply pointed handle was driven into the bound portion. — **(3) 1842** HONE *Diary* II. 140 They will sell their worthless swamps and barren hemlock lands at a good round price. **1874** *Vt. Bd. Agric. Rep.* II. 154 Hemlock land, light soil inclined to be scurfy, had been in pasture previous to 1871. — **(4) 1895** *Current Hist.* V. 349 The advance in leather began about the middle of April: the price of 'hemlock monacid' on April 13 was $17\frac{1}{2}$ cents per pound.

(5) 1786 WASHINGTON *Diaries* III. 9 Planted the Hemlock Pine. **1834** *S. Lit. Messenger* I. 97/2 Black spruce and hemlock pines, of dark funereal aspect, tower above the soil [in N.W. Md. & Va.]. — **(6) 1868** *N.Y. Herald* 1 July 9/3 The market for hemlock sole was tolerably active. **1881** *Chi. Times* 11 June, Hemlock sole has been quiet and unchanged. — **(7) 1781–2** JEFFERSON *Notes Va.* (1788) 39 Hemlock spruce fir. *Pinus Canadensis.* **1889** *Rep. Secy. Agric.* 131 Hemlock Spruce, *Abies Canadensis* [was used in specimen hedges]. — **(8) 1769** in R. SMITH *Four Great Rivers* (1906) 38 After traversing a deep Hemloc Swamp we encamped in the Evening 11 or 12 Miles from Croghans. **1881** *Harper's Mag.* Sep. 583/2 An owl hooted dismally from the hemlock swamp; but there was no wind, no star. — **(9) 1851** CIST *Cincinnati* 176 The leather, with the exception of a small portion of hemlock tanned sole, is all made in this city. **1854** *Mich. Agric. Soc. Trans. 1853* 56 Domestic Manufactures . . . 6 hemlock tanned calf skins.

(10) 1830 GALT *Lawrie Todd* I. 190 [At breakfast] we had hemlock-tea, a pleasant and salutary drink. *a*1862 THOREAU *Maine Woods* 292 The Indian made us some hemlock tea instead of coffee. — **(11) 1812** WILSON *Ornithology* V. 114 Hemlock Warbler. *Sylvia Parus.* . . . This is another nondescript, first met with in the Great Pine swamp, Pennsylvania. **1917** *Birds of Amer.* III. 137 Hemlock Warbler. . . . Wonder and delight . . . are inspired by the appearance of this gaudy little sprite of the deep forest.

As the last term in **alpine, Carolina, ground, mountain, poison, trailing hemlock.**

* **hemmer,** *n.* A sewing-machine attachment for hemming. — **1863** *Rep. Comm. Patents 1861* I. 252 Improvement in Hemmers and Folders. **1920** *Sears Cat.* (ed. 141D) 517 The set [of sewing-machine attachments] consists of one tucker, one ruffler, one shirring blade . . . and one set of four hemmers of different widths.

* **hemp,** *n.* In combs.: (1) **hemp bird,** the purple finch, also the American goldfinch; (2) **factory,** a factory in which hempen products are made; (3) **harvester,** (see quot. 1875); (4) **necktie,** a hangman's rope, also **hemp party,** a lynching, *colloq.*

(1) 1791 W. BARTRAM *Travels* 289 *F*[*ringilla*] *cannabina;* the hemp bird. **1858** *Atlantic Mo.* Oct. 595/2 The American Goldfinch, or Hemp-bird, (*Fringilla tristis,*) [is] one of the most interesting and delicate of the feathered tribe. — **(2) 1847** L. COLLINS *Kentucky* 44 Harrodsburg [contains] . . . one printing office, two hemp factories, two wool carding establishments. **1911** Persons *Mass. Labor Laws* 147 The older workers in the dusty room, at hemp as well as flax factories, are likely to become asthmatic and hoarse. — **(3) 1859** *Rep. Comm. Patents 1858: Agric.* I. 416 Improvement in Hemp-Harvesters. **1875** Knight 1100/1 Hemp-harvesters resemble those for corn in their adaptation to operate upon tall top-heavy stalks. — **(4) 1892** *Dispatch* (Columbus, O.) 6 Dec., If the incendiarist is found, a hemp party may result. **1940** Baber & Walker *Longest Rope* 34 We wanted to lynch Frank Canton, and if we had been allowed to hand him a hemp necktie right then, it would have saved a heap of good men.

b. *All right on the hemp,* a phrase used during the struggle over slavery in Kansas (see quot.). *Obs.* Cf. *To be right* (or *sound*) *on the goose, s.v.* ***goose, n. 4. a.***

1857 T. H. Gladstone *Englishman in Kansas* 256 In the northern districts, the piece of hemp was the more customary mark of those who were ready to use the halter in proof of the soundness of their views. 'Neither give nor take quarter,' and 'All right on the hemp,' were their two pass-words.

As the last term in **American, blossom, Indian, seed hemp.**

hemp hεmp, *v. tr.* To hang. *Slang. Obs.* — **1857** T. H. Gladstone *Englishman in Kansas* 264 'This infernal scoundrel will have to be hemped yet,' writes the editor of one of the Missouri journals, in commenting upon the acts of the Governor. **1885** L. W. Spring *Kansas* 50 Some talked of 'hemping' the scoundrel.

hen, *n.

1. *pl.* (See quots.) Cf. ***rooster, *n.* 5.**

1893 *Amer. Folk-Lore* VI. 138 *Viola Canadensis*, hens. Ferrisburgh, Vt. **1907** Lyons *Plant Names* 489 V[iola] canadensis L. Canada, south to N. Carolina, Nebraska and Arizona. Canada Violet, American Sweet Violet, June-flower, Hens. **1946** [see ***rooster, *n.* 5**].

2. In combs.: (1) **henbill,** (*a*) the American coot, (*b*) the dabchick; (2) **clam,** (*a*) any one of various species of large clams found on the eastern coast of North America, (*b*) (see quot.); (3) **fruit,** eggs, *jocular;* (4) **grass,** ?broom sedge, *rare;* (5) **hawk,** (*a*) =**blue hen hawk,** (*b*) (see quots.); (6) **minded,** (see quot.), *rare;* (7) **scratch,** a chicken feed made from grain for scattering in litter or on the ground to induce chickens to scratch; (8) **skin,** see as a main entry; (9) **-'s tracks,** written letters suggestive of tracks made by a hen, bad handwriting, cf. **quail tracks,** *colloq.* [cf. *EDD hens'-toes* in same sense]; (10) **yard,** a yard or inclosure in which poultry are kept.

(1) (*a*) **1844** *Nat. Hist. N.Y., Zoology* II. 273 The American Coot, *Fulica americana*, . . . has also received the popular names of Mud-hen, White-bill and Hen-bill. . . . Frequents low marshy spots near the coast. **1917** *Birds of Amer.* I. 214 Coot. *Fulica americana*. . . . [Also called] White-bill; Hen-bill; Crow-bill [etc.]. (*b*) **1888** Trumbull *Bird Names* 82 (*footnote*), The Pied-billed Grebe, *Podilymbus podiceps*, that lively little nuisance, familiar to us all . . . as Hen-bill, Hen-bill Diver, Hell-diver [etc.]. — **(2)** (*a*) **1877** Bartlett 784 *Hen-Clam.* The Broad Sea-clam. (*Macta gigantea.*) Common on the shores of New England. **1883** *Nat. Museum Bul.* No. 27, 231 *Mactra solidissima* . . . is known commonly as the 'sea,' 'surf,' or 'hen' clam. **1949** *Sat. Ev. Post* 25 June 52/4 He went after herring with a deep net, dragged for hen clams and harpooned tuna. (*b*) **1884** Goode *Fisheries* I. 708 Aboriginal money was made from the valves of the ponderous Hen Clam of southern California (*Pachydesma* [i.e., *Pachyderma*] *crassatelloides*). — **(3) 1854** *Harper's Mag.* VIII. 280/2 A young lady is said to have asked a gentleman at the table of a hotel 'down East' to pass her the 'hen fruit.' She pointed to a plate of eggs. **1945** *Everybody's Digest* Aug. 66 At the finish the egg is broken into a glass to show that there's no trick to it, as far as the hen fruit is concerned. — **(4) 1840** J. Buel *Farmer's Companion* 18 They will produce what we call hengrass, brown-straw and . . . a starveling pine or cedar bush.

(5) (*a*) **1806** Clark in *Lewis & C. Exped.* IV. (1905) 131, I have observed . . . a hawk of an intermediate size with a long tail and blewish coloured wings, remarkably swift in flight and very ferce. Sometimes called in the Un. States the hen Hawk. (*b*) **1869** *Amer. Naturalist* III. 393 This bird [the red-tailed hawk] is generally known as the Hen-hawk (*Buteo borealis*). **1916** Seton *Woodcraft Man.* 305 *Redtailed Hawk or Henhawk* (*Buteo borealis*). — **(6) 1892** Howells *Quality of Mercy* 6 She was really one of those hen-minded women, who . . . are made up of only one aim at a time, and of manifold anxieties at all times. — **(7) 1931** *Dly. News-Journal* (Murfreesboro, Tenn.) 15 April 4/2 Corn, per bu. . . . White oats, per bu. . . . Hen Scratch, per 100 lbs. . . . 2.00. — **(9) 1907** C. C. Andrews *Recoll.* (1928) 48 He wrote with a quill pen and used a great deal of ink, making regular hen's tracks.

(10) 1816 Weems *Letters* III. 166 Yr. Bible carts had been here as thick as weasels in a hen yard selling Bibles at nearly half price. **1918** Lincoln *Shavings* 130 My friends are like corn sprouts in a hen-yard, few and scatterin'.

b. In colloq. and slang phrases: (1) (*As*) *scarce as* (or *scarcer than*) *hen's teeth,* extremely scarce; (2) *a hen is on,* something important is in preparation; (3) *as mad as a wet hen,* extremely angry.

(1) 1863 E. Kirke *Southern Friends* 250 [Horses are] scarcer than hen's teeth round here. **1893** *Cong. Rec.* 2 Oct. 2044/1 North of Mason and Dixon's line, colored county officials are scarce as hen's teeth. — **(2) 1878** in *Wash. Hist. Quart.* XVIII. 192 Keep cool, boys, there's a hen on. **1908** McGaffey *Show-Girl* 211 Something has gone wrong, or there is a big hen on. — **(3) 1823** in *Amer. Sp.* XXI. (1946) 119/2 Every body that was not ax'd was mad as a wet hen. **1900** Munn *Uncle Terry* 68 He came in yesterday, mad as a wet hen, and wanted his money back.

As the last term in **blue, fool, freshwater marsh, grade, heath, Indian, marsh, meadow, moor, mud, pine, prairie, sage, saltwater marsh, saltwater meadow, sedge, small mud, speckled spruce, steam hen.**

hence hεns, *n.* [f. the *adv.*] Heaven, the next world, the future. *Humorous.* — **1884** Nye *Baled Hay* 26 All-wool delaine that was worn by one who is now in the golden hence. **1904** Lynde *Grafters* 233 Now suppose you hint darkly . . . that more . . . developments may be safely predicted in the immediate hence.

Henry, *n. [Benjamin Tyler *Henry* (1821–98). For some account of the Henry family of gunmakers see Dillin, *The Ky. Rifle,* 20.] (See quot. 1944.) Also attrib.

1869 in *Frontier* IX. (1929) 157 One of them . . . lost one of our Henry carbines. **1927** Russell *Trails* 71 From the copper rim-fire cattridges in his belt, I guess his weapon's a Henry. **1944** Adams *W. Words* 75 Henry An early repeating breech-loading, lever-action rifle first used by the Union Army in the Civil War. This type of rifle never became popular as a military weapon, but was used to some extent upon the frontier.

b. Esp. **Henry rifle.**

1859 in F. Hall *Hist. Colorado* II. App., Got Oake's Henry rifle for Phil. I take my old Hawkins. **1876** *Pioche* (Nev.) *D. Jrnl.* 23 Sep. 3/1

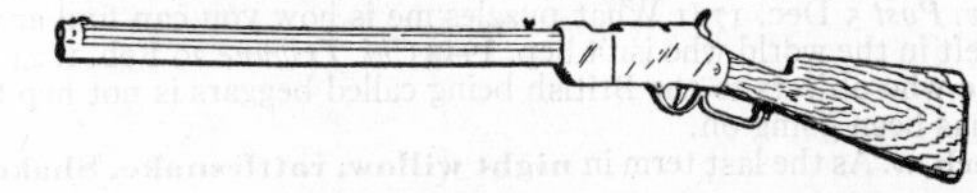

Henry rifle or carbine (*c*1865)

He carried a Henry rifle on the occasion. **1948** *Chi. Tribune* 7 March I. 38/5 Its predecessor was the Henry rifle, made by the New Haven Arms company, and grandfather of the repeating arms.

Henry Clay. [Amer. statesman (1777–1852).]

1. (See quots. 1893, 1949.)

1884 *Harper's Mag.* 647/1 The dealer . . . asked him if he would like to 'ave a 'Enry Clay. **1893** *Harper's Mag.* LXXXVIII. 34/1 And bring some cigars—Henry Clays. . . . My father was always a Henry Clay man, and I suppose that's why I like those cigars. **1949** *Chi. D. News* 30 April 2/2 The Russians, of course, have never heard of the popular cigar called 'Henry Clay.'

2. Henry Clay flag, a flag or banner used by the political supporters of Henry Clay. *Obs.*

1846 Emory *Milit. Reconn.* 61 One [Indian] had a jacket made o fa Henry Clay flag, which aroused unpleasant sensations, for the acquisition, no doubt, cost one of our countrymen his life.

3. Henry Clay whig, one of the whigs who in Congress during Tyler's administration supported Clay in his opposition to the President. *Obs.*

1855 Hambleton *H. A. Wise* 148 The proud, inflexible, consistent Henry Clay Whigs will never give up the banner of 'the old Clay Guard.' **1890** Howells *Boy's Town* 11 My boy's father restored his self-respect in a measure by being a Henry Clay Whig, or a Constitutional anti-slavery man. **1900** *Miss. Hist. Soc. Pub.* III. 77 A tabular view of the convention . . . shows that it was composed of 100 delegates among which were . . . 2 Henry Clay Whigs, 4 Old Whigs.

Henryite ˈhenrɪˌaɪt, *n. Hist.* One of those N. Eng. Federalists whose bitter, even incipiently treasonable, attitude during Jefferson's administration was reported on in letters written back to England by one John Henry. Also **Henryism.** *Obs.* — **1814** *Ann. 13th Congress* 1 Sess. I. 1126 Certain other terms frequently are [used] without any real or specific meaning, . . . such as Old tory, British gold, Henryism, &c. **1817** in Fearon *Sketches* (1818) 145 It is an unholy league between apostates and . . . blue-light men, the embargo-breakers, the Henryites, the men who in time of Peace cried out for War! War!

hen-skin ˈhɛnˌskɪn *n. W.* A comfort stuffed with feathers. *Slang.* Cf. ∗**sugan.**

1902 *Out West* June 620 Why don't you burn these henskins and get you a decent bed? **1939** ROLLINS *Gone Haywire* 62 If, as sometimes, the soogan was stuffed with feathers, it was termed a hen-skin. **1947** PRICE *Trails I Rode* 49, I didn't have much of a bed, just a few henskins and an old sougan.

Also **hen-skin blanket.**

1910 BRONSON *Remin. Ranchman* 98 It was a silent, surly group, with none of the usual jest and badinage over 'hen-skin blankets' and 'fat huldys' a cold morning usually inspired.

∗**Henslow,** *n.* [See quot. 1831.] **1. Henslow's bunting,** =next. **2. Henslow's sparrow,** a plain striped sparrow (see quot. 1917) found chiefly in the eastern states. Cf. **Eastern Henslow's sparrow.**

(1) **1831** AUDUBON *Ornith. Biog.* I. 360 Henslow's Bunting.... In naming it after the Rev. Professor Henslow of Cambridge, ... my object has been to manifest my gratitude for the many kind attentions which he has shewn towards me. **1874** COUES *Birds N.W.* 133 *Coturniculus Henslovii,* (Aud.) Bp. Henslow's Bunting [inhabits] ... Eastern United States to Massachusetts. West to the Loup Fork. — (2) **1870** *Amer. Naturalist* III. 632 Henslow's Sparrow. *Coturniculus henslowi.* This species must still be considered a rare summer visitor [in Mass.]. **1917** *Birds of Amer.* III. 28 Henslow's Sparrow. *Passerherbulus henslowi henslowi.* ... Other Name.—Henslow's Bunting.

hep hɛp, *interj.* and *a.* [In sense **1.** cf. Eng. dial ∗*hup.* In sense **2.** app. a different word.]

1. A call or exclamation used to assist marching soldiers to keep step.

1862 STRONG *Cadet Life West Point* 113 [We] followed in three squads, of thirty or more each, our music the euphonious 'hep, hep, hep,' of our instructors. **1918** in *Liberty* 11 Aug. (1928) 8/2 We slogged up a four kilometer hill to a so-called rest camp—hep, hep, hep—with that damned Frog music running 165 steps to the minute.

2. *To be hep to* (and variants), to be wise about, informed of. *Slang.*

[**1903** *Cin. Enquirer* 9 May 13/2 Hept—To get onto or next.] **1908** *Sat. Ev. Post* 5 Dec. 17/1 What puzzles me is how you can find anybody left in the world who isn't hep. **1948** *Chi. Tribune* 29 Feb. I. 24/1 Anyone who objects to the British being called beggars is not hep to what has been going on.

∗**herb,** *n.* As the last term in **night willow, rattlesnake, Shaker herb.**

Herbemont ˈhɝbəˌmɑnt, *n.* [Origin obscure.] A native American grape. *Obs.* — **1856** FERGUSSON *America* 272 Those which are chiefly cultivated are ... the Herbemont. **1859** MACKAY *Tour* I. 208 He again selected twelve as alone fit for the production of wine. These twelve were the Catawba, ... the Herbemont's Madeira ... and the Mammoth Catawba.

∗**Hercules,** *n.*

1. ∗**Hercules'-club,** (see quots. 1876, 1907).

1876 HOBBS *Bot. Hand-Book* 53 Hercules' club, Yellow prickly ash, Xanthoxylon clava Herculis. Prickly elder, Aralia spinosa. **1907** LYONS *Plant Names* 47 A[ralia] spinosa L. Gulf States to New York. Hercules'-club, Toothache-tree, Wild Orange. **1943** PEATTIE *Great Smokies* 282 At the lower elevations the Hercules'-club, second only to witch-hazel as the latest-blooming tree, becomes crowned with its showy whitish flowers.

2. Hercules powder, a powerful explosive used chiefly in mining.

1876 RAYMOND *8th Rep. Mines* 171 To blast the holes above mentioned 25,945 pounds of Giant and Hercules powder was used. **1880** *Amer. Inst. Min. Eng. Trans.* VIII. 417 Hercules powder ... contains a very large proportion of nitrate of soda ... the remainder of the dope being incombustible carbonate of magnesia.

∗**herd,** *n.* In combs.: (1) **herd boss,** one who is in charge of a herd of cattle; (2) ∗**boy,** *W.* a cowboy in charge of, or assisting in managing, a herd of cattle; (3) **broke,** (see quot. 1944); (4) **ground,** *W.* an extensive area over which cattle are ranged; (5) **guard,** *W.* one who guards or assists in guarding a herd of cattle; (6) **house,** in colonial times, a house used in connection with the keeping of a herd of cattle belonging to the town, *obs.;* (7) **law,** *W.* a law concerning the ranging or grazing of herds of cattle; (8) **-'s grass,** see as a main entry; (9) **walk,** the area over which a herd ranges, *obs.*

(1) **1920** HUNTER *Trail Drivers Texas* I. 361, I was herd-boss. — (2) **1865** G. HAMILTON *Skirmishes* 144 Herd-boys lie on the grass. **1901** WHITE *Westerners* 63 Then he allowed himself to be captured by the herd boys. — (3) [**1927** JAMES *Cattle Country* 16 They caught around four hundred head, which, after a lot of hard and ticklish riding, they herd-broke and trailed to the shipping point.] **1944** ADAMS *W. Words* 75 herd broke. Said of cattle when they become accustomed to traveling in a herd. — (4) **1860** GREELEY *Overland Journey* 230 The best of these islands is possessed by 'the church,' (Mormon) as a herd-ground, or ranche, for its numerous cattle. **1874** MCCOY *Cattle* 132 The herd is brought upon its herd ground and carefully watched during the day, but allowed to scatter out over sufficient territory to feed.

(5) **1929** J. PARKER *Old Army* 157, I sent one of the herd guard to the top of the mountain as a lookout.—(6) **1652** *Dedham Rec.* III. 204 Joh Partridg com to demande 5 s disbursed by him for the heardhouse. — (7) **1872** *Newton Kansan* 31 Oct. 2/5 We are indebted for the present efficient herd law. **1942** DALE *Cow Country* 36 The Kansas farmers believed equally strongly in the 'herd law,' or that livestock should be inclosed and fields left unfenced. — (9) **1662** *Dedham Rec.* IV. 47 Ther is like to be dammage ... by the reason of sume lettinge there cowes goeinge in the heardwalkes with out a Keeper. **1884** *Cent. Mag.* Jan. 443/2 In some places a peninsula was chosen for a 'herd walk,' and fenced at its junction with the mainland, to keep the cows in and the wolves out.

b. In phrases, chiefly western: (1) *on herd,* among cowboys, on duty watching or guarding a herd of cattle; (2) *to keep under herd,* to keep in a herd or group; (3) *to ride herd (on),* to guard cattle by riding on the outer edge of a herd, also to watch or keep anything under observation; (4) *to be the whole herd,* to be the one of chief importance, *colloq.*

(1) **1869** *Overland Mo.* III. 126 The various reliefs during the day and night speak of being 'on herd' or 'off herd.' **1920** HUNTER *Trail Drivers Texas* I. 146 The first relief was on herd. — (2) **1876** in WHILLDIN *Descr. W. Texas* 15 One man, ... with the assistance of a 'bell mare,' keeps the extra horses under herd. — (3) **1897** A. H. LEWIS *Wolfville* 29 'Cherokee makes me tired,' says Peets, who's ridin' herd on the play. **1945** *Reader's Digest* Sep. 109/1 Many a cowboy who thought he had been hired to ride herd found himself repairing windmills. **1947** *Chi. Tribune* 1 Nov. 16/2 Thought you was ridin' herd on the hotel desk in town. — (4) **1909** R. A. WASON *Happy Hawkins* 178 An' he was an athlete an' a quarter-back an' a coxswain—oh, he was the whole herd, the cousin was.

As the last term in **calf, close, cut, day, horse, loose, night, sheep, Texas herd.**

∗**herder,** *n.* As the last term in **cattle, horse, mule, night, sheep herder.**

herdic ˈhɝdɪk, *n.* [Peter *Herdic* (1824–88), Amer. inventor.] A small omnibus for public conveyance. Also attrib. Now *hist.*

1882 T. S. HUDSON *Scamper through Amer.* 74 Taking a herdick (small one-horse 'bus named after the inventor) we drove to the White House. **1883** E. M. BACON *King's Dict. of Boston* 207/1 The herdic-phaetons, or herdics as they are universally called, are little cabs of recent introduction (in 1881). **1897** FLANDRAU *Harvard Episodes* 32 He found a dumpy, patient-looking herdic cab drawn up to the curbstone. *Ib.* 268 In the chill of the small hours, a herdic load of boys from some dance in town would often stream in to gossip. **1948** *Neb. Hist.* March 16 The mud on the streets of Lincoln was so deep that it required four horses to pull a herdic.

herd's-grass ˈhɝdzˌgræs, *n.* Also **herd grass.** [The origin of the name is doubtful. See quot. *a*1736 and the context of the 1890 quot.] Timothy grass, *Phleum pratense,* or redtop, *Agrostis stolonifera major.*

*a*1736 J. SHOT *Essay Field Husband* (1760) 57 It is said that herdgrass was first found in a swamp in Piscatagua by one herd, who propigated the same. **1774** J. ADAMS *Diary* Works II. 326 Shall I try to introduce fowl-meadow, and herds-grass into the meadow? **1863** *Ill. Agric. Soc. Trans.* V. (1865) 862 Timothy grass, or Cat's Tail, or as it is called in New England, Herd's Grass—is the *Phleum pratense* of Linnaeus, a European species, introduced and we may say naturalized in this country, where it is highly valued as a pasture grass. **1890** *N. & Q.* VI. 8 Nov. 16 *Timothy,* or *Herd-grass.* ... Most botanists regard the plant as European rather than American.

∗**here,** *adv.* In colloq. phrases: (1) *here's at you,* an expression signifying assent or approval; (2) *here's where,* this is the point at which.

(1) **1835** LONGSTREET *Ga. Scenes* 27 But as I bantered you, if you say an even swap, here's at you. **1884** HARRIS *Mingo* 49 There was a little pause.... Then the response came,—'Here's at you!' — (2) **1921** R. D. PAINE *Comr. Rolling Ocean* xiv. 250 I've got a hundred dollars left, and here's where I slip it out to the old gink.

∗**Heresiarch,** *n.* A minor sect in the Mormon Church. *Obs.* — **1851** HOWE *Hist. Coll. Great West* 421 The '*Spiritual Wife System,*' is alone maintained by the *Heresiarch,* a small fragment of seceders from the main Mormon body.

∗ **hermit,** *n.*

1. Short for next. *Colloq.*

1943 DAMON *Sense of H.* 6 The hermit . . . seems after each song to listen to some unheard echo. **1948** *Green Bay* (Wis.) *Press-Gazette* 30 June 4/2 In a lonely, shaded spot in the woods we heard the hermit sound out its sweet flutelike notes.

2. hermit thrush, the American nightingale or solitary thrush, *Hylocichla guttata faxoni,* of eastern North America. Cf. **Monterey, Sierra hermit thrush.**

1812 WILSON *Ornithology* V. 95 The Hermit Thrush is rarely seen in Pennsylvania. **1895** *Outing* April 69/2 A hermit thrush . . . flew off with a querulous *pay* as if he wished me to recompense him for my invasion. **1948** *Pacific Discovery* March-April 17/1 A hermit thrush savored the grape-sized fruit of the persimmon tree.

3. hermit warbler, a small, conspicuously colored songbird, *Dendroica occidentalis,* of the Sierra Nevada forests.

1839 AUDUBON *Ornith. Biog.* V. 55 Hermit Warbler. *Sylvia Occidentalis.* **1917** *Birds of Amer.* III. 146/1 The yellow head, black throat, and white breast and belly of the Hermit Warbler are so characteristic that it can hardly be confused with any other bird within its range.

∗ **hero,** *n.*

1. Heroes of America, the name of a secret organization in N.C. during and just after the Civil War. *Obs.*

1871 *42nd Congress* 1 Sess. Sen. Rep. No. 1, I. 199 There was [in N.C.] an organization at the close of the war, which has existed since, called the Heroes of America, or the Red Strings. **1871** *Ku Klux Klan Rep.* II. 363 [In 1868] the republican party had three secret organizations in operation in the State [N.C.], the Union League, the Heroes of America, and the Red Strings. **1904** FLEMING *Doc. rel. Reconstruction* No. 3, 5 The dislike of the whites to the Union League was so great that the local bodies began to assume other names: 'Red Strings' and 'Heroes of America' in North and South Carolina.

2. Hero of New Orleans, a nickname for Gen. Andrew Jackson (1767–1845), in allusion to his victory over the British at New Orleans on Jan. 8, 1815.

1824 *Amer. Sentinel* (Georgetown, Ky.) 10 Sep. 2/3 In the west, all the advocates of Mr. Clay . . . joined those of the Hero of New Orleans, in denouncing this effort, as anti-republican. **1913** GOODWIN *As I Remember Them* 313 Of course the first thing was to drink to the health of the president; then to the memory of the hero of New Orleans.

3. Hero of Tippecanoe, Wm. Henry Harrison (1773–1841). *Obs.*

1840 *Ill. State Reg.* (Springfield) 5 Feb. 2/1 The dandy 'association' termed the 'Old Soldier' undertake to compare the Hero of Tippecanoe with the Hero of New Orleans.

Heroite ˈhiroˌaɪt, *n.* A political supporter of Andrew Jackson. *Obs.* — **1827** *Spirit of Seventy-Six* (Frankfort, Ky.) 29 Mar. 3/2 From the best information I can gather, there is no chance of the *Heroites* between the Potomac and Delaware. **1832** *Polit. Examiner* (Shelbyville, Ky.) 6 Oct. 3/3 It was supposed that a large number of the Heroites, collected from every quarter of the state, would be present.

∗ **heron,** *n.* As the last term in **blue, great blue, green, least, Louisiana, red-shouldered, snowy heron.**

∗ **herring,** *n.*

1. (See quots.)

1871 *Amer. Naturalist* V. 398 The 'Hickory Shad' (*Meletta Mattawocca*), the young called 'Herring' at that locality [N.J.]. **1884** ROE *Nature's Story* 197 These half-grown fish [shad] are . . . sold as herrings or 'alewives.'

2. In combs.: (1) ∗ **herringbone,** designating a fence or hedge the materials or supports of which form a zigzag pattern, *rare;* (2) **chopper,** a bluefish; (3) **driver,** (see quot.); (4) **hawk,** (see quot.); (5) **salmon,** a North American species of *Coregonus;* (6) **torching,** (see quot. and cf. **herring driver**).

(1) **1869** *Rep. Comm. Agric. 1868* 258 This form of thorn fence is similar to the old time 'herring-bone' rail and stake fence, and the name 'herring-bone hedge' would not be inappropriate. **1939** *L.A.* Map 117. — (2) **1894** *Youth's Companion* 22 Nov. 562/4 Sometimes it would happen that, in pursuit of food, a great dull-blue 'herring chopper' would work inshore. — (3) **1889** *Cent.* 2810/1 *Herring-driver*, . . . a fisherman engaged in the capture of herring by torchlight. (Maine, U.S.; Bay of Fundy.) — (4) **1709** LAWSON *Carolina* 138 The Herring, or Swallow-tail'd Hawk, is about the Bigness of a Falcon, but a much longer Bird. He is of a delicate Aurora-Colour. (5) **1836** RICHARDSON *Fishes* 180 The Herring salmon forms its [*sc.* the namaycush's] principal food in Lake Huron. — (6) **1884** *Nat. Museum Bul.* No. 27, 1030 Herring-torching. Photograph of a fishing crew engaged in 'driving' herring.

As the last term in **autumnal, blue, Californian, English, fall, glut, gold, lake, Long Island, mountain, Ohio gold, river, shad, shad fall, spring, Staten Island, summer, tailor, thread, wall-eyed herring.**

Herrite ˈhɛraɪt, *n.* [?G. *Herr* + *-ite*.] (See quot.) — **1923** ROSENBERGER *Pa. Germans* 125 The Reformed Mennonites, who were organized in Lancaster County in 1821, and are sometimes called 'Herrites,' or, at other times, 'New Mennonites.'

∗ **hesitation,** *n.* A form of waltz characterized by a hesitating or gliding movement at the pleasure of the dancers. In full **hesitation waltz.** — **1914** V. CASTLE *Mod. Dancing* 71 It is the Hesitation Waltz. **1919** G. D'EGVILLE *How & What to Dance* (1922) 46 The American 'Hesitation.'

∗ **Hessian,** *n.*

1. (See quot. 1877.) *Obs.*

1861 *Dly. Dispatch* (Richmond, Va.) 19 June 3/1 Just as the train was about to stop, the artillery fired a well directed shot from one of their guns, which raked the Hessians fore and aft. **1877** BARTLETT 284 *Hessian.* . . . During the late civil war, it was used at the South as a term of reproach towards the loyal United States citizens and soldiers. 'The Hessians of the North,' frequently said the 'Richmond Despatch.'

attrib. **1860** *Charleston* (S.C.) *Mercury* 24 Nov. 4/1 Raise the Palmetto flag . . . we can defeat Abolition Lincoln and his Hessian Douglas, with their united powers and chain-gang followers. **1861** *Richmond* (Va.) *Examiner* 17 Dec. 1/5 When he accepts a commission . . . to fight against his own people, the *Hessian Yankee* affords the strongest possible evidence that he has little principle or honour, and, therefore, he should not be trusted.

2. (See quot. 1877.) Also attrib.

1877 BARTLETT 284 *Hessian.* A hireling; a mercenary politician; a fighter for pay. Derived from the traditional dislike toward the Hessian soldiers employed by England against her American colonies in the war of the Revolution. **1905** *Springfield W. Republican* 13 Oct. 1 The extent to which the placing of state politics upon a Hessian basis has gone deserves to be exposed. **1909** *Fra* Feb. 67/2 Let Gompers use his Hessians.

3. (See quots.)

1936 *Amer. Sp.* Dec. 315 Hessian, n. A term of reproach, usually applied to a vicious or meddlesome old woman. It has no connection with nationality. [Ozark Mts.] **1944** *D.N.* Nov. 29 hayshant: A rascal; an annoying child. . . . E. Ky. Rare.

4. In combs.: (1) **Hessian bug,** =next, *rare;* (2) **fly,** a small dusky fly or midge very destructive to wheat; (3) **insect,** =prec., *rare.*

(1) **1787** *Amer. Museum* II. 459 (Th.), That pernicious insect commonly known by the appellation of the Hessian bug. — (2) **1786** *Virginia Gaz.* 18 Oct. (Th.), [He] recommends roasting of wheat . . . to prevent injury from the Hessian fly. **1925** G. W. HERRICK *Manual Injurious Insects* 317 The Hessian fly is an imported insect. It was first found in 1779 in the vicinity of Lord Howe's encampment on Long Island of three years before. It now occurs in all of the wheat-growing region of the United States. **1949** *Downers Grove* (Ill.) *Rep.* 31 Mar. 7/8 Wheat jointworm, ranking next to Hessian fly as causing heavy losses to the wheat crop, was present in many fields this past season. — (3) **1787** *Amer. Museum* I. 146/1 The Hessian insect deposits its eggs in October or May.

∗ **het,** *v. To het up,* to become angry or excited. Usu. *to get het up. Colloq.*

1886 S. W. MITCHELL *R. Blake* 17, I don't het up easy. **1902** LORIMER *Lett. Merchant* 59 You mustn't get yourself all 'het up' before you take the plunge. **1912** WASON *Friar Tuck* 291, I was so meek I wouldn't 'a' got het up over it.

heterophemy ˈhɛtərəˌfimɪ, *n.* [Gk. *hetero-* + *phēmē*, "the other voice, speech."] (See quots.) Also **heterophemous,** *a.*

1875 *Galaxy* Nov. 693 Another incident of its manifestation is that the assertion made is most often not merely something that the speaker or writer does not mean to say, but its very reverse, or at least something notably at variance with its purpose. For this reason I have called it heterophemy, which means merely the speaking otherwise, and which has relations to and illustrations in heterodoxy, heterogenous, and heteroclite. **1890** *Railways Amer.* 164 Richard Grant White gave a name to a mental habit which, in train-despatchers, has caused many fatal accidents. It is 'heterophemy,' or thinking one thing while saying, hearing, or reading another. *Ib.* 167 The despatcher was also 'heterophemous.' He *saw* 'K,' but he *thought* 'I,' and replied to the operator that the message was O.K.

hewed-log house. A house built of hewed logs.

1793 in L. COLLINS *Kentucky* (1847) 517 Every purchaser or purchasers of lotts . . . shall build thereon a hued log house, with a brick or stone chimney. **1843** *Amer. Pioneer* II. 148 Two small hewed-log houses had been erected. **1883** EGGLESTON *Hoosier School-Boy* xvi. 106 There's the old hewed-log house on the Indianny side. *a***1918** G. STU-

ART *On Frontier* I. 106 Here was a good hewed log house, stable, corral, and a small field fenced, but not a human being.

hewgag ˈhjuˌgæg, *n.* Also **hugag.** [Of fanciful origin]. A musical or noise-making instrument facetiously so called.

1850 *Calif. Courier* (S.F.) 6 Sep. 2/3 Beat the hong-gong; sound the hew-gag! **1879** *Glendale* (Mont.) *Atlantis* 28 Dec. 4/4 A Dutchman drove rapidly along Main Street, with a new shoo-fly attached to his wagon, making forty flips a second and striking back and forth with the vigor of a hewgag.

transf. **1858** in MERRIAM *S. Bowles* I. 295 Hanscomb sends a letter . . . , setting it out with the accompanying 'sound of hew-gag.' **1889** *Voice* 21 Nov., When a leading paper . . . sounds the hewgag, other papers take up the cry, and repeat it from one end of the country to the other. **1905** TARKINGTON *In Arena* 152 Professors and students all kow-towed and sounded the hew-gag before him.

hex hɛks, *n.* [*Hexe,* "a witch," is recorded in *EDD*, but the use here is from Pa.-G. *hex* (G. *Hexe*).]

1. A witch. Also attrib. *Colloq.*

1920 LEWIS *Main Street* 159, I couldn't talk to you without twenty old hexes watching, whispering. **1943** MENEFEE *Assignment* 29 Many natives of York still visit these 'Word-Healers' or Hex Doctors to be 'tried for' what ails them.

2. A magic charm or spell. Also *to put the hex on. Colloq.*

1909 *Sat. Ev. Post* 16 Jan. 7/1 'Old pal,' agreed J. Rufus, 'the hex is sure on me.' **1943** *Ib.* 3 April 59/1, I don't see how the cat put the hex on old dog.

Hence **hexerei,** witchcraft. *Colloq.*

1929 AURAND *Acct. Witch Murder Trial* 30 White men brought 'hexerei' to the hills where it blended with the Indian 'powwow.' **1942** WEYGANDT *Plenty of Penna.* 48 A share of it [folk medicine] came from 'Indian doctors,' who are responsible as well for some of our hexerei.

3. hex mark, a mark indicative or provocative of bewitchment. Also **hex-marked,** *a.*

1938 HARK *Hex Marks Spot* 21 It seemed reasonable to suppose they were originally hex marks, brought by older generations to this country and incorporated with other customs of the homeland into the new life on a foreign shore. **1948** *Time* 11 Oct. 21/1 Fall, with its memories of the American past, belonged to the country—to Pennsylvania's huge, hex-marked barns, to the aching distances of the Great Plains.

hex hɛks, *v.* [f. Pa.-G. Cf. **hex,** *n.*] *tr.* To place a spell on (someone). Also absol.

1857 WATSON *Ann. Phila.* I. 270 A decent shopkeeper once got him to hex for his wife, who had conceited that an old Mrs. Wiggard had bewitched her, and made her to swallow a piece of linsey woolsey. [**1882** GIBBONS *Pa. Dutch* 402 They still speak of horses and animals being bewitched (verhext).] **1948** *Dly. Ardmoreite* (Ardmore, Okla.) 7 April 7/3 John Henson says this reporter must have hexed him.

Hence **hexer,** *n.*

1938 HARK *Hex Marks Spot* 140 After that, the three strings used in 'measuring' were placed on the floor while the 'hexer' walked solemnly back and forth across them, repeating more magic words as she did so.

hiaqua hɪˈɑkwə, *n.* [See note.]

"This word, which has been variously spelled *haiqua, hioqua, hiqua, hykwa, iokwa, ioqua,* etc., and even *Iroquois,* is derived from the name for dentalium in the Chinook jargon" (Hodge).

Shell money and ornaments composed of strings of tusk shells or tooth shells used by Indians on the North Pacific Coast. Also attrib. Cf. **allocochick.**

*c***1816** ROSS *Adv. on Oregon* (1923) 103 The circulating medium in use among these people is a small white shell called higua, about two inches long, of a convex form, and hollow in the heart, resembling in appearance the small end of a smoking pipe. **1845** DUNN *Ore. Terr.* 95 They regulate the prices of their articles by *haiqua,* which is a milk-white round shell of extreme hardness. **1868** WHYMPER *Alaska* 182 The women's dress is more squarely cut; and they adopt very much a long ornament of Hy-a-qua shells.

b. (See quots.)

1831 COX *Adv. Columbia R.* 158 The Indians regulate the prices of their various articles by *haiqua;* a fathom of the best description. **1910** HODGE *Amer. Indians* II. 909/1 A string of 25 of these shells, which, placed end to end, reached one fathom or 6 ft, was called a *hiaqua.* . . . One *hiaqua* . . . would purchase as a rule one male and two female slaves: this was approximately £ 50 sterling.

hickety-crickety road. (See quot.) *Obs.* Cf. **corduroy road.** — **1870** MACRAE *Americans* II. 170 Another variety of sensation is enjoyed in swampy regions, on what are called 'Corduroy roads,' which consist of logs or trunks of trees laid transversely and close together, and which are distinguishable as Hickety-crickety or Hunker-chunker roads, according to the thickness of the logs.

hickey ˈhɪkɪ, *n.* A device or gadget. *Colloq.* — **1913** in WENTWORTH. **1932** *Atlantic Mo.* CXLIX. 665 We have little hickeys beside our seats to regulate the amount of air admitted through a slot in each window.

hickok ˈhɪkɑk, *n.* [See quot. 1896 and cf. Sp. *icaco, hicaco* in the sense shown here.] The coco plum, *Chrysobalanus icaco,* or its plum-shaped fruit. — **1837** WILLIAMS *Florida* 19 The ovino, custard apple, hickok, and huesco plumbs are abundant on the east bank of the Indian River. **1896** *Garden & For.* IX. 263 Hickok (*Chrysobalanus Icaco*).—Through Carib-Span., from *ikákoo,* the name of the plum-like fruit in the female dialect of the Caribs of the Lesser Antilles. Cocoa, in the name Cocoa-plum (Corker-plum in Fla.), is a variant of the word.

hickory ˈhɪkərɪ, *n.* and *a.* [See first group of quots., esp. quot. 1872, and cf. **pokahickory.**]

1. Any one of various American trees of the genus *Carya,* or the nut of such a tree.

(1) *c***1618** STRACHEY *Virginia* 112 Likewise the women plant and attend the gardeins, dresse the meate brought home, make their broaths and pockerchicory drinckes, make matts and basketts, . . . etc. **1634** *Relation of Beginnings of Md.* 8 The ground is couered thicke with pokickeries which is a wild Walnut very hard and thick of shell; but the meate (though little) is passing sweete. **1653** J. FERRAR *Reformed Va. Silk Worm* (*Cent.*), Popler, Plum, Crab, Oake, and Apple tree, Yea, Cherry, and tree called *Pohickery.* **1872** TRUMBULL in *Amer. Philol. Assoc. Trans.* 26 *Hickory* is from the Virginian *powcohickora* (Strachey) *pawcohiccora,* (J. Smith), the name neither of the tree nor the nut, but of 'a kind of milk or oily liquor pressed from the pounded kernels.' 'Pokickory' is named in a list of Virginian trees, in 1653, and this was finally shortened to 'hickory.'

(2) **1671** *S.C. Hist. Soc. Coll.* V. 333 This Land bears very good . . . Ash, Hickory, Popler, Beach [etc.]. **1705** BEVERLEY *Virginia* III. 15 The kernels of the Hiccories they [the Indians] beat in a Mortar with Water, and make a White Liquor like Milk, whence they call our Milk *Hickory.* **1792** IMLAY *Western Territory* 90 Several kinds of nuts grow in the forests, such as chesnuts, hickory, and black walnuts. **1831** PECK *Guide* 139 Of our nuts [in Illinois], the hickory, black walnut, and pecan deserve notice. **1947** *U.S. Dispensatory* 1386/2 There are six other common species of hickory which are indigenous to the United States and Canada.

b. The wood of a hickory tree, often used as firewood. Cf. **3.** below.

1676 GLOVER *Acc. Va.* in *Phil. Trans.* XI. 628 There is also another sort of Timber called Hickery, that is harder than any Oak. **1791** JEFFERSON in *Harper's Mag.* LXX. 535/2, 6 cord of hiccory last a fire place well the winter. **1816** *Ann. 14th Congress* 2 Sess. 1196 There may be small variations, according as . . . hickory . . . or any other wood is employed. **1880** *Scribner's Mo.* May 126/2 This ragged prickly shrub is full of 'grease,' and makes an exceedingly hot fire, which snaps and sputters like hickory. **1945** *Chi. Tribune* 13 May VII. 1/1 Donie Simms shoved the big iron skillet to the front of the cookstove and put another stick of dried hickory into the fire.

c. A switch, orig. one of hickory, used in chastising anyone, esp. children, urging horses forward, etc., in full **hickory switch.** *Colloq.* Cf. **hickory oil, stick** (*b*), **tea, towel,** in **8.** below.

1734 *N.J. Archives* XI. 359 Several Indians had seiz'd a Boy . . . whom they stripped and whipt with Hickery Switches. **1824** DODDRIDGE *Notes* 176 The master, then took two of the hiccories in his hand, and . . . lacerated the shoulders of the poor miserable sufferer. **1948** *Sat. Ev. Post* 11 Sep. 4/4 Just how often did each of these five brats experience the benefits of a sound whaling with a hickory switch?

fig. A rapid gait or clip. *Colloq.*

1839 WILLIS *A l'Abri* 135 'Wal!' said he, as we shot past, 'you're going a *good hickory,* Mister!' **1914** *Collier's* 10 Jan. II. 44/2 We be goin' pretty good hickory, pretty good hickory, Chief! **1949** *Sat. Ev. Post* 12 Feb. 125/1 You were going pretty good hickory.

d. A cane or walking stick. *Obs.*

1748 WEISER *Journal* 39 The French had very hard heads, & your Country afforded nothing but Sticks & Hickerys which was not sufficient to break them. **1833** S. SMITH *Major Downing* 185 The Gineral pulled his own chair up to the other side of the table and laid his hickory and hat down before him. **1857** *Harper's Mag.* Aug. 422/1 Tom . . . placed under his arm the gold-headed *hickory,* which was . . . his staff of office.

e. A baseball bat. *Colloq.* Cf. ∗**ash,** *n.* **1.**

1900 *Chi. Times-Herald* 6 May VI. 8/1 Chicago failed to accomplish anything in the inning and Cincinnati took on the turn at the hickory. **1911** *Chi. D. News* 1 April 6/1 Zimmerman also made himself conspicuous with his new hickory just out of the bat factory.

2. Designating areas where hickory is the prevailing growth, as (1) **hickory barren,** (2) **bottom,** (also as a place-name), (3) **field,** (4) **flat,** (5) **ground,** see as a main entry, (6) **land,** (7) **opening,** (8) **uplands.**

(1) **1799** ASBURY *Journal* II. 431 Wandering out of our way in the Hickory barrens, we made it thirty miles to Alexander Hill's. — (2) **1795** *Pittsburgh Gaz.* 26 Dec. 1/2 The supposed Thief . . . has resided for some time at the Hickory Bottom, near the Monongahela. **1896** READ *Jucklins* 41 We were upon . . . a hickory bottom, where squirrels were barking. — (3) **1869** *Harper's Mag.* Nov. 847/1 Barnabas was away off in the hickory-fields, chopping. — (4) **1912** COBB *Back Home* 38 The fair grounds lay in a hickory flat a mile out of town.

(6) **1674** *S.C. Hist. Mag.* XI. 83 Hickery land wth divers spatious savanas. **1741** TAILFER *True Narrative Ga.* 97 The Proportion of Pine Barren to either good Swamp or Oak and Hickory Land, is at least six to one. **1818** *Niles' Reg.* XV. 125/2 Many tracts of hickory land were offered at two dollars; which nobody would take. — (7) **1840** in *Mich. Agric. Soc. Trans.* VI. 272 Hickory openings [are] interspersed with plains of white, black and burr oak, and hickory. — (8) **1844** MOORE *Texas* 106 The 'Hickory Uplands' near Soda Lake, constitute one of the most beautiful and productive portions of Texas.

3. In expressions alluding to the use of hickory as firewood, often with reference to its use in cooking, curing, or smoking meat. Cf. **1. b.** above.

1777 *Jrnl. Nicholas Cresswell* (1925) 199 Nothing but hickory wood is burnt in these smoke-houses. **1828** in M. B. SMITH *Forty Yrs. Washington Soc.* (1906) 244 A rousing hickory fire blazed in the chimney. **1901** *Munsey's Mag.* XXV. 617/1 Have you forgotten how a hickory-cured ham sandwich tastes? **1940** WILSON *Wabash* 186 Fried chicken such as can be found nowhere else, . . . fiddler catfish . . . hickory barbecue . . . roasting ears. **1947** *Dly. Oklahoman* (Okla. City) 28 Dec. 5/6 The Andersons are not the only ones receiving a two-year-old hickory-cured ham.

4. Designating a member of a religious faith regarded as flexible, yielding, not perfectly orthodox, as **hickory Amish, Methodist, Mormon, Quaker.** *Colloq.*

The word *hickory* came into use as an adjective in the sense of "tough, firm, unyielding," and, sarcastically, in the opposite sense. See *Amer. Folk-Lore* XV. (1902) 245. Our 1949 quot. is app. an example of the earlier sense. Cf. **5.** below.

1940 *Sat. Ev. Post* 30 March 37/4 He is 'under the ban,' and referred to by the neighbors as a 'hickory Amish' because of some infraction not publicly mentioned, but most likely that of going to a movie. — [**1949** *Pacific Northwest Quart.* April 124 Missionary Baptists . . . have applied to them, on occasion, names such as 'hard shells,' 'iron sides,' 'iron jackets,' and 'hickory Baptists.'] — **1872** EGGLESTON *End of World* xxxix, 249 Any member of your class would do better to marry a good, faithful, honest New Light than to marry a hickory Methodist. — **1855** *N.Y. Herald* 12 Nov. 5/1 It is the wicked, half hearted, and what I call hickory Mormons that prevent a more extensive gathering of the saints. **1878** BEADLE *Western Wilds* 534 Among the young or 'Hickory Mormons,' there are about as many men as women. — [**1824** SINGLETON *Letters* 15 There are at present various species of this sect [i.e., Quakers]; the starch primitives in faith and practice; and the hickory, or half-blooded by intermarriages with the world's people.] **1831** *Boston Transcript* 12 Dec. 1/1 They accordingly hitched Botherem, the pony, and made two of this assemblage of *Shaking* Quakers, for so many of them proved, who were only *hickory* ones till they joined the sett. **1835** *S. Lit. Messenger* I. 551/1 Some years ago a kind of 'Hickory Quaker,' (as he called himself,) . . . found his way . . . from one of the middle States to Congress.

5. Used in expressions designating or relating to Andrew Jackson (1767–1845), popularly known as "Old Hickory," as (1) **hickory characteristics,** (2) **chivalry,** (3) **club,** (4) **Jackson,** (5) **man,** (6) **Unionist.** All *obs.* Cf. **hickory bush, pole, stick** in **8.** below.

(1) **1829** IRVING in P. M. Irving *Life W. Irving* (1873) II. 143 As to the old general [Jackson], with all his *hickory* characteristics, I suspect he has good stuff in him. — (2) **1848** *Campaign* (Wash., D.C.) 7 June 25/1 Our ticket is of the true hickory stamp. Both [men] have hickory chivalry and hickory principles. — (3) **1838** MAYO *Polit. Sk. Washington* (1839) 15 Your wicked Partisan Rulers, contrived to . . . gull the tolerant and confiding spirit of the people . . . to the end that their abused trusts and overgrown power be . . . perpetual—such as the establishment of a Central Hickory Club and other Juntos or Conspirators. **1876** *Arcola* (Ill.) *Rec.* 26 Feb. 8/1 There Pilcher, and greater and lesser lights of the Democracy, in conjunction with the old Hickory Club, schemed strategy to circumvent Old Hal and his followers. — (4) **1826** S. WOODWORTH *Melodies* 221, I s'pose you've read it in the papers how Packenham attempted To make old hickory Jackson run. **1861** *Vanity Fair* 2 Feb. 59/2 Hickory Jackson's dead! The rebels are going ahead!

(5) **1827** *Cin. Enquirer* 7 April 2/3 Congress has been exposed to some pretty severe sharp shooting from the people too—and the hickory men, as usual, have done the most execution. — (6) **1862** *N.Y. Tribune* 1 April (Chipman), Parson Brownlow. This hickory Unionist reached Cincinnati on Friday.

Also **Hickoryism,** *n.*

1834 *Sun* (N.Y.) 21 May 2/1 My cheeks are both Clay, though one of them carries the badge of Hickoryism—a dirty whisker, that covers a *ring-worm.*

6. In the names of trees: (1) **hickory elm,** the rock elm of eastern North America; (2) **pine,** (*a*) (see quot.), (*b*) the bristle-cone pine, *Pinus aristata*, of the western states; (3) **poplar,** (see quot.).

(1) **1884** SARGENT *Rep. Forests* 123 *Ulmus racemosa.* . . . Hickory Elm. — (2) (*a*) **1884** SARGENT *Rep. Forests* 199 *Pinus pungens.* . . . Table-mountain Pine. Hickory Pine. (*b*) **1897** SUDWORTH *Arborescent Flora* 18 Bristle-cone Pine. . . . Common names: Hickory Pine (Cal. lit.). **1948** *Pacific Discovery* Nov.–Dec. 18/1 They are the limber pine . . . ; the hickory pine (*P. aristata*) of the high desert ranges north of the Mohave Desert. — (3) **1893** *Amer. Folk-Lore* VI. 136 *Liriodendron tulipifera*, white, yellow, or hickory poplar. West Va.

7. Of or pertaining to a strong cotton fabric often used for shirts. *Colloq.* Cf. **hickory shirt, hickory shirting, hickory striped shirt,** in **8.** and **8. b.** below.

1857 *Jrnl. Discourses* IV. 205 (Th.), Get some good hickory cloth, or some buckskins, and let the sisters make dresses and garments that cannot be easily torn. **1885** *Cent. Mag.* April 834/1 In their blue shirts and hickory trousers they [*sc.* Indians] had nothing of the look of the savage about them, save their long hair. **1892** HARTE *Col. Starbottle's Client* 113 He was warming his hands and placidly ignoring his gaunt arms in their thinly-clad 'hickory' sleeves. *a***1918** G. STUART *On Frontier* I. 66 His pay for this would be one hickory cotton shirt which cost seventy-five cents.

8. In miscellaneous combs.: (1) **hickory bark,** see as a main entry; (2) **borer,** any one of various beetles, as *Goes tigrinus*, whose larvae live in the wood or under the bark of hickory trees; (3) **bottomed,** *a.* designating a chair having a bottom made of hickory splits; (4) **broom,**

Hickory broom

a broom made by shaving down a suitable piece of hickory and binding the folded-over shavings somewhat in the manner of a mop, *obs.* or *hist.*; (5) **bush,** a young hickory used as a political symbol by the political supporters of Andrew Jackson, cf. **5.** above; (6) **cake,** a cake in which hickory nuts are used; (7) **chair,** a chair made of hickory; (8) **faced,** *a.* hard-featured, *obs.* [this term and *hickory face* occur in *EDD*, app. interesting examples of American colloquialisms that made their way into British dialect]; (9) **horned devil,** see as a main entry; (10) **law,** lynch law, law administered with hickory switches, *obs.*, cf. **1. c.** above; (11) **oil,** a thrashing, *colloq.*, cf. **1. c.** above; (12) **pole,** a pole of hickory, esp. as a party emblem used by the supporters of Andrew Jackson, in allusion to his nickname of "Old Hickory," *obs.*, cf. **hickory bush** and see **5.** above; (13) **shad,** see as a main entry; (14) **shirt,** a shirt made of hickory shirting *q.v.* in **b.** below, also **hickory-shirted,** cf. **7.** above; (15) **stick,** (*a*) (see **hickory pole** and cf. **5.** above), *obs.*, (*b*) a switch for thrashing children, cf. **1. c.** above; (16) **striped shirt, = hickory shirt;** (17) **towel,** (*a*) a hickory switch for chastising a person, *obs.* [cf. **oaken towel*, **lead* *towel*, in *OED s.v.* **towel*, *n.* 3, and see **1. c.** above], (*b*) a towel of hickory cloth, cf. **7.** above.

(2) **1854** EMMONS *Agric. N.Y.* V. 262. **1911** *Dept. Agric. Yrbk. 1910* 349 The painted hickory borer is a close relative of the locust borer. — (3) **1847** ROBB *Squatter Life* 39 Seating himself upon a hickory bottomed chair, he took the widow's sickly little daughter upon his knee. **1943** *Nat. Geog. Mag.* Dec. 743/2 Homemade hickory-bottomed chairs were brought, and we all sat down. — (4) **1843** CARLTON *New Purchase* 119 Then the floor had been assaulted with stiff hickory brooms.

(5) **1827** *Spirit of Seventy-Six* (Frankfort, Ky.) 16 Aug. 3/3 The Jacksonians had a booth at one side of the court house, with their insignia, a hickory bush, and flag. — (6) **1846** BEECHER *Domestic Receipt-Book* 143 Almond, Hickory, or Coconut Cake. — (7) **1944** CLARK *Pills* 20 Leaning back against hundreds of kitchen walls in homemade hickory chairs, dramatic bumpkins repeated to their neighbors hair-raising stories. — (8) **1796** A. BARTON *Disappointment* I. i, He's a snug, hickory faced, dry dog.

(10) **1834** SIMMS *Guy Rivers* 87 The little touch of hickory law, with a dipping in the mire. — (11) **1827** *Amer. Sentinel* (Georgetown, Ky.) 21 April 3/2 *Hickory* oil is the grand restorative. **1857** *S. Lit. Messenger* XXV. 306/1 At school he is a disciplinarian of the strictest old-fashioned style; dosing small boys with hickory oil. **1916** MASSEY *Reminiscences* 47 Mr. Hennessee taught the 'three R's' very thoroughly, as was reported, by the lubrication of 'hickory oil'; but it never fell to my lot to have any of this knowledge dispensed by Mr. Hennessee. — (12) **1830** *Greensborough* (N.C.) *Patriot* 4 Aug. 2/4 They would *look* and act much better in throwing the weight of their votes against Jackson's re-election than they do in pulling down tavern signs and prostrating hickory poles! **1876** *Cattaraugus* (N.Y.) *Union* 31 Aug. 3/2 There will be a Hickory Pole raising at the Lattin School house, on Friday afternoon of this week. **1902** *Amer. Folk-Lore* XV. 245 After the hickory have been named the following: . . . hickory-pole (party emblem). — (14) **1850** RYAN *Adventures* II. 8 A little man, in a 'hickory shirt,' . . . darted out from some dark corner. *a***1861** T. WINTHROP *Canoe & Saddle* ii. 23 Three unsavory, hickory-shirted, mat-haired, truculent siwashes. **1946** *Reader's Digest* Jan. 110/2 The 'ballroom' was crowded with men in hickory shirts.

(15) (*a*) **1844** EMERSON *Poet* Essays 2 Ser., The cider-barrel, the log-cabin, the hickory-stick, the palmetto, and all the cognizances of party. (*b*) **1943** WOOD *W. Reed* 37 The schoolmasters . . . relied heavily on the hickory stick as an aid to learning. **1948** *Woman's Day* 96/1 He pushed one foot carefully ahead of the other and leant heavily on a hickory stick. — (16) **1944** CLARK *Pills* 208 Underneath jeans britches and hickory-striped shirts for most of the year were the red flannels. — (17) (*a*) **1834** CARUTHERS *Kentuckian* I. 30, I gin him a wink, as much as to let him know that . . . I would wipe him down with a hickory towel. (*b*) **1942** LILLARD *Desert Challenge* 241 Guests were glad to pay $4 for a paper-bound chamber that contained a bed, a cornhusk mattress, a washstand, a bar of soap, a hickory towel, and a kerosene lamp.

b. In combs. of obvious meaning or sufficiently explained in the quots., as (1) **hickory ashes,** (2) **dealer,** (3) **grass,** (4) **grub,** (5) **milk,** (6) **shirting,** (7) **tea,** (8) **withe.**

(1) **1777** *Jrnl. Nicholas Cresswell* (1925) 199 Some rub them [hams] with hickory ashes instead of salt petre, it makes them red as the salt petre and gives them a pleasant taste. **1836** *Franklin Repository* (Chambersburg, Pa.) 4 Oct. 1/3 Ever since these black stones were brought to town, the wood-sawyers and pilers, and then soap-fat and hickory ashes-men, has been going down. **1941** ALLEY *Random Thoughts* 495 Where now is the old ash-hopper that stood in the kitchen yard filled with hickory ashes from which the lye was extracted. — (2) *c***1820** in BARNARD *Retrospections of Amer.* (1887) 45 One of the class [of Yankee peddlers] called a 'hickory dealer,' or seller of wooden ware, came down to the South in summertime with a well-laden wagon. — (3) **1910** THORNBER *Grazing Ranges Ariz.* 261 The more important are salt-bush, . . . winter fat, . . . bear or hickory grass (*Nolina*). — (4) **1800** B. HAWKINS *Sk. Creek Country* 50 On the hillsides and their tops, hickory grub and grape vines.

(5) [**1705** BEVERLEY *Hist. Va.* III. 15 The Kernels of the Hiccories they beat in a Mortar with Water, and make a White Liquor like Milk, whence they call our Milk Hickory.] **1775** ADAIR *Indians* 409 An oily, tough, thick, white substance, called by the traders hiccory milk, and by the Indians the flesh, or fat of hiccory-nuts, with which they eat their bread. **1791** W. BARTRAM *Travels* 38 [The Indians] pound them [*sc.* hickory nuts] to pieces, and then cast them into boiling water, which, after passing through fine strainers, preserves the most oily part of the liquid: this they call by a name which signifies hiccory milk; it is as sweet and rich as fresh cream, and is an ingredient in most of their cookery. — (6) **1831** *N.Y. Tribune* 31 Dec. (Chipman), The ball was extracted [from his lung] a few days ago, along with a piece of hickory shirting which was used for packing. **1923** *D.N.* V. 235 hickory shirt, a work shirt made of cross-barred cotton cloth, which is called *hickory-shirtin'*. **1941** M. L. SMITH *God's Country* 37 Later one could buy the old hickory shirting. — (7) **1939** *Amer. Sp.* April 90 Hickory Tea. A whipping. 'The school teacher feeds hickory tea to the bad boys.' — (8) **1838** *S. Lit. Messenger* IV. 294 The roof was of clapboards, . . . tied fast with hickory withes. **1847** DARLINGTON *Weeds & Plants* 306 The tough sprouts, or seedling plants, are often employed as ligatures, in rural economy, under the name of hickory withes. **1944** DUNCAN *M. Graham* 35 But all such questions were soon forgotten in the splendid uproar of neighbors unpacking roast possum, turkey, squirrel, pigeon, pig, and deer from hickory-with creels on pack horses tethered about the dooryard.

Also *hickory ax handle, bough, bow, box, cane, chip, chunk, coal, handle, hoop pole, log, mast, post, rail, rod, splinter, split, staff, walking stick, woodpile, yoke,* etc.

As the last term in **balsam, barren, bitter, black, broom, common, downy, flying-bark(ed), hard-bark, hardshell, hognut, Illinois, nutmeg, oak and, Old, pale-leaf, pecan, puckery, red, scaly-bark, shad, shagbark, shellbark(ed), small-fruited, small nut, split, Springfield, swamp, sweet, switch, thick shellbarked, upland, water, white, white heart, Young Hickory.**

hickory ˈhɪkərɪ, *v.*

1. *tr.* =next. Also **hickorize.** Both *rare.*

1842 in *Amer. Sp.* XVIII. 125/1 We shall do our duty, and hope Old Hickory will do his, else, . . . We'll hickorize him, so that he won't forget us all his days. **1854** *Ib.* I. (1926) 292 You won't hick'ry your wife much more, ole hoss.

2. hickory-whip, to thrash or whip with a hickory switch. *Colloq.*

1871 *Cong. Globe* App. 4 April 293/2 They threatened me that if I ever came back they would take me out and hickory-whip me. **1934** VINES *Green Thicket World* 119 The merchant had tried to hickory-whip *Lattie.*

hickory bark. The bark of the hickory tree. Also attrib.

[**1716** in *Memoirs Huguenot Family* (1872) 276 They [Indians] make a roof with rafters, and cover the house with oak or hickory bark, which they strip off in great flakes, and lay it so closely that no rain can come in.] **1775** *Jrnl. Nicholas Cresswell* (1925) 103 We crossed the River in a Canoe made of Hickory Bark, stretched open with sticks. **1846** *N.O. Picayune* 31 Aug. 648/2 An Arkansas man dressed in a hickory-bark coat. **1946** WILSON *Fidelity* 147 Hickory-bark whips left over from the preceding spring . . . made the drudgery pretty hard.

b. hickory bark borer, a beetle, *Eccoptogaster quadrispinosa,* that burrows under the bark of some species of hickory.

1911 *Country Life* 15 Oct. 35/2 All of the white-banded trees are hickories of various kinds killed by the hickory bark borer.

hickory ground. 1. (*cap.*) A traders' name for an Indian town on the east bank of the Coosa River, in Elmore County, Ala. Also attrib. **2.** Ground or land upon which hickory is the prevailing growth.

(1) **1772** in *Travels Amer. Col.* 507 This Morning the Messenger Returned from Emistisguo desiring me to go to the Hickory Ground. **1796** B. HAWKINS *Letters* 44, I continued on up to the Coosau, 3 miles to the hickory ground. **1858** T. S. WOODWARD *Reminiscences* (1939) 37 But the Little Warrior being a Hickory-Ground Indian, set the Coosa Indians at variance with the Big Warrior. — (2) **1850** LYELL *Second Visit U.S.* II. 22 The soil of the 'hiccory grounds' is derived from the disintegration of granitic rocks, which are very felspathic here, and are decomposing in situ.

hickory horned devil. (See quot. 1891.) Also **hickory horn devil, horned hickory devil, hickory devil.**

1891 *Cent.* 6813/1 walnut-moth. . . . Any moth whose larva feeds on walnut, as the regal walnut-moth, *Citheronia regalis,* whose larva is known as the *hickory horned devil.* **1909** *Country Life* Oct. 652/3 The caterpillars emerged on the 27th of June, and bore the characteristic markings which are responsible for the common name 'Hickory Horn-devil.' **1912** *Ib.* 15 June 31 Regalis caterpillar, commonly called the horned hickory devil. **1938** BRIMLEY *Insects N.C.* 266 The larva is known as the 'hickory devil' or 'simmon bull' and feeds on cotton, hickory, sweet gum, walnut, pecan, persimmon, sourwood, Paulownia.

hickory nut. The fruit of the hickory tree. Cf. **Gloucester hickory nut.**

1670 *S.C. Hist. Soc. Coll.* V. 166 They brought also plenty of Hickery nutts, a wall nut in shape & taste onely differing in ye thickness of the shell & smallness of ye kernell. **1709** LAWSON *Carolina* 98 Hiccory Nuts have very hard Shells, but excellent sweet Kernels, with which, in a plantiful Year, the old Hogs, that can crack them, fatten themselves, and make excellent Pork. **1948–9** *N.W. Ohio Quart.* Winter 13 He had wandered nine days living entirely on hickory nuts.

attrib. **1876** *Wide Awake* 296/1 They made, for one thing, great loaves of Mr. Summer's favorite hickory-nut cake. **1947** *Atlantic Mo.* Dec. 112/2 Gone, too, with these luscious homemade loaves are other substantial and tasty favorites: . . . rolled oats and wheat flour bread . . . ; sweet hickory nut bread.

hickory-nutting ˈhɪkrɪˌnʌtɪŋ, *n.* Gathering hickory nuts; an excursion for this purpose. — **1845** KIRKLAND *Western Clearings* 111 It was a tale of such passionate protestation—such humble suing,—on the part of the hero of the hickory-nutting [etc.]. **1904** DARROW *Farmington* 163 Sometimes they went hickory-nutting or chestnutting with us.

hickory shad. Any one of various fishes, esp. the fall herring and the gizzard shad, the stomachs of which resemble hickory nuts.

1800 HAWKINS *Sk. Creek Country* 53 The fish taken here are, the hickory shad, rock, trout, perch. **1903** *N.Y. State Mus. Bul.* No. 60, 198 The name hickory shad is applied to this species (*Pomolobus Mediocris*) from the Chesapeake Bay region southward, and in some Georgia rivers this is abbreviated to hicks. **1947** DALRYMPLE *Panfish* 341 Then suddenly a big buck Shad of four or five pounds, or a small Alewife or Hickory Shad, will break away, dart out and smack the lure.

hicks hɪks, *n.* A local name for the hickory shad or fall herring. — **1884** GOODE *Fisheries* I. 608 The name 'Hickory Shad' . . . is used in the Chesapeake and in the Albermarle regions, and on the Ogeechee, Savannah, and Altamaha Rivers, where it is familiarly called 'Hicks.' **1911** *Rep. Fisheries 1908* 312 It is called 'hickory shad' and 'hicks,' particularly in the South.

Hicksite ˈhɪksaɪt, *n.* A member of the Religious Society of Friends, the body of American Quakers that in 1827–28, under the leadership of Elias Hicks (1748–1830), seceded from the Society of Friends.

1832 *Boston Transcript* 21 Jan. 2/1 Hendrickson, in his bill, charges the 'Hicksites' with seceding from the society—holding doctrines repugnant to Christianity, and to the principles of the church. **1905** *N.Y. Ev. Post* 1 June 14 The congregation was composed of liberal Quakers, or Hicksites, as they dislike being called.

Also **(a) Hicksite Friend, (b) Hicksite Quaker.**

(a) 1842 J. STURGE *Visit to U.S.* 6 He has been recently disowned by the 'Hicksite Friends' for his connection with the newspaper called the 'National Anti-Slavery Standard.' **1855** *N.Y. Wkly. Tribune* 16 June 1/3 The persons who took the lead in the new movement were for the most part seceders from the Genesee Yearly Meeting of (Hicksite) Friends. **1940** *Sat. Ev. Post* 17 Feb. 42/2 The differences between the orthodox and the Hicksite Friends were entirely doctrinal. — **(b) 1838** *Knickerb.* XII. 196 The Hicksite Quaker, with placid countenance, reposing . . . under the shadow of a great brim. **1871** *Cong. Globe* 22 Feb. 1492/3 If they can find a Hicksite Quaker, . . . [he] is put in charge of Indians.

hick town. A small country town. Also attrib. *Slang.*

1924 H. CROY *R.F.D. No. 3* 220 You ought to get out of this hick town. The city is the place for you. **1938** NIXON *Forty Acres* 41 Summer revivals and all-day singings 'with dinner on the ground' make strong appeal to hillbillies, farm villagers and hick-town men. **1949** *Sat. Ev. Post* 12 Feb. 21/2 More are resentful of the implication that 'Peoria' is synonymous with 'hick town.'

hidalgo hɪˈdælgo, *n.* [Sp., app. an Amer. borrowing.] A Spanish nobleman or landed proprietor in the West.

1842 in *Amer. Sp.* XVIII. 125/1 The hidalgo was dressed in a brown coat. **1881** BUEL *Border Bandits* 49 The place was swarming . . . with blood-craving hidalgoes and greasers. **1944** JOHNSON *As I Dare* 264 In such a neighborhood Alec would negotiate with some hidalgo in his mud house for replenishment of the buckboard.

Hidatsa həˈdɑtsɑ, *n.* [See note.] (See first quots.)

"The name Hidatsa, by which they now call themselves, has been said, with doubtful authority, to mean 'willows,' and is stated by Matthews to have been originally the name only of a principal village of the tribe in their old home on Knife r." (Hodge).

1907 HODGE *Amer. Indians* I. 547 Hidatsa. A Siouan tribe living, since first known to the whites, in the vicinity of the junction of Knife r. with the Missouri, North Dakota, in intimate connection with the Mandan and Arikara. **1909** CURTIS *N. Amer. Indians* IV. 129 The Hidatsa, commonly known under the inappropriate appellation 'Gros Ventres of the Missouri,' differed from most of the tribes of the northern plains in that they were a sedentary and semi-agricultural people, gaining part of their livelihood, of course, by the chase. **1941** in DE TROBRIAND *Army Life in Dakota* xxv, Fort Berthold was established much later, after the removal of the Mandans and Hidatsa to its vicinity.

Hiddenite ˈhɪdṇˌaɪt, *n.* [William Earl *Hidden*, (1832–1918), an Amer. mineralogist.] A variety of spodumene occurring in North Carolina and used as a gem.

1881 *Amer. Jrnl. Science* 3 Ser. XXI. 130, I therefore propose the name of *Hiddenite* [for emerald-green spodumene], after the indefatigable mineral explorer [W. E. Hidden] who has directed our attention to it. **1905** *N. Eng. Mag.* Nov. 365/2 Prof. W. E. Hidden, of Newark, N.J., whose mineralogical fame is embalmed in Hiddenite, . . . has made an extensive research into this coinage episode, and collected many of the coins. **1943** PEATTIE *Great Smokies* 211 True rubies and sapphires have been found there, and many semi-precious stones such as garnet, . . . and hiddenite, a sea-green stone of great beauty found in Alexander County.

* **hide,** *n.* In combs.: (1) **hide-bottomed,** *a.* denoting a chair having a bottom made of cowhide; (2) **buyer,** a purchaser of buffalo hides, *obs.;* (3) **camp,** a camp of those who slaughtered buffaloes for their hides, *obs.;* (4) **crop,** (see quot.); (5) **drogher,** a vessel used by a trader in hides, one employed on such a vessel, *obs.;* (6) **droghing,** transporting hides by means of a drogher, *obs.;* (7) **house,** (see quot. 1846); (8) **hunter,** one who hunts animals for their hides; (9) **out,** a hiding place; (10) **rick,** a pile of buffalo hides awaiting sale, *obs.*

(1) 1870 W. BAKER *New Timothy* 110 Mr. Long . . . seats himself on a hide-bottomed chair. **1883** SWEET & KNOX *Through Texas* xii. 149 We found . . . the same identical hide-bottomed chairs that are to be found in every little town in Texas. — **(2) 1907** COOK *Border & Buffalo* (1938) 193 Here I found Mr. Hickey, the hide-buyer, whom I had expected to find in Fort Griffin. — **(3) 1907** COOK *Border & Buffalo* (1938) 194 Hickey asked me where my hide camp was and how many hides I had. — **(4) 1929** DOBIE *Vaquero* 24 The cow people of the lower country came to speak of the 'skinning season' as naturally as they spoke of the 'branding season.' A settler short on a corn crop could count on a 'hide crop.' The cow outfits of summer became the 'skinning outfits' of winter.

(5) 1840 DANA *Two Years* xiv. 109 After falling in with a few other 'hide droghers,' and finding that they [the men] carried only one [hide on their heads] at a time, we 'knocked off' the extra one, and thus made our duty somewhat easier. **1891** *Cent. Mag.* Jan. 402/1 The whaling fleets and the hide drogers . . . half a century ago wintered on the coast [of Calif.]. — **(6) 1840** DANA *Two Years* xxv. 259 We did not believe that a French prison would be much worse than 'hide-droghing' on the coast of California. *Ib.* xxix. 340 The prospect of eighteen months or two years more of hide droghing seemed completely to break down his spirit. — **(7) 1840** DANA *Two Years* xvii. 151 We took possession of one of the hide-houses, which belonged to our firm. **1846** EMORY *Military Reconn.* 113 The hide houses are a collection of store houses where the hides of cattle are packed before being shipped. **1945** BOTKIN *My Burden* 111 The hidehouses was just long sheds, all open along the sides and covered over with cypress clapboards. — **(8) 1886** LODGE in *Cent. Mag.* July 345/1 If there was no riding to hounds, the fox would be run down with one or two sharp dogs by the local hide-hunter. **1947** *True* Nov. 39/2 The Indians did and the mountain men and the hide hunters, and, finally, the wolfers. — **(9) 1885** *Cent. Mag.* March 684 They tried fur ter mek me fight fur the Confed'ret States an' they never done hit . . . they guv my place the name o' Hide-out, an' they didn't conscrip' me, nuther. **1928** *Hearst's International* Aug. 74/2 It was going to be terrible to be in a hide-out where you couldn't laugh, talk, smoke, breathe. **1949** *Time* 4 April 27/1 She thought he had tipped off the cops to one of their hideouts.

(10) 1907 COOK *Border & Buffalo* (1938) 341 Several had their beds made down in the aisles of the big hide-ricks.

b. *hide and tallow factory, W.* a concern which in times of depression in the cattle trade slaughtered cattle for their hides and tallow. *Obs.*

1929 DOBIE *Vaquero* 21 The slaughter raged in scores of 'hide and tallow factories'—as the packeries were fittingly called —that dotted the coast line from Corpus Christi Bay to Galveston Island.

As the last term in **bull, cow, deacon, fallen, moose, parchment, rawhide.**

* **hide,** *v.* **1.** *intr. To hide out,* to go into hiding, to seek to baffle pursuit or discovery by hiding. Hence **hiding out,** *n. Colloq.* (Cf. **hide-out.**) **2.** *to hide the switch,* a children's game in which one hides a switch which the others compete with each other in finding.

(1) 1884 J. C. HARRIS *Mingo* 124 He 'lowed that the revenue fellers better not git too clost ter Hog Mountain, bekaze the hidin'-out bizness is done played. **1885** CRADDOCK *Prophet* 44 Loneliness had made his sensibilities tender, and 'hiding out' affected his spirits more than dodging the officers. **1924** BECHDOLT *Tales* 345 A man . . . could hide out and hold up his herd. — **(2) 1898** HARRIS *Tales of Home Folks* 278 She compared it in her mind to the game of hide-the-switch which the children play. **1909** CALHOUN *Miss Minerva* 108 'Le's play "Hide the Switch," ' suggested Billy.

***Hieronymus,** *n.* (See quots.) *Obs.* or *hist.* — **1891** QUINN *Fools of Fortune* 273 Hieronymus . . . is, perhaps one of the most successful games of dice—considered from the standpoint of the . . . gambling fraternity. **1938** ASBURY *Sucker's Prog.* 350 (*footnote*), Hieronymus was a dice game somewhat similar to Chuck-a-Luck, played with three dice and two wooden bowls, the smaller ends of which were connected by a hollow tube. . . . The dice were . . . placed in the upper bowl and permitted to fall through the tube and fall upon a tambourine upon which the lower bowl had been inverted.

* **high,** *a.*, *n.*, and *adv.*

1. *n.* In meteorology, an area where the barometric pressure is high.

1878 *Pop. Sci. Mo.* July 310 These high and low areas, or 'highs' and 'lows' as they are technically known, travel. **1898** *Outlook* May 349 If the high be a decided one, it will cover a territory one or two thousand miles in width, the weather within its influence will be cold and clear, and the wind will have a general tendency spirally outward from the center. **1947** *N.Y. Times* 12 Oct. v. 11/5 Very little movement is indicated for the weak high over New England.

2. Used colloq. with a prefixed term as a shortening of **high school.**

1928 *Boston Ev. Transcript* 30 March 15/7 I'm hardly more than a schoolboy, not so very long out of Dorchester High. **1948** *Sat. Ev. Post* 23 Oct. 63/1 That Morris High should offer perhaps the first instance of re-zoning to avert Jim Crowism is singularly appropriate.

3. *Stock exchange.* The highest point or price reached by a stock or commodity.

1926 *Chi. Tribune* 23 Jan. II. 9/1 Wheeling and Lake Erie issues resumed their advance, the common toward a new high at 40⅝. **1948** *Green Bay* (Wis.) *Press-Gazette* 12 July 22/1 Nickel Plate Railroad hit a 1948 high at one time but this was later wiped out.

4. *a.* and *adv.* Situated upwards on a river, far up or near the source of a river. *Colloq.*

1815 *Niles' Reg.* IX. 29/1 It will probably be the last of August before M. G. Kennerly arrives with the Indian high upon the Missouri and Mississippi. **1816** U. BROWN *Journal* II. 358 Up said River 3 Miles to John Rush's where we put up & was kindly treated, he being the highest setler up that River.

5. (See quots.)

1850 *Rep. Comm. Patents 1849: Agric.* 322 Tobacco should not be too moist, or 'high' as it is termed, when put in the stalk-bulks. **1863** *Ill. Agric. Soc. Trans.* V. 669 Care must be taken that the tobacco does not imbibe too much moisture, or get too high in case before it is bulked.

6. In noun and adjectival combs.

a. In expressions denoting persons: (1) **high banker,** in lumberjack usage, a pretentious person, *slang;* (2) **brown,** a Negro of a very light complexion, cf. **high yellow;** (3) **collar crowd,** the well-to-do; (4) **Dutcher,** (see quot.), *obs.*, cf. **d.** (3) below; (5) **grass constable,** a rural law officer, *slang, rare;* (6) * **light,** a social or intellectual bigwig, *humorous;* (7) * **man,** a leading man, in allusion to such expressions as high hook, high line *qq.v.;* (8) **minded (Federalist),** (see quot. 1885); (9) * **priest,** an American Indian having a place of leadership in the religious life of his tribe, *rare;* (10) **private,** a term used facetiously for one who is merely a private; (11) **protectionist,** = **high tariffite;** (12) **roller,** one who makes a display of reckless spending and fast living, *slang;* (13) **-stand man,** a college student whose standing in his class is high, *obs.;* (14) **tariffite,** one who advocates a high tariff, *rare;* (15) **yellow,** a mulatto of a light yellow complexion, *colloq.*

(1) *a***1904** S. E. WHITE *Blazed Trail* i. 8 Come on Jimmy. Don't be a high-banker. **1908** ——— *Riverman* i. 10 Are you going to let that old high-banker walk all over you? — (2) **1927** SANDBURG *Songbag* 29 Then come all you rounders, an' all you high-browns too. — (3) **1931** *Blue Valley Farmer* (Okla. City) 31 Dec. 3/4 So far as the poor class of people are concerned . . . they are recognized as a bunch of 'wild jackasses' by the high collar crowd any way. — (4) **1823** COOPER *Pioneers* viii, The Germans, or 'High Dutchers,' as they were called, to distinguish them from the original or Low Dutch colonists, were a very peculiar people.

(5) **1908** K. McGAFFEY *Show-Girl* 188 I'll have you know that I am only nicked by the best cops on Broadway, and not by any high-grass constable. — (6) **1908** MARK TWAIN *Capt. Stormfield* 268 (R.), They ain't any fonder of kissing the emotional high-lights of Brooklyn than you be. — (7) **1910** *Springfield W. Republican* 1 Dec. 16 For a number of years Alderman Bowman has been either high man or near-high man in the returns of election day. — (8) **1824** in MACKENZIE *Van Buren* 169 It is not very serviceable to talk much of Burrites, Lewisites, or the High minded. **1885** *Mag. Amer. Hist.* Feb. 201/2 *High Minded Federalists.*—A derisive term applied in 1820 to a few Federalists who supported Gov. Clinton, and were laughed at for their frequent use of the phrase 'high-minded.' — (9) **1835** SIMMS *Yemassee* I. 211 At this moment, surrounded by the chiefs and preceded by the great prophet or high-priest, Enoree-Mattee, came Sanutee.

(10) **1863** *Harper's Mag.* May 860/1 One of the high privates . . . found himself . . . in a situation demanding a reconnaisance. **1869** BROWNE *Adv. Apache Country* 280 There was a California volunteer in our party, holding the position of high-private. — (11) **1913** EATON *Barn Doors & Byways* 151 The State of Rhode Island is famed throughout the nation for Newport, high protectionists, and grasshopper-fed turkeys. — (12) **1881** *Reinbeck* (Ia.) *Times* 15 Sep. 1/6 California's Speculators who invest large sums are called 'high rollers.' **1909** WASON *Happy Hawkins* 105 Miller, the youngest capitalist, . . . was a bit of a highroller. **1949** *10 Story Western* May 57/2 They were high rollers, playing for big stakes, and hang the poor devil who came out on the short end. — (13) **1871** BAGG *At Yale* 640 Next beside him, in class and examination sat a high-stand man. **1893** POST *Harvard Stories* 7 He was not a very high stand man. — (14) **1841** *Cong. Globe* App. Jan. 153/1 The high tariffite, and the anti-tariffite—the distributionist, and the anti-distributionist— . . . were united against the Democracy.

(15) **1929** *Variety* 17 April 51/3 She looks like a genuine high-yaller (that being her make-up in buxom mammy fashion). **1943** OTTLEY *New World* 177 There are a scattering of organizations whose memberships consist entirely of fair-skinned or mulatto types, and where the blackball is rigorously employed against any crasher whose coloring is deeper than high yaller.

For **highbinder, -brow, hook, line,** see as main entries. For **high grader** see **high grade,** and for **hightoner** see **high tone** as a main entry.

b. In the names of, or with reference to, plants, fruits, and birds: (1) **high bean,** a now unidentifiable variety of bean, *rare;* (2) **-belia,** the great lobelia, *Lobelia syphilitica,* found in the eastern states; (3) **blackberry,** an American variety, *Rubus villosus,* of the blackberry; (4) **bush,** see as a main entry; (5) **cranberry,** the cranberry tree, the fruit of this; (6) **ground willow oak,** (see quots.); (7) **holder,** = next; (8) **hole,** [rationalization of * *highwale,* * *hewhole,* cf. *EDD haihow, high hoe,* used of a green woodpecker], the flicker, *Colaptes auratus;* (9) **land,** see as a main entry; (10) **tops,** apples of a now unidentifiable variety, *obs.;* (11) **water shrub,** see **high water,** as a main entry

(1) **1784** SAMUEL DEANE *Diary* (1849) 356 We planted melons, cucumbers, corn, high beans and potatoes. — (2) **1847** DARLINGTON *Weeds & Useful Plants* 207 The crimson Cardinal-flower . . . is sometimes used by the 'Indian doctors' under the name of '*High-belia,*' probably to distinguish it from '*Low-belia.*' **1931** CLUTE *Plants* 47 It must have been a cousin at least of this individual who, hearing the Indian tobacco (*Lobelia inflata*) called lobelia, named a taller species high belia. — (3) **1814** BIGELOW *Florula Bostoniensis* 122 High blackberry . . . is a tall bramble that spreads rapidly by its roots, and is often troublesome in pastures and fields. **1896** WILKINS *Madelon* 336 The high blackberries grew in great thorny thickets.

(5) *c***1805** R. PUTNAM *Memoirs* 19 We had northing to eat Sence morning, but Beech buds and a few high Cramberries. **1847** DARLINGTON *Weeds & Plants* (1860) 163 *Viburnum Opulus.* . . . Bush, or High-cranberry. — (6) **1894** COULTER *Bot. W. Texas* III. 417 *Quercus cinerea.* . . . (High-ground willow-oak.) . . . Sandy barrens, extending from the Gulf States to the valley of the Brazos. **1897** SUDWORTH *Arborescent Flora* 176 *Quercus brevifolia.* . . . Blue Jack. . . . Common Names: . . . Sand Jack (Tex.). High-ground Willow Oak (S.C.). Turkey Oak (S.C., Ga.). — (7) **1857** *Rep. Comm. Patents 1856: Agric.* 145 The golden-winged wood-pecker, called *Pic-bois jaune* in Louisiana, 'Yellow Hammer,' in New England, and 'High Holder,' 'Yucker,' and 'Flicker' in other parts of the Union. **1917** *Birds of Amer.* II. 164/2 One observer . . . has given the bird [the flicker] the name of High-hole or High-holder. — (8) [**1793** CAMPBELL *Travels* 30 Also shot two other beautiful birds, called *Hei-ho,* whose plumage is beautifully variegated.] **1808** WILSON *Ornithology* I. 53 [The Gold-winged woodpecker] has numerous provincial appellations in the different states of the Union, such as 'High-hole,' from the situation of its nest. **1941** SETON *Trail of Artist-Naturalist* 77 He had a golden-winged woodpecker that he had shot—he called it a high-hole.

(10) **1836** COX *Baptists* 399 The passengers . . . gathered some beautiful yellow apples, called 'high tops.'

c. In phrases: (1) *To have on one's high-heeled shoes,* (see quot.), *obs.*, cf. **d.** (6); (2) *how's that for high?* (see quot. 1871); (3) *high, wide, and handsome,* in a most grandiloquent manner, *slang;* (4) *to hit* (or *touch*) *the high spots,* see **high spot,** as a main entry; (5) *to give the high sign,* (see quot. 1944), *slang;* (6) *to go up on high,* to drive an automobile up a steep hill or slope in high gear; (7) *to break for high timber,* see * **timber.**

(1) **1859** BARTLETT 195 To say of a woman that she 'has on her *high-heeled shoes*' is to intimate that she sets herself up as a person of more

consequence than others allow her to be; or in other words, **that** she is 'stuck up.' New England. — **(2) 1871** DE VERE 326 The phrase, 'How is that *for high?*' [is] borrowed from a low game, known as Old Sledge, where the *high* depends, not on the card itself, but on the adversary's hand. Hence the phrase means, What kind of an attempt is that at a great achievement? It is of Western origin, having made its appearance in some of the Northwestern journals, but has spread, as weeds do, rapidly, all over the Union. **1887** F. FRANCIS *Saddle & Moccasin* xviii. 315 'How's that for high, boys?' concluded the narrator. . . . 'That's on top,' declared Black Jack; 'that takes the cake.' — **(3) 1907** WHITE *Arizona Nights* 35 Tim could talk high, wide, and handsome when he set out to. **1949** *Agric. Hist.* Jan. 42/1 Tree farm certificates were sometimes 'handed out high, wide and handsome during the initial months.'

(5) 1915 *Everybody's Mag.* June 694/2 Butter-ball showed up on his usual schedule and handed Blossom the hungry man's high sign. **1944** *D.N.* Nov. 34 *high sign, to give the:* phr. To signal a message with gestures. N.C. and other Southern states. Common. **1948** *Trail Riders Bul.* Dec. 18/1 The date is July 15, 1949 and we are seated in our saddles waiting for the high sign from our president, Ralph J. Mather. — **(6)** [**1921** HALL *Yosemite Nat. Park* 308 You may hear a driver boast that he made such and such a grade on 'high,' but that is merely an admission of poor judgment.] **1931** *K.C. Star* 8 Aug., Now [all they talk about is] whether or not they were able to go up Pikes Peak on high.

d. In miscellaneous combs.: (1) **high art,** of designs, clothing, etc., especially artistic or attractive; (2) **daddy,** ?designating something grand or elegant, *slang, obs.;* (3) **Dutchers,** (see quot. 1871), *obs.*, cf. **a.** (4) above; (4) **hat,** a tall hat, *fig.* as predicate adj., snobbish, cf. **7.** (3) below; (5) **headed,** proud, obstinate, *colloq.;* (6) **heeled,** snobbish, uppish, *slang*, cf. **c.** (1) above; (7) ∗**life,** carbon disulphide, *colloq.;* (8) ∗**life(d),** *a.* full of life or spirit, *colloq.;* (9) **lonesome,** a drunken spree, also attrib. denoting something excessive, cf. **7.** (4) below; (10) **prairie,** level upland; (11) **stoop,** denoting a house having a stoop higher than usual; (12) **studded,** of a room, having studs longer than usual, and thus having a high ceiling.

(1) 1885 E. S. PHELPS *Fourteen to One* (1896) 161 In Mrs. Salt's parlor was a carpet of a high-art pattern under reduced conditions. **1887** N. PERRY *Flock of Girls* 121 Of course these 'high art dresses' will never be common. — **(2) 1898** F. H. SMITH *C. West* 21 Now don't try any of your high-daddy tricks on me. **1904** *N.Y. Tribune* 22 Oct. 1 The Democratic press is trying to get up a regular high-daddy time over it. — **(3) 1837** *Knickerb.* IX. 289 Give me a satisfactory pair of *high-dutchers*, . . . the Delaware or Fair-Mount dam for my theatre, and I can enact more wonders [etc.]. **1871** DE VERE 608 *High Dutchers*, a cant term for skates, the blade of which is curled up high in front. — **(4)** [**1899** A. H. QUINN *Pa. Stories* 39 Houston . . . was under strong suspicion of having worn a high hat out to college that morning.] **1924** P. MARKS *Plastic Age* 149 Christmas Cove's a nice place; not so high-hat as Bar Harbor. **1931** *K.C. Times* 4 Sep., Many a high hat covers a low-brow.

(5) 1837 *S. Lit. Messenger* III. 86 It may suit my neighbor . . . to have one of them high-headed Roanoke planters to come here. **1909** WASON *Happy Hawkins* 10 You always was the most obstinate, high-headed, bull-intellected thin-skin 'at ever drew down top wages fer punchin' cows. — **(6) 1903** FOX *Little Shepherd* xxiv, Bein' so high-heeled that you was willin' to let him mighty nigh bust his heart. **1912** RAINE *Brand Blotters* 190 You're mighty high-heeled to-day, 'pears like. — **(7) 1906** *D.N.* III. 140 high life, *n. phr.* Bi-sulphide of carbon. 'Give me a dime's worth of *high life*.' **1947** *Democrat* 14 Aug. 6/2 Fumigate corn with carbon bisulphide (high life) about two weeks after it is put into the crib. — **(8) 1861** *Ill. Agric. Soc. Trans.* IV. 376 A long narrow-headed, high-lifed, brainless animal should be quietly handled. **1902** McFAUL *Ike Glidden* 70 Ike told him to be sure and hold the reins tight . . . because the colt was a high-life fellow. **1913** LONDON *Valley of Moon* III. xxi, 'She's used to spurs,' Billy called after. 'Spanish broke, so don't check her quick. . . . She's high-life, you know. — **(9) 1924** J. M. FRANKS *Seventy Yrs. in Texas* 111 Old Dad and Jim Day got on a high lonesome and started to paint the town red. **1946** *Reader's Digest* Feb. 96/1 And they're stacking the scenery behind at a high-lonesome pace.

(10) 1814 BRACKENRIDGE *Views of La.* 222 It is a high prairie; smooth waving hills, perfectly green with a few clumps of trees in the hollows. **1894** ROBLEY *Bourbon Co., Kansas* 45 There is the usual amount of bottom land along these streams, . . . but these lands are not especially desirable over those of the high prairie for farming purposes. — **(11) 1883** *Harper's Mag.* Sep. 561/1 People talk as if . . . the brown-stone high-stoop house with its bloated detail . . . had been done by educated architects. **1902** WILSON *Spenders* 181 It is the brown-stone, high-stoop house, guarded by a cast-iron fence. — **1(2) 1787** CUTLER in *Life & Corr.* I. 269 It is a very large chamber and high studded. **1884** HOWELLS *Silas Lapham* iii, Certainly, have the parlours high studded.

e. In similar but usu. less frequent combs. of obvious meaning or sufficiently explained in the quots., as (1) **high box dip,** (2) ∗**C,** (3) **finance,** (4) **fresh,** (5) **jamboree,** (6) **license,** (7) **river,** (8) **table,** (9) **-ti,** (10) **ticket.**

(1) 1859 G. W. PERRY *Turpentine Farming* 148 Solid box turpentine is called high box dip, but how high the box must be to merit the appellation has not yet been explained. — **(2) 1908** MULFORD *Orphan* iv. 40 I've reached the high C of rollicking progress too many times to be airy scairt at rumours. — **(3) 1905** *McClure's Mag.* 48 In other words, we could eat our cake and have it, too—which is one secret of high finance. — **(4) 1829** HALL *Travels* III. 216 But the flood-tide from the Atlantic was an overmatch for the river, though swoln nearly to its utmost height, or what is called a 'high fresh,' by the heavy rains in the interior of Georgia.

(5) 1890 HARTE *Waif of Plains* 57 The dance of High Jambooree, [is] evidently of remote mystical African origin. — **(6) 1883** *Harper's Mag.* Aug. 480/1 The Illinois Legislature passed a high license bill, and the governor signed it. **1891** *Cyclo. Temperance* 207/2 *High License*, the name given to that policy of American liquor legislation whose distinctive feature is the requirement that individual liquor-sellers shall pay relatively large annual fees into the State, municipal or county treasuries. — **(7) 1883** MARK TWAIN *Life on Miss.* 423 (R.), In high-river stage, . . . the water is up to the top of the inclosing levee-rim. — **(8) 1941** *Harvard Univ. Reg.* 38 At stated intervals all the members of a House dine together in some formality (called variously 'high table' or 'long table') and have as their guests the Associates and distinguished men from fields outside the University. — **(9) 1856** HALL *College Words* (ed. 2) 254 High-ti. At Williams College, a term by which is designated a showy recitation. Equivalent to the word *squirt* at Harvard College.

(10) 1850 in *Calif. Hist. Soc. Quart* VIII. 25, I see a painter [at Eliza City] lettering a sign, and for large ornamental letters he charges 6 dols per & common block 2 dollars each letter this I guess is a high ticket.

For ∗**highball, -falutin, five, grade, hook, line, post bedstead, pressure,** ∗**school, Sierra, time, tone, toned,** ∗**water,** see as main entries.

7. In slang verbal combs.: (1) **highball,** see as a main entry; (2) **grade,** *W. mining*, to steal valuable ore, also **high grading,** cf. **high grade** (as a main entry) **3;** (3) **hat,** to treat snobbishly, hence **high-hatting,** cf. **high hat** in **6. d.** above; (4) **lone,** to go alone without any incumbrance, *rare*, cf. **high lonesome** in **6. d.** and for ∗*highlone* as an adv. see *OED;* (5) **power,** to compel, force; (6) **pressure,** =prec.; (7) **tail,** to run at full speed, in allusion to the position of the tails of alarmed and running cattle, orig. western.

(2) 1904 *Alliance News* (S.F.) Oct. 8/3 Many miners . . . make snug little fortunes, and then, as a rule, they 'blow them in,' and continue to work and to 'high grade.' **1936** McKENNA *Black Range* 279 Oh, what high-grading, especially when we struck rich ore. Many a time the miners were forced to strip in a bath house to be gone over by searchers, who even combed the hair of their head looking for bits of ore. **1942** LILLARD *Desert Challenge* 278 A man who refused to high-grade was likely to lose his job on demand of the union. **1949** *L.A. Times* 23 May III. 16/3 High-grading then was so prevalent that a number of companies employed armed guards for protection of rich workings. — **(3) 1926** *Collier's* 8 May 32/4 Where do they get off to high-hat *you?* **1947** *Chi. Tribune* 16 Nov. (Comics) 5, I haven't noticed him doing any high-hatting. — **(4) 1760** WASHINGTON *Writings* (1889) II. 155 Mulatto Jack return'd home with the Mares he was sent for; but so poor were they, and so much abus'd had they been by my rascally overseer, Hardwick, that they were scarce able to highlone, much less to assist in the business of the plantations.

(5) 1931 *Blue Valley Farmer* (Okla. City) 24 Dec. 6/6 He tried to high-power his customers to save his job. — **(6) 1947** *Chi. Tribune* 22 June I. 12/2 The state introduced into evidence a letter written by Dr. Lewis, declaring the trustees had been 'high pressured' into voting against the condemnation proposal four days before. — **(7) 1927** JAMES *Cow Country* 239 Often they'd scatter like a bunch of antelope, at the sight of the rider, and hightail it any direction excepting the right one. **1948** *Reader's Digest* Dec. 154/2 Folks pouring out of every door; colt high-tailing through the pastures.

Highatans ˈhaɪətn̩z, *n. pl.* [See Hodge *s.v.* Ietan.] Any one of various western tribes of Indians, esp. the Utes. *Rare.* — **1821** J. FOWLER *Journal* 53 The Highatans amounting to about 350 lodges arived this day and camped with the others. *Ib.* 54 We soon understood that the hole nation ware at hand and that we head nothing to dred from the Highatans.

∗ **highball,** *n.* Also **high ball.**

1. A game of chance. *Obs.*

1881 C. M. CHASE *Editor's Run in N. Mex.* 134 Mexican monte, keno, faro, high ball, etc., are the prevailing games [in Socorro], and everybody indulges.

2. *Baseball.* (See quot. 1885.) Also **high ball hitter.**

1885 CHADWICK *Art of Pitching* 59 A High Ball is a ball legally delivered by the Pitcher, over the Home Base, higher than the belt of the Batsman, but not higher than his shoulder. **1912** MATHEWSON *Pitching* 221 Now, this guy is a high ball hitter.

3. A signal given a railway engineer to proceed.

No doubt the expression in this sense arose from the use on railroads of a semaphore signal of which a large ball formed a part. When the ball was high it was a signal to the engineer to go ahead. See quots. 1947 (in **b.**) and 1948 below.

Highball as used in railroading

1897 *Chi. Record* 1 Mar. 6/1 'Milk trains' . . . have 'rights' over the rails and get nothing but 'high balls.' **1938** in *Amer. Sp.* XIX. 34 We are informed that the signal the conductor waves to the engineer to go ahead is still known as the 'high-ball' on most lines. **1948** *Chi. Tribune* 8 Aug. 4/6 The term 'highball' also was introduced into America by railroaders, who used a ball about 2 feet in diameter to signal an engineer whether to stop at small stations.

transf. and *attrib.* **1920** HUNTER *Trail Drivers Texas* I. 68 We had a high ball trail from there on. *Ib.* 354 Mr. Butter and I told them [cowboys] . . . to strike a high ball to town.

b. In full **highball signal.**

1909 *Sat. Ev. Post* 26 June 9/1, I gave 'em the highball signal to go ahead. **1947** BEEBE *Mixed Train Dly.* 111 It is the last remaining region of the original highball signal, and the crossovers . . . are guarded by manually operated cross arms with halyards for raising metal globes as old in design as the mysteries of railroading itself.

4. An iced, spirituous drink, usu. served in a tall glass.

This use has been suspected of deriving from sense **3.** above, but conclusive evidence is lacking.

1898 *N.Y. Journal* 16 Sep. 4/2 Evening dress and khaki talked much sport and a little war over 'high balls' or chicken livers. **1949** *Lubbock* (Tex.) *Morn. Avalanche* 23 Feb. I. 7/7 He downed 'four or five highballs' and then went on the rampage.

b. highball glass, a glass for use in serving highballs.

1932 *K.C. Star* 16 Feb. 22 She added to her education by learning all about cocktail and highball glasses. **1944** *Sears Cat.* (ed. 189) 605 Heavy bottom, crystal highball glasses with frosted panel for writing name . . . 9-ounce capacity.

highball ˈhaɪˌbɔl, *v.*

1. a. *absol.* To give a locomotive engineer a signal to proceed. **b.** *tr.* To drive a locomotive rapidly on its way. *Slang.*

(**a**) **1934** LOMAX *Amer. Ballads* 24 The con high-balled, and the manifest freight, Pulled out on the stem behind the mail.—(**b**) **1945** *This Week Mag.* 14 July 19/2 He highballed the big locomotive down the tracks.

2. *intr.* To leave at top speed. Also transf.

1941 *Pop. Sci. Mo.* May 76 Its smooth power . . . is fully available, whether the giant is pulling away from a dead stop or highballing along at its maximum governed speed. **1946** *Sat. Ev. Post* 11 May 27/3 Everyone else had highballed . . . out of there. **1948** *Time* 9 Aug. 68/2 With Westinghouse at the throttle, it looked as if Baldwin was ready to highball.

highbinder ˈhaɪˌbaɪndɚ, *n.* [Origin obscure.]

1. A ruffian or rowdy. Orig. a member of one of various street gangs in New York City, but later applied more generally, often merely as a term of opprobrium. *Slang.* Cf. **Tammany highbinder.**

1806 *N.Y. Ev. Post* 26 Dec. 2 There has for some time existed in this city, and in and about George and Charlotte Streets, a desperate association of lawless and unprincipled vagabonds, calling themselves 'Highbinders.' **1835** *Knickerb.* July 65 He was one of our distinguished 'high-binders,' and deserved promotion, and a good office. **1919** WILSON *Ma Pettingill* 9 All the trout in the pool are knocked out and float on the surface, where this old highbinder gathers 'em in. **1948** *Popular Western* June 41/2 Yuh figger the ol' highbinder aims to feed us on—on mice?

2. A member of a band of Chinese criminals or terrorists located chiefly in California. Also attrib. Cf. **hatchetman.**

1879 *Cong. Rec.* App. 14 Feb. 92/2 It is shown by the testimony that coolies attempting to evade their debt contracts are subjected to violence by a special class of Chinese known as 'High-binders.' **1894** *S.F. Chron.* 14 Nov., The fear of a high-binder outbreak in Chinatown grows as the activity of the dreaded hatchetmen is observed. **1940** RIESENBERG *Golden Gate* 165 Their membership then included the feared highbinders, or hatchetmen, as they were better known, who stalked the streets and alleys of Chinatown, bringing swift punishment to any who opposed their tong.

highboy ˈhaɪˌbɔɪ, *n.* [Var. of ∗*tallboy.* Cf. **lowboy.**] A tall chest of drawers mounted on a base having legs from about eighteen inches to two feet high. Also attrib. and transf.

1891 *Scribner's Mag.* Sep. 353/2 These Lafayette plates had always been kept in the top drawer of a high chest of drawers, a 'high boy,' wrapped in a hand-woven 'flannel sheet.' **1906** *Harper's Mag.* Oct. 707 She brought out a fine white napkin from the highboy. **1947** *Newsweek* 6 Oct. 17/3 You know, we have a 'highboy' government in Washington—one bureau on top of another.

∗ **highbrow,** *n.* and *a.* A derisive term for a person who manifests an air of intellectual superiority. Cf. next and see ∗ **lowbrow.**

1908 *Sat. Ev. Post* 29 Aug. 27/1 It takes all sorts of men to make a party, and Mr. Hearst apparently led in a few prize-fighters with the other high-brows and reformers he accumulated. **1926** *Ladies' Home Jrnl.* July 27 No selected group of highbrows can inflict a classic on mankind. **1949** *Life* 11 April 99/1 We have a society of the intellectual elite, run by the high-brows.

b. *a.* Suitable for those of superior intellectual attainments. *Colloq.* Cf. next.

1920 LEWIS *Main Street* 86 The Jolly Seventeen as a separate entity guffawed at the Thanatopsis, and considered it middle-class and even 'highbrow.' **1947** *Denver Post* 20 Feb. 6/5 Nearly all agreed the program was too highbrow.

∗ **high-browed,** *a.* Intellectually superior, pretentious. *Colloq.* — **1908** R. W. CHAMBERS *Firing Line* ix, You were very much amused, I suppose—to see me sitting bras-dessus-bras-dessous with the high-browed and precious. **1948** *Time* 26 April 81/1 Some of America's highest browed literary critics had gathered to discuss just what a critic's job is.

∗ **high-bush,** *n. attrib.* Designating high or bushlike varieties of various plants or shrubs, or the fruit of these, as (1) **high-bush blackberry,** (2) **blueberry,** (3) **cranberry,** (4) **huckleberry,** (5) **laurel.**

(1) **1867** HOLMES *Guardian Angel* 230 High-bush blackberries and low-bush blackberries,—you understand,—just so everywhere,—high-bush here and there, low-bush plenty. **1947** *U.S. Dispensatory* 972/1 *Rubus argutus* Link, or high-bush blackberry, is an erect shrub growing wild from New England to Florida and Arkansas. — (2) **1913** EATON *Barn Doors & Byways* 179 There used to be a swamp into which we youngsters penetrated for a mile or so, finding high-bush blueberries, hornpout pools and wet feet. **1945** PEARSON *Country Flavor* 31 There is an area of high-bush blueberries, which mean juicy pies in late July. — (3) **1805** CLARK in *Lewis & C. Exped.* III. (1905) 169 They gave us High bush cramburies. **1949** *Mo. Bot. Garden Bul.* April 92 Some desirable shrubs which need very little care are Mento barberry . . . , highbush cranberry [etc.]. — (4) **1889** *Cent.* 2909/1 The common high-bush huckleberry or black huckleberry of the markets. **1938** MATSCHAT *Suwannee River* 33 Around the swollen bases of the trees grow high-bush huckleberries. — (5) **1860** CURTIS *Woody Plants N.C.* 65 Yellow Wood. (*Symplocos tinctoria.*)—Also called *Sweet Leaf* and *High Bush Laurel.*

∗ **higher,** *a.*

1. higher law, a divine or moral law; the dictates of conscience regarded as superior to man-made legislation.

W. H. Seward's use of the term (see quot. 1850) with reference to the compromise of 1850 and in allusion to slavery caused the expression to have considerable vogue.

1844 in *N. Eng. Quart.* II. (1929) 240 It is a violation of the higher law, printed by the finger of God on the heart of man, and our own consciences repeal and annul it. **1850** SEWARD *Memoir* (1891) II. 216 The Constitution devotes the domain to union, to justice, to defense, to welfare, and to liberty. But there is a higher law than the Constitution. **1886** POORE *Reminiscences* II. 29 He stood like a sturdy sentinel . . . pleading the 'higher law' in justification.

attrib. **1854** *Maysville* (Ky.) *Eagle* 4 Nov. 2/1 The 'higher law' doctrine . . . is neither more nor less than High Treason in the garb of Religion. **1860** *State Gaz.* (Austin, Tex.) 22 Sep., Committees should be set up throughout the State and prepare lists of 'Black Republicans, abolitionists, or higher-law' men of every class, and make accurate lists in every county. **1948** *Ohio State Arch. & Hist. Quart.* Jan. 45 The Mason committee . . . withdrew its charge, retaining in its report only the ideological attack that Giddings' 'higher law' doctrines had encouraged Brown to commit his deed.

transf. **1860** *Charleston* (S.C.) *Mercury* 15 Dec. 1/6 At the bidding of pelf—New England's 'Higher Law'—it would be as quickly broken as that on the fragments of which they are now trampling.

Hence **Higher Lawite,** *obs.*

1857 *Phoenix* (Sacramento) 13 Sep. 2/1 Black Republicans, and 'Higher Lawites' can do much, however, in their own families and circles.

2. higher money, money lent at a rate of interest higher than usual. *Rare.*

1899 *Dly. News* 31 March 3/5 New York . . . Higher money.

3. higher-up, one occupying a superior position. *Colloq.*

1916 C. SANDBURG *Chi. Poems* 61 Higher-ups among the con men of Jerusalem. **1949** *N.O. Times-Picayune Mag.* 3 July 13/2 Other 'higher-ups' in the Murrel clan were members of a grand council.

highfalute ˌhaɪfəˈlut, *v.* Also **highfalutin.** [App. f. **highfalutin,** *a., q.v.*] *tr.* and *intr.* To indulge in high-flown, bombastic oratory; to praise immoderately. *Slang. Obs.* — **1846** *Dollar Newspaper* (Phila.) 15 July 4/5 *Ef* my opponent has any idee of gittin a single vote down in the Bottom, . . . I'd advise him not to go down in the Bottom hifilutin on the Vic side. **1852** *So. Illinoisian* (Shawneetown) 29 Oct. 2/4 Did you not hurrah at his nomination, and have you not *highfaluted* him ever since.

highfalutin ˌhaɪfəˈlutn̩, *a., n.,* and *adv.* [Origin obscure.]

1. *n.* Discourse or phrases of a bombastic or high-flown sort. *Slang.*

1848 in BARTLETT (1859) 195 A good-looking, fat, rosy-looking man . . . ground out . . . a regular built fourth-of July . . . speech, making gestures to suit the highfalutens. **1858** *S.F. Bulletin* 28 Dec. 3/2 Judge Freelon appeared on the part of the defence, and wasted a great deal of hyfalutin on Grecian mythology. **1903** *Atlantic Mo.* Sep. 419 A high-erected vein which not seldom reaches to tall talk and high-falutin. [**1949** *N.Y. Times Book Review* 13 March 1/1 In an onlooker it would have been high fallutin'.]

2. *a.* and *adv.* Bombastic, highflown, in a pompous or pretentious manner. *Slang.*

1839 *Spirit of Times* 18 May 123/3 (We.), Them high-faluting chaps. **1889** HARTE *Heritage of Dedlow Marsh* 244 He talked high-faluten' o' the inflooence of the press and sech. **1948** *Popular Western* June 23/2 Such high-falutin' horseplay was enough to make a man's gorge rise.

high five. (See quot. 1938.)

1893 *Outing* Sep. 426/1 The gentlemen betook themselves to a shady spot on the beach to play 'High Five' or some such wicked game. **1931** *K.C. Times* 13 Dec. 20 Don't let the present bridge craze worry you. It isn't half the vogue that 'high five' was forty years ago. **1938** ASBURY *Sucker's Prog.* 323 At first the Nevadans used the room principally as a place in which to play Cinch, a variation of All-Fours which was also known as Double Pedro or High Five, but after a few years it was devoted almost entirely to Poker.

high grade.

1. In stock-breeding, an animal that approximates the breed of its purebred parent.

1882 *Rep. Maine Bd. Agric.* XXVI. 253 High-grades of either breed [Jersey or Guernsey] are undoubtedly as good for all practical purposes.

2. *attrib. W.* Designating ore or an ore vein that is especially rich.

1878 HINTON *Arizona* 161 The Metallic Accident is a large lode of low-grade ore, with a number of high-grade feeders. **1943** *Copper Camp* 42 High grade ore from Amalgamated mines, nonchalantly purloined from under their very noses, was hoisted through Heinze's mine shafts and smelted in his Meaderville smelter.

3. *W.* An ore thief. Also **high grader.** *Slang.*

1904 *N.Y. Sun* 14 Aug. 11 One of the pests of gold mining in Colorado is the high-grades, which is a polite term for the ore thief. The term high grades comes from the fact that they steal only high grade ore. **1904** *Alliance News* (S.F.) Oct. 8/3 Throughout this camp are men known to rumor as 'high graders,' in other words ore stealers. **1948** *Sat. Ev. Post* 13 Nov. 38/1 He is plagued by high-graders—men who enter other people's mines and help themselves.

high hook. (See quot. 1848.)

1848 *R.I. Words* (Bartlett MS), *High Hook,* the one who catches the largest or the greatest quantity of fish. **1899** VAN DYKE *Fisherman's Luck* 109 When we met to . . . compare notes . . . and make up the fish stories for the year, Beekman was almost always 'high hook.' **1939** CHAMBERLAIN *Nantucket* 11 Mr. James Wood . . . is the oldest man on the island, . . . and 'high hook' of Nantucket, a distinction coming from his feat of making the largest single catch of codfish on local record.

transf. **1848** in CUTLER *Greyhounds* (1930) 134 The schooner Velasco, another first rate vessel, will sail soon with a joint stock company of the 'right sort,' from Groton, who will come home, 'high hook' in the gold line.

* **highland,** *n.* and *a.*

1. Highland Indians, the Wappinger Indians of New York State. *Obs.*

[**1655** P. STUYVESANT in *Doc. Col. Hist. N.Y.* XIII. (1881) 52 What is to be done . . . about the captives, still in the hands of the *Wiequaskeck* and *Highland* Indians.] **1669** in *Doc. Col. Hist. N.Y.* XIII. (1881) 440, I believe I can resolve your doubt concerning what is meant by ye *Highland* Indians amongst us, ye *Wappingoes & Wickersheck* &c. have alwayes beene reckoned so. **1906** RUTTENBER *Indian Names* 39 'Highland Indians' was a designation employed by the Dutch as well as by the English.

2. highland moccasin, =**copperhead 1.** Cf. **upland moccasin.**

1842 HOLBROOK *N. Amer. Herpetol.* III. 45 The *Trigonocephalus altro-fuscus* . . . [is] called in Tennessee Highland Mocassin. **1928** BRADFORD *Ol' Man Adam* 6 Eve see a great big highland moccasin crawlin' long twarg her.

3. highland pond, (see quot. 1728). *Obs.*

1728 in *Amer. Sp.* XV. 273/1 All our Woodsmen call these flat Grounds High-Land-Ponds, and in their Trading Journeys are glad to halt at such Places for Several days together, to recruit their Jaded Horses, expecially in the Winter Months, when there is little or no Grass to be found in other Places. **1759** *Ib.*, Along the said Dowells line to a high land pond.

4. In the obs. or occasional names of plants, as **highland beauty, cotton, dogwood, meadow oat, willow oak.**

1754 CATESBY *Nat. Hist. Carolina* I. 22 *Quercus humilior Salicis folio breviori.* The Highland Willow Oak. This is usually a small Tree, having a dark coloured bark with Leaves of a pale green, shaped like those of a Wild oak. It grows on dry poor land, producing but few acorns, and those small. **1802** DRAYTON *S. Carolina* 62 Highland dogwood. (*Cornus Florida.*) . . . It is a strong tough wood, used some times for cogs in machinery. **1820** *Western Carolinian* 24 Oct., For ten years past I have been trying a grass called here the 'highland meadow oat, . . . the Egyptian oat, . . . and the Peruvian grass.' **1831** AUDUBON *Ornith. Biog.* I. 359 *Highland Cotton* is distinguished by its five-lobed leaves and herbaceous stem. **1883** *Harper's Mag.* Dec. 56/1 Our seedling apple, the Highland Beauty.

Highley's copper. A copper threepence formerly minted by John Highley of Granby, Conn. *Obs.* — **1858** J. H. HICKCOX *Amer. Coinage* 74 At Granby, Conn., about the year 1737, coppers circulated, called Highley's coppers.

high line.

1. The member of a fishing party who catches the most fish, or the fishing vessel that brings in the heaviest fare of the season. Also transf. and attrib.

1864 *Harper's Mag.* Feb. 367/2 Captain Aleck was determined to fish for 'high line' out of Chatham. **1885** J. S. KINGSLEY *Stand. Nat. Hist.* III. 196 The emulation to be 'high-line' for the day and for the season is extreme. *Ib.*, In a single day a high-line fisherman has caught from ten to fifteen barrels [of mackerel]. **1913** LONDON *Valley of Moon* II. xv, She was among the high-line weavers when the jute mills closed down.

Hence **high-liner,** *n.*

1914 STEELE *Storm* 56 On the grounds he was a great 'killer,' an unmerciful 'driver,' and for three years running now the 'high liner' of the Old Harbor fleet. **1947** *Chi. Tribune* 2 Nov. (Comics) 10 Such luck, on the heels of these record hauls was maddening! We'd have been the 'high liners' of the fleet!

2. A road over an elevated region or divide; the highest part of a mountain range.

1880 *Harper's Mag.* March 556/2 These Colorado builders . . . propose carrying the Colorado Central . . . over the 'high line' by which we came. **1883** RITCH *Illust. N. Mex.* 61 There are now eight [dailies], some of which in quality are equal to the best upon the high line of the continent.

high-muck-a-muck ˈhaɪˈmʌkəˌmʌk, *n.* [See note.]

Chas. J. Lovell in *Amer. Sp.*, April 1947, pp. 91 ff. has traced this term to its source in the Chinook Jargon. He has shown: the prevalence of the two elements in the word, *hiu*, plenty, a lot, and *muckamuck*, food, to eat, drink; their combination into the phrase *hiu muckamuck*, plenty to eat; and, finally, the emergence of the term in its sense of a "big bug," a person of importance. The earliest examples below, and the order of their arrangement, are derived from Lovell's article. Cf. **hyas kloosh.**

1. Plenty to eat.

The first two groups of quots. are included to indicate the prevalence of the two elements of which the term is composed. See note above.

(1) **1847** PALMER *Jrnl. of Travels* 147 High-You, Quantity; many. **1868** WHYMPER *Alaska* 21 The Chinook jargon . . . has no equivalent for 'glacier.' It could only be expressed by *hyu ice, hyu snow,*—plenty of ice and snow. **1939** COLBY *Guide to Alaska* xl, Some of the Chinook expressions still used in everyday speech . . . are given below: . . . *hiyu n.* (C.) plenty.

(2) **1838** PARKER *Jrnl. Exploring Tour* 338 Eat, mucamuc. **1847** —— *Jrnl. of Travels* 150 Muck-a-muck, Provisions, eat. **1853** T. WINTHROP *Letters* 13 June, We stopped once or twice for them to 'muck-a-muck,' which they are ready for forty times a day. **1889** EELLS *Hymns in Chinook Jargon Language* 8 Spose nesika muckamuck whiskey, Whiskey muckamuck nesika dolla. If we drink whiskey, Whiskey will eat up our money.

(3) **1853** *Oregonian* (Portland) 20 Aug. 2/6 (*advt.*), Thomas Pritchard, General Store: *Hiou Muckamuck* of all kinds, but *Halo Lum* [no rum]. **1872** LANGEVIN *British Columbia* 163 Hyui muckamuck, plenty to eat. **1946** R. PEATTIE *Pac. Coast Rangers* 235 *Hiu muckamuck* (lots of food) meant steady [logging] crews.

2. A "big bug," a pompous person, a person of importance. *Slang.*

1856 *Dem. State Jrnl.* (Sacramento) 1 Nov. 3/1 The professors—the high 'Muck-a-Mucks'—tried fusion, and produced confusion. **1880** NYE *B. Nye & Boomerang* 241 By the Great High-Muck-a-Muck of the Ute nation . . . I dassent tell a lie! **1947** *Chi. Tribune* 21 Dec. (Comics) 8 They's a highmuckymuck in th' radio business vacationin' here, so we gotta be good.

high-post bedstead. A bedstead with high corner posts, usu. supporting curtains.

1824 *Boston Indep. Chron.* 9 Oct. 3/2 High-post, field and French Bedsteads, of every description. **1835** INGRAHAM *South-West* II. 242 Why are you at the trouble and expense of having high-post bedsteads for your negroes? **1920** HOWELLS *Vacation of Kelwyns* 26 They had given them the rag carpets and the hooked rugs, the high-post bedsteads and splint chairs.

high pressure.

1. *attrib.* (See quot. 1875.)

1830 *Palladium* (Toronto) 29 Aug. 244/1 The man stirred up his team, and was soon under way, at a rate which would leave a common high pressure steamboat out of sight in no time. **1838** FLAGG *Far West* I. 13 The landing at the time was thronged with steamers, and yet the incessant 'boom, boom, boom,' of the high-pressure engines . . . gave notice of a constant augmentation to the number. **1875** KNIGHT 1102/1 High-pressure Engine. (Steam.) A steam-engine, condensing or non-condensing, in which the safety-valve is loaded with a weight equivalent to a boiler-pressure of, say, fifty pounds to the square inch. **1941** DORSEY *Master of Miss.* 72 Nathan Read, of Massachusetts, built a boat model with paddle-wheels driven by a high-pressure engine.

2. *transf.* Designating anything of an exceptionally urgent, intense, forceful sort. *Colloq.*

*c***1845** *Big Bear Ark.* 20 The fellow, I reckon, was made on the high-pressure system, and the lead sort of bust his biler. **1867** *N.Y. World* 26 Sep. 1/1 The Convention is to be ran in the high pressure Radical character—little or no show for anything or anybody that does not go the 'whole hog,' negro suffrage, heavy taxation, and all. **1947** *Hygeia* Nov. 856/1 With today's high pressure selling campaigns women and men are besieged from all sides to buy some special cosmetic preparation advertised with claims that promise almost everything except rejuvenation.

* **high school.** A school for pupils beyond the elementary stage; now one with a four-year curriculum to which students are admitted upon completion of six or eight elementary grades. Also attrib.

1824 *Boston School Comm. Minutes* 23 June, Voted, That the schoolhouse which the city is now building on Pickney Street be appropriated to the use and accommodation of the English High School. **1838** *Speeches of D. Barnard* 127 To unite to form a high-school district and establish a district high-school. **1855** BAXTER *America* 159 Those who make a creditable appearance during their curriculum, are advanced, if they choose, to the 'high' school, where they are taught all those branches which fit a young man for college. **1949** *Sat. Ev. Post* 9 April 80/4 Marian loved grade-school and high-school theatricals.

As the last term in **community, junior, senior, town high school.**

High Sierra. The main range of the Sierra Nevada mountains in California.

1869 MUIR *First Summer in Sierra* (1911) 100 The clouds of noon on the high Sierra seem yet more marvelously, indescribably beautiful from day to day as one becomes more wakeful to see them. **1890** *Silverton* (Colo.) *Miner* 1 Mar. 2/3 In the high Sierra . . . snow-shoe riding has been carried to a science. **1949** *Pacific Discovery* May–June 3/1 The High Sierra, like most of the rest of the world, is just getting too populous.

attrib. **1945** CLARKE *Pac. Crest Trailway* 47 The upper Merced River Basin with Mt. Lyell (13,090) group is splendid High Sierra country, offering interesting climbs and hard mountaineering under primitive conditions. **1949** *Sierra Club Bul.* Mar. 5/2 This conference is intended to include those whose interest in the High Sierra Wilderness is commercial . . . or recreational.

high spot.

1. An outstanding or prominent part or feature.

1928 *Wis. Alumni Mag.* Dec. 85 The high spot of the season was unquestionably the Iowa game. **1947** *West. Pa. Hist. Mag.* March–June 9 A high spot of his first professional season . . . was his famous eighth-inning home run on May 2, 1878, which defeated pitcher Tommy Bond and the Boston Nationals, 1 to 0.

2. *To hit* (or *touch*) *the high spots,* to go with great speed; to mention briefly. Also transf. *Colloq.*

1910 W. M. RAINE *B. O'Connor* 12 Here come your train a-foggin'—also and likewise hittin' the high spots. **1921** *Outing* Sep. 244/2 Two wiry, middle-aged Canadian alpine members . . . had come West for the sole intention of donning hobnail boots and hitting the high spots. **1948** *Pacific Discovery* May–June 31/2 The author handles the problem by concentrating intimately on the Cascades, where he is thoroughly at home, and only touching the high spots in the other mountains.

* **high time.**

1. A time of great hilarity or enjoyment. Also *pl.*

1833 C. A. DAVIS *Lett. J. Downing* (1834) 177 Just ater breakfast yesterday, I and the general had a high time [i.e., a heated argument] together. **1889** MARK TWAIN *Conn. Yankee* 338 (R.), High Times in the Valley of Holiness!

2. high old time(s), =prec.

1858 *Spirit of Times* 30 Jan. 345/1 Our friends in Northern New York, the Canadas, several New England and North-western States, are having a real 'high old time' generally, just now, in trotting on the ice. **1869** B. HARTE *Luck of Roaring Camp* (1871) 226 These are high old times, ain't they? **1941** SKINNER *Soap Behind Ears* 153 Nimrods who are out quaking happily away in gale-swept blinds and little boats that leak ice-water are having a high old time.

high tone. 1. *pl.* (See quot. and cf. * **chivalry.**) *Obs.* **2.** A lofty tone or manner, good form. Also attrib. and as adj.

(1) **1865** *Nat. Anti-Slavery Standard* (N.Y.) 23 Sep. 1/5 The 'high-tones,' as the Western soldiers call the 'chivalry,' make many asseverations of . . . loyalty. — (2) **1889** *Cent. Mag.* March 775/2 She took a high tone from the beginning. **1897** BRODHEAD *Bound in Shallows* 105 They was high-tone lookin' fellers, and I'd like 'em to brag up the house. **1898** *Christian Herald* 19 Jan. 44/4 The infernal delusion that it was not high-tone for women to learn a profitable calling.

Hence **hightoner.**

1876 BORNEMANN *Madame Jane Junk* 66 (*title*), Meeting with Hightoners.

* **high-toned,** *a.*

1. Of people: Of lofty character, superior. Often somewhat contemptuous.

1807 in *West. Pa. Hist. Mag.* (1947) March–June 56 The same editor also states that there were 'no Demo-Republicans in it, all high-toned gentlemen.' **1853** *S.F. Alta California* 18 May 2/2 Their deportment gave an unexceptional evidence of the high toned gentleman and thoroughly drilled soldier. **1947** *Sat. Review* 30 Aug. 5/1 My quarrel with publishers is that they are, if anything, too high-toned.

Also absol.

1866 *Washoe* (Nev.) *Eastern Slope* 11 Aug. 2/2 It is [necessary] when the high toned meet . . . for the purpose of cutting off debate, that they should be ready to raise the previous question at any moment.

b. Esp. of Southerners. *Obs.* Cf. **high tone 1.**

1862 *War Songs for Freemen* 37 A ripping, tearing gentleman of an uncommon kind. . . . A 'high-toned Southern gentleman,' one of the present time. **1865** BROWNE *Four Years in Secessia* 246 The provost pretended, as all the Southerners who have the least education do, to be a high-toned gentleman.

2. Excellent, of superior quality, pretentious.

1829 *Va. Herald* (Fredericksburg) 28 Mar. 2/3 He might be President if he liked; but this high-toned eulogy, he thought highly objectionable. **1875** *S.F. Ledger* 25 Aug. 1/4 He purchased 30 gallons of this high toned whisky and returned to his club rejoicing. **1946** *Chi. Sun* 29 Nov. 1/7 We don't think there is any place in Arizona for high-toned fox hunting.

* **high water.**

1. *attrib.* **a.** (See quot.) *Obs.* **b.** Designating shortened or rolled up pants.

(a) **1856** MARK TWAIN *Adv. T. J. Snodgrass* (1928) 9 (R.), Then some soldiers with bobtailed tin coats on—high water coats we used to call 'em in Keokuk—come in, then some gals, with high water dresses on. — (b) **1902** LORIMER *Lett. Merchant* 7 High-water-pants boys who take their college education and make some fellow's business hum with it. **1902** *Sears Cat.* (ed. 112) 357/3 The High Water Pants Cuffs . . . are made of good, substantial cloth, with elastic insertion. . . . By their use a pair of ordinary trousers are quickly transformed into bicycle, golf or riding breeches. **1946** T. JONES *Skinny Angel* 279 When she spoke of it, he quickly rolled them down again, smiling, but the next time she saw him it would be high-water pants again.

2. high-water shrub, any one of various salt-marsh shrubs of the genus *Iva.*

1814 BIGELOW *Florula Bostoniensis* 204 *Iva frutescens.* High water shrub. . . . A fleshy shrub, about the borders of salt marshes. **1892** COULTER *Bot. W. Texas* II. 208 Marsh elder. High water-shrub. . . . Shrubby coarse plants, with thickish leaves.

* **highway,** *n.* In combs.: (1) **highway commission,** a public commission having charge of the location, construction, maintenance, etc., of highways; (2) **commissioner,** one who serves on a highway commission; (3) **district,** in some states, a unit or district for administering the road system in a state; (4) **fund,** (see quot.); (5) **patrol,** a police organization for patrolling the highways to see that traffic laws are observed and enforced, also **highway patrolman,** a member of such a force.

(1) **1895** *Dept. Agric. Yrbk. 1894* 507 Said highway commission shall consider such petition and determine what the public necessity and convenience require in the premises. **1949** *Ill. State Reg.* (Springfield) 1 Feb. 4/2 The highway commission members have not agreed on many matters. — (2) **1869** *Mich. Agric. Rep.* VII. 458 An Act Authorizing the Locating, Establishing, and Constructing of Ditches, Drains, and Water-courses by Highway Commissioners of Townships. **1914** *Cyclo. Amer. Govt.* II. 123/1 The state highway commissioner is a necessary part of the good roads movement. — (3) **1850** *Mich. Gen. Statutes* I. (1882) 59 There shall be elected annually, . . . one overseer of highways for each highway district. — (4) **1879** *Mich. Gen. Statutes* I. (1882) 739 Such moneys shall constitute a 'general highway fund,' and shall be expended exclusively for working and improving the highways, streets, lanes and alleys of the village. (5) **1945** *E. Jefferson Sentinel* (Edgewater, Colo.) 26 July 5/2 Over the weekend Highway patrolmen were kept busy. **1947** *Steamboat* (Colo.) *Pilot* 2 Jan. 1/5 The governor asked that the budget for the Highway Patrol be increased.

As the last term in **country, national, shell, state highway.**

hijack ˈhaɪˌdʒæk, *v.* Also **highjack.** [Origin unknown.] *tr.* To rob one, esp. a bootlegger or rumrunner, of his stock of supplies. *Slang.*

1923 *Lit. Digest* 4 Aug. 51/3, 'I would have had $50,000,' said Jimmy, 'if I hadn't been hijacked.' **1927** J. BARBICAN *Confess. Rum-Runner* xvii. 181 So we landed the cargo as quickly as we could, and took the chance of the cargo being seized or hijacked on shore. **1948** *Chi. Tribune* 11 Jan. 1. 12/4 Figures show that truckloads of meats, butter, lard, cheese, candy, and innumerable other foodstuffs stolen or hijacked have doubled since prices started to climb.

Hence **hijacking,** *n.* and *a.*

1923 *Lit. Digest* 4 Aug. 55/1 So much for hijacking on the high seas. **1941** FERGUSSON *Southwest* 346 This highjacking of one people's practice by another has speeded up the interfusion which was going on anyway. **1948** *Green Bay* (Wis.) *Press-Gazette* 13 July 5/2 If the artillery fell into the hands of one of the heist and hijacking mobs around town, there was no telling what might happen.

hijacker ˈhaɪˌdʒækɚ, *n.* Also **highjacker.** [Origin unknown.] A holdup man, esp. one who robs rumrunners, bootleggers, etc. *Slang.*

1923 *Nation* 11 July 36 There was, of course, the rush of adventurers, oil promoters, highjackers (an oil-region term for murderous robbers). **1931** REEVE *Golden Age Crime* 39 The hijacker victimizes the racketeer himself. **1949** *Amer. Milk Rev.* May 42/1 The trucking companies have declared an all-out war against the hijackers.

hike haɪk, *n.*[1] [f. the verb.]

1. A laborious undertaking or task, esp. a long tramp or march. *Colloq.*

1865 SUSAN HALE *Lett.* (1919) 15 I've been engaged this week in a pecunious *heik;* to wit, getting money from the ladies of the Parish to get a new gown for Dr. Hedge. **1868** *Ib.* 45, *I* ascended the Grand Pyramid, Lucretia got half-way . . . and Susie didn't try. It is a fearful heik. **1871** *Ib.* 71 [Getting out the paper] was a great heik! and glad was I . . . when 'twas over. **1902** HANCOCK *Life West Point* 224 There are many marches—'hikes' the soldiers call them—where the pursuit of the enemy may require five days. **1946** *N. & Q.* April 12/1 Probably the earliest and most remarkable of all long American hikes was that of David Ingram, who in 1568 started his eleven months' walk from the Gulf of Mexico to the Bay of Fundy. **1949** *Sky Line Hiker* March 8/2 On Monday of our hike I had been caught in the hail storm and thoroughly soaked and chilled.

transf. **1949** *Ev. Northwestern* (Chi.) 11 April 2/2 Via this program Gamma Delta promotes acquaintance and fellowship among Lutheran students with bike hikes, picnics, skating parties.

b. *On the hike,* on the go.

1907 BEACH *Barrier* iv. 53 He's the feller that killed the gold-commissioner. Of course, that put him on the hike again.

2. An increase, a raise in pay, rent, price, etc. *Colloq.*

1931 *K.C. Star* 5 Aug., The hike was occasioned by the fact that cigarette butts . . . are now only a half inch. **1948** *Herald-Press* (St. Joseph, Mich.) 14 Aug. 3/1 There is enough unfilled demand for new cars to absorb a lot more price hikes.

Hike haɪk, *n.*[2] [Origin obscure. Cf. **kike.**] (See quots.) *Obs.* — **1896** *N.Y. Herald* 13 Jan. 3/4 The average Pennsylvanian contemptuously refers to these immigrants as 'Hikes' and 'Hunks.' The 'Hikes' are Italians and Sicilians. **1898** *Cent. Mag.* LV. 811 The Italians are termed Hikes.

* **hike,** *v. intr.* Of a garment, sail, etc.: To hang, be, or go up as if pulled or yanked upward, usu. with *up.*

*c*1873 DE VERE *MS Notes* 488 What makes y[ou]r dress hike up so? **1890** *D.N.* I. 61 The curtain hikes or hikes up. **1897** *Outing* XXX. 603/2 The west wind increased to such an extent that the heavy live ballast, 'hiked out' to windward as far as possible, could not keep her lee deck out of water. **1948** *Sat. Ev. Post* 4 Dec. 127/2 When I sit down, it hikes up.

* **hill,** *n.*

1. (Usu. *cap.*) The elevation on which the Capitol at Washington, D.C., stands. Cf. **Federal Hill.**

1848 *Literary Amer.* 15 July 31/1 Invalid though I be, I sometimes reach the *Hill;* and setting myself upon the steps of the capitol, take notes of passers by. **1915** LEUPP *Walks about Washington* 54 Washington has several hills, but 'the' hill is by universal consent the one on which the Capitol stands. **1947** *Democrat* 30 Oct. 1/2 If Johnny and I are wanted at home during the next few days—'Page us on the Hill.'

2. In combs.: (1) **hillbilly,** *S.* a southern backwoodsman or mountaineer, also attrib.; (2) **cat,** (see quot.),

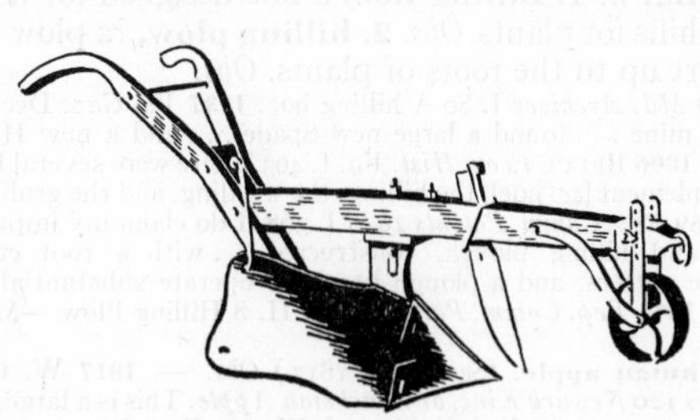

Type of hillside swivel plow

rare; (3) **city,** (see quot.), *rare;* (4) **claim,** *W.* a mining claim extending up a hill, *obs.*, cf. **hill diggings, hill mine;** (5) **clearing,** a clearing on a hill; (6) **diggings,** *W.* a place in a hilly region where gold is sought by digging, *obs.;* (7) **farm,** a poor farm in a hilly region; (8) **grape,** a now unidentifiable variety of grape found in a hilly region, *rare;* (9) **grass bird,** the buff-breasted sandpiper; (10) **lot,** a portion of public land in a hilly region allotted to a settler, *obs.;* (11) **mine,** *W.* a mine situated on a hill, *obs.;* (12) **road,** a road along or through hills; (13) * **-side,** denoting a type of plow (see quot. 1850).

(1) **1900** *N.Y. Jrnl.* 23 April 2/5 In short, a Hill-Billie is a free and untrammelled white citizen of Alabama, who lives in the hills, has no means to speak of, dresses as he can, talks as he pleases, drinks whiskey when he gets it, and fires off his revolver as the fancy takes him. **1949** *Amer. Cattle Producer* April 27/1 They began throwing out the old songs and mixing up the programs with hillbilly ballads and popular songs. — (2) **1860** MORDECAI *Va.* 290 If they see any young mountaineers (Hill-Cats as they call them) descending towards their valley, they immediately raise the war-cry. — (3) **1883** MARK TWAIN *Life on Miss.* xxxv. 375 We used to plow past the lofty hill-city, Vicksburg. — (4) **1865** in *Frontier* VIII. (1928) 131 A hill claim [in Elk Creek district, Deer Lodge Co., Mont.] shall be fronting two hundred feet and shall extend to the summit of the Hill.

(5) **1829** COOPER *Wish-ton-Wish* iii, The trainer from Hartford town struck the wild-cat on the hill clearing. — (6) **1852** *Calif. Express* (Marysville) 25 Aug. 2/2 The hill diggings are all but deserted, the miners prefering to work the river and bars adjacent. **1873** LAWRENCE *Silverland* 160 These extensive deposits of gold attracted the attention of the early adventurers in California, and were called 'Hill Diggings.' — (7) **1865** A. D. WHITNEY *Gayworthys* xxviii. 296 They knew, . . . at the hill-farm, how it was at the homestead. **1945** *Reader's Digest* Jan. 94/1 It was a hill farm in Alabama. — (8) **1806** *Ann. 9th Congress* 2 Sess. 1142 Black grape, hill grape, yellow grape, . . . and a variety of other vines. — (9) **1917** *Birds of Amer.* I. 249 *Tryngites subruficollis*. . . . [Also called] Hill Grass-bird. . . . Occasional on the Atlantic coast in fall.

(10) **1693** *Derby Rec.* 162 At the est end of the hill lots. — (11) **1871** RAYMOND *3rd Rep. Mines* 185 In the Blue Mountains, on the head of Grande Ronde River, good land has been found, and indications of extensive hill-mines.—(12) **1865** *Atlantic Mo.* April 404/2 Having entered the city by the hill-road, it was proposed to return along the Creek. **1929** SHELTON *Salt-box House* vii. 49 The hill-road and its riders were plainly seen.—(13) **1827** *19th Congress* 2 Sess. H.R. Doc. No. 27, 9 [Improvement] in the hill-side, double nosed, cast iron plough [patented April] 12 [by] John Shepherd. **1850** *N. Eng. Farmer* II. 107 *Hill-Side or Swivel Plough*. This plough is so constructed that the mouldboard may be easily changed from one side to the other while the team is turning, which admirably adapts it to ploughing on hill sides, as all the furrows are turned down hill. **1944** CLARK *Pills* 284 Competing with the thrifty pioneer Brinly, they entered the market with their famous 'hillside' turning plows and their 'bat wing' middle busters.

b. *A hill of beans*, something insignificant, small, trifling. *Colloq.*

1863 E. KIRKE *My Southern Friends* v. 80, [I] karn't take Preston's note—'taint wuth a hill o' beans. **1947** *Chi. Tribune* 23 Jan. 12/2 That oath he took here don't amount to a hill of beans.

c. *S. A hill of potatoes*, = **potato heap.**

1904 T. WATSON *Bethany* 11 Old people, even now, speak of the enormous numbers of hills of potatoes that stood in triple rows between his cow-lot and the Big Road. **1939** *These Are Our Lives* 68 We got a nice hill o' sweet potaters.

As the last term in **barn, beach, boot, Capitol, coal, corn, Federal, fool's, foot, gopher, huckleberry, Indian corn, manzanita, over, potato, prairie, river, sage, Sam, sand, scrub, short, tobacco, yam, Yankee hill.**

* **hilling,** *n.* **1. hilling hoe,** a hoe designed for use in making hills for plants. *Obs.* **2. hilling plow,** ?a plow that turns dirt up to the roots of plants. *Obs.*

(1) **1639** *Md. Archives* I. 80 A hilling hoe. **1737** *Va. Gaz.* Dec. 9 A Negro of mine . . . found a large new Spade . . . and a new Hilling hoe by it. **1896** BRUCE *Econ. Hist. Va.* I. 463 There were several kinds of this implement [*sc.* hoe], the hilling, the weeding, and the grubbing. — (2) **1859** *Rep. Comm. Patents 1858* I. 368, I do claim my improved weeding and hilling plough, constructed . . . with a root cutter, adjustable cutters, and a plough beam, to operate substantially as specified. **1871** *Rep. Comm. Patents 1869* II. 8 Hilling-Plow.—March 2, 1869.

Hinchman apple. (See quot. 1817.) *Obs.* — **1817** W. COXE *Fruit Trees* 120 *Newark King, or Hinchman Apple*. This is a large, fair, and handsome apple; called the Newark King in East-Jersey, and the Hinchman apple in Gloucester county, West-Jersey. **1859** ELLIOTT *Western Fruit Book* 161 Newark King. Hinchman. An old variety from Newark, New Jersey.

* **Hindooism,** *n.* The principles and practices of the Know-Nothing party after 1854. *Obs.* Cf. next. — **1855** *Chi. W. Times* 14 June 2/3 Nearly all the representatives of Western Hindooism in the Philadelphia convention, are persons unknown. **1856** *Louisville Democrat* 18 July 2/1 The said Gustavus Augustus Adolphus Scroggs, Esquire, . . . vouches for the orthodox investiture of said Fillmore with all the singular and mysterious rites of this modern Hindooism.

* **Hindoos,** *n. pl.* (See quot. 1859.) Also (in *sing.*) attrib. *Obs.*

1855 *N.Y. Wkly. Tribune* 20 Jan. 1/A The platform . . . will meet with a response that will appal your Hindoo Silver-Gray Know-Nothings. **1855** *Chi. Times* 27 Feb. 4/1 The signs of the times are anything but favorable to the American 'Hindoos.' *Ib.* 3 March 4/4 Secret Political Societies Startling disclosures: The Hindoo oaths and rituals. **1859** BARTLETT 196 *Hindoos*, a name given to the Know Nothing party, in consequence of their candidate for the presidency [error for governorship of N.Y.], Daniel Ullman, having been charged with being a native of Calcutta.

hindsight ˈhaɪndˌsaɪt, *n.*

1. The rear sight of a firearm.

1843 CARLTON *New Purchase* I. 130 Very good separate shots—yet proving want of . . . even a little experimenting with the edges of the hind sight. **1901** WHITE *Blazed Trail* 125 Indians never clean their rifles . . . and are deficient in the philosophy of hind-sights.

b. *fig. To knock, kick, the hindsights out, off* (*of* something), to demolish utterly. *Colloq.*

1834 CARUTHERS *Kentuckian* I. 21 As sure as you saw the fire at the muzzle of his gun, so sure he knocked the creter's hind sights out. **1850** GARRARD *Wah-To-Yah* xx. 248 They backed their ears preparatory to kicking the hindsights off the first man that struck them. **1892** *Cong. Rec.* 1 April 2843/1 The American producer, whether on the farm or in the shop, can knock the hind sights off the producer anywhere else on the face of the earth.

2. The capacity of looking back and seeing what should have been done. *Colloq.*

1866 C. H. SMITH *Bill Arp* 130 But then you know a man's foresight ain't as good as his hind sights. **1918** OWEN *Typewriting Speed* 108 That little saying about 'if our foresight was only as good as our hindsight' is just as applicable here [in education] as for the stock market! **1948** *Sierra Club Bul.* Mar. 18 The closing of the season on wolverine 22 years after the alarm was sounded is surely no more than conservation by hindsight.

* **hinge,** *n.* In combs.: (1) **hinge gun,** (see quot.), *obs.;* (2) **mud turtle,** a box turtle, *rare;* (3) **seat,** a seat provided with hinges so that it may be raised as the lid of a box, *obs.*

(1) **1883** *Nat. Museum Bul.* No. 27, 280 The darting-guns [used by whalers] of the original pattern were muzzle loading, but more recent inventions have developed the breech-loaders which are known as the 'screw gun' and the 'hinge gun.' — (2) **1851** *De Bow's Review* XI. 53 *Cooter, Hinge Mud Turtle*, or *Emys Clausa*, is also found here. — (3) **1845** JUDD *Margaret* I. xiv. 111 The noise of the hinge-seats . . . seemed to disconcert her. **1865** A. D. WHITNEY *Gayworthys* v. 50 Spice-cake . . . [was] stowed away carefully in sanctuary cupboards, under the hinge seats.

b. In phrases: (see quots.). *Colloq.*

1839 F. KEMBLE *Jrnl. Res. Ga.* (1863) 326 She (to use a most extraordinary comparison I heard of a negro girl making with regard to her mother) is as black as 'de hinges of hell.' **1912** LONDON *Smoke Bellew* 73 It's colder than the hinges of hell. **1944** BARBOUR *Eden* 117 In summer in this part of Florida it is hotter than the hinges of Gehenna.

Hingham bucket. A bucket made at Hingham, Mass. *Obs.* Cf. **bucketmaker.** — **1860** MORDECAI *Va.* 94 He proffered to him a bargain in apples, onions, fish, and Hingham buckets.

* **hip,** *n.* In combs.: (1) **hip boot,** a high boot, usually of rubber, reaching to the hip; (2) **flask,** a small whisky flask suitable for carrying in the hip pocket; (3) **pocket,** a rear pocket in a pair of trousers, first used as a place for carrying a weapon; (4) **shot,** *W.* one who fires a revolver from the hip without taking formal aim.

(1) **1893** *Outing* XXII. 124/2 Gossamer hip-boots are good if of reliable stock. **1946** *Washington Outdoors* June 10/2 The tools necessary for one to participate in this sport consists of a clam gun, surf sack and hip boots. — (2) **1923** ELIZ. MARBURY *My Crystal Ball* lxxi. 352 Let these same people frequent ballrooms . . . and they will find the hip flasks in evidence and the consequent conditions a sorry spectacle. — (3) [**1867** LATHAM *Black & White* 161 A large proportion of the men here [in New Orleans] carry arms; you see trousers hanging up in the tailors' shops with a pocket on the hip behind for knife or pistol under the skirt of the coat.] **1880** *Cimarron News & Press* 22 July 3/2 Lee snatched Armstrong's revolver from his hip pocket and pointed it at Armstrong. **1948** *This Week Mag.* 9 Oct. 22/2 People who carry their life savings in their hip pockets usually go down fighting. — (4) **1904** *McClure's Mag.* Feb. 362 None but the dwarf of Bar X could have lived, for he was the deadliest hip shot in the territory.

* **hip,** *v. tr.* To put (something) on the hip and carry (it) there. *Colloq.* — **1818** H. C. KNIGHT *Lett. from South* 93 Some mothers here [in Kentucky] hip their infants; as do the Sumatrans. **1843** CARLTON *New Purchase* I. 191 Each [log] is often carried by two persons; but oftener still each is hipped. And hipping is done by one man who . . . adroitly whips up the log on his hip, and trots off with it.

hipped hɪpt, *a.* [Prob. f. **hip*, abbrev. of **hypochondria*.] Excessively given to, fond of. *Slang.* — **1927** *Dly. Express* 24 Oct. 8 'New York,' as the manager of one of the largest hotels remarked lately, 'is badly "hipped" on dining in public.' **1949** *Reader's Digest*

July 77 A Sunday-school teacher was mildly hipped on the happiness theme.

∗**hippodrome,** *n.* **1.** (See quot.) **2.** A race or athletic contest in which it is arranged beforehand that a certain contestant shall win. *Slang.* Cf. next.

(1) **1866** *Wilkes' Spirit of Times* 7 April 83/1 As for the general belief that no one but Alexander could mount him, that's a hippodrome, or a stall, as Mike Walsh used to say. — (2) **1887** *Courier-Journal* 19 Jan. 5/1 No one calls the affair a hippodrome. The fight was to be for points, and the winner was to get 75 per cent. of the house receipts. *Ib.* 8 Feb. 5/2 A number in the audience pronounced the affair a hippodrome. **1915** *Everybody's Mag.* June 698/1 They bunted us dizzy, ran the bases hog-wild, and turned the game into a hippodrome before the inning was over.

hippodrome ˈhɪpəˌdrom, *v.* [f. the noun.]

1. *tr.* To arrange or "fix" a contest in advance so that in reality there is no competition. Also **hippodroming,** *n. Slang.*

1868 Woodruff *Trotting Horse* 288 [A mare] was hippodromed with a good deal. *Ib.*, 'Hippodroming' . . . has come more and more into fashion. **1896** Chadwick *Spalding's Base B. Guide* 54 After the opening game had been drawn, the Boston club defeated the Clevelands in the next four games, thereby utterly depriving the enemies of the professional class of any chance to cry 'hippodroming.' **1948** *Chi. Tribune* 1 Feb. (Grafic Mag.) 13/1 Cynics argue there is a great deal of hippodroming [in ice hockey].

2. To do (something) in a spectacular manner as if performing before a crowd in a hippodrome. Also *intr.* Hence **hippodroming,** *a.*

1898 *Cong. Rec.* 11 March 2736/1, I insist that I have the floor, and I will not be hippodromed from the floor. **1900** *Ib.* 17 Feb. 1899/2 My friend here goes hippodroming over the country comes back loaded with such nonsense as that. **1908** *Nation* 23 April LXXVI. 374/3 Mr. Root has certainly done better than that even in the season when he undertook his hippodroming junket round Cape Horn.

hipsesaw ˈhɪpsəsɔ, *n.* [Origin obscure. Cf. ∗*seesaw.*] (See quots.) *Obs.* — **1830** Watson *Philadelphia* 237 Hipsesaws and jigs were the common dances of the commonalty. **1832** ——— *Hist. Tales N.Y.* 145 The dances of that day among the politer class were minuets, and sometimes country dances; among the lower order hipsesaw was every thing.

∗**hire,** *v.*

1. *absol.* for *reflex.* To engage oneself as a laborer or hand for payment, usu. with *out. Colloq.*

a1772 Woolman *Works* (1774) 10 A man . . . asked me, if I would hire with him to tend shop and keep books. **1830** S. Smith *Major Downing* 35, I forgot to tell you that I had hired out here this summer. **1900** Drannan *Plains & Mts.* 306 This was no doubt their first experience in hir'ng out.

2. In phrases: (1) *To hire one's duty,* in the Army the offense, punishable by court-martial, of hiring another to do one's (an enlisted man's) duty; (2) *to hire one's (own) time,* of a slave, to pay one's master for the right to use one's time for one's own profit, *obs.*

(1) **1806** *Ann. 9th Congress* 1 Sess. 1245 Every such soldier found guilty of hiring his duty, as also the said party so hired to do another's duty, shall be punished at the discretion of a regimental court martial. — (2) **1845** F. Douglass *Narrative* 102, I decided to hire my time, with a view of getting money with which to make my escape. **1862** E. Kirke *Among Pines* 19 This lady . . . had since allowed him to 'hire his time,' and he then carried on an 'independent business,' as porter.

∗**hired,** *a.* Used esp. with (1) **girl,** (2) **hand,** (3) **help,** (4) ∗**man,** to denote free men and women engaged to assist their employers.

For a discussion of the social environment out of which *hired* with this slightly different connotation arose, see A. Matthews in *Trans. Col. Soc. Mass.* March, 1898, 225–56.

(1) **1818** J. Flint *Lett. from Amer.* 39 On Sundays it would be difficult to discriminate betwixt the hired girl and the daughter in a genteel family [in Phila.], were drapery the sole criterion. **1887** M. E. W. Freeman *Humble Romance* 64 The hired girl sat down at the table with David and his mother. **1943** Damon *Sense of H.* 36 Betsey was . . . obliging the hired girl to walk around on the wrong side.

(2) **1818** J. Flint *Lett. from Amer.* 98 They [i.e., laborers] are not *servants*, all are *hired hands.* **1862** *Ill. Agric. Soc. Trans.* V. 196 With the aid of two small boys and hired hand, with his good management he has succeeded. **1943** Menefee *Assignment* 9, I have seen—especially the farmers, who are short of hired hands.

(3) **1815** *Mass. Spy* 23 Aug. (Th.), If our friends knock at the door, our lady and gentleman 'hired helps' do not understand who is meant when their master is inquired for. **1896** *Nation* 3 Sep. 172/1 The immense majority of . . . [farmers] work with their own hands; sometimes not so hard as their hired help, but often a good deal harder.

(4) **1737** *Plymouth Rec.* 18 May, A hired man with me on a fishing voyage. **1819** J. Flint *Lett. from Amer.* 135 Last night a gentleman from Carolina lodged in the tavern here [at Jeffersonville, Ind.]. After a hired man had given him his slippers, and asked him for his boots to be blacked, he exclaimed, . . . 'I would not live in a free state, where one white man cleans the boots of another.' **1948** *Democrat* 11 March 4/3 The oldest daughter eloped with the hired man.

hireland ˈhaɪrˌlænd, *n.* (See quot.) *Colloq.* — **1889** *Amer. Folk-Lore* II. 229 *Hireland*, a renter or cropper. [Kentucky and Tennessee.]

∗**hiring,** *a.* **1.** ∗**hiring day,** a day set aside for the hiring out of Negro slaves for the ensuing year. **2. hiring ground,** *S.* a place where Negro slaves were formerly put up for hire. Both *obs.* — (1) **1861** H. Jacobs *Life Slave Girl* 25 Hiring-day at the south takes place on the 1st of January. On the 2d, the slaves are expected to go to their new masters. — (2) **1861** H. Jacobs *Life Slave Girl* 26 If he lives until the next year, perhaps the same man will hire him again, without even giving him an opportunity of going to the hiring-ground.

His Accidency, see **Accidency.**

∗**hissing snake.** (See quot. 1949.)

1778 Carver *Travels* 486 The most remarkable of the different species that infest this lake [Lake Erie], is the hissing-snake, which is of the small speckled kind, and about eighteen inches long. . . . Its spots, which are of various dyes, become visibly brighter through rage. **1807** Janson *Stranger in Amer.* 75 Mr. Carver's account of the *hissing snake* is supposed to be fabulous. **1949** *Scientific Mo.* Jan. 57/2 No gallery of American mythical snakes would be complete without mention of the celebrated blow snake, sometimes known as the 'hissing snake,' 'blowing viper,' 'spreading adder,' or 'puff adder.' This is none other than the common hog-nosed snake (*Heterodon contortrix*).

hist-a-boy ˈhɪstəˌbɔɪ, *interj.* Used as a command to incite or urge on. *Colloq.* Cf. **staboy.** — **1841** Emerson *Addr., Conservative* Wks. (Bohn) II. 276 He must cry 'Hist-a-boy' and urge the game on. **1860** ——— *Cond. Life, Illusions* 443 To . . . cry *Hist-a-boy!* to every good dog.

∗**hit,** *n.* In policy gambling, a winning number or combination of numbers; a ticket bearing a winning number. — **1847** C. White *Policy Players* (1874) 3 Some of my heaviest players are getting discouraged. . . . It would be a good idea . . . [to] let them get a hit, in order to keep their custom. **1856** *Porter's Spirit of Times* 20 Dec. 261/3 This [lottery ticket] was number 37149, and it was a hit for $3,000, if it had been genuine instead of bogus.

As the last term in **base, clean, fair, ground, pinch, place, sacrifice, scratch, three-base, two-base hit.**

∗**hit,** *v.*

1. *tr.* To arrive at (a place). *Colloq.*

1888 *Detroit Free Press* Oct. (F.), Professor Rose who hit this town last spring, is around calling us a fugitive from justice. **1910** Walcott *Open Door* 105 He had been telling his troubles to the telephone . . . ever since he hit the desk at ten o'clock. **1931** *K.C. Times* 24 Aug., It has always been the custom of this office to help a printer who, touring the country, hits the place hungry.

b. *To hit by,* to go or pass by. *Rare.*

1911 H. S. Harrison *Queed* vii. 86 I've seen you hit by the window many's the time.

2. To "strike," affect, or occur to (a person). *Colloq.*

1914 Atherton *Perch of Devil* 175 Lucky it hit him to buy the house and send that last five thousand. **1916** Bower *Phantom Herd* 68, I wanted to see how it would hit you.

3. In colloq. phrases: (1) *To hit it up,* to go along at high speed, to work hard; (2) ∗*to hit up,* to increase speed, or the stroke in rowing; (3) ∗*to hit it at* (a given speed), to travel rapidly at an indicated speed, also *to hit a clip,* to move at a certain speed; (4) *to hit on all four cylinders,* to run along perfectly, to be in good working condition, also *hitting on all six;* (5) *to hit the upgrade,* to advance, to begin to achieve one's goal; (6) *to hit one's stride,* to perform up to one's usual level; (7) *to hit the jackpot, trail,* see **jackpot,** *n.*, **trail,** *n.*

(1) **1893** Post *Harvard Stories* 146 When you are doing better than three and a half, you are hitting it up pretty well. **1908** Lorimer *J. Spurlock* 16 Off hitting it up again. — (2) **1893** Post *Harvard Stories* 300 These two could surely 'hit up' the stroke indefinitely. **1907** London *Road* 213 As the freight got out of Philadelphia she began to hit up speed. — (3) **1911** Harrison *Queed* 90 You'll never finish your book at all at the clip you're hitting now. **1911** J. C. Lincoln *Cap'n Warren's Wards* iii. 39 They nabbed us for speeding. . . . Said we were hitting it at fifty an hour. — (4) **1912** Mathewson *Pitching* xii. 269 So the best infielder takes time to fit into the infield of a Big League club and have it hit on all four cylinders again. **1928** *Sat. Ev. Post* 10 March 127/1 Modern science offers you a *natural* means to keep you 'hitting on all six'—every minute of the day.

(5) **1926** *N.Y. Times Mag.* 15 Aug. 6 The climber hit the upgrade in his 20th year, after lamplight study of shorthand and accounting. — (6) **1931** *K.C. Times* 13 Nov. 22 Mr. Southern has resumed his Solomon Wise column in the Examiner and is hitting his old stride again.

b. *To hit the bush, flat, park, pike, road, sod, ties,* to take to the places designated, to get going.

1889 BARRERE-LELAND I. 464/1 *Hit the flat, to* (cowboys), to go out on the prairies. **1891** RYAN *Told in Hills* 23 We'll hit the bush by and by. **1896** ADE *Artie* xiv. 127 A little more weather like this and we'll be hittin' the park. **1904** *Hartford Courant* 25 June 8 The La Follette convention, whose delegates were so summarily ordered to hit the pike by the national committeemen at Chicago. **1907** O. HENRY *Heart of West* x. 173, I hit the sod in the direction of the show. **1907** LONDON *Road* 130 It was up to me to hit the ties to Wadsworth. **1925** TILGHMAN *Dugout* 70 Well, I must hit the road. **1948** *Dly. Ardmoreite* (Ardmore, Okla.) 17 May 4 So the ol' boy has hit the road again!

c. * **hit-or-miss,** *attrib.* designating things not regular or symmetrical. Also fig.

1883 JACKSON *Ramona* 473 It's jest a kind er 'hit-er-miss' pattern we air all on us livin' on; 'taint much use tryin' ter reckon how 't 'll come aout. **1947** *Chr. Sci. Monitor* 15 Jan. 6/5 Such a carpet was a sure sign of elegance, replacing the hit-or-miss rag covering in many a Victorian home.

Esp. **hit-or(or -and)-miss carpet,** (see quot. 1848).

1848 in *Amer. Sp.* X. (1935) 40/2 Hit-or-miss-carpet. A carpet woven from strips of old cloth sewed together. **1897** W. E. BARTON *Hero in Homespun* 377 They ripped up the new hit-an'-miss carpet for horse blankets.

d. *To hit the booze, the pipe,* to drink liquor, to smoke opium. *Slang.*

1889 *Oregonian* (Portland) 14 Oct. 3/1 If Dasher gets a dozen or more customers with his own appetite for hitting the booze he will have no trouble making it go. **1902** *Chi. Record-Herald* 7 Sep. VI. 5/2 On each bunk two almond-eyed devotees of the drug may be seen 'hitting the pipe,' as opium smoking is termed. **1943** *Amer. Sp.* April 157/1 The fundamental locution is *hit the pipe*, which is (or at least for some time was) slang for smoking opium. **1949** *Sun. World-Herald Mag.* (Omaha) 3 April 2/1 Opium smokers are considered at a low level . . . but a guy who profits when he hits the pipe is the plumber.

e. *hit and run,* (1) in baseball, a play wherein a base runner starts with the pitcher's throw as the batter attempts a hit, a sacrifice hit, also attrib.; (2) of or pertaining to accidents of automobiles, trucks, etc., in which the driver seeks to avoid detection by not stopping.

(1) **1899** *Chi. D. News* 2 May 7/1 Chance and Callahan in the points, combined with Green, Lange, Everitt, Demont, McCormick and Wolverton, not to leave out Jimmy Ryan himself, is a rare combination for the hit-and-run game. **1904** BARBOUR *Sch. & Coll. Sports, Baseball* 188 *Team batting.* The best known example of this is what is called the sacrifice hit or 'hit and run.' *Ib.* 191 The 'hit-and-run' play may also be used when there is a man on third and a run is badly needed. **1909** *Amer. Mag.* May 35/1 Evers and Kling analyzed and discovered every hit and run signal used by the Cincinnati club. **1948** *Spokesman-Review* (Spokane, Wash.) 23 Sep. 14/1 Slaughter, running toward second on a hit and run play in the fourth inning, was struck hard on the bridge of the nose by Nippy Jones' liner.

(2) **1927** *Topeka Capital* 31 Jan., Reckless automobile driving and the odious hit-and-run practise of some automobile drivers. **1948** *Atlanta Constitution* 5 Dec. 1/1 They found the hit-run car hidden in an alley.

* **hitch,** *n.*

1. A particular time, esp. *this hitch,* this time. *Colloq.*

1835 TODD *Notes* 38 We shall clear up three load this hitch. **1835–7** HALIBURTON *Clockmaker* 1 Ser. ix. 169 She'll mind her stops next hitch, I reckon. **1842** UNCLE SAM *Peculiarities* I. 218 Put the leak into them this hitch, and I calckylate they won't blart out any more locofocoism from July to etarnity. **1845** HOOPER *Simon Suggs' Adv.* x, They're peart at the snap-game, they'selves; but they're badly lewed this hitch!

b. A period of enlistment, usu. four years, in the army or navy. Also transf.

1920 *Collier's* 15 May 4/3 It's commencin' to look kinda silly to the little pals of Alma Mater for them to toy with readin' and 'ritin' and 'rithmetic for a four-year hitch. **1947** *Woodlawn Booster* (Chi.) 3 Sep. 4/3 My son has recently entered the armed service and signed up for a 4 year hitch. **1948** *Pauls Valley* (Okla.) *D. Democrat* 2 July 2/7 Many young men will come back from a hitch in the army or navy better physically mentally and spiritually than when they left.

2. A mode of harnessing a team; the team itself.

1876 *Vt. Bd. Agric. Rep.* III. 143 If he can go best in one kind of a hitch, and, in that hitch, make the best time ever made by any horse, he is entitled to the credit of the best recorded time. **1905** *Springfield W. Republican* 22 Sep. 12 The coaching parade was started at 10.30. . . . There were also several other creditable displays, both single and double hitches. **1912** MULFORD & CLAY *Buck Peters* 201, I want a hitch of some kind . . . something with speed and bottom, and the sooner the better.

b. The action of "hitching" a sled to a moving vehicle. *Colloq.*

1880 *Harper's Mag.* March 525/1 With 'ducking' heads and muffled screams you ran the gauntlet [in the sleigh] past the school-house mob; saw them scrambling for 'a hitch.'

3. *To make a hitch of it,* to make a go of it, to get on well together. *Colloq.*

1898 WESTCOTT *D. Harum* 141, I thought we was goin' to make a hitch of it, an' he cert'nly hain't said nuthin' 'bout leavin'.

As the last term in **diamond, Kit Carson, pack, prospector's, sheep-herder's, squaw hitch.**

* **hitch,** *v.*

1. *tr.* To harness or yoke (a draft animal or team) to a vehicle, farm implement, etc. Usu. with *up.* Also in passive or absol. construction.

1817 PAULDING *Lett. from South* (1835) II. 201 Hitch up, . . . boys, and push on. **1846** EMORY *Mil. Reconnoissance* 15, I ordered my horses to be hitched up. **1877** CAMPION *On Frontier* 249 In three minutes' time we are 'hitched-up.' **1907** WHITE *Arizona Nights* 225 One day in the spring I hitched up . . . and druv over to the railroad. **1920** HOWELLS *Vacation of Kelwyns* 201 Kite was not there to hitch up the horse for him.

2. To tie up (a horse, mule, etc.) to a rack, post, fence, etc.

1827 *Mass. Spy* 24 Oct. (Th.), I reckon in futur you'll hitch your creter to the rack afore Patty Pott's door, she havin' larnt edification at boardin' school. **1885** CRADDOCK *Prophet* 20 Dorinda . . . marked how short a consultation resulted in dismounting and hitching the horses. **1902** HARBEN *A. Daniel* 72 Just then Pole Baker . . . rode up to the fence and hitched his horse.

transf. **1881** STODDARD *E. Hardery* 119 He had hitched his buggy in front of Dr. Edgerton's. **1895** BELL *Little Sister* 153 Tobe Manley hitched his wagon at a considerable distance from all the rest.

3. To attach (a vehicle) to a draft animal. Also transf.

1870 EMERSON *Soc. & Solitude* 25 That is the wisdom of a man, . . . to hitch his wagon to a star. **1872** *Cong. Globe* 11 April 2364/1, I think that on the whole I would rather not hitch up a buggy when I can get somebody else to do it.

b. To attach (any motive power) to a piece of machinery. *Colloq.*

1903 SHUMAN *Pract. Journalism* 11 With steam-power hitched to such a press the possibilities of journalism were becoming great.

4. Used in combs. in the sense of "hitching": (1) **hitch rack,** (2) **rail,** (3) **rein.** Cf. * **hitching,** *n. attrib.*

(1) **1903** A. ADAMS *Log Cowboy* xxi. 138 Tying our horses in a group to a hitch-rack in the rear of a saloon. **1945** *This Week Mag.* 15 Dec. 2/3 My father went among the people at the hitchracks asking if they knew where it was. — (2) **1906** H. D. PITTMAN *Belle of Blue Grass C.* xiii. 187 A slim-legged yellow girl . . . swinging by her arms from a hitch rail. **1948** *Range Riders Western* May 34/2 He saw Hank and Dusty separate at the hitch-rail. — (3) **1899** G. ADE *Doc. Horne* i. 7, I jumped off my horse and threw him one end of my hitch-rein and pulled him out.

b. hitch up, marriage, a married couple. *Rare.*

1898 WESTCOTT *D. Harum* 298 What a nice hitch up they'd make. *Ib.* 336, I putty much made up my mind to try another hitch-up.

5. In colloq. phrases: (1) *To hitch horses,* to get along together, to marry; (2) *to hitch teams together,* to join efforts, become partners.

(1) **1830** *Mass. Spy* 28 July (Th.), 'Your notions and mine don't agree; we can never hitch horses.' 'Who asked you to hitch horses?' **1862** LOWELL *Biglow P.* Poems (1890) II. 283 An' so we fin'lly made it up, concluded to hitch horses. — (2) **1892** MARK TWAIN *Amer. Claimant* 35 (R.), Give me your hand, my boy. . . . We'll hitch teams together, you and I.

Hitchcock chair. Any one of various chairs made by Lambert H. Hitchcock (1795–1852) or produced in his chair factory established in 1818 at Barkhamsted, Conn.

Such chairs are of many designs and sizes. In general they are characterized by strong front legs, curved-top backs, and seats (prob. orig. rush-bottomed) wider at the front than at the back.

*c*1828 in MOORE *Hitchcock Chairs* (1933) 5 Hitchcock chairs, . . . flag and wooden seats, warranted well manufactured. **1933** MOORE *Hitchcock Chairs* 3 The first Hitchcock chairs probably had the rush seat, but very soon were added the cane and solid wood seats. **1945** *Springfield* (Mass.) *Union* 13 Mar. 8/1 Hand-painted Hitchcock chairs, old fans from foreign countries . . . displayed the talents and hobbies of members of the Arts Club. **1949** *Cleveland Plain Dealer*

13 Feb. (Pict. Mag.) 9/1 The study . . . remains exactly as she left it at her death almost 75 years ago. The same wallpaper, and carpet, . . . and the dozen perfect Hitchcock chairs.

hitchhike ˈhɪtʃˌhaɪk, *n.* A journey made by securing rides in passing automobiles. *Slang.* — **1927** *New Masses* June 15/1 Most young janes have their heads full of a trip to Paris, or a hitch-hike thru New England. **1948** *Dly. Ardmoreite* (Ardmore, Okla.) 27 May 8 The shape our budget is in, we couldn't afford a one-way hitch-hike to the city limits!

hitchhike ˈhɪtʃˌhaɪk, *v. tr.* and *intr.* To make one's way by securing rides in passing automobiles, trucks, etc. Also **hitchhiking,** *n.* Also transf. *Slang.*

1923 *Nation* 19 Sep. 297/2 Hitch-hiking is always done by twos and threes. **1930** *Randolph Enterprise* (Elkins, W. Va.) 9 Oct. 4/3 Waddell . . . was said to be 'hitch-hiking' his way to Morgantown to see the big foot ball game. **1948** *Sky Line Trail* June 9/1 True, we may not all be Nelson Eddys and Lily Pons's but once our piano-accordionist gets his squeeze-box in motion our voices just can't resist hitch-hiking onto those strains of melody—for better or for worse.

Hence **hitchhiker,** *n.*

1943 PEATTIE *Journ. into Amer.* 5 Every time the door opens, letting in a truck driver, a bus passenger, a hitch-hiker, you can see a little farther into this nation. **1948** *Dly. Oklahoman* (Okla. City) 7 June 1/3 Over the weekend wheat harvest and summer lured hundreds of hitchhikers to the open road.

***hitching,** *n. attrib.* Designating objects to which horses and mules may conveniently be hitched, as (1) **hitching bar,** (2) **pole,** (3) **post,** (4) **rack,** (5) **rail.**

(1) [**1787** ATTMORE *Journal* 37 There was a place for horses to stand, composed of two posts set in the ground at about 15 feet distance from each other on the tops rested a cross piece with Pins at intervals for

Hitching post or horse post

fastening the Bridles, here stood a dozen horses.] **1877** CAMPION *On Frontier* 128 Beyond the fire, at a similar distance from it, a 'hitching-bar' was put up, to fasten horses and mules to. — (2) **1914** BOWER *Flying U Ranch* 63 [They] rode to the hotel, tied their horses to the long hitching pole there and went in. — (3) **1843** J. L. SCOTT *Journal* 68 When at the door they alighted, and he rode off to the 'hitching post.' **1948** *Newsweek* 30 Aug. 19/1 No ex-governors will put a halter or bridle on me and lead me to a hitching post. — (4) **1904** HARBEN *Georgians* 146 Eric rode up to a hitching-rack and dismounted. **1947** CHALFANT *Gold, Guns, & Ghost Towns* 69 There [he] saw tied to a hitching rack a horse to which he took a fancy, so he mounted it and rode off.

(5) **1920** J. GREGORY *Man to Man* 103 A dozen saddle-horses were tied at the hitching-rail. **1948** *Sat. Ev. Post* 21 Aug. 99/2 An hour later, he leaned on the hitching rail at the post office and wished he could simply die and have it over with.

b. Also (1) **hitching grounds,** an area near a store where customers usually hitch their teams; (2) **rein, strap,** a rein or strap with which to hitch a horse or mule; (3) **weight,** a weight which, when put on the ground and attached by a strap to a horse's bit, keeps the animal from going away.

(1) **1944** CLARK *Pills* 11 In many instances stores remained isolated with their hitching grounds worn deep by fifty years of scouring by wagon wheels, scuffing feet of mules and horses and by erosion. — (2) **1852** BRISTED *Upper Ten Th.* iii. 67 Benson leaped out, pulled a hitching-strap from under the seat, and fastened his off-horse very neatly to a lamp-post. **1883** SWEET & KNOX *Through Texas* viii. 107, [I] filed a counter-claim of a dollar and a half, covering the value of one of my spurs and the doctor's hitching-rein. **1909** STRATTON-PORTER *Girl of Limberlost* 131 He drove with the hitching strap tied to the railing of the dashboard. — (3) **1884** HOWELLS *S. Lapham* iii. 60 The Colonel turned from casting anchor at the mare's head with the hitching-weight.

hitchy ˈhɪtʃɪ, *a.* (See quot. 1889.) Hence **hitchily,** *adv.*, **hitchiness,** *n. Colloq.* — **1871** HOWELLS *Wedding Journey* 37 Things go more hitchily the first year [after marriage] than ever they do afterward. *Ib.* 38 You must be careful not to contradict me, or cross me in anything. . . . The great object is not to have any hitchiness. **1889** *Cent.* 2844/2 *Hitchy.* . . . Characterized by hitches or jerks; interrupted by temporary obstructions.

***hitter,** *n.* As the last term in **first ball, pinch, scratch, shoulder hitter.**

hittock ˈhɪtək, *n.* [Poss. imitative.] (See quot.) *Obs.* — **1808** WILSON *Ornithology* I. 53 The Gold-winged woodpecker . . . has numerous provincial appellations in the different states of the Union, such as . . . 'Hittock,' 'Yucker,' 'Piut,' 'Flicker.'

***hive,** *n.*[1]

1. (See quot. 1823 and cf. **bee,** *n.*[2]) *Obs.*

1823 HOLMES *Acct. U.S.* 358 For the clergy, in country places, once or twice a year, they have what they denominate a 'bee,' or 'hive.' On these occasions, the members of his congregation, and such others as choose, repair to the minister's dwelling, each person taking something, either an article of clothing or victuals. **1832** TRAILL *Backwoods* 93 We are, however, to call the 'bee,' and provide every thing necessary for the entertainment of our worthy *hive.* **1853** STRICKLAND *Twenty-seven Yrs.* I. 97 My hive worked well, for we had five acres logged and set fire to the same evening.

2. A local unit of a fraternal order known as the Maccabees.

1929 *Randolph Enterprise* (Elkins, W. Va.) 11 April 1/6 Eighty tents and hives in West Virginia will send delegates to the state convention of the Maccabees in Clarksburg April 22.

As the last term in **bee, dividing, observation hive.**

hive haɪv, *n.*[2] [See note.]

In **1.** app. from **hives*, a skin disease or croup, but poss. based upon **hive*, a variant of **heave*, to vomit. In **2.** the source of the first element is not clear.

1. hive sirup, a medicinal sirup composed of squill and used as an emetic.

1839 *S. Lit. Messenger* V. 65/2 There's nothing there but a few drops of peppermint . . . and some of the patent hive-syrup. **1850** LEWIS *La. Swamp Doctor* 127 From what does hive syrup derive its name?

2. hive-vine, (see quots.).

1889 *Cent. s.v.*, hive-vine. . . . The partridge-berry or squaw-vine, *Mitchella repens.* **1893** *Amer. Folk-Lore* VI. 140 *Desmodium rotundifolium*, hive vine. West. Va.

***hive,** *v.* **1.** *intr.* To shut oneself *up. Colloq.* **2.** *tr.* (See quot.)

(1) **1774** FITHIAN *Journal* I. 233 Come, Fithian, what do you mean by keeping hived up sweating in your Room? **1843** STEPHENS *High Life N.Y.* II. 45 Captin Doolittle will board there and help about when he hives up for the winter. **1858** GOVE *Letters* 127 We are hived up here without any knowledge of events outside our camp. — (2) **1871** OLIVER E. WOOD *West Point Scrap Book* 339 A Vocabulary of the Expressions and Phrases used in the Corps of Cadets. . . . To hive.—To appropriate—to take without permission.

hi-yi ˈhaɪjaɪ, *interj.* Used by drovers, cowboys, etc., in urging cattle on. — **1872** MARK TWAIN *Roughing It* iii. 31 The pattering of the horses' hoofs, the cracking of the driver's whip, and his 'Hi-yi! g'long!' were music.

hoary marmot, A large marmot, *Marmota pruinosa*, of the Northwest.

1781 PENNANT *Hist. Quadrupeds* II. 398 Hoary [marmot]. . . . Inhabits the northern parts of North America. **1829** J. RICHARDSON *Fauna Boreali-Amer.* I. 150 Hoary marmot, with long coarse fur, particularly on the chest and shoulders, where it is hoary. **1912** WHEELER *Selkirk Mts.* 47 Among their bases are caves once beardens, but since the advent of the tourist the home of the hoary marmot, whose sudden shrill resounding whistle with its uncanny human note is enough to make one's hair stand on end. **1949** *Sky Line Trail* March 5/1 We have now entered the domain of the hoary marmot and the ptarmigan.

***hoaxing,** *n.* (See quot.) *Obs.* — **1851** HALL *College Words* 162 At Princeton College, inducing new-comers to join the secret societies is called *hoaxing.*

***hob,** *n.*

1. *To play hob with*, to play the mischief with, to upset. *Colloq.*

1838 *N.Y. Mirror* 2 June 387/1 They say it's playing *hob* with the fellers in these here parts. **1916** WILSON *Somewhere* 120 He looked like one of them silly little critters that play hob with Rip Van Winkle . . . before he goes to sleep. **1948** *Sat. Ev. Post* 16 Oct. 54/4 The coming of people, utilities and the like have played hob with many of nature's workings.

2. *To raise hob*, to "raise the devil." *Colloq.*

1911 LINCOLN *Cap'n Warren's Wards* 88 Theoph's been raisin' hob because the Odd Fellows built on to their buildin'. **1918** ——— *Shavings* 127 Drop in there some evenin' and hear Gabe Bearse . . . raise hob with the Kaiser. **1949** *Chi. Tribune* 14 June II. 1/1 The change in time on the new quiz programs is raising hob with getting the evening chores finished.

∗**hobble,** *n.* **1. hobblebush,** a small caprifoliaceous shrub, *Viburnum alnifolium*, of the northern U.S. **2. hobblewood,** =prec.

(1) **1817–8** EATON *Botany* (1822) 510 *Viburnum lantanoides*, hobblebush, tangle-legs. . . . Stem very flexible and crooked. **1893** DANA *Wild Flowers* 49 Its straggling growth, and its reclining branches, which often take root in the ground, have suggested the popular names of hobble-bush, and wayfaring-tree. **1943** DAMON *Sense of H.* 194 The high-bush blueberry was in blossom and in damp places the hobble bush expanded its wide exquisite corymbs. — (2) **1813** MUHLENBERG *Cat. Plants* 32 *Viburnum lantanoides* (hobble-wood).

∗**hobble,** *v.* *To hobble out* (a horse), to turn (a horse) loose with hobbles on. *Rare.* — **1805** Dow *Journal* (1814) 236 We halted, hobbled out our horses immediately, . . . and proceeded to kindle up a fire.

∗**hobby,** *n.* A translation or "pony." *Obs.* — **1851** HALL *College Words* 162 Hobbies are used by some students in translating Latin, Greek, and other languages.

hob-grate, *n.* (See quot.) — **1936** MORSE *Furniture* 35 About 1750 the hob-grate was invented. . . . The bars, of course, are of iron for holding coal, and the sides of the grate are of brass. These were at first called 'cat-stones' to distinguish them from 'fire-dogs,' but later they were named 'hob-grates.'

hobo ˈhobo, *n.* [Origin unknown.] A migratory worker, a tramp. Also transf.

1889 *Ellensburgh* (Wash.) *Capital* 28 Nov. 2/2 The tramp has changed his name, or rather had it changed for him, and now he is a 'Hobo.' **1913** *Industrial Worker* 1 May 5/3 *n.*, Hobo is a much misunderstood word. It should not be confused with tramp or vagrant. It means a casual, migratory worker, either unskilled or a jack-of-all-trades. One who works at seasonable occupations or on construction projects. **1927** *Chi. Tribune* 2 Jan. II. 3/4 Finding enough food to live on is quite a job for the feathered hobos who are bumming around the country at this time. **1947** *Reader's Digest* Aug. 93 He wrote of clubmen, cabmen, thieves, policemen, touts, shopgirls, cashiers, hobos, actors, stenographers.

attrib. **1889** *Pasco* (Wash.) *Headlight* 6 Sep. 3/1 The hobo crop is more plentiful than ever before. **1898** *Boston Jrnl.* 22 Aug. 6/2 Mrs. S. J. Atwood calls herself the 'Hobo Hustler of the West.' . . . Her business is to gather up all the idle laborers she can find and put them to work on the Union Pacific Railroad. **1944** *Democrat* 14 Dec. 4/3 The objection we found to most hobo printers was that they were tired when they asked for a job.

b. (See quot.) *Rare.*

1907 LONDON *Road* 77 The 'Hobo' is that part of a prison where the minor offenders are confined together in a large cage.

c. hobo jungle, a camp or haunt of hobos.

1908 JOHNSON *Pacific Coast* 215 My companions spoke of the grove they were in as the 'Hoboes Jungle.' **1949** *Sat. Ev. Post* 9 April 152/4 To have fun doing nothing, whether in Palm Springs or a hobo jungle, you've got to be born that way.

d. hoboland, (see quot. 1896).

1896 *Atlantic Mo.* Jan. 58/1 By the 'ambulater' it [the underworld] is called Gypsyland, by the tramp Hoboland. **1933** *Variety* 14 Mar. 1/1 House located in the heart of hoboland on West Madison street, is playing to around 10,000–11,000 paid admissions weekly at 10c per head.

Also **hobodom, hoboism.**

1926 *Amer. Mercury* July 338/2 Even Bar-Room Bill is there, that monarch of the golden age of hobodom. **1930** *Publishers' Wkly.* 31 May 3736/2 Any hobo temporarily sober can find a publisher to place on the market with great éclat an epic of Hobodom. **1930** *19th Cent.* June 849 These were the high days of American hoboism.

hobo ˈhobo, *v.* [f. the noun.] *intr.* and *tr.* To live as a hobo, to make one's way in the manner of a hobo. Also **hoboing,** *n.*

1906 SINCLAIR *Jungle* xxv. 298 Then he explained how he had spent the last summer, 'hoboing it,' as the phrase was. **1907** LONDON *Road* 48 In all my hoboing it is the best bit of train-jumping I have done. **1939** *These Are Our Lives* 311 The boy left the country and was later killed while hoboing his way on a freight train.

Hobomoko ˌhɑbəˈmɑko, *n.* [Amer. Indian.] (See quots.) *Obs.*

1624 WINSLOW *Good Newes* 53 Another power they worship, whom they call Hobbamock, and to the norward of us Hobbamoqui; this as farre as wee can conceiue is the Deuill. **1634** WOOD *N. Eng. Prospect* II. viii. 76 In the night . . . [Indians] will not budge from their owne dwellings for feare of their *Abamacho* (the Devill) whom they much feare, specially in evill enterprizes. **1663** *Maine Hist. Soc. Coll.* III. 96 [The Indians] believed that all good came from Squantum (God) and all evil from Abbamocoko (the Devil). **1781** PETERS *Hist. Conn.* 161 Some few . . . declared that Putnam . . . was the first son of Hobbamockow. **1907** HODGE *Amer. Indians* I. 555/1 *Hobomoko*. . . . Mentioned by early writers as an evil deity of the Massachuset and closely related Algonquian tribes.

hobomok skipper. (See quot.) — **1909** *Cent. Supp.* 828/3 Mormon . . . an American hesperiid butterfly, *Atrytone hobomok*, which occurs from eastern Canada to the Mississippi valley. Its larvae feed on grasses. Also called *hobomok skipper*.

Hobsonizing ˈhɑbsn̩ˌaɪzɪŋ, *n.* [Richmond P. *Hobson* (1870–1937), "hero of the Merrimac" in consequence of which the girls "gave him a merry smack."] Flirting. *Rare.* — **1904** *Baltimore Amer.* 17 Aug. 6 The wild waves must have been saying some severe things at Atlantic City against the Hobsonizing on the beach, since flirting has been forbidden there by official decree.

hock hɑk, *n.*[1] [See note.]

The origin of this term is obscure. It may be the same word as ∗*hoc*, ∗*hock*, the name of an old card game (see *OED*), but see the spellings in the first group of quots. below. It may be the same word as **hock,** *n.*[2] below.

In faro: The last card remaining in the deal box after the deal. In full **hock card.** Cf. ∗**soda,** *n.* **1.**

(1) **1843** GREENE *Exposure of Gambling* 210 By hocklety and splitting, many men have experienced great disappointment on this same device of hocklety. *Ib.* 166 *Hockley*, signifies the last card but one, the chance of which the banker claims, and may refuse to let any punter withdraw a card when eight or less remain to be dealt. **1850** BOHN *Handbook Games* 336 Faro . . . *Hocly:* a certainty; signifies the last card but one, the chance of which the banker claims.

(2) **1859** MATSELL *Vocabulum* 113 *Hock*, the last card in the box. **1864** DICK *Amer. Hoyle* (1866) 205 The fourth nine remaining in the box, being the last, or 'hock.' **1897** A. H. LEWIS *Wolfville* 20 'Whatever's the hock kyard to all this?' he says to Jack Moore. **1931** WILLISON *Here They Dug Gold* 217 The next card is a loser, the next a winner, and so throughout the deck to the last card, the 'hock,' which likewise pays nothing.

b. (See quot.) *Obs.*

1898 DICK *Amer. Hoyle* (ed. 17) 347 As the game was originally played, the dealer took *hock*—that is, all the money which happened to be placed upon that card.

hock hɑk, *n.*[2] [f. Du. *hok*, hutch, hovel, dog house, prison.]

1. *In hock*, in difficulties, or the loser in a card game. *Slang.*

1859 MATSELL *Vocabulum* 113 When one gambler is caught by another, smarter than himself, and is beat, then he is in hock. Men are only caught, or put in hock, on the race-tracks, or on the steamboats down South. **1889** FARMER 299/1 To be caught in hock is a fate which befalls simpletons who venture into the toils of card sharpers. **1913** MULFORD *Coming of Cassidy* 118 If the four lay under the Queen, Cassidy lost; if not, he either won or was in hock.

b. In jail, hence *out of hock.*

1859 MATSELL *Vocabulum* 113 Among thieves a man is in hock, when he is in prison. **1887** *Courier-Journal* 25 Jan. 5/5 An Embezzler in Hoc [*sic*]. Sheriff James Ferguson, of Wyandotte, passed through this city yesterday with a prisoner . . . whom he had arrested . . . upon the charge of embezzling $10,000. **1902** HARBEN *A. Daniel* 199 Somehow I felt . . . ef they did git Jimmy out o' hock . . . without me a-chippin' in, I'd never be able to look at 'em without remorse. *Ib.* 234, I determined to have it by hook or crook, ef it killed me, or put me in hock the rest o' my life.

c. In pawn. Also *out of hock.* Cf. **2.** below.

1884 DOUGHERTY *Oratorical Stump Speaker* 26 (We.), My other coat's in hock. **1908** LORIMER *J. Spurlock* vii, I was doing him a favour in consenting to have my evening clothes taken out of hock. **1949** *Sun. World-Herald Mag.* (Omaha) 10 April 5/1 The determined builder 'has about everything in hock' to keep his venture going.

d. In debt.

1926 J. BLACK *You Can't Win* xxiv. 390, I was in hock to friends who saved me from a heavy sentence. **1948** *Sat. Ev. Post* 17 July 57/2 The board of trustees who were running the colony from England, and to whom it was in hock, coaxed the people to produce the silk, wine and drugs which England needed.

e. (See quot.)

1938 ASBURY *Sucker's Prog.* 15 In hock—The last card in the box was said to be in hock.

2. hock shop, a pawnshop. *Slang.*

1902 LIMERICK *B. Burgundy's Letters* 15 (We.), As a last resort fell into a hock-shop. **1903** ADE *People You Know* 96 Unless he could raise the Wind, it meant a Receiver over at the Works, his credit evaporated and the Pianola to the Hock-Shop. **1949** *This Week Mag.* 9 Jan. 5/4 As a result, some of their homes resemble hock shops.

hock hɑk, *v.* [f. **hock,** *n.*[2]] *tr.* To pawn or pledge. *Slang.*

1878 *S.F. Trade Herald* Aug. 2/2 To soak—to hock—Yer upper benjamin at yer uncle's, to get the 'sugar' for a good square meal. **1922** FOSTER *Adv. Trop. Tramp* 354, I've just hocked my camera, and all I've got is two dollars. **1948** *Good Housekeeping* Jan. 44, I hocked all my possessions and a few of the landlady's and was on a train to Grainbelt City.

hock-hack ˈhɑkhæk, *n.* Variant of **hackback.** *Obs.* — **1832** WATSON *Hist. Tales N.Y.* 16 The white skins first dealt out strong drink from a large hock-hack, (a gourd or bottle).

*** hod,** *n.* **1.** *** hod carrier,** =next. **2. hod elevator,** an elevator for raising mortar, stone, etc., from the ground to a mason working on a wall. Both *obs.* — **(1) 1864** NICHOLS *Amer. Life* I. 382 Steam hod-carriers [may be seen] in the large buildings. — **(2) 1867** *Rep. Comm. Patents 1865* I. 697 Hod Elevator. . . . This invention consists of a frame or cage, so shaped in a triangular form that the body of the hod will rest securely therein while being hoisted with brick or mortar.

*** hoe,** *n.*

1. *pl.* Short for "hoehands." *Colloq.*

1855 DAVIS *Farm Bk.* 160 The Hoes worked in the crab apple cut.

2. In combs. in some of which ***hoe** is of verbal origin: (1) **hoecake,** see as a main entry; (2) **dig,** a rollicking rustic dance, cf. **hoedown;** (3) **down,** see as a main entry; (4) **force,** *S.* a group of laborers engaged in hoeing, *colloq.;* (5) **hand,** *S.* a farm laborer employed in using a hoe, esp. in thinning out and cultivating cotton; (6) **harrow,** a triangular harrow, usu. with handles, for use between the rows of a growing crop, *obs.;* (7) **Negro,** a Negro slave who works with a hoe, *obs.*

(2) 1852 *Knickerb.* July 45 The company have generally to pay fifty cents admittance, for a couple, to a 'hoe-dig.' *Ib.* 46 At these 'hoe-digs' . . . are not Americans alone. . . . There is the Dutchman, all pipe, appetite, and stolidity; the Irishman, all dirt, fun, and flattery. **1944** ADAMS *W. Words* 77 hoe dig. A dance; also called *hoe down.* — **(4) 1852** in *Fla. Plant. Rec.* (1927) 66, I have bin thrown back a Little with the Hoe Force from choping cotton on the Account of the Hard rain washed up the Crop in Places.

(5) 1829 in COMMONS *Doc. Hist.* I. 231 Hoe hands finished rolling logs & burning brush, at an hour by sun. **1942** RAWLINGS *C. Creek* 129 Snow hinted that the man was starving, so we put him to work as a hoe-hand. — **(6) 1786** WASHINGTON *Diaries* III. 80 Finding the Hoe Harrow did not do good work in the drilled Corn, I ordered it to desist and the Bar share plow to be used. **1869** *Rep. Comm. Agric. 1868* 416 In the spring, when the ground had become sufficiently dry, a small garden hoe-harrow was run between the wide rows. — **(7) 1793** in *Pub. Col. Soc.* XI. 181, I have directed you to have him severely punished and placed under one of the Overseers as a common hoe Negro.

As the last term in **ax, bog, breaking-up, broad, clamshell, corn, cotton, gooseneck, grape, grubbing, hilling, Negro, sang, sprouting, tobacco, Virginia, weeding, wheel hoe.**

*** Hoe,** *n.* [Richard *Hoe* (1812–86), Amer. inventor.]

1. A Hoe printing press.

1883 *Harper's Mag.* Oct. 789/1 The spinning-wheel has given way to the factory, the hand-press to the magnificent 'Hoe.'

2. Used attrib. and in the possessive with reference to a high-speed, power-driven printing press in which the type is placed on a revolving cylinder.

[**1846** *Sci. Amer.* 5 Dec. 86/1 The above engraving represents one of R. Hoe & Co.'s double cylinder printing presses.] **1873** *Harper's Mag.* July 235/2 Then the Washington news goes through the hands of the compositors, the proof-readers, and the makers-up, to be rattling away in type or in stereotype on the 'turtles' of a Hoe's lightning press. **1876** *Chico* (Calif.) *Enterprise* 23 June 3/1 The Oroville *Mercury* has got a splendid new Hoe cylinder press. **1945** ADAMS *Album Amer. Hist.* II. 250 The Hoe cylinder press quickly replaced many used in this country.

*** hoe,** *v. To hoe (it) down* (or *off*), to execute a dance in the manner of a hoedown. *Colloq.*

1835 *Vade Mecum* (Phila.) 21 Mar. 3/5 'Pooh!' replied his panting rib, hoeing it off like a regular Juba, 'don't be a nigger all the days of your life.' **1874** MCCOY *Cattle* 139 He plunges in and 'hoes it down' at a terrible rate, in the most approved yet awkward country style; often swinging 'his partner' clear off of the floor. **1942** WARNICK *Dialect Garrett Co., Md.* 9 Hoe down, v. phr., to dance vigorously.

hoecake ˈhoˌkek, *n. S.* [See quot. 1789, but cf. **no-cake.**] A large flat cake of bread made of corn meal, water, and salt. See also **Indian hoecake, piki.**

1745 in *Pa. Mag. Hist.* XXXVI. 162 Got Breakfast on Tea & Hoe Cake. **1789** ANBUREY *Travels* II. 335 Hoe-cake is Indian corn ground into meal, kneaded into a dough, and baked before a fire, but as the negroes bake theirs on the hoes that they work with, they have the appellation of hoe-cakes. **1850** S. F. COOPER *Rural Hours* 162 The bread was made from their own wheat, and so were the hoe-cakes, and griddle-cakes from the Indian meal and buckwheat of their growth. **1948** DICK *Dixie Frontier* 290 This was called a johnnycake. Sometimes a hoe was used instead of a board and the product was known as hoe cake.

b. *By hoecake,* a mild expletive. *Rare.*

1850 LEWIS *La. Swamp Doctor* 83, I 'spected it [a tooth extraction] would make all things pop, by hoecake.

*** hoed,** *a.*

1. hoed crop, a row crop in the cultivation of which hoes are used.

1850 *Rep. Comm. Patents 1849: Agric.* 101 Barley always follows a hoed crop, as it seems to do best on a subdued soil. **1879** *Scribner's Mo.* Dec. 239/2 The owner has only to . . . give it a year of ordinary cultivation taking from it . . . some profitable hoed crop. **1945** *N. Eng. Homestead* 22 Sep. 16/3 We have some cause to worry because some hoed crops are beginning to suffer for lack of water.

2. hoed land, land that is broken up or cultivated with the hoe. *Rare.*

1643 *Plymouth Laws* 74 By ympróved lands are understood meddow land plowed land and howed lands.

hoedown ˈhoˌdaʊn, *n.* Orig. and chiefly *S.*

1. A lively and riotous kind of dance, a breakdown; also the music or tune played for this. See **Kentucky, Negro, Virginia hoedown.**

The first quot. may suggest the origin of the term. Cf. **hoe-dig.**

[**1807** IRVING *Salmagundi* 7 Mar. 98 As to dancing, no Long-Island negro could shuffle you 'double trouble,' or 'hoe corn and dig potatoes' more scientifically.] **1849** T. T. JOHNSON *Sights Gold Regions* iv. 38 One of our party commenced a regular hoe-down, knocking his shins with heavy boots. **1919** T. K. HOLMES *Man from Tall Timber* 84 Most of his playing was a medley of old-time hoe-downs and jig music. **1948** DICK *Dixie Frontier* 131 The usual type of dance was the square dance commonly known as a hoe-down or breakdown.

attrib. and *transf.* **1841** *N.O. Picayune* 14 Jan. 2/1 He looks and walks the character to the life, and some of his touches are of the genuine 'hoe down,' 'corn-field' order. **1893** *Outing* Mar. 125/1 For regular good old-time, hoe-down sport, 'bobbing' carries the palm. **1948** *Popular Western* June 72/2 Mac Conway tapped an accompaniment to an old hoe-down tune he was humming.

2. A party at which such dances are the chief source of entertainment. Also **hoedown party.**

1870 NOWLAND *Indianapolis* 33 Whar's Russell, with his fiddle? and we'll have a reg'lar hoe down. **1887** *Courier-Journal* 22 Jan. 3/6 We have an old Kentucky hoe-down twice a week. **1948** *Prairie Club Bul.* May 11 Once again Deer Grove Camp comes through with a grand old country-style Hoe-Down (Square Dance) Party. **1949** *Ib.* June 11 We will have the use of the hayloft for a hoedown.

*** hog,** *n.*

1. (See quots.) Now *hist. Slang.*

1859 MATSELL *Vocabulum* 42 Hogg, a ten-cent piece. **1889** FARMER 299/2 *Hogg* (Cant).—A ten cent piece (about 5d). **1948** FUNK *Hog on Ice* 153 A shilling in England or a ten-cent piece in the United States was at one time called a 'hog.'

2. =**hog engine.** *Slang.*

1888 *Walla Walla* (Wash.) *Union* 24 Nov. 3/4 The 'hog' will haul nine loaded cars up the heavy Alto grade, while the ordinary road engine had a hard tussel to haul four or five. **1949** *Boston Sun. Globe* 8 May (Fiction Mag.) 1/1 We have 2458, a big hog with eight drivers and lots of power.

3. In combs.: (1) **hogback,** =**hog frame,** cf. **5.** (1) below; (2) **call,** the calling of hogs, esp. in a contest, also **hog caller,** cf. **11.** (1) below; (3) **chain,** "a chain in the nature of a tension rod passing from stem to stern of a vessel, and over posts nearer amidships; designed to prevent the vessel from drooping at the ends" (Knight), also attrib.; (4) **cholera,** an infectious disease of hogs caused by a filtrable virus and characterized by intestinal ulceration, fever, etc., sometimes applied to other diseases (see quot. 1870), also attrib.; (5) **claim,** a claim to some of the hogs ranging in a particular region, *colloq.;* (6) **engine,** a powerful freight engine; (7) **fat,** *a.* as fat as a hog, *colloq.;* (8) *** head,** a railroad engineer, *slang;* (9) **Hogopolis,** Cincinnati, cf. **Porkopolis;** (10) **packing,** the action of killing and dressing hogs, also attrib.: (11) **proof**

fence, a fence that is hog-tight; (12) **season,** formerly winter, the time when hogs were slaughtered; (13) **sign,** a mark or trace left by a hog or by hogs; (14) **tie,** a way of tying an animal's feet together by securing them one on top of the other, cf. **11.** (2) below.

(1) 1886 *Waterbury* (Conn.) *Amer.* 2 April (*Cent.*), The strength of her hull and the solidarity of her hog-back. — **(2) 1927** *Sat. Ev. Post* 24 Dec. 28/3 On the paper I work for we once started a queer tempest indeed. This was in regard to the hog call. **1949** *Time* 7 Mar. 27/3 She echoed his ideas like an empty barrel on a hog caller's porch. — **(3) 1873** MARK TWAIN & WARNER *Gilded Age* iv. 43 They ran races up and down the deck; . . . 'skinned the cat' on the hogchains. **1907** STEWART *Partners* 9, I knew that one [*sc.* borehole] because that was where I threw the hog-chain bolt. — **(4) 1859** *Prairie Farmer* XX. 35 To Prevent Hog Cholera—Give from five to twenty grains of calomel to a hog. **1870** *Rep. Comm. Agric. 1869* 43 'Hog cholera' . . . popularly means any disease which sweeps off the species as an epizoötic. **1946** *Democrat* 13 June 3/1 We have in stock at all times Hog Cholera Serum.

(5) 1859 TALIAFERRO *Fisher's R.* 52, I had a hog claim over beyant Moor's Fork, and I concluded I'd take old Bucksmasher [his rifle], and go inter the big huckleberry patch, on Round Hill, in sarch for 'um. **1932** RANDOLPH *Ozark Mts.* 86 A hawg-claim was jest a piece o' paper made out like a deed, givin' th' bearer th' right t' kill so many hawgs, an' signed by th' feller whut sold th' claim. — **(6) 1888** *Walla Walla* (Wash.) *Union* 24 Nov. 3/4 A gigantic 'hog' engine, for use on the Starbuck hill, was taken up the road Wednesday. — **(7) 1924** R. CUMMINS *Sky-High Corral* 15, I got a hundred head more than my permit calls for—an' they're hog fat. **1929** E. W. HOWE *Plain People* 190 Later it [*sc.* a buffalo] became hog fat, and was finally sold to a committee preparing a barbecue. — **(8) 1931** *Illinois Central Mag.* June 30/2 To the initiated, a 'tallow-pit' is a locomotive fireman and a 'hoghead' is the engineer. **1948** *Railway Clerk* June 320/2, I recall once knowing a hoghead by th' name o' Witsaway. — **(9) 1872** *Borderer* (Las Cruces, N.M.) 3 July 2/1 This is not the first of his class from Hogopolis that has perambulated and deadheaded through this territory.

(10) 1870 O. LOGAN *Before Footlights* 254 Chicago is bounded . . . on the sou'-sou'-west by a hog-packing establishment. **1881** *Chi. Times* 14 May, The *Cincinnati Price Current* reviews the hog-packing returns as follows. — **(11) 1922** *Dly. Ardmoreite* (Ardmore, Okla.) 8 Jan. 7/1 He is putting 40 acres under hog proof fence. — **(12) 1835** in HOFFMAN *Winter in West* II. 117 (*footnote*), During the whole 'hog season,' this stream [near Cincinnati] . . . is running blood. — **(13) 1853** P. PAXTON *Yankee in Texas* 117 Nothing leaves a mark to him [a Texan], he only sees sign. . . . You hear of turkey sign, bear sign, hog sign, cow sign, Indian sign, etc. — **(14) 1910** BRONSON *Remin. Ranchman* 12 Before he could rise, Pete lit on him and soon had the wicked hind hoofs safely half-hitched, and all four feet securely bound in the 'hog-tie.' **1941** SETON *Trail of Artist Naturalist* 321 The two cowmen jerked loose the hog-ties, the broncos sprang to their feet, and of course ran away.

b. In similar combs. of obvious meaning or sufficiently explained in the quots., as (1) **hog age,** (2) **bite,** cf. **4. b.** (3) below, (3) **crop,** (4) **frame,** (5) **guessing,** (6) **Latin,** (7) *****leg,** (8) **tight,** *a.*, (9) **way,** (10) **wild,** usu. in phrases.

(1) 1848 J. MITCHELL *Nantucketisms* 40 *Hog age.* Between Boyhood & Manhood. **1893** FARMER & HENLEY *Slang, Hog-age*, the period between boyhood and manhood. — **(2) 1890** HOWELLS *Boy's Town* 72 [If] you began to sell out bites [of an apple] at three pins for a lady-bite and six pins for a hog-bite, and a boy bought a lady-bite and took a hog-bite, he was held in contempt. — **(3) 1847** *Sci. Amer.* 3 Jan. 147/4 The Hog Crop of the United States, this year, is three times the value of the cotton crop. **1855** *N.Y. Wkly. Tribune* 6 Jan. 1/2 The 'Hog crop' of this year would seem to be a very large one, in spite of the scarcity of grain. — **(4) 1864** WEBSTER 631/3 *Hog-frame.* A fore-and-aft frame, usually above deck, and forming, together with the frame of the vessel, a truss to prevent vertical flexure. Used chiefly in American river and lake steamers. Called also *hogging-frame.* **1875** KNIGHT 1108/1 The term 'hog-frame' has been adopted into carpentry and engineering in some forms of trusses for roofs and bridges.

(5) 1859 BARTLETT 198 *Hog Guessing*, a sport peculiar to Long Island. In the fall a fat hog is selected to be 'guessed for.' The chances are put at a given price as in a raffle, and at the time appointed each holder of a chance 'guesses' at the weight of the hog, which is then determined in the presence of all by the scales; the best guess, of course, takes the animal. — **(6) 1810** M. DWIGHT *Journey to Ohio* 53 He pass'd us on the road, singing & screaming, advising us to go back & learn hog-latin—alias German—or dutch. **1908** *D.N.* III. 321 *Hog-Latin*, dog-Latin, gibberish invented by school-children. — **(7) 1920** HUNTER *Trail Drivers Texas* I. 232 A 'hog-leg,' . . . better known as a six shooter gun. **1949** *10 Story Western* May 61/2 He too toted an upholstered hogleg as he came around the rumps of the two ponies. — **(8) 1859** BARTLETT 198 *Hog-tight and Horse-high*, always used together, of fences that are sufficient to restrain trespassing stock. Maryland. **1879** TOURGEE *Fool's Errand* xxx. 194 The split-board paling . . . was 'horse-high, hog-tight, and bull-strong.' **1947** *Steamboat* (Colo.) *Pilot* 13 Feb. 6/7, 250 acres land, 200 in cultivation, 120 fenced and cross fenced, woven wire, hog, sheep and cattle tight. — **(9) 1907** STEWART *Partners* 80 The deck [was] like a sidewalk all along each side; and them was the hogways. . . . When the hogways was all piled up with cordwood around the cabin, no Blackfeet Indians could shoot through that boat.

(10) 1904 *D.N.* II. 419 hog wild, adj. Wildly excited. 'I never saw such an excitement over a little thing in Arkansas as there was over that debate. They went *hog wild.*' **1915** *Chi. Tribune* 14 Oct. 9/5 If he had been hog wild like usual they couldent of hit so many runs. **1915** *Everybody's Mag.* Oct. 459/2, I'm going to take a round-house wallop at the first thing I see and run hog-wild on the bases.

4. In the names of, or with reference to, plants: (1) **hog corn,** corn of an inferior quality regarded as sufficiently good for feeding to hogs; (2) **peanut,** a fabaceous vine, *Amphicarpa comosa*, of the eastern U.S., producing one-seeded pods at the base of the stem; (3) *****potato,** (*a*) the manroot, *Ipomoea pandurata*, (*b*) (see quot.).

(1) 1751 MACSPARRAN *Diary* 58 We have but 51 Bushels of good, and 5 Ditto, of Hog Corn. **1800** MAUDE *Niagara* 34 Has produced, per acre, ninety bushels of marketable shelled Corn, (maize) exclusive of inferior or Hog-Corn. — **(2) 1857** GRAY *Botany* 106 *Amphicarpæa.* Hog Pea-nut. **1885** *Outing* VII. 180/1 A beautifully slender twining vine, bearing the euphonious title of hog-peanut. **1941** R. S. WALKER *Lookout* 58 The hog or wild peanut clings closely to waste places where moisture and rich soil are abundant. — **(3)** (*a*) **1800** HAWKINS *Sk. Creek Country* 21 In the old beaver ponds, in thick boggy places, they have the hog potatoe. **1820** in MORSE *Rep. Indian Affairs* (1822) II. 206 [The Chaneers] derive a portion of their subsistence regularly from the . . . Papaws, parsimmons, hog potatoes, and several other nutritious roots. (*b*) **1931** CLUTE *Plants* 98 The hog-potato (*Stenanthium graminium*) [is] a poisonous lily-wort.

b. Also (1) **hog apple,** (2) **berry,** (3) **bite,** cf. **3. b.** (2) above, (4) **brake,** (5) **cranberry,** (6) **fennel,** (7) **onion,** see quots.

(1) 1843 TORREY *Flora N.Y.* I. 35 *Podophyllum peltatum.* May-apple. Mandrake. Hog-apple. . . . Moist open woods and meadows, in rich soil. **1931** CLUTE *Plants* 98 The hog-apple (*Podophyllum peltatum*) a fruit which is little esteemed. — **(2) 1846** BROWNE *Trees Amer.* 519 *C*[*eltis*] [*occidentalis*] *crassifolia.* . . . Hack Berry, Hag Berry, Hog Berry, Hoop Ash, of the Anglo-American. . . . The fruit . . . is of a dark-brown, or nearly black colour. — **(3) 1894** *Amer. Folk-Lore* VII. 91 *Chondrilla juncea*, hog bite, Devil's grass. West Va. — **(4) 1891** *Amer. Folk-Lore* IV. 149 [In N.H.] *Pteris aquilina* was Hog Brake, probably because of the mucilaginous roots which the hogs eagerly sought for.

(5) 1894 *Amer. Folk-Lore* VII. 99 *Empetrum nigrum* . . . hog cranberry. Islands of Penobscot Bay, Me. **1931** CLUTE *Plants* 98 The hog cranberry (*Empetrum nigrum*) [is] an inedible fruit. — **(6) 1931** CLUTE *Plants* 97 The hog-fennel is another name for the familiar dog-fennel (*Anthemis cotula*). — **(7) 1894** *Amer. Folk-Lore* VII. 101 *Brodiaea capitata*, hog onion, Spanish lily. Santa Barbara Co., Cal.

For *****hognut, hog plum,** see as main entries.

5. In the names (sufficiently explained in the quots.) of fishes and other animals, as (1) **hogback,** (cf. also **3.** (1) above), (2) **bass,** (3) **bear,** (4) **choke,** (5) **choker,** (6) **clam,** (7) **molly,** (8) **sucker.**

(1) 1832 *N.H. Hist. Soc. Coll.* III. 86 The Hogback, or sunfish, as some call it, . . . is about as large as the Perch. **1880** *Rep. Supt. Yellowstone Nat. Pk.* (1881) 40 The hog-back, or real California grizzly, . . . is one of the largest, most powerful, ferocious and dangerous animals upon the continent. — **(2) 1820** RAFINESQUE in *Western Rev.* II. 56 Bass Hogfish, *Etheostoma calliura*, . . . has some similarity with . . . other River bass, wherefore it is called Minny-bass, Little-bass, Hog-bass, &c. — **(3) 1868** *Amer. Naturalist* I. 657, I had at one time two tamed [black bears, *Ursus americanus*]. . . . One was what is called the 'Ranger' Bear. . . . The other was what is called a 'Hog Bear,' and was shorter-legged and blacker. So I am sure the Hog Bear and Ranger are of one species. — **(4) 1857** *Harper's Mag.* March 442/1 The refuse fish commonly taken [in N.C.] are sturgeon, . . . hog-choke or flounders . . . and common eels.

(5) 1855 BAIRD in *Smithsonian Rep.* 350 [The New York sole] is familiarly known at Beesley's point under the name of hog-choker, as when seized by the hogs it doubles itself up, and, filling the oesophagus, obstinately resists by the scabrous nature of its scales all effort on the part of the animal to swallow it. — **(6) 1799** BENTLEY *Diary* II. 312 They are not the long large Clams of our Beaches, not the Quahoag, but really a larger species of the Hog or Common Clam, differing from the long or larger Clams. — **(7) 1889** *Cent.* 2852/2 *Hog-molly*, . . . the hog-mullet or hog-sucker, *Hypentelium nigricans.* (Local, U.S.) *Ib.* 2851/3 A darter, *Percina caprodes*, of the family *Percidæ* and subfamily *Etheostominæ*, inhabiting American fresh waters, [is] also called *hog-molly, log-perch*, and rockfish. **1933** *Amer.*

Sp. Feb. 49/2 Hogmolly, *n.* A fish of the sucker family. The term is in common use among the Choctaws in Oklahoma, according to a writer in *Outdoor Life* (Sep., 1928). — **(8) 1883** *Nat. Museum Bul.* No. 27, 478 *Catostomus nigricans*. . . . Hog Sucker. . . . United States from New York to Florida and westward to Alabama and Kansas; Great Lake region. **1935** ROLLINS *Disc. Ore. Trail* 130 The 'Sucker' was a catostomoid fish, *Catostomus* or *Hypentelium nigricans*, known also, in popular parlance, as Stone-roller, stone-lugger, sucker, hog-sucker and hog-molly.

For ∗**hogfish, hognose,** see as main entries.

6. Designating places for, frequented by, or associated with, hogs: (1) **hog bed,** a pile of straw, leaves, etc., made by a hog or by hogs as a place to lie at night; (2) **-bed prairie,** =**hog-wallow prairie,** *rare;* (3) **court,** a place or yard for hogs, *rare;* (4) **lot,** an inclosure for hogs; (5) **path,** a path through the woods made by hogs running at large; (6) ∗**pen,** see as a main entry; (7) **ranch,** a ranch or farm where particular attention is given to raising hogs; (8) **range,** an area suitable for hogs to range over; (9) **scald,** (see quot.), *colloq.;* (10) **trail,** =**hog path;** (11) **wallow,** see as a main entry.

(1) 1799 J. SMITH *Acc. Captivity* (Lexington, Ky.) 37, I made a bed like a . . . hog-bed. — **(2) 1834** *Visit to Texas* x. 91 The country in the rear . . . has a poor soil, of that sort which is called hog-bed Prairie. — **(3) 1639** *Md. Archives* IV. 110 It. for 10. daies work in railing in the hog-court. — **(4) 1854** DAVIS *Farm Bk.* 4 Rolled logs with the men & burned brush with the women till dinner in the hog Lot.

(5) 1866 MOORE *Women of War* 172 Know all the roads—don't you? and all the bridle paths, and even the hog paths—don't you? **1911** SAUNDERS *Col. Todhunter* 272 How far is it from town before you come to that hog-path, Abe? — **(7) 1869** BRACE *New West* 117 Another trail . . . follows up the divide between the Middle fork and Main river, joining the first-named trail at the 'Hog Ranch.' **1943** *Copper Camp* 3 Mrs. Fitzpatrick ran the 'Hog Ranch.' — **(8) 1857** BRAMAN *Texas* 29 This county has good cattle and hog ranges. — **(9) 1943** *Nat. Geog. Mag.* May 612/1 'Hog scalds' are favored spots along creeks where hogs are killed, scalded, and scraped.

(10) 1866 C. H. SMITH *Bill Arp* 76 A man can travel . . . any cow trail or hog trail and not meet from two to ten of the d-a-m cavalry.

7. Designating vehicles, tools, etc., used in raising or dealing with hogs: (1) **hog car,** a railroad car for shipping hogs; (2) **cart,** a cart with small wheels and a pig-pen body once used in New York City in rounding up hogs found going at large on the streets, *obs.;* (3) **fence,** a fence such as hogs cannot get through, *obs.;* (4) ∗**knife,** a large, strong knife such as is used at hog killings; (5) **scalder,** (see quot. 1867); (6) **scraper,** (see quots.); (7) **tamer,** a device placed on a hog's nose to prevent its

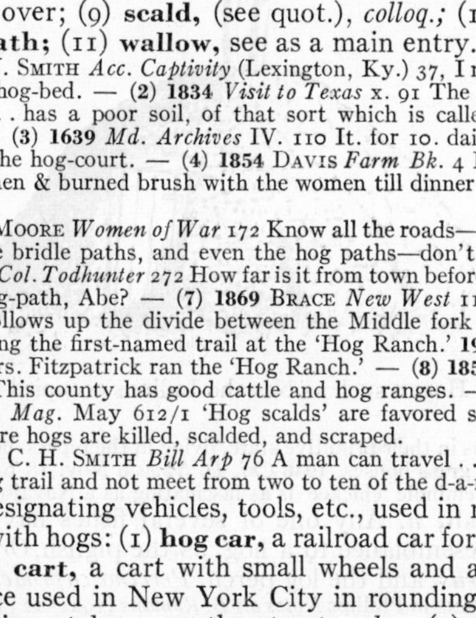

Type of hog tamer (*c*1870) to prevent rooting

rooting; (8) **waterer,** a container for a readily available supply of water for hogs; (9) **wire,** wire fencing suitable for inclosures for hogs (see quot. 1909).

(1) 1863 NORTON *Army Lett.* 135 If I get down so low as that, I would not be much to load down an ambulance or a hog-car, would I? **1865** in *Ohio Arch. & Hist. Quart.* XXXVIII. 711 Morning found us still packed in stock or hog-cars. — **(2) 1825** in T. F. DEVOE *Market Book* 482 We are glad to learn . . . that the hog-cart, so long a desideratum here, is making a tour of sequestration through the city, and collecting the unsightly and ferocious quadrupeds which have hitherto enjoyed free commons on our streets. — **(3) 1663** *Watertown Rec.* I. 79 The hogreiffes . . . p[re]sented a list of thos persons that weare deffective in hogge Fences. — **(4) 1848** in A. ALLEN *P. Brooks* (1900) I. 55, I lost my big large hog knife down in the pasture. **1945** *Story* May–June 40, 'I don't like Mr. Tubberville,' says Olivia Ann staunchly. 'I'll go get my hog knife.'

(5) 1867 *Rep. Comm. Patents 1865* II. 1018 Portable Hog Scalder. . . . This invention consists of a boiler and table attached, with a furnace underneath the table. **1936** *Sears Cat.* (ed. 173) 947 (Index). — **(6) 1873** *Pat. Off. Gazette* IV. 13/1 Rotary Hog-Scraper. . . . An adjustable rotary scraping device for dressing hogs, operated by a belt and shifting pulley. **1902** *Sears Cat.* 754/3 Hog Scraper. . . . Wood handle with bolt extending through scraper . . . made of No. 20 sheet iron . . . price, each . . . 8c. — **(7) 1868** *Iowa Agric. Soc. Rep. 1867* 233 Tousley's Hog-Tamer, or Snout-Rings for Swine. **1871** *Ill. Agric. Soc. Trans.* VIII. 236 He recommends cutting the nose with a hog tamer, to prevent rooting. — **(8) 1931** *Chi. Sun. Tribune* 18 Jan. II. 9/7 Hundreds of problems have been solved by this system . . . sanitary hog waterer, sheep feeding rack [etc.]. **1944** *Sears Cat.* (ed. 189) 878A This merchandise is not available in your Sears catalog this fall. . . . Hog Feeders, Oilers and Waterers. — **(9) 1909** WEBSTER 1024 *Hog wire*, barbed wire with four-pointed barbs and weighing about 400 lbs. per mile. *U.S.* **1945** *Hardin* (Mont.) *Tribune-Herald* 15 Feb. 7/5, 6 rolls of hog wire.

8. Denoting persons or groups having to do with hogs: (1) **hog combine,** a group of people financially interested in hogs; (2) **constable,** =**hogreeve,** *obs.;* (3) **drover,** one who owns or is in charge of a large number of hogs, *obs.;* (4) **grower,** one engaged in raising hogs; (5) **hayward,** =**hogreeve,** *obs.;* (6) **keeper,** =**hogreeve,** *obs.;* (7) **reeve,** *N. Eng.* a town officer having the duty of impounding stray hogs, appraising damage done by them, etc., cf. **field driver.**

(1) 1896 *Cong. Rec.* 21 Dec. 384/2 All the members of . . . the 'hog combine' were on their feet, deviling him and asking him questions. — **(2) 1683** *Groton Rec.* 82 Fo hog constiblls Samiwell Criptur goodman William Green. **1714** *Topsfield Rec.* 182 Dwaniel and Nathaniel Borman are chosen Hog constables. **c1849** PAIGE *Dow's Sermons* I. 199 It were a work of charity, indeed, if heaven, or some hog constable, would interfere in this business. — **(3) 1845** HOOPER *Simon Suggs' Adv.* 57 Simon could, of course, have no reasonable objection to being believed to be General Thomas Witherspoon, the rich hog drover from Kentucky. **1872** FLAGG *Good Investment* viii. 369/1 A park merchant . . . received him kindly, being used to deal with hog-drovers. — **(4) 1869** *Ill. Agric. Soc. Trans.* VII. 441 This table . . . will be found of value to the hog growers of the West.

(5) 1840 *N.Y. Mirror* 11 April 334/3 A 'town meeting' was to be held, and town officers to be appointed; among whose number, in old Connecticut, is an official designated a '*Hog-Hayward*.' — **(6) 1635** *Cambridge Rec.* 21 The Hog keeper begane to keepe one the first of April . . . at 10s. per Weeke. — **(7) 1636** *Boston Rec.* 13 At this meeting Richard Faireback is chosen for our Hog Reeve. **1839** *N.O. Picayune* 5 April 2/4 It is with no slight satisfaction we announce the important intelligence that Eben Carpenter has allowed himself to be put in nomination for hog-reeve. **1944** HOLTON *Yankees* 34 He had been elected hog-reeve by a large majority, or perhaps it was fence-viewer.

9. In the names of foods, dishes, etc., prepared from hogs: (1) **hog bosom,** hog meat, *jocular*, cf. **sow bosom;** (2) **jowl,** the jowl of a hog prepared as food; (3) **products,** (see quot. 1900); (4) **round,** (see quot. 1899); (5) **-'s cheese,** =next, *rare;* (6) **-shead cheese,** (see quot. 1859).

(1) 1905 BEACH *Pardners* ii. 55 'Bout to-morrer evening we'll be eating hog-bosom on Uncle Sam. — **(2) 1846** *Spirit of Times* 6 June 171/1 Our bill of fare was not very inviting. . . . Hog jowl served up with *greens, brains*, ditto, and 'biled ingons!' **1931** *Durant* (Okla.) *D. Democrat* 14 Jan. 1/7 Boiled turnips and hog jowl will be the principal items on the menu at the first meal. — **(3) 1891** *Times* (London) 23 March 5/2 The American negotiations with France for the resumption of the import of hog products . . . indicate that France will soon admit them. **1900** NELSON *A B C Wall St.* 145 Hog products. Speculatively they are pork, lard and shortribs. Other hog products are sides, hams, shoulders and bacon, comprising in all the American hog as he is marketed for domestic and foreign consumption. — **(4) 1819** *Amer. Farmer* I. 142 Bacon the hog round, 12 to 13 [dollars]. **1863** G. B. JONES *Rebel War Clerk's Diary* (1866) II. 35 Bacon is firm at $2 to $2.10 for hoground. **1899** GREEN *Va. Word-Bk.* 189 Hams, shoulders and middlings have different prices, but when taken all together at one price, it is so much *hog-round*.

(5) 1836 GILMAN *Recoll.* (1838) 25 Her hog's cheese (the English brawn) was delicacy itself. — **(6) 1859** BARTLETT 192 *Headcheese*, the ears and feet of swine cut up fine, and, after being boiled, pressed into the form of a cheese. In Maryland it is always called 'hogs-head cheese.' **1870** O. LOGAN *Before Footlights* 222 An inhuman and unearthly substance, yclept 'hogshead cheese,' constituted our breakfast at Nashville. **1947** *Pub. Amer. Dial. Soc.* No. 8, 32 *hog's head cheese:* Usually *head cheese.*

b. hog and hominy, pork and Indian corn prepared as food, also food in general, provender. *Colloq.*

1776 W. HOOPER in *Lett. from James Murray* (1901) 239, That I might enjoy in my own Cabin, eat my Hogg & Hominee without anything to make me afraid. **1843** CARLTON *New Purchase* II. 171 And all this was real American, United States' learning!—useful, practical stuff!—such as would enable a fellow to get his own bread and butter; or in New Purchase terms, his hog and hominy! **1948** DICK *Dixie Frontier* 290 Bacon or other pork products were such a common accompaniment of this kind of corn that the monotonous diet was often referred to as 'hog and hominy.'

Also **Hog and Hominy State,** (see quot.).

1946 *Agric. Hist.* April 86/1 A common nickname for the State of Tennessee has long been 'The Hog and Hominy State.'

10. In colloq. phrases of obvious meaning or sufficiently explained in the quots.

(1) **1857** *S.F. Call* 19 April 2/3 He don't appear to care nothing for nobody—he's 'as independent as a hog on ice!' [**1877** RUEDE *Sod-House Days* 181 About 8:30 we went for water, and had to break through an inch of ice in order to get it. Bub went sprawling round on the ice like a hog.] **1948** *Time* 9 Aug. 18/2 They like to think of themselves as independents—independent as a hog on ice. — (2) **1858** *Harper's Mag.* May 732/2 The negroes' hogs are always fatter than those of their master. 'Fat as a nigger's hog' has become a proverb with us in Virginia. — (3) **1878** *Cong. Rec.* 18 Dec. 288/1 He knows no more about Indian affairs than a hog does about a holiday. — (4) **1889** FARMER 300/2 *Hog in togs*, a well-dressed loafer.

(5) **1900** FLYNT *Tramping* 395 *On the hog*, on the tramp; also, 'busted,' 'dead broke.' **1904** O. HENRY *Cabbages & Kings* (1916) 155 'The man . . . used to be a railroad man. He's on the bum now.' . . . 'Railroader,' says I again, 'On the hog.' **1920** COOPER *Under Big Top* 229 This road's on the hog. — (6) **1939** *These Are Our Lives* 360, I can be independent as a hawg goin't to the wars when I wants to.

For *To root hog or die* see ∗**root,** *v.*

11. In verbal combs.: (1) **hog-call,** to call hogs, esp. to engage in contests with other hog-callers, hence **hog-calling,** *n.;* (2) **hog-tie,** to secure (an animal) by tying all four feet together, in allusion to the manner in which hogs are usu. tied, also transf.; (3) **hog-tight,** to make (a fence) hog-tight, *rare.*

(1) **1927** *Sat. Ev. Post* 24 Dec. 28/3 Noticing that there was to be a hog-calling contest in Omaha, . . . we feigned great ignorance of this branch of the vocal art. **1948** *Chi. Tribune* 14 Mar. I. 2/1 One of the farmers had awakened his pullman car by hog calling in his sleep. **1949** *Esquire* April 77/1 Farmers of the Midwest think so highly of their ability to call pigs that they honor the art with an annual hog-calling contest. — (2) **1894** *Harper's Mag.* Feb. 356/1 A cow was soon caught . . . and 'hog-tied,' which means all four feet together. **1906** *Out West* Feb. 137 Surely no hint here that a later Congress . . . would undertake to rope and hog-tie 'said Territory,' and drag it into the corral of a neighboring Territory. **1948** *Capital-Democrat* (Tishomingo, Okla.) 17 June 2/2 If the government can compete with and hogtie banking, it can compete with and control the grocer. — (3) **1913** CATHER *O Pioneers!* 140 Why don't you go over there some afternoon and hog-tight her fences?

As the last term in **game, ground, Hoover, Indian, Kentucky, land, Mexican, red, ribbon, river, road, sand, switch, tom, whole, wild, wood, yard hog.**

∗**hog,** *v.*

1. *tr.* To turn (an unharvested crop) over to hogs, also with *down* or *off. Colloq.*

1859 H. W. BEECHER *Pleasant Talk* 93 Some of the best farmers in this region hog their corn-lands. *Ib.* 94 Land being hogged, will be free from cut-worms. **1863** *Rep. Comm. Agric. 1862* 82, I was forced to hog down my crop this year. **1948** *Democrat* 19 Aug. 7/3 A good place to plant crimson clover and rye grass is where you hogged off peanuts.

b. (See quot.)

1915 *N. & Q.* 11 Ser. XII. 219 *Hog* (v.t.), to sow grain without ploughing.—'I just hogged my wheat into the stubble field.'

2. To steal or to take greedily in excess of one's share. *Slang.*

1884 MARK TWAIN *H. Finn* xxvi. 275 So, says I, s'pose somebody has hogged that bag on the sly? **1906** *Life* 4 Oct. 366 To bend oneself to the work of hogging everything in sight is an inglorious way to invest one's life. **1949** *Boston Globe* 10 July (Fiction Mag.) 8/5 You want to hog it all.

Hence **hogger, hogging game.**

1869 *New No. West* (Deer Lodge, Mont.) 15 Oct. 2/3, [I] am well acquainted with the party who struck the camp, and also with all of the '. . . hog-ers' and 'filers' from Lemki. **1880** *Pacific Metropolis* (S.F.) 12 June 6/1 The chief has made gambling an expensive luxury to the many professionals of both the square and 'hogging' games.

∗**Hogan** ˈhogən, *n.*[1] [See quot. 1848.] A variety of cotton, also **Hogan seed.** *Obs.*

1848 in TURNER *Cotton* (1865) 105 Hogan seeds were introduced into Mississippi by Mr. Wm. Hogan, who lives a few miles from me. **1851** *De Bow's Review* X. 568 The '*Hogan*' does better on thin land. **1865** TURNER *Cotton* 29 The fresher the land, and richer it is, the greater the distance; the Mexican seed requiring more distance than the cotton I have seen, which is called in a part of Mississippi, the Hogan seed.

hogan ˈhogən, *n.*[2] [f. Navaho *qoghan*, house.] A Navaho Indian lodge or wigwam, usu. built of earth walls kept in place by upright or slanting timbers. Cf. **summer hogan.**

1871 *Rep. Indian Affairs* (1872) 379 When a member of a family dies, in most cases they immediately leave their hogan (or wigwam) with the dead body in it. **1904** *N.Y. Ev. Post* 2 July 2 The North Amer-

Hogan such as Navaho Indians occupied

ican Indians in their primitive state, living in the tepees, hogans, sod-lodges and grass houses. **1948** *Chi. D. News* 9 Nov. 18/6 The palm-thatched Seminole 'chickee' is as fascinating as a Navajo 'hogan.'

∗**hogfish,** *n.* Any one of several fishes having some fancied resemblance to a hog, as the pigfish, *Orthopristis chrysopterus*, and the log perch, *Percina caprodes.*

1772 ROMANS in Phillips *Notes on B. Romans* (1924) 123 It Abounds here in fish of all kinds, . . . the Hog Fish, the Croaker, the Glen Fish, not unlike the Trout in Europe, and of the same Outward Appearance and so Called here. *c***1870** BAGBY *Old Va. Gentleman* 131 Another name for the nigger-knocker is hogfish, and it is by far the ugliest tenant of the Virginia waters. **1878** *Nat. Museum Proc.* I. 379 *Orthopristis fulvomaculatus.*—Hog-fish, Extremely common everywhere in the harbor. **1911** *Rep. Fisheries 1908* 308 Blunt-nosed Shiner (*Selene vomer*). . . . It is known in various places as 'hogfish.'

hog-killing ˈhɔgˌkɪlɪŋ, *n.*

1. The action of killing and dressing hogs. Also **hog-killing city** (see quot. 1848), **hog-killing day.**

1817 in ROYALL *Letters from Ala.* (1830) 36 It was hog-killing day at Wills. **1833** J. S. JONES *Green Mt. Boy* I. iii, I declare if she didn't look worse than a scalded shoat, on the last day o' hog-killin'. **1848** *Literary Amer.* 23 Dec. 451/3 In our wanderings the other day, we chanced to find ourselves among the pork-butcheries of this hog-killing city [Cincinnati]. **1943** *Democrat* 28 Oct. 2/2 Any day now is hog-killing day.

transf. **1933** *Amer. Sp.* Feb. 49/2 Hog-killing, n. Any sort of hilarious celebration or jollification. [Ozarks.]

2. hog-killing time, the time in winter when hogs are killed on the farm. Also transf., a time of jollification. *Colloq.*

*c***1862** BAGBY *Old Va. Gentleman* 96 They are the fixtures used at hog-killing time. **1948** *Dly. Ardmoreite* (Ardmore, Okla.) 27 May 3/2 All the neighbors used his scalding vat during hog-killing time.

hognose ˈhɔgˌnoz, *n.*

1. =next.

1888 *Pop. Science Mo.* XXXIII. 660 The blow-snake of Illinois is variously known in other localities as hog-nose, flat-head, viper and puff-adder.

2. hognose(d) snake, any one of various small, stout-bodied snakes of the genus *Heterodon*, esp. *H. contortrix*, the blowing adder.

1736 CATESBY *Carolina* II. 56 *Anguis Capite Viperino.* The Hog nose Snake, . . . [has] the Nose turning up like that of a Hog, his whole Visage being very ugly. **1842** *Nat. Hist. N.Y., Zoology* III. 51

The Hog-nosed Snake . . . is found frequently in dry sandy soils; . . . it is rather common in the southern parts of this State. **1949** *Scientific Mo.* Jan. 57/1 Since the hog-nosed snake is fairly common in sandy locations, where it preys upon toads, it is not a difficult matter to check on its bad reputation.

b. Also **hognosed sand viper,** (see quot.).

1878 HINTON *Arizona* 339 The *heterodon vasicus* (hog-nosed sand viper) was found as far south as Mineral Park.

c. hog-nosed skunk, a skunk, *Conepatus mesoleucus*, found in the Southwest, having a long, flexible snout with which it roots about in the manner of a hog.

1918 NELSON *Wild Animals N. Amer.* 584 The persistence with which the Hog-nosed Skunks hunt insects renders them a valuable aid to farmers. **1949** *Pacific Discovery* Jan.–Feb. 11/2 Hog-nosed skunks, in their search for grubs, plowed up the riverbottoms every night.

* **hognut,** *n.*

1. a. = **hognut hickory. b.** = **hog peanut.**

(a) 1814 BIGELOW *Florula Bostoniensis* 229 *Juglans glabra.* Pig nut. Hog nut. **1867** DEVENS *Pictorial Bk.* 117 The Legislature adjourned . . . by taking a square drink and a handful of 'hognuts.' — **(b) 1843** TORREY *Flora N.Y.* I. 164 *Amphicarpoea monica.* . . . Common Hognut. . . . Woods and thickets; common, August–September.

2. hognut hickory, a popular name for a species of hickory, *Carya glabra,* or its fruit. Cf. **pignut hickory.**

1810 MICHAUX *Arbres* I. 21 *Pig nut hickery, Hog nut hickery,* plus usitée dans quelques cantons de la Pensylvanie. **1832** BROWNE *Sylva* 182 This tree is generally known in the United States by the name of Pignut or Hognut Hickory.

* **hogpen,** *n.*

1. (See quots.) *Obs.*

*c***1775** in *S. Lit. Messenger* XXVII. 265/1 Our Army has been for some time arrested in its march to Norfolk by a redoubt or stockade, or hog-pen, as they call it here by way of derision. **1894** *McClure's Mag.* III. 112/2 The least ingenious or enterprising brand thief can cover . . . almost any mark, with a brand called the Hog-pen, or Window-sash.

2. *attrib.* Designating a creek or place where there is a pen for hogs. *Obs.*

1640 *Md. Hist. Mag.* V. 374 The Neck of Land called hog penn Neck, lyeing between thicketty Creek on the North, hog pen Creek on the South Chesapeak Bay. **1679** *Essex Inst. Coll.* XLIX. 26 Layd outt atta plaine Comonly Called Hogpen plaine and the medow lying within the upland. **1718** *N.H. Probate Rec.* II. 4, I give & bequeath unto my sone John Green . . . a lot of land lying by the hogpen meadow.

hog plum. A popular name for various wild plants or their plumlike fruit, esp. the Chickasaw plum *q.v.*

1876 HOBBS *Bot. Hand-Book* 53 Hog plum, Spondias entra. **1906** O. HENRY *Heart of West* 51, I was on my way over to take her a basket of wild hog-plums. **1949** *Chi. Tribune* 20 Feb. 30/3 Cedar and mesquite alone are costing Texas ranchers 115 million dollars a year. Add the sage and cactus, . . . catclaw, hog plum . . . and prickly pear and the toll is terrific.

* **hogshead,** *n.* As the last term in **crop, tobacco, trash hogshead.**

* **hogskin,** *n.*

1. (See quot. 1944.) In full **hogskin saddle.**

1858 SIMMONDS *Dict. Trade* 194/2 *Hog-skin Saddle,* a superior kind of saddle made from tanned hogskin. **1876** CROFUTT *Trans-continental Tourist* 53 The saddle of the plains . . . is a different article altogether from the Eastern 'hog skins.' **1944** ADAMS *W. Words* 77 hog skin. What the cowboy sometimes calls the small eastern riding saddle.

2. hogskin cap, app. a cap made of hogskin. *Obs.*

1849 *Hunt's Merch. Mag.* XX. 118 We except a large lot of that *unique* article of 'gentleman's wear' denominated hog-skin caps.

hogue hog, *v.* [Origin unknown.] (See quot.) *Rare.* — *c***1750** HUTCHINSON *Diary & Lett.* I. 46 It was part of the exercise of the scholars to read a verse or two each out of a Latin Testament into Greek every evening at prayer time [at Harvard College]; and it was a practice of some, to take a leaf of the Greek Testament, & put into the Latin Testament, which was termed *hogueing.*

hog wallow.

1. A muddy place where hogs wallow.

1829 DOW *Omnifarious Law Exemplified* 51 (Th. S.), It becomes a trespass to make a dam for a hog wallow. **1888** *Washington* (La.) *Argus* 21 June 2/2 Cesspools, hog wallows and duck ponds in close proximity to wells are liable to defile the water. **1894** *Cong. Rec.* Jan. 1036/1 At the back of the barn there was a pool which in the summer was a hog-wallow.

2. *W.* A depression in a prairie or plain (see quot. 1929).

1840 *Amer. Jrnl. Science* XXXIX. 212 From difference of surface, soil, and exposure, there arises a great diversity in the size, depth, and general appearance of the hog-wallows. **1883** SWEET & KNOX *Through Texas* 199 We came to a depression in the ground called a hog-wallow. **1929** DOBIE *Vaquero* 38 The very word 'hog-wallow' has produced no end of argument among people of the soil. A large number of them have stubbornly held that the depressions in the black lands of Central Texas were caused by the wallowing of early day razorbacks and thus properly acquired their name, hog-wallows.

attrib. **1858** *Texas Almanac 1859* 74 We have no stiff hog-wallow lands. **1883** SMITH *Geol. Survey Ala.* 494 The hog-wallow clay in dry weather packs very much after the fashion of the prairie soil of the Rotten Limestone. **1899** *U.S. Geol. Surv. Water Supp. Paper* 19, 37 They experienced great difficulty in preparing and cultivating the shallow , coarse, gravelly, hogwallow soil.

b. (See quots. and cf. quot. 1853 under **c.** below), app. from a misapprehension of the significance of "wallow."

1898 U.S. Geol. Surv. *Water Supp. Paper* 18, 36 Its surface is very generally besprinkled with the low mounds usually known in the West as hog-wallows. **1948** *Scientific Mo.* April 356/1 Hog-wallow land is the reverse of this: it is composed of mounds, not depressions, sprinkled over fairly flat or gently rolling areas.

c. A prairie region characterized by hog wallows, in full **hog wallow prairie.**

1840 *Amer. Jrnl. Science* XXXIX. 211 In Texas . . . I had full opportunity to study the phenomenon of hog-wallow prairies. **1853** P. PAXTON *Yankee in Texas* 95 The ground we were riding over, of the description known as 'hog-wallow,' being a succession of small mounds and corresponding hollows. **1883** SMITH *Geol. Survey Ala.* 494 Local patches of a tenacious clayey soil, called 'hog-wallow prairie,' are here and there met with in Cowikee lands.

3. hog-wallow mesquite, (see quot.).

*a***1877** *Emigrant's Guide* 44 (B.), *Hog-Wallow Mesquit.* A species of grass, used only to be found in the hog-wallows of Texas, but which is now rapidly spreading itself along the road-sides, and carpeting all the old roads and other spots and places of ground which have been denuded of other grasses, with a thickly crowded coat of extremely fine, nutritious pasturage for every type of graminivorous animals. In appearance, it closely resembles the Bermuda grass (*Cynodon dactylon*). Except on suitably moist grounds, it is not large enough to make hay of; as it does not, on ordinary soil, exceed three to six inches in height.

Hohokam ˌhoˈhokəm, *n. S.W.* [f. Pima Indian.] (See quots.)

1884 BANDELIER *Arch. Inst. Rep.* V. 80 The Casa Blanca and all the ruins of the Gila were the abode of the fore-fathers of the Pimas, designated by them as 'Vĭ-pĭ-sĕt' (great-grandparents), or 'Ho-ho-qom' (the extinct ones). **1912** FEWKES *Casa Grande, Ariz.* 153 The Pima name Hohókam may be adopted to designate this ancestral stock, to whom may be ascribed the erection of the casas grandes on the Gila. **1942** STEGNER *Mormon C.* 147 The Ho-ho-kim, the Old People Who Left, were the Nephites, the ruins were the ruins of their cities.

attrib. **1937** *Southwestern Lore* Dec. 54 As a result of investigations conducted at Winona Village certain archaeological discoveries have definitely explained the affiliation with the Hohokam Culture. **1941** FERGUSSON *Southwest* 116 What happened to the early Hohokam people is still in dispute. Some archaeologists believe they were the ancestors of the modern Pima and Papago folk who still live in brush shelters on the desert.

hoi-koh ˈhɔɪˈko, *n.* [?Native name.] (See quot.) — **1883** *Nat. Museum Bul.* No. 27, 418 *Oncorhynchus keta.* . . . Hoi-Koh; Dog Salmon. West coast of the United States from San Francisco northward.

* **hoist,** *n.* Short for Irish hoist *q.v. Colloq. Obs.* — **1859** ELWYN *Glossary* 59 *Hoist.* . . . We use it as the substantive, and say, 'he got the deuce of a *hoist,*' meaning a fall.

* **hoist,** *v.*

1. *tr.* (See quots.) Also **hoisting,** *n. Obs.*

1773 S. CHANDLER in *Harvard Graduates' Mag.* X. 381 After Dinner I was histed by Dunbar for eating before the Scholars came in. **1851** HALL *College Words* 162 It was formerly customary at Harvard College, when the Freshmen were used as servants, to report them to the Tutor if they refused to go when sent on an errand; this complaint was called a *hoisting,* and the delinquent was said to be *hoisted.*

2. In substantival combs., as **hoistaway, -door, -way, works,** (see quots. and cf. **hoisting works**).

1879 WEBSTER *Supp., Hoistway,* an opening in the floor of a wareroom for hoisting or lowering merchandise. **1881** WORCESTER *Supp.,* Elevator, a mechanical contrivance for raising persons and goods from the lower story of a building to the higher stories . . . called also lift and hoistaway. **1881** *Harper's Mag.* March 528/1 In the middle of the hall was the 'hoist-door,' through which the wheat was 'hoisted' up by a crane and stored in the loft. **1883** *Ib.* March 497/1 From the roof of the Grand Hotel you looked down at the shaft the hoist works, and heaps of extracted ore of the Vizina.

hoisting works. The mining machinery used in hoisting ore, etc., out of a shaft. — **1871** RAYMOND *3d Rep. Mines* 40 The great fire at the Empire mine in September . . . swept the company's milling and hoisting works out of existence. **1877** W. WRIGHT *Big Bonanza* 172 The incline hoisting-works stand a short distance from the building in which is contained the hoisting machinery of the vertical shaft.

hoja ˈohə, *n. S.W.* [Sp., leaf.] A corn shuck formerly used to roll tobacco in for smoking. *Obs.*

1834 A. PIKE *Sketches* 102 'Buy some tobacco, compadre,' said a voice from the sala, 'a hundred cigarrones, you know, of the best ojas, and of tobacco.' **1850** GARRARD *Wah-To-Yah* xi. 149 With saddle, lasso, hojas and ponche—corn shucks and tobacco—they seem content to lead this desultory life. **1866** MELINE *Two Thousand Mi. on Horseback* 156 An inferior tobacco, which grows much higher than our tobacco, [is] mostly used by the women, who, with *hojas* (corn-husks), neatly cut and trimmed, make their cigaritos at home, in the street, at the theatre or hall, and smoke them, too, then and there.

Ho Joe whisky. App. a kind of cheap whisky. *Obs.* Cf. prec. — **1867** *Terr. Enterprise* (Virginia, Nev.) 19 Feb. 3/4 While they were in full flight a man who had been indulging liberally in 'Ho Joe Whisky' passed along.

hokum ˈhokəm, *n.* [Prob. f. **hocus*, to hoax.] Bosh, stuff, nonsense. *Slang.* — **1917** *Lit. Digest* 25 Aug. 28/2 'Jasbo' is a form of the word common in the varieties, meaning the same as 'hokum,' or low comedy verging on vulgarity. **1946** *Pueblo* (Colo.) *Star-Journal* 30 June 8/2 That hokum has been definitely disproven.

Holbrookia holˈbrʊkiə, *n.* [J. E. *Holbrook*, (1794–1871), Amer. herpetologist.] A genus of lizards related to the horned toad. — **1851** C. GIRARD in *Amer. Assoc. Adv. Science Proc.* IV. 200 A new American Saurian Reptile. . . . I propose for it the generic name of *Holbrookia.* **1883** *Nat. Hist. Museum Bul.* No. 24, 49 [Specimens of] Holbrookia [were found in] . . . San Antonio, Tex., Santa Fé, N. Mex. [etc.].

***hold,** *v.*

1. *W. tr.* To keep together (a herd of cattle, etc.).

1888 ROOSEVELT in *Cent. Mag.* April 860/2 As the animals of a brand are cut out they are received and held apart by some rider detailed for the purpose, who is said to be 'holding the cut.' **1920** HUNTER *Trail Drivers Texas* I. 131, I was holding the herd while first relief was at supper.

2. a. To keep back (a letter) from delivery. **b.** To detain in custody, to keep under arrest. **c.** To delay or detain (a train).

(a) 1891 F. H. SMITH *Col. Carter* 135 [The letter] was held for postage. — **(b) 1903** *N.Y. Ev. Post* 19 Aug., The men were held for felonious assault, and the woman as a witness. **1922** TITUS *Timber* 32 'Why did he arrest you?' 'Oh, I dropped a cigarette out here in summer an' started a fire . . . an' he held me under the fire law.' — **(c) 1904** *N.Y. Times* 20 Aug. 1 Trains shall not be held for . . . taking on baggage after the regular time scheduled for stops has expired.

3. *To hold down* (*a claim* or *homestead*), to keep or retain a mining claim, to reside on and improve homesteaded land in order to acquire full possession of it.

1884 *Milnor* (Dak.) *Teller* 20 June, The claim-holder has broken up his five, ten, or fifteen acres around his shanty or shack, which is supposed to be solid enough to 'hold down' a 160 acre claim. **1910** J. HART *Vigilante Girl* 331 But he did not like the looks of the many miners he saw 'holding down' claims on lands which belonged to his clients, and making a transparent pretence of working them. **1916** BOWER *Phantom Herd* 31 Sounds most as exciting as holding down a homestead any way.

b. To occupy. *Jocular.*

1891 C. ROBERTS *Adrift Amer.* 92 Jumping an east bound freight . . . , I managed to hold it down or keep on it till I got to . . . Alameda. **1899** *Chi. Record* 26 Jan. 4/4 He is at once made welcome by that part of society which holds down the empty dry-goods boxes along the street.

c. To operate or manage (anything) well; to keep (a job). *Colloq.*

1893 *Harper's Mag.* Dec. 80/2 If a man is to 'hold down' a big ranch in northern Mexico he has got to be 'all man.' **1896** ADE *Artie* xiv. 129 That guy up in your place don't know nothin' on earth except how to hold down his measly job. **1930** *Randolph Enterprise* (Elkins, W.Va.) 2 Oct. 4/4 Br. Johnson is holding down a $4,500 per year job.

d. To keep an opposing team in check; in baseball, to play a designated position.

1897 *Boston Morning Jrnl.* 8 June 4/5 Put Callahan in centrefield and let Lange hold down third base. **1930** *Randolph Enterprise* (Elkins, W.Va.) 23 Oct. 1/6 The University Team played the powerful Detroit University machine on their own grounds and held them down much better than they did at Morgantown last year.

4. **To hold out*, to live, to "hang out." *Colloq.*

1855 *Knickerb.* XLVI. 100 Is this the place where the phrenologist 'holds out?'

b. To conceal or hold something back, usu. with *on. Colloq.*

1907 FIELD *Six-Cylinder Courtship* 71 If it wasn't for Bellows and Rooker, we'd hold out on him every time. **1911** HARRISON *Queed* 57 Surface, by clever juggling of his books, had managed to 'hold out' a large sum of money. **1944** JOHNSON *As I Dare* 339 Been holdin' out on me, have you?

5. *To hold over.* **a.** Of U.S. senators: To stay in office from one Congress or session into the next, either as a senator with an unexpired term or as one re-elected. Cf. **hold-over senator.**

1850 *Harper's Mag.* Dec. 123/2 The U.S. Senate will then stand thus: Holding over—18 Whigs, 23 Democrats. **1852** *Whig Almanac* 5/2 Twenty-four Senators, who also held over, did not accept this Constructive Mileage at the time [when an extra session immediately followed a regular session]. **1871** DE VERE 263 All the members who *hold over, i.e.*, are re-elected for a new Congress, are paid their full mileage as if they had returned to their home and then came back to Washington.

b. Of other officeholders: To remain in office from one term into the next.

1887 *Courier-Journal* 21 Jan. 3/3 The dispatch to the Times in regard to changes of officials in the Jeffersonville depots has created a stampede among the Republicans holding over there. **1895** *Denver Times* 5 Mar. 1/5 The Democrats elected three out of five aldermen. The mayor holds over.

c. Of actors: To continue on a program longer than scheduled. Also transf.

1896 *N.Y. Dramatic News* 11 July 3/4 Weber and Fields, Harry Gilfoil and the Nawns held over. **1911** *Chi. D. News* 30 Sep. 17/1 (*heading*), Attractions Held Over. **1949** *Sat. Ev. Post* 16 April 113/1 It was a good picture, and was held over for three weeks at the Roxie.

d. To have the advantage over (another). Originally a poker term. *Colloq.*

1872 MARK TWAIN *Roughing It* xlvii. 332 You ruther hold over me, pard. I reckon I can't call that hand. Ante and pass the buck. **1889** MUNROE *Golden Days* 127 Do we hold over Bowers?

6. **To hold up.* **a.** To put up or nominate (one) as a candidate for public office. *Obs.*

1789 in VAN SCHAACK *Life Peter Van Schaack* (1842) 429, I was talked of, but very early declared in explicit terms that I would *not* be held up. **1824** CLAY *Letters* (1855) 93 [Mr. Crawford] can no longer be held up for the presidency.

b. To restrain oneself, to check oneself in an action, to stop. *Colloq.*

1843 MAURY in Corbin *Life M. F. Maury* 46 The doctors said I was destroying myself with over-much headwork, and . . . I have had to hold up somewhat. **1887** CUSTER *Tenting on Plains* xii. 394 Some who came to us had held up [drinking] for a time.

c. To rob (a traveler, train, stage, etc.) at the point of a gun, to rob on the highway.

1851 *Oquawka* (Ill.) *Spectator* 5 Feb. 1/7 At St. Louis he *held up* . . . several men and got more or less money. **1879** *Chi. Tribune* 9 May 2/2 Later they took a jug of whisky away from a granger, maltreated a yearling colt, and 'held up' two men for their money. **1945** *Chi. Tribune* 27 Dec. 13/4 Edgar Black . . . was shot and killed . . . by police who saw him holding up a man.

d. By extension from prec.: To get money from (a person) by overcharging, imposing upon his sympathies, etc.

1890 *Stock Grower & Farmer* 19 April 3/3 Cattle inspectors of New Mexico were holding up trail herders for one and one-half cents per head for all cattle admitted into the territory. **1931** WILLISON *Here They Dug Gold* 86, I was often 'held up,' but I never found it profitable to kick about it.

e. Of a cow: To keep back (milk).

1856 *Porter's Spirit of Times* 22 Nov. 198/2 One of the best methods to prevent cows from holding up their milk, is to feed them at the time of milking. **1894** *Vt. Agric. Rep.* XIV. 70 When . . . a cow holds up her milk there is some disturbing element.

f. To obstruct or delay (something), to arrest the progress of.

1904 *Phila. Ev. Telegraph* 15 Nov. 1 Out of the 900 steerage passengers, 135 failed to pass the immigration inspectors, and were held up. **1906** *N.Y. Herald* 5 March 5 It is thought the Senate Finance Committee will seek to devise new excuses for holding up the investigation of the State Banking Department.

7. In noun and adjectival combs.: (1) ***holdfast,** the name of a drink, *slang, rare;* (2) ***out,** (*a*) a hide-out suitable for defense, also attrib., (*b*) a professional athlete, esp. a baseball player, who refuses to renew a contract for another season.

(1) **1844** UNCLE SAM *Peculiarities* I. 161 Give me a holdfast, or a timber-doodle; I don't care which: anything in the shape of stone-fence will suit my fancy. — (2) (*a*) **1924** BECHDOLT *Tales* 350 There was another hold-out place over in Castle Valley. **1929** A. ELLIS *Life* 56 Our place was a great hold out. (*b*) **1911** *Chi. D. News* 3 April 1/6 Hofman Again in Fold. Holdout Finally Attaches Name to Chicago National League Baseball Contract. **1938** *Rocky Mt. News* (Denver) 7 April 12/6 Whether it will be the offered $25,000 or the asked $40,000 Joe DiMaggio, Yankee holdout, is going to be ready to open the season.

See also ***holdback, *holdover, holdup,** as main entries.

For *to have* (or *hold*) *the age, to hold one's horses, to hold the sack,* see the nouns.

***holdback,** *n.*

1. A strap on the breeching of a horse's harness to be attached to the shaft of a vehicle so that the horse can hold it back. Also fig.

1850 *N.H. Hist. Soc. Coll.* VI. 220 The hold-backs of his harness gave way, and precipitated his gig upon the horse. **1874** B. F. TAYLOR *World on Wheels* 30 A harness with neither hold-back nor breeching is a dangerous thing. **1878** ——— *Between Gates* 147 You settle down in your holdbacks, and walk on your heels. **1920** HOWELLS *Vacation of Kelwyns* 186 Kelwyn found him there buckling the holdbacks of the harness round the shafts.

2. The act of holding back. Also attrib.

1852 *Mich. Agric. Soc. Trans.* III. 333 There are a few specimens of the hold-back and stand-still class occasionally seen. **1888** BUFFALO BILL *Wild West* 627 There was no brake on the wagon, and the horses were not much on the hold back.

Holden ˈholdən, *n.* [See quot. 1867.] A variety of apple, also **Holden sweeting.** *Obs.* — *a***1817** DWIGHT *Travels* I. 45 The varieties of apple-trees are: . . . Spitzenberg, Holden Sweeting, Fall pippin. **1867** DOWNING *Fruits of Amer.* 143 Holden. . . . Origin, Holden, Mass. A very strong, erect grower, good bearer.

***holder,** *n.* As the last term in **claim, copy, high, horse, job, policy, prospect holder.**

Holderness breed. A breed of dairy cattle. *Obs.* — **1893** G. W. CURTIS *Horses, Cattle* 146 Mr. Cole's herd has become justly celebrated; and by his skill and carefulness, he has won for himself a most enviable reputation as a patient and painstaking breeder, and as the originator of the American Holderness breed.

***holdover,** *n.*

1. A prison where persons awaiting trial are kept.

1888 *Missouri Republican* 24 Feb. (F.), Wilson was released from the hold over, where he had been held since Irwin's death.

2. One who stays on from one engagement or term of office into another. Also attrib.

1888 *Cong. Rec.* 1 June 4838/2 Assuming that these letters are written by Republican or 'hold-over clerks,' who were connected with the last administration, . . . why all this 'fuss and feathers.' **1895** *N.Y. Dramatic News* 9 Nov. 20 The holdovers consist of John Higgins . . . and the Ella Zuila troupe. **1898** *Chi. Times-Herald* 6 April 2/1 These are the holdovers who have never failed to sustain the mayor's veto of franchise grabs in an emergency. **1948** *Aurora* (Ill.) *Beacon-News* 7 Nov. 26/1 Those holdovers who had been influential in blocking the President will be in a much weaker position now.

b. hold-over senator, a senator whose term of office extends over an election at which other senators are elected.

1892 *Boston Jrnl.* 9 Sep. 4/1 The Indiana Democrats, anticipating that their gerrymander will be overthrown by the courts, and that with it will go the hold-over Senators who were elected under it. **1893** *Chi. Tribune* 28 April 4/1 Out of twenty-two hold-over Senators in districts outside of Cook County the Democrats have eleven and the Republicans have eleven.

3. An authorization to hold a prisoner over from one period of confinement to another.

1903 *McClure's Mag.* Nov. 97 If that old sport turns himself loose you're going to get 'life' three times and a holdover.

4. Something left over from a former time or period.

1904 *L.A. Express* 11 Aug. 12 Doing the best it could on crackers and cheese and holdovers. **1929** *Atlantic Mo.* Mar. 298 The little village of Washington in Connecticut, one of the most charming holdovers of the past that state possesses.

holdup ˈholdˌʌp, *n.*

1. A check or stoppage in the progress of a vehicle, a delay or obstruction.

1837 *Knickerb.* X. 439 The wheels of the coach are shod with the preparation of iron slippers, which are essential to a hold-up. **1904** *N.Y. Tribune* 15 May 2 Its efforts to end the hold-up of the railroad's application for a permit.

b. A cessation in a storm.

1913 A. B. EMERSON *F. Fielding at Snow Camp* 154 We got to sit down and wait for a hold-up.

2. A robbery made at the point of a gun; a robbery of a traveler, stage, train, etc. *Colloq.* Cf. **stage, train hold-up.**

1878 ROE *Army Lett.* 206 The driver is their only protector, and the stage route is through miles and miles of wild forest, and in between huge boulders where a 'hold-up' could be so easily accomplished. **1948** *Chelsea* (Mass.) *Rec.* 30 Nov. 1/5 Policemen . . . would be powerless to reach for their weapons in the event of a holdup.

attrib. **1880** NYE *B. Nye & Boomerang* 192, I did give him the grand bounce, and now he hath joined a hold-up outfit on the overland stage route. **1897** *Chi. Tribune* 12 July 7/5 (*headline*), Holdup Suspects in Jail. These hold up cases on our lines seem to be of a sporadic character. **1938** *Rocky Mt. News* (Denver) 23 April 1/3 Somewhere in Denver is a holdup man who bemoans his inability to pick victims.

b. One who commits or takes part in a robbery of this kind.

1885 *Harper's Mag.* April 695/2 Darkness . . . into which one ventured with grave apprehensions lest a 'hold-up' might be in waiting for him. **1947** *Rocky Mt. News* (Denver) 2 Mar. 5/1 Then the holdup fired a shot into the safe.

c. *fig.* Extortion.

1910 *Sat. Ev. Post* 27 Aug. 6/3 Our house . . . cost twenty-five thousand dollars, exclusive of the plumber's little hold-up and the Oriental rugs. **1914** S. H. ADAMS *Clarion* 201 Libel suits are generally 'hold-ups.'

***hole,** *n.*

1. A low, wet meadow or other place surrounded by uplands. Also in place-names. *Obs.*

1627 in *Amer. Sp.* XV. 274/1 Twelve acres of land . . . bounded . . . Westward on a Marsh called Tuckers hole. **1660** *Plymouth Rec.* 40 Graunted unto ffrancis Billington viz.: a Round Knowle of land lying and adjoyning to the hole of meddow belonging to the said ffrancis Billington on the south side of the Cartway. **1714** *Topsfield Rec.* 185 A Tree Standing by ye side of a round Hole or valley. **1722** *Providence Rec.* IX. 31 Att the place Called Dayles hole and at a pine stake set up and stones Layed about it.

b. *W.* (See quot. 1850.) Also in place-names.

For some comment on the use of the word in the West see *D.N.* III. 230.

1832 *Evening & Morning Star* (Independence, Mo.) Oct. 7/1 The company was attacked in Piers Hole, on the 12th of July last, by the Black feet Indians. **1850** HINES *Voyage* 323 The southern part of this third region . . . is distinguished by its steep and rugged mountains, deep and dismal valleys, called *holes*, by mountaineers. **1949** *Desert Mag.* June 19 Brown's Hole was a hidden valley 30 miles long, watered from the Green river.

2. *local.* A small bay, inlet or creek, often in place-names.

1639 in *Va. Hist. Mag.* III. 31 Yf the shipps be p'mitted to goe at pleasure and ride in every hole as is desired by them. **1651** *Plymouth Rec.* 33 [The land] being compased on the one side with the aforesaid hole or creeke. **1781–2** JEFFERSON *Notes Va.* (1788) II. 4 Rappahanock affords 4 fathom water to Hobb's hole, and 2 fathom from thence to Fredericksburg. **1900** *Amer. Geog. Soc.* XXXII. 37 Hole: A small bay, as Wood's Hole, Mass. Local in New England. **1949** *Time* 20 June 44/3 By month's end, in such unlikely pastures as Fish Creek, Wis. and Woods Hole, Mass., more than 200 summer playhouses will sprout across the land.

3. ?A quantity (of turnips) sufficient to fill a hole in which they are stored. *Rare.* Cf. **potato hole.**

1846 in *Minn. Farmers' Diaries* (1939) 70 We took up a hole of Turnips & put them in the Stable.

4. hole card, in stud poker, a card that is dealt face down. Cf. ***ace,** *n.* **2. c.**

1908 *Sat. Ev. Post* 5 Dec. 19/2 Scarcely glancing at his hole card Phelps let him take the pot, and it became Phelps' deal. **1920** *Amer. Mag.* Dec. 32/2, I figured six to one that I could pair my hole card—which was a king—so I put in one hundred and fifty, too. **1946** MOREHEAD & MOTT-SMITH *Penguin Hoyle* 127 Usually a player should drop out when his cards, including his hole card, are beaten by the showing cards of any other player.

5. *hole in the wall,* (see quots.). *Slang* or *colloq.*

1856 *Iroquois Republican* (Middleport, Ill.) 25 Dec. 2/3 A 'grocery'—a 'doggery'—a 'hole-in-the-wall'—is an 'odious damned spot' in any community. **1896** SHINN *Story of Mine* 51 Many lived in 'dug-outs,' which they called 'holes in the wall.' **1940** RIESENBERG *Golden Gate* 212 For the shipping of lumber, small brigs and brigantines were in wide use at first, craft that could go into the 'holes in the wall' along the ragged Pacific Coast.

attrib. **1949** *Sat. Ev. Post* 9 April 82/4 Jordan spent six months playing club dates or singing in hole-in-the-wall cafés.

6. *To be in the hole,* to be in debt.

See quot. 1892 for the prob. source of this expression.

1890 *Centralia* (Wash.) *Chronicle* 18 Sep. 3/2 His failure leaves a number of our local dealers in the hole for amounts ranging from $200 down. [**1892** QUINN *Fools of Fortune* 219 The 'take off' . . . is an amount taken by the proprietors out of the pots as a percentage due the 'house' on every hand 'called' and shown down; a pair of aces and another pair, and you must 'go to the hole' with a check. The 'hole' is a slot cut in the middle of the poker table, leading to a locked drawer underneath, and all checks deposited therein are the property of the keeper of the place.] **1947** *Atlantic Mo.* July 12/1 The Canadian balance of trade with the United States is currently running at a rate which, if maintained, would put the Dominion 900 millions in the hole by the end of the year.

b. Of a baseball player or team: To be in a difficult or tight spot.

1889 *Sporting Life* (Phila.) 5 June 1/3 Sure enough, the next day they ran the bases magnificently, and put Brooklyn in the hole, 5 to 4. **1909** *Amer. Mag.* Aug. 402/2 Sallee had the batters 'in the hole' all the time. **1949** *Athletic Jrnl.* Mar. 9/3 The right-handed batter who can get the pitcher into a hole, can step far enough away from the plate to wait for the groove ball.

c. (See quot.)

1943 *Sat. Ev. Post* 26 June 75/1 A single-track line, the freighters had to spend much time 'in the hole'—on sidings—while the priority trains passed.

As the last term in **air, alligator, apple, bean, bull, cat, cinder, clay, coal, corn, corporation, coyote, cradle, crawfish, dog, dry, fire, fishing, gopher, grass, grassy, grog, grub, high, mud, nine, nineteenth, pitch, pond, potato, prairie-dog, prospect, rum, salt, sink, snake, soup, spring, sunk, sweat, swimming, whisky hole.**

* **hole,** *v. tr.* To chase or drive (an animal) into its hole. Also transf. *Colloq.*

1838 DRAKE *Tales & Sk.* 151 A fierce little junior . . . had often signalized himself on the banks of Licking river, as the 'real thing,' in hunting 'coons' and 'holeing possums.' **1862** *Harper's Mag.* June 8/1 We've got him holed, any how! It won't take long to root him out. **1878** in SUMMERS *Ann. S.W. Va.* 1528 Each claiming that his dog 'holed' her [the wolf].

holia 'holɪə, *n.* [Origin obscure. Cf. Chinook *olallie,* the salmonberry.] The humpback salmon. — **1888** GOODE *Amer. Fishes* 80 On Frazer River it is known as 'Holia' or 'Hone' Salmon, and on Puget Sound as the 'Haddoh.'

* **Holiness,** *n. attrib.* Of or pertaining to any one of several small religious sects that place emphasis on evangelism and sanctification.

1888 *Calif. State Gaz.* 623/2 Pasadena . . . contains Methodist, Baptist, Presbyterian, . . . Friends, and Holiness churches. **1913** KEPHART *So. Highlanders* 271 In our day the same may be said of the Holy Rollers and Holiness People. **1928** *Amer. Mercury* Oct. 185/1 This . . . was first preached by the Straight Holiness sect in Kansas in the 1890's. **1947** THOMPSON *Amer. Daughter* 77 Oscar Olson told him of the Holiness Camp, a two-week religious festival held at Jamestown every June.

* **Holland,** *n.* In combs.: (1) **Holland pippin,** a variety of apple, *obs.;* (2) **Purchase,** land in western N.Y. purchased by the Holland Co. from Massachusetts after the satisfactory adjustment of conflicting claims to it by New York and Massachusetts, now *hist.;* (3) **-s acre,** formerly in N.Y., a land measure of slightly more than two acres.

(1) **1817** W. COXE *Fruit Trees* 109 Fall, or Holland Pippin. This is one of the finest, and most beautiful apples of the season. **1856** *Rep. Comm. Patents 1855: Agric.* 291 Of autumn apples, there are the Rambo, Holland Pippin. — (2) **1811** SUTCLIFFE *Travels* (1815) 177 After breakfast, my hospitable friends showed me into the land-office [in Batavia, N.Y.] of the Holland purchase. **1875** YOUNG *Hist. Chautauqua Co., N.Y.* 66 Robert Morris became seized of the preëmptive title to all the lands in the state west of the eastern boundary of the Holland Purchase. **1944** MAU *Central & Western N.Y.* 242 The four following engravings, and their descriptions, . . . were intended primarily to illustrate, in accurate detail, the progress of settlement of the Holland Purchase. — (3) **1645** *Doc. Hist. N.Y. State* I. 632 Gardens or orchards not exceeding one Hollands acre being excepted. **1658** *Hempstead Rec.* I. 43 Every inhabitant . . . [shall] give in to be inlisted by the towne-clerk all lands that was plowde . . . , excepting one Hollands Accre or morgen by patent allowed for each inhabitants allowance.

As the last term in **Nun's, shepherd('s) holland.** Also **tandem hollands.**

* **holler,** *n.* A yell or cry of protest. *Slang.* — **1896** ADE *Artie* xvi. 147, I put up a holler right at the jump. **1901** FLYNT *World of Graft* 133 Some gamblers were particularly loud in making their 'hollers,' and threatened to bring about an investigation.

* **holler,** *v. intr.* In a fight, to give up, to cry "Enough!" Also transf. *Slang.*

*c*1845 *Big Bear Ark.* 41 Who hollered? Which gave up? *a*1859 *Spirit of Times* (B.), Tige was using me powerful rough, and had done whipped me; but pshaw! I never did holler. **1859** BARTLETT 199, I once heard a Western man say he had 'hollered on drinking,' meaning that he had quit the practice. **1926** J. BLACK *You Can't Win* iv. 43 Holler before you're hurt; that's my motto.

Also * **hollering,** *n.* (see quots.). *Colloq.*

1917 H. GRANT *Two Sides of Atlantic* 77 Robert had taken to the profession of 'hollering for the Lord,' as they sometimes call Evangelism in that land [U.S.] of sweet expression. **1934** *Nat. Geog. Mag.* LXV. 624 By far the finest of all the musical gifts is the 'hollerin'.' This is yodeling at its best—no more to be likened to what is heard on the vaudeville stage than grand opera can be compared with the hurdy-gurdy. It is the grand opera of the Okefinokee, where it is a common possession of man, woman, and child.

* **hollow,** *a.*

1. hollow horn, a run-down condition in cattle popularly ascribed to hollowness of their horns. *Colloq.*

1805 PARKINSON *Tour* 87 There were a few half-starved cattle; in general standing shaking with cold, and many more complaining of what they call the hollow-horn. This arises from matter in the horn, which kills numbers. **1888** BUFFALO BILL *Wild West* 704 Though sick as a cow with hollow-horn myself [etc.]. **1932** RANDOLPH *Ozark Mt.* 32 It was holler-horn kilt her, I reckon, but Poly Bradford he figgered she was witched.

b. *To bore for the hollow horn,* (see quot. 1919). *Colloq.*

1852 J. WEIR *S. Kenton* 107 (Th.), I suppose you ain't had your ears bored for the hollow horn lately. **1887** *Courier-Journal* 21 Jan. 2/2 Congressman Cheadle . . . should be bored for 'hollow horn,' or idiocy, or some other dire disease. **1919** *D.N.* V. 34 A hole is bored in the horn [of a cow having hollow horn] with a gimlet. This custom gave rise to the epithet applied to people who have acted foolishly 'He ought to be bored for the *holler horn.*'

2. a. hollow iron, (see quot.). *Rare.* **b. hollow tail,** a run-down condition in cattle popularly thought to result from hollowness of their tails.

(a) 1809 KENDALL *Travels* I. 229 Not only the ordinary *hollow iron* or *hollow ware,* is manufactured, but also anchors and cannon. — **(b) 1849** in *Soc. Calif. Pion. Quart.* II. (1925) 121 Some (cattle teams) have the hollow horn. . . . They have another disease called the hollow tail; for that they split the tail where it is hollow.

* **holly,** *n.*

1. holly bay, (see quots.).

1833 EATON *Botany* (ed. 6) 161 *Gordonia lasianthus,* holly-bay. . . . Charleston, S.C. **1859** BARTLETT 250 Loblolly Bay (*Gordonia lasyanthus*), an elegant ornamental tree of the maritime parts of the Southern States, called also Holly Bay. Its bark is useful for tanning.

2. hollyleaf cherry, *Calif.* a cherry, *Prunus ilicifolia,* having hollylike leaves.

1897 SUDWORTH *Arborescent Flora* 247 Hollyleaf Cherry. . . . Common Names. Spanish Wild Cherry (Cal.), Islay (Cal.), etc. **1942** VAN DERSAL *Ornamental Amer. Shrubs* 151 Hollyleaf cherry is tolerant of alkali, resitant to drought, and will stand considerable abuse in handling.

3. holly rancher, (see quot.).

1930 *Sat. Ev. Post* 13 Dec. 37/3, I get it from a holly rancher near Puget Sound. Raising holly is quite a business out there.

As the last term in **California, Canadian, dahoon, desert, emetic, European, Florida, hedgehog, mountain, swamp holly.**

* **Holstein,** *n.* Also **Holstein-Friesian.** A dairy animal of a breed originally from northern Holland and Friesland. Also attrib.

1865 *Rep. Comm. Agric. 1864* 161 Holstein cattle . . . [have] not received that appreciation in this country to which they are entitled by reason of their pre-eminent dairy qualities. **1889** WARFIELD *Cattle-Breeding* 247 The Holstein-Friesians, the Ayrshires, and the Shorthorns all have their exclusive admirers. **1946** *Amer. Mag.* June 108/3 There she was, large-framed, sturdy—something like a Holstein.

* **holy,** *a.* In combs.: (1) * **Holy City,** (see quot.); (2) **horror,** a great fear or a feeling of repulsion; (3) **terror,** something in the extreme, one who is difficult to get along with or manage, *slang.*

For **holy laugh, Holy Roller, holy tone,** see as main entries. (1) **1848** ROBINSON *Santa Fe Exped.* (1932) 25 The flag of our country triumphantly waved over the battlements of the holy city [Santa Fe]. — (2) **1837** *S. Lit. Messenger* III. 668, I have a holy horror of gossips. **1882** MCCABE *New York* 123 The better class of New Yorkers have a holy horror of politics. — (3) **1886** THOMPSON *Banker of Bankersville* 265 (We.), To get it by means of such a holy terror of exhortation. **1920** LEWIS *Main Street* 248 She must be a Holy Terror to live with!

b. In mild oaths as (1) **holy Egypt,** (2) **Moses,** (3) **smoke.** *Colloq.*

(1) **1846** *Dollar Newspaper* (Phila.) 10 June 3/2 In I went, one leg, but—holy Egypt! out I cum again, howling! — (2) **1908** *D.N.* III 321 *Holy Moses,* interj. [e. Ala.]. **1944** *Harper's Mag.* June 25/2 Holy Moses! If you can't see the ball why do you try to play punchball? — (3) **1895** SULLIVAN *Tenement Tales* 210 Well, ho-lee smoke! You *be* a tough! **1948** *Sat. Review* 3 July 32/3 Holy smoke, they ought to listen to an American baseball game!

holy laugh. A laugh by one in a state of religious hysteria or fervor, usu. at camp meetings. Also **holy laughing.**

1829 *Western Mo. Rev.* II. 477 Dr. Roberts is very pointed in his testimony against the abominable practice of jumping, pointing, dancing, boreing. . . . Might he not have added the 'holy laugh?' **1847** R. DAVIDSON *Presbyterian Ch. in Ky.* 157 Hysterical Laughter was at first sporadic, but in 1803 we find 'the Holy Laugh' introduced systematically as a part of worship. **1853** J. R. DIX *Transatlantic Tracings* 199 There was maintained for some time the most edifying uproar of shouting, bellowing, crying, clapping and stamping, mingled with hysterical laughing, termed out there 'holy laughing,' and even dancing and barking! **1922** KEPHART *So. Highlanders* 345, I saw two Holiness exhorters prancing before a solemnly attentive crowd in the courthouse square, one of them shouting and exhibiting the 'holy laugh.' **1948** DICK *Dixie Frontier* 198 When it got started in an audience, everybody would be seized with hearty natural laughter. It would last for hours sometimes. This was known as the 'holy laugh.'

Holy Roller. A member of any one of various minor religious sects whose services are sometimes characterized by violent physical exercises. Usu. *pl.*, with reference to such a sect. Cf. **Sweezyites.**

1842 *So. Quart.* I. 400 It is a new species of religion, which sprang up . . . contemporaneously with the enthusiasm of the 'Holy Rollers.' **1893** LELAND *Memoirs* 216 The Holy Rollers under such circumstances rolled over and over on the floor. **1947** *Chi. D. News* 4 Feb. 8/3 I get awfully tired of people who keep saying that we have to like the Negroes or the Jews or the Mongolians or the Holy Rollers.

Also **Holy Rollerism.**

1928 *Amer. Mercury* Oct. 183/1 It was John Wesley himself who grandsired the modern cult by preaching sanctification in terms of what is now orthodox Holy Rollerism.

holy tone. A method of utterance, often used in their sermons by Primitive Baptist preachers, in which the sound "ah" occurs at the end of each breath pause and the taking of a fresh breath is intentionally made audible. Also **holy whine.**

[**1858** *Salem Advocate* 27 Jan. 1/2 You can no more get to heaven without it, than a jay bird can fly without a tail—ah!] **1881** H. W. PIERSON *In the Bush* 74 They would have gone away worse than disappointed—grievously outraged—if they could not have heard this sermon with the 'holy tone.' **1931** SWEET *Religion* 10 One of the peculiar mannerisms developed by the preachers was the 'holy whine,' a sing song method of speaking which seems to have arisen with outdoor preaching, and which continued to be practiced by the less educated Baptist ministers on the frontier for many years. **1948** DICK *Dixie Frontier* 191 Often the preacher had no idea what he would say from one 'ah' to the next. This 'holy tone' had charms for the audience and they preferred such a sermon to that by a learned college president.

hombre 'ɔmbre, *n.* [Sp., man.]

1. A man of Spanish descent; by extension, any man. *Colloq.* or *jocular.*

1846 MAGOFFIN *Down Santa Fe Trail* (1926) 93 Not only the children, but *mujeres* (women) and *hombres* (men) swarmed around me like bees. **1867** *Wkly. New Mexican* 27 April 2/2 Our music-loving citizens . . . were astonished at beholding four stalwart *hombres* zigzagging their devious way through the principal streets. **1948** *Sat. Review* 28 Aug. 37/1 He was a swarthy-skinned hombre, greasy and unkempt.

2. *S.W.* **hombre bueno,** [Sp. in same sense], an arbitrator. *Obs.* Cf. **goodman.**

1836 EDWARD *Hist. Texas* 161 United, the Alcalde and hombres buenos, . . . will hear as much as they wish to expound in their favor. **1844** GREGG *Commerce of Prairies* I. 234 [In N. Mex.] by a species of mutual agreement, the issues of a suit is sometimes referred to *hombres buenos* (arbitrators), which is the nearest approximation . . . to trial by jury.

b. hombre viejo, [Amer. Sp. *viejo* in same sense] (see quot.). Cf. **old man cactus.**

1897 SUDWORTH *Arborescent Flora* 304 *Cereus Schottii,* Schott Cactus. . . . [Commonly called] Hombre viejo [in Ariz. & N. Mex.].

* **home,** *n.*

1. A tavern or public house. *Obs.*

So called app. to avoid taxes on taverns and inns. Cf. **private entertainment.**

1836 WESTON *Visit* 194 An itinerant shoemaker . . . was about to erect a frame-house on the road side as a public-house, or home as it is termed. **1863** DICEY *Six Months* II. 126 The public-houses are homes, arcades, exchanges, or saloons.

2. *Baseball.* Short for "home run." *Obs.*

1856 *Spirit of Times* 8 Nov. 165/1 Dakin also made a home, and otherwise distinguished himself in striking.

3. In combs.: (1) **homebody,** one given to staying at home, *colloq.;* (2) * **-coming,** (*a*) (see quot.), (*b*) used attrib. with reference to the return of alumni to their school on special occasions, hence * **homecomer;** (3) **Department,** the name formerly applied to the Department of the Interior, both before and after its creation in 1849; (4) **guard,** a guard organized for the protection of the home while the standing army is in the field, often a local organization and usu. made up of those not qualified for regular army service; (5) **industry,** industry within the U.S. as contrasted with foreign industry; (6) **labor,** labor of domestic, as contrasted with that of foreign, workers; (7) **log,** the backlog of a fire, *colloq.;* (8) **protectionist,** one who favors a protective tariff; (9) **run,** in racing, the homestretch, *rare,* cf. **b.** (9) below; (10) **secretary,** the Secretary of the Interior, *obs.,* cf. **Home Department;** (11) **seeker,** one who is looking for a place to settle down permanently, a homesteader; (12) **-spun ball,** (see quot.), *obs.*

(1) **1821** COOPER *Spy* xi. Marry him I don't think I will, unless he becomes steadier and more of a homebody. **1852** EASTMAN *Aunt Phillis's Cabin* 146 She was rather a homebody; yet she reproached herself with having neglected poor old Peggy. — (2) (*a*) **1902** CLAPIN 230 *Home-bringing.* In the North of New Jersey, the entertainment given at the house of the bride-groom after the marriage. Similarly, in Southern New Jersey, they will say *home-coming.* (*b*) **1935** *Chronicle-News* (Trinidad, Colo.) 16 Oct., A 'Homecoming Dance' at the Trinidad high school will be held Saturday evening following the Trinidad-Salida football game. **1947** *Chi. Tribune* 1 Nov. 19/5 Illinois' embattled players . . . adjourned to the Champaign Country club for last inspection and to escape a horde of homecomers who are flooding this university community. — (3) **1789** *Ann. 1st Congress* I. 370 Mr. Vining thought the gentleman should have added another department, viz: the Home Department. **1849** *Statutes at Large* IX. 395 An Act to establish the Home Department. . . . There shall be created a new executive department of the government of the United States, to be called the Department of the Interior. — (4) **1861** *Richmond* (Va.) *Examiner* 6 Sep. 2/4 The Secessionists, 4,500 strong, attacked the 430 Home Guards and Federal troops in the entrenchments at Lexington. **1945** BOTKIN *My Burden* 94 They was getting up a home guard because the Yankees done got down in Alabama not far away.

(5) **1842** *Niles' Reg.* 12 Feb. 384/2 A state convention is to be held on the 17th instant, at Hartford, Connecticut, to adopt measures for laying before congress the claims of home industry. **1848** POLK in *Pres. Mess. & P.* IV. 657 The protective tariff . . . was to protect 'home industry' and furnish a steady market for the farmer. — (6) **1828** in *Bankers Mag.* (Oct., 1846) I. 217 The creation and subdivision of home labor must bring new wealth to this country. — (7) **1880** F. L. OSWALD *Summerland Sk.* 173 Broke a piece of timber . . . for a home-log, as they say in North Carolina. *Ib.* 173 We put the home-log on the fire. — (8) **1882** *Jrnl. of Freedom & Rights* (S.F.) 3 Sep. 3/1 The Republican plank was not all that the Home Protectionists desired, but it was a stepping stone to something better. — (9) **1841** *N.O. Picayune* 10 Dec. 2/2 The grey filly brushes at Sarah near the head of the home run, but she k.k.k.—(kan't kum it kwite.)

(10) **1849** *Whig Almanac 1850* 23/1 Congress, last session, created . . . a home secretary, at $6,000. — (11) **1889** *Advance* 7 March 191 Its chief constituents were the home-seekers of the 19th Century Pilgrim Fathers. **1916** THOBURN *Stand. Hist. Okla.* II. 722 There were fine race horses used by many of the more enterprising homeseekers [in the race of 1889 for homestead claims]. — (12) **1865** SALA *Diary*

II. 195 The grand entertainments, however, were the 'Homespun Balls,' at which the ladies of Dixie wore only dresses of coarse homespun of their own weaving.

See **home demonstration, economics, -made, -stake, -steader, -stretch,** as main entries.

b. In expressions relating to athletics, chiefly to baseball: (1) **home-and-home,** designating contests between teams from two towns, the games being played alternately in each town; (2) **base,** see as a main entry; (3) **battery,** the pitcher and catcher of a home-town baseball team; (4) **club,** a home-town baseball club; (5) **grounds,** the playing ground in the town or city which an athletic team regards as home; (6) **nine,** a baseball team at its home ground as distinguished from a visiting team; (7) **plate,** in baseball, a marker, now usu. of whitened rubber, beside which the batter stands, often used as the equivalent of home base *q.v.;* (8) **player,** a member of a home team; (9) **run,** a hit that enables the batter to make a complete circuit of the bases without the benefit of an error by the opposing players, cf. **3.** (9) above, and see **clean home run;** (10) **slugger,** a member of a home-town baseball team; (11) **team,** =**home nine.**

(1) **1856** *Spirit of Times* 13 Sep. 28/1 This was what is termed a home and home match, and . . . a very large and gay attendance was present to see the sport. **1867** *Ball Players' Chron.* 6 June 3/3 The Union Club of Morrisania, in response to a challenge from the Irvington Club, visited that interesting . . . place . . . to play their first game with the Irvingtons and the first of a home and home series between them. **1948** *Alva* (Okla.) *Review-Courier* 2 July 1/4 The Sunday matches will be the first of a home-and-home affair, with Alva golfers to go to Anthony at a later date. — (3) **1888** *Outing* May 117/1 The home battery comprised Zettlin and Ferguson. — (4) **1884** *Milnor* (Dak.) *Teller* 22 Aug., So far as a home club is concerned Milnor boasts of the best nine in the Northwest. **1910** *Spalding's Base Ball Guide* 362 The choice of innings shall be given to the captain of the home club.

(5) **1890** *Spokane Falls* (Wash.) *Globe* 26 July 1/3 Six hundred baseball cranks witnessed yesterday one of the prettiest exhibitions of ball playing that ever took place on the home grounds. — (6) **1875** *Chi. Tribune* 16 Sep. 8/4 The home nine . . . punished the parabolic curve with a relish pleasant to see. **1889** *S.F. Bulletin* 29 July 1/7 The home nine up to last Thursday had to their credit 200 base steals. — (7) **1875** *Chi. Tribune* 3 Aug. 7 He stole third . . . and reached the home-plate. **1948** *Dly. Ardmoreite* (Ardmore, Okla.) 10 May 6/3 The tying run was cut off at home plate. — (8) **1897** *Chi. Record* 4 Mar. 10/3 The fans in some of the cities won't know when to root until after a few games have been played and they have learned the home players. — (9) **1856** *Spirit of Times* 4 Oct. 86/1 On the Eagle Club taking the bat they soon placed 4 to their credit, and would have done better, but for an injudicious attempt on the part of Mr. Gelston to get a home run. **1948** *This Week Mag.* 1 May 14/2 A home run would give the Giants victory.

(10) **1892** *Courier-Journal* 4 Oct. 5/1 The home sluggers . . . made six runs clean off the stick's end. — (11) **1889** *Seattle Post-Intelligencer* 3 July 1/8 The home team played an up hill game, but . . . won the third game of the series from Boston. **1948** *Chi. Sun* 27 Jan. 23/1 The home team has won 20 out of 23 games in the first half of the league scramble.

c. Designating places where persons, cattle, etc., are at home, as (1) **home corral,** (2) **county,** (3) **forty,** (4) **house,** (5) **lot,** see as a main entry, (6) **place,** (7) **ranch,** (8) **range,** (9) **share,** (10) **state,** (11) **station,** (12) ***-stead,** see as a main entry, (13) **town.**

(1) **1869** MUIR *First Summer in Sierra* (1911) 6, I saw the silly sheep bouncing one by one through the narrow gate of the home corral to be counted. **1947** *Sierra Club Bul.* May 53 The string tendency of pack and saddle animals to drift back to the home corral or to lower elevations during chilly nights has led to the construction of many drift fences and trail bars in the high country. — (2) **1910** J. HART *Vigilante Girl* 384 But this is Tower's home county, and I know his home people better than you do. — (3) **1934** VINES *Green Thicket World* 34 Early in the morning the voice carried over the whole home forty. **1945** *Chi. Tribune* 22 July VII. 1/5 A rabbit jumped in the woods along the Home Forty is almost sure to make a run for the woodpile. — (4) **1786** WASHINGTON *Diaries* III. 4 Took an Acct. of the Tools about the home house. **1866** S. ANDREWS *South Since War* 98 De home-house might come to me, ye see, sah, in de dewision.

(6) **1736** *N.H. Probate Rec.* II. 625, I give & bequeath . . . my Dwelling and Devise to my Son . . all my land . . . Known by the name of my home place. **1885** *Wkly. New Mexican* 12 Feb. 4/3 They are connecting D. D.'s outlying ranches with the home place. **1946** FOREMAN *Last Trek* 91 They continued in their attachment to the old home place. — (7) **1869** MUIR *First Summer in Sierra* (1911) 8 The home ranch from which we set out is on the south side of the Tuolumne River near French Bar. **1949** *Time* 21 Feb. 66/2 After seven months, Rupert returned to his home ranch, full of penicillin, assorted hormones and vitamin C. — (8) **1884** W. SHEPHERD *Prairie Exper.* 205 Stock are always restless at first on a drive, and are striving to get back on their home-ranges. **1939** ROLLINS *Gone Haywire* 62 The ol' man's bin steadily enlargin' his home range till now it includes mos' all the headwaters o' Elk Prairie Crick **1949** *Boston Sun. Globe* 1 May (Fiction Mag.) 2/5 He never went back because the only folks on his home range who had treated him white were wild fellas and boys who wanted to be wild, and girls who didn't give a damn. — (9) **1643** *Providence Rec.* II. 2 Matthew wesen shall haue that hom share of ground. **1670** *Ib.* III. 181 A home share of land Containeing of five acres. **1701** *Ib.* IV. 220 Bounding . . . on ye southerne part with a house Lott or home share of land.

(10) **1908** LORIMER *J. Spurlock* vi. 127, I was the possessor of a thousand Bibles . . . which I proposed to make a powe'ful means fo' good in my home State. **1948** *Time* 8 March 20/1, I come from your home state of Idaho. — (11) **1867** *Harper's Wkly.* 15 June 373/4 'Look's Ranche' on Spring Creek is a 'home station' for the overland mail. **1930** BANNING *Six Horses* 400 *Home stations,* where often the station-master dwelt with his family, were also the dwellings of stage drivers and other line employees off duty, and were prepared to supply meals for passengers, and fresh teams for the stages as they arrived. — (13) **1912** *Top-Notch Mag.* 1 Aug. 64/2 He was killed in a pool-room row in my home town up the state. **1945** *New Yorker* 10 Mar. 54/2, I was busy writing a lot of notices for home-town newspapers.

d. *Home of the brave,* the United States, in allusion to the use of this phrase in "The Star-Spangled Banner."

1894 MARK TWAIN *Tom Sawyer* 355 (R.), With the Desert's bulk you could cover up every last inch of the United States. . . . Yes, sir, you could hide the home of the brave . . . clean out of sight under the Great Sahara.

As the last term in **country, county, dugout, farm, funeral, log, soldiers' home.**

home base. A small area suitably marked to serve as the fourth base in baseball (see also quot. 1867). Also fig. and transf.

1856 *Spirit of Times* 4 Oct. 86/1 He was headed off and put out on the home base. **1867** *Ball Players' Chron.* 4 July 5/1 The first three bases must be canvas bags covering a foot square of surface, and the home base a *flat* iron quoit. **1920** LEWIS *Main Street* 300 He invariably decided that coming confinement-cases or land-deals would prevent his 'getting away from home-base for very long this year.' **1948** *Parents' Mag.* March 92/3 No matter how good the field work may be, you can't win the game unless home base is covered by both parents.

home demonstration. *attrib.* Designating an *agent* who gives instruction to country women in the arts and skills of homemaking. Also used of a *club* composed of women receiving such instruction.

1928 *Dly. Ardmoreite* (Ardmore, Okla.) 4 March 15/1 Miss Maude Andrews, home demonstration agent, took an active part in the show. **1947** *Ib.* 14 Nov. 7/2 The County Agent and Home Demonstration Agent furnish supervision and assistance to 4-H Club boys and girls and farm men and women's clubs. **1948** *Durant* (Okla.) *D. Democrat* 1 July 5/1 A new home demonstration club has been formed in the county, the 46th such club.

home economics. The science or art of homemaking, including the knowledge needed in selecting and preparing food and clothing, caring for children, etc., often as the subject of a course in school or college. Usu. attrib.

1926 *Chi. Drovers' Jrnl.* 5 May 3/3 Here all of the home economics work, which has been scattered in half a dozen buildings, will be housed. **1946** *Okla. Dly.* (Norman) 22 Aug. 4/3 For the past three years, she has been a home economics teacher in the Guthrie school system. **1948** *Chi. Tribune* 8 Feb. (Pict. Sec.) 12 He is a third year student in forestry, she a sophomore in home economics.

Hence **home economist.**

1943 LYON *So to Bedlam* 262 The young woman who made the masterpiece [a chocolate cake] was a graduate home economist. **1949** *Chesterton* (Ind.) *Tribune* 28 April 13/2 The manufacturer of a food product selects the home economist to head its food service with great care.

home lot. A lot on which a home is built, as distinguished from land used for other purposes.

1635 in J. H. BENTON *Warning Out* (1911) 10 All the hoame lots . . . shall have right to the Commons. **1734** *Mass. H. Rep. Jrnl.* 137 Lay out the said Township, as also the first division or home Lots in as defensible a manner as conveniently may be. **1782** CRÈVECOEUR *Letters* 126 For that purpose [i.e., of making a town] they surveyed as much ground as would afford to each what is generally called here a home-lot. **1947** LUMPKIN *Southerner* 26 From his father's estate my grandfather bought the 'home lot,' a piece comprising over six hundred acres.

transf. **1898** *Mo. So. Dakotan* I. 52 Just beyond the field of grain, in the distance, stood the home lot—a humble cluster of sod buildings.

home-made ˈhomˈmed, *n.*

1. A garment or cloth made in the home. *Obs.*

1823 COOPER *Pioneers* xi, The thick coat of brown 'home-made,' that was concealed beneath, preserved a proper degree of warmth. **1847** in H. HOWE *Hist. Coll. Ohio* 192 Home-made was the common wear of the people of Kentucky, at that time: sheep were not yet introduced into the country.

2. home-made Yankee, (see quot. 1866). *Obs.*

1866 MOORE *Women of War* 308 One half the balance were loyal southerners, or, as the rebels contemptuously called them, 'home-made Yankees.' **1884** CRADDOCK *Where Battle Was Fought* 367 That opprobrious epithet 'home-made Yankee' had been stricken from his Vocabulary.

* **homer,** *n.* A home run in baseball.

1868 *N.E. Base-Ballist* 6 Aug. 3/1 The second inning saw a change as the Champions went out for two runs, one of these a 'homer' by Franklin. **1894** *Advance* 23 Aug., 'What do you call that [a home run]?' . . . 'A homer.' **1948** *Chi. Tribune* 12 Mar. III. 1/1 He was in 140 contests last season and smacked 35 homers.

homestake ˈhomˌstek, *n.* (See quot. 1915.) Also transf.

1878 HART *Sazerac Lying Club* 67 Many a man made a home-stake . . . by standing in line till he got up pritty close to the winder, and then sellin' out his chance . . . to fellers as had more money than time. **1885** *Wkly. New Mexican* 5 Feb. 4/1 At last he reached 'his homestake' and died about March 1881. **1915** KINGSBURY *Hist. Dakota Terr.* III. 23 'Hank, this is surely a homestake.' This term was then [1876] in common use and merely meant enough money to take a fellow where he wanted to go—back to the states.

* **homestead,** *n.*

1. A place where a family makes its home, including a plot of land, the house, and other buildings.

1638 *Charlestown Land Rec.* 3 Ezechell Richardson hath in the high ffeilde one homesteede, containing three Acres by esteemation . . . butting to the south upon the high-way. **1715** *Providence Rec.* XVI. 75 Fifty acres of Land It being parte of my home stead. **1900** *Cong. Rec.* 26 Jan. 1234/1 New England . . . has sent forth her children . . . and bequeathed to them the imperishable riches of the old homestead. **1946** *Reader's Digest* March 134/1 Ownership of these homesteads was decided by a claim-staking race.

attrib. **1704** *Providence Rec.* VII. 210, I give . . . my homestead place to him. **1749** *N.H. Probate Rec.* III. 741, I give to my Son . . . all my Homestead Land. **1934** VINES *Green Thicket World* 57 He had seen every spot of their loved homestead forty.

b. The house or its garden.

1769 *Cambridge Prop. Rec.* 361 The piece of common Land . . . bordering on Mr Danforths Garden or Homestead. **1856** *Harper's Mag.* Jan. 163/1 She looked mournfully around at each familiar object. The old homestead, with its chunked and daubed walls. **1872** *Vt. Bd. Agric. Rep.* I. 62 The old apple trees . . . showered their luscious bounties, ruddy and golden, about the door-stones of our old homesteads.

2. A tract of land taken up from the public domain by a settler under the homestead laws; the developed farmstead established on such land.

Ordinarily 160 acres each, these tracts were as large as 640 acres in mountainous or semiarid regions.

1846 *Quincy* (Ill.) *Whig* 21 March 3/1 He asked and obtained leave to introduce a bill granting to 'every maid, widow or man who was at the head of a family, a homestead not exceeding one hundred and sixty acres of land.' **1900** *Cong. Rec* 4 Jan. 647/1 A man has not secured title to a homestead without paying for it. **1945** *Roundup* (Mont.) *R.-Tribune* 15 Feb. 1/3 The Butlers formerly lived on a homestead on Cameron creek above Sahara.

b. The action of taking up land under the homestead laws.

1885 *Milnor* (Dak.) *Teller* 24 April 2/5 White persons . . . claim . . . that it [Okla.] was public domain, subject to pre-emption and homestead.

3. homestead exemption clause, law, a clause in a state constitution, or a state law, exempting a homestead from attachment or sale for certain kinds of debt.

1849 COOPER *Sea Lion* xxix, That plausible and impracticable desire of a false philanthropy, which is termed the Homestead Exemption Law . . . was not yet dreamed of. **1853** in *Mich. Agric. Soc. Trans.* VII. 299 Michigan . . . was the first State to pass a homestead exemption law. **1877** JOHNSON *Anderson Co., Kans.* 128 There were two hundred and six votes in favor of the homestead exemption clause in the [Wyandotte] constitution, and one hundred and nine against.

b. In combs. (sense **2.**) of obvious meaning, as (1) **homestead act,** (2) **bill,** (3) **claim,** (4) **entry(man),** (5) **grant,** (6) **law,** (7) **right,** (8) **settlement,** (9) **settler,** (10) **State.**

(1) 1881 *Rep. Indian Affairs* p. xxv, Extending to the Indians the benefits of the provisions of the homestead act of May 20th, 1862. **1948** *Antioch Rev.* Fall 333 This was the period of the Homestead Act and the period when the Negro became free, a citizen, and a voter. — **(2) 1859** *Harper's Mag.* March 543/1 The House on the 18th of February . . . passed the Homestead Bill of Mr. Grow. It provides that any citizen of the United States . . . shall be entitled to enter any quarter section of unoccupied land, and to hold the same, on condition of actual settlement. **1948** *Pacific Spectator* Spring 151 When the Democratic President Buchanan vetoed a homestead bill in 1856 the issue was drawn with clarity. — **(3) 1883** in *Frontier* X. (1930) 255/2, I want to build me a house next month . . . on my homestead claim. **1941** WILDER *Little Town on Prairie* 2 Laura thought of the town, and of the homestead claim. **1949** *L.A. Times* 21 June 8/1 The men . . . learned that the land was owned by the State of Tennessee, and was subject to homestead claim. — **(4) 1917** *Statutes at Large* XL. I. 248 An Act For the relief of homestead entrymen or settlers who enter the military or naval service of the United States in time of war. — **1930** HEBARD *Washakie* 221 The ceded land of 1904 mainly given to the government for the purpose of opening unused lands on the reservation for homestead entry.

(5) 1884 MULHALL *Dict. Statistics* 231 *Homestead Grants.* In 1862 the United States law was passed to encourage settlers from Europe, whereby lots of ¼ square miles or 160 acres are given to immigrants, on condition of 5 years' occupation. — **(6) 1850** *Quincy* (Ill.) *Whig* 7 May 1/3 The N. York Legislature has enacted a *Homestead Law.* **1913** *Indian Laws & Tr.* III. 557 The lands shall be reoffered for sale and entry under the provisions of the homestead law. **1948** DICK *Dixie Frontier* 76 As early as 1803, settlers of Mississippi sent a memorial to Congress asking for a homestead law. — **(7) 1881** *Mich. Gen. Statutes* I. (1882) 387 Any person being a freeholder or a holder of lands by homestead right within the township [etc.]. **1949** *Canadian Alpine Jrnl.* May 79, I think it *would* have been easy had not a young bear claimed his homestead right behind the Icefield Chalet. —**(8) 1900** *Cong. Rec.* 26 Jan. 1222/1 [Had] this land . . . ever been open to homestead settlement? — **(9) 1880** LAMPHERE *U.S. Govt.* 199/2 A homestead settler may, at any time after a six months' residence on the homestead, pay for it with cash, warrants [etc.].

(10) 1901 *Outlook* 17 Aug. 910/2 Some one has called Oklahoma 'the Homestead State.'

homestead ˈhomˌstɛd, *v.* [f. the noun.] *tr.* and *intr.* To take up and settle on (land) in accord with the homestead laws, to become a settler on homesteaded land.

1872 *Newton Kansan* 12 Sep. 3/3 [He] had homesteaded the southeast quarter of sec. 14, rg. 5 west, tn. 21. **1877** RUEDE *Sod-House Days* 123 If he homesteads, you would have to be here inside of 6 months; a married man is required to have his family on his claim, even though he is away at work. **1948** *Milwaukee Jrnl.* 18 July 6/5 It was Alice's grandfather, George Keeler, who back in the eighties homesteaded 40 acres of land close to the shore of Pelican lake.

b. Hence **homesteading,** *n.* and *a.*

1943 HOLT *Carver* 50 But he kept it strictly for his own enjoyment, violating unwritten homesteading law by refusing to share his delicacies. **1948** *Range Riders Western* May 23/2 In new territories open to homesteading, Reese had seen many like it. **1949** *Sat. Ev. Post* 5 Mar. 72/4 The company . . . concluded that the homesteading doctor had accidentally hit a hidden ancient lake.

homesteader ˈhomˈstɛdɚ, *n.* A settler who takes up public land under the homestead law.

1872 TICE *Over Plains* 80 As far as the eye can reach the plain is dotted with new shanties of the homesteaders and pre-emptioners. **1900** *Cong. Rec.* 20 Feb. 1978/1 The State, in selecting these lands for grazing near to the ranches of homesteaders, . . . will render irrigation and reclamation possible. **1947** *Steamboat* (Colo.) *Pilot* 13 Feb. 8/5 Many of the water holes have been taken by homesteaders and wheat fields now take the place of the open range.

homestretch ˈhomˈstrɛtʃ, *n.* The last part or lap of a racecourse.

1841 *N.O. Picayune* 19 Jan. 1/6 At the head of the home stretch Cowboy overtook him and after a pretty brush beat him out by a length. **1860** *Yale Lit. Mag.* XXV. 83 (Th.), The first boat in is the winner of the race, so round they turn, and 'beef her' for the home stretch. **1947** *This Week Mag.* 8 March 14/4 He hired a plane to swoop low over the tightly bunched racers in the homestretch.

transf. **1866** *Wilkes' Spirit of Times* 9 June 231/1 A noteworthy feature of the play of the Harvards is that they improve as they trench upon the home-stretch. **1948** *Capital-Democrat* (Tishomingo, Okla.) 3 June 1/4 General primary candidates will swing political campaigning into the home stretch the next three weeks.

hominy ˈhɑmənɪ, *n.* [See **rockahominy.**]

1. A food prepared from grains of Indian corn freed of their hard outer coverings, and often broken up into a coarse meal, and boiled in water or milk. Cf. **hulled corn.**

1634 *Rel. Beginnings of Md.* 17 Their ordinary diet is Poane and Omine, both made of Corne. **1784** J. SMYTH *Tour U.S.* I. vi. 48 Hommminy is an American dish, made of Indian Corn, freed from the husks, boiled whole, along with a small proportion of a large kind of French beans, until it becomes almost a pulp. **1807** WILSON *Travels* 52 The chief food of the negroes was Indian corn, which they bruised in mortars they had for the purpose and then boiling it in water, made a sort of hasty pudding. They ate their *hominy*, as they called it, sometimes with salt, sometimes without. **1845** LEWIS *Impressions* 151 Even the *hominy*, a dish prepared of Indian corn, and used with milk, like Scottish stir-about, and which makes quite as good a breakfast for young or old, has disappeared. **1945** *Las Cruces* (N.M.) *Citizen* 15 Feb. 3/4 Browned, cooked hominy goes nicely with pork chops in the place of potatoes.

b. small hominy, (see quot. 1849).

1708 E. COOK *Sot-Weed Factor* 5 Syder-pap is a sort of Food made of Syder and Small Homine, like our Oatmeal. **1750** I. WALKER *Journal* 41 Having purchased half a Busshell of meal and as much small Homcny we set off and Lodged on a small Run between Peak and Reedy Creek. **1849** *Rep. Comm. Patents: Agric.* 153 When meal is ground for bread, the mill is set rather wide, that the flinty part of the grain may not be cut up too fine, this being sifted out for 'small hommony'; the farinaceous part of the grain is left for bread.

c. Preceded by other qualifying terms as **big, great, milk, thin hominy,** (see quots.). *Obs.* See also **corn, fried, lye, sour hominy.**

1629 J. SMITH *Travels* (1910) 886 [The Virginians'] servants commonly feed upon Milke Homini, which is bruized Indian corne pounded, and boiled thicke, and milke for the sauce; but boiled with milke the best of all will oft feed on it. **1746** E. KIMBER *Itinerant Observ.* 34 Great Homine has Meat or Fowl in it. **1751** J. BARTRAM *Observations* 60 This repast consisted of 3 great kettles of Indian corn soop, or thin homony, with dry'd eels and other fis1 boiled in it. **1836** *Knickerb.* VIII. 45 We were compelled to pick up our meals at the houses of the scattering planters . . . where corn-cake and 'big hominy' is the universal provender. **1943** POWELL *Home Again* 194 They buy their . . . big hominy . . . already prepared, in cans from the grocery store.

2. In combs.: (1) **hominy bean,** (see quot. 1805 and cf. quot. 1784 in **1.** above), *obs.;* (2) **beater,** (see quot. 1871), *obs.;* (3) **bird,** (see quot.), *rare;* (4) **corn,** corn esp. suitable for making hominy; (5) **eaters,** a term used jocosely to refer to Negro children, *obs.;* (6) **man,** formerly a vendor who sold hot hominy in the streets; (7) **snow,** ?snow in a somewhat granular form suggestive of hominy grits, *obs.*

(1) **1785** *Lower Norfolk Co. Va. Antiquary* I. 53 A parcel old Casks and some hominy beans. **1805** PARKINSON *Tour* 341 The hominy-bean is a sort of kidney-bean, and very productive. — (2) **1824** SINGLETON *Letters* 71 The dish is so popular in Virginia, that they have a river named Chicka*hominy;* and also an insect called the hominy-beater. **1871** DE VERE 42 From some fancied resemblance to a kernel thus hulled, a snapping-beetle, or Elater, of Pennsylvania, is called the 'Hominy-beater.' (S. S. Haldeman.) — (3) **1859** TALIAFERRO *Fisher's R.* 102 Some folks are allers gwine the long way, but that ain't me. I gits right inter it, like a homminny-bird (humming-bird) inter a teche-me-not flower. — (4) **1763** (tr.) DUPRATZ *Hist. La.* II. 3 Louisiana produces several kinds of *maiz*, namely *flour-maiz*, which is white, with a flat and shrivelled surface . . . [and] homony corn, which is round, hard, and shining. **1775** ADAIR *Indians* 407 The second sort is yellow and flinty, which they call 'hommony-corn.' **1895** *Amer. Antiq. Soc. Proc.* April 160 These . . . were known to the whites as hominy corn, bread corn and six-weeks corn.

(5) **1859** MACKAY *Tour* I. 328 The General declared them to be 'hominy-eaters' and not workers. — (6) **1893** LELAND *Memoirs* 11 Also the quaint old Hominy-man: 'De Hominy man is on his way.' — (7) **1857** in *Kans. Hist. Quart.* III. 162 It then snowed a coarse hominy snow till the ground was white.

b. In the names of utensils used in connection with hominy, as (1) **hominy block,** (2) **mill,** (3) **mortar,** (4) **pot,** (5) **sifter.**

(1) **1791** in JILSON *Dark & Bl. Ground* 109 The hominy block is one of the best I have seen anywhere. **1824** Z. F. SMITH *Kentucky* (1886) 395 The hominy block . . . was made of a large block of wood about three feet long, with an excavation burned in one end, wide at the top and narrow at the bottom, so that the action of the pestle . . . threw the corn up to the sides toward the top of it, from whence it continually fell down into the centre. **1948** DICK *Dixie Frontier* 249 The earliest and crudest mill was the hominy block. — (2) **1821** *16th Congress* 2 Sess. H.R. Doc. No. 46, 7 Hominy mill . . . [patented May 8, 1820, by] Nathan Read, Belfast, Maine. — (3) **1827** COOPER *Prairie* ii, Others . . . [were] plying the heavy pestle of a movable hominy-mortar. **1837** PECK *New Guide* 126 The hominy mortar and hand-mill, are in use in all frontier settlements. The first, consists of a block of wood, with an excavation burned at one end, and scraped out with an iron tool [etc.]. **1949** *Tenn. Hist. Quart.* March 22 Such aids to cookery as pots, skillets, Dutch ovens, hominy mortars, . . . and bread trays were put into use by the mother of the family. — (4) **1687** CLAYTON *Acct. Va.* in *Phil. Trans.* XLI. 159 At all Hours of the Night, whenever they [Indians] awake, they go to the Hominy-pot, that is, Maze dressed in a manner like our pilled Wheat. **1853** SIMMS *Sword & Distaff* 181 The hominy pot . . . now stood in the centre, resting upon a barrel-head into which its three legs burned regular sockets. **1945** MOLLOY *Pride's Way* 21 She poked her head into the kitchen where Jennie was stirring the hominy pot.

(5) **1638** *Md. Council Proc.* 76, I have seised . . . 1 hominie sifter.

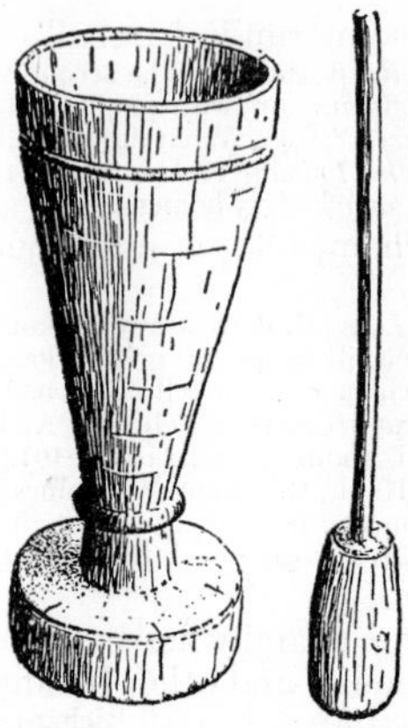

Hominy mortar and pestle

c. In the names of foods: (1) **hominy bread, cake,** (see quot. 1941); (2) **corn-pone,** hominy bread in the form of pones, *obs.;* (3) **grits,** coarsely ground corn meal.

(1) **1711** *N.C. Col. Rec.* I. 765 The planter here . . . dare not allow himself to partake of his own creatures except it be the corn of the Country in hominy Bread. **1876** M. F. HENDERSON *Cooking* 70 Hominy Cake . . . is a very nice breakfast cake. **1941** F. M. FARMER *Boston Cook Book* 109 Corn Meal or Hominy Cakes. Make of cooked corn meal or hominy grits. Serve in place of potato or other starchy vegetable. — (2) **1889** *Hood's Cook-Book* No. 2, In the preparation of hominy corn-pone the yellow kind of corn-meal is used. — (3) **1876** M. F. HENDERSON *Cooking* 71 When the milk is salted and boiling, stir in the hominy grits, and boil twenty minutes. **1949** *Time* 31 Jan. 19/1 They ate Missouri ham and hominy grits.

Homogenized milk. (See quot. 1909.)

[**1904** *Sci. Amer.* 16 April 315/2 To the many methods of purifying . . . and preserving milk must now be added a process for *homogenizing* so that it will keep almost indefinitely without change in its physical condition.] **1909** *Cent. Supp.* 596/1 Homogenized milk, a trade-name for milk which has been heated to 185° F. and forced by heavy pressure through a number of very fine openings, the jets impinging upon a porcelain plate. **1949** *Chesterton* (Ind.) *Tribune* 7 April 14/5 Infants, children and adults, known as 'milk shunners,' drink Homogenized Milk with self-evident enjoyment.

honda ˈɔndə, *n. W.* [See note.] (See first quots.)

Usu. regarded as f. Sp. *honda*, a sling, but more likely f. Sp. *hondón*, an eyelet, the eye of a needle. See the first quot.

1887 *Scribner's Mag.* II. 508/2 The common [cowboy] terms are . . . *heel*, to lariat an animal by the hind leg, *hondou* (derivation unknown, though probably from the Spanish *honda*, the eye of a needle), the slip-knot of the lariat. **1922** ROLLINS *Cowboy* 138 This hondo, or, as often called, 'honda,' was sometimes a cunningly devised, knotted or spliced eyelet . . . sometimes a metal ring. **1948** *Popular Western* June 52/1 He dropped the hondo over his head and cinched it tight around his lean, hard middle.

* **hone,** *v. tr.* (See quot.) *Obs.* — **1836** W. O'BRYAN *Travels* 57 As I went on from Jericho to New York, some men were honing the turnpike, as they call it. This is done to scrape the mud off, by a drag made to draw obliquely, by a train of cattle along on one side the road.

* **honest,** *a.* and *adv.*

1. Used as an intensive, esp. to emphasize the truth of a statement. *Colloq.*

1876 MARK TWAIN *Tom Sawyer* ix, Tell me, Joe,—*honest* now, old feller—did I do it? **1901** MERWIN & WEBSTER *Calumet 'K'* 160 Honest, Hilda, I don't see how he does it. **1921** PAINE *Comr. Rolling Ocean* 105 He is not so bad as he sounds, honest, Jud.

b. With embellishments in the same sense (see quots.).

1912 MATHEWSON *Pitching* 233 A really true, on-the-level, honest-to-jiminy jinx can do all sorts of mean things to a professional ball-player. **1914** BOWER *Flying U Ranch* 192 Honest to grandma, a little gore would look better to me right now than a Dutch picnic before the foam's all blowed off the refreshments. **1916** ——— *Phantom Herd* 43 The real honest-to-goodness-twelve-months-in-the-year West . . . has been mighty little used in the films. **1948** WESTON *Mother Lode* 72 Old-timers insist [this cabin] was the 'honest-to-John' hideaway used by the famous California bad man, Joaquín Murieta, during his frequent stays in Tuolumne County.

Honda on a lariat

2. Used in various expressions with reference to Abraham Lincoln (see quots.). Cf. **Old Honest Abe.**

1858 *Chi. D. Press & Tribune* 2 Nov. 1/3 One hundred cheers for Honest Abe Lincoln! **1860** G. W. BUNGAY *Bobolink Minstrel* 54 All the *rail*ing accusations, Honest Abraham occasions, Greet our ears as pleasant chimes. **1860** in *Dly. Times* (Chi.) (1941) 14 Feb. 43 Republicans Rally! Old Madison Must & Shall Be Redeemed. Rally For Honest Old Abe! **1865** RICHARDSON *Secret Service* 312 All over the country people began to ask about this 'Honest Abe Lincoln.'

3. honest Indian, (see quot. 1892).

[**1676** in JUDD *Hist. of Hadley* (1905) 169 We sent 27 women and children to Norwich under conduct of some of those we call honest Indians.] **1851** in *Pioneer* (S.F.) (1854) July 25 Instead of simply asking you if it is true, he will invariably nod his head interrogatively, and almost pathetically address you with the solemn adjuration, 'Honest Indian?' **1892** WALSH *Lit. Curiosities* 485 *Honest Injun*, in colloquial American, is equivalent to the English 'honor bright,' and is often heard among school-boys as a pledge of faith. Originally, no doubt, the reference to Indian honesty was sarcastic. **1946** *Chi. D. News* 5 July 7/1 It's all over—no more firecrackers—all gone, see, Honest Injun—come on out.

* **honey,** *n.* In combs.: (1) **honey balls,** (see quots.); (2) **bean,** (see quot.); (3) **box,** (*a*) a box in which wild honey is gathered, *obs.*, (*b*) a box so attached to a hive as to induce the bees to make honey in it; (4) * **dew,** a kind of tobacco in the processing of which molasses is used, *obs.;* (5) **dram,** a spirituous drink sweetened with honey, *obs.;* (6) **gum,** a bee gum, *obs.;* (7) **locust,** see as a main entry; (8) **mesquite,** the common mesquite, so called because of its edible pods, also attrib.; (9) **-moon car,** (see quot.), *obs.;* (10) **shucks,** honey locust, *Gleditsia triacanthos*, or the beans in the pods of this; (11) * **sucker,** (see quot.), *rare;* (12) * **-suckle,** see as a main entry; (13) **tree,** (*a*) honey locust, *Gleditsia triacanthos*, (*b*) a tree in which bees have stored honey.

(1) **1909** WEBSTER, honey-balls. . . . The nectar-yielding flower heads of the buttonbush. *Southern U.S.* **1931** CLUTE *Plants* 60 Among other names that seem to be more fanciful than real are . . . honey-balls for *Cephalanthus occidentalis.* — (2) **1867** DE VOE *Market Ass't* 378 Honey bean or sweet locust-fruit. . . . The fruit or pod is flat, crooked, and long, of a reddish brown color, and full of hard seeds, enveloped in a sweet pulpy substance, much like honey. — (3) (*a*) **1853** *Knickerb.* XLII. 368 In October, Venison, myself, his honey-box, and axes, set out 'a bee-hunting,' as he called it. (*b*) **1859** *Rep. Comm. Patents 1858* I. 343 Nor do I claim spare honey-boxes C applied to the hives B, for these are commonly used. — (4) **1843** LUMSDEN *Amer. Mem.* 14 My next communication will probably contain full details of the methods adopted by the Virginian planters in the manufacturing of the nigger-head, . . . pig-tail, honey-dew, and other varieties of the stimulating and soothing herb. **1854** GREATREX *Whittlings* 52 He patronised a quiet bit of 'honey-dew' occasionally, however, for I saw him take out his box, and push a portion of its contents surreptitiously into his cheek.

(5) **1834** NOTT *Novellettes* I. 75 He handed to Singularity a sheet of paper, on which was neatly charged . . . bitters, gin-slings, mint julaps, honey drams, and a variety of other small refreshments. **1842** BUCKINGHAM *Slave States* I. 197 Among those comforts he numbered his 'honey-dram before breakfast,' and his 'mint julap or sling, when the weather required it.' — (6) **1840** SIMMS *Border Beagles* 317 With the grace and felicity of a black bear at a honey-gum. — (8) **1890** *Cent.* 3727/2 Mesquite. . . . Also called *honey-mesquite, honey-locust, honey pod.* **1940** CASSADY & GLENDENING *Revegetating Semi-desert Range Lands* 2 New Mexico . . . sand dune lands . . . [are] characterized by . . . sandy soil supporting honey mesquite bushes, soapweed, shinnery oak, and similar shrubs. **1946** *So. Sierran* Nov. 2/3 The principle tree of the desert is . . . the 'honey mesquite.' — (9) **1874** B. F. TAYLOR *World on Wheels* 57 The Union Pacific Company . . . have just begun to run a lunatic asylum with every San Francisco train, but they give it an astronomical name. They call it a 'honeymoon car.'

(10) **1884** SARGENT *Rep. Forests* 59 *Gleditschia triacanthos.* . . . Black Locust. Three-thorned acacia. Sweet Locust. Honey Shucks. **1904** GLASGOW *Deliverance* 501 I've a powerful taste for trash . . . since the time I overate ripe honey-shucks when I was six months old. **1917** *Lit. Digest* 15 Dec. 22/2 Honey-locust pods, often locally called 'honey-shucks,' contain a sweetish, thick, clear pulp, which is often eaten. — (11) **1857** *Ladies' Repository* XVII. 446/2 Bees were found in great abundance in all the timbered portion [of Ill.]. The early inhabitants used to cut down the trees and eat the honey. From this they were first styled 'honey-suckers.' In course of time 'honey' was left out and the term 'sucker' continued in use. — (13) (*a*) **1705** BEVERLEY *Virginia* II. 21 The Honey and Sugar-Trees are likewise spontaneous, near the Heads of Rivers. The Honey-Tree bears a thick swelling Pod, full of Honey. **1737** BRICKELL *N. Carolina* 71 The Honey Tree is so like the Locust that there is scarce any Difference between them, only the Honey Tree is more prickly than the former; and are a Species of the Locust. (*b*) **1831** HOLLEY *Texas* (1833) 42 Frequent mention was made, in conversation, of honey trees. . . . Hollow trees, in which the bees deposit their honey, are so called. **1901** *Harper's Mag.* Dec. 49/2 Our Johnny found a honey tree yesterday.

b. honey and hug, manifestation of affection. Also as verb. *Colloq.*

1833 NEAL *Down-Easters* I. 82 All honey an' hug a minit ago; an' now . . . what a change. **1896** HARRIS *Sister Jane* 21 She won't git a thrip of it [*sc.* money] when she comes a-bringin' a young feller around here a-honeyin' and a-huggin'.

As the last term in **maple, rock honey.**

honeyfuggle ˈhʌnɪˌfʌgl, *v.* [App. a var. of * *connyfogle* in same sense. See *EDD.*]

1. *tr.* To deceive, hoodwink, cheat (a person); to obtain by duplicity. *Slang.*

1829 *Va. Lit. Museum* 30 Dec. 458 *Honeyfuggle*, to quiz, to cozen. *Kentucky.* **1866** C. H. SMITH *Bill Arp* 119 I can't be honeyfuggled as to how my money comes and how it goes. **1905** PHILLIPS *Plum Tree* 278 Goodrich . . . was posting to make peace on whatever terms he could honeyfugle out of my conciliation-mad candidate.

2. *intr.* To act in an ingratiating manner so as to deceive or cheat. *Slang.*

1856 *Cong. Globe* App. 22 July 965/1 Pardon me for using the word; but Sharp '*honey-fuggled*' around me. **1906** *Nation* 22 Feb. 140 'Don't honey-fugle,' he advised the committee, 'but go to the bottom in any way possible.'

honey locust. An ornamental tree, *Gleditsia triacanthos*, having a spiny trunk; any one of various trees, as the clammy locust, black locust, and mesquite, resembling this.

1743 CLAYTON *Flora Virginica* 194 *Gleditsia*, . . . Honey-locust. **1784** FILSON *Kentucke* 23 The honey-locust is curiously surrounded with large thorny spikes, bearing broad and long pods in form of peas, has a sweet taste, and makes excellent beer. **1872** TICE *Over Plains* 25 Two species of the honey locust (*Gleditchia triacanthos*, and *G. monosperma*) . . . occurred occasionally [between Leavenworth and Fairmont]. **1884** SARGENT *Rep. Forests* 62 *Prosopis juliflora.* . . . Mesquit. Algaroba. Honey Locust. Honey Pod. **1949** *Nat. Hist.* May 223/2 Persimmon belongs in the class of the very strong woods and is surpassed in our sylva only by honey locust and black locust.

attrib. [**1756** KALM *Resa* II. 205 Honey-Locust-trä.] **1770** *Md. Hist. Mag.* XIII. 72 You may get Honey Locust Pods at Mrs. Ogles. **1847** DRAKE *Pioneer Life Ky.* iii. 67 Even a great honey-locust stump . . . had decayed and disappeared.

b. (See quot.) *Obs.*

1856 FERGUSSON *America* 274 The difficulty of climbing a tree of this kind has given rise to a western proverb. They say, 'Such a one is ugly enough to scare a bear up a honey-locust, stern foremost'

* **honeysuckle,** *n.* **1.** (See quots.) **2. honeysuckle apple,** = **swamp apple 2.**

(1) **1833** FERGUSSON *Notes Tour U.S.* 216 The *Kalmia latifolia* (Mountain Laurel), here [at Mt. Vernon, Va.] called Honey suckle, in a luxuriance and beauty which baffle description. **1891** *Amer. Folk-Lore* IV. 147 Aquilegia we always called Honey-suckle [in N.H.]. — (2) **1878** STOWE *Poganuc People* xix. 209 The woods . . . were full of the pink and white azalea, and she gathered . . . stores of what were called 'honeysuckle apples,' that grew upon them—fleshy exudations not particularly nice in flavor, but crisp, cool, and much valued by children.

As the last term in **bush, cinnamon, clammy, coral, hairy, Indian, swamp, trailing, trumpet, wild, yellow honeysuckle.**

honk hɔŋk, *n.* [Imitative.]

1. A wild goose, doubtless *Branta canadensis. Obs.* Cf. **cohonk.**

1800 BOUCHER *Glossary* p. xlix, Wild-geese, . . during their annual migrations, constantly utter a cry, resembling *Cohonc*. . . . The animals themselves, by natural onomatopoeia, were also called *Honc*.

2. The cry of a wild goose, or a noise, esp. that of an automobile horn, somewhat resembling this.

1854 THOREAU *Walden* 267, I heard the tread of a flock of geese, or else ducks, . . . and the faint honk or quack of their leader as they hurried off. **1869** BARNUM *Struggles & Triumphs* 413 The man has got a natural honk, I tell you; . . . when the flocks are flying over he goes out and honks and the geese, supposing that some goose has settled and is honking . . . all fly towards the ground. **1906** *N.Y. Ev. Post* 9 June 5 The first intimation the passengers had that anything was wrong was the 'honk' from the motorman's box. **1946** THOMPSON *Amer. Daughter* 12 Now and then the silence was broken by the clear notes of a meadow lark on a near-by fence or the weird honk of wild geese.

honk hɔŋk, *v.* [Imitative.]

1. *tr.* To entice (ducks, geese) within range by making a noise similar to a honk.

*a***1835** in AUDUBON *Ornith. Biog.* IV. 10 They [ducks] could readily be brought within range by 'honking' them when flying. **1856** *Spirit of Times* 6 Dec. 226/2 The moment when your guide descries the circular pinion-beat of a gaggle of geese, far off across the amber sky, and begins to *hawnk* them, follow his example with all your might, especially if they begin to answer him.

2. *intr.* and *quasi-tr.* Of wild geese: To utter a characteristic cry.

1868 HOLMES *Old Vol. of Life* 169 As the air grows colder, the long wedges of geese flying south, with their 'commodore' in advance, and *honking* as they fly, are seen high up in the heavens. **1911** J. F. WILSON *Land Claimers* 22 Wild geese honked their way overhead. **1944** DUNCAN *M. Graham* 120 The cranes flew south early, and wild geese honked by before November.

Hence **honking,** *n.*

1846 ABERT *Rep. N. Mexico* 28 Oct., The wild geese are flying about us in great numbers, and keep up an incessant 'honking.'

3. *tr.* To sound (the horn of an automobile). Also *intr.*

1895 REMINGTON *Pony Tracks* 256 The irrepressible Dan begins to 'honk' on his horn. **1948** *Time* 9 Aug. 30/2 Motorists honked their horns. **1949** *Chi. Tribune* 7 July IV. 1/1 He honks his horn even if no one is ahead of him when the traffic light changes.

Hence **honking,** *n.*

1903 *Cin. Enquirer* 23 May 14/2 That honking isn't from wild geese—it's the horns of the automobiles on the boulevard, two squares away. **1949** *Trail Riders Bul.* March 19/1 There is no honking of automobile horns.

honker 'hɔŋkɚ, *n.* [f. **honk,** *v.*] A wild goose. Cf. **Canada honker.**

*a***1841** W. HAWES *Sporting Scenes* I. 178 We have killed wild geese . . . and we know what it is to bring down a glorious gaggle of honkers to our stool. **1879** WILLIAMS *Pacific Tourist* 275/2 Three varieties are common, the white and speckled breasted brant, and the hawnker. **1948** *Time* 11 Oct. 21/2 Honkers were winging their way south in high Vs and deer were beginning their migration from high country. *transf.* **1891** *Outing* Oct. 43/1 Though a fair honker, I cannot successfully imitate the constantly varying note of the snow goose.

b. honker duck, a duck. *Rare.*

1887 *Virginia* (Nev.) *Rep.* 18 Nov. 3/3 Sportsmen report slathers of honker ducks over at Little Washoe Lake.

honky-tonk 'hɔŋkɪˌtɔŋk, *n.* [Origin unknown.] A cheap burlesque show, a place of low amusement. Also attrib. *Slang.*

1894 *Dly. Ardmoreite* (Ardmore, Okla.) 24 Feb. 1/4 The honk-a-tonk last night was well attended by ball-heads, bachelors and leading citizens. **1927** SANDBURG *Songbag* 232 It was moaned by resonant moaners in honky tonks of the southwest. **1947** *Haverford News* (Ardmore, Pa.) 5 Nov. 1/1 The play's locale is laid in the honky-tonk atmosphere of Nick's North Pacific Street Saloon. **1949** *Boston Globe Mag.* 29 May 7/3 Across the narrow street a honkatonk orchestra blared from the open door of a saloon.

honor system. *Educ.* (See quot. 1904.) — **1904** *Pittsburgh Gaz.* 3 Dec. 4 The most successful plan of combating the tendency of college students to cheat in examinations has been some form of an 'honor system' by which the pupil is implicitly trusted and his statement accepted that he used no dishonest aids. **1942** *Vanderbilt Univ. Bul.* 314 For the successful operation of the Honor System the cooperation of every student is essential.

hooch hutʃ, *n.* [Short for next.] Whisky, esp. that which is surreptitiously made or handled. Also attrib. *Slang.* Cf. **hoochinoo,** sense **2.**

1898 *Klondike Nugget* (Dawson) 20 July 1/1 The race was a short one, and upon being overhauled, boat 232 proved to contain another six kegs of the forbidden joy dispensing 'hooch.' **1923** C. J. DUTTON *Shadow on Glass* 200, I thought of our modern 'hooch ships' that were doing the same thing. **1948** *Chi. D. News* 18 Mar. 20/7 We bought the pueblo from some of your people for a cask of hooch and some glass beads.

hoochinoo 'hutʃɪˌnu, *n.* Also **Hootzenoo, Hootznahoo, Kootznahoo, hootchinoo,** etc. [A var. of *Hutsnuwu*, "grizzly bear fort." See quot. 1890 below.]

1. (*cap.*) An Indian of a small tribe on the western and southern coasts of Admiralty Island, Alaska. In *pl.*, the tribe. Also attrib.

1878 DENNIS in Morris *Pub. Service Alaska* (1879) 122 On top of this there came a fight among the Hootzenoo Indians here—*friends* of mine. **1880** JACKSON *Alaska* 242 Tuesday we reached Angoon, the chief town of the Hootznahoos. . . . But we did not remain long, as the whole town was drunk. **1890** BALLOU *New Eldorado* 321 We pass the Indian village of Kootznahoo, occupied by a tribe of the same name, a people who have always proved to be restless and aggressive, requiring a strong hand to control them. **1915** MUIR *Travels Alaska* (1917) 211 They were about to set out on an expedition to the Hootsenoos to collect blankets as indemnity or blood-money for the death of a Chilcat woman from drinking whiskey furnished by one of the Hootsenoo tribe.

2. An intoxicating liquor made by or among the Hoochinoo Indians.

1877 *Puget Sound Argus* (Pt. Townsend, Wash.) 23 Nov., I have frequently seen soldiers go to the Indian ranch for their morning drink of kootznehoo. **1878** *S.F. Chronicle* 30 Sep., After much negotiating, $250 and a plentiful supply of 'hoochenoo' was agreed upon as the ransom of the two white men. **1883** WRIGHT *Among Alaskans* 222 For if molasses, then hoochinoo; if hoochinoo, then fights. **1945** MENCKEN *Supp.* I. 310 On the advent of Prohibition this *hoochino* began to appear in the Northwestern coast towns, and soon its name was shortened to *hooch*, which quickly penetrated to all parts of the country.

b. (See quot. 1883.) In full **hoochinoo still.**

1879 *Chi. Tribune* 14 May 6/3 We accidentally dropped upon a hootchenoo still in full operation. **1883** WRIGHT *Among Alaskans* 150 Mr. Dennis had appointed the most reliable Indians as policemen, giving them authority, under United States revenue customs laws, to seize and destroy the hoochinoos or whisky-stills. **1935** *Glimpses Alaska* 18 Imported liquors and the product of the hootchenoo stills, operated by Indians and whites alike, were in abundance.

* **hood,** *n.*

1. The covering over the motor of an automobile.

1906 *Collier's* 22 Dec. 31/1 Ford Model 'N' Runabout . . . vertical motor under hood at front. **1948** *Savings News* Nov. 9/1 The gradual disappearance of hoods has aided in increasing vision as the driver looks toward the road.

2. hoodwort, = **mad-dog skullcap.** Cf. **fall hoodwort.**

1784 CUTLER in *Mem. Academy* I. 463 *Scutellaria*. . . . Hoodwort. Blossoms blue. By fences in Sandwich. August. **1832** WILLIAMSON *Maine* I. 131.

As the last term in **class, fire, muskmelon, pumpkin hood.**

* **hooded,** *a.* In the names of birds: (1) **hooded merganser,** a small merganser, *Lophodytes cucullatus*, the adult male of which species has a hoodlike crest on the head; (2) **oriole,** any one of various subspecies of an oriole, *Icterus cucullatus*, found in the Southwest, also **Sennett's hooded oriole,** cf. **Arizona hooded oriole;** (3) **sheldrake,** = **hooded merganser;** (4) **warbler,** a

warbler, *Wilsonia citrina*, the male of which species has a hood-shaped marking about the head and neck.

(1) **1823** in JAMES *Exped.* I. 267 *Mergus cucullatus*—Hooded merganser. **1944** *Mass. Audubon Soc. Bul.* Dec. 260 The Hooded Mergansers which appeared again this year at Leverett Pond in late October have been attracting the usual amount of attention. — (2) **1869** *Amer. Naturalist* III. 186 The most peculiar birds in Calif. not yet mentioned are . . . the Little Vireo (*Vireo pusillus*) and Hooded Oriole (*Icterus cucullatus*), also migratory [etc.]. **1917** *Birds of Amer.* II. 255 Sennett's Oriole, *Icterus cucullatus sennetti*, . . . [also called] Sennett's Hooded Oriole. — (3) **1844** *Nat. Hist. N.Y., Zoology* II. 320 The Hooded Sheldrake, *Mergus Cucullatus*, . . . it breeds from Carolina, . . . to high northern latitudes. **1883** *Nat. Museum Bul.* No. 27, 163 *Lophodytes cucullatus*. Hooded Sheldrake. . . . Whole of North America. **1917** *Birds of Amer.* I. 112. — (4) **1844** *Nat. Hist. N.Y., Zoology* II. 107 The Hooded Warbler, . . . *Wilsonia mitrata*, . . . builds in low bushes. . . . A bold, courageous bird, feeding on insects which it takes on the wing. **1917** *Birds of Amer.* III. 164/1 The black domino of the Maryland Yellow-throat is replaced in the male Hooded Warbler by a broad yellow mask.

hoodlum 'hudləm, *n.* [Prob. f. G. dial. (Bavarian) *hodalum, huddellump*. See J. T. Krumpelmann in *Mod. Lang. Notes*, 50 (1935) 93 ff., and *Amer. N. & Q.* I. (1888) 16 June, 83.]

1. A young street rowdy or loafer.

1871 *Cin. Commercial* 6 Sep. (Supp.) 2/5 Surely he is far enough away here in this hideous wild of swamp, to escape the bullying of the San Francisco 'hoodlums.' **1881** MARSHALL *Through Amer.* (1882) 270 The hoodlums of San Francisco are young embryo criminals—regularly organized gangs of boys and girls. **1948** *So. Wkly.* 3 July 3/2 This mob of cowardly hoodlums aroused the girls' camp in the dead of night.

transf. **1917** *Birds of Amer.* III. 17 English Sparrow. *Passer domesticus*. . . . Other Names.—European House Sparrow; Gamin; Tramp; Hoodlum.

attrib. **1876** *Dutch Flat* (Calif.) *Forum* 17 Aug. 4/3 Should farmers discard their Chinese helpers and give boys a chance, the hoodlum element would soon cease troubling municipal authorities. **1882** *Ill. Republican* (Taylorville) 22 Nov. 5/2 About a dozen other hoodlum bums are customarily hangers on around the depot. **1943** MENEFEE *Assignment* 14 It ended with the hoodlum warning, 'Johnny Doughboy has a date with America's fighting Jew.'

2. *W.* An extra wagon used on a roundup to carry grain, extra bedding, wood, water, etc. In full **hoodlum wagon.**

1908 *Sat. Ev. Post* 31 Oct. 39/2 The jolting of the hoodlum-wagon now focused the herd's attention. **1909** *Ib.* 20 March 9/2 The outfit was engaged in packing the chuck-wagon and the hoodlum, shoeing the work-horses, straightening ropes, . . . and shaking bedding. **1944** ADAMS *W. Words* 78/2 hoodlum wagon A slang name for the bed-wagon.

Also **hoodlum driver.**

1909 *Sat. Ev. Post* 20 Feb. 10/1 'He's done opsot all my ideas of things,' he complained, addressing himself to the hoodlum driver.

hoodlumism 'hudləm,ɪzəm, *n.* The acts and practices of hoodlums. — **1872** *Newton Kansan* 14 Nov. 4/1 The Rev. Dr. Cunningham in a recent sermon traced the history of 'Hoodlumism.' **1949** *Forecast* (Chi.) 5 May 2/4 Recent rope-cutting and egg-throwing smacks more of hoodlumism than anything else.

hoodoo 'hudu, *n.* [See note.]

This term, widespread in colloq. use, is app. a variant of **voodoo.** If **Hoodoo Bar** (see **2. c.** below) was so named as early as 1850 (see the quots.), this name is the earliest evidence so far found for "hoodoo."

1. One who practices voodooism.

1875 HEARN *Amer. Miscellany* (1924) I. 127 Supposing you fall in love with a girl and can't get her, and that you go to one of these hoodoos, he will do something awful to her with charms. **1881** *Harper's Mag.* April 736/1 Who seed yo' las' moon-risin' w'en Hoodoos met? *Ib.* 738/2 Suddenly she . . . rushed forward with an African yell and joined in the dance as wild as any Hoodoo among them. **1947** TALLANT *Voodoo in N.O.* 16, I heard people say hoodoos was cannibals and used to eat babies.

attrib. **1875** HEARN *Amer. Miscellany* (1924) I. 127 Well, in that case, she would die, of course, unless she could get some other hoodoo doctor to take the charm away by a counter charm. **1881** *Harper's Mag.* April 738/1 All her blood fired when she heard that the Hoodoo priest had called a meeting of his devotees. **1945** *N. & Q.* July 58/2 He cites the example of 'love powders,' sold in New Orleans drugstores or obtainable from 'hoodoo doctors.' **1946** TALLANT *Voodoo in N.O.* 195, I got Adele to a good hoodoo woman and she uncrossed her.

b. A malignant spell, something which causes bad luck

1893 *Chi. Tribune* 2 July 15/3 You could kill the hoodoo of a cross-eyed man or woman by burning the stage properties. **1901** M. E. RYAN *Montana* 16 If it's a hoodoo, as you thought, why not throw it away? **1903** *Cin. Enquirer* 14 Feb. 1/8 The double hoodoo presided to-day. The date is the 13th of the month and the day Friday. **1947** FISCHER *Focs'le Days* 48 There seemed to be a hoodoo over the ship.

c. A person who causes bad luck.

1900 GARLAND *Eagle's Heart* 226, I'm a hoodoo, Cory; nobody is ever in luck when I'm around.

d. *attrib.* Designating things under a spell, or that exercise a malignant influence.

1881 *Harper's Mag.* April 737/2 'De Hoodoo meetin' is my drink,' said Dulcie . . . 'an' somethin' pulls an' pushes till I git dar.' **1889** *Sporting Life* (Phila.) 5 June 3/3 It cost me $5 for transportation yesterday, and it is going to cost me $15 to-day, but I won't have any tarnation hoodoo 'bus taggin' after me. **1904** *N.Y. Globe* 2 April 1 It is hard to find a crew for a 'hoodoo' ship. Men desert from a vessel with an uncanny reputation. **1914** GERRY *Masks of Love* 168 Kansas City had always been a 'hoodoo town' for Newbold's productions. **1945** BOTKIN *My Burden* 30 That's how the niggers say Old Bab Russ used to make the hoodoo hands he made for the young bucks and wenches.

2. *W.* One of the weirdly shaped spectral masses resulting from erosion observable in the Yellowstone River region. Also **hoodoo land.**

1879 WHITMAN *Spec. Days* 148, I had wanted to go to the Yellowstone river region—wanted specially to see . . . the 'hoodoo' or goblin land of that country. **1880** *Rep. Supt. Yellowstone Nat. Pk.* (1881) 8 Actual observation is absolutely necessary to adequately impress the mind with the wild unearthly appearance of these eroded Hoodoos of the Goblin Land. **1940** *Places to See in Wyo.* xii/2 Silver Gate, composed of white granite blocks, ends in the Hoodoos, oddly shaped gray travertine lumps.

b. In proper names.

1880 *Rep. Supt. Yellowstone Nat. Pk.* (1881) 7, I pushed on some three miles to explore the Hoodoo Mountain and its labyrinths. **1882** WYLIE *Yellowstone Nat. Pk.* 71 Hoodoo Basin. This singular locality, lately discovered, is fifty miles southeast from Baronet's Bridge. . . . This Hoodoo region is not, as the name 'Basin' would indicate, a low flat place surrounded by hills or mountains, but is itself situated high upon a mountain. **1949** *Travel* April 21/2 The Hoodoo Rocks in the Red Deer River Valley are mushroom-shaped stone formations among which remains of prehistoric animals have been found.

c. Esp. **Hoodoo Bar,** (see quot. 1946).

1888 BANCROFT *Hist. Calif.* VI. 361 Intermediate [i.e., between 1849, 1852] rose in 1850 St Joe, Nigger Slide, Ranty Doddler, Hoodoo, Cut Throat or Woodville, and Slaughter bars. **1946** HANNA *Dict. Calif Land Names* 125 Hoodoo Bar. . . . A mining site of 1850 on the north fork of the Yuba River. **1948** JOHNSTON *Gold Rush* 40/2 Ranty Doddler Bar and Hoodoo Bar were close by. The origin of the latter name is ascribed to the peculiar enunciation by an Indian of the salutation 'How do you do?' rendering it 'Hoodoo.'

d. (See quot.) *Obs.*

1882 *Harper's Mag.* April 691/1 Besides the larger houses, inhabited by the engineers, foremen, etc., you will see [in mineral region of southwest Colorado] numbers of little huts about three logs high, roofed flatly with poles, brush, and mud . . . or into a side-hill will be pushed small caves, with a front wall of stones and mud, and a bit of canvas for a door. . . . So substantial are most of these 'hoodoos,' however [etc.].

e. hoodoo stick, a divining rod used in finding rich ore. Cf. **doodle-bug b.**

1905 *Out West* Sep. 209 There was a man could locate silver nuggets with the hoodoo-stick, every time. **1936** MCKENNA *Black Range* 111 My hoodoo stick twirled like a top there on the summit of Old Kentuck.

hoodoo 'hudu, *v.* [f. the noun.] *tr.* To bewitch, put under a spell. *Colloq.* Cf. **voodoo,** *v.*

1886 *Harper's Wkly* 25 Dec., The surest way to provide against being 'hoodooed,' as American residents call it, is to open one's pillow from time to time. **1903** BROWN *How to Beat Game* 30 Kill a black cat on the last quarter of the moon, and place it upon the door-step of the person you desire to hoodoo. **1848** JOHNSTON *Gold Rush* 17/2 Thereafter it was regarded as 'hoodooed,' and fit only for exhibition as a relic.

b. To expel, drive away. *Colloq.*

1889 *Walla Walla* (Wash.) *Union* 12 Jan. 3/5 Over the head of the man preparing the [Chinese] lottery tickets was hanging a bundle of chicken claws, which the reporter was informed were placed there for the purpose of 'hoodooing' the spirits. **1895** *Chi. Strike of 1894* 107 As soon as you are found out to be a member of the American Railway Union you were . . . hoodooed away from the property as quick as possible.

c. To make a commotion or "ado" about something. *Colloq.*

1900 *Cong. Rec.* 27 Feb. 2336/2, I will tell you what they [the Democrats] . . . are hoodooing about.

hoodooism ˈhuduˌɪzəm, *n.* (See quot. 1881.) Cf. **voodooism,** *n.* — **1881** *Harper's Mag.* April 737/1 'What *is* Hoodooism anyhow?' 'It's de ole African r'ligion, honey. It's jes' like white folk's r'ligion on'y it's heathenism, an' dey worships de debbil.' **1921** *Double Dealer* July 22/1 The white folks gaze at the negro with incredulous eye and wonder what amazing story of hoodooism will come from his lips.

hooey ˈhuɪ, *n.* [?Fanciful.] Humbug, blarney, claptrap. *Slang.*

[**1889** FARMER 308/1 Huey.—In American pugilistic slang *Huey* represents the *National Police Gazette* published in New York.] **1924** P. MARKS *Plastic Age* 100 My prof's full of hooey. He doesn't know a C theme from an A one. **1948** *Chi. Tribune* 3 April 1. 4/7 Mr. Truman told a news conference last week he considered daylight saving a lot of hooey unless it was followed on a national scale.

* **hoof,** *n.* In combs.: (1) **hoof ail,** = **hoof rot;** (2) **-and-mouth disease,** the foot-and-mouth disease, a contagious disease esp. of cloven-footed animals; (3) **rot,** foot rot, a disease affecting the feet of sheep and cattle and characterized by inflammation of the tissues, ulceration, and sometimes loss of the hoof.

(**1**) **1838** in *Rep. Comm. Agric. 1884* 246 A number of the 'Farmer and Gardener' . . . contains an article on the 'Hoof-ail' of cattle. **1871** *Ill. Agric. Soc. Trans.* VIII. 182 The most damaging disease, because the most difficult of eradication, is that known as Foot-Rot—sometimes called Hoof-Ail. — (**2**) **1884** DOWELL *On Democracy* 5 Would it account for the phylloxera, and hoof-and-mouth disease, and bad harvests . . . and the German hands? **1947** *Chi. D. News* 10 Feb. 9/1 Fear of another outbreak of hoof and mouth disease that closed the Union Stock Yards and cut off meat supplies in November, 1914, stirred Packingtown today. — (**3**) **1863** RANDALL *Pract. Shepherd* 25 These miserable animals brought along with them scab and hoof-rot, those dire scourges of the ovine race. **1869** *Ill. Agric. Soc. Trans.* VII. 458 A large number of sheep suffering either from scab or hoof-rot.

b. In phrases: (1) *on the hoof,* of beef cattle, alive, under their own motive power; (2) *to sell corn on the hoof,* to convert corn into money, not by direct sale, but by feeding it to hogs or cattle later to be sold alive; (3) *heating of the hoof, W.* the initial stage of hoof rot, once regarded as the onset or cause of Texas cattle fever, *obs.*

(**1**) [**1752** *N.C. Morav. Rec.* I. (1922) 39 Many cattle are also sold outside of North Carolina. . . . They are . . . driven to Virginia and sold on the hoof.] **1817** *Niles' Reg.* XII. 287/1 An ox, bred at Springfield, Mass. weighs on the hoof, 3,100 lbs. **1890** *Stock Grower & Farmer* 4 Jan. 4/2 [Monroe] shipped on the hoof, and did all of his killing near the large cities which he supplied. — (**2**) **1902** LORIMER *Lett. Merchant* 78 It seems to take a farmer a long time to learn that the best way to sell his corn is on the hoof. — (**3**) **1878** J. H. BEADLE *Western Wilds* xxviii. 438 The tramp of from three to eight hundred miles to the border causes 'heating of the hoof,' and the poisonous matter exuding therefrom is left upon the grass. Hence, say the Kansians, the 'Texas cattle fever.'

hoofed locust. *W.* (See quot. 1939.)

1869 MUIR *First Summer in Sierra* (1911) 75 Sheep, like people, are ungovernable when hungry. Excepting my guarded lily gardens, almost every leaf that these hoofed locusts can reach within a radius of a mile or two from camp has been devoured. **1939** ROLLINS *Gone Haywire* 82 The sheep—'hoofed locusts'—actually were a menace to the raising of other live stock. Nibbling the bunch grass to its roots and, with their sharp hoofs, chopping these roots into sterility, they converted into a semi-desert any locality they frequented. **1947** *Sierra Club Bul.* 3 Ardent lover of flowers and trees that he was, he noted the destructive effects of those 'hoofed locusts' on the wild gardens and forests through which they passed.

hoofer ˈhʊfɚ, *n.* A dancer. *Slang.* — **1925** *Sat. Ev. Post* 4 July 17/2, I didn't know you had rose above hoofers. **1949** *Sat. Ev. Post* 16 April 110/3 He thought of himself as a dancer of a superior kind; certainly not an example of the breed known vulgarly as hoofers.

* **hook,** *n.*

1. A bend in the course of a river or channel.

This use is equally early in British English, but the Amer. currency of the term may be the result of a borrowing here from the Du. *hoek,* a corner, nook (of land). The word is common in place-names in eastern N.Y. See *Amer. Sp.* V. 162.

1670 *Doc. Col. Hist. N.Y.* XII. 474 A Plantation with proporcon of meadow ground for Hay for their cattle on Verdrietiges or Trinity Hook at Delaware. **1781** *Deane Papers* 161, I am just informed that the British Fleet have again sailed from the hook. **1848** BARTLETT 179 *Hook.* (Dutch, *hoek,* a corner.) This name is given in New York to several angular points in the North and East rivers; as, *Corlear's Hook, Sandy Hook, Powles's Hook.* **1895** *Educational Rev.* Nov. 357 This . . . forming an array of mud-flats . . . hooks and deltas.

b. (*cap.*) A district in N.Y. City. *Obs.*

1851 GREELEY in *Whig Almanac 1852* 12/2 The 'Five Points' is the most 'Democratic' district of our city [New York]; 'The Hook' follows not very far behind it. [**1859** see * **hooker 1**].

2. In combs.: (1) **Hook and Eye Baptists,** ? = next, *rare;* (2) **Hook and Eye Dutch,** (see quot. 1903 and cf. * **hooker,** *n.* **3.**); (3) **hook and ladder,** see as a main entry; (4) * **and line,** used attrib. in the sense of completely, fully equipped, also as adv., *colloq.,* cf. (6); (5) * **-bill,** a local name for the large-mouthed black bass; (6) **line and sinker,** completely, without reservation, *colloq.;* (7) **slide,** in baseball, a slide to a base by a runner who thrusts one foot directly into the bag and throws his body to one side to avoid the baseman; (8) **stick,** (see quot.); (9) **tender,** the foreman of a yarding crew of loggers, esp. one who directs the attaching of the cable to logs; (10) **worm,** (see quot. 1909).

(**1**) **1898** *Philistine* Feb. 66 The East Aurora Hook & Eye Baptists as yet have not Meeting Houses of their own, holding services every Sunday at the residence of some member. — (**2**) **1903** *N.Y. Times* 9 Sep., He was a member of the Amish sect, commonly known as the Hook and Eye Dutch, for the reason that they wear hooks and eyes in preference to buttons on their clothes. **1947** *Amer. Sp.* Feb. 72/2 Consequently these 'hook and eye Dutch' were often the butt of fun-making by the other school-children. — (**4**) **1834** C. A. DAVIS *Lett. J Downing* 44 Its all over with you and the Bank—you'll all go 'hook and line.' **1900** BACHELLOR *E. Holden* 215 When we came back, 'hook an' line' for another vacation, the fields were aglow with color.

(**5**) **1897** *Rep. Comm. Fisheries* 185 The conspicuous development of the under jaw in the males led to the local names of 'hawk-bill' and 'hook-bill'; the silvery sides of the fish in summer gave rise to that of 'white trout.' — (**6**) **1838** in BARNES *Memoir of T. Weed* (1884) 60 (We.), We are gone, hook, line and sinker. **1947** BASKINS *Dr. Has Baby* 46 Most mothers, I discovered in comparing notes over the back fences, swallowed the books hook, line, and sinker, and gladly wore themselves out in the service of their young. — (**7**) **1917** MATHEWSON *Sec. Base Sloan* xi. 145 A dexterous hook-slide that kept him far out of reach of the baseman's sweep. — (**8**) **1917** KEPHART *Camping* I. 228 A hook for lifting kettles is a hook-stick. — (**9**) **1893** *Atlantic Mo.* Feb. 196/1 Each man, being hired for a definite purpose, as chopper, hook-tender, barker [etc.], . . . keeps closely to his own job. **1924** SHEPHARD *P. Bunyan* 160 He'd said he was goin' to show that hooktender, Joe, and he certainly showed him all right.

(**10**) **1903** *Pop. Sci. Mo.* Feb. 382/2 The other anemia, preeminently a disease of the sandy regions, is caused by a parasitic 'hookworm' (*Uncinaria americana*) which lives in the intestines and which is not affected by quinine. **1909** *Cent. Supp.* 598/1 hook-worm, . . . n. An intestinal parasite, *Uncinaria americana* or *Ankylostoma duodenale:* so called originally from the presence of rays or ribs, interpreted as hooks, in the membranous expansion or caudal bursa, at the hinder end of the male worm. **1949** *Democrat* 10 Feb. 1/6 Hookworm is one of our most common diseases, and one of the easiest to dispose of.

b. *On* (or *upon*) *one's own hook,* upon one's own authority, responsibility, or initiative. *Colloq.*

Cf. Du. *op zijn eigen houtje,* on one's own risk, responsibility, authority, where *houtje* app. refers to a notched stick upon which a reckoning is kept. See *WNT s.v. hout,* 1176.

1812 *Boston Gaz.* 23 Nov. (Th.), [Commodore] Rodgers himself says that he went upon his own hook. **1896** HARRIS *Sister Jane* 339, I allowed I'd git my head took off over here, an' I come primed to do some talking on my own hook. **1907** WHITE *Arizona Nights* 52, I joined the trail crew; and somehow or another the Honourable Timothy got permission to go along on his own hook.

As the last term in **boot, brier, bush, car, cat, cotton, fid, gang, high, mat, mud, pin, pot, potato, pulling, swamp, tow, trap, wolf hook.**

* **hook,** *v.*

1. *tr.* To make (a rug) by looping strips of cloth, yarn, etc., through a burlap back; to crochet. *Colloq.* Cf. **hooked rug.**

1879 HOWELLS *Lady of Aroostook* 20 That's a rug she hooked. **1898** *Boston Ev. Transcript* 16 April 14/5 A Detroit lady joyfully boasted: 'I have just hooked my husband a lovely pair of mittens.' **1945** MACDONALD *Egg & I* 66 A time to repair machinery, hook rugs, patch quilts, mend harness and perform other leisurely tasks.

2. *To hook Jack,* "to play truant. New England" (B. '77). *Colloq.*

1905 J. C. LINCOLN *Partners of Tide* iv, The boy 'hooked Jack' for a whole day.

3. hookup, *n.* A connection or combination of apparatus, resources, etc., esp. of radio broadcasting facilities.

1903 A. H. Lewis *Boss* 116 It'll put us in line for a hook-up with th' reform bunch in th' fight for th' town next year. **1911** H. Quick *Yellowstone N.* vii. 191 The Golden Fountain . . . had no lawyer against us. It was a funny hook up. **1948** *Sat. Ev. Post* 9 Oct. 25/1 And then he had to do it, national hookup or not, and said with all joy bubbling over in his throat, 'How'm I doin', Maggie?'

hook and ladder. A fire-fighting truck which carries ladders. In full **hook-and-ladder carriage, truck.**

1831 *Boston Ev. Transcript* 10 May 2/2 The chief engineer's communication respecting placing a hook and ladder carriage in High-street . . . [was] referred to the committee on the Fire Department. **1882** McCabe *New York* 603 There are employed in the service of the department 42 steam fire-engines, . . . and 18 hook and ladder trucks. **1948** *Sat. Ev. Post* 20 Nov. 42/1 Hook and Ladder No. 26 responded in record time as tenants of the four-story building collected on the sidewalk. **1949** *L.A. Times* 18 May 8/1 The Fire Department obligingly backed up a hook-and-ladder truck.

b. Also **hook-and-ladder company, house, man.**

1821 *Boston Selectmen* 187 Mr. George G. Channing . . . declines taking command of the Fire Hook & Ladder company. **1825** in Brayley *Boston Fire Dept.* (1889) 156 The engineers, the firemen and hosemen, and hook and laddermen are competent to manage all the machines. **1834** *Sun* (N.Y.) 3 June 2/2 In the Park, . . . a roofed wooden building is now erecting for the purpose of a hook and ladder house. **1923** Watts *L. Nichols* 68 The only clean place in the vicinity was the Bald Eagle Engine-House and Hook-and-Ladder Company 17.

c. Hook-and-Ladder Democrat, (see quot.). *Rare.*

1855 Weld *Vacation Tour* 282 The number of political associations in America is as extraordinary as the strange names which they bear. . . . Hook and Ladder Democrats, Dumb Democrats, &c.

hooked rug. A rug that is handmade of yarn or strips of cloth hooked back and forth through a burlap back. Cf. ***hook,** *v.* **1.**

1880 Howells *Undisc. Country* 415 Hooked rugs and embroidered tidies, were as worthy a place in Mrs. Ford's simple house as most of the old-fashioned things. **1894** ——— *Traveler from Altruria* 163 Home-made hooked rugs, in rounds and ovals, [were] scattered about the clean floor. **1949** *Amer. Photography* April 236/2 Don't forget . . . the hooked rugs hanging out for sale in the Carolinas, or Indian blankets similarly displayed through the southwest.

***hooker,** *n.*

1. (See quot.)

1859 Bartlett 201 *Hooker.* A resident of the Hook, i.e. a strumpet, a sailor's trull. So called from the number of houses of ill-fame frequented by sailors at the Hook (i.e., Corlear's Hook) in the city of New York.

2. A cow that hooks, or attacks with the horns.

1866 *Harper's Mag.* May 816/1 He . . . asked 'Why that pipe [*sc.* a hookah] was like a cow?' having in mind the obvious answer that it was a *hooker.* **1885** Craddock *Prophet* 48 The red cow jes' hooked down the bars, bein' a turrible hooker. **1902** Lorimer *Lett. Merchant* 84 Of course, you want to . . . learn to distinguish between a cow that's a kicker, but whose intentions are good if she's approached with proper respect, and a hooker, who is vicious on general principles.

3. (See quot. 1880.) Also attrib.

1880 *Harper's Mag.* May 810/1 The stricter Mennonites regarded them [*sc.* buttons] as a worldly innovation, and, adhering to the use of hooks and eyes, were called 'Hookers,' in distinction from the more lax brethren, who were called 'Buttoners.' **1913** *Proc. Pa.-Ger. Soc.* XXII. 82 The inn was the first public house west of Philadelphia, kept by a 'Hooker' Mennonite.

4. (See quot. 1881.)

1881 Ingersoll *Oyster Industry* 245 *Hooker,* . . . in sponging, the man who hooks up the sponges from the bottom. (Florida reefs.) **1883** *Nat. Museum Bul.* No. 27, 125 As soon as a Sponge is sighted, the boat is quickly stopped, and the 'hooker' thrusts down his spear and fastens into it.

5. =**lumber hooker.**

1946 Newton *P. Bunyan* 76 Its capacity was equal to that of ten ordinary lumber carriers, or 'hookers,' as they are called in the Lake Superior country.

hooky ˈhʊkɪ, *n.* [App. f. **hook, v.*, to make off.] *To play hooky,* to play truant, to remain away from school without permission. Also transf.

1848 Bartlett 180. **1870** Mark Twain *Sk., New & Old* 56 He would not play hookey, even when his sober judgment told him it was the most profitable thing he could do. **1906** *Corning* (Calif.) *New Era* 17 Mar. 4/4 The report of the truant officer . . . showed a growing tendency among the boys to play 'hookey.' **1948** *Ore. Hist. Mag.* March 79 Like many another soul, he 'played hookey' from man-made books in order that he might delight his soul in the God-made books.

Hence **hooky-player.**

1947 Baskins *Dr. Has Baby* 174 'Feeling like a bride?' . . . 'Not exactly. . . . More like a hookey-player.'

***hoop,** *n.*

1. A wooden shoulder-yoke for use in carrying pails. *Obs.* See **neck yoke, sap yoke.**

1851 Cist *Cincinnati* 102 There are many still living who associate 'toting' water by hoop and buckets with their reminiscences of a washing day. **1857** E. Stone *Life J. Howland* 25 It fell to the lot of the boys, some of whom were negroes . . . to go with two pails and a hoop, across the bridge for a supply.

2. In combs.: (1) **hoop dress,** =next, *obs.*; (2) **skirt,** a skirt that is expanded near the bottom and held out by hoops, also fig.; (3) ***wood,** the black ash, *Fraxinus nigra,* or the winterberry, *Ilex laevigata;* (4) **wood buckeye,** a now unidentifiable tree or shrub, *rare.*

For **hoop-and-pole, hoop ash, hoop pole, hoop snake,** see as main entries.

(1) **1842** in *Amer. Sp.* XVIII. 125/2 Who, anywhere but in this strange country, would have thought of mounting a horse in a hoop-dress? — (2) **1857** Underhill & Thompson *Elephant Club* 193 Lady with hoop-skirt hails the driver. **1906** *Springfield W. Republican* 19 July 1 Populism was a 'hoopskirt' article of statesmanship, perhaps, but it produced no thieves. **1949** *Nat. Geog. Mag.* Feb. 207 Hoop Skirts Swish Again in Majestic Stanton Hall's Driveway. — (3) **1770** Washington *Diaries* I. 429, I also marked . . . an Ash and hoopwood for the Beginning of another [corner] of the Soldiers Survey. **1821** J. Fowler *Journal* 21 We Set out at our ushal time at ten miles pased a point of Rocks and a Hoop wood tree on them. **1854** Bancroft *Hist. U.S.* VI. 379 He would . . . set his mark on a maple, or elm, a hoop-wood, or ash, as the corner of a soldier's survey. — (4) **1787** in *Amer. Sp.* XV. 163/1 Beginning at a hoopwood Buckeye and red oak standing in Cave.

As the last term in **ear, grace, head, set, wagon hoop.**

hoop-and-pole. An Indian game played in any one of many ways (see quots. 1858, 1907). Also **hoop-and-stick.** *Obs.*

1823 James *Exped.* I. 186 The men in the mean time amuse themselves with hunting, playing with the hoop and stick, cards, dancing, &c. **1858** *Harper's Mag.* Sep. 463/1 Some of the young men selected a

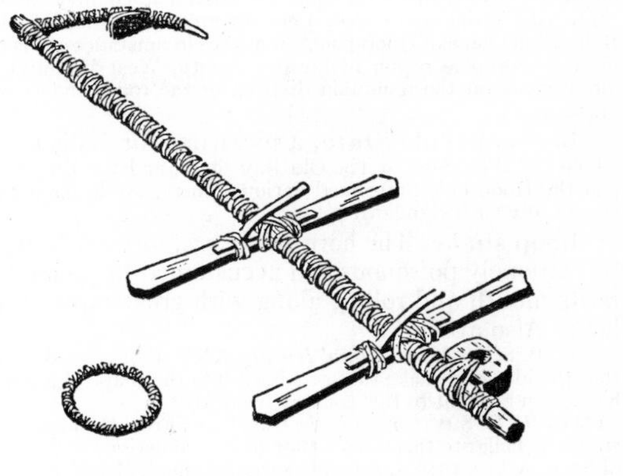

Articles used in one form of the Indian hoop-and-pole game

level spot, forty paces in length . . . and amused themselves with their favorite game of hoop-and-poles. . . . Rolling the hoop from one end of the course towards the other, two of the players chase it half-way, and at the same time throw their poles. He who succeeds in piercing the hoop wins the game. **1907** Hodge *Amer. Indians* I. 485 *Hoop-and-pole.*—A widely distributed athletic game in which a hoop or ring, frequently covered with network, is rolled along the ground and shot at with arrows or javelins, the counts being determined by the way in which the latter fall with reference to the ring.

hoop ash. 1. The black ash, *Fraxinus nigra.* **2.** Any tree of the genus *Celtis.*

(1) **1763** in Durrett *Louisville* (1893) 132 [Boundaries] Beginning at a hoop-ash and buckeye, the lower corner of Major Edward Ward's land. **1916** Seton *Woodcraft Man.* 295 Black Ash, Hoop Ash, or Water Ash (*Fraxinus nigra*) A tall forest tree of swampy places; 70, 80, or rarely 100 feet high. — (2) **1787** Sargent in *Mem. Academy* II. I. 157 Black Ash, three feet diameter. White Ash, to five feet diameter. Hoop Ash, of three, and three and a half feet diameter. **1810** Michaux *Arbres* I. 38 *Hackberry tree,* . . . *Hoop ash,* sur les bords de

l'Ohio. **1921** Deam *Trees Indiana* 148 *Celtis occidentalis* . . . was formerly often known as hoop ash.

hoopee 'hupi, *n.*[1] *local.* [Origin obscure.] (See quot.) — **1903** Austin *Land of Little Rain* 128 By the south corner, where the campoodie stood, is a single shrub of 'hoopee' (*Lycium Andersonii*), maintaining itself hardly among alien shrubs.

hoopee, *n.*[2] See **whoopee.**

hoopid salmon. (See quot.) — **1883** *Nat. Museum Bul.* No. 27, 474 *Oncorhynchus kisutch*. . . . Hoopid Salmon. . . . Pacific coast of North America from San Francisco northward to Bering Strait.

hooping crane, see **whooping crane.**

hoop-la 'hupla, *interj.* and *n.* **1.** (See quot.) **2.** Fervor, excited delight. *Slang.*

(1) **1877** Bartlett 294 Hoop-la. A stage-driver's ejaculation to his horses. — (2) **1877** *N.Y. Tribune* 1 March (B.), The Stock Exchange to-day commenced its business of speculation with a grand 'hoop-la,' regardless of the closing prices of yesterday. **1948** *Carpenter* March 16 Organized some three years ago amid a great hoopla of Communist propaganda and promotion, it has creaked along in a very erratic and unpredictable manner.

hoople 'hupl̩, *n.* (See quot.) *Obs.* — **1848** Bartlett 180 *Hoople.* (Dutch, *hoepel.*) The boys in the city of New York still retain the Dutch name *hoople* for a hoop.

hoop pole.

1. A small sapling, esp. a young hickory or whiteoak, having a smooth straight stem or stock suitable for making a hoop for a cask.

1645 *Dedham Rec.* III. 112 Sam Milles hath libtie to cut 400 lengthes of hoope poles on the common. **1703** *Suffield Doc. Hist.* 145 It was agreed . . . to impose a fine . . . upon any person, that shall presume hereafter, to cut . . . and carry away hoop-polls, from off any of our commons. **1835** Bird *Hawks of Hawk-H.* I. vi. 76 There was a bundle of green hoop-poles, at a cooper's shop. **1884** *Rep. Comm. Agric.* 140 In some counties the mania for hoop poles has played havoc with young hickory and white oak.

2. *attrib.* Designating a place or region where such poles are abundant.

1859 *Harper's Mag.* Oct. 712/1 Uncle Jim . . . saw a huge fellow . . . who hailed from the hoop-pole county of Marshall, Virginia, coming up Main Street. **1880** *Ib.* May 907/1 One day I accompanied the doctor on a long drive through the 'hoop-pole country' as certain timbered district was called. **1894** Searight *Old Pike* 162 Gideon Bolton (nicknamed 'Hoop-pole,' from the circumstance of his coming from a hoop-pole region in Preston county, West Virginia), drove many years on the mountain division of the road, and is well remembered.

b. Hoop-Pole State, a nickname for Indiana.

1906 *Out West* Jan. 59 The Old Bay State, and the Empire State, and the Hoop-Pole State, and various others, would have cause to lament any such standard.

hoop snake. The horn snake *q.v.*, formerly alleged to be extremely poisonous and accustomed to taking its tail in its mouth and rolling along with great rapidity like a hoop. Also attrib.

K. P. Schmidt in *Natural History* XXV. (1925) 76–80 suggests that the idea of a snake that gets itself into the shape of a hoop may have been brought to this country from Africa.

1784 J. F. D. Smyth *Tour in the U.S.* I. 265 From the above circumstance, peculiar to themselves, they have also derived the appellation of hoop snakes. **1840** *S. Lit. Messenger* VI. 380/2, I never believed in the existence of hoop-snakes neither, until I went out into the western country. **1949** *Scientific Mo.* Jan. 52/1 There appears to be no classical or European analogue of the American hoop-snake story.

hoosegow 'husgaʊ, *n.* [Sp. *juzgado*, often pronounced as if *juzgao*, a court or tribunal.] A jail or prison. Also transf. *Slang.*

1920 *Public Opin.* 560/3 Only the keeper and the kept in the hoosegow knew it. **1943** *Reader's Digest* Dec. 50/1 Despite this national nutrition crisis, margarine is still cooped up in a legislative hoosegow. **1948** *Dly. Ardmoreite* (Ardmore, Okla.) 13 April 1/1 The bonafide stranger gets a summons and shows up at the hoosegow and is let go with a kindly warning.

hoosier 'huʒɚ, *n.* [See note.]

The most plausible of the many theories about the origin of this term is that advanced by Jacob Piatt Dunn (see his *Indiana and Indianians* II. 1121–55) who relates it to the Cumberland dialect word *hoozer* (see *EDD*) used of anything unusually large. Dunn was no doubt correct also in thinking the term had a general application before being applied specifically to an Indianian, but no evidence for such use is now available.

1. (*cap.*) A nickname for a resident or native of Indiana. Also transf.

1826 in *Chi. Tribune* (1949) 2 June 20/3 The Indiana hoosiers that came out last fall is settled from 2 to 4 milds of us. **1831** in J. P. Dunn *Indiana* (1919) II. 1154 He [a horse] is stabled however in Indianapolis, the center of the race track, he has been corned, littered and kept in Indiana and may be called a 'Hoosher.' **1832** *Ind. Democrat*, Ask for our 'hoosiers' good plantations. **1885** *Outing* Nov. 152/2 Did you notice that young Hoosier and his bride who sat opposite me at breakfast? **1947** *Harper's Mag.* Jan. 67/2 Other Hoosiers ridicule them as hillbillies.

b. A big, burly, uncouth specimen or individual, a frontiersman, countryman, rustic. Cf. **mountain hoosier.**

1832 in J. P. Dunn *Indiana* (1919) II. 1153 A Real Hoosier.—A sturgeon, who, no doubt, left Lake Michigan on a trip of pleasure . . . being brought on terra firma, and cast into a balance, he was found to weigh 83 pounds. **1857** Godkin in R. Ogden *Life E. L. Godkin* I. 157 The mere 'cracker' or 'hoosier,' as the poor [southern] whites are termed. **1900** Flynt *Tramping* 394 *Hoosier*, a 'farmer.' **1948** Dick *Dixie Frontier* 310 Before it was used to designate the citizens of Indiana, the term 'Hoosier' was used in the South to describe a rough or uncouth person.

c. A way of speaking characteristic of Hoosiers. *Rare.* Cf. **Hoosierism.**

1871 Eggleston *Hoosier Schoolm.* iv. 41 The 'big road' (Hoosier for *highway*) ran along the north-west side.

d. (See quots.)

1926 *Amer. Mercury* Jan. 64/2 The word *hoosier* is applied to anyone who is incompetent. **1944** *N. & Q.* March 188 Its advertisements . . . were answered by a number of Indianans who knew little or nothing about the lumbering business; hence the word *hoosier* in the lumber trade came to mean 'a man who doesn't know his job.'

2. In combs.: (1) **Hoosier bait,** a kind of gingerbread (see quot. 1919 and cf. next), *obs.;* (2) **cake,** (see quot. and cf. prec.), *obs.;* (3) **dinner,** (see quot.); (4) **frog,** (see quot.); (5) **land,** Indiana, a nickname; (6) **Poet,** James Whitcomb Riley (1849–1916), a poet of Indiana; (7) **State,** a nickname for Indiana.

(1) **1833** in Dunn *Indiana* (1919) II. 1127 My pockets are so shrunk of late I can not nibble 'Hoosher bait.' **1919** J. P. Dunn II. 1141 The man said, 'I guess you want hoosier-bait,' and when he produced it I found that he had the right idea. . . . The gingerbread referred to was cooked in square pans—about fifteen inches across. . . . A quarter-section sold for a fip, which was 6¼ cents. — (2) **1859** Bartlett 202 Hoosier Cake, a Western name for a sort of coarse gingerbread, which, say the Kentuckians, is the best bait to catch a hoosier with, the biped being fond of it. — (3) **1856** Fergusson *America* 324 We reached Seymour about half-past twelve, and had a 'Hoosier' dinner at the M'Callum house . . . plenty of dishes, but miserably cooked, and worse served. — (4) **1883** *Amer. Naturalist* XVII. 945 The Mink or Hoosier Frog. . . . This frog (*Rana septentrionalis*) seems comparatively unknown, and is found in localities far apart.

(5) **1834** in *Indiana Hist. Soc. Pub.* IV. No. 2, 10 The poet *laureat* of Hoosierland and editor of the Richmond Palladium has threatened to 'cut acquaintance with B. of the Democrat!!' **1948** *Chesterton* (Ind.) *Tribune* 28 Oct. 7/1 (*heading*), This Week in Hoosierland. — (6) **1925** *Lit. Digest* 10 Oct. 40/1 The Hoosier Poet likes to choose his own company. **1945** *Chi. Sun Book Week* 23 Sep. 3/5 Children from all sections of Indiana, coming to plant a rosebush in the front yard of the beloved Hoosier poet—the adored Children's Poet. — (7) **1833** *Indiana Democrat* 12 Jan., [John W. Davis gave the toast] 'The Hooshier State of Indiana.' [**1853** *Ore. Statesman* 23 April 1/4 In the State of Hoosierana, in the year 1844, there were 'all sorts' of excitement concerning the doctrines and prophecies of that arch deceiver, Miller. **1856** *Spirit of Times* 15 Nov. 179/3 Not long since we went to White River in the State of Hoosier, to catch a fish or two.] **1949** *Chi. D. News* 29 March 10/5 In my native Hoosier state, the only thing wrong with cutting in on party lines is that it interferes with the housework.

Also *Hoosier boy, commonwealth, court, manners, schoolmaster,* etc.

Hoosierdom 'huʒɚdəm, *n.* The West, also a nickname for Indiana.

1848 *Cong. Globe* App. 7 Aug. 1119/3 In the West, every political thingumderry . . . does his little best to produce confusion in Hoosierdom. **1850** *Quincy* (Ill.) *Whig* 9 July 2/5, I say, my friend, you are from Hoosierdom, I suppose. **1910** *Morrison's Chi. Wkly.* 1 Dec. 46/1 'Doc Bird' is a Hoosier from Hoosierdom, and proud of it. **1947** *Chi. Tribune* 9 Nov. iv. 23/2 His book is focused on the strife rather than the serenity of Hoosierdom.

Hoosierina ˌhuʒə'rinə, *n.* A woman or girl who lives in Indiana. *Obs.* — **1843** Carlton *New Purchase* II. 5 And what could have deceived our Hoosierina? **1844** *Yale Lit. Mag.* IX. 264 Advancing to the door, I was met by a dame of goodly proportions, surrounded by some ten or twelve young Hoosiers and Hooshierina's.

Hoosierism ˈhuʒɚˌɪzəm, *n.* A word, phrase, or idiom peculiar to the speech of Indianians (see also quot. 1948). Now *hist.*

1843 CARLTON *New Purchase* I. 63 Thus the cabin lady kept on doing up her small stock of English into Hoosierisms and other figures. **1878** BEADLE *Western Wilds* i. 18 The native of Indiana finds . . . that he must drop some of his 'Hoosierisms.' **1948** MENCKEN *Supp.* II. 142 In those days *Hoosierism* was used almost as frequently as *Westernism* to designate one of the novel and usually uncouth locutions that flowed eastward across the mountains.

Hoosierize ˈhuʒɚˌaɪz, *v. tr.* To render (a person) like the people of Indiana. — **1852** *S. Lit. Messenger* XVIII. 435/1 He was built after the model and structure of Bolingbroke in his youth. *Americanized* and *Hoosier-ized* a little by a 'raising in,' and an adaptation to, the Backwoods. **1940** WILSON *Wabash* 187 The Hoosier is sometimes called 'the typical American'; for he has somehow managed to Hoosierize them all.

Hoosieroon ˈhuʒəˌrun, *n.* A Hoosier; originally a child of Hoosier parents, a little Hoosier. *Obs.*

*c*1833 in J. P. DUNN *Indiana* II. (1919) 1126 Where half a dozen Hoosheroons, With mush and milk, tincups and spoons . . . Seemed much inclined to keep their places. **1834** *Knickerb.* IV. 390 A few remote Kentuckians, or Indiana Hoosheroons. **1853** *Dly. Morning Herald* (St. Louis)27 April (Th.), He looks like a Hoosieroon; all he lacks is a chunk of gingerbread in his fist.

hoosiery ˈhuʒɚɪ, *a.* (See quot.) *Colloq.* — **1919** J. P. DUNN *Indiana* II. 1140 In that region it [*sc.* 'Hoosier'] always carried the idea of roughness or uncouthness, and it developed a derivative—'hoosiery'—which was used as an adjective or adverb to indicate something that was rough, awkward or shiftless.

hoot hut, *n.* Short for **hooter,** *n.*[1], usu. in negative phrases. *Colloq.*

1883 BEADLE *Western Wilds* xxxviii. 615, I got onto my reaper and banged down every hoot of it [wheat] before Monday night. **1928** *Sat. Ev. Post* 4 Feb. 84/4, I don't give a hoot what you like to see. **1947** *Chi. Sun* 4 Nov. 5/1, I do not give a hoot if it's colder, and I do not give two hoots what any given cabbie thinks about it.

hootchy ˈhutʃɪ, *n. attrib.* Short for next.

1903 *Cin. Enquirer* 1 May 6/5 And the peacherines from Turkey, In the dance you learned to like, We will see the hoochy jerky When we all come down The Pike. **1911** *Cosmopolitan* Jan. 231/2 Hit up the hoochie music, you Black-Handers. **1947** *Denver Post* 20 Feb. 18/3 Wearing his false forms and wig, Cook joined a carnival show in Tennessee as a 'hootchy' dancer.

hootchy-kootchy ˈhutʃɪˈkutʃɪ, *n.* [See note.] A burlesque, suggestive or indecent dance, usu. regarded as of Oriental origin (see also quot. 1949). Also attrib.

The origin of this term is obscure. The name and the dance are often said to have originated at the Chicago World's Fair in 1893, but quot. 1890 below shows an earlier occurrence of the term, and the dance may have been earlier also.

[**1890** BIFF HALL *Turnover Club* 75, I have been told that one night 'Hoochy-Coochy' Rice, the minstrelman, . . . entered Hoyt's room with a dark lantern.] **1899** *Mr. Dooley in Peace & War* 18 He's seen th' hootchy-kootchy an' th' Pammer House barber shop. *Ib.* 36 Hootchy-kootchy girls dancin' before him. **1937** *Fortune* Dec. 143/1 Along the south edge of the campus runs the Midway, . . . where Little Egypt once danced the hootchy-kootchy for the raucous World's Fair crowds of 1893. **1949** *Time* 25 July 13/1 Musicians swung informally into *The Hootchy-Kootchy,* Little Egypt's tune at the 1893 World's Fair.

b. In full **hootchy-kootchy dance.**

1901 *Everybody's Mag.* Oct. 437/2 The Doctor was too professional to relish the hootchie cootchie dance. **1948** *Hoosier Folklore* March 9 Charley Chaplin went to France, To learn the girls the hootchie-kootchie dance.

Hence **hootchy-kootchy dancer.**

1928 *Wkly. Dispatch* 6 May 15/2 Don't forget to take in the Midway of the Chicago Fair of 1893, with its five hundred glittering lights, its great wheel, and its hootchy-kootchy dancers! **1948** *Time* 11 Oct. 21/1 Autumn was also the time for county fairs—for merry-go-round music, spun sugar, and the sight of prize cakes, prize cattle and sullen hootchy-cootchy dancers.

hooter ˈhutɚ, *n.*[1] [Origin obscure (see quot. 1859).] A very small bit, a whit, usu. in negative phrases. *Colloq.*

1839 *Havana* (N.Y.) *Republican* 21 Aug. (Th.), Now the Grampus (a vessel) stopt, and didn't buge (budge) one hooter. **1859** BARTLETT 202 *Hooter.* Probably a corruption of *iota.* Common in New York in such phrases as 'I don't care a *hooter* for him,' 'this note ain't worth a *hooter.*' **1900** DIX *Deacon Bradbury* 202 'Do you mean that you don't know anything about the matter at all?' . . . 'Not a hooter.'

hooter ˈhutɚ, *n.*[2] [Origin obscure.] A kind of dance. *Rare.* **1845** *Lowell Offering* V. 270 We could dance . . . an eight-handed reel, and an eight-handed 'hooter.'

***Hoover,** *n.* [Herbert C. *Hoover* (1874——), 31st President of the U.S. (1929–33). Cf. next.] Used colloq. in derivatives and combs.: (1) **Hoover apron,** a reversible apron or house dress; (2) **Hoovercrat,** (see quot.); (3) **Hooverette,** a woman's or girl's smock worn to protect the regular clothes; (4) **Hoover hog,** (see quot.); (5) **Hooverian,** *a.* of or pertaining to Herbert Hoover; (6) **Hooverville,** a village of cheap makeshift houses.

(1) **1946** *Reader's Digest* May 130/1 Only a very poor girl would go to a public park in a hoover apron. — (2) **1939** *Newsweek* 7 Aug. 31 'Hoovercrat!' This was the epithet flung at Frank Ramsay McNinch back in 1928 when the lawyer from North Carolina, a lifelong Democrat, voted for the Republican candidate. — (3) **1935** *Montgomery Ward Cat.* (ed. 123) 49 Vat-dyed Percale Hooverette—sturdy, well made, full cut, so it won't bind. **1948** *Chi. Tribune* 11 Jan. (Pict. Sec.) 9 Washable block check Hooverettes $3. — (4) **1945** MATHEWS *Talking* 6 He might resort to eating 'Hoover hogs,' which was the name given to rabbits by the valley farmers.

(5) **1929** *Amer. Mercury* June 176/1 The genesis of the Hooverian outlook on life is rooted deep in history. — (6) **1933** *New Republic* 24 May 40/1 Hoovervilles are in a separate nation, with separate codes, though the men who live in them are still subject to a sort of imperalist intervention. **1949** *Sat. Review* 6 Aug. 116 They called them 'Hoovervilles.' Evicted families lived in tin-and-cardboard shacks.

Hooverize ˈhuvɚˌaɪz, *v.* [f. Herbert C. *Hoover,* U.S. food commissioner (1917–19), and later (1929–33) President of the U.S.] *intr.* To economize in the use of food. *Colloq.* — **1918** *Lit. Digest* 12 Jan. 14/2 Hooverizing is commonly regarded as something new, but the Lawrence *Journal-World* found this in Proverbs 15:17, 'Better is a dinner of Herb's.' **1932** *Blue Valley Farmer* (Okla. City) 7 Jan. 5/6 Once before he made us Hooverize When Wilson had his war.

***hop,** *n.* In combs.: (1) **hop butterfly,** a butterfly, *Thecla humuli,* that feeds upon the heads of the hop plant; (2) **louse,** an aphid, *Phorodon humuli,* very destructive to the hop plant, also **hop plant louse;** (3) **ranch,** a ranch or farm upon which hops are raised; (4) **rising,** =**hop yeast;** (5) **sage,** a low shrub of the saltbush family, *Grayia* (after Asa Gray) *spinosa,* of desert regions from Wyoming to California; (6) **tree,** a small tree, *Ptelea trifoliata,* bearing a fruit somewhat resembling hops; (7) **yeast,** a homemade preparation made from hops and used for leavening, also attrib., *obs.,* cf. **sots.**

(1) **1854** EMMONS *Agric. N.Y.* V. 262. — (2) **1868** *Rep. Comm. Agric. 1867* 238 The wheat midge, fruit blight, potatoe rot, black knot and hop louse were unknown. **1888** *Amer. Naturalist* XXII. 68 The Hop Plant-louse, *Phorodon humuli,* . . . passes the winter on plum trees. — (3) **1889** *Seattle Post-Intelligencer* 24 Sep. 8/2 Emery Flynn, in a scuffle at a hop-ranch near Snoqualmie . . . fell on a scythe and nearly cut off his left hand. — (4) **1836** TRAILL *Backwoods* 137 She must know how to manufacture *hop-rising* or *salt-rising* for leavening her bread. **1941** *L.A.* Map 290.

(5) **1925** JEPSON *Flowering Plants Calif.* 329 G[rayia] spinosa . . . Hop Sage. **1940** JAEGER *Calif. Deserts* 169 Associated with the creosote bush . . . is the spiny hop sage. — (6) **1857** GRAY *Botany* 75 *Ptelea.* Shrubby Trefoil. Hop-tree. **1885** HAVARD *Flora W. & S. Texas* 458 Of the Rutaceae, two shrubs are common: the Hop-tree (*Ptelea trifoliata*) along the river [San Antonio] and the Prickly Ash. **1942** TEHON *Native Ill. Shrubs* 152 There are only three species of hop-trees, all natives of the United States and Mexico. — (7) **1836** TRAILL *Backwoods* 194 The *salt-rising* makes beautiful bread to look at, being far whiter and firmer than the hop-yeast bread. **1884** *Harper's Mag.* Oct. 789/1 Then she made hop yeast and sold that.

***hop,** *v.tr.* To jump onto (a moving vehicle), to obtain (a ride) in this way. *Colloq.* — **1909** *Springfield W. Republican* 18 March 16 Hopping a freight cost Edward Monahan both feet. **1929** *Lit. Digest* 30 Nov. 30/2 Boys are predominantly the ones who 'hop' rides on trucks, trains and other vehicles.

***hope,** *n.*

1. hope chest, a chest in which a girl accumulates articles, esp. linens and clothing, for use in a home of her own after marriage.

1920 *N.Y. Tribune* 23 Oct. 15/2 (*heading*), Bride Accused as Burglar Charged With Looting Sister-in-Law's Hope Chest. **1948** *Aurora* (Ill.) *Beacon-News* 7 Nov. (Supp.) 12/2 The modern bride never thinks of her 'hope chest' as a dowry in the old time sense of the word.

2. *Hope of Israel,* formerly, *c*1855, an organization of Mormon boys in which they were taught camping, woodcraft and military maneuvers.

1942 STEGNER *Mormon C.* 17 That outfit known as the 'Hope of Israel,' antedated the Boy Scout movement by fifty years.

* **Hopewell,** *n.* [See quot. 1892.] *Anthropol.* **Hopewell culture,** a stage of aboriginal culture exhibited by the Indians in the Ohio Valley during the second burial mound period *c*900–1300.

[**1892** MOOREHEAD *Primitive Man in Ohio* 184 From September 1, 1891, until the middle of January of the following year, we were investigating the tumuli and village sites of Mr. Cloud Hopewell's farm, one mile west of Anderson, in the interests of the World's Columbian Exposition.] **1916** MILLS *Explor. Tremper Mound* 216 Spool-shaped ear ornaments of copper are generally present in burials of the Hopewell culture. **1947** MARTIN *Indians* 267 Southern Ohio was the center of the Hopewell culture, although there were subsidiary centers in Michigan, Ohio, Pennsylvania, New York, Tennessee, Indiana, Illinois, Wisconsin, Iowa, and Kansas.

Also **Hopewell mound, village.**

1938 *Rochester Mus. Arts & Sci. Research Rec.* No. 4, 137 Some or most of the 'non-Hopewell' features observed in the New York tumuli could evidently be duplicated in Hopewell mounds of Ohio, Indiana, Illinois and Wisconsin. **1947** MARTIN *Indians* 267 Hopewell villages and ceremonial centers were located along rivers and streams. **1949** *Highway Traveler* April 38/3 This figure, built along a high rocky cliff, overlooking a creek, seems to have been built for ceremonial purposes alone and has been called a Hopewell mound.

Hence **Hopewellian,** *a.*

1949 *Ill. State Arch. Soc. Jrnl.* April 30/2 The foremost incentive was Hopewellian artifacts.

Hopi ˈhopɪ, *n.* [f. a native name meaning "peaceful ones."] "A body of Indians, speaking a Shoshonean dialect, occupying 6 pueblos on a reservation of 2,472,320 acres in N.E. Arizona" (Hodge). Cf. **Moqui.**

1877 *Buffalo Soc. Nat. Sci. Bul.* 170 The title of '*Moquis*' has been applied to this confederacy by its enemies, and signifies the dying race. I understand that they usually speak of themselves as '*Ho-pees*' (our people). **1893** DONALDSON *Moqui Pueblo Indians* 13 The name which they call themselves by is Ho-pi, or Ho-pi-tuh-lei-nyu-muh, meaning 'peaceful people.' **1907** HODGE *Amer. Indians* I. 654/2 The Hopi are rather small of stature, but muscular and agile. . . . In mental traits the Hopi are the equal of any Indian tribe. **1947** *Dly. Ardmoreite* (Ardmore, Okla.) 13 Aug. 13/7 In the land of the Hopis some wedding ceremonies still last for weeks.

attrib. **1933** HARRINGTON *Gypsum Cave, Nev.* 159 Finally we come to 'cotton,' which is cotton and nothing else, probably of the variety now called 'Hopi cotton' (*Gossypium hopi*) long raised by the Hopi Indians and by ancient Pueblo peoples. **1945** *Pueblo* (Colo.) *Star-Journal* 3 June 8/2 The program this year will include the Hopi snake dance. **1948** *Our Dumb Animals* May 5/3 We moved about like Hopi Rain Dancers.

hopine hɑˈpin, *n.* [Prob. f. **hops*+*-ine*]. (See quots.) *Obs.* — **1888** *Texas Siftings* (F.), We don't get beer precisely but they sell a drink out there called hopine . . . the sale of which is not a violation of the liquor law. **1902** CLAPIN 232 Hopine. A name given to malt-liquor, which, for all practical purposes, is genuine beer, it being however so called to evade the provisions of the Prohibition Act.

Hopkinsian hɑpˈkɪnzɪən, *a.* and *n.* [See **Hopkinsianism.**]

1. *n.* A believer in the doctrines of Hopkinsianism. *Obs.*

1795 BENTLEY *Diary* II. 139 The minister is what is called an Hopkinsian. It is the unsocial character of the professors of this sect which makes them odious. **1882** SCHAFF *Religious Encycl.* I. 82/1 Some of the Hopkinsians would have preferred a larger modification of the catechism [than that of the 'Andover Theology'].

2. *a.* Of or pertaining to the theological system of Hopkinsianism. *Obs.*

1797 BENTLEY *Diary* II. 213 The Hopkinsian opinions are distinguished, not so much by their intrinsic character as by the opposition of the Clergy, & the divisions in all the societies consequent upon that opposition, encouraged or patronised. **1853** M. BLAKE *Mendon Association* 53 The religious history of this town might be made to testify the practical workings of Hopkinsian theory. **1886** *Encycl. Brit.* (ed. 9) *Amer. Supp.* III. 339/2 [Samuel Hopkins] was also noted as the founder of 'Hopkinsian divinity,' a modification of Calvinism.

Hopkinsianism hɑpˈkɪnzɪənˌɪzəm, *n.* The Calvinistic theological system of the Reverend Samuel Hopkins (1721–1803), a celebrated New England divine, which, although opposing the Calvinistic doctrines of original sin, stressed unselfish submission to the will of God.

1811 E. S. ELY (*title*), Contrast between Calvinism and Hopkinsianism. **1850** WHITTIER *Writings* VI. 131 Hopkinsianism, as a distinct and living school of philosophy, theology, and metaphysics, no longer exists. **1882** SCHAFF *Religious Encycl.* I. 82/1 [The 'Andover Theology'] on the whole, adopts the substance of Calvinism as well as the substance of Hopkinsianism.

Hopkinsonian ˌhɑpkɪnˈsonɪən, *n.* A Hopkinsian. Also **Hopkinsonism.** *Obs.* — **1838** in *Spirit XIX Cent.* (1842) June 285, I should wholly despair of ever seeing the Presbyterian church, 'arise and shine,' her 'light' being 'one,' if a door for *Hopkinsonians* is left open. *Ib.*, What is the mind of the leaders of our reformation, about admitting any more *Hopkinsonism* into our church, on any terms?

Hopkintonian ˌhɑpkɪnˈtonɪən, *a.* and *n.*

1. *n.* =**Hopkinsian,** *n.*

1788 BENTLEY *Diary* I. 104 Such are the exertions of a certain class of Preachers, called Hopkintonians that weekly, & almost daily, lectures are established in many towns of Essex.

2. *a.* =**Hopkinsian,** *a.*

1796 S. HOPKINS *Sk. Life* (1805) 97 In the latter end of the year 1769, or beginning of 1770, Mr. William Hart of Saybrook published a dialogue. . . . And soon after there was a small pamphlet published, which was doubtless by the same Mr. Hart. . . . To disgrace me before the public, he called them [my doctrines] *Hopkintonian* doctrines. This is the original of this epithet. **1883** SCHAFF *Religious Encycl.* II. 1634/2 [New England divines] announced a few principles, which were called 'New-Light Divinity,' or 'New Divinity.' When a few more principles were added to their system, it was called 'Hopkintonian,' or 'Hopkinsian.'

hoppas ˈhɑpəs, *n.* Also **hoppers, hoppus, hoppis.** [Origin obscure.] A receptacle used by Indians in carrying various objects. Also **hoppas strap.** *Obs.*

1803 in CRISWELL *Lewis & Clark* (1940) 48 Dress'd lether for Hoppers-Straps. **1823** *Ib.* 46 At the age of four or five years, she is taught the use of the *hoppas*. . . . This shell is taken with the band to all the national hunts, and is transported by means of a hoppas on the back of a man. **1824** J. DODDRIDGE *Notes* 309 When night came on, the fire was covered up, the boys pinioned and made to lay down together, the Indians then placed their hoppis straps over them, and laid down, one on each side of them, on the ends of the straps. *c***1826** T. ALDEN in *Mass. H.S. Coll.* 3 Ser. VI. 151 They however killed a buck, the best part of which they carried in a kind of hopper, made of his skin. . . . In the dialect of our hunters—a hoppus.

* **hopper,** *n.*

1. *pl.* A hobble for a horse. *Rare.*

1847 in HOWE *Ohio* 366 The first object of a new comer after selecting a location, and putting the 'hoppers' on the horse, . . . was to cut some poles or logs, and build a cabin.

2. =**hopper car.**

1862 *N.Y. Tribune* 10 June 8/2 Of the 57 hoppers thrown over Opequan Bridge, one half can be put into serviceable order again. **1909** *Sat. Ev. Post* 13 March 16/3 Then if any 'gonds' and 'hoppers' survived the process of elimination, Robbie was told to place the remainder.

3. In combs.: (1) **hopper-bottom car,** =**hopper car;** (2) **boy,** a mechanical device for spreading freshly ground meal to cool; (3) **car,** an open-top railroad freight car the bottom of which is provided with hoppers that are dropped to discharge the contents; (4) **dozer,** a contrivance consisting essentially of a large shallow pan for kerosene mounted on wheels or runners so as to be pushed or drawn over a field to catch and destroy grasshoppers; (5) **grass,** see as a main entry; (6) **mine,** an early form of machine gun used in the Civil War, *obs.*, cf. **Gatling gun.**

(1) **1890** *Railways of Amer.* 146 It would require a separate article to give even a brief description of the different kinds of cars which are now used. . . . Hay-car, Hopper-bottom car, Horse-car. — (2) **1787** in *Rep. Comm. Patents 1849* 574 The other [device], denominated an hopper-boy, so constituted as to spread the meal over the floor of a mill to cool. **1822** *Niles' Reg.* 27 April XXII. 131/1 It is stated, that Oliver Evans' patent right to the Hopper-boy has been declared, by a late decision of the supreme court, . . . 'void as a patent for improvement.' — (3) **1862** *N.Y. Tribune* 10 June 8/2 There were 183 iron hopper cars recovered and in a condition to be restored. **1947** *Dly. Ardmoreite* (Ardmore, Okla.) 14 Nov. 1/7 It has received orders from the Atchison, Topeka and Santa Fe railroad for 250 ballast cars and 200 triple hopper cars. — (4) **1880** *Lib. Universal Knowl.* IX. 123 One of the most efficient pieces of apparatus [for destroying locusts] is the coal-tar pan, known as 'Robbins's hopperdozer.' **1932** *Chieftain* (Tecumseh, Nebraska) 5 May, Mechanical 'hopperdozers' have some value in the control of grasshoppers on fairly level fields of alfalfa or on short field crops early in the season.

(6) **1903** STILES *Four Years* 76 Then, too, the enemy had opposite to us several rapid-firing guns of those early models which we dubbed 'the hopper-mine.'

As the last term in **ash, bell, gin, leaf hopper.**

hoppergrass ˈhɑpɚˌgræs, *n.*

1. A grasshopper. *Colloq.*

1829 *Va. Lit. Museum* I. 458 *Hoppergrass.* This word is often used in the south for grasshopper. **1899** CHESNUTT *Conjure Woman* 10 My mammy tol' me dat tale w'en I wa'n't mo' d'n knee-high ter a hopper-grass. **1939** ROLLINS *Gone Haywire* 242 Hopper-grasses in Kansas, a drought in Nebrasky, an' now this here present drought that's here, an' we lost our cows an' can't get our sheep. **1949** *N.O. Times-Picayune Mag.* 17 July 9/1 Fact is, Bankston makes a good thing out of the hoppergrasses.

2. (See quot.) *Rare.*

1875 *Chi. Tribune* 16 Aug. 2/6 This grass [in w. Mo.] is without a name. Since the hoppers brought a little good into the country [by bringing grass seeds from plains] . . . why not call it 'hopper-grass'?

hoppine hɑˈpin, *n.* Also **hoppeny.** [App. Indian name.] (See quots.) *Obs.* — **1825** WM. BIGGS *Narr. Captivity* 34 The Indians had nothing to eat the last week I was with them, but Indian potatoes—some people call them hoppines, that grew in the woods, and they were very scarce. **1834** *Mass. H.S. Coll.* 3 Ser. VI. 150 It was further agreed that Bisquittam should spend some time in a meadow, a little below the fire of the two women, in digging hoppenies [i.e., groundnuts]. *Ib.*, Gibson should return that way with the horse and venison, and take the hoppenies and meat home.

hopping John. *S.* A dish consisting of meat, as bacon, ham or pork knuckles, and peas cooked together and seasoned with red pepper. *Colloq.*

1838 GILMAN *Recollections* xviii. 124 Before me, though at the head of many delicacies provided by papa, was an immense field of *hopping John.* **1856** OLMSTED *Slave States* 506 The greatest luxury with which they are acquainted is a stew of bacon and peas, with red pepper, which they call 'Hopping John.' **1948** *Chi. D. News* 23 Feb. 12/7, I fought a losing battle with an infernal concoction called Hopping John, which seems to be compounded of cow peas and melted horse's hoofs, back in North Carolina.

hoppy ˈhɑpɪ, *a.* Of bread: Leavened with hop-rising, or hop yeast. *Obs.* — **1893** *Harper's Mag.* Feb. 458 'Jest so it don't tas'e hoppy, I ain't pertic'lar; but from hoppy bread *de*liver me!'

hoptoad ˈhɑpˌtod, *n.* A toad. Also **hop-toady.** *Colloq.*

1827 *Mass. Spy* 28 Nov. (Th.), An inhabitant of the Middle States talks of 'hop-toads,'—as if all toads were not hoppers. **1899** *Animal & Plant Lore* 62 Hop-toad, and hop-toady, *Bufo lentiginosus.* [Name] somewhat general [in the U.S.]. **1938** DAMON *Grandma* 139 And scratched with adoring straw the warty backs of hoptoads, who seemed to me to have found out some secret of life I didn't know.

Horatio Alger. A poor but honest boy who by hard work and sobriety achieves success, in allusion to a type of hero who appeared repeatedly in the fiction of Horatio Alger (1832–99), whose books enjoyed wide popularity. Usu. attrib.

[**1902** *Sears Cat.* (ed. 112) 135/1 Mr. Alger's books are not only interesting as stories, but they stimulate and encourage every boy in his efforts to rise in the world.] **1935** *Lit. Digest* 9 March 39/1 (*heading*), The Horatio Alger of Basketball. **1940** *Amer. Mercury* Sep. 100/1 The lowly beginnings are there, and the obstacles overcome, but actually this is a Horatio Alger story in reverse. **1942** LILLARD *Desert Challenge* 24 It had its Horatio Alger heroes and its robber barons, but no empire builders.

* **horizontal,** *a.* Of tariff rates: Applied equally or uniformly to all articles. Hence **horizontal tariff.**

1842 *Cong. Globe* 17 March 331/1 If they [members of the Ways and Means Committee] undertook . . . to depart from the plain horizontal line of a tariff, . . . they should be able to justify themselves before this House. *Ib.* Was it expected that this committee would send in a horizontal tariff? **1890** *Cong. Rec.* 9 May 4392/2 The Democratic bill made a horizontal cut of 20 per cent. **1909** *Nation* 18 March 278/1 The proposition to frame a horizontal tariff, in which a uniform rate of duty was imposed on all articles, was ridiculed.

horizontal ˌhɔrəˈzɑntl̩, *v. tr.* To terrace (land). Hence **horizontaler,** *n. Obs.* — **1860** *So. Cultivator* XVIII. 109/1 The most skillful horizontaler cannot . . . horizontal land on a level by the eye. **1862** *Ill. Agric. Soc. Trans.* V. 518 Side-hills were generally 'horizontaled,' that is, laid out in ridges as above described, running around the hill.

horizontalize ˌhɔrəˈzɑntl̩ˌaɪz, *v. tr.* =prec. Hence **horizontalizing,** *n. Obs.*

1858 *So. Cultivator* July 214 Yours of the 16th ult., containing the names of those who wish to engage me to . . . horizontalize their cultivated hills, is before me. **1862** *Ill. Agric. Soc. Trans.* V. 518 This 'horizontalizing' is only required when the soil is loose. **1883** SMITH *Geol. Survey Ala.* 386 This damage [done to the hillsides by heavy rains] has been checked to some extent by horizontalizing.

* **horn,** *n.*

1. The pommel of a saddle.

1847 PARKMAN in *Knickerb.* XXIX. 394 My long heavy rifle encumbered me, and the low sound it made striking the horn of my saddle startled him. **1882** BAILLIE-GROHMAN *Camps in Rockies* 5 The frontiersman when on horse-back usually carries his rifle in front of him across the Mexican saddle, attached by a simple leather arrangement to the 'horn.' **1947** *Harper's Mag.* July 42/1 He took off his battered old gray hat and rested it on the horn of his saddle.

2. *Mining.* "A spoon or scoop of horn, in which washings are tested in prospecting" (Knight). *Obs.* Cf. * **horn,** *v.* **2,** and * **horn spoon.**

1869 J. R. BROWNE *Adv. Apache Country* 412 There was as nice a little deposit of pure gold in the bottom of the horn as ever I saw taken at random from any mine. **1896** SHINN *Story of Mine* 78 The quartz prospector prefers the horn, because he only pans out a few ounces of powdered rock, and the flakes are so much finer that a more manageable tool is required than in the case of the placer prospector.

3. In combs.: (1) **horn ail,** any one of various diseases of horned cattle, esp. hollow horn *q.v.*, the seat or root of which is supposedly in the horns; (2) **blow,** (*a*) the blowing of a horn as a rising signal in the morning, (*b*) also in phrasal use (see quot.), *colloq.;* (3) **bowed,** *a.* of spectacles, having bows of horn; (4) **breeze,** (see quots.), *obs.;* (5) **distemper,** =**horn ail,** *obs.;* (6) * **flint,** a gunflint of horn, allegedly an article sold by Yankee peddlers, also **horn gunflint,** *obs.;* (7) * **spoon,** see as a main entry; (8) **spree,** at Princeton, a procession of students creating discord and confusion by blowing upon fish horns, *obs.;* (9) **string,** (see quot. 1944).

(1) **1831** *Boston Transcript* 22 June 2/4 Our cow died of the 'Horn-ail' on Wednesday morning last, after a few days suffering. **1902** L. RICHARDS *Mrs. Tree* 165 Wasn't he the man that tried to cure Peckham's cow of the horn ail, bored a hole in her horn and put in salt and pepper,—or was it oil and vinegar? — (2) (*a*) **1880** MARK TWAIN *Tramp Abroad* xxviii, We had missed the morning horn-blow, and slept all day. **1902** WHITE *Blazed Trail* 68 Dyer should have been out of bed at first horn-blow. (*b*) **1906** F. LYNDE *Quickening* 243 First and fo'most, the majority ain't the majority, not by three sights and a horn-blow. — (3) **1845** JUDD *Margaret* I. 103 She provided him with a pair of broad horn-bowed bridge spectacles. **1893** *Columbus* (O.) *Dispatch* 28 Sep., The old man . . . slapped his horn-bowed spectacles upon his nose. — (4) **1878** *Buffalo Hist. Soc. Pub.* IX. 405 [Since] there was no harbor at Buffalo of sufficient depth . . . , [the steamboat] was obliged to wait for a 'horn breeze,' as the sailors term it; by hitching on eight or ten pair of oxen [etc.]. **1891** WELCH *Recoll. 1830–40* 18 It was not necessary for vessels or steamboats to be launched and towed up against the current of the river by twenty Yoke of Ox-(s)team power (then called a 'Horn Breeze').

(5) **1843** *Knickerb.* XXI. 254 Hence it is as important to keep the bee-moth out of hives as the horn-distemper out of cattle. — (6) **1925** *Mem. Charles Mathews* III. (1839) 520 The other [saddlebag] crammed of course, with wooden nutmegs, horn gunflints [etc.]. **1861** *Crisis* (Columbus, O.) 26 Dec. 6/3 We have often heard of Yankee Blue Laws, Yankee Blue Lights, wooden nut megs, horn flints, beech hams, &c. — (8) **1879** HAGEMAN *Hist. Princeton* I. 281 A college horn-spree, in the year 1855, . . . was so disorderly that constable David Hullfish . . . attempted . . . to quell it. **1888** J. MCCOSH *20 Yrs. Princeton College* 36 We had horn-sprees and foolish bonfires kindled in the campus. — (9) **1931** DOBIE *Coronado's C.* 130 In less time than it takes to draw a six-shooter he had the horn string around his rope loose and a loop shaken out. **1944** ADAMS *W. Words* 79 horn string A leather or buckskin string, fastened to the horn of the saddle and used for securing a rope to it.

b. In the names of plants and animals: (1) **hornbine,** =**hornbound tree,** *colloq.;* (2) * **blower,** (see quot. 1909); (3) **-bound tree,** a black gum, *obs.*, cf. **hornbine;** (4) **bug,** any one of various beetles, esp. the *Passalus cornutus*, having long jaws or hornlike processes on their heads; (5) **fly,** see as a main entry; (6) **frog,** =**horned toad;** (7) * **pipe,** =**hornbine;** (8) **pout,** see as a main entry; (9) **snake,** see as a main entry; (10) **toad,** =**horned toad;** (11) **worm,** either one of two common larvae of hawk moths that feed upon the tobacco plant.

(1) **1793** *Mass. H.S. Coll.* 1 Ser. III. 167 The timber here growing is . . . spruce, beech, buttonwood, hornbine, and sassafras. **1894** *Amer. Folk-Lore* VII. 90 *Nyssa sylvatica*, . . . horn-bine, horn-pipe. Southern States. — (2) **1850** *Rep. Comm. Agric. 1849* 320 The greater portion of the first *glut* reappear the same year as *Hornblowers* and breed myriads. **1909** *Cent. Supp.* 599/2 horn-blower. . . . In *entom.*, a southern United States tobacco-growers' name for the tobacco sphinx-moth, *Phlegethontius carolina*, the parent of the horn-worm of tobacco. — (3) **1634** WOOD *N. Eng. Prospect* (1865) 19 The Horne-bound tree . . . requires so much paines in riving as is almost incredible. **1684**

Duxbury Rec. 60 Beginning at a white oak tree, . . . and so to another horn bound tree. **1714** *Ib.* 93 Thence upward to a hornbound tree marked, viz a hornbound sapling standing in said swamp. — **(4) 1776** J. TRUMBULL *McFingal* (Th.), Thought horn-bugs bullets, or, through fears, Muskitoes took for musqueteers. **1878** STOWE *Poganuc People* 110 That Bill is saassy enough to physic a horn-bug. **1899** *Animal & Plant Lore* 63 Horn-bugs, May-bees, May-flies, June-bugs *Lachnosterna*. Bernardston, Mass.

(6) 1807 PIKE *Sources Miss.* (1810) ii. 156, I have seen the Wishtonwish, the rattle snake, the horn frog, . . . and a land tortoise all take refuge in the same hole. **1949** *Nat. Hist.* Feb. 87/1 Although these lizards are common throughout much of the Lone Star State, the natives know them as 'little ol' horn frogs.' — **(7) 1894** [see **hornbine**].

(10) 1853 P. PAXTON *Yankee in Texas* 24 He gave vent to a profusion of strange backwoods oaths, which involved in one common anathema all sorts of reptiles and insects—musquitoes, fleas, and horn-toads being included in the general ruin. — **(11) 1676** GLOVER *Acct. Va.* in *Phil. Trans.* XI. 635 When the [tobacco] plant is well grown they suffer damage by a Worm that devours the leaf, called a *Hornworm* (an *Eruca* or Caterpillar). **1784** SMYTH *Tour* II. 132 The other [species] is the horn-worm, . . . of a vivid green colour, with a number of pointed excressences [*sic*], or feelers, from his head like horns. **1863** *Rep. Comm. Agric. 1862* 125 The larva [of the sphinx Carolina moth] . . . is sometimes called the horn worm. **1946** *Reader's Digest* Sep. 10/1 It has also registered failures against the tobacco hornworm, the cabbage seedpod weevil, the tomato russet mite, the chigger, the poultry mite and sundry others.

c. In colloq. phrasal expressions: (1) *a horn of gunpowder*, (see quot.), *obs.;* (2) *to haul in one's horns*, to recede from a position, to modify one's pretensions; (3) **to lock horns*, *fig.* and *transf.* to engage in combat, to compete; (4) *to go round the horn*, (see quot.), *obs.* See also **hornblow,** above, and ***horn spoon** as a main entry.

(1) 1830 *Zion's Advocate* (Portland, Me.) 26 Aug. 4/5 Tipplers call their idol . . . 'a slug of blue fishhooks,' 'a horn of gun-powder,' 'essence of lock-jaw.' — **(2) 1833** *Polit. Examiner* (Shelbyville, Ky.) 23 Mar. 2/1 The old man hauled in his horns, and marched off shamed enough. **1871** Goss *Soldier's Story* iii. 67 But we told him we had 'hauled in our horns' considerably since our capture, which accounted for their not being visible. — **(3) 1836** *Hist. Virgil A. Stewart* (N.Y.) 23 They are enemies, and let them lock horns. **1948** DICK *Dixie Frontier* 311 A minister on arriving at a certain appointment found the meeting-place where he was to preach occupied that evening by a secret society. The church people commented that the two appointments 'locked horns.' — **(4) 1869** *Alaska Times* (Sitka) 18 June 2/3 Going round the horn is a game of Dice which many of the inhabitants of this city indulge in, simply for the drinks or cigars.

As the last term in **big, birch, blowing, boat, breakfast, broad, buck, buck's, buffalo, bug, clam, dinner, elk, farm, fire, fish, hollow, long, lop, moose, prong, prospecting, river, saddle, scout, short, spike, stag, tin, unicorn's horn.**

* **horn,** *v.*

1. *To horn off* (or *out*), to ward off or drive away. *Colloq.*

1850 in *Calif. Hist. Soc. Quart.* VIII. (1929) 268 Sutter is wanting to horn out some squatters off what he calls his property which they deny & say they squat on the Government land. **1851** HOOPER *Widow Rugby* 69 You horned me off to get a chance to get gaming witnesses out of the way. **1881** *Phila. Times* 5 June (Th.), There are others who believe that MacVeagh is trying his best to horn Blaine out of the Cabinet herd, just as young buffalo bulls horn out the old ones from the herd when they get superannuated.

2. *Mining.* (See quots. and cf. ***horn,** *n.* **2,** and ***horn spoon** as a main entry.) Also **horning,** *n.*

1867 *Terr. Enterprise* (Virginia, Nev.) 1 Jan. 1/4, I found lots of quartz, and pounded and horned and panned, and panned and horned and pounded it, till ready to curse all creation. **1896** SHINN *Story of Mine* 78 This process is called 'horning a prospect,' or 'assaying with a spoon.' **1949** WYNN *Desert Bonanza* 258 When cow horns were no longer used and horn spoons became a thing of the past, the old timers still frequently called the process horning.

3. *To horn in*, to intrude, butt in. *Slang.*

1912 C. MATHEWSON *Pitching* x. 213 Many of them try hard to 'horn in' with the men who have made good as Big Leaguers. **1944** *Chi. D. News* 1 June 10/2 The silver producers are anxious to enlarge their field and horn in on the international agreement. **1949** *Boston Globe* 3 July (Fiction Mag.) 9/2 All you'll get is a kick-out, though, if you horn in.

* **horned,** *a.* In combs.: (1) **horned bug,** a horn bug, *rare;* (2) **dace,** any one of various American fishes resembling the carp, esp. *Semotilus astromaculatus;* (3) **frog,** = **horned toad;** (4) **grebe,** a common small-crested grebe, *Colymbus auritus;* (5) **lizard,** = **horned toad;** (6) **pout,** any one of various catfish of the genus *Ameiurus*, esp. *A. nebulosus*, often called bullhead, bullpout; (7) **rattlesnake,** the sidewinder, a rattlesnake, *Crotalus cerastes*, found in the sandy plains of the West and Southwest, so called from the horn-like projections between its eyes; (8) **snake,** (*a*) the horn snake *q.v.*, or a snake thought to resemble this, (*b*) = **horned rattlesnake;** (9) **toad,** *W.* and *S.W.* any one of various small lizards having hornlike protuberances on their bodies.

(1) 1778 CARVER *Travels* 493 The Horned Bug, or as it is sometimes termed the Stag Beetle, is of a dusky brown colour. — **(2) 1842** *Nat. Hist. N.Y., Zoology* IV. 199 The Horned Sucker is common in most of the fresh-water streams of this State. . . . It is known under the various popular names of *Barbel, Dace*, and *Horned Dace.* **1884** GOODE *Fisheries* I. 617 The Horned Dace—*Semotilus corporalis*. This species abounds in all small streams and ponds from Western Massachusetts to Nebraska and southward. — **(3) 1804** *Fredericktown* (Md.) *Herald* 14 July 3/4 They carry with them to the President one of the curious horned frogs, which a late ingenious discoverer described as living in association with ground squirrels and snakes. **1942** PHILIPS *Big Spring* 9 It was so hot and dry it would sunburn a horned frog. — **(4) 1823** JAMES *Exped. Rocky Mts.* I. 266 *Colymbus* (*Podiceps*, Lath.) *cornutus.* Horned grebe. **1917** *Birds of Amer.* I. 5 Horned Grebes are commonly known as 'Hell-divers' or 'Water-Witches.'

(5) 1806 CLARK in *Lewis & C. Exped.* IV. (1905) 325 The Horned Lizzard is also common. **1948** *Pacific Discovery* March–April 10/2, I collected western fence lizards . . . and California horned lizards. — **(6) 1867** HAWTHORNE *Amer. Note-Bk.* (1883) 65 The fish caught were . . . three horned pouts. **1890** WIGGIN *Timothy's Quest* 126 The baby horned-pouts rustled their whiskers drowsily. — **(7) 1870** COOPER in *Proc. Calif. Acad. Sci.* IV. 67 The region bordering this valley on the west may be called the Desert, most of it being destitute of trees. . . . The following do not occur west of this region . . . Horned Rattle-snake . . . Sheep-nosed Snake . . . Glass Snake. **1922** J. VAN DENBURGH *Reptiles* II. 953 Horned rattlesnake[s] . . . were often found in pairs and were doubtless mating. — **(8)** (*a*) **1775** ADAMS *Works* (1850) II. 426 Every dip of his pen stung like a horned snake. **1851** WOODS *Gold Diggings* 134 It answers the description of the horned snake. It is said that, taking the end of its tail in its mouth, it will form a perfect hoop with its body, rolling rapidly over till it reaches the object at which it aims. (*b*) **1903** AUSTIN *Land of Little Rain* 19 It is a question whether it is not better to be bitten by the little horned snake of the desert that goes sidewise and strikes without coiling, than by the tradition of a lost mine. — **(9) 1806** *Mass. Spy* 16 July (Th.), A venerable Philosopher . . . surrounded by piles of . . . stuffed squirrel skins, and horned toads. **1869** CRONISE *Nat. Wealth Calif.* 482 A 'Horned Toad,' of more slender form is found in the southeastern regions. **1947** *Time* 25 Aug. 23/2 Even the Texas Boy Scouts in Paris knew that it was no good for them to have horned toads unless the other boys had enough penknives to swap. **1949** *Nat. Hist.* May 209/2 This 'horned toad' is one of two or three species of lizards that feeds voraciously on the fiery-stinged agricultural ants.

* **hornet,** *n.*

1. In contexts allusive to the ill-humor of hornets, esp. *mad as a hornet. Colloq.*

1833 *Md. Hist. Mag.* XIII. 347, [I] broke his bridle—mad as a hornet—rode out to Mitchells mine. **1855** LONGFELLOW *Hiawatha* 224 Words of anger and resentment, Hot and humming, like a hornet. **1893** *Harper's Mag.* Feb. 378/1 They slap about and climb and snap with their jaws with the activity and malice of so many hornets. **1932** W. KELLEY *Inchin' Along* 194 The war worker was a northerner—energetic gentleman from whom words flowed with the rapidity of maddened hornets bailing from a disturbed nest.

2. ***hornet's nest,** = **guayave.** In full **hornet's nest bread.** *Obs.*

1846 J. S. ROBINSON *Jrnl. Santa Fe Exped.* 60 [We] found the inhabitants still friendly, giving us to eat of their pepper dishes and hornet's nest bread. **1849** *31st Congress* 1 Sess. Sen. Doc. 64, 62 When folded and rolled together, it [a guayave] does not look unlike (particularly that made from the blue corn) a 'hornet's nest'— a name by which it is sometimes called.

As the last term in **bald-faced, paper, sand, white-faced hornet.**

hornety ˈhɔrnɪtɪ, *a.* Angry. *Colloq.* — **1834** C. A. DAVIS *Lett. J. Downing* 126 The Gineral got as hornety as all nature at this.

horn fly. (See quot. 1909.)

1708 KERSEY *Horn-fly*, an American Insect. **1889** *Secy. of Agric. Rep.* 17 The horn fly, a pest to horned cattle newly imported from Europe. **1909** *Cent. Supp.* 599/5 horn-fly. . . . An injurious muscid fly, *Haematobia serrata*, common to Europe and the United States: named from its habit of clustering on the horns of cattle. **1946** *Democrat* 4 July 2/4 Cows can't and won't give you full milk production if they are constantly annoyed by house, stable or horn flies.

∗**horning,** *n.* (See quots.) *Colloq.*

1889 *N. & Q.* IV. 81 The neighbor was engaged in giving him what is called in the despatches a 'charivari,' but is more idiomatically known in some of the rural parts of our country as a 'horning.' **1896** *Chi. Record* 12 Feb. 2/4 'Horning' is peculiar to Dartmouth, and is much in the line of hazing. Feb. 1 the sophomore class howled beneath the windows of Prof. Foster's study and hurled snowballs and coal at them, breaking the glass. **1949** *Time* 25 July 34/2 The custom of noisily serenading a couple on their wedding night is called a . . . *horning* in Rhode Island.

horn pout. = **horned pout.**

1798 *Gaz. U.S.* Aug. (Th.), The company concluded to go, for the sake of seeing a horn pout—when at last I drew one up—and behold! what was it, but a cat fish! **1832** *N.H. Hist. Soc. Coll.* III. 87 On each side of their body and close to the head is a formidable weapon, called a *horn*, and hence the name of *Horn*-pout. **1943** DAMON *Sense of H.* 22 First he brought her a mess of horn pouts he had caught.

horn snake. A harmless snake, *Farancia abacura*, found in the southern states, formerly alleged to have an extremely poisonous horn stinger at the end of its tail. Cf. **bastard horn snake, hoop snake.**

1688 CLAYTON *Acct. Va.* in *Phil. Trans.* XVIII. 134 The Horn-Snake is, as they [= Virginians] say, another sort of deadly Snake. **1764** in FRIES *Rec. Moravians in N.C.* II. 581 It is said that when the Horn Snake gets angry it will drive its sting into a tree, and the tree will die within twenty-four hours. **1896** P. A. BRUCE *Econ. Hist. Va.* I. 129 Other varieties of snakes were common, such as the puff adder, the moccasin, the corn, the black, the water, and the horn. **1949** *Scientific Mo.* Jan. 53/1 When we speak of the hoop snake, horn snake, or stinging snake, a single species, *Farancia abacura*, is implied.

∗**horn spoon.** = ∗**horn,** *n.* **2.**

1855 *Golden Era* (S.F.) 6 May 2/7 They appear to have prospected pretty well, in this way, though with very inferior tools—horn spoon, wooden bowl, and quicksilver, being a full inventory. **1897** Chi. Record *Klondike* 107 The horn-spoon is a very simple contrivance used in some places by prospectors instead of a pan. **1942** LILLARD *Desert Challenge* 172 His equipment included a pick, shovel, gold pan, canteen, great horn spoon, an ax [etc.].

b. *By the great horn(ed) spoon, see* ∗**great 8.** (3).

hornswoggle ˈhɔrnˌswagl, *v.* [A fanciful formation.] *tr.* To hoax, deceive, bamboozle. *Slang.*

1829 *Va. Lit. Museum* 30 Dec. 458 *Hornswoggle.* 'To embarrass irretrievably.' Kentucky. **1866** C. H. SMITH *Bill Arp* 133, I'll be hornswaggled if the talkin and the writin and the slanderin has got to be done on one side any longer. **1948** *Chi. Tribune* 9 March 22/2 The farmer . . . came into the Central police station and reported he was hornswoggled out of $180.

Hence **hornswogglement,** *n.*

1868 POMEROY *Nonsense* 253 (We.), It's a humbug . . . a-a-a hornswogglement.

hornyhead ˈhɔrnɪˌhɛd, *n.* Any one of various American fish of the family Cyprinidae, the heads of which at certain seasons are covered with hornlike processes.

1838 *S. Lit. Messenger* IV. 405, I don't 'spect to cetch any thing vut a few horny-heads no how, vut I'll fish on a while longer. **1883** HARRIS *Nights* (1911) Brer Wolf 'low he gwine ter fish fer horneyheads. **1944** WILSON *Passing Inst.* 41 And Old Maud stood hitched to a sycamore and snorted at the scent of the scaly, bony little sunfish and hornyheads that we threw excitedly on the bank.

∗**horse,** *n.*

1. In the game of policy, four numbers appearing anywhere on the list to be selected from.

1872 CRAPSEY *Nether Side N.Y.* 106 A player had a 'saddle' when any two of the numbers he selects are drawn, . . . and a 'horse' when the four appear. **1938** ASBURY *Sucker's Prog.* 93 *Horse*—Four numbers to appear anywhere on the list. Odds, 680 to 1.

2. Short for Charley horse *q.v.*

1910 *Amer. Mag.* April 786/1 Rubbing with volatile oils and steady massaging serve to press the muscle back to position, but the 'horse' returns at the next serious strain.

3. In miscellaneous noun and adjective combs.: (1) **horse-and-buggy,** used attrib. in the sense of old-fashioned, outmoded, *colloq.;* (2) **billiards,** shuffleboard, a game usu. played aboard ships; (3) **cake,** (see quot. 1899), *colloq.;* (4) **disease,** an epidemic influenza affecting horses, *obs.;* (5) ∗**fly,** a jocular or familiar term of address, a fellow or guy, *colloq.;* (6) ∗**herd,** *W.* a herd of horses; (7) **jockeying,** trafficking in horses; (8) **mail,** mail carried on horseback; (9) **post,** a hitching post; (10) **-'s neck,** (see quot. 1909); (11) **thieving,** the stealing of horses, also as adj.; (12) **trade,** a horse swap; (13) **trail,** a trail made by the passage of horses or a path which can be followed by horses, also attrib.

(1) 1927 EUBANK (*title*), Horse and Buggy Days. **1949** *This Week Mag.* 9 Jan. 5/1 Wherever this horse-and-buggy court is held, your chances of going scot-free are slim. — **(2) 1869** MARK TWAIN *Innocents Abroad* iv. 39 Horse-billiards is a fine game. **1897** ——— *Following Equator* iv. 69 The short-voyage passenger gets his chief physical exercise out of 'horse-billiards'—shovel board. — **(3) 1826** in *W. & M. Coll. Quart.* 2 Ser. VIII. 89, I presume it is the same Old gentleman (Mr. Aubry of Richmond, Virginia) of whom I bought so many horse-cakes, & sugar-strawberries. **1899** GREEN *Va. Word-Book* 192 Horse-cake, *n.* Gingerbread fashioned into the shape of a horse. — **(4) 1872** *Newton Kansan* 21 Nov. 2/1 The notorious epizootic, or horse disease, continues to work its way westward. **1875** *Chi. Tribune* 4 Nov. 3/3 The horse-disease, commonly called the 'Epizootic,' prevails throughout the entire country.

(5) 1846 *Quincy* (Ill.) *Whig* 29 Jan. 2/3 Sure of dat, hoss fly? **1851** *Polly Peablossom* 50 Did you ever hear how that hoss-fly died? **1859** *No. Californian* (Union) 2 Mar. 1/2 Look-a-here, Jess, hoss-fly, you ain't a gwine to put your old Uncle Josey in that, is yer? — **(6)** [**1733** in *S.W. Hist. Quart.* XLIV. 88 The Apaches . . . have continued their incursions upon the horse-herds and the missions.] **1884** *Cent. Mag.* May 141/1 Joseph and his elder daughter were . . . among the horse-herd, when the first charge was made. **1903** ADAMS *Log Cowboy* 80 Byler had come in with a horse herd from the Nueces. — **(7) 1783** in S. E. BALDWIN *Simeon Baldwin* 129 The conversation was upon News —horsejockeying—& other indifferent subjects. **1809** IRVING *Knickerb.* IV. iii, He swore that he would have nothing more to do with such a . . . cider-watering, horse-jockeying, notion-peddling crew. — **(8) 1825** *Catawba Jrnl.* 21 June, A horse mail will answer every purpose on the route between Salisbury and Raleigh. **1837** W. JENKINS *Ohio Gaz.* 54 The *post office* . . . is supplied by a horse mail twice a week. — **(9) 1852** STOWE *Uncle Tom* vi, Sam and Andy . . . flew to the horse-posts, to be ready to 'help mas'r.' **1903** *Smart Set* IX. 96 Go out and argue with a wood pile, or a horse-post, or anything else that can't get away from you!

(10) 1909 WEBSTER, horse's neck. . . . A beverage of ginger ale flavored with lemon peel, sometimes with whisky added. **1925** J. METCALFE *Smoking Leg* 138 A tall young man in a grey suit whose drink was horse's neck in summer and Burbon in the winter. **1938** *Rocky Mt. News* (Denver) 30 April 8/2 Don't paper the walls of a cocktail lounge with exotic flower prints, but pictures of horses' necks, side cars, [etc.]. — **(11) 1835** BIRD *Hawks of Hawk-H.* II. xiii. 137 Down you rogue, or I'll indict you for horse-thieving. **1874** GLISAN *Jrnl. Army Life* 463 These men are never so happy as when . . . in pursuit of a band of fleeing, horse-thieving, prairie Indians. — **(12) 1846** *Knickerb.* XXVIII. 361 He was employed in . . . an action brought by a man against another for cheating him in a 'horse-trade.' **1948** *Time* 6 Dec. 93/3 As angry as a loser in a sharp horse trade. — **(13) 1824** MARSHALL *Kentucky* I. 348 Captain Herndon . . . gave pursuit—and coming on the horse trail, took that, being the easiest followed. **1913** LONDON *Valley of Moon* III. vii, The road was badly washed and gullied. . . . 'It peters out altogether farther down,' Billy said. 'From there on it's only horse trails.' **1946** *Sierra Club Bul.* Dec. 119 At the horse trail bridge, follow the creek and talus up the left of the fall as far as possible.

b. In less frequent, often obs. or rare, combs.: (1) **horse ail,** some unidentifiable ailment or distemper of horses; (2) **bone limestone,** (see quot.); (3) **book,** a book of information about horses and their diseases; (4) **card,** a currycomb; (5) ∗**chestnut,** a color like that of a horse chestnut; (6) **dam,** (see quot.); (7) **dance,** an Indian dance in which, app., horses were imitated; (8) **duty,** ?signals or calls blown on a trumpet for a cavalry company; (9) **hunting,** (see quot.); (10) **jog,** designating something slow or old-fashioned; (11) **lawyer,** a lawyer without ability or standing; (12) **piano,** a calliope; (13) ∗**piece,** a horse drama; (14) **rail,** a horse rack; (15) **rattle,** prob. a bull-roarer; (16) **round-up,** *W.* the bringing together of horses on a ranch; (17) **shedder,** (see quot.), cf. **8. b.** (2) below, and see **horse shedding** as a main entry; (18) **smoke,** (see quot.); (19) **trumpet,** ?a very large trumpet.

(1) 1872 HOLMES *Poet* iii. 75 Something like horse-ail, very likely—horses get it, you know, when they are brought to city stables. — **(2) 1870** *Rep. Comm. Agric.* 551 By leaching and concretion it sometimes forms a singularly irregular, perforated rock, known in Alabama as the 'bored,' and in Mississippi, where it also occurs, as the 'horse-bone,' limestone. — **(3) 1643** *Essex Prob. Rec.* I. 30, I give to him my horse booke alsoe a pitchforke. — **(4) 1832** *Louisville Pub. Advt.* 3 March, Whittemore's cotton and horse cards.

(5) **1897** Mark Twain *Following Equator* 622 (R.), There is every shade of complexion: ebony, old mahogany, horse-chestnut, sorrel. — (6) **1905** *Forestry Bureau Bul.* 61 B, Horse dam. A temporary dam made by placing large logs across a stream, in order to raise the water behind it, so as to float the rear. (N.F.) — (7) **1899** H. B. Cushman *Hist. Indians* 499 Then followed the fun-making dances, such as chicken dance, horse dance. — (8) **1777** *N.J. Archives* 2 Ser. I. 327 A man well acquainted with blowing the trumpet, and capable of teaching the horse duty on that instrument. — (9) **1708** Oldmixon *Brit. Empire in Amer.* I. (1708) 293 [The Virginians] also have other sorts of Hunting, as Vermine-hunting, and Horse-hunting; the latter is much delighted in by young People, who pursue wild Horses with Dogs, and sometimes without them.

(10) **1853** Fowler *Home for All* 53, I leave you to either proceed in the old horse-jog mode of building, or adopt this new railroad style. — (11) **1890** *Cong. Rec.* 1 July 6900/2 If you speak of John McSweeney as a horse lawyer, God knows what will become of Missouri. — (12) **1920** C. R. Cooper *Under Big Top* 202 The calliope player takes him along on parade and tells him the story of steam, to the accompaniment of the screaming notes of the howling, screeching 'horse piano.' — (13) **1856** *Chi. Democrat* 22 Oct., The stage is so constructed that it can be used to the best advantage for the exhibition of what are termed 'horse pieces.' — (14) **1861** Tallack *Friendly Sk.* 41 On arriving at the meeting-house, the horses are not usually taken out from their vehicles, but merely 'hitched up' to a tree, or 'horse-rail.'

(15) **1858** *Harper's Mag.* June 133/1 A 'horse-rattle' which he was whirling round and round to the disturbance of the town.—(16) **1927** Siringo *Riata & Spurs* 15, I had to attend the horse round-up . . . to brand up the W. B. G. colts. — (17) **1846** Cooper *Redskins* xiv, Your regular 'horse-shedder' is employed to frequent taverns where jurors stay, and drop hints before them touching the merits of causes known to be on the calendars. — (18) **1807** in Pike *Sources Miss.* II. App. 22 The chief . . . filled a calumet, which several different Indians took from him, and handed the Osages to smoke. This was called the *horse-smoke*, as each person who took the pipe from the chief intended presenting the Osages a horse. — (19) **1850** H. C. Watson *Camp-Fires Revol.* 254 Bill Hurley had also brought with him an old horse-trumpet.

For ***horseback, bill, drama, fiddle, *hair, high, opera, *race, rack, sense, shedding, *shoe, show, swap, trading, trotting,** see as main entries.

4. In expressions, usu. obs., designating devices, machines, etc., operated by horses, as (1) **horse broom,** (2) **drill,** (3) **ferryboat,** (4) **flat,** (5) ***gin,** (6) **locomotive,** (7) **mower,** (8) **-power Pullman,** (9) **rail-car,** (10) **railroad,** (11) **railway,** (12) **rake,** (13) **road,** (14) **scraper,** (15) **shovel,** (16) **sled.**

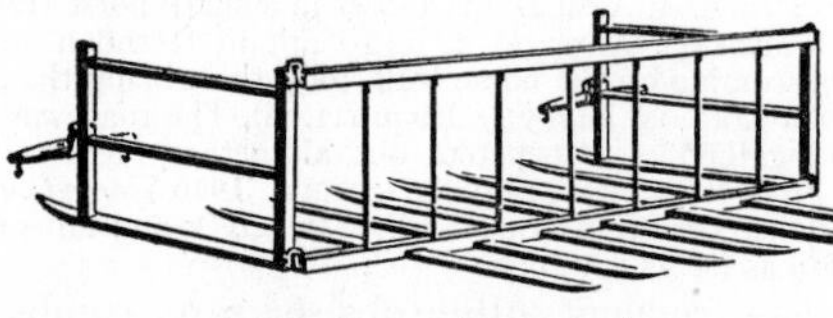

One form of horse rake

(1) **1840** *N.O. Picayune* 22 Aug. 2/5 A new thing has appeared in the streets of New York in the shape of a horse broom for street sweeping. — (2) **1848** *De Bow's Review* VI. 133 The *Horse-Drill* will plant wheat, rye, Indian corn, &c. [**1936** *Sears Cat.* (ed. 173) 936 Sears Reliable One-Horse Drill.] — (3) **1833** J. Stuart *Three Years N. Amer.* I. 51 The horse-ferry-boat over the river is, I believe, peculiar to America,—certainly an American invention. **1838** H. Martineau *Retrospect* I. 109 We crossed, as every body does, by a horse ferry boat; a device so cruel, as well as clumsy, that the sooner it is superseded the better. I was told that the strongest horses, however kept up with corn, rarely survive a year of this work. — (4) **1803** *Steele P.* I. 395 A new Horse flatt not yet launched sufficiently large to take in a loaded Waggon & Team.

(5) **1944** Clark *Pills* 177 As late as 1898 slaves were still feeding horse gins and rolling bales of cotton around the wharf at New Orleans. — (6) **1833** *Amer. R.R. Jrnl.* II. 673/3 Would not this make a very simple *horse locomotive?* — (7) **1867** J. Meline *Santa Fe & Back* 298 Huge horse-mowers . . . are seen in the fields. — (8) **1906** *McClure's Mag.* XXVI. 87 The first of these 'Hoss-power Pullmans' reached Denver May 17, 1859—six days for the 665 mile journey. — (9) **1856** *Porter's Spirit of Times* 268/1 If she could have gone through it [the Louvre] in a horse rail-car, she would have liked it very well.

(10) **1857** *Mich. Gen. Statutes* (1882) I. 856 The said companies shall have the right to charge . . . fair compensation for the use of its said road and tunnel by the railroad companies or horse-railroad companies. **1927** Benét *J. B.'s Body* 101 Tecumseh Sherman, . . . [was the] untidy ex-president of a little horse-railroad. — (11) **1863** Whitman *Specimen Days* 31 Campbell hospital, out on the flats, at the end of the then horse railway route, on Seventh street. **1883** *Harper's Mag.* Sep. 648/1 The President of one of Boston's horse railways is trying to apply the civil service reform rules to his employes. **1948** *Neb. Hist.* March 23 A hundred and fifty sugar factory workers in Grand Island boycotted the local horse railway for several weeks. — (12) **1817** *Ill. Hist. Soc. Trans. 1910* 147 The ground has to be cleared of the Cornstock by . . . cutting them down and drawing them together with a horse Rake. **1906** *Indian Laws & Tr.* III. 204 The net proceeds . . . shall be expended . . . in the purchase of stock cattle, horse teams, . . . horserakes [etc.]. — (13) **1868** *Comm. & Fin. Chron.* 832/3 We are always in a position to furnish all sizes . . . for both steam and horse roads. **1882** McCabe *New York* 240 Some of the horse roads . . . are beginning to experience a return of their old prosperity. — (14) **1846** *De Bow's Review* II. Sep. 135, I now scrape, with a horse scraper, leaving the drill an inch wide.

(15) **1889** *Cent.* 2893/2 *Horse-shovel*, . . . a road-scraper. — (16) **1745** in *Mass. H. S. Coll.* 6 Ser. X. 54 Advised, that orders be given . . . to take one foot, cord measure, of wood from every horse sled load brot into ye city. **1782** *Broadside Verse* (1930) 107/3 The corpse of the murderer . . . was placed on a horse-sled, dragged to an obscure place and buried. **1848** Thoreau *Maine W.* (1894) 37 A horse sled made of saplings.

See also ***horse boat, horsecar** as main entries.

5. In the names of plants: (1) **horse apple,** see as a main entry; (2) **balm,** an American plant of the genus *Collinsonia* having an exceptionally strong odor; (3) ***bean,** (see quots.); (4) **brier,** (see quots.); (5) **devil,** the wild indigo, *Baptisia tinctoria*, a tumbleweed; (6) **fly-weed,** (see quot. 1931); (7) **gentian,** (see quot. 1931); (8) **laurel,** the great rhododendron of the eastern states; (9) **-mane oat,** (see quots.); (10) ***mint,** any one of various American coarse plants of the genus *Monarda;* (11) **nettle,** a weed, *Solanum carolinense*, also known as Carolina nightshade; (12) **-shoe violet,** see ***horseshoe** as a main entry; (13) **sugar,** the sweetleaf, *Symplocos tinctoria*, of the southern states; (14) ***tooth,** see as a main entry; (15) **weed,** any one of various American weeds, as the troublesome composite plant, *Leptilon canadense*, the horse balm, and the great ragweed.

(2) **1787** *Columbian* (Phila.) Dec. 807 *Horse balm*, or *Ox-weed*, smells like balm, but more mild, grows in moist, rich, new grounds and woods, to the height of two feet, or more. **1894** *Harper's Mag.* March 562/2, I passed a luxuriant clump of the plant known as 'horse-balm.' — (3) **1909** *Cent. Supp.* 600/2 horse-bean. . . . In the southwestern United States, either of two species of palo verde, *Parkinsonia aculeata* and *P. microphylla*, the twigs of which are eaten by horses. **1942** Castetter & Bell *Pima & Papago Agric.* 60 Of somewhat less importance were the seeds of . . . Jerusalem thorn or horsebean (*Parkinsonia aculeata*). — (4) **1839** in *Mich. Agric. Soc. Trans.* VII. 419 *Smilax rotundifolia*. Horse brier. Green brier. **1949** *Amer. Photography* April 245/2 The one best known to anyone who has ever tramped through woods is the catbrier, greenbrier, or horsebrier (*Smilax rotundifolia*).

(5) **1869** Fuller *Flower Gatherers* 261 The whole plant forms a globular mass, which, when dry, breaks away from the soil and rolls about in the wind, . . . greatly to the discomfiture of horses; for which reason it has acquired the bad name of Horse-devil. — (6) **1847** Darlington *Weeds & Plants* 108. **1931** Clute *Plants* 102 The horse-fly weed (*Baptisia tinctoria*) receives its name from the belief that the fresh branches attached to the harness will keep the flies away from the horses. — (7) **1843** Torrey *Flora N.Y.* I. 301 Horse Gentian. . . . It has long been a popular medicine. **1931** Clute *Plants* 70 The horse gentian (*Triosteum perfoliatum*) belonging to the honeysuckle family and unrelated to the gentians. — (8) **1894** *Amer. Folk-Lore* VII. 93 *Rhododendron maximum*, horse-laurel, White Haven, Pa. — (9) **1838** *Mass. Agric. Survey 1st Rep.* 33 The Tartarian, or as some call it, the Horse-Mane Oat, from the grain hanging together on one side of the panicle, is sometimes cultivated. **1862** *Ill. Agric. Soc. Trans.* V. 196 Four bushels of seed to the acre, of black Tartarian, or, as sometimes called, horse mane or side oats.

(10) **1784** Cutler in *Mem. Acad.* I. 460 Horse mint. Blossoms blue. By brooks, and in wet meadows. **1858** Thoreau *Maine Woods* 108 Horehound, horsemint, and the sensitive fern grew close to the edge. **1943** Peattie *Great Smokies* 196 There was a lilac fleck here and there from the downy horsemint. — (11) **1817–8** Eaton *Botany* (1822) 463 *Solanum carolinense*, horse-nettle. **1868** *Mich. Agric. Rep.* VII. 181, I discovered along the side of the railroad track . . . a plant . . . known in Virginia and Carolina as horse nettle. — (13) **1847** Darlington *Weeds & Plants* 218 The *Symplocos* (Hopea) *tinctoria*, the 'Horse Sugar' of the South, . . . [is] a favorite food of cattle. **1913** Morley *Carolina Mts.* 47 Horse sugar, the only North American member of its family, which otherwise lives in South America, Asia, and Australia, is another early blossoming shrub.

(15) **1791** *Amer. Philos. Soc.* III. 114 *Collinsonia canadensis* (Horse-weed, Knot-root), *Hydrophyllum canadensis* (Scaly-root). **1874** J. W. LONG *Wild-Fowl* 239 The hunter usually selects a position . . . amongst the high 'horse-weeds' bordering the field. **1947** *Atlantic Mo.* June 61/1 Mr. Henry he pushed down through the hoss weeds thar by the river bank.

b. In the names of fishes, crabs, etc.: (1) **horse clam,** a coarse clam of the north Pacific Coast; (2) **conch,** a univalve mollusk or its shell; (3) **crevalle,** (see quot. 1889); (4) ***head,** a moonfish, *Argyreiosus vomer,* or a related fish, cf. **Jersey horsehead;** (5) ***racer,** (see quot.), *obs.;* (6) **snake,** (see quot. and cf. **horse racer**), *obs.;* (7) **sucker,** (see quot.).

For ***horsefish,** ***foot, guard,** ***hair,** ***shoe,** see as main entries.

(1) **1940** SMITH *Puyallup-Nisqually* 187 Children were allowed all sorts of tidbits such as the necks of dried horse clams, nuts and acorns. **1948** *Nat. Hist.* April 164/2 These were Horse Clams (*Schizothaerus*)—much smaller than a geoduck and too scrawny to be interesting as food. — (2) **1869** *Amer. Naturalist* III. 464 At low tide can be collected . . . the Horse Conch (*Fasciolaria gigantea*). **1881** INGERSOLL *Oyster Industry* 245 *Horse Conch,* the largest species of Triton. (Florida reefs.) — (3) **1884** GOODE *Fisheries* I. 323 The Cavally of the Gulf of Mexico and Eastern Florida—the 'Horse Crevallé' of South Carolina—occurs abundantly on our Southern coast. **1889** *Cent.* 2891/1 horse-crevalle. . . . A carangoid fish, *Caranx hippos,* the cavally: so called in South Carolina, in contradistinction to the pompano, there known as *crevalle.* — (4) **1883** *Nat. Museum Bul.* No. 27, 438 *Selene argentea.* . . . Horsehead. . . . Atlantic coast of the United States. **1884** GOODE *Fisheries* I. 323 In the Chesapeake this fish is often called by the names 'Horsehead' and 'Look-down.'

(5) **1833** BROOKS *Zóphiël (footnote),* The ring necked serpent is still sometimes seen in North America. . . . From the extreme swiftness of its movement, it received from the English settlers the name of horse-racer. — (6) **1852** FLEISCHMANN *Wegweiser* 251 Andere Schlangen sind nicht gefährlich, z.B. die schwarze Schlange, wegen ihrer schnellen Bewegungen auch Renner genannt (*Black Snake, Racer, Horse snake, Coluber constrictor Linn.*). — (7) **1820** RAFINESQUE in *Western Rev.* II. 303 Red-tail Sucker. *Catostomus erythrurus.* . . . Vulgar names Red-horse, Red-tail, Horse-fish, Horse Sucker, &c.

6. Designating places where horses are kept or found: (1) **horse barn,** a barn or stable in which horses are kept; (2) **beat,** ?= **horse stamp,** *obs.;* (3) **corral,** a corral for horses; (4) **exchange,** an establishment where horses are kept for trading, *obs.,* cf. **exchange stable;** (5) **farm,** a farm on which horses are raised, cf. **Morgan horse farm;** (6) **Horse Heaven,** a place in the Northwest where droves of cayuse ponies formerly roamed; (7) **lick,** a place to which horses go to lick the ground for saline particles, cf. ***lick,** *n.;* (8) **lot,** an inclosure for horses; (9) **pen, ranch,** see as main entries; (10) **range,** an area over which horses range; (11) **restaurant,** (see quot.); (12) **stamp,** a place where horses usu. stand, an inclosure for horses, *obs.*

(1) **1854** M. J. HOLMES *Tempest & Sunshine* xix. 266 I'd as soon be married in the horse barn as there. **1948** *Minneapolis Morn. Tribune* 28 Sep. 11/1 Shortly before midnight Sunday fire broke out in a $2,500 horse barn. — (2) **1736** *Smithtown Rec.* 299 May the 15 day 1736, then layd out to Job Smith a certain tract of land . . . by the place called the Horse beat. — (3) **1912** MULFORD *Buck P.* 192 The flimsily constructed horse corral swarmed with . . . punchers. **1946** UNDERHILL *First Penthouse Dwellers* 99 Only Domingo, the unofficial capital of the Keres, remains barricaded between its network of horse corrals and its rich fields. — (4) **1879** *Bradstreet's* 6 Dec. 8/1 A horse exchange is being established in New York. **1890** *Stock Grower & Farmer* 12 April 3/2 A horse exchange [at Albuquerque] will be a feature of the enterprise.

(5) **1883** *Harper's Mag.* Oct. 717/2 [He] has made the best [fortune] of all . . . by his high-grade horse farm. — (6) [**1824** *Microscope* (Albany, N.Y.) 22 May 43/2 (Th.), [Our filthy streets emit] such savoury exhalations as may be supposed to arise from skunk's purgatory, if there is such a place, and we know of no reason why there should not be as well as a horse-heaven.] **1888** *Walla Walla* (Wash.) *Union* 18 Feb. 3/2 J. N. Armstrong, of the Horse Heaven country, will plant a hop yard this spring in Klickitat county. **1947** *Mazama* Dec. 15/2 Here was a sign pointing back the way I had come saying 'Horse Heaven 6 Miles.' Very 'confoosin.' — (7) **1714** in *Amer. Sp.* XV. 275/1 To a white Oak Standing by a horse lick on ye sd. Branch. — (8) **1847** in THOMPSON *M. Jones* (1872) 230 Down the street she went a tearin, Pete pullin and sawin at the reins—round Uncle Josh's house, with half a dozen dogs barkin at her heels, through the horse-lot. **1892** HARRIS *U. Remus & Friends* 7 Dis make Brer Rooster laugh twel you mought er heered him squeal all over de hoss lot.

(10) **1808** PIKE *Sources Miss.* 256 [We] came on eight miles further to a horse range of the marquis's. — (11) **1856** *Herald of Freedom* (Lawrence, Kans.) 5 April 1/7 In California they call a livery stable a 'Horse Restaurant.' Very refined! — (12) **1791** BARTRAM *Travels* 355 A horse-stamp, where was a large squadron of those useful creatures. **1797** B. HAWKINS *Letters* 226 They have made free with the horses of the traders and some of the Indians who have horse stands or stamps. **1837** BIRD *Nick of Woods* II. 122, [I know] all the parts injacent and outjacent circumsurrounding the hoss-stamp.

7. Designating those having to do with horses: (1) **horse drover,** one in charge of a drove of horses; (2) **fighter,** a bronco buster *q.v., rare;* (3) **guard,** see as a main entry; (4) **herder,** *W.* one in charge of a herd of horses; (5) **holder,** a cavalry soldier detailed to hold the horses of his comrades when they fight on foot; (6) **hunter,** one who hunts horses; (7) **Indian,** see as a main entry; (8) ***jockey,** a trafficker in horses, a sharper or knave, also attrib.; (9) **plunger,** ?a reckless gambler on horse races, *rare;* (10) **pusher,** one who accompanies and cares for a carload of horses, *rare;* (11) **rustler,** *W.* a horse wrangler, a horse thief; (12) **swapper,** one who frequently swaps horses; (13) **thief,** see as a main entry; (14) **trader,** one who engages in trading or swapping horses; (15) **wrangler,** see as a main entry.

(1) **1835** *S. Lit. Messenger* I. 645 Of the most conspicuous '*minora sidera,*' the Kentuckian horse-drover, the horse-jockey, the gander-puller, might be mentioned. — (2) **1927** RUSSELL *Trails* 165 Talkin' about bronc twisters, . . . there's some difference between hoss fighters to-day an' them I knowed years ago. — (4) *a***1918** G. STUART *On Frontier* I. 154 This boy we employed as a horse herder. **1920** HUNTER *Trail Drivers Texas* I. 131 The horse herders were going to relieve Dan.

(5) **1873** CUSTER in *Boots and Saddles* App. 282 The entire squadron (except the horse-holders) was dismounted and ordered to fight on foot. **1903** FOX *Little Shepherd* xxii, A horse-holder ran up from the rear, breathless, and announced that the Yankees were flanking. — (6) **1827** in *Ashley-Smith Explor.* (1918) 225 Five of our best horses (are) missing. . . . The horse hunters returned without finding them. **1924** BECHDOLT *Tales* 248 The young horse-hunter went about his business. — (8) **1784** *Deane P.* 204 Ship Building is carried on with Vigor in this State, & the Horse Jockey business flourishes. **1865** *Atlantic Mo.* XV. 667/1 His father's tavern [was] a great resort for horse-jockeys, cattle-dealers [etc.]. **1905** LINCOLN *Partners* 145 His brother Sol . . . would skin the eye-teeth out of a Down-East horse jockey. — (9) **1891** WELCH *Recoll. 1830–40* 156 Bill Lockwood, a noted horse plunger, who quite recently 'passed in his chips.'

(10) **1895** REMINGTON *Pony Tracks* 22 Two scouts and a young 'horse-pusher' from St. Louis helped me to load. — (11) **1920** HUNTER *Trail Drivers Texas* 63, I told the cook and horse rustler to take the wagon and camp it up the river. *Ib.* 208 We thought '*horse rustlers,*' now commonly called horse thieves, had attacked the camp. **1940** BABER & WALKER *Longest Rope* 32 No one envied a horse rustler, and nobody but a horse lover got any reward for the long time and hard work it took to trap and gentle them. — (12) **1883** ZEIGLER & GROSSCUP *Alleghanies* 94 A unique character, who frequently mingles with the crowd, is the 'nat-ral-born hoss-swopper.' **1926** ROBERTS *Time of Man* 43 Do you-all know whe'r they's any gypsies a-campen down the roads or not? Any horse-swappers? — (14) **1806** *Western Amer.* (Louisville) 6 Mar. 2/4 A young man from Kentucky in character of a horse trader, did in open day, with a pole-axe beat out the brains of a young man named John Dixon. **1948** *Washington Post* 5 Dec. 6C/4 The men who have replaced the horse trader as shrewd bargainers converged on Minneapolis today for their annual carnival of buying and selling baseball talent.

8. In colloq. phrases: (1) *To sing psalms to a dead horse,* to do something entirely useless or in vain, *rare;* (2) *hold your horses,* don't be disturbed, be patient; (3) *horse and horse,* "equally divided or matched; no one better than the other" (*Cent. Supp.*) (see also quot. 1920); (4) *to face the horses,* (see quot.), *obs.;* (5) *to play horse,* (*a*) of children, to ride something in play, as if upon a horse, (*b*) to act in a violent manner, to play the fool, to ridicule or bamboozle [for the use of this expression among college students see *D.N.* II. 49]; (6) *the man on the horse,* the person in authority, cf. **horseback 2. b.**

(1) **1836** CROCKETT *Adventures* 81 He mought just as well have sung psalms to a dead horse. — (2) **1844** *N.O. Picayune* 16 Sep. 241/4 Oh, hold your hosses, Squire. There's no use gettin' riled, no how. **1948** *Reader's Digest* Dec. 147/1 Now hold yore horses, Jerry. I didn't

promise. — (3) *a*1846 *Quarter Race Ky.* 91 (We.), Yes, 'hoss and hoss,' and my deal! **1908** Lorimer *J. Spurlock* 3 It was horse and horse between the professors. **1920** Webster, *horse and horse*, a form of gaming, esp. dice throwing, in which the winner has to win a majority of rounds. When each player has won the same number of rounds the match is said to stand at horse and horse; hence, on even terms. — **(4) 1874** Knight 481/2 The back of a car seat is usually reversible, so as to adapt it for the passengers in either direction of motion of the car, the preference being to 'face the horses,' as it is called.

(5) (*a*) **1885** *Santa Fe Wkly. New Mexican* 9 July 4/3 His bright little son 'playing horse' on the arm of the chair. (*b*) **1892** Crane *Maggie* (1896) 24 Curious faces appeared in doorways, and whispered comments passed to and fro. 'Ol' Johnson's playin' horse agin.' **1907** O. Henry *Heart of West* 311 I'll drop the tanglefoot and the gun play, and won't play hoss no more. — **(6) 1887** *Pall Mall Gaz.* 21 July 1/1 The man on the horse, . . . to use the picturesque American phrase, is not now Lord Salisbury.

b. In verbal expressions: (1) **horse fiddle,** to serenade with horse fiddles; (2) **horse shed,** (see quot. and cf. **horse shedder** in **3. b.** above and **horse shedding** as a main entry).

(1) **1863** *Young Parson* 98 The last time [I went on a spree] was when Strapiron got married; then a parcel of us fellers did horse-fiddle him. — **(2) 1901** *Cong. Rec.* 4 Feb. 1918/1 (Th.), There was no opportunity, as Mr. Lincoln used to say, to 'horse-shed' them before they were brought in,—before their counsel or attorneys had had any opportunity to change their minds.

As the last term in **all, American, basket, black, brush, buffalo, buggy, calico, California, Californian, Canadian, carrying, cattle, cayuse, Charley, Chickasaw, chopping, cornstalk, courting, cow, cut, cutting, dark, death, devil's, devil's rear, devil's riding, draw, family, fancy, fast quarter, frow, gone, grade, half, harness, helper, Indian, iron, Kentucky, light, Mexican, Morgan, mud, mustang, night, old, one, paint, Pawnee, Pennsylvania, pinto, plantation, plug, pole, prairie, range, rear-, red, running, sea, shaving, shingle, short, skunk, smoke, Snake, Spanish, stake, standard bred, stick, stud, tobacco, Vermont, wheel, white, wood horse.**

horse apple. An exceptionally productive large yellow summer apple suitable for cooking and for eating.

1852 Fleischmann *Wegweiser* 171 Für die Breitengrade von Mississippi eignet sich besonders der Limber-Twig und Horse-apple. **1870** *Dept. Agric. Rep. 1869* 185 Horse Apple. Origin, Nash County, North Carolina; fruit, large; form, roundish oval. **1940** Mencken *Happy Days* 90 Unfortunately, the brakemen, in their dudgeon and alarm, mistook the horse apples for rocks, and conceived the theory that they were being beset by homicidal tramps.

b. (See quot.)

1915 *D.N.* IV. 226 horse-apple, n. The Bois d'arc apple. [w. Texas.]

* **horseback,** *n.*

1. A low, sharp ridge, a hogback. *Colloq.*

1851 Springer *Forest Life* 41 The pumpkin Pine is . . . also [found] on abrupt ridges, called horsebacks, where the forest is dense. **1884** in D. Hurd *Hist. Norfolk Co., Mass.* 561/2 In various parts of [Weymouth, Mass.] . . . are unusually fine examples of the sharp, linear hills, called horse-backs or kames. **1942** Cannon *Mountain* 38 He'd gone a little out of his way up onto a horseback.

2. In combs.: (1) **horseback mail,** mail transported on horseback, cf. **horse mail;** (2) **opinion,** opinion given off hand without full consideration, *colloq.;* (3) **outfit,** *W.* an outfit that travels on horses; (4) **post route,** a route over which mail is carried on horseback; (5) **work,** work, as that of a cowboy, done on horseback.

(1) **1894** Robley *Bourbon Co., Kans.* 64 Three times a week they had a horseback mail from Westpoint, Montevallo and Sarcoxie, Mo. — **(2) 1879** *Cong. Rec.* 23 April 728/1, I am not here as a judicial authority or oracle. I can only give horseback opinion. — **(3) 1895** Remington *Pony Tracks* 1 Before accepting an invitation to accompany an Indian commission into the Northwest I had asked the general quietly if this was a 'horseback' or a 'wagon outfit.' — **(4) 1877** H. C. Hodge *Arizona* 204 Two great stage lines have been in operation in Arizona for many years, and several minor ones, and horseback post routes.

(5) 1891 *Harper's Mag.* Aug. 364/1 This breeds the universal habit of horseback work.

b. *The man on horseback,* the one in authority, applied particularly to Gen. U. S. Grant and Theodore Roosevelt. *Colloq.*

1879 *Cong. Rec.* 25 June 2324/2 An Army under President Hayes, or 'the man on horseback' if he should come back into power. **1904** *Courier-Journal* 21 July 4 This is the lay-out. It is Parker, the Jurist and Patriot, against Roosevelt, the would-be Man-on-Horseback. **1948** *Time* 19 July 22/3 In short, let Ike go before the country as a Man-on-Horseback—who would, incidentally, carry the rachitic Democratic Party to safety.

horse bill. A handbill advertising the qualities and location of a stallion available for breeding purposes. *Obs.*

[**1829** *Va. Herald* (Fredericksburg) 18 Mar. 3/4 The Beautiful Horse Tariff, Will continue at his former Stable, the present year, at his former prices. Particulars will be seen in Handbills. **1864** *N.Y. Tribune* 7 May 3/5, I suggested 'stud-horse type' [?from its use in horse bills] as an appropriate means of conveying to your readers something of the sensation created here by Garibaldi.] **1873** *Newton Kansan* 6 March 2/2 Parties desiring horse bills for the coming season can have the same neatly printed at this office. **1886** Mark Twain *Speeches* 185 (R.), I can see that printing office of prehistoric times yet, with its horse bills on the wall.

* **horse boat.** A boat propelled by horses that are aboard it. *Obs.*

1823 I. Holmes *Account* 315 One of the horse-boats which cross the North river to Mohawken, is of a very peculiar construction. **1897** Robinson *Uncle Lisha* 257 They wended their way to the ferry just in time to see the horse boat come splashing into port, the four horses plodding their unprogressive journey on the revolving wheel. **1928** *Old-Time N. Eng.* April 161 Before the wreck of the *Belknap* a new type of freighter, the horse-boat, appeared on the lake. The first one of its kind was built on Long Island in 1838. It was an open scow propelled by paddle-wheels, the motive power being supplied by a pair of horses tramping a treadmill.

horsecar ˈhɔrsˌkɑr, *n.*

1. A streetcar or railroad car drawn by a horse or by horses. Now *hist.*

1833 Coke *Subaltern's Furlough* v, We entered the several horse-cars, according to the numbered tickets we had received. **1886** *Cent. Mag.* May 237/1 Horse-cars . . . leave Bowdoin Square, Boston, every half-hour for Mt. Auburn. **1944** Kahn *Cable Car Days* 24 By 1875 the horsecars had reached the crest of their popularity. Their service had been good and was appreciated by the riding public.

One type of horsecar

attrib. **1867** *Harper's Mag.* Dec. 36/2 Sell the house and take a smaller one out of town, on a horse-car route. **1871** Howells *Wedding Journey* 45 They seemed to have dreamed of a long horse-car pilgrimage. **1876** *Scribner's Mo.* April 912/1 There are round-eyed, wondering infants . . . in the cradles of to-day who are to be the horse-car conductors and passinjares of the next generation. **1900** *Scribner's Mag.* Sep. 369/1 From the tracks on Brattle Street, came the drowsy tinkle of horse-car bells.

b. horsecar driver, one who drives a horsecar.

1885 Crawford *Amer. Politician* 55 The horse-car drivers on Tremont Street rang their bells furiously. **1926** Cooper *Oklahoma* 3 A horse-car driver suddenly twirled taut his brake, pulled his bony horses to a sudden halt.

c. horsecar line, a transportation line or route upon which horsecars are used. *Obs.*

1880 Ranous *Diary of Daly Débutante* 207 Their horse-car lines [i.e., in Boston] are simply maddening. **1894** *Vt. Agric. Rep.* XIV. 93 Electricity has displaced the horse-car lines. **1905** *McClure's Mag.* XXIV. 347 A scheme to buy up, equip with electricity, and not only run, but finance, the old horse-car lines of Providence.

2. A railroad car fitted up for carrying horses.

1890 *Railways of Amer.* 146 It would require a separate article to give even a brief description of the different kinds of cars which are now used. . . . Hay-car, Hopper-bottom car, Horse-car. **1944** *Reader's Digest* Oct. 93/1 Although service men may be forced into old rolling stock or forced to sleep on coach floors, luxurious horse cars still roam the land attached to fast passenger trains.

horse drama. A form of drama in which trained horses are used. Cf. **equestrian drama.**

1868 *Boston Ev. Transcript* 7 May 2/2 The horse drama at the Howard is attracting very large audiences. **1901** CLARA MORRIS *Life on Stage* 109 Mr. Robert E. J. Miles . . . was starring at that time in the Horse Drama, doing such plays as 'The Cataract of the Ganges,' 'Mazeppa,' 'Sixteen-String Jack,' etc. **1944** *N. & Q.* 140/2 John F. Robinson, circus man of the mid-nineteenth century, was interested in the horse dramas of that period.

horse fiddle. Any one of various noise-making contrivances.

1807 in *Ind. Hist. Soc. Pub.* X. 164 The French . . . convened around the house of the new couple . . . ringing cow bells, striking on old kettles, playing on horse fiddles, night after night. **1872** E. EGGLESTON *End of World* 294 It is called in the West a horse-fiddle, because it is so unlike either a horse or a fiddle. **1907** *D.N.* III. 83 horse-fiddle, *n.* A tin can with a resin-smeared thread passed through a hole punctured at the bottom. Pulling the string produces ear-splitting noises. [n. w. Ark.] **1941** *L.A.* Map 409.

* **horsefish,** *n.*

1. A variety of sea clam. *Rare.*

1643 WILLIAMS *Key* (1866) 140 *A Horse fish.* . . . This the English calls Hens, a little thick shel-fish, which the Indians wade deepe and dive for.

2. Any one of various American fishes in some way suggestive of a horse.

1672 JOSSELYN *N. Eng. Rarities* 96 Blew fish, or Horse . . . are as big usually as the Salmon, and better Meat by far. **1884** GOODE *Fisheries* I. 322 This fish [*Selene setipinnis*], [is] known on some parts of the coast as the 'Horse-fish.' *Ib.* 424 The 'Sauger,' [*Stizostedium canadense*, is] known also as the . . . 'Horse-fish.' **1947** COFFIN *Yankee Coast* 48 Tuna?—Maybe to you. But he is plain horse-fish, horse-mackerel, to the Maine coast man.

* **horsefoot,** *n.*

1. Short for next.

1672 JOSSELYN *N. Eng. Rarities* 13 They feed . . . upon a shell-fish called a Horse-foot. **1802** *Mass. H.S. Coll.* 1 Ser. VIII. 189 The horse-foot, or king crab, was formerly much used for manuring land. **1855** P. PAXTON *Capt. Priest* 15 The exodus of the water also discloses . . . quantities of muscles, horsefeet, and fiddlers. **1911** *Rep. Fisheries 1908* 311.

2. horsefoot crab, a king crab.

1870 *Amer. Naturalist* IV. 257 This crustacean . . . bears also the popular names Horse Foot Crab, Horseshoe, and King Crab. **1918** LINCOLN *Shavings* 159 They walked along the beach, picked up shells, inspected 'horsefoot' crabs, jelly fish and 'sand dollars.'

3. horsefoot snipe, (*a*) the ruddy turnstone, (*b*) the American knot, *Calidris canutus rufus.*

(*a*) **1813** WILSON *Ornithology* VII. 32 On the coast of Cape May and Egg Harbour this bird [the turn-stone] is well known by the name of the Horse-foot Snipe. **1917** *Birds of Amer.* I. 268 Ruddy turnstone. . . . Other Names. . . . Stone-pecker; Horsefoot Snipe; Brant-bird [etc.]. — (*b*) **1888** G. TRUMBULL *Names of Birds* 179 Knot: Red-breasted Sandpiper: Red Sandpiper [etc.]. . . . At Pleasantville [N.J. it is called] . . . Horse-Foot Snipe. **1917** *Birds of Amer.* I. 231 Knot. . . . Other Names. Red Sandpiper; . . . Horsefoot Snipe [etc.].

* **horse guard.**

1. A fly that preys upon horseflies. Cf. * **guard,** *n.* **3.**

1796 HAWKINS *Letters* 46 A large flie called the horse guard come at the same season. **1845** LEWIS *Impressions* 276 The Creator . . . has provided the prairie with another fly, called 'the horse guard,' the scourge of the prairies, who seizes the green-head, whilst gorging himself on the traveller's horse, and carries him to his den in the ground.

2. One or more men detailed to keep watch over horses.

1828 in *Mo. Hist. Rev.* VIII. 187 An Irish sentinel of the horse guard, about 10 o'clock, mistook one of the company for an Indian; he fired, and then challenged. **1865** PIKE *Scout & Ranger* (1932) 91 He sent his horses down into the bed of the stream, at the same time motioning me to go with the horse guard. **1907** COOK *Border & Buffalo* (1938) 279 The horse-guard brought in the horses.

* **horsehair,** *n.* **1. horsehair bonnet,** (see quot.). *Obs.* **2. horsehair snake,** (see quots.).

(**1**) **1830** WATSON *Philadelphia* 176 Another hat, not unlike it in shape, was made of woven horse hair, wove in flowers, and called 'horse-hair bonnets.' — (**2**) **1897** *Outing* XXX. 434/2 The creature referred to as a mystery is what is termed the 'horsehair snake,' in reality, a hairworm. **1949** *Scientific Mo.* Jan. 56/2 Another mythical serpent, confined to the rural scene, is the horsehair snake . . . the worm *Paragordius varius.*

horse high. As high as a horse; in the colloq. phrase *horse-high, bull-strong, and pig-tight,* to describe a fence that is sufficient to restrain horses, cattle, and hogs. Cf. * **bull,** *n.* **9.** (**15**), **hog tight, pig tight.**

1873 BEADLE *Undevel. West* 40 A 'lawful fence' required five [strands of wire], which, the local courts consider, will make it 'horse-high, bull-strong, and pig-tight.' **1896** WHITE *Real Issue* 147 In the summer the field stood horse-high with corn. **1905** PRINGLE *Rice Planter* 176 The fence . . . is neither 'horse high, bull strong, nor pig tight,' and my cattle do not regard it at all. **1941** ALLEY *Random Thoughts* 260 These fences were built 'horse-high,' bull-strong, and pig-tight.

horse Indian. A Plains Indian accustomed to horses and to horseback riding.

1839 MARRYAT *Diary in Amer.* II. 85 They are *Horse* Indians, as those who live on the prairies are termed. **1887** *Cent. Mag.* Jan. 448/2 There are no bettter horsemen in the world than our horse-Indians. **1944** ROSS *Westward* 94 The Shoshone tribe were Horse Indians, and they knew every trail and pass in the region of the Continental Divide.

horse opera.

1. A circus entertainment featuring horses.

[**1857** *Spirit of Times* 19 Dec. 256/2 The denizens of the Bowery, who prefer the equine opera, will do well to make the most of present opportunities.] **1864** *Washoe* (Nev.) *Herald* 2 July 3/1 Those fond of 'horse opera'—and who is not?—will have an opportunity to gratify themselves—by visiting the Pavilion. **1867** *Territorial Enterprise* (Virginia, Nev.) 18 July 3/1 Of course all our people, old and young, will visit the 'horse opera.'

2. A cheap movie depicting western scenes, cowboys, bandits, etc. Also attrib.

1941 FERGUSSON *Southwest* 327 Chain stores, with familiar fronts and window displays, alternate with bars and movie houses advertising double features of 'horse operas' and their popular stars. **1947** *Sat. Ev. Post* 14 June 20 Bill Boyd remains the exciting darling of horse-opera fans. **1948** *This Week Mag.* 16 Oct. 20/2 A horse-opera hero gets a once-over lightly.

horse pen. An inclosure for horses. Also **horse-penning.** *Obs.*

1738 in CHALKLEY *Scotch-Irish Settlement Va.* II. 376 One of ye corners of Col. Carter's Horsepen. **1773** in SUMMERS *Ann. S.W. Virginia* 592 Ordered that John Crockett and John Adams . . . view the nighest and best way from the horse pen to Captain Crockett in the Cove. **1884** *Harper's Mag.* Dec. 107/2 The logs for the horse-pen had been provided days before. *Ib.* 106/1 It was the day fixed for the 'horse-penning' on Assateague Island.

* **horse race.** A narrow passage or defile. Usu. as a proper name.

1836 WOODCOCK *Journal* 6 We now enter the High Lands [on the upper Hudson River] by a narrow passage called the Horse race. **1882** HUBBARD *Moosehead Lake* 119 For a mile and a quarter below the dam the bed of the brook is a mass of boulders without pretence of having any channel, and has the name of 'horse-race.' **1901** THOMPSON *In Maine Woods* 32 Below is the Horserace, two miles of strong, broken rips, with ledges, that require a skilled guide to run.

horse rack. A hitching place for horses, usu. a pole or heavy beam placed upon posts and provided with nails, hooks, etc.

1824 SINGLETON *Letters* 90 There is commonly in the front yard a horse-rack, with bridle pins over head for a dozen of steeds. **1910** C. HARRIS *Eve's Husband* 17 There was long line of horse-racks on the north side of the square. **1943** POWELL *Home Again* 13 Scattered about on the Square, . . . were the horse racks, to which the people from the country hitched their horses, mules, or oxen, when they came to town.

horse ranch. *W.* A ranch upon which horses are raised.

1887 I. R. *Lady's Ranche Life Mont.* 13 One afternoon we drove up to the horse-ranche. **1890** *Stock Grower & Farmer* 8 March 4/4 Horse ranches in the Rocky mountains are improving the stock in that region. **1927** SIRINGO *Riata & Spurs* 221, I learned that Harvey Logan, alias Kid Curry, had a half-interest in a horse ranch with a man I will call Jim Thompson. **1949** WYNN *Desert Bonanza* 235 We drank a toast to the horse ranch in Kentucky.

Hence **horse-ranching,** *n.*

1912 WHEELER *Selkirk Mts.* 127 Now, as then, there is good fishing in the creek; now, as then, deer are running in the forests; but the mining places are given over mainly to horse-ranching.

horse sense. Practical common sense.

1832 PAULDING *Banks of Ohio* II. 215 (Th.), He's a man of good strong horse sense. **1850** *Quincy* (Ill.) *Whig* 12 Nov. 3/2 Thos. Ewing is simply a man of great good sense; what the Western people call 'horse sense.' **1949** *Downers Grove* (Ill.) *Rep.* 31 Mar. 1/7 The use of a little old-fashioned 'horse sense' will go a long way toward cutting down the toll that will be taken by swimming accidents this summer.

horse shedding. (See quots. 1856, 1888.) Also attrib. *Obs.* Cf. **horse shedder** *s.v.* ∗**horse,** *n.* **3. b.** (17).

1846 COOPER *Redskins* xiv, The private discussions that were held between pairs under what is called the 'horse-shedding' process. **1856** HALL *College Words* (ed. 2) 258 *Horse-shedding.* At the University of Vermont, among the secret and literary societies, this term is used to express the idea conveyed by the word *electioneering.* **1888** BITTINGER *Hist. Haverhill* 361 Sometimes a little business was initiated [between services on Sunday], incipient steps taken toward purchases or trades. . . . The hour was a sort of exchange time, when seller and buyer . . . would talk, saying, 'If it was to-morrow, what and so.' This was generally . . . known as 'horse-shedding.'

∗**horseshoe,** *n.*

1. A horsefoot crab. In full **horseshoe crab.**

1775 ROMANS *Nat. Hist. Florida* 302 It was no other than a crab of the kind called . . . to the northward a horse-shoe. **1797** BENTLEY *Diary* II. 234 A smaller number than usual of the Horse Shoe or Molucca Crab, tho' abundance of the small crab. **1901** *Cosmopolitan* July 310/2 That rooster thought he could eat King Philip [a pet lobster] jest as if he was a ordinary horseshoe, what chickens is so fond of. **1948** *Time* 14 June 1 The underside of this strange sea dweller is shaped like a horseshoe—hence the name horseshoe crab.

2. horseshoe violet, a local name for the birdfoot violet.

1892 *Amer. Folk-Lore* V. 92 *Viola pedata,* horseshoe violet, Concord, Mass. Crowfoot violet. New England. horse violet. New England.

horse show. A competitive public exhibition of horses and horsemanship. Also, rarely, **horse-and-corn show.**

1856 *Porter's Spirit of Times* 181/2 The performances at the horse show . . . were very interesting. **1921** *Rural Organization* 98 In several communities there are such committees as these: . . . exhibit committee to look after horse-and-corn show. **1945** *Chi. D. News* 10 Sep. 15/4 Sept. 17, 18 and 19 are dates of a society horse show and harness and running races here.

horse swap. An exchange of horses. Also **horse-swapping,** *n.*

1800 TATHAM *Agric. & Commerce* 80 The trade of *horse-swapping* is nearly as unlimited as the circle of society whose occasions this noble animal accommodates. **1813** *Wheeley's Baptist Ch. Min.* Dec. (N.C. Univ. MSS), Brother Wills Lay in another Charge against Brother Whalock Concerning a horse Swap took place between him & James Millenner. **1870** MACRAE *Americans* I. 283 The fair, however, has degenerated of late years; roughs and vagabonds from all quarters attend it; and its principal features now are gambling, drinking, and what they call 'horse-swopping.'

horse thief. One who steals a horse or horses. Also attrib. Cf. Du. *paardendief.*

1768 *Boston Chron.* 10 Oct. 388/3 People . . . who have assembled . . . with the view of driving all horse thieves . . . from amongst them. **1869** J. R. BROWNE *Adv. Apache Country* 133 It [Tucson] became during the few years preceding the 'break-up' quite a place of resort for traders, speculators, gamblers, horse-thieves [etc.]. **1948** *Green Bay* (Wis.) *Press-Gazette* 12 July 2/5 It is the first activity on the part of horse thieves reported here in several years. **1949** *10 Story Western* May 11/2 He'd been ordered to quit the Dominion of Canada and never return unless he wanted to stand trial for being connected with a horsethief gang.

∗**horsetooth,** *n. attrib.* Designating a variety of corn (see quot. 1887 and cf. ∗**dent**).

1868 G. BRACKETT *Farm Talk* 100 'Southern corn, I s'pose?' 'Yes; or rather western—the large "horsetooth" variety.' **1887** J. KIRKLAND *Zury* 45 The 'dent' which occurs in the top of each kernel [of Indian corn] produces a withered appearance and gives it the name of 'horse-tooth' corn. **1894** R. E. ROBINSON *Danvis Folks* 36, I druther hev a peck o' Dutton corn, yis, er Tucket, than a bushel o' their hoss-tooth corn.

∗**horse-trading.** The swapping or exchange of horses. Also transf.

1826 FLINT *Recoll.* 64 Horse-trading . . . seems to be a favorite and universal amusement. **1913** LONDON *Valley of Moon* III. xiii, As extra man at the biggest livery stable, Billy's spare time was so great that he drifted into horse-trading. **1941** STUART *Men of Mts.* 345 Great horse-tradin goes on here durin the Association. **1948** *Time* 3 May 17/1 Like any other national program, this one, in the end, was going to be put together by the usual method of horse-trading, wrangling and compromise.

horse trot. A trotting match. Also **horse-trotting.**

1858 HOLMES *Autocrat* 38 Horse-*racing* is not a republican institution; horse-*trotting* is. **1864** *Maine Agric. Soc. Ret. 1863* 40 On the second day of the Fair, had the inevitable horse trot. **1918** RIDEOUT *Key of Fields* 262 [The tin peddler] used to . . . win money on horse trots at the fairs.

horse wrangler. *W.* A herdsman having charge of the horses of a ranch or "outfit."

The suggestion by Bentley, p. 216, that this expression is a partial translation and partial taking over of Amer. Sp. *caballerango* (listed by Santamaría and defined as a "mozo de estribo") appears more probable than that the word here dealt with is an extension in meaning of the English ∗*wrangler.*

1888 ROOSEVELT in *Cent. Mag.* April 851 There are two herders, always known as 'horse wranglers'—one for the day and one for the night. [**1925** W. JAMES *Drifting Cowboy* 80 (Bentley), The cavy-wrango had brought the horses in.] **1949** *10 Story Western* May 10/1 The horse wrangler was in his early twenties.

hose company. A company of men who bring and have charge of the hose in firefighting.

1806 *Mass. Spy* 21 May (Th.), The efforts of several hose and fire companies at length prevailed. **1835** *Vade Mecum* (Phila.) 31 Jan. 3/3 The Fire Department of Boston has twenty Engines, twenty-five Hose Companies, and twelve hundred and fifty men. **1948** *N.O. Times-Picayune Mag.* 5 Dec. 21/2 The next and last contestant is Sound Point Protection Hose Company Number One!

hoskin gloves. ?Gloves of horse skin. *Obs.* — **1827** *National Gaz.* (Phila.) 7 Aug. 3/5 (*advt.*), Tan and coloured Hoskin gloves. **1827** *National Palladium* (Phila.) 25 July 3/5 (*advt.*), Kid and hoskin gloves. **1829** *Amer. Advertiser* (Phila.) 29 July 2/2 (*advt.*), Hoskin gloves and mits.

∗**hospital,** *n.* As the last term in **county, insane, marine, shoe, state hospital.**

hospital steward. Formerly, the highest noncommissioned officer in the Hospital Corps of the U.S. Army (see quot. 1865).

1856 GLISAN *Jrnl. Army Life* 350 Besides the sick, hospital steward, hospital attendants, and some three others, there will be no troops. **1865** KELLOGG *Rebel Prisons* 247 Hiram Buckingham . . . was detailed as hospital steward, or Doctor's clerk. **1895** *Outing* Dec. 255/2 The non-commissioned staff comprises a sergeant-major, a quarter master-sergeant, a commissary-sergeant, and a hospital steward.

hosteen hasˈtin, *n. S.W.* (See quot. 1910.) Usu. *cap.*

1910 Franciscan Fathers *Ethnol. Dict. Navaho Lang.* 110 The word hastqṳ́n which is often prefixed corresponds to our 'Mister.' **1938** *Southwestern Lore* Sep. 37 Hosteen Nez smoked store tobacco while Hosteen Yazzie used Zilth-Nut-To—mountain tobacco. **1948** *N.M. Hist. Rev.* April 85 In fact to this day Chee is addressed by his tribe not so much Chee as Hosteen Adicai, meaning, 'Mr. Interpreter.' **1949** *Desert Mag.* April 23/2 Hosteen Many Horses was buried in the Country of the Standing Rocks.

∗**hostile,** *a.* and *n.*

1. *pl.* Short for next.

1838 *N.Y. Mirror* 27 Jan. 245/3 Yesterday five Delaware chiefs, who had gone from the main army to the stronghold of the hostiles, reappeared with four Indians. **1880** MCELRATH *Yellowstone Valley* 39 The only 'hostiles' who have been in the Valley within three years have been small bands of horse thieves. **1947** *Westerners' Brand Book* 27 General Terry . . . issued an order demanding the Indians return to the reservations by January first or they would be treated as hostiles.

2. hostile Indians, Indians unfriendly to the whites.

1796 *Pittsburgh Gaz.* 16 Jan. 1/4 It would form a barrier between the United States and the hostile Indians. **1876** *White Pine* (Nev.) *News* 22 July 2/4 The hostile Indians are, according to my advices, encamped on the Little Horn. **1948** *Pacific Discovery* Sep.–Oct. 31/1 Fatigue, hardship, disease, danger from hostile Indians—all these were secondary to the problem of sufficient water.

∗**hot,** *a.*

1. In baseball, designating a ball batted or thrown very hard. *Slang.*

1867 *Ball Players' Chron.* 6 June 3/4 The hot one he sent to pitcher being missed by Walters, Stockman and Sweezy, Abrams reached his 2d by the muffing. **1871** *N.Y. Herald* 4 Aug. 7/3 The way he pulled the hot tips off the bats of the Flyaways was really a treat to all who saw him. **1905** *Chi. D. News* 26 July 6/2 The next time up he pulled a hot one over first that Harry Davis fortunately got and the game was ended. **1917** MATHEWSON *Sec. Base Sloan* 125 The players . . . had not handled a ball since the summer before and the 'hot ones' made them wince and yell.

2. In constant use, as if heated by friction. *Colloq.*

1888 *Harper's Mag.* Oct. 679/2 The New York and Washington wire is kept 'hot' for eight hours every night. **1900** *Cong. Rec.* 31 Jan. 1343/2 The Government had kept the cable wires hot in its efforts to secure bidders for those bonds in Europe.

3. Involved in a labor strike, as **hot cargo, hot section.** *Slang.*

1901 *Denver Republican* 19 Aug. 1/1 (*headline*), Non-Union Men Invading 'Hot' Section. **1940** RIESENBERG *Golden Gate* 312 One hundred ships were tied up and docks had become dangerously congested, for the teamsters joined with the I.L.A., refusing to haul 'hot cargo.' **1947** *Chr. Sci. Monitor* 22 May 1/2 Unions use 'hot cargo' or secondary-boycott practices against firms for which they have no grievance other than that they are buying or handling products of a firm where there is a strike and a picket line.

b. Of a check: Worthless, drawn to defraud. *Slang.*

1922 *Dly. Ardmoreite* (Ardmore, Okla.) 6 Jan. 6/5 Hot Check Artist En Route Ardmore. **1948** *Credit World* May 19/2 There are enough [checks] of the 'hot' type to warrant caution. **1948** *Durant* (Okla.) *D. Democrat* 4 July 3/6 We have cleaned up burglaries, stolen cars, hot check artists, dope addicts, shoplifting and various other law violations.

c. hot oil, oil produced in excess of a quota established by law. *Slang.*

1935 *Amer. Mercury* May 71/2 The hot oil producer believes in rugged individualism. **1948** *Chi. Tribune* 20 June (Grafic Mag.) 23/2 It was charged in Congress that these loans were secured from men interested in 'hot oil' cases then being pressed by the department of justice.

4. Most remarkable, highly attractive, exciting. *Slang.*

1911 E. Ferber *Dawn O'Hara* xxi. 301 I'll give you the hottest assignment on my list. **1932** *Blue Valley Farmer* (Okla. City) 28 Jan. 2/3 For president he's not so hot. Business won't support him. **1948** *Sat. Ev. Post* 9 Oct. 54/4 You're the hot news, Farmer. Please say something. **1949** *L.A. Times* 17 June 21/8 Two new [oil] developments on Tejon ranch yesterday sent that region into the picture as one of the hottest areas in the State.

5. In special combs.: (1) ***hot air, blood,** see as main entries; (2) **box,** a journal box, esp. on a railroad coach, overheated by friction, also transf.; (3) ***foot,** prompt or rapid action, *slang;* (4) ***house,** see as a main entry; (5) **spell,** a time of very warm weather; (6) **-spur State,** (see quot.); (7) **Water War,** Fries's Rebellion in March, 1799, in eastern Pennsylvania, occasioned by a direct federal tax on houses, *obs.;* (8) **wave,** a period of hot weather, cf. **heat wave, hot spell.**

(2) **1848** *Hunt's Merch. Mag.* XIX. 656 Such a thing as a 'hot box' to a car has not been known, even at the greatest speed, since the sprinkler has been in use. **1948** *Sat. Ev. Post* 25 Dec. 69/3 The brakie . . . looks outside from time to time with a sharp eye for indications of dragging brake beams or hot boxes. **1949** *Ib.* 2 July 19/1 Barkley . . . was father of the Railway Labor Mediation Act—a law which has developed some hotboxes lately. — (3) (*a*) **1869** *Cong. Globe* 15 Jan. 389/3 The honorable Senator . . . admonished us of the importance of hot-foot in this business. **1915** H. L. Wilson *Ruggles of Red Gap* ii. (1917) 27 We'd better report to her before she does a hot-foot over here.

(5) **1830** *Phila. Inquirer* 9 Sep. 2/3 Yesterday was a warmer day than we have had since the 'hot spell.' **1949** *Boston D. Globe* 7 Jan. 1/3 Bostonians found themselves 'sweltering' in an unseasonable hot spell that saw the mercury reach 59 at one point. — (6) **1883** J. Fiske in *Harper's Mag.* Feb. 425/1 After the union of the States under the Constitution the political conduct of South Carolina was so imperious and so unreasonable that she was not uncommonly known as the 'Hotspur State,' or as the 'vixen sister.' — (7) **1799** *Aurora* (Phila.) 3 May (Th.), The tale of a tub begat the hot water war, and that begat the devil among the tailors. **1800** *Ib.* 11 June (Th.), Three citizens were condemned to death for participating in this hot water war. **1892** W. S. Walsh *Literary Curiosities* 495 Hot-Water War. . . . When the officers came to make the necessary measurements, the women deluged them with hot water, whence the disturbance became known as the Hot-Water War. — (8) **1888** J. D. Whitney in *Encyl. Brit.* XXIII. 805/1 The occasional occurrence of 'hot waves' which sweep over large areas of country, raising the temperature much above its normal height, is one of the most . . . disagreeable features of the [U.S.] climate. **1901** Mark Twain *Letters* 711 (R.), We have heard of the hot wave every Wednesday, per the weekly paper.

b. In the names of, or with reference to, foods and drinks: (1) **hot biscuit,** a biscuit fresh from the oven; (2) **potato,** *fig.* something extremely unpleasant or embarrassing, often in the phrase *to drop like a hot potato, colloq.;* (3) **Scotch,** a drink consisting of a small amount of Scotch whisky to which hot water has been added; (4) **slaw,** (see quot. *a*1870); (5) **sling,** a drink of warmed spirituous liquor, *obs.;* (6) **water tea,** **=cambric tea.**

For **hot cake, corn, dog, stuff, tamale,** see as main entries.

(1) **1806** Wm. Dunlap *Diary* II. (1931) 387 At Mr. Love's (Washington, D.C.) we had usually three kinds of Bread at Breakfast & tea (or supper) Vizt Bakers. . . . Hot biscuit home made & hoe cake (or as they call it Corn bread). **1944** Clark *Pills* 164 Southerners generally loved hot biscuits. **1949** *Boston Globe* 3 July (Fiction Mag.) 9/5 Hot biscuits were Spike's favorite dish. — (2) **1886** Poore *Reminiscences* I. 448 They dropped him like a hot potato when they learned that he had accepted a place on the Republican Committee of his State. **1948** *Sat. Ev. Post* 4 Dec. 25/3 Doctor Jones, the great evangelist, had hold of a hot potato that in the next year or two will burn a good many hands. — (3) **1882** Howells *Modern Instance* xxiv, The bar-keeper said there was nothing like a hot-scotch to make you sleep. **1891** Welch *Recoll. 1830–40* 368 The thirsty could slake their thirst, or lunch, by visiting the saloon within the theater, taking their 'mug of ale,' 'hot Scotch,' or 'julep.' — (4) *a***1870** Chipman *Notes on Bartlett* 205 *Hot-slaw.* Cabbage minced and heated with vinegar; and thus named to distinguish it from *Kool Slaa* (mistakenly etymologized into Cold Slaw). **1905** *N.Y. Ev. Post* 23 Sep. 2 Mince pie, hokey-pokey ice cream, over-ripe watermelon, frankfurters with hot slaw—all the less expensive and less desirable articles of diet go to stunt the gamin's growth.

(5) **1827** J. Howe *Journal* 17 Here I had some hot sling and a warm breakfast. **1856** Goodrich *Recoll.* I. 63 Under the influence of this advent of new notions, some took . . . to hot slings. — (6) **1897** Terhune *Old Field* 54 'Hot-water-tea' (*i.e.*, milk-and-water sweetened) had not offended her taste yesterday, or ever before. Now they were disgusting and humiliating.

***hot air.** Empty boasting, talk, bombast. Also attrib. *Slang.*

1873 Mark Twain & Warner *Gilded Age* xliv. 399 The most airy scheme inflated in the hot air of the Capital only reached in magnitude some of his lesser fancies, the by-play of his constructive imagination. **1910** *Sat. Ev. Post* 2 July 13/3 'Hot-air artists' was a phrase uncoined; the farmer called them 'jawsmiths.' **1916** *Out West* Sep. 117/1 People in California have forgotten Warden, the hot air town created by Pat C. Lavey, who came from Oklahoma to carve out a fortune and landed in prison. **1948** *Chi. Sun-Times* 14 Oct. 88/1 It's all just a lot of hot air.

b. hot air vessel, a projected vessel to be driven by a caloric engine. *Rare.*

1853 *Hunt's Merch. Mag.* XXVIII. 282 *Hot-air* vessels are to take the place of steamships.

hotblood ˈhɑtˌblʌd, *n.* One who is extremely impetuous or hot-blooded.

1798 Woodworth *Spunkiad* 17 O dire disgrace! some hot-bloods would exclaim. **1860** *Lawrence* (Kans.) *Republican* 22 Nov. 2/2 The hot-bloods propose, now, to wait until some overt act of oppression is committed by Lincoln. **1948** *Chi. Tribune* 14 Mar. (Comics) 10 The man comes from a long line o' hot-bloods!

hot cake. [Cf. Du. *heetekoek*, a pancake.]

1. Orig. a freshly baked corncake, but now a griddle-cake.

1683 Penn *Select Works* (1782) IV. 309 Their entertainment was . . . twenty bucks, with hot cakes of new corn, both wheat and beans, which they make up in a square form, in the leaves of the stem, and bake them in the ashes. **1791** W. Bartram *Travels* 241 Fine Corn flour . . . being fried in the fresh bear's oil makes very good hot cakes or fritters. **1914** Bower *Flying U Ranch* 89 Patsy was lumbering about the stove frying hot-cakes. **1929** *Sunset* Feb. 47/1 Its griddles are removable, making it possible to have hot cakes as well as waffles.

2. Often attrib. or in phrases with reference to something that goes off well. *Colloq.*

1839 in *Amer. Sp.* XXI. (1946) 117/2 'You had better buy 'em, Colonel,' said Mr. Lummocks, 'they will sell like hot cakes.' **1852** *Ore. Statesman* 6 Jan. 2/3 They 'go off like hot cakes.' **1856** *Iroquois Republican* (Middleport, Ill.) 31 July 2/2 Our pleasant neighbor and co-worker . . . addressed the citizens of Concord on Saturday last, and we understand went off in his regular hot-cake style. **1946** *Fort Collins Coloradoan* 16 June 1/5 Ice cream sold like hot cakes Saturday, and hot cakes didn't sell at all, as the temperature began to climb early in the morning and kept it up until 4:30 p.m.

***Hotchkiss,** *n.* A small rapid-fire cannon of a type designed by Benjamin B. Hotchkiss (1826–85), an American inventor. Also attrib. Now *hist.*

1886 *Harper's Mag.* Oct. 793/2 The types adopted by the United States navy are the Hotchkiss revolving cannon and rapid-firing single-shot guns. **1902** Moore *Songs & Stories* 178 It required more skill to fire it without killing everybody on each side of it than it now requires to properly fire a Gatling or a Hotchkiss. **1916** Eastman *From Deep Woods* 107 We distinctly heard the reports of the Hotchkiss guns.

hot corn. Freshly boiled ears of Indian corn. Also attrib.

1788 Schöpf *Reise* I. 456 Sie [i.e., roasting ears] werden gekocht, oder in der Asche gebraten, und mit Salz und Butter genossen; und in den Städten zum Verkauf, warm (hot Corn) ausgeruffen. **1813** *Cramer's Alman. 1814* (Pittsburgh) 52 There are . . . the melon merchants, a numerous band, and as noisy as the *hot-corn* women of

Philadelphia. **1844** in THOMPSON *M. Jones* (1872) Take some of them good hot-corn muffins. **1944** *Chi. D. News* 13 July 21/3 A good menu consists of an India relish cold plate, hot corn on the cob, rye bread and butter.

hot dog.

1. A heated frankfurter or wienerwurst, esp. one placed in a split roll and garnished to taste with mustard, onion, etc. *Slang.*

[**1903** *Cin. Enquirer* 1 May 6/5 And will we eat the 'Hot! Hot! Hot!' and 'Bum, bum' stuff? Sure, Mike.] **1909** *Sat. Ev. Post* 24 April 6/3 Couple of hot dogs, Steve, give 'em a touch of mustard. **1949** *Friends* April 16/2 The hot dog was introduced by Charles Feltman, a Coney Island baker.

attrib. **1920** LEWIS *Main Street* 304 Lining one block of Main Street were the 'attractions'—two hot-dog stands . . . a merry-go-round, and booths. **1929** *Chi. Tribune* 13 Feb. 3/7 (*heading*), Oil Men Declare War On Hot Dog Filling Stations. **1945** *Athol* (Mass.) *D. News* 8 June 2/2 Guests enjoyed a hot-dog roast, and games were played during the evening.

2. Used as an interjection to express surprise or approval. *Slang.*

1924–5 FOSTER *Larry* (1930) 40 Hot dog, ain't I got the definite plans for the future though? **1948** *Chi. Tribune* 25 Mar. III. 4/2 Hot dog! Another double ringer!

* **hotel,** *n.*

1. Formerly at the University of Virginia, a dining hall for students. *Obs.* Cf. **hotel keeper.**

1820 *N. Amer. Review* X. 117 Besides this, it is proposed to have, for the dieting of the students, *hotels* of a single room for a refectory, and two rooms for tenants charged with this department. **1829** *Va. Lit. Museum* 336/1 The Proctor is required to make a monthly report to the Chairman of the Faculty [of the Univ. of Va.], of the state of the dormitories, hotels, and public buildings.

2. In combs.: (1) **hotel barge,** a large vehicle for conveying travelers to and from a hotel; (2) **bus,** a bus operated by a hotel for the convenience of its guests; (3) **car,** (see quot. 1890), cf. **Pullman hotel car;** (4) **clerk,** a hotel employee who assigns rooms to guests and attends to their comfort; (5) **coach,** a coach operated by a hotel for the convenience of its guests; (6) **hop,** a ball attended by those occupying a social position below that of the elite, *obs.;* (7) * **keeper,** formerly at the University of Virginia one in charge of a "hotel" for students, *obs.,* cf. **hotel 1;** (8) **office,** the place where the business of a hotel is transacted, the lobby; (9) **parlor,** a room in a hotel suitably arranged and equipped for conversation, rest, reception of visitors, etc.; (10) **piazza,** the veranda or porch of a hotel; (11) **privilege,** the privilege or right to erect and operate a hotel; (12) **register,** a book in which the guests of a hotel register their names; (13) **runner,** (see quot. 1903), cf. **runner.**

(1) **1881** HOWELLS *Modern Instance* xxvii. 328 Marcia watched him drive off toward the station in the hotel barge. — (2) **1878** *Harper's Mag.* Jan. 194 The traveller reaches his stopping-place by hotel 'bus, carriage, or by the democratic street cars. — (3) **1870** W. F. RAE *Westward by Rail* 29 The Hotel Car is divided into sections, forming state rooms. . . . At the rear [of the car] is a kitchen, which, though small, contains every appliance necessary for cooking purposes. **1890** *Railways of Amer.* 244 The Pullman Company now introduced the hotel-car, which was practically a sleeping-car with a kitchen and pantries in one end and portable tables which could be placed between the seats of each section and upon which meals could be conveniently served. — (4) **1856** OLMSTED *Slave States* 333 An easy and gentleman-like employment as that of hotel-clerk and bar-keeper. **1945** TRYON *Poor Man* 185, I suppose the actor is better trained than most of us at inventing stratagems for getting past the hard and watchful eyes of hotel clerks.

(5) **1882** LATHROP *Echo of Passion* ix, He was careful to ride in the hotel coach, while she went to the station in a carriage. — (6) **1865** SALA *Diary* II. 153 We don't call such things as those 'balls.' We call them 'hotel hops.' — (7) **1829** *Va. Lit. Museum* 336/1 The Proctor is required to make a monthly report . . . of any matters relating to the students or hotel-keepers which may be worthy of being noticed. *Ib.*, The hotel keepers are required to furnish a list of such of their boarders as are absent from breakfast. — (8) *a***1861** WINTHROP *C. Dreeme* 77, I heard here at the hotel-office [etc.]. **1912** NICHOLSON *Hoosier Chron.* 243 Harwood waylaid Allen in the hotel office a moment after Marian had gone to her room. — (9) **1853** *Harper's Mag.* Jan. 193/1 There were several of the sedate groups that Nature always permits in hotel-parlors, to preserve the balance—so much lead to so much elixir. **1913** LA FOLLETTE *Autobiog.* 144 Sawyer said that he had been unable to secure a room and requested me to go with him to the hotel parlors on the second floor.

(10) **1898** CANFIELD *Maid of Frontier* 126 Standing upon his hotel piazza, . . . Hornung thought of the tremens, and the small houses in the ardent sun danced fantastically before his eyes. — (11) **1884** *Cong. Rec.* 27 May 4550/2 'Do I understand the Senator from Missouri that there are seven hotel locations in the [Yellowstone] park?' . . . 'Yes, sir; seven hotel privileges.' **1886** *Ib.* 2 Aug. 8354/2 There was a lease drawn up . . . that did give a monopoly both of transportation and hotel privileges [in Yellowstone Park]. — (12) **1860** in *A. Lincoln Quarterly* (1949 Mar.) 262 When I went to breakfast this morning I found the name of Mr Bates on the hotel register. **1897** HOWELLS *Open-eyed Conspiracy* vi, Shall I go round exploring hotel registers for a victim to such a divinity as that? — (13) **1848** JUDSON *Mysteries N.Y.* II. 57 Many of our readers may have noticed the almost professional look . . . of an outside hotel-runner. **1903** LEWIS *Boss* 11 A special trade had grown up among the piers; the men to follow it were called hotel runners. These birds of prey met the ships to swoop on newcomers with lie and cheat, and carry them away to hostelries whose mean interests they serve. **1910** *Sat. Ev. Post* 23 July 13/1 Usual jumble and jangle and tangle, Mixup of baggage, hotel-runners' wrangle.

As the last term in **apartment, depot, European, floating, log, palace, pine, Raines law, summer hotel.**

* **hothouse,** *n.* Among American Indians, a cave or hut which may readily be heated for winter residence or for taking sweat baths. *Obs.*

1643 R. WILLIAMS *Key* (1766) 211 This Hot-house is a kind of little Cell or Cave, . . . [and] into this frequently the men enter after they have exceedingly heated it. . . . Here doe they sit . . . sweating together. **1702** C. MATHER *Magnalia* (1853) I. 558 Their hot-house is a little cave, about eight foot over, where, after they have terribly heated it, a crew of them go sit and sweat and smoke for an hour together, and then immediately run into some very cold adjacent brook. **1833** FLINT *D. Boone* 147 The waiter . . . placed a couple of blocks of wood . . . opposite the door of a circular cabin, called the hot-house, in the centre of which was the council fire.

hot stuff.

1. Spiced rum. *Obs.*

[**1841** HONE *Diary* II. 103 We were treated with coffee, spiced rum (known in the Dutch nomenclature as hot stuff), nice bread and butter, Dutch cheese, herrings, doughnuts, New Year's cookies, crullers, mince pies, and waffles.] **1853** BALDWIN *Flush Times Ala.* 162 Cave, . . . refreshing himself with about a pint of hot-stuff, rose, turned his back to the fire, and . . . began. **1866** *Beadle's Mo.* March 279/2 She has a fine table set out down-stairs, and plenty of hot-stuff for her friends.

2. Anything violent, extreme, grandiloquent. *Slang.*

1895 REMINGTON *Pony Tracks* 208 'That's that outpost of the Twenty-seventh guarding the building.' . . . It fairly crackled now—'giving 'em hot stuff.' **1932** *K.C. Star* 6 Jan. 20 Lay on a few trowels of hot stuff about his town and he beams all over.

hot tamale. A Mexican food consisting of highly seasoned ground meat coated with corn meal and steamed in cornhusks. Also transf. and attrib.

1893 *Outing* April 27/2 Nice hot *tamales!* dear little *tamales!* very nice, very hot! **1896** *Cin. Enquirer* 21 Aug. 6/7 Thomas Gates [was arrested] . . . on the charge of passing a counterfeit silver dollar on . . . an old colored hot tamale man. **1936** MCKENNA *Black Range* 163 Some of the young miners . . . gave it out that she was 'a red-hot tamale.' **1948** *Coronet* July 42/2 Such Mexican female characters as escape half-caste roles are presented as 'hot tamales from below the Rio Grande,' with the social graces of a Kansas tornado.

* **hound,** *n.*

1. (*cap.*) *pl.* A gang of rowdies and desperadoes formerly active in San Francisco. *Obs.*

1850 W. RYAN *Adv. Calif.* II. 257 Amongst the most prominent and notorious disturbers of the public peace figured an association . . . known by the cognomen of the 'Hounds.' . . . They were a desperate set of brawlers, gamblers, and drunkards. **1872** MCCLELLAN *Golden State* 133 The 'Sydney Ducks' and 'Hounds'—classes of desperadoes —were ever on the alert for booty.

2. In colloq. combs.: (1) **hound dog,** a hound, esp. a male hound; (2) **pup,** a young hound.

(1) **1649** *Dedham Rec.* 162 That care be taken that the young hound doges be in time taught to hunt. **1768** WASHINGTON *Diaries* I. 293 She was shut up with a hound dog, old Harry. **1949** *Chi. D. News* 6 July 14/3 He's got about nine houn' dawgs. — (2) **1857** OLMSTED *Journ. Texas* (1861) 52 The child . . . five miles from a neighbor; . . . [with] hound-pups and negroes for playmates. **1878** J. H. BEADLE *Western Wilds* xxviii. 439 What he wouldn't steal, a hound pup wouldn't pull out of a tan-yard. [**1949** *Democrat* 5 May 8/4 Two hound puppies from my deer hound, 3 months old.]

As the last term in **bird, coon, drag, gray, Negro, possum, pot, sleuth, tea, track, turkey hound.**

* **hour,** *n.*

1. Used in phrases to indicate the position of the sun above the horizon. *Colloq.*

1637 *Essex Inst. Coll.* IX. 66 The keeper . . . [is] to take the Cattle at the pen at Sun halfe an hour highe. **1700** SEWALL *Diary* II. 14 Set out for Salem about an hour by sun. **1822** J. FOWLER *Journal* 101 [We] set out the Sun about one Hour High. **1907** M. H. NORRIS *Veil* 3 The sun was an hour high when he entered a narrow road overgrown with grass.

2. A unit of credit in college and university work.

1918 *D.N.* V. 25 Hour, n. A unit of credit. 'I'm taking twenty *hours* this semester.' College communities. **1942** *Vanderbilt Univ. Bul.* 69 Each course at this level is one term in length and gives five hours credit. **1949** *Sooner Mag.* May 8/1 Treadwell . . . lacked six hours to reach senior standing which the fellowship requires.

As the last term in **five-cent, morning, noon, nooning, rush, semester, study, ten hour.** See also **bank hours, store hours.**

hourly 'aurlı, *n.* (See quot. 1877.) *Obs.*

1832 *Boston Transcript* 29 May 2/1 One thing is very certain that, at present, the patrons of the Hourlies are only partially accommodated. **1877** BARTLETT 299 *Hourly*, formerly used in and about Boston for an omnibus. **1881** *Harper's Mag.* Feb. 388 The terrors of the 'hourly' or omnibus.

* **house,** *n.*

1. A quantity of tobacco sufficient to fill a curing house. *Rare.*

1770 in *Md. Hist. Mag.* XIII. 61 We expected a frost last night & cut all our tobo yesterday which was standing viz. about half a House.

2. Either of the two branches of the Congress of the U.S.

1787 *Constitution* ii. § 3 [The President] may, on extraordinary Occasions, convene both Houses, or either of them. **1857** BENTON *Exam. Dred Scott Case* 108 Mr. Benton, fearing the loss of the Oregon bill in the disagreement between the two Houses, moved that the Senate recede from its amendment. **1894** *Harper's Mag.* Oct. 802/1 After a six month's debate on the floors of both Houses and in Conference Committee [etc.].

3. (*cap.*) = **House of Representatives** *q.v.* as a main entry.

1789 *Ann. 1st Congress* I. 17 The Senate have appointed one of their members to sit at the Clerk's table to make a list of the votes as they shall be declared; submitting it to the wisdom of the House to appoint one or more of their members for the like purpose. **1849** J. DIXON *Tour through U.S.* 27 On leaving the Senate, we entered the House, as it is called, meaning the House of Representatives. **1949** *Time* 11 July 15/1 The House took up a temporary stand across the street in the new House Office Building.

4. Either of the two branches of a state legislature.

1793 *Pa. Gen. Assembly Jrnl. of Senate 1793–5* 45 All bills, orders, resolutions, votes, and amendments of either House . . . shall be presented to the other. **1839** *Indiana H. Rep. Jrnl.* 208 Resolved, That, whereas a communication has been made to the Legislature of Indiana by Dr. I. Coe, one of the canal fund commissioners relative to the property received by said commissioners from the Cohens, . . . that the Senate be respectfully requested to transmit to this House, a copy. **1945** *Chi. D. News* 4 Jan. 11/5 A deadlock over election of a speaker for the North Dakota House was broken by Representative C. T. Olson.

5. Short for "house of ill fame," a brothel.

1865 *Detroit Tribune* 6 Oct. 3/1 Efforts have time and again been made by the police force to break up the house so as to rid society of the nuisance. **1930** FERBER *Cimarron* 175 Why didn't you tell me that when she married him she was a girl out of a—out of a—house! **1943** *Copper Camp* 182 Each house, operated by a bediamonded 'madame,' had a score or more of attractive, well-groomed girls.

6. A gambling establishment, business house, institution, etc. *Colloq.*

1901 *Denver Republican* 26 Aug. 3/4 Whenever a player cashes in his checks, provided he is fortunate enough to secure any, the 'house' orders a drink. **1938** ASBURY *Sucker's Prog.* 122 Comparatively, the house was honest.

7. *local.* (See quot.)

1938 MATSCHAT *Suwannee River* 34 They [flooded marshes] are dotted with wooded islets, commonly called 'houses' because they have enough dry land to furnish camp sites for the hunters.

8. In combs.: (1) **house Amish,** the most conservative element in the Amish community; (2) **burning,** of tobacco, suffering from the disease known as poleburn during the curing process, cf. **house burn,** *v.;* (3) **car,** = **dormitory car;** (4) **coat,** a lounging robe; (5) **detective,** a detective employed by a hotel, business house, etc.; (6) **dick,** = prec.; (7) **dress,** a dress, usu. washable, for wear while working in or around the house; (8) **father,** a man who occupies to some extent the place of a father to young men living in the same boarding or rooming house with him, cf. * **house mother;** (9) **frame,** the frame of a wooden house; (10) **gang,** formerly a group of Negro slaves who worked in the vicinity of the master's home, *obs.;* (11) **girl,** a girl, esp. a Negress, who does domestic work in a home for pay; (12) **help,** = prec., *obs.;* (13) * **mother,** in some schools, sororities, fraternities, etc., a woman who occupies to some extent the place of a mother to the students; (14) **mover,** one whose business is to move houses; (15) **organ,** (see quots.); (16) **plot,** = **house lot,** *obs.;* (17) **porch,** the veranda of a house; (18) **-raised,** *a.* of a Negro before the Civil War, brought up in the master's house in contrast with raised in the "quarters," *obs.;* (19) **share,** = **house lot,** *obs.;* (20) **-smith,** a smith or ironworker who assists in doing the iron and steel work in buildings; (21) **tent,** (see quot.), *rare;* (22) **yard,** a yard adjoining a dwelling.

(1) 1938 HARK *Hex Marks Spot* 228 That's why, too, they were called 'House Amish,' as distinguished from 'Church Amish.' **1940** *Sat. Ev. Post* 30 March 40/3 Here, again, we run into the difference between the most conservative, the house-Amish, and the less conservative, the church-Amish. — **(2) 1772** *Md. Hist. Mag.* XIV. 291 Every day we have had very damp foggy mornings, fiers Have been kept to prevent House burning. **1850** *Rep. Comm. Patents 1849: Agric.* 324 In this crop every leaf was saved, none lost by worms, nor by 'house-burning,' (that is, suffering, or even rotting from being hung too thick). — **(3) 1856** FERGUSSON *America* 338, I was glad to withdraw myself and my stool within the doorway of a house-car, as the covered freight-trucks are called. **1890** *Railways of Amer.* 155 Under the bridge supervisor are organized 'bridge gangs,' each consisting of a competent foreman with carpenters and laborers skilled in bridge work and living in 'house' or 'boarding' cars. — **(4) 1942** RAWLINGS *C. Creek* 103, I put on a house-coat and went to the front door. **1944** *Chi. D. News* 18 Dec. 17/5 You will be glad to know of a collection of reasonably priced housecoats and brunch coats shown in a local store.

(5) 1898 *McClure's Mag.* X. 525/2 A house detective [had] observed the whole transaction. **1949** *This Week Mag.* 30 April 4/2 Today's house detective is no comic in a derby hat. — **(6) 1943** LYON *And So to Bedlam* 255 He must have been the one that called Mr. Casey here, and ten to one he's the fellow that tipped off you house dicks. **1946** *Chi. D. News* 12 Aug. 3/1, I wonder if it is the house dick. — **(7) 1897** *McClure's Mag.* X. 66 She looked charming in her long, soft house-dress. **1943** LYON *And So to Bedlam* 32 Flashing-toothed young men selling house dresses from the rear end of trucks. **1949** *World-Herald Mag.* (Omaha) 3 July 6/2, I change into a house dress and hunt up fresh clothes for those who can't find where they took their duds off. — **(8) 1901** WASHINGTON *Up From Slavery* 97 The special work which the General desired me to do was to be a sort of 'house father' to the Indian young men. — **(9) 1824** in *N.H. Hist. Soc. Coll.* I. 246 A new two-story house frame nearly covered . . . and two barns, were blown down.

(10) 1792 in *Pub. Col. Soc.* XI. 117 If you conceive that the House gang, with such aids as you can derive from River Plantation [etc.]. — **(11) 1851** *Knickerb.* XXXVIII. 394 The baker stops a moment to chatter with the house-girl. **1945** BOTKIN *My Burden* 55 Part white children sold for more than black children. They used them for house girls. — **(12) 1835** in *Amer. Sp.* XXII. 203/2 Well, he roared like a bull, till black Lucretia, one of the house helps, let him go. — **(13) 1909** WEBSTER. **1948** *Seattle Times* 26 Sep. 4/1 There Nancy met the housemother, a sorority alumna and the house president. — **(14) 1838** STEVENSON *Sketch* 316 Mr. Brown mentioned that he and his father, who was the first person who attempted to perform the operation, had followed the business of 'house-movers' for fourteen years. **1948** *Chi. Maroon* 9 April 16/1 'Yust a little job,' said Chris, 55 years a house mover.

(15) 1926 *Ladies' Home Jrnl.* April 107 A house organ is not, as Phyllis had supposed, a musical instrument, but a periodical published by the company to incite employes to further effort. **1949** *Sat. Ev. Post* 25 June 62/3 The paste pot on his desk was for affixing to letters pertinent items snipped from his newspapers, most of which were house organs of well-known penitentiaries. — **(16) 1636** *Boston Rec.* (1877) II. 12 William Hudson hath sould an housplott and garden. **1662** *Providence Rec.* III. 7 Betweene the said home share and the afore said howse plott. — **(17) 1899** MARK TWAIN *How to Make Hist. Dates Stick* 144 (R.), From the house-porch the grounds sloped gradually down to the lower fence. — **(18) 1854** THORPE *Master's House* 256 From the vicinity of Colesburg, Dixon had for many years, through his agents, purchased a large part of the choicest 'house-raised' negroes, which he offered for sale in New Orleans. — **(19) 1643** *Providence Rec.* II. 7 All the land that he hath lying in the Bounds of prouidence excepting his house share and housing.

(20) 1903 *McClure's Mag.* Nov. 33/2 In 1897 the housesmith received $2.50 a day. In 1903 he receives $4.50 a day. **1904** *N.Y. Ev. Post* 29 Mar. 6 The so-called builder sublets the work to the masons, the housesmiths, the marble workers, the steamfitters and to the other 20 or 25 trades employed in constructing a modern skyscraper. — **(21) 1871** COOKE *R. E. Lee* 205 The headquarters tent, at this time (December, 1862), as before and afterward, was what is called a 'house-tent,' not differing in any particular from those used by the private soldiers of the army in winter-quarters. — **(22) 1863** MITCHELL *My Farm* 26 An ample stream . . . came with a gushing fulness upon the very margin of the quiet little houseyard that compassed the dwelling. **1893** *Harper's Mag.* Feb. 350/1 Apples as they fell to the ground could be heard on every side in the quiet houseyards.

For **house joiner, log, lot, Negro, raising,** see as main entries.

b. In phrases with "of" (see also **9.** below): (1) **house of assignation,** =**assignation house;** (2) **of employment,** (see quot. and cf. **bettering house**), *obs.;* (3) **of entertainment,** see as a main entry; (4) **of students,** (see quot.), *obs.*

(1) **1834** *Sun* (N.Y.) 10 April 2/2 Such men as Samuel Q. Wright, (a bank man) the keeper of a notorious house of assignation, and prostitution. **1943** OTTLEY *New World* 158, I don't believe it would be an exaggeration to say that on nearly every other street in Negro neighborhoods there is at least one brothel or house of assignation maintained for the almost-exclusive patronage of white men. — **(2) 1788** SCHÖPF *Reise* I. 99 Unweit des Hospitals [in Philadelphia] ist noch ein anderes öffentliches Gebäude. . . . Es ist das Arbeitshaus, (Bettering- or Working-house, sonst auch House of Employment genannt.) — **(4) 1871** CUTTING *Student Life at Amherst* 93 In the summer term of 1828, a legislative body was formed in college, known as the 'House of Students.' Its object was to enact such laws . . . as the good of a college community would seem to require. **1895** TYLER *Hist. Amherst Coll.* 74 A legislative body, called the 'House of Students,' enacted laws for the protection of the buildings, for the security of the grounds, for the better observance of study hours, and similar matters.

9. In expressions relating to politics or government: (1) **House bill,** a bill that originates in the House or lower branch of Congress or of a state legislature; (2) **caucus,** (see quot.); (3) **of Assembly,** the legislative body of certain of the colonies and states, one, usu. the lower, of the two houses of a state legislature; (4) **of Burgesses,** in colonial times, the representative assembly of Virginia, now *hist.;* (5) * **of Commons,** the name given to the lower branch of the North Carolina legislative body from 1776 to 1868; (6) * **of Delegates,** in some states, esp. Virginia and Maryland, the lower house of the legislature; (7) * **of Lords,** (see quot.), *sarcastic, rare;* (8) **of Representatives,** see as a main entry; (9) **page,** a boy serving as a page in the House of Representatives at Washington, cf. **page.**

(1) **1868** *N.Y. Herald* 2 July 3 Mr. Loughbridge . . . reported the House bill for the relief of the grantees of Ann D. Durelling. **1945** *Las Cruces* (N.M.) *Citizen* 15 Feb. 2/3 He did learn something about it, though, when the bill came up for reading. It was House Bill No. 200. — **(2) 1888** BRYCE *Amer. Commw.* II. III. lxxiii. 596 What the Americans call '*House caucuses,*' *i.e.* meetings of a party in the larger House of the legislature, are not uncommon in England. — **(3) 1653** *Va. House of Burgesses* 88 By the Unanimous Opinion of the House of Assembly. It is ordered that John Baldwin shall . . . keep his place. **1790** *Ky. Petitions* 154 [He] Continued in publick, Business . . . either as a Deligate in the House of Assembly or as a melitia officer in the Jersey State. **1914** *N.J. Legisl. Minutes of 138th Gen. Assembly* 245, I am directed by the Senate to inform the House of Assembly that the Senate has passed the following bills. — **(4) 1658** *Va. House of Burgesses* 111 The Burgesses . . . are not dissolvable by any power now extant in Virginia, but the House of Burgesses. **1766** in *S. Lit. Messenger* XXVII. 117/2 [The chair] shall have no influence, whether I am in or out of the House of Burgesses. **1948** *Chi. Tribune* 9 May 1. 24/3 From here he was elected to the house of burgesses.

(5) 1776 *N.C. Col. Rec.* X. 1007 The legislative Authority shall be vested in two distinct Branches, . . . to wit, a Senate and House of Commons. **1867** *N.C. Senate Journal* 23 Jan. 187 A message was received from the House of Commons, informing the Senate . . . that the House was ready for the transaction of business. — **(6) 1783** STOKES *View* 98 The two distinct branches, called 'The Senate,' and 'The House of Delegates,' form a complete Legislature, and are named 'The General Assembly of Virginia.' **1814** *Ann. 13th Congress* 1 Sess. I. 620 The Legislature of Maryland is composed of two branches. . . . The House of Delegates are annually elected. **1918** *Va. Acts of Assembly* 788 Resolved, by the senate, the house of delegates concurring [etc.]. — **(7) 1890** *Stock Grower & Farmer* 10 May 3/3 Our ornamental house of lords, the senate, never should have existed and now ought to be abolished. — **(9) 1886** ALTON *Among Law-Makers* 20 The House-pages are double in number those of the Senate.

b. *To clean house, fig.* to set right, cleanse from corruption. *Slang.*

1934 WEBSTER. **1948** *Chi. Tribune* 23 June 8/3 (*heading*), Women Urged to Aid G.O.P. in Cleaning House.

Hence * **house-cleaning,** *n.*

1928 FOY & HARLOW *Clowning Through Life* 294 The Chicago horror was a blessing in one respect—namely, in that it brought about a country-wide house-cleaning. **1948** *Time* 25 Oct. 21/1 We're going to start the biggest and best and healthiest house-cleaning this government ever had.

10. In the names of birds, snakes, etc.: (1) * **house builder,** (see quot.), *rare;* (2) **finch,** any one of various small red-headed finches of the genus *Carpodacus;* (3) **snake,** the milk snake or spotted adder, *Lampropeltis triangulum;* (4) **wren,** the common American brown wren, *Troglodytes aedon.*

(1) **1898** *Mo. So. Dakotan* I. 97 It was in the early morning that a yellow striped hornet commonly known as 'the house-builder' was poising itself in the air and darting every now and then around a full grown tea plant. — **(2) 1869** *Amer. Naturalist* III. 183 About the gardens [in California] are the House Finch . . . the Black Pewee (*Sayornis nigricans*) [etc.]. **1917** *Birds of Amer.* III. 7 House Finch. . . . Other names [include] Crimson-fronted Finch; Red-headed Linnet; Linnet; Burion; Red-head. — **(3) 1807** *Mass. H.S. Coll.* 2 Ser. III. 54 The milk or house snake, speckled like a rattlesnake. **1884** MARK TWAIN *H. Finn* xxxix. 396 [We] grabbed a couple of dozen garters and house-snakes. — **(4) 1808** WILSON *Ornithology* I. 129 House Wren. *Sylvia Domestica.* **1850** S. F. COOPER *Rural Hours* 90 Among all the varieties of birds flitting about our path during the pleasant months, there is not one which is a more desirable neighbor than the house-wren. **1949** *Sat. Ev. Post* 9 April 122/4 The house wren builds in a sack of rags.

As the last term in **accommodation, apartment, ash, assignation, back, bag, baggage, balloon, barber, bark, barrel, basement, bath, bathing, beaver, berry, bettering, big, bird, bit, blade, block, board, boarding, book, boom, bough, bound, box, breakfast, brown, brush, bug, bunk, bush, camp, cane, canvas, car, carpet, carriage, cart, cat, chapter, cheese, chicken, China, church, clapboard, coach, cob, commission, community, company, corn, cotton, county, court, coyote, crap, curing, dance, derrick, devil's, dining, dog, dollar-a-day, double, dry, dry-goods, dumping, egg, English, federal, fifteen-cent, fire, flat, fodder, forcing, fort, forwarding, fourth, frame, frat, freight, frog, full, garrison, gin, government, Graham boarding, gray, great, guard, gull, gun, hardware, hash, herd, hide, home, hot, Humboldt, hunting, Indian, inspection, issue, jail, jobbing, ladder, light, line, log, log dwelling, long, mail order, manor, martin, medicine, meeting, ministry, minstrel, molasses, muskrat, musquash, Negro, noon, notion, oil, one-and-a-half story, open, ore, out, overseer(s), oyster, oyster packing, package, packing, palmetto, panel, parlor, passenger, pent-, picket, pigeon, pilot, pine, play, plate, pole, pork, possession, pot, potato, precinct, president's, private boarding, purging, rag, ranch, receiving, relay, rock, rolling, rooming, rough, round, Sabbaday, Sabbath-day, salmon, salt, saltbox, sap, scale, school, scrap, scrape, section, shaft, shake, ship, shuck, skookum, slaughter, smoke, social, sporting, spring, squatter, stage, state, station, steam, store, storm, strong, sugar, sweat, tail, third, tithing, tobacco, tobacco curing, trade, trading, truck, try, upper, wash, Washington, watch, wheel, whipping, whisky, White, wire, work house.**

house burn, *v. intr.* Of tobacco: To become injured by poleburn during the curing process. Also *tr.*

1640 *Md. Archives* 98 Bad Tobacco shall be judged ground leafes Second Crops leafs notably brused or worm eaten or leaves house burnt sun burnt. **1772** *Md. Hist. Mag.* XIV. 363 For 3 weeks past the Weather has been very unfavourable for the tob[acc]o Cured by fier very much & I suppose has House burnt all tob[acc]o not fierd. **1820** *Amer. Farmer* I. 395 If hung too close it will 'house burn' and the leaves drop off from the stalk. **1879** *Bradstreet's* 25 Oct. 1/4 Some of the leading growers report several crops as 'house burnt' and inclined to rot.

house joiner. A carpenter. *Obs.*

1785 WASHINGTON *Diaries* II. 378 One Richd. Boulton, a House joiner and undertaker, recommended to me. **1803** LEWIS in *L. & Clark Exped.* VII. (1905) 288 Among the party from Tennessee is a blacksmith and House-joiner—these may be of service in our present situation. **1852** REYNOLDS *Hist. Illinois* 316 He learned the trade of a house-joiner, or carpenter.

house log. A log for use in building a log house.

1824 in *Mo. Hist. Soc. Coll.* VI. 54 Get a party detailed to cut House logs to build a house for Sutler. *a***1918** G. STUART *On Frontier* I. 263 The nearby mountains furnished an abundance of house logs . . . and soon log houses made their appearance on all sides. **1941** STUART *Men of Mts.* 171 When the corner of the long house log was pulled upon the frame of logs, Wilburn hollered, 'Steady, men, steady!'

house lot. A lot of land suitable for the erection of a dwelling.

1636 *Springfield Rec.* I. 158 It is agreed that no man except Mr. William Pynchon shall have above 10 acres for his house lott. **1703** *Manchester Rec.* 105 One half of a common rite which hous lot is now in the possession of Ezekiell knowlton purcheser. **1885** HOLMES *Mortal Antipathy* Introd., He can add as many acres as he will to the narrow house-lot.

house Negro. Before the Civil War, a Negro slave who worked in the master's house. Now *hist.*

1711 *Boston News-Letter* 21 May 2/2 (*advt.*), A Young House-Negro Wench of 19 Years of Age that speaks English to be Sold. **1880** HARRIS *U. Remus* (1884) 116 Dey er mighty biggity, dem house niggers is, but I notices that dey don't let nuthin' pass. **1945** BOTKIN *My Burden* 107 Then a house nigger come out from Old Mistress on a hoss.

house of entertainment. An inn, tavern, or other house providing accommodations for travelers. Also **house of public** (or **private**) **entertainment,** prob. so called to avoid taxes on inns and taverns. *Obs.*

1638 *R.I. Col. Rec.* I. 55 Will. Balston shall erect and sett up a howese of entertainment. **1671** *Boston Rec.* 58 A house of publique Entertainment for the sellinge of Coffee & Chuchaletto. **1830** *Va. Lit. Museum* 597/1 My friend proposed we should stay all night at a small house of private entertainment in the neighborhood. **1865** *Nation* I. 557, I came to a large white house with several outbuildings. . . . Knowing it to be professedly a house of entertainment, I preferred a request for lodging.

House of Representatives. The lower house of certain colonial and state legislatures and of the U.S. Congress.

1692 *Mass. Acts & Resolves* I. 65 [No] member of the house of representatives . . . shall be chosen to the office of constable. **1775** CUTLER in *Life & Corr.* I. 52 Was in the galleries to hear the debates in the House of Representatives [in Mass.]. **1787** *Constitution* i. § 1 All legislative Powers herein granted shall be vested in a Congress of the United States, which shall consist of a Senate and House of Representatives. **1948** *This Week Mag.* 16 Oct. 38/2 The election would have to be referred to the House of Representatives.

b. (See quot.) *Obs.*

1838 *Representative* (Belleville, Ill.) 20 Jan. 4/1 The legislative powers, wholly rested in the Senate and House of Representatives, styled the Congress of the republic of Texas.

house-raising. A community gathering for assisting a neighbor in erecting a house. Also atrrib.

1704 *Essex Jrnl.* Aug. 29 (Th.), A dispute having arisen between Mr. C. S. and myself, at a house-raising last year, in which we both got warm and angry. **1832** *Polit. Examiner* (Shelbyville, Ky.) 2 June 3/2 What then . . . are we to do? Simply to meet as men do at musters, log-rollings, house-raisings, &c; try the relative strength of these worthy candidates, and agree to unite upon the two strongest. **1948** DICK *Dixie Frontier* 27 He cut logs and notched them, and the house was put up at a house-raising. **1949** *Time* 2 May 22/2 It was just like an old-fashioned house-raising bee, except that it took place in the age of the assembly line and the publicity man.

Houstonia hus'tonɪə, *n.* [Wm. *Houston* (?1695–1733), Eng. botanist.] A genus of American plants of the madder family, also (not *cap.*) a plant of this genus.

1762 CLAYTON *Flora Virginica* 18 Houstonia primo vere ubique florens, floribus infundibuliformibus dilute cœruleis, soliis parvis adversis in caule paucis. **1814** BIGELOW *Florula Bostoniensis* 35 *Houstonia longifolia.* Long leaved Houstonia. . . . Flowers purplish. . . . June, July. **1851** HAWTHORNE *Notebooks* II. 189 The Houstonias seem quite to overspread some pastures, when viewed from a distance. **1932** HARVEY *Wild Flowers Amer.* 69 Large Houstonia (*Houstonia purpurea*), is slightly hairy and its leaves vary from heart-shaped to lance-shaped.

Houstonize 'hjustənˌaɪz, *v. tr.* To beat up (a congressman). In allusion to a beating administered by Sam Houston to Representative William Stanberry, April 13, 1832. *Rare.* — **1837** *Cong. Globe* App. 13 Oct. 326/1 The president pronounced us liars all the way from Washington to the Hermitage, and said here we ought to be Houstonized.

* **how,** *adv.*

1. An interrogative used in asking for the repetition of something not quite understood.

1815 in *Amer. Sp.* XXII. 283 *How?* An interrogative very often used in Kentucky & North Carolina when a person does not distinctly hear or understand what is said to him, for '*what do you say.*' **1879** HOWELLS *Lady of Aroostook* 123, 'I suppose the young men of South Bradfield are both serious and earnest.' 'How?' asked Lydia. 'The young men of South Bradfield.' **1943** in WENTWORTH.

2. *How are you off for* (or *in*) (something), how well supplied are you with (something). *Colloq.*

1776 C. LEE in Sparks *Corr. Rev.* II. 485 How are you off in the article of intrenching tools? **1848** *R.I. Words* (Bartlett MS), 'How are you off for money or anything else' simply meant how much have you.

3. *How come,* (see quot. 1848). *Colloq.*

1848 BARTLETT, How-Come? rapidly pronounced *huc-cum*, in Virginia. Doubtless an English phrase, brought over by the original settlers, and propagated even among the negro slaves. The meaning is, How did what you tell me happen? How came it? **1930** *Sat. Ev. Post* 8 March 12/1 These firms assert blandly to pressmen and journalists who ring them up, wishful to know how come, [that] they have nothing against women.

4. *And how!* a colloq. or slang expression used as an intensive.

1932 J. W. DRAWBELL *Good Time!* xvii. 3 'You mean it, Peggy?' 'And how!'

how haʊ, *interj.* [See quot. 1911, and cf. Sioux *hâo*, Omaha *hau.*] An ejaculation, orig. used by western Indians in a variety of applications (see quots.).

1817 BRADBURY *Travels* 95 We were interrupted by one of the chiefs crying 'How,' signifying amongst the Indians 'Come on,' or 'let us begin.' **1882** STEELE *Frontier Army* (1883) 90, I have seen long conversations carried between very communicative specimens of copper-color and officers of the army, only prefaced by the word 'how' and a most demonstrative and cordial shaking of hands. **1911** *N.Y. Ev. Post* 28 Jan. (Supp.) 3 The expression 'How,' used by army men in giving a toast, is equivalent to the expression, 'Here's to your health.' Some think it is merely the Indian corruption of 'How d'ye do?' abbreviated by the Indian to 'How.' Others believe the expression is derived from the Indian language direct. **1949** *Sat. Ev. Post* 21 May 145/1 This Clevelander, when he came face to face with his first Taos Indian, raised his hand, palm out, and said 'How!'

howel 'haʊəl, *n.* [LG. *höwel*, a plane. See Berghaus, *s.v. hövel.*] (See quot. 1875.)

1805 LEWIS in *L. & Clark Exped.* II. (1904) 140 To be deposited in this cash: . . . some chisels, a cooper's Howel, some tin cups [etc.]. **1870** *Rep. Comm. Patents 1868* II. 447/1 The howel and croze are so combined that the work of both may be done with one tool. **1875** KNIGHT 1138 *Howel.* (Coopering.) A plane with a convex sole, used for smoothing the insides of barrels and casks.

howeling 'haʊəlɪŋ, *n.* The action of smoothing with a howel. Also attrib.

1847 *Rep. Comm. Patents 1846* 339 What I claim therein as new . . . is the attaching the howeling, crozing, and chamfering cutters. **1850** *Ib. 1849* 386, I also claim the apparatus for chamfering and howelling and crozing. **1870** *Ib. 1868* 447/1 The howeling tool . . . may be used without the croze.

huajillo wɑ'hijo, *n. S.W.* [Amer. Sp. *guajillo* (dim. of *guaje* f. Nahuatl), the name of a kind of acacia and of various other plants.] (See quot. 1937.)

1905 BRAY *Sotol Country in Texas* 21 On the eastern border of the sotol country . . . huajillo and Parkinsonia texana give the vegetation aspect in places where one would expect the sotol and lechuguilla. **1932** *Ariz. Agric. Exp. Sta. Bul.* 141, 24 The more valuable of these are . . . blue and green canutillo or Mormon tea, . . . catsclaw, and huajillo or fairy duster. **1937** PARKS *Valuable Plants Texas* 57 *Pithecolobium brevifolium* Benth. Gulf Coast Guajillo . . . must not be confused with the prairie Guajillo. *Ib.* 45 *Acacia Berlandieri* Benth. Guajillo. The most famous honey plant of Texas. **1949** *Nature Mag.* April 165 Down around Uvalde, in Texas, they boast they have the best honey in the world—that's made from cat's-claw and huajillo.

Hualapai, *n.* See **Wallapi.**

huaracho wɑ'rɑtʃo, *n.* Also **huarache.** [Amer. Sp. *huarache, guaracho*, etc., in same sense.] A form of sandal.

1892 *D.N.* I. 190 huaracho, -s: a kind of sandals worn by Indians and the lower classes generally. Used generally in the plural only. **1894** *Scribner's Mag.* May 604/1 He complacently wears the sandals, or 'guarachis,' which so many of his neighbors still affect. **1948** *Ariz. Republic* (Phoenix) 29 Feb. II. 1/1 He stopped to remove a small rock from his guaraches.

***hub**, *n.*

1. The State House at Boston, Mass., or the city itself, thought of as being the center of culture and progress. Often *cap.* and in phrases, as *Hub of the Solar System* (or *Universe*, etc.). Cf. **Hubbite.**

1858 HOLMES *Autocrat* vi. 143 Boston State-House is the hub of the solar system. **1862** F. MOORE *Rebellion Rec.* V. II. 600 One might imagine as he left the metropolis and journeyed eastward toward the 'Hub of the Universe,' he were going away from the action of the centrifugal forces to where the people never went off in tangents, or got excited. **1860** *Charleston* (S.C.) *Mercury* 15 Nov. 3/2 Boston assumes to be the intellectual 'hub' of the republic, if not of 'creation.' **1948** *New Yorker* 25 Sep. 55/1 Boston hopes to regain its old position as Hub of the Universe by having a World Series between the Braves and the Red Sox.

b. Applied to places other than Boston. Also **hub city.**

1833 *Harper's Mag.* July 263/1 Cincinnati is 'the hub of the universe.' **1887** *Courier-Journal* 8 May 5/3 Take Massachusetts, the 'hub' of free schools, free labor, and boasted intelligence, as a fair representative. **1949** *Sat. Ev. Post* 16 April 24/1 The citizens of nearly every hub city, or zenith city, or queen city must sometimes be upset by the outsider's inability to understand the importance of their community in the cosmic scheme.

2. hub-deep, *a.* Of mud: So deep that a wheel will sink in it up to the hub. *Colloq.*

[**1814** in *Amer. Sp.* XXII. 274 Up to the hub—deep in anything.] **1833** S. SMITH *Major Downing* 192 The longer horses and waggons stand knee and hub deep in mud, the less able they'll be to git out on 't. **1897** H. PORTER *Campaigning with Grant* xxvi. 415 The mud was nearly hub-deep.

3. *From hub to tire,* completely, entirely. *Colloq.*

1899 E. E. HALE *Lowell & Friends* 161 In the war the magazine was loyal from hub to tire.

Hubbard squash. A well-known dark-green or golden-yellow winter squash.

1868 *Mich. Agric. Rep.* VII. 349 Thos. Smith, Hamtramck, [exhibited] 8 Hubbard squashes. **1919** CADY *Rhymes of Vt.* (1923) 100 To raise a head of Hubbard squash. **1948** *Fargo* (N.D.) *Forum* 28 Sep. 2/1 A giant hubbard squash was the pride of the youngsters at the Children's hospital.

Hubbardston ˈhʌbərdstən, *n.* [See quot. 1849.] A well-known winter apple of superior quality. Also **Hubbardston nonesuch.**

1846 B. ALCOTT *Journals* 176, I set out six apple trees. . . . They were Hubbard Stone, Nonesuch, Bell Flower, and Hood's Early Sweeting. **1849** *N. Eng. Farmer* I. 25 The Hubbardston Nonsuch is one of our best late fall apples. . . . Origin, Hubbardston, Mass. **1895** A. BROWN *Meadow-Grass* 211 The Hubbardston, a portly creature—quite unspoiled by the prosperity of growth, and holding its lovely scent and flavor like an individual charm.

Hubbite ˈhʌbaɪt, *n.* A Bostonian. *Colloq.*

1868 *N. Eng. Base-Ballist* 6 Aug. 1/3 In the evening the 'Hubbites' were entertained in a handsome manner by the victors. **1881** *Detroit Free Press* 22 Sep. 6/2 The lively Wolverines again compelled the Hubites to engage in leather hunting today, this being the last game of the Boston series. **1905** *Chi. D. News* 19 July 6/2 It is a long and thorny path the Hubites will have to travel to overtake the Naps.

***hubbub,** *n.* A noisy game somewhat like dice, played by Indians in colonial New England (see quot. 1887). Now *hist.*

1634 WOOD *N. Eng. Prospect* II. xiv. 85 The Indians . . . have two sorts of games, one called *Puim*, the other *Hubbub*, not much unlike Cards and Dice, being no other than Lotterie. **1764** HUTCHINSON *Hist. Mass.* I. 470 Another game they call hubbub, the same the French called jeu de plat, the game of the dish among the Hurons. **1887** *N. & Q.* 11 June 472/2 Hubbub was a game played by the Indians . . . which was accompanied by a continual shouting of 'Hub-hub!' or 'Hubbub!' **1935** DOW *Every Day Life* 110 The Indians indulged in similar sports and played 'hubbub,' a game resembling dice, with much shouting of 'hub, hub, hub,' accompanied by slappings of breasts and thighs.

hubbly ˈhʌblɪ, *a.* [Prob. a var. of Eng. dial. *hobbly*, but cf. Du. *hobbelich, hobblig*, as possible source of Amer. borrowing.] Rough, uneven. *Colloq.* Cf. next.

*a***1870** CHIPMAN *Notes on Bartlett* 206 *Hubbly.* Said of the surface of ice on roads and streams. . . . N[ew] E[ngland]. **1896** *N.Y. Wkly. Witness* 23 Dec. 4/1 Where the snow had been swept off the ice by the wind, some places were hubbly. **1903** *Springfield W. Republican* 9 Oct. 8 Stumbling as over a hubbly field. **1949** *Consumer Rep.* Jan. 8/1 Pick out a hubbly surface or a 'washboard' gravel road . . . and keep your eye on that nifty plastic hood ornament.

hubby ˈhʌbɪ, *a.* =prec. *Colloq.* — **1848** BARTLETT 183 *Hubby.* Applied to rough roads, particularly when frozen; as, the road is hubby. In the Craven Dialect of England the word hobbly is applied to rough or stony roads. **1889** *Oregonian* (Portland) 16 Dec. 5/1 The ground was too rough or 'hubby' to make driving pleasant, and out in the country the mud was not frozen hard enough to bear a horse or wagon.

huckleberry ˈhʌklˌberɪ, *n.* [See note.]

App. a variant of ***hurtleberry.** Usu. regarded as an Americanism but G. C. Druce, *Flora of Bucks* (1927), regards it as a Buckinghamshire expression brought here early by those who settled Woburn, Mass.

1. The fruit or berry of any one of various species of *Gaylussacia*, esp. *G. baccata;* the bush or shrub which produces this.

1670 DENTON *Brief Descr. N.Y.* (1937) 4 The Fruits natural to the Island, are Mulberries, Posimons, Grapes great and small, Huckelberries. **1775** CRESSWELL *Journal* 98 Rode up to the Laurel Mountain with some Young Girls to get Huckleberries. They are the same as our Bilberries, only grow in clusters. **1807** JANSON *Stranger in Amer.* 281 A feast is prepared of dog's flesh, boiled in bear's grease, with huckleberries. **1948** *Country Gentleman* May 175/2 He brought us dewberries, huckleberries and wild gooseberries.

2. *fig.* A small amount, degree, or extent. *Colloq.*

1832 PAULDING *Westward Ho!* I. 182, [I once got] within a huckleberry of being smothered to death. **1839** *Spirit of Times* 27 July 247/1 (We.), A Moose hunt is an affair just a huckleberry over any American Field Sport short of Buffalo hunting. **1920** BOK *Americanization* 165 He always kept 'a huckleberry or two' ahead of his readers.

b. A person, esp. one of no consequence. *Slang.*

[**1835** *Vade Mecum* (Phila.) 22 Aug. 2/4 Orson, the wild man of the woods is nothing to him—not a circumstance—not a huckleberry.] **1868** *N. Eng. Base-Ballist* 3 Sep. 17/1 Now then, my huckleberry, look sharp! you're wrong! **1889** BARRERE-LELAND I. 479 'Liger just got in his chariot, cut 'er loose, and flew. Dat's wot kind of a huckleberry 'Liger was. **1906** F. LYNDE *Quickening* 199 You know the whites—Welshmen, Cornishmen, and a good sprinklin' o' 'huckleberries.'

3. In combs.: (1) **huckleberry apple,** =**swamp apple;** (2) **bush,** any one of various American shrubs or bushes of the genus *Gaylussacia;* (3) **heaven,** an imaginary place of perfect bliss; (4) **johnnycake,** (see quot. and cf. **johnnycake**), *rare;* (5) **oak,** an oak or species of oak, *Quercus vaccinifolia*, found in the West; (6) **pie,** a pie made of huckleberries; (7) **pudding,** a pudding made of huckleberries; (8) **road,** a road upon which a huckleberry train *q.v.* operates; (9) **train,** a train that makes poor time, allegedly because of frequent stops to permit passengers to pick huckleberries, *humorous.*

(1) *a***1862** THOREAU *Cape Cod* vii. (1894) 155 That kind of gall called Huckleberry-apple. — **(2) 1846** THORPE *Myst. Backwoods* 182 [A 'cat'] instantly leaped to the ground from a height of over forty feet, . . . throwing a sort of rough somerset, and then starting off as sound in limb and wind as if he had leaped off a 'huckleberry bush.' **1947** COFFIN *Yankee Coast* 6 The huckleberry bushes were in full scarlet cry of the ending year. — **(3) 1856** W. G. SIMMS *Eaton* 403 He'll make as good a husband for the gal as she'll find 'twixt here and huckleberry heaven. — **(4)** *c***1880** T. R. HAZARD *R. I. Jonny-Cake P.* (1888) 41 The huckleberry jonny-cake, . . . to be first rate, must be made half and half of meal and fresh gathered ripe berries.

(5) 1921 HALL *Yosemite Nat. Park* 128 At about the 6000-foot contour . . . the golden oak becomes replaced by the dwarf huckleberry oak. **1947** PEATTIE *Sierra Nevada* 142 Sometimes dwarf forms of such trees as huckleberry oak, buckeye, and California laurel take over completely. — **(6) 1775** FITHIAN *Journal* II. 68 We have . . . boil'd potatoes, & huckleberry-pie. **1867** G. W. HARRIS *Sut Lovingood* 120 Yu cud onkiver a huckleberry pie wif a case-knife. **1947** *Mazama* Sep. 1/1 Smell that turkey, those roasting ears, and the huckleberry pies? — **(7) 1828** NEAL *R. Dyer* 210 You'll never eat another huckleberry-puddin' in this world. **1857** UNDERHILL & THOMPSON *Elephant Club* 235 His complexion bore a close resemblance to the outside of a huckleberry-pudding. — **(8) 1871** *Harper's Mag.* Oct. 799/2 A gentleman . . . took the train a few days since on what is termed 'the huckleberry road,' running between Avon and Mount Morris. **1891** *N.Y. Herald* 7 April 7/5 High Tammany officials seem to be much interested in the 'Huckleberry Road.' — **(9) 1881** MARSHALL *Through Amer.* (1882) 65 Should you be travelling by a 'huckleberry train,' or one that stops at every station, the chances are you are liable to have your ticket examined pretty frequently. **1901** MERWIN & WEBSTER *Calumet 'K'* xv. 296 You'd have thought he was running a huckleberry train from the time he took.

b. Designating places or regions where huckleberries abound, as (1) **huckleberry bog,** (2) **cut,** (3) **hill,** (4)

island, (5) **land,** (6) **pasture,** (7) **patch,** (8) **plantation,** (9) **slash,** (10) **swamp.**

(1) **1888** MUIR *Picturesque Calif.* 6 You will be delighted with the . . . translucent purple and crimson of huckleberry bogs. — (2) **1856** DAVIS *Farm Bk.* 23 Planted cotton in the Huckleberry cut, then the Beach Homack. — (3) **1749** *N.H. Probate Rec.* III. 751 The Remender . . . is to be Made up from the Marked pine tree on the fare Huckellberry hill streght to the head of Allon Andorsons uper Meadow. **1865** WHITTIER *Poetical Works* (1895) 404/1 Dread Olympus at his will Became a huckleberry hill. — (4) **1682** *Topsfield Rec.* 40 An Iland Caled hocellbarey Iland.

(5) **1751** J. BARTRAM *Observations* 13 The land hereabouts is middling white oak and huckleberry land. **1941** DANIELS *Tar Heels* 54 Just up the road in Sampson in huckleberry land they used to say you could tell the ages of the children by the blue rings around their legs. — (6) **1854** LOWELL *Writings* I. 70 The greater part of what is now Cambridgeport was then (in the native dialect) a 'huckleberry pastur.' **1878** STOWE *Poganuc People* xiv. 157 Widder Brown . . . lives up by the huckleberry pastur'-lot. — (7) **1855** *Shasta Courier* (Redding, Calif.) 3 Nov., All that is necessary is to clear the way through a level, timbered country as far as the 'Huckleberry Patch' at the head of Shasta Valley. **1947** *Mazama* Sep. 2/1 An easy 10 mile round trip over a good trail to the largest huckleberry patch we've ever seen. — (8) **1868** *N.Y. Herald* 20 July 4/2 Mr. Hill gave an exposition of the principles and purposes of the republican party, as understood among the 'huckleberry plantations.' — (9) **1699** in *Amer. Sp.* XV. 275/1 One Tract of land . . . binding upon a Huckleberry Slash. *c*1729 W. BYRD *Hist. Dividing Line* (1866) I. 58 Betwixt this and Edenton there are many thuckleberry Slashes, which afford a convenient Harbour for Wolves and Foxes.

(10) **1636** in *Amer. Sp.* XV. 275/1 Along a great swamp called Huckleberry Swamp. **1833** E. T. COKE *Subaltern's Furlough* xxvi, My steed, which having served a long apprenticeship, carried me safely through the huckleberry swamps and forests. **1939** HARRIS *Purslane* 118 The men cut across the huckleberry swamp straight toward the Sally Baker woods.

Also *huckleberry county, district, field, knob, point, pond, region, season*, etc.

c. In colloq. phrases: (1) *As thick as huckleberries*, very thick; (2) *to be one's huckleberry*, to be particularly suited or adapted to one; (3) *to get the huckleberry*, to be laughed at, to incur ridicule.

(1) **1833** S. SMITH *Major Downing* 167 Congressmen . . . we shall have them here as thick as huckleberries. — (2) **1881** HAYES *New Colorado* v. 68 The first words that we heard him speak settled his nationality, for . . . he sententiously remarked, 'Hi'm 'is 'uckleberry.' **1908** LORIMER *J. Spurlock* 72 If she were looking for a kind, considerate, thoughtful husband . . . you were her huckleberry. — (3) **1883** *Cent. Mag.* June 280/2 He got the huckleberry, as we used to say in college, on that particular text.

For phrases involving "huckleberry" and "persimmon" see **persimmon.**

As the last term in **bear, black, blue, box, choke, hairy, squaw, sugar, swamp, tree, winter huckleberry.**

huckleberrying ˈhʌklˌbɛrɪ·ɪŋ, *n.* The seeking or gathering of huckleberries; an outing for this purpose.

1779 T. B. HAZARD *Nailer Tom's Diary* (1930) 9/2 Went ahuckling Berring. *c***1845** *Big Bear Ark.* 103 Who went blackberryin and huckleberryin with me? **1884** ROE *Nature's Story* 336 A party of children who were out huckleberrying on the mountain were separated from home by the swollen brook. **1943** *L.A.* Map 671.

huddup ˌhʌdˈʌp, *interj.* [?Var. of "get up."] Get up! A word of command to a horse. *Colloq.* — **1858** HOLMES *Poetical Works* (1895) 160/1 'Huddup!' said the parson.—Off went they. **1891** COOKE *Huckleberries* (1896) 329 Huddup, Whitey!

***Hudson,** *n.*

1. *attrib.* In the names of various plants and birds (see quots.).

1784 J. SMYTH *Tour U.S.* II. 129 There are seven different kinds of tobacco, particularly adapted to the different qualities of the soil on which they are cultivated, and each varying from the other. They are named Hudson, Frederick [etc.]. *a***1817** DWIGHT *Travels* I. 43 The *Hudson Strawberry* is the sweetest of all the fruits which bear this name. **1882** E. K. GODFREY *Nantucket* 241/2, I have met with the following specimens . . . Hudson Curlew (*Numenius Hudsonicus*). **1916** SETON *Woodcraft Man.* 318 It is well known in the winter woods of eastern America up to the Canadian region where the Brown-capped or Hudson Chickadee takes its place.

2. Hudson Dusters, a gang of New York City rowdies and criminals. *Slang.* Now *hist.*

1928 FOY & HARLOW *Clowning Through Life* 165 Regular gang organizations grew up among the hoodlums, and they could have given pointers to New York's Dead Rabbits or Hudson Dusters. **1943** *Chi. D. News* 12 June 6/2 Exploited Pennsylvania produced its Molly Maguires . . . New York had its Hudson Dusters, its Monk Eastmans and now its 'muggers.'

Hudsonia hʌdˈsonɪə, *n.* [After Wm. *Hudson* (1730?–93), an English botanist.] A genus of tufted or matted shrubs of the rockrose family with showy yellow flowers, common in sandy or rocky soils in eastern North America. Also (not *cap.*) a plant of this genus. Cf. **beach heather, poverty grass.**

1845 LINCOLN *Botany* 112/2. **1864** THOREAU *Cape Cod* 20 A moss-like plant, *Hudsonia tomentosa* . . . called 'poverty-grass,' because it grew where nothing else would. **1942** TEHON *Native Ill. Shrubs* 206 The Woolly Hudsonia is a shrub of sandy regions and in them is distributed from New Brunswick to Manitoba and south to North Carolina and North Dakota.

Hudsonian hʌdˈsonɪən, *a.*

1. In the names of birds (see quots. and cf. next).

1858 BAIRD *Birds Pacific R.R.* 744 *Numenius Hudsonicus.* Short-billed or Hudsonian Curlew. . . . Atlantic and Pacific coasts of North America. **1887** RIDGWAY *Man. N. Amer. Birds* 564 *P[arus] hudsonicus* Hudsonian Chickadee. **1948** *Chi. Tribune* 25 June 16/3 The rare bristle-thighed curlew looks much like the Hudsonian curlew, which is common along the shores of the South Atlantic states.

b. Esp. **Hudsonian godwit,** the American black-tailed godwit, *Limosa haemastica.*

1835 AUDUBON *Ornith. Biog.* III. 726 The Hudsonian Godwit. *Limosa Hudsonica,* . . . is scarcely ever found farther south along the coast than the State of Maryland. **1874** COUES *Birds N.W.* 494 *Limosa Hudsonica,* Hudsonian or Black-tailed Godwit. **1942** Nat. Pk. Service *Fading Trails* 157 The Barren Grounds is the breeding country for Hudsonian godwits.

2. Designating, or with reference to, the life-zone next above the Canadian. Cf. **Canadian zone.**

1871 *Harvard Mus. Comp. Zool. Bul.* II. 401 The Hudsonian Fauna doubtless embraces outlying islands of the Canadian Fauna, as the upper part of the White Mountains, and the summits of some of the higher peaks in the Adirondacks. **1894** *Nat. Geog. Mag.* 29 Dec. 236 The distinctive temperatures of the three Boreal Zones (Arctic, Hudsonian and Canadian) are not positively known. **1940** *Mt. Hood Guide* 11 The heaviest timber growth is in the Canadian and Hudsonian zones, between 2,000 and 4,000 foot altitude. **1948** *Sierra Club* (So. Calif. Chap.) *Sched.* 127, 93 Do you know what a Hudsonian Island is?

hudsonite ˈhʌdsnˌaɪt, *n.* =**cortlandtite.** — **1842** BECK *Min. N.Y.* 405 Hudsonite . . . was found by Dr. Horton in a vein of quartz. **1868** DANA *Min.* (ed. 5) 216 Aluminous Iron-Lime Pyroxene; Hudsonite.

***Hudson River.** *attrib.* (See quots.) — **1842** *Nat. Hist. N.Y., Zoology* IV. 322 The Hudson-river Sea-horse. *Hippocampus hudsonius.* . . . We believe that the animals of this genus stand alone among the fishes, in having a prehensile tail. **1862** *Rep. Comm. Patents 1861: Agric.* 167 We are told that on the Hudson river fields are planted with a variety of the Red Antwerp, which has received its American cognomen from that stream, the Hudson River Red Antwerp. **1894** *Chi. Record* 1 May 13/2 Connecticut shad are regarded by many as a much more delicious fish than either the Hudson river shad or its Potomac river prototype.

***Hudson's Bay.** Also ***Hudson Bay.**

1. *attrib.* Designating birds and animals found in the region about Hudson's Bay.

1826 GODMAN *Nat. Hist.* II. 138 The Hudson's Bay Squirrel . . . is very common in the northern and western parts of this Country. **1839** PEABODY *Mass. Birds* 402 The Hudson Bay Titmouse, *Parus Hudsonicus,* . . . has been found . . . in Brookline. **1855** in SCHMIDT *Briefe* 146 Die gefrässige *Wolverene* (Gulo luscus), auch Quick-hatch und Hudsonsbai-Bär genannt, lebt an der altantischen Küste bis zu sehr hohen Breiten hinauf.

2. In the names of articles sold by the Hudson's Bay Company.

1888 SHERIDAN *Memoirs* I. 61 The fugitive was armed with only an old Hudson's Bay flint-lock horse-pistol which could not be discharged. *a***1918** G. STUART *On Frontier* I. 241 We bought four fine Hudson's Bay shirts from him @ $3.00 each. **1949** *Sat. Ev. Post* 19 March 25/1, I was dressed in the height of style—golf knickers and a red Hudson's Bay jacket.

huero ˈwero, *n. S.W.* [Sp. in Amer. Sp. sense shown here.] (See quots.)

1847 RUXTON *Adv. Mexico* 43 (Bentley), From the caprice of human nature, the guero is always a favorite of the fair sex. **1929** DOBIE *Vaquero* 50 (Bentley), In person he was a huero, or red-complexioned man. **1932** BENTLEY *Sp. Terms* 147 Huero English modification guero. . . . A person of fair or 'sandy' complexion and light or red hair.

***hug,** *n.* As the last term in **close, death, Indian hug.**

huge paw.

1. A man who has large hands, hence a common working man, a farmer. Often *pl.* and *cap.*

Daniel Webster was app. the originator of this expression. See quot. 1842 in the first group of citations below.

(1) [**1834** *State Advocate* (Vandalia, Ill.) 19 Oct. 3/3 We shall endeavor to enlarge our paper to the size of the 'Huge Paw' of the Boston Courier. **1838** *Quincy* (Ill.) *Argus* 1 Dec. 3/1 A farmer with his Huge Paw on the statute book, what can he do? As well might a blacksmith attempt to mend a watch as a *farmer to legislate*. **1842** *Wasp* (Nauvoo, Ill.) 1 Oct. 2/1 Daniel Webster had stated that the farmer ought not to put his Huge Paw on the statute book.]

(2) **1839** *Eastern Argus* (Portland, Me.) 24 Sep. 2/3 (Th.), How do you account for this, Mr. Huge Paw? **1844** *Quincy* (Ill.) *Herald* 19 April 2/2 Mr. Woodson, . . . in a long speech endeavored to show to the 'huge paws' of Pike that they must have a U.S. Bank, a high tariff, &c. **1923** POAGE *Henry Clay & Whig Party* 24 Ewing is with & of the people—the huge paws—as well as the monied interest of the Country have confidence in him.

b. Hence **huge-pawed boys,** some of the frontiersmen and backwoodsmen of Illinois. *Obs.*

1847 T. FORD *Hist. Illinois* 88 Since the butcher knife has been disused as an article of dress, the fashion has been, to call this class of people 'the bare-footed boys,' 'the flat-footed boys,' and 'the huge-pawed boys.'

2. Huge Paws, (see quot. 1848). Now *hist.*

1846 *N.Y. Herald* 7 Oct. (B.), The huge paws ought to have another meeting at Tammany Hall before they make their nominations. **1848** BARTLETT 183 Huge Paws, a nickname given to the working-men of the Loco Foco party in New York. **1941** A. W. READ in *Sat. Review* 19 July 3/2 On March 11, 1840, the Locofoco newspaper, the New York *New Era*, listed the clubs as follows—the Butt Enders, the Tammany Temple, the Indomitables, the Huge Paws (named for their symbol, a muscular arm grasping a hammer).

hug-me-tight ˈhʌgmɪˌtaɪt, *n.*

1. A close-fitting knitted vest or jacket worn by women.

1860 *Godey's Lady's Bk.* Dec. 544 Hug me tight. A garment to be worn under a cloak. **1910** *N.Y. Ev. Post.* 24 Dec. (Supp.) 3 Hug-me-tights and mittens, all knit at home by grandmother. **1943** *Time* 4 Oct. 6/7, I take off my hat to any female who has the fortitude to wear one of those zebra-striped hug-me-tights.

2. A buggy having a narrow seat barely sufficient for two passengers, in full **hug-me-tight buggy.** *Colloq. Obs.* or *hist.*

1901 HARBEN *Westerfelt* 6, I seed 'em takin' a ride in his new hug-me-tight buggy yesterday. **1902** ——— *A. Daniel* 42 He's got a new buggy—a regular hug-me-tight. **1948** *Amer. Folk-Lore* April–June 212 Those roads were so bad . . . that they kept making the buggies narrower and narrower. . . . Some of them got so narrow they used to call them 'Hug-Me-Tights.'

huisache wiˈsɑtʃe, *n.* [Amer. Sp. (<Nahuatl) in same sense.] A thorny shrub, *Acacia farnesiana*, found in the tropical parts of the U.S. Cf. **cassie.**

1838 TEXIAN *Mexico vs. Texas* 231 The rose-geranium shook its elegant perfume, and the yellow-bloomed *guisache* embalmed the air with odours equal to those of the blossoms of the grapevine. **1892** *D.N.* I. 190 *Huisache* (also *huaji, guaje*): a small tree or shrub with very sweet smelling yellow flowers (*Acacia Farnesiana*). From Mexican *huaxin*. Texas. **1941** FERGUSSON *Southwest* 55 Now and then a lone huisache sprays scent from its wide and lacy tent of bloom. **1949** *Boston Sun. Globe* 1 May (Fiction Mag.) 3/2 He discovered another rider sitting his horse in a clump of huisache north of the trail.

hula ˈhulə, *n.* [Hawaiian.] A native Hawaiian dance performed by women. Usu. **hula hula,** and attrib.

1868 *Terr. Enterprise* (Virginia, Nev.) 29 Aug. 3/1 We have borne ourselves with calm fortitude at a Sandwich Island *hula-hula*. **1894** *Concord* (Calif.) *Sun* 17 March 1/5 The hula-hula dancers filled amply their carriages. **1894** *S.F. Midwinter Appeal* 24 Feb. 1/1 She called in the leading American citizens and danced the hula hula until the police closed the place. **1948** *Chi. D. Times* 17 Jan. 12/1 Oh, anybody can do the hula.

Hull hʌl, *v.*[1] *tr.* To defeat, in allusion to the surrender of Detroit to the British by Gen. Wm. Hull (1753–1825), during the war of 1812. *Obs.* — **1812** *Conn. Courant* 22 Sep. (Th.), Should Gen. Dearborn enter the territory, he ought, if he means not to be Hull'd, or defeated, to have 25 or 30,000 men. **1814** *N.Y. Herald* 30 March (Th.), With the paltry force now marching . . . we shall most certainly get Hull'd.

∗**hull,** *v.*[2] *tr.* (See quots.) Cf. **hulled corn 2.** — **1859** BARTLETT 398 To Shell Corn. To remove the grains of Indian corn from the cob. In the South the phrase 'to hull corn' is used in the same sense. *a***1870** CHIPMAN *Notes on Bartlett* 398 *To Shell Corn.* . . . In the South, and in the North, too, the phrase 'to hull corn' is used in the same sense.

hulled corn.

1. (See quot. 1877.)

1788 *Mich. Hist. Coll.* XI. 556 Q. What did he pay for these Goods. A. Two thousand Wampum, two & a half bushels of huld corn [etc.]. **1877** BARTLETT 302 *Hulled Corn.* Indian corn scalded or boiled in lye, until the hulls come off. It is then rinsed and boiled, making a most palatable dish. **1904** WALLER *Wood-Carver* 136 Twiddie rushed in with . . . a bowl of fresh hulled-corn. **1944** JOHNSON *As I Dare* 7 Only in parts of New England do beans and brown bread come always for Saturday supper. . . . Hulled corn is peculiar to Massachusetts.

b. Also **hull-corn man,** a vendor of hulled corn. *Rare.*

1922 CADY *Rhymes* (1926) 40 The hull-corn man will come next week.

2. Corn that has been shelled from the cob. Cf. ∗**hull,** *v.*[2]

1948 *Reader's Digest* Sep. 110/2 He . . . threw it into Mother's big kettle of hulled corn.

hull-gull ˈhʌlˌgʌl, *n.* (See quot. 1899.) *Colloq.* — **1833** GREENE *Dod. Duckworth* I. 30 There was no obstruction to the pleasant games of . . . hull-gull. **1899** GREEN *Va. Word-Book* 195 Hull-gull, *n.* A guessing game for children. One player takes a number of chinkapens in his closed hand, saying '*hull-gull*.' Another says: 'Hand full.' Then the first says: 'How many?' The other player then guesses at the number, taking all if the guess is correct, otherwise making up the discrepancy. They play alternately.

Hull's Victory. A dance named in honor of Captain Isaac Hull (1773–1843) in commemoration of his victory in the U.S.S. "Constitution" over the British ship "Guerriere" on Aug. 19, 1812. *Obs.* — **1891** WELCH *Recoll. 1830–40* 376 At the balls and parties the popular figures in dancing, were the 'Contra Dances,' viz. . . . 'Hull's Victory,' 'Triumph' [etc.].

∗**human,** *n.* In combs.: (1) **human chattelism,** slavery, *obs.;* (2) **fly,** one who engages in spectacular climbing; (3) **scab,** (see quot.).

(1) **1855** *Kans. Free State* (Lawrence) 24 Sep. 4/1 They proclaim their purpose to curse Kansas with human chattleism, and defy any and every opposition. **1875** *Scribner's Mo.* 275/2 The system of human Chattelism does not enter here. — (2) **1919** *Alameda* (Calif.) *Times-Star* 11 Jan. 1/3 Besides being a 'Human Fly,' Williams has other unusual accomplishments. **1948** *So. Sierran* Jan. 2/3 Walking like human flies up the vertical trail to the ski lodge atop Mt. Abel, the group settled for a frozen food lunch. — (3) **1869** *Overland Mo.* III. 131 Then there is another phrase, 'human scabs,' for money.

humbird ˈhʌmˌbɜd, *n.* =**hummingbird 1.**

1634 WOOD *N. Eng. Prospect* I. viii. 28 The Humbird is one of the wonders of the Countrey, being no bigger than a Hornet. **1806** *Mass. Spy* 1 Jan. (Th.), Rattlesnakes are frequent and humbirds common in New England. **1891** COOKE *Huckleberries* (1896) 167, I never see a humbird fuller o' buzz.

humble-come-tumble. An admirer or beau. *Humorous.* — **1806** T. G. FESSENDEN *Orig. Poems* 139 Her humble-cum-tumble. . . . Who loves her so well he could eat her. **1898** HARRIS *Tales* 134 As long as I'm in town, with nothin' much to prey on my mind, I might as well drop in an' tell her I'm still her humble-come-tumble.

humbo ˈhʌmbo, *n.* [Origin obscure.] (See quots.) *Colloq.*

The Ling. Atlas (map 307) lists from Webster, N.H., a word for thick maple syrup that would app. be written *larbo* or *larbow*. The informant who supplied the form is described, however, as "not entirely trustworthy."

1895 GERARD in *N.Y. Sun* 30 July, Humbo, a name in New Hampshire for maple syrup, cited by the Boston *Commonwealth* as an Indian word. **1907** HODGE *Amer. Indians* I. 578 Humbo. A New Hampshire word for maple syrup. Horatio Hale sought to bring it into relation with *ombigamisige* in Chippewa and closely related Algonquian dialects, a term signifying 'he makes the maple syrup boil' or 'boiled sugar drink,' the chief element being the radical *omb*, 'to boil.' **1947** *Amer. Sp.* XXII. 307 *Humbo* is a New Hampshire word for maple sirup, from the Algonquian radical *omb*, to boil.

∗**Humboldt,** *n.* **1. Humboldt house,** (see quot.), app. so called from the Humboldt River in Nevada. *Obs.* **2. Humboldt's lily,** a lily, *Lilium humboldti*, found in California.

(1) **1869** MARK TWAIN *Innocents Abroad* 286 We built a Humboldt house. It is done this way. You dig a square in the steep base of the mountain, and set up two uprights and top them with two joists. Then you stretch a great sheet of 'cotton domestic' from the joists to the ground; this makes the roof and front of the mansion; the sides and back are the dirt walls your digging has left. A chimney is easily made by turning up one corner of the roof. — (2) **1888** LINDLEY *Calif. of South* 330 Humboldt's [lily], the greatest of all, must be looked for in open glades of the Sierra Madre foot-hills.

humdinger ˈhʌmˈdɪŋɚ, *n.* [Origin obscure.] A person or thing of superior excellence. *Slang.* — **1916** BOWER *Phantom Herd* vi. 100 That pit'cher's a humdinger! **1943** LYON *And So to Bedlam* 16 But whoever thought them up is a humdinger.

*** humility,** *n.* In New England, any one of various kinds of snipe, prob. so called because of their teetering or bowing habit, but cf. quot. 1917.

1634 W. WOOD *N. Eng. Prospect* (1635) 26 The Humilities or Simplicities (as I may rather call them) bee of two sorts, the biggest being as big as a greene Plover, the other as big as birds we call Knots in England. **1832** WILLIAMSON *Hist. Maine* I. 149 The *Humility* [*Tringa interpres*] has long yellow legs, long neck, is gray spotted, . . . and is nearly as large as a pigeon. **1870** *Amer. Naturalist* III. 638 Black-necked Stilt . . . is well known to the gunners of Ipswich, who occasionally meet with it, and by whom it is ironically named 'Humility.' **1917** *Birds of Amer.* I. 247 And yet this forward creature has been nicknamed 'Humility,' because it probes for worms in the humble mud in the intervals between the periods when it lifts up the voice on high.

*** hummer,** *n.* = **hummingbird 1.**

Quot. 1871 is in error. The mango hummingbird is not *Trochilus colubris* but *Anthracacothorax mango*, nor does it occur in the U.S.

1871 DE VERE 377 The tiny *Mango* Humming-bird (*Trochilus colubris*) . . . [is] known familiarly . . . as *Hum-bird* or *Hummer* simply. **1874** COUES *Birds N.W.* 269 The Hummers constitute a very large family of very small birds. **1898** *N.Y. Observer* 14 July 34/2 Today I saw one of the 'old-gold hummers' have a fight with one of our common hummers. **1948** *Pacific Discovery* March–April 14/2 Both species of hummer have been known to nest and rear their families in the court or nearby.

hummingbird ˈhʌmɪŋˌbɜd, *n.*

1. Any one of various American birds of the family Trochilidae, noted for their small size and brilliant plumage.

1632 T. MORTON *N. English Canaan* 50 There is a curious bird to see to, called a hunning [*sic*] bird, no bigger than a great Beetle; that out of question lives upon the Bee, which he eateth and catcheth amongst Flowers. **1763** in W. ROBERTS *Nat. Hist. Fla.* 101 Of their feathered kind are the curosoe, the maccow, the quam, and humming-bird. **1874** COUES *Birds N.W.* 270 Wilson knew but one North America Humming-bird. . . . In 1872 I was able to recognize eleven species. **1949** *Nat. Geog. Mag.* Aug. 232/2 We thought of 'snappin' turkles,' but it was a hummingbird.

transf. **1854** TROWBRIDGE *M. Merrivale* 1 The winter of calm judgment had not yet come to chill and drive away those bright-winged humming-birds of fancy.

b. hummingbird moth, (see quot. 1899).

1850 S. F. COOPER *Rural Hours* 202 The whole tribe of hawk-moths are now sometimes called humming-bird moths, from these same insects. **1899** *Animal & Plant Lore* 63 Humming-bird moth, any large sphinx moth, family *Sphingidæ*. General in the United States. **1936** *Univ. Ariz. Gen. Bul.* 3, 118 The striped humming bird moth with its oblique red and white bars on its wings may be seen any evening flitting over the petunias.

2. In the names of flowers: (1) **hummingbird sage,** the crimson sage, *Ramona grandiflora*, of the western states; (2) **-'s dinner-horn,** a species of Penstemon, *P. centranthifolius*, having long tubular flowers attractive to hummingbirds; (3) **-'s trumpet,** (see quot. 1909).

(1) **1911** RICHTER *Honey Plants Calif.* 1021 *Salvia spathaceae* Greene. Humming Bird Sage. Crimson Sage. **1947** *So. Sierran* May 4/2, I had been especially impressed by the Hummingbird Sage, deep crimson in hue. — (2) **1914** SAUNDERS *With Flowers & Trees* 117 The bees have no monopoly on its sweets, for upon it hummers levy special tribute—a fact that has given rise to another pretty name, hummingbird's dinner-horn. — (3) **1888** LINDLEY *Calif. of South* 332 A type of faithfulness, a tiny shrub, blooms through every month in the year, *Zeuschneria* [*sic*], the 'humming-bird's trumpet.' **1909** *Cent. Supp.* 603/1 Humming-birds' trumpet. Same as *California fuchsia*.

As the last term in **Anna, black-chinned, broad-tailed, calliope, purple throat, Rivoli, ruby-throated hummingbird.**

*** hummock,** *n.*

1. A tract of land somewhat higher than an adjacent marsh, swamp, creek, etc., and usu. well wooded. Cf. *** hammock.**

1589 in FRIEDERICI (1947) 303/2 It is all of plaine lande, and full of trees and certaine woodie homocks, and among them certaine heapes of sand. . . . In the mouth of the river of S. Peter and S. Paul are two homockes of white sand. **1635** *Boston Rec.* 9 There stands 3 homocks, with pyne trees upon the south side of the marsh neare the water. **1669** in *Amer. Sp.* XV. 270/1 Includeing into these bounds two Humocks of trees & marish adjoyneing, ye one Humock Commonly known by ye name of Oake Island, the other by ye name of pond Island. **1766** in DARLINGTON *Mem. Bartram & Marshall* 438, I thrice visited the River St. John, often landed upon each shore, exploring the swamps and hummocks, pine barrens, and sand barrens. **1883** C. F. ADAMS in *Prince Soc. Pub.* XIV. 11 Tradition still points out a small savin-covered hummock . . . as his [an Indian's] subsequent dwelling-place. **1945** *Reader's Digest* Oct. 36/1 On every hummock, fear-crazed poisonous snakes struck and writhed among the survivors.

2. *W.* A portion of land, usu. inferior in fertility, higher than the surrounding prairie.

1869 *Overland Mo.* III. 130 There is the 'chocolate' prairie, . . . the 'hummock,' (yielding principally small honey-locusts) and the 'wire grass.' **1919** L. F. CODY *Buffalo Bill* 325 Below can be seen . . . the hills of Colorado and hummocks of Wyoming.

3. hummock land, = **hammock land.** Cf. **river hammock land.**

1812 STODDARD *Sk. Louisiana* 123 Hummock land . . . rises in tufts or small mounts among the pines. **1883** SMITH *Geol. Survey Ala.* 21 These Second Bottom deposits, or hummock lands, are always above overflow, and vary in thickness from sixty feet and upwards in the central parts of the State, to less than ten near the gulf. **1939** *L.A.* Map 30.

*** hump,** *n.*

1. In a switchyard *q.v.*, an artificial mound down which cars run by gravity to appropriate tracks.

1901 *Railroad Gaz.* 4 Jan. 2/1 All that was necessary to take advantage of this mode of distributing cars, was to put a 'hump' in the switching track. **1906** DROEGE *Yards & Terminals* 104 It is now a common proceeding to throw up humps on a level prairie or even bottoms and make a gravity yard. **1949** *Chi. Tribune* 24 June III. 4/8 Many of the railroads own their yards—some with humps and some without.

2. hump rib, in a buffalo, a rib immediately adjacent to the hump. Also transf.

1834 in *Ore. Hist. Soc. Quart.* XVII. 126 The tongue, the heart, the marrow bones and the hump ribs is all they use when meat is plenty. **1848** BRYANT *California* vii. 96 The choice pieces of a fat cow, are . . . the hump-ribs; and . . . the 'marrow-gut.' **1850** GARRARD *Wah-To-Yah* ix. 123 Perchance astonishing with the recital of the number of 'Yutes' whose 'humpribs' have been savagely tickled.

3. *To get a hump on,* to hurry. *Colloq.*

1892 *Harper's Mag.* Feb. 487/2 'We went fast enough then.' 'We do seem to be gittin' a leetle less hump on oursel's than we did then.' **1940** WILSON *Wabash* 231 'Let's git a hump on, Allen,' Abe said; and the two boys dipped their oars deeper into the brown water.

*** hump,** *v. tr.* and *intr.* To hurry or hasten; to put forth one's best efforts. Usu. with *it*, or reflexively. *Colloq.*

*c***1845** *Big Bear Ark.* 126 He was breathin' sorter hard, his eye set on the Governor, humpin' himself on politics. **1884** MARK TWAIN *H. Finn* xxix. 307, I never hunted for no back streets, but humped it straight through the main one. **1908** LORIMER *J. Spurlock* v. 92 Back to Broadway for yours, Ferdinand, and hump yourself. **1923** *D.N.* V. 211 *hump*, v. To hurry. 'I'll shore have t' hump m'se'f if I git thar on time.' [Mo.]

transf. **1882** BAILLIE-GROHMAN *Camp in Rockies* 57 'That yar white powder as makes bread git up and hump itself,' as an old trapper called it. **1896** *N.Y. Wkly. Witness* 2 Dec., Would make the liver hump and get, This sulphur and molasses.

*** humpback,** *n.*

1. Any one of various whales of the genus *Megaptera*. In full **humpback whale.**

1725 DUDLEY in *Phil. Trans.* XXXIII. 258 Both the Finbacks and Humpbacks are shaped in Reeves longitudinal from Head to Tail on their Bellies and their Sides. . . . The Bunch or humpback Whale is distinguished from the right Whale, by having a Bunch standing in the Place where the Fin does in the Finback. **1832** WILLIAMSON *Maine* I. 164 Such [whales] as we now see, are the *Humpback*, which are the most common, . . . severally yielding from 15 to 25 barrels of oil. **1868** *N.Y. Herald* 1 July 9/3 Of fish oils the sales were very light . . . humpback whale at 80¢.

2. A species of salmon, *Oncorhynchus gorbuscha*. In full **humpback salmon.**

1881 *Amer. Naturalist* XV. 177 The fact that the hump-back salmon runs only on alternate years in Puget sound . . . is well attested. *Ib.* 182 The hump-back, taken in salt water about Seattle, shows the same peculiarities. **1891** *Fur, Fin, & Feather* 151 The salmon most plentiful in the Alaska waters is known as the humpback or garbusche. **1945** *Md. Conservationist* 8/1 There are five species of Pacific salmon: . . . the coho or silver salmon; the humpback or pink salmon.

3. (See quot.)

1911 *Rep. Fisheries 1908* 318 The common whitefish . . . is found in the Great Lakes region and is known as 'humpback,' 'bowback,' and 'highback' whitefish.

* **hump-backed,** *a.* In the names of fishes and whales (see quots. and cf. * **humpback,** *n.*).

1807 tr. GARYTSCHEV *Voyages* 28 We managed . . . to lay in a stock for ourselves of the hump-backed salmon, and other such fish. **1816** *Niles' Reg.* X. 199/1 On the 26th of March, two hump-backed whales were killed and caught by the crew of two boats. **1884** GOODE *Fisheries* I. 323 The Blunt-nosed Shiner . . . is a frequent summer visitor all along the coast as far north as Wood's Hole, Massachusetts, where it has a peculiar name . . . the 'Hump-backed Butterfish.' **1896** JORDAN & EVERMANN *Check-List Fishes* 241 *Xyrauchen cypho.* Razor-back Sucker; Hump-backed Sucker.

humper ˈhʌmpɚ, *n.* [f. * **hump,** *v.*] A thing which "humps" or goes along at a rapid clip. *Colloq.* Cf. **squaw humper.** — **1895** *Columbus* (O.) *Dispatch* 27 March 1/3 We were coming along on time. Engine 586 is a humper, and Rankin, my fireman, was keeping her hot.

* **hunch,** *n.* A hint, an intuitive premonition. *Slang.* — **1899** ADE *Fables in Slang* (1902) 123 She didn't know how to make a Showing, and there was nobody in Town qualified to give her a quiet Hunch. **1947** *Sat. Ev. Post* 15 March 16/3 The prediction was based upon a mystical, or seat-of-the-pants, hunch.

* **hundred,** *n.* In phrasal combs.: (1) *hundred-and-sixty,* a tract of land containing one hundred and sixty acres; (2) *hundred-percenter,* one who is volubly, often offensively, patriotic, hence *hundred-percentism;* (3) *hundred-yard red-eye,* an esp. fiery brand of cheap liquor, cf. * **forty rod.**

(1) 1945 M. JAMES *Cherokee Strip* 3 His whole hundred-and-sixty was under fence, and a good half of it broken and in crops. — **(2) 1928** *N.Y. Observer* 4 March 13/2 Perhaps New York is not the place for the Hundred-per-centers. I certainly never met any. *Ib.* 8 April 8/2 He is really another victim of hundred-per-centism. — **(3) 1856** *S.F. Call* 25 Dec. 1/1 Then I came up, and felt as if I had been drinking 'hundred-yard red-eye'; and dragged through a hole as big as nothing.

As the last term in **five, four hundred.**

* **Hungarian,** *a.*

1. Hungarian grass, Italian millet, *Setaria italica,* valued as fodder when cut young. Also attrib.

1861 *Ill. Agric. Soc. Trans.* IV. 319 Hungarian grass is a sure preventive. **1863** *Mich. Statutes* I. (1882) 447 Fifty pounds for a bushel of millet or Hungarian grass seed. **1901** MOHR *Plant Life Ala.* 135 Cattail millet, Hungarian grass and the so-called Johnson grass . . . furnish green forage and hay crops throughout the summer.

2. Hungarian partridge, a name given the European partridge, *Perdix perdix,* introduced into, and now widely established in, the U.S. and southwestern Canada.

1913 *Conn. State Geol. & Nat. Hist. Survey* Bul. 20, 184 As the majority brought to the United States came from Hungary, this bird has become commonly known as the Hungarian Partridge. **1947** *Collier's* 29 March 92/2 The true European partridge does exist in this country; but it is known as the Hungarian partridge.

hunk hʌŋk, *n.*[1] and *a.* [Du. *honk,* LG. *hunk,* "home," in a game.]

1. *n.* (See quots.)

1848 BARTLETT 185 *Hunk.* (Dutch, *honk.*) A goal, or place of refuge. A word much used by New York boys in their play. **1891** *Amer. Folk-Lore* IV. 222 Tag is sometimes rendered more complicated by certain places which are called 'hunks' or 'homes' being agreed upon where the players may find refuge when closely pursued.

2. *a.* In a safe place, all right, "hunky-dory." *Colloq.*

1847 FIELD *Drama in Pokerville* 50 Well, I allow you're just *hunk,* this time, then. **1856** *N.Y. Tribune* 30 Dec. (B.), Now he felt himself all hunk, and wanted to get this enormous sum out of the city. **1903** LEWIS *Boss* 181 'Do you approve my proposition?' . . . 'The proposition's all hunk.' **1949** *Boston Globe* 12 June (Fiction Mag.) 2/4 Suppose I show you how to get hunk with the cheapskates?

Hunk hʌŋk, *n.*[2] [LG. "Ein ungeschliffener Mensch" (Berghaus).] (See quots. and cf. **bohunk,** *n.,* **hunky,** *n.*) *Slang.* — **1896** *N.Y. Herald* 13 Jan. 3/4 The average Pennsylvanian contemptuously refers to these immigrants as 'Hikes' and 'Hunks.' The 'Hikes' are Italians and Sicilians. 'Hunks' is a corruption for Huns, but under this title the Pennsylvanian includes Hungarians, Lithuanians, Slavs, Poles, Magyars and Tyroleans. **1898** *Cent. Mag.* 811 The other foreigners are grouped under the inelegant name 'Hunks.'

Hunker ˈhʌŋkɚ, *n.* [Prob. from **hunk,** *n.*[1] as is more clearly indicated under Old Hunker *q.v.* But see quot. 1888 below.]

1. *pl.* Conservative Democrats, esp. those who in New York politics opposed the Barnburners *q.v.* Now *hist.*

1843 in WEED *Autobiog.* 553 Let the 'Hunkers' and 'Barn-burners' contend. **1849** *N.Y. Ev. Post* 11 July (B.), He is now the leader of the hunkers of Missouri. **1888** M. LANE *Pol. Catch-Words* 15 Hunkers.—A division of the New York Democracy that arose in opposition to Governor Wright in his disagreement with President Polk. . . . By sharp management the administration faction packed the state convention and nominated a complete ticket for their faction; or, as a Wright man said, took the whole 'hunk.' From this expression they took the name of 'Hunkers.' **1909** *N.Y. Ev. Post* 1 Nov., In 1847, Tammany, weakened by the factional fight between Hunkers and Barnburners, was defeated by the Whig candidate. **1944** HOLTON *Yankees* 124 The town wasn't strictly speaking solidly Republican, for there were a few Democrats, we called them Hunkers.

b. Also **Hunker Democrat, majority.** *Obs.*

1848 *Whig Almanac 1849* 9/1 At the Syracuse Convention . . . one of the last acts was the laying on the table by the Hunker majority a resolution proposed by the Barnburners. **1855** *N.Y. Wkly. Tribune* 20 Jan. 1/4 Its election so triumphantly is a great victory of the friends of Freedom over the factious efforts of the Silver-Gray Whigs and Hunker Democrats. **1884** R. GRANT *Average Man* 225, I'm a Hunker Democrat, and Stoughton's a Dyed-in-the-wool Republican.

2. (not *cap.*) A conservative, an old fogy. Also transf. *Colloq.* Cf. **hunkerish,** *a.*

1900 *Cong. Rec.* 1 Feb. 1408/1 There has never occurred a change for the higher and better forms of life without arousing the hostility of some . . . conservative hunker, who will prate of those fairer and better days of old. **1932** *N.Y. Times* 9 Nov. 18/4 To show that New Ashford is no hunker, one vote was given to the Socialist and one to the Communist candidate for Governor.

Hence **Hunkerdom,** *n. Obs.*

1855 *N.Y. Wkly. Tribune* 3 Feb. 1/6 Although this Territory is comparatively new, there is as much genuine Hunkerdom or old fogyism as one will find in any portion of our Union. *Ib.* 21 April 4/1 The religious Germans are either Catholics, and so, inclined to Hunkerdom, or Lutherans, with proclivities for Free-Soilism.

hunker-chunker road. (See quot.) *Colloq. Obs.* — **1870** MACRAE *Americans* II. 170 Another variety of sensation is enjoyed in a swampy region, on what are called 'Corduroy roads,' which consist of logs or trunks of trees laid transversely and close together, and which are distinguishable as Hickety-crickety or Hunker-chunker roads, according to the thickness of the logs.

hunkerish ˈhʌŋkərɪʃ, *a.* [f. **Hunker,** *n.*] Conservative, old-fashioned, slow. *Colloq.* — **1857** *Lawrence* (Kans.) *Repub.* 2 July 3 This has in times past, been considered rather a hunkerish neighborhood. **1905** *Springfield W. Republican* 8 Sep. 1 Intelligent forward movements in legislation are met and hampered by the hunkerish conservatism which Mr. Cannon and the Senate stand for.

Hunkerism ˈhʌŋkɚˌɪzəm, *n.* The political philosophy of the Hunkers, extreme conservatism. *Obs.* Cf. **Old Hunkerism.**

1843 *Western New Yorker* (Rochester, N.Y.) 23 Oct. 1/4. **1847** *Semi-Wkly. News* (Fredericksburg, Va.) 21 Oct. 2/2 But for . . . the cunning Hunkerism in the 'democratic party,' . . . this overwhelming Whig majority . . . would be shown in every election. **1865** S. ANDREWS *South Since War* (1866) 186 The cold hunkerism of this people, however, stands immovably in his way, and gives him [*sc.* the Negro] little chance.

Hunkpapa ˈhʌŋkˌpɑpə, *n.* [f. a native expression of uncertain meaning. See Hodge.] A small warlike tribe or division of Teton Sioux of which Sitting Bull was the best-known chief.

1823 in *So. Dak. Hist. Coll.* I. 210 On the 28th came to where two bands of the Sioux Indians, the Sciones and Akkpapat had pitched their lodges. **1937** HYDE *Red Cloud's Folk* 82 Part of the Miniconjous and Hunkpapas were hunting buffalo west of the Black Hills. **1942** SANDOZ *Crazy Horse* 6 The others were the Minneconjou, Hunkpapa, No Bow, Two Kettles, and Blackfoot.

attrib. **1825** in *Treaties Between U.S. & Indian Tribes* (1837) 351 The United States agrees to receive the Hunkpapas band of Sioux into their friendship.

hunky ˈhʌŋkɪ, *n.* Also **Hunky.** [Poss. an extension of **Hunk,** *n.*[2], but cf. **bohunk.**] An unskilled or poorly skilled laborer of foreign birth, esp. a Hungarian. *Colloq.* or *slang.*

1910 *Sat. Ev. Post* 3 Sep. 18/1 Almost every . . . Hunky or Dutchman who lands in New York has in his 'kick,' or wallet, the written address of some boarding-house. **1916** C. SANDBURG *Chi. Poems* 25 The hunky and his wife and the kids. **1948** *Sat. Review* 31 July 5/3 There are chapters on Bayou French, Ozark hillbillies, Navajo Indians, Milwaukee Hunkies, and Minnesota lumberjacks.

hunky ˈhʌŋkɪ, *a.* [?f. **hunk,** *a.*] Fine, first-rate, all right, usu. **all hunky.** *Slang.*

1861 ARTEMUS WARD in *Vanity Fair* 15 June 273/1 He (Moses) folded her to his hart, with the remark that he was 'a hunkey boy.'

1894 Mark Twain *Those Twins* vii, We're all hunky, after all. **1902** Harben *A. Daniel* 242 It's all hunkey, an' my opinion is that it'll never be wuth less. **1910** *Sat. Ev. Post* 16 July 15/3, I want to get hunky with the Sanitary boss.

hunky-dory ˌhʌŋkɪˈdorɪ, *a.* [Origin unknown. See quot. 1930.] Fine, quite satisfactory. *Colloq.*

1868 in Odell *Annals N.Y. State* VIII. 390 [Even Samuel Slater admitted that Tostee, when and if she sang] was hunky-dory. **1930** Wittke *Tambo & Bones* 185 'Josiphus Orange Blossom,' a popular song with many disconnected and futile stanzas, in a reference to Civil War days, contained the phrase, a 'red hot hunky dory contraband.' The Christy's made the song so popular, that the American public adopted 'hunky dory' as part of their vocabulary. **1948** *Chi. D. News* 26 March 3/1 The election that's supposed to 'make everything 100 per cent hunky-dory again' approaches.

* **hunt,** *n.*

1. In the fur trade, the pelts, etc., secured by hunting. *Obs.*

1813 Luttig *Journal* 118 We found him shot in the Belly and Breast his hunt laid a little ways off. **1849** McLean *Notes* I. 171 In the course of the winter five Indians came in with their 'hunts' and agreeably to their usual practice encamped close by.

2. hunt club, a club composed of those interested in hunting. Also attrib.

1886 Lodge in *Cent. Mag.* July 342/1 In Livingston county, New York, in the valley of the Genesee, from which it takes its name, there is a hunt-club. **1894** *Harper's Mag.* June 157/1 He is working on the Hunt Club ball committee. **1895** *Cent. Mag.* Aug. 625/1 Hitherto the hunting has been done individually. Now hunt clubs are being formed. **1928** *Amer. Mercury* Sep. 69/2 The prisoners regained composure and washed themselves in the manner of men at a hunt club. **1949** *Life* 4 July 74/2 A mule . . . embarrassed the horsy set half to death by winning the jumper classic of the Camp Carson Hunt Club.

3. hunt sergeant, in Massachusetts in colonial times, one in charge of hunts, carried on with dogs, for hostile Indians. *Obs.*

1706 *Prov. Mass. Bay Acts* (ed. Goodell) I. 599 Persons who shall . . . have them [hounds] at all times in readiness to attend the hunt serjeant.

As the last term in **bear, beaver, bee, camp, cattle, circle, coon, cow, fall, fire, gold, gospel, jack, man, meat, mustang, pigeon, possum, raccoon, ring, self, snipe, spoon, squirrel, still, tallow hunt.**

* **hunt,** *v.*

1. *tr.* To seek (land) suitable for settling upon. *Obs.* Cf. **land hunter, land hunting.**

1767 Washington *Writings* II. (1889) 222 Any person, therefore, who neglects the present opportunity of hunting out good lands . . . will never regain it. **1818** Fordham *Narr. Travels* 221 The next day I shall cross the Little Wabash to 'hunt land.' **1834** *Visit to Texas* i. 10 An old Tennessean and his wife with their sons . . . were going 'to hunt land' as the familiar term is for exploring new regions, for a place to form a settlement.

2. *To hunt one's bed* (or *blanket*), to retire, go to bed. *Colloq.*

1891 Ryan *Told in Hills* 309 All were sleepy enough to hunt beds early. **1903** A. Adams *Log Cowboy* iii. 38 Flood . . . suggested that all hands hunt their blankets and turn in for the night.

* **hunter,** *n.*

1. Short for "bee hunter." *Obs.*

1830 Ray *Letter*, Our hunter brings us plenty of honey, which he gets from the 'honey-trees.' **1887** *Cent. Mag.* Jan. 443/1 The hunters set out shortly after breakfast, Mr. Wimpy, besides his professional tackle, carrying the biggest bucket for the spoil.

2. In combs.: (1) **hunterman,** a huntsman, *colloq.;* (2) **Hunters' Association,** (see quot. and cf. **Hunters' Lodge**), *obs.;* (3) **hunter's case,** of a watch, a hunting case, *rare;* (4) **Hunters' Lodge,** an organization, or one of its branches, formed in Vermont in May, 1838, to aid in securing the independence of Canada after the failure of the rebellion of 1837, *obs.;* (5) **Hunters of Kentucky,** the people of Kentucky, in allusion to a song of this title written by S. Woodworth and brought into popularity during the War of 1812, *rare;* (6) **hunter spider,** a tarantula.

(1) 1891 Mark Twain *Slovenly Peter* 12 (R.), Behold the dreadful hunterman, In all his fateful glory stand! **1933** *Amer. Sp.* Feb. 50/1 Hunterman, n. Hunter. One often sees this in country newspapers. (Cf. Charles A. Cummins, Springfield, Mo., *Press*, Nov. 18, 1931, p. 7). Comparable to jewellerman, groceryman, etc. — **(2) 1846** F. Wyse *America* I. 232 And which soon after gave birth to a society, or organization of American citizens, along the entire northern frontier, under the name of the *'Hunters' Association'*; with branches in the several States. — **(3) 1890** Trowbridge *Kelp-Gatherers* 80 It had a hunter's case, which, if it had so far kept it from being broken, would probably preserve it still. — **(4) 1849** W. Brown *America* 51 When the Rebellion was raging in Canada, caused mainly by the emissaries from the States, the sympathisers in the various cities bordering upon that country formed themselves into lodges, called Hunters' Lodges, of which there was one in Cleveland.

(5) 1888 Norton *Reminiscences* 33 The 'Hunters of Kentucky' will be found true to the great Whig party of the Union — **(6) 1867** *Amer. Naturalist* Oct. I. 409 This very large hunter-spider makes its appearance in Texas some years as early as the twenty-fifth of May.

As the last term in **bear, beaver, bone, bug, cattle, coon, cow, crust, ditch, fire, fur, gold, hide, horse, Indian, jack, land, long, market, moose, muskrat, mustang, Osage, pie, pocket, prairie, prairie-dog, raccoon, scalp, skin, snake, spoils, squirrel, still, turkey hunter.**

* **hunting,** *n.* In combs.: (1) **hunting bag,** a bag carried by a hunter for his shot, powder, etc.; (2) **boat,** a boat used by hunters, esp. by those engaged in fur hunting, *obs.;* (3) **cow,** (see quot.), *rare;* (4) **dance,** a dance indulged in by Indians in connection with hunting, *obs.;* (5) **expedition,** an expedition for the purpose of hunting, *obs.;* (6) **frock,** = **hunting shirt,** *obs.;* (7) **jacket,** = **hunting shirt,** *obs.*, cf. **deerskin hunting shirt;** (8) **knife,** see as a main entry; (9) **path,** a path made or followed by hunters; (10) **rifle,** a rifle designed for use by hunters; (11) **right,** the right or permission to hunt over a particular region, *obs.;* (12) **root,** angelica, the odor of which, the Indians thought, attracted deer, *rare;* (13) **shirt,** see as a main entry; (14) **snow,** a snow which makes hunting more successful, *obs.;* (15) **trail,** = **hunting path,** cf. **Osage hunting trail;** (16) **voyage,** = **hunting expedition,** *rare;* (17) **wagon,** a light wagon suitable for use by a hunter.

(1) 1790 David Zeisberger *Diary* II. (1885) 131 At his side were his tobacco-pouch, fire-tongs, pipe, and knife, his hunting-bag and powder-horn. **1836** Crockett *Exploits* 131 She placed it in his hunting bag. — **(2) 1828** *Western Mo. Rev.* I. 577 In autumn the passengers of the hunting boats . . . saw him. — **(3) 1936** Crissey *A. Legge* 43 Eventually the wild geese and ducks became more cautious. Then the boys trained a 'stalking cow' to permit them to shoot over its back. This was then [*c*1885 in Wisconsin] a common practice; nearly every large ranch had one or more of these 'hunting cows.' — **(4) 1846** Farnham *Prairie Land* 345 Their hunting-dances are no more seen at evening!

(5) [**1703** Lahontan *New Voyages* II. 84 This great Calumet is likewise made use of by the Confederate Savages, that demand Passage thro' the Country of their Allies . . . in pursuance of Warlike or Hunting Expeditions.] **1801** A. Mackenzie *Voyages* 45 We . . . found three men, three women, and two children, who had been on an hunting expedition. **1846** Sage *Scenes Rocky Mts.* xii, A hunting expedition that included my self with six others. — **(6) 1794** in *Amer. Pioneer* II. 222 Dressed in a hunting frock, breechcloth and leggins. **1835** Hoffman *Winter in West* I. 257 A tall backwoodsman, in a fringed hunting-frock, was stretched on several chairs. **1870** O. Optic *Field & Forest* 287, I had dressed myself in my best clothes, discarding forever my hunting frock and skin cap. — **(7) 1857** Strother *Virginia* 61 Hunting-jackets have a rowdy look, so Miss Minnie thinks. — **(9) 1820** in *Minn. Hist.* XXIII. (1942, Sep.) 249 On the evening of the third day we found to our inexpressible joy, a hunting path which our guides told us led directly to Sandy Lake. **1821** Nuttall *Trav. Arkansa* 167 The cane brake . . . we here crossed by a hunting path.

(10) 1856 in *Kans. Hist. Coll.* IV. 504 The marauders were well armed with muskets, and Sharps carbines, hunting rifles, revolving pistols, bowie-knives, etc. **1886** Roosevelt in *Outing* March 615 No hunting-rifles in the world possess greater accuracy. — **(11)** [**1721** in *Mich. Hist. Coll.* XXXIII. 672 M. de La Mothe thinks he has good reason for asking for the concession of all Detroit . . . together with the hunting, fishing and trading rights.] **1762** *Huntington Rec.* II. 450 [We] do fully & absolutely give . . . unto them the said trustees . . . all the Soyl Right Planting and Hunting right and all the remainder. — **(12) 1687** Clayton *Va.* in *Phil. Trans.* XLI. 157 And I have since learned from others, that the [Virginia] Indians call it the Hunting-root. — **(14) 1824** Doddridge *Notes* 61 Hunting snows usually commenced about the middle of October.

(15) 1840 *Knickerb.* XXVIII. 419 For years I hung upon their hunting-trails, sometimes hundreds of miles from the most western settlement. **1843** N. Boone *Journal* (1917) 192 Followed until 2 O'clock the great Osage hunting trail until it left the waters of the creek. — **(16) 1805** *Ann. 9th Congress* 2 Sess. 1102, I set off . . . in company with a party of young Indian men, . . . on a hunting voyage, and to procure horses. — **(17) 1854** *Pa. Agric. Rep.* 98 Quinn & Palmer . . . for neat hunting wagon.

b. Designating regions frequented by hunters, as (1) **hunting ground,** see as a main entry, (2) **land,** (3) **place,** (4) **range,** (5) **swamp.**

(2) **1745** BRAINERD *Journal* (1902) 104 It was supposed a great part of their [*sc.* Indians'] hunting lands was much endangered, and might speedily be taken from them. — **(3) 1648** ROGER WILLIAMS *Letters* (1874) 157 They hope you will not countenance him to rob Ninigret of those hunting places which the commissioners gave him to make use of. **1775** ADAIR *Indians* 346 They scouted off . . . to the hunting place, both for their own security, and to give the alarm. — **(4) 1886** Z. F. SMITH *Kentucky* 7 This region was known as the common park, or hunting range.

(5) **1648** *Portsmouth Rec.* 39 To have 30 acres of lande . . . by the huntinge swampe. **1707** *Cambridge Prop. Rec.* 257 The Ninth Squadron is a tract of Land called hunting Swamp.

c. Designating headquarters or temporary abodes of Indians engaged in hunting, as (1) **hunting cabin,** (2) **quarters,** (3) **town.** All *obs.* Cf. **hunting camp, hunting house,** as main entries.

(1) **1751** J. BARTRAM *Observations* 23 We lodged within about 50 yards of a hunting cabin, where there were 2 Men, a Squaw and a child. **1760** CROGHAN *Journal* 109, I met three Indians who informed me that the Deputys I sent from Fort Pitt had passed by their hunting Cabin Eight days agoe. — **(2) 1697** *Md. Hist. Mag.* XV. 116 Their time of moving to their hunting Quarters was in June. **1714** *N.C. Col. Rec.* II. 140 Ye same [land] is reserved for hunting Quarters for some of ye Tuskurora Indyans. — **(3) 1608** SMITH *Works* (1884) I. 18 The next night I lodged at a hunting town of Powhatams. **1751** GIST *Journals* 69, [I] encamped on the SW Side about 1 M from a small Hunting Town of the Delawares from whom I bought some Corn.

As the last term in **bear, beaver, bee, candle, cow, crust, fall, fire, gold, horse, Indian, jack, land, moose, porgy, possum, raccoon, snipe, still, timber hunting.**

hunting camp. The temporary headquarters of a party of hunters, esp. Indian hunters.

1751 GIST *Journals* 71 We lodged at a hunting Camp of an Indian Captain named Oppaymolleah. **1808** PIKE *Sources Miss.* 44, [I] dispatched Miller and Huddleston to the lower hunting-camp. **1929** McCLINCHEY *Joe Pete* 76 One day he stopped in to ask her if she would go over to the hunting camp and clean it.

hunting ground. A region over which hunting is carried on; esp. *pl.*, the areas over which Indians roamed in search of game.

[**1656** VAN DER DONCK in *N.Y. Hist. Soc. Coll.* 2 Ser. I. 198 In the fall and winter, when venison is best, they (Indians) retire to the woods and hunting grounds.] **1710** in *Amer. Sp.* XV. 275/1 The Wyanokes . . . bought all ye Hunting Ground from thence to the mouth of Roanoke River. **1825** KEATING *Exped. St. Peter's River* I. 173 The hunting grounds of the Potawatomis appear to be bounded on the north by the St. Joseph. **1946** FOREMAN *Last Trek* 135 They had moved over into their hunting grounds in Iowa. **1949** *Tenn. Hist. Quart.* March 3 The Indians of the Five Civilized Tribes used Middle Tennessee as a common hunting ground.

As the last term in **happy, Indian hunting ground.** See also **Pawnee, Rocky Mountain hunting grounds.**

hunting house. A hunting cabin.

1608 SMITH *Works* (1884) I. 22 In certaine olde hunting houses of Paspahegh we lodged all night. **1765** ROGERS *Acct. N. Amer.* 247 The Indian hunting houses are generally but the work of half an hour at the most. **a1817** DWIGHT *Travels* II. 21 It was called his hunting-house because he spent the summer here in hunting.

hunting knife. A large, strong knife suitable for a hunter's use.

1803 in *Minn. Hist.* XXI. (1940, June) 126 When the defendant came to pierce his tent with his hunting knife . . . the larger part of the goods had already been moved to the spot agreed upon. **1884** *Cent. Mag.* Oct. 803/2 Northern and Southern soldiers were alike in their fondness for hunting-knives and revolvers. **1946** *Sears Cat.* 609 4½-inch Hunting Knife. Saber ground. Keen-edged. **1949** *Chi. Tribune* 22 June II. 1/4 A policeman took a 6 inch hunting knife from the waist of one of the white boys.

hunting shirt. A long, loose, coatlike frock often made of deerskin and ornamented with fringe. Now *hist.* Cf. **deerskin hunting shirt.**

1774 in PEYTON *Adv. Grandfather* (1867) 132 Providing myself, Charles and Annetta with good rifles . . . ammunition and Indian dresses, consisting of hunting shirts, buckskin leggins and moccasins. **1842** *Amer. Pioneer* I. 274 The hunting shirt . . . was made of dressed buckskin, and in the same way ornamented with the fringe down the outside of the arms, around the collar, cape, belt and tail. **1949** *Canadian Alpine Jrnl.* May 32 The leader of the expedition described himself in a cream buckskin hunting shirt.

attrib. **1775** FITHIAN *Journal* II. 31 This town in arms. All in a hunting-shirt uniform & bucks tale in their hats. **1835** HOFFMAN *Winter in West* II. 183 There is a group of the white beaver and hunting shirt gentry collected at this moment around a blood-horse, whose points a groom is showing off. **1838** J. McDONALD *Biog. Sketches* 187 This short pathetic speech, found its way to the sympathetic hearts of his leather-hunting-shirt comrades.

b. In an exclamatory phrase. *Rare.*

1824 *Free Press* (Halifax, N.C.) 17 Sep., Bobtails and hunting shirts! you are a set of d——d ignorant fellows.

Hunting shirt or rifle coat

Also **hunting-shirted,** *a.*, clad in a hunting shirt.

1833 *Knickerb.* I. 310 A shout of irrepressible joy . . . was instantly responded to by a body of hunting-shirted soldiers.

Huntington root. A coarse variety of beet, mangel-wurzel. *Obs.* — **1788** *Amer. Museum* IV. 100/2 Mr. Laurens has now growing at Mepkin plantation upwards of 1600 plants of the Huntington (or scarcity) root, all in flourishing condition. *Ib.* 436/2 The Huntingdon (or scarcity) root.

Hupa ˈhupə, *n.* [f. a native word of doubtful meaning.] *pl.* and *collect.* "An Athapascan tribe formerly occupying the valley of Trinity r., Cal., from South Fork to its junction with the Klamath, including Hupa valley" (Hodge).

1853 SCHOOLCRAFT *Indian Tribes* III. 139 The lower Trinity tribe is, as well as the river itself, known to the Klamaths by the name of Hoopah. **1872** *Overland Mo.* Aug. 157/1 The Hoopas closely resemble the Cahrocs in *physique.* **1903** JAMES *Indian Basketry* 53 On the lower Trinity River are the Hupas, the main reservation being in the Hoopa Valley. **1924** CURTIS *N. Amer. Indians* XIII. 16 For transportation the Hupa had cedar canoes purchased from the Yurok.

In full **Hupa Indians.**

1885 *Rep. Comm. Indian Affairs* 6 It would be a benefit not only to the Government but to the Hoopa Indians, if their reservation were abandoned. **1948** *Amer. Folk-Lore* Oct.–Dec. 348 The Hupa Indians of northwestern California have a great variety of non-mythical narratives which they are fond of telling.

* **hurdy,** *n. attrib.* Short for hurdy-gurdy, or hurdy-gurdy house *qq.v. Colloq.*

1870 *Boise* (Ida.) *Statesman* 22 Oct. 3/3 What is the reason Ada county does not collect her hurdy licenses? **1894** *S.F. Midwinter Appeal* 7 Jan. 1/4 For some time the old hurdy joint down at Forks Flat has been the only place where a miner could enjoy social life after a hard days' work. *Ib.* 19 May 3/3 Leaving the hurdy-house . . . we struck out to see the sights.

* **hurdy-gurdy,** *n.*

1. *W. Mining.* A water wheel operated by the impact of a stream of water on its radially-placed paddles. In full **hurdy-gurdy wheel.** *Obs.*

[**1868** *Alta California* (S.F.) 11 Jan. 2/5 The water swept into the old 'hurdy' headquarters, and riddled the building of floor-beams, etc., depositing a large quantity of mud and rock in the same.] **1871** RAYMOND *3d Rep. Mines* 86 An eight-stamp mill, run by a 'hurdy-gurdy' wheel 8 feet in diameter, using 75 inches of water under a pressure of 75 feet. **1882** *47th Congress* 1 Sess. H.R. Ex. Doc. No. 216, 628 The actuating power of the derrick is, generally, a hurdy-gurdy. This is a peculiar kind of impact wheel made to utilize water under high pressure.

2. =hurdy-gurdy house.

1876 BOURKE *Journal* 8 Sep. 22 Close by these were 'hurdy-gurdys,' where the music from asthmatic pianos timed the dancing of painted, padded, and leering Aspasias. **1926** J. BLACK *You Can't Win* xv. 216, I put in the winter investigating the cheap dives, hurdy-gurdies, and dance halls.

attrib. **1863** *Gold Hill* (Nev.) *News* 2 Dec. 3/1 A girl belonging in one of the hurdy gurdy establishments was on C street in a state of derangement or stupor, last night. **1869** J. R. BROWNE *Adv. Apache Country* 346 Organ-grinders are grinding their organs and torturing consumptive monkeys; hurdy-gurdy girls are singing. **1897** CLOVER *Paul Travers' Adv.* 34 Dance halls, hurdy-gurdy saloons, cheap clothing stores . . . constituted the 'substantial' buildings. **1946** ADAMS *Album Amer. Hist.* III. 218 'Hurdy-gurdy' girls, hired by the saloon keepers to dance with all comers, provided feminine society for the lonely miners.

3. hurdy-gurdy house, a place of low resort featuring cheap liquor, noisy music, lascivious dancing, and prostitution.

1866 *Beadle's Mo.* Oct. 280/1 Hurdy-gurdy houses, with dancing-girls, music, and long bars, where whiskey was sold at fifty cents a drink, and champagne at twelve dollars a bottle, were filled with visitors. **1874** ALDRICH *P. Palfrey* vii, Sunday was a gala day. The bar-rooms and the gambling-saloons were thronged; at sundown the dance-house would open, — the Hurdy-Gurdy House, as it was called. **1944** ROSS *Westward* 127 Women who frequented dance halls, hurdy-gurdy houses, and other social centers of mining-camp days were bound to see some fancy shooting and some fancy characters.

Huron ˈhjʊrən, *n.* [See note.]

"From French *huré*, 'bristly,' 'bristled,' from *hure*, 'rough hair' (of the head). . . . So it is quite probable that the name was applied to the Indians in the sense of 'an unkempt person,' 'a bristly savage,' 'a wretch or lout,' 'a ruffian' " (Hodge).

An Indian belonging to any one of four confederated tribes formerly occupying a region adjacent to Lake Huron. In *pl.*, this confederation of tribes.

[**1632** *Relat. Jésuites* (1858) I. 14 Ie vy arriuer les Hurons.] **1658** GORGES in *Maine H.S. Coll.* II. 67 The Hiroons, who being neuters are friends both to the one [the Iroquois] and the other [the French]. **1721** *Mass. H. Rep. Jrnl.* III. 111 The Algonquins, The Hurons, The Mikemaks, The Mountainiers on the North-side. **1826** COOPER *Mohicans* iv, He is one of those you call a Huron. **1841** ——— *Deerslayer* x, The Iroquois, or Hurons, as it would be better to call them, were entirely ignorant of the proximity of her lover. **1949** *Newsweek* 25 July 36/3 Iroquois of the Mohawk tribe and descendants of the scattered Hurons gathered in full regalia.

attrib. **1786** *Mem. Acad.* II. I. 125 The Huron, or Wyandot language having no affinity to the Shawanese, Delawares, and other nations. **1888** *Amer. Naturalist* XXII. 803 Jerusalem Artichoke, *Helianthus tuberosus*, . . . was cultivated by the Huron Indians.

Huronian hjʊˈronɪən, *n.* [*Huron*+*-ian*.] (See quot. 1889.)

1883 *Virginias* Jan. 11/2 The Huronian seems to occur in long narrow strips, enclosed by the gneisses, and possessing a complex synclinal structure. **1889** *Cent.* 2924/2 Huronian. . . . In geology the term is applied to a division of the azoic or archaean series, as indicated by the Canadian geologists. It is a lithological division exclusively, since it contains no fossils, so far as known. . . . The epithet has no satisfactory basis, and has been abandoned by most geologists.

* **hurrah,** *n.* [Poss. f. various sources in the examples here shown.] In colloq. combs.: (1) **hurrah boy,** see as a main entry; (2) **bush,** *S.* the fetterbush or shining fetterbush, *Neopieris nitida*, also attrib.; (3) **place,** a disorderly or lawless place; (4) **-'s nest,** see as a main entry.

(2) **1853** SIMMS *Sword & Distaff* 81 We're in a pretty close thick, you see of gall and 'hurrah-bushes.' *Ib.*, The wild, matted, tangled, tough, and altogether indescribable shrub, which the woodman described as the 'hurrah-bush,' and for which we have no better name, constitutes, in poor soil . . . one of the most formidable . . . of forest-walls. *c***1945** HOPKINS *Okefenokee* 16 We wrapped stout twine around the bottoms of trouser legs making the trousers a more difficult target for thorny vines and 'hurrah bush' stubble. — (3) **1883** SWEET & KNOX *Through Texas* xix. 257 [A railroad terminus in w. Texas] is what is called, in the classic vernacular of the country, 'a hoorah place.'

b. Zest, uproariousness. Usu. attrib. or as adj. designating a group, gathering, etc., characterized by zest, noise, joyfulness, confusion, etc. *Colloq.*

1889 *Sporting Life* (Phila.) 5 June 1/2 Aspen has jumped from tail-end to second place and is playing a rattling hurrah game of ball. **1890** *Stock Grower & Farmer* 22 March 4/2 A hurrah convention does nothing to promote the cattle interests. **1903** *N.Y. Ev. Post* 30 Oct. 16 Added to this solid element is the hurrah crowd whose enthusiasm has a venal tone. **1913** *Collier's* 13 Dec. 26/2 There was an old-fashioned 'Hurrah' to Western football this season. **1927** SIRINGO *Riata & Spurs* 31 One shot hit me in the calf of my left leg, and the scar remains to this day, as a reminder of Wichita's hurrah days. **1932** *Blue Valley Farmer* (Okla. City) 18 Feb. 1/5 He soon falls in with the 'hurrah' or criminal element.

hurrah boys.

1. Blindly enthusiastic partisans. *Colloq.*

1835 *Franklin Repository* (Chambersburg, Pa.) 2 June 2/3 The New York delegation cared nothing for principles! To them . . . the men who would secure for the ticket and for *Martin Van Buren* the *hurra boys* was every thing! **1836** *Cong. Globe* App. 17 Feb. 115/1 Some have declared that his election had been brought about by the '*hurrah boys*,' and those who knew just enough to shout 'hurrah for Jackson.'

2. A noisy attack or melee. *Colloq.*

1841 COOPER *Deerslayer* xi, [A squall] came down upon us night afore last, in the shape of an Indian hurrah-boys! **1885** HOWELLS *S. Lapham* xiv, When there's such a hurrah-boys as there was then, you can't tell which is which. **1899** A. BROWN *Tiverton Tales* 183 They say you'll repent it if you stay, an there'll be a hurrah-boys all round.

3. (See quot.)

1903 *D.N.* II. 298 hurrah boys . . . *interj*. A general exhortation. 'As soon as a new minister comes, then it's *hooraw boys* and everybody goes to meeting.'

hurrah's nest.

1. A place of disorder and confusion.

1829 LONGFELLOW in S. Longfellow *H. W. Longfellow* I. 164 A queer looking Dutchman, with a head like a 'hurra's nest' and a great wooden pipe. **1895** A. BROWN *Meadow-Grass* 134, I'll clear up this kitchen; it's a real hurrah's nest, if ever there was one. **1910** WALCOTT *Open Door* xxvi. 337 Here's this room looking like a hurrah's nest. **1948** *Chi. Tribune* 8 Feb. (Comics) 1 Your hair looks like a hurrah's nest!

2. (See quots.)

1889 *Cent. Mag.* Aug. 503/1 The old lumberman pointed quietly to a 'hurrah's nest' . . . a mass of leaves left by a freshet in the crotch of the divergent branches of a bush. **1916** W. L. MCATEE in *Torreya* XVI. 235, I might add that on this island [i.e., Matinicus Island, Me.] I heard the fungoid malformation of trees, known as witches' broom, called hoorah's-nest. **1917** KEPHART *Camping* I. 213 Observe the more or less continuous line of dead grass, leaves, twigs, mud, and other flotsam or hurrah's-nests left in bushes along the water-front.

* **hurricane,** *n.*

1. An area devastated by a hurricane. *Colloq.* See also **Pennsylvania hurricane.**

1735 HEMPSTEAD *Diary* 291 The Stack . . . was made in the Hurrycane this Side the Swamp. **1824** *Missouri Intelligencer* 2 Feb. (Th.), Hurricanes are so called from the appearance of the land when stripped by a violent wind. **1891** SWASEY *Early Days Calif.* 15 In Missouri, cause and effect had been blended in the common designation of 'hurricane.'

attrib. **1775** ADAIR *Indians* 337 They had passed over a boggy place of the creek, upon an old hurricane-tree. **1775** ROMANS *Nat. Hist. Fla.* 307 Travelled chiefly through pine land, and some hurricane ground. **1837** WETMORE *Gaz. Missouri* 80 That part of the county of Howard commonly termed the hurricane-hills is rich and picturesque; and the track of the tempest and the whirlwind, marked by the bare and branchless trunks of scathed oaks, lends a thrilling interest to the scenery. **1855** SIMMS *Forayers* 255, I was in a 'harricane thick,' on the butt-eend of an almighty big tree. **1891** SLOAN *Fogy Days* 176 Now back to the mill pond, where he tries to loose them in the hurricane thicket.

2. hurricane roof, a hurricane deck.

1839 *N.O. Picayune* 29 March 2/2 The snag went through the guards, cabin and hurricane roofs, destroying six or seven berths. **1883** *Cent. Mag.* June 222/1 The tall, broad, frail-looking steamers . . . hidden to their hurricane roofs in cargoes of cotton bales.

hurricane deck. The upper deck of a river steamer.

1833 *Niles' Reg.* XLIV. 261/1 The hull of the boat sunk, leaving a part of the hurricane deck . . . floating on the surface. **1855** BAXTER *America* 39, I have stood on the hurricane or upper-deck of one of these floating palaces, going so fast that the resistance of the air made it impossible to face the bow without shelter. **1945** *Reader's Digest* Oct. 13/2 Until the last gong of the midnight sailing, Marjorie was on the hurricane deck with her medical student.

transf. **1857** *Lawrence* (Kans.) *Republican* 11 June 3 The New York Second Avenue Railroad Company have placed on the route some cars with an upper or 'hurricane deck.' **1876** *Silver City* (Ida.) *Avalanche* 7 March 2/2 Leaving Salubria on the hurricane deck of a cayuse, your correspondent wended his doleful way across the snow to the Little Weiser. **1948** *Kananaskis Ranch Cat.* 5 You can jam your oldest and stoutest clothing into a duffle bag, watch your cowboy guide pack them with many boxes of grub onto the hurricane deck of some wild-eyed cayouse.

∗ **hurry,** *n. attrib.* Denoting something to be dealt with in a hurry. Esp. **hurry-call,** an urgent call for action or help. *Colloq.*

1900 E. A. DIX *Deacon Bradbury* 72 I'd been down at th' store, that evenin', t' mark up a 'hurry' consignment of goods. **1901** *Munsey's Mag.* XXIV. 798/1 If it was a hurry call, she would send them to Gilchrist. **1924** A. J. SMALL *Frozen Gold* i. 39 It's generally a frantic hurry-call from some little dog-eared show or other that has just been cleaned up.

b. hurry-wagon, (see quot.). *Slang.* Cf. **hurry-up wagon.**

1908 LORIMER *J. Spurlock* 36 Rawden, the human hurry-waggon, smelled rough-house of some sort starting.... So he came running.

hurrygraph ˈhɜɪˌgræf, *n.* A hurried writing, sketch, or picture. *Colloq.*

Under *-graph OED* has "jocular nonce-words, like *hurrygraph* for 'a hurried sketch,' are occasionally met with," but no evidence is given.

1851 *Oquawka* (Ill.) *Spectator* 3 June 1/1 Just as we are 'putting up' this hurry graph a flat boat is passing up First street laden with several hundred sacks of grain. **1879** WHITMAN *Prose Wks.* (1892) 502, I set out on the following hurrygraphs of a breezy early-summer visit to New-York City. **1918** *Hist. Amer. Lit.* I. iii. 242 Fleeting impressions, 'dashes at life,' ephemera, 'hurrygraphs' were his forte.

hurry-up ˈhɜɪˌʌp, *a.*

1. Involving or requiring haste. *Slang.*

1902 WILSON *Spenders* 466 He would not be compelled to seek one of those 'hurry-up' lunch places with its clamour and crowd. **1916** B. HALL & J. J. NILES *One Man's War* (1929) 191 He had to ... wait for some hurry-up repairs. **1930** *Dixon* (Ill.) *Ev. Telegraph* 24 Sep. 2/2 It is hoped there will be a large attendance at the 'hurry-up' meeting this evening. **1949** *Sun. World-Herald Mag.* (Omaha) 13 Feb. 5/2 It is often necessary to make a hurry-up call to a registered donor who is known to have the right type of blood.

2. hurry-up wagon, a police van. *Slang.*

1893 W. K. POST *Harvard Stories* 118 The manager ... told him to send for a hurry-up wagon, and run us all in. **1943** *Copper Camp* 191 A frantic bartender called the police and Callahan was once more looking out of the hurry-up wagon on his way to the City Hall.

∗ **hurtleberry,** *n.* = **huckleberry.**

1607 in *Amer. Antiq. Soc. Trans. & Coll.* IV. (1860) 61 The soyle [near mouth of James River] ... naturally yeelds mulbery-trees, cherry-trees ... goosberyes, strawberyes, hurtleberyes [etc.]. **1682** M. RAWLINSON *Narr. Captivity* 69 [She had] nothing to eat or drink but water, and green Hirtle-berries. **1774** FITHIAN *Journal* I. 195 Every Day [we have] good fruit for Dinner, caudled Apples, Hurtle-Berries with milk. **1903** *Old Dartmouth Hist. Sk.* III. 13/2 Church's party proceeding by the old Plymouth trail, ... found Indians picking hurtleberries.

attrib. **1654** *Boston Rec.* 27 More or lesse lately the land of William Curtiss called hurtlebury hill. **1677** *Plymouth Rec.* I. 153 The Towne have Graunted unto Thomas hewes a Certaine swamp Called hurtleberry swamp.

Hence **hurtleberrying,** gathering hurtleberries.

1830 in *N. Eng. Mag. 1895* Nov. 319/2 Aug. 21 Cool, ahurtleberrying, tired.

∗ **husband,** *n.* As the last term in **budget, budgeted, ship's husband.**

husbandman's tree. (See quot.) *Obs.* — **1857–8** *Ill. Agric. Soc. Trans.* III. 481 The ash ... is called the 'husbandman's tree,' and thrives well in a deep, rich, calcareous soil.

∗ **hush,** *v. intr.* Used imperatively to denote enthusiastic approval or appreciation. *Colloq.* — **a1846** *Quarter Race Ky.* 88 Oh hush! It makes my mouth water now to think what a beautiful row we had. **1898** DUNBAR *Folks from Dixie* 62 'Then you can sell chickens and eggs, and we'll go halves on the profits.' 'Hush, man!' cried 'Lias in delight.

hush puppy. *S.* (See quots.) Also attrib. *Colloq.*

1918 *D.N.* V. 18 *hushpuppy*, a sort of bread prepared very quickly and without salt. [N.C.] **1947** *This Week Mag.* 4 Oct. 27/1 What's a hush puppy? You mean you don't know that Southern fried bread like a miniature corn pone—but glorified? It's made of the white cornmeal of the South, smooth and fine as face powder. Florida and Georgia women like their pones scented with onion. In the Carolinas and Virginia, they prefer them plain. **1949** *N.O. Times-Picayune Mag.* 15 May 10/2 Fishing parties, dances, hush-puppy suppers and fish fries left the MGMers almost too pleasantly busy to proceed with their filming.

∗ **husk,** *n.*

1. The bracts or outside covering of an ear of corn. Cf. **corn husk, shuck,** *n.*

1677 WINTHROP in *Phil. Trans.* XII. 1067 The Husks about the Ear are good Fodder, given for change sometimes after Hay. **1823** JAMES *Exped.* I. 194 [Among the Omaha Indians] the poor who have no kettles, place the ear, sufficiently guarded by its husk, in the hot embers until properly cooked. **1899** *Mo. So. Dakotan* I. 175 In the corn field the dry blades beating, the crackling husks and creaking stalks made deafening confusion. **1944** *N. & Q.* IV. 57 Hunter also recalls that in 1828 William Cobbett had the title page and contents leaf of his London-printed book *A Treatise on Corn* done on paper made from the husks of corn which he himself had grown.

b. (See quots.)

1824 SINGLETON *Letters* 81 What we [in N. Eng.] call cob, they [in Va.] call husk; as also the external envelope of the kernel, which cannot be reduced to meal, and which makes the bran. **1856** FERGUSSON *America* 128 'Husk' is the name given to the enamelled skin of the individual seeds [of corn]. **1894** EGGLESTON in *Cent. Mag.* April 851/1 Husk is applied in the middle belt and in the South to the bran of corn-meal.... In this sense the word has largely lost its final letter.

c. *local.* (See quot.)

1881 INGERSOLL *Oyster Industry* 245 *Husks.*—Oyster shells.

2. In combs.: (1) **husk bed,** a bed having a husk mattress; (2) **collar,** a horse collar made of corn husks, cf. **shuck collar;** (3) **hackler,** (see quot.), *obs.;* (4) **mattress,** a mattress stuffed with corn husks; (5) **tomato,** = **strawberry tomato.**

(1) **1849** in *Mo. Hist. Rev.* XXXVII. 248 *Husk Beds.* Now [the husking season] is the time to secure the best and most durable underbeds. All the inner husks of the corn should be saved for this purpose. **1881** *Harper's Mag.* Sep. 579/1 You may hanker after more black-flies, and mosquitoes, ... and baked beans, and husk beds, and so forth. — (2) **1857** *Ill. Agric. Soc. Trans.* II. 361 In these aboriginal times [*c*1800] husk collars were mostly used [in southern Ill.]. — (3) **1875** KNIGHT II. 1143/1 Husk-hackler. A machine for tearing corn-husks into shreds for stuffing for mattresses, pillows, cushions, etc. — (4) **1832** *Amer. R.R. Jrnl.* I. 70/3 Mr. Cobbett is making an effort to introduce the use of husk mattresses. **1941** LEE *Stagecoach North* 4 The Vermont could boast of good husk mattresses. (5) **1895** *Standard* 1899/1. **1941** WILDER *Little Town on Prairie* 128 The husk-tomatoes were covered with a smooth dull-brown husk. When this was opened there lay the round, bright-purple tomato.

∗ **husk,** *v. tr.* To strip the husks from (corn). Cf. ∗ **shuck,** *v.*

1624 J. SMITH in Lefroy *Mem. Bermudas* I. 158/1 The good husbands husked it [corn], and with much labor hung it up. **1771** PATTEN *Diary* 274, I husked out the Remainder of what corn we got in on last monday. **1836** GILMAN *Recoll.* (1838) iv. 35 Joseph, when a boy, was employed in tying fagots, driving cows, husking corn, hoeing potatoes, etc. **1944** DUNCAN *M. Graham* 78 The corn had not yet been husked, and the Grahams 'invited in' to a husking bee.

b. (See quot.)

1881 INGERSOLL *Oyster Industry* 245 *Husk.*—To remove the shells from an oyster or 'open' it. (Georgia.)

huskanaw ˈhʌskəˌnɔ, *n.* ["The word is ... from the Powhatan equivalent of the Massachuset *wuskenoo*, 'he is young' " (Hodge).] (See quot. 1907.) — **1705** BEVERLEY *Virginia* III. 41 The *Appamattucks*, formerly a great Nation, tho' now an inconsiderable People, made an *Huskanaw* in the year 1690, and brought home the same number they carried out. **1907** HODGE *Amer. Indians* I. 592 Huskanaw, an Algonquian word applied to certain initiation ceremonies of the Virginia Indians, performed on boys at puberty, which were accompanied by fasting and the use of narcotics.

huskanaw ˈhʌskəˌnɔ, *v.* [f. the noun.] *tr.* To subject (an Indian youth) to a huskanaw. Also transf. *Obs.*

1705 BEVERLEY *Virginia* III. 39 The choicest and briskest young men of the Town, and such only as have acquired some Treasure by their Travels and Hunting, are chosen out by the Rulers to be *Huskanawed;* and whoever refuses to undergo this Process, dares not remain among them. **1733** BYRD *Journey to Eden* (1901) 326 And the Joy of meeting my Family in Health made me in a Moment forget all the Fatigues of the Journey, as much as if I had been husquenawed. **1788** JEFFERSON *Writings* V. (1895) 43 Luzerne ... is a good man, too, but so much out of his element, that he has the air of one huskanoyed.

husker ˈhʌskɚ, *n.* One who husks corn. Cf. **corn husker, hand husker.**

1780 E. PARKMAN *Diary* 279 Breck was very generous in treating ye Huskers with Liquor. **1888** BITTINGER *Hist. Haverhill* 360 Then unhusked corn was piled in a heap, ... and the huskers ... sat around the fire on the floor. **1944** *Reader's Digest* Oct. 63/2 Drop down into the great midlands and hear the song of the corn on the bangboard of the husker's wagon.

∗ **husking,** *n.*

1. = **husking bee.** Cf. **corn husking.**

1693 C. MATHER *Wonders Invisible W.* 142 At another time this deponent was desired by the Prisoners to come unto an Husking of Corn. **1713** in KITTREDGE *Old Farmer* 172 The Riots that have too often accustomed our *Huskings*, have carried in them, fearful Ingratitude. **1834** C. D. ARFWEDSON *United States* I. 205 The entertainment, which is called 'husking,' is given by every farmer to his neighbours. **1903** W. E. CURTIS *True Abraham Lincoln* 66 The guest of honour at dinners, receptions, quiltings, huskings, weddings, and other entertainments.

attrib. **1828** *Yankee* May 147/1 A husking supper was composed of Indian pudding, and pork-and-beans baked, and a dessert of apple-pie and cheese. **1841** *Lowell Offering* I. 292 Farewell, the merry husking-night, Its pleasant after scenes.

2. In special combs.: (1) **husking ballad,** a ballad often sung at a husking, *obs.;* (2) **bee,** a community gathering of friends and neighbors at the home of a farmer for assisting him to husk his corn; (3) **feast, festival,** (see quot. 1805), *obs.;* (4) **frolic, =husking bee,** *obs.;* (5) **match,** a competition in husking corn; (6) **party, =husking bee,** *obs.;* (7) **pin,** a pin or peg worn on the hand by a husker to aid in husking.

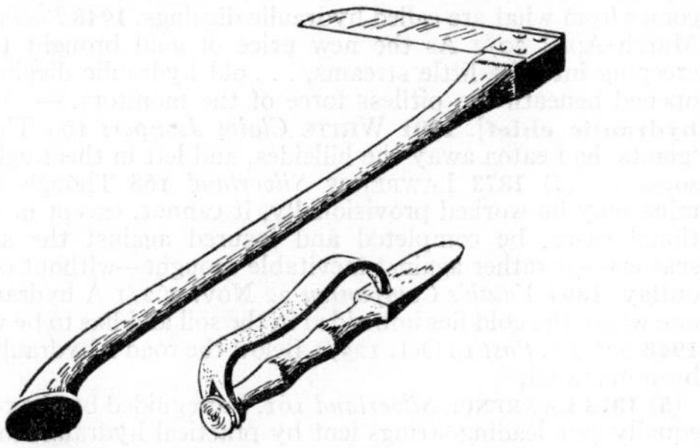

One type of husking pin and corn knife

(1) **1850** WHITTIER *Poetical Works* (1895) 364/1 The master of the village school . . . a husking-ballad sung. — (2) **[1791** in *Admiral James' Journal* 193 During our stay at this place we saw and partook of the ceremony of husking corn, a kind of 'harvest home' in England, with the additional amusement of kissing the girls whenever they met with a red corn-cob, and to which is added dancing, singing, and moderate drinking.] **1836** R. WESTON *Visit* 218, I was invited to many . . . husking bees, in the neighbourhood. **1948** *Chi. Tribune* 24 Oct. 36/3 A few hundred city folks, most of them strangers to corn without butter, learned recently why the corn husking bee probably will outlast the double feature. — (3) **1805** PARKINSON *Tour* 331 They have generally a husking-feast; when all the neighbours come and help to husk; and, after they have done, they have a supper, smoke segars, and drink whiskey. **1829** COOPER *Wish-ton-Wish* iv, Mutton will not be wanting for the husking-feast. **1855** *Pioneer* (S.F.) Jan. 37 This old clock . . . had seen many a 'paring bee,' and ticked away the small hours of many a husking festival. — (4) **1755** in *N. Eng. Quart.* II. (1929) 67 The character of its entertainments is portrayed by Bailey, November 6, 1755, in 'A Description of a Husking Frolic Lately Celebrated by the Beaux and Belles of Kingston.' **1822** J. WOODS *English Prairie* 300 This is a high day with the Americans, and is called a Husking Frolic; plenty of whiskey is generally to be found at one of these frolics. **1887** TOURGEE *Button's Inn* 50 She went with him and his mother to a husking-frolic.

(5) **1853** THOMAS *J. Randolph* 97 After this, we got to the husking-match safe. **1885** HOLMES *Mortal Antipathy* ix, Carpet of her room looked like a barn floor after a husking-match. — (6) **1830** *Workingman's Gaz.* (Woodstock, Vt.) 28 Oct. 33/2 There is not a pleasanter thing in this whole round of country life, than the good old fashioned husking party. **1831** *Boston Transcript* 17 Aug. 2/2 Mrs. Thimblebury, and a few other of the topping-folks, wouldn't invite poor Mrs. No-tea to their husking and quilting parties. — (7) **1862** *Rep. Comm. Patents: 1861 Agric.* 642. **1870** *Rep. Comm. Agric. 1869* 328 It is a matter of doubt whether with the aid of any one of them [hand-huskers] a man could husk more corn per hour than with the old-fashioned husking pin. **1948** JACOBS *We Chose Country* 136 Katherine and I fell into the routine quickly—a jab with the husking pin at the silk end of the cob, tearing back the husk, then a half-twist of the ear to break it from the stalk, and a long toss to the basket.

Husky ˈhʌskɪ, *n.* Also **husky.** [Of uncertain origin, but poss. f. a name, Tinne *ŭskimi*, meaning Eskimo. See Hodge.]

1. An Eskimo, or the language of the Eskimos.

1864 C. F. HALL *Life among Esquimaux* I. 66 Carl Petersen no speak Husky . . . quick. **1894** *Outing* Feb. 366/2 When we came up to our husky, his face beamed joyously as he pointed with great pride to his game. **1945** SERVICE *Ploughman* 426 I don't like huskies. The men get mad at you if you won't sleep with their wives, and the damn women stink so there's no fun in it.

2. An Eskimo dog.

1886 *Col. & Indian Exhibition* (London) (*Cent.*) 75 The original Husky has always been an animal requiring firm treatment. **1948** *Sat. Ev. Post* 21 Aug. 71/3 Nine out of ten people, they say, think the Husky is a brute, mean, vicious, unpredictable, ready to tear his master to pieces at the first chance.

attrib. **1941** *Yankee* Dec. 28/1 Mrs. Milton Seeley with a Husky pup, at Chinook Kennels. **1947** *Reader's Digest* Oct. 162/2 They had to bring their 22 Husky dogs with them.

∗ **husky,** *a.* Strong, vigorous. *Colloq.*

1869 STOWE *Oldtown Folks* xvii. 191 Them wild Injuns, . . . they're so kind o' wild, and birchy, and husky as a body may say. **1912** LONDON *Smoke Bellew* 133 Thirty-eight men he counted, a wild and husky crew, all frontiersmen of the States or voyageurs from upper Canada. **1932** W. KELLEY *Inchin' Along* 45 He, a common, husky buck, was one of the chosen people of the Lord.

b. *absol.* A strong, powerful person. *Colloq.*

1864 *Old Piute* (Virginia, Nev.) 17 May, He demanded to see the Charter of the concern, which was read by the Rev. Geo. Birdsall, in his usual impressive manner, and the 'husky' accepted the apology. **1884** MARK TWAIN *H. Finn* xxix. 281 That big husky had me by the wrist. **1945** *Jefferson Co. Republican* (Golden, Colo.) 26 Sep. 1/3 One faculty member who strayed too close to the Washington Avenue bridge was picked up bodily by ten huskies and tossed in the murky waters below.

∗ **hustle,** *n.* Energetic effort, briskness, animation. *Colloq.*

1892 *Home Missionary* (N.Y.) July 120 The hustle and stir of our day. **1906** *N.Y. Ev. Post* 7 Sep. 6 What the Kaiser hopes from Herr Dernburg is what is popularly known as American 'hustle'—the ability to go right to the point, to decide quickly, to act aggressively by means of simple and direct methods. **1923** *Nation* 26 Sep. 313/2 A country with no 'pep,' no 'hustle.' **1949** *Sat. Ev. Post* 25 June 32 The business [is] now headed by his grandson, who displays all the founder's hustle but eschews the whiskers.

∗ **hustle,** *v.*

1. *tr.* To get *up*, obtain. *Colloq.*

1840 *S. Lit. Messenger* VI. 414/2 Can't you go out to the woodpile and hustle me up a few chips to start this fire? **1914** GRAU *Theatre of Science* 80 He had to write his own scenarios, direct the productions and 'hustle props.' **1948** *Sat. Ev. Post* 11 Sep. 36/1 She hustled circulation, advertising and news for the weekly newspaper.

2. *intr.* To exert oneself briskly, often with *for.*

1889 *Boston Jrnl.* 31 Dec. 2/4 He says he can't begin to hustle as his father used to. **1906** O. HENRY *Four Million* 62 Do you think I'm going to let you hustle for wages while I philander in the regions of high art? **1931** *K.C. Star* 11 Aug., These farm girls know how to hustle.

Hence **hustling,** *a.*

1887 *Courier-Journal* 16 Feb. 6/1 The snort of the iron horse now awakens the echoes of that hustling little town. **1947** *Steamboat* (Colo.) *Pilot* 16 Jan. 1/4 It . . . was a hustling silver camp where many fortunes were made.

∗ **hustler,** *n.* (See quot. 1899.)

1886 *Publishers' Wkly.* 18 Dec. 965/1 Young man, a 'hustler' in every respect, wants a strictly first-class position with a 'live' book house. **1899** ADE *Doc' Horne* 238 In the United States of America a hustler is one who is busy, persistent, resourceful and combative, usually that he may accumulate money. **1947** *Denver Post* 2 March A-11/5 There are more hustlers and salesmen there than in any Chinese marketplace.

∗ **hut,** *n.* As the last term in **baby, bark, birchbark, booby, brush, bush, clapboard, fishing, fodder, Indian, log, Negro, palmetto, picket, tule hut.**

∗ **Hutchins,** *n.* [Thomas *Hutchins* (d. 1790), English attaché of the Hudson's Bay Co.] **Hutchins' goose,** (see quot. 1917).

1835 AUDUBON *Ornith. Biog.* III. 526 Hutchins's Goose. *Anser Hutchinsii.* . . . I have no doubt that it is the very species which has been named in honour of Mr. Hutchins, and that its periodical appearance along our eastern coast will ere long be fully established. **1917** *Birds of Amer.* I. 160/2 Hutchins's Goose (*Branta canadensis hutchinsi*) is precisely like the Canada Goose in everything except size. . . . It breeds in the Arctic region of North America and migrates south in winter chiefly through western United States and the Mississippi valley. **1947** *Beaver* June 3/2 Hutchins' goose is now considered a species in its own right, though in colour it closely resembles the Canada goose.

Also **Hutchins' brant.**

1865 *Wilkes' Spirit of Times* 16 Dec. 243/1 Hutchins' goose, or, as it is sometimes called, Hutchins' Brant, greatly resembles the Brant goose.

huttonweed ˈhʌtn̩ˌwid, *n.* The wild teasel. — **1894** *Amer. Folk-Lore* VII. 90 *Dipsacus sylvestris*, . . . Indian thistle, Huttonweed, English thistle, water-thistle, West Va.

***hyacinth,** *n.* =**water hyacinth.** — **1944** KANE *Bayous of La.* 28 Men like him went to Congress a few years after the hyacinths became prevalent, and since then millions of dollars have been spent by the government to wipe them out. **1949** *Sat. Ev. Post* 25 June 79/3 He heard a black bass smack a floating island of hyacinths.

hyas kloosh. Variously spelled. *N.W.* [Chinook *hya*, very, great; *kloshe*, good. Cf. **high-muck-a-muck.**] Very good, fine.

1869 *Alaska Times* (Sitka) 25 Dec. 1/2, I . . . gave him another dose for two grown persons and a small boy. As this went down he seemed satisfied and expressed himself in the poetical language of his tribe 'Hi-as-kloosh!' **1876** *Avalanche* (Silver City, Ida.) 8 March 3/1 We inquired after a certain gentleman's gentleman's health this morning and he replied, 'hi-as-cloosh,' which it seems is the Chinook term for 'very good.' *a***1915** MUIR *Travels Alaska* (1917) 214 All said that Monday would be *hyas klosh* for the starting-day.

hyas tyee. *N.W.* [Chinook. See prec.] A great chief. — **1878** *Puget Sound Argus* 25 Jan., Old Shoe-Stacks, who professes to be a 'hyas tyee,' . . . has letters of recommendation from nearly every military and naval officer that has been at Wrangel. **1897** *Land of Sunshine* May 248 He was Hyas Tyee of the Duwanish,—and Quo-doultz was his name.

***hybrid,** *a.* Denoting corn produced by crossing selected varieties. Also absol.

1944 *Nat. Geog. Mag.* June 688 Idaho produces nearly 85% of all hybrid sweet corn seed in the United States. Its crop amounted to more than 5,300,000 pounds in 1942. **1948** *Savings News* Jan. 7/1 He went upstairs to the storeroom, selected the finest ears of hybrid, dropped them in a gunny sack and started for town. **1948** *Fargo* (N.D.) *Forum* 19 Sep. 23/2 Plans call for harvesting rows of the hybrid corn and piling the yields at the ends to permit easy comparison.

***Hydra,** *n.* An officer in the first Ku-Klux Klan organization. *Obs.* — **1867** in LESTER & WILSON *Ku Klux Klan* 136 The officers . . . shall consist of a Grand Wizard of the Empire and his ten Genii; a Grand Dragon of the Realm and his eight Hydras [etc.].

hydrant ˈhaɪdrənt, *n.* [f. *hydr-* (combining form, before vowels, of Gk. *hydōr*, water)+*-ant.*]

1. An upright cylinder or street fixture from which water may be drawn from a city main. Cf. **fire hydrant, public hydrant.**

1806 *Phila. Ordinances* (1812) 197 If any person . . . shall wilfully injure . . . the hydrants . . . [he] shall forfeit . . . five dollars. **1948** *Capital-Democrat* (Tishomingo, Okla.) 24 June 2/1 With scores of hydrants running, it is extremely difficult to keep pressure up.

attrib. **1809** *Phila. Ordinances* (1812) 229 The watering committee . . . is directed on application made by any fire associations, to grant . . . a permit for the use of the hydrant water, for the purpose of . . . preparing their hose. **1878** PINKERTON *Strikers* 270 There stood a ruffian on a hydrant-head with his arm about a lamp-post. **1904** *Dly. Pub. Opinion* (Watertown, S.D.) 28 Dec. 1/3 A bunch of bills was allowed, covering hydrant rental from July to January, six months, at $2,504.

b. Any one of various, usu. smaller, outlets for water; a faucet.

1846 COOPER *Redskins* xxiii, I knew that a hydrant stood in the kitchen itself, which gave a full stream of water. **1890** *Cent. Mag.* Dec. 227 Then there is an old-fashioned hydrant, with a half-spiral crank of a handle on its top. **1905** *D.N.* III. 83 hydrant . . . Faucet. 'You can get a drink at the *hydrant* in the hall.' Common. [nw. Ark.]

2. A fire engine. Also **hydrant company.** *Obs.*

1851 J. H. ROSS *In New York* 31 The department contains thirty-four engine companies, forty-seven hose companies, nine hook and ladder companies, three hydrant companies. **1859** MACKAY *Tour* I. 50 The men . . . spend large sums in the ornamentation of their favourite engines, or hydrants, as already mentioned. **1889** BRAYLEY *Boston Fire Dept.* 219 Nearly all the companies were reorganized, and a new ladder company and two hydrant companies put in commission.

***hydraulic,** *a.* and *n.*

1. *n.* =**hydraulic monitor.** Cf. **monitor.**

1856 *S.F. Call* 5 Dec. (Th.), I've used them things enough in the mines to know that that 'ere all-fired machine is not '*hydrollicks*.' **1872** MCCLELLAN *Golden State* 259 The pan gave way to the rocker, the rocker to the sluice and shovel, and finally to the use of powder and the hydraulic. **1885** M. A. LEESON *Hist. Montana* 231 The pan, the rocker, the bumper, the Long Tom, the sluice, and the hydraulic have succeeded each other in the order named.

2. A ditch or flume for water. *Obs.*

1890 HOWELLS *Boy's Town* 2 Then it had a Hydraulic, which brought the waters of Old River for mill power through the heart of town, from a Big Reservoir. *Ib.* 3 Grist-mills on the rivers and canal, cotton-factories and saw-mills on the Hydraulic.

3. *a. W.* Of or pertaining to mining gold by means of water under high pressure.

1869 J. R. BROWNE *Adv. Apache Country* 310 Put you through the hydraulic process after your arrival at Placerville, and your washings are worth $14 per ounce. **1883** RITCH *Illust. N. Mex.* 129 A hydraulic company . . . is expected to have twelve miles of pipe down and arrangements complete for extensive placer washing. **1949** *Nat. Geog. Mag.* Oct. 514 Hydraulic mining near Fairbanks frequently uncovers frozen prehistoric animals.

4. In special combs. relating to mining gold by means of powerful jets of water with which auriferous earth is disintegrated, as (1) **hydraulic chief,** (2) **diggings,** (3) **giant,** (4) **mine,** (5) **miner,** (6) **mining,** (7) **monitor,** (8) **nozzle,** (9) **washing.**

(1) **1876** RAYMOND *8th Rep. Mines* 97 The company has nine hydraulic chiefs or giants, the streams from which are forced out under a pressure of 250 feet of water. . . . These giants under the former pressure with seven-inch nozzle will throw 1,000 inches of water. — (2) **1869** BRACE *New West* 163 The greater part of this destruction comes from what are called hydraulic diggings. **1948** *Pacific Discovery* March–April 20/2 As the new price of gold brought the dredges creeping into the little streams, . . . old hydraulic diggings were re-opened beneath the pitiless force of the monitors. — (3) **1876** [see **hydraulic chief**]. **1901** WHITE *Claim Jumpers* 169 The hydraulic 'giants' had eaten away the hillsides, and left in them ugly unhealed sores. — (4) **1873** LAWRENCE *Silverland* 168 Though a hydraulic mine may be worked provisionally, it cannot, except in very exceptional cases, be completed and insured against the accidents of seasons—or rather against inevitable drought—without considerable outlay. **1894** *Youth's Companion* 22 Nov. 562/1 A hydraulic mine is one where the gold lies imbedded in the soil and has to be washed out. **1948** *Sat. Ev. Post* 16 Oct. 125/1 Below the road a hydraulic mine had been operated.

(5) **1873** LAWRENCE *Silverland* 161, I am guided by the rougher, but equally safe leading-strings lent by practical hydraulic miners. **1876** DODGE *Black Hills* 72 There is no doubt but that the gold on this creek will richly pay the hydraulic miner.—(6) **1856** *Porter's Spirit of Times* 22 Nov. 194/2 Near San Juan North . . . hydraulic mining is very successful. **1873** RAYMOND *Mines & Mining* xvii. 390 Hydraulic mining in California—The origin of this branch of mining dates back as far as the spring of 1852. **1946** FAIR *Crows Can't Count* 181 They have some very fine properties that can be worked by hydraulic mining. — (7) **1883** *Cent. Mag.* Jan. 325 The hydraulic monitor . . . resembles nothing so much as a piece of ordnance. **1948** *Pacific Discovery* Sep.–Oct. 29/1 The damage caused by hydraulic monitors and dredges is far greater than the value of the gold 'recovered.' — (8) **1871** RAYMOND *3d Rep. Mines* 55 The most important improvements in mining . . . are the improved hydraulic nozzles and the new drilling and boring machines. **1948** *Life* 2 Feb. 47/2 Man-made canyons near Nevada City resulted when huge hydraulic nozzles washed away entire hillsides between 1860 and 1880. — (9) **1856** *Spirit of Times* 6 Sep. 13/1 For some kinds of labor, such as tunneling, hydraulic washing, blasting, &c., much higher wages are paid. **1869** BRACE *New West* 161 Since the enormous hydraulic washings in the Foot Hills, or the Sierras, this has all been changed, on account of the filling up of the mountain streams with gravel and soil.

b. Also (1) **hydraulic (dry) dock,** a form of dock in which hydraulic pressure is used to raise vessels so that their hulls may be inspected and repaired; (2) **privilege,** (see quot.), *obs.*; (3) **telegraph,** app. some relatively inefficient device for channeling water to a desired spot.

(1) **1833** *Amer. R.R. Jrnl.* II. 521/1, I visited the hydraulic dry dock. **1838** STEVENSON *Sketches* 30 The last of those methods to which I have alluded, is an apparatus called the Hydraulic-dock, a beautiful application of the principle of Bramah's press, to produce a power capable of raising vessels of 800 tons burden. — (2) **1829** MACTAGGART *3 Yrs. in Canada* I. 198 These engines he obtains by procuring for himself, in the first place, a *mill-seat*, or what the Yankees call a *hydraulic privilege*. — (3) **1857** *Hutchings Mag.* May 520/1 [The new hose] is not only much better, and much cheaper than the old fashioned clumsy wooden 'penstock' and 'hydraulic telegraph,' but is perfectly water-tight, and will bear a much greater pressure.

hydraulic haɪˈdrɔlɪk, *v. W.* [f. the noun.] *tr.* (See quot. 1883.)

1883 KNIGHT *Dict. Mech. Supp.* 481 Most of the water thus distributed is used, as it is said, *to hydraulic*, that is, to wash banks of auriferous earth by throwing a stream of water upon them through a hose and pipe. **1892** LUMMIS *Tramp Across Continent* 122 Another company expended $750,000 in the laudable scheme to run a fifteen-mile pipe-line from the Sandias to Golden, and thus bring water to hydraulic the enormous areas of gold-bearing gravel. **1947** CHALFANT *Gold, Guns, & Ghost Towns* 33 From which it was said the owner hydraulicked $90,000 worth of gold.

Also **hydraulicer, -ing.**

1880 Ingham *Digging Gold* ix. 243 Two steam pumps have been in operation near the city, forcing water from French Creek up to these dry diggings for hydraulicing, and with most satisfactory results. **1882** *47th Congress* 1 Sess. H.R. Ex. Doc. No. 216 Reed's Hydraulic mine . . . is being refitted for hydraulicing the coming spring. **1949** *Nat. Geog. Mag.* Oct. 507/2 A recent find made by 'hydraulickers' in this prehistoric deep freeze near Fairbanks was part of a young mammoth.

hydraulion haɪˈdrɔlɪən, *n.* A form of hydraulic engine used by fire fighters. Also attrib. Now *hist.*

1826 *Va. Herald* (Fredericksburg) 13 Sep. 2/1 Why, sir, they will pick the bones of a man and horse sooner than a Cossack; and certainly the sucker of a modern mosquito draws stronger than the hose of a hydraulion, when it is worked by thirty-four men. **1830** *Mass. Statutes* 9 March, The number of enginemen shall not exceed fifty to every hydraulion or suction engine. **1845** *Transcript & Chronicle* (Providence) 8 Jan. 2 The Annual Meeting of 'The Providence Association of Firemen for Mutual Assistance' will be held at Hydraulion house, No. 1. [**1937** Lincoln *Wilmington, Del.* 124 The third [fire] company in the Borough itself was formed on April 22, 1819. . . . The hose was carried on a two-wheeled gig, and instead of buckets, they decided to use a box mounted on wheels called a *hydraulin*.]

∗ **hydrographic,** *a.* **1. Hydrographic Bureau,** = next. **2. Hydrographic Office,** a bureau under the direction of the Navy Department having charge of charts and studies of the geography of the sea.

(1) **1873** *Republic* I. 23 The Hydrographic Bureau . . . takes cognizance of the geography of the sea. — (2) **1866** *Statutes at Large* XIV. 69 There shall be a hydrographic office attached to the bureau of navigation in the Navy Department. **1948** *Milwaukee Jrnl.* 18 July 2/3 In the Pacific the United States hydrographic office branch at Honolulu was designated as the agency to collect and disseminate all mine information.

Hylodes haɪˈlodiz, *n.* [Gk., woody, wooded.] A large genus of New World frogs; also (not *cap.*) a frog of this genus. — **1839** Storer *Mass. Reptiles* 240 *H[ylodes] Pickeringii.* Pickering's Hylodes. **1852** Thoreau *Autumn* 57, I hear a hylodes (?) from time to time. **1858** —— *Maine Woods* 139 We also heard the hylodes and tree-toads.

∗ **hymn,** *n. W.* (See quot. 1939.) See also **camp meeting, penny-royal, whoop hymn.** — [**1891** *Outing* Mar. 411/1 Back and forth and around the sleeping pilgrims go the guard, singing to the uneasy ones quaint old lullabies, some learned in their childhood days, some picked up, some like Topsy, with no parentage.] **1939** Rollins *Gone Haywire* 170 The night herders, as they circled around the bedded beasts, constantly crooned songs or chants, which when so used were entitled 'hymns.'

hyper ˈhaɪpɚ, *v.* [Origin obscure.] *intr.* (See quot. 1867.) *Colloq.*

1867 Lowell *Biglow P.* II. p. lviii, A few phrases not in Mr. Bartlett's book which I have heard [include] *Hyper:* to bustle; 'I must *hyper* about an' git tea.' **1894** R. E. Robinson *Danvis Folks* 218 I'll hyper over and git the dawg. **1928** *Sat. Ev. Post* 12 May 27/2 I'll hyper on ahead to see the way's all clear.

∗ **Hyperion (tea).** *n.* (See quots. 1895, 1917.) *Obs.*

1759 Brooks *Days of Spinning-Wheel* (1886) 11 The use of Hyperion or Labradore Tea, is every day coming into more general vogue among people of all ranks. **1895** Coffin *Daughters of Revolution* 116 Strawberry and other domestic teas were called by the high sounding name Hyperion [in 1769]. **1917** in *Pub. Col. Soc.* XIX. 194 Hyperion or Labrador tea was a decoction of the leaves of the common 'red root' and is described as 'something like wild rosemary,' with a 'very physical taste, of a deep brown color, and generally disliked by those who taste it.'

∗ **hyphenated,** *a.* Denoting persons whose nationality is designated by a hyphenated form, as Irish-American, German-American, etc.; hence of a person whose patriotic allegiance is assumed to be divided.

1893 Farmer & Henley *Slang, Hyphenated American,* a naturalised citizen, as German-Americans, Irish-Americans, and the like. **1904** *Westm. Gaz.* 3 Jan 3/2 American politics, where men who call themselves Irish-Americans, German-Americans, Dutch-Americans, and so on, are contemptuously referred to as 'hyphenated Americans.' **1915** *Lit. Digest* 4 Sep. 462/1 Hyphenated residents will continue to insist that American newspapers should be strictly neutral. **1941** Fergusson *Southwest* 8 For centuries few people have arrived from Spain to become hyphenated Americans.

∗ **hyssop,** *n. local.* Any one of several species of *Artemisia.*

1807 P. Gass *Jrnl.* 79 There is a great quantity of hysop in the vallies. **1812** Brackenridge *Views La.* (1814) 29 There are other places . . . producing nothing but hyssop and prickly pears. **1817** J. Bradbury *Trav. Amer.* 116 A species of Artemesia, common on the prairies, and known to the hunters by the name of Hyssop.

hystericky hɪsˈtɛrɪkɪ, *a.* Hysterical, given to having hysterics. *Colloq.*

1823 Cooper *Pilot* II. xiv. 239 In order that the women need not be 'stericky in squalls. **1867** Holmes *Guardian Angel* xi. 127 That queer woman, the Deacon's mother,—there's where she gets that hystericky look. **1894** Wilkins in *Harper's Mag.* Sep. 605/2 You'd better go to bed, Sophy Anne; you're gittin' highstericky.

I

*I, *n.* Abbreviation of Incest, which, in the form of a badge, those convicted of that crime in colonial New England were sentenced to wear. Now *hist.* Cf. *A, *n.*

1743 *Suffolk Co.* (Mass.) *Files* 557 That he forever after wear a capital I, two inches long and of a proper proportionate bigness, cut out in cloth of a contrary color to his coat, and sewed upon his upper garment on the outside of his arm, or upon his back in open view. **1895** *Proc. Amer. Antiq. Soc.* April 106 The penalty [for incest] was in substance the same, the only change being that the letter which the convict was ordered to wear upon his upper garment was an I instead of A. **1947** DOWNEY *Lusty Forefathers* 123 *F* was the brand of forgery or of fornication, and *I* of incest, guilty ones being also whipped on a gallows.

***ibex,** *n. W.* A name formerly, and still occasionally, used for the mountain goat and Rocky Mountain sheep.

1805 CLARK in *Lewis & C. Exped.* II. (1904) 297, I killed a Ibix. *Ib.* III. (1905) 105 The women dress in a Shirt of Ibex or Goat (Argalia) Skins. **1812** STODDARD *Sk. Louisiana* 358 Among other animals incident to the country may be noticed the Ibex, or Antelope of California, called by the Spaniards mountain sheep. **1860** in A. D. SMITH *Narrative Sam. Hancock* 64 We also saw a large Ibex, the first I ever saw, between the sizes of an elk and mountain goat, with very large horns. **1912** *Outing* Nov. 249/1 Idaho enjoys the proud distinction perhaps of being the only state in the Union that has found it necessary to enact a law protecting ibex.

***ibis,** *n.* As the last term in **red, scarlet, white, wood ibis.**

Ibo ˈibo, *n.* Often **Ebo.** A Negro of the Ibo tribe in the Niger delta (see also quot. 1895). Usu. attrib. *Obs.*

1732 *S. C. Gazette* 20/1 Stolen . . . an old Ebo Negro Man; . . . had on a blue Negro Cloth Frock, and new Oznaburgh Trowsers. **1755** *Va. Gaz.* (Williamsburg) 17 Oct. 3a, Ran away from the Subscriber . . . *Jemmy*, an *Eboe* Negroe . . . very sly and crafty, speaks seldom, tho' tolerable good *English.* **1822** *Amer. Beacon* (Norfolk, Va.) 3 Sep. 2/1 (Th. Supp.), Monday Gell is an Ebo, and now in the prime of life. **1895** *Cent. Dict. Names* 523 The chief town, also called Ibo, is an emporium of the palm-oil trade. All the slaves exported from the Niger used to be called Ibos in North America.

b. Ibo-shin, a Negro. *Slang. Obs.*

1856 *Western Citizen* (Paris, Ky.) 4 April 2/1 In the Enquirer this morning it read *ebo skin.* Don't Virginians at this day know what an '*ebo-shin*' is? **1866** J. E. COOKE *Surry* 195 They charge him with leaving behind his own wounded to make room in his wagon for the ebo-shins.

***Icarian,** *a.* and *n.*

1. *n.* A follower of the French communist Étienne Cabet (1788–1856). *Obs.*

The Icarians came from France to the United States in 1848–49. Settling at first in Texas, they removed (1849) to Nauvoo, Ill. Subsequently they settled in Iowa.

[**1851** in CABET *Colonie icarienne aux Etats-unis d'Amérique* (1856) 51 Les Icariens forment entre eux une véritable Société.] **1867** DIXON *New Amer.* II. 217 The Socialists had to quit New Lanark; the Rappists had to sell Harmony; the Icarians have been swept from Nauvoo. **1873** BEADLE *Undevel. West* xxxii. 694 After the Mormons came a people even more curious than they, but quite harmless: the Icarians, or French 'Fraternal Society' of Communists. **1904** *Harper's Mag.* Dec. 142/2 For several months the Icarians huddled together in New Orleans while their agents searched for a location.

2. *a.* Of or pertaining to the Icarians. *Obs.*

1851 *Ill. Private Laws* 114 Etienne Cabet, J. Pendant, P. J. Tavard, Andre Thebant, Alfred Pignnard and Jean J. Witzig . . . are hereby constituted a body politic and corporate, by the name and style of the 'Icarian Community.' **1875** NORDHOFF *Communistic Soc. U.S.* 393 The Icarian system is as nearly as possible a pure democracy. **1895** in HINDS *Amer. Communities* (1902) 351 The Icarian Community is dissolved. **1904** *Harper's Mag.* Dec. 146/2 So perished in 1895 the last vestige of the great Icarian movement.

Icarianism aɪˈkɛrɪənˌɪzəm, *n.* Communism as taught by Étienne Cabet. *Obs.* — **1883** ELY *Fr. & German Socialism* iii. 50 The apostles of Icarianism should . . . convert the world by teaching, preaching . . . and by setting good examples.

***ice,** *n.* In combs.

1. In miscellaneous expressions: (1) **ice-bridge,** an ice formation bridging a stream [cf. Du. *ijsbrug*]; (2) **carnival,** a carnival held on the ice; (3) ***cream,** see as a main entry; (4) **crop,** the yield of natural ice in a season; (5) **cube,** a small cube of ice such as a mechanized refrigerator produces, also attrib.; (6) **farm,** a place where ice as a commercial product is secured in winter, cf. **ice farmer;** (7) **gorge,** see as a main entry; (8) **gull,** (see quots.); (9) **harbor,** a harbor for ships available for use when other harbors are closed by ice; (10) **party,** a skating party; (11) ***plant,** a manufacturing plant where ice is made; (12) **pond,** a pond from which ice is cut in winter; (13) **road, storm,** see as main entries.

(**1**) **1874** R. H. COLLINS *Kentucky* I. 76 Breaking up of the ice-bridge in the Ohio river. **1880** MARK TWAIN *Tramp Abroad* xl. 460 (R.), A young porter disengaged himself from the line and started across an ice-bridge which spanned a crevasse. — (**2**) [**1866** *Wilkes' Spirit of Times* 3 Feb. 356/3 (*heading*), Academicians on Ice—Carnival in the Moonlight.] **1913** *Outing* Jan. 456/2 So far there is but one place in the United States where winter sports are thoroughly organized and where an ice and snow carnival is a feature. — (**4**) **1853** BUNN *Old Eng. & N. Eng.* 28 The 'ice-crop' (as it is drolly called) proved to be a fair average one. **1906** *Country Life* Sep. 560/2 In locations where the winter is severe enough to make the ice crop a certainty ice can be purchased from neighboring ponds at a cost of from one to two cents a cake.

(**5**) **1930** *Municipal Sanitation* Aug. 429/1 The small ice cube and the gas filling station are symbols of American progress. **1935** *Sears Cat.* (ed. 170) 549 The freezer unit with two ice cube trays. **1945** GARDNER *Golddigger's Purse* 23 Della returned from the kitchen with glasses, ice cubes, scotch and soda. — (**6**) **1889** *Pall Mall Gaz.* 6 Feb. 3/1 When the winter fairly sets in the scene on an ice-farm is a busy one. — (**8**) **1899** *OED*, ice-gull, a name given in N. America to the glaucous gull and the ivory gull. **1917** *Birds of Amer.* I. 41 Glaucous Gull. *Larus hyperboreus.* . . . [Also called] Ice Gull; Harbor Gull. — (**9**) **1876** *Cong. Rec.* 17 July 4655/1 When the ice forms in the river, it is necessary that the shipping coming in from the ocean should have some place of refuge. Hence that ice-harbor at that point was established. *Ib.*, With reference to the ice-harbor at New Castle, we have but comparatively very little commerce at that point. **1884** *Ib.* 10 June 4967/1 The establishment of an ice-harbor at Bellaire [Ohio] is a matter of interest to all.

(**10**) **1884** *Cent. Mag.* July 339/2 The wonderful, brilliant New York winter, . . . the sunset on the snow, the ice-parties in the frosty clearness, the bright, hot, velvety houses. **1905** WIGGIN *Rose* 91 Claude . . . was very much in evidence at the Saturday evening ice parties. — (**11**) **1900** *Cong. Rec.* 3 Feb. 1477/2 Every article of commerce is produced there, from a paper bag to the huge ice plants and cotton and sugar presses scattered everywhere. **1948** *Ice & Refrigeration* Sep. 19/2 A course in the rudiments of ice plant operation and engineering will be offered at Michigan State College. — (**12**) **1851** *S. Lit. Messenger* XVII. 687/1 The waters which flow past Norfolk into the sea, divide . . . the ice ponds of the North from the cotton fields at the South. **1949** *Cleveland Plain Dealer* 13 Feb. (Pict. Mag.) 2/2 [For skating] we had to be content with Fogle's ice pond and icy streets.

b. In less frequent, now obs., expressions: (1) **ice apple,** (see quot.); (2) **barren,** an ice-covered tract or region; (3) **coffin,** app. a coffin or coffin-box so made as to permit the use of ice in keeping or transporting corpses, cf. **7.** (2) below; (4) **embargo,** stoppage of navigation because of ice; (5) **gush,** in a glacier, ice and water at the bottom of a crevasse; (6) **palace,** an edifice made of ice; (7) **quarry,** a place, as a pond, where natural ice is harvested; (8) **shove,** the upward thrust or heave of ground by alternate freezing and thawing; (9) **station,** a place to which ice is brought for shipment.

(1) **1891** WELCH *Recoll. 1830–40* 411 The trees of which seemed loaded with the sparkling winter fruit of the place called 'ice apples.' (frozen balls of snow). — (2) **1897** MARK TWAIN *Following Equator* xlix. 461 (R.), The ice-barrens of Greenland. — (3) **1882** McCABE *New York* 233 The charge for ice coffins varies from $12 to $18. — (4) **1876** *The Dalles* (Ore.) *Tribune* 29 Jan. 3/2 We have the satisfaction of knowing that the winter is now two thirds gone; and that the ice-embargo cannot last a great while longer.

(5) **1904** *Franklin Inst. Jrnl.* Oct. 304 Never once did one [horse] . . . refuse to climb out of an ice gush when called upon to do so. — (6) **1886** *Outing* March 712/1 The emulative people of St. Paul, Minn., manifest pardonable pride in their ice palace, which is gradually assuming grand proportions. **1888** *St. Paul Globe* 22 Jan., If every man in St. Paul would only do a little booming for the coming ice palace the amount of good it would do is almost incalculable. — (7) **1860** HOLMES *Professor* (1902) 212 The east wind . . . clasps a clear-eyed wintry noon on the chill bridal couch of a New England ice-quarry. — (8) **1865** PARKMAN *Champlain* xi. (1875) 334 He built a wall of bricks . . . in order to measure the destructive effects of the 'ice-shove' in the spring. — (9) **1866** LOSSING *Hudson* 304 Rockland Lake village . . . [is] the most extensive ice-station on the [Hudson] river.

2. Designating persons or groups having to do with ice: (1) **ice baron,** an opulent ice dealer; (2) **company,** a company that deals in ice; (3) **cutter,** see as a main entry; (4) **dealer,** one who sells ice; (5) **farmer,** one who harvests ice from lakes, ponds, etc.; (6) **harvester,** =prec.; (7) * **man,** a man who delivers ice to customers, or one who harvests ice from ponds, streams, etc.; (8) **merchant,** an ice dealer; (9) **monger,** an ice dealer, *rare;* (10) **trust,** a trust that controls the price of ice.

(1) **1906** *N.Y. Ev. Post* 29 June 7 The ice 'barons' of this city have again raised the price of ice to the dealers. — (2) **1834** *Cong. Deb.* 14 Feb. 544 He then read the prices of various stocks of banks, ice companies, . . . at the South. **1900** *Nation* 29 Nov. 421/2 The petitioner claimed that an action should be brought to annul the certificate of the Ice Company. — (4) **1851** CIST *Cincinnati* 50 [In Cincinnati there are three] ice dealers. **1948** *Ice & Refrigeration* Oct. 36/2 (*heading*), Ice Dealer Charged With Violation of Sanitary Code.

(5) **1937** COFFIN *Kennebec* 172 The Kennebec ice farmers heaped great towers of the harvest outside their houses and covered them with spruce boughs and sawdust, for extra measure. — (6) **1880** *Scribner's Mo.* Aug. 490/1 The ice had moved up thirty feet, the width of the ice-harvester's canal above, and had stopped. — (7) **1844** *Maysville* (Ky.) *Eagle* 7 Sep. 1/3, I do wish an ice man would come this morning. **1854** THOREAU *Walden* 209 Though . . . the ice-men have skimmed it once, it is itself unchanged, the same water which my youthful eyes fell on. **1944** *Time* 21 Aug. 86/2 He has set up an 'education department' to train icemen to make friends with women. — (8) **1855** *Amer. Inst. N.Y. Trans.* 374 In building ice houses . . . the best thing, as has been fully proved by Mr. Tudor, the great ice merchant of Boston, is hollow walls, containing a statum [*sic*] of air. **1905** THWAITES *Early Western Travels* XXI. 12 Wyeth finally . . . settled down to the humdrum role of ice-merchant in Cambridge. — (9) **1838** *N.Y. Advertiser & Exp.* 24 Feb. 4/5 The ice-mongers need not have felt alarm on account of the warm weather the early part of the Winter.

(10) **1900** *Outlook* 9 June 328/2 The leaders of Tammany Hall became connected with the ice trust, and that trust advanced prices one hundred per cent.

3. Designating tools used in connection with ice: (1) **ice chisel,** a tool used in cutting and breaking ice; (2) **cutter,** see as a main entry; (3) **marker,** (see quot. and cf. **ice plow**); (4) **pick,** a sharp-pointed implement for breaking ice into small pieces; (5) **plane,** (see quot. 1875); (6) **plow,** an implement for cutting grooves in pond ice to facilitate its fracture or cleavage into rectangular blocks.

(1) **1791** in *Pub. Champlain Soc.* XXI. 498 They met them coming towards the Slave Lake House as they supposed to Trade as they had a few Beaver skins with them, with hatches, Ice chisels. **1891** *Memphis Appeal-Avalanche* 26 April 3/2 Steel Ice Chisels and Picks, 10c each. **1904** *Harper's Wkly.* 9 Jan. 561 Expert users of long-handled ice-chisels stab down where division lines should be. — (3) **1909** *Cent. Supp.*, ice-marker . . . , n. A plow-shaped device for marking a groove in ice which is to be cut into blocks. It is guided by a gage which runs in the last-plowed groove. — (4) **1879** STOCKTON *Rudder Grange* i, It is not probable that I can sell that ice-pick after you have used it for ten years. **1949** *Chi. D. News* 12 May 14/7 A professional killer . . . pushes icepicks into business rivals for a stated fee.

(5) **1848** *Amer. Almanac 1849* 180 If snow falls so heavy as to bring the water above the surface of the ice, it is removed, after it has congealed into snow-ice, with the 'ice-plane,' which takes off about 2 inches in depth and 22 inches wide of its surface. **1875** KNIGHT 1169 Ice-plane. 1. A tool for dressing the surface of ice-blocks before stowage in bulk. 2. An instrument for shaving off fragments of ice for cooling drinks. — (6) **1873** *Leisure Hour* 552/2 Where a few weeks before magnificent passenger steamers were racing at the rate of twenty miles an hour, the ice-plough is at work. **1945** PEARSON *Country Flavor* 111 Rectangular blocks . . . have previously been marked out by the horse-drawn ice plow.

4. Denoting vehicles, etc., for use on ice or in connection with ice: (1) **ice bicycle,** a form of bicycle adapted for use on ice, *rare;* (2) **brogans,** brogan shoes for use on ice, *rare;* (3) **car,** (see quot.); (4) **cart,** a vehicle used in cities in delivering ice to customers; (5) **chair,** a chair fitted with runners so that it may be propelled easily upon ice, *obs.;* (6) **creeper,** a fixture with iron points to

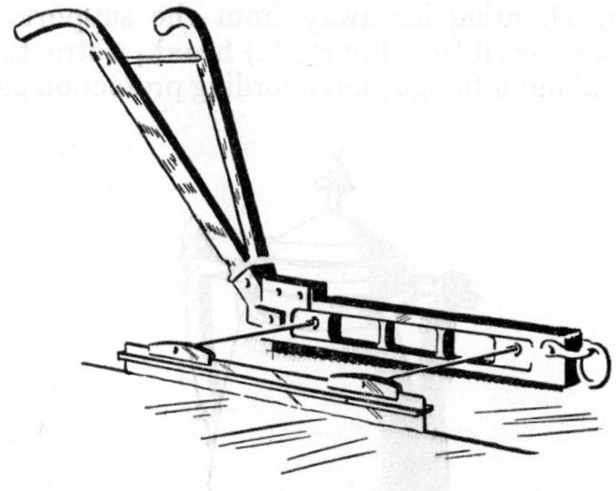

Ice marker

be worn on a shoe to prevent slipping on ice; (7) **scooter,** (see quot.); (8) **stage,** (see quot.); (9) **wagon,** a wagon used for delivering ice to customers.

(1) **1897** *Outing* XXIX. 343/2 Ice-bicycles, in which a runner is substituted for the front wheel, and the rear wheel is bound with a steel or iron rim, set with sharp teeth. — (2) **1852** *Knickerb.* March 290 We heard one [cobbler singing] . . . while [we were] waiting for 'Young Knick.'s' ice-brogans, 'on tap' at that period. — (3) **1895** WAIT *Car-Builder's Dict.* 69 Ice-car. A car for transporting ice, usually constructed with double roofs, floors and sides, filled in with sawdust or other non-conducting substance. — (4) **1842** *Knickerb.* XX. 205 Before an omnibus or hotel or restaurant or ice-cart had assumed its popular cognomen. **1870** O. LOGAN *Before Footlights* 275 Towards the close of the day, the shaking of the ice-cart, together with [etc.] . . . quite wear out the temper of the tired school-girl.

(5) **1861** *Index of Patents.* **1913** A. B. EMERSON *R. Fielding at Snow Camp* 88 The boys took turns in pushing her about in an ice-chair. — (6) **1875** KNIGHT 1162 Ice-creeper. A socket for the heel of a boot, having spurs on it to prevent slipping on ice. **1933** *Old-Time N. Eng.* July 5/2 Nearby is a group of toilet articles, featuring . . . equipment for inclement weather, such as umbrellas, ice creepers. — (7) **1909** *Cent. Supp.* 620–1 Ice-scooter. . . . These scooters may be run alternately through water and over ice. — (8) **1872** F. POOLE *Queen Charlotte Islands* 2 The ice-stage is a square-built conveyance, in form resembling a colossal packing box, in that the sides are composed of wind and waterproof curtains, instead of wood-work. It slides over the ice upon wooden runners shod with steel. — (9) **1865** *3 Yrs. Among Working Classes* 304 The ice-waggons may be seen with their crystal loads flying about the towns in all directions from May to the end of September. **1949** *Time* 28 Feb. 21/1 About the only rule was that a boy mustn't hang on to the back of ice wagons.

5. Designating places or receptacles where ice or ice water is kept, or where a low temperature is maintained: (1) **icebox,** see as a main entry; (2) **cellar,** a storage cellar for beer, meat, etc., that is kept cool with ice, cf. Du. *ijskelder*]; (3) **chest,** an icebox [cf. Du. *ijskast*]; (4) **closet,** a closet in connection with an ice house, *obs.;* (5) **cooler,** a receptacle for ice water; (6) **pitcher,** a pitcher for ice water, orig. a metallic one having a nonconducting interval between its double sides.

(2) [**1771** J. R. FORSTER tr. Kalm *Travels into N. Amer.* III. 232 Some of the people of quality [in Quebec] make use of ice-cellars, to keep beer cool in, during summer, and to keep fresh flesh. . . . These ice-cellars are commonly built of stone, under the house.] **1810** *Columbian Centinel* 20 Jan. 4 A new green-house and ice-cellar. **1883**

Harper's Mag. July 261 [In Cincinnati] I visited one of the largest whiskey distilleries, and also one of the largest beer factories, and took copious notes about . . . the ice cellars colder than Siberia ever dared to be. — **(3) 1841** CIST *Cincinnati (advt.)*, Manufacturer of Packing-boxes, Ice-chests, Trunk and Segar Boxes, &c. **1947** ROBINSON *Great Snow* 167 It had been his plan to . . . take a piece of cold meat from the ice chest. — **(4) 1823** *N. Eng. Farmer* II. 125, I herewith hand you a sketch of my ice closet attached to my ice house.

(5) 1892 *Harper's Mag.* Feb. 441/2 What's the matter with the ice-cooler? — **(6) 1865** *Nation* I. 159 At this season of the year nothing adds more to one's c mfort than to drink freely of the contents of our new pattern richly double-plated ice-pitchers. **1912** COBB *Back Home* 321 On opposite sidewalks they [2 Negroes] stood, sweating like brown stone china ice pitchers. **1918** LINCOLN *Shavings* 138 'Uncle Jed' . . . got a handle to it but it ain't so much like the handle to an ice pitcher as Mister is.

6. Designating structures constructed as safeguards against ice in winter: (1) **ice apron,** a pointed structure which by shunting ice away from the supports of a bridge preserves it from injury; (2) **break,** a structure, as cribbing, about a bridge pier, affording protection against

Ice pitcher

ice; (3) **breaker,** see as a main entry; (4) **guard,** (see quot.).

(1) 1871 *Scribner's Mo.* II. 170 It [has been] necessary to construct enormous breakwaters, having ice-aprons of strong oak timber. **1875** KNIGHT 1161/1 The ice-aprons of the Eads's St. Louis Railway Bridge are 200 feet long and 60 feet wide. — **(2) 1884** *Lisbon Star* 30 May, A crib has been built around the piles in the centre of the river and filled with stone, thereby forming a good and substantial ice-break. — **(4) 1905** *Forestry Bureau Bul.* No. 61, 40 *Ice guards.* Heavy timbers fastened fan shaped about a cluster of boom piles at an angle of approximately 30 degrees to the surface of the water. They prevent the destruction of the boom by ice, through forcing it to mount the guards and be broken up. (N[orthern] F[orest].)

7. In colloq. phrases: (1) *On ice,* safely assured, "in the bag," also *to put on ice,* to make sure of; (2) *on the ice,* used of a corpse that is being preserved with ice, *obs.,* cf. **ice coffin;** (3) *to keep on ice,* to hold in reserve; (4) *to cut ice,* to have importance or effect, usu. in negative contexts; (5) *to chop one's own ice,* to look after one's own interests; (6) *to crack the ice,* variant of "to break the ice."

(1) 1890 GUNTER *Miss Nobody* xx. 231 For Election. Gussie de P. Van Beekman. . . . On ice! **1945** *Chi. D. News* 4 Oct. 12/1 They started in and accumulated enough runs in the first inning to put the game on ice. **1949** *Dly. Ardmoreite* (Ardmore, Okla.) 23 Feb. 14/5 Lone Grove tried desperately to gain control of the ball but Dickson froze the ball to put the game on ice.—**(2) 1892** MARK TWAIN *Amer. Claimant* i. 23 (R.), Having departed this life five days ago . . . he is on the ice yet, him and his brother. . . . I shall take immediate occasion to have their noble remains shipped to you. — **(3) 1894** FORD *P. Stirling* 328 They say she's never been able to find a man good enough for her, and so she's keeping herself on ice. — **(4) 1896** ADE *Artie* xi. 96 But that cuts no ice in our set. **1948** *Time* 19 Jan. 20/3 The eight New Hampshire delegates would cut little ice at the Republican convention.

(5) 1904 *Dly. Ev. Telegraph* 20 June 6 Do not think that Teddy Roosevelt is making any mistake in chopping his own Presidential ice. — **(6) 1932** *Blue Valley Farmer* (Okla. City) 3 March 1/1 He has cracked the ice and other men of public life are now following his courageous action.

As the last term in **anchor, camphor, Dry, field, glare, mush, trash, Wenham ice.**

icebox 'aɪsˌbɑks, *n.*

1. An insulated box or boxlike structure in which a low temperature is maintained, either by the use of ice or by a cooling system operated, usu., by gas or electricity.

1846 *St. Louis Reveille* 9 Sep. 4/5 Everything requisite for funerals, such as Hearse, Carriages, Crape, Gloves, Scarfs, Ice, Ice-boxes, &c. **1862** T. F. DEVOE *Market Book* 485 This year [1830] also was first introduced 'ice-boxes or refrigerators' into the public markets, and in 1843 the Croton water. **1948** *L.A. Times* 5 Dec. (Home Mag.) 5/1 Electric stove and icebox are neatly fitted into one unit with work table between.

2. *attrib.* Designating cookies or rolls the dough for which is chilled in an icebox or refrigerator before cooking.

1929 *Ladies' Home Jrnl.* Feb. 66/1 The ice-box cookie is the new and improved 1929 model home-made cookie. **1942** RAWLINGS *C. Creek* 211 We have a wonderful recipe in these parts for ice-box rolls, whose yeast-rising dough may be prepared in advance, kept in the icebox, and brought out to be raised and baked when needed. **1949** *Sun. World-Herald Mag.* (Omaha) 3 April 18/1 There is ice cream on Sunday, ice box rolls [etc.].

icebreaker 'aɪsˌbrekɚ, *n.*

1. (See quot. 1889.) Cf. Du. *ijsbreker* 4 in *WNT*.

1816 THOMAS *Travels Western Country* (1819) 247 Notwithstanding these precautions, and that of placing *ice-breakers* to the south, [the bridge] was only saved from destruction the ensuing winter by the intrepidity of James Bennett, one of the proprietors. **1833** *Niles' Reg.* XLIV. 179/1 The ice breaker had been enlarged during the season to an extent of 575 feet in length by 60 in breadth. **1889** *Cent.* 2966/2 Ice-breaker, . . . a structure of masonry or timber (as a pier or row of piles) for the protection of bridge-piers or of vessels in dock from moving ice.

attrib. **1924** *Collier's* 2 Feb. 3/4 Rod in hand, Chicky stepped on the ice-breaker log and walked it, balancing carefully, down to the heads of the spiles that held it.

2. (See quot. 1875.) Cf. Du *ijsbreker* 2 in *WNT*.

1875 KNIGHT 1161/2 An ice breaker for harbors is a steam-vessel provided with means for opening or keeping open a channel for ships. **1902** LORIMER *Lett. Merchant* 114 You'll find that you can't push within a mile of her even on a Soo ice-breaker. **1945** *Business Wk.* 20 Jan. 34/2 The Mackinaw is said to be the most powerful icebreaker afloat—able to churn through heavy, solid ice at a steady speed of ten knots.

fig. **1883** MARK TWAIN *Life on Miss.* xxxix. 412 (R.), They closed up the inundation with a few words—having used it, evidently, as a mere ice-breaker and acquaintanceship-breeder—then they dropped into business.

* **ice cream.** In combs.: (1) **ice cream cake,** (see quot. 1883); (2) **cone,** a conical wafer, about five inches long, with a small amount of ice cream served in it, also attrib.; (3) **freezer,** a device used in freezing ice cream, also fig., cf. * **freezer;** (4) **pants,** white pants, cf. **ice cream suit;** (5) **parlor,** a shop which specializes in selling ice cream; (6) **saloon,** =prec.; (7) **sociable, social,** =**ice cream supper;** (8) **soda,** soda water to which ice cream has been added; (9) **stand,** a stall or booth where ice cream is sold; (10) **store,** a store or shop where ice cream is sold; (11) **suit,** a white suit; (12) **sundae,** a serving of ice cream to which sirup, crushed fruit, etc., have been added; (13) **supper,** a social gathering at which ice cream is sold for some benevolent purpose.

(1) 1883 *Practical Housekeeping* 83 Ice-Cream Cake. . . . Make good sponge-cake. . . . When cold, cut a round hole in top . . . fill with ice-cream just before serving. **1947** *Red Book* (Chi.) 137/1 Ice Cream Cakes Decorated for Any Occasion. — **(2) 1909** *Sat. Ev. Post* 15 May 11/2 The remainder is about equally divided among popcorn, ice cream cones, and candy. **1915** *Amer. Mag.* Aug. 23/2 One's name is Jake Nathan, he's got a ice-cream-cone business. **1945** *This Week Mag.* 19 May 19/1 First they'd walk to the corner and get an ice cream cone. — **(3) 1854** *Pa. Agric. Rep.* 363 Three ice cream freezers. **1873** *Winfield* (Kans.) *Courier* 14 Aug. 1/7 Flirts are always pretty, have big hearts, and when once caught you'll find them worth a dozen iceberg girls, who are only useful as icecream freezers. **1945** *Progressive Grocer* May 85 The ice cream freezer, one of the earliest gadgets patented in America, (No. 3,254), was the invention of a woman, Mrs. Nancy Johnson, of Philadelphia. — **(4) 1908** *Sat. Ev. Post* 5 Sep. 15/1 About half-past eight Johnny ambled up, decorated with a blue coat, white vest an' ice cream pants, an' his hair all slicked down. **1947** *Chi. Tribune* 25 May 12 (Comics), All the fellers have to come in dark coats, ice-cream pants an' white shoes.

(5) **1884** *Milnor* (Dak.) *Teller* 27 June, An ice cream parlor where the dudes and dudines sip . . . congealed milk and sugar. **1949** *Sat. Ev. Post* 22 Jan. 100/4 There's a convenient ice-cream parlor downstairs. — **(6) 1847** *Ill. State Reg.* (Springfield) 1 July 3/4 He has fitted up a room in the State House, superior to any in the city, for an 'Ice Cream Saloon.' **1906** BELL *C. Lee* 276 We took every child on the scene . . . to an ice-cream saloon and treated them. — **(7) 1873** *Winfield* (Kans.) *Courier* 15 May 3/2 The Ladies of the Congregational church will hold an Ice Cream Sociable at the residence of Capt. John Lowrey. **1898** *Dly. Ardmoreite* (Ardmore, Okla.) 15 July 3/3 The ladies of the Methodist Church . . . gave an ice cream social last night on the lawn at the parsonage. **1948** *News-Palladium* (Benton Harbor, Mich.) 14 Aug. 2/4 They only needed to follow the crowd to find that the occasion was an ice cream social. — **(8) 1886** *Mobile* (Ala.) *D. Reg.* 23 April 2/3 (*advt.*), Drink Ice Cream Soda. **1948** *Ice Cream Trade Jrnl.* Oct. 80/2 Sales are discouraged as the result of a poor quality ice cream soda. — **(9) 1876** *Nevada State Jrnl.* (Reno) 12 Aug. 3/7 The following awards [were] made: fruit stand to A. Jose, ice cream stand to A. Jose, and the music to Chas. Bock of Virginia. **1921** *Outing* July 160 'John' had paddled across the Pond and asked 'Jim' to take care of his ice cream stand for a while.

(10) 1887 *Courier-Journal* 11 Jan. 3/4 Annie Heinrich . . . clerked for . . . the proprietress of an ice-cream and confectionery store. **1948** *Savings News* Nov. 5/1 In Hollywood, an ice-cream store is doing something about the public's yen to create its own exotic treats (?) by permitting Amateur Night, behind the counter each Thursday. — **(11) 1890** *Road* (Denver) 19 April 1/3 Tenderness of heart perchance warns him against dragging a light colored ice cream suit into the ides of November with its chilling blasts. **1948** *Sat. Ev. Post* 11 Sep. 76/3 She hasn't had that ice-cream suit of hers off for twenty-four hours. — **(12) 1915** CAMPBELL *Proving Virginia* 106 Viviette insisted on stopping at Anderson's for ice-cream sundaes. **1945** SERVICE *Ploughman* 387 Give me the American way of life—the corner drug store, hot dogs and ice-cream sundaes. — **(13) 1892** *Canebrake Herald* 1 July 3/1 A delightful ice cream supper was given by the ladies. **1946** WILSON *Fidelity* 98 Ice-cream suppers were long used as a means to raise money for churches and schools.

b. In less frequent combs. and derivatives: (1) **ice cream cactus,** =**pitahaya;** (2) **candy,** ?candy consisting of a fondant which suggests ice cream; (3) **ice creamer,** a vendor of ice cream; (4) **ice creamery,** an ice cream parlor; (5) **festival,** a social gathering where the eating of ice cream is the chief diversion; (6) **foundry,** an ice cream parlor; (7) **garden,** a place of leisure or amusement which specializes in selling ice cream; (8) **party,** =**ice cream festival;** (9) **plant,** (see quot. 1949); (10) **table,** a table for customers in an ice cream parlor.

(1) 1894 *Scribner's Mag.* May 597/1 There is an almost unvarying succession of the . . . 'pitahaya,' or ice-cream cactus. — **(2) 1873** BAILEY *Life in Danbury* 273 And a package of ice-cream candy. — **(3) 1901** *Scribner's Mag.* XXIX. 484 Every low-down Neapolitan ice-creamer in the town. — **(4) 1851** W. K. NORTHALL *Curtain* 121 Niblo's was crowded from pit to dome with a larger and more brilliant audience than was ever collected before within the walls of that magnificent ice-creamery.

(5) 1893 *Harper's Mag.* March 593 The groups gathered here and there enjoy themselves about as they do at church sociables and ice-cream and strawberry festivals in their home villages. — **(6) 1889** *Road* (Denver) 28 Dec. 4/3 Ice cream and lemonade foundries did a rushing business. — **(7) 1853** *Harper's Mag.* VII. 567/2, I was sitting in an ice-cream garden, pretending to lick an ice-spoon. — **(8) 1904** M. KELLY *Little Citizens* 203 They expected some word of farewell—perhaps even an ice-cream party. — **(9) 1939** *Univ. Idaho School Forestry Bul.* 9, 38 In addition, elderberry is considered to be an 'ice cream' plant by the Forest Service of Region 4. **1949** *Pacific Discovery* Jan.–Feb. 7/1 In the parlance of U.S. deer managers this would put mahogany in the class of an 'ice cream plant'—one so favored by deer that it is commonly overbrowsed regardless of the balance between deer and the total available forage.

(10) 1898 *K.C. Star* 18 Dec. 3/6 (*advt.*), We will show (occupying the space formerly used by our ice cream tables) the handsomest lot of Christmas Candy Novelties ever brought to the West.

As the last term in **Neapolitan, Philadelphia, scuppernong ice cream.**

ice cutter.

1. Any one of various tools for cutting or breaking up ice.

1791 LONG *Voyages* 120 The fishing party consisted of . . . natives of Canada, who, being provided with axes, ice-cutters, and fishing materials, set off. **1884** *Nat. Museum Bul.* No. 27, 1053 Ice-cutter. A flat chisel-shaped piece of steel, with saw-like teeth on the lower edge. . . . Used for chopping up ice for the purpose of packing fresh fish.

b. An ice marker or ice plow *qq.v.*

1848 *Amer. Almanac 1849* 180 These grooves should be parallel to each other, and to make them so, the 'ice-cutter' has a guide, which is placed in the last groove made. **1940** R. O. CUMMINGS *American & His Food* 38 This ice-cutter [invented *c*1827] was in form not unlike a plow with a shear of sawlike cutting teeth which bit into the ice, making a deep groove. **1947** DOWNEY *Lusty Forefathers* 190 More recently a plow-like ice cutter had been devised to harvest ice from lakes and streams.

2. One who cuts or harvests ice from the surface of ponds, streams, etc.

1854 THOREAU *Walden* 315 These ice-cutters are a merry race, full of jest and sport. **1917** MCCUTCHEON *Green Fancy* 45 Jim Roudebush,—one of our leadin' ice-cutters.

3. (See quot.)

1894 SEARIGHT *Old Pike* 110 To get down an icy hill with safety, it was necessary to use an ice cutter. . . . The ice cutter was of steel or iron, in appearance like a small sled, fitted on the hind wheels, which were first securely locked.

***iced,** *a.* **iced coffee, tea,** coffee or tea chilled with ice. Also **iced-tea spoon,** a long-handled teaspoon.

1880 *Amer. Punch* Jan. 4/1 Some were talking of . . . the cooling and invigorating influences of 'iced tea.' **1918** *Sears Cat.* (ed. 136) 624 Iced tea spoons . . . set of six $1.68. **1944** JOHNSON *As I Dare* 200 There was iced tea and iced coffee, with beer for the less regenerate.

ice gorge. An accumulation of ice-blocks choking the bed of a river. Also transf.

1862 *Cong. Globe* 24 June 2896/1 [League] Island is below the bend of the Delaware, and hence mainly out of danger from ice gorges. **1890** *Cong. Rec.* 5 Feb. 1329/2 The closing days of the session, when there is a perfect ice gorge of measures contending for precedence. **1938** in MENCKEN *Supp.* I. (1945) 184 Snow and ice melt and ice gorges sometimes cause floods in Northern rivers.

ice road. [Cf. Du. *ijsbaan.*]

1. A road from an ice pond to an ice house. *Obs.*

1879 *Harper's Mag.* July 211 The old ice-road, which leads from the house to the pond, . . . was cleaned out [and] gravelled.

2. A road the surface of which is ice.

1881 *Harper's Mag.* Jan. 231/2 There was a track over the ice. . . . Beyond these there were no other ice roads. **1884** DAWSON *Canada* 122 The ice-roads [across the St. Lawrence in the Province of Quebec] are always marked-out by spruce-trees stuck in the snow. **1946** NEWTON *P. Bunyan* 102 Then he ordered the cookees to pump the gravy into a water tank which we used to sprinkle the ice roads in winter.

ice storm. A storm in which rain freezes on the objects it falls upon (see also quot. 1886).

1877 MARK TWAIN *Speeches* (1910) 63 (R.), One feature . . . compensates for all its bullying vagaries—the ice-storm: when a leafless tree is clothed with ice from the bottom to the top . . . and becomes a spraying fountain, a very explosion of dazzling jewels. **1886** GEIKIE *Outline Geol.* 50 Should one [ice-laden tree] be overthrown it collides against its neighbour, and this in turn falls upon another, until shortly the trees are seen crashing to the ground in all directions. This is what is known in North America as an ice-storm. **1947** COFFIN *Yankee Coast* 317 We have days in January, after an ice-storm, when living in Maine is living inside a diamond with all the walls cut and polished so they flame.

ictas 'ɪktɑs, *n. pl.* [Chinook.] Goods, things, merchandise. *Colloq.*

1856 *Dem. State Jrnl.* (Sacramento) 4 Oct. 3/1 The probability is, they are getting short of blankets and other *ictas.* *a***1861** WINTHROP *Canoe & Saddle* (1913) 44 My motley retinue followed me humbly, bearing 'iktas,' my traps and their own plunder. **1900** *Everybody's Mag.* Dec. 539/1 A white man, I told them, always has a good heart, but always does what he chooses with his own *ictas.*

Idahoan 'aɪdəˌhoən, *n.* A native or inhabitant of Idaho.

1918 REES *Ida. Chronology* 46 Idahoans feel proud of a name which signifies such a noble and expressive thought as the 'Gem of the Mountains.' **1923** *Nation* 13 June 693/2 The absence of class solidarity is a marked characteristic of Idahoans. **1944** ROSS *Westward* 135 'Times aren't so different,' said an old Idahoan who had made and lost a series of fortunes in sheep, mining, and saloonkeeping.

***idea,** *n.* A small drink. *Colloq. Obs.* See also **big, Broadway, Ohio idea.** — **1830** *Ky. Gazette* 20 Aug., [I] ventured a tiff of Bramin and an idea of water. **1836** CROCKETT *Exploits* 129 'Let us take an ideer.' So we walked up to the bar, [and] took a nip.

Illini ɪ'laɪˌnaɪ, *n. pl.* [See **Illinois.**] The Illinois Indians. Also the inhabitants of Illinois.

1932 MATHEWS *Wah' Kon-Tah* 91 In the cities, squat, hairy men from the islands of Greece; Germans, Slavs and Italians had taken the place of the Missouri, the Kansa, the Illini, the Osages and the ravaging Pawnees. **1945** *Chi. D. News* 12 July 12/1 We Illini would become wards of the Great White Father. **1949** *Chi. Tribune* 20 Feb. (Grafic Mag.) 14/4 These Indians called themselves *Illini* (the native word for men) but the French called them *Illinois*.

Illinoian ˌɪləˈnɔɪən, *a.* and *n.*

1. *n.* An Illinoisan.

1835 HOFFMAN *Winter in West* II. 204 Why now, squire, the Yankees are becoming great people here north of us, in Michigan and so on, and they call us old Illinoians 'Suckers.' **1867** RICHARDSON *Beyond Miss.* xi. 132 Most readers have heard Ohioans spoken of as 'Buckeyes.' . . . Illinoians as 'Suckers.'

2. *a. Geol.* Of or pertaining to one of the stages of the Pleistocene epoch when the interior of North America was glacial.

1899 *U.S. Geol. Surv. Water Supp. Paper 21*, 10 The sheet which forms the surface of much of the glaciated portion of Illinois, and which is known as the Illinoian drift sheet, is exposed only in a few counties of Indiana. **1947** *Midland Naturalist* July 6 The Illinoian till plain of southwestern Ohio, with similar conditions of soil moisture and acidity, has vegetation similar to the Patuxent swamps.

Illinois ˌɪləˈnɔɪ, *n.* ["*Iliniwek*, from *ilini* 'man,' *iw* 'is,' *ek* plural termination, changed by the French to *ois*" (Hodge).]

1. *pl.* The Algonquian Indians composing a confederacy that embraced parts of northern Illinois, southern Wisconsin, and parts of Iowa and Missouri.

1722 COXE *Carolana* 16 Forty miles above the Yellow River, on the East side is the River *Chicagou* or the River of the *Alinouecks*, corruptly by the French call'd *Illinois*. **1766** ROGERS *Ponteach* II. ii, This same Chekitan a Captive led The fair Donanta from the Illinois. **1834** PECK *Gaz. Illinois* 102 [Marquette and Joliet] were hospitally [*sic*] received by the Illinois, a numerous nation of Indians who were destitute of the cruelty of savages. **1907** HODGE *Amer. Indians* I. 598/2 In addition to the principal tribes or divisions above mentioned, the following are given by early writers as seemingly belonging to the Illinois. **1949** [see **Illini**].

b. Also **Illinois Indians.**

[**1670** *Relations des Jésuites* (1858) 86 Les Illinois peuples tirans au Sud, ont cinq grands Bourgs.] **1770** PITTMAN *Present State* 51 The principal Indian nations in this country are, the Cascasquias, Kaoquias, Mitchigamias, and Peoryas; these four tribes are generally called the Illinois Indians. **1948** *Chi. Tribune* 26 June I. 7/8 Starved Rock obtained its name from a legend which says that a band of Illinois Indians perished there in 1769.

2. a. Short for "Illinois country." **b.** An Illinoisan. Both *rare.*

(**a**) **1818** in *R.I. Hist.* I. 31 Jenckes and myself went across the river on the 9th (of January) with an intention of going to see the grand prairie in the Illinois. — (**b**) **1838** *Boston Wkly. Mag.* 17 Nov. 84/1 Add to this an Alabamian who sang negro songs; a Rock-River Illinois, who whooped like an Indian, a Texian [etc.].

3. In special combs., chiefly obs.: (1) **Illinois grazier,** (see quot.); (2) **lands,** (see quot.); (3) **mange,** the itch or an affliction resembling this; (4) **river note,** allegedly one of the derisive terms for paper currency after the panic of 1837; (5) **rowdy,** (see quot.); (6) **Territory,** the Northwest Territory.

(**1**) **1836** in HALL *Statistics of West* x. 149 The Illinois grazier, a most useful race of sheep, . . . is a short-legged, stout sheep, with a long-stapled soft wool. — (**2**) **1946** FOREMAN *Last Trek* 21 At the time of the Revolution the Indians of the Illinois Confederacy had been recognized as owners of a vast area of what were known vaguely as 'Illinois Lands' lying on both sides of the Mississippi. — (**3**) [**1815** DRAKE *Cincinnati* 185 The *Itch*, and a breaking-out which nearly resembles that complaint, are the most common.] **c1845** *True Picture* 26 Part of it we were obliged to spend in sulphur, to cure what is called the Illinois mange, from which we were all suffering. — (**4**) **1930** *Amer. Sp.* V. 409 'Soft' money, variously called 'shinplasters,' 'rag money,' . . . 'red-dogs,' 'plank road,' 'Illinois river' notes, etc., might work great harm.

(**5**) **1819** W. FAUX *Memorable Days* 277 The hunters, or Illinois Rowdies, as they are called, are rather troublesome. — (**6**) **1819** THOMAS *Travels* 170 From a bluff ten miles above Turtle Creek, we had a most charming prospect of *La Motte Prairie*, west of the river in the Illinois Territory.

b. In the names of, or with reference to, plants and animals: (1) **Illinois coffee,** (see quot.); (2) **corn,** a now unidentifiable variety of corn; (3) **hickory,** (see quots.); (4) **nut,** a pecan; (5) **parrot** the Carolina parakeet, now extinct; (6) **strawberry,** (see quot.).

(**1**) **1863** *Ill. Agric. Soc. Trans.* V. 869 *Cicer Arietunum* . . . has again been heralded as a valuable acquisition upon the prairies under the name of *Illinois coffee*, or 'Australian coffee.' — (**2**) **1849** EMMONS *Agric. N.Y.* II. 265 Illinois, or Lady-finger corn, . . . is an unproductive kind, bearing sometimes four ears upon a stalk. — (**3**) **1785** MARSHALL *Amer. Grove* 69 *Juglans pecan*. The Pecan, or Illinois Hickery. This tree is said to grow plenty in the neighborhood of the Illinois river. **1867** DE VOE *Market Ass't* 400 Pecan nuts—These nuts are brought from the South and West, and are taken for a species of the *Hickory Nut*, known by some as the *Illinois Hickory*. — (**4**) **1781–2** JEFFERSON *Notes Va.* (1788) 37 Paccan, or Illinois nut. . . . It grows on the Illinois, Wabash, Ohio, and Missisipi. **1884** SARGENT *Rep. Forests* 132 *Carya olivæformis*. . . . Pecan. Illinois Nut.

(**5**) **1811** WILSON *Ornithology* III. 97 The Carolina, or Illinois Parrot, (for it has been described under both these appellations) is thirteen inches long, and twenty-one in extent. — (**6**) **1862** *Rep. Comm. Patents 1861: Agric.* 190 *Fragaria Illinoiensis*—Illinois strawberry.

c. In nicknames applied to Abraham Lincoln, as **Illinois baboon, gorilla, rail-splitter, Xerxes.** All *obs.* or *hist.*

1861 *Dly. Dispatch* (Richmond, Va.) 1 Aug. 2/3 The consternation in Washington, upon the arrival there of the 'Grand Army' of the Illinois Xerxes, was indescribable. **1865** RICHARDSON *Secret Service* xxiv. 355 [*The Appeal*] was noticeably free from vituperation, calling the President 'Mr. Lincoln,' instead of the 'Illinois Baboon.' **1866** CARPENTER *At White House* 120 The newspapers announced the nominee as the 'Illinois Rail-splitter,' and . . . it seemed to many people a very extraordinary qualification for the Presidency. **1866** W. REID *After the War* 30 The Rebel owner has the satisfaction of . . . calculating the profits which might have gone into his own pockets, but for the frantic determination . . . never to submit to the tyrannical rule of the Illinois gorilla.

Also *Illinois bed, cabin, country, farmer, hoosier, Indian, man,* etc.

Illinoisan ɪləˈnɔɪsən, *n.* Also **Illinoisian.** A native or inhabitant of Illinois.

1836 *Public Ledger* 14 Oct. (Th.), The Illinoisans are called Suckers. **1855** *N.Y. Tribune* 31 Dec. 6/1, I had told him I was an Illinoisian, and an editor. **1948** *Aurora* (Ill.) *Beacon-News* 7 Nov. 3/1 The Illinoisan . . . boarded the Truman victory special at Union station here to welcome the President home.

***illuminate,** *v. tr.* (See quot.) *Slang. Obs.* — **1851** HALL *College Words* 167 *Illuminate*, to interline with a translation. *Ib.*, Illuminated books are preferred by good judges to ponies or hobbies, as the text and translation in them are brought nearer to one another.

***illuminator,** *n.* A highly polished convex reflector placed behind a light to intensify it. *Obs.* — **1851** GLISAN *Jrnl. Army Life* 77 The slow procession . . . moves onward with burnished muskets flashing their reflected light . . . like so many calcium illuminators. **1897** BRODHEAD *Bound in Shallows* 90 Buck Sherrer's house, with an illuminator behind the oil lamp on its porch, flashed in sight.

immediate government. An expression formerly used for the faculty at Harvard. Now *obs.* or *hist.*

[**1723** in *Pub. Col. Soc.* XVI. 492 When Such Laws are made the *Ordinary Execution* of them belongs to the Presidt and Tutrs residing in the House, who are in the Immediate Governmt of it, and for this Service among others they rec-v their Salary.] **1781** *Ib.* XV. xcix, Voted—That the immediate Government of the College be desired to dispose of Stoughton Hall as it now stands, on the best terms they can, to some person who will engage to remove it from the ground as soon as may be after the building shall be sold. **1823** *Ib.* XXVII. 89, I am fully aware of the necessity of maintaining, and of vindicating the authority of the immediate Government of the University. **1928** *Ib.* 65 It was the class of 1823, however, which gave the Immediate Government of the University most trouble and which started what is known in college history as the 'Great Rebellion.'

***immediatism,** *n.*

1. The proposal or policy of abolishing slavery at once. Now *hist.*

1835 H. G. OTIS in *Liberator* V. 144 [Abolitionists] have enriched the nomenclature with a new word, *immediatism.* This . . . is the opposite of *gradualism*, another new coinage. **1880** O. JOHNSON *W. L. Garrison* 45 Mr. Garrison had learned the doctrine of immediatism from Dr. Beecher. **1941** BUCKMASTER *Let My People Go* 73 Colonization versus Immediatism was debated with such glow, such fervor . . . such sweet persuasion that the hearts of those who listened were wrung.

2. Millerism. *Obs.*

1896 HASWELL *New York* 281 Thus, the Rev. Dr. Beman of Troy, N.Y. . . . delivered a course of lectures on the 'Second Coming of Christ,' which showed some advanced views, though he disclaimed belief in Miller's Immediatism.

immediatist ɪˈmidɪətɪst, *n.* **1.** One who favored the immediate abolishment of slavery. **2.** A Millerite *q.v.*, cf. ***immediatism 2.** Both *obs.*

(**1**) **1835** H. G. OTIS in W. P. & F. J. Garrison *W. L. Garrison* I. (1885) [Christ] was not an immediatist. **1852** W. GOODELL *Slavery & Anti-Slavery* 424 [Some] professed to be opposed to slavery, and in favor of its gradual removal, while they only deprecated the imprudent measures of the *immediatists*. — (2) **1888** *Andover Rev.* Oct. 361 The gospel of the Immediatist,—work while the day lasts.

immigrant ˈɪməgrənt, *n.* [L. *immigrans*, f. *immigrare*, to go into.]

Pickering discussed *immigrate, immigration,* and *immigrant*, ascribing all of them to Dr. Belknap and saying "they do not appear to have been found necessary." See A. Matthews in *Nation* LXX. 10.

1. One who has come from a foreign country to settle in the U.S. Cf. **emigrant.**

1789 Morse *Amer. Geog.* 253 There are in this state [N.Y.] many immigrants from Scotland, Ireland, Germany, and some few from France. **1809** Kendall *Travels* II. 252 *Immigrant* is perhaps the only new word, of which the circumstances of the United States has in any degree demanded the addition to the English language. **1896** C. W. Ernst in *Proc. Bostonian Soc.* 26 The word 'immigrant' is likewise a Boston coinage. . . . Boston men once went so far as to have a society for the encouragement of immigrants. **1947** *Chi. D. News* 12 March 1/2 (*heading*), Immigrant Kills Himself 'Too Old' to Learn English, He Said.

attrib. **1835** Cooper *Monikins* xxiv, The 'immigrunt interest,' as Noah termed it, had actually carried a candidate on each of the two great opposing tickets. **1911** Persons *Mass. Labor Laws* 175 In the investigation of immigrant women, evidence was obtained [etc.].

2. One who has migrated from one part of the U.S. to another, as from the East to newly opened territory in the West.

1798 *Doc. Hist. N.Y. State* I. 675 New England had not been settled so long as to produce Native Immigrants when E. Hampton [L.I.] was first settled. **1874** Glisan *Jrnl. Army Life* 481 The more sensible immigrants took up claims in the beautiful Willamette Valley. **1945** *Chi. D. News* 18 Dec. 1 (*caption*), Vets, Eastern Immigrants Jam California.

3. In special combs., now obs.: (1) **immigrant cattle,** *W.* cattle brought into a range from a distance; (2) **fund,** (see quot.); (3) **train,** (*a*) a railroad train that carried immigrants at reduced fare, now *hist.*, (*b*) a long succession of wagons carrying settlers going to the West; (4) **wagon,** one of the wagons making up an immigrant train.

(1) **1888** Roosevelt in *Cent. Mag.* XXXVI. 837/1 They were mostly Texan *doughgies*,—a name I have never seen written; it applies to young immigrant cattle. — (2) **1903** *Statutes at Large* XXXII. 1. 1213 Money thus collected [by a head-tax on entry of aliens] . . . shall constitute a permanent appropriation to be called the 'immigrant fund.' — (3) (*a*) [**1854** in Schmidt *Briefe* 28 Es giebt in der Regel nur eine Wagenclasse; auf einigen Bahnen—ich glaube auf allen nach dem Westen führenden—findet man eine zweite Classe, die für die sogenannten Emigrantenzüge bestimmt.] **1947** *N. & Q.* April 11/2 On June 28, 1864, . . . an immigrant train plunged through the open draw into the Richelieu River. (*b*) **1900** *Cong. Rec.* 31 Jan. 1354/1 In 1849 . . . many immigrant trains crossed the great plains through Arizona Territory. — (4) **1867** Richardson *Beyond Miss.* 26 A confused picture of immense piles of freight, horse, ox, and mule teams receiving merchandise from the steamers, scores of immigrant wagons, and a busy crowd of whites, Indians [etc.].

***immigration,** *n.*

1. A (or the) body of immigrants.

1852 Stansbury *Gt. Salt Lake* 126 In the autumn, another large immigration arrived under the president, Brigham Young, which materially added to the strength of the colony. **1857** *Lawrence* (Kans.) *Republican* 2 July 2 The whole immigration of this season . . . was excluded from the ballot-box. **1857** *Ill. Agric. Soc. Trans.* II. 365 The immigration [into Ill.] was generally a moral, correct people. . . . They emigrated from the various old states. **1948** *Sat. Review* 17 July 20/1 A far vaster immigration . . . began pouring through the city portals.

2. In combs. of obvious meaning as (1) **immigration boom,** (2) **department,** (3) **report,** (4) **service,** (5) **society.**

(1) **1890** *Stock Grower & Farmer* 22 Feb. 3/2 This territory has never had an immigration 'boom.' — (2) **1890** *Stock Grower & Farmer* 25 Jan. 7/2 Col. Edward Haren, of the immigration department of the Santa Fe, is in the city on his return from Albuquerque. — (3) **1872** *Atlantic Mo.* April 456/1 Natives of Europe and the British Provinces who came from and through Canada and New Brunswick . . . not included in the immigration reports were [etc.]. — (4) **1903** *Statutes at Large* XXXII. 1. 1217 The United States Public Health and Marine-Hospital Service shall be reimbursed by the Immigration Service for all expenditures incurred in carrying out the medical inspection of aliens. **1948** *Time* 1 Nov. 38/2 The U.S. State Department, after privately landing on the Immigration Service with both feet, composed an apologetic note that made the Mexicans feel happier.

(5) **1879** *Bradstreet's* 10 Dec. 2/3 It is our idea that immigration societies are doing us no good. [**1896** C. W. Ernst in *Proc. Bostonian Soc.* 26 Boston men once went so far as to have a society for the encouragement of immigrants, and they secured an act of incorporation on June 25, 1795. It is needless to add that they disbanded in 1798.]

imperial ɪmˈpɪrɪəl, *n.* [F. *impériale*, in same sense.] A form of goatee.

1841 *Knickerb.* XVII. 460 Two wigs, moustaches, an imperial, a gay vest. **1896** Haswell *New York* 69 A full beard, or even an imperial or goatee, was unknown [in N.Y. *c*1816], except when a native of an Eastern country would appear with the former. **1946** *N. & Q.* May 31/2 The 'Imperial' of Napoleon III was widely copied in this country, and popularized by William F. Cody (Buffalo Bill). It was adopted in the South, especially among 'Kentucky colonels' after the Civil War.

***imperial,** *a.*

1. In the names of plants, trees, fruit, birds. *Obs.*

1815 *Lit. & Phil. Soc. N.Y. Trans.* I. 172 Our Dutch forefathers . . . introduced . . . wall flowers, tulips, imperial flowers, the white lily. **1839** Audubon *Ornith. Biog.* V. 313 Imperial Woodpecker. *Picus Imperialis.* **1862** *Rep. Comm. Patents 1861: Agric.* 197 Imperial Crimson [strawberry] . . . Imperial Scarlet [strawberry]. *Ib.* 541 Of plums, Jefferson, imperial gage and purple gage [succeeded best]. **1892** Apgar *Trees Northern U.S.* 127 *Paulownia imperialis.* (Imperial Paulownia.)

2. a. imperial cake, a cake resembling a pound cake but having in it nuts and raisins. **b. Imperial Palace,** a grandiloquent term for the headquarters of the Ku-Klux Klan. **c. Imperial Wizard,** the highest officer in the Ku-Klux Klan.

(a) **1888** L. Hargis *Graded Cook Book* 359 Imperial Cake. . . . One and one-half cups well-creamed butter, ten eggs beaten separately [etc.]. — (b) **1923** *Imperial Night-Hawk* 29 Aug. 4 Published Weekly From The Imperial Palace, Atlanta, Georgia, by The Knights of the Ku Klux Klan. — (c) **1946** *Coronet* Oct. 5/2 The Imperial Wizard . . . had disbanded the hooded hoodlums. **1949** *Chi. D. News* 12 March 8/3 The senior Senator from the state of the Talmadges and the Imperial Wizard of the Ku Klux Klan can offer no such defense.

imphee ˈɪmfi, *n.* [Zulu (Africa) *imfe.*] Any one of several African varieties of sorghum. *Obs.*

1859 *Ill. Agric. Soc. Trans.* IV. 108 A meeting was convened . . . for the purpose of discussing all matters of interest connected with the culture and manufacture of the Chinese Sugar Cane and Imphee. **1867** *Iowa Agric. Soc. Rep.* 177 The African Imphee is raised to some extent. **1880** *Vt. Agric. Rep.* VI. 222 Sixteen varieties of sorghum [introduced] from Africa . . . received the general name of Imphees.

implete ɪmˈplit, *v. tr.* To fill. *Obs.* — **1862** *N.Y. Independent* 31 July 4 It was the purpose of Mr. Calhoun . . . to implete the Government silently with Southern principles. **1886** Beecher in *Homiletic Rev.* May 421 [God] impletes all lands, all breadths, above, below, everywhere.

implied power. Power not specifically granted by the U.S. Constitution but implied from enumerated powers. Usu. *pl.*

1791 *Ann. 1st Congress* 1909 He did not pretend that it [i.e., the last paragraph of Section 8 of the Constitution] gives any new powers; but it establishes the doctrine of implied powers. **1819** Marshall in *Supreme Ct. Rep.* XVII. 357 The implied powers of the constitution may be assumed and exercised, for purposes not really connected with the powers specifically granted, under color of some imaginary relation between them. **1883** Waite in *Supreme Ct. Rep.* CX. 432 Otherwise the assertion and exercise by Congress of any implied power, irrespective of facts or circumstances, would destroy all limitations, and give to the implied powers a greater force than the express powers themselves.

***import,** *n.* A system of taxation on imported articles. *Obs.* — **1789** in *S. Lit. Messenger* Jan. 36/1, I am sorry that the opinion of those who wished to adopt the plan of Import, of [17]83, had not been followed; . . . the Legislature would have had leisure to digest a proper law of Import. **1802** *Steele P.* I. 259, I do not believe that the Import will produce the sum which he estimates.

impost ˈɪmpost, *v. tr.* (See quots.) Also **imposter,** *n. Obs.* — **1884** *Harper's Mag.* June 57/2 The entry papers . . . [are] sent to an official who imposts them, or, in other words, classifies the articles therein described in separate columns according to the rate of duty that each is liable to pay. *Ib.*, From the imposter the entries pass to other hands. *Ib.*, Again they pass into the hands of the imposting and statistical clerks.

impressional ɪmˈprɛʃənl, *a.* Related to impressions, impressionable. *Obs.* — **1860** Emerson *Conduct of Life* 111 He must be musical, Tremulous, impressional, Alive to gentle influence Of landscape and of sky. *a***1882** Quincy *Figures of Past* (1883) 279 The resemblance

. . . could scarcely be called physical, and I am loath to borrow the word impressional from the vocabulary of spirit mediums.

***improve**, *v.* [See note.]

The senses here shown seem to be of American origin, but the *OED* has quite early British examples of "improvement" in corresponding senses, and likewise early examples (1649——) of "improver" corresponding to sense **1.** The only one of the senses here given that has persisted and spread beyond N. Eng. is that shown in **1.** Pickering has an interesting discussion of this verb.

1. *tr.* To use or do work upon (land) in such a way as to increase its value.

1632 *Mass. Bay Rec.* I. 94 If the . . . said John Winthrop shall . . . suffer the said ileland to lye wast, and not improue the same, then this present demise to be voide. **1675** *Pa. Mag.* VI. 87 Every one must joyn their Hands, first in Building the Houses, and next in Improving the Land. **1777** *Va. State P.* I. 279 He settled and Improved a Plantation on the Monongahela River. **1906** BELL *C. Lee* 293, I could refuse an offer to improve my land, denuded and mortgaged as it is.

2. To employ (a person) in a designated manner. *Obs.*

1640 *Conn. Hist. Soc. Coll.* VI. 11 The Townsmen [shall] haue liberty to Improue men for the killing of woolfs. **1722** in B. PEIRCE *Hist. Harvard Univ.* (1833) 232 Voted . . . that Mr. Judal Monis be *improved* as an instructor of the Hebrew language in the College. **1789** FRANKLIN *Writings* X. 76 A deceased Country Gentleman . . . had been for more than 30 years *improved* as a Justice-of-Peace. This Use of the Word *improved* is peculiar to New England. **1829** *Va. Lit. Museum* 30 Dec. 458 To improve. 'To occupy, make use of, employ'—as to 'improve as a tavern'—'to improve as a schoolmaster,' 'to improve their children in labour &c.' New England.

3. To make use of (a house or part of a house), usu. for an indicated purpose. *Obs.*

1647 *Conn. Probate Rec.* I. 17 It being my will that . . . my sayd Howsing & Lande . . . bee improved by the overseers of this my will for the maintenence and education of my children. **1751** *Boston Rec.* 259 Forty six years ago Mr. Thomas Hunt occupied & improved a Blacksmith's Shop. **1782** *R.I. Col. Rec.* IX. 512 Josiah Flagg . . . [shall] have the liberty of improving the cellars under the state house in Providence, as repositories for the public stores. **1828** WEBSTER *s.v., Improve.* . . . To use; to occupy; to cultivate. The house or farm is now improved by an industrious tenant. This application is perhaps peculiar to some parts of the U. States. **1862** HAWTHORNE in *Atlantic Mo.* Dec. 712/2 The hall . . . has come to base uses in these latter days,—being improved, in Yankee phrase, as a brewery and wash-room.

***improved**, *a.* Of land: In use, under cultivation, fenced and provided with farm buildings. Cf. **unimproved land.**

1643 *Plymouth Laws* 74 By ymproved lands are understood meddow land plowed land and howed lands. **1703** *N.J. Archives* III. 20 A hundred or Fifty Acres of improved Land (as it's call'd). **1832** WILLIAMSON *Maine* II. 159 The school tax was from a half-penny to a penny per acre on improved lands. **1870** *Dept. Agric. Rep. 1869* 8 The vague and meaningless distinctions of 'improved' and 'unimproved' land should be replaced by more . . . useful divisions. **1949** *Lubbock* (Tex.) *Morn. Avalanche* 23 Feb. II. 8/5 $230 per acre. Fully improved, all conveniences.

b. Also **improved farm.**

1787 in *Mag. Amer. Hist.* I. 435 Stopped at a very beautiful improved farm . . . where one Craig lives in an excellent stone house.

***improvement**, *n.*

1. *pl.* Buildings, fences, clearings, etc., made or put upon land.

1640 in *New Haven Col. Rec.* 43 If they remove, to sell nothing butt improvements. **1748** *Va. Mag. Hist. & Biog.* V. 279 The County Court . . . ordered John Savage . . . to make a new Survey, . . . having Regard to the Buildings and Improvements then standing. **1818** FEARON *Sketches Amer.* 219 The price of land varies very much, according to situation and the proximity of townships. Farms which are called *improved* can be bought at from 8 to 30 dollars per acre; the *improvements* often consist of the erection of rough log buildings, and about from 12 to 20 acres under middling cultivation. **1908** *Indian Laws & Tr.* III. 382 Any person who . . . shall be an actual resident upon any one such lot and the owner of substantial and actual improvements thereon. **1949** *Lubbock* (Tex.) *Morn. Avalanche* 23 Feb. II. 3, 320 A. near Shallowater, good 8 inch irrigation well, large loan, good improvements, possession.

b. The latest household conveniences in plumbing, heating, lighting, etc.

1859 GRATTAN *Civilized Amer.* I. 104 The absences of what American delicacy called 'modern improvements' . . . give to the generality of houses in the United States a half-finished and half-furnished appearance. **1875** *N.Y. Tribune* 10 Aug. 9/2 Will be rented very low to a good tenant, a desirable house, with all the modern improvements near depot. **1918** *N.Y. Times* 15 Jan. 21/5 Delightful home built to order; owner moved to California; a sacrifice for a fine semi-bungalow; 7 rooms and bath; all up-to-date improvements.

c. The paving of roads and sidewalks, the laying of water pipes, sewers, etc., in a town or town site.

1884 *Cent. Mag.* March 648/1 The rights of property-owners were disregarded, and they were assessed for 'improvements' when their property was ruined. **1948** *Downers Grove* (Ill.) *Rep.* 21 Oct. 11/1 (*advt.*), 7 room home just south of Fairview depot, bath and a half, 60 ft. frontage, all street improvements in and paid including paving.

2. Employment. *Obs.* Cf. ***improve**, *v.* **2.**

1703 SEWALL *Letter-Book* I. 282 Very few gray hairs are to be found in the Colony, in civil or sacred improvement. **1736** *Suffolk Co.* (Mass.) *Rec.* XXXII. 207 As to the rest and residue of my Estate both Real and Personal I give the Improvement benefit and Income thereof to my Dear Wife Elizabeth Davenport during her Natural Life.

3. In combs.: (1) **improvement cabin,** a cabin erected on public land in partial fulfillment of the requirements for a title of ownership, *obs.;* (2) **circle,** a group of people interested in their personal and cultural improvement, *obs.;* (3) **company,** a company engaged in building or in developing real estate, transportation, etc.; (4) **district,** (see quot.), *obs.;* (5) **lease,** a lease or permission to use land on condition that certain improvements will be made upon it; (6) **loan,** ?a loan granted a settler to enable him to make certain improvements upon land which he has entered, *obs.;* (7) **money,** money paid to a settler for improvements he has made upon a certain piece of land, *obs.;* (8) **right,** a right or title to public land secured by making certain improvements upon it, *obs.;* (9) **society,** a group of persons working together for the betterment of local conditions; (10) **title,** =**improvement right,** *obs.*

(1) 1886 Z. F. SMITH *Kentucky* 29 The men dispersed . . . to build on such locations improvement cabins. — **(2) 1847** *Hunt's Merch. Mag.* XVI. 361 Besides these, clubs are formed, that are denominated 'Improvement Circles.' **1855** BAXTER *America* 116 The numerous 'Improvement Circles,' or literary societies, at which so many of the workers spend their leisure time . . . bear ample testimony to the existence of mind among the Spindles.' — **(3) 1880** E. KIRKE *Garfield* 57 The Credit Mobilier Company is . . . authorized by its charter . . . to make advances of money and credit to railroad and other improvement companies. **1884** MATTHEWS & BUNNER *In Partnership* 150 There was already an Avoca Improvement Company, building a big hotel, advertising right and left, and prophesying that the day of Saratoga and Sharon and Richfield was ended. — **(4) 1883** *Ill. Rev. Statutes* 265 Any city or village . . . may lay off such city or village . . . into what shall be known or called improvement districts.

(5) 1849 CHAMBERLAIN *Indiana Gaz.* 34 They rented land on improvement leases, by which they were to have the use of from ten to twenty acres from seven to ten years, and often at the end of that time they were able to buy land for themselves. — **(6) 1839** *Indiana H. Rep. Jrnl.* 368 An amount may be realized sufficient . . . to discharge the entire amount of interest on the improvement loans down to the year 1850. — **(7) 1850** GARRARD *Wah-To-Yah* i. 3 [He] was to receive ten thousand dollars improvement money for his farm in Ohio. — **(8) 1876** *Ill. Dept. Agric. Trans.* XIII. 330 Succeeding the systems of commons and common fields came the grants of 'head rights' of 400 acres each, 'improvement rights' of 250 acres, and 'militia rights' of 100 acres, under acts of congress. — **(9) 1880** *Harper's Mag.* Dec. 147 The village improvement societies are signs of the wish to remedy congenital defects of rural communities. **1894** *Ib.* June 156/1 The president of our improvement society.

(10) 1794 *Ann. 4th Congress* 2 Sess. 2803 The people in the western counties . . . complained of the decisions of the State courts, which discountenanced improvement titles, and gave the preference to paper titles.

As the last term in **internal, tomahawk improvement.**

inaugural ɪnˈɔgjərəl, *a.* and *n.*

1. *n.* Short for **inaugural address.**

1832 *Cong. Deb.* 5 May 2778 The President, in his inaugural, . . . [hoped for] 'instruction and aid from the co-ordinate branches.' **1845** *Quincy* (Ill.) *Whig* 20 Nov. 2/4 Mr. Polk, . . . it is understood, will repeat to Congress, the declaration in his Inaugural, that 'our title to Oregon is clear and unquestionable.' **1947** *Life* 10 Feb. 66/2 He [Lincoln] was dressed immaculately as he delivered the immortal words of the second inaugural.

transf. **a1861** WINTHROP *Open Air* 134, I must give them a little sharp talk by way of Inaugural.

b. The ceremony of inaugurating the President of the U.S.

1913 *Chi. D. News* 3 March 2/1 (*heading*), Noise For Inaugural. Seating of New President Is to Be Marked Here by Din of Whistles and Bells. **1948** *Washington Post* 5 Dec. 19M/7 The Freedom Train . . . will wind up its tour of the country with a weeks' stay here during the inaugural.

2. inaugural address, the speech made by a President of the U.S., or the governor of a state, at his inauguration.

1804 *Fredericktown* (Md.) *Herald* 19 May 3/1 The promises of the Inaugural Address, with the wanton and continued breaches of those promises, they mind not. **1864** *Wkly. New Mexican* 10 June 1/4 The oath of office was administered, and the Governor then delivered his inaugural address. **1949** *Chi. D. News* 26 April 12/2 His program, as outlined in his inaugural address and messages to the 81st Congress, is virtually sunk.

b. The speech made by Jefferson Davis upon his inauguration as President of the Southern Confederacy. *Obs.*

1884 BLAINE *20 Years of Congress* I. 256 In his message to the Confederate Congress, Mr. Davis apparently attempted to cure the defects of his Inaugural address.

3. a. inaugural ball, a ball on the occasion of the inauguration of a President of the U.S. **b. inaugural day,** the day on which a President of the U.S. is inaugurated.

(a) 1913 *Outlook* 15 March 567/2 A vast concourse of people enjoyed the unprecedented display, surely a much more democratic pleasure than attendance, limited by pecuniary considerations only, upon an inaugural ball. **1948** *Washington Post* 5 Dec. S 1/4 The festivities are scheduled as follows: January 19, the Gala Concert; the Inaugural and Inaugural Ball on the 20th and Hospitality Day on the 21st. — **(b) 1909** *Forum* Dec. 533 The adoption of a different inaugural day would perhaps necessitate an amendment to the twelfth article of the Constitution.

***inauguration,** *n.* In combs.: (1) **inauguration ball,** see as a main entry; (2) **cake,** an elaborate cake made on the occasion of the inauguration of a President of the U.S., *rare;* (3) ***Day,** see as a main entry; (4) **week,** the week during which the inauguration of a President of the U.S. takes place.

(2) 1841 *N.O. Picayune* 21 Feb. 2/2 An Inauguration Cake has been prepared at Georgetown, D.C., which is a model of the Capitol at Washington. — **(4) 1849** *Knickerb.* XXXIII. 368 A friend who was present gives us an amusing description of matters and things in Washington during 'inauguration-week.'

inauguration ball. A ball given on the occasion of the inauguration of a state governor or of the President of the U.S. Also transf.

1817 in MORISON *Life H. G. Otis* (1913) II. 206 A grand inauguration Ball in the even'g [for Monroe's inauguration]. **1841** *N.O. Picayune* 8 Dec. 2/1 The Inauguration Ball in honor of the opening of the St. Louis Hotel, will take place to-night, in the Ball-room. **1852** *Knickerb.* XL. 52 Ten years after, I was present at an inauguration-ball at Milledgeville. **1885** *Wkly. New Mexican Rev.* 11 June 2/6 The inauguration ball to be given in Santa Fe when our new governor is inaugurated will be the grandest ever witnessed in the territory.

Inauguration Day. The day upon which the President of the U.S. is inaugurated.

The 20th of January in every year next after a year divisible by four is now Inauguration Day, but before 1934 the ceremony was held on the 4th of March of such years.

1829 in M. BAYARD SMITH *Forty Yrs. Washington Soc.* (1906) 288 On the Inauguration day when they went in company with the Vice-President's lady. **1893** WIGGIN *Polly Oliver* (1894) xvii. 185 As it chances to be a presidential year, we will celebrate Inauguration Day. **1948** *Denison* (Tex.) *Herald* 1 July 4/3 That was when Inauguration Day was changed from March 4 to January 20, for Roosevelt's second term.

b. The day upon which a state governor is inaugurated (see quot. 1887).

1886 J. H. TRUMBULL *Memorial Hist. Hartford Co., Conn.* 189 It was the duty of a selected company . . . to escort the governor on 'Election Day' as inauguration day was always styled [in Conn.]. **1887** *Narragansett Hist. Reg.* V. 343 The day upon which state officers are engaged—the day called in other states [than Rhode Island] Inauguration day.

Inc., *a.* Abbreviation of "incorporated." — **1906** *Country Life* May 16/1 (*advt.*), The Engleside Company, Inc., Owners. **1945** *Red Book* (Chi.) March 312 Meyer Engineering Co. Inc.

Inca dove. A small dove, *Scardafella inca*, found from southern Arizona to Central America. — **1887** RIDGWAY *Manual N. Amer. Birds* 216 *S[cardafella] inca*. . . . Inca Dove. **1917** *Birds of Amer.* II. 52 The little Inca Dove . . . often seems very tame or very stupid. . . . One cannot live in Tucson for a day without making the acquaintance of the little Inca Dove.

incense cedar. "The white or post cedar, *Libocedrus decurrens*, a native of the Pacific coast of the United States, from Oregon south, growing on the mountains. It is a large tree with light, soft, but durable wood" (*Cent.*).

1869 MUIR *First Summer in Sierra* (1911) 27 Another conifer was met to-day,—incense cedar (*Libocedrus decurrens*), a large tree with warm yellow-green foliage in flat plumes like those of arborvitæ. **1923** SAUNDERS *So. Sierras Calif.* 42 Silver firs, yellow pine, and incense cedars four and five feet in diameter made a contemplative twilight. **1948** *So. Sierran* April 1/3 An Incense Cedar just above Idyllwild near the Fern Valley road has a girth of 30 feet.

***inch,** *n.* **1. inch plant,** the wandering Jew. **2. inchworm,** a measuring worm.

(1) 1892 *Amer. Folk-Lore* V. 104 *Tradescantia crassifolia*, . . . inch-plant. — **(2) a1861** WINTHROP *Open Air* 123 All the green inchworms vanish on the tenth of every June. **1949** *Sat. Ev. Post* 12 March 33/1 One evening the Main Line local hunched its cars together like an inchworm and skidded to a halt at Merion station.

incienso ɪnsɪ'ɛnso, *n. S.W.* [Sp. "incense," in Amer. Sp. applied to various trees and shrubs.] (See quot. 1931 and cf. **brittlebush** and **Encelia.**) — **1925** JEPSON *Flowering Plants Calif.* 1082 E[ncelia] farinosa Gray. Incienso. **1931** DAYTON *Western Browse Plants* 164 Other vernacular names include brittlebrush, golden hills, incienso, starchy encelia, tohafs (Pima), and whitebush.

***incline,** *n.* =next.

1880 *Harper's Mag.* Dec. 52 The nerve-trying 'inclines' . . . scale the bold cliffs of Coal Hill. **1883** *Ib.* Aug. 328/2 The Portage Railroad. . . . received travelers by the canal route . . . and conveyed them over the mountain by inclines and stationary engines. **1948** *Sierra Club* (So. Calif. Chap.) *Sched.* 128, 43 Here we will view the ruins of the once famous Incline, hear our echo at Echo Point and bask in the sunshine.

incline(d) railway. A cable-car line used on a steep incline.

1833 COKE in *Select Circulating Library* II. 398/2 A melancholy accident occurred to a party of four gentlemen . . . upon the inclined railway connected with the quarries, by the chain to which the car was attached suddenly breaking. **1906** LYNDE *Quickening* 311 He took an electric car . . . on the line connecting with the inclined railway running up the mountain to Crestcliffe Inn. **1948** *Sierra Club* (So. Calif. Chap.) *Sched.* 129, 83 The trail . . . leads up Echo Mountain to the abandoned powerhouse of the old Incline Railway, up around Sunset Point.

incommunicado ˌɪnkəˌmjunɪ'kɑdo, *a.* [Sp. *incomunicado*, in same sense.] Without means of communication, usu. said of prisoners in solitary confinement.

1844 KENDALL *Santa Fe Exped.* II. 255 Now that I was incomunicado—now that all intercourse with my friends was cut off, . . . my situation became irksome in the extreme. **1931** *Nation* 24 June 689 (Bentley), As the courts are closed, one . . . may be held for three days incommunicado before being arraigned in court. **1949** *Sat. Ev. Post* 16 April 71/2 The only possible thing I can think of would be to arrest those men on a murder charge and hold them incommunicado until the option time runs out.

***incorporator,** *n.* One who participates in the formation of a town corporation or of a business corporation.

1877 *Mich. Gen. Statutes* I. (1882) 1013 An affidavit made by three or more of the incorporators, that the signatures to such articles and consent and agreement are genuine. **1898** PAGE *Red Rock* 209 Among the incorporators were himself, Hiram Still, Still's son, and Mr. Bolter.

Also **incorporatorship.** *Rare.*

1873 MARK TWAIN & WARNER *Gilded Age* xlii, It would be more money in my pocket, in the end, than my brother-in-law will get out of that incorporatorship, fat as it is.

***incurve,** *n.* In baseball, a pitched ball which curves toward a right-handed batter. — **1886** CHADWICK *Art of Pitching* 14 It is essential to change the direction of the curve from an 'out-curve' to an 'in-curve,' and from an 'up-shoot' to a 'down-shoot.' **1906** *Spalding's Base Ball Guide* 112 An In-curve . . . is a ball which curves in towards the batsman as he stands in his position.

indeedy ɪn'didɪ, *adv.* A jocose or slang variant of "indeed."

1856 *Knickerb.* Dec. 620 'Is thy eye not opened?' 'Yes, indeedy,' says I. **1917** KEPHART *Camping* II. 134 Whiskey warms the hearts of otherwise disobliging natives—yes indeedy. **1949** *Canning Trade* 21 March 28 Do you like the long train on my gown? Yes indeedy.

indemnity lands. Lands granted to a state by the federal government in lieu of those set aside for parks, Indian reservations, etc. — **1908** *Indian Laws & Tr.* III. 380 The State of Montana has not heretofore received indemnity lands. **1911** *Okla. Session Laws* 3 Legisl. 208 And of any indemnity lands granted in lieu thereof the following amounts.

*indent, *n.*

1. A certificate of indebtedness formerly issued by a state or by the federal government.

1786 *Jrnls. Cont. Congress* XXX. 431 The board . . . are of opinion, that the continuation of the issue of indents in that state [Pa.] would not be improper. **1801** *Hist. Review & Directory* I. 188 It may be discharged in certificates (called *indents*) granted for interest due on continental governmental securities. **1809** MARSHALL *Writings Fed. Const.* (1839) 124 The indents issued upon them [state bonds] for interest, were drawn by David Rittenhouse.

2. indent of interest, an indent issued by the federal government for interest on the public debt. *Obs.*

1790 *Statutes at Large* I. 140 The sums which shall be subscribed . . . [shall] be payable in . . . [certificates] issued for the payment of interests, commonly called indents of interest. **1822** *Ib.* III. 697 [All] indents of interest, which . . . shall be outstanding, may be presented at the treasury.

***independence,** *n.*

1. (*cap.*) Short for next. Also attrib. *Obs.*

1799 J. COWLES *Diary* 28 Thursday. Independence, which they celebrate. **1835** ABBOTT *N. Eng.* 151 In the country village, not a few of the farmers' wives and daughters are found with their husbands or gallants, helping them 'keep independence.' **1865** B. ALCOTT *Journals* 372 Emerson comes and spends Independence evening.

2. Independence Day, the anniversary of the adoption of the Declaration of Independence, July 4, 1776.

1791 HILTZHEIMER *Diary* (1893) 4 July 170 This being Independence Day, the Governor invited several of the neighbors to dine with him. **1841** *Knickerb.* XVII. 276 The enthusiasm which is annually rekindled . . . by the return of 'Independence day.' **1949** *Chi. D. News* 2 July/5 There will be no issue of the Daily News Monday, Independence Day.

***independent,** *a.* and *n.*

1. *n.* One who has separated from the Mormon Church. *Rare.*

1862 *N. Amer. Rev.* July 221 In the catalogue of Mormon members, M. Remy reckons two thousand 'schismatics' and 'independents' in Texas, Pennsylvania, and Michigan.

2. One who is not a member or adherent of a political party, or who does not regularly support the measures advanced by his political party.

1882 *Nation* 27 July 63/2 Some time ago he [Alexander H. Stephens] was spoken of as the candidate of the 'Independents' in Georgia. **1886** ALTON *Among Law-Makers* 20 [The Senate occasionally includes] a few Independents—men who talk and vote sometimes with the Democrats and sometimes with the Republicans. **1949** *Sat. Ev. Post* 19 March 31/3 There were among them Republicans, dissatisfied Democrats and independents.

b. (*cap.*) =**Independent Republican 2.** *Obs.*

1876 *Dallas* (Ore.) *Itemizer* 9 Sep. 2/1 The Indiana Independents are a plain speaking people. **1882** ROOSEVELT *Wks.* (1926) XIV. 14, I now wish to speak for a moment to those Republicans who call themselves the Independents and work outside of the party. **1888** *Amer. Almanac* 204 The [Dakota] Legislature of 1887–88 stands: . . . House, . . . 7 Democrats, 3 Farmers' Alliance, 1 Independent.

3. *pl.* Those engaged in a business enterprise outside the combine or trust which dominates the field.

1904 TARBELL *Hist. Standard Oil Co.* I. 93 The independents [in oil-selling] . . . demanded open rates, with no rebates to anyone. **1948** *Time* 19 July 90/2 [This is] the first time a large-scale oil operation has been undertaken in the Middle East by independents.

4. In combs. chiefly obs.: (1) **independent company,** a military company having no official connection with forces directly under some form of government supervision; (2) **Day,** =**Independence Day;** (3) **Democrat,** (see quot.); (4) **fireman,** app. a volunteer firefighter not belonging to a regular fire company; (5) **paper,** a newspaper that does not give allegiance to any particular political party; (6) **Republican,** see as a main entry; (7) **ticket,** a ticket containing the names of those political candidates not affiliated with a regular political party; (8) **trader,** a fur trader not connected with a fur company.

(1) 1732 *Cal. State P., Amer. & W. Indies* 280 Proposes W. Dick, Capt. of one of the Independent Companies, in the place of Alexander in the Council of New York. **1777** CUTLER in *Life & Corr.* I. 61 The old Council and House, escorted by the Independent Company from the State House to the Meeting House. **1842** *Vt. Militia Act of 1842* Sec. 14, In such manner, however, as to retain the several independent companies, with their officers, now raised and organized. — **(2) 1803** E. S. BOWNE *Life* 161 We are in expectation of great entertainment on fourth of July—Independent day! as they laugh at us Yankees for calling it. **1850** DANA *Two Years* xxxi. 383 Monday, July 4th. This was 'independent day' in Boston. — **(3) 1882** COOPER *Amer. Pol.* I. 54 The main plank of the platform of the Abolition party (or Independent Democrats, as they were called) was for the nonextension and gradual extinction of slavery. — **(4) 1892** MARK TWAIN *Amer. Claimant* xvi. 164 (R.), One is an old 'independent' fireman.

(5) 1876 *Humboldt Reg.* (Winnemucca, Nev.) 21 July 3/3 As for Governor Hayes and Samuel J. Tilden, there is not an Independent paper in the State of New York that will not support Governor Hayes as a matter of patriotic duty. — **(7) 1876** *Wkly. Bee* (Portland, Ore.) 26 May 2/2 Those composing the so-called Independent ticket are able gentlemen. — **(8)** *c***1908** F. M. CANTON *Frontier Trails* 162 He was an independent trader.

b. *Independent as a wood-sawyer's clerk,* see **wood-sawyer;** *independent as a hog on ice,* see ***hog,** *n.* **10.**

Independent Republican.

1. A member of the Democratic-Republican party in Pennsylvania after the division of *c*1805. *Obs.*

1818 FEARON *Sketches* 139 The moderate democrats [are] called by the several names of 'Independent Republicans,' 'Democrats of the Revolution,' and 'Old Schoolmen.'

2. A member of the group in the Republican party who refused to support James G. Blaine for the presidency, a Mugwump. Also **Independent Republicanism.**

1884 ROOSEVELT *Wks.* (1926) XIV. 41 The most bitter foes of the very principles which Independent Republicanism has so stoutly upheld. **1888** BRYCE *Amer. Commonw.* II. III. lvi. 379 The Independent Republicans of 1884 did not venture to start a programme or candidate of their own.

***index,** *n.* **1. index board,** a signboard put up on streets and roads to give information to wayfarers. *Obs.* Cf. ***signboard. 2. index forest,** (see quot.).

(1) 1830 WATSON *Philadelphia* 725, I remember very well that when a boy, about the year 1800, we first saw index boards on the walls, to show the streets. **1858** *Texas Almanac 1859* 23 It is made the duty of overseers . . . to put up index-boards at the forks of public roads, pointing to the most noted places to which the roads lead. — **(2) 1905** *Forestry Bureau Bul.* 61, Index forest. The forest which in density volume and increment reaches the highest average which has been found upon a given locality.

***Indian,** *n.* Also (*dial.*) **Ingen, Injun,** etc. (see (2) below).

1. A member of one of the native tribes found in what is now the U.S.

(1) **1602** BRERETON *Virginia* 6 We saw manie Indians, which are tall big boned men. **1711** *Boston News-Letter* 14 May 2/2 Several of the Inhabitants of Cocheco . . . were way-laid by a small Company of Indians. **1812** MARSHALL *Kentucky* 38 White men in their wars against the Indians, became themselves Indians in practice. **1947** *Chi. Tribune* 16 July 19/2 Don't you think we should give the country back to the Indians while there is anything left?

(2) **1670** *E.-Hampton Rec.* I. 330 Obadia the engiane was hiered to keepe the cattell. **1680** *N.H. Hist. Soc. Coll.* VIII. 55 The ingens have showed themselves. **1758** *Essex Inst. Coll.* XLVI. 211 A hous wass Burnt down a littell while afore by the Indjons. **1825** NEAL *Bro. Jonathan* I. 104 Where's the injunn? what's become o' him? **1889** MUNROE *Golden Days* 118 No more attention was paid to the shooting of an 'Injun' than if he were a coyote. **1949** *Sat. Ev. Post* 18 June 140/3 Her cow and chickens were still there, but the Injun had been prowling right enough.

fig. and *transf.* *a***1861** WINTHROP *J. Brent* xxii. 242 But these yer fall storms is reg'lar Injuns. **1905** N. DAVIS *Northerner* 173 Watson . . . sat erect, staring at Falls silently. . . . 'You—you old Indian!'

b. (See quots.)

1674 JOSSELYN *Voyages to N. Eng.* (1865) 111 An English woman suffering an Indian to have carnal knowledge of her had an Indian cut in red cloth sewed upon her right arm, and was injoyned to wear it twelve months. **1947** DOWNEY *Lusty Forefathers* 123 She showed them the clearly recognizable silhouette of an Indian warrior, cut from red cloth. 'A white woman must wear yon image a twelve-month upon her right arm if she cohabits with one of the red savages,' Justice Brand expounded.

2. Any one of the languages spoken by the Indians.

1637 *Mass. H.S. Coll.* 4 Ser. VI. 215 He came from a trading howse . . . & can speake much Indian. **1775** D. JONES *Jrnl. Visits Indians* (1865) 90 The proper pronunciation in Indian is *Mooskingung,* i.e. Elk Eye River. **1894** EELLS *Father Eells* 91 A school was also kept in Indian, the lessons being prepared on paper, hung up on the side of the house and read and recited. **1946** STANWELL-FLETCHER *Driftwood Valley* 114 Be that as it may, I have pronounced and spelled it, just as we do all the various other localities, as it sounds to us in Indian.

3. Short for **Indian corn,** or **Indian meal. Cf. rye and Indian.**

1641 *Dorchester Rec.* 286, I Re[ceive]d in wheate and Indein 3l. 8s. **1780** E. PARKMAN *Diary* 200 Elias went today with a Bushel of Indian. **1849** COOPER *Sea Lions* xxiii, There were . . . a few barrels of cornmeal, or 'injin,' as it is usually termed in American parlance. **1894** *Cent. Mag.* April 849 The newcomer from another part of the country, when first he crosses the Connecticut River, is startled at being asked by an innocent-looking girl waiter in a village tavern if he will have some 'fried Indian.' **1942** CANNON *Mountain* 63 You need a few quarts of Indian to plant when you've girdled.

4. A white man disguised as an Indian for the purpose of committing violence, used esp. of participants in the Boston Tea Party, and later of the Anti-Renters in N.Y.

1774 *Boston Gaz.* 3 Feb. 3/1 A Tribe of Indians met at Col. Watson's and Boot-cap'd Mr. Hutchinson's Sley. **1844** *St. Louis Reveille* 19 Dec. 1/6 Fire-arms were loaded, and hot water was prepared for the besiegers, by Mr. Livingstone and the inmates of the house, as the 'Indians' seemed to be making arrangements for an attack. **1882** *Amer. Univ. Cyclo.* I. 534 During . . . 1845 some alarming outrages were committed by 'Indians' of the anti-rent associations. **1948** *Chi. Tribune* 12 Dec. 1. 26/3 On that momentous evening about 90 'Indians'—professional and business men and young mechanics—emptied the tea chests into the sea.

attrib. **1901** STILLMAN *Autobiog. Journalist* I. 31 My mother had taken me to visit one of her brothers, a farmer in the western section of New York, soon after made famous by the anti-rent war, in which my uncle was one of the 'Indian Chiefs.'

5. Temper, "dander." *Colloq.*

1888–90 BARRERE-LELAND I. 487 Irish, Indian, Dutch (American), all of these words are used to signify anger or arousing temper. But to say that one has his 'Indian up,' implies a great degree of vindictiveness, while Dutch wrath is stubborn but yielding to reason. **1893** LELAND *Memoirs* 320 It woke Colonel John Forney up to the very highest pitch of his fighting 'Injun,' or, as they say in Pennsylvania, his 'Dutch.'

6. In phrases: (1) *To sing Indian,* to act as one who defies death, in allusion to the conduct of Indians under torture, *obs.;* (2) *to do* (or *play*) *the sober Indian,* (see quot. 1832), *obs.;* (3) *to play Indian,* (*a*) to make no display of one's emotions, in allusion to the stoicism of Indians, *obs.,* (*b*) of children, to pretend to be Indians; (4) *seeing Indians,* (see quot.), *obs.;* (5) *to turn Indian,* to revert to a state of nature, *obs.*

(1) **1829** *Western Mo. Rev.* II. 467 A native young Kentuckian, . . . warmed with the idea of getting rid of death and the doctor, began to sing Indian, after reading this. — (2) **1832** FERRALL *Ramble* 221 During these drinking fits, there is always one at least of the party who remains sober, in order to secure the knives, &c. Hence the Americans derive the cant phrase of 'doing the sober Indian' which they apply to any one of a company who will not *drink fairly.* **1876** MILLER *First Families* xxi. 184 He had had his carouse, and was now playing sober Indian. — (3) (*a*) **1840** *Knickerb.* XVI. 265, I tried to keep my countenance, and to play Indian, but it would not do. (*b*) **1907** *St. Nicholas* XXXIV. 641/1 Both boys and girls delight in 'dressing up' and playing Indian. **1948** *Sat. Ev. Post* 20 Nov. 94/4 Children . . . decide to play barbershop, beauty parlor, Indian or Dick Tracy quietly, in the middle of the night. — (4) **1850** LEWIS *La. Swamp Doctor* 118 In one of the upper apartments was a private patient, labouring under the disease indifferently known as the blue-devils, red-monkeys, seeing injuns, or man-with-the-poker.

(5) **1862** *Rep. Comm. Patents 1861: Agric.* 356 The oft-quoted proverb of reclaimed swamps turning Indian was rehearsed for my especial benefit.

As the last term in **agency, Alabama, Alaska, Anglo-, annuity, bad, beaver, blanket, blood, border, Brothertown, buck, bulldog, carrier, cat, Catawba, Cayuse, Choctaw, Christian, church, cigar-sign, college, creek, Dakota, English, Esaw, field, Flathead, Florida, foreign, forest, French, friend, good, hat, honest, horse, inland, Iron, Laguna, Lake, Maherin, mission, Missouri, Mohave, Mohawk, Mohican, Moravian, Navaho, New York, Nez Percé, Osage, Pawnee, plains, prairie, praying, Rocky Mountain, river, road, Sac, Seminole, Seneca, settlement, Sioux, Southward, Spanish, stage, Stockbridge, tame, Taos, tobacco, treaty, upland, Ute, Wabash, Welsh, western, whisky, white, wild, wood, wooden Indian.**

Also in the *pl.,* in **Eastern, Eastward, Fall, grasshopper, great belly, highland, severalty, Snake, Stone, Sunapee Indians.**

* **Indian,** *a.* and *attrib.*

The combinations, most of them of course now obs., in which this adjective appears are far too numerous to be illustrated fully here. An effort has been made to include a reasonably large number of those that appear to possess at least some historical significance, and to refer, without giving quots., to others of a perhaps less significant nature. Those felt to be of most importance or interest are given as main entries.

1. In the names of, or with reference to, plants: (1) **Indian bell,** the white mariposa, *Calochortus albus;* (2) **fig,** the fruit of the prickly pear; (3) **millet,** common sorghum, also mountain rice; (4) **plantain,** any one of various leafy herbs of the genera *Mesadenia* and *Synosma;* (5) **plume,** the Indian paintbrush, or the Oswego tea; (6) **posy,** the pearly everlasting *q.v.*

(1) **1890** HEALY & BIGELOW *Kickapoo Indians* 156/2 The Indian Bell . . . is one of the components of Indian Sagwa. **1925** JEPSON *Flowering Plants Calif.* 238 C[alochortus] albus Dougl. White Globe Lily. . . . Also called Snow-drops, Indian Bells, and Satin Bells. — (2) *c***1622** in *John Pory's Lost Description of Plymouth Colony* (1918) 25 The fruite it selfe is likened to a fig in respect of the thicknes and softnes of the rinde, and because of the graines within it, and hence it hath beene fitlie called the Indian-figge. **1877** CAMPION *On Frontier* 304 Tunas are the fruit of the prickly pear or Indian fig. — (3) **1876** HOBBS *Bot. Hand-Book* 57 Indian millet, Coffee corn, Sorghum vulgare. **1888** *Dept. Agric. Bot. Div. Bul.* No. 6, 53 *Oryzopsis cuspidata* (Indian millet) . . . has a wide distribution through all the interior region of Utah, Nevada, New Mexico, Texas, Colorado, and Nebraska to the Missouri River. It is a perennial, growing in dense tufts, whence its common name of bunch grass. — (4) **1876** HOBBS *Bot. Hand-Book* 153 Cacalia tuberosa, Indian plantain. **1947** *Iowa Acad. Sci. Proc.* LIV. 29 The conspicuous plants are: . . . phlox (*Phlox pilosa*), Indian plantain (*Cacalia tuberosa*) [etc.].

(5) **1888** LINDLEY *Calif. of South* 329 Here, too, is *Castilleia,* the painter's brush or Indian plume, identical with that of the East. **1907** LYONS *Plant Names* 307 M[onarda] didyma . . . Red or Scarlet Balm, Mountain Mint, Horsemint, Indian's-plume, Sweet-Mary. — (6) **1846** *Knickerb.* XXVII. 287 [On one end of the island] were scattered dwarf cedars, interspersed with golden-rods, lobelias, Indian posies. **1907** HODGE *Amer. Indians* I. 606/2.

b. In less frequent plant names: (1) **Indian date,** the persimmon; (2) **gooseberry,** the dangleberry, *Gaylussacia frondosa;* (3) **gravelroot,** joe-pye weed, *Eupatorium purpureum;* (4) **hand,** the root of polypody, in allusion to its branching habit; (5) **head-root,** the purple coneflower, *Echinacea purpurea;* (6) **soap plant,** the chinaberry, *Sapindus drummondi.*

(1) **1838** FLAGG *Far West* II. 177*n.,* Indian date, by the French called Placiminier, *Diosporus Virginiana.* — (2) **1785** MARSHALL *Amer. Grove* 158 *Vaccinium frondosum.* Leafy Vaccinium, or Indian Gooseberry. — (3) **1894** *Amer. Folk-Lore* VII. 92 *Eupatorium purpureum,* . . . quill-wort, Indian gravel root. West Va. — (4) **1830** *Huntingdon* (Pa.) *Courier* 15 Sep. 4/5 Female Fern or Indian Hand, (Polyp. Canadensis.)

(5) **1940** EARLY *N. Eng. Sampler* 317 Another remarkable weed is Echinacea (*Indian Head-root* or *Nigger-head*), a powerful drug, and an American cure-all for nearly three hundred years. — (6) **1931** MATTOON *Forest Trees Okla.* 95 This species, sometimes called Indian soap plant, grows on moist clay soils or dry limestone uplands.

c. In other plant names sufficiently explained in the quots.: (1) **Indian apple,** (2) **balm,** (3) **bark,** (4) **basket grass,** (5) **brier,** (6) **creeper,** (7) **cup,** (8) **ginger,** (9) **hippo,** (10) **lettuce,** (11) **mozemize,** (12) **pear,** (13) **poke,** (14) **root,** (15) **sage,** (16) **salt,** (17) **wickape.**

(1) **1847** PARKMAN in *Knickerb.* XXIX. 310 The rich flowers of the Indian-apple were there in profusion. **1931** CLUTE *Plants* 35 The May-apple (*Podophyllum peltatum*) was known to the settlers as Indian apple, but it is really a berry. — (2) **1866** *Treas. Bot. s.v. Trillium,* The plant *T. erectum* or *pendulum* is also called Indian Balm. **1907** HODGE *Amer. Indians* I. 605/1 *Indian balm.*—The erect trillium, or ill-scented wake-robin (*Trillium erectum*). — (3) **1876** HOBBS *Bot. Hand-Book* 56 Indian bark, Sweet bay, Magnolia glauca. — (4) **1922** *Country Life* June 45/2 We camped two days . . . in the ghost forest beyond the glorious and fragrant cream-white spikes of the Indian basket grass. **1938** THOMPSON *High Trails* 86 The bear grass flower . . . is also listed as . . . Indian basket grass.

(5) **1892** TORREY *Foot-Path Way* 80 The common greenbrier (cat-brier, horse-brier, Indian-brier) of my boyhood. — (6) **1924** DEAM *Shrubs Indiana* 289 Trumpetcreeper . . . is also called Indian-creeper. — (7) **1876** HOBBS *Bot. Hand-Book* 56 Indian cup plant, Silphium perfoliatum. **1931** CLUTE *Plants* 37 Nor is it likely that the

hollow leaves of the pitcher plant (*Sarracenia purpurea*) were used as cups by the Indians, though they are known as Indian cups. Possibly these are plants mentioned only to their disparagement. — **(8) 1876** HOBBS *Bot. Hand-Book* 56 Indian ginger, Canada snake root, Asarum Canadensis. **1931** CLUTE *Plants* 37 We cannot imagine a real use by the aborigines of Indian ginger (*Asarum Canadense*). — **(9) 1876** HOBBS *Bot. Hand-Book* 57 Indian hippo, Indian physic, Gillenia trifoliata.

(10) 1791 BARTRAM *Travels* 42 A very singular and elegant plant, of an unknown family, called Indian Lettuce, made its first appearance in these rich vales. **1907** HODGE *Amer. Indians* I. 606/1 *Indian lettuce.*—The round-leaved wintergreen (*Pyrola rotundifolia*). — **(11) 1893** *Amer. Folk-Lore* VI. 141 *Pyrus Americana*, Indian mozemize, . . . Ferrisburgh. **1907** HODGE *Amer. Indians* I. 606 *Indian mozemize*, or moose misse.—The American mountain-ash or dogberry (*Sorbus americana*). — **(12) 1832** J. MCGREGOR *British Amer.* I. 90 The fruit called Indian pear, is of the most delicious flavor. **1907** HODGE *Amer. Indians* I. 606/1 *Indian pear.*—The service-berry (*Amelanchier canadensis*), called also wild Indian pear. — **(13) 1784** CUTLER in *Mem. Acad.* I. *Veratrum.* . . . White Helebore. Poke-root. Indian Poke. Common in wet meadows and swamps. June. **1907** HODGE *Amer. Indians* I. 606/1 *Indian poke.*—(1) American white hellebore (*Veratrum viride*). (2) False hellebore (*V. woodii*). — **(14) 1775** A. ADAMS in *J. Adams' Fam. Lett.* (1876) 96, I should be glad of one ounce of Indian root. **1907** HODGE *Amer. Indians* I. 606/2 *Indian root.*—The American spikenard (*Aralia racemosa*).

(15) 1847 DARLINGTON *Weeds & Plants* 170 *E[upatorium] perfoliatum.* . . . Perfoliate Eupatorium. Thorough-stem. Boneset. Indian Sage. — **(16) 1881** *Harper's Mag.* March 526/1 He saw moving with the wind a quantity of Indian salt commonly known as sumac, which when ripe presents a red appearance. — **(17) 1832** WILLIAMSON *Maine* I. 112 *Leatherwood* or *Indian Wickape* is a small tree which grows on the best hardwood land and none other: . . . even when dry, it is sufficiently limber and flexible to be used in lieu of twine or cords. . . . Its roots are emetic, and its fruit, which consist of small oval, red, one-seeded berries, are quite narcotic.

d. In plant names of doubtful meaning: (1) **Indian all-heal,** (2) **olive,** (3) **onion,** (4) **purge,** (5) **silk.**

(1) 1737 BRICKELL *N. Carolina* 23 The herb Mastick, Indian-all-heal, Cinquefoil. — **(2) 1791** BARTRAM *Travels* 41, I observed . . . some very curious new shrubs and plants, particularly the Physic-nut, or Indian Olive. . . . The fruit is yellow when ripe, and about the size of an olive. The Indians, when they go in pursuit of deer, carry this fruit with them, supposing that it has the power of charming or drawing that creature to them. — **(3) 1890** HEALY & BIGELOW *Kickapoo Indians* 54/1 The Indian Onion . . . contributes its leaves and root to the great Kickapoo Sagwa remedy. — **(4) 1687** CLAYTON *Va.* in *Phil. Trans.* XLI. 150 There is another Herb, which they [i.e., Virginians] call the Indian Purge. This Plant . . . bears yellow Berries round about the Joints.

(5) 1800 TATHAM *Communications* 136 There is a species of wild plant, which among the people of the country, is vulgarly called *wild hemp*, sometimes *wild silk, Indian hemp, Indian silk, silk grass*, &c.

Also see as main entries **Indian arrow, bean, cherry, chief, corn, cucumber, currant, grass, hemp, kale, maize, medicine, paint, pea, peach, physic, pine, pink, pipe, plum, potato, rice, shoe, tea, tobacco, turnip, weed, wheat.**

2. In the names of animals, or denoting animals belonging to Indians: (1) **Indian cattle,** (2) **chub,** (3) **devil,** see as a main entry, (4) **dog,** (5) **hen,** see as a main entry, (6) **hog,** (7) **horse,** (8) **pony,** (9) **pullet,** (see quots.).

(1) 1849 in *Sci. Hist. Assoc. Pub.* VI. (1902) 292 Here [notch near Rio Grande] as before when marching up the river we fell in with Indian cattle. **1872** *Newton Kansan* 3 Oct. 2/2 No person shall be allowed to drive . . . any cattle from the country south of Kansas, commonly known as Indian cattle, or Texas cattle. **1882** *Nation* 9 Nov. 392/3 Any one who has grown rich as an Indian-cattle and Star-route contractor. — **(2) 1820** RAFINESQUE in *Western Rev.* II. 238 Kentuckian Shiner, *Luxilus Kentuckiensis.* . . . Vulgar names, Indian Chub, Red tail, Shiner, &c. — **(4) 1672** JOSSELYN *N. Eng. Rarities* 15 The Indian Dog is a Creature begotten 'twixt a Wolf and a Fox, which the Indians lighting up on, bring up to hunt the Deer with. **1836** *S. Lit. Messenger* II. 367 The embers of the council fire have gone out, and the bark of the Indian dog has ceased to echo in the forest. **1944** S. P. YOUNG *Wolves of N. Amer.* 183 He refers to the Indian dog as a wolfhound.

(6) 1806 ASHE *Travels Amer.* 157, I also took notice of a small aboriginal animal, called the ground or Indian Hog—whose sensibilities are so little refined that no attention or caresses, can ever force from it a reciprocity of manners. — **(7)** [**1756** in *Mem. of Moravian Ch.* I. (1870) 276 For shoeing 1 Indian horse.] **1805** CLARK in *Lewis & C. Exped.* III. (1904) 16 The Indian horses pass over those clifts hills beds & rocks as fast as a man. **1887** *Cent. Mag.* Jan. 448/2 [The Indians' horses] were undersized, as compared with our thoroughbreds, though larger than the average Indian horse. — **(8) 1752** in *Travels Amer. Col.* 314 He is given us for an Indian poney in his place. **1850** HAYES *Pioneer Notes* (1929) 60 Got in August 10th, with their broken-down Indian ponies. **1949** *No. Dak. Hist.* Jan. 14 Spotted Indian ponies grazed on the hillside. — **(9) 1835** AUDUBON *Ornith. Biog.* III. 275 [In S.C. the night heron] is named 'the Indian Pullet,' in Lower Louisiana the Creoles call it '*Gros-bec*,' the inhabitants of East Florida know it under the name of 'Indian Hen,' and in our Eastern States its usual appellation is 'Qua Bird.'

3. Denoting articles of food prepared from Indian corn: (1) **Indian bannock,** (2) **batter,** (3) **battercake,** (4) **chop,** (5) **dab,** (6) **dumpling,** (7) **flapjack,** (8) **hoecake,** (9) **johnnycake,** (10) **mush,** (11) **pone,** (12) **porridge,** (13) **poundcake.**

(1) 1806 R. B. THOMAS *Farmer's Almanack for 1807* 2–4 Jan./2 Now for a good broiled sausage, a dish of pancakes, or an Indian bannock, if you please, with a little butter, *if you have it.* **1935** DOW *Every Day Life* 41 Indian bannock, made by mixing corn meal with water and spreading it an inch thick on a small board placed at an incline before the fire and so baked, was a common form of bread. — **(2)** *c***1859** in *Ohio Arch & Hist. Pub.* XIII. (1904) 516 Dar's buckwheat cakes an' Injin batter, Makes you fat or a little fatter. **1929** *Randolph Enterprise* (Elkins, W.Va.) 4 April 1/6 Ingin batter Inspires West Virginians to grow fine and fatter. — **(3) 1867** *Common Sense Cook Book* 8 [Recipe:] Indian Batter Cakes. — **(4) 1840** *N.O. Picayune* 21 Aug. 2/5 The homminy is nothin' but Ingin-chop.

(5) 1877 BARTLETT 312 *Indian Dab*, a kind of battercake. Pennsylvania. — **(6) 1751** J. BARTRAM *Observations* 60 Last of all was served a great bowl, full of Indian dumplings, of new soft corn, cut or scraped off the ear. **1851** *Knickerb.* XXXVIII. 392 He scattered far and wide corn-meal, with recipes for making pone and Indian dumplings. — **(7) 1849** *N. Eng. Farmer* I. 386 [Recipe:] Indian Flap Jacks. — **(8) 1789** MORSE *Amer. Geog.* 131 He breakfasts . . . on three small indian hoe-cakes. — **(9) 1829** *Detroit Gaz.* XII. 5 March 4/2 Supper—hot Indian Jonnycakes. **1848** THOMPSON *L. Amsden* 22 Then came the fine meal Indian Johnny-cake, mixed with cream, eggs, and sugar . . . forming . . . the most delectable esculent of the bread kind, that ever gratified an epicure's palate.

(10) 1788 *Mass. Centinel* 18 Oct. 40/1 This milk may be used . . . either with bread, or rice or Indian mush. **1832** *Boston Transcript* 28 March 2/1 Most of the time he had lived upon Indian mush and grease for breakfast, and Indian mush and milk for supper. — **(11) 1881** TOURGEE *'Zouri's Christmas* v, The fish with its red-clay case and Indian-pone cover lay exposed upon her lap. — **(12) 1938** DAMON *Grandma* 11 To make 'injun porridge' perfectly—a very little 'injun' meal boiled a very long while in a vast amount of water. **1941** *L.A.* Map 288. — **(13) 1828** LESLIE *Receipts* 61 Indian Pound Cake.

b. Also (1) **Indian coffee,** (2) **flour,** (3) **liquor,** (4) **rum.**

(1) 1884 SHEPHERD *Prairie Exp.* 61 You let your visitor have whatever scraps were left over, and if the grouts have not been thrown out of the pot, water is poured on, and the liquid set to boil; this second decoction of the berry, much resented by the tardy cow-boy, goes by the name of Indian coffee. — **(2) 1860** CLAIBORNE *Life of Dale* 149, I set out the same night, taking with me only a blanket, my flint and steel, my pistols, and a wallet of Indian flour for myself and horse. — **(3) 1859** *Nat. Intelligencer* 10 July, A barrel of the 'pure Cincinnati' . . . is a sufficient basis upon which to manufacture one hundred barrels of 'good Indian liquor!' — **(4) 1793** in *Five Fur Traders of Northwest* (1933) 101 Mixed nine Gallons of Indian Rum it being customary for Bourgeois to wet the whistle of every Indian they met on the way. **1839** JOHN K. TOWNSEND *Narrative* (1839) 178 Indian rum, i.e. rum and water in the proportion of one part of the former to two of the latter.

c. Designating medicines and nostrums (see quots.).

1802 *Wash. Federalist* 19 July 4/2 A fresh supply has been received of the Patent Indian Vegetable Specific, prepared by Dr. Leroux. **1826** *Va. Herald* (Fredericksburg) 30 Sep. 4/5, I am now perfectly satisfied of the superior quality of the Vegetable Indian Specific, over every other medicine ever discovered in this country. **1845** *Quincy* (Ill.) *D. Morn. Courier* 22 Sep. 4/2 We have made use of Dr. D. Benjamin Smith's (Sugar Coated) Indian Vegetable Pills, and consider them far superior to any other pills offered to the public. **1877** BURDETTE *Rise & Fall of Mustache* 291 This 'Centennial Cordial and American Indian Aboriginal Invigorator' . . . has positively no equal for the cure of . . . salt rheum, teething, . . . pimples, tan and freckles, kleptomania, . . . tailor's bills, . . . and all other ills to which human flesh is heir. **1890** HEALY & BIGELOW *Kickapoo Indians* 14 Last year more than 5,000,000 bottles of Indian Sagwa alone were sold, nearly 3,000,000 bottles of Indian Oil, and over 1,000,000 packages of Indian Worm Killer. **1947** *Chi. D. Tribune* 4 July 6/2 Instead of being cast as a statesman, he should have been a vendor of Indian herb elixir.

Esp. **Indian oil,** a form of petroleum.

1835 *Vade Mecum* (Phila.) 14 Mar. 3/7 Indian Oil . . . for growth and general improvement of the Hair. **1948** *Sat. Ev. Post* 26 June 47/1 Long before the drilling of the Titusville well, the Howland of the legend had been sent samples of the 'Indian oil' of quacks and medicine men.

See also as main entries **Indian bread, cake, corn, meal, medicine, physic, pudding, sugar.**

4. Denoting articles of clothing used by or named for Indians: (1) **Indian apron,** (2) **breeches,** (3) **cap,** (4) **capote,** (5) **coat,** (6) **pac,** (7) **slipper,** (8) **stocking.**

(1) 1819 E. Evans *Pedestrious Tour* 103 An Indian apron ... was about eighteen inches square, covered with fine bear skin, trimmed with fur, and having over the lower part of it a net for game. — **(2) 1634** Wood *N. Eng. Prospect* (1865) 72 A paire of Indian Breeches ... which is but a peece of cloth a yard and a halfe long, put betweene their groinings, tied with a snakes skinne about their middles, one end hanging downe with a flap before, the other like a taile behinde. **1701** Wolley *Journal N.Y.* (1902) 35 Their ordinary habit is a pair of Indian Breeches. — **(3) 1755** in *Va. Hist. Soc. Coll.* XI. 211 We found here [Nicholas' Fort, Maryland] an Indian cap made of bear skin. — **(4) 1827** *McLoughlin Letters* (1941) 41 The outfit received this year is sufficient for the Indian trade except for Indian capots.

(5) 1634 in *Md. Hist. Soc. Pub.* No. 35 (1899) 23, I haue in ... Indian coates one rich fox skins coat, fower loose fox skins and one coat of martin skins. **1684** *E.-Hampton Rec.* II. 146 The towne of Easthampton is to pay ... for their payns and [*sic*] Indean coate, or the Vallew of it. — **(6) 1893** *Outing* Feb. 397/1 The feet of the boots were made like Indian 'pacs.' — **(7) 1856** Phillips *Kansas* 382 He struck at me again, when I caught the musket in my hands, and held on to it. He held the other end, and jumped on my body, stamping on my head and face; but, as he wore Indian slippers, he did not hurt me much. — **(8) 1647** *Conn. Rec.* I. 478 A pair of Indean stockins. **1755** in *Lett. to Washington* I. 89 Indian Goods at Fort Cumberland ... [include] 33p blue Indian Stockgs. **1793** *Mass. H.S. Coll.* 3 Ser. V. 152 Besides, they all have Indian stockings, made of woollen cloth.

b. In the names of other articles made or used by Indians: (1) **Indian ax,** (2) **bag,** (3) **basket,** (4) **beads,** (5) **belt,** (6) **bowl,** (7) **cradle,** (8) **curiosity,** (9) **drum,** (10) **gun,** (11) **shield,** (12) **sleigh,** cf. **hand sled,** (13) **tomahawk,** (14) **tray.**

One form of Indian cradle

(1) 1814 in *Pa. Mag. Hist.* XXXV. 287, I found on the road ... an Indian axe made of this stone (possibly quartz) ... a large one 6 inches long by 4. — **(2) 1645** *Early Conn. Prob. Rec.* I. 21 Lotham, William—A prticular of all debts ... a perre of pinsers, 2 hamers, a gymlett, 2 Indean baggs. **1841** Joseph Williams *Tour to Ore. Terr.* (1921) 33, I saw on the other side of the road a skin bag, full of something, which I then knew was an Indian bag. — **(3) 1642** *Md. Archives* IV. 94 Inventary ... 3 indian basketts. **1713** Sewall *Letter-Book* II. 22, I offer to your view a small Indian basket of summer fruit. **1880** *Harper's Mag.* Sep. 534/2 The ceilings [were] hung with ... Indian baskets filled with the family clothing. — **(4) 1640** *Mass. H.S. Coll.* 4 Ser. VII. 339 He carried one hundred twenty od yeards of Indians beades with him. **1856** John A. Sutter *Diary* (1932) 17 Every year the Russians was bound to furnish me with ... Indian Beeds.

(5) 1788 Manasseh Cutler in *Life and Corr.* I. (1888) 425 Mons. Vigo gave me a curious Indian belt, and a buffalo skin dressed with the hair on. — **(6) 1661** *Md. Archives* LIV. (1937) 227 Sold.... To Allexander Tourson on Smoathing Iron 3 Indian Bowles ... & on owld Cannoow. **1826** in *Overland to Pacific* II. (1933) 161 The Bales contain ... 2 Indian Bowls. — **(7) 1834** in *Wis. State H.S. Coll.* XIV. 435, I have recd from Miss Cadle a little indian cradle &c for Lill, & a bundle of bark, a canoe & an indian hat. **1837** in *Minn. Hist. Bul.* IV. (1922) 404 (At the ball) I beheld ... a number of ... mamas with their hopeful progeny straped on ornamented boards or Indian cradles, after the manner of the *natives.* — **(8) 1776** in *N.J. Hist. Soc. Proc.* 1 Ser. II. 116 Sir Wm. Johnson's picture ... was curiously surrounded with all kinds of beads of Wampum, Indian curiosities and trappings of Indian finery. **1853** Elizabeth Ellet *Summer Rambles* 104 The words 'Indian curiosities,' blazoned over several stores near the landings (at St. Paul, Minn.), create expectations seldom satisfied. — **(9) 1738** in *N.C. Hist. Comm. Pub.* XIX. (1929) 114 (The Indians) danct to ... an Indian-drum, that is, a large Gourd with a Skin bract tort over the Mouth of it. **1853** Strickland *Twenty-seven Yrs.* II. 70 The tewagan, or drummer, stood in the centre of the circle, and beat time manfully upon that odd-looking kind of instrument with one head, yclept an Indian drum.

(10) 1740 W. Stephens *Proc. Georgia* 574, I should give a light Indian Gun out of the Stores. **1755** *Lett. to Washington* I. 89, 4 Indian Guns. **1756** *Ib.* II. 4 Majr. Lewis will send You some Indn. Guns for the Catawbas. — **(11) 1890** Custer *Following Guidon* 7 An Indian shield ... is made of the thickest part of the buffalo-hide. — **(12) 1748** in Temple & Sheldon *Hist. Northfield Mass.* (1875) 259, I was forced to have it carried upon Indian sleys, there being no possible passing by land. **1794** A. Bradman *Narr. Sufferings R. Forbes* 4 They undertook to haul [it] on Indian sleighs, or handsleds. — **(13) 1705** Beverley *Virginia* III. 29 In another Mat, we found some Indian Tomahawks finely grav'd, and painted. **1835** in *Ohio Arch. & Hist. Quart.* XV. 236, I picked up (near Circleville, Ohio) half of an Indian tomahawk. — **(14) 1648** *Conn. Col. Rec.* I. (1850) 486 Item, 2 Indian trayes, 4 *s.*

c. In the names of objects allegedly used by Indians or in some way associated with them: (1) **Indian bridge,** (2) **kettle,** (3) **mortar,** (4) **well,** (5) **windmill,** (see quots.).

(1) 1763 *Plymouth Rec.* 132 Over Jones River by the Indian bridge by the herring weire. **1818** Harris *Remarks* 40 The Indian bridge (a large tree cut down in such a manner as to fall across the stream) carried away by the torrent. — **(2) 1904** *N.Y. Ev. Post* 18 June, On the grounds are a number of 'Indian Kettles,' or potholes in the rocks. **(3) 1902** Clapin 318 *Pot-holes,* naturally formed depressions in rock,—due to the action of water, and which, from being circular in shape, were at one time thought to have been made by the early aborigines for grinding and pounding corn in. Also called *Indian Mortars.* — **(4) 1641** [see **Indian barn** as a main entry]. **1925** in *Amer. Sp.* XV. 276/1 These homesteads are generally to be found near some old spring, in which, generations ago, hollow gum-logs were forced into the sand, forming the 'Indian Wells' which are spoken of in the countryside.

(5) 1889 Munroe *Golden Days* 120 [Acorns] were ground to a coarse meal, in the holes of the flat rock, which was called by the miners an 'Indian windmill.'

Also *Indian apparel, arms, boat, bow, canoe, clothing, coffin, dress, habit, hat, headdress, jewelry, leggings, mat, matchcoat, mitten, money, paddle, peag, petticoat, pot, pottery, rattle, shot pouch, wampum, ware, whip,* etc.

See also as main entries **Indian arrow, blanket, boots, hatchet, ladder, moccasin, pipe, raft, razor, saddle, shoe.**

5. In combs. relating to governmental dealings with Indians: (1) **Indian annuity,** an annual payment made by the U.S. Government to Indians; (2) **Bureau,** one of several terms used for the Bureau of Indian Affairs; (3) **claim,** the claim of ownership made by Indians to a piece of land, or the right to a piece of land acquired or alleged to have been acquired from Indians, also attrib.; (4) **factory system,** the system (1795–1822) intended to protect the Indians from exploitation and secure their friendship by having government-owned and operated stores among them where they could sell or buy goods at prices advantageous to them; (5) **float,** = ***float,** *n.* **1;** (6) **Homestead Act,** a congressional enactment enabling Indians to take up public land for homesteads; (7) **office,** a federal office through which transactions with the Indians are carried on; (8) **payment,** a payment or annuity paid by the federal government to Indians; (9) **police,** a police force of Indians under the supervision of white officers, for keeping order among Indians; (10) **present,** a present given to an Indian, esp. for creating good will or in return for land; (11) **rate,** a tax or assessment levied against Indians; (12) **right,** the claim or title to property, esp. land, possessed by an Indian; (13) **trust land,** land held in trust by the U.S. Government for the benefit of Indians.

(1) 1839 *Boston Wkly. Mag.* 12 Jan. 151/3 Several gentlemen present at the payment of the Indian annuities at Prairie du Chien, represent the affair to be managed in such a manner as almost entirely to deprive the Indians of any benefit from the payment. **1840** *Niles' Reg.* 11

April 95/1 The officers of the army employed in paying Indian annuities. — (2) **1831** CALEB ATWATER *Tour to Prairie du Chien* 142 Taking advantage of frauds committed on the Indians, by persons connected with the Indian bureau, the Factory system gave place to the present system. **1948** *Salt Lake Tribune* 17 Dec. 25/4 The secretary of the interior and the president are having difficulty finding the right man to head the Indian bureau. — (3) **1674** *Plymouth Laws* 172 Concerning Indian claimes that are . . . made to any lands within this Government; which are now orderly possessed by the English those which doe lay claime to them shall orderly comence and prosecute their claime as farre as hee or they are able. **1749** *N.J. Archives* 1 Ser. VII. 344 The other 5th [of the rioters] possess lands under the Indian Claim and not more than ⅕ of that ⅕ first settled the lands they possess on an Indian Title. **1873** *Winfield* (Kans.) *Courier* 26 June 1/7 An Indian Claim Agent. . . . If there is anything that an Indian agent will not do, it is that he will not treat his clients, the Indians, honestly. — (4) [**1831** see **Indian Bureau.**] **1854** BENTON *30 Years' View* I. 20/2 The experience of the Indian factory system is an illustration of the unfitness of the federal government to carry on any system of trade.

(5) **1857** *Lawrence* (Kans.) *Republican* 4 June 2 That the General Government will allow two or three men to jump a whole city of fifteen hundred or two thousand inhabitants, locate an Indian float and divide the town between them, I do not believe. — (6) **1881** *Rep. Indian Affairs* 13 It were better to encourage Indians . . . to take up the land under the 'Indian homestead act.' — (7) **1871** *Rep. Indian Affairs* (1872) 174 We then nominated Mr. Smith, who had been in the Indian office in Detroit. **1948** *Dly. Ardmoreite* (Ardmore, Okla.) 22 Jan. 2/4 Some Indians . . . had been unable to lease their lands for agriculture or oil development purposes due to lack of sufficient personnel at the Anadarko western Indian office. — (8) **1847** LANMAN *Summer in Wild.* 141 He was on his annual visit to the North, to attend the Indian payments. — (9) **1876** in CLARK WISSLER *Indian Cavalcade* (1938) 127 Clay Beauford . . . you are directed to take fifteen Indian police and ascertain the truth of these reports. . . . John P. Clum, United States Indian Agent. **1946** FOREMAN *Last Trek* 235 Congress, on May 27, 1878, authorized a force of Indian police.

(10) **1739** *Ga. Col. Rec.* XXII. II. (1913) 247 (Part of) which money has been paid in discharge of the account of Indian Presents. **1766** ROBERT ROGERS *Ponteach* 17 We are intrusted with these Indian Presents. A Thousand Pound was granted by the King. **1767** in *Amer. Sp.* XX. (1945) 272 His endeavours to reduce the expenses attending Indian presents, the exhorbitant amount of which gives him much uneasiness. — (11) **1682** *Plymouth Laws* 195 Overseers and Constables shalbe acomptable to the Treasurer for all Indian rates and fines. — (12) **1674** *Mass. Bay Rec.* V. (1854) 11 The Generall Court . . . haue confirmed patent rights, possession rights, toune rights, & Indian rights. **1700** *N.J. Archives* 1 Ser. II. (1881) 348 John Royce a great Asserter of the Indians sole Right, and a Ringleader of that faction, . . . did purchase a large Tract of Land from the Indians, containing about Twenty Thousand Acres. **1722** in *Md. Hist. Soc. Pub.* No. 34 (1894) 56 So hath it been allways ffound, a safe and suxsesfull Way, to purchase the Indians Right to Lands that are remote, and where any Considerable Settlements have been made. — (13) **1857** *Lawrence* (Kans.) *Republican* 28 May 2 The President . . . has issued his proclamation for the sale of the Indian Trust Lands in Kansas Territory.

b. In similar combs. of more obvious meaning: (1) **Indian Appropriation Act, Bill,** (2) **conveyance,** (3) **court,** (4) **deed,** (5) **subsidy,** (6) **treaty.**

(1) **1868** *N.Y. Herald* 17 July 8/3 So the Indian Appropriation bill was taken up. **1914** *Cyclo. Amer. Govt.* II. 161/1 The Indian appropriation act of 1869, following the exposure of some serious frauds in connection with the Government's Indian relations, authorized the President to organize a board of commissioners. — (2) **1683** *Mass. H.S. Coll.* 4 Ser. V. 106 The deed . . . was given and received only as a confirmation of the English title, long before truly made by purchase, but not so amply conformed by writing, which was not thought so necessary unto Indian conveyances until of later times. **1800** JEFFERSON *Notes* 139 From these regulations there resulted to the state a sole and exclusive power of taking conveyances of the Indian right of soil: since, according to them an Indian conveyance alone could give no right to an individual, which the laws would acknowledge. — (3) **1904** in *Indian Laws & Tr.* III. 37 For compensation of judges of Indian courts, twelve thousand dollars. — (4) [**1654** *Mass. Bay Rec.* IV. I. (1854) 190 This Court allowes ye Indians deed of sale of ye land formerly given them by this Court vnto Thomas Danforth.] **1664** *Brookhaven Rec.* 12 The Copey of the Indian Deydes vpon recorde. **1796** in *Pub. Col. Soc.* VI. 61 In a letter written 2 August, 1796, William Fraser said that the first deed he found 'was an Indian Deed from John Samoset [and] Unongoit, Indian Sagamores to John Brown.' **1832** WILLIAMSON *Maine* I. 365 Jeremisquam, Sebascodegan, and other islands . . . were purchased of the natives; when the practice of obtaining 'Indian Deeds' became fashionable, till nearly the whole patent was covered by them.

(5) **1831** *Boston Transcript* 3 June 2/4 The non-payment of Indian subsidies . . . might have provoked hostilities, and would certainly have caused trouble and discredit to the government. — (6) **1719** *Pa. Archives* 8 Ser. II. (1931) 1299 Ordered, That Richard Hill, Isaac Norris, and Clement Plumsted, do prepare and bring in the Bill for regulating Indian Treaties, and settling the Indian Trade. **1789** *Ann. 1st Congress* I. 61 The committee, to whom was referred the Message of the President of the 25th of May, with the Indian treaties and papers accompanying it, reported. **1946** FOREMAN *Last Trek* 17 It was this tribe with which our infant government in 1778 made its first Indian treaty.

Also see as main entries **Indian affairs, agency, Department, reservation, reserve, ring, service.**

6. Denoting Indians of some specified rank or function: (1) **Indian conjurer,** (2) **councilor,** (3) **emperor,** (4) **guide,** (5) **king,** (6) **magician,** (7) **minister,** (8) **physician,** (9) **priest,** (10) **runner,** (11) **sachem,** (12) **sagamore.**

(1) **1709** LAWSON *Carolina* 24 The Indian-Conjurer made a huge Lilleloo . . . howling very frightfully. **1812** in *Mich. Hist. Coll.* XV. 153 He then told me that two of the Indian Conjurors had dreamt that they should be successful that day, and that they were determined to fight. — (2) **1669** *Md. Archives* II. 197 [The Upper House thinks] each of these Indian Councellours here [should be given] a Present at parting.—(3) **1639** *Md. Archives* IV. 110 Administration . . . delivered to the Indian Emperour a great knife bought for him by the deceased. **1766** ROBERT ROGERS *Ponteach* 2 Ponteach, Indian Emperor on the great Lakes. — (4) **1609** *Va. Co. of Lon. Doc. Rec.* III. 17 This place [Ohonahorn] . . . if you seeke by Indian guides . . . you shall finde a braue and fruiteful seate euery way vnaccessable by a straunger enemy. **1866** *Rep. Indian Affairs* 125, I have made several trips to different parts of the Territory, accompanied by Indian guides, in the endeavor to have an interview with Black Hawk. **1947** *Atlantic Mo.* Sep. 22/1 Our Indian guide is there, along with a half-dozen other Indians.

(5) **1621** *Va. Co. of Lon. Ct. Bk. Rec.* I. 50 The particular relations gave the Companie verie great content to heare . . . of a confirmation of a Peace, and of a League with the Indian Kinge. **1767** *Essex Hist. Coll.* LIII. 134 *Thomas Sommerville* . . . begs leave to acquaint all Gentlemen . . . that he still keeps The Indian King Tavern and London Coffee-House in Salem. — (6) **1899** CUSHMAN *Hist. Indians* 38 There was but little difference between the 'Indian Magician' and the Indian 'Medicine Man.' — (7) **1689** I. MATHER *Rel. State of N. Eng.* 17 In the Island of Martha . . . are two American Churches . . . more Famous than the rest, for that over one of them presides an Ancient Indian Minister, called *Hiacooms.* **1727** EXPERIENCE MAYHEW *Indian Converts* 76, I have instanced . . . a very considerable number of *Indian* Ministers, who have appeared to be truly godly. — (8) **1778** CARVER *Travels* 395 The Indian physicians always annex these superstitious ceremonies to their prescriptions. **1820** D. W. HARMON *Journal* 372 These Indian physicians do at times, however, perform distinguished cures. — (9) **1672** in GEORGE FOX *Journal* II. (1831) 136 There was also one of the Indian priests . . . who sat soberly among the people. **1769** RICHARD SMITH *Four Great Rivers* (1906) 67 The Indian Priest named Isaac sat in the Pulpit, and the Indian clerk, Peter, below him.

(10) **1725** *Travels Amer. Col.* 158 This morning I recd the following Letter . . . by one of the Indians runners. **1885** *Wkly. New Mexican Rev.* 5 Feb. 3/1 The Indian runners informed Lieutenant McDonald that more mutineers were coming. — (11) **1638** *New Haven Col. Rec.* 1 Momaugin ye Indian Sachem of Quinopiocke. **1838** *Boston Wkly. Mag.* 1 Dec. 109/3 In the year 1660, William Phillips of Saco, became proprietor of all this incalculable wealth, by purchasing the hills from an Indian Sachem. **1949** *N. Eng. Quart.* March 86 The island is supposed to owe its present name to an Indian sachem or chief named Tequenoman. — (12) **1631** *N.H. Doc. and Rec.* I. (1867) 104 An Indian Sagamore . . . and his company . . . having killed them [white settlers], burnt the house over them.

b. Denoting white people having to do with Indians: (1) **Indian constable,** (2) **countryman,** (3) **fighter,** (4) **inspector,** (5) **merchant,** (6) **superintendent.**

(1) **1682** *Plymouth Laws* 195 Such Indians . . . shall forthwith give notice of the said Runaway to the Indian Constable. — (2) **1858** WOODWARD *Reminiscences* (1939) 49 The Indian countryman, John Ward, died in 1813. **1948** DICK *Dixie Frontier* 11 'Indian countrymen' . . . were men who for various reasons had left civilization to live among the Indians long before the true American pioneer came. — (3) **1832** *Louisville Directory* 97 Our fellow townsmen . . . were no doubt animated by the hardy gallantry so universally characteristic of the backwoods hunters and Indian fighters, as they were termed in those days. **1947** *Sat. Ev. Post* 15 March 146/4 The first Killingworth had been a brilliant Indian fighter and colonizer. — (4) **1880** LAMPHERE *U.S. Govt.* 274/1 Indian inspectors [are appointed by the president]. **1946** FOREMAN *Last Trek* 249 On the thirtieth, E. C. Kemble, United States Indian inspector, arrived.

(5) **1705** BEVERLEY *Virginia* I. 69 Their Indian Merchants had lost a considerable Branch of their Trade they knew not how. **1747** *Ga. Col. Rec.* XXV. 168 It might be an easy matter to induce

the Indian Merchants to carry their Goods rather to Savannah than 150 Miles farther of [*sic*] to Charles-Town. — **(6) 1773** *Hist. MSS Comm.* 14th Rep. App. X. (1895) 140 Necessity there is for the appointment of an Indian Superintendent for the country west of Lake Huron. **1946** Foreman *Last Trek* 61 Some of the chiefs went to St. Louis to see the Indian superintendent.

Also *Indian brave, factor, killer, man-servant, master, medicine man, preacher, ruler, servant, slave, soldier, squaw, teacher, trailer,* etc.

See also as main entries **Indian agent, commissioner, doctor, hunter, interpreter, powwow, scout, trader, warrior.**

7. Denoting places owned or occupied by Indians: (1) **Indian farm,** (2) **ground,** (3) **hunting ground,** (4) **plantation,** (5) **praying village,** (6) **quarters,** (7) **ranch,** (8) **rancheria,** (9) **rancho,** (10) **range,** (11) **reservation,** see as a main entry, (12) **reserve,** (13) **settlement.**

(1) [**1750** Cammerhoff & Zeisberger *Diary* (1916) 24 May–4 June, In the afternoon we came to an Indian farm. An Indian . . . called to us to come over to him. He . . . had a plantation and a strange looking lodge.] **1758** in *Essex Inst. Hist. Coll.* XII. 142 Encamped at Col. Schuyler's Farm by some called ye great Indian Farms. **1885** *Rep. Indian Affairs* 122 When I say 'we' I mean the Indian as well as the agency farm. — **(2) 1657** *Conn. Hist. Soc. Coll.* XIV. 390 One parcell of Indian Ground lying in the South Meadow. — **(3) 1780** in *Mich. Pioneer Coll.* IX. 580 Their Route shall be to the Ohio, which they (special military forces) shall cross & attack some of the Forts, which surround the Indian Hunting ground in Kentuck. **1865** Pike *Scout & Ranger* (1932) 75 We were in a country celebrated as an Indian hunting-ground, and therefore it would be folly for us to proceed further. — **(4) 1639** *Mass. Bay Rec.* I. 277 The place desired by Mr Bellingham for his farme is on the head of Salem . . . there being in it a hill, with an Indian plantation, & a pond, & about a hundred or 150 acres of meadow. **1699** *God's Protecting Providence* 82 We went through a Kirt of wood into the Indian Plantation.

(5) 1674 in *Mass. H.S. Coll.* 1 Ser. I. 194, I have endeavoured particularly to describe these Indian praying villages within the jurisdiction of Massachusetts. — **(6) 1647** *Md. Hist. Mag.* VI. 372 The Easte side of St. Clements Bay, about 2 miles from Little Brittaine commonly knowen by the name of the Indian Quarters. — **(7) 1849** in *Calif. Hist. Quart.* XXI. 301 Toward evening arrived at a small Indian ranch, tolerable grass and water 15 miles from the creek. **1856** Glisan *Jrnl. Army Life* 344 The agent . . . got the commanding officer of this post to send out three of four men to examine the Indian ranches for arms, etc. — **(8) 1842** in *Calif. Hist. Soc. Quart.* XIX (1940) 199 As interesting as the visit to such an Indian ranchería was to me, I must confess that the impression was not at all cheering; the conditions are too beastly. **1864** in *N.M. Hist. Rev.* (1949) April 116 We are encamped in an old indian rancherie. — **(9) 1850** in *Soc. Calif. Pion. Quart.* VII. 12 They [boat crew] had been 7 or 8 miles into the country & had found an Indian rancho [near San Diego].

(10) 1828 in *Texas Hist. Assoc. Quart.* XIII. (1909) 65 This is the principal Indian range—many have been robbed of money and horses. — **(12) 1818** F. Hall *Travels* 131 The river Credit is an Indian reserve, well stocked with salmon. **1901** Duncan & Scott *Allen & Woodson Co., Kans.* 582 All of Woodson County and a small strip off the south side of Coffey County was included in the New York Indian Reserve. — **(13) 1705** Beverley *Virginia* III. 10 The method of the Indian Settlements is altogether by Cohabitation, in Townships, from fifty to five hundred Families in a Town, and each of these Towns is commonly a Kingdom. **1781** in *Hist. MSS Comm.* 9th Rep. App. III. II. (1910) 226 He had been industrious in passing the Indian settlements on the way to spread the alarm.

b. Designating other places in some way associated with Indians: (1) **Indian bed,** (2) **meadow,** (3) **orchard,** (4) **oysterbank,** (5) **ridge,** (6) **side.**

(1) 1848 Bartlett 188 An *Indian bed* of clams is made by setting a number of clams together on the ground with the hinge uppermost, and then kindling over them a fire of brushwood, which is kept burning till they are thoroughly roasted. — **(2) 1658** *Hartford Land Distrib.* 216 One parcell of Indian Meadow lying in the South Meadow. **1920** in *Amer. Sp.* XV. 275/2 When the white explorer came the Rockbridge area, like the Valley of Virginia in general, was largely occupied by tracts of prairie. These were known as Indian meadows, or as savanas, the word prairie having not yet come into the English language. — **(3) 1798** C. Williamson *Descr. Genesee* ii, The old Indian orchards had been dressed up, and the fruit secured from depredation. **1859** Bartlett 215 Indian Orchard, an old orchard of ungrafted apple-trees, the time of planting being unknown. New York. — **(4) 1798** *Amer. Philos. Soc.* IV. 439 The immense oyster-beds, which have been quitted by the ocean, are vulgarly called *Indian* oysterbanks.

(5) 1847 in *31st Congress* 1 Sess. H.R. Ex. Doc. No. 5, II. 731 The banks [of a stream] rise on either side . . . worn in some places into 'hog backs' or more like our 'Indian ridges,' being only two or three feet wide on the top and extending along the river for a considerable distance. — **(6) 1806** Ashe *Travels* 85 Little more than twenty years have elapsed since the whole of the right bank of the Ohio was called the Indian Country or the Indian Side. [**1842** *Amer. Pioneer* I. 102 The latter name was derived from its lying on the north or Indian side of the Ohio.]

c. Denoting structures or abodes occupied by Indians: (1) **Indian cabin,** (2) **dwelling,** (3) **house,** (4) **hunting cabin,** (5) **hunting lodge,** (6) **hut,** (7) **lodge,** (8) **pen,** (9) **pueblo,** (10) **tent,** cf. **bush tent,** (11) **tepee,** (12) **wickiup,** (13) **wigwam.**

(1) 1671 *Md. Archives* LIV. 492 Your deponent. . . . Mett With two men at An Indian Cabbin upon the Branches of Coursaca Creeke. **1877** Johnson *Anderson Co., Kans.* 18 When the first whites settled in Anderson county, . . . they found some of the Indian cabins. — **(2) 1811** Robert Sutcliff *Travels* 138 Under the piazza of a commodious Indian dwelling, I saw . . . the harness and yokes of horses and oxen. — **(3) 1622** Mourt *Relation* 26 They found seaven or eight *Indian* houses, but not lately inhabited. **1750** T. Walker *Journal* 43 In the Fork between Holstons and the North River, are five Indian Houses built with loggs and covered with Bark. **1883** Jackson *Ramona* 26 At that time there were long streets of Indian houses stretching eastward from the Mission. — **(4) 1766** John Bartram *Journey* 29 Here we found an Indian hunting cabin covered with palmetto-leaves. **1791** W. Bartram *Travels* 344, I saw an Indian hunting cabin on the side of a hill.

(5) 1809 A. Henry *Travels* 6 We arrived at a solitary Indian hunting-lodge built with branches of trees. — **(6) 1690** *Doc. Rel. Col. Hist. N.Y.* IX. 461 [It was] reported . . . that there . . . [were] no Indian huts . . . in the neighborhood of their route . . . although it was the usual hunting and fishing ground. **1797** Francis Baily *Journal* (1856) 371 We entered his habitation, which was a poor sorry place, little better than an Indian hut. **1839** *Boston Wkly. Mag.* 27 April 267/2 Sometimes, however, the halting place was an Indian hut. **1949** *Exciting Western* May 90/2 They reached Quivara and found Indian huts peopled by folk so poor and unlearned they didn't even use wooden plates like the commonest folk of Spain. — **(7)** [**1656** Van der Donck in *N.Y. Hist. Soc. Coll.* 2 Ser. I. (1841) 193 We seldom visit an Indian lodge at any time of the day, without seeing their sapaen preparing, or seeing them eating the same.] **1805** Lewis in *L. & Clark Exped.* II. (1904) 227 Passed a very extraordinary Indian lodge . . . formed of sixteen large cottonwood poles each about fifty feet long. *a***1918** G. Stuart *On Frontier* I. 125 We all lived in elk skin Indian lodges and were very comfortable. — **(8) 1813** Stuart *Narrative* 209 When finding an Indian Pen sufficient to screen us from the severity of the weather we stopped in it. — **(9) 1858** D. Peters *Kit Carson* 239 Near the mountains, to the east of Fernandez de Taos, is located an Indian Pueblo which is very interesting to the traveler.

(10) 1708 John Oldmixon *Brit. Empire in Amer.* I. 392 The Governour . . . , and others, travell'd on the Ice to Point Comfort, where were some Indian Tents, to buy what [illegible] could. **1797** Francis Baily *Journal* (1856) [illegible] pearance of rain, we formed a curious kind o[illegible] bark of some trees. **1837** *S. Lit. Messenger* III[illegible] side of the river several Indian tents made [illegible] **1859** in *Pac. N.W. Quart.* XXXI. 339 We ar[illegible] yds. of the Spokane river some few Indian te[illegible] March 2/2 Camps are made up of Indian te[illegible] and decorated by the Stony Indians who have a[illegible] at nearby Morley. — **(12) 1867** in *Frontier* XII. (1932[illegible] We camped in some willows, back by a small grove of trees . . . in this grove was an old Indian wickiup. — **(13) 1631** *Mass. Bay Rec.* I. (1853) 90 Every first Friday in every moneth there shalbe a generall traineing . . . att a convenient place aboute the Indian wigwams. **1674** in *Mass. H.S. Coll.* 1 Ser. I. 203 Certain Quakers . . . landing upon that island [Martha's Vineyard] went to some of the Indian wigwams. **1893** in *S. Dak. Hist. Coll.* I. 301 Still further on in the timber are the Indian wigwams.

d. Denoting ways, paths, etc., used by Indians: (1) **Indian carrying-path,** (2) **carrying-place,** (3) **crossing,** (4) **road,** (5) **trace,** (6) **trading-path,** (7) **trail.**

(1) 1765 Robert Rogers *Journals* 17 We lodged on the mountain, and next morning marched to the Indian carrying-path, that leads from Lake George to Lake Champlain. — **(2) 1765** Robert Rogers *Journals* 17 In our way we had a view of the French and Indians, encamped at the old Indian carrying-place, near Ticonderoga. **1832** Williamson *Maine* I. 47 Here was the Indian carrying place between Casco and Merry-Meeting bays. — **(3) 1831** Withers *Chron. Border Warfare* 206 Proceeding by forced marches to the Indian crossing at the mouth of the Sandy fork of Little Kenhawa, he remained there nearly three days. — **(4) 1730** *Md. Hist. Mag.* XVIII. 13 Ordered, that the Road formerly cleared from the long Calm to Mr. Gist's be continued into the road . . . called the old Indian Road. **1846** Stewart *Altowan* I. 221 A few hundred yards through the thick wood brought him back on the Indian road.

(5) 1810 Cuming *Western Tour* 238 An old Indian trace, now the post road from Louisville to Vincennes, crosses it. **1852** Watson *Nights in Block-House* 355 The track which he followed was only an old Indian trace. — **(6) 1728** in *N.C. Col. Rec.* II. 784 We ordered the horses to the Ford near a mile higher (than canoe landing on Roanoke), which leads to the Indian trading path. — **(7)** [**1753** in BEAUCHAMP *Moravian Jrnls.* (1916) 159 We thought it an Indian trail, but on careful examination it was a bear track.] **1812** STUART *Narratives* 158 We this day crossed a large Indian trail. **1948** *Sierra Club Bul.* Mar. 3 He plunged ahead and came back a few minutes later announcing that he had found an Indian trail.

e. Denoting lines of demarcation between the whites and Indians, as **Indian border, boundary, boundary line, fence, frontier, line.**

1873 BEADLE *Undevel. West* 804 It was then [1839] 'far up country,' on the Indian border. — **1835** HOFFMAN *Winter in West* I. 186, I am now within eight or ten miles of the Indian boundary. — **1773** *Ga. Hist. Soc. Coll.* III. II. (1873) 158 The Nearest Mountain is at Chote a Cherokee Town about 45 Miles above the Indian Boundary Line. — **1666** *Duxbury Rec.* 15 Beginning the measurement on the north side the Indian fence, from a red oak tree marked on four sides. — **1791** W. BARTRAM *Travels* 46 Excursions, through uninhabited wildernesses, and an Indian frontier. — **1706** *Duxbury Rec.* 80 From thence we ran about fifty five rods by John Boneys line, to the Indian line, then we ran by the Indian line near South.

See also as main entries **Indian barn, camp, country, field, fort, grave, land, mound, path, territory, town, village.**

8. Denoting organizations, institutions, etc., formed to promote civilizing influences among Indians: (1) **Indian Aid Society,** (2) **charity school,** (3) **church,** (4) **company,** (5) **corporation,** (6) **free school,** (7) **industrial school,** (8) **manual labor school,** (9) **peace association.**

(1) 1872 *Rep. Indian Affairs 1871* 182 Indian aid societies have been formed. — **(2) 1763** *Hist. MSS Comm.* 14th Rep. App. X. (1895) 12 And present State of the Indian Charity School at Lebanon in Connecticut. — **(3) 1670** JOHN ELIOT *Progress of Gospel* (1671) 4 We had the Sacrament of the Lords Supper celebrated in the *Indian Church.* . . . A Foundation is laid for two Churches more. **1702** C. MATHER *Magnalia* VI. 61/2 The Indian Church at Natick (which was the first Indian Church in America) is since blessed Eliot's Death, much diminish'd and dwindl'd away.—**(4) 1715** in *Va. Hist. Soc. Coll.* ns. II. 138 The late erected Indian Company have built a fine School house at one of the Indian towns.

(5) 1712 in *Harvard Coll. Rec.* I. (1925) 401 That the Comissionrs of the Indian Corporacon do afford them Such Support & Encouragmt as shal be Iudg'd suitable. **1746** *Ib.* II. 754 That Part of the Honble Mr. Boyle's Donation wch is in the Hands of the Commissioners of the [illegible]ian Corporation. — **(6) 1674** in *Mass.* [illegible] *Coll.* 1 Ser. [illegible]
[illegible] Comfor[illegible],
[illegible] dry'd Meat he
[illegible]31 There being an ap-
[illegible] Indian tent out of the
[illegible]. 689 We saw on either
[illegible]f straw mats. — **(11)**
[illegible] within a few hundred
[illegible]is. **1949** *Sky Line Trail* [illegible] [*sic*] clothing,
[illegible]epees, construct[illegible]
[illegible] reservatio[illegible]

See al[illegible] 155[illegible] **college, school.**

9. In misce[illegible] combs.: (1) **Indian Bible,** the Bible translated by John Eliot (1604–90) into a dialect of the Massachusetts Indians, first published in 1663 at Cambridge, Mass.; (2) **harvest,** a harvest of Indian corn; (3) **line,** =**Indian file;** (4) **money,** beads made of shells and used by the Indians as money; (5) **poker,** =**stick poker;** (6) **purchase,** the sum or amount involved in a purchase made from Indians, the transaction itself; (7) **store,** a store maintained for trade with the Indians; (8) **wrestling,** wrestling after the manner of Indians (see quot. 1946 and **cf. Indian hug** as a main entry).

(1) 1663 EBENEZER HAZARD *Hist. Coll.* II. (1794) 489 Mr. Simon Bradstreet and Mr. Danforth are Requested to take care for the preparation of an epistle to the Indian Bible dedicatory to his Majestie and cause the same to bee printed. **1674** I. MATHER *Diary* (1900) 41 Marmaduke Johnson the Printer died in Boston. He had just fitted his press to go to work. He was to have printed [the second ed. of] the Indian bible. **1718** SEWALL *Diary* III. 180, I gave her 10s to give her sister Weld for her Indian Bible. — **(2) 1639** *Md. Hist. Soc. Pub.* No. 7 (1874) 73 To the hope of the Indian harvest, are to be added also no mean fruits reaped from the colony and its inhabitants. **1780** *N.H. Hist. Soc. Coll.* IX. 188, [I] went on with Indian Harvest. — **(3) 1839** AUDUBON *Ornith. Biog.* V. 255 Far away to seaward we spied a flock of Flamingoes advancing in 'Indian line,' with well-spread wings. — **(4) 1705** in *Amer. Sp.* (1948) April 110/1 To send . . . with a Belt of their Indian money. **1940** SMITH *Puyallup-Nisqually* 205 They spoke also of a lot of 'Indian money' being buried with the person.

(5) 1876 *Stanislaus Co. Wkly. News* (Modesto, Calif.) 30 June 1/4 A Piute sport from Stillwater came over a few days ago, and tackled the Austin Indians in a game of Indian poker. **1878** HART *Sazerac Lying Club* 232 These stalwart Piutes were engaged in a game of Indian poker, the stakes of which were chewing-gum. — **(6) 1642** *Springfield Rec.* I. 170 If ye Indian purchase be payd. **1682** *Huntington Rec.* I. Twenty shillings . . . is the Indian purchas for the whole forme. **1777** *Va. State P.* I. He was further fixed in his Determination not to be concern'd in any Indian Purchase whatever. — **(7) 1798** C. WILLIAMSON *Descr. Genesee* i, At the Genesee River I found a small Indian store and tavern. **1878** I. L. BIRD *Rocky Mts.* 162 The Indian stores and fur stores and fur depôts [in Denver] interested me most. — **(8) 1913** LONDON *Valley of Moon* 8 She's got that Indian wrestlin' down pat, an' she's built for it. **1946** *Chi. D. News* 8 Nov. 1/3 He broke his arm while 'Indian wrestling' with a 220-pound bartender in a down-town lounge. They locked hands, rested their elbows on the bar and each was trying to force the other's hand down. **1949** *Sat. Ev. Post* 19 March 103/2 He pulled me forward like in Indian wrestling and slammed me across the back with his free arm.

b. In similar combs. sufficiently explained in the quots.: (1) **Indian gift,** (2) **giver,** (3) **giving,** (4) **hunting,** (5) **shell.**

(1) 1764 HUTCHINSON *Hist. Mass.* I. 469 An Indian gift is a proverbial expression, signifying a present for which an equivalent return is expected. — **(2) 1848** BARTLETT 189 *Indian Giver.* When an Indian gives anything, he expects an equivalent in return, or that the same thing may be given back to him. This term is applied by children in New York and the vicinity to a child who, after having given away a thing, wishes to have it back again. **1949** *Chi. Tribune* 9 Jan. 6/1 Those who use the term 'Indian giver' slightingly have never heard of Pokagon, wise and beloved chieftain of the Pottawatomies. — **(3) 1837** IRVING *Bonneville* II. 71 Captain Bonneville was suitably affected by this mark of friendship; but his experience in what is proverbially called 'Indian giving,' made him aware that a parting pledge was necessary on his own part, to prove that this friendship was reciprocated. **1911** SAUNDERS *Col. Todhunter* 103 But you're sure about it, too, ain't you? She ain't doin' no Injun-giving in your case? — **(4) 1818** FORDHAM *Narr. Travels* 179 He has killed more men than Boon has, and most of them in single fights, or Indian hunting, as it is called. **1869** W. MURRAY *Adventures* 225 Jack Murdock . . . learned his horsemanship from buffalo and Indian hunting on the Plains.

(5) 1794 *N.Y. State Soc. Arts* I. 134 The remaining two acres I manured with shells called Indian shells, that is, the shells of clams, oysters, wilks and scollops, collected by Indians, and by length of time settled under the surface of the ground, and so dissolved as to be broken in pieces and mixed with the earth.

c. In other combs. of obvious meaning: (1) **Indian alarm,** (2) **dance,** (3) **fashion,** (4) **scalp,** (5) **scare,** (6) **whoop,** (7) **yell.**

(1) 1745 in FRANKLIN *Indian Tr.* (1938) 309 Andrew Van Petton the low Dutchman . . . had been accused of being the Author of the Indian Alarm last Winter. **1829** COOPER *Wish-ton-Wish* i, Indian alarms, as they were termed, were not infrequent. — **(2) 1705** BEVERLEY *Virginia* III. 22 Antique Indian Dances, perform'd both by Men and Women, and accompany'd with great variety of Wild Musick. **1893** *Harper's Mag.* April 761/1 Dolly had announced her intention of going with them to see the Indian dance. — **(3) a1738** BYRD *Secret Hist.* (1929) 115 They offer'd us no Bedfellows, according to the good Indian fashion, which we had reason to take unkindly. **1949** *Sat. Ev. Post* 26 Feb. 26/3 His moccasined feet pointed outward, Indian fashion, from the iron stirrups of a battered saddle. — **(4) 1690** SEWALL *Letter-Book* I. 113 Writt to Cousin Hull per Mr. Sergeants Ketch sent 4 Ind. Scalps in Barrals mark'd with Ink. **1871** *Scribner's Mo.* II. 386 British troops [in 1775] . . . expected to send home Indian scalps as trophies gathered in the wilds of Cape Cod.

(5) 1882 *N. Mex. Terr. Rep.* (1884) 101 By this time the Indian scare was over with, and I can assure you . . . if they had come along they would have had a warm reception. **1912** DAWSON *Pioneer Tales Ore. Trail* 163 Nothing of serious consequence occurred during this Indian scare. — **(6) 1761** NILES *Indian Wars* II. 578 The Indian whoop went directly after from front to rear of the line of both flanks. **c1845** *Big Bear Ark.* 15 We were startled most unexpectedly by a loud Indian whoop, uttered in the 'social hall,' that part of the cabin fitted off for a bar. — **(7) 1764** HUTCHINSON *Hist. Mass.* I. 78 No sound that was ever made can be more horrid than the Indian yell. **1848** J. S. ROBINSON *Jrnl. Santa Fe Exped.* (1932) 46 In the midst of these exciting [hunting] scenes they [Navahos] indulge in the wild Indian yell, or shout of triumph.

Also *Indian army, battle, cry, custom, expedition, feast, festival, fighting, funeral, fur trade, market, massacre, outrage, raid, tribe, trouble,* etc.

Also see as main entries **Indian council, goods, language, nation, sign, summer, sweat, title, trade, trading, war, war whoop.**

Indian ˈɪndɪən, *v. intr.* To move about stealthily like an Indian. *Rare.* — **1869** Stowe *Old-town Folks* 189 Jack Marshall and me has been Indianing round these 'ere woods more times 'n you could count. **1871** ——— *Sam Lawson* 55 Lordy massy! when a feller is Indianin' round, these 'ere pleasant summer days, a feller's thought gits like a flock o' young partridges.

Indiana ˌɪndɪˈænə, *n.* [The name of a state, f. ***Indian** + *-a.*] *attrib.* Of or pertaining to the state of Indiana.

1856 Brewerton *War in Kans.* 128 As for the animal motive power, we had a couple of rat-like 'Ingianny' horses, of which our driver seemed particularly proud. **1908** Phillips *Old Wives* 22 It is one of these—a square, brick house trimmed with Indiana limestone—that we enter. **1949** *Chi. D. News* 27 Oct. 28 (*heading*), Strike Relief Drains Indiana Towns' Tills.

Indian affairs.

1. Matters relating to Indians. *Obs.*

1647 Roger Williams in *Mass. H.S. Coll.* 3 Ser. IX. 269 Sir—concerning Indian affaires—Reports are various: Lyes are frequent. **1714** Sewall *Diary* II. 433 Discours'd Mr. Mayhew largely of the Indian affairs. **1873** *Newton Kansan* 6 Feb. 1/5 In the present state of Indian affairs we cannot afford to allow the bad Indians to score a victory against the government.

2. In the names of governmental bodies or offices that deal with matters affecting the relationship of Indians with the colonies and with the U.S.

1703 Sewall *Letter-Book* I. 287 The Commissioners for the Indian Affairs, are to have a Meeting at the Council-chamber. **1822** *Ann. 17th Congress* 1 Sess. I. 137 The petition was read and referred to the Committee on Indian Affairs. **1947** *Chi. Sun. Tribune* 6 July I. 3/1 The office of Indian affairs has worked out a program for an irrigation project.

Indian agency. The office of an Indian agent or the headquarters of such an agent.

1822 Morse *Rep. Indian Affairs* 1. 39 Should the Government establish a military post here it will be very important . . . that . . . an Indian agency should be planted, at the same time, near it. **1866** *Rep. Indian Affairs* 73 [The Grande Ronde] reservation [in Ore.] consists of two townships and two fractional townships . . . and upon it is located the oldest Indian agency in the superintendency. **1948** *Dly. Ardmoreite* (Ardmore, Okla.) 5 May 3/4 He is acting head of the Indian agency for this district.

Indian agent. A white man who represents the government in its dealings with Indians.

[**1712** *Jrnl S.C. Bd. Comm. Indian Trade* (1926, Salley) 43 Law Directs. . . . That no Trader receive or take any present . . . from any Indian . . . but shall direct him or them to ye Agent with ye Same.] **1766** in Rogers *Journals* (1883) 216 As Commandant and Indian Agent, it will be extremely difficult to check him, or detect him. **1946** Underhill *First Penthouse Dwellers* 97 There were Indian agents, first for all New Mexico, later for groups of pueblos.

attrib. **1949** *Sat. Ev. Post* 2 April 125/1 The Office of Indian Affairs then began an examination of tribal rolls, Indian-agent and Army reports in the National Archives.

Indianaite ɪndɪˈænəˌaɪt, *n. Min.* A kind of white clay found in Indiana. — **1875** E. F. Cox in *Geol. Surv. Indiana* 15 Owing to the mode of its formation and other features to be mentioned beyond, I have thought proper to give to this porcelain clay the name of *Indianaite.*

Indianan, see **Indianian.**

Indian arrow.

1. An arrow used by the Indians. Also attrib.

1654 Johnson *Wonder-w. Prov.* 50 He felt something brush hard upon his shoulder, which was an *Indian* arrow shot through his Coat, and the wing of his buffe-Jacket. **1765** J. Bartram *Diary* 8 Sep., I asked one that rode A mile with us if he had not often found in yᵉ fields Indian arrow points & flint knives & hatchets. **1860** Holmes *Professor* 308 At Cantabridge, near the sea, I have once or twice picked up an Indian arrowhead in a fresh furrow. **1947** Peattie *Sierra Nevada* 55 Indian arrows put an end to his remarkable career in 1831.

2. Wahoo or burning bush, *Euonymus atropurpureus.* Also **Indian arrowwood.**

1815 Drake *Cincinnati* ii. 77 [Plants growing in Miami country include] Indian arrow-wood. **1843** Torrey *Flora N.Y.* I. 141 Burning-bush, Indian arrow, . . . [grows in] moist woods and along rivers, in the western part of the State. **1892** *Amer. Folk-Lore* V. 94 *Euonymus atropurpureus,* Indian arrow. Salem, Ind.

Indian barn. (See quot. 1736.) *Obs.*

1634 *Mass. Bay Rec.* I. 121 What hurt the swyne of Charlton hath done amongst the Indean barnes of corne. **1641** *Southampton Rec.* I. 22 Any Indian Barnes or welles lyeing open . . . the owners or overseers of such Lotts shall fill up all such Barnes and welles. **1736** Gyles *Mem. Captivity* 11 We put some into Indian Barns, i.e. in Holes in the Ground lin'd and cover'd with Bark, and then with Dirt. **1898** J. R. Trumbull *Hist. Northampton Mass.* I. 173 Evidence . . . exists that they had receptacles for storing corn and other articles, 'Indian barns,' the settlers called them.

Indian bean.

1. Any one of various edible beans found in colonial times in use among the Indians. *Obs.*

[**1622** Mourt *Relation* 30 Wee went to another place, which we had seene before, and digged, and found more corne, viz. two or three Baskets full of Indian Wheat, and a bag of Beanes.] **1637** *Conn. Rec.* I. 9 Weathersfeild [is to provide] 1 bushell of Indian Beanes; Windsor 50 peeces of Porke. **1779** Hewatt *Hist. Acct.* 461 For a whole month, they had no other subsistence but the flesh of lean horses and dogs, and a small supply of Indian beans, which some friendly Cherokee women procured for them by stealth. **1793** *Mass. H.S. Coll.* 3 Ser. V. 129 His Indian beans [were] ready to be eaten as stringed beans.

2. The catalpa or its fruit.

1843 Torrey *Flora N.Y.* II. 25 *Catalpa syringæfolia* Catalpa. Indian Bean. . . . About habitations. . . . The Catalpa is more esteemed for ornament than for use. **1931** Clute *Plants* 36 The slender cylindrical fruits of the catalpa tree (*C. speciosa*) are often known as Indian beans and Indian cigars. **1938** Mowry *Ornamental Shrubs* 29 *Catalpa bignonioides.* . . . Catalpa. Indian Bean.

Indian blanket. A blanket made by or for Indians, a matchcoat. *Obs.*

1764 in *N.J. Archives* 1 Ser. XXIV. 350 There are a blue Great Coat, and an Indian Blanket missing. **1765** in Chalkley *Scotch-Irish Settlement Va.* I. 450 One rifel gun . . . one snafel bridle, and one Indian blanket. **1807** Irving *Salmagundi* iii. 58 The shawl scarlet . . . thrown over one shoulder, like an Indian blanket, with one end dragging on the ground. *a*1861 T. Winthrop *Canoe & Saddle* iii. 33 Hickory shirts and woolen blankets are worn instead of skin raiment, mat aprons, and Indian blankets.

Indian boots. (See quots.) *Obs.*

1744 Moore *Voy. Georgia* I. 120 Those who walk the woods much, wear what they call Indian boots, which are made of coarse woolen cloths, much too large for the legs, tied upon their thighs and hang loose to their shoes. **1784** J. Smyth *Tour U.S.* I. xxiii. 180 On their

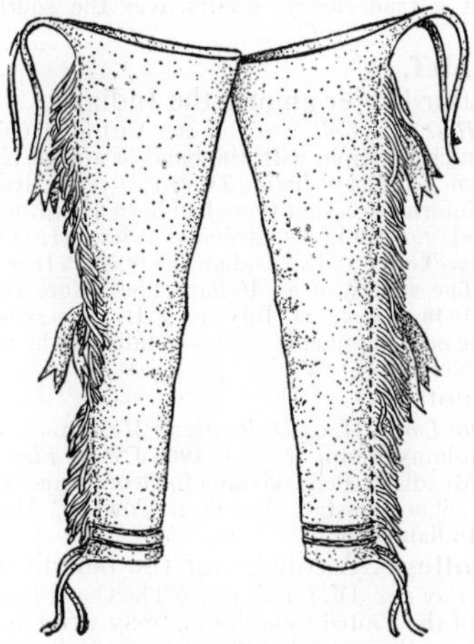

Indian boots (Sac and Fox)

legs they [backwoods riflemen] have Indian boots or leggings, made of coarse woolen cloth, that either are wrapped round loosely and tied with garters, or are laced upon the outside, and always come better than half way up the thigh. **1855** Simms *Forayers* 81 Sinclair, wearing Indian boots—moccasins and leggins of buckskin—awoke no echoes by his tread.

Indian bread.

1. Bread made of the meal of Indian corn. *Obs.*

1654 Johnson *Wonder-w. Prov.* 84 The want of English graine . . . proved a sore affliction to some stomacks, who could not live upon Indian Bread. **1765** Timberlake *Memoirs* 30 Fried meats of several kinds, and very good Indian bread, baked in a very curious way. **1863** *Rio Abajo Press* 26 May 4/1 Indian Bread.—Take two quarts of Indian meal, pour on boiling water enough to make the meal quite wet [etc.]. **1949** *Amer. Sp.* April 110/1 Indian Bread, *n.* Corn bread prepared in pones (large, hand-shaped loaves, cooked two to a spider or Dutch oven). [Nassau Co., Fla.]

2. In the names of plants (see quots.).
1848 BARTLETT 366 *Tuckahoe*. . . . The Virginia truffle. A curious Vegetable, sometimes called by the name of Indian bread, or Indian Loaf, found in the Southern States, bordering on the Atlantic. **1903** *D.N.* II. 318 Indian bread or Indian pone. A hard, perhaps fungous, growth found in the woods. It is black outside and white within and nearly globular. Is said to have been used for food by Indians. **1917** KEPHART *Camping* II. 379 *Potato, Prairie*. Prairie turnip. Indian or Missouri Breadroot. The *pomme blanche* of the voyageurs. *Psoralea Esculenta*. . . . Often sliced and dried by the Indians for winter use. Palatable in any form. **1931** CLUTE *Plants* 30 A species of *Psoralea* otherwise known as Indian bread-root (*P. esculenta*), is the Cree potato.

Indian cake. Corn bread or hoecake.
1607 WINGFIELD *Discourse Va.* (1860) 25 And hee (as Mr Pearsie sent me worde) had bought some witnesses' handes against me to diuers artycles, with Indian cakes . . . perswations, and threats. **1719** in *N.J. Hist. Soc. Proc.* 3 Ser. X. 103 The Indians supplied them [the Reading company] with Indian cakes. **1835** ABBOTT *N. Eng.* 232 Two or three steaming Indian cakes, hot from the fire, send up their clouds of incense from the centre of the table. **1896** WILKINS *Madelon* 45 Madelon . . . put pieces of Indian cake into her untasting mouth.

Indian camp. An encampment of Indians (see also quot. 1775).
1775 FITHIAN *Jrnl.* II. 81 We saw many 'Indian Camps,' small crotched Sticks covered with thick Bark. **1807** GASS *Journal* 42 [We passed] an old Indian camp, where we found some of their dog-poles, which answer for setting poles. *c***1908** CANTON *Frontier Trails* 59 Every thing was quiet as a graveyard, not even a dog barking, which seemed singular in an Indian camp. **1948** *Pacific Spectator* Summer 316 They were successful in locating the Indian camp and approaching it just before daylight.

Indian cherry. (See quot. 1909.)
1705 BEVERLEY *Virginia* II. 13 Of Cherries natural to the Country, and growing wild in the Woods, I have seen Three Sorts. . . . The Third sort is call'd the Indian Cherry, and grows higher up in the Country, than the Others do. **1763** in *Amer. Sp.* XX. (1945) 48 The small cherries, called *Indian* cherries, are frequent in this country. **1909** *Cent. Supp.* 233/2 Indian cherry, (*a*) The Carolina buckthorn, *Rhamnus Caroliniana*. (*b*) The service-berry, *Amelanchier Canadensis*. **1930** MATTOON *Forest Trees Okla.* 96 The Indian cherry, which, however, is not a true cherry, occurs over the southern United States.

Indian chief.

1. A chief or leader among the Indians.
1641 in *N.Y. Hist. Soc. Coll.* 2 Ser. I. 262 An Indian chief . . . came to the fort in much triumph, with the hand of a dead man hanging on a stick. **1758** in FRANKLIN *Indian Tr.* (1938) 313/1 George Croghan came and gave information that there had been a great meeting of the Indian chiefs today. **1780** in *Pa. Archives* 2 Ser. XI. (1895) 603 Reviewed by his Excellency and six Indian chiefs. **1835** HOFFMAN *Winter in West* I. 61 The speech of an Indian chief before the council of Pennsylvania. **1948** *Parade* 11 July 12/3 It all serves a purpose, though, even the odd chinquapin seed — a talisman he received from an old Indian chief.

2. (See quots.)
1894 *Amer. Folk-Lore* VII. 94 *Dodecatheon Meadia*. . . . Indian chief, Rockford, Ill. Johnny jump, So. Cal. **1908** LYONS *Plant Names* 168 D[odecatheon] Meadia L. Pennsylvania to Georgia and west to Texas and Manitoba. Shooting-star, American Cowslip, Mosquito-bells, Pride of Ohio, Indian-chief.

Indian college. A college for the benefit of Indians.
1658 in *Mass. Bay Rec.* IV. I. (1854) 336 The Court judgeth . . . the commissioners of the Vnited Colonjes . . . may write to the corporation in England for the procuring of twenty pounds worth of letters for the vse of the Indian Colledg. **1674** in *Mass. H.S. Coll.* I Ser. I. 176 A means intended for the good of the Indians . . . was the erecting a house of brick at Cambridge in New-England, which passeth under the name of the Indian college. . . . It is large enough to receive and accommodate about twenty scholars with convenient lodgings and studies. **1698** SEWALL *Diary* I. 480 The old Brick College [at Harvard] commonly called the Indian College, is pulled down to the ground. **1822** MORSE *Rep. Indian Affairs* II. 315, I should think this the place for the ultimate establishment of the Indian College. **1948** *Chi. Tribune* 25 April VII. 3/5 The council finances a boy student at Bacone Indian college in Oklahoma.

Indian commissioner. A white man or an Indian who negotiates officially in behalf of his government or people.
1713 C. MATHER in *Mass. H.S. Coll.* 7 Ser. VIII. 233 Besides my drawing up Instructions for Agents to go from the Indian-Commissioners to *Martha's Vineyard*, I must prevent some indirect Proceedings in *Connecticot*. **1817** in *Essex Inst. Hist. Coll.* VIII. 235 Whilst we were in Pittsburg we had an interview with twelve Indian Commissioners, with their chief. **1946** MCWILLIAMS *So. Calif. Country* 152 President Hayes appointed Albert Keith Smiley to the board of Indian commissioners on which he served until his death.

Indian corn.

1. Maize, *Zea mays*, a cereal grass which Europeans found in use here among the Indians. Also the ripened ears or seeds of this.
1617 *Va. Co. of Lon. Doc. Rec.* III. 71 English wheate, barly, Indyan Corne, Tobacco greate plenty in the ground. **1713** *Boston Town Rec.* VIII. 101 Voted. That five thousand bushalls of Indian Corn be purchaced and Layd up on Some Convenient place or places. **1855** BAXTER *America* 218 The best judges prefer as food for horses the leaves of the Indian corn, bruised, and sprinkled over with its meal. **1948** *Chi. Tribune* 8 July 12/4 As pioneers pushed westward across the country, it was the fields of Indian corn that helped them eat and live.

2. In combs.: (1) **Indian corn crop,** (2) **dance,** (3) **field,** (4) **harvest,** (5) **hill,** (6) **patch.**
(1) **1806** *Balance* V. 268/1 Principles in Agriculture, Leading to the improvement of land by the mode of culture . . . and the application of it to the Indian Corn crop. — (2) **1878** JACKSON *Travel at Home* 149 You will be invited to an Indian-corn dance, too, if you can read the Indian language. — (3) *a***1738** BYRD *Secret Hist.* (1929) 209 We encampt near one of these Indian Corn Fields, where was excellent Food for our Horses. **1776** *Battle of Brooklyn* II. i, We was standing by the end of a side of an Indian cornfield, up yonder a piece. **1943** BENÉT *Western Star* 145 On the hill's slope, where the Indian cornfield grew, For there, God be thanked, is cleared ground. — (4) **1642** *Essex Inst. Coll.* V. 219/2 Other poore people shalbe repayed . . . at the next Indian corne harvest.
(5) *a***1870** CHIPMAN *Notes on Bartlett* 213 *Indian Corn-Hills*. . . . In Essex Co., M[as]s., plot of ground where hummocks look like the hillocks in which maize has grown. — (6) **1818** FRANCIS HALL *Travels Canada & U.S.* 196 The traveller . . . suddenly mounting a little rise, close to a poor cottage with its Indian corn patch . . . finds himself opposite to the Capitol of the Federal city.

b. In the names of foods or preparations of corn for use as food, as (1) **Indian cornbread,** (2) **flour,** (3) **meal,** (4) **mush,** (5) **soup,** (6) **stirabout.**
(1) **1799** WELD *Travels* (1800) I. 183 Indian corn bread . . . is a coarse, strong kind of bread, which has something of the taste of that made from oats. **1864** NICHOLS *Amer. Life* I. 117 The long narrow table through the centre of the cabin is covered with Yankee luxuries —hot Indian-corn bread, milk-toast, hot rolls [etc.]. — (2) **1701** WOLLEY *Journal N.Y.* (1902) 40 The Price of Provisions: . . . Indian Corn Flower fifteen shillings a hundred. — (3) **1778** in *Pa. Mag. Hist.* XXVI. 32 Went into winter quarters in Newport, in old empty houses . . . and the food worse,—little bread and that made of rice and Indian corn meal. **1836** W. O'BRYAN *Travels* 140 Johnny-cake is made with Indian corn meal tempered, laid on a board about two feet long and about 9 inches wide. — (4) **1888** WHITMAN *Nov. Boughs* 412 On the floor of the big kitchen, toward sundown, would be squatting a circle of twelve or fourteen 'pickaninnies,' eating their supper of pudding (Indian corn mush) and milk.
(5) **1751** JOHN BARTRAM *Travels Pa. to Onondaga* 60 This repast consisted of 3 great kettles of Indian corn soop, or thin homony, with dry'd eels and other fish boiled in it. — (6) **1856** in *Amer. Legion Mag.* XXIII. 58/2, 2 families gave out, being frightened at getting nothing for 3 days but Indian corn stirabout.

Indian council. A council or deliberative assembly of Indians.
1745 in FRANKLIN *Indian Tr.* (1938) 309 The Indian Council met the Governor again in the Evening and gave their Answer to what the Governor had sayd yesterday. **1847** LOWELL *Biglow P.* I Ser. iv. 60 Town Meetings, . . . Parliaments, Diets, Indian Councils, Palavers, and the like. **1886** *Cent. Mag.* Nov. 11/2 The same ground being often claimed by a dozen different persons or companies under various grants from the crown or from legislatures, or through purchase from adventurers or Indian councils.

Indian country. A region in the possession of Indians. Cf. **Digger Indian country.**
[**1664** *Wyllys P.* 29 Aug. 159 We being wel entertayned of ye Lord in ye Indians Countrie, Ought to offer the Gospell . . . to them.] **1697** *Doc. Rel. Col. Hist. N.Y.* IV. 283 He then presented to their Lordships a Draught of the Indian Country above Albany towards the great Lake on one side, and Quebec on the other. **1855** *Wkly. Gaz.* (Santa Fe) 8 Dec., The Mormons have no right to intrude in the Indian country, and if they are caught there they must expect rough treatment from the red men. **1946** FOREMAN *Last Trek* 59 The necessity was realized also for some federal authority in the Indian country.

Indian cucumber. A liliaceous plant, *Medeola virginica*, the tuberous rootstock of which has the taste of a cucumber. Also **Indian cucumber-root.**
1784 CUTLER in *Mem. Acad.* I. 437 *Medeola*. . . . Indian Cucumber. The roots . . . are esculant and of an agreeable taste. The Indians made them a part of their food. **1814** PURSH *Flora* I. 244 Medeola

virginica. . . . This plant is known by the name Indian Cucumber; the roots have a strong resemblance in taste and flavour to cucumbers, and are eaten by the natives. **1902** PARSONS *According to Season* 91 Another wood plant, a little less fastidious, perhaps, in its choice of locality, is the Indian cucumber-root, or *Medeola*. **1947** *Midland Naturalist* July 37 Indian Cucumber-root [is] common in terrace forest; occasional in seepage swamps and bluff forest.

Indian currant. =**coralberry.**

1785 MARSHALL *Amer. Grove* 82 *Lonicera Symphoricarpos*. Indian Currants, or St. Peter's Wort. This hath a shrubby stalk, which rises from four to five feet high. **1931** CLUTE *Plants* 37 We cannot imagine a real use by the aborigines of . . . Indian currant (*Symphoricarpus orbiculatus*). **1948** *So. Sierran* Feb. 2/2 'Indian currant' was also in bloom.

Indian Department. The department or office of the federal government having to do with the Indians, the Bureau of Indian Affairs.

1776 in *Mich. Hist. Coll.* X. 264, I shou'd have no objection to his being appointed an assistant in the Indian department provided you [Lieut. Gov. Hamilton] find the service require it. **1887** *Amer. Missionary* Oct. 283 Nor do we question the motives of the heads of the Indian Department. **1948** *Sat. Ev. Post* 23 Oct. 25/3 The agent furnished by the Indian Department decided everything.

Indian devil. The wolverine or the cougar.

1851 SPRINGER *Forest Life* 66 A dangerous specimen of the feline species, known by woodsmen as the 'Indian devil,' had prowled from time immemorial. **1901** THOMPSON *In Maine Woods* 60 The cougar, or 'Indian devil,' is sometimes seen, but only rarely. **1942** Nat. Pk. Service *Fading Trails* 83 The wolverine's physical and mental traits have earned for it such names as 'skunk bear,' 'carcajou,' 'glutton,' and 'Indian devil.' **1949** *Sat. Ev. Post* 22 Jan. 98/2 Once the Indian Devil has found the line he will give up his wider wanderings and settle down to working it as persistently as the trapper, and several days earlier.

Indian doctor. An Indian medicine man, or a white man who follows Indian methods of healing.

1670 *S.C. Hist. Soc. Coll.* V. (1897) 201 The Indian Doctor tells us that where he liues is exceedinge rich and fertill generally of a red mould . . . and abundantly stored with Mulberries. **1818** J. PALMER *Travels U.S.* 113 Though termed Indian doctors they are whites; it is because they practise after the Indian manner, that they are so called. **1890** *Aberdeen* (Wash.) *Herald* 23 Oct. 8/1 [His daughter] became ill and died, . . . so the Indian doctor was soon consulted. **1948** DICK *Dixie Frontier* 215 The settlers doctored themselves or sometimes secured the services of Indian doctors.

Indianesque ˌɪndɪənˈɛsk, *a.* Like or resembling Indians.

*a*1861 WINTHROP *J. Brent* iv. 45 This was the Indianesque Saxon who greeted me. **1882** STEELE *Frontier Army* (1883) 84 In all that is peculiarly Indianesque, she excels her master. **1942** *Chi. Tribune* 15 Nov. (Pict. Sec.) 6/2 (*caption*), Indianesque.

Indian field. (See quot. 1902.)

1631 in *Amer. Sp.* XV. 275/2 Three hundred acres . . . comonly called by the name of Indian ffield. **1791** BARTRAM *Travels* 50 An ancient Indian field, verdured o'er with succulent grass. [**1902** in *Amer. Sp.* XV. 275/2 When the country was first discovered, there were considerable openings of the land, or natural prairies, which are called 'the Indian old fields' to this day.] **1942** WEYGANDT *Plenty of Penna.* 48 On a ridge of poor soil above the Delaware in Bucks County there is an 'Indian field' which in the memory of men still alive bore good crops because a shad, or a half shad, was planted to each hill under six grains of flint corn.

Indian file. Single file, so called in allusion to the way groups of Indians traveled through the woods.

1758 in *Mass. H.S. Proc.* 1 Ser. XVII. 244 Set out for Fort Edward in an Indian file, Major Putnam in the front. **1841** *N.O. Picayune* 19 Jan. 2/3 Cross over, turn round, forward two, dos-a-dos, Indian file, promenade. **1946** RICHTER *Fields* 236 The six trooped in, Indian file.

Indian fort.

1. A place of defense erected by Indians.

1651 JOHN WILSON in *Strength ovt of Weaknesse* (1652) 18 Other particulars . . . of the *Indian* Fort and buildings in Mr *Eliots* Letter . . . are here supplyed. **1775** *Mass. H.S. Coll.* 2 Ser. II. 231 At Norridgewalk are to be seen the vestiges of an Indian fort and chapel. **1939** EVANS *Pigwacket* 38 The Indian fort thus established soon came to be looked upon by the English as a menace.

2. (See quots.)

1831 FOWLER *Jrnl.* 170 In many parts are still very visible the remains of what are called Indian forts. . . . In some of these places have been found accumulations of spear-heads, axes [etc.]. **1877** BARTLETT 312 Indian Fort. Enclosures, usually by banks of earth three or four feet in height, found in Western New York, Pennsylvania, Ohio, and other Western States. They were found by the early settlers, and are apparently of great antiquity.

Indian goods. Goods used in trading with the Indians. *Obs.*

1685 *N.J. Archives* 1 Ser. I. 504 Which money [i.e., four pounds in beaver pay] wee disbursed ffor indean trade which sayd indean goods went to the purchase of the . . . land. **1786** E. DENNY *Jrnl.* 78 Captain O'Harra . . . arrived with a large cargo of Indian goods and stores for the commissioners. **1871** *Rep. Indian Affairs* (1872) 458 All goods of the character denominated 'Indian goods' have been excluded [from the agency trading house].

Indian grass. Any one of various wild grasses, esp. *Sorghastrum nutans*. Cf. **finger Indian grass.**

[**1749** PETER KALM *Travels N. Amer.* I. (1937) 269 A grass which grows in great plenty here [Pa.], . . . the English call Indian grass and the Swedes wildgrass.] **1764** HUTCHINSON *Hist. Mass.* I. 480 The natural upland grass of the country commonly called Indian grass, is poor fodder. **1894** COULTER *Bot. W. Texas* III. 494 *Chrysopogon nutans*. (Indian Grass.) . . . Common in rather dry soil throughout the United States, but more abundant in the South. **1941** R. S. WALKER *Lookout* 49 Indian grass is a tall wild grass, quite ornamental, and grows in various places on the side of the mountain near the base.

attrib. **1810** CUMING *Western Tour* 137 In an Indian grass hammock, lay Mr. Hunt.

Indian grave. The grave of an Indian; also a hillock or barrow popularly supposed to be such a grave.

1677 I. MATHER *Early Hist. N. Eng.* (1864) 64 They . . . saw where there had been Corn planted, and found Indian Graves &c. **1818** J. FLINT *Lett. from Amer.* 101 By the road side are many conical mounds of earth, called Indian graves. **1913** EATON *Barn Doors & Byways* 156 The Indian graves are still green on Indian Burying Hill, overlooking the great salt marshes and the sea.

Indian hatchet. An Indian tomahawk.

1677 WM. HUBBARD *Troubles with Indians* I. (1865) 116 Robert Dutch, of Ipswich, having been sorely wounded by a Bullet . . . and then mauled by the Indian Hatchets, was left for dead by the Salvages. **1702** C. MATHER *Magnalia* II. (1820) 545 On July 27 [1694] about break of day *Groton* felt some surprizing blows from the *Indian hatchets*. **1812** MARSHALL *Kentucky* 166 Some of the men were overtaken in the way, and fell beneath the stroke of the Indian hatchet. **1885** *Wkly. New Mexican Rev.* (Santa Fe) 19 March 4/5 Mr. Mat Breeden has picked up several fine Indian hatchets at the penitentiary quarry.

Indian hemp. (See quot. 1907.)

1619 *Va. House of Burgesses* 10 For hempe also both English & Indian . . . wee doe require . . . all householders . . . to make tryal thereof. **1830** WATSON *Philadelphia* 444 The Indians made their ropes, bridles, and twine for nets, out of a wild weed, growing abundantly in old corn fields, commonly called Indian hemp—(i.e. *Linum Virginianum*). **1907** HODGE *Amer. Indians* I. 605/2 *Indian hemp.*—(1) The army-root (*Apocynum cannabium*), called also black Indian hemp. (2) The swamp milkweed (*Asclepias incarnata*) and the hairy milkweed (*A. pulchra*), called also white Indian hemp. (3) A West Virginia name for the yellow toad-flax (*Linaria linaria*). (4) The velvet-leaf (*Abutilon abutilon*), called also Indian mallow. **1933** HARRINGTON *Gypsum Cave, Nev.* 41 Near the surface where two pieces of string, one of Indian hemp and one of sinew.

Indian hen. The American bittern, *Botaurus lentiginosus*.

1781–2 JEFFERSON *Notes Va.* (1788) 73 *Ardea stellaris Americana* . . . [is known as] Brown bittern [and] Indian hen. **1825** KEATING *Exped. St. Peter's River* I. 171 Mr. Say observed, among others, the mallard, . . . stellate heron or Indian hen, (Ardea minor), &c., &c. **1932** A. H. HOWELL *Fla. Bird Life* 110 Indian Hen. . . . The birds usually alight on the ground and fly with neck drawn in and legs extended.

b. (See quot.)

1933 *Amer. Sp.* Feb. 50 Indian hen, n. The pileated woodpecker, also known as the woodhen.

Indian hug. A style of wrestling in which the opponents begin by facing each other, each grasping the other with both arms around the body. Also attrib. and transf.

1825 NEAL *Bro. Jonathan* I. 257 Giving out his challenge . . . in a loud voice, for 'Indian hug'; half hug [etc.]. **1853** *S. Lit. Messenger* xix. 471/2 To start in medias res . . . to give out and prove the law . . . to wrestle with the subject Indian-hug fashion . . . to speak in plain English . . . these qualities were possessed in an eminent degree. **1916** DU PUY *Uncle Sam* 46 Like a flash his head was in the tall man's chest, all his strength was in his arms, and he was administering that treatment known in his youth as the 'Indian hug.'

Indian hunter. An Indian huntsman.

[**1656** VAN DER DONCK in *N.Y. Hist. Soc. Coll.* 2 Ser. I. (1841) 226 Beavers were found not far from my residence, and several were brought to me by the Indian hunters.] **1740** *Ga. Col. Rec.* IV. 666 Each Indian Hunter is reckoned to get three hundred Weight of Deer-

Skins in a Year. **1884** Roe *Nature's Story* 134 Adjacent buildings are for the storage of furs, bear-meat, and the accommodation of Indian hunters. **1941** Taggard *Here We Are* 193 Did he really think he could out-track an Indian hunter?

Indianian ˌɪndɪˈænɪən, *n.* Also **Indianan.** A native or resident of Indiana. Cf. **hoosier 1.**

1833 Hoffman *Winter in West* I. 190 The term 'Hooshier' . . . bears nothing invidious with it to the ear of an Indianian. **1894** *Pittsburg Press* 9 Sep. 7/7 The Indianians, unable to withstand such odds, were compelled to fall back. **1944** *N. & Q.* March 188 Its advertisements . . . were answered by a number of Indianans.

Indian interpreter. One who served as an interpreter between white people and Indians.

1647 John Eliot *Day-Breaking of Gospel* (1903) 4 But this wee perceived, that a few words from the Preacher were more regarded than many from the *Indian* Interpreter. **1788** Franklin *Autobiog.* 400 George Croghan, our Indian interpreter, join'd him [i.e., Braddock] on his march with one hundred of those people. **1894** *Harper's Mag.* Feb. 467/1 This young man . . . was evidently . . . Indian interpreter, ambassador, topographer, and guide.

Indianish ˈɪndɪənɪʃ, *a.* Like an Indian. *Obs.* — **1759** *N.J. Archives* XX. 342 Run away. . . . An Irish Man Servant, . . . wore when he went off his own Indianish long slim Hair. **1856** W. A. Phillips *Conquest of Kans.* 13 The Potawattomies, Kaws, Sacs, and Foxes, and several other lesser tribes, are of the Indians, Indianish.

Indianism ˈɪndɪənˌɪzəm, *n.* The customs and culture of the American Indians. Also transf. *Obs.*

1652 *Strength ovt of Weaknesse* 37 All the while I went on in Indianisme I was going from God. **1710** Sewall *Letter-Book* I. 401 Though some of their aged men are tenacious enough of Indianisme. **1871** *Rep. Indian Affairs* (1872) 181 We were in our original Indianism. **1887** *Longfellow's Prose Wks.* (Camelot) p. xiii, Those who stood between the culture of *Hyperion* and *Kavanagh*, and the wild Indianism of Almard and Cooper.

b. A word or expression of Indian origin. *Rare.*

1855 Bristed in *Cambridge Essays* 68 The term ['Yankee'] is therefore additionally remarkable, as being the only Indianism that has found a place among Americanisms.

Indianize ˈɪndɪənˌaɪz, *v.*

1. *intr.* To adopt the ways of Indians. *Obs.*

1689 C. Mather *Way to Prosperity* 27 How much do our people Indianize? **1702** ——— *Magnalia* (1853) II. 400 We have shamefully Indianized in all those abominable things.

2. *tr.* To make Indian in manners or appearance. *Colloq.*

[**1745** in *Moravian Jrnls. Rel. Central N.Y.* (1916) 7 Bro. Joseph also went over to the island, to visit Madam Montour from Canada, who lately with her family had become Indianized.] **1837** Bird *Nick of Woods* I. 49 A bad thing for her, to have an Injunized father. **1879** *Mass. H.S. Coll.* 5th Ser. VI. 375 More than one hundred of the whites have been 'Indianized' to each Indian who has been civilized. **1941** *U. of Maine Bul.* Nov. 84 The fort and trading house here had made the name of *George's* so familiar that it was early adopted and Indianized.

Indian kale. Any one of various arums having edible rootstocks.

1810 Cuming *Western Tour* 297 He made me observe some ginger in a thriving state, and the cullaloo or Indian kail. **1817** S. Brown *Western Gaz.* 236 Most kinds of tropical fruits flourish here, such as the sweet orange, guinea corn, [and] Indian kail. **1876** Hobbs *Bot. Hand-Book* 147 Arum esculentum, Indian kale.

Indian ladder. (See quot. 1859.)

1715 in *N.J. Hist. Soc. Proc.* 3 Ser. X. 41 S. G. and I went up . . . to a rock which shoots from the hill . . . about 20 foot high, against which we set an Indian ladder. **1791** Bartram *Travels* 247 Having provided ourselves with a long snagged sapling, called an Indian ladder. **1859** Bartlett 214 Indian Ladder, a ladder made of a small tree by trimming it so as to leave only a few inches of each branch as a support for the foot. Southern. **1929** L. P. Summers *Ann. Southwest Va.* 1517 It is very easy to ascend and descend, as the limbs usually begin at the ground, and being cut off about a foot from the trunk, a very convenient 'Indian ladder' is formed.

Indian land. Land belonging to or recently acquired from the Indians.

1658 *Conn. Hist. Soc. Coll.* VI. 121 One acker of ye Indian land which Belonges to ye Towne. **1802** Drayton *S. Carolina* 93 The Yamassee resided in that part of Beaufort district, which is still known by the name of *Indian land.* **1885** *Cent. Mag.* Jan. 447 The Indian lands are scattered through the valley among the farms of the whites. **1946** Foreman *Last Trek* 22 It was against public policy to permit the sale of Indian land to private individuals without a treaty.

attrib. **1947** *Christian Cent.* 8 Oct. 1204/1 Substantial progress was being made in clarifying and confirming Indian land titles in southeastern Alaska.

Indian language. Any one of various languages used by American Indians.

1642 *Md. Hist. Soc. Pub.* No. 7 (1874) 80 Father Roger went to a new settlement . . . in order to learn the more easily the Indian language. **1707** *Boston News-Letter* 24 Feb. 2/2 She speaks good English, not very perfect of the Indian Language. **1947** *Reader's Digest* April 92/1 Having picked up much of the Indian language, Smith desperately began to talk for time.

Indian maize. Corn.

1637 Morton *New Canaan* 72 The black bird . . . is a small sized Choffe that eateth the Indian maisze. **1676** B. Thompson *Poet. W.* 49 The dainty Indian Maize Was eat with Clampshells out of wooden Trayes. **1849** *S. Lit. Messenger* XV. 414/1 A delicious food which has been known among the Choctaws as the sweet *ton-cha* or Indian maize. **1948** *Sat. Review* 27 March 26/2 The hybrid-corn makers . . . took Indian maize . . . [and] produced the hybrids.

Indian meal.

1. The meal of Indian corn.

[**1609** *Doc. Hist. of N.-Y.* III. 5 They [Indians] eat dried Indian meal which they steep in water like porridge.] **1635** *Mass. Bay Rec.* I. 140 Noe person whatsoeuer shall from henceforth transport any Indean corne or meale out of this jurisdiccon, till the next harvest. **1743** Brainerd *Diary* (1902) 112 Through divine goodness I had some Indian meal, of which I made little cakes and fried them. **1832** *Polit. Examiner* (Shelbyville, Ky.) 19 May 2/3 Strewing Indian meal on cucumber hills will prevent insects from approaching the vines. **1929** Shelton *Salt-box House* 91 The bag pudding of Indian meal boiled for several hours till it gained a ruddy color.

2. *attrib.* (See quots.)

1797 Asbury *Journal* II. 344 My diet is chiefly tea, potatoes, Indian-meal gruel, and chicken broth. **1841** Eliza R. Steele *Summer Journey* 128 They soon placed upon the table cloth . . . nice indian meal cakes, eggs, milk, cheese, cucumbers, butter, bread, and 'chicken fixens.' **1895** *Yearbook Dept. Agric. 1894* 285 A phycitid moth allied to the preceding and known as the Indian-meal moth is widely distributed and injurious to a great variety of edibles.

Indian medicine.

1. A plant or plants such as Indians used in their medications. *Obs.*

1799 James Smith *Remarkable Occurrences* 64, I ordered him to search for Indian medicine, and told him to get me a quantity of bark from the root of a Lynn tree. **1843** in *Utah Hist. Quart.* II. (1929) 117 The Mission buildings are good wooden edifices. . . . Timber pine and oak. Singular Indian medicine for the sick.

2. Any one of various nostrums alleged to be cure-alls and usu. sold by traveling peddlers. Also attrib.

1830 *Mechanics' Press* (Utica, N.Y.) 15 May 210/3 He deals in 'yerbs' and Indian medicine. **1929** F. E. McClinchey *Joe Pete* 263 After a time he ceased worrying about her stubbornness and let her use the ointments she got from the Indian medicine man. **1943** Crow *Amer. Customer* 165 Medical quacks who traveled about the country selling nostrums with their Indian medicine shows sold a lot of this oil.

Indian moccasin. A moccasin or covering for the foot worn by Indians.

1756 in *N.J. Archives* 1 Ser. XX. 55 A Dutch servant man. . . . Had on when he went away . . . a pair of Indian mockosens, with buckles in them. **1784** J. Smyth *Tour U.S.* I. 181 On their feet they . . . generally wear Indian moccosons, . . . which are made of strong elk's, or buck's skin. **1847** J. S. Hall *Book of Feet* 146 The Indian moccasin was the boot or shoe worn by the aborigines of America. **1935** *Amer. Mercury* May 108/1 The Indian moccasin is fine for the Indian in open country.

Indian mound. Any one of numerous earthen mounds found chiefly in the Gulf States, the Mississippi Valley, and the Great Lakes region, erected by Indians as altars, effigies, burial places, fortifications, etc.

1791 *Mass. H.S. Coll.* 1 Ser. III. 24 There is an Indian mound, the base of which is about three hundred paces round, and rises in a conic form about one hundred feet. ***c*1845** *Big Bear Ark.* 22 'It's full of cedar stumps and Indian mounds,' said he, '*and it can't be cleared.*' 'Lord,' said I, 'them ar "cedar stumps" is beets, and them ar "Indian mounds" ar tater hills.' **1949** *Ill. State Arch. Soc. Jrnl.* Jan. 7/2 When the term, 'Indian Mound,' is mentioned, one naturally thinks of a large ceremonial Mound which covers one to three acres of ground and is perhaps five or ten or even 20 feet in height.

Indian nation.

1. A tribe of Indians.

***c*1622** Pory *Plymouth Colony* (1918) 44 They of New Plymmouth relate an Indian nation of man-eaters called Monhacke, who goe armed against arrowes with jacks made of cordage. **1676** I. Mather *Hist. War with Indians in N.-Eng.* 26 Those three *Indian* Nations are become abominable to the other *Indians.* **1835** Simms *Yemassee* II. 27

Did it include the Indian nations generally—twenty-eight of which, at that time, occupied the Carolinas?

2. =**Indian territory 2.**

1855 BARNUM *Life* 173 We were obliged to travel eighty miles through a very thinly settled and desolate portion of country known as the 'Indian Nation.' **1897** HOUGH *Story of Cowboy* 5 In 1867 a venturous drover took a herd across the Indian Nation, bound for California. **1948** *Dly. Ardmoreite* (Ardmore, Okla.) 18 July 24/1 The homestead of the last chief executive of the Indian Nation was placed on the block for sale.

Indianologist ˌɪndɪənˈɑlədʒɪst, *n.* A student of, or an authority on, the American Indians.

1894 *Nation* 31 May 417/3 His ears, in the view of Indianologists, were a sure mark of aboriginal origin. **1923** *Arrow Points* 5 Feb. 40 This work should be of especial value to Indianologists in this Southern country. **1947** *Time* 3 March 37/1 The R.D.C. preferred the route that followed the old telegraph line strung diagonally across the great Brazilian plateau by General Candido Nariano Rondon, a famed Indianologist.

Indian paint.

1. (See quots.)

1826 DARLINGTON *Flora Cestrica* 57 *Sanguinaria canadensis. . . . Vulgo*—Red-root. Blood-root. . . . Indian Paint. **1899** *Animal & Plant Lore* 119 *Lithospermum canescens* is called 'Indian paint,' because the Indians are said to have used it in painting themselves. [s.w. Mo.] **1931** CLUTE *Plants* 26 Possibly the original puccoon was the bloodroot (*Sanguinaria Canadensis*), because of its red juice. The plant is also called puccoon-root, Indian paint.

2. Indian paintbrush, the painted cup *q.v.*

1892 *Amer. Folk-Lore* V. 101 *Castilleia coccinea. . . .* Indian paintbrush. Mass. **1946** *Mazama* Dec. 35/2 An acre or more of the steep hillside was thickly carpeted with blue lupines, red and orange Indian paint brushes, and asters.

Indian path. A path made by Indians.

1634 WOOD *N. Eng. Prospect* (1865) 79 An Indian path (which seldome is broader than a Cart's rutte). **1798** C. WILLIAMSON *Descr. Genesee* i, There was no access to the country but by Indian paths. **1898** EARLE *Customs Old N. Eng.* 205 Ere the days of turnpikes, the old Indian paths witnessed many a sad and pathetic parting. **1939** EVANS *Pigwacket* 3 To the consideration of this important gateway, through which the old Indian path entered Pigwacket, further attention will be directed.

Indian pea. (See last quots.) *Obs.*

1649 *Descr. Va.* 4 They have store of Indian Pease, better then ours, Beans, Lupines, and the like. **1805** PARKINSON *Tour* 341 What are termed Indian peas, are a sort of kidney-bean; the bunch-bean is the same, and produces abundantly. **1822** J. WOODS *Eng. Prairie* 221 Here are a few Indian peas in growth, leaf and blossom, much like a kidney-bean; the pods are very long, and contain from nine to sixteen peas in each.

Indian peach. (See quot. 1907.)

1709 LAWSON *Carolina* 110 Of this sort we make Vinegar; wherefore we call them Vinegar-Peaches, and sometimes *Indian* Peaches. **1881** *Harper's Mag.* April 745/2 A robe of gauze the color of an Indian peach garlanded with pale clear blooms. **1907** HODGE *Amer. Indians* I. 606 *Indian peach.*—Ungrafted peach trees, according to Bartlett, which are considered to be more thrifty and said to bear larger fruit. In the South a specific variety of clingstone peach. **1949** *Amer. Sp.* April 110/1 Indian Peach, *n.* Clingstone peach. [Lexington Co., S.C.]

Indian physic. Any one of various plants used as a purgative (see quot. 1907).

1738 BYRD *Dividing Line* (1901) 113 In the Stony Grounds . . . we found great Quantity of the true Ipocoanna, which in this part of the World is call'd Indian-Physick. **1814** PURSH *Flora Amer.* II. 382 *Magnolia auriculata. . . .* The bark of this and some of the foregoing species is esteemed a valuable medicine, particularly in intermitting fevers; from which circumstance it is known in some places by the name of Indian Physic. **1843** TORREY *Flora N.Y.* I. 200 *Gillenia trifoliata. . . .* Indian Physic. Bowman's-root. . . . [The root] acts as an emetic or a cathartic, according to the dose. **1907** HODGE *Amer. Indians* I. 606/1 *Indian physic.*—(1) The bowman's-root (*Porteranthus trifoliatus*), called also Indian hippo. (2) American ipecac (*Porteranthus stipulatus*). (3) Fraser's magnolia, the long-leaved umbrella-tree (*Magnolia fraseri*).

b. A concoction prepared from some such plant.

1914 APPLEGATE *Recoll. Boyhood* (1934) 28, I have thought that if Socrates instead of the cup of hemlock, had had to take a dose of 'Injin Fizic,' he . . . would have skipped, not to save his life, but to avoid the dose.

Indian pine. (See quots. 1860, 1907.)

1806 SHECUT *Flora Carolinæensis* I. 122 Almiggim wood, supposed to be the Indian Pine. **1860** GREELEY *Overland Journey* 268 In Ruby Valley, they have one [mail-station cabin] of red or Indian-pine. **1907** HODGE *Amer. Indians* I. 606/1 Indian pine.—The loblolly, or old-field pine (*Pinus taeda*).

Indian pink.

1. =next.

1738 CATESBY *Carolina* II. 78 The Indian Pink. . . . This Plant rises usually with four or five stalks, of about twelve or fourteen inches in height; every one of which has three or four pair of sharp-pointed leaves, set opposite to each other. **1890** *Cent.* 3179/3 The cypress vine, Indian pink, American red bell-flower, or sweet-william of the Barbadoes . . . is now widely naturalized. **1939** *Nat. Geog. Mag.* Aug. 232/1 The family name changed accordingly to Dianthaceae, which counts among its members the clove pinks or carnations, Indian pinks, and other attractive garden or florists' plants.

2. Indian pinkroot, the pinkroot, *Spigelia marilandica.*

1765 J. BARTRAM *Diary* 5 Sep., The *Spegelia*, or *Indian* pink-root. **1835** AUDUBON *Ornith. Biog.* I. 361 The Indian Pink-root or Worm-grass. . . . This plant is perennial, flowers in the summer months, and grows in rich soil by the margins of woods, in the Middle States.

Indian pipe.

1. A pipe such as the Indians used.

1791 J. LONG *Voyages* 46 The calumet, or Indian pipe, which is much larger than that the Indians usually smoke, is made of marble, stone or clay. **1846** DE SMET *Ore. Missions* (1847) 240 We . . . smoked together the friendly Indian pipe.

2. The wax plant, *Monotropa uniflora.* Also **Indian pipestem.**

[**1785** MARSHALL *Amer. Grove* 147 This is called Indian Pipe Shank, from the pithy stems being used by the natives for that purpose.] **1817–8** EATON *Botany* 357 *Monotropa uniflora*, birds nest, indian-pipe. . . . Whole plant ivory-white at first. **1869** *Amer. Naturalist* III. 6 The Indian Pipestem (*Monotropa uniflora*) will be found rarely in low woods [in central Ill.]. **1938** THOMPSON *High Trails* 152 In the woods below we may find some Indian pipes, queer, colorless, pipelike parasites which live in the moist deep woods of the west slope.

Indian plum. 1. The persimmon. **2.** The blueberry. **3.** (See quot.)

(1) 1705 BEVERLEY *Virginia* II. 14 The Persimmon is by Hariot call'd the Indian Plum. — **(2) 1850** *N. Eng. Farmer* II. 346 Will you be so good as to give us the correct name of the shrub known here, with some by the name of *bilberry*, with others by that of *Indian plum?* — **(3) 1920** *D.N.* V. 82 *Indian plum.* Osmaronia cerasiformis [i.e., the osoberry]. [Northwest.]

Indian potato. (See quots. 1931, 1940.)

[**1705** BEVERLEY *Virginia* II. 28 Besides all these, our Natives had originally amongst them, Indian Corn, Peas, Beans, Potatoes, and Tobacco.] **1737** WESLEY *Journal* I. (1909) 402 In Fresh pineland [in Ga.], Indian potatoes grow well—which are more luscious and larger than the Irish. **1827** WEST *Journal* 109 There is a root which is found in large quantities, and generally called by the settlers, the Indian potatoe. It strongly resembles the Jerusalem artichoke, and is eaten by the natives in a raw state; but when boiled it is not badly flavoured. **1931** CLUTE *Plants* 35 Among the more useful of the Indian's food plants are the Indian potatoes (*Apios tuberosa, Helianthus giganteus*, and *H. tuberosus*). These even the white man has used on occasions. **1940** SMITH *Puyallup-Nisqually* 250 Wappato or Indian potatoes grew only in land flooded by fresh water.

Indian powwow. 1. An Indian priest or medicine man. *Obs.* **2.** A noisy frolic or a discussion.

(1) 1649 ELIOT *Glorious Progress* 3 The Indian Pawwawes gave him over for a dead man. **1693** C. MATHER *Wonders Invis. World* 74 The Indian *Powawes*, used all their Sorceries to molest the first Planters here. — **(2) 1826** FLINT *Recoll.* 366 If I could describe its Indian powwows, its Spanish fandangos, its French balls, and its American frolics. **1947** *N.Y. Times Mag.* 12 Oct. 18/4 In this matter, as in all other questions that arose, we held an Indian pow-wow and found the best way out.

Indian pudding. A pudding composed principally of Indian meal, milk, and molasses.

1722 *N.-Eng. Courant* 19–26 March 2 A Plain Indian Pudding, being put into the Pot and boil'd the usual Time, it came out of a Blood-red Colour, to the great Surprise of the whole Family. **1856** GOODRICH *Recoll.* I. 371 As to her Indian puddings—alas, I shall never see their like again. **1944** HOLTON *Yankees* 246 And you would top off with Indian pudding, half a dozen kinds of pie, and as many varieties of cake, all the time drowning yourself in strong coffee with thick cream.

Indian raft. A form of raft used by Indians. Also **Indian raft-boat.** *Obs.*

1804 in *Lewis & Clark Journals* VII. (1905) 56 Saw an Indian raft. **1836** IRVING *Astoria* II. 55 They followed down [the Snake R.] for a short distance, in search of some Indian rafts made of reeds, on which they might cross. **1876** *Nat. Museum Bul.* No. 6, 43 Methods of Transportation. . . . Indian raft-boats, Launches.

Indian razor. Orig. a pair of clam shells with which Indians pulled out their hair, later a metal device for this purpose obtained from traders.

1775 Adair *Amer. Indians* 6 Holding this Indian razer between their forefinger and thumb, they deplume themselves, after the manner of the Jewish novitiate priests. **1776** Hadden *Journal* 13 The sprouts [of hair] on a certain part are carefully pulled out with what is called an Indian Razor. This resembles a cork Screw except in having many more turns; and being made of wire when compressed together lays hold of the devoted Hairs. [**1937** Lincoln *Wilmington, Del.* 13 They

Types of Indian razors

[men of the Lenni-Lenapes tribe] plucked out their beards with tweezers made of mussel shells, in order that they might lay the paint on more smoothly.]

Indian reservation. An area set apart by the government for the occupancy of Indians.

1819 David Thomas *Travels* 12 The flats here [Genesee River] are chiefly on the west bank, nearly one and a half miles wide, and very fertile. This tract is an Indian Reservation. **1821** Nuttall *Travels Arkansa* 103 On the opposite side, or Indian reservation, the hills approach within six or eight miles of the river. **1882** *Cent. Mag.* XXIV. 864 As a rule the Indian reservations take the best part of the Western country. They are absurdly large. Nearly half of Montana is Indian territory to-day. **1949** *Kans. Hist. Quart.* Feb. 2 They learned that Council Grove was situated on an Indian reservation and was not available for settlement.

Indian rice. (See quots.)

1843 Torrey *Flora N.Y.* II. 416 *Zizania aquatica*.... Tuscarora Rice. Water Oats. Indian Rice.... The grain of this plant is a favorite article of food among the Indians, and cattle are very fond of the herbage. **1901** Mohr *Plant Life Ala.* 362 *Zizania aquatica*.... Wild Rice. Indian Rice.... Copious in water ... in the estuaries of the rivers emptying into Mobile Bay. **1940** Jaeger *Calif. Deserts* 165 Indian rice (*Oryzopsis hymenoides*) is frequent in porous soils, particularly on blown sand.

b. Also **Indian rice grass.**

1948 *Ecological Monographs* April 171/1 Indian rice grass, *Oryzopsis hymenoides*, is common in certain small areas.

Indian ring. A group of conniving politicians, contractors, etc., who conspired to rob the Indians in connection with annuities paid them by the government.

1873 J. H. Beadle *Undevel. West* xix. 361 Fuller had been engaged in some questionable transactions with the Indian ring. **1891** Swasey *Early Days Calif.* 248 The general ... was in bad odor with the 'Indian Ring' and the 'Army Contractors.' **1946** *Sat. Review* 8 June 41/3 He fought as stoutly for them against the grafting politicians of the Indian Ring.

Indian saddle. A somewhat crude form of saddle used by Plains Indians.

1817 John Bradbury *Travels Amer.* 123 Mr. Hunt ... tried by arguments to dissuade me.... He represented to me ... the fatigue of riding on an Indian saddle, &c. *c***1908** Canton *Frontier Trails* 53 The hunters again appeared ... leading a pinto pony, on which was an Indian saddle packed with a beef hide. **1923** J. H. Cook *On Old Frontier* 52 We took some of the Indian saddles and blankets ... for we knew that squaw-saddles were better than none at all.

Indian school. A school for the benefit of Indians.

1660 John Eliot *Progress of Gospel* 36 Peter Fouldger ... for many years taught the Indian School in Mr Mayhu's life time. **1732** in *W. & M. Coll. Quart.* 2 Ser. VIII. 239 We have a very convenient room for a library over the Indian School. **1948** *Dly. Oklahoman* (Okla. City) 16 May E. 26/5 Nearly every day fullbloods are to be seen transacting business at the Indian schools and Indian agencies.

Indian scout.

1. An Indian serving as a scout.

1676 *Mass. Bay Rec.* V. (1854) 96 Captain Daniel Hinchman .... by sending out partjes, discouered the ennemy by our Indian scouts. **1758** *Newport Mercury* 19 Dec. 3/1 On the 24th at Night, we were informed by one of our Indian Scouts, that he had discovered a Cloud of Smoke above the place. **1837** Irving *Bonneville* II. 18 Rising ground ... might betray his little party to the watchful eye of any Indian scout. **1923** J. H. Cook *On Old Frontier* 169, I am Lieutenant Gatewood, and these men are Indian scouts.

b. A white man who serves as a scout against Indians.

1838 *S. Lit. Messenger* IV. 294 He became an Indian scout or ranger, and passed his days upon the frontier. **1947** *True* Nov. 90/1 The wolfer did not make the picturesque figure that the Buffalo Bill type of Indian scout did.

2. A scouting expedition against Indians.

1852 Watson *Nights in Block-House* 147 John Whetzel and Veach Dickerson associated to go on an Indian scout. **1866** *Wkly. New Mexican Rev.* 25 May 1/3 Captain Krause's men have returned from their Indian scout.

Indian service.

1. Missionary service among the Indians. *Obs.*

1710 Samuel Sewall *Letter-Book* I. (1886) 401 It will be necessary to take off those persons from their Ministry among the Indians, who are of all men the most essential to the Indian Service. *c***1749** in D. Brainerd *Journal* (1902) 237 The Correspondents ... prevailed with Mr. Azariah Horton ... to devote himself to the Indian service.

2. =**Indian Department.** Also attrib.

1846 Polk *Diary* I. 323 During my walk this evening I met Senator Turney, who resumed the conversation about an appointment in the Indian Service. **1941** Fergusson *Southwest* 294 The enemy, the Indian Service, embodied everything the artist most loathes: discipline, formalized education, religious intolerance. **1947** *Newsweek* 22 Dec. 21/1 The Navajos told their problem to Indian Service officials.

3. Military service against the Indians. *Obs.*

1866 Moore *Women of War* 112 She is now with the detachment that has crossed the great plains and the Rocky Mountains for Indian service on the distant western frontier.

Indian shoe.

1. An Indian moccasin. *Obs.*

1674 in *S.C. Hist. Soc. Coll.* V. (1897) 460 Finding severall flakes of Isinglass in ye paths, ye soales of my Indian shooes in which I travelled glistened like sylver. **1711** Buckingham *Land Exped.* 120 This proved an Indian shoe, or part of one, in which he found a leaded ink-case. **1803** J. Davis *Travels* 33 Mocossins are Indian shoes, made of deer-skin. **1931** [see **2.** below].

2. (See quots.)

1764 Reuter *Wachau, Lady Shoes*, some call it *Indian Shoes*. It is a Snakeroot, and the Indians know how to use it for many things. Has a yellow or white blossom which is exactly the shape of a wooden shoe. Grows in rich Uplands. [**1931** Clute *Plants* 36 It requires perhaps less fancy to see in the blossoms of *Cypripedium parviflorum*, an Indian shoe or moccasin.]

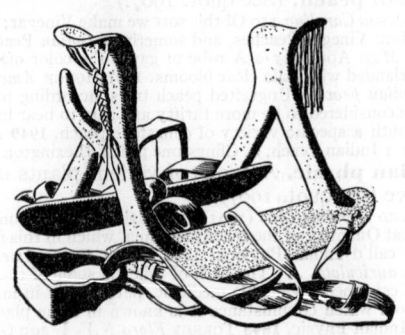

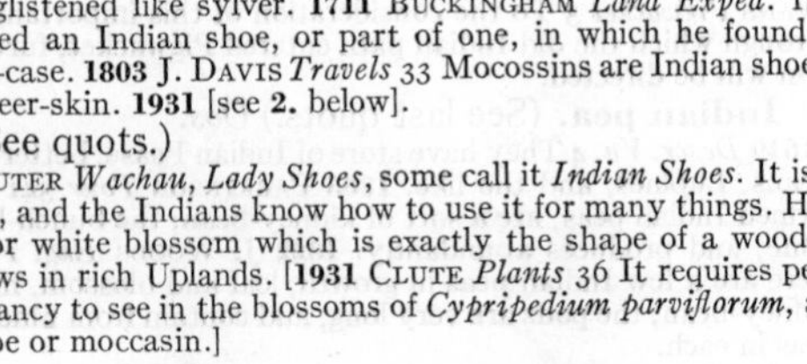

Indian saddle (Blackfoot)

Indian sign.

1. A track, trace, or other indication of the presence of Indians.

1807 Gass *Journal* 93 We see a great many fresh Indian tracks or signs as we pass along. **1892** Duval *Young Explorers* 84, I was purty shore it was Injin sign from the start, fur the trail didn't hardly scatter enough fur mustangs. *a***1918** G. Stuart *On Frontier* 115 Plenty of Indian signs, saw signal fires on the mountains to westward.

2. A signal or token used or relied upon by Indians.

1906 Mark Twain *Horse's Tale* 327 (R.), I know some of the Indian signs—the signs they make with their hands, and by signal-fires at night and columns of smoke by day. **1942** Cannon *Mountain* 100 That's an Indian sign.

3. *To hang* (or *put*) *the Indian sign on* (someone), to get the better of (someone), to leave marks of battle upon. Also allusively. *Colloq.*

1946 *N. & Q.* July 55/1 What is the meaning and origin of the phrase 'to hang the Injun sign' [on someone]? **1946** NEWTON *P. Bunyan* 153 Paul put the Indian sign on them before he went away, and now they rarely bother anyone after the Fourth of July in this part of the country. **1948** *Sat. Ev. Post* 25 Sep. 122/2 How's chances of briefing me on the personalities around this place—who has the Indian sign on whom, and stuff?

Indian sugar. Maple sugar.

1784 in VAN SCHAACK *Life Peter Van Schaack* (1842) 360 Little Cornelius is her favorite; she convinces him of her affection by giving him a small present, as Indian sugar, cookies, etc. **1835** HOFFMAN *Winter in West* I. 191 The usual settlers' dinner of fried bacon, venison cutlets, hot cakes, and wild honey, with some tolerable tea and Indian sugar,—as that made from the maple-tree is called at the West,—was soon placed before us. **1947** *St. Louis Globe-Democrat* 18 May, The extraction of maple sugar, once known as Indian sugar, was an art probably learned from the aborigines.

Indian summer. [See note.]

Many theories, none of them convincing, have been advanced to account for this expression. For the most competent discussion of the term see Albert Matthews in the *Monthly Weather Review* for Jan. and Feb., 1902.

1. A period of mild, warm weather in late October or early November, after the first frosts of autumn. Cf. **smoke summer.**

1778 CRÈVECOEUR *Sk. 18th Cent. Amer.* (1925) 41 A severe frost succeeds [the autumn rains] which prepares it [*sc.* the earth] to receive the voluminous coat of snow which is soon to follow; though it is often preceded by a short interval of smoke and mildness, called the Indian Summer. **1832** *Boston Transcript* 8 June 1/2 The Indian summer is so called because, at the particular period of the year in which it obtains, the Indians break up their village communities, and go to the interior to prepare for their winter hunting. **1948** *Richmond* (Va.) *News Leader* 26 Oct. 19/3 Four days of Indian summer were on tap for Richmond today.

attrib. **1832** KENNEDY *Swallow Barn* II. 92 The foggy tint which is said . . . to spread such a charm over an Indian-summer landscape. **1898** FORD *Tattle-Tales* 89 The young couple had enjoyed . . . a recurring Indian-summer honeymoon of two months in front of their own fireside. **1944** *Reader's Digest* May 127/1 Vacation would be nearing its end with the gentle melancholy which hung like an Indian summer haze.

b. *transf.* A period of happiness, serenity, or good fortune occurring toward the end of a life, career, etc.

1843 WHITTIER *Poetical Works* 387/1 The warm light of our morning skies,—The Indian Summer of the heart! **1881** *Harper's Mag.* Jan. 273/2 Perhaps in the Indian summer of his life he may put his heart into a poem. **1944** ROBSJOHN-GIBBINGS *Goodbye* 63 Far be it from me to cast a gloom over this brave Indian summer of the decorating and antique world.

2. Indian-summerish, like Indian summer.

1852 THOREAU *Autumn* 79 It is a warm, Indian-summerish afternoon. **1898** *Advance* (Chi.) 12 May 627/2 [Psalms] in the cradle-like rock of the Hebrew parallelisms . . . which . . . so calm body, mind & soul, that your thoughts become *Indian* summerish. *a*1915 MUIR *Travels Alaska* (1917) 370 The hazy air, white with a yellow tinge, gives an Indian-summerish effect.

Also **Indian-summery,** *a.*

1881 WHITMAN *Spec. Days* 189 Out here on a visit—elastic, mellow, Indian-summery weather.

Indian sweat.

1. A sweat bath of the kind common among Indians. Also transf. *Obs.*

1797 WEEMS *Letters* II. 83. This moment I have got out of an Indian sweat of fright. **1807** GASS *Journal* 219 We gave him an Indian sweat and he is some better. **1812** STUART *Narratives* 153 We had no more medicine, but had recourse to an Indian Sweat, which had a good effect.

2. Indian sweat house, a temescal *q.v.*

[**1784** *N.C. Morav. Rec.* V. (1941) 1981 The Colonel soon came creeping out of an Indian sweat-house, and welcomed me in very friendly fashion.] **1861** *Napa Co.* (Calif.) *Rep.* 6 April 1/4 He may have been here since '49, may have seen 'slugs' as plenty as two bit pieces are now . . . but if he has not been present at a dance, in an Indian Sweat House, he is emphatically 'nowhar.'

Indian tea. Any one of several plants used for making a drink similar to tea, esp. a species of holly, *Ilex vomitoria*, common in the southern states. Also **Indian tea tree.** Cf. **black drink, yaupon.**

1709 LAWSON *Carolina* 91 This plant is the Indian Tea, us'd and approv'd by all the Savages on the coast of Carolina, and from them sent to the Westward Indians, and sold at a considerable Price. **1737** BRICKELL *N. Carolina* 87 The Indian-Tea Tree, which in their Language is called Yaupan, and Cassena, grows in great plenty in this Province. **1925** HEMING *Living Forest* 131 That evening, while we were talking about bears, the old woodsman infused some of the Indian tea he had gathered.

Indian territory.

1. Any one of several areas set aside for, or recognized to be, the residence of Indian tribes.

1677 WM. HUBBARD *Troubles with Indians* I. (1865) 105 Lying upon the Head of the principal Indian Territories, they [five sachems] were divided into . . . small Parties. **1792** *Ann. 2nd Congress* 1037 A great part of this is within the Indian territory. **1834** J. HALL *Sk. of West* (1835) I. 103 The United States claims the right of navigation on all navigable rivers which pass through an Indian territory.

2. (*cap.*) The territory, orig. approximately that of the present state of Oklahoma, set aside by the federal government for the Five Civilized Tribes of Indians. Also attrib.

1828 in *Kans. Hist. Quart.* V. (1936) 260, I am inclined to hope for a mission Station, & perhaps the seat of government of the Indian Territory, say from 30 to 70 miles due west of Missouri. **1887** *Courier-Journal* 14 Feb. 6/2 An Indian Territory special says: 'Reports from the Territory show that stock have wintered well.' **1948** *Chickasha* (Okla.) *D. Express* 4 July 1/2 When he was one year old his parents brought him to the Indian territory.

b. (See quot.)

1846 *Indian Adv.* (Louisville) May 51/1 Another matter prayed for in our memorial is, that something be done towards establishing a second Indian Territory, located west of the Rocky mountains.

Indian title.

1. The legal right or claim which the Indians had to the land which they occupied.

1660 *Dedham Rec.* IV. 26 Lieft Fisher & Sergent Ellice are deputed to treat . . . with the Indians . . . and cleere the place from all Indians title. **1800** JEFFERSON *Notes* 138 The lands prayed for were already cleared of the Indian title. **1899** CUSHMAN *Hist. Indians* 433 It was now falsely claimed that the Indian title was extinguished east and south of the Ohio River. **1937** KINNEY *Continent Lost* opp. 351 Some agreements and acts provided that surplus lands in excess of allotment requirements should be ceded to and paid for by the United States, all Indian titles to such land being extinguished.

2. A legal right to the possession of land, derived from the original Indian owners.

1683 *Mass. H.S. Coll.* 4 Ser. V. 107 He purchased no propriety unto himself or unto any other, but only procured the confirmation of the common right, from the Indian title, to his own and to every other particular inhabitant's lands and possessions. **1765** ROGERS *Acct. N. Amer.* 33 Being not satisfied with their Indian title, they this year obtained a grant from the aforesaid company. **1883** *Cent. Mag.* Sep. 657/2 One of the most interesting things with regard to the relations between the whites and the Indians is the occasional appearance, to this day, in the Massachusets law reports . . . of suits relating to Indian titles.

Indian tobacco. Any one of various American plants, esp. *Lobelia inflata*, *Nicotiana rustica*, and any variety of *Antennaria*.

1764 REUTER *Wachau*, *Indian Tobacco* has leaves much like Brown Betonia, though rougher. **1830** J. F. WATSON *Philadelphia* 470 The ancient Swedes . . . called the mullein plant the Indian tobacco; they tied it round their arms and feet, as a cure when they had the ague. **1947** *Midland Naturalist* July 60 Indian-tobacco [is] occasional in abandoned fields, pine fields, and wood margins.

b. (See quot. and cf. **kinnikinnick.**)

1928 LONG LANCE *Long Lance* 241 He dispatched a runner to the Crow chief, who was coming with his band more than one hundred miles away, with a present of Indian tobacco—*kinikinik*.

c. Indian tobacco pouch, a tobacco bag *q.v.* such as Indians used. *Obs.*

1775 in CRESSWELL *Journal* (1925) 116 Mr. Douglas gave me an Indian Tobacco pouch made of a Mink Skin adorned with porcupine quills.

Indian town. A town established and occupied by Indians.

1608 JOHN SMITH *Virginia* (1925) B, I was sent . . . to Kegquouhtan an Indian Towne, to trade for Corne. . . . The Towne conteineth eighteene houses, pleasantly seated upon three acres of ground. **1792** *Mass. H.S. Coll.* 1 Ser. I. 113 Tatnuck and Boggochoag hills are remarkable for having formerly had Indian towns on them. **1872** HOLLAND *Marble Prophecy* 107 Straight up the river an Indian town Filled the soft air with its musical hum. **1914** APPLEGATE *Recoll.* (1934) 35 We came up on the south side of the Caw River and camped below and near an Indian town of the Caw tribe.

Indian trade. Trade with the Indians.

1644 *Conn. Rec.* I. 113 The propositions of the Commissioners concerneing a generall Indean trade (except corne, fishe and venison)is also approued. **1790** R. PUTNAM in *Memoirs* 235 All the beef, pork, & mutton . . . will come to the seaports of Verginia, Maryland & Pennsylvania to market, as will also most of the furs skins, etc. obtained by the Indian Trade to those places & New York. *a***1918** G. STUART *On Frontier* I. 149 Another French Canadian moved in with a stock of goods for the Indian trade. **1937** KINNEY *Continent Lost* 17 Prior to 1748 the English Government had exhibited little interest in land titles or Indian trade in America.

Indian trader. One who engages in trade with the Indians.

1696 SCOTTOW *Massachusetts* 42 The first English Blood-shed was of an Indian trader. **1788** FRENEAU *Misc. Works* 128 At this instant an Indian trader alighted at the door. **1947** *Sierra Club Bul.* May 36 Partnerships and corporations sent technical specialists—trappers and Indian traders—into the West to bring out the furs.

b. (See quot.) *Obs.*

1835 LONGSTREET *Ga. Scenes* 222 *Indian-traders* (a long, cheap, but sometimes excellent kind of gun, that Mother Britain used to send hither for traffic with the Indians).

Indian trading. *attrib.* Of or pertaining to trade with the Indians. *Obs.*

1676 I. MATHER *King Philip's War* (1862) 99 [Resolved] that the Indian Trading-houses, whereby the Heathen have been debauched and scandalized against Religion, be suppressed. **1738** in *Ga. Col. Rec.* IV. (1906) 156 An Indian Trading Boat arrived, laden with the usual Traffick of those Nations . . . ; and it was said that she had no less than eight thousand Weight of Skins. **1807** WILSON *Travels* 108 All the places held by the English, French, Spaniards, and Americans, were supplied with guns, made on purpose for the Indians, called Indian trading guns. **1821** in *Ore. Hist. Quart.* XXXIII. 367 Along the west side [of North West Company's fort, Columbia River] stands a range of stores, tailor's shop, and Indian trading shop. **1822** MORSE *Rep. Indian Affairs* I. 62 The Indian Trading Fund of $300,000, now yielding no income to the Government, and no substantial benefit of the Indians . . . would be withdrawn.

Indian turnip. (See quot. 1907.)

1806 in *Ann. 9th Congress* 2 Sess. 1142 Persicaria, Indian turnip, wild carrot, wild onion, . . . and bastard indigo [grow near the Ouachita R.]. **1907** HODGE *Amer. Indians* I. 606/2 *Indian turnip.*—(1) The jack-in-the-pulpit (*Arisaema triphyllum*), also called three-leaved Indian turnip. (2) The prairie potato, or pomme blanche (*Psoralea esculenta*). **1949** *Nature Mag.* April 178 A few of these, like Indian turnip or jack-in-the-pulpit, cowslip and milkweed, may be considered mildly inedible.

Indian village.

1. A village of Indians.

[**1544** DE SOTO in *La. Hist. Coll.* II. (1850) 99 On the bank of a river was an Indian village.] **1674** in *Mass. H.S. Coll.* 1 Ser. I. 220 There is an Indian village, within twenty eight or thirty miles of Boston. **1839** HOLMES *Explor. Aroostook River* 7 The point formed by the junction of these rivers was not long ago the site of an Indian village. **1947** PEATTIE *Sierra Nevada* 53 The party named the Merced River and penetrated the foothills at one point to an Indian village called Pizcache.

2. A group of Indians composing such a village. *Obs.*

1843 FRÉMONT *Explor. Rocky Mts.* 55 We reached a place where the Indian village had crossed the river. **1846** SAGE *Scenes Rocky Mts.* xxxii, The Indian village . . . on its way in quest of buffalo, visited the fort.

Indian war. A war carried on between white people and Indians or between different groups of Indians.

1668 WINTHROP *Letters* (1882) 127 The impossibility almost that full discoveries [of minerals] should be made, while these Indian warrs continue. **1707** *Cal. Va. State P.* I. 110 We are strangely alarmed in the uper parts of King and Queen . . . for fear of an Indian Warr. **1860** GREELEY *Overland Journey* 92 Indian wars with each other are . . . fitted to excite only disgust. **1948** *Sat. Review* 22 May 18/3 It was exactly this type of man who caused the Indian wars.

Indian warrior.

1. An Indian brave or fighting man.

[**1683** HENNEPIN in *La. Hist. Coll.* IV. 118 The youngest of these Indian warriors danced the calumet to four or five of their chiefs till midnight.] **1690** in *Hist. Dig. Prov. Press* Mass. Ser. I. 32 Twenty Kennebeck Indian-Warriors went to look further after the business, who never yet returned. **1744** in FRANKLIN *Indian Tr.* (1938) 45 In the back Parts of Virginia, [there was a skirmish] between some of the Militia there, and a Party of the Indian Warriors of the Six Nations. **1851** GLISAN *Jrnl. Army Life* 59, I marched into garrison as proudly as an Indian warrior with his dozen scalps dangling to the breeze.

b. A white man skilled in fighting Indians. *Rare.*

1775 CRESSWELL *Journal* (1925) 64 Went with Captn. Douglas to Captn. John Stephenson's. This Gentleman is a great Indian Warrior, but appears to be a good-natured man.

2. *W.* Any one of various louseworts, esp. *Pedicularis densiflora*, having fernlike leaves and a thick spike of red flowers.

1902 *Out West* May 512, I love your flaming crest, Your smouldering indignation, Stern 'Indian warrior,' with fierce lips compressed, Stalking your reservation. **1937** *Range Plant Handbook* W 142 Several species of *Pedicularis*, such as elephanthead (*P. groenlandica*), Indian-warrior (*P. densiflora*), and sickletop (*P. racemosa*), have fairly well-standardized common names. **1946** *Sierra Club Bul.* Dec. 21 Here were brilliant masses of Indian warrior.

Indian war whoop. The war cry of an Indian. Also transf.

1794 S. WILLIAMS *Nat. Hist. Vt.* 144 The Indian warwhoop is the most awful and horrid. **1821** S. F. AUSTIN in *Texas Hist. Quart.* VII. 304 At the lower end (of the lake) the Indian war whoop was raised. **1883** MARK TWAIN *Life on Miss.* 44 When he was done they all fetched a kind of Injun war-whoop.

Indian weed.

1. (See quot.) *Rare.*

1687 CLAYTON *Va.* in *Phil. Trans.* XLI. 145 The Indians . . . have indeed various very good Wound-herbs, as an Herb commonly called Indian-weed, which perhaps may be referred to the Valerians, and be said to be *Plantani foliis*.

2. Tobacco.

1730 E. COOK *Sotweed Redivivus* 10 Leaving behind, to raise up Seed, And tend a stinking Indian Weed, Scotch, English, and Hybernians wild. **1844** *Knickerb.* XXIV. 394 The '*Experiences of a Tobacco Smoker*' will suggest to the lover of the Indian weed . . . some important truths. **1900** WINCHESTER *W. Castle* vi. 124 You know that smoking and chewing the vile Indian weed are great evils. **1907** HODGE *Amer. Indians* I. 606/2 *Indian weed.* An early term for tobacco.

Indian wheat.

1. Corn or maize. *Obs.*

1609 in *N.Y. Hist. Soc. Coll.* I. (1841) 325 The people of the country came aboard of us, making show of love, and gave us tobacco and *Indian* wheat, and departed for that night. **1674** JOSSELYN *Two Voyages* 56 Their Summer is hot and dry proper for their *Indian* Wheat; which thrives best in a hot and dry season. **1746** E. KIMBER *Itinerant Observ.* 43, I have known them [*sc.* horses] to go six Days Journey without a Feed of Corn, having nothing but the Stalks of Indian Wheat, and such other Litter as they could pick up.

2. Tartarian buckwheat. *Obs.*

1838 *Mass. Agric. Survey* 1st Rep. 33 [Tartarian buckwheat] is known under the name of Indian wheat. **1868** GRAY *Field Botany* 289 *F[agopyrum] tartaricum*, Tartary or Indian Wheat. Cult[ivated] for flour on our N.E. frontiers and N.

3. (See quots.)

1839 HOLMES *Explor. Aroostook River* 60 The variety called Indian wheat in Kennebec, but more commonly in this region, 'Rough Buckwheat,' is very extensively cultivated . . . on the Aroostook. **1910** THORNBER *Grazing Ranges Ariz.* 264 The native plantains known widely as Indian wheat, rank next in importance.

* **India rubber.**

1. *pl.* Overshoes made of rubber. *Obs.*

1840 *Knickerb.* XVI. 207 He gave such answers as suited him to the gentleman in the India-rubbers, taking especial care not to invite him to alight. **1877** HALE *G.T.T.* 143 She took also her cloak, her india-rubbers which she had not time to put on, and her carpet-bag.

2. An eraser made of rubber. *Rare.*

1857 M. J. HOLMES *Meadow-Brook* v. Taking my India-rubber, I erased it [the writing] while my scholars were settling the matter of seats.

3. In combs., now obs., denoting things made partially or entirely of rubber, as **India rubber boat, cloth, overcoat, overshoes, poncho, shoe.**

1843 FRÉMONT *Explor. Rocky Mts.* 11 The carts had been unloaded and dismantled, and an India-rubber boat, which I had brought with me for the survey of the Platte river, placed in the water. **1858** D. PETERS *Kit Carson* 181 Among the rest of the forethought supplies, there was an India-rubber boat. — **1833** *Niles' Reg.* XLIV. 420/2 The India rubber cloth may be obtained on application to George Spring. **1847** *Rep. Comm. Patents* 212 The outsides of boats have been made of India-rubber cloth. — **1895** M. A. JACKSON *Memoirs* xxi. 428 He was wearing at the time an india-rubber overcoat over his uniform. — **1896** HASWELL *New York* 244 About this period [*c*1830] India-rubber overshoes first appeared; the exact date I cannot give. They were wholly made of pure rubber, and were very rough and unsightly in fashion. — **1888** SHERIDAN *Memoirs* I. 325 There was but little clothing to be obtained in Chattanooga, and my command received only a few overcoats and a small supply of India-rubber ponchos. — **1827** Mrs. BASIL HALL *Aristocratic Journey* (1931) 49, I paddled along in a pair of india rubber shoes which Mrs. Ford . . . lent to me. They are very much worn here in wet weather. **1870** F. FERN *Ginger-Snaps* 182 Yesterday I went out with only one India-rubber shoe on.

***indication,** *n. Mining.* Evidence of the presence of profitable ore. Usu. *pl.*

1855 *So. Californian* (Los Angeles) 28 Mar. 1/7 Mineral indications in Southern California . . . differ in many respects with the mineral indications of the earth's surface in Central, or Northern California. **1861** *Harper's Mag.* Jan. 157/1 That's a speculator from San Francisco. See how wildly he grasps at every 'indication,' as if he had a lease of life for a thousand years. **1884** HARTE *Story of Mine* 394 Luckily the fertile alluvium of these valleys . . . offered no 'indications' to attract the gold-seekers. **1948** *Duncan* (Okla.) *D. Banner* 2 July 1/3 The location was one of three staked by the Ohio Oil Co. on indications given by the Palmer No. 1 Leard-Amerada.

Indienne ˈændjɛn, *n.* [F.] A light printed cotton cloth of a kind orig. made in India. — **1880** CABLE *Grandissimes* 247 There bounded into the ring the blackest of black men, . . . in breeches of 'Indienne' —the stuff used for slave women's best dresses.

indignation meeting. A public meeting held to express indignation at something regarded as an abuse.

1842 *Spirit of Times* 5 March 1/2 We have held an 'indignation meeting' and passed strong resolutions against Mexico. **1905** N. DAVIS *Northerner* 53 Indignation meetings were held daily at the different houses of the officials of the societies and guilds. **1948** *Sat. Ev. Post* 3 July 16/1 Mothers were holding indignation meetings about the schools.

***indigo,** *n.*

1. (*cap.*) A jocose term for a "blue." *Obs.* Cf. ***blue,** *n.* **3.**

1842 *Dartmouth* IV. 117 Success to every student. That rooms in Dartmouth Hall, Unless he be an Indigo, Then, no success at all. **1851** HALL *College Words* 169 *Indigo.* At Dartmouth College, a member of the party called the Blues.

2. In combs.: (1) **indigo bird,** =next; (2) **bunting,** a small finch, *Passerina cyanea,* the male of which is notable for its deep blue color; (3) **bush,** (*a*) false indigo, (*b*) a showy southwestern shrub or small tree, *Parosela spinosa;* (4) **cotton,** cheap cotton cloth dyed with indigo, *rare;* (5) **farm,** a farm upon which indigo is the principal crop, *obs.;* (6) **finch,** =**indigo bunting;** (7) **plantation,** a plantation upon which indigo is the principal crop, *obs.;* (8) **planter,** the owner of an indigo plantation, *obs.;* (9) **shrub,** =**indigo bush** (*a*); (10) **snake,** the gopher snake of the southern states; (11) **weed,** any wild plant popularly regarded as a kind of indigo, esp. the wild indigo, *Baptisia tinctoria;* (12) **work,** a building in which indigo dye is extracted from plants, *obs.*

(1) 1785 PENNANT *Arctic Zool.* II. 365 The Americans call it [the indigo bunting] the Indigo bird. **1917** *Birds of Amer.* III. 72 The Indigo Bird is one of our most valuable species and should be given rigid protection. — **(2) 1783** LATHAM *Gen. Synopsis Birds* II. 205 Indigo B[unting]. . . . It is common at New York. **1887** RIDGWAY *Manual N. Amer. Birds* 448 Eastern United States and more southern British Provinces, west to edge of Great Plains. . . . *P[asserina] cyanea.* Indigo Bunting. **1948** *Green Bay* (Wis.) *Press-Gazette* 13 July 11/4 Birds that sang in the afternoon were the . . . scarlet tanager, indigo bunting, red-eyed vireo and crested flycatcher. — **(3)** (*a*) **1860** CURTIS *Woody Plants N.C.* 104 *Indigo bush* (*Amorpha fruticosa.*) A very pretty shrub. . . . It is said to have been used for the manufacture of Indigo, but, I imagine, with not much profit. (*b*) **1897** SUDWORTH *Arborescent Flora* 257 Dalea spinosa Gray. Indigo Bush. **1947** *So. Sierran* May 4/2 We were thrilled by the fine display of Indigo Bush. — **(4) 1896** WILKINS *Madelon* 11 Not a girl . . . could wear a gown of brocade with the grace . . . with which Madelon Hautville wore indigo cotton.

(5) 1874 *Rep. Comm. Agric. 1873* 260 In the county of Orangeburgh, S.C., there are six indigo-farms, carried on by some of the older men of the county. — **(6) 1828** BONAPARTE *Ornithology* II. 91 Female Indigo Finch. *Fringilla Cyanea.* **1917** *Birds of Amer.* III. 71. — **(7) 1757** *Lett. to Washington* II. 174 What adds to make this Place at present disagreeable is that most of the Gent of Note are out at their Indigo Plantations, so that We have nothing left but a Set of trading Ones. **1797** IMLAY *Western Territory* (ed. 3) 253 It is also scarce possible to keep any animal on an indigo plantation in any tolerable case, the fly being so troublesome, that even poultry thrive but little where indigo is made. — **(8) 1772** HABERSHAM *Letters* 202 We have had a great Quantity of Rain fall, which must hurt the Indigoe Planters. **1880** CABLE *Grandissimes* vi. 37 Old De Grapion . . . married her . . . to young Nancanou, an indigo-planter on the Fausse Rivière. — **(9) 1935** ROLLINS *Disc. Ore. Trail* 225 [A] title for this same stream . . . given because the birdwood or indigo shrub, *Amorpha fruticosa,* was common along its banks.

(10) 1885 *Riverside Nat. Hist.* III. 367 *Spilotes cooperi* . . . is of a deep black, shading into yellow on the throat. It is known by the negroes as the indigo or gopher-snake. **1948** *Atlantic Mo.* Feb. 87/1 The others—the hog-nosed viper, the indigo or gopher snake, the ringneck, the assorted grass and water snakes—we never got around to naming. — **(11) 1784** CUTLER in *Mem. Acad.* I. 473 *Indigofera* . . . Indigoweed. . . . A durable pale blue may be obtained from the leaves and small branches. Fomentations of the plant, it is said, will abate the swelling, and counteract the poison in the bite of rattlesnakes. **1852** *Mich. Agric. Soc. Trans.* III. 197 My timber is generally oak, with some hickory, indigo weed, tea weed. — **(12) 1687** BLOME *Isles & Terr. in Amer.* 14 There [are] already above eighty Indico-Works. **1797** IMLAY *Western Territory* (ed. 3) 252 An indigo work should always be remote from the dwelling-house.

As the last term in **pit-coal, prairie, stone coal, wild indigo.**

Indomitables ɪnˈdɑmətəblz, *n. pl.* A faction in the Democratic party in N.Y. *c*1840. Now *hist.* — **1840** *Boston Transcript* 15 April 2/1 When the Registry Law was first spoken of, the tail of the Democratic party, the roarers, butt-enders, ringtails, O.K.'s, (flat burglary this latter title) and indomitables, talked strong about nullification and all that. **1941** *Sat. Review* 19 July 3/2 On March 11, 1840, the Locofoco newspaper, the New York *New Era,* listed the clubs as follows—the Butt Enders, the Tammany Temple, the Indomitables.

indoor baseball. A form of baseball that can be played in rinks and halls by the use of a larger, softer ball than is used in the outdoor game. Also the ball used in this game.

1890 *Harper's Wkly.* 8 Mar. 179/4 In-door base-ball has not the slightest resemblance to parlor croquet. **1920** *Outing* July–Aug. 209/1 She strolled to a small pine and picked up the coveted indoor baseball at its foot. **1922** RAINWATER *Play Movement in U.S.* 56 Indoor baseball was invented in Chicago as a substitute for regular practice by professional ball teams during inclement weather. **1949** *Dly. Ardmoreite* (Ardmore, Okla.) 23 Feb. 18/2 The explosive charge weighs in the neighborhood of 20 to 30 pounds and occupies a sphere of three or four inches—about the size of an indoor baseball.

***industrial,** *a.* and *n.*

1. (*cap.*) A member of any of various sporadic groups of unemployed who in the manner of Coxey's Army *q.v.* organized marches on Washington, D.C., demanding work for all unemployed, restriction of immigration, legislation against aliens, etc. Also **Industrial Army.** *Obs.*

1894 *Chi. Record* 16 March 1/5 The industrial army received accessions to-day, bringing its estimated forces up to 850 men. *Ib.* 2 May 2/3 The industrials took breakfast at the fashionable hour of 10 a.m., for provisions did not come in at a lively rate. **1919** HOUGH *Sagebrusher* 14 We been hearing a long while about the free Industrials . . . Hobos, I call them, no more.

2. *Industrial Workers of the World,* a labor organization formed at Chicago in 1905 to organize all workers into one big union in order to gain control of economic activities. Usu. abbreviated **I.W.W.** Cf. **wobbly,** *n.*

1912 *Cent. Mag.* July 473/1 Counsels of violence were emphatically rejected, despite the opposition of the ideas of the Industrial Workers of the World. **1942** LILLARD *Desert Challenge* 90 The labor militancy that made the IWW of Tonopah and Goldfield first-page news is thirty years past. **1946** *Craig* (Colo.) *Empire-Courier* 10 April 2/3 The Industrial Workers of the World held a convention in Chicago last week. There are now forty of them, whereas 30 years ago, 100,000 were on the membership rolls.

***industry,** *n.* As the last term in **home, infant, maple-sugar industry.**

***infant,** *n.* **1. infant industry,** (see quot. 1914). **2. infant manufacture,** =prec.

(1) 1870 *Cong. Globe* App. 29 March 240/3 But, argue our defenders of monopoly, let us protect our infant industries, and when they have grown to manhood, . . . they will need no further protection. **1914** *Cyclo. Amer. Govt.* II. 176 Infant Industry. This term is applied to the need of protecting new industries in order to give them opportunity to compete with older foreign establishments. — **(2) 1789** *Ann. 1st Congress* I. 106 Some [duties are] calculated to . . . protect our infant manufactures. **1831** PECK *Guide* 81 Were protection to the sugar making business to be wholly abandoned, . . . the result would be more disastrous to the south and west, than the influx of foreign goods was to the infant manufactures of the north, and to the whole country.

***infield,** *n. Baseball.* (See quot. 1867.) Also attrib.

1867 CHADWICK *Base Ball Reference* 138 The In-Field.—That portion of the field within the base lines. **1926** *N.Y. Times* 6 Oct. 16/1 The Cardinals clinched their victory by scoring again on two clean hits and an infield out. **1946** *Chi. D. News* 6 June 33/1 The Bucs . . . appeared for batting practice but failed to take their infield drill.

For **inferior post office,** see **post office 3.**

b. *collect.* The players who perform in the infield.

1867 *Ball Players' Chron.* 13 June 1/1 The Independents have a very fine catcher and a good in-field. **1889** *Glenrock* (Wyo.) *Graphic* 13 Sep. 7/1, I have seen in the public prints, occasional allusions to 'a famous Chicago stonewall infield.' **1944** *Reader's Digest* Dec. 71/2 He'll toss the fish to some other sea lions, who catch it and flip it around, like an infield warming up.

infielder ˈɪnˌfildɚ, *n. Baseball.* A player stationed in the infield. — **1867** *Ball Players' Chron.* 27 June 2/1 These 'safe hits' . . . [were] balls sent over the heads of the in-fielders, and yet not far enough out to be caught by the out-fielders. **1947** *Chi. D. News* 1 Nov. 13/1 The youngster was one of the most promising infielders he had seen.

infielding ˈɪnˌfildɪŋ, *n. Baseball.* Playing in the infield. — **1866** CHADWICK *Base-Ball Player* 27 On the activity and judgment of the Short Stop depends the greater part of the in-fielding. **1875** *Chi. Tribune* 12 Dec. 12/4 A quick ball reduces infielding to a minimum.

infit ˈɪnˌfɪt, *v. local. tr.* To supply (a seaman) with necessaries for shore life, usu. on credit. Hence **infitter,** *n.* — **1887** GOODE *Fisheries* II. 226 The merchant is as anxious to 'infit' as he was to 'outfit' him, but the man must now bring an order from the agent or owner of the vessel. *Ib.*, The outfitters are also 'infitters,' that is, they furnish the men with such supplies and articles of clothing as they may need when the vessel returns.

***inflation,** *n.* Of money and prices: Overexpansion. Also attrib.

1838 *Speeches of D. Barnard* (Albany) 195 The property pledge can have no tendency whatever to prevent an inflation of the currency. **1870** W. W. FOWLER *Ten Years Wall St.* 315 Used ten thousand shares of the new stock to load up the bulls at these inflation prices. **1949** *Newsweek* 7 Feb. 19/1 The nation . . . worried increasingly about the danger of runaway inflation.

inflationist ɪnˈfleʃənɪst, *n.* One who favors inflation of the currency. Also as adj. — **1870** *Nation* 3 March 129 The work of inflation by adding fifty million dollars to the currency . . . is part of an arrangement between the Western inflationists, who want more greenbacks, and the Eastern tariff men, who are opposed to a reduction of duties. **1918** *Ib.* 7 Feb. 129/1 There is a pretty obvious inflationist trend to the proposal.

***influence,** *n.* The ability to secure political office or other favors. Also, rarely, the person exercising such power. *Colloq.*

1792 in BOWERS *Jefferson & Hamilton* 161 Favoritism, influence and monopoly. **1888** BRYCE *Amer. Commonw.* III. IV. lxxxviii. 177 This position gave him a vast amount of 'influence,' which he continued to use for his own advantage until the board was abolished in 1870. **1904** DERVILLE *Other Side of Story* 49 Asked me how I liked Washington, how I liked my work, how old I was and who was my influence.

Ingersollian ˌɪŋgɚˈsəlɪən, *a.* Favoring the views of Robert Green Ingersoll (1833–99), a well-known American anti-Christian propagandist. *Obs.*

1892 STEVENSON & OSBOURNE *Wrecker* xi, I don't know if you quite believe in prayer, I'm a bit Ingersollian myself. **1898** *Mo. So. Dakotan* I. 117 Then follows an analysis of the several petitions of the Lord's prayer, which, were the author not redeemed from the charge by his earnestness and by his final deductions would lead the reader to set him down as a scoffer of the Ingersollian school.

Hence **Ingersollism,** *n.*, **Ingersollistic,** *a.*, **Ingersollite,** *n.* All *obs.*

1883 G. R. WENDLING (*title*), Ingersollism; from a Secular Point of View. **1898** *Dly. Ardmoreite* (Ardmore, Okla.) 9 May 3/3 Hear Judge Dickson tonight at the Presbyterian church on 'The Fallacies of Ingersollism.' — **1896** *Advance* (Chi.) 2 April 477/3 We could wish that the expressions had been less ambiguous and seemingly ingersollistic. — **1883** *Home Missionary* Nov. 281 Nowhere is skepticism more prevalent. . . . Many of our ablest men . . . are Ingersollites.

ingrain carpet. A carpet dyed in the grain, i.e., in the yarn, before it is woven.

1836 *Penny Cyclo.* VI. 314/1 Kidderminster or Scotch carpet, or, as the Americans more descriptively term them, *ingrain carpets.* [**1863** M. HARLAND *Husks* 20 Sarah's carpet was common ingrain, neither pretty nor new.] **1905** LINCOLN *Partners* 29 There were two or three straight-backed chairs set squarely in their places on the ingrain carpet.

Also **ingrain carpeting,** the fabric from which these carpets are made.

1847 *Rep. Comm. Patents 1846* 75 Letters patent have been granted for improvements in looms for weaving ingrain carpeting. **1861** *Vanity Fair* 1 June (*advt.*), Three Ply and Ingrain Carpeting, Rugs, Mats, . . . at a great Reduction in Prices.

***inhabitant,** *n.*

1. *pl.* In colonial times, a region or district settled or inhabited by colonists. *Obs.*

1753 WASHINGTON *Diaries* I. 43 In company with those persons [I] left the Inhabitants the Day following. **1784** ELLICOTT in Mathews *Life A. Ellicott* 23 Tomorrow we shall set off for the Inhabitants.

2. *Law.* One who technically resides in a particular area or jurisdiction. Cf. **back, Seminole inhabitant.**

1787 *Constitution* i. § 2 No person shall be a representative who shall not . . . be an inhabitant of that state in which he shall be chosen. **1834** *Cases Contested Elections 1789–1834* (H. Comm. on Elections) 411 An inhabitant of a State, within the meaning of the . . . constitution, is one who is *bonafide* a member of the State, subject to all the requisitions of its laws, and entitled to all the privileges . . . which they confer. **1883** E. CHANNING *Town & County Govt. Eng. Col. N. Amer.* (1884) 12 To this [parish] meeting all those who had benefit of the things there transacted might come; that is to say, all householders, and all who manured land within the parish. Such were technically termed inhabitants, even though they dwelt in another town.

inhalator ˈɪnhəˌletɚ, *n.* An apparatus for administering an anesthetic, oxygen, etc., by inhalation, an inhaler. Also attrib.

1929 *Lit. Digest* 30 March 79/2 The most effective arrangement of all is to see that the city fire or police department and the hospital ambulances have inhalators. **1947** *Chi. Tribune* 17 July 32/2 Inside the ambulance is an inhalator. **1949** *Chi. D. News* 4 May 1/4 (*legend*), [He] is administered oxygen by members of Inhalator Squad 2.

initiation fee. The fee one pays upon being initiated into a society or organization.

1865 PIKE *Scout & Ranger* (1932) 125 The initiation fee to this degree was but one dollar. **1913** *Industrial Worker* (Spokane) 27 Mar. 4/3 What's the initiation fee? **1948** *Mazama* June 1/1 The income from initiation fees and dues fell $1,500.00 short of equaling the running expenses.

***ink,** *n.* In combs.: (1) **inkberry,** the gallberry, *Ilex glabra*, a shrub of the holly family, also the berry of this; (2) **jerker,** =**ink slinger;** (3) **pencil,** (see quot.), *obs.;* (4) **shedder,** =next; (5) **slinger,** (see quot. 1877), also **ink slinging,** *colloq.*

(1) **1765** J. BARTRAM *Diary* 11 Oct., Little & poor grass mixed with dwarf mirtle . . . ink berries & chinkapin. **1858** WARDER *Hedges & Evergreens* 275 The *Prinos glaber* or Winter-Berry, is a handsome shrub, growing three or four feet high, and bearing black berries, called ink-berries. **1949** *Amer. Photography* Feb. 115/2 A third species, inkberry or evergreen winterberry (Ilex glabra), sometimes grows to a height of fifty feet. — (2) **1865** *Harper's Mag.* 683/2 This rattle-brained scribbler, this miserable ink-jerker. — (3) **1939** GILBERT *Forty Yrs.* 4 Once, with great boldness, I wrote on it, 'I think I ought to have an ink pencil for this.' I longed beyond words for one of these pencils. There was no ink in them, but you pressed one end and it opened its mouth at the other end and let out a large blue lead, upon which it clamped its teeth. — (4) **1868** *Harper's Mag.* Aug. 428/2 The marriage question, viewed from the pecunious viewpoint, has become the topic of so many ink-shedders abroad as well as at home. (5) **1877** BARTLETT 786 *Ink-Slinger*, one who habitually writes for publication; particularly an editor or reporter of a newspaper. **1896** *Spectator* 7 Nov. 619 There is . . . no picturesque ink-slinging, as the happy American phrase goes. **1943** *Copper Camp* 94 They didn't dare press the search too closely for fear . . . any suspicious action might disclose the secret to the ink slingers.

As the last term in **blind, pokeberry ink.**

***inland,** *a.* In combs.: (1) **inland alewife,** (see quot.); (2) **cotton,** upland cotton, *rare;* (3) **Empire,** a name applied to the region around Spokane, Washington; (4) **Indian,** an Indian from the interior of the country as distinguished from one living near the coast, *rare;* (5) **sea,** one of the Great Lakes, *obs.;* (6) **swamp,** (see quots.), *obs.*

(1) **1884** GOODE *Fisheries* I. 594 The Inland Alewife or Skipjack . . . is abundant throughout the Mississippi Valley in all the larger streams. — (2) **1803** J. DAVIS *Travels* 78 Of cotton there are two kinds; the sea-island and inland. The first is the most valuable. — (3) **1878** (*Newspaper title*), The Dalles [Ore.] Inland Empire. **1890** *Oregonian* (Portland) 17 Jan. 5/2 The Chinook winds, which visit the Inland Empire during the months of January and February, take the same general course as do the northwesterly winds of summer. **1947** *Sports Afield* Dec. 28/2 The water transportation people, proposing

to save the wheat growers of the Inland Empire many thousands of dollars annually on freight to the coast, insist that the dams in the lower Columbia are essential for slack water navigation to Lewiston, Idaho. — (4) **1675** Richard Smith, Jr. *Letter* (1937) 111 As to the Naragansets, here are maney inland Indyans come hither, as they pretend, to shelter themselufe for feare of the Einglish sowders.

(5) **1819** Thomas *Travels* 17 The term of 'Inland Seas' may be used here with much propriety; and, from its general excellence, the soil that surrounds them, must one day support a vast population. **1840** Cooper (*title*), The Pathfinder; or, The Inland Sea. — **(6) 1802** Drayton *S. Carolina* 116 The plantations which produce this grain [rice], are of two kinds, *river swamp*, and *inland swamp*. The first are immediately connected with fresh water rivers; the latter are situated on low inland swamp, unconnected with tides or navigation. **1842** Buckingham *Slave States* I. 38 There are no less than six classes or kinds of soil in this territory: the first of these is the tide swamp, near the sea; the second is the inland swamp, above the reach of the tide-water range.

* **in-lot,** *n.* A lot within a town, village, or new settlement. Now *hist.*

1779 *Ky. Petitions* 51 We pray that every Actual settler . . . may be entituled to Draw a free lott; . . . the lotts to consist of half acre in lott and five acre out lott. **1815** Drake *Cincinnati* iii. 139 Bonfires, and all other conflagrations on the streets or in-lots, are . . . forbidden. **1841** Cist *Cincinnati* 16 As an inducement to settlers the new proprietors agreed to give an in lot six rods by twelve . . . and an out lot. **1948** Dick *Dixie Frontier* 148 The area in and around one of these stations was plotted and each settler could hold one or more 'in lots' or building plots on the townsite and one or more 'out lots' or farming areas.

* **inning,** *n.* In baseball, the period of play in which both sides have a turn at bat.

"In *Cricket, Base-ball*, and similar games (in Great Britain always in *pl.* form *innings* whether in sing. or pl. sense)" (*OED*).

1856 *Spirit of Times* 6 Dec. 229/1 After the first inning is played, the turn commences at the player who stands next to the one on the list who lost the third hand. **1873** *Chi. Tribune* 4 June 1/7 Hatfield made a clean home run in the third inning by a magnificent hit to centre field. **1948** *St. Paul Dispatch* 17 Sep. 1/1 The Tribe handed Washington its 16th straight loss 6–3 on a five-run first inning.

* **innocence,** *n.* The common bluet, *Houstonia caerulea.* Cf. **prairie innocence.**

1821 Barton *Flora* I. 119 Fairy-flax-Bluett. Innocence. Venus' Pride. **1838** *Boston Wkly. Mag.* 22 Sep. 17/1, I must not omit a passing notice of that most exquisite little flower, known by the names of 'Venus' Pride' and 'Innocence.' **1893** *Outing* July 286/1 We see a little brook of clear water . . . with a tangle of blackberry vines, and a small patch of 'innocents' growing beside it.

* **inquiry,** *n.* **1. inquiry meeting,** (see quot. 1835). **2. inquiry room,** a room, usu. in a church, in which persons troubled about their prospects of salvation may ask for information and guidance. Both *obs.*

(1) **1835** Reed & Matheson *Visit* II. 15 *Conference or Inquiry Meetings.*—These are instituted for those persons who have become anxiously concerned for their salvation; and who need the more exact guidance and encouragement, which discreet conversation can best supply. **1850** Gallaher *Western Sketch-Book* 242 A church was organized. . . . I appointed an inquiry meeting, to be held early in the morning. — (2) **1850** Gallaher *Western Sketch-Book* 243 He came into the inquiry room, and told me, very frankly, that he had been living in sin, and that unmerited grace alone had held him up from a deserved hell. **1877** *Boston Bul.* Feb. (B.), They had a tough subject in the inquiry-room this week. Moody wrestled with him, and Sankey sang with him, but the man seemed to despair of forgiveness.

* **insane,** *n.*

1. insane asylum, a public asylum, usu. state-supported, for the insane.

1830 *Mechanics' Press* (Utica, N.Y.) 9 Jan. 69/3 He proceeded at large to mention the Orphan, Deaf and Dumb, and Insane Assylums [*sic*]. **1884** *Lisbon* (Dak.) *Star* 31 Oct. 3/2 It is more than likely that he is kept out of the way in some insane asylum. **1948** *Chi. Tribune* 24 Mar. III. 7/5 Right now Buck is a good candidate for an insane asylum.

2. insane hospital, =prec.

1828 Webster, Insane . . . 2. Used or appropriated to insane persons; as, an insane hospital. **1842** *Niles' Reg.* 16 July 318/3 The bill to establish an insane hospital in the District of Columbia was read a third time and passed.

* **insect,** *n.* As the last term in **Hessian, spittle, wheat insect.**

in-shoot ˈɪnˌʃut, *n.* =**in-curve.** — **1892** *Outing* Jan. 302/1 An old ball player . . . taught Harry to pitch and to try some curves and 'in shoots' of his own device. **1940** Mencken *Happy Days* 230 When I ventured on an inshoot it was apt to be recovered, not by the catcher, but by the third baseman.

inshore cod. (See quot. 1884.) — **1884** Goode *Fisheries* I. 201 [Cod] fish which live near the shores, but which are less closely limited to the reefs . . . are called 'Shoal-water Cod,' 'Shore Cod,' 'Inshore Cod' [etc.]. **1889** *Cent.* 1082/2 *Clam-cod*, inshore cod which feed on clams.

* **inside,** *n., a., adv.,* and *prep.*

1. That which is secret or confidential. *Slang.*

1904 W. H. Smith *Promoters* v. 101 I'll give it to you straight, for I happen to know the inside.

2. a. (See quot.) **b.** Short for "inside of." *Colloq.* Cf. **3. b.** (3).

(a) 1878 Hinton *Arizona* 168 A genuine Arizona pioneer always speaks of going 'inside' if he is about to visit California. — **(b) 1924** A. J. Small *Frozen Gold* i. 39, I hear all about it inside twenty-four hours.

3. In combs.: (1) **inside ball,** see as a main entry; (2) **cut,** =next; (3) **dope,** inside or confidential information, *slang;* (4) **history,** confidential or secret history; (5) * **man,** one who has confidential information, as one employed within a building who connives with a burglar or robber, *slang.*

(2) **1879** *Bradstreet's* 19 Nov. 8/1 Some people who claim to have the 'inside cut' of the iron trade, prophesy a decline in prices. — **(3) 1924** Croy *R.F.D. No. 3* 157, I knew a fellow on the inside and we used to pal around together and I got a lot of inside dope. — **(4) 1894** Leavitt *Our Money Wars* 11 A few lines of inside history are worth whole books of that usually printed. **1912** Mathewson *Pitching* ix. 184 Behind this game is some 'inside' history that has never been written.

(5) **1912** Dreiser *Financier* 43 There was . . . a George Waterman, a brother, aged fifty, who was the confidential inside man. **1924** Henderson *Keys to Crookdom* 98 The bank robber may have an inside man who is giving him information or he may be simply working from 'hunches.'

b. Used fig. in colloq. and slang phrases: (1) *To have the inside track,* see **inside track** as a main entry; (2) *to be (on the) inside,* to be in possession of confidential information; (3) *inside of,* within.

(2) **1870** *Cong. Globe* 3 Feb. 1022/1, 'I ask the gentleman from Ohio to name the ships which he says have been sold for a song. The gentleman is inside on all these matters.' . . . 'I am no more inside than [Mr. Eldridge].' **1924** [see **inside dope**]. — **(3) 1839** *Spirit of Times* 27 July 246/1 (We.), There are dozens of horses . . . that can trot their mile in harness inside of three minutes. **1925** *Sat. Ev. Post* 10 Oct. 144/3 It was too big to resist, and inside of twenty-four hours we had everything set. **1941** Smith *Gang's All Here* 146 (We.), Inside of a month I was in circulation.

inside ball. In baseball, the game played with careful attention to an exploitation of the finer, more skilful aspects of the sport, and with less reliance on a reckless, bludgeoning type of play. Also **inside baseball.**

1912 *Sat. Ev. Post* 3 Aug. 49/2 Hughie Fullerton, the original exponent of inside baseball, is another baseball reporter. **1912** C. Mathewson *Pitching* 282 For eight and one-third innings the Giants had played 'inside' ball, and I had carefully nursed along every batter who came to the plate, studying his weakness and pitching at it. **1949** *Dly. Worker* 1 May 12/4 Finally the team is smarter with Durocher, Frisch and Fitzsimmons working steadily on inside baseball and helping especially such things as pitching, baserunning, defensive cut-offs, hit and run, et al.

insider ɪnˈsaɪdɚ, *n.*

1. (See quot. 1848.) Also anyone who has confidential information or "pull."

1848 W. Armstrong *Stocks* 7 Insiders are those by whom and through whom all transactions are made in and about the Exchange. **1892** *Courier-Journal* 1 Oct. 11/2 The only other important change for the day was in Distillers, which is taken care of by the insiders. **1902** H. L. Wilson *Spenders* xxx. 355 Shepler's back of all three [stocks]. The insiders are buying up now, slowly and cautiously, so as not to start any boom prematurely. **1931** *Blue Valley Farmer* (Okla. City) 12 Nov. 1/7 The Post Office Department simply hands over contracts and subsidies to 'insiders.'

2. An inside passenger on a stagecoach. *Obs.*

1853 B. F. Taylor *Jan. & June* 170 'No Room For Two!' was the exclamation of some insider, the other morning. **1892** *Harper's Mag.* Jan. 257/1 The exhilarating pace, the smooth roads, and the juxtaposition of the insiders tended, in a high degree, to the promotion of enjoyment.

inside track. *To have the inside track, fig.* to have a favored or advantageous position.

1857 *Richmond W. Whig* 5 Sep. 2/1 In a word, *'Gizzard-Foot'* has the inside track for the Senatorship, and means to keep it. [**1864** *Mercantile Gaz.* (S.F.) 1 April 3/1 These tales, we say, are becoming pretty well understood by persons who have their eye teeth cut and know how things are managed on 'the inside track.'] **1914** ATHERTON *Perch of Devil* ii. 361 When a woman knows where she stands, and has the inside track, . . . the man has no show whatever. **1945** *Steamboat* (Colo.) *Pilot* 19 July 2/3 There is a general feeling that labor has had the inside track for the past five or six years.

insinuendo ɪnˌsɪnjuˈendo, *n.* (See quot. 1913.) — **1885** MATTHEWS in *Longman's Mag.* Dec. 151 Could I not damn with faint praise and stab with sharp insinuendo?—to use the labour-saving and much-needed word thoughtlessly invented by the sable legislator of South Carolina. **1913** *Boston Transcript* 9 July 16/6 'Portemanteau' Words. . . . Insinuendo—a compound from innuendo and insinuation.

***inspect,** *v. intr.* To prove or turn out to be upon inspection. *Rare.* — **1865-6** *Ill. Agric. Soc. Trans.* VI. 638 All Flour that inspects 'Sound' and full weight shall be branded.

***inspection,** *n.*

1. Short for inspection house *q.v. Rare.*

1860 S. MORDECAI *Virginia* 330 The Tobacco Warehouses or Inspections in Richmond, fifty years ago were, *Shockoe*, a mere cluster of wooden sheds.

2. In combs.: (1) **inspection car,** (see quot. 1895); (2) **house,** a house in which tobacco is inspected and

Inspection car

graded, *obs.;* (3) **law,** a law providing for the inspection of various articles of commerce to determine their fitness for transportation or sale, *obs.*

(1) **1890** *Railways of Amer.* 146 It would require a separate article to give even a brief description of the different kinds of cars which are now used. . . . Hotel-car, Inspection-car, Lodging-car [etc.]. **1895** WAIT *Car-Builder's Dict.* 70 Inspection-car. A car used for inspecting track of a railroad. In inspecting the track it is pushed in front of a locomotive. — (2) **1773** *Md. Hist. Mag.* II. 358 To compel all the Owners or Makers of Tobacco to send it to certain Inspection Houses whence it cannot be again removed till it is put on Board a Ship. **1818** *Niles' Reg.* XV. 139/2 Adjoining the inspection house, on Queen street [in Baltimore], two frame dwellings . . . were burnt to the ground. — (3) **1753** *Md. Hist. Mag.* III. 366 Which made me apprehend they intended some Opposition to the Inspection Law. **1773** *Ib.* XV. 286 Prohibiting their Delegates from Proceeding to Business unless the inspection Law was Previously obtained. **1790** MACLAY *Deb. Senate* 188 Read the law for giving effect to the inspection laws of the States.

***inspector,** *n.*

1. An official who examines various articles, as brick, tobacco, etc., to determine their suitableness for sale or their conformity to regulations.

1685 *Boston Rec.* 173 Inspectors of Bricke. **1763** *Md. Hist. Mag.* 171 Mr. John Johnson, Inspector at St. Leonard's Creek warehouse . . . was seized with an apoplectic fit. **1840** *Niles' Reg.* 26 Sep. 64/2 Inspectors attention! We have complaints from England that the tare of barrels are fraudulently marked. **1948** *Ice Cream Trade Jrnl.* Oct. 166/2 In drawing samples of fruit, which is done constantly, the inspector endeavors to get the most representative sample possible.

2. An official appointed to see that an election is conducted in a lawful manner.

1800 *Phila. Ordinances* 100 An act to . . . choose two inspectors of the general election for each . . . of the said wards. **1875** *Mich. Gen. Statutes* I. (1882) 708 The inspectors of such election, after the close of the polls, shall canvass the ballots.

3. (See quots.) *Obs.*

1814 *Harvard Coll. Laws* 58 One of the members of the Immediate Government shall have the office of Inspector of the College. His duty shall be from time to time to examine the exterior and interior State of the College public buildings . . . and to cause such repairs of them to be made as may to him appear necessary or proper. **1851** HALL *College Words* 171 *Inspector of the college.* At Yale College, a person appointed to ascertain, inspect, and estimate all damages done to the College buildings and appurtenances, whenever required by the President.

4. (See quot.)

1944 NUTE *Lk. Superior* 210 The camps had 'inspectors,' too. This was the lumberjack's name for hoboes.

As the last term in **car, cattle, deer, flour, food, road, state, steamboat, stock, timber inspector.**

***instal,** *v. tr.* (See quot. 1828.)

1788 *Presb. Church Constitution* 405 The presbytery shall . . . ordain and install him pastor. **1828** WEBSTER *s.v.*, To install a clergyman or minister of the gospel, is to place one who has been previously ordained, over a particular church and congregation, or to invest an ordained minister with a particular pastoral charge. **1874** ALDRICH *P. Palfrey* xi, The Rev. James Dillingham was formally installed pastor of the Old Brick Church.

***instalment,** *n.*[1] The action of installing an ordained minister in a new charge. *Obs.* — **1759** *Essex Inst. Coll.* XLIX. 2, I went to an Instalment at Stoneham where Mr. John Serls took upon him the pastoral Charge of the Church. **1788** *Presb. Church Constitution* 405 When a call shall be presented to any minister or candidate, it shall always be viewed as a sufficient petition from the people for his instalment.

***instalment,** *n.*[2] In combs.: (1) **instalment house,** a large store where goods may be bought on the instalment plan; (2) **man,** a man who collects payments from purchasers of goods on the instalment plan; (3) **plan,** the plan or method of paying for goods in instalments, also transf. and attrib.

(1) **1886** *Stand. Guide Washington* 194 The Washington Installment House is the place to buy your furniture, carpets, bedding, stores, &c. — (2) **1887** *Courier-Journal* 18 Jan. 3/7 Installment men and agents generally will find just what they need by addressing Installment Dealers' Supply Co. **1909** O. HENRY *Roads of Destiny* 47 The poor . . . when they get money . . . exhibit a strong tendency to spend it for stuffed olives . . . instead of giving it to the instalment man.— (3) **1876** *L.A. Dly. Herald* 4 Oct. 3/6 Lots for Sale on the Installment Plan or Cheap for Cash. **1910** *Sat. Ev. Post* 24 Sep. 15/3 Most beaver dams are built on the instalment plan—are the result of growth. **1949** *Mo. Hist. Rev.* April 209 The story is the first satire on installment plan buying.

***institute,** *n.*

1. A school or college, often of a specified type. Also the building used by such an institution. Cf. **Smithsonian Institute.**

1830 WATSON *Philadelphia* 248 The simple, unassuming apellation [*sic*] of 'scnool' was the universal name till about the year 1795; after that time 'academies,' 'seminaries,' 'lyceums,' 'institutes,' &c. were perpetually springing up in every quarter among us. **1882** LATHROP *Echo of Passion* i, The Institute was a large, nondescript wooden building with an immense colonnade. **1948** *Chi. Sun-Times* 28 Oct. 30/5 Ground was to be broken Thursday for a new two-story building to house the Institute of Gas Technology on the campus of the Illinois Institute of Technology.

2. A short period of instruction for teachers, librarians, etc. Cf. **farmers', state teachers', teachers' institute.**

1890 J. G. FITCH *Notes Amer. Sch. & Training Coll.* 90 By an 'Institute' is meant a sort of normal class, held periodically for the teachers of a district, and furnishing instruction in the art and practice of education, and an opportunity for the discussion of methods. Institutes are, in fact, migratory and occasional academies. **1910** BOSTWICK *Amer. Pub. Library* 27 Library extension [is encouraged] by means of . . . the maintenance of schools, classes, or 'institutes' for library instruction. **1948** *West Va. Hist.* Oct. 9 The Patrons soon noted that when institutes were held in the neighborhood of active granges they were 'of the very highest character.'

***institution,** *n.* The practice or system of keeping slaves. *Obs.* Cf. **peculiar institution.**

1833 *Ill. Patriot* (Jacksonville) 19 Oct. 4/1 And what do they propose to do with this institution? **1835** CHANNING *Slavery* iii, There are masters who . . . see slavery as it is. . . . They deplore and abhor the institution. **1857** *So. Illinoisian* (Shawneetown) 1 May 2/1 They begin to tremble and quake with fear for the stability of the 'institution' even in the Old Dominion. **1881** *Cong. Rec.* 28 April 418/2 Down with it [defeated South] . . . went the institution, and there ended that 'irrepressible conflict.'

As the last term in **manual labor, moneyed, Smithsonian, state institution.**

***institutor,** *n.* A bishop or one who acts for him in instituting a minister into a church or parish. *Rare.* — **1808** *P.E. Ch. Bk. Comm. Prayer* (1823) 674/2 Then shall the Priest who acts as the Institutor receive the Incumbent within the rails of the Altar.

***instruct,** *v.* **1.** *tr.* To direct (an elected representative) how to vote in a particular matter coming before the body to which he is elected. **2.** *To instruct out,* of a state legislature: To direct a U.S. senator to vote in a way that is so repugnant to his own views as to result in his resignation. *Rare.*

(1) **1817** CALHOUN *Wks.* II. 177 This doctrine of implied instruction . . . is very different . . . from the old doctrine, that the constituents have a right to assemble and formally to instruct the representative. **1904** *N.Y. Times* 31 March 8 A delegation instructed for Judge Parker will go to St. Louis from this State. — (2) **1862** *N.Y. Tribune* 22 Jan. 4/6 Mr. Tyler . . . opposed the removal of the U.S. deposits from the U.S. Bank by General Jackson's order, and was in 1836 instructed out of the Senate on that issue.

***instruction,** *n.* The giving by an electorate, a state legislature, convention, etc., of specific voting directions to one whom they elect or delegate; also, *pl.*, the directions themselves.

See Kenneth Colegrove, "New England Town Mandates," in *Pub. Col. Soc. Mass.* XXI. (1919) 411–99, and cf. quot. 1919 below.

1640 in *Pub. Col. Soc.* XXI. 414 As well to acquaint them with what is p[ro]pounded or enacted at the Court, as to receive instruccons for any other business they would haue done. **1817** CALHOUN *Works* II. 177 The ear of this House [i.e., House of Representatives] . . . is closed to truth and reason. What has produced this magic spell? Instructions! . . . Have the people of this country snatched the power of deliberation from this body? **1841** *Cong. Globe* App. 9 June 74/2 Minorities may petition, majorities enjoy the higher right of instruction. **1919** *Pub. Col. Soc.* XXI. 416 Altogether, there are records of eighteen votes of instructions by Boston town-meetings previous to the Revolution of 1689.

instructive ballot. (See quot.) — **1897** *Cong. Rec.* 18 Feb. 1970/1 The law of Illinois provided, also, that accompanying these ballots should be eight 'instructive ballots'—ballots prepared for the instruction of the voters, sample ballots.

***instructor,** *n.* A college teacher, usu. one whose rank is below that of professor. See also **moral instructor.**

1722 in PEIRCE *Hist. Harvard Univ.* 232 Voted . . . that Mr. Judal Monis be *improved* as an instructor of the Hebrew language in the College. **1846** *Knickerb.* XXVIII. 10 We think that the power which the corporation possess, but which they do not exercise, should be vested in the instructors of the college. **1943** *U. of C. Announcements* 88 Ruth Blair, Ph.D., Instructor in Home Economics.

***insurance,** *n.* As the last term in **endowment, title insurance.**

***insurrection,** *n.* As the last term in **Texas, whisky insurrection.**

insurrecto ɪnsəˈrɛkˌto, *n.* [Sp. in same sense.] A rebel or insurgent. — **1910** *Sat. Ev. Post* 15 Oct. 17/2 I'll declare an amnesty for him and all his insurrectos. **1947** *Ib.* 8 March 18/3 Later he saw a bit of the fighting in the Philippines, north of Manila, against Aguinaldo's insurrectos.

inswamp ɪnˈswamp, *v. intr.* and *reflex.* To take refuge in a swamp. *Obs.* — **1676** *Conn. Rec.* II. 458 Who presently inswamped themselves in a great spruce swamp. **1775** ADAIR *Amer. Indians* 315 The violent exercise of running a great distance under the violent rays of the sun . . . would not allow him to inswamp. *Ib.* 386 [They] take an oblique course, till they inswamp themselves again, in order to conceal their tracks.

intangibles, *n. pl.* (See quots.) Also **intangible property.** — **1888** BRYCE *Amer. Commonw.* II. II. xliii. 129 The largest part of a rich man's wealth, consists in what the Americans call 'intangible property,' notes, bonds, book debts, and Western mortgages. At this it is practically impossible to get, except through the declaration of the owner. **1914** *Cyclo. Amer. Govt.* III. 496/1 The term 'personal property' . . . includes . . . visible property and intangibles.

***intelligence office.**

1. An employment bureau for household servants and domestic help.

1768 *Boston Gaz.* 25 July. **1830** WATSON *Philadelphia* 220 Intelligence Offices. These offices for finding places for servants, began within a very few years and upon a very small scale. **1876** SCUDDER *Dwellers* i. 19, I keep an intelligence-office. . . . I have unrivaled means for securing the most valuable help from all parts of the world. **1904** *N.Y. Ev. Post* 2 March 5 The intelligence offices in New York city supply fully one-half of the families having household help.

2. (See quot. 1828.)

1828 WEBSTER, *s.v. Intelligence-office,* an office or place where information may be obtained. **1857** *Lawrence* (Kans.) *Republican* 28 May 1 General Land Agency, and Emigrant's Intelligence Office.

intendente ˌɪntɛnˈdɛntɪ, *n. S.W.* [Sp. in same sense.] A government officer of high rank. *Obs.*

1803 M. CUTLER in *Life, Jrnls. & Corr.* (1888) II. 121 The violation of the Spanish treaty by the Governor and Intendent at New Orleans. **1849** T. T. JOHNSON *Sights Gold Region* ix. 85 We received . . . the utmost attention and kindness from the natives . . . as well as from Señor Don Mariano Arossemena, the Intendente of that department. **1850** W. COLTON *Deck and Port* viii. 257 The demand, after the responsibility of the case had been shuffled from the intendente to the prefect, and from him to the criminal judge, was complied with.

interchange paper. =**exchange paper.** *Obs.* — **1831** *Boston Transcript* 20 May 2/1 A friend . . . 'just dropt in' to look over our interchange papers and 'set things to rights.'

***inter-class,** *a. Educ.* Carried on between classes. — **1929** *Playground & Recreation* July 227/1 In inter-class competition . . . the under classes come to a new sport, and consequently the upper class teams have the edge because of longer competition. **1947** *This Week Mag.* 4 Jan. 2/1 Girl athletes on our cover are Wellesley College youngsters engaged in a tough inter-class game.

intercourse law. A law regarding intercourse or trafficking between certain groups; esp. a federal enactment of June, 1834, that sought to protect Indians from unscrupulous land seekers. *Obs.*

1846 M'KENNEY *Memoirs* I. 194 My inability to make a certain account, amounting to some sixty thousand dollars square with the provisions of either the intercourse law of 1802, or with my conscience. **1866** *Rep. Indian Affairs* 166 Are not such acts on the part of steamboat men in direct violation of our intercourse laws? **1871** *Ib.* 407 The Indians are placed on a reservation, and ample power given to enforce the 'intercourse law.'

***interest,** *n.*

1. A plantation or landed estate. *Obs.*

1663 *Charlestown Land Rec.* 84 Fencing Stuffe from of our wood interest on Maulden Common. **1700** in *Md. Hist. Mag.* XX. 185 Johns Interest.

2. interest lands, lands set aside to secure the payment of interest on bonds. *Rare.*

1859 *Ill. Central Railroad Lands* 16 The Company's lands are respectively designated as Construction, Free-lands, and Interest Lands.

As the last term in **log, middling, planting, rum, short, sugar interest.** Also *pl.* in **cotton, liquor, special, transportation interests.**

***interfere,** *v. Football. intr.* To assist a teammate who is carrying the ball by shielding him from tacklers. Hence ***interferer,** *n.* — **1920** W. CAMP *Football* 51 The full-back and the right half must interfere for their companion. **1923** D. CANFIELD *Rough-Hewn* xxv, Neale could see Rogers rock a second, undecided, on tip-toe; side-step an interferer; and then shoot his body like a projectile into the play.

***interference,** *n.*

1. In football, the action of interfering with a tackler so as to clear the way for the player carrying the ball. Also a player whose function it is to safeguard the runner.

1894 *Outing* XXIV. 112/2 The special feature of American Rugby arises from the principle of interference to aid the man running with the ball. **1920** *Chi. Herald & Examiner* 2 Jan. 14/1 The gangling Church took the direct pass . . . and . . . outran his able interference. **1949** *Time* 7 March 40/3 As any football player knows, to win a game you have to have good interference.

attrib. **1894** *U. of Chi. Wkly.* 1 Nov. 49/1 An improvement in interference play was noticeable, and the tackling in most cases was good.

b. The act of interfering with a runner in baseball—now barred by the rules of the game.

1927 H. G. SALSINGER in *Secrets of Baseball* 147 Interference plays, too, are scored as they probably have been made.

2. *attrib.* Of or pertaining to conflicting claims to prior right in a patent.

1888 *Scribner's Mag.* Aug. 190/2 An application for a patent which, after an interference litigation with Edison, was finally issued to Maxim. **1903** *Cong. Directory* (58th Congress Extra. Sess.) 251 The Commissioner of Patents, . . . has appellate jurisdiction in the trial of interference cases.

inter-fraternity ˈɪntɚfrəˌtɜnətɪ, *a.* Taking place between fraternities in school. — **1900** *Cap & Gown* (Chi.) 221 The Inter-Fraternity and Inter-House Meet was held on June 9, 1899—Junior Day.

Interior Department. =**Department of the Interior.**

1859 BUCHANAN in *Pres. Mess. & P.* V. 543 According to a report from the Interior Department . . . the lands given to the States amount to 6,060,000 acres. **1917** S. MATHER in *Nat. Park Service Rep.* 16 The Interior Department . . . will control the destinies of the Sand Dunes National Park. **1945** MATHEWS *Talking* 213 On the way to the Interior Department, I looked at the paper John had given me.

interline ˈɪntəˌlaɪn, *a. Railroad.* Of or pertaining to two or more lines or roads. — **1897** *Columbus* (O.) *Dispatch* 26 Feb. 9/3 Among the subjects [for discussion] will be . . . uniform contract for interline ticket. **1903** E. JOHNSON *Railway Transportation* 124 If the shipment made is to be through freight, a 'joint' or 'interline' way-bill of merchandise is used.

∗**interlinear,** *n.* A book containing a text in a foreign language with a translation between the lines. — **1850** THAXTER *Poem before Iadma* 20 Then [he] devotes himself to study, with a steady earnest zeal, And scorns an 'Interlinear,' or a 'Pony's' meek appeal. **1851** HALL *College Words* 171 *Interlinear*, a printed book, with a written translation between the lines.

∗**interliner,** *n.* =prec. *Obs.* — **1832** *Tour through College* 25 Ponies, Interliners, Ticks, Screws, and Deads (these are all college verbalities) were all put under contribution. **1852** FELTON *Mem. J. S. Popkin* p. lxxvii, He was a mortal enemy to translations, 'interliners,' and all such subsidiary helps in learning lessons.

∗**interlock,** *v. intr.* Of the heads or sources of rivers that flow in different directions: To lie or be situated between or adjacent to each other. Also *tr.*

[**1693** T. CLAYTON in *Phil. Trans.* XVII. 791 The Heads of the Branches of the Rivers interfere and lock one within another . . . after the manner that an Indian explained . . . to me, when . . . he clapt the Fingers of one hand 'twixt those of the other, crying, they meet thus.] **1749** in J. WINSOR *Miss. Basin* (1895) 241 The Branch [of the Susquehanna] interlocks with the Branches of Allegeny and the North Branch of Potomack. **1796** MORSE *Univ. Geog.* I. 718 A branch of the Hiwassee, called Amoia, almost interlocks a branch of the Mobille. **1840** BANCROFT *Hist. U.S.* III. 122 The journey, by way of the Ottawa and the rivers that interlock it, was one of more than three hundred leagues.

∗**interlocutor,** *n.* In a group of Negro minstrels, the performer who usu. occupies the middle place in a row, converses with the end men, and acts as chairman.

1880 E. JAMES *Negro Minstrel's Guide* 2 An Amateur Negro Minstrel band . . . arranged on the stage as follows: Interlocutor or Middle Man, in the Center [etc.]. **1915** MATTHEWS in *Scribner's Mag.* June 756/1 The dignified interlocutor took his place in the middle of the semicircle. **1949** *Chesterton* (Ind.) *Tribune* 28 April 1/6 Ralph was script writer, interlocutor and director, and received a wrist watch for doing a lion's share of the work.

intermediate school. (See quots. 1911, 1945.)

1866 *Rep. Indian Affairs* 252 The branches usually taught in primary and intermediate schools receive attention here. **1911** MONROE *Cyclo. Educ.* II. 430/2 In the North Atlantic group of states, the term 'intermediate school' is frequently still retained to designate the upper primary and the lower grammar grades of the elementary school. **1945** C. V. GOOD *Dict. Educ.* 223 intermediate school: a school that enrolls pupils in intermediate grades, usually comprising the fourth, fifth, and sixth years of schoolwork.

intermontane ˌɪntəˈmɑnten, *a.* Also **intermountain.** Between or amid mountains.

1807 MEASE *Geol. Acct. U.S.* 59 Whatever of saline . . . the soil of the upland contains, is thus floated or rolled along to the low lands, and constitutes with proportional diversity and mixture, the intermontane soil. **1893** *Harper's Mag.* April 700/2 The irresistible tendency of emigration to the intermontane regions of the West, and the Northwest, already dedicated to freedom. **1907** *Springfield W. Republican* 13 June 2 The opposition in the intermountain states will not find anything comforting in the president's remarks.

intern ˈɪntɜn, *n.* [F. *interne.*] A doctor, recently graduated from a medical school, who is serving a prescribed period in a hospital as a requirement for license to practice. Also **interne.**

1879 WEBSTER *Supp.* 1563/1. **1914** GERRY *Masks of Love* 123 The young interne, standing before them, very trim in his white uniform, had alarmed them. **1923** WYATT *Invis. Gods* II. v. 85 The older man . . . became . . . attached to the young surgical interne. **1948** *Amer. Jrnl. Nursing* Dec. 743/3 Santa, usually a pediatrics intern, is on hand for parties in the children's department.

Hence **internship,** *n.*

1924 *Scribner's Mag.* Feb. 183/1, I was at that time just finishing my internship. **1949** *Newsweek* 13 June 47/3 [His] direct acquaintance with the sick was limited to a brief internship after getting a degree.

∗**internal,** *a.*

1. Of taxes: Levied upon or derived from commerce and industry, etc., within the U.S.

1792 HAMILTON *Works* III. (1850) 298 There can surely be nothing in the nature of an *internal duty* on a *consumable* commodity, more incompatible with liberty, than in that of an external duty, on a like commodity. **1838** *U.S. Mag.* I. 145 That ascendency, which launched our American Government on a sea of troubles, in the midst of such rocks of the *British channel* as a funding system, national bank, internal taxation, soon stranding Washington's administration on the quicksands of civil war. **1914** H. E. SMITH *U.S. Federal Internal Tax Hist.* 291 The people of the United States, as a whole, did not oppose the internal taxes.

2. internal improvement, the improvement at public expense of conditions within the country, as by building of roads, canals, etc.; an improvement of this kind. Usu. *pl.* Also attrib.

1818 in *Amer. Sp.* XXI. (1946) 306/1 These are some of the future advantages connected with this branch of our Internal Improvements. **1832** BENTON *30 Years' View* I. 219/1 The Bank of the United States . . . wields at its pleasure, the whole high tariff and federal internal improvement party. **1874** GLISAN *Jrnl. Army Life* 484 The effect of these internal improvements has been to stimulate all branches of industry. **1944** CLARK *Pills* 57 Garrulous politicians and impractical visionaries poured forth eloquent words on 'internal improvements.'

3. internal revenue, governmental revenue derived from excise taxes, income taxes, etc., as distinguished from customs duties. Also attrib.

1796 *Ann. 4th Congress* 1 Sess. 379 Mr. W. Smith moved the order of the day on the report of the Committee of Ways and Means on the Internal Revenue. **1873** *Newton Kansan* 2 Jan. 2/1 The most important bills . . . are those reducing the internal revenue force. **1914** *Cyclo. Amer. Govt.* III. 214/1 The collection of internal revenue is made by a bureau of the Treasury Department.

internation ˌɪntəˈneʃən, *n.* [f. ∗*intern*, *v.* to send (merchandise, goods, etc.) into the interior of a country.] Sending goods into the interior of a country. *Rare.* — **1885** *U.S. Const. Rep.* No. 53½. 282 (*Cent.*), Importations and internations which are made from the 1st of April . . . through the frontier custom-house of Paso del Norte.

international novel. (See quot.) *Obs.* — **1885** *Phila. American* 14 Nov., 'International novel:' . . . By that term we have come to designate a class of books in which the contrasts of character and habit between Americans and Europeans define the situation, and the clashing of idiosyncrasies supplies the incidents and in large measure take the place of the plot.

internist ɪnˈtɜnɪst, *n.* A doctor who has specialized in internal medicine. — **1904** *Science* 29 April 696/1 Many internists ('general physicians') of experience and authority. **1947** *Hygeia* Nov. 941/2 For these reasons we must conclude that the internist has not replaced the surgeon in the treatment of toxic goiter.

interstate ˌɪntəˈstet, *a.*

1. Carried on between the states of the U.S., pertaining to the interrelation of the states.

1844 J. J. WEBB *Memoirs* 163 All goods sold there were free from 'consumers' or interstate duty. **1890** *Stock Grower & Farmer* 4 Jan. 3/1 A call has been made for an interstate convention of cattlemen, bankers, and merchants. **1948** *Time* 29 Nov. 22/2 He will recommend . . . a law against segregation and discrimination in interstate transportation.

2. interstate commerce, commerce among the states of the U.S.

1872 *Sup. Ct. Rep.* LXXXII. 272 The question . . . calls upon us to trace . . . the power and duty of the Federal government to protect and regulate interstate commerce. **1913** LA FOLLETTE *Autobiog.* 461 My valuation measure . . . had been bottled up in the Committee on Interstate Commerce.

b. Interstate Commerce Commission, an administrative board, with quasi-judicial powers, established in 1887 for the regulation of transportation and communication between the states.

1887 *Statutes at Large* XXIV. 383 A Commission is hereby created and established to be known as the Inter-State Commerce Commission. **1949** *Lubbock* (Tex.) *Morn. Avalanche* 23 Feb. I. 10/7 He is awaiting approval from the Interstate Commerce Commission on his application for abandoning the line.

c. interstate commerce law, a federal law regulating commerce among the states.

1887 *Courier-Journal* 5 May 4/3 He is greatly disappointed in the criticisms being made by the press and the public on the interstate commerce law. **1903** *McClure's Mag.* Nov. 110/1 Congress . . . in 1887 passed an interstate commerce law forbidding railroad discrimination.

interterritorial ˌɪntəˌterəˈtorɪəl, *a.* Pertaining to relations among territories of the U.S. — **1888** *Philadelphia Ledger* 4 Dec. (*Cent.*), A call for an inter-territorial convention of the four northwestern Territories—the two Dakotahs, Montana, and Washington.

1903 in THOBURN *Stand. Hist. Okla.* II. 755 At a nonpartisan interterritorial statehood convention held in this city today . . . the following resolutions were unanimously adopted.

interurban ˌɪntəˈɜbən, *a.*

1. Carried on between or connecting cities or towns, usu. of electric railroads.

1883 *Harper's Mag.* May 927/1 [The] increasing volume of interurban commerce. **1906** H. QUICK *Double Trouble* 140 The core of their ambitious project of interurban lines connecting half a dozen cities. **1910** *Salt Lake Tribune* 27 Nov. 21/1 The roadbed has been so improved within the last two months that the big interurban cars run over it like a boat gliding through calm water.

2. *absol.* An interurban electric railroad, or a car or train on such a road.

1912 *Out West* Mar. 204/1 There is no more beautiful road (through the orange groves) than the Los Angeles interurban through Azusa. **1948** *Dly. Ardmoreite* (Ardmore, Okla.) 11 April 1/6 Fifty persons were hurt, five seriously, when two interurbans smashed head-on in Dallas county today.

Also **interurban motorman.**

1945 *Jefferson Co. Republican* (Golden, Colo.) 25 July 1/2 The alertness of an interurban motorman probably saved the life of a two-year-old Golden boy last Saturday night.

***interval,** *n.* [See note.]

As a topographical term "interval" was first used of land occupying an *interval*, as that between a river and the high ground adjacent to it. Later the last element was confused with "vale" resulting in "intervale" *q.v.* These terms in the senses here shown have rarely been used outside New England. See A. Matthews in *Mass. Col. Soc. Pub.* VI. (1899–1900), 137–51.

1. Short for **interval land.**

1647 *Suffolk Deeds* I. 85 Fifty Acres of Interval. **1771** J. ADAMS *Diary* Wks. (1850) II. 273 When I first came into the town, . . . there opened before me the most beautiful prospect of the river, and the intervals and improvements on each side of it. **1841** W. KENNEDY *Texas* I. 142 The term 'bottom' is used throughout the West to designate the alluvial soil on the margins of rivers, usually called 'intervals' in the eastern States of the Union. **1942** CANNON *Mountain* 96 Logs would be easy to snake down this hillside. . . . A man could probably girdle every tree on that interval in a day—if he worked.

attrib. **1736** GYLES *Mem. Captivity* 14 We cross'd a large Interval-Corn-Field. **1780** E. PARKMAN *Diary* 255 Elias carrys one Load of ye Interval Hay to Capt. Fisher. **1863** *Rep. Comm. Agric. 1862* 98, I have grown it on interval or alluvial soil. **1892** *Vt. Agric. Rep.* XII. 132 From Hardwick to Fairfax nearly all of our interval farms are under a high state of cultivation.

2. interval land, low alluvial land along a stream or between hills. Also a particular piece of such land. Cf. **alluvion.**

1683 in TEMPLE & SHELDON *Hist. Northfield, Mass.* (1875) 95 Every person that has 60 acres granted of interval land, shall settle two inhabitants upon it. **1789** J. MORSE *Amer. Geog.* 141 These vallies, which have received the expressive name of *interval lands*, are of various breadths, from two to twenty miles. **1942** CANNON *Mountain* 63 Interval land with wild hay aplenty.

***intervale,** *n.* [See note to ***interval.**]

1. Short for **intervale land.**

1653 *Lancaster Rec.* 29 We Covenant . . . to proportion to every ten pounds three acors of Land two of vpland and one of Entervale. **1746** in *N.H. Hist. Soc. Coll.* IV. 203 Then . . . marched to a River . . . and there camped in the Intervale. **1817** *Niles' Reg.* XII. 92/1 The ground on the Wabash was wholly unfit, the highland being destitute of water, and the intervale (or bottom land as it is called) being without wood. **1949** *Pacific Spectator* Spring 232 It was the intervale where the low-bush blueberries grew.

attrib. **1653** *Lancaster Rec.* 29 He which hath now more then his estate Deserveth in home Lotts and entervale Lotts shall haue so much more. **1730** in *N.J. Archives* (1894) XI. 226 To be sold. . . . A Plantation . . . having nearly fifty Acres of very good intervale Meadows, which is most of it ploughable. **1799** *Poughkeepsie* (N.Y.) *Jrnl.* 31 Dec. 1/1 Belle Vale . . . consists of four hundred and six acres of land, of which above one-third is . . . intervale meadow. **1942** RAWSON *N.H. Borns a Town* 14 Before it has journeyed too far toward the sea to lose the beauty of its intervale farms.

2. intervale land, =**interval land.**

1653 *Early Rec. Lancaster, Mass.* (1884) 27 Wee doe Allowe Covernant and Agree that there be laid out Stated and established . . . thirty acors of vppland and fortie acors of Entervale Land. **1795** WINTERBOTHAM *Hist. View* II. 4 These valleys, which have received the expressive name of *intervale lands*, are of various breadths. **1884** S. E. DAWSON *Hand-Bk. Domin. Canada* 108 The spring freshets flood these wide valleys, and produce what is called 'intervale land' of great fertility.

***interventor,** *n.* (See quots.) — **1803** in *Ann. 8th Congress* 2 Sess. 1521 The interventor superintends all public purchases and bargains. **1889** *Cent.* 3157/2 *Interventor*, . . . an inspector in a mine, whose duty it is to report upon the works carried on, and upon the use made of supplies. Gregory Yale. (Western U.S.)

***interview,** *n.* A meeting between a writer, usu. for current publications, and another person, in which the former secures information for publication. Also the article resulting from such a meeting.

1869 *Nation* 28 Jan. 67 The 'interview,' as at present managed, is generally the joint product of some humbug of a hack politician and another humbug of a newspaper reporter. **1894** SHUMAN *Steps into Journalism* 68 The newspaper interview is peculiarly an American product. **1948** *Time* 29 Nov. 24/1 He donned a proper hand-painted necktie, submitted cheerfully to interviews.

***interview,** *v. tr.* To have an interview with (a person).

1870 LONGFELLOW in S. Longfellow *H. W. Longfellow* III. 144 A northwest newspaper, in which I have been 'interviewed,' and private conversation reported to the public. **1881** MARSHALL *Through Amer.* (1882) 36 He would . . . be formally 'interviewed' during his progress up the Bay towards the Empire City. **1948** *Time* 6 Dec. 14/3 Miss Sulzberger interviewed dozens of producers, stage managers, actors, writers, etc.

Hence **interviewing,** *n.*

1869 *Nation* 28 Jan. 66 'Interviewing' is confined to American journalism. **1874** *Cin. Enquirer* 2 July 2/1 Having begun the task of interviewing, I resolved to persevere.

***interviewer,** *n.* One who seeks to obtain information by interviewing. Cf. **newspaper interviewer.**

1869 *Nation* 28 Jan. 67/2 'Interviewing' helps to establish the curious device of looking on the correspondent, whether interviewer or not, as . . . not at all under editorial control. **1919** W. G. BLEYER *Feature Articles* 57 In studying an interview article, one can generally infer what questions the interviewer asked. **1949** *Time* 31 Jan. 64/2 *Interviewer:* Are you continuing to go to church? *Wife:* Oh, yes.

***intolerant,** *a.* Of vegetation: Unable to endure heavy shade. — **1898** PINCHOT *Adirondack Spruce* 22 If the intolerant species can get the start, . . . they may hold their position by growing above the other trees about them, as do Tamarack and Pine. **1905** *Forestry Bureau Bul.* No. 61, 14.

intrastate ˌɪntrəˈstet, *a.* Within a state.

1903 E. JOHNSON *Railway Transportation* 370 In 1886 the Supreme Court in the Wabash decision . . . limited the authority of the State strictly to the intrastate traffic and excluded that moving from one State to another. **1931** *Randolph Enterprise* (Elkins, W.Va.) 19 March 1/3 Prohibiting the grouping of inter-state and intra-state bridges. **1949** *Lisle* (Ill.) *Eagle* 31 March 1/5 The company states that it is currently in the red in its Indiana intrastate operations.

***introduce,** *v. tr.* To offer (a new product) for sale. — **1899** ADE *Doc' Horne* 203 He found employment as a house-to-house salesman and 'introduced' a new kind of soap.

***invalid,** *n.* In combs.: (1) **invalid chair,** a reclining chair, usu. on wheels, designed for the use of invalids; (2) **pension,** a pension paid to a former soldier on account of invalidism, *obs.;* (3) **pensioner,** a former soldier to whom the federal government has granted a pension because of ill health, *obs.;* (4) **-'s table,** (see quot. 1856), *obs.*

(1) **1865** WHITNEY *Gayworthys* 336 Jane Gair [was] sitting in her invalid chair, with her invalid gown and cap on. **1944** *Sears Cat.* (ed. 189) 565 A practical invalid chair for all around use. — (2) **1793** *Ann. 2d Congress* 804 An engrossed bill to regulate the claims to Invalid Pensions was read. **1887** *Courier-Journal* 2 Feb. 1/2 Representative Taulbee, for the Committee on Invalid Pensions, today reported adversely the Senate bill to pension the widows of Gen. Logan and Gen. Blair. — (3) **1782** *N.H. Comm. Safety Rec.* 307 Ordered that Lt. Joseph Huntoon & Capt. Chase Taylor continue on Quarter instead of Half pay, as Invalid Pensioners. **1809** *Steele P.* II. 604 Sherwood Haywood Agent for Invalid pensioners. — (4) **1847** J. MITCHELL *Scenes & Characters* 117 It was extremely difficult to obtain permission to board out. . . . To take away all pretext for it, an '*invalid's table*' was provided. **1856** HALL *College Words* (ed. 2) 267 Invalid's table. At Yale College, in former times, a table at which those who were not in health could obtain more nutritious food than was supplied at the common board.

***inventory,** *v. intr.* To prove to be worth upon inventory. — **1902** G. H. LORIMER *Lett. Self-made Merchant* ix. 113 The last time I saw her, she inventoried about $10,000 as she stood. **1905** *Springfield W. Republican* 20 Oct 12. The late Senator Platt left an estate which inventories at $20,880.

inverted T. Used of, or with reference to, what is now known as a T rail *q.v.* — **1837** *Civil Engineer* I. 39/2 The pattern . . . is by American engineers called the inverted T. rail. **1839** *Amer. R.R. Jrnl.* IX. 83 Edge rail of the inverted T pattern.

Invisible Empire. The Ku-Klux Klan.

1870 W. H. Holden *Proclamations Gov. N.C.* 31 There is a widespread and secret organization in this State, partly political and partly social in its objects; . . . known . . . as 'The Invisible Empire.' **1924** Mecklin *Ku Klux Klan* 108 Here is a large and powerful organization offering to solace his sense of defeat by dubbing him a knight of the Invisible Empire for the small sum of ten dollars. **1947** Lumpkin *Southerner* 90 Who can say with certainty . . . what went on in middle Georgia at the time this Invisible Empire was sending out its unknown men to perform its unnamed missions?

involuntary servitude. Forced employment, esp. Negro slavery. — **1845** *Whig Almanac 1846* 44/1 North of said Missouri compromise line, slavery, or involuntary servitude (except for crime,) shall be prohibited. **1864** in Fleming *Hist. Reconstruction* I. 121 Involuntary servitude is forever prohibited, and the freedom of all persons is guaranteed in said State.

* **Io,** *n.* (See quots. 1873, 1889.) Also **Io moth.**

1873 Riley *5th Ann. Rep. Mo. State Entom.* 133 The Io Moth . . . is one of our most beautiful moths, receiving its name from two conspicuous eye-spots on the hind wings, in allusion to the ancient Greek heroine, Io. **1889** *Cent.* 3178/1 Io. . . . A showy and beautiful moth of North America, *Hyperchiria io*, or *Saturnia io*, of yellow coloration, with prominent pink and bluish eyes on the hinder wings. **1912** Stratton-Porter *Moths of Limberlost* 207 Mr. Eisen presented me with a pair of Hyperchiria Io. . . . Because the Io was yellow, I wanted it.

Iowa ˈaɪəwə, *n.* [App. f. Dakota *Ayuba*, sleepy ones, applied to the Iowa Indians in ridicule. The *pl.* is either Iowa or Iowas.] An Indian of a Siouan tribe formerly occupying parts of Minnesota, Iowa, and Missouri, but now on reservations in Kansas and Oklahoma. Usu. *pl.* with reference to the tribe.

1805 Pike *Sources Miss.* (1810) App. to I. (1810) 2 This place would be a central position for a trading establishment, for the Sacs, Reynards, Iowas of the de Moyen. **1857** *Richmond* (Va.) *W. Whig* 5 Sep. 2/3 The Iowas realized about 185 thousand dollars. **1907** Hodge *Amer. Indians* I. 612/2 The Sioux have a tradition . . . that when their ancestors first came to the falls of St. Anthony, the Iowa occupied the country about the mouth of Minnesota r. **1942** Priest *Uncle Sam's Stepchildren* 139 Agent Lightfoot of the Iowas reported the appointment of tribal police in 1869.

attrib. **1810** *Ann. 12th Congress* 1 Sess. II. 1858 An Iowa Indian informs me, that two years ago this Summer, an agent from the British arrived at the Prophet's town. **1839** Van Buren in *Pres. Mess. & P.* III. 512 Lay before you . . . a treaty concluded with the Omaha, Ioway, and Otoe tribes of Indians. **1944** *Sat. Ev. Post* 9 Sep. 82/3 One treaty made with the Iowa Indians in 1836 agreed 'to erect for the Ioways five comfortable houses, to enclose and break up for them two hundred acres of ground.'

b. *pl.* Cattle from Iowa. *Rare.*

1884 *Harper's Mag.* July 298/2 They were driven away before a splendid pen of corn-fed 'Iowas' near by had found a purchaser.

c. In the names of plants and trees associated with the state of Iowa.

1853 *Knickerb.* XLII. 202 Then hoe the corn, (Iowa-white, an esteemed present, that hung all winter long from the buck-horns in our town-sanctum,) which is now higher than our head by four inches. **1862** *Rep. Comm. Patents 1861: Agric.* 190 *Fragaria Iowensis*—Iowa strawberry. **1897** Sudworth *Arborescent Flora* 209 *Pyrus ioensis.* . . . Iowa Crab.

d. Iowa marble, (see quot.).

1852 Owen *Geol. Survey Wis.* 79 To the imbedded specimens of this beautiful, star-like polypifer is a portion of the Iowa limestone indebted for that appearance of great beauty, when highly polished, which has procured it the name of 'Iowa marble.'

Iowan ˈaɪəwən, *n.* and *a.*

1. *n.* A native or inhabitant of Iowa.

1856 N. H. Parker *Iowa as It Is* 56 Our ferry is busy all hours in passing over the large canvas-backed wagons densely populated with becoming Iowaians. **1909** Parker *G. Cleveland* 134 Delegations of Iowans . . . had come to town in great force. **1948** *Sat. Ev. Post* 10 July 68/3 Calmer heads shushed the rampant Iowans back into their seats.

2. *a.* Of or pertaining to Iowa; also, in geology, with reference to one of the subdivisions of the Glacial period.

1894 J. Geikie *Gt. Ice Age* (ed. 3) 735 The chief track of the current from the Hudsonian centre was down the Dakotan and central Iowan basins. **1899** *U.S. Geol. Surv. Water Supp. Paper 21*, 10 The Iowan drift sheet may be present underneath later drift sheets in the northern portion of Indiana. **1948** *Canadian Alpine Jrnl.* June 3 At that time Glacier was full of patient, sodden Iowan mountaineers with whom, I couldn't help thinking, I should probably be glad to exchange lots in a day or two.

ipecac ˈɪpɪˌkæk, *n.* [f. * *ipecacuanha.*] Any one of various North American plants (see quot. 1931), the roots of which have emetic properties; also a medicinal preparation from roots of one of these or from the South American ipecacuanha. Cf. **wild ipecac.**

1710 Byrd *Secret Diary* (1941) 133 My daughter . . . had a fever, for which I gave her a vomit of the tincture of ipecac. **1788** Cutler in *Life & Corr.* I. 409 Examined several vegetables, the Pawpaw, Ipecac, Redbud, Spanish Oak, Honey-locust. **1852** *Fla. Plant Rec.* 80 It seames Like Nothing will brake the Fever hear Except Calomel, Ippecac and Qinine. **1876** Habberton *Jericho Road* 12 One day he was half mad with whisky, and went to the drug-store and ordered two ounces of arsenic, but the clerk gave him ipecac. **1931** Clute *Plants* 124 Six plants are called ipecac and none of them is the true one. . . . The two more important of these are *Gillenia trifoliata* and *Triosteum perfoliatum.*

attrib. **1772** in *W. & M. Coll. Quart.* XIII. 221 Perhaps a little Ipecac tea . . . w'd have saved the child. **1803** *Med. Repository* 18 He then took an ounce of Ipecac. wine, which operated three times.

* **ipecacuanha,** *n.* =prec.

*c***1729** Catesby *Carolina* I. 24 *Anapodophyllon Canadense Morini* Tournef. The May Apple. This Plant grows about a Foot and half high. . . . The root is said to be an excellent Emetic, and is used as such in Carolina; which has given it there the Name of Ipecacuana, the stringy Roots of which it resembles. **1788** Cutler in *Life & Corr.* I. 427 Found vast quantities of Ipecacuanha on a hill. **1896** *Garden & Forest* IX. 282 Ipecacuanha. . . . A name for several North American plants, of which the roots, like those of the officinal *Cephaëlis*, possess emetic qualities (*Podophyllum, Euphorbia, Gillenia,* etc.).

b. ipecacuanha spurge, a spurge, *Tithymalopsis ipecacuanhae*, found in the eastern states.

1832 Williamson *Maine* I. 125 *Ipecacuanha-spurge* has a large pulpous root. . . . It is a powerful emetic.

Ipswich sparrow. (See quot. 1917.) — **1892** Torrey *Foot-Path Way* 54 The Ipswich sparrow . . . I have now seen at Nahant . . . from October to April. **1917** *Birds of Amer.* III. 24 Ipswich Sparrow, *Passerculus princeps*, . . . is a songless Sparrow which . . . seems to have been first discovered near Ipswich, Mass, in 1868.

irene aɪˈrin, *n.* (See quot.) *Obs.* — **1853** *Alta California* (S.F.) 25 April 1/7 These watches are made of an alloy called here 'Irene,' which is a corruption from 'airain,' French for brass.

* **Irish,** *a.*

1. Of places: Settled by Irish immigrants. *Obs.*

1800 Tatham *Agric. & Commerce* 150 That powerful extent of rich and fertile vales, called the Irish Tract, that populous country which is situated between the Blue and Allegany ridges. **1809** Cuming *Western Tour* 177 Passing Millersburgh, and one of the first settlements, called the Irish station, . . . I spurred my horse past Nicholasville Court house.

2. In special combs.: (1) **Irish-American,** see as a main entry; (2) **dividend,** (see quot.), *rare;* (3) **grey,** a variety of Irish potato, *obs.;* (4) **hint,** a very broad hint, *rare;* (5) **hoist,** an awkward fall (see quot. 1843), *colloq.;* (6) * **man,** (see quot.), *obs.;* (7) **pendant,** (see quot.), *obs.;* (8) **spoon,** a shovel, *humorous;* (9) **trot,** (see quot.), *obs.*

(2) **1881** *Harper's Mag.* May 805/2 Members [of the N. Y. Philharmonic Society] found themselves in debt and obliged to declare an 'Irish dividend' to make the accounts balance. — (3) **1852** Regan *Emigrant's Guide* 255 The early whites were ripe full two weeks sooner than any of the others, the Meshanocks next, then Irish greys, then pink-eyes. — (4) **1834** Nott *Novellettes* I. 8 Various young men, . . . intimated, in what might be called Irish hints that they had espied the worthy Mr. Hunt.

(5) *c***1800** *Boston* 120 In this amusement they not only often get what they call an 'Irish hoist' themselves, but are the occasion of dangerous falls to all who are obliged to pass such places. **1843** *Yale Lit. Mag.* VIII. 363 Ephraim . . . projected him from the extremity of his indignant foot, through a curved line, which has received the technical appellation, 'Irish hoist,' but what its mathematical properties are, has never yet been discovered. — (6) **1709** Lawson *Carolina* 159 The flat or mottled Pearch are shaped almost like a Bream. They are called Irish-men, being freckled or mottled with black, and blue spots. — (7) **1840** Dana *Two Years* xxii. 221 There was no rust, no dirt, no rigging hanging slack, no fag ends of ropes and 'Irish pendants' aloft. — (8) **1862** Norton *Army Lett.* 73 One company just passed armed with 'Irish spoons,' going out to work in the trenches. — (9) **1824** J. Doddridge *Notes* 158, I remember to have seen once or twice, a dance which was called 'The Irish Trot' but I have long since forgotten its figure.

b. *As black as an Irish spinning wheel*, quite black. *Rare.*

1837 *S. Lit. Messenger* III. 387 A few half dead coals . . . seemed to be expiring with despair at the idea of being expected to kindle a few round pine logs laid above them which looked as comfortless aye and as black too as an *Irish spinning-wheel.*

Irish-American, *a.* and *n.*

1. *n.* A person born in Ireland who becomes a U.S. citizen; the child of such a citizen.

1836 T. Power *Impressions Amer.* I. 185 The accent of the Irish American . . . differ[s little] from that of the settler of a year. **1900** *Cong. Rec.* 14 Feb. 1799/1 Out on the prairies of that great State [Missouri], . . . we do not hear any such terms as German-American, Irish-American . . . or French American. Such terms are, and ought to be, offensive. **1947** *Chi. Tribune* 4 July 3/1 More than 20,000 Irish-Americans are expected to attend the fete.

b. Language such as Irish-Americans use.

1910 *Sat. Ev. Post* 27 Aug. 35/2 Father Tieren . . . spoke Calabrian Italian almost as well as he spoke Irish American.

2. *a.* Of or pertaining to Irish immigrants in the U.S.

1832 *N.-Eng. Mag.* June 490 Irish-American Literature. **1900** *Cong. Rec.* 15 Jan. 805/1 The great body of our German and Irish American citizens are in favor of it.

***iron,** *n.* and *a.*

1. The rails of a railroad. Cf. **iron car.**

1833 *Amer. R.R. Jrnl.* II. 532/2 All the iron would have been on. **1851** *De Bow's Review* X. 339 The iron for the entire road . . . is at the depot. **1885** *Santa Fe Wkly. New Mexican* 30 July 4/3 Nearly a mile of iron has been laid on this end of the Los Angeles & San Gabriel valley railroad.

2. In combs.: (1) **iron belt,** a region throughout which iron is produced; (2) **car,** a car on which railroad rails are transported in track-laying operations; (3) **county,** a county in which iron is extensively produced; (4) **fence,** a fence made of iron rods, bars, etc.; (5) **horse,** a locomotive, also transf.; (6) **Indian,** the iron figure of an Indian used as the figurehead of a steamboat, *obs.;* (7) **king,** one who has become wealthy in the iron industry; (8) **knuckles,** =**brass knuckles,** *obs.;* (9) **lock office,** app. a small, often rural, post office not provided with a rotary lock such as is used for registered mail; (10) **lung,** a large metal cylinder arranged to encompass the trunk of a patient whose powers of respiration are impaired, rhythmic alternations of air pressure within the cylinder simulating normal respiratory movements, used esp. in certain cases of infantile paralysis; (11) **ore baron,** =**iron king;** (12) **road,** a railroad, esp. one serving an iron-producing region; (13) **-sides,** *fig.* designating Primitive or Hard-Shell Baptists, *rare,* cf. **Old Ironsides;** (14) **store,** a store dealing in iron products; (15) **-tooth harrow,** a harrow the teeth of which are of iron; (16) **trail,** a railroad.

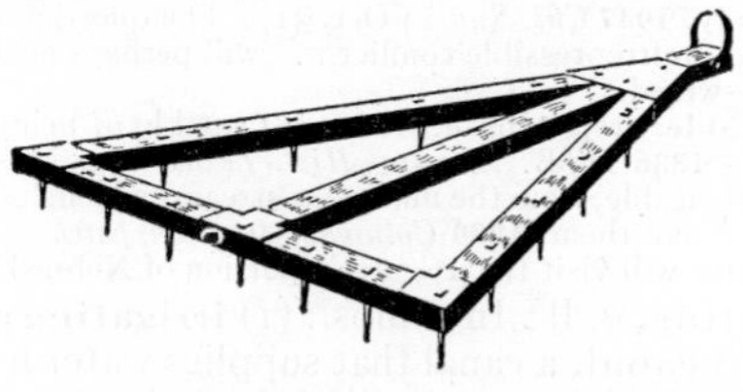

Iron-tooth harrow

(1) **1902** Harben *A. Daniel* 137 She said she knew one [branch railroad] in the iron belt in Alabama that didn't own a car or an engine. — (2) **1872** Huntington *Road-Master's Ass't* 23 It is customary, with most track-layers, to curve iron by dropping it as it is drawn from the iron cars, when laying it. — (3) **1844** *Whig Almanac 1845* 5/1 Mr. Polk received large majorities in nearly every Iron County of New-York, New-Jersey and Pennsylvania. — (4) **1847** *Santa Fe Republican* 24 Sep. 1/4 Iron Fences are becoming common in the U. States, and will soon be made cheap. **1949** *Nat. Geog. Mag.* Feb. 207 It once sold for less than the cost of the iron fence which surrounds it.

(5) **1839** March *Yankee Land* (1840) 24 While other steeds must be champing hay, Must repose by night, and be fed by day, Let the Iron Horse have his level way, And he asks for only his fire and water. **1949** *L.A. Times* 26 April 20/3 These Iron Horses that have their noses stuck in the roundhouse are all styles and sizes. — (6) **1908** S. E. White *Riverman* xxvi. 227 [A steamboat] two-storied, with twin smokestacks, an iron Indian on her top. **1911** ——— *Bobby Orde* i. (1916) 27 In a moment appeared the *Lucy Belle,* . . . Bobby could make out . . . the swaying iron Indian with bent bow. — (7) **1887** *Courier-Journal* 20 Jan. 4/3 If the correspondent will look around Washington, . . . he will find plenty of kings—lumber kings, coal kings, iron kings. — (8) **1868** *N.Y. Herald* 30 July 8/1 Oscar Bass was arrested . . . on the charge of having secreted in his coat pocket a pair of iron knuckles. **1895** *Chi. Strike of 1894* 293, I arrested this man and found on him a policeman's club and a pair of iron knuckles. — (9) **1887** *Postal Laws* 418 If such a pouch, properly labeled, is left by mistake at an iron-lock office, it should be forwarded unopened by first mail to destination.

(10) **1936** *Dly. Oklahoman* 6 Dec. 12/5 The boy, encased in the lately-installed 'iron lung' at St. John's hospital, died after a heart attack. **1949** *Newsweek* 9 May 52/3 As yet doctors considered it too early to reach any conclusions as to the value of the new device in replacing the iron lung. — (11) **c1888** *Chi. Inter-Ocean* (F., p. 40/2), I have observed in all the 'steam rail baron's' reply to 'fair trade' that he calls upon the 'iron ore barons,' . . . to aid him. — (12) **1851** E. S. Wortley *Travels U.S.* 142 As to the cows, they seem to think the iron-road was especially intended for them. **1880** *Harper's Mag.* Oct. 722/2 On all the iron roads the freight trains were made . . . to be concentrated on the lines leading into Chicago. — (13) **1901** *Scribner's Mag.* XXIX. 398/2 Mountaineers . . . are for the most part Methodists and Baptists—sometimes Ironsides—feet-washing Baptists. — (14) **1837** W. Jenkins *Ohio Gaz.* 138 There are . . . 3 hardware stores . . . 3 wholesale and many retail grocery stores, 1 iron store [etc.]. **1849** Chamberlain *Ind. Gazetteer* 199 There are now in Covington fourteen dry goods stores, two drug stores, four groceries, two iron stores.

(15) **1850** in Turner *Cotton* (1865) 32 There will be a narrow ridge of earth, not covered by the fresh earth, but I invariably run an iron-tooth harrow along the ridge, so as to break clods, and rake off pieces of stalk and to leave the ridge fresh. — (16) **1923** J. H. Cook *On Old Frontier* 215 The story . . . would have added so much to our knowledge of the Indian life west of the Missouri River before the building of wagon roads and iron trails through the land of the Sioux. **1927** James *Cow Country* 143 Pretty soon there was plenty of wagon tracks to be seen; them wagon tracks had branched out both ways from the iron trails and was scattering out on their range, bringing settlers.

b. In combs. sufficiently explained in the quots., as (1) **Iron City,** (2) **Iron-Jacket Baptist,** (3) **Iron State.**

(1) **1853** Bunn *Old Eng. & N. Eng.* 100 We told you . . . that New York was one of the dirtiest places we ever happened to have been in, but the Iron City (as Pittsburg is called), . . . throws it completely into the shade. **1887** *Courier-Journal* 8 May 16 (*advt.*), The Iron City! . . . South Pittsburg, Tenn., . . . is the manufacturing center of the world-famed Sequachee Valley. — (2) **1885** *Cent. Mag.* March 678 He kin preach all round any o' yer Meth'dist bible-bangers 'at ever I see, don't keer ef ye do call 'im a Hardshell, an' a Forty-gallon, an' a' Iron-Jacket Baptus. — (3) **1846** *Knickerb.* XXVII. 205 Large numbers [of Moravians] came to Pennsylvania, and the civilization of the Iron State is not a little indebted to the simple-hearted Hernhutters. **1854** *Locomotive Sk.* 104 Pennsylvania may well be called the Iron State of the Union.

c. In the names of plants and animals: (1) **ironhead,** (*a*) the goldeneye duck, (*b*) the wood ibis, *Mycteria americana;* (2) ***oak,** any one of various American oaks, as the post oak, *Quercus stellata,* cf. **white iron oak;** (3) **wood,** any one of various North American trees, esp. the hornbeam and the hop hornbeam, also attrib.

(1) (*a*) **1888** G. Trumbull *Names of Birds* 79 At Morehead, N.C. [the American goldeneye, *Glaucionetta clangula americana,* is called] Iron-head. (*b*) **1917** *Birds of Amer.* I. 179 'Goard Head,' 'Iron Head' and 'Gannet' are the appellations given to these birds by many swamp-dwellers to whom the name Wood Ibis is unknown. — (2) **1814** Pursh *Flora Amer.* II. 632 The Upland White Oak, or Iron Oak is a spreading tree about fifty or sixty feet high; its timber is of great value in ship-building. **1897** Sudworth *Arborescent Flora* 154 *Quercus minor* . . . [called] Iron Oak (Del., Miss., Nebr.).—(3) **1762** Clayton *Flora Virginica* 151 Nostratibus Iron-wood, Belgis Noveboracensibus Yzerhout. **1814** Pursh *Flora* II. 624 Ostrya virginica. . . . It is generally known under the name of Iron-wood; in some parts they call it Lever-wood. **1942** Cannon *Mountain* 2 There were weeds now, but there weren't any seedlings—poplar, witch hazel, and iron-wood bushes.

For ***ironclad,** ***ironman, iron mountain,** ***ironweed,** see as main entries.

As the last term in **Baltimore, band, blazing, fire-bed, flip, hollow, marking, medicine, Northwestern, plow, railroad, running, sand, sheet, shooting, spiegel, stone coal, strap, talking, waffle iron.**

***iron,** *v. tr.* To provide (a railroad roadbed) with rails. *Obs.* or *hist.* — **1833** *Amer. R.R. Jrnl.* II. 532 The road is now ironed a distance of 100 miles. **1945** *Ala. Hist. Quart.* Spring 38 The land received by the Mobile and Ohio was valued at approximately two million dollars—a sum said to be sufficient in that day to 'iron' the road.

*** ironclad,** *a.* and *n.*

1. *n. transf.* (See quots.)

1867 EDWARDS *Shelby* 483 The West Pointers were the iron-clads in our wooden navy. **1889** MARK TWAIN *Conn. Yankee* xxxix. 503 Things began to look serious to the ironclads [i.e., knights in armor]. **1892** O. F. WHITNEY *Hist. Utah* I. 547 The ravages of the 'iron-clads' [i.e., grasshoppers] were wide-spread and far-reaching.

2. *a.* Of plants and trees: Able to resist cold.

1872 *Vt. Bd. Agric Rep.* I. 54 Currants and gooseberries are iron clad as regards climate. **1882** *Maine Bd. Agric. Rep.* XXVI. 336 It is an early winter fruit, the tree not perfectly 'iron clad,' notwithstanding its origin, yet hardy enough for most places.

3. ironclad oath, (see quot. 1914).

[**1865** *Civilian & Telegraph* (Cumberland, Md.) 2 Nov. 2/4 He went through all the oaths but the 'iron-clad.'] **1866** *Cong. Globe* 14 Feb. 835/1 Traitors never would be troubled with the 'iron-clad oath,' for they never would have a chance to take it. **1914** *Cyclo. Amer. Govt.* II. 239 *Iron-Clad Oath,* a name given the stringent oath of office prescribed by Congress in 1862 and applied at the close of the Civil War for office holders in the reconstructed states. It aimed at the exclusion of all who had participated in the 'rebellion.'

b. *transf.* (See quots.)

1873 MILLER *Amongst Modocs* xxvi. 304 Some hard, iron-clad oaths and then shot after shot. **1900** *Cong. Rec.* 25 Jan. 1207/1 Members-elect . . . could be kept out by the exaction of an iron-clad oath.

*** iron man.**

1. A petrified man. *Rare.*

1847 *Fredericksburg* (Va.) *Semi-Wkly. News* 11 Oct. 2/3 On Saturday week a gentleman brought into Portsmouth, [Ohio] from the Bloom Furnace, Scioto county, a portion of an *iron man,* found in the *ore bed.*

2. A dollar. *Slang.*

1915 *Everybody's Mag.* Oct. 450/2 If we win will he come through with transportation back to that dear Southern California and two hundred large iron men on the side. **1945** *This Week Mag.* 21 April 15/2 When I'd given the boys back their dough I had a nice little profit of two hundred iron men.

3. A man of superior endurance, used esp. of baseball pitchers (see quot. 1931). *Slang.*

1914 *Collier's* 31 Jan. 28/2 He took pride in his mastery of the pitching art, in the reputation he bore as 'the iron man.' **1931** *Atlantic City News* 7 Aug. 20/1 The term 'iron-man' is applied solely to pitchers and refers to those hurlers who have shown the stamina and power to pitch either a double-header or two games in successive days. **1938** *L.A. Times* 9 Aug. 13/1 Charles Melhorn of U.C.L.A., Ray Wood of the Pasadena 'Y' and Charles Lovell of Pasadena are the other iron men in the contest to date.

iron mountain. A mountain rich in iron ore.

1838 *Boston Wkly. Mag.* 24 Nov. 91/1 Having visited the Iron Mountain in Missouri in October last I am happy to add my testimony to that of numerous observers by whom I have been preceded, respecting the remarkable deposites of iron ores. **1846** *Sci. Amer.* 12 Dec. 90/1 The new blast furnace at the iron mountain is again in blast. **1854** WHIPPLE *Prelim. Rep. Explor. Ry. Route* 13 The iron mountains [of Ark.] near the Missouri line are alone worthy a railroad.

*** ironweed,** *n.* Any one of various plants of the genus *Vernonia.* Cf. **devil's, western ironweed.**

1816 D. THOMAS *Travels Western Country* (1819) 231 The *iron-weed,* which I first saw above Pittsburgh, extends on clayey lands all the way to the Wabash. **1835** AUDUBON *Ornith. Biog.* III. 56 Locusts . . . were gathered by boys from the trunks of trees and the 'iron weeds,' a species of wild hemp very abundant in that portion of the country. **1949** *Chi. Tribune* 9 Jan. VI. 5/8 In September there are the iron-weed, goldenrod, and composite groups.

b. ironweed aster, a frost flower.

1913 EATON *Barn Doors & Byways* 259 They held little blue asters, sometimes called iron weed asters, . . . which flower after the frost, [and] hold a faintly faded blue of summer in their tiny petals.

Iroquoian ˌɪrəˈkwɔɪən, *a.* Of or pertaining to the Iroquois.

1917 MOOREHEAD *Stone Ornaments Amer. Indian* 170 A surface find in the Iroquoian area in New York is no sure indication that the artifact is Iroquoian. **1943** PEATTIE *Great Smokies* 22 The Cherokees belong to the Iroquoian linguistic stock. **1946** *Nat. Geog. Mag.* Jan. 54/1 The Iroquoian language was represented in the Southeast principally by the important Cherokee tribe, which inhabited the southern Appalachians from northern Georgia and Alabama to West Virginia, and by the Tuscarora confederation of North Carolina.

Iroquois ˈɪrəˌkwɔɪ, *n. sing. & pl.* [F. (note the *-ois* suffix) f. Algonquin *Irinakoiw,* real adders.]

1. The Five Nations *q.v.* or an Indian belonging to one of the tribes included in this.

[**1603** CHAMPLAIN *Œuvres* (1870) II. 9 Lesdicts Irocois . . . sont en plus grand nombre que lesdicts Montagnés.] **1826** COOPER *Mohicans* v, Every Indian who speaks a foreign tongue is an Iroquois, whether the castle of his tribe be in Canada, or be in York. **1854** *S. Lit. Messenger* XX. 396 The Iroquois never made themselves felt south of the northern border of Virginia. **1949** *Nat. Geog. Mag.* Aug. 155/2 A few tribes, among them the Hidatsa, Manda, Omaha, Pawnee, Ponca, and Iroquois, have been known to grow sweet corn.

attrib. **1666** *Doc. N.Y. Col. Hist.* III. 134 The Irocquois Indians should not comit any Act of hostilety. **1764** H. GRACE *Hist. Life & Sufferings* 31 We crossed the River to the Iroquois Nation. **1896** WILKINS *Madelon* 11 The first Hautville . . . had espoused an Iroquois Indian girl. **1949** *Chi. D. News* 25 March 45/4 The Iroquois Confederacy . . . was also known as the Five Nations and later as the Six Nations. According to tradition the Confederacy was formed by Hiawatha about the beginning of the 15th century.

b. In phrasal use (see quot.). *Obs.*

1872 W. H. VENABLE *School Hist. U.S.* 19 To say 'as savage as an Iroquois warrior' is to exhaust the power of simile.

2. The Iroquoian language. Also attrib. *Obs.*

1713 in SWIFT *Works* XVI. (1883) 27 Lest you should not have your Iroquoise Dictionary at hand, 'Brother, I honour you and all your tribe.' **1722** COXE *Descr. Carolana* 55 The name of this Lake [Ontario] in the *Irocois* Language (that Nation bordering upon it to the south) signifies that pleasant or beautiful Lake, as it may be deservedly stil'd. **1836** J. HALL *Stat. West* ii. 22 The idea . . . that the word Ohio is derived from the Iroquois language, is not correct. **1851** *Harper's Mag.* Aug. 390/2 He fancied he heard her mutter in Iroquois one word—'revenged!'

*** irredeemable,** *a.* Of paper money: Not convertible into cash.

1790 HAMILTON *Works* II. 78 The subscriber . . . [is entitled] to have the whole sum funded at an annuity or yearly interest of four per cent., irredeemable by any payment exceeding five dollars per annum. **1837** D. WEBSTER *Works* (1851) I. 374, I abhor paper; that is to say, irredeemable paper, paper that may not be converted into gold or silver at the will of the holder. **1884** BLAINE *20 Years of Congress* I. 429 A government cannot . . . maintain a state of solvency by the continuous issuing of irredeemable paper.

*** irrepressible,** *n.*

1. One who believed that the conflict over slavery was irrepressible. *Rare.* Cf. next.

1860 *S.F. Times* 9 June 1/2 We know of but one way to beat Seward, and that is to take Lincoln, as Lincoln is an 'irrepressible,' like Seward.

2. irrepressible conflict, the conflict between freedom and Negro slavery; the Civil War. Also transf.

1858 SEWARD *Works* IV. 292 This collision . . . is an irrepressible conflict between opposing and enduring forces, and it means that the United States must . . . become either entirely a slaveholding nation, or entirely a free-labor nation. **1881** *Cong. Rec.* 28 April 418/2 Another 'irrepressible conflict' has arisen in this country . . . between the people for their liberties, and arrogant, bloated corporate power and monopoly. **1947** *Chi. Sun* 14 Oct. 31/1 The question of whether or not it was an irrepressible conflict . . . will perhaps never be satisfactorily answered.

irrigatable ˈɪrəˌgetəbḷ, *a.* Of land: Capable of being irrigated, irrigable. — **1836** D. B. EDWARD *Hist. Texas* i. 40 Most of these lands are irrigatable, from the numerous streams which flow down the mountains above them. **1889** *Columbus* (O.) *Dispatch* 24 July, The sub-committee will visit the irrigatible portion of Nebraska.

*** irrigating,** *a. W.* In combs.: (1) **irrigating acequia,** =next; (2) **canal,** a canal that supplies water for irrigating farm lands; (3) **ditch,** a ditch for irrigating a field.

(**1**) **1883** W. G. RITCH *N. Mex.* 78 At other periods the volume of water is so depleted by irrigating acequias and by evaporation, as to render steam . . . necessary [for power]. — (**2**) **1866** *Rep. Indian Affairs* 120 The first thing necessary to insure success is an irrigating canal. **1948** *Chi. D. News* 3 Jan. 7/6 The valley is a network of bright green fields latticed by 3,000 miles of irrigating canals. — (**3**) **1854** *Harper's Mag.* April 582/2 The numerous irrigating ditches . . . are the inseparable assistants of New Mexican agriculture. **1912** *Out West* May 309/1 Ben Larkin was busy repairing a break in one of his irrigating ditches.

*** irrigation,** *n.*

1. *W.* Refreshment by means of alcoholic liquor. *Slang. Obs.*

1856 DERBY *Phoenixiana* 162 Being of a naturally arid disposition, and perhaps requiring irrigation at that particular moment, you unguardedly invite Brown, and your new friend Jones of course, to step over to Parry and Battens, and imbibe.

2. In combs. relating to irrigating lands in the West, as (1) **irrigation bill,** (2) **district,** (3) **ditch,** (4) **pump,** (5) **rancher,** (6) **valley.**

(1) **1909** O. HENRY *Roads of Destiny* 91 Senator Kinney had an irrigation bill that he wanted passed. — (2) **1945** *Dly. Sentinel* (Grand Junction, Colo.) 27 Nov. 6/5 Property owners under the Orchard Mesa Irrigation district will elect a member of the board. — (3) **1870** HUNT *Own Story* (MS) 1 Irrigation ditches were dug for as much of the land as could be covered with water. **1949** *Lubbock* (Tex.) *Morn. Avalanche* 23 Feb. 1. 10/3 The cash boxes were . . . buried in a hole . . . near an irrigation ditch along a fence row on Watts' farm. — (4) **1890** *Stock Grower & Farmer* 22 March 6/2, 75,000 gallons of water raised 20 feet at an expense of 100 lbs. of soft coal seems wonderful. The Greely Irrigation Pump does it, just the same.

(5) **1910** PINCHOT *Fight for Conservation* 31, I have been impressed with the peculiar advantages which surround the irrigation rancher. — (6) **1913** LONDON *Valley of Moon* III. xvi, Let them hunt their white sparrows in the Sacramento islands and the irrigation valleys.

irrigationist ɪrəˈgeʃənɪst, *n.* One who favors the extension of irrigation, or who employs irrigation in growing crops.

1887 *Detroit Free Press* 21 May 2/4 Of interest to irrigationists. **1926** BRANCH *Cowboy* 114 'Nesters'—irrigationists and dry-farmers—had not preempted lands. **1949** *S.F. News* 14 March 14/1 Three state officials . . . have appeared before Congress in favor of legislation which would have the effect of greatly increasing the cost to irrigationists of Central Valley water.

* **Isabella,** *n.* [See quot. 1832.] A cultivated variety of the northern fox grape, *Vitis labrusca*, or the fruit of such a variety. Also attrib. In full **Isabella grape.**

1831 *Boston Transcript* 22 Sep. 2/1 *Mr. David Fosdick,* Charlestown; [exhibited] White Muscadine and Isabella Grapes. **1832** *Ib.* 7 July 2/2 The Isabella vine . . . was introduced into Brooklyn, from North Carolina, by Mrs Isabella Gibbs, the lady of George Gibbs Esq, now of St Augustine, Florida. **1846** *Knickerb.* XXVII. 419 A snaky-looking vine . . . from which glorious bunches of Catawbas and Isabellas may be gathered. **1890** HOWELLS *Shadow of Dream* 49 Over staggering trellises the grape-vines clung, and dangled imperfect bunches of Isabellas and Concords. **1949** *Amer. Photography* April 244/1 *Vitis labrusca* . . . has furnished the catawba, . . . the Concord, . . . and the Isabella.

* **isinglass,** *n.* **1.** (See quot.) **2. isinglass land,** (see quot.). Both *obs.*

(1) **1776** in *Boston Pub. Lib. Bul.* (Oct., 1902) 427 People *here* [Boston] don't mind giving the most extravagant prices for Goods and seem uneasy untile they have exchanged their *Oacum & Issinglass*, as it is called, meaning the Continental Money, for Articles which in their Opinion are of more sure worth. — (2) *c***1800** STRICKLAND *Observations* 14 Inland of this tract in Jersey and Pennsylvania, is a dry, rising, irregular country, consisting chiefly of what is here called isinglass land, a sandy soil full of micaceous particles, glimmer, and tale.

* **island,** *n.*

1. A piece of ground rising from a level tract, a hill. *Obs.*

1638 *Dedham Rec.* III. 51 Abraham Shawe selleth vnto Ferdinando Adam one portion of Grownd called an hill or Iland as it lyeth to his home lott. **1703** *Providence Rec.* V. 61 A little Island of upland in sd meaddow. **1802** *Mass. H.S. Coll.* 1 Ser. VIII. 112 There are on it [a ridge] one or two hills, which the neighboring inhabitants call islands.

2. A grove or clump of trees in a plain or prairie.

1656 *Southold Rec.* I. 42 Ten acres of meadow . . . buting against a little creeke at the east end, and to an Island of trees on the West. **1853** F. W. THOMAS *J. Randolph* 61 Here and there, arising from the immense body of the prairie, were what are called islands—that is, great clumps of trees, covering sometimes many acres. **1902** S. E. WHITE *Blazed Trail* ix. 63 The pine there grew thick on isolated 'islands' of not more than an acre or so in extent,—little knolls rising from the level of a marsh. **1948** *Sat. Ev. Post* 4 Dec. 34/1 The fall-cast green earth ran off in the gentle meadow vistas, here and there interrupted by low knobs and little islands of timber.

3. In combs.: (1) **Island City,** New York City; (2) **island cotton,** (see quot.), *obs.;* (3) **grape,** (see quot.), *obs.;* (4) **money,** interest-bearing paper money authorized in March, 1780, by the Pennsylvania assembly (see quots.), *obs.;* (5) **State,** Rhode Island, *rare.*

(1) **1848** *Literary Amer.* 23 Sep. 189/1 You remember how gloriously the sun sent forth his rays, this morning, over the Island City. **1855** M. THOMPSON *Doesticks' Letters* 57, I left . . . the sweet retiracy of the swamps of Michigan, to become a denizen of the Island City. — (2) **1802** DRAYTON *S. Carolina* 134 That raised on lands adjacent to the sea and salt water, called *island* or *sea shore cotton*, being black seed, is preferred to the *green seed* cotton. — (3) **1775** CRESSWELL *Journal* 115 Went over the Alligany River with Mr. Douglas to get Island Grapes. This is a small grape and grows on low vines on the gravelly beeches and Islands in River. — (4) **1874** SCHUCKERS *Finances & Paper Money of Rev. War* 89 The assembly set apart as a further security a number of city lots in Philadelphia and the Province Island. . . . Hence the emission was called 'the Island money.' **1892** W. G. SUMNER *Financier & Finances of Amer. Rev.* I. 97 The so-called 'island money' of Pennsylvania became as good as specie or better, because it bore interest, and the amount of it which was issued was not equal to the value of the tract of land which was pledged as security for it.

(5) **1870** WHITTIER *Poetical Works* 229/1 Once more the Island State repeats The lesson that he taught her.

As the last term in **floating, grass, huckleberry, prairie, ragged, Rhode, Rogue's, sea, Staten, swamp, willow, wooden island.**

* **islander,** *n.* As the last term in **Long, off, Rhode Islander.**

islay izˈlaɪ, *n.* [Amer. Sp. in same sense.] A California plum tree, *Prunus ilicifolia*. Also its cherrylike fruit or the juice of this.

1857 HAYES *Pioneer Notes* (1929) 230 Somebody has gathered for Miss Schiller the branches of the *islaya*, now in bloom, and very pretty. **1893** *Amer. Folk-Lore* VI. 140 *Prunus ilicifolia*, islay. S. Cal. and W. Arizona. **1910** JEPSON *Silva of Calif.* 253 Islay grows in the Southern Coast Ranges from San Diego to the San Jacinto River.

* **islet,** *n.* = * **island 2.** *Obs.*

1791 W. BARTRAM *Travels* 117 Interspersed with hommocks or islets of evergreen trees. **1814** BRACKENRIDGE *Views La.* 110 To the left, we behold the ocean of prairie, with islets at intervals. **1844** MOORE *Texas* 101 The remainder of the county consists of small prairies, interspersed with islets of timber.

* **isolation,** *n.* A policy on the part of the U.S. of not participating in the affairs of other nations.

1862 in J. B. MOORE *Digest International Law* VI. (1906) 23 Since that period [the time of Washington] occasions have frequently happened which presented seductions to a departure from what, superficially viewed, seemed a course of isolation and indifference. **1940** *Amer. Pol. Sci. Rev.* June 539 About the middle of the nineteenth century, interventionists, desirous that 'Young America' help actively Europe's revolutionary liberalism, called upon those less rash than themselves for an abandonment of 'isolation.'

Hence **isolationism.**

1922 *19th Cent.* Nov. 731 Her isolationism . . . discovered that the strain of a formidable advance against freedom was more than it could bear. **1948** *Time* 1 Nov. 60/2 She also broke with her father, editorially, on his isolationism.

isolationist ˌaɪsəˈleʃənɪst, *n.* One who favors a policy of political isolation for the U.S. with respect to other governments.—**1899** *Press* (Phila.) 25 March 8 Their consent ought to have been obtained first, according to the creed of the isolationists. **1949** *Newsweek* 8 Aug. 22/3 To some sensitive American isolationists this fact has made the UN itself suspect.

issuance ˈɪʃuəns, *n.* The sending out or emission of proclamations, notes, documents, etc.

1863 *National Almanac* 545/2 A proclamation of neutrality . . . was issued [May 13, 1861] by Victoria, Queen of England. . . . A brigade of British Volunteers [which] had been enlisted in the North, . . . disbanded after its issuance. **1914** *N.Y. Herald* 4 April 13/1 The definition of an American legal term caused confusion among the Appeal Judges in the High Courts [London] yesterday. . . . The President, Judge Sumner, explained that 'issuance' was a word that originated in the United States and was quite new to him. **1925** BRYAN *Memoirs* 218 In the New England States . . . the Grange . . . [demanded] the issuance of greenbacks by the Federal Government.

* **issue,** *n.*

1. The act of issuing government supplies to soldiers or Indians; supplies so issued.

1861 *Army Regulations* 283 His descriptive list, . . . on which the surgeon shall enter all payments, stoppages, and issues of clothing to him in hospital. **1881** *Rep. Indian Affairs* x, They agreed to go as soon as the issue of beef (which was in progress) had been made. **1942** DALE *Cow Country* 163 They [Indians] could not subsist upon the present issue of eighty thousand pounds a week.

2. Short for **issue cattle.** *Rare.*

1911 H. QUICK *Yellowstone* xii. 321 She hove in sight of the issue.

3. In combs.: (1) **issue cattle,** cattle given, or to be given, by the U.S. Government to reservation Indians; (2) **day,** the day upon which government supplies are issued, esp. to Indians; (3) **house,** a storehouse from which supplies are issued by the government to Indians; (4) **room,** a room in which issues of government supplies

are made to Indians; (5) **tobacco,** tobacco issued by the government to Indians.

(1) **1916** EASTMAN *From Deep Woods* 117 Moreover, the Government herd of 'issue cattle' was found to be greatly depleted. — (2) **1874** GLISAN *Jrnl. Army Life* 447 They gave the white physicians much annoyance by coming for medicine only on issue or ration day. **1915** YOUNG *Hard Knocks* 130 This ended issue day at Red Cloud Agency. — (3) **1878** *Rep. Indian Affairs* 39 Other mechanics are putting up new store and issue-houses. **1923** GARLAND *Amer. Indians* 1 The sun blazed hot in the roadway which ran between the licensed shops, the office and the issue house. — (4) **1877** *Rep. Indian Affairs* 60 A new issue room, 22 by 120 feet.

(5) **1924** *Scribner's Mag.* Dec. 651/2 He traded issue tobacco for three gallons of wine.

As the last term in **cattle, graveyard, Kansas, old, race, steamer issue.**

***it,** *pron.* In emphatic predicate use (see quots.). *Colloq.*

1900 *D.N.* II. 42 Did he know his Greek? I should say so. He was *it*. **1906** *Dly. Chron.* 5 Mar. 6/6 There is in America a curious use of the word 'it' conveyed by emphasis. Pre-eminently Roosevelt is 'it.' Next after Roosevelt an American would say 'Shaw is it.' **1915** IAN HAY *First Hundred Thousand* xx, You can't go anywhere in London without running up against him. He is It.

***Italian,** *a.* In combs., chiefly obs.: (1) **Italian-American,** a U.S. citizen of Italian birth or ancestry; (2) **chair,** (see quot. and cf. next); (3) **chaise,** (see quot.); (4) **mulberry,** (see quot. 1743), also **Italian white-fruited mulberry;** (5) **squash,** a dark-green summer squash of a long, slightly curved cylindrical shape.

(1) **1915** *Chi. Tribune* 13 Oct. 5/1 The one absolutely certain way of bringing this nation to ruin . . . would be to permit it to become a tangle of squabbling nationalities, an intricate knot of . . . Scandinavian-Americans, or Italian-Americans. **1947** *Sat. Ev. Post* 15 March 142/2 Mrs. Lodge appeared before Italian-American rallies and led them in the old songs of the homeland. — (2) **1754** *S.C. Gazette* 15–22 Jan. 2/3 Two new genteel Italian chairs, with iron axle-trees, red wings, and lined with worsted coffoy [will be sold]. — (3) **1775** BURNABY *Travels* 114 Return home in Italian chaises, (the fashionable carriages in this [N.Y.] and most parts of America, Virginia excepted, where they make use only of coaches, and these commonly drawn by six horses). — (4) **1743** CATESBY *Carolina* App. p. xxi, The Italian or silk-worm mulberry . . . [was] introduced into Virginia by Sir William Berkley. **c1790** T. COXE *View U.S.* 45 We have a large nursery of the white Italian mulberry established here this summer. **1846** BROWNE *Trees Amer.* 444 *Italian White-fruited Mulberry; Mûrier d'Italie*, of the French; with lobed leaves.

(5) **1926** *Ladies' Home Jrnl.* Nov. 149/1 Italian squash which is found in many markets at present is most satisfactory.

***itch,** *n.* As the last term in **buckwheat, ground, Kansas, prairie, seven-year, Tennessee, Texas, trigger itch.**

***item,** *n.* As the last term in **city, local, news, newspaper item.**

itemize ˈaɪtəmˌaɪz, *v. tr.* "To state in items, or by particulars; as, to *itemize* the cost of a railroad" (W. '64).

1857 PAYNE *Rep. Railroads Tenn.* 13 Itemized Cost of Road . . . Bridges and trestles, [$]340,367.23. **1919** *Detective Story Mag.* 25 Nov. 14 'Was the list itemized?' 'Not entirely. In some instances several articles were grouped under a single item.'

Hence **itemizing,** *n.* Also, rarely, in the sense of utilizing items in a newspaper.

1875 C. F. WINGATE *Views & Interviews* 190 Once, in the rage for itemizing, in '68, he told me to fill up the first page with items. **1903** *Nation* 3 Dec. LXXVII. 448/3 As *real* children display a spirit of mischief, some itemizing of pranks was called for by the title [Betty Sage's *Rhymes of Real Children*].

itemizer ˈaɪtəmˌaɪzɚ, *n.* **1.** One who writes "items" for a newspaper. **2.** One who interprets or applies single passages from the Bible without consideration of their contexts. Both *obs.* — (1) **1860** *Congregationalist* 21 Sep. (Chipman), An itemizer of the *Adams Transcript*. — (2) **1887** *Bible Soc. Rec.* Feb. 27/2 The itemizers have often been huge misinterpreters of the gospel.

Ithuriel's spear. [f. *Ithuriel*, an angel in Milton's *Paradise Lost*.] (See quot. 1889.) — **1889** *Cent.* 3203/3 Ithuriel's-spear. . . . The Californian liliaceous plant *Brodiæa* (*Triteleia*) *laxa*. **1915** M. ARMSTRONG *Field Bk. West. Wild Flowers* 24 Ithuriel's Spear. Very much like Harvest Brodiaea but rather taller. . . . Common on hillsides and in adobe fields.

***ivory,** *n.* In combs.: (1) **ivorybill,** short for **ivory-billed woodpecker;** (2) **-billed coot,** (see quot. 1889); (3) **-billed woodpecker,** the largest of the North American woodpeckers, *Campephilus principalis*, now almost extinct but surviving to some extent in central Fla.; (4) **-bill woodcock,** =prec., *obs.;* (5) **plum,** the wintergreen, *Gaultheria procumbens*, or its fruit, also the creeping snowberry, *Chiogenes hispidula*, or its fruit; (6) **tower,** *fig.* a secluded place for study and meditation [James's use of this expression (see below) was prob. inspired by F. *tour d'ivoire* which alludes to "Thy neck is a tower of ivory," in Song of Solomon 7 : 4]; (7) **type,** (see quot. 1875).

(1) **1787** *Ellicott Alman. 1788* (Winchester, Va.) B2ʳ The land fowls [of Ky.] are turkeys, pheasants, . . . the perraquet, ivory-bill, woodcock, and the great owl. **1937** *Bird Lore* Jan.–Feb. 21/2 No species of wild bird left in North America so completely personifies the spirit of the primeval forest as does the Ivory-bill. — (2) **1889** *Cent.* 3205/2 *Ivory-billed coot*, the common American coot or whitebill, *Fulica americana*. **1917** *Birds of Amer.* I. 214 Coot. *Fulica americana*. . . . Other Names. . . . Pond Hen; Mud Coot; Ivory-billed Coot. — (3) **1811** WILSON *Ornithology* IV. 20 Ivory-billed Woodpecker: *Picus principalis* . . . [has] a distinguished characteristic in the superb carmine crest and bill of polished ivory. **1946** *New Yorker* 2 March 75/1 He started his book with a 'motto,' something I thought had become almost extinct, like the ivory-billed woodpecker. — (4) **1784** FILSON *Kentucke* 26 The ivory-bill wood-cock, of a whitish colour with a white plume, flies screaming exceeding sharp. It is asserted, that the bill of this bird is pure ivory.

(5) **1828** NEAL *R. Dyer* 55 The more brilliant ivory-plumbs or clustered bunch-berries rattled among the withered herbage. **1891** *Amer. Folk-Lore* IV. 149 *Gaultheria procumbens* seems to have an almost endless variety of epithets. . . . In South Berwick, Me., . . . the berries are called *Ivory Plums*. **1892** *Ib.* V. 99 *Chiogenes serpyllifolia*, ivory plums. Washington Co., Me. — (6) **1917** HENRY JAMES (*title*), Ivory Tower. **1946** *Chi. D. News* 20 Feb. 18/3 'Marching Blacks' will be the object of much criticism both within and without the Negro race by those who see their ivory towers falling. — (7) **1860** *Charleston* (S.C.) *Mercury* 11 Dec. 1/5 In the same building I noticed very handsome specimens of ivory types and photography from Pugh Bros. & Wood. **1875** KNIGHT 1207/2 *Ivorytype*, . . . a kind of picture in which two finished photographs are taken, one light in color, made translucent by varnish, tinted on the back, and placed over a stronger picture, so as to give the effect of a photograph in natural colors.

***ivy,** *n.*

1. The mountain laurel.

1743 CLAYTON *Flora Virginica* 160 *Andromeda*. . . . The common Laurel, vulgarly called Ivy. **1832** WILLIAMSON *Maine* I. 116 [The lambkill] has been called *mountain Laurel, Spoonwood, Ivy* and *Calico Bush*. **1888** WARNER *On Horseback* 29 In this region the rhododendron is called laurel, and the laurel (the sheep-laurel of New England) is called ivy. **1943** PEATTIE *Great Smokies* 196 They assert that the great-leaved common kind is laurel, while what I call mountain laurel they call ivy.

2. Poison ivy.

1788 MAY *Jrnl. & Lett.* 65, I have been clearing land for eight days, and now begin to feel the effects of poison—from ivy, doubtless. **1848** PARKMAN in *Knickerb.* XXXI. 4 In the morning Shaw found himself poisoned by ivy.

3. ivyberry, a local name for the wintergreen.

1849 *S. Lit. Messenger* VI. 518/2 There were the fringed polygala, the butter-cup, wild geranium, bunch-plum, ivy-berry. [**1892** *Amer. Folk-Lore* V. 100 *Gaultheria procumbens*, ivy-berry. N.B.]

As the last term in **American, beach, Canadian, English, European, five-fingered, mountain, poison, spoonwood ivy.**

I.W.W., see *Industrial Workers of the World*.

iztle ˈɪstlɪ, *n. S.W.* [Amer. Sp. (<Nahuatl).] A form of obsidian once used by Indians in the Southwest for making knives, arrow points etc. — **1888** WALLACE *Land of Pueblos* 50 The old arrowheads are mainly obsidian, (*iztli*) usually black, sometimes a smoky or brown tint. *Ib.* 104 Among many trinkets offered, I chose a little looking-glass of *iztli*, and an amulet of *chalchuite* from the ruins of a prehistoric city near El Paso.

J

jacal haˈkal, *n.* Also **jackall, hackal,** etc. *S.W.* [Amer. Sp. (<Nahuatl) in sense **1.**]

1. A Mexican or Indian hut, usu. built of upright poles or sticks and plastered with mud; an adobe house or hogan. Cf. **shack,** *n.*

1838 TEXIAN *Mexico vs. Texas* 249 It was a little jacal, or cabin, built with large unburnt bricks, called *adobes,* in the language of the country. **1877** H. F. McDANIELD & N. A. TAYLOR *Coming Empire* 124 These edifices are called *jacels* . . . but the Americans call them hayricks. **1886** *Outing* IX. 111/1 Two or three miles from the line we passed an old *hackel,* or Mexican hut. **1947** *Chi. Sun Bk. Week* 8 June 2/2 But in the back alleys . . . are to be found . . . primitive jacals where human beings exist on a plane somewhat lower than that on which self-respecting farmers keep their livestock.

Also (*dim.*) **jacalito.**

1925 O. P. WHITE *Them Was Days* 214 He wended his way to his own *jacalito.*

b. A temporary shelter, similarly constructed, used by sheep herders.

1849 AUDUBON *Western Journal* (1906) 54 The ranchos are forlorn 'Jacals' (a sort of open-work shed covered with skins and rushes and plastered with mud, here so full of lime and marl that it makes a hard and lasting mortar). **1894** *Cong. Rec.* 18 Jan. 1011/1 Sheep-herders, many of whom doubtless exist in jacals, men whose employment compels them to be out on the hills among the cacti.

Jacal

2. The material or method used in building such a hut or shelter. Also **jacal built.**

1850 AUDUBON *Western Journal* (1906) 230 We . . . saw a comfortable (for this country), log and jacal built house. **1885** *Santa Fe Wkly. N. Mexican* 10 Dec. 2/6 Found on the land a very miserable shanty of jackall, unfit to be a hog pen for a fourth-class clerk. **1894–5** *Amer. Bureau Ethnol. Rep.* 108 This method is known to the Mexicans as 'jacal,' and much used by them. It consists of a row of sticks or thin poles set vertically in the ground and heavily plastered with mud.

***jack,** *n.* [See note.]

No effort is made here to relate all the senses and combinations which follow to their etymologically proper source word. For convenience of reference they are grouped together. The *OED, s.v. jack,* lists ten substantives, the ultimate origin of some being quite obscure.

1. Short for "jackass."

1785 WASHINGTON *Diaries* II. 458 Dispatched at his own reqt. the Spaniard who had the charge of my Jack from Spain. **1864** *Ohio Agric. Rep.* XVIII. 3 Ordered, that the class of Jacks and Mules be changed so as to read as follows. **1944** *Democrat* 2 Nov. 3/4 For Sale—One Tennessee jack, 12 to 14 years old, weight about 700 pounds, $250.

2. (*cap.*) = **Jacksonian,** *n. Rare.*

1830 *Boston Transcript* 31 Aug. 2/2 The masons, as the antis say, are clearly unfit for office—the Jacks are just as bad.

3. Short for "flapjack" or "applejack." *Obs.*

1832 KENNEDY *Swallow Barn* I. 57 She was usually occupied in paring apples to be baked up into tough jacks for our provender. **1850** W. RYAN *Adv. Calif.* I. 238, [I soon] set to work upon the 'jacks.' **1894** *D.N.* I. 331 In Salem, Sussex, and Burlington counties [N.J.], where apple whiskey is made, it is commonly called 'jack.' **1946** *Reader's Digest* Aug. 160/1 A New Year party for me and you with a side of beef and a gallon of jack to wash it down.

4. (See quot. 1889.)

1839 *Knickerb.* XIII. 43 The body was brought on deck, laid on the lee-gangway-board, and covered with a jack. **1889** *Cent.* 3208/3 In the United States naval service the jack is a blue flag with a white five-pointed star for each State in the Union. It is hoisted on a jack-staff at the bow-sprit-cap when in port, and is also used as a signal for a pilot when shown at the fore.

5. (*cap.*) Short for Jack Mormon *q.v. Obs.*

1845 *Quincy* (Ill.) *Whig* 25 Nov. 2/1 The Mormons and Jacks, will doubtless attempt to create the impression that the contrary is the case. **1846** *Ib.* 21 Mar. 2/4 It is asking too much of a high-minded and honest people, to retain among them a gang of thieves and rascals, that the Register and a few Jacks, may be benefited by their votes and influence in elections.

6. A portable light (see quots.) used at night by hunters and fishermen. Cf. **Jack hunt, lamp, light, shooting.**

1853 STRICKLAND *Twenty-seven Yrs.* I. 75 The usual way of catching them [i.e., salmon] is by spearing, which is done as follows.—An iron grate—or jack, as it is called by the Canadians—is made in the shape of a small cradle, composed of iron bars three or four inches apart. **1859** *Harper's Mag.* July 175/1 'A jack' composed of a bit of tin, acting as a reflector on one side and as a shade on the other, is bent round a piece of wood holding a candle. **1902** WHITE *Blazed Trail* 61 On soft moccasined feet they stole about in the evening with a bull's eye lantern fastened on the head of one of them for a 'jack.'

7. Short for jack rabbit, *q.v.*

1864 in *Kans. Hist. Quart.* VII. 9 Went to the bluffs (western Nebr.) hunting. . . . Started one 'jack' and a flock of chickens. **1948** *Life* 23 Aug. 101 Now this was corn, he was exclaiming as the jack went lolloping off.

8. (*cap.*) Short for Jack rose *q.v. Rare.*

1888 *Scribner's Mag.* Dec. 757/2 'What roses?' said Mrs. Van Corlear. 'Why, I ordered some Jacks this morning. Didn't they come?'

9. Any one of various American fish (see quots.).

1897 *Outing* XXIX. 231/2 Other game fishes of Florida are the 'jack,' or crevallé, also called carvalho. **1911** *Rep. Fisheries 1908* 311 *Jack.*—A name applied to the common pickerel (*Esox reticulatus*) in the South, to the bocaccio (*Sebastodes paucispinis*) on the Pacific Coast, and to the wall-eyed pike (*Stizostedion vitreum*) in the South. **1947** DALRYMPLE *Panfish* 271 Any one species may be a Jack, a Pickerel, a Pike, a Green Pike, Blue Pike, Grass Pike, and so on for pages.

10. Short for **lumberjack.**

*c*1900 FRANZ RICKABY *Ballads & Songs of Shanty-Boy* (1926) 97 Every jack's a cant-hook man; no others can be found. They do some heavy loggin', but they do it best in town. **1947** *Sat. Ev. Post* 8 March 20/1 The red-bearded jack came on again, head low and shielded.

11. Money. *Slang.*

App. a new development and not connected with much earlier **jack* meaning a farthing. Possibly connected with *to make one's jack, q.v.* under **12. d.** below.

1922 *Short Stories* Feb. 95/2 This Charles was a big bird. . . . He had a pile of jack. **1948** *Dly. Oklahoman* (Okla. City) 4 June 10/7 In our cockeyed civilization, there's not much jack for the jack-of-all-trades.

12. In combs.: (1) ***jackass,** a picture or representation of a donkey used as a symbol of the Democratic party, *rare,* cf. ***donkey,** *n.* **2;** (2) ***chain,** (see quot.); (3) **hammer,** *W.* a type of rock-drill used in mining; (4) **hunt,** a hunt carried on at night by means of a jack light, also **jack hunter, hunting;** (5) **knife,** see as a main entry; (6) **lamp,** =**jack light;** (7) **leg,** an incompetent workman, shyster, also attrib.; (8) **legged,** *a.* incompetent, contemptible, *slang;* (9) **legging,** (see quot.), *slang;* (10) **light,** =**jack,** *n.* **6,** cf. **jack-light,** *v.;* (11) **Jack Mormon,** a non-Mormon who is friendly toward Mormons, a half Mormon, also **Jack Mormonism;** (12) **pie,** an apple pie, *rare;* (13) **pot,** see as a main entry; (14) **rock,** *local* (see quot.); (15) **shooting,** shooting at night with a jack light; (16) **train,** a mule train.

(1) 1870 *Harper's Wkly.* 15 Jan. 48/1 [A cartoon by Thomas Nast showing a donkey, labelled 'Copperhead papers,' kicking a lion, E. M. Stanton, with the caption] A Live Jackass kicking a Dead Lion. — **(2) 1905** *Forestry Bureau Bul. 61* Jack chain. An endless spiked chain, which moves logs from one point to another, usually from the mill pond into the sawmill. — **(3) 1929** *Amer. Sp.* V. 147 The small rock-drill is a *jack-hammer* or a *plugger.* — **(4) 1881** *Harper's Mag.* Oct. 690/2 It is the only way to get venison in that season of the year which intervenes between Jack-hunting and still-hunting. **1888** *Ib.* Sep. 510/1 The jack-hunter hears them [*sc.* caribou] prowling among the bushes. **1901** W. J. STILLMAN *Autobiog. Journalist* I. 255 We had no other opportunity for the 'jack-hunt.'

(6) 1888 *Harper's Mag.* Sep. 510/1 Occasionally a caribou is killed at night by the light of a jack-lamp. — **(7) 1850** *Amer. Rev. Mag.* XI. 465/2 A party of some twenty of the most notorious rode up, headed by what is there [in Texas] known as a 'jack-leg' lawyer, who acted as leader and speaker for the party. **1853** in *Amer. Sp.* XIX. 44 In the Texan vocabulary, all men who have a mere inkling of any trade or profession are called 'jack-legs.' **1943** OTTLEY *New World* 86 The cultists were augmented by a number of herb doctors, clairvoyants, and 'jackleg' preachers. — **(8) 1839** *Cong. Globe* App. 19 Jan. 127/3 That party contains no *jack-legged pettifogging* lawyers. **1892** *Cong. Rec.* 27 May 4777/1 He goes away, and a jack-legged [army] officer could do nothing. — **(9) 1918** LINCOLN *Shavings* 133 After an hour of what he called 'putterin' and jackleggin',' he hung it [the timepiece] up again.

(10) *a***1841** W. HAWES *Sporting Scenes* I. 228 A stranger . . . presented in the glare of the jack-light an object of fear and admiration. **1883** *Chi. Advance* 30 Aug., William sat just behind the jack-light for two long hours. *Ib.*, Once after that in a jack-light hunt. **1949** *Pacific Discovery* Jan.–Feb. 11/2 We never saw them during the day and had to collect specimens at night with a jack-light.—**(11) 1845** *Quincy* (Ill.) *Whig* 30 Oct. 2/1 Jack Mormons, and sympathizers abroad may croak and groan over the poor Mormons to their heart's content, but their sympathies will not shield the scoundrels collected at Nauvoo from the just indignation of the people of Illinois. **1870** J. H. BEADLE *Life in Utah* 197 From 1850 to 1862, 'jack-Mormonism' ruled at Washington. **1947** *Time* 21 July 21/1 The number of backsliding 'jack-Mormons' is increasing. — **(12) 1857** *Harper's Mag.* Sep. 446/1 The groom went out and presently returned with ten or twelve turnovers, or Jack-pies. — **(14) 1920** THOMAS *Ky. Super.* 263 A 'bull-rock,' also called a 'jackrock' (a small round rock), in the ashes keeps hawks away from chickens.

(15) 1869 W. MURRAY *Adventures* 170 It was settled that we should go jack-shooting up Marion River.—**(16) 1870** *Colo. Gazetteer* 163 For this purpose 'jack-trains' are used in some districts, and 'chutes' in others.

b. In the names of animals: (1) **jackash,** [app. f. Indian name], (see quots.); (2) **-ass rabbit,** =**jack rabbit;** (3) ∗**-daw,** one of several varieties of American grackle, esp. the boat-tailed grackle, also **purple jackdaw;** (4) ∗**fish,** a name used locally for any one of various American fishes (see quots.); (5) **mackerel,** (see quot.); (6) **pike,** (see quot. 1819); (7) ∗**rabbit,** see as a main entry; (8) **salmon,** the wall-eyed perch.

(1) 1889 *Cent.* 3209/3 jackash. . . . The mink or vison of North America, *Putorius vison.* **1895** GERARD in *N.Y. Sun* 30 July, Jackash, a name among the fur traders of British America for the common mink. — **(2) 1847** HENRY *Campaign Sk.* 61 [We] started a number of hares (called jackass rabbits) and had no little amusement in witnessing some animated runs; their speed is wonderful. **1911** *Chi. D. News* 16 Sep. 15/3 The figures have reached 4,500,000 and are jumping along like a jackass rabbit pursued by a pack of wolves. — **(3)** *c***1728** CATESBY *Carolina* I. 12 *Monedula purpurea.* The Purple Jack-Daw. . . . At a distance they seem all black, but at a nearer view, they appear purple. **1884** COUES *Key to Birds* (ed. 2) 412 Boat-tailed Grackle, Jackdaw. Of large size, with long, much keeled and graduated tail. **1917** *Birds of Amer.* II. 270 Boat-Tailed Grackle. . . . This is the 'Jackdaw' of the South. . . . It got its popular name from the early settlers of the country on account of its superficial resemblance to the European Jackdaw. — **(4) 1884** GOODE *Fisheries* I. 313 The Amber-fish—*Seriola carolinensis* . . . is . . . rather common on the Carolina coast, where it is known as the 'Jack-fish.' **1917** KEPHART *Camping* II. 410 Here in the Carolina mountains the natives call it [*sc.* mascalonge] the 'jackfish.' **1947** BROWN *Outdoors Unlimited* 168 Up in Canada they call him the jackfish and despise him as most fishermen despise the carp.

(5) 1882 G. C. EGGLESTON *Wreck of Red Bird* 18 They call them blue fish up North, I believe, but we call them skip-jacks or jack-mackerel. — **(6) 1819** THOMAS *Travels* 212 The *Jack pike* or *pickerel* is an excellent fish, and weighs from six to twenty pounds. **1949** *Esquire* March 88 One day he was quietly fishing and contemplating his catch when a four-pound jack pike struck his lure. — **(8) 1871** *Pa. Laws* 276 The species commonly known as Susquehanna salmon, pike, perch, jack salmon, and by the scientific name of *stigostedium americanum,* shall henceforth not be taken . . . during their spawning time. **1920** *Outing* May 118/2 We always hope . . . to catch a few jack salmon.

c. In the names of plants: (1) **jack bean,** any one of various tropical American plants of the genus *Canavalia,* having purple and white blossoms and white seeds in long pods, also attrib.; (2) **brush,** (see quot.); (3) **bush,** ?short for "blackjack bush," *rare;* (4) **grape,** ?the muscadine, *rare;* (5) ∗**-in-the-pulpit,** see as a main entry; (6) **oak,** the blackjack oak or shingle oak *qq.v.,* also attrib.; (7) **pine,** any one of various North American pines, as *Pinus banksiana,* hickory pine, lodgepole pine, etc.; (8) **rose,** the General Jacqueminot (hence the name) rose, a hybrid rose of a deep red color.

(1) 1885 CRADDOCK *Prophet* 280 He sat upon the cabin porch beneath the yellow gourds and the purple blooms of the Jack-bean. **1888** —— *Despot* 69 The jack-bean vines that hung above her head blossomed lilack and white. — **(2) 1921** HALL *Yosemite Nat. Park* 251 An allied species is the Jack Brush (*Ceanothus divaricatus*). — **(3) 1812** J. CUTLER *Topographic Descr. Ohio* 96 The land in this distance is mostly clothed with jack bushes and tall woods. — **(4) 1848** *Rep. Comm. Patents 1847* 465 The Ohio, I believe to be a native, and may be the same as the jack grape of the Mississippi.

(6) 1816 U. BROWN *Journal* I. 266 Ugly Hills . . . abounded with pines of a scruby kind, Jack Oaks and other Scrub Wood. **1945** *Chi. Tribune* 28 Oct. VII. 1/7 The dogs sniff for rabbits in the dripping jack oaks. — **(7) 1888** in EARL C. BECK *Songs of Michigan Lumberjacks* (1941) 186 We are swamping out the jack pines, And I'll tell you it's no fun. **1949** *Reader's Digest* May 122/1 He scurried up a jack pine, cut loose a green cone with his teeth, then came scampering to earth. — **(8) 1883** *Harper's Mag.* Jan. 241/1 The box contained a . . . nosegay, with a 'Jack' rose in the centre. **1902** BANKS *Newspaper Girl* 252 The village florist he says the roses is what you call 'Jack roses.'

d. In phrases: (1) *To make one's jack,* to succeed in one's endeavors, become rich, *slang;* (2) *to tear up* (or *raise*) *jack,* to make a disturbance, also *to be full of jack,* to be full of mischief, *colloq.*

(1) 1778 in TEMPLE BODLEY *Kentucky* I. (1928) 153/2 My greatest Pleasure here [Harrodsburg] is thinking I shall make my Jack here if I can preserve my Night-Cap. **1853** in *Mo. Hist. Rev.* XXXVI. 257 We are inclined to think now is the time for them to make their 'jack.' **1901** H. ROBERTSON *Inlander* 25 You've come here to make your jack. — **(2) 1845** *Lowell Offering* V. 104 The mill has been started on sometime now, and the girls always tear up Jack, in my absence. **1867** S. HALE *Letters* 23 The street is narrow, so it looks quite deep,—and full of Arabs raising Jack all the time. **1872** *Ib.* 96 Mr. Holmes . . . and James Lowell were full of Jack, chaffing each other and going on.

As the last term in **apple, black, blue, boot, California, dancing, fence, fire, five-leaved, flap, jumping, lamp, loading, log, lumber, mountain, river, sand, sign, single, skip, slap, supple, Tennessee, Tom-and-, wagon, whisky, whistling, wood, Yellow Jack.**

∗**jack,** *v.*

1. *intr.* To hunt or fish at night with the aid of a jack (sense **6.**). Also *tr.*

*a***1841** HAWES *Sporting Scenes* I. 219 Not a man on Long Island can clam, crab, jack, shoot, or draw a net for bony fish with the skill and success of those who have inherited the honorable name of 'Smith.' **1885** *Outing* Oct. 80/1 'Sportsmen' . . . had 'still-hunted,' 'jacked,' and 'drove.' **1930** *Scientific Mo.* XXXI. 65/2 Henry R. Carey and I had experimented with 'jacking' gators on the old logging canal.

Hence **jacking,** *n.*

1885 ROOSEVELT *Hunting Trips* 168 The streams are not suited to the floating or jacking with a lantern in the bow of the canoe. **1894** *Cent. Mag.* Jan. 354/1 'Jacking' or 'floating,' for moose is seldom practiced, from the difficulty found in getting near enough to flash the light on the game. **1902** *N.Y. American* 21 Dec. 64/1 'Jacking' for deer . . . is hunting it by the aid of a strong lantern which has a brilliant reflector . . . attracting the game up to it, so that it may be easily shot.

b. *W.* (See quot.) *Obs.*

1871 DE VERE 211 Any owner of a large herd considers himself authorized to brand a maverick which he finds on or near his ranche, and this operation is called *to jack a maverick.*

2. ∗*To jack up,* **a.** To call to account, to bring (a person) to a sense of his duty. **b.** To suspend in disgrace. **c.** To raise or increase, force up. All *slang.*

(a) **1896** ADE *Artie* xii. 107 He was goin' to clean the streets and jack up the coppers. **1914** S. H. ADAMS *Clarion* 100, I think I'll jack up our boys in the city room by hinting that there may be a shake-up coming under the new owner. — **(b) 1898** HAMBLEN *Gen'l Manager's Story* 298 The engineer was, of course, discharged; and the head brakeman . . . was jacked up for thirty days. — **(c) 1904** *N.Y. Tribune* 8 May 10 The management thought it saw a chance to jack up rents, and made a sudden announcement of a raise. **1948** *Time* 1 Mar. 11/1 The country's biggest steelmakers decided to jack up some of their prices again.

*__jacker,__ *n.* (See quot. 1895.) *Obs.* — **1887** *Courier-Journal* 24 Jan. 2/4 Fortune varied one way and then another and finally they played a jacker in which the opener was promptly raised $500. **1895** *Thompson Street Poker Club* 6 *Jacker*—Jack-pot—The combined contributions of all who play, each one contributing the same amount.

* **jacket,** *n.*

1. (See quot. 1889.)

1843 in *W. & M. Coll. Quart.* 2 Ser XVI. 554 As the Dept. [of State] does not need a bearer of despatches, it cannot pay any thing for that service; but it is a very common practice to give to citizens whose interests strongly require it . . . a letter or jacket of papers. **1888** *Cong. Rec.* 12 June 5174/1 You can not get that information by taking one case or several cases, and taking the jacket down and getting an abstract. **1889** *Cent.* 3210/2 *Jacket,* . . . a folded paper or open envelop containing an official document, on which is indorsed an order or other direction respecting the disposition to be made of the document, memoranda respecting its contents, dates of reception and transmission, etc.

2. *attrib.* Of or pertaining to a suitably printed and ornamented detachable paper cover issued with a bound book.

1921 *Double Dealer* April 157/1 Concerning jacket eulogies of novels and writers, he said: 'That is one of the curious things I notice in America.' **1929** M. HOLLAND *Industrial Explorers* 3 As colorful as a futuristic jacket design of a best seller. **1944** *Sat. Review* 23 Sep. 27/3 There is a gay jacket cover, designed in black and white and red by Hugh Lofting. **1948** *Pacific Discovery* May–June 31/2 The title is provocative and the jacket design adds to the lure.

As the last term in **barrel, deerskin, frontiersman, gray, hunting, lumber, mackinaw, pea, sea pea, smoking, sport, stone, war, Yankee, yellow jacket.**

jacket ˈdʒækɪt, *v. tr.* To file with related material in a folder or envelope. *Rare.* — **1888** *American* 16 May (F.), Another record was made in the book of the office of letters received and jacketed.

* **jack-in-the-pulpit.** Any one of various American plants, esp. the Indian turnip *q.v.*

1847 WOOD *Botany* 519 Jack-in-the-Pulpit. . . . A curious and well-known inhabitant of wet woodlands. **1949** *Nature Mag.* April 194/2 Jack-in-the-pulpit is the plant so commonly used by smart alecks to carry out what they think a practical joke.

b. jack-in-the-pulpit rock, (see quot.).

1879 WILLIAMS *Pacific Tourist* 117/1 Going a little farther, you notice what is called 'Jack-in-the-Pulpit-Rock,' at the corner of a projecting ledge.

jackknife ˈdʒækˌnaɪf, *n.* [App. f. "*jackleg knife," but see *OED Jockteleg*, a large clasp knife, and *EDD jackalegs.*]

1. A large, strong pocketknife. Also attrib.

1711 *Springfield Rec.* II. 42 Eleven iron handled Jack knives. [**1759** *Newport* (R.I.) *Mercury* 26 June 4/2 Imported . . . and to be sold. . . . Pen and Jack-Spring Knives.] **1879** B. F. TAYLOR *Summer-Savory* 138 Here is the wooden bench beside the stove, covered with jack-knife sculptures. **1949** *Sat. Ev. Post* 9 April 138/4 He had in his pocket a waterproof match container and a jackknife.

b. Such a knife allegedly given as a prize for ugliness. *Obs.*

1804 FESSENDEN *Orig. Poems* 31 Peter Grievous, and his black wife, Though they both have had the jack-knife. **1846** *Knickerb.* XXVII. 470 They have a practice at the west of giving to the ugliest man in all the 'diggin's' round about, a jack-knife.

2. (See quots.)

1883 KNIGHT *Supp.* 510/1 *Jack-knife,* . . . a form of commutator used in telephone central stations. **1889** *Cent.* 3211/1 jack-knife, . . . a form of terminal used for making connections in central telephone-stations.

3. A form of dive in which the diver, while in the air, assumes a folded position, then straightens out just before entering the water. In full **jackknife dive.**

1922 *Country Life* July 60/3 All variety dives fall into four main groups—somersaults, twists, gainers, jack-knives. *Ib.* Aug. 61/1 In any jack-knife dive you must enter the water within six feet of the board, or three points will be taken off in a contest. **1943** *Copper Camp* 140 Here was a revel of swan dives, jackknives and belly-floppers.

jackknife ˈdʒækˌnaɪf, *v.* **1.** *tr.* To cut (someone or something) with a jackknife. **2.** *intr.* To double up like the folding blade of a jackknife.

(1) 1806 *Balance* V. 228/2 A sailor . . . Jacknifed (as he termed it) the poor creature in several places about the head. **1889** *Amer. Annals Deaf* Oct. 277 Some of the class-rooms had desks ink-stained and jack-knifed like those of a country school. — **(2) 1888** *Cent. Mag.* June 251/2 The practice, for instance, of dodging shots, 'jackknifing' under fire, proceeds from a nervousness which is often purely physical. **1946** *Reader's Digest* Aug. 171/2 Mrs. McGill jackknifed into her chair.

jack-light, *v. tr.* To hunt (deer, etc.) at night with the aid of a jack light. Hence **jack-lighting,** *n.*

1883 *Chi. Advance* 30 Aug., By night, it is called 'jacklighting' the deer. **1895** *Outing* XXVI. 63/2 Dark banks so suggestive of jack-lighting experiences. **1942** Nat. Pk. Service *Fading Trails* 30 We have come a long way since the days of market hunting, . . . of legal jack-lighting, and of using snares and many-barreled guns.

Jack hunter with a jack or jack-light

jack pot.

1. In poker, a pool opened only when some player has a hand containing a pair of jacks or better; a game in which such a pot or pool is used. Also **progressive jack pot.** Also transf. or fig.

1884 *Virginia* (Nev.) *Chron.* 1 Oct. 3/3 Old Bill [the warden] just lays back until there is a good jack-pot of trout in hand, and then he makes a bold bluff and walks off with it. **1887** KELLER *Draw Poker* 38 The result is the progressive jack pot, viz.: If a pot is not opened on the first deal the opening hand for the next deal increases from jacks, or better, to queens or better; . . . on the second deal . . . from queens, or better, to kings, or better. **1903** *Cin. Enquirer* 30 May 13/4 It was his deal in a big jack pot. **1947** *Steamboat* (Colo.) *Pilot* 16 Jan. 1/5 The largest pension payments ever made at one time in the United States are being distributed in the form of a 'jackpot,' or accumulated yearend bonus, of $220.80 to each pensioner on the rolls.

b. In colloq. or slang phrases: (1) *To be in* (or *get into*) *a jack pot,* to be in or get into a difficulty or straits; (2) *to hit the jack pot,* to have extremely good luck.

(1) 1902 McKEE *Land of Nome* 123, I was flattered to know that on the occasion of his getting into a 'jack-pot' (some trouble) he had hunted Nome after me for legal advice. **1948** *Neb. Hist.* March 14 Maybe you' ll catch me in a jack-pot some day when I'll need help. — **(2) 1944** *Newsweek* 25 Dec. 67/1 The 'Vick's Vaper' had indeed hit the jack-pot. **1949** *Obstetrical & Gynecological Survey* Feb. 96 One is justified in assuming that sooner or later, if other factors are normal, the jackpot is hit.

2. (See quot.)

1905 *Forestry Bureau Bul.* No. 61, 40 *Jackpot.* 1. A contemptuous expression applied to an unskilled piece of work in logging. (N [orthern] F[orest].) 2. An irregular pile of logs. (App[alachian] F[orest].)

* **jack rabbit.** A rabbit of any one of several varieties of long-legged, long-eared hares found in the West and Southwest. Also transf. and attrib. Cf. **black-tailed jack rabbit.**

1863 in *Colo. Mag.* XVII. (1940) 69 We saw wolves, buffalos, antelopes, jack-rabbits, prairie-dogs innumerable, deer, and birds of various kinds. **1910** *Sat. Ev. Post* 16 July 8/3 'Now, shake your wheels, ye castiron ould jack-rabbit!' he goes on to the ingine. **1931** *Durant* (Okla.) *D. Democrat* 26 Jan. 1/6 Huntsmen gathered here today for a jack rabbit drive near Cambridge. **1948** *Okla. City Times* 14 June 15/1 Like so many other jackrabbits Mitchell without his fleetness afoot would be just another average ballplayer.

* **Jackson,** *n.*

1. *attrib.* Designating persons and things dominated by or related to Andrew Jackson (1767–1845), seventh President of the U.S. (1829–37). *Obs.*

1824 *Amer. Sentinel* (Georgetown, Ky.) 10 Sep. 2/3 You would much oblige a subscriber by inserting . . . the address of the Jackson Convention at Louisville, published on the 18th August, 1824. **1827** *Spirit of Seventy-Six* (Frankfort, Ky.) 7 June 3/1 They are intelligent and zealous *Jackson Republicans.* **1839** T. BROTHERS *United States* 57 These are two *real democratic banks*, commonly called, on account of their sterling worth, 'Jackson Banks,' meaning that they belong to the Jackson party. **1844** *Henry Clay Bugle* (Maysville, Ky.) 2 May 1/2 Hickory Clubs, Jackson Clubs and Democratic Associations are formed, but no Van Buren Clubs.

Also *Jackson candidate, committee, democrat, electoral ticket, measure, meeting, paper, ticket,* etc.

b. Designating articles of clothing named for President Jackson. *Obs.*

1832 *Boston Transcript* 3 July 2/3 *High* top or Jackson boots, double precontracted Camboo travelling stick, and dark pumps with white gaiters, shall constitute his livery. **1834** *Albany Ev. Jrnl.* 8 Aug. 2/1 Our very habiliments may bear some evidence of the impress of his bloated reputation. We have Jackson hats, and Jackson coats, and Jackson jackets, and Jackson trousers, and Jackson boots, and Jackson shoes, and Jackson slippers.

2. In special combs.: (1) **Jackson ball,** ?a confection named for President Jackson, *obs.;* (2) **banquet,** a banquet held in connection with a celebration in commemoration of Jackson's defeat of the British at New Orleans on Jan. 8, 1815; (3) **cracker,** (see quot.), *obs.;* (4) **Day,** Jan. 8, celebrated, esp. by Democrats, in commemoration of Jackson's victory at New Orleans on Jan. 8, 1815, also **Jackson Day dinner,** an occasion upon which Democratic leaders dine together, hear speeches from outstanding party members, and outline such action as best promotes party solidarity and success; (5) **dinner,** a dinner enjoyed together by the political followers and admirers of Gen. Andrew Jackson, *obs.;* (6) **funeral,** (see quot.), *rare;* (7) **man,** a supporter of Andrew Jackson, or of the political beliefs attributed to him, a member of the Jackson party, now *hist.;* (8) **money,** (see quots.), *obs.;* (9) **party,** the political following which elected Andrew Jackson to the presidency of the U.S., later an unofficial title for the Democratic party, also **Jackson-Van Buren party,** *obs.;* (10) **Purchase,** (see quot.).

(1) **1889** MELLICK *Story Old Farm* 9 Dusty jars tempt the school children to barter eggs for sticks of peppermint and wintergreen, or the succulent Jackson-ball. — (2) **1884** *N.Y. Herald* 9 Jan. 3/4 The annual 'Jackson' Banquet . . . took place at the Parker House this afternoon. — (3) **1877** BARTLETT 319 *Jackson crackers.* Fire crackers. South-western. — (4) **1885** *N.Y. Herald* 9 Jan. 2/3 The Iowa democrats observed Jackson's Day in old fashioned style. **1909** *Springfield W. Republican* 14 Jan. 1 'Jackson day' has always been January 8—a day seldom celebrated in this part of the country. **1949** *Chi. D. News* 28 Feb. 10/7 Why do these persons on the government payroll spend $100 a plate for the Jackson Day dinners?

(5) **1827** *U.S. Telegraph* (Wash., D.C.) 7 Aug. 2/4 Those who attended the Clay dinner at Noble's, declared there were three times as many at the Jackson dinner. **1837** in ANNIE H. ABEL *Chardon's Journal* (1932) 121 Charboneau gave us a Jackson dinner, of Pot pye, and pudding. — (6) **1860** *Harper's Mag.* Jan. 280/1 During the summer of that year the Democrats got up 'a Jackson funeral'; and as the members of that party were death on the General in his lifetime, they were, of course, enthusiastic in their funeral ovations. — (7) **1826** *Norfolk Co. Gaz.* (Roxbury, Mass.) 20 July 3/1 The President of the meeting, who was of the Jackson party, and other Jackson men, . . . declared they had never before understood the matter, but had been entirely deceived. **1906** W. MACDONALD *Jacksonian Democracy* 34 It was not until some years later [than 1826] that the name 'Jackson men' was generally relinquished in favor of 'Democrats.' — (8) **1834** M. CHEVALIER *Society, Manners & Politics* 147 Gold is called *Jackson money.* **1842** UNCLE SAM *Peculiarities* I. 289, I always pay cash, in hard Jackson money, at auctions. — (9) **1827** *Spirit of Seventy-Six* (Frankfort, Ky.) 3 May 1/4, I cannot close this address without one further mention, as to the coalition formed by the leaders of the Jackson party in this State. **1839** MAYO *Polit. Sk. Washington* p. v, The Jackson-Van Buren party, is . . . made up of odds and ends of all parties. **1843** in HAMBLETON *H. A. Wise* (1856) 40 This same republican portion of the Whig party was that fragment of the old Jackson party that had gone off under the white flag of '36.

(10) **1946** WILSON *Fidelity* 1 It came into existence almost overnight when the Jackson Purchase, the area between the Tennessee and Mississippi Rivers, was opened for settlement.

As the last term in **anti-, hard, Old Mad Jackson.**

Jacksonian dʒæk'sonɪən, *a.* and *n.*

1. *n.* A political supporter of Andrew Jackson or of his policies.

1824 *Amer. Sentinel* (Georgetown, Ky.) 18 Oct. 3/1 At Mountsterling . . . they collected together six Jacksonians. **1896** *Emporia* (Kans.) *Gaz.* 15 Aug., We have an old mossback Jacksonian who snorts and howls because there is a bath-tub in the state house. **1946** *Newsweek* 17 June 106/2 His book can be read by Jeffersonians, Jacksonians, and Hamiltonians alike without shock.

2. *a.* Pertaining to or characteristic of Andrew Jackson or his political supporters.

1824 *Commentator* (Frankfort, Ky.) 23 Oct. 3/2 The Louisville Advertiser . . . working with the old Jacksonian aristocratic leaven of the Adams faction, has been able to produce some little agitation. **1894** *Life* 11 Oct. 238/1 Every town has . . . one Jacksonian Democrat. **1948** *Chi. Sun-Times* 7 Sep. 31/4 The so-called Jacksonian revolution marked the end (with the exception of some Southern states) of the restricted franchise.

b. Jacksonian democracy, the democratic political ideals reflected in the administrative policies of President Andrew Jackson; also, *collect.*, the supporters of these policies.

1838 MAYO *Polit. Sk. Washington* (1839) 49 The reader is enabled to appreciate the sacrifice I have made . . . in pursuing the phantom of 'Jacksonian-democracy.' **1879** *N.Y. Herald* 9 Jan. 4/4 The Jacksonian democracy were the determined foes of monopoly. **1913** A. C. COLE *Whig Party in South* 31 [The Whig party's] object stood out clearly from the beginning—to check Jackson and Jacksonian democracy, to 'cure the sea of Jacksonism.'

Jacksoniana ˌdʒæksonɪ'ænə, *n.* The name of a state proposed in 1841 (see quot.). — **1841** *Tenn. Senate Jrnl.* 15 Dec. 345 The expediency . . . of ceding that portion of this State lying west of the Tennessee River . . . for the purpose of being formed into a separate . . . State to be called Jacksoniana. *Ib.*, The disposition of said States [Ky. and Miss.] to cede . . . a portion of their territory, to be embraced in and form a part of the contemplated State of Jacksoniana when formed.

Jacksonianism dʒæk'sonɪənˌɪzəm, *n.* =next. *Obs.* — **1827** *Spirit of Seventy-Six* (Frankfort, Ky.) 12 July 3/3 Jacksonianism and Clintonianism, it intimates, compose a draught too bitter for any Republican to swallow. **1830** *Greensborough* (N.C.) *Patriot* 4 Aug. 2/4 This is no very striking exemplification of the increase of Jacksonianism in that quarter.

Jacksonism 'dʒæksn̩ˌɪzəm, *n.* The political principles and policies advocated by Andrew Jackson and his followers. Now *hist.*

1827 *Amer. Sentinel* (Georgetown, Ky.) 16 Feb. 2/3 These attempts are evidently but the stages that precede the *dissolution* of Jacksonism in Pennsylvania. **1846** MCKENNY *Memoirs* I. 200 General Green . . . remained [in exile] till recalled by his ancient friend and ally in the cause of Jacksonism, Mr. Tyler. **1922** MCCORMAC *Biog. Polk* 130 Admiration for the man had obscured the vision of many who would otherwise have been quick to detect the inherent evils of Jacksonism.

Jacksonist 'dʒæksn̩ɪst, *n.* =**Jackson man.** *Rare.* — **1842** in *Amer. Sp.* XVIII. 126/1 Away with the wild Kentuckian. . . . Take this barbarian from my sight! This Jacksonist—away!

Jacksonite 'dʒæksn̩ˌaɪt, *n.* =**Jackson man.** *Obs.*

1827 *Amer. Sentinel* (Georgetown, Ky.) 28 April 2/4 Some opposition was manifested by the Jacksonites against Messrs. Barker and Whipple. **1830** J. Q. ADAMS *Memoirs* VIII. 247 Although counteracted by a double opposition, federalist and Jacksonite, I have received nearly three votes in four, throughout the district. **1902** CLAPIN 242 *Jacksonites.* Said of the followers of general Andrew Jackson (1821–32). Their opponents were called Adamites.

Jacksonize 'dʒæksn̩ˌaɪz, *v. local. tr.* To defeat or overwhelm in battle, in allusion to Jackson's decisive victory at New Orleans. *Obs.* — **1815** *Niles' Reg.* IX. 64/2 But the Sacs and Foxes, west of the Mississippi, it is thought, must be brought to a sense of justice through feeling—they must be *Jacksonized*, as the saying is in the west.

* **Jacob,** *n.* [The source of "Jacob" in (1) and (3) is obscure.] In combs.: (1) **Jacob Evers,** (see quot.), *rare;* (2)

*Jacob's ladder, any one of various American flowers, esp. the toadflax, *Linaria vulgaris;* (3) **plow,** a now obsolete type of plow; (4) ***staff,** (see quot.).

(1) **1770** in PHILLIPS *Notes* 123 It Abounds here in fish of all kinds. . . . Principally the Jacob Evers, or Jew Fish. — (2) **1817–8** EATON *Botany* (1822) 462 *Smilax peduncularis,* jacob's ladder. **1945** *Chi. Tribune* 5 April 10/2 Distinctive small green leaves of Jacob's ladder may be seen all thru the same lot. — (3) **1848** *De Bow's Review* V. 143 It requires four mules, with a Jacob's plow. *Ib.* VI. 55, I have tried such land successively with the centre draft of Jacob's, Cary, and others. — (4) **1891** COULTER *Bot. W. Texas* I. 33 *Fouquiera splendens* . . . [is] common on rocky mesas from the Colorado to the Pecos and westward. Known as 'Jacob's staff' or 'Ocotillo.'

***Jacobin,** *n.* and *a.*

1. *n.* One opposed to the political beliefs and practices of the Federalists, an Antifederalist. Now *hist.*

1798 CUTLER in *Life & Corr.* II. 8 Mr. Gerry . . . was at first little noticed by the first Federal characters, but attended by almost all the Jacobins. **1867** *N.Y. Tribune* 27 Dec. 4/5 To this, it may be answered that the *mis*management of the Government was in the hands of those Jacobins. **1948** *Dly. Ardmoreite* (Ardmore, Okla.) 6 May 9/1 In fact, the very word 'democrat' was synonymous with 'Jacobin.'

2. *a.* Of or pertaining to Jacobins or Antifederalists.

1803 *Fredericktown* (Md.) *Herald* 30 April 2/2 Whoever stops short of the utmost point of Jacobin fury, falls a sacrifice to Jacobin vengeance. **1868** *N.Y. Herald* 10 July 6/2 The delegates . . . were called together by pure patriotism and by a resolve to stand by the constitution, now threatened by Jacobin revolutionists.

***Jacobinic,** *a.* Also **Jacobinical.** Characteristic of or pertaining to the American Jacobins. Now *hist.*

1794 *Balt. D. Intelligencer* 25 Aug. 3/1 It appears that our patriotic tars dare express . . . their *Jacobinical* principles even under the nose of his Britannic majesty. **1802** HAMILTON *Works* VII. 325 If his [Jefferson's] plan has been to rise to power on the ladder of Jacobinic principles [etc.]. **1822** J. Q. ADAMS *Diary* 282 Archer was a Radical and inclined to be Jacobinical. **1878** STOWE *Poganuc People* 105 The Rev. Mr. Coan rejoiced in the result of the election. Not that he was by any means friendly to the ideas of the Jacobinical party by whose help it had been carried. **1941** MOTT *Amer. Journalism* 133 Thomas Adams and his brother Abijah . . . suffered under the Sedition Act for their 'jacobinical' assaults on local Federalists.

***Jacobinism,** *n.* The principles and policies of American Jacobins, or those attributed to them. *Obs.*

1792 JEFFERSON *Writings* VIII. 444 They endeavored . . . to conjecture up the ghost of antifederalism, and to have it believed that this and republicanism were the same, and that both were Jacobinism. **1804** *Fredericktown* (Md.) *Herald* 25 Feb. 3/2 We find it absolutely necessary . . . to descend as often as we can in justice to other subjects down among the wretches of Jacobinism. **1869** STOWE *Oldtown Folks* 222 We are both stanch Federalists, and make the walls ring with our denunciations of Jacobinism and Democracy.

***Jacobinize,** *v. tr.* To win to the cause or support of the Antifederalists. *Obs.* — **1801** F. AMES *Works* (1854) I. 291 Great efforts will be made to jacobinize Massachusetts, and to elect Gerry [governor].

***jagged,** *a.* Intoxicated, drunk. *Slang.* — **1737** *Pa. Gazette* 13 Jan. 1/3 He's Jagg'd. **1907** O. HENRY *Trimmed Lamp* 162 What I want is a masterful man that slugs you when he's jagged and hugs you when he ain't jagged.

***jail,** *n.* In combs.: (1) **jail bleach,** (see quot. 1888), also **jail bleached;** (2) **house,** a jail; (3) **wagon,** a patrol wagon, *rare.*

(1) **1871** HAY *Pike Co. Ballads* (1880) 33 Shadowed by his jail-bleached hair. **1888** CRADDOCK *Despot* 29 A man with that singular pallor acquired by years of indoor life, and known as 'jail bleach.' — (2) **1812** ASBURY *Journal* III. 399 We left our lodging in the jail-house, and came away to Green Hill's. **1937** SUTHERLAND *Professional Thief* 4 He will render assistance to a professional burglar in fixing cases, securing bonds, or escaping from a jailhouse. — (3) **1868** *Harper's Mag.* Sep. 515/1 To secure this we have brought with us the jail-wagon, and we must request you to put the sick man into it.

As the last term in **country, county, log jail.**

***jake,** *n.*[1] Short for **country jake.** *Colloq.* — **1895** *D.N.* I. 389 *Jake:* a rough, uncouth country fellow. N.C., Tenn., Mo., Kan. **1915** *Ib.* IV. 199 He's no jake even though he did come from a Nebraska farm.

jake dʒek, *n.*[2] [App. in allusion to Jamaica ginger.]

1. An alcoholic liquor, consisting largely of Jamaica ginger, sometimes used during the prohibition era (1920–33) as a beverage. *Slang.* Cf. **ginger jake.**

1931 *K.C. Star* 1 Oct., It must have been 'lit up' with some of that Wichita 'jake' about which we read so much not long ago. **1948** *Dly. Ardmoreite* (Ardmore, Okla.) 11 Aug. 1/1 The popular bootleg beverage of the addicts was a mysterious drug popularly called 'jake.'

2. A form of paralysis caused by drinking this or some other alcoholic preparation. In full **jake-leg.** *Slang.*

1931 I. L. REEVES *Ol' Rum River* 351 Much of the present liquor being poisoned, as a result of the Government's own acts, and thus directly responsible for thousands of cases of blindness, paralysis, 'jake,' and death. **1932** *K.C. Star* 4 Jan. 16 If one goes to a social party there is great danger of acquiring jake-leg. **1947** *Democrat* 22 May 4/5 That stuff not only gives you the jake leg, it gives you 'jake legs.'

jake dʒek, *a.* [Origin obscure.] Fine, first-rate. *Slang.*

1921 *Collier's* 15 Jan. 11/1 If he'd step into the dressin' room with the handlers everything would be jake. **1924** MARKS *Plastic Age* 247 She said the whole college seemed jake to her. **1948** *Dly. Ardmoreite* (Ardmore, Okla.) 21 July 6/1 Last heard news was to the effect that everything was jake with the program.

jalopy dʒəˈlɑpɪ, *n.* [Origin obscure.] (See quots. 1929, 1936.) *Slang.*

1929 HOSTETTER & BEESLEY *It's a Racket* 229 Jaloppi—A cheap make of automobile; an automobile fit only for junking. **1936** *Amer. Sp.* XI. 306 A *jalopy* is an old, battered automobile. The word was used in Chicago about 1925; in western and northern Pennsylvania about 1934; in an Associated Press dispatch from Landisville (Lancaster Co., s.e. Pa.) in 1935. **1948** *Chi. Sun-Times* 20 April 3/4 In their earlier statements to police they had said the jalopy struck the girl.

***jam,** *n.*

1. An accumulation, esp. of timber, blocking a stream. Cf. **center, log, side jam.**

1805 SIBLEY in *Ann. 9th Congress* 2 Sess. 1076 Its overflowing [is] occasioned by a jam of timber choking the river. **1850** JUDD *R. Edney* xvi. 199 At the head of the pond was probably also a jam of ice. **1882** HUBBARD *Moosehead Lake* 153 An Indian . . . was killed there in May, 1882, in a 'jam' of logs. **1944** *Nat. Geog. Mag.* June 672/2 Priest River . . . made a striking picture with a jam of logs stranded on its sandbars.

transf. **1910** *Sat. Ev. Post* 3 Sep. 58/2 If the traffic's light, and there's no chance to get pinched in behind a jam, the usual thing is to pull up to the curb and tinker with some imaginary engine trouble.

attrib. **1879** *Lumberman's Gaz.* 1 Oct., From the jam-boom to the head of the sorting works is a distance of seven miles. **1902** WHITE *Blazed Trail* 358 Down at the booms the jam crew received the drive as fast as it came down. **1905** *Forestry Bureau Bul.* No. 61, 39 An expert river driver who, during the drive, is stationed at a point where a jam is feared . . . [is called] a jam cracker. (P[acific] C[oast] F[orest].) **1926** RICKABY *Ballads* 235 *Jam-pike.* An implement consisting of a pole or shaft twelve or fifteen feet long, with a combined spike and hook at one end.

2. A social gathering or party. *Obs.* Cf. **gam,** *n.*[1]

1827 LONGFELLOW in S. Longfellow *H. W. Longfellow* I. 123, I have been several times to her evening jams; but, as it was Lent, there was no dancing. **1851** *Chi. D. Jrnl.* 19 Feb. 3/1 Party succeeds to party, from a quiet little 'social' to the pretending and fashionable 'Jam,' where 'wheeling about and turning about' is the order of the evening. **1889** HALE *Letters* 213 We left at ten-thirty, and might have gone on to Mrs. Secretary Whitney's jam.

3. A difficulty or tight spot. *Colloq.*

1929 HOSTETTER & BEESLEY *It's a Racket* 4 Such organizations employ expensive legal counsel to defend their members in the event of a 'jam' with the law. **1948** *Sat. Ev. Post* 4 Dec. 140/2 Let a jam come up, and the headwaiter starts screaming for the houseman in six languages.

jam dʒæm, *a.* and *adv.*

1. Short for next. *Obs.*

1832 *Boston Transcript* 6 Aug. 1/1 Do you like jam spruce beer, Miss? **1839** F. TROLLOPE *Domestic Manners* xxix. 272 There they go, that's jam! and now we must set to slick. *Ib.* 273 Say no more, that's a jam gal.

2. jam-up, fine, first-rate, excellent. *Colloq.*

1841 *S. Lit. Messenger* VII. 54/2 Reaching him a hand, Received him, introduced him to 'the jam-up little company' in his command. **1856** *Spirit of Times* 8 Nov. 159/1, I tuck a steam-boat at Louisville —one of your real jam-up boats. **1931** *K.C. Times* 21 Aug., This . . . perchance truthful comment . . . has been quoted approvingly by . . . other jam-up papers.

b. Also as an adverb: Fully, closely pressed, pressing close upon. Also with *against. Colloq.*

1825 NEAL *Bro. Jonathan* II. 52 He had been sitting, for two or three hours, without opening his mouth, 'jam up' in a back seat. **1845** *Quincy* (Ill.) *Whig* 4 Nov. 1/5, I am glad, girl, that you have this time made choice of a man who knows how to pettifog, jam-up, without being too lazy to work on a farm. **1874** EGGLESTON *Circuit Rider* xvi. 142 Jam up fifty miles, and over tough roads. **1932** *K.C. Star* 24 May 18 His Chevrolet . . . [ran] jam up against a house on a neighboring lot.

*jam, *v.*

1. *intr.* Of logs, floating ice, etc.: To collect in an immovable mass, blockading a stream.

1706 SEWALL *Diary* II. 156 The Ice jam'd and made a great Damm. **1877** *Lumberman's Gaz.* Dec. 362 The logs which follow are halted one after another, . . . jamming into what seems to the unpracticed eye an inextricable mass. **1905** *Forestry Bureau Bul.* No. 61, 40 *Jam, to break a,* to start in motion logs which have jammed.

transf. **1946** *Reader's Digest* Sep. 167/2 The audience was jamming up outside.

2. *tr.* (See quots.)

1860 *Harper's Mag.* April 607/1 No amount of judgment can select with any certainty a favorable location for 'jamming' or turning a river. **1909** *Cent. Supp.* 665/3 *Jam,* . . . to push (a bill or measure) through the regular routine of a legislative body by the brute force of a majority controlled by 'the machine,' without proper consideration or discussion. (Political slang.) *N.Y. Com. Advertiser,* April 11, 1901.

***Jamaica,** *n.* **1. Jamaica buckthorn,** (see quot.). **2. Jamaica fish,** (see quots.). *Obs.*

(1) **1889** *Cent.* 707/1 Jamaica buckthorn, the Cherokee rose (*Rosa lævigata*), used for hedges. — (2) **1792** BELKNAP *New-Hampshire* III. 214 The fish of the summer and fall fares is divided into two sorts, the one called merchantable, and the other Jamaica fish. **1800** *Mass. H.S. Coll.* VII. 249 The summer codfish, called Jamaica fish, which goes to the West Indies, is about three dollars a quintal.

***jamb,** *n.* **1. jamb pike,** a form of pike used by loggers in driving logs down a stream. (Cf. **driving pike,** and quot. 1926 *s.v.* ***jam,** *n.*) **2. jamb stove,** a five-plate stove *q.v.* (see also quot. 1931).

(1) *c*1870 in E. C. BECK *Songs of Michigan Lumberjacks* (1941) 39 With jamb pikes and with peaveys These brave men nobly go. **1926** *Old-Time N. Eng.* July 27 Several others, as part of the equipment, . . . relate to log and lumber transport by water, namely, the Jamb Pike. — (2) **1830** J. F. WATSON *Philadelphia* 198 The first idea of those ten plate stoves was given by C. Sower, the printer, of Germantown, who had every house in that place supplied with his invention of jamb-stoves,' roughly cast at or near Lancaster. **1931** *Old Time N. Eng.* Oct. 71/2 They were called 'Five-Plate' or 'Jamb Stoves,' and were made up of two sides, a back, a bottom, and a top, the whole bolted together.

jambalaya ˌdʒæmbəˈleə, *n.* [See note.]

"The actual source is Modern Provencal *jambalaia,* which Mistral, II, 152, renders by 'ragoût de riz avec une volaille'" (W. A. Read in *Zeitschrift* LXI. 76).

A New Orleans dish composed of rice together with shrimp, crabs, oysters, chicken, turkey, etc. Also transf.

1872 *N.O. Times* 28 June, Those who brought victuals, such as gumbo, jambalaya, etc., all began eating and drinking. **1885** *La Cuisine Creole* i, In this compilation will be found many original recipes and other valuable ones heretofore unpublished, notably those of Gombo file, . . . Jambolaya, . . . Cray-fish a la Creole. **1948** *Sat. Ev. Post* 11 Sep. 50 One of the most famous of traditional Creole dishes is Jambalaya.

transf. **1945** *Democrat* 25 Oct. 2/2 The above might very well be called typesetter's hash, or compositor's jumbalaya.

jambone ˈdʒæmbon, *n.* [Origin unknown.] (See quot.) *Obs.* — **1864** DICK *Amer. Hoyle* (1866) 83 Jambone is a word unknown to Webster, but, as applied to Euchre, means that a party who plays Jambone plays a lone hand with his cards exposed upon the table.

jamboree ˌdʒæmbəˈri, *n.* [Origin unknown.] **1.** (See quot.) **2.** An unrestrained celebration or merrymaking. Also transf. Cf. **high, whoop jamboree.**

(1) **1864** DICK *Amer. Hoyle* (1866) 85 Jamboree signifies the combination of the five highest cards, as, for example, the two Bowers, Ace, King and Queen of trumps in one hand, which entitles the holder to count sixteen points. — (2) **1868** *N.Y. Herald* 10 July 8/3 The Seventh regiment has gone on a jamboree to Norwich, Connecticut. **1937** *Lit. Digest* 3 July 28/2 An international army of peace and brotherhood—an army of 27,000 boys—gathered from twenty-five nations for America's first National Boy Scout Jamboree. **1947** *Chr. Sci. Monitor* 1 March 10/4 The club will make its presentation at its football jamboree at the close of each grid season.

James River.

1. Tobacco grown in the James River region of Virginia. Also attrib. *Obs.*

1785 in *S. Lit. Messenger* XXVIII. 37/2 Some very low sales of tobacco from Britain has much reduced the price here; James River to about 4 d. and Rappahannock to a Guinea. **1818** *N.-Eng. Palladium* (Boston) 28 Sep. 4/3 Parker & Stevens . . . have for sale . . . 19 hds. James' River Leaf Tobacco. **1892** DUVAL *Young Explorers* 113 Uncle Seth pulled out a plug of James river from his pocket, from which he cut slivers, then immediately stuffed them first into one side and then the other of his mouth.

2. James River fever, (see quot.). *Obs.*

1866 MOORE *Women of War* 39 Here were hundreds and hundreds languishing with that low, dull fever that overcame so many who shared in that [Peninsular] campaign, and which was called in the army the 'James River fever.'

Jamestown ˈdʒemzˌtaʊn, *n.* **1. Jamestown lily,** a term used locally for the jimson weed. **2. Jamestown weed,** the original name of the jimson weed first observed at Jamestown, Va.

(1) **1894** *Amer. Folk-Lore* VII. 95 *Datura Stramonium* . . . stinkweed, West Va.; Jamestown lily, Lincolntown, N.C. — (2) **1687** J. CLAYTON *Acct. Va.* in *Phil. Trans.* XLI. 160 The Soldiers . . . lighting in great Quantities on an Herb called James-town-weed, they gathered it; and by eating thereof in plenty, were rendered apish and foolish, as if they had been drunk, or were become Idiots. **1812** *Cramer's Alman. 1813* (Pittsburgh) 26 James'-town weed, from James'-town, on James' River, in Virginia, where the plant seems to have first attracted notice. It is also known by the name of Jimson, and Thorn-apple. **1904** GLASGOW *Deliverance* 273 Well, you must persuade her to use a liniment of Jamestown weed steeped in whisky.

jams dʒæmz, *n. pl.* Jim-jams, delirium tremens. Also transf. *Obs.* — **1888** *Boston Globe* 4 March (F.), My fader's de best doctor in Boston, an' . . . keeps de medicine to stave off de jams already mixed. **1894** WISTER in *Harper's Mag.* July 208/1 That's the kind of clock gives a man the jams. Sends him crazy.

janitorship ˈdʒænətɚˌʃɪp, *n.* The office or position of janitor. Also attrib. — **1878** HARTE *Drift from 2 Shores* 144 A desire for rural repose led him to seek the janitorship of Doemville Academy. **1893** *Columbus* (O.) *Dispatch* 12 July, The janitorship fight is expected to rear its 'hideous form' in the meeting of the Board of Education tomorrow night.

January thaw. A thaw or spell of mild weather occurring in January.

1832 WILLIAMSON *Maine* I. 100 'The January thaw,' when the rain sometimes freezes as it falls [and] covers the face of the earth with a glare ice. **1873** BEADLE *Undevel. West* 711 No 'January thaw' need be apprehended. **1948** *Cong. Rec.* 1327/3 The January thaw up our way is the only measure of relief we have so we can build up our meager stock piles.

***Japan,** *n.*

1. a. Japan clover, a clover-like plant introduced into the U.S. before 1846 from Japan. **b. Japan lily,** any one of several large-flowered lilies introduced into the U.S. from Japan.

(a) **1868** *Rep. Comm. Agric. 1867* 253 The Japan clover (*Lespedeza striata,*) . . . has already extended over large districts in the more southern States, proving itself to possess extraordinary merit, both for fodder and grazing. **1889** VASEY *Agric. Grasses* 95 *Lespedeza striata* (Japan Clover) . . . was introduced in some unknown way, over forty years ago, from China into the South Atlantic States. — (b) **1836** LINCOLN *Botany* App. 111 [*Lilium*] *japonicum,* (Japan lily,) corolla elongated into a tube; flowers very large, pure white, with a streak of blue. **1899** GOING *Flowers* 204 The white day or Japan lily opens about sundown, giving forth an alluring sweetness.

2. Also **Japan allspice, fowl, Judas tree, maple, pea, persimmon, plum,** (see quots.).

1854 *Pa. Agric. Rep.* 73 For pair Japan fowls, $2.00. **1855** BROWNE in *Amer. Inst. N.Y. Trans.* 597 Japan pea . . . has been since cultivated with remarkable success. **1856** DAVIS *Farm Bk.* 39 Got some Japan Peas for Mr Le Vert. **1865** RICHARDSON *Secret Service* 39 Japan plums hung ripe. **1868** GRAY *Field Botany* 131 Japan Allspice, . . . *Chimonanthus fragrans.* Shrub with long branches, . . . hardy S. of Penn. **1879** *Scribner's Mo.* May 55/1 One of the very best on our lawn, is the Japan Judas-tree. **1889** *Rep. Secy. Agric.* 29 Tests have been made . . . with olives, Japan persimmons, pine-apples, etc. **1892** APGAR *Trees Northern U.S.* 88 There are a great number of Japan Maples, many of them probably varieties of this species [*Acer palmatum*].

Japanese-American, *n.* A citizen of the U.S. of Japanese ancestry. Also attrib. or as adj.

1907 *Collier's* 12 Oct. 14/2 K. K. Kawakama, a Japanese-American journalist married to an American woman, told me of an extreme example. **1948** *Sat. Review* 4 Sep. 12/2 In December 1941 there were 126,000 Japanese-Americans in the continental United States.

b. Of or pertaining to Japan and the United States.

1920 *Pacific Review* Dec. 421 The present crisis is the most serious and delicate which has been known in Japanese-American relations. **1925** *Inquiry* April 15/2 A Japanese newspaper owner, K. Abiko, has drawn up a suggestive scheme for a Japanese-American Friendship Campaign.

Japonicadom dʒəˈpɑnɪkədəm, *n.* (See quot. 1859.) *Obs.*

1851 A. O. Hall *Manhattaner* 123 The general society of New Orleans is still in a chaotic state, and she has no located, acknowledged empire of Japonicadom. **1859** Bartlett 219 *Japonicadom* [is] a word invented by N. P. Willis to denote the upper classes of society. *a***1870** Chipman *Notes on Bartlett* 219 *Japonicadom*. . . . Allusive to the flower known as the Japonica lily.

jaquima ˈhækɪmə, *n. S.W.* [Sp. *jáquima*, in same sense.] (See quots.) Cf. **hackamore.** — **1877** Bartlett 321 *Jaquima*, . . . the head-stall of a halter, used in Texas and California for breaking wild horses. **1894** *D.N.* I. 324 *Jáquima:* the headstall of a halter; often pronounced somewhat like *hackamore*.

jar dʒɑr, *n.* [See note.]

The source or sources of the word as used in the following examples are obscure. In **jarfly** there may be an allusion to the folk observation that the noise of some of the creatures to which the name is given can be temporarily stopped by slightly jarring the trees in which they are singing. The spelling "jarr" in **2.** (3) may be significant.

1. (See quot. 1863.)

1863 Randall *Pract. Shepherd* 73 Those usually short, detached, not very coarse, glistening particles of hair found in the fleece, termed 'jar,' are very objectionable. **1878** *Ill. Dept. Agric. Trans.* XIV. 239 The jar is coarse hair invariably found in the wrinkled fleeces.

2. In combs.: (1) **jarfly,** any one of various cicadas or harvest flies which make strident noises; (2) **head,** (see quot. 1918), *slang;* (3) **raisin,** (see quot. 1789), *obs.*

(1) **1880** M. Allan-Olney *New Virginians* I. 110 There is the thing they call the 'jar-fly,' for instance. . . . It makes a noise like a watchman's rattle. **1940** Stuart *Trees of Heaven* 48 There is the singing of jarflies among the soapy poplar trees. — **(2) 1918** *D.N.* V. 18 *jarhead*, a mule. [N.C.] **1946** *Sierra Club Bul.* Dec. 50 Few of our motor-minded city-bred soldiers knew the fuel consumption, rated-load capacity, and first echelon maintenance of a jarhead. — **(3) 1761** in E. Singleton *Social N.Y.* 364 To be sold, wholesale and retail . . . Sugar Plumbs and Carraway; Confects, Jarr Raisins and Cask ditto [etc.]. **1789** *Philos. Soc. Trans.* I. 262 Jarr Raisins or Raisins of the Sun curing the most perfect manner, so as to retain their full flavor, and keep long without candying, is done in the following manner. **1872** Ellet *Cyclo. Domestic Econ.* 476/2 Have half a pound of stoned jar-raisins chopped as fine as possible.

As the last term in **cooky, fruit, Mason, slop jar.**

jarabe hɑˈrɑbe, *n. S.W.* [Sp. in Amer. Sp. sense shown here. Cf. Santamaría.] (See quots.) *Obs.* — **1834** A. Pike *Sketches* 103 In the jarabes, or singular dances of the fandango, her first partner was always Rafael. **1910** J. Hart *Vigilante Girl* 157 The fandango was danced by the lower orders, generally combined with the jarabe, a Mexican dance.

jargon book. A dictionary of the Chinook Jargon. *Rare.* — **1862** *Walla Walla* (Wash.) *Statesman* 22 Nov. 2/4 By all means let the Rev. get a jargon book and a pack of cards and come along.

jasm ˈdʒæzəm, *n. local.* [Origin obscure. Poss. the same word as *gism*, semen, see Wentworth. Cf. **jazz.**] Energy, enthusiasm. — **1860** Holland *Miss Gilbert* xix. 350 If you'll take thunder and lightning and a steamboat and a buzz-saw and mix 'em up and put 'em into a woman, that's jasm. **1886** *Harper's Mag.* Sep. 579/2 Willin', but hain't no more jas'm than a dead corn-stalk.

***jasmine,** *n.* The Carolina jessamine, *Gelsemium sempervirens.* Cf. **Confederate, yellow jasmine.**

1802 Drayton *S. Carolina* 6 Their undergrowth is covered with a profusion of shrubbery; and jassmines. **1846** Thorpe *Myst. Backwoods* 166 The roe eat up the dahlias, jasmines, or other choice flowers of the neighbouring gardens. **1912** N. Woodrow *Sally Salt* 113 The odor [was] shaken from the insignificant green bells of a night-blooming jasmine by a wandering breeze.

***jasper,** *n.* A country fellow, a hick. *Slang.* — **1914** Bower *Flying U Ranch* 174 Some uh you boys help me rope him—like him and that other jasper over there done to Andy. **1948** *Range Riders Western* May 64/1 These buyin' jaspers claimed they was goin' to ship to the eastern packin' houses.

***Java,** *n.*

1. A breed of chickens or a chicken of this breed. Also **Java fowl.**

1849 *N. Eng. Farmer* I. 386 *Java* fowls were shown by John Giles. **1871** Lewis *Poultry Book* 70 The Black Javas. This species of birds are said to be among the most valuable breeds of this country. **1889** *Cent.* 3222/1 The javas are of good size and broad and deep shape, and rank well for utility.

2. Coffee grown in Java, or a drink prepared from this. Also coffee in general. *Colloq.*

1850 Garrard *Wah-To-Yah* xiii. 169 Partaking of the nectar-like Java, . . . we smoked. **1853** *Harper's Mag.* VII. 276/1 Sh'd be glad to sell you a lot of damag'd Java . . . very cheap. **1947** *Chi. Tribune* 20 July (Comics) 1 Another cup of Java, sister.

javalina hɑvəˈlinə, *n.* Also **havalena.** *S.W.* [Sp. *jabalina*, wild sow.] The peccary, a piglike animal found in the Southwest.

1822 Dewees *Lett. from Texas* 25 Bears are very plenty, but we are obliged to use great care when hunting for them, lest the *havalenas* (meaning the peccary) kill our dogs. **1892** Duval *Young Explorers* 96 Cudjo came rushing out with half a dozen Mexican hogs or 'javalinas' in hot pursuit of him.

Also as *pl.*

1941 Fergusson *Southwest* 10 In Death Valley. . . . Mountain sheep still defy the hunter from barren crags, and javelina (peccary) root for acorns among scrub oak and cactus. **1948** *Ariz. Republic* (Phoenix) 3 March 16/7 Many hunters were out and from the number of shots fired there must have been plenty of javelina.

***jaw,** *n.* In combs.: (1) ***jawbone,** see as a main entry; (2) ***breaker,** (*a*) a kind of hard candy, *colloq.*, (*b*) =next (*a*); (3) **crusher,** (*a*) a machine for breaking ore, (*b*) =**jawbreaker** (*a*); (4) **smith,** (see quot. 1889).

(2) (*a*) **1875** *Chi. Tribune* 21 Nov. 2/6 Each one had grown tired of jaw-breakers and popcorn balls. **1946** T. Jones *Skinny Angel* 173 She treated all the first grade nice girls to licorice whips and jaw breakers. (*b*) **1877** Raymond *8th Rep. Mines* 421, I speak of the rolls as more applicable for completing the crushing of the ore as it comes in small pieces from the jaw-breaker. — (3) (*a*) **1877** Raymond *8th Rep. Mines* 420 The jaw-crusher, and also the rolls, . . . simply break up the ore. (*b*) **1944** *Vogue* 1 Oct. 178 Army men on every front, Navy men on every sea, ask for . . . hard candy (the lemon and lime jaw crushers are good travellers). — **(4) 1887** *Chi. Tribune* 13 May 5/2 George Schilling, Socialist and jawsmith, says [etc.]. **1889** *Cent.* 3222/3 jawsmith. . . . One who works with his jaw; especially, a loud-mouthed demagogue: originally applied to an official 'orator' or 'instructor' of the Knights of Labor. *St. Louis Globe-Democrat*, 1886. [Slang, U.S.] **1905** *Belleville* (Ill.) *News-Democrat* 8 Dec. 1/7 The jawsmith must stand aside and wait for some other and more favorable opportunity to spit out enunciated atmosphere.

As the last term in **big, drop, lump(ed), Morocco, muffle, wring jaw.**

***jawbone,** *n.*

1. (*cap.*) A once popular minstrel song or tune. *Obs.* Cf. **Walk jawbone.**

1826 *Constitutional Advocate* (Frankfort, Ky.) 3 Feb. 3/3 They then toasted Massa, . . . after which they all patted *Jawbone* very *soft* and slow. **1839** *Observer & Reporter* 24 Aug., No more shall he enliven the negro quarters on Saturday nights . . . or sing 'jaw bone' at the corn shucking.

b. jawbone talk, (see quot.). *Obs.*

1895 *Chi. Record-Herald* 10 Nov. 35/1 The jawbone talk was a droning song game, in which those engaged sat in a ring and made a rhyme to the prevailing tune by turns. But if one hesitated when his turn came the next one took up and the the failing one was ruled out.

2. Castanets or a jew's harp. Also **jaw-bone lute.** *Obs.*

1844 Cist *Cincinnati Misc.* 14 Fowler . . . found the truant as he expected at a dance house on Columbia st, with his slippers off, dancing and playing the *jaw bones* or Castanets. **1845** *Knickerb.* XXVI. 336 The frequent sound of the violin, banjo, or jaw-bone lute is . . . an indication. **1869** Dumont *Benedict's Cong. Songster* 50, I can play the old jawbone, and can use the fiddlebow.

3. a. Talk without action. **b.** (See quot.) Both *slang.*

(a) 1898 *Voice* (N.Y.) 24 March 4/1 Jawbone is cheap, and there is plenty of it; backbone is something rare. — **(b) 1900** *Nation* 4 Oct. LXXI. 270/1 A common slang among American soldiers for the word 'credit' is 'jawbone.' . . . The soldier asks . . . the native keeper . . . to sell him a bottle of beer . . . 'on jawbone.'

***jay,** *n.* As the last term in **blue, blue-fronted, California, Canada, city, country, Florida, mountain, mountain blue, piñon, pine, Sierra (Nevada), Steller's jay.**

***jay,** *a.*

1. Rustic, countrified, naïve. *Slang.*

1889 *S.F. Bulletin* 13 July 1/6 Smith has a poor opinion . . . of St Joseph, which he alludes to as a 'jay' town of the worst description **1894** *Life* 19 April 256/1 People of taste and refinement . . . haven't any 'pull,' and the jay vote is the one to consider in matters of an artistic nature. **1916** Wilson *Somewhere* viii. 348 He puts it up with the press agent of this big hotel to have the poor things [Indians] sleep up on the roof, . . . so them jay New York newspapers would fall for it, and print articles about these hardy sons of the forest.

2. jay-bird stallion, a scrub stallion. *Rare.*

1887 *Courier-Journal* 2 May 6/5 The man who has one or more good mares to breed can . . . make a very ridiculous ass of himself . . . in using some jay-bird stallion to breed them to.

jayhawk ˈdʒeˌhɔk, *n.* [Origin obscure.] **1.** =**jayhawker 1. 2.** (*cap.*) *attrib.* Of or pertaining to Kansas as the Jayhawker State.

(1) **1858** in *Kans. Hist. Coll.* V. 552, I detached them in small posses, sent them in different directions to watch the movements of the 'Jayhawks,' as they are termed. **1907** C. D. STEWART *Partners* 269 We was just jayhawks and greenhorns that had been picked up everywhere and didn't know nothing about war. **1948** *Dly. Ardmoreite* (Ardmore, Okla.) 15 Jan. 6/8 Allen was 'all wet' when he said the Jayhawks were suffering from a lack of experience. — (2) **1944** *Chi. D. News* 14 Feb. 8/3 We [in Kansas] have Jayhawk theaters, Jayhawk restaurants, Jayhawk lumber yards; the fabulous Jaykawk is the insignia not only of our state university, but of scores of other concerns.

jayhawk ˈdʒeˌhɔk, *v.* [App. f. the noun.] *tr.* and *intr.* To steal (something), to harass (someone), to act as a jayhawker. *Slang.*

1874 *Chi. Times* 1 Jan. 5/5 George Jones jayhawked a turkey from a stall on South Clark street on yesterday. **1875** D. W. WILDER *Annals of Kans.* 190 [1858] November 12.—On the three following days and nights several persons in Linn county are jayhawked. **1901** DUNCAN & SCOTT *Allen & Woodson Co., Kans.* 595 About this time lumber was obtained for a new school house, but I am told the greater portion of it was 'jayhawked' by a wagon maker who had a shop near by. **1912** COBB *Back Home* 94 He was jayhawkin' back and forth along the State line here, burnin' folks' houses down over their heads.

Hence **jayhawking,** *n.*

1855 SPRING *Kansas* 252 Legislative action . . . brought the territorial jayhawking era substantially to a close. **1897** BARTON *Hero in Homespun* 218 The 'jay-hawking' might now be looked for at every foot of the way.

jayhawker ˈdʒeˌhɔkɚ, *n.* [Origin unknown.]

1. Orig. a free-stater who took part in the irregular war (1854–60) waged in Kansas over slavery; during the Civil War, a free-lance soldier, freebooter, or guerrilla operating in Kansas; any lawless marauder or robber.

1858 in *Kans. Hist. Coll.* V. 559 Mr. Fossett also stated that two of the 'jayhawkers' [i.e., anti-slavery men] stayed all night with him . . . that he was afraid to refuse the 'jayhawkers' to stay. They left early in the morning. **1894** ROBLEY *Bourbon Co., Kans.* 137 From that day both communities drew a clearer line between 'jayhawkers' and good citizens. **1900** GOODLANDER *Fort Scott* 8 We may be attacked by the Jayhawkers before morning, and you must use it [a gun].

attrib. **1888** *St. Louis Globe-Democrat* 20 Jan. (F.), He was connected with what is known as the Jayhawker war that raged on the borders of Kansas about twenty-five years since.

transf. **1889** *Cent.* 3223/1 jayhawker. . . . A large spider or tarantula, as species of *Mygale.* (Western U.S.)

b. (See quot. 1862.) *Obs.*

1862 *Lawrence* (Kans.) *Republican* 11 Sep. 4/1 That faction of the Democracy who sympathise with the rebels are known . . . in Kansas as 'jayhawkers,' in Kentucky as 'bushwhackers,' and in Indiana as 'copperheads.' **1878** GUILD *Old Times* 374 A parcel of 'bummers' and 'scalawags' . . . impose heavy and onerous taxation . . . to feed and pamper a parcel of 'jay-hawkers.'

attrib. **1862** *Knickerb.* LIX. 392 Guess she must a-had Secesh beaux And gone to Jayhawker parties from her youth up.

2. (*cap.*) A nickname for a native of Kansas. Also attrib.

1875 *Chambers's Jrnl.* 13 March 171 Kansas . . . is occupied by Jayhawkers. **1890** *Opelousas* (La.) *Democrat* 14 June 3/2 Some did not understand what was meant by 'Jay-hawker'. . . . This is the name that is applied to all citizens of Kansas. **1947** *N. & Q.* June 40/1 One small boy . . . was no doubt inspired by my brother's Jayhawker accent.

b. Jayhawker State, Kansas.

1885 *Santa Fe W. New Mexican* 3 Sep. 4/3 Mr. Hutchinson . . . has seen the Jayhawker state rise from an arid waste. **1907** *Boston Transcript* 9 Nov., A list of the popular names of the States: . . . Jayhawker—Kansas.

jaywalk ˈdʒeˌwɔk, *v.* [f. **jay*, a stupid person, + **walk, v.*] *intr.* To cross streets at unauthorized places or in an unusual manner, esp. to go from one street corner to another on a diagonal. Also **jaywalking,** *n.*

1919 LEWIS *Free Air* 257 He had . . . been cursed by a policeman for jaywalking. **1935** MITCHELL *America* 125 Don't jay walk. That is, don't cross a road except at the proper crossing places. **1948** *Dly. Ardmoreite* (Ardmore, Okla.) 21 April 8/1 The 'angels' . . . distributed pamphlets telling how many fatal accidents are caused by jay-walking.

Also **jaywalker,** *n.*

1917 *Harper's Mag.* June 70/2 The Bostonian, supposedly sesquipedalian of speech, has reduced 'a pedestrian who crosses streets in disregard of traffic signals' to the compact *jaywalker.* **1946** *Jefferson Co. Republican* (Golden, Colo.) 8 May 1/7 Jaywalkers in Golden can be fined as much as $300 for crossing the street at Twelfth and Washington against the red light.

jazz dʒæz, *n.* [See note.]

The source of this word is not clear. It is often regarded as being of African or Creole origin. See the first group of quots. under the verb, and cf. *Amer. Sp.* I. 513–18 and Mencken *Supp.* II. 708/9. See also **jasm,** *n.*

1. Music, esp. for dancing, based upon ragtime, characterized by syncopated rhythms and varied themes, melodies, and orchestral coloring.

[**1913** *Harper's Wkly.* 11 May 11/3 The music they made had the . . . rhythm of African tom-toms, . . . or of ragtime down on the levee—the swaying, sensuous syncopation that is characteristic of the music of the black man everywhere.] **1917** *Lit. Digest* 25 Aug. 28/2 To-day the jazz bands take popular tunes and rag them to death to make jazz. **1922** *Sat. Ev. Post* 15 July 74/2 Oh, mother can't play jazz. **1949** *Democrat* 5 May 3/2 A band plays far better jazz than you can hear in a British club.

b. A piece of jazz music. *Obs.*

1920 *Harvey's Wkly.* 24 July 14/2 That isn't a keynote; it's a jazz. **1921** *Ladies' Home Jrnl.* Jan. 50 All the latest popular hits . . . all this season's jolliest jazzes.

2. Also attrib. or as adj. Characterized by jazz style, pertaining to jazz music.

1917 *Lit. Digest* 25 Aug. 28/2 Jazz music is the delirium tremens of syncopation. **1929** *Etude* Sep. 699/2 The radio is bringing to my ears a celebrated jazz-ensemble in New York City. **1949** *Chi. D. News* 25 March 33/2 One of his ambitions reportedly was to sit in on a jam session with some of our jazz musicians.

b. Lively, unconventional, "peppy."

1922 *Ardmore* (Okla.) *D. Press* 3 Jan. 4/1 Jazz life, like crime, is the exception. **1923** *Birmingham* (Ala.) *News* 20 April 6/6 (*advt.*), Jazz Suits. See the new ones that have just come to town—all the smart dressers are wearing them. **1938** S. M. BESSIE (*title*), Jazz Journalism; the Story of the Tabloid Newspapers.

c. Sophisticated, pervaded by the jazz spirit.

1919 *Current Opinion* Aug. 98/3 Boston is only slightly Jazz.

3. In special combs.: (1) **jazz age,** the early nineteen twenties, also attrib.; (2) **baby,** a flapper, *obs.;* (3) **band,** a dance orchestra which plays jazz and which includes such instruments as the piano, guitar, and saxophone.

(1) **1922** FITZGERALD (*title*), Tales of the Jazz Age. **1938** *Life* 26 Dec. 50/3 Whiteman did more than any other musician to make the Jazz Age. **1950** *Birmingham* (Ala.) *News* 8 Jan. D. 1/1 The nation's fashion editors . . . will rub their eyes to be sure they're not seeing a playback of a jazz age movie. — (2) **1920–1** FITZGERALD *Tales of Jazz Age* (1922) 21 Marylyn and Joe followed, singing a drowsy song about a Jazz baby. **1931** F. L. ALLEN *Only Yesterday* 101 The producers of one picture advertised 'brilliant men, beautiful jazz babies.' — (3) **1916** in *Lit. Digest* (1919) 26 April 48/1 On account of the big expense of hiring Bert Kelly's Jazz Band for the entertainment of our patrons, it has been necessary to raise the price as follows. **1939** *Life* 18 Dec. 27 His well-disciplined band is selling more records right now than any other jazz band in the business.

jazz dʒæz, *v.* [See note.]

The source of this verb is as obscure as that of the noun. It is not clear which use, noun or verb, is the earlier. If the noun is related to jasm *q.v.*, it prob. preceded the verb. The relatively early verb use ascribed to Hearn in quot. 1926 below is not available for this entry. The quots. in the first group below may have some bearing on the source of the term.

1. *tr.* To speed up, enliven, "pep up." Often with *up. Slang.*

(1) **1917** *Lit. Digest* 25 Aug. 28/2 The phrase 'Jaz her up' is a common one to-day in vaudeville and on the circus lot. When a vaudeville act needs ginger the cry from the advisers in the wings is 'put in jaz,' meaning add low comedy, go to high speed and accelerate the comedy spark. **1917** in *Amer. Sp.* I. 514/2 In the old plantation days, when the slaves were having one of their rare holidays and the fun languished, some West-Coast African would cry out, 'Jas her up,' and this would be the cue for fast and furious fun. **1926** *Amer. Sp.* I. 514 Lafcadio Hearn found the word jazz in the creole patois and idiom of New Orleans (presumably in the late seventies or early eighties of the last century). He wrote that it had been taken by the creoles from the negroes, that it meant 'to speed things up,' and that it was 'applied to music of a rudimentary syncopated type.' **1938** *News Letter & Wasp* (S.F.) 17 March 5 Mr. Slattery . . . had heard the word jazz in crap games around San Francisco. It is a creole word and means, in general, to speed up.

(2) **1919** *Amer. Mag.* Nov. 69/1 For ways that is dark and tricks which is vain, the daughters of Eve is peculiar, to jazz up a line of Bret Harte's. **1922** *Collier's* 2 Sep. 5/1 What is these up-to-date nifties, anyway, but the old stuff jazzed up? **1931** IRWIN *Amer. Tramp & Underworld Slang* 109 Jazz.—To speed up.

b. Esp. to play (an instrument) or render (music) in the manner of jazz.

1920 *Collier's* 3 Jan. 13/3 You jazzes a waltz, de grandes' dance dey is. **1921** *Ladies' Home Jrnl.* Aug. 16/3 Familiar hymn tunes can be jazzed until their original melodies are hardly recognizable. **1922** *Sat. Ev. Post* 15 July 74/2 Oh, I tell you who we could have in to jazz up the piano. **1938** *Life* 26 Dec. 49/2 He jazzed *Liebestraum, Dance of the Hours.* **1948** *Chi. Maroon* 20 Feb. 4/4 Two bugs on the edge of the larynx Were jazzing a ragtime tune.

Also *intr.*

1919 *Lit. Digest* 26 April 28/1 While society once 'ragged,' they now 'jazz.' **1920** *Collier's* 17 Jan. 15/3 Who can picture Josef Hofmann and Rudolf Gany jazzing cyclonically?

2. *intr.* To copulate, engage in coition. Also *tr.* and *to jazz up*, to make pregnant. *Slang.*

1927–8 WOLFE *Look Homeward Angel* (1929) 166 Jazz 'em all you like, . . . but get the money. **1942** [see ***knock up** (*a*)]. **1948** MENCKEN *Supp.* II. 709 *To jazz* has long had the meaning in American folk-speech of to engage in sexual intercourse. [**1949** ELLIOT PAUL *My Old Kentucky Home* 92 That was the first time I had heard the word 'jazz' applied to music.]

3. *To jazz around*, to gad about, to seek pleasure. *Slang.*

1920 *Rank & File* (S.F.) 1 May 1/2 The boys are 'jazzing' around waiting for the proper word. **1942** BERREY & VAN DEN BARK *Amer. Thesaurus Slang* 342 Go pleasuring, go about among 'em, jazz around, kick around.

4. In slang derivatives: (1) **jazzer,** *n.* one who plays jazz; (2) **jazzing,** *n.* playing jazz or rendering in the manner of jazz; (3) **jazzist,** *n.* **=jazzer;** (4) **jazzy,** *a.* like jazz, spirited, lively.

(**1**) **1919** *Current Opinion* Aug. 99/3 The 'klaxon' in particular . . . as one of the Jazzers explains, . . . reminds them that they have an automobile. **1932** *Forum* April 235/2 The jazzers, weary of the stenciled refrain . . . have made up their mind to break through this cage. *Ib.*, I have in mind the tin-pan jazzers at their daily task. — (**2**) **1919** *Lit. Digest* 26 April 28/1 The negro loves anything that is peculiar in music, and this 'jazzing' appeals to him strongly. **1938** *Life* 26 Dec. 52/2 In Pasadena, Whiteman's new-fangled jazzing of the classics. — (**3**) **1929** *Etude* Sep. 655/2 But the jazzists have woven some novel patterns with the rhythmic threads. **1941** *New Yorker* 1 March 44/2 Basie makes effective use of tone-shading, a technique which some of our noisier jazzists might do well to cultivate. — (**4**) **1920** *Collier's* 13 March 57/2 Bergstrom's two-piece orchestra was in the throes of its jazziest foxtrot number. **1938** *Life* 6 June 14 Carefree, jazzy and extremely likeable, Kenneth had to think hard. **1949** *Amer. Mercury* July 86/1 The youthful composer astonished the professors and undergraduates with his jazzy *passacaglias* and improvisations.

Jean Crapeau. =Johnny Crapaud. *Obs.* — **1834** HOFFMAN *Winter in West* (1835) II. 246 The whimsical application of *soubriquets* is . . . religiously kept up, . . . the Tuckahoes and Coheese of Virginia, on either side of the Blue Ridge, complimenting each other with as much amiability as do John Bull and Monsieur Jean Crapeau.

Jebacco boat. Variant of Chebacco boat *q.v. Obs.* — **1799** BENTLEY *Diary* II. 304 We had an opportunity of seeing the fashion of mooring Boats commonly called Jebacco Boats. **1817** *Ib.* IV. 478 The sight of Jebacco boats building for the bay fishery . . . was very impressive.

jeep jip, *n.* [See note.]

The history of this term is obscure. The word is app. a fanciful coinage by Elzie Crisler Segar in a comic strip ("Popeye") where on March 16, 1936, he introduced Eugene the Jeep, a small animal of supernatural powers. The word has been used of various devices. Its application to the Army vehicle may have been a verbalizing of GP (general purpose) inspired by a knowledge of its earlier use in the comic strip. See *Amer. Sp.* Feb. 1943, 68 f.; *Amer. N. & Q.*, June 1944, 43; and Mencken *Supp.* II. 782 ff.

A small, light motor vehicle orig. designed for, and widely used in, the U.S. Army, noted for its four-wheel drive and ruggedness. Also attrib.

1941 DANIELS *Tar Heels* 47 Beer wagons moved on the road with the brown jeeps of soldiers and marines. **1945** *Pueblo* (Colo.) *Chieftain* 18 June 5/4 Everything from X-ray films to jeep tires hastened victory over Germany. **1948** *Salt Lake Tribune* 17 Dec. 16/5 They were in a black jeep with a metal top.

Jeff Davis.

1. Short for Jefferson Davis (1808–89), President of the Southern Confederacy (1861–65), and in some circles a symbol of unpopularity. *Rare.*

1870 O. LOGAN *Before Footlights* 202, I thought perhaps they imagined I was a female Jeff Davis, and were going to make a '*charge a la bayonette*' instanter.

2. In obs. combs.: (1) **Jeff Davis box,** (see quot.); (2) **coffee,** during the Civil War, wheat used as a coffee substitute, cf. **Lincoln coffee;** (3) **Grays,** name of a Confederate regiment; (4) **money,** Confederate money.

(**1**) **1871** DE VERE 283 The *Musical-Box* of the Confederates was also known as *Jeff Davis' Box:* it was the humorous name given by the men to the lumbering, ill-built army-wagons, which were apt to creak horribly for want of greasing. — (**2**) **1941** M. L. SMITH *God's Country* 13 My folks parched wheat and we called it 'Jef Davis Coffe.' — (**3**) **1865** *Atlantic Mo.* June 746/1 Jeff-Davis Grays . . . fired with patriotism and whiskey, proud to be in Richmond. — (**4**) **1941** M. L. SMITH *God's Country* 13 Of course every one had some Jef Davis money. That was the confederate money. But it wasnt worth any thing after the war.

Jeffdom ˈdʒɛfdəm, *n.* The Confederate States of America. *Rare.* — **1861** *N.Y. Tribune* 11 July 4/4 To attempt to issue a Union journal . . . in any city of Jeffdom, would be . . . stark mad.

***Jefferson,** *n.* [Thomas *Jefferson* (1743–1826), third President of the U.S. (1801–9).]

1. *attrib.* Designating a type of shoe or boot. Also absol. *Obs.*

1821 *Gen. Reg. for Army* 344 Each cadet [at Military Academy at West Point] shall keep himself at all times supplied with . . . two pairs of Jefferson shoes, rising above the ankle joint, under the pantaloons. **1834** in *Mil. & Naval Mag. of U.S.* III. June 282 My boots, my boots . . . my Jeffersons, good Longfield, the Jeffersons you promised me. **1847** J. S. HALL *Book of Feet* 144 The Jefferson boot, which was introduced at about the time when Mr. Jefferson came into the presidency, . . . and which that gentleman was himself fond of wearing, was laced up in front, as high as the ankles, in some instances perhaps higher. **1861** *Army Reg.* 482 Boots: . . . For all Officers—ankle or Jefferson.

2. A variety of plum. *Obs.*

1862 *Rep. Comm. Patents 1861: Agric.* 163 Plums are very productive, and those that are most prominent are the Green Gage, the Damson, and the Jefferson.

3. A name proposed for the territory that later became the state of Colorado. Also **Jefferson Territory.**

1860 *N.Y. Tribune* 7 April 6/3 The people of the Gold Region, however, have selected for their embryo body politic the name and style of 'the Territory of Jefferson.' **1931** WILLISON *Here They Dug Gold* 22 The gold fields remain subject to two . . . sets of authorities till '61 when Congress organizes them as the Territory of Colorado, spurning the name Jefferson as smacking too much of Democracy, then fatally identified with the slave-holding South. **1947** *Staff Lookout* (Denver Pub. Lib.) Winter 6/2 Eight were members of the convention which drafted the Constitution of Jefferson Territory.

b. Similarly used with reference to the state of Montana and the Indian Territory.

1889 *N.Y. Semi-Wkly. Tribune* 2 Aug. 9 It has been proposed in the Montana Constitutional Convention that the name of the State be made Jefferson. **1900** *Dly. Ardmoreite* (Ardmore, Okla.) 4 May 2/2 Congressman Moon of Tennessee, today introduced a bill providing a territorial form of government for the Indian Territory, under the name of Jefferson Territory.

4. In special combs.: (1) **Jefferson Bible,** (see quot. 1928), also **Jefferson's Bible;** (2) **Day,** a day observed by Democrats for rallying party supporters; (3) **-'s giant sloth,** (see quot.), *obs.;* (4) **-'s Manual,** a popular name for a manual of parliamentary practice drawn up by Thomas Jefferson and published in 1800, orig. for the use of the Senate of the U.S.

(**1**) **1928** STIMPSON *Nuggets of Knowledge* 71 The *Jefferson Bible* is a compilation made by Thomas Jefferson, consisting of passages from the four gospels cut out and pasted in a book according to a scheme of his own. . . . He used all the words attributed to Jesus. . . . The original book is in the National Museum at Washington, D.C. **1936** SIMMS *Bible in Amer.* 264 Comparatively few, perhaps, know anything about what is called 'Jefferson's Bible.' . . . It was published in 1904 . . . at the direction of Congress. — (**2**) **1936** *Young Democrat* (Okla. City) IV. No. 10, 2/1 [He] sent delegates . . . away from Baltimore's huge Jefferson Day regional rally. [**1949** *Chi. D. News* 26 March 6/3 Senators traveled around the country to speak at Lincoln-Jefferson-Jackson Day dinners.] — (**3**) **1826** GODMAN *Nat. Hist.* II. 197 Jefferson's Giant Sloth. *Megatherium Jeffersonii.* . . . The only fragments yet obtained of the skeleton of this extinct species were discovered in a salt-petre-cave, . . . in Green Briar county, Va. — (**4**) **1837** *Cong. Deb.* 15 Sep. 626 The rules of parliamentary practice comprise Jefferson's Manual, and shall govern the proceedings of the House in all cases in which they are not inconsistent with the rules of the House. **1900** *Cong. Rec.* 1 Feb. 1375/2 The Secretary will read what Jefferson's Manual says in relation to it.

Jeffersonia ˌdʒɛfəˈsonɪə, *n.* (See quot. 1879.) — **1816** D. THOMAS *Travels Western Country* 222 *Jeffersonia diphylla* two leaved Jeffersonia. **1879** WEBSTER *Supp.* 1563/3 *Jeffersonia*, . . . A genus of American plants of the barberry family, bearing a handsome white flower, an inch in diameter; found in woods from Western New York to Wisconsin, and southwards, and named in honor of Thomas *Jefferson.*

Jeffersonian ˌdʒɛfəˈsonɪən, *a.* and *n.*

1. *n.* A political follower or supporter of Thomas Jefferson, an advocate of political principles attributed to him, a Democrat. Now *hist.*

1803 *Fredericktown* (Md.) *Herald* 30 April 3/3 Osborne Sprigg Esq. (a thorough going Jeffersonian . . .) was the democratic candidate. **1880** *Lib. Universal Knowl.* I. 91 The Jeffersonians were eager for discrimination against England. **1948** *Antioch Review* Spring 10 American Federalists openly sympathized with British Tories and American Jeffersonians with French Girondists.

2. *a.* Of or pertaining to Thomas Jefferson, or to the political doctrines held by or attributed to him.

1799 *Spectator* (N.Y.) 3 April (Ernst). **1803** *Fredericktown* (Md.) *Herald* 28 May 1/3 What else can reconcile the book of Jefferson with Jeffersonian ministry? **1854** BENTON *30 Years' View* I. 224/2 It was a message of the Jeffersonian school. **1948** *Time* 3 May 23/1 He has a Jeffersonian view of the importance of the people's voice.

3. In special combs.: (1) **Jeffersonian classification,** a system, devised by Thomas Jefferson and based upon Bacon's classification of the sciences, for classifying books in a library, *obs.;* (2) **Democrat,** a member of the Democratic party who believes in the principles of government advocated by Thomas Jefferson; (3) **Mobocracy,** a contemptuous term for the body of political followers of Thomas Jefferson, *obs.;* (4) **Republican,** a Democratic Republican who followed the leadership of Thomas Jefferson; (5) **simplicity,** the absence of pomp and ceremony in political and social matters.

(1) 1872 *Harper's Mag.* Dec. 47/1 The new library hall [of the Library of Congress] was ready for occupancy on the first of July, 1853, and the books were again arranged in accordance with the ponderous Jeffersonian classification. — **(2) 1804** *Fredericktown* (Md.) *Herald* 4 Feb. 3/1 Randolph, and his immediate followers, who may be especially styled *Jeffersonian Democrats*, may wish entirely to subvert the judiciary of the United States. **1948** *Time* 23 Feb. 23/1 In Mississippi last week, 5,000 local rebels gathered to brandish the Confederate flag and issue a secession call for all 'true, white Jeffersonian Democrats.' — **(3) 1807** JANSON *Stranger* 201 As this man is the leader of what is termed the *Jeffersonian Mobocracy*, I shall add another note from the same pen. — **(4) 1805** *N. Eng. Palladium* 18 an. 1/2 He would have been *no monarchist*, but a *good christian* and a fine *Jeffersonian republican.* [**1836** N. N. SCOTT *Memoir H. L. White* (1856) 354 My political friends who have placed my name before the public, are Jeffersonian Jackson Republicans. . . . Deprive the people of their right of suffrage, by throwing over him the name of a 'good old Jeffersonian democratic republican.'] **1900** *Cong. Rec.* 6 Feb. 1587/2 Randolph, Jeffersonian Republican, said that the power to settle disputes as to boundaries involved the power of extending boundaries.

(5) 1886 *Cong. Rec.* 29 June 6302/2 (Th. Supp.), What would a man wedded to 'Jeffersonian simplicity' do with $16,000 worth of new furniture? **1914** *Cyclo. Amer. Govt.* II. 251 *Jeffersonian Simplicity.* An expression denoting the dislike and disregard for display, . . . [which] has been used to denote principles of democratic equality and simplicity.

Jeffersonianism ˌdʒɛfəˈsonɪənˌɪzəm, *n.* The political principles and doctrines advocated by or attributed to Thomas Jefferson. — **1876** H. C. LODGE in *N. Amer. Rev.* July 137 Ultimately, Jeffersonianism must have prevailed, but at the time of its actual triumph it came too soon. **1945** *Nation* CLX. 17 March 307/2 Various types of monopo ists have been trying to hide behind the phrase 'Jeffersonianism' and 'states' rights' ever since the time of Theodore Roosevelt.

Jeffersonite ˈdʒɛfəsnˌaɪt, *n.* [Named in 1822 after Thomas *Jefferson.*] A variety of pyroxene containing some zinc and manganese. — **1822** *Amer. Jrnl. Science* V. 402 Jeffersonite . . . has a great resemblance to pyroxene. **1889** *Cent.* 3224/2 *Jeffersonite* . . . is peculiar in containing some zinc and manganese. It occurs, with franklinite, zincite, etc., at Franklin Furnace, Sussex county, New Jersey.

Jeffite ˈdʒɛfaɪt, *n. attrib.* Designating a follower of Jefferson Davis. *Rare.* — **1861** *N.Y. Tribune* 11 July 5/4 Whispers . . . come up from Washington that his [Henry May's] mission has for its object a disgraceful and humiliating peace with the Jeffite traitors, upon their own terms.

Jeffrey pine. [John *Jeffrey*, a Scottish botanical explorer.] A long-needled pine, *Pinus jeffreyi*, found in the western states.

1897 SUDWORTH *Arborescent Flora* 22 *Pinus jeffreyi.* . . . Black Pine. . . . Jeffrey Pine. **1911** CHASE *Yosemite Trails* 55, I had noticed what appeared to be a sleeping place of particular excellence, . . . where a big Jeffrey pine had laid down a carpet of dead needles. **1948** *Pacific Discovery* Nov.–Dec. 20/2 Yellow pine cones are three to five inches long; those of the Jeffrey six to eight.

Jehovah's Witnesses. The members of the International Bible Students' Association, a society composed of the followers of Charles T. ("Pastor") Russell (1852–1916). — **1941** *Amer. Guardian* (Okla. City) 15 Oct. 7/1 Remember . . . the fifth column hunt directed at Jehovah's Witnesses trying to establish the Four Freedoms before F. D. R. got the idea. **1947** *Chi. Sun* 25 Nov. 14/5 The majority held valid a regulation issued by the director of Selective Service which prescribed tests for determining whether Jehovah Witnesses were entitled to exemption as ministers.

*__Jehu,__ *n.* **1.** Used attrib. app. in the sense of large. **2. Jehu Nimshi,** an exclamation. Both *rare.* Cf. ***Nimshi.** — **(1) 1837** CROCKETT *Almanac* 43 A coat of strong blue cloth of the Jehu cut, with white bone buttons of the Jehu size . . . served . . . to hide the neckcloth. — **(2) 1859** TALIAFERRO *Fisher's R.* 53 Jehu Nimshi! thar he [a snake] were right dab at my heels, head up, tongue out, and red as a nail-rod.

jell dʒɛl, *v.* [f. **jelly.*] *intr.* To congeal or jelly. Also transf.

1869 ALCOTT *Little Women* II. 60 The—the jelly won't jell—and I don't know what to do! **1890** *D.N.* I. 22 Jell, to harden, said of jelly: 'the jelly doesn't jell.' Is it used generally? The dictionaries seem not to recognize it. **1949** *Dly. Oklahoman* (Okla. City) 13 Feb. D. 16/2 These separate elements are never quite jelled into a coherent whole.

*__jelly,__ *n.* **1. jelly bean,** a bean-shaped piece of candy having a gumlike center. **2. jelly cake,** a layer cake having jelly between the layers.

(1) 1905 *Chi. D. News* 5 July 11/5 Jelly beans, assorted, per lb., 9c. **1948** *Carpenter* May 13/2 It says a pound of beans all right, but are you sure she meant jelly beans? — **(2) 1863** in CHESNUT *Diary* 249 Then we had a salad and a jelly cake. **1899** TARKINGTON *Gentleman from Ind.* xvii, Behind Miss Briscoe came Mildy Upton with glasses and a fat, shaking, four-storied jelly-cake.

Jemimaite dʒəˈmaɪməˌaɪt, *n.* Allegedly an adherent of Jemima Wilkinson, a Quakeress who in the late eighteenth century gained some repute in and around Providence, R.I., by dressing as a man and discoursing against marriage. — **1940** EARLY *N. Eng. Sampler* 189 And the people who came to hear her preach banded together, and called themselves Jemimaites.

*__Jenny Lind.__

1. a. (See quots.) **b.** A type of artificial fly used by anglers. **c.** (See quot. 1948 and cf. **Jenny Lind carriage.**)

Jenny Lind carriage

(a) 1862 *Rep. Comm. Patents 1861: Agric.* 186 Jenny Lind, and Burr's New Pine are good early strawberries. **1885** *Harper's Mag.* March 559/1 Some blocks [of granite] are polished by a great machine called a Jenny Lind. — **(b) 1882** HUBBARD *Moosehead Lake* 13 For spring-fishing additional varieties may be found good, such as the Jenny-Lind, the grizzle-king, the professor, and the gray-drake. — **(c) 1901** CHURCHILL *Crisis* 267 A 'Jenny Lind' passed them. Miss Belle recognized the carriage immediately. **1948** RITTENHOUSE

Vehicles 11 A 'Jenny Lind' was an early type of buggy with a fixed top. Named for the famous singer. Usually of elaborate design and painting. Body 30 inches wide; wheels 47 and 50 inches.

2. Used attrib. in allusion to Jenny Lind (1820–87), the famous Swedish operatic soprano who toured the U.S. in 1850–52, as (1) **Jenny Lind bed,** (2) **boot,** (3) **carriage,** (4) **house,** (5) **polka,** (6) **table.**

(1) **1929** *Sears Cat.* Fall 945 Quaint Jenny Lind Bed. — (2) **1857** *Lawrence* (Kans.) *Republican* 28 May 3 Ladies' Fine Kid Jenny Lind Boots . . . for sale. — (3) **1854** *Pa. Agric. Rep.* 128 To S. P. Hamilton, . . . for a Jenny Lind Carriage. — (4) **1941** *Chr. Sci. Monitor* (Wkly. Mag. Sec.) 3 May 11 But I do not find Jenny Lind house. The vertical-boarded unpainted houses which blend so well into the West Virginia hollers are called locally Jenny Lind houses. **1946** *March of Progress* Feb. 158/1 We lived in a rented, forty-year-old, Jenny Lind house on a side street.

(5) **1850** *S.F. Picayune* 26 Aug. 3/1 The band led by Mons. Bona were playin a Jenny Lind poker. **1948** *Time* 13 Dec. 44/1 The talented pair played a piano duet of the *Jenny Lind Polka.* — (6) **1874** *Gold Hill* (Nev.) *News* 21 April, A splendid Jenny Lind table in the saloon for players.

jerk dʒɜk, *n.*[1] Also **jirk.** [f. the verb.] Jerked meat, a piece of such meat. *Obs.*

1799 J. SMITH *Acct. Captivity* 65 This we kept to stew with our jirk as we needed it. **1831** BUTTRICK *Travels* 64 The venison for want of salt to preserve it, is cut in slices, dried and smoked, which makes what they call jerk. **1873** HAYCRAFT *Elizabethtown, Ky.* 16 The dried venison, called 'jirk,' was the bread; the fat, juicy bear the esculent, the bulky buffalo, the substantial.

***jerk,** *n.*[2]

1. *pl.* Involuntary spasmodic jerkings of the head or other parts of the body in one under the influence of strong religious emotion. Now *hist.* Cf. ***exercise,** *n.* **2, holy laugh.**

For some account of this affliction see *Ohio Archæological and Historical Pub.* XII. (1903) 248.

1805 L. DOW *Jrnl.* in H. Mayo *Pop. Superst.* (1851) 125, I have seen all denominations of religion exercised by the jerks—gentleman and lady, black and white, young and old, without exception. I passed a meeting-house, where I observed the undergrowth had been cut down for camp-meetings, and from fifty to a hundred saplings were left for the people who were jerked to hold by. I observed, where they had held on they had kicked up the earth, as a horse stamping flies. **1847** L. COLLINS *Kentucky* 109 The Baptists escaped almost entirely those extraordinary and disgraceful scenes produced by the jerks . . . which extensively obtained among some other persuasions of those days. **1948** DICK *Dixie Frontier* 197 The next most common phenomenon was known as 'the jerks.'

2. (See quot. 1927.) In full **jerk road.** *Colloq.*

1907 LONDON *Road* 26 By mistake I had missed the main line and come over a small 'jerk' with only two locals a day on it. **1927** *D.N.* V. 451 *jerk road,* n. A small, branch railway,

3. In combs.: (1) **jerk-line,** see as a main entry; (2) **neck,** (see quot.), *slang;* (3) **rein,** = **jerk-line;** (4) **water,** see as a main entry.

(2) **1927** RUSSELL *Trails* 43 We're drivin' these vehicles jerkneck, that is the trail pony's tied to the lead cart so one man can handle both. — (3) **1895** *Forum* June 475 The big freight wagon, with its six or eight mules guided by a single jerk-rein.

***jerk,** *v.*

1. *intr.* To move involuntarily and convulsively under the influence of religious excitement. *Obs.* Cf. ***jerk,** *n.*[2] **1.**

1807 MCNEMAR *Ky. Revival* 69 About the latter end of the year 1804, there were regular societies of these people in the state of Ohio; . . . praying, shouting, jerking, barking, or rolling. **1898** DUNBAR *Folks from Dixie* 12 Every now and then some mourner would spring half up, with a shriek, and then sink down again trembling and jerking spasmodically.

2. *tr.* To slipshuck (corn) by removing the coarser outer part of the husk. *Colloq.*

1859 T. D. PRICE *Diary* (MS) 4 Oct., Put up some corn. Jerked about one load for hogs. **1907** *Farmers' Bul.* No. 313, 17 The total amount of work required to jerk the corn and afterwards husk it is considerably greater than that required to husk it from the standing stalk.

3. To draw (beer, etc.) at a bar. *Slang.*

1884 MILLER *Memorie & Rime* 20 They stared at me, but went on jerking beer behind the counter. **1946** *This Week Mag.* 28 Dec. 4/3 Captain Derry . . . could not easily go back to jerking sodas in Bullard's Drug Store.

4. *To jerk up,* to arrest. *Slang.*

1901 MERWIN & WEBSTER *Calumet 'K'* 222 He'll probably try to make out a case of criminal carelessness against me, and get me jerked up. **1910** MCCUTCHEON *Rose in Ring* 122 The cops . . . jerk up a circus man on the slightest excuse.

***jerker,** *n.* **1.** One who in religious excitement has the jerks. **2.** (See quots.) Both *obs.*

(1) **1807** MCNEMAR *Ky. Revival* 62 Head dresses were of little account among the female jerkers. **1889** *Pop. Sci.* June 148 Examples of this [religious excitement] in America are seen in the 'Jumpers,' 'Jerkers,' and various revival extravagances. — (2) **1884** GOODE *Fisheries* I. 617 The 'Horny-head,' 'River Chub,' or 'Jerker' is one of the most widely-diffused of fresh-water fishes. **1889** *Cent.* 3226/3 *Jerker,* . . . a cyprinoid fish, *Hybopsis kentuckiensis:* same as *hornyhead.*

As the last term in **beer, ink, pan, soda, wire jerker.**

***jerking,** *n.*[1] **1.** Spasmodic and convulsive jerks and tremors induced by religious excitement. **2. jerking exercise,** = ***jerk,** *n.*[2]

(1) **1842** BUCKINGHAM *E. & W. States* II. 427 At a great Camp-Meeting in Kentucky . . . the women were seized with convulsions, called at that time 'jerkings.' **1949** *Newsweek* 18 July 62/3 These groups feature . . . seeing visions, falling into trances, jerking, dancing and experiencing ecstasies. — (2) **1847** HOWE *Ohio* 46 The phenomena of '*bodily exercises,*' then common in the west . . . have been classified by a clerical writer as 1st, the *Falling* exercise; 2d, the *Jerking* exercise. **1851** —— *Hist. Coll. Great West* 200 The most singular and alarming of those affections, was the 'Jerking Exercise,' which, although common to both sexes, was more frequent in vigorous, athletic men.

***jerking,** *n.*[2] Designating a *line* or *rack* used in preparing meat as "jerk." *Obs.* — **1851** W. REID *Scalp Hunters* xxvii. 201 Yonder goes the jerking-line! **1885** *Outing* VII. 79/2 In front of the shanty was a 'jerking rack'; two parallel poles, fifteen feet in length and three feet apart.

jerk-line ˈdʒɜkˌlaɪn, *n.* A line used in place of reins to guide the lead horse of a team. Also attrib.

1888 GRIGSBY *Smoked Yank* xix. (1891) 164 The driver rode on the near wheel mule and drove the leader with a jerk-line. **1943** *Copper Camp* 124 In their wake followed more; this time, long strings of freight wagons with jerkline skinners and six- and eight-horse teams. **1947** PRICE *Trails I Rode* 175 He had a jerk-line outfit.

b. jerk-line express, (see quot. and cf. ***jerk,** *n.*[2] **2.**).

1897 *Chi. Rec.* 1 March 6/5 The nearest postoffice was Ivanpah, Cal., and ore was shipped by the 'jerk-line express' to the Atlantic & Pacific road, 90 miles away.

jerkwater ˈdʒɜkˌwɔtɚ, *n.*

1. (See quots. 1905, 1945.) Also **jerkwater line, train.**

[**1878** HART *Sazerac Lying Club* 16, I wish I may be run over by a two-horse jerk-water if there was a sage-hen in sight as far as a man could see with a spy-glass.] **1905** *D.N.* III. 84 Jerkwater (train), n. Train on a branch railway. 'Has the *jerkwater* come in yet?' **1909** *Sat. Ev. Post* 15 May 9/3 The farther along Thorpe got in the list the more disgusted he became with the prospect of living on jerk-water trains. **1945** MARSHALL *Santa Fe* 68 The Santa Fe was the Jerkwater Line—because train crews, when the water got low, often had to stop by a creek, form a bucket brigade and jerk water from the stream to fill the tender tank.

2. Also attrib. or as an adj. in the general sense of small, insignificant. *Colloq.* or *slang.*

1897 *Chi. Tribune* 25 July 15/2 *Jerkwater,* insignificant. 'John J. Ingals regards the Swiss Mission as a jerkwater job, and would not take it if it were offered to him.' **1948** *Dly. Ardmoreite* (Ardmore, Okla.) 11 Aug. 1/1 Of course what it was was one of those little jerkwater, overland circuses we used to have.

jerky ˈdʒɜkɪ, *n.*[1] (See quot. 1917.)

1850 COLTON *3 Years Calif.* 298 A tin cup of coffee, a junk of bread, and a piece of the stewed jerky. **1917** KEPHART *Camping* I. 277 'Jerky' or jerked meat has nothing to do with our common word 'jerk.' It is an anglicized form of the Spanish *charqui.* **1948** *Sat. Ev. Post* 25 Dec. 13/3 The jerky which filled one side [of the saddlebag] he distributed in his pockets.

jerky ˈdʒɜkɪ, *n.*[2] *W.* [f. the verb **jerk.*] A wagon without springs.

1869 *New No. West* (Deer Lodge, Mont.) 3 Sep. 3/5 Hon. Simon Estes is carrying the United States mails between Virginia and Bannock—per 'jerkies.' **1890** *Outing* July 326/1, I myself am an 'old timer' enough to remember riding along it in a 'jerky' in 1877. *a***1918** G. STUART *On Frontier* II. 103 Here we changed for a covered jirky.

***jerry,** *a. To be jerry to,* to be "wise" to or cognizant of. *Slang.* — **1908** K. MCGAFFEY *Show-Girl* 200 She accepted the attentions of the comedian which his wife was not supposed to be jerry to. **1928** *Collier's* 29 Dec. 29/4 Now . . . you know I' m jerry to you.

* **Jersey,** *n.*

1. The colony or state of New Jersey, formerly often pl., usu. with reference to the colonies of East New Jersey and West New Jersey.

East New Jersey and West New Jersey, formed by division in 1670, were united in a royal colony in 1702.

(1) **1683** *N.J. Archives* 1 Ser. I. 429 We desired it may be examined . . . whether he had Power to sell . . . Land in Jersey's. **1707** *Boston News-Letter* 3 Nov. 2/2 The Assembly of the Jerseys are now sitting. **1809** CUMING *Western Tour* 186 Marshon is from the Jerseys. **1863** M. HARLAND *Husks* 37 She was a native of New Jersey, 'the Jarseys' she had heard it called in her father's house.

(2) **1784** HILTZHEIMER *Diary* (1893) 22 July 64 With my wife and son Thomas, set out for Jersey, and arrived at my friend Abraham Hunt's in Trenton. **1839** *N.O. Picayune* 5 March 2/2 We have seen land in Jersey that would not support more than three whippoorwills to the acre under the highest cultivation. **1905** *McClure's Mag.* 43 They already were running to Jersey for charters, and they were already getting all that they asked for.

attrib. **1839** *N.O. Picayune* 5 March 2/2 If they dont cost more than some Jersey farms are really worth the shawls are of no more value than Mackinaw blankets. **1884** MATTHEWS & BUNNER *In Partnership* 151 Winter was still on the Jersey flats on the last day of March. **1949** *Sat. Ev. Post* 12 March 17/2 Don't confuse the Pines with the Jersey Barrens, a like district sixty miles to the southwest, across a belt of rich farm lands.

Also *Jersey boy, brigade, clamboat, -made, station,* etc.

2. a. Short for **Jersey wagon.** *Obs.* **b.** English such as is used in New Jersey. *Rare.*

(a) 1834 SIMMS *Guy Rivers* 491 A small Jersey—a light wagon in free use in that section—contained all his wardrobe, books, papers, etc. **1845** SOL. SMITH *Theatr. Apprent.* 137 Off started the Jersey, with John standing up and lashing old Copp at every jump. — **(b) 1886** S. W. MITCHELL *R. Blake* 236 Uncle John and I will arrange all that on the 'mashes.' Isn't that good Jersey, Uncle John?

3. In special combs.: (1) **Jersey bird,** (see quot. and cf. **New Jersey mosquito**); (2) **blue,** see as a main entry; (3) **cider,** (see quot. 1866), *obs.;* (4) **Dutch,** (see quot.), *obs.;* (5) **horsehead,** any one of various New Jersey cents having a representation of a horse's head on them [see *The Standard Catalogue of U.S. Coins* (1938 ed.) 11 f.]; (6) **justice,** strict or severe justice; (7) **lightning,** a particularly strong kind of applejack, *slang;* (8) * **-man,** a native or resident of the colony or state of New Jersey; (9) **Red,** formerly a breed of red swine now part of the Duroc-Jersey breed; (10) **stone,** ?a building stone found in New Jersey, *rare;* (11) **whisky,** (see quot. and cf. **Jersey lightning**).

(1) 1931 *Atlantic City Press* 3 Aug., Has the Mosquito Commission gone on a strike, or are the 'Jersey Birds' breeding so fast they can't cope with them?—**(3) 1845** *St. Louis Reveille* 4 March 2/3 If one basket of champaigne is not sufficient, go the Jersey cider. **1866** *Comm. & Fin. Chron.* 11 Aug. 163/2 Champagne is most popular in America, and yet it is probably the least reliable of all liquors. So poor is its reputation that the common name given to it is 'Jersey Cider.' — **(4) 1896** HASWELL *New York* 91 A well-known and intelligent citizen of Hackensack being asked if the language he spoke (now known as Jersey Dutch) was alike to that of the Germans, he replied he did not know.

(5) 1903 *Nation* LXVI. 22 Jan. 76/3 Fifty years ago, boys gathered cents of the various dates, and 'Jersey horseheads.' — **(6) [1863** ROSE *Great Country* 48 In Jersey they seem to have some closer ideas of justice than elsewhere, and generally hang murderers.] **1903** *N.Y. Tribune* 18 Oct. 8 Even with a faithful judge . . . 'Jersey justice' did not shine as brilliantly as usual. **1948** *Collier's* 20 Nov. 78/3 Today, the Columbus Trust Company has been merged with another bank, and Pellecchia is having dealings with Jersey justice—from the nether side of the bench. — **(7) 1852** *Alta California* (S.F.) 23 Aug. 2/5 The rumsellers dealt out Jersey lightning by the gallon. **1892** *Boston Jrnl.* 14 April 8/1 Jersey lightning will still be distilled and sold to the honest, unsuspecting public as fine old French brandy. — **(8) 1679** *Boston Rec.* 58 Thomas Begretia [entertained] at James Wardens, Jersiman. **1839** *S. Lit. Messenger* V. 800/2 A Jerseyman is preëminently calculated to make a good traveller. **1949** *Hist. & Philos. Soc. Ohio Bul.* April 74 They were especially obnoxious to the Pennsylvanians and Jerseymen. — **(9) 1879** *Diseases of Swine* 120 Claims [of immunity to swine plague] were made in behalf of Chester Whites and Jersey Reds. **1893** G. W. CURTIS *Horses* 302 The old Jersey Red or Duroc was a coarse, heavy, raw-boned, lop-eared and 'lank-sided' animal.

(10) 1857 VAUX *Villas* 104 The window-dressings, angles, etc., may be of hard Jersey stone. — **(11) 1910** J. HART *Vigilante Girl* 207 It's made of whiskey and hard cider—Jersey whiskey at that.

b. Designating light vehicles suitable for use on the loose, sandy soil usual in New Jersey, as (1) **Jersey cart,** (2) **stage,** (3) **wagon.** *Obs.* or *hist.*

(1) 1850 BURKE *Reminisc. Ga.* 240 Chairs, tables, beds and bedsteads, cradles for babies, and coops for chickens, all heaped upon cotton Jersey carts. — **(2) 1800** WEEMS *Letters* II. 154 O that I had but a Jersey Stage and a couple of good strong horses! — **(3) 1811** SUTCLIFF *Travels* p. viii, Jersey waggons . . . are made very light, hung on springs with leather braces, and travel very pleasantly. **1859** *Ladies' Repository* Nov. 669 A horse was put in the Jersey wagon, pillows and cushions piled in for her. **1944** *Sat. Review* 14 Oct. 24/2 From the vagabond Reverend Mason Weems 'bumping along in his Jersey wagon,' . . . to suave Washington Irving driving in his open carriage . . . we meet here every kind of eccentric.

c. In the names of plants: (1) **Jersey pine,** the scrub pine, *Pinus virginiana;* (2) **tea,** New Jersey tea.

(1) 1743 CLAYTON *Flora Virginica* 191 The common Jersay-Pine. **1884** SARGENT *Rep. Forests* 546 The manufacture of pumps and water-pipes from logs of the Jersey pine (*Pinus inops*) at one time an important industry in Louisville, has . . . become unremunerative. — **(2) 1808** MUHLENBERG in Dunbar *Life* 203 Red Root or Jersey Tea we call the Ceanothus. americanus a little shrub with white Flowers, cordate leaves. Some times the sanguinaria is called so. **1850** *N. Eng. Farmer* II. 60 The Jersey Tea is a small shrub, found in dry soils. **1948** *Green Bay* (Wis.) *Press-Gazette* 13 July 11/4 On the prairie land we found . . . Jersey tea, the shrub whose leaves were the 'tea' used by the colonists after the Boston tea party.

Also **Jersey greening, oak, peach, pippin, sweet, sweeting.**

1817 W. COXE *Fruit Trees* 129 Jersey, or Rhode-Island Greening. Sometimes called the Burlington Greening. **1827** DRAKE & MANSFIELD *Cincinnati* 73 The durability of the boats built upon the Ohio has in some instances even surpassed that of boats constructed in the east, from the Jersey oak. **1838** C. NEWELL *Revol. Texas* 169 The so-much celebrated Jersey peach, found in Philadelphia and New York markets, will not compare with [the Texas peach]. **1830** *Illinois Mo. Mag.* 13 Every negro in New Orleans might afford to eat Jersey pippins. **1875** BURROUGHS *Winter Sunshine* 163 With a tree of the Jersey sweet . . . in bearing, no man's table need be devoid of luxuries. **1836** *Knickerb.* VIII. 58 He held forth his bony, knuckle-knobbed hand, in which was clasped . . . a green 'Jersey-sweetin.'

As the last term in **grade, New Jersey.**

Jerseyan ˈdʒɜzɪən, *n.* A resident of New Jersey. *Rare.* — **1854** SIMMS *Southward Ho!* 21 The courage and enterprise of the Jerseyans had plucked the rugged oyster from his native abodes.

Jersey Blue. Also **Jersey blue.**

1. A name at first applied to a colonial New Jersey soldier because of his blue uniform, later extended to any native or resident of New Jersey.

1758 *Essex Inst. Coll.* XVIII. 110 Excepting ye Yorkers and Jersey Blews all ye Provincials didn't loose more than 100 men. **1849** COOPER *Sea Lions* i, Distinctions . . . do certainly exist between the Eastern and the Western man, . . . the Buckeye or Wolverine, and the Jersey Blue. **1889** MELLICK *Story Old Farm* 333 The term 'Jersey Blues' had its origin in a volunteer company from the vicinity of Springfield. Its uniform furnished by some patriotic women of the township consisted of tow frocks and breeches dyed a bright blue.

b. In allusive use.

1866 LOWELL *Biglow P.* II. xi. 242 A Nothun Dem'crat o' th' ole Jarsey blue Born copper-sheathed an' copper-fastened tu.

c. (See quot.) *Rare.*

1902 CLAPIN 243 *Jersey blue,* the color of uniform worn by Jersey troops before the War of the Revolution.

2. A breed of chickens. Also attrib.

1850 BROWNE *Poultry Yard* 77 The Jersey-Blue Fowl.—This is another large mongrel of a bluish cast. **1897** *Farmers' Bul.* No. 51, 10 The Jersey Blues . . . are one of the largest breeds of poultry. **1942** WEYGANDT *Plenty of Penna.* 277 We have no native breeds of fowls in Pennsylvania as New Jersey had its Jersey Blues.

3. In rare combs.: (1) **Jersey Blue dog,** a term of contempt for a Jerseyman; (2) **Jersey blue sand,** app. a kind of sand found in New Jersey.

(1) 1798 *Aurora* (Phila.) 13 Dec. (Th.), They said I was a Jarzy Blue Dog, and they would cut my head off. — **(2) 1848** *Rep. Comm. Patents 1847* 117 A dry compost was sifted on it, composed of the following substances: . . . Jersey blue sand, . . . Peruvian guano [etc.].

Jerseyite ˈdʒɜzɪˌaɪt, *n.* A New Jerseyan.

1854 SIMMS *Southward Ho!* 21 Perhaps, the most exciting of recent events is the oyster war between the Gothamites and Jerseyites. **1896** *Home Missionary* July 133 There are but few real Jerseyites in the

Congregational Churches of New Jersey. **1949** *Sat. Ev. Post* 12 March 17/3 People from the Oranges or Montclair or Bernardsville or Hoboken are Jerseyites only to themselves and to New Yorkers.

***Jerusalem,** *n.*

1. Used alone or in phrases as a mild oath. *Colloq.*

1840 *Spirit of Times* 8 Aug. 276/2 (We.), By Jerusalem! **1888** *Outing* May 108/1, I tried . . . the very mildest [words] first. . . . After which I advanced to 'Great Caesar!' '*J*emima'! '*J*erusalem!' (prolonging the *je* in both cases). **1914** *N.Y. Herald* 21 May 3/7 All he said to Mr. Morgan over the phone was 'Jerusalem.'

2. Jerusalem wagon, (see quot.). *Rare.*

1877 in ADAMS *Pioneer Hist.* (1923) 295 One of the curiosities of this burg is a new Jerusalem wagon. . . . The wheels are six feet in diameter, the running gear is simply two racks. The wheels run between two perpendicular posts, as there is no axle.

3. In the names of plants: (1) **Jerusalem apple,** (see quot.), *obs.;* (2) **cherry,** either of two species of *Solanum*, cultivated as ornamental house plants and so called from their cherry-like berries; (3) **corn,** (see quots.); (4) **cucumber,** a species of gherkin (see quot.); (5) **wheat,** (see quots.).

(1) **1850** *N. Eng. Farmer* II. 288 The Tomato. This plant or vegetable, sometimes called *Love Apple*, or *Jerusalem Apple*, . . . was first found in South America. — (2) **1788** CUTLER in *Life & Corr.* I. 428 Landlady gave me Jerusalem cherries, and Vandaver's Apple. **1899** VANDERBILT *Flatbush* 290 There were other plants which were transplanted to the garden after being sheltered during the winter, such as. . . . Cape jessamine, a glossy-leaved plant bearing a bright-red fruit known as 'Jerusalem cherry,' and wax-plant. **1941** *Yankee* Dec. 33/2 Jerusalem cherries and Christmas peppers, old-fashioned favorites are very intolerant of illuminating and coal gas. — (3) **1894** COULTER *Bot. W. Texas* III. 494 *Sorghum vulgare*. . . . This species includes the many varieties cultivated as sugar sorghum, Kaffir corn, Jerusalem corn, and broom corn. **1909** *Cent. Supp.* 676/1 Some varieties—for example, red Kafir-corn—are adapted to use as forage; others, particularly that known as *Jerusalem corn*, furnish grain. — (4) **1847** DARLINGTON *Weeds & Plants* 140 *Cucumis Anguria*. . . . Prickly cucumber. Jerusalem Cucumber.

(5) **1805** in *Communications to Mass. Soc. for Promoting Agric.* (1806) 26 Several Gentlemen in this neighborhood [Portsmouth, N.H.] . . . have cultivated the new species of grain, which is here generally called Jerusalem wheat. **1877** RUEDE *Sod-House Days* 147 The Jerusalem wheat is the prettiest red spring wheat I have seen, and if I can get the ground ready in the spring I will sow a few acres.

b. Jerusalem cricket, =**sand cricket.** Cf. **niño de la tierra.**

1947 *Desert Mag.* Jan. 22/3 It appears that the Babyface is actually our old friend the yellow and black striped Jerusalem-cricket or sand-cricket.

***jessamine,** *n.*

1. The yellow jessamine or a related species. Cf. **Florida jessamine.**

1709 LAWSON *Carolina* 63 Myrtles, Jessamines, Wood-bines, . . . interweave themselves with the loftiest Timbers. **1889** DELAND *Fla. Days* 68 The grass is thick in the wet darkness along the walls under the tangle of jessamine. **1927** BENÉT *J. B.'s Body* 165 The men come out of the ground, . . . as the roots of the cow-pea, [and] the roots of the jessamine.

2. a. The matrimony vine, *Lycium halimifolium.* **b.** *S.W.* A low shrub of the family Apocynaceae having fragrant white flowers.

(a) **1892** *Amer. Folk-Lore* V. 101 *Lycium vulgare*, jessamine. Stratham, N.H. — (b) **1894** *Ib.* VII. 94 *Macrosiphonia brachysiphon*, . . . jessamine. Arizona.

***Jesse,** *n.*

1. *To give* (a person) *Jesse*, to scold, thrash, beat soundly. *Slang.* Cf. **particular jesse.**

1844 *Nauvoo Neighbor* 17 April (Th.), Lo, the Saints, the Mormons bless ye! Felt thy glory most severely, When Missouri gave them jesse. **1888** *Amer. Folk-Lore* I. 78 When two American boys are fighting together and a crowd is watching the mill, a spectator will often encourage one of the contestants by crying, 'Give him jessy!' **1946** *Amer. Sp.* April 153/1 Thornton's latest citation for *give him Jesse* is from 1865. . . . In February, 1946, I heard the expression used in a game of bridge by a player from Sidney, Nebraska.

2. Also in other phrases (see quots.). *Slang.*

1840 *Boston Transcript* 12 Feb. 1/1 If any of you ever come to Saco, I kalkilate you'll get *jesse*. **1846** *Spirit of Times* 4 July 223/3 One of the combatants 'caught Jessie.' **1847** ROBB *Squatter Life* 59 The afarr [affair] raised jessy in Nettle Bottom. **1858** VIELÉ *Following Drum* 172 General Harney . . . had come down . . . to administer 'jesse' generally to all delinquents. **1863** *Rocky Mountain News* 2 April (Th.), Wherever we go [after vaccination] we are sure to catch jesse on our sore arm.

***Jesuit,** *n.* **1.** A term of contempt applied to the Tories during the Revolution. *Obs.* **2.** ***Jesuit's bark,** a local name for the marsh elder.

(1) **1774** J. ADAMS *Works* IX. 337, I admire the Jesuits! . . . Bowing . . . to persons whom . . . they would gladly butcher. **1779** HAMILTON *Works* VII. 576 He has given up Dr. Gordon, of Jamaica Plains. You will remember the old Jesuit. **1878** *N. Amer. Rev.* May–June 504 One-fourth of all power is in these ignorant masses, and they are in the hands of the political Jesuits of the South. — (2) **1894** *Amer. Folk-Lore* VII. 92 *Iva frutescens*, . . . Jesuit's bark. N.Y.

***Jethro,** *n.* A variety or alleged variety of cotton. *Rare.* — **1851** *De Bow's Review* X. 568 '*Jethro*' I have not for sale.

jew dʒu, *v.*

1. *tr.* To overreach or cheat by sharp practice or trickery. *Slang. Obs.* Cf. **Yankee,** *v.*

1824 CHESTER HARDING [an Amer. artist in England] Diary 29 April in *Sketch* (1929) 75 He is a country clergyman; and, from his Jewing disposition, I should judge he had more taste in tithes than pictures. *a***1834** L. DOW *Dealings of God* (1849) 189 If they [the Jews] will *Jew* people, they cannot flourish among Yankees, who are said to '*out-jew*' them in trading. **1859** BARTLETT 220 To *Jew* a person, is considered, in Western parlance, a shade worse than to 'Yankee' him. **1888** BILLINGS *Hardtack* 204 It's just like that fraud of a quartermaster to jew a recruit out of a part of his outfit.

2. *intr.* To haggle and bargain by way of lowering a price. Also *tr. Colloq.* or *slang.*

1825 *Constitutional Adv.* (Frankfort, Ky.) 15 Dec. 3/1 We hope, for the honour and character of the state, that neither the legislature nor the people, will Jew the items of expence. **1872** *Chi. Tribune* 14 Oct. 8/2 The prices [for lodging] asked vary—the lodger being generally asked as much as it is thought he will give. If he jews, he will get it for comparatively little. **1890** *Stock Grower & Farmer* 19 April 7/1 Don't 'jew' the owner of a stallion in the price he asks for the service of his horse.

b. jew down, to bring (a payment or price) lower by haggling or bargaining, to argue (a person) into lowering the price of something. *Slang.*

1870 *Cong. Globe* 7 July 5340/1 This bill supposes that Congress . . . is ready to commence jewing down the pay of its General. *c***1895** NORRIS *Vandover* (1914) 259, I jewed him down . . . from twenty-five thousand I brought him right down to, say eight thousand. **1942** WARNICK *Dialect Garrett Co., Md.* 9 Jew down, v. phr., endeavor to purchase an article for less than originally asked for it (Slang).

jewelhead ˈdʒuəlˌhɛd, *n.* (See quot.) — **1884** GOODE *Fisheries* I. 370 Another name [for the fresh-water drum] used in the southwest is 'Jewelhead.'

***jewelry,** *n.* **1.** *W.* A cowboy's weapons, esp. his revolvers. *Slang.* **2. jewelry store,** a store in which jewelry is sold.

(1) **1877** in ROBERT M. WRIGHT *Dodge City* (*c*1913) 165 Suppose Hayes and Morton should get on a bender and put their jewelry in soak for booze, then it would be appropriate to say they 'got to the joint' by this means. — (2) **1847** COLLINS *Kentucky* 304 Frankfort contains . . . two hardware stores, two jewelry stores, four commission houses. **1948** *Sat. Ev. Post* 9 Oct. 86/4 None of the rings could be duplicated in jewelry stores and gift shops at the prices paid at the auction.

As the last term in **dollar, hair jewelry.**

jewelweed ˈdʒuəlˌwid, *n.* Either of two American plants of the genus *Impatiens*, "so called from the earring-like shape of the flower, and the silver sheen of the under surface of the leaf in water" (*Cent.*).

1817–8 EATON *Botany* (1822) 317 *Impatiens nolitangere*, jewelweed, touch-me-not. **1893** DANA *Wild Flowers* 154 Jewel-Weed. Touch-Me-Not. . . . *Impatiens pallida.* **1949** *Chi. Tribune* 9 Jan. VI. 5/7 Then come the trumpet vine, followed by wild hydrangea, pale and spotted jewel-weed, and several species of water leaf.

Jewett red. (See quots.) Also **Jewett's fine red.** — **1847** IVES *N. Eng. Fruit* 49 *Jewett's Fine Red.*—This apple originated in Hollis, N.H. . . . It is among the best native apples of our country. **1909** WEBSTER 1162 *Jewett red*, an American variety of apple, of round-oblate form, yellow color, and subacid flavor.

jewlark ˈdʒuˌlɑrk, *v.* [Origin obscure.] *intr.* To sport *round*, to play the lover. Also **jewlarker, jewlarkie,** *n. Colloq.*

1851 HOOPER *Widow Rugby* 59 Wonder if I'll ketch that rascal Jim Sparks jewlarkin' round Betsey, down at old Bob's. **1884** J. C. HARRIS *Mingo* (1893) 166 They wuz jewlarkers thar frum ever'-where's, an' they lookt like they wuz too brazen to live skacely. **1890** *D.N.* I. 230 jewlarky . . . sweetheart. 'I'm going to see my jewlarky.'

Ky. **1908** *Ib.* III. 324 jewlarker, *n.* A person of fine dress, manners, etc., a beau, a lover. East Ala. **1934** VINES *Green Thicket World* 164 They always have been settin' on their jewlarkies' knees . . . and their jewlarkies had rather die than not to have the sweet things there.

jibe dʒaɪb, *n.* [Origin obscure. Cf. **gybe, v.*] A sharp push or blow. *Colloq.*

1843 A. E. SILLIMAN *Gallop* 5 The river stretched tranquilly onwards, undisturbed save by the occasional jibe of the boom, or lazy creak of the rudder of some craft. **1851** SPRINGER *Forest Life* 66 After an untold number of stumbles over old windfalls, and jibes from the limbs, knots, and protruding boughs of trees, we reached [the log cabin]. **1870** *Scribner's Mo.* I. 58 Richard gave the boat an impatient jibe.

jicara ˈhikɑrɑ, *n. S.W.* [Amer. Sp. *jícara* (<Nahuatl), a cup, vase, bowl, esp. one made f. the fruit of the calabash tree.] A tightly woven basket (see also quot. 1909). — **1892** LUMMIS *Tramp Across Continent* 149 Each bore upon her head a big, flaring basket—the rush *chiquihuite* of home make, or the elegantly woven Apache *jicara.* **1909** *Cent. Supp.*, jicara. . . . Same as *calabash-tree.* . . . Same as *calabash.* . . . In *metal.*, a small bowl used in testing silver amalgam.

Jicarilla hikɑˈrilja, *n. S.W.* [Amer. Sp. *jicarillos* or *xicarillas* (little baskets) dim. of *jícara* (<Nahuatl) in sense shown here.] "An Athapascan tribe, first so called by Spaniards because of their expertness in making vessels of basketry" (Hodge). Also **Jicarilla Apache.**

1799 tr. in *Pac. R.R. Rep.* (1856) III. 119 The *Apaches Xicarillas* anciently inhabited the forests of that name in the far territory to the north of New Mexico. **1850** *31st Congress* 1 Sess. Sen. Doc. 64, 57 The vocabulary as distinctly shows the kindred character of the language of the Navajos and of the Ticorillas [*sic*] branch of the Apache. **1871** *Republican Rev.* 1 April 2/1 News also came on Sunday of the murder of Francisco, the lawyer of the Jicarilla Apache tribe. **1944** ADAIR *Navajo & Pueblo Silversmiths* 97 The Jicarilla Apache move down to the southern edge of their reservation in the winter.

***jig,** *n.* **1. jig juice,** whisky. *Slang. Obs.* **2. jig-time,** a short time. *Colloq.* **3. jig-water,** (see quot.). *Rare.*

(1) 1897 LEWIS *Wolfville* 70, I s'pose this yere bein' married is a heap habit, same as tobacco an' jig-juice. **1908** MCGAFFEY *Show-Girl* 121 We had to force the only jig juice in the crowd between his clinched teeth before he could be revived. — **(2) 1916** H. L. WILSON *Somewhere in Red Gap* vii. 314 Kate has about four more of 'em licked to a standstill in jigtime. **1949** *Time* 7 March 12 Well, I fixed up that car in jig-time. — **(3) 1888** *Boston Globe* 4 March (F.), A middle-aged countryman had just tottered away from the counter, over which fusil oil (jig-water) is dispensed.

As the last term in **squid, Virginia jig.**

***jigamaree,** *n.* (See quot. 1908.) *Colloq.*

1824 *Old Colony Memorial* (Plymouth) 6 March (Th.), O the wonderation, what a nation sight of jiggermarees! **1851** *Polly Peablossom* 71 One uv them er all-fired yankee pedlars come er long with er outlandish kind uv er jigamaree to make the wimmin's coat sorter stick out in the t'other eend. **1908** *D.N.* III. 324 jigamaree, *n.* A gewgaw, a thingumabob. [East Ala.]

***jigger,** *n.*[1] (See quot. 1889.) Cf. **chigger,** *n.*

1851 D. B. WOODS *At Gold Diggings* 22 We were ourselves likewise the sport of innumerable swarms of musquitoes, ticks, fleas, and jiggers. This latter insect, though very small, is the occasion, at times, of great inconvenience and suffering. **1889** *Cent.* 3232/3 *Jigger,* . . . in the United States, a name of sundry harvest-mites or harvest-ticks which, though normally plant-feeders, fasten to the skin of human beings and cause great irritation. **1917** KEPHART *Camping* I. 253 The *moquim* mentioned above answers the description of our own chigger, jigger, red-bug, as she is variously called.

***jigger,** *n.*[2] [It is not certain that all the senses listed here relate to the same word.]

1. A vessel of the smack type having a small sail and often used as a fishing boat.

1819 BENTLEY *Diary* IV. 570 Every Jiger takes out several dories. **1842** BUCKINGHAM *E. & W. States* I. 107 Vessels collectively he [the Bay of Fundy fisherman] calls *craft,* and subdivides them into *Pinkies, Pogies, Jiggers,* &c. **1880** *Harper's Mag.* Aug. 350/2 The jigger, a small schooner of perhaps forty feet long by ten feet beam, with a considerable hold, and a cabin of four bunks. **1890** BABSON *Hist. Gloucester* II. 572 At that time, the size of the Chebacco boats was increased; and it began to be common to furnish them with a bowsprit, and call them 'jiggers.'

2. *pl.* (See quot.) *Rare.*

1841 *S. Lit. Messenger* VII. 646/2 He then dressed himself, with more than ordinary care; . . . discarding his 'stitch downs' for his 'jiggers' (his pumps).

3. A drink or dram, usu. of whisky. Also a glass or other container holding this amount.

1857 *Harper's Mag.* March 443/1 Betsy . . . would drink numerous consecutive jiggers of raw whisky without winking. **1892** A. E. LEE *Hist. Columbus* (O.) I. 335 The 'jigger' was a dram of less than a gill, taken [5 times a day]. **1946** HOLDING *Innocent Mrs. Duff* 17 On a shelf there was a fine array of bottles, with jiggers of two sizes, swizzle sticks, glass mixers.

transf. **1909** *Sat. Ev. Post* 24 April 6/2 Say, you chaps, come over and have a jigger [i.e., an ice cream soda] on me.

b. jigger boss, (see quot. 1836). *Obs.*

1836 O'BRYAN *Narrative* 107 These canal labourers have a boy to supply them with whiskey, called a *Jiggar boss,* who goes on the canal and carries a half gill (half noggin) of Whiskey to every man sixteen times a day! **1905** VALENTINE *H. Sandwith* 6 'A black couple of days,' Joe the jigger-boss suggested, as he took the 'tin' from Uncle Billy.

4. A kind of heavy cart or dray. *Colloq.*

*c***1860** in Dow *Every Day Life* 65 The long jiggers now used are scarcely less objectionable than the old trucks.

5. (See quots.)

1889 *Cent.* 3232/3 *Jigger,* . . . a small street-railway car, drawn by one horse, and usually without a conductor, the driver giving change and the fare being deposited in a box. *Ib., Jigger,* . . . a machine now generally used in the produce exchanges of American cities, which exhibits on a conspicuous dial the prices at which sales are made as the transactions occur. The hand or pointer is controlled by electric mechanism connected with a keyboard. **1900** FLYNT *Tramping* 394 *Jigger,* a sore, artificially made, to excite sympathy.

jiggling board. (See quot. and cf. **joggling board.**) *Colloq.* — **1859** BARTLETT 221 *Jiggling-Board,* a board the ends of which are placed upon frames or stools, upon which a person stands and springs up—also called a jolly-board.

***Jim,** *n.*

1. Used, alone or in combinations, as a mild oath. *Colloq.*

1866 F. KIRKLAND *Book Anecdotes* 444 By Jim! Major, you got out of that snarl completely—slick! **1897** STUART *Simpkinsville* 56, I'd give every dog gone cent . . . ef I'd been raised to swear—jim-blasted ef I wouldn't. **1911** SAUNDERS *Col. Todhunter* 7, I'll be jim-swizzled if I don't believe [etc.].

2. Jim Crow, see as a main entry.

3. Jim-dandy, jim dandy, a. A person or thing that is unusually fine or admirable. Cf. **Dandy Jim. b.** As an adj. meaning unusually good or excellent. Both *colloq.*

(a) 1887 *Courier-Journal* 12 Jan. 2/1 Dear Sir: Though a stranger to you (yet a Democrat), let me say you are a 'Jim Dandy.' **1915** *Everybody's Mag.* Oct. 460/1 It was a Jim-dandy of a peg, neither too high nor too low, but just exactly right. — **(b) 1888** *Chi. Inter-Ocean* 14 Feb. (F.), George C. Ball came upon the floor yesterday arrayed in a jim-dandy suit of clothes. **1941** STUART *Men of Mts.* 154 He said the blue-tick hound was a jim-dandy possum dog.

4. Jim Swinger, (see quots.). *Colloq.*

1895 *D.N.* I. 389 *Jim-swinger:* long-tailed coat, especially a 'Prince Albert.' **1912** CRUMPTON *Two Boys* 78, I was a tall, slim, awkward lad, about eighteen years old, thin as a match, pale as a ghost and had on a long Jim Swinger.

jimberjawed ˈdʒɪmbɚˌdʒɔd, *a.* Also †**gimbal-jawed.** Having a lower jaw that is especially loose, as if mounted on gimbals. *Colloq.*

1830 *N.Y. Constellation* 11 Sep. 2/5 You jimber-jawed rascal. **1859** BARTLETT 169 Gimbal-Jawed or Jimber-Jawed. One whose lower jaw is loose and projecting. **1923** WATTS *L. Nichols* 290 [They] moved away, all but th' oldest girl, that there jimber-jawed one, remember her? **1949** *Sat. Ev. Post* 5 March 36/3 Make it fifty! You—you jimber-jawed Judas!

transf. **1904** STERLING *Belle* 256 They were a guard, flanking on each side an old 'jimber-jawed, wobble-sided' barouche, drawn by two raw-boned horses.

***Jim Crow.** [See note.]

This term is recorded in *EDD* in the sense of a street actor (1851). This sense app. accounts for its application to a Negro, orig. a singing or clowning one.

1. The name of an old Negro song or piece of music. Also the Negro character that appears in this. *Slang. Obs.*

1828 RICE *Jim Crow* i, My name's Jim Crow, Weel about, and turn about, And do jis so. **1835** *Vade Mecum* (Phila.) 28 March 2/7 'Ditanti Palpita,' 'Jim Crow,' 'Old Hundred,' with two or three waltzes played in *different* keys usually form the *Hotchpotchiana* of their delicious entertainment. **1838** *Harvardiana* IV. 299 'Zip Coon' and 'Jim Crow' . . . are hymns of great antiquity. **1840** *Boston Transcript* 25 Mar. 2/3 Tell 'em to play Jim Crow! **1841** *N.O. Picayune* 7 May 2/2 Rice was fond of riding, and frequently visited . . . a very droll negro hostler, who used to dance grotesquely and sing odd fragments of a song about one *Jim Crow.*

attrib. **1835** *Knickerb.* V. 47 Some jolly slaves . . . were waiting to take us into a ferry-boat, which they rowed, singing some Jim Crow song.

2. A stage presentation of a song and dance first performed by Thomas D. Rice, who copyrighted the song in 1828. Also the Negro character in this performance, or the actor playing his part. *Obs.*

1835 *Vade Mecum* (Phila.) 24 Jan. 3/7 Jim Crow is in the town, about to 'wheel about' for the edification of the Brandywine. Daddy Rice will surprise them. **1835** CROCKETT *Tour* 32 The landlord, Dorrance, and others were to go with me to see Jim Crow. **1867** *Atlantic Mo.* Nov. 608/2 As a national or 'race' illustration, behind the footlights, might not 'Jim Crow' and a black face tickle the fancy of pit and circle? **1926** *N.Y. Times* 26 Dec. VII. 8/2 From 'Old Jim Crow' to 'Black Bottom,' the negro dances came from the Cotton Belt, the levee, the Mississippi River, and are African in inspiration.

attrib. **1847** *Chi. Jrnl.* 7 Oct., We do not mean *Jim Crow* dances and poor songs worse sung. **1849** HOWE *Glee Book* 89 Toe and heel and away we go, Ah, what delight it is to know De fancy Jim Crow Polka.

b. A Negro. Also attrib. *Slang.*

1838 UNCLE SAM in *Bentley's Misc.* IV. 582 Don't be standing there like the wooden Jim Crow at the blacking maker's store. **1841** H. PLAYFAIR *Playfair Papers* I. 3 A portmanteau and carpet-bag . . . were snatched up by one of the hundreds of nigger-porters, or Jim Crows, who swarm at the many landing-places to *help* passengers. **1852** STOWE *Uncle Tom* xx, I thought she was rather a funny specimen in the Jim Crow line. **1884** SHEPHERD *Prairie Exper.* 60 The Crows are a tall race, given to brilliant blankets and Jim Crow head-dresses. **1948** *Sat. Review* 27 March 36/1 Jim Crow works at the depot.

c. *To jump Jim Crow,* (1) to jump or dance according to the routine of the Jim Crow stage piece; (2) to vacillate in political allegiance for private gain, *obs.*

(1) **1833** *Sketches D. Crockett* 41 She took me down de hill side to jump Jim Crow. **1893** OWEN *Voodoo Tales* 189 Everybody began to sing and 'jump Jim Crow.' **1930** WITTKE *Tambo & Bones* 23 It was as an interpolation between the acts of this play that Rice first sang and jumped 'Jim Crow.'

(2) **1840** *Log Cabin Song Book* 38 Fo he's the man to jump Jim Crow, And prove that black is white. **1842** *Juliet* (Ill.) *Courier* 2 Feb. 1/3 The Kentucky delegation jump Jim Crow to perfection. They found the people would not sustain them in their former course. **1844** *Republican Sentinel* (Richmond, Va.) 23 March 1/2 If they were *honest* in going for Harrison *and* a Bank in 1840, then never did any set of politicians jump Jim Crow more expeditiously.

d. (See quot.) *Obs.*

1875 KNIGHT 1216/1 The jim-crow planing-machine is furnished with a reversing tool, to plane both ways, and named from its peculiar motion, as the tool is able to 'wheel about and turn about.'

e. Jim Crow Rice, (see **2.** above).

1841 *Tazewell Rep.* (Pekin, Ill.) 23 June 1/4 (*heading*), Jim Crow Rice's new verse. **1889** A. W. BRAYLEY *Complete Hist.* 185 Quite a row occurred during the winter [c1833–4] in Tremont Theatre over 'Jim Crow' Rice. **1930** WITTKE *Tambo & Bones* 20 To 'Daddy' Rice or 'Jim Crow' Rice, as he was often called, properly belongs the title of 'father of American minstrelsy.'

3. Some kind of crude comb. *Rare.*

1899 CHESNUTT *Conjure Woman* 22 He wuk at it ha'f de night wid er Jim Crow.

4. (See quot.)

1931 *Amer. Sp.* VII. 48 [In lumberjack lingo] 'Tie men' are also known as 'Jim Crow men.' Their boss is called 'Captain Jim Crow.' These names are derived from the 'jim crows,' the small unsalable ties which they make.

5. Short for **Jim Crowism.** Also attrib. *Slang.*

1943 OTTLEY *New World* 69 Negro soldiers had suffered all forms of Jim Crow, humiliation, discrimination, slander, and even violence at the hands of the white civilian population. **1948** *Time* 13 Dec. 63/1 The Federal Council . . . went on record as opposing Jim Crow in any form.

6. In special combs.: (1) **Jim Crow bill,** a legislative bill that permits racial discrimination; (2) **car,** see as a main entry; (3) **law,** a law, esp. in the southern states, requiring the separation of white and colored people in public conveyances, at resorts, etc.; (4) **school,** (*a*) actors or minstrels of the Jim Crow type, *rare,* (*b*) a school for colored students.

(1) **1904** *Nation* 17 March 202 Writing of the 'Jim Crow' bills now before the Maryland Legislature, the Cardinal expressed his strong opposition. — (3) **1904** *Richmond Times-Dispatch* 25 May 10 The Norfolk and Southern Railroad was fined $300 to-day for violating the 'Jim Crow' law by allowing negroes to ride in the same car with whites. **1949** *Lubbock* (Tex.) *Morn. Avalanche* 23 Feb. I. 2/2 The Jim Crow law causes occasional difficulty, although the company does not post signs. — (4) (*a*) **1847** J. SPENCE *Ship & Shore* 88 Here . . . are two boys of the Jim Crow school, singing charcoal songs to a checkered crowd. (*b*) **1903** *N.Y. Sun* 29 Nov. 7 The members of the committee have arranged with the parents of negro children to send them all to the Jim Crow school, thus entirely separating the white and negro pupils. **1948** *Dly. Ardmoreite* (Ardmore, Okla.) 22 Jan. 1/7 What they call a 'Jim Crow' school cannot meet the federal court's requirements for equality under the 14th amendment.

b. In miscellaneous expressions denoting institutions, regulations, etc., practicing, resulting from, or catering to racial discrimination, as **Jim Crow church, -poor white system, presbytery, regulation.**

1904 *Churchman* 11 June 728 Many opposed it [a proposal at the Presbyterian Assembly for the organization of presbyteries for a special race] as constituting 'Jim Crow presbyteries.' **1910** *N.Y. Ev. Post* 2 June (Th.), An attempt to get the Supreme Court of the United States to pass on the authority of common carriers engaged in interstate commerce to make 'Jim Crow' regulations, met with failure to-day. **1943** *Christian Cent.* 29 Sep. 1101/2 He knows too many churchmen who approve Jimcrow churches. **1947** *Chi. Sun.* 20 Jan. 6/2 His very riddance at this moment in history would strengthen the fight against the Jim Crow-poor white system.

c. Used with the force of a common adjective in the sense of tricky, mean, contemptible. *Colloq.*

1838 *N.Y. Advt. & Exp.* 18 April 2/1 Gov. Marcy's message, Mr. Secretary Woodbury's Letter [etc.] . . . are Jim Crow performances. **1890** *Stock Grower & Farmer* 11. Jan. 3/4 The *Stock Grower* has refused to puff a fraudulent jim crow ditch scheme whose projectors have handled a big profit before the 'preliminary survey' was made. *Ib.* 3 May 7/4 Many people have become slaves to the vile opium habit from the use of that drug by these jim-crow physicians. **1897** A. H. LEWIS *Wolfville* 193 He hangs about Wolfville an' Red Dog alternate turnin' little jim-crow tricks for the express company.

Jim Crow, *v. tr.* To subject (a person) to discrimination because of race. *Slang.*

1923 *Nation* 15 Aug. 155 But they are not 'jim crowed.' **1924** *Amer. Mercury* Oct. 182/1 They said that their officers were more eager to Jim Crow them than to fight the Germans. **1944** *Reader's Digest* March 73 Even in Army uniform, George has been 'Jim Crowed.'

Jim Crow car. A railroad car for the exclusive use of Negroes. Also transf.

"The very phrase 'Jim Crow car' seems to have been first used in 1841 with reference to a railroad car in Massachusetts set apart for the use of Negroes" (*New Republic,* 27 Nov. 1915, 88/1).

1842 *Liberator* (Boston) 21 Jan. 10/1 It is this spirit that compels the colored man to set in the 'negro pew,' and ride in the 'Jim-Crow car.' **1861** H. JACOBS *Life Slave Girl* 265, I was now put into a 'Jim Crow car,' on our way to Rockaway. **1927** *Seattle Enterprise* 14 Jan. 1/2 The 'jim crow' car was made to humble the better class of Negro as well as to separate the humbler class. **1949** *Southwest Rev.* Spring 124/2 The Central Jurisdiction [of the reunited Methodist Church] is not geographic. It is an overlapping Jurisdiction, in a different dimension—the racial dimension. It is the Jim Crow car of the Methodist train.

Jim Crowism. Discrimination based upon race. *Slang.*

1837 *N.Y. Mirror* 7 Oct. 118/1 Then, to counterbalance this good, you have entailed upon those British islands the curse of Jim Crowism. **1925** *Amer. Mercury* Jan. 87/2 In his celebrated Atlanta speech he justified all the forms of Jim-Crowism. **1948** *Sat. Review* 24 July 16/3 It is to his eternal credit that he ripped through the Jim Crowism of our national game by giving a fine Negro athlete a chance to play in organized baseball.

jimmies 'dʒɪmɪz, *n. pl.* = **willies.** *Slang.* — **1900** J. C. HARRIS *On the Wing* 42 Take 'im to the hospital, Tim; 'tis the only way to clear the jimmies from his head.

***jimminy,** *n.* In various phrases used as mild oaths (see quots.). *Colloq.* Cf. **gee.**

1848 J. MITCHELL *Nantucketisms* 40 *By Jiminy Cricket,* an exclamation of surprise. **1887** *Cent. Mag.* April 854/2 'Great Jiminy Crimany!' Major Jimmy Bass would exclaim; 'don't we all know Little Compton like a book?' **1893** *Harper's Mag.* 67/2 Jiminy crackers! but I wush 't I'd 've knew it. **1898** F. H. SMITH *C. West* 288 Jiminy-whiz, but it's soapy out there! See 'er take that roller! Gosh! **1942** WARNICK *Dialect Garrett Co., Md.* 7 Geeminy criminy, interj., mild imprecation.

***jimmy,** *n.* **1.** "A freight-car used for carrying coal; a coal-car" (*Cent.*). **2.** A large crab. Both *colloq.* — (1) **1887** *N.Y. Semi-Wkly. Tribune* 18 March (*Cent.*), The express train . . . ran into a freight. . . . The second car on the freight was lifted from the rails and carried on top of two jimmies loaded with coal. — (2) **1942** DAVIS *Chesapeake Biol. Lab. Pub.* 53, 8 When a big 'Jimmy' gets into the pot, the little crabs . . . keep their distance.

jimmy-john ˈdʒɪmɪˌdʒɑn, *n. S.* A jocose variant of "demijohn." *Colloq.*

1884 HARRIS *Mingo* 28 Ole Marster he ain't say nothin', but he tuck a fresh grip on de jimmy-john. **1888** CRADDOCK *Despot* 200 Jes' ketch a-holt o' the handle o' that thar jimmy-john in the corner, an' haul it hyar. **1922** in WENTWORTH, *s.v. demijohn.*

jimpsecute ˈdʒɪmpsəˌkjut, *n. S.* [App. Eng. dial. *jimpsey*, neat, smart, + ∗**cute,** pretty, attractive. See *jimpsey* in *EDD* and *jimp* in *OED.*] (See quots.) *Colloq.*

[**1848** in *Amer. Sp.* X. (1935) 40/2 Cumsha kute. Excellent. Also Lumpsha kute.] **1869** *Overland Mo.* III. 131 When a Texan goes forth on a sparking errand, he does not go to pay his devoirs to his Amaryllis, . . . but . . . his 'jimpsecute.' **1891** *N. & Q.* VIII. 60 In the State of Mississippi, I several times heard the word jimpsycute used in the sense of 'sweetheart,' it being always, so far as I remember, applied to the young lady in the case.

jimson ˈdʒɪmsn̩, *n.* [f. **Jamestown (weed).**]

1. Short for next. Also attrib.

1812 *Cramer's Alman. 1813* (Pittsburgh) 26 James'-town weed, from James'-town, on James' River, in Virginia, where the plant seem to have first attracted notice. It is also known by the name of Jimson, and Thorn-apple. **1867** G. W. HARRIS *Sut Lovingood* 177 They makes soup outen dirty towels an' jimson burrs. **1943** PEATTIE *Great Smokies* 118 Jimson root for ulcers and to help palsy . . . they went to the woods for them.

2. jimson weed, a tall, coarse, poisonous weed, *Datura stramonium,* from the leaves of which the drug stramonium is obtained. Also **jimpson weed.**

1832 BENTON *30 Years' View* I. 256/2 An eagle . . . [was] by a pig under a jimpson weed . . . caught and whipt. **1875** *Cin. Enquirer* 5 July 8/1 Gympson weeds are ripe. **1948** *Nat. Hist.* April 147/2 These [narcotic plants] included Jimson weed (*D. stramonium*) and Ololiuhqui (*D. meteloides*), both used by the Aztec priests.

∗**jingle,** *n.*

1. (See quot.) Cf. **gold shell** (*b*).

1881 E. INGERSOLL *Oyster Industry* 245 *Jingle.*—Any species of *Anomia.* (Long Island sound.) **1887** GOODE *Fisheries* V. 543 A more fragile shell, such as a scallop, mussel, or jingle (*Anomia*) is certainly better.

2. jingle bob, *W.* (See quots.)

1890 *Stock Grower & Farmer* II. Jan 11/2 Ear marks, double jingle-bob left ear. **1913** BARNES *Western Grazing Grounds* 382 Jingle Bob.—An ear-mark made by cutting the ear on the upper side, so as to break the back of the ear. This allows it to hang down along the side of the face much as do the long ears of the Angora goat. **1920** HUNTER *Trail Drivers Texas* I. 15 Mr. Charles Goodnight went the western route . . . , afterwards trailing the 'Jingle Bobs' or the John Chissum cattle north. **1926** BRANCH *Cowboy* 24 Spurs might have 'jingle-bobs' to tinkle as the cowboy walked.

∗**jingled,** *a.* Confused with drink, fuddled. *Slang.* — **1908** G. H. LORIMER *J. Spurlock* xii. 315 Old Mrs. Corliss was purple with pleasure at having so plausible a pretext for getting comfortably jingled.

jinglet ˈdʒɪŋglɪt, *n.* **1.** (See quots. 1885, 1893.) **2.** A short, catchy piece of verse.

(1) **1881** *Sci. Amer.* XLIV. 323 This sand core, with the jinglet inside, is placed in the mould of the outside [etc.]. **1885** *American* IX. 350 The little iron ball [of the sleigh bell] is called 'the jinglet.' **1893** *Stand.* 964/3 Jinglet . . . any small jingling appendage, especially one shaped like a sleigh-bell. — (2) **1931** *K.C. Star* 5 Oct., A Kansas jinglet by Tom Thompson.

jingo ˈdʒɪŋgo, *v. tr.* To force into action by an aggressively chauvinistic policy. *Rare.* — **1898** *Westminster Gaz.* 28 Feb. 7/1 President McKinley is reported to have declared that he 'will not be jingoed into war.'

jinks dʒɪŋks, *n.* The checkerberry. *Colloq.* — **1892** *Amer. Folk-Lore* V. 100 *Gaultheria procumbens,* . . . jinks or chinks. N.H.; Mass.

jinx dʒɪŋks, *n.* [A form of ∗*jynx*, the wry-neck, a bird used in witchcraft, hence a charm or spell.] A person or thing that brings bad luck; esp. in sports, a hoodoo. Also attrib. *Slang.*

1911 *Chi. D. News* 19 Sep. 6/3 Dave Shean and 'Peaches' Graham . . . have not escaped the jinx that has been following the champions. **1928** *Wis. Alumni Mag.* Dec. 79 Once realizing that the jinx had been broken, . . . there was not hesitation. **1946** *Dly. Ardmoreite* (Ardmore, Okla.) 15 Dec. 12/4 Friday is supposed to be a jinx day but when the 13 comes with it it is really a jinx day and everything goes wrong. **1948** MENJOU & MUSSELMAN *It Took 9 Tailors* 96 There has never been such a jinx picture as that one.

Also **jinx,** *v. tr.*, to cast a spell on (someone).

1917 *Amer. Mag.* April 43/1 What do you mean—humming love songs when their darn pitcher is forcing in runs? You jinxed my ball club. **1928** *Collier's* 13 Oct. 20/3 The best way to jinx any team is to predict a winning season.

jitney ˈdʒɪtnɪ, *n.* [Origin obscure. Cf. F. *jeton*, a token or counter.]

1. (See quots.) *Slang.*

1903 *Cin. Enquirer* 2 May 11/5 [In St. Louis] a 'crown guy' is a policeman, a 'gitney' is a nickel, and 'mug's landing' is the Union Station. **1915** *Nation* 4 Feb. 142/1 The word 'jitney' . . . is the Jewish slang term for a nickel.

attrib. **1916** H. L. WILSON *Somewhere in Red Gap* ii. 59 He . . . sells these jitney pianos and phonographs and truck like that. **1946** *Grizzly Growl* (Yampa, Colo.) 20 Dec. 2/1 Many enjoyed the Jittney dance.

2. An automobile, esp. one covering a regular route and carrying passengers for a nickel, orig. **jitney bus.** Also transf. *Slang.*

1915 *Nation* 14 Jan. 50/3 (Letter of 28 Nov., 1914), This autumn automobiles, mostly of the Ford variety, have begun to run in competition with the street cars in this city [*sc.* Los Angeles]. The newspapers call them 'Jitney 'buses.' **1916** *Illust. World* (Chi.) 597 (*heading*), Woman Captain of a Jitney Boat. **1947** *Chi. Tribune* 9 Nov. I. 27/1 With flashlights they stopped the old 'jitney' I'd hired. **1949** *Chi. D. News* 14 June 14/6 Suggests Drivers Run Jitney Cars.

b. Also **jitney,** *v. intr.*, to travel by jitney.

1915 *Amer. Mag.* Dec. 21/3 Four masked men held up an omnibus in which seventeen men were jitneying to Salem, New Jersey, with their pay envelopes in their pockets.

Also *jitney driver, omnibus, operator, service,* etc.

jitters ˈdʒɪtɚz, *n. pl.* Extreme nervousness, the jimmies or willies. Also transf. *Slang.*

1931 *Charlottesville* (Va.) *Prog.* 23 March 12/8 Swift moving elevators and roller coasters also give her the jitters. **1945** *Chi. D. News* 31 Oct. 1/3 This, in brief, is the administration wage-price policy, long awaited by a nation with the reconversion jitters. **1949** *Lubbock* (Tex.) *Morn. Avalanche* 23 Feb. I. 11/7 His scream enhanced the drama, gave the crowd the jitters.

Hence **jittery,** *a.*

1931 *K.C. Times* 13 Nov. 22 The editors will go home all jittery unless the Junior League girls . . . quit parading around the mezzanine. **1949** *Wholesale Grocery News* April 14/3 There is no reason to be jittery.

∗**Joan,** *n.* App. a kind of cloth. Also **Joan's spinning.** *Obs.*

Cf. *OED* ∗*Joan,* "a close-fitting cap worn by women in the latter half of the 18th century," and note that quot. 1812 below may be in that sense.

1790 *Pa. Packet* 2 Jan. 1/4 A compleat assortment of Stuff Goods; such as, durants, tammies, Joan's spinning, calimancoes. **1793** *Mass. Spy* 16 May 3/3 New goods imported this Spring include: . . . wildbore, joans, black russel, black lasting. **1812** *Niles' Reg.* II. 9/1 Much of it [i.e., wool] . . . may be wrought into . . . joans.

∗**Job,** *n.*[1] The well-known name of the Biblical character used in the possessive in colloq. combs.: (1) **Job's cat,** a symbol of poverty, *rare;* (2) **coffin,** Delphinus, or the Dolphin, a northern constellation nearly west of Pegasus; (3) **oxen,** the oxen owned by Job, in allusion to their numbers, 500 yoke, *rare;* (4) **turkey,** used, in phrases, of something, particularly poverty, that is exceptionally great.

(1) **1854** SEBA SMITH *'Way Down East* 184, I should rather be as poor as Job's cat all the days of my life. — (2) **1883** WILDER *Sister Ridnour* 133, I chanced to get a glimpse of the stars in 'Job's coffin.' **1931** *Randolph Enterprise* (Elkins, W.Va.) 12 Nov. 2/2 We watch the Great Dipper, the Seven Stars, Jobs coffin and several others. — (3) **1830** S. SMITH *Major Downing* 24 It broke the Sinnet wheel right in tu, and left it so flat, that all Job's oxen never could start it. — (4) **1824** *Troy Sentinel* 22 May (Th.), We have seen fit to say 'the patience of Job's turkey,' instead of the common phrase, 'as patient as Job.' **1830** *Va. Lit. Museum* 496/2, I am left by my new house, Poor as Job's turkey, or a starv'd church mouse. **1948** *Sat. Review* 22 May 14/1 'Poor as Job's turkey,' for instance, illustrates our habit of extending a well-known simile for variety or humorous effect.

∗**job,** *n.*[2]

1. A more-or-less permanent position of employment, a situation. *Colloq.* Cf. **fence riding, rush job.**

*a***1861** WINTHROP *E. Brotherloft* 38, I will find you a fat job and plenty of pickings! **1945** *Nation* CLX. 476/2 For every job lost in a low-wage protected industry, one or more new jobs would be created in our high-wage export industries.

2. In combs.: (1) **job holder,** one who holds a political job, *colloq.;* (2) **legislation,** legislation designed to provide jobs for political party henchmen, *colloq.;* (3) **print, printing,** the printing of small pieces of work, as handbills, programs, etc., also attrib.

(1) **1904** CRISSEY *Tattlings* 275 There'll be a brass band and a lot of job holders waiting with glad hands at the station to meet me. — (2) **1854** BENTON *30 Years' View* I. 232/1 It seems to be nothing now ... when personal and job legislation have become the frequent practice. — (3) **1825** *New Lisbon* (Ohio) *Patriot* 29 Oct. 1/4 Job Printing, Neatly and expeditiously done at this office. **1921** MULFORD *Bar-20 Three* vi. 77 A hard-riding courier, relaying twice, carried the work of the job-print toward Mesquite. **1948** *Capital-Democrat* (Tishomingo, Okla.) 10 June 6/4 The job printing department of the Capital-Democrat is a busy place, turning out hundreds of different kinds of jobs.

***jobber,** *n.* As the last term in **real estate, stock jobber.**

jobbing house. A firm engaged in stock-jobbing. Also one which buys goods in bulk to sell to retailers.

1870 MEDBERY *Men Wall St.* 166 Mr. Fisk's maturity dates with his entrance as partner in a well-known Boston jobbing-house. **1878** *Harper's Mag.* April 760/2 We were all employed in the old jobbing-house down town. **1928** *Publishers' Wkly.* 30 June 2596 The service of a well-equipped and completely-stocked jobbing house ... is ... invaluable to the small bookseller.

***jobster,** *n.* A contemptuous term for one who gives or takes jobs in public service in return for political favors. — **1897** *N.Y. Times* 15 Nov., The Hawaiian jobsters are astir again, and they talk with buoyant confidence. They seem to feel sure of the administration. **1913** LA FOLLETTE *Autobiog.* 167 He was not in favor of the spoilsman or the jobster.

***jockey,** *n.*[1]

1. a. Short for *jockey cap.* **b.** A jacket. Both *obs.*

(**a**) **1759** *Boston Gaz.* 13 Aug., Sattin Jockeys with Feathers for Boys, brocaded silk, black sattin, and Russel Shoes. **1865** STOWE *House & Home P.* 165 That's my jockey, papa, with a plume *en militaire.* — (**b**) **1879** *Harper's Mag.* Dec. 67/1 The scissors ... changed the relic of stately awkwardness [a waistcoat] into a jaunty 'jockey' or jacket.

2. jockey stick, (see quots.).

1887 CUSTER *Tenting on Plains* 352 In driving a prairie schooner a small hickory stick, about five feet long, called the jockey-stick, not unlike a rake-handle, is stretched between a pilot [mule] and his mate. **1942** WARNICK *Dialect Garrett Co., Md.* 9 Jockey-stick, n., a stick fastened to the bridles of a team of horses to prevent crowding.

jockey ˈdʒɑkɪ, *n.*[2] [f. the verb.] A horse deal. *Colloq.* — **1867** LACKLAND *Homespun* II. 181 [The Tavern] served for their Exchange; and never did a dicker or a jockey occur, but the profit and the loss were each congratulated and consoled with sundry social drinks.

As the last term in **horse, Negro jockey.**

***Joe,** *n.* Also **joe, jo.**

1. (See quot. 1851.)

1847 in *N. & Q.* VI. (1946) 61/2 Feeling quite lively after my return, disguised myself, and went down and nailed up all the South College joe-doors! [At Amherst.] **1851** HALL *College Words* 271 *Joe,* a name given at Yale and Hamilton colleges to a privy.... The following account of *Joe-burning* is by a correspondent from Hamilton College. **1942** BERREY & VAN DEN BARK *Amer. Thesaurus Slang* 87.

2. In combs.

In some of the expressions included here there has apparently been confusion between **Joe,* the familiar form of Joseph, and **jo,* as a term of endearment, probably the same word as **joy.*

(1) **joe boat,** app. a small rowboat, *obs.*, cf. **John boat;** (2) **Joe Bunker,** app. a nickname for an American, also attrib., now *obs.* or *hist.;* (3) **joe dandy,** variant of jim dandy *q.v.*, one who or that which is of outstanding excellence, *slang;* (4) **darter,** a quick, smashing blow (see quot. 1908), *slang;* (5) **Joe Doakes,** a name for a fictitious individual regarded as representing a large class, a John-a-Nokes, *colloq.;* (6) **joe-fired,** denoting something unusual of its kind, *slang;* (7) **flogger,** (see quots.), *obs.;* (8) **-pye,** either of two tall perennial herbs of the genus *Eupatorium,* in full **joe-pye weed;** (9) **rocker,** (see quot.).

(1) **1874** R. H. COLLINS *Kentucky* I. 238, 5 persons, while crossing the Big Sandy river in Floyd co. in a joe boat, caught in the ice and drowned. **1887** *Courier-Journal* 15 Feb. 6/4 The Noise of the Midnight Hammer is Heard in the Land, Building 'Joe Boats' to Be Used in the Second-story of High Houses. — (2) **1787** in *Pub Col. Soc. Mass.* XXXII. 379 Huzza, my joe-bunkers! no taxes we'll pay! **1797** *Ib.*, No American felt injured by this appellation, no more than he did by being called a *Yankee,* a *Joe Bunker,* or a *leather-button Curse.* **1935** A. MATHEWS in *Pub. Col. Soc. Mass.* XXXII. 379 In a letter written from Boston in 1777 by William Gardiner of Gardiner, Maine, there is an allusion to 'a Joe Bunker justice.' ... I do not know exactly what the term means. — (3) **1890** *Juliaetta* (Ida.) *Gem* 9 Aug. 1/2 Ben is what is termed a 'Joe dandy,' and undoubtedly knows how to build grades in a rapid and workmanlike manner. **1926** BRANCH *Cowboy* 57 Mounted on a 'cutting pony' that was a 'Joe-dandy,' he made a figure for his boss. — (4) **1851** *Polly Peablossom* 151, I could hit him a jo-darter. **1904** O. HENRY *Heart of West* 113 That cussed little runt ... is the Jo-dartin'est hustler. **1908** *D.N.* III. 325 *joe darter,* n. phr. A very fine or excellent thing, a shrewd or smart person. 'He's a *joe darter* when it comes to trading.'

(5) **1945** *Nation* CLX. 28 April 480/1 John Doe and Joe Doakes, along with the Cabots and the Lowells ... will have very little idea whether the result should be a source of enthusiasm or despair. **1949** *Lisle* (Ill.) *Eagle* 10 March 6/5 As long as we have the Joe Doaks, the Bill Smiths, the Jack Browns and Mary Lees representing us at Washington, we will continue to have government 'of, for and by the people.' — (6) **1824** *Woodstock* (Vt.) *Observer* 24 Feb. (Th.), Whate'er joe fir'd racket they keep up. **1851** *Ore. Statesman* 2 Sep. 1/7, I don't write my name as handsome as some, but it's Joe-fired plain. **1925** KRAPP *Eng. Lang. in Amer.* I. 118 Phrases like *I swan ... all fired, jo fired* are quite safe though they still bear enough of the marks of their origin upon them to satisfy the needs of Puritan imprecation. — (7) **1852** *32nd Congress* 2 Sess. H.R. Ex. Doc. No. 23, 260 [The boat-fisherman of the Bay of Fundy] is kind and hospitable in his way; and the visitor ... is treated to *fresh smother, duff,* and *jo-floggers.* [Note:] Potpie of sea-birds, pudding and pancakes. **1889** MUNROE *Dorymates* 47 The cook made them [the crew] a great dish of Joe-floggers (peculiar pancakes stuffed with plums) for breakfast. — (8) **1817–8** EATON *Botany* (1822) *Eupatorium purpureum,* purple thoroughwort, joe-pye. **1893** DANA *Wild Flowers* 210 Joe-Pye-Weed. Trumpet-Weed. *Eupatorium purpureum.* ... 'Joe Pye' is said to have been the name of an Indian who cured typhus fever in New England by means of this plant. **1949** *Nature Mag.* April 187/2 Later the cowslips are replaced by purple loosestrife and that butterfly magnet, Joe-pye weed. — (9) **1884** GOODE *Fisheries* I. 774 In Vineyard Sound and Buzzard's Bay it [the green crab] is known to the fishermen as the 'Joe Rocker.'

b. Joe Brown's Pets, (see quot.), in allusion to Joseph E. Brown (1821–94), governor of Georgia during the Civil War. *Obs.*

1863 CUMMING *Hospital Life* (1866) 104/1 A young man came in and told Mrs. B. that the soldier was pretending that he was one of 'Joe Brown's Pets,' as the Georgia militia are called.

Joey ˈdʒo·ɪ, *n.* [App. f. **banjo.**] (See quot.) *Obs.* — **1884** ROWBOTHAM *Prairie-Land* (1885) 145 His opportunities of enjoying music, since the period when he left Sunday-school, had been confined to an occasional performance upon the 'Joey,' as the banjo is familiarly termed.

***jog,** *n.* A receding or projecting break in a surface or line, an abrupt bend in a road. *Colloq.* Cf. **horse jog.**

1845 JUDD *Margaret* I. xiv. 118 Directly on the right of the sun-setting was an apparent jog or break in the line of the woods and hills. **1892** MAHAN *Sea Power & Fr. Rev.* I. 80 [Spain's] maritime advantages were indeed diminished by the jog which Portugal takes out of her territory. **1928** F. N. HART *Bellamy Trial* 173 There is a jog in the road two or three hundred feet north of our house.

joggle board. =next. — **1905** DIXON *Clansman* 206 He took his seat on the joggle-board beside the door and awaited her return.

joggling board. (See quot. 1930.) *Colloq.*

1882 G. C. EGGLESTON *Wreck of Red Bird* 14 The best way to get acquainted with a joggling board ... is to get on it.... Don't be afraid. **1904** *K.C. Star* 18 Aug. (Th. Supp.), A 'Joggling-board' is the latest contrivance for exercise that has made its appearance in these parts and it is liable to become the poor man's horse. **1930** *D.N.* VI. 82 *joggling board,* n. phr. A thick, resilient plank, about twelve feet long, resting on two uprights, on which one sits and 'joggles' up and down. Formerly, everyone had a joggling board on his piazza. A few may still be seen, but they are not as popular as they once were. [Wedgefield, S.C.]

***John,** *n.*

1. A Chinese. *Slang.* Cf. **John Chinaman.**

1853 *Alta California* (S.F.) 20 April 2/2 The May Adams brought 118 'Johns' from the terrestrial kingdom of heaven. **1889** *Woodburn* (Wash.) *Independent* 7 Sep. 1/4 It will only be a matter of time when the demand for 'John' will be little or nothing ... for the whites do the work so much better. **1948** JOHNSTON *Gold Rush* 11/1 The despised 'Johns' were permitted to pan gold in peace, provided they paid their foreign miners' tax when it was due.

2. In combs.: (1) **John A. Grindle,** (see quots. and cf. **Grindle** and **Johnny Grindle**); (2) **Alden,** (see quot.); (3) **boat,** a flat-bottomed skiff, cf. **joe boat;** (4) ***Brown,** *attrib.* honoring or in allusion to John Brown (1800–1859), the abolitionist; (5) **Chinaman,** (*a*) a

Chinese, (*b*) (see quot.); (6) **Donkey,** a jackass, *colloq.;* (7) **Hancock,** an autograph or signature; (8) **Henry,** =prec.; (9) **Mariggle,** (see quot.); (10) **Paw,** the speckled hind, a common food fish found on the Florida coast; (11) **Q. Public,** a name for a fictitious typical citizen, also **John Q. Citizen, John Q. Voter,** *colloq.;* (12) * **the Baptist,** (see quot.), *rare, slang;* (13) **-the-Conqueror-root,** =**Conquer-John;** (14) **Yankee,** a typical Yankee, *rare.*

(1) **1896** Jordan & Evermann *Fishes N. Amer.* 113 Amia calva, Linnæus. (Mudfish; Dogfish; Grindle; 'John A. Grindle'; Lawyer; Poisson de Marais.) **1943** in *Amer. Sp.* XX. (1945) 69/1 The bowfin is a well-known fish . . . Virginians give it the dignified name of John A. Grindle. — (2) **1942** Rawson *N.H. Borns a Town* 118 Another of the typical New England center-chimney homes of great size, 'John Alden' or 'Duxbury barn' type, as 1941 calls them. — (3) **1905** *N.Y. Ev. Post* 2 Sep., Two men came down the Mississippi in an Illinois jon-boat, paddling slowly with rough-whittled boards. **1917** Kephart *Camping* II. 134 [We] hit upon what we conceived to be a brilliant scheme for transporting a gallon of whiskey inconspicuously in our John-boat. **1941** Stuart *Men of Mts.* 312, I bought me a john-boat. — (4) **1863** Dicey *Six Months* II. 188 With the 'John Brown year,' as the report of the Anti-Slavery Society termed the year 1860, a change came. **1865** *Atlantic Mo.* Feb. 252/1 The Bishop of Vermont must meditate a John Brown raid. **1874** Pinkerton *Expressman & Detective* 18, I had always been a man somewhat after the John Brown stamp, aiding slaves to escape, or keeping them employed, and running them into Canada when in danger.

(5) (*a*) **1834** *Amer. R.R. Jrnl.* III. 189/1 They are required to . . . ascertain the height of John Chinaman in a breath. **1913** London *Valley of Moon* III. v, There are . . . apple canneries and cider and vinegar factories. And Mr. John Chinaman owns them. **1943** *Copper Camp* 107 John Chinaman followed close on the heels of the first miners. (*b*) **1939** Rollins *Gone Haywire* 137 The only feasible menu . . . seemed at the moment to be beans, 'sow belly,' . . . 'saddle blankets' (griddle cakes), and 'john chinaman' (boiled rice with raisins). — (6) **1859** Taliaferro *Fisher's R.* 234 Some one passed the road with a long-eared animal, politely called a John Donkey. — (7) [**1846** Holmes in *Corr. R. W. Griswold* (1898) 221 Avoiding . . . the pretentious boldness of John Hancock . . . I subscribe myself Yours very truly.] **1948** *Sat. Review* 31 July 16/2 Every American old enough to sign a legal paper has sometimes referred to the act as 'putting on my John Hancock.' — (8) **1914** *D.N.* IV. 109 John Henry or John Hancock. Autograph. **1945** *Everybody's Digest* Aug. 87 'John Henry,' meaning signature, . . . rolled from the cowboy's language mint. — (9) **1896** Jordan *Check-List N. Amer. Fishes* 279 *Elops saurus* . . . [is called] Tenpounder . . . John Mariggle; Bony-fish; Bone-fish; Big-eyed Herring [etc.]; Common north to the Gulf of California and to Long Island on the Atlantic Coast.

(10) **1883** *Nat. Museum Bul.* No. 27, 503 *Epinephetus drummondhayi* . . . John Paw; Spotted Hind. — (11) **1945** *Suburban List* 8 Feb. 10/2 Who is going to represent and look out for the interests of John Q. Public as a lobbyist? **1947** *Denver Post* 25 Feb. 16/1 It makes no difference that thousands of plain John Q. Citizens are unable to buy tickets at any price. **1948** *Dly. Ardmoreite* (Ardmore, Okla.) 29 April 1/1 The political big shots are so sure of the way John Q. Voter will act they do not fret themselves over him at all. — (12) **1888** *Arkansaw Traveler* Oct. (F.), Mebbe he gwine ter gimme a John de Baptist' [*sic*]—dat's one cent. — (13) **1934** Carmer *Stars Fell on Ala.* 220 Mix John the Conqueror Root with a lodestone and it will draw dimes right off a store counter. **1946** Tallant *Voodoo in N.O.* 225 Thousands of Negroes carry Johnny the Conqueror roots. — (14) **1778** J. Adams in *Warren-Adams Lett.* II. 40, I never was however much of John Bull. I was John Yankee and such I shall live and die.

As the last term in **apple, blue, Bronze, hopping, rolling, Saddle-bag, whisky, wo-haw John.**

John Brown, *v. tr.* To darn. *Slang.* — **1869** in Mathews *Beginnings* 160 You need apprehend nothing dreadful, for boobies seldom 'John Brown' each other. **1942** Phillips *Big Spring* 1 I'll be John Browned if we didn't have a dry norther that would send you hunting for your long ones.

Johnkannaus 'dʒɔnkənaʊs, *n.* [App. related to Twi (spoken on the Gold Coast) *agyanka,* orphan, child bereft of its father.] (See quot.) *Obs.* — **1861** H. Jacobs *Life Slave Girl* 179 Every child rises early on Christmas morning to see the Johnkannaus. . . . These companies, of a hundred each, turn out early in the morning, and are allowed to go around till twelve o'clock, begging for contributions.

* **Johnny,** *n.* Also **Johnnie.**

1. ?A johannes, a Portuguese gold coin valued at about $8.81, once current in America. *Rare.*

1766 in Duane *Lett. to Franklin* (1859) 190, I shall be obliged to you for a Johney and the New England song.

2. A Chinese. *Colloq.*

1857 Gunn *N.Y. Boarding Houses* 275 He knows. He's seed the *Johnnies* goin' into that there doorway next block. **1884** W. Shepherd *Prairie Exper.* 140 The American atmosphere of independence . . . has breathed into Johnny the spirit of equality.

3. =**Johnny Reb.** Now *hist.*

[**1864** *Richmond* (Va.) *Examiner* 11 June 1/2 At the sound of cannon from the 'front,' these [Union sympathizers and spies] descant upon the probable fate of the campaign and the whereabouts of their Johnnies.] **1888** *Cent. Mag.* July 467/1 He spoke of the Confederate soldiers. as 'Johnnies.' **1927** Benét *J. B.'s Body* 257 The Johnnies is there!

4. (See quot.)

1884 Goode *Fisheries* I. 259 'Johnny' is applied only to very little Sculpins along the shore [of the Pacific], notably *Oligocottus maculosus.* The same name is given in the Ohio Valley to fishes of precisely similar habits, the *Etheostomatinae.*

5. (See quot.) *Colloq. Obs.*

1888 *Boston Rec.* 24 Sep. 1/4 A very large number of 'Johnnies' as small English schooners are called, were entered at the custom house this morning.

6. (See quot. and cf. **Johnny-jump-up.**) *Colloq.*

1892 *D.N.* I. 236 *Johnnies,* a popular name for violets [in Jackson Co., Mo.]. Also used in Michigan.

7. In combs.: (1) **Johnny Appleseed,** the nickname of John Chapman (?1775–1843), a celebrated eccentric who distributed appleseed throughout the Ohio Valley; (2) **board,** (see quot. 1918 and cf. **Johnnycake board**); (3) **bread,** =johnnycake, *q.v.* as a main entry; (4) **-come-lately,** one who has recently arrived at a place or position, *colloq.;* (5) **Congress,** a familiar term for Congress, *obs.,* cf. *cheap John Congress;* (6) **Crapaud,** a Frenchman, *colloq.* [cf. F. *crapaud,* toad]; (7) **Navaho,** *S.W.* formerly a colloq. name for the Navahos; (8) **-on-the-spot,** on hand, ready, also one who is on hand or prepared, *colloq.;* (9) **Reb,** during the Civil War, a Confederate soldier, now *hist.* or *allusive.*

(1) **1854** M. Busch *Wanderungen* I. 184 Ein anderer seltsamer Bewohner dieser Gegend war ein gewisser Jonathan Chapman, bekannter unter dem Spitznamen Johnny Appleseed. **1948** *Coronet* April 97/2 Today many an Ohio farmer swears that his apple orchard was planted by the hand of Johnny Appleseed — one of America's legendary heroes. — (2) **1918** E. Waller *Illinois* 76 Johnny-board, a smooth board to put dough on before the fire to bake bread. It was probably a corruption of Journey-board, a name given to it because they used it when they were moving. **1946** Richter *Fields* 145 Your mam's not settin' up with the johnny board waitin' for you. — (3) **1898** Earle *Customs Old N. Eng.* 67 One [wife], owing to her spouse's stinginess, had to use 'Indian branne for Jonne bred,' and never tasted good food. **1940** Mencken *Happy Days* 147 Himself an habitual snitcher of peanuts and Johnny-bread from poor Italians, he prohibited lifting a few cheap turnips or carrots from the baskets outside the stores of rich grocerymen. — (4) **1839** Briggs *Harry Franco* I. 249 'But it's Johnny Comelately, aint it, you?' said a young mizzen topman. **1949** *N.Y. Times Mag.* 3 July 23/1 He is no johnny-come-lately to the stream.

(5) **1817** *Guardian of Liberty* (Cynthiana, Ky.) 12 April 4/1 O! wo'nt you hear What roaring cheer, Was spent by Johnny Congress O! And how so gay They doubled their pay, And doubled the people's taxes O! **1827** *Western Mo. Rev.* I. 445 In the rural, but significant speech of the swains, this body is called Johnny congress. — (6) **1840** Cooper *Pathfinder* xvi, We are no Johnny Crapauds to hide ourselves behind a . . . fort on account of a puff of wind. **1886** *Harper's Mag.* Aug. 330/1 The Indian maiden soon learned to prefer Johnny Crapeau for a husband. — (7) **1863** *Rio Abajo Press* 17 Nov. 2/3, I must 'pitch in' and portray some of the characters now engaged in stirring up Johnny Navajo. **1865** *Wkly. New Mexican* 14 July 1/4 We'll first chastise then civilize bold Johnny Nav-a-jo. — (8) **1896** Ade *Artie* 24, I could see that a Johnny-on-the-spot with a big badge marked 'Committee' was tryin' to keep cases on her. **1947** *Hyde Park Herald* (Chi.) 29 May 3/3 They're 'Johnny on the spot' when the lights go out! — (9) **1865** *Nation* I. 584 They begun to talk to the old man, an' he talked too. They said he was a Johnny Reb. **1944** *Chi. D. News* 15 Jan. 3/3 President Roosevelt's Democrats, whether New Deal, win-the-war or Johnny Reb in category, are having unity troubles.

b. In the names of plants and animals: (1) **Johnny-cock-horse,** (see quot.); (2) **Grindle,** (see quot. and cf. **grindle** and **John A. Grindle**), *colloq.;* (3) **jump,** the shooting star; (4) **jumper,** (see quot.), *colloq.;* (5) **-jump-up,** any one of various American violets, also a popular name for the wild pansy or daffodil; (6) **jump-up-and-kiss-me,** (see quot.); (7) **smoker,** a local name for one of the geums; (8) **tuck,** (see quot.); (9) **Verde,** (see quots.).

(1) **1888** *Nature* 26 July 303/2 [The humming bird] was in the clutches of an insect, which he identified as a mantis, popularly known in those parts as 'Johnny-cock-horse.' — (2) **1884** Goode *Fisheries* I. 659 The Bowfin . . . is also abundant . . . in all parts of the Mississippi Valley, where it is variously called the 'Johnny Grindle,' 'Bowfin,' and 'Dogfish.' — (3) **1894** *Amer. Folk-Lore* VII. 94 *Dodecatheon Meadia,* Johnny jump. So. Cal. — (4) **1859** [see **Johnny-jump-up-and-kiss-me**].

(5) **1842** *Knickerb.* XIX. 115 Mr. Ketchup had now kissed little Chip and stuck a johnny-jump-up in his cap. **1945** Mathews *Talking* 61 These are the Johnny-jump-up, spring beauties, and hundreds of others that I cannot name. **1949** *Chesterton* (Ind.) *Tribune* 7 April 4/4 It takes me back to the times when each of us sought to be the first to find the first Johnny-jump-up. — (6) **1859** Bartlett 221 *Johnny Jump up and Kiss me. Johnny Jumper.* Names given to the Heart's Ease, or Violet. This name is also given to the breast-bone of a goose, with its two ends brought together by a twisted string held by a stick passing through it and stuck fast at the end by a piece of wax. — (7) **1893** *Amer. Folk-Lore* VI. 141 *Geum triflorum,* Johnny smokers. Rockford, Ill. — (8) **1937** *Range Plant Handbook* W136 *O. erianthus,* often called Johnny-tuck, or (less happily) butter-and-eggs, a relatively low species . . . is often very abundant in the foothills of California, frequently coloring wide stretches during April and May with gold-tinted streamlike bands. — (9) **1884** Goode *Fisheries* I. 413 The Johnny Verde—*Serranus nebulifer* . . . is common only from San Pedro southward to Magdalena Bay. **1911** *Rep. Fisheries 1908* 308 Cabrilla.—A name applied indiscriminately to several serranoid fishes of the southern coast of California. They are also called 'rock bass,' 'kelp salmon,' 'Johnny Verde,' etc.

johnnycake ˈdʒɑnɪˌkek, *n.* [See note.]

The origin of this term is obscure. The *EDD* records *Johnny-cake,* a noodle or simpleton (cf. **2.** below), but it is not easy to see any connection between this dial. expression and *johnnycake.* Any relationship with journey cake *q.v.* is likewise difficult to ascertain. The earlier and now obs. jonakin *q.v.* may account for the first element in johnnycake but no real evidence for this is available.

1. Corn bread in the form of a flat cake cooked on a board before an open fire, on a griddle, or in a pan in an oven.

1739 *S.C. Gazette* 22 Dec. 4/2 (Th. Supp.), New Iron Plates to cook Johnny Cakes or gridel bread on. **1805** Parkinson *Tour* 332 The lower class of people mix the flour . . . with water, make a sort of paste, and lay it before the fire, on a board or shingle, to bake, and generally eat it hot, as it is but very indifferent when cold. This is called a Johnny cake. **1834** Simms *G. Rivers* I. 119 There were eggs and ham, hot biscuits, hominy, milk, marmalade, venison, Johnny, or journey cakes, and dried fruits stewed. **1949** *Sat. Ev. Post* 12 March 52/4 Then she would make some pea soup with the liquor, and with johnnycake this was something to remember.

b. (*cap.*) (See quots.)

1867 Richardson *Beyond Miss.* 92 Another Delaware taken captive in war, escaped and made a long journey back to his own village, eating nothing on the way but a loaf of corn bread. He was immediately re-christened 'Journey-cake.' Several of his descendants yet survive and bear that family name, though the white settlers corrupt it into Johnny-cake. **1902** *Kans. Hist. Coll.* VII. 335 We stopped [in 1856] and stayed near the Indian chief's, Johnnycake, in a house. *Ib.* 495 There was then [in 1858] a nucleus of Christians in Kansas. . . . They were Methodist Indians. . . . Charles Ketchum and Charles and Isaac Johnnycake (if my recollection serves me) were of the same persuasion.

c. *land of johnnycake,* New England. *Rare.*

1844 *Lowell Offering* IV. 26 This was the mystery connected with his visit to the land of johnnycake and wooden nutmegs.

d. johnnycake board, a board upon which johnnycakes were baked. Now *hist.* Cf. **johnny board.**

1841 *N.O. Picayune* 16 Jan. 1/6 She's got *every thing* that ever was perduced for sich pupposes — . . . kittels, pots, a jonny-cake board, troth to mix rine-injin bread in, crock'ry of all sorts. *c*1880 Hazard *Jonny-Cake P.* (1915) 29 The red oak jonny-cake board was always the middle portion of a flour barrel from five to six inches wide. **1944** Duncan *M. Graham* 84 Cook pots and johnnycake board, noggins and wooden spoons, she made secure in a firkin suspended beneath the wagon.

e. *To be all smiles and johnnycake,* to be most affable. *Rare.*

1889 S. Hale *Letters* 227 Emily . . . was all smiles and johnny cake.

2. A New Englander. *Colloq. Obs.*

This may be nothing more than the *EDD Johnny-cake,* a noodle or simpleton. Cf. note above.

1840 Dana *Two Years* viii, 65, I've been through the mill, ground, and bolted, and come out a regular-built down-east johnny-cake. **1842** Dickens *Amer. Notes* 58 Down Easters and Johnny Cakes can follow if they please. I an't a Johnny Cake, I an't. I am from the brown forests of the Mississippi, I am.

As the last term in **corn, huckleberry, Indian, pumpkin johnnycake.**

***Johnson,** *n. attrib.* Designating a man, party, or Unionist loyal to Andrew Johnson (1808–75), seventeenth President of the U.S. (1865–69). *Obs.*

1866 *Wilkes' Spirit of Times* 3 March 8/1 He at once modified his ultra sentiments, besought the South, and conceived the notion of creating an universal Andrew Johnson party. **1866** *Wkly. New Mexican* 27 Oct. 2/2 In Pennsylvania the Johnson party has lost two members of Congress. **1867** Locke *Swingin' Round* 253 Vote ez a Johnson Unionist, or ez a Democratic Johnsonian–but vote. **1914** *Cyclo. Amer. Govt.* I. 402/1 The Conservatives or Johnson men were the adherents of President Johnson in his contest with Congress over the question of reconstruction.

Johnson grass. [W. *Johnson* of Ala., who introduced it about 1840.] A tall perennial European grass, *Sorghum halepense,* first planted for pasture and hay, but now often regarded as a pest. Also attrib.

1884 Vasey *Agric. Grasses* 51 *Sorghum halapense.* (Cuba grass, Johnson grass, Means grass, false Guinea grass, Evergreen millet, Arabian millet.) **1946** *Democrat* 11 July 3/2 Our first truck load of beautiful 1946 crop Johnson Grass Hay has just arrived. **1949** *Lubbock* (Tex.) *Morn. Avalanche* 23 Feb. II. 6/4 For Sale: . . . Five thousand bales fine black land Johnson Grass Hay.

***Johnsonian,** *n.* and *a.* **1.** *n.* A follower of Andrew Johnson. **2.** *a.* According to the policies of Andrew Johnson. Both *obs.*

(1) **1867** Locke *Swingin' Round* 212 There were twenty Johnsonians in this hamlet. **1867** *Harper's Wkly.* 14 Sep. 576 (*caption*), Whipping a Negro Girl in North Carolina by 'Unconstructed' Johnsonians. — (2) **1880** Tourgee *Bricks* 209 The Black Codes, which were adopted by the legislatures first convened under what has gone into history as the 'Johnsonian' plan of reconstruction, were models of ingenious subterfuge.

Johnsonite ˈdʒɑnsṇaɪt, *n.* = **Johnsonian.** *Obs.* — **1866** *Eastern Slope* (Washoe, Nev.) 13 Oct. 3/2 'We count on getting the larger part of the soldiers' vote for Clymer,' replied the Johnsonite.

***Johnsonize,** *v. tr.* and *intr.* To indoctrinate with the principles of Andrew Johnson; to become so indoctrinated. *Obs.*

1867 *Cong. Globe* 16 March 144/1 There are few Democratic negroes, and they cannot be Johnsonized. **1867** *Harper's Wkly.* 6 April 211/1 The freedman without a vote is a being to be treated as the laws of Johnsonized South Carolina treated him. **1913** Watkins *Hist. Neb.* III. 36/2 [That the nominees] had been turned down by the senate . . . may be accounted for by the fact that both of these men had 'Johnsonized.'

***joiner,** *n.* One particularly given to joining clubs, lodges, etc. *Colloq.*

1890 *Ann Arbor* (Mich.) *Rec.* 13 March, Ypsilanti is a good place for 'jiners.' There are an even 100 societies and organizations that a person can join—if they'll let him. **1894** Rittenhouse *Maud* 570 Miss Rittenhouse called me a 'jiner' last winter. Now that Christmas is past I seem doomed to be a jiner again. **1947** *Harper's Mag.* Jan. 70/2 This gregarious man is an inveterate joiner and belongs to 'every fraternal order in Muncie—Eagles, Moose, Elks, everything.'

***joint,** *n.*

1. In early N. Eng. buildings, the place where a stud joined a sill or plate. Now *hist.*

1644 *Springfield Rec.* I. 176 Cooper is to build ye house . . . 9 foote betwixt Joynts. **1723** *Manchester Rec.* 155 It was voted that a scool hous should be buelt forthwith of 24 foot Long 17 foot wide & 7 foot betwen Joynts. **1939** Shurtleff *Log Cabin* 98 The joints made by corner posts with the sills, girts, and plates. The phrase '9 foote betwixt Joynts' is equivalent to '9 foot stud.'

2. (See quots.)

1863 Randall *Pract. Shepherd* 74 When the change of condition [in a sheep] . . . takes place from a low and unhealthy state to a healthy and fleshy one—it generally occasions 'a joint' in the wool,—i.e., the place in the fibers where the change began, is so weak that a slight pull will detach the two parts. **1879** Vivian *Wanderings Western Land* 54 From these depôts, rafts, or, as they are called here, 'joints' are formed, which are towed down by steamers to the various saw mills on the banks of the river.

3. A low gathering-place or hangout, often illegal. *Slang.*

1883 *Harper's Mag.* Nov. 944/2, I have . . . smoked opium in every *joint* in America. **1902** *Chi. Record-Herald* 7 Sep. VI. 5/2 The joints for white people are, to the contrary, usually very luxurious. **1949** *Time*

21 March 25/1 If they were looking for slot machines, he could fetch them out of practically every self-respecting lodge hall in town as well as in the joints.

b. Used disparagingly for any place or establishment. *Slang.*

1887 *Lippincott's Mag.* Aug. 290 The student, upon reaching his 'joint,' as the club is called, hurriedly bolts a few mouthfuls of breakfast. **1947** *Chi. Tribune* 9 Nov. IV. 6/1 She has done a lot of hanging around hamburger stands, coffee joints, and bars, listening to people.

4. In combs.: (1) **joint ballot,** a ballot taken at a joint meeting of a legislative body; (2) **committee,** a committee made up of members of both houses of a legislative body; (3) **convention,** (*a*) a joint session of a legislative body, specifically convened to elect a public officer or to consider matters arising out of an election, (*b*) a political convention composed of delegates of two or more parties; (4) **resolution,** a resolution adopted jointly by the two houses of a legislative body; (5) **session,** a session of a legislative body in which the two houses sit together; (6) **shingle,** a short shingle fitting closely with those beside it instead of overlapping; (7) **vote,** in a political convention, a vote in which the delegates from a particular election district concur.

(1) **1780** *Const. of Mass.* II. ii. Sec. IV. § 1 [The Secretary, Treasurer and Receiver General, and the Commissary General, Notaries Public, and] Naval Officers, shall be chosen annually, by joint ballot of the Senators and Representatives, in one Room. **1885** *Wkly. New Mexican* 5 Feb. 3/1 The election of Governor Stanford [to the U.S. Senate] was confirmed today on a joint ballot [of the California legislature]. **1949** D. O. McGovney *Amer. Suffrage* 40 The two electors at large were elected solely by joint ballot of the two houses. — (2) **1778** *N.Y. Laws* 27 March, The joint Committee . . . [shall] canvas and estimate the votes. **1854** Benton *30 Years' View* I. 9/2 The joint committee acted, and soon reported a resolution. — (3) (*a*) **1844** *Ind. Senate Jrnl.* 166 Resolved, That the Senate be invited . . . in the Hall of the House of Representatives, to go into joint convention for the purpose of electing president judges in the 1st, 2d, and 3d judicial circuits. **1887** *Courier-Journal* 11 Jan. 1/2 The law does not require or contemplate a joint convention in counting the vote. (*b*) **1900** *Cong. Rec.* 14 Feb. 1801/2 In 1884 . . . our Republican gold-standard, gold-bond friends . . . made a bargain with our Greenback friends in the State, had a joint convention and gave to our Greenback folks half the electoral ticket. — (4) **1838** *Indiana H. Rep. Jrnl.* 85 Mr. Judah asked leave to introduce a joint resolution relative to postponing the election of United States' Senator. **1924** E. W. Hughes *Amer. Parliamentary Guide* 613 In recent years Congress has endeavored to restrict the use of joint resolutions in law-making to matters of minor importance.

(5) **1863** *Rio Abajo Press* 15 Dec. 2/2 Last Wednesday, about noon the Governor read his annual message to both Houses of the Legislature, in joint session, in the hall of the House of Representatives. **1948** *Salt Lake Tribune* 17 Dec. 1/6 Pres. Harry S. Truman will deliver his state of the union message in person to a joint session of the new congress. — (6) **1799** in Rothert *Muhlenberg Co.* 45 A joint shingle roof put on with pegs, except the outside rows with nails. **1806** *Austin P.* (1924) I. 105 Some Keggs Cut Nails for Joint Shingles and others for lathing of the smallest kind. — (7) **1851** Quentin *Reisebilder* II. 44 Man hat nun beide Candadaten zu einem sogenannten 'Joint Vote' zugelassen, ein merkwürdiger Vergleich, welcher dem Wahldistricte nur dann ein Votum gewährt, wenn, was kaum jemals sich zutragen kann, beide Vertreter in ihrer Ansicht übereinstimmen.

b. In the names of plants and animals: (1) ***joint grass,** a creeping grass, *Paspalum distichum;* (2) **pine,** any plant or shrub of the genus *Ephedra*, having a leafless jointed stem; (3) **snake,** =**glass snake;** (4) **weed,** a jointed, spikelike herb, *Polygonella articulata;* (5) ***worm,** the larva of any of several small chalcid flies of the genus *Harmolita*, such as *H. tritici*, which attack wheat.

(1) **1835** Simms *Partisan* 55 Rebellion grows like joint-grass when it once takes root. **1894** Coulter *Bot. W. Texas* III. 499 Joint grass. . . . Moist places throughout Texas and across the continent. — (2) **1903** Austin *Land of Little Rain* 234 Who taught them that the essence of joint pine (*Ephedra nevadensis*), which looks to have no juice in it of any sort, is efficacious in stomachic disorders. — (3) **1789** Morse *Amer. Geog.* 61 The Joint Snake is a great curiosity. Its skin is as hard as parchment and as smooth as glass. . . . When it is struck, it breaks like a pipe stem; and you may . . . break it from the tail to the bowels into pieces not an inch long. [**1892** Duval *Early Times Tex.* 113 To-day I came across a specimen of the jointed snake, the first I had ever seen.] **1899** *Animal & Plant Lore* 87 A snake known as the 'joint snake' can be broken into many pieces, which will then reunite into a living snake. — (4) **1817–8** Eaton *Botany* (1822) 401 *Polygonum articulatum*, joint-weed. . . . Very abundant on the sandy plains west of Albany. **1892** Torrey *Foot-Path Way* 60 [Plants in Mass. in Dec. include] two kinds of groundsel, fall dandelion, and jointweed.

(5) **1855** *Amer. Inst. N.Y. Trans.* 328 The Jointworm or, as naturalists generally call it, *Euritoma*, . . . has done much mischief [to wheat] this year, especially to the South. **1882** *Ill. Entom. Rep.* XI. 81, I have obtained another specimen of this species from a gall in a stalk, produced evidently by the regular joint-worm (*Isosoma hordii*). **1949** *Time* 20 June 77/1 The farmers blamed joint worms, rain and hail for cutting [the wheat crop] down.

As the last term in **blue, booze, bunko, chili, drinking, feed, flat, gambling, lunch, opium, poker, pool, rum, thick, whisky joint.**

***joint,** *v.* **1.** *tr.* (See quot. 1864.) *Obs.* **2.** *intr.* Of grain: To form nodes in growth.

(1) **1815** *Niles' Reg.* IX. 36/1 Two horses . . . with a man and a boy can dress and joint, in a superior manner, the staves necessary for one hundred barrels, hogsheads or pipes in twelve hours. **1864** Webster 728/2 Joint, . . . to prepare so as to fit closely; to fit together; . . . as, to *joint* boards. — (2) **1772** *Md. Hist. Mag.* XIV. 289, I am apprehensive it [the wheat and rye] will be too thick and Joint if the weather proves warme. **1904** *Topeka Capital* 1 June 8 Wheat has not done well, though it is jointing now.

jointist ˈdʒɔɪntɪst, *n.* **1.** The keeper of a "joint" or low dive. **2.** One interested in having both Arizona and New Mexico admitted into the Union as states, as contrasted with those desirous of having only New Mexico admitted. Both *obs.*

(1) **1889** in *Voice* (N.Y.) 5 Sep., The Grand Jury has found nineteen indictments against jointists. **1893** *Arena* 9 Mar. 467 In Kansas . . . the liquor seller is the sneaking bootlegger, skulking jointist, criminal and outlaw. — (2) **1906** *N.Y. Ev. Post* 18 Sep. 6 Arizona 'jointists' are to form an organization with joint Statehood as the only plank in its platform.

jojoba həˈhobə, *n. W.* [Amer. Sp. in sense shown here.] (See quots. 1925, 1942.)

1925 Jepson *Flowering Plants Calif.* 607 S[immondsia] californica. Nutt. Jajoba. Goat-nut. **1931** Dayton *Western Browse Plants* 94 The seeds of jojoba have an agreeable nutty flavor, and are a rather important source of food supply among certain Indians. **1942** Castetter & Bell *Pima & Papago Agric.* 26 On the lowest, drier level adjoining the desert are thickets of *jojoba* or coffeeberry (*Simmondsia californica*).

Jo. Johnson cap. Some now indefinable form of cap. *Obs.* — **1857** B. Young in *Jrnl. Discourses* V. 97 (Th.), [When I was a boy] my sisters would make me what was called a Jo. Johnson cap for winter.

***joke,** *n. To throw at the joke,* (see quot.). *Obs.* — **1833** Watson *Hist. Tales Phila.* 152 They used to have a play at the time of the fairs, called 'throwing at the joke.' A leather cylinder, not unlike a high candlestick, was placed on the ground over a hole. The adventurers placed their coppers on the top of the joke, then retired to a distance and tossed a stick at it.

***joker,** *n.*

1. little joker, a thing used in cheating, as the pea in thimblerig, or the game itself. Also transf. *Obs.*

1849 *N.O. Picayune* 9 May 2/2 In the meantime, the 'little joker,' that went off with the lead, meets with no obstacle in coming South. **1850** *Calif. Courier* (S.F.) 4 Nov. 2/5 In one house yesterday we actually saw a man trying to show under which of the thimbles the *little joker* was! **1856** Thompson *Plu-ri-bus-tah* 176 Yunga-Merrakah. . . . Knew the game of triple thimbles, Thimbles three and 'little joker.' **1868** *Terr. Enterprise* (Virginia, Nev.) 22 July 2/1 He certainly showed himself an adept at guessing, . . . about as much so as a 'thimble rigger' would in finding the 'little joker' under the long nail of his little finger.

b. A small rubber contrivance used by election officials for cheating in an election. Also a ballot marked by such a contrivance. *Obs.*

1888 in Fleming *Hist. Reconstruction* II. 86 Several hundred of these 'little jokers' bounced out and were counted just as though they had been honestly voted. **1895** *Rev. of Reviews* (London) Jan. 70/2 These little jokers were attached to the left thumbs of certain judges of election as the ballots were being counted. These jokers are made of rubber and have a cross on them. They are really rubber stamps. As these judges picked up the ballots they took hold of them in such a way that their left thumbs, with jokers attached thereto, pressed upon the squares opposite the name of the candidate they wished to aid.

2. In a deck of cards, an extra card that counts in certain games as a trump. Also allusively.

1885 GREENOUGH *Queen of Hearts* iii, The White Knight, called the Joker, otherwise the Best Bower. 1910 MULFORD *Hopalong Cassidy* 52 [They] began to back away, glancing around in an endeavour to locate the joker in the deck. 1931 *K.C. Star* 26 Aug., Why does a flush beat a straight even though in a game without a joker the odds favor making the former?

3. An unobtrusive clause inserted in a legislative bill or other document to affect its operation in a way not consistent with its apparent purpose.

1904 *N.Y. Ev. Post* 11. May 1 They are all nervous over the possibility that there may be a hitherto unperceived joker in the present bill. 1947 *Harper's Mag.* Nov. 441/1 The order also contains this crucial joker: The charges shall be stated as specifically and completely as . . . security conditions permit.

jollier ˈdʒɑlɪɚ, *n.* [f. the verb.] One who jokes and "kids." *Colloq.* — 1896 ADE *Artie* 78 He's one o'f [*sic*] the biggest jolliers that ever come over the hills. 1905 *N.Y. Ev. Post* 12 Oct. 2 He was talkative, and, as the attendants say, 'quite a jollier.'

* **jolly,** *v. tr.* To talk to or "kid" (a person) in a good-natured way so as to put him in good humor, often with *along* and *up*.

1890 H. PALMER *Stories Base Ball Field* 81, I jollied him along as strong as I could. 1892 GUNTER *Miss Dividends* 232 You've left her alone all to-day—you ain't been near to jolly her up. 1918 LINCOLN *Shavings* 129 My wife is pretty good at that, she jollies him along.

b. To succeed in raising, to work up. *Colloq.*

1921 R. D. PAINE *Comr. Rolling Ocean* xii. 206, I can jolly steam enough for a couple of pumps and a dynamo.

jolly board. See **jiggling board.**

Jonah crab. A large crab, *Cancer borealis*, found on the eastern seaboard. — 1883 *Nat. Museum Bul.* No. 27, 110 The Rock and Jonah Crabs (*Cancer irroratus* and *borealis*) are eaten only to a slight extent. 1911 *Rep. Fisheries 1908* 308.

jonakin ˈdʒɑnəkɪn, *n.* [Origin obscure. Poss. f. Amer. Indian. Cf. **johnnycake.**] (See quot. 1850.) *Obs.* — 1675 B. TOMPSON *N. Eng. Crisis*, Then times were good, merchants car'd not a rush For other fare than Jonakin and mush. 1850 COOPER *Rural Hours* 388 We have . . . Jonikin, thin, wafer-like sheets, toasted on a board; these are all eaten at breakfast, with butter.

* **Jonathan,** *n.*

1. A nickname orig. applied to an American patriot by the British and loyalists, at first with esp. reference to a New Englander, and finally used of any American.

The reason for the adoption of this nickname is obscure. The *EDD* records "Jonathan" in the sense of an awkward, stupid person, though only one example (of 1861) is cited. Note that the first clear evidence below is dated 1776, but quots. *c*1765, 1797 hint at earlier uses. Quot. 1724 is of obscure meaning but prob. has no connection with the use of "Jonathan" as a nickname. See * **Brother Jonathan** and the articles by A. Matthews there cited.

[1724 JONES *Virginia* 54 Except the last Sort [i.e., the deported convicts], for the most Part who are loose Villains, made tame by *Wild*, and then enslaved by his *Forward Namesake*. . . . These if they forsake their Roguery together with the other Kids [indentured servants] of the later Jonathan, when they are free, may work Day-Labour, or else rent a small Plantation for a Trifle almost.] [*c*1765 Alleged by J. Harriott (1815) to have been applied by sailors to 'all New-England men.' See *Pub. Col. Soc. Mass.* XXXII. 382.] 1776 in a London satirical political print reproduced in *Pub. Col. Soc. Mass.* XXXII. 376, I swear its plaguy Cold Jonathan; I don't think They'll Attack us, Now You. 1780 *Royal Gaz.* (N.Y.) 27 May 2/4 [The loyalists] also took and destroyed a piece of cannon, which the Jonathans in vain endeavoured to defend. 1797 in *Pub. Col. Soc. Mass.* XXXII. 379 'Jonathan' it is true in the year '70 was sometimes used by 'way of derision,' but no American felt injured by this appellation. 1849 WILLIS *Rural Letters* 157 The itching to be doing something, . . . in one shape or another, belongs to every genuine Jonathan. 1861 *Richmond* (Va.) *Examiner* 6 Sep. 1/4 The defeat of the Federalist forces at Bull Run will, it is said, lead to a change of the name of that rivulet [to] . . . Jonathan's Run. 1884 W. SHEPHERD *Prairie Exper.* 17 The Americans tell you that all Englishmen inherit money from their parents. . . . The great purpose of Nature is to relieve this plethora by transferring the cash into the pockets of Jonathan; this is called developing our resources by Eastern capital.

b. A country yokel. *Colloq.* Cf. note above.

1825 *N. Eng. Galaxy* (Boston) 5 Aug. 3/2 'I'll be darned,' said Jonathan, a raw boned fellow, in the costume of an up-country clown. 1857 *Lawrence* (Kans.) *Republican* 2 July 4 Among the arrivals was . . . a regular no-mistake Jonathan—with his eyes wide open at the novelties he met at every turn.

c. (See quots.) *Obs.*

1855 *Chi. Democrat* 3 May, The Jonathans are Anti-Slavery, but not against foreigners. 1855 *Prairie News* (Okalona, Miss.) 7 June 3/1 The [Know Nothing] Council is divided on the Jonathan and Sam question. . . . The Jonathans are anti-slavery, but will admit foreigners. They will admit all foreigners who disavow temporal allegiance to the Pope.

2. A late autumn variety of red eating apple, said to have been introduced in 1800 by P. Rick.

1842 *Cat. Fruits Cultivated in Garden of Hortic. Soc.* (ed. 3) 21 Apples . . . Jonathan. 1879 *Chi. Tribune* 3 May 10/3 Our best winter apples are . . . Jeniton, Jonathan, Red Canada, Wythe. 1948 *Chesterton* (Ind.) *Tribune* 28 Oct. 10/3 For Sale . . . 13 acre apple orchard, 70 bearing trees—varieties, Rome Beauty, Winesaps, Jonathans, Red and Yellow Delicious.

As the last term in **Brother, Kentucky, Yankee Jonathan.**

Jonathanism ˈdʒɑnəθənˌɪzəm, *n.* A tall story. *Rare.* Cf. **Brother Jonathanism.** — 1841 *N.O. Picayune* 4 Dec. 4/1 The original version, which is greatly superior in humor to those monstrosities called Jonathanisms, is, we believe, as follows.

Jonathanization ˌdʒɑnəθənɪˈzeʃən, *n.* Americanization. *Colloq. Obs.* — 1854 EMERSON *Corr. Carlyle & Emerson* (1883) II. 235 John Bull interests you at home. . . . Come and see the Jonathanization of John. 1894 *Sat. Review* 15 Dec. 652/1 The Jonathanization of John is going on . . . symptoms of American corruption and misrule.

joree dʒəˈri, *n.* [Imitative.] (See quot. 1945.) Cf. **grasset.** — 1884 HARRIS *Mingo* 179 We seem to agree, Brother Brannum, like the jay-bird and the joree,—one in the tree and t'other on the ground. 1945 *Democrat* 21 June 2/3 The joree, also called towhee and chewink, one of the finch family, is getting more plentiful in Montgomery.

jornada hɔrˈnadə, *n. S.W.* [See note.] An arid expanse or region, one which can be crossed in one day.

In Spanish the term means a day's journey. In American Spanish (see Santamaría) it has the added meaning, in the pl., of an arid prairie, and in Texas such an expanse as can be crossed in one day. Our examples, representing an independent borrowing made in this country, seem to show a mixture of these senses, and often refer to particular regions. See Bentley and Friederici.

1828 in *Mo. Hist. Rev.* VIII. (1914) 190 At 4 p.m. we entered *Jornada*. 1831 *Ib.* 179 This company . . . suffered extremely in the passage of the great Jornada, or day's journey, from one watering place to another. 1859 in FRIEDERICI 334 In some localities 50 or 60 miles, and even greater distances, are frequently traversed without water; these long stretches are called by the Mexicans '*journadas*,' or day's journeys. There is one in New Mexico called *Journada del Muerto*, which is 78½ miles in length, where, in a dry season, there is not a drop of water. 1880 *Cimarron News & Press* 15 April 2/3 The buckboard carrying the U.S. mail was taken by our braves last week near Aleman on the Jornado. 1947 *Sierra Club* (So. Calif. Chap.) *Sched.* 125, 56 The Journado will continue: To Dirty Devil River; To Land of Standing Rocks; To Robbers Roost.

b. (See quot.) *Rare.*

1846 HUGHES *Diary* 80 Wednesday, 18th. [Nov.]: Left camp and pursued our march down the River 12 miles, over lofty sand hills, and across a great many Jornadas or sand creeks.

josephinite ˈdʒozəfɪnˌaɪt, *n.* [f. *Josephine* Co., Ore.] A natural alloy of nickel and iron. — 1892 *Amer. Jrnl. Sci.* CXLIII. 509 Josephinite, a new Nickel-Iron. *Ib.*, The placer gravel, in which josephinite is found.

Josephite ˈdʒozəfˌaɪt, *n.* [f. *Joseph* Smith, the younger (1860–1914).] A member of the Reorganized Church of Jesus Christ of Latter Day Saints, which was established by Mormons who chose to follow the son of the prophet rather than Brigham Young. Also attrib. or adj. *Obs.*

1865 in *Kans. Hist. Quart.* VII. 39 Have a dance with the Mormon ladies, 'Brighamites' and 'Josephites.' 1890 *Cong. Rec.* 2 April 2933/1 The Josephites . . . live a sober life of monogamy, as much so as any class of people on this continent. 1912 BIRGE *Awakening Desert*, These dissenters were known as Josephites.

* **Joseph's coat.** Either of two ornamental plants (see quots.). — 1866 LINDLEY & MOORE *Treas. Bot.* I. 48/1 In the gardens of the Southern United States, these hues are so richly developed as to have procured for it [*Amaranthus tricolor*] the appellation of Joseph's coat. 1894 *Amer. Folk-Lore* VII. 96 *Coleus Blumei*, Joseph's coat. general.

* **Josh,** *n.* [Short for * *Joshua*. See note to **2.**]

1. (See quots.) *Obs.*

1869 *Overland Mo.* III. 129 The cant designation in the Rebel army for a man of Arkansas was 'Josh.' . . . Just before the battle of Murfreesboro, the Tennesseeans, seeing a regiment from Arkansas approaching, cried out, . . . 'Thar come the tribes of Joshua!' 1870 MEDBERY *Men Wall St.* 136 *Josh*, a word shouted at the Exchange in order to wake up a sleepy member.

2. (not *cap.*) A joke, jest, badinage. *Slang.*

This use app. comes from the verb josh *q.v.* and note the earliness of the evidence there.

1878 HART *Sazerac Lying Club* 57 Be there anything in this . . . or aint it only one of them 'joshes' they gets up in the *Reveille* sometimes? **1919** CADY *Rhymes of Vt.* (1923) 101 And all you get is jest a josh As off he lugs your Hubbard squash. **1948** *Sat. Review* 12 June 19/1 We found him tired-eyed and peaked, overcome with yawns after months of fifteen-hour quiz-days—not a man for josh or chatter.

josh dʒaʃ, *v.* [See note.]

The origin of this term is obscure. The derivation from *Josh* Billings, pen name of Henry Wheeler Shaw (1818–85), noted Amer. humorist, suggested in the *OED* is untenable because it was not until *c*1860 that this writer gained any public notice.

tr. and *intr.* To joke, banter, ridicule. *Colloq.*

1845 *St. Louis Reveille* 19 April 2/4 Look out in future, and if you must *Josh*, why, give a *private* one. **1852** *Lantern* (N.Y.) I. 199/2 'Wall,' says he, snickering till I tho't he'd split, or choak, or suthin', 'the squint eyed chap's been jossin' ye.' **1878** HART *Sazerac Lying Club* 144 Oh, boys! you don't mean it! You're only joshing me, I know. **1945** *Newsweek* 5 Feb. 19/2 Those in White House circles say that F. D. R. is going to josh Stalin about the timing of the present Soviet offensive on the eastern front.

Hence **joshing,** *n.* and *a.*

1864 in *Ohio Arch. & Hist. Quart.* LII. 175 The Bay was rough; thirty minutes out and the boys began to get sick. There was a good deal of joshing. **1948** *Sat. Review* 3 July 7/1 What John was doing was running the chatty, homespun, joshing sort of thing that actually goes on in a town.

josher ˈdʒaʃɚ, *n.* [f. **josh,** *v.*] One who joshes. *Slang.* — **1899** G. ADE *Doc Horne* 172 Gerty, you're lively company an' a very neat josher. **1913** LONDON *Valley of Moon* II. vii, 'He's just teasing you,' Saxon soothed. 'He always was a josher.'

***Joshua,** *n.* A small tree, *Yucca brevifolia*, found in some desert regions in the western states. Also **Joshua palm, tree, yucca.**

1875 *Amer. Naturalist* IX. 141 We recognized one of the principal objects of our journey in the singular forms of that remarkable desert production, *Yucca brevifolia* Engel. This is universally known among the Mormon settlers under the name of '*The Joshua.*' **1897** SUDWORTH *Arborescent Flora* 106 *Yucca arborescens*. . . . Joshua Yucca. . . . Common Names. . . . The Joshua (Utah). Joshua Tree (Utah, Ariz., N. Mex.). **1946** GARDNER *D. A. Breaks Seal* 3 Joshua palms, thrusting up grotesque spine-covered arms, made the scenery resemble some fantastic reconstruction of life on another planet. **1949** *Time* 18 April 69/1 The mountain-ringed desert, with its mourning Joshua trees, has a kind of austere beauty.

b. In the name of a national monument in southeastern California, near San Bernardino.

1947 *Desert Mag.* April 12/1 Flowers should be at their best in Joshua Tree national monument during April.

josie ˈdʒozɪ, *n.* [Short for **joseph*, a cloak or greatcoat.] A close-fitting outer waist worn by women, a bodice. *Obs.* — **1848** BARTLETT 192 A garment made of Scotch plaid, for an outside coat or habit, was worn in New England about the year 1830, called a *Joseph*, by some a *Josey*. **1894** CHOPIN *Bayou Folk* 170 She wore a coarse white cotton 'josie,' and a blue calico skirt.

jour dʒɜ, *n.* Short for "journeyman," one who has learned a craft or trade. Also attrib. *Obs.*

1835 *Vade Mecum* (Phila.) 27 June 3/1 The *jours* are in the habit of *spouting* their work from one week to another. **1854** SHILLABER *Mrs. Partington* 146, '*I* wouldn't be so bothered about *my* meals,' said a jour printer to a brother typo. **1898** *Milwaukee Sentinel* 16 Jan. II. 2/7 Where the hundreds of old time-honored 'jours' . . . have gone to, no one seems able to determine.

***journal,** *n.* As the last term in **copper, yellow journal.**

***journalism,** *n.* As the last term in **college, yellow journalism.**

journey cake. =**johnnycake 1.**

The evidence here, which is somewhat later than that for johnnycake *q.v.*, is not sufficient to support the suggestion that *journey cake* is the original form of that word. For neither of the words, however, can the evidence be regarded as complete. Both terms may be rationalized forms of jonakin *q.v.*

1754 in FRIES *Moravians in N.C.* II. 531 We kept a Lovefeast with the Journey Cakes, and afterwards a blessed Communion. **1868** G. G. CHANNING *Recoll. Newport* 25 The 'journey-cake,' vulgarly called *Johnny-cake*—how can I sufficiently extol it? **1903** K. M. ABBOTT *Old Paths & Legends* 463 The 'real Johnie-cake' or 'journey' cake, made of Rhode Island meal ground by the mills on Aquidneck Isle, is a unique breakfast delicacy. **1948** *Nat. Geog. Mag.* Aug. 169/1 Finding the meal handy to carry on long journeys, they called the cakes it made 'journey cakes.' Time made it 'jonny cake,' and even 'johnny cake.'

b. journey-cake board, =**johnnycake board.** *Obs.*

1852 REYNOLDS *Hist. Illinois* 265 The bread used at these frolics, was baked generally on jonny, or *journey*-cake boards.

jovite ˈdʒovaɪt, *n.* [f. *Jove*, Jupiter.] (See quot. 1898.) *Obs.* — **1897** *Current Hist.* VII. 646 Recent tests of the explosive known as 'jovite' indicate its great promise as to its effectiveness for navy shells. **1898** *Boston Transcript* 25 June 24/6 The explosive employed in her projectiles is wet guncotton. Before long . . . she will use 'jovite' instead. . . . Jovite is the invention of a Swede named Blomen. It is a mixture of certain coal-tar products with a metallic nitrate.

joy ride. A pleasure ride in an automobile, often a surreptitious and reckless one taken with a party. Also transf. *Colloq.*

1909 *N.Y. Ev. Post* (semi-weekly ed.) 15 July 2 [The Acting Mayor vetoed the ordinance passed last week to prevent city officers from taking 'joy rides.' **1916** *Out West* Dec. 250/2 *The Birth of a Nation* . . . is a joy-ride through history; . . . a college education crammed into a night. **1919** *Richmond Rec.* (S.F.) 26 April 1/3 The tragedy was the culmination of a joy-ride participated in by five women and two men. **1947** *Chi. Tribune* 16 Nov. I. 23/1 Delegates today voted to hold the 1948 United Nations general assembly in Europe over . . . protests that they were voting themselves a joy ride.

Also as a verb. Hence **joy rider, joy riding.** *Colloq.*

1910 *N.Y. Ev. Post* 13 June (Th.), Judge Dike remarked that the next joy-rider who was brought before him would be sentenced to Sing Sing. **1913** *Collier's* 27 Dec. 9 (*heading*), With the Joy-Riding Fleet. **1915** *Amer. Mag.* Oct. 28/2 You take your dago friend 'n' joy ride with the gang all night. **1942** LILLARD *Desert Challenge* 40 Reno was 'a roadhouse for matrimonial joy riders.' **1949** *Sat. Ev. Post* 23 April 17/1 Under the circumstances, five Federal cases involving joy riders were not prosecuted.

juba ˈdʒubə, *n.* [Origin obscure.]

1. =**juba dance.** Usu. *to dance* (or *pat*) *juba.*

1834 CARUTHERS *Kentuckian* I. 113 A man looks so unromantic with his teeth, and his hands, and his feet all in motion like a negro dancing 'Juba.' **1838** *Lexington Observer & Rep.* 8 Aug., A darky got . . . well sweetened . . . while 'patting Juba.' **1867** *N.Y. World* 14 Dec. 2/2 Then came a break down, none of your city jubas, done in burnt cork by a professional. **1944** DUNCAN *M. Graham* 171 Negro deck hands 'patted juba' and 'popped corks' between wharves.

2. juba dance, a noisy, rollicking dance formerly popular among Negroes.

1850 *Calif. Courier* (S.F.) 11 Nov. 2/4 The negroes have appropriated a sort of 'Red Row' near the City Hall, for juba dances, double-shuffles, and 'break-downs' generally. **1900** SMITHWICK *Evol. State* 20 A regular series of hand-claps going on . . . naturally reminded us of the 'Juba' dance among the negroes.

b. Also **Juba minstrels.** *Obs.*

1852 *Lantern* (N.Y.) II. 215/1 Time was when 'Juba' minstrels struck the lyre—*i.e.*, 'picked the banjo'—in rapturous praise of 'Hog and Hominy.'

juberous ˈdʒubərəs, *a.* *S.* [App. f. **dubious.*] Doubtful, hesitant. *Colloq.*

1845 HOOPER *Suggs* (1928) 70 Sometimes I sorter think it would, and then agin it looks sorter jubous. **1892** HARRIS *U. Remus & Friends* 105 Ole Brer Elephen flop his years en shake his snout like he sorter jubious. **1932** RANDOLPH *Ozark Mt.* 40 Th' ol' man he pondered a while, a-shakin' of his head kinder juberous.

Jubilee Singers. A group of singers at Fisk University who go on singing tours in the interests of their school. Also **Jubilee song.**

1872 T. F. SEWARD (*title*), Jubilee Songs as Sung by the Jubilee Singers, of Fisk University. **1881** *Harper's Mag.* May 804/1 Thomas's Symphony concerts and the . . . Jubilee Singers all find an appreciative audience. **1949** *Reader's Digest* May 97/1 In two triumphal tours the Jubilee Singers took Europe by storm.

transf. **1946** HOLBROOK *Lost Men* 133 The Chautauqua offered no such strong meat as the Lyceum, but went in for bell ringers, jubilee singers, preachers, William Jennings Bryan, and assorted stuffed shirts.

***judge,** *n.*

1. (*cap.*) Used as a mere title of respect or courtesy. *Colloq.*

1800 J. MAUDE *Visit Niagara* 74 Captain Williamson was himself here best known as 'the Judge.' **1850** *Quincy* (Ill.) *Whig* 3 Dec. 4/2, I asked the driver if the man he spoke to was surely a Judge? 'Certainly, sir,' he replied. 'We had a cockfight last week, and he was named a judge for the occasion!' **1905** *N.Y. Ev. Post* 18 March, The title of 'Judge' stuck to him from the time he was a justice of the peace. **1936** DRURY *Editor on Comstock* 21 All lawyers and leading saloon-keepers were also Colonels, excepting those called Judge.

2. In combs.: (1) **Judge Colt,** *W.* a Colt revolver as the symbol of law enforcement, *rare;* (2) **Lynch,** the personification of lynch law.

(1) **1941** *Nat. Geog. Mag.* March 300/2 During that period 'Judge Colt was the Law and the Winchester rifle was Order.' — (2) **1835** *Vade Mecum* (Phila.) 25 July 2/4 These tumults are an eastern branch of Judge Lynch's western courts, and the time is not far off when appeals from the decisions must be made with the bullet and the bayonet. **1900** *Cong. Rec.* 25 Jan. 1205/1 When Judge Lynch decides that a man ought to be hanged, he decides, too, that the method of procedure is immaterial. **1948** WESTON *Mother Lode* 30 One of the Mexicans robbed a sluice and Judge Lynch stepped in.

b. *Judge of probate,* **=probate judge.**

1707 SEWALL *Diary* II. 205 Some desire that it may be put in the Bill that Mr. Leverett Lay down all his Civil offices; as Judge of Probat, and judge of the Superior Court. **1877** *Mich. Gen. Statutes* I. (1882) 233 The judge of probate of such county may, on application of the officer so elected, approve of the bond and sureties thereto. **1945** *Bristol Enterprise* 15 Feb. 3/2 The subscriber has been duly appointed by the Judge of probate.

c. *judge of election,* one appointed to see to the carrying out of laws relating to an election.

1839 MARRYAT *Diary in Amer.* I. 298 In an action by Wm. Fogg, a negro, against Hiram Hobbs, inspector, and Levi Baldwin and others, judges of the election, for refusing his vote. **1901** DUNCAN & SCOTT *Allen & Woodson Co., Kans.* 12 On the 19th of August, 1856, the Board met and appointed judges of election for the first Monday in October for members of the Territorial legislature.

d. *Judge of the Plains,* in California, a county official appointed annually to decide disputes as to the ownership of cattle and to have supervision over cattle, sheep, hogs, etc., driven through his jurisdiction.

1851 *Calif. Laws* 515 Whenever any dispute arises respecting the ownership, mark, or brand of any horse, mule, jack, jenny, or horned cattle, it shall be the duty of the Judges of the Plains to decide on such dispute.

As the last term in **circuit, county, district, flower pot, midnight, parish, patrol, president, presiding, probate, salary, side, state, trial judge.**

***judger,** *n. judger of fence,* **=fence viewer.** *Obs.* — **1689** *Tisbury Rec.* 22 John Manter and Thomas Look shall stand in the place of savairs [=surveyors] and judgers of fence for this following year.

***judicial,** *a.* **1. judicial circuit,** a district through which a judge travels at definite intervals to hold court. **2. judicial district,** =prec.

(1) **1841** (*title*), Document showing the testimony given before the Judge of the fifth judicial circuit of the State of Missouri, on the trial of Joseph Smith and others for high treason, and other crimes against that State. **1946** *Democrat* 21 Feb. 7 Three new names appear this week. . . . Judge Joe M. Pelham, Jr., for reelection as Judge of the First Judicial Circuit [etc.]. — (2) **1841** *Diplom. Corr. Texas* III. (1911) 1333 Henry J. Jewett Attorney of the republic for the third Judicial district. **1914** *Cyclo. Amer. Govt.* I. 503 Courts of common pleas are now to be found in New Jersey, Pennsylvania, Delaware and Ohio, one or more counties forming a judicial district for such courts.

judiciary committee. In a legislative body, a committee having supervision of matters affecting the judiciary. — **1789** *Ann. 1st Congress* I. 19 Mr. Carroll and Mr. Izard were added to the Judiciary Committee. **1911** PERSONS *Mass. Labor Laws* 25 These petitions were referred as received, in January and February, to the judiciary committee.

Judy,** *n.* (See quot.) *Obs.* — *a1870** CHIPMAN *Notes on Bartlett* 222 *Judy,* . . . a lamp formerly used in N[ew] E[ngland] for burning blubber.—Eastern Mass.

***jug,** *n.* In combs.: (1) **jug-fishing,** (see quot. and cf. ***jug,** *v.* **2.**); (2) ***handle,** (*a*) **=jug-handled,** *obs.,* (*b*) (see quot.); (3) **handled,** one-sided, not evenly proportioned, *colloq.;* (4) **head,** (see quot. 1944), also transf.; (5) **swallow, =cliff swallow;** (6) **trade,** trade involving whisky shipped in jugs.

(1) **1889** *Cent.* 3249/2 Jug-fishing . . . [is a] method of fishing with empty jugs or bottles, which are corked and thrown overboard to serve as buoys, carrying a line, at the end of which is the hook. — (2) (*a*) **1846** SOL. SMITH *Theatr. Apprent.* 118 Not perceiving the entire justice of this arrangement, it being somewhat on the jug-handle principle, all on one side. *a*1882 in MCCABE *New York* 85 This jug-handle style of architecture has become so universal that we have grown accustomed to it. (*b*) **1913** BARNES *Western Grazing Grounds* 382 *Jug Handle.*—A mark made in cattle by slitting the dew lap about 4 inches so that the outside strip hangs free from the animal. — (3) **1881** *Cong. Rec.* 8 Dec. 60/2 English reciprocity in pleasure travel, however, like their often proposed commercial reciprocity, is comparatively jug-handled. **1904** *Boston Herald* 28 Sep. 6 At the present time the trade between Canada and the United States is distinctly jug-handled, with the handle altogether on the side of our people. — (4) **1936** in WENTWORTH. **1944** ADAMS *W. Words* 85/2 jughead A horse which lacks intelligence and has to be pulled around considerably before he is made to understand what is wanted of him. **1946** *Chi. D. News* 18 March 8/3, I don't know whether most of our primary teachers are jugheads. **1949** *Amer. Dial. Soc. Pub.* April 23 jughead. . . . 1. A horse or mule with a large, long head. . . . 2. A stupid or slow person.

(5) **1868** *Amer. Naturalist* II. 217, I had nailed a board . . . under the eaves of a barn to form a resting-place for the nests of the Cliff or Jug-swallow. **1917** *Birds of Amer.* III. 84 Cliff Swallow. . . . Other Names.—Eave Swallow; Jug Swallow. — (6) **1887** *Courier-Journal* 1 Jan. 2/4 (*caption*), The Prohibitory Law at the Health Resort Results in a Boom in the Jug Trade. **1908** *Amer. Rev. of Reviews* April 468/2 The jug trade from the 'wet' into the 'dry' counties [in Ga.] became so great and annoying [etc.].

***jug,** *v.* **1.** *tr.* To preserve (fruit) in a jug. *Rare.* (Cf. **can,** *v.* **1.**) **2.** *intr.* To catch fish by attaching a baited hook and line to a jug filled with air which in time tires out the fish and brings it to the surface, usu. **jugging.**

(1) **1862** T. D. PRICE *Diary* (MS) 13 Aug., Picked 1/2 bushel of cherries to jug and dry; stored them, put up two jugs and dried balance. — (2) **1872** *Kans. Mag.* Feb. 178 Jugging for catfish in the chutes of the Missouri and the Kaw. **1947** *Life* 15 Sep. 155 The boys go jugging for catfish. They tie their fishing lines to jugs and haul them in when the jug bobs in the water.

***jugful,** *n. By a jugful,* by a great deal, usu. with a negative. *Colloq.*

1831 *Boston Transcript* 14 Nov. 2/1 'Vote on your side!' says another; 'Not by a jug full.' **1893** *Cong. Rec.* 2 Oct. 2048/1 Take the Republicans one at a time and they are very clever sort of gentlemen . . . , but take them en masse and they will not do to tie to, by a jugful. **1949** *Boston Sun. Globe* 1 May (Fiction Mag.) 2/2 You ain't been havin' all the fun, Cot, not by a jug full.

***juggler,** *n.* (See quots.) *Obs.* — **1808** T. ASHE *Travels* xxxii, 273 A juggler is a mixed character representing a mamae, physician and priest. **1845** DE SMET *Ore. Missions* (1847) 92 Chalax, that is to say the *White Robe,* surnamed the Juggler or great medicine man. *Ib.,* Chalax had acquired great celebrity *as a juggler,* and in predicting future events.

***juice,** *n.* Electric current. *Slang.*

1896 *Boston Herald* 25 Dec. 4/5 Now we know what a blessing the trolley is—when the juice isn't turned off. **1908** *Sat. Ev. Post* 18 July 10/2 'Cable cars all stopped,' he said; ''lectric cars all stopped; no juice, no nothing, everything stopped.' **1948** *Great Falls* (Mont.) *Tribune* 18 Sep. 12/1 Turn on the juice to this elevator, and do it now.

As the last term in **bug, caper, corn, cornstalk, cow, jig, palmetto, pokeberry, tarantula juice.**

juicery 'dʒusərɪ, *n.* (See quot. 1853.) *Slang. Obs.* — **1853** J. G. BALDWIN *Flush Times Ala.* 325 We took Jefferson with us, in the recess of court, over to a place of departed spirits . . . we mean, an evacuated doggery, grocery or juicery, as, in the elegant nomenclature of the natives, it was variously called. **1892** DUVAL *Young Explorers* 7, I stepped up to one of the crowd collected around this 'juicery' and enquired if anything unusual had happened.

juke dʒuk, *n.* [See note.]

This term is no doubt of African origin. L. D. Turner found "juke house," a disorderly house, a house of ill repute, in well-established use among the Gullahs *c*1930. He finds in Wolof and Bambara clear antecedents of the Gullah term "juke."

1. Short for **juke box** or **juke joint.** Cf. **2.** *Slang.*

1942 KENNEDY *Palmetto Country* 183 These jooks are tough joints. They'll murder you, caress you, and bless you. **1947** *Sat. Ev. Post* 8 March 91/1 As I watched, a man came from the direction of the bar and fed the juke a nickel. **1948** *Ib.* 9 Oct. 136/3 Here on the 'Gold Coast,' a squalid collection of jooks and honky-tonks, liquor may be bought openly by the case.

attrib. **1942** KENNEDY *Palmetto Country* 190 Jook organs are seldom quiet; bleary-eyed customers who take a fancy to a particular tune have been known to keep it playing continuously until dawn. **1947** *Chi. D. News* 16 Jan. 4/2 (*heading*), Juke Operator Surrenders in Shooting Quiz.

2. juke box, a nickel-in-the-slot electrically operated record-playing music box. Often attrib. Also **juke joint,** a place of low resort. *Slang.* Cf. **Negro juke (joint).**

1946 *Trail & Timberline* April 52/2 Back at the cars, the group decided to explore Crested Butte, an expedition which wound up behind high-collared glasses of beer in a Slovene Juke Joint. **1946** *N.Y. Times Mag.* 14 April 31/2 The price of most juke boxes is about $300—varying from $150 to $700. **1948** *Chi. D. News* 24 Feb. 1/7 [He was] erstwhile 1st ward Democratic committeeman and juke box boss of the Loop and surrounding territory. **1949** *Ib.* 16 June 18/3 Most of the new automobiles look like animated juke boxes.

Jukes dʒuks, *n. pl.* Descendants of the "Jukes sisters" who lived in N.Y. State in the eighteenth century [a fictitious name used by R. L. Dugdale (see 1st quot.) in a study of the persistence through successive generations of tendencies to crime, immorality, disease and poverty]. Sometimes *sing.* Cf. **Kallikaks.**

1877 DUGDALE *Jukes* (1891, ed. 3) 13 To this day some of the 'Jukes' occupy the self-same shanties built nearly a century ago. **1912** GODDARD *Kallikak Family* 57 So far as the Jukes family is concerned, there is nothing that proves the hereditary character of any of the crime, pauperism, or prostitution that was found. **1947** *Sat. Ev. Post* 15 Mar. 151/1, 'I adore you,' he said, 'and would, if you were a Kallikak, Joad or Juke.'

transf. **1947** CROY *Corn Country* 191 Scientist Shull thought it would be interesting to see what would happen if he mated corn to itself, that is, kept it in the family—a sort of cornfield Juke.

∗**julep,** *n.* A sweetened spirituous drink, often artificially cooled and flavored with mint. Cf. **mint julep.**

1787 *Amer. Museum* I. 215 [A middle-class Virginian] rises in the morning about six o'clock. He then drinks a julap, made of rum, water, and sugar, but very strong. **1834** *Knickerb.* III. 350, I had never fancied their amusements of riding to the Lamb tavern for a julep. **1900** ROBERTSON *Red Blood & Blue* 134 [At] Syracuse, . . . the most elegant ladies not only drank juleps with him, but they drank julep for julep.

attrib. **1841** *Spirit of Times* 193/1 (We.), Julep drinkers. **1849** G. G. FOSTER *N.Y. in Slices* 4 Let us hurry . . . past this palatial refectory cooled by a julep-fountain in the basement.

Hence **julepize,** *v. intr.*, to indulge in juleps. *Rare.*

1840 *N.O. Picayune* 26 Aug. 2/4 Neither the joy nor the sorrow of the order will prevent folks from julepising.

∗**julienne,** *n. attrib.* Of or pertaining to vegetables cut in strips.

1909 FARMER *Boston Cook Book* 116 Julienne Soup. **1941** *Dly. Oklahoman* (Okla. City) 9 Oct., Cut green beans, Julienne style (lengthwise of the beans) and cook them uncovered in boiling salted water only until they are tender. [**1947** BEROLZHEIMER *Regional Cookbook* 208 Arrange potatoes cut as chips or Julienne in a potato-basket mold or between 2 strainers, for frying.]

jumbo ˈdʒʌmbo, *n.* [See note.]

This term appears to be of African origin (cf. Gullah *jamba*, elephant), and to have been introduced into this country by slaves. But see *OED s.v.*

1. (See quots. and cf. **2.** below.)

1808 C. SCHULTZ *Jrnl. Travels* (1810) II. 142 The fifth was another joint of cane closed at both ends, with a narrow strip out from end to end, over which was extended a strong deer sinew; which being set in vibration by the thumb, produced a dull monotonous sound, something like the lowest string of the African jumbo. **1846** *Knickerb. Mag.* XXVII. 511 And so we walk up to the 'jumbo,' an old-time schooner with a monstrous heap of quarter-deck. **1863** DICEY *Six Months* II. 149 There are still many traces in this part of the Mississippi of the early French settlements. . . . The inhabitants are a queer race, 'jumbos,' as the American settlers call them—half French, half negro, and half Indian. **1901** *Everybody's Mag.* Oct. 394/1 In the historical exhibit in the Electricity Building there may be seen the famous old Edison 'jumbo' dynamo. **1908** *Sat. Ev. Post* 7 Nov. 11/3 Nearest the portal was the 'jumbo,' a great, movable platform through which the 'muckers' dumped their barrow-loads to cars beneath.

b. A trade-mark name for a shade of gray like that of an elephant. *Obs.*

1882 *Phila. Ev. Star* 2 May, 'Jumbo' is a new gray hue.

2. Anything large of its kind. Often attrib.

Barnum's huge elephant (6½ tons), Jumbo, purchased from the London Zoölogical Gardens in 1882, no doubt inspired this application of the word, though the notion of large size seems present in some of the quots. under **1.**

1883 *Harper's Mag.* Oct. 705/2 It is the Jumbo of Crickets, and just as black. **1916** *Amer. City* April 373/1 Large jumbo peanuts were bought, instead of culls. **1921** *Peanut Promoter* Jan. 79/1 Jumbos in the shell are meeting with considerable demand. **1946** *Reader's Digest* July 141/2, I saw jumbo strawberries, tearless onions, fuzz-free peaches. **1949** *Sat. Ev. Post* 2 April 116/3 Davis . . . is a jumbo-sized (six feet two, 202 pounds) man of forty-six with graying hair.

∗**jump,** *n.* In colloq. phrases: (1) *From the jump*, from the beginning; (2) *(at a) full jump*, at full speed; (3) *on the (keen) jump*, at once, abruptly; (4) *to put* (one) *over the big jump*, to kill; (5) *to get the jump on*, to forestall.

(1) **1831** *Maysville* (Ky.) *Eagle* 12 July, I'll give you a history of Henry Clay, from the *first jump* of him. **1911** FERBER *Dawn O'Hara* 32 Asked for you, right from the jump. — (2) **1854** M. J. HOLMES *Tempest & Sunshine* i. 12 What you ridin' Prince full Jump down the pike for? **1870** KEIM *Sheridan's Troopers* 39 The irate quadruped made for our party, coming at a 'full jump.' — (3) **1859** *S. Lit. Messenger* XXVIII. 143, I run down stream, an I meets Bill on the jump. **1861** *Atlantic Mo.* Sep. 293/1 De tar-kittle's a-bilin' on de keen jump, Mas'r Mellasys. **1913** LONDON *Valley of Moon* II. xii, The receivin' hospital went outa commission on the jump. — (4) **1920** WILSON *Red Gap* 353 Everybody was kind of glad he'd got off and kind of satisfied that he'd put this bad Injin, with his skull-duggery, over the big jump.

(5) **1939** *These Are Our Lives* 227 Mr. Hunter's got the jump on us. Hub ain't got nothing good in sight right now.

As the last term in **cross, johnny, squirrel's jump.**

∗**jump,** *v.*

1. *tr.* In hunting, to cause game to start from cover, also with *up*.

1836 GILMAN *Recoll.* (1838) 211 The boys were ordered to stick close to the dogs, and if they jumped the buck, to catch him. **1900** DRANNAN *Plains & Mts.* 58 We jumped up a band of fifty elk, which was considered a small herd then. **1947** *Chi. Tribune* 16 Nov. II. 7/1 You jump a rabbit and are forced to make a quick shot before it dives into protective cover.

transf. **1891** *Harper's Mag.* Nov. 883/1 He kept ever on the trail . . . going from camp to camp to 'jump' whiskey peddlers and gamblers. **1937** CALDWELL *Their Faces* 35 If that nigger out there in the woods gets jumped before the sheriff finds him, it will all be over and done with by sundown, and everybody will be satisfied.

2. To take possession of or occupy without legal procedure.

1836 in *Wis. Hist. Mag.* XIX. 446 The quarter (near Plainfield, Ill.) that I claimed originally myself has been 'jumped' by a person with whom reasoning is of no avail. **1866** *Eastern Slope* (Washoe, Nev.) 17 Feb. 2/2 The opposing claimants have recently located, or as is commonly termed, 'jumped' the premises. **1949** *Sat. Ev. Post* 26 Feb. 27/1, I will not jump another man's land.

b. Used esp. of a claim to a mining area. Cf. **claim jumper, claim jumping.**

1846 *Ore. Spectator* 29 Oct. 2/3 Although a neighbor may, as it is commonly termed, jump your claim, be not alarmed. **1877** JOHNSON *Anderson Co., Kans.* 59 He jumped the claim made by one Card. **1949** *No. Dak. Hist.* Jan. 21 The Ward Brothers, who jumped claims in Ramsey County, were shot by a band of the vigilantes.

3. In checkers, to pass over and so take an opponent's man.

1864 E. LESLIE *Amer. Girl's Book* 144 Two men, if left unprotected, can be jumped over and taken at one move, but then there must be a vacant space diagonally behind each. **1887** *Lippincott's Mag.* Sep. 350 If your checkers are jumped off the board so fast, you won't get any in the king-row. **1949** *Chi. Tribune* 3 April (Comics) 13 Look, ya dope—ya got a move there that'll jump t'ree of his men!

4. To quit (something), leave (a place or thing). Also absol.

1876 MILLER *First Families* 94 Even the head man of the company . . . jumped a first-class poker game . . . to come in and weigh out dust. *a***1904** WHITE *Blazed Trail* ii. 30 The men, discouraged, . . . would begin to 'jump,' would ask for their 'time.' **1910** *Sat. Ev. Post* 3 Sep. 19/1 Then, just as I had a private job in hand, I had to jump the town. **1945** SERVICE *Ploughman* 201 The monkey-faced man collected our blankets and checked them through. This was to prevent us from jumping the train on the way.

b. Esp. of a sailor: To leave (a ship) with no intention of returning to duty aboard it.

1883 *American* VI. 40 This evasion of imperative duty affords impunity to the men, if they jump the boat on the route. **1897** CLOVER *Paul Travers' Adv.* 146 The lad, . . having signed articles for Sydney, was amenable to discipline if detected in an attempt to 'jump the ship.' **1947** *Sat. Review* 11 Oct. 42/2 Jumping ship, this novelist spent two years on a Pacific island before being picked up by a whaler.

5. To get aboard (a train) surreptitiously as a tramp or hobo. *Slang.*

1891 C. ROBERTS *Adrift Amer.* 123, I jumped a freight here, and not being able to get into a car I rode the drawheads. *a***1910** O. HENRY *Rolling Stones* 118 I've grabbed my hat and jumped a freight and rode 200 miles to identify him.

6. To elevate (an officer) in rank; to place (someone) in a particular position; to pass above (another) on being promoted.

1897 C. A. DANA *Recoll. Civil War* 96 He was jumped almost at a stroke, without much previous service, to be a lieutenant general. **1902** WISTER *Virginian* xvii, But I'd happened to come along, and he jumped me into the vacancy. **1903** *N.Y. Sun* 20 Nov. 12 Four hundred and 94 officers are jumped by Gen. Wood.

7. In substantival, usu. colloq., combs.: (1) **jump butt,** a defective portion of the butt end of a tree trunk cut off and left in the woods by log sawyers, cf. **butt cut;** (2) **gully,** a dilapidated vehicle, *rare;* (3) **off,** a place where there is a precipitous descent, cf. **jumping-off**

place; (4) **rocks,** (see quot.); (5) **seat,** (see quots.); (6) **seed,** the Virginia knotweed; (7) **up,** (see quot.), *rare;* (8) **-up Johnny,** (see quot. and cf. **Johnny-jump-up**).

(1) **1942** *Democrat* 1 Oct. 1/2 Three colored men . . . overturned the jumpbutt of an old poplar log and found underneath 22 rattlesnakes. — (2) **1901** *Cong. Rec.* 17 Jan. 1147/1 [The rural mail ought not to be] carried over this country, as it is now, in a jump-gully, with one wheel turned one way and another, drawn by a Texas pony worth about a dollar and a half. — (3) **1873** BEADLE *Undevel. West* 490 In this bayou we encountered dangerous whirls and jump-offs. **1934** VINES *Green Thicket World* 136 The bluffs were small, but many of the rocks were great, and straight up and down so that there was only one jump-off. — (4) **1889** *Cent.* 3252/2 jump-rocks. . . . A catostomine fish, *Moxostoma cervinum,* with a 3-lobed air-bladder, from 10 to 12 dorsal rays, and a very slender body, rarely attaining a foot in length. It inhabits the South Atlantic States from the James to the Chattahoochee river. Also called **jumping-mullet.**

Jump butt, butt cut, or butt log

(5) **1864** WEBSTER, *Jump-seat,* a carriage constructed with a movable seat; . . . a movable carriage-seat. *Ib., Jump-seat, a.,* having a movable seat; as, a jump-seat rockaway. **1875** KNIGHT *Dict. Mech.,* Jump-seat, . . . a kind of open buggy which has a shifting seat or seats. . . . It may be arranged as a double or single seat vehicle. — (6) **1931** CLUTE *Plants* 137 Not so the jump-seed (*Tovaria Virginica*). This has a trigger arrangement which needs only a touch to set things going. — (7) **1855** in *Wis. Hist. Mag.* XXII. 210 There seems to be a sort of *'jump up,'* or dancing-school here (Erie Co., Penna.) this evening. — (8) **1899** VANDERBILT *Flatbush* 287 Pansies were abundant, but they were very small, and, under the common name of 'jump-up Johnnies,' crept out from the garden-bed to the grass-plot.

b. In phrases: (1) *To jump bail,* to abscond while at liberty under bail; (2) *to jump one's bill, board,* to depart without paying; (3) *to jump a bounty,* to obtain a military bounty by enlisting and then deserting the service, *rare.*

(1) **1859** MATSELL *Vocabulum* 47 *Jumped his bail,* run away from his bail. **1911** VANCE *Cynthia* 177 He's jumped bail on a bigamy indictment. — (2) **1879** *Amer. Punch* Oct. 109/2 The circus springboard vaulter never gets arrested for 'jumping his board.' **1888** *Chi. Herald* (F.), He arose at early dawn and jumped his bill. — (3) **1884** *Cong. Rec.* 28 March 2388/1, I shall not vote for this bill until I am ready to put the man upon the pension-roll 'who broke his leg attempting to jump a bounty.'

c. With adverbs: (1) ***jump off,** (see quot. and cf. **jumping-off place**); (2) ***jump up,** (*a*) of a town or village, to arise or spring up, *obs.,* (*b*) to obtain without particular effort.

(1) **1847** PARKMAN in *Knickerb. Mag.* XXIX. 316 It was resolved to remain one day at Fort Leavenworth, and on the next to bid a final adieu to the frontier; or in the phraseology of the region, to 'jump off.' — (2) (*a*) **1818** *Niles' Reg.* XIV. 310/2 The improvements in the navigation of this important river [the Roanoke] has [*sic*] caused new towns and thriving villages to 'jump up' as suddenly as in any part of the western country. **1833** *Ib.* XLIV. 198/1 A new and flourishing town of fifty houses, called Amsterdam, has jumped up on the Big Black river. (*b*) **1843** in BLAIR *Amer. Humor* (1937) 333 The company was jest about as good a one as could be jumped up for sich a occasion.

***jumper,** *n.*

1. A sled or sleigh, often of a crude type.

1823 COOPER *Pioneers* xxiv, He was seen drawing one of those jumpers that they [*sc.* pioneers] carry their grain to mill in. **1898** *N. Eng. Mag.* June 455/1 My pulse quickens as I recall the glorious times with our 'jumper,' and the hair-breadth escapes from posts and barberry bushes, in our swift descent upon the ice. **1944** DUNCAN *M. Graham* 154 Many New Salem folk had jumpers (sleighs) that might be borrowed by an ingratiating young man or rented in exchange for a day's work.

2. (See quot.) *Rare.*

1850 BROWNE *Poultry Yard* 71 *Jumpers,* from their halting gait, are rather to be considered as accidental deformities collected from unhealthy families of Bantams, than as constituting any distinct variety.

3. One who jumps a claim. Cf. ***jump,** *v.* **2. b.**

1851 A. T. JACKSON *Forty-Niner* (1920) 67 They are good friends of ours and will keep the jumpers off [our claim]. **1925** TILGHMAN *Dugout* 102 She stopped there, rather than at the house, because the road ran by it, and there the jumpers would first reach the claim. **1948** JOHNSTON *Gold Rush* 34/1 Clame Notise—Jim Brown of Missoury takes this ground; jumpers will be shot.

4. A teamster or driver. *Colloq.*

1882 HUBBARD *Moosehead Lake* 106 During the summer season, a team and 'jumper' are constantly on hand to haul canoes and luggage over to Mud Pond. **1947** CHALFANT *Gold, Guns, & Ghost Towns* 82 Many shots were exchanged, one of which killed jumper Snell.

5. (See quot.)

1884 GOODE *Fisheries* I. 401 In Kentucky it [the large-mouth black bass, *Micropterus salmoides*] is called 'Jumper.' *Ib.,* The Smallmouth [black bass, *Micropterus dolomiei*] shares with the Large mouth in the Southern States the names 'Jumper,' 'Perch,' and 'Trout.'

6. A contrivance upon which fire hose is wound. Also attrib.

1889 BRAYLEY *Boston Fire Dept.* 326 The new-style hose-carriage, or wagon, was fast taking the place of the old-fashioned 'jumper,' or reel. **1903** *N.Y. Ev. Post* 17 Oct., Next came firemen's day—a long eight hours of flashing uniforms, . . . of sudden dashes by swift hose 'jumper' men.

7. = ***jerker,** *n.* **1.** *Obs.*

1889 *Pop. Sci. Mo.* June 148 Examples of this [religious excitement] in America are seen in the 'Jumpers,' 'Jerkers,' and various revival extravagances.

8. One who has quit his job. *Rare.*

1903 WHITE *Blazed Trail* ii. 33 Silver Jack . . . took one of the 'jumpers' in the cutter with him.

9. A plural voter. *Slang. Obs.*

1903 *N.Y. Tribune* 27 Oct. (*Cent. Supp.*), There are more 'jumpers' than there were two years ago. These 'jumpers' vote in widely separated parts of the city.

10. A boy who delivers packages from a delivery wagon.

1905 *Washington Star* 24 Nov. 20 (*advt.*), Wanted—boys for jumpers on delivery wagons.

As the last term in **baby, bounty, bridge, claim, land, lot, ox, Yankee jumper.**

***jumping,** *a.* and *n.*

1. (See quot. 1879), used esp. of mining claims. *Obs.* Cf. ***jump,** *v.* **2. b.**

1850 HINES *Voyage* 198 Here was no jumping of claims, . . . all were satisfied to select from that part of the vast surface of the whole around which lines had not been run. **1879** *Scribner's Mo.* Oct. 806/1 Next came a period of 'jumping,' that is, getting forcible or fraudulent possession of property. **1907** MULFORD *Bar-20* 356 The first operation was simple, being known . . . as 'jumping.'

Jumping alligator, piney woods rooter, Carolina racehorse, or land pike

2. In combs.: (1) **jumping alligator,** a humorous term for a razorback hog, *obs.;* (2) **bean,** the seed of any one of various Mexican euphorbiaceous plants containing the larva of a moth the movements of which cause the seed to roll and jump about, cf. **Mexican jumping bean;** (3) **cactus,** =next; (4) **cholla,** a spiny cactus found in the Southwest, so called because of the ease with which the spines are detached; (5) **deer,** =**mule deer;** (6) **exercise,** = ∗**jerk,** *n.*² **1,** *obs.;* (7) ∗**jack,** (see quot.); (8) **jingoes, jings,** (see quot.); (9) ∗**mouse,** =**kangaroo mouse;** (10) **mullet,** the jumprocks or a related fish; (11) **-off place,** see as a main entry; (12) **rat,** =**kangaroo rat;** (13) **seed,** =**jumping bean.**

(1) 1872 *Harper's Mag.* April 663/2 An infernal beast with long legs, a bristling back, and immense proboscis . . . frightened Miss Lilly dreadfully. She told me it was a 'ridge-back'—a 'jumping alligator,' a 'sub-soiler.' — **(2) 1889** *Cent.* 3252/2 *Jumping seed.* . . . Also called *jumping-bean, devil-bean.* **1896** *Chambers's Jrnl.* 18 April 249 A new botanical curiosity . . . has lately been brought into notice in England under the name of 'A Jumping Bean.' **1946** *This Week Mag.* 26 Oct. 2/1 [He] is the world's Jumping Bean King. — **(3) 1939** PICKWELL *Deserts* 65/1 So notorious is Cholla that in the desert it is known by many different names: 'Silver Cactus' (the new stems at the top are silvery in color . . .), 'Jumping Cactus' (when the loose stems on the ground are touched their needles may cause the whole stem to leap) [etc.]. **1947** J. W. HILTON *Sonora Sk. Bk.* 180 They put a fellow in a ring covered with joints of cholla cactus (you know what the stuff is—Americans call it 'jumping cactus,' the orn'riest thing that grows from the ground). — **(4) 1942** CASTETTER & BELL *Pima & Papago Agric.* 25 The heaviest stands, for the most part, consist of a single species, the jumping cholla (*Opuntia fulgida*). **1946** *Desert Mag.* April 29/1 This distinctive tree-like cactus commonly is called Jumping Cholla.

(5) 1831 R. COX *Adv. Columbia R.* 319 The jumping-deer, or chevreuil, . . . frequent the vicinity of the mountains in considerable numbers. — **(6) 1834** *Biblical Repertory* VI. 349 We saw another who had, what was termed, 'the jumping exercise;' which resembled that of the jumpers in Wales. — **(7) 1861** *Ill. Agric. Soc. Trans.* V. 416 There is scarcely an individual . . . to be found who is unacquainted with the 'Spring-beetles,' or as they are often termed, 'Jumping-Jacks.' — **(8) 1815** HUMPHREYS *Yankey* 106 *Jumping jings, jingoes,* expletives indicative of confirmation. — **(9) 1826** GODMAN *Nat. Hist.* II. 95 The jumping-mouse is found in this country from Canada to Pennsylvania, and no doubt still farther south. **1949** *Pacific Discovery* May–June 16/2 Our favorites . . . were three young jumping mice that my wife captured in a patch of wild strawberries.

(10) 1766 J. BARTRAM *Journal* 35 Saw a mullet jump three times in a minute or two, which they generally do before they rest, so are called jumping-mullets. — **(12) 1867** *Amer. Naturalist* I. 394 The *Saccomyinæ* . . . are known in the vernacular as 'Kangaroo' or 'Jumping' Rats and Mice, and are entirely confined to Transmississippian regions. — **(13) 1876** *Field & Forest* II. 53 We have recently had the pleasure of examining . . . these so-called jumping seeds received from California. **1889** [see **jumping bean**].

As the last term in **bounty, claim, land, lot jumping.**

jumping-off place.

1. A derogatory designation for a place thought of as being the farthest limit of civilization.

1826 FLINT *Recoll.* 366 Being, as they phrase it, the 'jumping off place,' it is necessarily the resort of desperate, wicked, and strange creatures who wish to fly away from poverty, infamy, and the laws. **1907** STEWART *Partners* 15, I couldn't see what a high-toned man like him was going up to that jumping-off place for. **1946** *Sunshine Mag.* Jan. 3 The little town of Sun Ridge was the jumping-off place.

2. A place at the end of a given portion of a journey as a point of departure for further travel. Also fig.

1834 BRACKENRIDGE *Recoll.* x. 111, I had no jumping off or jumping up place, like those who prepare their exordium and perorations, and leave the body of the speech to take care of itself. **1841** *N.O. Picayune* 28 May 2/2 To-morrow I set out for Austin, which may be considered the 'jumping off place,' as from there we leave the settlements altogether. **1949** *Chi. D. News* 9 March 18/7 That any European state will allow its territory to be used as a jumping-off place for a blitz on the Soviet union is preposterous.

3. The extreme limit of the earth, the end or edge of the world. Also fig.

*c***1845** PAULDING *Amer. Comedies* (1847) 197, I have hunted all over them parts, almost clean out to the jumping off place of creation. *a***1862** THOREAU *Maine Woods* 178 He . . . only reached the jumping-off place of his wonder at white men's institutions. **1870** KEIM *Sheridan's Troopers* 224 Religious superstition also teaches that the earth is a great plain, and that there is a jumping off place. **1902** WISTER *Virginian* 17 The men were on the ragged edge, the very jumping-off place, of mutiny and possible murder. **1934** VINES *Green Thicket World* 169 He would follow Morgan to the jumping-off place.

∗**junco,** *n.*

1. =**allthorn.**

1849 in *Amer. Antiq. Soc. Proc.* ns. XLI. 382 You speak of a 'dry berry' which I sent you as seed of the junco (green-thorn-shrub). I aimed . . . to send . . . large branches of these berries. **1871** *Overland Mo.* VI. 555/1 The *junco* has absolutely no foliage, except immense, horrid, green thorns. **1934** *N.M. Agric. Exp. Sta. Press Bul.* 714, 1 Another green-stemmed leafless shrub found in many parts of southern New Mexico is the all-thorn, crown of thorns, or junco.

2. Any one of various small American finches, a snowbird.

1887 RIDGWAY *Manual N. Amer. Birds* 422–4 [Gives eight U.S. species.] **1947** *Sports Afield* Dec. 132/2 Equally unafraid are the other winter birds, the chickadees and juncos.

As the last term in **Oregon, slate-colored junco.**

∗**June,** *n.* In combs.: (1) **June berry,** any one of various American shadbushes or the fruit of one of these; (2) ∗**bug,** see as a main entry; (3) **butter,** butter made in June; (4) **corn,** early corn suitable for table use in June; (5) **freshet,** =**June rise;** (6) **grape,** (see quot.); (7) **grass,** =**blue grass,** also a tufted grass, *Koeleria cristata,* found in prairie regions, cf. **prairie June grass;** (8) **pear,** a pear that ripens in June; (9) **plum,** (see quot.); (10) **rise,** (see quots.).

(1) 1810 MICHAUX *Arbres* I. 32 *June berry,* nom donné à cet arbre [*Mespilus arborea*] dans tous les Etats du milieu. **1821** *Jrnl. Science* III. 275 Found the apple . . . trees, the iron-wood, june-berry [etc.] . . . in flower. **1949** *Ward Co. Independent* (Minot, N.D.) 21 July 1/1 There will be a fair crop of juneberries and chokecherries in the Kenmare area this season. — **(3) 1839** *Mass. Agric. Survey 2d Rep.* 71 June butter . . . and September butter . . . are generally of a superior quality to that made at other seasons. **1902** *Boston Ev. Globe* 18 Feb. 4/5 Gathered cream butter in June 20 to 21 cents; renovated and best June butter, after being in cold storage, 23 cents. — **(4) 1943** *Democrat* 3 June 2/6 Some June corn planted in the garden now will give some roasting ears later on.

(5) 1844 GREGG *Commerce of Prairies* I. 65 The 'June freshets,' however, are seldom of long duration. — **(6) 1819** NUTTALL *Travels Ark.* (1821) 98 A species of *Vitis,* called the June grape, from its ripening at that early period, was also nearly in bloom. — **(7) 1855** *Mich. Agric. Soc. Trans.* VI. 160 One tree of the damson variety, standing in a stiff June grass sod plat. **1870** *Rep. Comm. Agric. 1869* 169 The best grasses for permanent lawns are red top (*Agrostis vulgaris,*) and June grass (*Poa pratensis*). **1919** *Maine My State* 336 How fair her fields when June-grass waves! — **(8) 1760** WASHINGTON *Diaries* I. 146 Grafted 10 of a pretty little early (June) Pear from Collo. Mason's. — **(9) 1832** in WILLIAMSON *Maine* I. 109 [The wild plum tree, *Prunus sylvestris,* is] called also pomegranate, wild pear, and June-plum.

(10) 1847 ROBB *Squatter Life* 134 The varmint's [a rival's] countenance looked as riled as the old Missouri in a June rise. **1880** MCELRATH *Yellowstone Valley* 33 The satisfaction of the journey is materially enhanced by availing one's self of that season of high water known technically as the 'June rise.'

june dʒun, *v.* [Origin unknown.] *intr.* and *tr.* To go rapidly, drive briskly. *Colloq.*

1869 *Overland Mo.* III. 127 A trig, smirk little horse is a 'lace-horse,' and he often has to 'june,' or 'quill.' **1889** FARMER 328/1 *June, To* (Texas).—To go. Probably from the German *gehen.* **1903** A. ADAMS *Log Cowboy* 228 To june a herd of cattle across in this manner would have been shameful.

∗**June bug.** Any one of various large beetles of the genus *Phyllophaga* and related genera. Also the fig-eater *q.v.*

1835 LONGSTREET *Ga. Scenes* 78 You'll see me down upon him like a duck upon a June-bug. **1872** *Harper's Mag.* Nov. 803/2 Phemie Bonner whirled him round like a June-bug tied to a string. **1948** *Chi. Tribune* 26 June 1. 10/3 A familiar nuisance of summer nights, the June bug, has not yet manifested itself.

attrib. **1857** STROTHER *Virginia* 110 [A Negro], dressed in his holiday suit, with a ruffled shirt of red calico, a June-bug breast-pin, a brass-headed cane [etc.]. **1909** O. HENRY *Options* 129 He spent his life seining the air for flying fish of the June-bug order, and then sticking pins through 'em and calling 'em names.

Juney bug. =**June bug.** — *c***1866** BAGBY *Old Va. Gentleman* 45 The humming-birds and the bumble-bees and Juney-bugs, which knew them [*sc.* butterflies] once shall know them no more. *c***1870** *Ala. Hist. Soc. Trans.* IV. 484 Why a hog has no more chance to live among these thieving negro farmers than a juney bug in a gang of puddle ducks.

∗**jungle,** *n.* A hobo camp. *Slang.* Cf. **hobo jungle.** [**1908** JOHNSON *Pac. Coast* 215 My companions spoke of the grove they were in as the 'Hoboes Jungle.'] **1945** *New Yorker* 25 Aug. 28, I was a bum, but a dreamy-eyed idealistic bum, and holing up in jungles outside a town, I'd recite verses by the hour.

***junior,** *a.* and *n.*

1. A student in the third year of a four-year academic course, formerly called a junior sophister *q.v.*

c1764 in WOOLSEY *Hist. Disc. Yale* (1850) 55 A Senior may take a Freshman from a Sophimore, a Bachelor from a Junior, and a Master from a Senior. **1842** *Yale Lit. Mag.* VIII. 46 The aspiring Junior is already anticipating the high enjoyments, and, perchance, the *ease* of Senior year. **1948** *Great Falls* (Mont.) *Tribune* 18 Sep. 5/4 Of the 471 students enrolled in the high school, 116 are freshmen, 105 sophomores, 119 juniors and 131 seniors.

b. (See quots.)

1847 WEBSTER 635/2 *Junior*, . . . one in the first year of his course at a theological seminary. **1889** *Cent. Mag.* Jan. 403/1 When the trade-school course is finished and he has proved by an examination held by a committee of master mechanics that he has profited by it, he is to enter a workshop as a 'junior.'

2. In combs.: (1) **junior bachelor,** (see quot. 1851), *obs.;* (2) **class,** see as a main entry; (3) **college,** a college, operating as a separate institution or as part of a standard college, which does not offer courses more advanced than those of the sophomore year; (4) **dean,** a subordinate dean in a college; (5) **exhibition,** a program designed to display the literary and, sometimes, the musical and dramatic talents of members of the junior class, usu. **Junior Ex.;** (6) **high (school),** a school usu. including the seventh, eighth, and ninth grades and affording pupils departmentalized instruction and some choice in the selection of subjects, also attrib.; (7) **preacher,** in the Methodist Church, a minister subordinate in rank to another serving with him; (8) **prom,** a formal ball or dance given by a junior class, a promenade; (9) **Republic,** (see quot. 1948); (10) **senator,** a senator who has been in Congress a shorter time than the other senator from his state; (11) **sophister,** see as a main entry; (12) **year,** the third year of a school or college course requiring four years for its completion.

(1) **1790** *Harvard Laws* 19 No Junior-bachelor shall continue in the College, after the Commencement in the summer vacation. **1851** HALL *College Words* 176 *Junior Bachelor*, one who is in his first year after taking the degree of Bachelor of Arts. — **(3) 1899** *Univ. of Chi. Reg. 1898–99* 37/1 The Faculties of the Schools of Arts, Literature, and Science have been organized as follows: (1) The Faculty of the Junior Colleges; (2) The Faculty of the Senior Colleges [etc.]. **1949** *Chi. D. News* 1 April 3/4 Jimmy came home and entered junior college. — **(4) 1944** *Chi. D. Tribune* 14 Nov. 12/6 He was . . . junior dean of the college.

(5) 1851 HALL *College Words* 45 At Hamilton College, it is customary for the Sophomores to appear in a class cap on the Junior Exhibition day. **1920** *Albion* (Mich.) *Recorder* 15 April (*advt.*), Junior Ex. Big Program and 3 act Comedy 'Tommy's Wife.' — **(6) 1909** *Ann. Rep. Bd. Educ.* (Columbus, O.) 168 The Board has declared itself in favor of the Junior High School System. **1948** *Dly. Ardmoreite* (Ardmore, Okla.) 12 Oct. 10/1 They met in the ninth grade in junior high and a romance began that ended in marriage. — **(7) 1846** *Indiana Mag. Hist.* XXIII. 242 Elliott being only a probationer in the conference and Brown being an elder of some years' standing, he thought his dignity invaded by being a junior preacher under a probationer, so that the elder deemed it expedient to change him with the junior preacher on Lawrenceburg circuit. **1874** EGGLESTON *Circuit Rider* 194 He had, therefore, sent him as 'second man' or 'junior preacher' on a circuit. — **(8) 1893** *Outing* Feb. 391/2 'Ah, let me see,' they overheard him ask her, 'This is your —' 'Twentieth Junior Prom.' **1914** GERRY *Masks of Love* 79 [Her tears] were a tribute not only to the lover but to all the years of sheltered sweetness with which he was associated, . . . her 'junior prom' at college [etc.]. — **(9) 1935** *Hist. Soc. So. Calif. Pub.* XVII. 19 The Butterfield route . . . followed a direct course past what is now the administration building of the California Junior Republic. **1948** *Amer. Butter & Cheese Rev.* Dec. 33/2 The George 'Junior Republic,' founded 52 years ago at Freeville, N.Y., near Ithaca to help 'problem' boys and girls grow up to good citizenship, is the birthplace of youth self-government.

(10) 1885 CRAWFORD *Amer. Politician* 142 The junior senator for Massachusetts died this morning, and there may be an election at any moment. **1900** *Cong Rec.* 11 Jan. 766/2 The details of the amendment offered by the junior Senator from Massachusetts . . . might be considerably extended. — **(12) 1884** R. GRANT *Average Man* 10 It was the end of my Junior year, and I was feeling terribly blue. **1948** *Sat. Ev. Post* 4 Dec. 154/4 War was in the air during Tukey's junior year in college.

junior class. A class in a college or high school made up of students in the third year of the school course.

1720 D. NEAL *Hist. N.-Eng.* I. 185 At Harvard the Junior Class are called fresh Men the first Year. **1842** *Knickerb.* May 433 The junior class is the natural ally of the freshman class. **1945** *Kansan* (Concordia) 8 March 6/4 A packed house witnessed the performance . . . which was presented by the Junior class of the high school.

b. (See quot.) *Obs.*

1816 *Ann. 14th Congress* 2 Sess. 270 Those in the militia between the age of twenty-one and thirty-one years of age, shall be called the junior class.

junior sophister. (See quots. 1654, 1847.) *Obs.*

1654 H. DUNSTER (Harvard Univ. MS), Ad 3m deinde pervenientes Annum termino Paschali Juniores Sophistae appellantur. [Those reaching the third year, from the Easter term on are called Junior Sophisters.] **1708** *Broadside Verse* (1930) 23 A Solemn Lacrymatory for the Grave of Jonathan Marsh, Junior-sophister: Who Deceas'd at Harvard College. **1818** *N. Amer. Rev.* March 423 The following are . . . the several classes [at Harvard]: . . . Freshmen . . . Sophomores . . . Junior sophisters . . . Senior sophisters. **1847** WEBSTER 635/2 *Junior*, . . . one in the third year of his collegiate course in an American college, formerly called *Junior Sophister*.

***juniper,** *n.* Used loosely for any one of various coniferous American trees resembling juniper.

1622 MOURT *Relation* 10 They found it to be a small neck of Land [near Cape Cod Bay] . . . all wooded with Okes, Pines, Sassafras, Iuniper, Birch. [**1748** H. ELLIS *Hudson's Bay* 138 They are commonly of Fir, or Larch, which the English there call Juniper.] **1834** in *Atlantic Mo.* XXVI. 491/2 Hemlock trees, exactly what we in Louisa [Co., Va.] have called juniper, on river hills. **1894** *Amer. Folk-Lore* VII. 99 *Larix Americana*, . . . juniper, Penobscot Co., Me., Grand Lake region of Penobscot River, Me.

attrib. **1773** in *Amer. Sp.* XV. 278/1 A Tract of Land . . . . well timbered with White Oak and old Pine, and joins a Juniper Swamp.

As the last term in **alligator (bark), desert, Sierra, thick-barked, Utah juniper.**

***junk,** *n.* [Some of the senses here may be of different words.]

1. A tobacco pipe. *Obs.* Cf. **junk tobacco.**

1704 S. KNIGHT *Journal* 29 Having 'litt, he makes an Awkerd Scratch with his Indian shoo, and a Nodd, sitts on ye block, fumbles out his black Junk, dipps it in ye Ashes, and presents it piping hott to his muscheeto's, and fell to sucking like a calf, without speaking. **1723** *N.-Eng. Courant* 15–22 July 1/1 The Engine whence ascends this fragrant Funk [tobacco smoke], Modern Interpretations render *Junk*.

2. Miscellaneous secondhand or discarded articles of little or no value.

1842 *Cong. Globe* 23 Feb. 261 Champagne was charged for under the head of 'old junk.' **1924** *Publishers' Wkly.* CVI. 545/1 In secondhand bookshops junk is a term for books that have practically no commercial value. **1948** *Sat. Ev. Post* 4 Dec. 40/3 The old mills will simply be dismantled and most of the machinery sold for junk.

3. In combs.: (1) **junk bottle,** (see quot. 1848); (2) **cart,** a cart used by a junkman; (3) **dealer,** a dealer in marine stores, one who busy and sells secondhand or cast-off articles; (4) **heap,** a rubbish heap; (5) **man,** = **junk dealer;** (6) **shop,** a shop in which miscellaneous secondhand or discarded articles are kept for sale, also fig.; (7) **store,** = prec.; (8) **tobacco,** ?smoking tobacco, pipe tobacco, *obs.*, cf. **junk,** *n.* **1;** (9) **yard,** an area or inclosure where secondhand or worn-out articles are collected.

(1) **1786** *Conn. Courant* 29 May 3/3 (*advt.*), *Drugs, Medicines and Groceries* . . . Junk Bottles, Corks . . . &c. &c. **1848** BARTLETT 192 Junk-bottle, the ordinary black glass porter-bottle. **1898** HARPER *S. B. Anthony* I. 36 It was said that great numbers of junk bottles had been laid under the floor to give especially nice tone to the fiddles. — **(2) 1880** ALDRICH *Stillwater Tragedy* xvii. 199 He would rather drive a junk-cart. — **(3) 1866** W. DAVIDGE *Footlight Flashes* 168 A marine or junk dealer's is a well ordered collection when compared with it. **1948** *Chelsea* (Mass.) *Rec.* 30 Nov. 1/4 The board of aldermen last night voted passage of an ordinance controlling the issuance of new licenses to junk dealers. — **(4) 1920** ALSAKER *Eating for Health* 195 You and I have to conform to the laws of nature, or else we are thrown into the junk heap.

(5) 1872 CRAPSEY *Nether Side N.Y.* 39 They pull away to a point convenient to the shop of a junkman selected beforehand as the purchaser of the plunder. **1948** *Washington Post* 5 Dec. 25M/1 The Russian-born former junkman . . . became boss of Hollywood's biggest film factory and drew the Nation's biggest salary. — **(6)** *c***1849** PAIGE *Dow's Sermons* I. 256 Trash that wouldn't fetch two cents in the market of heaven, and but a trifle more in the junk-shops of hell. **1907** M. C. HARRIS *Tents of Wickedness* 398 Those trunks full of papers . . . worth just so much per pound as waste papers in the junk-shops. — **(7) 1882** McCabe *New York* 583 They gather up whatever they can find, and sell it to the junk and rag stores. **1888** *St. Louis Globe Dem.* 10 March (F.), A Junk Store Rifled. The second-hand store of Joseph Laschkowtz . . . was rifled of a large lot of goods early yesterday morning. — **(8) 1817** *Conn. Courant* LIII. 10 June 4/5 (*advt.*), For Sale . . . Junk and paper Tobacco. — **(9) 1880** Cable *Grandissimes* 192 You may still here and there see one [villa] standing . . . among founderies, cotton and tobacco-sheds, junk-yards, and longshoremen's hovels. **1948** *Sat. Review* 3 July 6/2 Wonderful in its day, the old press was ready for the junk yard.

junk dʒʌŋk, *v.* [f. ***junk,** *n.* **2.**] *tr.* To scrap, cast aside as useless. Also transf. *Slang.* — **1916** B. Hall *One Man's War* (1929) 196 When he got home his ship was a complete wreck. It will be junked. **1947** *Chi. D. News* 14 June 6/3 Telling his audiences that he's a Roosevelt New Dealer and advising them to junk the Democratic party if it does not drop the Truman Doctrine.

junker ˈdʒʌŋkɚ, *n.* [f. **junk,** *v.*] (See quot.) — **1889** *Boston Herald* 3 Feb. 3/4 What was termed the junkers, parties who buy up old vessels and anything they think there is a little money in.

***junket,** *n.* (See quot. 1886.) Also transf. and attrib.

1886 *Detroit Free Press* 4 Sep. 4/2 The term 'junket' in America is generally applied to a trip taken by an American official at the expense of the government he serves so nobly and unselfishly. **1912** Mathewson *Pitching* 229 At last, after the long junket through the South . . . is ended, comes a welcome day, when the new uniforms are donned. **1947** *Chi. Tribune* 19 July 3/1 Several rules committee members have opposed the resolutions on the ground that they would provide 'nice junket trips' for committee members

***junketer,** *n.* An official who takes part in a political junket. — **1862** *N.Y. Tribune* 14 June (*Cent.*), On what principle . . . are these junketers . . . allowed the use of steamboats at an expense of from $300 to $500 per day? **1892** *Columbus* (O.) *Dispatch* 20 Oct., It would have been a matter of selfish precaution for the State and Legislative junketers to invite Dr. Probst to accompany them to Chicago.

***junketing,** *n.* A political feast, trip, etc., enjoyed at public expense. Also as adj. Cf. **tea junketing.**

1809 Irving *Hist. N.Y.* (1927) III. ii. 123 They were . . . graciously permitted to eat, and drink, and smoke, at all those snug junkettings and public gormandizings. **1843** *Pathfinder* 22 April, After all the parades, junkettings and speeches, . . . is there a single man who can honestly say that his lot has been improved by the result [of the election]? **1899** *Chi. Record* 27 Jan. 2/2 The commission takes the place of the junketing committees that have hitherto visited the institutions.

***junto,** *n.* As the last term in **county, Essex Junto.**

***jury,** *n.* In combs.: (1) ***jury box,** a box in which the names of prospective jurors are placed; (2) **commissioner,** a member of a jury commission charged with the duty of preparing jury lists; (3) **fixer,** see as a main entry; (4) **lawyer,** a trial lawyer; (5) **wheel,** a revolving device to assure the operation of chance in drawing the names of jurors.

(1) 1738 *Boston Selectmen* 159 [The names of] Persons . . . Qualified and lyable to Serve on the Petit Jury, . . . may be put into the Jury Box, as the Law directs. **1843** *Knickerb.* XXI. 190 He had read . . . the names which had been put into the jury-box. — **(2) 1911** *Okla. Session Laws* 3 Legisl. 58 The board of jury commissioners of Pontotoc County shall make three lists of names of two hundred (200) persons each who shall possess the qualifications of jurors. — **(4) 1902** Whitlock *13th District* 53 General Bancroft . . . was the best jury lawyer we ever had there.

(5) 1882 S. D. Thompson & E. G. Merriam *Juries* 624 The jury wheel shall be secured against tampering [by being sealed]. **1940** Stuart *Trees of Heaven* 313, I could have all the names called in the jury wheel and it would be the same.

b. *jury of view,* (see quot.). *Obs.*

1895 Craddock *Myst. Witch-Face Mt.* 96 This engine of the law . . . consist[ed] of one road commissioner and two freeholders, the trio still . . . denominated a 'jury of view.'

As the last term in **blue ribbon, Indian, police, sheriff, sheriff's jury.**

jury fixer. One who bribes or attempts to bribe or otherwise illegally influence a juror. Also **jury-fixing.**

1882 *Washington Post* 18 March (Th.), There was an idea abroad that there might be some scope in the proceedings before the Grand Jury for a 'jury fixer.' **1887** *Library Mag.* April 531/2 Bribery and jury-fixing would speedily disappear. **1931** *Blue Valley Farmer* (Okla. City) 24 Dec. 1/6 Fill the town with secret service men to catch the jury fixers. **1946** McWilliams *So. Calif. Country* 245 Then began the long and sordid aftermath, involving jury-fixing, bribery, and murder.

***just,** *adv.* Used before a demonstrative or an interrogative introducing a subject clause. — **1884** Goode *Fisheries* II. 543 Just what makes the best lodgement for oyster spawn . . . has been greatly discussed. *Ib.* 544 Just how many bushels a man will place on an acre depends upon both his means and his judgment. **1900** *School Rev.* June 322 Just this happened in Latin.

***justice,** *n.*

1. One of the judges of a state or federal court.

1839 *Knickerb.* XIII. 2 In this city [New York] alone, are three law courts; a superior court with three justices. **1910** J. Hart *Vigilante Girl* 307 He could not continue to appear in the case before the circuit court with his uncle as presiding justice.

b. *Justice of the Supreme Court,* a judge in the supreme court of a state or of the U.S.

1789 Morse *Amer. Geog.* 180 The salaries of governor and justices of the supreme court, cannot be diminished. **1894** *Harper's Mag.* April 797/1 His father is justice of the Supreme Court. **1948** *New Yorker* 6 Nov. 65/1, I saw a justice of the Supreme Court of the United States drink one in a Washington barroom in 1886.

2. a. Justice Department, =**Department of Justice. b. justice weed,** (see quots.).

(a) 1944 *Newsweek* 25 Sep. 69/1 In its determined drive against cartels the United States Justice Department has sent Federal Bureau of Investigation agents . . . to dig up evidence. **1949** *Lubbock* (Tex.) *Morn. Avalanche* 23 Feb. I. 11/1 The Justice Department, I recalled moodily, had warned us there were none [corroborating witnesses]. — **(b) 1907** Lyons *Plant Names* 189 E[upatorium] leucolepis T. & G. New Jersey to Florida and Louisiana. Justice-weed, White-bracted Thoroughwort. The name Justice-weed is applied also to E. hyssopifolium L., Massachusetts to Texas. **1909** *Cent. Supp.* 675/3 justice-weed. . . . Either of two American species of *Eupatorium, E. leucolepis* and *E. hyssopifolium.*

As the last term in **county, Jersey, seat of, trial justice.**

***juvenile,** *n.* In combs.: (1) **juvenile asylum,** a refuge for vagabond or homeless children; (2) **court,** a court, or a special part of a court, in which children's cases are tried.

(1) 1856 *Porter's Spirit of Times* 18 Oct. 108/2 'The New York Juvenile Asylum' . . . [is designed] to provide a refuge for all the little vagabond children of both sexes, found prowling about the streets. **1856** MacLeod *F. Wood* 289 Thus sat the Hon. Fernando Wood, Mayor of the City of New-York, . . . Director of the New-York Juvenile Asylum, Member of the Board of Trustees of the Astor Library, in his chair of state. — **(2) 1899** *Ill. Laws* 132 A special court room, to be designated as the juvenile court room, shall be provided . . . , and the court may, for convenience, be called the 'Juvenile Court.' **1947** *Newsweek* 24 Feb. 30/2 In Juvenile Court, the maximum sentence would be reform school.

juzgado huzˈgɑ·u, *n.* *S.W.* [Sp., court, tribunal.] A hoosegow *q.v.*

1919 C. G. Raht *Romance of Davis Mountains* 168 As the prisoners were being led to the *juzgado*, they cast longing eyes across the River. **1931** *Lariat* April 122 (Bentley), And I had to stay in the nearest *jusgado* for three days. **1935** *So. Calif. Hist. Soc. Pub.* March 10 The southern part of the adobe, formerly separated from the rest by a narrow passageway, was the old *Juzgado*, or court room of the pueblo.

K

ka-, see **ca-** and cf. **ker-**.

Kachina kɑˈtʃinə, *n.* [See quot. 1890.]

1. (See quots.)

1889 in DONALDSON *Moqui Pueblo Indians* (1893) 67 The whole Moqui heavens are filled, too, with Katcina, angels, or, literally, 'those who have listened to the gods.' All of the great dead men of the Moqui nation at some time before they died saw Katcina and received messages from them. **1890** *Arch. Inst. Amer. Papers* IV. 151 The origin of the word is found in the Tehua language, where 'Ka-tzin-a' signifies the spirits of the fetiches of game. **1893** DONALDSON *Moqui Pueblo Indians* 53 These gods are not, properly speaking, gods at all, but represent different Cachinas (or Katcheenas), who are but semi-gods and intermediaries between the Moquis and their principal deity. **1907** HODGE *Amer. Indians* I. 638/1 Kachina. A term applied by the Hopi to 'supernatural beings impersonated by men wearing masks or by statuettes in imitation of the same.'

attrib. **1890** in DONALDSON *Moqui Pueblo Indians* (1893) 17 This, the Moquis say, was the origin of their numerous religious or Katcheena societies. **1922** CURTIS *N. Amer. Indians* XII. 99 All Hopi boys and many girls are initiated into the Kachina order and thus become capable of participating as masked dancers in the various summer dances.

2. a. Kachina dance, among the Hopi Indians, a masked dance to honor or invoke the Kachina. **b. Kachina doll,** (see quot. 1948).

(a) 1888 WALLACE *Land of Pueblos* 47 Their Te Deum after victories, and most sacred and beloved rite, is the *cachina* dance, which they celebrate at certain seasons of the year with great rejoicings. **1944** ADAIR *Navajo & Pueblo Silversmiths* 166 These pieces may be seen to best advantage during the Zuñi ceremonies, especially during the summer Kachina dances. — **(b) 1944** JOHNSON *As I Dare* 329, I discovered later . . . that a white man who had been having some success in the sale of spurious cochina dolls . . . had picked up some of my carved bones and had at once begun reproducing them. **1948** *Seattle Sun. Times* (Mag.) 26 Sep. 3/4 'Katchina' dolls . . . are play-things with a most serious purpose, and show in miniature ornaments, headdresses, masks, and clothes worn by the masked dancers who impersonate deities, or katchinas, in the great rain rites and rituals. **1949** *L.A. Times* (Home Mag.) 16 Jan. 7/1 These katchina dolls are collected by the artist.

kadoodle kəˈdudl̩, *v.* [Fanciful variant of ∗*doodle, v.*] *intr.* To sport, play. *Rare.* — **1875** HOLLAND *Sevenoaks* 232, I have a little game with a rovin' angel that comes kadoodlin' round me.

Kaeding's petrel. [Henry B. *Kaeding* (1877–1913), mining engineer and bird lover.] A species of petrel, *Oceanodroma leucorhoa kaedingi*, found on the Pacific Coast.

1898 *Auk* XV. 37 Kaeding's Petrel [is found] . . . from Socorro and Clarion Islands to Southern California. **1917** *Birds of Amer.* I. 86 On Three Arch Rocks off the Oregon coast, we found both the Forked-tailed and the Kaeding Petrels nesting. **1922** *U.S. Nat. Museum Bul.* 121, 147 We know very little about the distribution and practically nothing about the habits of the Kaeding petrel.

Kaffeeklatsch ˌkɑfeˈklɑtʃ, *n.* [G.] An informal social gathering for drinking coffee and talking. — **1935** SANDOZ *Old Jules* 195 The neighbor women invited her to their homes, asked her to join their *Kaffeeklatsche.* **1948** *Amer. Sp.* April 108 As the name suggests, the activities of a *kaffee klatsch* consist of the drinking of coffee and of light conversation (gossip).

kaffir corn-er. (See quot.) *Obs.* — **1913** BARNES *Western Grazing Grounds* 89 During the past few years a new type of settler, the dry farmer or 'kafer corn-er,' as he is often called, has worked great changes in the western ranges, especially in the Great Plains region lying east of the Rocky Mountains.

Kaintuck, see **Kentuck.**

Kalapooian ˌkæləˈpujən, *a.* Of or pertaining to a linguistic family of Indians that formerly lived in Oregon. — **1907** HODGE *Amer. Indians* I. 187 Calapooya. The name . . . of a division of the Kalapooian family formerly occupying the watershed between Willamette and Umpqua rs., Oreg. **1940** *Ore. Guide* 34 One of the most important families was the Kalapooyan.

∗**kale,** *n.* Money, orig. **kale seed.** *Slang.* Cf. *OED* ∗*coal*, ∗*cole*, in same sense.

1902 MUNN *Rockhaven* 4 'Wal,' he says, pullin' out a roll o' bills. . . . 'Here's the kale seed.' **1911** *Chi. D. News* 16 Sep. 28/1 He was out for the Kale, if you know what I mean. **1946** FAIR *Crows Can't Count* 272 Murindo, the illiterate mining manager, had a bunch of kale in the banks.

Kallikaks ˈkælɪˌkæks, *n. pl.* [Gk. *kalli-* (combining form of *kallos*, beauty) + *kakos*, ugly, bad.] The fictitious name for the members of a family the history of which showed that heredity, rather than environment, was the cause of feeble-mindedness, as well as of intelligence and respectability. Also **Kallikak family.** Cf. **Jukes.**

1912 GODDARD *Kallikak Family* 71 There are Kallikak families all about us. They are multiplying at twice the rate of the general population. **1948** *Dly. Ardmoreite* (Ardmore, Okla.) 22 April 16 Jumping blue blazes . . . it's the Kallikak family!!

transf. **1947** PERRY *Cities of Amer.* 179 For those Boston visitors who look upon the cod and the bean as the Jukeses and Kallikaks of human fare, it's worth noting that the Hotels Vendome and Copley Plaza have genuinely gifted French chefs.

Kalmia ˈkalmɪə, *n.* [f. Peter *Kalm* (1715–79), Swedish botanist.] A genus of North American evergreen shrubs of the family Ericaceae, the principal species being the mountain laurel, *K. latifolia*. Also a plant or flower of this genus.

1765 J. BARTRAM *Diary* 6 Sep., Here grows our most northward trees here except . . . white pine & our 3 calmias. **1838** *Boston W. Mag.* 22 Sep. 17/2 The *Rhodora* is followed in succession by the *Honeysuckles*, the *Kalmias* or *Laurels*, the *Azalea*, . . . and many others not less important as ornaments of our native landscape. **1949** *Mo. Bot. Garden Bul.* April 91 Kalmia and Rhododendron do well in regions of abundant moisture.

b. With distinguishing adjectives.

1785 MARSHALL *Amer. Grove* 72 Narrow leaved Kalmia . . . delights in moist or swampy places. *Ib.*, Broad leaved Kalmia. **1821** *Amer. Jrnl. Science* III. 276 Visited the bog in Goshen, [Mass.] where I found . . . the glaucous kalmia.

kalsominer ˈkælsəˌmaɪnɚ, *n.* One whose business is kalsomining. — **1873** *Winfield* (Kans.) *Courier* 11 Jan. 1/2 Painting, Sign-writing, Kalsomining, Paper hanging and all kinds of work in the painting line. Paper-hangers, Kalsominers and Gilders. **1916** WILSON *Somewhere in Red Gap* 128 He was a painter and grainer and kalsominer and paperhanger.

kamas, see **camass.**

kamik ˈkɑmɪk, *n.* [Eskimo.] =**mukluk.**

1894 *Outing* Feb. 367/2 The hide is used by the Eskimos to make soles for their boots, or kamiks. **1900** *Scribner's Mag.* Sep. 297/1 Seal-skin kammicks, or top boots. **1910** PEARY *North Pole* xiv. 128 The kamiks, or boots, of sealskin, soled with the heavier skin of the square-flipper seal.

Kamloops ˈkæmlups, *n.* [f. *Kamloops*, a village in British Columbia.] (See quot. 1909.) In full **Kamloops trout.**

1896 JORDAN & EVERMANN *Fishes N. Amer.* 499 Salmo gairdneri kamloops (Jordan). (Kamloops Trout; Stit-tse.) **1909** *Cent. Supp.* 1381/3 Kamloops trout, *Salmo gairdneri kamloops*, of the Fraser and upper Columbia rivers. **1947** *Field & Stream* June 19/1 He makes his favorites, the sea-run steelheads and the Kamloops trout, which he knows well, appear to be magnificent fish.

Kanaka kəˈnækə, *n.* [Polynesian word for man.] A Hawaiian or South Sea Islander.

1838 PARKER *Exploring Tour* 354 The Sandwich islanders, or kanakas, as the common people are called, have less activity of mind and body than the Indians of our continent. **1850** COLTON *Deck & Port* 338 My kanacka brought me his horse this afternoon at the hour. **1945** *Reader's Digest* Oct. 50/2 Kanakas and Portuguese began to replace the vanishing New England crews, who were deserting.

b. Kanaka Ranch, (see quot.).

1948 *Utah Humanities Rev.* Jan. 1 There were forty families . . . in this Hawaiian community, which naturally was called 'Kanaka Ranch' (ranch of the Hawaiian people).

Kanawha kəˈnɔwə, *n.* [A native word of unknown significance.] A name proposed for the state of West Virginia, after one of its rivers.

1826 *Va. Herald* (Fredericksburg) 13 Sep. 3/1 The Western Virginian, a paper printed in Charleston, Kanawha. **1861** *Richmond* (Va.) *Examiner* 20 Dec. 1/5 This proposal amounts to nothing more nor less than the wiping out of the rebel State of Virginia, and the parcelling out of its territory among the loyal States of Kanawha (Western Virginia), Maryland and Delaware. **1933** AMBLER *Hist. West Va.* 325 Some objected to 'Kanawha' because of its alleged difficulties in spelling.

* **kangaroo,** *n.* In combs.: (1) **kangaroo convention,** an irregular or unauthorized convention; (2) **court,** an unauthorized or irregular court conducted with either a disregard for or a perversion of legal rights and procedure, as a mock court held by prisoners in a jail, or an irregularly conducted court in a frontier district; (3) **mouse,** a term applied loosely to various mice and rats, esp. the deer mouse and the kangaroo rat; (4) **rat,** any one of various pouched burrowing rodents of the genus *Dipodomys*, found in dry regions in the West.

(1) **1868** *Sonora Democrat* (Santa Rosa, Calif.) 1 Feb. 1/1 Among those who are reflecting infamy on Virginia in the Kangaroo Convention at Richmond is a nigger named Lewis Lindley. — (2) **1853** P. PAXTON *Yankee in Texas* 205 By a unanimous vote, Judge G. . . . was elected to the bench, and the 'Mestang' or 'Kangaroo Court' regularly organized. **1949** *Democrat* 24 Feb. 17 Harrell . . . blamed outcries heard coming from the jail on a 'kangaroo court' conducted by the prisoners in the jail. — (3) **1857** *Rep. Comm. Patents 1856: Agric.* 96 This animal is known as the 'Long-tailed Deer Mouse,' 'Fob-tailed Mouse,' 'Kangaroo Mouse.' **1909** WEBSTER 1171/3 They [jumping mice] undergo true hibernation in winter. Called also, erroneously, *kangaroo mouse*. — (4) **1867** *Amer. Naturalist* I. 394 They are known in the vernacular as 'Kangaroo' or 'Jumping' Rats and Mice, and are entirely confined to Transmississippian regions. **1948** *Pacific Discovery* March–April 9/1 On those nights our delight was to watch the kangaroo rats, those long-tailed elves of the great sand wastes, at their play and fighting.

Kankakees ˌkæŋkəˈkiz, *n. pl.* [Native name.] (See quot.) *Obs.* — **1827** *Spirit of Seventy-Six* (Frankfort, Ky.) 31 May 3/4 The *Kankakees*, a tribe of Indians, living on the head branches of the Illinois river, are said to be in a state of the utmost wretchedness.

Kansa ˈkænsə, *n.* [See note.]

This native name is of uncertain meaning. See Hodge for variants of the name and for earlier non-English references. The *pl.* is either Kansa or Kansas.

A member of a tribe of Siouan Indians formerly in Kansas but now in Oklahoma. Also, *pl.*, this tribe.

1741 COXE *Descr. Carolana* 11 Upon the river Ousoutiwy . . . dwell . . . the Kansae, Mintou Erabacha and others. **1804** CLARK in *Lewis & C. Exped.* I. (1904) 64 We camped after dark . . . opposit the 1st old village of the Kanzes. **1848** BRYANT *California* 41, I asked him if he was a Kansas. **1907** HODGE *Amer. Indians* I. 654/1 The Kansa figured but slightly in the history of the country until after the beginning of the 19th century. **1947** MARTIN *Indians* 317 Perhaps the Omah, Ponca, Osage, Kansa, and others should be included as Oneota tribes.

attrib. **1806** WILKINSON in Pike *Sources Miss.* 108 You may attach to this deputation . . . the same number of Kanses chiefs. **1831** in *Kans. Hist. Coll.* XVI. 228 There are about 1,500 souls in the Kanzas tribe. **1947** D. COYNER *Lost Trappers* 41 They were informed of the trade made by Captain Williams and the chief of the Kansas village.

Kansan ˈkænzən, *n.* and *a.*

1. *n.* One who lives in Kansas.

1868 J. N. HOLLOWAY *Hist. Kansas* 574 At a favorable opportunity the Kansans seized the Ruffians, . . . and held them for trial. They gave them a drum-head trial. **1888** D. D. FIELD *Speeches, Arguments* (1890) III. 369 Nebraskan, Kansan, Arkansan, Minnesotan, are the true designations of the citizens of those flourishing States, from whose names they are derived. **1948** *Galveston* (Tex.) *News* 14 June 4/5 The Kansan is leaving public office on no note of pessimism.

2. *a.* (See quot. 1909.)

1909 *Cent. Supp.* 678/1 Kansan. . . . In *geol.*, noting an epoch or subdivision of the glacial period of which the deposits are found in Kansas. **1916** *Iowa Acad. Sci. Proc.* XXIII. 139 The Kansan drift was weathered and eroded to its present state before the loess in this locality was deposited. **1948** *Pacific Discovery* March–April 32/2 Four glacial stages are recognized in North America, from oldest to youngest, respectively: Nebraskan, Kansan, Illinoian, and Wisconsin.

Kansas ˈkænzəs, *n.* [f. **Kansa.**] The name of a territory and state used in combs.: (1) **Kansas Aid Society,** a society for aiding those involved in the struggle over slavery in Kansas, *obs.*; (2) **Conflictionist,** ?one involved in the conflict in Kansas over slavery, *obs.*; (3) **free stater,** one who favored having Kansas as a free state; (4) **issue,** the question of whether Kansas should be a free or a slave state, *obs.*; (5) **League,** an organization for furthering participation in the struggle over slavery in Kansas, *obs.*; (6) **Legion,** (see quot. and cf. prec.), *obs.*; (7) **-Nebraska Bill,** an act passed by Congress in 1854 providing for local option on the slavery question in Kansas and Nebraska and thus nullifying the Missouri Compromise of 1820, now *hist.*; (8) **War,** the struggle (1854–58) over slavery in Kansas, *obs.*

(1) **1901** DUNCAN & SCOTT *Allen & Woodson Co., Kansas* 20 Many of the settlers . . . were rescued from actual starvation only by the timely arrival of supplies sent out by the numerous 'Kansas Aid' societies which were organized throughout the East. — (2) **1858** *N.Y. Tribune* 15 Nov. 6/2 Not so the 'Kansas Conflictionists.' They are jealous of every emigrant for fear he will 'jump their claim,' and howl around his cabin like so many famished wolves. — (3) **1944** *Chi. D. News* 14 Feb. 8/3 It [Jayhawk] was a name intended to ridicule the Kansas Free Staters. — (4) **1859** WILMER *Press Gang* 123 Is the Kansas issue, your favorite hobby, or the principle which it is supposed to involve?

(5) **1856** BREWERTON *War in Kans.* 285 Ultra men boasted in our Legislative Assemblies, that if they could not defeat these bills in one way they would in another, and returned to their homes to organize 'Emigrant Aid Societies,' and 'Kansas Leagues.' — (6) **1856** PHILLIPS *Kansas* 142 The most important . . . was the Kansas Legion. Its object was to enroll men to be ready at any moment for the defence of the territory. It also had signs and passwords, by which one member could appeal to others for assistance in case he was attacked by the common enemy. — (7) **1854** in *West. Pa. Hist. Mag.* VI. 48 The Kansas-Nebraska bill, which has now become a law, has excited the wrath of the Whigs and Abolitionists beyond measure. **1907** ANDREWS *Recoll.* 73 The year 1854 was memorable for the reopening of the slavery agitation by the passage of the Kansas-Nebraska bill, repealing the Missouri Compromise. **1948** *Pacific Spectator* Spring 152 Speakers attacking Stephen A. Douglas' Kansas-Nebraska Bill in 1854 still linked the exclusion of slavery from the Western territories with the need for facilitating American contact with the Orient. — (8) **1858** GOVE *Letters* 351 Thus was peace made —thus was ended the 'Mormon war,' which mirabile dictu, was much less sanguinary and direful than the 'Kansas war,' and may thus be summarily historized;—killed, none; wounded, none; fooled, everybody.

b. In other combs., usu. obs., of obvious meaning or explained by the quots., as (1) **Kansas aristocracy,** (2) **banana,** (3) **boom,** (4) **brick,** (5) **City money,** (6) **itch,** (7) **marble,** (8) **scenes,** (9) **scrip,** (10) **stable,** (11) **wintered,** (12) **zephyr.**

(1) **1848** BRYANT *California* iv. 47 We counted, . . . on our arrival, to be received and entertained by the female *élite* of the Kansas aristocracy. — (2) **1931** *K.C. Star* 9 Oct., Pawpaws, known also as the Kansas banana, and persimmons are ripening already, before the first frost. — (3) **1898** *K.C. Star* 18 Dec. 2/3 After the Kansas boom collapsed the property of Mr. Collins shrank. — (4) **1877** RUEDE *Sod-House Days* 39 Snyder broke a lot for us this a.m. and we began laying up the wall. It is 20 inches thick. These 'Kansas brick' are from 2 to 4 inches thick, 12 wide and 20 long, and the joints between them we fill with ground. **1888** *Harper's Mag.* July 235/1 A house built of squares of sod taken from the prairie—Nebraska or Kansas brick, as they are facetiously termed.

(5) **1877** RUEDE *Sod-House Days* 5 Travelers west should take care how they spend money here in Kansas City, because they have what they call 'Kansas City money,' which is worth only 80 cents on the dollar, and is hard to get rid of, as the people don't care about taking it. — (6) **1877** RUEDE *Sod-House Days* 92 Another nuisance here is what people call 'Kansas itch,' which attacks nearly everybody within a short time after arrival here; few are immune. Not all are affected alike; some scratch a few days, other are affected for months. — (7) **1857** DANA *Great West* 201 This Kanzas marble exists in abundance, and makes very beautiful and substantial buildings. — (8) **1856** *Porter's Spirit of Times* 25 Oct. 126/1 In our happy and beautiful Territory [Minnesota], where we have no bloody Kansas scenes to deplore, there yet roam the buffalo and the elk. — (9) **1856** BREWERTON *War in Kans.* 341 Kansas scrip is a peculiar currency whose market value is . . . difficult to quote.

(10) **1885** *Harper's Mag.* June 5/1 Near by [was] the 'Kansas stable,' with its one horse only sheltered as to its head. **1886** EBBUTT *Emigrant Life Kans.* 199 The stables were of the kind known as '*Kansas stables*,' that is built with a few forked posts stuck into the ground, with poles laid across, and the roof and sides built up with sods, brush, manure, and rubbish of all sorts. — (11) **1922** T. A.

McNeal *When Kansas Was Young* 186–8 The Texan 'called' with an even 250 straight Kansas wintered Texas half-breed steers. — (12) **1888** *Harper's Mag.* June 39/2 People speak of its strongest gales as 'Kansas Zephyrs.'

Kansian ˈkænzɪən, *n.* =**Kansan.** *Obs.* — **1855** Whitman *Leaves of Grass* 58 Not only the free Utahan, Kansian, or Arkansian. **1879** ——— *Spec. Days* 141 We found a train ready and a crowd of hospitable Kansians to take us on to Lawrence.

Kanuck, see **canuck.**

kanyon, see **canyon.**

Karankawa kəˈrænkəˌwɔ, *n.* (See quot. 1907.) Also attrib.

1807 Dunbar *Travels* 44 Carankouas . . . are irreconcilable enemies to the Spaniards. **1823** Dewees *Letters* (1852) 30 During their absence the Carancoway Indians attacked the vessel. **1892** Duval *Early Times in Tex.* 26 Here we found encamped a band of the Caranchua tribe of Indians. **1907** Hodge *Amer. Indians* I. 657/1 Karankawa. A term that seems to have been given originally to a small tribe near Matagorda bay, Texas, but its application has been extended to include a number of related tribes between Galveston bay and Padre id. The signification of the name has not been ascertained. **1948** *True* May 126/2, I hear the Carancahuas been putting on war paint down south of here.

karimption kəˈrɪmpʃən, *n.* [Origin obscure. Cf. "rimption," used in the same sense in the southern states. See Wentworth *s.vv. rimption, rimptions.*] An abundance, a crowd. *Colloq. Obs.* — **1859** *Cairo* (Ill.) *Times* (B. '59), A whole karimption of Dutch emigrants were landed here yesterday.

Karok kaˈrɑk, *n.* [f. a native word *karuk,* upstream. See quot. 1851.] "The name by which the Indians of the Quoratean family have, as a tribe, been generally called. They lived on Klamath r. from Redcap cr. to Indian cr., N.W. Cal." (Hodge).

1851 in Schoolcraft *Indian Tribes* (1853) III. 151 They do not seem to have any generic appelation for themselves, but apply the term 'Kahruk,' up and 'Youruk,' down, to all who live above or below themselves. **1872** *Overland Mo.* April 328/2 The Cahrocs are probably the finest tribe of Indians in California. **1903** James *Indian Basketry* 53 The Karoks (often spelled Cahrocs) are a fine, vigorous people. **1924** Curtis *N. Amer. Indians* XIII, The Karok depend on the same plants and animals for food as did the Hupa. **1940** *Ore. Guide* 34 The southern part of Oregon was occupied by . . . two 'spillovers' from California—the Shastas and Karoks of the Kohan family.

Kaskaskia kæsˈkæskɪə, *n.* [f. a native name or word of obscure significance.] "Once the leading tribe of the Illinois confederacy, and perhaps rightly to be considered as the elder brother of the group" (Hodge). Also **Kaskaskia Indians.**

1722 Coxe *Descr. Carolana* 17 Besides the Illiconecks, are the Nations Prouaria, the great Nation Cascasquia and Caracontanos. **1759** *Newport Mercury* 10 July 1/1 The Chickesaws . . . were removing from a Settlement they had made near the Halbanna Fort, to join a Nation of other Indians called Causcoskees. **1799** *Guardian Of Freedom* (Frankfort, Ky.) 30 May 3/2 The people of the Illenois settlements appear much alarmed, as also the Kaskaskia Indians. **1949** *Chi. Tribune* 20 Feb. (Grafic Mag.) 17/3 The Kaskaskias sought refuge on the top of the rock, so an Indian legend tells, and were besieged by the Sacs and Foxes.

Hence **Kaskaskian,** a member of this tribe.

1947 *Chi. Maroon* 25 July 3/1 According to the most authoritative rumors the last Kaskaskian was seen in the year 1680, about where Buffalo Rock State Park is now located.

katowse kəˈtaʊs, *n.* (See quot.) *Obs.* — **1859** Bartlett 224 *Katowse,* (Germ. *Getöse,*) a din, tumult, rumpus; as, 'What a *katowse* you are making!' New England.

katydid ˈketɪˌdɪd, *n.* [Imitative.] Any one of several large, green, arboreal, orthopterous insects of the family Locustidae which produce a noise suggestive of the name.

In the first group of quots. variant forms of the name are shown. Cf. **b.** below.

(1) **1751** J. Bartram *Observations* 70 It was fair and pleasant, and the great green grass-hopper began to sing (*Catedidist*) these were the first I observed this year. **1804** Lewis in *L. & Clark Exped.* (1905) VI. 127 The green insect known in the U.' States by the name of the sawyer or chittediddle, was first heard to cry on the 27th. of July. **1827** *Western Mo. Rev.* I. 451 Not the slightest noise was heard, but the never ending creakings of the catadeds. **1831** Paulding *Dutchman's Fireside* I. 69 (Th.), [He was] as busy as a bee, as noisy as a catydid, and as merry as a cricket.

(2) **1784** J. F. D. Smith *Tour U.S.* II. 387 There is a very singular insect in this island [L.I.], which I do not remember to have observed in any other part of America. They are named by the inhabitants here *Katy did's.* **1845** Kirkland *Western Clearings* 58 The katydids are high in their eternal disputations. **1949** *Nat. Hist.* June 258/3 Of course, we must use our imaginations a bit in transforming the katydid's rasping call into words.

transf. **1905** *Forestry Bureau Bul.* No. 61, 42 *Logging wheels,* a pair of wheels, usually about 10 feet in diameter, for transporting logs. . . . Syn.: big wheels, katydid, timber wheels.

b. Also **katydidn't.**

1849 Colman *European Life & Manners* II. 109 We landed amidst . . . a jabbering of voices which can only be rivalled among the Katydids and the Katydidn'ts of Connecticut. [**1909** *Springfield W. Republican* 16 Sep. 1 All around the globe people are like katydids, saying he did and he didn't in an endless reiteration.]

katzenjammer ˈkætsn̩ˌdʒæmɚ, *n.* [G. in same sense.] Headache, nausea, etc., following a drinking carousal. Also transf. *Colloq.*

1849 *Pres. Mess. Cong.* II. 733 Some of Mr. Hale's men had kept up a drunken frolic all night, general kakenjammer, therefore all day. **1877** Burdette *Rise & Fall of Mustache* 291 This 'Centennial Cordial and American Indian Aboriginal Invigorator,' . . . has positively no equal for the cure of . . . rattlesnake bites, jim-jams, katzenjammer, tight boots, bad breath. **1948** *Life* 5 April 111/2 The cause was an unrequited love affair, the result one of the most colossal *Katzenjammers* ever recorded.

Kaw kɔ, *n.* The Kansa Indians. In full **Kaw Indians.**

1823 in *Mo. Hist. Rev.* IV. 79 Among the Caw Indians we were treated hospitably. **1841** *N.O. Picayune* 13 June 2/4 Should the Pawnees take vengeance it is to be feared the Caws and their allies will be driven across the river and be compelled to seek refuge in the settlements. **1872** *Newton Kansan* 26 Sep. 2/1 [The Quaker Indians] are something like the Kaws. **1873** *Ib.* 10 April 2/1 The Kaw Indians are to be removed south to the new reservation.

kazoo kəˈzu, *n.* [Origin obscure.] A crude musical instrument used by children, consisting of a tube, inside of which is stretched a piece of catgut which vibrates and makes a sound when one hums or sings into the tube. Also transf.

1884 *Lisbon Dak. Star* 31 Oct. 3/2 When you hear a noise like the combined sound of a fish-horn and a runaway . . . it is only the small boy amusing himself peaceably with his kazoo. **1904** *N.Y. Sun* 2 Sep. 5 Dear Edna sang as usual out of tune and with a quality of voice that resembled a solo on the gentle kazoo. **1947** *Chi. Tribune* 1 Nov. 15/3 The New Deal is now playing hearts and flowers thru a kazoo instead of a Stradivarius.

attrib. **1948** *Dly. Ardmoreite* (Ardmore, Okla.) 21 March 19/4 The 'Prairie Queen Kazoo band' furnished background music.

Kearneyism ˈkɑrnɪˌɪzəm, *n.* [Dennis *Kearney* (1847–1907), Irish-American labor agitator.] (See quot. 1914.) *Obs.* Cf. **sand lot.**

1879 *Cong. Rec.* App. 28 Jan. 51/1 Kearneyism, with all that the term implies, is not the cause of the discontent and clamor coming from the Pacific coast. **1880** *Chi. Tribune* 1 April 4/3 This means the end of Kearney and Kearneyism in San Francisco. **1914** *Cyclo. Amer. Govt.* I. 277/1 *Kearneyism,* a term signifying the policy of driving out Chinese laborers by violent measures if necessary.

Kearneyite ˈkɑrnɪˌaɪt, *n.* (See quot. 1885.) Cf. **sand lotters.** — **1885** *Mag. Amer. Hist.* Feb. 201/2 *Kearnyites.*—Followers of one Dennis Kearny, a Communist, who a few years since commanded quite a strong faction among discontented working men. For a time he made his headquarters in what were known as the 'Sand Lots,' near San Francisco. **1947** Chalfant *Gold, Guns, & Ghost Towns* 46 Without provisions, their bottles empty, the summer sun of that sandy basin pouring down on them, and the keen edge of mob spirit worn off, the Kearneyites were a sorry lot.

keel kil, *n.*[1] [Prob. a back formation from keelboat *q.v.* and not a continuation of the earlier British use.]

1. =**keelboat.** Now *hist.*

1785 Denny *Journal* 57 Our fleet now consists of twelve small keels and batteaux. **1810** Cuming *Western Tour* 75 The navigation of the Allegheny is easy for boats called *keels* from fifty to seventy feet long, sharp at both ends, drawing little water, carrying a good burden, and calculated to be set against the stream, so as to surmount it from eight to twenty miles a day in proportion to the strength of the current operating against them. **1883** Mark Twain *Life on Miss.* i, Some hundreds [of rivers subordinate to the Mississippi] . . . are navigable by flats and keels. **1941** Baldwin *Keelboat Age* 45 The burden was not always rated by tons, and on the upper Allegheny, keels were sometimes spoken of as carrying sixty or one hundred barrels of salt.

2. keelboat, a large flat-bottomed river boat formerly extensively used on western rivers. Now *hist.*

Bense is prob. correct in regarding the American use of this term as a borrowing of *kiel-boot* from early Dutch settlers.

1786 in *Mag. Amer. Hist.* I. 176 Great numbers of Kentucke and keel boats passing every day; some to the Falls, others to Post Vincent—Illinois Country &c. **1818** PALMER *Jrnl.* 50 Steam-boat, ark, Kentucky, barge, and keel-boat building, is carried on [at Pittsburgh] to a considerable extent. **1843** *Amer. Pioneer* II. 271 This . . . led to the introduction of keel-boats. These boats were long and narrow, sharp at bow and stern, and of light draft. They were provided with running boards, extending from bow to stern, on each side of the boat. **1949** *Indiana Hist.* June 147 The first keelboat on the St. Joseph River, the 'Fair Play,' arrived at South Bend July 1, 1832.

Hence **keelboater, keelboating.**

1883 MARK TWAIN *Life on Miss.* iii, Then keelboating died a permanent death. *Ib.* xxxix, [Natchez, Miss.] had a desperate reputation, morally, in the old keelboating and early steamboating times. **1912** COBB *Back Home* 296 [He was] the roughest of them all, . . . rougher even than the keel-boaters and the trappers.

b. keelboatman, one who operates or helps to operate a keelboat. Now *hist.* Cf. **ex-keelboatman.**

1839 *Knickerb.* April 344 It was not until a year after, that a long-armed, high-shouldered keel-boatman . . . saw a steam-boat gallantly paddling up against the centre current of that 'Father of Rivers.' **1898** CUSHMAN *Hist. Indians* 479 Under the disguise of keeping a store for the accommodation of keel and flat-boatmen, he enticed them into his power. **1941** DORSEY *Master of Miss.* 129 Keelboatmen and 'broadhorn' pushers eyed it with suspicion.

***keel,** *n.*[2] A yacht having a keel instead of a centerboard. — **1883** *Harper's Mag.* Aug. 443/2 Two keels are being laid down to every centre-board designed.

* **keel,** *v.*

1. *intr.* To collapse, faint, fall, usu. with *over. Colloq.*

1832 S. SMITH *Major Downing* 98 [The horse] keeled up and couldn't go another step. **1857** HAMMOND *Northern Scenes* 225 The bear keeled over onto his back with a jerk. **1861** NEWELL *Orpheus C. Kerr* I. 20, I only keeled for the shake of a tail. **1946** GARDNER *D. A. Breaks Seal* 29 A man keeled over with heart failure.

2. *tr.* To upset, capsize, kill (a person or thing). *Colloq.*

1843 STEPHENS *High Life N.Y.* II. 208, I wish to gracious the old shote had got up and keeled me over with both fists tu once. **1872** EGGLESTON *End of World* 239 S'posin' they was a woodpecker on that air stump, wouldn't I a keeled him over? **1873** *Cin. Commercial* 3 March 3/3 A few hours in the wind at such a temperature would keel a man up.

* **Keeley,** *n. attrib.* Designating a *cure* or *treatment* for alcoholism according to a system developed by Dr. Leslie E. Keeley (1832–1900), an American physician. Also fig.

1895 *N.Y. Dramatic News* 6 July 8 Keeley Cure Not Certain. The treatment for dipsomania invented by Dr. Leslie A. Keeley does not appear to be universally efficacious. **1922** *Collier's* 29 April 3/2 A little event which come to the pass whilst we are carving out our farewell picture was the Keeley Cure for me as far as believing in signs is concerned. **1948** *L.A. Times* 26 Dec. I. 10/2 The Keeley Treatment can be arranged so as to prevent loss of time from work or normal conditions.

b. Keeley institute, an institution for giving patients the Keeley treatment for alcoholism.

1892 *S.F. Enterprise* 12 May 4/1 A son of the late lamented Boss graduated from a Keeley institute and went directly on a howling drunk.

* **Keely,** *n. attrib.* Of or pertaining to a perpetual motion device or "vibratory generator" operated by "etheric force," devised by John Worrell Keely, a Philadelphia inventor. *Obs.*

1886 *Lippincott's Mag.* Oct. 414 The writer, one would say, really loves the Keely motor, and the worship and cult thereof, and the philosophy appended kite-tailwise thereto. **1894** *Arena* (Boston) Aug. 387 Deserted and stigmatized by physicists, Keely's only hope in the line of utilizing this unknown energy lay in the men who had in 1872 organized a Keely Motor Company. **1899** *Cosmopolitan* April 633/1 Millions of money sprang to the assistance of the Keely motor project when in the zenith of its quarter-of-a-century existence.

Hence **Keelyism, Keelyist.** *Obs.*

1886 *Lippincott's Mag.* Oct. 415 It is not safe to do otherwise in the neighborhood of Keelyism. **1899** *Cosmopolitan* April 640/2 To all intents and purposes this stock company is still intact, but the action of the Keelyists did not restrain one holder of a hundred shares of stock from disposing of his certificates for a few dollars.

keener ˈkinɚ, *n.* A person or thing in some way superior. *Slang.* — **1839** *Spirit of Times* 27 April 90/3 (We.), The filly is a keener, but looked out of fix. **1859** BARTLETT, Keener, a very shrewd person, one sharp at a bargain, what in England would be called 'a keen hand.' Western.

* **keep,** *n.*

1. Formerly in N. Eng., one having the care of animals, a herdsman. *Obs.*

The examples are doubtful, as the manuscripts may have an abbreviation for *-er.* Cf., however, **barkeep, cowkeep,** and see **easy keep, room keep.**

[**1638** *Dorchester Rec.* 32 The rest [are] to bring their Cowes be yound Mr. Stoughtons dore or elce the keep' [is] to driue away the heard not to stay for the rest.] **1641** *Boston Rec.* 60 If any goates shall be found without a keep after the 14th day of the next moneth, . . . the owners of them shall forfett for every goate soe found halfe a bushell of Corne. **1643** *Ipswich Rec.* 25 March, The keeps are to have iijs iid by the head, for soe long as the keeps attend the herd.

2. *For keeps,* in full measure, to the limit, for good and all. *Colloq.*

1889 *Sporting Life* (Phila.) 5 June 1/5 Joe Kappel is hitting the ball for keeps. **1949** *Sat. Ev. Post* 12 March 30/1 The snow suddenly gave way and I plunged into the depths of the glacier. *This time,* I thought, *it's for keeps.*

b. *To play keeps,* or *for keeps,* to play marbles with the understanding that the players keep their winnings.

1861 *Ladies' Repository* Oct. 627/1 Pay him! Nothing. He and I played for 'keeps,' and I was the best player and won all his. **1876** MARK TWAIN *Tom Sawyer* xvi. 135 Next they got their marbles and played 'knucks' and 'ring-taw' and 'keeps.' **1932** *K.C. Star* 4 March 30 We suppose dad will whip Willie for playing keeps while the old man plays every slot machine in town.

* **keep,** *v.*

1. *intr.* Of a school: To be in session. Cf. **2.** (2) below.

1845 *Knickerb.* XXVI. 277 One afternoon, when 'school didn't keep,' some one got into the house. **1882** THAYER *From Log-Cabin* iii. 53 School will keep through the winter. **1908** FREEMAN *Shoulders of Atlas* 68 School ain't going to keep to-day.

2. In colloq. phrases: (1) *To keep a stiff upper lip,* to persevere in one's efforts in the face of difficulties, to endure whatever comes; (2) *not to care whether school keeps or not,* not to care what happens; (3) *to keep tab on,* to keep account of, to keep close watch upon; (4) *to keep the log rolling,* see **log.**

(1) **1815** *Mass. Spy* 14 June (Th.), I kept a stiff upper lip, and bought [a] license to sell my goods. **1931** *K.C. Star* 24 Aug., Keep a stiff upper lip. — (2) **1852** in *Amer. Sp.* XX. (1945) 8, I was aout on a time, marm, and I didn't care a darn whether school kept or not, as the boy said to his boss. **1946** *Chi. D. News* 8 Oct. 13/1 They've got a few dollars and they don't care if school keeps or not. — (3) **1888** *Mo. Republican* 15 Feb. (F.), [As] the conductor . . . did not keep tab on the party Maloney travelled free. **1938** ASBURY *Sucker's Prog.* 15 Keeping tabs—Making this record . . . on which the players noted the cards they won or lost.

***keeper,** *n.* In colonial New England, a town officer who looked after the livestock of townsmen who paid for such service. *Obs.* — **1635** *Cambridge Rec.* 20 Itt is ordered Every man shall put his Goats to the keeper before the 20th of March. **1658** *Dedham Rec.* IV. 2 In case the Town . . . cannot attayne a keeper . . . ther is common land . . . [where] our drye Cattell might be put thether.

As the last term in **baggage, bar,** ***book, calf, camp, case, cow, cowpen, dive, doggery, gin, grocery, groggery, ground, hog, hotel, Sabbath, saloon, score, spring, storekeeper.**

***keeping,** *n.* As the last term in **camp, cow, school, storekeeping.**

keet kit, *n.* (See quots.) *Colloq.* — **1859** BARTLETT 184 *Guinea-Keet,* or simply *Keet,* a name given in some localities to the Guinea fowl and probably derived from its cry. **1899** *Animal & Plant Lore* 61 *Keets,* young Guinea fowls. Chestertown, Md.

***keg,** *n.* As the last term in **dandy, nail keg.**

keister ˈkistɚ, *n.* [Origin uncertain. Cf. G. *kiste,* a box, chest.] A box, trunk, or similar receptacle.

1882 PECK *Sunshine* 227 The boy took the Knight's keister and went to the elevator. *Ib.* 229 He looked around at them, picked up his boots and keister and started for the door. **1910** MCCUTCHEON *Rose in Ring* 80 Ruby Noakes . . . was directing the contortionist in his efforts to construct a table out of three 'blue seats' and a couple of property trunks, or 'keesters,' as they were called. **1947** *Chi. D. News* 21 July 12/7 The little guy in the Kremlin had better pack his keister and get ready for a long trip.

Keithian ˈkiθɪən, *n.* [Geo. *Keith* (?1639–1716), an English Quaker.] (See quots.) Also **Keithian Quaker.** *Obs.*

*a*1854 in BOWDEN *Hist. Soc. Friends in Amer.* II. 102 The Keithian Quakers ended in a kind of transformation into Keithian Baptists. **1882** SCHAFF *Relig. Encycl.* II. 1230/1 Keith was condemned by the Annual Meeting, but formed a body of his own, known as the 'Christian Quakers,' or 'Keithians.' **1888** *Cent. Mag.* May 115/1 He managed . . . to rend the little newly planted Pennsylvania world into two parties, leading out in 1691 a sect of those who modestly distinguished themselves as the *Christian* Quakers, but who were popularly known as Keithian Quakers.

Kellogg oak. [Albert *Kellogg* (1813–87), Amer. botanist.] (See quots.) Also **Kellogg's oak.**

1897 SUDWORTH *Arborescent Flora* 169 *Quercus californica*. . . . California Black Oak. . . . [Commonly called] Kellogg's Oak ([in] Cal.). **1923** SAUNDERS *So. Sierras Calif.* 127 The Kellogg oak . . . keeps alive the memory of a kindly old Forty-Niner, Dr. Albert Kellogg. **1947** PEATTIE *Sierra Nevada* 97 The leaves on the Kellogg oaks are pink and silver.

kellupweed ˈkɛləpˌwid, *n.* [Var. of ∗*kelpweed*.] A local name for the oxeye daisy. — **1894** *Amer. Folk-Lore* VII. 91 *Chrysanthemum leucanthemum*, Kellup weed, Rhode Island clover, Montpelier, Vt.

kelly ˈkɛlɪ, *n.*[1] [Prob. f. ∗*callow*, the equivalent term in England.] The topsoil removed in securing clay for brick-making. Also as a verb (see quot.). — **1884** C. T. DAVIS *Manuf. Bricks* 103 This vegetable soil is called in brickyard parlance, 'kelly,' and the operation of removing it termed 'taking off the kelly.' *Ib.*, The operation of placing the soil upon the places where the bricks are moulded is termed 'kellying the floors.'

kelly ˈkɛlɪ, *n.*[2] [Origin obscure.] A derby or other stiff hat. *Slang.* — **1922** *Collier's* 4 March 8/2, I have got to wear a brass Kelly on my head which weighs at least ten pounds. **1948** *Dly. Ardmoreite* (Ardmore, Okla.) 25 April 1/1 A ring was drawn and some brawny gent who felt his strength, would toss his kelly into the circle.

Kelly pool. A form of pool in which the player draws a number and in his play tries to pocket the ball the number of which corresponds to his.

[**1909** *Cent. Supp.* 1037/3 Keeley pool, an American version of ball-pool.] **1918** *Amer. Mag.* Aug. 38/1 There's fortunes which would make the Vanderbilts and Astors look like public charges . . . awaitin' those which will quit playing Kelly pool some night and invent a new way to do *anything*. **1948** MENJOU & MUSSELMAN *It Took 9 Tailors* 29 The only sports I cared to indulge in personally were Kelly pool and bowling.

kelp crab. A spider crab, *Epialtus productus*, found in California. — **1887** GOODE *Fisheries* II. 657 The kelp crab . . . is eaten by the Indians.

Kemble Jackson rein. (See quot.) *Obs.* — **1896** HASWELL *New York* 522 Horses' tails were seldom 'docked'; occasionally 'pricked' and, in the teams of a few young men, their ears were sometimes clipped, but that cruel device, a 'Kemble Jackson' rein, was unknown [*c*1858].

Kemmler process. The process of executing a condemned criminal by means of electricity, in allusion to Wm. Kemmler, the first criminal to be so executed, in Auburn prison, N.Y., Aug. 6, 1890. Also **kemmlerization.** *Obs.* — **1890** *Cong. Rec.* 9 Aug. 8375/1 That the gentleman . . . should be 'electrocuted' by the Kemmler process recently adopted in the state of New York. **1890** *Boston Jrnl.* 22 Oct. 2/3 He tied their heads together with a copper wire, turned on the spark, and presto, the cats were deader than Kemmler, and now he is to apply for a patent on the process of kemmlerization of cats.

∗**kench,** *n.* [?Var. of *EDD canch*, a small rick, stack of bricks, firewood, etc., piled up together.] A box or bin in which fish or skins are salted.

[**1852** SABINE *Fisheries* 207 The fish taken are split, salted, and put in 'Kenches' or piles.] **1874** SCAMMONS *Marine Mammals* 161 The [seal] skins are all taken to the salt-houses, and are salted in kenches, or square bins. **1887** GOODE *Fisheries* V. 370 Sliding planks, which are taken down and put up in the form of deep bins, or boxes—kenches, the sealers call them.

Kennebunker ˈkɛnəˌbʌŋkɚ, *n.* [f. *Kennebunk*, Me.] (See quots.) — **1895** *D.N.* I. 390 Kennebunker: valise in which clothes are put by lumbermen when they go into camp for a 'winter operation.' **1902** *Amer. Folk-Lore* XV. 245 *Kennebunker*, a word of comparatively recent origin used to denote 'the valise (for clothes) which Maine lumbermen take with them to the woods.'

keno ˈkino, *n.* [Cf. F. *quine*, five winning numbers.]

1. A gambling game in which the players cover numbers on their cards as those numbers happen to come from the keno goose *q.v.*, or from a wheel of chance, the first five numbers in a row on a card winning the prize. Also attrib.

1814 B. F. PALMER *Diary* (1914) 70, I employ'd in washing & mending my messmate playing keeno. **1845** NOAH *Gleanings* 133 They were employed at a game called *lotto* or *kino*—the master drew the numbers from a wheel, while the company covered such as appeared on small placards before them, and when they obtained a certain number, they claimed and took the purse. **1871** *Figaro* 15 April, The police pulled every Keno establishment in the city. **1936** ASBURY *French Quarter* 218 In later years lotto became known as keno, and although it is seldom heard of now, for more than half a century it was by far the most popular of all games among the lower and middle classes of New Orleans and other Mississippi River cities. **1949** *L.A. Times* 23 June 21/1 Bingo, Keno and allied games are gambling and lotteries, and may not be licensed by individual cities.

Also **kenoist,** *n.*

1873 *Cin. Commercial* 2 March 4/4 The interference with the Sycamore street kenoists was simply a hint to the dens on Vine and Race streets that there was a large amount of blackmail due.

b. *To make (a) keno*, in playing keno, to secure five numbers in a row.

1874 CARTER *Comm. Rollingpin* 243 Hey, take up the cards, I've made a Keno! **1878** HART *Sazerac Lying Club* 224 He launched a vicious kick at it, and uttering the ejaculation used by a keno-player when some other fellow makes keno, he turned on his heel and left.

c. keno goose, a receptacle from which numbered balls used in keno are taken.

1887 *Courier-Journal* 20 Jan. 6/2 (*headline*), Fred Therwanger Manipulates a Keno Goose for Edification of the Court. **1938** ASBURY *Sucker's Prog.* 51 A purely percentage game with no betting,

Keno goose

Keno was properly played with a large globe called 'Keno goose,' ninety small ivory balls numbered from 1 to 90, and Lotto cards, which were sold to the players at whatever price might be fixed by the operator of the game, who was known as the 'roller.'

2. The exclamation given when a player has winning numbers; also transf., an exclamation of approval or satisfaction.

1868 *Terr. Enterprise* (Virginia, Nev.) 30 Sep. 3/2 When they thus got three beans in a row they were to call out 'Keno!' and rake in the pot. **1907** MULFORD *Bar-20* 193 He wants to know where th' cards are stacked an' why he can't holler 'Keno.' **1920** in HUNTER *Trail Drivers Texas* I. 205 Shake yer spurs an' make 'em rattle! Keno! Promenade to seats.

Kensington stitch. Crewel stitch, or crewelwork. — **1883** *Cent. Mag.* Sep. 787/1 They know little of Kensington stitch or of Eastern-woven portières. **1884** *Ib.* Jan. 473/2 In the 'woman's department' it is half smothered by the Kensington stitch.

kenticoy, see **cantico.**

Kentuck kɛnˈtʌk, *n.* Also **Kaintuck.**

1. The territory or state of Kentucky. *Obs.*

1776 FITHIAN *Journal* II. (1934) 166 We will return & go on as far as Can-Tuck; or Transylvania. **1795** J. & E. PETTIGREW *Lett.* 25 May (Univ. N.C. MS), They expect to set off for Caintuck about the first of september. **1835** *Vade Mecum* (Phila.) 22 Aug. 2/4 Though his father can lick any man in all Kentuck, he can *lick* his father! **1854** M. J. HOLMES *Tempest & Sunshine* iv. 52 Kentuck hain't many like her, nor never will have.

b. In figurative and allusive contexts: An ideal place. *Obs.*

1826 FLINT *Recoll.* 64 Heaven is a Kentuck of a place. **1834** CARUTHERS *Kentuckian* I. 190 [New York is] a real Kentuck of a place.

c. ?A cigar made of Kentucky tobacco. *Rare.* Cf. **Kentuck twist.**

1851 *Polly Peablossom* 117, [I] was a sittin' on a log, smokin' a Kaintuck regaly.

d. A Kentucky rifle *q.v.*

1920 SAWYER *Our Rifles* 12 Because 'Kaintucks' were accurate within sporting range—about 100 yards—they were said to shoot point blank.

2. An inhabitant of Kentucky. Now *hist.*

1826 FLINT *Recoll.* 15 You learn the received opinion, that a 'Kentuck' is the best man at a pole. **1856** M. J. HOLMES *L. Rivers* viii. 93 How do you git along down amongst them heathenish Kentucks & niggers? **1941** BALDWIN *Keelboat Age* 61 Even the Americans admitted that the Creoles were the best oarsmen, though they considered a 'Kentuck' best at the setting poles.

3. In combs., now obs., as **Kentuck bill, boat,** [cf. **Kentucky boat**], **boy, fashion, Negro, rifle,** [cf. **Kentucky rifle**], **screamer, settlement, twist.**

1850 LEWIS *La. Swamp Doctor* 85 Here's a five dollar Kaintuck bill, take your pay and gin us the change. — **1786** in *Mag. Amer. Hist.* I. 176 Great numbers of Kentucke and keel boats passing every day; some to the Falls, others to Post Vincent-Illinois Country &c. **1842** *Amer. Pioneer* I. 343 A Kentuck boat has landed at the creek. — **1834** CARUTHERS *Kentuckian* I. 25 When we Kentuck boys gits at it, it won't all end like a log rollin'. — **1872** FLAGG *Good Investment* 544/1 If you and I should ever have the pleasure of meeting again, you must expect me to defend myself *Kaintuck* fashion. — **1852** STOWE *Uncle Tom* x, Them plantations down thar, stranger, an't jest the place a Kentuck nigger wants to go to. — **1855** *Amer. Inst. N.Y. Trans.* 583 Seventy years ago, some American made rifles in the Western country, . . . which soon bore the name of *Kain Tuck rifle*. — **1852** WATSON *Nights in Block-House* 27, I say, you Kentuck screamer, . . . what kind o' livin' had you while you were up the stream? — **1778** in FRIES *N.C. Morav. Rec.* III. (1926) 1227 Day before yesterday two men arrived from Kentuck Settlement, going as Deputies to the Assembly. — **1834** CARUTHERS *Kentuckian* I. 24, I gets a quid of the real Kentuck twist . . . into my mouth.

Kentuckian kən'tʌkɪən, *n.* and *a.*

1. *n.* An inhabitant or native of Kentucky.

1779 G. R. CLARK *Campaign in Ill.* (1869) 85 If not deceived by the Kentuckyans, I should still be able to compleat my design. **1827** *Hallowell* (Me.) *Gaz.* 20 June 2/2 This venerable *conscript Father* is, we infer, a real Kentuckian. **1948** DICK *Dixie Frontier* 255 The Kentuckians particularly liked peaches.

b. (See quot.) *Obs.*

1807 SCHULTZ *Travels* II. 21 All the inhabitants on the Ohio are here called *Kentuckians*.

c. A Kentucky-bred horse. *Rare.* Cf. **Kentucky horse.**

1835 HOFFMAN *Winter in West* I. 111 There was . . . the sleek spongy-looking Ohio horse, and the clean-limbed quickly-gathering Kentuckian.

2. *a.* In, from, belonging to, or pertaining to, Kentucky.

1804 C. B. BROWN (tr.) Volney *View* 71, I have observed the Kentuckian bank of the river to be formed of similar ridges. **1822** WOODS *English Prairie* 110 The best boat channel to pass the Falls is on the Indiana side, it is called the Indian shoot; . . . the other the Kentuckian shoot. **1885** BAYLOR *On Both Sides* 145 A handsome carriage . . . drawn by a beautiful pair of Kentuckian thoroughbreds.

Kentucky kən'tʌkɪ, *n.* [Amer. Indian. The original meaning is uncertain.]

1. Short for Kentucky rifle *q.v.*

1920 SAWYER *Our Rifles* 130 The workmanship of the inside of the barrel is nowhere near up to that of the best Kentuckies of the same period. **1948** *Outdoor Life* June 46/2 Many hunting models lacked decorations because these might reflect the sun and frighten game, but other Kentuckys made liberal use of brass on the side plates, buttplate, . . . and trigger guard, as well as on the patch box.

2. In obs. combs. designating things or actions characteristic of, found in, or coming from, Kentucky, as (1) **Kentucky ax,** (cf. **Collins ax**), (2) **bagging,** (3) **bite,** (4) **fence,** (5) **ham,** (6) **harvester,** (7) **leggings,** (8) **marble,** (9) **note,** (10) **petroleum,** (11) **Revival,** (12) **tavern,** (13) **yell.**

(1) **1848** C. L. FLEISCHMANN *Nordamerikanische Landwirth* 306 Sie werden von verschiedener Grösse, Schwere und Form gemacht; die sogenannte Kentucky-Axt . . . und die Yankee Heavy-Ax . . . sind die besten und gesuchtesten. — (2) **1854** *Harper's Mag.* March 456/2 By previous arrangement, strong Kentucky bagging has been so placed as to cover the upper and lower side of the pressed cotton. — (3) **1830** N. AMES *Mariner's Sk.* 147 It was not difficult to perceive that in the Indian hug or Kentucky bite, I should stand no chance at all. — (4) **1837** PECK *New Guide* 318 Fencing it [the Ill. farm] into four fields, with a Kentucky fence of eight rails high, with cross stakes.

(5) **1855** *N.Y. Wkly. Tribune* 26 May 1/2 We were regaled with Kentucky ham, eggs, excellent coffee, and corn bread. **1903** FOX *Little Shepherd* xvii, A great turkey supplanted the venison, and last to come . . . was a Kentucky ham. — (6) **1858** *Texas Almanac 1859* 67 The Kentucky Harvester is most used, and is generally preferred. — (7) **1817** FORDHAM *Narr. Travels* 158, I had on . . . a pair of Kentucky leggings. — (8) **1847** L. COLLINS *Kentucky* 156 It is in these cliffs of the Kentucky river, and in the adjacent country that we find what is called Kentucky marble. — (9) **1807** *Ann. 10th Congress* 1 Sess. I. 429 Blannerhasset paid me off in Kentucky notes.

(10) **1904** TARBELL *Hist. Standard Oil Co.* I. 5 'Seneca Oil' . . . was followed by a large output of Kentucky petroleum sold under the name 'American Medicinal Oil.' — (11) **1841** BUCKINGHAM *America* II. 68 In that year [1805] a very remarkable excitement or agitation of the public mind on the subject of religion took place in Kentucky, and is known by the name of the 'Kentucky Revival.' . . . The excitement was occasioned by the preaching of some Presbyterian missionaries who had been sent into the Western States from New-England. — (12) **1852** STOWE *Uncle Tom* xi, You have an idea of the jollities of a Kentucky tavern. — (13) **1845** SOL. SMITH *Theatr. Apprent.* xviii. 119 A still louder laugh . . . presently increased into a real *Kentucky yell*.

b. Designating livestock bred in Kentucky, as **Kentucky cattle, hog, horse, mule,** (also, *slang*, in the sense of * white mule *q.v.*), **ox, porker, stock, thoroughbred.**

1858 D. K. BENNETT *Chron. N.C.* 86 On our way down we meet 373 head of Kentucky cattle in one drove. — **1834** H. TUDOR *Tour* II. 9 About two thousand large Kentucky hogs, which we unluckily encountered in one of the very narrowest defiles of the mountains. — **1839** *N.O. Picayune* 17 March 2/2 Through the whole mile Wagner continued to gain on the Kentucky horse. **1925** BRYAN *Memoirs* 273 We watched as he rode out on Governor, his shiny black Kentucky horse. — **1878** CONKLIN *Arizona* 57 There was another arrival not a little important to the completion of the company, in the shape of eight large stalwart Kentucky mules. **1948** *Sat. Ev. Post* 26 June 86/4 Ford reaches for a bottle and passes around a drink compared to which Kentucky mule is soda pop. — **1882** *Cong. Rec.* 22 June 5229/2 The fatted calf—the Kentucky ox—was killed for the returning prodigals. — *c*1845 PAULDING *Amer. Comedies* (1847) 190 Like a real Kaintucky porker a-rootin' in the woods. — **1881** *Harper's Mag.* April 728/2 Such horses as awaited them! Kentucky stock full-blooded and fit for warriors. — **1900** *Outing* Sep. 645 The Master of Woodburn did more to improve the Kentucky thoroughbred . . . than all of his contemporaries combined.

c. Designating persons living in or native to Kentucky, as **Kentucky corn-cracker, fellow, horseman, Indian fighter, major, man.**

1868 *N.Y. Herald* 6 July 3/3 Kentucky 'corn-crackers' and Illinois 'suckers' might have joined labors yesterday. — **1847** PARKMAN in *Knickerb.* XXIX. 162 The parties of emigrants . . . professed great disinclination to have any connexion with the 'Kentucky fellows.' — **1887** *Southern Bivouac* V. 576/2 An accomplished Kentucky horseman like James B. Clay. — **1886** POORE *Reminiscences* I. 153 There were several other prominent men in the House: Richard Mentor Johnson, a burly and slightly educated Kentucky Indian-fighter. — **1895** G. KING *New Orleans* 246 A kind-hearted Kentucky major. — **1792** *Amer. Museum* (Phila.) Jan. 13 The great boast of a Kentucky-man is the quantity of corn that the land will raise upon an acre. **1845** DUNN *Ore. Terr.* 223 Richardson, a Kentuckyman . . . [is] one of the most astute and *dare-devil* traders of the mountains.

d. With **broadhorn, man, ship,** = **Kentucky boat.** *Obs.*

1788 MAY *Jrnl. & Lett.* 33, I was obliged to put my stores and baggage on board a small ferry-boat in order to put them on board the Kentucky man. *Ib.* 66 The house . . . I am in hopes to raise in eight or ten days; for I am not very comfortable on board my Kentucky ship. **1884** *Harper's Mag.* June 124/2 There was the Kentucky 'broad-horn,' compared by the emigrants of that day to a New England pig-sty set afloat, and sometimes built one hundred feet long, and carrying seventy tons.

3. In special combs., chiefly obs.: (1) **Kentucky beauty,** a quilt or coverlet design; (2) **breakfast,** (see quot.); (3) **burgoo,** (see quot.); (4) **Colonel,** one upon whom the unofficial title of "Colonel" has been conferred in Kentucky; (5) **Derby,** the classic of American horse races, run since 1875 at Churchill Downs, Louisville, Ky., also transf.; (6) **flat,** (see quots. and cf. **Kentucky boat**), now *hist.*; (7) **Futurity,** a futurity *q.v.* held in Kentucky; (8) **Jonathan,** a rural Kentuckian; (9) **oyster,** (see quot.); (10) **reel,** (see quot. 1832), *obs.*

(1) **1889** *Harper's Mag.* Jan. 269/2 There was a very handsome one [coverlet] in crimson, done in wavy lines and bizarre figures, that was called the Kentucky Beauty. — (2) **1882** *Cent. Mag.* April 884/2 His morning meal was a simple Kentucky breakfast—'three cocktails and a chaw of terbacker.' — (3) **1947** BEROLZHEIMER *Regional Cookbook* 167 'Kentucky Burgoo' is the celebrated stew which is served in Kentucky on Derby Day, at Political Rallies, Horse Sales and at other outdoor events. — (4) **1889** OPIE READ (*title*), A Kentucky Colonel. **1947** *N. & Q.* April 8/2 No Kentucky colonel, in our time, takes his title seriously.

(5) **1875** *Courier-Journal* 18 May 4/3 The second race was the event

of the day—the Kentucky Derby, a dash of $1\frac{1}{2}$ miles for three-year olds, fifty dollars entrance, p.p., the Association adding $1,000. **1948** *Time* 1 Nov. 44/2 It was dogdom's Kentucky Derby. **1949** *Cue* 30 April 10/2 This race . . . reopens the whole question of the Kentucky Derby. — **(6) 1812** STODDARD *Sk. Louisiana* 374 Most of the produce of the upper country is floated to market in what are called Kentucky flats, or arks. These are of various size, generally from forty to sixty feet long, and from twelve to fifteen broad, with roof of thin boards to secure their cargoes from the water. **1936** ASBURY *French Quarter* 74 Huge flatboats or barges, known in the vernacular as arks, broadhorns, and Kentucky flats. — **(7) 1913** *N.Y. Times* 8 Oct. 12/2 The Kentucky Futurity for three-year-old trotters . . . was won by Etawah, . . . driven by Ed. F. ('Pop') Geers. — **(8) 1830** *Alexandria* (Va.) *Phenix Gaz.* 23 June 1/1 After many fruitless inquiries of the passing craft, he met with a Kentucky Jonathan. — **(9) 1898** DUNBAR *Folks from Dixie* 103 There was hog jole and cold cabbage, ham and Kentucky oysters, more widely known as chittlings.

(10) **1824** OWEN *Diary* 119 Afterwards in the course of the evening, we danced a Kentucky reel. **1832** BUTLER *Jrnl.* I. 290 Danced sundry quadrilles; and, finally, what they called a Kentucky reel, — which is nothing more than Sir Roger de Coverly turned Backwoodsman. **1834** *Sun* (N.Y.) 24 May 1/2 Several Kentucky reels were played, anon, the sweet breathings of a melodious voice sung 'Sweet —sweet home.'

b. In the names of, or with reference to, plants and birds: (1) **Kentucky bluegrass,** a grass, *Poa pratensis,* which grows particularly well in Kentucky and is highly valued for pasturage and hay; (2) **cardinal,** a local name for the cardinal bird, *Richmondena cardinalis;* (3) **coffee,** see as a main entry; (4) **warbler,** a warbler, *Oporornis formosus,* common in the eastern part of the U.S.

(1) **1849** EMMONS *Agric. N.Y.* II. 68 An earlier kind of grass than timothy, is the Spear grass, Meadow grass, or Kentucky blue grass. **1945** *Chi. D. News* 29 May 6/1 Round about Chicago and down in the Kentucky bluegrass we yet have lordly mansions and estates inhabited by criminals. [**1948** *Chi. Tribune* 5 Dec. III–2 6/4 It is not good practice to place a mulch over the lawn for the permanent grass, like Kentucky blue.] — **(2) 1894** *Harper's Mag.* May 926 (*title*), A Kentucky Cardinal. **1944** DUNCAN *M. Graham* 87 Everywhere the color was as brilliant as Brush Creek, and the Kentucky cardinal was singing. — **(4) 1811** WILSON *Ornithology* III. 85 The Kentucky Warbler, *Sylvia Formosa*, . . . inhabits the country whose name it bears. It is also found generally in all the intermediate tracts between Nashville and New Orleans. **1939** LINCOLN *Migration* 171 The offshore route is used by . . . Kentucky warblers.

c. In less frequent terms, chiefly obs., of a similar kind, as **Kentucky clover, corn, queen, red, rose, tobacco, white-bearded wheat.**

1785 WASHINGTON *Diaries* II. 426 Also sowed about a tablespoonful of the Buffalo or Kentucke Clover. — **1849** EMMONS *Agric. N.Y.* II. 265 Kentucky corn . . . Kernel white, somewhat shrivelled, elongated and pointed. — **1870** *Rep. Comm. Agric. 1769* 186 Buckingham. Synonyms. . . . Kentucky Queen, Lexington Queen etc. — **1856** *Rep. Comm. Patents 1855: Agric.* 290 The 'Tennessee Milam,' and 'Kentucky Red,' are our best early winter apples. — **1846** *Knickerb.* XXVIII. 38 The Kentucky rose is not excelled by any plant in America for the plenitude of its blossoms. — **1868** *N.Y. Herald* 1 July 9/4 Kentucky tobacco has been less active during the past month. — **1849** EMMONS *Agric. N.Y.* II. 139 Kentucky White-bearded, Canada Flint, Hutchinson Wheat. In Western New York, it has become a favorite variety.

For **Kentucky ark, boat, jean, Resolutions, rifle,** see as main entries.

Kentucky ark. =**Kentucky boat.** Now *hist.*

1824 BLANE *Excursion U.S.* 102 [Boats] of about 150 tons' burthen . . . are called Kentucky Arks, and indeed they contain almost as great a medley of eatables, furniture, animals, &c. &c. as ever Noah could have stored in his miraculous vessel. **1852** E. F. ELLET *Pioneer Women* 180 [They] arrived at Marietta, coming down the Ohio in 'Kentucky arks,' or flatboats. **1941** DORSEY *Master of Miss.* 9 These flatboats were dubbed 'Kentucky arks,' or, more generally, 'broadhorns.'

Kentucky boat. (See quots. 1818, 1847.) Now *hist.*

1785 E. DENNY *Journal* 57 Our fleet now consists of twelve small keels and batteaux, besides two large flats called Kentucky boats. **1818** PALMER *Jrnl.* 56 Our conveyance was one of the long Kentucky boats, in common use here for transporting produce and manufactures *down* the Ohio; they are shaped something like a box, forty or fifty feet long, having a flat bottom, with upright sides and end. Three-fourths of the boat nearest the stern is roofed in; two oars are occasionally worked at the bows; and a large sweep on a pivot serves as a rudder. **1847** in H. HOWE *Ohio* 210 Boats similarly constructed on the northern waters, were then called *arks*, but on the western rivers, they were denominated *Kentucky boats.* **1948** DICK *Dixie Frontier* 109 These were often known on Western waters as Kentucky boats. Farther north and east they were called arks.

Kentucky coffee. The seed of a tall, handsome tree, *Gymnocladus dioica,* sometimes used as a substitute for coffee. Also **Kentucky coffee tree.** Cf. ***mahogany 1,** ***nicker tree.**

1785 WASHINGTON *Diaries* II. 360 Eight Nuts from a tree called the Kentucke Coffee tree. **1859** BARTLETT 227 *Kentucky Coffee.* The fruit of *Gynonoclades* [*sic*] *canadensis.* A large tree, resembling the locust tree, bearing a pod with berries which are used for coffee. **1871** DE VERE 416 The Coffee-tree (*Gymnocladus canadensis*), often called Kentucky Coffee-tree, or Kentucky Locust, derives its name from the fact that in the days of early settlements the seeds were frequently used as a substitute for coffee, a practice renewed during the late Civil War. **1900** H. L. KEELER *Native Trees* (1902) 109 Kentucky coffee tree, stump tree. **1941** SETON *Trail of Artist-Naturalist* 242, I got one of the pods—some kind of locust or Kentucky coffee tree.

Kentuckyism kən'tʌkɪˌɪzəm, *n.* A word or way of speaking characteristic of Kentuckians. *Rare.* — **1832** *Polit. Examiner* (Shelbyville, Ky.) 17 Nov. 4/1 Mr. Littlejohn is well sustained, and Mr. Bushfield is made to utter Kentuckyisms with great volubility.

Kentuckyize kən'tʌkɪˌaɪz, *v. tr.* To make like Kentucky or Kentuckians. *Rare.* — **1840** *Knickerb.* XVI. 262 It was Sir Charles Grandison, however, Kentuckyized.

Kentucky jean. A fabric, usu. homemade, formerly quite popular, esp. in Kentucky where it was extensively made, having a cotton warp and a wool weft with about 27–30 threads per inch. Often *pl.* Now *hist.*

1835 WM. F. GRAY *Diary* (1909) 10 They also make Kentucky jeans . . . a great number of women and girls employed. **1882** THAYER *From Log-Cabin* xviii. 262 He would wear Kentucky Jean just as quick as broadcloth. **1944** CLARK *Pills* 205 In fact, frontier Kentucky jeans early made a national reputation for itself.

attrib. **1843** CARLTON *New Purchase* I. 73 He had on a Kentucky-jean vest.

Kentucky Resolutions. Resolutions passed by the Kentucky legislature (1798–99) defining the strict constructionist view of the relative powers of the state and the federal governments. Sometimes associated with the Virginia Resolutions in the phrase *Kentucky and Virginia Resolutions.*

1798 JEFFERSON *Writings* X. 62, I enclose you a copy of the draught of the Kentucky Resolutions. **1856** *Democratic Conv. Proc.* 25 *Resolved,* . . . That the Democratic party will faithfully abide by and uphold, the principles laid down in the Kentucky and Virginia resolutions of 1798. **1886** *Southern Bivouac* March 581/1 The first seven of the Breckinridge or Kentucky resolutions are the same as these numbers of the Jefferson draft, . . . but the 8th and 9th of the Breckinridge or Kentucky set are radically different from these numbers in the Jefferson series. **1948** *So. Weekly* 20 Oct. 7/3 Barkley happens to be a Kentuckian, and as a Kentuckian must be familiar with such a principle of State and party policy as Kentuckians of yore engraved into history: The Kentucky Resolutions.

Kentucky rifle. An extremely accurate, double-sighted, long-barreled, small caliber flintlock rifle of a type used by the first white hunters and settlers in Kentucky. Now *hist.*

The British evidence (1838 below) for this term is slightly earlier than has been found in American sources, but the term is included here because it is intrinsically American.

[**1838** J. R. PLANCHÉ *Extravaganzas* II. 25 But in a moment he or she is picked off As by a long Kentucky rifle.] **1839** HOFFMAN *Wild Scenes* 132 The British bayonet was no match then for the Kentucky rifle. **1892** DUVAL *Early Times Tex.* 14, I purchased a good Kentucky rifle. **1949** *Chi. Sun. Tribune* (Grafic Mag.) 20 March 13/1 Most of their kind in those days were expert with the long rifle, the flintlock muzzle-loader which was perfected by Pennsylvania gunsmiths and later came to be termed the Kentucky rifle.

***ker-.** The first element in echoic formations, usu. for heightening the idea of impact or sound.

The *OED* ascribes this term and its use as shown here to the U.S. The term, variously spelled, has been popular on a colloq. level in this country but it may not have originated here. The *EDD* records *curflummox*, and the *Supp.* has British evidence for *kersmash, kerplunk.* Other expressions not illustrated here are *kerbim, -chunk, -flop, -plumpus, -swallop, -tush, -whop,* and there are no doubt many more.

1843 CARLTON *New Purchase* I. 268 In he splash'd kerslush, like a hurt buffalo bull. **1859** *Harper's Mag.* Aug. 318/2 In his eagerness to grasp a magnificent lily, [he] was plunged 'ker swop!' . . . to the muddy bottom of the lake. **1884** MARK TWAIN *H. Finn* xxiii. 234 Long come de wind en slam it to, behine de chile, ker-*blam!* **1945**

Democrat 31 May 2/1 The operators . . . are coming over to Clarke County and sink a well right kersmack in the middle of it.

b. kerlaraping, cavorting. *Rare.*

1878 GUILD *Old Times* Busiris was still 'kerlaraping.' 'Hold him, Jesse. Don't let him break down the fence.'

Keresan ˈkɜəsən, *a.* [f. the native name of unknown significance.] Of or pertaining to a linguistic family of Pueblo Indians formerly found in north central New Mexico.

1893 DONALDSON *Moqui Pueblo Indians* 91 The Queres group (Keresan stock) are the Pueblos of Santa Ana, San Felipe, Cochiti, San Domingo, Acoma, Zia, and Laguna. **1946** UNDERHILL *First Penthouse Dwellers* 70 Even the relationship of the Keresan language is still in doubt. *Ib.* 98 Keresan children up to the age of thirteen have just as much schooling as white children.

kermis bed. [Du.] (See quots.) *Obs.* — **1885** *Cent. Mag.* April 877/2 The pallet on the floor—'the kermis bed,' as the Dutch called it—was an occasional resort even in good houses. **1913** JAMES (tr.) *Danckaerts Jrnl.* (1679–80) 54 It was very late at night when we went to rest in a kermis bed, as it is called [Shake-down, bed on floor], in the corner of the hearth, along side of a good fire.

kernite ˈkɜnaɪt, *n.* A form of sodium borate found in Kern County, Calif., hence the name. — **1934** WEBSTER. **1949** *Sat. Ev. Post* 5 March 72/4 A geologist . . . identified the stuff as colemanite and kernite, both rich in borax.

kerosene ˈkerəˌsin, *n.* [Irreg. f. Gk. *keros,* wax+ *-ene.*]

1. A mixture of liquid hydrocarbons, distilled from mineral wax, bituminous shale, etc., or from petroleum; coal oil.

1855 *Rep. Comm. Patents 1854* 462 This [fluid] the inventor calls *A. Kerocene.* **1866** *Beadle's Mo.* Jan. 29/2 The words *telegram, revolver, humbug, placer miner, petroleum, kerosene, crinoline,* are all very new, and all, save the last, are of American origin. **1945** *Reader's Digest* Jan. 65/1 I'm buying the kerosene.

2. In combs. of obvious meaning, as (1) **kerosene can,** (2) **lamp,** (3) **lantern,** (4) **oil.**

(1) **1882** PECK *Sunshine* 40 [He] calls for the kerosene can, and pours a little oil into the crevice. **1945** *Nat. Geog. Mag.* Sep. 293 They have little interest in the white man's civilization except for his cotton goods and kerosene cans. — (2) **1860** *So. Cultivator* XVIII. 391 It

Kerosene lamp

produces a clear burning fluid, . . . affording a good light in an ordinary kerosene lamp. **1948** *Capital-Democrat* (Tishomingo, Okla.) 24 June 1/3 A single kerosene lamp throws light on the words from a small Bible during night services. — (3) **1939** *These Are Our Lives* 135 It was winter time when we first went there and we started to work by lantern light and quit by lantern light, the kerosene lanterns swinging down from the ceiling. **1945** PEARSON *Country Flavor* 81 No chapter in that history would be more revealing than the story of the service of the humble kerosene lantern. — (4) **1858** *Boston Directory* 114/2 Downer, Samuel, kerosene oil, 76 Water. **1944** CLARK *Pills* 41 Kerosene oil was forever getting into the sugar or the lard or the meat box, and sometimes it reached the liquor barrel.

Also *kerosene factory, heater, light, refinery, refrigerator, stove, works,* etc.

Kerrite ˈkɜaɪt, *n.* [W. C. *Kerr* (1827–85), Amer. geologist.] A kind of vermiculite found in North Carolina (see quots.). — **1873** *Amer. Philos. Soc.* XIII. 396 Kerrite . . . consists of innumerable fine scales, which under the microscope do not present a definite shape. **1890** *Cent.* 3277/1 *Kerrite,* named after W. C. Kerr, a State geologist of North Carolina.

Kerry pippin. A variety of apple. *Obs.* — **1847** IVES *N. Eng. Fruit* 38 *Kerry Pippin.*—Fruit of medium size; the form oblong, flattened at the eye and stalk.

keta ˈkitə, *n.* [Russian *kita,* in same sense.] (See quot. 1909.)

1896 JORDAN & EVERMANN *Fishes N. & Middle Amer.* 479 The usual order of salmon running in the streams of Oregon and Washington is *nerka, tschwytscha, kisutch, gorbuscha,* and *keta.* **1909** *Cent. Supp.* 682/2 keta. . . . A vernacular name in Kamchatka of the dog-salmon, *Oncorhynchus keta.* This fish is one of the smaller of the Pacific salmon and is found from San Francisco to Kamchatka, ascending all streams in the fall and spawning at no great distance from the sea. **1948** *Consumer Rep.* Jan. 27/2 Chum or Keta (*O. keta*) is the cheapest species packed.

Ketan ˈkitn̩, *n.* [Amer. Indian.] A name given by some of the Indians of New England to their god. *Obs.*

[**1624** WINSLOW *Good Newes* 34 This all of them concluded to be very well, and said, they beleeued almost all the same things, and that the same power that wee called God, they called Kietitan. *Ib.* 52 For as they conceived of many diuine powers, so of one whom they call Kiehtan, to be the principall and maker of all the rest, and to be made by none.] **1634** WOOD *N. Eng. Prospect* II. xii. 82 Ketan . . . is their good God, to whom they sacrifice (as the ancient Heathen did to Ceres) after their garners bee full with a good croppe. **1637** MORTON *N. Eng. Canaan* 50 They are perswaded that Kytan is hee that makes corne growe, trees growe, and all manner of fruits. **1764** HUTCHINSON *Hist. Mass.* I. 473 They acknowledged a God, whom they mentioned by the word Ketan. **1857** ELLIOTT *N. Eng. Hist.* I. 313 There is no doubt of their belief in Manitou or Manit (or Kiehtan) . . . and to him some seem to have referred all good.

***kettle,** *n.* **1.** =**war kettle.** *Rare.* **2. kettle bail,** a local name for a dredge used in taking scallops. **3. kettleman,** in sugar-making, one who attends a boiling pot.

(1) **1710** in J. W. LYDEKKER *Faithful Mohawks* (1938) 27 We hung on the Kettle and took up the Hatchet. — (2) **1881** INGERSOLL *Oyster Industry* 245 *Kettle Bail.*—A dredge used in catching scallops, which has the blade adjusted to swing in the eyes of the arms, in order to prevent its sinking into the mud of the soft bottom on which it is used. (Rhode Island.) — (3) **1833** B. SILLIMAN *Man. Sugar Cane* 15 The manner in which the hands are distributed during the cutting season is the following . . . forty hands with knives . . . six kettle men.

As the last term in **bake, Boston, croup, dye, farina, Indian, open, process, sap, war, wash kettle.**

kettled ˈketld, *a.* **1.** Rendered in kettles. **2.** *Geol.* Worn into kettle-shaped hollows. — (1) **1869** *Ill. Agric. Soc. Trans.* VII. 432 Kettled lard . . . sold at 16 c.—(2) **1898** *Amer. Geologist* Nov. 298 Crevasses and moulins would be formed . . . producing such a profusely kettled surface as in the Glacier Garden.

Keweenawan ˌkiwəˈnɔən, *n.* [f. *Keweenaw* Point, Michigan.] (See quot. 1889.) Also the geological system of which these rocks form a part. — **1889** *Cent.* 3278/1 Keweenawan. . . . The name given to the series of trappean rocks and their interbedded sandstone and conglomerates in which the Lake Superior copper-mines are worked. **1913** A. P. COLEMAN *Proterozoic Can. Shield* (1915) 151 The volcanic eruptions so characteristic of the later Keweenawan.

kewpie ˈkjupɪ, *n.* [f. **Cupid.*] A chubby, winged baby fairy with a topknot such as originally drawn by Rose O'Neill (d. April 6, 1944), also (*cap.*) the trademark name of a doll patterned after this drawing. Also attrib.

1912 *Ladies' Home Jrnl.* Oct. 109 The kewpies were invented by Rose O'Neill. They are always doing good, helping Dotty Darling and her Baby Brother to have a good time. . . . So Rose O'Neill has made the Kewpie Kutouts. **1931** *K.C. Star* 7 Aug., Why do the movie producers insist on playing Nancy Carroll's kewpie-doll face in tragic parts? **1947** *Atlantic Mo.* Oct. 52/1 Familiar as the substance of fountain pens and kewpie dolls, they [plastics] turn up in bomber noses and auto finishes, toothbrush bristles and parachutes.

***key,** *n.*

1. The matter used in keying an advertisement. See ***key,** *v.*

1905 CALKINS & HOLDEN *Mod. Advt.* xi. 266 A variation of the 'key' in advertising is the coupon.

2. In combs.: (1) **key basket,** a small basket in which keys are kept; (2) **City,** (see quot.); (3) **log,** in a log jam, the log the release of which will break the jam; (4) **man,** (*a*) one who seeks out and dislodges the key logs in a jam, (*b*) a telegrapher; (5) **noter,** one who makes a keynote speech; (6) **note speech,** a speech, usu. at a political gathering, which presents the principal issues in which those present are interested; (7) **State,** (see quot.); (8) * **stone,** see as a main entry; (9) **West,** the name of a city in Florida, used attrib. in the names of birds (see quots.).

(1) **1836** GILMAN *Recoll.* (1838) 172 Mama had carefully placed hers in her key-basket. **1889** *Cent. Mag.* April 841/1 A mob-cap covering her grey hair, and key-basket in hand, the wife of Washington must have offered a pleasant picture. — (2) **1859** *Ladies' Repository* XIX. 51/2 Dubuque, Iowa, is the 'Key City,' as it is said to open the doors of trade to the north-west and the Pacific. — (3) **1851** SPRINGER *Forest Life* 166 It may be thought best to cut off the key-log, or that which appears to be the principal barrier. **1947** *Sat. Ev. Post* 8 March 56/4 The key log was partly out of water, one end sticking out at an angle. — (4) (*a*) **1851** in WILSON *Aroostook* (1937) 104 The key man then commences prying while they are pulling. If the jam starts, or any part of it, . . . he is drawn suddenly up by those situated above. (*b*) **1907** *Washington Star* 30 Sep. 9 Some of the leading keymen are sounding as their shibboleth the cry of 'government ownership of the telegraph systems.'

(5) **1932** *K.C. Star* 30 April 26 Senator Dickinson of Iowa has been chosen keynoter of the Republican national convention. **1948** *Time* 26 April 22/1 In 1940, at 33, he was keynoter of the G.O.P. convention in Philadelphia. — (6) [**1886** in T. ROOSEVELT *Wks.* XIV. 75 My Democratic friends are advancing one argument in this campaign, and it is the key-note of their campaign.] **1913** LA FOLLETTE *Autobiog.* 441 He was able to elect himself chairman, make the keynote speech. **1949** *Sat. Ev. Post* 2 July 67/1 Barkley, at the Philadelphia convention, cut loose with his keynote speech. — (7) **1851** J. F. W. JOHNSTON *Notes on Amer.* II. 326 With more dignity, those of New Hampshire speak of their home as the Granite State, . . . of New York as the Empire State; of Pennsylvania as the Key State; and of Virginia, proudly as the Old Dominion! — (9) **1858** BAIRD *Birds Pacific R.R.* 607 Key West Pigeon. . . . Key West, Florida, and West Indies. **1917** *Birds of Amer.* III. 110/2 The Small White-eyed Vireo . . . is similar in color to the Key West Vireo.

As the last term in **bow, Florida, mail, night, oxbow, wet, Yale key.**

* **key,** *v. tr.* To include in (an advertisement) material designed to identify answers to it. — **1905** CALKINS & HOLDEN *Mod. Advt.* xi. 264 The advertiser likes to know which particular mediums pull best. To accomplish this the advertising is 'keyed.' Some form of address is used which can be varied in each magazine. **1948** JACOBS *We Chose Country* 77 Katherine inserted a discreetly keyed ad in the Middleton weekly paper.

* **Keystone,** *n.*

1. Short for Keystone State *q.v.* Also attrib.

[**1803** in HOWARD M. JENKINS *Pennsylvania* II. 186 As Pennsylvania is the Keystone of the democratic arch, every engine will be used to sever it from its place.] **1844** *Cong. Globe* App. 4 June 662/3 The old Keystone has never furnished the Union with either President or Vice President, and it causes her to feel badly. **1899** *Success* 6 May 391 They emigrated to the Keystone commonwealth when the northern portion of the state was howling wilderness. **1948** *Time* 21 June 22/3 That was why the control of keystone Pennsylvania was one of the big question marks of the convention.

b. Keystone City, (see quot.). *Obs.*

1846 WYSE *America* II. 114 General Fritz, was . . . a working stonecutter, in this 'keystone city,' as Philadelphia is often called.

2. Keystone State, Pennsylvania, in allusion to its central position in the thirteen original states (see also quot. 1885).

1836 *S. Lit. Messenger* II. 277 The little German farmer . . . in the Key Stone State . . . would not wish the property of the country to be thrown in jeopardy. **1885** *Cent. Mag.* Feb. 635/2 Pennsylvania was once the 'Keystone State' of the political arch, but its citizens . . . transferred their State contest to November. **1948** *Dly. Ardmoreite* (Ardmore, Okla.) 27 April 6/2 Republican aspirants matched strength in the politically important keystone state.

transf. **1860** *Charleston* (S.C.) *Mercury* 6 Nov. 2/4 Georgia . . . is at once the 'Empire' and the 'Keystone State' of the South.

K. G. C. Abbreviation for **Knights of the Golden Circle.** Also attrib. *Obs.*

1860 *So. Enterprise* (Thomasville, Ga.) 11 April 2/3 (*heading*), The Alleged K. G. C. Imposition. **1861** *Cong. Globe* 23 Jan. 532/1 The K. G. C.—A secret and oath-bound association the members of which call themselves the Knights of the Golden Circle, has existed for many months throughout the cotton States. **1865** *Nation* I. 66 Wendell Phillips and Barnwell Rhett are relieved from the suspicion of being K. G. C.'s.

kibbling ˈkɪblɪŋ, *n.* [Probably f. * *kibble, v.*, to crush into small pieces, but cf. Du. *kibbels, kibbeling.*] (See quots.) *Obs.*

1843 in GOODE *Fisheries* v. (1887) 160 Metal hooks baited with parts of small fish (by us called kiblings). **1848** BARTLETT 194 Kiblings. Parts of small fish used by fishermen for bait on the banks of Newfoundland. **1889** *Cent.* 3282/1 kibbling. . . . A part of a small fish used as bait by fishermen on the banks of Newfoundland. Also spelled *kibling.*

kibitz ˈkɪbɪts, *v.* [f. **kibitzer.**] *tr.* and *intr.* To watch, look on as an outsider, and usu. to offer gratuitous advice. Also **kibitzing,** *n. Slang.*

1928 *Amer. Sp.* IV. 159 It defines 'kibbitzing' as a slang expression used to indicate the act of offering gratuitous advice by an outsider. **1939** H. M. LYDENBERG *Lett. to Editor,* As I passed an excavation on 42nd Street [N.Y.] I saw a sign painted on the protecting wooden enclosure reading as follows: 'Air Lines Knot-Hole Club To Kibitz the erection of the world's largest air terminal.' **1948** *Chi. Herald-Amer.* 22 May 7/2 If you would care to kibitz you are more than welcome to peer over our shoulders.

kibitzer ˈkɪbɪtsɚ, *n.* Also **kibbitzer.** [Yiddish modification of colloq. G. *kiebitzen,* to look on at cards, f. *Kiebitz,* a meddlesome looker-on, lit. a lapwing or plover. Cf. **pewit,** and see Mencken *Supp.* I. 433.] One who looks on, as at a card game, and offers gratuitous advice. *Colloq.*

1928 *Amer. Sp.* IV. 159 The trade journal . . . devotes an editorial . . . to the 'kibbitzer.' **1938** WHITE *One Man's Meat* 2 Two kibitzers stopped to attend the deal, and the El train went off down the block, chuckling. **1949** *N.Y. Times Mag.* 3 April 25 (*legend*), The prime entertainers of the Big Show go for a game of rummy, assisted by the usual kibitzers.

Kichai ˈkaɪtʃaɪ, *n.* [f. their native name.] "A Caddoan tribe whose language is more closely allied to the Pawnee than to the other Caddoan groups. In 1701 they were met by the French on the upper waters of the Red r. of Louisiana and had spread southward to upper Trinity r. in Texas" (Hodge).

1842 *Texas Times* (Galveston) 4 March 2/1 A warlike expedition has been plotted by several frontier tribes—Shawnese, Delawares, Caddos and Kyches, for an invasion of the Comanche country this spring. **1934** FOREMAN *Five Civilized Tribes* 119 The Kichai tried to settle on the Washita River against their opposition. **1946** FOREMAN *Last Trek* 303 Kichai, a small Caddoan tribe, were first known in Texas.

* **kick,** *n.*

1. A vigorous complaint or objection, esp. in the phrase *to have a* (or *no*) *kick coming. Slang.*

1839 *Chemung* (N.Y.) *Democrat* 25 Dec. (Th.), So take the hint without a kick, and shut the open door. **1863** in *Mont. Hist. Soc. Contrib.* III. (1900) 326 As the coat belonged to him, I had no kick coming. **1948** *Gainesville* (Tex.) *D. Reg.* 3 July 6/2 The admission price will be upped to six-bits, which shouldn't draw any kicks from fans, since they're seeing games this season at cut-rate prices, anyway.

2. A sharp stimulating effect, a pleasurable thrill. *Slang.*

1903 *Dly. Chron.* 16 Jan. 5/1 With cayenne and mustard (to give their food the missing 'kick' [*sc.* of alcohol]). **1948** *Dly. Racing Form* (Chi.) 29 June 2/4 We used to get a kick out of the stuff we read in the papers about Sande.

* **kick,** *v.*

1. *tr.* To reject (a suitor). *Colloq.*

1809 MRS. ANN SIMONS in *Singleton P.* in *So. Hist. Coll.* (at U. of N.C.) 1 Sep., A lady whom I met . . . affirmed that poor Ashby had been kicked by you. . . . She insisted upon the fact and concluded by saying, he still wished to renew his suit. **1848** in THOMPSON *M. Jones* (1872) 215 Jest as everybody expected, after encouragin the feller long enough to make him believe he had the thing dead, she kicked him flat. **1895** *Outing* XXVII. 74/2 Some years ago . . . a Suffolk gal kicked me. **1948** DICK *Dixie Frontier* 314 If his suit was rejected, it was said: 'She kicked him.'

2. *intr.* To walk, go, or be *around* or *down. Slang.*

1839 KIRKLAND *New Home* xxv. 195 We heard that he was better, and would be able to 'kick around' pretty soon. **1908** MCGAFFEY *Show-Girl* 47 The other evening I kicked down to a show I once worked in. **1945** *New Yorker* 10 March 20/1 The ancient Egyptians, of course, kept their dead kicking around indefinitely.

3. *tr.* To set (a railroad car) in motion in a desired direction, as onto a switch, by giving it a smart bump with the engine. Also **kicking,** *n. Slang.*

1898 *McClure's Mag.* X. 211/1, I was about to step directly in front of a rapidly approaching car which an engine had kicked in on that track. *Ib.* 212/1 A conductor . . . pulled the coupling pin on the crippled car, and gave his engineer a signal to kick it in. . . . The kicked car fetched up. **1912** DROEGE *Freight Terminals & Trains* 97 There are many yards in which cars are dropped onto the tracks of a separating or classification yard during many months of the year by gravity, without the assistance of poling, a summit, or 'kicking.'

4. *To kick oneself,* (see quot. 1892). *Colloq.*

1891 *Voice* 29 Jan., In the absence of any of the committee to kick I went home kicking myself, and it wears on the constitution to be both kicker and kickee at the same time. **1892** WALSH *Lit. Curiosities* 584 To kick one's self, often used with an infinite variety of adjuncts, —*i.e.*, to kick one's self 'all over the house,' 'all over the place,' etc.,—means to feel or express violent dissatisfaction with one's self, to be mortified or chagrined.

5. *To kick in,* to contribute, pay what is due or exacted. *Slang.*

1908 MCGAFFEY *Show-Girl* 45 The lawyer guy kicked in with the balance of the ten thousand. **1948** *Lawton* (Okla.) *Constitution* 2 July 8/1 The spectators 'kicked in' with a little cash to show their appreciation.

6. In substantival combs.: (1) **kick-back,** an amount or portion returned, *slang;* (2) **off,** (see quot. 1916), also the ball so kicked; (3) **out,** *football* (see quot.); (4) **switch,** (see quot.); (5) **up,** (*a*) a dance, *obs.,* (*b*) (see quot.); (6) **wheel,** a potter's wheel operated by the foot.

(1) **1940** RIESENBERG *Golden Gate* 308 Longshoremen were finding it tougher than ever to get jobs, even through kick-backs of pay, bottles of liquor, and cigars. **1948** *Salt Lake Tribune* 18 Dec. 19/6 Utah cities, towns and counties still are a long drink away from a full $1,000,000 liquor profit kickback allowed them annually by the 1947 legislature. — (2) **1887** *Cent. Mag.* Oct. 892/2 He may be quite ignorant of many of the more minute points, of the difference between a 'kick-off' and a 'kick-out,' . . . or between a 'kick-over' and a 'touch-down.' **1916** BANCROFT *Handbook* 220 Kick-off. Act of kicking the ball from the 40-yard line at the beginning of the game or after each touchdown. **1948** *Aurora* (Ill.) *Beacon-News* 7 Nov. 31/1 First he ran the kick-off back 58 yards to the Aggie 37 then on the 12 he faked a pass and sped around left to a touchdown. — (3) **1887** *Outing* Oct. 85/2 Kick-out must be a drop-kick or place-kick from not more than twenty-five yards outside the kicker's goal. — (4) **1918** *Dyke's Automobile & Gasoline Engine Encycl.* (ed. 6) 277/2 Kick switch means, the switch can be kicked from one side to the other by foot.

(5) (*a*) **1778** *Md. Hist. Mag.* III. 116 We Collected the Girls in the neighbourhood and had a kick up in the Evening. **1804** FESSENDEN *Orig. Poems* (1806) 30 See what lasses we can pick up For our famous village kick up. (*b*) **1909** H. LOUIS *Dressing of Minerals* 451 In larger mines it is more usual to use cars with fixed sides and to use some form of 'Tippler' or 'Tumbler' for turning the car over and thus emptying out its contents. Tipplers are of two kinds: end tipplers or 'Kick-ups' and side tipplers. — (6) **1923** E. A. BARBER *Pottery & Porcelain U.S.* xii. 250 Such wares . . . were produced in large quantities by negro men and boys, who employed the old-fashioned 'kick-wheel' in their manufacture.

Kickapoo 'kɪkəpu, *n.* [Native word for "he stands about" or "he moves about, standing now here, now there." See Hodge.]

1. A member of an Algonquian tribe found orig. in southern Wisconsin, but now, to the number of about 800, on reservations in the West; also *pl.,* the tribe itself.

1670 *Relations des Jésuites* (1858) 100/1 A quatre lieues d'icy sont les Kikabou, et les Kitchigamich. **1722** COXE *Descr. Carolana* 50 Nations to the West of this Lake, besides the beforemention'd, are Part of the Outogamis, Mascoutens, and Kikpouz. **1835** HOFFMAN *Winter in West* I. 276 The Indians that frequent the neighbourhood of Chicago, . . . are chiefly Pottawattamies and Ottawas, with a few Chippewas . . . , and a straggling Kickapoo or Miami. **1948** *Salt Lake Tribune* 17 Dec. 39/3 Those Kickapoos we drove out without too much work!

attrib. **1776** in J. HALL *Sk. of West* (1835) II. 245 It will most certainly be the terror of our savage enemies, the Kickeboos Indians. **1876** *Nev. State Jrnl.* (Reno) 12 Aug. 1/4 A small command under Lt. Butler found the Kickapo and Lipan camp in Texas, attacked it, killed two and captured four Indians. **1890** HEALY & BIGELOW *Kickapoo Indians* 6 Better than cure is prevention, and one of the functions of *Kickapoo Indian Sagwa* is to serve as a guard against disease. **1912** *Indian Laws & Tr.* III. 544 Said sum to be paid to the treasurer of a corporation to be known as the Kickapoo community of Mexico.

2. Kickapoo ranger, during the struggle over slavery in Kansas, a violent proslaver. *Obs.*

[**1856** PHILLIPS *Kansas* 13 The Kickapoos, unlike the 'Rangers' of the same name, are comparatively civilized; but it is Indian civilization at best.] **1856** in *Kans. Hist. Soc.* IX 141 At Lawrence, May 21, 1856, Atchison made this kind of a speech: 'Boys, this day I am a Kickapoo ranger, by G—d. This day we have entered Lawrence with Southern rights inscribed upon our banner, and not one d——d Abolitionist dared to fire a gun.'

* **kicker,** *n.* One who complains, rebels, or makes "kicks" (see quot. 1885). *Colloq.*

1876 *Chi. Tribune* 6 Aug. 7/5 One 'kicker' in a nine will spoil the other eight. **1885** *Mag. Amer. Hist.* Feb. 202/1 *Kicker.*—One who revolts against party discipline—kicks over the traces, as it were. **1924** R. CUMMINS *Sky-High Corral* 71 His people had been kickers—they had kicked over the grub, and the cooking and the camp sites.

b. In poker, a card held with a pair, either as a bluff, to make others think one has three good cards, or in hope of improving one's hand. Also transf.

1902 LORIMER *Lett. Merchant* 234 The Augustus was just a fancy touch, a sort of high-card kicker. **1946** MOREHEAD & MOTT-SMITH *Penguin Hoyle* 127 To keep an ace or other high card as a 'kicker' seriously decreases the chances of improving.

As the last term in **log, sidekicker.**

* **kicking colt.** The spotted jewelweed. *Colloq.* — **1892** *Amer. Folk-Lore* V. 93 *Impatiens fulva,* a kicking colt. N. Mass.

* **kid,** *n.*

1. (See quots.) *Obs.*

1724 JONES *Virginia* 53 The Ships . . . often call at Ireland to victual, and bring over frequently [to Va.] white Servants which are . . . bound by Indenture, commonly call'd *Kids,* who are usually to serve four or five Years. **1898** EARLE *Customs Old N. Eng.* 96 These indentured servants were in three classes: 'free-willers' or 'redemptioners,' or voluntary emigrants; 'kids,' who had been seduced through ignorance or duplicity on board ships that carried them off to America; and convicts transported for crime. **1940** ELEANOR EARLY *N. Eng. Sampler* 6 Convicts and kids were sold into virtual slavery.

b. "A kidnapper" (Chipman). *Rare.*

1862 *N.Y. Tribune* 9 April 6/4 Attempted Kidnapping in Washington. The kidnappers Caught and Locked up. . . . The 'Kids' were . . . sent into town to the Provost Marshal's office.

2. Applied as a familiar or intimate term to any young person. *Colloq.*

1884 *Cheyenne* (Wyo.) *Sun* 3 Nov. 3/1 There were some strange pranks played by the Cheyenne 'Kids' on the occasion of the 'Halloween' which occurred last Friday night. **1896** *Emporia Gaz.* 15 Aug., Then we have discovered a kid without a law practice and have decided to run him for attorney general. **1920** SANDBURG *Smoke & Steel* 89 Do you love me, kid?

3. kid curler, a small device, made of wire covered with soft leather, used for curling the hair.

1936 *Sears Cat.* (ed. 173) 103 Favorite 'Kid' Curlers Flexible, leather covered. Make tight curls or loose ones. **1945** MAXWELL *Folded Leaf* 193 Hope Davison, with her hair in brown kid curlers, leaned over the banister.

4. *With kid gloves,* gently, with tact, without roughness. Also allusively. *Colloq.*

1864 in *Wkly. New Mexican* 3 June 2/3 We have handled the Yankees with kid gloves far too long for our good. **1888** BRYCE *Amer. Commonw.* II. III. lviii. 410 The Americans who think that European politics are worked, to use the common phrase, 'with kid gloves.' **1949** *Western Polit. Quart.* March 100 It is difficult to determine what losses, if any, the Republicans suffered because of these kid-glove tactics.

5. kid-glove orange, a tangerine.

1881 BARBOUR *Florida* 246 The Mandarin or Tangierine orange . . . is sometimes called the 'kid-glove orange,' because you can break the skin and peel it without using a knife or staining the fingers. **1886** I. D. HARDY *Oranges & Alligators* 38 Both these varieties known as 'kid-glove oranges' from the ease with which one can pull the 'sections' apart, and eat them without soiling a light glove.

kiddy car. A small vehicular contrivance for a child. — **1918** *Sears Cat.* (ed. 137) (Index). **1948** *Atlantic Mo.* Jan. 61/2 At noon Mary discovered that she could sit down in the shallow water and be pushed along like a kiddy car.

* **kidney,** *n.* In combs.: (1) **kidney-leaved crowfoot,** the common buttercup of the eastern states, so called from the shape of its basal leaves; (2) **punch,** a blow just over the kidneys; (3) **root,** (see quots.); (4) **seed cotton,** a variety or reputed variety of cotton, *obs.;* (5) **shot,** a shot through the kidneys.

(1) **1843** TORREY *Flora N.Y.* I. 13 *Ranunculus abortivus.* . . . Kidney-leaved Crowfoot. . . . A common species in rocky woods,

meadows, etc.; beginning to flower towards the end of April, and continuing through May. — (2) **1896** ADE *Artie* 3 Miller gave him a friendly blow known to ringside patrons as a 'kidney-punch.' — (3) **1898** BRITTON & BROWN *Illust. Flora Northern U.S.* III. 307 *Eupatorium purpureum*. Joe-Pye or Trumpet-weed. . . . Called also Kidney-root, Queen of the Meadow. **1931** CLUTE *Plants* 124 Others are mildly tonic or possess some faint medicinal value. . . . Familiar examples are . . . Kidney-root (*Hepatica triloba*). — (4) **1829** SHERWOOD *Gaz. Georgia* (ed. 2) 266 The kidney seed cotton . . . was tried. (5) **1923** J. H. COOK *On Old Frontier* 85, I kept on and was soon close enough to the big bull to give him what was called a 'kidney shot.'

b. Also **kidney-fern, -leaf violet, -liverleaf, weed,** (see quots.).

1817–8 EATON *Botany* (1822) 517 *Woodwardia angustifolia*, kidney-fern. . . . About a foot high. — **1821** *Mass. H.S. Coll.* 2 Ser. IX. 158 Plants, which are indigenous in the township of Middlebury [Vermont, include] . . . *Viola asarifolia*, Kidney-leaf violet. — **1829** EATON *Botany* (ed. 5) 241 *Hepatica americana*, kidney-liverleaf. . . . Grows chiefly in woods, prefering [*sic*] the south side of hills and mountains. — **1819** *Western Rev.* I. 92 As a striking instance . . . I shall select . . . *Cacalia reniformis*, Kidney weed.

kike kaɪk, *n.* [See quot. 1926 and cf. **Hike,** *n.*[2]] A contemptuous term for a Jew. Also attrib. *Slang.*

1917 CAHAN *Rise David Levinsky* 407 You know who Mr. Levinsky is, don't you? It isn't some kike. It's David Levinsky, the cloak-manufacturer. **1926** *Amer. Sp.* I. 322/1 Since the names of so many of these eastern European Jews ended in 'ki' or 'ky,' German-American Jewish traveling men designated them contemptuously as 'kikis,' a term which, naturally, was soon contracted to 'kike.' . . . I heard the term 'kikis' for the first time at Winona, Minnesota, about forty years ago. **1949** *Time* 7 Feb. 15/2, I do not love Roosevelt and all his kike boy friends.

Kilham Hill. A variety of apple. *Obs.* — **1847** IVES *N. Eng. Fruit* 38 *Kilham Hill.*—Originated on the farm of Doctor Kilham, in Wenham, Essex county, Mass. The size is sometimes large, the form round, a little oblong.

kilhig ˈkɪlhɪg, *n.* [Origin unknown.] In logging, a stout pole used to force a tree to fall in a desired direction. — **1905** *Terms Forestry & Logging* 41. **1913** R. C. BRYANT *Logging* 83 Kilhig or sampson. . . . It consists of a pole . . . either sharpened or armed on one end with a spike.

kill kɪl, *n.* [Du. *kil*, early mod. Du. *kille*, channel, river bed.]

1. (*cap.*) Locally used as the name of a strait.

1639 in STEPHENS JENKINS *Story of Bronx* (1912) 177 The Kil which runs behind the Island of Manhattan, mostly east and west. **1771** FRANKLIN *Autobiog.* 250 A squall . . . tore our rotten sails to pieces, prevented our getting into the Kill and drove us upon Long Island. **1828** *Englishman's Sketch-Book* 25 We took the right hand passage round Staten Island, called the Kills. **1888** *Newark Advt.* (F.), The new Baltimore and Ohio bridge across the Kills, below Elizabethpoot [*sic*], commences to assume imposing proportions.

2. A channel, stream, creek, often in place-names.

1669 *Doc. Col. Hist. State N.Y.* XII. 464, I doe hereby graunt ye said request upon condition that . . . a Draught be taken of ye Land lying in ye said Kill & a returne thereof be made unto me. **1705** in TAYLOR *Hist. Great Barrington, Mass.* (1882) 3 Northerly to a Creek or Kill that comes out of the woods called Wata-pick-aak. **1879** BURROUGHS *Locusts & Wild Honey* 169 Kills and dividing ridges. **1921** *Outing* April 12/1 It rained again as the tent went up on the gravel edge of a small 'Kill' in the pasture.

3. killweed, (see quot.).

1931 CLUTE *Plants* 16 There is also the kill-weed (*Lythrum salicaria*) which at first glance appears to be a terrible species, but which is quite harmless and in all probability is named for the kills or creeks along which it delights to dwell.

* **kill,** *v.*

1. Used in the infinitive form after another verb with adverbial force: To a great or impressive degree. *Colloq.*

1840 *Boston Transcript* 12 Feb. 1/1 A young fellar, dressed to kill, in spick and span new broadcloth, comes in and pacifies the old man. **1848** BARTLETT 194 *To kill.* To do anything *to kill*, is a common vulgarism, and means to do it to the uttermost; to carry it to the fullest extent; as 'He drives *to kill*'; 'She dances *to kill*.' **1895** *N.Y. Dramatic News* 9 Nov. 13/1 Directly in front of them was a picturesque young 'Johnny,' dressed to kill. **1948** *Sat. Ev. Post* 17 July 106/4 Girls who dress fit to kill not infrequently cook that way too.

2. *tr.* In printing, to cancel or delete (matter) before publication.

1865 *Wilkes' Spirit of Times* 16 Dec. 256/1 Two galleys of equal length, one being marked 'Must,' the other 'Kill this.' **1887** *Courier-Journal* 29 Jan. 5/4 Please kill the deer story sent by Associated Press this morning. **1947** *Time* 29 Dec. 51/3 Publisher Forsberg decided to kill the editorial page.

transf. **1924** *Publishers' Wkly.* CVI. 188 *Dead matter*—type which has been 'killed,' i.e., not to be included in the printing. **1941** *Amer. Guardian* (Okla. City) 15 Oct. 9/4 Maybe that is why newspapers use the word 'killing' instead of stopping when they remove subscribers from their lists.

3. To wreck (a boat), to put (an engine) out of working order, to make (a gasoline engine) go dead, as by putting on it a load that is too great. *Colloq.*

1883 MARK TWAIN *Life on Miss.* 106 It seems incredible that Mr. Bixby should have left the poor fellow to kill the boat, trying to find out where he was. **1886** *Phila. Ev. Telegraph* 20 March (*Cent.*), The hose was cut, fire dumped out, . . . pins removed, and engines *killed* so that it will take days to bring them to life again. **1907** FIELD *Six-Cylinder Courtship* 9, I lost no time in starting. What a blessing that I hadn't killed my engine!

4. The verb stem used in substantival combs.: (1) * **kill-cow,** (see quot.); (2) * **devil,** (see quot.), *obs.*; (3) **lamb,** the lambkill; (4) **-me-quick,** whisky, *slang*; (5) **preacher,** (see quot.), *rare.*

(1) **1894** *Amer. Folk-Lore* VII. 103 *Eleocharis tenuis*, poverty-grass, kill-cow, West Va. — (2) **1882** *Narragansett Hist. Reg.* I. 215 They furnished a lamp, which consisted of a wick drawn through an iron ring and elevated to burn, the other end drawing from an open vessel of grease or oil in an open pot, which contrivance was called a 'Kill Devil.' — (3) **1832** CHILD *Frugal Housewife* 28 [Winter evergreen] resembles the poisonous kill-lamb, both in the shape and the glossiness of the leaves. **1869** FULLER *Flower Gatherers* 65 One of the Andromedas, with *deciduous* or falling leaves has acquired the bad name of 'Kill-Lamb,' because it is thought to poison sheep if they eat it. *a***1870** CHIPMAN *Notes on Bartlett* 228 *Kill-Lamb*, C[onnecticu]t Usage. See Lamb-Kill. — (4) **1861** NEWELL *Orpheus C. Kerr* I. 236, I druv down to the tavern . . . and the fust feller I see was hisself, a standin' in the door, and sippin' kill-me-quick. (5) **1890** D'OYLE *Notches* 24 He spread through all that section yet another name for whisky—'Kill Preacher.'

As the last term in **calf, lamb, winter kill.**

killcu ˈkɪlku, *n.* [Echoic.] (See quot.) — **1888** TRUMBULL *Names Birds* 168 [The greater yellow-legs, *Totanus melanoleucus*] in New Jersey at Dennisville, Cape May C.H., and Cape May City, [is called] *Kill-cu;* this name being used by many of the gunners for [the yellow-legs, *T. flavipes*] . . . as well.

killdee ˈkɪldi, *n.* = next.

1781–2 JEFFERSON *Notes Va.* (1788) 74. **1789** MORSE *Amer. Geog.* 59 The following catalogue [of Amer. birds] is inserted: . . . The Chattering Plover or Kildee [etc.]. **1848** *Oquawka* (Ill.) *Spectator* 25 Oct. 4/1 There the land's so poor that it takes two kildeas to say 'kildea.' **1867** J. N. EDWARDS *Shelby* 206 One tall, kill-dee of a looking fellow darted out from the brush. **1917** *Birds of Amer.* I. 239 Kill deer. . . . [Also called] Kildee.

b. (See quot.)

1835 AUDUBON *Ornith. Biog.* III. 193 To 'run like a kildee' is to move with the utmost possible agility.

killdeer ˈkɪlˌdɪr, *n.* [Echoic.] The largest and commonest of the American ring-plovers, *Oxyechus* (syn. *Aegialitis*) *vociferus*. In full **killdeer plover.**

1731 *Phil. Trans.* XXXVII. 176 The Chattering Plover. In Virginia they are called Kildeers, from some resemblance of their Noise to the Sound of that Word. **1813** WILSON *Ornithology* VII. 73 Kildeer Plover. . . . This restless and noisy bird is known to almost every inhabitant of the United States. **1941** LOFBERG *Sierra Outpost* 74 Among the flock of Brewer's blackbirds, spotted sandpipers dipped and dug, and over there were four killdeers. **1949** *Nat. Hist.* May 233/1 The pantomime of a broken wing will usually be enacted. . . . Killdeer and nighthawks often alternate injuries from side to side and thus spoil the illusion.

b. The note of this bird.

1924 *Frontier* Nov. 7 'Kill-deer, kill-deer,' The snipe's wail rose and fell harshly in the hot quiet.

* **killer,** *n.*

1. (*cap.*) *pl.* A Philadelphia gang of thugs somewhat on the order of the Dead Rabbits *q.v. Obs.*

1846 *Dollar Newspaper* (Phila.) 16 Sep. 2/2 This would really appear like a connivance on the part of the Moyamensing authorities with the gang of rowdies in that district, whose name, the 'Killers,' is enough to show the disgraceful character of the association. **1849** in *Amer. Sp.* XXI. (1946) 116/2 It is now well known to the police that several persons from Philadelphia, known as 'Killers' and 'Church Burners,' were in the city participating with the rioters on Thursday night. **1850** *Quincy* (Ill.) *Whig* 26 Nov. 2/6 This dangerous tool, as used by the Killers, is a leaden ball of two pounds weight, fastened to a string cord four feet in length, and attached to the right wrist.

2. A criminal who recklessly or wantonly kills others. *Slang.*

1885 *Wkly. New Mexican Rev.* 5 Feb. 2/6 Aragon is an old time killer and numbers fully a dozen men on his dead list. **1948** *N.O. Times-Picayune Mag.* 19 Dec. 2/2, I ran toward the sound of the shooting, and, rounding a corner, bumped headlong into the killer, waving a gun.

b. A slaughterer, a butcher.

1883 SWEET & KNOX *Through Texas* 584 The killer, as he is called, rides as near to the herd as he can without alarming the buffalo. **1898** *K.C. Star* 20 Dec. 8/3 A bunch of . . . lambs which were covered with mud sold to the killers at $4.65.

As the last term in **ant, cow, dog, fool, locust, man, mosquito, mule, Negro, pain, rattlesnake, salmon, snake, tarantula killer.**

killhag ˈkɪlhɑg, *n.* [See quot. 1902.] (See quot. 1848.)

1848 BARTLETT 194 *Killhag,* (Indian,) a wooden trap, used by the hunters in Maine. **1864** *Bradford Times* (De Vere), The first furs were brought into town yesterday, and already a number of killhags have been put up everywhere. **1902** *Amer. Folk-Lore* 245 Killhag. This name of a sort of wooden trap used by hunters in the Maine woods is probably a corruption of some Micmac or Passamaquoddy word.

killie ˈkɪlɪ, *n.* =next. Also transf.

1848 BARTLETT 403 *Killifish,* . . . a small fish found in the salt water creeks and bays. . . . They are often called *killies.* **1897** *Cong. Rec.* 6 Jan. 518/1 While you are feeding country 'killies' to great newspaper sharks, you ought . . . to have some regard for the great publishing interests. **1898** HAMBLEN *Gen'l Manager's Story* 243 Frank had remained for a bit seated on a stone behind me, watching the 'killies' swimming in the shallow water.

killifish ˈkɪlɪˌfɪʃ, *n.* [Prob. f. Du. *kille,* (older form of *kil,* a channel or stream)+*visch* or *fish.*] Any one of several minnowlike cyprinodont fishes of the genus *Fundulus* or allied genera, esp. *F. heteroclitus,* found on the eastern and southern coasts of the U.S.

1814 MITCHILL *Fishes N.Y.* 441 Sheep's-Head Killifish. *Esox ovinus.* . . . Length about an inch and a half; and remarkably large in the girth. **1856** *Spirit of Times* 27 Dec. 274/1 The young shad are hauled ashore, without thought, and left to perish, high and dry, by thousands, the destroyers, probably, not distinguishing them from ordinary small-fry, killy fish, shiners, and the like. **1949** *This Week Mag.* 23 April 22/2 One female killifish beat her would-be husband so severely a glass plate had to be put between them.

killikinick ˌkɪlɪkɪˈnɪk, *n.* =**kinnikinnick.**

1792 POPE *Tour S. & W.* 63 Killicanic or Sumac Leaves, which when mixed with Tobacco, emit a most delightful Odour from the Pipe. **1865** *Nation* I. 209 The windows of half the shops make a display of earthen pipes, bundles of tobacco [etc.]. . . . One is everywhere attracted by such titles as 'the Celebrated Killikinnick.' **1889** MUNROE *Golden Days* 284 Put that in your pipe and smoke it, along with your killikinick.

***killing,** *n.*

1. The action of shooting or knifing a man to death. Also attrib. *Slang.*

1875 *Chi. Tribune* 28 July 2/2 A killing scrape occurred at Johnson City. **1890** *Stock Grower & Farmer* 12 July 6/1 No, son, there ain't no murderin much on the range. There's a heap of killin', which is different, killin' being moral an' decent. **1911** ROLT-WHEELER *Boy with Census* 9, I thought the Kentucky 'killings' had stopped ten or fifteen years ago. **1928** SIRINGO *Riata* 145, I had got into a killing scrape in Texas, and had gone to Oklahoma to hide out.

2. A financial coup, a clean-up. *Slang.*

1891 *Appeal-Avalanche* (Memphis) 26 April 5/2 The race was a killing for the books, as everybody believed Philora would win in a walk. **1947** *Time* 21 July 84/3 He made his first killing in a gas pipeline.

3. ***killing time,** on farms, the season or time of year when animals are usu. slaughtered.

1666 *E.-Hampton Rec.* I. 244 A barrell of beef Merchantable to be paid unto the aforesaid Mr. Stanbrough att killinge time. **1841** LYELL *Trav. N.A.* (1845) I. 157, I was told it was 'killing time,' this being the coldest season of the year. **1891** *Harper's Mag.* Oct. 824/1 Sausages (after 'killing-time') were hung to dry. **1938** *Cattleman* May 10/3 The hogs usually ran wild, eating acorns, and were rounded up only at killing time.

As the last term in **hog, winter killing.**

Kilmarnock willow. (See quots.) — **1869** *Rep. Comm. Agric. 1868* 202 Kilmarnock willow (*Salix caprea,* var. *pendula*) . . . becomes one of the most distinct of the hardy weeping plants which we possess. **1892** APGAR *Trees Northern U.S.* 166 The Goat-willow [*Salix caprea*] is the one generally used for the stock of the artificial umbrella-formed 'Kilmarnock Willow.'

kiln-dryer. A kiln for drying freshly ground meal. *Obs.* — **1808** *Niles' Reg.* III. Add. 7/2 The machinery invented . . . consisted of . . . an improved *kiln dryer. Ib.* V. Add. A. 16/1 The Kiln-Dryer.—To kiln-dry the meal after it is ground.

***Kimball,** *n. attrib.* Designating a coach or wagon of a type made in the 1870's by the Kimball Mfg. Co., of San Francisco. Now *hist.* — **1879** WILLIAMS *Pacific Tourist* 315/2 It is well, therefore, to see a photograph of the coach, and know beforehand whether it is to be a 'mud-wagon,' or a 'Concord coach,' or an open 'Kimball wagon.' **1947** BEEBE *Mixed Train Dly.* 181 The coming and going of its bright yellow and green Kimball coaches and high-stepping ten-wheelers is possessed of a flourish, a display of pioneer elegance.

Kinderhook ˈkɪndɚˌhuk, *n.* The name of the village in N.Y. where Martin Van Buren (1782–1862) was born, used attrib. or allusively with reference to him. Also in the name of a political club. *Obs.* or *hist.* Cf. **O.K.** — **1840** *New Era* (N.Y.) 7 April 3/1 The Simon Pures, Kinderhook Club, and all others friendly to the good cause, are expected to attend. **1941** *Sat. Review* 19 July 3/2 In papers of the time Van Buren was referred to in such terms as 'the magician of Kinderhook,' 'Your cunning Kinderhook Fox,' and 'the Kinderhook pony.'

kinepox ˈkaɪnˌpɑks, *n.* The cowpox, which when communicated to persons, as by vaccination, affords protection from smallpox.

1800 BENTLEY *Diary* II. 357 The use of the Kine Pox has not been unequivocally successful, & we hear that Waterhouse has written to some patients. **1815–6** *Niles' Reg.* IX. (Supp.) 182/1 This excellent woman did more in establishing the credit of the *Kine Pox Inoculation* in America, than is generally known. *c***1887** in *Amer. Sp.* (1948) April 113/2 Vaccinating with the small-pox instead of the kine-pox.

kinetograph kəˈnɛtəˌgræf, *n.* [f. *kineto-,* combining form of Gk. *kinetos,* movable, +*-graph,* written.] A camera for taking pictures of objects in motion. *Obs.* — **1891** *Times* (London) 29 May 5/1 [Mr. Edison said] the kinetograph is a machine combining electricity with photography. **1894** *Voice* 5 April, Edison has recently invented what he calls a kinetograph and a kinetoscope.

kinetoscope kəˈnɛtəˌskop, *n.* [f. *kineto-* (see prec.)+*-scope.*] A series of pictures or a machine for projecting such a series. Now (*cap.*) used as a trade-mark name for a particular make of such machine.

1864 WEBSTER 739/2 *Kinetoscope,* . . . a sort of movable panorama. **1894** *Dly. Telegraph* (London) 18 Oct. 5/3 With his [Edison's] kinetoscope . . . he reproduces most realistically the movements of a Spanish ballet-girl. **1908** LORIMER *J. Spurlock* i. 9 That was where the bear came into the kinetoscope. **1948** *New Yorker* 16 Oct. 40/1 A spectator peering into a Kinetoscope would push a button, and a fifty-foot strip of film would pass between a light and a rapidly revolving shutter and thus produce a small and very flickering motion picture.

Hence **kinetoscopic,** *a.*

1894 DICKSON *Life Edison* 311 A popular and inexpensive adaptation of kinetoscopic methods. *a***1906** O. HENRY *Trimmed Lamp* 215 The fluttering leaves of the trees made a dim kinetoscopic picture of them in the moonlight.

***king,** *n.*

1. One who is an outstanding leader or pre-eminent in some indicated activity. *Colloq.*

1846 J. G. SAXE *Progress* (1847) 28 How would she [the Muse] strive, in fitting verse, to sing The wondrous Progress of the Printing King! **1862** *Rep. Comm. Patents 1861: Agric.* 185 He has been called the 'Strawberry King' . . . [because of] unquestionable pre-eminence in this branch of fruit culture. **1908** HORNBLOW *Profligate* 13 There were multi-millionaires, social leaders, actresses, kings of finance, captains of industry [etc.]. **1947** *Newsweek* 24 Feb. 57/1 Babe Ruth, 52, former home-run king, walked out of a New York hospital.

2. A favored man at a **king ball.** *Obs.*

1844 *N.O. Picayune* 19 Feb. 1/3 The bawl cum on, and wus opened as usual by the kings and thar queens. **1856** *Spirit of Age* (Sacramento) 20 Oct. 3/1 These balls were reigned over by four kings and four queens, who reigned for one night only, and then appointed their successors.

3. A variety of cotton.

1910 TYLER *Varieties Amer. Upland Cotton* 20 This group is composed of King and its derivatives and some other cottons developed in North Carolina and Tennessee.

4. In combs. (often *cap.*): (1) **King Alcohol,** liquor, whisky, *colloq.;* (2) **ball,** (see quot. 1856), *obs.;* (3) **beat,** (see quot.), *obs.;* (4) ***bee,** a leader, ruler, foremost personage, *slang;* (5) **Caucus,** a congressional caucus *q.v.,* in allusion to the great political power it once wielded, now *hist.;* (6) **Cotton,** a popular personification of cotton in allusion to its economic supremacy in the South; (7) **full,** in poker, a hand in which there are three kings and a pair of other cards; (8) **George man,** (see quots.), now *hist.;* (9) **hill,** (see quots.); (10) ***John I,** a nickname for

John Adams (1735–1826), second President of the U.S. (1797–1801), *rare;* (11) **Kleagle,** an officer of the Ku-Klux Klan after World War I, cf. **Kleagle;** (12) ***pin,** *fig.* a person or thing of prime importance, *colloq.;* (13) **-'s arm,** a gun such as was once used by those in the service of the King of England, *obs.,* or *hist.;* (14) **-'s base,** a children's game; (15) **-'s cure-all,** (see quot.); (16) **-'s ex(cuse),** (see quots.); (17) **-'s gift,** (see quot.), *obs.;* (18) **-'s man,** one who supported the English cause at the time of the American Revolution, now *hist.;* (19) **-'s Mountain Day,** (see quot.).

(1) 1845 *Quincy* (Ill.) *Whig* 20 Nov. 2/2 Would it not be a good idea to call together the Washingtonians of the city, and let the friends as well as the enemies of Temperance, see what impression King Alcohol has made upon our ranks during the past Summer? **1947** DOWNEY *Lusty Forefathers* 299 King Alcohol was tottering on his throne. — **(2) 1832** HALL *Leg. of West* 153 He continued to make a voyage of three or four months annually, and spent the remainder of his time in cultivating his crop, smoking his pipe, attending the king-balls, and playing the fiddle. **1856** *Spirit of Age* (Sacramento) 20 Oct. 3/1 A custom prevailed in the West, of keeping up during the winter, a series of weekly festivals, called 'king balls,' to which all the beauty and valor of the vicinity were invited. — **(3) 1902** CLAPIN 249 *King-beat,* in newspaper parlance, exceedingly important news which have been obtained in advance of other papers. — **(4) 1895** MARK TWAIN *Personal Recoll. Joan of Arc.* (R.), He was king-bee of the little village.

(5) 1824 *Boston Indep. Chron.* 9 Oct. 1/5 A new paper in the State of New-York, called the *Warren Recorder,* . . . has sworn obedience to *King Caucus.* **1902** E. C. MEYER *Nominating Systems* 15 The congressional caucus was doomed. The people had won a decisive battle. King Caucus was dethroned. **1948** *Time* 14 June 15/1 By 1832 the revolution against King Caucus was complete. — **(6) 1860** R. H. STODDARD in *Vanity Fair* (1861, 8 June) 269/1 Ye slaves, of curs begotten, Hats off to great King Cotton! **1949** *Land Economics* Feb. 11/1 Fertilizer contributed to the hold which King Cotton had over the South. — **(7) 1849** *N.O. Picayune* 14 July 1/4 The game proceeded with the usual fluctuations for some length of time . . . when it happened that an 'ace-full,' was out against a 'king-full,' and Mr. Hancock . . . found himself loser $200 more. **1923** *Sunset* March 22/3 One of them had a king full, the second four treys. — **(8) 1860** in A. D. HOWDEN SMITH *Narr. S. Hancock* (1927) 154, I informed them we were King George men, (Englishmen) who were lost from a ship. **1946** R. PEATTIE *Pac. Coast Ranges* 190 The long-lived Indians out on the coast could have heard from their grand-parents of the coming of the 'King George men,' the English, and the 'Bostons,' the American traders. — **(9) 1888** PURDY *Legends of Susquehanna* 125 We planted our corn on the tenth of May, And carefully made, ere we went away, The great 'King-hill' for the squirrel and bird. **1942** WEYGANDT *Plenty of Penna.* 96 For him [i.e., the crow], and for the chipmunks and red squirrels, was planted 'the great King-hill,' in the corner of the field. . . . It was thickly planted with kernels of corn, perhaps a quarter of a peck, in the hope the varmints would confine their attentions to it.

(10) 1798 *Aurora* (Phila.) 27 Aug., Whether any of them may be induced to swear to support the cause of monarchy or to enter into the pay of King John I is 'a horse of another color.' — **(11) 1923** *Imperial Night-Hawk* 29 Aug. 6/1 When trouble seemed unavoidable the King Kleagle of Pennsylvania is said to have ordered the marchers to return to the hill. **1931** F. L. ALLEN *Only Yesterday* 66 The country was divided into Realms headed by King Kleagles, and the Realms into Domains headed by Grand Goblins. **1949** *L.A. Times* 21 May 7/2 Gus Price in the early 1920s was King Kleagle of the California Ku Klux Klan. — **(12) 1867** *Harper's Wkly.* 14 Sep. 590/2 His best position was as a batter. He was a 'King-pin' there. **1948** *Dly. Ardmoreite* (Ardmore, Okla.) 21 March 3/4 Wheat—kingpin in the commodity price structure—skidded to a low closing point for the year. — **(13) 1860** WHITTIER *Home Ballads* 49 When each war-scarred Continental, Leaving smithy, mill, and farm, Waved his rusted sword in welcome, And shot off his old king's arm. **1929** SHELTON *Salt-box House* xvi. 125 Then Jube took the old king's arm from its place behind the kitchen door. — **(14) 1883** EGGLESTON *Hoosier School-Boy* xxv. 165 They agree to play that favorite game of Greenbank. . . . It is called 'king's base.'

(15) 1893 *Amer. Folk-Lore* VI. 142 *Oenothera biennis,* king's cure-all, Southern States. — **(16) 1890** *D.N.* I. 65 *King's excuse.* . . . Abbreviated to *king's ex.* In playing base, when a boy falls down, to keep from being caught he says, 'King's ex.' [Ky.]. **1948** *N. & Q.* Aug. 73/1 King's-Ex. . . . This is a widely used expression, for I have seen records of it from Alabama, Arkansas . . . Kansas, Louisiana, Missouri, Nebraska, Ohio, and Virginia. — **(17) 1800** HAWKINS *Sk. Creek Country* 66 These negroes were, many of them, given by the agents of Great Britain to the Indians, in payment for their services, and they generally call themselves 'King's gifts.' — **(18) 1797** FRENEAU *Poems* (1809) II. 11 Whate'er some angry king's-men say, You play a game that must be won. **1857** *Ladies' Repository* XVII. 83/1, I never feed kingsmen if I can help it. **1949** *Sat. Ev. Post* 2 April 98/4 You may conclude that I am neither king's man nor rebel. — **(19) 1909** *N.Y. Ev. Post* (s.-w. ed.) 7 Oct. 8 'King's Mountain Day,' the anniversary of the battle of King's Mountain, S.C., in which 900 'mountain men' won a victory over a British force numbering 1,200, on October 7, 1780.

b. In the names of animals: (1) **king rail,** a large, long-billed American rail, *Rallus elegans;* (2) **salmon,** =**quinnat salmon;** (3) **snake,** a large, harmless colubrid snake, *Lampropeltis getulus,* found in the southern states, also used of various other snakes, cf. **chain snake.**

(1) 1835 AUDUBON *Ornith. Biog.* III. 28 Hunters . . . now and then obtained a few of these birds, which they considered as very rare, and knew only by the name of 'King Rails.' **1944** *Nat. Geog. Mag.* June 310 The bird's brown color more nearly resembles that of the King Rail than the familiar Clapper Rails of the eastern coast of the United States. — **(2) 1881** *Amer. Naturalist* XV. 177 These species may be called the quinnat or King salmon . . . or *Oncorhynchus chouicha.* **1948** *Pacific Discovery* Sep.–Oct. 2/1 Very large runs of king salmon were seen in 1945. — **(3) 1709** LAWSON *Carolina* 132 The King-Snake is the longest of all others, and not common. **1827** WILLIAMS *West Fla.* 28 The king snake kills them [*sc.* poisonous snakes] whenever they cross his path. **1949** *Scientific Mo.* Jan. 55/1 When pursued by an enemy such as a king snake or some mammal, the lizard attempts to slip away.

c. In occasional allusion to males of various animals, etc., as **king buffalo, eagle, rattler, tumbleturd.**

1901 RYAN *Montana* 93 You're strong as a mountain lion, or an old king buffalo. — **1862** in F. MOORE *Rebellion Rec.* V. II. 245 The old man, game as a king-eagle, begged to be permitted to drive the rebels home. — **1904** STRATTON-PORTER *Freckles* 293 She's just about where the old king rattler crosses to go into the swamp. — **1748** CATESBY *Carolina* App. 11 *Scarabæus pilaris Americanus.* The Tumble-Turds. . . . [The males] are commonly called King Tumble-Turds, tho' by what appears, they assume no pre-eminence.

For ***kingbird,** ***king crab,** ***kingfish,** see as main entries.

d. In the names of plants: (1) **king cactus,** ?the giant cactus, *rare;* (2) ***devil,** a local name for a hawkweed introduced from Europe; (3) **grass,** (see quot.), *rare;* (4) **nut,** see as a main entry; (5) **Philip corn,** (see quots.).

(1) 1846 EMORY *Military Reconn.* 77 In one view could be seen . . . the cactus, (king) cactus, (chandelier) green wood acacia, &c. — **(2) 1891** *N. & Q.* VI. 162 There is a rather rare and curious weed growing in Northern New York, which is locally known as king-devil. — **(3) 1878** in KILLEBREW *Tenn. Grasses* 209 Japan Clover, or King Grass, *Lespedeza striata,* . . . seems especially adapted to the Southern states.

(5) 1856 *Rep. Comm. Patents 1855: Agric.* p. xi, The Improved King Philip or Brown Corn . . . was extensively disseminated in all the States north of New Jersey, and throughout the mountainous districts of Pennsylvania, Maryland, and Virginia. **1917** WILL & HYDE *Corn Among Indians* 22 The well known and widely diffused King Philip corn is one of the surviving varieties of the pioneer New England flints.

As the last term in **bonanza, cattle, coal, Indian, land, lumber, Mohawk, money, paint, pork, railroad, railway, silver, steamship, sugar, wheat king.**

***kingbird,** *n.* Any one of various tyrant flycatchers, esp. the common kingbird, *Tyrannus tyrannus,* often called a bee martin *q.v.* See also **Arkansas, olive-sided kingbird.**

1778 CARVER *Travels* 475 The King Bird is like a swallow, and seems to be of the same species as the black martin or swift. **1820–32** J. P. KENNEDY *Swallow Barn* II. 121 How spiteful these little king-birds take after and worry a crow. **1948** *Reader's Digest* Dec. 149/1 They saw a bee martin that some folks call a kingbird.

***king crab.** Any one of various large marine arthropods, esp. *Xiphosurus sowerbyi,* found on the eastern and southern coasts of the U.S.

1698 *Phil. Trans.* XX. 394 The Molucca Crab *Mus. Regal. Soc.* 120 In *Virginia* and several parts of the Continent of *America,* they call it, *The King Crab.* **1796** MORSE *Univ. Geog.* I. 227 King Crab, or Horse Shoe *Monoculus polyphemus.* **1884** GOODE *Fisheries* I. 829 The curious form of marine animal called 'Horseshoe Crab' [and] 'King Crab' . . . is not, however, a true Crab. . . . Some naturalists regard it as a low type of crustacean, while others place it among the *Arachnida,* or scorpions and spiders. Its nearest allies all occur as fossils. **1935** LINCOLN *Cape Cod Yesterdays* 154 Hallett ignored and did not trouble himself to dip out . . . king crabs.

***kingfish,** *n.*

1. The cero, *Sierra cavalla.* Also the spotted cero or pintado, *Scomberomorus regalis.*

It is not clear what fish is referred to in the 1st. quot.

1775 ROMANS *Nat. Hist. Fla.* App. 7 Groopers are in great plenty, king-fish, Spanish mackrel and Barrows are often caught towing. **1884** GOODE *Fisheries* I. 316 It is more than likely that this [*Scomberomorus regalis*] and the preceding species [*S. cavalla*] are both included by the Key West fishermen under the name 'King-fish.' **1948** *Galveston* (Tex.) *News* 14 June 7/7 The visiting anglers . . . asked numerous questions in regards to kingfish, tarpon and other big fish that are likely to be encountered during the two-day stay.

2. Any one of various marine sciaenoid fishes of the genus *Menticirrhus*, esp. *M. saxatilis*, found on the Atlantic Coast.

1814 MITCHILL *Fishes N.Y.* 408 King-fish, *Sciaena nebulosa*. . . . Length sixteen or eighteen inches. **1897** *N.Y. Forest, Fish, & Game Comm. 2d Rep.* 243 Kingfish . . . was formerly abundant in Gravesend Bay, but it seldom makes its appearance there now.

3. (See quots.)

1884 GOODE *Fisheries* I. 380 The Queen-fish—*Seriphus politus*. This species is known as 'King-fish' or 'Queen fish.' **1890** *Cent.* 3290/3 *Kingfish*, . . . a sciænoid fish, the little roncador, . . . common on the coast of California: so called in the San Francisco markets.

king nut.

1. =**mockernut.**

1884 SARGENT *Rep. Forests* 134 *Carya tomentosa*. . . . Whiteheart Hickory. King Nut. **1894** *Amer. Folk-Lore* VII. 98 *Carya alba*, king-nut, West Va. **1945** DARLINGTON *Higher Plants Mich.* 25 Some of these are not at all common, such as blue ash . . . , king-nut.

2. The big shellbark hickory, *Carya laciniosa*, of the eastern states. In full **king nut hickory.**

1897 SUDWORTH *Arborescent Flora* 114 *Hicoria laciniosa*. . . . Common Names [include] . . . Thick Shellbark Hickory (N.C., Ark.). King Nut (Tenn.). **1931** MATTOON *Forest Trees Okla.* 32 The king nut hickory becomes a very large tree and is found in the rich bottom land forests of the eastern part of the State.

***kink,** *n.*

1. *fig.* An odd notion or quirk, a whimsical mental twist. *Colloq.*

1803 JEFFERSON *Writings* VIII. (1897) 280 Should the judges take a kink in their heads. **1890** *Pomona* (Calif.) *Times-Courier* July, If she gets some highfulutin kink in her head, it is . . . the proper thing for her to hand him over to some other girl. **1948** *So. Folklore Quart.* March 102 A few minutes with John Tasker Howard's *Our American Music*, edition of 1946, would have straightened out the African 'kink' in the editor's music-historical concepts.

2. A twist, angle, device, fad, an individual or clever way of doing a thing. *Colloq.*

1825 NEAL *Bro. Jonathan* III. 291 There he goes, now!—there! there!—that's a new kink! **1910** *Sat. Ev. Post* 24 Sep. 64/1 Learn this little kink and your collar troubles are over. **1932** *K.C. Times* 27 Feb. 24 This is a new kink on the old racket.

b. An imperfection or difficulty.

1868 *Cong. Globe* 16 May 2492/2 There would have been kinks in it [the Arkansas bill], and somebody would have wanted to send it back. **1948** *Time* 3 May 65/1 At an estimated cost of $20,000 a week, it had hired 350 typists and other extra help, and set up a special staff . . . to iron the kinks out of the new process.

c. *To come the kink*, (see quot.), *obs. To come out of the kinks*, to turn out surprisingly well. *Colloq.*

1863 BROWNE *Four Years in Secessia* (1865) 288 'Coming the kink' was to steal a negro from the country, and dispose of him in town. . . . Those fellows would steal the Ethiop and sell him again; and sometimes they had bartered away the same darkey seven or eight times in one month. — **1892** DUVAL *Young Explorers* 230 Well, it does beat all natur the way that nigger has come out'n the kinks.

***kink,** *v. tr.* To confuse with odd notions. *Rare.* — **1801** JEFFERSON *Writings* X. 189 A head, entangled and kinked as his is.

***kinkajou,** *n.* "An American step-dance" (*OED Supp.*). *Obs.*

See the "animal" dances listed in quot. 1947 *s.v.* **bunny hug.**

1927 *Bulletin* 22 Sep. 5/5 The Kinkajou's Coming. . . . It is . . . a lively variation on the fox trot. **1928** *Dancing Times* Jan. 643/2 Mr. Casani and Miss José Lennard gave demonstrations of the Yale and also the Kinkajou, to the 'Kinkajou Strut,' both dance instructions and dance music having been received over the Atlantic 'phone the previous week.

kinky ˈkɪŋkɪ, *a.* Of hair, esp. of Negroes: Full of kinks or short tight curls. Often in combination with *hair(ed)*, *headed.*

1844 *Cong. Globe* App. 6 Jan. 42/3 [The Negro's] skull is as thick, his hair is as kinkey, . . . and his skin as black, as they were the day he was first introduced. **1861** in F. MOORE *Rebellion Rec.* I. III. 137 A marked distinction is laid Between the rights of the mistress, And those of the kinky-haired maid. **1921** PAINE *Comr. Rolling Ocean* 252 This kinky-headed, limber-tongued, son-of-a-sea-cook of a Mendosa is aboard this ship as a fireman. **1947** TALLANT *Voodoo in N.O.* 5 They sell toilet articles and beauty aids, products 'guaranteed' to straighten kinky hair and make dark skin light.

kinnikinnick ˌkɪnɪkəˈnɪk, *n.* ["The word . . . is derived from one of the Cree or Chippewa dialects of Algonquian. The literal signification is 'what is mixed' " (Hodge).]

1. Dried sumac leaves used alone or with other ingredients for smoking (see quot. 1907). Cf. **killikinick.**

1817 BRADBURY *Travels* 91 They did not make use of tobacco, but the bark of *Cornus sanguinea*, or red dog wood, mixed with the leaves of *Rhus glabra*, or smooth sumach. This mixture they call kinnikineck. **1835** FEATHERSTONHAUGH *Canoe Voyage* I. 265 He only smoked the *kinnekinnic*, which is a mild preparation of the inner bark of the willow, mixed with a little tobacco. **1907** HODGE *Amer. Indians* I. 692/1 Kinnikinnick. An Indian preparation of tobacco, sumac leaves, and the inner bark of a species of dogwood, used for smoking by the Indians and the old settlers and hunters in the W. The preparation varied in different localities and with different tribes. **1948** *N.W. Ohio Quart.* Jan. 40 The council fire was lighted and the calumet of Kinnekanick (tobacco) was passed from chief to chief.

attrib. **1805** ORDWAY in *Jrnls. Lewis & O.* 199 Some Indians had hung up . . . a Scraper a paint bag with ½ an ounce in it, kinikaneck bags, flints [etc.].

2. Any one of various plants supplying the leaves or bark for such mixtures.

1817–8 EATON *Botany* (1822) 178 *Arbutus uva-ursi*, bear berry, kinnikinnick. . . . Dry, barren sand plains. **1876** *Atlantic Mo.* Dec. 683/2 The little mound is kept green with the faithful kinnikinnick vines. **1931** CLUTE *Plants* 28 One of the kinnikinniks is still known as Indian tobacco (*Lobelia inflata*). **1938** THOMPSON *High Trails* 86 As we climb into the Hudsonian zone we find extensive carpets of kinnikinnick.

Also *kinnikinnick bark, berry, brush, seed.*

kinspeople ˈkɪnzˌpipl, *n. pl.* Persons of the same kin, relatives. — **1866** HOWELLS *Venetian Life* xviii, Kinspeople of herself or her husband. **1891** WINSOR *Columbus* v. 86 Here his kinspeople ruled.

Kiowa ˈkaɪəwe, *n.* [" 'Principal people,' their own name" (Hodge).]

1. A member of a warlike tribe of plains Indians apparently of a distinct linguistic stock; *pl.* the tribe of these Indians.

1808 PIKE *Sources Miss.* II. App. 16 The only nations with whom the Pawnees are now at war, are the Tetaus, Utahs, and Kyaways. **1848** RUXTON *Life Far West* vii, The Kioway loves the pale-face, and gives him warning. **1945** M. JAMES *Cherokee Strip* 10 Away back, the Gov'mint had taken it from the Comanches and their friends the Kiowas.

attrib. **1821** J. FOWLER *Journal* 64 The Kiawa cheef with his nation had stoped and intended we shold stop with them. **1865** PIKE *Scout & Ranger* (1932) 57 This wild region we well know to be a favorite resort for Comanche and Kiowa hunters. **1948** *Lawton* (Okla.) *Constitution* 4 July 2/6 Featured in the . . . midway attraction are . . . the ever-popular troupe of Kiowa Indian dancers.

2. *Geol.* A formation of the Lower Cretaceous in Kansas. Also attrib.

1895 *Amer. Geol.* XVI. 162 The Kiowa shales. *Ib.*, The upper part of the Kiowa. **1924** PIRSSON & SCHUCHERT *Text-Book of Geol.* II. 541 The change from the Kiowa or Denison fauna to the Woodbine of the Upper Cretaceous shows little if any greater contrast [etc.]. **1947** *Geol. Survey Kans. Bul.* 66, 35 The combined total of the Dakota formation, the Cheyenne sandstones, and the Kiowa shale in Scott County is approximately 550 feet.

kip kɪp, *n.* [f. **kilo*+**pound*.] (See quot.) — **1914** H. R. THAYER *Struct. Design* II. 87 Shear in Kips. [Note:] 1 Kip=1000 lbs. Moments in Kip Feet. *Ib.* 250 Maximum shear 110 kips. . . . Maximum moment 9140 kip in[ches].

kirmess ˈkɜmɪs, *n.* [Du. *kermis*, an Amer. borrowing, cf. **kermis*, the usual form in England.] A fair characterized by much noisy merrymaking, usu. got up for a charitable purpose. *Obs.* — **1885** *Boston Jrnl.* 16 April 2/3 The kirmess which opened yesterday in New York is a festival which originated in the Netherlands many years ago. It is supposed that the word is derived from kerk, the Dutch for church, and maesse, feast, and was originally a church festival. **1888** *Ib.* 12 Dec. 1/8 Salem Mechanic Light Infantry Kirmess . . . is destined to prove a brilliant success.

***Kirtland,** *n.* [J. P. *Kirtland* (1793–1877) Amer. naturalist.] **1. Kirtland's owl,** =**saw-whet owl. 2.**

Kirtland's warbler, a rare warbler, *Dendroica kirtlandi*, that breeds in Michigan.

(1) **1871** *Amer. Naturalist* V. 119 Occurrence of Kirtland's Owl in Maine.—A characteristic specimen of the *Nyctale albifrons* Cassin, was shot at Norway, Me. **1917** *Birds of Amer.* II. 107 Saw-Whet Owl. ... [Also called] Kirtland's Owl. — (2) **1858** BAIRD *Birds Pacific R.R.* 286 Kirtland's Warbler.... Of this species but a single specimen is known to be extant. It was killed by Dr. Kirtland ... in May of 1851. **1942** Nat. Pks. Service *Fading Trails* 262 Kirtland warblers nest in Michigan where jack pines grow after fires.

Kirtland money. Currency issued by a Mormon bank in Kirtland, Ohio, about 1830. *Rare.* — **1845** *S. Lit. Messenger* XI. 477/2 'Kirtland money' was as plenty in the West at that time as have been the issues of similar equally well-founded institutions since that period.

kiskatomas ˌkɪskəˈtaməs, *n. local.* [Amer. Indian. Cf. Cree *kiskisikatew*, "it is cut or gnawed."] The mockernut hickory, shellbark hickory, or a nut of one of these. Also **kiskatomas nut.**

1809 RITSON *Poetical Picture* 161 Their nuts, black walnuts, persimins, Kiscatoma nuts, and Chinquapins. **1810** MICHAUX *Arbres* I. 20 *Shell bark hickery* [*sic*], ... nom le plus en usage dans tous les Etats-Unis.... *Kiskythomas*, par les Hollandois du New-Jersey. *a***1817** DWIGHT *Travels* IV. 58 On these grounds, grow the chesnut, the shag-bark or Kiskatoma, and several other trees. **1832** BROWNE *Sylva* 184 The Dutch settlers ... near the city of New York, call it [shellbark hickory] Kisky Thomas Nut. **1894** *Amer. Folk-Lore* VII. 98 *Carya alba*, kiskytom, Otsego Co., N.Y.

* **kiss,** *n.* and *v.* In combs. and phrases.

1. kiss joke, a party ticket printed on very thin paper to permit a dishonest voter to cast several of them folded within a large ballot. In full **kiss-joke ticket.** Also **kiss-joker, kiss-joking.** *Obs.*

1879 *Cong. Rec.* 24 April 843/1 In many States ... ballot-stuffing, kiss-joking, bulldozing, and murder have been ... unrestrained. *Ib.* 844/1 In 1878 it [Charleston, S.C.] cast for a democrat ... 22,707 votes, kiss-joker and all, and for a republican 14,096. **1880** *Ib.* 26 May 3809/1 Only upon rare occasions was one of these 'kiss-jokes' destroyed. It was a neat and safe way to establish a democratic majority—to put in a few hundred extra fraudulent democratic votes and then take out and destroy the same number of republican votes. *Ib.*, Then [in 1878, in Charleston] came in those kiss-joke tickets, printed on very thin tissue paper.

2. kiss me, (see quot.).

*a***1870** CHIPMAN *Notes on Bartlett* 230 *Kiss-me.* Used, as is 'Thank-you-Ma'am,' for a ridge or hollow place across a roadway; a jolting obstruction to vehicles.—N[ew] E[ngland].

3. kiss-me-if-you-dare, (see quots.). *Obs.*

1846 *Ore. Spectator* 20 Aug. 3/2 [The kiss-me-quick] is the opposite of those long looking poker-bonnets which are called 'Kiss-me-if-you-dares.' **1857** *Spirit of Times* 26 Sep. 55/3 A few years ago, the ladies wore a very handy sort of hood, which was called, 'Kiss-me-if-you-dare' hood.

4. kiss-me-quick (-before-mother-sees-me), (see quot. 1846). *Obs.*

1845 *Knickerb.* XXV. 375 Seen from the Bowery, it [a church] looks like a barn with a 'kiss-me-quick' hood on. **1846** *Ore. Spectator* 20 Aug. 3/2 The Lynn ladies wear a style of bonnet, sitting not much back from the face, and called by the expressive name of 'Kiss-me-quick-before-mother-sees-me.' **1852** [see **Kossuth hat**].

b. (See quot.) *Obs.*

1880 FARRAR *Five Years Minn.* 133 A bright streamer of cerise-coloured ribbon, known, I think, by young ladies of the period as a 'kiss-me-quick,' completed his headdress.

5. (See quots. and cf. **2.** above.)

1931 CLUTE *Plants* 129 In the hop-growing regions of central New York, ... a vine ... twines back upon itself, thus forming a loop which, in the rough and informal parlance of the hop-yards, is known as a 'kiss-me-quick.' **1945** *Amer. Sp.* April 156 Although *kiss-me-quick* does not seem to appear in the dictionaries with the meaning of ridge or depression in a roadway, it does have that meaning for many people in the southeastern part of the United States.

6. kiss-the-Bible, a solemn oath sworn on the Bible. *Rare.*

1884 MARK TWAIN *H. Finn* xxviii. 283, I don't want nothing more out of you than just your word—I druther have it than another man's kiss-the-Bible.

7. kiss verse, an amatory verse such as those on the wrappers of confections known as kisses. *Obs.* Cf. * **motto, motto candy.**

[**1831** *Nat. Intelligencer* (Wash., D.C.) 27 4/5 The printed mottoes which now envelope the kisses and comfitures ... are ... devoid of taste.] **1848** in THOMPSON *M. Jones* (1872) 216 If he ketched him sendin any more love letters and kiss verses to his daughter by his nigger galls, he'd make one of his boys give him a alfired cowhidin.

As the last term in **red-ear, sugar, wheelbarrow kiss.**

* **kissing,** *a.* and *n.*

1. kissing bee, a party or social gathering of young people. *Colloq.*

1853 *Turnover* 6 (Th.), [He was about] to shave and dress for a 'party' or 'kissing-bee.' **1900** DRANNAN *Plains & Mts.* 188, I sat in a corner like a homely girl at a kissing-bee, and had nothing to say.

2. Kissing Bridge, (see quots.). *Obs.*

1783 *Polite Traveller* 62 In the way is a bridge, distant about three miles from New York, which ... is called the Kissing-Bridge, where it is part of the etiquette, for the gentleman to salute the lady who has put herself under his protection. **1807** IRVING *Salmagundi* II. 19 He particularly noticed a worthy old gentleman of his acquaintance, who had been somewhat of a beau in his day, whose eyes brightened at the bare mention of Kissing-bridge.

3. kissing bug, any of several hemipterous insects that sometimes bite the lip, causing a painful sore.

1899 *Pop. Sci. Mo.* Nov. 33 Several persons suffering from swollen faces visited the Emergency Hospital in Washington and complained that they had been bitten by some insect while asleep.... Thus began the 'kissing bug' scare. *Ib.* 35 The kissing bug, in its own way and in the short space of two months, produced almost as much of a scare as did the San Jose scale in its five years of Eastern excitement. **1936** *Univ. Ariz. Gen. Bul.* 3, 113 When houses are built in the desert these kissing bugs transfer their affections to people.

* **kit,** *n.* Used in various colloq. phrases referring to a number of persons or things taken together as (1) *the whole kit and biling*, (2) *the whole kit and boodle*, (3) *the whole kit and caboodle*, cf. **caboodle,** (4) *the whole kit and tuck.*

Cf. in British use *the whole kit*, 1785——.

(1) **1859** BARTLETT 32 The phrase the *whole* (or more commonly *hull*) *kit and bilin*, means the whole lot, applied to persons or things. **1941** TAGGARD *Here We Are* 246 'Twas the hind-quarters of the sorrel I bet on. He was the only one in the hull kit and bilin' of 'em that his quarters didn't fall away. — (2) *a***1861** WINTHROP *J. Brent* xxviii. 296, I motioned we shove the hul kit an boodle of the gamblers ashore on logs. **1946** *Newsweek* 16 Sep. 32/2 It gave the farm and the whole kit and boodle to Stanley. — (3) **1888** *Boston Globe* 5 Feb. 1/3 If say 'railroad lobbyists' cast reflections on his character he would wipe out the whole kit and caboodle of them. **1939** ROLLINS *Gone Haywire* 64 Soon's we receive, we's got to skedaddle west with th' hull kit an' caboodle. **1949** *Time* 18 July 13/2 There was no longer any point to the whole kit & caboodle of anti-inflation controls which he had been demanding. — (4) **1871** EGGLESTON *Hoosier Schoolm.* iv. 50 He'll beat the whole kit and tuck of 'em afore he's through.

As the last term in **camp, signal kit.**

Kit Carson hitch. [Christopher (or *Kit*) *Carson* (1809–68), noted plainsman.] =**diamond hitch.** — **1882** BAILLIE-GROHMAN *Camps in Rockies* 45 You have at last managed the famous 'diamond' or 'Kit Carson' hitch to the lash rope.

* **kitchen,** *n.*

1. (See quots.) *Rare.*

In 1st. quot. app. a trans. of Du. *keuken* used for a small house in which the living room and the cookroom are the same. See *WNT*, 2588.

1824 DODDRIDGE *Notes* 174, I saw that the slaves and convicts [in Md.] lived in filthy hovels called kitchens. **1903** FOX *Little Shepherd* xv, He was told that in everything but mathematics he must go to the preparatory department until the second session of the term—the 'kitchen' as it was called by the students.

2. In combs.: (1) **kitchen back,** the back of a two-story house in which the kitchen is of only one story, *obs.;* (2) **cabinet,** see as a main entry; (3) **car,** a railroad car in which food is prepared for patrons of the dining car; (4) **caucus,** a private caucus held by persons without official status in the government, *obs.;* (5) **chamber,** a chamber over, or adjacent to, a kitchen; (6) **dance,** a dance held in a kitchen; (7) **gardening,** growing garden vegetables for the kitchen (see also quot. 1893, and cf. next); (8) **garten,** a class for children in cooking, sewing, etc., *rare*, cf. * *kindergarten;* (9) **mule,** a pack mule that carries kitchenware; (10) **oyster,** (see quot.), *obs.;* (11) **police,** in the army, soldiers detailed to assist the cooks, also their work, also transf., often abbreviated **K.P.;** (12) **rocker,** a rocking chair kept in a kitchen; (13)

shower, an occasion upon which the friends of an engaged couple assemble sociably bringing gifts of various kitchen utensils for the latter's future use; (14) **wood,** = **stove wood.**

(1) **1787** in *Mag. Amer. Hist.* I. 382 These houses add much to the beauty of [Fort Harmar, near Pittsburgh]. . . . The Colonel's is two story high, with a kitchen back. — (3) **1867** *Harper's Mag.* June 6/2 The middle or kitchen-car is placed transversely across the track. **1948** *New Yorker* 25 Sep. 27/1 The dining car, which is serviced from a kitchen car, . . . has a continuous serpentine leather sofa. — (4) [**1825** *Harbinger* (Frankfort, Ky.) 1 June 4/1 No, he was not in that caucus, *but the governor was present when they held the* first *meeting*, in the speaker's room, *over the kitchen*.] **1826** *Spirit of Seventy Six* I. 322 Your adversaries, the friends and agents of king and kitchen caucus, have assumed many names. **1831** *Boston Transcript* 14 Nov. 2/1 We learn also, that something was said by one of the disaffected, about '*kitchen caucuses*.'

(5) **1649** *Conn. Rec.* I. 497 An Inventory of the Estate of Mr. William Whiting: . . . In the kitching chamber . . . a bid, . . . In the Kittching . . . 2 brass pots. **1780** E. Parkman *Diary* 227 Ye Fire, . . . kindled in ye Kitchen Chamber. **1865** A. D. Whitney *Gayworthys* xxxvii. 346 The kitchen-chamber at the head of the 'end staircase,' was what had been Joanna's room. — (6) **1880** *Harper's Mag.* Dec. 89/2 The younger people had their berrying frolic, sleigh-rides, kitchen dances, nuttings, and the like. — (7) **1867** De Voe *Market Ass't* 320 By the progress of the science brought to bear upon that branch we now term 'kitchen-gardening,' markets are supplied with the asparagenous plants, spinaceous plants [etc.]. **1893** *Dly. News* (London) 26 Jan. 5/5 'Kitchen-gardening' is the curious name bestowed upon their labours by the ladies of an American city, who teach a class of poor children to sew, cook, dust, sweep, make beds, and wash clothes. — (8) **1893** Barrows *World's Parl. of Religions* II. 1483 Kindergartens, kitchengarten, and nightschools [etc.] . . . are among the methods employed [by the Woman's Home Missionary Society]. — (9) **1873** in Abbott *C. Carson* 296 He met the first animal, which happened to be the kitchen mule. He was so called, because he had very large open bags or panniers into which we put all our cooking utensils. **1880** *Scribner's Mo.* May 128/1 When a bread-pan is taken, it is lashed bottom up on the top of the kitchen-mule's pack.

(10) **1881** Ingersoll *Oyster Industry* 245 *Kitchen Oyster.*—Small oyster for cooking. (New Orleans.) — (11) **1930** F. A. Pottle *Stretchers* 31 A cook or K.P. stands by to see that the dishes are decently scraped before they go into the pail. *Ib.* 33 Before first call, six or more unfortunates crept out of bed and went on kitchen police. **1942** Philips *Big Spring* 164 K P on a ranch wasn't any more popular than K P in the army. **1949** *L.A. Times* 13 July II. 21/2 American husbands admitted sheepishly today that the little woman often puts them on KP. — (12) **1903** Wiggin *Rebecca* 218 Miranda removed the shawl from her head and sank into the kitchen-rocker. — (13) **1924** Croy *R.F.D. No. 3* 89 It was a 'kitchen shower.' The glittering array was piled high, like a special sale in a racket store—dishpans, saucepans, pie pans . . . and so on. — (14) **1902** Moore *Songs & Stories* 15, I ain't got nuffin' ter do but to tote the kitchin wood in fer mammy.

As the last term in **buffet, candy, cellar, diet, Hell's, log, Negro, shed, summer, tin, wash kitchen.**

kitchen cabinet. A coterie of personal, unofficial advisers of President Andrew Jackson (1829–37). Also attrib.

1832 in A. C. Cole *Whig Party in So.* (1913) 13 If there be no other mode of preventing its [a mission's] being given to the most despicable of all the Protegees of the Kitchen Cabinet [i.e., Van Buren.] **1842** Uncle Sam *Peculiarities* I. 212 We will hurl the Kitchen cabinet tyrants from their stools. **1867** *Wkly. New Mexican* 30 March 2/2 [Gov.] Mitchell [of N.M.] having failed in his 'kitchen cabinet' diplomacy, Perea turned his eyes upon the Senate. **1948** *Sat. Ev. Post* 10 July 19/2 The bright idea of overriding this opposition by a well-managed convention originated with Maj. W. B. Lewis, a member of Jackson's 'Kitchen Cabinet.'

transf. **1886** *Cong. Rec.* 9 June 5721/2 Don't you think Mr. Adams, of New York, is one of the members of that kitchen cabinet? **1948** *Chi. D. News* 4 Dec. 4/4 One of the most important members of Gov. Stevenson's kitchen cabinet will be the new head of the State Department of Labor.

kitchenette ˌkɪtʃɪn'ɛt, *n.* A small, compactly arranged kitchen and pantry combined. — **1911** *Country Life* 1 Dec. 43/2 The kitchenette is a model of convenience. **1948** *Durant* (Okla.) *D. Democrat* 2 July 1/6 On each of the second and third stories will be a cleaning and pressing room and a kitchenette in each wing.

b. kitchenette apartment, an apartment having a kitchenette.

1929 *Sears Cat.* Fall 925/1 It is complete in equipment and is particularly adapted to one or two-room kitchenette apartments. **1945** Maxwell *Folded Leaf* 31 Mr. Peters and Lymie had lived first in cheap hotels and then in a series of furnished kitchenette apartments, all of them gloomy like this one.

***kite,** *n. Higher than a kite*, very high, with unusual force. Also *higher than Gilderoy's kite. Colloq.*

E. C. Brewer, in *Notes and Queries* (7 Ser. V. 357/1), suggests a Scottish ballad as the possible source of *Gilderoy's kite*.

1867 *Wkly. New Mexican* 24 Aug. 2/2 The Cleverites have thrown him higher than a kite. **1869** Mark Twain *Innocents* xxv. 256 She squandered millions of francs on a navy . . . , and the first time she took her new toy into action she got it knocked higher than Gilderoy's Kite—to use the language of the Pilgrims. **1903** Brown *How to Beat Game* 53 This theory, however, like many others, is often knocked higher than Gilderoy's kite when put to the test of practice.

As the last term in **everglade, Mississippi, swallow-tailed, white-tailed kite.**

***kite,** *v. intr.* To go up in price. *Colloq.* — **1870** W. W. Fowler *Ten Years Wall St.* 504 Would send to be enough to start a panic, or send the market 'kiting' up among the tall figures. **1902** Wilson *Spenders* 355 The stock is bound to kite.

***kitefoot,** *n.* A kind of tobacco once extensively produced in Maryland, in full **kitefoot tobacco,** app. so named from its bright-yellow color when cured, suggestive of the color of a kite's foot. *Obs.* Cf. **Maryland kitefoot.**

[**1688** Clayton *Va.* in *Phil. Trans.* XVII. 943 Aranoko Tobacco, whose Scent is not much minded, their . . . aim being . . . to procure it a bright Kite's-foot colour.] **1788** *Mass. Centinel* 4 June 94/2 Crowley & Clark Have just received a quantity of Kitefoot Tobacco, of a *superior quality* for smoking. **1835** Todd *Notes* 50 The adjacent state of Maryland produces . . . the Bright Kite's Foot Tobacco.

kit fox. A small fox, *Vulpes velox*, found on the western plains, or a related species found in the Southwest.

1805 Lewis in *L. & Clark Exped.* II. (1904) 216 The party who were down with Capt. Clark also killed a small fox. . . . It is so much like the comm[on] small fox of this country commonly called the kit fox that I should have taken it for a young one of that species. **1917** *Mammals of Amer.* 77 The Kit Foxes might be considered as Red Foxes that had left the timbered regions to dwell in open, semi-arid areas and had become bleached out by exposure to the hot sun, as well as suffering a reduction in size. **1947** Cahalane *Mammals* 235 The kit fox has been extirpated from large sections of its natural range.

Kittatinny ˌkɪtə'tɪnɪ, *n.* [*Kittatinny* Mountains of New Jersey and Pennsylvania.] A garden variety of blackberry. Also attrib. — **1874** *Dept. Agric. Rep. 1873* 187 Six years ago he planted ten rows of Kittatinny and ten of Wilson. . . . None of the Kittatinny canes bore fruit. **1928** Bailey *Cyclo. Horticulture* 510/2 The varieties most commonly grown are Agawam, Kittatinny, . . . and Snyder.

***kitten,** *n.* As the last term in **Maltese, mud, painter kitten.**

kittly-benders 'kɪtlɪˌbɛndəz, *n. pl.* [Poss. f. **kittle*, ticklish, perilous, + **bend*, a leap, bound. See *EDD kettlebend*, surpass, outdo, and *bendy-leather* (*s.v. bend*, sb.¹), thin ice, and cf. **tiddledies.**] "Thin bending ice; act of running over such ice" (W. '09). Also fig. *Colloq.*

1854 Thoreau *Walden* 353 Let us not play at kittlybenders. **1858** G. M. Dallas *Series of Lett. from London* (1869) II. 7 This will enable our ministers here to walk, on this treacherous element of dress, as on thick ice, not as heretofore on what boys call 'kiddly benders.' **1872** E. E. Hale *How to Do It* iii. 46 You will, with unfaltering step, move quickly over the kettle-de-benders of this broken essay. [**1944** Johnson *As I Dare* 20 In the winters we skated on the half-frozen river, or 'ran benders' on the cove.]

kiva 'kivə, *n. S.W.* [Hopi Indian, lit. "old house or man house."] An assembly chamber of the Pueblo Indians for the observance of religious rites. Cf. **estufa.**

1871 in *Utah Hist. Quart.* VII. (1939) 54 Found pieces of pottery and arrowheads. . . . Also saw a 'kiver' or underground 'clan room.' **1893** Donaldson *Moqui Pueblo Indians* 55 An estufa is a large room underground, called by the Indians 'kiva' (keva or keevah), meaning 'man house,' a place where men hold their private councils. **1948** *N.M. Quart. Rev.* Autumn 273 Men, naked and painted, filed out of the sacred kivas to dance in the dusty plazas.

Kiwanian kə'wanɪən, *n.* [See next.] A member of a Kiwanis Club. — **1922** *Dly. Ardmoreite* (Ardmore, Okla.) 16 Jan. 8/4 Local Kiwanians will . . . have a program in keeping with those being given throughout Kiwanism. **1949** *Milwaukie* (Ore.) *Rev.* 4 Aug. 1/5 All the Kiwanians and their wives then shared in the festivities by being served some of the cake.

Kiwanis Club. [See note.]

Any one of various local clubs designed to promote civic interests and good fellowship, and patterned on the first such organization formed at Detroit in 1915.

The first element in this name is said to be based upon a Michigan Indian term meaning "to make oneself known, to impress oneself."

1922 *Collier's* 29 April 5/2 It had a civic association, and Rotary, Kiwanis, and Lion clubs. **1948** *Dly. Ardmoreite* (Ardmore, Okla.) 30 March 3/1 A class of older girls recently entertained the local Kiwanis club.

ki-yi ˈkaɪjaɪ, *n.*[1] [Imitative. Cf. the *v.*]

1. An exclamation of joy. *Colloq.*

1831 *Boston Transcript* 21 Feb. 2/4 He forthwith changed his tune to '*Cui-i, cui-i, ki-i, ki-i,*' to the increased sport of the school and still greater indignation of the master. **1836** *Crockett's Yaller Flower Almanac* 17 Oh cricky! What lots of fun, ki eye! **1867** *Chi. Times* 27 July 5/2 Every muff was received with a ki-yi and a yell. **1895** Remington *Pony Tracks* 27 The men from Tongue River greeted the men from Pine Ridge . . . with *ki-yis* of delight.

Pueblo Indian kiva or estufa

2. A bark or yelp as of a coyote or dog. Also transf., a dog.

1869 Muir *First Summer in Sierra* (1911) 32 Even the howls and ki-yis of coyotes might be blessings if well heard, but he hears them only through a blur of mutton and wool, and they do him no good. **1904** *Buffalo Express* 20 June 4 A butcher in Brussels made sausage of the carcass of a zoo elephant which had been killed. Doubtless the Brussels kiyis yelped for joy. **1913** London *Valley of Moon* I. x, But them sickenin', sap-headed stiffs, with the grit of rabbits and the silk of mangy ki-yi's, a-cheerin' me—*me!* **1949** *Sat. Ev. Post* 12 March 56/4 The loud barking of the aggressor would change to a ki-yi of pain as the wheel ran him down and went over him with a bump, bump.

b. (*cap.*) *attrib.* Of or pertaining to the Know-Nothings. *Obs.*

1855 *Butte Rec.* (Bidwell, Calif.) 1 Dec. 2/4 The Kye Eye papers are loud in their professions about the purity of the ballot box.

kiyi ˈkaɪjaɪ, *n.*[2] [Origin obscure. Poss. Algonquian Indian.] A lake herring *q.v.* — **1896** Jordan & Evermann *Fishes N. Amer.* 469 Argyrosomus hoyi, Gill. (Moon-eye Cisco; Cisco of Lake Michigan; Kieye of Lake Michigan.)

ki-yi ˈkaɪjaɪ, *v.* [Imitative.] *intr.* To howl or yelp, said of dogs. *Colloq.*

1850 Garrard *Wah-To-Yah* vii. 95 The poor victim to savage appetite . . . ki-yi-ed until his little canine spirit departed for elysium. **1869** Stowe *Oldtown Folks* 332 But hang him (the dog) we did, and he ki-hied with a vigor that strikingly increased the moral effect. **1943** Peattie *Great Smokies* 111 The dogs tuk to kiyi-in' and yippin' and stickin' their tails betwixt their legs and lightin' out for home.

transf. **1894** *Harper's Mag.* Sep. 642/2 One of those little Skye-terrier tugs . . . began to ki-yi right under our stern.

K. K. Abbreviation for **Ku-Klux** or **Ku-Kluxer.** — **1870** B. Yocum in *Report on Public Frauds, S.C.* (1878) 26 If the governor is going to arm the white K. K.'s to operate against them, he, the Gov., can take back the guns and commissions that has been already sent to this county. **1898** Page *Red Rock* 322 You better watch out for de K. K.'s.

K. K. K. Abbreviation for **Ku-Klux Klan,** or **Ku-Klux Klansman.** Also attrib.

[**1846** *Dollar Newspaper* (Phila.) 8 April 3/3 Definitions . . . K.K.K. Kuba, Kalifornia and Kanada.] **1872** in Fleming *Hist. Reconstruction* II. 132 We advanced upon the supposed K.K.K.'s with an intrepidity that reflected credit upon the troops. **1921** in Fry *Modern Ku Klux Klan* (1922) 55 You gentlemen at headquarters will probably be pleased to know what rapid strides the K.K.K. is making in this State [Miss.]. **1949** *Newsweek* 25 July 20/2 It discovered that one of the jurymen was a KKK member.

Klamath ˈklæməθ, *n.* [f. a native term of uncertain significance. The pl. is usu. with *-s.*] *pl.* A tribe of Indians formerly found along the Klamath River in California and Oregon.

1902 *Out West* March 273 The pappoose basket of the Pomos is a neat piece of weaving, but was never so ornate as those of the Klamaths. **1924** Curtis *N. Amer. Indian* XIII. 238 The capture of slaves was almost an industry with the Klamath. **1948** *Ore. Hist. Mag.* March 91 'How Christmas Came to the Klamaths' is an account completed from interviews with aged members of the tribe.

In full **Klamath Indians, tribe.**

1826 *McLoughlin Lett.* (1941) I. 33 Mr. Ogden [goes] . . . thence towards Lac Sale makes a Circuit West and comes Out above the Clamet tribe. **1851** in Schoolcraft *Indian Tribes* (1853) III. 133 The goods destined for the Klamath Indians had been sent to Trinidad. **1855** *N.Y. Herald* 29 Nov. 2/1 In Rogue River valley, the Shasta, Klamaths and Applegate Indians have combined.

b. The language of these Indians.

1890 Gatschet *Klamath Indians* I. 209 *Triphthongs* are not infrequent, since Klamath has a greater tendency to accumulate consonants than vowels.

c. Klamath weed, (see quot. 1922).

1922 Smiley *Weeds of Calif.* 54 (Hypericum perforatum L.) English names: (1) Common St. John's-wort; (2) Speckled John; (3) Herb of St. John; (4) Klamath Weed. **1949** *Sun. World-Herald Mag.* (Omaha) 1 May 10/1 Klamath weed probably can be controlled or destroyed chemically.

Klan klæn, *n.* =**Ku-Klux Klan.**

1868 *Cent. Mag.* XXVIII. 409/1 The Klan now, as in the past, is prohibited from doing such things. **1884** *Ib.* July 399/1 During the entire period of the Klan's organized existence Pulaski continued to be its central seat of authority. **1949** *Memphis Commercial-Appeal* 26 June 1/1 The Klan has been accused of being involved in a wave of floggings, cross burnings, and threats in this area in recent weeks.

b. klansman, a member of the Ku-Klux Klan.

1905 Thomas Dixon (*title*), The Clansman. **1948** *Ariz. Republic* (Phoenix) 4 March 12/3 Some 300 hooded and robed klansmen paraded here last night.

Klaxon ˈklæksn̩, *n.* [Gk. *klazō*, "I make a sharp piercing sound."] A trade-mark name for a kind of horn often used on automobiles; also the horn denoted by this. — **1910** *Sat. Ev. Post* 17 Sep. 48 The Klaxon has never taken a life; it has saved thousands. **1949** *Reader's Digest* April 140/2 It was a gray Pierce Arrow, equipped with two bulb horns and an electric Klaxon.

Kleagle ˈkligl̩, *n.* [Origin unknown. ?Poss f. *Kl*(an)+*eagle.*] An official in the present Ku-Klux Klan. Cf. **King Kleagle.** — **1924** Bynum *Personal Recoll.* 8 The Kleagle showed considerable irritation in the conversation which followed. **1949** *Time* 13 June 24/1 Samuel Green, the Grand Dragon of the Ku Klux Klan, was frantically exhorting his Kleagles and Cyclops to mass for a big night of cross-burning and hate-spieling.

Klieg klig, *n.* Also **Kleig.** [f. A. and John *Kliegl*, experts in stage lighting.] **1. Klieg eyes,** (see quots.). **2. Klieg light,** an intense incandescent light rich in actinic rays used in taking motion pictures.

(1) **1923** *Sci. Amer.* Oct. 243/1 The burning of the eyeballs by the ultra-violet rays is a form of conjunctivitis. . . . This malady occurs so freely among motion-picture actors—stars and supers alike—that a name, 'Kleig eyes,' has been coined for it. **1929** Dorland *Amer. Ill. Med. Dict.* (ed. 12) 453/2 Klieg e[ye], a condition marked by conjunctivitis, lacrimation, and photophobia due to exposure to the intense lights (Klieg lights) used in making moving picture photographs. — (2) **1929** [see prec.]. **1948** *Ada* (Okla.) *Ev. News* 4 July 1/4 Kleig lights, had they been used, would have been subdued by the number of luminaries that gathered in the banquet room.

Klikitat ˈklɪkɪˌtæt, *n.* Also **Klickitat.** [f. a Chinook word meaning "beyond," with reference to the Cascade Mts.] *collect.* and *pl.* A small Shahaptian tribe formerly living in and near Klickitat County in Washington, and now on the Yakima Reservation in that state.

1833 Catlin *N. Amer. Indians* II. 113 In the vicinity of the mouth of the Columbia, there are, besides the *Chinooks*, the *Klick-a-tacks.*

Cheehaylas, Na-as, and many other tribes. **1855** *N.Y. Herald* 12 Nov. 2/2 The Clikitats are divided. **1903** JAMES *Indian Basketry* 261 The Klikitats have been styled the 'Iroquois of the Northwest.' They were robbers and marauders. The very word Klikitat means robber. **1907** HODGE *Amer. Indians* I. 713/2 The Klikitat were always active and enterprising traders, and from their favorable position became widely known as intermediaries between the coast tribes and those living E. of the Cascade range.

attrib. **1838** PARKER *Exploring Tour* 240 The Klicatat nation count with different words up to ten. **1892** BOSTON TILICUM *Puyallup Indians* 19 His mother was a Klickitat woman. **1914** APPLEGATE *Recoll. Boyhood* (1934) 95 This son of an African sire, and a native daughter of the Walla Walla, Cayuse, Klickitat, Chemomichat, Spokane or Wascopum tribe, had an immense shock of grizzly, almost curly hair.

Klondike ˈklɑndaɪk, *n.* ["Klondike is a corruption of the name of this stream [i.e., a tributary of the Yukon] in one of the Athapascan dialects prevailing in that region" (Hodge).]

1. *attrib.* Of or pertaining to a region in Yukon Territory to which a famous gold rush was made in 1897–99.

1898 *Cent. Mag.* March 695 During the rush of 1897 only two routes into the Klondike country were followed. *Ib.* 697/2 These men made their way home, as best they could, out of the wreckage of the first Klondike rush. **1898** *K.C. Star* 21 Dec. 7/3 For the first time, though, there are a number of military dolls and quite a number of Klondike dolls. **1948** *Life* 2 Feb. 49/3 78-year-old Emil J. N. Ott, . . . a veteran of the Klondike Rush, who smelts rough gold into ingots.

2. *Cards.* A form of solitaire resembling Canfield, with which it was originally identical. Cf. ***Canfield.**

1902 McKEE *Land of Nome* 163 All the games were going—roulette, vingt-et-un, faro, poker, stud-poker, Klondike, and craps. **1946** MOREHEAD & MOTT-SMITH *Penguin Hoyle* 174 Klondike is probably the most widely known solitaire game.

Klondiker ˈklɑndaɪkɚ, *n.* An inhabitant of the Klondike or one who prospects for gold there. — **1898** *Dly. Ardmoreite* (Ardmore, Okla.) 12 July 2/1 Klondikers returning from the fields report plenty of gold. **1904** G. BURGESS & IRWIN *Picaroons* 102 The Story of the Returned Klondyker.

klootch klutʃ, *n. N.W.* [Chinook Jargon *klootchman*, female, woman.]

1. =next.

1945 SERVICE *Ploughman* 176 On one side of me I had a klootch with a papoose tied to her back. **1949** *Boston Globe* 15 May (Fiction Mag.) 6/4 One-armed John's out back helpin' the klooch smoke some meat.

2. klootchman, an Indian woman, squaw.

1865 STUART *Montana As It Is* 83 Oregon is the place to hear the 'Chinnook' in all its glory; it has 'played' the English language 'square out' in that land of rain, fir-trees, 'cloockmans' and camus. **1890** *Aberdeen* (Wash.) *Herald* 2 Oct. 1/2 Usually a canoe is manned by an Indian and his klootchman—the siwash sitting in the stern and the klootchman in the bow. **1945** SERVICE *Ploughman* 176 In the old days he had taken up with a klootchman, and had written home, saying he was married to an Indian Princess.

Klucker ˈklʌkɚ, *n.* =**Ku-Kluxer.** *Rare.* Cf. **Kluxer.** — **1879** TOURGEE *Fool's Errand* xxvii. 141 Ef dere's any mo' Kluckers raidin' roun' Burke's Corners, dar'll be some funerals tu. **1944** PENNELL *Rome Hanks* 176 Are you a Klucker, Mr. Ocamb?

Klu Klux. Erron. variant of **Ku Klux.** — **1872** *Cong. Globe* 21 May 3707/3 Since 1868, when we handled this organization without gloves, we have had no Klu Klux in Arkansas. **1924** *Imperial Night Hawk* 14 Feb. 8 We understand that a member of your firm ran for Mayor on the Klu Klux ticket.

Kluxer ˈklʌksɚ, *n.* =**Ku-Kluxer.** *Colloq.* — **1923** *Nation* 21 Nov. 570 We are not much impressed with the desireability of organizations specially formed to fight the 'Kluxers.' **1948** *Dly. Ardmoreite* (Ardmore, Okla.) 25 July 20/4 Some 20 more noted Kluxers, anti-Semites, anti-Negroes, anti-foreigners and similar ragtag and bobtail were on hand.

K. N. [Abbrev. for **Know-Nothing.**] *attrib.* Of or pertaining to the Know-Nothing party. Also **K. N.'ism.** *Obs.* Cf. **Cayenne.**

1855 *Chi. W. Times* 2 Sep. 1/2 The Philadelphia *Sun*, an original K.N. organ, draws a picture of the greedy office seekers among the Hindoos. **1856** *Ill. State Reg.* 8 May 3/1 The subtile management of the k.n. fusionists proved abortive. *Ib.* 26 June 1/3 Having taken such decided grounds in favor of K. N.'ism, we will not feel surprised if he should obtain both nominations.

knackaway ˈnækəwe, *n.* [See quot. 1896.] The anaqua, a tree or shrub found in the southwestern part of the U.S.

1884 SARGENT *Rep. Forests* 114 *Ehretia elliptica.* . . . Knackaway. Anaqua. **1896** *Garden & Forest* IX. 282 *Knackaway* (*Ehretia elliptica*), a corruption of the Mex.-Span. anaqua, shortened from anacahuite, which is from Aztec *nanahuaquahuitl*, 'lues venera tree,' so called from the medicinal use of its roots. **1902** CLAPIN 18 *Anaqua* . . . (Sp.), a tree or shrub of the borage family (*Ehretia elliptica*), found in South-Western Texas. Also called *knackaway*.

knapsack ˈnæpˌsæk, *v. intr.* To travel across country, camping en route and living from the contents of a knapsack. Also *tr. Colloq.*

1913 *Outing* Feb. 636/2 In addition, there are overnight trips for those who wish to take a longer trip or to 'knapsack it.' **1916** *Out West* July 41/1 To one toughened to knapsacking this makes an ideal way to see the 'big country.' **1946** *So. Sierran* Dec. 2/2, I knapsacked the entire John Muir Trail last summer. **1948** *Sierra Club Bul.* March 21 True, I did learn how the other half lives by knapsacking quite a bit, but that was a few years back.

Hence **knapsacker,** *n.*

1947 *Sierra Club Bul.* March 5/1 Knapsackers are the most independent of mountain travelers. **1949** *Canadian Alpine Jrnl.* May 81 Keep a sharp lookout for any knapsackers or parked cars within the next seven miles.

***knee,** *n.*

1. (See quot. and cf. **butting pole.**) *Obs.*

1791 in JILLSON *Dark & Bl. Ground* 109 The knees are pieces of heart timber laid above the butting poles to prevent the poles rolling off.

2. A cone-like process on the roots of the cypress and tupelo. Cf. **cypress knee.**

1823 C. VIGNOLES *Florida* 91 The *cypress galls* have firm sandy bottoms, and are only troublesome from the multitude of sprouting knees. **1889** *Science* XIII. 177/1 At this stage . . . if the crown be permanently wet, the knees [of the tupelo] become an extremely conspicuous feature. **1938** MATSCHAT *Suwannee River* 12 Their attention was fixed on a big cottonmouth basking on a cypress root—knee, the swampers call it.

3. In combs.: (1) **kneebunt,** (see quot.); (2) **crop,** a crop in the cultivation of which labor performed on the knees is required; (3) **sprung,** having overstrained or bent knees, bow-legged; (4) **trousers,** trousers coming no lower than the knees.

(1) **1892** *Amer. Folk-Lore* V. 146 Kneebunt.—Another coasting term, used to denote the side-saddle fashion of riding the sled. — (2) **1928** *Sat. Ev. Post* 10 March 170/2 He does heavy field work—particularly in the so-called 'stoop crops' and 'knee crops' of vegetable and cantaloupe production. — (3) **1875** HARTE in *Scribner's Mo.* XII. 208 Particularly when that animal's foundered and knee-sprung. **1907** STEWART *Partners* 204 Old John, which was the second cook, was so kneesprung you could see through his apron. — (4) **1899** T. HALL *Tales* 162 Since she was a little girl in short dresses and he a boy in knee trousers.

b. *knee-high to a frog*, etc., used, esp. in comparisons, to emphasize smallness, youthfulness, or remoteness in past time. *Colloq.*

1814 *Portsmouth Oracle* 2 April 3/2 One . . . who, as farmer Joe would say, is 'about knee high to a toad.' **1824** *Microscope* (Albany, N.Y.) 12 June 55/1 (Th.), He has lived with me ever since he was 'knee high to a musquitoe.' **1833** *Louisville Herald* 20 March, It is really the best version of an old story we have heard 'ever since we were knee-high to a frog.' **1851** *Democratic Review* XXVIII. 301 You pretend to be my daddies; some of you who are not knee-high to a grasshopper! **1911** SAUNDERS *Col. Todhunter* 275 Lawdy massy! I done know him since he wa'n't mo'n knee-high to a duck, suh! **1947** *Harper's Mag.* Aug. 133/2 Fatigue was gone forever when, knee-high to nothing, I caught my first trout.

***knee,** *v.* **1.** *tr.* To renew (the knees of a garment). **2.** To urge (a horse) on by pressing the knees against its sides. Both *rare* or *obs.*

(1) **1847** HOWE *Ohio* 348 After wearing out their woollen pantaloons, [they] were obliged to have them seated and kneed with buckskin. — (2) **1924** MULFORD *Rustler's Valley* iii. 33 Then he . . . turned his own animal southward and kneed it forward. **1926** ——— *Cassidy's Protege* x. 133 The herder, . . . kneeing his horse, rode swiftly back and forth several times for a hundred feet each way.

Knickerbocker ˈnɪkɚˌbakɚ, *n.* [See note.]

Diedrich Knickerbocker was alleged by Irving to have been the author of his *A History of New York.* Irving's ascription was no doubt in jesting allusion to his friend Herman Knickerbocker of Schaghticoke, near Albany.

1. A New Yorker, esp. one descended from the original Dutch settlers. Cf. **Old Knickerbocker.**

1809 IRVING *Hist. N.Y.* II. 108 Lastly came the Knickerbockers, of the great town of Scaghtikoke, where the folk lay stones upon the houses in windy weather, lest they should be blown away. **1831** *Boston Transcript* 29 Oct. 2/1 Some [masqueraders] were quakers and some Knickerbockers—some were Indians, more frightful than the Sioux. **1886** *Harper's Mag.* March 642/1 He would not selfishly keep New England to himself, but he shares it with the hapless Knickerbockers. **1945** *Sat. Review* 24 Feb. 19/3 To the Knickerbocker this Yankee interloper was a sly, scheming, unprincipled rascal . . . a liar, a boaster, a hypocrite.

b. (See quot. 1881.)

1857 *Harper's Mag.* March 451/1, I am an Albany Knickerbocker—a Dutchman of purest Belgic blood—and I justly claim to be heard. **1881** *Ib.* March 533/1 It has become common to speak of the *élite* of Albany as Knickerbockers—a name derived from Knik-ker-bak-ker (pronounced as spelled), a baker of knickers [marbles].

c. (See quot.) *Rare.*

1880 CABLE *Grandissimes* 101 The Creoles—the Knickerbockers of Louisiana.

2. Often attrib., as (1) **Knickerbocker game,** (2) **literature,** (3) **name,** (4) **social compact,** (5) **stock,** (6) **style.**

(1) **1857** *Spirit of Times* 31 Jan. 357/1 Base Ball . . . is the old Knickerbocker game, and ought to be looked upon in this country with the same national enthusiasm as Cricket and Foot Ball are regarded in the British Isles. — (2) **1878** *Harper's Mag.* Jan. 307/1 That 'Knickerbocker literature' which the Nation pungently described some years ago. — (3) **1903** *N.Y. Times Sat. Rev.* 7 Nov. 790 A young woman who bears a Knickerbocker name beginning with Van. — (4) **1830** WATSON *Philadelphia* App. 39 It was one of the grand links of union in the Knickerbocker social compact.

(5) **1893** *Outing* Jan. 243/2 Everything and anything not strictly of Knickerbocker stock they frowned upon . . . as either trivial or wicked. **1935** PEEL *Political Clubs N.Y. City* 34 In 1834, Tammany Hall elected to the office of mayor, C. W. Lawrence, a quiet, unassuming gentleman of Knickerbocker stock. — (6) **1884** *Cong. Rec.* App. 25 June 343/1 Upon mattresses laid on the bare ground within this tent twenty-five of us were 'bundled' in true Knickerbocker style, without regard to sex, side by side.

b. Also in derivatives, as **Knickerbockerdom, Knickerbockic.** *Obs.*

1856 *Porter's Spirit of Times* 15 Nov. 176/2 We feel a degree of old Knickerbockic pride, at the continued prevalence of Base Ball as the National game of the region of the Manhattanese of these diggings. **1864** *Alta California* (S.F.) 2 Feb. 1/5 Knickerbockerdom has really outdone itself.

***knife,** *n.* As the last term in **barlow, belt, big, bowie, bush, butcher, cane, case, Congressional, corn, cotton, crook, frog-sticker, great, hog, jack, leg, long, pie, pocket, scalp, scalping, sharp, tobacco knife.**

***knife,** *v.*

1. *Polit. tr.* To strike at or try to defeat (a candidate, ticket, etc.) in an underhand manner. *Slang.*

1888 *Nation* 10 May 375/1 The strongest men in the party cannot be nominated, because they are hateful to the Blaine faction, and are certain to be knifed in the Convention in case Blaine does not get the nomination. **1911** HARRISON *Queed* 323 What chance'd there be of namin' to lead the party in the city the man who had knifed the party in the State? **1948** *Chi. D. News* 10 May 12/3 What Stassen did . . . was to enter certain districts in Ohio where the labor vote is predominant and try to knife Senator Taft.

Hence ***knifer,** *n.*

1888 *Nation* 22 March 227/3 This third may be called the 'knifers,' for, should any other candidate than Blaine be nominated, they would see to it that he was never elected.

2. *intr.* (See quot.)

1920 W. CAMP *Football without Coach* 107 If any of these three center men lunges through—'knifes' through, as it is called—he opens the door on either side of him. . . . The hole that the man in the line has left by knifing through now becomes a yawning cavity. *Ib.* 116 The first caution to be given a guard on defense is not to knife through.

knife man. (See quots.) *Obs.* — **1643** R. WILLIAMS *Key* (1866) 66 Whence they call English-men Cháuquaquock, that is, *Knive-men.* **1764** HUTCHINSON *Hist. Mass.* I. 478 The French [writers] speak of others [Indians], viz. that, at certain repasts, they never make use of knives; it is not probable they ever had any to use, on any occasion, until they were brought to them from Europe, they called the first English, Knifemen.

***knight,** *n.*

1. (*cap.*) A member of one of the secret orders given in **2.** below.

1865 PIKE *Scout & Ranger* (1932) 125 He explained to us that the Knights were organized with three degrees—the military, the financial, and the legislative. **1908** *Sat. Ev. Post* 31 Oct. 3/2 Most of the voters thought the Knights were some kind of a secret order with an insurance clause attached. **1947** *Newsweek* 29 Dec. 21/3 What made the Knights so irate were six Christmas cards. **1949** *Agric. Hist.* Jan. 13/1 The Democrats . . . accepted the planks offered by the Knights but treated the Alliance cavalierly.

2. Used in the pl. in the names of, or with reference to, various secret organizations, as (1) *Knights of Columbus,* a society of Roman Catholic men, founded in 1882; (2) *of King Arthur,* (see quot.); (3) *of Labor,* an organization founded in 1869 to safeguard the rights of workingmen, also the members composing this, now *hist.;* (4) *of Pythias,* a society founded in Washington, D.C., in 1864, for social and benevolent purposes, the members composing this order; (5) *of the Circle,* =next, *obs.;* (6) *of the Golden Circle,* an organization founded in Cincinnati in 1854, which, during the Civil War, became an avowed advocate of the southern cause, the members of this organization, now *hist.,* cf. **American Knights;** (7) *of the Invisible Empire,* =next, *obs.;* (8) *of the Ku-Klux Klan,* members of the Ku-Klux Klan organized after World War I; (9) *of the White Camelia,* a name applied to various local organizations that sprang up in the South soon after the Civil War, the members of this organization.

(1) **1901** *N.Y. Tribune* 22 July 3/4 Wednesday the Knights of Columbus of Columbus and Utah will unite their forces; on Thursday another double-header. **1948** *Green Bay* (Wis.) *Press-Gaz.* 12 July 16/7 Members of the Green Bay lodge Knights of Columbus were reminded today that the annual fish fry will be held at the Shorewood Country club next Tuesday. — (2) **1907** *Springfield W. Republican* 3 Jan. 14 This modern and in a measure revived institution of chivalry—the Knights of King Arthur—inaugurated so quietly and unassumingly in the parsonage of a Congregational clergyman, numbers now, at the end of its 14th year, 750 local branches or castles. — (3) **1885** *Cent. Mag.* Sep. 802 The Knights of Labor have a scheme on foot in some of the Western States by which tracts of land are to be purchased by the State. **1947** *Atlantic Mo.* June 72/2 The Knights of Labor revolted in the 1880's against the labor policies of big business. — (4) **1864** in SHACKLEFORD *Knight's Armor* (1869) 41 It was resolved, that this Order be styled the Knights of Pythias. **1945** *Somerset News* 12 April 1/3 Local Knights of Pythias will hold a special Ladies Night at the Parish House Monday evening. **1948** *Dly. Oklahoman* (Okla. City) 1 July 8/1 He is a member of the American Legion, Knights of Pythias, . . . and the Spencer Methodist church.

(5) **1865** *Nation* I. 67 A charge, which the Abolition Knights of the Circle could readily substantiate. — (6) **1861** in LOGAN *Great Conspiracy* 250 A Conspiracy for the overthrow of the Government through the military organizations, the dangerous secret order, the 'Knights of the Golden Circle,' 'Committees of Safety,' Southern leagues [etc.]. **1948** *Sat. Ev. Post* 7 Aug. 116/2 Carrington was sent from Washington to help . . . stamp out the Knights of the Golden Circle. — (7) **1931** F. L. ALLEN *Only Yesterday* 65 Here was a chance to dress up the village bigot and let him be a Knight of the Invisible Empire. — (8) **1923** *Imperial Night-hawk* 29 Aug. 2/1 The time has now come when the Knights of the Ku Klux Klan should take the leadership. **1924** *Ib.* 2 Jan. 7/3 They passed through the sublime gates of the Invisible Empire, Knights of the Ku Klux Klan, and were knighted. — (9) **1870** *Cong. Globe* 19 April 2794/3 The society called the Knights of the White Camelia . . . [wanted] to maintain the integrity and superiority of the white race. *Ib.,* Its individual members . . . coöperated with the Democratic party . . . as Democrats, and not as 'K. W. C.'s,' or Knights of the White Camelia. **1877** DIBBLE *Why Reconstr. Failed* 21 Thousands of men . . . sought relief . . . through the agency of . . . the Knights of the White Camelia, Regulators, . . . and such kindred secret organizations. **1904** FLEMING *Doc. rel. Reconstruction* No. 1, 5 The Knights of the White Camelia aimed to extend their organization over the entire United States.

***knitting,** *n.* **1. knitting bee,** a social gathering of girls and women to knit for some helpful or charitable purpose, *obs.* **2. knitting frolic,** =prec., *obs.*

(1) **1855** *Chi. Times* 19 March 2/6 This girl had been at a knitting bee, at the house of a friend. **1880** *Harper's Mag.* Sep. 508/1 In winter they sometimes had knitting bees. — (2) **1818** FEARON *Sketches* 223 [The women who have sent gifts] are invited to the preacher's house, to partake of a supper. . . . This is termed a knitting frolic.

b. *To get down, stick close* (or *attend*) *to one's knitting,* to get well into one's task, to persevere in one's efforts. *Colloq.*

1891 SLOAN *Fogy Days* 127 We were just getting down properly to our knitting in what is called the cyclone movement, when the music suddenly ceased. **1906** *Washington Post* 22 May 4 If the Senate sticks close to its knitting, . . . then it is not improbable for Congress to adjourn about June 20. **1931** *Randolph Enterprise* (Elkins, W. Va.) 9 July 1/2 Nevertheless, the house attended to its knitting and passed the bill.

* **knob,** *n.*

1. (*cap.*) *pl.* As the name of a particular region.

[**1804** MICHAUX *Voyage à l'Ouest* 256 Cet arbre s'élève rarement au-dessus de quarante pieds, et croît de préférence sur les Knobs, espèces de petits monticules.] **1817** BROWN *Western Gaz.* 44 You are not sensible of *ascending* to the height at which you find yourself, on the summit of the 'Knobs,' from which you have a boundless prospect to the east. **1873** MARK TWAIN *Gilded Age* i. 17 (R.), The district was called the 'knobs' of East Tennessee. **1906** in MARK TWAIN *Autobiog.* (1924) II. 268 (R.), His boyhood was spent up there among the knobs'—so called— of East Tennessee. **1928** *Mt. Life* (Berea, Ky.) Oct. 11/2 Stratigraphically, the rocks of the Knobs are of Siluric, Devonic, Mississippian, and occasionally Pennsylvanian ages.

2. knobcone pine, a pine, *Pinus attenuata,* found on the Pacific Coast.

1884 SARGENT *Rep. Forests* 196 *Pinus tuberculata.* . . . Knobcone Pine. **1897** SUDWORTH *Arborescent Flora* 25 *Pinus attenuata.* . . . Knobcone Pine. **1948** *Pacific Discovery* Nov.–Dec. 20/1 The knobcone pine (*Pinus tuberculata*) reseeds itself in the ashes of the parent trees.

As the last term in **beech, cedar, flint, pine, prairie knob.**

***knobby,** *a.* Covered with knobs or hills, hilly. *Colloq.* — **1869** MARK TWAIN *Innocents Abroad* xxvi. (1899) II. 327 It is as knobby with countless little domes as a prison door is with bolt-heads.

* **knock,** *v.*

1. *S. tr.* To break down (cotton stalks) by striking them with a stout stick preparatory to planting a new crop. *Colloq.*

1847 *Fla. Plant. Rec.* 216, 15 hand knocking cotton stalks.

2. To surpass, beat, cure. *Slang.*

1853 *Knickerb.* XLII. 55 He 'knocked' all the adjacent male population, native and imported, in the matter of looks. **1877** BURDETTE *Rise of Mustache* 19 Your boy . . . has a formula . . . [which] will cause warts to disappear from the hand, or, to use his own expression, will 'knock warts.' **1887** J. KIRKLAND *Zury* 112 Them [i.e., the physicians] 's kin tell what'll knock all complaints, they station in the big cities.

3. To criticize harshly. Also absol. *Slang.*

1896 G. ADE *Artie* xii. 110 He's got to make good with 'em to keep 'em from knockin. **1910** *Sat. Ev. Post* 23 July 13/3, I don't like to knock, friend; in fact, I'm a booster. **1949** *Dly. Ardmoreite* (Ardmore, Okla.) 25 Jan. 5/3, I am not knocking any of our out-of-town bakeries that come in here, but I am saying that we need not go to Texas for good bread.

4. In verbal expressions: (1) * **knock down,** see as a main entry; (2) * **off,** to auction off, *colloq.;* (3) * **out,** (*a*) of a hound, to discontinue the trail or scent in a chase, *rare,* (*b*) *fig.* to eliminate, get rid of something; (4) * **up,** (*a*) to render pregnant, *slang,* (*b*) to round up, *rare,* (*c*) to prepare (food) quickly.

(2) **1747** *Boston Selectmen* 15 April, He being the highest bidder, the same was knocked off to him. **1843** STEPHENS *High Life N.Y.* II. 35, I'll jest go down to the bar-room and see when the critter is going to be sold, and what madam it is that's going to knock her off. **1883** HOWELLS *Woman's Reason* v. 98 The auctioneer intoned his chant . . . varied with a quick 'Sold!' as . . . he knocked off this lot or that. — (3) (*a*) **1835** LONGSTREET *Ga. Scenes* 187 When the game was up, she soon 'knocked out' and went in quest of cold trails. (*b*) **1883** MARK TWAIN *Life on Miss.* 465 (R.), The religious feature has been pretty well knocked out of it [i.e., Mardi-Gras at New Orleans]. **1904** *N.Y. Sun* 5 Aug. 4 In power, the Democrats wouldn't knock out protection if they could. — (4) (*a*) **1836** CROCKETT *Adventures* 97 Negro women are knocked down by the auctioneer, and knocked up by the purchaser. **1942** BERREY & VAN DEN BARK *Amer. Thesaurus Slang* 130 Impregnate . . . jazz up, knock up. (*b*) **1844** GREGG *Commerce of Prairies* I. 63 If any animals are found 'staked' beyond the 'chartered limits,' it is the duty of the guard to 'knock them up' and turn them into the *corral.* (*c*) **1869** ALCOTT *Little Women* II. v. 61 Don't cry, dear, but just exert yourself a bit, and knock us up something to eat. **1890** *Harper's Mag.* May 894/2, I jest killed a chicken, and knocked up a few biscuit.

b. *To knock the socks off,* to beat decisively. *Slang.*

1864 *Harper's Mag.* Feb. 427/1 The good-natured people . . . predicted that when he took his seat in the House he would 'knock the socks' from some who had more reputation than he. **1883** *State Republican* (Colo. Springs, Colo.) 24 Sep. 3/1 Harvey & Parker's 'Burro' 'knox the sox' off all other cigars.

For to *knock down and drag out* see ***knock down,** *v.;* *to knock cold,* see ***cold;** *to knock the spots off,* see **spot;** *to knock out of the box,* see ***box.**

5. In noun and adj. combs.: (1) **knock about,** (*a*) a small pleasure boat or yacht, (*b*) a rough-and-tumble fight, *colloq.;* (2) **around,** a spree or frolic, *rare;* (3) **down,** see as main entry; (4) **-'em-stiff,** liquor, *slang;* (5) * **out,** see as a main entry.

(1) (*a*) **1897** *Outing* XXX. 497/1 The cat-boat, knock-about, and special classes of small yachts are well filled. **1904** *N.Y. Ev. Post* 21 May 6 There are numerous knockabouts and other small yachts in the Pawcatuck River. (*b*) **1903** LEWIS *Boss* 316 He was all for th' strong-arm, an' th' knock-about! It's a bad system. Nothin's lost by bein' smooth, Gov'nor. — (2) **1837** J. C. NEAL *Charcoal Sk.* (1838) 175 The protegé . . . longed to indulge himself in that which he classically termed a 'knock-around.' — (4) **1859** TALIAFERRO *Fisher's R.* 18 With most of the people a rifle, shot-pouch, butcher-knife, and an article they dubbed 'knock-'em-stiff' were of vastly more importance than 'larnin'.' **1905** VALENTINE *H. Sandwith* 5 Ah jedge thez plenty a knockem stiff fer the crowd.

* **knockdown,** *a.* and *n.*

1. *n.* A person or thing of some stunning or overwhelming quality. *Slang. Rare.*

1843 *Knickerb.* XXI. 484 'Tom and Jerry' ushered before a Park audience the scientific Mr. T. Belcher Kay, one of the great knock-downs of foreign celebrity.

2. The careening of a ship under the impact of heavy seas. Cf. * **knocked down 2.**

1888 *Scribner's Mag.* May 526/1 Every bit of that water came in through the hatch at the time of the knock-down.

3. (See quot.) *Rare.* Cf. **5.** below.

1875 KNIGHT *Dict. Mech.* 1239/2 *Knock-down,* a piece of furniture or other structure adapted to be disconnected at the joints so as to pack compactly.

4. An introduction. *Slang.* Cf. * **knock down,** *v.* **3.**

1896 G. ADE *Artie* vi. 59 Now, I did n't expect no knock down to his girl. **1945** *Chi. D. News* 7 Sep. 31/3, I know her well! I'll sell you a knockdown to her for two-bits.

5. *a.* Constructed so as to be easily taken apart for packing or shipment.

1795 WINTERBOTHAM *Hist. View* III. 305 Articles of exportation were . . . 231,776 Barrels of dried and pickled fish . . . 48,860 Shook or knock-down casks. **1888** *Sci. Amer.* LIX. 187 To make a knock-down wigwam, the framing should be lashed together with ropes or twine, and the bark tied to the rafters with twine. **1948** *Sierra Club* (So. Calif. Chap.) *Sched.* 129, 56 Permanently assembled but collapsible construction. Can be set up in 10 sec. Knockdown size.

6. Of or pertaining to knocking down at an auction.

1888 *Harper's Mag.* Nov. 934/2 Bills for knock-down fees are presented for payment to auctioneers every month. *Ib.* 937/2 The knock-down book records the price, buyer, and all particulars of every sale in the Auction-room.

* **knock down,** *v.*

1. *tr.* To bring down (game) with a shot.

1733 BYRD *Journey to Eden* (1901) 311 We pursued our Journey thro' uneven and perplexed Woods, and in the thickest of them had the Fortune to knock down a young Buffalo, 2 Years old. **1809** WEEMS *Marion* (1833) 100 Many a family goes without dinner, unless the father can knock down a squirrel in the woods.

2. Of a conductor, ticket-taker, etc., to steal or appropriate (fares, money, etc.). Also **knocking down.**

*a***1855** KELLEY *Humors* 86 No knocking down, sir! **1860** HOLLAND *Miss Gilbert* xii. 220 Now tell a feller: is there any chance to knock down? **1904** *N.Y. Ev. Post* 5 April 9 Two conductors on surface cars were convicted of petit larceny to-day. The men were accused of 'knocking down' fares on their cars. **1922** *Collier's* 2 Sep. 25/1 The only thing you ever knocked down in your life is nickels when you was a street car conductor.

3. (See quot.) Cf. * **knockdown,** *n.* **4.**

1916 *D.N.* IV. 325 *Knock down,* to introduce (one person to another). [Kan.] Also Pa. as early as 1890, both *v.* and *n.* (an introduction). I was knocked down to about a dozen girls at the dance. Also Mass.

4. *To knock down and drag out,* to vanquish utterly. Also transf. *Colloq.*

1842 *Knickerb.* XX. 491 If the wife ran in debt, or . . . knocked down and dragged out a fellow-citizen, the man and wife were one. **1882** C. B. LEWIS *Lime-Kiln Club* 291 To say that the prominent members were pleased, gratified, knocked down and dragged out, would not cover the case.

b. Hence *knock-down and drag-out*, a free-for-all, rough-and-tumble fight. Also transf. and with adjectival and adverbial force. *Colloq.*

1827 COOPER *Prairie* iv, It was thinking of what you call consequences . . . that prevented me from . . . making it a real knock-down and drag-out. **1834** *Amer. R.R. Jrnl.* III. 304/1 He was one of our careless unconcerned knock down and drag out looking sort of fellows. **1932** *Tulsa D. World* 13 March v. 2/3 It now looks as though a knock-down-and-drag-out battle between Roosevelt and Smith forces would feature the Democratic primaries.

***knocked down. 1.** =**knockdown,** *a.* and *n.* **5. 2.** (See quot. and cf. **knockdown,** *a.* and *n.* **2.**)

(1) 1776 *R.I. Col. Rec.* (1862) VII. 571 Shaken or knocked down casks. **1924** MCCONNELL *Frontier Law* 13 A few days after my arrival at camp we received a big load of harness, 'knocked down'; that is, the parts had not been put together. — **(2) 1891** PATTERSON *Illust. Naut. Dict.* 104 *Knocked down,* said of a vessel when, by the force of the wind acting upon her sails and spars, she is careened to such an extent that she does not recover herself.

***knocker,** *n.* One who "knocks" (sense **3.**); a fault-finder (see also quot. 1909). *Slang.* Cf. **Negro knocker.**

1900 *Everybody's Mag.* II. 585/2 Knocker—n. One who 'knocks.' A discontented actor who generally receives less than $40. a week. **1909** *Washington Post* 20 Feb. 1 The 'Knockers' are an organization of Cincinnati's most prominent business men. . . . The business of the 'Knockers' is to knock hard and effectively everything tending to hinder the material advancement of the city. **1945** *Chi. D. News* 22 March 10/4 Not desiring to be a knocker; yet I fail to see improvement in Chicago's transportation.

***knockout,** *n.*

1. *Polo.* (See quots.)

1894 in M. H. HAYES *Mod. Polo* (1896) 314 When the ball goes out ends, the side defending that goal is entitled to a knock out from the point at which it crossed the line. When the player having the knock out causes unnecessary delay, the Referee may throw a ball on the field and call play. **1897** *Outing* XXX. 486/2 The ball . . . is the property of the side defending that goal, the captain of which team is entitled to a knockout from the point at which the ball crossed the line.

2. A striking or outstanding success. *Slang.*

1909 *Sat. Ev. Post* 5 June 17/2 A knockout. . . . Pronounced success. **1917** MCCUTCHEON *Green Fancy* 342 The gross was $359. The instant that fact became known to Mr. Rushcroft he informed Barnes that they had a 'knockout,' a gold mine, and that never in all his career had he known a season to start off so auspiciously.

b. Esp. an extremely beautiful or attractive woman.

1926 *Ladies' Home Jrnl.* Nov. 13 Only it isn't very exciting for him, and I'm no knock-out to introduce around. **1931** *K.C. Star* 28 Sep., Her nose is long and she has gray-green eyes and blond hair. She's a knockout in her clothes and a grand cook. **1949** *Sat. Ev. Post* 27 Aug. 85/2 You shouldn't let the fact that she's a knockout stand in your way.

3. knockout drops, drops of some powerful stupefying drug slipped into one's drink preparatory to robbing him. *Slang.*

1896 HASWELL *New York* 309 Neither were there any . . . rum and policy shops . . . where 'knock-out drops' . . . were administered to a casual patron. **1947** *Chi. D. News* 14 Jan. 4/3 Do girls now use tear gas instead of knockout drops?

4. knockout man, a criminal who uses knockout drops. *Slang.*

1903 *N.Y. Ev. Post* 18 Sep. 7 He may be one of the new sort of 'knockout men' discovered this week. **1928** *Sat. Ev. Post* 12 May 90/2 They're murderers and knockout men and they never play a straight game.

***knot,** *n.* In combs.: (1) **knot bowl, dish,** a bowl or dish made from a knot, *obs.;* (2) **root,** (see quot.); (3) **-root grass,** an American grass, *Muhlenbergia mexicana,* valued as hay and as a soil preserver.

(1) 1733 BENJAMIN LYNDE *Diary* (1880) 45, I paid Mrs. Hewins for cedar baskets, knot bowls and broom, 55s. **1769** PATTEN *Diary* 228, I turned a knot dish that holds about 2 quarts in the forenoon and in the afternoon john and I went to the meadow. [**1826** COOPER *Mohicans* vi, He tendered . . . the venison in a trencher, really carved from the knot of the pepperage.] — **(2) 1837** DARLINGTON *Flora Cestrica* 349 Canadian Collinsonia. *Vulgo*—Knot-root. Horse Balm. — **(3) 1895** *Dept. Agric. Yrbk. 1894* 434 *Knot-root grass* is very common along river banks, usually where the soil is somewhat sandy.

As the last term in **black, forty, goat, lightwood, love, pine, pitch, tar, topknot.**

***knotting,** *n.* (See quot.) *Rare.* — **1867** *Ill. Agric. Soc. Trans.* VII. 505 *Knotting,* or hardening of the fruit, is a disease not very prevalent [in the pear].

***know,** *v.* In colloq. expressions: (1) *I want to know,* well, well! do tell! is it possible? (2) *as I know on,* so far as I know; (3) *what do you know about that?* isn't that amazing? well, I never.

(1) 1833 NEAL *Down-Easters* I. 45, I *want* to know! exclaimed the other down-easter. Well you *do* know, replied the southerner. **1921** PAINE *Comr. Rolling Ocean* 169 And you come from North Dakoty! I want to know. — **(2) 1835** *Jrnl. Excursion U.S. 1834* 159 A few of the Yankeeisms [are] . . . a tarnal lie—not as I know on [etc.]. **1887** WILKINS *Humble Romance* 72, I don't know what you mean as I knows on. — **(3) 1914** ATHERTON *Perch of Devil* I. xvii. 103 What do you know about that? **1916** B. M. BOWER *Phantom Herd* ii. 33 Now what do you know about that, Mig?

know-how ˈnoˌhaʊ, *n.* The ability to do something. Also attrib. *Colloq.*

1857 *Spirit of Times* 26 Dec. 270/3 'No, no, Massa,' replied the gentleman from Africa, 'charge fifty cents for killing, and fifty for the know how.' **1898** *Me. Exp. Sta. Ann. Rep.* 170 Patience and a little of the 'know how' will overcome all of these. **1904** *Dly. Public Opinion* (Watertown, S.D.) 28 Dec. 8/6 Wanted—A 'know how man' for the Kellogg House, Hazel, S.D. A good place for one that can keep a good hotel. **1949** *Chi. D. News* 18 Feb. 5/2 But this authority needed, and still needs, Germans to apply the know how.

***Know-Nothing,** *n.*

1. A member of the Know-Nothing party. Now *hist.*

1854 *Cong. Globe* 10 July 1667/2 That misguided and proscriptive faction, called 'Native Americans' or 'Know-Nothings.' **1872** *Newton Kansan* 3 Oct. 4/3 Mr. Wilson was a Know-Nothing. **1948** *Chickasha* (Okla.) *D. Express* 4 July 7/3 Members of the American party, called the Know-Nothings, had forcibly seized the records of the society and assumed control.

attrib. **1854** *S. Lit. Messenger* XX. 540/1 This Know Nothing movement will prove to be . . . a giant evil. **1888** *N.Y. World* May (F.), During the days of Know Nothing excitement he was an active sympathizer with that party. **1948** *Chi. Tribune* 4 Jan. 1. 4/4 Millard Fillmore received Maryland's 8 electoral votes on the American, or Know Nothing, ticket.

b. (See quot.), said to be in allusion to a governor of the Know-Nothing party who secured the passage of a law compelling trains to stop at such crossings. *Obs.*

1885 *Mag. Amer. Hist.* XIII. 202 A curious local meaning is found in Massachusetts, where the crossing of two railroads at grade is termed a 'Know Nothing.'

2. Know-Nothing party, the popular name for a secret political party composed chiefly of those who were alarmed about the increasing influence in political affairs of newly arrived foreigners and Roman Catholics. Now *hist.* Cf. **Dark Lantern party.**

In this short-lived party (*c*1852–55) membership was divided into three classes. Members of the third class were pledged to reply "I don't know" to all questions about the party, hence the name. In 1855 the official title "American party" was adopted.

1854 *S. Lit. Messenger* XX. 542/2 The great Know Nothing party desire a presidential candidate. **1893** *Chi. Record* 3 July 9/2 The American Protective association . . . is the old know-nothing party revived, being intensely anti-catholic in its aims and objects. **1945** BOTKIN *My Burden* 185 He belonged to the Know Nothing party, and he was a real leader in it.

***Know-Nothingism,** *n.* The principles of the Know-Nothing party. Now *hist.*

1854 *Maysville* (Ky.) *Eagle* 21 Nov. 2/4 Know Nothingism. . . . Character, Principles, and Objects of the Native American Party. **1876** *Dly. Silver State* (Union, Nev.) 4 Oct. 2/1 The Alliance is a new name for the . . . secret political organization, which was generally known as Know Nothingism. **1903** *N.Y. Ev. Post.* 28 Oct. 4 Irishmen who were fixed for life in the Democratic party by the bitter Knownothingism of years ago.

Know-Something. A member of a projected political party in opposition to the Know-Nothings. *Obs.* — **1855** *N.Y. Wkly. Tribune* 26 May 4/5 In the meantime the Know-Somethings are making sad ravages among the fold of Sam. **1856** (*title of broadside*), Platform of principles of New York know somethings.

***knuck,** *n.* [In sense **1.** cf. *OED knucker,* a pickpocket.]

1. A pickpocket; a thug who uses brass knucks. *Slang.*

1865 *Sun. Mercury* (Phila.) 3 Sep. 4/2 The knuck's plan of pulling away a watch or a pocket-book requires considerable skill. **1893** *Cong. Rec.* H.R. Rep. 2242/2 They employ knucks, bounty-jumpers, pocketbook-droppers, plug-uglies, heelers . . . and all other criminal vermin.

2. *pl.* =**brass knuckles.**

1913 *Sat. Ev. Post* 17 May 50 The fat fist armed with a set of murderously heavy knucks. **1947** *Chi. Tribune* 21 July 22 One kid landed a pretty good punch, but I shook 'em off with the 'knucks.'

***knuckle,** *n.*

1. *pl.* Short for brass knuckles or iron knuckles *qq.v.*

1860 G. C. Lewis *Letters* (1870) 380 A most formidable weapon, similar to the steel knuckles of the Yankees. **1895** *Morning Patriot* 7 July 11/3 These visitors were armed with pistols, knives, and knuckles.

2. In combs.: (1) **knuckle ball,** in baseball, a slow ball in throwing which the pitcher grasps the ball so that the knuckles of the first joints of his three middle fingers press firmly upon it; (2) **dabster,** (see quot.); (3) **duster,** (*a*) (see quot. 1858 and cf. **brass knuckles**), (*b*) a small derringer designed for use also as a kind of brass knuckles.

(1) **1910** *Amer. Mag.* Jan. 382/2 Summers possesses the art of pitching the most marvelous 'knuckle ball' ever delivered. **1949** *Chi. D. News* 5 March 15/1 'Leonard may never lose a game in Wrigley Field,' he said, 'if you got a catcher who can hold that knuckle ball.' — (2) **1890** Howells *Boy's Town* 82 You could use a knuckle-dabster of fur or cloth to rest your hand on [in playing marbles], but it was considered effeminate. — (3) (*a*) **1858** *Times* (London) 15 Feb. (F. and H.), Knuckle-duster, . . . a formidable American instrument, made of brass, which slips easily on to the four fingers of the hand, and having a projected surface, across the knuckles, is calculated, in a pugilistic encounter to inflict serious injury on the person against whom it is directed. **1949** *N.O. Times-Picayune Mag.* 3 April 25/2 A glorious free-for-all ensued, a primitive battle of fists, clubs, rocks, knuckle-dusters and steel bars. (*b*) **1948** *Chi. Tribune* 7 March 1. 38/5 Allen fashioned a multi-barreled gun, which, in even more curious form, came out as 'the knuckle duster.'

***knuckle,** *v.* **To knuckle* (*down*), to apply oneself earnestly and seriously *to* something. *Colloq.*

1864 Webster 743/3 *To knuckle to*, . . . to apply one's self vigorously. **1882** in *Frontier* X. (1930) 249/1 The work is awful hard but I am going to nuckle down to it and put it through. **1948** *Atlantic Mo.* March 40/2 He insists that they knuckle down to business about all the time.

***knuckler,** *n.* =**knuckle ball.** — **1928** G. H. Ruth *Baseball* vi. 79 Eddie used to toss 'knucklers' until he had the hitters blue in the face. **1948** *N.Y. Times* 23 May v. 3/1 Casey, a fast ball pitcher, . . . also throws a sweeping curve and a knuckler with surprising efficiency.

K.O. A Whig perversion of **O.K.** *Rare.* — **1840** *N.Y. Times* 6 April 2/2 The K.O. system is working admirably. It was first put in operation at Masonic Hall on Friday night, March 27th, where the bullying O.K.'s, who attempted to disturb and break up a peaceable meeting of citizens were Kicked Out.

Koasati koə'sɑtɪ, *n.* [f. a native word or words of unknown significance. The form here is also used as a pl., but that with *-s* is more common.] (See quot. 1907.)

1817 *N.Y. Herald* 24 Sep. 2/4 The Coshattes, Tankawahs and Caddo's of Red river, and the Cherokees of the Arkansas, complain that the Osages are perpetually sending strong war parties into their country. **1907** Hodge *Amer. Indians* I. 719/2 Koasati. An Upper Creek tribe speaking a dialect almost identical with Alibamu and evidently nothing more than a large division of that people. **1934** Foreman *Five Civilized Tribes* 104 The Chickasaw had been annoyed by roving bands of Delawares, Shawnees, Kickapoos, . . . and Koasati.

b. The language of these Indians.

1949 *Int. Jrnl. Amer. Linguistics* April 122/2 Koasati has three main paradigmatic classes.

Kodak 'kodæk, *n.* Also **kodak.** [Coined as a trademark by George Eastman. See Mencken, *Supp.* I. 342.]

1. A small camera made by the Eastman Kodak Company. Also erroneously used of small cameras of other makes.

1888 *Patent Off. Gazette* XLIV. 1072/1 Photographic Cameras and Sensitized Plates and Film Therefor.—The Eastman Dry Plate and Film Company. . . . 'The word "Kodak."' **1899** *Scribner's Mag.* XXV. 65 (*advt.*), There *is* no Kodak but the Eastman Kodak. 'Kodak' is a Trade Name applied by us to cameras and other goods of our manufacture. We originated and registered the word 'Kodak.' The trade-mark is our exclusive property. **1943** Crow *Amer. Customer* 227 The bicycle and the Kodak flourished together.

attrib. **1890** *N. & Q.* April 12 (*advt.*), New Kodak Cameras. 'You press the button, we do the rest.' **1894** *Forum* June, The Kodet is the youngest member of the Kodak family. **1912** Nicholson *Hoosier Chron.* 323 This item was among the 'Kodak Shots' subjoined to the 'Advertiser's' account of the convention.

2. A small picture made with a kodak. In full **kodak picture.**

1898 *N.Y. Observer* 3 March 258/1 Some of the rest took kodaks of us. **1906** L. Bell *C. Lee* 244, I enclose the kodak I took of it, for I know you won't believe me else. **1914** *Sunset* Jan. 81/1 In the office of the captain of detectives in the city of San Francisco there used to be upon the captain's desk a framed enlargement of a kodak picture.

3. Kodak Convention, (see quot. and cf. quot. 1890 under **1.** above). *Obs.*

1914 *Cyclo. Amer. Govt.* III. 324 Snappers. A nickname applied to the machine Democrats in New York in 1892, who, under the leadership of David B. Hill, held a very early state convention on short notice, called a 'snap' convention (Feb. 22, 1892). . . . This convention was also called the 'Kodak Convention'—the boss manipulator pressing the button and the obedient 'snapper' delegates doing the rest.

4. kodak girl, a pretty girl, one worth "kodaking." *Colloq.*

1912 Nicholson *Hoosier Chron.* 450, I reckon you can hardly call Marion a kodak girl. **1943** Crow *Amer. Customer* 225 There was a chorus of Kodak girls and two of them sang a song.

kodak 'kodæk, *v. tr.* and *intr.* To photograph with a kodak.

1891 *Int. Ann.: Anthony's Photog. Bul.* IV. 59 A next door neighbor, who is just beginning to 'kodak.' **1894** *Outing* Feb. 369/1 A walrus seized our commander Prof. Heilprin's oar as he was about to kodak the animal. **1904** O. Henry *Cabbages & Kings* 8 The tintype man, the enlarged photograph brigand, the kodaking tourist . . . carry on the work.

kolf baan. [Du.] (See quot. 1931.) *Obs.*

1788 *Charleston City Gaz. & Advt.* 18 Sep., There is lately erected that pleasing and genteel amusement, the Kolf Baan. Any person wishing to treat for the same at private sale, will please apply to David Denoon. [**1931** A. J. Barnouw in *Netherland-Amer. Foundation Mo. Letter* 4 In the eighteenth century the game [kolf] began to be played on specially prepared kolf courses or malls. . . . These malls were usually covered by a tiled wooden roof, but open on the sides. The length of the course was no more than eighty feet, and its width seldom more than twenty. A stake in the shape of a huge ninepin stood at either end, and the ball was driven from one to the other across a course of loam mixed with mortar and beaten into a hard, smooth surface.]

Kootenay 'kutə͵ne, *n.* [f. their native name.] *collect.* and *pl.* (See quot. 1907.) Also attrib. Cf. ***long knife c.**

1826 *McLoughlin Letters* (1941) I. 28 Between the Kootonais and Flat Heads their is an Increase of three hundred and Eighty Beaver. **1855** *N.Y. Wkly. Tribune* 15 Sep. 6/1 Gov. Stevens has effected treaties with the Flat Head, Kootenah, and Kalispee tribes of Indians. **1907** Hodge *Amer. Indians* I. 740/2 Kutenai. . . . A people forming a distinct linguistic stock, the Kitunahan family of Powell, who inhabit parts of s.e. British Columbia and n. Montana and Idaho. **1938** Thompson *High Trails* 137 In olden days the Flatheads and Kootenais came this way each year to get their buffalo for pemmican.

Also **Kootenay Indians.**

1947 *Trail Riders Bul.* Feb. 2/2 For one of its forks is worn deep by the cavalcades of Stoney and Kootenay Indians. **1948** *Sierra Club Bul.* Sep.–Oct. 12/1 Trees more than two hundred years old can be found growing in trails made by the Kooteni Indians, trails still uneroded in dense timber.

kooyah 'kujɑ, *n.* (See quot. 1907.) Also attrib.

1843 T. Talbot *Journals* 45 We traded some Kooyah or Black root . . . a black, sticky, suspicious looking compound, of very disagreeable odor. . . . It is a very palatable and soon a favorite mess. **1843** Frémont *Exped.* 135, I ate here, for the first time, the *kooyah*, or tobacco root, (*valeriana edulis*,) the principal edible root among the Indians who inhabit the upper waters of the streams on the western side of the mountains. **1845** *Ib.* 273 The kooyah plant . . . is the best remedial plant known among those Indians. **1907** Hodge *Amer. Indians* I. 725/2 Kooyah. A root (*Valeriana edulis*), also known as 'tobacco root,' from which a bread is made by some of the Indians of the Oregon region. The word is from one of the Shahaptian or Shoshonean dialects.

korl kɔrl, *n.* [Origin unknown.] (See first quot.) Also attrib. — **1861** *Atlantic Mo.* April 435/1 In the neighboring furnace-buildings lay great heaps of the refuse from the ore after the pig-metal is run. *Korl* we call it here [in the iron mills]: a light, porous substance, of a delicate, waxen, flesh-colored tinge. *Ib.* 450/2 A wan, woful face, through which the spirit of the dead korl-cutter looks out.

***kosher,** *a. fig.* Fine, all right, legitimate. *Slang.*

1924 *Cosmopolitan* Nov. 104/2 It don't sound kosher to *me!* **1926** *Collier's* 19 June 6/4 Barbara agrees with him and it was kosher with me too. **1948** *Milwaukee Jrnl.* 18 July 6/1 Four game wardens checked the lakes in one fell swoop, for licenses. Everything kosher, including residents and non residents.

Kossuth hat. [Louis *Kossuth* (1802–94), Hungarian patriot who visited the U.S. in 1851.] A hat having an oval, flat-topped crown and a roll brim. *Obs.*

1852 G. W. BUNGAY *Crayon Sk.* (1854) 372 She wears . . . a Kossuth hat instead of a 'kiss-me-quick.' **1870** O. LOGAN *Before Footlights* 194 But it was funny, wasn't it, to see a charger all out of drawing, carrying a rider, whose only really distinguishable article of apparel was a Kossuth hat. **1905** VALENTINE *H. Sandwith* 8 Davis Sandwith, entering the shed, shaking the sparks from his Kossuth hat.

kouse kaʊs, *n.* [See quot. 1896.] = **cowish.** Also attrib. with *root.* — **1896** *Garden & Forest* IX. 282 *Kouse, or Kouse-root.*—From *kowish*, the Nez-Perce (Shahaptian) name of the root, which is used by these and other Indians for bread making. **1907** HODGE *Amer. Indians* I. 728 Kouse. A plant (*Peucedanum ambiguum*) used by the Indians of the Columbia-Oregon region for making bread.

K.P., see **kitchen police.**

krieker ˈkrikɚ, *n.* (See quot. 1888.)

1866 R. B. ROOSEVELT *Game-Birds N. States* 160 Krieker Meadow Snipe Fat Bird Short Neck Jacksnipe. **1888** G. TRUMBULL *Names of Birds* 176 At Newport, R.I., on Long Island . . . , and at Barnegat, N.J., [the pectoral sandpiper is called] Krieker. . . . It was not applied . . . because of the bird's creaking note, but because of its crouching or squatting habit—German *Kriecher*, a cringing person. [*c*1937 C. A. URNER *Christmas Poems* 14 You have seen Cock Robin's striking head; The Krinkers in the grass.]

Kriss Kringle. [G. *Christkindl, -del,* dim. of *Christkind.*] Santa Claus. Also attrib.

1830 WATSON *Philadelphia* 242 Every father in his turn remembers the excitements of his youth in Belsh-nichel and Christ-kinkle nights. **1864** *Sacramento Union* 7 Jan. 5/2, I do not know whether the good Saint Nicholas rejoices in your locality in the name of Santa Claus, as he does here [N.J.], or whether he answers in those regions to the musical title of Kriss Kringle, as in the Queen City. **1947** *Chi. Tribune* 20 July IV. 3/1 It is the story of an old man whose name was Kris Kringle and who believed he really was Santa Claus.

kroosken ˈkroskən, *n.* [Dim. of Du. *kroes*, mug, jug. See *kroos* in *Br. Wtb.*] A small mug or jar. *Rare.* — **1829** in *Amer. Sp.* XXI. (1946) 117/2 After the barbacue was over and Mr. Clay had washed down the pig and a kroosken of apple-toddy, he mounted a porch and said grace in a speech.

krummholz ˈkrʊmholts, *n.* [G., "crooked wood."] A region, usu. alpine, characterized by a growth of stunted or scrub trees. — **1908** *Bot. Gaz.* May 333 The Krummholz is composed of two trees only, *Pinus flexilis* and *Picea Engelmanni*, the former on the ridges, the latter in the cañons. **1942** PEATTIE *Friendly Mts.* 162 The upper part of the spruce slope dwindles to a 'scrub' forest, or 'krummholz.'

kudzu ˈkʊdzu, *n.* [Jap.] (See quot. 1909.) Also **kudzu vine.** — **1909** WEBSTER, kudzu vine. . . . A fabaceous plant of China and Japan (*Pueraria thunbergiana*) widely cultivated for its ample foliage and spikes of fragrant purple flowers. The stems yield the fiber known as kohemp. **1948** *Atlantic Mo.* Nov. 60/1 Kudzu, a coarse, rapidly growing legume of incredible efficiency in checking gullies, restoring drainage, and storing nitrogen, came from Japan.

Ku-Klux ˈkjuˌklʌks, *n.* [Gk. *kyklos*, circle.] Short for Ku-Klux Klan *q.v.* Also *collect.* or *pl.*, the members of this.

1868 in CLARK *Pills* (1944) 62 We are inclined to think he is somewhat disloyal, and may be in sympathy with the Ku Kluxes. **1876** *Moving Ball* (Marlin, Tex.) 23 March 2/5 Bell was murdered by the ku-klux. **1922** *Dly. Ardmoreite* (Ardmore, Okla.) 8 Jan. 7/4 In Ponca City the Ku-Klux have subscribed $50 to the annual budget of the Humane Society. **1946** *Negro Digest* Aug. 30/2 The Ku Klux will get you if you don't watch out.

attrib. **1868** *Independent Monitor* (Tuscaloosa, Ala.) 1 Sep. 2 He is a cur with a contracted head, downward look, slinking and uneasy gait; sleeps in the woods, like old Crossland, at the least idea of a Ku-Klux raid. **1872** *Atlantic Mo.* March 386 The first step consisted of an arrest of the governor and his confederates under the Ku-Klux Act. **1945** *Somerset News* 15 March 1/2 Men willing to face defeat at the polls if they have stood for principles of law not exactly favored in Ku Klux circles.

b. Also, rarely, **Ku-Kluxic, Ku-Kluxish.**

1873 *Newton Kansan* 5 June 3/4 This morning a tall . . . Ku Kluxic looking stranger arrived here. **1948** *So. Wkly.* 3 July 13/3 A member of the 'Black Raiders,' a Ku Kluxish outfit that took it upon itself to flog folks whose ways it didn't like down in the vicinity of Atlanta, was sentenced to a year in prison.

Ku-Klux ˈkjuˌklʌks, *v.* Also **ku-klux.** *tr.* To treat (one) after the fashion of the Ku-Kluxers.

1871 *Ku Klux Klan Rep.* VI. 107 [The Negro] supposed . . . that he was going to ku-klux the Ku-Klux. *Ib.* 364, I considered that I had done nothing to be Ku-Kluxed for. **1882** *Atlantic Mo.* July 106/2 It made the Ku-Klukers feel sorter solemn when the niggers tuck to Ku-Klukin' *them.* **1945** BOTKIN *My Burden* 251 He says, 'That damn rascal ought to be Ku Kluxed.'

Ku-Kluxer ˈkjuˌklʌksɚ, *n.* Also **Ku-Klucker.** A member of the Ku-Klux Klan.

1880 TOURGEE *Bricks* 274 Jes let 'em come . . . Ku Kluckers or sheriffs, it don't make no difference which. **1887** *Cent. Mag.* XXXIV. 550/1 He run'd en tole Mars . . . dat de Kukluckers wuz atter 'im. **1948** *So. Wkly.* 3 July 13/2 The recent raid by a gang of Ku Kluxers on a Girl Scout camp near Birmingham . . . was one of the most vicious, dastardly and stupid outrages of its kind that has been committed in the South in years.

Ku-Kluxers (*c*1872)

Ku-Kluxery ˈkjuˌklʌksərɪ, *n.* Conduct such as that of Ku-Kluxers, underhanded skulduggery and connivings in general.

1876 *Harper's Wkly.* 5 Aug. 631/2 The negro slaughters, and every kind and degree of Ku-Kluxery, are not due to negro insults and outrages, but to the deep and deadly contempt and hatred of the negroes upon the part of brutalized whites. **1926** *Amer. Mercury* Jan. 127/1 But the facts that he has amassed will not be disposed of by such Ku Kluxery. **1942** *Va. Quart. Rev.* XVIII. 71 Forgetting them for a time in favor of the primary problems of the world may do something to save the South from a mess of Communism and Ku Kluxery after the war.

Ku-Kluxism ˈkjuˌklʌksɪzəm, *n.* The principles and practices of the Ku-Klux Klan. *Obs.*

1868 *N.Y. Herald* 30 July 5/2 A Bill to Punish Ku-Kluxism—Selection of Electors. **1880** TOURGEE *Invisible Empire* 491 It was in a soil thus prepared that Ku-Kluxism struck its roots wide and deep. **1923** *Nation* 4 July 18 Ku Kluxism in the Schools. **1949** *Sat. Ev. Post* 18 June 96/3, I shall simply continue to oppose Ku Kluxism, imperialism, fascism and communism whether in America, Indonesia or behind the Iron Curtain.

Ku-Klux Klan ˈkjuˌklʌksˈklæn, *n.* Also **Ku Klux Klan.** [See **Ku-Klux,** *n.*] A secret organization that arose in the South immediately after the Civil War, designed chiefly to preserve native white supremacy in the South.

"The Ku Klux Klan was one of the secret revolutionary organizations of southern whites, whose objects were to oppose what the founders believed to be the chief objects of the congressional plan of reconstruction. The name of this organization was also applied in popular usage to all of the secret political orders existing in the South from 1865 to 1877" (*Cyclo. Amer. Govt.* II. 282/2).

1868 *N.Y. Herald* 1 July 6/4 If the Democratic Convention can only be induced . . . at the dictation of the Knights of the Golden Circle and the Ku Klux Klan, to place upon their tickets some copperhead opponent of the war, the radicals will have a clear track next November. **1890** *Cent. Mag.* Dec. 306, I was warned against the Ku Klux Klan, that's all. **1949** *Reader's Digest* March 23/1 At a time when the Ku Klux Klan was riding in the South, my father refused to hate any man.

b. A secret fraternal order incorporated in Georgia in 1915, based on the earlier Klan and advocating native white Protestant supremacy. Also any one of various local organizations modeled on or inspired by this.

[**1920** *N.Y. Times* 11 Oct. 1/2 The old Ku Klux Klan has been reorganized and is regularly chartered under the laws of Georgia.] **1949**

L.A. Times 13 June 10/1 These bums, hoodlums and cutthroats, otherwise known as the Ku Klux Klan, are on the prowl again.

c. Hence (1) **Ku-Klux Klaner,** (2) **Klanism,** (3) **Klansman.**

(1) **1923** *Nation* 11 July 35 He will help his fellow Ku Klux Klaners. — (2) **1924** J. M. MECKLIN *Ku Klux Klan* 98, I have yet to come in contact with the first trace of Ku Klux Klanism. **1943** MENEFEE *Assignment* 61 The Louisiana Legislature called upon the FBI and the Dies Committee to investigate this new form of Ku Klux Klanism, but without results when this was written. — (3) **1868** in HORN *Invisible Empire* (1939) 335 Let every Ku Klux Klansman heed The General Order of General Meade. **1948** *Time* 15 March 29/2 Last week Georgia's Grand Dragon Samuel Green carefully explained that Ku Klux Klansmen wore masks to protect themselves against the prejudice of Jews, Catholics and foreigners.

kunzite ˈkʊntsaɪt, *n.* [Named after George F. *Kunz* (1856–1932), a N.Y. mineralogist.] (See quot. 1909.)

1909 *Cent. Supp.* 693/2 kunzite. . . . A transparent pink-and-purple lilac variety of spodumene. It is found in crystals near Pala, San Diego county, California, and affords gems weighing from 1 to 200 carats each. **1916** *Sunset* Oct. 68/2 In America it is known as the Kunzite and in England as the California Iris. **1949** *Rocks & Minerals* March–April 177 Kunzite. A perfect pear shaped stone of good color, 4.70 carats, $50.00.

kyack ˈkaɪæk, *n. W.* [Origin obscure. Prob. f. an Indian or Sp. term.] A form of packsack consisting of two hollow containers swung on either side of a packsaddle.

1907 WHITE *Arizona Nights* 17 We skirmished around and found a condemned army pack saddle with aparejos, and a sawbuck saddle with kyacks. On these we managed to condense our grub and utensils. **1913** *Outing* Jan. 425/2 The alforjas are constructed of heavy duck and leather, and of the same dimensions as the kyack. **1948** *Sierra Club Bul.* Dec. 2/2 He must therefore plod on trails engineered for stock that don't like a steep ascent and don't mind getting wet up to the kyacks at a stream crossing.

L

* **L,** *n.*

1. A fifty-dollar bill. *Obs.*

1839 *Spirit of Times* 13 April 66/3 (We.), I had no idea of betting more than an 'L,' or a 'C.' **1845** *St. Louis Reveille* 2 May 2/1 'You are as lucky as a jailor,' I remarked, as my friend began to smooth down the V's, X's, L's and C's.

2. *attrib.* Short for "elevated," with reference to trains and railroads. *Colloq.* Cf. **El.**

1879 *N.Y. Herald* 19 Sep. 8/4 The crowds at the Park place station of the Metropolitan 'L' road, . . . have apparently been unprecedently large. **1899** *Chi. D. News* 15 May 1/2 Through trains to Oak Park over the Lake street 'L' extension are now running. **1946** *Ib.* 24 May 1/2 The 'L' jam was further complicated as riders found earlier tickets voided by the increase in fares.

labor ˈlebɚ, *n.*[1] [See note.]

App. f. F. *labour.* Cf. 1694 *Dict.Fr. Acad.*, "Labouré, -ée, participe. *Champ labouré. Terres labourées*"; also 1769 Richelet, *Dict. Langue Frçse.* "Labour. . . . Une terre qui est en labour." The presence here of Huguenots may account for the word.

A piece of plowed land. Also attrib. *Obs.*

1694 *N.C. Col. Rec.* I. 410 Ordered that the dividing line between the sd Benjamin Gidion and the sd Orphan shall begin about the length of a chaine up the swamp from a little house built upon Alexander Speeds labour and shall run paralel with Cornelius Lerrys side line. **1816** U. BROWN *Journal* I. 269 Finds ½ a ⅓ & ⅔ Labor Lots taxed in the name of George Dyke.

labor ləˈbor, *n.*[2] [Sp. in Amer. Sp. sense shown in **1.**]

1. (See quots. 1905, 1948.)

1824 DEWEES *Lett. From Texas* 50 Every single man, who receives land under the Mexican government, on marrying, is entitled to an augmentation of his claim, to a league and labor of land. **1905** *Forestry Bureau Bul.* No. 62, 33 Under the law to which reference was made the unit of measurement was a vara (about 331-3 inches); a square of land measuring 1,000 varas on a side was a labor (about 177 acres). **1948** *True* May 123/2 The land was apportioned to the settlers at the rate of . . . one *labor* (177 acres) to each family that preferred dirt farming.

2. (See quot.)

1890 *Cent.* 3317/1 *Labor*, . . . in the quicksilver-mines of California any place where work has been or is going on; especially, in the plural, those parts of the mine from which ore is being extracted in some quantity; workings.

* **labor,** *n.*[3]

1. Among the Shakers, the dancing used in their ceremonies of worship. *Obs.*

1832 WILLIAMSON *Maine* II. 699 The Shakers live in families, having . . . a house of public worship, which they call their *Temple*. Here both sexes join in acts and exercises of devotion, which they denominate 'labor.' **1841** BUCKINGHAM *America* II. 60 The assembly then formed itself into another order for the dancing, which is called by them 'labour.'

2. In combs.: (1) **labor baron,** a man of influence and power among laborers; (2) **boss,** one who "bosses" or controls labor, *colloq.;* (3) **Bureau,** see as a main entry; (4) **candidate,** a person nominated for office by a labor party; (5) **convention,** a convention held by a labor party; (6) **Day,** a day established as a holiday in honor of labor, now the first Monday in September; (7) **party,** any one of various U.S. political parties claiming to represent especially the interests of labor, cf. **Union Labor party;** (8) **pass,** a railroad pass to a place where labor is needed, as to harvest fields; (9) **reform,** see as a main entry; (10) **union,** a union of laborers, esp. of those engaged in a particular craft, a trade union.

(1) *a*1889 *Chi. Inter-Ocean* (F.), I have observed in all the 'steam rail baron's' reply to 'fair trade' that he calls upon the 'iron ore barons' and the 'labor barons' to aid him in meeting European competition. — (2) **1903** *McClure's Mag.* Nov. 40/1 The arrogance of the Labor Boss, . . . is largely traceable to this courting of the labor monopoly by both parties. — (4) **1888** *Amer. Almanac* 222 Of the scattering votes, . . . 4,434 [were] for the Labor candidate for Governor.

(5) **1872** *N.Y. Herald* 23 Feb. 10/1 The National Labor Convention reassembled at ten o'clock this morning. — (6) [**1884** *N.Y. Herald* 2 Sep. 3/3 This . . . is a day that should be honored above all others. It is in honor of the greatest of saints—St. Labor. . . . What we want is to have the 1st of September set apart every year as a holiday for workingmen.] **1887** *Oregon Laws* 86 The first Saturday of June of each and every year [shall] be . . . set apart and declared to be a public holiday under the name and title of Labor day. **1948** *Chi. D. News* 11 June 16/3 As things stand now, only the Labor Day holiday always falls on a week-end. — (7) **1886** *Public Opinion* 13 Nov. 1/1 These voters wish to be considered the Labor party, as if there were no other. **1913** LAFOLLETTE *Autobiog.* 17 A Labor party was organized to agitate the problems of capital and labor. [**1949** *Sat. Ev. Post* 22 Jan. 17/1 The Democrats are the labor party.] — (8) **1891** ROBERTS *Adrift Amer.* 194 Knowing that there was a chance of getting sent out on a 'labour pass' to almost any part of the States from Kansas City in Missouri, I determined to go there.

(10) **1883** HAY *Bread-Winners* 183 The labor unions have ordered a general strike. **1948** *Dallas Morning News* 5 Dec. 1. 1/2 That would prevent individual states from going beyond the federal law with strong regulations of labor unions.

As the last term in **free, hard, home, Knights of, manual, Negro, organized, Secretary of, white labor.**

Labor Bureau. 1. A department in a state government concerned with the problems of labor. **2. Bureau of Labor,** the department or office in the federal government now known as the Department of Labor *q.v. Obs.*

(1) **1872** *Bur. Stat. Labor 4th Rep.* 13 Industrial partnerships and cooperation are the most important subjects for inquiry by . . . the Massachusetts Labor Bureau.—(2) **1884** *Statutes at Large* XXIII. 60 There shall be established in the Department of the Interior a Bureau of Labor, which shall be under the charge of a Commissioner of Labor. **1888** *Ib.* XXV. 183 The Bureau of Labor, as now organized and existing, shall continue its work as the Department of Labor, until the Department of Labor shall be organized in accordance with this act.

laborite ˈlebəˌraɪt, *n.* A supporter of the interests of labor in politics, used first of the Populists. *Colloq.*

1889 *Denver Press* 9 Aug. 4/2 I believe that only two of the laborites were for prohibition. **1922** *Tom Mooney's Mo.* (S.F.) Nov. 3/6 [He] was well-known as a radical laborite and his petition has always been refused. **1949** *Time* 14 March 64/2 At least one powerful group of Catholic laborites, the Association of Catholic Trade Unionists, last week took sharp issue with His Eminence.

labor reform. Reform in the working conditions of laborers. Also used attrib. to designate organizations seeking such reforms.

1847 (*title*), Conditions of Labor. An address to the Members of the Labor Reform League of New England by one of their number. **1872** *Atlantic Mo.* June 771 The size of the vote caused a good deal of wonder, as no one supposed that Labor Reform, as an independent political movement could muster so many supporters. **1911** PERSONS *Mass. Labor Laws* 107 This later convention seems to have assembled under the auspices of the Labor Reform party. *Ib.* 109 The Labor Reform Association was reorganized in 1867, as a result of a mass meeting in which Wendell Phillips was the leading spirit.

b. labor reformer, one associated with a labor-reform organization.

1872 *Atlantic Mo.* June 771 It was in great measure to the discontent of the Crispins . . . that the heavy vote thrown at the Labor-Reformers was at that time attributed. **1883** *Cent. Mag.* Oct. 901/1 'We are Labor Reformers,' said the spokesman.

* **Labrador,** *n.*

1. =**Labrador tea.** *Obs.*

1766 in J. T. BUCKINGHAM *Newspaper Lit.* (1850) I. 34 Procure a good store of the choice Labradore. **1767** *Newport Mercury* 28 Dec. 3/3 Where . . . noxious Bohea sheds a pois'nous Stream, There let balsamic Labrador regale.

2. In combs.: (1) **Labrador auk,** (see quot.); (2) **brown-capped chickadee,** (see quot.); (3) **duck,** a black and white sea duck, *Camptorhynchus labradorius*, now extinct; (4) **pine,** =**jack pine;** (5) **tea,** see as a main entry; (6) **twister,** (see quot.).

(1) **1917** *Birds of Amer.* I. 18 Puffin. . . . [Also called] Labrador Auk. — (2) **1917** *Birds of Amer.* III. 213/2 Another subspecies is the so-called Labrador Brown-capped Chickadee (*Penthestes hudsonicus nigricans*). — (3) **1869** *Amer. Naturalist* III. 383 The Pied or Labrador duck . . . is a very interesting bird to the naturalist. — (4) **1803** LAMBERT *Descr. Genus Pinus* 7 Labrador Pine. . . . Habitat in Americâ septentrionali. **1917** KEPHART *Camping* I. 239 The gray (Labrador) pine or jack pine is considered good fuel in the far North.

(6) **1877** MINOT *Land-Birds & Game-Birds N. Eng.* 405 Those very small wiry, compactly feathered, weather-tanned birds [woodcocks] . . . are called, perhaps locally, Labrador twisters.

Labrador tea.

1. Tea made with the leaves of an evergreen (see next). *Obs.*

1768 *Boston Gaz.* 9 May, They took Labradore Tea and Coffee for their Support, and finished their work . . . long before night. **1828** SHERBURNE *Memoirs* iii. 69 We were driven into store houses, and furnished with a kind of tea, which they called Labrador tea.

2. The evergreen shrub, *Ledum groenlandicum.*

1784 CUTLER in *Life & Corr.* I. 103 There were large beds of what is called the Labrador tea, of a very aromatic taste and smell. **1870** *Amer. Naturalist* IV. 217 Labrador Tea . . . with its delicate white clusters and leaves rusty-woolly beneath, is likewise full of beauty. **1946** STANWELL-FLETCHER *Driftwood Valley* 196 The marshes and bogs of Trail Lake are . . . bright with the tender reds and greens of young leaves of Labrador tea.

labrick ˈlebrɪk, *n. Mo.* [Origin unknown.] A fool. *Slang.* — **1889** MARK TWAIN *Conn. Yankee* xxx. 382 As a rule, a knight is a lummux, and sometimes even a labrick. **1893** ——— *P. Wilson* i, He's a labrick—just a Simon-pure labrick, if ever there was one.

lace flower. Queen Anne's lace, the wild carrot. — **1894** *Amer. Folk-Lore* VII. 89 *Daucus Carota,* lace-flower, Philadelphia, Pa. **1899** GOING *Flowers* 349 There are places west of the Mississippi where wild-carrots, despised intruder on Eastern lawns, is cosseted and extolled under the appropriate alias of 'lace flower.'

lacrosse ləˈkrɔs, *n.* [F. *la crosse*, a hooked stick.] A field game originating with the Indians, similar to hockey, the ball being caught, carried, and thrown with long-handled rackets by the players. Also attrib. Cf. **bagataway, ball-play, crosse,** *n.*

[*a***1716** PERROT *Mémoire des Sauvages de l'Amérique* (1864) 43 Il y a parmy eux un certain jeu de crosse qui a beaucoup de raport avec celuy de nostre longue paume.] **1718** in BECKWITH *Ill. & Indiana Indians* 168 They play a good deal in La Crosse in summer, twenty or more on a side. [**1808** PIKE *Sources Miss.* 18 Passed the Racine river, also a prairie called Le Cross, from a game of ball played frequently on it by the Sioux Indians.] **1886** *Outing* March 665/2 Lacrosse . . . is the offspring of the American savage. It was born and bred upon the plains of the South and West. **1892** *Outing* Oct. 77/1 Outside of the Indians, who are not outclassed by the whites, there are no professional lacrosse-players. **1948** *Dly. Ardmoreite* (Ardmore, Okla.) 12 April 8/3 Dick expects to . . . join the lacrosse team for the second quarter.

***ladder,** *n.* In combs.: (1) **ladder company,** a unit of a fire-fighting company consisting of the men who operate a ladder truck, cf. **hook-and-ladder company;** (2) **house,** a building where a ladder truck is kept; (3) **man,** a member of a ladder company; (4) **pole,** a long pole for use in making a ladder; (5) **truck,** a vehicle for carrying fire ladders and hooks.

(1) **1889** BRAYLEY *Boston Fire Dept.* 173 On September 21 the members of the ladder company were provided with caps like those worn by the enginemen. — (2) *Ib.* 139 Almost the first act of this board was . . . the enlargement of the ladder-house. — (3) *Ib.* 297 Ladder companies [included]: foreman, assistant foreman, and twelve laddermen. — (4) **1678** *Springfield Rec.* II. 160 To Goodm[an] Mirricke for ladder Poles . . . 2 [shillings].

(5) **1889** BRAYLEY *Boston Fire Dept.* 466 They had a narrow excape [*sic*] from a collision with Ladder Truck No. 8.

b. In the names of woodpeckers (see quots.).

1869 *Amer. Naturalist* III. 474 The resident species not found westward of this valley [the Colorado Valley in Calif.] were the Ladder Woodpecker (*Picus scalaris*) [etc.]. **1884** COUES *Key N. Amer. Birds* (ed. 2) 485 *Picoides americanus*. . . . Ladder-backed Three-toed Woodpecker. **1917** *Birds of Amer.* II. 149/1 The Ladder-back Woodpeckers are divisible into three regional varieties, the American, the Alaska (*Picoides americanus fasciatus*), and the Alpine (*Picoides americanus dorsalis*). **1948** *Ecological Monographs* April 171/2 Typical nesting residents include the Gambel quail . . . , the Yuma ladder-backed woodpecker . . . , and the desert sparrow.

c. *To see through a ladder*, to see something that is obvious. *Colloq.*

1834 *Sun* (N.Y.) 13 May 2/3 The prisoner was found in the street at a late hour last night, so drunk that—(as he admitted himself) he could not see a hole through a ladder. **1897** BRODHEAD *Bound in Shallows* 86, I can see through a ladder when the rungs ain't too close together.

As the last term in **extension, fish, foot, hook and, Indian, Jacob's, log, love's ladder.**

ladies' day. A day upon which special privileges are given to women (see also quot. 1882).

1787 WASHINGTON *Diaries* III. 225 Dined with a Club. . . . The Gentlemen . . . met every Saturday . . . accompanied by the females every other Saturday. This was the ladies' day. **1882** MCCABE *New York* 329 January 2d . . . is 'Ladies' Day,' and is devoted by the fair sex to calling upon each other. **1906** *Amer. Mag.* Oct. 595 Ladies' Day in Carbury Mine. **1948** *Dly. Ardmoreite* (Ardmore, Okla.) 23 May 13/3 The league-leading Cleveland Indians recorded a 7 to 0 victory before a ladies' day crowd of 28,997.

ladino lɑˈdino, *n. S.W.* [Sp., crafty.] (See quot. 1891.) — **1891** *D.N.* I. 191 *Ladino*. In Spanish, learned, knowing Latin; then crafty, cunning. In Texas as a noun, a vicious, unmanageable horse, full of cunning and tricks. **1929** DOBIE *Vaquero* 14 (Bentley), They were all outlaws, ladinos, as wild as bucks, cunning, and ready to fight.

***Ladle,** *n.* (See quot. 1833.) *Colloq.* Cf. ***dipper,** *n.* **3.** — **1833** BURRITT *Geog. of Heavens* (1839) 85 Ursa Major. The great Bear.—This constellation is readily distinguished from all others by means of a remarkable cluster of seven bright stars, forming what is familiarly termed the *Dipper* or *Ladle*. **1841** *Lowell Offering* I. 26, I was just endeavoring to point out to my cousins the constellation vulgarly called 'The Ladle.'

ladrone ləˈdron(ɪ), *n. S.W.* [Sp. *ladrón*, in same sense.] A thief.

Prob. used somewhat earlier by British writers with reference to Spain, but in U.S. use a new borrowing from the Spanish of the Southwest.

1838 *N.Y. Mirror* 6 Jan. 217/3 No ladrone in Mejico dare attack a party guarded by myself and brother soldiers. **1867** *Wkly. New Mexican* 6 April 1/4 The soldiers would not be able to discriminate the good Indian from the ladrone. **1947** *Westerners' Brand Book* 99 The pursuers tracked them finding every place where the ladrones stopped signs of other offenses against law—the killing of beef.

b. ladronism, in the Philippines, organized resistance to law or authority among the native population.

1902 *Outlook* LXXII. 298/1 A local police and an insular constabulary system have been created, and ladronism, or organized robbery and brigandage . . . has almost disappeared.

***lady,** *n.*

1. In miscellaneous combs.: (1) **lady cake,** a kind of butter cake, also **Lady Baltimore cake;** (2) **chair,** (*a*) a kind of seat improvised by two persons who face each other, each grasping one of his wrists and the opposite wrist of the other, (*b*) a light, armless chair with especially graceful lines; (3) **lobbyist,** (see quot.).

(1) **1849** G. G. FOSTER *N.Y. in Slices* 72 It would be sacrilege to eat any thing heartier than ice-cream and lady-cake till the crisis comes off. **1883** HOWELLS *Woman's Reason* viii, In a plated basket in the center of the table was a generous stack of freshly-sliced lady-cake. **1913** *Ladies' Home Jrnl.* Oct. 47/2 [Menu:] Tomato Bouillon, Welsh Rarebit, Lady Baltimore Cake, Whipped Cream. **1948** *Chi. Tribune* 15 Jan. 4/6 Lady Baltimore Cakes, 85c–$1.10. 4 white, fine grained layers, filled and iced with butter cream. Glace fruit decoration. — (2) (*a*) **1869** STOWE *Oldtown Folks* 298 Tina . . . insisted upon it that we should occasionally carry her in a lady-chair over to this island. (*b*) **1937** LANGDON *Everyday Things* 34 As the wife usually sat in one of these, they were called, especially in Connecticut, 'Lady Chairs.' — (3) **1938** ASBURY *Sucker's Prog.* 143 To influence Congressmen who were immune to the fascinations of Faro Pendleton utilized the services of women who were politely referred to by journalists as 'lady lobbyists,' a term which by no means fully describes their activities.

b. Often pl. and in the possessive: (1) **Ladies' Aid Society,** (*a*) during the Civil War, a women's organization devoted to sending garments, bandages, etc., to the soldiers, *obs.*, (*b*) a society of church women devoted to raising money for the church; (2) **choice,** a dance, during a program of dancing, for which the ladies choose their partners; (3) **day,** see as a main entry; (4) **entrance,** an entrance to a public building, esp. a saloon or bar, for ladies alone or with escorts; (5) **fair,** a bazaar held by women for some charitable purpose; (6) **Loyal Legion,** a women's auxiliary of the Loyal Legion *q.v.;* (7) **night,** a night at a theater, men's club, or the like, when a special program is given for ladies; (8) **ordinary,** a meal served for ladies and their escorts, *obs.;* (9) **parlor,** a lounge for women; (10) **room,** =prec.; (11) **table,** in a restaurant, a table for ladies and their escorts, *obs.;* (12) **twist,** pig-tail tobacco, *obs.*

(1) (*a*) **1866** MOORE *Women of War* 214 Mrs. Wittenmeyer, as president of the Ladies' Aid Society of Iowa. (*b*) **1893** THANET *Stories* 185 The furnishing of the church . . . is in charge of the Ladies' Aid Society. **1945** *Estes Park* (Colo.) *Trail* 9 Nov. 1/4 The dinner was served at the Community church by the members of the Ladies Aid society. — (2) **1914** BOWER *Flying U Ranch* 202 He had been invited to dance 'Ladies' choice' with the prettiest girl in the crowd. — (4) **1893** *Voice* 20 July, No respectable drinking man of mature years favors the ladies' entrance. **1908** DAVENPORT *Butte Beneath X-Ray* 58 If we had a little more of this in Butte's high society there might be more babies, less automobiling out to the road-houses to meet some other man, less 'Ladies' Entrance' traffic, less divorce cases.

(5) **1829** *Va. Herald* (Fredericksburg) 25 April 3/4 The Ladies' Fair, For the benefit of the Female Charity School of Fredericksburg, will be held at the Town-Hall, on Friday & Saturday, the 8th & 9th of May. **1855** THOMPSON *Doesticks* 132 There was soon to be a ladies' fair, in aid of the poor, given by the benevolent ladies of the Church. — (6) **1886** *San Jose* (Calif.) *Mercury* June 9/3 There are five Masonic bodies, . . . and a Ladies' Loyal Legion. — (7) **1875** *Chi. Tribune* 8 July 7/6 Adelphi Theatre Thursday Evening, July 8—Ladies Night. **1949** *Ill. State Reg.* 1 Feb. 5/3 The Rotary club will hold a special ladies night program on Feb. 14. — (8) **1851** QUENTIN *Reisebilder* I. 2 Das Diner der einzelnen Herren (Gentlemen's Ordinary) um 3 Uhr, das 'Ladie's Ordinary' um 4 Uhr Abends gereicht wird. **1859** GRATTAN *Civilized Amer.* II. 57 They breakfast, dine, and sup from the tenderest age at the table *d'hôte*, or, as it is called, 'the ladies' ordinary.' — (9) **1851** QUENTIN *Reisebilder* I. 2 Unsere Freunde empfangen wir in den prachtvoll decorirten, mit allen erdenklichen Bequemlichkeiten versehenen Gesellschaftszimmern (Ladie's Parlors) [of a New York hotel]. **1876** INGRAM *Centennial Exp.* 639 There were also committee-rooms, a ladies' parlor, invalids' room, . . . and gentlemen's parlor in the [Ind. State building].

(10) **1870** O. LOGAN *Before Footlights* 266 Past the ladies' room, now tenantless. **1885** *Harper's Mag.* March 552/2 They took possession of the ladies' room, which Anastasia, who had seen many pronounced a very good one. — (11) **1841** BUCKINGHAM *America* II. 441 At the Tremont House in Boston . . . about the same number of persons dined at what is called the ladies' table, and where gentlemen (but only those who are accompanied by ladies) sit. — (12) **1824** *Shipping & Comm. List* (Pettigrew P.) 31 July, Tobacco . . . Ladies' Twist, Cavandish, Sweet scent. **1864** E. BURRITT *Walk from London to John O'Groat's* 290 An American tobacco-chewer, of fifty years' standing would not have asked a cut from a neighbor's 'lady's twist,' or 'pig-tail' in more perfect good faith.

Also designating a railroad **car, carriage,** or **coach** esp. suitable for the use of women.

1864 DALY in J. F. Daly *A. Daly* 62 Brutes and blackguards in the so-called ladies' car! **1887** CUSTER *Tenting on Plains* i. 35 There was a ladies' car, to which no men unaccompanied by women were admitted. — **1861** BERKELEY *Sportsman* 94 Attached to all trains there is what is termed a lady's carriage, in which smoking is prohibited; into this, when it is not full, men of respectable exterior are permitted, and at times men get in there whose looks are decidedly the reverse. — **1876** *Wkly. Ranchero* (Brownsville, Tex.) 27 Aug. 6/3 The passengers hurt were in [the] smoking car and ladies coach.

2. In the names of plants: (1) **lady finger corn,** (see quot.), *obs.;* (2) **-'s delight,** any one of several species of wild pansy; (3) ∗**-'s eardrop,** any one of certain American plants such as the spotted jewelweed, balsamweed, etc.; (4) **-'s slipper,** the garden balsam, *Impatiens balsamina,* see also **gay, showy, yellow lady's-slipper;** (5) **-'s thumb,** the common persicary, *Polygonum persicaria;* (6) **Washington lily,** =**Washington lily.**

(1) **1849** EMMONS *Agric. N.Y.* II. 265 Illinois, or lady finger corn . . . is an unproductive kind, bearing sometimes four ears upon a stalk. — (2) **1841** CHILD *Lett. New York* I. 14, I am like the Lady's Delight, ever prone to take root. **1895** A. BROWN *Meadow-Grass* 254 Dorcas . . . remembered he loved ladies'-delights. — (3) **1887** WILKINS *Humble Romance* 195 He cut lavishly sprays of dioletra, or lady's ear-drop, snowballs, daffodils. **1931** CLUTE *Plants* 74 On the other hand . . . lady's ear-drop (*Impatiens biflora*), lady's purse . . . and many others have a more mundane origin, though some may have been named because of their blooming at Lady-tide. — (4) **1836** LINCOLN *Botany* 101 The Impatiens of the garden is sometimes called *Ladies'-slipper*, sometimes *Balsamine*. **1892** *Amer. Folk-Lore* V. 94 *Impatiens fulva*, Lady's slipper. Plattsburg, N.Y.; Mansfield, O.

(5) **1837** DARLINGTON *Flora Cestrica* 249 Lady's Thumb. Spotted Knot-weed. **1931** CLUTE *Plants* 74 Lady's thumb (*Polygonum persicaria*) is so named to explain the dark markings on the leaves which are reputed to be the marks of Our Lady's thumb. — (6) **1859** *Calif. Acad. Sci. Proc.* II. (1863) 13 Dr. Kellogg also exhibited a drawing and growing specimens of a new species of lily from the Sierra Nevada. *L. washingtonianum*, (Kellogg) Lady Washington Lily. **1937** MCFARLAND *Garden Bulbs in Color* 155 The name [Lilium washingtonianum] . . . seems not to be associated with the state, but rather with the compliment paid to the wife of George Washington by the early miners who found it and called it 'The Lady Washington Lily.'

3. *Lady of the White House*, the presiding lady in the White House, usu. the wife of the President.

1841 *N.O. Picayune* 20 April 2/3 The Lady of the White House.—A daughter of the venerable Thomas Cooper, Esq., . . . will now, it is said, be presiding lady at the President's Mansion in Washington. **1881** L. C. HOLLOWAY *Ladies of White House* 3 The Ladies of the White House have had no biographers.

For *to dress the lady*, see ∗**dress,** *v.*

As the last term in **British, chair, first, fore, Grecian, old, sales, Shaker, Spanish, speckled, wash lady.**

∗**Lafayette,** *n.*

1. The spot, *Leiostomus xanthurus*.

1842 *Nat. Hist. N.Y., Zoology* III. 69 The Lafayette . . . visits us in almost incredible numbers at irregular . . . intervals. One of these visits happened to coincide with the arrival of . . . La Fayette at New York, in the summer of 1824. **1884** GOODE *Fisheries* I. 370 The Lafayette, or 'Spot,' . . . is found along our coast from New York to the Gulf of Mexico. **1903** *N.Y. Sun* 15 Nov., The fish are small—something like Lafayettes.

2. The butterfish or dollar fish.

1890 *Cent.* 3329/3 *Lafayette*, . . . a stromateoid fish, *Stromateus triacanthus*. **1896** JORDAN & EVERMANN *Fishes No. & Mid. Amer.* I. 967 *Rhombus Triacanthus* . . . (Dollar-fish; Harvest-fish; Butter-fish; La Fayette.) . . . Maine to Florida; very abundant northward. **1910** *Sat. Ev. Post* 13 Aug. 7/3 On another [day] I'd stroll down to the dock near where I lived and try my luck on the tomcods and lafayettes.

3. *attrib.* Designating articles of food and dress.

1824 *Free Press* (Halifax, N.C.) 3 Dec., Mrs. S. expects to receive . . . an elegant assortment of *La Fayette Bonnets*. *Ib.*, La Fayette gloves, belts, buckles, &c.—all of which will be sold at the lowest *Petersburg prices*. **1828** LESLIE *Receipts* 67 [Recipe for] Lafayette Gingerbread. **1947** DOWNEY *Lusty Forefathers* 296 Remaining nooks and crannies of stomachs were filled by confectionery in the form of almond macaroons, Lafayette cake, kisses.

b. *Geol.* (See quots.)

1896 CLENDENIN *Fla. Parishes E. La.* 187 The geologic age of the Lafayette formation has not been exactly determined. **1909** *Cent. Supp.* 550/2 Lafayette group, a division of the Tertiary rocks, now regarded as of Pliocene age in the Gulf region of the United States, lying above the Floridian series and regarded as equivalent to the Lagrange, the Orange sand, and the Appomattox groups of this region.

Lafittes lə'fits, *n. pl.* The followers of Jean Lafitte (d. *c*1825), a French pirate who operated in the Gulf of Mexico. *Rare.* Cf. **Baratarian.** — **1817** *Niles' Reg.* XIII. 289/1 The Barratarians, among whom the Lafittes may be classed foremost, and most actively engaged in the Galvezton trade.

lager 'lɑgɚ, *n.* [G. *lagerbier*. Cf. **2.** below.]

1. Short for next. Cf. ∗**grizzly 2.**

1855 COOKE *Ellie* 13 He was rotund, red and solemn—'lager' was written in his eyes. **1883** MARK TWAIN *Life on Miss.* 260 Give an Irishman lager for a month and he's a dead man. **1942** LILLARD *Desert Challenge* 213 He soaked up life and lager, leaned against doorways watching people and listening to them, and unconsciously stored up data for future books.

2. lager beer, a beer which is slowly fermented at a low temperature and stored for some months.

The *OED*'s 1853 quotation refers to Germany.

1854 *Calif. Chronicle* 16 May 7/3 We do not suppose lager bier to be an earthly nectar. **1901** CHURCHILL *Crisis* 117 [In] South St. Louis . . . lager beer took the place of Bourbon, and black bread and sausages of hot rolls and fried chicken. **1948** *Amer. Sp.* April 108 Other common terms are *hausfrau*, *lager* beer, *bock* beer, and *frankfurter*.

3. Often attrib., as **lager beer brewery, cask, cellar, garden, restaurant, saloon, schooner, shop, wagon.**

1856 *Sacramento Union* 24 March 3/2 A fight occurred at the lager-beer brewery in Auburn on Wednesday evening. — **1855** THOMPSON *Doesticks* xxxi, 272 Within the American shield, two lager-bier casks supporting a rum-bottle rampant. — **1854** *Town Talk* (S.F.) 25 Nov. 1/4 Lager bier cellars, and other ordinary soup houses, I have no doubt, are sufferers. **1894** HOWELLS in *Harper's Mag.* LXXXVIII. 818/2 He could tell me of Pfaff's lager-beer cellar on Broadway. — **1868** M. H.

SMITH *Sunshine & Shadow* 214 Saloons, 'free-and-easies,' and immense German lager beer gardens are here [in the Bowery in N.Y.] located. — **1870** MEDBERY *Men Wall St.* 244 On Williams Street . . . is a basement floor, now radiant with the brass-mounted counters of a flourishing lager-beer restaurant. — **1856** *N.Y. Wkly. Tribune* 14 July 6/3 There are already stores, taverns, German lager-beer saloons, and other signs of growth in abundance. **1882** *Wheelman* I. 173 [The] enlivening interchanges of sentiment which take place in . . . city lager-beer saloons may also be freely overheard. **1910** PRESCOTT *Early Day Railroading* 56 A Dutchman finally opened a lager beer saloon on Milwaukee Avenue. — **1889** *San Juan Prospector* (Del Norte, Colo.) 27 July 4/1 With the lager beer schooner departed the last vestige of our American shipping. — **1861** *Atlantic Mo.* April 433/1 The long rows of houses, except an occasional lager-bier shop were closed. — **1869** *Overland Mo.* III. 53 Who has not met graduates of the German Gymnasia, all through this country, in the capacity of wood-sawyers, organ-grinders, . . . [and] drivers of lager-beer wagons.

Lager beer wagon

lagniappe læn'jæp, *n.* [See note.]

Read in *La.-Fr.*, 142, thinks this word is composed of the French *la*, "the" and a French adaptation of Spanish *ñapa*, which is taken from Kechuan *yapa*, a present made to a customer. But Santamaría regards the base of the word as being of ultimate African, not South American, origin. See *Amer. Sp.* XIV. 93–6, *Zeitschrift* LXI. 77, and Santamaría.

A small present given when a purchase is made; a gratuity. Also transf. and attrib.

1849 *Knickerb.* XXXIV. 407/1 Ime sum pumkins in that line; but he's a huckleberry above my persimmon, and right smart lanyope too, as them creole darkies say. **1927** BENÉT *J. B.'s Body* 231 They come back with a scraping of this and a scrap of that and try to remember old lazy, lagnappe days. **1948** *Travel* Nov. 10/1 The Cajuns of Louisiana call it [Spanish moss] a 'lagniappe' crop. **1949** *N.O. Times-Picayune Mag.* 24 April 9/3 Mack is the old loquacious type of business man of 50 years ago and he will not only sell you one or 100 pictures, but give you the history of each vessel depicted there for lagniappe.

Laguna lə'gunə, *n. S.W.* [Sp., pond or lagoon, on account of a large pond west of the pueblo.] "A Keresan tribe whose principal pueblo, which bears the same popular name, is situated on the s. bank of the San José r., Valencia co., N. Mex., about 45 m. w. of Albuquerque" (Hodge). Also **Laguna Indians, people.**

1776 in *Catholic Church in Utah* (tr.) (1909) 201 The Indians who live in this vicinity (San Jose valley) . . . are extremely timid, and different from the Lagunas and the bearded Indians. **1777** *Ib.* 242 We offer this journal, with a description of the regions of the lakes mentioned in it, and of the Laguna Indians. **1907** HODGE *Amer. Indians* I. 753/1 The Laguna people numbered 1,384 in 1905.

laid work. Couched work, embroidery made by couching. — **1884** *Harper's Mag.* Aug. 346/1 [A silk-canvas foundation for tapestry] resembles, in effect, 'laid-work,' or 'couching,' as seen in the grounds of so many old embroideries. **1891** WILKINS *N. Eng. Nun* 95 When Liddy was married she had a whole chistful of clothes, real fine cotton cloth, all tucks an' laid-work.

* **lake**, *n.*

1. *pl.* The Great Lakes.

1759 P. COLLINSON in Darlington *Mem. J. Bartram & H. Marshall* 217, I don't remember ever reading of any [goats] in the country about the lakes, nor with you. **1847** *Ill. State Reg.* (Springfield) 8 June 2/4 The following letter . . . gives an idea of the demand for transportation and the course of commerce on the Lakes and Erie Canal. **1888** *Forum* June 421 The story of the lakes is not completely told by explaining the origin of their basins.

2. In combs.: (1) **Lake City,** Chicago, Ill.; (2) **fever,** (see quot. 1937), now *hist.;* (3) **front,** a situation fronting upon a lake; (4) **Indian,** a Laguna Indian, or one from the region of the Great Lakes, *obs.;* (5) **port,** a port, harbor, or town on the shore of a lake, esp. on one of the Great Lakes; (6) **sailor,** one employed as a sailor on a boat operating on the Great Lakes; (7) **State,** see as a main entry; (8) **steamer,** a steamer operating on a lake, esp. on one of the Great Lakes.

(1) **1867** *Harper's Wkly.* 12 Jan. 19/4 A project has been started to run it [sewage] southward, and thus manure the prairies of Illinois with the 'slops' of the 'Lake City.' — (2) **1829** J. MACTAGGART *Three Years* II. 208 There is an oily substance, of a brown colour, found floating on the surface of the lakes in the warm weather; it has not yet been fairly analyzed, but is thought to be an antidote against the *lake fever.* **1841** BONNYCASTLE *Canadas* II. 78 The lake fever is more prevalent in marshy districts, or on the immediate borders of Erie and Ontario, if the locality be not well drained. **1937** ELLIOTT *W. Scott* 108 He died at Fort George of the terrible 'lake fever' from which the army suffered constantly. This scourge, which was simply typhoid fever, contracted by drinking the polluted lake and river water without boiling it, was to devastate the American and other armies for a hundred years to come. — (3) **1880** MARK TWAIN *Tramp Abroad* xxv. 245 (R.), The lake-front is walled with masonry like a pier. **1948** *Green Bay* (Wis.) *Press-Gazette* 12 July 18/4 The Cook county fair will run from Aug. 27 through Sept. 6 in Soldier field and adjacent space on the lake front. — (4) **1776** in W. R. HARRIS *Catholic Church in Utah* (1909) 184 We found them [nearby Indians] as kind and gentle as the lake Indians. **1781** in *Hist. MSS Comm.* 9th Rep. App. III. II. 230 The Lake Indians showed them a very good example.

(5) **1872** *Atlantic Mo.* April 455 There is no difficulty in determining the number who landed at our sea-ports and the lake-ports since October 1, 1819. **1893** *Advance* 10 Aug. 606/3 [Work like that of the Boston Seaman's Friend Society] ought to be inaugurated in every seaport and lakeport of considerable size. — (6) **1881** *Harper's Mag.* Jan. 219/2 The poor parson's cooking was passed from one incompetent hand to another—lake-sailors' wives, wandering emigrants, moneyless forlorn females [etc.]. **1922** PARRISH *Case & Girl* 244 Neither Hogan, nor the man Mark, bore any resemblance to a lake sailor. — (8) **1847** *Knickerb.* XXX. 456 He has been inspired by looking down through the iron foot-grating of a great lake-steamer. **1946** FOREMAN *Last Trek* 91 They were transferred from lake steamer to canal boats.

b. In the names of fishes: (1) **lake bass,** any one of several basses found in lakes, cf. **white lake bass;** (2) **cusk,** (see quot.); (3) **herring,** any one of several species of cisco found in the Great Lakes, esp. *Leucichthys artedi* (see also first quot.); (4) **lawyer,** (see quots.); (5) **salmon,** a species of large trout, *Cristivomer namaycush;* (6) **sheepshead,** (see quot.); (7) **whitefish,** (see quot.); (8) **whiting,** =prec.

(1) **1795** J. SCOTT *U.S. Gazetteer, s.v. Vermont,* The rivers are stored with a great variety of fish, as . . . a species of fish called lake bass. **1883** *Cent. Mag.* July 376/2 The black bass . . . have received names somewhat descriptive of their habitat, as, lake, river, marsh, pond, . . . and Oswego bass. — (2) **1884** GOODE *Fisheries* I. 236 The Burbot is known as . . . 'Lake-cusk' in Lake Winnepiseogee. — (3) **1842** *Nat. Hist. N.Y., Zoology* IV. 267 The Lake Moon-eye, *Hyodon clodalis,* . . . is common in Lake Erie. At Buffalo and Barcelona, it is called Moon-eye, Shiner, and Lake Herring. **1875** *Amer. Naturalist* IX. 135, I received . . . a collection of deep-water 'Siscoes.' . . . Compared with Coregonus most of the species have a more slender form; hence their popular name of 'lake herrings,' although their resemblance to the sea herring is quite superficial. **1902** *Amer. Folk-Lore* XV. 243 [The name *cisco* is] applied to certain species of fish found in the Great Lakes and adjoining waters, . . . [including] the lake herring (*Coregonus artedi*). — (4) **1838** in *Nat. Hist. N.Y., Zoology* IV. 270 The *Dog-fish* is found in Lake Erie, where it is frequently called '*The Lake Lawyer.*' **1848** BARTLETT 198 Lake Lawyer . . . [or] the Western Mud-fish . . . is found in Lakes Erie and Ontario, where it is known by the name of Dog-fish. **1871** DE VERE 383 The Lake-Lawyer (*Amia*) is the Mud-Fish of Western waters, so called from its 'ferocious looks and voracious habits.'

(5) **1842** *Nat. Hist. N.Y., Zoology* IV. 239 The well known Lake Salmon . . . appears to possess all the coarseness of the halibut, without its flavor. **1940** SMITH *Puyallup-Nisqually* 236 These smoked lake salmon would keep as well as any smoked salmon. — (6) **1842** *Nat. Hist. N.Y., Zoology* IV. 73 The Lake Sheepshead, *Corvina oscula,* . . . is a very common fish in Lake Erie. — (7) **1863** *Rep. Comm. Agric. 1862* 55 The fishes of Maine . . . which are known to spawn in

fresh water [are] . . . lake trout, *Salmo confinis;* lake white fish, *Coregonus albus* [etc.]. [**1920** LEWIS *Main Street* 414 He was the guest of honor at the Commercial Club Banquet . . . an occasion for . . . soft damp slabs of Lake Superior whitefish served as fillet of sole.] — **(8) 1883** *Nat. Museum Bul.* No. 27, 422 Lake Whiting, Great Lake Region; lakes of the Adirondacks.

As the last term in **alkali, blind, dry, great, Illinois, mud, saleratus, salt, sand-hill, tule, walled lake.**

* **laker,** *n.*

1. A lake trout or species of lake trout, esp. the lake salmon.

1823 COOPER *Pioneers* xxiv, I see a laker there, that has run out of the school. **1882** HUBBARD *Moosehead Lake* 55 White-fish and 'lakers' of considerable size are often caught. **1949** *Reader's Digest* April 98/2 Pike and perch's gotten in and there's few lakers left.

2. One who navigates on lakes, esp. the Great Lakes.

1838 COOPER *Home as Found* xix, After fishing a few hours, the old laker [Captain Truck] pulled the skiff up to the Point. **1900** FLYNT *Notes Itinerant Policeman* 157 [The] rough element . . . is composed largely of 'lakers,' men who work on the lakes during the open season.

3. A lake steamer, esp. one operating on the Great Lakes.

1882 *Tenth Census* VIII. IV. 221 A representative laker is the Boston, a fine steamer, carrying 83,000 bushels of wheat. **1887** *Cent. Mag.* Aug. 484/2 A twenty-foot laker can slip through any lock without scratching her paint.

4. (See quot.)

1905 *Forestry Bureau Bul.* No. 61, 41 *Laker,* a log driver expert at handling logs on lakes. (N[orthern] F[orest].)

Lake State.

1. (See quots.)

1871 DE VERE 660 Michigan, surrounded by the four magnificent lakes . . . derives from this position also the name of *Lake State.* **1886** *Chi. W. News* 29 April 4/3 Michigan, which borders on four great lakes, is the Lake state, and its people are Wolverines. **1894** *N.Y. Wkly. Tribune* 7 March 4/3 Michigan means the 'lake country'; sobriquets, State of Wolverines, or the 'Lake State.'

2. Lake States, those states that border on the Great Lakes.

1845 *S. Lit. Messenger* XI. 578/1 The Lake States will be there, with their plans for the common defence and their own safety in war. **1933** CHELEY *Camping Out* 255 Most familiar of all [are] the hardwood and hemlock forests that clothe our Appalachian hills and extend westward to the prairies and north to the Lake States. **1947** *Sports Afield* Dec. 81/1 He had heard that Georgia had a lake and river inhabited by the vicious fish from the lake states.

lallygag ˈlɑlɪgæg, *v.* Also **lollygag.** [Origin unknown.] *intr.* To fool around, dawdle, waste time. *Colloq.* or *slang.*

1870 *No. Vindicator* 19 Feb., The weather once more is 'salubrious' and balmy, and indicates that winter will not lollygag in the lap of spring. **1910** *Sat. Ev. Post* 30 July 19/1 Frank lally-gagged through the first term and came back for the second. **1944** DUNCAN *M. Graham* 127 The children begged for cracklins and ate them while they lallygagged around under the table.

Hence **lallygagging,** *a.* and *n.* (see quots.).

1868 *No. Vindicator* 30 Dec., The lascivious, lolly-gagging lumps of licentiousness who disgrace the common decencies of life by their love-sick fawnings at our public dances. **1869** *Tidal Wave* (Silver City, Ida.) 15 Jan. 3/2 They are too pious to encourage dicing, and the feature of their entertainments may be what the boys call 'lally-gagging.' **1949** *Amer. Folk-Lore* Jan.–Mar. 63 'Lally-gaggin'' was Grandmother's word for love-making.

Lamanite ˈlemənˌaɪt, *n.* According to the *Book of Mormon,* an American Indian, represented as being a descendant of Laman, a prophet who led a company of his fellow Jews from Jerusalem to America in 600 B.C.

1830 *Book of Mormon* (1920) Jac. 3 : 5 The Lamanites your brethren . . . ye hate because of their filthiness and the cursing which hath come upon their skins. **1883** *Harper's Mag.* Oct. 710/1 The gesture gave rise to much 'how-howing' among the Lamanites (such is the name given to the Indians in the Book of Mormon.) **1944** *Utah Hist. Quart.* Jan.–Apr. 2 Because of disobedience a part of the people were cursed with dark skins, and were known as 'Lamanites.'

Hence **Lamanite brethren, Lamanitish.**

1844 HUNT *Hist. Mormon War* 119 Their 'Lamanite' brethren, under General Black Hawk, were about that time commencing a war upon the whites. **1853** *Harper's Mag.* April 609/2 It was immediately revealed to the Prophet that the skeleton was that of a Lamanite; . . . that the arrow was a Lamanitish one.

* **lamb,** *n.*

1. * **lambkill,** the sheep laurel, *Kalmia angustifolia,* or the stagger bush *q.v.*

1814 BIGELOW *Florula Bostoniensis* 103 *Kalmia angustifolia,* . . . a low shrub with rose coloured flowers, very common in low grounds, and known by the names *sheep poison, lambkill, low laurel,* &c. **1823** WILLIAMSON *Maine* I. 116 Lamb-kill . . . has been called mountain laurel, Spoonwood, Ivy and Calico Bush. Its wood is dense and hard. **1939** *Nat. Geog. Mag.* Aug. 255/1 Other poisonous members of the heath family are the kalmias, frequently called 'lambkill' from the effect they have on grazing animals.

2. * **lamb's tongue,** a local name for any one of several plants such as the yellow adder's tongue.

1873 MILLER *Amongst Modocs* x. 128 [Winter] cut down the banners of the spring that night, lamb-tongue, Indian turnip and catella. **1894** *Amer. Folk-Lore* VII. 102 *Erythronium Americanum,* lambs' tongues, Banner Elk, N.C.

As the last term in **buck, kill, mountain, pet, Staten Island lamb.**

* **lambrequin,** *n.* A narrow valance for hanging from a shelf or from a casing at the top of a window.

1872 *Rep. Comm. Patents 1870* 40/2 Claim.—The construction of lambrequins in sections, which can be adjusted to windows of different sizes. **1929** A. ELLIS *Life* 152, I made a crazy-work lambrequin. **1942** THOMAS *Blue Ridge* 120 (Wentworth), I want a lamberkin all scalloped deep.

* **lame,** *a.*

1. lame distemper, (see quots). *Obs.*

1733 *S.C. Gazette* 221/2 A Receipe, being an effectual Cure for all Distempers arising from an inveterate Scurvy, such as the Yawes, Lame Distemper [etc.]. **1775** ROMANS *Nat. Hist. Fla.* 249 The chronic diseases are . . . among blacks the leprosy, elephantiasis, and body yaws; which last in Carolina is called the lame distemper.

2. * **lame duck,** an officeholder who has not been re-elected, esp. a defeated member of the short session of Congress after a November election. Cf. **dead duck.**

1863 *Cong. Globe* 14 Jan. 307/1 In no event . . . could it [the Court of Claims] be justly obnoxious to the charge of being a receptacle of 'lame ducks' or broken down politicians. **1910** *Springfield W. Republican* 8 Dec. 1 The Congress which assembled Monday for its last session is full of what they call 'lame ducks,' or representatives who failed of re-election in November and senators who will fail when the Legislatures meet. **1947** *Chi. D. News* 23 Jan. 14/1 Volstead, then a congressional lame duck, did take a lawyer job in the legal end of prohibition enforcement.

b. Also attrib., as **Lame Duck Alley, amendment, bill, Congress, session.**

1910 *N.Y. Ev. Post* 8 Dec. 8 'Lame Duck Alley' . . . is the name they [*sc.* reporters] have given to a screened-off corridor in the White House offices, where statesmen who went down in the recent electoral combat may meet. — **1925** *Independent* 21 Feb. 213/1 The proposed Constitutional amendment . . . has been usually designated as the 'lame-duck' amendment. **1949** *L.A. Times* 13 July II. 4/2 Usually the amending process is slow—repeal of prohibition and the lame duck amendments being notable exceptions. — **1930** *Randolph Enterprise* (Elkins, W.Va.) 27 Nov. 4/1 Norris also demands that his 'Lame Duck' bill . . . be enacted into law. — **1924** *Outlook* 17 Dec. 627/1 A 'lame duck' Congress is not likely to be very competent, because it is not really representative. **1948** *Chi. Tribune* 25 April I. 24/6 However, a 'lame duck' congress . . . was ordered by them to annul the elections. — **1932** *Dly. Ardmoreite* (Ardmore, Okla.) 16 Feb. 1/4 A resolution proposing to the states a constitutional amendment to abolish the 'lame duck' session of congress. **1948** *Ib.* 6 July 1/1 Congress, you recall, changed its schedule of activities not so long ago to eliminate what history calls 'lame duck' sessions.

* **lamp,** *n.* In combs.: (1) **lamp district,** ?a municipal administrative district, *obs.;* (2) **jack,** (see quot. 1884); (3) * **lighter,** see as a main entry; (4) **mat,** an ornamental mat on which to set a lamp; (5) * **post,** (see quot.), *obs.;* (6) **rubbing,** "burning the midnight oil" in study, *rare.*

(1) 1867 *Comm. & Fin. Chron.* 22 June 775 The principal disbursements were an account of . . . lamp districts $120,922.21. — **(2) 1884** KNIGHT *Supp.* 526 *Lamp jack* (Railway), a hood over a lamp chimney on the roof of a car. **1895** WAIT *Car-Builder's Dict.* 80 Lamp-cover, or lamp-protector (English). American equivalent, *lamp-jack.* — **(4) 1842** *Spirit of Times* 15 Oct. 389/2 (We.), Also to Miss Waterman . . . [a diploma] for various specimens of her exquisite work of lamp mats. **1893** MARK TWAIN in *Harper's Mag.* CIV. 602/1 Wall-paper and framed lithographs, and bright-colored tidies and lamp-mats, and Windsor chairs.

(5) **1885** *Cent. Mag.* XXX. 449/2 The gun-boats . . . opened fire, . . . throwing those awe-inspiring shells familiarly called by our men 'lamp-posts,' on account of their size and appearance. — **(6) 1842** A. LINCOLN in B. Binns *Life* (1927) 88 The success of your 'lamp rubbing' might possibly prevent you passing the severe physical examination, to which, etc.

As the last term in **arc, astral, bug, cigar, drop, head, jack, kerosene, lard, phoebe, rag, student, study, thermolamp.**

***lamp,** *v. tr.* To see. *Slang.* — **1916** H. L. WILSON *Somewhere in Red Gap* 198 Stella . . . was standing on the centre table by now, so she could lamp herself in the glass over the mantel. **1923** J. L. VANCE *Baroque* viii. 50 Nobody even lamped its number.

***lamper,** *n.* (See quot.) *Colloq. Obs.* — **1886** *Pall Mall Gaz.* 23 Sep. 12/1 In Philadelphia, women make a good living as professional 'lampers.' They contract to call each day, and trim and keep in perfect order the lamps of the household.

***lamper eel.** The eelpout or mutton fish, *Zoarces anguillaris.*

[**1709** *N.H. Hist. Soc. Coll.* III. 53 Edward Taylor was slain by the Indians at Lamper-eel river.] **1834** C. A. DAVIS *Lett. J. Downing* 23 Mr. Van Buren hung on like a lamper-eel, till he was kinder jerked up like a trounced toad. **1897** *Outing* Aug. 440/1 The lamprey, or lamper-eel, may once have been considered a delicacy.

***lamplighter,** *n.*

1. A slim roll of paper or similar device for lighting lamps.

1833 NEAL *Down-Easters* II. 115 One side is clean, said she—and it will do for lamplighters! **1893** *Harper's Mag.* April 760/1 Mrs. Franklin . . . knocked off a chair accidentally the lamplighters which she had just completed. **1938** DAMON *Grandma* 25 On every mantelpiece stood a vase filled with 'lamplighters.' These were cunningly twisted papers (no envelope fell to the floor that Grandma did not take notice of it).

2. Any one of various fishes (see quots.).

*a***1876** *Ohio Fish Comm. 1st Rep.* 77 *P[omoxis] hexacanthus* . . . Strawberry Bass; . . . Lamp-lighter, of Kirtland. **1892** LUMMIS *Tramp Across Continent* 33 For three years I had been fairly starving for a bout with these beauties—a hunger which the catfish and 'lamplighters' of Ohio had utterly failed to satisfy. **1947** DALRYMPLE *Panfish* 84 Here, my friend, are the various names by which you would address that little gamester, the Crappie, depending on where you happened to be at the moment: Bachelor, . . . Lake Bass, Lake Erie Bass, Lamplighter.

***lance,** *n.* **1.** A slender, tapering pole. **2. lance rod,** a form of fishing rod. — **(1) 1902** *Sci. Amer.* 27 Dec. 459/1 The second truck is loaded with four or five hundred lances of well-seasoned cypress or spruce, each a trifle over fourteen feet in length. — **(2) 1885** *Outing* Oct. VII. 74/1 He . . . then untied, and fondly handled the several joints of a lance-rod.

***land,** *n.* In combs.

The number of combinations and phrases into which this term has entered is large. The more significant or interesting are here given. Many of them, usu. indicated by the dates of the quots., are either *obs.* or *hist.*

1. In miscellaneous combs.: (1) ***land bank,** =**federal land bank;** (2) **bank bill,** a note issued by the land bank organized in Massachusetts in 1740; (3) **-board,** [formed on the analogy of **seaboard*], the land bordering on the western frontier, *rare;* (4) **claim,** see as a main entry; (5) ***crab,** a landlubber, *slang;* (6) **district,** one of the districts into which a territory or state is divided for convenience in the disposition of public land; (7) **fence,** ?a fence on land as distinguished from a water fence, *rare;* (8) **fever,** a powerful urge to acquire title to public land, used esp. of the speculations of *c*1835; (9) ***-grave,** see as a main entry; (10) **hunger,** an intense desire for the acquisition of land, also **land hungry,** *a.;* (11) **list,** (see quot.); (12) **loafer,** [cf. G. *landlaufer*, land trotter, and see **loafer**], an idler, a good-for-nothing; (13) ***mail,** mail sent overland, *rare;* (14) **-mark Baptist,** (see quot.); (15) **Pitches,** a body of Ute Indians that formerly occupied a region in central Utah, *obs.;* (16) **plaster,** "rock-gypsum ground to a powder for use as a fertilizer" (*Cent.*); (17) **poor,** possessing ample land but lacking cash because of large tax payments, interest, etc., also attrib.; (18) **Reform,** *ellipt.* a party or movement that advocated a policy of homesteading public lands free to actual settlers, usu. attrib.; (19) **security,** land used as security for the issuance of currency; (20) **slide,** see as a main entry; (21) **state,** a state in which there are public lands open to homestead; (22) **tacks,** see as a main entry; (23) ***way,** "a road giving access to land" (*OED*).

(1) 1916 MYRICK *Fed. Farm Loan System* 67 All directors of the land bank must have been residents of the district for at least two years. — **(2) 1740** in Dow *Every Day Life* 173 One of these notes preserved in the cabinets of the Massachusetts Historical Society has written on its back, in old-time handwriting, 'A Land Bank bill reserved as a specimen of ye mad humour among many of ye people of ye Province, 1740.' — **(3) 1790** JEFFERSON *Writings* XVII. 306 If Great Britain establishes herself on our whole land-board our lot will be bloody and eternal war. **1793** *Ib.* III. 277 The position and circumstances of the United States leave them nothing to fear on their land-board. . . . But on their sea-board they are open to injury.

(5) 1861 *New Haven Palladium* 26 Dec. (Chipman), We 'Old Whales' . . . are not supposed by some 'land-crabs' to have much of a taste for the feathery tribe done up brown. — **(6) 1812** *Ann. 12th Congress* 2 Sess. 28 The Board of Land Commissioners, for the western land district in the State of Louisiana. **1831** PECK *Guide* 257 For the convenience of sale, the State is divided into land districts, which are designated by congress. **1883** *Rep. Indian Affairs* 187 An Act to create three additional land districts in the territory of Dakota. — **(7) 1644** *Southampton Rec.* I. 34 The little common shall be sufficiently fenced . . . both for land fence and for water fence. — **(8)** [**1801** HULL *Remarks* 29 He has . . . caught the fever and ague, and what is infinitely worse, that horrid disorder which some call the *terra-phobia.*] **1839** *N.O. Picayune* 23 April 2/2 Then came the *land fever*, which swept over the country like a pestilence. **1946** HODGINS *Mr. Blandings Builds Dream House* 16 Then, suddenly the land fever had seized them.

(10) 1862 J. M. LUDLOW *Hist. U.S.* vi. 221 The land hunger of the South now outstripped even the ambition of conquest of Mr. Polk. **1949** *Time* 4 July 13/1 The city gulped in armies of aging Iowans, land-hungry Oklahomans and dazzled tourists. — **(11) 1911** *Okla. Session Laws* 3 Legisl. 332 The assessor shall keep a book to be known as the 'land list.' — **(12)** [**1785** GROSE R^r, Land Lopers, or Land Lubbers. Vagrants lurking about the country, who subsist by pilfering.] **1836** *Knickerb.* VII. 21 'T would be too bad . . . to be . . . laughed at int' the bargain by every yaw-hawing land-loafer, about the borough. **1856** *Porter's Spirit of Times* 18 Oct. 113/1 Squirrels . . . may still be . . . ignobly plundered with shot-guns by land-loafers. — **(13) 1835** *Diplom. Corr. Texas* I. (1908) 53 You will write in duplicate and order one to be forwarded by the Land Mail by way of Fort Jessup. — **(14) 1905** *D.N.* III. 85 *Landmark Baptist.* Name used by and of that Baptist sect which stresses what it regards as the ancient landmarks or original principles of Baptist Christianity. [N.W. Ark.]

(15) 1839 FARNHAM *Travels West. Prairies* (1841) 107 Here live the 'Piutes' and 'Land Pitches,' the most degraded and least intellectual Indians known to the trappers. — **(16) 1887** *Courier-Journal* 24 Jan. 6/2 It is important that land plaster be sown early enough in the season to have it thoroughly dissolved by rains. **1894** *Vt. Agric. Rep.* XIV. 177 In order that the manure be all saved . . . sprinkle a little land plaster on the platform to absorb all moisture. — **(17) 1873** BEADLE *Undevel. West* 781 In the country, the old settlers are 'land-poor'—so rich that they can not pay their taxes. **1914** *Collier's* 31 Jan. 22/2 The land-poor farmer is a well-known institution in the Middle West. — **(18) 1846** *Whig Almanac 1847* 45/1 [Election return in N.Y.] *Land Reform.*—Governor, (Masquerier) 550. **1848** *Ib. 1849* 59/1 In New York and Ohio, 2,656 votes were given to the Land Reform Electors. — **(19) 1714** *Mass. Bay Currency Tracts* 134 Our Fathers about Twenty eight years ago, entred into a Partnership to Circulate their Notes founded on Land Security, stamped on Paper, as our Province Bills.

(21) 1900 *Cong. Rec.* 4 Jan. 648/1 [The bill] will give to the land States . . . 5 per cent . . . upon all lands that were disposed of by bounty land laws. — **(23) 1638** *Charlestown Land Rec.* 4 Ten acres of woodland . . . butting west upon the drift way towards the north river to the east upon the land way bounded on the south by Ed Convers. **1899** D. P. COREY *Hist. Malden* 90 The land-way and drift-way along the five acre lots ended at the head of the North River.

2. Designating individuals having to do with land: (1) **land agent,** see as a main entry; (2) **banker,** one who advocated or supported the Massachusetts land bank of 1740; (3) **boomer,** one who extols the virtues of a certain area of land, usu. because of his own interests in it; (4) **booster,** a real estate speculator; (5) **claimer,** one who holds a land claim; (6) **commissioner,** the officer in charge of the Bureau of Land Management in the federal government; (7) **contractor,** ?one who procures tracts of public land with the intention of finding settlers for it; (8) **grabber,** one who seizes land unfairly or selfishly; (9) **hog,** one who destroys the fertility of land by improper farming; (10) **hunter,** one who searches for public land for speculative purposes or with the intention of settling on it; (11) **jumper,** one who acquires the land of another by dishonest means; (12) **king,** one who holds large tracts of land; (13) **lawyer,** a lawyer who specializes in land law *q.v.;* (14) **layer,** a town official in New England whose duty it is to lay out land for occupancy, *rare,* cf. **layer-out;** (15) **leaguer,** a member of an association of Kansas settlers on the Osage ceded lands organized to fight the railroads' claims to their land; (16) **locator,** one who seeks out or locates land, usu. for others; (17) **looker,** see as a main entry; (18) **officer,** an officer in a land office; (19) * **pirate,** a person who pirates or appropriates by dishonest means land to which he is not entitled; (20) **prospector,** =**land hunter;** (21) **scout,** (see quot.); (22) **seeker,** one who seeks land on which to settle; (23) * **shark,** one who gets control of large tracts of public land or other land for speculative purposes, a land grabber, cf. **6.** (5) below; (24) **speculator,** one who speculates in land.

(2) 1741 B. LYNDE *Diary* 162 Election, where most of the number were Land Bankers, Capt. Watts for Speaker and negatived. — **(3) 1898** *Scribner's Mag.* XXIV. 425/1, I should have suspected a land-boomer in the doctor had there been anything aggressive or boastful in his manner. **1946** FOREMAN *Last Trek* 228 But they were suddenly menaced by the intrusion of land-boomers. — **(4) 1927** JAMES *Cow Country* 147 The old cowman had his suspicions of what these two gents was, the minute they got out of the horseless rig; they was land-boosters.

(5) 1911 J. F. WILSON (*title*), Land Claimers. — **(6) 1937** in M. D. WOODWARD *Checkered Years* 9 In 1883, according to the report of the land commissioner in Washington, eight million acres of government land had been disposed of to private persons within the year. **1949** *Western Polit. Quart.* March 119 J. O. Gallegos, defeated candidate for land commissioner, announced his support of Manuel Lujan for governor. — **(7) 1846** MACKENZIE *Van Buren* 260 He was a land contractor.—**(8) 1860** *Richmond* (Va.) *Enquirer* 7 Aug. 1/7 (Th.), Is not John Bell an outrageous land-grabber? **1942** LILLARD *Desert Challenge* 16 Nevada fell into the hands of the usual ego-minded land-grabbers of the frontier. — **(9) 1913** LONDON *Valley of Moon* 432 'Land hogs,' he snapped. 'That's our record in this country.'

(10) 1816 U. BROWN *Journal* I. 367 This John Hall was a Land Speculator & a Land Hunter & Informed him of the Vacancy. **1894** *Outing* June 172 Four or five rough-looking men—evidently land-hunters. — **(11) 1896** *Cong. Rec.* 16 March 2840/2 [Many men have had] to spend all they have . . . to purchase the claims of professional land jumpers. — **(12) 1884** *Mills' Mexico* (Las Vegas, N.M.) 1 June 45/2 There are some of these land kings who will lease their land for a term of years, and furnish the stock to stock it. — **(13) 1894** *Cong. Rec.* 11 July 7339/2 This bill is in the interest of land lawyers, and no other class of citizens. No . . . honest man can afford to support it. — **(14) 1673** *Essex Inst. Coll.* XXXVII. 22 Any two of those aforesayd land layers may act according to order from the town.

(15) 1878 BEADLE *Western Wilds* 432 It [1873] was the year of Grangers, *land leaguers* and war on the railroads. **1882** *Phila. Inquirer* 13 July, Rossa is stated to have sent instruction yesterday to select no Land Leaguers, but only disciples of his school. — **(16) 1816** U. BROWN *Journal* I. 364 Those present Land Locaters Surveys will hold good. **1839** *Cong. Globe* App. 23 Jan. 265/1 Land hunting soon became a distinct and profitable profession. Hence, sir, in the legal vocabulary of the day, the land 'locator' was as familiarly known by his name as the attorney and clerk of the court by their respective titles. — **(18) 1814** *Niles' Reg.* V. 322/1 The land officers in these districts are progressing to a close in ascertaining the character and extent of the private claims. **1905** *Indian Laws & Tr.* III. 606 A homestead entry duly allowed by the local land officers. — **(19) 1849** in *Amer. Sp.* XIX. 70/1 Viele, sehr viele [immigrants] sind noch übeler berathen gewesen und den sogenannten 'Land-piraten' in die Hande gefallen [etc.]. **1852** *Western American* (S.F.) 1 March 1/1 Land pirates and brazen faced swindlers may go on in their work of iniquity for a time with impunity, but retributive justice is sure to overtake them. **1948** *Sat. Ev. Post* 24 April 88/4 For a long time Little Rock had been a jumping-off-place for various land pirates who'd gone down to conquer Texas by force.

(20) 1887 *Courier-Journal* 2 Feb. 5/4 The country is full of land prospectors. — **(21) 1741** *Ga. Hist. Soc. Coll.* II. 114 That the indented servants . . . when their time of servitude was expired, were under the necessity of listing in the service of a bad paymaster, or starving, because there was a land scout and water scout to keep them from leaving the place by land or water. — **(22) 1845** HOOPER *Simon Suggs' Adv.* (1928) 30 He overtook the land-seeker. **1892** *Aberdeen* (S.D.) *Sun* 6 Oct. 5/1 The land-seekers who are now going into the state are of a desirable character. **1946** MCWILLIAMS *So. Calif. Country* 126 They sold prospective settlers so-called 'land seekers' tickets,' under an arrangement whereby the fare could later be applied on the purchase of railroad land. — **(23) 1829** in *Ohio Arch. & Hist. Quart.* XLVIII. 331 The Counsel is sure to be supported by the presiding Judges . . . & thus the Property of Society is Confiscated Legally between these *Land Sharks.* **1881** BARBOUR *Florida* 301 One class of persons against whom the immigrant must be on his guard is the 'land-shark.' — **(24) 1798** I. ALLEN *Hist. Vermont* 24 Lawyers and land speculators called on Mr. Allen. **1898** *McClure's Mag.* X. 523/1 The land speculators were in the habit of giving free excursions occasionally to prospective purchasers. **1948** *Reader's Digest* May 124/1 He was ill-educated, selfmade, an incurable land speculator.

b. Designating groups in some way interested in land: (1) **land association,** an association that invests money in land and land mortgages; (2) **company,** a company which deals in land, esp. in promoting the settlement of new lands [The *OED, s.v. land* II. 11, records one example, 1630, app. sporadic, of this expression; the Amer. use prob. represents an independent formation.]; (3) **emigrating company,** a company that sells land to emigrants.

(1) 1874 *Pa. Laws* 99 All land and building associations are hereby authorized to make sale of . . . the ground-rents created as aforesaid. — **(2) 1805** *Ann. 8th Congress* 2 Sess. 1044 Having never thought of purchasing any land from the Georgia land companies, I made no inquiry. **1909** RICE *Mr. Opp* 107 Mr. Opp . . . set to work to call a meeting of the Turtle Creek Land Company. **1949** *Pa. Hist.* April 124 The land companies later used as their main support the next proviso of the act [etc.]. — **(3) 1841** *Diplom. Corr. Texas* III. (1911) 247 The preliminary arrangements Mr. Burnley and myself have made with certain land emigrating companies.

3. Denoting, or in allusion to, governmental enactments, etc., with reference to public land: (1) **land bill,** a legislative bill relating to the sale or the granting of public lands; (2) **bounty act,** an act providing for the distribution of land by the government as a form of premium; (3) **certificate,** a negotiable certificate guaranteeing to the grantee the ownership of a certain tract of public land; (4) **day,** a day formerly set aside for the sale of public land; (5) **entry,** public land acquired by filing a claim, cf. **desert land entry;** (6) **grant,** see as a main entry; (7) * **law,** a law relating to the ownership of land, esp. to the proving up of a land claim, cf. **land lawyer;** (8) **office,** see as a main entry; (9) **patent,** a patent conferring ownership of a tract of public land; (10) **receipt,** ?a land warrant; (11) **relief bill,** a legislative bill making it possible for purchasers of public land to postpone payments; (12) **scrip, warrant,** see as main entries.

(1) 1710 BYRD *Secret Diary* (1941) 264, I went to the capitol . . . the Governor came to us and I endeavored to soften him concerning the passing of the land bill, but in vain. **1833** *Niles' Reg.* XLIV. 1/1 If the land-bill fails in the house, some also believe that the tariff bill will hardly pass the senate. **1873** *Newton Kansan* 27 Feb. 2/1 The soldiers' bounty land bill has been adversely reported. — **(2) 1854** BENTON *30 Years' View* I. 116/2 He voted against . . . all the modern revolutionary pensions and land bounty acts. — **(3) 1837** in GOUGE *Fiscal Hist. Texas* (1852) 70 The acting paymaster-general had issued upwards of thirty thousand acres of land-certificates for discharged soldiers. **1883** *Rep. Indian Affairs* p. xxv, Payne issues 'land certificates' to persons who do not desire to go down themselves by which he guarantees them 160 acres of land in the 'Oklahoma Colony.' — **(4) 1763** HABERSHAM *Letters* 10 The Governor [of S.C.] . . . has issued Warrants the last Land Day to the amount of four hundred thousand acres.

(5) 1814 *Steele P.* II. 728, I have sealed and placed it [the certificate] to the credit of your Accot. in payment for the Land-Entry above mentioned. — **(7) 1800** JEFFERSON *Notes* 139 They therefore thought it better to establish general rules, according to which all grants should be made, and to leave to the governor the execution of them, under these rules. This they did by what have been usually called the land laws, amending them from time to time. **1886** *Cent. Mag.* Nov. 12/1 The land laws of Kentucky had reduced to something like order the chaos of conflicting claims arising from the various grants. — **(9) 1841** *Niles' Reg.* 27 Feb. 412/3 On leave, Mr. Lincoln reported a bill to confirm land patents. **1884** BLAINE *20 Years of Congress* I. 459 They had their land patents, which were certificates of patriotic service in the Revolutionary war.

(10) **1814** *Steele P.* II. 730, [I] am hurried by those who wish land Receipts &c. and therefore do not recollect any other business done by the Assembly which would be new to you. — (11) **1854** Benton *30 Years' View* I. 12/2 The passage of this land relief bill was attended by incidents which showed the delicacy of members at that time.

4. Denoting activities concerned with acquiring public land: (1) **land finding,** the locating of land to be settled; (2) **hunting,** seeking out desirable tracts of public land for speculative purposes or with the intention of settling upon it; (3) **looking,** seeking land on which to settle or locating and appraising tracts of timber, also attrib.; (4) **lottery,** (*a*) a business in which land is disposed of by a lottery, (*b*) a lottery in which the prizes are land; (5) **opening,** an occasion when public land is made available for individuals to purchase and settle it, cf. ∗**opening,** *n.* **4;** (6) **rush,** a rush to occupy public land recently thrown open to settlement; (7) **speculation,** speculation in land, legitimate or illegitimate activities in the purchase and sale of unsettled land for profit, a single deal of this kind.

(1) **1845** Kirkland *Western Clearings* 2 A friend . . . became quite a proficient in the mysteries of land-finding. — (2) **1839** *Cong. Globe* App. 23 Jan. 265/1 Land hunting soon became a distinct and profitable profession. **1948** Dick *Dixie Frontier* 64 Several hundred persons were engaged in this business, known as land-hunting or land-looking. — (3) **1840** Thompson *Green Mt. Boys* II. x. 260 Remington seemed . . . convinced that it would not be prudent to proceed any further in the land-looking excursion. **1902** W. Hulbert *Forest Neighbors* (1903) p. xiii, Some thirty years ago, while out on one of his landlooking trips in the woods of Northern Michigan, my father came upon a little lake. **1948** [see **land hunting**]. — (4) (*a*) **1808** Ashe *Travels* iv. 34 He could purchase a share in a capital house; or he might buy a land-lottery. (*b*) **1832** Williamson *Maine* II. 530 Another expedient, which met with some success, was a *land-lottery.*

(5) **1914** *Sunset* April 766/2 They [in Idaho] filed on the water, made a new survey, . . . started work on dams and ditches and held the first of the famous 'land openings' at which lots were drawn to determine which buyer of a water right should have first choice in the selection of land. — (6) **1927** Sandburg *Songbag* 114 In the first Oklahoma land rush in the late 'Eighties. **1949** *World-Herald* (Omaha) 15 May F. 8/4 There was a mild land rush to buy the lots. — (7) **1821** Nuttall *Travels Arkansa* 103 General Calamees and his brother, two elderly men out on a land speculation. **1860** Greeley *Overland Journey* 36 The twin curses of Kansas . . . are land-speculation (whereof the manufacture of paper-cities and bogus corner-lots . . . is not half so mischievous as the grasping of whole townships by means of fraudulent pre-emptions and other devices . . .) and one-horse politicians. **1885** Howells *S. Lapham* xx, He's been dabbling in . . . patent-rights, land speculations.

b. Also with reference to unfair or illegal acquisition of land: (1) **land gobble,** =next, *rare;* (2) **grab,** the acquiring of large areas of land, frequently by dishonest means, cf. **land grabber;** (3) **grabbing,** =prec.; (4) **jumping,** the acquiring of another's land dishonestly, cf. **land jumper;** (5) **piracy,** the pirating or stealing of land, *obs.*, cf. **land pirate;** (6) **trap,** a dishonest land scheme, *rare.*

(1) **1873** *Newton Kansan* 9 Jan. 2/2 It beats all the land gobbles and swindles that the country has ever yet seen. — (2) **1876** W. M. Fisher *Californians* 114 'Land Grabs,' 'mining grabs,' etc. . . . are enabling a few persons 'to fill themselves with gold as a sponge fills itself with waters.' **1947** *Sierra Club Bul.* May 39 The immediate objectives make this attempt one of the biggest land grabs in American history. — (3) **1851** *S.F. Picayune* 19 Sep. 2/4 We can imagine the dismay . . . with which this future Knickerbocker will commence that chapter in his history, which will treat of land grabbing in San Francisco. **1884** Hill *Colo. Pioneers* 22 Pike subsequently indulged quite heavily in a kind of appropriation peculiar to the West, called 'land-grabbing.' — (4) **1910** Hart *Vigilante Girl* 46 His opinion was asked by a street tribunal over a 'land-jumping.'

(5) **1852** *Western American* (S.F.) 1 March 1/1 The citizens of this city and county assembled on the Plaza, for the purpose of taking into consideration the subject of Land-Piracy and Illegal Rents. — (6) **1801** *Spirit Farmers' Mus.* 205 He bought lands in Boston at the time all their great men got caught in the Georgia land trap.

5. In obsolete designations of vehicles, as **land ark, carriage, clipper, packet.**

*a***1861** Winthrop *J. Brent* 98 The great blue land-arks, each roofed with its hood of white canvas stretched on hoops. — **1800** Hawkins *Sk. Creek Country* 30 Wood for fuel is at a great and inconvenient distance, unless boats or land carriages were in use. **1859** *36th Congress 1 Sess.* H.R. Rep. No. 648, 740 A temporary contract has recently been awarded . . . for the conveyance of the United States mail . . . in steamships, steamboats, and land carriages. — **1853** *Shasta Courier* (Redding, Calif.) 17 Sep., A certain express friend of ours who took hurricane deck passage on one of them, says they [i.e., stage-coaches] are the greatest land clippers that he has yet seen. — *a***1846** *Quarter Race Ky.* 115 [Uncle Billy] was well known as the captain of a 'land-packet'—in plain terms, the driver of an ox-team.

6. In the names of animals: (1) **land-locked salmon,** one of several varieties of salmon which do not leave inland waters, esp. *Salmo sebago* of northern New England; (2) **moccasin,** =**highland moccasin;** (3) **otter,** an otter of the subfamily Lutrinae, inhabiting rivers and lakes; (4) **pike,** see as a main entry; (5) ∗**shark,** (see quots.), cf. **2.** (23) above; (6) **terrapin,** a land turtle.

(1) **1869** *Rep. Comm. Agric. 1868* 324 The taking of trout and land-locked salmon by any other means than by hook and hand-line is prohibited. **1901** Thompson *In Maine Woods* 7 Nowhere in Maine can the landlocked salmon . . . be found more plentiful than at Sebec and Onama lakes. — (2) **1836** Holley *Texas* 104 Land and water moccasin, coach whip, and copper heads are the only venomous snakes, besides the rattlers. — (3) **1844** Lee & Frost *Oregon* 71 Beaver was valued at two dollars per skin, though worth five dollars; land otter at fifty cents, though worth five dollars. **1947** Cahalane *Mammals* 200 The river or land otter has the outline of a small seal or a very big weasel.

(5) **1840** *Cultivator* VII. 81 That vile race of animals which infest the country, and which, before the discovery of the name of 'land sharks,' used to be known by the name of hogs. **1860** *Indiana Bd. Agric. Rep. 1858–9* 303 Hogs.—All kinds of mixtures, consisting in part of Grazier, Berkshire, Russian and China, together with the original 'elm pealers,' or land sharks. — (6) **1709** Lawson *Carolina* 133 The Land-Terebin is of several Sizes, but generally Round Mouth'd and not Hawks-Bill'd, as some are.

7. In grandiloquent or high-flown phrasal designations of America or of the U.S.

1770 *Boston Chron.* 1 March, The said horse . . . was not imported from England, but manufactured in this land of liberty. **1817** Paulding *Lett. from South* II. 209 He heard of America, the Sweet Land of the Exile, where the industrious stranger is ever welcome. **1825** Neal *Bro. Jonathan* II. 67 America—as everybody knows, *there*—is the land of liberty and equality. **1857** [see **8.** below]. **1861** Newell *Orpheus C. Kerr* I. 196 Our Union, my boy—our Land of the Eagle—is stricken sorely. **1885** Baylor *On Both Sides* 10 Even in the 'land of the free,' . . . there was something about her that made Bridget stammer when asking if she was the woman that wanted a 'gurl.' **1926** *Amer. Sp.* I. 277 America has been well named the Land of Hope; the United States is known throughout the world as the Land of Freedom.

b. Designating a particular state or region, sometimes cap. and often of only occasional application, as (1) *land of abstractions,* (see quot.); (2) *baked beans,* New England; (3) *blood,* (see quot.); (4) *Blue Grass and Bourbon,* Kentucky; (5) *corn dodgers,* (see quot.); (6) *cotton,* the South; (7) *Flowers,* Florida; (8) *gold,* California; (9) *Legree,* the South, in allusion to Simon Legree, the brutal slave dealer in *Uncle Tom's Cabin;* (10) *lumber,* Maine; (11) *perpetual youth,* (see quot.); (12) *pork and beans,* Massachusetts; (13) ∗*Promise,* the West; (14) *pumpkins,* Connecticut; (15) *Red Apples,* (see quot.); (16) *the Redwoods,* (see quot.); (17) *Setting Suns,* (see quot.); (18) *Silver,* (see quot.); (19) *Steady Habits,* see as a main entry; (20) *the honeybee,* Utah, cf. **Deseret;** (21) *the Sky,* the Great Smoky Mountain region of North Carolina; (22) *the Web-feet,* Oregon.

(1) **1845** *Cong. Globe* App. 11 Jan. 295/3 We have had bold messages from the land of abstractions [*sc.* Va.]. — (2) **1882** Steele *Frontier Army* (1883) 50 Here is the down-east Yankee, oblivious of all the ideas of the land of baked beans and hard cider, turning his native cunning to account at poker. — (3) **1826** *Spirit of Seventy-Six* I. 31 Look abroad, and Kentucky is rechristened in derision, the land of blood! Our fame is gone; our credit is destroyed. — (4) **1879** *Amer. Punch* Oct. 119/1 The following conundrum from the land of Blue Grass and Bourbon.

(5) **1850** Garrard *Wah-To-Yah* 140 Their hatred was of the deepest dye toward these unfortunate wights, so far from the 'land o' corn dodgers'—Missouri. — (6) **1859** in Moore *Rebellion Rec.* I. III. 92/2 I wish I was in de land o' cotton. — (7) **1867** Muir *Thousand-Mile Walk* (1916) 87 To-day, at last, I reached Florida, the so-called 'Land of Flowers.' — (8) **1857** *Spirit of Times* 25 April 117/1 I'm safely out of the land of gold now, 'pile' and all, thank Providence. **1887**

Three (S.F.) Aug. 3/2 Let the California Amateurs all join hands and cry, 'Hurrah for our land of gold!' **1948** in A. B. HULBERT *Forty-Niners* p. vii, Even the latter part of the emigrant road which left the true Oregon Trail and swung southward to the Land of Gold had split and branched. — **(9) 1855** *N.Y. Wkly. Tribune* 5 May 5/4 A slave named S——, with his wife and child, . . . were proceeding from 'the land of Legree and the home of the *slave*.'

(10) 1868 *N.Y. Herald* 2 July 4/2 From Maine, the land of lumber, there is a respectable share of a delegation. — **(11) 1883** WILDER *Sister Ridnour* 110 Adeline had the pleasure . . . of seeing Evangeline and her mother start for the land of perpetual youth [*sc.* Florida]. — **(12) 1852** *Deseret News* (Salt Lake City) 4 Sep. 1/1 There made his appearance a long-legged, lean, lank specimen of human nature whose *tout ensemble* bespoke him from the land of 'pork and beans.' — **(13) 1817** PAULDING *Lett. From South* I. 83 The prospect . . . will allure many of the young ones of the East, to the Land of Promise in the West. — **(14) 1829** *Mechanics' Press* (Utica, N.Y.) 5 Dec. 28/1 Ever since her husband had won her, as a 'strapping gal,' in the land of pumpkins, she had made it her duty to 'see to things.' **1832** *Boston Transcript* 20 Feb. 2/3 The most confirmed drunkard we ever knew, was an old man in the 'land of punkins.'

(15) *c***1873** DE VERE *MS Notes* 661 *Oregon* =Land of Red Apples. — **(16) 1888** MUIR *Picturesque Calif.* 460 The term 'Land of the Redwoods' is used to distinguish the long forest strip beginning near Santa Cruz and skirting the line of hills between mountain and sea as far north as the Oregon line. — **(17) 1881** MARSHALL *Through Amer.* (1882) 257 Upon their first arrival in this 'Land of Setting Suns,' as California has been peculiarly and distinctively named. — **(18) 1876** POWELL *Nevada* 49 Nevada—'The Land of Silver,'—but for *her* mineral wealth would, to-day, be the same cheerless waste that, prior to the development of her great silver treasures, she had been from time immemorial!

(20) 1853 *Harper's Mag.* April 612/2 When the Mormons left Nauvoo for the land of the Honey Bee, they had expended almost a million of dollars upon this temple. **1947** *Time* 21 July 21/1 After a hundred years there is milk and honey in the land of the honeybee.— **(21) 1898** *Epworth League Cook Book* 20 (*advt.*), The Line to Asheville, N.C. 'The Land of the Sky.' **1912** *Country Life* 1 April 45 In the 'Land of the Sky,' not far from Asheville, Grandfather Mountain looks dreamily down upon Linville Gap several thousand feet below. — **(22) 1862** *S.F. Bulletin* 22 Sep. 1/2 Others who have not been quite so successful, swear that . . . they will never return to the land of the 'Web-feet.'

For *land of mañana, of wooden nutmegs*, see **mañana, wooden nutmeg.**

8. In colloquial exclamatory phrases in some of which "land" is used euphemistically for "Lord." Cf. **landy.**

1825 NEAL *Bro. Jonathan* I. 108, I know *you;* don't care for *you;* land o' liberty; walk *into* you, any time, for half a sheet o' gingerbread. **1857** *Spirit of Times* 19 Dec. 243/3 Land of Freedom! how she looked, with a red bandana round her head, her hair all broke loose. **1865** A. D. WHITNEY *Gayworthys* 324 Land alive! Why, Grace, child, what's happened you? **1885** JACKSON *Zeph* 17 Land o' the livin'! What a hole! **1886** STAPLETON *Major's Christmas* 95 When I told her how I'd come to see Miss May Pennock, she says, 'Good land a mercy, she's been gone to New York these three months!' **1916** EATON *Idyl of Twin Fires* 152 'Land o' Goshen!' said Mrs. Bert. 'I ain't got no fit clothes.' **1939** *These Are Our Lives* 374 My lands, she works out in that garden from sun-up till night come without stopping for more than a spitting spell. **1948** *Reader's Digest* Dec. 145/2 'Land of Goshen,' said Granny, 'it never entered my head to show my weavin' at a county fair.'

b. Esp. (*for*) *land sakes*, and variants, as a mild oath.

1834 C. A. DAVIS *Lett. J. Downing* 232 'For the land's sake,' says, I 'jist look at it.' **1906** *Harper's Mag.* Nov. 887 'Land sakes!' ejaculated her sister-in-law. 'Why, Mehetabel Elwell, where'd you git that pattern?' **1948** *Sat. Ev. Post* 21 Aug. 92/2 Land's sakes, I guess the papers here will be full of it.

As the last term in **back, bad, barren, bay, beach, beech, bench, birch, bitter, black, bluff, bottom, bounty, branch, brush, buckshot, burnt, buttermilk, cabbage, canal, cane, cattle, cherry, chestnut, coal, Congress, corn, cotton, country, cow, crawfish, creek, ditch, divided, donation, dry, fast, ferry, field, fire, flowed, French, Frenched, fresh, gang, glade, gold, good, goose-nest, government, grapevine, hammock, hard, head, hemlock, high, hire, hobo, Hoosier, huckleberry, hummock, Indian, interval, intervale, isinglass, low, lumber, maiden, maple sugar, meadowish, Miami, military, mineral, ministry, mission, mixed, mixture, mow, mowing, muck, new, new-born, No Man's, non-resident, oak, Ohio, oil, Oklahoma, old, old field, out, over, overflowed, patent, patented, patroon, peach, pine, plains, post oak, prairie, pre-emption, premium, province, provision, public, public school, railroad, riddle, river, sagebrush, school, scrub, seated, second-hand, shell, shell hammock, silver, slave, social, sod, sold, soldier's, soldier's bounty, South, spotted, sprout, state, sucker, sugar, sunken, swamp, tax, timber, tobacco, town, trap, trembling, trust, tule, turpentine, ungranted, university, vacant, village, voodoo, warranted, white oak, wild, Yankeeland.**

Also *pl.* as the last term in **beaver, between, green, half-breed, Indemnity, interest lands.**

land agent.

1. In Massachusetts and Maine, an official who administers public lands. Now *hist.*

1828 *Maine Laws* III. (1831) 243 The Land Agent . . . is hereby authorized to execute deeds [etc.]. **1833** in *Pres. Mess. & P.* III. 423 A letter . . . complaining of the 'conduct of certain land agents of the States of Maine and Massachusetts in the territory in dispute between the United States and Great Britain.' **1937** WILSON *Aroostook* 85 Maine's land agent, Rufus McIntyre, . . . headed for far Aroostook, leading a force of two hundred militiamen.

2. An agent in charge of a government land office. Also a broker or agent who helps settlers acquire title to public or private land. Cf. **general land agent.**

1829 BASIL HALL *Travels N. Amer.* I. 144 A settler . . . sets about finding what are the marks upon the stakes nearest to him, and by reference to these, the land-agent, who has maps before him, can at once lay his hand upon the very spot. **1847** ROBB *Squatter Life* 124 The Land Agent . . . informed the unsuspecting squatter, that the stranger had . . . entered the claim. **1890** *Stock Grower & Farmer* 22 Feb. 8 Upson and Garrett, Land Agents and Conveyancers, Roswell, New Mexico. **1941** *Yankee* Dec. 48/2 In 1802, John Black, an important land agent, imported brick from Philadelphia.

b. An agent of a land-owning railroad.

1883 *Harper's Mag.* Nov. 943/2 To read the 'land agents' literature of the railroads which have land to sell in it [Missouri] one would think it a veritable land of Goshen. **1948** JOHNSTON *Gold Rush* vi/1 It was named in fact for B. B. Redding, first land agent of the Central Pacific Railroad Company.

land claim. A claim to a given portion of public land, based on the claimant's conforming to the requirements of the land law. Cf. ***claim,** *n.* **1.**

1812 *Steele P.* II. 695 In the prosecution of several very valuable land claims in Tennessee, I have to encounter a set of men well practiced in the art of forging. **1877** JOHNSON *Anderson Co., Kansas* 110 In November, 1858, a Free State squatters' court was organized . . . for the trial of contested land claims, etc. **1907** C. C. ANDREWS *Recoll.* (1928) 84 There is a store there, and a registry of land claims has been established there by the squatters. **1949** *Minn. Hist.* March 30 The Sioux disputed the German colonists' right to establish land claims on the site.

b. In areas that were formerly Spanish, a claim on land based upon a Spanish or Mexican grant. *Obs.*

1825 *Austin P.* (1924) II. 1061 He advises his son to not sell his land claims in Texas. **1860** *Statutes at Large* XII. 71 The private land claims in the Territory of New Mexico . . . are hereby confirmed.

c. A certificate or document embodying a claim to land.

1847 ROBB *Squatter Life* 117 Dick Kelsey's Signature to his Land Claim.

landeritt chaise. Also **landright.** [Origin unknown.] A now undefinable kind of chaise. *Obs.* Cf. **landau*, **landaulet(te)*. — **1760** *Boston Gaz.* 14 April 3/3 Isaac Hawes . . . has to sell 2 second-hand chaises, one a fall-back, the other landright. **1761** *Boston Post Boy* 1 June 4/2 A new Landeritt Chaise . . . to be sold.

land grant.

1. A grant of public land made to a railroad or school.

The first federal land grant to a railroad was to the Illinois Central R.R. in 1850. (Cf. **canal land, school land.**)

1862 *N.Y. Tribune* 21 March (Chipman), Some years since, the movement for a Pacific Railroad, attended by an enormous land-grant, assumed proportions that indicated the probable success of the movement. **1895** *Dept. Agric. Yrbk. 1894* 91 After the passage of the Morrill act of 1862 the legislature of New York voted to give the whole of New York's share of the land grant to the 'People's College.' **1948** *Milwaukee Jrnl.* 18 July 1/5 The company had trouble selling the land grant and the bonds it was forced to issue.

2. In areas formerly Spanish, a grant of land made by the Spanish or the Mexican government.

1865 *Santa Fe Wkly. New Mexican* 16 June 2/2 Any man who can't see it, is an enemy to wholesale swindles in land grants, to speculation upon 'lo! the poor Indian.' **1877** H. C. HODGE *Arizona* 47 Near the upper part of the San Pedro Valley is one old Spanish-Mexican land-grant, said to be the only one in the Territory which is legal and valid. **1900** *Cong. Rec.* 3 Jan. 637/2 Also, a bill . . . to confirm to the city of Albuquerque, in the county of Bernalillo and Territory of New Mexico, the Villa de Albuquerque land grant.

3. In combs.: (1) **Land Grant Act,** the Morrill Act of 1862 "donating public lands to the several states and territories which may provide colleges for the benefit of agriculture and mechanic arts [etc.]"; (2) **Bill,** a bill proposing the granting of public lands; (3) **college,** a state college created by the Land Grant Act; (4) **company,** a railroad company receiving a land grant; (5) **railroad,** a railroad built on public land donated for that purpose; (6) **road,** =prec.; (7) **sinking fund bond,** a sinking fund bond issued by a railroad receiving a land grant.

(1) **1895** *Dept. Agric. Yrbk. 1894* 96 The shares of the several States under the land grant act of 1862 ranged from 24,000 acres for Alabama to 990,000 acres for New York. — (2) **1884** *Cong. Rec.* 27 June 5695/2 The vote by which the Backbone Railroad land grant bill had failed to pass. — (3) **1889** *Cent. Mag.* Jan. 404/2 The land-grant colleges graduate men fitted to superintend farms and workshops. **1948** *Time* 12 July 37/1 It also supervises the spending of federal funds by land-grant colleges.— (4) **1900** *Cong. Rec.* 4 Jan. 648/2 Patents subsequently issued from the Government to the land-grant company.

(5) **1873** *Republic* I. 47 There are sixty-seven land-grant railroads in the United States. **1947** *Harper's Mag.* Dec. 560/1 He picked up cheaply vast holdings descended from a plundering land-grant railroad. — (6) **1873** *Newton Kansan* 13 March 2/1 The trunk lines are mainly land-grant roads. — (7) **1869** *Kansas Pacific Ry. Gold Loan* 5 Dabney, Morgan & Co. [etc.] . . . have accepted the Agency of the Kansas Pacific Railway Company for the sale of its new Seven Per Cent. Gold-bearing Railroad and Land-Grant Sinking Fund Bonds.

***landgrave,** *n.* In the Carolina colonies, a county nobleman. *Obs.* or *hist.*

1669 *Fundamental Constitutions of Carolina* ix, There shall be just as many landgraves as there are counties, and twice as many casiques, and no more. **1738** Byrd *Dividing Line* (1901) 77 Neither land-graves nor Cassicks can procure one drop for their wives. **1884** *Cent. Mag.* Jan. 437/1 Smith was raised to the rank of landgrave, and made governor of the colony three years after the success of his rice-patch. **1910** *S.C. Hist. & Geneal. Mag.* XI. 75 A 'barony' was the estate of a Landgrave or a Cassique.

Hence **landgraveship,** *n. Obs.*

1732 in *Cal. State P.* Amer. and W. Indies 218 Except the patents subsisting from the late proprietors for landgraveships and baronys which people have purchased under.

***landing,** *n.*

1. (See quot. 1882.) Cf. **3.** (*b*) below.

1851 in Wilson *Aroostook* (1937) 102 In forming a landing on the margin of such streams, the trees and bushes are cut and cleared out of the way for several rods back, and a considerable distance up and down, according to the number of logs to be hauled into it. **1882** Hubbard *Moosehead Lake* vii, A 'landing' is a term used by lumbermen to denote a place cleared of bushes and trees on the bank of a stream or pond, to which the logs cut in winter are hauled, in anticipation of the spring floods. **1902** Wm. F. Fox *Hist. Lumber Industry N.Y.* 25 Logs . . . were hauled . . . to the shore of some stream, where they were piled in huge tiers on the 'banking grounds' as they were called on the Susquehanna, or 'landings' or 'rolling-banks,' in northern New York. **1949** *Timberman* Feb. 51/1 Curves must be banked and surfaces must be smooth so truck drivers can maintain tight time schedules from landing to dump.

2. landing day, any of various days commemorating the first landing in America of certain explorers or colonizers. *Obs.*

1832 Watson *Hist. Tales N.Y.* 19 The memorable *landing day* of the discoverer [Henry Hudson] and his crew was on the 3d September, 1609. **1845** —— *Philadelphia* I. 15 The arrival, or *landing day* of Penn [Oct. 27, 1682], as a commemorative occasion, is but a modern institution, originally got up in 1824.

3. ***landing place,** (*a*) a town at which river boats regularly stop, (*b*) = ***landing 1.** Cf. **buffalo landing place.**

(*a*) **1791** *N.Y. Mag.* Dec. 702, I arrived at *Limestone* [Ky.] which is the general landing-place for people coming by water from the United States. **1837** *S. Lit. Messenger* III. 3 It had now become a regular landing place for a steamboat. (*b*) **1837** *Niles' Reg.* 29 April 142/3 The main roads . . . run from the camps to the landing places, or some stream of sufficient size to float down the logs on the spring freshet. *Ib.* 143/3 The owner . . . is obliged to make one contract to have the timber cut and hauled to the landing places, and another to have it run down.

As the last term in **boat, farm, steamboat landing.**

landlooker ˈlændˌlʊkə, *n.*

1. A person claiming to have looked at and appraised all the land in a given area (see quot.). *Obs.*

1840 *Knickerb.* XVI. 206 Another class of operators . . . became popularly known as 'land-lookers.' These met you at every turn, ready to furnish 'water power,' 'pine-lots,' 'choice farming tracts,' or any thing else, at a moment's notice.

2. One employed to look for valuable timberland. Cf. ***cruiser,** *n.* **1.**

1887 *Courier-Journal* 2 Feb. 5/4 Most of these land-lookers come from the great Northwest. **1902** White *Blazed Trail* 116 This is the usual method of procedure adopted by landlookers everywhere. **1946** Newton *P. Bunyan* 152 For many years after that Cap Fisher, who was once a land looker for Paul Bunyan, served delicious maple syrup from the lake.

land office.

1. A government office where business concerning public land is transacted, or an office where the business of a privately owned land company is carried on. Cf. **general land office.**

1681 *Md. Archives* VII. 242 An Act relating to the Land Office also passed in these words. **1784** Filson *Kentucke* 37 After the entry is made in the land-office, there being one in each county, the person making the entry takes out a copy of the location. **1811** Sutcliff *Travels* (1815) 177 My hospitable friends showed me into the land-office of the Holland purchase. **1884** W. Shepherd *Prairie Exper.* 6 Sometimes railways or land offices pretend to supply information. **1949** *Desert Mag.* June 11/3 The excuse the inspector from the state land office made was that his men could not make desert inspections during the hot weather.

b. A building which houses such an office. Also attrib.

1838 Flagg *Far West* I. 38 The buildings . . . are a very conspicuous bank, courthouse, and a land-office for the southern district of Illinois. **1873** *Newton Kansan* 9 Jan. 2/3 The land office was fortunately saved. **1949** *World-Herald Mag.* (Omaha) 3 July 8/3 Antique dealers and curio peddlers hold forth in old buildings that once accommodated gold assayers, land offices and mining machinery dealers.

2. In combs.: (1) **land office business,** a thriving business like that of a land office in boom times, *colloq.;* (2) **certificate,** a certificate of ownership of a tract of public land issued by a land office; (3) **lawyer,** a lawyer employed by a land office; (4) **money,** (see quot.), *obs.;* (5) **(treasury) warrant,** a warrant entitling its holder to ownership of certain land when given conditions are fulfilled.

(1) **1839** *N.O. Picayune* 2 April 2/3 A practical printer . . . could do a land-office business here. **1949** *Sat. Ev. Post* 25 June 33/1 One [customer] in a small Atlantic seashore community . . . was doing a land-office business in home-made clam chowder. — (2) **1839** *Indiana H. Rep. Jrnl.* 263 The fee simple of any tract of land is vested in the holder of a land office certificate to the land therein described. — (3) **1873** Eggleston *Myst. Metrop.* 92 He is a land-office lawyer. — (4) **1822** Woods *English Prairie* 256 The paper money is of two kinds, called land-office and current money; land-office money is bank paper that will pass at the land-office, but this money frequently changes.

(5) **1824** *Ky. Petitions* 180 There issued from the Land office of this commonwealth, a Land office Treasury Warrant . . . for 1462 acres. **1824** Doddridge *Notes* 99 Building a cabin and raising a crop of grain . . . entitled the occupant to four hundred acres of land, and a preemption right to one thousand acres more adjoining, to be secured by a land office warrant.

Land of Steady Habits.

1. Connecticut, app. in allusion to the strict morals of its inhabitants. Cf. **blue law(s).**

1805 *Intelligencer* (Lancaster, Pa.) 20 Aug. (Th.), The significant Essay of the Hero of the *Land of Steady Habits.* **1904** Morgan *Conn. as Colony & State* III. 106 Never had such a political cyclone swept over the 'land of steady habits.' **1945** Webster *Town Meeting Country* 223 This is the land of steady habits, and the landscape must not be too lushly rich.

2. (See quots.) *Obs.*

1831 *Boston Transcript* 4 Jan. 3/2 In the good old days of our fathers. . . . New England was *truly* the land of steady habits. *c***1873** De Vere *MS Notes* 661 New England—The 'Land of Steady Habits.'

land pike.

1. The hellbender *q.v.*

1687 Blome *Isles & Terr. in Amer.* 50 A Land-Pike is another strange Reptile, so called from its likeness to that Fish; but instead of Fins it hath four Feet. **1706** Phillips *New World of Words* (ed. 6), *Land-Pike,* a Creature in America, like the Fish of the same Name, but having Legs instead of Fins.

2. A hog of an inferior breed. Also attrib. Cf. **jumping alligator.**

1841 *Cultivator* VIII. 152, I am anxious that he should soon get rid of his land-pikes and alligators at such prices as will enable him to buy a better breed. **1842** *Ib.* X. 37 Hogs, Landpike variety, are so cheap that stealing them is no longer petit larceny. **1879** *Diseases of Swine* 189, I have not learned of a single person [in St. John's Co., Fla.] having an improved breed of pigs. All depend on the 'razor-back' or 'land pike.' **1890** *N. & Q.* V. 21, I think the term *land-pike* more frequently designates a thin, lank, half-wild swine.

***landscape,** *n.* **1. landscape architect,** one who practices landscape architecture. **2. landscape architecture,** (see quot. 1909).

(1) **1879** *Chi. Tribune* 3 May 1/3 (*advt.*), H. W. S. Cleveland, Landscape Architect. **1949** *Ib.* 1 Sep. 18/1 Altho he was a graduate landscape architect, he went to work in the old west park system as a laborer in 1884. — (2) **1909** *Cent. Supp.* 703/1 Landscape architecture, a term introduced to denote the treatment of landscape in a formal way, with groups of trees, flights of steps, vases, statues, etc. It implies a more formal style of work than *landscape-gardening.* **1949** *Agric. Hist.* Jan. 45/1 She received her B.S. and M.S. in landscape architecture at Pennsylvania State College.

land scrip.

1. A land certificate issued to a person or land company.

1834 JACKSON in *Pres. Mess. & P.* III. 52 Mr. St. Clair . . . had permitted the clerk in his office to be the agent of speculations in land scrip. **1900** *Cong. Rec.* 4 Jan. 648/2 All of said lands . . . which hereafter may be sold, located, or disposed of by the United States for cash or bounty land warrants, or land scrip. **1943** L. V. HAMNER *Short Grass* 174 Surveyors . . . bought up a lot of land scrip for almost nothing.

2. Scrip entitling states having insufficient public lands to certain amounts of land in public land states. See **college scrip, land grant college.**

1862 *Statutes at Large* XII. 504 The Secretary of Interior is hereby directed to issue to each of the States in which there is not the quantity of public lands . . . land scrip to the amount in acres for the deficiency of its distributive share. **1874** *Dept. Agric. Rep. 1873* 321 The amount already received by the colleges of the several States from the sales of the congressional land-scrip is $10,560,264.

landslide ˈlænd͵slaɪd, *n.*

1. The slipping of an embankment or of a mass of earth and rocks off a hill or mountain side; the place where such a slipping has occurred.

1838 *Niles' Reg.* 6 Oct. 96/1 *Land slide in Vicksburg.* . . . An avalanche or sinking of the earth on the margin of the landing at Vicksburg . . . threatens serious damage to the front street of that city. **1903** *N.Y. Ev. Post* 17 Sep. 12 The trains are now running as usual, all washouts and landslides having been repaired. **1949** *L.A. Times* 22 May 7/1 Several persons were killed by landslides.

transf. **1893** M. TWAIN *Traveling With Reformer* (1900) 353 (R.), It would bring down a landslide of ridicule upon him. **1895** *Cent. Mag.* March 734 There was then a great landslide of votes for McClellan. **1948** *Sat. Review* 5 June 5/1 The bull market in Wall Street, stimulated by obvious inflation and an almost-certain Republican landslide in November, will revive all luxury lines.

2. (See quots.)

1913 O. A. ROTHERT *Hist. Muhlenberg Co.* (Ky.) 113 In the early days, and even until comparatively recent times, some of the farmers used a ground-sled or a 'landslide' for short hauls. It was built on the principle of a sled, and so used during all seasons. **1948** DICK *Dixie Frontier* 308 When horses were available much hauling was done with a ground sled known as a 'landslide.' Built like a sled, it was used at all seasons, even as a family vehicle.

land tacks. *pl.* In phrase (orig. nautical), *to take* (*our*, etc.) *land tacks on board,* to travel by land. *Colloq.*

1776 *Mass. H.S. Coll.* 2 Ser. II. 304 Maj'r Meigs & I agree'd to take our Land-Tacks on board and quit the boat. **1813** *Salem Gaz.* 1 Oct. 3/3 The farms of Nantucket men were formerly upon the ocean, but Madison's war has obliged them to take land tacks on board, and pass the mountains. **1814** *Boston Spectator* 16 April 63/3 Are you lately arrived from a voyage? Yes, sir, and the longest voyage [i.e., a trip on land] I ever made with my land tacks aboard.

b. *To take a land tack,* to make a trip by land.

1937 EDWARD M. CHAPMAN *N. Eng. Village Life* 167, I took a 'land-tack' with them in a ramshakle wagon.

land warrant.

1. A negotiable warrant authorizing a surveyor or a land officer to grant to the holder a given amount of unlocated public land; a warrant wherein the land is described. Also attrib. Cf. **land office (treasury) warrant, military land warrant, warrant.**

1742 *Md. Hist. Mag.* XX. 261, I will give him Eighty pounds sterling. . . . Conditional he allso Assigns the fifty Acres Land wa[rra]nt **1826** BRADFORD *Ky. Notes* 66 Virginia having passed a law opening a land office for the sale of land warrants. **1866** *Internal Revenue Guide* 69 Any person shall be regarded as a land-warrant broker who makes a business of buying and selling land-warrants, or of furnishing them to settlers. **1948** DICK *Dixie Frontier* 8 Big speculators bought up the land warrants for a fraction of their actual value.

b. Preceded by designating terms: (1) **executed land warrant,** a land warrant the instructions of which have been executed by a surveyor; (2) **unlocated land warrant,** a land warrant granting an amount of land, but not specifying its location.

(1) **1788** WASHINGTON *Diaries* III. 398 A Mr. Oconnor, D. Surveyor in the Western Country, came here with some executed Land Warrants. — (2) **1787** T. JEFFERSON *Writings* II. (1853) 334 Individual speculators and sharpers had duped so many with their unlocated land-warrants.

2. In phrases: (1) *To locate a land warrant,* see ***locate 2. b;** (2) *to survey a land warrant,* to survey land as described in a land warrant.

(2) **1834** M. BUTLER *Hist. Ky.* 20 Land warrants were actually surveyed on the Kenhawa as early as 1772. **1949** *Tenn. Hist. Quart.* March 14 A man received or purchased a land warrant, surveyed it where he liked.

landy ˈlændɪ, *interj.* A euphemism for *Lordy. Slang.* Cf. ***land 8.**—**1877** JEWETT *Deephaven* x. 194 'Landy!' said she, 'if it ain't old Parson Lorimer!' **1909** STRATTON-PORTER *Girl of Limberlost* iv. 70 'Landy, ain't I a queen?' she murmured.

***lane,** *n.* **1.** On an improved highway, a strip of road sufficient for a single line of traffic. **2. lane snapper,** (see quot. 1876).

(1) **1926** *Amer. City* April 358/1 One of the most recent developments in highway design is the so-called super-highway where eight or more traffic lanes are provided for on the same right of way. **1930** *N.Y. Times* 2 Feb. 1/4 (*heading*), Cost of Six-Lane Vehicular Tunnel From West St. Is Put at $58,300,000. **1947** *Rocky Mt. News* (Denver) 2 March 23/2 The road . . . can be widened to four lanes at a minimum cost. — (2) **1876** GOODE *Fishes of Bermudas* 17 *Salpa purpurescens variegata* (The Lane Snapper) I cannot place. **1911** *Rep. Fisheries 1908* 316 The silk snapper . . . [and] the lane snapper . . . [are] fishes of food value common in the West Indies and southern Florida.

As the last term in **cow, devil's, farm, fire, picket lane.**

***language,** *n.* As the last term in **American, Chinook, Creek, Federal, Mohegan, Navaho, sign language.**

***lantern,** *n.* As the last term in **beach, crab, kerosene, yellow lantern.** See also **Dark Lantern.**

***lap,** *n.*

1. ?A small piece (of a skin). *Obs.*

The provenience of the quots. suggests that in this sense the term may be a borrowing from Du. *lap,* in the sense of a piece as contrasted with the whole. See *WNT, s.v. lap* (1) 1087. With **lapcloth** in **b.** below cf. Du. *lappendeken* in *WNT.* The only quot. in the *OED* for *lapcloth,* a covering for the lap, is of 1849.

1673 *N.J. Archives* I. 132 They presented about 20 deer skins, 2 @ 3 laps of Beaver, and 1 string of Wampum. **1687** *Doc. Hist. State N.Y.* I. 164 The custom @ duty upon every beaver skin commonly called a whole Beaver, nine pence. And that all other furs @ peltry bee valued accordingly that is for two half beavers nine pence, for four lapps nine pence.

b. lapcloth, ?a cloth to serve as a cover for the lap, or a large piece of cloth made up of smaller pieces sewn together. *Obs.*

1675 *Doc. Col. Hist. N.Y.* XII. 524 The Gov. present them [*sc.* Indians] with 4 Coates & 4 lappcloathes.

2. The space of ground inclosed in an angle of a rail fence. *Obs.*

1787 WASHINGTON *Diaries* III. 213 In the laps of the fence Inclosg. it 139 pumpkin hills were Planted.

3. In railroad euchre, points scored in excess of the number necessary for winning a game, so called when the excess is applied to the player's score in a subsequent game. Also **lap game.**

1864 DICK *Amer. Hoyle* (1880) 70 The *lap* . . . is simply counting upon the score of the ensuing game [etc.]. *Ib.,* When the Lap game is played, it is usual to count four points [etc.]. **1944** *Pocket Book of Games* 187 Laps. Points beyond 5 won in a game are carried forward to the next game.

4. A lapstreak boat. Cf. **5.** (3) below.

1867 *Harper's Mag.* Oct. 654/2 In the next boat-house you see two more [shells], besides three or four 'laps.' **1876** TRIPP *Student-Life* 130

A few choice spirits . . . [would] buy an old 'lap.' from one of the upper classes.

5. In combs.: (1) **lap robe,** a blanket or covering spread across the lap to cover the legs and feet, freq. used in carriages, sleighs, etc., cf. **buggy robe;** (2) **rug,** =prec.; (3) **-streak,** in a boat, a board so laid that its edge overlaps that of another board in the manner of clapboards, also attrib. and comb. passing into adj.

(1) **1866** [Ernst annotation]. **1875** STOWE *We & Neighbors* 373 He took her to ride in such a stylish carriage, white lynx lap-robe, and all! **1948** *Chi. Tribune* 15 Jan. 3/2, I loved the sleighrides too—snuggled under great buffalo hide lap robes. — (2) **1876** A. D. WHITNEY *Sights & Insights* I. 27 On a sea voyage. . . . She has a brown leather belt and reticule, and a brown veil and a sealskin-jacket, and a beautiful brown-shaded lap-rug. — (3) **1771** *Boston Gaz.* 11 March (Th.), Whale-boats and all sorts of Lap-streak Boats. **1815** *Essex Inst. Coll.* II. 60/2 [The boat] was lap-streak built and carried 3 lateen sails. **1874** LONG *Wild-Fowl* 89 The siding is put on commencing at the bottom in lap-streaks. **1897** *Outing* XXX. 113/1 The *Wanderer* was a sixteen-foot yawl, lap-streak, copper-riveted and built for salt water.

b. Used with reference to eating from dishes held on the lap, as **lap party, supper, tea.**

1866 LOWELL *Biglow P.* 2 Ser. p. lviii, A few phrases not in Mr. Bartlett's book which I have heard [include] . . . *Laptea;* where the guests are too many to sit at table. **1889** *Cent. Mag.* April 853/2 [As the] last act of this woful tragedy [of over-eating], which, till now, had been what is innocently called in the Colorado vernacular a 'lap-party'—the guests were summoned to 'a *full* supper.' **1920** LEWIS *Main Street* 12 They made a specialty of sandwich-salad-coffee lap suppers.

* **lap,** *v. intr.* Of a bear, to obtain fruit, nuts, etc., from a tree by pulling off the branches. Also **lapping season.**

1853 P. PAXTON *Yankee in Texas* 18 Just you sight that muscadine vine, whar one of the varmint's [a bear] been a lappin'. **1868** *Amer. Naturalist* May 122 [Bears] climb in order to 'lap,' as the hunter says, described by Mr. Clapp as drawing in branches to get the fruit. **1881** *Scribner's Mo.* Oct. 858/2 The fall . . . is called the lapping season, as he [the bear] ensconces himself in a tree-lap and breaks the limbs to pieces, in gathering fruits and nuts.

b. lapboard, *n.* a contrivance (see quot.) designed to induce wolves, coyotes, etc., to lap up a poisonous preparation. *Colloq.*

1892 LUMMIS *Tramp Across Continent* 159 A dozen augur-holes, bored almost through, were filled with lard, in which were a few grains of strychnine, and then the surface of the board was similarly smeared. . . . Any carnivorous animal that comes to a lapboard stays there—licking the lard from the board.

* **lapland,** *n.*

1. = **laplander.** *Obs.*

1887 *Cent. Mag.* Nov. 16/2 A procession of little darkies at Mount Vernon, Va. . . . supporting plates of hot . . . griddle-cakes, love-puffs, beaten biscuit, laplands.

2. (*cap.*) In combs. in the names of birds and plants: (1) **Lapland azalea,** a dwarf plant, *Rhododendron lapponicum;* (2) **longspur,** a long-clawed Arctic bird, *Calcarius lapponicus;* (3) **rosebay,** = **Lapland azalea;** (4) **snowbird,** (see quot.); (5) **waxwing,** the Bohemian waxwing, *Bombycilla garrula pallidiceps.*

(1) **1892** TORREY *Foot-Path Way* 31 The splendid Lapland azalea . . . is to be seen in all its glory upon the Mount Washington range in middle or late June. — (2) **1828** BONAPARTE *Ornithology* II. 53 [The] Lapland Longspur, *Emberiza Lapponica*, . . . long since known to inhabit the desolate Arctic regions of both continents, is now for the first time introduced into the Fauna of the United States. **1947** *Iowa Acad. Sci. Proc.* LIV. 381 Lapland Longspur . . . comes down from the north with more or less regularity during the winter. — (3) **1857** GRAY *Botany* 257 *R[hododendron] Lapponicum.* (Lapland Rose-bay.) . . . Alpine summits of the high mountains of Maine, New Hampshire, and New York. — (4) **1844** *Nat. Hist. N.Y., Zoology* II. 177 The Lapland Snow-Bird. *Plectrophanes Lapponicus.* . . . This rare arctic bird is not an unfrequent visitor in this State during the extreme cold of winter.

(5) **1917** *Birds of Amer.* III. 95 Bohemian Waxwing. . . . [Also called] Lapland Wax-wing.

* **laplander,** *n.* A kind of quick bread resembling a popover. *Obs.* — **1882** OWENS *Cook Book* 133 Laplanders. One egg, one cup of milk, one cup of flour, pinch of salt; beat well. . . . No baking powder required.

La Plata potato. (See quots.) *Obs.*

1838 *Mass. Agric. Survey 1st. Rep.* 33 The kinds [of potato] raised [in Essex Co.] are . . . the Biscuit potato . . . ; the La Plata, or long red, well known; and the Chenango. **1839** *Ib. 2d Rep.* 90 In the starch manufactory at Williamstown, they have found the long red or La Plata potato unfit for their purposes until the spring. *c***1887** in *Amer. Sp.* (1948) April 115/1 Then came the River la Plate, a large red variety.

la platte. = ***bowl,** *n.* **1.** *Obs.* Cf. ***platter.** — **1808** PIKE *Sources Miss.* II. App. 16 The third game [played by the Pawnees] alluded to, is that of La Platte, described by various travellers, and is played at by the women, children, and old men, who like grasshoppers crawl out to the circus to bask in the sun, probably covered only with an old buffalo robe.

larb lɑrb, *n.* [Origin unknown.] The bearberry, *Arctostaphylos uva-ursi.* Cf. **kinnikinnick.**

1846 SAGE *Scenes Rocky Mts.* xxvii, Frequent clusters of larb, richly laden with its deep red berry. *Ib.*, The larb-berry is of a deep red color, and somewhat larger than the common currant. **1871** *Rep. Comm. Agric. 1870* 413 Bearberry (*arctostaphylos uva-ursi.*)—This plant is the killikinick of the Indians and larb of hunters. **1877** STANLEY *Rambles in Wonderland* 143 The moose feeds upon willow, 'larb,' and various other shrubs and branches of trees.

* **larch,** *n.* As the last term in **American, black, black American, European, German, red, western larch.**

larder beetle. A dark-colored insect, *Dermestes lardarius*, the larva of which feeds on dried meat, fur, etc.

1868 *Amer. Naturalist* II. 165 *Ptinus fur* . . . is destructive to cloth, furs, etc., resembling the Larder-beetle (*Dermestes*) in its habits. **1895** COMSTOCK *Manual Insects* 539 The Larder Beetle, *Dermestes lardarius*. . . . This pest of the larder is the most common of all the larger members of this family [Dermestidae]. **1905** KELLOGG *Amer. Insects* 264 The larder- or bacon-beetle, *Dermestes lardarius*, . . . is about ⅓ inch long.

lard lamp. An illuminating device consisting of a receptacle containing lard and provided with a wick. *Colloq.* — **1852** EASTMAN *Aunt Phillis's Cabin* 53 The lard-lamp . . . lit up everything astonishingly. **1898** N. E. JONES *Squirrel Hunters of Ohio* 292 The man . . . did his reading at night by the light of the furnace or a 'log-cabin luminary,' a lard lamp.

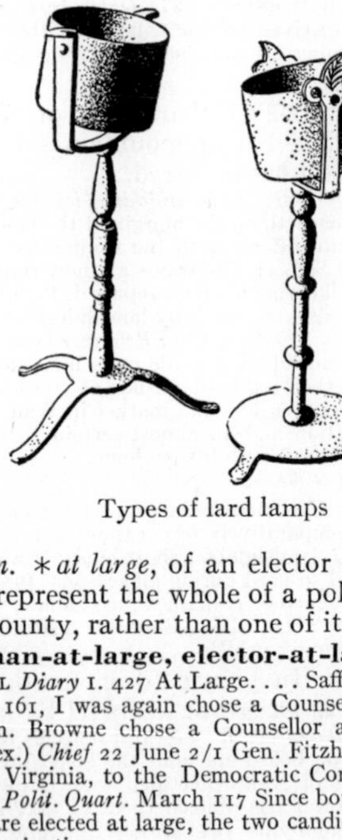

Types of lard lamps

* **large,** *n.* * *at large*, of an elector or representative: Chosen to represent the whole of a political unit such as a state or county, rather than one of its subdivisions. Cf. **congressman-at-large, elector-at-large.**

1696 SEWALL *Diary* I. 427 At Large. . . . Saffin 39. **1741** B. LYNDE *Diary* (1880) 161, I was again chose a Counsellor in ye 1st 18, and my Coz. Wm. Browne chose a Counsellor at Large. **1876** *Wkly. Comanche* (Tex.) *Chief* 22 June 2/1 Gen. Fitzhugh Lee is a delegate-at-large from Virginia, to the Democratic Convention at St. Louis. **1949** *Western Polit. Quart.* March 117 Since both United States Representatives are elected at large, the two candidates leading the field receive the nomination.

* **large,** *a.* In combs.: (1) **large bread,** ?bread in loaves in contrast to rolls, also attrib.; (2) **-mouth,** = next; (3) **-mouth(ed) (black) bass,** a species of black bass, *Huro floridana* or *Micropterus salmoides;* (4) **-toothed aspen,** (see quot. 1892); (5) **tupelo,** a southeastern variety of the tupelo, *Nyssa aquatica.*

(1) **1837** *S. Lit. Messenger* III. 660/1 [In New York] there are for sale hats, boots and shoes, . . . large bread, jewelry . . . : every thing on earth. **1876** SCUDDER *Dwellers* 7 There was a large-bread bakery at Skotos. — (2) **1884** GOODE *Fisheries* I. 401 The Large-mouth is known in the Great Lake region . . . as the 'Oswego Bass.' **1897**

Outing XXX. 219/2 [He] has killed Florida large-mouths weighing well up in the 'teens.' — (3) **1883** *Cent. Mag.* July 376/2 There are but two well-defined species, the large-mouthed bass and the small-mouthed bass. **1893** *Outing* XXII. 94/1 In the fresh pond above Nag's Head . . . are found the large-mouth black-bass. **1947** Edminster *Fish Ponds* 89 The largemouth bass . . . can be used in a pond. — (4) **1858** Thoreau *Maine Woods* 98 Its banks were . . . densely covered with . . . mountain ash, the large-toothed aspen [etc.]. **1892** Apgar *Trees Northern U.S.* 168 *Populus grandidentata,* (Large-toothed Aspen,) . . . [is] a large tree . . . with rather smoothish gray bark. **1938** Brown *Trees Northeastern U.S.* 149 Like the Large-toothed Aspen, this species is valuable as a cover-tree, establishing itself quickly in slashes and burns.

(5) **1810** Michaux *Arbres* I. 29 *Large tupelo,* . . . nom le plus général dans les Etats du sud. **1832** Browne *Sylva* 222 The large tupelo . . . attains the elevation of 70 or 80 feet. **1892** Apgar *Trees Northern U.S.* 113 (Large Tupelo.) . . . In water or wet swamps; Virginia, Kentucky, and southward.

b. Also in the names of or denoting plants, trees, and birds that are large of their kind, as (1) **large brown crane,** (2) **buttonwood,** (3) **buckeye,** (4) **flowered button snakeroot,** (5) **flowered magnolia,** (6) **fruited shagbark** (or **shell-bark**) **walnut.**

(1) **1844** *Nat. Hist. N.Y., Zoology* II. 218 The Large Brown or Whooping Crane has not been observed by me in this State. — (2) **1785** Marshall *Amer. Grove* 105 *Platanus occidentalis.* American Plane Tree or Large Button Wood. — (3) **1832** Browne *Sylva* 226 The large buckeye attains the height of 60 or 70 feet. — (4) **1843** Torrey *Flora N.Y.* I. 325 *Liatris scariosa.* Large-flowered Button-Snakeroot. . . . Sandy, moist bushy places; Long Island, particularly in Suffolk County. *Fl.* August–September.

(5) **1846** Browne *Trees Amer.* 2 Of all the trees . . . the Large-flowered Magnolia is most remarkable for the . . . beauty of its flowers. — (6) **1813** Muhlenberg *Cat. Plants* 88 *Juglans compressa* [or] *squamosa macrocarpa,* large-fruited shell-bark [or] shag-bark walnut.

c. Esp. **large-leaved,** as (1) **large-leaved cucumber tree,** (2) **magnolia,** (3) **maple,** (4) **umbrella tree,** (5) **Virginia mulberry tree,** (6) **Virginia snakeroot.**

(1) **1884** Sargent *Rep. Forests* 21 *Magnolia macrophylla.* . . . Large-leaved Cucumber tree. — (2) **1810** Michaux *Arbres* I. 34 Large leaved magnolia, . . . nom donné par moi. **1911** *Storrs* (Conn.) *Agric. Exp. Sta. Bul.* 69, 470 The Cucumber Tree . . . differs . . . from the Large-leaved Magnolia by the smaller size of its buds. — (3) **1892** Apgar *Trees Northern U.S.* 86 Large-leaved or California Maple. . . . Cultivated; from the Pacific coast. — (4) **1883** Hale *Woods & Timbers N.C.* 112 Large-leaved umbrella tree (*M. macrophylla*). . . . Its leaves and flowers surpass in size those of any tree or shrub in this country.

(5) **1785** Marshall *Amer. Grove* 93 *Morus rubra.* Large-leaved Virginian Mulberry Tree. — (6) **1901** Mohr *Plant Life Ala.* 480 Birthwort Family . . . [includes] Virginia Snakeroot, . . . Large-leaved Pipe Vine [etc.].

lariat ˈlærɪət, *n.* [Amer. cowboy adaptation of Sp. *la reata,* the rope.] A long rope, made of rawhide, horse hair, or hemp, used for lassoing or tethering animals; a long halter; a lasso. See **hondo,** and cf. **hair, rawhide lariat,** and **riata.**

1832 in H. L. Ellsworth *Washington Irving* (1937) 84 The Lariat is [a] long braided leather thong made of strips of Buffaloe hide of sufficent [*sic*] strength to hold the strongest horse. **1849** *31st Congress* 1 Sess. Sen. Ex. Doc. No. 64, 85 The sergeant, however, soon ascertained that the horse was an American one, and had a *lariat* (a long halter) upon him. **1948** *Popular Western* June 52/1 He dashed for the river, scooping up his own lariat as he surged into the water.

attrib. **1850** Garrard *Wah-To-Yah* i. 9 The lariat noose is sure to fall on their [the mules'] unwilling necks. **1875** *Chi. Tribune* 14 Oct. 7/1 The old camp-sites are marked by . . . lariat-stakes . . . to which the ponies have been attached. **1884** Hill *Colo. Pioneers* 195 Around his waist hung a raw-hide lariat, which he said was useful, in more ways than one. If he ran out of provision he made 'lariat soup' for dinner, drew it through his mouth for supper, and chewed it for breakfast.

b. lariat pin, a pin or stake, to be driven into the ground, and to which a lariat is secured. Cf. **picket pin.**

1881 *Rep. Indian Affairs* 93 [Manufactured] by the blacksmith: twenty-three beetle-rings, . . . one hundred and fifty lariat pins [etc.]. **1913** Cather *My Antonia* 39 He patted her flanks and talked to her in Russian while he pulled up her lariat pin and set it in a new place.

c. lariat rope, a lariat.

1859 W. P. Tomlinson *Kansas in 1858* 246 A lariet rope was coiled about his graceful neck. **1879** Williams *Pacific Tourist* 175/2 He took a piece of railroad iron and tied some lariat ropes to it (about 160 feet), and could find no bottom in the deepest springs he sounded with that length of rope. **1947** Price *Trails I Rode* 87, I wired the seat to the wagon bed, fastened the neck-yoke to the tongue so it couldn't come off, put Spanish hobbles on the bronc, with a lariat rope fastened to the hobbles.

lariat ˈlærɪˌæt, *v.* [f. the noun.]

1. *tr.* To catch with a lariat, to lasso.

1846 *Spirit of Times* 4 July 222/2 [The horse] has never been backed or before *lariated.* **1847** Henry *Campaign Sk.* 85 One of the men was evidently lariated, and was probably choked to death before he was pulled off his horse. **1886** *Outing* IX. 104/2 A mustang was lariated, saddled, and . . . we were *en route* for the mountains.

2. To stake out (an animal) on a tether. Freq. with *out.*

1849 in *Wagons West* (*c*1930) 125 When we stop early enough, for the cattle to fill themselves before night . . . we larriet (tie with long ropes to stakes) them till just at daylight when they are turned loose. **1852** *Laws of Utah* 93 They are carried from place to place packed upon horses or mules lariated out to subsist upon grass roots or starve. **1900** *Kans. Hist. Coll.* VI. 255 He . . . lariated his horse and lay down on the grass.

transf. **1869** *Overland Mo.* Aug. 127, I have even heard a Texan speak of land which he 'lariated out,' meaning thereby that he had just bought it from Government, but not occupied it yet.

larigo ˈlɑrəgo, *n. W.* [Poss. a cowboy modification of latigo *q.v.*] (See quot. 1894.) Also **larigo ring.** — **1894** *D.N.* I. 325 larígo: a ring at each end of the cinch . . . through which the *latigos* . . . are passed and wound to fasten the saddle. **1932** Bentley *Sp. Terms* 154 This [the largo or latigo] is secured and fastened at one end to the cinch ring (or larigo ring) on the saddle.

***lark,** *n.* In combs.: (1) **lark bunting,** the prairie bobolink, *Calamospiza melanocarys,* the state bird of Colorado, cf. **painted lark bunting;** (2) **finch,** =next; (3) **sparrow,** a sparrow, *Chondestes grammacus,* widely distributed west of the Alleghanies.

(1) **1869** *Amer. Naturalist* III. 296 That pretty and musical bird of the high plains, the Lark Bunting (*Calamospiza bicolor*), also occurred [along the upper Missouri R.]. **1944** *Mass. Audubon Soc. Bul.* Dec. 261 Miss Dorothy E. Snyder identified a Lark Bunting on October 24 at South Egremont, a first record for Berkshire County. — (2) **1825** Bonaparte *Ornithology* I. 47 [The] Lark Finch, *Fringilla Grammaca,* . . . frequent the prairies, and very seldom, if ever, alight on trees. **1877** *Field & Forest* III. 51 A pair of lark finches were seen and identified by Mr. Ridgway. — (3) **1887** Ridgway *Manual N.A. Birds* 414 *C*[*hondestes*] *grammacus.* . . . Lark Sparrow. **1917** *Birds of Amer.* III. 31 Lark Sparrow. . . . Other Names.—Quail-head; Road-bird; Lark Finch; Little Meadowlark.

b. *To catch the larks,* to prosper. *Slang.*

1857 *Spirit of Times* (N.Y.) 3 Jan. 294/1 Your farm kingdom must not, if you would *catch the larks,* be limited to one, two, or three products.

As the last term in **brown, eastern meadow, meadow, med, Missouri sky, mud, old field, prairie, shore, sky, Sprague's lark.**

larmon ˈlɑrmən, *n.* [f. Abnaki *oulamon,* the name for vermillion (red hematite), f. *oule,* good, pretty.] (See quot.) *Colloq.* — *a***1862** Thoreau *Maine Woods* 301 'What is that which ladies used?' he asked. 'Rouge? Red vermilion?' 'Yes,' he said, 'that is *larmon,* a kind of clay or red paint, which they used to get here.'

Larrea lɑˈreə, *n. W.* [J. A. H. de *Larrea,* a Spanish patron of art and science.] A small genus of American desert shrubs belonging to the family Zygophyllaceae. Also (not *cap.*) a plant of this genus, esp. the creosote bush.

1846 Emory *Military Reconn.* 77 In one view could be seen clustered, the larrea Mexicana, the cactus, (king) cactus, (chandelier) green wood acacia &c. **1861** Newberry *Geol. Rep.* 31 The slopes and gravel mesas contain a few clumps of cactus, *Larrea* and other desert-loving shrubs. **1893** Coville *Death Valley Exped.* 76 The dead branches of *Larrea* remain for many years without decomposing. **1925** Jepson *Flowering Plants Calif.* 604 Larrea [is] . . . very abundant in desert valleys and mesas in the Mohave and Colorado deserts.

larrigan ˈlærɪgən, *n. Me.* [Origin unknown.] (See quot. 1889.) Also **larriganed,** *a.*

1889 *N. & Q.* III. 308 A *larigan,* or *larrigin,* in Maine and New Brunswick, is a kind of boot or moccasin of yellow leather, having a long leg reaching above the knee. It is worn by lumbermen in the deep snows of winter. **1915** *Outing* Oct. 27/2 A 'shoe-pac' or 'larrigan' is a beef-hide moccasin with eight to ten-inch top, and with or without a light, flexible sole. **1922** *Short Stories* Feb. 129/1 [The dogs] clipped fangs at Cherriman's larriganed legs.

lashorn ˈlæʃɚn, *n.* Also **lash-horn.** [Origin unknown.] The Fraser balsam fir, *Abies fraseri*, of the Appalachian mountains. Also attrib.

1878 CHAS. B. COALE *Life & Adv. Wm. Waters* 18 The lashorn of White Top is peculiar to that locality, and of the thousands that have been transplanted, not one has ever been known to grow, though some have lived several years. **1889** *Auk* Jan. 51 The extreme summit is covered with a species of balsam known locally as the lashhorn. **1943** PEATTIE *Great Smokies* 197 The 'heath balds' . . . can only be compared to . . . the chaparral of California, and the *Krummholz* of the Alps, or the 'lashorn thickets' of dwarf spruce on the high mountains of Virginia, all of which are practically impenetrable growths of scrub.

lash rope. A rope used for lashing or securing a pack on a horse, sledge, or the like.

1806 LEWIS in *L. & Clark Exped.* V. (1905) 114 Sergt. Gass, McNeal, Whitehouse and Goodrich accompanyed them [*sc.* Indians] with a view to procure some pack or lash ropes. **1893** ROOSEVELT *Wilderness Hunter* 178 A skilful professional packer . . . adjusts the doubles and twines of the lash-rope so accurately, that everything stays in place. **1946** *Sierra Club Bul.* Dec. 5 Tying a loop on a lash rope, I made a throw.

'lasses ˈlæsɪz, *n. pl.* Short for "molasses." Also attrib. *Humorous* or *colloq.*

1775 *Broadside Verse* (1930) 141/1 The 'lasses they eat every day, Would keep an house a winter. **1854** M. J. HOLMES *Tempest & Sunshine* 317 Get along Jack, pokin' your fingers into the 'lasses cup. **1909** CALHOUN *Miss Minerva* 174 Aunt Minerva's in the kitchen right now makin' me a 'lasses custard. **1948** *Chi. Tribune* 14 March VII. 17/2 Now, come spring, it's ''lasses time' right over the border and 'sap's a-bilin',' Um! Um!

b. Esp. **'lasses candy.**

1807 IRVING *Salmagundi* x, This manufacture is called by the Bostonians *lasses candy.* **1856** *Porter's Spirit of Times* 18 Oct. 109/1 The one who could object to so harmless an amusement [as trotting for purses at a horse fair], would deprive his baby of 'lasses' candy on a Sunday, for conscience' sake.

lasset ˈlæsɪt, *n.* [F. *lacet*, in same sense.] A lasso. *Obs.* —**1848** ROBINSON *Santa Fe Exped.* (1932) 19 Five hundred frightened horses (with their lassetts and pickets flying about them) ran wildly down the Arkansas.

lasso ˈlæso, læˈsu, *n.* [Sp. *lazo*, in same sense. An Amer. borrowing.] A long rope, often of rawhide, having a running noose at one end and used chiefly for catching cattle and horses. Also attrib. Cf. **rope lasso.**

1819 *Petersburg* (Va.) *Republican* 5 Oct. 3/1 He was equipt with a *lassau*, a long knife, and sword; mounted on a high pummeled saddle. **1833** CATLIN *Indians* I. 253 The laso is a long thong, of rawhide. **1844** in *Amer. Sp.* XVIII. 126/2 The Mexican troops disbanded, like wild herds of mustangs, pursued in the prairie by the lasso-hunter. **1940** MENCKEN *Happy Days* 284 They lay in wait in dark Greene street with their dreadful hooks, saws, lassos, and knives.

lasso ˈlæso, læˈsu, *v.* [f. the noun.] *tr.* To catch with, or as with, a lasso. Also fig.

An Amer. borrowing. The *OED* has earlier evidence with reference to South America.

1831 BEECHEY *Voyage to Pacific* II. 62 Two or three men are dispatched for a wild bull, which they lasso in an equally dexterous manner. **1888** J. J. WEBB *Adventures* 212 There was a man in the corral lassoing a mule. **1945** *Chi. D. News* 30 Aug. 5/4 Trucks blocked the animal. James Givonda . . . then lassoed him.

transf. **1860** HOLMES *Professor* ii. 55 A country-boy, lassoed when he was a half-grown colt, just as good as a city-boy, and in some way, perhaps better. **1949** *Chi. Tribune* 21 Feb. I. 28/2 Dr. Hutchins announced his success in lassoing three renowned foreign scholars for appearance on the program.

lassoer ˈlæsoɚ, læˈsuɚ, *n.* One who lassoes. — **1883** SWEET & KNOX *Through Texas* xli. 584 Juan Gonzales . . . is said to be the champion lassoer in the world. **1884** W. SHEPHERD *Prairie Exper.* 52 There are few good lassoers in this part of the country.

lassoing ˈlæsoɪŋ, læˈsuɪŋ, *n.* [f. the verb.] Catching with a lasso. — **1838** TEXIAN *Mexico v. Texas* 48 The men were collecting the mules, and when these were driven together, the lassoing began. **1860** in *Narr. of Samuel Hancock, 1845–1860* (1927) 91, I here witnessed for the first time the operation of lassoing, which was expertly done.

* **last,** *n.* and *a.*

1. The last part (of the week, month, etc.), the last days.

1929 L. F. CARR *Amer. Challenged* 194 (Horwill), The corn will be hard by the last of August. **1931** A. E. MARTIN *Hist. U.S.* ii. 24 (Horwill), By the last of May he had formulated his plan and on the 29th he issued two proclamations.

2. a. *the last of pea time(s)*, see **pea time. b.** *last-rose-of-summer*, the New England aster.

(b) **1931** CLUTE *Plants* 140 The New England aster (*Aster Nova* [*sic*] *Angliae*), which lingers long in the fields and fence corners, is further distinguished as last-rose-of-summer. When this plant blooms, the Indian surveys it soberly and sighs 'It-brings-the-frost.'

latania ləˈtenɪə, *n.* Also **latinier.** [See quot. 1939.] The cabbage palmetto *q.v.* (see also quot. 1939).

1684 tr. JOUTEL *Journal* (1719) 14, I could see from the Ships . . . [an] Abundance of that Sort of Palm-Trees, in French call'd *Lataniers*, fit for nothing but making of Brooms, or scarce anything else. **1799** CUMING *Western Tour* 336 Some . . . cabins [were] covered over with a shrub like a large fan, called latania. **1848** *De Bow's Review* VI. 56 They are well pointed, without poles, and topped with latania. **1939** W. A. READ in *Zeitschrift* LXIII. 1–11. 46 *Bâche*, f. 1. The Dwarf Palmetto, *Sabal adansonii* Guerns.—Bayou Lafourche region; city of Lafayette. The usual term in Louisiana-French for this palmetto is *latanier*, m., a derivative of Carib *aláttani*, a name recorded by Breton for a West Indian palm with fan-shaped leaves.

attrib. **1868** *Putnam's Mag.* I. 594/1 Here and there . . . is a 'latanier-hut,' with adobe walls and a roof thatched with . . . palmetto.

* **latch,** *n.*

1. An earmark for domestic cattle to denote ownership. Also attrib. *Obs.*

1665 *Hempstead Rec.* I. 188 One brindled two yeere old heifer marcked on the neer ear with a latch marke. **1689** *Ib.* 433 Jeams Jackson his eare marcke is a slot in ye neere eare and a lach on ye uppor side of ye eare. **1745** *Smithtown Rec.* 85 Samuel Smith his ear mark is a latch under the left ear.

2. * **latchstring,** in various contexts having reference to leaving the latchstring out as a sign of hospitality and welcome. Also fig.

1858 *Ill. Agric. Soc. Trans.* III. 342 The people of the west . . . are always to be found with 'their latch strings out.' **1912** *Out West* March 213/2 The latch-string is always out, and we're making hundreds of new friends every year. **1948** *Salt Lake Tribune* 18 Dec. 10/3 The attorney general said the latchstring was out at the department of justice to corporations or their counsel to discuss the problems related to the antitrust laws.

* **lateral,** *a.* and *n.*

1. In a system of irrigation, a ditch leading directly out of the main canal or water supply.

1887 *Pall Mall Gaz.* 22 June 5/2 Ilissus . . . would not make a lateral for an irrigating ditch in Colorado. **1913** LONDON *Valley of Moon* III. xiv, A five-inch stream of sparkling water . . . flowed away across the orchard through many laterals. **1948** *Newsweek* 3 May 36/2 From there it would course through miles of canals and laterals and into the immemorially dry earth.

2. lateral (rail)road, a branch railroad. *Obs.* Cf. **coal lateral.**

1833 *Amer. R.R. Jrnl.* II. 786/1 The arrangements . . . would be equally available for the lateral road. **1834** *Ib.* III. 742/3 [It] was estimated in my report upon the Washington Lateral Railroad.

late unpleasantness, see **unpleasantness.**

latigo ˈlætɪgo, *n. W.* [Sp. *látigo*, in same sense.] A strap which secures the end of a cinch to the saddle. Also **latigo strap.** See **larigo.**

1889 *Cent.* 3367/1 latigo-strap. . . . A strong tapering leather strap used for tightening the cinch or girth in packing. [Western U.S.] **1894** *D.N.* I. 325 Latígo: a thong; used mostly in the plural. The two ends of the cinch . . . terminate in long, narrow strips of leather—*latigos*—which connect the cinch with the saddle and are run through an iron ring called *larigo.* **1948** *Popular Western* June 48/2 Shorty chattered as he tugged the latigo tight around the pinto's resisting belly.

* **Latrobe,** *n.* [f. J. H. B. *Latrobe*, its inventor.] A stove which may be used in a fireplace in a lower room in such a way as to heat also the room above it. In full **Latrobe stove.**

[**1846** *Sci. Amer.* 6 Nov. 49/4 A List of Patents. . . . To John H. B. Latrobe, of Baltimore, for improvement in Stoves. Patented 5th Sept. 1846.] **1905** *Washington Star* 24 Nov. 21 (*advt.*), We have for exchange for your old houses, with latrobe, furnace heat and basement kitchens, choice new homes. **1940** MENCKEN *Happy Days* 63 Our house in Hollins street, as I first remember it, was heated by Latrobe stoves, the invention of a Baltimore engineer.

* **latter,** *a.*

1. Latter-Day Brethren, the Mormons. *Obs.*

1845 *Quincy* (Ill.) *Whig* 13 Dec. 2/2 Some Mormon on a visit to Cincinnati, keeps the editor of the Commercial of that city, constantly primed with all the late, strange and wonderful news, movements, and so on, of the Latter Day Brethren at Nauvoo.

2. Latter-Day Saint, a member of the Church of Jesus Christ of Latter-Day Saints, a Mormon. Also attrib.

1834 *Ev. Star* (Kirtland, Ohio) Aug. 183 The church of Christ, recently styled the church of the Latter Day Saints, contumeliously called 'Mormons,' or 'Mormonites,' has suffered many privations. **1855** *N.Y. Herald* 4 Dec. 4/3 The Mormon, a Latter Day Saint paper, [is] published in this city. **1884** *Cent. Mag.* May 114 It was a Mormon elder, come to preach . . . the strange doctrines of the Latter-Day Saints. **1948** *Amer. Folk-Lore* Jan.–Mar. 21 To this day the Latter-Days Saints Church takes pride in asserting the child-like naïveté of the Prophet.

Also **Latter-Day Saintship.**

1882 BUEL *Metropolitan Life Unveiled* 415 This lady . . . prefaces her exposure of the Endowment rites with an absorbingly interesting story of how she became a convert of Latter-day Saintship.

∗**laughing,** *n.* An hysterical fit of laughter or involuntary facial distortion which formerly sometimes afflicted those who were under the stress of strong religious excitement. Also **laughing exercise.** *Obs.* Cf. **holy laugh.** — **1824** R. H. BISHOP *Hist. Church Ky.* 353 *Falling* . . . was succeeded by involuntary convulsive *laughing*, by the *jirks* [etc.]. *c***1843** B. W. STONE *Biography* (1847) 41 The laughing exercise was frequent, confined solely with the religious.

∗**laundry,** *n.* As the last term in **auto, Chinese, frame, hand, Troy laundry.**

∗**laurel,** *n.*

1. Any one of various American trees resembling or suggesting the European laurel, as: The evergreen magnolia; any one of various shrubs of the genera *Kalmia* and *Rhododendron;* the madrona, *Arbutus menziesi.* Also attrib. with *tree.* Cf. **noble laurel tree.**

1637 T. MORTON *New Canaan* 92 There are divers arematicall herbes . . . , Balme, Lawrell, Hunnisuckles, and the like. **1682** ASH *Carolina* 6 There are many other Fragrant smelling trees, the Myrtle, Bay and Lawrel, several Others to us wholly unknown. **1765** J. BARTRAM *Diary* 22 Sep., Wee observed our north laurel of Kallmia grow plentifully near ye falls. *a***1918** G. STUART *On Frontier* I. 59 There were also . . . some beautiful madrona or laurel trees. **1943** PEATTIE *Great Smokies* 266 They are, in reality, extremely dense tangled growths of rhododendrons (called 'laurel' by the mountain people), with some amounts of mountain laurel, blueberry, smilax, and occasionally sand myrtle.

2. In combs.: (1) **laurel almond,** the cherry laurel, *Laurocerasus caroliniana,* found in the South; (2) **brake,** a dense growth of laurel, cf. **canebrake;** (3) **hell,** =prec., cf. ∗**hell,** *n.* **1;** (4) **magnolia,** the evergreen magnolia, *Magnolia grandiflora,* or the sweet bay, *M. virginiana;* (5) **oak,** see as a main entry; (6) **slick,** (see quot. 1917); (7) **swamp,** a swamp having a dense growth of laurel; (8) **thicket,** =**laurel brake;** (9) **tulip,** a species of the tulip tree.

(1) **1827** *Western Mo. Rev.* I. 252 The handsomest of the family, is the laurel Almond, *laurus Caroliniensis.* — (2) **1853** KENNEDY *Blackwater Chron.* 73 A man could walk about for a week . . . if he got into a big laurel-brake. **1893** *Outing* Oct. 61/2 Only in the wilds of the backwoods, . . . or in the mountains where tracts of laurel brakes give refuge against men and dogs, do the Virginia deer hold their own. — (3) **1920** *Outing* June 190/2 From lookout cliff on northwest side of Siler's, a little below summit, you get a good view of laurel 'hells.' — (4) **1817** S. BROWN *Western Gaz.* 145 The laurel magnolia is the beauty of the forest. **1850** S. F. COOPER *Rural Hours* 476 The small Laurel Magnolia, or Sweet Bay, is found as far north as New York, in swampy grounds.

(6) **1917** KEPHART *Camping* II. 24 Those great tracts of rhododendron . . . cover mile after mile of steep mountainside where few men have ever been. The natives call such wastes 'laurel slicks.' **1943** PEATTIE *Great Smokies* 266 Such areas are known locally as 'laurel slicks.' — (7) **1788** SCHÖPF *Reise* II. 242 In den tiefern Stellen der Wälder finden sich überall Sümpfe voll meist immergrünender Gewächse (Evergreen or Laurel Swamps). — (8) **1750** T. WALKER *Journal* 49 Just at the foot of the Hill is a Laurel Thicket. **1945** *Mass. Audubon Soc. Bul.* Jan. 274 It was June 25 when I sat on a log in a laurel thicket. — (9) **1744** MOORE *Voy. Georgia* 98 The trees in the groves are mostly bay . . . American ash, and the laurel tulip.

As the last term in **American, bay, big, broad-leaved, California, Catawba, deer-tongued, dog, European, great, ground, horse, mountain, pale, sassafras, sheep, swamp, tulip, umbrella laurel.**

laurel oak. Either of two American oaks, *Quercus laurifolia* and *Q. imbricaria,* having glossy, laurel-like leaves.

1810 MICHAUX *Arbres* I. 23 *Laurel oak,* . . . dénomination secondaire dans les Etats à l'ouest des Monts Alléghanys. **1832** BROWNE *Sylva* 271 West of the [Allegheny] Mountains . . . it is called Jack Oak, . . . and sometimes from the form of the leaves, Laurel Oak. **1884** SARGENT *Rep. Forests* 154 *Quercus imbricaria.* . . . Shingle Oak. Laurel Oak. **1901** MOHR *Plant Life Ala.* 131 Between Bon Secour and Perdido Bay low, sandy hills . . . support a high forest . . . of laurel oak and Cuban and long-leaf pine. **1949** COLLINGWOOD & BRUSH *Knowing Your Trees* 201/1 Laurel oak has been widely used, especially in the South, as an ornamental, particularly as a shade or street tree.

laurier almond. =**laurel almond.** — **1818** DARBY *Emigrant's Guide* 80 The most important vegetable productions [include]: . . . *Celtis crassifolia,* Hackberry, *Cerasus caroliniana,* Laurier almond [etc.]. **1829** *Western Mo. Rev.* III. 57 An area of three acres, shaded with laurier almond, and Bois d'arcs, the most beautiful trees of the American forest.

∗**law,** *n.*

1. A policeman (see also quot. 1930). *Slang.*

1835 *Vade Mecum* (Phila.) 17 Jan. 3/6 A dreadful uproar is heard in the domicile of the Simpkinses. The law opens the house and the belligerent couple are extracted like an oyster from its shell. **1930** *Durant* (Okla.) *D. Democrat* 30 Dec. 3/5 'The law west of Pecos' has ever been a phrase of highest salutation and respect for the peace officers of that broad expanse. **1949** *Boston Sun. Globe* 1 May (Fiction Mag.) 3/5 If the law comes around, just leave 'em to me. . . . I know lots of ways to make a good law out of a bad one.

2. Law and Order (party), the party or group in Rhode Island who opposed the Dorrites. *Obs.*

1846 *Nat. Intelligencer* 24 March 3/4 The 'Law and Order' party has clearly fulfilled, and excellently fulfilled, its public mission. **1846** *Quincy* (Ill.) *Whig* 16 April 2/4 The Rhode Island election has resulted in the triumph of the 'law and order' party, by a majority of 173 for Governor.

b. (See quot. 1914.)

1855 *N.Y. Wkly. Tribune* 8 Dec., We, the Law-and-Order party, the Union-loving patriots, and State Rights party of Kansas Territory, . . . pledge ourselves to support and maintain Gov. Shannon. **1857** *Lawrence* (Kans.) *Republican* 6 Aug. 2 In order to get this class of Northern men to act with them, the pro-slavery party agreed . . . to change the name of the party from pro-slavery to the law and order party. **1914** *Cyclo. Amer. Govt.* II. 312 *Law and Order Party,* a name taken by the pro-slavery party in Kansas during the struggle for the control of that territory following the Kansas-Nebraska Act . . . of 1854.

c. A group in San Francisco who opposed the Vigilance Committee in that city. *Obs.*

1856 *Sacramento Union* 5 Aug. 3/1 E. Cohen and N. Koshland, representatives, the one of Law and Order, the other of Vigilancism, became excited on Saturday in discussing the relative merits and demerits of their respective parties.

d. A name assumed by political groups wishing to appeal especially to law-abiding citizens.

1879 *N.Y. Herald* 17 Sep. 5/2 The law and order party of Newark, led by a number of Presbyterian, Methodist, and Baptist clergymen, have resolved to nominate an independent ticket for Mayor and Aldermen.

3. In combs.: (1) ∗**lawman,** an Indian councilman, *obs.;* (2) **office,** the office of a lawyer; (3) **school,** a school, operating independently or as part of a university, in which instruction in law is given.

(1) **1857** *Herald of Freedom* (Lawrence, Kans.) 31 Jan. 1/2 When any one shall be elected to be a lawman he must not refuse to serve, unless he shall pay five dollars in order that he may be excused. . . . The lawmen are required to be present at the Councils wherever held on the Ottawa land—sickness only may hold them back. — (2) **1819** in MACKENZIE *Van Buren* 155, I considered it absolutely impossible for him to confine himself to so irksome an employment as a clerkship in a law office. **1949** *Sat. Ev. Post* 2 July 68/2 At one time he worked in the Paducah law office of old Judge Bishop. — (3) **1818** *N. Amer. Rev.* March 428 A Law School is established at the University, under the superintendence of the University Professor of Law. **1855** *N.Y. Wkly. Tribune* 21 July 6/4 The first institution of its character in the New-England States was the Litchfield Law School established in 1782 by Tapping Reeve. **1949** *Sooner Mag.* June 24/1 He is attending law school at Wayne University.

As the last term in **Alien and Sedition, Audubon, black, blue-sky, donation, fence, fifteen gallon, Fugitive Slave, gag, Granger, hat, health, herd, hickory, higher, homestead, homesteading, inspection, Interstate Commerce, Jim Crow, land, liquor, Logan black, Lynch('s), Maine, Maine liquor, mountain, National banking, non-importation, non-intercourse, nullification, organic, out, oyster, padlock, paleface, patrol, prairie, pre-emption, primary, prohibition,**

prohibitory, Raines, registry, scaling, school, Scott, sedition, Sherman Anti-trust, snap, squatter, stand-up, state, stay, steamboat, stock, stop, swamp law. Also pl. in **blue, Cherokee, Duke's laws.**

Lawler wheat. [f. James *Lawler*, who brought it to Va. from Chester Co., Pa.] (See quot.) *Obs.* — **1817** *Niles' Reg.* XIII. 239/2 It appears, by many certificates of respectable gentlemen in Virginia, that for several years past they have cultivated a species of wheat, called by them the 'Lawler wheat,' that effectually resists the attack of the Hessian fly. **1826** *Va. Herald* (Fredericksburg) 30 Aug. 2/1 Lawler wheat, carried from Pennsylvania to Virginia, was cried up for some time, in the latter state, as being proof against the insect.

lawn grass. (See quot.) — **1889** *Rep. Secy. Agric.* 389 *Paspalum platycaule*, called lawn grass or Louisiana grass, usually grows on low rich land, but is perfectly at home in poor pine land. As a pasture grass it can not be excelled, and is also an excellent lawn grass.

***Lawrence,** *n.* [George Newbold *Lawrence* (1806–95), Amer. ornithologist.] Used in the possessive in bird names (see quots.).

1858 BAIRD *Birds Pacific R.R.* 181 *Myiarchus lawrencii.* Lawrence's Flycatcher. **1869** *Amer. Naturalist* II. 185 Other birds observed [near Cajon Pass, Calif.] were a flock of Pigeons . . . , Lawrence's Goldfinch (*Chrysomitris Lawrencii*), and the Western Bluebird. **1887** RIDGWAY *Manual N. Amer. Birds* 486 Northwestern United States (New Jersey, etc.). *H[elminthophila] lawrencei.* Lawrence's Warbler. **1901** *Land of Sunshine* May 376 They are termed, by those who know them intimately, Willow goldfinch, Arkansas goldfinch, and Lawrence's goldfinch.

***Lawson,** *n.* [John *Lawson*, d. 1712.] **Lawson's cedar, cypress,** the Port Orford cedar, found in the West.

1874 HITTELL *Resources Calif.* 360 Lawson's cedar (*Chamaecyparis lawsoniana*) is a tree of little value in the forest, but as an ornament it is highly prized. **1884** SARGENT *Rep. Forests* 179 *Chamaecyparis Lawsoniana.* . . . Port Orford Cedar. . . . Lawson's Cypress. Ginger Pine. **1897** SUDWORTH *Arborescent Flora* 82 (*Chamæcyparis lawsoniana*. . . . [Commonly called] Lawson's Cypress (Cal., Oreg.). **1928** BAILEY *Cyclo. Horticulture* 730/2 Lawson's Cypress . . . is one of the most beautiful conifers and very variable, about 80 garden forms being cult[ivated].

Lawton blackberry. A variety of blackberry introduced by Lewis A. Seacor of New Rochelle, N.Y., in 1834.

1847 DARLINGTON *Weeds & Plants* 128 The kind known as the 'Lawton' or 'New Rochelle Blackberry,' is a splendid fruit, and is now becoming abundant in the markets of our cities. **1860** *Ill. Agric. Soc. Trans.* IV. 446 There is more danger the Lawton Blackberry will become a pest. **1928** BAILEY *Cyclo. Horticulture* 510/2 The varieties most commonly grown are . . . Lawton and Snyder.

***lawyer,** *n.*

1. As a name for birds: **a.** The American avocet. **b.** The blacknecked stilt.

(a) 1813 WILSON *Ornithology* VII. 126 American Avoset: *Recurvirostra Americana;* . . . from its perpetual clamour and flippancy of tongue, is called by the inhabitants of Cape May, the Lawyer. — **(b) 1844** *Nat. Hist. N.Y., Zoology* II. 265 The Lawyer, *Himantopus nigricollis*, . . . is known under the various popular names of Tilt, Stilt, Longshanks and Lawyer. **1917** *Birds of Amer.* I. 223 Black-necked Stilt. *Himantopus mexicanus*. . . . [Also called] Longshanks; Lawyer.

2. Used locally for various fishes, as the American burbot, *Lota maculosa*, the bowfin or mudfish, or the gray snapper, *Lutianus griseus*.

1857 HAMMOND *No. Scenes* 45 That . . . is a species of ling; we call it in these parts a *lawyer.* **1885** J. S. KINGSLEY *Stand. Nat. Hist.* III. 97 *Amia calva*, the bowfin . . . or lawyer. **1897** *N.Y. Forest, Fish, & Game Comm. 2d Rep.* 246 *Lota maculosa*. . . . Ling; Lawyer. . . . One of the most difficult of the fresh-water fishes to transport. **1948** *Wis. Fishing Reg.* 4 Carp, dogfish, garfish, lawyers or eelpout . . . when taken in any manner cannot be returned to the water.

As the last term in **constitutional, cornstalk, corporation, horse, jury, lake, land, land office, patent, Philadelphia, prairie, railroad, sea, self-made, ship's, shyster, trial lawyer.**

***lay,** *n.*

1. Price or rate, terms or conditions of a sale, contract, employment, etc. (see also quot. 1902). *Colloq.*

1703 *N. Eng. Hist. & Gen. Reg.* (1880) XXXIV. 92 So soon as wee delivered him the particulars wisht for, wee supplyed the Indians at a very moderate lay. **1772** WASHINGTON *Diaries* II. 81 Agreed with my Overseer . . . to continue another year on the same lay as the last. **1816** PICKERING 121 *Lay*, terms or conditions of a bargain; price. . . . *A low word. New England.* **1902** *D.N.* II. 238 *Lay*, advantage afforded by a contract, situation or employment, as 'A good lay'—'A poor lay.' [Southern Ill.]

2. The plowshare of a moldboard plow.

1868 *Iowa Agric. Soc. Rep. 1867* 266 There is no clogging and the mould and lay are so hardened that they scour readily.

3. (See quots. 1871, 1901.)

1871 DE VERE 303 A kind of limited partnership is, in the West, not unfrequently called *to go on lays.* **1901** GRINNELL *Gold Hunting in Alaska* 90 A 'lay' is a lease given by a claim owner to a party to work a claim for a certain percentage of the outcome. **1909** O. HENRY *Roads of Destiny* 322 We five are on a lay. I've guaranteed you to be square, and you're to come in on the profits equal with the boys.

b. layman, one who engages with others in mining operations for a share of the entire gains.

1899 *Harper's Wkly.* 8 April 344/1 The lay-men struck it the first hole, and out of thirty burnings took out $40,000. **1908** BEACH *Barrier* 190 Some of his laymen are quitting work. They've cross-cut in half a dozen places and can't find a color.

***lay,** *v.*

1. ***lay-by,** the final flooding of a growing rice crop. Also **lay-by flow, water.**

1854 in COMMONS *Doc. Hist.* I. 262 This is called the lay-by flow. Up to the time of this flow, is about ninety days for Rice sown the first week in April. **1859** *Harper's Mag.* Nov. 728/2 The 'lay-by water' . . . is kept on until the rice is fully headed and the blossoms have dropped. **1940** E. M. COULTER *T. Spalding* 77 In the last flowing, called the lay-by, the water was kept on the field until the rice stalks had borne their fruits.

b. lay-by time, *S.* the time in summer when the cultivation of crops ceases. *Colloq.* Cf. **4.** below and see **laying by.**

1945 *Amer. Sp.* Dec. 306/2 This prized interim, called by all classes and colors *lay-by time.*

2. In other noun and adj. combs.: (1) **lay-down,** designating a collar that folds over; (2) **off,** the period during which an employee is absent from work or is "laid off," *colloq.;* (3) **out,** see as a main entry; (4) **over,** (*a*) a stop or a break in a journey, cf. **7.** below, (*b*) a transplanted oyster.

(1) 1870 LOGAN *Before Footlights* 375 Master Dolly in a jacket and lay-down collars, home from school for the Christmas holidays. — **(2) 1889** *Gallup* (N.M.) *Gleaner* 27 March 1/3 Fred Diamond is taking a lay-off. **1949** *This Week Mag.* 12 March 21/2 When he resumes work after a layoff he finds he gets dizzy speeding around the wall of a small bowl. — **(4)** (*a*) **1873** BEADLE *Undevel. West* 756 Two invalids and myself . . . applied for a 'lay over,' unable to go further. **1947** *Sierra Club Bul.* May 60 During layover days the pack train is sent back to pick up a relay of supplies or forward to establish a cache for a new camp. (*b*) **1891** *Scribner's Mag.* Oct. 472/1 Young oysters so treated are termed 'lay-overs.'

3. **To lay away*, to bury.

1866 WHITTIER *Snow-Bound* l. 205 Who, hopeless, lays his dead away. **1885** M. E. WILKINS in *Harper's Mag.* March 594/1 It was hardly six months since my poor sister was laid away.

4. **To lay by*, *S.* to cultivate (a crop) for the last time. *Colloq.* Cf. **1. b.** above and see **laying by.**

1759 in *W. & M. Coll. Quart.* 1 Ser. XI. 106 Mowing oats & laying by corn. **1864** in EASTERBY *S.C. Rice Plant.* (1945) 289, I have got the Rushes out of the Rice and am now laying by the up land Crop. **1947** *Democrat* 25 Dec. 3/4 This year when the corn was 'laid-by' the crotalaria came up voluntarily.

5. **To lay down*, to deliver (a commodity) at a given point or destination.

1865 *Atlantic Mo.* June 695/1 Grain can be laid down in New York ten cents a bushel cheaper than it now is done. **1885** *Santa Fe Wkly. New Mexican* 17 Sep. 2/7 The animal [a stallion] is 4 years old, and 'laid down' there [in Albuquerque] cost the carpet king $1,500.

b. To submit to, give up, cease trying, fail to function. *Colloq.*

Cf. *EDD lie down* in a related sense, i.e., to give up, turn tail.

1898 *Scribner's Mag.* XXIII. 453/2, I swear I hate to lay down to such a nincompoop. **1901** MERWIN & WEBSTER *Calumet 'K'* 64 You've never had to lay down yet, and you don't now. **1911** HARRISON *Queed* 87 Your body's got to carry your mind around, and if it lays down on you [etc.]. **1923** WATTS *L. Nichols* 157 The engine had laid down, he didn't know what was the matter.

6. *To lay off*, to mark off (a field) with rows or furrows preparatory to planting.

1787 WASHINGTON *Diaries* III. 187 Brought another of the Muddy hole-plows home from French's, and set it to laying off the 20 acre cut designed . . . for Carrots. **1847** *Fla. Plant Rec.* 223, 2 [slaves] laying off cotton land in Redoak field.

b. To plan or intend (to do some specified thing). *Colloq.*

1842 in THOMPSON *M. Jones* (1872) 48 I'd been laying off to go to see Miss Mary, but my nose wasn't quite well whar I blazed it on that dratted grape-vine, and so I thought I mought as well go long with 'em. **1941** STUART *Men of Mts.* 144 (Wentworth), For the last 34 years I've laid off to go back.

c. To desist from, to cease annoying or bothering. *Slang.*

1919 *Amer. Mag.* May 42/2 If you guys don't lay off of me I'll bounce the two of you. **1926** J. BLACK *You Can't Win* vii. 87 Hey, kid, lay off o' that. **1931** IRA L. REEVES *Ol' Rum River* 289 My deductions at the time were that his original purpose was to try to get me to 'lay off' Dugan. **1949** *Life* 4 July 14/3 To some articulate businessmen everything would be fixed but quick if the government would just cut taxes and lay off business generally.

7. * *to lay over,* to postpone.

1838 *Speeches of D. Barnard* 132 Whether the suggestions of the committee shall be acted upon at all, at the present session, or whether the subject shall be laid over for such consideration as the community may see fit to bestow upon it. **1890** *St. Nicholas Mag.* Sep. 920/1, I know of tennis matches . . . that have been laid over for hours because of a sprained ankle.

b. = * *to lie over, q.v.*

1841 *Cultivator* VIII. 152 The stage lays over here this day. **1900** DRANNAN *Plains & Mts.* 224 Here we laid over three days to let our horses rest up a little.

c. To excel or surpass. Also *to lay it all over. Slang.*

1865 MARK TWAIN *Sk., New & Old* 33 All said he laid over any frog that ever *they* see. **1911** J. F. WILSON *Land Claimers* xiii. 179 He let on as how anybody . . . could lay it all over you. **1923** WATTS *L. Nichols* 210 In Luther's own language, she laid over the whole bunch.

d. To place under restrictions.

1890 *Standard* 20 Nov. 5/2 Great regions were 'laid over.' They were taboo to the hunter until the fur animals had time to recover themselves.

8. * *To lay up,* to put up (a log building). *Obs.*

1788 MAY *Jrnl. & Lett.* (1873) 86 To-day finished laying up the house, and put on the roof. **1847** in HOWE *Ohio* 377 A block-house . . . was laid up of large beech logs, and rather open.

b. To take out of operation. Also to stop, "lie up," said of a train.

1860 HANCOCK *Five Years* 184 The monster steamboats are 'laid up' for the season. **1864** *Santa Fe Wkly. New Mexican* 25 Nov. 3/2 Large trains have been compelled to 'lay up' on the road.

9. *To lay* (something) *up against* (someone), to hold something against a person. *Colloq.*

1856 M. J. HOLMES *L. Rivers* vi. 63 The poor critter is sick, and I shan't lay it up agin her. **1903** WILKINS *Six Trees* 61, I hope you won't lay it up against her.

For *to lay fence-worm,* see ***fence,** *n.; to lay pipe,* see ***pipe,** *n.*

***layer,** *n.*

1. layer cake, a cake made of two or more layers between which jam or some other sweet filling is used. Also fig. Cf. **Washington pie.**

1882 OWENS *Cook Book* 188 (*heading*), Layer Cake. **1905** *N.Y. Ev. Post* 16 Dec., In the mixing of this literary layer cake most of the humor rose to the top. **1946** WILSON *Fidelity* 172 Once in a great while a new recipe got loose in our neighborhood: new brands of teacakes, or layer cakes, or cake icings.

2. layer-out, in colonial times, one appointed to lay out or measure off lands, roads, etc. *Obs.*

1635 *Essex Inst. Coll.* IV. 90/1 Overseers & layers out of lotts of ground for this presinct of Salem. **1740** *East-Hampton Rec.* IV. 114 The passing highways above mentioned were allowed for . . . by us the layers out, as witness our hands.

As the last term in **Confederate, land, lot, pipe, track layer.**

laying by. (See quot. 1800.) Also **laying-by time.** Cf. ***lay,** *v.* **4.**

1800 TATHAM *Communications* 56 What is termed the *laying by* of the crop in autumn; that is, the last ploughing and hoeing which it requires before it is suffered to remain at rest and ripen like other fruits of the earth. **1850** *Rep. Comm. Patents 1849: Agric.* 169 Between the 'laying by' of the crop of cane and the rolling season, it grows luxuriantly. **1939** *These Are Our Lives* 76 At layin'-by time in July we gen'ly has some time off but since we been makin' 'backer dis is not always de case.

layout ˈleˌaʊt, *n.* [f. the verb.]

Cf. ***outfit,** *n.* **3.** Many of the extended meanings of **layout** and **outfit** are identical.

1. A laying out; the order, arrangement, or disposition of a city, land, etc.

1850 J. H. TRUMBULL in *Conn. Col. Rec.* I. 203 (*note*), The remainder of the volume consists of records of Wills and Inventories, and of conveyances of land and lay-outs of grants to individual proprietors. **1888** *Harper's Mag.* July 285/1 Although the conception of its lay-out dates back nearly half a century, the tree planting that has added so much to Washington was begun only in 1872. **1890** *Conn. Rec.* XV. 448 The lay-out [of the grant of land] is recorded in *Col. Record of Deeds.* **1908** *Sci. Amer.* 22 Aug. 119 The construction of the new layout of the tracks called for some heavy and costly work.

b. The make-up of a newspaper, book, or the like (see quot. 1924).

1924 *Publishers' Wkly.* CVI. 121/1 *Layout.* Practically, the working diagram for the printer to follow. Usually marked to show the general grouping of a job and specifying the sizes and kinds of type to be used. **1949** *Amer. Photography* Jan. 29/1 A picture story will generally run from about twelve to fifteen shots in the first layout.

2. The general setup or arrangement of a gambling device (see also quots. 1864, 1890). Also transf. Cf. **monte layout.**

1850 *S.F. Picayune* 10 Sep. 3/1 As the fellars say at monte, he was a 'lay out' I didn't want to bet on. **1864** DICK *Amer. Hoyle* (1866) 456 He deals out two [cards], one at a time, and places them side by side upon the table, with their faces up. This is called the 'lay-out' and upon these cards the players place their bets. **1890** *Cent.* 3382/2 *Faro lay-out,* the thirteen cards of a suit, which are fastened to the faro-table, and on or near which the stakes are placed. They are usually arranged in two rows of six cards each, ace to six in one, and eight to king in the other, in reversed order, and the seven at the end next to the six and eight. **1948** *Sat. Ev. Post* 10 July 74/3 Professional gamblers will not buck a new game until they have carefully studied the layout and have assured themselves it is on the level.

3. An "outfit," situation, "setup." *Colloq.*

1869 MCCLURE *Rocky Mts.* 219 They get up a most expensive 'layout' for him. **1890** *Stock Grower & Farmer* 26 April 3/1 Mr. Armour's daughters must have struck their pa for a new layout of spring clothes and somebody had to be squeezed. **1929** *Variety* 1 May 53/1 Well we walk right into this arrangement without knowin a thing about the layout.

b. A number of articles laid out for use or display; equipment or apparatus for use in some particular business or pursuit. *Colloq.*

1890 *Saginaw Courier-Herald* 4 July, A fine layout of fruits and vegetables at C. Rimmele's, 122 North Hamilton. **1894** *S.F. Midwinter Appeal* 10 Feb. 1/5 Do you fellows want a coffee and doughnut lay-out and ride on brake-beams. **1947** FAIR *Fools Die on Friday* 100 It's a good-looking layout. Nice furniture. Nice suite of offices.

4. A group or party of people; somewhat derogatorily, a family. *Colloq.*

1869 *Overland Mo.* Aug. 128 Several persons in our 'lay-out' (*i.e.,* our company) in New Mexico 'swapped' good American horses for mustangs. **1904** HARBEN *Georgians* 20, I hain't never seed nothin' good in him nur his layout. **1927** RUSSELL *Trails* xiii, I tell you they was a pretty sad lookin outfit. They sho was a lonesome layout.

***lazuli,** *n.* In combs.: (1) **lazuli bunting,** =next; (2) **finch,** *Passerina amoena,* found in the West; (3) **painted bunting,** =prec.

(1) **1887** RIDGWAY *Man. N. Amer. Birds* 447 Western United States, east to Great Plains, south, in winter, to western Mexico, *P*[*asserina*] *amœna.* . . . Lazuli Bunting. **1917** [see **lazuli painted bunting**]. — (2) **1825** BONAPARTE *Ornithology* I. 61 Lazuli Finch. *Fringilla Amœna.* **1839** AUDUBON *Ornith. Biog.* V. 64 The Lazuli Finch, one of the handsomest of its tribe, and allied to the Indigo Bird, . . . was added to our Fauna by Thomas Say. **1874** COUES *Birds N.W.* 170 The prettily-colored and delicate little Lazuli Finch is found to be common. — (3) **1917** *Birds of Amer.* III. 72 Lazuli Bunting *Passerina amœna.* . . . [Also called] Lazuli Painted Bunting.

***lazy,** *a.*

1. *W.* Of a type of brand or of letters and figures in a brand: Lying on the side.

1887 *Scribner's Mag.* II. 508/2 Words used in connection with . . . life on the plains: . . . *flying-brand; lazy-brand* [etc.]. **1921** F. S. HASTINGS *Ranchman's Recoll.* 232 Strange stories drifted in about a certain outlaw speckled yearling on the Lazy 7 Ranch—he had thrown every boy with rodeo aspirations who had tried to ride him. **1947** *Steamboat* (Colo.) *Pilot* 9 Jan. 4/7 Strayed—Two white face cows and calves, branded Bar lazy AC.

2. In combs.: (1) ***lazy-back,** (see quot. 1875), also **lazy-back chair;** (2) **bird,** the cowbird, the female of which lays her eggs in the nests of other birds; (3) **board,** (see quot. 1930), also transf.; (4) **Susan,** (*a*) (see quot. 1947), (*b*) also designating a tiered and revolving hat rack.

(1) **1875** KNIGHT 1268/1 *Lazy-back,* . . . a high back-bar to a carriage seat. It is sometimes made shifting, so as to be removed at will.

1887 *Pop. Sci. Mo.* XXX. 748 A lazy-back chair makes a capital observing-seat. **1902** *Sears Cat.* (ed. 112) 537/2 Narrow Lazy Backs. Complete, as shown in illustration. — (2) **1917** *Birds of Amer.* 243 Cowbird, *Molothrus ater ater*. . . . Other Names: Cow Blackbird . . . Lazy Bird [etc.]. — (3) **1894** SEARIGHT *Old Pike* 138 Samuel Trauger, an old wagoner, fell from his lazy board while descending Laurel Hill. **1930** OMWAKE *Conestoga Teams* 18 The driver, instead of having a seat inside, rode on the lazy board, a sliding board of strong white oak that was pulled out on the left-hand side of the wagon body. **1948** *Sat. Ev. Post* 25 Dec. 69/3 Then, warmed and comfortable, Kemp pulls himself up into the cupola and stretches out on the lazy boards in the darkness. — (4) (*a*) **1934** WEBSTER. **1947** *Savings News* Dec. 9 A gleaming maple Lazy Susan with copper base contains two spacious removable compartments for hors d'oeuvres and crackers, a plain surface for cheese, cold cuts and sandwiches, center bowl for cottage cheese or salad spreads, mustard jar and salt and pepper set. (*b*) **1945** *Chi. D. News* 6 Sep. 32 The 'Lazy Susan' hat rack is a rotating plastic tree which keeps each headdress on a separate level within view and reach.

One form of Lazy Susan

leached ashes. Ashes that have been leached, used as fertilizer. *Obs.*

1813 *Yankee* 14 May 4/2 The manure of leached ashes has been much used on Long-Island. **1839** BUEL *Farmer's Companion* 74 *Leached ashes* are in many cases beneficial, particularly within the influence of the marine atmosphere. **1868** *Mich. Agric. Rep.* VII. 130, I propose, also, to test leached ashes in the same way, to ascertain from whence comes the beneficial action of wood ashes.

leachy ˈlitʃɪ, *a.* [f. the verb.] Of soils: Of a loose or sandy formation, porous. — **1846** EMMONS *Agric. N.Y.* I. 247 [The soil] is rarely sufficiently tight to retain manures well, and yet they are not excessively leachy. **1886** *Harper's Mag.* Sep. 533/2 The subsoil is too loose and leachy.

∗**lead,** *n.*[1] In combs.: (1) **leadback,** the red-back sandpiper, so called because of its winter coloration; (2) **-colored gnatcatcher,** a western gnatcatcher related to the blue-gray gnatcatcher (see quot. 1869); (3) **pipe cinch,** a sure thing, also attrib., *slang;* (4) **plant,** a shrub of the genus *Amorpha*, esp. *A. canescens*, found in the West and reputedly indicating the presence of lead ore in the soil.

(1) **1917** *Birds of Amer.* I. 237 Red-Backed Sandpiper, *Pelidna alpina sakhalina*. . . . Other Names. . . . Lead-back. — (2) **1869** *Amer. Naturalist* III. 474 Resident species not found westward of this valley [of the Colorado R.] were . . . the lead-colored Gnatcatcher (*Polioptila plumbea*), Malherbe's Flicker [etc.]. **1881** *Ib.* XV. 214 Later, in Arizona, I noticed the remaining species of gnatcatcher peculiar to our fauna, the Arizona or lead-colored gnatcatcher. — (3) **1904** W. H. SMITH *Promoters* v. 102 He was one of the lead-pipe-cinch kind, . . . and what he once buckled to he never let get away from him. **1921** *Outing* July 183/1 It is a double-barrelled lead-pipe cinch that you'll be more anxious to get it back than you ever were about a $10 loan overdue. — (4) **1833** EATON *Botany* (ed. 6) 15 *Amorpha canescens*, lead plant. . . . Somewhat woody. **1918** VISHER *So. Dakota* 71 Gravelly areas are blotched with the low shrubs of the lead plant where the matrix is loam. **1939** *Nat. Geog. Mag.* Aug. 220/1 Chief among the peas is a group of close relatives: lead plant, . . . prairie clovers, together with indigo plant.

∗**lead,** *n.*[2]

1. In mining, a lode or vein. Also transf. and fig.

1814 BRACKENRIDGE *Views La.* 148 Leads, (or loads) are the smaller fissures that connect with the larger, which are called by the miners, *caves*. **1869** S. BOWLES *Our New West* vii. 136 A quaint old miner of the valley, who, 'prospecting' for society that day, had struck a 'lead' in us. **1875** *Scribner's Mo.* July 277/1 The genuine Californian never says he has made a fortunate investment; but he has 'struck a lead.' **1903** AUSTIN *Land of Little Rain* 73 He was a perfect gossip of the woods, this Pocket Hunter, and when I could get him away from 'leads' and 'strikes' and 'contacts,' full of fascinating small talk.

2. In baseball, the distance from base taken by a runner preparatory to running to the next base.

1893 CAMP *College Sports* 216 The runner should be coached to take as great a lead as he can with security. **1911** *Chi. D. News* 1 April 6/1 [He] anticipated an infield hit and took a good lead as he knew he would have to hurry to make the plate. **1948** *Dly. Ardmoreite* (Ardmore, Okla.) 15 July 12/3 He scored one run and got in the hair of the Duncan pitcher with his long leads off bases.

3. (See quot.)

1905 *Forestry Bureau Bul.* No. 61, 41 *Lead*, a snatch block with a hook or loop for fastening it to convenient stationary objects, used for guiding the cable by which logs are dragged. (P[acific] C[oast] F[orest].)

4. In combs.: (1) **lead harness,** relatively light harness for the animals that work at the head of a team; (2) **mule,** a mule that works on the left side in a pair, or at the head of a team or pack train.

(1) **1871** *Atlantic Mo.* Nov. 574 Conversation sprung up on 'lead harness,' [and] the 'Stockton wagon that had went off the grade.' **1944** *Democrat* 26 Oct. 3/2 For the log men we now have leather collars, lead harness, load binders. — (2) **1857** in *Annals of Wyoming* XI. (1939) 83 The carriage sustained no injury, but one of our lead Mules became detached from the wagon. **1860** GREELEY *Overland Journey* 169 The Frenchman . . . took one of our lead-mules by the halter. **1887** CUSTER *Tenting on Plains* 352 A broad piece of leather . . . divides over the shoulders of the lead or pilot mule. **1936** MCKENNA *Black Range* 194 When he turned to climb into his wagon seat he noticed that one of the lead mules showed excitement.

As the last term in **blind, blue, mother, oil, quartz, surface, Virginia lead.**

∗**lead,** *v.*

1. *intr.* In boxing, to launch or direct a blow at one's opponent. **2.** ∗*to lead out*, to set out.

(1) **1887** *Courier-Journal* 29 Jan. 5/3 Both sparred cautiously, looking for an opening. Danforth led for Harding's head with his left, but was short. **1895** T. ROOSEVELT *Works* (1926) 205 If you are going to 'lead freely' you have got to 'take punishment,' if you will allow me to speak in the language of those who box. — (2) **1894** *Harper's Mag.* Feb. 354/2, I 'led out' for the casa at a rate of speed which the boys afterwards never grew weary of commending. **1903** A. ADAMS *Log Cowboy* xx. 312 The cattle led out as if walking on a wager.

∗**leader,** *n.*

1. A short line of strong material, preferably transparent, used to attach a hook or bob to the casting line.

1848 *Knickerb.* XXXII. 80 The bending-on of leaders and hooks, and the adjustment of sinkers and floats, was soon completed. **1882** HUBBARD *Moosehead Lake* 14 Six foot leaders are long enough. **1947** *Field & Stream* June 116/2, I may snap the leader, but I won't let another fish snap the hook.

2. An article of major importance in trade; an article specially featured or displayed and usually lowered in price to attract trade.

1851 CIST *Cincinnati* 319 These articles are the leaders, as they are called, in commercial transactions, with the west. **1888** *Chi. Tribune* 29 April 4/7 Goods advertised and sold below cost are technically known as 'leaders.' **1903** *Sears Cat.* (ed. 113) 14/3 We do not make a leader of sugar, coffee, crackers, or other well known items, and depend upon the balance of your order to make the transaction profitable to us. [**1948** *Chi. Tribune* 24 Oct. 17/3 In New York high schools a lunch costing 36 cents is sold for 20. This meal is known as the 'loss leader' in New York.]

3. *S.* A slave exercising authority under an overseer. *Obs.* Cf. ∗**driver 2.**

1855 DAVIS *Farm Bk.* 180, I find my mules getting out of condition —this is neglect on my part and my leaders and this must be stratened up. *c***1862** *Ib.* 10 The overseer is expected to have and name as many leaders as there are divisions of work.

4. A downspout. Also **leader pipe.** *Colloq.*

1868 *Putnam's Mag.* I. 21 Then, without stay or stopping, My first and last eaves-dropping, By leader-pipe I sped. **1941** *L.A.* Map 349 [Shows *leader* used in this sense in Hartford and New London, Conn.]

As the last term in **bell, cheer, floor, Tammany leader.**

*leading, *n.*

1. An inner spiritual prompting to proper action.

1879 HOWELLS *Lady of Aroostook* 3 It's an opportunity; you might call it a leadin', almost, that it would be flyin' in the face of Providence to refuse. **1889** M. C. LEE *Quaker Girl Nantucket* 8 Ann Millet . . . began to have 'leadings' at the age of four years.

2. leading way, (see quot. 1665). *Obs.*

1641 *Dedham Rec.* III. 79 Lay out a Cart way to our Water Mill for a common leading way. **1665** *Ib.* IV. 108 Whether the said space of grounde be onely a leading waye. That is for Cartes and teams. or Cattell kept in hand. or a Common drift waye for loose Cattell to goe at liberty in.

leadoff man. In baseball, the player who is first in the batting order. — **1922** *Ardmore* (Okla.) *D. Press* 6 May 3/3 His ability to judge close ones, as attested to by the fact that he drew seventy-seven passes last season, make[s] him an ideal leadoff man. **1948** *Chi. Maroon* 7 May 18/1 Luther . . . took the lead in the fourth on a home run over the left field by the lead-off man, Gresens.

***leaf,** *n.* In combs.: (1) **leaf concert,** (see quot.); (2) ***cutter,** a paper cutter, *rare;* (3) **hopper,** any one of various small leaf-sucking insects.

(1) **1876** *Wide Awake* 193 Many Sunday-Schools have in the Autumn, what is called the 'Leaf Concert,' when the church is beautifully decorated with Autumn leaves. — (2) **1850** WARNER *Wide, Wide World* iii, Mrs. Montgomery . . . went on further to furnish the desk with an ivory leaf-cutter, a paper-folder [etc.]. — (3) **1852** T. W. HARRIS *Insects Injurious Veg.* (1862) 220 Leaf-hoppers . . . live mostly on the leaves of plants. **1945** *Athol* (Mass.) *D. News* 5 July 5/4 Leaf hoppers . . . are responsible for more reduction in yield than any other potato pest.

As the last term in **arrow, bay, blow, bonnet, broad, buckeye, cabbage, carpenter's, cigar, curl, curled, currant, cut, fall, gold, ground, heart, heavy, leather, liver, long, mesquite, mint, palm, rattlesnake, saddle, sassafras, seed, shin, speaking, sweet, trumpet, umbrella, velvet leaf.**

***leafy,** *a.* In names of plants: **leafy meadow grass, raspberry, vaccinium** (see quots.).

1785 MARSHALL *Amer. Grove* 158 Leafy Vaccinium or Indian gooseberry. **1833** EATON *Botany* (ed. 6) 310 *Rubus frondosus,* leafy raspberry. **1878** in KILLEBREW *Tenn. Grasses* 229 *Poa alsodes,* . . . Leafy Meadow Grass, . . . is a scattered growing grass.

league lig, *n.*[1] *S.W.* [See note.]

In sense **1.** app. a borrowing of Sp. *legua,* in the Amer. Sp. sense of 5,000 varas. For sense **2.** cf. Sp. *legua cuadrada.*

1. A linear measure, prob. about two and a half miles. *Obs.*

1810 *Amer. Republic* (Frankfort, Ky.) 19 Oct. 3/3 Westward of that line, we will establish a distinct territory of thirty leagues on either side of the line. **1849** *Placer Times* (Sacramento) 12 May 2/2 Bear creek and dry diggings (distant a few leagues) are worked, and to advantage, it is said by those who *do* work. **1885** *Santa Fe Wkly. New Mexican* 24 Sep. 1/2 The legal league contains 100 cordels, or 5,000 varas. **1949** *L.A. Times* 3 July II. 6/4 Don Joaquin Estrada was granted the four square leagues of the Santa Margarita [Rancho].

2. In areas formerly a part of Mexico, a measure of land, approx. 4,400 acres.

1824 DEWEES *Lett. from Texas* 50 Every single man, who receives land under the Mexican government, on marrying, is entitled to an augmentation of his claim, to a league and labor of land. **1857** OLMSTED *Journey through Texas* 360 A gentleman from Alabama had recently purchased a league (4,400 acres). **1943** DALE *Cow Country* 23 In so far as they [Texans] thought of the Kansans at all, it was to regard them as narrow, intolerant, penny-pinching, Yankee abolitionists inhabiting a land where each family was confined to a petty hundred-and-sixty-acre claim, while in their own country every man measured his land by leagues or square miles.

***league,** *n.*[2]

1. Short for: **a. Union League. b. =Loyal League.** *Obs.*

(a) **1865** in FLEMING *Hist. Reconstruction* I. 135 Some of the most prominent men of the League ask of you an interview. **1871** *Ku Klux Klan Rep.* VIII. 227 The negroes . . . had half a dozen league rooms. — (b) **1880** TOURGEE *Bricks* 145 The colored men should be encouraged to consider and discuss political affairs. . . . The League gives them this opportunity.

2. An association of baseball clubs. Freq. attrib. Cf. ***class 2. b.**

1879 *Chi. Tribune* 17 May 7/5 A misunderstanding has arisen as to the condition of the Cleveland Club, and its inability to play, which will end in an appeal to the League. **1884** *N.Y. Wkly. Tribune* 3 Sep. 4/4 Baseball . . . as now played by the League nines is undoubtedly good sport for the onlookers. **1949** *Lisle* (Ill.) *Advt.* 11 March 1/1 The Lisle Baseball team was admitted into the Fox Valley League on Tuesday.

As the last term in **baseball, big, bush, colored, Epworth, Farmers', Kansas, Lie-all, Liquor, Loyal, Lucy Stone, major, minor, National Negro, Non-Partisan, southern Union, White league.**

***leaguer,** *n.* As the last term in **big, bush, land, Loyal, Non-Partisan, Texas, White leaguer.**

***lean,** *v. intr.* To run away, to "make tracks." *Colloq.* — **1833** CATLIN *Indians* I. 98 He darts forth . . . wraps his robe around him and 'leans' as fast as possible for home. **1851** *Polly Peablossom* 109 Lean, Sam, . . . she's goin' to rip, sartin.

leana li'ænə, *n.* **=Lea's oak.** *Colloq.* — **1904** *N.Y. Ev. Post* 2 Nov. 4 A variety of oak the 'leana,' which is confined almost wholly to central Ohio.

lean streak. A stretch of poor, stony land. *Colloq.* — **1860** HOLMES *E. Venner* xxxi, Hiram [was] the man from the lean-streak in New Hampshire. **1880** *Harper's Mag.* March 556/1 The 'loafers' hung around as if this were a sleepy agricultural town on a 'lean streak' in New Hampshire.

leap year party. A party during leap year, to which women invite men. — **1880** *Cimarron News & Press* 26 Feb. 3/2 As the Leap Year party was given up some of the enterprising gentlemen of town, . . . got up an impromptu affair on Tuesday night. **1883** RITTENHOUSE *Maud* 266 Early in the evening had given note to Elmer asking to take him to the leap year party next Thursday.

***lease,** *n.* As the last term in **grazing, improvement, yellow-dog lease.**

Lea's oak. A hybrid oak, *Quercus leana,* said to be a cross between the shingle oak and the black oak. — **1875** *Year in Nat. Hist.* IX. 390 The scarlet oak and Spanish oak are probably the least common, except Lea's oak which occurs in Fulton county [Illinois].

***least,** *a.* Used in the names of birds regarded as the smallest of their kind: (1) **least bittern,** the dwarf bittern, *Ixobrychus exilis,* found in the temperate parts of North America; (2) **bush titmouse,** (see quot.); (3) **flycatcher,** the chebec, *Empidonax minimus,* found chiefly in eastern U.S.; (4) **golden crown thrush,** ?the oven bird; (5) **heron, =least bittern;** (6) **petrel,** the *Halocyptena microsoma* of the West Coast; (7) **sandpiper,** a sand peep, *Pisobia minutilla,* a common marsh and shore bird; (8) **tern,** the little striker or minute tern, *Sterna antillarum;* (9) **tit, =least bush titmouse.**

(1) **1813** WILSON *Ornithology* VIII. 37 Least Bittern: *Ardea exilis;* . . . is commonly found in fresh water meadows. **1944** *Sat. Ev. Post* 9 Sep. 13/1 Sometimes the bays are occupied by ponds or fresh-water marsh, the haunt of king rails and least bitterns. — (2) **1881** *Amer. Naturalist* XV. 213 At Colton, Cal., I first found the nest of that diminutive little bird, the least bush titmouse [*Psaltriparus minimus*]. — (3) **1874** COUES *Birds N.W.* 254 The Least Flycatcher is . . . numerous during the breeding season along the Red River of the North. **1939** LINCOLN *Migration* 63, I found in a refuse can the bodies of 88 warblers, . . . besides Red-eyed Vireos, . . . and Least Flycatchers. — (4) **1796** MORSE *Univ. Geog.* I. 209 Least Golden Crown Thrush.

(5) **1917** *Birds of Amer.* I. 182 Least Bittern. . . . [Also called] Least Heron. — (6) **1917** *Birds of Amer.* I. 87 The Least Petrel, a Pacific Ocean form, [is] seen occasionally off the coast of California. — (7) **1858** BAIRD *Birds Pacific R.R.* 721 Least Sandpiper. . . . Entire temperate North America. . . . Specimens from western localities seem to be slightly larger. **1917** *Birds of Amer.* I. 236/1 The tiniest atom of its tribe, the Least Sandpiper, . . . is still with us, . . . thanks to the outlawry of shooting them. — (8) **1858** BAIRD *Birds Pacific R.R.* 864 The Least Tern . . . Texas to Labrador; western rivers. **1917** *Birds of Amer.* I. 65/1 The most dainty of all the American seabirds is the Least Tern. — (9) **1858** BAIRD *Birds Pacific R.R.* 397 Least Tit. . . . Pacific coast of United States.

b. least chipmunk, (see quot. 1917).

1917 *Mammals of Amer.* 193/2 Least Chipmunk.—*Eutamias minimus minimus* (Bachman). Smallest of the Chipmunks, length 8 inches. Colors very pale. A desert form. Bad Lands and plains of Dakota, Montana and Wyoming. **1946** STANWELL-FLETCHER *Driftwood Valley* 42 Sometimes he and the least chipmunks . . . play hide-and-seek round boxes and trees.

***leather,** *n.* In combs.: (1) ***leather apron,** (see quot. and cf. **maple wax**); (2) **back,** the ruddy duck; (3) **breeches,** *S.* (see quots.); (4) **canoe,** a canoe made of leather, *obs.;* (5) **face,** a hard, emotionless face, also attrib., *colloq.;* (6) **-faced,** hard-featured, emotionless, *colloq.;* (7) ***head,** see as a main entry; (8) **jacket,** one who wears a jacket made of leather, *obs.;* (9) **lodge,** an

Indian lodge or tepee made of buffalo skins; (10) **-stocking,** see as a main entry; (11) **store,** a store in which leather goods are sold.

(1) **1939** WOLCOTT *Yankee Cook Book* 346 Some people call the [maple] syrup [boiled down and poured on snow] 'sheepskins'; others refer to it as 'leather aprons' or 'maple wax.' — (2) **1917** *Birds of Amer.* I. 152 Ruddy Duck.... [Also called] Leather-back. — (3) **1913** KEPHART *So. Highlanders* 292 Beans dried in the pod, then boiled 'hull and all,' are called leather-breeches (this is not slang, but the regular name). **1943** R. CHASE *Jack Tales* viii, Stringing beans for canning, or threading them up to make the dried pods called 'leather britches' [in mts. of N.C.]. — (4) **1772** in *Travels Amer. Col.* 561 The water . . . often rises twenty feet above its present Surface, which Obliges the Traders to Carry leather Canoes along with them.

(5) **1842** in *Amer. Sp.* XVIII. 126/2 He had the impassable leather-face of the pilgrims of Plymouth. **1884** MARK TWAIN *H. Finn* 287 You ain't one of these leather-face people. — (6) **1834** SIMMS *G. Rivers* I. 77 What's to hinder us now, you leather-faced Jew? — (8) **1842** in *Amer. Sp.* XVIIII 126/2 'Free country, neighbor,' replied the leather-jacket. — (9) **1807** GASS *Journal* 254 A great many of the Chien . . . encamped here, in large handsome leather lodges. **1825** in *19th Cong.* 1 Sess. H.R. Doc. 117 (1826) 8 The Yanctons . . . live by the chase alone. . . . They cover themselves with leather tents, or lodges, which they move about from place to place, as the buffalo may chance to range.

(11) **1941** LEE *Stagecoach North* 13 One went to the leather store to find a lace tassel.

b. In the names of plants: (1) **leatherbark,** any one of various tough-barked trees of the genus *Dirca;* (2) **flower,** the *Clematis viorna* of the southeastern U.S.; (3) **leaf,** a shrub, *Chamaedaphne calyculata,* with tough coriaceous leaves; (4) **root,** *Calif.* (see quot. 1937); (5) **wood,** see as a main entry.

(1) **1751** J. BARTRAM *Observations* 28 Leather-bark or *thymelea* . . . is plentiful in all this part of the country. **1855** *Mich. Agric. Soc. Trans.* VI. 149 The shrubs are crab-apple, . . . leather bark, elder [etc.]. **1933** SMALL *Southeastern Flora* 919 D[irca] palustris. . . . Leatherwood. Swamp-wood. Moose-wood. Leather-bark. — (2) **1817–8** EATON *Botany* (1822) 241 *Clematis viorna,* leather flower; . . . flowers solitary, bell-form. **1937** *Range Plant Handbook* B58 The clematis genus includes the plants known as leatherflower, travelers-joy, and virgins-bower. — (3) **1817–8** EATON *Botany* (1822) 173 *Andromeda calyculata,* leather leaf. **1945** MCATEE *Pheasant* 137 This gives a spreading or rambling shrub like leather-leaf, ground juniper, or shrubby cinquefoil a much higher score than if the measurement were made at the surface. — (4) **1923** SAUNDERS *So. Sierra Calif.* 336 Hard by another wilding of famous fragrance grows—the leather root. **1937** *Range Plant Handbook* W157 The roots of leatherroot (*P[soralea] macrostachya*) furnished a tough fiber prized by the Pomos and other native Indian tribes.

c. *To pull leather, W.* to hold on to the saddle with the hands in an effort to retain one's place on a bucking horse. Also transf. *Colloq.*

1918 MULFORD *Man from Bar-20* 22, I manages to stick on th' job by pullin' leather. **1923** J. H. COOK *On Old Frontier* 16 He certainly made me 'pull leather,' and I clung to his mane as well in order to keep in close touch with him. **1924** RAINE *Troubled Waters* 190 Stick to the saddle, Mac. Don't you pull leather, old scout.

As the last term in **Adam's, apple, bridle, Creek, Napa, patch, patent, peach, Union leather.**

***leatherhead,** *n.*

1. (*cap.*) *pl.* (See quots.)

1845 *St. Louis Reveille* 14 May 2/4 The inhabitants of . . . Pennsylvania [are called] Leatherheads. **1886** *Chi. W. News* 29 April 4/3 Pennsylvania is the Keystone state from its position in the middle of the arch of the original thirteen states, but its people are Leatherheads for some unknown reason.

2. A watchman or policeman. Now *hist.*

1846 *N.O. Delta* 2 Sep. 2/4 *Watchman.*—He said as how I was a leather-sconced corporate reality, and that we leatherheads were the only real offering of chartered rights. **1868** M. H. SMITH *Sunshine & Shadow* 148 The guardians of the city were watchmen . . . and were known as leather-heads, from the leather cap they wore. **1888** *N.Y. Mercury* 21 July (F.), The old police or leatherheads tried to restrain them. **1947** CRANE *Sins of N.Y.* 11 The town called these watchmen 'leatherheads' because of the heavy helmets they wore on duty, not unlike those that adorn a fireman in action today.

3. (*cap.*) One who is not a copperhead *q.v.* (sense **2.**). *Rare.*

1863 in *Pub. Col. Soc. Mass.* XX. 217 'Copperhead' stock is rising and 'Leatherhead' falling.

Leatherstocking ˈlɛðɚˌstɑkɪŋ, *n.* A wearer of stockings or leggings made of leather, usu. with particular reference to Natty Bumppo, the hero of Cooper's *Leatherstocking Tales,* whose sobriquet was "Leather-stocking."

1823 COOPER *Pioneers* xxxiii, The Leather-stocking made his appearance, . . . under the custody of two constables. **1829** *Va. Herald* (Fredericksburg) 11 March 2/4 Simeon Kendall, of Ohio, who is represented as the prototype of Cooper's inimitable Leatherstocking, has applied to Congress for a pension. **1831** HOLLEY *Texas* (1833) 43 The dress of these hunters is usually of deer-skin. Hence the appropriate name *Leather Stocking.* **1948** *Southwest Rev.* Summer 280/1 Young, handsome, and actually or potentially genteel trappers and hunters are almost as numerous [in Western fiction] as the older hunters who are replicas of Leatherstocking.

leatherwood ˈlɛðɚˌwʊd, *n.*

1. A small shrub or tree, *Dirca palustris,* having tough, pliant branches and stem. Cf. **marsh leatherwood,** and see **moosebush, moose tree, moosewood.**

1743 CLAYTON *Flora Virginica* 155 Unde Leather-wood appellatur. **1843** TORREY *Flora N.Y.* II. 163 Leather-wood. . . . The branches of this shrub are so tough that the Indians use them for making cords. **1949** *Jrnl. N.Y. Bot. Garden* March 59 Leatherwood is easily raised from seeds sown in sandy peat that is kept constantly moist.

attrib. **1784** SMYTH *Tour U.S.* I. 275 My journey . . . brought me to a large water-course, named Leatherwood Creek. **1787** *Mem. Amer. Acad. Sciences* (1793) II. 159 Leather Wood bark is an excellent substitute for cord. **1852** ELLET *Pioneer Women* 232 The harness consisted mostly of leatherwood bark, except the collar.

b. In full **leatherwood bush.**

1787 *Mem. Amer. Acad. Sciences* II. I. 159 Leather Wood Bushes. Leather Wood bark is an excellent substitute for cord . . . : it grows only in low and very rich lands. **1808** ASHE *Travels* 225 There were nine species of bark, spice, and leather wood bushes. **1887** EGGLESTON *Graysons* xiii, Bob now went to the brookside and cut up and stripped three or four leatherwood bushes.

2. The ironwood, *Cyrilla racemiflora.*

1901 MOHR *Plant Life Ala.* 122 Swamp dogwood . . . interspersed with titi . . . , leatherwood . . . , holly . . . and blue palmetto.

***leaved,** *a.* As the last term in **entire, heart, long, maple, parsley leaved.**

Lebkuchen ˈlɛbkukən, *n.* [G.] A form of sweetcake, usu. containing fruit peel.

1909 WEBSTER. **1938** HARK *Hex Marks Spot* 187 Then, there are . . . *lebkuchen* (spice cakes), and chocolate drops, and nut kisses, and Scotch cakes. **1948** *Chi. Tribune* 12 Dec. (Grafic Mag.) 22 These Christmas cookies are: rum balls, lebkuchen, cherry queens, sandbakkels, pecan patty cakes.

lechuguilla ˌlɛtʃuˈgijə, *n.* [Sp. in Amer. Sp. sense here.] Any one of several agaves found in the Southwest.

1844 GREGG *Commerce of Prairies* II. 78 One of the most useful plants to the people of El Paso is the lechuguilla, which abounds on the hills and mountain sides of that vicinity. **1905** BRAY *Sotol Country in Texas* 4 Mr. Vernon Bailey . . . estimates that the area covered by lechuguilla in Texas would exceed twenty thousand square miles. **1937** PARKS *Valuable Plants Texas* 16 *Agave heterocantha* Zucc. One of the common Lechuguillas.

b. lechuguilla pocket gopher, a pocket gopher, *Thomomys aureus lachuguilla,* that feeds upon the starchy heart of this plant.

1931 BAILEY *Mammals N. Mex.* 238 The little desert Lechuguilla pocket gophers are common in the gulches of the lower foothills of the Franklin and Organ Mountains.

Lecompton ləˈkɑmptən, *n.* [*Lecompton,* Kans.]

1. *attrib.* Of or pertaining to the political situation growing out of the struggle over the adoption or rejection of the Lecompton Constitution. *Obs.* or *hist.* Cf. **anti-Lecompton.**

1858 *N.Y. Tribune* 17 May 6/1 Even the 'Lecompton half-breeds,' as they are called, see the ruin of any scheme connected with the Lecompton Constitution. **1861** in LOGAN *Great Conspiracy* 178 The Pro-Slavery Party in Kansas perpetrated, and the President and the South accepted, the Lecompton fraud. **1886** LOGAN *Great Conspiracy* 86 The split in the Democratic Party, between the Lecompton and Anti-Lecompton Democracy, was widened.

2. Lecompton Constitution, a constitution for the state of Kansas drawn up by proslavery leaders at Lecompton in 1857. *Obs.* or *hist.*

1858 LINCOLN in Logan *Great Conspiracy* 56 The Lecompton Constitution connects itself with this question [of popular sovereignty], for it is in this matter . . . that . . . Judge Douglas, claims such vast credit. **1886** POORE *Reminiscences* I. 532 The racket in the House of Representatives commenced with a struggle as to whether the President's Message or the Lecompton Constitution of Kansas should be referred to the Democratic Committee on Territories or to a select committee of fifteen. **1948** *Sat. Review* 12 June 17/3 A fraud was perpetrated in the Lecompton constitution, a trick to impose a proslavery instrument by a misleading referendum that gave no valid opportunity for a free-state vote.

3. Used in now obs. derivatives, as **Lecomptoner, Lecomptoniad, Lecomptonian, Lecomptonism, Lecomptonist, Lecomptonite.**

1858 *N.Y. Tribune* 26 April 5/3 The Lecomptoner paid the liquor and sloped. — *Ib.* 22 Feb. 6/5 The Territorial Legislature has just passed a law for punishing usurpation under the Calhoun Lecomptoniad. — *Ib.* 6/6 This law indicates the fate that will probably befall the Lecomptonians, whether under its provision or not. — *Ib.* 20 July 5/5 We, in common with our brother laborers all over the county, have been characterized by the haughty dictation of Lecomptonism as 'mud-sills' in society, and unworthy the consideration of the Government. — *Ib.* 1 April 3/3 (Th.), Lecomptonists and the 'anti-Lecompton' Democracy of Lecompton went off on this bolt, doing it secretly. — *Ib.* 31 July 4/3 The Lecomptonite opponents of the Hon. John B. Haskin opened their campaign on Wednesday last with all the rustic and radiant festivities of a pic-nic. **1859** BARTLETT 239 *Lecomptonite*, an upholder of the pro-slavery constitution for Kansas promulgated at the city of Lecompton.

***Leconte,** *n.* [John Lawrence *Le Conte* (1825–83), Amer. entomologist.] Used in the possessive in the names of birds: (1) **Leconte's bunting,** =**Leconte's sparrow;** (2) **mockthrush,** =**Leconte's thrasher;** (3) **sparrow,** a small sparrow, *Passerherbulus caudacutus*, of the Southwest; (4) **thrasher,** a thrasher of the desert regions of the Southwest.

(1) **1873** COUES in *Amer. Naturalist* VII. 748 LeConte's bunting (*Coturniculus LeContei*) long remained among our special desiderata. — (2) **1869** *Amer. Naturalist* III. 188 The only peculiar bird known is Leconte's Mock-thrush (*Harporhynchus Lecontei*), which is also of a pale grayish brown. — (3) **1874** COUES *Birds N.W.* 134 *Coturniculus Lecontei.* Leconte's Sparrow. **1917** *Birds of Amer.* III. 29 On the prairie marshes of the Mississippi valley . . . is another . . . species, known as Leconte's Sparrow (*Passerherbulus lecontei*). — (4) **1917** *Birds of Amer.* III. 184 Leconte's Thrasher. *Toxostoma lecontei lecontei.* . . . It is a pity that this fine bird does not select a habitat more habitable for man. **1940** JAEGER *Calif. Deserts* 92 The LeConte and Crissal thrashers . . . are able to go for long periods without dipping their beaks in water.

***lecture,** *n.* In combs.: (1) **lecture agent,** one who arranges for a lecture or a lecture series; (2) **committee,** a committee in charge of arranging for a lecture or a lecture series; (3) **system,** the system of providing lectures, usually in courses, for popular audiences; (4) **time,** in colonial New England, the time when a periodical lecture was given, *obs.*

(1) **1873** MARK TWAIN & WARNER *Gilded Age* lviii. 527, I am a lecture-agent. — (2) **1864** NICHOLS *Amer. Life* I. 67 There are towns where a lecture-committee would not dare to invite Beecher or Phillips to lecture. — (3) **1854** *Harper's Mag.* Feb. 415/1 We can not . . . look abroad over the varied panorama of life and society in our country, and not mark so striking a fact as the Lecture-system. **1875** *Scribner's Mo.* Dec. 281/2 The 'lecture system' . . . is declining in its usefulness and interest. — (4) **1674** SEWALL *Diary* I. 3 News of Peace in Lecture time. **1702** *Ib.* II. 63 Got home in Lecture-time. After Lecture Council sets. **1779** STILES *Lit. Diary* II. 328, I had no Lecture to day, as just at Lecture time this Aft. a Brigade of 500 Contin. Troops came into Town to be stationed here.

As the last term in **century, moral, preparatory, singing lecture.**

lecturizing rod. ?A lightning rod. *Rare.* — **1768** *Boston Gaz.* 25 July 2/2 All Sorts of Lecturizing Rods, for Town or Country.

***ledge,** *n.* As the last term in **bull, gold, panther, pay ledge.**

ledgy ˈlɛdʒɪ, *a.* Abounding in ledges or rocky ridges. — **1779** *N.H. Hist. Soc. Coll.* VI. 355 This swamp is not level, but has some considerable hills and ledgy mountains in it. **1895** CRADDOCK *Myst. Witch-Face Mt.* 124 The shadowy woods stood dense about the little open ledgy space on three sides.

***leech,** *n.* (See quot.) — **1890** *Stock Grower & Farmer* 5 July 7/1 Liver flukes are called by some western shepherds 'leeches,' and are treated with charcoal and salt.

***left,** *n.*

1. Short for **left field.** *Colloq.*

1867 *Ball Players' Chron.* 18 July 3/1 John Grum went in to pitch, Swandell to catch, Nelson short stop, Fesler to right field, and Mills to left. **1909** *Amer. Mag.* LXVIII. May 36/2 O'Leary and Crawford opened Detroit's half of the fourth inning with line singles to left. **1948** *Tishomingo* (Okla.) *Capital-Democrat* 17 June 5/5 Dean's triple to left cleaned the bases.

2. In combs.: (1) **left center,** in baseball, that portion of the outfield slightly to the left of center field; (2) **field,** see as a main entry; (3) **fielder,** the player who covers left field; (4) ***-hander,** in baseball, a left-handed pitcher, cf. **southpaw;** (5) **tackle,** in football, the player whose position is between the left guard and the end.

(1) **1875** *Chi. Tribune* 3 Aug. 7/3 Pike's difficult fly to left-centre was muffed by Eggler after a desperate effort. **1948** *Minneapolis Star* 17 Sep. 30/8 Williamson drove a hard smash into left center to score Haase. — (3) **1867** *Ball Players' Chron.* 6 June 2/1 What with the rough field and the close proximity of the crowd, the left fielders, on both sides, had a poor show for catches. **1946** *Life* 23 Sep. 108 The Boston Red Sox . . . last won a championship in 1918, the year in which Ted Williams, their slugging left fielder, was born. — (4) **1887** *Courier-Journal* 27 May 2/4 The big fellows . . . made twenty hits off the famous left-hander. **1912** MATHEWSON *Pitching* 30 He became the greatest lefthander in the country.

(5) **1891** *Cent.* 5278/1 When eleven players are on each side, the rushers are known, according to their positions in the rush line, as *right end, right tackle . . . left tackle.* **1940** WHITE *One Man's Meat* 185 But in doing so had broken the neck of Army's left tackle, E. A. Byrne, and the player had died on the field.

***left,** *a.*

1. leftover, something remaining, esp. food left over from a meal.

[**1892** M. TWAIN *Amer. Claimant* xii. 119 (R.), Irish stew made of the potatoes and meat left over from a procession of previous meals.] **1897** R. M. STUART *Simpkinsville* 64, I try to keep the Potter's field a-bloomin' with my left-overs. **1905** *St. Louis Globe-Democrat* 2 July (Mag. Sect.) 9/6, I also give a few suggestions for using the 'left-overs' from the Fourth of July feast. **1947** *Sierra Club Bul.* March 18/1 When the Forest Service acquired the lands which it now administers, those lands were primarily 'left-overs' from the original extensive areas of public domain.

2. *To get* (or *be*) *left*, to be left behind, "left in the lurch," be disappointed in something. *Colloq.*

1882 *Chi. Tribune*, Destiny won't get left any in the mean time. **1899** QUINN *Pa. Stories* 69 We determined not to be left entirely, and so we laid a plan to steal theirs in return. **1914** ATHERTON *Perch of Devil* 174 They tried to corral your mine . . . but got left.

left field. In baseball, that portion of the outfield to the left of the batter as he faces the pitcher. Also the position played by the left fielder.

1857 *Spirit of Times* 29 Aug. 404/3 Enterprise Club. Maxfield, catcher; . . . Webber, left field. **1867** CHADWICK *Base Ball Reference* 51 Suppose, also, that a ball similarly hit to the right or left fields [etc.]. **1949** *Minot* (N.D.) *D. News* 22 July 8/8 Marinari spoiled Lettau's chance for a no-hitter, lining a solid single to left field in the fifth frame.

b. *To play* (or *fill*) *left field*, to play as a left fielder.

1874 WRIGHT *Boston Base Ball Club* 12 He will probably play left field. **1897** *Outing* June 299/2 Greenway or Tearey can fill left field well. **1910** *Sat. Ev. Post* 27 Aug. 34/1 Within a week he had been fined his first two days' pay 'for tossin' in the ball, it might be once or twice,' otherwise playing left field for more than half an hour with the Young Dukes.

***leg,** *n.*

1. The case or housing in which the vertical conveyor belt of a grain elevator operates.

1881 *Harper's Mag.* April 708/2 Iron buckets [of grain] . . . travel up a sort of chimney, called a 'leg,' to this roof chamber. **1901** MERWIN & WEBSTER *Calumet 'K'* 212 Harahan Company are building the Leg.

2. In combs., usu. obs.: (1) **leg knife,** a heavy knife carried in the legging or boot; (2) **man,** one who does leg work, as a newspaper reporter, or one who serves in some capacity that necessitates his going from place to place, *colloq.;* (3) **treasurer,** used facetiously for a treasurer who takes leg bail or absconds; (4) **work,** work that involves considerable walking, *colloq.*

(1) **1835** HOFFMAN *Winter in West* II. 69 Leg knife . . . worn beneath the garter of the leggin, and carried in addition to the larger knife which the western hunter always wears in his girdle. — (2) **1923** *Nation* 24 Oct. 454/2 Newsboys and 'legmen' and a foreign news service keep the streets of Mecca aware of all that goes on. **1949** *Newsweek* 2 May 56/2 The soft-spoken Edson comes naturally by his regard for legmen. — (3) **1840** *Mercantile Journal* (Boston) 12 March 2/2 The weather last week was 'just the thing' for the sap, and the way it ran was a caution to buckets and leg-treasurers. **1844**

Henry Clay Bugle (Maysville, Ky.) 2 May 1/2 His old friend, the leg treasurer, will return . . . to fatten again upon the public plunder. — (4) **1891** *D.N.* I. 207 Reporters characterize a task in which there is more running than writing by the expressive compound *leg-work.* **1947** *Time* 15 Dec. 24/1 Dave will relieve me of some of my travel and leg work.

b. Used in allusion to theatrical entertainment giving actresses opportunity for displaying their legs, as **leg business, drama, performer, shop, show.**

1870 LOGAN *Before Footlights* 90 Newspapers which defend the indecencies of the leg-business. — **1872** *Chi. Tribune* 8 Dec., The history of the leg-drama, so well known under the title of *The Black Crook.* — **1870** LOGAN *Before Footlights* 584 But these leg-performers were so few in number . . . that the evil did not assume such frightful proportions as it subsequently did. — **1871** M. TWAIN *Screamers* 144 (R.), They're playing 'Undine' at the Opera House, and some folks call it the leg shop. — **1895** *N.Y. Dramatic News* 7 Dec. 3/3 The entertainment was a sort of Zozo leg show, cut on a smaller pattern and called Zero. **1949** *Chi. Tribune* 26 Nov. 10/3, I began to run around the playhouses as an eager young searcher for the good, the true, the beautiful and the leg shows.

c. In slang phrases: (1) *To show leg,* to run away; (2) *to have by the leg,* to have at a great disadvantage.

(1) **1837** BIRD *Nick of Woods* I. 120, I'll fight for you, or run for you, take scalp or cut stick, shake fist or show leg. — (2) **1894** *Cong. Rec.* 9 April 3556/1 To use the language imputed to the President [Cleveland], 'the banks have got the country by the leg.'

As the last term in **black, boot, hog, jack, paper, red, tangle, yellow leg.**

***leg,** *v. intr.* To bestir oneself (for someone or something). *Colloq.* — **1844** *Lexington Observer* 30 Nov. 3/5 There are a number of men here 'legging' for the Colonel. **1902** HARBEN *A. Daniel* 74 Durin' election . . . he was leggin' fer a friend o' his'n.

***legal,** *a.* **1. legal cap,** ruled writing paper made in long sheets folded at the top and often used for legal documents. **2. legal holiday,** a holiday established by a state statute or a governor's proclamation during which government and other business is usu. suspended.

(1) **1874** KNIGHT 455/2 *Cap-paper* . . . [Ruled] with red lines to form a margin on the left hand, and made to fold on the top, it is *legal cap.* **1904** HARBEN *Georgians* 104 Abner . . . drew out several sheets of legal-cap paper pinned together at the top. — (2) **1867** *Santa Fe Wkly. New Mexican* 30 March 1 New Jersey makes a legal holiday of President Lincoln's birthday. **1949** *Dly. Ardmoreite* (Ardmore, Okla.) 23 Feb. 15/4 Classes were resumed today at Carter seminary after the legal holiday Tuesday, due to Washington's birthday.

***legged,** *a.* As the last term in **bare, bench, yellow-legged.**

***legger,** *n.* Short for bootlegger *q.v.,* and as the second element in such terms as **booklegger, liquor legger, sheetlegger, steaklegger,** suggested by this. *Colloq.*

For *foodlegger, gaslegger, tirelegger, votelegger* see *Amer. Sp.* Feb., 1943, p. 63.

1929 *Variety* 5 June 58/2 Leggers claim the tonic is as potent as a fifth of gin selling for three times the price. **1932** *Ib.* 15 March 59/3 (*heading*), Publishers Talk Printing Own Song Sheets to Eradicate Sheetleggers. **1934** *Time* 29 Jan. 49/1 Hundreds of U.S. citizens have smuggled copies through the customs or bought them from bookleggers. **1937** *Ib.* 4 Jan. 11/2 Unlike Prohibition's liquor 'leggers,' they are not growing rich. **1945** *Chi. D. News* 12 July 12/2 Most of the counterfeits have been used by steakleggers down East.

leghorn flat. A broad-brimmed, low-crowned hat made of leghorn, worn by women. *Obs.* — **1830** WATSON *Philadelphia* 176 Other articles of female wear . . . [include] a 'skimmer hat,' . . . of a very small flat crown and big brim, not unlike the present Leghorn flats. **1891** WELCH *Recoll. 1830–40* 174 The ladies shopping, visiting or driving in summer . . . wore leghorn flats, shaped into bonnets according as the fashion dictated.

***Legion,** *n.* = **American Legion.** Also attrib.

1919 G. S. WHEAT *Story of Amer. Legion* 32 The organization of the Legion was duly heralded in the press. **1941** S. V. BENÉT *Listen to People* (1942) 471 There are the veterans and the Legion Post. **1948** *Chelsea* (Mass.) *Rec.* 30 Nov. 4/2 The Legion will not have its national convention in Boston next year.

As the last term in **American, European, Foreign, Kansas, Loyal, Nauvoo Legion.**

***legionnaire,** *n.* A member of the American Legion. — **1921** *Alton* (Ill.) *D. Times* 8 Nov. 1/6 He was assisted by several other Legionaires and then fun began—fun to the perpetrators. **1949** *St. Paul Pioneer Press* 12 Aug. 1/5 Legionaires escorted the mothers to seats of honor inside.

***legislation,** *n.* As the last term in **job, liquor, Negro, state legislation.**

Legislative Assembly. [Cf. F. *assemblée législative* (1791).] The title of any one of various territorial and state legislatures.

[**1836** *S. Lit. Messenger* II. 408 His [Madison's] second reason for having a Senate, or second branch of the Legislative Assembly, is thus stated.] **1855** *Santa Fe. Gaz.* 8 Dec., The legislative Assembly of the Territory of New Mexico convened in the Palace, in Santa Fe. **1889** *N.D. Constitution* ii. § 29 The Legislative Assembly shall fix the number of Senators. **1943** *Statesman's Year Book* 612 The Legislative Assembly [of North Dakota] consists of a Senate of 49 members . . . and a House of Representatives of 113 members. *Ib.* 619 The Legislative Assembly [of Oregon] consistes of a Senate of 30 members . . . and a House of 60 Representatives.

legislative caucus. A party caucus in a state legislature. *Obs.* — **1816** *Ann. 14th Congress* 2 Sess. 351, I come now to the last and great complaint. . . . The deformity of a legislative caucus—State intrigues [etc.]. **1846** MACKENZIE *Van Buren* 190 Martin Van Buren having procured himself to be made Senator of the United States by the legislative caucus . . . then directed the following appointments to be made.

Legislative Council.

1. A territorial legislature. *Obs.*

1787 in *Sp. & Doc. Amer. Hist.* I. (1844) 41 The Legislative Council shall consist of five members, to continue in office five years. **1836** *Niles' Reg.* 24 Sep. 62/2 [Appropriations.] For arrearages of the expenses of the legislative council of the territory of Michigan, 3,553.40. **1882** SALA *Amer. Revisited* II. 302 (*footnote*), Mr. Cannon has been frequently a member of the Legislative Council of Utah.

2. The upper house of the New Mexico territorial legislature. *Obs.*

1867 *Santa Fe Wkly. New Mexican* 9 March 1/4 The Legislative Assembly convened . . . and with the unanimous consent of the Legislative Council, I was appointed and commissioned as Attorney General.

3. A council whose function is to investigate problems before the meeting of a state legislature (see quot.). Also attrib.

1945 *Bk. of the States* 148 Since the first legislative councils were established in Kansas and Michigan, in 1933, seven other states . . . have adopted this device to provide advance consideration of important problems facing state legislatures. *Ib.* 149 The legislative council plan is only 10 years old; it is not easy to gage accurately its success in fostering legislation.

***legislature,** *n.*

1. The body or assembly of constituted representatives of a colony, state, or territory, vested with authority to make laws for the governance of the body politic.

1729 FRANKLIN *Writings* II. 147 It would behove the Legislature most carefully to contrive how to prevent the Bills issued upon Land from falling with it. **1836** *Niles' Reg.* L. 371 All the states choose [electors] by general ticket except South Carolina, which chooses by the legislature. **1891** O'BEIRNE *Leaders Ind. Territory* vi/1 The legislature convenes annually at Tishomingo, the capital. **1942** *Life* 2 Nov. 27 The Legislatures in most of these States have divided them into new Congressional districts.

2. The federal Congress. Also *Legislature of the United States. Obs.*

1788 *Federalist* II. 150 All the local information and interests of the state [i.e., each state] . . . may easily be conveyed by a very few hands into the legislature of the United States. **1798** *Ann. 5th Congress* I. 599 Any person . . . [who shall] traduce or defame the Legislature of the United States . . . shall be punished by a fine. **1866** *Nation* II. 423/2 The present conflict between the legislature and the Executive possesses much political importance.

As the last term in **granger, National, state legislature.**

lemita lə'mitə, *n.* [Prob. f. Sp. *limonita,* in allusion to its use.] Any one of various sumacs the acidulous fruits of which are used in making a refreshing drink. Cf. **lemonade berry, sumac,** *s.v.* ***lemonade.**

1904 WOOTON *Native Ornamental Plants N.M.* 27 Lemita. Three-Leaved Sumach. (*Rhus trilobata*) . . . is a many-stemmed shrub which grows upon our dry mesas. **1913** —— *Trees & Shrubs N.M.* 112 The Lemitas (*Schmaltzia trilobata* and *S. emoryi*) are widely branching shrubs with trifoliate leaves on long slender stems. **1931** DAYTON *Western Browse Plants* 96 The most valuable of the sumacs from a forage viewpoint are the lemonade sumacs, sweet-sumacs, or lemitas. **1942** VAN DERSAL *Ornamental Amer. Shrubs* 137 Other common names are squawbush and lemita.

***lemon,** *n.*

1. A worthless person or thing. *Slang.*

1863 DAVIS *Young Parson* 222 She was what the knowing ones denominated 'a lemon.' **1909** *Sat. Ev. Post* 20 Feb. 38/2 The wheel goes around; wherever the little indicator at the point of the pin stops, there is your prize—or your lemon. **1947** *Dly. Oklahoman* (Okla. City) 28 Dec. 6/4 Lemon Sale. . . . Not fruit but buyers mistakes. Join the throng and enjoy the fun for it's real fun buying these lemons.

2. In combs.: (1) **lemon butter,** any one of various spreads made of butter and lemon, with or without other ingredients such as sugar and eggs; (2) **lily,** (see quots.); (3) **pie,** a pie with a filling flavored with lemon; (4) **sour,** see ***sour;** (5) **squeezer,** see as a main entry.

(1) **1882** F. OWENS *Cook Book* 265 *Lemon Butter*. Use as sauce, filling for tarts, or as jelly for layer cake. **1947** *Chi. Tribune* 1 July 10/6 Allie, before I forget it, I want a recipe for your lemon butter. — (2) **1909** *Cent. Supp.* 729/2 Lemon-lily, the day-lily, *Hemerocallis fulva*. **1947** *So. Sierran* Aug. 2/2 The Nature Section guide . . . decided . . . to go to Little Jimmy Springs . . . just over the divide where Lemon Lilies (lilium parryi) were reported to be in full bloom. — (3) **1846** HOWLAND *N.E. Econ. Housekeeper* 44 Lemon Pie. **1947** FAIR *Fools Die on Friday* 35 A woman doesn't put arsenic in the lemon pie unless there's a boy friend.

As the last term in **smell, wild lemon.**

***lemonade,** *n.* **lemonade berry, sumac,** (see quots. and cf. **lemita**).

1907 LYONS *Plant Names* 397 R[hus] integrifolia (Nutt.) . . . is called Lemonade-berry and Mahogany. R. ovata Wats. of Southern California is called Lemonade-and-sugar tree. **1931** DAYTON *Western Browse Plants* 96 Lemonade sumac (*Rhus trilobata*), . . . ranges from Alberta to Missouri, northern Mexico, and southern Oregon. **1942** VAN DERSAL *Ornamental Amer. Shrubs* 139 The lemonade sumac, *Rhus integrifolia*, is another strictly Californian species.

lemon squeezer. A device for expressing the juice from lemons. Also transf.

1781 *Salem Gaz.* 3 July, Isaac Greenwood . . . makes Flutes, . . . Billiard-Balls, Maces, Lemon Squeezers. **1857** UNDERHILL & THOMPSON *Elephant Club* 118 One . . . had been hit over the head with a lemon-squeezer. **1902** *Sears Cat.* 774 Malleable Iron Lemon Squeezer, fully tinned. . . . Price, each . . . 8c. . . . Glass Lemon Squeezer. The best made for private use; fits any ordinary size tumbler. Each . . . 5c. **1949** *Nat. Geog. Mag.* Aug. 235 Knapsack's a Nuisance in the 'Lemon Squeezer' [i.e., a narrow defile].

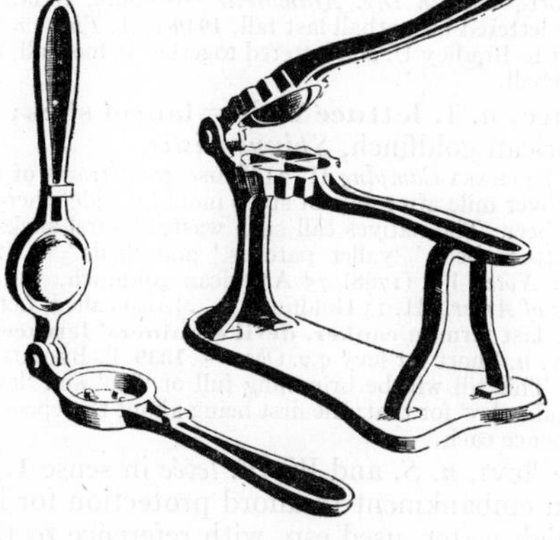
Types of lemon squeezers

Lenape ˈlɛnəˌpi, *n. Collect.* or in the *pl.*: The Leni-Lenape Indians.

1728 in *Pa. Archives* I. 230 Our Lenappys or Delaware Indians know nothing of it. **1892** A. E. LEE *Hist. Columbus* (O.) I. 67 The Lenapes . . . paternally styled the other Algonquins as children or grandchildren. **1946** FOREMAN *Last Trek* 17 The Lenape, or Delaware proper, included three principal tribes—the Munsee, Unami, and Unalachtigo.

attrib. **1839** MORTON *Crania Americana* 188 The Lenapé nations have a common tradition that they came from the far west. **1949** *Nat. Hist.* May 223/3 The name of persimmon is old; the Lenape Indians with whom William Penn treated, called it *pasimenan*.

***length,** *n.* As the last term in **box, rail, stove length.**

lengthily ˈlɛŋkθəlɪ, *adv.* At length, fully.

1787 JEFFERSON *Writings* VI. 394, I have written somewhat lengthily to Mr. Madison. **1827** *Blackw. Mag.* XXI. 729 Informing her very lengthily,—to borrow an Americanism . . . that her father has promised her hand. **1894** *Columbus* (O.) *Dispatch* 23 March, Justh . . . lengthily extolled Kossuth's services.

lengthy ˈlɛŋkθɪ, *a.* Long, protracted or prolonged, not brief.

"*Rare* exc. U.S. and *tech.* of animals" (*OED*). *EDD* records *lengthy*, meaning "tall," in the North Country in 1846.

1689 *Mass. H.S. Coll.* 4 Ser. VIII. 370, I very much fear a dreadfull, lengthy, wasting Indian war. **1769** *Boston Gaz.* 6 March, We have received sundry Pieces, some of which came so late, and others so lengthy, that we are obliged to postpone them. **1816** PICKERING 123 This word . . . is applied by us, as Mr. Webster justly observes chiefly to writings or discourses. Thus we say, a *lengthy* pamphlet, a *lengthy* sermon, &c. **1949** *Lubbock* (Tex.) *Morn. Avalanche* 23 Feb. I. 10/8 The entire investigation—lengthy as it was—was 'hurried along because of the alertness of a service station operator who took the precaution to copy down a license number of a car.'

b. Used with reference to physical length.

1760 *N. Eng. Hist. & Gen. Reg.* IX. 341 There is an Hill . . . the most steep and lengthy to ascend which I have ever seen. **1787** CUTLER *Life* (1888) I. 244 The attention of travelers is principally engaged by a very lengthy brick building, just above the town. **1849** THOREAU *Week on Concord* (1894) 248 Many a lengthy reach we've rowed. **1944** *Chi. D. News* 24 June 2/4 The operator . . . celebrated his 38th birthday by shearing our lengthy locks just behind the lines.

lengthy ˈlɛŋkθɪ, *adv.* At length, fully. *Rare.* — **1775** J. HANCOCK *J. Hancock His Book* (1898) 199 Do acquaint me every Circumstance Relative to that Dear Aunt of Mine; write Lengthy and often.

Leni-Lenape ˌlɛnɪˈlɛnəpɪ, *n. Collect.* or in the *pl.* (See quot. 1907.)

1781–2 JEFFERSON *Notes* (1803) 140 Delawares, or Linnelinapies (Croghan, 1759). . . . Between Ohio and Lake Erie and the branches of Beaver creek, Cayahoga and Muskingum. *c***1824–38** G. FURMAN *Antiquities of L.I.* 13 The Mohegans and Lenni Lenapi were of the same origin. **1907** HODGE *Amer. Indians* I. 385/1 They called themselves Lenâpe or Leni-lenape, equivalent to 'real men,' or 'native, genuine men'; the English knew them as Delawares, from the name of their principal river.

***leopard,** *n.*

1. leopard frog, a common American frog, *Rana pipiens*, green with black markings on the back which suggest the spots of a leopard.

1839 STORER *Mass. Reptiles* 237 *Rana halecina* . . . [is] better known in this state as the leopard frog from its ocellated appearance. **1938** MATSCHAT *Suwannee River* 66 Among the choristers the leopard frogs were close by. **1948** *Sierra Club Bul.* March 140 Migration is a part of the story of the American merganser, hibernation of the leopard frog.

2. leopard lily, (see quots. 1938, 1949).

1902 *Out West* Sep. 349 The leopard-lily lights the heather dun. **1938** McFARLAND *Garden Bulbs* 136 Lilium pardalinum. Sometimes called the Western Tiger Lily, this highly esteemed California native also has the common names of Leopard Lily and Panther Lily. **1949** MOLDENKE *Amer. Wild Flowers* 323 A great favorite of the Southeast is the leopard lily or pine lily, L. catesbaei, found in pinelands and acid swamps on the coastal plain from North Carolina to Florida and Louisiana.

lepero ˈlɛpəro, *n. S.W.* [Amer. Sp. *lépero* in sense shown here.] A low character, a villain, one of the rabble. *Obs.*

1836 EDWARD *Hist. Texas* 122 The lower and poor sort of Creoles, however, [are] called *Leperos*. **1847** RUXTON *Adv. in Mex. & Rocky Mts.* 67 (Bentley), Leperos whine and pray for alms, and lavenders for your clothes to wash. **1856** HAYES *Pioneer Notes* (1929) 134 They are generally picked up in Mexico among the class called *leperos*.

Lespedeza ˌlɛspəˈdizə, *n.* [D. *Lespedez*, Sp. governor of Fla.] A variety of Japan clover, used for forage in the South.

[**1803** A. MICHAUX *Flora Boreali-Americana* II. 70 Lespedeza. D. Lespedez, gubernator Floridæ, erga me peregrinatorem officiosissimus.] **1937** PARKS *Valuable Plants Texas* 54 There are ten other species of Lespedeza, all of which are called Bush Clover. **1949** *Mo. Bot. Garden Bul.* Feb. 51 As is commonly true of many lespedezas, this species seems well adapted to soils of low fertility.

***lesson,** *n.* (Usu. *cap.*) *Christian Science.* A passage taken from the Bible and from the Christian Science textbook, *Science and Health with Key to the Scriptures*, by Mary Baker Eddy, read in Christian Science church services. In full **Lesson-sermon.**

1899 EDDY *Church Manual* (ed. 10) 24 The readers must devote a suitable portion of their time to preparation for reading the Sunday lesson,—a lesson on which the prosperity of Christian Science largely depends. *Ib.* 25 [The readers] shall make no remarks explanatory of the Lesson-Sermon at any time during the service. **1949** *Chi. D. News* 7 March 12/3 The lesson-sermon consists always of alternate passages from the Bible and from that textbook [i.e., *Science and Health with Key to the Scriptures*].

As the last term in **back, heart lesson.**

∗**let,** *v. tr.* and *intr.* In colloq. phrases and expressions.

1. *To let up on* (someone or something), to grant respite to, to desist from further activity against or concerning. *Colloq.*

1857 *S.F. Call* 21 Feb. (Th.), Our spicy contemporary must 'let up' on us for this error of omission. **1875** MARK TWAIN *Old Times Miss.* iii. 52 [When the wheel on the steamboat] fights strong . . . let up on her a trifle. **1889** RILEY *Pipes o' Pan* 62 Then you 'let up' on that suicidal talk of marrying. **1932** COOLIDGE & LORD *Archibald Cary Coolidge* 334 (Horwill), He never let up on his main hobby of planting trees.

2. ∗*To let out*, of school or a meeting: To dismiss, break up. Also **letting out.**

1867 LACKLAND *Homespun* 325 No impatient chap in school looks forward more wistfully to the 'letting out.' **1888** EGGLESTON *Graysons* x, [He] would meet her at the door of the Mount Zion tent when the meeting should 'let out.' **1898** N. BROOKS *Boys of Fairport* 173, I'll lick you when school lets out. **1948** DICK *Dixie Frontier* 175 When time for 'letting out' approached, the whole school was summoned to line up and spell for 'head marks.'

b. To release or excuse (someone) from further responsibility.

1871 HARTE *Luck of Roaring Camp* 44, I ran the whole way, knowing nobody was home but Jim,—and—and—I'm out of breath—and—that lets me out. **1904** *Montgomery W. Advt.* 29 July 4 A Chinese name is bad enough and a Russian is worse, but now they are going the limit by making one word out of parts of a Russian and a Chinese one. That lets us out.

c. *To let out the links*, to move along at a great rate. *Colloq.* or *slang.*

1868 WOODRUFF *Trotting Horse* 282 Lancet . . . in the third heat, let out the links in such a manner that he trotted it in 2m. 25½s. **1880** BURNETT *Old Pioneer* 110 [The buffaloes] let out a few more links, and ran much faster.

3. ∗*To let down*, to diminish.

1926 *Publishers' Wkly.* 20 Feb. 563 Sales are increasing instead of letting down.

b. *To let down the bars*, to cast off all restraints, to remove restrictions or obstructions.

1869 *Cong. Globe* 22 March 199/1 Why should we thus 'let down the bars' the first time a vacancy occurs? **1890** *Cong. Rec.* 8 May 4322/2 We have tried the experiment of 'letting down the bars.'

4. *Let it go at that*, let matters remain as they are, say no more about it.

1898 WESTCOTT *D. Harum* 306 'Very well,' said John, 'we will let it go at that.' **1917** FARNOL *Definite Object* ii. 19 Eleven will do as well as any other time—let it go at that.

5. *To let rip*, see ∗**rip.**

Letheon 'liθɪɑn, *n.* [Irreg. f. ∗*Lethe*, forgetfulness+ *-on*, poss. influenced by ∗obliv*ion*.] (See quot. 1880.) *Obs.* Cf. **anesthesia,** *n.*

Dr. Morton, after the successful demonstration of the use in surgery of an anesthetic agent, on Oct. 16, 1846, at Massachusetts General Hospital, was anxious to keep secret the means he had employed. A few weeks after he had selected the name "Letheon" for the agent he had used, the fact came out that this agent was nothing more mysterious than ether, and as a result "Letheon" promptly fell out of use.

1848 *Santa Fe Republican* 12 Feb. 1/3 The Letheon is used successfully in Mexico in surgical operations. Dr. Barton has introduced it. **1880** *Lib. Universal Knowl.* X. 241 Dr. [W. T. G.] Morton [of Boston] obtained a patent for the use of ether [as an anesthetic], under the name of 'letheon,' in 1846. **1891** HODGES *Intro. of Sulphuric Ether* 56 The term 'letheon,' commonly adopted immediately after the American patent was secured, had its origin in a meeting at the house of Dr. Gould. . . . Returning to his [Dr. Morton's] office, he said, 'I have found a name for the discovery, and am going to call it Letheon.'

∗**letter,** *n.*

1. The initial or initials of a school, college or camp presented as an award for achievement, usu. in athletics, and worn on a sweater. Cf. **letterman.**

1915 *Chi. D. Maroon* 10 June 1/4 The Board of Athletic Control will meet today to award letters to this year's members of the track, baseball, tennis and gymnastic teams. **1944** *Eng. High School Cat.* 43 The athletic letter or insignia in any sport, major or minor, shall not be awarded to any boy who is ineligible to participate in the last scheduled contest of the season. . . . Football and baseball letters may be awarded at the end of the season.

2. In combs.: (1) **letter A tent,** =**A tent;** (2) **drop,** a slit or opening through which letters are dropped in mailing; (3) **mail,** postal matter consisting of letters; (4) ∗**man,** an athlete who has been awarded a letter (sense **1.**); (5) **missive,** in the Congregational Church, a letter bidding a church send a representative to a council.

(1) 1873 *Forest & Stream* 23 Oct. 186/2 A letter A tent is the greatest luxury in camping. — **(2) 1890** *Cent.* 3421/3 *Letter-drop*, . . . on a postal or mail railroad-car, a plate with an opening closed by a hinged flap, for receiving letters for the post along the route of the train. **1904** WALLER *Wood-Carver* 52 The letter-drop is a simulated squirrel-hole. — **(3) 1817** *Niles' Reg.* XII. 177/1 Three entire letter mails . . . did not even arrive. **1860** BUCHANAN in *Pres. Mess. & P.* V. 597 In consequence of the diversion of a large part of the letter mail to the overland route, the postages derived from the California service have been greatly reduced. — **(4) 1926** *Chi. Tribune* 19 Sep. II. 5/4 The letter men in the line are Wolf and Neff, guards, and Rouse, center. **1949** *Telephone Reg.* (McMinnville, Ore.) 4 Aug. 1/1 With the flock of lettermen we have, every team will be pointing for us.

(5) 1798 M. CUTLER in *Life Jrnls.* (1888) II. 4 We jointly addressed letters missive to eleven churches, all of whom complied, and the council was formed at my house. **1880** H. M. DEXTER *Congregationalism* x. 527 In what manner Councils are regularly called. This has been uniformly done by a form of written request, which has received the technical name of a Letter-Missive.

b. *letter of transmittal*, "an official letter in which the recipient is informed that certain documents are transferred to his custody" (*OED*).

1861 *Army Reg.* 339 No letter of transmittal required. **1879** *Postal Laws & Reg.* Sec. 79 A letter of transmittal should accompany each deposit [of postal funds].

As the last term in **box, bucket, by, check, church, drop, fashion, form, mash, Morey, public, scarlet, single, triple, way letter.**

∗**letter,** *v. intr.* To obtain a letter (sense **1.**) in some school or college sport. — **1928** *Dly. Ardmoreite* (Ardmore, Okla.) 6 March 6/5 Drake lettered in football last fall. **1949** *L.A. Times* 8 May 26/1 They went to Bradley U. and lettered together in football, basketball —and baseball.

∗**lettuce,** *n.* **1. lettuce bed,** =**laurel slick; 2. bird,** the American goldfinch, *Spinus tristis.*

(1) 1917 KEPHART *Camping* II. 24 Those great tracts of rhododendron . . . cover mile after mile of steep mountainside where few men have ever been. The natives call such wastes 'laurel slicks,' 'woolly heads,' 'lettuce beds,' 'yaller patches,' and 'hells.' — **(2) 1781–2** JEFFERSON *Notes Va.* (1788) 75 American goldfinch. Lettuce bird. **1917** *Birds of Amer.* III. 13 Goldfinch. . . . [Also called] Lettuce-bird.

As the last term in **canker, devil's, miners' lettuce.**

lev lɛv, *n.* Short for levy *q.v. Obs.* — **1839** T. BROTHERS *United States* 228 This till will be brimming full of 'fips' and 'levs'; a 'fip' for this, and a 'lev' for that; the first being about threepence, and the other six-pence each.

levee 'lɛvɪ, *n. S.* and *W.* [F. *levée* in sense **1.**]

1. An embankment to afford protection for lowlands during high water, used esp. with reference to the lower Mississippi River. Also attrib.

[1719 in WINSOR *Narr. & Crit. Hist.* V. 39 Devant la ville [New Orleans] il y a une levée et par derrière un fossé.] **1766** H. GORDON in *Travels Amer. Col.* 481 [They] are obliged to have Levée's of Earth to keep off the Floods. **1851** A. O. HALL *Manhattaner* 4 New Orleans . . . is walled by flat boats, . . . wrinkled with levee crevasses, and dotted with shipyards. **1891** *Memphis Appeal-Avalanche* 23 April 1/3 Our levee board constructed a small run-around at one of these places some weeks ago and had under construction their new protective levee. **1949** *Chi. D. News* 25 March 18/2 The swirling river was biting out great chunks of the levee.

b. A small dike or terrace built to utilize and control to best advantage irrigation water on particular areas.

1855 *N.Y. Wkly. Tribune* 16 June 2/2 We . . . found two hundred stalwart men and women engaged in repairing a break of some hundred feet in length in one of the levees or mud dams which surround each division of the field to regulate the flow of water. **1898** U.S. Geol. Survey *Water Supp. Paper 18*, 80 In alfalfa fields the levees inclosing them are often made so flat and low that farming implements can pass over them. **1941** *Dly. Oklahoman* (Okla. City) 30 Sep., In addition to crop losses, farmers feared heavy damage from erosion, loss of levees and irrigation canals.

c. A low ridge or sandbar formed by a stream.

1870 in CRAMTON *Early Hist. Yellowstone Nat. Pk.* 129 Passing over a sand levee, grown up with sagebrush, we found ourselves on the open beach of the great Yellowstone Lake. *Ib.*, 137 The shore line is bordered by a levee of obsidian, lava pebbles, and calcareous fragments, cutting off and inclosing ponds of water behind it. **1936** CRONEIS & KRUMBEIN *Down to Earth* Pl. 14, Levees, another stream deposit, aid in preventing floods, when breached; destruction may result.

2. A landing place, a dock or quay.

1813 *Cramer's Alman. 1814* (Pittsburgh) 52 This class confine themselves to the levee and levee street principally. **1842** H. CASWALL *City of Mormons* 3 The landing-place [at St. Louis] (or levée, as it is denominated) was literally swarming with life. **1949** *Time* 5 Sep. 58/2 For eleven weeks, St. Louis playgoers had gone down to the *Goldenrod's* mooring by the cobblestoned levee and paid 75¢ a head to sass the actors in his hokum-logged version of *Hamlet*.

b. levee rat, =**wharf rat.** *Slang. Obs.*

1856 *Sacramento Union* 13 Aug. 3/1 On the suggestion of a friend, [he] took board at the Atlantic Bar, as being the resort of 'levee rats and bummers.' **1856** *Dem. State Journal* (Sacramento) 10 Sep. 2/4 Hugh Early, formerly one of the peculiar class regularly styled 'levee rats,' entered a saloon on J street yesterday, and insisted upon abusing the landlord.

3. A vice district, with esp. reference to Chicago. Also attrib. Cf. ***dive,** ***n.* 1. b.**

1882 *Chi. Tribune* 25 Jan. 8/2 Maggie Moore, one of the old-time residents of the levee, was arrested last night . . . upon charges of abduction and keeping a house of ill-fame. **1892** *Scribner's Mag.* July 10/2 'The Dive' is only half a mile south of it, and 'The Levee,' 'The Bad Lands,' 'Chinatown,' etc., are still nearer. **1903** *N.Y. Sun* 8 Nov. 3 Three levees, one for each of the three leading parts of the city, are to be sanctioned by the city of Chicago. **1948** *Chi. Sun-Times* 11 Aug. 2/5 [His] beat was the infamous old Chicago Levee District.

levee ˈlɛvɪ, *v.* [f. prec.] *tr.* To provide (land, a river, etc.) with a levee. Also *to levee off*. Also fig.

1837 WILLIAMS *Florida* 45 Where there is clay enough in the soil, to form good embankments, the waters might be leveed off. **1847** PALMER *Rocky Mts.* 225 Several islands in the river might be leveed and successfully cultivated. **1869** M. TWAIN *Innocents Abroad* xv. 147 (R.), He ought to be damned—or leveed, I should say. **1877** W. H. BURROUGHS *Taxation* 75 An act incorporated certain persons for the purpose of leveeing and draining a district.

***level,** *n.* and *a.*

1. *n. On the level*, in a fair, straightforward manner, honestly. *Colloq.*

1875 BURNHAM *Three Years* p. vi, On The Level, meeting a man with honorable intentions. **1923** VANCE *Baroque* 40 No, on the level; if it hadn't been for luck we'd still be guessin'. **1948** *Minneapolis Star* 17 Sep. 24/5 On the level, aren't there some really big, important exposes to make?

2. *a.* Well balanced or poised, possessing common sense. Said usu. of the head, regarded as the seat of understanding or judgment.

1870 *Orchestra* 12 Aug. 331/1 To tell a woman her head is level is apparently a compliment in America. **1872** MARK TWAIN *Sk., New & Old* 180 With a great brain and a level head reminding the bar-keeper not to forget the strawberries. **1907** M. C. HARRIS *Tents of Wickedness* 136 Commend me to common sense . . . and a level head.

3. Used with superlatives in imitation or after the manner of ***level best.** Also **levelest.** *Colloq.*

1884 M. TWAIN *H. Finn* xxviii, He was on hand and looking his level pisonest. **1891** *Harper's Mag.* July 208/2 The pony will not do his level worst again. **1898** CANFIELD *Maid of Frontier* 97 She told me . . . that she was goin' to do her levelest to make our little home comfortable.

4. In combs.: (1) **level head,** a person possessed of common sense and poise; (2) **headed,** (*a*) having good common sense and judgment, (*b*) of a horse, steady, not skittish; (3) **headedness,** (*a*) of a horse, steadiness, (*b*) the quality of good judgment and sound reasoning.

(1) 1906 O. HENRY *Four Million* 204 James Williams belonged among the level heads. — **(2)** (*a*) **1879** TOURGEE *Fool's Errand* 8 Clear-headed, or, as they would now be called, level-headed, were these children of the Berkshire hills. **1893** *Boston Jrnl.* 6 Jan. 6/1 Hon. William C. Whitney is a level-headed man, and . . . doesn't want to imperil his political future. (*b*) **1884** *N.Y. Herald* 27 Oct. 1/3 Wanted—Sound, Level Headed Horse. — **(3)** (*a*) **1876** *Vt. Bd. Agric. Rep.* III. 156 That same steadiness, or, in horse parlance, level-headedness, . . . is quite as essential on the race track . . . as any where else. (*b*) **1886** *New Englander* (New Haven, Conn.) Feb. 179 This unexampled success is due . . . to the levelheadedness of its clerical guardians.

***lever,** *n.* In combs.: (1) **lever bit,** a severe curb bit; (2) **man,** one employed to work the levers in a railway signal box; (3) **wood,** the American hop hornbeam.

(1) 1834 *Visit to Texas* vi. 60 [A rider puts] the terrible lever bits into his mouth. **1836** CROCKETT *Exploits* 183 Lever bits of the harshest description, able to break the jaws of their animals under a very gentle pressure. — **(2) 1901** *Daily News* (London) 12 Jan. 6/2 A saving . . . has been effected in the wages of lever men. **1949** *Chi. Tribune* 4 Sep. III. 3/4 A railroad man with model railroading as a hobby . . . is Richard H. Radford of Hammond, a lever man for the Indiana Harbor Belt railroad. — **(3) 1755** *N.H. Hist. Soc. Coll.* II. 102 In this meadow, they left a bow, made of lever wood, and several arrows. **1843** TORREY *Flora N.Y.* II. 185 Hop Hornbeam . . . is often used for levers, and is hence called *Lever-wood* in some places. **1938** BROWN *Trees Northeastern U.S.* 177 Hop Hornbeam, Ironwood, Leverwood.

levis ˈlivaɪz, *n. pl.* [See note.] Bibless overalls, orig. and properly applied to those of heavy blue denim reinforced at strain points with copper rivets and made by Levi Strauss and Company.

Orig. such overalls were known as *Levi's*, the maker's trade-mark name, from *Levi* Strauss, a pioneer overall manufacturer in the West.

1941 *Yankee* Dec. 39/1 Red-flannel underwear, Peavey axes, copper-riveted Levi's, etc. **1949** *Rocks & Minerals* May–June 226/2 This garb may consist of . . . miner's dress, Levis and gay colored shirt, or any dress that will enable the contestant to look the part.

levy ˈlɛvɪ, *n.* [Shortening of *eleven pence*, the approx. value of the coin.] A Spanish real or its equivalent; one eighth of a dollar. Now *hist.* Cf. **fip.**

1829 in *Amer. Sp.* XVI. (1941) 28 Levies, Fips, so werden abgekürzt in den westlichen Staaten die sogenannten 12½ and 6¼ Centstücke (genannt). **1835** *Vade Mecum* (Phila.) 17 Jan. 3/6 Fips and levies are not as plentiful as snowballs. **1855** *Monterey* (Calif.) *Sentinel* 14 July 1/2 What are its denominations? Coppers, boges, and Bungtown cents, fourpence ha'penys, levys. **1883** G. M. TUCKER in *Trans. Albany Inst.* X. 336 The 'shilling' of our own State [New York] is the 'levy' of Pennsylvania, the 'bit' of San Francisco, the 'ninepence' of old New England, and the 'escalon' of New Orleans. **1928** *Bur. of Mint Cat. Coins U.S.* 10 The Secretary of the Treasury prescribed the rate at which the 'Levy' and the 'Bit' . . . should be received in exchange.

b. levy shirting, ?cloth for shirts ordinarily selling for a levy a yard. *Obs.*

1859 J. B. JONES *Southern Scenes* 161 Levy shirting is now a quarter of a dollar; and they say it'll soon be fifty cents.

levy court. In Delaware and formerly in other places, a body of county officials who administer the affairs of the county. — **1788** *Md. Laws* II. Nov. iv. 3 Every person . . . who shall produce a certificate as aforesaid . . . at the levy court, shall, for every old wolf's head be allowed five pounds current money. **1891** *Del. Rev. Statutes 1893* 78 The Levy Court of each county shall meet at the court house . . . three times in every year.

***Lewis,** *n.* [Capt. Meriwether *Lewis* (1774–1809), Amer. explorer.] Used in the names of plants and fish found in the western part of the U.S., as **Lewis' barberry, Lewis grass, Lewis' trout,** (see quots.).

1813 MUHLENBERG *Cat. Plants* 36 *Berberis pinnata*, Lewis's Barberry. **1859** BARTLETT 268 Mesquit Grass (*Stipa spata*), a fine, short grass, called also Lewis Grass, which grows with great vigor and beauty on the western prairies. **1869** *Amer. Naturalist* III. 125 Lewis' Trout (*Salmo Lewisii Girard*) . . . abounds in the headwaters of the Missouri.

b. Lewis(') woodpecker, *W.* the black or crow woodpecker, *Asyndesmus lewisi.*

1811 WILSON *Ornithology* III. 31 Lewis's Woodpecker, *Picus Torquatus*, . . . was eleven inches and a half [long]. **1880** *Cimarron News & Press* 23 Dec. 1/4 Another remarkable inhabitant of the mountains and cañons is the Lewis woodpecker, its head, back and wings black, with a bronzy-green iridescence. **1940** GABRIELSON & JEWETT *Birds Ore.* 375 The striking red and dark bronzy green Lewis's Woodpecker is an exceedingly familiar sight in Oregon.

c. *Lewis and Clark Centennial Exposition*, an exposition commemorating the one-hundredth anniversary of the Lewis and Clark Expedition (1804–6).

1947 *Democrat* 6 Nov. 7/2 The first cross-laminated panels using Douglas fir veneer were made in a veneer plant in Portland, Ore., in 1905 and exhibited that year at the Lewis and Clark Centennial exposition in that city.

Lewisia luˈɪsɪə, *n. W.* [See prec.] A large genus of herbs of the family Portulacaceae found in the western states. Also a plant of this genus.

1917 SAUNDERS *Western Wild Flowers* 52 The large root of *Lewisia* is a conspicuous feature. **1920** RICE *Calif. Wild Flowers* 89 In California the plant [bitterroot] is more commonly called by its scientific name

'Lewisia.' **1947** *Nat. Geog. Mag.* July 60/1 The Bitter Roots (*Lewisia*); how some of them resent being moved!

Lewisite ˈluɪsˌaɪt, *n.* (See quot. 1888.) *Obs.*—**1804** *Mass. Spy* 2 May (Th.), Both Burrites and Lewisites are very polite to the Federalists. **1888** M. LANE in *America* 11 Oct. 16 Lewisites.—Followers of Morgan Lewis, Governor of New York, in 1804. It was too exclusive and aristocratic a faction to gain much popularity or to live long.

* **liberal,** *n.*

1. One holding liberal rather than orthodox views on theological matters.

1821 *Mass. Const. Convention Jrnl.* (1853) 589 What the ultra liberals and the ultra royalists in religion had acquiesced in, seemed to be a point at which we ought to stop. **1925** W. P. MERRILL *Liberal Christianity* 11 [Machen] has even gone so far as to deny to liberals the right to be considered Christians at all.

2. A member of the Liberal Republican party. *Obs.*

1872 *Newton Kansan* 17 Oct. 4/2 What pleases the Liberals, displeases the Rebels and Copperheads. **1885** *Mag. Amer. Hist.* Feb. 202/2 *Liberal.*—This term acquired its recent significance from a movement headed by Carl Schurz in Missouri, in 1870, and resulting in a division of the local Republicans into 'Liberals' and 'Radicals.'

* **liberal,** *a.*

1. Used freq. in religious contexts to characterize Unitarians and Universalists.

1823 (*title*), The Liberal Christian. **1846** HOLMES *Poetical Works* (1899) 56/2 Thine eyes behold A cheerful Christian from the liberal fold. **1876** FROTHINGHAM *Transcendentalism* 128 Liberal Christianity or Unitarianism.

2. In combs.: (1) **liberal construction,** a construction of the federal Constitution that ascribes to the federal government powers not expressly granted by the Constitution but reasonably necessary for carrying out the powers that are expressly granted, cf. **strict construction;** (2) **party,** =**Liberal Republican party;** (3) **Liberal Republican,** a member of the Liberal Republican party, also attrib.; (4) **Republican party,** a party formed 1870–72 by Carl Schurz, B. Gratz Brown, and other Republicans desirous of securing various reforms; (5) **ticket,** the ticket of this party.

(1) 1791 *Ann. 1st Congress* II. 195 If we look at their [=Congress'] acts under the existing Constitution, we shall find they are generally the result of a liberal construction. **1854** BENTON *30 Years' View* I. 24/1 It has been shown, after the most liberal construction of all the enumerated powers of the general government [etc.]. — **(2) 1872** *Newton Kansan* 21 Nov. 2/4 It seems . . . that the 'Liberal' party would sweep over the country like an avalanche. — **(3) 1872** in *Fla. Hist. Quart.* (1949) Jan. 224 We cordially take the hand of Liberal Republicans and accord to them the same honesty we claim for ourselves. **1900** *Cong. Rec.* 14 Feb. 1800/1 The Liberal Republican element got control of the State of Missouri in 1870. **1949** *Social Studies* May 218/1 They had about the same effect upon Truman's victory as the Liberal Republicans had upon Grant's reelection in 1872. — **(4) 1882** COOPER *Amer. Pol.* I. 199 An issue raised in Missouri gave immediate rise to the Liberal Republican party. **1899** BREEN *Thirty Years* 409 The outgrowth of this sentiment was the organization of what was known as the Liberal-Republican party, of which Carl Schurz, Senator Trumbull, and other prominent Republican leaders were exponents.

(5) 1872 *Chi. Tribune* 9 Oct. 1/4 Cincinnati elects the Liberal ticket by 4,000.

***Liberator,** *n.* A nickname for Abraham Lincoln. *Obs.* Cf. ***Emancipator 2.** — **1869** TOURGEE *Toinette* (1881) xlii, The Liberator had signed that proclamation [etc.].

* **liberty,** *n.*

1. Ease or facility of expression in preaching or praying.

1794 in W. W. SWEET *Religion on Amer. Frontier* IV. (1946) 206 Had some liberty in preaching and a comfortable class meeting. **1872** BRACE *Dangerous Classes N.Y.* 277 He had held forth with peculiar 'liberty' on the sin of thieving.

2. In combs.: (1) **Liberty Bell,** the bell in Independence Hall, Philadelphia, regarded as a symbol of liberty; (2) **Bond,** one of the interest-bearing bonds issued by the U.S. Government during World War I; (3) **Boys,** see as a main entry; (4) **bush,** the pinkster flower; (5) **cabbage,** (see quots.); (6) **Elm,** the Liberty Tree in Boston; (7) **Hall,** the area under the Liberty Tree in Boston, *obs.;* (8) **head nickel,** a five-cent coin having on one side a representation of the head of the goddess of liberty bordered with stars, coined from 1883 to 1913; (9) **man,** see as a main entry; (10) **nickel,** =**Libertyhead nickel;** (11) **party,** see as a main entry; (12) **pin,** (see quot.), *obs.;* (13) **pole,** see as a main entry; (14) **song,** during the Revolutionary period, a song popular with American patriots; (15) **stump,** the stump of the Liberty Tree in Boston; (16) **tea,** (see quots.); (17) **Tree,** see as a main entry.

(1) 1852 B. J. LOSSING *Pictorial Field-Bk.* II. 272, I ascended to the steeple, where hangs, in silent grandeur, the 'Liberty Bell.' **1943** PEATTIE *Journey into Amer.* 18 And the Liberty Bell is the great voice of this people, which no other on earth can shout down or command to be still. — **(2) 1919** HOUGH *Sagebrusher* 195 Told me three times he had bought fifteen thousand dollars' worth of Liberty Bonds. **1947** *Time* 1 Sep. 76/2 He made his first killing in 1921, buying up depressed Liberty Bonds. — **(4) 1839** AUDUBON *Ornith. Biog.* V. 70 The Liberty bush, *Azalea nudiflora*. . . . Occurs in dry situations in most parts of the United States, from their northern limits to Florida.

(5) 1927 *Haldeman-Julius Quart.* July–Sep. 7/2 Here we were, . . . doing everything we were told to do: eating rye bread instead of wheat, calling sauerkraut 'Liberty cabbage.' **1948** *True* May 52/2 The feeling against anything that sounded German . . . was so strong [in World War I] that the name of sauerkraut was changed to Liberty cabbage. — **(6) 1769** *Boston Chron.* 22 May, All persons . . . are . . . to call and receive their respective dues of T. Chase, at the venerable Liberty-Elm. — **(7) 1768** *Boston Rec.* 312 The Sons of liberty request all those who . . . would promote the peace . . . to assemble at Liberty Hall under Liberty tree on Tuesday. **1768** in TUDOR *Life J. Otis* (1823) 221 (*footnote*), It has since been adorned with an inscription, and has obtained the name of Liberty Tree, as the ground under it has that of Liberty Hall. — **(8) 1932** *Durant* (Okla.) *D. Democrat* 10 Feb. 6/3 He also pointed out that 1913 Liberty head nickels (not the present Indian head, or Buffalo type) have a distinct valuation to collectors. **1949** *Sat. Ev. Post* 5 Feb. 33/1 One of Mehl's most famous stunts . . . was advertising an offer of seventy-five dollars for every 1913 liberty-head nickel sent to him.

(10) 1948 *Forest Way* (Chi.) May–June 9 Liberty Nickels—1912S $1.25. — **(12) 1863** in *Pub. Col. Soc.* XX. 226 The 'Copperhead,' or Liberty Pins, were another noticeable emblem in the procession. Strange to say, the wearers of these things seemed wholly unconscious of *treason* (as defined in the Constitution) in thus exhibiting them. — **(14) 1769** J. ADAMS *Diary* Wks. II. 218 We had also the Liberty Song—that by the farmer, and that by Dr. Church, and the whole company joined in the chorus. **1774** FITHIAN *Jrnl.* I. 96 There were parties in Rooms made up, some at Cards; . . . some singing 'Liberty Songs' as they call'd them.

(15) 1782 *Broadside Verse* (1930) 107 Sold near Liberty-Stump and next the Swan-Tavern. **1824** *Amer. Sentinel* (Georgetown, Ky.) 17 Sep. 2/3 Another beautiful arch was thrown across the same street at the site of the old Liberty Stump opposite Boylston Market. — **(16) 1837** *N.H. Hist. Soc. Coll.* V. 84 During the Revolution many adopted the use of what was called *Liberty tea*, as a substitute for the Chinese herb. It was made of four-leaved loosestrife. **1898** *Essex Antiq.* II. 33 With the Revolution came the refusal to drink the tea of commerce, and our four-leaved loosestrife, being dried and steeped, was used in its stead. This was known as 'Liberty tea.'

As the last term in **shield of, Sons of Liberty.**

Liberty Boys. Active supporters of the American Revolution. Now *hist.*

1774 in ASPINALL-OGLANDER *Admiral's Widow* (1942) 51 They are distinguished here by the name of Tories, as the Liberty Boys—the tarring feathering gentry—are by the title of Whigs. **1872** *Harper's Mag.* April 692/2 The close of the revolutionary war found New York politically in the hands of the Whigs of that day, who were controlled by the Liberty Boys, the most radical of their number. **1938** HART *New Yorkers* 23 Washington stormed at the organization of the people in the Democratic party by the Liberty Boys, caustically styling their local groups 'self created societies' which he apparently believed dammed them completely.

b. Those interested in freeing Texas from Mexican rule. *Obs.*

1858 *Texas Almanac 1859* 33 The Liberty boys, always on hand on an emergency, joined Austin's Company.

Liberty man. Also **liberty man.**

1. a. During the Revolution, one who was loyal to the cause of the colonists. **b.** (See quot.) Both *obs.*

(a) 1774 HUTCHINSON *Diary & Lett.* I. 111 Some of the highest Liberty men begin to see they have carried the matter too far. **1855** SIMMS *Forayers* 139 But what's it to you, ef I'm king's or liberty man! — **(b) 1867** DIXON *New Amer.* II. 243 One party [of Perfectionists] putting freedom before holiness, were known as the 'Liberty men'; another putting sanctity before freedom were known as the 'Holiness men.'

2. A member of the Liberty party, a Free-Soiler. *Obs.*
1843 *Philanthropist* (Cin.) 18 Jan., [We hereby invite] the Liberty men of the United States to meet in convention at Buffalo, . . . on the 28th day of June, 1843, . . . to take into consideration the subject of that nomination [etc.]. **1848** *Free Soil Minstrel* 20 For conscience whigs and liberty men, And every true barnburner, Here join to stay proud slavery's curse, And from free soil to spurn her.

Liberty party.

1. A political party organized *c*1840, having as its main object the abolition of slavery. Now *hist.* Cf. **Free-Soil party, Personal Liberty party.**
1842 *Greene Co. Torchlight* (Xenia, O.) 6 Jan. 2/3 The above convention, which assembled at Columbus on the 29th, nominated Judge King of Trumbull county, as the candidate of the 'liberty party,' as they denominate themselves. **1922** McCormac *Biog. Polk* 263 In August, 1843, the Liberty party had nominated James G. Birney, of Michigan, on an anti-slavery ticket. **1948** *Ohio State Arch. Quart.* April 165 The chieftains of Ohio's Liberty Party were laboring with that purpose in mind from the very inception of the party.

2. A political party in revolt against existing "old line" parties.
1932 *N.Y. Times* 9 Nov. 17/6 William H. (Coin) Harvey, standard bearer of the Liberty party, . . . admitted that he did not expect to be elected and gloomily added that 'it made no difference which of the two—Hoover or Roosevelt—is elected under the present financial system.'

Liberty pole. A tall pole or mast, usu. having a cap or banner on it, and serving orig. as a rallying place for the Sons of Liberty. Now *hist.*
1770 in *Mag. Amer. Hist.* (1890) Aug. 91 Our city [N.Y.] is yet in a ferment, and last Saturday night a party of soldiers attempted to cut down or blow up the liberty pole. **1794** *Balt. D. Intelligencer* 8 Sep. 3/2 They threaten to march to Middle-Town and Funks-Town, and put up Liberty-poles at those places. **1858** *N.Y. Tribune* 16 Nov. 7/4 The famous 'iron' Liberty-pole to be raised in West Broadway is to be of wood after all. It is over 200 feet high. **1945** McLean *Moment of Time* 17 It's a liberty pole, child.
attrib. **1774** in *Copley-Pelham Lett.* 281 The demolition of Liberty-Pole-Committee,—we could not come to, on that Day.

Liberty Tree.

1. An elm in Boston upon which, during the excitement over the Stamp Act (1765), unpopular persons were hanged in effigy. Now *hist.*
1766 *Boston Selectmen* 26 March 212 Complaint being made by a number of Inhabitants that the Chimnies of a House. . . . Situate in Newbury Street near *Liberty Tree* . . . are Insufficient and dangerous. **1776** A. Adams in *Familiar Letters* 180, I ventured just as far as the stump of Liberty Tree. **1889** Brayley *Boston Fire Dept.* 68 Engine 8 . . . was ordered to be removed to a piece of ground near . . . the 'Liberty Tree.' **1924** *Pub. Col. Soc.* XXVI. 37 Coffin was one of the addressers of both Hutchinson and Gage. . . . It is said that it was one of his sons who in August, 1775, helped cut down the Liberty Tree, when the British had complete control of the town.

2. Any tree dedicated to, or serving as a symbol of, liberty.
1823 Tudor *Otis* 223 In Providence, an inhabitant gave a deed to the Town of a small piece of ground containing a large tree, to be used as a 'Liberty Tree' forever. **1895** *N. Eng. Mag.* Dec. 503/2 'Liberty trees' were planted in many of the towns, whose branches waved in freedom's breezes years after the strife was ended. **1944** Adams *Album Amer. Hist.* I. 361 Almost every American town had a Liberty Tree, under which patriots gathered or organize and protest.

* **library,** *n.* In combs.: (1) **Library Association,** see as a main entry; (2) **Company,** =prec.; (3) **school,** a school in which professional training for librarians is given.
(2) **1745** Franklin *Writings* II. 296 Our Library Company sends for about twenty pounds sterling worth of books yearly. **1877** *Harper's Mag.* April 723/1 This [subscription] library . . . exists today in the Philadelphia Library Company. — (3) **1907** *Springfield W. Republican* 18 April 16 The New York state library school at Albany is regarded as one of the most exacting fitting schools for librarians in the country. **1942** *Gen. Cat. U. of Wis.* 85 Practical work in an approved library, preferably in a public library, for a year or more before entering a library school is very desirable.
As the last term in **Carnegie, Congressional, Ohio school, parish, rental, school district, social, state library.**

Library Association. An organization composed of those who make contributions for founding and maintaining a library.
1848 *Santa Fe Republican* 29 Jan. 2/1 The citizens of Santa Fe have taken an interest in the establishment of a Library Association. **1881** Rittenhouse *Maud* 1 We were first introduced to the Social Science and Cairo Auxiliary, and the Woman's Club and Library Association. **1910** Bostwick *Amer. Pub. Library* 343 The American Library Association was organized in Philadelphia on October 6, 1876.

* **license,** *n.* As the last term in **grocery, high, liquor license.**

licitation ˌlɪsɪˈteʃən, *n.* [Sp. *licitación*, an Amer. borrowing.] In parts of the U.S. formerly under Spanish rule, an auction at which property jointly owned is released for sale. *Obs.* — **1820** in Martin *La. Term Rep.* VII. 89 The sale made by the parish judge . . . was a cant or licitation between the parties for the purpose of dividing the property, which had been held in common by their ancestors. **1887** Merrill *Amer. & Eng. Encycl.* II. 721 Cant, or Licitation.—A mode of dividing property held in common by two or more persons.

* **lick,** *n.*

1. A salt lick.
1747 in *Amer. Sp.* XV. 280/2 Crossing the said Run above a Lick. **1858** *Porter's Spirit of Times* 6 March 4/2 When you have killed a deer in a lick, it will not be frequented any more until after a heavy rain. **1948** Dick *Dixie Frontier* 33 The earliest hunters waited at the licks and killed a few as the animals came for salt.

b. In place-names.
1774 D. Jones *Journal* (1865) 86 As I passed a certain place called the *Great Lick*, saw the last flock of parrots. **1777** *Va. State P.* I. 276 [They] had left their women and children . . . at the Blue Licks on Kentucke River. **1781–2** Jefferson *Notes Va.* 32 The area of Bullet's lick is of many acres. **1791** W. Bartram *Travels* 35 We sat [*sic*] off from Augusta, early in the morning, for the Great Buffalo Lick, on the Great Ridge. **1838** Ellsworth *Valley of Wabash* 6 Near the French lick . . . freestone . . . may be readily obtained.

c. Also **buffalo lick, clay lick.**
1749 in *Amer. Sp.* XV. 161/2 My Land called the Buffalo Lick on both Sides of James River. **1850** *Ib.*, I have seen several places which were noted Buffalo licks, where the earth had been eaten away by long usage. **1888** Roosevelt in *Cent. Mag.* XXXVI. 209/1 These clay licks were mere holes in the banks.

2. * **big lick,** (see quot.). *Obs.*
1865 Sala *Diary* II. 72 A giant ferry-boat, crowded with people who didn't say a word, but sat solemnly side by side from stem to stern of this Noah's ark, chewing the cud of sweet 'big lick' or bitter 'pigtail,' and spitting in mournful unison.

3. A turn *of work. Colloq.*
1868 *Putnam's Mag.* June I. 715/1 The father . . . cultivated a little patch of corn, and did an occasional 'lick of work' for some well-to-do neighbor. **1906** H. D. Pittman *Belle of Blue Grass C.* xv. 224 I'll have to take care of the whole gang, and never get a lick of work out of one of them.

4. (See quots.) *Slang.*
1909 *Sat. Ev. Post* 20 March 9/1 The range boss, Uncle Henry and Maize trifled with bits of biscuit and 'lick' so that he might not be uncomfortable sitting alone. **1927** *Ib.* 23 July 36/2 The chuck box also holds lick—sirup—pieces of salt pork and all the main things to sort of season the grub with. **1943** L. V. Hamner *Short Grass* 113 Over here you all say . . . 'lick' for syrup.

5. *To put in big* (or *best*) *licks*, and variants, to put forth maximum or continued and substantial effort. *Colloq.* Cf. **good lick**(**s**).
1835 *Vade Mecum* (Phila.) 14 Feb. 3/4 When you come to put in the scientific licks, I squat. **1847** Robb *Squatter Life* 106 He was puttin' in the biggest kind a licks in the way of courtin'. **1851** *Polly Peablossom* 111, I saw comin' my gray mule, puttin' in her best licks, and a few yards behind her was a grizzly. **1907** *Springfield W. Republican* 22 Aug. 3 It is a time for those interested in the city's welfare to wake up and put in some solid licks for good government. **1949** *News-Herald* (Marshfield, Wis.) 19 July 4/1 The power lobby got in its licks through a subcommittee of the Senate Appropriations Committee passing on the bill for funds for the Department of Interior.
As the last term in **cattle, clover, deer, elk, fair, horse, long, mud, pine, salt, solid, suck, sugar, sulphur lick.**

* **lick,** *v.*

1. lickblock, a block of hard salt put out for stock to lick.
1878 in Summers *Ann. S.W. Va.* 1602 A gang of horses had come in from the range to the lick-blocks, about one hundred yards from the house.

2. lick-log, (see quot. 1889).
1852 G. W. L. Bickley *Hist. Tazewell Co., Va.* 226 Capt. Moore, who had previously distinguished himself at Alamance, was at a lick log, . . . salting his horses, of which he had many. **1889** Roosevelt *Winning West* II. 212 To provide for the latter [farm stock] a tree was chopped down and the salt placed in notches or small troughs cut in the bark, making it what was called a lick-log. **1948** Dick *Dixie Frontier* 105 Small troughs were cut in the trunk of a fallen tree and occasionally salt was placed there, making what was known as a 'lick log.'

b. *To stand (up) to one's lick-log,* to meet something fairly and courageously, as an unpleasant duty. *Colloq.* Cf. *To stand up to the rack, s.v.* ∗**rack,** *n.*

1834 Crockett *Narr. Life* 170, I was determined to stand up to my lick-log, salt or no salt. **1840** Haliburton *Clockmaker* 3 Ser. xii, I like a man to be up to the notch, and stand to his lick-log.

lickety ˈlɪkətɪ, *adv.* Used colloq. in various adverbial expressions to denote rapidity of movement, quickness or impulsiveness of going: **lickety brindle, click, cut, liner, split, switch.**

Wentworth records a large number of such expressions as these, and also has compounds with *lippity, nickety,* etc. In *EDD s.v.* ∗*like* 12 the following expressions are recorded: *lick-a-to-lick, likatee-lik,* all alike, all of one mind.

Lick-log for cattle

1876 *Wide Awake* 236/2 You can't describe a boy running down hill without saying he went 'lickety split,' or 'lickety brindle.' **1901** *Kans. Hist. Coll.* (1902) VII. 61 We had only revolvers with us, and away they came lickety brindle. **1847** Robb *Squatter Life* 116 Away they started, 'lickety-click,' and arrived at the winning-post within touching distance of each other. — **1831** *Boston Transcript* 4 June 2/2 He ran down the street licketty cut, and is probably at home by this time. **1898** E. N. Westcott *D. Harum* 175, I up an' put fer the village lickity-cut. — **1859** Bartlett 243 *Lickety Split.* Very fast, headlong. . . . *Lickety cut* and *lickety liner* are also used. — **1843** in *Ore. Hist. Soc. Quart.* I. 399 The candidates [for Ore. emigrant leaders] stood up in a row . . . and at a given signal they wheeled about and marched off, while the general mass broke after them 'lick-a-ty-split.' **1949** *Sat. Ev. Post* 2 April 42/3 Down the street came little Annabelle on her new roller skates, lickety-split. — **1858** *Harper's Mag.* May 766/2 There they had it, lickety-switch, rough-and-tumble, till Cephe give in. **1894** *Ib.* April 693/2 She's goin' down street lickety-switch—her arms full of flower-pots agin.

∗**licking,** *n. attrib.* Designating places to which animals resort to lick the ground for salt, as **licking hole, place, pond.** Also transf. Cf. **salt lick.** See also **boot-licking.**

1727 in *Amer. Sp.* XV. 281/1 Thence to the Licking place, and from the Licking place across the Meadow and old Field to a Corner Tree. **1736** *Ib.,* Thence . . . to two Corner red Oaks and a black Oak by a Licking Hole. **1751** J. Bartram *Observations* 27 We found a *Liching* [*sic*] *Pond,* where we dined, the backs [*sic*] parts of our country are full of these liching ponds. **1840** Marryat *Diary* 44 'Why,' replied he, pointing to an hotel opposite, 'that is his *licking place,*' (a term borrowed from deer resorting to lick the salt).

licorice root. Wild licorice, *Glycyrrhiza lepidota,* or its root (see also quot. 1870). Cf. **Chinook licorice.**

1870 Dall *Alaska* 438 [The Indians pick] the roots of *Hedysarum Mackenzii,* the 'liquorice root' of the trappers. **1883** Mark Twain *Life on Miss.* xliv, The shopman . . . gives the child a bit of licorice-root. **1893** *Harper's Mag.* Feb. 459/1 She slipped a piece of licorice-root from her pocket to her mouth as she began a circuit of the room, chewing vigorously the while. **1940** Early *N. Eng. Sampler* 310 Lydia Pinkham's *Vegetable Compound* was (and still is) made from herbs the Indians used—Life Root, Pleurisy and Licorice Roots.

∗**lid,** *n.* In various slang or colloq. phrases, usu. with *down, off,* with reference to the enforcing (or non-enforcing) of laws (cf. quots.). Also transf. Cf. ∗**blow,** *v.* **6.** (6).

1904 *Phila. Pub. Ledger* 12 Sep. 16 He has taken frequent occasion to deny that the 'lid' was off, to use the slang definition of a lax police administration. **1915** *Lit. Digest* 4 Sep. 467/1 In fact, excepting the ordinary saloons . . . the 'lid' is down, secure and tight. **1945** *Chi. D. News* 10 Sep. 1/8 (*heading*), Radio News Lid Tightened.

∗**lie,** *v.* In phrases: (1) *To lie around loose,* or be in an unattached, scattered, or neglected condition, *colloq.;* (2) ∗*to lie out,* of land, to remain in an uncultivated condition; (3) ∗*to lie over,* to interrupt a journey by stopping for a time, cf. **lay over,** *s.v.* ∗**lay,** *v.* **2.** (4).

(1) **1856** *Knickerb.* XLVII. 617 One of the effects of their refreshment was to make things lie around loose in a promiscuous manner. **1879** *Cong. Rec.* 21 Jan. 609/2 The cipher dispatches were suffered to 'lie around loose.' — (2) **1805** Parkinson *Tour* 717 Two years' laying out . . . put the land in a fit state to receive those two crops again. **1850** *Rep. Comm. Patents 1849: Agric.* 402 After the corn crop, do not suffer the land to 'lie out.' **1945** Botkin *My Burden* 74 They never had a hand left there on that great big place, and all that ground laying out. — (3) **1849** *31st Congress* 1 Sess. Sen. Ex. Doc. No. 64, 186 But I shall make an early drive and 'lie over' to-morrow at the first water. **1903** A. Adams *Log Cowboy* 181 We overtook a number of wagons loaded with wool, lying over, as it was Sunday.

Lie-all League. A contemptuous name for the Loyal League, which aided Negroes set free after the Civil War. *Rare.* — **1868** Rose *Great Country* 382 'White Boys in Blue' are organising as an opposition to the G.A.R., while the Kuklux will attend to the Lie-all League.

Liederkranz ˈlidɚˌkrɑnts, *n.* [G. in same sense.] A singing society made up of men of German extraction. Also **Liederkranz (Singing) Society.**

1858 *Harper's Wkly.* 11 Sep. 586/1 On this elevation the orchestra and members of the New York Harmonic Society, . . . and the Liederkranz societies were seated. **1866** *Wilkes' Spirit of Times* 21 July 332/2 The ball commenced and was continued with unflagging spirit until sunrise, varied at intervals with pyrotechnical displays and grand choruses, executed in their usual admirable style by the Liederkranz Society. **1948** *Amer. Sp.* April 108 *Liederkranz* is devoted to a variety of social activities, and, until recently at least, had its own Liederkranz Hall in Belleville [Ill.]. **1949** *Sat. Ev. Post* 12 Feb. 123/3 Peoria harbors something called the I Too Reform Progress Society and the Liederkranz Singing Society.

Hence **Liederkranzer,** a member of such an organization.

1871 *N.Y. Herald* 28 July 5/4 The festival . . . was nevertheless somewhat marred by the threatening aspect of the heavens and the continuance of the lightning, which seemed at times so glaring as to mock the artificial illuminations of the Liederkranzers.

lie detector. An instrument used by the proper authorities on those under suspicion of guilt or complicity in an effort to ascertain their guilt or innocence through changes in their blood pressure, respiration, etc., upon being questioned. Also attrib.

1931 *Durant* (Okla.) *D. Democrat* 13 May 1/1 Defense attorneys announced that Kirkland would again testify and would submit to an instrument known as a lie detector. **1945** *Chronicle-News* (Trinidad, Colo.) 16 Oct. 8/1 A lie detector test holds no legal weight in Colorado. **1949** *This Week Mag.* 5 March 5/4 He said that he wanted to arrange for an immediate test on a lie detector.

lienor ˈliənɚ, *n.* One who holds a lien. — **1890** *Law Times* LXXXIX. 165/1 If the lienors may insure, so may the owners of the injured ship and cargo. **1907** *N.Y. Rep. Supp.* CIII. 679 Where a mechanic's lien has been discharged by the giving of a bond, the lienor may do either one of two things.

∗**lieutenant,** *n.* In combs.: (1) **lieutenant commander,** a navy officer below a commander and above a lieutenant; (2) ∗**general,** (see quot. 1890), now *hist.;* (3) ∗**governor,** a state official ranking below the governor and succeeding him in case a vacancy occurs in the governorship.

(1) **1839** in Sturge *Visit to U.S. in 1841* xxxiii, This means of expressing in some slight degree, their thankfulness and obligation to Lieut. Com. T. R. Gedney, and the officers and crew of the U.S. surveying brig Washington. **1883** *Harper's Mag.* Nov. 950/1, I was a young lieutenant-commander. **1949** *Sat. Ev. Post* 26 March 62/2 Their commander, Lt. Comdr. Lance E. Massey, had worked his way within a mile of the Akagi. — (2) **1639** *Md. Council Proc.* 89 A high Constable . . . [is] to arrest all offenders against the peace and them to send or bring to Our Lieutenant General. **1890** *Cent.* 3441/2 *Lieutenant-general,* . . . in the proprietary government of Maryland, the deputy of the proprietor, who acted as governor of the province for him. — (3) **1775** in *Hist. MSS Comm.,* 14th Rep., App. X. 306 As the Lieut Gov. is constantly at his country house waiting with anxious impatience for the arrival of Lord William Campbell. **1924** Croy *R.F.D. No. 3,* 3 The Lieutenant Governor was to officiate [at a dedication ceremony]. **1948** *Dly. Ardmoreite* (Ardmore, Okla.) 4 May 1/1 Instead, elect the key office holders—governor, lieutenant governor, judges [etc.].

As the last term in **county lieutenant.**

∗**life,** *n.* In combs.: (1) **life car,** a watertight vessel moved by ropes, by means of which persons can be brought from wrecked ships through heavy seas; (2) ∗**everlasting,** see as a main entry; (3) ∗**guard,** one employed at a beach or swimming pool to prevent bathers' drowning; (4) **net,** a large, strong net held, usu. by firemen, so that persons trapped in a burning building may jump into it; (5) **-of-man,** see as a main entry; (6) **saving station,** a building or establishment on a shore or coast, with apparatus and a crew of men for preventing loss of life by drowning; (7) **station,** =prec.

(1) **1851** *Harper's Mag.* July 162/1 The Life-Car is a sort of boat. **1882** GODFREY *Nantucket* 344 The best and finest apparatus for saving life . . . , consisting of . . . floats, life-cars and lines, has been placed on this [island]. — (3) **1896** HOWELLS *Impressions & Exper.* (1909) 159, I came out almost before the life-guard could get ready to throw me a life-preserver. **1949** *Milwaukie* (Ore.) *Rev.* 4 Aug. 3/1 A life guard was on duty. — (4) **1911** in LIMPUS *Hist. N.Y. Fire Dept.* (1940) 307 'Life nets?' commented Battalion Chief Worth at the ensuing investigation. 'What good were life nets?' **1947** *Chi. Tribune* 20 July (Comics) 4 Let's see some action—grab that life net!

(6) **1858** *Statutes at Large* XI. 320 Twenty-eight life-saving stations on the coast of New Jersey. **1908** *Suburban Life* July 46/3 The life-saving stations, of which there are four, are a source of much interest to the sojourner. — (7) **1856** *Statutes at Large* XI. 97 For compensation of two superintendents for the life-stations on the coasts of Long Island and New Jersey, three thousand dollars. **1886** S. W. MITCHELL *R. Blake* 217 Uncle John is the captain of the life-station on Five Mile Beach.

b. In colloq. phrases: (1) *To save one's life,* for the life of one, used as an intensive; (2) *bet your (sweet) life,* see ***bet,** *v.;* (3) *not on your life,* by no means; (4) *life of Riley,* usu. *to lead* (or *live*) *the life of Riley,* to live a carefree life, usu. with opportunity for physical pleasures.

(1) **1863** HOPLEY *Life in South* II. 151, I could not help laughing, 'to save my life,' in Virginia phraseology. — (3) **1895** GORE *Student Slang* (We.), Not on your life: By no means, not at all. **1940** BOWER *Spirit of Range* 17 (We.), Not on your life! — (4) **1942** STEGNER *Mormon C.* 128 He instituted polygamy and lived the life of Riley. **1948** *Reader's Digest* March 87/2 Here, truly, I could lead the life of Reilly, swinging comfortably in my hammock. **1949** *Chi. D. News* 12 May 7/4 (*heading*), GIs in Germany Content With Their Life of Riley.

As the last term in **high, prairie, preacher, squatter, western life.**

***life everlasting.** A species of *Gnaphalium,* cudweed, widely distributed throughout the U.S. See **rabbit tobacco.**

1629 PARKINSON *Paradisus* 374 *Argyrocome siue Gnaphalium Americanum.* Liue long or Life euerlasting. This siluer tuft or Indian Cotton weede, hath many white heads of leafes. **1784** CUTLER in *Mem. Acad.* I. 480 Life-Everlasting. Blossoms white. In pastures and fields. September. **1883** *Cent. Mag.* Nov. 45/1 The antiquated cottage that used to 'squat right down upon the sidewalk, as do those Choctaw squaws who sell bay and sassafras and life-everlasting,' was ruthlessly torn away. **1946** WILSON *Fidelity* 91, I do not like the taste of burning Life Everlasting ('rabbit tobacco') or corn-silks or grapevine.

life-of-man, *n.*

1. The American spikenard, *Aralia racemosa.*

1784 CUTLER in *Mem. Acad.* I. 431 *Aralia,* . . . Pettymorrel. Life of Man. . . . It is aromatic. The berries give spirits an agreeable flavour. **1795** WINTERBOTHAM *Hist. View* III. 397 Among the native and uncultivated plants of New-England . . . employed for medical purposes . . . [is] Pettimorrel, or life of man. **1832** WILLIAMSON *Maine* I. 126 Life-of-man . . . bears clusters of purple berries, large as shot and wholesome; its root is excellent in a poultice. **1894** *Amer. Folk-Lore* VII. 90 *Aralia racemosa,* life-o'-man, Fryeburg, Me.

2. A plant of the stonecrop family, *Sedum telephium.*

1893 *Amer. Folk-Lore* VI. 142 *Sedum Telephium* life of man. Concord, Mass. **1931** CLUTE *Plants* 134 A more agreeable side is given to the picture by that cheerful and persistent plant, the live-for-ever (*Sedum purpureum*) whose other name, life-of-man, makes plain who is to do the living.

***lift,** *n.* **1.** The difference between the maximum and the minimum depths of water in a lock. **2. lift lock,** a lock in a canal or stream for raising or lowering boats.

(1) **1829** J. MACAULEY *Hist. New York* I. 170 This [canal] lock has an extent within the gates of one hundred and fourteen feet, with a breadth of thirty—the lift is nine feet. **1840** TANNER *Canals & R.R. U.S.* 252 The difference between the levels is termed the *lift of the lock,* which ranges from 3 to 30 feet. — (2) **1828** in *Williams's N.Y. Ann. Reg. 1830* 125 From the mouth of the Rondout . . . to Port Jervis, near the Delaware river, are 60 lift locks and one guard lock. **1881–5** McCLELLAN *Own Story* 193 The lift-locks, above and below, are all large enough for the ordinary boats.

***lift,** *v.*

1. *tr.* To please or satisfy. *Rare.*

1825 *Austin P.* (1924) II. 1120, I was very much lifted with your country.

2. (See quots.) Also **lifting,** *n. Obs.*

1829 *Va. Lit. Museum* 98/1 The stone is not to be laid on in shovel-fulls, but to be scattered over the surface, one shovel-full following another and being spread over a considerable space. This preparation of the road for the receipt of small stones is called *lifting. Ib.* 98/2 In some cases it would be unprofitable to *lift* and relay a road, even if the materials should have been originally too large.

3. To pay off or redeem (a note, mortgage, etc.).

1834 CROCKETT *Narr. Life* 45, I would set in and work out the note so as to lift it for him. **1868** BEECHER *Sermons* (1869) I. 190, I want to lift a mortgage, and two hundred dollars would lift it. **1908** *N.Y. Ev. Post* (s.-w.) 2 April 5 It is naturally the desire of the club to lift this debt as soon as possible.

b. To take back (a claim made for public land). *Rare.*

1825 *Austin P.* (1924) II. 1184 If anything has taken place that may in any wise effect my land Claims in Texas I would like to lift one or both and locate them anew.

For *to lift the hair,* see ***hair,** *n.* **1. b.**

***lifter,** *n.* As the last term in **beet, chicken, cow, hair, stove lifter.**

***light,** *n.* and *a.* [In the combs. here listed the 1st element is from various sources.] In combs.: (1) **light boat,** a boat equipped with a bright light or lights and often with signals or other warning devices and anchored where it can serve as a lighthouse; (2) ***bread,** *S.* wheaten bread leavened with yeast as distinguished from corn bread; (3) ***horse,** a mounted police guard among some of the western Indians, also **light horseman;** (4) ***house,** *transf.* (see quot.), *slang;* (5) **house board,** (see quot. 1880); (6) ***house district,** an area of coastal or interior waters under the supervision of a superintendent in the U.S. Lighthouse Service; (7) **housekeeping,** housekeeping on a limited scale in restricted quarters; (8) **opera,** opera with a "light" plot, not tragic; (9) **wood,** see as a main entry.

(1) **1831** *Statutes at Large* IV. 491 Ten thousand dollars for building a light-boat to be stationed in the strait connecting Lakes Huron and Michigan. **1863** in MOORE *Rebellion Rec.* V. I. 10 The Commodore Perry found the lantern from the light-boat at the mouth of Roanoke River. — (2) **1821** *Western Carolinian* 27 March, Crackers and light Bread will always be found in his shop. **1945** *Chi. Tribune* 18 Nov. VII. 1/6 Ma spread thick slices of her homemade 'light bread' with golden butter. — (3) **1820** in MORSE *Rep. Indian Affairs* (1822) II. 172 The Cherokee Nation shall be laid off into Eight Districts . . . , and one company of light horse [is] to accompany each Circuit Judge on his official duties in his respective districts. **1842** BUCKINGHAM *Slave States* II. 102 Each district has two judges, and two sheriffs (who are called 'light-horse-men,' because their long journeys require them to be well mounted). **1899** CUSHMAN *Indians* 217 A company of armed and mounted police, called *'Light Horse Men,'* were organized from each district. — (4) **1900** FLYNT *Tramping* 386 'Lighthouse' . . . means a man who knows every detective of a town by sight.

(5) **1852** [see **lighthouse district**]. **1880** LAMPHERE *U.S. Govt.* 79/2 The Light-House Board consists of nine members, three of whom are civilians, three naval officers, and three officers of the Corps of Engineers of the army. — (6) **1852** *Statutes at Large* X. 119 The Light-house Board . . . [shall arrange] light-house districts. **1880** LAMPHERE *U.S. Govt.* 80/2 The following will give the limits and bounds of the 14 Light-House Districts. — (7) **1904** DERVILLE *Other Side of Story* 119, I think I'll move to a place where I can try light housekeeping, too. **1923** WATTS *L. Nichols* 213 There were plenty of furnished rooms for light housekeeping. — (8) **1882** F. M. A. ROE *Army Lett.* 309 During the summer four of us found much pleasure in practicing together the light operas.

b. *To disappear between two lights,* to depart between sundown and sunup. *Colloq.*

1859 A. CARY *Country Life* 188 The feller what brought her, had shortly afterwards disappeared between two lights, leaving her with a limited amount of chink.

As the last term in **arc, blue, bug, bush, day, dead, drop, fan, fishing, flash, forest, head, high, jack, leading, moon, New, Palatine, torch, tumbler, weather light.**

***light,** *v.* With advs. and preps. in colloq. phrases: (1) *To light down on* (someone), to take someone to task; (2) *to light in(to)* (someone, something), to attack, to go at; (3) *to light on,* =prec.; (4) *to light out,* to depart in haste, to "make tracks."

(1) **1884** R. GRANT *Average Man* 3 She was in love with Willis Blake, but her stern parent lit down on her. — (2) **1878** J. H. BEADLE

Western Wilds xii. 187 They double-quicked into town and lit in generally. **1917** FREEMAN & KINGSLEY *Alabaster Box* 3 He'll light into those hot doughnuts. — (3) **1837** CROCKETT *Almanac* 2 I'll lite on him like a martin. **1865** M. TWAIN in Paine *Biog.* I. 275 (R.), Tom Maguire, Roused to ire, Lighted on McDougal; Tore his coat, Clutched his throat, And split him in the bugle. — (4) **1870** D. B. R. KEIM *Sheridan's Troopers* 65 Leaving the guard, the General had brought with him to protect the train, we mounted and 'lit out,' as rapid locomotion is called in that locality. **1925** HEMING *Living Forest* 103 Silently wheeling about, I lit out for camp as if all the animals in the forest were after me and fairly flew among the trees.

lighterd 'laɪtəd, *n. S.* A dialect form of **lightwood.** Also attrib.

1842 in THOMPSON *M. Jones* (1872) 19 Well, she sot on one side of the fire-place, and I sot on tother, so I could spit on the hath, whar ther was nothin but a lighterd chunk burnin to give light. **1899** CHESNUTT *Wife of His Youth* 225 Well, I declar' if I ain't done fergot ter tote in dat lighterd. **1942** RAWLINGS *C. Creek* 6 Sometimes black Henry passes with a mule and wagon, taking a load of lighter'd home to Old Boss.

***lighting,** *n.* As the last term in **fire, moon lighting.**

***lightning,** *n.*

1. Whisky of inferior quality. In full **lightning whisky.** See **chain lightning 2,** and **Jersey, Taos, white lightning.**

Cf. *OED* **lightning*, meaning gin, and *s.v.* **flash*, note *flash of lightning*, meaning a glass of gin.

1858 *Calif. Spirit of Times* (S.F.) 7 Aug. 1/4 Having in his possession a few kegs of liquid lightning upon which he was avariciously desirous of reaping a speedy profit [he] . . . retailed it out to the almost famished men. **1863** *Harper's Mag.* July 283/2 Providing himself with a small lot of ginger-cakes and a disproportionately large stock of 'lightning whisky' he located upon an eligible site near the field. **1876** HEARN *Amer. Miscellany* (1924) I. 188 'Guess he must have got struck,' observed Knox. . . . 'By lightning?' queried Patsy Brazil. . . . 'Lightning whisky,' said Officer Knox. **1949** *Sat. Ev. Post* 30 April 23/3 Believe I'll have a slight stroke of that Old Lightning.

2. A decisive political upset, sudden political success or failure. *Colloq.*

1879 *Cong. Rec.* 25 April 920/2 No danger of that kind of lightning in my district. **1891** *Ib.* 5 Jan. 925/1 When the doctrine of practical reciprocity is applied the lightning will strike next time somewhere about Arkansas.

3. The political policy of winning at all costs, even by the use of violence and fraud if necessary, used esp. with reference to Alabama when that state was being wrested from carpetbag control after the Civil War. Also attrib. *Obs.*

1876 *Cin. Enquirer* 12 June 4/3 Nothing but the 'lightning' principle will help Hayes, and when only a majority is needed, the opportunities for a 'lightning' candidate are hopelessly small. **1883** *Cent. Mag.* July 397 The figures, as thus amended by the lightning process, went into the official returns of the State. **1887** in *Cong. Rec.* 3 June (1890) 5547/2 [In 1886] the issue in the Democratic party between aspirants for the office of probate judge was understood to be 'honesty or the lightning process at elections.' **1890** *Cong. Rec.* 3 June 5548/1 The Progress was founded in May, 1887, . . . as an advocate of the lightning Democratic creed of 1880. *Ib.*, Before we went into lightning session Colonel Gaillard withdrew. *Ib.*, It was lightning in 1880; it was lightning in 1886.

4. In special combs.: (1) **lightning bug,** the firefly, also transf.; (2) **calculator,** an adept at rapid calculation; (3) **conductor,** (*a*) =**lightning rod,** also transf., (*b*) *W.* a revolver, *slang, obs.;* (4) **express,** see as a main entry; (5) **line,** a telegraph line, or a railroad that runs lightning express trains; (6) **pilot,** a pilot on a river steamer who attains all the speed possible for his boat; (7) **pitching,** in baseball, the pitching of exceptionally fast balls; (8) **rod,** see as a main entry; (9) **train,** a lightning express train; (10) **wood,** =**lightwood,** *rare.*

(1) **1778** CARVER *Travels* 491 The Lightning Bug or Fire Fly is about the size of a bee. **1842** *S. Lit. Messenger* VIII. 199/2 It will never do to tell *us* that there is any humbug in this business, or even that it is a mere *lightning-bug.* **1947** *Chi. Tribune* 21 June 2/4 He asserted that to 'talk about Henry Wallace intimidating Harry Truman on the veto is like describing a lightning bug as blotting out the rays of the sun.' — (2) **1883** *Cent. Mag.* July 397 One of the board, commonly known as the 'lightning calculator' from his expertness in this sort of rascality, deliberately changed 2000 to the wrong column. **1949** *Time* 27 June 81 Talk about lightning calculators! International Business Machine Corporation has an electronic calculator that does 50 multiplications a second of 14 digit numbers! — (3) (*a*) **1792** in ROOSEVELT *Amer. Backlogs* (1928) 61 The lightning conductor was at the mast-head. **1868** *Mich. Agric. Rep.* VII. 362 N. Brittan & Co., Coldwater, [exhibited] 1 continuous copper stick lightning conductor. **1902** *Chi. Record-Herald* 4 Sep. 9/2 Yes! The red-headed one. I know! She's a daisy—reg'lar blizzard—lightnin' conductor! (*b*) **1867** *Prescott* (Ariz.) *Gaz.* 31 July 3/1 They were armed with shot-guns, revolvers and pocket 'lightning' conductors.

(5) **1846** *Dollar Newspaper* (Phila.) 11 March 2/4 The New Jersey Railroad Company having assented to the extension of the Telegraph from Newark along their route to Jersey City, the 'lightning line' will doubtless be constructed to the latter point. **1873** W. MATHEWS *Getting On in World* 242 Now . . . people travel by 'lightning lines,' going from New York to Chicago in twenty-nine hours. — (6) **1875** MARK TWAIN *Old Times* 41 By the Shadow of Death, but he's a lightning pilot. — (7) **1867** *Ball Players' Chron.* 15 Aug. 5/3 The Nationals . . . commenced the game with rather long faces, as they were to stand up to Ball's 'lightning' pitching, which was something they were not posted in. — (9) **1862** LOWELL *Biglow P.* 2 Ser. iii. 109 An' ary man thet's pop'lar's fit to drive a lightnin'-train. **1893** *Harper's Mag.* April 788/2 This first experience in a lightning train was by no means unalloyed bliss.

(10) *c***1820** in *Knickerb.* XXIX. 472 There's in the rottenness of sin something that shines like lightning-wood.

lightning express. A telegraph line, or a fast train.

1846 *Sci. Amer.* 31 Oct. 45/4 We learn from a New Orleans paper that a citizen of that place has completed his arrangements to have the 'lightning express' from Philadelphia to New Orleans. **1853** BUNN *Old Eng. & N. Eng.* 160 You have direct communication from [Buffalo] . . . with New York . . . by what they term 'lightning expresses.' **1909** M. TWAIN *Letters* (1917) II. xlvii. 833 (R.), A tramp stealing a ride on the lightning express.

Also attrib. and transf.

1860 HOLMES *Professor* vi. 163 The scenery of a long tragic drama flashed through his mind as the lightning-express-train *whishes* by a station. **1880** MARK TWAIN *Tramp Abroad* 456 The passenger-part of this glacier,—the central part,—the lightning-express part, so to speak,—was not due in Zermatt till the summer of 2378. **1889** MUNROE *Golden Days* 114 All the lightning express eating-houses in the States would get left so quick as would make 'em dizzy.

lightning rod.

1. A pointed, properly grounded metallic rod, usu. of copper, placed on a building or other structure as a protection against lightning.

1789 *Ann. 1st Congress* I. 688 John McPherson . . . [petitioned for] an exclusive privilege . . . to make and vend lightning rods upon an improved construction. **1825** PAULDING *J. Bull in Amer.* 164 They likewise boast of one Franklin, . . . one of the first manufacturers of lightning rods. **1946** HODGINS *Mr. Blandings Builds Dream House* 122 Mr. Simms has forgotten lightning rods on the chimney!

fig. **1872** EGGLESTON *End of World* 24 Julia . . . erected what she imagined might prove a conversational lightning-rod. **1948** *Chi. D. News* 15 July 9/2 Meanwhile Senators O'Mahoney of Wyoming and McMahon of Connecticut had their lightning rods up.

2. In combs. of obvious meaning: **lightning rod agent, business, company, dispenser, man, peddler, salesman.**

1894 *Outing* June 205/1 If you see a lightnin' rod agent up the road, ask him how he feels. — **1883** *Cent. Mag.* Oct. 889/2 The young woman told who *he* was—in the lightning-rod business in Kalamazoo. — **1869** *Boyd's Business Directory* 586 Lightning Rods. Hawley's Patent Lightning Rod Co. **1938** WHITE *One Man's Meat* 5, I got a letter from a lightning rod company this morning trying to put the fear of God in me. — **1881** CARLETON *Farm Festivals* 89 This railroad smash reminds me . . . of a lightning-rod dispenser that came down on me one day. — **1873** BAILEY *Life in Danbury* 253 There were letters from nine different lightning-rod men. — **1891** GARLAND *Main-travelled Roads* (1922) 73 Guessed Bill had got hooked onto by a lightnin'-rod peddler, or somethin' o' that kind. **1921** *Frontier* Nov. 5, I sat into a poker game with Smith and a lightning-rod peddler who had come in from Salt Lake way. — **1942** PHILIPS *Big Spring* 114 The lightning-rod salesman would say he had decided he better not try to get on to the next ranch.

Also **lightning rodder.** — **1879** STOCKTON *Rudder Grange* xiii, They'd go to fightin', and leave me to settle with some blood-thirsty lightnin'-rodder. **1927** BENÉT *J. B.'s Body* 71 And if any more of those lightning-rodders come around, We don't want no more dum lightning-rods.

***lightwood,** *n.*

1. *S.* The dead, thoroughly dried heart of a tree of any one of several species of pine; also a dead root, knot, or limb of this. Used for fuel or kindling. Cf. **fat pine, lighterd.**

1705 BEVERLEY *Virginia* III. iii. 12 [The Indians] generally burn Pine or Lightwood, (that is, the fat Knots of dead Pine). **1859** G. W.

PERRY *Turpentine Farming* 37 Lightwood is produced by the soaking or penetrating of the spirits through the pine. **1949** *Yrbk. Agric.* 286/1 The product from stumps, lightwood, and pulp mills is called wood naval stores.

2. In combs. of obvious meaning, as **lightwood brand, fence-post, fire, knot** (also attrib.), **soot, spike, splinter, stump, torch.**

1853 SIMMS *Sword & Distaff* 458 M'Kewn . . . [was] satisfied with the sufficient blaze of the lightwood brands cast upon the fire. — **1946** *Democrat* 9 May 4/4 Wanted—1,000 lightwood fence posts 5½ feet long. — **1863** E. KIRKE *Southern Friends* 290 An iron kettle filled with tar was already simmering over a light-wood fire. — **1800** HAWKINS *Sk. Creek Country* 80 They covered him with lightwood knots, burnt him [etc.]. **1897** TERHUNE *Old-field School* 27 The windows of a room on the ground-floor were red with the flame of a 'lightwood knot' fire. **1944** *Democrat* 20 July 2/2 Chunk movers and lightwood knot floaters are two names which the Journal omitted. — **1709** LAWSON *Carolina* 183 Their Faces dawb'd over with Light-wood Soot, (which is the same as Lamp-black). — **1725** in *Travels Amer. Col.* 150 [The Ditch] is Stuck full of light wood Spikes. — *c***1845** THOMPSON *Chron. Pineville* 165 He had gone to the kitchen and lit a few light-wood splinters. **1939** HARRIS *Purslane* 110 Uncle Hen left the lot and went to the woodpile to cut an armful of lightwood splinters to start morning fires. — **1847** *Knickerb.* XXIX. 534 A 'quantity' of children were gathered round the fire of a light-wood stump. — **1709** LAWSON *Carolina* 210 [The] Indian Boys go in the Night, and one holding a Lightwood Torch, the other has a Bow and Arrows. **1884** HARRIS *Mingo* 192 When Aunt Tabby . . . started for her cabin after dark, she was accompanied by a number of little negroes bearing lightwood torches.

***like,** *prep.* **1.** *like everything*, rapidly. **2.** *like a little man*, in a manly, straightforward manner. Both *colloq.*

(1) 1875 MARK TWAIN *Old Times Miss.* 284 (R.), The banks are caving and the shape of the shores changing like everything. — **(2) 1884** *Las Vegas* (N.M.) *Gaz.* 6 Dec. 4/1 [The] street car driver made [him] walk up to the front of the car like a little man and deposit the almighty nickel. **1915** *Amer. Mag.* Nov. 91/1 Are you going to endorse this draft like a little man or am I stuck? **1949** *Sat. Ev. Post* 11 June 127/1 Joe is halfway through a large wedge [of pie] he has been eating like a little man.

***like,** *suffix.* As the last term in **ark, Barnum, deacon, scow, tublike.**

***lilac,** *n. Pacific Coast.* A shrub of the genus *Ceanothus*, esp. the blue myrtle, *C. thyrsiflorus.* Cf. **blue, California lilac.**

1872 MCCLELLAN *Golden State* 163 In the State [of Calif.] are the wild nutmeg, . . . lilac, cherry, plum, grape-vine, vine-maple, and sequoia. **1896** *Amer. Folk-Lore* IX. 184 Rhamnaceæ . . . *Ceanothus divaricatus*, Nutt., lilac, Santa Barbara County, Cal. **1937** *Range Plant Handbook* B39 Probably the names in most general use have been bluebush (or bluebrush), buckbrush, lilac, and myrtle.

***lily,** *n.* In combs.: (1) **lily pad,** the broad flat leaf of the water lily, also attrib.; (2) **padded,** strewn with lily pads; (3) **white,** (*a*) a cosmetic made chiefly of chalk, *obs.*, (*b*) designating or pertaining to organizations composed of those desirous of drawing the color line against Negroes, esp. a group of Republicans in the South desirous of excluding Negroes from the party and from political activities in general, also **lily whiter,** *n.*, cf. **black and tan.**

(1) 1814 BIGELOW *Florula Bostoniensis* 132 *Nymphoea advena.* Yellow water lily. . . . The floating leaves of this . . . are well known to anglers under the name of lily pads. **1947** *Field & Stream* June 6/3 Its depth varies from shallow, lily-pad coves to 85 feet of water near the west side. — **(2) 1859** *Harper's Mag.* April 610/1 The lake . . . was not one of ordinary lily-padded lagoons, overrun with tall rank rushes. **1933** CHELEY *Camping Out* 255 [It is] a country of . . . placid and lily-padded lakes, where the fighting bass and the 'musky' lurk. — **(3)** (*a*) **1858** *Harper's Mag.* Sep. 566/2 Notable ladies . . . used lily white (prepared chalk), and made faces for themselves such as Nature had denied them. **1861** *Vanity Fair* 23 Feb. 85/2 There was the fresh pot of lily-white and the bottle of liquid rouge, just to touch up her cheeks. (*b*) **1903** *N.Y. Times* 23 Sep., The report that the President was seeking reconciliation with the 'Lilywhite' faction, which eliminated the negro from the last State Convention. **1932** LEWINSON *Race* 110 The 'lily white' movement in the Southern Republican party was another indication of the South's opposition to Negro suffrage. **1948** *Chi. Maroon* 22 Oct. 4/3 Our attitude derives from the past 'lily white' tradition of the clubs. **1949** *World-Herald Mag.* (Omaha) 18 Sep. 26/1 In that year, their control of the Texas Republican Party was broken by 'lily-whiters,' who supported Cecil Lyons of Sherman.

As the last term in **bullhead, chaparral, corn, desert, dog, Easter, fairy, flag, Florida, frog, glade, Humboldt's, Jamestown, Japan, Lady Washington, lemon, liver, mariposa, meadow, pond, prairie, red, ruby, rush, sand, sego, Shasta, snake, Southern red, spider, spring, swamp, toad, Washington, yellow lily.**

***limas,** *n. pl.* Short for "lima beans." *Colloq.* — **1856** COZZENS *Sparrowgrass P.* 85 Put the Limas to the right . . . and as for the rest of the seeds, sweep them into the refuse basket. **1870** WARNER *Summer in Garden* ix, I put up the most attractive sort of poles for my limas.

***limb,** *n. Out on a limb*, at a disadvantage. *To go out on a limb*, to take a stand. *Colloq.* — **1897** LEWIS *Wolfville* 59 Seven of us . . . seein' whatever can we tie down an' brand, when some Mexicans gets us out on a limb. **1945** *Democrat* 12 April 1/1 The editor went out on a limb last week and stated that if he didn't kill a turkey on Fred Stimpson's preserve, he wouldn't have an alibi left.

***limb,** *v. tr.* (See quot. 1839.) — **1839** HOLMES *Explor. Aroostook River* 53 The best mode undoubtedly is, to fall the trees and '*limb*' them, (that is, cut off the limbs,) in June. **1889** *Harper's Mag.* Jan. 231/1 It seemed to be built principally of alder poles well limbed off and placed, roughly speaking, side by side. **1949** *Business Week* 24 Sep. 74/2 When you use the saw manually without the pole, it will fell or limb trees up to 2 ft. in diameter.

***limber,** *a.*

1. limber pine, a pine, *Pinus flexilis*, found chiefly on the Pacific Coast of the U.S.

1897 SUDWORTH *Arborescent Flora.* **1917** EATON *Green Trails* 53 Over her, dwarfed like a print by Hiroshige, a twisted limber pine flaunted its pink cone buds. **1938** *Famous Trees* 73 A limber pine (*Pinus flexilis*) 18.8 feet in circumference at breast height, and 67 feet tall, is on the Huerfano district of the San Isabel National Forest.

2. Limber-twig, a kind of inferior winter apple. Also attrib.

1852 FLEISCHMANN *Wegweiser* 171 Für die Breitengrade von Mississippi eignet sich besonders der Limber-Twig und Horse-apple. **1924** J. M. FRANKS *Seventy Yrs. in Texas* 122 They were small, but good eating—the Limber Twig. **1947** *Democrat* 6 Feb. 4/1 It was a cluster of three which she had just pulled from a Limbertwig tree.

***lime,** *n.* **1. lime sink,** (see quot. 1845 and cf. **limestone sink**). **2. lime store,** a store in which lime is sold.

(1) 1837 J. L. WILLIAMS *Florida* 9 Ponds and lime sinks are numerous. **1845** LYELL *Travels N. Amer.* I. 176 Lime-sinks or funnel-shaped cavities, are frequent in this country arising from natural tunnels and cavities in the subjacent limestone. **1883** SMITH *Geol. Survey Ala.* 286 [The] Lime Sink Region . . . embraces an area of 6,570 square miles. — **(2) 1889** BRAYLEY *Boston Fire Dept.* 111 It was occupied by Elijah Loring as a lime-store.

***lime-juicer.** A British sailor or ship (see also quot. 1936). *Slang.*

Regarded as an Americanism (see quot. 1945 below), but the Australian use to designate an emigrant newly arrived from England is as early as 1859. See *OED.*

1884 *Pall Mall Gaz.* 26 Aug. 11/1 They would not go on a 'lime-juicer,' they said, for anything. **1907** LONDON *Road* 13 He had sailed always on French merchant vessels, with the one exception of a voyage on a 'lime-juicer.' **1936** MENCKEN *Amer. Lang.* 295 The American language offers. . . . For Englishman: *lime-juicer* or *limey.* [Note:] A term borrowed from Navy slang. It refers to the fact that, beginning in 1795, lime-juice was issued in the British Navy (and later in the merchant marine) as an anti-scorbutic. **1945** BAKER *Australian Lang.* 185 The Australian use for any Englishman is taken from the U.S. slang *limey* and *limejuicer* for a British sailor.

***limestone,** *n.* In combs.: (1) **limestone belt,** a relatively narrow area over which limestone prevails; (2) **bluff,** a bluff composed of limestone; (3) **fence,** a fence made of blocks of limestone, *obs.;* (4) **prairie,** a prairie over which limestone occurs near the surface of the ground; (5) **sink,** (see quot. 1854 and cf. **lime sink**).

(1) 1873 RAYMOND *Silver & Gold* 56 The limestone belt, on which are found the early placers noted for their immense yield. — **(2) 1831** PECK *Guide* 14 The remainder [of the Mississippi Valley] is made up of abrupt hills, flint and limestone ridges, bluffs, and ravines. — **(3) 1892** J. L. ALLEN *Blue-Grass Region* 28 One hears of fewer lime-stone fences of late years. — **(4) 1821** FOWLER *Journal* 14 At 6 miles over High Rich lime stone pirarie We Camped. **1945** MATHEWS *Talking* 18 The dramatic processes of the earth have made of it an open-woods country of limestone prairie and sandstone ridges.

(5) 1817 *Md. Hist. Mag.* XI. 371 They will thrive much better than taking their drink from them Nasty filthy Lime Stone Sinks that you pen up & keep from one rain to another. **1854** BARTLETT *Personal Narrative* I. 110 (B. '77), Leaving the Pecos, we stopped to look at some limestone sinks near the road. The earth and stones had caved in, or sunk, in spots varying from ten to thirty feet in diameter.

As the last term in **bastard, bird's-eye, blue, cliff, Niagara, rotten limestone.**

limey ˈlaɪmɪ, *n.* [f. **lime-juicer.**] A Britisher, orig. a sailor. Also attrib. *Slang.*

1924 *Chi. Tribune* 18 Oct. 1/5 Midway Signs Limey Prof. to Dope Yank Talk. **1940** EASTMAN *Expectant Motherhood* 52 In 1854 a law was passed in England requiring that fruit juice be rationed out daily on long voyages, and it was because of this dole of lemon juice that English sailors began to be called 'limeys.' **1944** CARRINGTON *Safe Convoy* 78 There was no scurvy when they arrived twenty-three weeks later and from that day to this British sailors are known as 'limeys.'

* **limit,** *n.* The very extreme, the last stage, the worst imaginable. Often *to go the limit. Colloq.* or *slang.* Cf. **fire, yard limit.**

1885 *Cong. Rec.* 18 Jan. 712/2 (Th. Supp.), [The Alabama Legislature might] increase their salaries to $4,000, which I believe is the limit that we have ever gone. **1904** *Montgomery W. Advt.* 26 Aug. 4 We can always depend on Kansas to go the limit in the freak line. **1928** C. A. BEARD *Amer. Party Battle* 5 The Jeffersonians used federal powers to the limit in purchasing Louisiana. **1948** *Nat. Geog. Mag.* Aug. 235/1 Geologists climbing up that railroad cut for pieces of rock were the limit.

***limitarian,** *n.* = **strict constructionist.** Also **limitarianism.** *Obs.* — **1829** *Amer. Turf Reg.* Sep. 41 The Virginians, you know, have always been great *limitarians* as to constitutional matters. **1833** *Polit. Examiner* (Shelbyville, Ky.) 9 Feb. 1/4 At the present time, when in the extreme of limitarianism, Mr. Calhoun is yet more obnoxious than in 1824.

* **limited,** *a.* and *n.*

1. A limited train. Often in the names of particular trains.

1887 *Pop. Sci. Mo.* March 577 Let . . . the limited crash through a trestle. **1944** *Santa Fe T. Table* 12 Nov. 6 On the following trains table d'hote meals . . . are offered in addition to a la carte service: . . . The California Limited. . . . The Grand Canyon Limited [etc.]. **1948** *Chi. D. News* 17 Aug. 1/3 Cars of the Great Northern Railway's westbound Oriental Limited left the tracks.

2. In combs.: (1) **limited express,** a fast train making few stops, in full **limited express train;** (2) **ticket,** of a railroad ticket, one not allowing all the privileges of an ordinary ticket; (3) **train,** (see quot. 1940).

(1) 1879 STOCKTON *Rudder Grange* ix, Time flew like a 'limited express' train. **1904** *Dial* 16 Oct. 238 It is not a book for the limited express. — **(2) 1888** LINDLEY *Calif. of South* 376 This rate is for a limited ticket. The purchaser is not allowed to stop over until he crosses the Missouri River. **1899** MUIRHEAD *Baedeker's U.S.* p. xxi, A distinction is frequently made between 'limited' and 'unlimited' tickets. — **(3) 1890** *Harper's Mag.* Aug. 409/1 Coming up by the limited train, Miss Lee was not favorably impressed. **1940** *Quiz* [Quest.] 182 A limited train has been defined as a passenger train meeting one or more of the following specifications: (1) bearing a distinctive trade name; (2) operating at an overall speed of 40 miles per hour or more for distances of over 200 miles; (3) operated for distances over 300 miles with scheduled stops at intervals averaging not less than 50 miles each.

***limits,** *n. pl.* As the last term in **city, corporate, corporation, railroad limits.**

***limping,** *a.* (See quots.) *Obs.* — **1900** *Cong. Rec.* 14 Feb. 1766/1 We are on what is sometimes called the limping silver standard and sometimes the limping gold standard, for it is neither a silver nor a gold standard, and it is not true bimetallism. *Ib.*, The United States was not on the gold standard, but on the limping standard. **1914** *Cyclo. Amer. Govt.* I. 132/1 Not being able to maintain a fixed ratio between the two metals, bimetallism necessarily establishes what has been called a limping standard, that is an alternation now of one standard and then of the other, the cheaper metal always serving in that capacity.

limpkin ˈlɪmpkɪn, *n.* [f. **limp, v.*+**-kin.*] The carau *q.v.*, so called from its peculiar halting gait. Cf. **crying-bird.**

1871 J. A. ALLEN *Mammals & Winter Birds* 362 Its popular name in Florida is 'limpkin.' **1883** *Nat. Museum Bul.* No. 27, 156 Limpkin. . . . Greater Antilles, Florida, and coasts of Central America. **1947** Nat. Pk. Service *Fading Trails* 169 Except where their presence is made known by a 'song' consisting of a series of caterwaulings and wailings, the limpkins are shy and inconspicuous birds.

* **Lincoln,** *n.*

1. In obs. combs. of obvious meaning in allusion to Abraham Lincoln and the North during the Civil War period: (1) **Lincoln Brotherhood,** (2) **coffee,** (3) **flag,** (4) **hireling,** (5) **navy,** (6) **platform,** (7) **pup,** (8) **skin** (9) **spy,** (10) **troops.**

(1) 1885 in FLEMING *Hist. Reconstruction* II. 20 In order to work the negro with greater facility in the interest of Osborn and his gang, this secret league was named the Lincoln Brotherhood. **1892** WALSH *Lit. Curiosities* 637 *Lincoln Brotherhood,* political associations of negroes in the South after the close of the civil war, to protect their rights of suffrage. — **(2) 1867** SCOTT *Partisan Life* 313 Mosby's men felt like gods, with dimpled Hebes to give them nectar in the likeness of Lincoln coffee—no bad substitute either to hungry and toil-worn soldiers. — **(3) 1861** *Charleston* (S.C.) *Mercury* 4 June 1/4 He it was who cut down the Lincoln flag at Occoqua, in spite of threats that he would be shot if he did. — **(4) 1861** *Dly. Dispatch* (Richmond, Va.) 31 May 1/5 The town has been taken possession of by the Lincoln hirelings. **1890** LANGFORD *Vigilante Days* (1912) 94 His tall form, rendered more conspicuous by the loud and inspiring voice with which, to the cries of . . . 'Lincoln hirelings,' he shouted back . . . 'copperheads' [etc.].

(5) 1861 *Dly. Richmond* (Va.) *Enquirer* 20 July 2/5 The amount appropriated for the Lincoln navy during the current year is upwards of $40,000,000. — **(6) 1866** SHANKS *Recollections* 272 He [Granger] did, however, give Sherman his rations—of the plainest materials he could gather—'Lincoln platform' (hard bread) and rye coffee. — **(7) 1865** *Erie* (Pa.) *Wkly. Gaz.* 5 Oct. 1/7, I called the soljers 'Linkin purps,' and the orfisers sholder trapt hirelin's and I meant it. — **(8) 1877** BARTLETT 356 Lincoln Skins. Fractional currency. South Carolina. **1923** ADAMS *Pioneer Hist.* 852 A neighbor bought 10 yards of common sheeting and crash for two towels and it took a $10 greenback (called 'Lincoln skin' by the 'copperheads,' rabid Democrats of the North,) to pay for them. — **(9) 1861** *Charleston* (S.C.) *Mercury* 4 June 1/5 A Lincoln spy, named Lambert, was arrested at Manasas Junction.

(10) 1861 *Alexandria* (Va.) *Gaz.* 27 April 1/5 The military authorities . . . are using their utmost endeavors to obtain possession of all the Surgical instruments in this city . . . for the use of the Lincoln troops.

b. Also **Lincoln badge, club, meeting.**

1860 *Chi. Tribune* 23 Feb. 2/4 The party went into the contest with the name of Lincoln on all their banners, instituted Lincoln clubs, wore Lincoln badges, and held Lincoln meetings at almost every school house in the State.

2. Lincoln cent, penny, a penny, first issued in August, 1909, having on its obverse the portrait bust of Lincoln done by Victor D. Brenner.

1909 *Chi. D. News* 12 Aug. 8/1 Lincoln pennies are quoted at 100 per cent premium by the newsboys. **1909** *Harper's Wkly.* 21 Aug. 24/1 It was the new Lincoln cent, born into a world of 1,650,000,000 cents with Indian heads, all struggling for that survival of the fittest predicated by Darwin. **1948** *Chi. Tribune* 8 Feb. (Comics) 2 Well, what d'you know—it's a brand new Lincoln penny!

3. Lincoln's Birthday, (see quot.).

1898 *N.Y. Wkly. Tribune* 23 Feb. 5/3 Legal holidays . . . February 12, Lincoln's Birthday—In Illinois, Minnesota, New-Jersey, New-York, and Washington (State).

4. Lincoln's finch, sparrow, a small North American sparrow, *Melospiza lincolni,* named by Audubon for Thomas Lincoln (1812–83), who accompanied him on an expedition to the coast of Labrador and secured specimens of this bird.

1834 AUDUBON *Ornith. Biog.* II. 539 Lincoln's Finch, *Fringilla Lincolnii.* . . . I named it *Tom's Finch,* in honour of our friend [Thomas] Lincoln, who was a great favorite among us. **1870** *Amer. Naturalist* III. 581 In avoiding the North-eastern states it resembles . . . *Melospiza Lincolnii* (Lincoln's Sparrow). **1940** GABRIELSON & JEWETT *Birds Ore.* 590 Lincoln's Sparrow is a breeding bird of the open meadows of the higher ranges.

Lincolndom ˈlɪŋkəndəm, *n.* [See **Lincolnite.**] During the Civil War, a nickname used in the South for the northern section of the U.S. Cf. **Davisdom.** — **1861** *Richmond* (Va.) *Dispatch* 13 Nov. 3/1 The city is infused with Yankee speculators, whose bodies are here and whose souls are in Lincolndom. **1862** *N.Y. Tribune* 14 June 2/3 We hope our [Confederate] Government will soon find some means of marching an army into that State [Ky.]. . . . A more serious blow could not be struck at Lincolndom.

Lincolnian lɪŋˈkonɪən, *a.* Characteristic of Abraham Lincoln. — **1910** WILLIS *Stephen A. Douglas* 283 [This was] a characteristic Lincolnian anecdote which the speaker applied to the repetition of the 'stale fraud' of the Springfield resolutions.

Lincolniana lɪŋˌkonɪˈænə, *n.* Books, letters, relics, etc., relating to Abraham Lincoln. — **1921** *Double Dealer* Feb. 67/1 Another notable essay in Lincolniana appears with the imprint of Walter M. Hill of Chicago—'The Assassination of Lincoln' by E. W. Coggeshall. **1949** *Ill. State Hist. Soc. Jrnl.* June 137 The volume is one of the few in the vast area of Lincolniana that influenced later research and publications.

Lincolnism ˈlɪŋkənˌɪzəm, *n.* [See **Lincolnite.**] The political principles and policies of Abraham Lincoln. *Obs.*

1861 *Dly. Dispatch* (Richmond, Va.) 30 April 1/1 There are here and there . . . gallant remnants and faithful exponents of the true and original faith, who have not bowed the knee to the Baal of Lincolnism. **1862** in MOORE *Rebellion Rec.* V. II. 183 The city [of Memphis] is conquered, but her people are not crushed, or converted to Lincolnism.

b. A story in parable form of the type for which Lincoln was noted. *Rare.*

1861 *Crisis* (Columbus, O.) 26 Dec. 6/3 Some things are so far beneath criticism, (to say nothing of Lincolnisms), that no one can get down to the work.

Lincolnite ˈlɪŋkənˌaɪt, *n.* [Abraham *Lincoln* (1809–65).] A believer in the political principles and policies of Abraham Lincoln; a Northern soldier or sympathizer in the Civil War.

1861 *Dly. Dispatch* (Richmond, Va.) 22 July 1/4 Woe to the Lincolnites when they meet those chivalrous sons of Carolina in battle array. **1861** *Richmond* (Va.) *Examiner* 2 Dec. 2/4 The Lincolnites are loud and bitter in their denunciation of the South Carolinians. **1906** in *Kans. Hist. Soc.* IX. 437 They shouted: 'That's right, you old Lincolnites, come in and surrender; we welcome you.'

Also attrib. or as adj.

1862 in MOORE *Rebellion Rec.* V. II. 181, I leave this office to any Lincolnite successor. **1863** RUSSELL *Diary* II. 12 They denounced Sam Houston as a traitor, but admitted there were some Unionists, or as they termed them, Lincolnite skunks, in the State.

* **line,** *n.*

1. A system of communication or transportation operated over a particular route or way, also the public conveyances used in operating such a system.

1781 JEFFERSON *Writings* IV. 390 A Quartermaster is employed in establishing a similar line from hence to the army before Portsmouth. **1786** *Boston Centinel* 11 Jan. 3/1 (Ernst), A line of stages. **1818** in ALBION *Square-Riggers* (1938) 23 Arrived since our last, Ship Courier, Bowne, (the first of the new line of Packets) 47 days from Liverpool. **1835** *Vade Mecum* (Phila.) 30 May 3/3 The new steam boat Constitution took her station on the Baltimore Rail Road Line on Tuesday last. **1949** *Lubbock* (Tex.) *Morn. Avalanche* 23 Feb. I. 10/7 The Wichita Falls & Southern railway, a 169-mile line, is on the market.

b. Also **line boat, packet.**

1819 *Niles' Reg.* XVII. 112/1 A late Nashville paper notices the *arrival* there of . . . 'Line boat, No. 11.' **1898** HARPER *S. B. Anthony* I. 47 The journey from here to Rochester was made . . . on a 'line boat' instead of a 'packet.' — **1842** EMERSON *Transcendentalist* 347 The storm-tossed vessel at sea speaks the frigate or 'line-packet' to learn its longitude.

2. The boundary between the U.S. and Canada or between the U.S. and Spanish possessions or Mexico.

1809 KENDALL *Travels* III. 259 The earlier counterfeiters . . . had commenced their business in Canada, or as it is here called, on the other side of *the line*. **1878** HINTON *Arizona* 121 South of Ostrich mill and towards the line more than sixty claims have been recorded. **1947** *So. Sierran* Nov. 3/2 Then there is some wonderful mountain country in the Sierra Madre over the line in Mexico.

b. Short for **Mason and Dixon's line.**

1845 F. DOUGLASS *Narrative* 101 We owe something to the slaves south of the line as well as to those north of it. **1949** *Sat. Ev. Post* 26 March 38/2 The critic thunders, and below 'the line' the shades of Marse Robert and Jeff Davis inevitably are summoned forth to meet the charge.

3. The frontier, often *pl.* (see also quot. 1851).

1840 COOPER *Pathfinder* xxviii, I do not think a truer-hearted lad lives on the lines than Jasper Western. **1849** *Pres. Mess. Congress* II. 1129 There has been an increase of grocery establishments near the lines of the nation. **1851** W. KELLY *Across Rocky Mts.* (1852) 45 And proceeded over twelve miles of magnificent country to the Line: I don't mean the great globular girdle . . . but the line of demarcation between the pale-face and the Indian: the extreme margin of civilization. **1912** DAWSON *Pioneer Tales* 130 On May 16, 1849, this company of intrepid men . . . started out upon the long, overland trail to California, and by night had crossed the 'line' and were in the Indian country.

4. = **telegraph line.**

1846 *De Bow's Review* I. 138 An arrangement was accomplished in November, 1845, for the construction of a line from New York to Boston. **1847** *Sci. Amer.* 30 Jan. 149/3 The New York and Baltimore line of telegraph has earned its stockholders ten per cent on their investment for the last six months.

5. A series of traps (see quot. 1857).

1857 HAMMOND *Northern Scenes* 331 We talk about a *line* of traps, because we blaze a line of trees, sometimes for miles, and set a trap every twenty or thirty rods. **1920** *Outing* Sep. 287/3 The trapper . . . had used snow shoes to follow up his line of traps. **1949** *Sat. Ev. Post* 22 Jan. 98/2 It is usually a glum day for the trapper when he pays his periodic visit to his line and sees in the snow the tracks of a wolverine joining the tracks that he made himself on his previous swing around.

6. = **pipe line.**

1881 *Mich. Gen. Statutes* I. (1882) 954 Any number of persons, not less than five, may form a company for the purpose of constructing and operating . . . a line or lines of pipes (pipe), for the conveying and transporting therein of brine. **1902** *Out West* Jan. 98 Our illustrations show a few portions of the line where the pipe was laid on fills and could not be covered. **1949** *Ill. State Reg.* (Springfield) 1 Feb. 6/5 The line broke early this morning, turning loose millions of cubic feet of gas a short distance from a heavily populated Orange suburb.

b. = **power line.**

1901 *World's Work* May 744/1 Starting in the Blue Lake region of California, one of these lines will transmit 60,000 volts 152 miles overland to San Francisco. **1949** *Dly. Ardmoreite* (Ardmore, Okla.) 25 Jan. 2/5 A half-mile stretch of the line from the west was on the ground—buried by ice and snow.

c. Short for "receiving line." *Rare.*

1903 *N.Y. Tribune* 4 Oct. She has had several years' experience 'behind the line,' and will doubtless be of great assistance to Mrs. Roosevelt.

7. In football, the players lined up even with the ball before the action of a down begins.

1887 *Cent. Mag.* Oct. 891/2 The two players on the ends of the line, the 'end-rushes,' stand slightly back of the main line. **1898** *N.Y. Tribune* 30 Oct. 1/2 The work of the Pennsylvania ends . . . has made it clear that the gains of the Harvard backs will have to be through the line. **1948** *Downers Grove* (Ill.) *Rep.* 21 Oct. 1/6 Once again as in previous games the line more than held its own.

b. Also (1) **line bucker, bucking,** (2) ***-man,** (3) **play,** (4) **plunger.** For **line drive** see **9.** (4) below.

(1) 1893 *Outing* Sep. 456/1 He is a heavy man and a capital 'line-bucker.' *Ib.* 456/2 The Berkeley men relied solely upon the 'wedge,' and Hunt did some very clever 'line bucking.' — **(2) 1907** *St. Nicholas* Sep. 1013/2 There was some discussion last year as to whether a line man could run from his position in the line and take the ball from the quarter. **1913** *Collier's* 13 Dec. 27/1 He was an aggressive, hard-fighting, and alert lineman, who did his best work under fire. — **(3) 1894** *U. of Chi. Wkly.* 4 Oct. 6/2 The team then resorted to line play and lost on downs. — **(4) 1948** *Syracuse* (N.Y.) *Herald-Journal* 16 Oct. 9/2 And with football ability as the solution, it looks like Cornell, the team with the better line and with the fastest ball carriers as well as the most successful line plungers.

8. Glib talk, used esp. in phrases. *Slang.*

1910 *Out West* Jan. 45 Butterick Rutherford Tay, real estate agent, spent several days absorbing the principles of lot selling, and he developed a line of talk which was pronounced strictly paralyzing. **1925** *Boston Transcript* 25 Nov. IV. 8/2 Anita Loos had done some highly original work in the character . . . of her little 'gold digger,' who hands out a very successful line. **1949** *Lincoln Co. News* (Oceanlake, Ore.) 4 Aug. 4/5 Every American male is convinced that his line is unique, devastating and sure-fire, and that it effectively disguises the inner wolf.

9. In special combs.: (1) **line ball,** (see quot. 1888 and cf. ***liner,** *n.* **4.**); (2) **breeding,** (see quot. 1879); (3) **camp,** *W.* temporary quarters for line riders on a ranch; (4) **drive,** (*a*) in football, a charge or plunge into an opponent's line, (*b*) = **line ball;** (5) **fence,** a fence on a boundary line between two properties; (6) **field,** ?a field bordering on a town or colony line; (7) **gale,** = **line storm;** (8) **house,** *W.* a house serving as a line camp; (9) **officer,** in the army or navy, an officer in the combat or fighting force as distinguished from a staff officer; (10) **place,** the place at which the boundary of a colony was fixed, *obs.;* (11) **rider,** *W.* one engaged in line riding, also a fence rider; (12) **riding,** *W.* patrolling on horseback the boundaries of a ranch, cattle drift, etc., cf. **fence riding;** (13) **road,** a road running along a section line or boundary line; (14) **shot,** a shot in which the bullet or projectile strikes in line with the target; (15) **tub,** (see quot. 1883).

(1) 1867 *Ball Players' Chron.* 25 July 2/3 The 9 [runs] obtained by the Nationals in this inning was almost entirely the result of effective batting, sharp line balls [etc.]. **1888** CHADWICK *Base Ball* 42 A line ball is one sent from the bat, or thrown by a fielder on a line with the fielder to whom the ball is hit or thrown. — **(2) 1879** WEBSTER *Supp.* 1565 *Line-breeding*, . . . the breeding of animals with reference to securing descent from a particular family, especially in the female line. **1889** W. WARFIELD *Cattle-Breeding* 105 Some breeders . . . have adopted a modified view of the general theory generally called 'line breeding.' — **(3) 1888** *Cent. Mag.* March 667/2 The men in the line camps lead a hard life. **1949** *10 Story Western* May 12/2 He had been telling them all how he was going to winter here at the Buffalo Crossing line camp. — (4) (*a*) **1920** *Cap & Gown* 353 The line stiffened and held Illinois in four line drives. (*b*) **1931** *Randolph Enterprise* (Elkins, W.Va.) 9 July 5/3 Boyles turned in the star catch of the day by racing . . . to pull down a line drive with one hand.

(5) **1854** HAMMOND *Hills, Lakes* 250 Later still, the old line fence was pulled away. **1946** *Chi. D. News* 23 March 1/8 He got into an argument with the boy's parents over the building of a line fence between their properties. — (6) **1638** *Charlestown Land Rec.* 1 Eight acres of earable land by estimation, more or lesse, scituate in the line feilde. — (7) **1836** *Knickerb.* VII.17 That blamed line gale has kept me in bilboes such a dog's age. — (8) **1913** MULFORD *Coming of Cassidy* 201 We had only two line houses. **1924** C. E. MULFORD *Rustlers' Valley* vi, You'll live in th' line house with him. — (9) **1850** in GLISAN *Jrnl. Army Life* (1874) 2 July 1/2 This rank . . . avails its possessor . . . in everything except commanding troops when a line officer is present. **1884** BLAINE *20 Years Cong.* I. 76 The line-officers appointed from civil life behaved gallantly.

(10) **1680** *Derby Rec.* 118 The Towne . . . impower[s] ye sd men to Conclude ye line place & places. — (11) **1888** ROOSEVELT in *Cent. Mag.* April 835/2 If the line-riders are caught in a blizzard [etc.]. **1942** DALE *Cow Country* 119 This by no means did away with the work of the line rider, though it was made somewhat easier. — (12) **1884** ALDRIDGE *Life on Ranch* 64 In order to make this line-riding, as it is called, easier, we divided our forces. **1928** *Sat. Ev. Post* 4 Feb. 138/3 Applicants . . . should be capable and willing to perform the arduous and frequently dangerous work incident to what is known as 'line riding' in the rough and mountainous country along the Mexican border. — (13) **1881** *Mich. Gen. Statutes* I. (1882) 389 Whenever a line road shall have been laid out. **1948** *Democrat* 19 Aug. 4/2 [She] lives near the intersection of the Line Road and the Grove Hill-Monroeville highway. — (14) **1883** SHIELDS *S. S. Prentiss* 72 General Foote fired first, his ball striking the ground immediately in front of Prentiss,—a line shot. **1910** J. HART *Vigilante Girl* 301 His bullet entered the ground some nine feet from where he stood, making a line shot.

(15) **1839** *Knickerb.* XIII. 382 Line-tubs, water-kegs, and wafe-poles, were thrown hurriedly into the boats. **1883** *Nat. Museum Bul.* No. 27, 302 Line tubs. Receptacles for the whale-line.

For **line back, shooting, storm, tree,** see as main entries.

b. In phrases: (1) *In line for*, in the running for; (2) *in line with*, in accord with.

(1) **1903** *Forum* Oct. 166 Senator Gorman's victory in Maryland placed him in line for the Democratic nomination for the Presidency. — (2) **1904** L. O. BRASTOW *Representative Modern Preachers* 233 The terms in which he characterizes sin are not theological, nor are they in line with Biblical representations of it.

For other phrases, *to* **get** *a line on*, **fight** *it out on this line*, **ride** *the line*, **run** *a line*, see the terms in boldface.

As the last term in **accommodation, air, anchor, banana, base, bay, bead, bee, belt, bread, by, Canada, captive, car, chalk, colony, color, confirmation, corporation, county, Creek, cross, danger, date, dead, dividend** (or **divident**), **division, drag, drop, drum, dry-goods, end, evening, express, fall, farm, fever, fire, foul, freight, general, guard, guide, hack, head, high, hook and, horsecar, jerk, Indian, Indian boundary, lightning, lot, low, main, Mason and Dixon's, Missouri Compromise, morning, mourners', night, old, old state, opposition, out, owl, packet, parting, party, patent, pea, Pennsylvania, pipe, pole, pony express, power, province, race, random, range, rush, sand, scenic, section, shore, shuttle, side, squaw, stage, state, steamboat, tape, telegraph, through, tight, timber, town, trap, treaty, tree, trolley, trunk, tump, Virginia, water, way, White line.**

***line,** *v.*

1. *tr.* To trace (wild bees) to their hive by observing their line of flight, to locate (a bee tree) in this way.

1827 COOPER *Prairie* v, May I never hear the hum of another bee, or . . . fail in sight to line him to his hive! **1917** KEPHART *Camping* II. 354 A backwoodsman's way of 'lining' bees . . . is to capture one of the insects and fasten to it, or stick into it, a small, downy feather . . . or some other light thing by which he can distinguish the insect in its flight; then he liberates it, and follows it as far as he can by sight. The bee . . . goes home for help. **1933** T. WILLIAMSON *Woods Colt* 218 No trackin' ham-meat, no *linin'* a bee tree, no nothin'.

transf. **1827** COOPER *Prairie* xiv, We have lined the squatter into his most secret misdoings.

2. In logging (see quot. 1890). Also **line up.* Cf. ***liner,** *n.* **2.**

1853 STRICKLAND *Twenty-seven Years* II. 280 As soon as the tree is felled, a person, called a liner, rosses and lines the tree on each side. **1890** W. J. GORDON *Foundry* 116 Then if the trunk is to be squared it is 'lined.' The string is fastened at one end, and, mounting the tree, the foreman moves the line about until he finds what branches should be cut away to trim the trunk to the best advantage. **1941** M. L. SMITH *God's Country* 30 When H. H. would get the log ready to line up we would take that cup [of black dye] and run to the log that he had scored ready to line up so he could hew it well. Before we could get both sides lined our string would be frozen.

3. (See quot.) *Obs.* Cf. **side-hobbled, side-line.**

1871 DE VERE 131 Mules . . . are *lined* [rather than hobbled], that is, the forefoot is tied to the hindfoot on the same side.

4. To straighten (railroad track).

1872 HUNTINGTON *Road-Master's Ass't* 66 Many suppose that after track is once well lined it needs no further attention.

5. To assign or accustom (a person) to a particular type of work. *Rare.*

1886 *Phila. Times* 21 March (*Cent.*), No actor of American birth and training can be lined to this class of work.

6. (See quot.) *Rare.*

1891 *Fur, Fin, & Feather* March 190 The lost camper . . . [should] look straight ahead and fix his eyes on some object on a line with him. Having walked to that object, he should line himself to another, and so on.

7. *intr.* To fish with a line. *Rare.*

1833 J. V. C. SMITH *Mass. Fishes* 262 The [squeteague] is taken both by lining and seining.

8. To guide or control a boat or canoe from the bank of a river by means of a rope. *Rare.*

1923 L. R. FREEMAN *Colo. R.* 356 The low stage . . . gave them room to work below instead of lining from a ledge, eighty feet above the water.

9. **To line out*, in baseball, to hit (a ball) so that it follows a more-or-less low, straight line for a considerable distance, also, *intr.*, to be put out by hitting a liner (sense 4.) that is caught.

1887 *Courier-Journal* 26 May 2/6 He smashed the first ball that came over the plate, and lined out a beautiful hit past second base. **1948** *Dly. Ardmoreite* (Ardmore, Okla.) 28 April 8/1 He . . . lined out to centerfield and walked twice in five trips to the plate.

b. Of football players: To get in position for playing. *Obs.*

1893 CAMP *College Sports* 105 As the players 'line out' they assume as nearly as possible the regular formation.

c. To leave or depart *for* a place.

1897 LEWIS *Wolfville* 90 Them towerists . . . lines out for Tucson.

d. (See quot.)

1905 *Forestry Bureau Bul. 61* Line out. To transplant seedlings from the seedbed to rows in the forest nursery.

10. *To line up*, to take a stand *for*, to side *with*, to go on record. *Colloq.*

1900 GARLAND *Eagle's Heart* 119 He made a serious social mistake when he 'lined up' with the truck farmers. **1903** *N.Y. Times* 18 Sep. 2 The Fusion cause is not likely to lose many of the independent Democratic voters who lined up for it in the last campaign. **1932** GRAYSON *Leaders* 53 And the wealthy southern planters, urged on by a desire to protect their far-flung possessions, lined up for once in favor of a highly centralized national government.

b. Also transitively.

1906 *Forum* Oct. 253 The university president must refuse to be lined up by any clique or party.

11. *To line with*, to border or form a line with something.

1881 *Harper's Mag.* Feb. 433/2 Three hundred acres of good fresh land, lining, on the east side, . . . with the Booker estate.

line back. An animal of the cow kind having a stripe down its back. Also attrib.

1856 M. J. HOLMES *L. Rivers* viii. 93 Our old line back cow has got a calf. **1893** G. W. CURTIS *Horses* 154 Kerry cattle are . . . black, but this is only a fashionable point of the last 10 or 15 years, so that black and white—'line backs'—are still found. **1947** BARRY SCOBIE *Old Fort Davis* 77 Some Longhorns, with all sorts of mixtures—red, black, spotted, lineback.

***linen,** *n.* In combs.: (1) **linen duster,** a duster or light-weight coat made of linen, cf. **duster;** (2) **shower,** a shower or party at which the hostess and guests present a bride-to-be with linen for her new home; (3) **wedding,** a twelfth wedding anniversary.

(1) **1868** *N.Y. Herald* 2 July 4/2 They arrived yesterday about three o'clock with, not carpet bags, but valises and linen dusters. **1949** *Chi. D. News* 11 Feb. 21/3 Grandma was a fashion plate in her smart linen duster for Sunday motoring. — (2) **1919** CUNNINGHAM *Chronicle* 24 Victor Kline had run away, on the eve of a linen shower for his fiancée. — (3) **1873** BAILEY *Life in Danbury* 39 And next night still another silver wedding, and then a linen wedding, followed by a wooden wedding [etc.].

As the last term in **baling, grass, tow, union linen.**

∗liner, *n.*

1. A vessel plying regularly between certain points, esp. one belonging to a regular line, often **ocean liner.**

1836 T. Power *Impressions of Amer.* (ed. 2) I. 17 A work of impertinent supererogation to describe at large an American packet-ship, together with the method of living on board a regular *Liner.* **1930** Cutler *Greyhounds* 62 Whirling, biting snow ushered in that long ago morning of the 5th of January, 1818, which was to witness the sailing of the first 'ocean liner.' **1947** *Chi. Tribune* 20 July I. 18/3 This year we went down on a steamer equal in luxury to the ocean liners.

b. A canal boat that traveled day and night. *Obs.*

1874 B. F. Taylor *World on Wheels* 25 The mighty fleet of white-decked 'liners,' looking like . . . ant's eggs with windows in them [etc.]. **1893** *Outing* Sep. 466/2 Two hours before, a 'liner' had passed southward, a boat towed by the company's mule-relays, and traveling day and night.

2. One who lines trees. Cf. **∗line,** *v.* **2.**

1853 [see **∗line,** *v.* **2.**]. **1880** *Lumberman's Gaz.* 28 Jan., The scorers and liner fell the trees and roughly trim the two opposite sides.

3. One who lives on a dividing line or boundary.

1867 *Ala. Laws 1866–7* 175 James M. Norwood, a liner, between the counties of Chambers and Lee, . . . is hereby declared a citizen of the County of Lee. **1901** *Ala. H. Rep. Jrnl.* 1200 Hugh W. Hardy . . . is a liner between Dallas and Lowndes counties.

4. In baseball, a batted ball that travels in a straight line (see also last part of first quot.).

1867 Chadwick *Base Ball Reference* 137 A Liner.—A ball sent swift and straight from the bat without rising in the air; or one thrown similarly to a base. **1949** *Fargo* (N.D.) *Forum* 23 July 8/1 Bickford . . . was carried off with a possible left instep fracture after being struck by Clyde McCullough's liner.

As the last term in **Atlantic, black, grub, head, high, lickety, Main, old, side, ten, White liner.**

line shooting. (See quot. 1843.) *Obs.* — **1836** *Knickerb.* VIII. 575 We went out to practise, and the major soon put me in the way of line-shooting. **1843** Carlton *New Purchase* I. 129 Each man had three shots. And provided the three were within the circle, each was to be measured by a line from the centre of the diamond to the near edge of the bullet hole—except a ball grazed the centre, and then the line went to the centre of the hole—and then, the three separate lengths added were estimated as one string or line, the shortest securing the prize. This is called line shooting.

line-storm ˈlaɪnˌstɔrm, *n.* "A storm popularly supposed to occur at the time the sun crosses the equator; hence, any heavy storm that occurs within a week or ten days of the equinoxes; an equinoctial storm" (*Cent.*). Chiefly *N. Eng.*

1850 Kingsley *Diary* 115 A fine day with a strong West wind; rather think the line storm is over. **1892** S. Hale *Letters* 274 It poured guns and blew blazes, the regular 'Line Storm.' **1948** Jacobs *We Chose Country* 71 A certain line storm caught us in dead center, spun the wheel and fan around three times, and snapped the chain like string.

line tree. A tree located on the line or boundary of a survey.

1743 *N.J. Archives* 1 Ser. VI. 161 Lett the line trees be markt with your notches on two sides where the line cutts them. **1832** *Louisville Directory* 107 The practice of blocking out the chops on the corner and line trees of surveys, has been universally adopted. **1899** Jewett *Queen's Twin* 176 The light axe . . . Isaac had carried to blaze new marks on some of the line-trees on the farther edge of their possessions. **1942** Cannon *Mountain* 89 He worked to his left for a few minutes and picked up a line tree.

line-up ˈlaɪnˌʌp, *n.* [f. the verb.]

1. A list of participants in a game together with the position played by each. Also transf.

1896 *Boston Jrnl.* 29 Dec. 3/2 The line-up for this game of ice-polo is complete. **1911** *Chi. D. News* 2 March 1/6 Here is the lineup of the regulars as they appeared to-day. **1947** *Dly. Ardmoreite* (Ardmore, Okla.) 14 Nov. 8/1 Of the seniors only five will probably be in the starting lineup.

b. A "ganging up," a formation of persons or groups having a common purpose.

1904 *Springfield W. Republican* 3 June 1 Thus we have a line-up of corporations against the people. **1913** La Follette *Autobiog.* 184 It was a rigid line-up against the bosses.

c. *To get a line-up,* see **∗get,** *v.* **7. a.**

2. A line of persons, esp. a line of prisoners for inspection.

1907 London *Road* 89 Then came the line-up, forty or fifty of us, naked as Kipling's heroes. **1928** A. G. Hays *Let Freedom Ring* 289 The prisoners were brought before witnesses—not in a line-up with others of the same general type but separately. **1930** *Publishers' Wkly.* 21 June 3003/1 There may be a line-up on the first tee.

∗linnet, *n. W.* The house finch, *Carpodacus mexicanus.* Cf. **blue, pine linnet.** — **1805** Lewis in *L. & Clark Exped.* II. (1904) 130, I observed among them the brown thrush, Robbin, turtle dove linnit goaldfinch [etc.]. **1883** *Harper's Mag.* Oct. 707/1 The sage-brush abounded in the nests of . . . the linnet, pipit, and blackbird kinds.

linotype ˈlaɪnəˌtaɪp, *n.* [f. *line of type.*] A typesetting machine which sets matter in solid lines or slugs, orig. a trade-mark name. In full **linotype machine.** Cf. **Mergenthaler linotype.**

1890 *Detroit Free Press* 5 July, The Linotype. . . . The Linotype Machine made by this company under its patents, is now for lease or sale; is capable of an average speed of 8,000 ems per hour. **1930** Ferber *Cimarron* 277 She was proud of the linotype machine. **1949** *Dly. Oklahoman* (Okla. City) 13 Feb. D. 4/2 She can hand set type and run the press but not the linotype.

attrib. **1947** *Chi. D. News* 21 Nov. 3/1 An office rule at all Chicago papers is that linotype operators put their name on type they set. **1949** *N.C. Hist. Rev.* 30 This house maintains a complete plant, linotype department, . . . press room, and bindery.

b. A bar of type that has been cast by such a machine.

1888 *Pat. Off. Gaz.* XLV. 1103/2 The linotype . . . [has] on its side face two or more ribs extending from top to bottom.

linotyper ˈlaɪnəˌtaɪpɚ, *n.* [f. prec.] One who operates a linotype machine.

1896 *Typographical Jrnl.* IX. 31 Mr. H. H. Murphy, an Express linotyper and treasurer of No. 172, . . . will spend the summer in Missouri. **1913** Biggers *Seven Keys to Baldpate* 150 One of 'em . . . flies back to New York with a ten-page story of my vicious career all ready for the linotypers. **1947** *Time* 1 Dec. 30/3 The linotyper, on his way home from work, paused amid the happy, shabby throngs.

linotyping ˈlaɪnəˌtaɪpɪŋ, *n.* [f. **linotype,** *n.*] The act or process of setting up matter on a linotype machine. — **1902** *U.S. Census Bul.* No. 242, 73/2 A new departure in the art of linotyping is the patent to Brott.

linotypist ˈlaɪnəˌtaɪpɪst, *n.* [f. **linotype,** *n.*] =**linotyper.** — **1931** *K.C. Star* 15 Aug., That paper is published by C. L. Rose and T. R. Bartley and Ruth E. Neiswanger is linotypist. **1947** *Newsweek* 20 Oct. 60/1 A linotypist walked up to the foreman and demanded his time.

∗lint, *n.*

1. The fiber surrounding the seed of unginned cotton.

1835 Ingraham *South-West* II. 289 The teeth of the saws catch and carry through the lint from the seed. **1911** *Dept. Agric. Yrbk.* 57 Some of the new types produce larger bolls and longer lint than any of the varieties now generally cultivated in Texas.

2. In combs.: (1) **lint box,** in a cotton press, a large boxlike structure in which the lint is pressed into bales; (2) **-dodger,** =next; (3) **-head,** one who works in a cotton mill, *slang;* (4) **room,** a room for storing cotton from which the seed has been removed.

(1) **1901** Cable *Cavalier* xxi, The lint-box of the old cotton-press was covered with wet morning-glories. — (2) **1941** Daniels *Tar Heels* 213 She is not just a lintdodger but a girl. — (3) **1934** Carmer *Stars Fell* xiii, Hill-billies and niggers, poor whites, and planters, Cajans and Lintheads are sometimes aware of the intangible net that encompasses them. **1948** *Time* 31 May 18/3 The 'lint-heads' in the Tennessee and Carolina mills . . . were showing signs of kicking over the belts and bobbins. — (4) **1845** *Ga. Messenger* 25 Sep. 1/4 The Cotton Packing Press may be placed in an ordinary Gin House, or Lint Room. **1866** W. Reid *After the War* 284 In the lint-room were stacks of muskets.

linter ˈlɪntɚ, *n.* **1.** (See quot.) **2.** *pl.* The fiber and fuzz remaining on cottonseed after the first ginning, and later recovered by a closer ginning and delinting process.

(1) **1890** *Cent.* 3469/3 *Linter,* . . . a machine for stripping off the short-staple cotton-fiber which adheres to cotton-seed after ginning, preparatory to extraction of oil from the seed. . . . Also *linter-machine.* — (2) **1904** Lamborn *Cottonseed Products* 50 The purpose of delinting is to remove more completely the short fibres which form the 'linters.' **1947** *Dly. Ardmoreite* (Ardmore, Okla.) 11 Aug. 6/6 Oil mills of the cotton belt have facilities to produce more than twice as much stock feed, oil and linters as can be obtained from the present supply of cottonseed.

Lintonite ˈlɪntṇaɪt, *n.* [f. Laura A. *Linton* (1853–1915).] A form of thomsonite. — **1880** *Amer. Jrnl. Sci.* 3 Ser. XIX. 122 On Lintonite and other forms of Thomsonite; A preliminary notice of the Zeolites of the vicinity of Grand Marais. **1909** *Cent. Supp.* 735/3 lintonite. . . . [Named after Miss L. A. *Linton,* who analyzed it.] A variety of thomsonite, occurring in green spherical forms, derived from the amygdaloid of Grand Marais, Lake Superior.

* **lion,** *n.* In combs.

1. a. lion dollar, (see quot. 1889 and cf. **dog dollar**). Now *hist.* **b. Lion's Den,** (see quots.). **c.** * **lion-skin,** a heavy woolen cloth. Also attrib. *Obs.*

(a) 1697 *Va. State P.* I. 52 Dollers, commonly called Lyon or Dog Dollers, have no vallue ascertained whereby they may pass currantly amongst the inhabitants of this Country. **1723** *Doc. Hist. N.Y. State* I. 714 The Current Cash being wholly in the Paper Bills of this Province and a few Lyon Dollars. **1889** *Cent.* 1725/1 *Lion dollar,* . . . a Dutch (Brabant) coin in circulation in the province of New York in colonial times. **1934** *Univ. Wis. Studies Soc. Sci.* XX. 205 The lion dollar was especially in evidence in 1693.

(b) 1846 *Warrock's Alman. 1847* (Richmond, Va.) 22 Tennessee, Lion's Den [State]. **1949** *Amer. Sp.* Feb. 28 *Whelp* was apparently suggested by *Lion's Den,* an early nickname for Tennessee.

(c) 1803 *Lit. Mag.* (Phila.) Nov. 153 Three of them wore lion-skin great-coats, the other had a coattee and boots on. **1812** *Niles' Reg.* II. 9/1 The *flushings* or *lion skins* for great coats . . . are nothing more than good tweeled blanketing. **1850** JUDD *R. Edney* 139 He wore a blue, shaggy lion-skin overcoat margined with black.

2. *lion of the west,* a frontier ruffian or bully. Also (usu. *cap.*) a nickname for Henry Clay (1777–1852). *Obs.*

1828 RICE *Jim Crow* viii, I wip de lion ob de west, I eat de Allegator. **1830** *Shelbyville* (Ky.) *Public Ledger* 14 July 2/2 The 'young lion of the west,' with Frank Granger on his back, is shaking his mane, and roaring, and there will be no attempt to check him, from Buffalo to Herkimer. **1848** COOPER *Oak Openings* I. 37 The time is at hand when the Lion of the West will draw his own picture.

3. In the names of flowers: (1) * **lion's foot,** a plant of the genus *Prenanthes,* as the gall of the earth, *P. serpentaria,* or the rattlesnake root, *P. altissima;* (2) * **-'s heart,** the dragonhead or the false dragonhead, also * **lionheart.**

(1) 1814 PURSH *Flora Amer.* II. 499 *Prenanthes Serpentaria* . . . is known by the inhabitants under the name of Lion's-foot, and is in high esteem as a specific in curing the bite of the rattlesnake. **1850** S. F. COOPER *Rural Hours* 283 These plants are sometimes called lion's-foot, rattlesnake-root, &c., but the name of Bird-bell is the most pleasing. **1931** CLUTE *Plants* 104 One of our autumn snakeroots, *Prenanthes serpentaria,* is known as lion's foot. — **(2) 1789** MORSE *Amer. Geog.* 315 Lyons hart . . . is a sovereign remedy for the bite of a serpent. **1847** WOOD *Botany* 426 *P[hysostegia] Virginiana.* . . . Lion's Heart. . . . A beautiful plant, native in Penn., S. and W. States. **1931** CLUTE *Plants* 104 In such a list, the king of beasts naturally comes first, and we find two related species known as lionhearts (*Dracocephalum parviflora* and *Physostegia Virginiana*).

As the last term in **California, Mexican, mountain, red, sea lion.**

Lipan lɪˈpɑn, *n.* [Amer. Sp. *Lipanes, Lipanis, Lipans.* Note variant spellings in our quots.] *collect.* and *pl.* (See quot. 1907.) Also an Indian of this tribe.

[**1776** GARCES *Diary* (E. Coues tr.) (1900) II. 404, I asked if the Yabipais Lipan were good, and they said to me, 'Yea.'] **1810** PIKE *Exped.* App. to III. 9 The nation (Nanahaws) . . . speak the language of the Appaches and Le Panis. *Ib.* 29 The Lee Pawnees are a nation who rove from the Rio Grande to some distance into the province of Texas. **1878** *McAlester* (Indian Terr.) *Star-Vindicator* 26 Oct. 2/1 The Mexican authorities claim to have settled the hash with the Lipans and Kickapoos who have been raiding into Texas. **1907** HODGE *Handbook* I. 768 *Lipan.* . . . An Apache tribe . . . which at various periods roamed from the lower Rio Grande in New Mexico and Mexico eastward through Texas to the Gulf coast. . . . The name has probably been employed to include other Apache groups of the southern plains, such as the Mescaleros and the Kiowa Apache.

lipstick ˈlɪpˌstɪk, *n.* A stick or pencil of pomade or rouge for use on the lips. Also attrib.

1880 E. JAMES *Negro Minstrel's Guide* 4 Prepared burnt cork, ready for use, 25 and 50 cents per box; lip sticks, 25 cts. *Ib.* 8 An application of lipstick . . . around the natural part of the lips will extend that feature to a size quite remarkable. **1919** WILSON *Ma Pettingill* 93 Metta was even using a lip stick! **1949** *Sat. Ev. Post* 10 Sep. 42/1 Please bring wave lotion, curl pins, . . . and if you won't be too sore, just a little lipstick pomade.

b. Hence **lipstick,** *v. tr.*, to paint (the lips) with a lipstick.

1926 *Ladies' Home Jrnl.* April 24 She . . . had recently lipsticked a red mouth into startling contrast to her natural pallor. **1944** PENNELL *Rome Hanks* 149 The lips were lipsticked a dark red following the curled outlines of a child's lips.

* **liquidator,** *n. Liquidator of vessels,* (see quots.). — **1884** *Harper's Mag.* June 58/1 The accounts of each vessel are put into the hands of a class of officials known as liquidators of vessels. . . . They examine the accounts of the liquidators of entries. **1909** *Cent. Supp.* 737/1 *Liquidator of vessels,* one of a number of officials belonging to the New York Custom-house.

* **liquid fire.** Whisky. *Colloq.* — **1830** *Workingman's Gaz.* (Woodstock, Vt.) 11 Nov. 53/1 What I consider a bit remarkable, I have not taken cold since I stopt taking the *liquid fire.* **1857** *Lawrence* (Kans.) *Republican* 28 May 4 Having just opened a commodious shop for the sale of 'liquid fire,' . . . on Saturday next I shall commence the business.

* **liquor,** *n.* In combs.: (1) **liquor doings,** see * **doings;** (2) **grocery,** = * **grocery,** *n.* **2,** now *hist.;* (3) **saloon,** = **saloon;** (4) **store,** a store in which liquor is sold; (5) **trade,** trade or traffic in liquor.

(2) 1849 G. G. FOSTER *N.Y. in Slices* 79 We believe the Liquor Groceries (by which we mean family groceries where grog is retailed) are the most pernicious. **1941** ASBURY *Gem of Prairie* 37 The liquor groceries and tippling houses were frequented by 'rowdies, blacklegs, and other species of loafers.' — **(3) 1863** *S.F. Bulletin* 29 Sep. 3/2 At 1 o'clock they went into a liquor saloon kept by a woman on Kearny street. **1895** SULLIVAN *Tenement Tales* 45 Of the common pattern of corner tenements, its ground floor is a liquor-saloon. — **(4) 1815** *Ann. Reg., Chron.* 46 Mr. Henry Beer's liquor store [re. Port Royal, Jamaica]. **1825** PICKERING *Inquiries Emigrant* 31 The roads leading to a town in America are full of houses on their sides, called 'taverns,' or 'liquor' . . . or 'grocery,' stores. **1949** *Courier-Journal* (Louisville, Ky.) 3 Sep. 9/5 Six liquor-store and pawnshop owners wish they had looked more carefully at the money they took in.

(5) 1859 WILMER *Press Gang* 172 The Liquor Trade has become a moneyed and political power.

b. Designating persons or groups interested in the sale of liquor, as (1) **liquor forces,** (2) **interest,** (3) **league,** *obs.*, (4) **man,** (5) **peddler.**

(1) *c***1919** in BRYAN *Memoirs* 466 Your voice . . . has sent the shock of alarm throughout the ranks of the liquor forces. — **(2) 1884** *Cent. Mag.* Nov. 126 Something in the past history of a public man is supposed to give him the best chance to capture the 'soldier' vote . . . or the liquor or the anti-liquor interest. **1905** *McClure's Mag.* 42 He accepted the support of the liquor interests. — **(3) 1859** WILMER *Press Gang* 172 The 'Liquor League,' the avowed object of which is to 'put down' the friends and advocates of temperance. — **(4) 1884** *Cent. Mag.* April 861/2 The liquor men . . . pay the taxes of their colored allies in order that their votes may be counted. **1891** *N.Y. Wkly. Witness* 11 Nov. 4/4 The liquor-men will hold on to the bitter end.

(5) 1850 JUDD *R. Edney* 81 He broke the bottles of the liquor-pedler with a religious zeal.

c. Used with reference to liquor as an object of political action, as (1) **liquor law,** cf. **Maine, prohibitory liquor law,** (2) **legislation,** (3) **license,** (4) **question,** (5) **ticket.**

1852 *Boston Bee* 29 July (B. '59), The Life Boat . . . takes the Bee to do, for its course in relation to the Liquor law. **1885** WELLS *Pract. Economics* 233 The prevalent . . . delusion, that liquor laws can be made different in principle from all other laws. — **(2) 1883** *Cent. Mag.* July 337/2 The effect of the liquor legislation is that a man who would ordinarily be satisfied with a mug of beer must buy a whole bottle. **1914** *Cyclo. Amer. Govt.* II. 356/1 The temperance movement has set a lasting mark upon all modern liquor legislation. — **(3) 1850** *Hunt's Merch. Mag.* XXII. 87 (*caption*), Statistics of Liquor Licenses in New York City. **1884** WELLS *Pract. Economics* (1885) 174 The number of those who take out similar liquor licenses in those States where prohibition has been engrafted on the constitution . . . appears to increase. — **(4) 1882** *Nation* 14 Sep. 221/2 The moral power of the nation 'is not, on the liquor question, arrayed against a few thousand brewers and rumsellers' simply. **1918** STELZLE *Why Prohibition!* 291 Michigan was about to vote on the liquor question.

(5) 1910 C. HARRIS *Eve's Husband* 148 There was less excuse for his running on the liquor ticket.

As the last term in **anti-, blockade, corn, cornstalk, cut-, Indian, wildcat liquor.**

* **liquor,** *v. intr.* To drink alcoholic liquor. Also with *up. Slang.*

1831 *Boston Transcript* 24 June 2/4 Come, let's liquor again. **1850** A. W. THAXTER *Poem before Iadma* 7 Hast 'liquored up' at Parker's? **1904** *McClure's Mag.* Feb. 359/1 'Let's liquor,' he said.

liquorite ˈlɪkəraɪt, *n.* One who approves of the use and sale of liquor. *Obs.* — **1888** *Voice* 19 Jan. 8 The Democracy of the State will hold only the rabid liquorites and the debauched element of the Negro race. **1908** *Home Herald* (Chi.) 13 May, The liquorites welcome and use such preachers and such preaching.

* **liquorize,** *v.* **1.** *intr.* To drink liquor. **2.** *tr.* To supply with liquor. Both *slang* and *obs.*

(1) 1819 *Ky. Almanac 1820* 30 Behind him was a Mister McBeth, who seemed to have been liquorising you may depend. **1840** *S. Lit.*

Messenger VI. 510/2 Friends, you liquorize too freely—its a bad thing. — (2) **1895** *Nat. Temp. Advocate* Jan. 6/1 The proposition to invest saloons with a legal right to liquorize the community on Sundays.

* **list,** *n.*^{1} An enumeration or description of property subject to taxation.

1646 *Va. Statutes* I. (1823) 329 To the prejudice of many who have duely and according to law presented their lists. **1809** Kendall *Travels* I. 187 The listers or assessors are to retain the lists in their possession till the last day of December annually. **1930** *Rep. Vt. State Tax Comm.* 6 The grand list of the individual taxpayer is one per cent of the appraised value of his taxable real and personal estate and the amount of his taxable poll.

b. * **listmaker,** = **lister,** *n.*^{1}

1663 *Conn. Rec.* I. 392 The said Towne of N. London to be more carefull in their choyse of List makers, for the future. **1692** *Ib.* IV. 81 Persons . . . [are] to give in a true acct. of theire stocks . . . to the list makers according to law.

As the last term in **alarm, batting, check, decommission, diet, exchange, form, free, land, mailing, poll, rank, salary, voting list.**

* **list,** *n.*^{2} A ridge of earth thrown up by a moldboard plow or hoe.

1768 Washington *Diaries* I. 267 Began to cross gd. at Muddy hole . . . , having Run only a single furrow for a list. **1833** Silliman *Man Sugar Cane* 20 The cotton beds are shaved down into the alleys, covering the trash, &c. and forming a wide list. **1886** *Amer. Philol. Assoc. Trans.* 40 *List,* 'a bed,' . . . (of a cotton row) . . . is common in South Carolina.

* **list,** *v.*^{1} *tr.* To record or enter for purposes of taxation. Cf. * **list,** *n.*^{1} — **1658** *Va. Statutes* I. (1823) 454 All negroes imported . . . and Indian servants . . . being sixteen years of age, to be listed and pay leavies as aforesaid. **1877** Burroughs *Taxation* 214 Assessors are to list such lands only as are situate [etc.].

* **list,** *v.*^{2} *tr.* and *absol.* To form lists or ridges on (land), formerly with hoes but now with plows, while cultivating, or preparatory to planting, a crop. Also with *up.* Cf. * **listing,** *n.*

1768 Washington *Diaries* I. 267 Began plowing at Doeg for Corn—that is to list. **1770** *Ib.* 374 Finished listing Ground for Corn at Muddy hole. **1835** Ingraham *South-West* II. 281 Several ploughs are kept constantly running . . . in 'listing up' corn and cotton ground. **1926** *K.C.* (Mo.) *Star* 8 May, Virtually no corn has been planted in this county, farmers being unable to list in the dry ground.

Also * **listed,** of corn: Planted with a lister. Cf. * **lister,** *n.*^{2}

1888 *Sci. Amer.* LVIII. 298/1 A fender for cultivators has been patented, . . . being designed more particularly for use on growing check-rowed and listed corn.

listable ˈlɪstəbl̩, *a.* [f. the noun.] Subject to enlistment for military service; taxable or assessable.

1665 *R.I. Col. Rec.* II. 115 Their sones and sarvants that are listable, which are to be listed, and to traine. **1688** *N. Eng. Hist. & Gen. Reg.* XXXIV. 371 An Accot. of the lystable Estates in the towne of Lyme. **1895** *Columbus* (O.) *Dispatch* 23 Nov. 13/5 [Such certificates] will be—of a nature and form not listable for taxation.

* **listen,** *v. intr.* To sound in a certain way. *Colloq.*

[**1844** *St. Louis Reveille* 20 Dec. 2/2 Dr. McDowell . . . never fails to deliver a very listen-to-able lecture.] **1908** K. McGaffey *Show-Girl* 78 That listened very well indeed, and we all climbed into a cabbage and vamped over. **1921** R. D. Paine *Comr. Rolling Ocean* xiv. 250 How does it listen to you? **1945** Mencken *Supp.* I. 317 It has been suggested . . . that *it listens well* may be from *es hört sich gut an.*

* **lister,** *n.*^{1} One who makes out returns on taxable property, an assessor. Also attrib.

1682 *Derby Rec.* 8 Dec. 130 The Town have chosen . . . John Hubbel & Abel Gun listers & rate makers. **1779** *Vt. State P.* (1823) 296 The listers shall add the sum total of such additions [etc.]. **1847** in Howe *Ohio* 197 The total amount of taxable property returned by the 'listers,' was $393.04. **1922** Cady *Rhymes* (1926) 36 No lister men that lean-to seek, Or 'round about it poke or peek.

* **lister,** *n.*^{2} A middle-buster *q.v.*, esp. one provided with a subsoiling attachment used in planting corn deep in regions of little rainfall. Also attrib.

1887 *Sci. Amer.* LVI. 6/3 When grain is planted by the so-called 'combined lister and drill,' the listing forms a ditch or furrow several inches deep, in which the seed is deposited. **1946** *Harper's Mag.* Oct. 307/2 In my day a lister cost $20—a great deal of money, indeed. **1949** *Lubbock* (Tex.) *Morn. Avalanche* 23 Feb. II. 6/4 Lister shares for any make tractor $3.50 each.

Listerine ˈlɪstəˌrin, *n.* [After Sir Joseph *Lister* (1827–1912), English surgeon.] A trade-mark name for an antiseptic solution manufactured since 1879 (see quot. 1889). Also attrib.

"*Listerine,* of course, is derived from the name of Lord Lister, the English surgeon who brought in aseptic surgery, but it was coined in the United States. Lord Lister objected to the use of his name, but in vain" (Mencken, *Amer. Lang.* 4th ed. 172).

1889 *Syd. Soc. Lex., Listerine,* a solution containing the antiseptic constituents of thyme, eucalyptus, baptisea, gaultheria, and mentha arvensis, with two grains of benzo-boric acid in each drachm. **1909** Farmer *Boston Cook Book* 591 Listerine is an excellent disinfectant to use for the mouth and throat. **1945** *Life* 17 Sep. 7 (*advt.*), We think you'll see what we mean when you squeeze just a fraction of an inch of Listerine Shaving Cream on your brush.

* **listing,** *n.* **1.** The action of making lists on land in farming. **2.** The action of planting corn with a lister.

(1) 1805 Parkinson *Tour* 165, I was near two months getting a plough made, therefore I hired for the listing (as they call it). **1862** *N.Y. Tribune* 19 Feb. 6/5 Manure is carted upon the land . . . , and left in heaps, . . . to be spread at the time of listing. — **(2) 1887** *Sci. Amer.* LVI. 6/3 The drawback to this listing is due to the fact that close to the edges of the furrow on each side, a row of weeds springs up.

* **literary,** *n. local.* (See quot. 1916.) — **1916** *D.N.* IV. 325 Literary, n. A kind of literary society or club; a gathering of persons, esp. in rural districts at the schoolhouse, nearly always in winter, and in the evening, where a program is presented, such as reciting or declaiming poetry or prose selections, reading selections, engaging in dialogues (committed to memory); debating propositions, reading original papers, essays, etc. Sometimes contests in spelling are included and even burlesque trials. **1936** Barnard *Rider* 157 We spent a happy winter at this work and visiting our neighbors and going to the 'literaries' and dances.

* **literary,** *a.* **1. Literary Emporium,** a nickname for Boston, Mass. *Obs.* **2. literary piano,** (see quot.). *Rare.*

(1) 1822 in *Mem. Chas. Mathews* III. 348 This [Boston] is more like an English town than any in America. . . . Kean, in one of his speeches from the stage, called it the literary emporium. **1843** *Lowell Offering* III. 24 The literati of our Literary Emporium comprises but a small proportion of its inhabitants. — **(2) 1867** *Sci. Amer.* 6 July 3/1 The weary process of learning penmanship in schools will be reduced to the acquirement of the art of writing one's own signature and playing on the literary piano above described [a typewriting machine invented by Mr. Pratt, of Ala.], or rather on its improved successors.

lithograph city. A projected city having only a pictured existence. *Obs.* Cf. **paper city.** — **1839** Briggs *H. Franco* I. 90 Augustus had travelled in foreign parts, for he had drummed in Arkansas, and collected in the lithograph cities of the west. **1846** N. F. Moore *Hist. Sk. Columbia Coll.*, 23 These streets, probably, like those of many lithograph cities of recent date, existed only upon paper.

* **lithographic,** *a.* Designating a projected city or town having only a fictitious existence. *Obs.* — **1837** W. Jenkins *Ohio Gaz.* 147 We believe it never existed except on paper; and that the forest retains undisputed possession of a lithographic city. **1846** Saxe *Progress* (1847) 11 You deem he puffs some lithographic town.

* **little,** *a.* In combs.: (1) **little American,** one who wishes to restrict the dimensions and responsibilities of the U.S., also **little Americanism,** *rare,* cf. * *little Englander;* (2) **giant,** = * **giant 1,** *obs.,* cf. **b.** (2) below; (3) **noon,** (see quot.); (4) **Osage,** one of the three tribes of Osage Indians; (5) **recess,** (see quot.); (6) **red schoolhouse,** see **red schoolhouse;** (7) **shot,** one who is not a big shot *q.v., slang;* (8) **theater,** a small theater, usu. one in which amateurs give performances, also attrib.; (9) **woman,** an affectionate or appreciative designation for a wife, *colloq.*

(1) 1904 *Phila. Press* 11 Aug. 6 Judge Parker's whole contention is that of the little American. . . . His little Americanism invites fuller discussion. — **(2) 1884** *N.Y. Wkly. Tribune* 16 Jan. 8/4 The whole superincumbent mass of earth, sometimes from sixty to one hundred feet deep, is washed down with 'Monitors' and 'Little Giants' carrying a six-inch stream with a pressure sufficient to bore a hole in a stone wall. — **(3) 1870** *Nation* 28 July 56/2 Recess, as we say now, the young 'micher' of fifty years ago called 'little noon,' while 'big noon' was the interval between the forenoon and afternoon sessions of the school. — **(4) 1804** *Lewis & Clarke Exped.* (1814) 15 The inroads of the same tribe [the Sauks] compelled the Little Osage to retire from the Missouri a few years ago, and establish themselves near the Great Osages. [**1812** *Niles' Reg.* II. 400/1 A deputation of Indians from the Big, Little and Arkensaw tribes of *Osages* have arrived at Washington city, to visit the president.] **1910** Hodge *Amer. Indians* II. 156 Geographically speaking the tribe consists of three bands: the Pahatsi or Great Osage, Utsehta or Little Osage, and Santsukhdhi or Arkansas band.

(5) **1903** Fox *Little Shepherd* iii, When the first morning recess came —'little recess,' as it was called—the master kept Chad in and asked him his name. — (7) **1931** Reeve *Golden Age Crime* 115 The millenium of Prohibition has passed for the Little Shots. **1949** *Time* 19 Sep. 11/1 Maragon 'continued to live like a little shot in a lower-middlebrow home in McLean, Va.' — (8) **1918** *Amer. Mag.* Jan. 27/3 We have four 'high-brow' little theaters, four universities, and dozens of colleges. **1930** Carew *Hist. Pasadena* I. 511 The Pasadena Community Playhouse [is] the most widely known of the Little Theatres in America. **1948** *Chi. Sun-Times* 18 March 55, I understand they're a little theater group!! — (9) **1881** *Harper's Mag.* June 110/2 When he died, his 'little woman' would be quite equal to carrying on the business. **1944** *This Week Mag.* 25 Nov. 2/1 There's no 'little woman.' She wouldn't like the barge—he wouldn't like being tied down.

For **little Coos, little dipper, little joker, little Mingoes,** see the nouns.

b. In nicknames, usu. obs.: (1) **Little Egypt,** = ***Egypt;** (2) **Giant,** a nickname for Stephen A. Douglas (1813–61), cf. (2) above; (3) **Isaac,** (see quot.), *rare;* (4) **Mac,** a nickname for Gen. George B. McClellan (1826–85); (5) **Magician,** a nickname for Martin Van Buren (1782–1862); (6) **Matty,** =prec.; (7) **Phil,** a nickname for Gen. Philip H. Sheridan (1831–88); (8) **Rhody,** a nickname for the state of Rhode Island; (9) **Robes,** a division of the Piegan Siksika Indians; (10) **Van,** =**Little Magician;** (11) **Volstead,** (see quot. and cf. **Volstead Act**).

(1) **1947** *Chi. Tribune* 9 Nov. IV. 20/1 H. Allen Smith ... makes a safari to the scenes of his childhood in 'Little Egypt' (Cairo, Illinois) and comes back with a new book full of mirth. — (2) **1838** *Quincy* (Ill.) *Whig* 24 Nov. 3/2 He has received a letter from the 'little giant,' in which he avows such an intention. **1844** *Quincy* (Ill.) *Herald* 16 Feb. 2/4 'The Little Giant' ... is a *sobriquet* very happily bestowed by our neighbors of Illinois upon ... Judge S. A. Douglass. **1948** *Sat. Ev. Post* 10 July 68/4 At their Charleston convention, Douglas, the Little Giant, obtained a bare majority, but not two thirds. — (3) **1781** S. Peters *Hist. Conn.* 262 It is from the singing of the tree-frog that the Americans have acquired the name of *Little Isaac.* — (4) **1871** [see **Little Phil**].

(5) **1832** *Polit. Examiner* (Shelbyville, Ky.) 1 Dec. 2/5 None even of his most intimate associates and advisers (save it be the little magician himself) can foresee his next political movement. **1885** Poore *Reminiscences* I. 130 He invariably extricated himself by artifice and choice management, earning the sobriquet of 'the Little Magician.' — (6) **1840** *Ill. State Reg.* (Springfield) 13 March 2/5 He don't ride about in fine carriages like little Matty, but is the log cabin candidate. **1840** *Niles' Reg.* 7 Nov. 157/1 Little Matty's days are number'd, number'd, number'd. — (7) **1871** De Vere 250 General McClellan was *Little Mac* or *Young Napoleon,* ... and Sheridan is still *Little Phil.* — (8) **1851** Johnston *Notes* II. 326 Arkansas is content to be called the Bear State, and Rhode Island with the affectionate familiarity of Little Rhody. **1948** *Nat. Geog. Mag.* Aug. 138/2 Texas is more than 220 times as big as Little Rhody. — (9) **1850** Culbertson in *Smithsonian Rep.* 144.

(10) **1840** *Niles' Reg.* 7 Nov. 156/3 And with them we'll beat little Van. **1868** *N.Y. Herald* 10 July 6/5 In cutting Cass out of the vote of New York and defeating him 'Little Van' [Martin Van Buren] had full satisfaction against the regular Democratic Convention. — (11) **1942** Lillard *Desert Challenge* 10 Nevada was caught in the propaganda wave of Prohibition and passed its own freedom-hampering 'little Volstead' a few months before the Eighteenth Amendment was adopted.

c. In the names of plants and animals: (1) ***little boy's breeches,** =**Dutchman's breeches;** (2) **chief hare,** =**pika;** (3) **Frederic(k),** (*a*) a kind of tobacco, (*b*) a kind of cotton, *rare* or *obs.;* (4) **neck (clam),** a small clam of any one of various species, esp. on the Atlantic Coast the young of the quahog or round clam; (5) **owl,** (*a*) the screech owl, *Otus asio,* or a related bird, also **little horned owl,** (*b*) the Acadian owl or saw-whet, *Cryptoglauca acadica;* (6) **striker,** the least tern, *Sterna antillarum;* (7) **sugar pine,** (see quot.); (8) **turk,** the plum curculio, *Conotrachelus nenuphar.*

(1) **1893** *Amer. Folk-Lore* VI. 137 *Dicentra cucullaria,* little boy's breeches. Central Iowa. — (2) **1868** *Proc. Calif. Acad. Sci.* IV. 6 Lagomys princeps Richardson—'Little Chief Hare;' Rat-rabbit. **1947** Cahalane *Mammals* 581 The attitude reminds one of a tiny old Indian huddling on a rock, drawing an imaginary blanket closer around the bent shoulders. It seems little wonder that some imaginative naturalist has given the animal the title of 'little chief hare.' — (3) (*a*) **1800** W. Tatham *Tobacco* 4 The different species of the genus have been in former days distinguished in Virginia by the names of Oronoko, sweet scented, and little Frederic. (*b*) **1843** in Turner *Cotton* (1865) 63 And so the cotton, without the ... manure, will be found, as is too common, the *little Frederick!* — (4) **1853** *Nat. Museum Bul.* No. 27, 234 Another name [for the small round clam] is 'Little Neck,' derived originally from a neck of land on the north shore of Long Island, known as Little Neck, whose clams had a superior flavor. **1903** *N.Y. State Museum Bul.* No. 71, 5 The little-neck clam, *Venus mercenaria,* grows most abundantly below the low tide line. **1935** Lincoln *Cape Cod Yesterdays* 49 After all, everyone eats oysters and Little Necks *au naturel.*

(5) (*a*) *c*1728 Catesby *Carolina* I. 7 *Noctua Aurita Minor.* The Little Owl, is about the size of, or rather less than, a Jack-daw. **1917** *Birds of Amer.* II. 109 Screech Owl, *Otus asio asio.* ... [Also called] Little Horned Owl; Gray Owl [etc.]. (*b*) **1811** Wilson *Ornithology* IV. 66 Little Owl: *Strix passerina* ... makes up in neatness of general form and appearance for deficiency of size. **1839** Peabody *Mass. Birds* 275 The Acadian or Little Owl, *Strix acadia,* is found in Massachusetts. — (6) **1917** *Birds of Amer.* I. 65 Least tern. ... Other names. ... Little Striker [etc.]. — (7) **1948** *Pacific Discovery* Nov.–Dec. 20/1 Because of its cones the silver pine is sometimes called the 'little sugar pine.' — (8) **1863** *Prairie Farmer* June 373/1 The crescent under fig. 1 is the cut made by the 'little Turk' in depositing its egg. **1879** *Vt. Bd. Agric. Rep.* I. 57 Jarring the trees every morning, which causes the little turk to drop upon a sheet spread to receive him.

* **live,** *a.* In combs.: (1) **live beat,** (see quot.), *rare;* (2) **fence,** =**live hedge,** also **live fencing;** (3) **gang,** (see quot.); (4) **hedge,** a hedge of growing shrubs or trees; (5) **paper,** (see quots.); (6) **shout,** (see quot.), *obs.;* (7) **steam,** (see quot.); (8) ***stock,** (*a*) Negro slaves, *obs.,* (*b*) **livestock king,** a wealthy cattle-raiser; (9) **wire,** a person having energy, ideas, and initiative, also attrib.

(1) **1889** Farmer 45/2 A *live beat* is anybody or anything that surpasses another, and the sense is not derogatory in the least. — (2) **1804** J. Roberts *Pa. Farmer* 84 When the hedge is full grown, then there is a perfect live fence. **1829** *Mass. Spy* 25 March (Th.), Messrs. G. Th. and Son have imported 75,000 hawthorns, for 'live fencing.' **1885** *Cent. Mag.* March 795 The cuts will be protected from snow-drifts, and long lines of 'live fences' be secured. — (3) **1875** Knight 1337/2 *Live-gang,* a gang-saw mill, so arranged as to cut through and through the logs without previous slabbing. — (4) **1835** Hoffman *Winter in West* I. 184 A great many English emigrants settled upon this prairie ... are successfully introducing here the use of live hedges instead of fences in farming.

(5) **1877** Bartlett 788 *Live Paper,* a term applied to business notes-of-hand. The banks, in discounting, prefer *'live paper,'* meaning notes that will be paid at maturity, and not such as will be renewed, or their payment prolonged. **1895** E. Carroll *Principles Finance* 299 *Live paper.* Unmatured promissory notes, in contradistinction to matured, dead, or protested paper. — (6) **1760** T. Brown *Plain Narr. Sufferings* 9 The Indians made a Live-Shout, as they call it when they bring in a Prisoner alive. — (7) **1875** Knight 1337/2 *Live-steam.* ... 1. Steam from the boiler at its full pressure; in contradistinction to *dead-steam.* 2. Steam from the boiler; in contradistinction to *exhaust-steam.* — (8) (*a*) **1842** Buckingham *Slave States* I. 454 Negro slaves which sold formerly at 1,000 dollars, now sell for 500 dollars. There was not so much depreciation in the value of the 'live stock,' as these are called, as in the land. **1852** Stowe *Uncle Tom* xii, The trader waked up bright and early, and came out to see his live-stock. (*b*) **1915** Young *Hard Knocks* 86 He also rode pony express in early days, but later became the 'Live Stock King' of Wyoming. — (9) **1909** *Sat. Ev. Post* 13 March 24/1 As a legislator, ... he was probably known to many people as an aggressive 'comer' of the live-wire kind. **1949** *Ib.* 1 Jan. 46/1 They wanted a 'live wire' who could put the pieces together again and bring some order into the White House routine.

b. In the names of trees: (1) **live ash,** a now unidentifiable tree, *obs.;* (2) **chestnut oak,** (see quot.); (3) **oak,** see as a main entry; (4) **sumach,** (see quot.).

(1) **1856** *Mich. Agric. Soc. Trans.* VIII. 729 The sturdy oak, elm, basswood or live-ash and hickory predominate [in Ottawa Co.]. — (2) **1813** Muhlenberg *Cat. Plants* 87 Yellow oak, or live chesnut Oak. — (4) **1885** Havard *Flora W. & S. Texas* 510 *Rhus virens.* (Live Sumach). Shrub found in shady arroyos and on lower slopes of mountains, west of the Nueces River.

* **live,** *v.*

1. * **Live forever,** (see quot.). *Obs.*

1859 Bartlett 247 *Live forever,* the name of a fanatical sect in Kentucky whose principal article of faith was that those who had 'faith' would never die.

2. In phrases: (1) *To live off,* (*a*) to live at the expense of (another), (*b*) *to live off the country,* of a military force, to secure subsistence from the country or region in which operations are being carried on; (2) *to live out,* (*a*) to be employed as a domestic servant, (*b*) to consume by the process of living; (3) *where one lives,* at one's most vital or vulnerable spot, *slang.*

(1) (*a*) **1886** HOWELLS *Minister's Charge* 38 Was he afraid that Barker wanted to come and live off him? (*b*) **1884** *Cent. Mag.* Feb. 503/1 In his marches he had been obliged to live, to a great extent, off the country. **1949** *Milwaukie* (Ore.) *Rev.* 4 Aug. 1/4 The main cause for the Communist army success was the fact that it was well fed, living off the country as it marched through China. — (2) (*a*) **1839** F. J. GRUND *Aristocracy in Amer.* II. 152 They will rather become tailoresses . . . than degrade themselves by 'living out.' **1882** M. HARLAND *Eve's Daughters* 200 The settled purpose of catching husbands whose wages will relieve them from the necessity of 'living out.' (*b*) **1894** WILKINS *Pembroke* 277 She's lived out her place, an' the town's jest took it. — (3) **1860** HOLLAND *Miss Gilbert* 386 When that little wife of mine says, 'Tom, you're a good feller, God bless you,' it goes right in where I live. **1886** HOWELLS in *Cent. Mag.* Feb. 511/1 If I could only have reached him where he lives, as our slang says!

* **lively,** *a.* **1.** Of land: Fertile, fruitful. **2.** Of a ball: Elastic, bouncing or rebounding quickly.

(1) **1770** WASHINGTON *Diaries* I. 426 A pretty lively kind of Land grown up with Hick[or]y. **1863** MITCHELL *My Farm* 119 The result [of harrowing] has been a compact lively sod. — (2) **1867** *Ball Players' Chron.* 20 June 1/4 When a lively ball gets on the cobble stones a home run is inevitable. **1948** *Dly. Ardmoreite* (Ardmore, Okla.) 1 July 14/1 Many experts blame the dead-arm pitching to the 'lively ball' with all the batters swinging for distance.

live oak.

1. Any of various American evergreen oaks, the most important of which are the *Quercus virginiana* of the South and various species of the Pacific Coast, esp. *Q. agrifolia.* In full **live oak tree.** Cf. **canyon, coast live oak.**

1610 *Estate of Va.* 54 Sarsafrase, liue oake, greene all the years, Cedar and Firre. **1695** *Duxbury Rec.* 68 A straight line to an elm or live oak tree marked. **1709** LAWSON *Carolina* 92 Live-Oak chiefly grows on dry, sandy Knolls. This is an Ever-green, and the most durable Oak all America affords. **1845** FRÉMONT *Exped.* 241 The prevailing tree [among the oaks in the country west of the Sierra Nevadas] was the evergreen oak, (which, by way of distinction, we shall call the *live oak*). **1949** HERTRICH *Huntington Bot. Gardens* 52 During the month of February we put through a program of transplanting 650 live oaks from the canyon.

b. Wood or building material obtained from this. Also attrib.

1735 *Ga. Col. Rec.* III. 130 Received four large Pieces of Live Oak Timber, sent to be tried if fit for the use of the Navy. **1774** in P. L. PHILLIPS *Notes on B. Romans* (1924) 20 There is a Scandalous illicit Trade Carried on between the inhabitants . . . & the Spanjards at Orleans the former. . . . Supplying the latter with Pitch, Tarr, Charcoal, Live Oak & Cattle. **1886** *Harper's Mag.* June 4/2 This vessel . . . was built of seasoned live-oak.

c. live-oak penny-a-grab, a kind of cheap cigar. *Colloq. Obs.* Cf. **oak-leaf cigar.**

1856 BREWERTON *War in Kans.* 253 [In the grocery there was] a box marked *Havanas,* which, were but too evidently 'live-oak penny-a-grabs.'

* **liver,** *n.* In combs.: (1) **liverberry,** = **twisted-stalk;** (2) **-leaf,** a plant of the genus *Hepatica* having heart-shaped three-lobed leaves; (3) **lily,** = **blue flag;** (4) **pad,** a pad worn over the region of the liver.

(1) **1894** *Amer. Folk-Lore* VII. 102 *Streptopus amplexifolius, Streptopus roseus,* liver-berry, St. Francis, Me. — (2) **1817–8** EATON *Botany* (1822) 304 *Hepatica triloba,* liverleaf. **1939** *Nat. Geog. Mag.* Aug. 225/2 Among the earliest of flowers, hepaticas . . . which are commonly called 'liverleaf,' sometimes come into bloom in December in the warmer parts of the country. — (3) **1892** *Amer. Folk-Lore* V. 103 *Iris versicolor* . . . liver-lily. — (4) **1879** PECK *Peck's Fun* 38 (We.), A boarder at a Leadville hotel investigated his beef-steak and found that it was a fried liver pad. **1889** *Internat. Ann., Anthony's Photog. Bul.* II. 72 Used as a liver pad or a plaster that is meant for chest protection.

liverwurst ˈlɪvəˌwɜst, *n.* [f. G. *leberwurst.*] Sausage consisting largely of liver. Also attrib.

1869 *Atlantic Mo.* Oct. 483/1 Instead, our Dutch neighbors make *liver-wurst* ('woorsht') or meat pudding, omitting the meal, and this compound stuffed into the large intestines, is very popular in Lancaster market. **1943** *Copper Camp* 249 Great platters of bologna, liverwurst, anchovies, summer sausages, . . . frankfurters and a half dozen other varieties of cold cuts gleamed. **1948** *Sat. Ev. Post* 17 July 40/3, I feel like a liverwurst sandwich.

* **livery,** *n.*

1. A livery stable, a public stable where horses and carriages are let.

1888 FERGUSON *Forty-Niner* i. 15 We placed our horses in a livery on Third street. **1902** HARBEN *A. Daniel* 29, I could 'a' gone to a livery an' ordered out a team.

attrib. **1845** F. DOUGLASS *Narrative* 16 His stable and carriage-house presented the appearance of some of our large city livery establishments. **1872** *Newton Kansan* 22 Aug. 3/6 If you want to hire a good saddle horse or livery team call at A. Shuster's Livery, Sale and Feed Stables. *Ib.* 26 Sep. 3/2 For a good livery rig . . . go to Shuster's stable. **1891** O'BEIRNE *Leaders Ind. Terr.* 43/2 He has been running a large livery business, which he sold out about August 8, 1890. **1926** COOPER *Oklahoma* 34 Go to Jake's livery barn. **1936** BARNARD *Rider* 210 They met a traveling man who was driving a good livery team to a buckboard.

2. A conveyance obtained from a livery stable.

1911 LINCOLN *Cap'n Warren's Wards* 8 Of course I shall share the expense of the livery.

* **living room.** A family sitting room.

1860 OLMSTED *Back Country* 237 The interior consisted of one large 'living-room,' and a 'lean-to,' used as a kitchen. **1910** C. HARRIS *Eve's Husband* 310 She occupied one chair in the living room all day. **1949** *Sat. Ev. Post* 9 July 88/2 A beautiful birch paneled living room boasting period treatment and many home-like refinements are typical of the luxuries found in trailers.

liza ˈlizə, *n.* [Sp. in same sense.] A gray mullet. — **1883** *Nat. Museum Bul.* No. 27, 449 *Mugil brasiliensis.* . . . White Mullet: Liza. Atlantic coast from Cape Cod to South America. **1911** *Rep. Fisheries 1908* 312/2 Mullet (*Mugil cephalus* and *M. curema.*) . . . Local names are . . . 'blue-back mullet,' 'liza,' or 'josea.'

* **lizard,** *n.*

1. (*cap.*) A nickname for a native or inhabitant of Alabama.

1845 *St. Louis Reveille* 14 May 2/4 The inhabitants of . . . Alabama [are called] Lizards. **1948** *Dly. Ardmoreite* (Ardmore, Okla.) 11 July 21/5 The residents of Alabama have been called 'Lizards.'

2. (See quots.) *Colloq.*

1870 NOWLAND *Indianapolis* 16 One end was placed on a sled called a 'lizard,' to which the horse was hitched. **1906** in *Amer. Sp.* VI. 465 Down in Texas a sledge or jumper is evidently called a lizzard. An effort is now being made to locate a lizzard made by Davy Crockett . . . in 1835. **1948** DICK *Dixie Frontier* 106 A type of sled used in Missouri before the era of the wagon was known as a lizard. It was made of a V-shaped forked tree and furnished with a bed of brush to haul a load.

attrib. **1917** KEPHART *Camping* II. 64 The logs were twitched to the nearby 'lizard road,' where they were loaded on lizards (forks of timber used as sleds).

As the last term in **fence, green, horned, lounge, pine, scorpion, slough, spring, striped, wood lizard.**

* **Lizzie,** *n.* = **tin Lizzie.** *Jocular.* — **1923** *Frontier* May 9 Lizzie appeared minus one headlight, with a distorted fender. **1947** PERRY *Cities of Amer.* 117 He had pieces of tin running a human gauntlet, and by the time they reached the end of it, they deserved the exalted name of Lizzie, would run like a spotted-bottomed ape—and with about as much grace.

llano ˈlɑno, *n. S.W.* [Sp. in same sense. An Amer. borrowing.] An extensive treeless plain, steppe, or prairie. Also attrib.

1846 SAGE *Scenes Rocky Mts.* xxxiii, A continuous chain of hills . . . plainly points out the cheerless *llanos* of the Great American Desert. **1885** HARTE *Maruja* 40 Your government, Captain, handed over ten leagues of the llano land to the Doctor West. **1895** REMINGTON *Pony Tracks* 83 The horse herds were moved in from the *llano* and rounded up in the corral. **1949** *Newsweek* 18 July 34 (*legend*), This 360-pound tiger (actually a jaguar) was killed recently in the Costa Rican llanos.

b. Llano Estacado, the Staked Plain, a high arid plateau of forty thousand square miles, situated in Texas and New Mexico. Cf. **yarner.**

1834 A. PIKE *Sketches* 42 The Llano Estacado, on whose borders we then were encamped, and which lay before us like a boundless ocean, was mentioned with a sort of terror. **1891** *Memphis Appeal-Avalanche* 22 April 1/3 Great interest was also shown in the subsequent destruction of the Llano Estacado. **1947** *Westerners' Brand Book* 68 The man of the Llano Estacado accepted the challenge.

lluvia de oro. *S.W.* [Sp., shower of gold. In Amer. Sp. applied to various plants.] = **palo verde.** — **1901** VAN DYKE *Desert* 134 Even such a tree as the lluvia d'oro has needles rather than leaves. **1946** *So. Sierran* Nov. 2/3 In April the Colorado desert is ablaze with the lemon-yellow bloom of the Palo verde (Parkinsonia Torreyana), sometimes called 'lluvia de oro' and 'naked tree.'

L. M. An abbreviation for "lawful money." *Obs.* — **1773** *Mass. Col. Soc. Pub.* VI. 115 He now promises a Reward of Ten Pounds

L.M. to any who shall give Information. **1788** CUTLER in *Life & Corr.* I. 429 Oated and had my hair dressed. Bill, 9d., L.M.; barber, 7d., L. M.

Lo lo, *n.* [f. Pope's well-known line "Lo, the poor Indian."] An American Indian. Also attrib.

1871 *Republican Rev.* 2 Sep. 1/4 Cowardly Lo prefers to attack none but very small parties of teamsters, farmers, or lone mail riders. **1873** *Forest & Stream* 13 Nov. 211/2 Is it longer a matter of astonishment that the Lo's are passing so rapidly from the face of the earth? **1912** F. J. HASKIN *Amer. Govt.* 86 The result is that Lo is given to understand that no amount of false swearing will serve to disprove his signature. **1947** COFFIN *Yankee Coast* 220 He caught a cold in captivity, . . . succumbed and went to join Lo, the Poor Indian on the Happy Hunting Grounds.

*__load,__ *n.* As the last term in **buck, canoe, car, flat, schooner, scow, sleigh, top, tote load.** Also **dead loads.**

*__loader,__ *n.* **1.** A small measure holding just the quantity of powder suitable for charging a muzzle-loading gun. Cf. **charger. 2.** (See quots.)

(1) **1843** CARLTON *New Purchase* I. 105 A powder horn, and its loader of deer horn. *Ib.* 199 A black, surly looking rifle, with the appurtenances of horns, pouches, loaders, tomahawks and knives. — (2) **1875** KNIGHT 1337/2 *Loader*, a machine attached to a wagon, as a *hay-loader* or *stone-loader*. **1883** ——— *Supp.* 552/1 *Loader*, an instrument for re-loading cartridge shells.

As the last term in **beet, hay, steam, top loader.**

*__loading,__ *n. attrib.* Designating devices for putting livestock or logs aboard railroad cars, as **loading board, chute, jack.**

1910 RAINE *B. O'Connor* 36 The loading board was lowered and the horses led from the car. — **1890** *Stock Grower & Farmer* 25 Jan. 6/1

Loading chute or stock chute

The loading chutes have been enlarged and remodelled. **1948** *Durant* (Okla.) *D. Democrat* 4 July 5/3 George has one of the best stock pens and loading chutes we have seen. — **1905** *Forestry Bureau Bul.* No. 61, 41 Loading jack, a platformed framework upon which logs are hoisted from the water for loading upon cars. (N[orthern] F[orest].)

*__loaf,__ *n.*[1] As the last term in **corn, Indian, oyster, peach, salt, sugar loaf.**

loaf lof, *n.*[2] [f. **loaf,** *v.*] A time spent in loafing. *Colloq.*

1860 WHITMAN *Leaves of Grass* 39 The farmer stops by the bars, as he walks on a First-day loafe, and looks at the oats and rye. **1897** *Outing* XXX. 374/2 We have . . . the holiday camp, in which a restful loaf is the principal object.

b. loaf day, a day when regular work is not done, a holiday.

1881 *Scribner's Mo.* XXII. 217/2 On 'loaf-days' the hands occupy themselves with making the neat cans which it is their . . . business to fill.

loaf lof, *v.* [Origin unknown. Cf. **loafer.**] *intr.* To stroll or saunter aimlessly; to loiter, linger, dawdle, to "lie down on the job." Often with *about* and *around.*

1835 *Vade Mecum* (Phila.) 16 May 3/4 On the contrary, the propensity to loaf is confined to no rank in life. **1844** GODLEY *Letters from A.* II. 146 There were . . . a number of people 'loafing' about. **1846** COOPER *Redskins* v, We were lounging around—loafing around is the modern Doric. **1890** *Boston Jrnl.* 30 June 4/1 Tennyson does the greater part of his literary work . . . between breakfast and lunch, and loafs the rest of the day. **1948** *Reader's Digest* January 105/1 Most of the people on the river loaf during the rainy season.

b. Also *loaf in, loaf out.*

1884 *N.Y. Wkly. Tribune* 16 July 3/4 One pair of high boots, surmounted with flannel shirt, rough beard and pipe, loafed in, lounged against the wall for a few minutes, and loafed out again.

loaf cake. Cake baked in the form of a loaf.

1828 LESLIE *Receipts* 62 Loaf Cake. **1878** COOKE *Happy Dodd* 344 I've give one boy . . . three doughnuts, a big slice o' loaf-cake and two cookies. **1941** FARMER *Boston Cook Book* 624 Loaf and Layer Cakes.

loafer ˈlofɚ, *n.*[1] [Short for land loafer *q.v.* Cf. also *EDD louper*, a vagabond, and *to loup the tether*, to ramble.] One given to loafing, an idler or lounger, one too lazy to work.

1830 *Mechanics' Press* (Utica, N.Y.) 10 July 274/1 Nor are they topers at taverns, or *benchers* at groceries, or loafers who 'chase misfortune o'er the tow path.' **1839** *N.O. Picayune* 12 April 2/2 The word 'Loafer,' says the Boston Post, was employed as long ago as 1794, in a work on banking by John Taylor of Philadelphia. It was used to signify what we now term a black leg. **1889** BRAYLEY *Boston Fire Dept.* 198 A gang of stout boys and loafers . . . had followed the firemen. **1947** *Denver Post* 9 Jan. 10/4 Will someone tell me what purpose this empty square serves other than for loungers, loafers, dog walkers and discarded lunch papers?

attrib. **1835** *Knickerb.* July 66 His decease—for he was a royal ragamuffin,—spread universal sorrow throughout all ranks of the loafer community. **1865** *Three Yrs. Among Working Classes* 49 Worse still, these loafer squads are generally above the law. **1888** BRYCE *Amer. Commonw.* II. III. lvii. 397 The 'loafer' class . . . have votes but no reason for using them one way more than another.

b. loafer rake, =**bull rake.** *Colloq.*

1913 *D.N.* IV. 56. **1942** CANNON *Mountain* 4 Even old David Gillmor was haying, but he couldn't mow or pitch this year; he was pulling a loafer rake.

c. Loafers' Hall, prison. *Slang. Obs.*

1861 *Dly. Richmond* (Va.) *Enquirer* 20 July 3/2 Yet for only this, he was compelled to retire for awhile from the gaities of society into the retirement of 'Loafers' Hall.'

As the last term in **coffee house, dock, land, log cabin, park, saloon loafer.**

loafer ˈlofɚ, *n.*[2] [f. Sp. *lobo*, wolf.] The gray or timber wolf. Cf. **lobo.**

1877 MCDANIELD & TAYLOR *Coming Empire* 314 The Mexicans call these big wolves 'lobos' and the Texans call them 'loafers' which is a corruption of the Mexican word. **1891** O'BEIRNE *Indian Territory* I. 209 The 'loafer,' or large mountain wolf, is very plentiful. **1908** *Sat. Ev. Post* 4 July 16/3 One of the loafers had run in, leaping out of the black like a streak of gray light from where no light had shone before. **1948** *Sat. Ev. Post* 10 July 80/3 With loafers, . . . mountain lions or bears, he was absolutely ruthless.

loaferdom ˈlofɚdəm, *n.* [f. **loafer,** *n.*[1]] An aggregation of loafers; the state of being a loafer. — **1856** *Butte Rec.* (Bidwell, Calif.) 2 Feb. 2/5 The present legislature started off with any amount of economical professions, but nevertheless loaferdom is victorious. **1894** *Forum* May 276 The steps from enforced idleness down into loaferdom, drunkenness, vagrancy, and crime, are short and near together.

loaferess ˈlofərɪs, *n.* [f. **loafer,** *n.*[1]] A female loafer. — **1835** *Knickerb.* July 63 My hero did actually come into the world by the connivance of Susan and Samuel Smith, loafer and loafress of this burgh . . . with the auspicious light of a brown, sputtering candle. **1885** *Advance* 16 July 458 The loafers and loaferesses . . . stared at her with unanimous admiration.

loaferish ˈlofərɪʃ, *a.* [f. **loafer,** *n.*[1]] Of, pertaining to, or like a loafer.

1841 *N.O. Picayune* 14 Jan. 2/1 You are rather a loaferish looking customer, but I aint particular about my company, at this time of night. **1895** SULLIVAN *Tenement Tales* 137 It was the loaferish fellow who had been with his pursuers. **1902** *Kans. Hist. Coll.* VII. 416 That lecture of Prentis's was a disgrace. It was loaferish and undignified.

b. Hence **loaferishness,** *n.*, **loaferishly,** *adv.*

1877 *N.Y. Tribune* 9 Oct. (B.), That town may rejoice in a population which, for grotesque stupidity, comical or stale vulgarity, and general loaferishness of man, woman, and child, has never been equalled or even imagined. **1902** CLAPIN 261 Loaferishly. In a way becoming the true loafer.

loaferism ˈlofəˌrɪzəm, *n.* [f. **loafer,** *n.*[1]] The practice of loafing. Cf. **Creole loaferism.** — **1836** *Knickerb.* VIII. 407 There is a moral sublimity in . . . his calling; but it is not the sublimity of loaferism. **1889** *Home Missionary* Dec. 362 As long as I am in charge here, loaferism and blackguardism . . . will find an unwholesome atmosphere.

loaferizing ˈlofəˌraɪzɪŋ, *n.* [f. **loafer,** *n.*[1]] =next. *Rare.* — **1838** *N.Y. Advt. & Exp.* 14 Feb. 1/2 The loafers, after wearing for a while a 'swashing and martial outside,' have sunk back into insignificance and *loaferizing*.

loafing ˈlofɪŋ, *n.* Idling about, doing nothing. Also attrib. and as adj.

1835 *Vade Mecum* (Phila.) 17 Jan. 3/6 Loafing's dull at this season of the year. **1835** *Knickerb.* July 63 He considered [this world] as an unbounded loafing-ground. **1841** *Loco-Foco* (Chester, Pa.) 17 April 15/1 If they'd let me apply my talent to loafin', I never need to do no vork. **1853** *Deseret News* (Salt Lake City) 15 Oct. 1/1 Joe Tucker, . . . a do-nothing, a loafing, cigar-smoking good-natured fellow, owned a dog. **1948** *Chi. D. News* 7 Jan. 16/7, I have just finished a long loafing session.

b. loafing place, a place where one habitually loafs.

1838 J. C. NEAL *Charcoal Sk.* III. ii. 34 One night Mr. Dabbs came home from his 'loafing' place. **1938** ASBURY *Sucker's Prog.* 442 Shanley's Grill was famous for its thick and juicy steaks, but for several years it possessed an even greater attraction—it was the favorite loafing place of the celebrated Bat Masterson.

***loan,** *n.* In combs.: (1) **loan certificate,** a form of paper money issued by some of the states after the collapse in value of the Continental paper currency, *obs.;* (2) * **office,** see as a main entry; (3) **officer,** one in charge of a government loan office, *obs.;* (4) **shark,** one who lends money at an exorbitant rate of interest, also attrib.

(1) **1777** *Boston Town Meeting* 26 May 285 If this could be accomplished, and the Money redeemed by Loan-Certificates, it would operate doubly in favor of the States. **1788** SCHÖPF *Reise* I. 606 Nach dem Verfall des Kongressgeldes, erhielt sich hier in Pensylvanien und einigen andern Provinzen nur noch das sogenannte Staatsgeld und die Loan certificates in einigem Werth . . . Leztere sind Staats-Schuldscheine, für dem Publiko geliehenes Geld, gethane Lieferungen und andere geleistete Dienste. — (3) **1737** *N.Y. Col. Laws* II. (1894) 1040 An Act to facilitate and Explain the duty of the Loan officers in this Colony. **1806** in J. T. BUCKINGHAM *Newspaper Lit.* I. 277 Benjamin Austin, Loan Officer, . . . has circulated an infamous falsehood concerning my professional conduct. — (4) **1913** *Munsey's Mag.* Nov. 218/1 In New York the loan-sharks were doing a business of twenty million dollars per annum. *Ib.* 221/1 At the convention of the Legal Aid Society in Pittsburgh, the same year, the loan-shark evil was discussed. **1946** *Reader's Digest* Jan. 103/2 For years they've paid heavy interest to loan sharks.

As the last term in **call, improvement loan.**

***loan office.**

1. An office that put province and state funds out on loan. *Obs.*

1758 in *Amer. Sp.* XXI. (1946) 118/1 The Trustees of the General Loan-Office of the Province of *Pennsylvania*, do hereby give Notice to the Mortgagors who are in Arrears. **1848** *Indiana Gen. Ass. Doc. 1848–9* II. 285 The amount of funds in the loan office is given by the Auditor of State, in his annual report of the Legislature.

attrib. **1777** *N.J. Archives* 2 Ser. I. 481 Many people object to receive the New-Jersey Paper Currency, called the Loan-office money, dated in March 1776, because . . . supposed to be of no value. **1854** PIERCE in *Pres. Mess. & P.* V. 294 The amount so found due was . . . entered by his order on the loan-office books of South Carolina.

2. One of various offices set up by the Revolutionary Continental government in various states to facilitate subscriptions to government loans. Also attrib. *Obs.*

1776 *Jrnls. Cont. Congress* V. 854 For the convenience of the lenders, a loan office [shall] be established in each of the United States, and a commissioner, to superintend such office, be appointed by the said states respectively. **1780** FRANKLIN *Writings* VIII. 56 The Reports you tell me prevail at Cadiz that the Loan Office Bills payable in France have not been duly honoured are wicked falsehoods. **1874** BANCROFT *Hist. U.S.* X. 223 An act of a previous session had directed debts due to British subjects to be paid into the loan office of the state.

b. loan office certificate, a certificate issued by such a loan office. *Obs.*

1778 *Mass. Spy* 29 Oct. 4/2 The Loan Office Certificates, which may issue for prizes of the second class of the lottery of the United States, shall bear an interest of six per centum per annum. **1794** *Ann. 3d Congress* 1430 No claim shall be allowed for the renewal of Loan Office certificates destroyed before the fourth day of March.

***lobby,** *n.*

1. *Collect.* Those who frequent the anteroom of a legislature to influence the actions of the legislators.

1808 *Ann. 10th Congress* 1 Sess. II. 1536 If we move to Philadelphia we shall have a commanding lobby. **1903** A. B. HART *Actual Govt.* 247 Another force is the lobby, by which is meant those men, and sometimes women, who make it a business to argue with congressmen and to solicit their votes. **1945** *Nation* 17 March 303/2 One of the most effective 'economy' lobbies in the country, has urged the state legislature to raise the Governor's salary.

2. In combs.: (1) **lobby agent,** =**lobbyist;** (2) **fund,** the fund to pay the expenses of a lobbyist; (3) **member,** =**lobbyist;** (4) **operator,** one who operates a lobby.

(1) **1864** NICHOLS *Amer. Life* I. 260 There were lobby agents, male and female, ready to give the influence they boasted of for a consideration. **1886** POORE *Reminiscences* I. 492 Mr. Simonton was correct when he stated that 'a corrupt organization of Congressmen and certain lobby-agents existed.' — (2) **1890** *Stock Grower & Farmer* 25 Jan. 3/4 Suppose . . . they agree to contribute a cent for each head of cattle in the United States to form a 'lobby fund' for legislative purposes. — (3) **1819** VERPLANCK *State Triumvirate* 67 There is a class of men . . . generally known by the name of Lobby members. **1869** *Overland Mo.* III. 63 He attended the California Legislature as a lobby member. — (4) **1865** *Three Yrs. Among Working Classes* 46 The one was a merchant of a pliable morality, and the other a notorious lobby operator.

Also *lobby force, interest, roster, system, tribe,* etc.

As the last term in **farm, railroad, senate lobby.**

lobby ˈlɑbɪ, *v.* [f. the noun.] *tr.* To solicit (a legislative body) in the lobby or elsewhere; to promote or secure (legislative action) by such means; to exert pressure on legislators in behalf of (something). Also *intr.*

*a*1848 *N.Y. Tribune* (B.), There is a quarrel in Philadelphia about Mr. W——'s appointments. Some of the Loco-focos have come out to lobby against him. **1849** LYELL *Second Visit* II. 28 A disappointed place-hunter . . . had been lobbying the Houses of Legislature. **1947** *Life* 13 Jan. 80/2 He left his farm and lobbied single-handed against reckless railroad operations.

Also with *through.*

1888 *Nation* 31 May 448/1 Leave Congress to launch upon the country whatever vagaries or political jobs may be lobbied through that body. **1949** *Time* 7 March 65/1 Bing lobbied through a state law banning the publication of such odds.

Hence **lobbying,** *n.*

1832 in MACKENZIE *Van Buren* (1846) 237 Perhaps I shall have a case of congressional lobbying, by which I can make it a jaunt of pleasure and profit. **1947** *Chi. Tribune* 21 July 1/3 New Dealers rejoiced in the victory as a triumph in lobbying.

lobbyer ˈlɑbɪɚ, *n.* [f. **lobby,** *v.*] =**lobbyist.** — **1841** BUCKINGHAM *America* II. 96 In one of these instances, the parties employing a Mr. Hillyer, of New-York, as a 'lobbier,' to promote the passing of a bill through the Trenton legislature . . . refused to pay him. **1882** WHITMAN *Spec. Days* 259 The members . . . were . . . lobbyers.

lobbyist ˈlɑbɪˌɪst, *n.* [f. **lobby,** *v.*] One who frequents the lobby of a legislative chamber in order to influence legislative action. Cf. **railroad lobbyist.** — **1863** *Cornhill Mag.* Jan. 96 There [was] a Representative listening to a lobbyist. **1949** *News-Herald* (Marshfield, Wis.) 19 July 4/2 Among the lobbyists and special pleaders were highly placed Democrats who claimed to have the ear of the President.

***loblolly,** *n.*

1. A miry puddle or mudhole (see also quot. 1946). *Colloq.*

1865 *Memphis* (Tenn.) *D. Argus* 19 Nov. 3/1 We noticed a party of two or three men attempting to clean off one of them, at the intersection of Main and Adams, but as fast as they cleaned away the lob-lolly, the lob-lolly rolled back again. **1899** ADE *Doc' Horne* 6 In those days a mud-hole with this deceptive dry crust on top was called a 'loblolly.' **1946** *Atlanta Jrnl. Mag.* 3 March 9/4 So is the word loblolly, which describes a semi-liquid state, a good word. The word itself shakes in pronunciation like jelly, which is most nearly what it describes.

2. loblolly bay, a small evergreen ornamental tree, *Gordonia lasianthus*, of the South. Also a marshy area in which this grows. Cf. **tan bay.**

*c*1730 CATESBY *Carolina* I. 44 The Loblolly-Bay . . . grows in Carolina; but not in any of the more Northern Colonies. **1766** J. BARTRAM *Journal* 24 Jan., After we rowed higher up we saw narrow cypress-swamps, loblolly-bays, and some few oak hammocks. **1897** SUDWORTH *Arborescent Flora* 272 *Gordonia lasianthus.* . . . Loblolly Bay (N.C., S.C., Ga., Ala., Fla., Miss., La.).

3. loblolly pine, a long-leaved pine, *Pinus taeda*, that grows in swampy and sterile soils in the South, the wood of this. Also attrib. Cf. **black-slash pine.**

1760 *Ga. Gen. Ass. Acts* 219 Squared Timber . . . made of swamp or loblolly pine and Shipped or offered to Sale. **1905** *Forestry Bureau Bul.* No. 64, 7 This preservative treatment made it possible to utilize loblolly pine for cross-ties. **1947** *Newsweek* 24 Feb. 28/3 It's easy to recognize the wool-hat boy on the red clay roads and around the cotton fields and in the loblolly pine lands.

lobo ˈlobo, *n. W.* [Sp., wolf.] The gray or timber wolf. In full **lobo wolf.**

1854 MARCY *Explor. Red River* 186 Large Lobos wolf. Above Cross-Timbers. **1856** WHIPPLE *Explor. Ry. Route* I. 101 Wolves (coyotes and lobos) are also numerous, and live by preying upon their weaker neighbors. **1945** *Everybody's Digest* Aug. 85 Youthful and 'lively as a lobo with a knot in his tail.'

transf. **1903** O. HENRY *Heart of West* 220 I'm not one of them lobo wolves . . . who are always blaming on women the calamities of life. **1928** STANSBERY *Passing of 3D Ranch* 31 It was his night to howl and any loboes from up the creek could not run a dance down there.

b. lobo stripe, (see quot.). Cf. **line back.**

1944 ADAMS *W. Words* 92 Lobo stripe. The white, yellow, or brown stripe running down the back from neck to tail, of a line-back animal, a characteristic of many Spanish cattle.

***lobster,** *n.*

1. *attrib.* Of or pertaining to newspaper workers who go on duty after the morning paper has gone to press and remain until the day staff comes.

1930 *N.Y. Telegram* 3 May 1/4 Munday was the 'lobster trick' reporter at Police Headquarters for the Evening World. [**1947** *Chi. Sun* 25 Nov. 3/4 Chicago Typographical Union No. 16, in meeting assembled Sunday, Nov. 23, 1947, adopted a wage scale of . . . $106 per week nights and lobster.] **1949** *Sat. Ev. Post* 2 April 34/2 It was six o'clock of a June morning in 1937 when the lobster editor of the New York World-Telegram called Murray Davis.

2. ***lobster('s) tail,** a gastropod, esp. a chiton.

*a*1884 in GOODE *Fisheries* I. 701 These shells have been called by different names, . . . such as 'Rattle-snake's Tail,' 'Lobster's Tail,' 'Sea-bug,' and 'Sea-caterpillar.' **1911** *Rep. Fisheries 1908* 315/2 Sea snails (*Gasteropoda*) . . . are found on all our coasts, and are known as . . . 'wood-lice,' 'lobster tails,' 'sea-bugs,' etc.

***local,** *a.* and *n.*

1. A news item of interest chiefly to those living in the place where the paper is published.

*a*1869 W. CARLETON *Farm Ballads* 83 So long as the paper was crowded with 'locals' containing their names. **1885** E. W. HOWE *Mytery of Locks* 142 John Bill was so situated that he did little else than write paid locals. **1949** *Sat. Ev. Post* 30 April 43/3 By the time she was fifteen the Paddleford girl was writing locals for the Manhattan, Kansas, Daily Chronicle.

b. =local editor.

1862 *Dly. Richmond* (Va.) *Enquirer* 3 Feb. 3/4 The 'Local' departed for that city shortly before Christmas. **1866** *Harper's Mag.* Aug. 368/1 A good local must combine the loquacity of a magician with the impudence of the d——l. **1889** *Gallup* (N.M.) *Gleaner* 27 March 3/3 The modest *local* of the Democrat blushed more than the bride when he saw her in the diaphanous costume he describes.

2. A train that makes all the stops on its run.

1879 WEBSTER *Supp.* 1565/2 *Local,* . . . an accommodation railway train, which receives and deposits passengers and freight along the line of the road. **1948** *Chi. Tribune* 12 Dec. I. 9/1 One slow train a day left Chicago for Louisville, Ky., connecting at Monon, Ind., with an equally slow branch line local for Indianapolis.

transf. **1948** *N.Y. Times* 2 May X. 3/3 Transports will span the country with three or four stops and the smaller planes will make the crossings as 'locals.'

b. A passenger riding on such a train. Cf. **local passenger.**

1887 GEORGE *40 Yrs. on Rail* 35 Even when tickets began to creep into use, they were at first sold only to through passengers, while the 'locals' had to pay cash.

3. Postal matter bearing a local instead of an officially recognized post-office address.

1882 *U.S. Offic. Postal Guide* 681 Locals and nixes. Matter addressed to places which are not post offices is unmailable.

4. A local branch of a trade-union.

1888 *Nation* 3 May 356/3 The Knights of Labor have locals of engineers and firemen. **1949** *Newsweek* 18 April 29/1 The local announced . . . miners would refuse to work in the pits with him.

5. In combs.: (1) **local accommodation train,** =***local 2;** (2) **agent,** a local freight agent; (3) **column,** the column in a newspaper devoted to items of local news; (4) **editor,** on a newspaper, the editor of the local news; (5) **freight,** freight sent on a local railroad line, also the train carrying such freight; (6) **item,** =**local 1;** (7) **passenger,** =***local 2. b,** also attrib.; (8) **road,** a railroad serving towns in a limited area; (9) **room,** the reporters' room in a newspaper office; (10) **station,** a station at which local trains make a regular stop; (11) **ticket,** in an election, the list of candidates for office in a local unit of government; (12) **traffic,** the traffic on a local road or railroad.

(1) **1882** *Rep. Ala. R.R. Comm.* II. 35 There are two kinds . . . the through, and local accommodation trains. — (2) **1843** *Hunt's Merch. Mag.* VIII. 193 The freight must be paid to the way-conductor by the local agent forwarding the same. — (3) **1856** *Louisville Democrat* 10 July 3/2 What took place at the Fillmore meeting is thus briefly narrated in the local columns of the Star. **1862** *First Minnesota* (Berryville, Va.) 11 March 4/1 Our short residence in Berryville, and sudden absquatulation of the local editor, is our apology for the meager variety in the local column. — (4) **1862** [see prec.]. **1894** *U. of Chi. Wkly.* 18 Oct. 3/1 'Throw that box of cigarettes in the fire,' came from the local editor.

(5) **1881** *Rep. Ala. R.R. Comm.* I. 65 Earnings from local freight . . . $425,717.58. **1891** *Appeal-Avalanche* (Memphis) 27 April 1/1 The local freight picked him up. **1902** MACGOWAN *Last Word* 11 The 'local freight' . . . pulled up at the station. — (6) **1864** *Gold Hill* (Nev.) *News* 14 April 5/2 Dan de Quille hath made the price of hay, and pack-trains of mules and Washoe city an inexhaustible theme for local items. **1923** ADAMS *Pioneer Hist.* 524 Of course politics was discussed column length and the industrial matters in 'local items,' but one gets the picture of the past, nevertheless. — (7) **1846** *Hunt's Merch. Mag.* XV. 240 The local passenger fare was fixed at three cents per mile. **1881** *Rep. Ala. R.R. Comm.* I. 64 Earnings from local passengers . . . $273,900-00. — (8) **1852** *De Bow's Review* XII. 203 Short and local roads are everywhere . . . of very doubtful success. **1866** *Comm. & Fin. Chron.* III. 71/1 This is almost entirely a local road, having no branches or connections, except at the eastern end. — (9) **1890** DAVIS *Gallegher* 7 We were all talking about it one night . . . in the local room. **1948** *Chi. Tribune* IV. 18 Jan. 2/3 When you see a newshound bent over his typewriter after hours oblivious to the usual banter that goes on in a local room after presstime, you can wager that he is writing stories on his own.

(10) **1891** *N.Y. Bd. Rapid Transit R.R. Comm. Rep.* 60, I also wish to commend the proposal . . . to locate gradients on the approaches to local stations. — (11) **1912** NICHOLSON *Hoosier Chron.* 247, I tell them to . . . try to get good men on local tickets. — (12) **1891** *N.Y. Bd. Rapid Transit R.R. Comm. Rep.* 71 The double-deck system [of subway construction] favors the local traffic at the expense of the express.

***localize,** *v. intr.* To work on a newspaper as a reporter of local items. Also **localizer,** *n.* — **1872** *Newton Kansan* 22 Aug. 3/1 This quiet season . . . furnishes poor food for localizers. **1877** *Alta California* (S.F.) 13 May 1/2 Sam. Clemens, when localizing for the *Enterprise,* always had an account with the balance against him.

locate 'loket, *v.* [f. L. *locātus,* pp. of *locāre,* to place, or poss. a back formation f. *location.*]

1. *intr.* To take up one's residence or quarters, to settle.

1652 *Va. Mag. Hist. & Biog.* V. 35 Divers Indians from the Town of Oanancocke . . . [have] suffered us to locate upon their land. **1843** CARLTON *New Purchase* I. 100 Families having bought lands at the government price from Uncle Samuel, have actually *located* on it. **1874** R. GLISAN *Jrnl. Army Life* 481 Concluded to locate in the very midst of the Oregon forest. **1947** PRICE *Trails I Rode* 103, I was in a barber shop one day and told the barber I was going to San Diego to locate there.

b. Of a minister in a Methodistic church: To withdraw, usu. temporarily, from service. Also transf. Cf. **5.** below.

1846 *Indiana Mag. Hist.* XXIII. 268 Philip Gatch, who was a traveling preacher as early as 1774, . . . traveled four years, and then located. **1853** BALDWIN *Flush Times Ala.* 132 He had long felt a call to the law, and he now resolved to 'locate,' and apply himself to the duties of that . . . profession. **1859** *Ladies' Repository* XIV. 318/1 Becoming master of Hunter's Lodge, he locates! *a*1870 CHIPMAN *Notes on Bartlett* 251 *To Locate,* . . . to cease being itinerant: to leave the itinerancy. **1942** R. W. ALBRIGHT *Hist. Evangelical Church* 148 And it must also be remembered that many of those who located to care honorably for their families did so temporarily.

2. *tr.* To appoint the region or locality in which (a tract of land) is to be set apart; esp. to enter a claim to (a tract of land) by determining its exact location with reference to a survey, to take up (land).

1701 in *Mem. Hist. Soc. Pa.* (1840) Oct. 29 IV. I. 204 Lands, some of which are not located and some want Confirmation. **1764** COLDEN in *Colden P.* (1877) I. 399 It was concluded . . . that the most advantageous place for locating 100,000 acres both as to goodness of the soil & conveniency of transportation, would be on the East side of the waters, between Crown Point & Ticonderoga. **1897** HOUGH *Story of Cowboy* 125 The *hidalgo* was pretty sure to locate his grant upon the best water he could find. **1929** J. PARKER *Old Army* 135 They followed closely, taking up . . . and 'locating' the Indian lands thrown open for settlement.

b. To determine the exact location, and to enter a claim thereto, of a quantity of public land granted in (a land warrant or scrip).

1754 *Md. Archives* VI. 58 The method always followed here of Locating Land Warrants . . . has left the Land . . . [in] irregular small & incommodious Parcells. **1783** in *Travels Amer. Col.* 662 Mr. Jno. May desired me to give him any warrants I had to locate and he would locate it for me. **1863** *Mass. Statutes* clxvi, To locate . . . all the land scrip.

c. To make and file a claim of ownership to the mining rights of (a defined area of land). Usu. *to locate a claim.* Also transf.

1869 BROWNE *Adv. Apache Country* 485 Andrew Veatch, an enterprising explorer, . . . had discovered and located a claim called the 'Comet.' **1872** MCCLELLAN *Golden State* 246 The fortunate finder of a stranded whale generally 'locates' a 'claim' upon him. **1901** DUNCAN & SCOTT *Allen & Woodson Co., Kans.* 70 C. L. Colman located a claim joining Geneva on the northeast. **1949** *Tenn. Hist. Quart.* March 15 Robertson was to survey and locate the claims; as compensation he received one fourth of the lands.

d. To obtain ownership of (springs or streams) by filing claim to the land on which they are situated.

1883 RITCH *Illust. N. Mex.* 48 There are in many places small streams and springs, which supply water to large herds of stock. These are located under the homestead laws, or otherwise obtained, with a view to controlling the lands for miles around. **1885** *Santa Fe Wkly. New Mexican* 17 Sep. 4/4 These springs and the land adjacent were located under the homestead law some months ago.

3. To lay out or determine the line of (a road).

1739 in PARMENTER *Hist. Pelham, Mass.* (1898) 26 A Committee [was appointed] To see ye same [road] located in the most Suitable place. **1877** JOHNSON *Anderson Co., Kans.* 31 This was the first road located in the county. **1949** *Sierra Club Bul.* March 11/2 It seems unlikely that a road would be built through the area since the road to Big Pines and the Angeles Crest Road are adequate and better located.

4. To fix or establish (a town, school, tribe, etc.) in a place.

1786 CUTLER in *Life & Corr.* I. 190 Much attention ought to be paid in forming a good plan for locating the first settlements. **1821** DWIGHT *Travels* II. 485 These . . . agree, that the College should be located where the largest contributions were made. **1894** ROBLEY *Bourbon Co., Kans.* 5 About 1825 the government began locating the various tribes of the more nearly civilized Indians from the East and South on reservations. **1948** *Chi. Tribune* 5 Dec. I. 24/4 Charleston, like New York and Boston, had been located to be accessible to the sea and defensible on the land side.

5. In the ministry of Methodistic churches, to permit a minister to withdraw from active duty. Cf. **1. b.** above.

*a***1814** T. COKE in Southey *Wesley* (1820) II. 464 It is most lamentable to see so many of our able married preachers . . . become located merely for the want of support for their families. **1894** H. GARDENER *Unofficial Patriot* 46 He had asked the presiding elder to locate him as a married man for the next year since he was about to marry.

6. To ascertain or find out the exact location or place of (somebody or something).

1816 *N. Amer. Rev.* Sep. 359 To locate a *noise* and locate a *quotation* . . . are expressions that violate the rules of propriety and taste. **1902** WILSON *Spenders* 13 Locating old Peter Bines at this season of the year was a feat never lightly to be undertaken. **1949** *Pa. Mag. Hist.* Jan. 24, 1756 small print . . . 100 copies known to have been printed. None located.

7. *reflex.* To settle down or establish a place of residence. Also *passive*, to live or be established in a place.

Frequently *is located*, as in quot. 1826, has little more force than *is*.

1819 F. WRIGHT *Soc. & Manners in Amer.* (1821) 128 Of all European emigrants, the Dutch and the German invariably thrive the best, *locate* themselves, as the phrase is here, with wonderful sagacity. **1826** *Monthly Mag.* II. 149 He is now 'located' here [i.e., in N.Y.]. **1923** BLAISDELL *F. T. Comm.* 139 Some mills were uneconomically located, and others were technically inefficient. **1948** *Kankakee* (Ill.) *D. Jrnl.* 5 June 2/2 The farm is located a mile north of the village of Cullom.

located ˈloketɪd, *a.* [See note.]

The *OED* records a 1689 example, app. sporadic, of "located" as the opposite of "dislocated." Our use no doubt represents an independent formation from the verb.

1. Of land: Fixed, determined, or agreed upon as to location. Cf. ***locate**, *v.* **2.**

1764 in FRANKLIN *Writings* IV. (1906) 325 The located uncultivated Lands belonging to the Proprietaries shall not be assessed higher than the lowest Rate [etc.]. **1799** J. SMITH *Acct. Captivity* 121, I took a journey westward, in order to survey some located land I had on or near the Youhomany. **1832** WILLIAMSON *Maine* II. 287 To facilitate the meetings of '*proprieties*,' a law was passed giving them equal privileges, whether their lands were within or without a *located* township.

2. Of a Methodist minister, stationed permanently in a particular charge. Cf. **locate,** *v.* **1. b.**

1843 CARLTON *New Purchase* I. 68 Mr. Parsons, like most *located* and *permanent* pastors of a wooden country, received almost literally nothing for ecclesiastical services. **1874** EGGLESTON *Circuit Rider* 297 [He] was directed to the double-cabin of a located preacher.

***location,** *n.*

1. The locating or fixing of the bounds of a tract or area of land. Cf. **Indian scrip location.**

1718 *N.J. Archives* IV. 379 Lands . . . Scituate on ye same Passiak by an actual Survey or location before the date of that Agreemt. **1873** *Newton Kansan* 24 April 2/1 Would it not be well for our commissioners to look after the location of this township and county line just now?

b. Surveying or laying out (a road); establishing or fixing upon a suitable site for a college, town, etc.

1808 *Ann. 10th Congress* 1 Sess. II. 2746 They have completed the location, gradation, and marking of the route from Cumberland to . . . the Monongahela river. *a***1817** T. DWIGHT *Travels* II. 113 The object, which first demanded attention, was the location of the College. **1847** *Sci. Amer.* 13 Feb. 163/4 Charles B. Stewart has been appointed chief engineer of location and survey. **1881** AVERY *Hist. Ga.* 530 The location of the capital at Atlanta or Milledgeville was left to the people to decide by an election. **1948** *Sierra Club Bul.* Dec. 6/2 The Crocker Ridge location also should give fine views of the peaks of the northern Yosemite.

2. (See quot. 1909.) Used esp. of New Hampshire.

1792 BELKNAP *Hist. New-Hampshire* III. 14 The lines of towns and locations . . . in so small a draught could not be introduced without confusion. **1816** *N. Eng. Jrnl. Med. & Surgery* V. 324 The road from Lancaster passes through Jefferson, . . . Bretton woods and Nash and Sawyer's location, to the Notch of the mountains. **1909** WEBSTER, Location. A subdivision of a county, in some of the United States.

3. The situation or position, with respect to natural advantages, of a tract of land or a town site.

1804 C. B. BROWN tr. Volney *View* 76 Considering its location, we shall perceive that it chiefly prevails in the lower basin of these two rivers. **1872** *Ill. Dept. Agric. Trans.* 173 It is one of the most lonely locations in the State. **1919** HOUGH *Sagebrusher* 14 This is one of the best locations in the valley.

4. A tract or grant of land intended for occupancy by settlers. Also attrib.

1809 E. A. KENDALL *Travels* III. 173 *Location* is a modern term, for a tract of land, of which the limits are defined, and the property conveyed to a purchaser. The same thing was formerly called a *plantation.* **1820** A. HODGSON *Lett. from N. Amer.* (1824) II. 44 When an emigrant has chosen the township in which he wishes to settle, and has complied with the necessary formalities, he receives, by lot, a location-ticket for a particular hundred acres. **1871** *Harper's Mag.* Sep. 581 The files of the Land office, . . . show that, under this law of relief, five hundred and fifteen 'location certificates' were issued. **1898** *Mo. So. Dakotan* I. 14 There were made more than one hundred locations of 160 acres each. **1949** *10 Story Western* May 71/2 I'll get the location notices out of the pack saddles.

b. The land or area embraced in a claim, esp. a mining claim or the site of a proposed oil well. Also attrib.

1846 *Spirit of Times* 6 June 175/1 Everywhere there were trout, apparently; but there are some choice 'locations,' as the copper speculators say. **1880** *Cimarron News & Press* 26 Feb. 1/5 Location stake notices were treated with contempt. **1910** *Sat. Ev. Post* 13 Aug. 5/1 All persons purposing to jump or contest this claim are requested to leave with their location papers written instructions as to disposition of remains. **1945** *Greeley* (Colo.) *D. Tribune* 13 Aug. 3/8 The rig for the well has been dismantled at Bunker Hill, Wyo., and is being trucked to the location.

5. In the Methodist ministry, a pastoral charge.

1846 *Indiana Mag. Hist.* XXIII. 268 [Preachers'] locations are not mentioned on the *Minutes* until the next year.

6. A place or site for the carrying on of a business or enterprise.

1861 *Chi. Tribune* 19 July 1/8 Wanted—A Partner with a small cash capital, to take half interest in a light and profitable business in one of the best locations in the city. **1875** *Ib.* 8 July 3/4, I have a good stock of groceries and fixtures, but not a good location.

7. In moving pictures, a place not in the studio where a movie or part of a movie is "shot." Also attrib.

1914 *Scribner's Mag.* March 276/1 It was his duty . . . to pick out 'locations,' as are called the scenes and backgrounds of a moving-picture play. **1923** *Amer. Mag.* Oct. 104/2 A location manager must know where to find every imaginable kind of scenery. **1947** *Sierra*

Club Bul. July 5/1 This time the project will embody one of the mightiest location treks in Hollywood's history.

***locator,** *n.* One who locates anything, esp. land or a mining claim. Cf. **land locator.**

1784 FILSON *Kentucke* 38 Prior locators may have time and opportunity to enter a caveat. **1825** *Austin P.* (1924) II. 1016 The locaters have property that suits you. **1876** RAYMOND *8th Rep. Mines* 62 The former owners and locators have washed by hydraulic process and mined away the top or red gravel. **1947** CHALFANT *Gold, Guns, & Ghost Towns* 50 While the names of the original locators were undecipherable, 'Sheepherder' as the name of the claim was plain, and the same name was put on the new notice.

***lock,** *n.*

1. A heavy rail slanted as a prop against the "lock" or corner of a rail fence. *Rare.*

1887 TOURGEE *Button's Inn* 54 The drifts had hidden the fences, save . . . where the 'locks' and 'riders' rose above the rounded hillocks.

2. lock tender, a lock keeper.

1821 in *Amer. Sp.* XXI. (1946) 306/1 For erection of houses for collectors and lock-tenders . . . [$]1407.45. **1900** WINCHESTER *W. Castle* vii. 148 [He] controlled a section of the canal and the hiring and discharging of all the lock-tenders and the laborers who kept the waterway in repair.

As the last term in **bank, ear, foot, goat, gray, guard, iron, lift, patent, plume, rotary, rough, scalp, soap, steamboat, weigh lock.**

***lock,** *v.*

1. *tr.* To furnish or equip (a canal or stream) with a lock or locks.

1792 *Mass. H.S. Coll.* 1 Ser. I. 285 There is only twenty-three miles to cut and lock, in order to carry commerce by water. **1898** B. H. YOUNG *Jessamine Co., Ky.* 143 It is locked and dammed to the extreme limits of Jessamine county.

2. *intr.* Of the branches of cotton plants: To mingle or intertwine. *Colloq.*

1855 *Fla. Plant Rec.* 129 The cotton on the fresh Land is Locking between the Roes in places.

3. In combs.: (1) **lock box,** a box or boxlike receptacle that can be locked, esp. in a post office a mail box that may be rented; (2) **cock,** a cock which may be locked; (3) **down,** (see quot. 1905); (4) **mail,** (see quot.); (5) **seat,** the excavation on a river or a canal intended to contain a lock; (6) **tortoise,** =**box turtle.**

(1) **1872** CRAPSEY *Nether Side N.Y.* 150 Picking up the last number of a journal which they patronize, I casually light upon the advertisements of . . . a rural rascal who calls himself C. H. Chester, M.D., Lock Box 4, Reading, Pa. **1916** DU PUY *Uncle Sam* 229 The writer of these letters gave his address as a lock box. . . . More letters came . . . from a lock box. **1949** *Time* 28 March 22/1 It's still back there in those lock-boxes, at least $8 or $9 million of it. — (2) **1814** *Sporting Mag.* XVIII. 112 Beer . . . which stood in a corner of his front parlour, with a lock-cock to it. — (3) **1881** T. B. WALKER *Letter* 4 June, A string of logs as customarily made for rafting is when the logs are fastened together by means of poles and 'Lock Downs.' **1905** *Forestry Bureau Bul.* No. 61, 41 Lock down, a strip of tough wood with holes in the ends, which is laid across a raft of logs. Rafting pins are driven through the holes into the logs, thus holding the raft together. (N[orthern] F[orest].) — (4) **1894** SEARIGHT *Old Pike* 168 There was a 'Lock mail' in leather pouches, and a 'Canvass mail,' the latter very frequently called 'the second mail,' carried in alternate months by the respective lines.

(5) **1789** MORSE *Amer. Geog.* 363 The work is nearly completed; except sinking the lock-seats. **1794** WASHINGTON *Lett.* Writings (1892) XIII. 1 Mr. Western's opinion, respecting the lock-seats at the Great Falls of that river. — (6) **1842** *Nat. Hist. N.Y., Zoology* III. 25 The Common Box Tortoise, *Cistuda carolina*, . . . is designated . . . in the west by the name of *Lock Tortoise*.

Loco ˈloko, *n.*[1] Short for **Locofoco.** Also attrib. Now *hist.*

1838 QUITMAN in Claiborne *Life & Corr.* I. 165, I thus claim to be a true Loco and Nullifier. **1843** *Whig Almanac 1841* 42/2 The Loco Members held a jollification. **1848** *N.Y. Tribune* 4 March (B.), The South-western and Western Locos . . . will cave in. **1947** DOWNEY *Lusty Forefathers* 253 *Stuff and guff!* Let the Locos read their history.

loco ˈloko, *n.*[2] and *a. W.* [Sp., crazy.]

1. *n.* =**locoweed.**

1844 *St. Louis Reveille* 8 Dec. 2/4 He was girt about the neck with a leather bridle, and his meat was locos and wild onions. **1884** ALDRIDGE *Life on Ranch* 187 It is a curious fact respecting the loco that it has been more than once analysed by chemists in the Eastern States, and they have never been able to discover any poisonous qualities in the plant. **1937** *Range Plant Handbook* W41 A large number of plants, chiefly of the genera *Astragalus* and *Oxytropis*, have, at one time or another, been called loco, because of their poisonous effects on domestic animals. **1942** [see **locoism**].

b. A distemper resembling madness manifested by cattle that have eaten locoweed. Also attrib. and transf.

1890 *Stock Grower & Farmer* 15 March 6/2 Loco threatens to be worse than last year. Range overstocked. **1890** *Cent.* 3499/2 *Loco-disease*, . . . a disease of horses resulting from eating the loco-weed or crazy-weed. **1916** *Sunset* Jan. 29 Mrs. Vera Harkins . . . has obeyed the 'miner's loco' for thirty-three years in Colorado.

c. An injurious preparation made from locoweed or possessing the properties of this. *Slang.*

1897 LEWIS *Wolfville* 59 She once saws off a thimbleful of loco on a captain in some whiskey . . . an' he goes plumb crazy. **1907** WHITE *Arizona Nights* 141 They had seen that white quartz with the gold stickin' into it, and that's the same as a dose of loco to miner gents. **1928** *Dly. Ardmoreite* (Ardmore, Okla.) 16 March 4 Keep that big ugly pan o yore'n away from that bottled loco.

2. *a.* Crazy.

1887 *Outing* X. 7/1 You won't be able to do nuthin' with 'em, sir; they'll go plumb *loco*, that's what they will. **1911** *Chi. D. News* 16 Sep. 9/4 If you go loco y' won't mind livin' in New York. **1948** *Sat. Review* 28 Aug. 37/2 Why not wait until he and the boys could handle this loco puncher in their own way?

3. In combs.: (1) **loco country,** (see quot. and cf. **hoodoo land, voodoo land**); (2) **plant,** =**locoweed;** (3) **weed,** any one of various weeds, esp. of the genus *Astragalus*, the eating of which causes stock to act as if they were drugged or intoxicated, cf. **crazy weed.**

(1) **1912** LONDON *Smoke Bellew* 120 That's loco country you're bound for. The hoodoo's sure on it. — (2) **1884** *Amer. Naturalist* XVIII. 1148 Experiments . . . prove that *Crotalaria sagittalis*, the Rattle-box, is a 'loco-plant.' **1913** BARNES *Western Grazing Grounds* 256 The loco plant is found generally over the entire Rocky Mountain region. — (3) **1879** *Diseases of Swine* 211 The losses among cattle, caused by eating the poisonous loco weed, will perhaps not exceed 1 per cent. **1897** HOUGH *Story of Cowboy* 210 The animal has been eating the 'loco weed,' against which instinct gives it apparently no protection. **1948** *Miami* (Okla.) *News-Rec.* 30 June 8/2 Little is heard today of the once troublesome loco weed.

loco ˈloko, *v.* [f. the noun.] *tr.* To poison with a locoweed. Also **locoed,** *a.* Also transf.

1884 ALDRIDGE *Life on Ranch* 191 Cattle occasionally get locoed, but much more rarely than horses. **1897** LEWIS *Wolfville* 119 Wolfville intelligence is too well founded to let any law loco it or set it to millin'. **1912** *Out West* May 312/2 Darley has locoed a good many by his sperit round-ups, but he's flunked by the cow-punchers, you bet! **1938** G. BALCH *Tiger Roan* 229 You're locoed, man, plumb locoed.

locofoco ˌlokoˈfoko, *n.* [Origin uncertain. Bartlett (1859) thought *loco-* was suggested by *locomotive*, popularly thought to mean "self-moving"; *foco* is app. derived from It. *fuoco*, fire.]

1. A match or cigar capable of self-ignition. In full **locofoco match, cigar.** Now *hist.*

1835 *Vade Mecum* (Phila.) 31 Jan. 3/1 The last 'kick' in the way of luxury and convenience that has been announced to the world, is the invention, by a Mr. Marck, of New York, of the *loco-foco* or self-lighting segars. **1843** BRANDE *Dict. Science* 677/1 Lucifers (which in America are termed *locofocos*). **1859** BARTLETT 252 In 1834, John Marck opened a store in Park Row, New York, and drew public attention to two novelties. One was . . . a self-lighting cigar, with a match composition on the end. These he called *'Loco-foco'* cigars. **1944** *Chi. D. News* 8 May 10/1 The night that the Moore match monopoly boom fizzled out like an old-time sulphur 'locofoco,' the city's rich men gathered at the home of old Phil Armour.

2. (*cap.*) Orig. a member of the Locofoco or Equal Rights party, a faction of the Democratic party in New York State; later (*pl.*) applied to Democrats in general. Now *hist.* Cf. **Loco,** *n.*[1]

The explanation of the origin of the term given in quotation 1856 is the one currently accepted.

1835 *Nat. Intelligencer* 9 Nov. 3/2 The *Agrarians*, the *Loco Focos*, and the *Ragamuffins*, are . . . the same people with whom they were . . . *glove* and *hand*—last year. **1856** *Spirit of Age* (Sacramento) 23 Oct. 4/1 The term 'Loco-foco,' a nickname given by the Whigs to the Democrats, originated from the fact of one section of Democrats, who, hearing of a plot to put the lights out at a Democratic meeting, held in Tammany Hall, 22nd October 1835, brought stores of loco-foco matches in their pockets, by which light was restored, and the scheme baffled. Putting their leader in the chair, the bearers of the loco-foco matches adopted an equal rights testimonial, and passed sundry resolutions against banks and paper money. The term Locofoco was applied to them by the opposing section. **1898** N. BROOKS *Boys of Fairport* 211 In those days there were only two large parties in the whole country—Whigs and Democrats. The latter was stigmatized as Loco-Focos. **1947** DOWNEY *Lusty Forefathers* 252 Many of the campaign log cabins, the Locofocos charged, were rum holes.

b. In combs. of obvious meaning, as (1) **Locofoco administration,** (2) **candidate,** (3) **luminary,** (4) **party.**

(1) **1841** *Louisville Journal* 31 May 1/1 Some of the supporters of the Locofoco Administration charged the present most tolerant Administration with 'horrible proscription.' — (2) **1852** *S.F. Bugle* 17 Sep. 2/2 One of the locofoco candidates for a State office called on one of the democratic bolters from the Benicia nominees. — (3) **1838** IRVING in P. M. Irving *Life W. Irving* III. (1863) 120 Those locofoco luminaries who of late have been urging strong and sweeping measures. — (4) **1844** *Henry Clay Bugle* (Maysville, Ky.) 11 April 3/4, I cooperated with the Loco Foco party under the delusion that it adhered or intended to adhere faithfully to the good old Democratic faith. **1892** WALSH *Lit. Curiosities* 654 The *Courier and Enquirer*, the Whig-paper, immediately nicknamed the Anti-Monopolists the Locofoco party. The faction thus nicknamed ultimately became dominant in the Democratic party in the State of New York.

Also *Locofoco doctrine, Excellency, -like, pow-wow, ticket, ward meeting*, etc.

c. Used also in now obs. derivatives, as **locofocodom, locofocoish, locofocoism, locofocracy.**

1846 *Quincy* (Ill.) *Whig* 21 March 2/5 He thinks the worst possible thing Congress could have, is a Chaplain, as prayers are totally out of place in Loco-focodom, which party always say their prayers backward. **1856** *Western Citizen* (Paris, Ky.) 19 Sep. 3/2 All Locofocodom ... seems in a flurry at this time about the State of Kentucky. — **1848** *Field Piece* (Chi.) 6 Sep. 4/4 They are very Locofocoish to be sure. **1857** BUNGAY *Off-Hand* 130 In personal appearance, he is a tall, spare man, with a 'locofocoish' look, somewhat round-shouldered, and stoops a little when he walks, as though he had to bear upon his back the responsibility of the party he lately rejuvenated. — **1838** *N.Y. Advertiser & Exp.* 17 Jan. 2/1 Loco Focoism, make the best of it, is Agrarianism, Fanny Wrightism, Equality of all races, colors, breeds, and tribes. **1855** *Herald of Freedom* 23 June 1/8 The South, allied with Locofocoism, has been the most despotic tyrant ever known in this country. — **1840** *Niles' Reg.* 26 Sep. 56/3 Every one present must have had a feeling of pity for the Ajax of locofocracy in Ohio [Senator Allen].

locofoco ˌloko'foko, *a.* [f. the noun.] Imbued with the principles of the Locofoco or Equal Rights party. *Obs.*

1837 HONE *Diary* I. 266–7 The President's message is loco-foco to the very core. **1838** *N.Y. Advertiser & Exp.* 6 Jan. 4/1 There was ... a company somewhat less Loco Foco, Slamm, Bang-ish than was usual with the Ex-President. **1846** CORCORAN *Pickings* 61 The coat of a third, he being half whig and half locofoco, had divided, and was split up the back center seam to the collar.

locoism 'lokoˌɪzəm, *n.* (See quot. 1909.)

1909 *Cent. Supp.* 742/1 locoism. ... A disease of cattle in the semi-arid region of the Western United States, due to eating certain weeds known as loco-weeds, and characterized by peculiar nervous symptoms which are followed by paralysis, emaciation, and finally death. **1937** *Range Plant Handbook* W36 A considerable number of species in the large *Astragalus* genus are recognized as poisonous to livestock; those which cause locoism are known as locos. **1942** *Stand. Plant Names* 30/3 The species [of Astragalus] causing locoism are called Loco.

locomobile 'lokəməˌbil, *n.* [App. f. F. *locomobile*, a portable steam engine.]

1. ?A portable steam engine. *Rare.*

1896 SCHLICH *Man. Forestry* V. 748 The elevator and macerating cylinder are driven by a locomobile *m*.

2. (*cap.*) The trade-mark name of an automobile of a particular make.

1900 *Sci. Amer.* 27 Jan. 54/1 The steam carriage which is popularly and commercially known as the 'Locomobile.' **1919** LEWIS *Free Air* 361 She didn't take the limousine, but merely the seven-passenger Locomobile with the special body. **1948** MENJOU & MUSSELMAN *It Took 9 Tailors* 42 One day a big Locomobile pulled up in front of our place.

b. Hence **locomobling,** automobiling. *Obs.*

1900 *N.Y. Journal* 11 Nov. 28/1 Perhaps the most popular fad of the week was 'bubbling.' This you know is the fashionable slang for automobling or locomobling or whatever you choose to call it.

locomote ˌlokə'mot, *v.* [Back formation f. *locomotive.*] To go or proceed. *Slang. Obs.* — **1834** *Knickerb.* IV. 20 Who but our author would represent him [a bard], 'locomoting' on a long, dog-trot over the bogs of his neighborhood? **1860** *Harper's Mag.* March 566/2 [Their] attention was attracted to the parson by his peculiar style of locomoting (being partially paralysed).

locomotive,** *n.* In combs.: (1) **locomotive cab,** =cab;** (2) **clause,** (see quot.), *obs.;* (3) **depot,** a passenger depot, *rare;* (4) **engineer,** =**engineer,** *n.;* (5) **runner,** =prec., *obs.;* (6) **yam,** a long, knotty yam potato, *rare.*

(1) **1940** *Quiz* [Quest.] 354 When was the locomotive cab introduced? — (2) **1880** *Bradstreet's* 20 Nov. 1/3 Wild-cat companies ... had both a locomotive and an india-rubber clause in their charters, permitting them at pleasure to change the character of their risks as well as their headquarters. — (3) **1841** STEELE *Summer Journey* 25 Two fine horses ... dragged us out of the barn into open day—up through the square, over the hill, to the Locomotive Depot. — (4) **1843** *Hunt's Merch. Mag.* IX. 480 Daniel Mathews, chief locomotive-engineer, receives a salary of $1,200 per annum. **1890** M. N. FORNEY in *Railways Amer.* 134 Locomotive engineers and firemen.

(5) **1890** M. N. FORNEY in *Railways Amer.* 137 Locomotive runners and firemen. — (6) **1864** *Wilkes' Spirit of Times* 10 Dec. 227/3 His arms and legs were unduly bloated at irregular intervals, giving them the appearance of locomotive yams.

As the last term in **Atlantic type, electric, horse, logging, mountain, pole locomotive.**

***locust,** *n.*

1. Any one of various North American trees or species of trees of the genus *Robinia*, as the black locust, *R. pseudoacacia;* also the honey locust, *Gleditsia triacanthos.* Cf. **squeak-bean.**

[**1640** PARKINSON *Theater of Plants* 1552 The second [of the trees] is called Locus by our Nation resident in *Virginia.*] **1670** DENTON *Brief Descr. N.Y.* 13 There grows black Walnut and Locust, as their doth in *Virginia.* **1671** ALVORD & BIDGOOD *Trans-Allegheny Region* 192 Weeds and small prickly locusts and Thistles [grew] to a very great height. **1709** LAWSON *Carolina* 49 Our whole Company ... set out from the Sapona-Indian Town, after having seen some of the Locust, ... the same Sort that bears Honey. **1835** *Vade Mecum* (Phila.) 18 April 3/3 A great deal of the locust is also raised in Tennessee, and the west generally. **1947** *Democrat* 25 Sep. 4/2 Here it is for what it's worth: pine, oak, ... wild cherry and locust.

attrib. **1700** *Md. Hist. Mag.* XIX. 352, 120 acr. Sur[veyed] ... on the west side of Delph Creek at a Locust Stump. **1718** *Ib.* VI. 347 Thomas Williams brought in his Accts. for ... setting up & painting four new Locust Posts & a new Locust Sill. **1888** DELAND *J. Ward* 18 A spring bubbled out of the hillside, and ran singing through a hollowed locust log. **1904** STRATTON-PORTER *Freckles* 47 He climbed on the locust-post and ... held a finger in the line of the moth's advance up the twig. **1949** *Sky Line Trail* March 17/1 Raise your wretched self from beneath that locust tree and attend to the General.

b. A policeman's club made of locust wood. Also transf. *Colloq.*

1865 SALA *Diary* II. 211 The New York policeman wears a handsome uniform. At his side hangs a club or bludgeon. ... This club is made of 'locust wood,' ... and by rowdies the policeman is often generically called (with the addition of a frightful expletive) a 'locust.' **1904** *N.Y. Tribune* 19 June 4 The policemen did not carry their 'locusts.'

2. The migratory Rocky Mountain grasshopper, *Melanoplus spretus.*

1823 FAUX *Memorable Days* 137 Grasshoppers, so called, but in fact a species of locust about the length of my little finger, swarm in countless millions. **1893** *Harper's Mag.* April 711/2 A succession of droughts and hot winds ... were re-enforced by swarms of locusts, which descended from the torrid mesas of New Mexico and the sterile Piedmont of Colorado and Wyoming. **1949** *L.A. Times* 6 July 19/5 The present horde, only known migratory band of locusts in the United States, will begin laying eggs within the next few days.

3. In special combs.: (1) **locust borer,** the locust beetle, *Cyllene robiniae*, the larvae of which bore into the wood of the locust tree; (2) **bush,** (see quot.); (3) **killer,** ?the *Stizus speciosus*, (see quot.); (4) **tree,** a tree belonging to one of several species of American locust; (5) **treenail,** a treenail made from locust wood; (6) **year,** a year when seventeen-year locusts are prevalent.

(1) **1839** *Mass. Agric. Survey 2d Rep.* 100 Locust-Borer.—Allen C. Metcalf of Lenox, washed his locust trees with spirits of turpentine, and in that way ... compelled the borer to leave them. **1930** MATTOON *Forest Trees Okla.* 83 It is severely attacked by the locust borer which has destroyed large numbers of the trees. — (2) **1834** A. PIKE *Sketches* 56 The valley ... was full of ... mesquito [*sic*] bushes, that is, a kind of prickly, green locust bush, which bears long narrow beans in bunches. — (3) **1868** *Amer. Naturalist* June 217 The Locust Killer. ... The 'killer' had seized one of our August locusts, and was endeavoring to rise from the ground with it. — (4) **1640** PARKINSON *Theater of Plants* 1550 The *Virginian* Locus tree ... hath

beene sent and brought us out of *Virginia*. **1792** *N.Y. State Soc. Arts* I. 26 The locust-tree (*Robinia Pseudacacia*) is one of the most valuable trees now cultivated. . . . Their greatest use is for ship-trunnels, fence-posts, mill-cogs and fire-wood. **1948** WESTON *Mother Lode* 124 Locust trees draped their fragrant blossoms over the little store in springtime like a lacy mantilla.

(5) **1797** *Ann. 4th Congress* 2 Sess. 2791, 1,200 locust trennails, of 36 inches [were sold]. — **(6) 1778** CARVER *Travels* 494 The years when they [locusts] thus arrive are denominated the locust years. **1931** *Randolph Enterprise* (Elkins, W.Va.) 16 April 4/3 This is 'Locust Year' and next month the locust will be here in full force.

As the last term in **bastard, black, blue, clammy, differential, dog day, honey, hoofed, pea, red, red-thighed, Rocky mountain, rose-flowering, seven-year, seventeen-year, sweet, thirteen-year, water, white, yellow locust.**

***lode,** *n.* In combs.: (1) **lode claim,** a mining claim to an area where the mineral occurs in lodes or veins; (2) **mining,** the taking out of ore that occurs in lodes, also attrib.; (3) ***stone,** (see quot.), *colloq.*, cf. **madstone.**

(1) 1874 RAYMOND *Statist. Mines & Mining* 365 Brown's Gulch . . . contains the following lode claims. **1935** *Rocky Mt. News* (Denver) 1 Jan. 17 There were numerous minor scale operations by owners of lode and placer claims. — **(2) 1874** RAYMOND *Statist. Mines & Mining* 363 Concerning the lode-mining interest of the county there is but little to report. **1945** *Gunnison* (Colo.) *Courier* 26 July 2/4 Gunnison County was the purchaser of . . . Bullion King, lode mining claim, . . . situate in the Ruby Mining District. — **(3) 1938** MATSCHAT *Suwannee River* 89 A lodestone from a deer (a hard substance sometimes found in a deer) . . . gives the power to produce twins at will.

As the last term in **blind, mother, pay lode.**

***lodge,** *n.*

1. An Indian lodge. Also transf.

1804 ORDWAY in *Jrnls. Lewis & O.* 172 They had a place fixed across their green from the head chiefs house across abt 50 yds to the 2 chiefs lodge. **1835** SIMMS *Yemassee* I. 71 Ishiagaska has looked upon the white chief in the great lodge of his Spanish brother. **1948** *N.W. Ohio Quart.* Jan. 42 The scalps of our enemies are drying in our lodges.

b. Often used in an inclusive sense with reference to the size of an Indian population, village, party, etc.

1804 CLARK in *Lewis & C. Exped.* (1904) I. 92 His party was Small Consisting only of about 20 Lodges. **1855** *N.Y. Wkly. Tribune* 6 Oct. 2/5 A band of forty or fifty Brule lodges were encamped on Blue Water Creek. **1901** DUNCAN & SCOTT *Allen & Woodson Co., Kans.* 9 They found about four hundred lodges of Osage Indians encamped in the timber. **1947** DEVOTO *Across Wide Missouri* 305 A village of Bannocks, sixty lodges, came up and camped three miles away.

2. In combs.: (1) **lodge mound,** the site of a former Indian lodge, *obs.*; (2) **pole,** see as a main entry; (3) **trail,** =**lodgepole trail.**

(1) 1898 *Mo. So. Dakotan* Nov. 112/2 Away from the village, there are many isolated lodge mounds scattered throughout the valley for several miles in either direction. — **(3) 1845** FRÉMONT *Exped.* 114 We resumed our journey . . . following an extremely good lodge-trail. **1855** *So. Dak. Hist. Coll.* I. 391 A reconnaissance made from Chantier River to the Cheyenne, a distance by the road we took (a lodge trail) of forty miles.

b. In combs. of obvious meaning, as (1) **lodge cloth,** (2) **cover,** (3) **covering,** (4) **fire,** (5) **frame,** (6) **skin,** (7) **timber.**

(1) 1871 *Rep. Indian Affairs* (1872) 526 The article of duck or lodge-cloth among the Indian annuities was the source of universal rejoicing. — **(2) 1878** BEADLE *Western Wilds* 137 [Buffaloes] furnished them with food, clothing, lodge-covers, bow-strings, and a dozen other conveniences. — **(3) 1847** PARKMAN in *Knickerb.* XXX. 234 The squaws of each lazy warrior had made him a shelter . . . by stretching . . . the corner of a lodge-covering upon poles. — **(4) 1837** IRVING *Bonneville* I. 111 Knots of gamblers will assemble before one of their lodge fires, early in the evening. **1889** *Cent. Mag.* Jan. 334/1 Cheyenne Indians . . . were well versed in that tribal legend which is rehearsed by the lodge fire in the long winter nights.

(5) **1852** MARCY *Explor. Red River* (1854) 78 It is only two years since they removed from here, and their lodge frames are still standing. — **(6) 1826** in M. S. SULLIVAN *Travels J. Smith* (1934) 4 They [Indian lodges] do not smoke except from a sudden change of wind and then no longer than it takes a squaw to spread a smoke wing of the Lodge skin . . . to the windward of the aperture at the top. **1891** *Cent. Mag.* March. 776/2 We had already devoured our moccasin soles, and a small sack made of smoked lodge skin. — **(7) 1805** ORDWAY in *Jrnls. Lewis & O.* 179 The Squaws from the 1st village are cutting their lodge timber on the opposite side of the River from the Fort.

As the last term in **bark, beaver, big, birchbark, blue, brush, canvas, cow, dirt, grass, Hunters', hunting, Indian, medicine, pony, prayer, skin, soldier's, sweat, sweating, trading lodge.**

lodgepole ˈlɑdʒˌpol, *n.*

1. *W.* A pole used by Indians in erecting a lodge.

1805 LEWIS in *L. & Clark Exped.* II. (1904) 88 Found a new indian lodge pole today which had been brought down by the stream. **1878** HART *Sazerac Lying Club* 126 Slung at the sides of the animals, with one end trailing on the ground, were the lodge-poles. **1946** FOREMAN *Last Trek* 242 They pulled down the lodges of three of their villages and sold the lodgepoles and lumber.

2. In combs.: (1) **lodgepole pine,** a western tree, *Pinus murrayana*, or one of a similar species; (2) **trail,** (see quots. 1860, 1876), *obs.*; (3) **vehicle,** a travois *q.v.*, *rare.*

(1) 1859 G. A. JACKSON *Diary* (MS) 4 Cut the top off a small lodge pole pine. **1905** *N.Y. Ev. Post* 29 April, The lodgepole pine, which is known in the Sierras of California as tamarack pine, and in Colorado and Montana is sometimes called white pine, . . . bears the common name of 'lodgepole' from the fact that the Indians used its long slender trunks as supports for their wigwams or lodges. **1949** *Sierra Club Bul.* June 6 Lodgepole pines, singing birds and scampering chipmunks, . . . and white, dancing water—all familiar elements of the mountain scenes—pass slowly behind and below the travelers. — **(2) 1848** RUXTON *Adventures* 241, I followed a very good lodge pole-trail. **1860** GREELEY *Overland Journey* 121 The Arapahoes say that a good 'lodge-pole trail'—that is, one which a pony may traverse with one end of the lodge-poles on his back, the other trailing behind him—exists from this point to the open prairie. **1876** DODGE *Black Hills* 137 There is not one single tepee or lodge-pole trail, from side to side of the Hills, in any direction, and these poles, when dragged in the usual way by ponies, soon make a trail as difficult to obliterate as a wagon road, visible for many years, even though not used. — **(3) 1851** WM. KELLY *Across Rocky Mts.* 139 Our cortege was an imposing one, for the Snakes packed up and accompanied us with their horses, and dogs drawing their lodge-pole vehicles.

lodgepoling ˈlɑdʒˌpolɪŋ, *n.* Among Indians, a sound thrashing or drubbing, as if with a lodgepole. *Obs.* or *hist.*

1848 RUXTON in *Blackw. Mag.* LXIV. 139 Nor are they [*sc.* squaws] so schooled to perfect obedience to their lords and masters as to stand a 'lodge poleing.' **1860** GARRARD *Wah-To-Yah* x. 131 She receives at the hands of her imperious sovereign a severe drubbing . . . or no very light lodgepoling. [**1947** DEVOTO *Across Wide Missouri* 101, I lodgepoled her at Colter's Creek and made her quit.]

***lodging,** *n.* **1. lodging car,** (see first quot.). Cf. **dormitory car. 2. lodging hall,** a lodging house.

(1) 1890 *Cent.* 3502/2 *Lodging-car*, . . . on a railroad, a car fitted with bunks, used as a sleeping- or dwelling-place for employees. (U.S.) **1890** *Railways of Amer.* 146 It would require a separate article to give even a brief description of the different kinds of cars which are now used. . . . Hotel-car, Inspection-car, Lodging-car. — **(2) 1860** HOLLAND *Miss Gilbert's Career* xii. 208 We left Arthur Blague . . . sitting on his bed in the lodging-hall at Huckleberry run. *Ib.* xvi. 293 Cheek was . . . led to the trunk-room of the lodging-hall.

***loft,** *n.* As the last term in **fodder, rigging loft.**

***log,** *n.*

1. (See quots.)

1875 KNIGHT 1348/1 *Log* . . . (Steam-engine.) A tabulated summary of the performance of the engines and boilers, and of the consumption of coals, tallow, oil, and other engineers' stores on board a steam-vessel. **1876** INGRAM *Centennial Exp.* 351 'Logs' . . . exhibit complete diagrams of the height and fluctuations of the steam within the boiler.

2. Denoting habitations made of logs: (1) **log cabin,** see as a main entry, (2) **dwelling,** (3) **home,** (4) **hotel,** (5) **house,** see as a main entry, (6) **hut,** (7) **inn,** (8) **pen,** see as a main entry, (9) **shack,** (10) **shanty,** (11) **tenement,** (12) **tent.**

(2) [**1794** *N.C. Morav. Rec.* VI. (1943) 2522 A log dwelling house was laid up at the mill.] **1835** HOFFMAN *Winter in West* II. 38 Descending another ravine [we] were comfortably housed . . . in the log dwelling of a miner. **1885** *Harper's Mag.* June 73/2 It looked down upon a . . . score or two of log dwellings. — **(3) 1944** LANKS *Alaska* 19 The original frame and log homes and the few business houses were almost lost among the new building operations. — **(4) 1880** INGHAM *Digging Gold* 342 Some poor fellows were tired out and sick, and compelled to lay by at our log hotel from this cause.

(6) [**1781** CHASTELLUX *Voyage de Newport* 146 Je trouvai dans ces bois de nouveaux *improvements* & plusieurs *lug-hutts*.] **1792** in *Amer. Museum* XI. 15 A new emigrant . . . (generally builds) a little log hut. **1947** DOWNEY *Lusty Forefathers* 165 The billet assigned me was a small log-hut of only two rooms. — **(7) 1836** E. L. WILLSON *Journey N.J. to Ohio* (1929) 25 We put up at a log inn [in Ohio]. — **(9) 1941** STUART *Men of Mts.* 35 Soon I saw the log-shack under the oaks

where Roosevelt Reffitt lived. **1949** *Nat. Geog. Mag.* June 802 (*legend*), [They] sit on the stoop of their log shack, its chinks calked with moss.

(**10**) [**1835** see **4.** (1) below]. **1907** Lillibridge *Trail* 7 She turned toward the rough log shanty unemotionally. — (**11**) **1829** Cooper *Wish-ton-Wish* xxii, The log-tenement, the stacks, and the out-buildings of Reuben Ring . . . were sending forth clouds of murky smoke. — (**12**) **1746** in Shurtleff *Log Cabin* (1939) 73 Some of the People were employed in cutting Fire-wood, others in building Log-Tents. This is a Contrivance borrowed, as I suppose, from the Natives. **1774** in *Pub. Champlain Soc.* XXI. 125 Dark cloudy Weather with a little Rain the Carper and People Empd adding 16 feet more to the Loggtent for Part of the People to live in. **1939** Shurtleff *Log Cabin* 73 This agrees with the Jesuit fathers' description. Log tents, still used as temporary shelters in the north woods, are of much simpler construction than log cabins.

b. Denoting buildings of other types made of logs: (1) **log barn,** (2) **chapel,** (3) **church,** (4) **corncrib,** (5) **courthouse,** (6) **crib,** see **4.** (3) (*a*) below, (7) **kitchen,** (8) **meetinghouse,** (9) **schoolhouse,** (10) **stable,** (11) **store,** (12) **tavern,** (13) **warehouse.**

(**1**) **1795** *Pittsburgh Gaz.* 6 June 1/2 To be Sold at Private Sale . . . two cabins, a log barn, 80 bearing apple trees [etc.]. **1836** in *West. Pa. Hist. Mag.* XVI. 290 The buildings . . . consist of . . . a large log barn and 6 or 7 other log buildings. **1948** *Time* 11 Oct. 21/1 Autumn [was] . . . the season which somehow best suited a country which still remembered Indians, wild turkeys, log barns and the long, westward crawling of wagon trains. — (**2**) **1810** F. Asbury *Jrnl.* (1821) III. 298 Saturday, at William Adams's log-chapel I preached to a small assembly. — (**3**) **1847** Parkman in *Knickerb.* XXIX. 313 We found the log-church and school-houses belonging to the Methodist Shawanoe Mission. **1895** M. A. Jackson *Memoirs* 382 The little log church is so full that the men were said to be packed like herrings in a barrel. — (**4**) **1847** Howe *Ohio* 240 Seventy or eighty feet of the enclosure was composed of a row of log corn cribs.

(**5**) **1798** Allen *Hist. Vermont* 22 A log Court House and Goal were erected at the latter place. **1885** *Harper's Mag.* June 73/2 It looked down upon a log court-house. — (**7**) **1874** Eggleston *Circuit Rider* 56 The wide old log-kitchen, with its loom in one corner. **1948** *Fla. Hist. Quart.* July 40 Close to many of the larger houses were log kitchens where cooking and eating took place. — (**8**) **1823** *Baptist Mag.* IV. 74 We have a good log meeting house on Salt Creek. **1844** Lee & Frost *Oregon* xxi. 249 This was the roof he finished during the summer, besides helping . . . in laying up a log meeting-house. — (**9**) **1869** Tourgee *Toinette* xiii. 154 She had managed to pick up . . . 'a tolerable English education,' . . . from one of the log school-houses. **1947** *Dly. Ardmoreite* (Ardmore, Okla.) 27 July 9/4 I . . . went to school at Iron Top school house when it was a log school-house.

(**10**) **1834** *S. Lit. Messenger* I. 120 The log stable belonging to Mr. Austin. — (**11**) **1873** *Winfield* (Kans.) *Courier* 11 Jan. 1/1 Millinery and Ladies Furnishing Goods. . . . One door north of Log Store. **1916** Eastman *From Deep Woods* 113 We found in a log store near by several who were badly hurt. — (**12**) **1809** Cuming *Western Tour* 44 We stopped to feed our horses at a small log tavern. **1874** Eggleston *Circuit Rider* 147 Morton was conducted three miles down the river to a log tavern. — (**13**) **1881** *Harper's Mag.* April 706/1 Juneau's log ware-house was the headquarters for gossip.

c. Denoting places of security made of logs, as (1) **log barrack,** (2) **cache,** (3) **fort,** (4) **guard,** (5) **jail,** (6) **pen,** see as a main entry, (7) **prison.**

(**1**) *a*1861 Winthrop *Open Air* 32 All the residents of Damville dwelt in a great log-barrack. — (**2**) **1944** Lanks *Alaska* 39 There was, too, as in all these north-woods homes, a little log cache on stilts. — (**3**) **1831** *Boston Transcript* 19 March 2/3, I have seen the rise and progress of Western . . . civilization, from . . . the sites of old log-forts and fortifications, [to] towns and cities rising in importance. **1858** Peters *Kit Carson* 14 The Carson family, with a few neighbors, lived in a picketed log fort. — (**4**) **1809** T. Ashe *Travels Amer.* 123 The town itself has in its centre the remains of an old log-guard.

(**5**) **1885** *Harper's Mag.* June 73/2 It looked down upon a log court-house, a log jail, and a score or two of log dwellings. — (**7**) **1845** Kirkland *Western Clearings* 212, I went to prison; nothing but a log-prison. **1847** *Knickerb.* XXX. 241 A young chief and his squaw . . . were now lying in the log-prison which by courtesy was termed the guard-house.

d. Designating miscellaneous structures made of logs, as (1) **log blind,** (2) **breastwork,** (3) **bridge,** see as a main entry, (4) **building,** (5) **causeway,** (6) **corral,** (7) **fence,** see as a main entry, (8) **pound,** (9) **raft,** (10) **still,** (11) **wall.**

(**1**) **1893** in Philips *Making of Newspaper* 200 They waylaid him from behind one of the old log 'blinds' they were so deadly at manufacturing. — (**2**) **1840** Cooper *Pathfinder* xxiv, We carried their log breastwork by storm. — (**4**) **1806** Pike *Sources Miss.* I. App. 36 [The fur-trading establishment] at Lower Red Cedar Lake . . . consists of log buildings.

(**5**) **1836** E. L. Willson *Journey N.J. to Ohio* (1929) 24 We pass sandhills where they have had to make log-causeways over them.— (**6**) **1916** Eastman *From Deep Woods* 15 It was my first task each morning to bring them [*sc.* ponies] into the log corral. — (**8**) **1737** *N.H. Hist. Soc. Coll.* VII. 358 [In 1737 was built] a log pound, . . . with a good gate. — (**9**) **1828** in Sullivan *Travels J. Smith* (1934) 69, I took some small presents and was ferried over the river by the indians on their log rafts. **1905** *Forestry Bureau Bul.* 61, Brail. A section of a log raft, six of which make an average tow.

(**10**) **1816** *Ann. 14th Congress* 2 Sess. 1190 Modern contrivances, such as log stills, rectifying vats, and some other utensils. — (**11**) **1840** *Knickerb.* XVI. 247, I looked around on the bare log-walls and ceiling. **1948** *Reader's Digest* March 143/2 We covered the roof with sod and chinked every crack between the log walls with arctic moss.

For **log road** see **4.** (9) (*a*) below.

e. Designating things made of a log or portion of a log, as (1) **log bench,** (2) **canoe,** see as a main entry, (3) **cradle,** (4) **ladder,** (5) **pipe,** (cf. **pump log**), (6) **skiff,** (7) **trap,** see as a main entry.

(**1**) **1882** Thayer *From Log-Cabin* 63 He had never undertaken to perform the feat of sitting bolt upright upon a log bench without a back. — (**3**) **1881** *Harper's Mag.* May 876/1 The guide is born not made. . . . He rolls out of his log-cradle into a pair of top-boots. — (**4**) **1855** in *Calif. Pion. Soc. Quart.* V. (1928) 18 At the end of the R. R. (leading to a quicksilver mine) a shaft is sunk, & descended upon a log ladder, i.e., a log with notches cut in it for steps.

Log bench

(**5**) **1896** Haswell *New York* 36 The water furnished by this company was raised from a well in Reade, near Centre Street, by a sun and planet wheel steam-engine, constructed in England, and thence was driven into a reservoir on Chambers Street, and distributed in some streets through log pipes. **1942** Harlow *Trees Eastern U.S.* 25 The ends of the log pipes could be fitted together without restraining iron bands (which would soon rust). — (**6**) **1838** Flagg *Far West* I. 30 The birch caïque of the Indian, and log skiffs, gondolas, and dug-outs of the pioneer [were] without name or number.

f. Denoting towns in which the buildings are made of logs: (1) **log city,** (2) **town,** (3) **village.**

(**1**) **1817** S. R. Brown *Western Gaz.* 106 Vangeville,—A log city, . . . has fifteen or twenty old log houses. — (**2**) [**1790** Freneau in *N.Y. Daily Advt.* 19 Feb., Lines Descriptive of a Tavern at Log-Town, a small Place in the Pine Barrens of North-Carolina.] **1836** Hildreth *Dragoon Campaigns* I. 70 The remains of a log-town long since evacuated, that had formerly been the settlement of a tribe of the Delawares. — (**3**) **1943** Benét *Western Star* 70 The log-village that hunters can leave behind.

3. In combs. relating to logging or lumbering operations: (1) **log beam,** (2) **birling,** (3) **boom,** (4) **booming,** (5) **buttings,** (6) **camp,** (7) **crop,** (8) **cut,** (9) **drive,** (10) **driving,** (11) **dump,** (12) **interest,** (13) **kicker,** (14) **mark,** (15) **measurer,** (16) **mule,** (17) **pocket,** (18) **riding,** (19) **rule,** (20) **stamp,** (21) **station,** (22) **yard.**

(**1**) **1883** Knight *Supp.* 558/2 *Log Beam,* the traveling frame in which a log lies and travels in a saw-mill. — (**2**) **1944** *P. Bunyan's Quiz* [Quest.] 33 What is log birling? The art of rolling a floating log under foot without falling off. This is the 'river hog's' game and is practiced as a competitive sport. **1947** *Chi. Tribune* 4 July 1/5 The beards of Traverse City and, of course, some of the other events, such as log birling contests, street dancing, pageantry, . . . have drawn 25,000 visitors to town. — (**3**) **1878** *Lumberman's Gaz.* 6 April, An addition to the wharf and log boom are being made. — (**4**) **1850** Judd *R. Edney* xiv. 180 He practiced log-booming in summer, and sawing in winter.

(**5**) **1879** *Lumberman's Gaz.* 15 Oct., A machine that would utilize . . . Log Buttings. — (**6**) **1858** Thoreau *Maine Woods* 136 My companion inclined to go to the log-camp on the carry. **1882** Hubbard *Moosehead Lake* 49 A good log-camp, however, just above the mouth of the brook, is not altogether uninviting. — (7) **1879** *Lumberman's Gaz.* 7 May, The delivery of the log crop of Michigan. — (8) **1882** *Uncle Rufus & Ma* 33 The log cut of 1879–'80 was 153,500,000 feet. — (9) **1904** *N.Y. Ev. Post* 3 May 2 The annual log-drives have begun in the upper Hudson watershed. *a***1904** S. E. WHITE *Blazed Trail Stories* ii. 25 He started up river for the log-drive.

(10) **1851** SPRINGER *Forest Life* 137 We were improving [the channel of the stream] by the removal of large rocks which obstructed log-driving. **1879** *Lumberman's Gaz.* 19 Dec., The dam will be used for flowage and log-driving purposes. **1905** *Forestry Bureau Bul.* No. 61, 34 *Cut off*, an artificial channel by which the course of a stream is straightened, to facilitate log driving. (N[orthern] F[orest].) — (11) **1905** *Forestry Bureau Bul.* No. 61 41 *Landing*, . . . a place to which logs are hauled or skidded preparatory to transportation by water or rail. . . . [Also called] banking ground, log dump, rollway, yard. — (12) **1881** *Mich. Gen. Statutes* I. (1882) 980 Nothing in this act shall be construed as conferring upon the log interest any paramount rights. — (13) **1922** R. C. BRYANT *Lumber* 44 Logs which are elevated into the mill by an endless chain are thrown or rolled upon the deck by means of log kickers of various types. — (14) **1859** *Mich. Rep.* VI. 270 The Mill Company had given a list of log-marks under section eight of the act.

(15) **1875** KNIGHT 1349/1 *Log-measurer*, a device for gaging logs, taking the round measure with the allowance for the squaring, and giving the results in board measure of the ascertained square in running feet of the log. — (16) **1944** *Democrat* 13 April 4/4 For Sale —Chevrolet Truck. . . . Also one log mule, weight 1200 pounds. — (17) **1877** *Lumberman's Gaz.* 17 Nov., A dam has been built across the river, forming a log pocket. — (18) **1905** WIGGIN *Rose* 154 Mr. Wiley narrated the sorts of feats in log-riding, . . . and the shooting of rapids that he had done in his youth. — (19) **1905** *Forestry Bureau Bul.* No. 61, 15 *Log rule*, . . . a tabular statement of the amount of lumber which can be sawed from logs of given lengths and diameters.

(20) **1878** *Lumberman's Gaz.* 5 Jan., Wyburn's improved log stamp is convenient for marking logs with the exact number of feet. — (21) **1861** WINTHROP *Open Air* 29 Our dessert of raspberries grew all along the path, and lured us on to a log-station by the water. — (22) **1883** SMITH *Geol. Survey Ala.* 370 'Log-yards' are established at every convenient bluff along the river.

For **log chain, jam, running, scale,** see as main entries.

b. Denoting vehicles, roads, or ways used in logging or lumbering: (1) **log car,** (2) **carriage,** (3) **chute,** (4) **railway,** (5) **road,** see **4.** (9) below, (6) **sled** (cf. **go-devil,** *n.* **2. d.**), (7) **sleigh,** (8) **slide,** (9) **train,** (10) **wagon,** (cf. **saw log**), (11) **way,** see as a main entry.

(1) **1881** *Chi. Times* 11 June, The track upon which runs the log-car. **1897** BRODHEAD *Bound in Shallows* 218 Above the scream of the saws and the splash of the log car. — (2) **1853** P. PAXTON *Yankee in Texas* 251 What did that enormous saw and log-carriage mean? **1874** KNIGHT 479/2 The *log-carriage* of a sawing-machine. — (3) **1878** JACKSON *Travel at Home* 150 A 'log-shoot' . . . is made of two split logs, laid lengthwise, close, smooth side up. Down this, logs are sent sliding into the river. — (4) **1858** THOREAU *Maine Woods* 94 Hinckley . . . appeared with a truck drawn by an ox and a horse over a rude log-railway through the woods.

(6) **1878** *Lumberman's Gaz.* 2 Feb. 89 He has constructed a road of ice . . . on which the log-sleds slip along readily. **1926** *Old-Time N. Eng.* July 22 Log Sled A massive home-made wooden sled, with wooden runners unshod with iron, which, when backed under the pried up log end, reduces friction in the winter transport of a log thus lifted at one end. — (7) **1893** *Scribner's Mag.* June 706/2 The log-sleighs have ten, twelve, and even fourteen-foot bunks. **1902** WHITE *Blazed Trail* 72 Eight log-sleighs . . . the carpenter had hewed from solid sticks of timber. — (8) **1887** HARTE *Phyllis of Sierras* i He would have come upon some rude wagon track, or 'log-slide,' leading from a clearing on the slope. **1946** NEWTON *P. Bunyan* 176 We sluiced our tons and tons of berries over it, using the old log-slide on the slope of Kill-Devil hill. — (9) **1886** *San Jose* (Calif.) *Mercury* June 3/1 On a flat road the trees must not only be peeled, but the skids must be greased to facilitate the sliding of the log train. **1946** *Nat. Geog. Mag.* Sep. 294/1 This log train loads for the mills of the Crossett Lumber Company.

(10) **1779** *N.J. Archives* 2 Ser. III. 69 To be sold . . . a good log waggon and four horses.

c. Denoting persons having to do with logging: (1) **log cuffer,** (2) **cutter,** (3) **driver,** (4) **maker,** (5) ∗**man, roller,** see as main entries, (6) **scaler,** (7) **watch.**

(1) **1941** *Time* 21 July 57/1 Once, 40 years ago two log cuffers . . . birled for two days . . . before one got a ducking. — (2) **1893** *Scribner's Mag.* June 710/2 At night he must get from the log-cutters their count for the day. — (3) **1850** JUDD *R. Edney* xviii. 220 This flood was both spring-time and harvest for log-drivers, boom-gatherers, and lumber-men generally. **1917** KEPHART *Camping* I. 144 The woolen cloth called kersey . . . is the favorite among . . . the log-drivers and lumberjacks generally. — (4) **1880** *Lumberman's Gaz.* 7 Jan. 28 Next come the 'log makers,' working in gangs of three or four, each with its 'chief.' **1944** *P. Bunyan's Quiz* [Quest.] 162 What is a bucker? A 'log maker'; his job is to saw the felled trees into specified log lengths.

(6) **1944** *P. Bunyan's Quiz.* [Quest.] 183 As it enters the mill, a log scaler measures it with a scale stick and records the volume in board feet. The log is kicked over on a sloping deck by a steam operated, arm-like device, where it awaits its turn to be sawn. — (7) **1905** *Forestry Bureau Bul.* No. 61, 39 *Head driver*, an expert river driver who, during the drive, is stationed at a point where a jam is feared. . . . [Also called] log watch (N[orthern] F[orest]).

4. In miscellaneous combs.: (1) **log-built,** *a.* built of logs; (2) **college,** see as a main entry; (3) **crib,** (*a*) a log house for storing corn, (*b*) = ∗**crib,** *n.* **3;** (4) **crossing,** ? =**foot log,** *rare;* (5) **furnace,** a smelting furnace in which logs are used as fuel; (6) **heap,** see as a main entry; (7) **pen,** see as a main entry; (8) **raising,** =**log cabin raising,** *obs.*, cf. **bull-push log raising;** (9) **road,** (*a*) a corduroy road, (*b*) a logging road, (10) **rolling, trap, work,** see as main entries.

(1) **1835** HOFFMAN *Winter in West* I. 79 We stopped to breakfast at a low log built shantee. **1925** BRYAN *Memoirs* 213 The logbuilt home has vanished. — (3) (*a*) **1872** POWERS *Afoot & Alone* 66 [Alabama] is . . . a land of log-cribs, high and spindling, and full of snow-white corn. (*b*) **1902** WHITE *Blazed Trail* 209 The steamboat . . . moved slowly toward the wharf of log cribs filled with stone. — (4) **1899** CUSHMAN *Hist. Indians* 227 When the spirit of a bad person arrives at the log-crossing of the fearful river, it is assailed by wakeful guards.

(5) **1819** SCHOOLCRAFT *Mo. Lead Mines* 94 This furnace is called the *Log Furnace*, and is peculiar to this [Mo. lead-mining] country. It is of very simple construction, consisting of an inclined hearth, surrounded by walls on three sides, open at top, and with an arch for the admission of air below. **1850** *Western Jrnl.* IV. 412 Messrs. Tingle & McKee . . . have raised about 50,000 pounds [of ore], and are now smelting in a log furnace. — (8) **1864** E. KIRK *Down in Tennessee* iii. 43 In April 1862, he and his band came upon a party of neighbors collected at a log raising in Fentress county. **1897** BRODHEAD *Bound in Shallows* 169 Law, the log-raisin's and corn-huskin's they used to have! — (9) (*a*) **1819** F. WRIGHT *Views* (1821) 234 A log road, or causeway, as it is denominated, is very grievous to the limbs. **1837** MARTINEAU *Society in Amer.* I. 331 The news was that a bridge in the middle of a marsh had been carried away by a tremendous freshet; and with how much log-road on either side, could not be ascertained. (*b*) **1880** INGHAM *Digging Gold* 367 We started on a gallop up the hill on a log road. **1893** *Scribner's Mag.* June 699/1 Banking-grounds [were] prepared, and log-roads made, all preliminary to the work of cutting and hauling logs.

b. In the names of animals and plants: (1) **logcock,** see as a main entry; (2) **fish,** (see quot.); (3) **perch,** =**hogfish;** (4) **wood,** the bluewood, *Condalia obovata*, of Texas.

(2) **1884** GOODE *Fisheries* I. 334 The Black Rudder-fish—*Lirus perciformis*. This fish is also called by the fishermen 'Log-fish' and 'Barrel-fish.' — (3) **1882** *Nat. Museum Bul.* No. 16, 499 *P. caprodes*. . . . Log Perch; Rock-fish. **1945** MCATEE *Nomina Abitera* 20 Log-perch (Percina caprodes)—This species, and also other darters . . . are called 'Oklahoma son-of-a-bitch' in that state. — (4) **1884** SARGENT *Rep. Forest* 4 Blue Wood, Log Wood, Purple Haw. **1891** COULTER *Bot. W. Texas* I. 58 *Condalia obovata*, . . . known as 'brasil' and 'logwood' [is] one of the common 'chaparral' plants of western Texas. **1897** SUDWORTH *Arborescent Flora* 297.

5. In colloquial phrases: (1) *As easy as rolling* (or *falling*) *off a log*, extremely easy; (2) *to split the log*, to explain a matter; (3) *to keep the log rolling*, to keep things moving, "to keep the ball rolling," cf. ∗**ball,** *n.*[1] **3. b;** (4) *to sit like a bump on a log*, to remain stupidly inarticulate; (5) *in the log*, in an unfinished state; (6) *to ride a log*, see ∗**ride,** *v.* **4.** (6).

(1) **1839** *N.O. Picayune* 29 March 2/2 He gradually went away from the Lubber, and won the heat 'just as easy as rolling off a log.' **1905** N. DAVIS *Northerner* 115 It will be just as easy 'as falling off a log.' **1948** *Green Bay* (Wis.) *Press-Gazette* 13 July 14/7 Then there are tricks that are as easy as falling off a log—or slipping between them. — (2) **1832** PAULDING *Westward Ho!* I. 183 No? well then, I'll split the log for you. [**1948** DICK *Dixie Frontier* 124 One of the most interesting methods of 'banking' gold and silver was to bore holes in large blocks of wood, fill the holes with coins, and drive tightly fitting pegs into them. Then the pegs were sawed off short. This left no way to remove the money except by splitting the log.] — (3) **1850** H. C. WATSON *Camp-Fires Revol.* 55 We must keep the log rollin'. [**1948** *Time* 6 Dec. 25/1 Through it one could hear the faint humming sound of platitudes being rubbed together, of logs being rolled, of whitewash being slapped across naked raw spots on international dispute.] —

(4) **1889** K. D. WIGGIN *Birds' Christmas Carol* 47 Ye ain't goin' to set there like a bump on a log 'thout sayin' a word ter pay for yer vittles, air ye?

(5) **1850** SEYMOUR *Sketches of Minn.* 200 Besides at the lowest estimate, six or seven million feet of lumber rafted in the log.

b. log and husk rubber, a heavy, long-handled mop consisting of a rectangular block of wood having holes bored in it and filled with corn husks, used in scrubbing floors.

1902 EGGLESTON *Dorothy South* 82 When Arthur came down stairs the next morning he found the maids busily polishing the snow-white floors with pine needles and great log and husk rubbers.

As the last term in **back, bark, basswood, bed, board, boom, bottom, buckeye, butt, carry, Choctaw, chop, cross, crossing, dock, double, down, drumming, face, fence, foot, fore, gas, home, house, key, lick, locust, mill, pump, round, salt, saw, saw-mill, soapstone back, trap, water, way log.**

*log, *v.*

1. *absol.* (See quot. 1905.)

1717 *Mass. H. Rep. Jrnl.* I. 272 Bridger [is trying] . . . to compel the inhabitants . . . to pay him forty shillings for each team they send to log and get timber. **1878** *Mich. Rep.* XXXVII. 408 He was logging on the . . . Manistee River. **1905** *Forestry Bureau Bul.* No. 61, 42 *Log, to,* to cut logs and deliver them at a place from which they can be transported by water or rail, or, less frequently, at the mill. **1948** *Milwaukee Jrnl.* 18 July 6/5 By 1889 he had built a farm home and 'tourist home' from timber he had cut and logged himself.

b. *tr.* To deprive (an area) of logs, to cut (a tree, or timber) into logs. Also with *up.* Cf. **logged off, over.**

1843 *Yale Lit. Mag.* VIII. 406 What a nation sight of bother **it** would be to log up a clearing in these parts. **1902** WHITE *Blazed Trail* 5 We own . . . five million on the Cass Branch which we would like to log on contract. **1917** KEPHART *Camping* I. 113 With this one tool a good axeman can . . . quickly fell and log-up a tree large enough to keep a hot fire before his lean-to throughout the night. **1949** *Mazama* Jan. 3/2 Had these mountain slopes not been logged so severely, the flood would have been much less serious.

2. *tr.* To protect (a structure) with logs. Also with *in* and *up.*

1743 in KERCHEVAL *History* (1833) 235 Ordered, that the sherif of this county build a twelve foot square log house, logged above and below, to secure his prisoners. **1786** *Md. Hist. Mag.* XIX. 268 Thomas Yates engaging to logg in, and wharf Jones's falls. **1798** *Smithtown Rec.* 351 The dam [is] to be logged up against where the saw mill shall stand. **1888** BILLINGS *Hardtack* 49 But by far the most common way of logging up a tent was to build the walls 'cob-fashion,' notching them together at the corners.

logan ˈlogən, *n.* =**pokelogan.** Cf. **bogan.**

1881 *Harper's Mag.* Nov. 826 Is it merely a coincidence that the sheet of water the Indians call logan, we name lagoon, from the Italian lagune. **1903** *Amer. Folk-Lore* April–June 128 (*Cent. Supp.*), Now curiously enough, exactly the same thing is generally called in Maine a logan—which must be another form of the same word [*pokologan*]. These words [*bogan* and *logan*] are in good local use, and occur in articles on sporting, etc. **1905** *Forestry Bureau Bul.* 61 *s.v.*, Logan. A bay or pocket into which logs may float off during a drive. **1942** RICH *We Took to Woods* (1948) 2 The country is criss-crossed with ridges, dotted with swamps and logans, and covered with dense forest.

loganberry ˈlogənˌbɛrɪ, *n.* [J. H. *Logan* (1841–1928), Amer. jurist and horticulturist.] A variety of red berry, or the plant producing it (see quot. 1894).

1893 *Calif. Agric. Exper. Sta. Bul.* No. 103, 3 The Logan Berry . . . [has] the shape of a blackberry, the color of a raspberry, and a combination of the flavors of both. **1894** *Garden & Forest* VII. 465/2 The Loganberry originated several years ago [1881] in the garden of Judge J. H. Logan, of Santa Cruz, from self-grown seeds of the Aughinbaugh [a blackberry]. . . . The other parent is supposed to be a Raspberry of the Red Antwerp type. **1948** *L.A. Time* 5 Dec. (Home Mag.) 29/2 The blackberry family that includes young, boysen, nectar and loganberries, should have five or six of the most vigorous canes of this year's growth saved.

attrib. **1949** *Canning Trade* 28 March 20/1 Boysenberry jam is priced at $1.65 and Loganberry jam at $2.25.

Logan black law. [After Gen. John A. *Logan* (1826–86).] (See quot.) — **1906** in *Kansas Hist. Soc.* IX. 393 Then the 'abolitionist' was an abomination to Logan: he 'smote them hip and thigh'; he was the reputed author of what was familiarly known as the 'Logan black law' of Illinois, being 'An act to prevent the immigration of free negroes into this state.' (Session Laws, February 12, 1853, p. 57.) This law provided severe penalties for any one who brought to or harbored in the state of Illinois a free negro.

log bridge. A bridge built of logs.

1664 *Springfield Rec.* I. 316 Foure acres of low lands Northwestrly from the logg bridge. **1842** *Lowell Offering* II. 275 How natural is that rude log bridge, so carelessly thrown over the crystallized brook! **1915** ATKINSON *Johnny Appleseed* 185 These young pioneers knew . . . how to . . . build blockhouses and log bridges. **1949** *Sierra Club Bul.* June 2 One could stand on a massive log bridge and watch the Kings River gliding and dancing and flashing in the sunlight between overarching green boughs.

log cabin.

1. A cabin built of logs. Cf. **double log cabin, log house.**

H. R. Shurtleff in *The Log Cabin Myth* (1939) shows that the only colonists who brought to this country a log house technique were the Swedes who began to settle on Delaware Bay in 1638. (See quot. 1709, *s.v.* **log house.**) He believes that the Scotch-Irish invented the term "log cabin" about 1750.

1770 in SHURTLEFF *Log Cabin* (1939) 25 The court [of Botetourt County in Va.] doth appoint . . . to agree with a workman to build a log cabbin twenty four feet long and twenty wide for a Court House, with a clapbord roof with two small sheads, one at each end for jury rooms. **1877** *Rep. Indian Affairs* 61, I trust that in a few years this entire tribe will substitute the log cabin for the cloth lodge now used by them. **1949** *Nat. Geog. Mag.* Oct. 507/1 Sturdy log cabins . . . crouched beneath the trees.

b. With particular reference to the presidential campaign of 1840, esp. *Log Cabin and Hard Cider.* Cf. **3. b.**

1840 HONE *Diary* II. 33 Never did the friends of Mr. Van Buren make so great a mistake as when by their sneers they furnished the Whigs those powerful weapons, 'log-cabin' and 'hard cider.' **1852** *So. Illinoisian* (Shawneetown) 29 Oct. 2/2 The same party, in the same year, resorted to building and *worshipping* log cabins and drinking hard cider made *harder.* **1944** ROSS *Westward* 137 During the dramatic 'log cabin and hard cider' campaign of William Tyler Harrison she stood on a stump in an Illinois village. **1947** *Sat. Review* 22 Nov. 40/2 Webster made a two-hour oration before some twenty thousand Vermonters at one of the mass rallies of the frenzied log-cabin and hard-cider campaign of 1840.

2. A quilt pattern suggestive of a cabin built of logs. Cf. **3. c.**

The meaning of the term in quot. 1846 is not clear.

[**1846** *Quincy* (Ill.) *Whig* 19 March 3/3 The subscribers have just rec'd their stock of New Spring Goods, consisting in part of the following:—Broad-cloths, . . . Log-cabin, linens, cottonades, gambroons.] **1898** E. C. HALL *Aunt Jane* 57 There seemed to be every pattern that the ingenuity of woman could devise and the industry of woman put together,—'four-patches,' 'nine-patches,' 'log-cabins,' 'wild-goose chases,' 'rising suns.' **1938** MATSCHAT *Suwannee River* 121 The names were enchanting: Wild Goose Chase, . . . Buzzard's Roost, Star of the East, Log Cabin. **1943** PEATTIE *Great Smokies* 129 The old coverlet patterns had life running through them; Log Cabin, Castle City, Blooming Leaf, Martha Washington, Lee's Surrender, . . . and Rose in the Wilderness.

3. In obs. combs.: (1) **log-cabin bonnet,** ?a bonnet of a design suggesting the structure of a log cabin; (2) **loafer,** a backwoods loafer, *rare;* (3) **luminary,** (see quot.); (4) **raising,** a community gathering for the purpose of helping a neighbor raise a log cabin, cf. **house raising.**

(1) **1856** ROBINSON *Kansas* 161 There were some with log-cabin bonnets of black silk, or cotton velvet, and dress of plain coarse stuff. — (2) *c***1845** W. T. PORTER *Big Bear Arkansas* 120 He's as ramstugenous an animal as a log-cabin loafer in the dog days. — (3) **1898** N. E. JONES *Squirrel Hunters of Ohio* 292 The man . . . did his reading at night by the light of the furnace or a 'log-cabin luminary,' a lard lamp. — (4) **1840** *N.O. Picayune* 12 Aug. 2/1 The cars were at the time full of people going to a log-cabin raising in Jersey City.

b. In allusion to the "Log Cabin and Hard Cider" campaign of 1840 (see **1. b.**), as **log-cabin boy, candidate, carpet, cologne, fan, state.** *Obs.*

1840 *Boston Atlas* 11 Sep. (Th.), The log-cabin boys Of old Tippecanoe. **1841** *Greene Co. Torchlight* (Xenia, O.) 16 Sep. 2/2 The only duty remaining now, is, to see that every Log Cabin boy votes. — **1840** *Rough Hewer* 26 March 45/1 The supporters of Harrison have staked their existence as a party, upon the fact that their candidate resides in a log cabin, and that he is therefore, a log cabin candidate. — **1888** NORTON *Reminiscences* 365 Log-cabin carpets were brought into use, and ink-stands, cane heads and quilts and various other emblems and devices were to be met with in the homes of Harrison men in all the States. — **1840** *N.O. Picayune* 2 Oct. 2/3 A druggist is selling log cabin cologne in Boston. — **1841** *Greene Co. Torchlight* (Xenia, O.) 1 July 4/1 The stock consists, in part of. . . . Threads, tapes, pins, needles, thimbles and Log Cabin Fans. — **1840** *Niles' Reg.* 28 Nov. 208/3 Here [Pa.] Harrison was started, and here his 'log cabin' first started also. After this, who will doubt our claim to the title of the log cabin state?

c. With reference to a quilt with a log cabin design (see **2.**), as **log-cabin bed quilt, comforter, patchwork, pattern, quilt.**

1920 Lincoln *Mr. Pratt* 214 Most everything was sold but a log cabin bed quilt. — **1935** Lincoln *Cape Cod Yesterdays* 109, I ducked my tousled head under the layers of sheet, blanket, 'crazy quilt,' 'log-cabin comforter' and . . . fell asleep. — **1890** *Stock Grower & Farmer* 10 May 3/1 If Uncle Jerry will furnish our farmer's wives with a good design for a log cabin patchwork or Prairie Sunflower quilt, the deed is done. — **1905** *McClure's Mag.* XXV. 602, I know the Log Cabin pattern, and the Mexican-Feather pattern, and I think I could make out to tell the Hen-and-Chickens pattern of quilts, but that's as much as ever. — **1887** *Harper's Mag.* Dec. 36/1 She slipped her book under the log-cabin quilt. **1900** H. Robertson *Red Blood & Blue* 192 She took the pipe from her mouth and led the way into the best room, which . . . was furnished with a few split-bottomed chairs; a high bed, covered with a bright 'log-cabin' quilt.

Also *log cabin boarder, hotel, inn, mill, period, pioneer, schoolhouse, slang, style, village*, etc.

log canoe. =**dugout,** *n.* **1.**

1752 in *Travels Amer. Col.* 315 An officer and ten soldiers . . . brought us in two log canoes. **1840** Thompson *Green Mt. Boys* I. 12 [Four men] were seen occupying a large log canoe near the eastern shore of the lake. **1944** Footner *Rivers of East. Shore* 104 A log canoe, the *Methodist*, was built for him, and it became famous among the islands, and as high up the rivers as it could go.

log chain. A long chain such as is used in logging operations. Also attrib.

1672 *Oyster Bay Rec.* I. 68, 1 loge chaine. **1741** Hempstead *Diary* 381, [I] got my Logg Chain mended. **1857** Underhill & Thompson *Elephant Club* 233 Overdale expatiated upon [it] at some length as an extensive log-chain factory. **1948** Jacobs *We Chose Country* 71, I got bigger chains, and longer periods of quiet in my progression from dog chain to log chain, but nothing ever lasted.

logcock ˈlɔgˌkɑk, *n.* **1.** The pileated woodpecker, *Ceophloeus pileatus*. **2.** =**ivory-billed woodpecker.**

(1) **1806** Lewis in *L. & Clark Exped.* IV. (1905) 132 The large woodpecker or log cock, the lark woodpecker and the small white woodpecker with a read head . . . are found exclusively in the timbered country. **1945** McAtee *Nomina Abitera* 46 To me the logcock repeats 'cack, cack,' or 'puck, puck,' with no touch of divinity about the performance. — (2) **1811** Wilson *Ornithology* IV. 24 The more intelligent and observing part of the natives . . . distinguish them [the ivory-billed and the pileated woodpeckers] by the name of the large and lesser *Log-cocks*. **1917** *Birds of Amer.* II. 138 Ivory-billed Woodpecker. *Campephilus principalis*. [Also called] Logcock [etc.].

log college. A school conducted in a log house, orig. applied in derision to a Presbyterian school founded by Wm. Tennent (1673–1746), near Philadelphia, for the training of candidates for the ministry. *Obs.* Cf. **New Light, New Side.**

1795 Freneau *Poems* 374 On the Demolition of a Log-College. **1850** Foote *Sk. Virginia* 393 The Smiths came to Virginia to commence log colleges in the 'Ancient Dominion.' **1884** Schaff *Religious Encycl.* III. 2316/1 Log College was the first of the literary and theological institutions of the Presbyterian Church in America, the parent of those in Princeton, N.J., and, indeed, of them all. **1949** *Wm. & Mary Coll. Quart.* Jan. 44 Tennent's Log College contributed both leaders and a plan of study to Princeton.

log fence. A fence in which logs are used as rails (see quot. 1828).

1651 *E. Hampton Rec.* I. 13 Those men that are behind in the Logg fence . . . shall Doe their worke betweene this & the 3 of May. **1790** S. Deane *N.-Eng. Farmer* 89/1 In the new plantations of this country, log fences are most used. **1828** Cooper *Notions* I. 343 (*footnote*), The 'log-fence' . . . is formed by laying the trunks of trees in a line, with their ends doubling for a couple of feet. **1880** *Scribner's Mo.* Feb. 504/2 The log fence was a structure of more substance than either the pole or brush fence. **1948** *Chi. Tribune* 8 Aug. 4/5 Little girl enjoys visit to Aspen, Colo., in heart of Colorado Rockies in a precarious stroll along log fence.

b. App. a fence in which the logs are stood upright in the fashion of a palisade.

1846 Durivage & Burnham *Stray Subjects* 32 We went so fast that the posts and rails by the road-side looked like a log fence. **1902** White *Conjurer's House* 39 The storehouse [is] surrounded by a protective log fence.

logged lɔgd, *a.* **1.** Built of logs. **2. logged off, over,** of land, denuded of logs.

(1) **1784** Washington *Diaries* II. 294 A Logged dwelling house with a punchion Roof. **1834** *Knickerb.* III. 32 Immediately on the road, appeared a large rude double logged cabin. — (2) **1909** *Nat. Conservation Cong. Proc.* 66 Investigating the methods of utilizing the logged-off lands of western Washington. **1947** *Sierra Club Bul.* June 20 There is precious little fringe of forest remaining—a narrow buffer strip between logged-over areas and snow peaks. **1948** *Ib.* May 6/1 Butano Forest . . . is now in immediate danger of being logged off.

logger ˈlɔgɚ, *n.* [f. ∗**log,** *v.*] One engaged in logging, a lumberman.

1732 *Cal. State P.* 122 Mr. Byfield's proceedings, of which he complained, have so animated the loggers that more waste has been committed this last winter than for many years past. **1848** Thoreau *Maine Woods* 18 The loggers' camp is as completely in the woods as the fungus at the foot of a pine in a swamp. **1948** *Sierra Club Bul.* March 15 If the loggers of the Olympic Peninsula are granted permission to cut their remaining virgin timber, they will do so.

Log fence

∗**loggerhead,** *n.*

1. =**loggerhead shrike.**

1803 J. Davis *Travels* 81 The red-bird is imitated with nice precision by the mocking-bird; but there is a bird [in S.C.] called the loggerhead that will not bear passively its taunts. **1917** *Birds of Amer.* III. 100/1 When seen the Loggerhead is usually occupying a perch on the top of some small tree, stake, telephone pole, or fence post.

2. A diamondback terrapin, or one of a related species. In full **loggerhead terrapin.**

1877 Bartlett 367 *Loggerhead Terrapin*, the large fresh and salt water tortoise. *Ib.* 699 The most celebrated is the diamond-back; there are also the yellow-bellies, red-bellies, loger-heads, snuff-boxes, etc.

3. (See quot.) *Obs.* Cf. ∗*loggat* in *OED.*

1871 G. R. Cutting *Student Life Amherst* 112 The pitching of 'loggerheads' and 'quoits' has been, at different times, quite common. As the game of 'loggerheads' has become obsolete, in this part of the country at least, a brief description of it may not prove uninteresting. A 'loggerhead' was a spherical mass of wood, with a long handle, and the game consisted of an attempt to hurl this towards a fixed stake, in such a manner as to leave it as near as possible.

4. (*cap.*) *pl.* During the Civil War, a nickname for Federal soldiers from Pennsylvania.

1888 Whitman *November Boughs* 70 Those soldiers from . . . Pennsylvania, [were called] Logher [*sic*] Heads.

5. =**loggerhead turtle.**

1807 Janson *Stranger* 312 The swamps produce a variety of what may be denominated land turtles. The natives call them loggerheads, tarapins [etc.]. **1931** Read *La.-French* 136 Owing to the remarkable size of its head, which may measure nearly or quite twenty-five inches in circumference, the alligator turtle is commonly known as a 'loggerhead.'

6. a. loggerhead shrike, the common shrike, *Lanius ludovicianus*, of the Southeast. **b. loggerhead turtle,** =**snapping turtle.**

(a) 1811 Wilson *Ornithology* III. 57 Loggerhead Shrike. . . . This species inhabits the rice plantations of Carolina and Georgia. **1938** Matschat *Suwannee River* 262 The bird was a loggerhead shrike, smoke gray and black, with white underneath. — **(b) 1842** *Nat. Hist. N.Y., Zoology* III. 8 The Snapping Turtle . . . is one of our largest turtles. . . . In other sections, it is known under the names of Loggerhead, Alligator Turtle and Couta. **1948** *Highway Traveler* Dec. 8/2 Huge loggerhead turtles frequent the beaches of the Keys.

loggery ˈlɔgərɪ, *n.* A log dwelling or building. *Obs.* — **1839** Kirkland *New Home* 261 These find no fault with their bare loggeries. **1882** *Harper's Mag.* Aug. 337/2 The old 'loggery' . . . still fronts the river on the island side.

logging ˈlɔgɪŋ, *n.* [f. the verb.]

1. The cutting and getting out of logs from a forest.

1706 *N.H. Prov. Papers* III. 337 Those whose livelihood chiefly consists in Logging and working in the woods. **1845** Cooper *Chainbearer* xiii, For the heavier . . . work, such as the logging, he [the axman] called on his neighbors for aid. **1948** *Sierra Club Bul.* May 5/1 San Mateo County officials found it necessary to rouse a judge from his bed at night to get court action to halt logging in Pioneer Grove.

2. =**logrolling 2.** *Obs.*

1817 JEFFERSON *Writings* XV. 134 The barter of votes . . . which, with us, is called 'logging,' the term of the farmers for their exchanges of aid in rolling together the logs of their newly-cleared grounds.

3. A quantity of felled logs, heavy timbers, planks, etc.

1823 COOPER *Pioneers* xvii, His piles, or to use the language of the country, his logging. **1896** SHINN *Story of Mine* 236 The other end [of the spragg], slightly sharpened, is against heavy planks, called logging.

4. The process of clearing off and piling for burning the small logs, timber, underbrush, etc., from a piece of land intended for cultivation; the area or land so cleared. *Obs.*

1827 COOPER *Prairie* xi, Show me . . . a set of boys who will . . . sooner chop a piece of logging and dress it for the crop, than my own children. **1828** ——— *Notions* I. 342 With the exception of such trees as are selected for lumber, the whole are piled in heaps of sufficient size to ensure their consumption by fire. The latter process is called logging. **1872** YOUNG *Hist. Wayne Co., Ind.* 37 Next followed the proceeding of *log-rolling*, or, as it was in some places called, 'logging.'

5. In special combs.: (1) **logging bee,** =**logrolling 1;** (2) **berth,** the scene of logging operations, as a logging camp; (3) **bob,** a bobsled used in logging; (4) **camp,** temporary or seasonal quarters established by loggers and lumbermen; (5) **chance,** a location in a forest suitable for a single logging operation.

(1) **1836** C. P. TRAILL *Backwoods of Canada* 192 We called a logging-bee. **1893** *Advance* 16 Nov., A logging bee has been described quite in detail. — (2) **1851** *Harper's Mag.* Sep. 521/2 Such annoyances from these migrating beasts in the vicinity of logging berths . . . are of recent date. — (3) **1919** CADY *Rhymes of Vt.* (1923) 19 While other 'toys' that help him do His work with neatness and despatch, Are logging bobs. — (4) **1832** WILLIAMSON *Maine* I. 141 The Whetsaw . . . frequents logging camps. **1947** *Canadian Alpine Jrnl.* June 91 Four miles to the south at the edge of the mountains is Doyle's camp, an abandoned logging camp.

(5) **1860** *Harper's Mag.* Feb. 296/2 An elderly man—a woodsman—came to the camp. . . . Two of his sons, he said, had started . . . to search in the woods for a 'logging chance,' and had not returned.

b. In combs. in which the meaning is obvious or is explained by the quots.: (1) **logging boots,** (2) **boss,** (3) **branch railroad,** (4) **chain,** (5) **company,** (6) **country,** (7) **crew,** (8) **establishment,** (9) **expedition,** (10) **locomotive,** (11) **mule,** (12) **operation,** (13) **path,** (14) **railroad,** (15) **railway,** (16) **river,** (17) **road,** (18) **shirt,** (19) **sled,** (20) **sledge,** (21) **swamp,** (22) **weather,** (23) **wheels.**

(1) **1946** *Sat. Ev. Post* 11 May 43/1 Logging boots were what every boy in camp wanted. — (2) **1919** CADY *Rhymes of Vt.* (1923) 131 They even set it so Jerome, The logging boss, would be at home. — (3) **1895** *Outing* XXVI. 393/1 We had traveled for the last twenty miles, on a logging branch railroad. — (4) **1905** *Forestry Bureau Bul.* No. 61, 36 logging chain. A levered chain grab hook attached to the evener to which a team is hitched in loading logs. **1949** *Sat. Ev. Post* 15 Jan. 71/2, I rushed around to the toolbox, dragged out one of the heavy logging chains.

(5) **1903** HART *Actual Govt.* 326 Logging companies buy up immense areas of land for timber. **1948** *Time* 9 Feb. 36/3 Logging companies protested it was a poor policy to rob them of 800 loyal, trained workers when there was a shortage of labor. — (6) **1945** *Reader's Digest* Aug. 87 We live in a logging country, and one of the big events of the year is the spring drive, when the pulpwood which has been cut during the winter is floated 50 miles down the chain of lakes to the mills. — (7) **1878** *Lumberman's Gaz.* 9 Feb., Logging crews are coming out of the woods there, on account of lack of snow. **1900** BRUNCKEN *N. Amer. Forests* 82 He may have charge of a logging crew as foreman. — (8) **1851** SPRINGER *Forest Life* 67, I have seldom taxed my judgment as severely on any subject as in judiciously locating a logging establishment. — (9) **1838** *Knickerb.* XII. 293 The lumbermen are . . . starting into the wilderness, on a logging expedition.

(10) **1905** *Forestry Bureau Bul.* No. 61, 33 *Corkscrew,* a geared logging locomotive. (P[acific] C[oast] F[orest].) — (11) **1945** *Democrat* 15 March 4/1 For Sale—1 pair logging mules. — (12) **1944** *P. Bunyan's Quiz* [Quest.] 74 Protection from forest fires during and after logging operations, forest fire patrols, and shutdowns during days of high wind and low humidity are saving millions of acres of seedlings from fire. — (13) *a***1862** THOREAU *Maine Woods* 218 [We] were soon confused by numerous logging-paths. — (14) **1893** *Scribner's Mag.* June 711/1 Finally with a large capacity came large enterprises, great lumber-mills, logging railroads, and finally great fortunes. **1949** *Nature Mag.* April 188/1 The logging railroad has less than two miles to go to reach the crucial units.

(15) **1888** MUIR *Picturesque Calif.* 460 It is moved from camp to camp by the 'logging' railway. **1944** *P. Bunyan's Quiz* [Quest.] 152 How much does it cost to build a logging railway? Some logging roads cost as much as $25,000 per mile. — (16) **1900** BRUNCKEN *N. Amer. Forests* 79 Booms are not the only structures used on the logging rivers to facilitate the 'driving.' — (17) **1839** HOLMES *Explor. Aroostook River* 27 Judging from the camps and logging roads which we occasionally met with, the lumbermen had been there operating on their own high responsibility. **1948** *Sat. Ev. Post* 24 Jan. 43/1 Timber companies are assured . . . a considerable saving in the construction of logging roads. — (18) **1834** TRAILL *Backwoods* 209 He learns to chop down trees, . . . dressed in a coarse over-garment of hempen cloth, called a logging-shirt. — (19) **1741** *N.H. Prov. Papers* VI. 349 Sent our Baggage on loging sleds to Rochester from Cochecho. **1905** *Forestry Bureau Bul.* No. 61, 42 Logging-sled road, a road, leading from the skidway or yard to the landing. (N[orthern] F[orest].) **1945** *Athol* (Mass.) *D. News* 26 May 7/2 Horse, harnesses, oil stoves, kerosene stoves, logging sled [etc.].

(20) **1944** W. BLAIR *Tall Tale Amer.* 169 But there was still the problem of turning logging sledges around. — (21) **1851** SPRINGER *Forest Life* 46 We have sometimes heard the voice of prayer even in the logging swamps. **1860** *Harper's Mag.* March 440/2 All these are but the preparatory duties of the 'logging swamp,' to be completed before winter. — (22) **1929** F. E. MCCLINCHEY *Joe Pete* 37 It was again very cold, the ideal logging weather. — (23) **1905** *Forestry Bureau Bul.* No. 61, 42 Logging wheels, a pair of wheels, usually about 10 feet in diameter, for transporting logs.

log heap. A heap or pile of logs, esp. one resulting from logrolling *q.v.*

1819 E. DANA *Geog. Sk.* 36 The Creoles never having before smelted, except by throwing the ore into log heaps. **1888** GRIGSBY *Smoked Yank* (1891) 201 He was building up a great log-heap of dry logs, with 'fat' pine for kindling. **1948** DICK *Dixie Frontier* 126 At a given signal they lifted it and carried it to the log heap.

log house. A house built of logs, orig. used for a prison. Cf. **double log house, log cabin.**

1662 in SHURTLEFF *Log Cabin* (1939) 80 As fare Westwardly as the logg house, formerly built, and now standing there [i.e., at Cape Porpoise, Me.] bounded with the sayd logg house. **1663** *Md. Archives* 490 Be itt Enacted . . . that A Logg howse be built Twenty foot Square . . . for a Prison. [**1709** LAWSON *Carolina* 215 A certain Indian, . . . one rainy Night, undermin'd a House made of Logs, (such as the Swedes in America very often make, and are very strong).] **1741** TAILFER *Narr. Georgia* (1835) 24 He threatned every Person . . . who . . . claim'd their just Rights and Privileges with the Stocks, Whipping-Post, and Logg-House. **1861** *Sacramento Union* 7 Dec. (Supp.) 4/3 The old jail was a little, uncomfortable log house, one of the relics of Mormondom. **1948** *N.W. Ohio Quart.* April 91 All but one of the Ohioans ran to a log house and barricaded themselves inside.

b. In combs. of obvious meaning, as **log house cottage, grocery, office, prison, quarters.**

1669 *Md. Archives* II. 224 That there be a Logg house Prison Twenty ffoot Square Built . . . in the Baltemore County. **1832** WILLIAMSON *Maine* I. 605 They seemed to exult . . . in their log-house cottages. **1844** KENDALL *Santa Fe Exped.* I. 25 Our log-house quarters, however, were closely 'chinked and daubed.' **1854** *Harper's Mag.* VIII. 422/1 A little log-house grocery stood on the near bank. **1906** LYNDE *Quickening* 352 There was a sharp crisis to the fore in the old log-house office at the furnace.

log jam. A number of saw logs which, impeded in passing down a stream, have formed a compact entangled mass. Also transf.

1886 DORSEY *Midshipman Bob* I. 73 His father got killed in a log-jam the year Robertin . . . was born. **1900** BRUNCKEN *N. Amer. Forests* 85 A 'log jam' is formed, usually at one of the rapids with which most logging rivers abound. **1907** *Springfield W. Republican* 14 Feb. 8 The congressional log-jam which held back all legislation for nearly a week was finally broken Thursday afternoon. **1947** *Chi. Sun* 30 June 4/5 Congress came up to the end of the government's fiscal year today facing one of the worst appropriations logjams in history.

***logman,** *n.* One engaged in getting out logs, a lumberer.

1851 SPRINGER *Forest Life* 159 It would be a match for 'Dame Nature' to locate a handsome Pine-tree beyond the grasp of the logmen. **1904** *Springfield W. Republican* 9 Sep. 11 The logman, as soon as he had been paid off at Mt. Tom, . . . [visited] Sobotsky's store. **1947** *Democrat* 11 Sep. 5/3 Axes, Saws, Peavies, Loading Chain, . . . and other supplies for the Log Man.

logo-fogie ˌlogoˈfogɪ, *n.* =**locofoco 2.** Also **logo-fogieism** *Rare.* — **1837** NEAL *Charcoal Sk.* (1838) 220 It's a logo-fogie! . . . a right down logo-fogie! *Ib.* 221, I'm pretty clear you're a logo-fogie—you talk as if your respect for me and other venerable institutions was tantamount to very little. *Ib.* 221 You sort of want to cut a piece out of the common veal by your logo-fogieism in wishing to 'bolish laws.

log pen.

1. A log cabin, esp. a poor one. *Obs.* or *hist.*

1789 WEEMS *Letters* III. 418, I lodged in a log-pen. **1836** *Quarter Race Ky.* (1846) 24, I went to town last night to the confectionary, (a whiskey shop in a log pen fourteen feet square). **1853** P. PAXTON *Yankee in Texas* 124 When he'd nothing else to do, [he] lazed about anybody's log-pen that he pleased. [**1948** *Fla. Hist. Quart.* July 40 A hip-roofed house had a roof at right angles to it and lowered from that over the single log pen first set up, which served to cover one or more so-called back rooms.]

2. A pen or inclosure made of logs.

1832 *Louisville Directory* 102 The ditch was surmounted by a breast work of log pens filled with the earth obtained from the ditch. **1836** B. TUCKER *Partisan Leader* (1861) 297 At the point where the stream ... swept away around the shoulder of the platform, was placed a small log pen. **1948** DICK *Dixie Frontier* 105 They [sheep] were kept at night in a strong log pen beside the house.

b. Such an inclosure used as a prison. *Obs.*

1854 SIMMS *Southward Ho!* 30 The whole foraging party ... were driven into an extemporary logpen.

logroll ˈlɔgˌrol, *v. fig. tr.* and *intr.* To engage in log-rolling, esp. to connive politically, to promote or carry through (legislation) by such means. *Colloq.*

1835 CROCKETT *Tour* 120 My people don't like me to log-roll in their business, and vote away pre-emption rights to fellows in other states, that never kindle a fire on their lands. **1854** T. FORD *Hist. Illinois* 186 The friends of the canal were forced to log-roll for that work by supporting others which were ruinous to the country. **1870** *Cong. Globe* 14 April 2700/2 If you vote for my interest I will vote for yours. That is the way these tariffs are 'log-rolled' through. **1949** *Time* 22 Aug. 88/3 An 'internal improvements' bill, calling for the expenditure of $10 million or $12 million on railroads and waterways, gave them their chance to logroll.

logroller ˈlɔgˌrolɚ, *n.*

1. A lumberer. *Rare.*

1830 *Cong. Deb.* 10 May 932/1 The log-roller, showing the amount of his lumber.

2. A politician, usu. of a cheap, conniving kind, who engages in political logrolling. *Colloq.*

1821 *Pa. Intelligencer* 16 Jan. (Th.), We shall see how the 'log-rollers' will unite their strength. **1883** *Cent. Mag.* Aug. 631/1 The caucus is fast drifting into the hands of wire-pullers and log-rollers. **1901** *McClure's Mag.* Dec. 152 He is ... a log-roller, willing to vote for this man's measure if the man will help Platt with some patronage scheme.

3. A birler. See ∗**birl,** *v.*

1941 *Time* 21 July 57/1 In birling, two surefooted log-rollers ... try to spin it so as to roll each other off.

logrolling ˈlɔgˌrolɪŋ, *n.*

1. An occasion when a group of neighbors assist one of their number in piling for burning, or otherwise disposing of, logs that hinder him in his farming operations.

*a***1792** MONETTE *Miss. Valley* (1848) II. 8 The standard dinner dish at log-rollings, house-raisings, and harvest days, was a large pot-pie. **1847** ROBB *Squatter Life* p. ix, When he [the western squatter] encounters his fellow man at a barbeque, election, log-rolling, or frolic. **1904** T. E. WATSON *Bethany* 131 His flying trips to corn-shuckings, to log-rollings, to church-meetings. **1948** *Fla. Hist. Quart.* July 41 Frolics also followed log-rollings and rail-splittings.

b. Also **logrolling frolic.**

[**1781** *View of N. Amer.* 93 Another capital frolic, but of a more laborious nature, and totally performed by men, is, the rolling, or heaping for burning, all the deadned trees which have fallen down in a field through the course of the winter.] **1847** DRAKE *Pioneer Life Ky.* 36 In due time a 'log-rolling' frolic was gotten up.

c. =**log cabin raising.** Now *hist.*

1835 C. J. LATROBE *Rambler in N. Amer.* I. 136 A family comes to sit down in the forest.... Their neighbours ... lay down their employments, shoulder their axes, and come in to the 'log-rolling.' They spend the day in hard labour, ... and then retire ... leaving the new-comers their good wishes, and an habitation. [**1843** *Amer. Pioneer* II. 121 A gang of fifteen men will get together, cut down the trees and divide them into suitable lengths, notch the ends, and, with skids, roll them up into cabins.] **1931** BEARD *Amer. Govt.* 285 In olden times pioneers on the frontier helped one another to cut trees and roll up logs for their cabins. This process was known as 'log-rolling.' **1949** *Américas* Aug. 9/1 A man often had to fight his own battles, still his own whiskey, and help a neighbor build a house at a community 'log-rolling.'

2. The exchanging of assistance by political schemers or factional leaders to secure their individual ends. Also transf.

1812 N. EDWARDS *MS letter* 17 Mar., Scenes of intrigue or to use a Kentucky term loggrolling will constantly present themselves. **1849** *Corr. R. W. Griswold* (1898) 246 Several clever persons in Boston have been spoiled by this log-rolling in literature. **1947** R. K. LEAVITT *Noah's Ark* 11 These included wide travel to sell his books, lecturing and logrolling to promote them. **1949** *Chi. D. News* 16 March 22/1 The assumption that a term in the Senate qualifies a man thereafter for any or all appointive posts is simply a form of log-rolling.

attrib. **1837** *U.S. Mag.* I. 23 His sense of obligations to the people ... [was] too unbending for the log-rolling honesty of factious demagogues. **1860** MORDECAI *Virginia* 303 The log-rolling system of Virginia has diverted her energies from the completion of any one useful work. **1885** *Wkly. New Mexican Review* 2 July 4/3 Territorial supreme courts have long since become known as a kind of log-rolling machine, in which the judges enter in the business of 'you tickle me and I will tickle you.' **1947** *Newsweek* 17 Feb. 22/1 An old-time log-rolling bee is threatened in the Senate.

3. In logging operations, rolling logs or allowing logs to roll to a desired spot, as into a river.

1848 THOREAU *Maine Woods* 15 Occasionally there was a small opening on the bank, made for the purpose of log-rolling.

4. Birling. Cf. ∗**birl,** *v.*

1893 *Westminster Gaz.* 16 May 5/1 For the special benefit of the distinguished spectators ... an elaborate display of log-rolling was given. **1948** *Hyde Park Herald* (Chi.) 1 Jan. 4/3 Canadian woodsmen ... will participate in log rolling, canoe tilting and other water and woods thrillers.

log running. Floating or guiding logs down a stream. Also attrib.

1878 *Lumberman's Gaz.* 6 April, The Green Bay *Advocate* of March 28 says that log-running is commencing all around. **1879** *Mich. Gen. Statutes* I. (1882) 550 Each log running or booming company doing business on any waters on which the logs or timber are floated or run. **1901** WHITE *Westerners* 199 In the log running Michail Lafond was the man always called upon to skim over the bobbing logs.

log scale. The contents, expressed in board feet, of a log or number of logs (see also quot. 1883).

1877 *Mich. Rep.* XXXVI. 168 It happens that the scale of the manufactured lumber exceeded the log scale. **1883** KNIGHT *Supp.* 559/2 *Log-scale*, a table which gives the quantity of lumber, one inch thick, board measure, which may be obtained from a round log, the length and the diameter below the bark being given. **1946** *Democrat* 26 Dec. 1/1 In stronger trees, the deduction in log scale for defect from canker is a serious cash loss.

log trap. A deadfall made of a heavy log. *Obs.*

1784 BELKNAP *Tour White Mts.* 13 Along this road ... we saw the culheags, or log-traps, which the hunters set for sables. **1840** EMMONS *Mass. Quadrupeds* 41 The Pine Marten ... is taken in a log trap, made and baited in such a way, that it cannot reach the meat without passing under the dead fall. **1851** *S. Lit. Messenger* XVII. 544/2 The skins of the game ... caught in log-traps.

b. A square pen made of fence rails into which wild turkeys are enticed by baiting. *Obs.*

1856 REID *Desert Home* 276 He had been keeping his eye upon the wild turkeys; and, for the purpose of securing some of them alive, he had constructed, not far from the house, a species of pen—which is known in America by the name of 'log trap.'

logway ˈlɔgˌwe, *n.*

1. A sloping chute, trough, slide, or inclosed passage for logs (see quot. 1905).

1779 in F. CHASE *Hist. Dartmouth Coll.* I. 562 The Trustees ... think fit to maintain said mills by repairing ... the log way and necessary mill houses. **1877** W. WRIGHT *Big Bonanza* 240 Such log-ways ... are so contrived that the logs leap from them into water of great depth. **1905** *Forestry Bureau Bul.* No. 61, 38 *Gangway*, ... the incline plane up which logs are moved from the water into a sawmill. ... [Also called] log jack, log way, slip.

2. A stretch of corduroy road.

1821 Z. HAWLEY *Tour* 94 In one place the traveller passes over a most fatiguing log-way, through which the horse occasionally thrusts his foot. **1874** B. F. TAYLOR *World on Wheels* 245 Over the old road, ran the yellow, mud-stained coach; laboring up its hills, and pitching along its log-ways.

∗**logwork,** *n.* Construction or building by the use of logs. Also a structure, barricade, etc., made of logs.

1721 in *N. Eng. Hist. & Gen. Reg.* XXI. 57 All Hands went briskly to work, to finish ye log-work in ye Lower Block-house. **1856** OLMSTED *Slave States* 111 The chimney is ... commonly of lath or split sticks, laid up like log-work and plastered with mud. **1895** in M. A. JACKSON *Gen. Jackson* 547 Lane . . . had not placed a single picket on the right of the log works, behind which his men were then standing.

***loin,** *n.* As the last term in **strip, tenderloin.**

lolapaloosa ˌlɑləpəˈluzə, *n.* Also **lallapaluza,** etc. [Origin obscure.] A person or thing very striking or unusual. *Slang.*

1909 CALHOUN *Miss Minerva* 204 You sho' is genoowine corn-fed, sterlin' silver, all-wool-an'-a-yard-wide, pure-leaf, Green-River Lolapaloosas. **1920** LEWIS *Main Street* 414, I met the meanest kind of critter that God ever made—meaner than the horned toad or the Texas lallapaluza! **1948** *Capital-Democrat* (Tishomingo, Okla.) 24 June 2/3 He's always using the word, 'lolapacooler.' We hate to disillusion him, but the word is 'lallapaloozer,' and you may lay to that.

lollygag, *v.* See **lallygag,** *v.*

loma ˈlomə, *n. S.W.* [Sp. in same sense.] A small hill or elevation. Often in place-names.

1849 *N.O. Picayune* 4 May 2/3 [They] were riding quietly along the Loma Blanca, (white hill,) when they came suddenly upon a party of eight or ten Indians. **1863** *37th Congress Sp. Sess.* Sen. Ex. Doc. No. 1, 20 The new road is to follow the bottom at the edge of the *lomas.* **1923** SAUNDERS *So. Sierras Calif.* 75 All about are rounded hills, or lomas, rising in baldness. **1941** *Harper's Mag.* Oct. 498/1 Stand on the 'knoll' at Yucca Loma, drink in the desert, and then look down at your feet.

***London,** *n. The London of America, of the States,* (see quots.). *Obs.* — **1832** FERRALL *Ramble* 19 Having determined on quitting 'the London of the States,' as my friends the Yankees call New York, I had bag and baggage conveyed on board a steamer. **1834** C. A. DAVIS *Lett. J. Downing* 191 They used to call Philadelphy the London of America.

Lone Star. Also **lone star.**

1. The flag of the Texas Republic. Also fig.

1843 DEWEES *Lett. from Texas* 246 The lone star of Texas shall continue to wave proudly in the air as long as one brave Texan remains to defend it. **1872** MORRELL *Flowers & Fruits* 20 Sam. Houston was then in Texas . . . intending . . . to set in motion 'a little two-horse republic under the Lone Star.' **1886** POORE *Reminiscences* I. 315 It took him only from February 28th to April 12th to conclude the negotiation which placed the 'Lone Star' in the azure field of the ensign of the Republic.

b. A nickname for Texas, derived from the Texas flag and seal.

[**1855** PIERCE in *Pres. Mess. & P.* V. 347 Who would rejoice to hail Texas as a lone star instead of one in the galaxy of States?] **1856** *Democratic Conv. Proc.* 56 The Democracy of the 'Lone Star' do battle for that favorite, noble son of the 'Keystone of the Arch.' **1907** *Boston Transcript* 9 Nov., Little Rhody. Rhode Island. Lone Star—Texas.

c. Used in various transferred applications (see quots.).

1849 A. MACKAY *Western World* I. 180 A little to his left . . . is the good-humoured face of Mr. Pendleton, familiarly known as the 'Lone Star,' being the only Whig in the whole delegation of Virginia. **1855** *N.Y. Tribune* 31 Dec. 6/2 There were two or three banners flying with different devices, but the large flag, with the Lone Star on it, was over the center of the camp, being the symbol of the great secret, blue band of Western Missouri, of which Atchison and Stringfellow are the leaders. **1944** WILSON *Passing Inst.* 187 All the [quilt] patterns . . . as elaborate as the 'Lone Star,' which might have taken all the time of a seamstress for a whole season.

2. The state flag of South Carolina. Cf. **Palmetto banner.**

[**1856** PHILLIPS *Kansas* 307 About this time a banner was seen fluttering in the breeze over the office of The Herald of Freedom. Its color was a blood-red, and a lone star in the centre, and South Carolina above.] **1860** *Charleston* (S.C.) *Mercury* 14 Nov. 2/8 We this day unfurl the 'State Rights Red Flag' of South Carolina—the Lone Star —emblematic of her pure unsullied name; the evergreen Palmetto, of her faithfulness. *Ib.* 13 Dec. 3/1 The lone star floats in almost every town and hamlet in our State.

3. In combs.: (1) **Lone Star Association,** an association of men favoring the annexation of Cuba to the U.S., *obs.;* (2) **banner,** the flag of the Texas republic, later of the state of Texas; (3) **flag,** see as a main entry; (4) **rattler,** a rattlesnake found in Texas; (5) **Republic,** that portion of the present state of Texas which won its independence from Mexico in 1836, remaining independent until it was annexed to the U.S. in 1845, the state of Texas; (6) **State,** Texas; (7) **Stater,** an inhabitant or native of Texas.

(**1**) **1853** *Harper's Mag.* VI. 267/1 The doctrine urged in favor of Filibustering expeditions and Lone Star Associations is also at war with some of our most popular professions. *c***1855** ROBERTSON *Few Months* 91 All southern men are not in favour of the annexation of Cuba, and are not members of the 'Lone Star' Association. — (**2**) **1846** SAGE *Scenes Rocky Mts.* xxix, Right gladly did I hail the Lone Star Banner. **1884** SWEET & KNOX *Through Texas* xxix. 385 They ran up the Lone Star banner of the Texas republic. — (**4**) **1943** *Democrat* 23 Sep. 2/2 Texans are proud of the part the Lone Star rattlers are playing in the war effort.

(**5**) **1865** *Louisville D. Democrat* 30 Sep. 1/8 He came out a young rover from Missouri in 1841 as one of a secret filibustering party, who intended to . . . join California to the then 'lone star' republic of Texas. **1910** J. HART *Vigilante Girl* 131 One of those veterans . . . turned over to the United States the Lone Star Republic as a Lone Star State. **1945** *Amer. Sp.* April 81 For the soft-spoken citizens of the Lone Star republic are avidly patriotic and their sons have leaped into World War II with glee. — (**6**) **1846** *Warrock's Alman. 1847* 22 Texas, Lone Star [State]. **1949** *Chesterton* (Ind.) *Tribune* 7 April 10/4 The other members of the party had all traveled in the Lone Star state of colorful history. — (**7**) **1873** BEADLE *Undevel. West* 805, I am proud to find him in honor and position among the 'Lone Star Staters.'

Lone Star flag. Any one of various flags (see quots.) having a single star in their devices.

1860 *Charleston* (S.C.) *Mercury* 25 Dec. 3/7 The Lone Star flag was raised here [Petersburg, Va.] to-day amid the exultant shouts of a tremendous multitude. **1861** *Ib.* 22 Jan. 3/3 At the lower end of the table a 'Lone Star flag' fluttered in the breeze, made up for the occasion from a red flannel shirt. **1899** *Success* 6 May 392 There should be a general amnesty, a general blotting out of the past, and a clean page for the future, for all who wish to live under the Lone Star flag [of Cuba]. **1936** ARTHUR *Old New Orleans* 174 It [i.e., the Stars and Stripes] was hauled down to make way for another banner—a strange flag it was, the 'Lone Star' flag of the state of Louisiana. **1941** FERGUSON *Southwest* 49 Texas was a republic for ten years, and on February 16, 1846 it entered the United States, the Lone Star flag came down, and Texans fought in the Mexican War. [**1948** *Chi. D. News* 1 May 6/4 A 6-foot Texas buck sergeant showed his pocket size Lone Star State flag to a Frenchman.]

***long,** *a.* and *adv.*

1. *Stock exchange. To be long* (*in* or *on*), to be well supplied with (products or securities). Also transf.

1849 *Hunt's Merch. Mag.* XXI. 118 'Long' means when a man has bought stock on time, which he can call for at any day he chooses. He is also said to be 'long' when he holds a good deal. **1870** M. H. SMITH *20 Years Wall St.* 68–9 *Long in Stocks:* — A broker buys stocks for a customer, pays the full value, and carries it. A man through his broker buys a thousand shares of New York Central at 117. The broker pays for it and keeps it. The customer is 'long' in Central. **1882** PECK *Sunshine* 48 Millions of Bibles were shipped to this country by the firm that was 'long' on Bibles. **1894** *Harper's Mag.* Feb. 351/1 The ranch bookkeeper [was] a young man 'short' on experience and 'long' on hope.

b. Of commodities: Held for a rise in price.

1892 *Courier-Journal* 1 Oct. 11/5 There was a considerable quantity of long oats thrown upon the market.

c. Of transactions: Based on long-term credit.

1902 MCFAUL *Ike Glidden* 139 He bought on the short side for cash and sold on the long side on credit at twelve per cent interest.

2. In miscellaneous combs.: (1) **long calm,** a stretch of calm water, *obs.;* (2) **chance,** a chance involving considerable uncertainty or risk, also attrib.; (3) **eighteen,** ?a cigar twice as long as a long nine *q.v.*, *obs.;* (4) * **field,** in baseball, the outfield, also **long-fielder,** *obs.;* (5) * **range,** a kind of liquor, *obs.*, cf. **forty-rod;** (6) **reach,** ?a wagon with an unusually long body, *obs.;* (7) **rifle,** a rifle having a long barrel, often sixty inches, as distinguished from firearms, often for military use, with shorter barrels; (8) * **session,** before the passage of the 20th Amendment (1934), the session of Congress beginning on the first Monday in December of odd numbered years; (9) * **talk,** a speech made at a conference between white people and Indians, also used allusively, *obs.;* (10) **term,** a full term of office as distinguished from a short term, *q.v.*

(**1**) **1728** *Md. Hist. Mag.* XVIII. 12 Luke Stansbury appointed overseer to clear a road according to law from the long calm of Gunpowder Falls to Edward Reston's plantation. **1730** *Ib.* XVIII. 13 Ordered, that the Road formerly cleared from the long Calm to Mr. Gist's be continued into the road . . . called the Old Indian Road. — (**2**) **1907** WHITE *Arizona Nights* I. xiii. 191 He's plumb scared at the prospect of suffering anything, and would rather die right off than take long chances. *Ib.* II. iv. 262 He's one of those long-chance fellows. — **(3) 1831** *Boston Transcript* 13 Aug. 2/2, I tried a segar; a long eighteen, and puffed myself blind and sick. — **(4) 1856** *Spirit of Times* 6 Dec. 229/1 He strikes with great force, but by raising the ball he gives many chances to the long field. **1857** *Ib.* 7 Feb. 373/1 Mr. Monson Hoyt, one of their long fielders, has no equal in his position on the field. **1867** CHADWICK *Base Ball Reference* 139 A *Home Run*, a run made from home to home from a hit to long-field.

(5) **1875** *Fur, Fin, & Feather* 111 They [hogs] were fed on slops from a distillery where they manufactured 'Long Range.' — **(6) 1899** A. BROWN *Tiverton Tales* 118 Passing the window, she saw the selectmen, in the vehicle known as a long-reach, waiting at the gate. — **(7) 1829** B. HALL *Forty Etchings* No. XX, The central figure is a Backwoodsman of the State of Indiana, with a long rifle in his hand. **1883** J. W. STEELE *Frontier Army Sk.* 284 The long rifle that now has a place in museums but which has made a larger subordinate figure in American history than all the Winchesters and Sharps. **1949** *Chi. Tribune* 20 March (Grafic Mag.) 13/1 Most of their kind in those days were expert with the long rifle. — **(8) 1851** QUENTIN *Reisebilder* I. 32 Eine Erledigung der Zollfrage, während der laufenden, ersten Sitzungs-Periode (long session) kaum zu erwarten ist. **1886** ALTON *Among Law-Makers* 13 There is one regular session every year, commencing on the first Monday of December, thus making two regular sessions in a Congress, known as the 'long session' and the 'short session.' **1903** PIDGIN *Quincy Adams Sawyer* 279 This is the long session, and my friends will be in Washington. — **(9) 1832** WILLIAMSON *Maine* II. 272 'Long talks,' were followed by re-assurances from the chiefs, of their wishes to live in tranquillity. **1876** *N.Y. Tribune* 5 July 1/6 The Hon. Fernando Wood gave the 'Long Talk.'

(10) 1855 *N.Y. Wkly. Tribune* 10 Nov. 4/2 We think Samuel L. Selden, who was placed on the tickets of the Hards, Softs, Liquor men and Half-Shells, is chosen for the long term.

b. In similar combs., usu. obs., of obvious meaning or sufficiently explained in the quots., as (1) **long arms,** (2) **beards,** (3) **bit,** (see ∗**bit,** *n.* **2. c.** (2)), (4) **food,** [cf. Du. *langvoer*, hay or grass], (5) **geared,** (6) **hairs,** (7) ∗**horn,** (cf. **Texas longhorn**), (8) **John,** (9) **lick,** (10) **room,** (11) **season,** (12) **short,** (13) **socks,** (14) **sugar.**

(1) 1675 *Conn. Rec.* II. 270 Such Troopers as shall neglect to prouide themselues with long armes, viz. a carbin or muskett, . . . shall be disbanded and attend the foot company. **1695** SEWALL *Diary* I. 405 Capt. Smith of Hampton meets us with 12. by Govr. Usher's order, long Arms. — **(2) 1742** *N.J. Archives* XII. 138, I think that while the Enthusiastical *Moravians* and *Long-Beards* or *Pickists*, are uniting their Bodies, . . . it is a Shame that the Ministers . . . should be divided and quarrelling. **1812** STUART *Narratives* 12 They [Indians] esteem it very uncooth and impolite to have a beard, calling the whites by way of reproach, the long beards. — **(4) 1823** in COMMONS *Doc. Hist.* I. 256 As much corn or oats and hay and fodder as our horses can destroy (usually half a bushel of grain and a rackful of long food).

(5) 1891 *Harper's Mag.* July 208/2 One of the most successful bronco riders . . . was a long-geared, lank Texas lad. — **(6) 1907** WHITE *Arizona Nights* 5 The old man was one of the typical 'long hairs.' He had come to the Galiuro Mountains in '69. **1944** ADAMS *W. Words* 93 Long-hairs. A slang name for the men of the early West who wore their hair long. — **(7) 1905** *N.Y. Times* 28 May (Th. Supp.), There was a big chief on the range, an old longhorn called Abraham, and his lil' ole squaw. **1921** THOM *Book of Cheese* 230 Size of Cheese Hoops, Weight, and Terms Applied to Cheese . . . Tabers 5–7 in. Height of Cheese 10–14 in. Weight of Cheese Pounds 10–16. Long Horn. — **(8) 1884** *N.Y. Wkly. Tribune* 23 July 11/1 'Quack grass can be killed by ploughing deep, but how can we beat this Long John?' The plant referred to is Camelina sativa, a member of the mustard family commonly known as wild or false flax. — **(9) 1898** F. T. BULLEN *Cruise Cachalo* 6 A pot of something sweetened with 'longlick' (molasses), made an apology for a meal. **1924** *D.N.* V. 286 Few grocers outside of Cape Cod would know what to produce when someone asked for a gallon of 'Porty Reek long lick.' But a real Cape Codder would know that a gallon of Porto Rico molasses was desired.

(10) 1870 MEDBERY *Men Wall St.* 22 A chamber is provided at the Exchange, where members may bargain with members at any hour throughout the day. This is known as the Long Room. **1885** *Harper's Mag.* Nov. 830 On the left, or Broad Street side, is the Long Room devoted to telegraphic apparatus and subscribers who pay $100 per annum for the privilege of using it. — **(11) 1800** W. TATHAM *Tobacco* 14 The term, *season* for planting, signifies a shower of rain of sufficient quantity to wet the earth to a degree of moisture which may render it safe to draw the young plants from the plant bed, and transplant. . . . These seasons generally commence in April, and terminate with what is termed the *long season in May.* — **(12) 1840** *Knickerb.* XVI. 22 A buxom, rosy-cheeked girl, with a blue-striped long-short . . . was busied around the fire-place. **1859** BARTLETT 256 *Long Short*, a gown somewhat shorter than a petticoat, worn by women when doing household work. — **(13) 1859** BARTLETT 204 *Hose*, the Western term for 'stockings,' which is considered extremely indelicate, although 'long socks' is pardonable. — **(14) 1729** BYRD *Dividing Line* (1866) 57 Their molasses comes from the same country, and has the name of 'Long Sugar' in Carolina, I suppose from the Ropiness of it.

For **long distance, green,** ∗**house, Hunters, Island, Islander,** ∗**knife, nine, sweetening, Tom,** see as main entries.

3. In the names of, or with reference to, plants: (1) **long corn,** ?corn of normal size as contrasted with nubbins, *obs.;* (2) **cotton,** =**long-staple cotton;** (3) ∗**grass,** designating a prairie region, also the country, the "sticks," *slang;* (4) **moss,** =**black moss;** (5) **sauce,** (see quot. 1859), *obs.;* (6) **shucks,** (see quot. and cf. **short shucks,** and see **longschat pine** as a main entry); (7) ∗**stalk,** (*a*) a variety of apple, (see quot.), (*b*) **long-stalk willow,** (see quot.), *obs.;* (8) ∗**-stalked,** used in the names of American plants (see quots.); (9) **-staple cotton,** cotton having an exceptionally long staple or fiber, esp. sea-island cotton, also attrib.; (10) **straw (pine),** =**long-leaf pine.**

(1) 1786 WASHINGTON *Diaries* III. 143 Measured at the latter 19 Barrls. of long Corn and 6 of Short. **1894** ROBLEY *Bourbon Co., Kans.* 153 They were a little short on big pumpkins and long corn, but the show of live stock and fancy work was very good. — **(2) 1854** in COMMONS *Doc. Hist.* I. 272 Among the diseases to which Long Cotton is subject blight, rust and blue may arise from some defect in the soil. — **(3) 1850** GARRARD *Wah-To-Yah* (1927) xxvi. 305 We were grateful for the sweet prairie-flowers, and the greensward, for we were again in the long-grass country. **1928** *Chambers's Jrnl.* XVIII. Feb. 118/2 I'm for the long grass, where I'll hide my head. — **(4)** [**1744** MOORE *Voy. Georgia* 105, I observed here a kind of long moss I had never seen before.] **1781–2** JEFFERSON *Notes Va.* (1788) 39 Long moss, *Tillandsia Usneoides.* **1896** BRITTON & BROWN *Illust. Flora Northern U.S.* I. 374 *Tillandsia usneoides.* Long Moss. Florida Moss.

(5) 1809 IRVING *Hist. N.Y.* (1927) III. vii. 161 To this end he takes unto himself for a wife, some dashing country heiress . . . deeply skilled in the mystery of making apple sweetmeats, long sauce and pumpkin pie. **1859** BARTLETT 255 *Long Sauce*, beets, carrots, and parsnips are *long sauce.* Potatoes, turnips, onions, pumpkins, etc. are *short sauce.* — **(6) 1897** SUDWORTH *Arborescent Flora* 26 *Pinus tæda*, Loblolly Pine. . . . Common names [include] Longshucks (Md., Va.), Black Slash Pine (S.C.), Frankincense Pine (lit.). — **(7)** (*a*) **1709** LAWSON *Carolina* 108 The Red-streak thrives very well. Long-stalk is a large Apple, with a long Stalk, and makes good Summer Cider. (*b*) **1897** SUDWORTH *Arborescent Flora* 119 *Salix occidentalis longipes.* . . Longstalk Willow. — **(8) 1813** MUHLENBERG *Cat. Plants* 87 *Quercus filiformis*, Long-stalk'd oak. **1814** BIGELOW *Florula Bostoniensis* 241 *Smilax peduncularis.* Long stalked Smilax. . . . A rank, herbaceous, climbing plant. . . . June. Perennial. **1833** EATON *Botany* (ed. 6) 155 *Geranium columbinum*, long stalked geranium. **1843** TORREY *Flora N.Y.* II. 268 *Microstylis ophioglossoides.* Long-stalked Adder's-mouth. — **(9) 1802** *Steele P.* I. 341 Black Seed or Long Staple Cotton is in demand. **1943** MENEFEE *Assignment* 255 The Arizona ranchers, who produce a rare type of longstaple cotton that is particularly needed in the manufacture of observation balloons and parachutes. **1949** MURRAY *This Our Land* 188 Long-staple cotton seed was brought to the colonies from the Bahama Islands soon after the settlement of Charleston.

(10) 1897 SUDWORTH *Arborescent Flora* 26, 31. **1949** COLLINGWOOD & BRUSH *Knowing Your Trees* 54 *Pinus palustris* . . . is commonly known as 'longstraw' pine.

See also **long green, leaf, leafed, neck,** as main entries.

4. In the names of, or with reference to, birds, fishes, etc.: (1) ∗**long-billed,** see as a main entry; (2) **clam,** the soft clam or the razor clam; (3) **-eared sunfish,** one of two species of sunfish, *Lepomis auritus* or *Xenotis megalotis;* (4) **-finned,** *a.* designating various American fishes having particularly long fins; (5) **-legged sandpiper,** the stilt sandpiper, *Micropalama himantopus*, frequently found along the Atlantic Coast; (6) **neck,** see as a main entry; (7) **-nosed gar (pike),** (see quot. 1889); (8) ∗**shanks,** the black-necked stilt, *Himantopus mexicanus;* (9) ∗**spur,** any one of several long-clawed birds, usu. of the genus *Calcarius*, found chiefly in the plains regions of the U.S., cf. **chestnut-collared, Lapland, McCown, longspur;** (10) ∗**-tailed,** see as a main entry; (11) **-toothed flounder,** (see quot.).

(2) 1843 J. E. DE KAY *Mollusca N.Y.* 240 *Mya Arenaria* . . . is known under the various appellations of *Long Clam* and *Piss Clam*, to distinguish it from the common *Round Clam* (*V. mercenaria*). **1887** GOODE *Fisheries* II. 614 Under the name of 'long clam,' 'knife-handle,' and 'razor-clam,' they are occasionally seen in New York Market. — **(3) 1884** GOODE *Fisheries* I. 406 The Long-eared Sun-fish—*Lepomis auritus*. This species . . . is found in all the coastwise streams from Maine to Louisiana. **1903** T. H. BEAN *Fishes N.Y.* 480 The long-eared sunfish . . . is an excellent food fish. — **(4) 1842** *Nat. Hist. N.Y., Zoology* IV. 194 The Long-finned Chubsucker, *Labeo cyprinus*, . . . is common in the Susquehannah. **1896** JORDAN & EVERMANN *Check-List of Fishes* 340 *Germo alalunga*. Long finned Albacore; Albecor . . . Mediterranean; San Francisco; Santa Barbara Islands.

(5) 1828 BONAPARTE *Synopsis* 316 The Long-legged Sandpiper . . . inhabits the middle states in summer and autumn. **1917** *Birds of Amer.* I. 230 Stilt Sandpiper. . . . [Also called] Long-legged Sandpiper. — **(7) 1884** GOODE *Fisheries* I. 663 The Long-nosed Garpike *Lepidosteus osseus* . . . is found in the Great Lakes, and throughout the Mississippi Valley, as well as in all the streams of the South from Mexico to New Jersey. **1889** *Cent.* 2453/3 *Long-nosed gar, Lepidosteus osseus*, the common garpike or bill-fish. — **(8) 1813** WILSON *Ornithology* VII. 50 Long-legged Avoset: *Recurvirostra himantopus*; . . . arrives on the sea coast of New Jersey about the twenty-fifth of April. . . . The name by which this bird is known on the sea coast is the Stilt, or Tilt, or Long-shanks. **1917** *Birds of Amer.* I. 223 Black-necked Stilt. . . . [Also called] Longshanks. — **(9) 1874** COUES *Birds N.W.* 122 *Plectrophanes Ornatus*, . . . Chestnut-collared Bunting: Black-bellied Longspur. **1939** *Nat. Geog. Mag.* March 354 In North America the representatives of this group are enrolled in three subfamilies, one of which, the Emberizinae, includes the towhees, sparrows, juncos, longspurs, and snow buntings. **1949** *Chi. Tribune* 14 Sep. 1/5 Small flocks of pipits and longspurs may be seen even after winter has closed in.

(11) 1855 BAIRD in *Smithsonian Rep.* 349 The long-toothed Flounder, *Platessa ocellaris*, . . . is generally found on sandy bottoms.

* **long-billed.** A qualifying term in the names of various American birds having long bills.

1822 FOWLER *Journal* 148 We Hear for the first time Seen the long Billed Bird [i.e., chaparral cock] . . . — the Bill about one foot in length. **1869** *Amer. Naturalist* III. 74 Long-billed Nuthatch. . . . Common in the Rocky Mountains. **1917** *Birds of Amer.* I. 205 Virginia Rail. . . . [Also called] Long-billed Rail. **1940** GABRIELSON & JEWETT *Birds Ore.* 264 The Long-billed Dowitcher is a regular but not abundant migrant in Oregon.

b. long-billed curlew, the hen curlew, *Numenius americanus*.

1813 WILSON *Ornithology* VIII. 23 Long-billed Curlew: *Numenius longirostra*; . . . is an inhabitant of marshes in the vicinity of the sea. **1917** *Birds of Amer.* I. 251/1 From being an abundant species on the south Atlantic coast a century ago, this interesting, spectacular species, the Long-billed Curlew, is now almost unknown in the eastern United States. **1940** GABRIELSON & JEWETT *Birds Ore.* 249 About the nesting ground the Long-billed Curlews are noisy birds.

c. long-billed marsh wren, a species of marsh-frequenting wren, *Telmatodytes palustris palustris*, or one of its regional varieties.

1856 BAIRD *Birds Pacific R.R.* 364 Long-billed Marsh Wren . . . North America from Atlantic to Pacific. **1945** *Nat. Geog. Mag.* June 740 Anywhere else the Long-billed Marsh Wren is unhappy and it has no use for bushes and trees or even for meadows.

long distance.

1. Short for next.

1905 TARKINGTON *In Arena* 128, I had it by the long distance an hour ago, from your own home. **1925** *Amer. Mag.* Dec. 5/1 Nixon . . . was called on long distance by an excited secretary in his Cleveland office. **1945** MENCKEN *Supp.* I. 474 The first recorded English example of *long-distance* is from American usage.

2. long distance telephone, a telephone or system of telephony which enables one to communicate with those who are far away, esp. in another city or town.

[**1884** *Whitaker's Almanack* 385/1 In America some remarkable trials of long distance telephoning have taken place, one in particular between New York and Chicago, a distance of 1,000 miles.] **1886** *Scientific Amer.* 2 Oct. 208/2 There is a popular belief that the long distance telephone is crowding the telegraph to the wall. **1912** NICHOLSON *Hoosier Chron.* 484 He watched her attack the problem by long-distance telephone. **1946** *Trail & Timberline* May 74/1 The first long distance telephone in Colorado Territory was installed that same year between Georgetown and Central City.

attrib. **1925** BRYAN *Memoirs* 487 After the meal he made several long distance telephone calls. **1948** JOHNSTON *Gold Rush* 38/2 It was at French Corral that construction of the world's first long distance telephone line was begun in 1878.

3. Often used with reference to telephony in expressions of obvious meaning, as (1) **long distance call,** (2) **connection,** (3) **line,** (4) **wire.**

(1) 1947 *Chi. Tribune* 2 Nov. (Grafic Mag.) 18/1 The demand for tickets was unbelievable . . . and we had to stop taking long-distance calls. — **(2) 1912** *Out West* March 173/2 He had wired some people in Los Angeles to get a long distance connection with Ogden by the time we got there as we would stop twenty minutes. — **(3) 1908** *Sat. Ev. Post* 26 Sep. 15/3 A long distance line can only be used by one person at a time. **1949** *Dly. Ardmoreite* (Ardmore, Okla.) 25 Jan. 2/4 Long distance lines in nearby Marshall and Bryan counties were down in many places. — **(4) 1909** A. C. RICE *Mr. Opp* 279, I know it ain't right to repeat anything I hear over the long-distance wire.

longevity pay, ration. (See quot. 1909.) Cf. ***fogy.** — **1879** *Cong. Rec.* 25 April 907/2 The meaning of it [the bill], then, is that the officer is to have pay allowed him computing all the time of service while in the Army . . . in addition to what is called the fogy ration, or longevity ration? **1909** *Cent. Supp.* 956/1 *Longevity pay*, additional pay given to officers for long service in the United States army and navy.

long green.

1. A variety of tobacco having unusually large, long leaves, home-grown. In full **long-green tobacco.**

1788 SCHÖPF *Reise* II. 115 Long-green Tobacco hat grosse, fette und lange Blätter, und liebt festen Boden. **1897** *Outing* XXX. 380/2 It seems that they were out of tobacco, and had been able to get only the 'long green' that the mountaineers used. **1933** T. WILLIAMSON *Woods Colt* 18 He pulls out a twist of long green, wrenches off a mouthful, and chews in silence.

2. Whisky. *Slang. Obs.*

1837 *Knickerb.* X. 413 The disturber, known by the name of 'long green' and 'blue ruin,' in Pennsylvania, . . . was happily beyond their reach.

3. Paper money, greenbacks. *Slang.*

1891 MAITLAND, Long green (Am.) Counterfeit bills of large denominations. **1896** G. ADE *Artie* 110 He's gone right down into his kick and dug up the long green. **1946** NEWTON *P. Bunyan* 63 We'll be there tomorrow afternoon with Napoleon and the long green.

* **long house.** Among the Indians, esp. the Iroquois, an exceptionally long wigwam or cabin serving as a communal dwelling and council house.

1643 R. WILLIAMS *Key* (1866) 197 [In the] *Long house*, sometimes an hundred, somtimes [*sic*] two hundred foot long . . . many thousands, men and women meet. **1826** COOPER *Mohicans* Pref., One branch of

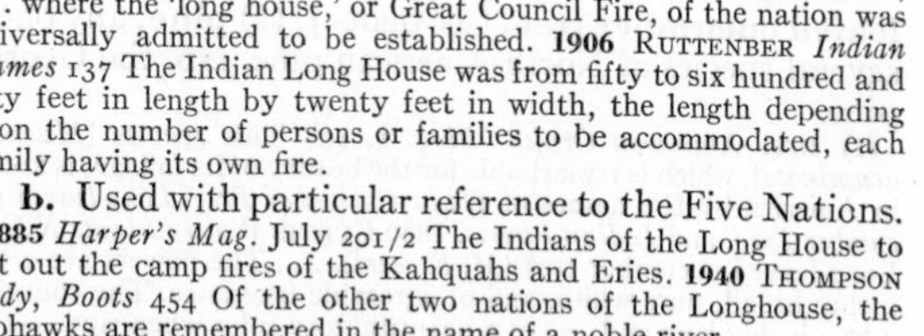

Long house of the Indians

this numerous people [the Delawares] was seated on a beautiful river, . . . where the 'long house,' or Great Council Fire, of the nation was universally admitted to be established. **1906** RUTTENBER *Indian Names* 137 The Indian Long House was from fifty to six hundred and fifty feet in length by twenty feet in width, the length depending upon the number of persons or families to be accommodated, each family having its own fire.

b. Used with particular reference to the Five Nations.

1885 *Harper's Mag.* July 201/2 The Indians of the Long House to put out the camp fires of the Kahquahs and Eries. **1940** THOMPSON *Body, Boots* 454 Of the other two nations of the Longhouse, the Mohawks are remembered in the name of a noble river.

Long Hunters. (See 1st quots.)

1792 IMLAY *Western Territory* 9 Certain men, called Long Hunters, from Virginia and North Carolina, by penetrating these mountains . . . were fascinated with the beauty. **1824** H. MARSHALL *Hist. Kentucky* (ed. 2) I. 9 Nine of this party, led on, by the present, Colonel James Knox, reached Kentucky; and from the time they were absent from home, obtained the name of the long hunters. **1949** *Tenn. Hist. Quart.* March 4 Mansher and a group of 'long hunters' discovered French Lick, the present site of Nashville.

Long Island. In combs.: (1) **Long Island cake,** a cake resembling poundcake leavened with potash, *obs.*; (2) **herring,** the fall herring or the mossbunker *qq.v.*; (3) **pike,** (see quot.).

(1) 1799 *Monthly Mag.* VIII. 873 The cake under consideration is called *pot-ashcake*, because pot-ash is one of the articles which enter into the composition of it. They call it likewise . . . *Long-Island cake*, upon a supposition that the inhabitants of that large and pleasant island, in the state of New York, were particularly addicted to the use of it. — **(2) 1814** MITCHILL *Fishes N.Y.* 451 Long-Island Herring,

Clupea mattowacca, . . . is caught most commonly in autumn. **1898** *N.Y. Journal* 26 July 14/7 Thousands of bunkers, otherwise known as 'Long Island herring,' floated lifeless on the surface of the water. — (3) **1856** *Spirit of Times* 29 Nov. 209/2 The little Long Island Pike, *Esox Fasciatus*, . . . is called the Long Island Pike, not because no other pike are found in the waters of that famous sporting region, . . . but because he is found nowhere else.

Long Islander. A native or resident of Long Island.
1637 *Mass. H.S. Coll.* 4 Ser. VI. 208 [As] for the Long Ilanders themselues & Wequashcuck, they will not medle with them. **1856** *Porter's Spirit of Times* 22 Nov. 193/1 Long life to the Long Islanders; and may their shadows never be less. **1894** WARNER *Golden House* xviii, Perhaps it would be best to get some Long-Islander to buy it for them.

***long knife.** An Indian designation for a white settler or frontiersman, esp. a Virginian. Usu. *pl.* Cf. **Big Knife.**
1774 in PEYTON *Adv. Grandfather* (1867) 141 The Indians . . . deliberately prepared to crush the force of 'Long Knives,' as they called the Virginians under Lewis. **1822** in MORSE *Rep. Indian Affairs* II. 246 My people have never struck the whites, and the whites have never struck them. . . . Mine is the only nation that has spared the long knives. **1923** J. H. COOK *On Old Frontier* 230 Red Cloud's popularity waned as others who were more belligerent led the young men on the trail against the 'long knives.' **1948** *N.W. Ohio Quart.* Jan. 38 They looked forward to their meeting with the 'Long Knives' (She-no-ke-man), as a holiday experience.
attrib. **1895** *Kans. Hist. Coll.* (1896) V. 95 This episode somewhat dampened diplomatic relations between the wily warriors and the 'long-knife chief.'

b. (See quot.) *Rare.*
1805 L. DOW *Travels* Wks. (1806) II. 67 But they [the Indians] being afraid of Long-knife, (i.e. Congress) refrained from violence.

c. long-knife tribe, =**Kootenay.**
1874 *Field & Stream* 20 Aug. 18/2 This region is occupied exclusively by the Kootenay, or long-knife tribe of Indians.

***long leaf.**

1. =next.
1860 CURTIS *Woody Plants N.C.* 22 It affords a good deal of Turpentine, which is less fluid than that from the *Long-leaf.*

2. longleaf pine, =**Georgia pine.** Also attrib.
1796 HAWKINS *Letters* 24, [I] came to the long leaf pine and open land. **1841** GREGG *Diary & Letters* (1941) I. 92 The 12 or 15 first miles of today was through a flat long leaf pine country. **1949** *N.O. Times-Picayune Mag.* 14 Aug. 5/2 They felled virgin long-leaf pines from their own tract.

3. longleaf yellow pine, the lumber of the longleaf pine. Also attrib.
1908 *Ill. Bureau Labor Statistics Ann. Coal Rep.* 349 The head frame is built with long leaf yellow pine lumber. **1924** CROY *R.F.D. No. 3* 197 The lumber is full of knots; he sold it to me for long-leaf yellow pine. . . . Is that long-leaf?

***long-leafed, long-leaved,** *a.* In combs.: (1) **long-leafed cucumber tree,** (see quots.); (2) **pine,** any one of several species of North American pine, esp. the Georgia pine.
(1) **1831** AUDUBON *Ornith. Biog.* I. 198 This species [*Magnolia acuminata*], which is remarkable for the beauty of its foliage, is known in America by the names of *White Cucumber Tree, Long-leaved Cucumber Tree*, and *Indian Physic.* **1860** CURTIS *Woody Plants N.C.* 68 Long-leaved cucumber tree (*M. Fraseri*). . . . The flowers are 2 to 4 inches broad, pure white, and of agreeable fragrance. The cones are 3 to 4 inches long and . . . of a beautiful rose color when ripe. — (2) **1765** J. BARTRAM *Diary* 11 July, Trees which naturaly grows there is . . . very fine long-leaved pine pitch pine yapon fartle berry chinkapin. **1867** MUIR *Thousand-Mile Walk* (1916) 131 The live-oaks of these keys divide empire with the long-leafed pine and palmetto. **1916** SETON *Woodcraft Man.* 267 Long-leaved Pine, Georgia Pine, Southern Pine, Yellow Pine, or Hard Pine (*Pinus palustris*). A fine tree, up to 100 feet high; evergreen; found in great forests in the Southern states; it supplies much of our lumber now; and most of our turpentine, tar, and rosin.

***longneck.**

1. *local.* (See quot.)
1888 G. TRUMBULL *Names of Birds* 39 At Pleasantville and Atlantic City we hear Long-neck [used as a name for the pintail duck].

2. long-neck clam, (see quot.).
1903 *N.Y. State Museum Bul.* No. 71, 22 The soft or long-neck clam, Mya, is capable of locomotion only when very small.

3. long neck(ed) squash, a variety of squash, *Cucurbita verrucosa*, having long necks and warty surfaces; a squash of this variety.
1835 *Vade Mecum* (Phila.) 10 Jan. 3/4 The editor of the National Eagle . . . offered a couple of long necked squashes, a huge pumpkin, and flour enough to make them into pies, for the best New Year's Address. **1868** GRAY *Field Botany* 160 C[*ucurbita*] *verrucosa*, Warty, Long-neck, and Crook-neck Squash, Vegetable Marrow, &c.

long nine.

1. A cheap cigar. In full **long-nine cigar.** *Obs.*
1830 *N.Y. Constellation* 11 Sep. 2/5 Some tugged at the bottle, some smoked long-nines. **1834** *Sun* (N.Y.) 20 May 3/1 His sugar-loaf cap was decorated with bunches of long-nine cigars for tassels. **1879** *Bradstreet's* 31 Dec. 3/3 Boys smoke 'long nines' while they still wear jackets.
transf. **1840** BIRD *Robin Day* 47 He demanded . . . what the devil I was doing with my long nine (meaning the duck gun).

2. (See quot. 1865.) Now *hist.*
1840 *Ill. State Reg.* (Springfield) 11 Jan. 3/4 One of the long-nine (Mr. Baker) who was not in the Legislature when the Internal Improvements law passed, took to himself great merit . . . because he was not in the *scrape* of his colleagues on that question. **1865** in DUNCAN *M. Graham* (1944) 252 In 1836 he [i.e., A. Lincoln] was again a candidate for the legislature and was elected and was one of what is called 'the long nine'—two tall senators and seven tall representatives from Sangamon who moved the capital of the state of Illinois from Vandalia to Springfield. **1949** *Time* 22 Aug. 88/3 By 1836, however, Lincoln had become the leader of the Sangamon County delegation of nine Whigs—'the Long Nine' whose aggregate height was exactly 54 feet.

longschat pine. [f. **long*+"schat." See **shats.**] (See quots.) — **1897** SUDWORTH *Arborescent Flora* 27 Pitch pine. . . .Common names . . . Long-leaved Pine (Del.), Longschat Pine (Del.), Hard Pine (Mass.). **1908** N. L. BRITTON *N. Amer. Trees* 31 Pitch Pine . . . is known by many names, such as Hard pine, Long-leaved pine, Longschat pine, Yellow pine, Black pine [etc.].

long sweetening. (See quots.) Now *hist.* Cf. **long lick, long sugar, long-tailed sugar.**
1714 *N.C. Col. Rec.* II. 132 Let who will go unpaid. Rum long sweet'n alias Mollasses, glystr. Sugar must be had. **1869** BOWLES *Our New West* viii. 170 The writer won his glory and victual by making the 'long-sweetening,' i.e. white sugar melted into a permanent syrup. **1943** CROW *Amer. Customer* 175 Sorghum molasses was more commonly used and was known as 'long sweetening.' Sugar was 'short sweetening.' **1948** DICK *Dixie Frontier* 291 The so-called 'long sweetening' was honey obtained from bee trees.

***long-tailed,** *a.*

1. In the names of American birds (see quots.).
1823 JAMES *Exped.* I. 265 *Tetrao phasianellus*—Long-tailed grouse. **1869** *Amer. Naturalist* III. 186 [Among] the most peculiar birds [in California is] . . . the Long-tailed Mocking-bird (*Mimus caudatus*). **1873** in COUES *Birds N.W.* 230 *Parus atricapillus* var. *septentrionalis*, Long-tailed Titmouse. **1917** *Birds of Amer.* III. 163/2 The Long-tailed Chat (*Icteria virens longicauda*) of the western United States is similar to the Yellow-breasted Chat. **1940** GABRIELSON & JEWETT *Birds Ore.* 432 The Long-tailed Chickadee is a species of the cottonwoods and river bottoms.

b. (See quots.)
1857 *Rep. Comm. Patents 1846: Agric.* 95 Long-tailed Jumping Mouse. . . . *Jaculus labradorius. Ib.* 96 This animal is known as the 'Long-tailed Deer Mouse.' . . . 'Wood Mouse,' and other names. **1881** FARROW *Mt. Scouting* 197 The *long-tailed deer* are found very high up in the Rocky Mountains, and are distinguished by their very long tails.

2. long-tail(ed) blue, a blue coat with long tails, part of the typical garb of a black-face comedian. *Obs.*
*c***1827** Atwater Music Saloon N.Y., *Long Tail Blue*, I wear a jacket all the week, And Sunday my long tail blue. **1835** *Vade Mecum* (Phila.) 21 Feb. 3/2 Pierre's coat—he has but one—a faithful follower—is a long-tailed blue: perhaps the origin of the celebrated bravura of that name. **1860** CLAIBORNE *S. Dale* 27 The negro wore a 'long-tail blue,' the skirts flying out as he fled. **1889** *Harper's Mag.* June 139/2 The first colored gentleman to wear 'The Long-tailed Blue' was Barney Burns, who broke his neck on a vaulting board in Cincinnati in 1838.

b. A dandified Negro or black-face comedian wearing such a coat. Also the title of a minstrel song often sung by such an actor.
1844 UNCLE SAM *Peculiarities* II. 170 A dandy nigger, technically termed a 'long-tailed blue,' [is] dancing Jim Crow's pattern dance. . . . The passengers . . . are laughing at 'long-tailed blue.' **1867** *Atlantic Mo.* Nov. 610/2 'Clar de Kitchen' soon appeared as a companion piece, followed speedily by 'Lucy Long.' . . . 'Long-Tail Blue,' and so on.

3. long-tailed sugar, (see quot.). *Obs.*
1868 WHYMPER *Alaska* 175 Molasses (known by us as 'long-tailed sugar'), and coffee, pleased our Russian friends well.

Long Tom. Also **long tom.**

1. A variety of apple. *Obs.*

1817 W. COXE *Fruit Trees* 125 Bullocks Pippin, or Sheep Nose. This is one of the finest apples in New-Jersey. . . . It is sometimes called the Long Tom. **1830** *Western Agriculturist* 318 Red fall Russet, or Long Tom, October and Nov.

2. *Mining.* A form of trough used for washing gold-bearing dirt. Cf. ∗**cradle,** *n.* **1.**

1839 *Amer. R.R. Jrnl.* VIII. 98 The Long Tom . . . consists merely of a trough. **1880** INGHAM *Digging Gold* 58 The 'Long Tom' . . . is placed at an incline and a stream of water introduced into the upper end. **1949** [see **gold rocker**].

3. A rifle of large caliber (see quot. 1944).

1849 *N.O. Picayune* 13 May 2/1 How to begin to describe our gun, puzzles us. There is no use in calling it a 'long tom,' for that would convey no idea at all. **1907** COOK *Border & Buffalo* (1938) 236 Jimmie had a condemned army gun, the old Long Tom. **1944** PYLE *Brave Men* 240 A 'Long Tom'—or 155 rifle—was the unwitting instrument.

4. (See quot.) *Obs.*

*a***1870** CHIPMAN *Notes on Bartlett* 256 *Long Tom.* . . . (From a not wholly fanciful resemblance to a cannon.) A long cigar—usually of a quality inversely proportioned.

∗**loo,** *n.* As the last term in **grab, prairie, shoemaker loo.**

∗**look,** *v.* In combs.: (1) **lookdown,** the horsehead, cf. **moonfish;** (2) **in,** a share of attention, *slang;* (3) ∗**out,** see as a main entry; (4) **outer,** one who looks out, a cautious person, *rare;* (5) **-up,** (see quot.).

(1) **1884** GOODE *Fisheries* I. 323 In the Chesapeake this fish is often called by the names 'Horse-head' and 'Look-down.' **1903** T. H. BEAN *Fishes N.Y.* 436 The lookdown is found on both coasts of tropical America and in temperate parts of the Atlantic north to Cape Cod. — (2) **1913** *Collier's* 6 Dec. 18/3 Why, you wheelbarrow men ain't got a look-in. **1916** *Lit. Digest* 1 Jan. 7/2 Between Colonel Roosevelt and the diplomatic correspondence of this epoch the dictionary business is getting a look-in all right. — (4) **1841** COOPER *Deerslayer* iii, Hutter is a first-rate look-outer, and can pretty much scent danger as a hound scents the deer.

(5) **1844** *Nat. Hist. N.Y., Zoology* II. 226 The American Bittern is also familiarly known under the names of . . . Look-up, Stake-driver, and in Louisiana Garde-soleil.

b. In phrases: (1) *To look at the bottom of the glass,* to finish a drink, *colloq.;* (2) *to look to, toward,* to tend toward, point in the direction of; (3) *to look good,* see ∗**good,** *a.* **3. g.**

(1) **1842** in *Amer. Sp.* XVIII. 126/2 Moreland . . . seemed to have looked pretty often at the bottom of the glass. — (2) **1904** *McClure's Mag.* 621 (Horwill), The South regarded jealously any teaching of the Negroes which looked toward equality. **1932** GRAYSON *Leaders* 278 His theory, and it still has much to recommend it, was that the thing to do was to take no precipitate action looking toward resumption, and without increasing the legal tenders, to let them stay about as they were.

∗**looker,** *n.*

1. One who is handsome or good looking. *Colloq.*

1898 WESTCOTT *D. Harum* 322, I was alwus a better goer than I was a looker. **1949** *Sat. Ev. Post* 9 April 56/4 Sure I remember them. They had Table Twenty-nine. Girl was a looker, all right.

2. looker-out, = ∗**lookout 3.**

1864 W. B. DICK *Amer. Hoyle* (1866) 202 The dealer sits at a table prepared for the purpose, with an assistant or 'looker-out' at his right hand.

As the last term in **best, good, land, timber, tree looker.**

looking glass prairie. Apparently a beautiful, somewhat circular prairie. Often (*cap.*) applied to a particular prairie of this kind. *Obs.*

1829 B. HALL *Travels N. Amer.* III. 385 Amongst which was one [prairie] particularly beautiful of its kind, and named . . . the Looking-Glass Prairie. **1831** PECK *Guide* 288 The prairies are High, Ridge, . . . and Looking-glass prairies. **1851** WORTLEY *Travels* 111 The Looking-glass Prairie, I fear, is too far off to attempt to go in this cold, bleak, unpropitious weather.

∗**lookout,** *n.*

1. A station or structure affording an extensive view; a tower or elevated structure on a building affording such a view. Cf. ∗**observatory.**

1700 *S.C. Statutes at Large* II. (1837) 161 The Look-out formerly built on Sullivan's Island . . . is by a late storm overthrown to the ground. **1766** W. STORK *Acct. E. Fla.* 33 To the back part of the house is joined a tower, called in America a look-out, from which there is an extensive prospect towards the sea. **1861** TALLACK *Friendly Sk.* 49 It is surprising how neat and comfortable the American wooden houses are. Many of them have good porches, galleries, and verandahs. Some of the larger ones have neat railed 'look-outs,' or 'observatories,' rising from their roofs. **1945** *Plymouth* (N.H.) *Rec.* 15 Nov. 2 One of his post-war projects is a 2500 mile hike over the crest of the Sierra Nevada and Cascade Ranges, from Tecate Lookout, on the Mexican border, to Hope, B.C.

b. A reconnoitering boat or vessel. Also **lookout boat.** *Obs.*

1761 *Descr. S. Carolina* 36 Eight Look-outs, which are laid aside. **1777** *Jrnl. Nicholas Cresswell* (1925) 212 And we had two armed lookout boats to escape, which makes our situation very dangerous.

c. (See quot.)

1895 WAIT *Car-Builders' Dict.* 22 Cabooses are made with a lookout for displaying train signals to the locomotive and trains following, and to give the trainmen a view of the train.

2. *W.* One who seeks out grazing land in advance of a herd.

1888 ROOSEVELT in *Cent. Mag.* Feb. 498/2 These lookouts or forerunners having returned, the herds are set in motion as early in the spring as may be. **1934** *Rocky Mt. News* (Denver) 30 Jan. 9/6 The vaquero was a 'lookout,' some distance in advance of the thundering herd.

3. An attendant at a gaming table to oversee the conduct of the game. Cf. **looker out.**

1851 in CRAPSEY *Nether Side N.Y.* (1872) 99 Any person or persons acting as 'look-out' or gamekeeper for the game of faro, shall be taken and held as a common gambler. **1888** *N.Y. Ev. Post* 24 Feb. (F.), The look-outs were held in 700 dols. bail each for examination to-morrow. **1938** ASBURY *Sucker's Prog.* 14 Lookout—The dealer's principal assistant, the one who paid and collected bets and kept a watchful eye on the players.

looloo 'lulu, *n.* Also **lulu.** [Origin unknown.]

1. Anyone or anything regarded as exceptionally fine or pleasing, a "honey." Also as adj. *Slang.*

1857 *Porter's Spirit of Times* 4 April 68/2 Well, *he* had a daughter; and she, O Bob! she was then, in my eyes, the looliest looly of the loolies, she was. Her hair was a beautiful auburn, and hung in ringlets; fair complexion; and a figure—such a figure! **1889** A. DALY *Great Unknown* 13 Oh, that's lulu! It'll suit mamma right down to the ground. **1947** *Sierra Bul.* May 81 Alas, there is no record that such a trip took place; but what a lulu it would have been.

2. (See quot. 1896.)

1896 LILLARD *Poker Stories* 85 'A looloo?' he repeated. 'What is a looloo, anyway?' 'Three clubs and two diamonds,' coolly replied the miner. . . . He jerked his thumb toward a pasteboard sign which ornamented the wall of the saloon. It read: *A Looloo Beats Four Aces.* **1938** ASBURY *Sucker's Prog.* 30 The most famous of all eccentric hands, the Looloo, is said to have been invented in a saloon in Butte, Montana, during the 1870's in a game between a stranger and a Butte miner.

∗**loon,** *n.* In various colloq. phrases (see quots.).

1830 *Ky. Intelligencer* (Flemingsburg) 29 May. 4/5 Patton informed me that McLaughlin had just gone from Elizabethville, and was 'drunk as a loon.' **1834** C. A. DAVIS *Lett. J. Downing* 42, I saw thru' it in a minute, and made it all as strait as a loon's leg. **1858** *Harper's Mag.* Sep. 487/2 'What do ye think he'll do,' says she, wild as a loon. **1877** ALDRICH *Queen of Sheba* 67 The fellow is mad! . . . as mad as a loon. **1880** *Harper's Mag.* Dec. 35 Miss Lois had been hunting the loon with a hand-net—a Northern way of phrasing the wearing of the willow.

b. Esp. *crazy as a loon,* quite crazy.

1845 KIRKLAND *Western Clearings* 83 'Why, you're both as crazy as loons!' was Mr. Ashburn's polite exclamation. **1888** FERGUSON *Forty-Niner* 121 The next morning Costler was as crazy as a loon—the mountain fever had attacked him. **1948** *Sat. Ev. Post* 4 Dec. 70/4 He's crazy as a loon.

∗**loop,** *n.* Orig. any completed turn in railroad or elevated tracks, then the territory inclosed by such tracks. Esp. the territory in downtown Chicago bounded by the elevated railway; hence transf. (esp. by Chicagoans), any business district. Also attrib.

1893 *Harper's Mag.* 814/2 Not quite the whole of the territory (now enclosed by the lower loop of the elevated railway) which lies south of the present Battery Place [in N.Y.]. **1897** *Chi. Record* 2 March 9/6 This will render likely the operation of the three elevated roads around the loop by June 1. **1920** COOPER *Under Big Top* 47 Through the loop district the entire cavalcade would have gone. **1923** WYATT *Invisible Gods* 109 Her permanent abiding place was a small frame cottage . . . situated some six miles from the loop on Lake Boulevard. **1944** *Chi. D. News* 10 Jan. 9/6 The students were treated to entertainment by several 'cowboys' from a Loop theater who gave lariat demonstrations, and sang.

b. The noose of a lasso. Cf. **wide loop.**

1907 White *Arizona Nights* 93 Some few whirled the loop, but most cast it with a quick flip.

***loose,** *a.* and *adv.*

1. Of horses, cattle, etc.: Allowed to run free in traveling and marching.

1843 in *Ore. Hist. Soc. Quart.* II. 191 About fifty wagons, with those who had large droves of loose cattle, now left. **1885** *Outing* Oct. 21/2 All drove pack and loose animals before them.

2. In special combs.: (1) **loose change,** coins such as one might carry loose in the pocket, money regarded as of little value; (2) **constructionist,** (see quot. 1892); (3) **hung,** gangling, lacking firmness in build, *colloq.*

(1) **1827** Sherwood *Gaz. Georgia* 112 It would be a kind of generous charity, to leave with the tavern-keepers . . . some of the loose change. **1927** Siringo *Riata* 53 That little burg saw the need of saloons and dance-halls to relieve the cowboy of his loose change. — (2) **1855** Barnum *Life* 358, 'I am always a loose constructionist' said Mr. Greeley. **1892** Walsh *Lit. Curiosities* 656 *Loose-Constructionists,* in American national politics, those who favor a liberal interpretation of the Constitution with regard to the powers delegated by that instrument to the federal government, and who are for the reading into it of large implied sovereign powers. — (3) **1890** Howells *Shadow of Dream* I. i, Faulkner stooped a little, and he was, as they say in the West, loose-hung.

b. loose herd, herding, *W.* (see quots.).

1881 Chase *Editor's Run in N. Mex.* 109 Loose herding prevailed; that is, everybody, after putting their mark upon their animals, turned them loose upon the prairie, to run where they would. **1925** Mulford *Cottonwood Gulch* 148 We've got to round-up, loose herd durin' the day, an' close herd nights.

***loosen,** *v. To loosen up,* to loosen the purse strings; to talk freely. *Slang.*

1908 K. McGaffey *Show-Girl* 125 Loosen up. . . . You've got to donate for a couple of tickets to the annual benefit. **1921** R. D. Paine *Comr. Rolling Ocean* xi. 187 Somebody will have to loosen up to pay for the damage to my nervous system. **1927** *Ladies' Home Jrnl.* Jan. 144 That is the first time he has ever loosened up.

***lop,** *v.*

1. *To lop down,* to sit or lie down, to "flop down." *Colloq.*

1839 Mrs. Kirkland *New Home* ii. 17 Jist come in, and take off your things, and lop down, if you're a mind to, while we're a getting supper. **1892** F. P. Humphrey *N. Eng. Cactus* 34 You'd best lop down to the lounge and get a nap.

2. In combs.: (1) **lop horn,** a horn that grows in a downward direction, also an ox having a horn of this kind; (2) **seed,** a perennial herb, *Phryma leptostachya,* having purplish flowers.

(1) **1850** D. Webster *Private Corr.* II. 405, I think your team a very good one; the old oxen, the starred steers, and the lop-horns. **1872** Powers *Afoot & Alone* 173 'Cut out that black fellow with the lop-horn,' he quietly orders one of the herdsmen. — (2) **1817–18** Eaton *Botany* (1822) 389 *Phryma leptostachia,* lopseed. **1840** Dewey *Mass. Flowering Plants* 173 Lopseed . . . grows along hedges and woods; July. **1901** Mohr *Plant Life Ala.* 696 Lopseed. . . . Alleghenian to Louisianian area.

lope lop, *n.* [f. **lope, v.*] A long, swinging, galloping stride, freq. of horses. Cf. **buzzard lope.**

1824 Horry & Weems *Life F. Marion* (1833) 111 He dashed off at a charging lope. **1833** J. Hall *Harpe's Head* 38 [The buck] came, at an easy *lope,* until he reached the top of a little knoll. **1869** McClure *Rocky Mts.* 302 The Western man always rides at a lope. **1945** MacDonald *Egg & I* 165, I broke into a lope and at last, panting and scared, I reached home.

***lope,** *v. tr.* To cause (a horse, mule, etc.) to go at a lope.

1885 Roosevelt *Hunting Trips Ranchman* (281) (*Cent.*), For seven or eight miles we loped our jaded horses along at a brisk pace. **1891** Thanet *Otto the Knight* 87, I lope dat mewl, an' I tell ye I . . . wen' so fas' we burnt de wind. **1902** Wister *Virginian* 175, I loped my cayuse full tilt by Mr. Snake.

***lord,** *n.* In combs.: (1) ***lord-and-lady,** the harlequin duck, also attrib.; (2) ***Lord God,** (see quot. and cf. **good god**); (3) **-'s fiddle,** (see quot.), *obs.*

(1) **1832** Williamson *Maine* I. 142 The *Lord and Lady,* or *Noddy* is as large as a pigeon, good for food. . . . Its perpetual whiffles with the wings when flying, give it name. **1835** Audubon *Ornith. Biog.* III. 612 To the south of the Bay of Boston the 'Lord and Lady Duck' is rarely seen on our coast. **1917** *Birds of Amer.* I. 142 Harlequin Duck. . . . Rightly are its little companies called the 'Lords and Ladies' of the waters. — (2) **1942** Rawlings *C. Creek* 260 At the Creek the pileated woodpecker is known as the Lord-God. — (3) **1878** Drake *Roxbury* 298 The bass-viol, or the 'Lord's fiddle,' as they called it, came in later and incurred far more serious opposition. Dr. Emmons left his church and refused to preach because the singers persisted in its use.

For **lord proprietary, lord proprietor,** see the second terms.

Lordy ˈlɔrdɪ, *interj.* [f. **Lord.*] An exclamation of surprise or astonishment. Also **Lordy me.**

1853 *S. Lit. Messenger* XIX. 602/2 On the sofa . . . you sank down and bounded up and said Lordy! **1898** Westcott *D. Harum* 178 'Lordy me!' sighed Mrs. Cullom. **1929** *Sat. Ev. Post* 12 May 20/3 But seven hundred dollars and his pocket piece back again! Phew! Lordy!

***lose,** *v.* In phrases: (1) *To lose off,* to come off, *colloq.;* (2) *to lose out,* (*a*) to be unsuccessful, to fail, (*b*) (see quot.).

(1) **1874** *Vt. Bd. Agric. Rep.* II. 717, I think that tin buckets are preferable for catching sap to wooden ones, as they have no hoops to lose off. — (2) (*a*) **1869** H. Bushnell *New Life* viii. 110 The child brought up a thief gets an infinite power of cunning . . . and loses out just as much in the power of true perception. **1931** *Blue Valley Farmer* (Okla. City) 3 Dec. 4/1 Down in the south and southwest, I am 'losing out.' (*b*) **1938** Asbury *Sucker's Prog.* 16 Losing out—Betting on a card which loses four times in one deal.

***lost,** *a.* In combs.: (1) **Lost Cause,** see as a main entry; (2) **lover,** used to designate a particular design or pattern of a quilt; (3) **moon,** (see quot.); (4) **river,** (see quot. 1843); (5) **rocks,** (see quots.); (6) **salmon,** (see quot.); (7) **stones,** =**lost rocks.**

(2) **1897** Brodhead *Bound in Shallows* 169 A great scarlet-and-white quilt, pieced in the 'Lost Lover' design, was spread on stretchers in the family-room. — (3) **1778** Carver *Travels* 250 Some nations among them [*sc.* the Indians] reckon their years by moons, and make them consist of twelve synodical or lunar months, observing, when thirty moons have waned, to add a supernumerary one, which they term the lost moon; and then begin to count as before. — (4) **1843** Carlton *New Purchase* I. 58 Out come the mole rivers that have burrowed all this time under the earth, and which, when so unexpectedly found are styled out there [in Ind.]—'lost rivers!' And every district a dozen miles square has a lost river. **1872** Raymond *Statist. Mines & Mining* 197 The great 'lost river' which bursts out of the vertical side of the cañon of the Snake—a torrent from the solid rock; a foundling rather than a lostling.

(5) **1831** Peck *Guide* 136 Scattered over the surface of our prairies are large masses of rock, of granitic formation, roundish in form, usually called by the people 'lost rocks.' **1857** *Ill. Agric. Soc. Trans.* II. 347 'Lost rocks' . . . are found on the surface of the earth in the middle and northern sections of Illinois. — (6) **1881** *Amer. Naturalist* XV. 178 Hump-back. . . . [Also called] holia, lost salmon, Puget Sound salmon. — (7) **1819** McMurtrie *Sk. Louisville* 29 Fragments of primitive rock . . . are said to be found . . . in the Illinois and Missouri territories, where they are denominated *lost stones,* from the evident circumstances, of their being strangers to the soil where they are found.

Lost Cause.

1. The cause of the South in the Civil War.

1866 E. A. Pollard (*title*), The Lost Cause. **1876** *Petaluma* (Calif.) *Argus* 11 Aug. 2/2 The Southern Democracy are at least consistent in honoring veterans who suffered for the lost cause. **1948** Kerwin *Civil-Military Relationships* 31 Their late adversaries, the United Confederate Veterans, licked their wounds and dwelt lovingly upon the Lost Cause.

transf. **1905** N. Davis *Northerner* 71, I don't mind doing a little proselyting now and then, for the political 'Lost Cause'!

2. The Confederate States, the South.

1886 Poore *Reminiscences* II. 526 They receive the representatives of 'the Lost Cause' with every possible honor. **1905** N. Davis *Northerner* 4 It is a sacred tribute to the heroes of what they call 'The Lost Cause,' meaning the under dog in the 'late unpleasantness!'

***lot,** *n.*

1. An inclosure for domestic livestock, usu. situated near a dwelling.

1831 Peck *Guide* 166 In autumn they [oxen] were shut up in a lot, fed with corn in the ear, . . . with water. **1886** *Harper's Mag.* Dec. 48/1 He heard some of his young mules galloping around the yard, and he made a sleepy resolve to sell them all, or to dismiss his overseer for letting them get out of the lot. **1948** *Democrat* 1 April 8/2 For Sale . . . one smoke house, two barns and lots, nice young orchard.

2. A burial plot in a cemetery.

1871 *Mich. Gen. Statutes* I. (1882) 1223 The said trustees . . . shall cause to be removed and again erected over the proper remains, all permanent fences around graves and lots, all tombstones and monuments. **1882** McCabe *New York* 234 At Greenwood each lot contains

378 square feet. **1949** *Desplaines Valley News* (Summit, Ill.) 8 April 12/1 For Sale—Six graves, Sec. 12A, Lot 125, Fairmount cemetery.

3. The grounds adjacent to a motion picture studio.

1921 *Ladies' Home Jrnl.* June 21/1 We have commenced our study of the films at the end, which is their projection before an audience, instead of at their source on 'the lot' of the studio where they are made.

4. In combs.: (1) **lot jumper,** one who appropriates another's lot; (2) **jumping,** the appropriation of a lot belonging to someone else; (3) **layer,** see as a main entry; (4) **line,** (see quot.); (5) **manure,** manure from a lot or lots for livestock; (6) **paling,** the paling around an inclosure for livestock.

(1) 1869 *Overland Mo.* III. 63 Then there had been a lot jumper's fight down at the end of the street. **1931** WILLISON *Here They Dug Gold* 241 Counterfeiters, lot-jumpers, mine-jumpers, road-jumpers, bunkosteerers and ruffians in general—none appear to have taken General Tabor very seriously. — **(2) 1928** FOY & HARLOW *Clowning Thro' Life* 136 Claim-jumping and lot-jumping had brought the community almost to a state of civil war. **1942** LILLARD *Desert Challenge* 258 Oh, there was petty theft, lot jumping, bunco steering. — **(4) 1853** STRICKLAND *Twenty-seven Yrs.* I. 88 Every township is laid out by the surveyor in parallel lines, sixty-six chains apart. These lines are sixty-six feet in width, and are given by government as road allowances, for the use of the public, and are called concession lines. Cross lines run at right angles with the former every thirty chains, and are called lot-lines: they subdivide the township into two hundred acre lots: every fifth cross line is a road allowance.

(5) 1848 *Fla. Plant. Rec.* 57, I dont think I will get done hawling out the lot manure under 3 weeks yet. — **(6) 1892** HARRIS *On Plantation* 66 Here come a big pack of dogs a-chargin' roun' the lot-palin's in full cry.

b. In colloq. phrases: (1) *across lots,* by a nearer or more convenient way, cf. **crosslots;** (2) *to go* (or *send*) *to hell* (or *the devil*) *across lots,* to go (or send) straight to hell (or to the devil).

(1) [**1848** LOWELL *Two Gunners* 21 Joe looked roun' An see (acrost lots in a pond . . .) A goose.] **1879** *Scribner's Mo.* June 334/1 'Good-night, Mr. Jordan!' said Evesham suddenly. 'I'm off across lots!' He leaped the fence, crashed through the alder hedge-row, and disappeared in the dusky meadow. **1947** CHALFANT *Gold, Guns, & Ghost Towns* 74 Palmer, Dexter, and one more man, each with Springfield rifle and fixed bayonet, went across lots to the bar of the Exchange Hotel. — **(2) 1853** B. YOUNG *Jrnl. Discourses* I. 83 (Th.), [I dreamed that] I cut one of their throats from ear to ear, saying, 'Go to hell across lots.' **1857** *Speech* (B.), I swore in Nauvoo, when my enemies were looking me in the face, that I would send them to hell across lots if they meddled with me. *a***1861** WINTHROP *J. Brent* xvii. 158 You may go to the devil across lots, on that runt pony of yourn, with your new friends, for all I care. **1942** STEGNER *Mormon C.* 211 Isaac in his sermons grew solemner and solemner, and surer in his mind that the Gentiles were going to hell across lots.

As the last term in **absent, back, barn, beach, berry, bottom, bounty, brush, building, burial, burying, bush, business, car, cedar, cellar, church, city, college, corner, cow, docking, donation, eighty-acre, family, farm, feed, feeding, ferry, fishing, forty-acre, front, garden, gospel, grain, grass, grave, hard, hay, hill, hog, home, horse, house, in-, marsh, meadow, ministry, mountain, mow, out, pasture, pine, planting, prison, sand, school, schoolhouse, scratch, spring, stable, stock, stump, sugar, swamp, sweepage, ten-acre, timber, tobacco, town, training, upland, vacant, village, water, wild, wood lot.**

***lot,** *v. To lot up,* to pen or confine (cattle) in a lot or inclosure. Cf. ***lot,** *n.* **1.**—**1874** J. C. McCOY *Hist. Sk. Cattle Trade* 171 In Central Illinois many of the most successful dealers in Southern Cattle, feed them upon the blue grass pastures, and never lot them up.

lot layer. An official appointed or selected in a town to lay out lots. Cf. next.

1636 *Ipswich* (Mass.) *Rec.* 20 Feb., Granted to Serjent French, ten acres of upland . . . to be laid out by the lott layers. **1716** *N.H. Prov. Papers* III. 654 (*footnote*), The Proprietors . . . shall run ye lines once in two years, the same to be done by ye Lot layers of each Town or Parish. **1882** in GODFREY *Nantucket* 90 It has been customary . . . for the proprietors' agents, or 'lot layers,' to set off the land to him.

***lotter,** *n.* =**lot layer.** *Obs.* See also **back lotter, sand lotter.** — **1640** *Portsmouth Rec.* 16 Itt is left to the discretion of the lotters to giue [part] of his Medowe adioyninge. **1672** *Ib.* 171 The Eight acres of Land . . . is now ordered to be layd out by the Lotters.

***lottery,** *n.* As the last term in **gift, land, Louisiana, road, state, Washington lottery.**

lottery cabin. A cabin assigned by lot (see quots.). Now *hist.* — **1874** R. H. COLLINS *Kentucky* I. 518 *The First Division of Cabins*—Lottery cabins, they called them—took place in June, 1774, . . . among a company of 31 explorers under Capt. James Harrod. **1886** Z. F. SMITH *Kentucky* 29 The men dispersed . . . to build on such locations improvement cabins. These latter were known as 'lottery cabins,' as they were apportioned among the men by lot.

lotteryite ˈlɑtərɪ aɪt, *n.* [f. **lottery.*] One favoring the Louisiana lottery. *Rare.* — **1890** *Columbus* (O.) *Dispatch* 10 June, That the lotteryites in Louisiana should attempt to back up their scheme.

***louder,** *adv.* Used imperatively to indicate to a public speaker that he is imperfectly heard, "speak up!" — **1880** *Dly. Inter-Ocean* (Chi.) 3 June 2/2 The spectators in the rear of the hall called 'louder,' and as the Senator could not make them hear, they crowded forward to catch the tones of his voice. **1948** *Dly. Ardmoreite* (Ardmore, Okla.) 6 April 4 My friends! I am reminded of the story about—Louder and funnier—whatta ya mean, *friends?*

Loudon whip. (See quots. 1894 and 1930.)

1888 in OMWAKE *Conestoga Teams* 134 And boot-jacks, slippers, tallow dips, And some great-coats and Loudon whips. **1894** SEARIGHT *Old Pike* 111 There was another whip, much used by old wagoners, known as the 'Loudon Whip.' The inner portion of this whip was an elastic wooden stock, much approved by the wagoners. It was manufactured in the village of Loudon, Franklin county, Pa. **1930** OMWAKE *Conestoga Teams* 127 The fame of Franklin County spread afar, because of the Loudon whip that was made especially for wagoners, at Fort Loudon.

Louisiana ˌluɪzɪˈænə, *n.* [f. *Louis* XIV of France.] The name of a southern state and, formerly, of the large region of which it was a part, used in combs.: (1) **Louisiana bit,** ?=**picayune,** *obs.;* (2) **cession,** see **Louisiana treaty;** (3) **flag,** a kind of iris found in the New Orleans region; (4) **grass,** (see quot.); (5) **heron,** an American species of heron, *Hydranassa tricolor ruficollis,* esp. abundant in the South; (6) **lottery,** a lottery, chartered by the Louisiana legislature in 1868 and continuing to 1895, which guaranteed the state a fixed sum annually; (7) **Purchase,** the purchase by the U.S. from France in 1803 of her territorial claims in North America; (8) **stock,** interest-bearing certificates issued in 1803 by the U.S. Government in payment for the Louisiana Purchase; (9) **tanager,** an American tanager, *Pironga ludoviciana,* found chiefly in the Rocky Mountain and Pacific Coast region; (10) **Territory,** the area acquired by the Louisiana Purchase, or that part of it lying outside the present limits of the State of Louisiana; (11) **treaty,** the treaty (1803) between the U.S. and France by which the Louisiana Territory was sold to the U.S., also **Louisiana cession;** (12) **water thrush,** the large-billed water thrush or wagtail, *Seiurus motacilla,* found throughout the eastern U.S.

(1) 1834 SIMMS *G. Rivers* II. 98 You know how he did that?—now, I'll go a York shilling 'gainst a Louisiana bit, that you can't tell to save you. — **(3) 1831** AUDUBON *Ornith. Biog.* I. 78 This plant [Iris] grows in the water, and in the neighbourhood of New Orleans, a few miles below that city, . . . and in bloom, in the beginning of April. Several flowers are produced upon the same stem . . . the name of *Louisiana Flag* is the one commonly given it. — **(4) 1889** VASEY *Agric. Grasses* 23 *Paspalum platycaule* . . . has sometimes been called Louisiana grass.

(5) 1813 WILSON *Ornithology* VIII. 13 Louisiana Heron: *Ardea ludoviciana;* . . . [is] found on the swampy river shores of South Carolina. **1917** *Birds of Amer.* I. 189/1 The Louisiana Heron ranks among the most abundant Herons in this country. — **(6) 1897** *Outing* Jan. 329/1 Fishing in Florida waters is so akin to playing the late Louisiana lottery that it would not surprise one to hear that our moral law-givers . . . had legislated it into the penal code. **1949** *Dly. Oklahoman* (Okla. City) 13 Feb. D. 8/4 Well integrated elements of the background picture are French cultural groups, Louisiana politics centering about the Louisiana lottery [etc.]. — **(7) 1898** *K.C. Star* 18 Dec. 6/2 Jefferson did not claim credit for that greatest of land trades, the Louisiana purchase. **1948** *Sat. Review* 26 June 13/1 In 1803, at the time of the Louisiana Purchase, some of these tribes had not even occupied the territories for which they were later paid. — **(8) 1812** *Ann. 12th Congress* 1 Sess. 1434 The Louisiana six per cent. stock is said to be generally from ½ to 1 per cent. below par. — **(9) 1811** WILSON *Ornithology* III. 27 Louisiana Tanager. . . . This bird, and the two others . . . were discovered, in the remote regions of Louisiana, by an exploring party. **1917** *Birds of Amer.* III. 78 [The name] Louisiana Tanager . . . is inappropriate now; for the bird is only a rare migrant in the Louisiana of to-day.

(10) 1806 *Ann. 9th Congress* 2 Sess. 1137 Nature has marked with a distinguishing feature, the line established by Congress, between the Orleans and Louisiana Territories. **1900** *Cong. Rec.* 19 Feb. 1947/2 The Louisiana territory, Florida, Texas, California, New Mexico,

Oregon, and Alaska have all been acquired under our Constitution. — (11) **1822** in *N. Amer. Rev.* XXIII. 408 Subjects of discussion between the two countries [France and the U.S. include] . . . *the question arising under the Louisiana treaty*. . . . I must object to uniting the Louisiana question to that of claims for indemnity. **1826** *Ib.* 410 Such is the subject of the controversy relative to the interpretation of the eighth article of the Louisiana cession. *Ib.* Discussion of the eighth article of the Louisiana treaty would carry us beyond our limits. — (12) **1831** AUDUBON *Ornith. Biog.* I. 99 The Louisiana Water Thrush. *Turdus Ludovicianus.* **1949** *Chi. Tribune* 9 Jan. VI. 5/8 These with the Louisiana water thrush, vultures, and thrashers are the most common.

Also *Louisiana clapper rail, cotton, everglades, flycatcher, gombo, hawk, lark, shrike,* etc.

Louisianian ˌluɪzɪˈænɪən, *n.* and *a.*

1. *n.* A native or resident of the region or state of Louisiana.

1775 ADAIR *Indians* 240 This will shew our southern . . . colonies what they may still expect from the masterly abilities of the French Louisianians. **1804** *True Republican* (Norwich, Conn.) 3 Aug. 1/2 Louisianians, you are no longer foreigners or strangers, but fellow-citizens. **1945** *Chi. D. News* 26 July 2/3 The slow but straight-talking Louisianian is extremely popular with his junior officers.

2. *a.* Of or pertaining to Louisiana.

*a***1808** in S. K. PADOVER *Jefferson* 355 Go, search with curious eye, for horned frogs, Mid the wild wastes of Louisianian bogs. **1901** MOHR *Plant Life Ala.* 430 Asiatic or Common Day-flower. . . . [Grows in] Carolinian and Louisianian areas.

lounge lizard. (See quot. 1925.) *Slang.*

1921 *Ladies' Home Jrnl.* Feb. 23/3 The dead man looked to him like what was at one time expressively called a 'lounge lizard.' **1925** KRAPP *Eng. Lang. Amer.* I. 117 Who will know a generation hence . . . that a crape-hanger is a reformer, or a lounge lizard one who suns himself eternally in good society. **1948** *Ariz. Republic* (Phoenix) 2 March 6/2 He is apparently a typical gold-plated lounge-lizard overwhelmed with a sense of his own superiority.

Loup lu, *n.* [F. *loup*, wolf.] *pl.* One of the tribes, the Skidi, which made up the Pawnee confederacy. Also **Loup Pawnees.** *Obs.* Cf. **Pawnee Loup.**

1780 *Cal. Va. State P.* I. 377 The Commander had engaged him to go with a party of Cheifs of the Loups. **1827** COOPER *Prairie* xxxiv, As it drew nigh, the partisan of the Loups was seen at its head, followed by a dozen younger warriors of his tribe. **1845** *St. Louis Reveille* 16 Feb. 2/4 The Grand Pawnees conspired to scalp and massacre him and his band, . . . and were only prevented from so doing by the Loup Pawnees, (or Wolf Pawnees) who happened to be present in considerable numbers.

loup-cervier ˌlusɛrˈvje, *n.* [Can. F.] The Canada lynx.

[**1744** A. DOBBS *Hudson's Bay* 41 The Loup Cervier, or Lynx, is of the Cat Kind, but as large as a great Dog.] **1791** *Mass. Laws 1780–1800* (1801) I. 509 No person . . . shall hereafter, in either of the months of June, July, August, or September . . . kill any Otter . . . Fisher or Black-Cat, Leusifee [etc.]. **1860** *Harper's Mag.* Feb. 302/1 'Keep still, Cap'n,' says I, 'he's after that lucive.' **1938** COFFIN *Kennebec* 233 The loup-cerviers were worse than the wolves, and lasted longer. The Maine folks pronounced them Lucy-V's. They were big wildcats.

***louse,** *n.* As the last term in **bark, corn, cornroot, cotton, grape, hop, oystershell bark, red louse.**

***lousy,** *a.*

1. Vile, contemptible (see quot. 1928). *Slang.*

1839 in R. W. GRISWOLD *Corr.* (1898) 24, I never will stand tamely by, and see the True Friends of Freedom assailed with lousy lies from any quarter. **1928** *Amer. Sp.* III. 345 'Lousy.' How long will the vogue of this unpleasant adjective continue? It is applied indiscriminately and means nothing in particular except that it is always a term of disparagement. **1948** *Chi. Maroon* 9 Jan. 9/1 The book was lousy; the movie was slightly less so.

2. *To be lousy with*, to have plenty of. *Slang.*

1850 JACKSON *Forty-Niner* 11 Wednesday I struck a crevice in the bed-rock on the rim of the creek and it was lousy with gold. **1856** *Dem. State Jrnl.* (Sacramento) 6 Oct. 2/3 The bed of the river is perfectly 'lousy' with gold. **1949** *Boston Globe* 15 May (Fiction Mag.) 4/1 He runs onto some crick which he claims is lousy with coarse gold.

***love,** *n.* In combs.: (1) **love-cracked,** foolish or irrational from being deeply in love, *colloq.;* (2) ***feast,** *transf.* a political jubilee, banquet, or occasion of common rejoicing; (3) ***knot,** =**cruller,** *obs.;* (4) **puff,** ?a kind of popover, *obs.;* (5) **-'s ladder,** a kissing game formerly popular at parties, *obs.;* (6) **tape,** *measuring love tape*, a kissing game formerly engaged in at parties, *obs.*

(1) **1843** *Yale Lit. Mag.* VIII. 328 The most general opinion was, that he was love-cracked, and free blame was bestowed upon Some inconsiderate hard-hearted beauty. **1891** WILKINS *N. Eng. Nun* 167 Christmas Jenny's kind of love-cracked. — (2) **1876** *Solano Republican* (Suisun, Calif.) 24 Aug. 2/1 A regular old-fashioned Democratic love-feast was engaged in by the many-scarred war-horses of the party. **1948** *Minneapolis Star* 17 Sep. 1/3 Senator Joseph H. Ball and Gov. Luther Youngdahl had a sort of love feast at the capitol Thursday. — (3) **1805** *Pocumtuc Housewife* (1906) 34 Crullers, Matrimony or Love Knots. — (4) **1887** *Cent. Mag.* Nov. 16/2 A procession of little darkies was seen to pass and repass, supporting plates of hot batter-cakes, . . . love-puffs, beaten biscuit, laplands [etc.].

(5) **1830–45** FURMAN *Customs* 13 At these merry making parties is another play, called 'Love's Ladder,' which is conducted as follows. — (6) **1830–45** FURMAN *Customs* 12 As is also 'measuring love tape,' which is done by a lad and girl . . . every time they stretch out their arms they bring their lips in contact and a kiss is the natural consequence.

b. Used colloq. in the names of flowers: (1) ***love entangled,** the common stonecrop; (2) **everlasting,** a cudweed of the genus *Anaphalis* or *Gnaphalium;* (3) **-in-a-puff,** the balloon vine, *Cardiospermum halicacabum;* (4) **-'s test,** (see quot.).

(1) **1892** *Amer. Folk-Lore* V. 96 *Sedum acre*, love entangled. N. Ohio. — (2) **1832** TRAILL *Backwoods* 93 The Americans ornament their chimney-glasses with garlands of this plant, mixed with the dried blossoms of the life-everlasting (the pretty white and yellow flowers we call love-everlasting). — (3) **1839** *S. Lit. Messenger* V. 751/2 A particular spot in his garden was appropriated to the culture of old maids, . . . and lady slippers, . . . and even love in a puff. **1944** *Seed Ann.* 35 Balloon Vine (Love-in-a-Puff). *Annual Climber.* White; 8 ft. The inflated seed-vessels are interesting. — (4) **1899** *Animal & Plant Lore* 104 The common everlasting (*Antennaria plantaginifolia*) is called 'love's test' and is used in love divinations.

As the last term in **free, puppy love.**

***lovely,** *a.* (See quots. 1841 and 1883.) *Obs.*

1766 in *Mass. Hist. Soc. Coll.* 3 Ser. V. 183 Two lovely young gentlemen . . . joined hand in hand, and flew away to the farther end of the pond. **1832** FERRALL *Ramble* 169 The judge is a wonderfully lovely fellow. **1841** BUCKINGHAM *America* I. 236 The term *lovely man*, is as frequent as that of lovely woman, and neither of them has the least relation to personal beauty, but mean always a combination of talent, virtue, and affability, in the person to whom it is applied. **1883** M. ARNOLD in Horwill *Dict. Amer. Usage* (1935) 195, I am staying with Mrs. Fields here—a *lovely* woman, as they say here—which means not a sweetly beautiful woman, but what we call a 'very nice' woman. **1899** MUIRHEAD *Baedeker's U.S.* p. xxx, *Lovely*, loveable.

***lover,** *n.* **1. lovers' lane,** a road, street, etc., to which lovers resort to be alone. **2. lover's walk,** (see quot.).

(1) **1881** *Golden Gate Gaz.* (S.F.) 26 Oct. 2/2 Sunday afternoon as a young lady and gentleman were promenading through 'Lovers' Lane' they were attacked by a ferocious dog. **1905** *St. Louis Globe-Democrat* 28 Aug. 1/5 For half an hour consternation reigned in lovers' lane, until finally a burly policeman arrested the youthful agitator. **1947** *Chi. D. Times* 28 Nov. 2/1 State police experts today were called to solve the mystery of the death of a pretty college girl whose nude body was found on a lonely lovers' lane.—(2) **1906** H. D. PITTMAN *Belle of Blue Grass C.* ii. 19 From a tangle of shrubbery near the gate, through which there was a labyrinthine maze, or 'lover's walk,' to the house, there came a voice.

As the last term in **free, lost, mother lover.**

***low,** *n.*

1. An area of low barometric pressure.

1878 *Pop. Sci. Mo.* July 310 These high and low areas, or 'highs' and 'lows' as they are technically known, travel. **1898** *Outlook* May 349 The low . . . is usually attended by clouds, rain or snow, and high winds. **1946** *Sierra Club Bul.* Dec. 18 At the same time to the south a deficiency of air created a 'low' that extended northward and westward from Arizona through California.

2. In the stock market, the lowest price for which a given stock has sold, esp. in the phrase *to hit a new low.* Also transf.

1911 *N.Y. Times* 20 Sep., Calumet and Hecla opened 17 points off at 373, which is 47 points above the established low of 1897. **1938** in MENCKEN *Supp.* I. 327 What the fate of psychology will be now that it has hit its new *low* is difficult to predict. **1948** *Minneapolis Morn. Tribune* 28 Sep. 18/1 During the downward movement there were 118 new lows for the year uncovered. **1949** *N.O. Times-Picayune* 6 Feb. 1/2 Many issues hit new lows for the past year or for longer periods.

***low,** *a.* and *adv.* In combs.: (1) **lowboy,** a low dressing table equipped with drawers, cf. **highboy;** (2) ***bridge,** a cry of warning given on approaching an obstruction overhead, orig. used on canal boats; (3) ***brow,** one who is not or does not claim to be intellectual or elegant, *slang*, cf. **highbrow;** (4) **down,** see as a main entry; (5) **downer,** *S.* a poor white or cracker, *colloq.;* (6) **flung,** =**low down;** (7) **line,** the one in a fishing party who catches the fewest fish, cf. **high line;** (8) **middling,** a grade used in estimating the quality of ginned cotton; (9) **-pressure hat,** prob. a soft hat as contrasted with a "stovepipe," *obs.;* (10) **-quarter shoe,** a shoe which does not reach above the ankle, a low shoe, also **low-quarters;** (11) **studded,** having short or low studs, built with a low ceiling; (12) **tea,** a plain tea as contrasted with high tea; (13) **-toned,** *a.* the opposite of high-toned *q.v.*

(1) 1899 *House Beautiful* Aug. 140 [Picture of] antique mahogany chair and low-boy. **1925** *Scribner's Mag.* July 92/1 Do you happen to have a lowboy? I would give anything for one. **1941** *L.A.* Map 339. — **(2) 1898** WESTCOTT *D. Harum* xxvii, Ev'ry man at the table, except the Englis'man, know'd what 'low bridge' meant from actial ex-

Lowboy with claw feet

perience. — **(3) 1909** *Sat. Ev. Post* 6 Mar. 19/1 The untiring but tiresome chase after what the highbrows call dross and the lowbrows call dough leaves us but a few moments to devote to the celebration of the noble qualities of our contemporaries. **1913** E. D. BIGGERS *Seven Keys to Baldpate* 21 My stuff is only for low-brows. **1948** *Dly. Ardmoreite* (Ardmore, Okla.) 27 May 8/6 Information that will even enable lowbrows to understand the atom is at last beginning to leak out.

(5) 1868 *Putnam's Mag.* I. 706/1 When . . . candidates refreshed their adherents by the barrelfull [*sic*] the low-downer enjoyed his periodical benders without expense. **1883** STEVENSON *Silverado Sq.* 131 They are at least known by a generic byword, as Poor Whites or Low-downers. — **(6) 1843** *Missouri Rep.* 11 April (Th.), Here we have a beautiful specimen of the dishonesty and low-flung slang of the clique. **1893** M. A. OWEN *Voodoo Tales* 64 Time someun teach dat low-flung red-head mannehs. — **(7) 1896** *N. Eng. Mag.* Feb. 680/2 Thus, if the high line caught 20,000 fish and earned $200, and the low line caught 10,000, he earned but $100. — **(8) 1848** *De Bow's Review* VI. 448 The absence of competition carried down prices in the early part of May to $4\frac{3}{4}$ *a* $5\frac{1}{4}$ cents for Low Middling to Good Middling. **1887** *Courier-Jounral* 17 Jan. 7/6 Cotton market was dull; middling 91–16c; low middling $8\frac{3}{4}$c. — **(9) 1852** J. H. EAGLE *Corr.* (Huntington Lib.) 28 June 3 Nearly the entire procession was dressed with flannel shirts, long boots with pants stuffed inside them, belts, and low-pressure hats.

(10) *c***1862** BAGBY *Old Va. Gentleman* 73 Give me a straw hat, an oznaburg shirt, no waistcoat, . . . and a pair of low-quarter shoes, moderately thick-soled. **1916** *D.N.* IV. 269 *Low-quarters*, Oxford shoes. — **(11) 1854** SHILLABER *Mrs. Partington* 16 A tall man could not stand erect in the low-studded room. **1897** F. C. MOORE *How to Build Home* 7 It is mistaken economy to have a low-studded cellar. — (12) **1883** HOWELLS *Woman's Reason* II. xviii. 133 The world . . . sent her invitations to little luncheons and low teas. — **(13) 1827** *Spirit of Seventy-Six* (Frankfort, Ky.) 8 Feb. 3/1 There is in circulation, a sleepy, low toned, but insidious pamphlet of ten pages, . . . *franked* from the City of Washington. **1861** *Charleston* (S.C.) *Mer.* 24 Jan. 2/6 Clay . . . comes from North Alabama, the lowest-tone place in the Cotton States. **1949** *Sat. Ev. Post* 5 March 124/2 Tomorrow's function . . . will be a low-toned flop.

b. In the names of, or with reference to, plants: (1) **low blackberry,** =**low-bush blackberry,** also attrib.; (2) **blueberry,** (see quot.); (3) **-bush blackberry,** any one of several species of dewberry; (4) **corn,** ?corn of poor quality, *obs.*, cf. **longcorn;** (5) **cornel,** a low plant of the dogwood family; (6) **-headed,** of trees, having a low head of foliage, also transf. and attrib.; (7) ***land,** a variety of cotton that does well on land that is low, *obs.;* (8) **-land chestnut,** a kind of chestnut growing in lowlands; (9) **-land Spanish oak,** (see quot.); (10) **maple,** a mountain maple, *Acer spicatum.*

(1) 1814 BIGELOW *Florula Bostoniensis* 122 ***Rubus trivialis.*** Low or running blackberry. Dewberry. . . . Fruit large, black, sweet. **1883** HOWELLS *Woman's Reason* ix, She was able to make several studies in color of the low blackberry-vine, now in its richest autumnal bronze. **1898** CREEVEY *Flowers of Field* 451 Low Blackberry. . . . It is a shrubby, trailing plant, growing in the dust by roadsides or in dry fields. . . . From Newfoundland to Virginia, and westward. — **(2) 1836** LINCOLN *Botany* App. 148 *Vaccinium pennsylvanica*, low blueberry. — **(3) 1857** GRAY *Botany* 122 *R. trivialis*, Michx. (Low Bush-Blackberry). **1891** COULTER *Bot. W. Texas* I. 104 Low bush blackberry. A southern blackberry, apparently common in eastern, southern, and western Texas. — **(4) 1788** WASHINGTON *Diaries* III. 452 The other hands compleated the Husking and measuring the Corn . . . qty. 46 barrls. of sound Corn, and 4 of what is called low Corn.

(5) 1850 S. F. COOPER *Rural Hours* 85 The low-cornel is opening. **1869** FULLER *Flower Gatherers* 72 The *canadensis* is an interesting species. It is usually called Low Cornel. — **(6) 1861** *Ill. Agric. Soc. Trans.* IV. 328 Plant dwarf, or dwarfed, low-headed cherries, only. *Ib.* V. 205 We have never . . . been identified with the ultra low headed orchardists. **1868** *Rep. U.S. Comm. Agric.* (1869) 201 The silk tree (*Albizzia julibrissin*) is a low-headed, spreading tree, possessed of the most graceful foliage. — **(7) 1828** PAULDING *New Mirror* 271 No uplands, nor lowlands, nor sea island, nor long staple, nor short staple? — **(8) 1815** DRAKE *Cincinnati* ii. 82 The most valuable timber trees are the . . . white, black, low-land chestnut and bur oaks. — **(9) 1785** MARSHALL *Amer. Grove* 123 This [Water Red Oak] is generally known by the name of water or Low Land Spanish Oak.

(10) 1813 MUHLENBERG *Cat. Plants* 95 Mountain maple or low maple. **1897** SUDWORTH *Arborescent Flora* 282 *Acer spicatum*. Mountain Maple. . . . [Also Called] Low Maple (Tenn.).

low-down ˈloˌdaᴜn, *a.* and *n.*

1. *n.* The real truth or facts, the "dope." *Slang.*

1926 FANNIE KILBOURNE *Dot & Will* (1929) 142 He . . . grinned through the black on his face, and gave the real low-down. **1948** *Chickasha* (Okla.) *D. Express* 4 July 16/2 Buzz him and he may consent to give you the lowdown on the battle.

2. *a.* Mean, degraded, contemptible. *Colloq.*

[**1850** *Cong. Globe* 25 April 821/1 The 'low down' Virginia Democracy had to yield to the western mountain Democracy.] **1865** *Nation* I. 586 His manners and conversation, showed him to be a good-deal above that class commonly called 'low-down, triflin' people,' or poor white trash. **1949** *Boston Globe* 19 June (Fiction Mag.) 4/1 His two low-down brothers swore lies; they didn't even see the fight.

Hence **lowdownest, lowdownness.**

1868 *Harper's Mag.* Sep. 488/2 He was turned out of their army for some low-down-ness. **1880** HARRIS *U. Remus* (1884) 46 He low'd, Mr. Buzzard did, dat Brer Rabbit wuz de low-downest w'atsizname w'at he ever run up wid.

***Lowell,** *n.* Also **lowell.** *S.* A cheap cotton cloth manufactured at Lowell, Mass. Also attrib. *Obs.* or *hist.*

1852 in STOWE *Key* 417 Ran away . . . a negro man . . . ; Had on, when he left, Lowell pants and cotton shirt. **1855** DAVIS *Farm Bk.* 251 Went to Marion—carried the wagon & bought supplies of merchandize for the season—such as Lowells—Calicoes. **1945** BOTKIN *My Burden* 90 They spinned the cloth what our clothes was made of, and we had straight dresses or slips made of lowell.

***lower,** *a.* In combs.: (1) **Lower Creeks,** see as a main entry; (2) **party,** during the Revolution, a faction among the Americans in New York favorable to the British; (3) **settlement,** (*a*) (*cap.*) *pl.* the settlements of the Cherokee Indians living in South Carolina and northeastern Georgia, (*b*) a settlement situated, or regarded as being, at a place lower than another or others, *obs.;* (4) **Sonoran,** (see quot. 1893); (5) **towns,** Indian towns in the region occupied by the Lower Creeks.

(2) 1789 ANBUREY *Travels* II. 482 What are termed these Upper and Lower Parties are mostly known to each other, and possess great inveteracy on both sides. **1831** SHERBURNE *Memoirs* App. 294 We asked him 'what party?' He replied 'the lower party.' — **(3)** (*a*) **1725** in *Travels Amer. Col.* 110 The head Men of the Lower Settlements had waited upon their King. (*b*) **1779** in *Hist. MSS Comm.* 9th Rep. App. III. II. 137 Such a concurrence of many of the respectable inhabitants in the lower settlements may be procured. **1825** *Austin P.* (1924) II. 1209 Could the men from the lower settlements be safely drawn from there? — **(4) 1893** COVILLE *Death Valley Exped.* 21 The Lower

Sonoran zone, which is a broad transcontinental belt, coincides in the desert region of southern California approximately with the distribution of *Larrea tridentata* and *Franseria dumosa*. **1938** *Southwestern Lore* Dec. 50 Since the Lower Sonoran bird forms do not occur in the area today, . . . we assume that the area was warmer, on the average, during Pueblo I than it is today. **1941** FERGUSSON *Southwest* 66 The Chisos Mountains, . . . whose varied flora runs from lower Sonoran cactus and leafless shrubs to Upper Canadian yellow pine, fir, and spruce.

(5) **1763** *Ga. Gazette* 7 April 2/2 All the Indians of the Lower-Towns do the same, except when they get rum from the settlements.

Lower Creeks. The Creek Indians who lived along the middle or lower Chattahoochee River on the Alabama-Georgia border. In full **Lower Creek Indians.**

1734 *Ga. Col. Rec.* III. 416 He has already, by Presents, attached the Lower Creeks to the Service of your Majesty. **1739** W. STEPHENS *Proc. Georgia* 421 He had the Friendship of the Lower and Upper Creek Indians secured to us. **1789** *Amer. State P.: Indian Affairs* I. 15 The Creeks are principally within the limits of the United States, but some of the most southern towns of the Lower Creeks, or Seminoles, are within the territory of Spain, stretching toward the point of Florida. **1949** *Wm. & Mary Quart.* Jan. 7 At first the company's activities were limited to East Florida and the Lower Creek Indians.

* **loyal,** *a.*

1. Faithful to, or in sympathy with, the North during the Civil War. *Obs.*

1863 MOORE *Rebellion Rec.* V. I. 57 Hundreds of citizens of the West and other portions of the loyal States fled into 'Canada like cravens, to escape the draft.' **1876** *N. Amer. Rev.* July 240 A refuge for the patriotism forbidden loyal Kentuckians within the limits of their own Commonwealth. **1884** BLAINE *20 Years of Congress* I. 435 The line of partisan division had been practically obliterated in the Loyal States.

2. In combs.: (1) **Loyal League,** a secret organization among the Negroes, toward the close of the Civil War and immediately thereafter, seeking to secure for them social and political rights, now *hist.;* (2) **Leaguer,** a member of the Loyal League, *obs.;* (3) **Legion,** an organization formed in 1865, membership in which was open to officers of the Union Army and Navy and to their eldest sons, cf. **Cincinnati.**

(1) **1865** *Nation* I. 194 The colored men are forming a Loyal League, which is likely to be a numerous body. **1947** LUMPKIN *Southerner* 81 But chiefly, Southern men cast the blame for the solid vote against them . . . on the Union or Loyal Leagues. — (2) **1864** G. SALA in *Dly. Telegraph* 23 Aug. (Th. Supp.), This last dirty move of the Loyal Leaguers to spite the Copperheads in view of the Chicago Convention. **1871** *Cong. Globe* 12 April 604/1 These outrages perpetrated by the Ku Klux and by the Loyal Leaguers. — (3) **1901** *Cleveland Leader* 8 Sep. 1/3 Out of the national tragedy of Lincoln's death grew the National Order of the Loyal Legion. **1948** KERWIN *Civil-Military Relationships* 30, I do not speak of the now-antiquated idea of a club 'for officers only' with hereditary notions, like the Cincinnati, Military Order of the Loyal Legion [etc.].

* **Loyalist,** *n.*

1. During the Revolution, an American who favored the British cause. Now *hist.*

1779 *N.J. Archives* 2 Ser. III. 291 These are worthies by Mr. Robertson, of New-York, in his Royal American Gazette of the 15th instant, called loyalists. **1821** COOPER *Spy*, The loyalists . . . adopted such measures as best accorded with their different characters. **1943** HICKS *Amer. Dem.* 87 The extremists, preferring the British connection to anything that resistance to the mother country had to offer, became the 'Tories' or 'Loyalists' of the American Revolution.

2. During the Civil War, an adherent of the Union or northern side. *Obs.*

1862 in MOORE *Rebellion Rec.* V. II. 4 The murderous bushwacker made an effort to deceive, by first saying they were Bill Richmond's company, a band of loyalists. **1866** LOWELL *Writings* V. 324 We have nothing to do with the number of actual loyalists at the South, but with the number of possible ones.

lubber grasshopper. (See quots.)

1877 *Field & Forest* II. 160 The 'Lubber' grasshopper [is the] large grasshopper *Romalia microptera*. **1885** KINGSLEY *Riverside Nat. Hist.* (1888) II. 194 The 'Lubber Grasshopper,' or the Clumsy Locust, of the plains, *Brachystola magna*, . . . [is] confined to the central portion of North America. **1889** *Cent.* 653/2 *B. magna* is a large clumsy locust, common on the western plains of North America, where it is known as the lubber grasshopper.

lubricator,** *n.* =greaser 1.** *Slang. Obs.* — **1872** C. KING *Mountaineering in Sierra Nevada* 285 'String him up!' 'Burn the dog-goned lubricator.'

* **luck,** *n.*

1. *attrib.* Designating a *ball* or *egg* used as a charm, fetish, or the like.

1893 M. A. OWEN *Voodoo Tales* 169 Aunt Mymee . . . [suffered] the loss of her most powerful fetich, the luck-ball she had talked to and called by her own name. **1899** *Animal & Plant Lore* 12 The small eggs dropped at the end of the laying season are kept under the name of 'luck eggs' to bring good fortune to the owner. Maine and Northern Ohio.

2. *A breeze of luck*, a spell of good fortune. *Colloq.*

1834 CROCKETT *Narr. Life* viii. 61, I now began to think we had struck a breeze of luck. **1850** LEWIS *La. Swamp Doctor* 83 I'se struck a breeze of luck, sure, to get it [a tooth] 'stracted without hurtin'.

As the last term in **bullhead, cat, chuck-a-, Negro, tough luck.**

***lucky bag.** "A receptacle on a man-of-war for all clothes and other articles of private property carelessly left by their owners" (*Cent.*). — **1840** *S. Lit. Messenger* VI. 233/2 Every man-of-war, you know, has her *lucky bag*, containing a little of everything, and something belonging to everybody.

* **Lucy,** *n.*

1. Lucy Long, the name of a minstrel song or walk-around (see quot. 1901). Now *obs.* or *hist.*

1844 *N.O. Picayune* 26 Feb. 9/1 [At the masquerade ball], Julius Caesar was holding a confidential chit-chat with Miss Lucy Long, while Rip Van Winkle was expatiating upon the virtues of cold water to Father Matthew. **1848** *New Negro Forget-me-not Songster* 7 Oh white folks I will sing to you Dis nigger's favorite song, I'll play it on de banjo To de tune ob Lucy Long. **1851** *S.F. Sun Clarion* 27 April 3/5 The whole [Ethiopian concert] to conclude with Lucy Long in character. **1901** *Cosmopolitan* Sep. 635/1 Dan Emmett wrote a long list of songs. 'Lucy Long' walk-around, if not the first, was among the first. **1930** WITTKE *Tambo & Bones* 45 All four performers sang and danced, . . . and did the 'Lucy Long Walk Around.'

b. Also *to dance Lucy Long. Obs.*

1860 in CHRISTY *Ethiopian Joke Book No. 3* viii, Mr. George Christy . . . danced his favourite 'Lucy Long' with such artistic grace and ease, as to draw the encomiums of the audience. **1869** *Atlantic Mo.* July 77/1 In addition to my jig, I . . . took the principal lady part in negro ballets, and danced 'Lucy Long.'

2. Lucy Stone League, (see quot. 1930), so named for Lucy Stone (1818–93), an advocate of women's rights.

[**1854** *Pioneer* (S.F.) April 214 From the Church, the civil law took its use, and circumscribed woman with a palisade of legal disabilities, over which a thousand Lucy Stones could never have made their way.] **1930** A. S. BLACKWELL *Lucy Stone* 177 The Lucy Stone League, organized in 1921, with the headquarters in New York, aims to promote the keeping of their own names by married women. **1945** MOLLOY *Pride's Way* 1 Charleston has a convention much older than the Lucy Stone League.

Hence **Lucy Stoner.**

1949 *Sat. Ev. Post* 12 Feb. 24/2 Some willfulness, almost an anger, stirred in Liz who, the Lord knew, was no Lucy Stoner. 'Actresses always keep their own names,' she said.

3. Lucy's warbler, a warbler, *Vermivora luciae*, of the Southwest and the Pacific Coast.

1861 *Proc. Calif. Acad. Sci.* II. (1863) 120 *Helminthophaga luciæ*—Lucy's Warbler. **1869** *Amer. Naturalist* III. 476 [Among] the first birds which I could consider as probably the leaders of the summer migration, . . . [was] *Helminthophaga Luciæ*, or Lucy's Warbler. **1917** *Birds of Amer.* III. 119/1 Lucy's Warbler frequents chiefly willow and mesquite thickets.

* **lug,** *n.*

1. *pl.* Airs, showy clothes, esp. in the phrase *to put* (or *pile*) *on lugs. Colloq.* or *slang.*

1889 MUNROE *Golden Days* 188 If you notice me . . . piling on any lugs [being overly proud] . . . you just bump me down hard. **1896** ADE *Artie* vi. 54 The family did n't put on no such lugs in them days. **1920** LEWIS *Main Street* 326 Oh, the lugs he puts on—belted coat, and piqué collar. **1941** *L.A.* Map 358.

2. A box or basket used in shipping fruit, containing usu. about 25 or 30 pounds.

1934 WEBSTER. **1949** *L.A. Times* 2 July 5/4 It takes an hour for a lug of grapes to pass through the [precooling] tunnel, which handles 768 lugs an hour.

luggage car. A baggage car. *Rare.* — **1841** *Knickerb.* XVII. 153 Your two pointer dogs . . . are locked up in the luggage-car.

* **lugs,** *n. pl.* The lower leaves of a tobacco plant; the poorest grade of tobacco.

1835 J. MARTIN *Descr. Va.* 175 An eminent tobacco manufacturer of Richmond has offered . . . to take all of their tobacco, (lugs included) at $10 a hundred. **1887** *Courier-Journal* 7 Feb. 7/1 The

Spanish buyer is the principal bidder for lugs. **1896** P. A. BRUCE *Econ. Hist. Va.* I. 442 The lowest grade [of tobacco] was known as lugs as early as 1686.

Luiseño ˌluɪˈsenjo, *n.* [See def. and quot. 1858.] "The southernmost Shoshonean division in California, which received its name from San Luis Rey, the most important Spanish mission in the territory of these people" (Hodge). Also attrib.

1858 *S.F. Bulletin* 5 Nov., The true native Americans of the wild forests—such as the Yumas, ... San Luiseños, Cahuillas, ... predominate. **1883** JACKSON *Ramona* 244 In the Luiseno tongue that is Majel; that was what I thought my people would have called you. **1903** JAMES *Indian Basketry* 59 The most populous of these is the San Luis Rey tribe, known as Luisenos. **1933** HARRINGTON *Gypsum Cave, Nev.* 117 Mr. Malcolm J. Rogers found one Gypsum Cave point ... on a fairly recent Luiseño village-site.

lulu, *n.* See **looloo,** *n.*

***lumber,** *n.*

1. Various pieces of wood, boards, etc.; any timber rough-sawn or finished into boards, staves, joists, etc.

In the first group of examples the word is used of articles left lying around to clutter up a road or street. These examples are interesting as showing the transfer in meaning of "lumber" from the general sense of anything that takes up room or is left lying about to the specific sense defined above. Quot. 1662 in the second group may belong with the first.

(1) **1663** *Boston Rec.* 16 Take care that noe wood logges, Timber stonnes or any other lumber be layed upon the flatts to the annoyance of any vesselles. **1701** *Ib.* 11 Nor shall any person incumber ... any Street, lane, or Alley ... by laying any Stones, Earth, Timber, boards, firewood and other Lumber, therein.

(2) [**1662** *Suffolk Deeds* IV. 50 [We] sayled in said ship, being freighted in Boston in New England with Beames, for houses boards, pipestaues tarr and other Lumber.] **1678** E. ANDROS in Toppan *Randolph* II. 303 The Comodityes of the Country to ye westward are wheate ... pipe staves, timber, lumber & horses. **1704** *Boston News-Letter* 13 Nov. 2/2 It's said, There are some Horses, Barrels and Lumber come on Shoar at *Nantucket* from some Vessel lately cast away. **1879** *Lumberman's Gaz.* Dec. 3 Ten cars of dressed lumber have been shipped from Gowen ... to parties in Nebraska. **1945** MATHEWS *Talking* 66, I had lumber left over from the building of the chicken and pheasant houses.

2. Growing timber that is suitable for lumber. Also **lumber tree.**

1855 in *S. Dak. Hist. Coll.* I. 411 There is no lumber on the Little Missouri River, three miles below this post. **1896** *Vt. Bd. Agric. Rep.* II. 161 The pine as a lumber tree is already a thing of the past.

3. In special combs.: (1) **Lumber Act,** a legislative act pertaining to lumbering, *obs.;* (2) **berth,** =**logging berth;** (3) **bill,** (*a*) (*cap.*) a legislative bill pertaining to lumber interests, *obs.*, (*b*) a bill rendered for the purchase of lumber; (4) **bush,** a tract of timber suitable for converting into lumber; (5) **hooker,** in the Great Lakes region, a sailing vessel converted into a barge to be "hooked to" and towed by a steam vessel; (6) **jack,** a man engaged in felling trees and getting them to market, also attrib.; (7) **jacket,** a jacket similar to those worn by lumberjacks, usu. made of leather; (8) **money,** ?a tax levied upon lumber; (9) **port**[1], "a port-hole cut in the bow or stern of a vessel for the passage of long pieces of timber" (*Cent.*); (10) **port**[2], a seaport where lumber is exported; (11) **trade,** (*a*) *collect.* commodities made of lumber, *obs.*, (*b*) the business of dealing in lumber; (12) **yard,** a yard in which lumber is kept for sale.

(1) **1721** *N.H. Prov. Papers* II. 834 A message to the house ... for repealing the lumber Act. — (2) **1851** SPRINGER *Forest Life* 56 Agricultural interests have invited men far into the interior in the vicinity of lumber berths. — (3) (*a*) **1694** *N.J. Archives* XIII. 215 A bill appointing officers for executeing ye lumber Bill &c. (*b*) **1941** WILDER *Little Town on Prairie* 26 There was the lumber bill for the new half of the house. — (4) **1850** *Knickerb.* XXXV. 22 (Th.), I had the misfortune to live in this town four years, my father having a lumber-bush there.

(5) **1929** F. E. McCLINCHEY *Joe Pete* 40 The logs were hauled down to the shore and piled ready for the loading on the lumber hookers. **1944** NUTE *Lake Superior* 126 Lumber 'hookers,' as they were termed, were the cheapest method of transportation ever devised for carrying forest products. — (6) **1896** *N.Y. Wkly. Witness* 30 Dec. 13/1 To lose the lumberjack vote meant to lose the election. **1902** WHITE *Blazed Trail Stories* 41 Typical native-born American lumber-jacks powerful in frame. **1948** *Chi. D. News* 11 June 16/7 He smokes a pipe and habitually wears moccasins and a checkered lumberjack shirt. — (7) **1939** *These Are Our Lives* 107 He was dressed in riding breeches and leather lumber-jacket. — (8) **1715** *N.H. Prov. Papers* II. 682 Mr. Treasurer Penhallow ... has an account of the lumber mony & excise mony. — (9) **1838** *Yale Lit. Mag.* III. 76 [He] found that the pirates had knocked out the lumber port, with the intention of sinking [the vessel].

(10) **1883** *Wheelman* I. 333 Calais [Me.], the great lumber port of this part of the country. — (11) (*a*) **1689** *Mass. H.S. Coll.* 3 Ser. I. 98 They are supplied ... with the lumber trade, deal boards, pipe staves, &c. (*b*) **1732** in *Cal. State P. Amer. & W. Indies* 201 The undertaker for the masting has and does carry on a greater lumber trade than any man in N. Engld. **1891** O'BEIRNE *Leaders Ind. Territory* 174/1 [He] engaged in the lumber trade on Red River close to the Harris Ferry. — (12) **1786** *Md. Journal* 4 April (Th.), Lumber-yard, at the head of Baltimore Bason. **1835** ABBOTT *N. Eng.* 218 Shops and wharves and lumber-yards multiply along the shore. **1949** *Ward Co. Independent* (Minot, N.D.) 21 July 1/3 T.T. left Minot in 1908 to establish a lumber yard in Wittenberg.

b. In combs. of obvious meaning: (1) **lumber business,** (2) **camp,** (3) **campaign,** (4) **flume,** (5) **mill,** (6) **raft,** (7) **shanty,** (8) **store,** (9) **town,** (10) **works.**

(1) **1792** BELKNAP *Hist. New-Hampshire* III. 211 Husbandry ... is much preferable to the lumber business, both in point of gain, contentment and morals. **1896** *Vt. Agric. Rep.* XV. 79 Gov. Woodbury has spent years as superintendent of the Burlington branch of J. R. Booth's gigantic lumber business. — (2) **1879** VIVIAN *Wanderings Western Land* 54 When the spring comes and the ice breaks up, the lumber camps are abandoned. **1948** *Great Falls* (Mont.) *Tribune* 18 Sep. 4/1 The forest service did not set an estimate of the damage in the lumber camp. — (3) *a***1861** WINTHROP *Open Air* 21 A Maine forest after a lumber-campaign is like France after a *coup d'état:* ... prosperous as ever, but the great men are all gone. — (4) **1877** W. WRIGHT *Big Bonanza* 240 In order to obtain a supply of water sufficient to run two lumber-flumes, a tunnel was run.

(5) **1830** *Cong. Deb.* 11 March 606/2 You will not find, in any other description of mills, such constant, unceasing labor as in our lumber mills. **1919** LEWIS *Free Air* 254 The pavement—the miles of it; the ruthless lumber-mills, with their thousands of workmen quite like himself. **1949** *Mo. Bot. Garden Bul.* June 140 The highway soon enticed a lumber mill which set up its saws in one of the flats of the creek. — (6) **1837** W. JENKINS *Ohio Gaz.* 62 The Hockhocking river ... furnishes ... a downward navigation for flat boats and lumber rafts. **1884** M. TWAIN *H. Finn* ix. 76 We catched a little section of a lumber-raft—nice pine planks. — (7) **1853** STRICKLAND *Twenty-seven Years* II. 285 The lumber-shanties are large, warm, and comfortable. **1857** HAMMOND *No. Scenes* 198 They generally keep a barrel of old rye in the lumber shanties. — (8) **1769** HILTZHEIMER *Diary* (1893) 9 Sep. 18 Last night Penington's lumber store burned down, caused by lime slacking. **1949** *Lincoln Co. News* (Oceanlake, Ore.) 4 Aug. 4/2 There are 12 important retail lumber stores in the county. — (9) **1880** *Harper's Mag.* Aug. 354/1 A cheerful little lumber town lying high among the hills.

(10) **1917** KEPHART *Camping* II. 44 An old 'lumber works,' where the trees have been chopped out ... is ... mean to flounder through.

c. Denoting persons and groups interested in lumber or in lumbering: (1) **lumber baron,** (2) **checker,** (3) **company,** (4) **cutter,** (5) **dealer,** (6) **gang,** (7) **jack,** see **3.** (6) above, (8) **king,** (9) **maker,** (10) **man,** (see **commercial, slave lumberman,** and cf. **lumberman** in **d.** (7) below), (11) **merchant,** (12) **scaler.**

(1) **1888** *N.Y. Life* 18 Feb. 27/2 One of the 'several times' a millionaire lumber 'Barons' of Michigan. **1948** *Time* 29 Nov. 24/1 In many ways he seemed a throwback to the lumber barons, the cattle kings and the mining magnates who had ruled the West before him. — (2) **1901** MERWIN & WEBSTER *Calumet 'K'* 11 Shake hands with Mr. Max Vogel, our lumber checker. — (3) **1839** *Spirit of Times* 6 April 49/3 (We.), Lumber Company. **1949** *Sierra Club Bul.* July 9/1 We feel that this is an emergency because the lumber company is now running a spur track into the Butano area. — (4) **1775** ROMANS *Nat. Hist. Fla.* 117 They planted their baronies in the pine barrens. There let the lords be lumber cutters!

(5) **1851** *Chi. D. Jrnl.* 16 Jan. 3/1 A petition ... had been circulated and signed in good faith, by the Lumber Dealers in this city. **1853** FOWLER *Home for All* 46 One other form of outside finish has been tried with success by Mr. Thornton, lumber dealer, in Pawtucket, R.I. — (6) **1904** STRATTON-PORTER *Freckles* 354 He joined one of my lumber gangs from the road. — (8) **1895** *N. Eng. Mag.* Sep. 71/2 One at least, Hon. Llewellyn Powers, may be entitled to the latter-day title of 'lumber king.' **1941** *Yankee* Dec. 19/3 They were, however Anderton's lumber kings; so nobody minded their smelling strongly of horses, even in the Methodist basement. — (9) **1778** *Jrnls. Cont. Cong.* X. 164 The Planters and Lumber Makers in the State of Georgia had large Quantities of Rice and Lumber.

(10) *a***1817** DWIGHT *Travels* II. 166 The lumbermen were without employment. **1949** *Pacific Discovery* Jan.–Feb. 29/1 'Western yellow

pine' is indicated as the correct name for *Pinus ponderosa* and ponderosa pine is indicated only as one encouraged by lumbermen. — **(11) 1789** *Boston Directory* 181 Dillaway Samuel, lumber merchant. **1864** *Harper's Mag.* Aug. 323/1 The lumber-merchants had found out these forests. — **(12) 1896** *N.Y. Wkly. Witness* 30 Dec. 13/1 A famous lumber-scaler should do the hustling.

d. Designating vessels and vehicles used in transporting lumber: (1) **lumber ark,** (cf. **lumber vessel,** quot. 1806), (2) **boat,** (3) **box,** (4) **car,** (5) **carrier,** (6) **droger,** (7) **-man,** (cf. **lumberman** in **c.** above), (8) **schooner,** (9) **sleigh,** (10) **sloop,** (11) **vessel,** (12) **wagon.**

(1) *a***1861** T. Winthrop *Canoe & Saddle* v. 83 It [a river] signifies navigation in birch-canoe, seventy-four, floating palace, dug-out, or lumber ark. — **(2) 1914** Steele *Storm* 261 The sound of a lanyard adrift on the forward shrouds of one of the lumber-boats . . . came distinctly to my ears. — **(3) 1834** Seba Smith *Lett. Major Jack Downing* 26, I want you to load up the old lumber-box with *bean poles*. **1862** *Cong. Globe* 31 March 1463/2 (Th. Supp.), Mr. White of Ind. moved to add pleasure sleighs to the tax-roll. Mr. Stevens of Pa. said he ought to . . . add 'pungs and lumber boxes.' — **(4) 1833** *Amer. R.R. Jrnl.* II. 325/2 [There are] 11 lumber cars, 8 on the line and 3 at the depository. **1895** Wait *Car-Builder's Dict.* 84 Lumber-car. A car of extra length, sometimes 40 ft. long, more particularly intended for carrying long timbers.

(5) 1700 *N.H. Prov. Papers* III. 104 Fees . . . for coasting vessels and lumber carriers going into the said Province. **1807** Janson *Stranger in Amer.* 13 The vessel, too, was not accommodated for passengers, being, in fact, a lumber-carrier. **1898** *Engineering Mag.* XVI. 98 Mr. Paulsen has applied for patents on his novel lumber carrier, and he expects his raft to occupy a place beside the whale-back. — **(6) 1848** Bartlett 123 *Droger,* lumber droger; cotton droger, etc. A vessel built solely for burden, and for transporting cotton, lumber, and other heavy articles. — **(7) 1850** *Knickerb.* XXXVI. 261 Business-like lumbermen, from 'down-east,' loaded deep in the water. **1863** *Boston Sun. Herald* 16 Aug. 3/3 (Ernst), The pilot of the oil boat signs as gaily as did the pilot of the lumberman. — **(8) 1856** Olmsted *Slave States* 155 He had once let him go to New York as cook of a lumber-schooner. **1947** Coffin *Yankee Coast* 240 Lumber schooners flocked from the coast and carried white-pine boards across all the seas. — **(9) 1823** Cooper *Pioneers* iv, A large lumber-sleigh, drawn by four horses, was soon seen dashing through the leafless bushes. **1853** Strickland *Twenty-seven Yrs.* I. 79 These are all for pleasure, but every farmer is obliged to have a lumber-sleigh for general use.

(10) 1857 *Harper's Mag.* May 741/2 He visited several taverns . . . near the river, and at length found the commander of a lumber sloop. — **(11) 1806** Webster 17/2 *Ark.* a lumber vessel or ship. **1835** Ingraham *South-West* I. 51 These vessels . . . are . . . usually loaded with shingles, masts, spars, and boards. — **(12) 1831** in *Mich. Hist. Mag.* XI. 472 Breakfast swallowed we stepped into our next rig, which was a lumber wagon drawn by two very good horses. **1948** *So. Sierran* Feb. 1/3 A lumber wagon was disassembled and packed in, as were an old Pelton water wheel, and saws to equip a sawmill.

e. Designating areas, regions, etc., where lumbering operations are or might be carried on: (1) **lumber country,** (2) **land,** (3) **plantation,** (4) **region,** (5) **state,** (also (*cap.*) as a nickname), (6) **tract,** (7) **woods.**

(1) 1848 *N.Y. Tribune* 22 May (B.), From Petersburgh I railed it through the North Carolina . . . lumber country. — **(2) 1834** Audubon *Ornith. Biog.* II. 463 While anxiously looking for 'lumber lands,' they ascended the eminences around. — **(3) 1787** in Commons *Doc. Hist.* I. 323 Great Encouragement will be given to an Overseer . . . to manage a Rice and Lumber Plantation. — **(4) 1896** *Vt. Agric. Rep.* XV. 82 The Maine Commissioner . . . has posted these notices of the new law, conspicuously throughout the lumber regions.

(5) 1846 *Warrock's Alman. 1847* 22 Maine, Lumber [State]. **1867** *Trübner's Amer. Lit. Rec.* Aug. 41 Maine is popularly known as *The Lumber or Pine-Tree State.* **1940** *Ore. Guide* 60 By 1890 . . . Oregon began to become prominent as a lumber state. — **(6) 1858** *Harper's Mag.* March 564/1 In the time of the great land-speculations in Maine, several . . . were carried away with the mania of buying lumber tracts. — **(7) 1940** Thompson *Body, Boots* 15 This sprightly grandfather learned many songs from his own Yankee father, memorized more of them in the lumberwoods, picked up several at singing school, and became a prince of balladeers.

Also *lumber district, dock, firm, grading, industry, job, market,* etc. As the last term in **hemlock, pine lumber.**

* **lumber,** *v.*

1. *intr.* To engage in the lumber business.

1809 Kendall *Travels* III. 73 The verb to *lumber* . . . has also the legitimate as well as technical sense, *to procure,* or even *to manufacture lumber:* a lumberer is one that *lumbers.* **1870** *Maine Rep.* LVI. 566 The plaintiff lumbered on his township called Holeb. **1937** Coffin *Kennebec* 9 They farmed while they fished, hunted while they hayed, lumbered while they manufactured.

2. *tr.* To cut (timber) and prepare it for the market; to clear (a region) of its timber. Also **lumbered,** *a.*

1850 Johnston *Notes* I. 52 We clean up two or three acres every year of the lumbered land (land from which the timber has been cut,) because it is unsightly. **1893** *Scribner's Mag.* June 711/1 They bought and lumbered timber on their own account. **1949** *Sierra Club Bul.* March 12/2 It took 2,000 years to grow the redwoods. . . . To lumber them takes a few months.

lumberer ˈlʌmbərɚ, *n.* One who fells forest trees and brings them to market; a lumberjack.

1809 Kendall *Travels* III. 33 To this mill, the surrounding *lumberers* or fellers of timber bring their logs. **1853** Strickland *Twenty-seven Yrs.* I. 22 Rough in manners, and often only half-civilized, the lumberer, as an individual, resembles little the woodsman of other lands. **1883** *American* VI. 297 The condition to which the lumberer and the farmer have brought the Ohio valley.

* **lumbering,** *n.* The business or action of cutting down forest trees and marketing them, the business of a lumberer. Also attrib.

1765 Samuel Deane *Diary* (1849) 309 An extraordinary good time for lumbering. **1839** Holmes *Explor. Aroostook R.* 40 Lumbering will probably be the order of the day upon it for many years. **1949** *Sierra Club Bul.* March 12/2 Even if lumbering companies should leave a seed tree, seedlings rarely survive where the forest is completely cut away as there is insufficient moisture and shade.

b. Also **lumbering business, camp, gang, party, port, season, town.**

1853 *Mass. Acts & Resolves* 690 The lumbering business, from the forest to the market. — **1858** Thoreau *Maine Woods* 108 Here were the ruins of an old lumbering-camp. — **1841** H. Playfair *Papers* II. 280 On the other sat three evidently married women boarders, whose husbands were far off in the wilderness directing some lumbering gangs. — **1832** J. MacGregor *British Amer.* II. 299 Several of these people form what is termed a 'lumbering party,' composed of persons who are . . . hired by a master lumberer. — **1885** Howells *Chance Acquaintance* 44 Ha-Ha Bay is a famous lumbering port. — **1893** *Scribner's Mag.* June 647/1 The out-put, for the last lumbering season, amounting to 9,000,000,000 feet.—**1902** White *Blazed Trail Stories* 181 A lumbering town after the drive is a fearful thing.

* **luminary,** *n.* As the last term in **locofoco, log cabin luminary.**

* **lump,** *n.*

1. Coal in lumps or large pieces as taken from the mine. Also screened coal of the size next larger than egg coal. In full **lump coal.**

1859 *Rep. Comm. Patents 1858* I. 704 The screen D retains and delivers the next size to 'lump,' known as the 'egg' coal. **1874** Knight 579 *Coal-breaker,* a machine for crushing lump-coal as taken from the mine. **1880** *Bradstreet's* 2 Oct. 5/4 The sizes used are 'lump,' 'steam-boat,' 'broken,' and 'pea.'

2. lump butter, butter not put up in a firkin. *Obs.*

1795 *Columbian Centinel* 10 Jan. 1/1 He has for sale . . . firkin and lump Butter, Capers [etc.]. **1818** *Boston Selectmen* 19 Persons . . . shall not . . . receive or sell on commission at Faneuil Hall market . . . lump butter, . . . [unless] with the express approbation of the Clerk of the Market.

* **lump,** *v. tr.* To put up with (something). Usu. in some variant of "if you don't like it, you can lump it." *Colloq.*

1791 *Columbian* (Phila.) Aug. 77 As you like it, you may lump it. **1878** Stowe *Poganuc People* 94 If anybody don't like it, why they may lump it, that's all. **1911** Saunders *Col. Todhunter* 166 And she can like it or lump it! **1948** *Chi. Tribune* 27 June (Comics) 3 Tell them the truth and let them lump it.

lumpy jaw. A disease among cattle and sheep causing suppurating tumors about the jaw. Also **lump jaw, lumped jaw.**

1890 *Ohio Agric. Exper. Sta. Bul.* III. 107 Actinomycosis, commonly called lump jaw, or lumped jaw, is not a new disease. **1913** Barnes *Western Grazing Grounds* 286 Big jaw, also called lumpy jaw and wooden tongue, is an infectious disease found generally all over the West. **1947** Cahalane *Mammals* 64 A very serious and frequently fatal malady is actinomycosis or 'lumpy-jaw.' This disease may be transmitted to man, and sometimes it is fatal.

transf. **1941** Seton *Trail of Artist-Naturalist* 307 When seeking some beef for wolf bait, we usually sought out a 'lumpy jaw.'

Hence **lumpy-jawed,** *a.*

1890 *Cong. Rec.* 29 May 5428/2 'Lumpy-jawed cattle' means cancerous cattle, cattle with cancer.

Luna moth. A large moth, *Tropaea luna,* having light-green wings. Also **Luna caterpillar.**

1855 Büchele *Landwirth* 32 Von Schmetterlingen, durch besonders Schönheit ausgezeichnet, die Mondmotte oder Königin der Nacht (*luna-moth*). **1869** *Amer. Naturalist* II. 679/2 Luna Moth. **1893** Ballard *Among Moths & Butterflies* 130 The Luna caterpillars are easily kept. **1911** *Country Life* 1 Aug. 66/3 The Luna moth is one of the most beautiful of North American insects. **1948** *Nat. Hist.* Dec. 451/1 The Hercules moth is a close relative of the well-known Luna moth.

attrib. **1909** Stratton-Porter *Girl of Limberlost* 321 [He] began examining a walnut branch for Luna moth eggs.

lunatic fringe. Those whose zeal in some cause, movement, matter, or "-ism" goes beyond reasonable limits. *Colloq.* or *slang.*

1913 *Outlook* 29 March 719/1 We have to face the fact that there is apt to be a lunatic fringe among the votaries of any forward movement. **1921** *Ladies' Home Jrnl.* April 40/1 What you see here is the lunatic fringe, the strutters, the peacocks, the cuff shooters. **1948** *Chi. Maroon* 19 Nov. 4/4 Hutchins debunked the attitude of those who consider the UC'ers are members of the 'lunatic fringe.'

Hence **lunatic fringer.**

1948 *Sat. Ev. Post* 24 July 17/2 It seemed ridiculous to gird our loins and charge into earnest battle against a handful of lunatic-fringers who spouted such gibberish.

***lunch,** *n.*

1. A lunch room. *Colloq. Obs.*

1835 *Vade Mecum* (Phila.) 24 Jan. 3/1 The *Terrapin Lunch,* under the American Museum, . . . is a fashionable and exceedingly well kept establishment. **1839** Briggs *Harry Franco* II. 49, I turned up a street towards the Park, and was tantalized by the savoury vapors which ascended from the Terrapin Lunch, beneath the American Museum. **1850** S. F. Cooper *Rural Hours* 468 As for the eating-houses . . . there are some dozen of them—Lunches, Recesses, Restaurants, &c.

b. =**free lunch.** *Obs.*

1844 *N.O. Picayune* 11 March 32/3 He is often hard set to get anything to eat. . . . He thinks that the man who invented lunches is a greater benefactor to mankind than Fulton or Arkwright. **1858** *Salem* (Ill.) *Advocate* 28 April 1/6, I saw one of the most brazen appropriators of small things (especially hard on lunch and drinks—free).

2. In combs.: (1) **lunch counter,** a counter or a restaurant at which people, usu. seated on stools, are served meals or refreshments; (2) **eater,** *local,* one who habitually partakes of free lunches given sometimes in saloons to those who purchase drinks, *obs.;* (3) **house,** =next; (4) **joint,** an unpretentious place where lunches are served; (5) **pail,** =**dinner pail;** (6) **room,** a restaurant that specializes in light meals quickly prepared, also attrib.; (7) **stand,** an eating place that serves light meals; (8) **wagon,** a wagon from which lunches are served.

(1) **1873** *Cottonwood Observer* (Alta, Utah) 16 July 3/5 Hirschman & Hunter's Lunch Counter, at the Swan Saloon, is stocked with the choicest Delicacies and Eatables. **1945** *Bent Co. Democrat* (Las Ani-

Lunch wagon

mas, Colo.) 27 July 2/2 The OPA has been accused of holding a high-grade restaurant to prices as low as those charged by lunch counters. — (2) **1856** *Spirit of Age* (Sacramento) 1 Sep. 2/2 The cities of California have become somewhat noted for a class of men known as 'lunch eaters.' **1869** *S.F. Tribune* 21 Dec. 4/6 The Lunch-Eater is a man of rather prepossessing means, but does not meanly possess anything that we are aware of. — (3) **1891** *Memphis Appeal-Avalanche* 22 April 4/3 Many of the finest business squares are . . . jagged with old shanties built in the days of the Chickasaws and now only fit to shelter a banana stand or a negro lunch house. — (4) **1886** *Calif. Maverick* (S.F.) 13 Feb. 1/3, I . . . wended my way to the lunch-joint to recuperate. — (5) **1891** Wilkins *N. Eng. Nun* 44 Matilda came in her voluminous alpaca, with her tin lunch-pail on her arm. **1901** Merwin & Webster *Calumet 'K'* 289 They slung their lunch pails on their arms and ate when and where they could. — (6) **1830** *N.Y. Mercantile Advt.* 16 Aug. 4/6 His Breakfast, Lunch and Dining rooms are capacious and comfortable. **1948** *This Week Mag.* 3 Jan. 2/3 In the days before dining cars, passengers had to eat at station lunch rooms. — (7) **1866** *Eastern Slope* (Washoe, Nev.) 13 Dec. 3/1 Kline has opened a lunch stand in the Bank Exchange saloon. **1944** *Sat. Review* 23 Sep. 15/3 He . . . winds up the day as a thoroughgoing individualist, dining al fresco at a Nedick lunch stand. — (8) **1894** *Life* 4 Oct. 215/1 'That, my dear,' responded Adalbert, 'is a lunch wagon.' **1947** Beebe *Mixed Train Dly.* 165 A car from the Silverton Northern may be seen today in Animas City where it stands beside the highway, a lunch wagon.

As the last term in **basket, dairy, Dutch, free lunch.**

lunge lʌndʒ, *n.* [f. **muskellunge.**] The namaycush, *Cristivomer namaycush.*

1851 *Vt. Laws* 49 Such person or persons shall forfeit and pay . . . the sum of one dollar for each trout or lunge so taken. **1857** *Porter's Spirit of Times* 11 April 86/3 The lower end of the lake . . . is supplied with the large catfish, small ditto, . . . Oswego, black, longe, greatbass, pike-perch, perch, &c. **1902** *Amer. Folk-Lore* 246 Longe or lunge. A common abbreviation of *muskelunge* (*maskalonge*) among English-speaking people in the region about the Great Lakes, especially the north shore of Lake Ontario.

***lunger,** *n.* **1.** One who has a tubercular disease. **2.** The cylinder of a gasoline motor. Both *slang.*

(1) **1893** Kate Sanborn *Truthful Woman So. Calif.* 14 The rainy season is hard for 'lungers' and nervous invalids. **1949** *Time* 2 May 54 Campbell joined the Thirteen Club ('All lungers—twelve of 'em died'). — (2) *a***1903** in Appel *Biog. J. Wanamaker* (1930) 154 The gasoline cars, one or two 'lungers,' as they were called.

lung fever. Pneumonia.

1747 in *Amer. Sp.* XV. 228/2 Peter Plumbs Daughter . . . died yesterday foren wth the Long fever. **1838** H. Martineau *Retrospect* III. 171 Breathing the frosty air of a winter's night, after dancing, may be easily conceived to be the cause of much of the 'lung fever' of which the stranger hears. **1899** Brown *Tiverton Tales* 227 Susan, do you remember that time I walked over to Pine Hill to pick you some mayflowers, when you was gittin' over the lung fever?

b. A lung disease among cattle.

1879 *Diseases of Swine* 195 Mitchell [County, Kansas]. Murrain, black-leg, and lung-fever have prevailed to some extent among cattle.

lunker ˈlʌŋkɚ, *n.* [Origin unknown. Cf. **slunker.**] Any particularly large fresh-water fish, esp. one usu. found at some depth. Also attrib.

1920 *Outing* July–Aug. 197, I said that I caught trout in a tin pan, and here's the proof. This old lunker of a rainbow gave me a bath. **1947** *Sports Afield* Dec. 21/1 A bronzed lunker came out of the shadowy depths and smashed the pigskin. **1947** Dalrymple *Panfish* 348 The first thought, of course, is in terms of lunker Bass, Pike, or Walleye.

lunkhead ˈlʌŋkˌhɛd, *n.* [Origin obscure. Note **lunk** in quot. 1867.] A thick-headed person, a blockhead. *Colloq.*

1852 A. T. Jackson *Forty-Niner* (1920) 150 Pard shut the book with a slam and said I was a lunkhead. [**1867** *Harper's Wkly.* 25 May 330/2 They're tigers, you thick-headed lunk.] **1949** *Time* 11 April 25/2 If them lunkheads is spies, I'm Mata Hari!

b. Also **lunk-headed,** slow-witted. *Colloq.*

1884 *Atlanta Const.* Sep., Her lunk-headed admirer has to turn squarely around, blocking up the side-walk. **1949** *Sat. Ev. Post* 16 April 143/2 Take it then, and be fast cleared out, for you're a lunk-headed moon-calf.

***lurch.** *n.* An inclination or penchant. *Colloq.* — **1794** *Mass. H.S. Coll.* IV. 48 He conceived a lurch for improvement in manufacturing spanish brown. **1878** in E. S. Phelps *A. Phelps* 219, I got from Professor Stuart and Albert Barnes . . . a lurch adverse to such work.

***lusty,** *a.* (See quot. 1839.) *Colloq. Obs.* — **1708** *Boston News-Letter* 15–22 Nov. 4/2 A Lusty Carolina Indian Woman fit for any Dairy Service, to be Sold on Reasonable Terms. **1839** in Kemble *Journal* (1863) 180, I came upon a gang of lusty women, as the phrase is here for women in the family-way.

lute lut, *n.* [Du. *loet.*] (See quots.) — **1875** Knight 1365/1 *Lute,* . . . a straight-edge employed to strike off the surplus clay from a brick-mold. **1889** C. T. Davis *Manuf. Bricks* (ed. 2) 142 There is a tool used for scraping off and levelling the moulding floor. . . . It consists of a piece of light pine board, . . . set upright, with a long light handle in the centre. . . . The tool is called a 'lute.'

***lyceum,** *n.*

1. An association which sponsors lectures, dramatic performances, debates, and the like; esp. the association started in 1826 by Josiah Holbrook in Millbury, Mass., which later had many branches. Also attrib. Cf. **Chautauqua.**

1818 *Detroit Gaz.* 23 Jan. 2/3 Lyceum.—The first meeting of this society was held on Tuesday evening last. **1835** *S. Lit. Messenger* I. 273 In all the cities, and many of the larger and middling towns . . . there are Lyceums. **1881** *Harper's Mag.* March 628/2 During the days of his lyceum lecturing, no man was more popular [than Dr. Chapin] upon the platform. **1898** M. TWAIN *Autobiog.* (1924) I. 151 (R.), By that verdict all the lyceums in the country determined the lecture's commercial value. **1948** *Sierra Club Bul.* March 51 We know of at least one lecture on 'American Scenery,' which he gave in 1835 before the New York Lyceum.

2. The program sponsored by a lyceum.

1854 O. OPTIC *In Doors & Out* (1876) 306 There were balls, parties, and lyceums in Tiptop. **1858** *Harper's Mag.* April 699/2 The Lyceum —or the course of miscellaneous winter lectures in towns and villages all through the country—has now become a fixed American institution. **1900** BACHELLER *E. Holden* 139 That there is talent in Faraway township . . . no one can deny who has ever attended a lyceum at the Howard schoolhouse.

3. In special combs. of obvious meaning: **lyceum association, bureau, hall, meeting, system.**

1865 *Atlantic Mo.* XV. 363 There are library associations or lyceum associations, composed generally of young men. — **1923** COBB *Kansas* 19 Fate, personated by the booking agency of a lyceum bureau, decreed that I should jump out of the Teutonic comforts of St. Louis clear over to a smallish community of interior Kansas. **1948** *Chi. Tribune* 25 Jan. IV. 6/3 They organized the Chicago Lyceum bureau in 1834 to listen to lectures and to provide the members with reading matter. — **1831** *Mass. Statutes* 4 March, They are hereby made a corporation, by the name of the Lyceum Hall, . . . for the purpose of affording means and facilities for the prosecution of literary and scientific studies. — **1834** *Amer. Ladies' Mag.* VII. (Boston) 202 The Lyceum meetings had ceased, as the evenings became shorter, and we rested upon the knowledge we had gained. — **1843** CARLTON *New Purchase* II. 174 The common school system, and the lyceum system.

***lyed,** *a.* Denoting corn or corn products prepared as food by a process involving the use of a weak solution of lye obtained from wood ashes. Cf. next and see **hulled corn.**

1788 *Mich. Hist. Coll.* XI. 585 The hull'd or Lied Corn he reserved for a more pressing occasion, when the Indians should according to custom arrive here in considerable numbers. **1793** in *Five Fur Traders of Northwest* (1933) 95 A full allowance to a voyageur while at this Poste is a Quart of Lyed Indian Corn or maize, and one ounce of Greece. **1814** BRACKENRIDGE *Views La.* 202 Their food consists of lied corn homony for breakfast. **1823** JAMES *Exped.* I. 114 Another very acceptable dish was called *leyed* corn. **1867** DE VOE *Market Ass't* 409 Since writing the above, I have found another kind, called lyed hominy, which is differently although easily prepared.

lye hominy. Hominy, so called from the use of lye in its preparation.

1821 DEWEES *Lett. from Texas* 20 Our subsistence was principally upon . . . a kind of lye hominy seasoned with hickory nut kernels. **1919** DUNN *Indiana* II. 1170 A woman situated like Mrs. McCoy, in her Indian boarding school, with no food but lye hominy in the house for weeks at a time, 'degraded her soul' by cooking lye hominy. **1948** DICK *Dixie Frontier* 290 Lye hominy was made by soaking the whole grains of corn in lye water to remove the hulls.

Lyman's long summer. A variety of apple. *Obs.* — **1847** IVES *N. Eng. Fruit* 48 *Lyman's Long Summer.* . . . A large and handsome American fruit introduced to notice by S. Lyman, of Manchester, Conn.

lynch lɪntʃ, *n.* Orig. ***Lynch.** *attrib.* Of or pertaining to lynching. See **lynch law,** as a main entry. Cf. ***regulator,** *n.* **3. a.**

1811 ELLICOTT in Mathews *Life A. Ellicott* 222, I should not have asserted it as a fact [that Capt. Lynch was the originator of Lynch law] had it not been related to me by Mr. Lynch . . . together with several other Lynch-men as they are called. **1835** GARRISON in W. P. & F. J. Garrison *W. L. Garrison* I. 519 The slave States . . . have organized Vigilance Committees and Lynch Clubs. **1852** CAZNEAU *Eagle Pass* 166 The press caught up and bruited the punishment as an evidence of the 'horrible license of the Lynch Code.' **1868** *N.Y. Herald* 29 July 4/5 The Indiana Lynch Murders. **1946** *Newsweek* 12 Aug. 34/2 A shocked nation flooded Washington and Atlanta with demands for apprehension of the lynch leaders.

As the last term in **Captain, General, Judge Lynch.**

lynch lɪntʃ, *v.* [See **lynch law.**] *tr.* Orig. to inflict severe bodily punishment upon (a person), as by whipping or tarring and feathering, without due process of law; later to hang or otherwise kill (a person) by mob action.

1835 in *Amer. Sp.* XXIII. (1948) 315/1 They were soundly flogged, or in other words, *Lynched,* and set on the opposite side of the river. **1836** *Niles' Reg.* 1 Oct. 69/1 Some personal friend of Mr. Broux . . . proceeded to the mansion of judge Bermudez, with a view to Lynch him, or to inflict some severe punishment upon his person. **1857** *Lawrence* (Kans.) *Republican* 28 May 1 The Rev. Pardee Butler had been lynched, tarred and feathered, and sent down the Missouri on a frail raft. **1882** *Nation* 5 Oct. 279/1 Rhodes, who brutally murdered an old man . . . near Charlottesville, Va., last February, was lynched near that town. **1946** *Chi. D. News* 22 Feb. 12/3 Men take the law into their hands and lynch alleged criminals without trial.

lyncher ˈlɪntʃɚ, *n.* Orig. **Lyncher.** [f. **lynch,** *v.*] One who lynches or helps to lynch.

1835 *Vade Mecum* (Phila.) 14 Feb. 3/2 He was then tied to a tree, and each Lyncher, being armed with a cow-hide, took turns in flogging him. **1851** *Ore. Statesman* 4 April 1/2 Col. Bill Borland was the *generalissimo* of the Texas Lynchers. **1949** *Antioch Rev.* Summer 215 He had the necessary powers to bring the lynchers to justice.

lynching ˈlɪntʃɪŋ, *n.* [f. **lynch,** *v.*]

1. The action of lynching a person.

1836 J. HALL *Statistics of West* p. xviii, The Lynching of these children in southern latitudes, is too often the terrible result of such early lessons. **1868** *N.Y. Herald* 22 July 5/2 The lynching was a premeditated affair. **1949** *Lubbock* (Tex.) *Morn. Avalanche* 23 Feb. I. 10/4 A bill defining and providing penalties for lynching was approved 9 to 3 tonight by the House Criminal Jurisprudence committee.

b. Also the treatment of being lynched.

1836 SIMMS *Mellichampe* 314 Had not Max Mellichampe pronounced me deserving of Lynching? **1900** *Cong. Rec.* 16 Jan. 847/1 Such legislation, . . . as will protect colored people from lynching and murder without the authority of law.

2. In combs.: (1) **lynching bee,** a gathering for the purpose of lynching someone; (2) **belt,** (see quot.), *rare;* (3) **corncracker,** a Southerner given to lynching, *rare;* (4) **mob,** a mob whose purpose is lynching; (5) **party,** =**lynching bee.**

(1) **1900** *Cong. Rec.* 31 Jan. 1369/1 They have sometimes had 'lynching bees,' . . . they have sometimes lynched men for murder, for arson, for rape. **1943** *Christian Cent.* 1 Dec. 1/2 Evidently there is a widespread and growing fear lest the United Nations . . . let loose in Europe what might turn out to be little less than a gigantic lynching bee. — (2) **1900** NICHOLSON *Hoosiers* 43 An attorney-general of the State . . . expressed his opinion that the right of way of the Baltimore and South-western Railway marked the [northern limits of the] 'lynching belt' in Indiana. — (3) **1839** HOFFMAN *Wild Scenes* 112 A disbanded regulator of the Georgia guard, with a Lynch-ing corncracker from that state, . . . had scented the contents of my master's saddle-bags. — (4) **1858** *N.Y. Tribune* 30 Sep. (B.), As gross a violation of justice as vigilance committee or lynching mob was ever guilty of. **1919** *30 Yrs. Lynching in U.S.* (N.A.A.C.P.) 7 From 1889 to 1918 . . . 3,224 persons have been killed by lynching mobs.
(5) **1851** *Ore. Statesman* 4 April 1/2 The district was one of the earliest settlements in Eastern Texas, where he became the chief of the Lynching party. **1948** WESTON *Mother Lode* 20 A low spreading oak . . . before long obligingly served for a lynching party and thereby became known as the Hang Tree.

lynch law. Also **Lynch law.** [Orig. Lynch's law *q.v.*]

Named after Captain William *Lynch* (1742–1820), of Pittsylvania County, Virginia, and later of Pendleton District, South Carolina. (See A. Matthews in *Mass. Col. Soc. Trans.* XXVII. 256–71 and quot. 1836 under **Lynch's law.**) The 1st quot. below is from the compact drawn up by Lynch and his neighbors.

The practice or custom by which persons are punished for real or alleged crimes without due process of law; the punishment so meted out.

[**1780** in *S. Lit. Messenger* (1836) II. 389 Whereas, many of the inhabitants of Pittsylvania . . . have sustained great and intolerable losses by a set of lawless men . . . that . . . we, the subscribers, being determined to put a stop to these iniquitous practices of those unlawful and abandoned wretches, do enter into the following association . . . and if they will not desist from their evil practices, we will inflict such corporeal punishment on him or them, as to us shall seem adequate to the crime committed or the damage sustained.] **1811** ELLICOTT in Mathews *Life A. Ellicott* 220 Captain Lynch just mentioned [residing on Oolenoy Creek, S.C.] was the author of the Lynch laws so well-known and so frequently carried into effect some years ago in the southern states in violation of every principle of justice and jurisprudence. **1835** *Md. Hist. Reg.* IX. 161 They then followed the example of the Vicksburg people in attempting to inflict the Lynch Law. **1902** LONDON *Daughter of Snows* 284 It's lynch law, you know, and their minds are made up. They're bound to get me.

attrib. **1840** GARRISON in W. P. & F. J. Garrison *W. L. Garrison* II. 365 [Several Englishmen] swore that Oxford 'ought to be strung up . . . ,' in true Lynch-law style. **1857** STIRLING *Lett. Slave States* 144 May not the Republicanism of Louisiana be characterized as a despotism, tempered by Lynch-law halters? **1887** *Macmillan's Mag.* March 348/1, I could hardly recognize the complacent judge of the afternoon, in the trembling creature who tried to assure his Lynch-law brother that Cobbett and Grobe had gone East.

Lynch's law. =prec.

In quot. 1836 the "annexed paper" refers to an agreement by William Lynch and others to take the law into their own hands to protect their community from horse-stealing, counterfeiting, and "other species of villany." An excerpt from this agreement is given *s.v.* **lynch law,** quot. 1780.

1782 C. LYNCH *Lett. to W. Hay* (MS) 11 May, They are mostly torys & such as [Capt.] Sanders has given Lynchs Law too for Dealing with the Negroes &c. **1836** POE in *S. Lit. Messenger* II. 389 Frequent inquiry has been made within the last year as to the origin of Lynch's law. . . . It will be perceived from the annexed paper, that the law, so called, originated in 1780, in Pittsylvania, Virginia. Colonel William Lynch, of that county, was its author. **1938** ASBURY *Sucker's Prog.* 216 In some of the smaller towns a few gamblers were caught up and used according to 'Lynch's Law'—that is, they were given from 40 to 300 lashes, tarred and feathered, and ordered to leave town within twenty-four hours.

Lynchy ˈlɪntʃɪ, *a.* and *adv.* In a manner suggestive of lynch law *q.v. Obs.* — **1835** *Vade Mecum* (Phila.) 14 Oct. 3/1 He was not interrupted; but in Boston, at the time announced for his lecture, a mob assembled having a very Lynchy look. **1840** HALIBURTON *Clockm.* 3 Ser. xiv. 202 People began to talk considerable hard and Lynchy about their galls comin' so often to a single man to tell their experience.

***lynx,** *n.* As the last term in **bay, Canada, Canadian, red lynx.**

lyscom ˈlɪskəm, *n.* [?f. proper name.] A variety of apple. *Obs.* — **1847** IVES *N. Eng. Fruit* 38 *Lyscom.*—This apple originated in Southboro', Mass. It is of medium size, rather oblong, and very regular. **1859** ELLIOT *Western Fruit Grower's Guide* 156.

M

ma'am school. A school conducted by a woman. *Obs.* Cf. **schoolma'am, schoolma'amish.** — **1856** GOODRICH *Recoll.* I. 39, I found a girl, some eighteen years old, keeping a ma'am school for about twenty scholars.

***macadam,** *n.* Also **McAdam.** A road made with successive layers of broken or crushed stone. Also fig. *Obs.*

1839 *Indiana H. Rep. Jrnl.* 216 Provided, . . . a good McAdam can be made on said route. **1848** *Yale Lit. Mag.* XIII. 281 Instead of plodding on foot along the dusty, well-worn McAdam of learning, why will you take nigh cuts on ponies? **1879** B. F. TAYLOR *Summer-Savory* 160 The streams . . . run along their rough McAdams. [**1897** *Outing* May 135/2 The width of the macadam is eighteen feet, while the crushed rock is ten inches deep.]

Macartney rose. A climbing rose, *Rosa bracteata,* imported originally from China. — **1856** *Rep. Comm. Patents 1855: Agric.* 315 The single white 'Macartney' rose, I find, in this region, forms an excellent hedge. **1930** BAILEY *Cyclo. Horticulture* 2996/2 Macartney Rose [is] . . . naturalized in Fla. and La.

maccarib 'mækərɪb, *n.* ["The old and original form from a cognate of which has been derived the Algonquian word *caribou*" (Hodge).] The caribou. *Obs.* — **1672** JOSSELYN *N. Eng. Rarities* 20 The Maccarib, Caribo, or Pohanc, a kind of Deer, as big as a Stag, round hooved.

McCarty mə'kɑrtɪ, *n.* Also **McCarthy.** [Amer. Sp. *mecate,* a rope.] (See quots.) Cf. **mecate.**

The identification of the name McCarty with the Spanish *mecate* can probably be attributed to the Eastern and Southern [mə'kɑ:tɪ].

1904 STEEDMAN *Bucking Sagebrush* 48 Everything was there, six-shooter and belt, McCarty (or hair rope), sombrero. **1927** RUSSELL *Trails* 166 They all rode an' broke broncs with a hackamore. It wasn't a rope one like they're usin' to-day, but one made of braided leather an' rawhide. Looped to this was about fifteen or twenty foot of hair rope called a 'McCarthy.' **1947** *Westerners' Brand Book* 55 We were to get these horses well reined, gentle, taught to stand 'ground tied' (with reins or McCarty on the ground).

***McClellan,** *n.* [Gen. George B. *McClellan* (1826–85).]

1. =**McClellan saddle.** Also **McClellan tree.**

[**1863** RUSSELL *Diary* II. 269 But M'Clellan is nevertheless 'the man on horseback' just now, and the Americans must ride in his saddle, or in anything he likes.] **1866** J. E. COOKE *Surry* 275, I found, from papers in the side-pockets of the 'McClellan tree' that the animal had belonged to a Lieutenant. **1889** *Outing* June 205/2, I like a Whitman or a McClellan better than I do a Mexican.

2. A type of military cap.

1888 BILLINGS *Hardtack* 277 [A] large number of the soldiers of '62 . . . did not wear the forage cap furnished by the government. They bought the 'McClellan cap,' so called, at the hatters' instead. **1922** HEBARD *Bozeman Trail* II. 68 As we looked toward the east we could see those glorious old McClelland caps on the heads of our comrades as they appeared in a long skirmish line.

3. McClellan saddle, a saddle of a type designed by General McClellan along the lines of the Hungarian saddle.

1865 SALA *Diary* I. 314 You know what the M'Clellan saddle is. *You* have a blanket put on the saddle, or you'll suffer. **1885** HOWELLS *S. Lapham* ii, A burly mounted policeman, bulging over the pommel of his M'Clellan saddle, jolted by. **1948** *Democrat* 19 Aug. 6/1 For Sale—Lawn mower, in good condition; also McClellan saddle, bridle and blanket.

***McCown,** *n.* [Captain John Porter *McCown,* born *c*1820.] Used in the possessive with *bunting* and *longspur* to designate a small bird, *Rhynchophanes mccowni,* related to the longspur family.

1856 CASSIN *Illust. Birds* 228 *Plectrophanes McCownii.* . . . McCown's Bunting. **1874** in COUES *Birds N.W.* 125 Maccown's Bunting . . . was abundant in the vicinity of Cheyenne in August. **1917** *Birds of Amer.* III. 22/1 McCown's Longspur (*Rhynchophanes maccowni*) . . . is found on the interior plains of North America, east of the Rocky Mountains.

McCoy mə'kɔɪ, *n.* [See note to **2.** below.]

1. Whisky or beer of a good quality. Also **attrib.** *Slang.*

1908 DAVENPORT *Butte Beneath X-Ray* 20, I took a good-sized snort out of that big bottle [of furniture polish] in the middle. . . . Have you none of the clear McCoy handy around the house? **1932** *Variety* 15 Nov. 41/5 Three McCoy centres that have been supplying New York with a not-bad brand of beer, will get a fraction of that price.

2. *The real McCoy,* the genuine article, the real thing. *Slang.*

This expression may have come into use as stated in quot. 1946 below, but in the earliest evidence so far found (cf. sense **1.** above) it refers to whisky. Note "clear McCoy" in quot. 1908 above. Quot. 1936 in **b.** below is typical of much that has appeared from time to time about the term. See also Mencken, *American Language,* 4th ed., 580*n.*

McClellan saddle

1922 *Collier's* 7 Oct. 26/2 'At's the real McCoy you got there, brother! . . . Comes right down from Canada! **1946** *N.O. Picayune* 24 March II. 2/2 'The real McCoy' came from the underworld. . . . The term originally was applied to heroin brought in from the island of Macao off the coast of China. . . . It was not cut. Dope addicts found out the stuff from Macao was the real Macao.

b. Also of persons.

1924 *Collier's* 4 Oct. 6/3 The lady guest was likewise the real McCoy, as soothin' to the eyes as belladonna. **1936** *Chi. D. News* 7 Dec. 18/1 A reader of The Daily News has sent us a bit from a ballad, current sixty years ago in Ireland, in which an irate wife proclaims herself the head of the household with the assertion, 'I'm the real McCoy.' **1949** *This Week Mag.* 30 April 5/1 If you meet the real McCoy in a corridor late in the evening, he'll have a lot more on his mind than smelling for smoke.

***macerator,** *n.* A pulping machine. — **1890** *Cent.* 3559/2 macerator. . . . Any suitable vessel in which substances are macerated. **1912** *Publishers' Circular* 12 Oct. 503 Then the macerator, the greatest consumer of contemporary literature, takes them [the books] to its bosom.

***MacGillivray,** *n.* Used in the possessive in the names of birds, esp. **MacGillivray's warbler,** Tolmie's warbler, *Oporornis tolmiei.*

1839 AUDUBON *Ornith. Biog.* V. 75 Macgillivray's Warbler, *Sylvia Macgillivrayi,* . . . is one of the most common summer residents of the woods and plains of the Columbia. **1887** RIDGWAY *Man. N. Amer. Birds* 69 *B*[*ulweria*] *macgillivrayi.* . . . Macgillivray's Petrel. **1917** *Birds of Amer.* III. 30/2 Macgillivray's Seaside Sparrow (*Passerherbulus maritimus macgillivraii*) is found on the Atlantic coast from South Carolina to Florida and, in winter, along the Gulf coast. **1940** GABRIELSON & JEWETT *Birds of Ore.* 509 This dark-headed little inhabitant of the brush patches, Macgillivray's Warbler, is a common bird in the Cascades.

McGuffey's reader. Any one of a series of widely used school readers, noted for their moral lessons and their selections from great English writers, edited by Wm. H. McGuffey (1800–1873). Also **McGuffey reader.**

1836 McGuffey (*title*), McGuffey's First Eclectic Reader. **1876** *Pioche* (Nev.) *D. Jrnl.* 23 Sep. 2/1 Fifteen years ago McGuffey's Fourth Reader sold for 27 cents apiece. **1948** *Forest Way* (Chi.) May 5 The most widely circulated American book of the past three centuries, the survey showed, is the McGuffey reader—125 million copies since 1834.

macheer məˈtʃɪr, *n.* [f. Sp. *mochila*, in the sense shown here.] =**mochila.** Also **macheer saddle.**

1847 *Calif. Star* (S.F.) 21 Aug. 2/3 [A] man declares his *macheres* (saddle cover) was stolen from under him, although seated upon his horse and his horse in motion. **1853** Brewerton *With Kit Carson* (1930) 49 Our saddles were of the true Mexican pattern, wooden trees covered with leathers called *macheers*. **1873** Miller *Amongst Modocs* 50 The Prince unfastened his cloak from the macheers behind my saddle. **1927** Russell *Trails* 166 I've seen bronc riders use an old macheer saddle with a Texas tree.

machero məˈtʃɛro, *n. S.W.* [Sp. *mechero*, in same sense.] A device for lighting a cigar or cigarette. — **1848** *Calif. Star* (S.F.) 18 March 2/2 Deliberately drawing from his vest pocket, his worn and soiled *machero*, he applies fire to a cigarito, which he thrusts in his mouth. **1889** *Outing* May 124/1 It should be long enough to hold the pipe and *machero*.

machete məˈtʃetə, *n. S.W.* [Sp. in same sense. An Amer. borrowing.] A knife, usu. a large, heavy one such as is used in cutting sugar cane.

1839 in Audubon *Ornith. Biog.* V. 354, I went immediately to the Fort [Vancouver], . . . and procured a matchette or large knife. **1854** J. L. Stephens *Central Amer.* 70 The Machete, or chopping-knife . . . varies in form in different sections of the country. **1893** *Outing* May 110/2 We had cut away the clinging vegetation with our *machetes*. **1949** *Américas* Sep. 22/1 Virtually all the cane is cut by hand, with machetes.

* **machine,** *n.*

1. A fire engine. Hence *to run with the machine*, (see quot. 1890). *Colloq. Obs.*

1848 *Glance at N.Y.* 9 I've made up my mind not to run wid der machine any more. **a1859** *Yankee Notions* 259 (B.), As for the machine, why, she's a pearl of the East. **1890** *Cent.* 3560/3 *To run with the machine*, to accompany a fire-engine to a fire, either as a member of the fire-company or as a hanger-on: a phrase used when the members of fire-companies (in large cities) were volunteers, and service at fires was gratuitous. (U.S.)

2. *Polit.* A factional, party, or personal organization that operates through a system of committees and individual workers in an effort to control nominations, appointments, elections, etc. See also **political machine.**

1865 *Phila. Sun. Mercury* 20 Aug. 3/7 Unworthy, dishonest men have his confidence, and have 'run the machine' to suit their own purposes. **1902** Meyer *Nominating Systems* 55 The convention is not the mouthpiece of the people, but of the 'machine.' **1949** *Time* 26 Sep. 24/1 The machine found itself running an investment banker and economist for controller, . . . a prominent lawyer for register of wills.

3. In combs.: (1) **machine card,** a perforated card of wood or metal, which may be attached to a loom to cause the warp-threads to be lifted in the proper succession to produce a figured design, a Jacquard card; (2) **oven,** (see quot.); (3) **shop,** a shop containing machines, such as lathes, planes, etc., where machines, parts of machines, or the like, are made, finished, or repaired; (4) **twist,** (see quot.).

(1) 1827 *Hallowell* (Me.) *Gaz.* 20 June 4/5 S. G. Ladd has for sale Winslow's Machine Cards at Factory prices. **1857** *Lawrence* (Kans.) *Republican* 28 May 3 Agents for the sale of James Smith & Co.'s superior Machine Cards. — **(2) 1890** *Cent.*, *machine-oven*, a bakers' oven, . . . or an oven for any other use, fitted with a . . . mechanical device for aiding the process of baking, or for economizing time or space. — **(3) 1827** *Aurora* (Phila.) 25 July 1/3 A Machine Shop, from 60 to 70 feet long and 20 feet wide, two stories high. **1947** Beebe *Mixed Train Dly.* 165 That longish low building . . . was his machine shop. — **(4) 1883** Knight *Supp.* 570 Machine Twist. A kind of silk thread made three-cord, and twisted from right to left. Made specially for use on the sewing machine. Sewing silk is two-cord, and twisted from left to right.

b. Also (sense **2.**) in combs. of obvious meaning, as (1) **machine boss,** (2) **man,** (3) **manager,** (4) **party,** (5) **politician,** (6) **politics,** (7) **ring,** (8) **rule,** (9) **slate,** (10) **ticket,** (11) **voting,** (12) **wing.**

(1) 1887 *Nation* 3 March 204/3 This is one of the prizes which the various Machine bosses are fighting to get 'a hack at.' **1949** *World-Herald Mag.* (Omaha) 12 June 4/1 That was only the usual prattle of a machine boss. — **(2) 1880** *Dly. Inter-Ocean* (Chi.) 1 June 2/3 They are good Republicans and 'machine men,' who always support the ticket. — **(3) 1896** *Chi. Record* 17 Feb. 4/1 The machine managers force the holding of primaries wherein their own candidates are put in nomination. — **(4) 1858** *N.Y. Tribune* 1 Nov. 716 Both of these alleged swindlers are prominent members of the 'Masheen' party of the First Ward.

(5) 1876 *Modesto* (Calif.) *Herald* 20 July 1/5 The fastidious malcontents of the Fifth Avenue Conference . . . threatened . . . to vote the Democratic ticket in case the 'machine politicians' captured the Cincinnati Convention. **1949** *Chi. D. News* 16 March 22/2 If he is a typical machine politician, the problem is simple. — **(6) 1876** *Cattaraugus Union* (Ellicottville, N.Y.) 31 Aug. 2/2, I am as sick of machine politics as I am of Grant. **1949** *Time* 5 Sep. 12/3 Shrewd, hard-bitten Bill Boyle believes in machine politics. — **(7) 1904** *N.Y. Ev. Post* 11 April 6 When he began his work in St. Louis as Circuit Attorney . . . he found that the criminals who were robbing the city were the machine ring. — **(8) 1882** *Nation* 10 Aug. 102/3 In politics he is chiefly known as having . . . dissatisfied the voters of his district by his obedience to 'Machine' rule. — **(9) 1944** *Chi. D. News* 15 Dec. 18/2 They elected Lucas. They played hob with machine slates generally.

(10) 1887 *Scribner's Mag.* May 625/1 If journalists and journals were in the market, . . . there would be no such widespread bolt against your machine ticket to-day. — **(11) 1866** *Cong. Globe* 18 Jan. 308/1 Machine voting is that by which a man puts a few hundred ballots in a district and demands of certain persons a certain number of votes when the poll is closed. — **(12) 1885** *Mag. Amer. Hist.* March 295/1 The 'machine wing of the Republican party came to be known as such under the leadership of Mr. Conkling.'

As the last term in **anti-, barrel, bogus, cockle, cotton, drilling, dry washing, eyeleting, folding, gas, harvesting, mowing, mud, nail, nail cutting, nickel-in-the-slot, nickelodeon, party, peanut, planing, political, rowing, sapping, sausage, seed, seeding, separating, sewing, shearer, sheep-shearer, shoe-pegging, street-scraping, stump, talking, type, typewriting, vote-getting, voting, washing machine.**

* **machinery,** *n.* As the last term in **party, road machinery.**

* **machinist,** *n.* A machine politician. *Obs.* Cf. **anti-, warrant machinist.** — **1880** *Scribner's Mo.* Oct. 908/1 'This,' says the political machinist, 'is an utter misconception of the whole case.' **1882** *Nation* 2 Nov. 371/3 Office-jobbing, and trading . . . are to-day making every Machinist in the country run to ask honest men what he must do to be saved.

machinize məˈʃinaɪz, *v.* [f. **machine*, *n.*] *tr.* To make like a machine; to organize into something like a machine. — **1856** Emerson *Eng. Traits* 41 The Times newspaper, . . . by its immense correspondence and reporting, seems to have machinized the rest of the world for his [the reader's] convenience. **1901** *Cong. Rec.* 8 Jan. 738/1 The real purpose of these rules is to machinize this House; to create a one-man power; to magnify the machine and minify the member.

* **McIntosh,** *n.* A variety of apple, so called after John McIntosh, a Canadian farmer who discovered the seedling in 1796. Also **McIntosh red.**

1913 *Boston Sun. Post* 23 Nov. 41 There are several hundred trees of Mackintosh reds. **1945** *Bristol* (N.H.) *Enterprise* 15 Feb. 1/1 (*advt.*), McIntosh, Cortland, Baldwins, Delicious Northern Spies. **1949** *Chi. Tribune* 18 Sep. II. 11/7, 1800 Full bearing Apple Trees, mainly McIntosh, Delicious, Winesaps, and Jonathons.

* **mackerel,** *n.* In combs.: (1) **mackerel goose,** (see quot.); (2) **gull,** any one of various terns; (3) **hawk,** =prec.; (4) **scad,** (see quot.); (5) **scales,** (see quot.); (6) **shark,** (see quot. 1839).

(1) 1917 *Birds of Amer.* I. 218 Northern Phalarope. Lobipes lobatus. . . . [Also called] Mackerel Goose. — **(2) 1796** P. A. Nemnich *Allgemeines Polyglotten-Lexicon* V. 820 Mackerel gull. *Larus ridibundus*. **1832** Williamson *Maine* I. 145 The mackerel gull is nearly as large as a goose. **1917** *Birds of Amer.* I. 60 Common Tern. Sterna hirundo. . . . [Also called] Mackerel Gull. — **(3) 1947** Coffin *Yankee Coast* 298 The mackerel . . . come in August with the mackerel-hawks, marked with the same markings and moulded into the same projectile-like bodies, crying and screaming over the fish. — **(4) 1897** *N.Y. Forest, Fish, & Game Comm.* 2nd Rep. 238 Decapterus macarelius, . . . Mackerel Scad, . . . was found common at Southampton, Long Island.

(5) 1933 Cheley *Camping Out* 184 'Mackerel scales,' which are *cirro-stratus clouds*, also indicate rain. — **(6) 1819** *Plough Boy* I. 135 The revenue cutter brought in two very strange fish, found eating a dead horse, supposed to be mackerel sharks. **1839** Storer *Mass. Fishes* 185 *Lamna punctata*. . . . As this species is generally seen following shoals of mackerel upon which it feeds, it is commonly known among the fishermen as the Mackerel Shark. **1949** *Fishes Western N. Atlantic* I. 117 Mackerel Sharks are often seen finning at the surface on calm days.

As the last term in **bull-eyed, chub, Easter, fall, jack, Monterey (Spanish), skip, spring, thimble-eye(d), yellow mackerel.**

mackerel ˈmækərəl, *v.* [f. the noun.] *intr.* To fish for mackerel. — **1877** JEWETT *Deephaven* vi. 108 When we were mackereling she never give us any trouble. **1881** MCLEAN *Cape Cod Folks* 62, I was going mackerellin' with ye myself that time.

Mackinaw ˈmækəˌnɔ, *n.* Also **mackinaw, mackinac.** [Can. F. *mackinac,* f. Ojibway *mitchimakinâk,* "great turtle." See note below.]

Mackinac is the name of the strait between Lake Michigan and Lake Huron. Mackinac Island lies in the Strait. Mackinaw City, on the northern tip of Michigan's lower peninsula, was once an important Indian trading post.

Andrew J. Blackbird, son of an Ottawa chief, and an interpreter for the U.S. Government, regarded the usual etymology (see above) of "Mackinaw" as entirely in error. See his *Complete History of Ottawa and Chippewa Indians* (1887), 11.

1. =**Mackinaw boat.** Now *hist.*

1842 *S. Lit. Messenger* VIII. 586/2 A party of six . . . had occasion about this time to ascend the Missouri, in a Mackinaw, with the purpose of trading with the Mandans. **1880** *Scribner's Mo.* May 124/1 All available space in the overladen mackinaws needed to be reserved for the indispensable whisky. **1936** ASBURY *French Quarter* 74 The traders of the western territories loaded their goods in an infinite variety of boats—canoes, keelboats, covered skiffs or Mackinaws [etc.].

b. =**Mackinaw blanket.**

1836 in *Mass. Hist. Soc. Proc.* 2 Ser. VII. (1892) 276 Covering, a cotton counterpane, a sheet, and a narrow short thin blanket, besides my own great coats and green Mackinaw. **1936** *Sears Cat.* (ed. 173) 499, 95% Wool Mackinaw for Rough and Tumble Service. . . . Not made for style, but strong, sturdy, and warm as a mackinaw coat.

c. A Mackinaw jacket or coat.

1902 WHITE *Blazed Trail* 375 A tall, slender, but well-knit individual dressed in a faded mackinaw and a limp slouch hat. **1949** *Boston Globe Mag.* 18 Sep. 10/5 The shoulder of his mackinaw was torn.

2. In combs.: (1) **Mackinaw blanket,** a thick blanket like those formerly distributed to Indians at Mackinac; (2) **boat,** a flat-bottomed boat, sometimes with oars and sails, formerly used esp. on the upper Great Lakes; (3) **coat,** (see quot. 1907); (4) **gun,** a type of gun distributed to the Indians at Mackinac, Michigan, *obs.;* (5) **hat,** a hat of a now unidentifiable type, *obs.;* (6) **jacket,** =**Mackinaw coat;** (7) **robe,** =**Mackinaw blanket;** (8) **shirt,** a plaid woolen shirt; (9) **skiff,** =**Mackinaw boat,** now *hist.*

(1) **1822** in *Wis. State H.S. Coll.* XX. 287 The heavy Mackinac blankets are almost impervious to the rain, and are universally worn by the Indians in this quarter (Mich.). They are large enough to cover an Indian completely. **1945** SERVICE *Ploughman* 157, I couched on the floor, lying on a buffalo-robe and wrapped in a mackinaw blanket. — (2) **1812** J. G. LUTTIG *Jrnl. of Exped.* (1920) 54 The Mackina Boat took 5 hunters to the Island. **1941** DORSEY *Master of Miss.* 47 He built a flatboat and bought a Mackinaw boat. — (3) **1902** WHITE *Blazed Trail* 16 They all wore heavy blanket mackinaw coats, rubber shoes, and thick German socks. **1907** *D.N.* III. 246 Mackinaw coat, a short, heavy, double-breasted plaid coat, the design of which is large and striking. Worn particularly by woodsmen, and, to a slight extent, by students of the University of Maine. **1944** NUTE *Lake Superior* 210 As for the lumberjack's dress—the most conspicuous item in it was the Mackinaw coat. It might be red, green, blue, or some other bright color, but it was always checkered in pattern. — (4) **1823** EDWIN JAMES *Expedition* I. 291 Mackinaw guns are greatly preferred to those which they [Indians] more commonly procure from our traders, being far more substantial and serviceable. **1824** KEATING *Narrative* (1825) I. 195 He was provided with a gun, of the kind distinguished by the name of Mackinaw gun.

(5) **1864** *Crisis* (Columbus, O.) 3 Feb. 15/5 Latest Styles. . . . Nutra Hats, Straw Hats, Mackinaw Hats. — (6) **1903** *Outlook* 7 Nov. 586 He caught up his Mackinaw jacket and his cap and mittens and hurried me out of the camp. — (7) **1909** LIPPS *Navajos* 88 The Mackinaw robes are worn by all 'blanket' Indians. — (8) **1917** KEPHART *Camping* I. 147, I usually discard the sweater in favor of a Mackinaw shirt, worn hunting fashion with tail outside. — (9) **1826** FLINT *Recoll.* 102, I have seen a Mackinaw skiff, carrying five tons, which came from the lakes into the Chicago of Michigan. **1941** BALDWIN *Keelboat Age* 50 The Mackinaw boat in use on the Missouri was an adaptation of the flatboat and of the Mackinaw skiff.

b. In the names of fishes: (1) **Mackinaw salmon,** (see quot.); (2) **shad,** any one of several small fish, esp. the *Decapterus macarellus;* (3) **trout,** a large lake trout, the namaycush.

(1) **1842** *Nat. Hist. N.Y., Zoology* IV. 240 The Mackinaw Salmon, *Salmo amethystus,* . . . [is] exceedingly voracious. — (2) **1838** *S. Lit. Messenger* IV. 28/1 Here I saw on the table d'hotel the Mackinaw shad, famous in those parts. — (3) **1840** *S. Lit. Messenger* VI. 604/1 The celebrated Mackinaw trout, so called after the town, near which they are found, is generally caught by the hook. **1940** *Places to See in Wyo.* xxix/1 Lake or Mackinaw trout in Jackson and Jenny Lakes are taken best by trolling.

* **McKinley,** *n.* [See **McKinleyism.**]

1. McKinley prosperity, the period of hard times following the passage of the McKinley tariff. *Obs.*

1897 *Boston Jrnl.* 11 Jan. 5/3 The urgent necessity for them will appeal to the people, groaning under the weight of 'McKinley prosperity.'

2. McKinley tariff, the tariff of 1890, during McKinley's administration, which raised duties to a high point.

1893 *Cyclo. Rev. Current Hist.* III. 265 The silver faction of the Democratic party favor making large modifications in the McKinley tariff. **1943** HICKS *Amer. Dem.* 528 Consumers found that the higher rates of the McKinley Tariff meant higher prices for what they had to buy.

McKinleyism məˈkɪnlɪˌɪzəm, *n.* [Wm. *McKinley* (1843–1901), representative from Ohio, later President of the U.S.] The policy of high protection, as exemplified by the McKinley Tariff Act of 1890. — **1892** *Peel City Guardian* 3 Dec. 8/6 One of the American papers . . . puts it second as a subject for congratulation on the defeat of McKinleyism. **1896** *Cong. Rec.* 19 March 2991/2 Before McKinleyism, we imported $54,772,000 more gold than we exported.

McKinleyite məˈkɪnlɪˌaɪt, *n.* One who supported McKinley's policy of protective tariffs. — **1891** *Ohio Falls Express* (Louisville) 11 July 2/4 It is therefore perfectly idle for the McKinleyites to pretend to be the foes of trusts and combinations to control prices. **1894** *Nation* 18 Jan. 39/3 Several of the McKinleyites were sent to grass in the course of the debate.

Maclura məˈklʊrə, *n.* [Wm. *Maclure,* Amer. geologist (1763–1840).] The genus of which the Osage orange, *M. pomifera,* is the single species; the Osage orange.

1818 NUTTALL *N. Amer. Plants* II. 233 *Maclura* (Bow-wood, Yellow-wood.) **1858** WARDER *Hedges & Evergreens* 32 For a fence of defence, the first in importance is the Maclura, Bodark (*Bois d'arc*) or Osage Orange; a native of Arkansas and Texas. **1929** BAILEY *Cyclo. Horticulture* 1961/2 [The osage orange] is sometimes described under Toxylon, but this name is replaced with Maclura under the 'nomina conservanda' of the international rules.

attrib. **1845** *Farmers' Cabinet* 15 June 338/2 The fields in future will be divided by hedges of *Maclura thorn.*

macock ˈmekak, *n.* Also †**macocqwer.** [Virginian *mawcawk, mahawk.*] A kind of melon.

1588 HARRIOT *Virginia* c b, Macócqwer, according to their seuerall formes called by vs, *Pompions, Mellions,* and *Gourdes,* because they are of the like formes as those kindes in England. **1612** SMITH *Virginia* 17 [The Indians plant] a fruit like vnto a muske millen, but lesse and worse; which they call *Macocks.* **1705** HARRIS *Navigantium atque itinerantium* I. 843 Macokes, which are like Musk-melons, but less, and not so well tasted, ripening in the beginning of *July* and continuing till *September.* **1902** *Amer. Folk-Lore* 247 The earlier writers cite the word in various forms, *macock, macokos, macocqwer,* etc., and it is doubtless derived from some dialect of the Maryland-Virginia region.

Macy wagon. (See quot.) *Obs.* — **1886** I. D. HARDY *Oranges & Alligators* 28 The buggy is the universal vehicle here [Florida] varied occasionally by the 'Macy waggon,' a light strong springless waggon with a movable spring seat.

* **mad,** *n.* In colloq. phrases with reference to becoming angry, as *to get one's mad up, to get over one's mad, to have a mad on.*

1867 GOSS *Soldier's Story* 258 The Colonel has got his mad up, and you'll be sent into the stockade. **1913** LONDON *Valley of Moon* 106 When he gets his mad up it's a case of get out from under or something will fall on you—hard. — **1941** *Sat. Ev. Post* 13 Sep. 54/3, I got to get over my mad. . . . I don't aim to get my mad up again. — **1943** *Ib.* 3 April 57/4 He ain't got a mad on anything in this world, except cats.

* **mad,** *a.* In combs.: (1) **mad-dog skullcap,** (see quot. 1843), cf. **hoodwort;** (2) **-dog stone,** a madstone *q.v.* as a main entry; (3) **-dog weed,** (*a*) the water plantain, (*b*) =**mad-dog skullcap;** (4) **-stone,** see as a main entry; (5) **tom,** any one of several species of fresh-water

catfish whose poisonous pectoral spines are capable of inflicting painful wounds, cf. **stone cat;** (6) **violet,** =**shooting star.**

(1) **1821** *Mass. H.S. Coll.* 2 Ser. ix. 156 *Scutellaria lateriflora*, Mad dog scull-cap. **1843** TORREY *Flora N.Y.* II. 72 *Scutellaria Lateriflora*. . . . Mad-dog Scull-cap. . . . Wet meadows and borders of small streams; common. About twenty years ago [believed an aid] in curing hydrophobia but is now quite neglected. **1894** *Outing* Nov. 180/1 A delicate little herb with dainty, blue flowers is called mad-dog skull-cap, from its imputed power of curing hydrophobia. — (2) **1822** in A. ROYALL *Lett. from Ala.* (1830) xlvii. 158 In this county [Madison] there is a stone called the mad-dog stone. **1824** SINGLETON *Letters* 70 Besides, near Loretto, they have a reputed remedy against canine rabiosity; two *mad-dog stones*, of long-extolled efficacy. . . . The stones are about an inch and a half cube; resembling a piece of bone, or hard soap; and are powerful astringents and absorbents. — (3) (*a*) **1821** *Mass. H.S. Coll.* 2 Ser. IX. 146 Plants, which are indigenous in the township of Middlebury, [Vt., include]. . . . Water plantain, mad-dog weed. **1833** EATON *Botany* 11 *Alisma . . . plantago* . . . water plantain, mad-dog weed. (*b*) **1818** *Amer. Jrnl. Science* I. 371, July 17. Mad dog weed (*Scutellaria lateriflora*) and purple vervain (*Verbena hastata*) in blossom.

(5) **1896** JORDAN & EVERMANN *Check-List Fishes* 234 *Schilbeodes insignis*. . . . Mad Tom. Pennsylvania to South Carolina. **1947** DALRYMPLE *Panfish* 290 In the Stonecat and Madtoms, this adipose fin is long and low, and usually connected in a continuous line with the tail, or caudal fin. — (6) **1931** CLUTE *Plants* 60 The name of mad violets given to the plants usually called shooting stars (*Dodecatheon meadia*), has all the ear-marks of being a made name.

b. In colloq. phrases (see quots.).

1823 DODDRIDGE *Dandy & Backwoodsman* 42 Every body that was not ax'd was mad as a wet hen, so that there was often a . . . great deal of mischief at a weddin. **1932** *K.C. Star* 26 March 14 'Did you think I was going to keep it?' snorted Old Bill, as mad as a wet hen. **1942** WARNICK *Dialect Garrett Co., Md.* 10 Mad enough to bite a tenpenny nail in two, adj. phr., very angry.

***madam,** *n.* Also ***madame.**

1. (See quot. 1809.) *Obs.*

1704 *Hist. Digest Press Mass.* (1911) 98 On Fryday died Madam Anne Paige. **1759** *Essex Inst. Coll.* XLIX. 4 Died at Danvers, Madam Hubard, mother to the Revd Mr Clarke's Lady. **1809** KENDALL *Travels* II. 44 Here [in Plymouth, Mass.], and in some of the neighboring places, it has been, and still is the practice, to prefix, to the name of a deceased female of some consideration, as the parson's, the deacon's or the doctor's wife, the title of *madam*.

2. A woman in charge of a house of prostitution.

1871 *N.Y. Herald* 29 July 6/2 The Madame . . . sent her to an infamous den in Forsyth street kept by a Mrs. Hines. **1933** ASBURY *Barbary Coast* 247 The mistress of such an establishment was always called Miss by the inmates, but the customers addressed her—and with considerable respect, too,—as Madame. **1949** *Newsweek* 18 July 19/3 She had committed perjury when she testified against the madame.

As the last term in **school madam.**

***made,** *a.* As the last term in **custom, home, Northern made.**

***Madeira,** *n.* **1. Madeira nut,** =**English walnut. 2. Madeira vine,** a vine with shiny leaves and white flowers *Boussingaultia basseloides.*

(1) **1817–8** EATON *Botany* (1822) 321 *Juglans regia*, madeira nut. . . . It is said that this variety is indigenous to North America. **1892** APGAR *Trees Northern U.S.* 141 *Juglans regia*. (Madeira Nut. English Walnut.) . . . Hardy as far north as Boston in the East, but needs protection at St. Louis. — (2) **1854** *S. Lit. Messenger* XX. 622/1 Behind so impervious a screen as honeysuckle and Madeira vine, . . . I can discern you. **1892** HARRIS *U. Remus & Friends* 255 Then she turned and began to pull down the dead Madeira vines that were still clinging to the strings on which they had run so bravely in the summer. **1928** BAILEY *Cyclo. Horticulture* 535/2 Boussingaultia . . . baselloides, HBK. Madeira Vine. Mignonette Vine.

***Madeleine,** *n.* A variety of summer pear. *Obs.*

1847 IVES *N. Eng. Fruit* 56 *Madaleine*.—This is the first good pear which ripens. **1858** *Ill. Agric. Soc. Trans.* III. 337, I once had a tree of the Madeline attacked [by blight] eight feet from the ground. **1928** BAILEY *Cyclo. Horticulture* 2514/1 The following is a list of a few of the most popular of these, arranged approximately in the order of maturity: Madeleine m[iddle] e[arly] July. Earliest good pear.

***mademoiselle,** *n.* (See quot. 1909.) — **1882** *Nat. Museum Bul.* No. 16, 570 *Sciæna punctata*. . . . Silver Perch; Yellow-tail; Mademoiselle. **1909** WEBSTER 1294/1 *Mademoiselle* . . . any of several sciænoid fishes which compose the genus *Bairdiella;* esp., *B. chrysura*, of the southern United States.

Madisonian ˌmædəˈsonɪən, *n.* [f. James *Madison* (1751–1836), fourth President of the U.S.] A supporter of the political policies or principles of James Madison. Also transf. *Obs.*

1809 *Ann. 10th Congress* 2 Sess. 1065 No Administration, even if composed of Adamites, Pickeronians, Jeffersonians, and Madisonians, . . . could uphold this navy system in time of peace. **1817** *N.Y. Herald* 22 March 1/4 It endeavors to stimulate the Madisonians by trying to recollect the conduct of Clinton in *times that tried men's souls*. **1866** *Dly. Richmond Enquirer* 16 Feb. 1/7 He was sole editor and proprietor of the *Madisonian*.

Madisonism ˈmædəsn̩ˌɪzəm, *n.* [See prec.] The political principles of James Madison. *Rare.* — **1812** *Salem Gaz.* 31 March 3/2 Madisonism . . . flat and daily declining.

Madison's war. The War of 1812. Now *hist.* — **1813** *Salem Gaz.* 1 Oct. 3/3 The farms of Nantucket men were formerly upon the ocean, but Madison's war has obliged them to take land tacks on board, and pass the mountains. **1941** BRANT *James Madison* 309 The war therefore became 'Madison's War' and a large section of the populace had their sympathies more with England than with the United States.

madrona məˈdronə, *n.* Also **madroño, madrone.** [Sp. *madroño*, in same sense.] Any one of various evergreen shrubs or trees of the genus *Arbutus*, as the *A. menziesi* of the West Coast and *A. xalapensis* found on the Mexican border. **Cf. Mexican madrona, mountain mahogany 2. b.**

[**1769** CRESPI *Diary* 5 Nov., En estas dos jornados ultimas, se han encontrado muchos madroños, aunque la fruta es mas chica que la de España pero si de la misme especie.] **1841** BIDWELL *Trip to Calif.* 2 Every kind of timber which I have seen, you will see in the following list. Oak, Cotton-wood, . . . Fir, Sicamore, Madrone, Laurel. **1892** COULTER *Bot. West. Texas* 253 A. Xalapensis HBK., var. Texana Gray. . . . Foothills of the mountains west of the Pecos, and known as 'madrona.' **1948** *Pacific Discovery* March–April 26/2 Our trail took off into the Sierra . . . through rough but highly interesting country to La Laguna, a pine forest with an association of oaks, madroños and other flora.

attrib. **1948** *Sierra Club* (So. Calif. Chap.) *Sched.* 127, 69 Noteworthy among the natural features are . . . the stands of Madrone trees.

madstone ˈmædˌston, *n.* A stonelike object obtained from the stomach of a deer (see quot. 1947), popularly believed to be efficacious if placed on the wound caused by the bite of an animal that has hydrophobia. Cf. ***lodestone, mad-dog stone.**

1834 *S. Lit. Messenger* I. 182 He should be able to form a concrete mass by means of beef gall and alkali, which would resemble and equal in virtue the madstone. **1883** ZEIGLER & GROSSCUP *Alleghanies* 158 The deer with a mad-stone in him is twice as hard to kill as one of the ordinary kind. **1947** CAHALANE *Mammals* 39 When a small hard object lodges in the stomach of any of the deer, calcium and other salts may be deposited around it, resulting in the formation of a hard, smooth, round 'stone' called a calculus or 'madstone.' **1949** *N.O. Times-Picayune Mag.* 19 June 5/2 Ernest Gravois . . . estimates over 4000 actual cases in which the application of the Mad Stone brought about instant relief and final cure of snake bites, black widow spider stings, bee stings, and mad dog bites, . . . and ailments resulting from poison infections in the blood stream.

magazinable ˌmægəˈzinəbl̩, *a.* [f. **magazine*.] Suitable for printing in a magazine; capable of writing material desired by magazine editors. *Colloq.* — **1906** *Nation* 11 Oct. 308/3 Since then, we may suppose, he [C. G. D. Roberts] has proved too 'magazinable' for his good. *Ib.* 22 Nov. 441 These tales have proved 'magazinable' for sufficiently obvious reasons.

***Magician,** *n.* A nickname for Martin Van Buren (1782–1862). Cf. **Great Magician, Little Magician.**

1832 *Boston Transcript* 1 Feb. 2/1 The nomination of Mr. Van Buren had been rejected. . . . The Vice President has 'broken the magician's wand over his own head.' **1844** *Republican Sentinel* (Richmond, Va.) 16 March 1/3 There is a power around the Magician—a power of thought, and a power of language, an extent of experience, and a brilliancy of reputation. **1941** *Sat. Review* 19 July 3/2 In papers of the time Van Buren was referred to in such terms as 'the magician of Kinderhook,' 'Your cunning Kinderhook Fox,' and 'the Kinderhook pony.'

magisterial district, see **district.**

***magistrate,** *n.* As the last term in **chief, first, gospel magistrate.**

***magnetic,** *a.*

1. Of a person: Possessing power to attract people.

This use may have originated in the U.S., but cf. Ben Jonson's *The Magnetick Lady* (1632), in which Lady Loadstone "draws unto her guests of all sorts."

1880 *Spectator* 3 Nov. 1437 The Americans have invented, and Englishmen are slowly adopting into their political vocabulary, a new word, intended to account for the otherwise unaccountable popularity of some politicians. They say they are 'magnetic.' **1899** BREEN *Thirty Years* 183 To carry out his plans, he secured the services of three men: a magnetic orator, a first-class talker from Brooklyn [etc.].

2. Designating a practitioner who employs electrical or electrical chiropractic treatment.

1881 RITTENHOUSE *Maud* 18 The Abbots came down yesterday for Agnes to be treated by the magnetic physician. **1894** *Stone's Davenport* (Iowa) *City Directory* 345 Daniel D. Palmer, magnetic healer, room 42 Ryan blk. **1905** WIGGIN *Rose* 127 She heard of a 'magnetic' physician in Boston.

3. magnetic telegraph, a type of telegraph invented by S. F. B. Morse (1791–1852). Also attrib.

1842 *Niles' Reg.* 25 Oct. 415/3 (*heading*), Magnetic telegraphs. **1844** *Lexington Observer* 1 June 3/2 The Baltimore papers of Saturday announce the connection of Morse's Magnetic Telegraph between Washington and Baltimore. **1848** *Whig Almanac 1849* 46/2 The trustees of the magnetic telegraph patents agreed with O'Rielly in 1845 that he should build certain lines. **1886** POORE *Reminisc.* I. 309 Another novel invention was the electric, or, as it was then called, the magnetic, telegraph.

***magnolia,** *n.*

1. A genus of large shrubs or trees of the family Magnoliaceae, noted for the beauty of their flowers and foliage; a tree of this genus.

Of the 35 or so species, about half are American, the other half Asiatic in origin. The chief American species are the evergreen magnolia, the sweet bay tree, the umbrella tree, the large-leaved magnolia, and the cucumber tree.

1748 *Phil. Trans.* XLV. 166 The Magnolia . . . tho' scarce in Virginia, has been since found to grow in great plenty in the North-West Parts of Penysylvania. **1784** FILSON *Kentucke* 24 Here is also found the tulip-bearing laurel-tree, or magnolia, which has an exquisite smell. **1860** HOLMES *Professor* x. 307 The magnolia grows and comes to full flower on Cape Ann. **1949** COLLINGWOOD & BRUSH *Knowing Your Trees* 236/1 The size and simple construction of the flower indicate that the magnolias are among the oldest of our broad-leafed trees.

attrib. and *transf.* **1948** *Pacific Discovery* March–April 15/2 The magnolia tree near the library window was the robins' choice for their nesting. **1949** *N.O. Times-Picayune Mag.* 13 Feb. 11/1 Over this, the inner walls, which are to be made of cherry, walnut or black magnolia paneling, will be placed.

b. With specifying adjectives.

1785 MARSHALL *Amer. Grove* 83 *Magnolia acuminata.* Long leaved Mountain Magnolia or Cucumber Tree. *Ib., Magnolia glauca.* Small Magnolia, or Swamp Sassafras. This grows naturally in low, moist, or swampy ground. **1850** S. F. COOPER *Rural Hours* 476 The small Laurel Magnolia, or Sweet Bay, is found as far north as New York, in swampy grounds. **1857** GRAY *Botany* 16 *M[agnolia] grandiflora*, the Great Laurel Magnolia, of the Southern States (a noble tree, remarkable for its deliciously fragrant flowers, and thick evergreen leaves, which are shining and deep green above and rusty-colored beneath). **1884** SARGENT *Rep. Forests* 534 This region differs . . . by the absence of the great magnolia (*M. grandiflora*). **1892** APGAR *Trees Northern U.S.* 63 *Magnolia grandiflora*. . . . Southern Evergreen Magnolia. . . . Splendid evergreen tree (50 to 80 ft.) in the Southern States.

2. A flower of the magnolia tree.

1822 *Holyoke Diaries* 177 We all went to Manchester to get Magnolias. **1900** *Louisiana Laws* 239 The Magnolia . . . is hereby selected and adopted as the State Flower. **1949** *Parade* 18 Sep. 14/3 Framed by magnolia, any little girl is lovely.

3. In special combs.: (1) **Magnolia City, State,** (see quots.); (2) **warbler,** the black-and-yellow warbler, *Dendroica magnolia.*

(1) **1899** *Sunset* Dec. 59/2 Ten years ago, the 'Magnolia City,' as Houston [Texas] is called by those who feel impelled to apply an endearing term, was a thriving village of 20,000 souls. **1934** SHANKLE *State Names* 127 The *Magnolia State* is given as a nickname to Mississippi because of the great number of magnolia trees growing within the State. — (2) **1887** RIDGWAY *Man. N. Amer. Birds* 498 Magnolia Warbler. . . . Eastern United States (west of Alleghanies). **1948** *Audubon Mag.* July–Aug. 235/1 Brilliantly hued magnolia, myrtle and Nashville warblers flitted from tree to tree.

As the last term in **cucumber, large-flowered, large-leaved, laurel, small, swamp, sweet, umbrella magnolia.**

magofer mə'gofɚ, *n.* [Poss. of Indian origin.] =**gopher 1.** *Obs.* Cf. **mungofa.**

1789 *Augusta* (Ga.) *Chron.* 11 July 4/2 (Th. Supp.), [The dog] expired by the mouth of a megopher's hole. **1795** *Gaz. U.S.* (Phila.) 16 March (Th.), He must be used like a magooffer, by putting fire on his back. **1840** *S. Lit. Messenger* VI. 509/1 I'd have taken a magofer's grip upon him, and not let go.

magotty bay bean. Also **magotty bay pea.** [Poss. f. *Magothy* River, Md., or *Magotha,* Va.] A fabaceous vine that grows along the seashore (see quot. 1829).

1786 WASHINGTON *Diaries* III. 127 The Overseer and two or three of the Weak hands . . . were gathering the Wild (or Mighty bay) Pea —a tedious operatn. **1788** *Phil. Soc. Trans.* III. 228 The Eastern-Shore-bean . . . is found in all parts of Virginia and Carolina. *Ib.* (*footnote*), Called also the Magotty-Bay-bean. **1829** *Va. Lit. Museum* 221 Whenever a field is not in cultivation, it puts up every where a rich luxuriant crop of a sort of wild vetch, called the magotty-bay bean, which shades the land while it is growing, and returns to it a rich coat of vegetable manure. **1893** *Amer. Folk-Lore* VI. 140 *Cassia Chamoecrista*, magotty boy [*sic*] bean, N.Y.

***magpie,** *n.* A kind of fly used in angling. Cf. **black-billed, yellow-billed magpie.** — **1897** *Outing* XXX. 223/1 Useful flies: silver doctor, magpie, Cheney, Chubb, oriole, . . . and some few others.

Maha 'mɑhɑ, *n.* [Var. of **Omaha.**] *collect.* or *pl.* The Omaha Indians.

1778 CARVER *Travels N.-Amer.* 109 Fort La Reine. . . . To this place the Mahahs, who inhabit a country two hundred and fifty miles south-west, come also to trade. **1804** CLARK in *Lewis & C. Exped.* I. (1904) 103 From this Lake to the Maha 4 days march. **1814** BRACKENRIDGE *Views La.* 76 Mahas, (or *Oo-ma-ha*) Reside on the Maha creek, about eighty leagues above the Platte, in their village, and raise corn. **1949** *Exciting Western* May 55/2 The Maha, or 'upstream people' as the name was translated, were responsible for the naming of Omaha, Nebraska.

attrib. **1804** CLARK in *Lewis & C. Exped.* I. (1904) 34 As we were pushing off this morning two Canoes Loaded with fur &c came to from the Mahas nation. **1811** BRACKENRIDGE in *Views La.* (1814) 230 Arrived . . . at some trading houses, near which, the Maha village is situated, about two miles from the river [Missouri]. **1825** in *N. Dak. Hist. Quart.* IV. (1929) 14 We are about opposite the Maha village.

mahala mə'hælə, *n. W.* [Yokuts (Indians of the Mariposan family in California) *muk'ela*, woman.] A squaw.

1850 *Calif. Courier* (S.F.) 31 Aug. 2/1 All this is the work of the squaws—or, as they call them—'Mo-hales.' **1903** JAMES *Indian Basketry* 227 Do not believe for a moment that a majella will furnish you goods of as fine a class as she makes for herself. **1916** WILSON *Somewhere* 338 That old mahala of mine, she not able to chew much now.

b. mahala mat, (see quots.). Cf. **squaw carpet.**

1907 HODGE *Amer. Indians* I. 786 Mahala mats. A California name of *Ceanothus prostratus*, also known as squaw's carpet. **1940** *Mt. Hood Guide* 17 Mahala mat, or squaw mat, is a dwarf creeper bearing dainty bells of lavender that blooms in May and June.

Maherin Indians. An "Iroquoian tribe formerly residing on the river of the same name on the Virginia–North Carolina border" (Hodge, I. 839). — **1703** *N.C. Col. Rec.* I. 570 It is the opinion of the Honble Council that it doth not appear that the Maherine Indians live within the bounds of the Province of Carolina. **1705** *Ib.* 615 It is Ordered that the clerk of the Council do not issue the Order of Council of 31st May to the Surveyor of Nansemond for laying out the Maherin Indians land.

Mahican. See **Mohegan.**

mahoganize mə'hagən,aɪz, *v.* Also **mahoganyize.** *tr.* (See quots.) — **1848** BARTLETT 219 *To Mahoganyize*, . . . to cause to resemble mahogany, as by staining. **1890** *Cent.* 3579/1 *Mahoganize*, . . . to cause to resemble mahogany, as by staining.

***mahogany,** *n.*

1. The Kentucky coffee tree. In full **mahogany tree.**

1780 in *Travels Amer. Col.* 633, I met with [the coffee tree] . . . , the bark something like a Cheery tree the wood when cut a crimson red and cald by some Mahogany. **1785** MARSHALL *Amer. Grove* 56 [In] Kentucky . . . this tree . . . is said to grow plenty, and is called the Coffee or Mahogany tree. **1825** *Catawba Jrnl.* 17 May, *American Mahogany.*—A tree, the growth of which is spontaneous in Florida, is said to answer all the purposes of mahogany for cabinet work.

2. A mountain mahogany of the West of the genus *Cercocarpus.*

1889 Union Pac. R.R. *Ore. & Wash.* 21 There are plenty of good timber lands, on which abound pine, fir, cedar, juniper and mahogany, in the mountains. **1949** *Pacific Discovery* Jan.–Feb. 7/2 Under present conditions it would be virtually impossible for the mahogany to reproduce, since seedlings would be eaten as fast as they appeared.

3. mahogany yard, a lumber yard where mahogany is the chief wood sold. *Rare.*

1818 FEARON *Sketches* 23 Mahogany yards are generally separate concerns.

As the last term in **curl-leaf, mountain, valley mahogany.**

Mahoneism məˈhonɪzəm, *n.* The principles of Gen. William Mahone (1826–95) (see quot. 1885). Also **Mahoneite, Mahonist.** *Obs.*

1880 *Dly. Dispatch* (Richmond, Va.) 3 Nov. 2/1 The Mahoneites owed their success to negro votes. **1885** *Mag. Amer. Hist.* March 295/2 *Mahonist.*—A follower of Gen. Mahone, late of the Confederate service, who organized a revolt against the 'Bourbon Democracy' in West Virginia in 1878. **1887** *Nation* 16 June 499/3 The Democratic party . . . fought a good fight against Mohoneism.

mahonia məˈhonɪə, *n.* [f. the genus name *Mahonia*, after Bertrand McMahon (*c*1775–1816), Amer. botanist.] Any one of various shrubs of the genus *Mahonia.* Cf. **algerita, Oregon grape.**

1846 ABERT *Exam. N. Mex.* 77 We saw a plant . . . called 'palmello angosta'; also a 'mahonia.' **1934** *N. Mex. Agric. Exper. Sta. Press Bul.* 713, 2 The Oregon grape, or to give it its common Spanish name—the Mohonia—is found in the high mountain sections. **1948** *Holland's Mag.* March 46/3 The brilliantly colored fruits of the nandinas, pyracanthas, mahonias, cotoneasters, and hollies reward the efforts of the considerate gardener.

* **maid,** *n.*

1. In the names of certain academic degrees conferred upon women. Usu. *cap. Obs.*

1882 in *Rep. Comm. Educ. 1882–3* 691 [Degrees conferred in 1882 on women] Maid of philosophy . . . [and] maid of science. **1885** D. C. GILMAN *N. Amer. Rev.* March 263 There are degrees devised by those who seem to think there is some incongruity in giving young ladies the title of Bachelor, viz.: . . . Maid of Philosophy, Maid of Science, Maid of Arts.

2. * **maid of honor,** in a wedding ceremony, an unmarried girl or woman who is the bride's principal attendant. Also transf. Cf. **matron of honor.**

1906 M. W. FREEMAN *Light of Soul* 348 Lily asked Maria to be her maid of honor. **1947** *Greek Star* (Chi.) 13 June 2/3 The Queen was Maid of Honor to the Ahepa Queen in 1945 and has attended Washington University where she majored in Psychology.

As the last term in **fair, old, second maid.**

* **maiden,** *n.* In combs.: (1) **maiden cane,** a creeping grass, *Panicum hemitomon,* of the southern coastal regions; (2) **land,** (see quot.), *obs.;* (3) * **-'s blush,** a variety of apple.

(1) **1806** LEWIS in *L. & Clark Exped.* V. (1905) 107 Among the grasses of this country I observe a large species . . . [which] has much the same appearance of the maden cain as it is called in . . . Ge[o]rgia. **1947** *Jrnl. Wildlife Management* Jan. 55/2 Maidencane (*Paricum hemitomon* . . .) eventually is the dominant plant. — (2) **1859** BARTLETT, Maidenland. Land that a man gets with his wife, and which he loses at her death. Virginia. — (3) **1817** W. COXE *Fruit Trees* 106 Maidens Blush. This is an apple of large size, and great beauty. **1944** *Chi. D. News* 25 Sep. 13/3 Right now Wealthies or Maiden's Blush are the choice varieties for cooking or pie.

As the last term in **paleface maiden.**

Maidu ˈmaɪdu, *n. pl.* [See quot. 1874.] "A tribe formerly dwelling in Sacramento valley and the adjacent Sierra Nevada in California" (Hodge).

1874 *Overland Mo.* Jan. 21/1 As you travel south from Chico, the Indians call themselves *meidoo* until you reach Bear River, but below that it is *neeshenam,* or sometimes *mana,* or *maidec,* all of which denote 'men' or 'Indians.' **1903** JAMES *Indian Basketry* 57 The proper names of these people are the Maidu . . . [and] the Nishinam. **1921** HALL *Yosemite Nat. Park* 51 Of such groups, there may be mentioned as neighbors: the Maidu to the north in the Sierra; the Yokuts to the south in the foothills.

attrib. **1880** DRAKE *Aboriginal Races N. Amer.* 756 The Meidoo nation formerly extended from Sacramento river to the snow-line, and from Big Chico creek to Bear river. **1948** JOHNSTON *Gold Rush* v/2 In the Maidu Indian language and in the southern Wintun Indian dialect *ono* means 'head.'

* **mail,** *n.*

1. A batch of letters, circulars, etc., already delivered to, or set aside for, a private family or a firm; a batch of private letters, etc., to be put into the mails.

*a***1844** M. C. FIELDS in Sol. Smith *Theatr. Apprent.* 204 He walks as if he had the missing mail in his pocket and an extra to issue immediately. **1906** *Harper's Mag.* March 577 Theodora took her mail and went on the back porch to read it. **1932** TARBELL *O. D. Young* 250 He must have an experienced secretary in the office handling his mail, organizing his day's engagements. **1949** *Sat. Ev. Post* 1 Jan. 47/1, I took a good look at the handwriting and said I would watch for any future letters and hold them out of the family's personal mail.

2. In combs.: (1) **mail-bag catcher,** = **mail catcher;** (2) * **box,** a box in which mail is deposited to be collected by the postal service, or in which private mail is left by a carrier; (3) **boy,** (*a*) a man who collects and distributes mail, (*b*) a clerk who sorts mail, *obs.;* (4) **carrier,** one who carries mail, as from one post office to another, or to families on a mail route; (5) **catcher,** in a mail car, a device used for catching bags of mail suspended from posts at way stations, cf. * **catcher 2;** (6) **day,** in remote or not readily accessible places, a day on which mail is distributed, chiefly in pioneer times; (7) **key,** a key that will open the lock of a mail pouch; (8) **matter,** letters, newspapers, etc., sent by mail; (9) **order,** see as a main entry; (10) **party,** *W.* a party of people traveling in a mail coach, *obs.;* (11) **pouch,** a mail bag, usu. of leather and provided with a key; (12) **rider,** a horseman charged with carrying mail, a mail carrier; (13) **robber,** one who robs the mails; (14) **robbery,** robbery of the mails; (15) **station,** *W.* a place along a mail route providing food and shelter for the drivers, passengers, and teams of a mail coach, *obs.*

(1) **1867** *Statutes at Large* XIV. 303 For mail bags and mail-bag catchers, one hundred thousand dollars. **1887** *Postal Laws* 21 The Mail-Bag Equipment Division . . . is charged with . . . the furnishing of . . . mail-bag cord-fasteners, and mail-bag catchers. — (2) **1872** *Rep. Comm. Patents 1870* II. 751/1 In a mail-box, the arrangement herein shown and described . . . for the purpose of guiding and holding the mail matter. **1923** DUTTON *Shadow on Glass* 170 There were but three mail boxes on the carrier's route. **1949** *Chi. D. News* 14 Feb. 1/3 The maid said she looked for Mrs. Kaplan at the mail-box. — (3) (*a*) **1842** in BUCKINGHAM *E. & W. States* II. 118, [I] saw descending the hill . . . the mail-boy on his horse at full speed. **1862** in HIGGINSON *Harvard Mem. Biog.* (1866) I. 112 The horrors of the battle-field I must describe to you in another letter, as the mail-boy calls for this. (*b*) **1874** *Cong. Rec.* 15 April 3099/1 Hitherto seven were known as mail-boys, and the others as mail-messengers. — (4) **1790** *Ann. 1st Congress* II. 1821 Mail-carriers should be . . . exempted [from serving in the militias of the several states]. **1855** HOLBROOK *Among Mail Bags* 195 The mail carriers . . . charged directly at the whole array of Indians. **1949** *Lubbock* (Tex.) *Morn. Avalanche* 23 Feb. 1. 11/5 Police designated a dog-bites-mail-carrier incident as, 'dog bite—occupational.'

(5) **1875** *Chi. Tribune* 18 Sep. 5/3 The Post-Office Department has introduced the use of a 'mail-catcher.' **1947** *Sat. Ev. Post* 1 Feb. 54/3 At one point on the northbound run—Bristol, Pennsylvania—Nemeth operates the mail catcher to pick up a pouch on the run. — (6) **1855** *Fla. Plant. Rec.* 131 People will be there [at the post office] every mail day. **1929** F. E. MCCLINCHEY *Joe Pete* 227 For the next three weeks she went to the store three times each week on the mail days, but there was no check from Simpson. — (7) **1839** *Diplom. Corr. Texas* 1. (1908) 392 The Texian Post Master . . . will furnish the United States post masters . . . with a Texian Mail key, and will be furnished with a United States mail key in return. **1887** *Postal Laws* 21 The Mail Equipment Division . . . is charged with the preparation of advertisements inviting proposals for the furnishing of . . . mail locks and keys, label cases [etc.]. — (8) **1839** *Diplom. Corr. Texas* 1. (1908) 392 He will charge himself with all unpaid U.S. postage on mail matter on hand in the Post offices of Texas. **1906** *Churchman* 10 Nov. 724 All mail matter for the secretary of the convention should be addressed [etc.].

(10) **1858** PETERS *Kit Carson* 517 A fatal adventure . . . once happened to a mail party while traveling this route. **1868** CUSTER *Following Guidon* 16, I send her to-night, by the mail party, to Fort Dodge. — (11) **1843** *P.O. Laws* 11. 57 All communications relating to portmanteaus, mail pouches and mail bags to be addressed . . . to the Inspection Office. **1903** E. JOHNSON *Railway Transportation* 173 The mileage traveled by the cars containing the mail-pouches . . . [was] 24,072,558. — (12) **1835** HOFFMAN *Winter in West* I. 121, [I] was glad . . . to be overtaken by a mail-rider, with his leathern charge, on horseback. **1893** *Harper's Mag.* Dec. 86/2 The mail-rider hev quit, 'count o' the rise in the ruver, an' thar's no way ter git word ter him. **1947** *Democrat* 18 Dec. 1/6 Mail Rider Finds Dead Negro Tuesday. — (13) **1855** HOLBROOK *Among Mail Bags* 375 The mail robber was committing depredations from day to day. **1931** KELLY *U.S. Postal Policy* 147 Postal inspectors went to Canada, Mexico, South America and Europe seeking the mail robbers. — (14) **1820** *Niles' Reg.* XVIII. 1/1 (*caption*), Mail Robberies. **1949** *Chi. Tribune* 4 Sep. 11. 8/8 (*heading*), 3 of 4 Held for Mail Robbery in Fox Lake Enter Guilty Pleas.

(15) **1867** in *S. Dak. Hist. Coll.* I. 451 The said bands do hereby cede to the United States the right to construct wagon roads, railroads, mail stations [etc.]. **1891** RYAN *Told in Hills* 130 The nearest mail station was twenty miles south.

b. Designating vehicles, boats, etc., used in transporting mail, as (1) **mail boat,** (2) **buckboard,** (3) ***car,** (4) **coach,** (5) **plane,** (6) **sledge,** (7) **sleigh,** (8) **stage,** (9) **steamer,** (10) **train,** (11) **truck,** (12) **wagon.**

(1) **1795** *Pittsburgh Gaz.* 8 Aug. 3/2 The Gazette is circulated . . . from Whelen by the Mail Boats to the settlements on the Ohio. **1946** STANWELL-FLETCHER *Driftwood Valley* 207 At the Landing J. waited a week for the mail boat. — (2) **1903** A. ADAMS *Log Cowboy* 130 The mail buckboard had reported us to the sutler as camped out back on a little creek. — (3) **1855** HOLBROOK *Among Mail Bags* 124 The man who couldn't ride in the mail car, [was] rather 'chop-fallen.' **1946** *Colo. School Jrnl.* Dec. 2/2 Once inside the mail car the letters are swiftly sorted for quick delivery. — (4) **1889** *Scribner's Mag.* March 271/1 The fifth . . . car, is the last mail coach on the train.

(5) **1931** KELLY *U.S. Postal Policy* 137 At the great airports may be seen the alert, efficient, young eagles who pilot the mail planes. **1947** *Sat. Ev. Post* 8 Feb. 37 The monthly arrival of the mail plane brings native Indians down to the beach at Tyonek to help unload. — (6) **1922** CURWOOD *Country Beyond* 147 He was usually reading the

Mail truck

wonderful little red volumes of history which he had purloined from the mail sledge up near the Barren Lands. — (7) **1799** BENTLEY *Diary* II. 300, 18 weeks the Mail sleigh successively passed through Keene, N.H. **1885** E. B. CUSTER *Boots & Saddles* xi. 122 It did not take long for the garrison to discover the poor mules . . . dragging the mail-sleigh into the post. — (8) **1792** *Ann. 2nd Congress* 361 The mail stage passes Merrimack river, about four miles above the old ferry. **1830** *Williams's N.Y. Ann. Reg.* 115 From Messrs. Thorps and Sprague's Western and New-York Mail Stage Office, corner of State and North Market-streets, Albany, three lines of post-coaches . . . depart every day for the West. **1949** *News-Rep.* (McMinnville, Ore.) 4 Aug. 1/5 When the horse-drawn mail stage came along it found him glumly standing by his defunct horseless carriage. — (9) **1845** POLK in *Pres. Mess. & P.* IV. 414 Proper measures have been taken in pursuance of the act of the 3d of March last for the establishment of lines of mail steamers between this and foreign countries. **1943** KEMBLE *Panama Route, 1848–1869* 86 Thus the Vanderbilt steamers became the 'mail steamers,' and the ships which had carried the mail for more than a decade passed into the position of 'opposition.'

(10) **1855** HOLBROOK *Among Mail Bags* 194 A usual 'mail train' consisted of three covered wagons, . . . each drawn by six mules, guarded by eight or ten men, and carrying perhaps as many passengers. **1931** KELLY *U.S. Postal Policy* 146 These men held up a mail train in Oregon on October 11th, 1923. — (11) **1924** *N.Y. Times* 25 Oct. 1/3 The chauffeur of the mail truck drove to the Beach Street Station, where he told detectives of the robbery. **1949** *Chi. Tribune* 17 Sep. 1/2 Pickets have been interfering with government mail trucks approaching or leaving the station. — (12) **1831** *Boston Transcript* 23 June 2/1 We were lost in the woods whilst crossing from Oysterville to Barnstable and Yarmouth and were carted thence in the mail waggon to Sandwich. **1910** J. HART *Vigilante Girl* 16 The mail-wagons passed.

As the last term in **air, canvas, express, fan, first-class, horse, horseback, land, letter, lock, overland, Pacific, through, way mail.**

mail mel, *v.* [f. the noun] *tr.* To post or send by mail. — **1827** *P.O. Laws* (1843) 1. 25 And be it further enacted, That one or more pieces of paper, mailed as a letter, and weighing one ounce, shall be charged with quadruple postage. **1944** *Sears Cat.* (ed. 189) 894 Simply write your order on a Sears Order Blank or plain paper and mail it to us.

mailability ˌmelǝˈbɪlɪtɪ, *n.* The quality or condition of being mailable. — **1883** *Official Postal Guide* Jan. 664 Mailability of Doubtful Matter. **1903** in *Publishers' Circular* (London) 3 March 275/3 As the card does not bear on the address side the words 'United States of America,' its mailability is not affected by my circular of the 16th ult.

mailable ˈmelǝbḷ, *a.* Acceptable for mailing.

1845 *Statutes at Large* V. 736 [No one shall] transport or convey, otherwise than in the mail, any letter or letters, packet or packages of letters, or other mailable matter [etc.]. **1896** *Harper's Wkly.* 8 Aug. 782 As to the cost of the initial movement of the mailable matter, that varies. **1944** *Sears Cat.* (ed. 189) 596 Dressing table mirror. . . . Plate glass. . . . Shipping weight, 17 pounds. Mailable.

mailer ˈmelɚ, *n.*

1. A mail boat.

1857 *Knickerb.* XLIX. 58 It is but a day-and-a-half to Halifax; thence by a British mailer across to those neighboring isles. **1883** *Cent. Mag.* Nov. 160/1 Showing the skill and good control on Transatlantic Mailers.

2. One who mails, esp. one who attends to the wrapping, addressing, etc., of periodicals for the mails.

1884 W. F. CRAFTS *Sabbath for Man* 328 Editors and compositors are kept up until the small hours on Sunday morning; pressmen and mailers for an hour or two later. **1917** D. C. ROPER *U.S. Post Office* 196 The responsibility for this delay [at Christmas time], however, is almost invariably with the mailer who has waited till the eleventh hour. **1947** *Chi. Sun* 25 Nov. 3/5 The ITU representatives informed us that any arrangement we might enter into with the typographers would be extended to the ITU's subordinate union of mailers.

3. A machine used for addressing mail.

1890 *Cent.* 3582/1 *Mailer*, . . . same as addressing-machine. **1931** *K. C. Times* 3 Nov., We must look over the mailer and see. Maybe we've lost 'em off our exchange list.

mailing ˈmelɪŋ, *n. attrib.*

1. Designating objects and places connected with, or involved in, the action of sending by mail.

1871 RINGWALT *Amer. Encycl. Printing* 292/2 Mailing Machines.—Contrivances of various descriptions to facilitate the operation of directing newspapers to subscribers. **1883** KNIGHT *Supp.* 575/2 *Mailing Table*, a table at which mail matter is distributed to the mail bags for the various routes of stations. **1887** *Postal Laws* 222 The cancellation of stamps at the delivery office which were not stamped at the mailing office. **1893** PHILIPS *Making of a Newspaper* 18 In this partial survey of the process and cost of making a 'mammoth newspaper,' no account has been taken of . . . the mailing room. **1902** LORIMER *Lett. Merchant* 16 The bottom in the office end of this business is a seat at the mailing-desk, with eight dollars [a week]. **1903** E. JOHNSON *Railway Transportation* 176 Mr. William A. Davis . . . was then chief clerk in the mailing department of the post-office.

2. mailing clerk, a clerk who addresses newspapers, letters, etc., for the mail.

1858 *So. Cultivator* XVI. 280/1 Our mailing clerk has attended to your request. **1902** LORIMER *Lett. Merchant* 69, [I] went for him pretty rough for having a mailing clerk so no-account as to be writing personal letters in office hours.

3. mailing list, a register of addresses to which goods and postal matter are sent.

1909 *Dly. Chron.* 12 Oct. 4/5 In the States there are 600,000 farmers on the mailing list. **1949** *L.A. Times* 15 May (Home Mag.) 34/4 Many enterprising growers let people come to their farms to pick fruit or berries and have mailing lists, informing their customers as to maturity dates.

mail order.

1. An order for merchandise, sent to a business house by mail. Also attrib.

1867 *Comm. & Fin. Chron.* V. 26/2 Mail and telegraph orders will receive our personal attention. **1898** *K.C. Star* 18 Dec. 5/2 The mail orders are quite heavy for holiday stock. **1915** *Printers' Ink* 23 Sep. 46/1 The mail-order firm urged that the mere use of such phrases in advertisements was not sufficient ground for claiming the measure of protection sought. **1948** *Carthaginian* (Carthage, Miss.) 19 Aug. 1/3 Look! I just got my new mail-order shoes, but all they had left in this style was size 12.

2. In special combs.: (1) **mail-order business,** business conducted by a mail-order house; (2) **catalogue,** a catalogue issued by a house which fills mail orders; (3) **cowboy,** (see quots.); (4) **house,** a business house whose customers order goods by mail; (5) **paper,** (see quot.).

(1) **1875** *Chi. Tribune* 8 July 6/3 Few buyers were present and the 'mail order' business also was light. **1944** JOHNSON *As I Dare* 183 The general publisher also does a direct mail-order business, it is true. — (2) **1888** *Chehalis* (Wash.) *Bee* 27 April 3/3 A new mail order shopping catalogue . . . can be had free by applying at once to Weinstock, Leuben & Co. **1947** *Nat. Geog. Mag.* Sep. 428/2 They listed them in mail-order catalogues to sell for $1. — (3) **1926** BRANCH *Cowboy* 17 The range came to expect and recognize the 'mail-order cowboy,' who arrived already fitted in cowboywear as he knew it from his reading and the assurances of some Middle Western store-keeper.

1944 ADAMS *W. Words* 95 Mail order cowboy. A tenderfoot, devoid of range experience, in custom made cowboy regalia. The average mail-order cowboy 'looks like he was raised on Brooklyn Bridge.' — (4) **1906** S. E. SPARLING *Introd. Business Organiz.* 280 Some of the business reasons which resulted in the organization of trusts, have also suggested the development of the mail-order houses. **1947** *Harper's Mag.* July 4/1 Mass-production principles were used for such jobs as the sorting and filling of orders in a mail-order house.

(5) **1942** ASHER & HEAL *Send No Money* 22 He was known as the largest buyer of advertising space in the 'mail order papers' (cheap story magazines of the day that are now extinct).

* **main,** *a.* In combs.: (1) **main divide,** = **Continental Divide;** (2) **stem,** the main line of a railroad, also transf.

(1) **1888** *Outing* Dec. 217 We follow it almost to its sources, before we come to Kicking-horse Pass, through the continental range, or Main Divide. **1903** ADAMS *Log of Cowboy* 380 We were sweeping across the tablelands adjoining the main divide of the Rocky Mountains. — (2) **1832** *Amer. R. R. Jrnl.* I. 804/2 The western fork . . . connects it with the main stem. **1906** *McClure's Mag.* Feb. 429 A railroad tax bill was introduced. It taxed second-class property (buildings and ordinary real estate) at local rates, but not the 'main stem' (the roadbed). **1945** WALLACE *Barrington* 62 The hog bounced us around and finally got back on the main stem.

For ***Main Line, road,** ***Street,** see as main entries.

Maine-iac 'menɪˌæk, *n.* An inhabitant of Maine, esp. in jocular allusion to the Maine law.

1852 *Lantern* (N.Y.) I. 145/2 On the 15th of April there is to be a great *Fast* throughout the State of Maine. The Mainiacs are to be *Fastmen,* which is a clear confession they are *loose* at present. **1856** *Santa Barbara* (Calif.) *Gaz.* 10 Jan. 4/2 Listen to the ravings of a Maine-ac. **1949** *Amer. Sp.* Feb. 26 Maniac is often applied jocosely to any Maine man.

Maine law. A law forbidding the sale or manufacture of intoxicating liquor in Maine, enacted in 1851. Also any state or local law enacted with similar provisions.

1852 *Lantern* (N.Y.) I. 119/2 Does the Maine Law, in abolishing the use of liquors, include the Cotton-Gin? **1897** *Encycl. Soc. Reform* 1107/1 Vermont in 1852, New Hampshire in 1855, and Connecticut in 1854, passed the Maine Law. **1920** *Collier's* 14 Feb. 42/4 For several years what was known as the 'Maine Law' was a party issue in most of the States.

attrib. **1855** *N.Y. Wkly. Tribune* 26 May 1/5 That plant [the strawberry] is one of the great water drinkers in the Maine Law army. **1866** *Wilkes' Spirit of Times* 17 March 33/2 At last they got their flasks filled with what purported to be *best Bourbon,* at a drug store, for *medicinal purposes,* this being the only dodge whereby a man can procure liquor openly in the Maine Law State of Iowa.

Also **Maine liquor law.**

1852 *Knickerb.* XXXIX. 570 'There is nothing new under the sun,' in the enclosed copy of a '*Maine Liquor-Law*' two hundred and sixteen years old. **1857** GRIFFITH *Autobiog. Female Slave* 295 His big nose, as red as a peony told the story that he was no advocate of the Maine liquor law.

b. In obs. derivatives, as **Maine lawism, lawite.** Cf. **Maine-iac.**

1855 *Chi. W. Times* 18 Oct. 2/3 It is a party erected by the fusion of Abolitionism, Maine Lawism, and all the other isms. **1862** *N.Y. Ev. Express* 15 April, All excellent, even the Whiskey, with the 'prophylactic doses' therein,—but what will the Maine Lawites say.

For *As Maine goes, so goes the nation* (or *union*), see ***go,** *v.* **6. s.**

Mainer 'menɚ, *n.* An inhabitant or native of Maine.

1879 *Harper's Mag.* April 799/2 An elder in his church was present, a way-down-East 'Mainer,' as they are called in this region. **1887** *Courier-Journal* 31 Jan. 4/4 The traducers of that great prohibition State assert that the Mainers get corned as often as they can. **1937** WILSON *Aroostook* 86 The Mainers marched north out of Bangor.

Mainite 'menaɪt, *n.* =prec. *Obs.* — **1857** *Spirit of Times* 3 Jan. 294/1 Would it be wise for the Maine-ites to leave their pines, lofty enough to make masts for 'tall admirals,' and do nothing but catch salmon, and out of season too? **1857** *Harper's Mag.* Sep. 538/2, I astonished a female Mainite by my inordinate capacity for sweet milk and pumpkin-pie.

* **Main Line.** The traditionally aristocratic district just outside Philadelphia, Pa., served by the main line of the Pennsylvania Railroad, often attrib. Also **Main Liner.**

[**1845** *Hunt's Merch. Mag.* XIII. 127 The main line of state works of Pennsylvania extends from the city of Philadelphia . . . to the city of Pittsburg. **1916** Rand McNally *Phila. Guide* 5 The most beautiful of these suburbs may be seen along the suburban section of the Main Line of the Pennsylvania Railroad.] **1941** *Time* 20 Jan. 77 f. (Wentworth), High life in Philadelphia's Main Line society. . . . Imperious daughter of a Main Line first family . . . a Main Liner to the last tweed. *Ib.* 3 Mar. 28/1 (Wentworth), A native of Philadelphia's archconservative 'Main Line.' **1947** SESSIONS *Cities of Amer.* 107 From what other city might one of its daughters, on being presented at court, reply to the queen's question as to where she lived: 'On the Main Line'?

main road. The principal road between two places, often having short branch roads.

1687 *Pa. Col. Rec.* I. 209 A late Order for ye Viewing and Discovering a maine Road from ye Center of Philadelphia ye Shortest way to ye falls. **1716** *N.C. Col. Rec.* II. 265 The main Road from the S.W. side of Middle neck Bridge to the S.W. side of ffrylys bridge. **1862** MOORE *Rebellion Rec.* V. II. 85 Our lines . . . were compelled to fall back to the woods across the main road. **1902** GORDON *Recoll. Lynchburg* 9 Sufficiently distant from the main road to impress the traveller . . . [are] sassafras bushes, and broom-straw.

* **Main Street.** *transf.* The most important street in any small American town regarded as typical and provincial. Usu. with reference to the novel by Sinclair Lewis. Also attrib.

[**1855** *N.Y. Tribune* 31 Dec. 4/4 It has risen to its present position of bloated arrogance and swaggering insolence by the liberal and unstinting patronage it has received from the full purses and free hands of Eastern men in Main street and elsewhere.] **1916** BOWER *Phantom Herd* 5 You'll have to let me weed out some of these Main Street cowboys. **1920** LEWIS (*title*), Main Street. **1948** *Time* 6 Dec. 20/3 Harry Truman has never lost his great respect for Marshall, nor is he unmindful of the prestige and authority Marshall carries on Main Street as well as in Moscow.

Hence **Main Streeter.**

1934 WEBSTER. **1945** *Sat. Review* 6 Oct. 8/2 His books started some Americans laughing at others and made it possible for people to realize that somebody else was a Main Streeter. **1947** *Time* 27 Jan. 4/3 It has raised the hope of this Mainstreeter from Podunk to its highest ebb since the era of Wendell Willkie's 'One World.'

b. (See quots.)

1927 *My Okla.* April 29/1. **1948** *Green Bay* (Wis.) *Press-Gazette* 30 June 1/4 'America's Main street' is the nickname often applied to U.S. Highway 66 [between Chicago and Santa Monica, Calif.]. **1949** *N.O. Times-Picayune Mag.* 11 Sep. 13 The Mighty Mississippi (Also America's Main Street).

* **maize,** *n.* In combs.: (1) **maize bird,** = **maize thief;** (2) **dance,** = **green corn dance;** (3) **harvester,** a machine for harvesting corn; (4) **thief,** the red-winged blackbird or the purple grackle, cf. **red-winged maize thief;** (5) **whisky,** = **corn whisky.**

(1) **1890** *Cent.* 3584/3 *Maize-bird,* . . . an American blackbird of the family *Icteridæ* and subfamily *Agelæinæ;* one of the troopials or marsh-blackbirds: so called from its fondness for Indian corn. — (2) **1873** COZZENS *Marvellous Country* 433 On the morrow the Zunis were to celebrate the 'Maize,' or 'Green-corn dance.' — (3) **1859** *Rep. Comm. Patents 1858* I. 417 Improvement in Maize-Harvesters. — (4) **1770** FORSTER tr. Kalm *Travels* I. 372 The laws of Pensylvania . . . have settled a premium of three-pence a dozen for dead maize thieves. **1811** WILSON *Ornithology* IV. 38 [Red-winged Starlings] are known by various names . . . ; such as the Swamp Blackbird, . . . Corn or Maize Thief, Starling, &c. **1917** *Birds of Amer.* II. 267 Purple Grackle. *Quiscalus quiscula quiscula.* . . . New England Jackdaw; Maize Thief; Keel-tailed Grackle.

(5) **1893** LELAND *Memories* 9 Maize-whiskey could be bought then [c1835] for fifteen cents a gallon [in Phila.].

As the last term in **forty-days, Indian, millo, red maize.**

* **major,** *a.* and *n.*

1. *n.* An informal title of respect.

1746 E. KIMBER *Itinerant Observer* 36 Wherever you travel in Maryland (as also in Virginia and Carolina) your Ears are constantly astonished by the number of Colonels, Majors, and Captains, that you hear mentioned. **1823** in *Mem. Charles Mathews* III. (1839) 385 On every road, even at the meanest pothouse, it is common to call out 'Major, bring me a glass of toddy.' **1884** *N.Y. Wkly. Tribune* 30 July 11/4 There are ten 'generals,' 500 'majors,' 600 'colonels,' and about a thousand 'belles of the season,' enjoying themselves at the White Sulphur Springs. **1909** CALHOUN *Miss Minerva* 42 He kilt 'bout a million Injuns and Yankees and he's name' Major 'cause he's a Confed'rit vetrun.

2. In some colleges and graduate schools: **a.** A course of specified length, usu. twice as long as a minor. **b.** The subject to which a student devotes special attention. Also a student who selects or pursues a major subject.

(a) **1890** in T. W. GOODSPEED *Hist. Univ. Chicago* (1916) 142 A subject taken as a major requires eight or ten hours' classroom work or lecture work a week. — (b) **1907** *Columbia Univ. Cat.* March, Open only to students taking a major in the Department of English. **1945** *Mass. Audubon Soc. Bul.* March 42 In 1913, he was graduated from Williams College with a biology major. **1948** *Democrat* 5 Aug. 1/7 Mr. Gray will receive the Bachelor of Science degree with a major in business administration. **1949** *Dly. Ardmoreite* (Ardmore, Okla.) 25 Jan 6/6 McLaurin is a Negro education major at the University of Oklahoma who is receiving instruction in a separate classroom.

3. *The majors*, in baseball, the major leagues.

1912 C. MATHEWSON *Pitching* 57 Many men, who shine in the minor leagues, fail to make good in the majors. **1931** *Durant* (Okla.) *D. Democrat* 25 July 6/3 It's becoming common-place in the majors today. **1949** *Newsweek* 18 July 64/3 The majors' youngest team (average age 24) might have its ups and downs.

4. major league, in baseball, either of the two principal associations of baseball clubs, the American League and the National League. Often attrib. Also **major leaguer.** Cf. **big league.**

1890 *Sporting Life* (Phila.) 31 July 1/3 They are liable to be represented on this Board by gentlemen of as great base ball acumen as some of the best of our major leaguers. **1906** *Cin. Enquirer* 1 April IV. 1/3 The Southern Class A organization has the advantage of witnessing the work of the youngsters being tried out by the major league clubs. **1948** *Time* 11 Oct. 16/2 In the major leagues, you just don't fall for tricks like that.

transf. **1949** G. AMBERG *Ballet* 94 They intended to compete in the major league and they knew that if the company were to survive it had to . . . meet any competition.

As the last term in **Georgia, Kentucky, sergeant major.**

***major,** *v. intr.* Of a college or university student: To specialize in, or devote special study to, an indicated subject. — **1927** *British Wkly.* 1 Sep. 470/2 He has already stood the examination, 'Majoring' in the Greek New Testament at Louisville. **1949** J. B. HERRICK *Memories* 27 The custom of 'majoring and minoring' that has been wisely adopted has helped remove some of the objections.

major-domo ˈmedʒɚˈdomo, *n.* [Sp. in Amer. Sp. sense shown in **1.** An Amer. borrowing.]

1. The overseer or manager of a mission, ranch, or hacienda.

1834 in *Calif. Hist. Soc. Quart.* VIII. 228 Four ranchos [near San Luis Rey], each one made up of an Indian village, a house for the *mayordomo* directing it, storehouses suitable for the harvests, and a very fine chapel. **1899** A. THOMAS *Arizona* 94 Pa . . . says you're the best Major Domo the ranch ever had. **1948** JOHNSTON *Gold Rush* ii, The precious metal was found earlier, on March 9, 1842, by Francisco Lopez, majordomo of San Gabriel Mission, in Placerita Canyon.

2. One in charge of an acequia.

1885 *Harper's Mag.* April 692/2 The *acequias* are public works, and in each place are under the control of the highly important local official called the *mayor domo.* **1902** NEWELL *Irrigation* 349 The ditches, as a rule, are owned in common by the farmers of each community, and one of the irrigators is annually elected superintendent, or majordomo. **1941** FERGUSSON *Southwest* 251 Every man owned so many days' ditch work under the elected mayordomo, ditch boss, who also doled out the water so the man living up the stream did not rob his down-stream neighbor.

***make,** *n. On the make*, eager to "get ahead," intent on profit or advancement. *Colloq.*

1869 J. R. BROWNE *Adv. Apache Country* 507 'I don't see what profit it is to me whether your ledge is worth two hundred thousand dollars or two cents.' 'Oh, you're on the make, are you?' . . . 'Why, yes, to be candid, I'd like to make fifty thousand or so.' **1920** *Amer. Mag.* Dec. 87/1 He has, as a matter of fact, gone far ahead of that figure and is still 'on the make.' **1948** DICK *Dixie Frontier* 84 Such a planter was 'on the make' and worked his slaves and himself hard.

***make,** *v.*

1. *tr.* To bring (a growing crop) to maturity; to produce (a crop). Also absol. for passive.

1714 *Boston News-Letter* 9–16 Aug. 2/2 We have had an extraordinary drought . . . which makes us apprehensive of a Scarcity of Corn, and little or no Tobacco like to be made. **1763** WASHINGTON *Diaries* I. Observed that my y[oun]g Corn was just beginning to show. . . . Quere, has it time to make or Ripen? **1818** *Wkly. Recorder* (Chillicothe, O.) 4 Dec. 135/1 There are great crops of corn made in this country. **1899** CUSHMAN *Hist. Indians* 222 He was allowed to return home and finish making his crop. **1949** MURRAY *This Our Land* 234 Maybe you make big cotton crop.

b. Of a crop, to amount to (a certain quantity).

1873 *Winfield* (Kans.) *Courier* 5 June 2/3 Most of the wheat over this way will make twenty-five bushels to the acre. **1949** *Ward. Co. Independent* (Minot, N.D.) 21 July 1/4 Wonderful oats that will probably make 75 bushels to the acre.

2. *Absol.* for "to make money," to profit. *Colloq.*

1852 STOWE *Uncle Tom* viii, I'd 'a gin Shelby eight hundred or a thousand, and then made well on her. **1902** HARBEN *A. Daniel* 213 Ef I knowed he had made by the bu'st I'd talk different, but I don't know it!

3. (See quot.) *Obs.*

1853 STRICKLAND *Twenty-seven Yrs.* II. 281 The same process is gone through, as before described, which finishes the operation of 'making,' as the lumber men term squaring the timber.

4. *Baseball.* To arrive safely at (a base).

1867 CHADWICK *Base Ball Player's Book* 130 When the batsman makes his first base. **1909** *Sat. Ev. Post* 6 March 5/3 Neumann gave a decorous imitation of a ball player 'making second' and then shot off at top speed to execute his orders.

5. Of a traveling salesman, to visit (a town) for the purpose of selling goods there.

1902 LORIMER *Lett. Merchant* 135, I hadn't more than made my first town . . . [before] I saw that business ought to be very good there. **a1910** O. HENRY *Rolling Stones* 112 When I used to sell hardware in the West, I often 'made' a little town called Saltillo, in Colorado.

6. To succeed in reaching or attaining (a place or position). Cf. **9.** (4) (*b*).

1916 H. L. WILSON *Somewhere in Red Gap* i. 25, I hurried home to get a bite to eat and dress and make the party. **1928** *Publishers' Wkly.* 24 Nov. 2184/2 Two books that almost made the Best Seller List are [etc.]. **1944** *Sat. Review* 8 July 16/2 Frederick was unconscious of the drama that had made page 1 of the morning paper.

b. Esp. of a prize fighter, to attain (a certain weight) for a match.

1904 *McClure's Mag.* April 668/2 The announcer shrieked from the two sides of the ring that both men had made the required weight. **1924** T. S. ANDREWS *Ring Battles of Cent.* 3 Champions . . . should be required to make weight for their matches.

7. *intr.* Of land, to extend in a certain direction.

1785 DENNY *Jrnl.* 58 Opposite the most prominent parts of the bottoms, hill makes in and forms what is called narrows. **1869** J. R. BROWNE *Adv. Apache Country* 251 This is little better than an open roadstead, protected slightly on the north-west by a sand-spit making out into the Gulf. **1875** MARK TWAIN *Old Times* iii. 46, I judge the upper bar is making down a little at Hale's Point.

8. Of ice, to form.

1784 N. WEBSTER in Ford *Notes* I. (1912) 88 Cold; ice makes in the river. **1890** *N.Y. Tribune* 12 Dec. 3/3 Several good guides . . . will assist him in an attempt to reach Kadiak Island by crossing Alaska Peninsula before the ice makes.

9. In various phrases: (1) **To make meat*, to jerk meat, *obs.;* (2) *to make change*, to give currency of a lower denomination in exchange for that of a higher; (3) *to make (good) time*, to cover a certain distance in a relatively short time, also fig.; (4) *to make it*, (*a*) in giving an order, to let it be, (*b*) to succeed in something, as in reaching a place, cf. **6.** above; (5) *to make tracks*, see ***track,** *n.;* (6) *to make oneself solid*, see ***solid;** (7) *to make to order*, to make in compliance with the wishes of the customer or user, *colloq.*

(1) 1846 SAGE *Scenes Rocky Mts.* vi, We commenced the process of 'making meat,' . . . cutting into thin slices the boneless parts of buffalo, or other meat, and drying them in the wind or sun. **1889** FARMER 362/2 *To make meat*, is the term by which the frontiersman denotes the process of drying thin slices of animal flesh for future use. — **(2) 1865** SALA *Diary* I. 237 'Making change' is quite an art, and persons who can 'make change' in a store or restaurant are advertised for every day in the newspapers. — **(3) 1861** *Remin. Locomotive Engineer* 12 My 'orders' were positive to use all due exertion to make time. **1870** MARK TWAIN *Sk., New & Old* 103 Vengeance Hopkins . . . made the best time on record, coming within one of reaching the Twelfth Auditor. **1949** *Chi. Sun-Times* 10 Feb. 59 Yeah! We've made good time this morning! — **(4)** (*a*) **1883** MARK TWAIN *Life on Miss.* 507 He softened, and said make it a bottle of champagne. **1944** JOHNSON *As I Dare* 242 It was possible for the *Ladies' Home Journal* to cable Rudyard Kipling that he must change certain lines in a story where the character was said to have taken a glass of wine. Kipling cabled back, 'Make it Malted Milk.' (*b*) **1885** HOWELLS *Silas Lapham* 108 He jumped on board the steam-boat. . . . 'Just made it,' he said. **1912** R. A. WASON *Friar Tuck* xxxvi. 187 Badger-face tried to raise himself on his elbow, but he couldn't quite make it. **1949** *Sky Line Trail* March 15/1 Here's hoping Shirley Rourke makes it this summer.

(7) 1838 ASBURY *Sucker's Prog.* 203 These cosmopolites . . . were made to order for the professional gambler.

***maker,** *n.* As the last term in **apple-butter, Basket, bogus, boom, bucket, cabinet, candy, canoe, cotton, fire, hay, home, list, log, lumber, maple sugar, money, peace, president, rate, sail, shake, slate, tie, wampum maker.**

***makings,** *n. pl.* Paper and tobacco for making a cigarette.

1907 S. E. WHITE *Arizona Nights* I. ix. 161 'Well,' agreed Rogers, 'pass over the "makings" and I will.' **1916** BOWER *Phantom Herd* viii.

116 Luck . . . trailed over to a table and gleaned 'the makings' from among the litter of papers . . . and rolled himself a much-needed smoke. **1949** *Sat. Ev. Post* 9 April 136/4, I got out his makin's and rolled him one.

As the last term in **maple sugar, moccasin, president, slate making.**

malashagany mɑlɑˈʃɑgənɪ, *n.* (See quot.) — **1896** GERARD in *N.Y. Sun* 30 July, Malashagany, a name of the sheepshead of Lake Huron, the 'bass' of the English of Canada, and the 'gros bossu' (from its rounded back) of the French of the same country. The name is, through Canadian French, 'malachegane,' from Nipissing 'manashigan,' 'the ill-formed bass.'

Malemute ˈmɑləˌmjut, *n.* [Native name.]

1. (See quot. 1907.)

1868 WHYMPER *Alaska* 143 The Malemutes and Kaveaks intermingle considerably, and have therefore been spoken of here as one people. **1907** HODGE *Amer. Indians* I. 794/2 Malemiut. An Eskimo tribe occupying the coast of Norton sd., n. of Shaktolik and the neck of Kaviak penin., Alaska.

2. An Eskimo dog of a breed originated by these Indians.

1898 *Klondike Nugget* (Dawson, N.W.T.) 20 July 3/2 After appointing a committee to keep stray Malamoots and donkeys off the diamond, the game was called. **1913** *Outing* Mar. 660/1 Muck-luck was a clear strain Malamute, courageous to the point of madness. **1945** SERVICE *Ploughman* 361 One day in early spring a malamute must have caught it, for I found its mangled body in a snowdrift.

attrib. **1913** *Outing* Feb. 521/1 Sitting among a litter of Malamute puppies we exchanged the news of the trial. **1948** *Chi. Tribune* 23 Feb. IV. 1/6 Along with the Eskimos will be a representation of the Malemute sled dogs that provide the only motive power available to Eskimos.

***mallow,** *n.* As the last term in **glade, poppy mallow.**

malpais ˈmælpaɪs, *n. W.* [Sp. *mal,* bad, and *país,* country.]

1. A rugged tract of volcanic ground; badlands. Also attrib. Cf. **mauvaise(s) terre(s).**

1844 KENDALL *Narr. Santa Fe Exped.* II. 384 We had crossed the mal pais, or bad country as it is called. **1885** *Harper's Mag.* April 692/1 These *mesas* are here of *mal pais* (bad lands), as the Mexicans call the ancient lava formations which are blotted in inky blackness over the Rio Grande landscape. **1942** KEARNEY & PEEBLES *Flowering Plants Ariz.* 17 Some of these are limestone areas, whereas others are volcanic, locally known as 'mallapy' (*mal pais*).

2. Basaltic lava. Also attrib.

1919 J. S. CHASE *Calif. Desert Trails* 193 The spur ran out at last in a tongue of yellowish rock of the malpais kind. **1949** *Chi. Tribune* 9 Jan VI. 3/3 They made manos and metates from malapai, in which they ground their meal.

* **malt,** *n.* **1. malt coffee,** a substitute for coffee made with malt. *Rare.* **2. malt tea,** (see quot. 1890).

(1) **1865** *Atlantic Mo.* XV. 676 The four children and herself breakfasted on bread and molasses with malt coffee. — (2) *a***1821** C. BIDDLE *Autobiog.* 329, I believe it was with malt tea she made the cure. **1890** *Cent.* 3598/3 Malt-tea, the liquid infusion of the mash in brewing.

b. malt shop, a shop where malted milk *q.v.* is sold.

1943 BAKER *Trio* (1946) 57 She was out of the gate and into a little section of bright lights—college clothes, bookstores, malt shops, the first block off any campus. **1949** *Time* 26 Sep. 25/1 The word was relayed through the drive-ins, malt shops and garages speckling the Los Angeles suburbs.

malted milk. [Orig. (*cap.*) a trade-mark name coined and registered by Wm. Horlick (1846–1936), Amer. manufacturer.] A powder made of evaporated milk and malted cereals; a drink made from this powder, now esp. one containing ice cream and flavoring as well.

1887 *Pat. Off. Gaz.* XLI. 358 Trade-Marks. . . . Food preparation for infants and invalids.—*Horlick's Food Company,* Mount Pleasant and Racine, Wis. . . . 'The words *Malted Milk* and the letters "M.M." ' **1901** *Everybody's Mag.* Oct. 433/1 There were honey-dew mince pie and malted milk and cheese. [**1948** *Chi. Tribune* 25 Jan. (Grafic Mag.) 15/2 Johnny and I 'fueled up' on cheeseburgers and malteds for the long ride to the beach.]

* **Maltese,** *a.* and *n.* Also, *colloq.,* **Maltee.**

1. *n.* A Maltese cat.

1857 HAMMOND *Northern Scenes* 120 One great Maltese, with eyes like tea-plates, and a tail like a Bologna sausage, grinned and sputtered, and spit. **1918** LINCOLN *Shavings* 45 Nate Rogers' old maltee never shed all that alone.

b. The color of a Maltese cat.

1897 STUART *Simpkinsville* 5 Maltee is a good enough color for a cat ef it's kep' true.

2. *a.* Denoting a breed of asses and a bluish-gray variety of domestic cats.

1787 WASHINGTON *Diaries* III. 284 On Saturday last brot. home the 2 Maltese Jennys, and 2 Mules. **1842** *Lowell Offering* II. 25 Josephine . . . came laughing and skipping into the kitchen, followed by a little Maltese kitten. **1857** *N. & Q.* 2 Ser. IV. 247/2 A New York merchant recently sent for a cargo of Maltese cats from that celebrated island. **1910** WHITLOCK *Gold Brick* 244 The fat Maltese cat . . . stretched herself again. **1946** STARRETT *Murder in Peking* 129 The gray roadster rushed across the Chinese countryside like a Maltese kitten.

mamelle mɑˈmɛl, *n. W.* [F. (a woman's breast), in the Amer. F. sense shown here.] A rounded hillock. Also **mammilla.** Cf. **teton.**

1819 NUTTALL *Travels Ark.* 126 Again to the south and south-west, . . . distinctly appeared the Mamelle. **1869** BOWLES *Our New West* 278 Mountains are always . . . rising and rounding out into innumerable fat mammillas. **1893** LERCH *Hills of La.* 61 Wherever these flats occur, low, well rounded mounds have been found associated with them, they have been termed very appropriately mammilae, from their peculiar form. . . . Their size varies, but averages 80 to 100 feet in diameter at base and 20 to 60 feet in height.

attrib. **1839** *Maysville* (Ky.) *Eagle* 18 Dec. 1/3 The ancient existence of an immense lake, where now lies the American Bottom, upon the east side of the Mississippi, and the Mamelle Prairie, upon the west side, . . . appears geologically demonstrable.

* **mammoth,** *n.* The American mastodon, remains of which have been found in various parts of the U.S.

1789 MORSE *Amer. Geog.* 55 The mammoth is not found in the civilized parts of America. . . . Skeletons of uncommon magnitude have been found at the salt licks, on the Ohio, in New Jersey, and other places. **1834** PECK *Gaz. Illinois* 52 Bones of a huge animal, but different from the Mammoth, have been recently found in St. Clair county. **1949** *Nat. Geog. Mag.* Oct. 514 Flesh of a mammoth, found recently, was flown to a New York museum.

mammoth ˈmæməθ, *a.* [See note.]

Thornton suggests that this adjectival use originated in the U.S. See also quot. 1842 below.

1. Huge, immense.

1802 *Balance* 19 Oct. 331 (Th.), No more to do with the subject than the man in the moon has to do with the mammoth cheese. **1802** *Port Folio* ii. 31 (Th.), A baker in this city offers *Mammoth bread* for sale. **1803** J. DAVIS *Travels U.S.A.* 329 (Th.), Its extraordinary dimensions induced some wicked wag of a federalist to call it the *Mammoth* Cheese. **1842** BUCKINGHAM *Slave States* II. 326 It [is] . . . the custom of this country to call every thing very large by the epithet of 'mammoth'; so that one hears of a mammoth cake, a mammoth pie, a mammoth oyster. **1949** *Dly. Ardmoreite* (Ardmore, Okla.) 8 Sep. 3/1 Bobby was one of the best dressed riders in the mammoth parade Wednesday.

b. *absol.* Anything of immense proportions.

1824 *Mass. Spy* 14 Jan. (Th.), The last load, as we Yankees say, was a 'Mammoth': . . . producing an aggregate of nearly twelve cords. **1947** *Nat. Geog. Mag.* July 105/2 Electric-drive mammoths are now being turned out by assembly line methods.

2. In special combs.: (1) **mammoth grove,** a grove composed of mammoth trees; (2) **powder,** (see quot.); (3) **sheet, =blanket sheet,** *obs.;* (4) **tree,** the giant sequoia.

(1) **1864** *Old Piute* (Virginia, Nev.) 27 Aug. 3/2 Two of the trees in Mammoth Grove have been respectively christened John Bright and Richard Cobden. — (2) **1875** KNIGHT 1040/2 For very heavy ordnance a much larger grained powder . . . called *mammoth* powder, was introduced by the late General T. J. Rodman. — (3) **1834** *Sun* (N.Y.) 16 May 2/2 The mammoth sheets will publish the report of the Committee on the Arsenal affair this morning. — (4) **1857** *S.F. Bulletin* 19 May 2/2 This is a most agreeable season of the year to visit the Grove of Mammoth Trees. **1897** SUDWORTH *Arborescent Flora* 62 *Sequoia washingtoniana.* . . . Bigtree. . . . [Also called] Mammoth-tree (Cal., and in Eng. cult.).

b. Also in names of fruits, flowers, and vegetables.

1852 FLEISCHMANN *Wegweiser* 176 Auf gutem Boden . . . der *Mammuth Tomato* wird nicht allein sehr gross, sondern auch äusserst schmackhaft und gut. **1859** MACKAY *Tour* I. 268 He again selected twelve as alone fit for the production of wine. These twelve were the Catawba, the Cape, . . . the White Catawba, and the Mammoth Catawba. **1868** *Rep. Comm. Agric. 1867* 305 Mr. Rogers also hybridized the Mammoth Grape (Vitis labrusca) with the pollen of the Black Hamburg. **1944** *Burpee's Seeds* 17 Mammoth Prize Long Red [Beets]. . . . Roots grow to a truly enormous size. *Ib.* 85 Alldouble Mammoth Peony Flowered [Petunias].

* **mammy,** *n. S.* A term of affection and respect used by white people, esp. children, to elderly Negro women,

esp. to those who have been their nurses. Cf. **black mammy.**

1803 J. Davis *Travels Amer.* 86 Children of the most distinguished families in *Carolina*, are suckled by negro-women. Each child has its *Momma.* **1835** Longstreet *Ga. Scenes* 110 'Aunt' and 'mauma,' or 'maum' its abbreviation, are terms of respect, commonly used by children, to aged negroes. *c***1898** Christian *Days* 42 He would take with him, Washington, your Mammy's son, as his body servant. **1948** *Chi. D. News* 23 Feb. 12/7 Mammy's little baby is a-wearying of short'nin' bread.

* **man,** *n.* In combs.: (1) **man drowner,** (see quot.), *obs.;* (2) **fashion,** in a manly way, in the manner of a man; (3) **hunt,** a hunt for a man, esp. a fugitive, also as verb, and allusive; (4) **hunter,** one who engages in a manhunt, also **man hunting;** (5) * **killer,** (*a*) a device, implement, or task that is especially severe or contrived to kill a man, (*b*) a person who does not scruple to kill another; (6) **school,** a school conducted by a man, *colloq.*, cf. **ma'am school;** (7) **tailor,** a tailor, esp. a woman, who makes clothes for men, *obs.*

(1) **1819** in Claiborne *Life Quitman* 42 We purchased a small canoe, here called a 'dug-out,' or 'man-drowner.' — (2) **1874** *Cong. Rec.* 1 April 2682/2 [If Senator Morton] is entirely confident that his opinions are sound, why so timid? . . . Why not walk up to this man-fashion? **1877** Bartlett 788 *Man-Fashion*, in a manly, straight-forward manner. Also, riding astraddle, in distinction from the feminine use of a side-saddle. — (3) **1841** *S. Lit. Messenger* VII. 769/1, I never strikes an officer—but I'll teach him how to man-hunt Jim Guest. **1846** *Hancock Eagle* (Nauvoo, Ill.) 10 April 3/1 A Whig paper gives an exceedingly humorous account of a man *hunt*, which came off in their town, a few days since. **1860** Greeley *Overland Journey* 84 Should one of these countless herds take a fancy for a man hunt, our riflemen would find even the express-wagons no protection. **1948** *Duncan* (Okla.) *D. Banner* 2 July 8/5 Southwest Missouri law officers continued an intense manhunt today for a youth who beat and attacked a 25-year-old farm wife. — (4) *c***1889** in Bowditch *Life & Corr.* (1902) 277 Around him the committee to call upon the man hunter would collect as if around a real slave catcher. **1922** Kephart *So. Highlanders* 226 It was also the first time I had ever appeared among them as a man-hunter. *Ib.* 233 How do you like this sport of man-hunting?

(5) (*a*) **1876** *Vt. Bd. Agric. Rep.* III. 614 Any man who ever held the old Kimball Rake, usually called the 'man killer,' or 'scratch rake.' **1903** *Cin. Enquirer* 3 Jan. 11/1 At a certain point and when a certain spring was touched by circumstances that man's arm would go up with presented pistol and reveal the 'man killer,' and the man who stood in front would have to be quicker or he would be dead. **1945** *Silverton* (Colo.) *Standard* 23 Feb. 3/1 This first column is a man-killer. (*b*) **1928** Breakenridge *Helldorado* 59 It had become the custom in these frontier towns to appoint as marshal someone . . . with a reputation as a man-killer. — (6) **1769** *Essex Inst. Coll.* XXI. 238 Voted to carry two Papers one for a man Scool and one for a woman Scool the most Signers to haue the use of the house. **1838** *U.S. Mag.* I. 404 [Kendall] went to a 'woman school' each summer for about two months, and to a 'man school' in the winter. — (7) **1789** *Boston Directory* 204 Woodman Abigail, stay-maker & man-taylor, creek-lane. **1796** *Ib.* 228 Bowns Martha, man-taylor, Sheaf street.

b. In the names of plants and animals: (1) * **man eater,** (see quot. 1884); (2) **gazer,** prob. the praying mantis, *obs.*, cf. **rear-horse;** (3) **-in-the-ground,** (see quots. and cf. **bigroot**); (4) **of the earth,** (*a*) the American morning glory, *Ipomoea pandurata,* (*b*) =next; (5) **root,** the long-rooted ipomoea of the western plains, also bigroot *q.v.*

(1) **1832** Williamson *Maine* I. 161 The Shark, among fishermen, is called the 'maneater,' 'the shovel-nose,' and 'the swingle-tail;' these being varieties of the species. **1884** *Amer. Naturalist* XVIII. 940 The 'Man-eater Shark,' *Carcharodon carcharias*. . . . The various descriptions given of this species are . . . imperfect and confusing. **1923** *N.Y. Times* 13 Sep. 23/7 (*heading*), Shark-Hunters Hook Man-Eater, Then Cut Line to Escape Him. — (2) **1742** Catesby *Carolina* App. p. xxxvii, The Grasshopper, The Man Gazer. **1789** Morse *Amer. Geog.* 62 Of the astonishing variety of Insects found in America, we will mention. . . . Man-gazer, Cock Roche, Cricket [etc.]. — (3) **1897** Parsons *Wild Flowers of Calif.* 26 Seeing its rather delicate ivy-like habit above ground, one would never dream that it came from a root as large as a man's body, buried deep in the earth. From this root, it has received two of its common names, 'big-root' and 'man-in-the-ground.' **1915** Armstrong *Western Wild Flowers* 518 This is also called Big-root and Man-in-the-ground. — (4) (*a*) **1833** Eaton *Botany* (ed. 6) 105 *Convolvulus panduratus*, mechoacan, wild potato vine, man of the earth. . . . A mild cathartic, and resembles rhubarb in its effects. **1933** Cheley *Camping Out* 527 The blossom of the man-of-the-earth looks like a morning glory and the plant grows in dry ground in the eastern United States. **1947** *U.S. Dispensatory* 593/2 The *I. pandurata* (L.) Meyer (commonly known as the wild-potato vine, man-of-the-earth or wild potato) is a native climber with a large perennial root sometimes two or three feet in length. (*b*) **1871** *Rep. Comm. Agric. 1870* 407 *Wild potato vine,* (*Ipomœa leptophylla.*)—This showy plant of the dry deserts of the West is commonly called man root, or man of the earth. . . . The Cheyennes, Arapahoes and Kioways roast it for food when pressed by hunger.

(5) **1846** Emory *Military Reconn.* 13 The principal growth is the buffalo grass, . . . and very rarely that wonderful plant, the Ipomea leptophylla, called by the hunter man root. **1902** Chesnut *Plants Used by Indians* 390 On account of its resemblance in size and shape to a man's head, it is not infrequently called 'man root.' **1949** Moldenke *Amer. Wild Flowers* 268 Because of this root the plant is often called bigroot or manroot.

c. In colloq. phrases, usu. explained in the quots.: (1) *man for breakfast,* (2) *man in the cars,* (3) * *Man of Destiny,* (4) *man at the pot,* (5) *Man of the Revolution,* (6) *Man of Sumter,* Gen. B. G. J. Beauregard (1818–93), the Confederate general in charge of the forces that began the bombardment of Fort Sumter, April 12, 1861.

(1) **1890** *Denver Republican* 4 May 24/3 For a long time there was no effort made to punish murderers, and we had a 'man for breakfast' nearly every day. **1947** *Westerners' Brand Book* 23 For many years after the American occupation of California, Los Angeles had its 'man for breakfast' as the morning report of the almost nightly murder was called. — (2) **1888** Bryce *Amer. Commw.* III. iv. lxxvi. 7 That representative of public opinion whom Americans call 'the man in the cars.' — (3) **1885** Siva *Man of Destiny* 78 Your own fame as a Man of Destiny, as you [Grover Cleveland] styled yourself . . . is the great stake for which you will pay. — (4) **1939** Rollins *Gone Haywire* 66 The nearest approach was an occasional cry of 'Man at the pot!' If in any cow camp a man rose to fill his coffee cup and that cry was given, it was his duty to go around with the pot and replenish all the cups held out to him.

(5) **1914** *Cyclo. Amer. Govt.* II. 390/2 *Man of the Revolution*, an affectionate nickname bestowed by the American people upon Samuel Adams . . . because of the leading part which he played in bringing about the War of Independence. — (6) **1870** Macrae *Americans* II. 139 Hence his sobriquet of 'The Man of Sumter,' by which he became known in Confederate history.

As the last term in **administration, all, Anglo-, ante-, ash, ax, backwoods, bad, baggage, band, bank, barn, base, bay, bear, best, blanket, blocking, border state, Boston, bow, bows, brake, brakes, buckra, buckskin, bunko, bushel, canoe, canvas, car, career, carry, cattle, chain, Chebacco, checker, chicken, Clay, collar, con, corner, cow, credit, dead, Dominion, Douglas, dry-goods, Dutch, eight-day, elevator, end, ends, entry, equal rights, Essex, Evening Post, express, federal, fence, fine, fire, fisher, flag, flatboat, floor, Four Minute, free, free-state, French, frontier, gag, galvanized, garbage, gas, Georgia, gin, gold, good, gopher, grain, Granite, grass, grip, grocery, gulch, gun, guns, hack, half, hall, hatchet, he-, head, high, high-stand, hired, hominy, hook-and-ladder, hull-corn, hunter, ice, inside, instalment, iron, Jackson, Jersey, Johnson, junk, Kentucky, kettle, key, King George, king's, knife, knockout, ladder, law, lay, leadoff, letter, lever, liberty, line, liquor, log, lumber, machine, mast, medicine, middle, Mingo, minstrel, minute, mortgage, motor, mountain, moving, mutual, New, New England, next, north, Northern, old, old school, pack, package, packhorse, palmetto, paper, parched corn, pasture, patent, patrol-, peanut, pit, plains, pliers, pod-, point, pond, poor, popcorn, prairie, press, prudential, railroad, ranch, red, remittance, Revival, rewrite, river, rod, rounds, saddle, salary, saloon, schooner, scout, scrub, second, select, self-made, shanty, share, sheep, shell, shirt, shores, silver, Sioux, sleigh, small potato, snowshoe, southern union, spear, spoils, sporting, squaw, stamp, steamboat, stock, strongarm, surf, tally, Tammany, tariff, telegraph, third, timber, tong, torpedo, transfer, traveling, trouble, truck, Tyler, union, venire, vigilance, voodoo, war, ward, wash, weather, Welsh, western, whale, wheel, wheelbarrow, wheels, whisky, white, wildcat, wildcat business, yegg, yes man.**

manada mǝˈnɑdǝ, *n. W.* [Sp. in same sense.] (See quot. 1877.)

1842 E. Vischer in *Calif. Hist. Soc. Quart.* XIX. 209, I was much interested in the lively scenes of a *remonta*, when at a designated place, the *remudadero*, a *manada* of thirty to forty horses, led by a man with a bell, is driven into a *corral*. The desired saddle-horses are then caught with a lasso. **1877** Bartlett 382 *Manada*, . . . a herd of cattle or drove of horses. In California, it is especially applied to breeding mares. **1888** Harlan *Calif., '46 to '88* 169 Alarm was given that the *manada* . . . had broken the hill-foot fences, and was widely scattered on the plain among the squatters' grain. **1934** White *Folded*

Hills 44 The greater part of two *manadas* had been driven off. **1949** *Boston Sun. Globe Mag.* 3 April 2/4 Matt has got four remudas and two manadas of bays on that range.

*__manager__, *n.* As the last term in **county, field, floor, general, machine, party, sales manager.**

managing editor. One of the chief editors of a newspaper or magazine.

1865 RICHARDSON *Secret Service* 18, I found the Managing Editor in his office. **1912** NICHOLSON *Hoosier Chron.* 94 You may tell your managing editor for me that if he doesn't print more of my stuff he can get somebody else on the job here. **1949** *Prairie Schooner* Spring 64 The managing editor informed me that I was to report to the . . . desk the following morning.

mañana məˈnjɑnə, *n.* Orig. *S.W.* [Sp. in same sense.] Tomorrow, the indefinite future. Also attrib.

[**1847** in G. B. MCCLELLAN *Mexican War Diary* (1917) 34 We . . . dreamed of a hard piece of work we had to commence on the morrow. Mañana por la mañana.] **1889** E. RIPLEY *From Flag to Flag* 165 Their *mañana* never came, never was intended to come. **1949** *Nat. Hist.* Feb. 64/3 To a certain extent the legendary 'mañana' complex of the country takes over, and I passed nest after nest, deciding to return on the morrow.

b. *Land* (or *kingdom*) *of mañana*, a land of postponement, specifically Mexico.

1885 *Harper's Mag.* Jan. 217/2 Is Cedar Keys just on the borderland of that vast region known as the kingdom of *Mañana?* **1895** REMINGTON *Pony Tracks* 103 He would show you the time within fifteen minutes of right, which little discrepancy could never affect the value of a watch in the land of *mañana*. **1903** A. ADAMS *Log Cowboy* 138 Flood had had years of experience in dealing with Mexicans in the land of *mañana*, where all maxims regarding the value of time are religiously discarded.

mananosay, see **maninose.**

Mandamus counsellor. A name opprobriously applied from 1774 to 1776 to a member of any colonial council whose appointment was by writ of mandamus. Chiefly in Massachusetts. Now *hist.* — **1774** J. ADAMS *Works* IX. 351 Our Alva, Gage, with his fifteen Mandamus counsellors, are shut up in Boston, afraid to stir, afraid of their own shades. **1876** BANCROFT *Hist. U.S.* IV. iv. 339 Councillors, called mandamus councillors from their appointment by the crown.

Mandan ˈmændən, *n.* [f. the native name, of uncertain significance.] An Indian of a Siouan tribe found chiefly in the Dakotas. Also, *pl.* or *collect.*, the tribe of such an Indian. Also attrib.

1794 in *Mass. H.S. Coll.* 1 Ser. III. 24 The tribes of Indians which he passed through, were called the Maskego Tribe . . . Mandon Tribe, Paunees, and several others. **1804** in *Wis. Hist. Coll.* XXII. (1916) 158 We Camped . . . at an old field where the Manden nation had raised corn the last Summer. **1805** LEWIS in *Ann. 9th Congress* 2 Sess. 1064 The bridlebits and blankets I have seen in the possession of the Mandans. **1916** EASTMAN *From Deep Woods* 41 My Uncle had been on the war-path against this tribe and had brought home two Mandan scalps. **1949** *Nat. Geog. Mag.* Aug. 155/2 A few tribes, among them the Hidatsa, Mandan, Omaha, Pawnee, Ponca, and Iroquois, have been known to grow sweet corn.

b. Mandan corn, a type of Indian corn, poss. sweet corn, found in use among the Mandans. *Obs.*

1818 *Wkly. Recorder* (Chillicothe, O.) 28 Oct. 64/1 The Mandan corn will find itself in its own climate at the mouth of the Yellow Stone. **1831** PECK *Guide* 41 A small species of maize called the Mandan corn, and produced by the Mandan and other Indians on the Upper Missouri, flourishes in this latitude. **1917** WILL & HYDE *Corn Among Indians* 302 It was called 'Mandan corn' and was spotted with white, blue and yellow seeds on each ear.

*__mandrake__, *n.* The May apple, *Podophyllum peltatum;* the fruit of this.

1778 CARVER *Travels* 118 In the country belonging to these people [the Pawnee Indians] it is said, that Mandrakes are frequently found, a species of root resembling human beings of both sexes. **1807** C. SCHULTZ *Travels* I. 144 The only fruits I have met with, with which you are unacquainted, are the mandrake and papaw. **1850** S. F. COOPER *Rural Hours* 91 The mandrakes, or May-apples, are in flower. **1949** *Amer. Photography* Aug. 484/1 On a shady hillside not far from a brook we find a patch of May apples, or mandrakes.

manga ˈmɑŋgə, *n. S.W.* [Sp. in Amer. Sp. sense shown here.] A cape, poncho, or mantle. Cf. **poncho,** *n.*

1834 in *Calif. Hist. Soc. Quart.* VIII. 247 To protect themselves from the cold, they have a cloak . . . with a hole for allowing the head to pass through, used in all the Spanish colonies of America, and . . . called, now *poncho* now *manga*. **1857** M. REID *War Trail* (B.), As the mustang sprang over the zequia, the flowing skirt of the manga was puffed forward. **1888** A. E. BARR *Remember the Alamo* 301 It was a grand moving picture of handsome men in scarlet and gold—of graceful mangas and waving plumes.

mangana mɑnˈgɑnə, *n. S.W.* [Sp. in same sense.] (See quot. 1944.)

1929 DOBIE *Vaquero* 262 In roping wild horses in the pen the *mangana* used to be employed constantly. **1939** WELLMAN *Trampling Herd* 240 The deadliest throw was called 'forefooting'. The noose caught the animal by the forefoot and spilled it. In the Southwest this was known as the *mangana*. **1944** ADAMS *W. Words* 96/2 mangana. . . . It is a throw which catches the animal by the forefeet and has come to mean *forefooting*.

*__mangler__, *n.* (See quot.) *Obs.* — **1875** KNIGHT 1383/2 *Mangler,* a machine for grinding meat, to render it more easy to masticate or to stew.

mangrove snapper. *a.* The bastard snapper; also the gray snapper.

1734 *Phil. Trans.* XXXVIII. 316 The *Mangrove Snapper* . . . is esteemed pretty good food. **1884** GOODE *Fisheries* I. 397 [*Lutjanus Stearnsi*] has as yet been found only on the Gulf coasts of the United States, where it is known as the 'Mangrove Snapper.' *Ib.*, The 'Mangrove Snapper' of Charleston, called at Pensacola the 'Bastard Snapper,' . . .is less vivid, being somewhat more russet. **1911** *Rep. Fisheries 1908* 316/2 The gray snapper or mangrove snapper (*L. griseus*), also known in Florida as 'lawyer,' is a most common species.

Manhattan mænˈhætn̩, *n.* [App. f. a native name for Manhattan Island, *manah*, island and *atin*, hill, i.e., "hill island."]

1. *pl.* or *collect.* An Algonquian Indian tribe formerly resident at the site of New York City.

1614 in *Doc. Col. Hist. N.Y.* (1856) (map), Manhattes. **1816** BOUDINOT *Star in West* 17 Mahatons, or Manhattons. **1907** HODGE *Amer. Indians* I. 800 The Manhattan had their principal village, Nappeckamack, where Yonkers now stands. **1949** *Sat. Ev. Post* 12 Feb. 39/3 It was one of the heftiest single packages of real estate to change owners in New York since the Manhattoes let the Dutch West India Company have their whole island for twenty-four dollars.

2. =**Manhattan water.** *Obs.*

1845 *Knickerb.* XXVI. 444 He abominates Croton water, and gives his preference to the delectable Manhattan, which his forefathers drank before him.

3. =**Manhattanese.** *Obs.*

1854 SIMMS *Southward Ho!* 4 My friend was a genuine Manhattan.

4. =**Manhattan cocktail.**

1894 WARNER *Golden House* v, He and old Fairfax sipped their five-o'clock 'Manhattan.' **1948** *New Yorker* 6 Nov. 65/1 The 'Dictionary of American English' traces the *Manhattan* only to 1894, but that is absurd, for I saw a justice of the Supreme Court of the United States drink one in a Washington barroom in 1886. **1949** *L.A. Times* 12 July 10/1 He has no preference as to type—Martinis, Manhattans, anything will do.

5. In combs.: (1) **Manhattan clam chowder,** (see quots.); (2) **cocktail,** a cocktail, sometimes sweetened, composed of whiskey, vermouth, and bitters; (3) **water,** the water used in New York City before the Croton River was utilized as a source of supply.

(1) **1940** EARLY *N. Eng. Sampler* 349 There is a terrible pink mixture (with tomatoes in it, and herbs) called Manhattan Clam Chowder, that is only a vegetable soup. **1949** *Chi. Tribune* 25 Feb. II. 4/4 One of the greatest gastronomic feuds is between devotees of New England clam chowder and Manhattan clam chowder (New England is made with milk, Manhattan with tomatoes). — (2) **1890** BIFF HALL *Turnover Club* 16 This order was as follows . . . the Actor, 'A Manhattan cocktail.' **1947** *Time* 10 March 106/1 The cause of world peace is advanced several notches when the Ambassador of X—— discloses to the Ambassador of Y—— the secret of his famous Manhattan Cocktails. — (3) **1862** DEVOE *Market Book* 210 In the month of June, 1800, some nine of the butchers in this market petitioned for the 'Manhattan Water' (which was just introduced through several of the streets) in this market, to make pickle and clean the market, and wish to bring it in at their own expense; which was granted to them.

Manhattaner mænˈhætn̩ɚ, *n.* =next. *Obs.* — **1851** A. O. HALL *Manhattaner* 82 *Manhattaner.* Is litigation attended here with much formality?

Manhattanese mænˌhætn̩ˈiz, *n.* One who lives on Manhattan Island; a New Yorker. Usu. collective.

1828 COOPER *Notions* I. 200 The New Yorkers (how much better is the word Manhattanese!) cherish the clumsy inconvenient entrances, I believe, as heir-looms of their Dutch progenitors. They are called 'stoops.' **1856** *Porter's Spirit of Times* 15 Nov. 176/2 We feel a degree of old Knickerbockic pride, at the continued prevalence of Base Ball as the National game of the region of the Manhattanese of these diggings. **1909** *Nation* 9 Sep. 238/3 Perhaps the most amusing thing in the book is an interpolated story based on a difference of opinion between New Englanders and Manhattanese on the subject of doughnuts and crullers.

Also **Manhattanite.**

1947 SESSIONS *Cities of Amer.* 25 If the average New Yorker is a Manhattanite, he's proud of the city, and of being a part of it. **1948** *Sat. Review* 27 March 5/2 Manhattanites never even felt it, and it was recorded only on the most delicately adjusted seismographs.

∗**mania,** *n.* As the last term in **Anglo-, gold, mulberry mania.**

∗**manifestation,** *n.* In spiritualism, the phenomenon by which the spirit is affirmed to make his presence known. *Obs.* — **1853** H. SPICER *Sights & Sounds* 88 In . . . 1850 . . . Cincinnati first became the scene of manifestations through recognised *media.* **1887** *Courier-Journal* 18 Jan. 1/7 Next came a spiritualistic seance which produced no 'manifestations.'

∗**manifest destiny.** The doctrine of the inevitability of Anglo-Saxon supremacy. A phrase used by those who believed that it was the destiny of the U.S. or of the Anglo-Saxon race to govern the entire Western Hemisphere. Often *cap.*

1845 in *Amer. Hist. Review* XXXII. (1927) 798 For the avowed object of thwarting our policy and hampering our power, limiting our greatness and checking the fulfilment of our manifest destiny to overspread the continent. **1870** O. LOGAN *Before Footlights* 260 The large number of railways . . . is a . . . sign of the great activity of the Universal Yankee Nation, which spreads its Aegis wings over our Manifest Destiny. **1923** R. MCELROY *Grover Cleveland* II. 73 On August 12th (1898), the very American flag which Grover Cleveland had caused to be hauled down was raised again [in Hawaii]. . . . 'Manifest Destiny' had triumphed at last. **1947** PAUL *Linden* 391 The standpatters . . . were sold on the 'white man's burden,' the 'little brown brother' in the Philippines, [and] the 'manifest destiny' of the United States as an imperial power.

attrib. **1856** *Spirit of Times* 13 Dec. 235/2 He was a 'manifest destiny' man.

Manifesto church. A Boston church, founded November 17, 1699, so called because of a manifesto issued by it setting forth its "aims and designs." *Obs.* — **1701** SEWALL *Diary* II. 48, I went to the Manifesto church to hear Mr. Adams. **1899** in *Pub. Col. Soc.* VI. 87 In 1699, he was a Founder of the Church in Brattle Square,—stigmatized as the 'Manifesto Church' by the Mathers, with whose church his own and his wife's family, the Hobbys, had previously been connected.

maninose ˈmænəˌnoz *n.* [See note.]

The spellings of this term are varied. See quots. The origin of it is unknown. It may be from an Indian word.

The soft clam, *Mya arenaria.* Cf. **long clam.**

1709 LAWSON *Carolina* 162 Man of Noses are a Shell-Fish commonly found amongst us. They are valued for increasing Vigour in Men, and making barren Women fruitful; but I think they have no need of that Fish; for the Women in *Carolina* are fruitful enough without their Helps. **1843** *Nat. Hist. N.Y., Zoology* V. 240 *Mya arenaria* . . . in some districts . . . still retains its ancient aboriginal appellation of *Maninose.* **1859** BARTLETT 84 The Soft Clam or Mananosay (*Mya arenaria*), obtained from the shores of tidal rivers by digging one or two feet in the loose sand. It has a long, extensible, cartilaginous snout, or proboscis, through which it ejects water. **1895** GERARD in *N.Y. Sun* 30 July, Mananosay, maninose (Maryland), man-of-noses (North Carolina), names for the round clam, from an Algonquian word meaning 'shellfish that one gathers by hand.'

manito ˈmænəˌto, *n.* Also **manitou, manetto,** etc. [Algonquian.] Among the Algonquin Indians, one of the deities or spirits, both good and bad, that dominate nature. Sometimes used allusively and figuratively.

1588 HARRIOT *Briefe & True Report* E2ᵛ They beleeue that there are many Gods which they call *Montoac,* but of different sortes and degrees; one onely chiefe and great God, which hath bene from all eternitie. **1671** *N.J. Archives* I Ser. I. 74 The Manetto hath kill'd my sister & I will go & kill the Christians. **1773** *Hist. Brit. Domin. N. Amer.* II. 241 They assert, there are two monetoes or spirits; that the one sends all the good things they have, and the other all the bad. **1828** *Western Mo. Rev.* Dec. 407 Their subordinate gods are called *manitous.* The manitou of waters is called *Michibichi,* whence, probably, Mississippi. **1946** *Progress* March 117/1 The Utes, in terror, prayed to their Great God, Manitou, whose gaze caused the giants and their beasts to turn to stone.

b. An image or idol of one of these deities.

1778 CARVER *Travels* 309 They place great confidence in their Manitous, or household gods, which they always carry with them. **1800** BOUCHER *Glossary* p. xlix, *Manitou;* an idol. **1949** *Chi. Tribune* 25 Sep. 18/4 Where the portages ended at lakes or rivers were manitous carved in the shape of human heads with caps of some bright material.

c. manito kump, (see quot.).

1944 FOOTNER *Rivers East. Shore* 137 They [the Nanticoke Indians] buried their dead and, after allowing the corpses to lie in the earth for some months, they exhumed them, cleaned the bones, and placed them in a sort of shrine they called 'manito-kump,' meaning 'place of the mystery-spirit.'

Mann Act. A congressional act of June 25, 1910, making it a federal offense to aid, cause, or in any way participate in the transportation across a state line of a girl or woman for immoral purposes. So called after Congressman Jas. R. Mann, of Illinois, who introduced the bill.

1913 *Survey* 23 Aug. 653/1 The Mann Act was, of course, upheld by the U.S. Supreme Court last February. **1924** *Collier's* 19 Jan. 21/1 What with the conflict an' confusion of divorce laws, almost every modern bridal trip comes under the Mann Act. **1949** *Real Detective* July 6/2 He was very probably liable for statutory rape and violation of the Mann Act.

∗**manned,** *a.* (See quot.) *Obs.* — **1818** H. B. FEARON *Sk. Amer.* 147 The ground was what is here called *manned;* that is, persons in the interest of the parties have written on their hat or breast, 'Federal Ticket,' or 'Democratic Ticket,' soliciting citizens as they approach the poll 'to vote their ticket.'

∗**manner,** *n.* As the last term in **border state, Boston, Indian manner.** Also, *pl.,* **plantation manners.**

mano ˈmɑno, *n.* [Sp. in similar sense. Cf. *mano de metate,—de piedra* in Santamaría.] A handstone used by Indians in grinding grain on a metate *q.v.*

1899 *Smithsonian Rep.* 37 The grinding-stone concordantly changes from a simple roller or crusher to a mano (or muller), and finally to a pestle, at first broad and short, but afterwards long and slender. **1922**

Mano and metate

Outing Nov. 83/1 Now she sits, or rather, squats, in a position impossible to one not trained from childhood, one foot extended to either side and her metate, or flat stone mill at her knees, grinding the parched wheat to a coarse meal or fine flour with her mano, or rubbing stone. **1947** *So. Sierran* March 4/1 A few metates (grinding bowls) and manos (grinders), arrow-points and other objects Mr. Edwards carefully charted.

∗**manor,** *n. S.* **1. manor house,** the dwelling on a manor plantation. **2. manor plantation,** the principal plantation of an ante-bellum landowner. Both *obs.*

(1) **1845** *Knickerb.* XXI. 42 He has but to call at the door of the manor-house next at hand . . . to receive all the kindness of an invited guest. **1897** *Outing* XXX. 70/1 He had heard of a manor-house back on the Rappahanock, in which lived a young girl. — (2) **1788** *Edenton* (N.C.) *Intelligencer* 9 April, The Manor Plantation will be Sold so as to Contain between two and three hundred Acres. **1806** *Pettigrew P.* (Univ. N.C. MS), I leave my dearly & well beloved Wife Mary Pettigrew in the full possetion of my House & mannor plantation.

∗**mansion,** *n.* As the last term in **executive, family, governor's, presidential mansion.**

manta ˈmæntə, *n. S.W.* and *W.* [Sp. in Amer. Sp. senses **1.** and **2.** shown here. An Amer. borrowing.]

1. Ordinary cotton cloth.

1848 *Santa Fe Republican* 16 Aug. 2/4 He also has on hand a well Assorted Stock of Merchandize, consisting of Lienzos, Manta, Prints [etc.]. **1858** IVES *Colo. River* (1861) 61 He promised before he left that evening that his people should bring some beans and corn to trade for manta and beads. **1946** UNDERHILL *First Penthouse Dwellers* 99 Dressed sometimes in moccasins and dark blue *manta,* . . . they bend over fireplace or stove.

b. (See quot.) *Rare.*

1887 *Outing* X. 5/1 We had some scrambling and sliding which cost me 200 pounds of flour, . . . and one manta, or pack cover.

2. (See quots.)

[**1860** *Eng. & Foreign Mining Gloss.,* Sp. Terms 109 *Manta,* a blanket, or horse cloth, used to contain ores or tools.] **1864** RAYMOND *6th Rep. Mines* 318 They pass through three rich streaks or *mantas.* **1890** *Cent.* 3617/1 *Manta,* . . . in mining, a blanket or sack of ore; a placer in situ. (Western U.S.)

manteca mæn'tekə, *n. S.W.* [Sp. in same sense. An Amer. borrowing.] Lard, butter, fat. — **1845** Green *Texian Exped.* 264 These sixty-two chunks . . . are boiled in water with six ounces of manteca, lard, with a sufficiency of salt and red pepper. **1890** *Cent. Mag.* Dec. 165 He brought me . . . a handful of *manteca*, which is used by Mexicans instead of lard.

mantelplace 'mæntl͵ples, *n. S.* A mantelpiece. — *a***1870** Simms *Last Wager* (De Vere), You have a very singular ornament for your mantle-place.

* **manual,** *a.* and *n.*

1. = **Jefferson's Manual.**

1900 *Cong. Rec.* 1 Feb. 1375/2 That is the only restriction which is laid down in the Manual, and there is no rule, of course, of the Senate relating to the matter.

2. *a.* In combs.: (1) **manual labor,** see as a main entry; (2) **training,** a course of training for the hands, esp. training in wood and metal work, basket-making, etc., also attrib.

(2) [**1880** *Bradstreet's* 11 Sep. 2/3 Washington University . . . has organized and opened an extensive department for the manual training of youths in . . . the mechanical manufacturing arts.] **1893** *Harper's Mag.* April 667/2 Manual training, as an adjunct to the schools, for the training of the eye and hand, he concluded to be . . . important. **1909** *Indian Laws & Tr.* III. 398 For equipment of manual training school, two thousand five hundred dollars. **1948–9** *N.W. Ohio Quart.* Winter 28 The lease for the use of the land called for the Manual Training School to furnish the pupils of the Central High School with manual training education.

As the last term in **sign, style manual.**

* **manualist,** *n.* One who uses manual methods to teach the deaf. — **1883** *Amer. Annals Deaf & Dumb* April 79 In the judgment of most manualists there can be no question that this fact alone, of prior speech, establishes such an important difference.

* **manual labor.** In combs.: (1) **manual labor college,** = **manual labor school** (*a*); (2) **school,** (*a*) a school in which students pay for their education in whole or part by doing manual labor, (*b*) an Indian school similarly conducted, see quot. 1866; (3) **tract,** a tract of land at an Indian manual labor school where labor is done.

(1) **1839** *Indiana H. Rep. Jrnl.* 210 [Resolved to appropriate] five hundred dollars . . . to aid the trustees of the Wabash manual labor college in the purchase of a library. **1853** *Harper's Mag.* Sep. 563/1 A cat . . . mischievously scratched up the corn and other seeds planted by the students of a manual-labor college situated in the neighborhood. — (2) (*a*) **1835** *S. Lit. Messenger* I. 274 *Manual Labor Schools* (on the Fellenberg plan) have not multiplied there [in New England], or grown in esteem, as might have been expected. **1895** *Dept. Agric. Yrbk. 1894* 87 Between 1830 and 1840 there was much talk about 'manual labor schools.' (*b*) **1850** Hines *Voyage* 95 At noon we arrived at . . . Chemekete, where the Oregon mission have commenced erecting mills, and where it is in contemplation to establish the Mission Manual Labor School. **1910** *Indian Laws & Tr.* II. III. 440 For support of two manual-labor schools, . . . ten thousand dollars. — (3) **1881** *Rep. Indian Affairs* p. lviii, The entire agency farm and mission manual-labor tract were inclosed in a substantial post and board fence.

b. Also (1) **manual labor institution,** (2) **plan,** (3) **system.**

(1) **1835** Hoffman *Far West* I. 6 The latter is a *Manual labour institution* (a term I need hardly explain to you), recently incorporated. — (2) **1837** W. Jenkins *Ohio Gaz.* 406 Here is a literary institution . . . on the manual labor plan in successful operation, where the silk culture is extensively engaged in. — (3) **1849** Chamberlain *Indiana Gazetteer* 48 From the beginning the manual labor system had prevailed, and the students . . . had paid a great part of their expense by their own labor.

* **manufactory,** *a.* Of or pertaining to the Manufacture Bank *q.v.*, or to its currency. *Obs.*

1740 in *Pub. Col. Soc.* VI. 171 A Letter to the Merchant in London, To Whom is Directed A Printed Letter relating to the Manufactory Undertaking, dated New England, Boston February 21st 1740. **1741** *Manchester Rec.* II. 34 Voted that manefactory mony shall pay town charges if it hath a Corincey. **1742** in Felt *Mass. Currency* (1839) 113 Some of our fellow-partners . . . have not nor will pay in their several shares and parts of the said Land Bank or Manufactory Bills. **1767** Hutchinson *Hist. Mass.* II. 392 A general dread of drawing in all the paper money . . . disposed a great part of the province to favor . . . the land bank or manufactory scheme. **1895** in *Pub. Col. Soc.* III. 11 These payments were to be made in Manufactory Notes, or in hemp, flax, cordage, bar-iron, cast-iron, and certain other enumerated commodities.

manufactural ͵mænjə'fæktʃərəl, *a.* Pertaining to industrial production through factories. *Obs.* — **1789** Morse *Amer. Geog.* 91 Pennsylvania has confessedly taken the lead . . . in manufactural improvements.

* **manufacture,** *n.* As the last term in **infant, steam-bonnet manufacture.**

* **manufacture,** *v. tr.* To grind (grain). *Obs.*

1771 Washington *Diaries* II. 12 Began to Manufacture my Wheat with the Water of Piney Branch. **1774** Fithian *Journal* I. 111 Mr. Carter's Merchant Mill begins to run to-day—She is calculated to manufacture 25,000 Bushels of Wheat a Year. **1834** Peck *Gaz. Illinois* 273 Lebannon has two steam mills, one for sawing lumber, and the other for manufacturing grain.

Manufacture Bank. The Massachusetts land bank of 1740, the bills of which were redeemable in twenty years in such produce and manufactured products as were enumerated in the scheme, i.e., cast-iron, bayberry wax, tanned leather, cordwood, etc. *Obs.* Cf. **land bank bill.**

By act of Parliament the scheme was stopped in 1741. For a full discussion of it see *Amer. Econ Assoc.* 3 Ser. II. No. 2, and *Pub. Col. Soc. Mass.*, III. 2–40.

1742 in Felt *Mass. Currency* (1839) 113 We the subscribers were partners in that unlucky and unfortunate scheme, called the Land or Manufacture Bank.

manufactured tobacco. Tobacco that has been processed and is ready for use. *Obs.* Cf. **Missouri manufactured.**

1835 *S. Lit. Messenger* I. 259 Among the items brought down may be enumerated . . . 2,230,900 lbs. of manufactured tobacco. **1862** *Statutes at Large* XII. 463 On tobacco, cavendish, plug, twist, fine cut, and manufactured of all descriptions . . . [there shall be a tax of] thirty cents per pound. **1884** Harris *Mingo* 87 'Manufactured' tobacco, in contradistinction to the natural leaf.

manufactury ͵mænjə'fæktʃərɪ, *n.* Manufacture. *Obs.* — **1721** *Mass. H. Rep. Jrnl.* II. 372 Encouraging the Produce and Manufactories of the Province. **1778** *N.H. Hist. Soc. Coll.* IX. 287 That all kinds of American manufactories & internal produce . . . be estimated at rates not exceeding 75 per Cent advance.

manumissionist ͵mænjə'mɪʃənɪst, *n.* An abolitionist. *Rare.* — **1841** J. Sturge *Visit to U.S. in 1841* cxvi, The writer of this pamphlet uniformly couples 'ultra-slave-holders' and 'northern manumissionists' in the same censure.

* **manure,** *n.* In combs.: (1) **manure distributor,** = next; (2) **spreader,** a device for spreading manure; (3) **tank,** a cesspool.

(1) **1857** *Rep. Comm. Patents 1856* I. 302 *Improved Manure Distributor.*—Patented October 14, 1856. . . . The amount of manure

One type of manure spreader

escaping through the open bottom can be regulated. — (2) **1888** *Vt. Agric. Rep.* X. 42 Implements . . . which reduce the cost of farm operating [include] . . . the hay tedder and the manure-spreader. **1949** *Time* 28 Mar. 21/3 Factory-bright tractors roared across the fields; loaded manure spreaders clumped and rumbled. — (3) **1857** Vaux *Villas* 46 We must . . . resort to the plan of a cess-pool or manure tank.

As the last term in **barn, chip, fish, lot, pond, swamp manure.**

many-millionaire. A multimillionaire. *Rare.* — **1893** *Harper's Mag.* March 498 That would be but little more unexpected than that a many-millionaire should use his means in this way.

manzanita ͵mænzə'nitə, *n.* [Sp. in Amer. Sp. sense shown here.] Any of various shrubs of the West Coast of the genus *Arctostaphylos*, esp. *A. pungens* and *A. tomentosa.* Also the fruit of such a shrub or of the madrona *q.v.* Cf. **mountain mahogany 2. a.**

1846 Bryant *California* (1848) 235 We have met occasionally with a reddish berry called by the Californians, *manzanita*, little apple,

1857 *33d Congress* 2 Sess. Sen. Ex. Doc. No. 78 VI. III. *Arctostaphylos glauca*. . . . Manzanita. . . . The manzanita has received the Spanish name which it bears from a fancied resemblance of its fruit to a little apple. 1946 *Sierra Club Bul.* Dec. 19 In fact some rare herbaceous species are not seen except after burns and it is only in the ashes of their parents that manzanitas and mountain lilacs germinate extensively.

attrib. 1851 *Harper's Mag.* June 101/1 Bruin . . . was seated . . . in front of a manzanita bush, making a repast on his favorite berry. 1869 BRACE *New West* xi. 144 These all had Manzanita apples and acorns, for stores. 1907 WHITE *Arizona Nights* 68 For the next day we planned a bear hunt afoot, far up a manzañita cañon. 1917 ABBOTT *Recollections* 192 The Indians make water-tight baskets, into which they put their food to cook,—whether it be beef, turkeys, or manzanita berries and grasshoppers. 1949 *Pacific Discovery* Jan.–Feb. 11/1 Preferred foods at this season were acorns, manzanita berries, and assorted greens.

* **map,** *n. To wipe off the map,* to annihilate. Also fig. *Colloq.* or *slang.* — 1904 W. H. SMITH *Promoters* 54 When she [Carthage] wouldn't let up, the only thing left was to wipe her off the map! 1928 FOY & HARLOW *Clowning Thro' Life* 104 The citizens of Dodge . . . had been hoping that the home boys would be permitted to wipe the D. & R.G. off the map.

As the last term in **canal, flat, section, weather map.**

* **maple,** *n.*

1. In combs.: (1) **maple borer,** (see quot.); (2) **bush,** (*a*) a shrubby maple, esp. *Acer spicatum,* (*b*) a grove of sugar maples; (3) **forest,** a forest in which the chief growth is maple trees; (4) **-leaved,** see as a main entry; (5) **orchard,** an orchard or grove of sugar maples; (6) **swamp,** a swamp in which the predominant growth is maple; (7) **timber,** timber consisting of maple trees, also **maple-timbered,** *a.*; (8) **worm,** the larva of a moth found on maple trees, see **green-striped maple worm.**

(1) 1890 *Cent.* 3623/1 *Maple-borer,* . . . one of the different insects which bore the wood of maples. — (2) (*a*) 1821 SCHOOLCRAFT *Narr. Travels* 162 Bark scraped off the small red twigs of the acer spicatum, or maple bush [is used by Indians as a substitute for tobacco]. 1845 LINCOLN *Botany* App. 69/1 *Acer spicatum,* (Mountain maple bush). (*b*) 1844 BROWN in *Edinburgh Jrnl.* I. 264 Mr Jones had also a maple bush, or a small wood containing sugar maple trees. 1919 CUNNINGHAM *Chronicle* 77 To the west, there is the little creek far down in its basin—Carle creek, where the old water mill used to stand—and beyond it the big maple bush, where three thousand pails are set out at sap-running time. — (3) 1840 *Knickerb.* XVI. 267 A small and beautiful lake [with] . . . a rich tract of maple forest on one side.

(5) 1868 BEECHER *Norwood* 399 The woods and maple orchards were filled with sounds of industry. 1884 *N.Y. Wkly. Tribune* 5 March 11/2 The owners of maple orchards will not be morally less responsible if they degrade their goods with this cheap diluent. 1949 *Highway Traveler* Feb. 17/1 The maple orchard owner may have you place covers over the buckets as you hang them. — (6) 1667 *Providence Rec.* V. 317 Standing on the west Side of a Maple Swampe. 1724 *N.H. Probate Rec.* II. 203 Twenty acres of swamp Land that was Layed out to me . . . in the mapell swamp so called. 1861 NEWELL *Orpheus C. Kerr* 326 A line about as regular as so many trees in a maple swamp. — (7) 1849 *Pres. Mess. Congress* II. 631 At 7½ a.m., went over good maple-timbered land to corner. 1854 MRS. KIRKLAND *Western Clearings* 3 He had purchased fine farming land and maple timber. — (8) 1873 *Winfield* (Kans.) *Courier* 24 July 1/5, I find the maple worm is a peculiarly Kansas institution. . . . Its body is constructed like a joint snake.

2. Designating products obtained or derived from the sap of sugar-maple trees, as (1) **maple beer,** (2) **candy,** (3) **crop,** (4) **honey,** (5) **molasses,** (6) **products,** (7) **sauce,** (8) **sirup,** cf. **tree maple sirup,** (9) **vinegar,** (10) **water,** (11) **wax,** (12) **wine.**

(1) 1788 in *Amer. Museum* IV. 350/1 *Maple beer.*—To every 4 gallons of water (while boiling) add a quart of maple melasses. 1857 D. H. STROTHER *Virginia Illust.* I. 23 The table was spread with the best in the house—cold bread and meat . . . maple beer. — (2) 1840 *N.Y. Mirror* 4 April 37/2 Your great dealers in Newtown pippins and maple candy tell you, to be sure, that they can't afford their *accommodations.* 1867 *Harper's Wkly.* 11 May 295/4 The 'Maple-Candy Man' brought his box and handed it around. 1947 *Chr. Sci. Monitor* 1 March III. 5 But to those who tap the maple trees, collect and boil the sap . . . for the lovers of maple sugar or candy there is a tidy sum to pay them for their work. — (3) 1939 WOLCOTT *Yankee Cook Book* 344 Today, thirty per cent of this country's maple crop comes from Vermont. There is a tendency for maple sugar to become stronger in flavor the farther north the region in which the trees grow. — (4) 1850 *Bentley's Miscellany* XXVII. 159 The uncrystalizable sugar which remains is called 'maple honey,' and with the addition of a small portion of alcohol, will keep for months without turning sour. This is esteemed as a great delicacy, and is much used in the consumption of buckwheat pancakes. 1941 *L.A.* Map 307 Maple honey, the older term for maple syrup.

(5) 1788 in *Amer. Museum* IV. 350/1 *Maple melasses* . . . may be made in three ways. 1857 *Knickerb.* Jan. 38 My more ordinary dissipation didn't generally go beyond buying two or three pennies' worth of . . . maple-molasses candy. 1930 *Lerna* (Ill.) *Wkly. Eagle* 21 March 4/1 Friday evening Geo. F. Grimes paid a visit to Lerna and brought along with him some of his famous maple molasses. — (6) 1939 WOLCOTT *Yankee Cook Book* 345 Maple products have been made for 45 years. — (7) 1939 WOLCOTT *Yankee Cook Book* 211 Maple sauce for vanilla ice cream. . . . Boil maple syrup. . . . Cool slightly and pour over ice cream. — (8) 1849 in *Mo. Hist. Soc., Glimpses of Past* I. 5 At the different houses they received sugar, coffee, lard, candles, flour, maple syrup [etc.]. 1949 *Chi. D. News* 12 May 14/3 Artur Rubinstein's piano playing makes me feel as if I were swimming around in a barrel of maple syrup. — (9) 1788 in *Amer. Museum* IV. 350/2 *Maple vinegar.*—Expose the sap of the maple to the open air, in the sun, and in a short time it will become vinegar.

(10) [1703 LAHONTAN *New Voyages to N.-Amer.* I. (1703) 249 Of this Sap [from maple tree] they make Sugar and Syrup, which is so valuable, that there can't be a better remedy for fortifying the Stomach. 'Tis but few of the Inhabitants [of Canada] that have the patience to make Mapple-Water.] 1886 Z. F. SMITH *Kentucky* 84 [They] visited a neighboring sugar-camp to drink of the maple water. — (11) 1883 SHIELDS *Rustlings in Rockies* 257 Oh, what a delicious bon bon is a dish of warm maple wax, pure and fresh from the woods! 1947 *Amer. Sp.* April 152 Maple wax. Sirup boiled to a density equal to that of hard sugar, but without stirring, and then poured over snow or ice to secure immediate cooling. — (12) 1788 in *Amer. Museum* IV. 350/1 *Maple wine.*—Boil four, five, or six gallons of sap (according to its strength) to one, and add yeast in proportion to the quantity you make.

As the last term in **ash, big-leaf, black, broad-leafed, broad-leaved, curl, curled, curly, English, goose-foot, green, hard, Japan, large-leaved California, low, moose, mountain, red, river, rock, round-leaved, scarlet, silver, soft, striped, sugar, swamp, sweet, upland, vine, water, white maple.**

maple-leaved ˈmepl̩ˌlivd, *n.* Used in the names of plants (see quots.).

1785 MARSHALL *Amer. Grove* 77 Maple-leaved Liquidamber Tree or Sweet Gum. 1797 IMLAY *Western Territory* (ed. 3) 277 The liquidambar, copalm, or maple-leaved storax, . . . affords a balm, the virtues of which are infinite. 1813 MUHLENBERG *Cat. Plants* 48 Maple-leaved Hawthorn. 1843 TORREY *Flora N.Y.* I. 306 *Viburnum acrifolium.* . . . Maple-leaved arrow-wood. . . . Dry open woods; very common. *Fl.* June *Fr.* September. 1907 HODGE *Amer. Indians* I. 394 *Dockmackie.* A name of the maple-leaved arrowwood (*Viburnum acerifolium*).

maple sugar.

1. Sugar obtained by evaporating the sap of certain maples.

[1705 HARRIS *Navigantium atque itinerantium* II. 929 The Maple Trees . . . yields a Sap. . . . Of this Sap they make Sugar and Syrup, which is so valuable, that there can't be a better Remedy for fortyfying the Stomach.] 1720 *Phil. Trans.* XXXI. 27 Maple Sugar is made of the juice of the Upland Maple, or Maple Trees that grow upon the Highlands. 1832 WILLIAMSON *Maine* I. 109 The method of making maple sugar . . . is learned from the Aborigines. 1947 *Amer. Sp.* April 152 Maple sugar. A further boiling of maple sirup produces a hard or creamy mass known as sugar. Usually molded into cakes.

b. A brown or brownish color.

1934 WEBSTER. 1936 *Sears Cat.* 397 [Colors:] Rose Pink, Maple Sugar, Alice Blue.

2. In combs. in which the meaning is obvious or is explained by the quots., as (1) **maple-sugar butternut candy,** (2) **cake,** (3) **camp,** (4) **capital,** (5) **eat,** (6) **industry,** (7) **land,** (8) **maker,** (9) **making,** also attrib., (10) **party,** (11) **sauce,** (12) **state,** (13) **works.**

(1) 1904 WALLER *Wood-Carver* 69 I'm waiting for the 'maple-sugar-butternut' candy and the spruce gum. — (2) 1941 LEE *Stagecoach North* 113 Their real unconfessed interest was focused on maple sugar cakes, dried whortleberries, fiddle music, and wild geese. 1949 *Downers Grove* (Ill.) *Rep.* 31 March 11/4 Maple sugar cakes (100 per cent pure) were made and real maple syrup was put into small bottles. — (3) 1884 ROE *Nature's Story* 156 We'll improvise a maple-sugar camp of the New England style a hundred years ago. — (4) 1943 *Nat. Geog. Mag.* April 405 Only town of its name in the United States, St. Johnsbury [Vt.] is the maple-sugar capital of the Nation.

(5) 1907 *Springfield W. Republican* 9 May 16 The Holyoke canoe club opened the river year with a maple-sugar eat at their club-house. — (6) 1880 *Vt. Agric. Rep.* VI. 112 My object is to give a brief history of the maple-sugar industry. — (7) 1797 IMLAY *Western Territory* (ed. 3) 151 A single family, . . . on the maple-sugar lands, between the Delaware and Susquehanna, made 1800 lbs. of maple-sugar in one

season. — (8) **1880** *Vt. Agric. Rep.* VI. 113 The present duty of maple sugar-makers is to educate consumers up to a higher standard. — (9) **1857** *Lawrence* (Kans.) *Republican* 11 June 4 Mr. Sloven electrified his family . . . with the announcement that he was going into the maple-sugar-making business. **1874** *Dept. Agric. Rep. 1873* 475 This letter is appended to the discussion on the subject of maple-sugar making.

(10) **1939** WOLCOTT *Yankee Cook Book* 347 For a real Vermont maple sugar party, doughnuts and pickles are necessary to complete the menu. — (11) **1939** WOLCOTT *Yankee Cook Book* 197 Maple sugar sauce. ½ pound maple sugar, 4 tablespoons hot water, ¼ pound butter. — (12) **1935** MITCHELL *America* 155, I wanted to buy some Vermont maple sugar to send to England and I wanted to buy it in Vermont so that I could truthfully say it came from the maple sugar state. — (13) **1814** *Niles' Reg.* VI. 152/1 A vermont statement of the maple sugar works is [etc.].

Maqua ˈmɑkwə, *n.* [f. the same source as Mohawk *q.v.*] A Mohawk warrior. Also attrib.

1616 in *N.Y. Doc. Col. Hist.* (1856) I. (map), Maquaas. **1690** *Mass. H.S. Coll.* 4 Ser. V. 258 Five of the Maquas are dead of the small-pox. **1826** COOPER *Mohicans* iii, Do the Maquas dare to leave the print of their moccasins in these woods? **1906** *Olde Ulster* July 203 A chief of the Maqua nation named Quaynant visited my father and they agreed that I should go with Quaynant to their country to learn the Maqua language.

maracock ˈmærəˌkɑk, *n.* [See **maypop.**] The maypop or the plant that produces it. *Obs.*

1612 SMITH *Virginia* 12 A fruit that the Inhabitants call Maracocks, . . . is a pleasant wholsome fruit much like a lemond. **1633** GERERD *Herball* 1591 Of the Maracoc or Passion-floure. . . . This Plant . . . is the same which the Virginians call *Maracoc.* **1705** BEVERLEY *Virginia* II. 17 The same Use is made also of . . . Squashes, Maycocks, Maracocks, Melons [etc.]. **1896** P. A. BRUCE *Econ. Hist. Va.* I. 98 In addition, there were muskmelons, . . . maracocks or mayapples, beans and pumpkins.

marais mɑˈre, *n.* [F. in the same sense.] (See quots.)

1839 *Maysville* (Ky.) *Eagle* 18 Dec. 1/3 Among these is one appropriatly named 'Clear Lake,' or the *Grand Marais.* **1853** in *Amer. Sp.* XIX. 44 Three miles below was a *marais* or slough. **1896** CLENDENIN *Fla. Parishes E. La.* 177 The bayous, 'marais' and 'coulees' that meander through or extend across this 'bluff' area are very unlike the hastily developed drainage system of this formation in West Feliciana. [**1945** G. STEWART *Names on the Land* 212 *Marais* they [the French] said, not for a marsh, but for a pool.]

maraud məˈrɔd, *n.* [f. **maraud, v.*] A raid. *On the maraud,* on a plundering expedition. *Obs.*

1837 IRVING *Bonneville* I. 136 While thus encamped, they were still liable to the marauds of the Blackfeet. **1855** —— *Wolfert's Roost* 18 He had an Indian's capacity in discovering when the enemy was on the maraud. **1884** *St. Nicholas* XI. 534 Certain neighboring tribes . . . make maraud upon them.

***marble,** *n.* **1. marble cake,** a cake made of both light and dark batter to produce a marble-like mottle. **2. marble yard,** a yard in which marble is stored or worked upon.

(1) **1882** F. E. OWENS *Cook Book* 174 Marble Cake. Light part—2 cups of white sugar. . . . Dark part—2 cups of brown sugar, 1 cup of molasses [etc.]. **1941** FARMER *Boston Cook Book* 635 Marble Cake. Add 1 square chocolate, melted, to half the mixture [for two-egg cake]. Fill cake pans by spoonfuls, alternating plain and chocolate mixtures. — (2) **1850** CIST *Cincinnati* 218 Seven marble yards and shops. **1870** MARK TWAIN *Sk. New & Old* 219 You have . . . littered up the floor with chips off your hams till the place looks like a marble-yard.

As the last term in **Athens, bird's-eye, candy, chocolate, dove, Kansas, Missouri, Potomac, shell, Tennessee marble.**

***marbled,** *a.* Used in the specific names of American (1) birds and (2) fishes (see quots.).

(1) **1828** BONAPARTE *Synopsis* 423 The Marbled Guillemot, *Uria marmorata,* . . . inhabits the north-western coasts of America. **1839** PEABODY *Mass. Birds* 371 The Marbled Godwit, *Limosa fedoa.* . . . In August they appear in large numbers, and many are shot for the table. **1909** WEBSTER 1317/1 *M[arbled] murrelet,* a small murrelet (*Brachyramphus marmoratus*) of the Pacific coast of North America. **1946** *So. Sierran* Oct. 4/1 Nearer shore were coots, grebes, the marbled godwit, and the Hudsonian curlew with his long, curved bill.

(2) **1884** GOODE *Fisheries* I. 173 The best known species [of the devil-fishes] are the Marbled Angler, *Pterophryne histrio,* and the Sea Bat, *Malthe vespertilio.* **1896** JORDAN & EVERMANN *Check-List Fishes* 374 *Mycteroperca bonaci.* Marbled Rockfish. West Indies, Pensacola to Brazil. **1903** T. H. BEAN *Fishes N.Y.* 89 *Ameiurus nebulosus marmoratus.* . . . Marbled Cat. . . . [Found in] lowland streams and swamps from New York to southern Indiana and Florida.

Marblehead turkey. [*Marblehead,* Mass.] (See quot.) *Jocular.* Cf. **Nantucket.** — **1859** BARTLETT 264 *Marblehead Turkeys,* cod-fish. So called in Massachusetts.

marbleized ˈmɑrblˌaɪzd, *a.* Colored in imitation of marble.

1868 *Mich. Agric. Rep.* VII. 355 J. B. Billings, Detroit, [displayed] specimens of marbleized slate, (mantels and panels). **1892** *Harper's Mag.* May 936/2 Strongly scented sweet soap of a marbleized reddish color lay wrapped in tin-foil. **1948** *Savings News* Nov. 12/2 Replace the upholstery with glass or dark marbleized or plain linoleum for a bedroom or small coffee table.

***march,** *n.*[1]

1. (See quots.)

1857 *Hoyles' Games* (Amer. ed.) 285 In case the party who makes the trump secures . . . all five tricks, it is called a 'march,' and counts two points. **1944** *Pocket Book of Games* 182 If he takes all five tricks, he scores a *march,* worth 2 points.

2. *W.* A cattle drive. *Rare.*

1869 *Overland Mo.* III. 126 Two men often 'bunch' on the march i.e., unite their herds for convenience in driving.

3. *march to the sea,* during the Civil War, the march of General Sherman's Union Army from Atlanta to Savannah, Georgia, November 15 to December 21, 1864.

1865 G. W. NICHOLS *Great March* 15 The March to the Sea . . . fills us with admiration . . . for the gallant heroes who pushed forward day by day, bearing . . . the Stars and Stripes. **1901** CHURCHILL *Crisis* 478 On our march to the sea, if the orders were ever given to turn northward, 'the boys' would get very much depressed.

4. *March of Dimes,* a drive for collecting funds for the aid of poliomyelitis victims.

1945 *Bristol Enterprise* 15 Feb. 4/1 (*heading*), March of Dimes. **1949** *Courier-Journal* (Louisville, Ky.) 3 Sep. 10/2 The campaign will be entirely apart from the foundation's regular March of Dimes appeal which will take place as usual next January.

***March,** *n.*[2] **1. March court,** a court session held in March. **2. March meeting,** in New England, the annual town meeting held in March.

(1) **1836** *S. Lit. Messenger* II. 302 But if court day be thus important, how much more so is March court! — (2) **1728** *Boston Rec.* 222 If the Money apropriated . . . at the last march meeting be Insoffcient . . . Henry Gibbon will advance and pay what falls Short. **1841** *Greene Co. Torchlight* (Xenia, O.) 19 Aug. 1/5 His people, . . . to show their *spunk,* on a certain March meeting, elected him *hog-reeve.* **1944** HOLTON *Yankees* 35 Town meeting was a big event in our community when I was growing up. We called it March Meeting then, and would have continued to do so if some busybody hadn't succeeded in shifting the date back to February.

Marcylite ˈmɑrsɪˌlaɪt, *a.* [Gen. R. B. *Marcy* (1812–87).] A decomposed form of copper pyrites. — **1853** in MARCY *Explor. Red River* (1854) 145 On subjecting the black ore to a close investigation, it proves to be a substance hitherto undescribed, and it affords me much pleasure to name it, in honor of the very enterprising and successful explorer to whom mineralogy is indebted for the discovery, *Marcylite.*

Mardi gras ˈmɑrdɪˌgrɑ, *n.* [F. ("fat Tuesday") in same sense.] Shrove Tuesday, the last day of carnival as celebrated in New Orleans; the festival ending on this day. Also attrib.

1832 *Boston Transcript* 13 June 1/3 Yesterday was '*Mardi Gras*'—the last day of the reign of Folly. **1899** ADE *Fables* in *Slang* (1900) 148 His Father was too serious a Man to get out in Mardi-Gras Clothes and hammer a Ball from one Red Flag to another. **1947** *Nation* 12 July 40/1 They come for the special holiday excitement, to take part in a Mardi Gras centering in a horse race.

b. A carnival or festival in imitation of the annual celebration in New Orleans.

1904 *N.Y. Ev. Post* 17 Sep. 3 At a special meeting of the Coney Island business men $25,000 was subscribed to pay the expenses of the semi-centennial celebration and mardi gras on September 21. **1930** *Dixon* (Ill.) *Ev. Tribune* 24 Sep. 1 (*heading*), Mardi Gras, Fireworks End Centennial Tonight. **1941** Z. GOLD in *Sat. Ev. Post* 15 March 14 Mardi Gras at Coney.

***mare,** *n.* As the last term in **bell, buggy, calico, devil's, grade, Morgan, Narragansett pacing, nightmare.**

***margin,** *v.* **1.** *tr.* and *intr. To margin up,* to deposit more margin with a broker when a stock is falling. **2.** *tr.* To cause the price of (a commodity) to come *down* by selling on margins.

(1) **1870** W. W. FOWLER *Ten Yrs. in Wall Street* 85 Put up your margin, say five hundred on a hundred shares, then keep margined up or they'll sell you out. **1902** NORRIS *Pit* (1922) x, It's always better

to keep our trades margined up. — (2) **1887** *Courier-Journal* 19 Feb. 7/4 Wheat is margined down under 75¢.

∗**marginal,** *a.* Of or pertaining to a margin in a stock market. — **1870** MEDBERY *Men Wall St.* 59 Nor is there any dissimilarity between the conditions of purchase in complete and in marginal transactions. *Ib.* 62 The broker . . . demands of his customer either Solid deposit of money or stocks, or marginal deposit of money.

Maricopa ˌmɑrəˈkopə, *n.* [The name, of unknown significance, applied to these Indians by the Pima. The pl. is usu. in *-s* (see quots.), but Hodge uses *Maricopa* with a plural verb.] *pl.* "An important Yuman tribe which since early in the 19th century has lived with and below the Pima and from about lat. 35° to the mouth of Rio Gila, s. Ariz." (Hodge).

1849 HAYES *Pioneer Notes* (1929) 45 The Maricopas, the interpreter says, number a thousand, in three villages. **1908** CURTIS *N. Amer. Indians* II. 81 The Maricopas are a small tribe of Yuman stock living as neighbors of the Pima. **1942** CASTETTER & BELL *Pima & Papago Agric.* 102 According to tradition, the first Pima pumpkin (called *rsâs katuk*) were obtained from the Yumas and Maricopas.

attrib. **1851** MILES *Overland Exped.* 23 Continued on our march to a village of Indian huts of the Maracopas tribe.

marijuana ˌmærɪˈwɑnə, *n.* [Amer. Sp. *marihuana*, in same sense.] The hemp, *Cannabis sativa*, or its leaves, used as a powerful narcotic, esp. when smoked in cigarettes.

1894 *Scribner's Mag.* May 596/2 [The] 'toloachi,' [and] the 'mariguan,' . . . [are] used by discarded women for the purpose of wreaking a terrible revenge upon recreant lovers. **1923** W. SMITH *Little Tigress* 102 (Bentley), The cockroach is unable to stagger around any more because he has no more marijuana to smoke. **1946** *Fort Collins Coloradoan* 11 June 1/7 One sack of seed, a sack containing dried plants, which may have been harvested only a few days ago and about 50 tobacco tins for packaging of the marijuana were obtained this morning.

attrib. and *transf.* **1935** *Amer. Mercury* Aug. 426/1 Such practices as adultery, marihuana smoking, gambling, . . . and rowdyism seldom worry the investigator. **1948** *Sat. Review* 19 June 24/3 One of the most cogent reasons for the success of the comics, is namely, that they are the marijuana of parents as well as of their offspring. **1949** *L.A. Times* 5 April 2/3 Two half-smoked marijuana cigarettes and debris from an ash tray indicating that other marijuana cigarettes had been smoked also were found.

∗**marine,** *a.* In combs.: (1) **marine armor,** a diver's suit, *obs.;* (2) ∗**Corps,** see as a main entry; (3) **court,** a federal district court trying a case under maritime law; (4) **hospital,** a hospital established by the federal government for seamen, also attrib.; (5) **railway,** an inclined railway running into the water, and provided with a cradle in which a vessel may be hauled; (6) **settlement,** (see quot.), *obs.*

(1) **1831** *Knickerb.* Oct. 373 One of the most interesting practical exhibitions . . . was that of the 'marine armor,' off the battery. **1840** *Niles' Reg.* 4 April 80/2 Mr. Taylor, with his marine armour, has succeeded in finding the wreck of the Lexington. — (3) **1830** *Williams's N.Y. Ann. Reg.* 238 The Justices of the Marine Court in the city of New York, are authorized to hold a court therein to be called 'The Marine court of the city of New York.' *a***1882** in MCCABE *New York* 122 The Marine Court has civil jurisdiction to the amount of $1000. — (4) **1798** *Statutes at Large* I. 606 Directors of the marine hospital of the United States. **1902** *Ib.* XXXII. 1. 75 The Secretary of the Treasury is authorized and directed to purchase . . . [land] for a marine hospital at Savannah, Georgia.

(5) **1824** *Mass. Laws* 319 Stephen Phillips, William P. Richardson, [and others] . . . are made a body politic . . . , for the purpose of making and supporting a marine railway in the town of Salem. **1874** KNIGHT 439/2 [The] Canal-lift . . . may be of the nature of the slip or marine railway, such as used on the Morris and Essex Canal, N.J. — (6) **1843** OLIVER *Eight Months* 178 A few miles to the north-east of Troy [?Illinois], we entered on the Marine Settlement. This settlement, which is situated on a large and beautiful prairie, consists of grants, which, we are told, had been made to retired officers of the American navy.

∗**Marine Corps.** An organization, authorized by Congress Nov. 10, 1775, made up of men serving on shipboard but trained as land soldiers, used esp. as landing forces.

1798 *Statutes at Large* I. 594 An act for the establishing and organizing a marine corps. **1807** *Ann. 10th Cong.* 1 Sess. I. 509 He grew importunate on the subject of the Marine corps, and asked me . . . how the Marine corps stood. **1834** *Sun* (N.Y.) 15 May 2/2 The Hon. Mr. Leigh of the Senate of the United States, accompanied by Col. Henderson of the Marine Corps, is on a visit to Virginia. **1949** *Chi. D. News* 4 Oct. 1/3 A former Navy and Marine Corps public relations officer.

∗**marionette,** *n.* **1.** (See quots.) **2. marionette theater,** a theater in which puppet shows are given.

(1) **1838** AUDUBON *Ornith. Biog.* IV. 217 Buffel-headed Duck . . . being known to these different districts by the names of . . . Marionette, Dipper, and Die-dipper. **1917** *Birds of Amer.* I. 140 Buffle-Head. *Charitonetta albeola.* . . . Also called Conjuring Duck; Marionette; Dipper [etc.]. — (2) **1878** *Harper's Mag.* Feb. 336/1 Along the beach [at Atlantic City] . . . there are photograph galleries, peep-shows, marionette theatres [etc.].

mariposa ˌmærəˈposə, *n.* [Sp., butterfly.]

1. (See quot. 1860.) *Obs.*

1860 in M. W. DISHER *Cowells in Amer.* (1934) 5 And have made two shawls . . . and one 'Maraposa' or Opera hood. **1862** *Harper's Mag.* Oct. 607/1 Constant relays of arrivals were successively denuding themselves of 'clouds' . . . 'Mariposas' and other dainty feminine wraps.

2. Short for Mariposa lily or Mariposa tulip *qq.v.*

[**1888** LINDLEY *Calif. of South* 330 Mariposa is the Indian word for butterfly, and butterfly-like, these flowers are poised upon their delicate stems, each cup a chalice, and every petal irised at its heart.] **1934** WHITE *Folded Hills* 198 Here also were . . . yuccas; chollas; mariposas; cascara and artemisia bushes from the mountains. **1947** *Nat. Geog. Mag.* July 60/1 And the Mariposas . . . mostly spurn permanent sanctuary with humans.

3. a. Mariposa lily, any one of various western plants of the genus *Calochortus.* **b. Mariposa tulip,** =prec.

(a) **1882** *Garden* 30 Sep. 291/1 The Mariposa Lily. **1947** *Mazama* Dec. 35/2 One of the most unusual was the Mariposa Lily found in California. — (b) **1869** MUIR *First Summer in Sierra* (1911) 43 Back from the bank most of the sunshine reaches the ground, calling up the grasses and flowers in glorious array, . . . monardella, Mariposa tulips, lupines, . . . glad children of light. **1920** RICE *Calif. Wild Flowers* 27 It would probably be more correct to say Mariposa Tulip than Mariposa Lily, for botanists place them in the tulip family.

∗**mark,** *n.* In criminal argot, a victim or intended victim. *Slang.*

1889 *Portland* (Ore.) *Mercury* 29 June 1/7 He is always quick to take a trick, and can size up a 'mark' as readily as any member of the profession. **1901** FLYNT *World of Graft* 165 Jervis Wilson and his 'mob' had a 'mark'—in their case, an easy bank to rob—in one of the Northern States. **1949** *Sat. Ev. Post* 17 Sep. 83/2, I usually get friendly with a mark before playing him, talk about the weather and then inquire in a casual way where he's from.

As the last term in **ax, corner, cost, country, dollar, double, easy, hash, head, log, noon, scalp, shoal, side, sleigh mark.**

∗**mark,** *v.*

1. *To mark up,* to raise (the price of goods).

1869 *Amer. Naturalist* III. 3 The prices of venison and other game was so far 'marked up' that gold . . . was charged for salmon. **1902** LORIMER *Lett. Merchant* 52 The clerks all knocked off their regular work and started in to mark up prices. **1948** *Sat. Ev. Post* 10 July 23/1 We can't mark up what we have to sell.

transf. **1947** *Sat. Ev. Post* 1 Feb. 56/4 Preference is given to veterans, who get a five-point mark-up on their exam.

b. *To mark down,* to lower (the price of goods).

1875 *Chi. Tribune* 2 July 5/6 We have selected over $30,000 of our elegant stock and marked them Down 50 per cent. **1925** DOS PASSOS *Manhattan Transfer* 103 Oy Oy Meester Solomon Levy with his best Yiddisher garments all marked down.

2. mark(ed) down sale, a sale of goods in which prices are lowered.

1880 (Boston newspaper), The success of our mark-down sales . . . has induced us to adopt the same means this year to introduce ourselves and stock to all new customers. **1908** *Sat. Ev. Post* 24 Oct. 13/1 At another store there is a marked-down sale of parasols.

∗**marker,** *n.*

1. A surveyor's helper who blazes trees, sets up landmarks, etc.

1743 *N.J. Archives* 1 Ser. VI. 154 You are to employ . . . an assistant surveyor if you think proper & also proper chainbearers & markers. **1813** *Steele P.* II. 702 Two common axemen who may serve as markers, 10/ each . . . 60. **1843** *Amer. Pioneer* II. 379 In running the back line of the survey, . . . I was about one hundred yards in advance of the chainmen and marker.

2. An agricultural implement for marking off rows.

1859 *Rep. Comm. Patents 1858* I. 479, I am aware that markers have been previously used and arranged similar to the ones described. **1871** *Ill. Agric. Soc. Trans.* VIII. 239 After the field has been thoroughly prepared, . . . proceed to check it off from east to west with a three-rowed marker. **1874** KNIGHT 628/1 *Corn-row Marker*, a sled with a gaged width between the runners for marking out rows in which to plant corn.

3. (See quot.)

1870 MEDBERY *Men Wall St.* 21 The 'marker' or black-board clerk writes off the prices upon the tablet.

4. In contexts suggesting comparisons: Anything of importance. Usu. in negative constructions. *Slang.*

1888 *Cong. Rec.* 12 Dec. 202/2, I can easily fancy what a cry would have been raised. . . . The waving of the bloody shirt would not have been a marker. **1904** W. H. SMITH *Promoters* 366 What little I've told you isn't a marker to other things he said.

5. A monument or stone that marks a place.

1906 *Springfield W. Republican* 15 Feb. 16 The committee appointed to investigate the matter of a marker for the Washington elm reported in favor of a granite marker. **1949** *Dly. Ardmoreite* (Ardmore, Okla.) 25 Jan. 8/3, I want to see a marker placed just south of the new Methodist church on highway 77 at Thackerville, marking the place of the last battle with the Comanche Indians in this country.

b. A highway sign.

1913 *Collier's* 6 Dec. 22/4 The route is marked with the official Lincoln Highway marker across many of the States.

6. *W.* (See quots.)

1913 BARNES *Western Grazing Grounds* 382 Markers.—The black sheep in a herd. Every herder knows exactly how many of such he has and by running over them occasionally he feels fairly sure that if they are all there he has lost no sheep. **1944** ADAMS *W. Words* 97 Marker. An animal with distinct coloration or other marks easily distinguished and remembered by the owner and his riders. Such an animal has frequently been the downfall of the rustler.

As the last term in **corn, ice, pie marker.**

* **market,** *n.* In combs.: (1) **market farm,** a farm where produce is raised for market; (2) **fish,** the margate fish; (3) **hunter,** one who hunts wild game for sale in the market; (4) **master,** an official who administers the law respecting the market or markets of a town; (5) **report,** a report on trading and market conditions, esp., *pl.*, the printed reports of prices for stocks, commodities, etc., sold on an exchange; (6) **reporter,** one who reports upon prices, trends, etc., in trading; (7) **shooter,** =**market hunter;** (8) **sieve,** a sieve for separating broken or small rice from the whole grains; (9) **truck,** (see quot. 1859); (10) **wagon,** a wagon in which produce is carried to a market place, often serving as a stand or booth for the sale of the produce.

(1) **1868** *Comm. & Fin. Chron.* VI. 457/1 The market farms established in East Florida for supplying northern cities with early fruits and vegetables will also become tributary. — (2) **1838** GOSSE *Letters* 18 There was another somewhat like this, but much larger, that they [on the coast of Fla.] denominated a market fish, of a ruddy silvery tint, with very large scales, the fins and tail bright crimson. **1911** *Rep. Fisheries 1908* 312 Margate-Fish (*Haemulon album*).—A grunt found in southern Florida, known also as 'porgy,' 'market fish.' — (3) **1874** LONG *Wild-Fowl* 185 Blue-winged teal . . . are much sought for by market-hunters. **1940** TRAUTMAN *Birds Buckeye Lake, Ohio* 170 According to former market hunters and old sportsmen, the Eastern Least Bittern was a most numerous transient and summering species between 1860 and 1900. — (4) **1851** CIST *Cincinnati* 87 A city treasurer, a marshal, a wharf and three market masters are elected. **1913** J. W. SULLIVAN *Markets for People* 104 The Pennsylvania markets usually get along with a single market-master, assisted by a laborer or two on market days.

(5) **1866** *Ore. State Jrnl.* 5 May 3/1 We have received late numbers of *McCracken Merrill & Co's Market Report.* **1880** MARK TWAIN *Tramp Abroad* 626 A child's handful of telegrams . . . ; letter-correspondence . . . ; market reports. . . . That is what a German daily is made of. **1902** WILSON *Spenders* 85 They're as matter-of-fact as market reports. — (6) **1853** B. J. TAYLOR *Jan. & June* 83 And so, as Market Reporters have it, 'we have movements to note.' — (7) **1897** *Outing* XXX. 293/2 The market-shooter . . . can sneak through the known haunts of the quail. — (8) **1761** *S.C. Hist. Coll.* II. 202 [Rice] is then sifted from the Flour and Dust made by pounding; and afterwards by a Wire-sieve, called a Market-sieve. — (9) **1784** *Md. Jrnl.* 14 Dec. (*advt.*) (Th.), He has also provided a large Room, with a Stove, for his Customers to lodge in, and deposit their Market-truck. **1859** BARTLETT 488 Truck, stuff; and especially, vegetables raised for market, called also market-truck.

(10) **1802** *Ann. 7th Congress* 1 Sess. 1027 In the State of New Jersey five hundred and forty two [of the carriages taxed] are . . . principally market-wagons. **1894** WARNER *Golden House* i, Here and there [was] a lumbering market-wagon from Jersey.

b. (1) *To hold the market,* (see quots.); (2) *to play the market,* to speculate on the stock exchange.

(1) **1870** MEDBERY *Men Wall St.* 136 Holding the market, is to buy sufficient stock at the Boards to keep the price from declining. **1900** NELSON *A B C Wall St.* 145 Holding the market. Moderate purchases skilfully distributed and designed to keep a market from declining. — (2) **1927** E. HUNTINGTON *Builders of Amer.* 215 The man who earns only a pittance in college may become a stockbroker; a pleasant manner and reasonable intelligence in playing the market may make him a millionaire.

As the last term in **bird, curb, fish, Fly, off, Pennsylvania, short, swimming market.**

marketer 'mɑrkɪtɚ, *n.* One who buys or sells in a market or shop.

1787 CUTLER in *Life & Corr.* I. 271 The marketers seemed to be all in and every thing arranged. **1851** *Polly Peablossom* 108 Two men from the interior, apparently marketers, halted at the corner. **1884** JAMES *Little Tour in France* xxiv, I sat down with a hundred hungry marketers, fat, brown, greasy men.

* **marking,** *n.*

1. marking iron, a surveyor's instrument provided with a die for marking trees, corner posts, etc.

1633 *N.H. Doc. & Rec.* I. 79, 1 markin iron. **1671** in ALVORD & BIDGOOD *Trans-Allegheny Region* 191 [We] went to the first tree which we marked thus with a pair of marking irons for his sacred majesty. **1697** SEWALL *Letter-Book* I. 188, I have sent . . . four Barrels of Pork marked with marking Iron SS. **1817** *Niles' Reg.* XII. 98/2 The numbers of the township and range, are marked with a marking iron (such as are used in mills and warehouses) on a bearing or other tree.

b. marking hammer, (see quot.).

1905 *Forestry Bureau Bul.* No. 61, 42 *Marking hammer,* a hammer bearing a raised device which is stamped on logs, to indicate ownership. . . . [Also called] marking iron.

Marking hammer and spud (see sense 1)

2. *marking of meat,* the infliction of severe bodily chastisement. *Rare.*

1824 SINGLETON *Letters* 100 Yet, slaves live with tenser skins in Kentucky, than in Virginia. There is no marking of meat here, as they say.

* **marl,** *n.* As the last term in **blue, plains marl.**

marlberry 'mɑrl,berɪ, *n.* [f. *marble-berry,* a name for *Ardisia crenulata.*] A small tropical American tree or shrub, *Ardisia paniculata.*

1884 SARGENT *Rep. Forests* 100 Marlberry. Cherry. . . . A small tree, sometimes 8 meters in height, . . . or often a shrub; reaching its greatest development in Florida. **1917** *Rep. Smithsonian Inst.* 384 In addition to these are the paradise tree or bitterwood; soapberry tree; . . . marlberry [etc.]. **1933** SMALL *Southeastern Flora* 1029.

* **Marlborough,** *n.* Used attrib. with **pie, pudding, pudding-pie,** (see quots.).

1805 *Pocumtuc Housewife* (1906) 24. **1869** STOWE *Old-town Folks* 340 Apple pies, Marlborough-pudding pies. **1893** HALE *N. Eng. Boyhood* 115 In any old and well-regulated family in New England, you will find there is a traditional method of making the Marlborough pie, which is a sort of lemon pie. **1919** DUNN *Indiana* II. 1170 Marlborough pudding pies. [Footnote:] A sort of apple pie.

* **marlin,** *n.* A local name for the godwit.

1886 ROOSEVELT in *Outing* Aug. 523 Yelper, Marlin, and Yellow Legs, are all occasionally found, although not plenty. **1893–6** NEWTON *Dict. Birds* 367 America possesses two species of the genus, the very large Marbled Godwit or Marlin, *L. fedoa*, . . . and the smaller Hudsonian Godwit. **1923** W. L. McAtee *Local Names Migratory Game Birds* 58 Marbled Godwit. . . . Vernacular Names . . . marlin (Long Id., N.Y., N.J., Va., Ill.).

marlinespike seamanship. ?Seamanship up to the standards of the old sailing days when marlinespikes were much in evidence. — **1888** *Harper's Mag.* July 170/1 Before this is ended he has learned a great deal of marline-spike seamanship. **1896** *United Service Mag.* 187 There is not nearly so much marlin-spike seamanship as in the days of our forefathers.

* **marmot,** *n.* =**prairie dog.** Also with defining adj.

1823 James *Exped.* II. 140 The high and barren parts of this tract [between the Loup fork and the Platte] are occupied by the numerous communities of the Prairie dog or Louisiana marmot. **1875** *Amer. Naturalist* IX. 148 'Marmot' is sometimes used [for prairie dog], the present species being the tawny marmot of some writers, but this is the name of the woodchucks (*Arctomys*). **1948** *Sierra Club Bul.* March 15 How long do the marmots hibernate, and what are the migration habits of the caribou?

As the last term in **hoary, Maryland, prairie, whistling marmot.**

* **maroon,** *n.* and *a.*

1. *S.* An extended camping trip or picnic. Also attrib. *Obs.*

1779 I. Angell *Diary* (1899) 59 Lt. Cook . . . Come from the Meroon frolick last night. **1785** *S.C. Hist. Mag.* XIII. 188 On Monday we form a maroon party to visit some saw mills. **1836** Gilman *Recoll.* (1838) 223 Feeling the necessity of refreshment, we alighted for a while beneath a tree by the roadside, for a maroon.

2. maroon cattle, (see quots.).

1842 in *Amer. Sp.* XVIII. 127 Large herds of (so-called) maroon-cattle had assembled in the forest and meadows of the canton, masterless and unmarked, had been chased and shot by the inhabitants. [**1931** W. A. Read *La.-French* 191 The French *marron*, thought to be an adoption of Spanish *cimarron*, 'wild,' signifies not only a fugitive slave, but also a domestic animal that has run wild.]

* **marooner,** *n.* **1.** A fugitive slave, a maroon. **2.** (See quot.) Both *obs.*

(1) **1738** Byrd *Dividing Line* (1901) 37 Not far from the inlet, dwelt a marooner. **1852** F. R. Goulding (*title*) (Roorbach), The Young Marooners. — (2) **1890** *Cent.* 3636/2 *Marooner*, . . . one who goes marooning; a member of a marooning party.

* **marooning,** *n.* **1.** (See quot.) **2. marooning party,** an extended picnic or excursion. Also **marooning expedition.** ?All *obs.*

(1) **1855** Haliburton *Nature & Human Nature* II. 283 He used to delight to go marooning. [Footnote:] Marooning differs from picnicing in this—the former continues several days, the other lasts but one. — (2) **1777** G. Forster *Voy. round World* I. 165 It may be curious to know the nature of our marooning parties, as the seamen called them. **1834** Caruthers *Kentuckian* I. 141 He entertained me with an account of his marooning expeditions. These are their excursions upon the Sea Islands for purposes of fishing and hunting. **1890** [see **marooner**].

marquee coop. A hencoop shaped like a tent. *Obs.* — **1850** Browne *Poultry Yard* 122 Another kind . . . is the marquee coop.

* **marrow,** *n.* In combs.: (1) * **marrow fat,** (*a*) a product resembling tallow or butter obtained by boiling down the marrow of buffaloes, (*b*) **marrow fat fraud,** (see quot.) *slang, obs.;* (2) **gut,** the chylopoietic duct of a buffalo, *obs.;* (3) **squash,** (see quot. 1864).

(1) (*a*) **1791** in *Pub. Champlain Soc.* XXI. 528 They broke the Bones of the Buffalo & made marrowfatt. **1888** *Cent. Mag.* Oct. 898/1 Then he slicked his hair with marrow-fat from a horn. (*b*) **1903** A. B. Hart *Actual Govt.* 75 The 'marrow-fat' fraud consists in a voter's putting in more than one ballot, while the clerk puts down fictitious names to cover the extra ballots. — (2) **1848** Ruxton in *Blackw. Mag.* LXIV. 585 If they pack along them *profits*, . . . who can make it rain hump-ribs and marrow-guts when the crowd gets out of the buffler range. **1894** *Harper's Mag.* Feb. 351/2 Inside of the cabin was William . . . , glowing with heat and pride over his corn cakes and 'marrow-gut.' — (3) **1864** Webster 814/3 *Marrow-squash*, a variety of squash having a soft texture and fine grain, resembling marrow. **1891** *Cent.* 5878/1 Other winter squashes are . . . egg-shaped and pointed at the ends, as in the (Boston) marrow, long a standard in America.

* **marry,** *v. intr. To marry out (of meeting)*, of Quakers, to marry one not of the Quaker faith. *Colloq.*

1842 *S. Lit. Messenger* VIII. 331/2 'Marrying out,' as the Friends call one of a different faith, is regarded by them with especial horror. **1898** Harper *S. B. Anthony* I. 10 The Quaker was not permitted to 'marry out of meeting.' **1946** Underhill *First Penthouse Dwellers* 149 The religious community of Taos sometimes reminds the student of the early Amish and Quakers in America and the tragedy of 'marrying out of meeting.'

* **marsh,** *n.* In combs.: (1) **marsh buggy,** a very high, relatively light motor-driven vehicle used in marshy or everglade regions, esp. by oil prospectors; (2) **grass,** any one of various grasses that grow in marshes, esp. those of the genus *Spartina;* (3) **harvester,** the trade-mark name of a type of grain reaping machine; (4) **leatherwood,** a small American shrub, *Dirca palustris;* (5) **lot,** a lot or allotment of land situated in a marsh, *obs.;* (6) **meadow,** a portion of marsh serving as grassland, *obs.;* (7) **mud,** soil from a marsh, used as fertilizer, *obs.;* (8) **prairie,** level land in a marshy area.

(1) **1944** Kane *Deep Delta Country* 255 The grotesque 'marsh buggies'! The latter are combinations of boat and automobile. — (2) **1785** *Md. Hist. Mag.* XX. 44 The Island . . . had flaggs or marsh grass growing on it. **1913** London *Valley of Moon* 259 She had even roofed the hole in rough fashion by means of drift wood and marsh grass. — (3) **1868** *Iowa State Agric. Soc. Rep. 1867* 228 Marsh Harvester. . . . The binders ride upon it while doing their work. . . . Two hundred sold in Iowa in 1867. **1923** Adams *Pioneer Hist.* 319 Until I was seven years old the sickle cut all the grain in the neighborhood; then the turkey-wing cradle, the grape-vine, the mully, the man rake-off reaper, the self raking reaper, the dropper, the marsh harvester [etc.]. — (4) **1785** Marshall *Amer. Grove* 41 Virginian Marsh Leather-wood . . . is a low shrub, growing in moist shady places. **1815** Drake *Cincinnati* 78 [Plants found in Miami County include] marsh leatherwood.

(5) **1638** *Essex Inst. Coll.* IV. 182/1 An acre & an half of vpland lying next to his marsh lott. **1672** *Ib.* LVI. 299 William Sargent . . . conveyed to Isaac Green . . . a marsh lot of Joseph Moyses [etc.]. **1740** in W. M. Sargent *Maine Wills* (1887) 530 Three Acres of Marsh to begin at the Westernmost End of my Marsh lot. — (6) **1638** *Essex Inst. Coll.* IV. 181/2 Granted . . . their proportions of marshe meadow. **1831** Smith *Life & Writings of Downing* 107 (We.), More than three quarters of the way, it was as bad as ploughing mash-meadow in April. — (7) **1789** Morse *Amer. Geog.* 48 He found . . . marsh grass, marsh mud, and brackish water. **1837** Williams *Florida* 107 No kind of manure has been found that will increase the quantity, without at the same time injuring the quality of the cotton, except it be sea-weeds, or marsh mud. — (8) **1818** Darby *Emigrant's Guide* 17 Some scattered clumps of trees are found along the shore, but the general surface of the little land that rises above the water is marsh prairie.

b. In the names of birds: (1) **marsh blackbird,** the red-winged blackbird or starling, *Agelaius phoeniceus*, cf. **red-shouldered marsh blackbird;** (2) * **goose,** (see quot.); (3) **hawk,** the American marsh harrier or mouse hawk, *Circus hudsonius;* (4) * **hen,** see as a main entry; (5) **quail,** =**meadow lark;** (6) **robin,** =**chewink;** (7) **snipe,** an American snipe, *Gallinago delicata*, which makes its nest in marshy ground; (8) **wren,** any one of various American wrens that breed exclusively in marshes, as the long-billed marsh wren, *Telmatodytes palustris palustris*, cf. **fresh-water, long-billed, prairie marsh wren.**

(1) **1811** Wilson *Ornithology* IV. 37 Starlings . . . are known by various names in the different states of the union; such as the Swamp Blackbird, Marsh Blackbird, Red-winged Blackbird. **1947** *Collier's* 29 March 92/2 There is the purple grackle which is most frequently known as the blackbird or as the crow blackbird, the marsh blackbird and the red-winged blackbird. — (2) **1890** *Cent.* 3640/1 *Marsh-goose* . . . Hutchins's goose, *Bernicla hutchinsi.* (North Carolina.) — (3) **1812** Wilson *Ornithology* VI. 67 Marsh Hawk: *Falco uliginosus;* . . . is most numerous where there are extensive meadows and salt marshes. **1949** *Nature Mag.* April 187/2 On cool, windy days in late September and through most of October there are often such aerial processions of buteos, accipiters, falcons, marsh hawks [etc.].

(5) **1750** J. Birket *Cursory Remarks* (1916) 32 Killd . . . some very pretty birds called Marsh quails, Something bigger than a field fare. **1821** *Amer. Jrnl. Science* III. 273 April 14. . . . The song of the marsh quail has been heard for a few days past. **1935** Lincoln *Cape Cod Yesterdays* 137 The Cape Cod market gunner of yesterday also shot upland birds for the market—quail, partridge, snipe, . . . 'marsh quail' and an occasional pheasant. — (6) **1874** Coues *Birds N.W.* 173 Ground Robin; Marsh Robin; Towhee Bunting; Chewink. . . . Eastern Province of North America to Minnesota. **1917** *Birds of Amer.* III. 58 Towhee. . . . [Also called] Marsh Robin. — (7) **1890** *Cent.* 3640/2 *Marsh snipe*, . . . the common American snipe; the meadow-snipe. (Maryland, U.S.) **1917** *Birds of Amer.* I. 227 Wilson's Snipe. Gallinago delicata. . . . Meadow Snipe; . . . Marsh Snipe; Bog Snipe. — (8) **1794** *Amer. Philos. Soc.* IV. 102 The great lark, the

marsh-wren, etc. **1923** *Frontier* March 12 Shall I ever again . . . hear the liquid call of the marsh wren?

c. In the names of other animals: (1) * **marsh frog,** = **pickerel frog;** (2) **pony,** = **marsh tack(e)y;** (3) **rabbit,** a rabbit, *Sylvilagus palustris,* slightly larger than the cottontail, found in the coastal lowlands of the southeastern states, also transf.; (4) **tack(e)y,** a small, wiry pony bred in marshy regions; (5) **tortoise,** the mud turtle; (6) **treader,** any one of various marsh insects of the order Hemiptera.

(1) **1745** E. KIMBER *Itinerant Observer* 12 (*footnote*), The Bull-Frogs, Lizards, Grasshoppers, Marsh Frogs [imitate city noises]. **1899** *Animal & Plant Lore* 61 Marsh frogs, smaller frogs, *Chorophilus triseriatus.* Pike Co., Ill. — (2) **1938** MATSCHAT *Suwannee River* 43 By the same mythology, the bands of marsh ponies that roam the coastal islands are declared to be descended from his [i.e., De Soto's] horses. — (3) **1869** *Amer. Naturalist* III. 343 It is clear that a Marsh Rabbit has passed this way. **1947** *N. & Q.* July 61/1, I am also told that muskrats are sometimes sold as 'marsh rabbits.' — (4) **1836** GILMAN *Recoll.* (1838) 131 An accident happening to my horse, I was obliged to hire one of the little animals called 'marsh tackies' to carry me over a creek. **1937** D. C. HEYWARD *Seed from Madagascar* 118 He could . . . gallop his 'marsh tackey' through thickets so dense that a rabbit could scarcely get through them.

(5) **1848** BARTLETT 230 *Mud-turtle,* the popular name of a reptile common in all parts of the United States. Marsh Tortoise and Mud Terrapin are other names for the same. — (6) **1902** L. O. HOWARD *Insect Book* 282 The Marsh Treaders. (Family *Hydrometridae.*)

As the last term in **bastard, blue, broken, cane, cranberry, dry, fresh-water, prairie, salt, salt-water, shaking, soft, swamp, tule, white marsh.**

* **marshal,** *n.*

1. In colonial times, an officer having various duties, as to serve writs, levy and collect fines, attend the sittings of courts, etc. Cf. **head marshal.**

1642 *Suffolk Deeds* I. 37 To the Marshall or his deputy By vertue hereof you are required to levy on the land. **1684** *Mass. H.S. Coll.* 4 Ser. V. 119 He ordered the Marshal to drop me at Captain Stileman's. **1774** in *Hist. MSS Comm. 14th Rep.* App. X. 211 The humble Memorial of James Ferguson Ranger of the Woods and Forrests, and Marshal of the Court of Admiralty in West Florida.

2. In a federal judicial district, a ministerial officer appointed by the President, with the concurrence of the Senate, to perform duties corresponding to those of a county sheriff. Also *marshal for* (or *of*) *the United States.*

1789 *Ann. 1st Congress* I. 86, I also nominate, for District Judges, Attorneys, and Marshals, the persons whose names are below. **1834** BAIRD *Valley Mississippi* xx. 257 There is . . . a Marshall for the United States. **1840** *Niles' Reg.* 21 March 47/2 A statement of the compensation received by district attorneys, clerks and marshals of the United States [was laid before the House]. **1946** *Chi. D. News* 19 Dec. 5/1 [He] surrendered to the U.S. marshal today on draft evasion charges.

b. A police officer or sheriff appointed by a territorial governor to have jurisdiction over a prescribed area.

1866 in DALE & RADER *Okla. Hist.* (1930) 363 [The governor of the territory of Oklahoma] shall have authority to appoint a marshal of said territory.

3. A person appointed to take, or to direct the taking of, a census. Cf. **census marshal.**

1814 *Niles' Reg.* 9 July 323 American Manufactures, exhibiting them by States, Territories, and Districts—so far as they are returned by the Marshals, and the Secretaries of Territories, and their respective assistants, in the autumn of the year 1810. **1840** *Ib.* 1 Aug. 352/1 The taking of the census will develop many curious facts. . . . In Queens county, New York, the marshall discovered a perfect albino . . . whose parents were negroes. **1873** *Mich. Gen. Statutes* I. (1882) 270 That the governor appoint marshals to take the census in the unorganized territory not otherwise provided in this act.

4. = **city marshal.**

1830 *Williams's N.Y. Ann. Reg.* 283 Common Council of Troy. Samuel McCoun, Mayor, Daniel Gardner, Recorder. . . . Justin Kellogg, Marshal. **1887** F. FRANCIS *Saddle & Moccasin* 298 The prisoner . . . was now returning in charge of the Marshal of Georgetown to be tried for killing the Deputy there. **1938** ASBURY *Sucker's Prog.* 342 Not until McCall had left Deadwood was it learned that he had been paid $200 by gamblers who feared that Hickok might be appointed Marshal of the town.

5. In combs. and phrases: (1) *Marshal at Arms,* the sergeant at arms of the House of Representatives, *rare;* (2) *Marshal of the day,* one charged with arranging or ordering exercises or proceedings on a public or ceremonious occasion; (3) **marshal general,** = **head marshal.**

(1) **1792** CUTLER in *Life & Corr.* I. 483 The Speaker of the House sent the Marshal-at-Arms to summons them to attend the House. — (2) **1811** *Niles' Reg.* I. 118/2 The whole was attended and regulated by the marshal of the day on horseback. **1868** *Western Mag.* Jan. (De Vere), The inhabitants within a radius of ten miles were invited to a chopping-bee. . . . The work was ordered by an elected marshal of the day. — (3) **1658** *Mass. Bay Rec.* IV. 326 To pay the marshall genll. three pence out of euery attachment by them [*sc.* the constables] served. **1690** SEWALL *Diary* I. 341 After Lecture Mr. Sam'l Gookin is Apointed by the Governour and Council to be Marshall Generall.

As the last term in **assistant, census, city, county, day, deputy, fire, head, night, provost, town, United States Marshal.**

* **marshal,** *v. tr.* To arrange (the cars of a freight train) in proper station order. Hence **marshaling yard,** a yard where freight trains are marshaled.

1880 WAIT *Car Builder's Dict.* **1945** *Reader's Digest* Aug. 81 Fritz Knickenberg, chief inspector of the great Hamm marshaling yards supervised 4000 railway men. **1948** *Sierra Club Bul.* 2/1 His proposal of hikers' trails would make the already well-covered Sierra a network somewhat like a railroad marshalling yard.

Marshallite ˈmarʃəˌlaɪt, *n.* [Robert *Marshall,* Presbyterian minister.] A member of an Arian faction in the Presbyterian Church in Kentucky in the early nineteenth century (see quot. 1856). *Obs.*

1834 *Biblical Reporter* VI. 339 There sprang up that fruitful crop of heresy and schism, that afterwards assumed the shape, as well as the name, of New Lights, . . . Marshallites, Unitarians, and Shakers. **1856** CARTWRIGHT *Autobiog.* 219 Arianism was rife through all that country [Kentucky], although they called themselves 'Christians,' and were called by the world, New Lights, Marshallites, or Stoneites. (These were two leading Presbyterian ministers, that in the time of a great revival in Kentucky, were disowned by the Synod of Kentucky.)

* **marshalship,** *n.* The office of a U.S. marshal.

1858 LINCOLN in Logan *Great Conspiracy* 74 They have seen in his round . . . face, Post-offices, Land-offices, Marshalships, and Cabinet appointments. **1898** *Outlook* June 433 The President appoints all important officers, beginning with the Governor and extending to the judiciary, the marshalship, and minor positions. **1948** *Popular Western* June 20/2, I have been offered the marshalship of Caprock, and I have accepted.

marshbanker ˈmarʃˌbæŋkɚ, *n.* [Du. *marsbanker.*] The menhaden. Cf. **mossbunker.**

1679 *L.I. Hist. Soc. Mem.* I. 100 Marsbanckers. **1803** *Med. Repository* 176 The fish which Mr. Latrobe describes is the *morsch-banker* of the Dutch settlers about New-York, and the *menhaden* of the Mohegan natives. **1814** MITCHILL *Fishes N.Y.* 453 Bony-fish, Hardheads, or Marsbankers . . . [are] about fourteen inches long. **1884** GOODE *Fisheries* I. 569 New Jersey uses the New York name with its local variations, such as 'Bunker' and 'Marshbanker.'

* **marsh hen.** Any one of various American rails, as the king rail and the American coot (see also quot. 1917). Cf. **fresh-water, salt-water marsh hen.**

1709 LAWSON *Carolina* 151 Marsh-Hen, much the same as in Europe, only she makes another sort of Noise, and much shriller. **1844** *Knickerb.* XXIV. 188 Next to this [hunting the turkey] perhaps, I prefer marsh-hens. **1917** *Birds of Amer.* I. 181 Bittern. *Botaurus lentiginosus.* . . . [Also called] Indian Hen; Marsh Hen; Poke. *Ib.* 214 Coot. *Fulica americana.* . . . [Also called] Water Hen; Marsh Hen; Moor-head.

martelle marˈtɛl, *n.* [f. **martel,* hammer + **-le,** app. with diminutive force.] A game resembling croquet. *Obs.* — **1867** *Ball Players' Chron.* 13 June 7/4 Martelle, the new field game, for which a patent has recently been issued, is already attracting great attention. **1867** *Harper's Wkly.* 29 June 403/4 But it is in many respects an improvement on Croquet, which is sometimes tedious and monotonous, Martelle being more varied in its play than the former game, more ingenious in its combinations, and more rapid in its movements.

Martha Washington. Used in combs.: (1) **Martha Washington armchair,** (see quot.); (2) **geranium,** (see second quot. 1890); (3) **sewing cabinet,** a low cabinet, usu. octagonal, with slender legs, deep receptacles for storing sewing material, and drawers.

(1) **1941** A. TRAIN, JR. *Story Everyday Things* 233 The Martha Washington armchair had a high, upholstered back and Hepplewhite arms and legs. — (2) **1890** WIGGIN *Timothy's Quest* 199 Timothy had insisted on putting a pink Ma'thy Washington geranium in her collar. **1890** *Cent.* 4361/2 Those [*sc.* flowers] of *P. grandiflorum* are

known specifically as pelargoniums or as Martha Washington geraniums. [1917 BAILEY *Cyclo. Horticulture* V. 2532/2 Lady Washington Geraniums (or Pelargoniums). This name distinguishes the garden types of florist's and fancy pelargonium.] 1949 *L.A. Times* 5 June (Home Mag.) 33/2 While the fish or horseshoe geraniums are the most common members of this group the Martha Washington geraniums definitely are the elect members of the family. — (3) 1935 *Montgomery Ward Cat.* (ed. 123) 375 Martha Washington Sewing Cabinet. Alcohol and water-proof top finish. Oak drawer interiors. 1945 *Sat. Review* 22 Dec. 34/2 John Drew has located a few diminutive Martha Washington Sewing Cabinets three fingers high with leaves that work as do the drawers.

* **martin,** *n.* In combs.: (1) **martin box,** a box set up for martins to nest in; (2) **gourd,** a gourd hung on a pole for martins to nest in; (3) **house,** a diminutive wooden house or houselike structure put up, usu. on a pole, for martins to nest in.

(1) [1822 J. WOODS *English Prairie* 292 The Americans frequently fix boxes on poles, or on the cabins, in which the black-martins build.] 1828 *Farmer's Alman. 1829* (Wendell, Mass.) F3ᵛ Whose house is that with white capped chimnies, black sashed windows, and a nice little marten [*sic*] box just an epitome of the State House? 1946 STUART *Plum Grove Hills* 85, I know what Mom is thinking when she looks at the martin boxes. — (2) [*c*1730 CATESBY *Carolina* I. 51 *Hirundo purpurea.* The Purple Martin.... They breed like Pigeons ... in gourds hung on poles for them to build in.] 1898 HARRIS *Tales* 151 No sign of life, save two bluebirds, the pioneers of spring, that were fighting around the martin gourds, preparing to take possession. 1948 *Democrat* 30 Sep. 8/1 Wanted.—About one dozen large sized gourds, suitable for martin gourds. — (3) 1835 BIRD *Hawks* I. 44 Here's ... the identical old Folly, with ... the pot in the chimney, and the old martin-house on a pole! 1949 *Chi. Tribune* 1 Sep. 7/5 The purple martins ... hardly had been gone 24 hours before their apartments in the martin houses were taken over by house sparrows.

As the last term in **bee, box, field, purple martin.**

Martini mɑr'tinɪ, *n.* Also **martini.** [App. f. a proper name.] A cocktail containing gin, vermouth, and orange bitters. In full **Martini cocktail.**

1899 *Collier's* 20 May 30/3 Choice of Manhattan, Martini, ... Vermouth, York or Whiskey is offered. 1908 LORIMER *J. Spurlock* ii. 24 So I stopped the cab and sopped up a dry Martini. 1910 WHITLOCK *Gold Brick* 244 Underwood watched Malachi Nolan mix his Martini cocktail. 1949 *Sun. World-Herald* Mag. (Omaha) 1 May 2/1 Where is the fellow who decided you must have an olive in the bottom of every martini?

Martling men. (See quot. 1890.) — [1812 PAULDING *Beaut. Bullus* 38 To ... play tricks for the entertainment of the Saints of Tammany and the *Moralists* of Martling.] 1890 *Cent.* 3043/2 *Martling-men.*... (So called from their habit of assembling in 'Martling's Long Room' in New York city.) In *U.S. hist.*, a coalition of two factions of the Democratic-Republican party in the State of New York, the Burrites and Lewisites, formed about 1807. The members afterward became known as *Bucktails.*

martynia mɑr'tɪnɪə, *n.* [John *Martyn* (1699–1768), Eng. botanist.] The unicorn plant, the fruit of which is used for pickles.

1753 in CHAMBERS *Cyclo. Supp.* 1796 H. HUNTER tr. *St. Pierre's Stud. Nature* (1799) II. 220 I did not know of what country the Martinia was a native. 1847 DARLINGTON *Weeds & Plants* 222 Long-beaked Martynia. Unicorn Plant.... This plant ... is cultivated for its singular fruit. 1942 CASTETTER & BELL *Pima & Papago Agric.* 73 While *Martynia* for some time has been grown for use in basketry, it is uncertain whether it was cultivated aboriginally.

Maryland 'mɛrələnd, *n.* [Named in 1632 by Charles I in honor of his queen, Henrietta *Maria.*] The name of a colony and state on the Atlantic seaboard, used in combs.: (1) **Maryland (beaten) biscuit,** =**beaten biscuit;** (2) **broadleaf,** a kind of tobacco, *obs.;* (3) **chicken,** (see quot.); (4) **end,** (see quot.), *obs.;* (5) **kitefoot,** a kind of tobacco, *obs.;* (6) **marmot,** an American marmot or woodchuck of the genus *Marmota,* esp. *M. monax,* the groundhog; (7) **parson,** (see quot.), *obs.;* (8) **pippin,** a variety of winter apple, *obs.;* (9) **yellowthroat,** the ground warbler, *Geothlypis trichas,* of the eastern U.S.

(1) 1872 ROE *Army Lett.* 35 There was no April fool about the delicate Maryland biscuits. 1941 FARMER *Boston Cook Book* 89 Maryland Beaten Biscuit. 1 pint flour, ⅓ cup lard [etc.]. — (2) 1864 *Ohio Agric. Rep.* XVIII. 148 The Maryland Broadleaf, as far as it has been tried, gives promise of being a valuable kind. [1867 SIMMONDS *Dict. Trade Supp., Maryland,* a mild kind of tobacco.] — (3) 1941 FARMER *Boston Cook Book* 376 Maryland Chicken.... Season chicken with salt and pepper, dip in flour, then in 1 egg, beaten slightly with 2 tablespoons cold water, then in soft bread crumbs. — (4) 1859 BARTLETT *Dict. Amer.* (ed. 2) *Maryland end,* said of the hock of the ham. The other is the Virginia end.

(5) 1834 CARUTHERS *Kentuckian* I. 24, I gets a quid of the real Kentuck twist or Maryland kite-foot into my mouth. — (6) [1781 PENNANT *Hist. Quadrupeds* II. 306–8 Marmot.... Maryland.... Inhabits Virginia and Pennsylvania.] 1823 JAMES *Exped.* I. 261 *Arctomys monax*—Maryland marmot. 1890 *N. & Q.* IV. 188 *Arctomys Monax* (Bear-Rat) ... commonly called 'Maryland marmot.' — (7) 1811 *Mem. Life Pa.* 93 Mr. L—— seemed in all respects to be what was then called in Pennsylvania a Maryland parson; that is, one who could accommodate himself to his company. — (8) 1830 *Ohio Phenix* (Marion) 2 Sep. 4/3 Sweet Bellybound, Maryland Pippin, Pearmain. — (9) 1702 J. PETIVER *Gazophylacii Nat.* I. 6 *Avis Mary-Landica gutture luteo.* The Mary-Land Yellow-Throat. 1896 *Atlantic Mo.* Feb. 199/1, I heard daily the singing of an orchard oriole, ... with sometimes the *fidgety, fidgety* of a Maryland yellow-throat. 1948 *N. & S. Dak. Horticulture* July–Aug. 106/1 From a nearby coulee came the odd but musical notes of the Maryland Yellow Throat.

Also *Maryland banknote, line, money, stock,* etc.

Marylander 'mɛrə͵lændɚ, *n.* A native or inhabitant of Maryland.

1662 *Wkly. Post Boy* 16 March, We congratulate the Marylanders on the safe Arrival of these *Recruits.* 1755 L. EVANS *Anal. Map Colonies* 14 The Sasquehannocks, after the great Defeat by the Marilanders, were easily exterminated by the Confederates. 1948 *Chi. Tribune* 9 May 3/2 Marylanders, used to disappointments, are keeping their fingers crossed.

b. A Maryland ham.

1838 COOPER *Homeward Bound* xii, This beef is not indigestible and here is a real Marylander, in the way of a ham.

Marylandian 'mɛrə͵lændɪən, *n.* =**Marylander.** *Obs.* — 1750 *Md. Hist. Mag.* X. 144 Most of our Marylandians do very well and they are said to be as good as any, if not the best boys in the house.

mascalonge, *n.* See **muskellunge.**

Mascoutens mæs'kutn̩z, *n. pl.* [f. native name meaning "little prairie people."] (See quot. 1907.)

1722 COXE *Descr. Carolana* 50 A little to the South-West of the Bottom of this Lake, and more to the North, [are] the *Anthontans,* and Part of the *Mascoutens,* near the River *Misconsing.* 1770 PITTMAN *Present State* 51 The Peanquichas, Mascoutins, Miamis, Kickapous, and Pyatonons, though not very numerous, are a brave and warlike people. 1907 HODGE *Amer. Indians* I. 811/1 Mascoutens.... A term used by some early writers in a collective and indefinite sense to designate the Algonquian tribes living on the prairies of Wisconsin and Illinois.... The name (*Mashkōtens*) is at present applied by the Potawatomi to that part of the tribe officially known as the 'Prairie band.'

* **mash,** *n.* In combs.: (1) **mash letter,** a sentimental "fan" letter, *slang;* (2) **note,** =prec.; (3) **trap,** a deadfall.

(1) 1880 *Diary Daly Débutante* 238 He had what is called a 'mash letter' from a schoolgirl fourteen years old. — (2) 1890 BIFF HALL *Turnover Club* 134 He is greatly afflicted by that dreadful bane of fine-looking actors, yclept the 'mash note' in the profession. 1899 *Chi. Record* 7 Jan. 4/6, I was writin' mash notes to myself. — (3) 1862 *N.Y. Tribune* 5 May 1/6 There is not the least danger that their precious carcasses will be caught under a mashtrap. *c*1866 BAGBY *Old Va. Gentleman* 48 [He must] set gums for 'Mollie-cotton-tails,' mash-traps and deadfalls for minks.

As the last term in **sour, squaw mash.**

* **mash,** *v.*

1. *tr.* To ogle, flirt with, or try to attract the amorous attention of (a person of the opposite sex). *Slang.* Cf. * **masher,** *n.*

1879 *Amer. Punch* Dec. 136/2 There was a young man in New Haven Who always was smoothly shaven. Without a mustache He never could mash The girls, and they thought him a craven. 1882 LELAND *Gypsies* 108 These black-eyed beauties by mashing men for many generations, with shafts shot sideways ... at last sealed their souls into the corner of their eyes. 1889 BARRERE-LELAND (1897) II. 44/1 About the year 1860 *mash* was a word found only in theatrical parlance in the United States. When an actress or any girl on the stage smiled at or ogled a friend in the audience, she was said to *mash* him. ... It occurred to the writer that it must have been derived from the gypsy *mash* (*masher-ava*), to allure, to entice. 1893 CRANE *Maggie* (1896) 95 Dere wasn't a feller come teh deh house but she'd try teh mash 'im. 1928 BRADFORD *Ol' Man Adam* 14 You tryin' to mash me?

2. *To get mashed on,* to become suddenly smitten with sentimental affection for; to be "gone on." *Slang.*

1883 PECK *Bad Boy* 99 An aunt of his ... got mashed on a Chicago drummer. 1894 HOYT *Texas Steer* (1925) III. 31 A dude who belonged to the British Legation got mashed on Dad's millions before we'd been here a week.

transf. **1880** NYE *B. Nye & Boomerang* 192, I wot ye art the damsel who erst was mashed [i.e., drunk] on Obejoyful.

∗ **masher,** *n.* A man who tries to flirt with, or make advances to, women in public places. *Slang.*

"The word was common in 1882 and for a few years after. It is said to have been introduced from the U.S." (*OED*).

1875 *Funny Fatherland* 56 (We.), The soldiers are great 'mashers' among the *dienst madchens.* **1904** *New Haven Reg.* 26 Oct. 3 'Mashers' have become such a nuisance in State street that all the dry goods stores have entered into an alliance to prosecute and drive them off the street. **1949** *Time* 4 July 13/3 Los Angeles . . . has hordes of critics, and they damn it like Victorian belles stabbing a masher with hatpins.

attrib. **1902** C. MORRIS *Stage Confidences* 171 Now and again . . . a man really falls in love with a woman whom he has seen only upon the stage; but no 'masher' proceedings are taken in such cases.

As the last term in **bug masher.**

∗ **mashing,** *n.* The action of a "masher" or flirt. Also attrib. *Slang.* — **1882** PECK *Sunshine* 130 There has got to be two parties to a mashing match, and one must be a woman. **1884** RITTENHOUSE *Maud* 306, I do try to make good honest friends but 'mashing' is altogether out of my line.

masked bobwhite. The Arizona bobwhite, *Colinus ridgwayi.* — **1887** RIDGWAY *Man. N. Amer. Birds* 189 Sonora and southern Arizona. . . . Masked Bob White. **1942** Nat. Pk. Service *Fading Trails* 259 The masked bobwhite formerly occupied a limited range in the United States near the Mexican boundary.

Mason and Dixon. The boundary line between Pennsylvania and Maryland as laid out (1763–67) by the English surveyors Charles Mason and Jeremiah Dixon, in full **Mason and Dixon's line.** In later times the entire southern boundary of Pa., and regarded as the line separating the free and the slave states, or as the boundary between the North and the South.

1779 in W. B. REED *Life & Corr. Joseph Reed* II. 134 The Virginia gentlemen offer to divide exactly the 40th degree with us. . . . Perhaps we [of Penna.] would be as well off with Mason and Dixon's line continued. **1834** C. A. DAVIS *Lett. J. Downing* 36 He tell'd me Georgia would go for me, arter the Gineral, as soon as any north of mason and dickson. **1861** *Vanity Fair* 25 May 251/2 Suffysit to say I got across Mason & Dixie's line safe at last. **1948** *Downers Grove* (Ill.) *Rep.* 21 Oct. 3/2 Two Dixiecrats, out of their element north of the Mason-Dixon, nevertheless registered their convictions on the States' Rights issue by giving their votes to James Thurmond.

transf. **1948** *Sat. Ev. Post* 30 Oct. 124/4 This same little band has long since adopted three war-ruined families in the old country—two in Bizonia, one on the other side of Europe's bitter Mason and Dixon's line.

Mason (fruit) jar. A fruit jar with a screw top used for home canning, esp. the early type with a porcelain-lined cap. Named for John Mason, who was granted the patent for such jars in 1858.

1885 *N.Y. Wkly. Tribune* 6 Aug. 13/2 The Illinois Agricultural Society calls attention to the fact that Mason fruit-jars have been sent to that State packed in straw foul with Canada thistle. **1888** L. HARGIS *Graded Cook Book* 472 Quince and apple butter. . . . Put a little of the mixture in a plate and invert, if it adheres the butter is done. Fill Mason jars and seal. **1947** *Nat. Geog. Mag.* June 822/1 His annual cherry crop amounted to one forlorn little cherry which he covered with a mason jar.

∗ **Masonic,** *a.* **1. Masonic temple,** a building serving as the headquarters or place of meeting for a Masonic lodge. **2. Masonic weed,** (see quot.), *obs.*

(1) **1854** MRS. C. A. MOWATT *Autobiog. of an Actress* 146, I was to read at the Masonic Temple [in Boston] for three successive nights. **1916** F. RIDER *N.Y. City* 438 East of the Masonic Temple, facing the abandoned cathedral, and extending to the northwest corner of Lafayette, . . . is the recently finished Queen of All Saints' Chapel. — (2) **1880** in FERGUS *Hist. Series* No. 13, 43, I have found the roots of what was called the 'Masonic-weed' thirty feet deep. . . . This weed, which is called in other localities the 'Devil's shoe-string,' grows luxuriantly over crevices . . . lead ore was found in these crevices. . . . This sign was at first known to but a few, and was tried by them to be kept as a secret, and hence the growth got the name of the 'Masonic-weed.'

Masonite ˈmesn̩ˌaɪt, *n.* The trade-mark name of a form of wood fiber pressed into sheets and used esp. in kitchens and bathrooms. — **1933** *Sci. Amer.* Jan. 39/1 Floors will be of Masonite cushioned flooring. **1948** *Dly. Ardmoreite* (Ardmore, Okla.) 23 May (Bldg. Sect.) 15/1 Masonite is now used mostly in bathrooms and kitchens with celetex and other forms of insulated wallboards being used in other rooms of the home in place of sheet rock.

∗ **mass,** *n.*

1. mass convention, an informal public meeting of political party members and leaders held primarily for discussing party interests and nominating party candidates.

1843 *N.Y. Herald* 13 Feb. 2/2 (Ernst), The Great Tyler mass Convention on the 15th of March, will be a screamer. **1900** *Cong. Rec.* 25 Jan. 1172/1 The nominations had been settled at primaries or mass conventions. **1907** *Old Dartmouth Hist. Sk.* XVI. 8/1 The Whigs of Massachusetts had issued a call inviting Whigs from all of the states of the Union to a mass convention.

2. mass meeting, a public meeting held for the purpose of discussing a common issue.

1733 BENJAMIN LYNDE *Diary* (1880) 39 Our mass meeting at which the village intend to urge their being a township. **1842** H. MANN *Oration* 4 July 64 The rival parties begin to play their game for the ignorant, and to purchase the saleable. Mass-meetings are held. **1948** JOHNSTON *Gold Rush* 9/1 For several days after the mass meeting, all was quiet.

transf. **1899** GOING *Flowers* 39 What looks like one blossom proves on examination to be a whole floral mass-meeting.

Massachuset ˌmæsəˈtʃusɪt, *n.* [Algonquian, "at or about the great hill."] *collect.* or *pl.* An Algonquian tribe of Indians formerly occupying the coastal region of Massachusetts Bay. Now *obs.* or *hist.*

1616 SMITH *Descr. N. Eng.* 26 The Countrie of the Massachusets . . . is the Paradise of all those parts. **1687** BLOME *Isles & Terr. in Amer.* 232 [The] Aberginians . . . consist of Mattachusets. **1845** *Cherokee Advocate* (Tahlequah, Okla.) 24 April 4/1 The tribe of the Massachusetts, even before the colonization of the country, had almost disappeared from the shores of the bay that bears its name. **1907** HODGE *Amer. Indians* I. 816/2 The Massachuset were more closely allied to the Narraganset than to any other of the surrounding tribes.

b. The language of these Indians.

1872 RUTTENBER *Ind. Tribes Hudson's River* 33 Earth, In Massachusetts, [is] *ahke;* in Mahican, *ahek.*

Massachusettensian ˌmæsəˌtʃusəˈtɛnsɪən, *n.* A native or inhabitant of the colony or state of Massachusetts. *Obs.*

[*c*1650 *Broadside Verse* (1930) 3/1 You English Mattachusians all Forbear sometime from sleeping, Let every one both great and small Prepare themselves for weeping.] **1702** MATHER *Magnalia* (1853) I. 132 The Massachusettensians had a Winthrop for their governour. **1787** J. ADAMS *Works* IV. 392 In this society of Massachusettensians then, there is . . . a moral and political equality of rights and duties among all the individuals.

Massachusetts ˌmæsəˈtʃusɪts, *n.* [f. **Massachuset.**] In combs.: (1) **Massachusetts Aid Society,** ?a society for aiding those who left Massachusetts for Kansas during the trouble there over slavery, *obs.;* (2) **ballot,** (see quot. 1914); (3) **claims,** see as a main entry; (4) **Fire Society,** (see quots. and cf. **Fire Society**); (5) **game,** see as a main entry; (6) **limitation,** (see quot.).

(1) **1856** BREWERTON *War in Kans.* 109 This club may be regarded as an humble imitation, which will, however, in all probability, accomplish quite as much as its progenitor, the Massachusetts Aid Society. — (2) **1891** *Nation* 30 April 360 The registering and cancelling ballot-box is an important feature of the Massachusetts ballot system. . . . Without the existing use of these boxes, the Massachusetts ballot law would be defective. **1914** *Cyclo. Amer. Govt.* I. 101/1 Fourteen states have the 'office-group' or 'Massachusetts' form of ballot, on which the several candidates for each office are grouped together, their names usually being arranged alphabetically, and each accompanied by the name of the party nominating him. **1949** *Time* 12 Sep. 21/3 The Taft forces got some 400,000 signatures on a petition to change to the 'Massachusetts ballot,' which requires voting for each separate office. — (4) **1794** *Mass. Acts & Resolves* VIII. 50 The persons above named, and their associates . . . are incorporated into . . . the Massachusetts Charitable Fire Society. **1904** KITTREDGE *Old Farmers* 149 The Massachusetts Charitable Fire Society . . . was organized in 1792, incorporated in 1794, and still exists.

(6) **1905** SHALER *Citizen* 207 In some states the voter must also show that he can read and write the English language. This is sometimes called the Massachusetts limitation, for the reason that it originated in that commonwealth.

Also *Massachusetts bank, man, pauper, pence,* etc.

Massachusetts claims. Claims made by the state of Massachusetts upon the U.S. Government in connection with the use of the Massachusetts state militia during the War of 1812. *Obs.*

At the time of the War of 1812, the right of Congress to employ state militia and the conditions under which such militia should operate caused debate. As a result of this confusion Massachusetts used and paid her state militia for service which benefited the American cause. Subsequently Massachusetts asked the federal government for reimbursement for the expense thus incurred. In 1870, these claims were settled by the payment of $678,362.42, regarded as the interest on the expenditures made by Massachusetts in behalf of the country as a whole.

1818 *Lynchburg* (Va.) *Press* 25 Dec. 3/4 The question regarding the Massachusetts Claims came up in the routine of business, yesterday. **1825** *Const. Advocate* (Frankfort, Ky.) 15 Dec. 1/2 The Georgia and Massachusetts Militia Claims will again be the topic of consideration. **1843** HAYWARD *Gazetteer of Maine* 83 The resources of the State, in 1842, consisted in its public lands; 21 shares of bank stock; one third portion of the Massachusetts claims, so called, against the United States for services of the militia during the war of 1812 with Great Britain.

Also **Massachusetts claim fund.**

1831 *Boston Transcript* 3 March 2/4 A portion of the 'Massachusetts Claim' fund could not be better invested, than in an enterprise of this nature.

Massachusetts game. A form of ball game somewhat resembling modern baseball. *Obs.* or *hist.* Cf. **New York game.**

1867 *Ball Players' Chron.* 6 June 1/1 It was in the year 1858, we believe, that the Massachusetts Association of Base Ball Players first met in convention to adopt a regular code of rules for the then popular game of ball of New England, known as the 'Massachusetts game.' **1912** *Collier's Mag.* 20 April 24/2 When Chicago was a village they knew only the old 'Massachusetts game,' first cousin to 'rounders.' **1939** *News Letter & Wasp* (S.F.) 14 April 5/1 Its [baseball's] immediate forbears include One, Two, Three and Four a' (old) Cat, Barn Ball, the Town Ball of Philadelphia, the Massachusetts Game and the New York game.

massasauga mæsə'sɔgə, *n.* [f. Ojibway *Missisauga*, the name of a tribe and of a river. Cf. **Missisauga.**] A prairie rattlesnake, *Sistrurus catenatus*, or a snake related to this. Also attrib. Cf. **ground rattlesnake.**

1840 KIRKLAND *New Home* 33 It's a rattlesnake; the Indians call them Massisangas [*sic*] and so *folks* call 'em so too. **1871** *Harper's Mag.* Nov. 821 In the grass the massasauga and other venomous reptiles lurked. **1947** *Chi. D. News* 23 Jan. 8/1 This is the massasauga rattler . . . and the woods around Chicago are full of them.

Massawomics mæsə'wɔmɪks, *n. pl.* =**Five Nations.** *Obs.*

*c*1612 STRACHEY *Virginia* (1849) 40 They can make well neare 600 able and mightie men, and are pallisadode in their townes to defend them from Massawomecks, their mortall enemies. **1629** SMITH *True Travels* (1819) 119 From thence returning we met 7 Canowes of the Massowomeks. **1831** WITHERS *Chron. Border Warfare* 39 That portion of the state lying north west of the Blue ridge, and extending to the lakes was possessed by the Massawomees. **1910** HODGE *Amer. Indians* II. 618/1 The Powhatan called them Massawomekes. The English knew them as the Confederation of the Five Nations.

Massena mə'sinə, *n.* [f. André *Masséna* (1758–1817), marshal of France.]

1. =next.

1857 *34th Congress* 1 Sess. Sen. Ex. Doc. No. 108 11. Birds 23 On being shot [the bird] proved to be a male massena. **1874** COUES *Birds N.W.* 444 What has been put on record concerning the habits of the beautiful Massena.

2. Massena partridge, any one of several varieties of quail, *Cyrtonyx montezumae*, found in the Southwest. Also a quail of such a variety.

1851 *Proc. Acad. Nat. Sci.* V. 222 The Massena Quail, or Partridge, . . . was not seen before crossing the San Pedro. **1853** SITGREAVES *Exped. Zuni & Colo. Rivers* 94 The Messena [*sic*] Partridge . . . are more sociable and not so shy as others of the same family. **1932** BENT *N. Amer. Gallinaceous Birds* 85 The favorite resorts of the Massena Partridge are the rocky ravines or arroyas that head well up in the mountains.

b. Massena quail, =prec.

1874 COUES *Birds N.W.* 443, I found no Massena Quail about Fort Whipple until a few days before my final departure. **1883** *Cent. Mag.* Aug. 484/1 Our partridges (viz. Bob White, the Mountain, Valley, and Massena quails, etc.) may be distinguished among American *Gallinæ*, by the foregoing characters.

* **mast,** *n.* In combs.: (1) * **masthead,** the statement printed in each issue of a periodical as to the title, ownership, subscription rates, etc.; (2) **man,** (see quot. 1890); (3) **pine,** the white pine, *Pinus strobus*, of the eastern states.

(1) **1838** *Hennepin* (Ill.) *Jrnl.* 22 Dec. 1/1 Many of our Whig friends in this and the adjoining counties were anxious that the Journal should . . . carry Whig colors at the mast-head. **1948** *Pacific Discovery* Jan.–Feb. 3/1 We have added a qualifying word indicative of the direction in which we plan to chart our course, and have placed at our masthead *Pacific Discovery.* — (2) **1839** BRIGGS *H. Franco* I. 236 All hands call him dismal Jerry, except Mike, the mast man, and he calls him Sergeant Longshanks. **1890** *Cent.* 3653/2 *Mastman*, . . . a seaman stationed at a mast in a man-of-war to keep the ropes clear and in order. — (3) **1792** BELKNAP *Hist. New-Hampshire* III. 103 [White pines] are distinguished by the name of mast-pine. **1832** W. D. WILLIAMSON *Hist. Maine* I. 111 The Hemlock in stature almost vies with the mast-pine.

* **master,** *n.* In combs.: (1) **master chopper,** one in charge of a gang of log-choppers; (2) **swamper,** one in charge of swampers or road makers in logging operations; (3) **wagoner,** one in charge of a wagon train; (4) **weed,** a plant thought to be useful as a cure for rattlesnake bites, *rare*, cf. **rattlesnake master;** (5) **wort,** (*a*) the American angelica, (*b*) =**cow parsnip.**

(1) **1851** SPRINGER *Forest Life* 92 Then [come] the choppers, meaning those who select, fell, and cut the logs, one of whom is master chopper. — (2) **1851** SPRINGER *Forest Life* 92 Next [come] the swampers, who cut and clear the roads through the forest to the fallen trees, one of whom is master swamper. — (3) **1848** PARKMAN in *Knickerb.* Oct. 312 He told Coates, the master-wagoner, that the commissary at the fort had given him an order for sick-rations. — (4) **1843** MARRYAT *M. Violet* xxiv, I removed . . . the poultice of master weed.

(5) (*a*) **1796** MORSE *Univ. Geog.* I. 189 Angelica or American Masterwort (*Angelica lucida*). (*b*) **1833** EATON *Botany* (ed. 6) 172 *Heracleum lanatum*, master-wort, cow parsnip, . . . A large umbelliferous plant of a white woolly appearance. . . . Meadows and other damp places. . . . Very poisonous. **1857** GRAY *Botany* 152 *H*[*eracleum*] *lanatum*. . . . A very large, strong-scented plant . . . in some places wrongly called *Masterwort.*

b. *Master of Life*, in Indian terminology or in imitation of this, the supreme manito or ruler over the forces of nature.

1822 MORSE *Rep. Indian Affairs* II. 21 The Master of life made us Indians. **1839** HOFFMAN *Wild Scenes* 88 The vengeance of the Master of Life overtook the wretch.

As the last term in **baggage, boom, check, crop, custom, depot, ferry, forest, harbor, market, old, path, poor, rattlesnake, road, sailing, say, section, settlement, snake, stunt, ticket, track, train, truck, vendue, water, wreck, yardmaster.**

* **masting,** *n.* The felling of trees for masts. Also attrib. *Obs.*

1718 *Mass. H. Rep. Jrnls.* II. 109 A Proclamation for . . . The Protection of His Majesty's good Subjects in their just Rights . . . of Logging, Masting and Tember. **1761** S. NILES *Indian Wars* II. 325 Colonel Hilton . . . was deeply engaged in the mashing [*sic*] business, and having fell[ed] several trees of value, . . . went with several men to peel off the bark. **1792** BELKNAP *Hist. New-Hampshire* III. 3 Persons who have been employed in surveying, masting, hunting and scouting.

b. masting pine, =**mast pine.**

*a*1752 W. DOUGLASS *Summary* II. 52 The Pines may be subdivided into the Masting, or white Pine [etc.]. **1832** WILLIAMSON *Maine* I. 110 So literally is this erect and lofty masting-pine the greatest ornament of our forests, that it was adopted as one of the emblems in the shield of our State coat of arms.

* **mastodon,** *n.* **1.** A variety of cotton, in full **mastodon cotton.** *Obs.* **2.** (See quot.)

(1) **1846** *De Bow's Review* I. 168 The name *mastodon* was given to it by myself [R. Abbey]—its nativity I have never learned. **1847** *Ib.* III. 18 There is no difficulty in pressing *mastodon* cotton. **1865** TURNER *Cotton* 46 The Mastodon cotton was tried here last season under unfavorable circumstances. — (2) **1898** *Boston Transcript* 21 June 3/6 Engines weighing eighty tons, called 'Moguls,' have long been in successful operation . . . in North and South America; the ninety-five ton monster is to receive the appropriate name of the 'mastodon.'

* **mat,** *n.* As the last term in **bear, drawn-in, lamp, mahala, saddle, shuck mat.**

matanza mə'tænzə, *n. W.* [Sp., slaughter, cattle for slaughter.] A slaughtering of cattle, a place where cattle are slaughtered for their hides and tallow.

1848 BRYANT *California* 446 The value of the hides and tallow derived from the annual *matanzas*, may be estimated at $372,000. **1929** DAVIS *Seventy-Five Yrs. in Calif.* 20, I found the enterprising man in the midst of his *matanza*, with more than a thousand steers slaughtered. **1941** CLELAND *Cattle on Thousand Hills* 89 Most of the tallow obtained in a matanza was sent to San Francisco or shipped to the eastern markets.

∗**match,** *n.* **1. match game,** a game agreed upon and played as a test of superiority by two rival teams, a match. **2. match race,** a race run as a match or competition in speed.

(1) **1857** *Spirit of Times* 26 Dec. 261/3 A match game of Base-ball came off, on Saturday last, between the Arctic and Superior. **1948** *Denison* (Tex.) *Herald* 1 July 4/6 He will reach Denison in time for the match game of baseball on the Fourth. — (2) **1804** CUTLER in *Life & Corr.* II. 172 Attended the races. First race I did not see. It was a match race of two two-year old colts for $1,000. **1948** *Chi. D. News* 1 Nov. 13/3 He whipped Sir Barton, a 4-year-old, in a memorable match race.

As the last term in **friction, hanging, husking, parlor, prairie, rifle, scratch, scrub, shooting, sleighing, solar, spelling, spinning, tickle, turkey, turkey shooting match.**

∗**match,** *v. To match (for),* to toss coins to determine a loser, esp. to determine who will pay for a treat. Also ∗**matching,** *n. Colloq.*

1894 *Life* 22 Feb. 113, I have twenty and no girl. I'll match you to see whether you take the twenty or I take the girl to the Opera. **1932** *K.C. Star* 15 Jan. 26 Matching for coffee has supplanted the old game of matching for cokes.

b. To engage in a guessing contest as to whether a particular digit, usu. the last, on two bills is odd or even, the one guessing correctly taking both bills.

[**1935** MAXWELL ANDERSON *Winterset* (Act III, stage direction), The two natty young men in serge and gray are leaning against the masonry in a ray of light concentrating on a game of chance. Each holds in his hand a packet of ten or fifteen crisp bills. They compare the numbers on the top notes and immediately a bill changes hands.] **1949** GRACE TULLY *F.D.R., My Boss* 154 His practice on the way to lunch was to match dollar bills with any financially solvent twosome, and he had a mysteriously high record as odd man.

matchacomoco ˌmætʃəˈkɑməko, *n.* [Amer. Indian.] (See quots.) *Obs.* — **1663** *Va. Statutes* (1823) II. 194 Be it further enacted that the king of Potomack be injoyned not to goe and hold Matchacomico with any strange nation without knowledge of the aforesaid officers of militia. **1705** BEVERLEY *Virginia* III. 24 When they are about to undertake any War, or other solemn Enterprize, the King summons a Convention of his Great men to assist at a Grand Council, which in their Language is call'd a *Matchacomoco.*

matchcoat ˈmætʃˌkot, *n.* [f. Chippewa *matshigote.*] A mantle of fur, feathers, etc., worn by American Indians, or a cloth garment somewhat resembling this obtained by the Indians from white traders. Now *hist.*

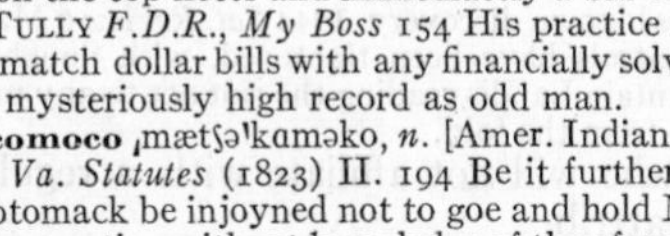

Matchcoat worn by an Indian

1638 *Md. Archives* IV. 30, 1. old match coate, 1. latin pott. **1705** BEVERLEY *Virginia* III. (1705) 5 Fig. 1 wears the proper Indian Match-coat, which is made of Skins, drest with the Furr on, sowed together, and worn with the Furr inwards, having the edges also gashed for beauty sake. **1760** HANSON *Captivity* 6 [We had] often nothing to eat but pieces of old beaver-skin match-coats. **1904** C. WEISER *Jrnl.* 32 A match-coat was a large loose coat worn by the Indians, originally made of skins, later of match-cloth.

matchet ˈmætʃɪt, *a.* [App. f. Amer. Indian.] (See quot. 1705.) *Obs.*

1676 B. THOMPSON *Poet. Wks.* 53 This no wunnegin, so big matchet law, Which our old fathers fathers never saw. **1682** MARY RAWLINSON *Narr. Captivity* 56 They said it were some Matchit Indian that did it. **1705** in *N. Eng. Co.* (1896) 88 But, at last, he entertained the distinction, that there were 'matchet' Englishmen as well as 'matchet' Indians, . . . matchet, that is to say, naughty or wicked.

match safe. (See quot. 1875.)

1864 *Hist. North-Western Soldiers' Fair* 81 [Donations include] 24 bottles perfumery, 1 match safe, 1 cigar case. **1875** KNIGHT 1410 *Match-safe,* a box to contain matches for use. Usually hung up near a gas-bracket or elsewhere within ready reach. **1893** *Outing* May 124/2 A water-tight match-safe . . . should be taken. **1902** *Sears Cat.* (ed. 112) 787/2 Twin Match Safes.

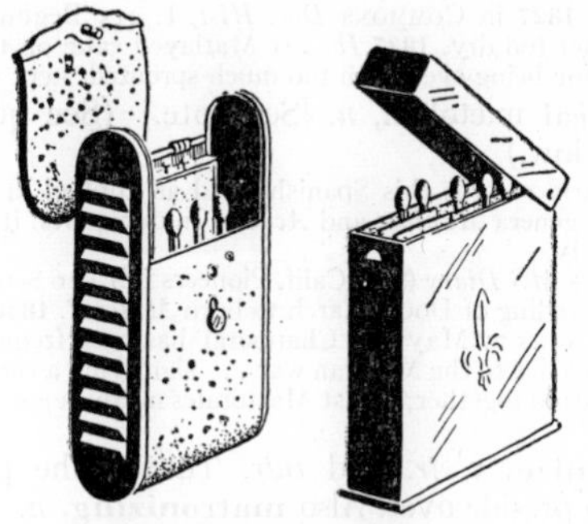

Types of match safes *c*1865

∗**mate,** *n.* "A point on tramway lines which is cast solid and pairs or 'mates' with the movable tongue or switch on the other rail; an 'open' or 'fixed' point. *Orig. U.S.*" (*OED Supp.*). — **1909** WEBSTER. **1922** *Glasgow Herald* 3 Oct. 8 The weight of the inserts varies from about 100 to 300 lb., depending on the angle of the crossing or mate.

As the last term in **bunk, cabin, class, desk, dory, rattlesnake's, room, running, sailmaker's, seat mate.**

∗**materialization,** *n.* In spiritualism, the appearance of a spirit in bodily form. — **1880** in WEBSTER *Supp.* **1892** M. TWAIN *Amer. Claimant* iii. 42 (R.), You have heard of materialization—materialization of departed spirits. **1949** *Chi. Tribune* 11 Dec. 29/2, I was anxious for a 'materialization' of my sister who had died in Duluth, Minn., in 1922.

∗**materialize,** *v. intr.* To appear, come to pass, become a reality.

1884 MATTHEWS in *Harper's Mag.* May 911/1 [The] ghosts . . . gave dark séances and manifested and materialized. **1885** CRADDOCK *Prophet* 18 Some fifteen or twenty hounds . . . suddenly materialized among the bee-hives and the althea bushes. **1904** *Omaha Bee* 28 June 4 How soon will those elevators and mills promised last winter materialize? **1945** *Bristol* (N.H.) *Enterprise* 15 Feb. 5/4 On Saturday snow again threatened but did not materialize.

materializee məˌtɪrɪəlaɪˈzi, *n.* [f. ∗**materialize,** *v.*] A "materialized" spirit. *Rare.* — **1892** M. TWAIN *Amer. Claimant* xvii. 175 (R.), The feeling . . . is not engendered by the mere conduct of the materializee.

materializer məˈtɪrɪəlˌaɪzɚ, *n.* [f. ∗**materialize,** *v.*] In spiritualism, a medium. *Rare.* — **1892** M. TWAIN *Amer. Claimant* ii. 28 (R.), One learned . . . that the Colonel was a Materializer, a Hypnotizer.

material train. A train that hauls materials for construction or repair work. — **1865** *Nation* I. 174/1 He was going up the road, he said, to see about the loading of a material train. **1902** GORDON *Recoll. Lynchburg* 42 The trip had to be made on the flats of a material train.

Mathiasism məˈθaɪəsˌɪzəm, *n.* A religious cult founded by Robert Matthias or Matthews of Hebron, N.Y., who *c*1831 proclaimed that he was Jehovah. *Obs.* — **1845** *Quincy* (Ill.) *Whig* 9 Dec. 2/3 We believe that Mormonism, like Millerism and Mathiasism, was conceived in sin and born in iniquity. **1846** *Dollar Newspaper* (Phila.) 28 Jan. 2/3 It is Mormonism and Mathiasism over again.

mat hook. [Du. *mat haak,* in sense shown here.] A device used by a reaper to hold together cut grain. *Rare.* — **1775** ROMANS *Nat. Hist. Fla.* 178, I would advise the introduction of the short scythe and hook, called in New York government segt and mat hook.

matilija poppy. [*Matilija* Canyon, Calif.] The giant poppy, *Romneya coulteri,* of California and the Southwest.

1902 *Out West* Feb. 165 (*title*), Matilija Poppies. **1920** RICE *Calif. Wild Flowers* 84 The most regally handsome poppy in the world is the giant white poppy, the stately Matilija, *Romneya coulteri,* which is native to the southern part of the State. **1949** *L.A. Times* 13 March (Home Mag.) 33 Matilija poppy . . . draws attention mostly because of the unusualness of a shrub bearing poppies, especially such huge, glistening, fragrant ones.

matlay ˈmætle, *n. La.* [F. *matelas*, mattress.] A pile or heap of sugar cane designed for seed, placed in mats or layers and covered with earth for protection from cold during the winter. Cf. **mattress.**

1853 *Harper's Mag.* Nov. 756/2 In the furrow, the cane preserved in the 'matlays' is laid in two or three parallel lines, and well lapped. [**1941** McDERMOTT *Miss. Valley French* 102 Matelas. . . . 'A layer of sugar canes kept to be planted.'] **1946** W. A. READ *Lett. to Editor* 4 Sep., I am quite familiar with *matelas*, a word which my French friends here [Baton Rouge, La.] use in such a phrase as 'un matelas cannes,' with the meaning assigned to *matlay* by the DAE.

matlay ˈmætle, *v.* [See prec.] *tr.* To place (sugar cane) in a matlay. *Obs.* — **1827** in COMMONS *Doc. Hist.* I. 215 Begun matlaying cane—weather too dry. **1837** *Ib.* 221 Matlayed cane on the 4th and 5th; these cane being even then too much sprouted, kept badly.

matorral mætəˈræl, *n.* [See note.] (See quots. and cf. note below.)

Santamaría records this Spanish word as applied in Mexico to plants of the genera *Manihot* and *Acacia*. In our quots. it appears to be used loosely.

1845 SUTTER *MS Diary* (Soc. Calif. Pioneers Lib.) 26 Sep., The boat started for Landing of Doct. March to burn *Matoral*. **1846** *New London* (Conn.) *News* 27 May 2/2 'Chapporal' has been frequently mentioned in reference to the Mexican war . . . signifying a compact mass of bushes matted together; whilst Mattorales means a good many not compact.

* **matronize,** *v. tr.* and *intr.* To act the part of a matron, to preside over. Also **matronizing,** *n.*

1866 MRS. WHITNEY *L. Goldthwaite* iv, They were to visit her next winter, and participate for the first time, under her matronizing, in city gayeties. **1877** *Rep. Indian Affairs* 7 The only individual to matronize is his family cook. **1897** HOWELLS *Landlord Lion's Head* 204 The lady who was matronizing the tea recognized him.

matron of honor. In a wedding ceremony, a married woman who is the bride's principal attendant. Cf. **maid of honor.** — **1903** *N.Y. Tribune* 20 Sep., Her only attendant, as matron of honor, wore pale blue crepe de chine. **1948** *Dly. Oklahoman* (Okla. City) 9 June 13/3 The bride and I wonder whether I should be called matron of honor or maid of honor.

* **matter,** *n.* As the last term in **front, mail, plate matter.**

mattowacca ˈmɑtəˌwɑkə, *n.* (See quots.)

1884 GOODE *Fisheries* I. 608 The name 'Mattowacca' is of Indian origin. **1896** JORDAN & EVERMANN *Check List* 281 *Pomolobus mediocris* . . . Tailor Herring; Mattowacca. **1911** *Rep. Fisheries 1908* 312 Mattowacca (*Dorosoma cepedianum*).—A poor food fish found on the Atlantic coast from Cape Cod to Florida, ascending rivers.

mattress ˈmætrɪs, *n.* [See **matlay.**] (See quot. 1829 and cf. **matlay.**) Also as a verb.

[**1814** *Niles' Reg.* VI. 200/2 This is done by putting them [stalks of sugar cane] into stacks (*morasses*) with all their leaves on.] **1829** SHERWOOD *Gaz. Georgia* (ed. 2) The stacks or banks in which seed cane is preserved during winter, are called mattresses. **1850** *Rep. Comm. Patents 1849: Agric.* 423 The cane was spoiled in the mattress, by the continued warm weather after it was mattressed.

As the last term in **husk, shuck mattress.**

* **maul,** *n. maul and wedges*, (see quot.). *Obs.* Cf. **church, ring maul.** — **1871** DE VERE 617 *Maul and wedges*, . . . used to denote the whole of a man's possessions, his movables.

* **maul,** *v. tr.* To split (fence rails) with a maul and wedges.

1677 in *Virginia Mag.* II. 168 (Th.), [The armed men] were . . . commanded to goe to work, fall trees and mawl and toat railes. **1784** SMYTH *Tour* I. 335 *Fence rails* . . . are made out of trees cut or sawed into lengths of eleven or twelve feet, which again are mauled or split into rails from four to six inches thick. **1880** HARRIS *U. Remus* (1884) 45 Brer Fox, he lammed away at dat holler tree, he did, like a man maulin' rails. **1948** DICK *Dixie Frontier* 313 Often people did not speak of splitting rails—they 'mauled' them.

* **mauler,** *n.* A rail-splitter. *Obs.* — **1788** WASHINGTON *Diaries* III. 306 The cutters and maulers had shifted to the East side of the Plantation in order to get Rails.

maul oak. An evergreen oak, *Quercus chrysolepsis*, found in California. Cf. **Valparaiso oak.**

1884 SARGENT *Rep. Forests* 146 Live Oak. Maul Oak. Valparaiso Oak. **1897** SUDWORTH *Arborescent Flora* 163 Cañon Live Oak. . . . [Commonly called] Maul Oak (Cal.). **1947** PEATTIE *Sierra Nevada* 145 Golden-cup oak—known by other names as well, such as maul oak, canyon oak, mountain live oak, etc.—is a tree of the talus slopes.

mauvaise(s) terre(s). [F. tr. of Sioux *Makochi Sika*, "bad lands."] = **badland 1.** Cf. **malpais.**

1843 *26th Congress* 2 Sess. Sen. Doc. 5 II. 41 The name of 'Mauvaises Terres' (bad lands) has been applied to districts cut up into deep and intricate chasms, from which the traveller could hardly hope to extricate himself without the assistance of a good guide, and that are doubtless due to the burning out of their pseudo-volcanoes. **1855** *S. Dak. Hist. Coll.* I. 382 Fort Pierre is situated in the country called 'Mauvaise Terre,' and for hundreds of miles around, there is no grass susceptible of being made into hay for winter food. **1939** ROLLINS *Gone Haywire* 25 The *mauvaises terres pour traverser* of the French-speaking explorers and pioneer fur traders, shortened by the early Americans into *mauvais terre*, became eventually and often misleadingly the 'Bad Lands.'

maverick ˈmævrɪk, *n.* [f. Samuel A. *Maverick* (1803–70), a Texas cattle owner who neglected to brand the calves of a small herd he once owned.]

1. *W.* A calf, cow, or steer bearing no brand and hence legitimately claimed by its finder. Also attrib.

1867 in *S.W. Hist. Ser.* VIII. (1940) 83 The term maverick which was formerly applied to unbranded yearlings is now applied to every calf which can be separated from the mother cow—the consequence is, the fastest branders are accumulating the largest stocks. **1881** ROMSPERT *Western Echo* 179 A calf that is following no cow, and is unbranded, is called a *mavorick;* and though by law these now belong to the state in some places, they used to belong to the man who first put his brand there. **1942** KENNEDY *Palmetto Country* 223 Most likely candidates for rustling are unbranded calves and cattle, called 'mavericks' in the West.

transf. **1890** *Cent.* 3666/1 *Maverick*, . . . anything dishonestly obtained, as a saddle, mine, or piece of land. (Western U.S.) **1893** *Cong. Rec.* 16 Dec. 291/1 [Mr. Raum's] successor in office . . . finds this charge as a kind of 'Maverick' wandering around, and he brands it and claims it as his own discovery. **1944** *Sat. Review* 6 May 21/1 In the first place, controls have been tightened, with doughty old Judge Kenesaw Mountain Landis reading the riot act to any mavericks who stray one step from the fold.

2. One who will not affiliate with a regular political party. Also attrib.

[**1886** *Calif. Maverick* (S.F.) 13 Feb. 4/1 If a man was unpronounced in his opinion on any subject, people would say, 'He holds maverick views,' meaning that his views were untainted by partisanship in the matter.] **1901** *McClure's Mag.* Dec. 147 Occasionally they found a maverick legislator, or traded for one. **1948** *Chi. D. News* 11 June 16/7 One Republican Senator, and not by any means a conspicuous maverick, pointed out that the Senate might have acted three months.

maverick ˈmævrɪk, *v.* [f. the noun.] *tr.* (See quot. 1890.) Also **mavericking,** *n.*

1889 *Glenrock* (Wyo.) *Graphic* 13 Sep. 1/3 Numerous cases are reported of cows having their throats cut so that the mavericking of the calf would be more easy. **1890** *Cent.* 3666/1 *Maverick*, . . . to seize or brand (an animal) as a maverick; hence, to take possession of without any legal claim; appropriate dishonestly or illegally; as, to *maverick* a piece of land. **1948** ROLLINSON *Wyo. Cattle Trails* 139 The artful practice of burning or working over brands was resorted to, with honest mavericking as a side line.

b. *intr.* To roam about at random. *Colloq.*

1940 RAINE *B. O'Connor* 203 It hadn't penetrated my think-tank that this was your hacienda when I came mavericking in.

mavericker ˈmævrɪkɚ, *n.* [f. the verb.] (See quot. 1944.) — **1889** *Denver Press* 26 July 2/5 Averill and his female companion were among the most notorious of the 'Mavericker.' **1944** ADAMS *W. Words* 97 Mavericker. A man who rode the ranges in the early days to hunt and brand mavericks.

* **mavis,** *n.* The brown thrasher or French mocking bird. Cf. **red mavis.** — **1865** BURROUGHS in *Atlantic Mo.* XV. 523/2 The Mavis, or Red Thrush, sneaks and skulks like a culprit. **1917** *Birds of Amer.* III. 170 Brown Thrasher. *Toxostoma rufum*. . . . [Also called] Mavis.

mawmouth ˈmɔˌmaʊθ, *n.* [Origin obscure.] (See quot. 1890.) Also attrib.

1840 SIMMS *Border Beagles* I. 213 Here . . . I find you, like a cursed maw-mouth that grows blind when he sees a worm wriggle. **1856**——— *Eutaw* 365 We could not withstand the bait, any more than a hungry mawmouth perch in mid-summer. **1890** *Cent.* 3666/3 *Mawmouth*, . . . the calico-, grass-, or strawberry-bass, *Pomoxys sparoides*, a centrarchoid fish. (Local, U.S.)

max mæks, *n.* [f. *max*imum.] (See first and last quots.) *Slang.* Cf. **cold max.**

1851 HALL *College Words* 197 At Union College, he who received the highest possible number of marks, which is one hundred, in each study, for a term, is said to *take Max* (or maximum); to be a *Max scholar*. *Ib.*, On the merit roll all the Maxs are clustered at the top. **1862** STRONG *Cadet Life W. Point* 64 [He was] working out an unmistakable 'max' in the mathematical section-room. **1937** KENDALL BANNING *West Point Today* 296 Cadet Lingo. . . . Max, *n.* A complete success in recitation; a maximum mark of 3.0.

max mæks, *v.* [See prec.] (See quots.) Also *to max it. Slang.* — **1871** OLIVER E. WOOD *West Point Scrap Book* 339 A Vocabulary of the Expressions and Phrases used in the Corps of Cadets. . . . To max it.—To make a perfect recitation. **1937** KENDALL BANNING *West Point Today* 296 Cadet Lingo. . . . Max, *v.* To make a 3.0 in recitation; to do a thing perfectly.

* **May,** *n.* In combs.: (1) **May basket,** see as a main entry; (2) **bird,** (*a*) in the South, the bobolink, (*b*) in the East, the knot or freckled sandpiper, *Calidris canutus;* (3) **cock,** (see quot.); (4) **corn,** on a grain exchange, corn to be delivered in May; (5) **court,** a session of court that meets regularly in May; (6) **fish,** (see quot.); (7) **sucker,** =**cutlips** (*b*); (8) **wheat,** on a grain exchange, wheat to be delivered in May.

(2) (*a*) **1823** in EASTERBY *S.C. Rice Plant.* (1945) 61 The field on the main next to Coachmans was ruined by the may-birds; there is scarcely any rice in it. **1940** E. M. COULTER *T. Spalding* 77 Winged destroyers whirled over the fields bent on destruction. These were the ricebirds, sometimes called May birds. (*b*) **1838** AUDUBON *Ornith. Biog.* IV. 132 In that country it is called the 'May Bird,' which, however, is a name also given to the Rice Bird. — (3) **1888** G. TRUMBULL *Names of Birds* 192 [The black-bellied plover is] known also at West Barnstable, Mass., as May cock. — (4) **1903** *Cin. Enquirer* 7 Jan. 9/9 May corn was up ¼ @ ½c higher. **1926** *Chi. Drovers' Jrnl.* 1 May 5/2 Holders of May corn proved to be free sellers as the near deliveries went to a further discount under the deferred months.

(5) **1836** *S. Lit. Messenger* II. 434/1 [The courthouse is] embosomed in a grove of locusts, which at the May Court fill the air with their balsamic odor. — (6) **1903** T. H. BEAN *Fishes of N.Y.* 309 The striped killifish, [is] also known as the . . . mayfish. — (7) **1884** GOODE *Fisheries* I. 614 The 'Rabbit-mouth,' 'Hare-lip,' 'Split-mouth,' or 'May Sucker' is found in abundance in many rivers of Tennessee. — (8) **1902** NORRIS *Pit* viii, I guess the visible supply of May wheat in the Chicago market is cornered. **1948** *Newsweek* 26 Jan. 22/1 He received his first memorandum from the brokerage house, informing him of his purchase of '10M May wheat.'

b. In the names of plants: (1) **May apple,** see as a main entry; (2) ***blossom,** =**mayflower,** *rare;* (3) **bush,** shadbush or June berry *qq.v.;* (4) ***cherry,** =prec.; (5) **flower,** see as a main entry; (6) **haw,** a small hawthorn, *Crataegus aestivalis;* (7) **star,** the star flower, *Trientalis americana;* (8) **wings,** =**gay wings.**

(2) **1871** *Scribner's Mo.* II. 102 Tenderest of all in yonder woods, where hepatica, and May blossoms, and Quaker ladies twinkle into life. — (3) **1831** AUDUBON *Ornith. Biog.* I. 309 The May-bush or Service. . . . This species is distinguished by its ovate, acuminate leaves, racemose flowers, linear-lanceolate petals, pubescent germens, and smooth calycine segments. — (4) **1884** SARGENT *Rep. Forests* 84 *Amelanchier Canadensis.* . . . Service Tree. May Cherry.

(6) **1868** *Amer. Naturalist* II. 468 [Deer] visit the ponds in which the May-haw grows, the fruit of which is juicy with the flavor of the apple. **1884** SARGENT *Rep. Forests* 83. — (7) **1850** S. F. COOPER *Rural Hours* 85 The elegant silvery May-star is seen here and there; by its side the tall, slender mitella. — (8) **1850** S. F. COOPER *Rural Hours* 86 As for the May-wings, or 'gay-wings,' they are in truth one of the gayest little blossoms we have. **1893** *Amer. Folk-Lore* VI. 140 *Polygala paucifolia,* May wings, Conn.; gay wings, Ferrisburgh, Vt.; N.Y.

As the last term in **Cape May.**

May apple.

1. An American plant belonging to any one of various species of the genus *Podophyllum,* esp. *P. peltatum;* also the fruit of such a plant.

1733 MILLER *Gard. Dict.* (ed. 2), *Anapodophyllon,* Duck's foot, or Pomum Maiale, i.e. May-apple. . . . This Plant was brought from America. **1737** BRICKELL *N. Carolina* 23 The May-Apple, so call'd from its having Apples in the Month of May. **1814** PURSH *Flora* II. 366 The fruit is the size of a common plum, green, eatable, and known by the name of May-apple. **1897–8** *Rep. Bur. Amer. Ethnol.* I. 420 The May-apple (*Podophyllum*), with its umbrella-shaped top, is [by the Cherokee Indians] called . . . 'it wears a hat.' **1947** *Collier's* 29 March 93/2 We have May apples and skunk cabbage. **1947** *U.S. Dispensatory* 907/2 The May apple is extensively diffused through the eastern United States.

attrib. **1886** *Harper's Mag.* June 58/2 A local store-keeper told the people . . . to go out and gather all the mandrake or 'May-apple' root they could find. **1899** GOING *Flowers* 56 The circular May-apple leaves have been folded back against their stalks.

2. (See quots.) Cf. **honeysuckle apple.**

1872 DE VERE 400 The same term of *May-Apple* is not unfrequently applied to a large, globular excrescence produced by the sting of a wasp on the miniature flowers of the Swamp Honeysuckle (*Azalea mediflora*), and, on account of its frequent occurrence, occasionally to the shrub itself. **1899** VANDERBILT *Flatbush* 293 May-apple, or 'Pinkster bloomitje,' as the Dutch people called it, was abundant early in the season.

3. A species of mallow found in Texas.

1891 COULTER *Bot. W. Texas* I. 43 *Malvaviscus Drummondii* . . . grows from the Rio Grande to the Colorado and northwestward. . . . Known as 'may apple.' The scarlet fruit, produced in late summer, is eaten both raw and cooked.

May basket. A small basket containing a gift, such as flowers or candy, left at a friend's door on May Day. Also transf.

1869 FULLER *Flower Gatherers* 43 We found the contents of the May-baskets carefully preserved in vases on the library table. **1911** LINCOLN *Cap'n Warren's Wards* 30, I know that there must be some reason bigger than 'implicit trust' and the other May-baskets for his appointing me in his will. **1920** ——— *Mr. Pratt* 115 She said he could . . . hang his Maybaskets on somebody else's door—or words to that effect.

maycock 'mekɑk, *n.* =**maypop.** *Rare.* — **1709** LAWSON *Carolina* 54/2 The Maycock bears a glorious flower, and apple of an agreeable sweet, mixed with an acid taste.

* **mayflower,** *n.*

1. Any one of various American spring-blooming plants, esp. the trailing arbutus, *Epigaea repens,* of the eastern U.S. Also attrib. Cf. **New England mayflower.**

1778 CARVER *Travels* 520 May Flowers, Jessamine, Honeysuckles, Rock Honeysuckles. . . . I shall not enter into a minute description of the flowers above-recited. **1884** HOWELLS *S. Lapham* iv, The tints of her cheeks and temples were such as suggested May-flowers and apple-blossoms. **1942** WHITE *One Man's Meat* 282 Mayflowers have been reported fifteen miles away in the mayflower country.

2. (*cap.*) Often used allusively with reference to those claiming descent from the colonists who reached Plymouth, Mass., in 1620, on the vessel known as the Mayflower. Also attrib. and transf.

1921 *Harper's Mag.* Jan. 138/1, I have talked to a number of people, literary, industrial, commercial, professional; . . . to *Mayflower* Americans, . . . to negroes, and to immigrants. **1925** *Woman's Home Companion* Nov. 34/1 They take no pride in being descended from a gentlewoman who came over in the Mayflower. **1930** FERBER *Cimarron* 361 Now it was considered the height of chic to be able to say that your parents had come through in a covered wagon. . . . As for the Run of '89—it was Osage's *Mayflower.*

Also **Mayflower family, stock.**

1854 THORPE *Master's House* 149 The best half of me is the very pith of the Mayflower stock. **1861** *Dly. Dispatch* (Richmond, Va.) 26 July 2/1 It must be acknowledged that from the beginning, Jonathan, (meaning by that term the Mayflower family, and no other race of the North,) has 'done' John Bull exceedingly brown in every business transaction.

* **Maynard,** *n.* **1. Maynard rifle,** a type of breech-loading rifle named for its inventor, Edward Maynard (1813–91). **2. Maynard's cuckoo,** (see quot.).

(1) **1899** WYETH *Forrest* 45 Forrest took a Maynard rifle from one of his men. **1933** *D A B* XII. 458 In 1851 he patented an improvement in

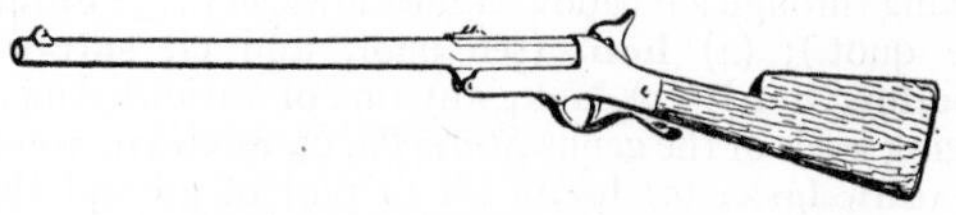

Early type of Maynard rifle

breech-loading rifles which, with subsequent improvements . . . , brought about the general adoption of the Maynard rifle by governments and sportsmen throughout the world. — (2) **1917** *Birds of Amer.* II. 130 The Mangrove Cuckoo . . . and the Bahama Mangrove, or Maynard's, Cuckoo (*Coccyzus minor maynardi*) are found in the Florida Keys and the West Indies south through Mexico to Central America.

* **mayoress,** *n.* A woman who holds the office of mayor.

1884 *Chi. Tribune* 5 May 4/3 She cannot under the laws monopolize the holding of nice special offices like Mayoress, . . . Public Librarianess, or Superintendentess of Education. **1895** *N. Amer. Rev.* Sep. 267 [One is] unable to conjecture what the results may be when women shall have become, not only *votresses,* but legisla*tresses,* mayor*esses,* and alder*women.* **1947** *Chi. Sun* 4 Nov. 16/5 The dish . . . will be delivered . . . later this week by Mrs. Margaret Craig, mayoress of Twickenham.

maypop ˈmepɑp, *n.* [See note.] The passion flower, *Passiflora incarnata,* or the fruit of this.

"Trumbull . . . considers that *maracock* is the Brazilian Tupi *mburucuia,* related to the Carib *merĕcoya* . . . , the fruit of a vine, the name and the thing having both come from South America. *Maypop* would thus ultimately represent, through *maracock,* this Tupi loan-word" (Hodge).

1851 *De Bow's Review* XI. 49 *May Pop, Passion Flower,* is also abundant here. **1896** W. R. GERARD in *Garden & For.* IX. 283 May-pop.—A name for the fruit of *Passiflora incarnata;* altered from may-cock (obsolete), a corruption of Powhatan (Algonk.) *maracock.* **1947** *Pub. Amer. Dial. Soc.* No. 8, 17 *May pop:* Usually meant the fruit of the passion flower (*Passiflora incarnata*), and by metonomy the vine itself.

attrib. **1880** HARRIS *U. Remus* (1884) 170 De drizzle w'at sets de tater-slips right Is de makin' er de May-pop vine.

mazuma məˈzumə, *n.* [Yiddish; see quot. 1926.] Money. *Slang.*

1907 MULFORD *Bar-20* viii. 90 When th' mazuma is divided up it won't buy a meal. **1926** *Amer. Sp.* I. 456 How many of those using the word *mazuma* know its meaning? As originally used by the Jewish people it is 'm'zumon' and is a Chaldean word meaning in literal translation the 'ready necessary.' It is employed in the Talmud which is written in Chaldean and not Hebrew. **1948** *Mazama* June 1/2 The Lodge Committee is now offering an opportunity to the younger members who may not have the necessary mazooma, to come up to the Lodge as Mazamas on official work trips once each month.

M.C. Abbreviation of *Member of Congress.*

1832 *Boston Transcript* 29 June 2/2 Two bundles were lately received at the Opeloasas post office, franked 'H. A. Bullard, M.C.' which contained two Marseilles vests for children in that parish. **1855** *N.Y. Wkly. Tribune* 17 Nov. 2/1 Messrs. Thomas R. Whitney and Bayard Clark, M.C.'s elect from this State, 'solicit' a meeting of the 'Members of Congress who have been chosen as Representatives of the American policy.' **1904** *N.Y. Ev. Post* 23 Sep. 5 John Wesley Gaines, M.C., made a careful study some years ago of the evils of a President's eligibility to reëlection.

* **mead,** *n.* (See quot. 1890.)

1883 *Cent. Mag.* July 419/2 The Creole boys drink mead. **1890** *Cent.* 3671/2 *Mead,* . . . a sweet drink charged with carbonic gas, and flavored with some syrup, as sarsaparilla. **1897** ROBINSON *Uncle Lisha* 297 Refreshments of mead, spruce beer, and great cards of good old-fashioned yellow gingerbread were temptingly displayed.

* **meadow,** *n.*

1. *W.* A level area of limited extent in a mountainous region, often grassy and usu. dry. Freq. in place-names. Cf. **mountain meadow.**

1870 *Amer. Naturalist* IV. 30 The meadows are bounded by Washoe Peak . . . by the Peavine Mountains . . . , and a range lying in the east. **1920** *Nat. Park Service Bul.: Rules & Reg.* 34 Through Gibbon Meadow, 4 miles from Norris, altitude 7,315 feet, are good camp sites. **1947** *Sierra Club Bul.* May 53 Concern has been growing for years over the continuing deterioration of most of the finest High Sierra meadows under the heavy grazing by pack and saddle animals.

2. (See quot. 1890.)

1877 [in **cod meadow**]. **1890** *Cent.* 3671/2 Meadow, . . . a feeding-ground of fish, as cod.

3. In combs., chiefly in the names of birds: (1) **meadow bird,** =**bobolink;** (2) **branch,** ?a branch flowing through a meadow or meadows, *obs.;* (3) **chicken,** (see quot.); (4) **hen,** (see quot. and cf. **salt-water meadow hen**); (5) **lark,** any one of various American singing birds of the genus *Sturnella,* cf. **eastern, western meadow lark;** (6) **lot,** a lot or plot of ground that is meadow land or part of a meadow, orig. such a tract allotted to a colonist; (7) **slash,** a slash having some of the features of a meadow; (8) **snipe,** (*a*) the pectoral sandpiper, *Pisobia melanotos,* (*b*) Wilson's snipe, *Capella delicata;* (9) **swamp,** low land partaking of the nature of both swamp and meadow; (10) **wink,** =**bobolink.**

(1) *c***1844** *Nat. Hist. N.Y., Zoology* II. 144 The Boblink . . . is known in others [i.e., states] by the various names of Reed-bird, May-bird, Meadow-bird [etc.]. **1917** *Birds of Amer.* II. 241 Bobolink. . . . [Also called] Meadow-bird. — (2) **1718** in *Amer. Sp.* XV. 283/2 Beginning at a Small meadow branch. **1721** *Ib.* 284/1 At a small drain or meadow branch. — (3) **1893** NEWTON *Dict. Birds* 539 *Meadow-chicken* and *Meadow-hen,* names given in North America to more than one species of Rail or Coot. — (4) *a***1841** HAWES *Sporting Scenes* I. 18 The principal inhabitants are gulls, and meadow-hens. **1893** [see **meadow chicken**].

(5) **1775** ROMANS *Nat. Hist. Fla.* 114 Meadow larks, fieldfares, rice birds, &c. &c. are very frequently had. **1948** JACOBS *We Chose Country* 161 Birds were everywhere, first killdeers, making a din in the fields at dusk, then meadowlarks, caroling in the morning sun. — (6) **1637** *Dedham Rec.* 28 Graunted to Samuell Morse yt necke of meadowe lying . . . towards the North to have it for a meadowe Lott. **1754** *Waterbury Prop. Rec.* 186 To Settle the bounds of the Meadow Lots. **1884** *Harper's Mag.* Feb. 413/2, I am very much in love with—the meadow lot. — (7) **1722** in *Amer. Sp.* XV. 284/1 Thence . . . to a corner in a meadow slash. — (8) (*a*) **1844** GIRAUD *Birds of Long Island* 235 To some of the residents of the Island, it is known by the name of 'Meadow Snipe.' **1917** *Birds of Amer.* I. 233/1. (*b*) **1890** *Cent.* 3672/1 Meadow-snipe. . . . The common American or Wilson's snipe, *Gallinago wilsoni* or *delicatula.* B. S. Barton, 1799. . . . (Local, U.S.). **1917** *Birds of Amer.* I. 227. — (9) **1655** *Suffolk Deeds* II. 156 A parcell of meadow swamp and vpland contayneing about Six Acres. **1720** *Amer. W. Mercury* 9 June 2/2 To be Sold by Mary Willson . . . good Corn Land with several parcells Meadow Swamps.

(10) **1884** COUES *N. Amer. Birds* (ed. 2) 400 *Dolichonyx oryzivorus.* . . . Bobolink. Meadow-wink. Skunk Blackbird.

b. In the names of plants: (1) **meadow beauty,** =**deer grass;** (2) **bout,** the marsh marigold; (3) **lily,** the Canada lily, *Lilium canadense,* or the lily of the valley, *Convalaria majalis;* (4) * **parsnip,** (*a*) the golden meadow parsnip, *Zizia aurea,* (*b*) any plant of the genus *Thaspium* with yellow flowers, often with defining adj.; (5) **pine,** (*a*) the Cuban pine, *Pinus caribaea,* (*b*) =**loblolly pine.**

(1) **1840** DEWEY *Mass. Flowering Plants* 51 Deer Grass, Meadow Beauty, . . . flowers in July, and grows in wet meadows. **1901** MOHR *Plant Life Ala.* 633 *Melastomaceae.* Melastoma Family. *Rhexia.* . . . Nine species. . . . Maryland Meadow Beauty [etc.]. — (2) **1784** CUTLER in *Mem. Amer. Acad. Arts. & Sci.* (1785) I. 459 Meadow-bouts. — (3) **1832** WILLIAMSON *Maine* I. 125 [We have] two varieties of meadow-lilies, . . . May-lily, or 'lily of the valley;' and nodding-lily. **1894** *Amer. Folk-Lore* VII. 102 *Lilium Canadense,* . . . meadow lily, nodding lily, N.Y. — (4) (*a*) **1833** EATON *Botany* (ed. 6) 401 *Zizia aurea,* meadow parsnip, alexanders. **1839** *Mich. Agric. Soc. Trans.* VII. 422 *Zizia aurea.* Meadow parsnep. (*b*) **1857** GRAY *Botany* 155. **1866** LINDLEY & MOORE *Treas. Botany* 1140 *Thaspium,* a genus of North American orthospermous *Umbelliferae.* . . . Its popular American name is Meadow Parsnip.

(5) (*a*) **1884** SARGENT *Rep. Forests* 202 *Pinus Cubensis.* . . . Slash Pine. Swamp Pine, Bastard Pine, Meadow Pine. **1898** SUDWORTH *Check List Forest Trees* 19 Pinus heterophylla. . . . Names in use.—Slash Pine (Ala., Miss., Ga., Fla.); . . . Meadow Pine (Fla., eastern Miss., in part). (*b*) *Ib.* 26 Loblolly Pine. . . . [Also called] Meadow Pine (Fla.).

As the last term in **bank, bayberry, beaver, bog, camass, cane, cranberry, dry, fresh, Indian, marsh, mountain, mowing, peat, river, salt, shaking, swamp, thatch, timothy, white, wild meadow.**

meadowish land. Land like or resembling a meadow. *Obs.* — **1668** *Springfield Rec.* II. 98 The Town granted unto Abell Wright . . . ffourteen acres of Meddowish Land up the little River. **1687** *Lancaster Rec.* 299 Ye land . . . bounded . . . westerly partly by a brook and partly by some ministeriall meadowish Land.

* **meal,** *n.*

1. =**Indian meal.**

In the first two quots. it is not clear whether or not the meal is made from Indian corn.

1623 *Va. House of Burgesses* 21 The allowance . . . for a man was only eight ounces of meale and half a pinte of pease. **1659** *R.I. Court Rec.* I. 57 The Sayd Indian . . . did one time this Summer steale a certaine parcell of meals out of George Laytons Mill to the quantity of three fower or five pecks of meale. **1775** in PUSEY *Road to Ky.* (1921) 42 [We] went on again to Brileys mill & suployed our Selves with meal. **1819** *Plough Boy* I. 115 A little meal of Indian corn and oats [was added]. **1948** *Dly. Ardmoreite* (Ardmore, Okla.) 20 April 3/3 He turns out fine White Wave flour and a meal that makes the best southern cornbread.

2. In combs., in some of which the first term is *meal* in the sense of a portion of food: (1) * **meal bag,** a bag used for conveying corn to, and meal from, a mill, cf. **mill bag;** (2) * **barrel,** a barrel in which corn meal is kept; (3) **moth,** a moth whose larva feeds on meal or flour (see quots.); (4) **pennant,** (see quot. 1890); (5) **-plum vine,** the bearberry, *Arctostaphylos uva-ursi;* (6) **sack,** =**meal bag;** (7) **snout-moth,** a kind of meal moth (see quots.); (8) **station,** a place where trains stop to allow passengers to secure meals, cf. **dinner station;** (9) **ticket,** a ticket which entitles the holder to a meal or to meals, also transf.

(1) **1644** *Essex Probate Rec.* I. 46 Too meal baggs. **1738** *N.H. Probate Rec.* II. 622 He knows of no meal Bag that his son had but what he borrowed of him. **1876** *Wide Awake* 72/1 She was bundled up so you would hardly have known her from one of the meal-bags. — (2) **1909** *Cent. Supp.* 329/1 *Cush*, (origin obscure) in North Carolina, the crumbs and scrapings of cracker or meal-barrels, fried with grease. — (3) **1842** T. W. HARRIS *Rep. Insects of Mass.* 343 The meal-moth (*Pyralis farinalis*), the caterpillar of which may be found in old flour-barrels, is often seen on the ceilings of rooms. **1909** *Rep. N.J. State Museum* 535 P[lodia] interpunctella Hbn. The 'meal moth'; common throughout the State in houses; the larva lives on meal, flour, dried fruits, etc. — (4) **1890** *Cent.* 3672/3 Meal pennant, meal pendant, in the United States navy, a red pennant displayed on ships of war during the time that the crew are at meals. **1899** *Scribner's Mag.* XXV. 89/2 The quartermaster . . . hauled down the meal pennant.

(5) **1882** in GODFREY *Nantucket* 36 The mealplum vine . . . gives true richness to the commons of Nantucket. — (6) **1860** in *Amer. Hist. Rev.* XXXIII. 602, I must tell you about those fatigue jackets. . . . Lieutenant McCook . . . is a great stickler for looseness and most of them looked as if they had meal sacks on. **1931** *K.C. Times* 18 Sep., A lady customer perched herself upon a meal sack. — (7) **1895** *Yearbook Dept. Agric. 1894* 286 The Meal Snout-Moth. (*Pyralis farinalis* Linn.) A moth belonging to the family Pyralidae often occurs in barns and other buildings wherever farinaceous products are housed. **1902** *Bureau of Entomology Bul.* ns. No. 4, 118 The Meal Moths. Two species of moths, in addition to the clothes moths, are habitual frequenters of the household, . . . the Indian-meal moth . . . [and] the meal snout-moth. — (8) **1895** CHAMBLISS *Diary* 324 The menu at the meal stations along through Texas and Arizona consists of white-leather steak, overdue eggs, bad-smelling butter, corn dodgers, and 'boot-leg' coffee. **1945** *Collier's* 17 Nov. 98/4 As the train approached a meal station the engineer blew a whistle code. — (9) **1870** O. LOGAN *Before Footlights* 248 The rather scrubby party who occasionally purchases . . . a 'Meal Ticket,' and thus gets entrance to the festive dining hall. **1903** G. ADE *People You Know* 189 When they got through with the living Meal Ticket he was as meek as an English Servant and ready to take orders from any one. **1949** *Sat. Ev. Post* 16 April 174/3 Places that cater to gentlemen of the fancy are decorated with any number of enlarged prints showing Louis exploding his meal ticket on the points of victims' chins.

b. In the names of foods and drinks prepared from corn meal, as **meal coffee, dumpling, mush, pudding.**

1909 *Pioneer Days Southwest* 253 Had nothing to eat but corn-bread and meal coffee. — **1868** G. G. CHANNING *Recoll. Newport* 19 The food given to us little children was bread and milk, and meal dumplings and molasses. — **1898** WESTCOTT *D. Harum* xxv, We had . . . potatoes, an' duff, an' johnny-cake, an' meal mush, an' milk emptins bread. — **1825** NEAL *Bro. Jonathan* II. 156 'Thee takes thy meal with me today?' 'Meal'; thought our hero; '. . . he means a meal pudding.'

As the last term in **acorn, bone, bread, brown, buckwheat, cob, corn, cornstalk, cottonseed, gluten, Indian corn, mesquite, nooning, parched, prayer, square, store meal.**

* **mealer,** *n.* One who has his meals at one place and his room or living quarters at another. *Colloq. Obs.* Cf. **haul mealer.**

1880 *Harper's Mag.* Sep. 619/2 The term 'mealer' is applied to those boarders living outside in the cottages, for whom, in wet weather, . . . [the buckboard] is sent by the hotel-keepers. **1896** *Boston Jrnl.* 24 Dec. 10/2 Boarders and mealers in this city owe a deep debt of gratitude to Dr. Harrington for his vigilance in the matter of oleomargarine. **1912** N. M. WOODROW *Sally Salt* 104 Besides the farm, I make something taking in mealers.

* **mean,** *a.*

1. * *To feel mean*, to feel ashamed, guilty. *Colloq.*

1839 MARRYAT *Diary in Amer.* II. 35, I never felt so mean in all my life. **1875** MARK TWAIN *Sk., New & Old* 88, I said I would feel mean to lie abed and sleep, and leave her to watch . . . our little patient. **1884** ———*H. Finn* xli. 421 [She] tucked me in, and mothered me so good I felt mean.

2. mean white, *S.* a "cracker" or "clay eater"; a member of the class known as "poor white trash." Also attrib.

1837 MARTINEAU *Society* II. 146 He told me that there was great excitement among the negroes in Augusta [about a lynching]; and that many had been saying that 'a mean white person' (a white labourer) would not have been hanged. **1869** TOURGEE *Toinette* ix. 104 There was no chance of patronizing this woman, if she was a 'mean white.'

* **meander,** *v. tr.* **1.** To follow the course of, or explore (a stream). **2.** Of a stream: To flow through (a tract of land). Both *obs.*

(1) **1821** in *Mo. Hist. Soc. Coll.* II. (1906) 61 We still continued meandering the Arkansas. **1839** LEONARD *Adventures* (1904) 69 We separated, each party to meander the rivers that had been respectively allotted to them. — (2) **1839** *Mich. Agric. Soc. Trans.* VII. 360 Branches of Swan creek meander this tract in such manner as to facilitate drainage.

* **means,** *n. pl. local.* (See quot. *c*1770.) — *c***1770** BOUCHER *Glossary* p. xlix, *Means;* medicines:—the means whereby sickness is relieved. **1835** LONGSTREET *Ga. Scenes* 209 First she took the ager and fever, and took a 'bundance o' doctor's means for that.

Means grass. = Johnson grass.

1858 *So. Cultivator* XVI. 57/2 We advise all our readers who are troubled with. . . . 'Means Grass,' . . . to give this place a fair trial. **1884** VASEY *Agric. Grasses* 51 *Sorgum halapense.* (Cuba grass, Johnson grass, Means grass, False Guinea grass, Evergreen millet, Arabian millet.) A tall perennial grass. **1887** W. J. BEAL *Grasses N. Amer.* I. 171.

* **Mearns,** *n.* [Dr. Edgar A. *Mearns* (1856–1916), army surgeon and naturalist.] Used, usu. in the possessive, in the names of animals: (1) **Mearns's coyote,** (see quot. 1917); (2) **quail,** a variety of the Massena quail *q.v.;* (3) **woodpecker,** a woodpecker, *Balanosphyra formicivora aculeata*, found in the Southwest.

(1) **1917** *Animals of Amer.* 66/2 Mearns Coyote.—*Canis mearnsi* Merriam. Size small, color bright, skull and teeth small. Southern Arizona. **1931** BAILEY *Mammals N. Mex.* 321 Specimens in the United States National Museum collection carry the range of Mearns's coyote across the Lower Sonoran valleys of New Mexico. — (2) **1903** *Condor* V. 113, I looked and became aware that I was staring at my first Mearns quail. **1949** *Pacific Discovery* Jan.–Feb. 11/1 Whereas turkeys had increased in the past decade, the Mearns quail had suffered a decrease of at least equal proportion. — (3) **1928** BAILEY *Birds N. Mex.* 387 The Mearns Woodpecker is the most abundant woodpecker in many parts of southern New Mexico.

* **measurably,** *adv.* To some extent, in a measure.

1756 WOOLMAN *Journal* (1840) 30 The public meetings were large and measurably favoured with divine goodness. **1869** MARK TWAIN *Innocents* 131 The ground ought to be measurably sacred by this time one would think. **1932** BECK *Wonderland* 10 The first necessity of the new government was to provide revenues, and this was measurably accomplished by the passage of the first tariff act.

* **measure,** *n.* As the last term in **Cape Cod, cornstalk coffin, log, new, southern, war measure.** See also **peace measures.**

* **measure,** *v.*

1. In slang expressions (see quots.).

*a***1890** *N.Y. Mercury* (B. & L.), He had been measured for a funeral sermon three times, he said, and had never used either one of them. **1890** BARRERE & LELAND (1897) II. 47 *Measured for a funeral sermon, to be*, . . to be near death's door. — **1896** FARMER & HENLEY IV. 296/2 *To have been measured for a new umbrella*. . . . (1) To appear in new but ill-fitting clothes; whence (2) to pursue a policy of doubtful wisdom.

2. *To measure up to*, to have the qualifications for, to fill the requirements for.

1910 *N.Y. Ev. Post* 16 Dec. 8 A man should be found for Senator who in ability and character will measure up to the just demands of such a situation. **1931** G. T. CLARK *Leland Stanford* 405 Stanford ever had in mind the problem of selecting someone who measured up to his ideal as president of his university.

measuring worm. The larva of a geometrid moth; a looper. — **1843** *Nat. Hist. N.Y., Zoology* VI. 41 It walks after the manner of some caterpillars called *Measuring worms.* **1946** *Nat. Geog. Mag.* Sep. 354/1 Who has not had himself measured, inch by inch, for a new suit by a green 'measuring worm' that had come down from a treetop to his shoulder.

* **meat,** *n.*

1. The flesh or body of a person. *Slang. Obs.*

1834 CARUTHERS *Kentuckian* I. 27 If I hadn't had so many inches, he'd have been into my meat. **1847** ROBB *Squatter Life* 59 Old Tom Jones' yell . . . gives my meat a slight sprinklin' of ager whenever I think on it.

2. One's quarry or victim. *Slang.*

1872 MARK TWAIN *Roughing It* I. 357 Come along—you're my meat *now*, my lad, anyway. **1902** HARBEN *A. Daniel* 141 As soon as he told me that I knew he was our meat. **1913** LONDON *Valley of Moon* 448 This young Sandow's my meat.

3. In combs.: (1) * **meat ax,** see as a main entry; (2) **bag,** the stomach, *slang, obs.;* (3) **baron,** a wealthy meat packer; (4) **barrel,** a strong, heavy barrel in which meat is packed; (5) **bird,** (*a*) **=Canada jay,** (*b*) **=Clark's crow;** (6) **biscuit,** (see quot. 1889); (7) **glacier,** (see quot.), *obs.;* (8) **hawk, =meatbird** (*a*); (9) **hunt,** a hunting expedition in search of game, as buffalo, also **meat hunter;** (10) **packing,** the business of slaughtering animals and preparing their meat for transportation and sale, also attrib., hence **meat packer;** (11) **party,** a hunting party sent out to procure meat; (12) ∗**pie,** see as a main entry; (13) **store,** a meat market; (14) **train,** on a military expedition, a supply train carrying meat, *obs.*

(2) **1848** Ruxton in *Blackw. Mag.* LXIII. 716 One [arrow] in his meat-bag, and two more 'bout his hump ribs. **1850** Garrard *Wah-To-Yah* iii. 46, I bet I make you eat dogmeat . . . and you'll say it's . . . the best you ever hid in your meatbag. — (3) **1932** *Blue Valley Farmer* (Okla. City) 3 March 2/5 Until recently 'meat barons' were among the loudest champions of 'less government in business.' — (4) **1778** *Jrnls. Cont. Congress* X. 249 Meat barrels, for packing beef, pork, or fish, each, 4/90ths of a dollar. **1833** A. Greene *Yankee among Nullifiers* 84 Bring a meat barrel and a half bushel of salt.

(5) (*a*) *a***1862** Thoreau *Maine Woods* 220 Three large slate-colored birds of the jay genus . . . , the Canada-jay, moose-bird, meat-bird, or what not, came flitting silently . . . toward me. **1917** *Birds of Amer.* II. 225. (*b*) *Ib.* 234 The Clarke Crow is very fond of meat, and for this reason he has often been called 'meat bird.' — (6) **1851** *De Bow's Review* X. 589, I sent you a pamphlet, giving an account of a useful invention, by a highly respected citizen of Texas, Gail Borden, Jr., termed, by the inventor, *Meat Biscuit.* **1889** *Cent.* 563/2 *Meat biscuit*, a preparation consisting of the matter extracted from meat by boiling, combined with flour, and baked in the form of biscuits. — (7) **1784–1812** D. Thompson *Narrative* (1916) 400 We made a Glacier for frozen meat. . . . In these meat glaciers, a layer of meat is laid on the ice, and then a layer of ice, and thus continued. — (8) **1857** *No. Scenes* 53 Small birds, of the size and general appearance of the cuckoo, save for their hooked beaks, . . . were called by our boatmen, 'meat hawks.' **1917** *Birds of Amer.* II. 225 Canada Jay. *Perisoreus canadensis canadensis.* . . . [Also called] Moose-bird; Meat-Hawk; Carrion Bird. — (9) **1907** Cook *Border & Buffalo* (1938) 80 In those days it was the custom of the Mexicans to go each fall to the border of New Mexico and Texas on meat hunts. *Ib.* 185 He thought the parties that had stolen the hides were meat-hunters from the edge of the settlement on the Clear Fork of the Brazos.

(10) **1873** *Iowa Agric. Soc. Rep.* 175 The panacea for all these ills is to be found in tanneries . . . meat packing and curing houses, glue factories [etc.]. **1903** E. Johnson *Railway Transportation* 131 The large meat-packers . . . own their own cars. **1943** Menefee *Assignment* 89 The meat packing industry suffered severely because wholesale and meat prices were held down. — (11) **1856** Kane *Arctic Explor.* II. 34 We long anxiously for weather to enable our meat party to start. — (13) **1920** Howells *Vacation of Kelwyns* 187 It was the best piece of steak in the meat-store. — (14) **1845** Frémont *Exped.* 234 The meat train did not arrive this evening.

b. In colloq. and slang phrases: (1) ∗*To make meat,* see ∗**make,** *v.* **9.** (1); (2) *to take meat,* to kill someone, *obs.;* (3) *meat in the pot,* (see quot. 1944).

(2) **1846** McKenney *Memoirs* I. 130 Red-Bird was called upon to go out, and 'take meat,' as they phrase it. — (3) **1869** *Overland Mo.* Aug. 126 Among names of revolvers I remember the following: Meat in the Pot, Blue Lightning, Peacemaker [etc.]. **1944** Adams *W. Words* 98 Meat in the pot. Slang name for a rifle, because this weapon is used by the hunter to secure meat for the camp.

As the last term in **bear, beat, bull, dark, ham, moose, mule, painter, shaved, sheep, sheep's, side meat.**

∗**meat ax.**

1. *fig.* A rough or crude method or means. *Colloq.*

1895 *N.Y. Dramatic News* 7 Dec. 3/2 For a lumbering, English melodrama it fills the bill, in spite of the editing Mr. Brady did with a meat-axe. **1902** Lorimer *Lett. Merchant* 41, I guess you'll see the point without my elaborating with a meat ax.

2. In phrases indicative of something in the extreme (see quots.). *Colloq.*

1834 C. A. Davis *Lett. J. Downing* 185 Its helve is of hickory—in Kentucky parlance, 'is as savage as a meat-axe.' **1838** Haliburton *Clockmaker* 2 Ser. ix. 141 She was as smart as a fox-trap, and as wicked as a meat-axe. **1856** *Western Citizen* (Paris, Ky.) 29 Feb. 4/1 Why you are as sharp as a meat axe.

∗**meat pie.** (See quot. *a*1870.)

1860 Holmes *E. Venner* vii, Mixed conversation chopped very small, like the contents of a mince-pie,—or meat pie, as it is more forcibly called in the deep-rutted villages. *a***1870** Chipman *Notes on Bartlett* 266 *Meat-pie.* A mince-pie. Occasionally, in this reference, heard in—N[ew] E[ngland]. **1894** *Harper's Mag.* Sep. 609/1, I dun'no' when I've eat a decent meat pie.

∗**meaty,** *a. fig.* Full of significance, weighty. *Colloq.* — **1865** Lowell *Biglow P.* 2 Ser. x. 213 Their talk wuz meatier, an' 'ould stay. **1896** Advt. of *Preacher's Complete Homiletic Commentary,* The Index suggests thousands of meaty themes for sermons.

mecate mə'kɑtɪ, *n.* [Amer. Sp. (<Nahuatl) in same sense.] (See quot. 1879.) Cf. **McCarty.**

1849 Revere *Tour of Duty Calif.* 260 Picketing our horses by the 'mecate,' we began telling stories, and some . . . of the party fell asleep. **1879** Webster *Supp.* 1566 *Mecate,* . . . a rope of hair or of the fiber of the maguey, used for tying horses, etc. (*Southwestern U.S.*) **1939** Rollins *Gone Haywire* 126 At the bottom of the heap lay chaparejos, a bridle, saddle, quirt, mecate, and a pair of spurs.

∗**mechanic,** *n.* **1. mechanic shop,** a shop in which some mechanical work is done. **2. Mechanics' ticket,** a political ticket supported by the "workies." *Obs.* Cf. **worky.**

(1) **1819** E. Dana *Geog. Sk.* 95 It . . . contains . . . two copper and tin manufactories, and a number of other mechanic shops. **1837** W. Jenkins *Ohio Gaz.* 102 There are . . . 10 mechanic shops. — (2) **1830** *Williams's N.Y. Ann. Reg.* 73 Senatorial and Judicial Districts. . . . First Senate District. . . . Webb 5125. . . . On Mechanics' Ticket.

∗**Mecklenburg,** *n.* [*Mecklenburg* Co., N.C.]

1. *Mecklenburg Resolves,* a series of resolutions passed May 31, 1775, at Charlotte, in Mecklenburg County, N.C., suspending the authority of the British government and making provision for local administration.

1775 in *Amer. Hist. Rev.* XIII. 19 You'll Observe the Mechlinburg resolves, exceed all other Committees, or the Congress itself. **1907** Hoyt *Mecklenburg Dec. Independence* 22 The Mecklenburg resolves of May 31, 1775, appeared in the *South-Carolina Gazette;* and *Country Journal* of Tuesday, June 13, 1775.

2. With *Declaration* (*of Independence*), etc.: Designating the resolutions (resembling those of the national Declaration of Independence of July 4, 1776) first published in 1819 as a document regarded as emanating from a convention in Charlotte on May 20, 1775.

The authenticity of this document has been questioned by many historians, who regard it as the result of false tradition based upon confusion with the Resolves (see **1.** above) of May 31, 1775. Cf. W. H. Hoyt *The Mecklenburg Declaration of Independence* (1907).

1819 J. Adams in Hoyt *Mecklenburg Dec. Independence* 11 The Mecklengburg Resolutions are a fiction. **1819** in *Dec. of Indep. by Citizens Mecklenburg Co.* (1831) 16, I then proceeded on to Philadelphia, and delivered the Mecklenburg Declaration of Independence of May, 1775. **1830** *Ib.* 27, I do certify that the foregoing statement, relative to the Mecklenburg Independence, is correct. **1831** *Ib.* p. vii, The striking similarity of expression in the concluding sentences of the Mecklenburg Declaration, and the Declaration by Congress on the 4th of July, 1776, has been repeatedly urged. **1949** *N.C. Hist. Review* Jan. 29 It is odd that no publications from the semi-centenary celebration of the Mecklenburg Declaration have come to light.

med mɛd, *n.* [Short for ∗*medical.*] (See quot. 1851.)

1851 Hall *College Words* 198 *Med., Medic,* a name sometimes given to a student in medicine. **1853** *Songs of Yale* 16 Take . . . Sixteen interesting 'Meds,' With dirty hands and towzeled heads. **1899** Quinn *Pa. Stories* 19 The Meds waited till the visitors were opposite them.

∗**medal,** *n.*

1. medal chief, an Indian chief possessing a medal given him in token of his rank, influence, etc. *Obs.*

1772 in *Travels Amer. Col.* 518 [Letter] to the Great and Small medal chiefs. **1800** Hawkins *Sk. Creek Country* 27 He is one of the great medal chiefs. **1813** *Niles' Reg.* V. 270/2 At this moment a medal chief of the *Choctaw* nation is soliciting to be employed.

2. Medal of Honor, =**Congressional Medal of Honor.**

1909 Webster. **1945** *Newsweek* 16 April 52/2 Except for the Purple Heart . . . American soldiers received only merit certificates for bravery until Congress established the Medal of Honor in 1862.

medeola mə'diələ, *n.* [Dim. f. L. *Medea* (the enchantress).] The Indian cucumber or the genus of plants to which it belongs.

1784 Cutler in *Mem. Acad.* I. 437 *Medeola* . . . Indian Cucumber. **1818** *Mass. H.S. Coll.* 2 Ser. VIII. 169 Among those, that flower in June, the most interesting are . . . two species of crowfoot, the blue-eyed grass, the medeola [etc.]. **1887** Burroughs in *Cent. Mag.* XXXIV. 323 Indian cucumber root, one of Thoreau's favorite flowers, is named after the sorceress Medea, and is called 'medeola.'

medialuna 'medɪə,lunə, *n.* (See quot.) — **1884** Goode *Fisheries* I. 395 The 'Half-moon,' more commonly known by its Spanish name, 'Medialuna,' *Scorpis californiensis,* . . . forms the greater part of the catch at San Pedro.

∗**median,** *a.* and *n.* (See quot. 1945.) — **1928** Henderson & Davie *Incomes & Living Lists of Univ.* 31 The median amount earned by extra teaching. **1945** C. V. Good *Dict. Educ.* 256 median: (*Md*) the point on the scale of a frequency distribution above which and below which 50 per cent of the observations occur; used as a measure of central tendency, but should not be confused with *mean* or *mode.*

* **medicine,** *n.*

1. (See quots.)

1805 LEWIS in *L. & Clark Exped.* II. (1924) 177 It is probable that the large river just above those great falls . . . has taken its name *Medicine river* from this unaccountable rumbling sound, which like all unaccountable things with the Indians of the Missouri is called *Medicine.* **1907** HODGE *Amer. Indians* I. 837/2 Among some tribes the term for medicine signifies 'mystery,' but among others a distinction is made between thaumaturgic practices and actual medicines. **1949** GORDON *Aesculapius Comes to Colonies* 8 The word 'medicine' itself is a good example of the American Indian's dualism of theology and medicine. . . . He employed the term not only for a drug or herb but also for some supernatural agency which may be invoked to cure disease or even insure the success of an undertaking.

b. = **medicine dance.** *Rare.*

1805 CLARK in *Lewis & C. Exped.* (1904) I. 245 A Buffalo Dance (or Medeson) for 3 nights passed in the 1st. Village, a curious Custom. . . . All this is to cause the buffalow to come near so that they may kill them.

c. A fetish, talisman, charm, deity, patron, etc., regarded as having supernatural power or potency. Also transf.

1807 GASS *Journal* 44 He told them . . . that he had more medecine aboard his boat than would kill twenty such nations in one day. **1899** CUSHMAN *Hist. Indians* 160 [When the ancient Indian] said it is 'good medicine,' he meant that the good spirit had the ascendency; and when he said it is 'bad medicine' he meant that the bad spirit had the ascendency. **1905** *N.Y. Ev. Post* 29 June 1 The coaches [were] talking 'race medicine' to the eight, who were already boated. **1929** F. E. MCCLINCHEY *Joe Pete* 101 This was the sign that the 'medicine' was strong and working, and requests could be heard.

d. = **medicine man.** *Obs.*

1827 COOPER *Prairie* II. xii, [The] release of the captives . . . was attributed by the hags to the incantations of the medicine. **1846** THORPE *Myst. Backwoods* 58 The whole tribe had . . . learned to respect him, and to look upon him as a great 'Medicine.'

2. Beaver bait, a mixture of beaver secretions, whisky, and various spices. Cf. **barkstone.**

1837 IRVING *Bonneville* II. 15 A small twig is then stripped of its bark, and one end is dipped in the 'medicine,' as the trappers term the peculiar bait which they employ. **1884** *Pop. Sci. Mo.* XXV. 20 The 'medicine' used as bait, sometimes denominated 'barkstone,' is the product of a gland of the beaver. **1947** DEVOTO *Across Wide Missouri* 157 The trapper . . . called it 'medicine,' 'castoreum,' or the like and carried it in a plugged horn at his belt.

3. In combs., now obs. or hist.: (1) **medicine arrow,** among American Indians, an arrow regarded as having magical powers; (2) **bag,** the bag in which an Indian

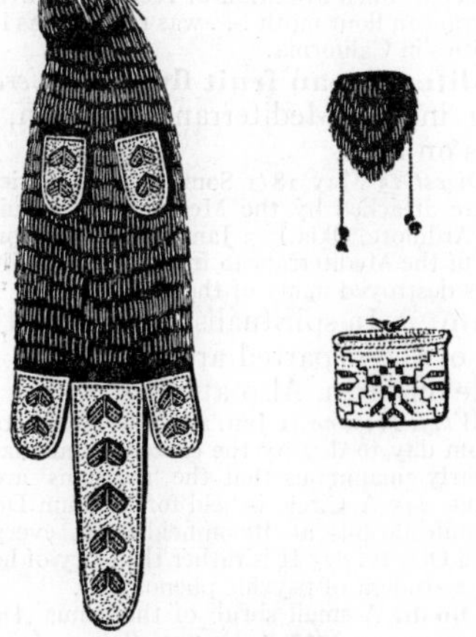

Medicine bags

carries his charms, fetishes, remedies, etc.; (3) **dance, a** dance engaged in by Indians to invoke or secure supernatural aid, cf. **grand medicine dance;** (4) **ground,** sanctified ground; (5) **man,** see as a main entry; (6) **pipe,** an Indian pipe used in various rites and ceremonies, also attrib.; (7) **show,** a cheap show or attraction at which medicine, sometimes represented as having originated among the Indians, is advertised and sold; (8) **stone,** see as a main entry; (9) **talk,** after the Indian manner of speaking, an important discussion or conference; (10) * **tree,** app. a species of California pine, *rare;* (11) **wolf,** among Plains Indians, the small prairie wolf or coyote; (12) **woman,** among the Indians, a female healer or diviner, cf. **medicine man.**

(1) 1863 J. L. FISK *Exped. Rocky Mts.* 5 Antoine Freniere described it to be a 'medicine arrow.' **1877** W. MATTHEWS *Ethnog. Hidatsa Indians* 69 They stuck their medicine-arrows in the ground. — **(2) 1805** CLARK in *Lewis & C. Exped.* III. (1905) 170 The Chief then directed his wife to hand him his medison bag which he opened and showed us 14 fingers . . . of his enemies which he had taken in war. **1947** B. HAILE *Prayer Stick Cutting* 39 These bundles of small medicine bags had been tied together by the singer and had their identification marks. — **(3) 1805** CLARK in *Lewis & C. Exped.* I. (1904) 245 We Sent a man to this Medisan Dance last night. **1949** GORDON *Aesculapius Comes to Colonies* 8 *The Medicine Dance* was engaged in alike by the Ojibwa, the Plains Cree, the central Algonkian and the Siouan tribes. — **(4) 1843** HAWKS *D. Boone* 78 Boone . . . drank the war-drink, and did not even leave the 'medicine-ground.'

(6) 1833 CATLIN *Indians* I. 111 With medicine-pipes in his hands and foxes tails attached to his heels, [he] entered Mah-to-he-hah. **1949** *Nat. Hist.* May 195/2 Chief Hind Bull was dressed for his Medicine Pipe Dance. — **(7) 1938** ASBURY *Sucker's Prog.* 355 Minnie and Colorado Charley then organized a medicine show with which they traveled through Mexico and Central America. **1949** *Chi. Tribune* 24 Sep. II. 1/1 Dr. Parker's medicine show is scheduled here for next Saturday night. — **(9) 1859** G. A. JACKSON *Diary* (MS) 12 Had a 'medicine talk' with them about diggings. **1924** BECHDOLT *Tales* 114 The punchers held a big medicine talk among themselves.

(10) 1851 D. B. WOODS *At Gold Diggings* 142 It is called the 'medicine-tree,' because its pitch is used as a balsam for all burns and bruises. — **(11) 1837** IRVING *Bonneville* II. 147 This little, whining, feast-smelling animal, is . . . called among Indians the 'medicine wolf.' **1848** RUXTON *Life Far West* iii. 117 The *wachunkamănet,* or 'medicine wolf' of the Indians, who hold the latter animal in reverential awe. — **(12) 1834** *Knickerb.* IV. 372 The mother evinced her sagacity, as a diviner or medicine woman. **1932** LINDERMAN *Red Mother* 9 Pretty-shield is a 'Wise-one,' a medicine-woman, of the Crow tribe.

b. In combs. of obvious meaning or sufficiently explained in the quots.: (1) **medicine bird,** (2) **buffalo,** (3) **bush,** (4) **chief,** (5) **dog,** (6) **drum,** (7) **hogan,** (8) **house,** (9) **Indian,** (10) **iron,** (11) **lodge,** see as a main entry, (12) **pole,** (13) **pouch,** (14) **rag,** (15) **rock,** (16) **sack,** (17) **smoke,** (18) **society,** (19) **song,** (20) **spear,** (21) **water.**

(1) 1833 CATLIN *Indians* I. 158 The mourning or turtle-dove . . . being, as they [*sc.* Mandans] call it, a *medicine-bird,* is not to be destroyed or harmed by any one. — **(2) 1848** RUXTON in *Blackw. Mag.* LXIV. 587 All they required was that they should give up their guns and ammunition 'on the prairie,' and all their mules and horses—retaining the 'medicine' buffaloes (the oxen) to draw their waggons. — **(3) 1863** in *Mont. Hist. Soc. Contrib.* III. (1900) 133 In the center of the lodge there was a bush planted,—the medicine bush. — **(4) 1851** M. REID *Scalp Hunters* 312 One was the medicine chief as I could tell by the flowing white hair.

(5) 1846 SAGE *Scenes Rocky Mts.* vi, The medicine-dogs (horses), bearing fire water (whiskey). — **(6)** *c***1834** in *Minn. Hist. Bul.* VI. (1925) 346 The Indian Cotanse is this Evening beating his Medicine Drum, & his wild Song echoes through the forest. He is preparing for a hunt. **1928** LONG LANCE *Long Lance* 50 We used to stand at a distance from the medicine-tepee and listen to the pounding of the big *Miteyawin* medicine-drum. — **(7) 1903** JAMES *Indian Basketry* 33 For nine days these ceremonies last, the first day being devoted to the building and dedication of a medicine hogan. — **(8) 1840** *Knickerb.* XV. 398 The 'Medicine-House,' that is to say, the temple, stood in the midst of the village. **1841** CATLIN *Indians* II. 232 Council or medicine-houses . . . are always held as sacred places. — **(9) 1923** *Frontier* March 9 Bow String Jack . . . had refused to become a 'Pistocal' or a 'Catlick' and remained true to the faith of his Fathers and was still just a 'Medicine Injun.'

(10) 1846 SAGE *Scenes Rocky Mts.* vi, Who shall then bring us medicine-irons [guns] to kill our meat? — **(12) 1833** CATLIN *Indians* I. 90 In the centre of the little mound is erected a 'medicine pole,' about twenty feet high, supporting many curious articles of mystery and superstition. **1876** BOURKE *Journal* 14 July, The oriflame of the tribe, the 'medicine pole' was borne along in the procession: the staff is about 12 feet long and decorated elaborately with feathers of the eagle. — **(13) 1855** LONGFELLOW *Hiawatha* 205 Then they shook their medicine-pouches O'er the head of Hiawatha. **1899** CUSHMAN *Hist. Indians* 41 [The Indian] has also been ridiculed as being an idiot for carrying with him his mystic Medicine-pouch, and relying on it for safety both in seen and unseen dangers. — **(14) 1875** BOURKE *Journal* 28

May, An Indian medicine rag was found this evening . . . in form like a banner or 'marker,' about 14 inches by 25. . . . It had emblazoned in black upon one side the representation of over 75 horseshoes.

(15) 1869 *Amer. Naturalist* II. 646 Two squaws passed through the fire to their places beneath the two medicine rocks. — **(16) 1858** in *Minn. Hist. Bul.* II. (1918) 505 The medicine sack [of the Dakotas] . . . is presented to new members at the time of their reception. This is sometimes an otter skin . . . a mink . . . a fisher, or other skin. It holds their medicine. **1883** MARK TWAIN *Life on Miss.* App. D, You see my medicine-sack, and my war-club tied to it. — **(17) 1848** PARKMAN *Knickerb.* XXXI. 331 The pipe . . . was passing from the left hand to the right around the circle; a sure sign that a 'medicine-smoke' of reconciliation was going forward. — **(18) 1846** LANMAN *Summer in Wild.* (1847) 105, I had an opportunity of witnessing a Medicine Dance, and of obtaining some information with regard to the Medicine Society. **1910** HODGE *Amer. Indians* II. 838/2 Besides these two chief classes of healers there existed among some tribes large medicine societies, composed principally of patients cured of serious ailments. This was particularly the case among the Pueblos. At Zuni there still exist several such societies, whose members include the greater part of the tribe and whose organization and functions are complex. — **(19) 1791** LONG *Voyages* 74 They then smoke the pipe of peace, and have their dog feast: they also sing the grand medicine song. **1923** *Bureau Ethnology Bul.* No. 80, 149 We are only told that it is the 'medicine song' of Old Dog, a prominent chief of the old days, and that he sang it before a battle.

(20) 1832 CATLIN *Indians* I. 40 In one hand he shook a frightful rattle, and in the other brandished his medicine spear or magic wand. — **(21) 1847** RUXTON *Adv. Rocky Mts.* (1848) 243 The Indians regard with awe the medicine waters of these fountains.

c. In phrases: (1) *To make medicine,* to engage in an incantation or ritualistic ceremony in an effort to invoke the favor of the spirits or unseen powers, also transf.; (2) *to take one's medicine,* to submit to something unpleasant or disagreeable, *colloq.;* (3) *to give* (a person) *a dose of his own medicine,* see * **dose.**

(1) 1841 CATLIN *Indians* II. 248 [For] nearly every animal they hunt for, . . . they 'make medicine' for several days, to conciliate the bear (or other) Spirit, to ensure a successful season. **1925** TILGHMAN *Dugout* 22 The medicine men of the Cheyennes had built prayer lodges and were industriously making medicine. [**1946** *Reader's Digest* May 87/1 The greatest opportunity in Wisconsin history for the brewing of individual political medicine seemed at hand.] — **(2) 1896** *Cong. Rec.* 7 Jan. 512/1, I fought . . . and was licked out of my boots. I took my medicine like a man. **1904** W. H. SMITH *Promoters* 224 Let them take their medicine like men if the luck is against them.

As the last term in **bad, beaver, big, black, Cherokee, grand, Indian, snake, squaw, store, war medicine.**

medicine lodge. (See quot. 1852.) Cf. **sweat lodge.**

1814 BRACKENRIDGE *Views La.* 258 A great number of young girls were collected before the medicine lodge or temple, prizes were exhibited [etc.]. **1852** MARCY *Explor. Red River* (1854) 116 In every village may be seen small structures, consisting of a frame-work of slight poles, bent into a semi-spherical form, and covered with buffalo-hides. These are called medicine-lodges, and are used as vapor-baths. **1922** *Outing* April 301/1 The quaint and unbelievable ceremony of raising the Medicine Lodge was carried out before our fascinated eyes. **1947** *Westerners' Brand Book* 27 The Indians began leaving the reservations and heading north to hold a 'Medicine Lodge' with their allies, the Northern Cheyennes in the Big Horn Mountains.

medicine man. Among North American Indians, one who practices healing; a priest, prophet, magician, etc. Cf. **Panisee.**

Indian healers or physicians were of two classes. One class was composed of those who made use of herbs, sweatings, and other practical remedies. The other was made up of those who depended upon charms, fetishes, exorcism of evil spirits, etc. Members of this class served also as priests, prophets, magicians, conjurors, etc.

[**1709** LAWSON *Carolina* 213 You must know, that the Doctors or Conjurers, to gain a greater Credit amongst these People, tell them that all Distempers are the Effects of evil Spirits.] **1806** ORDWAY in *Jrnls. Lewis & O.* 349 Everry fiew minutes one of their warries made a Speech . . . which was all repeated by another meddison man with a louder voice. **1847** LANMAN *Summer in Wild.* 105 A medicine man would sooner die, than divulge the secrets of his order. **1949** *Nat. Geog. Mag.* Oct. 475/1 The most influential individuals among them were the shamans, or medicine men.

b. The chief character in a medicine show *q.v.*

1947 *Chi. D. Tribune* 2 Nov. IV. 4/2 He was one of the great fraternity of medicine men who went up and down the land, prior to the pure food and drug act. **1948** DICK *Dixie Frontier* 164 Each act closed at a most exciting point, giving the dapper, professional-looking medicine man an opportunity to sell various panaceas without fear of the crowd's dispersing.

medicine stone.

1. (See quot. 1823.) *Obs.* Cf. **medicine rock.**

1805 CLARK in *Lewis & C. Exped.* I. (1904) 264 Several men of their nation was gone to consult their Medison Stone. **1823** JAMES *Exped.* I. 252 The Me-ma-ho-pa or medicine stone of the *Gros ventres,* or Minnetarees, . . . is a large, naked, insulated rock. . . . The Minnetarees resort to it, for the purpose of propitiating their Man-ho-pa or Great Spirit.

2. (See quots.)

1885 HENSHAW in *Amer. Jrnl. Archæol.* I. 110, I was told they were 'medicine or sorcery stones' used by the medicine-men [among San Buenaventura Indians] in making rain, in curing the sick, and in various ceremonies. **1890** *Cent.* 3684/3 *Medicine-stone,* . . . a smooth stone found among American prehistoric remains. It was probably used as a sinker or plummet for fishing.

medio ˈmedɪo, *n. S.W.* [Sp. in same sense.] An obsolete Mexican coin worth half a "real fuerte" (see quots.). *Obs.* — **1844** G. W. KENDALL *Santa Fe Exped.* II. xii. 239 One of the lads [handed] each of the unfortunate prisoners a medio [six and a quarter cents] and a small bunch of paper cigars. **1845** GREEN *Texian Exped.* 203 A medio, the sixteenth of a dollar. *Ib.* 246 One medio would buy a leaden rivet. *Ib.* 272, I have known a whole 'medio' bet upon a race.

* **Mediterranean,** *a.* and *n.*

1. Designating a *duty* or *fund* formerly levied or set aside by the U.S. for use in defending its commerce from the Barbary powers. *Obs.*

1807 *Ann. 10th Congress* 1 Sess. I. 1208 The duties constituting what was generally called the Mediterranean fund would expire on the first of January. *Ib.* 1209 He had no objection to the continuance of the Mediterranean duties. **1811** *Ib.* II. 2052 An addition of fifty per cent. to the present amount of duties, (together with a continuance of the 'Mediterranean Fund,') will be sufficient.

2. *To fit like a Mediterranean pass,* (see quot.). *Obs.*

1848 J. MITCHELL *Nantucketisms* 40/2 'Fits like a Mediteranean [*sic*] Pass.' Fits well. A Mediteranean Pass, or Passport, is severed by the government in two pieces, the line where it is cut being undulating, the larger part, about 4/5, is issued to vessels, the small retained. When they are placed together of course they fit exactly.

3. A species of wheat introduced from the Mediterranean region. In full **Mediterranean wheat.** *Obs.*

1842 *Farmers' Cabinet* 15 Aug. 33/1 After trying five different varieties within a few years, he now sows none but the Mediterranean. *Ib.* 15 Oct. 90/1 Six years ago . . . the Mediterranean wheat was first introduced into this section of the country. **1850** *Rep. Comm. Patents 1849: Agric.* 204 The golden straw [wheat] and Mediterranean have lately been introduced. **1856** *Ib. 1855* 192 The 'Mediterranean' is generally used for seed, and certainly answers well.

4. Mediterranean flour moth, the common flour moth, the larva of which feeds on flour and meal.

1895 *Dept. Agric. Yrbk. 1894* 283 The Mediterranean Flour Moth . . . has attracted much attention of recent years. **1903** *Ib. 1902* 87 The Mediterranean flour moth . . . was reported as injurious in mills in new localities in California.

5. Mediterranean fruit fly, a fly, *Ceratitis capitata,* originating in the Mediterranean region, the larva of which lives on fruit.

1929 *Lit. Digest* 25 May 18/1 Some seventy varieties of fruit and vegetables are attacked by the Mediterranean fruit fly. **1948** *Dly. Ardmoreite* (Ardmore, Okla.) 23 Jan. 1/8 U.S. customs officials, fearing a spread of the Mediterranean fruit fly, have halted delivery and in some cases destroyed many of the parcels.

* **medium,** *n.* In spiritualism, a person through whom the spirits of the departed are thought to communicate with people on earth. Also attrib.

1852 *N.Y. Wkly. Tribune* 31 Jan. 4/5 The Manifestations have been witnessed from day to day by the citizens of all classes, whose conclusion is nearly unanimous that the 'mediums' are *not* impostors. **1871** DE VERE 245 A Circle is held for Medium Developments and Spiritual Manifestations at Bloomfield-street every Sunday. **1949** *Chi. Tribune* 2 Oct. IV. 8/5 It is rather the story of how she became a medium and a student of psychic phenomena.

medlar bush. A small shrub of the genus *Amelanchier,* often found in swamps. — **1817–8** EATON *Botany* (1822) 181 *Aronia ovalis,* medlar bush. **1869** FULLER *Flower Gatherers* 31 Another species of the Aronia, or Amelanchier, is known as the 'Medlar Bush.'

medlark ˈmedˌlark, *n.* Short for **meadowlark.** — **1859** *Harper's Mag.* April 603/2 He had angled for sunfish and bull-pouts, and hunted gophers and med'larks in Connecticut. **1917** *Birds of Amer.* II. 251 Meadowlark. . . . [Also called] Medlark.

medregal ˈmɛdrəˌgæl, *n.* Also **madregal.** [Amer. Sp. in same sense.] An amber fish.

1884 GOODE *Fisheries* I. 331 This fish, called in Cuba the 'Medregal' and in Bermuda the 'Bonito,' has been observed in South Florida and along the coasts of the Carolinas. It is apparently exceedingly rare in the waters of the United States. **1896** Jordan & Evermann *Check-List Fishes* 344 *Seriola fasciata*. . . . Madregal. West Indies, north to Charleston, South Carolina. *Ib., Seriola falcata*. . . . Madregal; 'Rock Salmon.' West Indies, north to Florida and Carolina.

medrick ˈmɛdrɪk, *n.* Also **madrick, medrake.** [Origin obscure.] A small gull or tern.

1832 Williamson *Maine* I. 145 We suppose there are with us four species of gulls . . . 4. the swallow-tail Gull, or Medrake. **1855** Lowell *Poet. Works* (1869) 361/2 The medrick that makes you look overhead With short, sharp scream, as he sights his prey. **1890** *Cent.* 3687/2 Medrick, madrick, . . . the tern or sea-swallow.

* **meet,** *v.* **1.** *tr.* To be introduced to (a person), usu. in the imperative. **2.** *To meet up with,* to overtake or fall in with. *Colloq.*

(1) **1920** Mulford *J. Nelson* vi. 37 'Meet th' Doc, Nelson,' said Dave. Johnny turned. 'Glad to meet you, Doctor.' **1926** A. A. Thomson (*title*), Meet Mr. Huckabee! — (2) **1837** Sherwood *Gaz. Georgia* (ed. 3), *Met up with,* for overtook. **1889** Munroe *Golden Days* 96 They'd meet up with you somewheres along Coloma way. **1916** H. L. Wilson *Somewhere in Red Gap* ix. 376 Ben Sutton had met up with his old friend Jake Berger.

* **meeting,** *n.*

1. * **meeting house,** a name used locally for the columbine.

1892 *Amer. Folk-Lore* V. 91 *Aquilegia Canadensis,* meeting-houses. New England.

2. meeting seed, any one of various dry seeds eaten as dainties (see quot. 1851). *Colloq.*

1851 *Knickerb.* XXXVIII. 372 Some people call it 'caraway' and 'anise seed,' but we call it 'meetin'-seed,' 'cause we cal'late it keeps us awake in meetin'. **1905** Valentine *H. Sandwith* 25 [He] sat contentedly munching 'meeting seed' which Molly Tucker, the family seamstress, had given him as entertainment on the drive. **1940** Early *N. Eng. Sampler* 319 In old New England herb gardens there grew three plants called *Meetin' Seed*—Fennel, Dill, and Caraway.

3. *attrib.* Designating clothes or articles of clothing worn by persons going to church. Cf. **go-to-meeting.**

1775 *Broadside Verse* (1930) 141/2 He got him on his meeting clothes. **1856** M. J. Holmes *L. Rivers* 30 Nobody'd think any better of them for being rigged out in their very best meetin' gowns. **1866** Lowell *Biglow P.* 2 Ser. p. lxxix, Her new meetin'- bunnet Felt somehow thru' its crown a pair O' blue eyes sot upon it. **1887** Wilkins *Humble Romance* 139 An' thar was Israel in his meetin' coat, an' me in my best gown. *Ib.* 300 Hatty in her . . . white meeting-hat . . . was not pretty.

b. *To speak out in meeting,* and variants: To express oneself frankly regardless of circumstances; "to speak one's mind." *Colloq.* Cf. **experience meeting.**

[**1830** N. Ames *Mariner's Sk.* 41 [Bengalese] children . . . shall 'speak in meeting,' and 'relate their experience.'] **1830** *Mass. Spy* 23 June (Th.), O dear, I spoke out in meeting, said she. **1875** *Chi. Tribune* 20 Aug. 7/3 These are the Indians that 'spoke out in meetin'.' **1906** in *Springfield W. Republican* 13 Sep. 8, I do not think the president will think any the less of me for speaking right out in meeting and saying that I am not for it.

c. *To marry out of meeting,* see * **marry,** *v.*

As the last term in **abolition, alumni, anxious, basket, body, brush, bush, call, called, camp, experience, faculty, family, four-day, grove, indignation, inquiry, lyceum, March, mass, Methodist big, miners', Negro, Negro camp, pep, primary, protracted, ratification, school, school district, Shaker, singing, squatter, Sunday-go-to-, tented, town, union, ward, wood meeting.**

megaphone ˈmɛgəˌfon, *n.* [Gk. *mega,* great, +*phōnē,* sound.]

1. (See quot. 1890.)

1878 *Scientific Amer.* XXXIX. 111/3 Now, at last, we have a megaphone, which is to the ear almost what the telescope is to the eye. **1890** *Cent.* 3691/2 *Megaphone,* . . . an instrument devised by Edison for assisting hearing, adapted for use by deaf persons or for the perception of ordinary sounds at great distances. It consists essentially of two large funnel-shaped receivers for collecting the sound-waves, which are conducted to the ear by flexible tubes.

2. A large speaking-trumpet.

1879 G. Prescott *Speaking Telephone* 561 One of the most interesting experiments made by Mr. Edison . . . is that of conversing through a distance of one and a half to two miles, with . . . a few paper funnels. These funnels constitute the megaphone. **1901** *Everybody's Mag.* Oct. 428/1 The barker grabbed his megaphone. **1946** *New Yorker* 4 May 18/3 He sat beside the driver with his back to the windshield and barked through an old-fashioned brown megaphone.

Also as a verb.

1920 *Cosmopolitan* Aug. 99/2 The girls with the flat-soled Shoes had stood out in the Timothy Hay and megaphoned what they were going to do to the Toddy.

megaphonist ˈmɛgəˌfonɪst, *n.* [f. prec.] One who uses a megaphone. *Rare.* — **1906** O. Henry *Four Million* 203 'What's eatin' you' demanded the megaphonist.

melada meˈlɑdə, *n.* [Sp. *melado,* in sense shown here.] (See quot. 1875.)

1861 *Ill. Agric. Soc. Trans.* V. (1865) 166 We found it to be quite a thick crude sugar or malada. **1875** *Statutes at Large* XVIII. 340 Melada shall be . . . defined as an article made in the process of sugar-making being the cane-juice boiled down to the sugar point. **1892** *Mod. Lang. Notes* Nov. 393 *Masse cuite,* or sometimes *cuite* only—a synonym of *melada* . . . as much more frequently used in this country.

melainotype məˈlenəˌtaɪp, *n.* Also **melanotype.** [Gk. *melano,* black, +*type.*] A ferrotype or tintype. Also attrib. Now *hist.*

1856 *Spirit of Times* 6 Dec. 232/3 Daguerrotypes, Ambrotypes and Melainotypes taken in all weather. **1890** *Internat. Ann. Anthony's Photog. Bul.* III. 302 These tin or melainotypes were taken everywhere. **1946** Adams *Album Amer. Hist.* III. 62 *Opposite* we have a Melainotype view of the affair made by J. C. Elrod of Lexington.

* **Melchizedek,** *n. attrib.* Designating the greater or higher order of priesthood in the Mormon Church.

1842 Kidder *Mormonism* 125 These pulpits were alike in each end of the house, and one was for the use of the Melchisedec, or higher priesthood, and the other for the Aaronic, or lesser priesthood. [**1852** Gunnison *Mormons* 100 The Melchisedek the Eternal one, which had two orders, the high priests and priests out of which was taken the Apostles and Council.] **1905** *Out West* Sep. 242 It requires the imposition of hands by those holding the higher or Melchisedek Priesthood, to bestow the Holy Ghost and induct the convert into the spiritual concerns of the kingdom.

meld mɛld, *n.* [G. *Meld,* in same sense.] (See quot. 1909.) Also as a verb.

1898 Dick *Amer. Hoyle* (ed. 17) 204 When a player melds any combination he must lay down the cards of which his meld consists face upwards on the table beside him. *Ib.* 205 No melds are permitted until he has led a card for the first trick. **1909** *Cent. Supp.* 784/1 meld. . . . In *penuchle,* the announcement of any counting combination in the hand: as, a meld of 60 queens; in card-games in general, a declaration. **1949** *Chi. Tribune* 8 June III. 11/2 To make the first meld for his side, a player must be able to meld at least 50 points.

mellow bug. =apple smeller. — **1894** Harris *Mr. Thimblefinger* 140 Why, I expect it *is* a mellow bug. . . . I used to catch them when I was a girl and put them in my handkerchief. They smell just like a ripe apple. **1947** *Jrnl. N.Y. Entom. Soc.* Sep. 205 Mellow-bugs and sugar-bugs are names of the same origin.

melodeon məˈlodɪən, *n.*[1] [Gk. *melos,* song, +*odeion* (F. *odeon*), a music hall.] A music hall, usu. (*cap.*) with reference to a particular place. Also **Melodeon Hall.** Now *hist.*

1840 *Boston Transcript* 1 Jan. 3/1 A grand vocal and instrumental concert will be given by Mr. John Bartlett, at the Melodeon, Washington street, on Saturday evening. **1884** *N.Y. Wkly. Tribune* 5 March 2/4 The International Dog Show begins here to-day in Melodeon Hall. **1948–9** *N.W. Ohio Quart.* Winter 19 Parker occupied Cleveland's Melodeon again on June 12, 1854, when he delivered 'The Progress of Mankind' to a 'crowded house.'

melodeon məˈlodɪən, *n.*[2] [A quasi-L. formation on * *melody.*] A type of reed organ. Cf. **parlor melodeon.**

1847 in Hammond *Remembrance of Amherst* (1946) 183 (We.), Under the lead of Goodale with his melodeon [they] sing 'Sparkling and Bright.' **1863** Massett *Drifting About* 246 I had a 'Melodeen' in those days (as pianos were difficult to obtain). **1883** *Harper's Mag.* July 296/2 The girls had the melojun, and the boys had everything from a willow whistle to a fiddle. **1949** *Hobbies* Sep. 68/1 They were no doubt the melodeons or portable organs carried around like a suitcase.

Hence **melodeonist,** *n. Obs.*

1875 Kingsbury *Kingsbury Sk.* 68 (We.), Miss Spraker, melodeonist.

* **melody,** *n.* As the last term in **plantation, slave melody.**

* **melon,** *n.* Profits available for distribution to stockholders, or to others who have participated in an enterprise. Hence *to split a melon,* to distribute such funds. *Slang.* — **1911** *Chi. D. News* 16 Sep. 18/2 They are at any rate no worse than the similar inventions regarding 'deals,' and 'melons' and 'extra dividends' and 'inside buying' which were distributed through Wall Street in 1906 and 1909. **1948** *Aurora* (Ill.) *Beacon-News* 7 Nov. (Supp.) 39/2 This year, a record number of your friends and neighbors will split a record 'melon' in our 1948 savings clubs.

As the last term in **citrus, coyote, nutmeg, pie, watermelon.**

melon loco. *S.W.* [Amer. Sp. *melón loco*, in the sense shown here.] (See quot. 1904.) — **1896** *D.N.* I. 191 The plant called *melon loco* is a gourd about the size of an orange. **1904** WOOTON *Native Ornamental Plants N. Mex.* 36 The Melon Loco (*Apondanthera undulata*) is a coarse, rough, creeping vine with circular crisped leaves, three or four inches in diameter, and gourd-like fruit.

Melungeon məˈlʌndʒən, *n.* [See quot. 1940.] A member of a group of people of mixed Indian, white, and Negro blood found in some parts of the mountainous portions of Tennessee and western North Carolina.

1889 *Boston Traveller* 13 April (*Cent.*), They resented the appellation Melungeon, given to them by common consent by the whites, and proudly called themselves Portuguese. **1891** *Arena* III. 470 The Malungeons believe themselves to be of Cherokee and Portuguese extraction. **1940** *Amer. Sp.* XV. 46 Perhaps from the French *mélangé*, mixed, or *mélange*, mixture, comes *melungeon*, current in eastern Kentucky and western North Carolina for a person of mixed Negro, Indian, and white blood. **1948** MENCKEN *Supp.* II. 235 There are many similar groups of mixed bloods, always of low economic status, in the Eastern States, notably . . . the Malungeons of southwestern Virginia, eastern Kentucky and Tennessee.

*****member,** *n.*

1. *Member of* (*the*) *Congress*, a legislator in either branch of Congress.

This term is frequently used to mean a representative as distinct from a senator (see quot. 1900). In quot. 1774 it refers to the Continental Congress.

[**1774** WASHINGTON *Writings* II. 438 Dined at the State House, at an entertainment given by the city [of Philadelphia] to the members of the Congress.] *a***1800** TWINING *Visit* (1894) 32, I asked a person in the street where the Members of Congress put up when they arrived from the different States. **1900** *Cong. Rec.* 15 Feb. 1847/2 Members of Congress and Senators, if given the opportunity to furnish a particular kind of man, furnish that kind. **1949** *Sooner Mag.* June 22/3 Before joining the Foreign Service he was Secretary to a member of Congress for a year.

2. member-elect, one who has been elected, as to the U.S. Congress or to a state legislature, but has not taken up the duties of his office.

1805 *Phila. Ordinances* (1812) 108 In case of the indisposition of the mayor, . . . it shall . . . be lawful for the recorder . . . to administer an oath . . . to each of the members elect of the select and common councils. **1900** *Cong. Rec.* 10 Jan. 748/2 Hon. William L. Greene, a member of the Fifty-fifth Congress and a member-elect to the Fifty-sixth Congress.

3. member bank, (see quot. 1914).

1914 *Federal Reserve Act* § 1, The term 'member bank' shall be held to mean any national bank, state bank, or bank or trust company which has become a member of one of the reserve banks created by this Act. **1923** *Accountant's Handbk.* 865 Member banks may rediscount short-time commercial notes with federal reserve banks.

As the last term in **abolition, carpetbag, lobby, secesh, State rights, Tammany member.**

memorandum check. (See quot. 1859.)

1835 *Mass. Rep.* XXXIII. 540 The word 'memorandum,' or 'Memo.' . . . was placed there as an admission or declaration on the part of the maker, . . . distinguishing them, as memorandum checks, from other checks which were to be presented for payment. **1859** BARTLETT 267 *Memorandum Check*, a check intended not to be presented immediately for payment; such an understanding being denoted by the word 'mem' written on it. **1880** *Amer. Encycl. Commerce* II. 722/2 If a Memorandum Check is indorsed, it is valid like any other check in the hands of the indorsee.

*****Memorial Day.** =**Decoration Day.** Also attrib.

In most states May 30 is the date of this observance. The Confederate celebrations in the southern states, however, vary in date from April 26 to June 3.

1869 *G.A.R.* (R.I. Dept.) *3d Encamp. Proc.* 32 Those patriotic men and women . . . gave their aid . . . to make successful this National Memorial day. **1897** FLANDRAU *Harvard Episodes* 181, I was thinking of all the horrible . . . Baccalaureate Sermons and ghastly Memorial Day orators that are allowed to go on. **1904** *N.Y. Ev. Post* 30 May 2 Thousands of people gathered this morning to witness the Memorial Day parade of civil war veterans. **1949** *This Week Mag.* 28 May 2/2 On Memorial Day, this lesson is poignant and clear.

*****memorist,** *n.* A memorizer; one with a keen memory. *Obs.* — **1872** *New Cyclo. Illust. Anecdote* 9/2 Fame has given me the report of being a memorist. **1890** *Cent.* 3705/3 *Memorist*, . . . one who has a retentive memory.

*****memorize,** *v. tr.* To commit to memory.

1838 GOSSE *Letters* 110 'Good,' is used in the sense of 'well;' . . . . To learn a thing by heart is to 'memorize' it. **1878** W. H. DANIELS *That Boy* 140 He had even taken the pains to memorize a number of hymns and sonnets. **1949** *Reader's Digest* April 145/2 None of us was allowed to touch the new typewriter until we had memorized the letters in each line forward and backward.

memory book. A scrapbook in which clippings, programs, snapshots and the like are pasted. — **1931** *Publishers' Wkly.* 14 Feb. 843/1 Another demand . . . is that for inexpensive memory books used by grammar school children. **1936** *Sears' Cat.* (ed. 173) 714 Limp brown suede leather memory book . . . 128 blue pages, 8×10 in. Boxed.

*****men,** *n. pl.* As the last term in **Clinker right, dollar store, Dorr, Finality, lynch, Martling, praying, red, seven, twelve men.**

*****mendment,** *n.* =*****amendment,** *n.* **1.** *Obs.* — **1738** *Southampton Rec.* III. 127 The mendment of meadow belonging to No. 33, Lies on a poynt of Segg near the beach. **1745** *Ib.* 77 There is a path or passing Rode between the lot and the mendment.

menhaden mɛnˈhedn̩, *n.* [Of Algonquian origin. App. the root idea is "fertilizer."] A marine fish of the family Clupeidae, *Brevoortia tyrannus*, abundant on the eastern coast of the U.S. (see also quot. 1890). Cf. **gulf menhaden.**

Cf. **bunker, marshbanker.** For a list of the popular names of this fish see *Amer. Naturalist* XII. (1878), pp. 735–9, where some thirty are listed. See also *Cent. s.v.*

1643 WILLIAMS *Key* 136 Aumsûog, & Munnawhatteaûg. *A Fish somewhat like a Herring.* **1792** *N.Y. State Soc. Arts* I. 57 This addition to making manure has been made by green sea-weed taken directly from the creeks and bays . . . and by the fish called menhaden or mosbankers. **1890** *Cent.* 3707/3 The name *menhaden* extends in literary use to all the other species of *Brevoortia*, of which there are several as *B. patronus* of the Gulf of Mexico; and it is locally misapplied to the thread-herring, *Opistonema thrissa.* **1949** *This Week Mag.* 10 Sep. 35/2 What is America's No. 1 fish today? The menhaden. The . . . menhaden yielded some $10,000,000 worth of oil, meal and dry scrap last year.

attrib. **1865** *Wilkes' Spirit of Times* 8 July 300/2 They have erected a very large ice-house and filled it with ice in order to preserve their menhaden bait. *a***1877** *Sag Harbor Express* (B.), During the last two weeks, the bunker or menhaden fishery has been very brisk. **1882** *Harper's Mag.* Sep. 588/1 A deck-load of brick for a menhaden oil-works had been dumped [on the wharf]. **1949** *Nat. Geog. Mag.* June 822 (*legend*), An Indoor Mountain of Menhaden Meal Is Bulldozed Down to Size. . . . Cattle, swine, and poultry are the consumers.

Mennist ˈmɛnɪst, *n.* [Du.] A Mennonite.

1771 TAYLOR *Voyage* 170 In the City of *Philadelphia* you see *Churchmen, Quakers, Lutherans, Calvinists, Moravians, Catholics, Menists* [etc.]. **1869** *Atlantic Mo.* Oct. 474/1 The Mennists in many outward circumstances very much resemble the Society of Friends. . . . In the interior of the Mennist meeting, a Quaker-like plainness prevails. **1889** HOWELLS *Hazard of Fortunes* I. 208 Aren't they [Dunkards] something like the Mennists?

Menominee məˈnɑməˌni, *n.* [f. the Chippewa name of the wild rice.]

1. An Indian of an Algonquian tribe first encountered by Europeans near the mouth of the Menominee River. Also attrib.

1762 in *Mich. Hist. Mag.* X. 369, I delivered the same Message to the Meynomeneys that I had done to the Sax and Reynard Nations And gave them a Belt of Wampum. **1834** HOFFMAN *Winter in West* (1835) II. 3 The Mè-nó-mé-né, or wild-rice-eaters, is a broken band that served with effect against the Sauks and Foxes in the Indian difficulties of 1832. **1909** *Indian Laws & Tr.* III. 421 Conferring jurisdiction upon the court of claims in certain cases against the Menominee Indians. **1948** *Green Bay* (Wis.) *Press-Gazette* 12 July 19/8 Sunday the group went on a conducted tour of the Menominee Indian reservation.

2. A small whitefish, *Prosopium quadrilaterale*, found in northern lakes. In full **Menominee whitefish.**

1884 GOODE *Fisheries* I. 541 *Coregonus quadrilateralis.* The only name which I have heard applied to this fish is that of 'Menomonee Whitefish.' **1903** T. H. BEAN *Fishes N.Y.* 221 Other names are Menominee whitefish, roundfish, shad-waiter, pilotfish and chivey. **1944** NUTE *Lake Superior* 186 Menominees, a kind of whitefish, are listed at 14,940 pounds, all caught in American waters.

3. (not *cap.*) =**wild rice** (*a*).

1945 *Nature Mag.* Nov. 466 Not to the Menominee alone was menomin of great value, but to all the tribes of the wild rice country. **1949** *Boston Globe* 14 Aug. (Fiction Mag.) 8/2 Wild ducks rose from the sloughs in the marsh where wild rice grew, the menominee of the Indian tribe of that name.

Menzies spruce. The Sitka spruce *q.v.*, so named for Archibald Menzies (1754–1842), surgeon and botanist of the Vancouver expedition to the Pacific Northwest who discovered the tree in 1792. (See also quot. 1949.)

1869 BREWER *Rocky Mt. Lett.* 46 The trees [were] most Menzies spruce. *a*1915 MUIR *Travels Alaska* (1917) 254 We spread our blankets beneath a Menzies spruce on moss two feet deep. 1949 COLLINGWOOD & BRUSH *Knowing Your Trees* 77 For a time it was known as Menzies spruce, *Picea menziesii*, but botanists now accept the geographical name, *Picea sitchensis*, in which the French botanist recognized the heavy stands of this tree in the vicinity of Sitka, Alaska.

*mercantile, *a.* 1. mercantile inspector, in some states, an official who inspects business establishments to see that they are operated in accordance with state labor laws. 2. mercantile store, a retail store. — (1) 1911 PERSONS *Mass. Labor Laws* 240 The exemption of the factory inspector and mercantile inspector, . . . is in line with the usual exclusion of important executive officers from the civil service. — (2) 1814 BRACKENRIDGE *Views La.* 123 There is a printing office, and twelve mercantile stores.

***Mercer,** *n.* A variety of potato developed in Mercer County, Pa. In full **Mercer potato.** *Obs.*

1839 *Mass. Agric. Survey 2d Rep.* 34 The Chenango [potato], sometimes called the Mercer, or Pennsylvania Blue. 1839 *Niles' Reg.* 22 June 269/2 John Gilky . . . of Mercer county, Pa., . . . produced from seed the justly celebrated Mercer potatoe. 1889 MELLICK *Story Old Farm* 236 Potatoes were a staple, as were in their season cabbages, beans and Indian corn, but tomatoes, cauliflower, Mercer potatoes, okra, lettuce, sweet corn, egg-plant and rhubarb had not yet been heard of.

***merchandise,** *n.* **1. merchandise car,** a railroad car in which merchandise is shipped. **2. merchandise depot,** a depot for storing merchandise. **3. merchandise lumber,** (see quot. 1905).

(1) 1850 *Hunt's Merch. Mag.* XXIII. 355 For repairs of merchandise cars. — (2) 1847 *Hunt's Merch. Mag.* XVI. 211 A merchandise depot just completed, is 124 by 84 feet. — (3) 1682 *Mass. Bay Currency Tracts* 5 A Proposal for erecting a Fund of Land . . . in the nature of a Money-Bank; or Merchandise Lumber, to pass Credit upon, by Book-Entries. 1905 *Pub. Col. Soc.* X. 85 Security of the 'deposit in Land, real, dureable & of secure value' was evidently preferred to what was then termed the 'Merchandise Lumber.' [footnote:] A phrase frequently used by the pamphleteers of the day, Lumber being intended for Lombard, the name of a well-known street in London, and the whole expression meaning simply a pledge of merchandise.

***merchant,** *n.* In obs. combs.: (1) **merchant flour mill,** =next; (2) **mill,** a mill where grain is bought, ground, and resold, cf. **country mill;** (3) **miller,** one who operates a merchant mill; (4) **note,** a note issued by a company of individual merchants, redeemable for a stated sum at a given date; (5) **-'s bag,** (see quot.); (6) **-'s watch,** (see quots); (7) **train,** a train or series of wagons or pack animals conveying the goods of merchants or traders.

(1) 1843 *Hunt's Merch. Mag.* IX. 156 There are three mills for planing boards, two white-lead factories, three oilmills, and six merchant flourmills. — (2) 1774 FITHIAN *Journal* I. 111 Mr. Carter's Merchant Mill begins to run to-day. 1851 CIST *Cincinnati* 194 It proposes to perform in a small compass, with less expense, greater safety and equal efficiency, the work of a merchant mill. 1877 JOHNSON *Anderson Co., Kansas* 252 In the spring of 1874 Chris. Bouck . . . immediately commenced the construction of a first-class merchant mill. — (3) 1838 *Speeches of D. Barnard* 163 It is not money which the merchant-miller wants; it is wheat. — (4) 1734 *Mass. H. Rep. Jrnl.* 77 On a motion made and seconded by divers members respecting the Circulation of Merchant Notes so called. 1895 *Pub. Col. Soc.* III. 29 In April, 1735, the Assembly of the Province of Massachusetts Bay passed an Act restraining the circulation of the New Hampshire Merchants' Notes emitted the preceding year.

(5) 1836 O'BRYAN *Narrative* 32, I had only to say we were safe arrived, &c seal them and put them into the post office, or Merchants' bag.—[footnote:] Merchant vessels are allowed to carry letters,—they advertise what ship is about to sail and there is a large bag hung up in the Merchant's office, with the ships name on it; so the person goes and throws in the letter as into a post office. — (6) 1733 *Boston Rec.* 52 The Town would alow Something toward the Charge of A watch at the Dock called the Merchants Watch which has hitherto bin Supported by a Number of Merchants. 1736 *Boston Selectmen* 301 The Watchmen supported at the Charge of the Merchants, and usually called *The Merchant's Watch.* — (7) 1847 JOHN T. HUGHES *Doniphan's Exped.* 16/1 The annual caravan or merchant train, of 414 wagons, heavily laden with dry goods for the markets of Santa Fé and Chihuahua, lined the road for miles. 1860 GREELEY *Overland Journey* 206 The road, though much traversed by Mormons as well as emigrants and merchant-trains, is utterly abominable.

As the last term in **board, British, dry-goods, forwarding, general, ice, Indian, lumber, pork, produce merchant.**

merchantable pay. =***pay,** *n.* **1.** *Obs.* — 1679 *N.H. Probate Rec.* I. 236, I Doe Give unto . . . our . . . pastor the some of five pound To be payd To him in Good merchenteble pay. 1714 *Essex Hist. Coll.* XLIX. 353 £44. 17 s. 1 d. to be paid in Courand money of New England or in any Currant Merchantable pay ye Growth of ye Country or in Such goods as the foresd Hill hath had.

merchanter 'mɜtʃəntɚ, *n.* Also **merchanteer.** A trading vessel; a merchantman. — 1829 MARRYAT *F. Mildmay* xiv, I'll fit out a privateer, and take some o' your merchanters. 1890 *Public Opinion* 30 Aug., A departure from the merchanteer type [of ship] was the immediate result.

***Mergenthaler,** *n.* [f. Ottmar *Mergenthaler* (1859–99), Ger.-Amer. inventor.] A typesetting machine. In full **Mergenthaler linotype.** Also attrib. Cf. **linotype.**

1896 *Internat. Typog. Union Proc.* 44/2 Otis stands ready to furnish any paper with an unlimited number of Mergenthaler operators at short notice. 1898 *Ib.* 54/2 There were no Mergenthalers in Quincy. 1923 *Linotype Decorative Material* 1 Mergenthaler Linotype Company. 1948 *Dly. Ardmoreite* (Ardmore, Okla.) 9 July 10/1 Within six months the Oklahoman had established a limited bank credit and ordered its first Mergenthaler.

***merger,** *n.* The merging or consolidation of different corporations or business concerns into one organization. Also attrib. Cf. **bank merger.**

In strict usage, *merger* indicates a combination in which the identity of every combining company but one is lost in that one; *consolidation* indicates a combination in which a new company absorbs the identity of every one of the combining companies.

1889 *Boston Jrnl.* 17 April 4/3 Ample powers of consolidation and merger, transfer and absorption of stock and kindred franchises are given. 1903 *Chi. Chronicle* 11 April 2 The stockholders will receive their profits from . . . the two roads, the joint stock of which is held by the merger corporation. 1949 *Time* 3 Oct. 13/1 He turned on the great Andrew Carnegie himself and fought a battle for power which ended in the mergers that became U.S. Steel Corp.

transf. 1905 *Springfield W. Republican* 1 Sep. 2 The people of Arizona are so hostile to a merger with New Mexico that they are now content to remain a territory for an indefinite period. 1949 *Commercial Appeal* (Memphis) 6 Feb. 1/4 The United Church of Christ was formed Saturday with the merger of the Congregational Christian Churches of America and the Evangelical and Reformed Church.

***meridian,** *n.* In land surveying, a north and south line forming right angles with its corresponding base line. In full **meridian line.** Cf. ***base,** *n.* **2.** (3).

1761 *Holyoke Diaries* 23 Drew a Meridian line for Mr. Mascarene. 1852 REGAN *Emigrant's Guide* 286 For the sake of easy reference, a line is first run due north and south, called *the meridian.* 1862 *New Amer. Encycl.* XV. 204/2 Each great survey is based upon a meridian line run due N. and S. 1945 *Calif. Highways* Jan.–Feb. 27/3 Some were named for rivers, as the Willamette, and the Gila and Salt River meridians.

As the last term in **guide, principal, second principal meridian.**

***merino,** *n.* A variety of potato. In full **merino potato.** *Obs.* Cf. **Saxon, Spanish merino.** — 1849 EMMONS *Agric. N.Y.* II. 41 Merino Potato. . . . Not highly esteemed for the table. 1887 TOURGEE *Button's Inn* 178 He picked up the potatoes . . . —delicate white 'Kidneys' . . . and coarse red 'Merinoes.'

***merit,** *n.* **1. merit fish,** (see quot.). **2. merit system,** the system of making appointments and promotions in the Civil Service on the basis of ability to pass qualifying examinations. Cf. **spoils system.**

(1) 1884 GOODE *Fisheries* I. 456 The Green Smelt of the Connecticut coast, *Mendia notata,* is also called . . . about Watch Hill the 'Merit-fish.' 1911 *Rep. Fisheries 1908* 316. — (2) 1879 *46th Congress* 2 Sess. H.R. Ex. Doc. No. 1, VII. 264 Under President Grant a trial, beginning January 1st, 1872, was made of the merit system in a limited way. 1943 MENEFEE *Assignment* 36 Government workers under the merit system are an above-average lot of people drawn from every part of the nation.

merluccio mɚ'lutʃɪo, *n.* [It., "sea pike."] A hake, *Merluccius productus,* of the Pacific Coast. — 1884 GOODE *Fisheries* I. 243 The California Hake . . . is most commonly known along the coast by its Italian name, 'Merluccio.' 1911 *Rep. Fisheries 1908* 312.

mermaid weed. Any water plant of the genus *Proserpinaca.*

1817–8 EATON *Botany* (1822) 410 *Proserpinaca palustris,* mermaid weed. 1840 DEWEY *Mass. Flowering Plants* 49 Mermaid Weed. Two species, *P. palustris,* and *P. pectinata,* grow in wet grounds, and round marshy places. 1940 DEAM *Flora Indiana* 712 Mermaid Weed [occurs] . . . in the low sedge borders of lakes, in swamps, dried-up ponds and sloughs, and cypress swamps.

***Merriam,** *n.* [Clinton Hart *Merriam* (1855–1942), Amer. scientist. Cf. Canadian zone.] Used, usu. in the possessive, in the names of animals: (1) **Merriam's**

chipmunk, (see quot. 1917); (2) **elk,** an elk, *Cervus merriami*, formerly found in the mountains of western New Mexico and eastern Arizona but now extinct; (3) **turkey,** one of the five usually recognized species of turkey, *Meleagris gallopavo merriami*, or a turkey of this species.

(1) **1907** MEARNS *Mammals Mex. Boundary* 296 We found the Merriam chipmunk ranging from Mountain Spring and the lower slopes of the Coast Range over the highest peaks. **1917** *Mammals of Amer.* 193/2 Merriam's Chipmunk.—*Eutamias merriami merriami* (Allen). Size large; colors pale; stripes not strikingly contrasted. California. — (2) **1907** MEARNS *Mammals Mex. Boundary* 213 Cervus. merriami Nelson. Merriam Elk. **1936** *Univ. Ariz. Gen. Bul.* No. 3, 62 Merriam's elk which was native to the Mogollon Plateau and White Mountains was hunted until the species became extinct. — (3) **1900** *Auk* XVII. 120 Meleagris g. merriami, Merriam's Turkey. **1936** *Univ. Ariz. Gen. Bul.* No. 3, 84 The most magnificent of all American game birds (hardly surpassed in the world) is that known as the Merriam turkey.

Merrimac ˈmɛrəˌmæk, *n. attrib.* Designating cotton fabrics formerly manufactured at Lowell, Mass., on the Merrimac River. Now *hist.*

1843 *Knickerb.* XXI. 496 There was a dull sale for 'Merrimack blues.' **1843** *Lowell Offering* III. 166 We would willingly wear 'Merrimack print' henceforth. **1873** M. HOLLEY *My Opinions* 205 The 'postal Paul didn't have to buy 40 or 50 yards of merrymac calico and factory cloth every year. **1891** WELCH *Recoll. 1830–40* 354 Calicos— of which the 'Merrimac' and 'Dover' were the choice prints of that day, were then quoted at 14 cts. for 'Dover,' and 16 cts. for 'Merrimac.' **1948** *Chi. Tribune* 25 Jan. VII. 14/1 Cooking stoves were not made then, nor Merrimac calicoes.

mesa ˈmesə, *n. S.W.* and *W.* [Sp. in same sense. An Amer. borrowing.] An elevated tableland. Cf. **prairie mesa.**

Mesa is applied to two phenomena: an isolated flat-topped hill with abrupt and steep sides, and a comparatively flat plateau extending back from the abrupt ridges of a valley.

1759 tr. VENEGAS *Nat. Hist. Calif.* II. 260 The squadron was obliged to run close in with the land, under some lofty black mountains, on the top of which were large plains. These they called Mesas de San Cypriano, or St. Cyprian's tables. **1840** JOSIAH GREGG *Diary* I. (1941) 53 Came today about 20 miles . . . over this very level *mesa* almost as firm and more smooth than a turn-pike. **1949** *Pacific Discovery* Jan.–Feb. 11/2 Band-tailed pigeons raced low over the mesas on their regular flights to water.

attrib. **1866** *Rep. Indian Affairs* 109 A mesa formation, rising abruptly from twenty to thirty feet, and more occasionally from the bottom. **1875** PHILLIPS *Letters From Calif.* 34 The city is built at the base of the mesa lands of the mountains. **1949** *Nat. Geog. Mag.* Sep. 392 Covered with thick forage, the mesa top makes a fine fenceless cattle range.

b. mesa oak, an oak or species of oak (see quot. 1925) found in the West in mesa regions.

1925 JEPSON *Flowering Plants Calif.* 274 Q. engelmannii Greene. Mesa Oak. **1945** *Travel* May 8/1 A two-hundred-year-old mesa oak with a spread of one hundred feet covers the path to the original mansion of the Huntingtons which now serves as the art gallery.

mescal mɛsˈkæl, *n.* [Amer. Sp. (<Nahuatl) in senses **1.** and **3.**]

1. Any species of *Agave* or a plant of the species; also the peyote or peyotl plant, *Lophophora williamsi*.

1702 LOCKMAN tr. *Travels of Jesuits* (1762) I. 399 On the Mountains grow Mescales, a fruit peculiar to the Country, and is gathered all the Year round. **1808** SHALER *Journal* (1935) 53 They also have a plant called the mixcal. **1846** EMORY *Military Reconn.* 59 This afternoon I found the famous mezcal, (an agave,) about three feet in diameter, broad leaves, armed with teeth like a shark. **1948** *Sierra Club* (So. Calif. Chap.) *Sched.* 127, 67 On the sides of the canyons you will find many mescal in blossom.

2. A food prepared from some variety of *Agave.*

[**1759** tr. VENEGAS *Nat. Hist. Calif.* I. 44 The mountains and forests yield the mezcal, . . . the root of which boiled is a principal ingredient of the mexcalli.] **1831** PATTIE *Personal Narr.* 63, I afterwards ascertained, that it was a vegetable, called by the Spanish mascal. **1890** *Arch. Inst. Amer. P.* III. 185 Vegetable food was limited mostly to wild fruits, . . . to stalks of the Maguey baked into a sweet conserve called Mexcal [etc.].

3. A colorless spirituous liquor made from the juice or baked heads of plants belonging to some species of *Agave* (see also quot. 1881). Also attrib.

[**1828** H. G. WARD *Mexico* I. 59 A strong kind of brandy called mexical, or Aguardiente de Maguey.] **1829** *Western Mo. Rev.* May 659 It is of this juice they make a kind of whiskey, called *vino meschal.* **1869** BROWNE *Adv. Apache Country* 133 Soldiers, teamsters, and honest miners lounging about the mescal-shops, soaked with the fiery poison; . . . these are what the traveller sees. **1881** *Amer. Naturalist* XV. 875 The main and paramount use of sotol is in the making of a spirituous liquor known as 'mescal' along the border, but in the interior of Mexico, to avoid mistaking it for a similar product from maguey, called sotol mescal. **1949** *Pacific Spectator* Spring 159 The man rationed a drink of *mezcal* to go with the chicken.

4. In special combs.: (1) **mescal bean,** prob. by confusion, a mesquite bean; (2) **bud,** the flowering stalk of the agave; (3) **button,** see as a main entry; (4) **ceremony,** among some of the Plains Indians, a ceremony in which mescal is drunk; (5) **head,** = **mescal button;** (6) **pit,** (see quot.); (7) **rattle,** a symbolic gourd rattle used in the mescal ceremony, zigzag lines on the rattle indicating the voice rising in song; (8) **thread,** a thread or fiber secured from mescal.

(1) **1856** DERBY *Phoenixiana* 46 A solitary antelope, picking up mescal beans. **1946** FOREMAN *Last Trek* 258 Two societies of mescal-bean eaters were organized. — (2) **1914** SAUNDERS *With Flowers & Trees* 139 The mescal buds are capable of making by distillation one of the fieriest intoxicants known, as hot, in 'bad man' parlance, as 'a sulphuric acid cocktail with a cactus-joint for a cherry.' — (4) **1930** FERBER *Cimarron* 293 Ruby was just teaching me one of the Mescal Ceremony songs.

(5) **1885** *Outing* Oct. 24/2 The old and young squaws . . . had brought down from the hillsides donkey-loads of mescal heads. **1933** SPIER *Yuman Tribes* 55 The mescal heads were baked in a pit. — (6) **1919** C. G. RAHT *Romance of Davis Mts.* 71 A peculiar class of rocky mounds are found, known as mescal pits. — (7) **1892** *Amer. Anthrop.* V. 64 [On] a Kiowa mescal rattle . . . two zigzag red lines, running the whole length of the gourd . . . represent the mescal songs, the same device of zigzag lines being frequently used in the Kiowa pictograph system. — (8) **1759** tr. VENEGAS *Nat. Hist. Calif.* I. 74 When they cannot procure sedge, they make use of an apron, or petticoat made of the mescal threads hanging down in the same manner.

mescal button. (See quot. 1909.)

1895 *N.Y. Dramatic News* 7 Dec. 3/2 For introducing brilliant coloring into dreams it is as efficacious as the nerve stimulant known as the mescal button, contributed to science by the Kiowa Indians. **1909** *Cent. Supp.* 789/2 *Mescal-buttons*, . . . the dried tops of a succulent, spineless, turnip-shaped cactus growing in the arid regions of Texas and northern Mexico, known botanically as *Lophophora Williamsii*, and called by the natives in various localities *peyote*, *hikuli*, and *wokowi*. **1930** FERBER *Cimarron* 295 She held out her hand, shaking a little, the mescal button crushed in her palm. **1948** *Travel* Nov. 16/2 Peyote or mescal 'buttons' are the dried disc-like tops of the small spineless Mexican cactus.

b. mescal button cactus, the peyote.

1948 *Holland's Mag.* June 18/2 Mescal button cactus . . . contains an alkaloid that causes the person who eats it to see gorgeous dreams in riotous colors.

Mescalero ˌmɛskəˈlero, *n.* [Amer. Sp. in same sense.] **1.** *pl.* (See quot. 1844.)

1844 GREGG *Commerce of Prairies* I. 290 Those [Apaches] that are found east of the Rio del Norte are generally known as *Mezcaleros*, on account of an article of food in use among them, called *mezcal*, . . . the baked root of the *maguey*. **1854** J. R. BARTLETT *Personal Narr.* I. 106 They could tell the footprints of . . . the Mescaleros. **1907** CURTIS *N. Amer. Indians* I. 83 The Civil War necessitated the withdrawal of the troops from the frontier, leaving the way open to the devastation of the country by the Navaho and Mescaleros.

2. In combs., as (1) **Mescalero Apache,** (2) **buck,** (3) **country,** (4) **Indian,** (5) **nation.**

(1) **1936** MCKENNA *Black Range* 57 Now, here you have messages left only yesterday—one by a Navajo, one by a Mescalero Apache, and a third by a White Mountain Apache. **1948** *Desert Mag.* Feb. 33/2 Percy Bigmouth was born on the Mescalero Apache Indian reservation 58 years ago, and never has left it. — (2) **1885** *Wkly. New Mexican Rev.* 12 March 3/5 Mescalero bucks . . . are expert horse thieves, and would like to go into Chihuahua or Sonora to steal horses, but they are afraid of the agent. — (3) **1855** *N.Y. Wkly. Tribune* 31 Mar. 1/4 An article in *The Santa Fe Gazette*, the 24th ult., discusses at length an excursion through the Mescolero country. — (4) **1913** WOOTON *Trees & Shrubs N. Mex.* 112 The stems of this species . . . are used by the Mescalero Indian women in making baskets.

(5) **1799** tr. in *Pac. R.R. Rep.* (1856) III. 119 The *Mescalero* nation inhabit the mountains on both banks of the river Pecos.

mescalism ˈmɛskəlˌɪzəm, *n.* The practice of taking mescal. — **1902** *Amer. Anthrop.* Oct.–Dec. 789/1 Through mescalism one seems almost to 'attain an objective knowledge of one's own personality.'

***mesh,** *v.* Also ***mash.** *intr.* (See quot. 1859.)

1849 *Rep. U.S. Comm. Patents* (1850) 155 What I claim as new ... is ... the shaft H, with the pinions i, mashing into racks II. **1859** BARTLETT 265 To Mash. In machinery, one wheel is said to *mash* into or with another, i.e. to 'engage' with it. This is, apparently, a corruption from *mesh*, which is sometimes used in the same sense. **1875** KNIGHT 1383/2 Mangle-rack, a rack having teeth on opposite sides engaged by a pinion which meshes with the opposite sides alternately. **1895** *Outing* XXVII. 55/1 Wooden cogs, which meshed into a horizontal wheel. **1910** *Sat. Ev. Post.* 3 Sep. 57/1 One of the gears is out of whack. It won't mesh.

transf. **1949** *U.S. News* 18 Nov. 19/1 U.S., highly centralized, industries closely meshed, is more vulnerable to atom bombs than Russia.

mesilla meˈsijə, *n. S.W.* [Sp. in Amer. Sp. sense shown here.] (See quot. 1859 and cf. note.)

Santamaría gives the definition, "Meseta elevada. Usual principalmente en Estados Unidos, en lo que antes fuera territorio mejicano."

1859 BARTLETT 268 Mesilla. (Span. dim. of *mesa.*) A small tableland. **1864** *Rocky Mt. News* (Denver) 3 Aug. 3/2 [They] are untiring in their efforts for the improvement of the means of popular travel between the marts of the Missouri and the mines and *mesillas* of New Mexico and Arizona. **1880** *Cimarron* (N.M.) *News & Press* 15 April 1/4 'Indignation meeting.' The people of the county of Doña Ana are urgently requested to join in a public meeting in the Mesilla plaza.

meson meˈson, *n. S.W.* [Sp. in same sense.] An inn.

1826 T. FLINT *F. Berrian* I. 94 In occasional stops at the *haciendas* and *mesons*, the time passed rapidly. **1845** T. J. GREEN *Texian Exped.* 188 Here we were quartered in an unfurnished room in the *meson* (inn). **1910** SANTLEBEN *Texas Pioneer* 164 Meson means an inn or hostelry.

mesquite mɛsˈkit, *n. S.W.* [Amer. Sp. *mezquite* (<Nahuatl).]

1. A species of deep-rooted, shrublike tree, *Prosopis juliflora*, often growing in dense clumps or thickets, or any species of this genus; also a tree of one of these species, or the wood of such a tree or shrub.

1759 tr. VENEGAS *Nat. Hist. Calif.* I. 100 Their most usual device was to hold up in their hands some little tablets of wood made with great labour, for want of iron, tools or mesquite, or another hard wood called Una de Gato, on which were painted some grotesque figures. **1805** LEWIS in *Ann. 9th Congress* 2 Sess. 1083 [With] a bean that grows in great plenty on a small tree resembling a willow, called masketo; the women cook their buffalo beef. **1859** *No. Californian* (Union) 7 Sep. 3/2 The troops took possession in a grove of mosquite, where the ground was clear of undergrowth. **1907** MULFORD *Bar-20* 339 'What is that thorny shrub just ahead?' she asked. 'That's mesquite,' he replied eagerly. **1948** *Reader's Digest* January 70/1 Anywhere in America has its particular hearth perfume—. .. mesquite floating out of desert chimneys in the Southwest.

2. *ellipt.* =**mesquite thicket.**

1834 A. PIKE *Sketches* 63 We emerged from the broken hills into the mesquito. **1945** *New Yorker* 25 Aug. 26 A railroad bull came walking along the tops of the cars and kicked me into the mesquite.

b. =**mesquite grass.**

1847 *Western Texas* 7 In grasses the glory of the State is the *musquit*, found only in Western Texas. **1899** M. GOING *Flowers* 153 The running mesquit of Arizona and the alkali-grass of the plains help to hold in place the shifting soils of the great thirst-lands.

3. (See quot.)

1869 *Overland Mo.* Aug. 130 Texas is notable for the number of its soils. In Montgomery County there is ... the 'mezquite,' (producing chiefly mesquite, both bush and grass) [etc.].

4. In special combs.: (1) **mesquite bean,** the fruit of the mesquite tree or shrub, which grows in a long pod similar to that of a string bean; (2) **chaparral,** a clump or thicket of mesquite bushes; (3) **grass,** any one of various pasture grasses, esp. those of the genus *Bouteloua*, affording superior pasturage; (4) **meal,** (see quots.); (5) **pasture,** a pasture of mesquite grass; (6) **prairie,** a prairie upon which mesquite grass grows; (7) **root,** the root of the mesquite tree used for fuel; (8) **thicket,** a chaparral of mesquite; (9) **tree,** a tree or shrub, *Prosopis juliflora*, common in the Southwest and Mexico; (10) **wood,** a mesquite tree or shrub, or the hard durable wood of this.

(1) **1846** in *Calif. Hist. Soc. Quart.* XXI. 217 My riding mule was the most refractory of all. I however succeeded at last in making him drink, by covering the water with the musquite bean. **1929** DOBIE *Vaquero* 3 There the curly mesquite grass, which cures like hay for winter, and mesquite beans keep horses fat the year round and as strong as corn would make them. — (2) **1849** in *31st Congress* 1 Sess. Sen. Ex. Doc. No. 64,20 Our present camp is a mezquite chaparral in a bend of the river. **1865** O. W. NORTON *Army Lett.* 271 Part of the way the road lay through mesquite chaparral. — (3) **1823** DEWEES *Lett. From Texas* 35 The musquite grass grows very thick and about three feet high, and looks very much like a blue grass pasture. **1949** *Boston Sun. Globe* 1 May (Fiction Mag.) 1/2 He walked his horses daily over the curly mesquite grass that carpeted the prairie. — (4) **1834** A. PIKE *Sketches* 56 We bought some meat and mesquito meal, made by grinding the beans between two stones. **1881** *Amer. Naturalist* XV. 30 Moreover, the 'mezquit meal,' which Indians and Mexicans manufacture by drying and grinding these pods and their contents, is perhaps the most nutritious breadstuff in use among any people.

(5) **1905** A. ADAMS *Outlet* 16 The horses had run idle during the winter in a large mesquite pasture. — (6) **1828** in *Texas Hist. Assoc. Quart.* XIII. (1909) 69 We enter upon what is here called Musquite prairie ... a very thin soil producing a short nutritious grass. **1857** D. BRAMAN *Inf. Texas* i. 22 Emigrants ... want good and cheap lands, with plenty of mesquite prairie for stock range. — (7) **1864** *Wkly. New Mexican* 28 Oct. 1/3 [Navajos] now at the Bosque are carrying mesquit roots, on their backs, from eight to ten miles, ... to cook their food. **1941** FERGUSSON *Southwest* 15 Mesquite roots make a fine, hot bed of coals, and many a man would have died of thirst if he had not known how to get water from a cactus. — (8) **1845** T. J. GREEN *Texian Exped.* 32 Dawson selected his position in a mesquet thicket favourable for his rifle-shooting. **1941** FERGUSSON *Southwest* 55 Along the streams are oak groves and mesquite thickets. — (9) **1827** DEWEES *Lett. from Texas* 63 The country is mostly a prairie country, the prairies being mostly covered with shrubs, musquit trees, and prickly pear. **1944** JOHNSON *As I Dare* 264 The dull brown dry earth, spotted with the green of many-shaped cacti, gave place to brighter green groves of low prickly mesquite trees.

(10) **1817** DARBY *Louisiana* 198 There are in the Parish of Nachitoches, two very distinct species of the robinia; one a tree of considerable size, the other a shrub, the latter is known by the name of musquito wood. **1846** *Phila. Pub. Ledger* 2 July 1/5 On the outside of the market house were numerous and various sized bundles of muskeet wood tied together with raw hide thongs. **1903** *N.Y. Herald* 8 March (Ernst), The bed of the carreta is made of open cross sections of mesquite wood.

Also *mesquite branch, brush, bush, coal, dagger, fire, flat, forest, fruit, grove, gum, leaf, pitch, plain, stump, timber, twig, valley,* etc.

As the last term in **barbed, curly, grapevine, hairy, hogwallow, screw, screwpod, vine mesquite.**

***mess,** *n.*

1. A group of Congressmen who take their meals together. Also **Congressional mess.** *Obs.*

1790 in *Jrnl. William Maclay* (1927) 253 This was a day of company at our mess. **1821** in *N. Eng. Hist. & Gen. Reg.* XXX. 191 Here a number of members [of Congress], vulgarly called a 'Mess,' put up, and have a separate table. **1886** POORE *Reminiscences* I. 61 Whist was regularly played at many of the 'Congressional messes.'

2. Short for "mess beef."

1855 *N.Y. Wkly. Tribune* 6 Jan. 5/4 Our market is again lower, and is dull for Mess and Prime Mess, while Prime is in short stock and is firmly held. **1884** *Harper's Mag.* July 299/1 [Chicago] The average weight of the class of animals used for 'mess' and 'canning' is 950 pounds.... The division [of the carcasses] is made into ... pieces ... viz. loins, ribs, mess, plates, chucks, rolls, rumps [etc.].... 'Extra mess' is composed of chucks, plates, rumps, and flanks.

3. In combs.: (1) **mess box,** a box or receptacle on a chuck wagon for storing food and cooking utensils; (2) **pork,** salt pork made from the shoulders and sides of hogs and put up in barrels; (3) **shack,** in a camp of laborers, the building in which the men eat.

(1) **1859–60** MRS. WITTER *Letters* (MS) 3 We had what we call a mess box which contained all our cooking utensils. **1913** BARNES *Western Grazing Grounds* 116 One can still find the old-time 'chuck wagon' and the great mess box with its hospitable lid and cranky cook. — (2) **1818** *N.-Eng. Palladium* (Boston) 28 Sep. 3/2 Isaac McClellan & Co.... Have for Sale ... 12 Bbls. Mess Beef—10 do. Pork. **1841** *S. Lit. Messenger* VII. 774/2 The meat served out to them consists generally of bacon cured on the farms, to which ... is added Western bacon or mess pork. **1902** LORIMER *Lett. Merchant* 33 He had better turn his attention to the stocks of mess pork. — (3) **1929** W. HEYLIGER *Builder of Dam* 209 A great log fire was roaring in the fireplace at the head of the mess-shack.

As the last term in **blind, clear, steerage mess.**

***message,** *n.* As the last term in **presidential, President's, veto message.**

***messenger,** *n.*

1. In the Plymouth colony, an officer who served as a constable, jailer, town crier, etc. *Obs.*

1633 *Plymouth Laws* 34 It is order that all measures be brought to the Messenger or Constable of Plym. to be sealed. **1637** *Plymouth*

Col. Rec. I. 54 Josua Pratt was sworne the Messenger for the whole government. **1644** *Ib.* II. 45 That the Messenger henceforth be styled or called by the Name of Marshall.

2. In ecclesiastical use, one sent as a delegate to a convention, synod, or the like.

1646 *Mass. Bay Rec.* II. 155 To assemble the churches, or their messengrs., upon occasion of counsell. **1712** SEWALL *Diary* II. 347 Declar'd that the Elders and Messengers of Churches had appointed him to give the charge. **1829** in SWEET *Religion* 245 To the Ministers and Messengers Composing the Illinois Association. **1947** *Christian Cent.* 21 May 648/2 The Southern Baptist Convention is an assemblage, not of representatives, but of messengers and visitors from local churches.

3. (*cap.*) A horse of a breed especially valued for riding (see quot. 1873).

1857 HERBERT *Forester's Horse & Horsemanship of U.S.* 151 It was the abiding hope of the breeder to obtain the . . . perfect symmetry of a Baronet, with the speed, power, and will of a Messenger. [**1873** *Harper's Mag.* XLVII. 604/1 In May, 1788, a gray horse, fifteen hands three inches high, was landed from England at the foot of Market Street, Philadelphia. This horse was called Messenger.] **1879** TOURGEE *Fool's Errand* 61 The horse of which he spoke was a bay Messenger. [**1908** *Sat. Ev. Post* 29 Aug. 32/1 John Wallace . . . showed that the imported thoroughbred or running horse, Messenger, was the potent sire whose blood furnished the first basis of this trotting branch of a great breed of horses.]

attrib. **1857** *Spirit of Times* 11 April 88/1 The stock horse, Young Morrill, has about an equal share of the Bulrush Morgan and Imported Messenger blood. *Ib.* 16 May 172/2, I have a splendid gray stallion of the Messenger stock. Morse Gray, jr. (now my horse) is out of a Messenger mare by Morse Gray, of New York.

4. = **express messenger.**

1881 BUEL *Border Bandits* 89 The messenger was forced to open the safe. **1948** JOHNSTON *Gold Rush* 46/1 Through that street passed the daily stages with strongboxes full of virgin gold—under the escort of armed messengers.

As the last term in **bank, express, shotgun messenger.**

Messiah craze, war. (See quot. 1940.) Cf. **ghost dance.**

1907 CURTIS *N. Amer. Indians* I. 20 Since the beginning of the present 'messiah craze' all baskets display the sacred symbols believed to have been revealed to Das Lan by Chuganaai Skhĭn—a combination of the cross and the crescent. **1923** J. H. COOK *On Old Frontier* 199 In the fall of 1890—just about the time the Messiah Craze started among the Sioux—a number of the old head men of the Ogallallas came from Pine Ridge Reservation on a hurried visit to my home. **1940** ADAMS *Dict. Amer. Hist.* III. 379 The Messiah War (1890–1) was an outgrowth of the Ghost Dance excitement which so affected the Sioux Indians that R. F. Royer, the agent at Pine Ridge, S. Dak., wired for troops.

mestang ˈmɛstæŋ, *n.* **1.** = **mustang. 2. mestang court,** = **kangaroo court.**

(1) **1834** A. PIKE *Sketches* 74 Lewis and Irwin obtained young and unbroken wild horses, (or, as the hunters call them, mestangs). **1853** P. PAXTON *Yankee in Texas* 120 Thar hit [it] stuck, just like one of them dern Comanches on a mestang. — (2) **1853** P. PAXTON *Yankee in Texas* 205 By a unanimous vote, Judge G. . . . was elected to the bench, and the 'Mestang' or 'Kangaroo Court' regularly organized.

***metal,** *n.* As the last term in **hard, pot, white metal.**

metallic tractors, see ***tractor 1.**

***metaphysical,** *a.* **1. metaphysical healer,** a Christian Science practitioner. **2. metaphysical healing,** = **Christian Science.**

(1) **1876** B. ALCOTT *Journals* 466 A wider acquaintance with idealism in its various phases will be serviceable to these 'Metaphysical Healers' and 'Christian Scientists' as they call their school. — (2) **1884** EDDY in *Christian Science Jrnl.* 2 Feb. 2 Metaphysical healing, or Christian Science, is a demand of the times. **1886** —— *Science & Health* (ed. 16) 11 In the year 1866 I discovered metaphysical healing, and named it Christian Science.

metate məˈtatɪ, *n. S.W.* [Amer. Sp. (<Nahuatl) in same sense.] The lower or bed stone, often rectangular in shape, used by the Indians in the Southwest in grinding corn, coffee, beans, etc. Also attrib. See **mano.**

[**1780** CLAVIGERO *Storia della Messico* II. 218 Gli Spagnuoli chiamino il Metlatl *Metate*.] **1834** in *S.W. Hist. Quart.* XLV. 330 Mrs. Roark had a Mexican utensil for grinding corn, called a *metate*. It was a large rock which had a place scooped out of the center that would hold a peck of corn. It had a stone roller. **1882** *Atlantic Mo.* Oct. 550/1 The muller, or rubbing stone, and the metlatl, or mill, of sandstone or volcanic rock . . . are used for grinding. **1893** LUMMIS *Land of Poco Tiempo* 49 Each brought to an appointed house her metate and sack of corn. . . . One of these *metate* songs . . . is as follows. **1949** *Desert Mag.* June 15/2 Several metates were strewn over a considerable area nearby.

b. metate stone, = prec.

1847 HENRY *Campaign Sk.* 134 The eldest was on her knees at the medatstone grinding corn, making it up into cakes, and baking tortillas on a plate of sheet-iron. **1877** H. C. HODGE *Arizona* 60 The Indians collect large quantities of both varieties, which when dried they grind into flour on their metat stones.

***meter,** *n.* As the last term in **parking, short meter.**

***Methodism,** *n.* As the last term in **Free, Southern Methodism.**

***Methodist,** *n.* In combs.: (1) **Methodist big meeting,** see **big meeting;** (2) **Episcopal Church,** the American Christian denomination organized in Baltimore in 1784, derived from the British organization founded by John and Charles Wesley in 1729; (3) **Episcopal Church, North,** (see quots. and cf. next); (4) **Episcopal Church, South,** the organization established in 1845 by southern Methodists who, because of the slavery issue, withdrew from the Methodist Episcopal Church (see also quot. 1943); (5) **Protestant,** a member of a nonepiscopal church or denomination founded in 1830 by Methodists dissatisfied with the administrative organization of the Methodist Episcopal Church, also **Methodist Protestant Church.**

(2) **1784** WHATCOAT in Phoebus *Memoirs* (1828), 24th [Dec.], we rode to Baltimore; . . . at 10 o'clock we began our Conference, in which we agreed to form a Methodist Episcopal Church, *in which the Liturgy* (as presented by the Rev. John Wesley) *should be read*, Sacraments to be administered by a Superintendent, Elders, and Deacons, who shall be ordained by a Presbytery, using the Episcopal form (as prescribed in the Rev. Mr. Wesley's Prayer-Book.) **1834** PECK *Gaz. Illinois* 273 There is [in Lebanon] a large society of the Methodist Episcopal Church. **1924** *M.E. Gen. Conference Jrnl.* 201 The Twenty-ninth session of the delegated General Conference to the Methodist Episcopal Church convened in the Auditorium, Springfield, Massachusetts. — (3) [**1864** in FLEMING *Hist. Reconstruction* II. 238 There is no such church as the Methodist Church North. Ours is the Methodist Episcopal Church. We are not sectional.] **1890** *Cent.* 3741/1 In the United States, the Methodist Episcopal Church exists in two geographical divisions, the *Methodist Episcopal Church* (*North*), and the *Methodist Episcopal Church* (*South*). — (4) **1860** *Charleston* (S.C.) *Mercury* 29 Dec. 3/1 We ministers of the Alabama Conference of the Methodist Episcopal Church South . . . believe African slavery, as it exists in the Southern States of this republic, to be a wise, humane and righteous institution. **1943** *Yearbook Amer. Churches* 67 Methodist Episcopal Church, South. This is the continuing M.E. Church, South . . . and is composed of congregations that declined to be a party to the merger of the M. E. Church. The M. E. Church, South and the Methodist Protestant Church with The Methodist Church. **1949** *Southwest Rev.* Spring 124/2 The Central Jurisdiction . . . was set up . . . as a sop to the M. E. Church, South, when race and segregation threatened to stand as barriers to the plan of union.

(5) **1831** PECK *Guide* 258 The Reformers, or Methodist Protestant church. **1851** STOWE *Key* 192 Some were professors of religion—Presbyterians, Episcopal Methodists, and Methodist Protestants. **1943** *Yearbook Amer. Churches* 63 In April, 1939, the Uniting Conference forming The Methodist Church was held by representatives of the Methodist Episcopal Church, the Methodist Episcopal Church South and the Methodist Protestant Church.

b. Denoting a *bonnet* or *cap* of a type formerly worn by Methodist women. *Obs.*

1844 *Lowell Offering* IV. 172, I have not seen one of the old 'Simon Pure' Methodist bonnets since I have been here. **1852** EASTMAN *Aunt Phillis's Cabin* 61 She had a black-satin Methodist bonnet, very much the shape of a coal hod. — **1853** STOWE *Key* 156/1 A plain Methodist cap shades her face, and the plain white Methodist handkerchief is folded across the bosom.

As the last term in **American, Dutch, Episcopal, Free, German, hickory, Otterbein, Protestant, Republican, shouting, Southern, United Otterbein Methodist(s).**

metif meˈtif, *n.* [F. *métif*, in same sense.] A person of mixed blood. Also attrib. Cf. next.

1808 PIKE *Sources Miss.* 203 The hospitality and goodness of the Creoles and Metifs began to manifest itself. **1821** NUTTALL *Travels Arkansa* 99 Mr. Drope remained at the Bluff, trading . . . with the two or three metif families settled here. **1884** G. P. LATHROP *True* ii. 14 She was not of octoroon or metif parentage.

metis meˈtis, *n.* [F. *métis*, in same sense.] A person of mixed blood, esp. a half-breed of white and Indian extraction (see quots. 1841 and 1885). Also, locally, an octoroon. Cf. prec.

1839 *Penny Cyclo.* XV. 158/2 The mixed race [in Mexico] is mostly composed of the descendants of the Europeans and the aboriginal tribes: these are called *Metis* or *Mestizos*. **1885** *Boston Herald* 29 Nov., The paternal ancestors of the Metis were the former employes of the Hudson Bay and Northwest Fur Companies, and their maternal ancestors were indian women of various tribes. **1902** WHITE *Conjuror's House* 5 Everywhere was gay color—the red sashes . . . the beaded moccasins and leggings of the *mètis*.

* **metropolis,** *n.* As the last term in **ancient, Great Metropolis.**

metump mə'tʌmp, *n.* [?f. Abnaki, *madumbi.*] (See quot. 1778.) Also **metump line.** *Obs.* Cf. **tumpline.** — **1754** in *N. H. Hist. Soc. Coll.* I. 279 There was next to their [Indians'] skin tied a number of small metump lines. **1778** CARVER *Travels* 331 The Indians draw these carriages with great ease be they ever so much loaded, by means of a string which passes round the breast. This collar is called a Metump.

Mex mɛks, *a.* and *n.* Colloquial shortening of "Mexican."

1853 BREWERTON *With Kit Carson* (1930) 154 The United States Hotel upon the *plaza* provided 'chicken fixin's and corn doin's' or, if a stranger wanted 'Mex livin',' *frijoles* and *tortillas* to boot. **1906** *McClure's Mag.* June 121/1 'Where'd you get the coat?' I asked the Mex. **1929** J. PARKER *Old Army* 246 He was evidently not one of those who looked with pleasure upon 'Mex' officers.

* **Mexican,** *a.* and *n.*

1. =**Mexican dollar.** *Obs.*

1827 COOPER *Prairie* v, A foal that is worth thirty of the brightest Mexicans that bear the face of the King of Spain. **1845** HOOPER *Simon Sugg's Adv.* 76 There's an old friend of mine . . . that's got three or four hamper baskets-full o' Mexicans.

2. =**Mexican cotton.** Also attrib. *Obs.*

1827 *Western Mo. Rev.* I. 82 The kinds of cotton which are chiefly cultivated are Louisiana, green seed, or Tennessee, and recently Mexican. **1850** in TURNER *Cotton* (1865) 125, I think, or rather fear, that the introduction of the great variety of seed will ruin the Mexican. . . . At present, it is almost impossible to get a genuine article of Mexican seed.

3. *pl. S.W.* A variety of sheep; wool obtained from sheep of this variety. *Obs.*

1878 I. L. BIRD *Rocky Mts.* 173 The flocks are made up mostly of pure and graded Mexicans. **1883** RITCH *Illust. N. Mex.* 45 Prices [of wool] this year, however, have been from 15 cents per pound for the lowest grade of Mexican, to 24 cents for the choicest. **1887** *Scribner's Mag.* II. 511/1 The season comes for the shearing of Southdowns or rough-fleeced Mexicans.

4. In special combs.: (1) **Mexican dollar,** the Mexican peso; (2) **packsaddle,** =**aparejo,** *obs.;* (3) **poncho,** =**poncho;** (4) **saddle,** a heavy saddle having, usu., a high pommel and cantle, heavy leather skirts, and wooden stirrups; (5) **spur,** a spur of a type favored by Mexican riders, often having large rowels and silver ornaments; (6) **War,** the war carried on by the U.S. and Mexico (1846–48), also attrib.

(1) **1831** in *Overland to Pacific* II. (1933) 180 The circulating medium of Missouri now consists principally of Mexican dollars. **1912** *Outing* Oct. 34/2 He was a short, chunky man, all gray hair and bushy whiskers, with a pair of round spectacles the size of Mexican dollars. — (2) **1858** IVES *Colo. River* (1861) 115 Several that I was unable to supply with the Mexican pack-saddle, or arapaho, have had to carry army pack-saddles. — (3) **1861** *Alexandria* (Va.) *Gaz.* 14 May 1/1 It [blanket] has a slit in the middle, so as to serve as a Mexican ponchar. — (4) **1839** MURRAY *Travels in N. Amer.* I. 380 Seated in a Mexican peak-saddle, covered with a wolf-skin, he seemed a part of the animal which he bestrode. **1846** in *Calif. Hist. Soc. Quart.* XXI. (1942) 203 Many of them [Indians] had Mexican saddles, cartridge boxes, and different parts of the Mexican dress. **1910** HART *Vigilante Girl* 345 She galloped on in her high-peaked Mexican saddle.

(5) **1865** PIKE *Scout & Ranger* (1932) 22 Imagine two hundred men . . . mounted on wiry, half wild horses, with Spanish saddles and Mexican spurs. **1944** ROSS *Westward* 112 They would sit jingling their Mexican spurs until the housewife appeared. — (6) **1846** *Dollar Newspaper* (Phila.) 27 May 3/1 (*heading*), The Mexican War. **1884** *N.Y. Wkly. Tribune* 30 July 6/3 Pensions for Mexican War veterans are demanded. **1947** *Steamboat* (Colo.) *Pilot* 2 Jan. 7/2 He had been with Winfield Scott in the Mexican war.

b. Also in combs. of more obvious meaning or explained in the quots.: (1) **Mexican ax,** (2) **bit,** (3) **blanket,** (4) **pioneer,** (5) **shilling,** (6) **sombrero.**

(1) **1858** PETERS *Kit Carson* 239 The Mexican axe . . . resembles as much the common pick of our laborers as it does the axe used by American woodsmen. — (2) **1874** KNIGHT I. 383/2 In the Mexican bit the curb-chain and its strap are replaced by a curb-ring. **1884** CABLE *Dr. Sevier* liii, A large dark horse . . . stood champing his Mexican bit in the black shadow of a great oak. — (3) **1834** A. PIKE *Sketches* 74 We gave him a red and gaudy Mexican blanket. **1894** *Harper's Mag.* Jan 299/1 He had parted with Pedro for forty dollars, a striped Mexican blanket, and a pair of spurs. — (4) **1872** MCCLELLAN *Golden State* 455 The Bay and the present site of San Francisco was first discovered . . . by Governor Portala, the Mexican pioneer.

(5) **1889** *Cent.* 567/1 *Bit,* . . . in parts of the United States, [the name] of a silver coin formerly current (in some States called a *Mexican shilling*), of the value of 12½ cents. — (6) **1848** EDWIN BRYANT *California* 239 Some of them were dressed in white shirts and pantaloons, with the Mexican sombrero, or broad-brim hat. **1913** BARNES *Western Grazing Grounds* 116 The broad-brimmed Stetson or Mexican sombrero has gone.

c. In the names of animals: (1) **Mexican badger,** a western species of the common American badger; (2) **bean beetle,** a spotted beetle, *Epilachna corrupta,* which feeds on the leaves of various beans; (3) **bluebird,** the

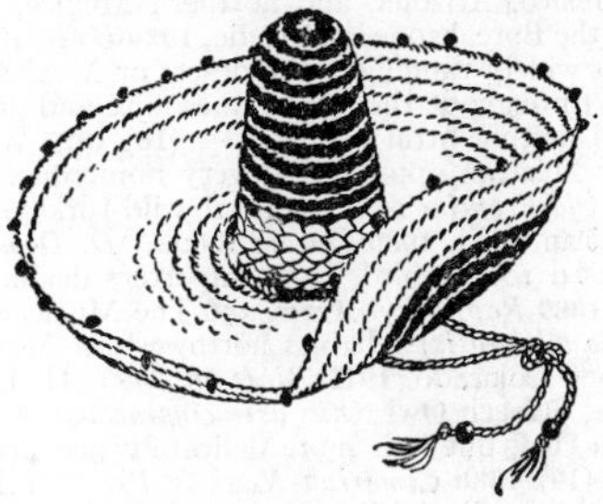

Mexican sombrero

western bluebird *q.v.;* (4) **bronco,** =**bronco;** (5) **chickadee,** (see quot.); (6) **cotton-boll weevil,** =**boll weevil;** (7) **cougar,** (see quot. 1907); (8) **eagle,** Audubon's caracara, *Polyborus cheriway auduboni,* found in the southern states; (9) **flycatcher,** a flycatcher found in Mexico; (10) **fruitfly,** a small fly, *Anastrepha ludena,* the larva of which is injurious to citrus fruit and mangoes; (11) **hog,** the Texas peccary, *Pecari angulatus;* (12) **horse,** =**bronco;** (13) **jaçana,** (see quots.); (14) **lion,** the cougar or puma; (15) **mule deer,** (see quots.); (16) **opossum,** a large opossum of a species found in the Southwest; (17) **quail,** a quail found in Mexico, esp. the Texas bobwhite; (18) **screech owl,** (see quots.); (19) **woodpecker,** the red-shafted flicker of the West; (20) **wren,** (see quot.).

(1) **1885** *Amer. Naturalist* Sep. 1922 The Mexican badger, two specimens of which are found in Central Kansas. — (2) **1924** *Science Supp.* 26 Dec. xii/2 The Mexican bean beetle . . . now makes the third unwelcome immigrant that has reached this country from Mexico. **1945** *Athol* (Mass.) *D. News* 9 July 2/7 The Mexican bean beetle is one of the most troublesome garden pests. — (3) **1846** ABERT *Exam. N. Mex.* 89 During the morning . . . we had killed eight Mexican blue birds, 'sialla occidentalis.' — (4) **1881** CHASE *Editor's Run* 83, I never saw a Mexican broncho hang his head lower.

(5) **1934** *Nat. Geog. Mag.* LXV. 580 The Mexican chickadee (*Penthestes sclateri eidos*) . . . occurs from the mountains of southern Arizona into Mexico. — (6) **1896** *Dept. Agric. Yearbook 1895* 51 The insect . . . had been brought across from Mexico, and so was commonly called the Mexican cotton-boll weevil. **1910** *Science* 28 Jan. 151/1 The Mexican Cotton Boll Weevil . . . works in such a manner that it has seemed beyond the usual means that have been followed in insect control. — (7) **1907** MEARNS *Mammals Mex. Boundary* 201 The Mexican cougar or mountain lion (*Felis oregonensis aztecus*) destroys great numbers of deer. **1936** *Univ. Ariz. Gen. Bul.* No. 3, 71 The Mexican cougar ranges throughout the state with the exception of the open treeless valleys and mesas. — (8) **1835** in *S.W. Hist. Quart.* XXVIII. 190 The most common birds and fowls found [in Texas] are the Mexican eagle, the hawk, the crow [etc.]. **1858** BAIRD *Birds Pacific R.R.* 45 The Mexican Eagle . . . [inhabits] Florida, Texas, Mexico. **1936** *Univ. Ariz. Gen. Bul.* No. 3, 92 This is sometimes called for want of knowledge of it a Mexican eagle. It is not an eagle but a hawk, the Audubon caracara. — (9) **1869** *Amer. Naturalist* III. 473 A solitary Mexican Fly Catcher . . . gave a specimen of the summer group of migrants.

(10) **1934** WEBSTER. **1944** *U.S. Govt. Man.* Summer 350 It [the Bureau of Entomology and Plant Quarantine] enforces plant quarantine to prevent the spread of plant pests which have gained a limited foothold, cooperating with States . . . to control the pink bollworm . . . the Mexican fruitfly, and the white-fringed beetle. — (11) **1821** NUTTALL *Travels Arkansa* 155 The *Sus tajassu* or Mexican hog, is not uncommon some distance higher up Red river. **1901** *Amer. Rev. of Reviews* Sep. 309/1 An otherwise magnificent grazing country . . . is frequented by wild Mexican hogs, panthers [etc.]. — (12) **1844** KENDALL *Narr. Santa Fe Exped.* II. 362 There is a little 'go-ahead' in a spirited, showy, well-trained Mexican horse. **1872** TICE *Over Plains* 140 The Mexican horses, or *bronchos*, will also winter out during the winter like the cattle. — (13) **1883** *Nat. Museum Bul.* No. 27, 154 Family Parridæ. — The Jaçanas . . . Mexican Jaçana. Middle America, north to Lower Rio Grande Valley in Texas. **1887** RIDGWAY *Man. N. Amer. Birds* 183 *J[acana] gymnostoma* (Wagl.). Mexican Jacana. — (14) **1903** O. HENRY *Heart of West* 250 It is well to be reasonably watchful when a Mexican lion sings soprano along the arroyos. **1932** JAMES GREER (ed.) *Texas Ranger* 52 He [a large puma] was what some are pleased to call a Mexican lion.

(15) **1907** MEARNS *Mammals Mex. Boundary* 191 Odocoileus hemionus canus Merriam. Mexican Mule Deer . . . inhabits southwest Texas, New Mexico, Arizona, and northern Mexico, ranging from the Sonoran to the Boreal zone in altitude. **1936** *Univ. Ariz. Gen. Bul.* No. 3, 63 Most widely ranging is the desert or Mexican mule deer, which is found throughout the cactus, mesquite and grassland areas in southern and south central Arizona. — (16) **1827** WILLIAMS *West Florida* 26 The Mexican oppossum is very numerous. — (17) **1923** J. H. COOK *On Old Frontier* 27 There were wild turkeys by the thousand: also Mexican quail. **1930** *Durant* (Okla.) *D. Democrat* 14 Nov. 7/2 We purchased 10,000 birds from importers dealing in Mexican quail. — (18) **1889** *Rep. Secy. Agric.* 376 The Mexican Screech Owl (*Megascops asio trichopsis*) inhabits northwestern Mexico, Arizona, New Mexico, and Colorado. **1917** *Birds of Amer.* II. 111 The Mexican, or Arizona, Screech Owl (*Otus asio cineraceus*) is similar to the Aiken's Screech Owl, but it is more delicately penciled both above and below. — (19) **1880** *Cimarron News & Press* 23 Dec. 1/4 The last member of this family is the red-shafted or Mexican woodpecker . . . the underparts lilac-brown with numerous circular black spots.

(20) **1874** COUES *Key* 28 *Catherpes Mexicanus* . . . Mexican Wren; White-throated Wren.

d. In the names of plants: (1) **Mexican (black) bean,** =**frijol;** (2) **jumping bean,** =**jumping bean.**

(1) **1850** *N. Eng. Farmer* II. 295 This is the true name of the Mexican Black Bean. **1901** *Amer. Rev. of Reviews* Sep. 313/1 The list [of provisions] includes Mexican beans, oatmeal . . . and canned tomatoes and corn. — (2) **1947** *Field & Stream* June 180/3 What makes a Mexican jumping bean jump?

e. In plant names of more obvious meaning or sufficiently defined in the quots.: (1) **Mexican banana,** (2) **buckeye,** (3) **cardinal flower,** (4) **clover,** (5) **cocoa,** (6) **four o'clock,** (7) **madrona,** (8) **mulberry,** (9) **persimmon,** (10) **(prickly) poppy,** (11) **tea.**

(1) **1884** SARGENT *Rep. Forests* 219. **1889** *Cent.* 437/1 Mexican banana, a name sometimes given to a species of Yucca, *Y. baccata*, of northern Mexico and the adjacent United States, which bears a large, juicy, edible fruit. — (2) **1891** COULTER *Bot. W. Texas* I. 66 *Ungnadia speciosa* Mexican buckeye. A shrub or very small tree common . . . from the valley of the Trinity through western Texas to New Mexico. **1931** DAYTON *Western Browse Plants* 104 Mexican-buckeye (*Ungnadia speciosa*), known also as monillo, Spanish buckeye, and New Mexican buckeye, is a monotypic genus. — (3) **1869** FULLER *Flower Gatherers* 237 It was marked *Lobelia fulgens*, or Mexican Cardinal flower, and had retained its superb color for years. — (4) **1889** VASEY *Agric. Grasses* 103 *Richardsonia scabra* (Mexican Clover; Spanish Clover; Florida Clover; Water Parsley [etc.]). **1901** MOHR *Plant Life Ala.* 135 The so-called Mexican clover . . . furnish[es] abundant, spontaneous crops of nutritious hay.

(5) **1890** WEBSTER 272/1 *Mexican cocoa*, an American herb (*Richardsonia scabra*), yielding a nutritious fodder. Its roots are used as a substitute for ipecacuanha. — (6) **1829** EATON *Botany* (ed. 5) 296 Exotic. *Mirabilis dichotoma*, Mexican four o'clock. **1836** LINCOLN *Botany* App. 117 *Mirabilis . . . dichotoma*, (Mexican four-o'clock.) — (7) **1897** SUDWORTH *Arborescent Flora* 312 Arbutus Xalapensis, . . . Mexican Madrona. . . . Common names. Manzanita. Madrona. — (8) **1884** SARGENT *Rep. Forests* 128 *Morus microphylla*. . . . Mexican Mulberry. — (9) **1885** HAVARD *Flora W. & S. Texas* 523 Mexican Persimmon; the Chapote of the Mexicans. Shrub or small tree 10 to 20 feet high. **1907** MEARNS *Mammals Mex. Boundary* 67 The Mexican persimmon was abundant in the region surrounding Fort Clark, in Kinney County, Texas.

(10) **1846** ABERT *Exam N. Mex.* 25 The Mexican poppy was abundant. **1901** MOHR *Plant Life Ala.* 520 *Argemone mexicana*. . . . Mexican Prickly Poppy. . . . Carolinian and Louisianian areas. Adventive sparingly in North Atlantic ports, frequent on the South Atlantic and Gulf coast. — (11) **1843** TORREY *Flora N.Y.* II. 135 *Ambrina Ambrosioides*. . . . Mexican Tea. . . . Road-sides and waste places; common near New-York and along the Hudson. **1901** MOHR *Plant Life Ala.* 488 Mexican Tea. . . . Carolinian and Louisianian areas. **1940** JAEGER *Calif. Deserts* 169 Species of ephedra or Mexican tea occur in similar situations.

As the last term in **Franco-, New, Spanish Mexican.**

Mexicanization ˌmɛksəkənəˈzeʃən, *n.* The process of rendering Mexican; the state or condition of being Mexicanized. *Rare.* — **1890** *Cong. Rec.* 5 June 5655/1 Gentlemen, do you know what a single silver standard means in this country? It means Mexicanization.

Mexicanize ˈmɛksəkənˌaɪz, *v. tr.* To make (a person or thing) like a Mexican or like Mexico. Also **Mexicanized,** *a.*

1844 GREGG *Commerce of Prairies* II. 119 To this great ball, however, no Americans were invited, with the exception of a Mexicanized denizen or two. **1846** ——— *Diary & Letters* I. (1941) 231 Dr. Davis . . . married a Mexican and has, in fact, perfectly Mexicanized himself. **1910** *N.Y. Ev. Post* 13 Oct. 8 Some object to describing the Roosevelt plan as one to Mexicanize our government. But that is precisely what it is.

Mexico piece. A Spanish piece of eight, used in Mexico. In full *Mexico piece of eight. Obs.*

1660 WINTHROP *Letters* 66 Mexico peices will passe for 5s. apeice. **1688** SEWALL *Diary* I. 240, I gave an oblong Mexico piece of Eight. **1741** *N.J. Archives* 1 Ser. VI. 118 Mexico pieces of eight, seventeen penny weight twelve grains, four shillings and six pence.

Miami maɪˈæmɪ, *n.* [Amer. Indian. Poss. f. a Chippewa term meaning "people who live on the peninsula."]

1. *pl.* An Algonquian tribe of Indians who, when first encountered by Europeans, lived in what is now eastern Wisconsin and northern Illinois and Indiana. In full **Miami Indians.**

[**1671** *Relations des Jésuites 1670* (1858) 90/2 L'on passe ensuite chez les Miamioüek, et on arrive par de grands deserts aux Ilinois.] **1722** COXE *Descr. Carolana* 49 Near the Bottom of the Bay . . . is the fair River of the Miamihas (so call'd because upon it lives Part of a Nation bearing the same Name). **1792** *Ann. 2d Congress* 1048 [The] aggressions of the Miami and Wabash Indians . . . are solely the causes of the war. **1896** *Harper's Mag.* April 711/1 When a boy of twelve he had been captured by the Miamis.

b. *sing.* An Indian of this tribe. In full **Miami Indian.**

1808 BARKER *Indian Princess* II. iii, The insolent Miami has braved your king, and defied him with the crimson tomahawk. **1812** *Ann. 12th Congress* 1 Sess. II. 1861 It has been reported by a Miami Indian . . . that twenty-four Indians of the Shawanese Prophet's band, . . . passed his camp. **1835** HOFFMAN *Winter in West* I. 276 The Indians that frequent the neighbourhood of Chicago . . . are chiefly Pottawattamies and Ottawas, with . . . a straggling Kickapoo or Miami.

2. In combs. of obvious meaning, as **Miami chief, confederacy, country, land, reserve, tribe, village.**

1791 *N.Y. Mag.* Dec. 737 At this place, which I judged to be about 15 miles from the Miami village, I had determined to throw up a flight work. **1797** in Soc. Friends, Phila. Yrly. Meeting *Acct. Comm.* (1806) 47 The Miami chief, Little Turtle, . . . is anxious to cooperate. **1815** DRAKE *Cincinnati* 80 Forest trees . . . of the Miami country. **1838** VAN BUREN in *Pres. Mess. & P.* III. 507, I transmit, for the consideration and constitutional action of the Senate, a treaty concluded with the Miami tribe of Indians. **1840** in *Ib.* IV. 1842 The Miami lands were very valuable. **1849** CHAMBERLAIN *Indiana Gaz.* 251 This county, lying entirely in the Miami Reserve, has only been settled about six years. **1945** *Chi. D. News* 2 Aug. 10/2 The Indians—Delawares, Shawnees, Wyandots and those of the Miami Confederacy—gave up all title to lands in southern Ohio. **1945** ADAMS *Album Amer. Hist.* II. 35 On the banks of the Maumee River sat, brooding, a Miami chief by the name of Little Turtle.

***Michaux,** *n.* [Andre *Michaux* (1746–1802), a French botanist and traveler.] Used in the possessive in the specific names of plants (see quots.). — **1843** TORREY *Flora N.Y.* II. 339 *Cyperus Michauxianus*. . . . Michaux's Galingale. . . . Borders of salt marshes: common in the neighborhood of New-York, and on Long Island. **1901** MOHR *Plant Life Ala.* 409 *Arenaria stricta*. . . . Michaux's Sandwort. . . . Canadian zone to Carolinian area.

Michigamea ˌmɪʃəˈgæmɪə, *n.* [f. Algonquian *michi*, great, +*guma*, water, prob. with ref. to Big Lake, Ark., where these Indians once lived.] (See quot. 1907.)

1770 PITTMAN *Present State* 51 The principal Indian nations in this country are, the Cascasquias, Kaoquias, Mitchigamias, and Peoryas. **1907** HODGE *Amer. Indians* I. 856/2 Michigamea. . . . A tribe of the Illinois confederacy, first visited by Marquette when he descended the Mississippi in 1673. **1949** *Chi. Tribune* 20 Feb. (Grafic Mag.)

14/4 The subtribes making up the confederation were the Kaskaskia, Peoria, Tamaroa, Cahokia, Moingwena, Mitchegamea, and others.

Michigan ˈmɪʃəgən, *n.* [Name of one of the Great Lakes and of a north central state, f. Algonquian.]

1. A card game resembling newmarket.

1944 *Pocket Book of Games* 80 Michigan is a simple game, yet rewards careful attention. **1946** Ford *Honolulu Story* 176, 'I want to play hearts. On the floor.' 'Michigan,' Mary said. 'Michigan it is.'

2. In combs.: (1) **Michigan (double) plow,** a heavy double-moldboard plow used for breaking, subsoiling, etc., *obs.;* (2) **grayling,** the *Thymallus tricolor,* a game fish related to the trout; (3) **itch,** prob. the Illinois mange *q.v.*, or some similar affliction.

(1) **1857** *Ill. Agric. Soc. Trans.* III. 496 For this purpose [subsoiling] the Michigan double or subsoil plow is used. **1862** *Rep. Comm. Patents 1861: Agric.* 279 This ploughing may also be done by a double team with the Michigan plough. **1874** Knight 728/2 In England and in the United States another form of this plow has been used in which the precedent portion is not merely a flange on the colter, but is a regular moldboard plow of small proportions, higher than and in front of the main plow. This is known in Ohio as the 'Michigan doubleplow,' and is an efficient implement requiring four horses. — (2) **1884** Goode *Fisheries* I. 505 It is, however, the Michigan Grayling which is at present most interesting to the angler. — (3) **1855** M. Thompson *Doesticks' Letters* 97 One was afflicted with the measles, and the other had the Michigan itch.

b. Also in combs. of more obvious meaning, as (1) **Michigan fish,** (2) **herring,** (3) **oak,** (4) **pine,** (5) **road,** (6) **well.** Chiefly *obs.*

(1) *a*1862 Thoreau *Maine Woods* 210, [I] caught several small somewhat yellowish sucker-like fishes, which the Indian at once rejected, saying that they were Michigan fish (i.e. soft and stinking fish). — (2) **1883** *Nat. Museum Bul.* No. 27, 423 *Coregonus artedi* ... Lake Herring, Michigan Herring. Great Lakes and northeastward. — (3) **1883** *Cent. Mag.* Oct. 814/1 The butts are made of Michigan oak. — (4) **1922** Titus *Timber* 12 Didn't Michigan Pine build th' corn belt?

(5) **1838** Colton *Indiana Delineated* 26 A rail road is located from Madison to Indianapolis, and the great Michigan road through the state commences here. — (6) **1942** Sears Roebuck *How to Get Running Water* 8/1 Open end driven wells ... are usually used only in localities where fine sand extends from the surface of the ground to the point where water is found, such as in country where sand dunes abound, usually around large lakes. Because such conditions are found in a state like Michigan, they are commonly known as Michigan wells.

Michigander ˈmɪʃəˌgændɚ, *n.* A native or inhabitant of the state of Michigan.

1835 in *Hist. Soc. N.W. Ohio* VII. (1935) 29 Aug. 3 Horner was not acceptable to the Michiganders and acting Governor Mason continued in office. **1903** *Mich. Ornith. Club Bul.* March 28 Cole writes that he still considers himself a Michigander, and expects to be with us during our Summer outings. **1949** *Readers' Digest* May 37/1 My husband and I had ... always been impressed by the state pride of the native-born Texans, Michiganders and Wisconsinites.

Michiganese ˌmɪʃəgənˈiz, *n.* Those who live in Michigan. — **1837** *N.Y. Mirror* 1 July 7/3 The fair *Michiganese,* compared with the Buckeye daughters, 'exceed them in beauty as the first of May doth the last of December.' **1888** Field *Speeches, Arguments* (1890) III. 369 Why not say Ohiese, Michiganese, and Vermontese?

Michigania ˌmɪʃəˈgenɪə, *n.* Michigan. *Rare.* — **1819** *Detroit Gaz.* II. 5 March 3/3 They combine the property of the Irish potatoe, and the merit of being raised in 'Michigania.'

Michiganian ˌmɪʃəˈgenɪən, *n.* = **Michigander.** *Obs.*

1813 *Niles' Reg.* V. 185/2 The Michiganians. **1835** Hoffman *Winter in West* I. 163 The pride of a Michiganian, in the beautiful land of his adoption, is ... strong. **1837** Martineau *Society* I. 65 The Michiganians were in the singular position of having a state government in full operation, while they were excluded from the Union.

Michiganite ˈmɪʃəgənˌaɪt, *n.* A native or inhabitant of Michigan. — **1894** *U. of Chi. Wkly.* 6 Dec. 107/2 The grand stand and bleachers were crowded with a crowd of loyal Michiganites or Chicagoans.

Mick mɪk, *n.* [f. proper name *Michael.*] An Irishman. Also attrib. *Slang.*

1856 *Butte Rec.* (Oroville, Calif.) 20 Sep. 3/3 One of the 'bucks' jerked something from his belt, ... and made for a Mick. **1894** Ford *P. Stirling* 369 Fortunately it's a Mick regiment, so we needn't worry over who was killed. **1946** *Sat. Ev. Post* 3 Aug. 48/3 The tourist will find that the people of Pittsburgh, who in earlier days were somewhat ungenerously thought of as Polaks, Hunkies, Wops, and Micks, ... are today mostly second and third generation Americans.

mico ˈmaɪko, *n.* Also **meiko.** [Muskogee *miko,* chief.] A chief or ruler among the Muskogee Indians. Cf. **mingo,** *n.*[3]

1737 Wesley *Journal* 2 Dec., Nor have they any kings or princes ... ; their meikos, or headmen, having no power either to command or punish. **1800** Hawkins *Sk. Creek Country* 68 Every town has a chief who presides over the whole; he is their Mic-co, called by the white people, 'King.' **1854** *S. Lit. Messenger* XX. 399 They had no doubts of the perfect worth of their young chief, to be the Great Mico, or King of the Catawbas! **1932** C. C. Lovell *Golden Isles Ga.* 59 Melatch, a Creek chieftain, ... visited Frederica with sixteen other micos or kings.

* **mid,** *a.* In combs.: (1) **mid-America,** the central part of the U.S.; (2) * **-night,** see as a main entry; (3) * **-shipman,** a toadfish of the genus *Porichthys,* so named because of the likeness of phosphorescent organs on the belly to the buttons of a midshipman's uniform; (4) * **-way,** see as a main entry; (5) **-west,** (often *cap.*) = **Middlewest,** also attrib.; (6) **-western,** *a.* (often *cap.*) = **Middle-western;** (7) **-westerner,** one who lives in, or is a native of, the Middlewest; (8) **-year,** *a.* occurring at the half-way point in an academic year of nine months; (9) **years,** examinations at the middle of an academic year, *colloq.*

(1) **1926** *Amer. Mercury* July 326/2 So much blood and meat in Mid-America! **1944** *Survey Graphic* June 280/2 Here is something distinctly of mid-America. — (3) **1882** Jordan & Gilbert *Synop. Fishes N. Amer.* 751 *Porichthys porosissimus*—Midshipman.

(5) **1923** *Collier's Mag.* 25 Aug. 24/3 One of the economic causes of Mid-Western discontent is the feeling that the Mid-West is the object of discrimination. **1949** *Chi. Tribune* 8 Sep. 24/3 Oak Wilt ... is invading the forests and woodlots of Illinois and several other midwest states. — (6) **1923** *Collier's Mag.* 25 Aug. 5/2 These Mid-Western states are almost entirely rural. **1948** *Ariz. Republic* (Phoenix) 29 June 18/4 The break in oats prices is attributed largely to midwestern rains over the past week. — (7) **1927** *Scribner's Mag.* Oct. 480/2 These midwesterners are alike unto Americans in other rural areas. **1947** *Dly. Ardmoreite* (Ardmore, Okla.) 18 Aug. 1/2 Midwesterners and their parched corn broiled from the heat Monday after the third consecutive torrid weekend. — (8) **1897** Flandrau *Harvard Episodes* 226 The midyear examinations have an unpleasant habit of disturbing the even academic tenor early in February, as their name suggests. **1912** Nicholson *Hoosier Chron.* 218 In the midyear recess of her sophomore year she visited one of her new friends in Boston. — (9) **1896** Moe *Harvard* 45 And thus Massachusetts Hall arose on the spot where it still stands, a pride to the College, and an abhorrence at the 'midyears' and 'finals.'

* **middle,** *a.* and *n.*

1. *n.* In a cultivated field, the strip of unplanted ground between the drills or rows of corn, cotton, etc. Usu. *pl.*

1829 in Commons *Doc. Hist.* 238 Two Ploughs breaking middles in Popular tree cut. **1909** *D.N.* III. 295 I've been bustin' out middles this week. **1946** *Democrat* 11 April 1/5 Two and three year old kudzu stands that have not covered the middles will be greatly helped if the middles are broken out.

2. In combs.: (1) **middle-buster,** (see quot. 1907); (2) **colonies,** *pl.*, the American colonies situated between those of New England and the southern ones, also **middle British colonies;** (3) **field,** formerly in baseball, the position of the center fielder; (4) * **ground,** (see quot.), *obs.;* (5) * **man,** (*a*) an oarsman in the middle of a boat, (*b*) in Negro minstrelsy, the actor in the middle of a line or semi-circle of performers; (6) **piece,** = * **middling 1,** also attrib.; (7) **states,** see as a main entry; (8) **tenor,** (see quot.); (9) **thaw,** (see quot.), *obs.;* (10) **West,** the north central portion of the U.S., embracing, approximately, the area north of the Ohio River and its latitude from the Rocky Mountains to the Alleghanies, also attrib., cf. **American Middlewest;** (11) **Western,** *a.* of or pertaining to the Middlewest; (12) **Westerner,** one who lives in the Middlewest.

(1) **1907** T. Hunt *Forage in Amer.* 352 (Th. Supp.), Or by means of a middle 'buster,' which is a double moldboard plow. **1944** Clark *Pills* 283 In the warerooms or crowded along the aisles in the stores themselves were the assembled implements such as middle busters, turning plows, side harrows, spring tooth cultivators, corn and cotton planters. — (2) **1775** in *Hist. MSS Comm.* 14th Rep. X. (1895) 308 And the Bill restraining the Trade of the Five Middle Colonies, filled

up, and a Clause added. **1776** (*title*), A Topographical Description of such parts of North America as are contained in the annexed map of the middle British colonies. **1821** JEFFERSON *Writings* I. 19 The people of the middle colonies (Maryland, Delaware, Pennsylsvania, the Jerseys and New York) were not yet ripe for bidding adieu to British connection. **1893** DRAKE (*title*), The Making of Virginia and the Middle Colonies. — **(3)** **1857** *Spirit of Times* 26 Dec. 261/2 They occupy the following positions: catcher, pitcher, 1st, 2d, and 3d base; short stop, right, left, and middle-field. — **(4)** **1784** FILSON *Kentucke* 8 The fertile region, now called Kentucke, then but known to the Indians, by the name of the Dark and Bloody Ground, and sometimes the Middle Ground.

(5) (*a*) **1839** TOWNSEND *Narrative* 355 The middle-men ply their oars. (*b*) **1870** O. LOGAN *Before Footlights* 248, I give it up, Brudder Bones as the middle man at the minstrels always does the end man's conundrums. **1915** MATTHEWS in *Scribner's Mag.* June 756/1 The device for immediate and boisterous laughter, this putting down of the middle-man by the end-man, the Negro minstrels appear to have borrowed from the circus. — **(6)** **1902** E. L. BANKS *Newspaper Girl* 161 Your Boston beans done in an earthern pot with the middle-piece pork just rightly browned. — **(8)** **1895** *Pub. Col. Soc.* III. 8 In 1737 there was a simultaneous issue in Massachusetts of two classes of Province Bills, one being identical in form with those which were already in circulation, while those of the other class stated that they were to be received on the basis of twenty shillings for three ounces of silver, troy weight. Bills of these forms were for a time thereafter distinguished under the titles of 'old tenor' and 'new tenor.' The latter are however, after 1741, sometimes designated 'middle tenor bills.' — **(9)** *c***1837** HAZLITT *Diary* I. 41 Here [near Boston] is also, about February, what they call a middle thaw, when the weather is mild for a week or two, and the snow seems to have vanished.

(10) **1898** M. H. CATHERWOOD (*title*), Heroes of the Middle West. **1949** *Lisle* (Ill.) *Eagle* 10 March 4/2 This Middlewest section has been . . . fortunate. — **(11)** **1909** O. HENRY *Options* 310 'I'm only a little Middle-Western girl,' went on Ileen. **1944** *New Yorker* 11 Nov. 87/1 It [is] a chronicle of small town Middle Western life. — **(12)** **1921** *Lit. Digest* 5 March 46/1 The unbridled enthusiasm with which the Middle-Westerner devotes himself to his work was an unending source of wonder to the Englishman. **1946** HOWE *We Happy Few* 81 Two of our best friends in Cambridge are Middle Westerners.

b. ∗*middle-of-the-road*, of or pertaining to those members of the Populist party who in 1896 and 1900 opposed joining with the Democrats. Also *Middle-of-the-Road Populists*. Also transf.

[**1892** in F. E. HAYNES *J. B. Weaver* 468 Side tracks are rough, and they're hard to walk, Keep in the middle of the road.] **1904** *N.Y. Tribune* 3 June 1 The committee has extended invitations to the Middle of the Road Populists. **1949** *Ill. State Reg.* (Springfield) 1 Feb. 4/1 It is not the brand of middle-of-the-road politics that shuns all positive commitments.

Hence *Middle-of-the-Roader*, a Middle-of-the-Road Populist. Also transf.

1896 *N.Y. Tribune* 21 July 2/2 If the Bryan faction predominates, the Middle-of-the-Roaders will bolt and nominate another candidate. **1904** *N.Y. Ev. Post* 5 July 3 The middle-of-the-roaders had secured all the officers of the convention. **1948** *Chi. Tribune* 1 Feb. 6/3, I can't see him in first place, because he is such a middle-of-the-roader, a liberal when among liberals and a conservative when among conservatives.

middle states.

1. The states—usu. New York, New Jersey, Pennsylvania, Delaware, and sometimes including Maryland—which in early times occupied a middle position between the northern or northeastern and the southern states. Also attrib.

1784 WASHINGTON *Diaries* II. 326 The middle States with the Country immediately back of them. *a***1800** TWINING *Visit* 398 The character of the Middle States, New York, Philadelphia, the Jerseys, and Maryland, seems to be a modification of the extremes. **1868** BEECHER *Norwood* 1 If we should employ a scientific method, and speak of a Western genus, and a Southern genus, and a Middle State genus [etc.]. **1912** NICHOLSON *Hoosier Chron.* 59 A region where there had been an infusion of population from New England and the Middle States. **1948** *Western Polit. Quart.* Sep. 244 The *Herald* . . . was probably the most valuable paper to any Northern men needing middle state and Southern votes.

2. The states situated between the Alleghany Mountains and the Mississippi River.

1856 *Western Citizen* (Paris, Ky.) 28 March 2/1 A light cloth overcoat, much lighter than I wore in the Middle States, . . . kept me entirely comfortable. **1902** McKEE *Land of Nome* 1 The remarkable discoveries of gold at Cape Nome, Alaska, . . . naturally created more excitement in the Western and mining sections of the country than in the Middle States and the 'effete East.'

∗ **middling,** *a.* and *n.*

1. *n.S.* and *S.W.* A portion of meat comprising the middle or side of a hog between the ham and the shoulder. Also pork or bacon cut from this piece. Cf. **middle piece.**

1777 *Va. State P.* I. 288 Bakin in hams, midlings, shoulders, &c. **1840** *S. Lit. Messenger* VI. 385/2 This anniversary she is in the habit of celebrating by a dinner of fried middling and ash-cake. **1904** GLASGOW *Deliverance* 51 She has had to fry the middling in the kitchen, and mother complains of the smell.

2. Tobacco or timber of an intermediate grade.

1793 WASHINGTON *Writings* XII. 382 The middlings and ship stuff may be sold to answer the money calls which you will have upon you. **1839** J. F. COOPER *Home as Found* ii, One of my own [trees] out of which the sawyers made a thousand feet of clear stuff, to say nothing of middlings.

3. A grade of cotton which in quality comes up to the standard or basic grade upon which market quotations are based, also cotton of this grade.

1851 in BASSETT *Plantation Overseer* 229 We received . . . your crop of cotton . . . of which 56 bales are in quality a high order of 'middling' to 'good middling.' **1864** in W. LAWRENCE *A. A. Lawrence* 194 Cotton has sold at 165 cents a pound for 'middling.' **1948** *Capital-Democrat* (Tishomingo, Okla.) 17 June 9/4 This basic loan rate for 1948-crop cotton will apply to Middling ⅞ inch cotton at average location.

4. middling interest, the middle class. Also attrib. *Obs.*

1857 E. STONE *Life of Howland* vii. 137 He resolved on attempting to arrest this hospitality by creating . . . a correct public sentiment, and by overlaying it with what is . . . denominated a 'middling interest' influence. *a***1859** *Conn. Courant* (Bartlett), Men of the middling interest class are now the best off. . . . They have felt they belonged to the middling interest, and have resolved to stay there, and not cope with the rich.

As the last term in **good, low middling.** Also **cross middlings.**

∗ **middy,** *n.* A loose blouse with a sailor collar, often extending below the waistline, worn chiefly by girls. In full **middy blouse.**

1919 *Sears Cat.* (ed. 138) 30 Stylish Middy Blouse Made of . . . cotton material. **1919** CUNNINGHAM *Chronicle* 280 She dressed for the day in dark brown skirt and middy. **1935** *Montgomery Ward Cat.* 140 The black tie is included with this smartly tailored white Middy Blouse.

attrib. **1949** *Chi. Tribune* 20 Feb. II. 12 He trimmed the middy collars, tailored a zipper into the V neck—and came up with these wonderful all around shirts.

∗ **midget,** *n.* = **punkie.** *Obs.* — **1851** J. S. SPRINGER *Forest Life* 56 One species of fly commonly called the midget . . . is so small as to be almost imperceptible. **1872** DE VERE 392 The *Midget* of Canada and some of the Northern States, is the Sand-fly of Europe.

∗ **midnight,** *n.* In combs.: (1) **midnight appointment,** (see quot.); (2) **caucus,** a caucus held at midnight; (3) **judge,** (see quot. 1914).

(1) **1889** *Cent.* 275/3 *Midnight appointments*, in *U.S. politics*, appointments made during the last hours of an administration; specifically, those so made by President John Adams. — **(2)** **1825** *Harbinger* (Frankfort, Ky.) 1 June 4/2 The bill to abolish the court of appeals . . . was . . . the work of a midnight caucus. **1842** *Greene Co. Torchlight* (Xenia, O.) 6 Jan. 1/5 Thus, we see the interests of the State in the hands of a *midnight caucus*, in which Boyington and McNulty are master spirits. — **(3)** **1855** *Cong. Globe* App. 10 Jan. 89/1 The term 'midnight judges' . . . has become a popular phrase; a phrase suggested for purposes of odium. **1914** *Cyclo. Amer. Govt.* 430 Midnight Judges. A disparaging nickname bestowed by the Jeffersonian Republicans, in 1801, upon the judges whose commissions were signed by the retiring President, John Adams, just before midnight, March 3. It was again applied by the Whigs to the judges appointed by Martin Van Buren at the close of his administration, March 1841.

∗ **midway,** *n.*

1. (*cap.*) Orig. a boulevard area connecting Washington and Jackson parks in Chicago, in which the amusement section of the Columbian Exposition of 1893 was situated. In full **Midway Plaisance.**

1871 *Chi. South Park Comm. Rep.* 25 The plan of the Midway Plaisance is shown on drawing No. 2. *Ib.* 26 Three streets are proposed to be carried across the Midway besides these at its end. **1949** *Chi. D. News* 6 July 14/7 Far to the south was the Midway and the University of Chicago's ivy-grown Gothic masses.

b. Used allusively with reference to the University of Chicago, which is situated on this Midway. Also attrib.

1911 *Chi. D. News* 18 Sep. 3/1 Practice at the Midway is scheduled to start next Wednesday, when Stagg will meet his charges for 1911.

1937 *Fortune* XVI. Dec. 146 The Midway rushing season brings out cars and sporty clothes. **1948** *Chi. Tribune* 15 Feb. VII. 2/4 Several of the foreign students on the Midway will be guests of the University of Chicago Settlement league at its meeting tomorrow in Ida Noyes hall.

2. At a fair, exposition, circus, etc., an avenue along which the amusement devices, fakirs, side shows, and the like are located.

1893 *Outing* Dec. 208/1 The waiters were the hardiest set on the Midway, and when they scowled at a man and asked him what he would have, it required considerable courage to answer 'Nothing.' **1901** *World's Work* Aug. 1097/2 Nowadays we frankly admit that the Midway is the strongest magnet of a big fair. **1949** *Sat. Ev. Post* 17 Sep. 25/1, I have worked in . . . big-time railroad shows whose midways had the glitter of a handful of diamonds.

attrib. **1901** *Everybody's Mag.* Oct. 427/1 A mile and a half of ker-whango and clash—That is the Midway show. **1944** HOLTON *Yankees* 110 There were some midway concessions.

b. Any place of cheap amusement.

1901 *Everybody's Mag.* Oct. 424 Can I arrange with you for placing a first-class Midway on your grounds? **1947** CRANE *Sins of N.Y.* viii, Most Americans probably regard New York as a glorified midway, much tamer than Cranford Falls on a Saturday night.

* **midway,** *adv. Midway of*, in the middle of. *Colloq.*

*a*1811 HENRY *Camp. Quebec* 192 About midway of the horn [of the moose] . . . there is a broad flat part of the horn. **1903** *Nation* 17 Sep. 234 He died midway of his 70th year. **1927** *Sat. Ev. Post* 24 Dec. 44/3 She stopped midway of her sentence.

miggle ˈmɪgl, *n.* [Orig. unknown.] (See quots. 1891 and 1895.)

1891 *D.N.* I. 76 Miggles is the generic name for marbles, also meaning the commonest clay marbles. **1895** *Stand.* 1123/1 *Miggle*, . . . a common playing-marble; in the plural, the game of marbles. **1906** *Amer. Illust. Mag.* March 562/1 Boys garner birds' eggs, door-knobs, chalk, and miggles. **1949** *Amer. Dial. Soc. Pub.* April 24 miggle: *n.* A marble; a non-agate marble.

migrant shrike. (See quot. 1917.) — **1917** *Birds of Amer.* III. 101 The Migrant, or Northern Loggerhead, Shrike (*Lanius ludovicianus migrans*) is practically identical with the Loggerhead in coloration. **1945** *Mass. Audubon Soc. Bul.* Feb. 19 Arkansas Kingbirds and the Migrant Shrike—Western birds—are usually seen up from the shore in the fall.

migration station. "A station or post for observing facts concerning the migration of birds" (*Cent.*). — **1884** *Science* IV. 374/2 Migration-stations now exist in every state and territory of the Union, excepting Delaware and Nevada.

* **migratory,** *a.* In combs.: (1) **migratory pigeon,** =**passenger pigeon,** *obs.*; (2) **squirrel,** the gray squirrel, *Sciurus carolinensis, obs.*; (3) **thrush,** (see quots.).

(1) **1810** WILSON *Ornith.* II. 293 *Columba migratoria.* . . . Migratory Pigeon. . . . The wild pigeon of the United States. **1835** AUDUBON *Ornith Biog.* III. 71 They flew high in close bodies. . . . much in the manner of the Migratory Pigeon. — (2) **1857** *Rep. Comm. Patents: Agric. 1856* 63 The migratory squirrel . . . is the most abundant of our American squirrels. — (3) **1839** AUDUBON *Ornith. Biog.* V. 442 American Robin or Migratory Thrush, *Turdus Migratorius.* **1917** *Birds of Amer.* III. 236 Robin. . . . [Also called] Migratory Thrush.

* **Mikado,** *n.* A type of heavy freight locomotive designed in the U.S. and first used in Japan in 1897. In full **Mikado locomotive.**

1909 WEBSTER. **1947** BEEBE *Mixed Train Dly.* 99 It is a stately Mikado with an enormous headlight located just above the pilot beam. **1949** *Travel* Mar. 27/1 About one o'clock in the afternoon the first train rolls out of Tiquisate behind a big mikado locomotive.

Mikasuki ˌmɪkəˈsukɪ, *n.* [App. a native word of unknown significance.] (See quot. 1907.) Also attrib.

1827 *Spirit of Seventy-Six* (Frankfort, Ky.) 25 Jan. 3/4 The Mickasuky tribe, who muster about two hundred warriors, and the discontented Creeks, it is believed, have madly determined on hostilities. **1827** *Amer. Sentinel* (Georgetown, Ky.) 26 Jan. 1/4 Several murders have been committed on the west side of the Ocilla river, . . . supposed to be by some of the Mickasuky Indians. **1839** *Ky. Observer* (Lexington) 27 July 3/3 There are 261 Micasuky warriors now in Florida. **1907** HODGE *Amer. Indians* I. 860/2 Mikasuki. A former Seminole town in Leon co., Fla., on the w. shore of Miccosukee lake, on or near the site of the present Miccosukee. The name has been applied also to the inhabitants as a division of the Seminole. **1948** *Fla. Anthropologist* Nov. 61 In 1750 Chief Seacoffee rejected Creek authority and, together with the Mickasukies, set the Seminoles up as a separate tribe.

* **mile,** *n.* **1. mileboard,** =next. Also fig. **2. milepost,** one of a series of posts set up a mile apart to mark the distance to or from a place. Also transf.

(1) **1857** *Harper's Mag.* Nov. 734/2 The ninth mile-board from Burnsville is past. **1894** CABLE *J. March* xxiv, If you'd made me just your first mile-board. — (2) **1768** *Md. Hist. Mag.* II. 317 As we returned (besides the Mile Posts) we erected Marks on the Tops of all the High Ridges. **1873** BAILEY *Life in Danbury* 164 He was standing on the platform, and had caught his coat on a mile post. **1948** *Chi. D. News* 4 May 12/2 It is merely a milepost on the road to establishing the principles that dues collected from union members are not the personal property of union officials.

As the last term in **car, Choctaw, passenger, Pennsylvania mile.**

* **mileage,** *n.*

1. An allowance of a fixed amount per mile to cover the expenses of traveling. Orig. for members of legislative bodies. Cf. **constructive mileage.**

1754 FRANKLIN *Writings* III. 197 Members' Pay . . . milage for travelling expenses. **1776** H. GATES in Sparks *Corr. Revol.* I. 281 The militia were promised their mileage and billeting-money. **1874** *Internat. Typog. Union Proc.* 41 None but delegates shall vote or receive mileage and per diem. **1945** MENCKEN *Supp.* I. 294 Of the political terms not already discussed or listed, *mileage*, signifying a legislator's allowance for traveling expenses, is probably the oldest.

2. In combs.: (1) **mileage allowance,** =**mileage;** (2) **book,** a book of mileage tickets; (3) **ticket,** a ticket entitling the holder to travel a specified number of miles on a given railroad without restriction as to route or destination.

(1) **1935** *Time* 27 May 16/1 It rejected with one of the loudest *viva voce* votes on record, a proposal . . . to abolish Congressmen's mileage allowance. — (2) **1909** O. HENRY *Options* 277 'And you came mighty near missing the train!'. . . says she, with a laugh that sounded as good as a mileage-book to me. — (3) **1882** *Rep. Ala. R.R. Comm.* II. 207 We quit selling mileage tickets. **1898** *Boston Morn. Herald* 16 April 8/3 (Ernst).

* **military,** *a.*

1. Of or pertaining to land given as compensation for military service. Cf. **military bounty, land, tract,** as main entries.

1780 in *Travels Amer. Col.* 652, 500 acres part of a military Warrant for one thousand [acres]. **1855** PIERCE in *Pres. Mess. & P.* V. 340 The aggregate amount of public land sold during the last fiscal year, located with military scrip or land warrants, taken up under grants for roads, . . . is 24,557,409 acres. **1915** COCKRUM *Underground Railroad* 313 On the fifteenth day of the next November he did sell him to a neighbor for four head of horses, ten head of cattle and one hundred acres of miltary donation land. **1945** *Calif. Highways* Jan.–Feb. 27/3 The New York State Militia lands were laid out in townships 10 miles square, and the Ohio Military and Connecticut Reserves, five miles.

2. In special combs.: (1) **military academy,** see as a main entry; (2) **bounty,** see as a main entry; (3) **district,** during the Reconstruction period, a district created by the federal government for the administration of civil affairs of those areas conquered by the North; (4) **governor,** a military officer who administers the civil or executive affairs of a state or region occupied, usu. temporarily, by military forces; (5) **land,** see as a main entry; (6) **reservation,** an area set aside by the government for occupation by a military force; (7) **school,** a military academy; (8) **schottische,** =**barn dance;** (9) **tract,** see as a main entry.

(3) **1866** in *Doc. & Sp. Amer. Hist.* (1943) III. 30 Sentenced to be hanged by a military commission organized under the direction of the military commander of the military district of Indiana. — (4) **1864** LINCOLN in Fleming *Hist. Reconstruction* I. 113 Military governors will be appointed, with directions to proceed according to the bill. **1872** MCCLELLAN *Golden State* 108 Kearney, from this date, entered upon the duties of his new office as Military Governor of California. **1905** DEVINS *Observer in Philippines* 74 On July 4, 1901, Judge Taft . . .was inaugurated Civil Governor of the Philippine Islands, and General A. R. Chaffee, Military Governor under him.

(6) **1850** E. S. SEYMOUR *Sk. of Minn.* 105 The Military Reservation embraces, it is said, an area of about ten miles square, of which Fort Snelling is near the center. **1946** FOREMAN *Last Trek* 97 They first camped on the Fort Leavenworth military reservation. — (7) **1777** *Jrnls. Cont. Congress* VII. 288 Resolved, That a Corps of Invalids be formed . . . to serve as a Military School for Young Gentlemen. **1862** in STRONG *Cadet Life W. Point* p. xv, Near by are seen the Cavalry

Stables . . . belonging to the Military School. **1912** Nicholson *Hoosier Chron.* 478 Blackford's course at the military school he had chosen for himself. — (8) **1894** E. Scott *Dancing* 134 The Military Schottische or Barn Dance was known to and danced by the Americans long before it became generally popular over here.

military academy. A school for boys and young men which emphasizes military training and discipline, orig. (*cap.*) with particular reference to the national school at West Point, N.Y., for the training of army officers.

This expression is not recorded in the *OED*, but an English example of 1805 occurs in *Letters of John Orrok*, p. 79. American priority in usage is therefore doubtful.

1776 *Jrnls. Cont. Congress* VI. 860 Resolved, That the Board of War be directed to prepare a plan for establishing a continental Laboratory and a Military Academy. **1827** Drake & Mansfield *Cincinnati* 96 The plans of education respectively pursued at West Point, and at Captain Partridge's Military Academy, at Middletown, are generally admitted to be of the most excellent kind. **1864** Penniman *Tanner-Boy* 37 The Military Academy at West Point is a national institution supported by the Government of the United States. **1925** *Harper's Bazaar* July 19 New York Military Academy, a school of distinction, Cornwall-on-Hudson, New York.

attrib. **1877** *Harper's Mag.* March 627/1 The Military Academy Appropriation Bill was passed by the House January 12.

b. (See quot.) *Obs.*

1802 *Ann. 7th Congress* 1 Sess. 1312 The said corps [of engineers] when so organized, shall be stationed at West Point . . . and shall constitute a military academy.

military bounty. Public land given as compensation for military service. Also attrib.

1792 *Ann. 2d Congress* 1036 The second reservation covers . . . grants to . . . Commissioners for laying out the military bounties; and to guards, chain-carriers [etc.]. **1812** Marshall *Kentucky* 105 Many surveys had been executed upon military bounty warrants, under the proclamation of George the third . . . bearing date in October, 1763. **1817** *Ann. 14th Congress* 2 Sess. 44 The President communicated a report . . . concerning the progress made in surveying military bounty lands. **1856** Fergusson *America* 417 Then for eighty miles, the route is diagonally through what is known as the Military-bounty tract.

military land. Public land set aside for allotment to soldiers. Also attrib.

1796 in *Sp. & Doc. Amer. Hist.* (1944) 217 That the part of the said Lands, which . . . may not be appropriated for satisfying military land bounties, and for other purposes, shall be divided . . . [etc.]. **1797** *Ann. 5th Congress* I. 431 Mr. Bayard moved to strike out the exception in favor of patents for military lands. **1852** *Whig Almanac 1853* 14/1 This act makes all warrants for military or bounty-land . . . assignable by deed or instrument of writing. **1946** Foreman *Last Trek* 36 The land designated for this purpose, and which became known as 'military lands,' was included in the cession.

b. Esp. **military land warrant,** a government warrant for a specified amount of public land, granted a soldier in payment for military service.

1789 *Ky. Gazette* 21 Feb. 2/4 The Subscribers have now . . . likewise a quantity of military land Warrants for sale. **1865** *Chi. Tribune* 15 April 1 Military and Agricultural Land Warrants for sale and bought at best rates. **1930** Henry *Conquer. Plains* 180 Besides, there existed the Military Land warrants, popularly called Soldiers' Claims, enabling any veteran of the Civil War to receive a Warrant from the Government for a specified part of the public domain without payment.

military tract. A tract of public land where veterans of the Revolution were allowed to locate their landscrip, and where veterans of the War of 1812 were given land grants. Also, *cap.*, with reference to a particular tract of this kind. Cf. **Central Military tract.**

1798 Putnam in *Memoirs* 422 Two of the Surveyors employed in runing out the Military tract had completed there work in the woods. **1834** *Sangamo Jrnl.* (Springfield, Ill.) 18 Nov. 3/2 They were bound for the military tract. **1852** Regan *Emigrant's Guide* 96 What is called the 'Military Tract,' runs through the centre of the State [Illinois], east and west, and consists of grants of land to the soldiers of the Revolution, and of the war with Great Britain in the early part of the present century. **1947** *Amer. Sp.* XXII. 207 The author left his home in Scipio, near the center of the 'Military Tract' in the Finger Lakes country of Central New York, lying between Owasco and Cayuga Lakes, and between the cities of Auburn on the north and Ithaca on the south.

* **militia,** *n.* The whole body of adult male citizens capable of bearing arms.

1705 Beverley *Virginia* IV. 34 Every Freeman . . . from sixteen, to sixty years of age, is listed in the militia. **1800** Jefferson *Notes* 94 Every able bodied freeman, between the ages of 16 and 50 is enrolled in the militia. **1890** *Cent.* 3761/2 *Militia*, . . . the whole body of men declared by law amenable to military service, without enlistment, whether armed and drilled or not.

b. (See quot. 1930.) *Obs.* or *hist.*

1888 in *Pa. Dutchman* 23 June (1949) 7/3 They bore their proud and lofty heads, And always thought themselves above The homespun, plain, Militia-men, Who wagoned only now and then. **1930** Omwake *Conestoga Teams* 100 At the time of year when farmers were not busy on their farms, they often carried freight in their wagons, and they were called by the regular wagoners, militia or sharpshooters.

c. militia muster, a gathering of militia forces for review, inspection, drill, etc.

1809 Cuming *Western Tour* 209 On the road I met . . . above fifty horsemen with rifles, who had been in Morristown at a militia muster. **1884** Harris *Mingo* 238 They could remain at home, so to speak, and attend the militia musters.

As the last term in **cornstalk, mixed, state militia.**

* **milk,** *n.* In combs.: (1) **milk car,** (see quot. 1895); (2) **condensery,** a place where milk is condensed; (3) **conductor,** the conductor on a milk train, *rare;* (4) **evil,** =**milk sickness,** *obs.;* (5) **pea,** a plant of the genus *Galactia;* (6) **plant,** =prec.; (7) **poison,** =**milk sickness,** *obs.;* (8) **purslane,** the spotted spurge, *Euphorbia maculata*, a prostrate milky-juiced weed found in the eastern states; (9) **ranch,** *W.* a dairy farm; (10) **route,** a route along which milk is collected from producers or delivered to customers; (11) **shed,** a region that supplies a particular community with milk; (12) **sick,** see as a main entry; (13) **snake,** a harmless snake, *Lampropeltis triangulum*, often found about milk houses; (14) **sociable,** a sociable at which milk is drunk, *facetious;* (15) **train,** a train transporting milk to market; (16) **weed,** see as a main entry.

(1) **1890** *Railways of Amer.* 146 It would require a separate article to given even a brief description of the different kinds of cars which are now used. . . . Mail-car, Milk-car, Oil-car [etc.]. **1895** Wait *Car-Builder's Dict.* 88 Milk-car. A car for carrying milk in cans, usually built with platforms similar to baggage cars, and equipped with passenger-car trucks. They are usually provided with tight-doors, ice racks or boxes, and insulation.—(2) **1930** *Randolph Enterprise* (Elkins, W.Va.) 13 Feb. 1/3 The farm bureau of Hoover origin advises West Virginia diary men to produce less milk, Pro beneficio milk candensories. — (3) **1897** *Chi. Record* 1 March 6/1 At Maple Park the milk conductor gets aboard and . . . takes up the tickets. — (4) **1843** Oliver *Eight Months* 103 In some parts, there is a most formidable disease called milk evil, or milk sickness, which is not only fatal to the cows, but also to the people who use the milk of the infected animals.

(5) **1843** Torrey *Flora N.Y.* I. 162 *Galactia.* . . . Milk Pea. . . . Flowers purplish. **1898** Creevey *Flowers of Fields* 318 Milk-pea. *Galactia glabella.* . . . From southern New York to Florida, and westward to Mississippi. — (6) **1836** Lincoln *Botany* App. 99 *Galactia . . . mollis.* . . . Milk plant. Pine barrens. **1861** Tallack *Friendly Sk.* 66 The large-leaved 'milk plant' . . . resembles a euphorbia. — (7) **1878** Guild *Old Times* 17 The second year after my father settled on Bledsoe's creek, there appeared in that section a dreadful malady called the milk-poison. — (8) **1843** Torrey *Flora N.Y.* II. 176 Milk Purselane. Small Spurge. . . . Fields, cultivated grounds and roadsides, usually in dry soils. **1847** Darlington *Weeds & Plants* 288 *E[uphorbia] maculata.* . . . Spotted Euphorbia. Milk Purslane. Spotted Spurge. — (9) **1856** *Calif. Pathfinder* (S.F.) 13 Nov. 2/4 The milk ranch that burned down beyond the Mission yesterday morning, was the property of G. S. Hall, whose loss is about $1000. **1899** *Mo. So. Dakotan* I. 194 [A man from Mo.] brought in a herd of cows and established a milk ranch on Slate creek.

(10) **1874** *Dept. Agric. Rep. 1873* 246 The most economical method of managing the delivery of milk at the factory is by establishing milk routes. **1948** *Chi. Tribune* 7 March IV. 5/1 Given the early morning setting available to her in the milk route, she could have used that as a constant base from which to reveal character. — (11) **1926** *Nation* 30 June 713/1 In the milkshed the Diarymen's League—a cooperative agency of farmers—played a dominant, and on the whole an efficient role. **1948** *Amer. Butter & Cheese Rev.* Dec. 47/1 Dairy farmers will be paid uniform prices of $5.52 a hundredweight for their November deliveries to 432 pool-approved plants in the six-state New York milkshed. — (13) **1800** J. Maude *Niagara* 41 Kane killed two Garter and one Black Snake; saw Milk Snake dead on the road. **1948** *Nat. Hist.* April 186/2 The milk snake has a pattern of brownish blotches margined with black, and a checkered belly. **1949** *Scientific Mo.* Jan. 55/2 It seems to be common knowledge that the thief among snakes is the milk snake. — (14) **1907** Neil Munro *Daft Days* vi. 41 Why, great Queen of Sheba! I was only joshing you: it was calm on that ship as a milk sociable.

(15) **1853** *Knickerb.* XLII. 532 The '*milk-train*' still had the right of way. **1948** *Chi. Tribune* 23 May 24/8 The carriers make it as discouraging as possible by limiting passes to the milk trains that leave town at 2 a.m.

b. In the names of, or with reference to, foods and drinks prepared with milk, as (1) **milk cracker,** (2) **emptins,** see as a main entry, (3) **gravy,** (4) **shake,** cf. * **shake,** *n.* 4, (5) **toast,** (see quots.).

(1) **1938** DAMON *Grandma* 49 Boss 'milk crackers' by the barrel. — (3) **1805** *Pocumtuc Housewife* (1906) 6 Pork and apple with a milk gravy, with Irish potatoes boiled, are always handy. **1944** *Amer. Sp.* April 123/4, I feel sure that *milk gravy* is the American name of an American thing. — (4) **1889** *Harper's Bazaar* 4 May 330/3 You needs some milk shake, dat's wat you does an' I got some nice new w'iskey to putt in. **1948** *Hungry Horse News* (Columbia Falls, Mont.) 24 Sep. 4/2 His diet, mostly ice cream and milk shakes, is the envy of all the kids in the neighborhood.

(5) [**1817** J. PALMER *Jrnl. of Travels* (1818) 241 One or two dishes are peculiar to New England, and always on the table, toast dipped in cream and pumpkin pie.] **1855** BESTE *Wabash* II. 260 Large platters of milk toast. This delicacy is made of slices of toast, buttered and sprinkled with pepper and salt, and laid in a dish of warm milk, which serves as a sauce to the rest. **1941** FARMER *Boston Cook Book* 163 Milk toast. 1 pint scalded milk, 2 tablespoons butter, 2½ tablespoons bread flour [etc.]. . . . Any thin white sauce may be used.

c. In colloq. phrases: (1) *milk and cider,* roan in color; (2) *milk-and-molasses,* of a color between white and dark brown, also fig.; (3) *the milk in the cocoanut,* the crux, secret, or crucial fact of a matter or situation; (4) *to bring* (a person) *to his milk,* to bring a person to a proper realization of his duty, condition, etc.

(1) **1738** *Va. Gazette* 12 May A . . . Roan colour'd Horse (commonly distinguished by a Milk and Cyder Colour). **1832** *Cattle Sent to Range* (MS in J.D. Davidson Coll., McCormick Hist. Assoc.) 1 A milk & cider steer 3 years old. — (2) **1833** NEAL *Down-Easters* I. 96 The people of this country, . . . are of two colors, black and white . . . or halt-and-half sometimes at the south, where they are called milk-and-molasses. **1868** *N.Y. Herald* 2 July 5/1 Then it will be of a purer color than the platform of the radicals, which is of milk and molasses hue. — (3) **1840** *Spirit of Times* 21 March 25/2 All of 'vich' . . . fully accounts . . . for the milk in the cocoa-nut. **1893** *Cong. Rec.* 28 Feb. 2299/1 Here is the milk in the cocoanut! A frank confession it is. — (4) **1857** HOLLAND *Bay-Path* 209 There ain't anything that'll bring you to your milk half so quick as a good double-and-twisted thrashin.

As the last term in **bull's, condensed, consolidated, evaporated, hickory, malted, skim, swill milk.**

* **milk,** *v.*

1. *tr.* To tap (a pine tree) for turpentine. *Obs.*

1746 *Mass. Acts & Resolves* III. (1878) 307 Any liberty obtained . . . for cutting off any timber, wood, hay, milking pine-trees, . . . shall not be any bar. **1789** *Mass. Laws* I. 442 No liberty . . . for cutting off any wood, timber or hay, milking pine-trees [etc.].

2. To manipulate (stocks, markets, etc.) in such a way as to obtain unfair and exorbitant financial gains. Hence **milking,** *n. Colloq.*

1870 M. H. SMITH *20 Years Wall St.* 69 Stocks are rushed up and down rapidly. In the excitement the combination reap a golden harvest. They have milked the street. **1883** *Harper's Mag.* May 820/2 What fabulous sums besides . . . the individual managers made by the ingenious process of 'milking the market.' **1936** LUNDBERG *Imperial Hearst* 326 All this is what is known to Wall Street as 'milking.'

b. (See quot.) *Slang. Obs.*

1843 GREENE *Exposure of Gambling* 179 To prevent splitting, the [faro] dealer will 'milk' the cards; that is, draw at the very same time one card from the top and one from the bottom, until the whole pack has been run through in this manner; then one half will win and the other half will lose, and cutting them does not in any wise alter the matter.

milk emptins. Also **milk emptyings.** A form of homemade yeast prepared from milk, *colloq.* Cf. **emptins.** Also attrib.

1824 KIRKLAND *Forest Life* I. 23 A tumble-down log-house, with its appropriate perfumes of milk-emptins, bread, and fried onions. **1857** YOUMANS *Household Science* 261 Milk is often used for mixing the flour, instead of water; the product is then called 'milk-emptyings bread.' **1880** *Scribner's Mo.* Jan. 426/1 The whole feminine conclave launched out into a . . . discussion of the relative merits of salt-risin's, milk-emptin's, and potato yeast. **1941** *L.A.* Map 290.

milk sick.

1. Short for **milk sickness.**

1818 *Missouri Gaz.* 14 Aug. 3/3 *Milk-Sick.* A disease called by the above name prevails along the marshes of the American Bottom, in Illinois territory, and in certain spots on the Missouri. . . . We have no doubt but this disease in cattle is occasioned by . . . Water Hemlock. **1898** *Dly. Ardmoreite* (Ardmore, Okla.) 12 July 3/5 The milk sick up in north Georgia is a terrible thing. **1946** G. HUTTON *Midwest at Noon* 16 Thousands fell by the wayside, victims of agues, 'the shakes,' the plagues like the fearful 'milk-sick' which prematurely carried off Abraham Lincoln's exhausted mother.

attrib. **1885** CRADDOCK *Prophet* 47 Baker Leal . . . let down the bars of the milk-sick pen, one day las' fall, an' druv' Jacob White's red cow in.

b. milk-sick plant, (see quot.).

1931 CLUTE *Plants* 125 The milk-sick plant (*Eupatorium ageratoides*) is an abundant wild species that is often introduced into the flower garden.

2. milk sickness, a disease affecting livestock, esp. cattle, that eat of certain plants, and transmitted to persons who consume the flesh or dairy products of such cattle. Now *hist.* Cf. **trembles.**

1823 JAMES *Exped.* I. 76 Along the Missouri R. They have a disease called the *milk sickness:* it commences with nausea and dizziness. **1840** in RABB *Tour* (1920) 141 When a person gets the milk sickness it is very hard to get rid of; some say it will always remain in the blood, producing what is known as 'the tires.' The person will feel pretty well, but can stand very little fatigue; he fails in strength and feels always tremulous. **1919** DUNN *Indiana* II. 804 From 1836 to 1856, the disease known as 'Morbo Lacteo,' or 'milk sickness,' was encountered in numerous localities. . . . Humans who partook of the milk or butter of diseased cows contracted the disease. **1942** CANNON *Mountain* 315 The flies and the rattlesnakes, the wolves and the Indians, milk sickness in summer 'n measles in March, all them 're a nuisance.

transf. **1842** *S. Lit. Messenger* VIII. 200/1 Writers . . . have inoculated a numerous population with . . . a sort of epidemic 'milk sickness,' or rather milk-and-water disease.

* **milkweed,** *n.*

1. Any one of various American plants, esp. of the genus *Asclepias,* having abundant latex.

[**1761** in FRIES *N.C. Morav. Rec.* I. (1922) 236 Careful survey was made of the native herbs, with an eye to their medicinal value, and several useful ones were found. . . . 'Squasweed' for rheumatism, 'Milkweed' for pleurisy.] **1814** BIGELOW *Florula Bostoniensis* 62 *Asclepias Syriaca,* Common Silk weed or Milk weed, . . . is used as a substitute for feathers, fur, cotton, &c. **1923** CATHER *Lost Lady* 17 The silvery milkweed was just coming on.

attrib. **1871** STOWE *Sam Lawson* 43 Wal, that was the reason why Jeff Sullivan couldn't come it round Ruth tho' he was silkier than a milkweed-pod. **1934** *N. Mex. Agric. Exp. Sta. Press Bul.* 717/2 The milkweed (*Asclepias*) vine also grows at the lower elevations and has whitish clove-scented flowers. **1947** *Sports Afield* Dec. 26/3 The web of a big black and gold spider, strung between two milkweed blossoms, barred his next step.

2. In special combs.: (1) **milkweed butterfly,** the monarch butterfly, *Danaüs archippus;* (2) **moth,** a gray moth, *Euchaetes egle,* the larva of which feeds on milkweed; (3) **silk,** the fiber contained in a milkweed pod.

(1) **1880** *Boston Soc. Nat. Hist. Mem.* 10 In the milkweed butterfly the colon is somewhat pyriform in the female, . . . but is longer and more cylindrical in the male. **1948** *Nat. Hist.* April 154 (*caption*), A Monarch, or milkweed butterfly. — (2) **1854** EMMONS *Agric. N.Y.* V. 262 Milkweed-moths, 227. **1903** HOLLAND *Moth Book* 135 Euchætias egle Drury. . . . (The Milk-weed Moth.) — (3) **1869** STOWE *Oldtown Folks* 121 That's milkweed silk. . . . 'Tain't good for nothin'.

As the last term in **green, poke, swamp milkweed.**

* **mill,** *n.*[1]

1. (See quot. 1890.)

1879 HARTE *Drift from Two Shores* 75 No work was done in the ditches, in the flumes, nor in the mills. **1890** *Cent.* 3764/1 *Mill,* . . . in *mining,* a passage or opening left for sending down stuff from the stopes to the level beneath.

2. *W.* A circling movement engaged in by a large herd of cattle deflected from a straight course.

1897 HOUGH *Story of Cowboy* 146 By shouts and blows he did all he could to break the 'mill and get the cattle headed properly. **1903** A. ADAMS *Log of Cowboy* xviii. 286 By the time the herd had covered a scant mile, we had thrown them into a mill. **1942** DALE *Cow Country* 55 Those behind them would follow and a 'mill' would be established in which the animals would swim around and around in a circle until they drowned unless it were quickly broken up and the leaders again headed for the opposite shore.

3. In combs.: (1) **mill bag,** = **meal bag,** cf. **go-to-mill bag;** (2) **boom,** a boom for impounding logs at a sawmill; (3) **carriage,** in a sawmill, the carlike conveyor upon which the logs are brought up to and past the saw; (4) **chain,** a chain for drawing saw logs from a pond up into a mill house, used attrib.; (5) **creek,** a creek upon which a mill is situated; (6) **cut,** the amount of lumber cut by a mill; (7) **log,** a log suitable for sawing in a saw mill; (8) * **pond,** (*a*) the Atlantic Ocean, *humorous,* (*b*) (see quot. 1905); (9) **privilege,** the right to operate a mill or to use adjoining land for storing lumber, also a piece of land for such a purpose, cf. **privilege;** (10) **right,** the right to set up or establish a mill; (11) **run,** see as a main entry; (12) **saw,** a saw such as is used in a sawmill; (13) **seat,** = **mill site;** (14) **site,** a site or location for a water mill; (15) **slash,** a slash on or near which a mill is located, *obs.;* (16) **town,** a town the industrial life of which centers about a mill or mills, also attrib.; (17) **yard,** an open area adjacent to a sawmill where lumber is piled or logs assembled.

(1) 1851 in R. Glisan *Jrnl. Army Life* (1874) 58, **I . . .** endeavored to throw [it] in a mill-bag style over my saddle. — **(2) 1878** *Mich. Rep.* XXXVI. 165 The mortgagees were to deliver at the mill-boom fifty-five million feet of merchantable pine saw logs. — **(3) 1881** *Harper's Mag.* Sep. 584/1 It [an eel] . . . leads the captor a ten minutes' dance over logs . . . and mill carriages. — **(4) 1850** Judd *R. Edney* 42 The logs lay in the water ready to be drawn in and by the aid of the tooth of the mill-chain dog, to be hauled to the bed of the mill.

(5) 1651 *Boston Rec.* 4 Granted unto Capt. John Leveret . . . free liberty of egresse and regresse in and out of the Mill Creeke. **1776** *Battle of Brooklyn* II. iii, The poor souls yonder . . . attempt to cross the mill creek. — **(6) 1902** S. E. White *Blazed Trail* vii. 49 Small stuff like that always over-runs on the mill-cut. — **(7) 1795** Thomas B. Hazard *Nailer Tom's Diary* (1930) 171/2, I helpt brother Robert flote mill logs to mill. **1850** Judd *R. Edney* i. 17 Perhaps a mill-log would be as agreeable for him to kneel upon as a hassock. — **(8)** (*a*) **1812** Paulding *J. Bull &Bro. Jon.* 5 He put himself in a boat, and paddled over the mill-pond to some new lands. **1885** G. Allen *Babylon* 79 How was our other friend Hiram Winthrop employing his time beyond the millpond? (*b*) **1850** E. S. Seymour *Sk. of Minn.* 125 Two long and narrow islands, extending from the western end of the dam nearly a mile up the river, form a secure harbor, or mill-pond, for an immense number of logs. **1905** *Forestry Bureau Bul.* No. 61, 42 *Mill pond,* the pond near a sawmill in which logs to be sawn are held. — **(9) 1734** *N.H. Probate Rec.* II. 508, I also give unto my son . . . the one half of my Mill Priviledge on the southerly side of ye River. **1892** *Vt. Agric. Rep.* XII. 134 Many mill privileges with excellent water power are afforded.

(10) 1794 *Mass. H.S. Coll.* I Ser. 147 The principal object of the original settlers being lumber, the more attention was paid to mill-rights than to the soil. *c***1845** Paulding *Amer. Comedies* (1847) 262 There's a man at Jack O'Lantern's that owns land and mill-rights. — **(12) 1790** *Pa. Packet* 2 Jan. 4/2 To be sold by Poultney and Wistar. . . . Mill, crosscut, hand, pannel, tennant, . . . compass, and keyhole saw. **1897** Brodhead *Bound in Shallows* 66 All the mill saws were silent.— **(13) 1770** Washington *Diaries* I. 365 Mr. Bellendine and myself leveled Doeg Run in ordr. to fix on a Mill Seat. **1855** Simms *Forayers* 487 They were in possession of an old mill-seat, on the Caw-caw. — **(14) 1831** Peck *Guide* 196 There are but few good mill sites in the State. **1896** Shinn *Story of Mine* 81 Water claims and mill sites were taken up almost as soon as work had fairly begun on the Comstock.

(15) 1680 in *Amer. Sp.* XV. 285/1 At the Marked tree . . . by the Mill slash. — **(16) 1848** D. P. Thompson *L. Amsden* 199 [The paper] came into town all damp from the press of Mill-Town Emporium. **1944** *Reader's Digest* Dec. 16/1, I used to live, years ago, in a mill town in the Deep South. — **(17) 1824** *N.H. Hist. Soc. Coll.* I. 246 A saw mill torn down and twelve thousand of boards in the mill-yard carried away. **1841** Buckingham *America* III. 49 This 'millyard,' as it was also called, had passed from the original purchasers into the possession of Sir William Pultney.

b. *Mill boy of the slashes,* (see quot. 1885).

1844 *Louisville Pub. Advt.* 17 Feb. 1/3 The picture of a bare-head, bare-footed boy on a bob tailed horse . . . is intended to represent 'the mill boy of the slashes.' **1885** *Mag. Amer. Hist.* March 296/1 *Mill Boy of the Slashes.* — A nickname for Henry Clay, who in his youth tended a mill in a region known as 'the Slashes,' near his birthplace.

As the last term in **bait, band, beer, bone, cane, cattle, clipper, coffee, corn, cornstalk, country, dope, feed, floating, floating grist, flouring, flutter, gang, gin, gospel, gossip, gravel, grinding, guano, hominy, lumber, merchant, movable, nail, nut, ox, pan, pecker, peckerwood, planing, pounding, rice, roller, rum, samp, screw auger grist, seed oil, shaving, shingle, smut, sorghum, steam, steam lumber, steam planing, stepping, stock, stone, sweat, tub, wampum, whisky, wood, wood-grinding mill.**

mill mɪl, *n.*[2] [f. L. *mille,* a thousand, or *millesimum,* a thousandth part.] One-thousandth of a dollar; one-tenth of a cent.

1796 *Ann. 4th Congress* 2 Sess. 2781 There is due for wastage . . . eighteen hundred and forty-five dollars ninety-five cents and five mills. **1856** *Mich. Agric. Soc. Trans.* VII. 770 The Society have received . . . the amount of the 1-10 of a mill required to be raised. **1911** *Okla. Session Laws* 3 Legisl. 201 The city council . . . may levy a tax not to exceed two mills on the dollar annually. **1949** *Telephone Reg.* (McMinnville, Ore.) 4 Aug. 1/8 It is an increase of 2.5 mills for the city.

b. mill tax, a tax of one mill per dollar of assessed valuation. Also **four mill tax.**

1848 *Indiana Hist. Soc. Pub.* III. 514 The former will pay on a mill tax $200. **1903** *Scribner's Mag.* Oct. 486 They support the Universities by a direct mill tax levied upon the assessed valuation of the State. **1949** *Ward Co. Independent* (Minot, N.D.) 21 July 1/7 The money would be raised by an additional four mill tax levy each year.

* **mill,** *v.*

1. *tr.* To put (stale or inferior butter) into marketable condition by reworking and recoloring it. Hence **milled butter.** *Obs.*

1877 *Vt. Dairymen's Assoc. Rep.* VIII. 79 Most grades of cheap butter and much stale old butter is now 'milled' in all the large dairy markets. . . . 'Milled Butter.' . . . The term is applied in some of the Eastern and in the St. Louis markets to butter which has been re-worked and re-colored, and put into a more marketable condition.

2. *intr.* Of cattle, to move around in a circular course. Also transf. Cf. **milling.**

1888 Roosevelt in *Cent. Mag.* April 862/1 The cattle may begin to run, and then get 'milling'—that is, all crowd together into a mass like a ball, wherein they move round and round. **1910** Raine *B. O'Connor* 227, I expect you were able to make out, even if I did get the letters to milling around wrong. **1949** *Nat. Humane Review* Sep. 29/2 Generally the large flock [of geese] . . . milled about over the refuge and then dropped back unharmed.

3. *tr.* and *intr.* To mull.

1911 H. Quick *Yellowstone N.* v. 127 The main thing the matter was that failure o' this a-millin' through his mental facilities. **1921** R. D. Paine *Comr. Rolling Ocean* xvii. 298 Judson, on guard in the cabin, was milling this problem over.

millage ˈmɪlɪdʒ, *n.* The rate of taxation in mills per dollar. Cf. **mill,** *n.*[2] — **1891** *Columbus* (O.) *Dispatch* 20 Feb., As great millage as [in] Toledo is not presented in the tables. **1949** *Telephone Reg.* (McMinnville, Ore.) 4 Aug. 1/8 The millage rate is an increase of 2.5 mills for the city over last year's figure.

* **miller,** *n.* As the last term in **bee, gin, merchant, moth, white miller.**

millering ˈmɪlərɪŋ, *n.* The work or occupation of a miller. Also attrib. *Obs.* — **1776** *N.J. Archives* 2 Ser. I. 119 Robert Colebrook . . . says he understands the millering business. **1818** Cobbett *Year's Residence* III. 582 Any of the men, however, could do the millering very well.

Millerism ˈmɪlərɪzəm, *n.* [See next.] The doctrines of the Millerites. Now *hist.*

1843 *Quincy* (Ill.) *Herald* 24 Feb. 1/4 The spread of Millerism has a tendency to illuminate the subject. **1886** Poore *Reminiscences* I. 309 Mr. Houghton thought that Millerism (a religious craze then prevalent) should be included in the benefits of the appropriation. **1943** *N. Eng. Quart.* XVI. 593 Millerism in Boston centered in a frame tabernacle . . . erected on Howard Street.

Millerite ˈmɪləraɪt, *n.* A believer in the teachings of William Miller (1782–1849), who predicted that the second coming of Christ would occur in 1843. Now *hist.* Cf. **Second Advent, Millerite.**

1842 *Niles' Reg.* 6 Aug. 368/2 The Millerites held a convention at Concord . . . to consider the fulfillment of prophecies. **1865** *Nation* I. 330 There have been conventions of . . . teetotallers and of anti-tobacconists, of Millerites. **1945** *Christian Cent.* 7 March 304/2 And they have chosen to emphasize that 'the major mistake' of the Millerites was in their interpretation, not in setting the time.

* **millet,** *n.* As the last term in **cattail, evergreen, Indian, Morocco, pearl, Texas millet.**

millinerize ˈmɪlənəraɪz, *v. intr.* To work as a milliner. Also **millinerizing,** *n. Rare.* — **1892** Mark Twain *Amer. Claimant* xxi, She couldn't design nor millinerize with any heart for thinking of him. Never before had millinerizing seemed so devoid of interest to her.

millinery store. A store or shop kept by a milliner, a hat store. — **1830** Watson *Philadelphia* 218 Millinery Stores. It is still within the memory of the aged when and where the first store of this kind was introduced into the city. **1898** Westcott *D. Harum* 337 When I looked 'round, there was a mil'nery store in full blast an' winders full o' bunnits.

* **milling,** *n.*

1. The action of a herd of cattle in going round and round in a circle. Also transf. Cf. * **mill,** *n.*[1] **2,** and * **mill,** *v.* **2.**

1874 McCoy *Cattle* 101 Drovers consider that the cattle do themselves great injury by running round in a circle, which is termed in cow-boy parlance 'milling.' **1924** *Scribner's Mag.* Dec. 607 Jack . . . stood outside the door and watched the milling of the excited, hysterical women.

2. *attrib.* Pertaining to the process by which stale or inferior butter is reworked and improved. *Obs.*

1877 *Vt. Dairymen's Assoc. Rep.* VIII. 79 The advantage of the milling process over the old hand-working is that the various batches are so broken up and mixed as to make a homogeneous mass. *Ib.*, Two or three of these milling establishments . . . have made a large amount of money.

As the last term in **free, lumber milling.**

millionairism ˌmɪljənˈɛrɪzəm, *n.* The state of being a millionaire; the social order prevailing where millionaires are numerous. — **1865** *Atlantic Mo.* Jan. 62/1, I fancied myself rich, even to millionairism, in Cruikshankiana. **1901** *Nation* 14 March 222/1 Divisions of the book take up . . . millionairism, the spirit of social equality [etc.].

million-dollar weed. (See quot.) — **1921** *Discovery* Feb. 48/1 The water hyacinth . . . is a beautiful aquatic plant . . . but its spread in St. John's River and the enormous sums spent in attempting its suppression have earned it the name of the 'million-dollar weed.'

millionism ˈmɪljənˌɪzəm, *n.* The state of being a millionaire. — **1858** Holmes *Autocrat* 367 People in the green stages of millionism. **1876** Gladden *Working People & Employers* (1885) 183 Some of the indispensable conditions of attaining to millionism.

millish məˈlɪʃ, *n* Short for militia. *Colloq.* — **1862** *N.Y. Herald* 9 April (Chipman), The city 'millish' embracing some of our very best citizens, . . . have gone into camp at the Fair-Grounds. **1914** *Collier's* 24 Jan. 22/3 We're not out to bag dinky milish; we want to get our guerdon back.

mill run.

1. A run or stream upon which a mill is located. *Colloq.*

1652 in *Amer. Sp.* XV. 284/2 On the North side of the Mill run at the head of Warwick River. **1788** *Ib.* 285/1 On the South West branch of Mill Run a Draft of Pattisons Creek.

2. A given quantity of ore tested for its quality by actual milling, also the yield of such a test.

1874 Raymond *7th Rep. Mines* 292 The mill runs have been as high as 3 oz. gold with from 30 to 60 oz. in silver. **1878** Beadle *Western Wilds* 465 This estimate is from the mill-runs—the only honest test of a mine's capacity. **1882** in Ritch *Illust. N. Mex.* 138 A millrun two months since at Pueblo, of 2,200 pounds, returned 140 ounces silver and 50 per cent. lead.

3. Anything that is average or mediocre. Orig. designating lumber sawed to usual specifications. Cf. * **bill,** *n.*[1] **2.**

1881 *Chi. Times* 1 June, The supply of choice mill-run lumber was generally quite limited. **1928** Foy & Harlow *Clowning Thro' Life* 299 He thought himself far too good for the ordinary mill run of melodramas which prevailed at that house.

mill-run, *v. Mining. tr.* To yield (a stated amount) in terms of a mill run. *Obs.* — **1884** *Cent. Mag.* Nov. 57 The vein where it came from would mill-run not less than a thousand ounces.

Mills's money. Wildcat notes issued by a Mississippi bank, given value in Texas before the Civil War by the indorsement of R. & D. C. Mills, a rich commercial house. *Obs.* or *hist.* — **1852** Gouge *Fiscal Hist. Texas* 235 'Mills's Money,' as it was called, was regarded as being as good as gold and silver, or even better, inasmuch as it could more readily be carried from place to place. **1929** A. L. Carlson *Monetary & Banking Hist. Texas* 4 Until the outbreak of the Civil War, 'Mills Money' was the prevailing paper money in Texas.

milo ˈmaɪlo, *n.* [Bantu *maili.*] Any one of various grain sorghums derived from *Sorghum vulgare.* Usu., but erroneously, **milo maize.**

1884 *N.Y Wkly. Tribune* 17 Sep. 10/1 The very old and well-known Sorghum halepense . . . has frequently been distributed of late years under many different common names, among the most familiar being Green Valley grass, Johnson grass, Nisan's grass, evergreen millet and Milo maize. **1901** Mohr *Plant Life Ala.* 135 Various kinds of sorghum, known as durrha or kafir corn, millo maize, and pearl millet, . . . furnish green forage and hay crops. **1947** *Dly. Oklahoman* (Okla. City) 30 Dec. 2/1 Oats, corn, barley, milo and kafir all put dollar signs on new levels. **1949** *Sat. Ev. Post* 24 Sep. 125/2 By August there were foot-deep cracks in the low corners of milo maize and kaffir corn.

milpa ˈmɪlpə, *n. S.W.* [Amer. Sp. (<Nahuatl) in same sense.] A small cultivated field, usu. a cornfield. Also **milpita,** a little cornfield.

1844 Gregg *Commerce of Prairies* I. 150 The *labores* and *milpas* (cultivated fields) are often . . . without any enclosure. **1869** Browne *Adv. Apache Country* 164 Our houses were closely picketed in the milpas, or corn-fields, down by the river. **1912** Lumholtz *New Trails* 144 Most of the towns, consisting of two long streets of adobe houses, can be dimly discerned between clusters of trees and the many *milpas* (cultivated fields) that surround it. **1919** J. S. Chase *Calif. Desert Trails* 326 After a dozen miles or so we came to a clearing where Mexicans had cultivated their little patches of maize, milpitas, as they call them.

Milwaukee mɪlˈwɔkɪ, *n.* [*Milwaukee,* Wis.] *attrib.* Of or pertaining to Milwaukee. Usu. with reference to wheat.

1856 *Porter's Spirit of Times* 1 Nov. 149/3 Wheat is in firm market demand; sales of 33,000 bush. at $1,49 for white Michigan; and $1,31 for Milwaukie Club. **1881** *Harper's Mag.* April 710/1 Milwaukee wheat has from the first been subjected to a most rigorous and honest inspection. *Ib.* 710/2 Feeding this artery to supply the Milwaukee elevators are the Northern Pacific . . . and various other railways. **1908** *U.S. Brewers' Assoc. 48th Conv.* 147 If anything can excel the quality of Milwaukee beer, it is Milwaukee hospitality.

Milwaukeean mɪlˈwɔkɪən, *n.* A resident or a native of Milwaukee, Wisconsin. — **1945** *Milwaukee Jrnl.* 13 May 16/1 Prof. Brown is best known to Milwaukeeans generally for the pageantry of her Christmas plays. **1948** *Ib.* 18 July 6/1 A Milwaukeean, vastly pleased with his luck, told me he took 'about a hundred roach' out of Mud lake in a couple hours.

Mimbres ˈmimbres, *n.* [In **1.** f. Amer. Sp. *Mimbreños,* people of the willows, in allusion to the Mimbres Mountains in southwestern N. Mex. In **2.** f. *mimbre,* the usu. Sp. term for willow.]

1. A division of the Apache Indians now on reservations in New Mexico and Arizona.

1799 tr. in *Pac. R.R. Rep.* (1856) III. 119 The *Mimbreños* are a very numerous tribe, and take their name from the river and mountains of the Mimbres. **1864** Mowry *Ariz. & Sonora* 31 The Apache . . . are best classified under their modern names: the Mescaleros, east of the Rio Grande; the Mimbres, . . . Sierra Blanca, and the Tontos. **1934** Morris *Digging in Southwest* 68 To the Mimbres, though, must the palm be given for pottery.

attrib. **1924** *Smithsonian Misc. Coll.* 76 No. 8, 13 Animals with their mouths approximated are sometimes found on Mimbres wares. **1937** *Southwestern Lore* Dec. 49 The technical excellence of Mimbres bowls is not always as high as it might be, but for sheer boldness of conception and often rich beauty of design it has no equals in southwestern prehistoric art. **1949** *Desert Mag.* June 15/1 A bit of Mimbres black-on-white ware showed that the trail from the Mimbres mountain pueblos must have crossed here.

2. (See quot.)

1904 Wooton *Native Ornamental Plants N. Mex.* 26 The Desert Willow or Mimbres (*Chilopsis linearis*) has already been brought into cultivation.

Mimeograph ˈmɪmɪəˌgræf, *n.* [Gk. *mimeisthai,* to imitate, and *-graph.*] A trade-mark name for a device for duplicating written or printed matter by the use of a stencil; in popular use (not *cap.*), any such device.

1889 *Voice* 19 Sep., The 'mimeograph' and the 'autocopyist' . . . will give any number of copies of a letter. **1932** *K.C. Times* 27 Feb. 24 All he has is a second-hand typewriter and an 8×10 mimeograph to reproduce the little pages. **1949** *Gladewater* (Tex.) *Times-Tribune* 31 July II. 5/2 A. B. Dick Mimeograph taken in trade on new Liberator Speed-O-Print.

mimeograph ˈmɪmɪəˌgræf, *v. tr.* To make (copies of an original writing, drawing, etc.) on a Mimeograph or similar device. Often **mimeographed,** *a.*

1895 *Advance* 6 June 1290/2 The copies were mimeographed at last, thanks to her mother's help. **1928** *Sat. Ev. Post* 10 March 156/1 There are several mimeographed lists of alleged Hoover disabilities. **1947** *Sierra Club* (S. C. Chap.) *Sched.* 126, 9 Mimeographed copies of the list will be ready for distribution at the next meeting of the Section.

mincy ˈmɪnsɪ, *a.* [f. **mince, v.* But cf. *EDD mimsey,* prim, prudish.] Using an affected delicacy or daintiness, esp. in speech. *Colloq.* — **1913** Stratton-Porter *Laddie* xiii, She didn't stop to be mincy. She shot things at him like a man talking to another man.

* **mind your business.** [f. an inscription on the coin.] = **fugio.** *Obs.* — **1857** *N.Y. State Library Cat. 1856* 197 Mind Your Business, 1787 Copper.

* **mine,** *n.* In combs.: (1) **mine bank,** an area of deposits that can be worked by excavations above the water

level, also the ground at the top of a mining shaft, cf. **coal bank;** (2) **salter,** (see quot.), *obs.;* (3) **sickness,** (see quot.), *obs.*

(1) **1777** *N.J. Archives* 2 Ser. I. 389 The mine bank, situated at a mile's distance from the furnace, is thought to be inexhaustible. **1807** J. R. SHAW *Life* (1930) 81, I followed working at the mine-banks. **1905** VALENTINE *H. Sandwith* 28 The iron bell that announced the arrival of ore-laden wagons from the mine banks. — (2) **1890** *Cong. Rec.* 16 April 3443/1 (Tb.), [This is said] to be a bill to widen the market of the mine-salter, to remove the protection [now given] to the foreign capitalist by preventing him from being roped in by the gentlemen who 'salt' the mines, or who have non-paying mines and want to unload on the unsuspecting foreigner. — (3) **1819** SCHOOLCRAFT *Mo. Lead Mines* 31 There are however, some losses annually sustained by inhabitants of the mine tract, from the death of cattle, who die of the mine sickness. . . . This has been accounted for, by supposing that they inhale the sulphur which is so abundantly driven off in smelting lead.

As the last term in **bonanza, captive, golden, gravel, gulch, hopper, hydraulic, paper, placer, sluice, Washoe, wildcat mine.**

∗**miner,** *n.* In the possessive (usu. *pl.*) in combs.: (1) **miners' camp,** =**mining camp;** (2) **court,** an independent court of justice set up by miners remote from long-settled regions; (3) **inch,** (see quots. 1867, 1873); (4) **law,** law such as prevailed among the early miners in the West; (5) **lettuce,** an annual, *Claytonia perfoliata,* common along the Pacific Coast; (6) ∗**meeting,** a meeting of gold and silver miners in the West in connection with miners' courts; (7) **tent,** (see quots.).

(1) **1876** DODGE *Black Hills* 113 The beautiful valley of French Creek, near Custer City, was picturesque with miners' camps. — (2) **1870** *Colo. Gazetteer* 24 The miners' courts were organized at a general meeting of the inhabitants of a district; who enacted a code of laws, criminal and civil. **1884** HILL *Colo. Pioneers* 66 They were pursued, captured, brought back to the gulch, tried by a 'miners' court' and sentenced to be hanged. **1948** JOHNSTON *Gold Rush* 5/1 In some camps 'good and true men' were at once elected as *alcaldes,* or mayors; in others there was the direct intervention of 'miners' court.' — (3) **1867** J. A. PHILLIPS *Mineral. & Metall. Gold & Silver* 152 The miner's inch of water, in California, is the quantity which will flow through an opening one inch square under a mean head of six inches. **1873** LAWRENCE *Silverland* 167 A miner's inch is rather liberal measurement. It varies in different districts: generally an opening of one inch high and twenty four long, is made with a pressure of six inches, producing, as I am informed, an outflow of about 17,000 gallons in each twenty-four hours. **1949** HERTRICH *Huntington Bot. Gardens* 6 The purchasers of water rights had the additional privilege of sinking a well and pumping water not to exceed 30 miners' inches. — (4) **1851** in SCHOOLCRAFT *Indian Tribes* (1853) III. 148 The space allowed, by 'miner's law,' to each man, as his 'claim,' is thirty feet square.

(5) **1920** RICE *Calif. Wild Flowers* 88 Miners' Lettuce is an annual plant from six to twelve inches high. **1947** *Atlantic Mo.* Dec. 110/1 Your Farewell to Spring, Cream Cups, Baby Blue Eyes, and Miner's Lettuce have given up their whimsical little ghosts. — (6) **1870** *Colo. Gazetteer* 24 Stronger power than that emanating from a distant State capital was required; and this was found in miners' courts, and that superior court, a miners' meeting. **1876** DODGE *Black Hills* 112, I was present at the miners' meeting at Custer City, August 10th. **1949** *Boston Globe* 15 May (Fiction Mag.) 4/4 All he'll do is call a miners' meetin' and hang the four of you. — (7) **1916** KEPHART *Camping & Woodcraft* II. 82 There is nothing better than a pyramidal or 'miner's' tent. **1933** CHELEY *Camping Out* 287 Figure 9 shows a pyramid or miner's tent, both with and without walls.

As the last term in **gold, gulch, hydraulic, pan, placer, pocket, quartz miner.**

∗**mineral,** *n.* In combs.: (1) **mineral belt,** an extensive stretch or strip of country in which mineral resources are abundant; (2) **blossom,** (see quots.), cf. ∗**blossom,** *n.* **1;** (3) **claim,** a mining claim; (4) **entry,** the filing of a claim for public land to obtain the right to any minerals it may contain; (5) **land,** land that possesses considerable mineral wealth; (6) **rod,** a divining rod; (7) **sperm,** (see quot. 1875), in full **mineral sperm oil.**

(1) **1869** BROWNE *Adv. Apache Country* 507 The wonderful richness of the mineral belt could be fairly appreciated. **1883** RITCH *Illust. N. Mex.* 68 The usual combination of quartz and feldspar . . . [is found] within the mineral belt range proper. — (2) **1819** SCHOOLCRAFT *Mo. Lead Mines* 71 This variety of quartz . . . has acquired the popular name of blossom of lead, or mineral blossom. **1842** BUCKINGHAM *E. & W. States* III. 97 One of these ridges has its declivities almost covered with crystallized spar, which is called by the people of the country 'mineral blossom.' — (3) **1851** *S.F. Herald* 26 Feb. 2/1 We think too many of our public officials are more familiar with 'monte' than they are with money, and believe they have a better knowledge of 'twenty-one,' than they have of trespass on mineral claims. **1948** JOHNSTON *Gold Rush* 37/1 As mineral claims took precedence over all other titles, the huge monitors swept all before them. — (4) **1908** *Indian Laws & Tr.* III. 378 Nor shall any such lands be subject to mineral entry or location.

(5) **1840** *Niles' Reg.* 18 April 107/1 [Petition] by Mr. Norvell, . . . asking to be allowed to work the mineral lands of the U. States on the southern shore of Lake Superior. **1905** N. DAVIS *Northerner* 100 Eastern capitalists had been quick to read the South's sad astrology in . . . her empty fields, her undeveloped mineral lands. — (6) **1809** KENDALL *Travels* III. 101 The mysteries of the mineral-rods are many. **1931** DOBIE *Coronado's C.* 107 They possessed a 'gold monkey'—a mineral rod—and this instrument they took to the fort; it oscillated towards the west and made two locations. — (7) **1875** *Amer. Cyclo.* XIII. 371/1 Mineral sperm is the name given by Joshua Merrill, of the Downer kerosene oil company, to a petroleum product discovered by him. This is an illuminating oil. **1883** *Cent. Mag.* July 338/2 Obtained from petroleum by the refining process . . . [is] mineral sperm oil, a heavier oil for burning in lamps . . . employed on steamers and railroads.

As the last term in **gravel mineral.**

Mingo ˈmɪŋgo, *n.*[1] [Algonquian *ming-we,* stealthy, treacherous.]

1. An Indian belonging to the Iroquois or a cognate tribe (see quot. 1907). In *pl.,* the tribe or tribes composed of these Indians. Now *hist.*

[**1656** VAN DER DONCK *Descr. New Netherlands* 206 With the Minquas we include the Senecas.] **1753** WASHINGTON *Diaries* I. 51, I intend to send a Guard of *Mingo's.* **1840** COOPER *Pathfinder* ii, If any Mingos have seen our path below the falls, they will strike off towards this smoke. **1907** HODGE *Amer. Indians* I. 867 *Mingo,* . . . a name applied in various forms by the Delawares and affiliated tribes to the Iroquois and cognate tribes, and more particularly used during the late colonial period by the Americans to designate a detached band of Iroquois who had left the villages of the main body before 1750 and formed new settlements in Pennsylvania, on the upper Ohio r., in the neighborhood of the Shawnee, Delawares, and neighboring tribes. **1940** THOMPSON *Body, Boots* 49 They had long hated the Mengwe (Iroquois), who, regarding them as a defeated and subject race, called them 'The Women.'

b. Little Mingoes, the Hurons. *Obs.*

1750 CIST *Journals* 37 The Wyendotts or little Mingoes are divided between the French and English.

c. (See quot.) *Obs.*

1882 WEED *Autobiog.* 268 The 'Mingoes' (as we then [1828] called Masons) were on my trail.

2. In obs. combs.: (1) **Mingo bottom,** a name given to a region in which the Mingoes lived; (2) **tongue,** the language spoken by the Mingoes.

(1) **1824** DODDRIDGE *Notes* 270 They saw the rendezvous on the mingo bottom. — (2) **1751** GIST *Journals* 49 You send for one of your Friends that can speak the Mohickon or the Mingoe Tongues well.

b. Also **Mingo chief, man, name, war captain.**

1752 W. TRENT *Journal* (1871) 85 We met a Mingoe man called Powell. **1803** J. DAVIS *Travels* 299 A young *Mingo* War Captain, evinced by his actions that the spirit of chivalry may be found in the forests of barbarous tribes. **1834** DRAKE *Indian Biog.* V. 41 Logan was called a Mingo chief. **1945** KENNY *West. Va. Place Names* 8 Typical of the conjectural nature of these place name conclusions is the status of the Mingo names.

mingo ˈmɪŋgo, *n.*[2] [L. *mingo,* I make water.] A chamber pot or urinal. *Obs.*

1775 *Essex Inst. Coll.* XIII. 187, 5 Mingos and a Bed pan. **1795** C. PRENTISS in *Fugitive Ess.* (1797) 90 To him that occupies my study, I give . . . Another, handy, called a *mingo.* **1851** HALL *College Words* 207 *Mingo.* Latin. At Harvard College, this word was formerly used to designate a chamber-pot.

mingo ˈmɪŋgo, *n.*[3] =**mico.** Also in appositive construction. Now *hist.*

1771 MEASE *Narrative* 70 Here I found a party of Pascagoula Indians, whose Chief or Mingo had a Silver Medal. **1801** HAWKINS *Letters* 387 Minutes of a conference held at the Chickasaw Bluffs by . . . Commissioners of the United States, with the mingco chiefs. **1859** BARTLETT 273 *Mingo* (Creek Ind.), a native king among the Creeks, Choctaws, etc.

Miniconjou ˌmɪnɪˈkandʒu, *n.* [Given by Hodge as a native expression for "those who plant beside the stream."] *collect.* or *pl.* Indians comprising a division of the Teton Sioux, now located on Cheyenne River reservation in South Dakota.

1804 LEWIS & CLARK *Exped.* I. (1814) 61 Tetons Minnakenozzo, a nation inhabiting both sides of the Missouri above the Cheyenne river, and containing about 250 men. **1867** *Harper's Wkly.* 23 March 189/1 The most terrible massacre lately occurring was committed by the Mennecojous. **1876** *S.F. Wkly. Examiner* 24 Aug. 1/6 Medicine Cloud numbers the hostiles as consisting of Brules, Uncapapas, Tetons, Minneconjous, Sans-Arcs, Ogallas, Cheyennes, and Blackfeet. **1949** *10 Story Western* May 39/2 White Bull lived to become chief of the Miniconjou.

Also **Miniconjou Sioux.**

1855 *N.Y. Wkly. Tribune* 23 June 5/2 It is known that the Minecajoux Sioux are guilty of all the late robberies. **1917** WILL & HYDE *Corn Among Indians* 186 The Minniconjou Sioux, according to the information given by some members of the band, secured seed from the Arikaras almost sixty years ago and have raised this corn ever since. **1949** *10 Story Western* May 39/1 White Bull was the twenty-year-old son of Makes-Room, hereditary chief of the Miniconjou Sioux.

*** Minié rifle.** Also **Minnie rifle.** Whisky of a particularly cheap, fiery kind. In full **Minié rifle whisky.** *Slang. Obs.*

1858 *Marysville* (Calif.) *News* 19 Jan. 2/3 May Minie Rifle Whisky be your drink—your sweetest solace. **1859** *Los Angeles Star* 23 April 4/1 Minnie rifle, Knock-'em stiff and flaming red-eye—Such as kills 'em at the counter, Forty rods or any distance. *a***1865** BROWNE *Four Years in Secessia* 194 Its classic communities would turn their attention from imbibing Minié rifle whisky, and assassinating unarmed men, to the vile Yankee habits of healthful employment and general culture.

*** mining,** *n.* In combs., chiefly with reference to the West, and often *obs.* or *hist.*: (1) **mining burg,** =next, *rare;* (2) **camp,** a settlement, usu. temporary, composed of miners; (3) **captain,** one in charge of mining operations; (4) **claim,** an area of mining land held by a claimant by virtue of location and entry; (5) **company,** a group organized for carrying on mining operations; (6) ***district,** a definitely bounded geographical area registered by name in a government land office for use in determining the location of mineral claims; (7) **ditch,** a ditch for conducting water in mining, also attrib.; (8) **recorder,** in a mining camp, a person selected to keep a record of all mining claims and properties; (9) **rod,** a divining rod, cf. **mineral rod;** (10) **rush,** a rush or stampede to an area where gold was, or was thought to be, plentiful; (11) **shark,** a mining expert, *colloq.;* (12) **sluice,** =**mining ditch;** (13) **stock,** stock issued by a mining company; (14) **stream,** a stream made use of in mining; (15) **time,** (see quot.); (16) **town,** a town that has grown up adjacent to a mine.

(1) **1869** *Tidal Wave* (Silver City, Ida.) 19 Jan. 3/2 Carson possesses something of the appearance of an aged mining burg in California. — (2) **1866** *Rep. Indian Affairs* 119 For the purpose of securing employment they resort to the towns and mining camps in large numbers. **1947** *Amer. Wkly.* 2 Nov. 20/2 The law in the mining camps of those days was pretty wobbly and erratic. — (3) **1853** *Harper's Mag.* March 442/2 We are accompanied by Captain John Cox, the mining captain. **1883** FOOTE *Led-Horse Claim* iii. 30 West [was] the mining-captain of the Led-Horse. — (4) **1857** *Hutchings Mag.* May 486/1 Mr. Dawley is the owner of some mining claims on West Hill. **1947** *Steamboat* (Colo.) *Pilot* 13 Feb. 2/6 Beginning with the fiscal year July 1, miners will again be required to do $100 worth of work on each unpatented mining claim they wish to hold.

(5) **1863** *Mich. Gen. Statutes* I. (1882) 1028 The president and secretary of every such mining company . . . [shall] make under their hands, a return to the state treasurer. **1910** J. HART *Vigilante Girl* 329 A rich mining company had been buying up some of the old placer claims. — (6) *c*1861 in LILLARD *Desert Challenge* (1942) 196 In all actions respecting mining claims, proof shall be admitted of the customs, usages, or regulations established and in force in the mining district embracing such claim. **1876** DODGE *Black Hills* 118 Every man in this particular 'mining district' was interested in this town. **1948** *Pacific Discovery* March–April 21/2 After several years, a stream may run clear again and the fish may work down from the high country above the mining district or upstream from the river. — (7) **1873** RAYMOND *Silver & Gold* 45 It is made the duty of the county assessors to return each year to the surveyor general . . . a list of the quartz-mills and mining ditches. **1910** J. HART *Vigilante Girl* 90 Judge Tower is a large owner in the mining ditch properties. — (8) **1876** *White Pine* (Nev.) *News* 22 July 3/1 An election took place on Treasure Hill on Thursday for Mining Recorder. — (9) **1821** *Amer. Jrnl. Science* III. 102 Permit me to suggest . . . well authenticated facts on the use of 'mining rods' in discovering fountains of water underground.

(10) **1896** *Land of Sunshine* July 61 Few if any of them knew . . . that the first 'mining rush' ever known in California had been to the foot-hills of that same cow country. — (11) **1923** BOWER *Parowan Bonanza* 114 I'm no mining shark, but I reckon I better . . . see what you got. — (12) **1878** JACKSON *Travel at Home* 140 On all sides were old mining-sluices.—(13) **1870** MEDBERY *Men Wall St.* 10 Gold was the favorite with ladies. Clergymen rather affected mining-stock and Petroleum. **1903** O. HENRY *Heart of West* 211 There come to the town a young chap all affluent and easy, and fixed up with buggies and mining stock. — (14) **1882** *47th Congress* 1 Sess. H.R. Ex. Doc. No. 216, 12 Mining streams usually cannot carry all the débris washed into them.

(15) **1882** *Harper's Mag.* May 897/1 The very clocks are set to 'mining time,' half an hour faster than sun time. — (16) **1856** *Hutchings Mag.* July 33/2 [We had] to put the *apparahoes* on the mule, and make a 'pilgrim's progress' to the nearest mining town. **1944** ROSS *Westward* 133 She appeared in the mining town of Murray in 1884 with a packtrain from Thompson' Falls.

As the last term in **bar, drift, gulch, hydraulic, placer, pocket, sluice mining.**

***minionette,** *n.* (See quot.) — **1871** RINGWALT *Amer. Encycl. Printing,* Minionette, a very small size of type, used chiefly in small ornamental borders.

Minisink ˈmɪnəˌsɪŋk, *n.* [See **Munsee.**] The leading division of the Munsee *q.v.*, who once "lived on the headwaters of Delaware r., in the s.w. part of Ulster and Orange cos., N.Y., and the adjacent parts of New Jersey and Pennsylvania" (Hodge). Also attrib.

1663 in SCHUYLER *Col. Hist.* IV. 98 The Mennissinck sachems further said that one of their sachems and other Indians were gone to fetch beavor and pelteries which they had hunted. **1872** RUTTENBER *Ind. Tribes Hudson's River* 178 The *Minnisinks* hesitated at first to embark in this war. **1923** VAN BUREN *Ulster Co. Under Dutch* 5 Their principal band was the Minisinks . . . who occupied the southwest part of Ulster and Orange counties and the adjoining parts of New Jersey and Pennsylvania.

*** minister,** *n.*

1. The horned pout, *Ameiurus nebulosus*, or a related species.

1842 *Nat. Hist. N.Y., Zoology* IV. 183 The Common Catfish, Horn Pout, or Minister . . . occurs in the great lakes, and along the Atlantic States. **1884** GOODE *Fisheries* I. 628 The common 'Horned Pout,' 'Bullhead,' 'Bull-pout,' or 'Minister' of the Northern and Eastern States is the most generally abundant and familiar representative of this family [Siluridae].

b. (See quot.)

1870 CHIPMAN *Notes on Bartlett* 273 Minister, . . . a sculpin.—Mass.

2. (*cap.*) (See quot. 1847.)

1847 IVES *N. Eng. Fruit* 45 *Minister.*—This fine apple originated in Rowley, Mass. The size is large, the form oblong like the Bellflower. **1857** HOOPER *Western Fruit Bk.* 61 Minister. . . . Better for orchard culture in the East than in the West. Needs a deep, sandy loam. **1905** W. H. RAGAN *Nomenclature of Apple* 199.

3. minister resident, a diplomatic agent of the third rank representing the U.S. at a foreign seat of government.

1848 *Whig Almanac 1849* 21/2 Dabney S. Carr. Md. *Minister Resident*, Constantinople, Turkey, $6,000. **1893** *Statutes at Large* XXVII. 497 The minister resident and consul-general in Haiti shall also [be] accredited as chargé d'affaires to Santo Domingo.

As the last term in **cabinet, Indian, New England, secession, traveling minister.**

*** Ministerial,** *a.* Designating the armed forces sent to this country by England early in the Revolutionary War. Also **Ministerial army.** *Obs.*

1775 *Jrnls. Cont. Congress* III. 278 For the use of the ministerial army or navy in America. **1776** A. ADAMS *Familiar Lett.* 140 There have been some movements amongst the ministerial troops, as if they meant to evacuate the town of Boston. **1855** IRVING *Life Washington* I. 453 Many still clung to the idea, that in all these proceedings they were merely opposing the measures of the ministry, and not the authority of the crown, and thus the army before Boston was designated as the Continental Army, in contradistinction to that under General Gage, which was called the Ministerial Army.

b. Designating governmental services conducted in this country by England about the time of the Revolution.

1775 *Jrnls. Cont. Congress* III. 488 When . . . our enemies here are corresponding for our ruin, shall we not stop the ministerial post?

c. ministerial (land), (see quot.). *Obs.* Cf. **ministry land.**

1835 *Sentinel & Star in West* (Philomath, Ind.), The town [of Marietta, Ohio] is located on a section of land termed *ministerial*—because allcted by Congress to the support of the christian ministry—the annual income of the lease of which, is divided among the different religious societies.

* **ministerium,** *n.* (See quot. 1873.)

[**1748** *Hallesche Nachrichten* I. (1886) 210 (Petition from Pa.), Alle Aelteste aus denen Gemeinen . . . bitten es [den öffentlichen Gottesdienst] kürzer zu machen; überlassen es dem Ministerio was und wie selbige abzukürzen.] **1873** *Quart. Rev. of Evang. Luth. Ch.* V. 94 *Ministerium* is the term applied to the body of ordained ministers, when they hold a meeting alone, to transact business pertaining to the ministry, viz., the '*Examination, Licensure, and Ordination* of candidates *for the ministry*.' **1918** *Lutheran Ch. Year Book* 102/1 Ministerium of New York.—Pres., Rev. Fred. H. Bosch.

* **ministry,** *n.* In obs. combs.: (1) **ministry house,** a house for the minister, a parsonage; (2) **land,** land set apart for the use of ministers or for the maintenance of a church establishment, also attrib.; (3) **lot,** a lot set apart for the use of a minister.

(1) **1695** *Dorchester Church Rec.* 16 Mr. Davis—where ye minestry house now stands. **1731** *Manchester Rec.* I. 185 A Dead of sale . . . was formerly Completed for the minstry house. — (2) **1710** *Lancaster Rec.* 300 [It] butts southardly on a peice of ministry Land. **1763** *Essex Inst. Coll.* XLIX. 137 Building their half fence, between the said ministry land, and lot of land given by our commoners to the poor. — (3) **1714** *Manchester Rec.* I. 130 John knowlton should have the minestry lott in the west Devision the 22 lott.

minkery ˈmɪŋkərɪ, *n.* A place where minks are bred for commercial purposes.

1877 Coues *Fur-bearing Animals* 182 Mr. Resseque's minkery consists of twelve stalls. **1897** *Boston Transcript* 11 Sep. 24/3 Minks have been bred for their skins in so-called minkeries. **1916** *Proc. Iowa Acad. Sci.* XXIII. 285 There are at present in this 'minkery' thirty-seven individuals.

Minneapolitan ˌmɪnɪəˈpɑlɪtən, *n.* One who lives in Minneapolis, Minn. — **1905** *N. Eng. Mag.* Sep. 33/2 Father Hennepin . . . is notably remembered by Minneapolitans for naming the city's great water power.

Minnesotan ˌmɪnɪˈsotn̩, *n.* [f. the state name, derived f. an Indian term with some such meaning as "sky-blue water."] A native or resident of the state of Minnesota. — **1888** D. D. Field *Speeches, Arguments* (1890) III. 369 Nebraskan, Kansan, Arkansan, Minnesotan, are the true designations of the citizens of those flourishing States, from whose names they are derived. **1948** *Minneapolis Morn. Tribune* 28 Sep. 2/8 The first Minnesotan accused of violating the new selective service law will be arraigned today in federal district court here.

Minnesotian ˌmɪnəˈsotɪən, *n.* =prec.

1860 *Harper's Mag.* Oct. 581 Town lot speculators striving to have the Capitol elsewhere than at St. Paul (all but Minnesotians have forgotten the name of the town now.) **1891** *Appeal-Avalanche* (Memphis) 27 April 4/1 Even should the modest Minnesotians legislate against tights on the stage spectacular dramas need not fear the result. **1948** *So. Bend* (Ind.) *Tribune* 3 April 1/1 (*heading*), Maine Republicans Also Lean Toward Minnesotian.

Minnetaree ˌmɪnəˈtɑrɪ, *n.* [Mandan *minitari,* "they crossed the water."]

1. *pl.* The Hidatsa, a Siouan tribe.

1804 Clark in *Lewis & C. Exped.* I. (1904) 227 The Meneterias . . . were alarmed at the tales told them by the Mandans. **1862** Hayden *Ethnog. & Philol. Mo. Val.* 344 [The Atsinas] have also been confounded with the Minnetarees of the Missouri. **1947** DeVoto *Across Wide Missouri* 134 The Fort was a village square for neighboring downriver Arikaras and upriver Minnetarees.

attrib. **1854** Brownell *Indian Races N. Amer.* 466 The smaller Minitary tribes . . . speak the same language with the Crows. **1949** *Life* 4 July 41/1 Pehriska-Ruhpa, war chief of the Minnetaree tribe which lived on the Dakota plains, was portrayed from life in 1833 in this lithograph by Charles Bodmer.

2. *Minnetarees of the Prairie,* and variants, the Atsina, a branch of the Arapaho. Often confused with the Hidatsa.

1806 Lewis in *L. & Clark Exped.* V. (1905) 24 As we had not yet seen the black foot Indians and the Minnetarew of Fort de Prarie they did not think it safe to venture over to the Plains of the Missouri. **1862** Hayden *Ethnog. & Philol. Mo. Val.* 344 [The Atsina Indians] have received a great variety of names, as Paunch, . . . Minnetarees of the Prairie, &c.

3. *Minnetarees of Knife River,* (see quot. 1907).

1805 Lewis in *L. & Clark Exped.* II. 283 Our present camp is precisely on the spot that the Snake Indians were encamped at the time the Minnetares of the Knife R. first came in sight of them five years since. **1907** Hodge *Amer. Indians* I. 870 *Minnetarees of Knife River,* an unidentified Hidatsa division. . . . Possibly the Amahami.

minniebush ˈmɪnɪˌbʊʃ, *n.* [f. "Menzies' bush," so called after Archibald *Menzies* (1754–1842), a Scottish naturalist.] (See quot. 1909.) — **1909** *Cent. Supp.* 813/1 minnie-bush. . . . A shrub, *Menziesia pilosa,* of the heath family, found in mountain woods from Pennsylvania to Georgia. It bears elliptical or obovate leaves, and greenish-purple urn-shaped flowers in terminal drooping umbels. **1943** Peattie *Great Smokies* 197 Most of the associated shrubs like mountain laurel, blueberry, and minniebush are of the heath family.

* **minnow,** *n.* As the last term in **mud, red, rotgut, salt-water, smelt, top minnow.**

* **minny,** *n.* **1. minny bass,** the small-mouthed black bass. **2. minny gang,** a set of hooks or nets for catching minnows.

(1) **1820** *Western Mo. Rev.* II. 56 Bass Hogfish. . . . It has some similarity with . . . other River bass, wherefore it is called Minny-bass, Little-bass. — (2) **1857** Hammond *Northern Scenes* 57 Nobody in them days tho't of sich contrivances as trollin'-rods, reels, and minny-gangs. [**1883** *Fisheries Exhib. Cat.* 195 Spanish gut as imported for the manufacture of leaders; single, double, and twisted gut leaders, minnow gangs, brails, gangings, used in various sea fisheries.]

* **minor,** *a.* and *n.*

1. In colleges and universities operated on the quarter system, a course requiring approximately half the time spent on a major course. *Obs.*

1890 in Goodspeed *Hist. U. of Chi.* (1916) 142 The plan of majors and minors, announced in our bulletins and calendars, has been arranged in order to meet this difficulty. **1893** *U. of Chi. Reg.* 7/1 Courses of instruction in the University are classified as Majors and Minors. . . . The Minor, [calls] for four to five hours of class-room work, or its equivalent, each week. **1894** *U. of Chi. Wkly.* 29 Nov. 99/2 Three minors has been decided upon as the proper amount of work for a student each quarter.

b. A secondary subject of study, either graduate or undergraduate. Hence **minor subject, minor field.**

1909 Webster 1376/3 Minor, . . . a subject of study, usually nearly related to the major subject, pursued by the candidate for a higher degree, less time being devoted to it than to the major subject. **1911** *Cornell U. Graduate Sch. Announcement* 4 Candidates for the doctor's degree are required to select a major subject and two minor subjects. **1945** *U. of Chi. Cat.* (Coll. & Div.) June 146 The Departmental requirements are as follows. . . . The passing of a preliminary examination . . . in . . . language of a minor field [etc.]. **1948** *Ada* (Okla.) *Ev. News* 2 July 6/2 Alliene Pryor-Smith . . . will graduate at East Central in July, with a major in history and a minor in sociology.

2. *pl.* Minor leagues. Cf. next.

1890 *Sporting Life* (Phila.) 31 July 1/3 It is certain that the major leagues must depend upon the minors for their recruits. **1912** Cooke *Baseballogy* 19 You're slow! you're slow! Go back and join the minors! **1949** *Newsweek* 18 July 64/3 Manager Eddie Sawyer claims that . . . he'd like to be back in the minors.

b. minor league, in professional baseball, a league or association other than a major league *q.v.* Also attrib.

1889 *Sporting Life* (Phila.) 29 May 1/2 It will mean . . . the relegation of four-fifths of the men not in those leagues to the minor leagues. **1912** C. Mathewson *Pitching* 57 Many men, who shine in the minor leagues, fail to make good in the majors. **1948** *Kankakee* (Ill.) *D. Jrnl.* 5 June 1/2 Prior to that the former minor league baseball pitcher had coached at Ball Township high school.

fig. **1948** *Atlantic Mo.* Jan. 81/2 This is the class . . . into which we should put our own minor-league spiritualists, who put out the lights and then speak for the spooks of Indian chiefs and little girls.

Hence **minor leaguer,** a player in a minor league.

1906 *Cin. Enquirer* 1 April IV. 2/1 The Coast team is a strong aggregation, fit to cope with the best of minor leaguers.

* **minority,** *n. attrib.*

1. Designating a political party or platform which consists of, or is supported by, a minority.

1901 *N. Amer. Rev.* Feb. 271 The captors were able to defeat the minority platform. **1902** E. C. Meyer *Nominating Systems* 53 Great leaders came forward in the ranks of the minority, for the possibilities of a vigorous campaign stood out clearly. The minority party could thoroughly gauge its strength through its assembled delegates.

2. minority representation, representation in a legislative body according to a procedure that allows the voter, when he has, for example, three representatives to vote for, either to cast three votes for one candidate or to divide them as he sees fit.

1870 *Ill. Constitution* (Chi. 1870) 39 (*caption*), Minority Representation. **1872** *Atlantic Mo.* Feb. 255 Calling a constitutional convention devolves this winter on the Ohio Legislature, and one of the most important subjects which will come before that body will be minority representation.

* **minstrel,** *n.*

1. *pl.* A group or company of theatrical performers, either Negroes or, more usu., white men in blackface, who entertain with songs, dancing, jokes, and the like. Also in proper names. Cf. **Christy's Minstrels, Congo Minstrels.**

1843 in ODELL *Ann. N.Y. Stage* IV. 668 The Ethiopian Serenaders, or Boston Minstrels. **1902** WILSON *Spenders* 337, I got a good notion to get me one of them first-part suits—like the minstrels wear in the grand first part, you know. **1947** *Nat. Geog. Mag.* Sep. 528/2 Minstrels opened their performance by saying: 'Welcome from Waterbury, the land of eternal spring.'

b. *sing.* A member of such a group of actors.

1890 BIFF HALL *Turnover Club* 162 One poor minstrel wore a pair of very sheer trousers.

c. =next.

1943 *Life* 5 July 80 All minstrels followed a pattern. **1949** *Chesterton* (Ind.) *Tribune* 28 April 1/6 Much variety was evidenced in the 35 numbers of the minstrel, so that if one number didn't appeal to all, the next one was bound to send the audience rolling in the aisles.

2. minstrel show, an entertainment by minstrels or of the kind given by minstrels.

1870 O. LOGAN *Before Footlights* 414 A clever actor at the Arch, who wrote a burlesque . . . for a minstrel show, improved on this idea. **1896** *Chi. Record* 12 Feb. 1/6 Give a female minstrel show. . . . The ladies of West Chicago gave their long-talked-of and much-opposed 'burnt cork' entertainment to-night. **1949** *Lisle* (Ill.) *Advertiser* 11 March 1/1 You won't want to miss seeing the Minstrel Show, 'Kentucky Dream,' to be given next Thursday and Friday evenings at the Lisle Congregational church.

attrib. **1947** DEVOTO *Across Wide Missouri* 141 The chiefs looked like a minstrel-show cakewalk in heaven and they shoved out their chests and strutted, counting their coups competitively.

3. In special combs. of obvious meaning: (1) **minstrel ballad,** (2) **band,** (3) **entertainment,** (4) **house,** (5) **man,** (6) **performance,** (7) **performer,** (8) **stage,** (9) **troupe.**

(1) **1881** *Harper's Mag.* May 818/2 The plaintive slave songs and their echoes—the plantation songs and the minstrel ballad . . . are rapidly passing away. — (2) **1884** *Cent. Mag.* June 307/2 It is hard . . . for two women of refinement and taste to stand between two members of some burnt-cork minstrel band on the Lord's Day. — (3) **1870** *Chi. Tribune* 26 March, The Dearborn [is] probably the most successful minstrel entertainment in the country. — (4) **1865** *Chi. Tribune* 10 April 1 Buckley & Budd's minstrel house is in blast.

(5) **1890** BIFF HALL *Turnover Club* 75, I have been told that one night 'Hoochy-Coochy' Rice the minstrelman . . . entered Hoyt's room with a dark lantern. **1944** *Chi. D. News* 25 Oct. 12/6 [He] used to be a minstrel man and traveled with a medicine show. — (6) **1882** *Sheldon* (Iowa) *Mail* 26 Jan., Sprague's Original Georgia Minstrel performance, given in this city last night, is, as a fraud and humbug, entitled to the cake. — (7) **1887** *Courier-Journal* 11 Jan. 5/2 The wife of . . . the minstrel performer, to-day began suit for separation against her husband. — (8) **1929** *Amer. Sp.* IV. 209 The sources of these originally extraneous snatches are . . . antebellum minstrel stage [etc.]. — (9) **1884** MATTHEWS & BUNNER *In Partnership* 211 A stock of musical instruments large enough to fit out a strolling minstrel troupe.

* **minstrelsy,** *n.* The arts or practices of Negro minstrels. Cf. **Negro minstrelsy.**

1857 *Spirit of Times* 23 May 192/2 Bryant's Minstrels continue to monopolise a large share of the patronage of the admirers of Ethiopian minstrelsy. **1901** *Cosmopolitan* Sep. 639/2 That he [American Negro] reads his title clear is proved by his determination to share the rewards of minstrelsy with his white imitators. **1930** WITTKE *Tambo & Bones* 42 Minstrelsy was born in a decade when the fashionable American public had not yet become addicted to the theatre-going habit.

* **mint,** *n.* In combs.: (1) * **mint-drop,** (see quot. 1872), also **Benton's mint drop,** cf. **Bentonian shiner,** *obs.;* (2) **julep,** an iced and sweetened drink of whisky or brandy flavored with sprigs of mint, associated esp. with the South, also attrib.; (3) **leaf,** (see quot.), *slang;* (4) **sling,** a spirituous drink, prob. of gin, flavored with sprigs of mint, also attrib.; (5) **smash,** a mint julep or mint sling; (6) **stick,** a stick of candy flavored with peppermint.

(1) **1835** HAWTHORNE *Amer. Note Bks.* (1871) I. 7 The bar-keeper had one of Benton's mint drops for a bosom-brooch! **1872** DE VERE 291 When the Hon. T. H. Benton . . . put his whole strength forward . . . to introduce a gold currency, he accidentally called the latter mint-drops, with a slight attempt at a pun. . . . For many years gold coins were largely known as Benton's mint-drops. — (2) **1809** IRVING *Knickerb.* VII. ii, The inhabitants [of Maryland] . . . were notoriously prone to get fuddled and make *merry* with mint julep and apple toddy. **1945** *Chi. D. News* 1 Feb. 8/6 That ruddy mint-julep colonel in the whisky ads is strictly a phony. — (3) **1929** *Amer. Sp.* IV. 357 For bills as such, we may say, in addition to lettuce, just mentioned, frogskins, mint leaves . . . or yellow boys. — (4) **1804** *Balance* 15 March 86, 3 Mint Slings [figure in a Referees' Tavern Bill, Lancaster, Pa.]. **1840** *S. Lit. Messenger* VI. 508/1 Alighting at a miserable looking log-hut, they called for a 'mint-sling.'

(5) **1884** *Washington* (D.C.) *Critic* Sep., He proceeded to the barroom, [and] took a mint smash. **1903** ADE *People You Know* 14 Then the atmosphere began to be curdled with High Balls and Plymouth Sours and Mint Smashes. — (6) *a***1855** J. F. KELLY *Humors* 187 The streets are filled by holiday-looking people, children with toys and 'mint sticks.' **1863** A. D. WHITNEY *F. Gartney* xxxvi, Glory resigned the boy to his mint-stick, and was saying good-by.

As the last term in **cow, horse, mountain mint.**

* **minute,** *n.*

1. *attrib.* Consisting of minutemen of Revolutionary times. Now *hist.*

1775 in SPARKS *Corr. Revol.* I. 64 A Committee of Safety . . . [for] calling the minute-battalions and drafts from the militia into service. **1775** HULTON *Letters* 77 The People in the Country (who are all furnished with Arms & have what they call Minute Companys in every Town ready to march on any alarm), had a signal.

2. minuteman, during the Revolutionary period, an armed citizen or militiaman who agreed to be ready for military duty the minute he was called upon. Also transf. Now *hist.* Cf. **four-minute men.**

1774 J. ANDREWS *Letters* 60 Seven regiments . . . are call'd minute men, i.e., to be ready at a minute's warning with a fortnight's provision, and ammunition and arms. **1857** E. STONE *Life Howland* 49 Before and after the commencement of hostilities, Rhode Island had an organized militia known as 'minute men.' **1949** *Sat. Ev. Post* 5 March 12/4 If the idea is to re-enact some episode of history, why not trick out five or six Redcoats and we'll trick out five or six Minutemen and chase them back, and then we can all relax?

b. A member of any of various groups of men organized in the South, at about the time of the Civil War, for the purpose of instantly resisting any forces threatening southern interests. Now *hist.*

1860 *Richmond Enquirer* 2 Nov. 1/6 (Th.), The formation of companies of 'Minute Men' has actually begun. **1901** CHURCHILL *Crisis* 260 The guardians were the *Minute Men,* organized to maintain the honor and dignity of the state of Missouri.

c. (See quot. 1895.)

1890 WILLS *Twice Born* 70, I joined the fire department as 'minute man.' **1895** *Stand.* 1129/3 *Minute-man,* . . . a fireman stationed outside of an engine-house and employed at any occupation, but subject to call in case of fire.

d. In the Southwest *c*1875, a member of an organization of stockmen formed to resist border lawlessness. Also attrib.

1929 DOBIE *Vaquero* 76 These minutemen were never enrolled by the state, but if rangers deserve a pension some of the minutemen deserve it also.

e. Minute Man Flag, in World War II, a flag awarded by the Treasury Department to business concerns, schools, etc., in which more than 90% of the employees were regular subscribers to war bonds.

1943 MENEFEE *Assignment* 108 We were one of the first big plants to get the Minute Man Flag. **1944** *Chi. Sun* 20 May 6/3 The Treasury Department has awarded to The Chicago Sun the Minute Man Flag.

miraculous pea. (See quot.) *Rare.* — **1709** LAWSON *Carolina* 76 We have the Indian Rounceval, or Miraculous Pease, so call'd from their long Pods, and Great Increase.

miscegen ˈmɪsɪˌdʒən, *n.* [See next.] A person of mixed racial background. Also attrib. *Obs.* — **1864** S. S. COX *Eight Yrs. in Congress* (1865) 354 (Th.), A very sprightly suffragan of a miscegen stamp. . . . The result would be an average miscegen and a superior patriot.

miscegenation ˌmɪsɪdʒəˈneʃən, *n.* [L. *miscere,* to mix, and *genus,* race.] Mixture of races by intermarriage or interbreeding, esp. such mixture on the part of white people and Negroes. Also fig.

This term is said to have been "invented" by David Goodman Croly, of New York, in a pamphlet which he copyrighted in 1863, and published anonymously in 1864, entitled *Miscegenation: the Theory of the Blending of the Races, Applied to the American White Man and Negro.* See *Amer. Sp.* Dec. 1949, 267.

1864 *Chi. Tribune* 18 March 2/1 Miscegenation. Such is the newly invented term to express the mingling of races generally, and specially the mingling of the white and black races on the continent as a consequence of the freedom of the latter. **1900** *Cong. Rec.* 8 Jan. 674/2 The choice of a negro, by an arbitrary law, to such an office is a political marriage and miscegenation. **1949** *N.Y. Times Book Rev.* 20 March 10/2 We'll have to wait a while longer for the good novel about miscegenation.

miscegenationist ˌmɪsɪdʒəˈneʃənɪst, *n.* [See prec.] One who favors miscegenation. Also **miscegenationalist.** *Obs.* — **1871** De Vere 289 A *Miscegenationist,* named Williams, was tarred and feathered. **1885** *Cent. Mag.* Sep. 689/1 The enemies of slavery getting from us such names as negrophiles, negro-worshippers, and miscegenationalists.

misplay mɪsˈple, *n.* A wrong play.

1867 *Ball Players' Chron.* 15 Aug. 4/3 But one misplay was made in the nine innings. **1889** *Columbus* (O.) *Dispatch* 1 Aug., A misplay of any kind would allow the score to be tied. **1894** *Outing* XXIV. 300/2 He was playing a steady, careful game, . . . apparently waiting for Hovey's misplays.

* **miss,** *n.* (See quot. 1851.) *Obs.* Cf. * **cut,** *n.* **4.**

1819 Peirce *Rebelliad* 62 Are there some who scrape and hiss Because you never give a miss. **1851** Hall *College Words* 208 *Miss,* an omission of a recitation, or any college exercise. An instructor is said *to give a miss,* when he omits a recitation. **1852** Felton *Mem. J. S. Popkin* p. lxxvii, One of the classes applied to the Doctor for what used to be called, in College jargon, *a miss.*

Miss America. A title bestowed as the result of a national beauty contest held to find the most beautiful girl in the U.S. Also the girl winning this title.

The first Miss America was chosen in 1921 in a contest involving eight girls, though the term was not used in connection with this contest. See *Amer. N. & Q.* IV. 61, 140.

1922 *N.Y. Times* 5 Sep. 19/6 Miss Margaret Gorman of Washington, winner of the 1921 contest, will be known as 'Miss America.' **1944** *N. & Q.* IV. 61, I have been told that the practice of selecting a 'Miss America' came from the Ziegfeld Follies; but I have not explored this source. **1949** *World-Herald* (Omaha) 11 Sep. 1/5 The new Miss America told the audience she plans to go to Stanford University to study dramatics.

miss-and-out, *n.* A contest in which a competitor who misses is out. — **1903** *Forest & Stream* 21 Feb. 159/3 A miss-and-out was . . . shot at live birds.

missey-moosey. A variant of **moosemise.** — **1892** *Amer. Folk-Lore* V. 95 *Pyrus Americana,* missey moosey. N.H. **1909** *Cent. Supp.* 815/3 Missey-moosey, . . . the American mountain-ash, Sorbus Americana.

* **missing,** *a.* and *n.*

1. *To be among the missing,* to be absent. *Colloq.*

1855 Haliburton *Nature & Hum. Nature* 17 (B.), If a person inquires if you are at home, the servant is directed to say, No, if you don't want to be seen, and choose to be among the missing. **1869** *Across the Desert* (F.), I tell you what, Jake, if this goes on I'll be among the missing before sundown.

2. *To come* (or *turn*) *up missing,* to fail to show up, to be absent. *Colloq.*

1869 Mark Twain *Letters* I. (1917) 164 (We.), But those extensions turned up missing every time. **1900** Drannan *Plains & Mts.* 503 The young man who had been riding in the middle, also four mules and their packs, as the saying is, 'came up missing.' **1942** Rawlings *C. Creek* 124 He has a trick of 'coming up missing.'

* **mission,** *n.*

1. A permanent diplomatic establishment or institution.

1805 *Amer. State P.: Foreign Relations* II. 669 As nothing was said in my communication respecting the ordinary mission, it remains of course in force. **1890** *Cent.* 3798/1 The members of the British mission at Washington.

2. In combs.: (1) **mission design,** a design or architectural style characteristic of the early Spanish mission buildings in the Southwest; (2) **family,** a family or association of families doing missionary work in a certain locality, *obs.;* (3) **farm,** a farm belonging originally to one of the missions in the Southwest; (4) **furniture,** furniture of a heavy, dark style with straight lines, said to have been modeled originally on the furniture of the Spanish missions in the Southwest, also attrib.; (5) **grape,** a variety of cultivated sweet wine grape introduced into this country from Mexico, presumably through the Spanish missions in California; (6) **Indian,** a member of any of various Indian tribes originally converted to Christianity by the Spanish Franciscan missionaries in California and governed by them until the secularizing of the missions in 1834 by the Mexican government; (7) **land,** land belonging to a mission; (8) **oil,** oil made from mission olives; (9) **olive,** a variety of olive grown in California; (10) **rocker,** a rocking chair of mission style; (11) **school,** (*a*) a school for Indian children conducted by missionaries or their helpers at an Indian mission, (*b*) a Sunday school at a city mission conducted by members of a church; (12) **sewing school,** a sewing school conducted by a mission school; (13) **station,** a place serving as the headquarters of missionary activities, esp. among the American Indians; (14) **style,** of a style like that of the Spanish missions in California; (15) **table,** a table made in the mission style of furniture.

(1) 1906 *Out West* Feb. 95 In the south these are handsome buildings of Mission design, in harmony with the character and traditions of the country. — **(2) 1822** Morse *Rep. Indian Affairs* I. 78 Education Families. I give this name to those bodies which have been commonly denominated *Mission Families.* **1875** Stowe *We & Neighbors* 375 A few Christian people had bought a house in which they had established a mission family, with a room which they use for a chapel. — **(3) 1861** Winthrop *J. Brent* 16 He had . . . bought a mission farm, and established himself as a ranchero. — **(4) 1900** *Harper's Bazaar* 28 April 388/1 She stumbled upon an artistic small shop filled to overflowing with what the salesman called Mission furniture. **1923** R. Herrick *Lilla* 213 It's Lawndale done in mission-furniture style. **1947** *This Week Mag.* 18 July 10/4, I looked at the spotted rug, the lifeless draperies, the mission furniture and nodded.

(5) 1868 *Iowa Agric. Soc. Rep. 1867* 205 The Mission grape is not as much esteemed as formerly. **1912** Saunders *Indian Terraced Houses* 28 There were loose clusters of sweet Mission grapes . . . and persimmon-like plums. — **(6) 1853** Hayes *Pioneer Notes* (1929) 94 Mr. Wilson goes to the Legislature, now in session, to obtain their co-operation in his plans for the Old Mission Indians. **1948** *Amer. Jrnl. Physical Anthrop.* March 82 Marked attrition was found to be common in the Texas Indians, except in Mission Indians who probably shared in European foodstuffs. — **(7) 1851** *Whig Almanac 1852* 18/2 The Commissioners are required to report to the Secretary of the Interior the tenure by which the Mission lands are held. **1883** *Cent. Mag.* Aug. 528/2 These Carmel Mission lands having been rented out, by their present owner, in great dairy farms. — **(8) 1883** *Cent. Mag.* Aug. 555/1 Residents of California have been accustomed to consider a small bottle of 'mission oil' for their salad as a treasure. — **(9) 1883** *Cent. Mag.* Aug. 555/2 The variety was the 'mission olive,' which has not been identified with any of the varieties now cultivated in Europe. **1929** Bailey *Cyclo. Horticulture* 2334/2 Like the Mission grape, the Mission olive has not been identified with any Old World variety and is probably a seedling.

(10) 1913 London *Valley of Moon* 491 They . . . found the big beautiful husband lying back reading in a huge Mission rocker. — **(11)** (*a*) **1822** in Morse *Rep. Indian Affairs* II. 171 There has been no particular information received from Elder Posey himself, superintendent of the mission schools at the Valley Towns. **1906** *Indian Laws & Tr.* III. 193 Mission schools on an Indian reservation may . . . receive for such Indian children duly enrolled therein, the rations of food and clothing. (*b*) **1871** Bagg *At Yale* 523 One of the most approved entrances to city society lies, oddly enough, through the doors of the 'Mission schools.' **1887** Rittenhouse *Maud* 387 This afternoon Harriet and I went down to the Mission-school, and I had my bright little boys once again. — **(12) 1877** *Harper's Mag.* Feb. 430/2 Ladies kindly take charge of these classes, which are managed much in the same way as the mission sewing schools of America. — **(13)** [**1844** *McDonough P.* 78 One of these young men . . . is now at the mission station at Settra Kroo, Liberia, keeping a school for the native youth. **1850** Hines *Voyage* 91 Our families found ourselves floating on the surface of the great Columbia, in two small canoes, on our way up to the mission station in the Wallamette settlement. **1871** *Rep. Indian Affairs* (1872) 535 As soon as the means are furnished to establish, permanently, mission-stations and school-houses. — **(14) 1911** *N.Y. Ev. Post* 1 March 8 The dignified . . . cement house, often in mission style with attractive tile roof. **1948** *Time* 9 Feb. 59/1 He lives in a charming mission-style house in San Marino.

(15) 1906 *Cin. Enquirer* 1 April 5, $3.98 for Mission Tables.

As the last term in **anti-, domestic, Oregon mission.**

* **missionary,** *n.*

1. *pl.* (*cap.*) Missionary Baptists. *Colloq.*

1865 *Nation* I. 395 The Missionaries, they holds to free grace.

2. In combs.: (1) **Missionary Baptist,** a Baptist who, unlike the Primitive or Hard-Shell Baptists, supports missionary work, also a church of such Baptists, also attrib.; (2) **barrel,** a barrel containing clothing and other articles of use to missionaries in their work; (3) **day,** a day upon which in certain churches missionary activities are stressed; (4) **ship,** ?a ship chartered for the sending of missionaries to foreign countries, *rare;* (5) **station,** the headquarters of a missionary, esp. one to the American Indians.

(1) **1849** Chamberlain *Ind. Gazetteer* 72 A large majority of this denomination are Missionary Baptists, and the minority is rapidly diminishing. **1888** J. Wallace *Carpetbag Rule in Fla.* 226 The freedmen prior to the emancipation knew nothing of any other churches than the Missionary Baptist, Primitive or foot-washing Baptist, and the Methodist Episcopal. **1944** Duncan *M. Graham* 91 But there was a 'regular' Baptist church at Clary's Grove, near by—missionary Baptist. **1949** *Sat. Ev. Post* 22 Oct. 122/4 He entered the Missionary Baptist ministry as a young man, and for ten years filled pastorates in the Carolinas. — (2) **1877** Phelps *Avis* 31 Some [people] take to zoology, and some take to religion.... John Rose says, in the Connecticut Valley, where he came from, it was missionary barrels. **1944** Holton *Yankees* 50 It would develop that Mabel had told her the dress she was wearing looked as if she had got it out of the missionary barrel, or that her Sunday hat made her look like a black calf under a new shed. — (3) **1944** Holton *Yankees* 16 Something like once a month, on missionary days, and always on such church festivals as Christmas, Easter and Children's Day, the Sunday school held a concert. — (4) **1854** Richards *V. Life* (1912) 47 Mr Noah T. Clarke told us in Sunday School last Sunday that if we wanted to take shares in the missionary ship, *Morning Star*, we could buy them at 10 cents apiece, and Grandmother gave us $1 to-day so we could have ten shares.

(5) **1835** N. P. Willis *Pencillings by the Way* (1942) 260, I confess I should not have gone far out of my way to visit a missionary station anywhere. **1899** Cushman *Hist. Indians* 464 She died and was buried at Monroe, the old missionary station.

As the last term in **anti-, Mormon, Shaker missionary.**

missionary ˈmɪʃənˌɛrɪ, *v. intr.* = **missionate.** *Obs.* — **1862** *Independent* 24 April 3/1 [The Rev. Stephen H. Tyng] was always fond of missionarying. **1884** Mark Twain *H. Finn* xix. 183 Preachin's my line, too, and workin' camp-meetin's, and missionaryin' around.

missionate ˈmɪʃənˌet, *v. intr.* To do the work of a missionary. *Obs.*

1815 in *Amer. Sp.* XXII. 284 *Missionate* (to perform the service of a missionary) a low ecclesiastical word—used in conversation, & American, I presume. **1836** L. Matthews *Lectures* 130, I have found the word *difficulted*, which I had classed with *missionate* in the lowest rank of unauthorized Americanisms, sanctioned by . . . Lord Thurlow. **1896** *Home Missionary* Oct. 303 To make professional visits, or to 'missionate' to the farmer, will not serve the purpose.

Missisauga ˌmɪsɪˈsɔgə, *n.* [Ojibway, "it has a large mouth," with reference to the Missisauga River.] An Indian of an Algonquian tribe which was originally a division or subtribe of the Ojibway. Also, *pl.*, the tribe itself.

[*a*1716 Perrot *Mémoire des Sauvages de l'Amérique* (1864) 132 Tout son monde estant assemblé, il envoya présenter le casse-teste aux Saulteurs, Missisakis et autres nations.] **1772** in *Hist. MSS Comm.* 14th Rep. App. X. (1895) 85 The Chippawaes and Mississagaes are by far the most numerous and powerful nation with whom we have any connection in North America. **1798** Barton *New Views* App. 4 The Messisaugers, or Messasagues. The language of these Indians is, undoubtedly, very nearly allied to that of the Chippewas. **1839** Morton *Crania Americana* 175 The northern group of the Algonquin-Lenapé embraces . . . the Crees, the Chippewas, the Ottawas, the Potawatomis, the Missasaugas, and the Algonquins proper. **1948** *Southwestern Jrnl. Anthrop.* Spring 100 These people, particularly the Missisaugas, seem to have occupied the southern end of the Park a century ago.

attrib. **1827** West *Jrnl.* 291, I proceeded in company with Mr. Brandt, to visit the Mississaugah Indians. **1831** A. S. Withers *Chron. Border Warfare* 299 Their force consisted of four thousand warriors, and was led on by a Missasago chief.

b. = **massasauga.**

1843 Oliver *Eight Months* 150 The inhabitants recognize two kinds of rattlesnakes, to wit, the wood- and the prairie-rattlesnake, or mississauga, of which the latter is much the smaller and less dangerous.

Mississip ˌmɪsəˈsɪp, *n.* [See next.] (See quot. 1859.) Also attrib. — **1834** Caruthers *Kentuckian* I. 218 If I was to meet that feller in a Mississip cane-brake. **1859** Mackay *Tour* I. 246 The Mississippi, or, as the people call it familiarly and affectionately, the 'Mississip,' was covered with floating ice.

Mississippi ˌmɪsəˈsɪpɪ, *n.* [The name (of Indian origin) of a river, a former territory, and a state.]

1. A kind of cotton. *Obs.*

1805 *Raleigh* (N.C.) *Reg.* 1 April, Common Georgia and Mississippi are quoted at 2s. to 2s.3d.

2. In combs.: (1) **Mississippi bond,** a bond issued by the state of Mississippi; (2) **bottom,** bottom land along the Mississippi River, also attrib. and transf.; (3) **broadhorn,** a kind of flatboat used on the Mississippi, *obs.*, cf. **broadhorn;** (4) **Bubble,** see as a main entry; (5) **butternut,** a Confederate soldier from Mississippi, *obs.;* (6) **coondom,** (see quot.); (7) **jager,** see as a main entry; (8) **plan,** the method followed in Mississippi just after the Civil War, for regaining political domination for the white population by the use of terror and force if necessary; (9) **rifle,** see as a main entry; (10) **(river) steamboat,** a large steamboat, often of a luxurious type, formerly in use on the Mississippi River; (11) **roarer,** a frontier rowdy of a type once common on the Mississippi, *obs.;* (12) **scheme,** = **Mississippi Bubble,** *obs.;* (13) **scraper,** a type of plow, *obs.;* (14) **states,** the states that border on the Mississippi River; (15) **territory,** a region east of the Mississippi River, embracing approx. the present states of Mississippi and Alabama, organized as a territory in 1798, now *hist.*

(1) **1851** *Ore. Statesman* 30 Sep. 1/2 Now if I do tell the hull story, I shall depend on your honor, (and I calkilate that is rather better than Mississippy bonds,) that you won't tell on me. — (2) **1818** Darby *Emigrant's Guide* 122 The three species of soil, Mississippi bottom, bluff, and pine woods, are to be found in Claiborne and Jefferson. **1866** W. Reid *After the War* 455 An investment in Mississippi bottom cotton plantations seemed to many business men very much like an investment. **1868** *Rep. Comm. Agric. 1867* 114 In De Soto are some 60 sections of 'Mississippi bottom' at $4 or less per acre. — (3) **1900** Smithwick *Evol. of State* 11 They are known in river parlance as 'Mississippi broadhorns,' the poor man's transfer.

(5) **1866** F. Kirkland *Bk. Anecdotes* 150 A brisk and spirited dialogue . . . took place between an East Tennesseean loyalist and a Mississippi 'Butternut.' — (6) **1913** A. C. Cole *Whig Party in South* 69 During the early forties the Whig party was frequently denounced as the aristocratic party of the slave-holders, the democracy of Mississippi designating the local organization as 'the empire of Mississippi coondom.' — (8) **1876** *Harper's Wkly.* 4 Nov. 886/3 The representative 'fire-eater' in the State was selected as a Democratic candidate to defeat the reform Republican, and by the familiar means, the 'Mississippi plan,' to secure the electoral vote for Tilden. **1893** *Cong. Rec.* 6 Oct. 2248/1 The Mississippi plan . . . is acknowledged to be the most efficacious of all known methods for eliminating the 'unwelcome voter.'

(10) **1832** Mrs. Trollope *Dom. Manners of Amer.* (ed. 2) I. 19 Let no one who wishes to receive agreeable impressions of American manners, commence their travels in a Mississippi steam boat. **1858** Vielé *Following Drum* 142 On a Mississippi river steamboat . .. he wounded . . . a fellow-passenger. **1896** Shinn *Story of Mine* 109 As distinct creations of adaptive and evolutionary genius as the . . . Mississippi River steamboat in days before railroads. — (11) **1847** Robb *Squatter Life* 64 Ben was an old Mississip' roarer—none of your half and half, but just as native to the element, as if he had been born in a broad horn. — (12) **1767** [see **Mississippi Bubble** as a main entry]. *c*1828 Benton *30 Years' View* I. 105/1 To give us a second edition, no doubt, of the celebrated '*Mississippi Scheme*' of John Law. — (13) **1852** *De Bow's Review* XII. 451 The first plowing of cotton should . . . be done with a sweep, Mississippi scraper, or some similar implement. — (14) **1804** C. B. Brown tr. Volney *View* p. xii, Disjunction of interests and views, and contrariety of habits, . . . separate the eastern from the southern, the Atlantic from the Mississippi states. **1890** Langford *Vigilante Days* (1912) 64 The intelligence spread through the Territories and Mississippi States like wildfire.

(15) **1799** J. Adams *Works* IX. 41 The organization of the government of the Mississippi territory . . . should perhaps be mentioned to Congress. **1857** Benton *Exam. Dred Scott Case* 47 Organizing the Mississippi Territory . . . was done by spreading the ordinance of '87 over it.

b. In the names of, or with reference to, plants and animals: (1) **Mississippi cotton tree,** a tree of the genus *Populus* common in the Mississippi region; (2) **guard,** = **horse guard,** *rare;* (3) **kite,** a kite, *Ictinia mississip-*

piensis, found throughout the southern states; (4) **moss,** =**Spanish moss;** (5) **nut,** (see quots.).

(1) **1814** PURSH *Flora* II. 619 Populus angulata. . . . It is known by the name of Mississippi Cotton Tree. — (2) **1828** *Central Watchtower* (Harrodsburg, Ky.) 19 Nov. 1/1 The herds of cattle would be compelled entirely to leave their pasture grounds were it not for the kind protection they receive from the Mississippi Guards. — (3) **1811** WILSON *Ornith.* III. 80 [The] Mississippi Kite, *Falco Mississippiensis*, . . . I first observed . . . a few miles below Natchez. **1937** BENT *N. Amer. Birds Prey* I. 68 The Mississippi kite feeds almost exclusively on the larger insects, such as cicadas, locusts, grasshoppers, katydids, dragonflies, and large beetles. — (4) *c***1826** STANLEY *Jrnl.* 243 (*footnote*), The Mississipi Moss, also called the Spanish Beard in its natural state resembles large masses of Vermicelli.

(5) **1775** WASHINGTON *Diaries* II. 179 Mississippi Nuts—[which] some think like the Pignut—but longer, thiner shell'd and fuller of meat. **1915** HAWORTH *G. Washington* 150 In March, 1775, he again grafted cherries and also planted peach seeds and seeds of the 'Mississippi nut' or pecan.

c. In miscellaneous combs., often occasional and obs., as **Mississippi alligator, delta, reconstruction, steamer, valley.**

1837 BIRD *Nick of Woods* II. 246 Leaving the land altogether, he . . . launched his broad-horn on the narrow bosom of the Salt, and was soon afterwards transformed into a Mississippi alligator. — **1880** CABLE *Grandissimes* 27 The pilgrim fathers of the Mississippi Delta . . . were taking wives. — **1868** *N.Y. Herald* 4 July 6/1 A committee of five, appointed by the Mississippi Reconstruction Convention, is in session. — **1847** ROBB *Squatter Life* 142 A select party of river cronies . . . were seated around him upon the boiler deck of a Mississippi steamer, as she sped along one bright June night. — **1839** *Niles' Reg.* 3 Aug. 368/1 The Mississippi valley, that is to say, country drained by the Mississippi and its tributaries, has been estimated at 1,400,000 square miles. **1942** FAIRCHILD *Cats* 115 This is the flea most frequently found annoying man in the Mississippi Valley, in Texas and westward to the Pacific Coast.

As the last term in **Father, trans-Mississippi.**

Mississippian ˌmɪsəˈsɪpɪən, *a.* and *n.*

1. A native or resident of the Mississippi region or state.

1775 ADAIR *Indians* 93 'The ugly yellow French,' (as they [*sc.* Indians] term the Missisippians). **1855** *S. Lit. Messenger* XXI. 4 At this period a new and interesting chapter opens in the career of this distinguished Mississippian. **1948** *Dly. Ardmoreite* (Ardmore, Okla.) 4 May 1/6, I recognize our Negroes, as do all good white Mississippians, as a part of our citizenry.

2. Mississippian pacer, (see quot. and cf. **Narraganset pacer**). *Obs.*

1835 INGRAHAM *South-West* II. 79 Of every variety of gaited animals . . . the Mississippian pacer is the most desirable.

3. *Geol.* (See quot. 1909.) Also **Mississippian age, time.**

1909 *Cent. Supp.* 815/3 Mississippian. . . . In the scheme of classification and nomenclature of the rocks adopted by the United States Geological Survey, the purely marine sedimentation of the early or Lower Carboniferous rocks of the interior or Mississippi basin. **1916** *Proc. Iowa Acad. Sci.* XXIII. 166 These formations were tilted to the southwestward and partly truncated in late Mississippian time. **1947** *Geol. Survey Kans.* Bul. 66, 32 During early Mississippian time there was extensive deposition of marine dolomitic limestone and some shale. **1949** *Photogrammetric Engineering* June 239 The lowlands are developed principally on the softer rocks of Lower Pennsylvanian . . . and Upper Mississippian (Windsor) age.

Mississippi Bubble. A financial scheme terminating disastrously, devised in France by John Law, who in 1717 formed a company and issued paper money based upon expected gains through colonization and trade in the Mississippi region, particularly Louisiana.

1767 FRANKLIN *Writings* V. 10 There have been . . . *Missisippi* and *South-Sea* Schemes and Bubbles. **1888** CABLE in *Cent. Mag.* Nov. 114/2 When John Law, author of that famed Mississippi Bubble . . . failed at his efforts of colonization on the Arkansas, his Arkansas settlers came down the Mississippi. **1947** *Chi. D. News* 22 Jan. 14/5 A nationally recognized authority on the law brushes the present storm aside by classifying it with the famous Mississippi bubble.

Mississippi jager. A heavy, long-barreled muzzle-loading rifle or musket of a type formerly popular among hunters of large game. *Obs.* or *hist.* Cf. next.

1858 GOVE *Letters* 294 One of their men came up with a United States rifle, popularly denominated a Mississippi yager. **1873** COZZENS *Marvelous Country* 168 To the saddles of four of the party was tied an old Mississippi yauger, of antiquated make and flint lock. **1910** SANTLEBEN *Texas Pioneer* 9 Every soldier was armed with . . . a Mississippi yager . . . loaded with a ball and three buckshot.

Mississippi rifle. 1. A large-bore muzzle-loading rifle formerly popular in Mississippi. **2. Mississippi Rifles,** the name of a Mississippi company in the Civil War. Both *obs.*

(1) **1851** GLISAN *Jrnl. Army Life* 92 The old Mississippi rifle, carrying a half-ounce ball, is a favorite with them. **1867** RICHARDSON *Beyond Miss.* 111, I have got twelve Mississippi rifles. — (2) **1943** DEVOTO *Yr. of Decision* 471 It was Jefferson Davis and the First Mississippi Rifles, above all it was the anonymous platoons, who won the battle.

Missouri məˈzʊrɪ, *n.* [See note.]

The name of the state is derived from the name of the river, which received its name at the hands of the French from a tribe of Indians dwelling near its mouth when Marquette visited them in 1673. The name probably meant "people of the big canoes."

1. An Indian of a tribe of the Sioux family, first encountered by Europeans near the mouth of the Missouri River; also, *pl.*, the tribe.

[**1703** LAHONTAN *New Voyage* I. 130 We . . . arriv'd on the 18th at the first Village of the Missouris.] **1807** GASS *Journal* 26 Six of them were made chiefs, three Otos and three Missouris. **1839** MORTON *Crania Americana* 65 Many nations east of the Rocky Mountains have the rounded heads so characteristic of the race, as the Osages, Ottoes, Missouris, Dacotas, and numerous others. **1947** *St. Louis Globe-Democrat* 16 March, The Missouris were a comparatively insignificant tribe, never formidable and steadily dwindling in numbers.

2. A form of dance. *Obs.*

1846 *Sun Weekly* (N.Y.) 8 Aug., I dances notin' now but de Missouri.

3. =**Missouri grape.**

1859 MACKAY *Tour* I. 208 He again selected twelve as alone fit for the production of wine. These twelve were the Catawba, . . . the Missouri [etc.].

4. In combs.: (1) **Missouri Act,** the Congressional enactment under which Missouri was admitted into the Union; (2) **Compromise,** see as a main entry; (3) **controversy,** the controversy that arose in Congress over the admission of Missouri into the Union; (4) **Pike,** an emigrant from Missouri, *obs.;* (5) **question,** the question in Congress of the conditions under which Missouri should be admitted into the Union, and problems regarding slavery that arose in this connection; (6) **raid,** a raid into Kansas during the Kansas struggle (1854–58) by Missourians trying to influence the stand taken by that state on slavery, *obs.;* (7) **rifle,** a heavy large-bore rifle of a type formerly used in the Missouri region, *obs.;* (8) **ruffian,** one of those taking part in the Missouri raids, also **Missouri ruffianism,** *obs.;* (9) **toothpick,** =**Arkansas toothpick;** (10) **weed,** chewing tobacco of a kind made or popular in Missouri, *obs.;* (11) **whisky invasion,** the entry into Kansas in 1890 of liquor dealers of Missouri who claimed that, in spite of Kansas' prohibition laws, it was legal to sell liquor there in its original packages.

(1) **1857** BENTON *Exam. Dred Scott Case* 107 It even went beyond the words of the Missouri act—entered its spirit. — (3) **1854** BENTON *30 Years View* I. 10/1 And thus ended the 'Missouri controversy,' or that form of the slavery question which undertook to restrict a State from the privilege of having slaves if she chose. — (4) **1885** *Harper's Mag.* May 832/1 Its fifteen or twenty male inhabitants represented every class of society from the Boston lawyer down to the Missouri Pike.

(5) **1819** J. ADAMS in Jefferson *Writings* XV. 236 The Missouri question, I hope, will follow the other waves under the ship, and do no harm. **1884** BLAINE *20 Years of Congress* I. 15 The 'Missouri question' . . . formally appeared in Congress in the month of December, 1818. — (6) **1872** TICE *Over Plains* 11, I also met . . . Gen. B. F. Stringfellow, conspicuous in the Missouri raids some sixteen and more years ago. — (7) **1853** *Harper's Mag.* Aug. 323/1 Lewis . . . carried a long Missouri rifle. **1856** *Ib.* Oct. 594/1 A Missouri rifle was slung across his back. — (8) **1855** in C. ROBINSON *Kansas Conflict* (1892) 141 Undoubtedly the mass of emigrants are in favor of making Kansas a free state, . . . and would do so if they were not under the dominion of Missouri ruffianism. **1877** JOHNSON *Anderson Co., Kans.* 38 These officers were in full sympathy with . . . the Missouri Ruffians. — (9) **1855** *Herald of Freedom* (Lawrence, Kans.) 9 June (Th.), We mistrust that the author of that statement saw a Missouri toothpick and was frightened out of his wits.

(10) **1847** ROBB *Squatter Life* 142 Tom squared himself for a yarn, wet his lips with a little corn juice, took a small strip of Missouri weed,

and 'let out.' — **(11) 1906** in *Kans. Hist. Soc.* IX. 424 On call of the governor and others, 3000 accredited delegates met in Topeka in June to register the popular protest against the 'Missouri whisky invasion' which was done in an address to the people and most vigorous resolutions on the subject.

b. In obs. combs. of obvious meaning or sufficiently explained in the quots., as (1) **Missouri bake,** (2) **Bird's Eye,** (3) **Indian,** (4) **manufactured,** (5) **marble,** (6) **ore blossom,** (7) **sail-top,** (8) **slope.**

(1) 1870 BEADLE *Utah* 222 Half the time our bread was 'Missouri-bake,' *i.e.* burnt on top and at the bottom, and raw in the middle.— **(2) 1850** *Western Jrnl.* IV. 123 Mr. Romel also exhibited a sample of red wine, which he calls the 'Missouri Bird's Eye.' — **(3) 1765** R. ROGERS *N. Amer.* 194 The inhabitants on this river are called the Missouri Indians. **1817** BRADBURY *Travels* 41 It is customary amongst the Missauri Indians to register every exploit in war, by making a notch for each on the handle of their tomahawks. — **(4) 1850** GARRARD *Wah-To-Yah* xviii. 216 He kept the pipe in his mouth . . . [and] cut from a solid plug of 'Missouri manufactured' a fresh pipe of strong tobacco.

(5) 1859 MACKAY *Tour* I. 232 The country around St. Louis contains not only these immense quantities of iron, but large mines of copper and lead, and some excellent quarries of what has been called 'Missouri marble.' — **(6) 1850** *Western Journal* IV. 123 The sample chosen by the committee as the best, was a specimen of white wine, the pure juice of the Catawba grape. This is the 'Missouri Ore Blossom.' — **(7) 1896** SHINN *Story of Mine* 109 One could see the famous conemaughs, Missouri sail-tops, lumbering ranch wagons, and other types of Eastern manufacture. — **(8) 1857** *Spirit of Times* 26 Sep. 54/1 The Missouri 'Slope,' is fast filling up with settlers from all parts of the Union.

c. In the names of, or with reference to, plants and animals: (1) **Missouri antelope,** =**antelope 1,** cf. **American antelope;** (2) **banana,** the pawpaw, which is quite common in Missouri; (3) **bear,** a hog, *slang, obs.;* (4) **breadroot,** =**Indian breadroot;** (5) **chipmunk,** (see quot.); (6) **currant,** =**buffalo currant;** (7) **flax,** an unidentifiable flax or flaxlike plant found in Missouri, *obs.;* (8) **grape,** a grape, *Vitis rubra,* growing in the southern and central U.S.; (9) **mule,** a mule bred in Missouri, long famous for its fine mules; (10) **silver tree,** (see quot.); (11) **skylark,** a variety of pipit, *Anthus spraguei,* found in the interior plains region of North America; (12) **striped ground squirrel,** =**Missouri chipmunk;** (13) **sucker,** =**gourdseed sucker;** (14) **willow,** (see quot.).

(1) 1805 LEWIS in *Ann. 9th Congress* 2 Sess. 1046 With the addition of the skins of the Missouri antelope, (called cabri by the inhabitants of the Illinois). *c*1810 *Rees's Cyclopædia* (Phila.) *s.v. Antelope,* The forked-horned or Missouri Antelope, so called by captain Lewis. — **(2) 1931** *K.C. Times* 16 Oct., Coming from Kansas, Mr. Garvin is not expected to have a taste for the Missouri bananas. — **(3) 1866** *Harper's Mag.* Oct. 674/2 It was quite common for the boys there to go out of nights and kill 'Missouri bears.' — **(4) 1917** KEPHART *Camping* II. 379 *Potato, Prairie.* Prairie turnip. Indian or Missouri Breadroot. The *pomme blanche* of the voyageurs. *Psoralea Esculenta.* . . . Often sliced and dried by the Indians for winter use. Palatable in any form.

(5) 1868 *Amer. Naturalist* II. 530 Missouri Chipmunk (*Tamias quadrivittatus*). This little Chipmunk I saw in the bare rocky hills of the Mauvaise Territory. — **(6) 1850** S. F. COOPER *Rural Hours* 117 They are extremely fond of the Missouri currant. — **(7) 1846** EMORY *Military Reconn.* 16 On these hills we found cedar growing, very stunted; Missouri flax, several varieties of wild currants. — **(8) 1856** FERGUSSON *America* 272 Those which are chiefly cultivated are the . . . Isabella, and the Missouri grape. — **(9) 1923** *Nation* 17 Oct. 432 Then there is the Missouri mule. He it was who won the war. **1947** *Time* 1 Sep. 17/3 The celebrated Missouri mule, isolationist by temperament, has been having some rude shocks, is due for more.

(10) 1814 PURSH *Flora* I. 114 Oleaster, or Missouri Silver tree. — **(11) 1858** BAIRD *Birds Pacific R.R.* 234 *Neocorys Spraguei,* Sclater Missouri Skylark. . . . This little known species has the general appearance of a titlark. **1941** SETON *Trail of Artist-Naturalist* 299 The strictly prairie birds were gone—of the Missouri skylark, for instance, I saw not one. — **(12) 1874** HITTELL *Resources Calif.* 384 The Missouri striped ground-squirrel has five dark-brown stripes on his back, separated by four gray stripes. — **(13) 1820** RAFINESQUE in *Western Rev.* II. 355 Black Suckrel . . . is also found in the Missouri, whence it is sometimes called the Missouri Sucker. **1911** *Rep. Fisheries 1908* 307 Black Horse (*Cycleptus elongatus*). — A sucker found in the larger streams of the Mississippi Valley. It is also called 'gourd-seed sucker,' 'Missouri sucker,' 'sweet sucker,' and 'suckerel.' — **(14) 1897** SUDWORTH *Arborescent Flora* 125 *Salix missouriensis* . . . Missouri Willow.

Also *Missouri boss, bottom, caravan, code, copper, expedition, fur cap, hunter, region, service, silica, way, whip,* etc.

d. *To be* (or *come*) *from Missouri,* to be extremely skeptical or unwilling to believe anything until it is demonstrated, also in allusive contexts. *Colloq.*

1900 *State Tribune* (Jefferson City, Mo.) 13 Dec. 4/1 Ex-Lieut.-Gov. Chas. P. Johnson thinks he knows the origin of the extensively-used expression: 'I'm from Missouri; you'll have to show me'; at least he can recall its use twenty years ago in Colorado. **1912** C. MCCARTHY *Wisconsin Idea* 291 In the words of the current slang phrase, every Wisconsin legislator 'comes from Missouri' and you have to 'show him.' **1912** *Out West* May 311/1 I'm open like a clam to conviction, but I'm from Missoury, and has got to be showed.

Missourian məˈzʊrɪən, *a.* and *n.*

1. *n.* A native or inhabitant of Missouri.

1820 *Ann. 16th Congress* 1 Sess. 945, I cannot believe that I or any other man or men, are better capable of governing Missourians than they are of governing themselves. **1896** *K. C. Star* 21 July 1/4 'I won't sit down,' said the Missourian, 'you can't make me sit down.' **1948** *Democrat* 2 Dec. 7/2 The 'missing' president is also a Missourian.

b. =**Missouri 1.** *Obs.*

1833 JACKSON in *Pres. Mess. & P.* III. 337 Treaty with the united bands of Ottoes and Missourians, made 21st September, 1833.

c. The English language as spoken in Missouri. *Colloq.*

1867 LUDLOW *Fleeing to Tarshish* 176 The rector's growing reputation for preaching busters, which is the Missourian for pulpit eloquence. **1929** DICKSON *Covered Wagon Days* 133 The border states furnished the bulk of the traffic, with Missouri in the lead Indeed, here was where one heard Missourian 'as she was spoke.'

d. the great Missourian, =**Missourium.** *Obs.*

1841 *Niles' Reg.* 23 Jan. 336/3, I went the other night to look at the greatest curiosity that I have ever seen. It is called *the great Missourian,* and is the skeleton of the greatest animal ever known.

2. *a.* Of or pertaining to Missouri, typical of Missouri.

1943 *Copper Camp* 205 He set the Missourian mule skinners who had been hauling waste to hauling ore instead. **1944** *Chi. Tribune* 30 April IV. 4/3 They must be shown; more Missourian than army mules. **1948** MENCKEN *Supp.* II. 173 D. S. Crumb . . . unearthed a great deal more than was specially Missourian.

As the last term in **ex-Missourian.**

Missouri Compromise. In the congressional act of March 6, 1820, admitting Missouri into the Union as a slave state, a proviso stipulating that slavery should be prohibited in all other states formed from that part of the Louisiana Purchase lying north of 36° 30′ north latitude, the southern boundary of Missouri. Also attrib.

1847 POLK *Diary* 183 He further expressed his willingness to extend the Missouri Compromise west to the Pacific. **1857** BENTON *Exam. Dred Scott Case* 9 There was no necessity, in deciding upon the question of freedom or slavery to Scott and his family, to decide upon the constitutionality of the Missouri Compromise Act. **1938** WHITE *One Man's Meat* 8 It was twelve or thirteen years after the Missouri Compromise had temporarily settled the slavery question that Webster had his first attack of the fever.

b. Missouri Compromise line, a line extending across the area of the Louisiana Purchase at 36° 30′ north latitude, the southern boundary of Missouri.

1820 in BENTON *Exam. Dred Scott Case* (1857) 102 The line is . . . nominated . . . by its popular descriptive appellation of 'the Missouri Compromise Line.' **1848** POLK in *Pres. Mess. & P.* IV. 641 Under menacing dangers to the Union, the Missouri compromise line in respect to slavery was adopted.

Missourium məˈzʊrɪəm, *n.* A specimen of the American *Mastodon giganteus* the skeleton of which was found in Missouri in 1840. Also transf. *Obs.*

1841 in *Nat. Hist.* XXXVII. 172 The Missourium. After minute investigation. . . . I have been led to conclude that the animal was a monster of the Tortoise Tribe. **1847** EMERSON *Rep. Men* (1849) 86 One of the missouriums and mastodons of literature, he [Swedenborg] is not to be measured by whole colleges of ordinary scholars. **1861** BERKELEY *Sportsman* 381 Dr. Kock continues: 'It was about one year after the excavation previously alluded to, that he found in Benton county, Missouri, in the bottom of the "Pomme de Terre river," about ten miles above its junction with the "Osage," several stone arrowheads mingled with the bones of the same nearly entire skeleton, mentioned above as the "Missouriam."'

misstep mɪsˈstɛp, *n.* [Cf. Du. *misstap.*]

1. The loss by a girl or woman of her virtue.

a1800 *Spirit Farmers' Mus.* 205 The 'Squire . . . can Sit on the Sessions, and fine poor Girls for natural missteps. **1892** *Harper's Mag.* June 152/2 Whatever we think of the first misstep of Tess in the immaturity of her girlhood. **1931** F. L. ALLEN *Only Yesterday* 101 The publishers of the confession magazines . . . concentrated on the description of what they euphemistically called 'missteps.'

2. A slip, or wrongly calculated step. Also fig.

1837 *Yale Lit. Mag.* III. 8 Forgetting the round door block, he made a misstep. **1894** *Outing* XXIV. 363/2 One misstep might have resulted in a clear fall of three thousand feet. **1949** *Sat. Ev. Post* 1 Oct. 20/3 Russians . . . turn sick with fear if they make the slightest little misstep.

***mistake,** *v. To mistake one's man,* to form an erroneous idea of the person with whom one has to deal. *Colloq.*

1794 *Mass. Spy* 16 April (Th.), If he supposes I am to be frightened by his pompous accusations, he has much mistaken his man. **1804** *Ib.* 5 Sep. (Th.), It seems that in one instance the General Committee have mistaken their man. **1841** J. Q. ADAMS in *Cong. Globe* 18 June 75/3 Gentlemen mistook their man if they supposed he was to be affected by the machinery of the political party.

mist flower. A composite plant, *Eupatorium coelestinum,* with violet heads, widespread in the warmer parts of the U.S.

1857 GRAY *Botany* 188 *Conoclinium.* Mist-flower. [1 species:] *C. cœlestinum.* **1901** MOHR *Plant Life Ala.* 765 Mist flower. . . . A common weed in cultivated and waste places, and on roadsides. **1949** MOLDENKE *Amer. Wild Flowers* 220 Related to the thoroughworts and bonesets is the mistflower, *Conoclinium coelestinum,* so well known to all travelers in the South.

***mistis,** *n.* In the speech of Negro slaves, mistress, i.e., a woman who owns or manages Negro slaves. Now *hist.*

1852 EASTMAN *Aunt Phillis's Cabin* 217 Master George, take it to mistis, and tell her de truth. **1885** *Cent. Mag.* Sep. 736/2, I ax your pardon, sir, but dis is *my* place, and I has my mistis' orders. **1901** JEWETT *Tory Lover* 84 Oh yis, mistis; her heart's done broke! **1925** MOORE *Old Mistis* 180 My Ole Mistis! My Ole Mistis! Whar you gwine?

***mistrial,** *n.* A trial in which the jury fails to reach a verdict. Cf. ***hang,** *v.* **2.** — **1889** *Boston Jrnl.* 3 May 1/5 Another Mistrial. A Seven Days' Trial of a Case Results in a Disagreement of the Jury. **1889** *Phila. Press* 1 July (*Cent.*), If there had been a mistrial, the colored jurymen voting to acquit and the white jurymen to convict.

mitasses mɪˈtɑs, *n. pl.* [F. *mitas, mitasse,* f. Indian.] (See quots.)

1807 tr. DU LAC *Two Louisianas* 45 Their clothing, which formerly consisted of a small apron, mitasses, and moksins, made of skins, has been exchanged for a dress of blue cloth, and mitasses either scarlet or blue. **1809** A. HENRY *Travels* 115 My legs were covered with *mitasses,* a kind of hose, made, as is the favourite fashion, of scarlet cloth. **1832** R. COX *Adv. Columbia R.* xi. 121 The dress of the men consists solely of long-leggings, called *mittasses* by the Canadians, which reach from the ancles to the hips, and are fastened by strings to a leathern belt round the waist. **1931** READ *La.-French* 97 Mitasses, *f. pl.* Leggings, puttees, as in *une paire de mitasses,* or in a transferred sense, as in *une poule à mitasses,* 'a hen with feathers on its legs.' The word is well known among the French of Louisiana.

mitchella mɪˈtʃɛlə, *n.* [John *Mitchell,* Amer. botanist (d. 1768).] A plant of the genus Mitchella, esp. the partridgeberry, *M. repens.*

1753 C. LINNAEUS *Species Plantarum* (1762) I. 161 *Mitchella.* 1. *Mitchella.* . . . Habitat in Carolina, Terra Mariana, Virginia. **1785** MARSHALL *Amer. Grove* 92 Creeping evergreen Mitchella. This is a small plant, growing upon mossy, northern, shaded banks. **1869** FULLER *Flower Gatherers* 100 This is the Mitchella, in honor of old Dr. Mitchell of New York. **1949** MOLDENKE *Amer. Wild Flowers* 172 The lovely partridgeberries, *Mitchella,* comprise another such genus.

***mite,** *n.* As the last term in **harvest, red, six-spotted mite.**

***Mitella,** *n.* A genus of American herbs of the family Saxifragaceae; also (not *cap.*) a plant of this genus.

1731 MILLER *Gard. Dict., Mitella.* . . Bastard American Sanicle. . . . American Mitella. **1882** *Harper's Mag.* Nov. 853/2 Why should the starry blossom of the fringed mitella seek the snow-flake as its model? **1949** MOLDENKE *Amer. Wild Flowers* 56 Visions of loveliness if examined closely, are the delicately fringed petals of the miterworts or bishopscaps (*Mitella*), resembling magnified snow flakes in their symmetrical and almost indescribable intricacy.

miterwort ˈmaɪtəˌwɜt, *n.* Also **mitrewort.**

1. The coolwort or false miterwort, *Tiarella cordifolia.*

1817–8 EATON *Botany* (1822) 487 *Tiarella cordifolia,* miter-wort, gem-fruit. **1847** WOOD *Botany* 280.

2. A plant of the genus *Mitella,* so called because the capsule resembles a bishop's miter.

1857 GRAY *Botany* 145 *Mitella.* Mitre-wort. Bishop's-Cap. **1898** CREEVEY *Flowers of Field* 363 Mitre-wort. Bishop's-cap. *Mitella diphylla.* . . . Range, from New England to North Carolina. **1942** PEATTIE *Friendly Mts.* 206 Down in the wet moss we find the rare little naked miter wort.

3. An herb, *Cynoctonum mitreola,* of the southern states.

1857 GRAY *Botany* 174 *Mitreola.* Mitre-Wort. . . . [1 species:] *M. petiolata.* . . . Damp soil, from Eastern Virginia southward. **1901** MOHR *Plant Life Ala.* 669 Miter-wort. . . . Central Pine belt to Coast plain.

Mite Society. A society whose object is to collect funds for some charitable purpose by securing small contributions. *Obs.* — **1822** *Missionary Herald* XVIII. 21 Female Mite Soc[iety] for Cher[okee] and Choc[taw] missions [gave $]25. **1883** WILDER *Sister Ridnour* 262 We call upon certain poor, we attend the 'Dorcas,' the socials, the festivals, and mite societies.

***mitt,** *n.*

1. A hand. *Slang.*

1901 H. MCHUGH *John Henry* 10 I'm sitting on the sofa with one mitt lying carelessly on the family album and the other bunched around a $1.70 cane. **1922** R. PARRISH *Case & Girl* 253 There was six to one, an' that 'Red' Hogan had a gun in his mitt.

2. *Baseball.* A form of heavy leather glove having on the palm side a thick pad for the protection of the user's palm.

1902 *Sears Cat.* (ed.115) 326 Boys' Canvas Mitt, made of canvas throughout; a good, cheap mitt for boys; well stuffed. **1949** *Nat. Geog. Mag.* June 738/1 On the ball field the Indians waved their mitts.

3. (See quot. 1903.) Also fortunetelling. Also attrib. *Slang.*

1903 *Dly. Chronicle* 27 May 7/2 'Mit' is the latest Americanese for a corruptionist who accepts a 'dip in the palm.' . . . The word also appears to be used for any very extensive municipal thievery. **1904** *Minneapolis Times* 18 May 5 One of the best known 'mitt' men of the Pacific coast has arrived in Minneapolis after being run out of St. Louis by San Francisco detectives. **1920** COOPER *Under Big Top* 60, I have seen a couple halt before a 'mitt joint' where a greasy Mexican or Syrian or anything else but a gypsy stands.

4. *To tip one's mitt,* to "squeal," to turn informer. *Slang.* Cf. *to tip one's hand, s.v.* **hand,** *n.* **6.** (4).

1908 K. MCGAFFEY *Show-Girl* 68 Some well-meaning Rube had tipped his mitt to the town marshall. *Ib.* 163 They are both wise people and neither tip their mitt.

mitten ˈmɪtn̩, *v.* [Prob. inspired by **to give* (someone) *the mitten,* in same sense.] *tr.* To reject (someone) as a lover. Also **mittening,** *n. Colloq.*

1873 CARLETON *Farm Ballads* (1882) 19 Once, when I was young as you, and not so smart, perhaps, For me she mittened a lawyer, and several other chaps. **1878** R. T. COOKE *Happy Dodd* 289 You a'n't set downright on mittenin' of him then? **1881** M. J. HOLMES *Madeline* 114 When she mittened him, it almost took his life. He was too old for her, she said.

Miwok ˈmaɪwɔk, *n.* [A native word meaning "man."] A division of the Moquelumnan family of Indians in central California, few members of which now survive.

1903 JAMES *Indian Basketry* 57 By far the largest nation of California was the Miwok. **1921** HALL *Yosemite Nat. Park* 51 The name Miwok is not strictly a tribal appelation; it is simply the word in the language of these Indians which means 'people.' **1949** *L.A. Times* 10 April II. 5/2 The name Yosemite was given to this valley by the Miwoks.

***mix,** *n.* **1.** Concrete consisting of a mixture of materials. **2.** Food consisting of various things mixed, also a mixture of ingredients sold in a package ready for cooking.

(1) **1911** *Amer. City* Nov. 289/1 The engineer of Ann Arbor, Mich., has had unqualified success with plain concrete 4½ inch substructure, 1–2–4 mix; superstructure 1–3 mix, suitably treated with a film of crude tar. **1928** BAUER *Highway Materials* 110 The chief advantage of the cold-application mixes is that they may be laid in communities where it is not profitable to institute the regular asphalt paving plant. — (2) **1917** *Ice Cream Trade Jrnl.* Jan. 20/2 The peaches should be prepared at least 14 hours before using in the ice cream mix. **1949** *World-Herald Mag.* (Omaha) 18 Sep. 4/1 Suggest to him that you can make Indian pudding from a packaged mix and the ensuing storm will make the pots and pans rattle on their hooks.

***mixed,** *a.* In combs.: (1) **mixed basis,** a basis for determining representation in Congress by taking into account the white population and the amount of taxable property in a given state, *obs.*, cf. **federal number;** (2) **blood,** see as a main entry; (3) **breed,** a crossbreed, also attrib.; (4) **farming,** farming carried on in conjunction with other pursuits of husbandry, as cattle-raising, fruit-growing, etc.; (5) **feed,** stock feed consisting of a mixture of corn, oats, wheat shorts, etc.; (6) **foursome,** a golf contest between two couples; (7) **militia,** militia consisting of both white men and Negroes; (8) ∗**school,** a school attended by white and by colored pupils; (9) **ticket,** see as a main entry; (10) **tomcod,** a variety of tomcod or frostfish, *Microgadus tomcod*, having mixed coloring; (11) **tribunal,** =**electoral commission.**

(1) **1830** *Va. Lit. Museum* 571/1 Mr. Doddridge moved to amend the amendment, by substituting for the federal number, the mixed basis of white population and taxation combined. — (3) **1775** in *S.C. Hist. and Geneal. Mag.* XVII. 98 It was with difficulty I could get away . . . after seeing his Indigo fields and Spiral Pumps, and breakfasting with his mixed breed daughters. **1838** *Mass. Agric. Survey 1st Rep.* 53, I have had some of the full-blood and some of the mixed breed. — (4) **1872** *Ill. Dept. Agric. Trans.* IX. 66 The majority of farmers, fruit-growers or others, generally succeed best by what is called mixed farming. **1892** *Vt. Agric. Rep.* XII. 132 Our hill farms . . . produce better crops of wheat and oats, and are better adapted to mixed farming.

(5) **1892** *York County Hist. Rev.* 61 A fine line of fine family flour and mixed feed as well as home-made bread. — (6) **1895** *Outing* Monthly Rec. Dec. 47/2 Mixed foursomes at Brookline, on October 26, brought out fourteen couples in a handicap in which Miss W. E. Andrews and G. E. Cabot won. — (7) **1868** *N.Y. Herald* 17 July 5/2 The temper of the body is decidedly against . . . mixed militia. — (8) **1868** *N.Y. Herald* 17 July 5/2 The temper of the body is decidedly against mixed schools. **1871** *Ann. Cyclo. 1870* X. 457/1 [We] raise no questions about mixed schools.

(10) **1814** Mitchell *Fishes N.Y.* 369 *Gadus tomcodus mixtus*, or mixed tom cod; with yet other modifications of colours, and with variations in the rays of the fins. — (11) **1877** *Nation* XXIV. 79 The count began on Thursday at one o'clock, but the Presidential dispute was almost immediately transferred to the Mixed Tribunal, on the papers in the Florida case.

b. In combs., chiefly obs., of obvious meaning or sufficiently explained in the quots.: (1) **mixed ale camp,** (2) **car,** (3) **convention,** (4) **currency,** (5) **forest,** (6) **land,** (7) **theatrical.**

(1) **1903** Owen Kildare *My Mamie Rose* 24 Several houses had well proven reputations as 'mixed ale camps,' meaning thereby places where certain cronies could meet nightly and 'rush the growler.' — (2) **1903** E. Johnson *Railway Transportation* 126 Oftentimes articles consigned to several places must be placed in the same car. Cars so loaded are called 'mixed' cars. — (3) **1902** E. C. Meyer *Nominating Systems* 15 There appeared in 1817 a new variation of our nominating machinery known as a 'mixed convention,' which was a popular convention of delegates from the counties in which the members of the legislature were to sit only in the absence of special envoys or delegates from their county. — (4) **1830** *Cong. Deb.* App. 29 March 100 A mixed currency of paper circulating with gold or silver . . . should always be exchangeable for gold and silver.

(5) **1859** [see **mixture land**]. **1905** *Forestry Bureau Bul.* No. 61, 15 *Mixed forest*, forest composed of trees of two or more species. — (6) **1741** in *Ga. Hist. Soc. Coll.* I. 158 Oak and Hickory, or Mixt Land. — (7) **1889** *Cent. Mag.* March 751/2 A new kind of amateur theatricals has in turn sprung up, called mixed theatricals, consisting of performances in which both professionals and amateurs take part.

mixed blood. 1. Descent from two or more races, as white and Indian, or white and Negro. Also **mixed-blooded,** *a.* **2.** A person of mixed blood.

(1) **1817** S. Brown *Western Gaz.* 244 About one half of the Cherokee nation are of mixed blood by intermarriages with the white people. **1866** *30th Congress* 1 Sess. Sen. Ex. Doc. No. 26, 52 The committee have not discovered . . . that the mixed-blooded slave has been elevated in the moral virtues of the white race as he advanced toward it in color. **1945** *Reader's Digest* Aug. 51 Census Bureau enumerators in 1940 were directed to list as Indians 'any person of mixed blood if one quarter or more.' — (2) **1858** Thoreau *Maine Woods* 137 The two mixed-bloods . . . went off up the river. **1947** *Amer. Sp.* April 81 To distinguish this type of mixed-bloods from mixed-bloods of biracial origin [etc.].

mixed ticket. 1. (See quot. 1871.) **2.** =**fusion ticket. 3.** (See quot.) *Obs.*

(1) **1871** De Vere 270 *Sticker* is the familiar name of a candidate printed on a slip of paper with the back gummed, to be pasted over the name of another candidate by those who wish to vote a *split* ticket; the term originated in 1860 in Pennsylvania as a *mixed* ticket. **1885** *Mag. Amer. Hist.* April 396/2 A 'Split ticket' represents different divisions of a party. A 'Mixed ticket' combines the nominees of different parties. — (2) **1872** *Newton Kansan* 10 Oct. 2/2 For our part we have rather favored a union or mixed ticket for our county officers. — (3) **1888** Lindley *Calif. of South* 376 There is also what is known as a 'mixed ticket,' viz., second class, to the Missouri River, and third class, from the Missouri River to the Pacific coast. The purchaser of a mixed ticket must carry his own blankets.

∗**mixer,** *n.*

1. A bartender.

1854 Longfellow *Poetical Works* (1893) 197/1 To the sewers and sinks With all such drinks, And after them tumble the mixer. **1919** T. K. Holmes *Man from Tall Timber* 93 [He] drank several insidious concoctions of the hotel's most famous 'mixer.'

2. A person evaluated as to his ability to get along with other people, esp. in groups. Orig. **good mixer.**

1896 Ade *Artie* 105, I'm a good mixer. **1902** Moore *Songs & Stories* 185 Being self-important and arrogant and a poor 'mixer,' he had met the fate of all such in this free country and been left in the ranks. **1945** Service *Ploughman* 309 He was a good mixer, oozed geniality, and had great gifts of chaff and humour.

3. A social gathering for making people acquainted with each other (see also quot. 1941). *Colloq.*

1929 *Dly. Maroon* (Chi.) 1 Oct. 1/2 All students are invited to an acquaintance mixer to be held tonight from 7 to 8 at Reynolds clubhouse. **1941** *Square Dance* (Ill. W.P.A.) 211 Mixers is the general terminology applied to round dances in which partners are constantly changed. . . . Miss Tucker or Old Dan Tucker. This is a mixer in which the two step is the basic dance. **1948** *Downers Grove* (Ill.) *Rep.* 21 Oct. 1/8 The Trojan Fathers Fall Mixer will take place Tuesday, Oct. 26 at the high school auditorium.

∗**mixings,** *n. pl.* Materials for mixing drinks. *Slang. Obs.* — **1862** Lowell *Biglow P.* 2 Ser. i. 21 Le''s liquor, Gin'ral, you can chalk our friend for all the mixins.

mixologist ˌmɪksˈɑlədʒɪst, *n.* A skilled mixer of drinks, a bartender. *Slang.*

1856 *Knickerb.* XLVII. 615 Who ever heard of a man's . . . calling the barkeeper a mixologist of tipicular fixins? **1908** Davenport *Butte Beneath X-Ray* 45 Brandy and cigarettes were furnished by an expert mixologist from the Thornton Hotel. **1948** *New Yorker* 6 Nov. 62/3 In 1901, the *Police Gazette*, then at the apex of its educational influence, attempted to revive and glorify *mixologist*, but the effort failed miserably.

mixture land. (See quot.) *Rare.* — **1859** Hillhouse tr. Michaux *Sylva* I. 169 In the district of Maine I have always found the Moose Wood most vigorous in mixed forests, or what are called *Mixture lands*.

∗**mobby,** *n.* The liquid, used as a beverage or for distilling, obtained by crushing apples or peaches (see quot. 1871).

1705 Beverley *Virginia* iv. 699 Others make a Drink of them [*sc.* peaches], which they call Mobby, and either drink it as Cyder, or Distill it off for Brandy. This makes the best Spirit next to Grapes. **1800** Boucher *Glossary* p. xlix, *Mobbie;* the liquid, as first expressed from the fruit, and which is afterwards distilled, and thus becomes peach or apple brandy. **1871** De Vere 507 *Mobee* or *Mobby* . . . is frequently applied in the South to what in England would be simply called a 'punch.'

Mobilian moˈbilɪən, *a.* and *n.* [f. an Indian word of doubtful meaning. Poss. related to Choctaw *moeli*, to row, paddle.]

1. An Indian of an extinct Muskhogean tribe whose early home was prob. Mauvila, or Mavilla, supposed to have been at or near Choctaw Bluff on the Alabama River.

1775 Adair *Indians* 318 [The Choctaws] killed the strolling French pedlars, — turned out against the Missisippi Indians and Mobillians. **1899** Cushman *Hist. Indians* 73 That the Mobilians, as they were called by the early writers, were a clan of ancient Choctaws there can be no doubt whatever. **1922** *Arrow Points* Jan. 14 In later years, the Mobilians inhabited that region near to the point settled by the French in 1701.

2. A native or inhabitant of Mobile, Ala.

1863 Cumming *Hospital Life* (1866) 79/1 Refugeeing . . . is not the best thing in the world. But Mobilians will have to do as others have done before in the world. **1887** *Courier-Journal* 19 Jan. 6/1 Mobilians are jubilant over the new route cotton is taking, and have big hopes of an increase in the business. **1949** *Chi. Tribune* 20 Feb. vii. 6/5 The story most generally accepted by Mobilians gives a homesick Frenchman credit for turning the city into a mecca for flower lovers.

3. (See quots.)

1907 Hodge *Amer. Indians* I. 916/1 The so-called Mobilian trade language was a corrupted Choctaw jargon used for the purposes of intertribal communication among all the tribes from Florida to Louisiana, extending northward on the Mississippi to about the junction of the Ohio. It was also known as the Chickasaw trade language. **1947** Martin *Indians* 68 In the Southeast a Choctaw jargon called 'Mobilian' was spoken from Florida to Louisiana and up the Mississippi River as far north as the Ohio.

Mobilianer moˌbɪlɪˈænɚ, *n.* [f. *Mobile*, Alabama.] A freshwater turtle, *Pseudemys alabamensis*, of the South. — **1842** Holbrook *N. Amer. Herpetology* I. 74 [In] the New Orleans market . . . it is known under the name Mobilianer. **1911** *Rep. Fisheries 1908* 317 The most common used for food are the 'red-bellied terrapin' (Pseudemys rugosa), the 'mobilianer' (P. mobiliensis), and the 'yellow-bellied terrapin' (P. scabra).

Mob Town. (See quots.) — **1889** Farmer 47 Mobtown.—The city of Baltimore. This place has always been, and still is, notorious for the gangs of roughs and rowdies which infest its streets. **1946** *Sat. Ev. Post* 11 May 15/2 Baltimore . . . in an earlier time when it was only moderately industrialized . . . was known, with good reason, as 'Mob-town.'

moccasin ˈmɑkəsn̩, *n.* [Algonquian.]

1. A soft-soled shoe, usu. made of skin, of a type worn orig. by American Indians.

1612 Smith *Works* (1910) I. 44 *Mockasins.* Shooes. **1709** Lawson *Carolina* 191 Sometimes, they wear Indian Shooes, or Moggizons, which are made after the same manner, as the Mens are. **1791** J. Long *Voyages* 36, I also made makissins, or Indian shoes. **1834**

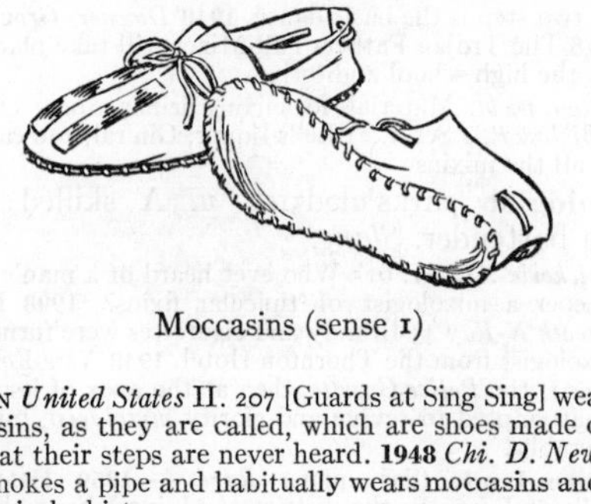

Moccasins (sense 1)

Arfwedson *United States* II. 207 [Guards at Sing Sing] wear on their feet mocassins, as they are called, which are shoes made of woollen yarn, so that their steps are never heard. **1948** *Chi. D. News* 11 June 16/7 He smokes a pipe and habitually wears moccasins and a checkered lumberjack shirt.

2. = **moccasin snake.**

1784 Smyth *Tour* I. 148 The more silent and dangerous moccossons also abound, especially in and near the swamps. **1855** Simms *Forayers* 549 [Have I] had the happiness to eat of the rattlesnake, the viper, the moccasin, or the boa-constrictor? **1948** *Nat. Hist.* April 188/1 Rattlesnakes, copperheads, moccasins, or coral snakes are not to be feared so much as they are to be respected.

3. A sleight-of-hand game resembling thimblerig played by American Indians (see quot. 1892). *Obs.*

1833 Catlin *Indians* I. 88 Groups [of Indians] are engaged in games of the 'moccasin,' or the 'platter.' **1892** *N. & Q.* VIII. 293 The game called Moccasin . . . was played by the use of three moccasins . . . together with the use of three leaden balls. The game was to shuffle the leaden balls and cover more than one ball with one moccasin and have it appear that each moccasin had a ball under it, when really one or more moccasins had no ball under it. This made a game of gambling among the Indians.

4. In combs.: (1) **moccasin awl,** an awl used in making moccasins, now *hist.;* (2) **carrier,** in an Indian war party, one having charge of the moccasins needed by the party, *rare;* (3) **fish,** (see quots.); (4) **flower,** see as a main entry; (5) **game,** = **moccasin 3,** *obs.;* (6) **Joe,** (see quot.); (7) **pac,** = **shoepack;** (8) **plant,** = **moccasin flower;** (9) **Rangers,** (see quot. 1866), *obs.;* (10) **snake,** any one of various pit vipers of the genus *Agkistrodon*, esp. *A. piscivorus*, also used of other snakes having a superficial resemblance to serpents of this genus; (11) **telegraph,** = **grapevine telegraph,** *colloq.*

(1) **1757** *Lett. to Washington* II. 80 Mocoson Auls . . . 16, Pounds of Thread . . . 8. **1886** Z. F. Smith *Kentucky* 746 [He had] no other instruments than a knife, a moccasin awl, and a pair of bullet-molds. **1948** Dick *Dixie Frontier* 295 The only tools necessary were a knife and a moccasin awl made from the back spring of an old clasp knife. — (2) **1812** Stuart *Narratives* 14 Some whose family have much influence may be indulged with the privilege of being mogsan carrier to a war party. — (3) **1807** J. Scott *Md. & Del.* 140 [In Harford County is] Swan creek, which affords an abundance of excellent fish called mockason, or sun fish, and herrings. **1889** Farmer 47 Mocasson fish.—In Maryland, the name given to a species of sun-fish. **1907** Hodge *Amer. Indians* I. 916 After the moccasin have been named moccasin fish (Maryland sunfish), moccasin flower [etc.].

(5) **1847** Lanman *Summer in Wild.* 123 The younger Indians commenced playing their favorite Moccasin game. **1870** McClung *Minnesota in 1870* 165 The moccasin game, being peculiarly an Indian invention, deserves to be here mentioned. — (6) **1893** Roosevelt *Wilderness Hunter* 265 The grizzly bear is known to the few remaining old-time trappers of the Rockies and the Great Plains . . . as 'Moccasin Joe' . . . in allusion to his queer, half-human footprints, which look as if made by some misshapen giant, walking in moccasins. — (7) **1917** *Outing* Jan. 515/2 These moccasin 'pacs' stand water, wear like iron, and *never* can hurt your feet. — (8) **1850** S. F. Cooper *Rural Hours* 111 We found also a little troop of moccasin plants in flower.—(9) **1862** *N.Y. Tribune* 3 June 5/1 This country of the Alleghenies is rife with stories . . . of the strength and exploits of the 'Moccasin Rangers.' **1866** F. Kirkland *Bk. Anecdotes* 406 Among the rebel guerrilla organizations, the most noted band was that known by the name of 'Moccasin Rangers.'

(10) **1765** J. Bartram *Diary* 5 Aug., We killed a Mocasine snake & toward noon it rained & thundred excedingly. **1904** M. D. Conway *Autobiog.* 12 A meadow we had to cross was the haunt of moccasin snakes. — (11) **1927** *Sat. Ev. Post* 23 July 3/3 That agency known to white men as the Moccasin Telegraph, by which odd bits of news are flashed from one isolated native camp to another. **1931** *Amer. Folk-Lore* XLIV. 3 The country schools that I know average about twelve pupils each, and these youngsters are the 'moccasin telegraph' by which the coming play party is announced. **1946** *This Week Mag.* 10 Aug. 17/3 And the word spreads through the woods by 'moccasin telegraph' that the Chief Forester has arrived.

Also *moccasin feet, making, print, string, track, trail,* etc.

As the last term in **beaded, canvas, ghost, highland, Indian, land, northern, swamp, upland, water, yellow moccasin.**

moccasined ˈmɑkəsn̩d, *a.* **1.** Of a foot: Clad or incased in a moccasin. **2.** (See quots.) *Slang.*

(1) **1928** Cooper *Wish-ton-Wish*, xxiv, The two chiefs left the piazza in the noiseless manner of the moccassined foot. **1947** *Chr. Sci. Monitor* 20 Dec. III. 5/3 Moccasined feet move with exquisite precision in intricate patterns. — (2) **1859** Bartlett 275 *Moccasoned,* intoxicated. South Carolina. **1871** De Vere 35 In the South a man made drunk by bad liquor is said to have been 'bitten by the [moccasin] snake,' or simply to be *mocassined.*

moccasin flower. The bastard hellebore, the lady's slipper, or any of various American orchids, as *Cypripedium acaule.*

1680 in Ray *Hist. Plant.* (1688) II. 1926/1 Helleborine flore rotundo luteo, purpureis venis striato. The Mockasine flower. **1700** Plukenet *Opera Bot.* III. 101 *Helleborine Virginiana.* . . . The Molkasin Flower. **1784** Cutler in *Mem. Acad.* I. 486 Lady's Slipper. . . . Catesby says, the flowers of this plant . . . were in great esteem with the Indians for decking their hair. They called it the Moccasin Flower. **1881** *Harper's Mag.* Dec. 20/2 All who love the hemlock woods will remember the common cypripedium, or moccasin-flower, also called lady's slipper. **1949** *Jrnl. N.Y. Bot. Garden* March 50 Through the drier area . . . are the pink slippers of the moccasin flower.

mochila moˈtʃilə, *n. W.* Also **machilla.** [Sp. in same sense.] A large piece of leather or skin covering a saddle. Now *hist.*

1856 *Harper's Mag.* Oct. 504/1 He rode a heavy black mule with bearskin *machillas.* **1913** G. D. Bradley *Story of Pony Express* 58 The *mochila* had four pockets called *cantinas* in each of its corners. **1946** Adams *Album Amer. Hist.* III. 95 Many riders and even more ponies carried the mail, but only the *mochila* made the entire trip.

mockbird ˈmɑkˌbɝd, *n.* = **mockingbird.**

1649 *Descr. Virginia* 15 We have . . . one Bird we call the Mockbird; for he will imitate all other Birds notes. **1791** W. Bartram *Travels* 11 Harbours and groves . . . filled with the melody of the chearful mockbird, warbling nonpareil. **1917** *Birds of Amer.* III. 175 Mockingbird. . . . [Also called] Mock bird.

* **mocker,** *n.*

1. = **mockingbird.** Cf. **French mocker.**

1773 *Phil. Trans.* LXIII. 286 From the attention which the mocker pays to any . . . sort of disagreeable noise, these capital notes would be always debased. **1886** *Cent. Mag.* Jan. 435/2 Ef a gal puts on a man's hat when she hears a mocker sing at night, she'll git married that year. **1947** *Democrat* 25 Dec. 1/5 My, isn't that just like the old mocker himself!

2. mockernut, a species of hickory, *Carya alba.* In full **mockernut hickory, mockernut tree.** Cf. **hardbark hickory,** and **square mockernut.**

In this word the origin of "mocker" is uncertain.
1804 MICHAUX *Voyage à l'Ouest* 17 L'on y observe cependant différentes espèces d'arbres, entr'autres, ... le *Juglans tomentosa*, Mocker-nut. **1810** ——— *Arbres* I. 20 *Mocker nut hickory* ... dans N.Y. et N.J. **1814** PURSH *Flora Amer.* II. 638 *Juglans tomentosa*.... This is known under the name of Mocker Nut, White-heart Hickory or Common Hickory. **1926** ROBERTS *Time of Man* 364 When I see you dance under the mockernut tree I says to myself, 'She's like a flower in bloom.' **1949** COLLINGWOOD & BRUSH *Knowing Your Trees* 152/1 Attaining maturity at 250 to 300 years, mockernut hickory sometimes reaches a height of ninety or a hundred feet.

Mochila

mockingbird ˈmɑkɪŋˌbɜd, *n.* Any one of various American birds having an aptitude for mimicry, esp. *Mimus polyglottos*, found chiefly in the eastern and southern parts of the U.S.
1676 *Phil. Trans.* XI. 631 There are also divers kinds of small Birds, whereof the *Mocking-bird*, the *Red-bird*, and *Humming-bird*, are the most remarkable. **1741** LUCAS *Jrnls. & Lett.* (1850) 11, I promised to tell you when the mocking bird began to sing. **1817** E. P. FORDHAM *Narr.* 47 The Mocking-bird which is here, as the Robin is in England, esteemed sacred, would scarcely avoid us. **1949** *Reader's Digest* Aug. 97/2 It is colored in bluish grays and white, rather like a mockingbird.
transf. **1890** *Stock Grower & Farmer* 19 July 4/4 Arizona Nightingale; Otherwise 'burro,' sometimes termed 'mockingbird.'

b. Mockingbird State, Florida.
1948 *Newsweek* 7 June 27/1 To the surprise of the Mockingbird State politicos, he ran a very close third.
As the last term in **English, French, ground, mountain, red, sandy, western mockingbird.**

mocking thrush. Any bird of the subfamily Miminae, esp. a thrasher. Also with a qualifying term. Cf. **Californian mocking thrush.**
1839 AUDUBON *Ornith. Biog.* V. 336 Townsend's mocking thrush ... [is] cinereous brown above, whitish below, with a long rounded tail. **1847** EMERSON *Poems* 144 A mocking thrush, a wild-rose, a rock-loving columbine, Salve my worst wounds. **1917** *Birds of Amer.* III. 175 Mockingbird.... [Also called] Mocking Thrush.

mocking wren. 1. =**Carolina wren. 2.** =**Bewick('s) wren.**
(1) **1844** *Nat. Hist. N.Y., Zoology* II. 55 The Mocking Wren. *Troglodytes Ludovicianus* ... is celebrated for his mimicry and powers of song. **1874** BAIRD *Hist. N. Amer. Land Birds* I. 142 The great Carolina or Mocking Wren, is found in all the Southeastern and Southern States from Florida to Maryland. **1917** *Birds of Amer.* III. 189. — (2) **1890** *Cent.* 3811/1 *Mocking-wren*, ... Bewick's wren (*T[hryothorus] bewicki*).

* **mock orange.**
1. The laurel cherry, *Laurocerasus caroliniana.*
1766 STORK in J. Bartram *Journal* 9 There is an evergreen sort of this Bird or Cluster-cherry, which grows about 30 feet high in S. Carolina, and from the beauty of its evergreen shining leaves is called the Mock-orange. **1893** *Amer. Folk-Lore* VI. 140 *Prunus Caroliniana*, mock-orange; wild peach. Southern States.
2. The Osage orange, *Maclura pomifera.* Also attrib.
1814 BRACKENRIDGE *Views La.* 59 There is particularly one very beautiful [tree], bois jaune, or yellow wood: by some called the mock orange. **1944** HARPER *Weeds* 93 *T[oxylon] pomiferum* Raf. (*Maclura aurantiaca*, Nutt.) known as Osage orange, mock orange, or bois d'arc. **1947** B. HAILE *Prayer Stick Cutting* 190 She carries a mock orange bow in her left hand.
3. Any gourd that resembles an orange.
1842 *Lowell Offering* II. 68 There were apples, pears, melons, a mock-orange, a pumpkin, and a crooked cucumber. **1892** *Amer. Folk-Lore* V. 96 *Lagenaria sp.*, mock orange. N. Ohio; Central Ill.
4. The snowbell, *Styrax grandifolia.*
1860 CURTIS *Woody Plants N.C.* 101 Mock Orange.... A very beautiful shrub.
5. The shaddock, *Citrus grandifolia.*
1868 *Rep. Comm. Agric. 1867* 142 The Shaddock ... is called ... sometimes in this country Mock-orange, or Forbidden Fruit.
6. (See quot. 1890.) Also attrib.
1890 *Cent.* 3811/1 mock-orange.... Any plant of the genus *Philadelphus*, but especially *P. coronarius*. Its fragrance in blossom resembles that of orange-flowers. **1945** *Barnum* (Colo.) *News* 20 July 1/3 The setting was made pretty by a huge basket of Peonies, and a large bouquet of Mock Orange blossoms.

mocock məˈkɑk, *n.* [Of Algonquian origin.] A container, made of birchbark and in various sizes (see quots. 1805, 1905), used for maple sugar.
1796 *Mich. Hist. Coll.* XII. 208 The Ottawas, Inhabitants of the Villages of L'Arbre Croche have this day presented in Council Forty four Makaks of Indian Sugar. **1805** in GATES *Fur Traders* 273 Margoe sent a Mocock Sugar 70 lb Net. **1846** LANMAN *Summer in Wild.* (1847) 71 Each of them presented me with a pair of moccasons, and placed before me whole mocucks of maple sugar. **1905** *N.Y. Ev. Post* 6 May, An old squaw stopped to offer a small mocock, a birch-bark box holding perhaps a pound of maple sugar. **1949** *Wis. Mag. Hist.* March 324 These cans went to market along with the birchbark *mokuks*, those bark boxes with rounded corners sewed on with basswood fiber and full of patty cakes of granulated sugar.

Mocock

* **model,** *n.*
1. Model A (Ford), a type of Ford car, later than the Model T, with a standard gearshift. Cf. next.
1927 *Ariz. Highways* Nov. 37 Carbon-forming oils got an awful blow when 'Model A' succeeded 'Model T.'! **1935** *Montgomery Ward Cat.* 603 Wards [*sic*] Auto Tops.... Tailored to Fit Your Open Car.... For Model A Fords state if Regular or De Luxe. **1948** *Shelby* (Mont.) *Promoter* 16 Sep. 3/6 Their little old 'Model A' covered 5,000 miles through the states of the southwest.
2. Model T (Ford car), an early type of Ford having only two speeds and a hand gasoline feed.
1918 A. R. BLESSING *Automobiles* 38 The Model T Ford car, its construction, operation and repair. **1949** *This Week Mag.* 28 May 11/2 He drove a Model T out on the Edwards Plateau on his first trip West.
b. *transf.* Anything that is outmoded. *Jocose.*
1947 *Reader's Digest* Jan. 119/1 Such simple demands as wages, hours and working conditions are strictly Model T. **1948** *Time* 1 March 66/2 The Nagasaki and Bikini bombs, now much improved, are called 'Model Ts' by atomic experts.

* **model,** *v. intr.* and *tr.* To serve as a model, to wear (dresses, coats, etc.) to show them to advantage to prospective customers. Also * **modeling,** *n.*
1927 *Cleveland Press* 4 March, Vivian, the heroine of The Press serial, will model Saturday in the shoe section of the Bailey Co. **1931** *Durant* (Okla.) *D. Democrat* 29 Oct. 3/2 See them [i.e., coats] modeled during style promenade tomorrow 10 to 11 A.M. **1949** *Chi. Tribune* 17 Feb. 10/3, I never thought of modeling as a career, anyway.

* **Moderators,** *n. pl.* **1.** Those who opposed the South Carolina Regulators (1767–69). **2.** In Texas and elsewhere, an illegal and often criminal group organized to oppose a band of regulators. Both *obs.*
(1) **1769** in GREGG *Hist. Ole Cheraws* (1867) 182 A new set of people, who call themselves Moderators, have appeared against the Regulators. — (2) **1842** J. STURGE *Visit to U.S. in 1841* 167 Late accounts from Texas inform us that gangs of organised deperadoes [*sic*] under the names of moderators and regulators, are traversing its territory, perpetrating the most brutal outrages. **1889** BANCROFT *Hist. No.*

Mexican States & Texas II. 355 A society which styled itself the Moderators was organized, and a kind of vendetta warfare was carried on [with the so-called Regulators] for three years.

Modoc ˈmodɑk, *n.* [In Hodge explained as f. Amer. Indian *Môatokhi*, southerners, but cf. quots. 1873, 1888.] An Indian of a small tribe formerly occupying a portion of the California and Oregon frontier. Also, *pl.*, the tribe of such an Indian. In full **Modoc Indians.**

1873 *Overland Mo.* June 535/1 Men best acquainted with this tribe, say that their true name is Moädoc—a word which originated with the Shasteecas, who applied it indefinitely to all wild Indians or enemies. **1888** BANCROFT *Calif. Inter Pocula* 446 Modoc is a Shasta word, signifying stranger, or hostile, and so was taken up and applied to these savages by white men hearing the Shastas speak of them. **1909** *Indian Laws & Tr.* III. 387 The Secretary of the Interior . . . is . . . directed to restore to the rolls of the Klamath Agency . . . those Modoc Indians now enrolled at the Quapaw Agency. **1947** DEVOTO *Across Wide Missouri* 310 Basil, who was killed by the Modocs at Klamath Lake, was one of the Pathfinder's favorites. **1949** *New Yorker* 2 April 25/2 Broncho Charlie's mother and father were killed by Modoc Indians when he was seventeen.

b. The language of these Indians.

1890 GATSCHET *Klamath Indians* I. xxiii, A smaller pine species, *Pinus contorta* (kápka, in Modoc kúga), which forms denser thickets near the water, is peeled by the Indians . . . to use the fiber-bark for food.

Mogollon ˌmogəˈljon, *n.* ["From the mesa and mountains of the same name in New Mexico and Arizona, which in turn were named in honor of Juan Ignacio Flores Mogollon, governor of New Mexico in 1712–15" (Hodge).] *pl.* Indians belonging to a subdivision of the Apache formerly living in western New Mexico and eastern Arizona. Also attrib.

1864 MOWRY *Ariz. & Sonora* 31 The Apache . . . are best classified under their modern names: the Mescaleros, . . . Mogollones, Chiracahuis, Coyoteros . . . , and the Tontos. **1937** *Southwestern Lore* Sep. 30 All of the pottery produced by the Hohokam people was fired in an oxidizing atmosphere, but so also was the early pottery manufactured by the Mogollones. *Ib.* Dec. 55 In the Mogollon and Pueblo cultures the walls of vessels were thinned by removing excess clay with a scraper.

mogote moˈgotɪ, *n. S.W.* [Sp. in Amer. Sp. sense shown here.] A thick patch of shrubbery. — **1929** DOBIE *Vaquero* 201 (Bentley), I worked for years in the *mogotes* of huisache and mesquite . . . and that brush is so bad that it could hardly be worse.

*** mogul,** *n.*

1. = mogul locomotive.

1883 KNIGHT *Supp.* 613/2 The Mogul is generally accepted as a type of engine especially adapted to the economical working of heavy-freight traffic. **1913** *Collier's* 20 Dec. 13 The great mogul struck the covered wall of the opposite embankment with terrific force. **1949** *Boston Sun. Globe* 8 May (Fiction Mag.) 3/4, I can see the big mogul waiting to take over our train and whip it on to the Coast.

attrib. **1880** *Railroad Gaz.* 27 Feb. 116/1 On another page are published engravings and descriptions of an American 'Mogul' type of locomotive. **1944** JOHNSON *As I Dare* 13 Those old-fashioned mogul engines today are as dinosaurs, and even their bones have rusted into nothingness.

2. mogul locomotive, a heavy passenger and freight locomotive; strictly, one having two pilot-truck wheels and six driving wheels, the driving rod being attached to the middle pair of drivers.

1877 FORNEY *Catechism of Locomotive* 432 'Mogul' locomotives are often used for ordinary freight service where heavy trains must be hauled, and also on steep grades. **1883** KNIGHT *Supp.* 613/1 Mogul . . . locomotives . . . originated in the Baldwin Locomotive Works with the 'E. A. Douglas,' built in 1867. **1947** ROBINSON *Great Snow* 29 Cobb saw a magnificent Mogul locomotive being detached from a long train it had drawn in from Buffalo.

moharra moˈhɑrə, *n.* [Sp. *mojarra*, in same sense.] Any fish of the family Gerridae, or one that is similar in appearance to this. — **1845** STORER in *Mem. Amer. Acad.* ns. II. 336 Gerres brasilianus . . . [is] called, at Porto Rico, 'Moharra.' **1911** *Rep. Fisheries 1908* 317 Surf-Fish (Embiotocidae).—The general name 'perch' is applied to them everywhere along the coast; they are also called . . . 'minny,' 'sparada,' 'moharra,' etc., along their northern range.

Mohave moˈhɑvɪ, *n.* [f. *hamok*, three, + *avi*, mountain, in allusion to the peaks near Needles, Calif., regarded by these Indians as the center of their old territory.] An Indian of a numerous and warlike tribe found along the Colorado River; occas., in *sing.* and *pl.*, the tribe.

1831 PATTIE *Personal Narr.* (1930) 143 We resumed our march, and on the 6th arrived at another village of Indians called Mohawa. **1852** SITGREAVES *Exped. Zuni & Colo. Rivers* (1853) 18 The appearance of the Mohaves is striking, from their unusual stature, the men averaging at least six feet in height. **1887** *Cent. Mag.* May 44/2 Pigments . . . are eagerly sought for temporary personal ornamentation, the Yumas and Mojaves even descending to stove-polish. **1945** MARSHALL *Santa Fe* 188 Southwest of Needles the Sacramento mountains lay stark and grim, and at their feet the low, brush-and-sand roofed hovels of the Mojaves.

attrib. **1858** *Harper's Mag.* Sep. 463/1 When the trading was concluded, the Mojave people sauntered about the camp. **1859** *Harper's Mag.* Oct. 695/2 In New Mexico the Mohave Indians have again broken out into open hostilities. **1879** WILLIAMS *Pacific Tourist* 289/2 The heated sand causes the wind to rush furiously, and early in the history of the road 'Mojave zephyr' was a well-fixed term. **1892** *Outing* April 13/2 The walls and doorways were hung with bright-colored and strange-figured Mojave and Navahoe blankets.

Mogul locomotive with pony truck

b. In the names of plants and animals found in the Southwest, as (1) **Mohave aster,** (2) **ground squirrel,** (3) **mariposa,** (4) **poppy,** (5) **rattler, rattlesnake,** (6) **yucca,** (see quots.).

(1) **1940** JAEGER *Calif. Deserts* 131 When it comes out in force on the gravelly mesas and rocky hills, the Mohave aster [*Aster abatus*] . . . presents an equally striking spectacle. **1949** *Desert Mag.* April 8/3 Golden bush and Mohave aster are in bloom among the rocks. — (2) **1938** HOWELL *Revision N. Amer. Ground Squirrels* 184 The Mohave ground squirrel [*Citellus mohavensis*] is remarkable for the limited extent of its range and for the fact that it has no near relatives. — (3) **1948** *Sierra Club Bul.* March 42 Mohave mariposas (*Calochortus kennedyi*) raise their flaming cups on valley flats below the snow-encrusted peaks. — (4) **1947** *Desert Mag.* July 22/2 You can't go far on the Mojave desert without seeing the Mojave Poppy [i.e., *Eschscholtzia glyptosperma*], often in lavish prodigality.

(5) **1936** *Univ. Ariz. Gen. Bul.* No. 3 104 The Mojave rattlesnake (*C. scutulatus*) occurs in much the same environment as *atrox*. **1940** JAEGER *Calif. Deserts* 88 The common olive-green rattlesnake of the open country in the Mohave Desert is the Mohave rattler (*Crotalus scutulatus*). — (6) **1940** JAEGER *Calif. Deserts* 174 On the high slopes of the New York Mountains and vicinity it consorts with junipers, Mohave yuccas [*Yucca schidigera*], tree yuccas, and piñons.

Mohavean moˈhɑvɪən, *a.* Pertaining to, or characteristic of, the arid plateau comprising the Mojave Desert region of Southern California.

1925 JEPSON *Flowering Plants Calif.* 12 The Mohavean Area [is] an area of the lower Sonoran Life-Zone, about co-extensive with the Mohave Desert. **1940** JAEGER *Calif. Deserts* 38 The Mohavean mesas and interior basins get their share too. *Ib.* 173 The most widespread Mohavean saltbush is *Atriplex confertifolia*. **1948** *Ecological Monographs* April 170/2 The area studied lies in the Mohavian Biotic Province.

Mohawk ˈmohɔk, *n.* [f. a native word. Cf. Narraganset *Mohowaúuck*, "they eat animate things."]

1. An Indian of the most easterly tribe of the Iroquois confederation, first encountered by Europeans in the Lake Champlain region. Also *pl.*, the tribe itself.

1634 WOOD *N. Eng. Prospect* II. i. 49 The very name of a Mohack would strike the heart of a poore Abergenian dead. **1751** *N.J. Archives* 1 Ser. VII. 598 The Susquahannah Indians only want leave from the Mohawks whom they call their Fathers in order to their accepting of a missionary. **1825** NEAL *Bro. Jonathan* I. 101 The Mohawks were a terrible race of Indians; a tribe, of whom all the other savages were afraid. **1948** *Green Bay* (Wis.) *Press-Gaz.* 30 June 16/5 One delegation of Mohawks is en route from New York, the original homelands of the Oneidas.

transf. **1911** HARRISON *Queed* 15 Eight sharp at the same place.—Go on you fat Mohawk you! **1948** *Chi. Tribune* 12 Dec. 1. 20/3 From its doorways surged the sham Mohawks the evening of Dec. 16, 1773.

b. In full **Mohawk Indian(s).**

[**1656** VAN DER DONCK in *N.Y. Hist. Soc. Coll.* 2 Ser. I. (1841) 169, I have also been frequently told by the Mohawk Indians, that far in the interior parts of the country, there were animals . . . of the size and form of horses . . . having one horn in the forehead.] **1705** in *Amer. Sp.* (1948) April 119/2 On the 22nd a Mahock Indian and his Squa being in Town and hearing of my design came & thus addrest us. **1775** *Jrnls. Cont. Congress* III. 365 The Commissioners for transacting Indian Affairs . . . [shall] be desired to obtain from the Mohawk Indians, and the corporation of Albany, a state of the controversy between them. **1947** DOWNEY *Lusty Forefathers* 70 Others set up a howling and a whooping like so many Mohawk Indians.

2. The language of the Mohawk Indians.

1754 EDWARDS *Works* (1808) V. 219 The question is not, whether what is said be . . . Latin, French, English or *Mohawk?* **1818** *Wkly. Recorder* (Chillicothe, O.) 18 Dec. 147/1 They have books containing hymns, prayers, and part of the Bible; English on one page, and Mohawk on the other. **1862** T. F. DEVOE *Market Book* 297 All were talking together, and creating a compound jargon of High-Dutch, Mohawk, and African, accompanied with laughter loud and long.

Also **Mohawk tongue.**

1774 in J. W. LYDEKKER *Faithful Mohawks* 136 With a large & plain Exposition of the Church Catechism & a compendious History of the Bible, all in the Mohawk Tongue.

3. In special combs.: (1) **Mohawk boat,** ?a boat similar to those built by the Mohawk Indians, *obs.;* (2) **corn,** (see quot.), *obs.;* (3) **weed,** (see quots.).

(1) **1794** in MATHEWS *Life Andrew Ellicott* 116 We have built a Mohawk boat, (which will be found very serviceable if we go on to Presqu'Isle), to which may be added a number of fine canoes. — (2) *c***1662** JOHN WINTHROP in *N. Eng. Quart.* X. (1937) 127 In the Northerly parts, and Uplands parts . . . they use a peculiar kind of that Corne which is called Mowhawkes Corne, which though planted in June will be Ripe in Season. — (3) **1907** LYONS *Plant Names* 479 U[vularia] perfoliata L., Canada and eastern U.S., Perfoliate or Mealy Bellwort, is called Mohawk-weed. **1931** CLUTE *Plants* 29 The Mohawk-weed (Uvularia perfoliata) is named for another tribe of central New York.

b. Also **Mohawk bean, brier, chief, children, congregation, king, village, warrior.**

1849 EMMONS *Agric. N.Y.* II. 280 Early Mohawk bean. — **1900** C. C. MUNN *Uncle Terry* 157, I lost my boat over back here on the shore, and have had a cheerful time among the Mohawk briers. — **1778** in J. W. LYDEKKER *Faithful Mohawks* (1938) 155 The Mohawk Chief Joseph Brant that was in London in 1776. — **1751** *Ib.* 70, I am informed that Sr Peter Warren has something under his direction for the education of some Mohawk children. — **1779** *Ib.* 163 Besides my Regimental Duty I continue according to my ability to serve the Mohawk Congregation as mentioned in my letter of May 1778. — **1766** ROGERS *Ponteach* II. i, The powerful Mohawk King Will ne'er consent to fight against the English. — **1782** in J. W. LYDEKKER *Faithful Mohawks* 173, I repaired to the Mohawk Village, & was welcomed very affectionately by my indian Flock. — **1870** M. H. SMITH *20 Years Wall St.* 391 That is Vanderbilt,—with nearly eighty winters upon him, yet as erect as a Mohawk warrior.

Mohawking 'mohɔkɪŋ, *n.* Masquerading as a Mohawk Indian and engaging in ruffianly conduct. Also **Mohawkism,** the quality of being a Mohawk. Both *obs.*

The terms here dealt with are puzzling. The *OED* shows that *Mohock* (note the spelling) was used by Swift (1711–12) to refer to a London ruffian or rowdy. The verb *Mohock,* "to assail or maltreat in the manner of Mohocks," is as early in British use as 1718, and *Mohockism* appeared in *Punch* in 1882.

Since *Mohock* is merely a variant spelling of *Mohawk,* it is not possible to show from the evidence at present available that the terms here given are entitled to be regarded as Americanisms. They are included because of the possibility that they may have been formed anew here directly on the noun *Mohawk.* If *Mohawk* was used in this country to mean a ruffian before 1711, we have no evidence of such a use.

1825 NEAL *Bro. Jonathan* I. 227 Does he ever go out 'a mohawking'? Peters alluded to a fashion—when a 'tory' was to be tarred and feathered . . . the people did it in the disguise of Indians. *Ib.* 229 Some loitering rascal who has been out a Mohawking, today. **1855** *Chi. Times* 13 March 3/1 That new implement in modern *Mohawkism*—brass knuckles.

Mohegan mo'higən, *n.* [f. Algonquian *maingan,* wolf.]

1. An Indian of either of two Algonquian tribes that formerly lived along the lower Connecticut River and on the upper reaches of the Hudson. Often, in *pl.,* either of these tribes.

The spellings of this word are varied (see quots.). According to Hodge, the Mahican Indians in early times occupied both banks of the upper Hudson River, while the Mohegan Indians app. had their chief seat orig. on the Thames River in Connecticut. The spellings indicate only a faint tendency on the part of writers to use Mahican and Mohegan consistently for the two branches of the Algonquian family mentioned above. Often, esp. in the attributives, it is not possible to tell which Indians are meant.

[**1612** SMITH *Wks.* (1884) I. 163 For remedy whereof, he sent presently to *Powhatan* to sell him the place called *Powhatan,* promising to defend him against the Monacans.] *c***1614** in *N.Y. Doc. Col. Hist.* I. (1856) (map), Mahican. **1637** J. HIGGINSON in *Mass. H. S. Coll.* 4 Ser. VII. 396 The multitudes of our enimies daily encrease by the falling of Mohigoners, Nepmets [etc.]. **1669** in *N.Y. Doc. Col. Hist.* XIII. 439 Ye Earnest desire of ye Maquases to conclude a firm peace with ye Mohicands. **1788** *Mass. H.S. Coll.* 2 Ser. X. 86 They, as well as the tribe at New London, are by the Anglo-Americans, called Mohegans. **1841** TRUMBULL *Autobiog.* 6 A small remnant of the Mohegans still exists . . . on the banks of the Thames. **1947** DOWNEY *Lusty Forefathers* 127 Its student body has grown to comprise twenty-nine Indian boys and ten Indian girls—Delawares, Mohawks, Oneidas, Montauks, Mohegans, and Narragansetts.

transf. **1829** ROYALL *Pennsylvania* I. 9 Gen. E. was a Bostonian, and had now in his possession the bowl in which the punch was made presented as a treat to the Mohicans (as they were called) who threw the tea overboard, at Boston. **1913** LONDON *Valley of Moon* 118 You're a Mohegan with a scalplock.

2. In miscellaneous combs., as **Mohegan councilor, Indian, language, sachem, sail, tomahawk, tongue.**

1647 in SHEPARD *Clear Sunshine* 26 The Mohegan Counseller . . . is counted the wisest Indian in the Country. — **1817** *Yankee Traveller* 61 He had hoped . . . to have made and cultivated an acquaintance with the celebrated Conundrum; but instead of that, he had been

Boat with Mohegan sail

turned over to an ignorant, frothy, gingling Doctor, who knew no more of philosophy than a Mohegan Indian. **1945** *New Yorker* 23 Feb. 24/1 Long before Bernard Gimbel and Gene Tunney, the U.N.O. site was populated by Mohegan Indians, wildcats, lynxes, beavers, moose, elk, and—according to the Mohegan Indians—unicorns. — **1832** WILLIAMSON *Maine* I. 459 That spoken by the Pawkunawkutts and the natives westward of them, is supposed to be the original *Mohegan* language. — **1637** *Mass. H.S. Coll.* VI. 207 Okace the Mohiganie Sachim had about 300 men with him on Pequt river. — **1894** *Outing* XXIV. 23/2 Fig. 7 shows the Mohican sail, a modification of the balance lug of sixty-five square feet area. — **1880** CABLE *Grandissimes* 25 The year 1682 saw a humble 'black gown' dragging and splashing his way . . . through the swamps of Louisiana, . . . backed by French carbines and Mohican tomahawks. — **1751** GIST *Journals* 49 You send for one of Your Friends that can speak the Mohickon or the Mingoe Tongues well.

b. *The last of the Mohicans,* the final representatives or survivors of a noble race or class, in allusion to the title of J. F. Cooper's well-known novel.

[**1826** COOPER (*title*), The Last of the Mohicans.] **1832** *Boston Transcript* 3 April 2/1 We have seen the last of the Mohigans and the last of the cocked-hats, and we pray that we may be able to say, on the morrow we have seen the last of the snow-storms. **1913** LONDON

Valley of Moon 155 D'ye know what we are?—we old white stock that fought in the wars, an' broke the land, an' made all this? I'll tell you. We're the last of the Mohegans. **1946** HOWE *We Happy Few* 7 You can't pay attention to a thing that John Calcott says because he is the perfect product of the school—our own special Last of the Mohicans.

***moke,** *n.*

1. A Negro. *Slang.*

1856 C. WHITE *Oh, Hush!* 9 Rose, don't you interfere, I'll show dis moke a sight. **1901** *Cosmopolitan* Sep. 637/2 Across the stage have paraded long processions of 'musical mokes,' 'knock-abouts' and 'monologists.' **1945** MENCKEN *Supp.* I. 635 *Moke* was thrown into competition with *coon* in 1899 by the success of 'Smokey *Mokes,*' a popular song by Holzmann and Lind, but is now heard only seldom.

2. (See quot.)

1900 *D.N.* II. 46 *Moke.* 1. An easy-going fellow; one in the habit of asking favors. 2. A moderate bore. Tu[fts College, Mass.].

Moki, see **Moqui.**

***molasses,** *n.*

1. A sweet sirup prepared by boiling down to a desired consistency any one of various vegetable juices or saps, particularly that of sugar cane.

1777 CUTLER in *Life & Corr.* I. 63 Boiled some cornstalk juice into molasses. **1842** *Niles' Reg.* 15 Oct. 112/1 Mr. Brown has four acres of corn which he planted expressly for the purpose of manufacturing mola-ses and sugar. **1925** TILGHMAN *Dugout* 21 The meal was ready; hot biscuits, coffee, molasses and meat. **1945** BOTKIN *My Burden* 55 A whole lot of boys was standing around and bet Green he couldn't tote that barrel of molasses a certain piece.

transf. **1902** G. C. EGGLESTON *Dorothy South* 136 He came and went as he pleased, . . . sometimes staying only long enough to advise Arthur to have a tobacco lot cut before a rain should come to wash off the 'molasses'—as the thick gum on a ripening tobacco leaf was called.

2. In combs.: (1) **molasses barrel,** a strong, well-made barrel for molasses; (2) **cake,** cake sweetened with molasses, also **molasses pound cake;** (3) **candy,** a kind of pulled candy made from molasses and sugar, butter, water, and flavoring boiled down; (4) **candy pulling,** a social gathering at which those present "pull" molasses candy, cf. **candy pull(ing);** (5) **cooky,** a cooky in the making of which molasses is used; (6) **corn-ball,** a confection made by pouring molasses over popcorn and then shaping it into a ball; (7) **fritter,** a fritter to be eaten with molasses; (8) **gate,** (see quots. 1875), cf. ***gate,** ***n.*** **2;** (9) **gingerbread,** gingerbread in the making of which molasses is used; (10) **house,** a building in which molasses is made; (11) **jug,** a jug in which molasses is stored; (12) **shook,** a stave of a kind used in making barrels or hogsheads for molasses; (13) **stew,** =**molasses candy pulling;** (14) **taffy,** =**molasses candy,** also attrib.; (15) **whisky,** (see quot.).

(1) 1846 CORCORAN *Pickings* 29 Isn't that cotton bale dancing a quadrille with the molasses barrel? **1904** TARBELL *Hist. Standard Oil Co.* I. 12 Turpentine barrels, molasses barrels, whiskey barrels . . . were added to new ones made especially for oil. — **(2) 1836** SIMMS *Mellichampe* xlvii, The negro broke his molasses-cake evenly between himself and the soldier, who did not scruple readily to receive it. **1903** M. E. WILLIAMS *Elements of Cookery* 267 Mixing molasses cakes.—Mix milk and molasses and stir them into the flour [etc.]. **1941** FARMER *Boston Cook Book* 642 Molasses Pound Cake. $\frac{2}{3}$ cup butter, $\frac{3}{4}$ cup sugar . . . $\frac{2}{3}$ cup molasses [etc.]. — **(3) 1809** IRVING *Knickerb.* VII. iii, Each . . . he patted on the head, . . and gave him a penny to buy molasses candy. **1945** *This Week Mag.* 15 Dec. 2/2 Cookies, molasses candy, popcorn balls and cider were brought out. — **(4) 1893** *Harper's Mag.* Feb. 441, I invited them all myself late this afternoon; and it is a molasses-candy pulling.

(5) 1887 ALDEN *Little Fishers* xxi, On shelves were displayed tempting pans of ginger cookies, doughnuts, molasses cookies, and soft gingerbread. **1949** *Sat. Ev. Post* 2 April 50/4 With every sizable order for bakestuff that she filled, she threw in half a dozen molasses cookies or as many lemon tarts, just for good will. — **(6) 1941** FARMER *Boston Cook Book* 704 Molasses Corn Balls. 3 quarts popped corn, 1 cup molasses [etc.]. — **(7) 1847** *Carolina Housewife* 119 Molasses Fritters. One quart of flour, one gill of molasses, a tea-spoonful of soda, two of cream of tartar. Fried in boiling lard. — **(8) 1875** KNIGHT 1458/2 *Molasses-gate,* a faucet with a sliding lip at the discharge end, to cut off the flow positively and prevent drip. **1902** *Sears Cat.* (ed. 112) 749 Molasses Gates. Stebbin's pattern. Size given indicates the size of the hole which should be bored. — **(9) 1832** CHILD *Frugal Housewife* 70 A very good way to make molasses gingerbread is to rub four pounds and a half of flour with half a pound of lard.[etc.].

(10) 1864 *Ill. Agric. Soc. Trans.* V. 317 A near neighbor of mine, . . . and his two sons, have a neat molasses house, with an engine to run the crushing mill. — **(11) 1839** *S. Lit. Messenger* V. 65/2 Behind the bar were . . . a molasses jug, a bottle of vinegar, and . . . decanters. **1906** LYNDE *Quickening* 111 The workmen's children . . . called her a mountain cracker when she went down to buy meal or to fill the molasses jug. — **(12) 1820** *Columbian Centinel* 1 Jan. 3/1 Isaac Winslow & Co. . . . Offer for sale. . . . Molasses Shooks, &c. — **(13) 1871** DE VERE 287 The people of the South had always been fond of *molasses stews,* in which the boiling molasses was pulled or tugged out into long strips.—**(14) 1927** BENÉT *J. B.'s Body* 113 And then an awful molasses-taffy voice Behind them yelled 'Halt!' **1946** PARTRIDGE & BATTMANN *As We Were* 13 Molasses taffy was cooked in a kettle on top of the kitchen stove and when ready for pulling was served out in gobs of a size to suit the manipulator.

(15) 1867 *Comm. & Fin. Chron.* 26 Jan. 105 It seems that the most common article produced by distillation is 'molasses whiskey,' or more properly 'rum.'

b. molasses and cabbage, a dish made by combining cooked cabbage and molasses.

1801 HANGER *Life* I. 86, I am not of opinion, because St. John fed upon locusts and wild honey, that a bishop's chief food should be molasses and cabbage, (which, by the by, is a famous dish in America).

As the last term in **cornstalk, maple, milk and, New Orleans, Orleans, pumpkin, sales, sorghum, sulphur and, tree molasses.**

***mole,** *n.*[1]

1. =**ground mouse.** (By error for ******vole.*)

1839 BUEL *Farmer's Companion* 99 Moles or ground-mice cannot penetrate. **1857** *Rep. Comm. Patents 1856: Agric.* 84 Many persons call them [*sc.* meadow mice] 'Moles,' though they are not in the least related to that family.

2. In combs.: (1) **mole bean,** (see quot.); (2) ***shrew,** (*a*) the short-tailed shrew, *Blarina brevicauda,* (*b*) the Gibbs's mole, *Neurotrichus gibbsi;* (3) **tree,** the caper spurge, *Tithymolus lathyrus.*

(1) 1939 *These Are Our Lives* 376 Nothing left now but that old hanging basket of moss and them mole beans. Castor beans, some calls them.They're supposed to keep a mole from rooting up your ground. **(2)** (*a*) **1884** J. S. KINGSLEY *Stand. Nat. Hist.* V. 148 The typical species, called the Mole-shrew, *Blarina brevicauda.* **1917** *Mammals of Amer.* 310 Short-tailed Shrew. *Blarina brevicauda.* . . . Other Name. —Mole Shrew. . . . Western Nebraska and Manitoba eastward to the Atlantic Coast. (*b*) **1890** *Cent.* 3823/1 *Mole-shrew.* . . . The name is also applied to *Neurotrichus gibbsi.* — **(3) 1847** WOOD *Botany* 487 Mole-tree. Caper Spurge. . . . Cultivated grounds and gardens. **1899** *Animal & Plant Lore* 119 'Caper-tree,' or 'mole-tree,' . . . is supposed [in n. Ohio] to keep moles out of flower-beds if planted there.

As the last term in **button-nose, ground, prairie, red, shrew, star-nosed mole.**

mole ˈmoli, *n.*[2] *S.W.* [Amer. Sp. (<Nahuatl) in same sense.] (See quots.) — **1932** BENTLEY 169 *Mole.* . . . A sauce used in Mexican cookery in connection with the serving of meats. Its chief ingredient is chile and sometimes *ajonjoli* (*benne*). . . . The unpalatability of *mole* to most Americans unaccustomed to *chile* gives it a certain notoriety. **1948** *Sat. Ev. Post* 2 Oct. 52/3 Señora Gonzalez does her stuff on such fabulous and sustaining dishes as chicken mole—boiled chicken bathed in a sauce of exotic Mexican spices, cinnamon, chili, mashed-up peanuts and even a dash of chocolate [etc.].

molecular (telephone). A projected type of telephone. *Obs.* — **1887** *Trial H. K. Goodwin* 11 Mr. Swan became connected with the Molecular Telephone Company. *Ib.* 110 He told you about this Molecular Telephone, didn't he? A. He was very enthusiastic about this Molecular; he thought it was the only telephone in the world.

***Moline,** *n. attrib.* Designating agricultural implements and vehicles made in Moline, Illinois. — **1876** *Ill. Dept. Agric. Trans.* XIII. 328 The barshare and shovel plow have been succeeded by . . . the Pekin, the Peoria, the Moline and a wonderful number of other earth turners. **1881** *Rep. Indian Affairs* 88, I used the leverage of the 50 Moline wagons and harness, as far as possible to make every wagon represent a new farm location.

***moll,** *n.* The blackfish, *Tautoga onitis.* — **1884** GOODE *Fisheries* I. 269 The Tautog or Black-fish . . . is called . . . on the eastern shore of Virginia 'Moll,' or 'Will George.' **1911** *Rep. Fisheries 1908* 317 Tautog (Tautoga onitis).—On the New York coast it is called . . . 'tautog' . . . ; on the Virginia coast, 'Moll.'

molligut ˈmalɪˌgʌt, *n. local.* [Origin unknown.] =**goosefish.** — **1884** GOODE *Fisheries* I. 173 The Goose Fish or Monk Fish *Lophius piscatorius.* . . . The names of the fish are many; . . . in Eastern Connecticut [it is called] 'Molligut.' **1911** *Rep. Fisheries 1908* 310.

***molly,** *n.* Also ***Molly.**

1. molly cottontail, =**cottontail.**

1835 LONGSTREET *Ga. Scenes* 188 When I went into the neighborhood . . . the common appellation of the rabbit was 'Molly Cottontail,' as it still is, elsewhere in Georgia. **1892** *Outing* Feb. 362/2 The prairie dog and jack rabbit have firmly established themselves, assisted by the screech owl, rattlesnake and the 'Molly cotton tail.' **1944** *This Week Mag.* 23 Dec. 5/4 You know that the little old molly cottontail does more crop damage than all other species of game combined.

2. Molly Maguires, members of a secret organization of miners who became notorious for criminal activities in the Pennsylvania coal region from 1865 to 1876. Now *hist.* Cf. **Blackspots, buckshot 2.**

1867 DIXON *New Amer.* II. 299 The judge who tried this murderer was elected by the Molly Maguires; the jurors who assisted him were themselves Molly Maguires. **1877** E. MARTIN *Hist. Great Riots* 462 Such is the region that has become notorious throughout the Union as the country of the Molly Maguires and the scene of their terrible crimes. **1947** CHALFANT *Gold, Guns, & Ghost Towns* 150 The union, or Molly Maguires as they were commonly termed, sent word to Williams that if he did not leave town he would be hanged.

Also **Molly Maguireism.** *Obs.*

1884 *N.Y. Wkly. Tribune* 24 Sep. 4/4 In Schuylkill County, the hot bed of Molly Maguire-ism, the society is reported to have appeared again.

As the last term in **hog, old molly.**

monadnock məˈnædnɑk, *n.* [Mt. *Monadnock*, N.H., f. Massachuset Indian "prominent mountain."] A hill or a rocky elevation on a plain that has been worn by erosion.

[1741 *N.H. Prov. Papers* (1881) XIX. 496 At the end of 292 Poles from where we began this Morning, we Ascended a large Mountain, *Grand Menadnuck* then being Northeasterly of us and distant near Twelve Miles.] **1894** *Nation* 9 Aug. 99/2 The White Mountains appear to be simply a cluster of Monadnocks, preserved by some peculiarity of structure or drainage not yet fully explained. **1946** *Sierra Club Bul.* Dec. 13 We grounded ourselves, walked around a final monadnock that had been blocking our view, and saw the lights of what could be Sierraville and its suburbs.

* **Monarda,** *n.* A genus of North American mints of the family Labiatae, or a species of this genus. Cf. **bee balm.**

1814 BIGELOW *Florula Bostoniensis* 7 *Monarda allophylla*, Soft Monarda. . . . Flowers, in terminal heads, blue or flesh coloured. **1887** BURROUGHS in *Cent. Mag.* July 328, I have never found it with its only rival in color, the monarda or bee-balm, a species of mint. **1937** *Range Plant Handbook* w-134 The volatile oil present in *monarda* yields . . . the valuable antiseptic drug, thymol.

* **money,** *n.* In combs.: (1) **money article,** in a newspaper, an article dealing with current quotations on stocks and bonds or financial affairs in general; (2) **baron,** =**money king;** (3) **belt,** a belt having convenient pockets or folds for money; (4) **bug,** a man possessing great wealth, *slang;* (5) **center,** a place of preeminent rank or importance in the financial affairs of a region or country, freq. with reference to New York; (6) **crop,** a readily salable crop, as cotton or tobacco, grown primarily for the market; (7) **digger,** one who seeks for buried treasure or is supposed to be an adept at locating it; (8) **digging,** (see quot.); (9) **finder,** (see quot.); (10) **king,** a man of great wealth who plays a dominant role in financial affairs; (11) * **maker,** a thing which is financially profitable; (12) **plank,** that part of a political party's platform embodying the views of the party concerning the proper management of the financial affairs of the country; (13) **price,** the price of an article stated in terms of money rather than in commodities accepted as money, *obs.;* (14) **shark,** a crafty, avaricious usurer, swindler, or extortioner, *colloq.*

(1) 1848 W. ARMSTRONG *Stocks* 18 Outsiders are influenced mostly by the 'money articles' in the leading papers of the day. **1888** KIRK *Queen Money* 197 Opening the second edition of the *Hesperus*, [he] turned to the money article. — **(2) 1932** *Blue Valley Farmer* (Okla. City) 18 Feb. 8/6 It would avoid the wrath of powerful money barons. — **(3) 1846** *St.Louis Reveille* 9 Sep. 3/2 The stock consists, in part, of Shirts, Collars, . . . Umbrellas, Money Belts. **1949** *Boston Globe* 5 June (Fiction Mag.) 4/5 He had a money belt around his waist with his stake in it. — **(4) 1904** O. HENRY *Cabbages & Kings* 304 The chief had got together the same old crowd of moneybugs with pink faces and white vests to see us march in.

(5) 1838 *Speeches of D. Barnard* 36 Composed of twenty-six local sovereignties, of all which New-York is the money centre, as London is the money centre of half the world. **1900** *Cong. Rec.* 17 Feb. 1897/2 At such times gilt-edged paper can be placed in the money centers at a small per cent. — **(6) 1881** *Harper's Mag.* Oct. 723/1 Cotton is the money crop, and offers such flattering inducements that everything yields to that. **1904** T. E. WATSON *Bethany* 5 They never failed to make it their object to produce on the farm the necessary supplies: tobacco or cotton being merely the surplus crop, the 'money' crop. — **(7) 1822** *Farmer's Diary 1823* (Canandaigua, N.Y.) C2r Every country has its money diggers, who are full in the belief that vast treasures lie concealed in the earth. **1897** ROBINSON *Uncle Lisha's Outing* 227 Sam recognized an old acquaintance, one of the money diggers of Garden Island. — **(8) 1848** *S. Lit. Messenger* XIV. 641/2 Joe . . . did no work; unless we dignify with that name an occasional turn at 'money digging,' a searching for hidden treasures. — **(9) 1831** *Illinois Mo.* Feb. 228 Christopher Colewort had recourse to one of those men who profess to discover hidden treasures, both of water and of metals, beneath the earth's surface, by means of the hazel rod—and are denominated water-wizards, or money-finders.

(10) 1838 *Speeches of D. Barnard* 106 To see him [the President] sit as a great money king over the nation. **1900** *Cong. Rec.* 7 Feb. 1610/1 Where ought control of the currency to rest? . . . At present the banks and the money kings wield this power. — **(11) 1899** ADE *Doc' Horne* 22, I expect to have an interest in the Neapolitan Dental Parlors, where I'm working now. It's a sure money-maker. **1941** FERGUSSON *Southwest* 349 He has instead snapped up his dances as money-makers. — **(12) 1894** LEAVITT *Our Money Wars* 221 February 22, 1878, the Greenback Labor Party . . . formulated an elaborate platform; the money planks of which have been much used by money reformers since then. **1900** *Cong. Rec.* 7 Feb. 1608/2 The money plank of the St. Louis convention . . . did the business. — **(13) 1647** *Suffolk Deeds* I. 88 Such Commodities as the sd Tho: . . . shall choose at any shopp in Boston at money prices. **1686** *Braintree Rec.* 24 Moses ffiske shall have the last yeare 90lb that is 40lb in money or corne at money price 50lb at Countrey rates prise. **1741** *N.H. Probate Rec.* III. 57, I give unto my Daughter Mehetiable Hains Fourty Pounds in Goods att money Prise. — **(14) 1844** *Cong. Globe* App. 20 Dec. 37/2 Banks . . . managed . . . by a set of irresponsible money sharks. **1900** *Cong. Rec.* 7 Feb. 1618/2 The idle few, the gold gamblers and the money sharks, may live, at the expense of the toiling masses in idleness.

b. *To pay one's money and take one's choice*, and variants, to proceed in a regular or orthodox manner. *Colloq.*

1864 *Sacramento Union* 18 Jan. 5/2 The reader 'pays his money and can take his own choice.' **1885** *Calif. Athlete* (S.F.) 19 Dec. 4/3 Well, sir, you pays your money and you takes your choice. **1937** *Trail & Timberline* April 59/2 If you 'pays your money,' you are bound to have a 'good choice.'

As the last term in **annuity, berry, big, black, Boston, bungtown, chicken, cob, commutation, Congress, corn, covered, cut, dog, eastern, egg, egg-and-butter, egg-and-chicken, entry, Ermatinger, fall, federal, fiat, first, folding, fractional, hand, hard, head, higher, improvement, island, Jackson, Jeff Davis, Kirtland, loan office, lumber, Mills('s), New York, old, old continental, parchment, Pennsylvania, powder, proc, proclamation, protection, rattlesnake, red, sale, scalp, school, shell, slush, soft, sound, state, tobacco, Turk's, Union, Virginia (paper), wildcat money.**

* **moneyed,** *a.*

1. moneyed corporation, (see quot. 1858).

1834 JACKSON in *Pres. Mess. & P.* III. 43 Were they bound . . . to subvert the foundationsof our Government and to transfer its powers from the hands of the people to a great moneyed corporation? **1858** *N.Y. Rev. Statutes* II. 526 The term 'moneyed corporation,' as used in this title, shall be construed to mean every corporation having banking powers, or having the power to make loans upon pledges or deposits, or authorized by law to make insurances. **1889** *Cent.* 1275/3.

2. moneyed institution, an institution rich in money.

1861 *Vanity Fair* 23 Feb. 96/1 The 'Presidents of Railroads and moneyed institutions' are stealing the Post Office and Custom House monies. **1900** *Cong. Rec.* 19 Jan. 992/2 A great moneyed institution which the court said had the right under the fundamental law of Louisiana to exist.

* **monger,** *n.* As the last term in **bank, ice, Negro, spoils, vote monger.**

* **mongrel,** *n.*

1. =**stilt sandpiper. 2. mongrel buffalo,** (see quot.).

(1) 1917 *Birds of Amer.* I. 230 Stilt Sandpiper. . . . Other names: Long-legged Sandpiper; Frost Snipe; Mongrel [etc.]. — **(2) 1911** *Rep. Fisheries 1908* 308 Red or Big-Mouthed Buffalo (Ictiobus cyprinella); Black or Mongrel Buffalo (I. bulbalus). These fresh-water suckers are common to the waters of the Mississippi Valley and sometimes weigh 30 to 40 pounds.

* **monitor,** *n.*

1. One appointed to maintain order or enforce rules (**a**) in a legislative assembly, (**b**) in a parish meeting. *Obs.*

(a) 1715 *Mass. H. Rep. Jrnls.* I. 3 Ordered, That Mr. John Stearnes [etc.] . . . be Monitors of the House to take care that the Orders thereof are duly observed. **1721** *Ib.* III. 90 Voted, That Mr. John Foster [etc.] . . . be the Monitors for this Sessions. — **(b) 1758** *Essex Inst. Coll.* XXI. 160 Voted that Frances Pool Joseph Thurston Junr. Nehemiah Grover be moneters for said meeting. **1786** *Ib.* XXII. 136 Chose Mr. Ebenezer Pool Mr. Joseph Thursten Mr. Ben Knights Monotors.

2. (*cap.*) The name of an ironclad naval vessel designed by John Ericsson in 1862. Also (not *cap.*) a war vessel made on the model of this.

1862 ERICSSON in Church *Life Ericsson* (1890) I. 255 The iron-clad intruder will thus prove a severe monitor to those leaders [*sc.* of the Confederacy]. . . . On these and many similar grounds I propose to name the new battery Monitor. **1863** KETTELL *Hist. Rebellion* II. 650 The iron-clads consisted of seven of the Ericsson monitors. **1865** *Harper's Mag.* Aug. 360/1 In anticipation of the conflict with the Monitors, great numbers of military men had flocked to the city [Charleston] from all parts of the South. **1947** *Chi. Tribune* 2 Nov. 22/3 The war with Spain made annexation necessary to enable the use of Hawaiian ports for American warships, particularly the double turreted monitor Monadnock on its way to Manila to make the American fleet preponderant in the bay.

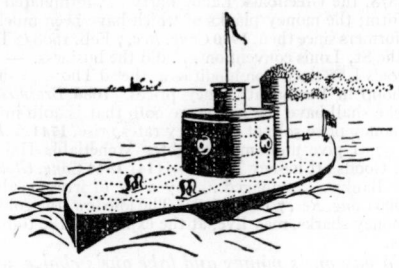

Monitor (sense 2)

b. A type of fortification formerly used in Indian warfare in the West (see quot.). *Obs.*

1868 *Harper's Mag.* Feb. 307/2 The mud Monitors are simply covered pits located a short distance from each corner of the ranch.

c. (See quot.)

1905 *Forestry Bureau Bul.* No. 61, 33 *Catamaran*, a small raft carrying a windlass and grapple, used to recover sunken logs. . . . [Also called] monitor, pontoon (P[acific] C[oast] F[orest]).

3. A raised roof or portion of a roof provided with openings and windows for light and ventilation. In full **monitor roof.** Also attrib.

1871 SNOW *Pathfinder* 2 'The roofs [of certain railroad passenger cars] are of the monitor pattern,' meaning slightly elevated along the centre, to make the car airy. **1889** *Cent. Mag.* Feb. 574/1 A large number of factories, . . . lighted with what are known as monitors, have been constructed in many parts of New England. **1923** NUTTING *Massachusetts* 294 The so called monitor roof which rises in a kind of clear story, is here and there found through the 18th century.

b. (See quot.)

1904 *Boston Sun. Globe* 28 Feb. 40/6 The monitor [of a caboose] is the square place with glass sides extending above the roof. There is a chair there . . . and the rear brakeman, or the conductor, may sit in it and see what is going on and where the train happens to be.

4. A nozzle capable of being turned completely around in a horizontal plane. Used in hydraulic mining.

1873 LAWRENCE *Silverland* 166 These pipes . . . connect with a powerful apparatus of cast iron, provided with an universal joint to which the outlet or 'nozzle' is attached, ending in a steel ring for the delivery of the stream, which varies from four to eight inches in diameter. This apparatus is sometimes called a 'monitor.' **1898** *Times* 22 Aug. 6/3 Hydraulic pressure exerted against the deposits by what are known as . . . 'Monitors,' huge squirts. **1948** JOHNSTON *Gold Rush* 24/2 The hills and mountains, torn and dismembered by the monitors, were carried piecemeal by lesser streams into the larger rivers.

* **monkey,** *n.* In combs.: (1) **monkey box,** (see quot.); (2) **business,** deceitful or crafty carryings-on, trifling, foolish conduct, also **monkey-doodle business,** *slang.;* (3) **rum,** *S.* (see quot.); (4) **shine(s),** monkey-like behavior, tricks, antics, capers, or pranks, freq. *to cut monkeyshines, slang;* (5) **show,** a show or exhibition of monkeys, also transf., *colloq.;* (6) **spoon,** (see quot. 1881), *obs.;* (7) **stove,** a small stove such as one uses in a home laundry; (8) **wire,** (see quot.), *slang;* (9) **work,** = **monkey business,** *rare;* (10) * **wrench,** see as a main entry.

(1) **1894** SEARIGHT *Old Pike* 164 Drivers and residents along the road called the passenger compartment of the early mail coach a 'monkey box.' — (2) **1883** PECK *Bad Boy* 109 There must be no monkey business going on. **1928** *Sat. Ev. Post* 12 May 41/2 They ought not to go abroad with such monkey-doodle business. **1946** *New Yorker* 5 Oct. 109/1 Let us nip this political monkey business in the bud before it sticks to us like a leech. — (3) **1941** DANIELS *Tar Heels* 255 Corn liquor and monkey rum (which in North Carolina was the distilled sirup of sorghum cane), were concoctions taken stoically, with retching and running eyes, for the effect beyond the first fusel oil belch. — (4) **1828** RICE *Jim Crow* iii, I cut so many munky shines, I dance de gallopade. **1930** J. W. JOHNSON *Black Manhattan* 64 After a good play the whole team would for a moment cut monkey-shines that would make the grand stand roar. **1948** *This Week Mag.* 1 May 6/2 A weak fence it is that separates civilized behavior from the complete monkeyshine.

(5) **1792** in *W. & M. Coll. Quart.* XX. 158 Of all the foolish monkey-shows I ever was at, a Levee is the most so. **1838** FLAGG *Far West* I. 102 A redoubted 'monkey show' . . . had wound its way over the mountains into the regions of the distant West. **1866** C. H. SMITH *Bill Arp* 125 Prouder to see him than a monkey show, I paddled the dugout over in double quick. — (6) **1749** [error for 1719] in DE VERE 507 To each of the eight bearers . . . a Monkey-spoon was given. **1881** *Harper's Mag.* March 530/1 A monkey-spoon. [Footnote:] Used for liquor, and so called from the figure of a monkey carved . . . on the handle. It had a circular and very shallow bowl. — (7) **1934** C. M. WILSON *Backwoods Amer.* 124 (Wentworth), The countryside . . . is free to . . . encircle patriarchal monkey-stoves as weather decides. **1944** STAFFORD *Boston Adv.* 38 He was sitting on the bench before the monkey stove, his head in his hands. — (8) **1929** *Amer. Sp.* IV. 289 'Monkey wires' are telegraph lines to 'the woods' or 'the sticks'—circuits connecting groups of small towns. . . . The stations usually are manned with the less skillful operators. Hence the derisive appellation. — (9) **1898** *McClure's Mag.* X. 541/2 'Mind you, any monkey work'll get you into more trouble.'

As the last term in **brass, English, gold, red, road, stuffed monkey.**

* **monkey,** *v. intr.* To act mischievously, to tamper, to fool *with*, to trifle *around. Colloq.*

1884 *Canon City* (Colo.) *Mercury* 22 Aug. 4/1 This reminds us of a sign in a Michigan planing mill, 'Dont Munkey with the Buz Saw.' **1909** STRATTON-PORTER *Girl of Limberlost* xviii. 349, I let her monkey with it until she said she had found 'my style.' **1942** STEGNER *Mormon C.* 264 It doesn't pay to monkey around too much. **1945** GARDNER *Golddigger's Purse* 157 I'm a bad man to monkey with.

Also **monkeying,** *n.*

1881 RITTENHOUSE *Maud* 39 Well, what with talking, running back and forth and general monkeying Clara slipped and fell.

* **monkey wrench. 1. Monkey wrench district,** (see quot.). **2.** *To throw a monkey wrench into* (something), to cause confusion, disaster, "to gum up the works." *Colloq.*

(1) **1902** CLAPIN 278 Monkey-wrench-district. The 3rd congressional district in Iowa was so called in 1890, from its resemblance in shape to a monkey-wrench. It has often been cited, by Democrats, as a flagrant case of Republican gerrymandering. — (2) **1929** ALLIGHAN *Romance of Talkies* 38 The Talkies threw several kinds of monkey wrenches into the machinery of production. **1947** *Chr. Sci. Monitor* 16 Jan. 1/7 It would throw another big monkey wrench into the already wobbly Japanese economy.

* **Monmouth,** *n. attrib.* Designating groups of citizens of Monmouth County, N.J., active in threatening or executing vengeance upon loyalists for injuries to rebels in the days of the Revolution. *Obs.* — **1780** *N.J. Archives* 2 Ser. IV. 545 This Committee will . . . retaliate on the Persons and property of the Disaffected within the County, for all Damages, & for all Injuries Sustained by any and Every of the Monmouth Associators. **1783** W. GORDON *Hist. Amer. Revol.* (1788) IV. 287 A set of vindictive rebels, known by the designation of *Monmouth retaliators*, associated and headed by one general Forman, whose horrid acts of cruelty gained him universally the name of *Black David*.

Mono ˈmono, *n.* [See quot. 1907.] An Indian belonging to any one of various Shoshonean tribes of southern California. Also *collect.* or *pl.*, the tribe of such an Indian.

1851 *Alta California* (S.F.) 14 June, On the morning of the 21st we discovered the trail of a small party of Indians traveling in the direction of the Monos' country. **1888** MUIR *Picturesque Calif.* 29 A good countenance may now and then be discovered among the Monos, but these, the first specimens I had seen, were mostly ugly. **1907** HODGE *Amer. Indians* I. 932/1 Mono. A general term applied to the Shoshonean tribes of S.E. California by their neighbors on the W. The origin and meaning of the name are obscure, its identity with the Spanish *mono*, 'monkey,' and its similarity, at least in certain dialects, to the Yokut word for 'fly' . . . are probably only coincidences. **1948** *Sierra Club Bul.* Mar. 22 Tommy Jefferson, a full-blooded Mono, had a tireless smile that let you know you were welcome to the land of his fathers.

attrib. **1903** James *Indian Basketry* 251 A few miles over the ridge, and the first of the Mono Indian rancherias was found. **1911** Chase *Yosemite Trails* 78 They were Mono Indians returning from the Yosemite to their valley on the eastern side of the mountains. **1921** Hall *Yosemite Nat. Park* 15 Old Tenaya had his skull crushed by a rock hurled from the hand of a Mono warrior. **1947** *Sierra Club Bul.* Nov. 49 The old Indian trail . . . descended Bloody Canyon to Mono Lake, in the land of the Mono Tribe of Indians.

monocrat ˈmɑnəˌkræt, *n.* [Gk. *monokratēs*, ruling alone.] One who favors monarchic rule, applied by Jefferson and his followers to Federalists, who sympathized with England rather than with France. Also attrib. *Obs.*

1792 Jefferson *Writings* VIII. 440 Mr. Ames, the colossus of the monocrats and paper men, will either be left out or hard run. **1793** *Ib.* IX. 75 Even the monocrat papers are obliged to publish the most furious philippics against England. **1839** *Ky. Observer* (Lexington) 4 May 2/2 'Republicans and monocrats,' the distinctive designation of American parties by Mr. Jefferson. The former recognize the supremacy of the popular, the latter of the Executive will. **1883** J. T. Morse *Jefferson* xv. 251 Here was an act, done by the great Republican doctrinaire-president, . . . monarchical, beyond what any 'monocrat' had ever dared to dream of.

monocycle ˈmɑnəˌsaɪkl, *n.* [* *mono-*, single, + * *cycle*, as in * *bicycle*.] A velocipede having one wheel. Cf. **unicycle.**

1869 *Velocipede* April 79 A New York mechanic has devised a monocycle or single machine. **1869** *Sci. Amer.* 22 May 330 The machine is evidently a monocycle. **1876** Knight 2698/1 The monocycle . . . is propelled by a hand-wheel, from which belts or ropes pass around pulleys on the axis of the main wheel, seen beneath the rider, which acts by friction. **1909** Webster, *monocycle*. . . . In one form the rider is seated inside the wheel.

* **monody,** *n.* (See quot. 1890.)

1849 Poe *Poems* (1917) 125 Hear the tolling of the bells—Iron bells! What a world of solemn thought their monody compels! **1885** Craddock *Prophet* 30 The vague, sighing voice of the woods rose and fell with a melancholy monody. **1890** *Cent.* 3839/1 *Monody*, . . . monotonous sound; monotonousness of sound.

Monongahela məˌnɑŋgəˈhilə, *n.* [Lenape *Menaungehilla*, "crumbling banks."] Whisky, orig. that made in the region of the Monongahela River in Pennsylvania. In full **Monongahela (rye) whisky.** Cf. **old Monongahela.**

1805 *Natchez* (Miss.) *Messenger* 1 July 3/1 *From Pittsburgh* . . . a Quantity of best Monongahela Whiskey for sale by the barrel. **1853** Brewerton *With Kit Carson* (1930) 185 He sorely tested my friendship by inviting me to join him in a 'horn of Monongahele' as he was pleased to term some of the most execrable 'corn whisky' which it has ever been my misfortune to taste. **1936** Asbury *French Quarter* 78 Their drink was Monongahela rye whisky, the universal tipple of the wilderness, known on the Mississippi simply as 'good old Nongela.' **1949** *Pa. Dutchman* 16 June 1/3 They indulged excessively in 'Old Rye' and 'Monongahela,' and died long before Volstead tried to suppress this habit with his 18th Amendment.

monopolistic məˌnɑplˈɪstɪk, *a.* Tending to create a monopoly. — **1883** *N.Y. Chr. Union* 30 August, The monopolistic 'railroad trunk-line fare-agreement.' **1948** *Jrnl. Polit. Econ.* Feb. 69/2 The theory of monopolistic competition treats only differentiation of goods at any given time.

* **monotype,** *n.*

1. (See quot. 1890.)

1882 *Artist* 1 Feb. 60/1 A very interesting collection of monotypes executed by Mr. Charles A. Walker of Boston. **1890** *Cent.* 3846/1 *Monotype*, . . . a print from a metal plate on which a picture is painted, as in oil-color or printers' ink. Only one proof can be made, since the picture is transferred to the paper. **1897** *Cent. Mag.* Feb. 517/1 The name 'monotype' was given to this form of art print by Mr. Charles A. Walker, of Boston who, in 1877, with no knowledge of the fact that the art was known and practised by painters in former times, discovered the process independently.

2. (*cap.*) A trade-mark name for a machine for setting type (see quot. 1949).

1895 *Cyclo. Rev. Current Hist.* V. 961 The Lanston Monotype . . . marks an important advance in the development of typographical art. **1949** *Manual of Style* 256 Monotype—A composing machine invented by Tolbert Lanston (1844–1913) and developed about 1890. In this machine a ribbon of paper, which is perforated on a keyboard, operates a casting machine by bringing the single matrices in contact in the proper order with a mold, so that the letters are cast one at a time and arranged in lines automatically spaced to the proper length.

attrib. **1929** Snyder *Blood Grouping* 156 The type must first be set; by the monotype method, there are two processes, the 'keyboarding' of the MS and the casting of the type from the perforated paper rolls thus produced.

* **Monroe,** *n.*

1. *pl.* Monroe shoes or boots. *Obs.*

1845 *Xenia* (O.) *Torch-Light* 23 Oct. 3/6 Adams & Cooper have just received . . . Men's Boots and Shoes: Coarse Brogans, Kip Monroes, Calf do, Calf Boots.

2. In combs.: (1) **Monroe boot,** = **Monroe shoe,** *obs.;* (2) **Doctor,** one who supports the principles of the Monroe Doctrine, *rare;* (3) **Doctrine,** see as main entry; (4) **shoe,** a kind of shoe or boot (see quot. 1825), *obs.*

(1) **1828** Sealsfield *Americans as They Are* 129 The dress of the planter during the summer months consists of a linen jacket, pantaloons of the same, Monroe boots, and a straw hat. — (2) **1905** *Nation* 2 Feb. 84/3 But we should think that the ludicrously unfulfilled prophecy we have cited ought to make our most angelical Monroe Doctors a trifle cautious in forecasting future troubles. — (4) **1825** *Gen. Reg. for Army* 382 Each cadet [at Military Academy at West Point] shall keep himself, at all times, supplied with . . . 2 prs. of Monroe shoes; rising above the ankle joint, under the pantaloons. **1888** P. H. Sheridan *Memoirs* I. 8 This requirement was a pair of '*Monroe shoes*.'

Monroe Doctrine. A policy or series of policies of the U.S. Government set forth in, or deduced from, President Monroe's message to Congress, Dec. 2, 1823.

The most significant points in President Monroe's message were (1) that the United States would regard "as dangerous to its peace and safety" any attempt on the parts of the allied European powers "to extend their system to any portion of this hemisphere"; (2) that the United States would view as an unfriendly act any interposition by any European power with the recently revolted Spanish American colonies for the purpose of repressing them "or controlling in any other manner their destiny"; (3) that the United States regarded the American continents as being no longer "subjects for any new European colonial settlement."

[**1848** *Cong. Globe* 29 April 711 The President [Polk] had the opportunity of reiterating a doctrine which was said to be the doctrine of Mr. Monroe.] **1853** *Hunt's Merch. Mag.* XXVIII. 160 Mr. Webster made one of the most eloquent speeches . . . defending the Monroe doctrine. **1949** *Time* 25 July 11/3 He suggested extending the Monroe Doctrine to Western Europe.

Monroeism mənˈro·ɪzəm, *n.* [See prec.] The principles set forth in the Monroe Doctrine. — **1903** *Nation* 19 March 219/1 The attempt has been made to place this doubtful contention under the aegis of Monroeism. Mr. Hay, however, refuses to strain the Monroe Doctrine in that way. **1905** *Ib.* 2 Feb. 84/2 Monroeism has since been getting on President Roosevelt's nerves.

Monroite mənˈro·aɪt, *n.* A political follower of James Monroe, fifth President of the U.S. *Obs.* — **1816** *Mass. Spy* 11 Sep. (Th.), It has been candidly confessed by at least one of the boasted sixty-five Monroites, in caucus, that [etc.]. **1817** *Ann. 14th Congress* 2 Sess. 795 That very numerous class of persons who at that time were staunch Federalists, and since that time have been staunch Jeffersonians, Madisonians, and Monroites.

monrolite mənˈrolaɪt, *n.* A variety of fibrolite, so named from *Monroe*, N.Y. — **1892** Dana *System of Mineralogy* 498 Bucholzite and monrolite are here included: the latter is irradiated columnar, and of the greenish color mentioned.

* **Monster,** *n.* A nickname for the second bank of the United States. *Obs.* — **1838** *Bentley's Misc.* IV. 586 Nicholas Biddle, the aristocratic Tory, democratic Whig, internal improvement president of the 'Monster,' or U.S. Bank.

As the last term in **Gila, great monster.**

Montana mɑnˈtænə, *n.* [Sp. *montaña*, mountainous region.] The name of a western state used in combs.: (1) **Montana black pine,** (see quot.); (2) **feathers,** a jocose designation for hay, *obs.;* (3) **junco,** = **Oregon junco;** (4) **pheasant,** (see quot.); (5) **tree,** ?a saddle tree of a type popular in Montana.

(1) **1897** Sudworth *Arborescent Flora* 20 *Pinus ponderosa* . . . Bull Pine, . . . [Also called] Montana Black Pine (var. *ambigua*) (Cal. lit.). — (2) **1918** Stuart *On Frontier* II. 146 A sergeant appeared at my door with an empty bed tick under his arm and told me that Mrs. Athey had sent him down to have it filled with 'Montana feathers.' — (3) **1917** *Birds of Amer.* III. 47 The Montana Junco . . . is one of the slaty-hooded and brown-backed Juncos. **1937** *Book of Birds* 283 Another one of this group is Montana junco. . . . It is found in summer in the Canadian zone elevations from southern Alberta to northwestern Montana, northern Idaho, and eastern Oregon. — (4) **1895** *Outing* XXVII. 43/1 The Montana 'pheasant' (the ruffed grouse) is the same as the bird found in the mountains of Virginia and the East.

(5) **1891** *Harper's Mag.* June 7/2 Their saddle is what is known as the Montana tree.

Montanan mɑnˈtænən, *n.* =next. — **1932** *Frontier* March 206/2 The better Montanan you are, in residence or out, the better American you will be. **1948** *Great Falls* (Mont.) *Tribune* 27 Sep. 10/6 Montana and Montanans played an important role today in the dedication of a copper international peace marker in Eastport.

Montanian mɑnˈtænɪən, *n.* A native or inhabitant of Montana.

1870 *Pick & Plow* (Bozeman, Mont.) 29 July 2/2 That desire to know, so prominently a characteristic of our countrymen, is perhaps enhanced among Montanians, by reason of their comparative isolation. **1878** BEADLE *Western Wilds* 358 The Montanian was gone before Manson had thought to ask. **1894** *Harper's Mag.* Aug. 482/1 (*caption*), The Unterrified Montanians.

Montauk mɑnˈtɔk, *n.* (See quot. 1907.) Also **Montauk Indian.**

1660 *East-Hampton Rec.* I. 175 Upon Petition ffrom ye Meantaquit Indians on Long Iland . . . occasioned by the Naragansets cruelty towards the said Indians & further threatening of them. **1795** DAVIS *Travels* (1803) 304 Directly the chin of this *Montauk Indian* became razorable, I put a razor into his hand, and taught him to shave. **1907** HODGE *Amer. Indians* I. 934/1 Montauk (meaning uncertain). A term that has been used in different senses, sometimes limited to the particular band or tribe known by this name, but in a broader sense including most of the tribes of Long Island, excepting those about the w. end.

monte ˈmɑntɪ, *n. S.W.* [Sp., in sense **1.**]

1. A card game of Spanish and Mexican origin, in which players bet upon a bottom and top layout of two cards each.

1841 *S. Lit. Messenger* VII. 77/2 At a short distance were seated the proprietors of this immense herd, busily engaged in the game of Monte. **1891** SWASEY *Early Days Calif.* 37 In the bar-room a crowd of Californians were playing monte. **1948** JOHNSTON *Gold Rush* 19/1 The miners . . . started games of poker, blackjack, and monte.

2. A chaparral region in the southern California foothills (see also quot. 1933).

1851 HAYES *Pioneer Notes* (1929) 79 An American coming from the Monte, whom he presently met, had seen no person on that road. **1855** *Santa Barbara* (Calif.) *Gaz.* 21 May 3/1 The course pursued by the citizens of the Monte, in lynching the men, is most unhesitatingly to be condemned. **1933** ROCKFELLOW *Log Ariz. Trail Blazer* 35 This was because of the dense mesquite brush or 'monte' through which the road ran.

3. In combs.: (1) **monte bank,** a table or a place where monte is played (see also quot. 1890), also attrib.; (2) **banker,** one in charge of a monte bank; (3) **dealer,** =**monte banker;** (4) **layout,** the layout of cards for the game of monte; (5) **sharp,** one who makes a practice of winning at monte by cheating; (6) **table,** a table or establishment at which monte is played; (7) **thrower,** a dealer of three-card monte.

(1) **1834** A. PIKE *Prose Sketches* 138, I saw the men and women dancing waltzes and drinking whiskey together; and in another room, I saw the monti-bank open. **1846** MAGOFFIN *Down Santa Fé Trail* 120 There was 'Dona Tula' the principal *monte-bank keeper* in Sant Fé [*sic*]. **1890** *Cent.* 3848/1 *Monte-bank*, . . . a gaming-table or an establishment where monte is played; also, the bank or pile of money usually placed in front of the dealer, and used in paying the stakes. — (2) **1864** [see **monte dealer**]. — (3) **1844** GREGG *Commerce of Prairies* I. 240 La Tules . . . [is] now considered the most expert 'monte dealer' in all Santa Fé. **1864** DICK *Amer. Hoyle* (1866) 456 The monte banker, or dealer, must have the whole of his bank, or money which he risks at the game, in sight upon the table. — (4) **1889** MUNROE *Golden Days* 20 A man who doesn't know a monte layout from a checker-board.

(5) **1851** *S.F. Herald* 1 Feb. 2/6 Our city continues to be infested with a certain class . . . usually termed 'Monte sharps.' *a***1918** G. STUART *On Frontier* I. 218 Our monte sharps are about to take the towns. — (6) **1847** RUXTON *Adv. Rocky Mts.* (1848) 190 Under the portales were numerous monté-tables, surrounded by Mexicans and Americans. **1869** BROWNE *Adv. Apache Country* 76 The city was built, bar-rooms and billiard-saloons opened, monte-tables established. **1948** JOHNSTON *Gold Rush* 50/1 The furniture in the latter consisted of a small bar of hand-sawed boards, a tin stove, and two monte tables. — (7) **1938** ASBURY *Sucker's Prog.* 122 Canada Bill Jones, a noted *Monte thrower*, once summed up the sharper's attitude when he said that suckers had no business with money anyway.

As the last term in **French, Pass, Spanish, three-card monte.**

Monterey ˌmɑntəˈre, *n.* [Sp. *Monterrey*, a place-name. A county, city, and bay in west central California.] In combs.: (1) **Monterey cedar,** prob. erroneous for next, under which see quot. 1874; (2) **cypress,** a species of cypress, *Cupressum macrocarpa*, indigenous to the region about Monterey Bay; (3) **halibut,** a flounder, *Paralichthys californicus*, found on the Pacific Coast; (4) **hermit thrush,** (see quot.); (5) **pine,** a tall, handsome pine, *Pinus radiata*, of southern California; (6) **(Spanish) mackerel,** a kind of mackerel, *Scomberomorus concolor*, found on the Pacific Coast.

(1) **1872** MCCLELLAN *Golden State* 450 The 'Monterey cedar,' a most beautiful ornamental tree, grows abundantly. — (2) **1874** HITTELL *Resources Calif.* 360 The Monterey cypress (*Cupressus macrocarpa*) is indigenous only on Cedar Point, at Monterey. **1948** *Pacific Discovery* July–Aug. 31/2 The Monterey cypress seems to have been the species most seriously affected. — (3) **1882** JORDAN & GILBERT *Synopsis Fishes N. Amer.* 821 *Paralichthys californicus*. . . . Monterey halibut; Bastard Halibut. — (4) **1917** *Birds of Amer.* III. 236/1 The Monterey Hermit Thrush (*Hylocichla guttata slevini*) is smaller, paler, and grayer than the Alaska. California is its home and the winter is spent in Mexico and Lower California.

(5) **1874** HITTELL *Resources Calif.* 358 The Monterey pine (*Pinus insignis*) is extensively cultivated as an ornamental tree. **1948** *Pacific Discovery* Nov.–Dec. 17/1 So, running to the very spray-line where sea winds distort it, bow and bend it, and cover its gnarled carcass with sand from the dunes, the Monterey pine is held in its narrow home. — (6) **1884** GOODE *Fisheries* I. 316 The Pacific species may be called the 'Monterey Mackerel.' **1911** *Rep. Fisheries 1908* 316/2 In California the Monterey Spanish mackerel . . . is a most excellent food fish.

* **Montezuma,** *n.*

1. *Land of the Montezumas*, New Mexico. A nickname. Cf. *Halls of (the) Montezuma(s)*, *s.v.* **hall,** *n.* **4. b.**

1871 *Republican Review* 25 March 2/1 While the mineral fields of California, Colorado and Mexico have attracted whole troops of miners, the land of the 'Montezumas' has been overlooked. **1885** *Weekly New Mexican Review* 8 Jan. 4/2 Journalism will henceforth prove a mighty power in the land of the Montezumas.

2. a. (See quot.) *Rare.* **b. Montezuma quail,** (see quot.).

(a) **1895** REMINGTON *Pony Tracks* 62 The punchers have dug down into these ruins, and found adobe walls, mud plastering, skeletons, and pits of woven goods. They call them the 'Montezumas.' — (b) **1917** *Birds of Amer.* II. 10 Mearns's Quail. *Cyrtonax montezumae mearnsi*. . . . Other names—Montezuma Quail; . . . Fool Quail; Fool Hen.

* **monument,** *n.*

1. An object fixed upon or erected by surveyors as a bound mark of a given piece of land or the limit of a survey.

1651 *Watertown Rec* I. I. 27 Make som Dureable Monements both at the fouer angles and pert[it]ion Line. **1724** *Talcott P.* 21 All the marks and monuments erected by the surveyors in it are utterly lost. **1885** *Rep. Indians Affairs* 147 Survey of the outward boundaries of . . . Reservations should be made and properly marked with suitable monuments.

2. A milepost. *Obs.*

1745 HEMPSTEAD *Diary* 438, I measured ye Road from ye Court house . . . to ye Millpond bridge . . . I made monuments at Every miles End.

3. (See quot. 1900.)

1900 *Amer. Geog. Soc.* XXXII. 38 Monument: A column or pillar of rock. Local in Rocky Mountain region. **1909** *Cent. Supp.* 827/1.

4. Monument City, =**Monumental City.**

1906 *Springfield W. Republican* 8 March 4 Baltimore has been known for years as the 'Monument City,' and some of these monuments are in reality works of art.

As the last term in **national, Washington monument.** Also **Sherman monuments.**

* **monumental,** *a.* **1. monumental cactus,** =**giant cactus. 2. Monumental City,** Baltimore, Maryland. **3. Monumental State,** Maryland. *Obs.*

(1) **1873** COZZENS *Marvelous Country* 233 Scattered here and there, growing apparently without any soil, rose to the height of forty or fifty feet grooved columns of the *Cereus grandes*, or monumental cactus, as it is sometimes called. — (2) **1827** *National Gaz.* (Phila.) 20 Nov. 213 The brave sons of Cincinnatus at the festival board in the 'monumental city.' **1904** *Baltimore Amer.* 5 Dec. 14 Detectives Hagan and Burns . . . have been working there [in Brooklyn] during the past week, and it is probable that they will return to the Monumental City to-day. **1949** *Business Week* 24 Sep. 101 'The Monumental City' is the nation's second largest seaport. — (3) **1846** *Warrock's Alman. 1847* 22 Maryland, Monumental [State].

moody ˈmudɪ *n.* [f. Ber*muda*.] A sweet potato. *Rare.* See ∗**Bermuda,** *n.* — **c1775** BOUCHER *Glossary* I. **c1800** *Ib.* 'Moodies; sweet potatoes first brought from the Bermudas.

moogadee ˈmugəˌdi, *n.* [f. Amer. Indian.] (See quots.) — **1909** *Cent. Supp.* 827/1 *Moogadee*, . . . A name applied by the Fort Hall Indians of Idaho to *Catostomus pocatello*, or sucker of the Snake River basin. **1911** *Rep. Fisheries 1908* 317 Sucker (Catostomidae). — The different species are known as . . . 'red horse,' 'mullet,' . . . 'moogadee,' etc.

∗**moon,** *n.*

1. A large round biscuit. *Obs.*

1847 C. WHITE *Policy Players* (1874) 3 Get me a buttered moon and a pickle. **1883** MARK TWAIN *Life on Miss.* lii, I spent my last 10 cts for 2 moons (*large, round sea-biscuit*).

2. =**moonshine whiskey.** *Slang. Rare.*

1928 *Collier's* 29 Dec. 8/2 Mister, this is good stuff. It's Leadville 'moon.' . . . The art of producing sugar 'moon' and aging it in charred casks . . . is becoming famous again.

3. In combs.: (1) **moon box,** (see quot. 1890); (2) **down,** the time when the moon goes down or sets; (3) **glade,** (see quot.); (4) ∗**light,** (*a*) (see quots.), also

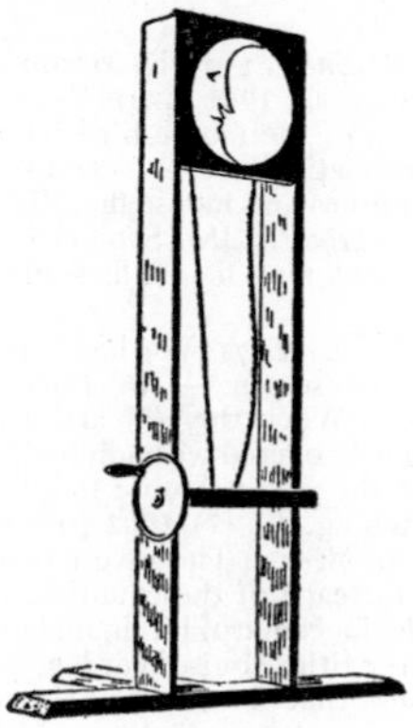

Moon box

attrib., *obs.*, (*b*) an excursion made in the light of the moon, *obs.;* (5) ∗**lighting,** exploding a charge of nitroglycerin in an oil well by night to start the flow afresh, *obs.;* (6) ∗**rise,** the time at which the moon rises; (7) ∗**shine,** see as a main entry; (8) ∗**shiner,** one who distils spirituous liquors without a government license; (9) ∗**shining,** the illicit distilling of whisky, cf. ∗**blockading,** *n.;* (10) **shower,** (see quot.).

(1) 1866 DAVIDGE *Footlight Flashes* 149 (*caption*), Moon Box. **1890** *Cent.* 3851/1 *Moon-box.* A theatrical device for displaying an imitation moon on the stage. — **(2) 1797** HAWKINS *Letters* 276 Last evening, just before moon down, his camp had been fired on by some men supposed to be Georgians. **1861** *N.Y. Tribune* 25 Oct. (Chipman), They landed at Santa Rosa Island, at about a quarter of an hour to moondown, or 11 o'clock, P.M. **1938** MATSCHAT *Suwannee River* 68 Four, five hours till moondown. — **(3) 1859** LOWELL in *Atlantic Mo.* Nov. 641/1 Moonglade: a beautiful word for the track of moonlight on the water. Massachusetts. — **(4)** (*a*) **1851** HALL *College Words* 210 *Moonlight.* At Williams College, the prize rhetorical exercise is called by this name; the reason is not given. **1854** *Boston Ev. Traveller* 12 July, In the evening comes the Moonlight Exhibition, when three men from each of the three lower classes exhibit their oratorical powers. **1860** DURFEE *Hist. Williams College* 104 Those who receive the appointment to speak for the prize have always . . . been called 'Moonlights.' (*b*) **1886** *Boston Jrnl.* 13 Aug. 3/7 To-night the fourth in the series of moonlights will be made.

(5) 1883 *Cent. Mag.* July 330/2 Sometimes well-owners 'torpedo' their wells stealthily by night to avoid paying the high price charged by the company. This operation is called 'moonlighting,' and many lawsuits have grown out of it. — **(6) 1877** BARTLETT. **1884** MARK TWAIN *H. Finn.* viii. 63 When it was good and dark, I slid out from shore about moonrise. — **(8) 1877** *N.Y. Ev. Post* 16 June 404 (B.), Nelson County, Kentucky, is the home of the Moonshiner. **1949** *Amer. Sp.* Feb. 4 This moonshiner of the Eastern mountains is as lethal as a water moccasin. — **(9) 1883** S. BONNER *Dialect Tales* 183 You can't stop moonshinin' 's long's there's an honest man in Old Hickory's State. **1946** WILSON *Fidelity* 54 He stoutly maintained that a regulated open saloon was to be preferred to the evils of moonshining and boot-legging.

(10) 1877 BARTLETT 404 Moonshower, a shower which descends from a cloud so situated as not to obscure the moon's rays. New England.

b. In the names of plants and animals: (1) **moonbill,** the ring-necked duck, *Nyroca* (or *Marila*) *collaris;* (2) ∗**eye,** see as a main entry; (3) **fish,** see as a main entry; (4) ∗**flower,** the evening-glory, *Calonyction aculeatum;* (5) **moth,** =**luna moth;** (6) **vine,** =∗**moonflower.**

(1) 1888 TRUMBULL *Names of Birds* 61, I am told by two well-informed gunners . . . of its being known to certain South Carolina duckers as the Moon-Bill. **1917** *Birds of Amer.* I. 137 Ring-necked Duck. *Marila collaris.* . . . [Also called] Ring-bill; Moon-bill; Marsh Blue-bill. — **(4) 1899** M. GOING *Flowers* 200 [Its] nocturnal habits are shared only by the moon-flower. **1928** BAILEY *Cyclo. Horticulture* 636/1 The moonflower . . . grows wild in swamps and thickets in peninsular Fla., and is probably indigenous there. **1948** *Good Housekeeping* Jan. 103/1 There used to be a thousand women like her from St. Johns Marsh to Fish Eating Creek; women that bloom like moonflowers that fade overnight.

(5) 1868 *Amer. Naturalist* II. 187 The pale-green, satin-robed Moon-moth (*Attacus luna*). **1870** *Ib.* IV. 52 The beautiful pale green Moon-moth (Actias Luna). — **(6) 1902** LESTER *So. N. Mex. Flower Garden* 15 Other climbing plants that grow well where a vine is desired are the ordinary hop, . . . the moonvine, and the Madeira vine. **1949** *L.A. Times* 3 April (Home Mag.) 32/4 The moon vine, Ipomoea grandiflora alba, is a rapidly growing perennial vine with handsome foliage and large pure white flowers that open during the evening.

As the last term in **goose, half, lost, strawberry, underground moon.**

moonack ˈmunæk, *n.* [Virginia Indian, "digger."]

1. The woodchuck, *Marmota monax*, or a related species.

1666 GEORGE ALSOP *Mary-Land* 9 The Monack, the Musk-Rat, and several others (whom I' le omit for brevity sake) inhabit here in *Mary-Land.* **1789** *Maryland Jrnl.* 13 Nov. (*advt.*) (Th.), A Monack or Ground-Hog, presented [to Peale's Museum] by Mr. Johnston. **1875** BURROUGHS *Winter Sunshine* 29 In Virginia, they [*sc.* Negro women] call woodchucks 'moonacks.'

2. *local.* (See quot.)

1871 DE VERE 151–2 It is presumed, though not proven, that the *Moonack*, a mythical animal known to negroes only, is also of African origin. The beast lives, according to their belief, in caves or hollow trees, and the poor negro who meets it in his solitary rambles is doomed. His reason is impaired, till he becomes a madman, or is carried off by some lingering malady. He dare not speak of it, but old, experienced negroes say when they look at him: 'He gwine to die; he seed the *moonack*.'

moonarian munˈɛrɪən, *n.* One whose planting, cultivating, etc., is done in accordance with the phases of the moon. *Colloq. Obs.* — **1800** in KITTREDGE *Old Farmer & His Almanack* (1904) 306 *Moonarians* have not neglected hauling up and destroying pernicious weeds before this day of the month! **1904** KITTREDGE *Old Farmer & His Almanack* 306 There is a rather pretty bit of irony which shows how he regarded the 'Moon-arians.'

∗**mooneye,** *n.* The toothed herring, *Hiodon tergisus*, or a related species. Also a small whitefish, *Leucichthys hoyi*, found in Lake Michigan.

1842 *Nat. Hist. N.Y., Zoology* IV. 267 The Lake Moon-eye, *Hyodon clodalis*, . . . is common in Lake Erie. At Buffalo and Barcelona, it is called Moon-eye. **1875** *Amer. Naturalist* IX. 135 This Indiana Argyrosomus appears to be quite distinct from the species found in Lake Michigan; *i.e.*, the shallow-water 'herring' . . . and the deep-water 'moon eye' (*A. Hoyi* Gill). **1911** *Rep. Fisheries 1908* 312 Moon-Eye, . . . a beautiful fresh-water food fish found in the Lake region and in the larger tributaries of the Mississippi. **1947** DALRYMPLE *Panfish* 325 The Mooneye is a perfect example . . . of a fish which, having little food value, has failed to get proper credit as a sport fish.

∗**moonfish,** *n.*

1. The spadefish, *Chaetodipterus faber.*

1842 *Nat. Hist. N.Y., Zoology* IV. 99 The Moon-fish, *Ephippus gigas*, . . . is rare on our coast, the mouth of the Hudson river being probably its northern limit. **1903** BEAN *Fishes N.Y.* 603 The moonfish has occasionally been taken as far north as Cape Cod.

2. The horsehead, *Argyreiosus vomer*, or a related fish.

1848 *Nat. Museum Proc.* I. 376 *Argyriosus vomer.*—Moon-fish. *Ib.*, *Selene argentea.*—Moon-fish. . . . Not common. **1903** BEAN *Fishes N.Y.* 436 Three individuals of the moonfish were obtained from Gravesend bay.

3. The horsefish, *Vomer setapinnis.*

1878 *Nat. Museum Proc.* I. 376 *Vomer setipinnis.*—Moon-fish; Sunfish. **1903** BEAN *Fishes N.Y.* 433 *Vomer setipinnis.* . . . Horsefish; Moonfish.

4. The opah, *Lampris regius.*

1896 JORDAN & EVERMANN *Check-List Fishes* 350 *Lampris luna* . . . Mariposa; Opah; . . . Gudlax; Moonfish.

* **moonshine,** *n.*

1. Any of several everlastings, esp. the pearly everlasting.

1850 S. F. COOPER *Rural Hours* 310 In our walk, this afternoon, observed a broad field upon a hill-side covered with the white silvery heads of the everlastings. The country people sometimes call these plants 'moonshine,' and really the effect in the evening upon so broad a field reminded one of moonlight. **1894** *Amer. Folk-Lore* VII. 92 Gnaphalium polycephalum, moonshine, Dorset, Vt. **1931** CLUTE *Plants* 60 More appealing names are moonshine for the silvery-white *Anaphalis margaritacea*, pussy toes for the soft fuzzy *Antennaria plantaginifolia* [etc.].

2. Liquor made by individuals, freq. in remote communities, having no license for distilling.

In British English the term is applied to smuggled liquor; in the U.S., to liquor illicitly distilled.

1892 J. L. ALLEN *Blue-Grass Region* 249 The manufacture of illicit mountain whiskey—'moonshine'—was formerly . . . a source of revenue. **1924** RAINE *Land of Saddle-Bags* 127 Why do those Mountaineers make moonshine? **1948** *Hoosier Folklore* March 1, I had a bottle of moonshine with me and was nipping it pretty heavy.

attrib. **1886** *Cent. Mag.* Jan. 432/1 He had a moonshine apparatus over on Sweetwater. **1920** *Outing* May 73/2, I was curious as to the moonshine industry. **1947** *Chi. D. News* 22 Oct. 10/6 The moonshine works was found in dense woods on the reservation near Thurmont.

b. moonshine still, a still in which moonshine whisky is made.

1891 *Cyclo. Temperance* 137/2 In this estimate no account is taken of the illicit whisky of the 'moonshine' stills. **1941** STUART *Men of Mts.* 35 I'll send him a carload of cracked-corn to feed his moonshine stills if he'll line up the votes just right. **1943** PEATTIE *Great Smokies* 45, I have been in several moonshine blockade stills.

c. moonshine whisky, =**moonshine 2.**

1875 E. KING *So. St. N. Amer.* 478 Producing from his pocket a flask of 'moonshine' whiskey, [he] invited us to drink. **1948** *Sat. Ev. Post* 25 Dec. 8/3 A pretty mountain girl of thirteen . . . announced her plan to wed a sullen character who trafficked in moonshine whisky.

3. Moonshine Bank, a nickname for the second bank of the United States. *Obs.*

1819 *Niles' Reg.* 9 Jan. 316/2 The president I mean, is not the president of the United States; he is president of the Moonshine Bank!

moonshine 'mun,ʃaɪn, *v. intr.* To make whisky without a license, to operate a moonshine still.

1902 W. N. HARBEN *A. Daniel* 209 Fred's always been a stanch friend to me. We moonshined it together two year, though he never knowed my chief hidin'-place. **1922** KEPHART *So. Highlanders* 143 When a man has promised not to moonshine, and then goes and does it, why that, by Jeremy, is a breach of contract. **1949** *N.O. Times-Picayune Mag.* 13 Feb. 6/2 Even a small operator can make fair living moonshining.

* **moor,** *n.* **1.** * **moor fowl,** the ruffed grouse. **2. moor head,** =next. **3. moor hen,** the American coot, or the Florida gallinule.

(1) **1791** W. BARTRAM *Travels* 331 The wary moor fowl thundering in the distant echoing hills. **1846** *N.J. Laws* 324. — (2) **1917** *Birds of Amer.* I. 214 Coot, *Fulica americana*. . . . Other names:—American Coot, Mud Hen . . . Moor-head [etc.]. — (3) [**1698** TONTI *LaSalle's Last Discoveries* 106 We saw in all their Ponds and Rivers vast quantities of Water-Fowl, Geese, Ducks, and Teal, Moor-hens, &c.] **1888** TRUMBULL *Names of Birds* 117 At Havre de Grace, Md., the American coot, [*Fulica americana*, is called] Moor-Hen, so termed by all.

moose mus, *n.* [App. f. some such native word as *moos, mos, mus,* he strips or eats off, "in reference to the animal's habit of eating the young bark and twigs of trees" (Hodge).]

1. A large forest-dwelling mammal, *Alces americana*, found in the northern U.S. and Canada.

1603 in FRIEDERICI (1947) 428/1. **1613** PURCHAS *Pilgrimage* (1614) 755 Captain Thomas Hanham . . . relateth of their beasts . . . redde Deare, and a beast bigger, called the Mus. **1775** ROMANS *Nat. Hist. Florida* 174 The Moose, or American Elk, found in the higher latitudes on the river, naturally leads a life . . . nearly approaching to a state of domestication. **1892** *Vt. Agric. Rep.* XII. 122 The last moose killed [in Essex Co.] . . . undertook a race with a railroad train on the Grand Trunk at Brighton, in 1858. **1949** *Nat. Geog. Mag.* Oct. 471/2 Moose and bear are fairly abundant.

transf. **1948** *Sat. Ev. Post* 16 Oct. 130/3 Schaeffer was a moose of a man.

2. (*cap.*) A member of the Loyal Order of Moose, a beneficiary, secret fraternal order founded in 1888 in Louisville, Kentucky. Also attrib.

1920 *Independent* 3 July 22/1 The Loyal Order of Moose has established there a home and school and town for the children of its deceased members. **1945** *Roundup* (Mont.) *R.-Tribune* 15 Feb. 5/1 The Royal Neighbors will hold their regular meeting Tuesday, Feb. 20, at 7:30 at the Moose hall. **1948** *Lewistown* (Mont.) *D. News* 2 Sep. 8/1 There will be a meeting of all Moose interested in bowling Thursday, Sep. 2, at the Moose hall.

3. In special combs.: (1) **moose bird,** =**Canada jay;** (2) **deer,** see as a main entry; (3) **fly,** a blackish fly, *Haematobia alcis;* (4) **horn,** see as a main entry; (5) **pen,** =**moose yard;** (6) **tick,** an American tick, *Dermacentor albipictus,* found on moose; (7) **trumpet,** =**moose horn 2,** cf. **moose call;** (8) **warden,** an official appointed to enforce the game law relating to moose, also transf. as a title; (9) **yard,** see as a main entry.

(1) **1832** WILLIAMSON *Maine* I. 150 The Moose-bird, which feeds on the berries of the moose brush. **1941** SETON *Trail of Artist-Naturalist* 270 Presently the wailing of the moose-bird fell on my anxious ear, and struck me with prophetic force. — (3) **1834** AUDUBON *Ornith. Biog.* II. 437 The musquitoes and moose flies did their best to render us uncomfortable. **1947** *Atlantic Mo.* Sep. 116/1 If the fishing was good, so were the flies; black flies, moose flies, mosquitoes, gnats, and their smaller cousins.

(5) **1854** HAMMOND *Hills, Lakes* 71 [We] had been down by the Saranac Lakes, beatin' up a moose pen. — (6) **1868** *Amer. Naturalist* II. 559 The Moose Tick. . . . When the cow arrived in New York, her sides and back were almost covered with adult ticks. **1869** *Ib.* III. 167 We have observed that the young Moose tick lived nearly a month without food after hatching. — (7) **1902** [see **moose horn 2**]. — (8) **1853** *Maine Acts & Resolves* 24 The governor shall . . . appoint one county moose warden for each of the counties. **1883** GOODE *Fishery Industries U.S.* 83 He had a canoe of birch, and on it he had burnt his name, and underneath the title 'Moose Warden,' and he said he would take care of all the moose that came within the reach of his rifle.

b. In the names of plants: (1) **moose berry,** =**hobblebush,** also the fruit of this; (2) **bush,** hobblebush or leatherwood **1,** *qq.v.,* cf. **black moosebush;** (3) **elm,** (see quots.); (4) **flower,** any one of various plants of the genus *Trillium;* (5) **grass,** (see quot.); (6) **maple,** an American variety of small shrubby maple, *Acer spicatum*, found in Maine and the St. Lawrence region; (7) **plum,** some now unidentifiable variety of plum, *obs.;* (8) **tree,** =**leatherwood 1;** (9) **weed,** =**pickerel weed;** (10) **wood,** see as a main entry.

(1) **1848** THOREAU *Maine Woods* 59 The cornel, or bunch-berries, were very abundant, as well as Solomon's seal and moose-berries. **1894** *Amer. Folk-Lore* VII. 90 *Viburnum lantanoides*, moose-berry, triptoe, hobble-bush, Franconia, N.H. **1942** PEATTIE *Friendly Mts.* 162 A small shadbush (*Amelanchier Bartramiana*) and the mooseberry (*Viburnum pauciflorum*) also make their appearance. — (2) **1784** CUTLER in *Life & Corr.* I. 102 The ground [was] covered with an underwood of moose bush. **1832** WILLIAMSON *Maine* I. 117 *Moose-bush* [footnote: 'or "Moose-wood," *Dirca palustris*'] is a small tree or large shrub, not uncommon in the forest. **1894** *Amer. Folk-Lore* VII. 90 *Viburnum lantanoides*, moose-bush, Buckfield, Me. — (3) **1810** MICHAUX *Arbres* I. 39 *Red Elm*, . . . *Slippery elm*, . . . [ou] *Moose elm*, . . . dans le haut de l'Etat de New York. **1832** BROWNE *Sylva* 311 This species of elm . . . bears the name of Red Elm, Slippery Elm and Moose Elm. **1949** COLLINGWOOD & BRUSH *Knowing Your Trees* 231 In the North the [slippery elm] tree is sometimes called moose elm because moose eat both twigs and bark. — (4) **1850** S. F. COOPER *Rural Hours* 73 The moose-flowers are increasing in numbers. **1894** *Amer. Folk-Lore* VII. 102 *Trillium*, sp., moose-flowers.

(5) **1938** THOMPSON *High Trails* 86 The bear grass flower . . . is also listed as pine grass, moose grass, Indian basket grass, and turkey beard. — (6) **1839** HOFFMAN *Wild Scenes* 38 We would come to a sort of plateau of swampy land, overgrown with moose maple. **1904** WHITE *Silent Places* 77 In the lucent, cool, green shadow of a thick clump of moose maples he felt . . . a certain warmth of tone. — (7) **1829** GREENLEAF *Survey Maine* 113 Prunus—(*Plum*)—several species, of little value, except the Moose-plum, or Kennebeck-plum. — (8) **1854** GREATREX *Whittlings* 119 Jacques caught up a sharp stone, and tried to saw it, but the thong, which was formed out of the tough bark of the moose-tree, would not yield. — (9) **1881** *Harper's Mag.* Oct. 684/2 The quiet bays and 'slews' are filled with . . .

patches of moose-weed, with lance-shaped leaves, and flowers of the brightest blue.

c. In miscellaneous combs. of obvious meaning or sufficiently explained by the quots.: (1) **moose beat,** (2) **call,** (3) **cat,** (4) **coat,** (5) **cow,** (6) **dog,** (7) **face,** (8) **ground,** (9) **hair,** (10) **hide,** see as a main entry, (11) **hunt,** (12) **hunter,** (13) **hunting,** (14) **meat,** (15) **muffle,** (16) **shanks,** (17) **sinew,** (18) **skin,** also attrib., (19) **suit,** (20) **swamp,** (21) **tongue,** (22) **trail,** (23) **woods.**

(1) **1838** *Knickerb.* XII. 293 The deer . . . tread the snow from around its branches [i.e., those of the ground hemlock], as often as it falls during the season. This spot is called the deer or moose *beat*, by the hunters. — (2) **1890** *Cent.* 3853/2 *Moose-call*, . . . a trumpet of birch-bark used by hunters in calling moose to an ambuscade or blind. **1902** *Amer. Folk-Lore* 249 After moose have been named the following: . . . moose-call, moose-horn, or moose-trumpet. — (3) **1926** RICKABY *Ballads* 212 *Moose-cat:* a slang expression, hard of translation but applied to anyone possessing great ability, strength, or what not. — (4) **1633** *N.H. Doc. & Rec.* 74, 16 mouse cootes, [£]16.

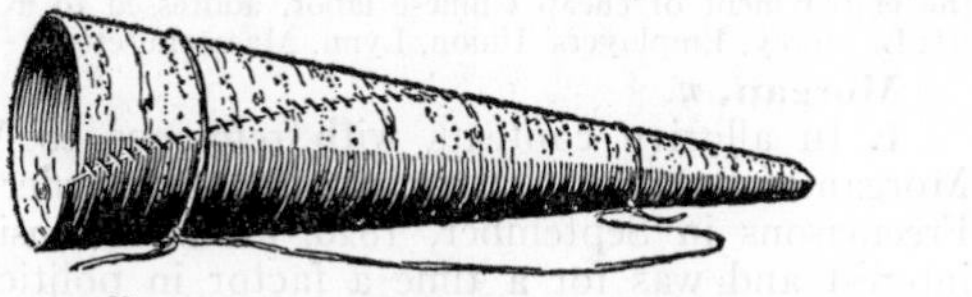

Moose call, moose trumpet, or moose horn (sense 2)

(5) **1942** *Nat. Geog. Mag.* May 613, I took motion pictures that afternoon of two moose cows swimming across the river. — (6) **1873** HOWELLS *Chance Acquaintance* 52 He is a moose-dog, and keeps himself in practice of catching the moose by the nose. — (7) **1859** MATSELL *Vocabulum* 56 Moose-face. A rich, ugly-faced man; a poor but handsome young girl who marries an old, wrinklefaced, ill-looking rich man, is said to have married a moose-face. — (8) **1837** *N.Y. Mirror* 28 Oct. 140/3 The broad west has no moose-ground so celebrated as that in our northern counties. — (9) **1820** D. W. HARMON *Journal* 317 From two points in this bow, equally distant from the board, two strips of leather . . . are suspended, at the ends of which, tassels, composed of moose hair, are fixed. **1845** *Knickerb.* XXV. 508 His attire . . . consisted of a hunting-frock of dressed deer-skin . . embroidered with dyed moose-hair.

(11) **1839** *Spirit of Times* 27 July 247/1 (We.), A Moose hunt is an affair just a huckleberry over any American Field Sport short of Buffalo hunting. **1886** *Outing* VII. 621/1 We start on our moose-hunt next. — (12) **1840** HOFFMAN *Grayslaer* I. 26 The moose-hunter was one of a hundred similar agents of frontier diplomacy. **1949** *Amer. Photography* Jan. 53/1 Thoreau once grumbled because it grew so abundantly in the Maine woods where only the moose and moose hunters could see it, and so rarely in Concord where philosophers dwelt. — (13) **1839** HOFFMAN *Wild Scenes* 58 The deepest snows of winter of course offer the best occasion for moose-hunting. *a***1861** WINTHROP *Open Air* 36 We . . . talked of the pine-woods, of logging, and of moose-hunting on snow shoes. **1886** *Outing* VII. 621 (*caption*), Moose-Hunting. — (14) **1845** *Knickerb.* XXV. 299 They ate the moose-meat which the Indians had left. **1949** *Highway Traveler* Feb. 39/2 She neglected to go to the spring for water in which to boil a piece of moose meat for her spouse's repast.

(15) **1917** KEPHART *Camping* I. 307 *Moose Muffle* (nose and upper lip).—Boil like pig's head. Add an onion. — (16) **1887** *Harper's Mag.* Feb. 458/2 'Moose shanks' are made by peeling the skin from the hind-legs of the animal. . . . The smaller end is then sewn up to form the toe; and thus a moose-hide stocking is formed. — (17) **1764** HUTCHINSON *Hist. Mass.* I. 464 Their bow-strings were made of Moose sinews. — (18) **1632** MORTON *N. Eng. Canaan* in Force Tracts II. 22 They have likewise another sort of mantels, made of Mose skinnes. **1775** *Mass. H.S. Coll.* 2 Ser. IX. 162 Donations; . . . 1 pair moose-skin breeches. **1903** *All Nations* March 73/1 Living a shivering life in moose-skin tents. — (19) **1645** *N. Eng. Hist. & Gen. Reg.* III. 82 The said Alexander Bradford have giuen to Robert Stowton his Moose Suite & a musket & Sworde.

(20) **1940** *Places to See in Wyo.* xii, The region between Mammoth and Norris Junction is one of lakes, meadows, and moose swamps. — (21) **1674** JOSSELYN *Two Voyages N. Eng.* 129 Their Diet is Fish and Fowl, . . . *Lampres* and dry'd *Moose-tongues.* *a***1862** THOREAU *Maine Woods* 289 Two or three large red chivin . . . , added to the moose-tongue, . . . made a sumptuous breakfast. — (22) **1890** G. O. SHIELDS *Big Game N. Amer.* 37 Just as I passed the point. . . . I found a Moose-trail. **1947** *Canadian Alpine Jrnl.* 95 The next day we followed a moose trail up the steep west side. — (23) **1856** *Spirit of Times* 6 Sep. 10/3 Rare and *racy* stories from all parts of the land will appear, from the Moose-woods of Maine, . . . off to the golden-sanded home of the grizzly bear in California.

As the last term in **American, black, bull, cow, gray, parchment, red moose.**

moose deer. = **moose 1.**

1672 JOSSELYN *N. Eng. Rarities* 44 Water Lilly, . . . the Moose Deer feed much upon them, at which time the Indians kill them, when their heads are under water. **1743** CATESBY *Carolina* II. p. xxiv, Beasts of the same genus, but different in species from those of Europe, and the Old World [include]. . . . The Panther, . . . Moose Deer, [and] Stag. **1842** BUCKINGHAM *E. & W. States* I. 162 The moose-deer . . . is as tall as an ordinary horse.

attrib. **1805** LEWIS in *Ann. 9th Congress* 2 Sess. 1070 Brown and grizzly bear, dressed elk and moose-deer skins, muskrat skins.

moose hide. The hide or skin of a moose. Also attrib.

[**1634** WOOD *N. Eng. Prospect* (1865) 73 (The Indians) weare shoes likewise of their owne making cut out of a Mooses hide.] **1708** OLDMIXON *British Empire in Amer.* I. 395 Every Man has commonly two Wives, whom they keep in great Subjection, and make 'em do all Slavery; as draw Sledds, cut Wood, make Fires, and dress Moose Hides. **1832** WILLIAMSON *Maine* II. 442 Some did not spare even their moose-hide breeches, moccasins and bayonet belts. **1916** EASTMAN *From Deep Woods* 170 The moose-hide drum, stretched upon a cylinder of bass-wood, was [more than forty years old]. **1949** *Sky Line Trail* March 19/1 Most hikers find a leather, buckskin or moosehide jacket ideal from the standpoint of both comfort and looks.

moose horn.

1. The horn of a moose, or a medicinal preparation similar to hartshorn prepared from this.

1672 JOSSELYN *N. Eng. Rarities* 19 Moose Horns better for Physick use than Harts Horns. **1847** PARKMAN in *Knickerb.* XXIX. 506 The walls are plentifully garnished, he told us, with moose-horns and deerhorns, bear-skins and fox-tails. **1942** *Nat. Geog. Mag.* May 607 Scattered moose horns and traces of old campfires marked the place.

2. A trumpet, usu. of birchbark, used by a hunter for calling moose within range. Cf. **moose call.**

1902 *Amer. Folk-Lore* XV. 249 After moose have been named the following: . . . moose-horn, or moose-trumpet (bark 'trumpet' used to imitate the note of the moose).

mooseling ˈmuslɪŋ, *n.* A young moose. *Rare.* — *a***1861** WINTHROP *Open Air* 56 Tame mooselings are exhibited.

moose-misse ˈmusmɪs, *n.* [Algonquian. Cf. Chippewa *monsomish*, moose shrub.] **1.** (See quot. 1909.) **2.** (See quot.)

(1) **1893** *Amer. Folk-Lore* VI. 141 *Pyrus Americana.* Indian mozemize. Ferrisburgh, Vt. **1909** *Cent. Supp.* 835/1 *Indian Mozemize*, the American mountain-ash, *Sorbus Americana.* — (2) **1902** *Amer. Folk-Lore* XV. 249 *Moosemise.* A name current in certain parts of New England (Vermont) for the *Pyrola Americana* or 'false wintergreen.'

moosewood ˈmusˌwʊd, *n.*

1. = **leatherwood 1.**

1778 CARVER *Travels* 507 The Moose Wood grows about four feet high, and is very full of branches. **1865** A. D. WHITNEY *Gayworthys* xxxvi, The moosewood grew with its tough-grained stems and broad thick leaves. **1931** CLUTE *Plants* 27 *Wicopy* . . . is used for the moose-wood (*Dirca palustris*) whose bark is so strong as to gain for it the common name of leatherwood.

2. The striped maple, *Acer pennsylvanicum.*

1792 BELKNAP *Hist. N.-Hampshire* III. 163 [The moose feeds] on the leaves and bark of a species of the maple, which is called moose-wood. **1814** PURSH *Flora Amer.* I. 267 *Acer striatum.* . . . A small tree with an elegant striped bark; known by the name of Striped-maple or Moose wood. **1902** *Amer. Folk-Lore* 249 After *moose* have been named . . . moose-wood (the striped maple, *Acer Pennsylvanica;* also the leatherwood, *Dirca palustris*, and the hobble-bush or *Viburnum tantanoides*). **1923** PEATTIE *Great Smokies* 265 Yellow birch, mountain ash, moosewood, red maple, mountain maple, Canadian hemlock, fire cherry, and others are common species.

moose yard. An area in the forest where moose herd in winter and keep the snow trampled down for protection and feeding. Cf. **winter yard.**

1800 D'ERES *Memoirs* 117 The animals are overtaken in their retreats (for they herd together, sometimes a large number, just as it happens) which is called the Moose yard, formed by them in trampling down the snow. **1839** HOFFMAN *Wild Scenes* 58 The sagacious animal, so soon as a heavy storm sets in, commences forming what is called a 'moose-yard'; which is a large area, wherein he industriously tramples down the snow while it is falling, so as to have a space to move about in, and browse upon the branches of trees. **1946** STANWELL-FLETCHER *Driftwood Valley* 137 We've seen old trails leading through the forest near a moose yard where the moose feed on tall dead grasses under thick spruces.

* **mop,** *n.*

1. A snuff stick or brush. *Colloq.*

1860 E. COWELL *Diary* 66 Each snuff dipper has her bottle and swab stick or box and mop.

2. The heavy mat of hair on the forehead of a buffalo.

1870 KEIM *Sheridan's Troopers* 40 On the forehead the bullet of the most powerful rifle has no effect whatever, the force being entirely expended on the immense mat or 'mop' of hair, eight or ten inches in length, between the eyes. **1938** GUYER *Pioneer Life West Texas* 5 The mop ... affords the buffalo protection from the ... cold.

3. A part of a dredge used by oystermen for removing starfish from oyster beds (see quot.).

1897 *Ann. Rep. Comm. Fisheries* 201 These mops are made of cotton twine, soft laid, and braided in ropes exactly like a mop for a kitchen floor, and, being attached to a triangle, are drawn by oyster steamers over the oyster beds, and the moment the mop touches a starfish the latter clings to it or is gathered up by it and lifted by steam hoist to the decks and the 'stars' are then taken ashore and buried.

4. mopboard, a baseboard or skirting board.

1853 FOWLER *Home for All* 159 After mop or base-boards are nailed on, ... fill in between these boards ... with stone or mortar. **1928** *Sat. Ev. Post* 12 May 114/2 Brant and Corbin were moving the desk slap up against the window to get the lamp cord out of the mopboard.

As the last term in **scrub mop.**

Moqui ˈmokɪ, *n. pl.* Also **Moquis.** [Tribal name, see quot. 1907.] A Shoshonean tribe of Pueblo Indians, the Hopi.

1780 in *N. Mex. Hist. Soc. Pub.* XXI. (1918) 17 The last news coming to me as to the condition of the Moquis is that the majority of them are taking shelter with the Carina Nation. **1831** J. O. PATTIE *Personal Narr.* 91 They had also met a tribe of Indians, who called themselves Mokee. **1907** HODGE *Amer. Indians* I. 560 *Hopi*. ... The name 'Moqui,' or 'Moki,' by which they have been popularly known, means 'dead' in their own language, but as a tribal name it is seemingly of alien origin and of undetermined signification. **1944** *Utah Hist. Quart.* Jan.–Apr. 24 With the death of George A. Smith, Jr., at the hands of the Navajos on his trip to the Moquis, the plan for moving the Indians was abandoned for some years.

attrib. **1848** RUXTON *Adventures* 195, I happened ... to enter the log hut of an old negro woman, being at the time in my mountain attire of buckskins, over which was thrown a Moqui or Navajo blanket, as it was wet weather. **1896** *Harper's Wkly.* 15 Aug. 801/1 This is the land of the Hopitah or Moki Indians—'the ancient province of Tusayan.'

b. The language of these Indians.

1882 *Atlantic Mo.* Oct. 547/1 They would repeat whole sentences, with marvelous truthfulness of sound, in Moqui, Zuñi, Navajo, Spanish, or English.

* **moral,** *n.* **1. moral dialogue,** a theatrical performance—a term used to disguise or make palatable dramatic exhibitions to a public opposed to the theater. Also **moral lecture.** *Obs.* **2. moral instructor,** (see quot.). *Obs.*

(1) *c***1761** in ODELL *Annals N.Y. Stage* I. 81 [Only the astute would recognize Othello ... in shape of] a Series of Moral Dialogues, in Five Parts, Depicting the Evil Effects of Jealousy and Other Bad Passions. *a***1789** in E. B. LEE *Sketches N. Eng. Village* 101, I have been to the theatre, or rather to the moral lecture, as they have named it here. ... This was ... a very amusing play, called the 'School for Scandal.' — (2) **1859** *First Impressions of New World* 178 There are chaplains, called here [penitentiary at Columbus, Ohio] Moral Instructors, who visit them and perform the service in the chapel.

moratorial mɔrəˈtorɪəl, *a.* Pertaining to, or payable in respect of, a moratorium. *Rare.* — **1914** *Economist* 7 Nov. 833/1 On the debts due to them and covered by the moratorium, they are entitled to a moratorial interest of 5 per cent.

* **Moravian,** *a.*

1. Moravian Indian, an Indian under the influence of, or converted by, Moravian missionaries. *Obs.*

1779 *N.H. Hist. Soc. Coll.* VI. 320 This place was settled by a denomination of people called Moravian Indians, by the Moravians having missionaries among them. **1831** WITHERS *Chron. Border Warfare* 232 The revengeful feelings ... towards the Moravian Indians ... were yet more deeply radicated by subsequent events.

2. Moravian town, a town composed chiefly of Moravian missionaries and their Indian converts. *Obs.*

[**1756** *N.C. Morav. Rec.* I. (1922) 168 Br. Christian Henrich ... explained that for a long time he had had it on his heart to suggest ... that the Hourly Intercession should be organized in Wachovia, as it was in Bethlehem and other Moravian towns.] **1791** WASHINGTON *Diaries* IV. 186 Arrived at Salem, one of the Moravian towns. **1831** WITHERS *Chron. Border Warfare* 160 Intelligence was conveyed to General Hand at Fort Pitt, by some friendly Indians from the Moravian towns.

moray ˈmore, *n.* [App. f. Pg. *moreia.*] Any one of various species of eels of the family *Muraenidae,* found in warm seas.

1624 SMITH *Gen. Hist. Va.* v. 172 Some of them yet knowne to the Americans, as the Prugoose, the Cauallo, The Gar-fish, Flying-fish and Marerayes. [*c***1733** CATESBY *Carolina* II. 20 The Muray [is found in the Bahama Islands].] **1897** *Outing* XXIX. 330/1 The murrey is not large, as Florida fishes go, but he is very red and excessively freckled.

morbo lacteo. = **milk sickness.** *Obs.* — **1919** DUNN *Indiana* II. 804 From 1836 to 1856, the disease known as 'Morbo Lacteo,' or 'milk sickness,' was encountered in numerous localities. It especially affected cattle, involving both flesh and milk.

Morey letter. (See quot. 1914.)

1884 *N.Y. Wkly. Tribune* 16 July 4/3 Our party is always well furnished with a garment of self-righteousness, and it needs no other; and truth, as represented by the Democratic party, will have a close-fitting Chinese fabric, known as the Morey letter. **1890** BIFF HALL *Turnover Club* 202 Is said to have been the author of the famous, or infamous, Morey letter of the Garfield campaign. **1914** *Cyclo. Amer. Govt.* II. 471 Morey Letter. A letter forged over the name of James A. Garfield, ... Republican presidential candidate, published in a New York paper called *Truth* shortly before the election of 1880, favoring the employment of cheap Chinese labor, addressed to a fictitious 'H. L. Morey, Employers' Union, Lynn, Massachusetts.'

* **Morgan,** *n.*

1. In allusive contexts with reference to William Morgan of Batavia, N.Y., whose alleged murder by the Freemasons in September, 1826, aroused considerable interest and was for a time a factor in politics. Usu. attrib. *Obs.* Cf. *good enough Morgan, s.v.* * **good 3. b.**

1827 *Hallowell* (Me.) *Gaz.* 20 June 3/3 An auctioneer in Utica, N.Y. advertises Grecian herrings, pitchforks, and lather-boxes, and Morgan mouse-traps, hats, and teapots. **1828** *Western Mo. Rev.* II. 253 There are [in Rochester] ... plenty of Morgan excitement, soda fountains, concerts, shows. **1849** *Commercial* (Wilmington, N.C.) 5 May 2/2 (Th. Supp.), The *Standard* has got it up as a 'very good Morgan' for political effect. **1867** *Harper's Wkly.* 24 Aug. 530/1 The nominating body ... are, if the expression may be permitted, looking about for Morgans.

b. Hence **Morganize,** *v. tr.,* to dispose of or kill secretly, as the Freemasons were alleged to have done in the case of Wm. Morgan. *Obs.*

1832 *Amer. R.R. Jrnl.* I. 165/3 Let him be *Morganized,* and his work suppressed by burning.

2. A horse of a superior breed the progenitor of which was a stallion owned by Justin Morgan (1747–98); also the breed of such a horse. Cf. **Vermont Morgan.**

Characteristics of these horses, esp. in early times, were: small heads and feet, short legs and backs, dark chestnut color, thick bright coats, curly manes and tails. They were good-tempered, energetic, and vivacious.

1855 in *Rep. Comm. Agric. 1862* 45 At present there are three breeds of horses that may be considered as being predominant in Maine, viz: Messengers, Morgans, and Black Hawks. **1901** MERWIN & WEBSTER *Calumet 'K'* 57 She was a tall, clean-limbed sorrel, a Kentucky-bred Morgan. **1945** MATHEWS *Talking* 185, I had a brown mare, half steel-dust and half black Morgan.

b. Often attrib., as (1) **Morgan blood,** (2) **breed,** (3) **colt,** (4) **foal,** (5) **horse,** (6) **mare,** (7) **stallion,** (8) **stock,** (9) **thoroughbred.**

(1) **1865** *Free South* (Newport, Ky.) 27 Sep. 1/7 There is no horse in the country in which there is a preponderance of Morgan blood. **1876** *Vt. Bd. Agric. Rep.* III. 173 This is precisely what the Morgan blood gives. — (2) **1841** *Spirit of Times* 24 July 246/3 (We.), Morgan breed. **1947** *Chi. Sun* (Bk. Week) 14 Sep. 4/2 The most debated chapter in all American horse history enters the story, too, with the ne'er-do-well Yankee, Justin Morgan, and his mysterious little red horse that stamped his likeness on the Morgan breed. — (3) **1876** *Vt. Bd. Agric. Rep.* III. 172 You can teach a Morgan colt anything. — (4) **1943** *Nat. Geog. Mag.* April 412 Morgan Mares and Foals Are Judged in Vermont.

(5) **1849** *N. Eng. Farmer* I. 314 There has never been a stock of horses in New England which has proved so generally useful as the Morgan stock of the original Morgan horse, raised by Justin Morgan, of West Springfield, Mass., in 1793. **1934** *DAB* XIII. 183 The establishment [in 1908] ... became the United States Morgan Horse Farm operated by the Department of Agriculture for the purpose of reviving and preserving the early Morgan type and distributing surplus stock of foreign and domestic breeders. **1949** *N.Y. Times Bk. Rev.* 5 June 26/3 There is a chapter also about the small, deep-chested, short-legged Morgan horse. — (6) **1945** PEARSON *Country Flavor* 107 The farmer and his boys hitched up the span of Morgan mares. — (7) **1857** *Ill. Agric. Soc. Trans.* III. 463 Our best roadsters are pro-

duced from a cross of the thoroughbred or Morgan stallions with grade mares. — **(8) 1913** LONDON *Valley of Moon* xxi. 516 They call her Ramona—some Spanish name: sired by Morellita out of genuine Morgan stock. — **(9) 1919** CUNNINGHAM *Chronicle* 141 A Morgan thoroughbred. Knows almost as much as a person.

Morgan cat. =**goujon.** *Colloq.* — **1920** FORBES & RICHARDSON *Fishes Ill.* 193 Leptops olivaris . . . is perhaps best known to the fishermen of the Mississippi River as the 'Morgan cat.' **1947** [see **goujon**].

morgen ˈmɔrgən, *n.* [Du. in same sense.] =**Holland's acre.**

[**1626** *Doc. Col. Hist. N.Y.* I. 37 The Island Manhattes . . . [is] 11,000 morgens in size.] **1681** *New Castle Court Rec.* 489, 300 Rod in all amounting to about 450 morgen. **1796** SMITH *Tour* 27 The Measures introduced originally by the Dutch are still in vogue [in n.w. New York]. A Morgan of Land contains somewhat more than Two Acres and a Skipple is about 3 Pecks. **1868** *Rep. U.S.Comm. Agric.* (1869) 151 Connected with this department of forestry are six thousand morgen of forest. **1891** *Financial World* Dec. 1 The assessed value of the real estate on this island of eleven thousand morgens [was] . . . set down officially for 1890 at $1,353,893,473.

* **morgue,** *n.*

1. A place for the bodies of the dead, esp. a place in which corpses of unknown persons found dead are exposed in order that they may be identified and claimed by relatives and friends.

1850 LEWIS *La. Swamp Doctor* 134 The morgue, in this institution [a hospital], was directly under the lecture room. **1880** *Dly. Dispatch* (Richmond, Va.) 3 Nov. 2/2 The remains were received at the Morgue. **1946** *Science Digest* Aug. 28/2 Grim statistics from the morgue prove that the great majority of those who are overweight die long before the average.

transf. **1900** *Dly. Ardmoreite* (Ardmore, Okla.) 3 May 4/3 The town is one vast morgue and every home a house of mourning. **1929** *Lit. Digest* 5 Oct. 66/2 In that capacity he had come upon a 'sick' letter which might eventually wind up in Uncle Sam's 'morgue'—the deadletter office.

2. In a newspaper office, a file of material to be used as needed. Cf. **newspaper morgue.**

1903 SCHUMAN *Practical Journalism* 103 This can be done with the aid of the 'morgue' or cabinet of biographical and obituary materials that is maintained in every wide-awake newspaper office. **1925** BENEFIELD *Chicken-Wagon Family* 94, I have written a column of assorted obituaries after having dug up enough material in the 'Transcript's' 'morgue' for six columns. **1949** *Boston Globe* 22 May (Sun. Mag.) 16/4 Newspaper libraries—morgues we call them—are interesting places.

attrib. **1912** *Outlook* 14 Sep. 84/1 In some newspaper offices the morgue man and his assistants—who sometimes number a dozen or more—work inside of steel cages, like bank clerks. **1923** BASTIAN *Editing Day's News* 10 The person in charge of the newspaper files, clippings, and pictures [is] called the 'morgue librarian.'

Mormon ˈmɔrmən, *n.* [f. personal name. See **1.**]

1. The alleged fourth-century prophet and author of the writings published in 1830 by Joseph Smith, the founder of the Church of Jesus Christ of Latter-Day Saints.

1830 *Book of Mormon* 518 And now I, Mormon, make a record of the things which I have both seen and heard, and call it the Book of Mormon. **1851** *Harper's Mag.* June 64/2 It professes to be an abridgement of the records made by the prophet Mormon. **1852** GUNNISON *Mormons* 13 The 'Latter-Day Saints' pretend to derive the word Mormon from the Gaelic and a branch of the Teutonic dialects: compounding it from Mor, *more* or *great*, and from Mon, signifying *good*, and therefore it imports—more good, great good. **1944** JOHNSON *As I Dare* 45 [He] . . . discovered the golden tablets of Mormon.

2. A member of the Church of Jesus Christ of Latter-Day Saints.

1830 *Mass. Spy* 22 Dec. (Th.), Elder Rigdon, one of the early Mormons, is described as having been 'a Campbelite leader of some notoriety.' **1883** RITCH *Illust. N. Mex.* 57 The Mormons have also gained a foothold on its [New Mexico's] domain. **1949** *Chi. D. News* 16 June 18/3 The prettiest girls in America are to be found among the Mormons of Salt Lake City.

transf. **1887** *Courier-Journal* 17 Feb. 6/7 A Dusky Mormon. Three Women Claim Richard Woods for a Husband. . . . Officers . . . arrested Richard Woods, colored. **1906** *Spectator* 3 Feb. 175/2 In distinction from the barnyard duck, who is a regular Mormon, the mallard is monogamous. **1922** *Lit. Digest* 10 June 40/1 Because a few of the inmates of the Hollywood film colony have 'married from time to time,' they are less to be censured as Mormons than pitied as morons.

Also **Mormonry,** in a collective sense.

1930 *Amer. Mercury* Jan. 6/1 The next step was an accident, one of a series that has displayed God's providence to Mormonry.

3. In combs.: (1) **Mormon battalion,** a company of soldiers enlisted from the Mormon camps in the territory of Iowa for service in the Mexican War, now *hist.*; (2) **Bible,** the *Book of Mormon*, those writings alleged by Joseph Smith to have been discovered and translated by him, and recognized by Mormons as having divine authority; (3) **Church,** the common but unofficial name for the Church of Jesus Christ of Latter-Day Saints; (4) **City,** Salt Lake City, Utah; (5) **expedition,** the expedition sent by the U.S. Government in 1857–58 to compel the Mormons in Utah to submit to federal laws, *obs.*; (6) **tea, trail, war,** see as main entries; (7) **weed,** the American jute or Indian mallow, *Abutilon theophrasti*.

(1) 1848 *Santa Fe Republican* 27 June 1/4 Capt. Hunt of the Mormon battalion, has left the Ciudad de Los Angelos for the Salt Lake. **1947** SESSIONS *Cities of Amer.* 36 The first detachment of the Mormon Battalion that had marched 2,000 miles to help in the Mexican War, and whose pay allotments had materially helped the Western migration, arrived in Salt Lake City. — **(2) 1838** WHITTIER in W. P. & F. J. Garrison *Life W. L. Garrison* II. 221 A discussion of the merits of animal magnetism, or of the Mormon Bible, would have been quite as appropriate. **1882** BUEL *Metropolitan Life Unveiled* 349 These three men have subscribed to an oath which will be found in all Mormon bibles. — **(3) 1838** *Niles' Reg.* 13 Oct. 103/3 We, and all the Mormon church, as we believe, entertain the same feelings and fears toward the Indians that are entertained by other citizens of this State. **1948** *Newsweek* 12 Jan. 38/2 Once a basic tenet of the Mormon Church, the doctrine of plural marriage was formally abandoned in 1890. — **(4) 1878** BEADLE *Western Wilds* 39 We got to the Mormon City all beat out.

(5) 1858 GLISAN *Jrnl. Army Life* 397 Our military friends of the Mormon expedition are perhaps barely sheltered under canvas tents on the snow-covered plains of Utah. — **(7) 1872** *Ill. Dept. Agric. Trans.* IV. p. ix, The Indian Mallow . . . [is] variously known as . . . 'velvet leaf,' 'butter print,' 'Mormon weed,' etc. **1907** LYONS *Plant Names* 8 Abutilon. . . . American Hemp, Indian Hemp, Mormonweed, Pie-marker, Pie-print, Sheep-weed.

b. In combs. of obvious meaning or sufficiently defined in the quots.: (1) **Mormon buggy,** (2) **coin,** (3) **cricket,** (4) **Destroying Angel,** (5) **elder,** (6) **flower,** (7) **fly,** (8) **hay press,** (9) **merchant,** (10) **missionary,** (11) **road,** (cf. **Mormon trail**), (12) **State,** (13) **Station,** (14) **store,** (15) **trading-train,** (16) **tree.**

(1) 1942 STEGNER *Mormon C.* 136 Buggies and wagons stood in line many of them the two- or three-seated light spring wagons with fringed white tops that the Gentiles already knew as 'Mormon buggies.' — **(2) 1860** *Mountaineer* (Salt Lake City) 14 Jan. 82/3 The Commanding Officer has been informed that there is a large amount of gold coin—several thousand of dollars, purporting to be worth five dollars, commonly called 'Mormon coin,' about to be put into circulation. — **(3) 1909** *Cent. Supp.* 314/1 Mormon cricket, a wingless American locustid, *Anabrus simplex*. **1948** *Yearbook Agric.* 274/2 The early Mormon settlers knew no satisfactory way of fighting the Mormon cricket. — **(4) 1872** MARK TWAIN *Roughing It.* xii. 106 [We] took supper with a Mormon 'Destroying Angel.' 'Destroying Angels,' as I understand it, are Latter-Day Saints who are set apart by the Church to conduct permanent disappearances of obnoxious citizens.

(5) 1884 *Cent. Mag.* May 114 It was a Mormon elder, come to preach in that conservative, comfortable-minded village. — **(6) 1878** JACKSON *Travel at Home* 19 This sunflower is called the Mormon flower, and is said to spring up wherever Mormons go. — **(7) 1845** F. N. MOORE *Diary* (1946) 46 Our boat and every thing about it is now covered with Mormon flies as they are called, being, I am told, peculiar to this neighborhood. I heard one of the deck hands a little while ago cursing 'these damned Nauvoo flies.' **1847** C. LANMAN *Summer in Wild.* 34, I noticed on . . . [the upper and lower rapids of the Miss. R.] a certain fly or miller which is found at the evening hour flying about in immense numbers. They are called the Mormon fly and I was told were found on these rapids alone. [**1909** *Cent. Supp.* 828/3 Mormon. . . . In *entom.*, an American hesperiid butterfly, *Atrytone hobomok*, which occurs from eastern Canada to the Mississippi valley. Its larvae feed on grasses. Also called *hobomok skipper*.] — **(8) 1872** EGGLESTON *Hoosier Schoolm.* xxvi. 178 His new red barn with its large 'Mormon' hay-press inside. — **(9) 1882** COYNER *Hand-Book of Mormonism* 90 Under the direction of the Church, 'Co-operative Mercantile Institutions' have been established . . . for the purpose of depriving Gentile and apostate Mormon merchants of the Mormon trade.

(10) 1855 *Santa Barbara* (Calif.) *Gaz.* 12 July 2/1 During the past three or four days, several parties of Mormon Missionaries have passed through our city. **1881** in COYNER *Hand-Book of Mormonism* (1882) 40 There is not a country on the globe where a Mormon missionary cannot be found. — **(11) 1850** *Jrnl. Birmingham Emig. Co.*

17 June, About noon we came to the forks of the road, the road turning to the left being the old mormon road, the other being what is called Sublets Cut-off. **1876** DODGE *Black Hills* 143 The old Mormon road furnishes a good route, preferable in every way to the Niobrara route, except that it is somewhat longer. **1942** STEGNER *Mormon C.* 35 The towns along the two transcontinental trails—the old Mormon Road through Las Vegas to Los Angeles, and the California Trail across the salt desert to Emigrant Pass, are partly Mormon yet. — **(12) 1881** CHASE *Editor's Run in N. Mex.* 109 Grant appointed Axtell governor, who . . . went so far as to lay plans to import Mormons and get the territory [of N. Mex.] admitted into the Union as a Mormon state. **1893** L. WAGNER *More about Names* 35 Utah, otherwise The Mormon State, is called by the Mormons themselves Deseret. — **(13) 1855** *N.Y. Wkly. Tribune* 15 Dec. 1/3 One of the wives of Elder Orson Hyde accompanied the above as far as the Mormon station in Carson Valley. **1877** W. WRIGHT *Big Bonanza* 20 To all who crossed the Plains, on their way to the goldfields of California, in the early days, Genoa [Nev.] was known as 'Mormon Station' a name it continued to bear for some years. **1942** STEGNER *Mormon C.* 65 He had sprung clear across the Great Basin deserts to locate the Mormon Station, now Genoa, under the shadow of the Sierra on the emigrant road to California. — **(14) 1888** ROE *Army Lett.* 385 Mormons . . . can purchase only at the mormon store, where the gentiles are ever cordially welcomed also.

(15) 1871 RAYMOND *3d Rep. Mines* 218 Far into the mining districts of other Territories went the Mormon trading-trains, carrying grain and vegetables. — **(16) 1942** STEGNER *Mormon C.* 21 These are the 'Mormon trees,' Lombardy poplars. Wherever they went the Mormons planted them.

Also *Mormon blanket, brake, conquest, country, cowboy, dog, emigrant, emigration, empire, fanatic, hater, pilgrim, prophet, rebellion, school, settlement, town, trade, trouble, village, vote,* etc.

As the last term in **anti-, basswood, hickory, Jack Mormon.**

Mormondom ˈmɔrməndəm, *n.* The region over which Mormonism prevails; Mormon country.

1845 *Quincy* (Ill.) *Whig* 8 Nov. 2/2 See how eagerly they snap up the articles of the Reveille and parade them before all Mormondom in their paper, as evidence that sympathy abroad is enlisted in their favor. **1887** *Courier-Journal* 21 Jan. 1/2 His experience in Mormondom satisfies him that the Latter Day Saints are a thoroughly incorrigible people. **1949** *Sat. Ev. Post* 12 Feb. 32/1 Not at all offended, the high prophet of Mormondom asked how much of a salary he could command.

Mormoness ˈmɔrmənˌɛs, *n.* A Mormon woman. — *a*1861 WINTHROP *J. Brent* 99 'What are those vermin about?' said Brent. 'Selecting, perhaps, a Mormoness to kidnap to-night or planning a burglary.' **1906** *Out West* May 405 (*title*), The Writer Lady and the Mormoness.

Mormonish ˈmɔrmənɪʃ, *a.* Of or like a Mormon or Mormons. *Obs.* — **1846** *Quincy* (Ill.) *Whig* 19 March 3/3 It would be desirable by all quiet citizens that they should be able to discover a complete evacuation of everything Mormonish in Nauvoo, before they hazard purchases in that place. **1852** *Ore. Statesman* 6 Jan. 2/6 Your course looks as Mormonish as anything I ever saw.

Mormonism ˈmɔrmənˌɪzəm, *n.* The doctrines and church polity of Mormons.

1831 *Niles' Reg.* 16 July 353/1 Mormonism. . . . Certain knaves . . . started a new religion. **1895** *Advance* (Chi.) 31 Jan. 617/1 With Mormonism . . . dominant in the one, and Catholic Mexicanism in the other. **1947** *Time* 21 July 21/1 Mormonism, with 74% of Utah's citizens, is still the greatest influence in the state's politics.

Mormonite ˈmɔrmənˌaɪt, *n.* A member of the Church of Jesus Christ of Latter-Day Saints; also, in *pl.*, the sect or entire body of believers in Mormonism. Also attrib.

1831 *Painesville* (Ohio) *Telegraph* 8 Nov. 1/3 'Being carried away in the spirit,' and 'I know it to be so by the spirit,' are well known phrases, and in common use in the Mormonite church. **1860** JOHNSON *New Comic Songs* 30, I wish I was a Mormonite, and lived in Utah State. **1947** DEVOTO *Across Wide Missouri* 185 The 'Mormonites' . . . had been driven into the unsettled lands of Clay County.

Mormonize ˈmɔrmənˌaɪz, *v. tr.* To render or make like a Mormon. *Rare.* — **1843** *Times & Seasons* (Nauvoo, Ill.) 1 Sep. 305/2 But do not think that I, even I, have been Mormonized, by what I write, for I say *Nay*.

Mormon tea. Any plant of the genus *Ephedra*. Cf. **Brigham.**

1910 THORNBER *Grazing Ranges Ariz.* 261 The more important are salt-bush, . . . winter fat, . . . and the green, rush-like twigs of . . . Mormon tea. **1931** DAYTON *Western Browse Plants* 12 All the species are known as a Mormon-tea, canatillo, Brigham tea, teamsters' tea, shrubby horsetail, and by other local names. **1949** *Chi. Nat. Hist. Mus. Bul.* April 8/1 Collections will be made of species of the Mormon tea plant, Ephedra, which is the dominant vegetation over large areas of the desert.

b. A drink prepared from a plant of this genus.

1937 NICHOL *Natural Vegetation Ariz.* 220 Among beverages commonly used and made from other than fresh fruits are the well-known Mormon tea (Ephedra) with its sennalike taste.

Mormon trail. The route followed by the Mormons in their emigration from the territory of Iowa to Utah in 1847.

1850 in *Annals of Iowa* 3 Ser. IX. 453 Here [near Chariton Point, Iowa] we struck the old Mormon trail. **1868** MARK TWAIN *Curious Dream* 45 The post route from Indian Gulch . . . changed partly to the old Mormon trail. **1949** *Kans. Hist. Quart.* Feb. 39 The War Department decided in 1854 to improve the Mormon trail from Omaha as far as New Fort Kearny.

Mormon war.

1. Any one of several struggles between the Mormons and their "Gentile" neighbors, esp. a series of such disorders at Nauvoo, Ill., 1844–46, which resulted in the departure of the Mormons for Utah. *Obs.*

1833 *Ev. Star* (Kirtland, Ohio) 118/1 (*heading*), 'The Mormon War.' **1839** *Columbian Reg.* (New Haven, Conn.) 19 March 4/4 The paymaster in Missouri, engaged in making out the pay rolls of the forces employed in suppressing the Mormon War, estimated . . . the whole expense not less than half a million of dollars. **1846** *Quincy* (Ill.) *Whig* 3 Feb. 2/4 He was a Major in the last '*Mormon War*.'

2. The conflict between the Mormons and the U.S. Government. Now *hist.* Cf. **Mormon expedition.**

1857 *S.F. Plaindealer* 10 Dec. 2/2 The Mormon war will furnish abundant material for Buncombe speeches. **1942** RISTER *Land Hunger* 8 Upon the outbreak of the 'Mormon War,' Dave and his older brother, Jack, rode away from their Indiana home to join the army of Johnston.

* **morning,** *n.* In combs.: (1) **morning boat,** a steamboat that begins a trip or passage early in the morning, cf. **day boat;** (2) **business,** in the Senate, legislative matters dealt with in the period immediately following the reading of the journal; (3) **-glory,** * **hour,** see as main entries; (4) **line,** a steamboat line operating boats which begin their runs in the morning.

(1) 1839 *Spirit of Times* 13 July 216/2 An immense crowd of persons embarked in the morning boats. **1871** HOWELLS *Wedding Journey* ii. 40 You had better go by the morning boat. — **(2) 1870** *Cong. Globe* 21 April 2862/3 After the privileged morning business shall have been concluded, the Calendar shall be taken up. **1900** *Cong. Rec.* 3 Jan. 632/2 Senators about me suggest that the bill might be called up to-morrow immediately after the morning business. — **(4) 1843** *Hunt's Merch. Mag.* IX. 97 These beautiful boats now form the morning line between New York and Albany. **1849** *Bankers' Mag.* IV. 89 Mr. Hays . . . returned to New York in the morning line.

morning-glory ˈmɔrnɪŋˌglorɪ, *n.* Any one of various plants of the genus *Ipomoea*, esp. *I. purpurea*. Also the blossom of such a plant.

1814 PURSH *Flora Amer.* I. 146 *Ipomoea Nil.* . . . Flowers beautiful pale blue, only open early in the morning, from which it has been called Morning-glory. **1873** ALDRICH *Marjorie Daw* 57 Dew . . . had been left from the revels of the fairies overnight in the cups of the morning-glories. **1945** *Chi. Tribune* 14 Oct. VII. 1/8 Red, white, and blue morning glories are climbing over their little trailer house.

transf. **1865** SALA *Diary* II. 76 The clinking of the glasses, as curious drinks—'morning glories' and 'Tom and Jerrys,' 'brandy smashes,' . . . are mingled at the bar. **1870** MACRAE *Americans* II. 306 You will see the barmen in their shirt sleeves hard at work compounding cocktails, morning-glories, tangle-legs, gin-slings, eye-openers, and other transatlantic refreshers.

b. *Attrib.*, sometimes in allusion to the shape or transitoriness of the blossom of the plant.

1871 STOWE *Sam Lawson* 75 She sat down in the mornin'-glory porch, quite quiet, and didn't sing a word. **1883** THAXTER *Poems for Children* 91 All clothed in bells of lovely blue, a morning-glory vine. **1920** *Harvey's Wkly.* 15 May 15/2 You have . . . sent one more morning glory statesman to limbo. **1947** COFFIN *Yankee Coast* 59 The owners . . . have to make guitars and banjos do. And accordions, phonographs with morning-glory horns, and, latterly, radios.

c. morning-glory stove, a parlor stove, poss. so called because of a morning-glory design on it. *Obs.*

1885 ROE *Driven Back to Eden* 74 A morning-glory stove gave out abundant warmth and a rich light which blended genially with the red colors of the carpet.

morning hour. (See quots.)

1876 *Cong. Rec.* 10 Feb. 1003/1, I desire to make a suggestion . . . that the morning hour for reports from committees for this day be dispensed with. **1889** *Cent. Mag.* March 793/1 In those days there used to be what was called a 'morning hour,' wherein committees reported bills and put them on their passage. **1946** *Newsweek* 28 Jan. 23/2 Under its rules, the senior legislative body was deep in its 'morning hour,' a period from noon till 2 p.m. reserved for introduction of bills, presentation of petitions and memorials, and other matters, during which debate is barred.

***Morocco,** *n.* In combs.: (1) **Morocco head,** =**dun diver;** (2) **jaw,** the surf scoter, *Melanitta perspicillata;* (3) **millet,** =**Johnson grass.**

(1) **1888** Trumbull *Names of Birds* 65 To some Atlantic City gunners, [the goosander is known as] Morocco-Head. **1890** *Cent.* 3862/1 *Morocco-head,* . . . the American sheldrake or merganser, (New Jersey.) **1917** *Birds of Amer.* I. 110 Merganser. *Mergus americanus.* . . . [Also called] Morocco-head (female). — (2) **1888** Trumbull *Names of Birds* 103 At Bellport, L.I., Morocco-Jaw and White-Head. **1917** *Birds of Amer.* I. 151 Surf Scoter. *Oidemia perspicillata.* . . . [Also called] Plaster-bill; Morocco-jaw; Goggle-nose. — (3) **1889** Vasey *Agric. Grasses* 36 *Sorghum halepense* (Johnson Grass: Mean's Grass) . . . has been called . . . Australian Millet, and Morocco millet.

moron 'moran, *n.* [Gk., neut. of *moros,* dull, stupid.]

1. A person possessing the highest degree of feeble-mindedness; an adult having the intelligence of a normal child between eight and twelve. Also attrib.

1910 Henry H. Goddard lett. 29 April in *Jrnl. Psycho-Asthenics* Sep.–Dec. 65 The other [suggestion] is to call them [feeble-minded children] by the Greek word 'moron.' It is defined as one who is lacking in intelligence, one who is deficient in judgment or sense. All this differentiates him too from the lower grade of whom we cannot say they are simply deficient in judgment, there is something more than that. **1926** *Chi. Tribune* 28 Jan. 14/1 Legislation to provide for a moron colony has the support of County Judge Edmund K. Jarecki. **1949** *Amer. Jrnl. Mental Deficiency* July 31/1 Approximately 75% of all mental defectives belong in the moron classification.

2. A degenerate, a fool, a brutish person. *Colloq.*

1922 Titus *Timber* iii. 37 So this backwoods moron, even, knew something about his affairs that John Taylor did not know. **1948** *Chi. Tribune* 4 April (Grafic Mag.) 20/3 We're intelligent and know what an optomist is, but how many of those morons are gonna know it's an eye doctor.

b. A sexual pervert.

1924 *Amer. Mercury* March 308/1 So long as morons are permitted to remain at large there will be crime waves. **1949** *Chi. D. News* 25 March 22/4 Removing shrubbery and lagoons will not improve the morals of a moron.

3. little moron, the feeble-minded hero of numerous jokes popular *c*1936.

1943 in Botkin *Amer. Folklore* 463 Did you hear about the little moron who cut his arms off? He wanted to wear a sleeveless sweater. **1948** *Savings News* March 18/3 There's the story about the little Swedish moron who heard about the atomic bomb and then went around the house throwing out all the pots of uraniums because they might split and blow up the place.

moronic mo'ranık, *a.* Like a moron.

1928 *Amer. Mercury* Sep. 66/1 Never was more moronic entertainment offered in American lodges. **1949** *Chi. Tribune* 1 Sep. 18/8 All the efforts have been shadow boxing to befuddle the moronic masses.

b. Hence **moronically,** *adv.*

1931 *Churchman* 14 Feb. 15 The philosophers go home considerably enheartened when they find Socrates moronically low in his I.Q. score. **1948** *Coronet* July 43/2 He was a thick-tongued 'worker type' and seemed moronically hypnotized by the Dodgers.

morral mo'ræl, *n.* [Sp. in same senses.] A knapsack or nose-bag.— **1931** Dobie *Coronado's C.* 161 The nigger reached into a morral (a fibre bag commonly carried on the horn of the saddle by horsemen of the Southwest), drew out a rock, and handed it to Reagan. **1932** Bentley *Sp. Terms* 169 Morral. . . . A nose-bag; a feed bag. *Morral* is widely current in the cattle country of the Southwest, particularly in Te^as.

***Morrill,** *n. attrib.* Designating a bill (later an act) introduced in Congress in 1857 by Representative (later Senator) Morrill of Vermont, providing for the founding of colleges of agriculture and mechanical arts in the different states.

1857–8 *Ill. Agric. Soc. Trans.* III. 565 If the Morrill bill, endowing industrial colleges in each state, passes the Senate next session, the farming public will gain a victory worth a thousand conquests. **1926** Gabriel *Pageant of Amer.* III. 245 Out of the Morrill Act, and the supplementary Act of 1890, have come the colleges of agriculture and the mechanical arts one or more of which are to be found in every state. **1948** *Miss. Valley Hist. Rev.* Dec. 442 In 1875 the company purchased fifty thousand acres of rich pine land that had originally been owned by Cornell University under the Morrill Act of 1862.

Morrisite 'mɔrɪsˌaɪt, *n.* [Joseph *Morris,* a Welsh convert to Mormonism.] A follower of Joseph Morris, the leader of a group of Mormons who seceded from the orthodox church about 1860 and established a communistic camp about thirty-five miles north of Salt Lake City.

1863 J. L. Fisk *Exped. Rocky Mts.* 31 On entering the mountains to the north of the Mormon settlements, we passed 'Soda Springs,' a small town of 'Morrisites,' seceders from Mormonism. **1883** Schaff *Relig. Encycl.* II. 1579/2 In Utah there have been Morrisites, reproaching Brigham that he was so barren of 'revelations.' **1942** W. Stegner *Mormon Country* 129 The Morrisites barricaded themselves and fought it out, but were eventually overpowered as ruthlessly as the Missourians had overpowered the Saints a few years before.

Morris' note. A note issued by the authority of Robert Morris (1734–1806), statesman and financier prominent in the financial affairs of the country in Revolutionary times. *Obs.* — **1787** *Maryland Gaz.* 1 June 1/3 Suitable to the present and ensuing seasons, which he is determined to sell on the most reasonable terms for Cash, Produce, Bills of Exchange, Bank and Morris's Notes only.

***Morse,** *n.* [S. F. B. *Morse* (1791–1872), Amer. inventor.]

1. *ellipt.* Telegraphic dispatches sent in Morse code.

1891 *Salt Lake Times* 18 April 1/1 The fearless, manly telegrapher is the man who sends even, well spaced Morse.

2. *attrib.* Designating articles used in the system of telegraphy invented by Morse.

1858 G. B. Prescott *Telegraph* 191 We work with Morse Key and detector. **1862** in Moore *Rebellion Rec.* V. II. 535 The following letter . . . gives an interesting account of the services of the Morse telegraph to the army. **1880** *Harper's Mag.* Oct. 727/2 Buyers . . . rap out their bids with the Morse instrument.

3. a. Morse alphabet, a system of dots, dashes, and spaces, invented by Morse, used in sending telegraphic messages. **b. Morse code,** =prec.

(a) **1873** *Harper's Mag.* Aug. 354/2 In each [instrument], holes representing the words of the message are first punched in a narrow strip of paper, which are the equivalents of the dot and dash of the Morse alphabet, and are translated into dots and dashes after transmission. **1890** *Ib.* Feb. 429/1 The expertness . . . made him one of the 'knights of the key,' as manipulators of the Morse alphabet delighted to call themselves. — (b) **1931** F. L. Allen *Only Yesterday* 13 For there is no such thing as radio broadcasting. Here and there a mechanically inclined boy has a wireless set, with which, if he knows the Morse code, he may listen to messages from ships at sea and from land stations equipped with sending apparatus. **1949** *Reader's Digest* April 149/2 We all knew the Morse code fairly well within a few weeks.

***mortar,** *n.* (See quot. 1881.)

1881 Raymond *Mining Gloss., Mortar,* . . . the receptacle beneath the stamps in a stamp mill, in which the dies are placed, and into which the rock is fed to be crushed. **1882** *47th Congress* 1 Sess. H.R. Ex. Doc. No. 216, 588 The gold goes in and out of the mortars continuously.

b. mortar bed, the inclined bottom of a stamp used in crushing ore.

1871 Raymond *3d Rep. Mines* 240 The battery-box is . . . cast in one piece with the mortar-bed. **1874** — *6th Rep. Mines* 353 The mortar-beds constitute a series of inclined terraces . . . ; and the pulp passing through the screens of one battery is discharged immediately into the one next in front, to be crushed still finer.

As the last term in **hominy, Indian, samp mortar.**

***mortgage,** *n.* As the last term in **chattel, crop, grab, snap mortgage.**

mortgage man. One of a group of men in Rhode Island claiming to have titles (prob. derived from Indians) to lands in the Narraganset country. *Obs.* — **1708** *R.I. Col. Rec.* (1859) IV. 50 The said committee met at the house of Capt. John Eldredge, and there heard the claims and pretended titles of those gentlemen called the mortgage men, and Atherton's associates.

mortician mɔr'tɪʃən, *n.* [f. **mort*uary and *-ician,* prob. influenced by **physician.*] An undertaker.

1895 *Columbus* (O.) *Dispatch* 14 Aug. (*advt.*), We, Mauk & Webb, are the only Morticians in the city who do not belong to the Funeral Director's Protective Association. **1932** Beck *Wonderland* 67 Some ambitious, but none too busy, mortician will feel that his ancient and honorable profession has been neglected. **1948** *Christian Cent.* 4 Feb. 146/1 Give the morticians credit—their cosmetic arts are highly skilled.

morus 'morəs, *n.* [L., mulberry tree.] **1. morus multicaulis,** =**multicaulis.** Also attrib. **2. morus plantation,** a plantation of white mulberry of the variety of multicaulis. *Obs.*

(1) **1833** *Niles' Reg.* XLIV. 332/2 A succession of crops of silk . . . can, by the Chinese *moras multicaulis*, be repeatedly cultivated and distributed throughout in this part of the new world. **1846** H. N. MOORE *Fitzgerald & Hopkins* 100 Before they invested all their capital in Vicksburg bank stock and morus multicaulis speculations. **1948** *Amer. Fabrics* No. 6, 65/1 In 1839 it was discovered that the 'morus multicaulis' was not a golden rooted tree, but a drug on the market. — (2) **1839** *S. Lit. Messenger* V. 753/1 She busied herself more than ever with her morus plantation.

Mosbyite ˈmozbɪˌaɪt, *n.* [John S. *Mosby* (1833–1916), a Confederate Colonel.] During the Civil War, one of the guerilla fighters under the leadership of Colonel Mosby. *Obs.* — **1867** J. M. CRAWFORD *Mosby* 286 In those expeditions he [a Northern officer] did nothing very damaging to us, except here and there picking up a Mosbyite and a horse or two.

* **Mose,** *n.* A "B'hoy." In allusion to a character in *A Glance at New York*, a play first presented in 1848. *Slang. Obs.*

[**1848** B. A. BAKER *Glance at New York* 9 *Mose.* [*Smoking; he spits.*] I've made up my mind not to run wid der machine any more.] **1851** NORTHALL *Curtain* 92 Mose, instead of appearing on the stage, was in the pit, the boxes, and the gallery. **1856** M. THOMPSON *Plu-ri-bus-tah* 222 Yunga-Merrakah determined To put off his Bowery notions, . . . To have done with Mose and 'Syksey.'

* **Moses,** *n.*

1. A ship's boat (see quot. 1769). In full **Moses boat.** *Obs.*

1705 *Boston News-Letter* 3 June, There was Stole, a Little Moses Boat from the side of the Sloop Larke. **1759** *Essex Inst. Coll.* II. 286/1 The Capt. sent our Moses (Boat) after them. [**1769** FALCONER *Dict. Marine* (1776) F4ᵛ A moses is a very flat broad boat, used by merchant-ships amongst the Carribee-islands, to bring hogsheads of sugar off from the sea-beach to the shipping.] **1774** ROMANS in P. L. Phillips *Notes on B. Romans* 19 It must Blow very hard before the Water begins to be too Rough for a Small Moses. **1812** *Boston Gaz.* 26 Oct. Supp. (Th.), On Saturday was picked up, on Dorchester Flats, a small Moses boat.

b. Also **Moses-built boat.** *Obs.*

1753 *S.C. Gazette* 5 Feb., Stolen, a New-England moses-built boat. **1770** *Boston Gazette* 12 March 3/2 (*advt.*) (Ernst), A Moses built Boat.

2. *Moses of the colored people*, Abraham Lincoln. *Rare.*

1870 MACRAE *Americans* I. 233 You lookin', sah, at President Linkum? We call him de Moses of de coloured people. He led us forth out of de land of bondage.

3. *To give particular Moses*, to scold or handle severely. *Slang. Obs.*

1850 LEWIS *La. Swamp Doctor* 52 The way a number ten go-to-meetin' brogan commenced givin' a hoss particular Moses, were a caution to hoss-flesh.

As the last term in **Holy Moses.**

mosey ˈmoʒɪ, *n. Pa.* [Pa.-Ger. (see quot. 1924). The ultimate origin is obscure.] (See quots.) Also **mosey sugar.** *Colloq.*

1849 W. DUANE *Lett. to Bartlett* 22 Jan. (MS), *Sugar Mosey* or *Mosey Sugar*, the name of a cake made of sugar, for children, in Harrisburgh Pa. **1870** *Nation* July 56/2 'Mosey-sugar' . . . was a black molasses candy—not cake, as Bartlett says—scalloped at the edges like our cakes of maple-sugar. **1916** *D.N.* IV. 338 Mozey, *n.* Molasses candy; also, nut candy. 'We stayed at home and made *mozey.*' (Pa.) [**1924** LAMBERT *Pa.-Ger.* 107 Mooschi, nooschi . . . m., taffy.]

mosey ˈmozɪ, *v.* [See note.]

This word may come from Spanish *vamos*. But *EDD* has *mose about*, "to go about in a dull, stupid manner," and *mouse* (with var. *mousey*), "to run quickly and stealthily like a mouse." It will be seen from the quots. here given that there has been some confusion as to whether the verb indicates fast or slow movement.

intr. To depart. Now, usu., to move along slowly, to amble, stroll; formerly, to move along fast, to "scram." *Colloq.*

1829 *Va. Lit. Museum* 30 Dec. 459 *Mosey.* To move off. *Kentucky.* **1859** TALIAFERRO *Fisher's R.* 60 Ev'ry time I'd strike the yeth the cussed sarpunt would peg away at me. At last the spell were broke, and I moseyed home at an orful rate. **1894** *D.N.* I. 332 Mosey. To leave suddenly, generally under doubt or suspicion. (New Jersey.) **1944** PYLE *Brave Men* 98 Italian men in old ragged uniforms moseyed through the arbors.

b. With adverbs.

1836 *Phila. Pub. Ledger* 2 Dec. (Th.), You'r not going to smoke me. So mosey off. **1870** MARK TWAIN *Curious Republic of Gondour* (1919) 57, I hain't got time to be palavering along here—got to . . . mosey along. **1923** J. H. COOK *On Old Frontier* 36 When that hyena comes to camp, you kind o' mosey around till he puts his gun down. **1949** *Chi. Tribune* 11 Sep. VI. Sec. 4. 8/2 You can also mosey around thru the furniture departments of stores to get your ideas.

moshay məˈʃe, *n.* [?F. *monsieur.*] (See quot.) *Rare.* — **1877** BARTLETT 408 *Moshay*, a slave who came from Florida at the beginning of the late civil war states that this is the name given there to the keeper of bloodhounds.

* **mosquito,** *n.* In combs.: (1) **mosquito box,** a derogatory term for cramped, uncomfortable quarters, *rare;* (2) **country,** (see quot.), *obs.;* (3) **hawk,** see as a main entry; (4) **killer,** a contrivance for killing mosquitoes, *rare;* (5) **proof,** of persons, not affected by mosquitoes or mosquito bites, *colloq.;* (6) **state,** a nickname for New Jersey; (7) **swamp,** a swamp infested with mosquitoes.

(1) **1887** N. PERRY *Flock of Girls* 224 Here you are in this poky little mosquito-box. — (2) **1778** CARVER *Travels* 106 All the wilderness between the Mississippi and Lake Superior is called by the Indians the Moschettoe country. — (4) **1870** *Rep. Comm. Patents 1868* II. 145/2 Mosquito Killer. . . . The head-piece is made of thin board covered with cloth of a loose nap.

(5) *a*1656 BRADFORD *Hist.* 196 They are too delicate . . . that cannot enduer the biting of a muskeeto; we would wish such to keepe at home till at least they be muskeeto proofe. **1818** FORDHAM *Narr. Travels* 216, I thought I was mosquito proof last year. — (6) **1930** in *Amer. Nicknames* (1937) 376 We get the scornful title, the *Mosquito State*, because we seem to have our share of these industrious and bloodthirsty insects. — (7) **1847** ROBB *Squatter Life* 70 Hoss Allen's Apology; or, The Candidate's Night in a Musquito Swamp!

b. Designating things used in keeping out or driving off mosquitoes, as **mosquito bar,** (see as a main entry), **canopy, curtain, dope, fire, frame, guard, trousers, veil.**

1857 *Rep. Comm. Patents 1856* 317 *Mosquito Canopy.* . . . The rods 8 and 9 which support the canopy [etc.]. — **1770** in *John Norton & Sons Merchants of London & Virginia* 119 Shall be glad you will see to the buying the . . . stuff for Musketo Curtains. **1803** *Lewis & Clark Exped.* VII. (1905) 234 Camp Equipage [includes]: . . . Muscatoe Curtains, 2 patent chamber lamps & wicks. **1863** WHITMAN *Spec. Days* 42 The mosquito-curtains of the adjoining cots obstructed the sight. — **1921** *Outing* Sep. 266/3 Mosquito dope may be made as follows. **1948** *Chi. Tribune* 11 July 7/1 New mosquito dopes are being tested by fishermen now that the insects are buzzing. — **1826** COOPER *Mohicans* xiv. The mists of Horican are not like the curls from a peace-pipe, or the smoke which settles above a mosquito-fire. — **1866** *Rep. Comm. Patents 1863* I. 294 An expanding mosquito frame formed of bars fitted so as to be increased or decreased in length to fit the window. — **1867** *Rep. Comm. Patents 1866* I, The deep frame . . . [and] the narrow fringe or edging—forming a mosquito guard for the face. — **1828** MRS. HALL *Letters* 261 We got her a pair of mosquito trowsers to save her poor little legs from being mangled in the way they have been during the last week. — **1843** *Nat. Hist. N.Y., Geology* I. 233 Although provided with thick gloves and musquito veils, myself and lady were much annoyed.

c. In place-names: (1) **Mosquito Cove,** (2) **Creek.**

(1) **1668** *Oyster Bay Rec.* I. 42 Joseph Carpenter of Muskeeto Cove. — (2) **1837** W. JENKINS *Ohio Gaz.* 323 Musketoe creek . . . was so called by the original surveyors of the Western Reserve, on account of the great numbers of Musketoes.

As the last term in **New Jersey mosquito.**

mosquito bar. [See **bar,** *n.*²] A framework covered with mosquito netting that may be fitted like a tent over a bed to protect a sleeper from mosquitoes, also mosquito netting that serves this purpose. Also attrib.

[**1682** in *S.C. Hist. Coll.* II. 136 There are few Insects in Carolina that can reasonably be complain'd of, except a sort of Gnats, which they call *Muscatoes* . . . for better Security, they make fine Gausework about their Beds, which keeps them off.] **1804** ORDWAY in *Jrnls. Lewis & O.* 87 Got mosquetoes bears from Capt Lewis to sleep in. **1805** LEWIS in *L. & Clark Exped.* II. (1904) 228, I sent a man to the canoes for my musquetoe bier . . . as it is impossible to sleep without being defended against the . . . insects. **1809** *Ann. 11th Congress* 2 Sess. II. App. 2448, 95 musquito bars, at 4½ and 7 dollars each. **1863** *Rep. Comm. Patents 1861* 443 Improved Mosquito-Bar Frame. . . . Frames of wood or other material . . . [which] when covered by a proper material . . . may be used as a protection against mosquitoes or as a tent. **1946** *Chi. D. News* 9 Aug. 12/1 That 'Iron Curtain' around Russia is beginning to look like a fly screen or a mosquito bar.

mosquito hawk.

1. A nighthawk.

1709 LAWSON *Carolina* 144 *East-India* Bats or Musquetc Hawks, are the Bigness of a Cuckoo, and much of the same Colour. **1850**

Conn. Public Acts 5 It shall not be lawful . . . for any person to shoot . . . the robin, blue-bird, swallow, . . . night or mosquito-hawk, whip-poor-will. [etc.]. **1917** *Birds of Amer.* II. 172.

2. *S.* A dragonfly.

1737 BRICKELL *N. Carolina* 163 The Muskeetoe-Hawks, are Insects, so called, from their continually hunting after Muskeetoes, and killing and eating them. **1949** *Time* 25 July 34/2 Yankees in some part of New England call it a *devil's darning needle*, while some Southern Coast people go for *mosquito hawk*.

* **moss,** *n.* In combs.: (1) **mossback,** see as a main entry; (2) **-backed,** extremely conservative or reactionary; (3) **backism,** the rule of mossbacks, *colloq.;* (4) **bass,** =**large-mouth(ed) (black) bass;** (5) **-draped,** draped with hanging-moss, also fig.; (6) **head,** (see quot. 1888); (7) **pink,** a mosslike plant, *Phlox subulata*, bearing white or pink flowers; (8) * **rose,** *W.* a false mallow, *Malvastrum coccineum.*

(2) 1900 *Speaker* 17 March 644 A few malcontents and mossbacked mugwumps. **1947** *Time* 3 Feb. 83/1 Actually, U.S. railroads are not as moss-backed as Bob Young sometimes seems to believe. — **(3) 1887** *Courier-Journal* 15 Feb. 6/6 The day of Mossbackism is over in Kentucky. — **(4) 1883** *Cent. Mag.* July 376/2 Black bass . . . have received names somewhat descriptive of their habitat, as, lake, . . . bayou, moss, grass, and Oswego bass. **1911** *Rep. Fisheries 1908* 307 Black Bass . . . is known in the Great Lakes region as 'Oswego bass,' in Indiana as 'moss bass.'

(5) 1901 C. MORRIS *Life on Stage* 240 We went quite wild with delight over the old moss-draped 'Il Trovatore.' **1932** W. KELLEY *Inchin' Along* 185 He set the small structure under a moss-draped live oak. — **(6) 1888** TRUMBULL *Names of Birds* 75 The colored women often use a large bunch of 'Florida Moss' . . . as a cushion for the heavy loads they carry upon their heads, and I am inclined to believe that 'Moss-head' [as a name for the hooded merganser, *Lophodytes cucullatus*] was suggested by this practice, rather than by any direct resemblance to moss in the bird's crest. [S.C.] **1917** *Birds of Amer.* I. 112. — **(7) 1857** GRAY *Botany* 332 Ground or Moss Pink. . . . Dry rocky hills and sandy banks, S. New York to Michigan and southward. **1938** DAMON *Grandma* 81 Clove pinks that smelled like the East India Spice Company, and moss pinks that crept great distances. — **(8) 1898** BRITTON & BROWN *Illust. Flora* III. 574/3 (Index), Moss-rose. [In text, II. 421:] *Malvastrum coccineum*. . . . Red False Mallow. . . . Prairies, Manitoba to Nebraska and Texas, west to British Columbia and New Mexico.

As the last term in **black, caribou, Carolina, cypress, ditch, Florida, hair-cap, hanging, long, Mississippi, New Orleans, pond, red-cup, Southern, Spanish, Texas moss.**

mossback ˈmɔsˌbæk, *n.* [See quot. 1888.]

1. A conservative, one hopelessly behind the times.

[1850 LEWIS *La. Swamp Doctor* 181 Here you sit, like a knot in a tree, with the moss commencing to grow on your back.] **1885** *Boston Jrnl.* 5 March 2/3 Everybody rejoices over the passage of the bill . . . except a few intense mossbacks, who were known during the war as copperheads. **1888** M. LANE in *America* 18 Oct. 16 Mossback . . . seems to have originated in the swamps of North Carolina, where a particular class of the poor whites were said to have lived among the cypress until the moss had grown upon their backs. **1948** *Chi. D. News* 25 Sep. 6/1 The 'mossbacks' in Congress, 'big business' and the 'gluttons of privilege' are his favorite targets.

transf. **1884** W. SHEPHERD *Prairie Exper.* 102 Three old bull buffaloes, 'moss backs,' from the faded tint of their shaggy manes, were feeding quietly with the tame herd in front of the ranch.

b. A member of a conservative faction of Ohio Democrats. *Obs.*

1885 *Mag. Amer. Hist.* March 296/1 *Mossbacks.*—A subdivision of the Democratic party in Ohio. **1895** MYERS *Bosses & Boodle* 187 The Washington end of the Ohio Democracy . . . wanted a 'Mossback' nominated upon a platform of National issues.

2. (See quot. 1890.)

1890 *Cent.* 3869/3 *mossback.* . . . A large and old fish, as a bass: so called by anglers, in allusion to the growth of seaweed, etc., which may be found on its back. **1946** *Democrat* 22 Aug. 2/2 Describing in detail how the big moss-backs fought, . . . he devoted the remainder of his story [etc.].

mossbunker ˈmɔsˌbʌŋkɚ, *n.* [f. Du. *marsbanker.* Now the form prevailing over marshbanker *q.v.*] =**marshbanker.** Cf. **bunker.**

1792 HOMMEDIEU in *Amer. Assoc. Proc.* XXVIII. 436 (*footnote*), The fish called menhaden or mosbanker. **1809** IRVING *Hist. N.Y.* (1927) VII. vii. 428 He saw the duyvel, in the shape of a huge Moss-bonker. **1893** *Outing* Aug. 355/1 All at once, rushing athwart our wake under our very stern, came a mighty school of moss-bunkers. **1949** *This Week Mag.* 10 Sep. 35/2 To extract this much money from the lowly 'mossbunker' requires a catch of 900,000,000 fish.

* **mossy,** *a.* In combs.: (1) **mossyback,** (*a*) =**mossbunker,** (*b*) (see quot.), *obs.;* (2) **-backed ranger,** (see quot.), *obs.;* (3) **cup (white) oak,** =**bur oak.**

(1) (*a*) **1871** DE VERE 67 In the State of New York the same fish appear under the name of *Mossy Back* or *Mossbunkers*. (*b*) **1871** DE VERE 283 The Mossybank [*sic*] . . . was the man of the South, who secreted himself in a remote forest, or an inaccessible swamp, in order to escape conscription. — **(2) 1876** *Cong. Rec.* 13 Jan. 411/1 [In the cotton states] those too cowardly to fight . . . were known as 'mossy-backed rangers' during the war, but came out fully fledged 'Union men' after the war. — **(3) 1810** MICHAUX *Arbres* I. 21 Q[uercus] muscosa, *Mossy cup oak. Mossy cup oak*, nom donné par moi à cette espèce, qui se trouve dans le Gennessée, (Etat de New-York) et près Albany. **1832** BROWNE *Sylva* 277 The flowers are succeeded by acorns of an elongated, oval form, and are inclosed in cups of nearly the same configuration. . . . From this peculiarity is derived the name of Mossy-Cup Oak. **1897** SUDWORTH *Arborescent Flora* 155 *Quercus macrocarpa*. Bur Oak. . . . Mossycup White Oak (Minn.).

* **moth,** *n.* **1.** (See quots.) **2. moth miller,** a miller or moth.

(1) 1867 *Harper's Wkly.* 6 April 222/2 For brown discolorations, called Moth and Freckles, use Perry's Moth and Freckle Lotion. **1922** COURTENAY *Physical Beauty* 26 The so-called 'moth spots,' brown spots or patches which appear after middle life, are due to this pigment. — **(2) 1865** *Harper's Wkly.* 25 Nov. 747/3 If there is *one* little hole in your linen or paper, some industrious moth-miller is pretty sure to discover it. **1899** JEWETT *Queen's Twin* 207 I'd looked more'n twenty times to see if there was any more moth-millers.

As the last term in **apple bud, bee, berry, buck, buffalo, butterfly, corn, cotton, fringe-tree, grape, half-looper, hawk, hummingbird, Io, Luna, meal, meal snout, Mediterranean flour, moon, Polyphemus, Promethea, rabbit, regal, royal walnut, tickle, walnut, yucca moth.**

* **mother,** *n.* In combs.: (1) **Mother Bank,** the second Bank of the U.S., *obs.*, see **national bank;** (2) **banker,** a note of the Mother Bank, *obs.;* (3) **Church,** =**First Church of Christ, Scientist;** (4) **country,** see as a main entry; (5) **ditch,** a main canal from which lateral irrigation ditches get water, cf. **acequia madre;** (6) **England,** England, the mother country; (7) **Hubbard overalls,** loose-fitting overalls, *humorous;* (8) **Hubbard sling,** =**switchel,** *slang;* (9) **lead,** =**mother lode 1;** (10) **lode,** see as a main entry; (11) **-s' Day,** [said to have been originated by Miss Anna Jarvis of Philadelphia in 1907, but such a day had been proposed three years before by Frank Hering of South Bend, Indiana], the second Sunday in May, celebrated in honor of mothers.

(1) 1833 in DUNN *Indiana* (1919) II. 1124 That Uncle Sam's 'old Mother Bank' Is managed by a foreign crank. — **(2) 1831** *Boston Transcript* 17 March 1/2 'Here's the five dollar bill,' says he, puttin a raal mother banker into the hands of one of the company. — **(3) 1889** EDDY in *Christian Science Jrnl.* April 13, I want to say, too, to my students everywhere . . . that they can become members of the 'mother church' here in Boston, and be received into its communion by writing without their personal presence. **1916** *Boston Transcript* 3 June 9/5 The First Church of Christ, Scientist. The Mother Church, Falmouth, Norway and St. Paul sts., Boston, Mass.

(5) 1844 GREGG *Commerce of Prairies* I. 151 One *acequia madre* (mother ditch) suffices generally to convey water for the irrigation of an entire valley. **1870** *Rep. Comm. Agric. 1869* 603 A large portion of the elevated plateaus bordering the Rio Grande may be irrigated from this stream, but this will require a considerable outlay in constructing the *acequia madre*, or mother ditch. — **(6) 1721** *Boston News-Letter* 28 Aug., People will take it for granted, they are a New Club set up in New-England, like to that in our Mother England. **1817** PAULDING *Lett. from South* I. 203 It is the production of one of the good ladies of Mother England. — **(7) 1897** *Outing* XXX. 555/2 The Doctor in brown 'Mother Hubbard' overalls. — **(8) 1919** CADY *Rhymes of Vt.* (1923) 185 Some used to call it 'sweetened water,' Some called it 'Mother Hubbard sling.' — **(9) 1874** RAYMOND *6th Rep. Mines* 342 The Mother lead is . . . taken up and named, on the supposition that it is the *mother-vein* of the country from which the ores of the Silver Flat and the Chloride districts are derived.

(11) 1908 *Cong. Rec.* 9 May 5971/1 The Secretary read the resolution submitted by Mr. Burkett [of Nebr.], as follows: *Resolved*, That Sunday, May 10, 1908, be recognized as Mothers' Day. **1949** *Democrat* 5 May 8/4 Call Pritchett's Flower-shop for your 'Mother's Day' flowers.

b. In phrases: (1) *Mother of Commonwealths*, the state of Virginia; (2) *Mother of her Country*, Martha Washington (1731–1802); (3) *mother of eels*, (*a*) the American burbot, *Lota maculosa*, (*b*) (see quot.); (4) *mother of floods*, (see quot.), *obs.*; (5) *Mother of Presidents*, (*a*) orig. Virginia, which furnished seven of the first twelve Presidents of the U.S., (*b*) (see quots.); (6) *Mother of States*, (*a*) the state of Connecticut, *rare*, (*b*) Virginia, in allusion either to its being the first settled of the original states, or to the fact that numerous states have been carved out of its original territory, also *Mother of States and Statesmen.*

(1) **1879** *Cong. Rec.* 10 Jan. 413/2 If it affords that gentleman any pleasure . . . to pour out the vials of his impotent wrath upon the 'Mother of Commonwealths,' . . . let him enjoy it. — (2) **1876** *Wide Awake* 158/1 She knew the couple in advance to be the Father and Mother of their Country, George and Martha Washington. — (3) (*a*) **1884** GOODE *Fisheries* 236 Professor Jordan gives the name 'Aleby-trout' and 'Mother of Eels' as in use in the Upper Great Lake region. **1903** T. H. BEAN *Fishes N.Y.* 702. (*b*) **1911** *Rep. Fisheries 1908* 313 Mutton-fish (*Zoarces anguillaris*). . . . It is also called the . . . 'mother-of-eels.' — (4) **1831** PECK *Guide for Emigrants* II. 24 'The Mother of Floods,' said to be the aboriginal meaning of Missouri.

(5) (*a*) **1827** A. SHERWOOD *Gaz. Georgia* 98 James Monroe . . . was born in Va., the mother of Presidents. **1904** *N.Y. Tribune* 12 June 8 Virginia concluded not to indorse any candidate. The 'Mother of Presidents' is a trifle particular. (*b*) **1897** *Chi. Record* 8 March 4/1 With the inauguration of William McKinley as president of the United States Ohio may claim to take rank with Virginia as a 'mother of presidents.' **1948** *Chi. D. News* 21 April 1/5 Ohio is the mother of Presidents, and Taft is one of her sons. — (6) (*a*) **1838** *Yale Lit. Mag.* III. 86 But to thee, Land of Steady Habits! to thee, Mother of States! to thee, good old Connecticut, do our praises most belong. (*b*) **1855** *S. Lit. Messenger* XXI. 675/1 Virginia . . . [was] hailed as 'the Mother of States,' . . . for where in all the West can we go without finding her children. **1861** *Chi. Tribune* 19 July 1/6 He went to Virginia, 'the mother of States.' **1896** *Cong. Rec.* 9 June 6342/2, That grand old Commonwealth of Virginia, the mother of States and statesmen, the mother of Presidents. **1915** EARLY *Heritage of South* 99 Enough men to fill the petty offices . . . could not be found in all the limits of that old commonwealth which has been designated 'the mother of states and statesmen.'

As the last term in **crazy, grand, house, Pilgrim mother.**

mother country.

1. England.

1617 ROBINSON & BREWSTER in Bradford *Hist.* 42 We [the Leyden Pilgrims] are well weaned from ye delicate milke of our mother countrie. **1747** FRANKLIN *Writings* II. 339 We have Numbers of the same Religion with those who of late encouraged the *French* to invade our Mother-Country. **1854** BENTON *30 Years' View* I. 217/1 The terms of the enjoyment are questions for the mother country. **1900** *Cong. Rec.* 20 Feb. 1995/2 The States that originally formed this Union were certain colonies which had revolted against the oppression of the mother country. **1949** GORDON *Aesculapius Comes to Colonies* 55 Massachusetts without interference from the Mother Country, has actually forbidden the use of the English Book of Common Prayer.

2. Any of various countries considered at one time or another as the source of certain American populations (see quots.).

1808 PIKE *Sources Miss.* 220 Malgares . . . deprecated a revolution or separation of Spanish America, from the mother country. **1836** *Diplom. Corr. Texas* I. (1908) 75 Please repair . . . to Washington City and there unite your exertions with those of our Commissioners in procuring a recognition from the government of our mother country. **1885** *Santa Fe Wkly. New Mexican* 9 July 1/2 Mexico is in trouble. . . . Will those of New Mexico . . . come to their mother country's relief now and at once! **1923** R. T. BROWN *Sidelights on European Tour* 7 The writer [a Negro] intended to visit Africa on the trip, but did not. . . . However, in the near future I hope to visit the mother country.

mother lode.

1. The principal vein of ore in a given place.

1883 BEADLE *Western Wilds* 561 What miners call a 'mother lode' is often like a tree in its upward development. **1947** *Mazama* Dec. 56/2 Polish up your geology to better understand the feelings of the gold rush crowd who followed traces into this region for the as yet undiscovered Mother Lode.

transf. and *attrib.* **1949** *Dly. Oklahoman* (Okla. City) 16 Jan. 2/1 It's been a long time since cars of casing and pipe backed up from Gainesville to Purcell, waiting to get onto the 30-mile road and go to the mother lode of black gold in Carter county. **1949** *L.A. Times* 23 May III. 16/1 Located in the Mother Lode area of Calaveras County, the Mt. Diablo embraces 1000 acres.

2. (*cap.*) The great quartz vein which runs from Mariposa to Amador in California.

1874 HITTELL *Resources Calif.* 337 The most remarkable vein of the State, and perhaps of the world—in extent, at least—is the Mother Lode of the Sierra Nevada. **1944** KAHN *Cable Car Days* 60 He went directly to the Mother Lode and started gold mining near the town of Columbia.

motocycle ˈmotəˌsaɪkl, *n.* [*motor* + *cycle.*] A horseless carriage, an automobile. *Obs.* or *hist.*

1895 *Chi. Times-Herald* 10 Nov. 34/3 Though the motocycle is a new thing under the sun, the horseless carriage is not. **1896** *Godey's Mag.* April 348/2 Let not the bicycle be confounded or too closely linked with the so-called 'motocycle.' **1945** *Chr. Sci. Monitor* 7 Nov. 9/6 Among other publicity stunts, he [*sc.* H. H. Kohlsaat, editor and publisher of the Chicago Times-Herald] held a contest to give a name to the new vehicle. Many were suggested, and 'motocycle' was chosen.

* **motor,** *n.* In combs. and derivatives: (1) **motor bike,** a bicycle equipped with a motor, or a light motorcycle; (2) **-cade,** a procession or parade of persons in automobiles; (3) **camp,** a place where, for a small fee, those traveling in automobiles may park their cars, prepare food, pitch a tent, and spend the night; (4) **car,** (see quot. 1890); (5) **court,** = **motor park;** (6) **man,** (*a*) a man who operates a trolley or a train on an electric railway, cf. **motorneer** as a main entry, (*b*) (see quot.); (7) **park,** a place provided with cabins, restrooms, and other conveniences, where those traveling in automobiles may spend the night.

(1) **1913** *Industrial Worker* (Spokane) 17 July 4/5 The Devil took a motor bike and got ketched at Minneapolis. **1948** *Carthaginian* (Carthage, Miss.) 19 Aug. 1/1, I do not believe a child under 16 years of age should be allowed or risked on the streets on a bicycle or motor bike. — (2) [**1928** *Amer. Mercury* Oct. 173/1 The Ottumwa Elks journey by motor cavalcade to put on an initiation in Oskaloosa.] **1932** *N.Y. World-Telegram* 11 Oct. 9/2 Plans were announced today for the invasion of 'dry' Congressional districts of New York State by a motorcade of advocates of repeal. **1948** *Time* 14 June 33/1 He rode off to the presidential palace in a horn-tooting, placard-plastered motorcade. — (3) **1925** *Sat. Ev. Post* 10 Oct. 98/1 The average motor camp is too well known to need any description. **1934** *Lit. Digest* 9 June 40/2 Tour-conscious Americans . . . will find . . . greater hospitality from proprietors of motor camps. — (4) **1890** *Cent.* 3874/3 *Motor-car*, . . . a car which carries its own propelling mechanism, as an electric motor. . . . Many such cars have sufficient power to draw other cars attached to them. **1903** *N.Y. Ev. Post* 4 Sep., As a crowded 6-car train was leaving the 16th Street station, the motor-car was discovered to be afire.

(5) **1936** *Pop. Mech.* LXVI. 674/1 The motor court is a recent development of the motor age. . . . It's not a tourist park, it's not an auto camp. . . . It's a collection of miniature homes clustered around a central service and administration building. **1949** *Nat. Humane Rev.* Sep. 30/3 This unusual directory lists hotels and motor courts which accept guests with dogs. — (6) (*a*) **1890** *Boston Jrnl.* 12 April 4/4 Has it . . . become the established policy of the West End road, from the late vice president to the motormen, that the public must learn that the electric cars cannot be fooled with? **1945** *Jefferson Co. Republican* (Golden, Colo.) 25 July 2/4 Motormen and conductors have the authority to enforce safety measures. (*b*) **1908** PHILLIPS *Old Wives* 351 He took an auto cab, said 'Up the Riverside Drive' to the motorman, threw himself back in the corner and forgot his surroundings. — (7) **1939** *New Yorker* 14 Oct. 72 The usual phrase for cabin colonies in California is 'auto court'; 'motor park,' perhaps copied from 'trail park.'

motorcycle cop. A member of the police force who patrols on a motorcycle. *Colloq.* — **1927** EUBANK *Horse & Buggy Days* 33 There's always some fool motor-cycle cop coming along to interfere and order you to move on. **1948** *Green Bay* (Wis.) *Press-Gaz.* 30 June 6/3 They're as impressionable as a motorcycle cop.

motorneer ˌmotɚˈnɪr, *n.* [By analogy with engi*neer.*] = **motorman** (*a*). *Obs.*

1890 *N. & Q.* IV. 275 A motorneer is the man who rides on the front of an electric car and handles the trolly, which runs on the wires overhead. **1899** *Boston Globe* (p.m.) 11 Aug. 4/3, I think the origin of this word can be claimed by the Rockland, Thomaston & Camden electric railway company of Maine. As far back as 1894 or 95 this company had painted on the platform of their cars 'Do not talk to the motorneer.' The word I think is a very appropriate one. **1936** M. R. EISELEN in *Yale Rev.* XXVI. 139 Similarly, there was the question of what to call the driver of the car. 'Chauffeur' met with disfavor. . . . Instead, 'motorneer' was advocated.

motte mɑt, *n. S.* and *W.* [Sp. *mata*, in same sense. Cf. Santamaría.] A clump or small grove of trees.

1839 WEBBER *Old Hicks* (1848) 52 Our course bearing west by north, over broken prairie, diversified by clumps or motts of scrubby growth.

1892 DUVAL *Young Explorers* 142 We've got the wind of them, and by keeping yon little 'mot' bertwixt them and us, we can git in three or four hundred yards of the drove. **1947** *Trail Riders Bul.* Feb. 20/1 They ain't no timber over thataway—nothin' more'n a motte o' two o' greasewood.

∗**mottled,** *a.* **1. mottled grampus,** (see quot). **2. mottled owl,** an American screech owl, so called when its plumage is in the gray phase.

(1) **1884** *Nat. Museum Bul.* No. 27, 639 *Grampus Stearnsii.* Mottled or White-headed Grampus. Pacific coast of North America. — (2) **1781** LATHAM *Gen. Synopsis Birds* I. I. 126 Mottled Owl. . . . The length of this species is eight inches and a half. The bill is brown: irides yellow. . . . Inhabits North America. **1878** *Nat. Museum Proc.* I. 134 *Scops asio.*—Little Mottled Owl; Screech. This Owl is quite abundant at Stockton. **1917** *Birds of Amer.* II. 109 Screech Owl. [Also called] Mottled Owl.

∗**motto,** *n.* **1.** A piece of candy wrapped in a paper inscribed with a motto or line of verse. *Obs.* Cf. ∗**cockle,** *n.*[2], **heart motto, kiss verse. 2. motto candy,** =prec. **3. motto mug,** a mug with a motto inscribed upon it. *Obs.*

(1) **1835** *S. Lit. Messenger* I. 358, I only ate . . . a few macaronies and mottoes. **1860** *North-West* (Port Townsend, Wash.) 5 July 3/3 Candies, Gum Drops, Mottoes. — (2) **1876** *Wide Awake* 90/2 [He] gave her motto-candies with the most complimentary verses he could pick out. [**1946** WILSON *Fidelity* 162 Many a verse found in these books had first come into the possession of the writer from the wrapper around a bit of candy, usually called a 'candy kiss.'] — (3) **1859** *Texas Almanac 1860* 248 Ornaments, Vases, Motto-Mugs, Card-Trays, etc.

mould mold, *n.* Short for ∗*mouldboard.* Cf. **waffle mould, doughboy moulds.** — **1858** *Ill. Agric. Soc. Trans.* III. 367 In fall-plowing we run the share and mould of the plow under the soil and invert it. **1868** *Iowa Agric. Soc. Rep. 1867* 266 There is no clogging, and the mould and lay are so hardened that they scour readily.

∗**mound,** *n.* Also **mount.**

1. A kind of extensive earthwork erected by the mound-builders, found chiefly in the Ohio and Mississippi valleys, the Gulf States, and the Great Lakes region.

1732 *Ga. Col. Rec.* III. 406 Half a Mile from Savannah is a high Mount of Earth, under which lies their chief King. **1775** in *Jrnl. Nicholas Cresswell* (1925) 71 The Indians' tradition is that there was a great Battle fought here and many great Warriors killed. These mounds were raised to perpetuate their memory. **1792** *Amer. Philos. Soc.* III. 217 On the low grounds of the Mississippi . . . is a very large mount encompassed by a number of smaller ones. **1884** COLANGE *Nat. Gazetteer* 674/2 Moundsville, W.Va. . . . Its name is derived from a remarkable mound in the vicinity, one of the largest of the ancient mounds in the U. States. **1948** *Chi. Tribune* 4 April VI. 4/4 This group of mounds is thus considered to be the most valuable undepleted group of mounds of the kind in existence.

2. In baseball, the slightly elevated ground from which the pitcher pitches.

1914 *Collier's* 7 Feb. 7/2 There's a pitcher who never has to be urged to go to the mound. **1948** *Capital-Democrat* (Tishomingo, Okla.) 17 June 5/5 Dean, coming to the mound from center field, got the side out with only one of the runners scoring.

3. In combs.: (1) **mound builder,** one of the aboriginal Indians who built burial and fortification mounds, formerly thought to have preceded the Indians as inhabitants of the Mississippi basin; (2) **building,** the action of building an Indian mound; (3) **City,** St. Louis, Missouri, so called from the Indian mounds that once occupied its site, also, rarely, **Mound Cityites;** (4) **prairie,** a piece of prairie land with Indian mounds or tumuli upon it, esp. such a region in the state of Washington; (5) **region,** (see quot.); (6) **-sman,** a baseball pitcher.

(1) **1838** FLAGG *Far West* I. 20 Here was fought the last battle between their race and the former dwellers in Kentucky—the *white mound-builders*—in which the latter were exterminated to a man. **1949** *West Va. Hist.* Jan. 126 The life and times of the mound builders and Indians, assuming they were different people, are all very interesting. — (2) **1853** LAPHAM *Antiq. Wisconsin* (1855) 89 These later tribes continued the practice of mound-building so far as to erect a circular or conical tumulus over their dead. — (3) **1846** *Quincy* (Ill.) *Whig* 12 Feb. 2/5 The Mound City can't be kept under, give her room, she's growing! **1858** *Cairo City* (Ill.) *Gaz.* 2 July 3/2 The Mound Cityites . . . displayed great foresight and a due regard to 'coming events.' **1929** *Cin. Enquirer* 1 Oct. 11/1 They dropped their first game in the Mound City. — (4) **1867** *Ore. State Jrnl.* 5 Jan. 1/3 The following extract is a description of the Mound Prairies which are in a few reach [*sic*] from Olympia. **1923** E. S. MEANY *Origin of Wash. Names* 173 Mound Prairie. . . . Many geologists have given different theories about the origin of the mounds which caused the name of this prairie.

(5) **1873** BEADLE *Undevel. West* 38 [Boscobel] is the centre of the 'Mound Region' of Wisconsin—so called from the many Indian mounds scattered about the valley. — (6) **1947** *Dly. Oklahoman* (Okla. City) 11 Aug. 13/1 Bogard, OCU moundsman, had brilliant help from his Gassers both afield and at bat. **1949** *Minot* (N.D.) *D. News* 22 July 8/4 Moundsman Frank Joyner worked for the Black Barons and the Chicago American Giants.

As the last term in **Indian, soda, wagon mound.**

∗**mount,** *n.*[1] A square tower fitted up for a sentry. *Obs.* — **1724** in TEMPLE & SHELDON *Hist. Northfield, Mass.* 202, 1 day's warding for a soldier which did work at the mount. **1748** J. NORTON *Redeemed Captive* 6 He kept two Men in the Northwest Mount, and some in the Great House.

∗**mount,** *n.*[2] A saddle horse, or a supply of such horses.

1906 *Out West* April 319, I suppose you noticed my mount today. **1907** S. E. WHITE *Arizona Nights* I. III. 53 He kept his own mount of horses, took care of them. **1949** *Sat. Ev. Post* 23 April 126/4 He used the gray plenty because Chaquaco was the only well-broken horse in his mount.

∗**mount,** *v. tr.* To "crawl," to tackle. *Slang.* — **1835** HOFFMAN *Winter in West* II. 186 Come out here, any ten of you, and I'll mount you one after another.

∗**mountain,** *n.* and *a.* Used extensively in combs.

1. In the names of plants: (1) **mountain balsam,** a coniferous tree, *Abies subalpina;* (2) **buckeye,** a species of buckeye found in mountainous regions, *rare;* (3) **cranberry,** (*a*) an evergreen shrub, *Vaccinium vitis-idaea,* also the dark red berry of this shrub, (*b*) (see quot.); (4) **crowder,** see ∗**crowder,** *n.* **1. b;** (5) **grape,** one of two grapes found in Texas, (*a*) the sweet mountain grape, *Vitis monticola,* and (*b*) the sand grape, *V. rupestris;* (6) **hemlock,** a hemlock, *Tsuga mertensiana,* that grows in mountainous regions; (7) **holly,** see as a main entry; (8) **ivy,** =**mountain laurel;** (9) **laurel,** see as a main entry; (10) **lilac,** a California shrub of the genus *Ceanothus;* (11) **mahogany,** see as a main entry; (12) **maple,** any one of several shrublike maples found in mountainous areas, as *Acer spicatum* of the eastern states and *A. glabrum* of the Rocky Mountains, also with defining term; (13) ∗**mint,** (*a*) Oswego tea, *Monarda didyma,* (*b*) an American mint of the genus *Pycnanthemum;* (14) **raspberry,** the cloud berry; (15) ∗**rice,** see as a main entry; (16) **snow,** =**snow-on-the-mountain;** (17) **tea,** see as a main entry; (18) **tobacco,** a species of *Arnica.*

(1) **1902** *Encycl. Brit.* XXXI. 263/2 The principal trees of the Rocky Mountains are aspen and . . . mountain balsam. — (2) **1873** BEADLE *Undevel. West* 751 In times of scarcity they eat . . . the balls of the mountain buckeye. — (3) (*a*) **1848** THOREAU *Maine Woods* 22 Mountain cranberries (*Vaccinium Vitis-Idaea*), stewed and sweetened, were the common desert. **1892** TORREY *Foot-Path Way* 72 Broad patches of bearberry showing at a little distance like beds of mountain cranberry. **1930** BAILEY *Cyclo. Horticulture* 3425/1 [Vaccinium] Vitis-Idæa, Linn. . . . Mountain Cranberry. Cowberry. Partridge Berry in the N. Foxberry. (*b*) **1894** *Amer. Folk-Lore* VII. 93 *Arctostaphylos Uva-ursi,* mountain cranberry, Southern Me.

(5) (*a*) **1862** *Rep. Comm. Patents 1861: Agric.* 485 *Vitis monticola* . . . is called the 'White or Mountain grape;' differs from *V. rupestris* in its trailing habit and long, slender branches. (*b*) **1885** HAVARD *Flora W. & S. Texas* 511 *Vitis rupestris,* Scheele, (Mountain Grape). . . . Said to grow on the hillsides of the Limpio and other mountains. **1891** COULTER *Bot. W. Texas* I. 63 In the Valley of Devil's River and westward into the mountains of the Pecos. Also called 'mountain grape.' — (6) **1884** SARGENT *Rep. Forests* 572 The timber on these ridges [in Shoshone Co., Idaho] was often small and scattered . . . with larch and red fir, balsam, hemlock, and sometimes the mountain hemlock (*Tsuga Pattoniana*). **1946** *Sierra Club Bul.* Dec. 27 Approaching Bond Pass I traversed one of the largest forest associations of mountain hemlock in the Sierra. — (8) **1817** S. BROWN *Western Gaz.* 322 [In n.e. Ohio are found] woodbine, . . . whortleberries, . . . mountain ivy, mountain laurel [etc.].

(10) **1911** CHASE *Yosemite Trails* 11 With them arrives the mountain-lilac (Ceanothus) in clouds of azure and white that emulate the very sky. **1948** *So. Sierran* March 2/3 The foothills should be white and blue with 'mountain lilac' (Ceanothus) this month. — (12) **1785** MARSHALL *Amer. Grove* 2 *Acer pennsylvanicum,* Pennsylvanian Dwarf Mountain Maple, . . . grows naturally upon the mountains in the back parts of Pennsylvania. **1897** SUDWORTH *Arborescent Flora*

284 *Acer glabrum.* Dwarf Maple. . . . Mountain Maple (Colo., Mont.). **1945** DARLINGTON *Higher Plants Mich.* 13 These in addition to the striped maple (*Acer pennsylvanicum*) and the mountain maple (*Acer spicatum*) are suggestive of the vegetation in parts of the upper peninsula. — **(13)** (*a*) **1817–8** EATON *Botany* (1833) *Monarda didyma*, mountain mint. (*b*) *Ib.* 415 *Pycnanthemum incanum*, wild basil, mountain mint. **1892** COULTER *Bot. W. Texas* II. 334. — **(14) 1805** T. M. HARRIS *Journal* 65 On these declivities [along the Ohio] grow the mountain raspberry . . . in great plenty. It is a handsome bush; and the flower, which is of a pale pink colour, . . . gives it a very ornamental appearance.

(16) 1888 CRADDOCK *Despot* 159 He mechanically noted . . . how the blooming 'mountain snow' brushed his mare's fine coat. **1913** BRITTON & BROWN *Illust. Flora* II. 469 *Euphorbia marginata*. . . . In dry soil, Minnesota to Colorado, south to Texas. Introduced into waste places in the Central and Atlantic States. Snow-on-the mountain. . . . Mountain-snow. — **(18) 1760** WASHINGTON *Diaries* I. 136 An order on Hunting Creek Warehouses for 7 Hhds. of my Mountain Tob[acc]o. **1947** B. HAILE *Prayer Stick Cutting* 52 Mountain tobacco is then dropped into the stick and the patient then symbolically lights it by motioning with rock crystal to the sun and touching the stick.

b. In similar combs. of obvious meaning or sufficiently explained in the quots.: (1) **mountain balm,** (2) **bird-cherry,** (3) **blueberry,** (4) **cherry,** (5) **chestnut oak,** (6) **flax,** (7) **foxtail,** (8) **fringe,** (9) **lover,** (10) **oak,** see as a main entry, (11) **pepper bush,** (12) **rose bay,** (13) **sage,** (14) **spurge,** (15) **sumach,** (16) **wild gooseberry.**

(1) 1887 *Overland Mo.* Aug., The low growth of shrubs . . . is made up of . . . *herba santa*, or 'mountain balm,' from which a medicine is prepared for pulmonary affections, and a few others. **1890** *Cent.* 3877/1 mountain-balm. . . . 1. An evergreen plant, *Eriodictyon glutinosum* (probably also *E. tomentosum*). Also called *yerba santa*. 2. The Oswego tea, *Monarda didyma;* so called in the drug trade. — **(2) 1785** MARSHALL *Amer. Grove* 113 *Prunus-cerasus montana*. Mountain Bird-Cherry-Tree. — **(3) 1847** WOOD *Botany* 369 *Vaccinium uliginosum*. Mountain Blueberry. . . . A low, alpine shrub, White Mts. . . . Berries oblong, deep-blue. — **(4) 1813** MUHLENBERG *Cat. Plants* 48 *Prunus montana*, . . . mountain cherry. **1871** *Harper's Mag.* Oct. 707 We must . . . gather mountain cherries (*Prunus cerasus*). **1909** WEBSTER 1413 Mountain cherry. A wild cherry (*Prunus angustifolia*) of the eastern United States.

(5) 1801 MICHAUX *Histoire des Chênes* 6 Chêne Chataignier (des montagnes). Mountain Chestnut Oak, Roky Oak. **1815** DRAKE *Cincinnati* 83 [The] fox grape and mountain-chestnut oak are still scarcer. **1821** NUTTALL *Travels Arkansa* 15 Much of the *Quercus Prinos monticola* (or mountain chestnut oak) presents itself on the mountain. — **(6) 1839** FARNHAM *Great Western Prairies* (1841) 99 The mountain flax . . . covered acres as densely as it usually stood in fields, and presented the beautiful sheet of blue blossoms. **1890** *Cent.* 3877/2 mountain flax. . . . A plant, *Linum catharticum* or *Polygala Senega*. **1930** BAILEY *Cyclo. Horticulture* 2738/1 [Polygala] Senega, Linn. Seneca Snakeroot. Mountain Flax. — **(7) 1889** VASEY *Agric. Grasses* 41 Mountain Foxtail . . . is called in some localities mountain Timothy. . . . It is of little value for grazing. — **(8) 1847** WOOD *Botany* 158 Adlumia. . . . A cirrhosa . . . *Mountain Fringe*. A delicate climbing vine, native of rocky hills, Can. to N. Car. **1893** *Stand. Dict.* 29/1 The climbing fumitory or mountain-fringe (A[dlumia] cirrhosa) of the eastern United States is the only species. — **(9) 1890** *Cent.* 3877/3 mountain-lover. . . . [Tr. NL. *Oreophila*, Nuttall's name of the genus. A proposed name for plants of the genus *Pachystima*.— Canby's mountain-lover, *P. Canbyi*, a shrub with deep-colored evergreen leaves, discovered in the mountains of Virginia in 1868. [**1941** R. S. WALKER *Lookout* 51 Among the most interesting species are brook parnassia near the water's edge and Mountain Lover pitcher plant.]

(11) 1860 CURTIS *Woody Plants N.C.* 100 Mountain Pepper-Bush. (*C*[*lethra*] *acuminata*.)—Quite an ornamental shrub, 10 to 15 feet high, growing in the mountains from Ashe to Cherokee. — **(12) 1941** R. S. WALKER *Lookout* 48 The most beautiful, perhaps, is rhododendron, known as mountain rose bay, which is in flower during the latter part of April and early May. — **(13) 1844** LEE & FROST *Oregon* 122 Toiling through immense tracts of mountain sage, or, more properly, wormwood. — **(14) 1941** R. S. WALKER *Lookout* 52 Pachysandra, or mountain spurge blooms in March and April in the rich soil in Lookout Mountain woods.

(15) 1813 MUHLENBERG *Cat. Pants* 32 *Rhus copallinum aestivale*, (mountain sumach). — **(16) 1785** MARSHALL *Amer. Grove* 132 *Ribes oxycanthoides*. Mountain wild gooseberry.

2. In the names of animals: (1) **mountain antelope,** =**Rocky Mountain goat;** (2) **badger,** the hoary marmot, used in transf. sense in quot.; (3) **boomer,** see as a main entry; (4) **caribou,** a species of caribou, *Rangifer montanus*, found in the Northwest; (5) **cat,** see as a main entry; (6) **deer,** a deer that lives in mountainous regions, esp. the mule deer, *obs.;* (7) **goat,** a goatlike animal, *Oreamnos montanus*, of the northwest mountains, the Rocky Mountain goat, also attrib.; (8) **lion,** the cougar; (9) * **rat,** a pack rat, *Neotoma cinerea*, of the West; (10) **sheep,** =**Rocky Mountain sheep;** (11) **trout,** (*a*) a trout that lives in mountain streams, as the brook or rainbow trout, (*b*) (see quot.).

(1) 1884 *Cent. Mag.* Dec. 193/2 As a popular name mountain antelope or antelope-goat might be suggested. — **(2) 1848** RUXTON in *Blackw. Mag.* LXIII. 728 The otter, . . . the mountain badger, . . . dangled their well-stuffed skins, and displayed the guardian 'medicine' of the warrior. — **(4) 1917** *Animals of Amer.* 27 The Blackfaced, or Mountain, Caribou of southeastern British Columbia is, in September, nearly black. **1942** Nat. Pk. Service *Fading Trails* 63 Occasionally mountain caribou enter Glacier National Park during the winter.

(6) 1820 EASTBURN & SANDS *Yamoyden* 18 He led them, fleet as mountain deer. **1834** A. PIKE *Sketches* 122 Around the tent two or three skins of the grizzly bear and of the mountain deer were stretched. — **(7)** *c***1837** CATLIN *Indians* II. 196 His leggings and shirt were of the mountain goat skin. **1844** LEE & FROST *Oregon* 98 These [moccasins] are of dressed skins of the deer, antelope, mountain-goat, and sheep. **1949** *Reader's Digest* June 15/1 His wife brought to the White House . . . the energy of a mountain goat. — **(8) 1859** G. A. JACKSON *Diary* (MS) 2 Killed a mountain lion today. **1949** *Pacific Discovery* July–Aug. 15/1 Elliott S. Barker, a cowman in the New Mexico mountains, has written one of the two best books on that elusive cat, the mountain lion. — **(9) 1885** *Outing* VII. 51/2 If the mountain rats hadn't eaten up my copy of Shakespeare, . . . I should have the very best of company. **1927** RUSSELL *Trails* 10 The floor's strewn with pine cones, an' a few scattered bones, showin' it's been the home of mountain-rats an' squirrels.

(10) 1802 in *Med. Repository 1803* 240 The mountain ram, or sheep, though not very often seen, is to be met with, in considerable numbers, in some parts of the mountains. **1893** ROOSEVELT *Wilderness Hunter* 17 The bighorn, or mountain sheep is found . . . from the Coast and Cascade ranges to the Bad Lands of the western edges of the Dakotas. **1947** *Trail & Timberline* Feb. 15/2 We saw moose, bear, caribou, mountain (Dall) sheep, and wolves almost every trip. — **(11)** (*a*) **1805** LEWIS in *L. & Clark Exped.* II. (1904) 15c These trout . . . resemble our mountain or speckled trout. **1948** *Trail Riders Bul.* July 6/1 Nor need they be sparing their optimism as the lake as well as nearby Cerulean and Sunburst are well stocked with scrappy and tasty mountain trout. (*b*) **1884** GOODE *Fisheries* I. 401 In Alabama, according to Professor Jordan, it [the small-mouth black bass, *Micropterus dolomieu*] is called the 'Mountain Trout.'

b. In similar combs. of obvious meaning or sufficiently explained by the quots.: (1) **mountain beaver,** (2) **buffalo,** (3) **fly,** (4) **grizzly,** (5) **herring,** (6) **mustang,** (7) **ram,** (8) **shad,** (9) **squirrel.**

(1) 1884 J. S. KINGLSEY *Stand. Nat. Hist.* V. 121 The 'Showt'l' or 'Sewellel' of the aborigines . . . [is] known to more prosaic hunters and trappers as the 'Boomer' or 'mountain Beaver.' **1943** CAHALANE *Meeting the Mammals* 98 'Boomer,' or the mountain beaver, is only a very remote relative of the real beaver, who lives in ponds, and is famous for his engineering. — **(2) 1868** *Amer. Naturalist* II. 538 'Mountain Buffalo.' . . . The Bighorn is sometimes called so. *Ib.*, I saw no difference in the skulls, indicating a different species, or 'Mountain Buffalo' of the hunters. **1884** DE VERE in *Encycl. Brit.* (ed. 9) *Amer. Supp.* I. 540/2 Buffaloes long inhabiting other localities than the open plains, their natural homes, acquire distinguishable varietal characters. They are known as 'wood-buffalo' and 'mountain-buffalo.' **1892** *Scribner's Mag.* Sep. 277/1 There are, besides the ordinary animal of the plains, the 'mountain buffalo,' . . . the 'wood buffalo' . . . , and the 'beaver buffalo.' — **(3) 1882** BAILLIE-GROHMAN *Camps in Rockies* 48 A scourge . . . swept down upon us when we struck the timbered foothills of the Rockies, i.e. the dreaded mountain flies—a species of mosquito. — **(4)** *c***1875** in *Frontier* X. (1930) 339/1 Other things of prey from the mountain grizzly to the rattlesnake fed well on the . . . ground squirrels that bored the valleys.

(5) 1884 GOODE *Fisheries* I. 542 This species is usually known as the White-fish; in Utah as the 'Mountain Herring.' — **(6) 1869** BRACE *New West* 82 Buy a mountain-mustang at one of the towns in the Foot Hills. — **(7) 1802** *Dly. Advertiser* (N.Y.) 4 Dec., The mountain ram, or sheep, though not very often seen, is to be met with, in considerable numbers, in some parts of the mountains. **1886** ROOSEVELT *Outing* May 131 One of my foremen shot a mountain-ram. — **(8) 1883** ZEIGLER & GROSSCUP *Alleghanies* 48 Some 'varmint' . . . [had eaten] a fine hundred-pound hog (otherwise known as a mountain shad). — **(9) 1857** *Rep. Comm. Patents 1856: Agric.* 67 This pretty and active little animal is well known through the Northern States, under the names of 'Red-Squirrel,' . . . and, sometimes, 'Mountain Squirrel.'

3. In the names of birds: (1) **mountain bluebird,** a western bluebird, *Sialia currucoides*, closely related to the eastern bluebird; (2) **chickadee,** a western titmouse, *Penthestes gambelli*, having a white stripe over the eye, also transf.; (3) **fowl,** =**dusky grouse;** (4) **mocking-bird,** the sage thrasher, also **mountain mocker;** (5) **partridge,** (*a*) =**ruffed grouse,** (*b*) =**mountain quail;** (6) **plover,** a small plover of the upland prairies of the West, *Eupoda montana;* (7) **quail,** a partridge of the Pacific Coast, *Oreortyx picta palmeri.*

(1) 1860 BAIRD in *Ives's Rep.* V. 5 *Sialia arctica*, Sw., Mountain blue bird. Fort Defiance, Fort Yuma. **1949** *Dly. Okahoman* (Okla. City) 13 Feb. D. 2/1 There are two kinds of bluebirds in Oklahoma in winter: the familiar eastern bluebird . . . and more rarely the exquisite, all blue mountain bluebird, a visitor from the timberline of our western mountains. — **(2) 1874** COUES *Birds N.W.* 22 Mountain Chickadee. . . . Common in various coniferous mountainous tracts in New Mexico and Arizona. **1937** *Bk. of Birds* II. 138 The calls of the mountain chickadee are closely similar to those of the blackcap species, but are uttered in a slightly slower, drawling tone, so that the note of the two may be distinguished by a practiced ear. **1947** *Sierra Club Bul.* April 5/2 You see, my little Mountain Chickadee, I want *all* children to be able to swagger up to a stranger some day and say with tremendous pride: 'This is *my* mountains!' — **(3) 1846** SAGE *Scenes Rocky Mts.* (1859) 169 A large bird called the mountain fowl. . . . This bird is rather larger than our domestic hen, and of a grayish brown color. — **(4) 1858** BAIRD *Birds Pacific R.R.* 347 *Oroscoptes Montanus*, . . . Mountain Mocking Bird. **1880** DENTON *Naturalist's Diary* (1949) 23, I got several nice birds, among them a mountain mocker.

(5) (*a*) **1728** in *N.C. Col. Rec.* II. (1888) 791 Our Indian shot a Mountain Partridge resembling the common Partridge in the plumage but as large as a hen. **1789** MORSE *Amer. Geog.* 60 American Birds [include the] . . . Pheasant or mountain Partridge, Water Pheasant, [and] Pelican. (*b*) **1887** RIDGWAY *Man. N. Amer. Birds* 191 Pacific coast district, from San Francisco North to Washington Territory. . . . O. pictus. Mountain Partridge. **1917** *Birds of Amer.* II. 5 Mountain Quail. *Oreortyx picta picta* . . . [also called] Mountain Partridge. — **(6) 1858** BAIRD *Birds Pacific R.R.* 693 Mountain Plover . . . is only known to inhabit the western countries of North America. **1917** *Birds of Amer.* I. 267 Mountain Plover. . . . Nest: On the open prairies; a depression in the ground, lined with leaves and grass. — **(7) 1858** BAIRD *Birds Pacific R.R.* 642 Plumed Partridge; Mountain Quail. . . . Mountain ranges of California and Oregon towards the coast. **1944** *Nat. Geog. Mag.* June 696/2 We did, however, secure some calls of the mountain quail and the chukar partridge.

b. In similar combs. of obvious meaning or sufficiently explained in the quots.: (1) **mountain duck,** (2) **grouse,** (3) **jay.**

(1) 1917 *Birds of Amer.* I. 142 Harlequin Duck. *Histrionicus histrionicus*. . . . [Also called] Mountain Duck. — **(2) 1844** in *Calif. Hist. Soc. Quart.* IV. 346 No animal Seen no fowl Save a few mountain grouse which can live in any region where vegitation can grow. **1917** *Birds of Amer.* II. 16 Franklin's Grouse. . . . [Also called] Mountain Grouse. — **(3) 1872** *Amer. Naturalist* VI. 398 The great-crested, Woodhouse's and the Canada jays were of frequent occurrence in the mountains, the former being familiarly known as the 'mountain jay.' **1938** THOMPSON *High Trails* 84 Of smaller birds the most showy is the mountain jay.

4. In miscellaneous combs.: (1) **mountain barren,** a tract of land in the mountains with little or no natural vegetation; (2) ***boy,** (*a*) a member of an informal military company of Vermont during the Revolution, cf. **Green Mountain Boy,** (*b*) a member of other military companies made up of men living in the mountains; (3) **day,** at certain colleges an annual holiday devoted to mountain climbing and hiking; (4) **division,** a division of a railroad in mountainous country; (5) **engine,** =**mountain locomotive;** (6) **feud,** among southern mountaineers, a continued state of strife between families; (7) **jack,** ?=**California jack,** *obs.;* (8) **locomotive,** a heavy locomotive especially suited for use in mountainous regions; (9) ***man,** a man skilled in going through, or living in, the mountains, as a mountain guide, trapper, or trader (see quot. 1910); (10) **mutton,** the flesh of the mountain sheep; (11) **ore,** ordinary iron ore, as distinguished from that found in bogs, *rare;* (12) **park,** =**mountain meadow,** cf. **mountain ranch,** and **park;** (13) **schooner,** a covered wagon or prairie schooner fitted up for travel through the mountains; (14) **time,** mean local time on the 105th meridian, adopted as the standard time in the Rocky Mountain area; (15) **trader,** one who traffiked among the Indians of the Far West, *obs.;* (16) **wagon,** see as a main entry.

(1) 1800 ASBURY *Journal* II. 470 We passed Montgomery-town and court-house among the mountain barrens. — **(2)** (*a*) **1777** HAMILTON *Works* VII. 522 Nixon's brigades, and Colonel Warner's mountain boys, to remain in and about Albany. **1815** *Niles' Reg.* IX. 171/1 In their hats [were] sprigs of ever-green, the ancient badge of the mountain-boys. (*b*) **1787** *Amer. Museum* II. Chron. 6/1 We may shortly expect to hear of . . . a new display of gallantry of the Mountain Boys. **1815** *Niles' Reg.* VIII. 39/2 At the most gloomy period of the war, these mountain boys of *Pennsylvania*, . . . organized themselves into a company. — **(3) 1845** *Williams Mo. Misc.* I. 555 Some, not content with a mountain day, carried their knapsacks and blankets to encamp till morning on the summit. **1887** *Springfield D. Republican* 14 Oct. 6/4 Yesterday was mountain day at Smith college and many students spent the day in the woods and upon the mountain. **1901** *Cosmopolitan* June 194/1 Tramping, too, is a favorite pastime, and in many of the colleges 'Mountain Day' is set apart for this purpose. — **(4) 1867** *Comm. & Fin. Chron.* 16 March 343 In the distance intervening between the two mountain divisions, $32,000 per mile.

(5) 1877 E. MARTIN *Hist. Great Riots* 130 The mountain engine was backed out of the round house. **1892** *Las Vegas* (N.M.) *Free Press* 5 Jan. 4/2 Mountain engine 280 is up from Lamy for repairs. — **(6) 1903** FOX *Little Shepherd* v, That night they tied up at Jackson—to be famous long after the war as the seat of a bitter mountain feud. — **(7) 1877** CAMPION *On Frontier* 25 Cards [were] brought out; seven-up, mountain-jack, and euchre had each their turn. — **(8) 1880** *Cimarron News & Press* 3 June 2/5 Mountain locomotives have two enemies —the falling rock and the snow slide. — **(9) 1847** RUXTON *Adv. Rocky Mts.* (1848) 217 The depreciation in the value of beaver-skins has thrown the great body of trappers out of employment, and there is a general tendency among the mountainmen to settle in the fruitful valleys of the Rocky Mountains. **1910** DOUGLAS ed. Parkman *Ore. Trail* 338 Mountainmen, a well-defined class of backwoodsmen, . . . versed in everything pertaining to life upon the plains and in the mountains. **1947** *True* Nov. 90/2 The wolfer's outfit was as simple as the original mountain man's.

(10) 1836 IRVING *Astoria* II. 165 Here they encamped for the night, and supped sumptuously upon their mountain mutton. **1847** COYNER *Lost Trappers* 152 What is commonly called mountain mutton . . . is very delicate and sweet. — **(11) 1734** *Doc. Hist. N.Y. State* I. 734 We have a great many Iron mines both of the bogg, and of the Mountain Oar. — **(12) 1883** RITCH *Illust. N. Mex.* 40 Excepting in several of the mountain parks, irrigation is more or less, a necessity. — **(13) 1869** BRACE *New West* 188 Coaches, wagons, and the stream of 'mountain-schooners' pour into it unceasingly. **1882** HARTE *Flip* 2 Anxious faces yearned toward it . . . from the blinding white canvas covers of 'mountain schooners.' — **(14) 1883** *N.Y. Herald* 18 Nov. 12/3 In the United States the standards will be known as the 'Eastern,' 'Central,' 'Mountain' and 'Pacific' times. **1949** *Sat. Ev. Post* 23 April 132/4 Set back your watches—this is Mountain time.

(15) 1847 ROBB *Squatter Life* 143 Old Fecho had been a mountain trader . . . and looked wicked as a tree'd bear.

b. In combs., often occasional, sufficiently explained by the quots.: (1) **mountain cholera,** (2) **company,** (3) **county,** (4) **Crow,** (5) **department,** (6) **hoosier,** (7) **lamb,** (8) **law,** (9) **lot,** (10) **meadow,** (11) **oyster,** (12) **ranch,** (13) **ridge,** (14) **saddle,** (15) **sprout,** (16) **stage,** (17) **stagecoach,** (18) **trapper,** (19) **vigilantes,** (20) **white.**

(1) 1903 FOX *Little Shepherd* ii, The mountain cholera had carried off the man and the woman who had been father and mother to him. — **(2) 1846** SAGE *Scenes Rocky Mts.* ii, A mountain company generally comprises some quaint specimens of human nature. — **(3) 1860** CURTIS *Woody Plants N.C.* 75 Gray Willow. . . . I have met with this insignificant plant only in the mountain counties. — **(4) 1880** *Rep. Supt. Yellowstone Nat. Pk. 1879* 11 Even these old Mountain Crows—as distinguished from those upon the Missouri—have long been well supplied with both horses and fire-arms.

(5) 1863 KETTELL *Hist. Rebellion* II. 504 It was finally determined to annex Eastern Tennessee and Kentucky to the department of Western Virginia, and erect it into 'the mountain department.' — **(6) 1902** HARBEN *A. Daniel* 164 Pole Baker, yo're nothin' but a rag-tag, bob-tail mountain Hoosier, an' he's a slick duck from up North. **1931** *Randolph Enterprise* (Elkins, W. Va.) 4 June 4/3 There is where us mountain hoosiers learned our letters. — **(7) 1902** CLAPIN 281 Mountain-lamb. In parts of New England, especially New-Hampshire, a common term for deer killed out of season. — **(8) 1851** M. REID *Scalp Hunters* 269 They believe themselves, according to mountain law, in the right. — **(9) 1700** *Waterbury Prop. Rec.* 52 Six acers on ye easter sid of his land on ye hill or mountain lot.

(10) 1868 H. M. FLINT *Railroads* 12 'The Glades' are the mountain meadows, a region on the high table land at the summit of the Alleghany mountains. **1947** *Sierra Club Bul.* May 57 At best, our mountain meadows are definitely limited in number and would gradually, though very slowly, change into drier forest areas through natural evolution. — **(11) 1890** *Cent.* 4219/1 Mountain-oyster, a lamb's testicle. **1944** *D. N.* Nov. 19 *mountain oysters:* n. Testicles of the boar, the bull, (or the sheep), whenever the highland gourmet partakes of these delicacies at the table. Heard also in Texas, (Va., N.C., S.C., Tenn.). — **(12) 1908** LORIMER *J. Spurlock* 306 Uncle Bill . . . runs a mountain ranch—one of those natural parks back in the range. — **(13) 1850** JOHNSTON *Notes* I. 257 The mountain-ridge, as it is called, formed by the outcrop of the Niagara limestone, has been long known to the inhabitants of western New York. — **(14) 1848** PARKMAN in *Knickerb.* XXXI. 357 Though aided by the high-bowed 'mountain-saddle,' I could scarcely keep my seat on horseback.

(15) 1891 SLOAN *Fogy Days* 103 The boys from near the South Carolina coast used to call us up-country fellows mountain sprouts, and we in turn called them sand-lappers. — **(16) 1910** J. HART *Vigilante Girl* 127 Their vengeance will probably take the practical form of . . . holding up the mountain stages for the express boxes. — **(17) 1896** SHINN *Story of Mine* 109 The wagons . . . were in their way as distinct creations of adaptive and evolutionary genius as the mountain stagecoach of the period. — **(18) 1837** IRVING *Bonneville* II. 61 Peak after peak had they to traverse, struggling with difficulties and hardships known only to the mountain trapper. **1848** PARKMAN in *Knickerb.* XXXI. 334 When winter sets in, . . . the mountain-trappers, returned from their autumn expeditions, often build their rude cabins in the midst of these solitudes. **1872** —— *Oregon Trail* (ed. 4) p. viii, The mountain trapper is no more. — **(19) 1910** J. HART *Vigilante Girl* 116 What class of men make up the Mountain Vigilantes?

(20) 1922 KEPHART *So. Highlanders* 152 Some of their descendants remained behind in the fastnesses of the Alleghanies, . . . and became, in turn, the progenitors of that singular race which, by an absurd pleonasm, is now commonly known as the 'mountain whites.' **1943** PEATTIE *Great Smokies* 33 The mountain whites formed a salient of Union sympathy deep in the heart of the Confederacy.

5. *Over the mountain(s)*, a phrase used on the eastern seaboard to designate a location west of the Appalachians. *Obs.*

1800 TATHAM *Agric. & Commerce* 150 Which (in common language) is called *over the mountains, universally*, by all the people who inhabit the Atlantic states. **1832** KENNEDY *Swallow Barn* I. 12 The generations . . . had been broken up, or, what in his conception was equivalent, had gone 'over the mountain.'

As the last term in **Green, iron, prairie, Rocky, salt, sand, snow-on-the, soda mountain.** Also, *pl.*, **back, sheep, Shining Mountains.**

mountain boomer.

1. The red squirrel, *Sciurus hudsonicus*. Cf. **boomer,** *n.*[1] **1.**

1858 D. K. BENNETT *Chronology N.C.* 94 The only inhabitants we saw in these high points were pheasants, cross bills, and mountain boomers, a sort of squirrel. **1922** KEPHART *So. Highlanders* 87 Out of a tree overhead hopped a mountain 'boomer.'

transf. **1859** TALIAFERRO *Fisher's R.* 33 A mountain 'Boomer,' [was] dressed in a linsey hunting-shirt down to his knees. **1922** KEPHART *So. Highlanders* 280 They call themselves mountain people, or citizens; sometimes humorously 'mountain boomers.'

2. (See quot. 1940.)

1912 in WENTWORTH. **1940** *Mt. Hood Guide* 21 The sewellel or mountain beaver, sometimes colloquially called 'mountain boomer,' . . . resembles the porcupine and marmot rather than the beaver.

mountain cat. A name given to various animals, as the cougar, the bobcat, and, in California, the cacomistle.

1709 LAWSON *Carolina* 118 The Mountain-Cat, so call'd, because he lives in the Mountainous Parts of America, . . . is a Beast of Prey, as the Panther is. **1842** *Nat. Hist. N.Y., Zoology* I. 51, I suppose the Mountain Cat described by Loskiel as having reddish or orange-colored hair, with black streaks, to have been the Bay Lynx. **1874** HITTELL *Resources Calif.* 382 The mountain cat, or striped bassaris (*Bassaris astuta*) is abundant along the western base of the Sierra Nevada, between latitudes 36° and 39°. **1917** *Animals of Amer.* 108 Ring-Tailed Cat. . . . Other names.—Civet Cat. . . . Mountain Cat [etc.].

∗**mountaineer,** *n. W.* **= mountain man.** Cf. **Green, Rocky Mountaineer.** — **1837** IRVING *Bonneville* I. 25 A totally different class has now sprung up, 'the Mountaineers,' the traders and trappers that scale the vast mountain chains. **1904** *Chi. Ev. Post* 23 Aug. 7 In it [a dunnage bag] the aspiring mountaineer may pack fifty pounds of necessities.

mountain holly.

1. = Oregon grape.

1806 LEWIS in *L. & Clark Exped.* IV. (1905) 274 Near the river we find . . . two speceis of mountain holley, & common ash. **1807** GASS *Journal* 135 There is also a small bush . . . which bears a bunch of small purple berries. Some call it mountain holly; the fruit is of an acid taste.

2. An upland holly of the eastern U.S., *Ilex dubia monticola*.

1817–8 EATON *Botany* (1822) 317 *Ilex canadensis*, mountain holly. . . . A shrub 3 to 5 feet high. **1901** MOHR *Plant Life Ala.* 71 Mountain holly (*Ilex monticola*) . . . extend[s] northerly on the lower of the western Alleghenian ranges to southeastern Kentucky. **1943** PEATTIE *Great Smokies* 161 Such are fire cherry, yellow birch, and serviceberry, mountain holly, beech, rowanberry, striped maple, and mountain maple.

3. An obovate-leaved shrub, *Nemopanthus mucronata*, found in the eastern U.S.

1843 TORREY *Flora N.Y.* II. 5 *Nemopanthes Canadensis*, Mountain Holly, . . . [is found] on the Catskill Mountains.

mountain laurel.

1. A glossy-leaved evergreen shrub, *Kalmia latifolia*, with rose-colored and white flowers. Cf. **Pennsylvania mountain laurel.**

1759 MILLER *Gard. Dict.* (ed. 7) *s.v. Kalmia*, Ever-green Rose Laurel . . . commonly called in America Mountain Laurel. **1832** BROWNE *Sylva* 191 The Mountain Laurel is a large shrub, which indifferently bears the name of Mountain Laurel, Laurel, Ivy, and Calico Tree. **1949** *Nat. Hist.* May 223/2 It falls in the class of the extremely hard woods, as hard as mountain laurel and surpassed only by ironwood and dogwood among the woods of our northeastern states.

b. (See quot.)

1785 MARSHALL *Amer. Grove* 127 *Rhododendrum maximum.* Pennsylvanianian Mountain Laurel. This grows to the height of about six or eight feet.

2. = California laurel.

1884 SARGENT *Rep. Forests* 120 Mountain Laurel. California Laurel. Spice Tree. **1889** *Cent.* 3373/1 The California laurel or bay-tree, the mountain-laurel of the West, is *Umbellularia Californica*.

mountain mahogany.

1. The sweet birch, *Betula lenta*, common in the eastern U.S.

1810 MICHAUX *Arbres* I. 26 *Sweet birch*, [ou] *Mountain mahogony*, dans Virginia. **1832** BROWNE *Sylva* 118 Black Birch: . . . [is known as] Mountain Mahogany in Virginia.

2. a. = manzanita. b. = madroña. c. The Pacific yew, *Taxus brevifolia*.

(a) 1860 GREELEY *Overland Journey* 268 There is a . . . small tree which a driver termed a mountain-mahogany and a passenger called a red haw. **1874** HITTELL *Resources Calif.* 365 The mountain mahogany is an evergreen found on the eastern slopes of the Sierra Nevada, at an elevation of 6,000 feet above the sea. The leaves are bright and glossy, the growth low, the trunk crooked, the wood red, very even in grain, hard, heavy, and susceptible of high polish. — **(b) 1885** *Outing* Oct. VII. 25/2 With this pine grew a little Mescal and a respectable amount of the 'madroña' or Mountain Mahogany. — **(c) 1897** SUDWORTH *Arborescent Flora* 103 *Taxus brevifolia*. . . . Pacific Yew. . . . Mountain Mahogany (Idaho).

3. *W.* Any of various western shrubs of the genus *Cercocarpus*, having gray bark and reddish wood. Also attrib.

1896 SUDWORTH *Check List Forest Trees* 69 Cercocarpus ledifolius Nutt. Mountain Mahogany. **1942** LILLARD *Desert Challenge* 110 Bearings made of mountain mahogany wood wear as well as metal ones. **1949** *Jrnl. N.Y. Bot. Garden* July 167/2 There is a lot of mountain mahogany around Grand Canyon and Bryce National Parks that would surely catch the visitor's eye.

mountain oak. Any one of various upland oaks (see quots.).

1817–8 EATON *Botany* (1822) 421 *Quercus montana*, rock oak, chestnut oak, mountain oak. **1883** SMITH *Geol. Survey Ala.* 296 On the high lands . . . are found . . . the mountain or tan-bark oak. **1897** SUDWORTH *Arborescent Flora* 153 *Quercus gambelii*. . . . Mountain Oak (Nev., Oreg.). **1949** COLLINGWOOD & BRUSH *Knowing Your Trees* 224 Sometimes this tree [*Quercus montana*, chestnut oak] is called rock oak or mountain oak because it grows on high, rocky slopes.

∗**mountain rice.** Any of various grasses of the genus *Oryzopsis*, as the Rocky Mountain species, *O. hymenoides*. Also with defining term.

1817–8 EATON *Botany* (1822) 370 *Oryzopsis asperifolia*, mountain rice. Woods and bushy fields. **1843** TORREY *Flora N.Y.* II. 432 *Oryzopsis melanocarpa*. . . . Black-fruited Mountain-rice. . . . Rocky woods, in the western and northern parts of the State. **1894** COULTER *Bot. W. Texas* III. 517 *O[ryzopsis] membranacea*. . . . (Mountain rice.) . . . Mountain regions of western Texas and northward. **1945** DARLINGTON *Higher Plants Mich.* 17 Common species of grass that furnish some nutrient to grazing animals in the early part of the season are wild oat-grass . . . , sheep fescue . . . , mountain rice.

mountain tea.

1. The wintergreen, *Gaultheria procumbens.*

1785 MARSHALL *Amer. Grove* 53 *Gaultheria procumbens.* Canadian Gaultheria, or Mountain Tea. . . . The leaves have been used as a substitute for Bohea Tea, whence the name of Mountain Tea. **1891** RYAN *Pagan* 65 As they reached the level above the cliff, the level carpeted with mountain-tea and rabbit-berries, . . . the mountaineer halted. **1941** STUART *Men of Mts.* 187, I would love to get out with you and get mountain tea from the knolls.

2. A beverage made by steeping the leaves of this plant.

1832 WILLIAMSON *Maine* I. 121 This 'mountain tea' [from checker-berries] promotes mammillary secretions. **1886** *Harper's Mag.* June 62/1 Another beverage is 'mountain tea,' which is made from the sweet-scented golden-rod and from winter-green.

mountain wagon. Any one of various vehicles particularly adapted for use in mountainous regions (see quots. 1873, 1948).

1867 DIXON *New Amer.* I. 170 On my return through the Bitter Creek country, I had the honour of riding in the mountain waggon with an old road-agent. **1873** BEADLE *Undevel. West* 255 We change

One type of mountain wagon

from the coach to a 'mountain-wagon'—so called—a street hack with three seats and no springs. **1896** SHINN *Story of Mine* 108 These trains of mountain wagons . . . contained dry goods, provisions, tools, machinery, and merchandise. **1948** RITTENHOUSE *Vehicles* 61 One of the chief features of the mountain wagon was its oversized brake. . . . The gear in general was more substantial. Some of these wagons could haul up to 6500 lbs. Body 10½ by 3½ feet; wheels 44 and 52 inches high.

* **mounted,** *a.* In combs.: (1) **mounted gunman,** a cavalryman armed with a gun, *obs.;* (2) **infantry,** infantry which moves from place to place on horseback but fights dismounted, *obs.;* (3) **ranger,** a man who ranges on horseback to patrol or protect an area.

(1) 1818 JACKSON in *Cong. Deb.* (1819) 11 Jan. 2361 Their [Seminoles'] war spirit must be put down. . . . To accomplish this, the aid of one regiment of mounted gunmen . . . is asked from West Tennesee. **1855** SIMMS *Forayers* 461 Pickens, with a force of mounted gun-men, was equally earnest in pressing upon the heels of Cruger. — **(2) 1792** *Ann. 2d Congress* 1134 General Harmar . . . detached . . . the mounted infantry, part of the cavalry, and a detachment of militia. **1862** MOORE *Rebellion Rec.* V. II. 599 The mounted infantry, or 'mule cavalry,' proved an entire success. . . . They move with the celerity of cavalry, yet fight as infantry. — **(3) 1812** *Ann. 12th Congress* 2 Sess. 195 [The Indiana Territory] had not enjoyed one hour of security and repose, from the protection of the one company of Mounted Rangers, which had been allotted for its defence. **1852** GOUGE *Fiscal Hist. Texas* 73 Treasury notes should be issued only to defray the expenses of the civil department, and those of the gun-men and mounted rangers.

* **mounting,** *n.* Designating the left side of a horse. *Obs.* — **1732** *S.C. Gazette* 5 Feb. 4/2 (Th. Supp.), A dark colour'd Horse, branded with M and a cross a top, on the mounting shoulder: . . . also a bay Horse . . . branded with H on the mounting buttock. **1794** *Ib.* 29 July 1/1 (Th. Supp.), A black gelding, . . . branded on the Mounting buttock C.

* **mourner,** *n.*

1. At a revival or camp meeting, one who publicly repents his sins.

1807 in *Va. Hist. Mag.* XXXIII. (1925) 284 One shouter, four mourners came to be prayed for. **1886** EBBUTT *Emigrant Life* 124 At the different meetings there was a row of seats in front for 'mourners,'—that is, those mourning for their sins and wishing to join the Church; and here a number of people got very excited, and there was a lot of weeping and shouting when a mourner 'found glory.' **1938** STUART *When Foxes Flirt* (Wentworth), Brother Spencer asks for mourners to come up & be saved.

2. mourners' bench, at a revival or camp meeting, a front seat reserved for the mourners. Also, rarely, **mourners' seat.** Cf. **anxious bench, anxious seat.**

1845 HOOPER *Simon Suggs' Adv.* 126 'Bimeby I felt so missuble, I had to go yonder'—pointing to the mourner's seat. **1848** *Ladies' Repository* VIII. 102 She loves the mourner's bench, for there she found peace and pardon. **1911** WRIGHT *Winning Barbara Worth* 20 When the rush for the mourners' bench come I unlimbered an' headed the stampede pronto. **1948** *Time* 13 Dec. 64/2 There was no public testimony of the saved, no mourners' bench nor sawdust trail.

transf. **1943** POWELL *Home Again* 166 Negroes, were brought from the jail and were seated just inside the bar rail, on what was colloquially called the 'mourners' bench.' **1949** *N.Y. Times Bk. Review* 10 April 3/3 What was the consequence of the vast effort of social Christianity to bring society to the mourner's bench?

b. mourners' line, (see quot.).

1904 *N.Y. Ev. Post* 10 March 12 The rush of people to the Tax Department to swear off taxes has set in. Yesterday the 'mourner's lines,' which ordinarily contains 10 to 15 persons, extended out into the corridor.

3. *To crowd the mourners,* see * **crowd,** *v.* **4.** (2).

* **mourning,** *a.* In combs.: (1) **mourning cradle,** (see quot. 1836), now *hist.;* (2) **dove,** the Carolina turtle dove, *Zenaidura macroura carolinensis,* or an allied bird of the West; (3) **granite,** (see quot.); (4) **piece,** a pictorial memorial of a person who has died, often showing a tomb, weeping willows, etc.; (5) **pole,** (see quot.), *obs.;* (6) **warbler,** a warbler, *Oporornis philadelphia,* of the East, also **mourning ground warbler.**

(1) c1836 CATLIN *Indians* II. 133 A *mourning cradle.* . . . If the infant dies during the time that is allotted to it to be carried in this cradle, it is buried, and the disconsolate mother fills the cradle with black quills and feathers, in the parts which the child's body had occupied, and . . . carries it around with her wherever she goes for a year or more, with as much care as if her infant were alive and in it. **1906** *N. Eng. Mag.* Feb. 714/1 The 'mourning cradle' of the Mississippi Sioux reveals one of the most curious and interesting customs of those strange people, and shows again the 'eternal feminine' in the savage woman. — **(2) 1833** CATLIN *Indians* I. 158 The mourning or turtle-dove, . . . being, as they [*sc.* Mandans] call it, a medicine-bird, is not to be destroyed or harmed by anyone. **1880** FARRAR *Five Years Minn.* 166 Mourning-doves fill every wood with their plaintive notes. **1949** *Democrat* 30 June 7/3 About 600 mourning doves have been banded in Alabama. — **(3) 1872** *Vt. Bd. Agric. Rep.* I. 669 Below this black marble is a layer of grey, or as has recently been named, mourning granite. — **(4) 1843** *Knickerb.* XXII. 189 The parlor . . . was ornamented . . . [with] the indispensable family mourning-piece. **1894** WILKINS in *Harper's Mag.* March 504/1 She worked a mourning-piece, and after that a great picture, all in cross-stitch.

(5) 1812 *Austin P.* I. (1924) 209 Mourning Poles were up. When an indian died his wives or relations put up a long Poll hung with hoops or wrethes of grape vine to which the friends of the deceasd cryd or howld night and morning. — **(6) 1810** WILSON *Ornithology* II. 101 The Mourning Warbler, *Sylvia Philadelphia,* . . . was shot in the early part of June, on the border of a marsh. **1871** BURROUGHS *Wake-Robin* (1886) 90 From his dark breast, the ornithologist has added the expletive mourning; hence the mourning ground-warbler. **1947** *Iowa Acad. Sci. Proc.* LIV. 379 A male Mourning Warbler in full male plumage was seen near George, Lyon County, Iowa.

* **mouse,** *n.*

1. A small rat *q.v.* for a woman's hair.

1866 *Ore. State Jrnl.* 30 June 1/4 Such little things as 'waterfalls,' 'nets' and 'mice,' and other head fixings we were prepared for. **1888** *Cent. Mag.* Sep. 769/1 The crescent shaped pillows on which it [hair] was put up, the startling names of which were 'rats' and 'mice.'

2. In combs.: (1) * **mouse bird,** a shrike (see quots.); (2) * **ear,** an American species of everlasting, *Antennaria plantaginifolia,* also **mouse-ear everlasting;** (3) **hawk,** = **marsh hawk;** (4) **proof,** *a.* safe against mice; (5) **squirrel,** a small squirrel-like rodent, as the chipmunk, *obs.*

(1) 1857 *Rep. Comm. Patents 1856: Agric.* 87 The Southern shrike, (*Lanius ludovicianus,*) . . . breeds largely in the prairie districts [of Ill.]. . . . Its destruction of arvicolae in summer is well known, and has gained for it the name of 'Mouse Bird,' in Central Illinois. **1917** *Birds of Amer.* III. 101 The White-rumped Shrike, or Mouse-bird

(*Lanius ludovicianus excubitorides*) . . . is found in the arid districts of western North America. — (2) **1833** EATON *Botany* (ed. 6) 159 *Gnaphalium plantagineum,* mouse ear, early life-everlasting. **1840** DEWEY *Mass. Flowering Plants* 125 Gnaphalium plantagineum. Mouse-Ear Everlasting. Rises early in the spring . . . flowers for a long time. **1869** FULLER *Flower Gatherers* 314 One species of the Everlasting, the Mouse-ear, blooms in early spring. — (3) **1812** WILSON *Ornithology* VI. 67 Marsh Hawk[s] . . . are usually known by the name of the Mouse Hawk along the sea coast of New Jersey. **1884** *Harper's Mag.* March 620/1 The marsh-hawk . . . is often called the mouse-hawk. **1917** *Birds of Amer.* II. 64. — (4) **1895** *Outing* XXVI. 365/2 A mouse-proof locker. **1897** F. C. MOORE *How To Build a Home* 47 The Store-Room . . . may be made rat- or mouse-proof at small expense.

(5) *c***1662** J. WINTHROP in *N. Eng. Quart.* X. (1937) 127 Some of them [i.e., hills of corn] are usually plucked up by . . . Mouse-Squirrells (a little creature, that doth much hurt in some Fields newly planted). **1674** JOSSELYN *Two Voyages* 86 There are three sorts, the mouse squirril, the gray squirril, and the flying-squirril. **1796** MORSE *Univ. Geog.* I. 203 The Striped Squirrel Linnaeus confounds . . . with a striped mouse squirrel.

As the last term in **beaver, bog, buck, bullheaded, cactus, dark wood, deer, fence, fobtailed, ground, jumping, kangaroo, pine, piñon, pocket, prairie, scorpion, tree, vesper mouse.**

∗ **mouse,** *v.*

1. *tr.* and *intr.* To hunt patiently and carefully. Also with *out.*

1864 *N.Y. Evangelist* 20 Oct. (*Cent.*), He . . . usually returned laden with boxes and bundles of literary odds and ends, moused from rural attics and bought or begged for his collection. **1870** H. STEVENS *Bibl. Hist.* Intro. 11 They are driven . . . to mouse out in foreign countries . . . what ought to be at home . . . in public libraries. **1949** *Boston Globe Mag.* 18 Sep. 5/4, I guess I'll hunt back toward camp, Dad. Get a bite and maybe mouse around the ridge.

2. *To mouse over,* to dip into, sample, "nibble at" (books). *Colloq.*

1808 IRVING *Salmagundi* xx. 546 With . . . a table full of books before me, to mouse over them alternately. **1864** TAYLOR in *Life & Lett.* II. 422, I have Little and Brown's 'British Poets' complete now, so you'll have wherewithal to mouse over. **1889** GRETTON *Memory's Harkb.* 137 He was . . . always 'mousing' over books.

∗ **mousing,** *a.* Denoting a person who mouses. *Colloq.*

1852 STOWE *Uncle Tom's Cabin* 53 The mousing man, who bore the name of Marks, . . . looked shrewdly at our new acquaintance. *a***1862** FELTON *Greece: Anc. & Mod.* II. 521 The dialects . . . will have become . . . obsolete curiosities for the researches of the mousing antiquarian. **1883** LODGE *D. Webster* 107 One Parker Noyes, a mousing, learned New Hampshire lawyer.

∗ **mouth,** *n.* In combs.: (1) **mouth-fallen,** down in the mouth, crestfallen, *rare;* (2) **harp,** =next; (3) **organ,** a small wind instrument which has two sets of free metallic reeds, one set being sounded by blowing, the other by inhaling; (4) **root,** =**goldthread.**

(1) **1825** in M. B. SMITH *40 Yrs. Washington Soc.* (1906) 200 La, Sir, I wish you had seen how disappointed and mouth fallen the fellow looked. — (2) **1903** G. ADE *In Babel* 40 I'd walked from Loueyville over to Terry Hut with a nigger that played the mouth-harp. **1943** *Post* (Morgantown, W. Va.) 21 June 6 (Wentworth), Swimmin', playin' a mouth harp, an' gittin' into trouble. — (3) **1866** LOCKE *Struggles Nasby* 314 He wuz . . . playin 'Hail to the Chief' on a mouth organ. **1946** *Reader's Digest* March 142/2 A man in a decrepit spring wagon, driving a 17-year-old horse and playing a mouth organ, rode through a line of vigilantes. **1949** *Chi. D. News* 6 July 14/3 He plays the French harp, or mouthorgan, on Saturday nights. — (4) **1784** CUTLER in *Mem. Acad.* I. 457 Mouth Root. . . . The roots are astringent. **1860** DARLINGTON *Weeds & Plants* 31 C[optis] trifolia. . . . In some places it is a domestic remedy for the sore mouths of children; whence the name 'Mouth-root.' **1931** CLUTE *Plants* 123 The canker-root (*Coptis trifolia*) or mouth-root, as it is called, belongs to a different order and continues to hold its place among medicines for the cure of sore mouth.

b. In colloq. phrases: (1) ∗*To make up one's mouth to,* to decide to accept (something); (2) *to have one's mouth made up for,* to have an expectant desire for, be ready for; (3) *to shoot off one's mouth,* (see ∗**shoot** *v.*).

(1) **1843** STEPHENS *High Life N.Y.* I. 110 Tu save my life, I couldn't make up my mouth to it. — (2) **1890** *Harper's Mag.* 715/2 No one who has his mouth made up for a laugh is prepared to relish a dose of reason. **1890** *Cent.* 3587/3 His mouth was made up for a chicken salad.

As the last term in **bad, big, cotton, dragon, flannel, large, pucker, red, small, smooth, snake, split, tickle, tin mouth.** Also, *pl.*, **blue mouths.**

∗**mouth,** *v. College slang. intr.* (See quot. 1851.) *Obs.* — **1835** J. TODD *Student's Manual* 115 Should you allow yourself to think of going into the recitation-room, and there trust to 'skinning,' as it is called in some colleges, . . . or 'mouthing it,' as in others. **1851** HALL *College Words* 211 *Mouth,* to recite in an affected manner, as if one knew the lesson, when in reality he does not.

movable mill. (See quot.) *Obs.* — **1898** N. E. Jones *Squirrel Hunters of Ohio* 20 Movable mills. [Note:] Mills erected on two boats, separated at an angle, with water wheel near the bow. The natural current of the stream passing between the boats turned the wheel that moved the machinery of the mill.

∗ **movement,** *n.* **1.** The activity of a commodity or stock in the market. **2.** (See quot.) *Slang. Obs.*

(1) **1847** *Knickerb.* XXX. 165 The over-reaching 'movements' in flour which were every moment vibrating between New-York and Buffalo. **1886** *49th Congress* 2 Sess. H.R. Ex. Doc. No. 2, I. 18 The total movement of bonds held for national banks was $87,967,300. **1895** *Stand.* 1158/3 An upward movement in stocks. — (2) **1888** in T. ROOSEVELT *Works* (1926) XIV. 83 Money spent, as has been asserted, in the effort to purchase blocks of votes, or 'movements' as they have been called in New York.

As the last term in **cyclone, Emmanuel, Free Soil, granger, secession movement.**

∗ **mover,** *n.*

1. An emigrant moving west to settle; a person participating in the tide of western migration.

1810 M. DWIGHT *Journey to Ohio* 29 It is a log hut built across the road from the tavern, for movers—that the landlord need not be bother'd with them. **1842** BUCKINGHAM *E. & W. States* II. 293 [Along the emigrants' road to the West] we saw several houses by the road-side, expressly for their use, with the signs 'Moovers' Accommodation'—others with more correct orthography, had 'House for Movers.' **1944** BLAIR *Tall Tale Amer.* 100 And instead of selling the seedlings from these nurseries . . . he'd . . . give them to the movers—free.

b. A tenant farmer who exhausts the original fertility of a piece of land and then moves on to repeat the process again and again.

1913 LONDON *Valley of Moon* 434 The 'movers' . . . lease, clean out and gut a place in several years, and then move on. **1945** MARSHALL *Santa Fe* 230 'Boomers' and 'movers' tried again and again to take up land, filtering down from Kansas and up from Texas along the Santa Fe track.

2. One whose business it is to move household goods, furniture, and the like from one place of residence to another. Cf. **house mover.**

1894 *Boston Directory* 1944 J. W. Cook & Son, . . . Movers of Pianofortes, Furniture, etc. **1948** *Dly. Ardmoreite* (Ardmore, Okla.) 25 April 20/2 No other mover . . . has a license to operate in seven states as he has.

3. a. movers' room, (see quot.). *Obs.* **b. mover's wagon,** a wagon in which a mover migrates west. *Obs.* Cf. **emigrant wagon.**

(a) **1895** HOWELLS *Recollections* 87 We stopped at a tavern, as was then the custom, only hiring the use of one room, on the first floor, known as the movers' room, and the privilege of the fire to make tea or coffee or fry bacon. — (b) **1883** HOWE *Country Town* (1926) 3 The building stood on the main road where the movers' wagons passed. **1889** *Harper's Mag.* Dec. 121/1 A mover's wagon with dingy cover was creeping slowly townward along the white road.

movie ˈmuvɪ, *n.* [f. *mov*ing picture.] A motion picture; a performance at which a moving picture is shown, often *pl.*

"The word *movie* appears to have come into the folk-tongue out of the gamin life of either New York or Chicago about 1906–1907. . . . By 1908 *movie* began to appear in the reports of social workers and contemporary newspaper accounts" (*Amer. Sp.* I. 357).

1913 *Lit. Digest* 4 Jan. 16/2 (*heading*), For More Brilliant 'Movies.' **1913** *Chi. D. News* 8 March 9/3 (*heading*), 'Movies' In A Small Town. **1949** *Reader's Digest* April 141/2 We . . . went to a movie, or bought tickets for a train or boat.

attrib. **1913** *Outlook* 5 April 784/1 The 'movie' fan lays himself open to overtired eye nerves, with the consequent headaches, indigestion, and general nervous complaints. **1917** *Chi. Defender* 22 Dec. 5 Watch for Our New Movie Palace to be Erected at a Cost of $250,000. **1918** *Current Opinion* Jan. 31 (*title*), Wonders of Camouflage that are Accomplished in Movieland. **1935** LINCOLN *Cape Cod Yesterdays* 268 There were no movie cameras for amateur use in those days. **1948** *Chi. Sun-Times* 20 April 3/2 Howard was an ardent movie fan, who especially enjoyed the blood-and-thunder murder mystery type of drama.

Also *movie colony, director, dude, game, house, palace, reel, show, star, theater,* etc.

*** moving,** *a.* In combs.: (1) **moving day,** a day on which leases expire and people who have not renewed theirs move to other quarters; (2) **man,** = *** mover,** *n.* **2;** (3) **school,** ?a school that meets in the homes of different pupils, *obs.;* (4) **van,** a van used by a mover (sense **2.**); (5) **wagon,** a wagon taking settlers westward, *obs.*, cf. *** mover,** *n.* **1.**

(1) **1832** WATSON *Hist. Tales* N.Y. 123 'Moving day' was, as now, the first of May. **1910** *Nation* 22 Sep. 259/2 A September Labour Day on which no manual labor is performed is less characteristic of us than our October moving day, . . . not without its realistic exhibits and its impressive parade. **1947** *Pasadena* (Calif.) *Star-News* 9 Sep. 16/6 Moving days are ahead for several county departments in the Hall of Records and Hall of Justice, Los Angeles. — (2) **1922** H. L. FOSTER *Adv. Trop. Tramp* xii. 179 While he shipped the furniture from the old place, I was to go down to the new one to see that the moving-men stole none of it en route. — (3) **1873** BLAKE *Hist. Warwick, Mass.* 37 At a town meeting convened at the meeting-house, March 7 [1768] . . . it was . . . proposed to the town, whether they would have a moving school? and it was voted in the affirmative. — (4) **1898** *K.C. Star* 21 Dec. 9/2 The moving vans and pie-wagons of New York are changing their pictures. Before the war of 1898 these vehicles were moving panoramas of scenes and incidents of the Revolutionary or the Civil War.

(5) **1817** in *Amer. Hist. Rev.* XXXVII. 74 About 10 moving waggons put up at the house where we stayed last night, all bound for Ohio and Indiana. *c***1835** in *Wis. State H.S. Coll.* XV. 271 We pass from 10 to 30 moving wagons a day, with droves of cattle & sheep, mostly going to Illinois.

*** mow,** *v.* **1. mow land,** =**mowing land. 2. mow lot,** a lot which produces grass for mowing. Both *obs.*

(1) **1845** JUDD *Margaret* II. 214 Women . . . [were] turning hay among alders and willows, that yet flourished in their best mowlands. **1874** *Vt. Bd. Agric. Rep.* II. 411 The breeding of wrinkled sheep is like a farmer who ridges up his level mow-land and seeds the ridges with an inferior grass. — (2) **1845** JUDD *Margaret* II. 325 They let me take the Colt; I kept him here in the mow-lot.

mow fly. An insect destructive to wheat. — **1859** *Harper's Mag.* Dec. 47/1 Next comes a very pretty Mow fly. . . . You will find her oftenest depositing her eggs near the joints [of wheat].

mowhackees mo'hækiz, *n. pl.* [Of Indian origin.] Dark wampum beads, twice as valuable in Indian trade as the regular white variety. Now *hist.*

1634 WOOD *N. Eng. Prospect* II. iii. 65 The Narragansets . . . are the most curious minters of their Wampompeage and Mowhakes, which they forme out of the inmost wreaths of Periwinkle-shels. **1672** JOSSELYN *N. Eng. Rarities* 36 A kind of Coccle, of whose Shell the Indians make their Beads called Wompampeag and Mohaicks. **1910** HODGE *Amer. Indians* II. 908/2 The Dutch applied the name *Sewan hacky*, 'Wampum land,' to Long-Island, perhaps in imitation of the natives. . . . In New England *mowhackees*, 'black beads,' was used.

*** mowing,** *n.*

1. *ellipt.* Land on which grass is grown for mowing. *Colloq.*

1741 *N.H. Probate Rec.* III. 71 One peice of Woodland . . . with about an Acre of mowing. **1838** *Mass. Agric. Survey 1st Rep.* 11 A considerable amount of this land . . . has been converted into profitable mowing. **1891** *N. & Q.* VI. 204 These rings were simply round patches of some kind of grass . . . amidst the richer grasses of a permanent 'mowing,' for we used to call a hay-field a 'mowing' in those days.

2. In combs.: (1) **mowing field,** = *** mowing 1;** (2) **ground,** see as a main entry; (3) **land,** = *** mowing 1;** (4) **machine,** a machine for mowing grass, alfalfa, weeds, etc.; (5) **meadow,** = *** mowing 1.**

(1) **1819** E. EVANS *Pedestrious Tour* 145 How many of our mowing fields are . . . shamefully poached and grubbed by horses and sheep! — (3) **1740** *Hartford Land Distrib.* 357 One parsell Called Swamp Now mowing land. **1745** *Boston News-Letter* 28 March, To be Sold . . . a Farm . . . which will make good Pasture and Mowing Land, and yields about 200 Cocks of Hay annually. **1858** FLINT *Milch Cows* 169 The grasses differ widely; and their value as feed for cows will depend . . . on the management of pastures and mowing-lands. — (4) **1823** *17th Congress* 2 Sess. H.R. Doc. No. 36, 6 Improvement in the mowing machine, Feb. 13, [1822,] Jeremiah Baily. **1945** WALLACE *Barington* 294 The double lanes of green mowing machines and red cultivators had given way to bright cooking ranges.

(5) **1799** WASHINGTON *Writings* XIV. 231 Although I am not sanguine enough to expect, that it will make good mowing meadow, I shall be much disappointed if it does not produce grass.

mowing ground. Grass-producing ground set aside by the early colonists for mowing, or ground on which a hay crop is produced (see also quot. 1790). *Obs.*

1634 *Cambridge Prop Rec.* 1 [The constable] shall make a surueyinge of the Houses backsids Corne ffeilds Moweing grounds and other lands. **1703** *N. H. Probate Rec.* I. 504, I give unto my son, Josiah, the use & Improvement of all my other marsh, & mowing ground. **1790** DEANE *N.-Eng. Farmer* 179/2 *Mowing-Ground*, a name commonly given in this country to land, which being fit for either mowing or tillage, is alternatively used for the one and the other. **1800** *Mass. H.S. Coll.* 1 Ser. VII. 245 [The Isles of Shoals] lie in common, except a few small inclosures for gardens and mowing ground.

*** Mozambique,** *n.* (See quot. 1875.) *Obs.*

1861 *Chi. Tribune* 15 April 1 Cheap Dry Goods. . . . Mozambiques, 6¼ cts. Yd. **1875** KNIGHT 1493/1 *Mozambique*, . . . an open dress-goods having a chain in which the cotton threads are associated in pairs, and the woolen filling is soft and fleecy. **1896** *Godey's Mag.* April 436/1 A new material of mohair and silk is known as Mozambique, and is semi-transparent and in rather straggling all-over designs; two tones are generally employed, such as brown and reseda.

mozo 'moso, *n. S.W.* [Sp. in same sense.] (See quot. 1944.)

1836 C. J. LATROBE *Rambler in Mex.* 49 (Bentley), The remainder were sent in advance under his domestics or mozos. **1923** WALLACE SMITH *Little Tigress* 5 (Bentley), An aged and stooping mozo came to answer his knocking. **1944** ADAMS *W. Words* 102 Mozo. Spanish, meaning *a young man, an assistant.* Americans usually use the word in speaking of the assistant of a pack train.

Also **moza,** an Indian girl or woman.

1934 WHITE *Folded Hills* 162 She wore the camisa and short skirt of the *moza*, and her legs were bare.

*** M.P.** Abbreviation of "Metropolitan Police." *Slang. Obs.* — **1872** BRACE *Dangerous Classes N.Y.* 176 They [street boys] could dodge an 'M.P.' as a fox dodges a hound.

Mr. John. *W.* Indians in general. *Colloq. Obs.* — **1870** DUVAL *Big-Foot Wallace* 86, I had gone but a little ways on the prairie when I picked up an arrow, and a few yards farther on, I came across one of our horses lying dead in the grass. . . . This satisfied me at once that 'Mr. John' had paid us a sociable visit during the night, and . . . had carried off all our stock when they left.

Mrs. Goff. (See quot. 1851.) *Obs.* — **1819** PEIRCE *Rebelliad* 21 Mrs. Goff has deign'd to weep. **1851** HALL *College Words* 211 *Mrs. Goff.* Formerly a cant phrase for any woman.

muchacho mu'tʃatʃo, *n. S.W.* [Sp. in same sense.] A boy; a male servant. Also attrib.

1823 *Nat. Intelligencer* (Wash., D.C.) 18 Jan. 4/4 The American opposition party, or the young men (*los muchachos,*) although more numerous possess neither the union, nor the energy, nor the means of their opponents. **1831** BEECHEY *Voyage to Pacific* II. 33 He amused himself by throwing pancakes to the *muchachos*, a number of little Indian domestics. **1849** JOHNSON *Sights Gold Region* 265 From thence our friendly *muchachos* conducted us to the shops of different jewelers. **1925** W. N. BURNS *Saga of Billy the Kid* 280 (Bentley), No, muchacho, protested Celsa.

muche 'mʌtʃi, *n.* [Du. *mutsje*, in same sense.] A liquid measure of about one fifth of a pint. *Obs.* — **1673** *Hempstead Rec.* I. 291 If any man shall Refuse to: go: . . . he shall pay six muches of Rume to them that goes [i.e., to run the bounds of the town].

*** mucilage,** *n.* A sticky solution of gum or a similar adhesive substance.

1859 *La Crosse Union* 15 Oct. 3/3 Mucilage, sealing wax, playing cards. **1923** WIGGIN *My Garden of Memory* 112, I bought pencils, crayons, and mucilage of the local stationers. **1936** *Sears Cat.* 726/2 Mucilage with Rubber Spreader Top.

attrib. **1870** M. TWAIN *Sk. New & Old* (1875) 237 (R.), There is a mucilage-bottle broken.

mucilaginous elm. The American elm, *Ulmus americana*, usu. planted for shade. — **1817** ROBIN *Florula Ludoviciana* 164 Ulmus americana. Mucilaginous Elm. **1819** DANA *Geog. Sk.* 245 A list of the most valuable forest trees growing . . . [includes] sycamore, white oak, black oak, linden, locust, mucilaginous elm and red elm.

*** muck,** *n.*

1. (See quots.) Cf. **black muck, swamp muck.**

1862 DANA *Man. Geol.* 614 *Muck* is another name for peat, . . . especially when the material is employed as a manure. **1897** LEONARD *Gold Fields Klondike* 180 The top 'muck,' as it is called by the miners, is, when thawed out, about two-thirds water and one-third sediment. **1914** ATHERTON *Perch of Devil* 148 His . . . hands were white with 'muck,' a mixture of rock-dust and water. **1949** *Nat. Hist.* Sep. 299/1 The gold-bearing gravels lie beneath a stratum of muck, which must be thawed and washed out of the way.

2. In combs.: (1) **muck bar,** in iron smelting, a bar of iron that has gone only through the muck rolls; (2) **raker, raking,** see as main entries; (3) **roll,** (see quot.).

(1) **1866** *Internal Revenue Guide* 104 On Steel made directly from muck-bar, blooms, slabs, or loops a tax of three dollars per ton. **1894** *Harper's Mag.* Feb. 421/3 The 'muck bar' is broken up, bunched together, raised to a welding heat, and again and again carried through the rolls. — (3) **1875** Knight, Muck-roll, the *roughing* or first roll of a rolling-mill train.

b. Also (1) **muck bed,** (2) **land,** (3) **swamp.**

(1) **1874** *Vt. Bd. Agric. Rep.* II. 553 Do not wantonly destroy a good muck bed. — (2) **1848** *Rep. Comm. Patents 1847* 358 They have been planted the present year, on deep muck lands. **1942** Kennedy *Palmetto Country* 16 After a total expenditure of twenty-two million dollars, thousands of acres of muckland were reclaimed and are now producing truck crops for Northern winter markets. — (3) **1870** *Rep. Comm. Agric. 1869* 270 The soil was . . . black mud or muck swamp, five feet deep, containing a mixture of sand.

muckamuck ˈmʌkəˌmʌk, *n.* [Chinook Jargon. See **high-muck-a-muck.**]

1. Food.

1847 Palmer *Jrnl. of Travels* 150 Muck-a-muck, Provisions, eat. **1852** *Oregonian* (Portland) 25 Dec. 2/3 The aborigine . . . 'put' for the settlement with a sort of legs-do-your-duty-for-the-body-is-in-danger resolution for his *muckamuck.* **1880** *Forest & Stream* 11 Nov. 285/2 We should have to come ashore and have some 'muck-a-muck.' **1939** Colby *Guide to Alaska* xl, Some of the Chinook expressions still used in everyday speech . . . are given below: . . . *muckamuck n.* (C.) food.

2. =**high-muck-a-muck.**

1914 *D.N.* IV. 113 Squeegee, *n.* A person of importance, muckamuck; used derisively. **1947** *Chi. Herald-Amer.* 15 Jan. 13/7 The supreme muckety-muck of the English army, the shy, bashful, retiring Montgomery, is in Russia, getting 21-gun salutes.

muckamuck ˈmʌkəˌmʌk, *v.* [See prec.] *intr.* To eat. *Colloq.*

1838 Parker *Jrnl. Exploring Tour* 338 Eat, mucamuc. **1853** Winthrop *Letters* 13 June, We stopped once or twice for them to 'muck-a-muck,' which they are ready for forty times a day. **1858** *Hutchings Mag.* May 527/1 One day no ketchum klicket; no muckamuck velly good. **1945** *Senior Scholastic* 23 April 19/3 *Muckamuck*—to eat food, to browse, etc. Muckamuck chuck, to drink.

muckawis ˈmʌkəwɪs, *n.* [Prob. of Algonquian origin. See quot. 1762.] The whippoorwill. *Obs.* — **1762** in Trumbull *Natick Dict.* (1903) 67/2 múckko-wheesce (Peq.), the whippoorwill. Stiles. **1837** Williams *Florida* 74 Muckawis. . . . This bird resembles the Whippoorwill in every thing but his note.

mucker ˈmʌkɚ, *n.*[1] [G., a sanctimonious bigot.]

1. A fanatical reformer. *Obs.*

1891 *Cyclo. Temperance* 269/1 The saloon-keepers then resolved to make 'the muckers take their own medicine,' and insisted that the Mayor should enforce the Sunday law against 'common labor.'

2. In a college town, a young townsman as distinguished from a college student. *Slang. Obs.*

1893 Post *Harvard Stories* 75 On the first corner . . . were stationed three or four small boys (the occasionally useful Cambridge muckers) employed as vedettes.

3. An unrefined or boorish person. *Slang.*

1899 Ade *Fables in Slang* 108 They were not Muckers; they were Nice Boys, intent on preserving the Traditions of dear old *Alma Mater.* **1904** *Phil. Public Ledger* 4 June 6 Cheering by the side benefited [by a misplay] was distinctly out of order; it was, in the elegant language of the campus, 'muckerish,' and the college which practiced it was composed of 'muckers.' **1921** Paine *Comr. Rolling Ocean* 99 He grumbles about the food and says the officers are dubs and most of the boys muckers.

* **mucker,** *n.*[2] **1.** A workman who removes gravel, hardpan, etc., in a mine or other excavation. **2.** A workman who handles muck bars *q.v.*

(1) **1899** *Harper's Wkly.* 20 May 498/1 The Company . . . paid $3. for miners and $2.50 for 'muckers,' or underground laborers. **1947** *Time* 1 Dec. 24/2 Rawhide Jim put Lew to work as a mucker in the mines at Jerome, where he started learning copper the hard way. — (2) **1906** Lynde *Quickening* 122, [I'll] go to work in the iron plant and be a mucker all the rest of my life, I reckon.

mucket ˈmʌkɪt, *n.* [?Blend of *mug* and *bucket.*] (See quot.) *Obs.* — **1862** Norton *Army Lett.* 64 Each of us has a small tin kettle holding three pints or so, fitted with a tight cover. We call them muckets for want of a better name. . . . I believe almost any of us would throw away a blanket before he would his mucket, they are so indispensable.

muckrake ˈmʌkˌrek, *v. tr.* To subject (public men, corporations, etc.) to vigorous and unscrupulous charges of misconduct and corruption.

The *OED* lists this term as an intransitive nonce-word in the sense of to rake refuse together. In Amer. use it is no doubt a new formation (from **muck* and **rake*).

1910 *N.Y. Ev. Post* 10 Dec. 8 Their knowledge of how it feels to be a muck-raked millionaire. **1943** M. Flavin *Journey in Dark* 193 The country has been muckraked from one end to the other.

muckraker ˈmʌkˌrekɚ, *n.* [f. **muckrake,** *v.*] One who makes sensational and undiscriminating charges of corruption on the part of public men, corporations, etc.

In a speech on April 14, 1906, Theodore Roosevelt used the figure of the "Man with the Muckrak" mentioned in *Pilgrim's Progress,* to describe persons given to charging individuals, corporations, and governments with corruption. Lincoln Steffens, who had already written several "muckraking" articles, and several of his friends seized upon this figure and *muckrake, muckraker, muckraking,* soon obtained wide currency.

[**1871** De Vere 618 *Muckrakes,* a slang term in politics for persons who 'fish in troubled waters,' from the idea of their raking up the muck to see what valuable waifs and strays they may find in it. The term is generally used in the form of *muckrakes and place-mongers.* **1906** *Cin. Enquirer* 15 April 4/4 The men with the muck-rakes are often indispensable to the well-being of society; but only if they know when to stop raking the muck, and to look upward to the celestial crown above them, to the crown of worthy endeavor.] **1906** *Collier's* 22 Dec. 30/2 The muck-raker . . . is the man who has dared to knock to pieces the great American mud god, 'Success.' **1949** *Register* (Denver) 5 June 1/3 He is a professional muckraker.

muckraking ˈmʌkˌrekɪŋ, *n.* Seeking out corrupt, or allegedly corrupt, practices and directing public attention to them.

1911 *N.Y. Ev. Post* 25 Jan. 14 The same articles brought President Roosevelt to the defence of the Senate, and led him to apply the word 'muck-raking' to the literature of higher exposure. **1945** *Chi. D. News* 8 Aug. 21/4 It sounds as though it might be muckraking but it isn't. **1948** *Time* 8 March 100/2 He left newspapering for magazine work, did notable muckraking on corrupt journalism.

attrib. [**1906** *Dly. Rec. & Mail* 19 Dec. 5 Few popular institutions in America have escaped violent attacks by muck-raking reformers.] **1912** *Out West* June 395, I have no 'muckraking' ability, and I am not skilled in the political arena. **1949** *Time* 4 April 65/3 By then most of McClure's muckraking fervor was spent and his health was failing.

* **mud,** *n.* In combs.

1. In the names of animals, chiefly fishes: (1) **mud bass,** (see quots.); (2) **bear,** (see quot.); (3) **cat,** see as a main entry; (4) **dabbler,** (see quot.); (5) **dauber,** see as a main entry; (6) **devil,** =**hellbender;** (7) * **fish,** see as a main entry; (8) **iguana,** the siren, *Siren lacertina,* of the South, *obs.;* (9) **kitten,** a mud cat, *humorous;* (10) **lump,** a lumpfish, cf. **4.** (9) below; (11) **minnow,** any small, pickerel-like fish of the genus *Umbra,* as *U. limi* of the Mississippi Valley; (12) **pike,** (see quot.); (13) **pout,** a catfish; (14) **puppy,** any of various American salamanders, as the hellbender; (15) **shad,** =**gizzard shad;** (16) **sucker,** any of various American fresh-water fishes of the family Catostomidae, which feed on the bottoms of streams and ponds; (17) **sunfish,** the fresh-water sunfish, *Acantharcus pomotis* (see also quot. 1909); (18) **terrapin,** =next; (19) **tortoise,** a mud turtle, esp. of the genera *Sternotherus* and *Kinosternon;* (20) **turtle,** see as a main entry; (21) **vampire,** (see quot.); (22) **wasp,** =**mud dauber 1.**

(1) **1884** Goode *Fisheries* I. 405 The Mud Bass—*Acantharchus Pomotis.* This species is found only in the coastwise streams of the lowlands from New Jersey to North Carolina. **1909** Webster 1417/3 *Mud bass,* . . . the large-mouthed black bass. . . . *Indiana.* — (2) **1880** *Rep. Supt. Yellowstone Nat. Pk.* (1881) 41 Wolverine, or long-tailed mud bear. — (4) **1877** Bartlett 410 *Mud-Dabbler,* a species of small fresh-water fish, of the same appearance as the *sucker,* although much smaller.

(6) **1825** *Amer. Jrnl. Science* XI. 278 *Menopoma Alleghaniensis.* . . . Hell-bender. Mud-devil. — (8) **1766** J. Ellis in *Phil. Trans.* LVI. 189 The natives [of S.C.] call it Mud-Inguana [*sic*]. **1796** Morse *Univ. Geog.* I. 224 The *Siren* or *Mud-iguana,* a fish of the order *Branchiostegi.* — (9) **1862** Bagby *Old Va. Gentleman* 92 [The water is] full of all manner of nasty and confounded 'mud-kittens,' 'snap'n' turtles,' and snake doctors.

(10) **1832** Williamson *Maine* I. 156 There are two varieties, if not species; the *mud* or *green,* and the red lump. — (11) **1870** *Amer. Naturalist* IV. 386 The Mud Minnow (*Melanura limi*) [is found in the Delaware at Trenton, N.J.]. **1897** *N.Y. Forest, Fish & Game Comm. 2d Rep.* 229 *Umbra limi.* . . . A number of mud minnows were shipped in wet moss from Caledonia, N.Y. — (12) **1870** *Amer. Naturalist* IV. 386 [The] Mud Pike (*Esox porosus*) [is found in the Delaware at Trenton, N.J.]. — (13) **1804** Fessenden *Orig. Poems* (1806) 132 Like an

otter that paddles the creek, In quest of a mud pout, or sucker. **1859** BARTLETT 72 [The catfish, genus *Prinelodus*] is also called by the name of Horned-pout, Bull-head, Mud-pout, Minister, or simply Cat. — **(14) 1882** *Amer. Naturalist* XVI. 325 Vitality of the Mud Puppy.—The observations on the Menopoma [etc.]. **1949** *Amer. Photography* Sep. 593/1 The best known is probably the common mud puppy or water dog (*Necturus maculosus*).

(15) 1883 *Nat. Museum Bul.* No. 27, 455 Gizzard Shad; Mud Shad; Hickory Shad. . . . The species has no commercial value. **1884** GOODE *Fisheries* I. 610 The 'Mud-Shad' . . . is abundant in brackish waters along the coast from Delaware Bay southward to Mexico. — **(16) 1820** *Western Rev.* II. 361 Toad Mudcat, *Pylodictis limosus*, . . . bears the name of . . . Mudsucker, and Toadfish. **1870** *Amer. Naturalist* IV. 113 The Mud-sucker (*Hylomyzon nigricans*). **1911** *Rep. Fisheries 1908* 317 The different species [of sucker] are known as 'May sucker,' 'mud sucker' [etc.]. — **(17) 1870** *Amer. Naturalist* IV. 102 Professor S. F. Baird, during the summer of 1854, discovered, in New Jersey, . . . the Mud Sunfish. **1883** *Nat. Museum Bul.* No. 27, 462 Mud Sun-Fish. Eastern United States from New York to South Carolina in sluggish streams. **1909** WEBSTER 1418/1 *Mud sunfish*, . . . the war-mouth. — **(18) 1842** *Nat. Hist. N.Y., Zoology* III. 23 The Musk Tortoise or Mud Turtle, Mud Terrapin or Stink-pot, . . . is to be found in most of our ponds and ditches. **1859** BARTLETT 284 *Mud-Turtle.* (*Sternothœrus odorata.*) The popular name of a reptile common in all parts of the United States. Marsh Tortoise and Mud Terrapin are other names for the same. — **(19) 1839** STORER *Mass. Reptiles* 210 *Sternothaerus odoratus*, the mud Tortoise, . . . is found burying itself in the mud in ditches and small ponds. **1890** *Cent.* 3887/3 *Mud-tortoise* . . . same as *mud-turtle*.

(21) 1843 MARRYAT *M. Violet* xliv, Among these [phenomena of rivers and bayous] is the mud vampire, a kind of spider leech. — **(22) 1824** *Old Colony Memorial* (Plymouth) 6 March (Th.), [He was] a sort of would-be dandy; having the bottom of his waist pinched up to the size of a quart pot, and thus resembling in shape what we call a mud wasp. **1881** *Amer. Naturalist* XV. 443 Baron Osten Sacken . . . records the breeding of *A[rgyramoeba] cephus* and *A. fur* from the nest of a Texan mud-wasp. **1939** *L.A.* Map. 239.

b. In the names of birds: (1) **mud coot,** (see quots.); (2) **dauber,** see as a main entry; (3) **dipper,** =**ruddy duck;** (4) **duck,** =**mud hen;** (5) **goose,** =**Hutchins' goose;** (6) ∗**hen,** any of various American birds of the family Rallidae, as the American coot, cf. **4.** (5) below; (7) **poke,** the shitepoke *q.v.*, cf. ∗**poke,** *n.*³ **2;** (8) **snipe,** (see quot.); (9) **swallow,** the cliff swallow or eaves swallow *qq.v.*, also transf. and attrib.

(1) 1890 *Cent.* 3886/3 *Mud-coot*, the common American coot, *Fulica americana.* **1917** *Birds of Amer.* I. 214 Coot. *Fulica americana.* . . . [Also called] Pond Hen; Mud Coot; Ivory-billed Coot. — **(3) 1888** TRUMBULL *Names of Birds* 110 [The ruddy duck, *Erismatura rubida*, is known] at Eastville, Va., as Mud Dipper. **1917** *Birds of Amer.* I. 152. — **(4) 1857** *Spirit of Times* 26 Sep. 54/2 There is duck of every quality, canvas-back, wood, mud, and various other species of ducks. **1903** *Forest & Stream* 21 Feb. 150/2 [Call ducks] are a cross between the mallard and ordinary mud duck.

(5) 1844 *Nat. Hist. N.Y., Zoology* II. 352 Hutchins's Goose . . . is not uncommon on the eastern part of Long island . . . and is known under the name of Mud Goose. **1917** *Birds of Amer.* I. 161 Throughout its range it [Hutchins' goose, *Branta canadensis hutchinsi*] is variously known also as Goose-brant, . . . Short-necked Goose, or Mud Goose. — **(6) 1813** WILSON *Ornithology* VIII. 62 Common Coot. . . . It is known in Pennsylvania by the name of *Mud-hen.* **1949** *Chi. Tribune* 20 Feb. II. 6/1 Each winter produces a pretty good concentration of these birds, plus thousands of mud hens. — **(7) 1809** IRVING *Knickerb.* VI. ii, Squatting himself down on the edge of a pond catching fish for hours together. . . . [Dirk Schuiler bore] no little resemblance to that notable bird ycleped the Mud-poke. — **(8) 1897** *Ann. Rep. Comm. Fisheries* 322 *Philohela minor* Gmelin. American woodcock. Popular synonyms: Bog-sucker; mud snipe; blind snipe. — **(9) 1873** LELAND *Egypt. Sketch-Bk.* 43 Those curious mud-swallow nests of little villages. **1898** DELAND *Old Chester Tales* 181 Mud-swallows had built their nests in the corners. **1917** *Birds of Amer.* III. 84 Cliff Swallow. *Petrochelidon lunifrons lunifrons.* . . . [Also called] Barn Swallow; Mud Swallow; Republican Swallow.

2. Designating things and places made of, or abounding in, mud, as (1) **mud brick,** (2) **butte,** (3) **creek,** (4) **fence, hole,** see as main entries, (5) **lake,** (6) **lick,** (7) **oven,** (8) **pike,** (9) **pipe,** (10) **playa,** (11) **road,** (12) **shanty,** (13) **slough,** (14) **town.**

(1) 1808 PIKE *Sources Miss.* II. App. 7 [Because of shortage of wood] houses [along the Kansas, Platte, and Arkansas rivers] would be built entirely of mud-brick (like those in New Spain) or of the brick manufactured with fire. **1881** *Amer. Naturalist* XV. 979 All of the houses [in Tucson] are built of . . . sun-dried mud bricks. — **(2) 1882** *Cent. Mag.* Aug. 510/2 Back of these mud buttes . . . are immense stretches of grazing country. — **(3) 1832** in *Overland to Pacific* IV. (1934) 166, I, with others of the company, quit the boat, and walked on for five days through woods, mud creeks, over prairies—in rain and shine.

(5) 1860 DEGROOT *Washoe Mines* 17/2 This latter is rather a shallow pond, drying entirely up in the summer, but in the winter covering a large extent of flat country with a few inches of water, converting it into what has been aptly named Mud Lakes. **1942** LILLARD *Desert Challenge* 105 Largest of all the mud lakes is Black Rock, . . . sixty miles long by twenty wide. — **(6) 1779** in *Amer. Sp.* XV. 287/2 Crossing a branch to a red oak near a mud lick. **1824** *Ib.*, On the bank of the Bee tree branch, about 200 yards above the mud lick. **1849** *Ib.*, To a white Oak and poplar near a mud lick. — **(7) 1850** GARRARD *Wah-To-Yah* xv. 180 In front of many dwellings is a mud oven, in shape like a cupping glass. **1872** POWERS *Afoot & Alone* 165 Here there is a mud-coop, there a mud oven. — **(8) 1860** MORDECAI *Virginia* 302 Some of them [*sc.* roads] soon acquired the name of *mud pikes*, the demand of toll being the only distinction by which to know them from country roads. — **(9) 1870** KEIM *Sheridan's Troopers* 140 He never failed to enjoy . . . lighting an old cob or mud pipe.

(10) 1942 LILLARD *Desert Challenge* 55 Nature . . . covered their bases with salty lakes, and then dried these up into alkali sinks and mud playas. — **(11) 1830** *Cong. Deb.* 30 March 717/2 A mud road can [not] be of any use after it is made. **1887** *Courier-Journal* 2 Feb. 1/1 They will arrive home as soon as the wretched state of the mud roads will permit. — **(12) 1868** in *Kans. Hist. Quart.* XIII. (1944) 201 The principal productions of this place [Kansas] are Negro soldiers and mud shanties. — **(13) 1851** SPRINGER *Forest Life* 61 We clamber, under our heavy burdens, over rocks, . . . and through mud-sloughs. — **(14) 1894** *Harper's Mag.* March 526/2 He had concluded . . . to create a business in a little mud town down the big road.

3. Denoting boats, vehicles, etc., used in muddy situations, or contrivances for dealing with mud, also in transferred senses, as (1) **mud boat,** (2) **cart,** (3) **machine,** (4) **scoop,** (5) **scow, wagon,** see as main entries.

(1) 1905 *Forestry Bureau Bul.* No. 61, 43 *Mudboat*, . . . a low sled with wide runners, used for hauling logs in swamps. — **(2) 1840** *N.Y. Mirror* 25 July 39/2 Nobody thinks nowadays of calling the conductor of a mud-cart on the rail-road, by any less dignified title than *an agent.* **1856** BREWERTON *War in Kans.* 34 It [the stagecoach] was what the Missourians call a 'mud cart'—a cross in fact between a second-hand bakers' wagon—and a hospital ambulance which had seen hard service. — **(3) 1806** *Balance* V. 162/3 The Mayor and Corporation of the city of New York will man their mud-machine. **1827** *Spirit of Seventy-Six* (Frankfort, Ky.) 14 June 3/2 From the extensive circulation of this 'Mud Machine,' and the total disregard to truth, which is observed in its columns, we had apprehended, that it was to have some influence in our Presidential contest. **1868** PAULDING *Book of Vagaries* 152 There was likewise an incorporated company, to build a mud-machine for deepening the river. — **(4) 1877** BARTLETT 411 Mud Scoop. A dredge; a dredging-machine or boat used in taking mud from the bottom of rivers.

4. In miscellaneous combs.: (1) **mud clerk,** see as a main entry; (2) **cracker,** (see quot.); (3) **geyser,** a geyser the waters of which are heavily impregnated with mud or mudlike silt; (4) **head,** (see quot.), *obs.;* (5) ∗**hen,** (see quot. and cf. **1. b.** (6) above), *obs.;* (6) ∗**hook,** a person's foot, *slang;* (7) **horse,** =**mudder;** (8) **Indians,** (see quot.), *obs.;* (9) **lump,** a phenomenon occurring in places where the water is shallow in the lower Mississippi River, caused by silt deposits that bear so heavily on the clays beneath that these flow under the pressure and break through at the surface, cf. **1.** (10) above, and ∗**mud volcano** below; (10) **ore,** (see quot.); (11) **plantain,** a North American plant, *Heteranthus reniformis*, growing in marshes; (12) **pot,** a potlike formation about a mud volcano; (13) **press,** a newspaper that besmirches people's characters by "throwing mud," *obs.;* (14) **River,** =**Big Muddy;** (15) **runner,** =**mudder;** (16) ∗**sill,** see as a main entry; (17) **snoot,** (see quot.), *obs.;* (18) **spring,** ?=**mud geyser;** (19) **stick,** a pole with a forked or widened end used in punting against a muddy bottom; (20) ∗**volcano,** =**mud lump.**

(2) 1877 BARTLETT 410 Mudcracker. A name given by boys to a fire-cracker which explodes with a dull report. — **(3) 1871** CAPT. J. W. BARLOW *Reconn. Yellowstone River* (1872) 15 We camped on the bank of the river, in the immediate vicinity of the mud geysers. — **(4) 1838** HALIBURTON *Clockmaker* 2 Ser. xix. 289 There's the hoosiers of Indiana, . . . the mudheads of Tennessee [etc.].

(5) 1877 BARTLETT 410 Mud-Hen. . . . The euphonious and rather peculiar epithet applied by brokers' clerks to that class of women that engage in the fascinating but uncertain game of stock speculations. The average 'mud-hen' is middle-aged, rather stout in person, as voluble in conversation as a stump-speaker, and possessed of an inordinate desire to become a 'stock-sharp.' — **(6) 1850** GARRARD *Wah-To-Yah* xx. 245 This 'mudhook' . . . hasn't a moccasin on for nuthin'. **1884** *Cent. Mag.* Dec. 283 The [soldier] boys called their feet 'pontons,' 'mud-hooks,' 'soil-excavators,' and other names not quite so polite. — **(7) 1890** *N. & Q.* V. 197 The expression 'mud horse' is often used in a sarcastic way. Thus, turfmen notice that certain steeds only win on a muddy track when the 'right odds'—say forty or fifty to one—can be obtained against them. — **(8) 1819** *W. Recorder* (Chillicothe, O.) 12 March 245/3 The Indians about the Illinois territory call them [the Comanches] the Mud Indians, on account of their coming to the trading posts, down the Missouri, at the season when that river is flooded by reason of there being not sufficient water for the passage of boats in the upper branches from whence they come, at other times. — **(9) 1868** *Putnam's Mag.* May 591/2 Small islands of bluish clay suddenly emerge from the water. . . . These are the famous *mud-lumps* of the Mississippi. **1944** H. T. KANE *Deep Delta Country* 132 The 'mud lumps' of the Mississippi are a phenomenon without counterpart.

(10) 1804 *Mass. H.S. Coll.* IX. 256 There is another kind found in bogs and swamps, which the workmen call swamp or mud ore; it is a ferruginous earth, or glebe, resembling black mould externally destitute of any metallick appearance; but being washed with water, small granulated particles of iron subside to the bottom. — **(11) 1817–8** EATON *Botany* (1822) 304 Mud-plantain . . . [is found] in muddy overflowed places. Very abundant in South Bay, below Hudson City. **1894** COULTER *Bot. W. Texas* III. 441 *Heteranthera* (Mud Plantain.) — **(12) 1897** *Outing* XXX. 164/2 The bank was honeycombed with miniature geysers and mud-pots. **1912** A. HAGUE *Geol. Hist. Yellowstone Park* 21 The number of geysers, hot springs, mud-pots, and paintpots scattered over the park exceeds 3,000. — **(13) 1846** MCKENNEY *Memoirs* I. 197 Jonathan Elliot, . . . had printed a paper in Washington, the quality of which had secured for it the title of 'the mud press.' — **(14) 1881** MARSHALL *Through Amer.* (1882) 105 It is separated from Omaha by the Missouri, or the 'Mud River,' twin sister of the Mississippi.

(15) 1905 *N.Y. Ev. Sun* 17 Aug. (*Cent. Supp.*), All the races . . . were won by the product of stallions that in their day were famous mud runners. — **(17) 1873** BAILEY *Life in Danbury* 34 Ruebens was prompted to call him a mud-snoot, a new name just coming into general use. — **(18) 1871** J. H. BARLOW *Reconn. Yellowstone River* (1872) 21 Across the plain to the west were found several mud-springs in a ravine near a small pond. — **(19) 1874** LONG *Wild-Fowl* 142 Now, you see, this mud-stick or setting-pole as we call it which I have exchanged the oar for, comes into use.

(20) 1902 *Smithsonian Rep. 1901* 71 Within the region [lower Colo. Valley] lie a number of 'mud volcanoes,' apparently analogous to the 'mud lumps' of the Lower Mississippi.

b. In phrases: (1) *mud-and-stick*, designating walls or chimneys made by plastering a frame of laths or sticks with mud; (2) *to pull mud*, to travel, *slang;* (3) *to sell for the mud*, to sell as worthless; (4) *his name is mud*, and variants, said of one who is extremely unfortunate or out of favor.

(1) 1817 S. BROWN *Western Gaz.* 65 Some [houses] have . . . a frame skeleton filled up with mud and stick walls. **1869** *Overland Mo.* III. 286 They build mud-and-stick chimneys. **1912** C. DAWSON *Pioneer Tales* 94 The chimney was a mud-and-stick construction. — **(2) 1884** *Cent. Mag.* 284 We took up our line of march, or, as Wad Rider expressed it, 'began to pull mud.' — **(3) 1906** M. TWAIN *Autobiog.* (1924) I. 276 (R.), His holding was sold for the 'mud'—so that he came out without anything. — **(4) 1902** *Out West* March 291 If there ever a man lived whose name ought to be Mud, 'twas Falk. **1948** *Chi. Tribune* 2 May (Comics) 7 Those early rising gossiping neighbors have seen me—whew—my name is Mud, now. **1948** *Time* 6 Dec. 27/1 His name is mud in all classes—they feel toward him as Americans felt toward Herbert Hoover in 1933.

As the last term in **blue, marsh, muscle, prairie, shad, stick-in-the-mud.**

*** **mud,** *v. tr.* To put clay or mud into (the chinks of a log building); to chink (a log house or cabin) with mud.

1818 BIRKBECK *Lett. from Illinois* 30 This cabin is built of round straight logs, . . . the intervals between the logs 'chunked,' . . . and 'mudded,' that is, daubed with a plaister of mud. **1842** KIRKLAND *Forest Life* II. 86 Even the house whose neat rustic appearance so charms her, has to be 'chunked and mudded.' **1905** *Forestry Bureau Bul.* No. 61, 42 *Mud*, to fill with soft clay the crevices between the logs in a logging camp. (N[orthern] F[orest].)

mud cat.

1. Either of two edible catfishes of the Mississippi Valley and the South, *Opladelus olivaris* and *Ameiurus platycephalus*.

1816 D. THOMAS *Travels Western Country* (1819) 211 The mud cat is covered with clouded spots, and is a very homely fish. **1897** *Outing* XXX. 439/1 The small 'mudcat,' or bull-head, also had these weapons [i.e., spikes in the fins] with a complete knowledge of their use. **1945** BOTKIN *My Burden* 27 The next is a mudcat; this kind of a fish likes dark trashy places.

b. (*cap.*) A native of Mississippi.

1871 [see **Mudcat State**]. **1945** *Chi. D. News* 16 Aug 10/7 While we are laying down surrender terms for the Japanese, how about a Declaration on Senator 'Dear Dago' Bilbo, the Mississippi mudcat?

c. Mudcat State, (see quot. 1871).

1871 DE VERE 660 Mississippi is occasionally spoken of humorously as the *Mudcat State*, the inhabitants being quite generally known as Mud-cats, a name given to the large catfish abounding in the swamps and the mud of the rivers. **1948** MENCKEN *Supp.* II. 630 *Mudcat State* . . . seems to be obsolescent.

2. mud catfish, the bullhead, *Ameiurus nebulosus*.

1842 *Nat. Hist. N.Y., Zoology* IV. 187 The Mud Catfish, *Pimelodus nebulosus*, . . . [is] recognized by the scarified and clouded appearance of its skin. **1870** *Amer. Naturalist* IV. 386 [The] Mud Cat-fish (*Amiurus DeKayi*) [is found in the Delaware near Trenton, N.J.].

mud clerk. (See quot. 1903.)

1872 EGGLESTON *End of World* 171 It was natural enough that the 'mud-clark' on the old steamboat Iatan should have taken a fancy to the 'striker.' **1903** *D.N.* II. 321 *Mud-clerk*, the second clerk of a river steamer. So called because it is his duty to go on shore (often at a mere mud bank,) to receive or check off freight. (Not facetious.) **1912** COBB *Back Home* 103 Even her two mud clerks, let alone her captain and her pilots, wore uniforms.

mud dauber.

1. Any one of various wasps of the genus *Sceliphron*, or related genera, which construct their cells of mud. Also transf.

1856 *Zoologists* XIV. 5030 The species of the genus *Pelopoeus* are popularly known as mud-daubers in America. **1866** M. TWAIN *Sk. New & Old* (1875) 297 (R.), The old mud-dobber tackled the piano, and ran his fingers up and down once or twice **1936** KROLL *Sharecropper* 90 Generations of mud-daubers had made the ceiling an unclean dingy gray.

b. In full **mud-dauber wasp.**

1949 *Time* 2 May 73/2 There he began to watch the mud-dauber wasp as she buzzed purposefully to the window sill, stretched her forefeet out like a kitten, and took a sun bath.

2. =**mud swallow.**

1899 *Animal & Plant Lore* 34 The building of the mud-daubers, or swallows, on the barn or house is a sign of prosperity to the occupants . . . Kansas. **1945** PEARSON *Country Flavor* 49 There was often a phoebe's home to explore and dozens of mud daubers' nests.

mudder ˈmʌdɚ, *n.* A horse that runs well on a muddy track. Also transf. *Slang.* Cf. **mud horse, mud runner.**

1905 *N.Y. Ev. Sun* 17 Aug. (*Cent. Supp.*), The third horse, Atholone, is by Handsel, a mudder himself and a son of a mudder. **1948** *Time* 1 Nov. 44/3 Halfback Jack Swaner, a superior mudder, had a big day, scoring all three touchdowns. **1949** *Ib.* 2 May 47/1 Capot, the second choice . . . and apparently no mudder, was six lengths back in third place.

*** **muddle,** *n.* A dish prepared variously but consisting chiefly of fresh fish; an occasion when friends gather and partake of this. Cf. **fish muddle.** *Colloq.* — **1833** *Amer. Turf. Reg.* April 403 Some years since, on my way to the post office at Weldon, I was overtaken by seven gentlemen, who insisted I should join them in a muddle, on the beach. **1890** *Cent.* 4654/3 *pottle*. . . . A dish made by Connecticut fishermen by frying pork in the bottom of a kettle, then adding water, and stewing in the water pieces of fresh fish. *Muddle*, made by Cape Ann fishermen, is the same dish with the addition of crackers.

*** **muddler,** *n.* (See quot. 1883.) *Colloq.* — **1855** *Chi. Times* 16 Jan. 4/1 Butter moulds and stamps, ladles, rolling pins, potato mashers, muddlers . . . wholesale and retail at Hollister's Bazaar. **1883** KNIGHT *Supp.* 621/2 *Muddler*, a churning stick for chocolate. A smaller one for mixing toddies.

muddling stick, *n.* =prec. *Obs.* — **1839** BRIGGS *H. Franco* I. 65 After a great display of nutmeg graters and muddling sticks, and of sousing and flourishing of tumblers. . . . the juleps were mixed.

*** **muddy,** *a.* **1. muddy breast,** *local,* =**golden plover. 2. Muddy (River),** the Missouri River. Cf. **Big Muddy.**

(1) 1888 G. TRUMBULL *Names of Birds* 196 At Newport, R.I., [the golden plover is called] Muddy-breast. — **(2) 1765** R. ROGERS *N. Amer.* 190 The Muddy River rises from the south of the central mountains . . . and runs south . . . till it meets the Mississippi. **1884** MARK TWAIN *H. Finn* 130 When it was daylight, here was the clear Ohio water inshore, sure enough, and outside was the old regular Muddy!

*** **muddying,** *n. S.* "A mode of fishing in which attendants stir up the muddy bottom of a lake or stream" (*Cent.*). — **1877** HALLOCK *Sportsman's Gaz.* 371 The season for muddying begins.

mud fence. A fence made of earth. Used chiefly in fig. expressions as a symbol of utter ugliness. *Colloq.*

1839 *Columbian Reg.* (New Haven, Conn.) 19 Feb. 4/3 There is a man down the street as ugly as a mud fence in a thunder storm. **1844** GREGG *Commerce of Prairies* I. 150 Mud fences, or walls of very large *adobes*, are also occasionally to be met with. **1941** M. L. SMITH *God's Country* 118 She was red headed as a wood pecker and was as ugly as a mud fence. **1948** *Chi. Tribune* 29 May 14/5 He didn't care whether she was as beautiful as Lana Turner or as homely as a mud fence.

* **mudfish,** *n.*

1. = **bowfin.**

1842 *Nat. Hist. N.Y., Zoology* IV. 269 The Western Mud-fish, *Amia occidentalis*, . . . is found in Lake Erie and Ontario. **1886** *Nat. Museum Proc.* VIII. 204 *Cobitis heteroclitus*. . . . The editor . . . has evidently been misled by the common name 'mud-fish' in referring number eleven to *Amia calva*.

2. (See quot. 1855.)

1855 BAIRD in *Smithsonian Rep.* 342, The Mud-Fish. *Melanura pygmæa*. . . . I have caught the Mud Fish . . . on the American shores of all the great lakes except Lake Superior. **1870** *Amer. Naturalist* IV. 99 Other streams, sluggish and thick, . . . are paradisiacal to the mud fish (*Melanura*).

3. = **mud minnow.**

1880 GÜNTHER *Fishes* 619 *Umbra limi*, locally distributed in the United States; called . . . 'Dog fish,' or 'Mud-fish' in America.

mudhole ˈmʌdˌhol, *n.*

1. A soft, muddy place in a road or street; a hole or depression filled with mud.

[**1753** *Moravian Diary* in MERENESS *Travels Amer. Col.* (1916) 346 Our wagon stuck fast in a mud-hole, and it took two hours to get it out. The tackle did us good service.] **1760** in COMMONS *Doc. Hist.* I. 310 As Soon as one Gets out It Rains on him or he Is In a large due or in a mud hole. **1838** H. MARTINEAU *Retrospect* II. 64 They told me, as an *on dit*, that a horse was drowned, last winter, in a mud-hole, in a principal street [of Charleston, S.C.]. **1870** MACRAE *Americans* II. 172 In Chicago . . . at the west end of Lake Street . . . a barrel floated over a mud-hole, with the warning intimation upon it No Bottom. **1948** *Capital-Democrat* (Tishomingo, Okla.) 24 June 7/4 He started to get in the wagon till they were past the mud-hole.

transf. **1949** *Time* 12 Sep. 24/1 [It] might help pull Britain out of the immediate financial mudhole in which she was floundering.

2. A small, insignificant town. Also as a proper name.

1784 in *Pa. Mag. Hist.* I. (1877) 51 The general curse of the country, disunion, rages in this little mud-hole [Uniontown, Pa.]. **1819** HULME *Journal* 62 In the evening, reach a place [in the Illinois country] very appropriately called Mud-holes. **1949** *Chi. D. News* 14 Feb. 10/3 He drags them out of their mudholes and into One World ideology.

b. mudhole in the prairie, a nickname for Chicago, Illinois. Now *hist.*

1938 ASBURY *Sucker's Prog.* 285 The population of Chicago was less than six hundred when 'the mud-hole in the prairie,' as envious St. Louisians called the new settlement, was incorporated as a town in 1833.

c. Great American Mudhole, see ***great 7.** (1).

3. "A soft spot in granite due to decomposition. Quarrymen's slang" (*Cent. Supp.*).

1898 *10th Rep. Geol. Survey* VI. (II). 230 Knots, streaks, and 'mudholes' must be carefully avoided in a conscientious selection of stock for monumental work.

mud scow. A barge or flatboat used in dredging.

1766 *Mass. Gazette* 20 Oct. 1/3 To Be Sold, a new Mud-Scow, 24 Foot long, and can carry 12 or 14 Tons Weight. **1836** THORPE *Life on Lakes* II. 239 Forward she looked exactly like a mud-scow; scarcely any deck, and an open hold exposed to the weather. **1945** *This Week Mag.* 10 March 18/2 He kept lookin' at this old hooker as if she was a mud scow.

b. (See quot.) *Humorous.*

1863 *U.S. Army & Navy Jrnl.* I. 180/2 Expensive shoes . . . are often thrown away unused, for the despised Government 'mudscows.' These 'mudscows' or 'gunboats' . . . are low-cut, stitched, very light, and very cheap. . . . The sole is very broad, and the heels broad and low.

* **mudsill,** *n.*

1. A member of the laboring classes, a term first applied in 1858 by Senator J. H. Hammond of South Carolina. Also attrib.

1858 HAMMOND in *N.Y. Tribune* 11 March 6/3 In all social systems there must be a class to perform the drudgery of life. . . . It constitutes the mud-sills of society. **1878** *N. Amer. Rev.* May 500 In Southern political articles of faith it was declared that the black laborer was a 'chattel,' and the white laborer a 'mudsill.' **1949** *Social Studies* May 215/1 An unpolished bucolic character named Lincoln, came into office, supported by what they called the greasy mechanics of the East and the mudsill farmers of the West.

b. Formerly often applied opprobriously by Southerners to Northerners. Also **northern mudsill.**

1860 STODDARD in *Vanity Fair* III. 269/1 White niggers, mudsills, Northern scum, Base hirelings, hear me, and be dumb. **1862** *Harper's Mag.* Nov. 856/2 In those days the penniless cadets of the Southern F.F.'s did sometimes condescend to marry the daughters of wealthy Northern 'mud-sills.' **1910** J. HART *Vigilante Girl* 125 They affect to look down on us of the North, and call us 'Yankees' and 'mudsills.'

2. (See quots.) Also attrib. *Obs.*

1858 *Marysville* (Calif.) *News* 8 July 2/2 The Mudsills are those Democrats who strike for the popular sovereignty doctrine of Senator Douglas, and who profess no faith in the President's Kansas policy. **1858** *S.F. Times* 16 Sep., David Jolson, late 'Mudsill' candidate for the Legislature, and badly beaten at that, values his reputation at five thousand dollars. **1885** *Mag. Amer. Hist.* March 296/1 *Mudsill*. . . . Assumed by certain political associations in California in 1858.

b. Mudsill Club, (see quot.). *Obs.*

1859 BARTLETT 284 *Mud-Sill Clubs*, The miners and working-men of California who support Broderick in his opposition to the Administration, are preparing for a vigorous campaign, and are already organizing themselves into associations which they style '*Mud-sill Clubs*.'—*New York Evening Post*, 1858.

mud turtle.

1. Any one of various fresh-water turtles, esp. one of the genus *Kinosternon*, or the snapping turtle, *Chelydra serpentina*. Cf. **hinge mud turtle.**

1785 T. B. HAZARD *Nailer Tom's Diary* (1930) 87/2 George found mudd tourtle. & I gave him ashilling for it. **1848** BURTON *Waggeries* 10 While the darkey was . . . snorin' himself sober, a mud tortle, about the size of our capting's epillitts, crawls right slick into his open mouth. **1945** BOTKIN *My Burden* 29 Another think he always have in the pocket was a little old dry-up turtle, just a mud turtle.

2. Used in comparisons and figurative contexts.

1857 STROTHER *Virginia* 32 'Looks more like he was embalmed,' cried another. 'A mummy! or a mud-turtle lying on his back! **1866** C. H. SMITH *Bill Arp* 129, I run like a mud turkel, lookin ahead of me at every step. **1896** MARK TWAIN *Tom Sawyer, Detective* xi. 527 (R.), A mud-turtle of a back-settlement lawyer.

b. App. some kind of dredging craft. *Obs.*

1818 in *Amer. Sp.* XXI. (1946) 237/1 A passage to the docks of Albany would be kept open across the river by mud-turtles. [**1871** MARK TWAIN *Screamers* 132 (R.), A pickaninny, mud-turtle-shaped craft of a schooner.]

c. = * **turtle,** *n.*[2] **1.** *Obs.*

1845 *Quincy* (Ill.) *Whig* 20 Dec. 1/4 The machine was towed into the stream, cast off, and 'Bije and his 'etarnal mud turtle' disappeared under water.

mud wagon. (See quot. 1948.)

1835 LATROBE *Rambler in N. Amer.* 259 We had to put up with an open 'mud-waggon,' with spring seats. **1896** SHINN *Story of Mine* 117

One type of mud wagon

[Stage drivers of the Nevada-California lines] drive 'mud-wagons' for the most part, that two or four horses can manage. **1948** RITTENHOUSE *Vehicles* 48 The 'mud wagon' was a type of stage-coach which might be called 'the poor man's Concord.' While it used thorough-braces, their method of attachment was simpler. One difference was in the body, with its flat sides and simpler joinery.

* **muff,** *n.*[1] As the last term in **ear, foot muff.**

* **muff,** *n.*[2] *Baseball.* A poor player, one who makes errors. Also **muffer.** *Obs.*

1867 *Ball Players' Chron.* 6 June 3/4 Of course, every player who makes a miss is regarded as a muff, and every decision that affects the side they bet on a rough one. *Ib.* 8 Aug. 2/3 The Times contented itself with claiming the defeat as a victory for Chicago, in proving themselves to be the greatest muffs in the country. **1867** *Harper's Wkly.* 14 Sep. 591/2 The President said he was not much on the catch; they would probably term him a 'muffer.' **1867** *Ball Players' Chron.* 24 Oct. 7/1 The 'muffers' are probably a much-abused class. The 'champion' muffer's experience is varied—always the last to be chosen on a side.

b. Hence **muffy,** *a.*, poor, awkward, inefficient. *Obs.*

1867 *Ball Players' Chron.* 15 Aug. 3/4 Three runs [were] . . . scored on muffy fielding, wild throws and passed balls, when good fielding would have led to a blank score.

* **muffin,** *n. Baseball.* (See quots.) *Obs.*

1867 *Ball Players' Chron.* 11 July 6/3 The muffins (poorest players) of the Trimountain Club played a match game of base ball on Friday afternoon on the South Boston common. **1868** CHADWICK *Base Ball* 42 Muffins.—This is the title of a class of ball players who are both practically and theoretically unacquainted with the game. . . . 'Muffins' rank the lowest in the grade of the nines of a club. **1871** BAGG *At Yale* 317 'Muffins,' or clubs which make no pretence to good playing, [use the practice ground].

attrib. **1867** *Ball Players' Chron.* 11 July 6/3 We noticed but one ball that was stopped, and that was by the fielder prostrating himself upon the approaching ball in genuine muffin style. **1867** *Norwich* (Conn.) *Bul.* 24 July, Even the old stand-bys catch the disease, and nothing but a muffin match will cure them. **1867** *Ball Players' Chron.* 7 Nov. 6/2 The Atlantics presented a 'muffin nine' to play the Athletics.

b. Hence **muffinism,** poor playing at baseball. *Obs.*

1865 *Sun. Mercury* (Phila.) 3 Sep. 4/2 Muffinism on their nine receives summary punishment. **1868** CHADWICK *Base Ball* 97 The alleged muffinism of the Excelsiors . . . did not benefit their opponents much.

mufflejaw ˈmʌflˌdʒɔ, *n.* Any of various American fresh-water fishes of the genus *Cottus*, as *C. ictalops* of the East, or *C. semiscaber* of the Rocky Mountains.

1882 *Nat. Mus. Bul.* No. 16,696 *U[ranidea] richardsoni*. . . . Miller's Thumb; . . . Muffle-jaw. . . . Middle and Northern States. **1884** GOODE *Fisheries* I. 259 In the lakes and streams of the Northern States are numerous species of *Uranidea* and allied genera, known in some localities . . . [as] 'Bull-heads,' 'Goblins,' 'Blobs,' and 'Muffle-jaws.' **1911** *Rep. Fisheries 1908* 315 Sculpin . . . in the lakes and streams of the Northern states [are called] . . . 'goblins,' 'blobs,' 'muffle-jaws,' etc.

* **muffler,** *n.* The mechanism that deadens or muffles the sound of the exhaust of a gasoline motor. Also fig.

1896 *Cosmopolitan* XX. 420 The noise of the exhaust is stifled in a muffler. **1916** BOWER *Phantom Herd* 310 Luck's heart began to pound so that he half expected his neighbors to tell him to close his muffler. **1931** *K. C. Star* 24 Oct., An Iola youth took the muffler off his motor car and put on a straight exhaust pipe instead.

* **mug,** *n.* A loving cup put up as a prize. Also comb. *Jocular.* See also **motto mug.** — **1883** *Harper's Mag.* Aug. 443/2 To the extreme mug-hunters [at yacht races] it [speed] meant [everything]. **1890** *Ib.* Sep. 593/1 The cruise is done and the mugs have escaped them. *Ib.*, He may be bitten by the tarantula of matches, be possessed of the fury of mug-hunting.

mug mʌg, *v.* [Origin unknown.] *To mug up,* to eat heartily. *Slang.* — **1897** KIPLING *Captains Courageous* v. 123 No reg'lar meals fer no one then. 'Mug-up when ye're hungry, an' sleep when ye can't keep awake.' **1901** *Scribner's Mag.* XXIX. 498/2 Let Martin and me mug up and get over near the fire to dry out.

mugger ˈmʌgɚ, *n.* [App. f. **mug*, hit, punch in the face.] A thief who leaves his victim helpless, as by taking his clothes away. Hence **mugging.** *Slang.*

1863 BROWNE *Four Years in Secessia* (1865) 340 The Muggers, like most bullies and ruffians, manifested a fine discrimination respecting the party they attacked, selecting those they thought they could rob with little resistance and entire impunity. **1946** *Life* 30 Dec., By day grimy youngsters play stickball in tenement-lined streets that at night are prowled by muggers, sluggers and white-slavers. **1949** *Sat. Ev. Post* 8 Oct. 171/2 The only things she reads in our newspapers are the murders and the muggings and the obituaries.

muggin ˈmʌgɪn, *n.* A mug. *Rare.* — **1872** *Cong. Globe* 20 March 1824/2, I, if I knew how to manufacture my little muggin of rum on Lake Michigan, had my drawback equally with the Yankees in New England.

muggs mʌgz, *n. Conn.* [Origin unknown.] (See quots.) — **1923** B. C. TROWBRIDGE *Old Houses of Conn.* 281 Built into a bank in the rear is a root-cellar called the 'muggs,' used for the preservation of roots and vegetables. **1947** *Amer. Sp.* April 155/1 The word is *muggs*, a singular noun. A muggs, in the old days (they still exist, but I doubt that one has been built in many a year) was a sort of outside root-cellar, an igloo-like structure. . . . In it were stored turnips and such, but especially potatoes, which the country people used for food during the long winters.

mugwump ˈmʌgwʌmp, *n.* [Algonquian *mugquomp*, a chief.]

John Eliot used the word in his Indian Bible (1663), e.g., in Genesis 36:15.

1. An important person; the high-muck-a-muck. Also transf. Used ironically.

1832 in *Nation* LII. 414/3 The secret bulletin . . . has extensively circulated among the Knights of Kadosh and the Most Worshipful Mug-Wumps of the Cabletow. **1835** D. P. THOMPSON *Adv. T. Peacock* 6 This village, I beg leave to introduce to the reader, under the significant appellation of *Mugwump*, . . . used at the present day vulgarly and masonically, as synonymous with greatness and strength. **1925** *N.Y. Times* 10 May, The royal red Indian mug-wump, the chief, was copiously red-blooded.

2. *Polit.* A member of the Republican party who bolted the party's presidential nominee, James G. Blaine, in 1884; more generally, any independent Republican.

1884 *N.Y. Ev. Post* 20 June (*Cent.*), We have yet to see a Blaine organ which speaks of the Independent Republicans otherwise than as Pharisees, hypocrites, dudes, mugwumps, transcendentalists, or something of that sort. **1948** *Time* 12 Jan. 13/1 The Mugwumps of 1884, for much the same reason deserted James G. Blaine and helped elect Democrat Grover Cleveland.

attrib. **1887** *Courier-Journal* 8 Jan. 4/5 The Mugwump War Department is a horse-power to the Republican machine. **1888** S. HALE *Letters* 202 If the Reps. win, . . . 't will be terrible facing the mugwump Churches and Democrat Osborns. **1904** *Grand Rapids Ev. Press* 7 June 4 The Democratic and mugwump press is making the most of it. **1944** *Harper's Mag.* June 44/2 Concern about the Mugwump vote speedily began to dampen the Republican rejoicing that followed Wisconsin primary.

b. A person who withdraws his support from any group or organization; an independent; a chronic complainer who doesn't take sides. Also transf.

1884 *Sat. Review* 22 Nov. 659/1 It maybe that in a few years . . . a little group of British Mugwumps . . . will arise in their might [etc.]. **1888** BILLINGS *Hardtack* 286 [The mule's] reputation as a kicker is world-wide. He was the Mugwump of the service. **1894** FORD *P. Stirling* 302, I'd have believed anything but that you [a Democrat] would be a dashed Mugwump! **1946** *Tuscaloosa* (Ala.) *News* 31 March 4/7 A few moments after Secretary Wallace made his pun, he hastened to add that he himself had been a mugwump.

mugwump ˈmʌgwʌmp, *v. intr.* To bolt a party or candidate. — **1889** *N.Y. Tribune* 10 March 1/6 E. D. Graves . . . 'Mugwumped to Cleveland,' in 1884 because he 'could not conscientiously support James G. Blaine.' **1911** *Springfield W. Republican* 2 Nov. 3 The Bay State voters do not mugwump very deep.

mugwumpcy ˈmʌgˌwʌmpsɪ, *n.* =next. *Rare.* — **1887** *Ohio State Jrnl.* 17 Aug, The people have resolved that Democracy and mugwumpcy must go!

mugwumpery ˈmʌgˌwʌmpərɪ, *n.* The views and practices of the mugwumps. *Colloq.*

1885 *Boston Jrnl.* 25 April 2/2 Has he [Cleveland] thrown this bombshell into the very citadel of Mugwumpery? **1906** *Nation* 16 Aug. 134/1 It is a revival or expansion of pure Mugwumpery that we are witnessing. **1948** *Dly. Ardmoreite* (Ardmore, Okla.) 29 April 1/1 They think this year will see a widespread exercise of the privilege of mugwumpery.

mugwumpian ˈmʌgˌwʌmpɪən, *a.* Of or pertaining to the mugwumps.

1885 *Boston Jrnl.* 21 Jan. 4/1 The college . . . must speak manly English and must not be too mugwumpian in its proclamation of free trade. **1887** *Voice* 1 Sep., Our esteemed Mugwumpian contemporary, the New York Times, is very solicitous for the Republicans to make concessions to the Prohibitionists. **1928** *Sat. Ev. Post* 4 Feb. 10/1 'There is no such thing as race,' says the first mugwumpian doctrine.

b. mugwumpian Democrat, a Republican who supported Grover Cleveland for President in 1884. *Obs.*

1885 *Boston Jrnl.* 21 Jan. 2/4 There is a row . . . between a Democrat and a mugwumpian Democrat.

mugwumpism ˈmʌgˌwʌmpɪzəm, *n.* Independent action in politics; mugwumpery. *Obs.* — **1886** *Cong. Rec.* 31 March 2968/1 That maudlin political sentiment which we recognize, for want of a better, under the name of 'Mugwumpism.' **1887** *Nation* 14 April 305/3 The municipal election in Jacksonville, Fla., last week was another victory for nonpartisanship, and showed that Mugwumpism is growing in the South as well as in the West.

mukluk ˈmʌklʌk, *n.* [f. Eskimo word for a large seal.] A sealskin. Also, more often, a sealskin boot. In full **mukluk boot.**

1868 WHYMPER *Alaska* 136 Their boots vary in length, and in the material used for the sides, but all have soles of 'maclock,' or sealskin, with the hair removed. **1902** MCKEE *Land of Nome* 159 One of the characters then at Nome, known and unmistakable from the Klondike down, was 'Mother' Woods, in her sunbonnet, abbreviated skirts, and 'mukluks' or native sealskin boots. **1947** *Chi. Tribune* 11 Dec. 20/3 He was presented with . . . a pair of mukluk boots made to order for Paul Bunyan. **1949** *Sat. Ev. Post* 4 June 142/2 The reindeer moss . . . was soft and springy beneath Brent's mukluks.

mulada mu'ladə, *n. S.W.* [Sp. in same sense.] A drove of mules.

1846 ABERT *Exam. N. Mex.* 22 Flocks of golden-headed troopials . . . mingled most socially with the common cow bird, and all in great glee were catching grass-hoppers in the vicinity of our 'mulada.' **1858** *Texas Almanac 1859* 143 We keep a mulada at Fort Yuma for our changes. **1944** ADAMS *W. Words* 102 Mulada. . . . A drove or herd of mules. Occasionally used by Americans as a convenience, since it is shorter than *mule herd*, or *herd of mules*.

* **mulatto,** *a.* Designating land or soil of a brownish color.

1741 in *Amer. Sp.* XV. 287/2 A Tract of rich Mulattoe Land, lying in that County. **1788** JEFFERSON *Writings* XVII. 260 The soil [is] a barren mulatto clay, mixed with a good deal of stone, and some slate. **1789** MORSE *Amer. Geog.* 447 It changes into what is called the mulatto soil, consisting of a black mould and red earth. **1883** SMITH *Geol. Survey Ala.* 435 The red or mulatto lands are much the best for cotton.

mulattress mə'lætrɪs, *n.* [fem. of **mulatto*.] A woman of mixed Negro and white blood. — **1805** *Amer. Pioneer* II. 234 The chief of the audience is formed of mulattresses and negresses. **1932** *DAB* VIII. 485 He lived openly with a mulatress and was only prevented from marrying her by the law against miscegenation.

* **mulberry,** *n.*

1. mulberry mania, the craze during the 1830's for planting mulberry trees in expectation of making profits in the silk industry. *Obs.*

1839 *S. Lit. Messenger* V. 115/2 If the mulberry mania should continue, we may have silk-worms fed on that . . . land. **1885** [see **multicaulis**].

2. Used in the names of insects, as **mulberry beetle, borer, wing.**

1854 EMMONS *Agric. N.Y.* V. 262 Index, Mulberry beetles, 93. [93. In Italy, the branches of the *Morus multicaulis* are perforated by the *Apate sexdentata*.] **1862** *Rep. Comm. Patents 1861: Agric.* 614 The mulberry tree in Pennsylvania has an enemy in . . . *Dorcaschema wildii*, (Uhler,) or 'mulberry borer.' **1909** *Cent. Supp.* 836/3 *Mulberry-wing*, an American hesperiid butterfly, *Poanes massasoit*, occurring in the eastern and middle United States, Texas, Nebraska, and Colorado.

As the last term in **English, Italian, Mexican, red, Virginia, Virginian mulberry.**

***mule,** *n.*

1. (See quot.) *Slang. Obs.*

1842 BUCKINGHAM *Slave States* I. 240 The first offspring of this young mother, produced after seven months' gestation, was 'a mule!' . . . This was a cant phrase [in Ga.] to denote a 'coloured child.'

2. = **mule meat.** *Rare.*

1843 in *Utah Hist. Quart.* II. (1929) 113 Camped at a small river. Grass so, so. Indians eating mule.

3. A tractor or locomotive for towing canal boats.

1903 *Elect. World & Engineer* 14 Nov. 795/2 The 'electric mule' . . . is a vehicle closely resembling a 'hog-back' mine locomotive.

4. In combs.: (1) **mule bear,** the grizzly bear, so called in the mistaken belief that he feasted on mules, *obs.;* (2) * **bird,** ? = **cow bird,** *obs.;* (3) **cavalry,** during the Civil War, a jocular name for the mounted infantry *q.v.;* (4) **deer,** a long-eared deer of the West, *Odocoileus hemionus*, cf. **black-tailed deer, desert mule deer;** (5) **driver,** a teamster who drives a mule team, or one in charge of a mulada; (6) **ear(ed) rabbit,** = **jackass rabbit;** (7) **killer,** see as a main entry; (8) **puncher,** = **mule driver;** (9) **rabbit,** = **jackass rabbit;** (10) **rush,** = **mule race,** *jocular;* (11) **skinner,** see as a main entry; (12) **skinning,** driving mules; (13) **train,** a train of wagons drawn by mules or a train of pack mules; (14) **whacker,** one who drives a team of mules.

(1) 1824 DODDRIDGE *Notes* 21 Being in the woods, he saw an old mule bear winding along after him. — **(2) 1867** J. MELINE *Santa Fé & Back* 8 The road is alive with the mule-bird, whip-poor-will, doves, plover, and meadow lark. — **(3) 1862** MOORE *Rebellion Rec.* V. II. 599 The mounted infantry, or 'mule cavalry,' proved an entire success. . . . They move with the celerity of cavalry, yet fight as infantry. — **(4) 1805** LEWIS in *L. & Clark Exped.* II. (1904) 21 With the mule deer the horns consist of two beams. **1893** ROOSEVELT *Wilderness Hunter* 16 The common blacktail or mule deer, which has likewise been sadly thinned in numbers, . . . extends from the great plains to the Pacific. **1945** *Mass. Audubon Soc.* Jan. 281, I was quite disappointed not to see a mule deer.

(5) 1850 P. ST. G. COOKE *Scenes & Adventures* (1857) 90 Sometimes a hundred or two [buffaloes] . . . would threaten a charge, which at best would have proved disastrous to the mule-drivers and their charge. **1882** *Wheelman* I. 176 The caution . . . administered to me . . . by a mule-driver, whose aspect was as uncouth and forbidding as that of the ideal tramp. **1909** O. HENRY *Roads of Destiny* 192 He had been mule-driver, cowboy, ranger, soldier, sheriff, prospector, and cattleman. — **(6) 1885** SIRINGO *Texas Cow Boy* 142, I had just eaten a mule-eared rabbit. **1889** H. H. MCCONNELL *Five Years* 56 The English hare . . . is not nearly so large as our jack or 'mule-ear' rabbit. — **(8) 1870** *Terr. Enterprise* (Virginia, Nev.) 21 April 3/1 Even a boss driver is liable to suffer the indignity of being called a 'mule puncher.' **1901** *Everybody's Mag.* June 582/1 Hickok was the only officer who was able to maintain order among the mule punchers, bull whackers, and tough soldiers at Hays City. — **(9) 1857** *Spirit of Times* 28 Feb. 414/3 Some of our expedition formed themselves into a 'Nimrod' party, and went farther out, for the purpose of fetching in some of the deer, bar, and mule rabbits aforesaid. **1877** COZZENS *Crossing Quicksands* 80 More commonly known as the 'mule' rabbit, so called on account of its enormous ears.

(10) 1883 M. TWAIN *Life on Miss.* xlv. 464 (R.), The most enjoyable of all races is a steamboat race; but next to that, I prefer the gay and joyous mule-rush. — **(12) 1880** NYE *B. Nye & Boomerang* 34 The closing ten years of the regular course might be profitably used in learning a practical knowledge of mule skinning, vocal music, horsemanship. **1945** MACDONALD *Egg & I* 50 If only I had studied carpentry or mule skinning instead of ballet. — **(13) 1849** in *Wagons West* (*c*1930) 116 The Indians . . . will not trouble us, so much as they will the mule trains—They will steal every mule . . . horse & oxen they can. **1866** *Rep. Indian Affairs* 125 The goods for the coming year [forwarded] by early mule trains . . . reached this point early in September. **1926** SHIPMAN *Taming Big Bend* 22 Mule trains could move much more quickly than ox-drawn trains. — **(14) 1873** BEADLE *Undevel. West* 88 The streets were thronged with motley crowds of railroad men . . . and mulewhackers. **1889** O'REILLY *50 Years on Trail* 357 The town was full of cow-punchers, mule-whackers [etc.].

b. In other combs. in which the meaning is obvious or sufficiently explained by the quots., as (1) **mule car,** (2) **cart,** (3) * **foot,** (4) **-footed,** (5) **guard,** (6) **herder,** (7) **litter,** (8) **load,** (9) **meat,** (10) **pack,** (11) **packer,** (12) **path,** (13) **picket,** (14) **race,** (15) **raising,** (16) **road,** (17) **route,** (18) **stage,** (19) **trail,** (20) **wagon,** (21) **way.**

(1) 1900 STOCKTON *Afield & Afloat* 53 Slowly the mule-car trundled along the shaded avenue. — **(2) 1847** PARKMAN in *Knickerb.* XXX. 228 Our little mule-cart was but ill-fitted for the passage of so swift a stream. — **(3) 1918** E. B. BABCOCK *Genetics* 527 We refer particularly to such characters as the polled condition in cattle, hornlessness in sheep, mule-foot in hogs. — **(4) 1913** O. A. ROTHERT *Hist. Muhlenberg Co.* (Ky.) 393 They are now not as well remembered on account of their connection with the mine as they are because they introduced into the neighborhood a breed of hogs known as 'mule-footed hogs.' **1918** E. B. BABCOCK *Genetics* 585 Our knowledge of factors is only extensive enough to apply this method of breeding to relatively simple problems, such as that of producing . . . mule-footed breeds of hogs.

(5) 1846 in *So. Hist. Ser.* VII. (1938) 158, I have . . . a mule guard of nine sentinels. — **(6) 1846** in *So. Hist. Ser.* VII. (1938) 158, I have directed (one of the New Mexicans) . . . to be employed . . . as a mule-herder. — **(7) 1888** BILLINGS *Hardtack* 315 Another invention for the transportation of the wounded from the field was the *Cacolet* or *Mule Litter*. — **(8) 1808** PIKE *Sources Miss.* III. App. 4 There are taken, to be coined, 100 mule-loads of bullion in gold and silver monthly. **1880** MARK TWAIN *Tramp Abroad* 491 We had plenty of company, in the way of wagon-loads and mule-loads of tourists—and dust. — **(9) 1846** SAGE *Scenes Rocky Mts.* xxx, We ended our fast of nearly seven days' continuance with a feast of mule meat. **1891** *Cent. Mag.* March 774 We made our Christmas and New Year's dinner on mule meat.

(10) 1911 QUICK *Yellowstone Nights* 309 A puncher . . . scooted through the British aristocracy . . . on the strength of a gold prospect an' the diamond hitch to a mule-pack. — **(11) 1923** J. H. COOK *On Old Frontier* 153 One of these was Arthur Sparhawk, an expert cargador or mule-packer. — **(12) 1834** A. PIKE *Sketches* 25 They would find a mule-path leading from the ford of the Canadian. — **(13) 1848** BRYANT *California* viii. 122 The ground is so hard that it is with difficulty that we can force our mule-pickets into it. — **(14)**

1883 M. TWAIN *Life on Miss.* xlv. 462 (R.), The ladies of New Orleans attend so humble an orgy as a mule-race.

(15)1867 *Rep. Iowa Agric. Soc.* (1868) 133 Robert Grant . . . mentions the names of several persons who give especial attention to mule-raising. — **(16) 1880** MARK TWAIN *Tramp Abroad* 445 We followed the mule-road, a zigzag course, now to the right, now to the left, but always up. — **(17) 1849** LANMAN *Alleghany Mts.* 58 The distance from Hubbard's Cabin . . . in a direct line, is eight miles, but by the ordinary mule-route it is thirteen. — **(18) 1849** *N.Y. Ev. Express* 17 Feb. 1/6 The conveyances used [on the route from Vera Cruz to Calif.] were generally mule stages. — **(19) 1944** JOHNSON *As I Dare* 332 Its citizens went by mule trail from Escalante.

(20) 1846 in *So. Hist. Ser.* VII. (1938) 69 There are three mule wagons to each company, beside six large ox wagons. **1885** CUSTER *Boots & Saddles* 66 It seemed to me preferable to die from accident, surrounded with friends, than to expire alone in the mule-wagon. — **(21) 1850** TYSON *Diary in Calif.* 24 [Down] the only pass . . . was a narrow mule-way.

As the last term in **bell, Brown, cotton, government, kitchen, lead, log, logging, Missouri, narrow gauge, pack, packing, pilot, riding, saddle, six, stage, white mule.**

mule killer. 1. (See quots.) **2.** (See quots.)

(1) 1847 PARKMAN in *Knickerb.* XXIX. 161 Almost hidden in this medley, one might have seen a small French cart, of the sort very appropriately called a 'mule-killer.' **1852** *Fla. Plantation Rec.* 67, I would call the New Waggon a nother Mule killer. — **(2) 1890** *Cent.* 3890/3 *Mule-killer*, . . . the whip-tailed scorpion, *Thelyphonus giganteus*. Also called *nigger-killer* and *grampus*. (Florida.) **1899** *Animal & Plant Lore* 63 Mule-killer, devil's war-horse, praying mantis. *Kansas.*

mule skinner. *W.* A mule driver.

1870 BEADLE *Utah* 224, I took to the plains with the train . . . in the capacity of a 'mule-skinner.' **1888** *Cent. Mag.* Feb 499 These prairie schooners usually go together, the brawny teamsters known either as 'bull-whackers' or as 'mule-skinners,' stalking beside their slow-moving teams. **1947** *Chi. Tribune* 14 Dec. IV. 8/3 He knew plenty of individuals who represented the types—muleskinners, cowboys, barkeeps.

b. A whip used in driving mules.

1912 WASON *Friar Tuck* 58 He would stand up an' yell, crack his mule-skinner, and send the ponies along on a dead run.

* **muley,** *n.*

1. = **muley saw.**

1846 *Davenport* (Iowa) *Gaz.* 25 June 1/3 The saw mill has but one saw, a 'muley,' constructed upon an improved principle . . . and capable . . . of turning out three thousand feet of lumber in twenty four hours. **1883** *Harper's Mag.* Jan. 208/2 If the log is of large size, it is sent at once against a 'muley,' or straight rip-saw, working perpendicularly, which splits it in two. **1887** *Courier-Journal* 22 Jan. 4/3 Sawyer goes to the Senate again from Wisconsin. Sawyer doesn't cut his logs with a muley.

2. muley saw, (see quot. 1875). Also attrib.

"The conjecture that *muley saw* is a perversion of G. *mühlsäge* mill-saw seems to be unfounded: see *Encycl. Brit.* (1886) XXI. 343/2 *note*" (*OED*).

1852 *Mich. Agric. Soc. Trans.* III. 487, 1 reaction water wheel and mully saw gearing. **1871** *Rep. Comm. Patents 1869* II. 165/2 Muley-Saw Mill. . . . The inclined guides D [etc.]. **1875** KNIGHT 1495/2 Muley-saw. A mill-saw (German, mühlsäge, mill-saw) which is not strained in a gate or sash, but has a more rapid reciprocating motion, and has guide-carriages above and below, called *muley-heads.* **1881** *Hist. Washington Co.* (Minn.) 196/2 May 13th, 1839, [a group of men] began work . . . , and in the fall of the same year, started their muley saw, thus becoming the pioneers in lumber in the St. Croix Valley. **1940** *Ore. Guide* 60 Water-powered mills with up-and-down mulay saws, cut the boards for Oregon's earliest houses.

b. muley twister, see * **twister,** *n.* **1.**

* **mull,** *v. tr.* To think (a thing) *over*, to consider (a subject) thoroughly (see also quot. 1879).

1873 FISKE in J. S. Clark *Life John Fiske* I. 488 [Huxley] hopes I will add the chapter on 'Matter and Spirit' which I have been mulling for a year back. **1879** WEBSTER *Supp.* 1568/3 *Mull*, . . . to work steadily without accomplishing much. **1932** GRAYSON *Leaders* 462 On this occasion he was lying ill in bed in his house on 55th Street, and of course mulling over the big deal which meant so much to him and his friends. **1949** *Chi. Tribune* 21 Jan. II. 4 It's an idea worth mulling over, Skeex.

* **mullein,** *n.* Also * **mullen. 1. mullein foxglove,** (see quot.). **2. mullein tea,** a tea made from the leaves of mullein. **3.** *To go to grass* (*and eat mullen*), see * **grass,** *n.* **4. a.**

(1) 1857 GRAY *Botany* 292 *S[eymeria] macrophylla.* (Mullein-Foxglove.) . . . Shady river-banks, Ohio, Illinois, and southwestward. — **(2) 1887** HARRIS in *Cent. Mag.* Aug. 551/2 She sent me word to make me some mullein tea. **1905** PRINGLE *Rice Planter* 275 Ruth's leg and foot . . . must be bathed twice a day with hot mullein tea and then rubbed dry.

As the last term in **turkey mullein.**

* **mullet,** *n.*

1. = **mullet sucker.**

1839 STORER *Mass. Fishes* 84 [Suckers] are occasionally brought into the city by the cartload, and palmed off upon the ignorant, as the mullet. **1884** GOODE *Fisheries* I. 614 The common 'Red Horse' or 'Mullet' abounds in most streams westward and southward of New York.

2. In combs.: (1) **mullethead,** a flat-headed freshwater fish; (2) **-headed,** stupid, *colloq.* [cf. *EDD mullhead*, "a dull, stupid fellow"]; (3) **sucker,** (see quot.).

(1) 1866 *Harper's Mag.* Sep. 537/1 Dat fish is a mullet-head; it hain't got any brains. **1873** BEADLE *Undevel. West* 102 A fish called the mullet-head, . . . cannot be intoxicated by any amount of liquor. It can even swim in that fluid. **1893** FORBES-MITCHELL *Great Mutiny* vi. 110 That fish, my son, is called a mullet-head: it has got no brains. — **(2) 1857** *Chindowan* (Quindaro, Kans.) 6 June 1/3 The men, for the most part sleepy, ignorant, mullet-headed looking wretches . . . were engaged in cooking provisions either in the shanties of the Irish, or out of doors on the hill side. **1884** MARK TWAIN *H. Finn* xxxix. 370 They're so confiding and mullet-headed they don't take notice of nothing at all. — **(3) 1842** *Nat. Hist. N.Y., Zoology* IV. 201 The Mullet Sucker, *Catostomus aureolus*, . . . at Buffalo passes under the various names of Mullet, Golden Mullet, and Red Horse.

As the last term in **golden, jumping, Utah, white mullet.**

mulligan ˈmʌlɪgən *n.* [Origin unknown. Poss. from proper name; said to have originated among tramps.] A stew or soup made of odds and ends of food, freq. leftovers. Also attrib. *Colloq.*

1907 LONDON *Road* vi. 169, I encountered hundreds of hoboes, whom I hailed or who hailed me, and with whom I waited at water-tanks, 'boiled-up,' cooked 'mulligans,' . . . and beat trains. **1926** J. BLACK *You Can't Win* xv. 198 He's crazy as a bed bug and the best 'mulligan' maker on the road. **1948** *Dly. Ardmoreite* (Ardmore, Okla.) 19 April 4 My senses tell me 'tis mulligan stew that gently strokes my nasal membranes with its soul-satisfying aroma.

Mulligan Letters. *Hist.* (See quot. 1914.)

[**1876** *Cong. Rec.* 5 June 3612/1 In regard to how Mr. Mulligan got possession of those letters, he says, . . . those letters were taken possession of and brought to the city of Washington by James Mulligan with the full consent and approbation of Warren Fisher.] **1884** *N.Y. Wkly. Tribune* 23 July 7/3 In 1876, with the Mulligan Letters on the table [etc.]. **1914** *Cyclo. Amer. Govt.* III. 474/2 Mulligan Letters. A series of letters between James G. Blaine and Warren Fisher of Boston, brought to public notice by Mulligan, Fisher's bookkeeper, for the purpose of confirming charges of corruption brought against Blaine in his alleged connection with the Little Rock and Fort Smith Railroad; and which became an important factor in the Republican nominating convention of 1876 and the presidential campaign of 1884. **1934** MUZZEY *James G. Blaine* 108 He had appealed to the confidence of his 44,000,000 fellow citizens as he read the Mulligan letters from his desk.

mulling ˈmʌlɪŋ, *n.* [Poss. f. **mull*, *v.*, to crush, grind.] Excitement, stir (see quot. 1866). *Colloq.* — **1845** JUDD *Margaret* I. 170 There has been a pooty consid'rable mullin goin on 'mong the doctors ever sen the Nommernisstortumbug come out. **1866** LOWELL *Biglow P.* 2 Ser. p. lvii, We have always heard *mulling* used for *stirring, bustling*, sometimes in an underhand way.

multicaulis ˌmʌltɪˈkɔlɪs, *n.* [f. the L. elements *multi*+*caulis*, "many stemmed."] A variety of white mulberry, grown esp. during the 1830's in the expectation of making profits in the silk industry. Also attrib. *Obs.* Cf. **morus multicaulis.**

1833 *Niles' Reg.* XLIV. 332/2, I had the first opportunity of receiving from Paris, . . . three rooted trees of the Chinese multicaulis. **1840** *Farmers' Cabinet* 15 May 326/2 The multicaulis *fever* has passed, and we are *shivering* under its effects. **1857** *Iroquois Republican* (Middleport, Ill.) 12 Feb. 3/1 The Sorghum will prove a valuable addition to our crops, if we don't render it odious by some Multicaulis foolery. **1885** *Harper's Mag.* March 610/2 This 'multicaulis' or mulberry mania still furnishes a world of humor to the 'elders.'

multicaulised ˌmʌltɪˈkɔlɪst, *a.* [f. prec.] (See quot.) *Slang. Rare.* — **1840** *Alexander's Wkly. Messenger* (Phila.) 27 May 1/5 New Word.—Multicaulised.—Run out—good for nothing—dished.

multimillionaire ˌmʌltəˌmɪljənˈɛr, *n.* A person having two or more million dollars. Also attrib.

1858 HOLMES *Autocrat* 288 The multi-millionaires sent him a trifle, it was said, to buy another eye with. **1893** *Advance* 3 Aug., On a salary of $5,000 per annum, [the Congressman] has become the multimillionaire owner of a marble palace. **1949** *Sooner Mag.* June 10/3 And somehow that sums up this dry, Baptist multimillionaire New Dealer who has always driven hard for the main chance.

b. Also **multi-billionaire.** *Humorous.*

1906 M. TWAIN *Chaps. from Autobiog.* 322 There would not be any multi-billionaire alive, perhaps, who would be able to buy a full set.

***multiplication,** *n. Multiplication, Division, and Silence,* (see quot.). *Obs.* — **1885** *Mag. Amer. Hist.* March 296/2 *Multiplication, Division, and Silence*—Ascribed to William M. Tweed (*circa* 1872), as his definition of the proper qualifications of a contractor, under the administration of the 'Ring.'

Multnomah mʌlt'nomə, *n.* [f. a native expression meaning "down river."] (See quot. 1907.) Also **Multnomah Indians.**

1804 LEWIS & CLARK *Travels to Source Mo.* (1817) III. 115 The women wear longer and larger robes than their neighbours the Multnomahs. *Ib.* 109 On reaching the Multnomah Indians, we learned, that although a great many words were the same, . . . yet there was a sensible variation of language. **1849** ROSS *First Settlers Ore.* (1923) 95 The Indian tribes inhabiting the country about the mouth of the Columbia may be classed in the following manner: (1) Chinooks; (2) Clatsop; (3) Cathlamux; . . . (9) Multnomas; and (10) Chickelis. **1907** HODGE *Amer. Indians* I. 856/1 Multnomah. . . . A Chinookan tribe or division formerly living on the upper end of Sauvies id., Multnomah co., Oreg. . . . The term is also used in a broader sense to include all the tribes living on or near lower Willamette r., Oreg. **1948** *Mazama* April 4/1 This nearby island . . . was once the home of the Multnomah Indians.

mumchimmee 'mʌmˌtʃɪmɪ, *n.* [Origin unknown.] ? = next. *Obs.* — **1807** *Mass. H.S. Coll.* 2 Ser. III. 57 The mumchimmee, a small fish, four or five inches long, resembling an eel in shape, is caught in summer.

mummichog 'mʌmɪˌtʃɑg, *n.* [Narraganset, "Moamitteaũg. A little sort of fish" (1643 Williams *Key* 141).] A name applied in the East to various killifishes.

1787 PENNANT *Arctic Zoology Supp.* 149 Inhabits New York, where it is known by the Indian name of Mummy Chog. **1883** *Nat. Museum Bul.* No. 27, 451 *Fundulus majalis.* . . . Mummichog. . . . Atlantic coast of the United States. **1911** *Rep. Fisheries 1908* 312 Mummichog (*Poeciliidae*).—These fish are found in the brackish waters along the Atlantic, Pacific, and Gulf coasts. **1939** *L.A.* Map 234.

* **mummy-cloth,** *n.* A modern fabric used especially as a base for embroidery, made in imitation of the cloths used by the Egyptians for wrapping mummies (see also quot. 1890).

1881 *Art Interchange* (N.Y.) 27 Oct. 93 Mantel scarfs . . . could be of . . . cretonne, momie cloth, plush [etc.]. **1887** *40th Congress* 2 Sess. H.R. Mis. Doc. No. 170, II. 652/2 [Textile fibers and fabrics in the U.S. National Museum include] Mummy cloth. **1890** *Cent.* 3897/3 *Mummy-cloth,* . . . a fabric resembling crape, having the warp of either cotton or silk and the weft of woolen; used for mourning when black on account of its lusterless surface.

mum social. A party at which everyone tries to keep silent until a certain time. *Obs.* — **1883** RITTENHOUSE *Maud* 253 Thursday night was the sociable here—a 'mum social.' I found the silence appalling and flew for refuge to my room, where I wrote poetry till Mr Davenport walked me down.

mung mʌŋ, *a.* [Origin unknown. Cf. *mungo,* "a reclaimed wool obtained by deviling rags" (1934 Webster).] **1.** (See quot.) **2. mung news,** false or out-of-date news. Both *obs.*

(1) **1859** MACKAY *Tour* I. 160 *Mung,* sham, false, pretended — (2) **1844** *Spirit of Times* (Phila.) 26 Sep. (Th.), Mung News [the heading of an item concerning news a year old]. **1849** *N.Y. Ev. Express* 17 Feb. 2/5 As there are many of our citizens who intend to go to California, who may possibly base their arrangements upon this kind of 'mung news,' we conceive it our duty to state, . . . that most of these letters are the silliest fictions.

***mungo,** *n.* **1.** Prob. the sewellel *q.v. Obs.* **2. mungo bass,** ? = **black bass.** *Obs.* — (1) **1806** LEWIS in *L. & Clark Exped.* (1905) IV. 185 This robe is made most commonly of the skins of a small animal which I have supposed was the brown Mungo. — (2) **1832** WILLIAMSON *Maine* I. 158 *Mungo Bass* is both smaller and much better fish [than the bass];—fat and fine flavoured as a salmon.

mungofa mən'gofə, *n.* = **magofer.** *Obs.* — **1836** HOLBROOK *N. Amer. Herpetol.* I. 41 *Testudo Polyphemus*—Daudin. Synonymes. . . . Gopher and Mungöfa, *Vulgo.*

* **municipal,** *a.* **1. municipal corporation,** an incorporated town. **2. municipal ownership,** ownership, esp. of a public utility, by a municipality.

(1) **1855** in HAMBLETON *H. A. Wise* 306 Let the States and your municipal corporations pass such laws as they please. **1877** JOHNSON *Anderson Co., Kans.* 174 On the 7th day of October, 1861, Charles Hidden, probate judge of Anderson county, . . . declared the town of Garnett a municipal corporation. — (2) **1891** *Advance Club* (Providence, R.I.) *Leaflets* No. 1, 12 Mayor Sargent of New Haven recommended with powerful arguments in his inaugural, municipal ownership of electric lighting. **1918** A. M. TODD *Municipal Ownership* 6 Our general judgment, considering the political and industrial conditions in this country, is in favor of municipal ownership.

municipality ˌmjunɪsə'pælətɪ, *n.* [App. a new borrowing of F. *municipalité.*] In New Orleans between 1836 and 1852, any one of the three districts into which the city was divided, each having a distinct local government. Now *hist.*

1840 *N. O. Picayune* 8 Aug. 2/6 The Police Prison of the Second Municipality. **1883** *Cent. Mag.* June 222/1 The city boundaries had been extended to take in both these faubourgs; and the three 'municipalities,' as they were called, together numbered one hundred and two thousand inhabitants. **1949** *N.O. Times-Picayune Mag.* 6 March 18/4 There were heard the shouts of municipality boatmen, offering free but limited transportation.

b. municipality paper, certificates of indebtedness issued by one of the municipalities of New Orleans. *Obs.*

1840 *N.O. Picayune* 28 July 1/4 A small Pocket-Book, containing $75 in city bank notes, $7 or $8 in Municipality paper, two $10 bills on the Canal Bank.

Munsee 'mʌnsi, *n.* [f. *Min-asin-ink* "at the place where stones are gathered together."] (See quot. 1907.) Usu. *pl.*

1660 tr. STUYVESANT in Ruttenber *Tribes Hudson R.* 140 On the intercession of the *Maquas,* the *Mahicans,* those of the Highlands, the *Minsis,* the *Katskills,* and other tribes, we concluded a truce with our enemies. **1855** SCHOOLCRAFT *Indian Tribes* V. 495 Tribes of Kansas, Indigenous and Removed from the Other States . . . Munceys, Christian Indians 250. **1907** HODGE *Amer. Indians* I. 957/1 Munsee. . . . One of the three principal divisions of the Delawares, the other being the Unami and Unalachtigo, from whom their dialect differed so much that they have frequently been regarded as a distinct tribe. **1942** WEYGANDT *Plenty of Penna.* 37 There have come to us from the Delawares and Munsees certain methods of farming and fighting, hunting and fishing, canoeing and woodcraft in general that are a part of what we are.

* **Munson,** *n. attrib.* Of or pertaining to shoes made on lasts designed by Surgeon-Major Munson of the U.S. Army.

1916 KEPHART *Camping & Woodcraft* 153 My advice is to get shoes made over the Munson last. **1921** HALL *Yosemite Nat. Park* 280 Shoes with broad toes and low, flat heels, of the Munson type of last, . . . are good for trail work and mountain climbing. **1922** *Outing* Jan. 168/3, I wore O.D. breeches (wool), leather puttees, and the Munson shoe with an extra heavy sole. **1947** *Chi. Tribune* 27 June 1. 30 Here's A Value Every Working Man Can't Afford to Pass. U.S. Army Munson Last Work Shoes. $2.99 per pair.

***mural,** *n.* A mural painting. — **1933** *DAB* XII. 645 He painted historical murals for the Minnesota and Wisconsin capitals. **1947** PERRY *Cities of Amer.* 242 On the cultural side, there's the great Huntington Museum, home of Gainsborough's Blue Boy, and, in the Public Library, the Dean Cornwell murals.

murrelet 'mɜlɪt, *n.* [**murre*+*-let.*] Any of several small sea birds of the family Alcidae, found chiefly on the Pacific Coast.

1872 COUES *Key to Birds* 344 *Brachyrhamphus marmoratus.* . . . Marbled Guillemot, or Murrelet. **1887** RIDGWAY *Man. N. Amer. Birds* 15 Southern California to Cape St. Lucas. . . . *B[rachyrhamphus] hypoleucus.* . . . Xantus's Murrelet. **1917** *Birds of Amer.* I. 22 Ancient Murrelet. *Synthliboramphus antiquus.* . . . Other Names.—Gray-headed Murrelet; Black-throated Murrelet. . . . *Ib.* 23/2 The Ancient Murrelet is another of the diving birds which fairly swarm on many of [the] islands along the southern coast of Alaska.

***muscadine,** *n.* As the last term in **early, southern muscadine.**

muscle 'mʌsḷ, *v. tr.* To overcome (a person) by physical violence. Usu. *to muscle in,* to force one's way into a business, "racket," etc., regardless of opposition. *Slang.*

1929 *Chi. Tribune* 18 Jan. 21/4 A certain gentleman in the illicit spirits business was accosted by two sinister characters, who 'muscled' him, . . . removing from his wallet the sum of $150. **1930** *Time* 14 July 28/3 A guy from Portland, Ore. tried to 'muscle in' on my game and I got his arms and legs busted for him. **1948** *Ib.* 16 Feb. 102/3 When he tries to muscle in, he discovers . . . that mere brute force is helpless against the intricacies of interlocking corporate structure.

* **mush,** *n.*

1. Porridge or hasty pudding made of cornmeal. Cf. **fried mush.**

1671 J. HARDY *Descr. Last Voyage to Bermudas* 11 Indian corn. . . . Which being groun'd and boyl'd, Mush they make Their hungry

Servants for to slake. **1724** JONES *Virginia* 40 This Grain is of great Increase and most general use, for with this is made good Bread, Cakes, Mush, and Hommony. **1847** HOWE *Ohio* 366 After the corn was sufficiently pounded, they sieved it, and took the finer portion for meal to make bread and mush of. **1944** BLAIR *Tall Tale Amer.* 107 Never eat a four-footed friend. . . . Just give me a little mush and a few pancakes.

2. In combs.: (1)**mushhead,** (see quot. 1888–90); (2) **ice,** water only partly frozen; (3) **note,** a love letter; (4) **pan,** a pan used for boiling mush; (5) **pot,** a pot used for boiling mush; (6) **sugar,** a crystalline sugar precipitating in or mixed with sirup; (7) **sirup,** =prec.

(1) **1888–90** BARRERE-LELAND II. 74 Mush-head. A stupid witless fellow. **1932** *Screenland* April 70/1 She has married the poor little mush-head that had been wished upon her. — (2) **1815** *Niles' Reg.* IX. 201/2 You may . . . take a pole sixty feet long, and . . . run it down the whole length, and find no termination of what is called the mush ice. **1959** ABBOTT-SMITH *We Pointed* 109 It was cold, and there was a lot of new ice along the banks, what we call mush ice. — (3) **1927** BENÉT *J. B.'s Body* 62 They wrote mush-notes to their girls and wondered how it would go. — (4) **1847** ROBB *Squatter Life* 59 Betsy Jones' Tumble in the Mush Pan. **1940** HATCHER *Buckeye Country* 173 When his self-made pasteboard hat fell to pieces . . . he covered his head with his mush pan.

(5) **1847** HOWE *Ohio* 432 Johnny, who wore on his head a tin utensil which answered both as a cap and a mushpot, filled it with water and quenched the fire. — (6) **1868** *Iowa Agric. Soc. Rep. 1867* 178 When sugar is contemplated, White Imphee is . . . the best, as all I have made went to thick mush sugar immediately. — (7) **1863** *Rep. Comm. Agric. 1862* 131 We have taken from one gallon of mush sirup . . . eight pounds of sugar.

b. *mush and milk* (or *molasses*), mush eaten with milk or molasses.

1745 E. KIMBER *Itinerant Observer* 34 The meaner Sort you find little else but Water amongst, when their Cyder is spent, *Mush* and Milk, or Molasses, *Homine*, Wild Fowl, and Fish, are their principal Diet. **1810** *Mass. Spy* 24 Jan. (Th.), They have mush and molasses twice a day. **1908** SINCLAIR *Metropolis* 162 [Common people] ate mush and molasses. **1945** SERVICE *Ploughman* 204 We were awakened for breakfast, which consisted of mush and condensed milk.

transf. and *attrib.* **1866** MARK TWAIN *Lett. Sandwich Is.* (1938) 151, I'm disgusted with these mush-and-milk preacher travels.

As the last term in **acorn, corn, Indian, Indian corn, meal, rye mush.**

mush mʌʃ, *v. N.W.* [Prob. f. *mush on*, inspired by F. *marchons*, let's go.] *intr.* To go on foot, esp. with a dog-sled across the snow. Also transf.

1862 KENNICOTT *Jrnl.* (1942) 130 My dogs are *dogs!* and we will *mouche* very likely, after all. **1902** MCKEE *Land of Nome* 32 The cry of encouragement to the dogs of 'Mush on' (dog French for *Marchons*) was heard frequently. **1906** O. HENRY *Four Million* 106, I never got off the train since I mushed out of Seattle, and I'm hungry. **1948** *Nat. Geog. Mag.* Aug. 235/2 We . . . then 'mushed on' to Dam No. 5.

b. *tr.* To cause (a dog team) to mush. Also transf.

1947 *Mazama* Dec. 6/2 Norris left Mt. McKinley Park station on 11 April and mushed his dog team to Base Camp arriving 15 April. **1948** *So. Sierran* Jan. 2/1, I mushed him up through more than a foot of snow to the top of Miller Peak yesterday.

musher ˈmʌʃɚ, *n.* [f. **mush,** *v.*] One who mushes. Cf. **dog musher.** — **1902** MCKEE *Land of Nome* 178, I felt that I had received a very high compliment, delicately expressed, when an old-timer in the party, with unnecessary calls on the Almighty, told me that I was a 'musher from hell.' **1948** *Time* 19 July 34/3 Klondike Mike, the greatest of the mushers, the sourdough who struck it rich and kept his poke, is a living legend.

* **mushroom,** *n. attrib.* Designating a (1) **city** or (2) **town** that has sprung up rapidly.

(1) **1910** J. HART *Vigilante Girl* 46 His second day in this mushroom city was an eventful one. **1948** JOHNSTON *Gold Rush* 42/1 By April, 1850, Downieville had become a mushroom city of large proportions with a population of about 5000. — (2) **1862** in MOORE *Rebellion Rec.* V. II. 309 One of those railroad mushroom towns, located in the pine woods of St. Helena parish—was to be the base of our operations. **1938** ASBURY *Sucker's Prog.* 310 The invasion reached its peak with . . . the building of the trans-continental railroads which the gamblers followed step by step, carrying on their thieving business in every mushroom town that sprang up along the route.

* **mushroom,** *v.* Of flames, to spread out.

"In Eng. the verb *mushroom*, in the fig. sense of *spread out*, is applied only to bullets. In Am. it may be used of fires also" (Horwill). **1903** *N.Y. Sun* 2 Nov. 3 The flames had gone up the stairs to the very top of the house, and had then 'mushroomed' out, as the firemen say. **1911** *Ithaca Jrnl.* 10 Aug., The flames mushroomed from the shaft on all floors above.

* **music,** *n.*

1. *local.* Liveliness, fun (see also quot. 1890). *Colloq.*

1859 BARTLETT 285 Jim is a right clever fellow; there is a great deal of music in him. **1890** *Cent.* 3907/3 *Music*, . . . diversion; sport; also, sense of the ridiculous. . . . (New Eng.).

2. a. music stand, a bandstand. **b. music store,** a store in which music, musical instruments, records, etc., are sold.

(a) **1861** *Ill. Agric. Soc. Trans.* IV. 7 A ring, well inclosed with posts and two planks . . . with music stand two stories high. **1880** *Cimarron News & Press* 30 Sep. 3/3 Sauntering down the street I found a square or plaza containing many fine, large trees and a music stand. — (b) **1815** *Intellectual Regale* 1 March 272 (We.), [This magazine] is removed to No. 8 South Fifty Street, nearly opposite to Mr. Blake's music store. **1941** LEE *Stagecoach North* 12 There were . . . liquor stores, . . . a shoe store, . . . and by 1840 even a music store. **1949** *Sat. Ev. Post* 26 Mar. 33/1 Across the street is the seventy-year-old music store of Arthur Winter.

3. *To face the music*, to meet an ordeal or rigorous test without flinching, to accept the consequences of one's actions without hesitation, to face facts. *Colloq.*

1850 *Cong. Globe* App. 4 March 324/3 There should be no skulking or dodging—. . . every man should 'face the music.' **1899** QUINN *Pa. Stories* 81 We'll all stand by him if he stays and faces the music. **1946** *This Week Mag.* 28 Dec. 13/3 I've been staying here to face the music.

As the last term in **dull, Negro pinkster, scalp music.**

* **musical,** *a.*

1. Of persons: Having a sense of humor, amusing, good-humored. *Colloq. Obs.*

1816 PICKERING 135 In some towns in the interior of New England, . . . they would say of a man of humour, He is very musical. **1846** WHITCHER *Bedott P.* vi. 61 Old Green's a musical old critter, you know.

b. Of a story or situation: Funny, amusing, puzzling. *Colloq. Obs.*

1842 *Life in West* 281 The rule is to 'gammon a stranger' who persists in asking questions, telling him something 'awfully musical.' **1878** COOKE *Happy Dodd* 344, I don't blame 'em none as I know of, but it's musical to see 'em do it. **1881** ——— *Somebody's Neighbors* 242 Why . . . I can't be left to do what I darn please is musical to me.

2. In combs.: (1) * **musical box,** (see quot.); (2) **burletta,** a comic sketch with music, *rare;* (3) **comedy,** a type of theatrical composition in which the plot is subordinated to musical numbers, comic dialogue, dancing, and similar vaudeville features; (4) **sardine box,** a flute harmonica, a wind instrument shaped like a small box, with a mouthpiece at one end and equipped with keys, *obs.;* (5) **steam engine,** a calliope *q.v.*, *obs.*

(1) **1871** DE VERE 283 The *Musical-box* of the Confederate was also known as *Jeff Davis' Box:* it was the humorous name given by the men to the lumbering, ill-built army-wagons, which are apt to creak horribly for want of greasing. — (2) **1895** *Boston Transcript* 1 Jan. 5/7 A Continuous Stage Show from 1 to 11 p.m. No waits. A Great Variety Bill. Funny Musical Burletta. — (3) **1890** BIFF HALL *Turnover Club* 29 'Twas in year of '83 When a party of six and me Went on the road with a show that's knowed As a musical com-i-dee. **1908** SINCLAIR *Metropolis* 145 The entertainment was another 'musical comedy' like the one he had seen a few nights before. **1949** *N.O. Times-Picayune Mag.* 2 Oct. 9 The movies explore colleges and find morons and musical comedies. — (4) **1880** E. JAMES *Negro Minstrel's Guide* 4 Flute harmonicas, or musical sardine box, $3.50.

(5) **1856** *Spirit of Times* 27 Sep. 55/3 There was a musical Steam Engine discoursing 'Pop goes the weasel' on a big scale.

musicale ˌmjuzɪˈkæl, *n.* [F. *soirée musicale.*] A social affair with music as the main feature; a private concert.

[**1846** *Dollar Newspaper* (Phila.) 1 July 3/4 It was about ten minutes before dark when he began his Soiree-Musicale]. **1872** ROE *Barriers Burned Away* xxx, He found soon himself involved in a round of sociables, musicales, and now and then a large party. **1907** *St. Nicholas* Oct. 1087/2 The plans for the musicale were running steadily on. **1948** *Vogue* 15 Feb. 107 His musicales . . . range from chamber music by members of the Boston Symphony Orchestra and gifted amateurs to boogie-woogie.

* **musk,** *n.* In combs.: (1) **musk beaver,** =**muskrat 1;** (2) **hog,** the peccary; (3) * **melon,** * **rat,** see as main entries; (4) **tortoise,** =next; (5) **turtle,** any one of various fresh-water turtles of the genera *Sternotherus* and *Kinosternon.*

(1) **1771** PENNANT *Synopsis Quadrup.* 259. **1842** *Nat. Hist. N.Y., Zoology* I. 75 The Musquash. *Fiber zibethicus*. . . . Musk Beaver. — (2) [**1773** *Gentl. Mag.* XLIII. 219 (*OED*), The Mexican Musk-Hog.] **1909** S. P. ELKINS *Pioneer Days* 277 In a moment out come an avaline or musk hog. **1923** COOK *On Old Frontier* 27 A javaline (musk hog) when in battle resembles more than anything else a 'ball of hair with a butcher knife run through it.' — (4) **1842** HOLBROOK *N. Amer. Herpetology* I. 134 *Sternothœrus Odoratus*. . . . Musk tortoise, or mud tortoise, *Vulgo*. **1884** GOODE *Fisheries* I. 154 Of the six species of Musk Tortoises inhabiting the United States, three are found only in Arizona and the Sonoran region generally, one in the Southern States, except lower Florida and Texas, and the remaining three in the Eastern and Southern States, and the central States westward to the extremities of the tributaries of the Mississippi.

(5) **1868** *Amer. Naturalist* II. 330 The Turtle which you sent . . . is the 'Musk Turtle,' *Aromochelys odoratus*. **1923** STEJNEGER *Rehabil. of Overlooked Species of Musk Turtle* 2 Three full-grown specimens of a musk turtle . . . [proved] to be true *Sternotherus carinatus*.

muskellunge ˈmʌskəˌlʌndʒ, *n.* [Ojibway *mashkinoje*, great pike.] A large pike, *Esox masquinongy*, of the Great Lakes. Also either of two other forms of this fish, *E. m. ohiensis*, of Chautauqua Lake and the tributaries of the Ohio River, and *E. m. immaculatus*, the great northern pike of Wisconsin and Minnesota. Cf. **musky.**

1789 ANBUREY *Travels* I. 274 It abounds with great quantities and variety of fish; sturgeon, black bass, masquenongez pike of an incredible size, and many others. **1798** I. ALLEN *Hist. Vermont* 13 Lakes and rivers in Vermont . . . are abundantly stored with fish . . . particularly sturgeon, salmon, salmon-trout, muskinunge, pike, &c. **1815** *Lit. & Phil. Soc. Trans. N.Y.* I. 496 The muscalinga, a species of pike, is greatly esteemed. **1891** *Outing* March 479/2 We speared this maskinonge in a quiet shallow. **1946** *Wis. State Jrnl.* 18 July 1/4 Gen. Dwight D. 'Ike' Eisenhower and his four brothers all continued their fishing luck Wednesday when they hit the jack pot with a muskellunge each, the limit in Pine lake, Vilas county.

Muskhogean ˌmʌsˈkogɪən, *a.* [f. **Muskogee.**] Of or pertaining to an important linguistic family of Indians formerly found in the Gulf States east of the Mississippi.

1907 HODGE *Amer. Indians* I. 962/2 The Muskhogean population at the time of first contact with Europeans has been estimated at 50,000. **1934** READ *Fla. Place-Names* 61 The term *Muskhogean* designates a large family of tribes in the southeastern United States, comprising the Alabama, Choctaw, Hitchiti, and other linguistic branches or groups. **1946** *Nat. Geog. Mag.* Jan. 53/2 Most important and most typical linquistic stock of the Southeast was the Muskhogean.

* **muskmelon,** *n.* **muskmelon bonnet, hood,** (see quot. 1830). *Obs.* Cf. **pumpkin hood.** — **1830** WATSON *Philadelphia* 176 The 'mush-mellon' bonnet, used before the Revolution, had numerous

Muskmelon bonnet or pumpkin hood

whale-bone stiffeners in the crown, set at an inch apart in parallel lines and presenting ridges to the eye, between the bones. **1891** EARLE *Sabbath* 91 The good wives' heads bore . . . hoods of all kinds and descriptions, from . . . 'muskmelon hoods,' to the warm quilted 'punkin hoods' worn within this century in country churches.

Muskogee mʌsˈkogɪ, *n.* [See note.]

"The name *Muscogee* is apparently of Algonquian origin. Compare Cree *muskeg*, 'swamp,' *muskagoo*, 'swamp Indian'; Ojibway *maskig*, 'swamp,' and Shawnee *muskiegui*, 'lake,' 'pond.'" (W. A. Read *Fla. Place-Names* (1934) 61).

An important linguistic family of southern Indians comprising the Creeks, Choctaws, Chickasaws, Seminoles, and others. Usu. pl. with reference to Indians of this family.

1775 ADAIR *Hist. Amer. Indians* 430 The Cherokees and Muscogees still observe that old custom. **1829** *Va. Herald* (Fredericksburg) 1 April 1/3 Superstition has throned upon the summit of these mountains a Malignant Spirit, the implacable foe of the Muscogees. **1860** CLAIBORNE *Life of Dale* 59 The Muscogee was once a mighty people. **1948** MATHEWS *Southernisms* 43 In general it may be said that the Muskogees occupied the territory [etc.].

attrib. **1775** ADAIR *Hist. Amer. Indians* 116, I had a conversation on this subject, with several of the more intelligent Muskohge traders. *Ib.* 392 A Muskohge warrior . . . got to a bramble swamp, and in that naked, mangled condition, reached his own country. **1839** MORTON *Crania Americana* 144 The Muskogee or Creek confederacy is composed of several nations or remnants of nations.

b. The language of these Indians.

1836 in *Trans. Amer. Antiq. Soc.* II. 94 The Muskhogees are the prevailing nation . . . the Hitchittees . . . speak a dialect of the Muskhogee. **1907** HODGE *Amer. Indians* I. 962/2 The recognized languages of the stock . . . are as follows: . . . Muskogee (including almost half of the Creek confederacy, and its offshoot, the Seminole).

* **muskrat,** *n.*

1. An aquatic rodent, *Ondatra* (syn. *Fiber*) *zibethicus*, having a long, laterally compressed tail. Cf. **musquash.**

1607 in SMITH *Works* (1910) I. p. lxix, There are Beares, . . . Muskats [*sic*] and wild beasts vnknowne. **1688** CLAYTON in *Phil. Trans.* XVIII. 123 Musk-rats in all things shaped like our Water-Rats, only something larger, and is an absolute Species of Water-Rats, only having a curious musky Scent. **1778** CARVER *Travels* 455 The Musquash or Musk-rat, is so termed for the exquisite musk which it affords. **1876** *Wide Awake* 55/1 Muskrats always . . . select a site for building purposes in a swamp, or the shallow parts of a pond, or on a marsh in the bend of a river. **1949** *Mazama* Jan. 3/2 About seventy percent of their habitat would be flooded out, along with much of that of musk rats, badgers and many lesser animals.

b. =**round-tailed muskrat.**

1917 *Mammals of Amer.* 256 While called a Muskrat, this less familiar animal occupies a group by itself, intermediate between the smaller Mice and its big cousin the common Musk-rat.

2. The fur or pelt of the common muskrat. Also attrib.

1666 ALSOP *Maryland* I. 66 Furrs and Skins, as Beavers, Otters, Musk-Rats, . . . were first made vendible by the Indians of the Country, and sold to the Inhabitant [*sic*]. **1822** in MCKENNEY *Memoirs* I. 288 Mr. Kennerly sold, of the parcel which was destined to this market . . . rackoon, muskrat, and beaver. **1916** EASTMAN *From Deep Woods* 101 We saw that they were colored troopers, wearing buffalo overcoats and muskrat caps. **1949** *Fur Trade Rev.* 28 April 1/1 Muskrat . . . is expected to be the leading fur for fall.

3. (*cap.*) A nickname for an inhabitant of a low-lying district, esp. a resident of Delaware.

1845 *Cincinnati Misc.* I. 240 The inhabitants of . . . Delaware [are called] Muskrats. **1890** *Cent. Mag.* July 369/2 Her grandmother . . . [had] a profound contempt for the 'muskrats' as the Flats people [near Detroit] are generally called. **1949** *Amer. Sp.* Feb. 26 To this list may be added . . . *Fox* for a Maine man, *Muskrat* for a Delawarean.

4. In special combs. of obvious meaning, as (1) **muskrat burrow,** (2) **colony,** (3) **house,** (4) **hunter,** (5) **pelt,** (6) **skin,** (7) **trail,** (8) **trap,** (9) **trapper.**

(1) **1870** *Amer. Naturalist* IV. 385 The fish, when the bank was carelessly approached, would withdraw to a deserted muskrat burrow. — (2) **1907** *St. Nicholas* Sep. 1041/2, I was sitting on the margin of a stream where there is a muskrat colony. — (3) **1837** IRVING *Bonneville* I. 174 About the beginning of April, they encamped upon Godin's river where they found the swamp full of 'muskrat houses.' **1867** MUIR *Thousand-Mile Walk* (1916) 88 There was a dry spot on some broken heaps of grass and roots, something like a deserted muskrat house. — (4) *a***1861** WINTHROP *Open Air* 78 Our muskrat-hunters . . . were visited with indescribable Nemesis.

(5) **1944** DUNCAN *M. Graham* 15 Patriotic pride grew under the stimulus of a new state constitution and the new mailboats and the new White House. Now, for only three muskrat pelts, you could send a letter clear back to the Monongahela. — (6) **1642** *Md. Archives* IV. 99, 2. musk-rat-skins. **1822** in ALCOTT *New Conn.* 234, I let my brother have $43, and he sends $100 worth of musk-rat skins by me. — (7) **1921** *Frontier* May 12 A mink had chanced upon a muskrat trail and had followed it up stream. — (8) **1835** HOFFMAN *Winter in West* I. 170 Some of the men were cleaning their weapons, and others were arranging their bundle of muskrat-traps. — (9) **1882** PECK *Sunshine* 261 Ask this red-headed muskrat trapper to sit on the other side of me. **1947** *Chi. Tribune* 21 Dec. (Grafic Mag.) 9/2 He reached his mission station by boat, arriving in March, when the muskrat trappers were returning from even remoter spots.

muskrateer ˌmʌskrəˈtɪr, *n.* One who hunts or traps muskrats. *Rare.* — *a***1861** WINTHROP *Open Air* 73 One of the muskrateers had relieved Cancut of his head-piece, and shot the lower rush of water.

muskratting ˈmʌskˌrætɪŋ, *n.* The hunting or trapping of muskrats. — **1822** *Niles' Reg.* 22 June XXII. 272/2 *Muskratting.* In the neighbourhood of Salem, N.J. one person has caught one hundred muskrats in one night and another caught two hundred and ten in two nights.

musky ˈmʌskɪ, *n.* Short for **muskellunge.** — **1894** *Outing* XXIV. 453/1 We were then all ready for old musky to begin his real fight. **1948** *Milwaukee Jrnl.* 18 July (Ed. Sect.) 6/5 By 1907 the summer guests had started to come, mostly fishermen seeking muskies in Pelican lake.

* **muslin,** *n.*

1. Any of various cotton cloths of medium to heavy weight. Used esp. for bedding and, formerly, for underwear. Also attrib.

1792 *Ann. 2d Congress* 1000 Great quantities of . . . jeans and muslins . . . are made in the household way. **1830** COLLINS *Guide* 176 Flannel is dear, and woollen goods. Calico is called muslin, and prints are called calicoes here. **1830** JOHNSON *Notes* II. 420 Something of the still youthful character and primitive habits of the females of New England and of New York State may be gathered from the fact that our twopenny or threepenny calico is usually called *muslin* among them. **1949** *Sears Cat.* (ed. 198) 470 We found dozens of ways to save money with muslin yardage!

2. In combs.: (1) **muslin-backed,** of paper, having a thickness of muslin glued to the back; (2) **ceiling,** a flimsy ceiling made of widths of muslin, freq. temporary, cf. next; (3) **-walled,** having walls made of widths of muslin, cf. prec.

(1) 1879 *Mich. Gen. Statutes* I. (1882) 432 Such map shall be made on sheets of good muslin-backed paper. — **(2) 1865** *Atlantic Mo.* Jan. 14/2 [We] found ourselves at last in a low room with a shaky floor and muslin ceiling. — **(3) 1878** JACKSON *Travel at Home* 104 Not that you cannot . . . live decently and with sufficient comfort for weeks in the muslin-walled bedroom.

musquash ˈmʌskwɑʃ, *n.* Chiefly *N.* [Algonquian.]

1. = * **muskrat 1.**

[**1588** HARIOT *Briefe & True Report* D2r *Saquenuckot & Maquo'woc;* two kindes of small beastes greater than conies which are very good meat.] *c***1612** STRACHEY *Hist. Travel Va.* (1848) 123 Muscascus is a beast black in collour, proportioned like a water ratt. **1791** *Mass. Laws* (1801) I. 509 No person . . . shall hereafter, in either of the months of June, July, August or September . . . kill any . . . Musquash or Wolverin. **1815** *Mass. H. S. Coll.* Ser. IV. 275 The skins of furred animals were formerly collected hereabout for exportation, as well as domestic use; rabbits, minks, and misquash are yet taken. **1942** CANNON *Mountain* 195 Two musquash and a mink were all he'd seen so far, and he hadn't thought them worth calling to Melissa's attention.

b. Attrib. with **cabin, fur, hole, house, skin, stew.**

1848 THOREAU *Maine Woods* 27 The Millinocket is a small shallow, and sandy stream . . . lined with musquash cabins. — **1876** GOODE *Anim. Resources U.S.* 74 Musquash fur used in felting. — **1835–7** HALIBURTON *Clockmaker* 1 Ser. xxiii. 222, I thought it was like Uncle Peleg's musquash hole, and that no soul could ever find the bottom of. — *a***1862** THOREAU *Maine Woods* 212 What increased the resemblance, was one old musquash house almost afloat. — **1633** *N.H. Doc. & Rec.* I. 72 Received by me . . . three racoon skins, and fourteene musquash skins. — **1882** HUBBARD *Moosehead Lake* 25 For duck, partridge, or musquash stew, cut the meat into small pieces, and place it in a pail, two thirds full of water, where it can boil gently.

c. *To talk musquash,* (see quots.).

1892 *Harper's Mag.* March 491 Talking business in the fur trade has always been called 'talking musquash.' **1942** Nat. Pk. Service *Fading Trails* 59 Many an aged Penobscot or Ojibway listening to the younger men endlessly 'talking musquash' (fur trade business) still wistfully awaits the day.

2. a. =next. **b. musquash root,** the water hemlock, *Cicuta maculata.*

(a) 1612 J. SMITH *Map of Virginia* 13 Musquaspenne is a roote of the bignesse of a finger, and as red os bloud. . . . This they use to paint their Mattes, Targets, and such like. **1722** BEVERLEY *Hist. Virginia* (ed. 2) 120 They have the Puccoon and Musquaspen, two Roots, with which the Indians use to paint themselves red. — **(b) 1807** *Mass. Spy* 22 July (Th.), Five children were lately poisoned in Scipio (Newyork) by eating Wild Parsnip, or *Musquash Root.* **1940** EARLY *N. Eng. Sampler* 309 The Indian had told his grandmother . . . of a decoction of Cowbane (called Musquash Root) that would make a woman forever sterile.

3. musquash weed, a. =prec. **b.** The fall meadow rue, *Thalictrum polygamum.*

(a) 1767 *Mass. Gazette* 21 May 3/1 Persons (especially Children) would do well to beware of this Weed: It is called wild Hemlock by some, and Musquash Weed by others: It grows in low Lands, especially by running Water. — **(b) 1892** *Amer. Folk Lore* V. 91 *Thalictrum polygamum,* muskrat-weed; musquash weed. **1907** LYONS *Plant Names* 457 T. polygamum. . . . Canada and eastern U.S. Tall Meadow-rue, Fall Meadow-rue, Celandine, Muskrat-weed, Musquash-weed.

musquash ˈmʌskwɑʃ, *v.* [f. the noun.] *intr.* To hunt or trap for musquash. — **1833** S. SMITH *Life J. Downing* 25 This was most capital fun, but it want quite equal to musquashing. **1843** STEPHENS *High Life N.Y.* I. 137 He mushquashed round in the woods till he got tired of that kind of fun.

* **muss,** *n.* As the last term in **plug, plum muss.**

* **mussel,** *n.* Also * **muscle.** In combs.: (1) **mussel cripple,** a low-lying area in which mussels thrive, *obs.;* (2) **digger,** the California gray whale; (3) * **eater,** (see quot.); (4) **farm,** a place for breeding mussels; (5) **mud,** (see quot. 1850); (6) **shoals,** *pl.* shoals where the shells of mussels accumulate, esp. (*cap.*) such shoals on the Tennessee River.

(1) 1678 *New Castle Court Rec.* 305, 800 acres Called the mussel Cripple. — **(2) 1860** *Merc. Marine Mag.* VII. 213 It being difficult to capture them, they have a variety of names among whalemen, as . . . 'muscle digger.' — **(3) 1890** *Cent* 3911/1 Mussel-eater, . . . the buffalo perch, *Aplodinotus grunniens,* of the Mississippi valley. — **(4) 1868** *Rep. U. S. Comm. Agric.* (1869) 320 A muscle farm near Rochelle has been cultivated, it is claimed, for hundreds of years.

(5) 1774 J. ADAMS in *Fam. Lett.* (1876) 18 But I long more still to see the procuring more seaweed, and muscle mud, and sand. **1850** JOHNSON *Notes* II. 151 Mussel-mud, as it is called, or sea-mud full of mussels, abounds in the Bay of St Andrews, and in some of the other smaller bays and creeks up the St Croix River. This is an excellent fertilising substance. . . . But the most apparently singular way of using it is to put it, with the mussels still living, into the turnip-drills, when it gives alone an excellent crop of turnips. — **(6) 1779** in RAMSEY *Tennessee* (1853) 200 After running until about 10 o'clock, [we] came in sight of the Muscle Shoals. **1812** *Niles' Reg.* III. 52/2 Above the muscle shoals, extends southeastwardly towards Coosahatcha, a branch of the Alabama. **1921** *Sci. Amer.* 7 May 364/1 The Federal Government finally decided to build a great nitrate plant at Muscle Shoals.

As the last term in **fan, ribbed mussel.**

* **must,** *n.* Newspaper matter that must be printed. Also **dead must.** Also attrib. — **1892** *D.N.* I. 205 An article marked with the word *must* is spoken of as a *must,* or emphatically—if there is absolutely no way of keeping it out of the paper—as a *dead must.* Moreover, as the word is usually accompanied on the copy with the initials of the man who makes the order, there follows a gradation, so that one hears of 'Mr. X's must,' 'Mr. Y's must.' **1912** NICHOLSON *Hoosier Chron.* 180 His gratification at being able to write 'must' matter for both sides of a prominent journal [etc.].

mustang ˈmʌstæŋ, *n.* [Sp. *mesteño,* in Amer. Sp. sense **1.** below.]

1. One of the wild horses of the western prairies and the Southwest, descendants of horses introduced by the Spanish. Cf. **bronco.**

1808 PIKE *Sources Miss.* 273 [We] passed several herds of mustangs or wild horses. **1836** EDWARD *Hist. of Texas* 74 The *mustang,* or wild horse, has almost deserted the lower prairies. **1923** J. H. COOK *On Old Frontier* 61 There were at that time hundreds of bands of Mustangs ranging Western Texas and the Plains Country.

b. Hence a horse of this breed broken to the saddle or harness; any tough, sturdy pony of the West; a cow pony.

1834 *Visit to Texas* 58 The small horses of the country, called mustangs, . . . are . . . purchased for three or four dollars, branded, hobbled, turned out again, and entirely abandoned to themselves until they are needed. **1883** SWEET & KNOX *Through Texas* 169 The horses are hardy mustangs, called cow-ponies. **1949** *Exciting Western* May 68/1 The mustang picked up his feet into a canter for the last few yards into the woods.

transf. The American P-51, a fighter plane.

1944 *Democrat* 23 Nov. 1/4 Not a bomber or Mustang was lost and 21 Nazi interceptors kayoed.

c. (See quots.) *Colloq.*

1836 EDWARD *Hist. Texas* 108 Hence the figure of speech so often used by the inhabitants of Texas, to denote any wild and uncultivated person: as wild as a mustang! **1862** *Harper's Mag.* June 16/2 She was a mustang in human shape. **1891** QUINN *Fools of Fortune* 283 Mustang . . . is substantially identical with 'grand hazard,' the only variations being, that differently inscribed dice are employed, . . . painted, respectively, with a club, a heart, a spade, a diamond, an anchor and a star.

2. = **mustang grape.**

1854 LONGFELLOW *Poetical Works* (1893) 196/2 The red Mustang, Whose clusters hang O'er the waves of the Colorado. **1862** *Rep.*

Comm. Patents 1861: Agric. 482 The Mustang is not a good table grape, but promises to be of great value for wine.

3. In combs.: (1) **mustang cattle,** wild cattle; (2) **cavalry,** (see quot. 1848), *obs.;* (3) **colt,** (*a*) the young of a mustang, (*b*) (*cap.*) a nickname for John C. Frémont (1813–90); (4) **court,** =**kangaroo court;** (5) **grape,** a woody grapevine, *Vitis candicans,* of the Southwest, also the light-colored pungent grapes of this vine; (6) **hunt,** a hunt for wild mustangs, *obs.;* (7) **hunter,** =**mustanger,** *obs.;* (8) **trail,** a trail made by mustangs; (9) **wine,** wine made from mustang grapes.

(1) **1889** *Oregonian* (Portland) 4 Oct. 5/1 A load of lively mustang cattle is coming up on Saturday, which with a number of untame broncos, will provide adequate material for the sport. — (2) **1848** GEORGE C. FURBER *Twelve Mo. Volunteer* 376 Any one that could raise the means to buy a long-eared burro [jackass], a mule, or old Mexican horse, or any such conveyance, immediately entered the mustang cavalry. **1872** POWERS *Afoot & Alone* 118 Ox-driving Eastern Texas furnished to the Confederacy several infantry regiments who were worth more than all the mustang cavalry together. — (3) (*a*) **1821** in *Texas Hist. Quart.* VII. 300 One mustang colt that got seperated from the gang (of mustang horses) came on with us. (*b*) **1856** *Ill. State Reg.* (Springfield) 24 July 1/7 It has chosen the *soubriquet* of 'Mustang Colt' for Fremont. **1856** *Republican Campaign Songster* 15 Then do your best with the old Gray hack. . . . The Mustang Colt will clear the track. — (4) **1853** P. PAXTON *Yankee in Texas* 205 By a unanimous vote, Judge G. . . . was elected to the bench, and the 'Mestang' or 'Kangaroo Court' regularly organized.

(5) **1846** GREGG *Diary & Letters* (1941) I. 239 There is a large species, called by the Americans, the *Mustang grape* which very much resembles the Muscadine of the western country, except in growing in large bunches or racemes. **1883** SWEET & KNOX *Through Texas* 72 The vine bearing the mustang grape assumes enormous proportions. **1948** *Sat. Ev. Post* 23 Oct. 104/2 Whole trees are enmeshed with vines bearing clusters of wild mustang grapes to be made into juice or jelly. — (6) **1923** J. H. COOK *On Old Frontier* 67, I never took any part in 'mustang hunts' of this type, but I watched the performance a few times. — (7) **1861** *Harper's Mag.* June 11/2 Horses then [in 1849] became valuable, and the mustang hunters made a good business of it. — (8) **1841** *N.O. Picayune* 8 June 2/3 The Indian trail discovered a few miles west of Austin, is likely to turn out nothing but a mustang trail. **1892** DUVAL *Young Explorers* 105 Occasionally we would fall into a buffalo or mustang trail — (9) **1862** *Rep. Comm. Patents 1861: Agric.* 483 Mustang wine is made in Texas by gathering the grapes in July, and passing them through a cog or cane-mill, or else they are placed in a cask open at one end and pounded. **1883** SWEET & KNOX *Texas Siftings* 45 The contents of the bottle was not the vile stuff called 'home-made mustang wine.'

b. Also **mustang girl, horse, persimmon, pond, pony, range.**

1831 HOLLEY *Texas* (1833) 89 These wild horses are called . . . Mustangs, and hence the figure of speech to denote anything wild and uncultivated, as a mustang girl, applied to a rude hunter's daughter. — **1821** in *Texas Hist. Quart.* VII. 300 Mustang horses very plenty saw at least . . . 150. **1942** PHILIPS *Big Spring* 149 The last of the mustang horses that roamed the plains were rounded up and captured along the spring of '98. — **1846** GREGG *Diary & Letters* (1941) I. 239 Among other wild fruits of this vicinity, that called by Mexicans chapote and generally by Americans, black persimmon (or Mexican or Mustang persimmon) a black fruit about half the bulk of the common persimmon, much the same shape, and of very pleasant sweet flavor, when ripe. — **1849** *31st Congress* 1 Sess. Sen. Ex. Doc. No. 64,207 This lake I have called 'Mustang pond.' — **1846** T. B. THORPE *Myst. Backwoods* 12 The mustang pony, the invariable companion of the inhabitants of the prairie, . . . is a little creature, apparently narrow-chested, and small across the loins. **1922** T. A. McNEAL *When Kansas Was Young* 188 The Texan 'called' with . . . fourteen Texas mustang ponies and the deed to a tract of land. — **1858** *Porter's Spirit of Times* 339/1 Leading his 'mustanging' horse [for use in capturing mustangs], the sportsman puts out for the mustang range.

As the last term in **calico, California, mountain, rolling, scrag-tailed mustang.**

mustanger ˈmʌstæŋɚ, *n. S.W.* One who makes a business of catching and selling mustangs.

1849 *N.Y. Wkly. Herald* 4 Aug. 245/6 The Indians had also attacked a party of Mustangers near San Patricio, killing two men and capturing three hundred mules and horses. **1929** DOBIE *Vaquero* 240 The professional mustangers were the only men who caught mustangs in considerable numbers. **1946** *Chi. D. News* 20 Aug. 12/6 It was a center for . . . mustangers, who hunted the wild horses, and for buffalo hunters.

***mustard,** *n.* In combs.: (1) ***mustard seed,** =next; (2) **-seed shot,** very small bird shot.

(1) **1844** *Knickerb.* XXIII. 440 None of the fine mustard-seed or robin, but the heavy duck-shot. **1874** COUES *Field Ornithol.* 8 A small bird . . . may be riddled with mustard-seed and yet be preservable. — (2) **1809** FESSENDEN *Pills Poetical* 8 Her single great gun loaded with mustard seed shot. **1846** THORPE *Myst. Backwoods* 180 A charge of mustard-seed shot, or a poke with a stick when at bay, will cause it [the 'cat'] to desert its airy abode.

b. In slang phrases: (1) *to be the* (*proper*) *mustard,* etc., to be the genuine article or the main thing; (2) *to be all* (or *so much*) *to the mustard,* to be very good; (3) *to cut the mustard,* to come up to one's expectations.

(1) **1903** A. ADAMS *Log Cowboy* 237 For fear they [two dogs] were not the proper mustard, he had that dog man sue him in court for the balance, so as to make him prove the pedigree. **1903** O. HENRY *Cabbages & Kings* 101, I'm not headlined in the bills, but I'm the mustard in the salad dressing just the same. — (2) **1907** O. HENRY *Trimmed Lamp* 217 Why don't you invite him if he's so much to the mustard? **1922** SANDBURG *Slabs Sunburnt West* 7 Kid each other, you cheap skates. Tell each other you're all to the mustard. — (3) **1904** O. HENRY *Heart of West* x. 163, I looked around and found a proposition that exactly cut the mustard. **1909** ——— *Roads of Destiny* 99 'She cut the mustard,' he said, 'all right.'

As the last term in **New England, tansy mustard.**

***muster,** *v.*

1. *To muster in,* to muster (a watch) at the time of going on duty.

1840 DANA *Two Yrs.* xxiii, The carpenter sometimes mustered in the starboard watch, and was an old sea-dog.

2. *To be mustered into* (or *in*) *the service,* to be enrolled into military service. Also **mustering-in,** *n.*

1848 *30th Congress* 1 Sess. Sen. Rep. No. 75, 36, I was present when the California battalion was mustered into the service of the United States. **1869** *Overland Mo.* III. 129 At the mustering-in no member was of a lighter weight than a hundred and eighty pounds. **1911** *Okla. Session Laws* 3 Legisl. 217 Before any ex-Confederate or ex-Union soldier or sailor shall be entitled to any of the privileges, he shall make an affidavit in writing that he was properly mustered in and served as a soldier or sailor in the army or navy of the Confederacy or United States prior to the year 1866.

3. *To be mustered out,* to be summoned to a muster in order to be discharged from service, to be discharged from service. Also in active voice.

1834 WAKEFIELD *Hist. Black Hawk War* (1907) 145 Lieutenant Anderson, of the United States army, . . . mustered us all out of the service of the United States. **1883** HAY *Bread-Winners* 242 I wouldn't muster out that army of yours till to-morrow. **1903** FOX *Little Shepherd* xxvii. 27 Chad got permission straightway to go back to Ohio and be mustered out with his old regiment.

b. *fig.* To be killed in action. *Rare.*

1866 KIRKLAND *Bk. Anecdotes* 629 The simple epitaph [read:]. . . . A Soldier of the Union Mustered Out.

***mustering,** *n. attrib.* Designating articles worn by soldiers or sailors on the occasion of a muster. *Obs.* — **1841** *S. Lit. Messenger* VII. 768/1 Who should I see . . . but Mr. Jim Guest himself, in . . . mustering jacket and trowsers, and tarpaulin hat. **1894** *Outing* XXIV. 468 (*legend*), Enlisted Men in Mustering Uniform.

muster out. The action of discharging a soldier or soldiers from service. Also attrib. — **1888** *Cent. Mag.* May 95/1 The muster-out rolls of this gallant regiment furnish the names from which the following abstract is made. **1903** FOX *Little Shepherd* xxv, The Commandant . . . ordered the muster-out of all State troops then in service.

mutch mʌtʃ, *n.* [f. MDu. *mutse,* in same sense. An Amer. borrowing.] (See quots.) *Obs.* Cf. **clockmutch.** — **1680** *New Castle Court Rec.* 404 His Wyfe had stole a mutch or Capp. **1704** S. KNIGHT *Jrnl.* 54 The Dutch . . . women, in their habitt go loose, were French muches wch are like a Capp and a head band in one, leaving their ears bare.

mutoscope ˈmjutəˌskop, *n.* [f. L. *mut*are, to change, +*-scope.*] A simple penny-in-the-slot device for viewing pictures made to appear animated (see quot. 1901). Cf. **kinetoscope, nickelodeon machine.** — **1901** *World's Work* Aug. 1057/2 Prints made from the film are mounted consecutively about a cylinder. As the cylinder is revolved the mounted pictures are held back by a stop, and snap past the eye so that the illusion is of a continuous motion picture. Encased in a box and with the automatic penny-in-the-slot attachment the mutoscope is ready for its common commerical use. **1948** *New Yorker* 16 Oct. 40/2 The Mutoscope justified its sponsors' faith in it, and before long the Kinetoscope had been all but driven out of business.

mutt mʌt, *n.* [f. **mutt*onhead.] An insignificant, stupid person, a fool. *Slang.*

1910 *Fra* Aug. 133/2 Make way for the mutt! **1913** *Industrial Worker* (Spokane) 27 March 3/2 You grease my wagon, you 'mutt,' And don't forget to screw the nut.

b. A dog, esp. a mongrel. *Slang.*

1911 R. W. CHAMBERS *Common Law* X. 310 Now fat old women . . . Arrive to exercise their various dogs; And ' round and 'round the little mutts all run. **1949** *Sat. Ev. Post* 16 April 44/2 That cat! That mutt! they fight it out And back and forth they shuttle.

* **mutton,** *n.* In combs.: (1) **mutton cane,** young tender sprouts of the large cane, *Arundinaria gigantea, colloq.;* (2) **corn,** (see quot.), *colloq., obs.;* (3) * **fish,** see as a main entry; (4) * **ham,** a kind of sail used on a fishing smack, hence **mutton ham boat.**

(1) **1901** MOHR *Plant Life Ala.* 103 These simple sprouts, which are known as 'mutton cane,' are tender and sweet and afford the best of pasturage. **1908** *Sat. Ev. Post* 8 Aug. 3/1 Through the gentle springtime he finds little to eat except bugs, ash-buds and tender shoots called 'mutton-cane.' — (2) *c***1850** in O'NEALL-CHAPMAN *Annals* 48 Ears of green corn (called in the upper country roasting ears, in the lower country, mutton corn,) boiled, were on the table at dinner. — (4) **1899** *Atlantic Mo.* Aug. 197 In a Mutton-Ham boat. *Ib.*, [The boat's] mutton-ham fluttered as white as new cotton around her single mast. I more than once sought to learn why Albermarle and Pamlico fishing smacks call their huge sails 'mutton-ham.'

As the last term in **mountain mutton.**

* **mutton fish.**

1. The pargo, *Lutianus analis.*

[*c***1735** CATESBY *Carolina* II. 25 *Anthea quartus Rondeletii.* . . . The Mutton Fish. . . . For the excellency of it's Tast it is in greater Esteem than any other at the Bahama Islands.] **1911** *Rep. Fisheries 1908* 313/1 Mutton-fish (*Zoarces anguillaris*). The name is also given to the snapper . . . of Florida.

2. A conger eel or kind of eelpout, *Zoarces anguillaris.*

1884 GOODE *Fisheries* I. 247 The Mutton-fish . . . is often seen near the shore north of Cape Cod. **1897** *N.Y. Forest, Fish, & Game Comm. 2d Rep.* 245 Mutton-Fish . . . never endures the warm water in summer. **1911** [see **1.** above].

3. (See quot.)

1885 J. S. KINGSLEY *Stand. Nat. Hist.* I. 93 One of the most abundant medusæ at times in the neighborhood of the Florida Keys is a Discophore, called by naturalists *Linerges*, and known to fishermen there as the 'thimble-fish,' 'mutton-fish thimble' [etc.]. *Ib.* (Index), Mutton-fish 93.

4. The mojarra, *Diapterus olisthostomus.*

1896 JORDAN & EVERMANN *Check-List Fishes* 392 *Gerres olisthostoma.* . . . Irish Pompano; Mutton-fish. West Indies, north to southern Florida.

muttonize ˈmʌtn̩ˌaɪz, *v. tr.* (See quot.) *Colloq.* — **1895** *Voice* 17 Oct. 7/5 'Muttonize' is the latest word in sheep-breeding. It means the introduction of the blood of meat-growing sheep into the wool flocks.

* **mutual,** *a.*

1. Designating various insurance companies in which the policy holders are the shareholders and elect the officers. Also absol.

1798 *Mass. Statute* 1 March, The Massachusetts mutual fire insurance Company . . . shall have power to choose . . . fifteen Directors . . . to manage the concerns of the said Corporation. **1881** *Harper's Mag.* Jan. 279/2 Insurance . . . companies should be strictly mutual. **1924** VALGREN *Farmers' Mutual Fire Insurance in U.S.* 11 Most of the early mutuals . . . were incorporated under special charters.

2. Designating various other societies organized so that the members are of assistance to each other.

1833 *Subaltern's Furlough* iii, There are . . . above one hundred and fifty mutual benefit societies, on the principle of the English clubs. **1864** NICHOLS *Amer. Life* I. 64 The mutual improvement and debating societies had their day. **1891** *Atlantic Mo.* June 814/1 The colored people have developed . . . Good Samaritan societies, and mutual benefit organizations. **1942** STEGNER *Mormon C.* 16 Every Mormon child from the age of twelve upward is a member of either the Young Men's or the Young Ladies' Mutual Improvement Association—the M.I.A., or Mutual.

3. mutual man, (see quot.).

1939 McILWAINE *Poor-White* 76 'Mutual men' were those who refused to join either side [in the Civil War].

* **mutualize,** *v. tr.* To reorganize (an insurance company) so that it will function according to the mutual system. *Rare.* — **1905** *Nation* 23 Feb. 147/1 An arrangement to 'mutualize' the equitable life became inevitable.

mux mʌks, *n.* [Origin unknown.] Any sharp-pointed metal instrument that may be used, according to its design, for boring holes, spearing fish, etc. *Obs.* — **1648** *Southampton Rec.* I. 51 In consideracon of twentie Coats, . . . one hundred Muxes, . . . we do give vp . . . all our right and interest in the sayd land. **1658** *Huntington Rec.* I. 17 Huntington . . . shall pay . . . twenty dutch howes, twenty duch knivis, two hundred of muxes.

muzzle-loading rifle. A rifle loaded at its muzzle.

1856 *Porter's Spirit of Times* 22 Nov. 192/1 A muzzle smaller than the chamber is a disadvantage to an ordinary muzzle-loading rifle, an advantage to a breech-loading piece. **1871** *Rep. Indian Affairs* (1872) 405 Nearly all the men are supplied with muzzle-loading rifles and Colt's revolvers. **1925** BRYAN *Memoirs* 36 We began the afternoon before . . . moulding the bullets for a muzzle-loading rifle.

* **myrtle,** *n.*

1. The trailing periwinkle, *Vinca minor.* Also **running myrtle.**

1890 *Cent.* 3923/3 Running myrtle, more often simply *myrtle*, a name of the common periwinkle. **1931** CLUTE *Plants* 65 Several plants have been named myrtle from their general likeness to the classical myrtle of Europe (*Myrtus communis*). First of these is the periwinkle (Vinca minor), a low spreading evergreen plant called running myrtle.

2. = **California laurel.**

1897 SUDWORTH *Arborescent Flora* 203 Umbellularia californica . . . Myrtle (Oreg.).

3. The moneywort.

1931 CLUTE *Plants* 65 Several plants have been named myrtle. . . . Some obtuse observer has transferred this name to the creeping moneywort (*Lysimachia nummularia*).

4. In combs.: (1) **myrtle bird,** = next; (2) **warbler,** a North American warbler, *Dendroica coronata;* (3) **wax,** see as a main entry.

(1) **1810** WILSON *Ornithology* II. 139 Thro the whole of the lower parts of the Carolinas, wherever the myrtles grew, these birds [*sc.* yellow-rumped warblers] were numerous. . . . In those parts of the country they are generally known by the name of Myrtle-birds. — (2) **1892** TORREY *Foot-Path Way* 95 Myrtle-warblers . . . manifest a particular fondness for the immediate vicinity of houses. **1947** *Iowa Acad. Sci. Proc.* LIV. 379 Myrtle Warbler . . . is often a late migrant, for a warbler.

b. myrtle-of-the-river, a shrub of the myrtle family (see quot. 1917).

1917 SAFFORD in *Smithsonian Rep.* 384 The myrtle-of-the-river . . . (*Calyptranthes zuzygium*) with opposite glossy leaves and clusters of fruit resembling blueberries. **1924** J. A. THOMSON *Science Old & New* v. 27 Even the names transport us into a land of pure delight—the paradise tree, the myrtle-of-the-river, the marlberry, and the boisfidele.

As the last term in **blue, candleberry, crape, sand, water myrtle.**

myrtle wax.

1. = **bayberry wax.**

1700 *Va. State P.* I. 68, 26 pounds of Mirtle-wax, 01.06.00. **1755** FRANKLIN *Writings* III. 263 I'll put in a few Cakes of American Soap made of Myrtle Wax. **1880** CABLE *Grandissimes* 414 He removed the lid and saw within . . . the image, in myrtle-wax.

2. myrtle-wax candle, a candle made of the wax from wax myrtles.

1732 *Cal. State P. Amer. & W. Indies* 59 Carolina. Messieurs Boone and Barnwell, then Agents for this Province in their answers to said queries etc. 1720 mentioned no manufactures except mirtle wax candles. **1770** PITTMAN *Present State* 23 The different articles are indigo, cotton, rice, maiz, beans, myrtle wax-candles, and lumber.

3. myrtle-wax shrub, = **candleberry myrtle.**

1766 STORK *Acct. E. Florida* 48 The myrtle-wax shrub is, without doubt, the most useful of the spontaneous growth of America. **1828** *Western Mo. Rev* I. 729 A description is given of the myrtle-wax shrub. We believe it to be the same with what is called *bayberry* in New England.

b. Also **myrtle-wax tree.**

1763 in *Amer. Sp.* XX. (1945) 46 The *Myrtle Wax-tree* is one of the greatest blessings with which nature has enriched *Louisiana.* **1836** EDWARD *Hist. Texas* 66 The shrubs . . . which he could designate, as . . . the Myrtle Wax-tree, the Wild Plum [etc.].

mystic testament. *La.* [F. *testament mystique.*] A will made under seal. Also **mystic will.** — **1839** BOUVIER *Law Dict.* II. 435/2 A mystic testament is also called a solemn testament, because it requires more formality than a nuncupative testament. **1891** *Amer. & Eng. Encycl. Law* XVI. 111 *Mystic Will.* In *Louisiana* a mystic will is a will under seal.

N

N. A. An abbreviation of "National Academician" or "National Academy."

1867 *Harper's Wkly.* 4 May 273 (*caption*), Eastman Johnson, N.A. **1883** *Harper's Mag.* Nov. 843/2 [G. H. Boughton] enjoys . . . the unusual distinction of being an N.A. and an A.R.A. **1924** *Who's Who in Amer.* XIII. 1706/1 Inness, George, Jr., painter; . . . A.N.A., 1895 N.A., 1899. **1949** *L.A. Times* 11 July 11. 4/2 [signature:] Hugo Ballin, N.A.

*nabob, *n.* (See quot. 1804.) *Obs.* — **1803** E. S. Bowne *Life* 151 Silk nabobs . . . are much worn. **1804** Fessenden *Orig. Poems* (1806) 36 Misses, squires, and gentlefolks, Call for Nabobs, hats, and cloaks. [Note:] Nabobs were a kind of outside garment formerly worn by the dashing belles of America.

***nag,** *n.* As the last term in **buggy, California, prairie nag.**

***nail,** *n.* In combs.: (1) ***nail cutter,** =next; (2) **cutting machine,** a machine that makes cut nails; (3) ***driver,** see as a main entry; (4) **factory,** a factory where machine-cut nails are produced; (5) **file,** (see quot. 1875); (6) **grab(s),** a tongs-like instrument used in stores for taking up nails to be weighed for a customer, also transf.; (7) **keg,** (*a*) a small, strongly made barrel in

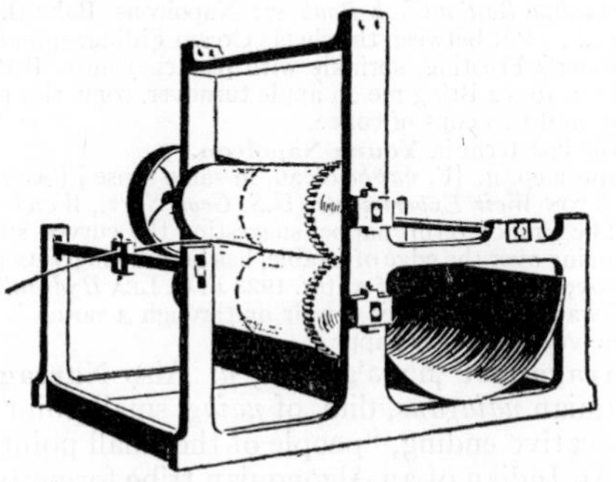

Nail cutting machine *c*1834

which nails are shipped, (*b*) *transf.* a hat somewhat resembling this in shape, *colloq.* [cf. *EDD nail box* with the same meaning]; (8) **machine,** see as a main entry; (9) **mill,** =**nail factory;** (10) **works,** =**nail factory.**

(1) 1875 Knight 1505/2 The American nail-cutter was the first to cut the nails and swage the heads at one operation. — **(2) 1816** *Mass. H.S. Coll.* 2 Ser. VII. 70 There were in the county of Hillsborough, in 1810 . . . 5 nail cutting machines, making 10 tons per annum. **1819** Flint *Lett. from Amer.* 125 The manufactories are . . . a grist-mill, a nail-cutting machine, . . . and a white-lead factory. — **(4) 1809** *Ann. 11th Congress* 2250 At Dover . . . [is a rolling and slitting mill] owned by the Boston iron and nail factory. **1864** Cumming *Hospital Life* (1866) 127/1 He said that he paid a visit to a nail factory.

(5) 1875 Knight 1506/2 *Nail-file*, a small, flat, single-cut file for trimming the finger-nails. **1936** *Sears Cat.* 190 LaCross Nail Files. . . . Triple Cut—5-in. with nail cleaning point . . . 23¢. — **(6) 1851** Hooper *Widow Rugby* 44 His mouth . . . looked as if it had been . . . made by gouging a hole in his face with a nail-grab! **1852** Mark Twain in *Hannibal Jrnl.* 16 Sep., 'Thar he sot,' . . . his 'nail-grabs' grasping a pew like grim death. — **(7)** (*a*) **1869** Browne *Adv. Apache Country* 402 Adobe-bricks, mud, . . . whiskey-barrels, nail-kegs, and even canvas, are the component parts [of chimneys]. **1905** Wiggin *Rose* 65 You can't drownd a Wiley, not without you tie nail-kags to their head an' feet an' drop 'em in the falls. (*b*) **1869** Mark Twain *Innocents* 269 [Americans] wear a comical hat termed a 'nail-kag.' **1909** *D.N.* III. 414 *nailkeg, n.* A silk hat. — **(9) 1850** *Rep. Comm. Patents 1849: Agric.* 93 Within . . . [the] present limits [of Bristol Co., Mass.] are about . . . seven rolling, slitting, and nail mills.

(10) 1913 London *Valley of Moon* 269 Saxon recognized . . . the shipyards, the nail works, Market street wharf.

b. *Nail City of the West*, Wheeling, W. Virginia. *Obs.*

1890 *Cong. Rec.* 9 May 4433/2 Down through the thriving city of Wheeling—the Nail City of the West—I could hear the rattling roll of machinery.

As the last term in **board, coffin, cut, heel, toe, trunk nail.**

***nail,** *v. intr.* To work as a carpenter. *Rare.* — **1885** Whitman in *N. Amer. Rev.* Nov. 434, 1st Conductor of a horse car, 'What did you do before you was a snatcher?' Answer of 2d Conductor, 'Nailed.' (Translation of answer: 'I worked as carpenter.')

***nail driver.** An excellent or superior thing, esp. a gun, from the frontier pastime of driving nails with rifle bullets in shooting matches. *Colloq.* Cf. ***drive,** *v.* **4.**

1823 Cooper *Pilot* viii, The cannon, above which were painted the several quaint names of 'boxer,' . . . 'exterminator,' and 'nail-driver.' **1878** Hickman *Brigham's Destroying Angel* 54, I had a nail-driver very swift and no end to his bottom. **1922** Kephart *So. Highlanders* 49 My rifle . . . was a nail-driver, and I, through constant practice in beheading squirrels, was in good form.

***nailer,** *n.* A machine for driving nails. — **1892** *York Co. Hist. Rev.*, A cigar-box factory is fitted out with the latest approved machinery, planers, tackers, nailers, presses etc.

nail machine. A machine for making nails.

1797 *Essex Inst. Coll.* LIV. 110 My Nail Machine consists of a cutting lever of the common form, which vibrates to cut, head & pound. **1819** E. Dana *Geog. Sk.* 77 Zanesville is on the east branch of the Muskingum, . . . whereon various mills are erected . . . [including] an oil mill, nail machine and woolen factory. **1883** *Cent. Mag.* Sep. 792/2 In mechanical trades there is a fear that such teaching will unfit the boy for tending a nail machine or a shoe-pegging machine.

naked bear. (See quot. 1818.)

1818 Heckewelder in *Mem. Hist. Soc. Pa.* XII. (1876) 255 (*footnote*), Probably alluding to a tradition which the Indians have of a very ferocious kind of bear, called the *naked bear*, which they say once existed, but was totally destroyed by their ancestors. **1855** Longfellow *Works* (1892) 262 Thus the wrinkled old Nokomis. . . . Stilled his fretful wail by saying, 'Hush! the naked bear will get thee.' **1929** McClinchey *Joe Pete* 16 Mabel put the drowsy baby in his basket, crooning an ancient Indian lullaby about the naked bear.

naked wood. a. ?The wild cinnamon, *Canella winterana.* **b.** (See quot. 1884.) **c.** (See quot. 1884.)

(a) 1837 Williams *Florida* 98 Wild Cinnamon.—Called by the inhabitants, Naked Wood. — **(b) 1884** Sargent *Rep. Forests* 42 *Colubrina reclinata.* . . . Naked Wood. Semi-tropical Florida, Umbrella Key, on the North end of Key Largo, and sparingly on the small islands south of Elliott's Key; through the West Indies. **1933** Small *Southeastern Flora* 834 C. reclinata. . . . Naked-wood. Soldier-wood. — **(c) 1884** Sargent *Rep. Forests* 88 *Eugenia dichotoma.* . . . Naked Wood. Semi-tropical Florida . . . ; in the West Indies. **1927** Sudworth *Check List Forest Trees* 211 Eugenia dicrana Berg. . . . Naked-wood(Fla.) Naked Stopper.

namaycush ˈnæmɪˌkʌʃ, *n.* [Algonquian Indian.] A large trout, *Cristivomer namaycush*, found in North American lakes. Cf. **Mackinaw trout.**

[**1787** Pennant *Arctic Zool.* Supp. 139 Naymacush. Inhabits the lakes of Hudson's Bay.] **1829** Richardson *Fauna Bor. Amer.* III. 179 The namaycush is the tyrant of the lakes. **1911** *Rep. Fisheries 1908* 311 *Cristivomer namaycush.* . . . The individuals vary greatly in color, size, and shape, and are known by the local names 'salmon trout,' 'namaycush,' 'togue,' 'tuladi' [etc.]. **1920** Forbes & Richardson *Fishes Ill.* 56 In our Illinois markets it is known almost wholly by the name of lake trout, but farther north the names of Mackinaw trout, salmon-trout, and namaycush are sometimes used.

***name,** *n.* As the last term in **Bay State, firm, first, office, war name.**

nanninose ˈnænɪˌnoz, *n.* =**maninose.**

1884 Goode *Fisheries* I. 707 Next upon the list comes the 'Soft Clam,' 'Long Clam,' or 'Nanninose' (*Mya arenaria*), dear to New Englanders. **1911** *Rep. Fisheries 1908* 308 Clam. . . . Various species, most of which are edible, are known by the names of . . . 'mananose,' 'nanninose' [etc.]. **1949** R. J. Sim *Pages from Past* 66 The soft-shell clam, or nanny-nose (*Mya arenaria*, Linn.), and often known by another name, lives in colonies in the sandy mud of the bare tidal flats.

∗**nanny,** *n.* **1. nannyberry,** =**sheepberry. 2. nanny-plum tea,** =**sheep nanny tea.** Both *colloq.*

(1) **1867** De Voe *Market Ass't* 384 Partridge-berries, or nanny-berries. These little black berries grow in clusters, on a tree-like bush, on uncultivated grounds or along hedges. **1945** McAtee *John and Joe* 5 So also do the smooth and staghorn sumacs, persimmon, nanny-berry, and black haw, not to mention several shrubs and vines. — (2) **1937** Coffin *Kennebec* 239 One remedy there is, peculiar to the heart of Maine, I hope. That is the laxative nanny-plum tea. You find nanny plums where the sheep have marched on their narrow track through the ferns. . . . It is, they say, efficacious.

Nanquitoche ˈnænkwɪˌtotʃɪ, *n.* [App. f. Amer. Indian.] A variety of tobacco formerly grown in Florida. *Obs.* — **1775** Romans *Nat. Hist. Florida* 149 There are present but two sorts of tobacco produced viz *Nanquitoche* and *Pointe coupée*, the first infinitely superior to the second.

Nanticoke ˈnæntɪˌkok, *n.* [f. native name meaning "tidewater people."]

1. *pl.* (See quot. 1910.)

1760 in *Mass H. S. Coll.* 4 Ser. IX. (1871) 258 Several Chiefs of the Delawares, Naaticokes & other Indians being on the Susquahanah, are gone to the great *Treaty* Congress of Indians. **1769** Smith *Tour* 83 Lower down on and near the Susquehannah there are yet remaining several Towns of various Tribes as Onondagoes Tuscarora's Nanticokes Delawares Shawanees and others. **1889** Morton *Crania Americana* 81 He saw a removing party of Nanticokes pass through that town, loaded with the bones of their dead friends. **1910** Hodge *Amer. Indians* II. 24/2 Nanticoke. . . An important Algonquian tribe living on Nanticoke r. of Maryland, on the E. shore. . . . They were connected linguistically and ethnically with the Delawares and the Conoy. **1949** *Pa. Hist. Mag.* April 154 Very little has been written about the Nanticokes in Pennsylvania.

2. A variety of bean, or its seed, native to the eastern states. *Obs.*

1709 Lawson *Carolina* 76 These are latter Pease, and . . . are very good; and so are the Bonavis, Calavancies, Nanticokes, and abundance of other Pulse . . . which we found the Indians possess'd of. **1737** Brickell *N. Carolina* 17 The Nanticoacks are another kind of Pulse, and resemble the Calivances.

Nantucket nænˈtʌkɪt, *n.* [Amer. Indian. Hodge has variants *Mantukes*, *Mantukett*, *Nantukes.*]

1. Whale oil. *Rare.*

1826 *Va. Herald* (Fredericksburg) 25 Oct. 2/3 Hymen began to pour a little pure Nantucket into his lamp.

2. *attrib.* Denoting people or things belonging to, or associated with, the island or the town of Nantucket, Mass. Often *humorous.*

1707 *Boston News-Letter* 7 April 2/1 The Nantucket Whale-boats came up with a Sloop that was overset. **1848** *Knickerb.* XXXI. 225 Who has not seen the eyes of the boarding-school boy almost suffused with tears as he gazed upon the cod-fish dinner, alias 'Nantucket owls?' **1882** Godfrey *Nantucket* 69 The Cap-Codders and the Vineyarders retaliated by calling the Nantuckers 'Scrap Islanders,' or 'Nantucket Scraps.' **1891** *Cent.* 5692/2 *Nantucket sleigh-ride*, the towing of a whale-boat by the whale.

Nantucketer nænˈtʌkɪtɚ, *n.* An inhabitant of Nantucket.

1857 Willis *Convalescent* 260 Hair still brown and thick, with the stubborn vitality of the un-killable Nantucketer. **1881** *Lippincott's Mag.* Sep. 307/2 Sixteen hundred Nantucketers lost their lives in one way or another during and on account of the Revolutionary War. **1948** *Sat. Ev. Post* 26 June 46/3 Russells also had played a part, along with Howlands and Rotches, who had been Nantucketers, in committing New Bedford to the gigantic gamble on whaling.

Also **Nantucketeer.**

1948 *Chi. Tribune* 11 July 18/3 The town clock in the tower of the Unitarian church has told Nantucketeers the time of day for generations.

Nantucketism nænˈtʌkɪtˌɪzəm, *n.* A word or phrase characteristic of Nantucketers. — **1848** J. Mitchell *Nantucketisms* 39/2 We have collected some words & phrases. . . . I do not claim them as Nantucketisms, except a very small part of them.

∗**nap,** *n.*[1] **1.** *pl.* Fabrics having a nap or pile. **2.** In phrases, as *to bring* (or *get*) *up one's nap*, to arouse one's temper or anger. *Colloq.*

(1) **1760** *Newport Mercury* 1 Jan. 3/2 To be Sold by King & Hagger . . . Naps of different Colours, . . . Gimp and small Trimmings. **1790** *Penna. Packet* 2 Jan. 1/3 A further supply of Seasonable Goods . . . Consisting of . . . Flannels Naps Frizes Halfthicks. — (2) **1845** Hooper *Taking Census* 155 This information brought our nap right up. **1849** Nason *Journal* 112 The bootblack, having got his nap up, came round very cautiously.

∗**nap,** *n.*[2] As the last term in **cat, dog nap.**

Napa ˈnæpə, *n.* [See note.]

"A name of doubtful Indian origin, now used to designate a county, a town, a river, and a creek in California. So far as can be learned it was not used as a village name by either the Wintun or the Yukian Wappo, the territories of both of which peoples embrace parts of Napa co. . . . Powers . . . lists it as a Patwin tribe" (Hodge).

Leather prepared from the skins of sheep or goats by a special tanning process. In full **Napa leather.** Also **Napa tannage.**

1897 C. T. Davis *Manuf. Leather* (ed. 2) 275 The staking machine . . . can be adjusted to any kind of leather, including napa. **1903** Flemming *Pract. Tanning* 49 The making of Napa leather. The cheapest tannage by which sheepskins are tanned is the Napa tannage, so called because it originated in Napa, Cal. **1928** *Daily Sk.* 7 Aug. 14/2 We can buy washable Nappa, suède, kid, and antelope.

∗**nap-at-noon,** *n.* (See quots.) — **1894** *Amer. Folk-Lore* VII. 92 *Tragopogon porrifolius* . . . nap-at-noon, Hennepin, Ill. **1931** Clute *Plants* 136 A cousin of this plant [goat's beard], the vegetable oyster (*Tragopogon porrifolius*) has the same habit and in consequence is often called nap-at-noon.

∗**napoleon,** *n.*

1. (*cap.*) A brass field gun adopted in France about 1856, under Napoleon III. In full **Napoleon gun.** *Obs.*

1862 in Moore *Rebellion Rec.* V. II. 405 [I propose] that the . . . smooth-bores . . . be exclusively the twelve-pound gun of the model of 1857, variously called 'the gun-howitzer,' the 'light twelve-pounder,' or the 'Napoleon.' **1897** *Outing* XXX. 80/1 These gun companies were each supplied with one 12-pounder Napoleon gun and one Gatling gun (new), and the men were armed with sabers. **1944** Pennell *Rome Hanks* 67 He saw the Massachusetts battery of Napoleons unlimbering.

2. (See quot. 1909.)

1909 Farmer *Boston Cook Book* 477 Napoleons. Bake three sheets of pastry. . . . Put between the sheets Cream Filling; spread top with Confectioner's Frosting, sprinkle with pistachio nuts. **1917** *Lit. Digest* 29 Dec. 102/2 Bring me an apple turnover, some rice pudding, a napoleon, and two cups of coffee.

As the last term in **Young Napoleon.**

nappe næp, *n.* [F. *nappe* d'eau, in same sense.] (See quots.) — **1906** Horton *Weir Experiments* (*U.S. Geol. Surv., Water-supp.* No. 150) 7 The French term 'nappe' suggesting the curved surface of a cloth hanging over the edge of a table, has been fittingly used to designate the overfalling sheet of water. **1923** F. C. Lea *Hydraulics* 81 The sheet of water flowing over a weir or through a notch is generally called the vein, sheet, or nappe.

Narraganset ˌnærəˈgænsɪt, *n.* Also **Narragansett.** [Algonquian *naiagans*, dim. of *naiag*, small point of land, +-*et*, locative ending, "people of the small point."]

1. An Indian of an Algonquian tribe formerly prominent in New England, esp. Rhode Island; often, *pl.*, the tribe of such an Indian. Also attrib.

1622 Mourt *Relation* 105 They told us that if they were Narrohiganset men they would not trust them. **1637** Morton *New Canaan* I. 163 The cause why these other Salvages of the Narohigansets came into these parts, was to see what strength we were of. **1682** M. Rawlinson *Narr. Captivity* 11, I was sold to him by another Narrhaganset Indian. **1809** Irving *Knickerb.* v. iv, He has been secretly endeavoring to instigate the Narrohigansett (o · Narraganset) . . . Indians. **1945** Webster *Town Meeting Country* 11 The principal Indian tribes were the Narragansetts on the west shores of Narragansett Bay and the Pequots in the lands around the Thames River.

2. A small, hardy horse, formerly used chiefly as a saddle horse, of a breed developed in Rhode Island in the region of Narragansett Bay. In the pl., the breed of such a horse. Also attrib.

1826 Cooper *Mohicans* ii, A breed of horses . . . were once well known in America by the names of the Narragansets. They were small, commonly of the color called sorrel in America. **1845** Judd *Margaret* III. 398 Nimrod . . . made us a purchase of some beautiful Narragansetts with draught and carriage horses. **1937** Langdon *Everyday Things* 288 The Narragansett horses were pacers, that came originally from Andalusia in Spain. **1943** Forbes *J. Tremain* 92, I never saw a horse his color before . . . Narragansett breed.

b. Narraganset pacer, a pacer of Narraganset breed. Also **Narraganset pacing mare.**

1777 J. Adams *Familiar Letters* 272 Narraganset pacing mares. **1809** Irving *Knickerb.* II. 57 They mounted their Narraganset pacers, and traversed back to the grand council. **1886** *Harper's Mag.* July 166/2 Colonial aristocracy . . . [were] perhaps best known for their breed of Narragansett pacers.

c. *transf.* A hog of an inferior breed. *Obs.*

1852 *Mich. Agric. Soc. Trans.* III. 332 Swine variously known as narragansetts, alligators, land sharks and flea breeders.

***narrow,** *a.* and *n.*

1. *n.* The narrowest part of a neck of land or of an island.

1668 in *Amer. Sp.* XV. 288/1 To an oake marked on three sides standing in the narrow of yt neck. **1747** STITH *Hist. Va.* 122 Sir Thomas Dale . . . pitched upon a Place for his new Town, on the Narrow of Farrar's Island, in Varina Neck.

2. A narrow pass or way between mountains. Usu. *pl.* Cf. ***notch.**

1779 in *R.I. Hist. Tracts* VII. 85 We soon entered another defile or narrows three-quarters of a mile in length . . . mountains on the east. **1808** PIKE *Sources Miss.* 175 We followed [the creek] through narrows in the mountains for about six miles.

3. *a.* In the names of plants and trees (see quots.).

1784 CUTLER in *Mem. Acad.* I. 436 *Rumex floribus hermaphroditis: valvulis dentatis nudis, pedicellis planis reflexis*. . . . Narrow Dock. . . . The fresh roots bruised and made into an ointment, or decoction, cure the itch. **1785** MARSHALL *Amer. Grove* 124 *Quercus phellos angustifolia*, Narrow willow-leaved oak. **1801** MICHAUX *Histoire des Chênes* 6 *Quercus prinus* (*acuminata*), Chêne chataignier (des Illinois). Narrow Live Chesnot Oak. **1897** SUDWORTH *Arborescent Flora* 25 *Pinus attenuata*. Lemmon. Knobcone Pine. . . . [Also called] Narrow-cone Pine (Cal. lit.).

4. In special combs.: (1) **narrow ax,** an ordinary ax primarily for chopping, as distinguished from a broadax for hewing, *obs.;* (2) **gauge,** see as a main entry; (3) **track,** standard-gauge railroad track, in contrast to extra broad gauge, *obs.*, cf. **narrow gauge.**

(1) **1641** *Conn. Rec.* I. 444 A broad axe, 2 narrow axes, wimbell & chessells. **1755** *Lett. to Washington* I. 136 Broadaxes are wanted, narrow axes I have been obligd to order some to be made. **1854** THOREAU *Walden* 46, I went on for some days cutting and hewing timber, and also studs and rafters, all with my narrow axe. — (3) **1846** *Hunt's Merch. Mag.* XIV. 37 An oscillating motion from side to side [is] common on the narrow track.

***narrow gauge.** In ellipt. use, a narrow-gauge railroad or train.

The early British *narrow gauge* of 4 ft. 8½ in. (as opposed to their early *broad gauge* of greater width) became the standard gauge of Great Britain. Contrariwise, the American *broad gauge* of 4 ft. 8½ in. (so called since the Civil War in contradistinction to the *narrow gauge* of lesser width) has become the standard gauge. In the early history of American railroading, *broad gauge* was also applied to gauges wider than the standard gauge.

1872 TICE *Over Plains* 24 Amongst those under contract and in a state of progress, the most important is a narrow gauge to Denver, thence to Santa Fe. **1909** O. HENRY *Roads of Destiny* 205 Watch our front window after the narrow-gauge gets in. **1946** *Trail & Timberline* May 67/1 The narrow gauge crossed the Continental Divide three times between Denver and Gunnison.

b. *fig.* Small-minded, insignificant, provincial, limited in view or vision. *Colloq.* Cf. ***broad-gauge.**

1872 *Harper's Mag.* March 637/2 This infamous proposition was combated by a narrow-gauge member from the 'outsquirts' of the Territory. **1902** WISTER *Virginian* xii, That young come-outer, and his fam'ly that can't understand him—for he is broad gauge, yu' see, and they are narro' gauge. **1906** BELL *C. Lee* 249 His ideas were on too narrow-gauge a plan to admit the suggestion now.

c. Designating members of the Prohibition party in 1896 who favored restricting the platform to the liquor issue, with no free-silver plank.

1896 *Chi. Times-Herald* 27 May 5/1 The narrow-gauge men won a big victory over the silver people at to-night's meeting of the national committee. **1896** *Prohibition Party Campaign Text-Book* 21 Governor St. John . . . wanted to see the platform as narrow as the narrow gauge men wanted it.

Hence **narrow gaugers.**

1896 *Chi. Times-Herald* 27 May 5/1 Judging from the talk of Chairman Dickie the narrow gaugers will hedge on money. **1944** BURDICK *Farmers' Political Action in N. Dakota* 125 This faction was called the 'Narrow Gaugers.'

d. narrow-gauge(d) mule, a jack rabbit. *Humorous.*

1930 HENRY *Conquer. Plains* 294 Thus Quibbs informed himself on the Plains as to its famous narrow-gauged mules, of which he had heard so much.

nary red (cent). Not a cent. *Slang.*

1849 *N.O. Picayune* 6 May 2/6 I'm goin' teu get my breakfuss yere, and not pay 'nary red' till I deu! **1856** DERBY *Phoenixiana* 125 Playin at billiards and monte Till they've nary red cent to ante. **1876** *Wide Awake* 236/2 These young folks . . . talk about the 'cops,' and 'plug-uglies,' say 'nary red,' and 'going on the straight,' like the low roughs.

nasaump nəˈsɔmp, *n.* [See note.] =**samp.**

It has been suggested that this Narraganset Indian term may have been borrowed by the Indians from French (*à*) *la soupe*. See *Language* XXI. (1945), 40–45.

1643 WILLIAMS *Key* (1866) 40 Nasàump, a kind of meale pottage, unpartch'd. From this the English call their Samp, which is the Indian corne, beaten and boild, and eaten hot or cold with milke or butter. **1764** HUTCHINSON *Hist. Mass.* I. 465 *n.* The Indian corn boiled, after being a little broken, they called Nasaump. The English call it Samp. **1832** DURFEE *Whatcheer* 23 Waban's nausamp and venison shall be free, . . . when his store shall fail.

Nashville ˈnæʃvɪl, *n.* [Capital of Tennessee, named for Gen. Francis *Nash*, a Revolutionary War hero.] **1.** =next. **2. Nashville warbler,** a yellow-breasted, olive-green warbler, *Vermivora ruficapilla*, common in eastern North America.

(1) **1896** *Atlantic Mo.* Feb. 202/1 The absence of the Nashville was a matter of wonderment to me. — (2) **1811** WILSON *Ornithology* III. 120 [The] Nashville warbler, *Sylvia Ruficapilla*, . . . [was] shot in the state of Tennesee, not far from Nashville. **1917** *Birds of Amer.* III. 120 The Nashville Warbler was discovered by Alexander Wilson at Nashville, Tennessee, and . . . has ever since borne the name Nashville Warbler. **1944** *Mass. Audubon Soc. Bul.* Dec. 261, I got 'kicks' out of seeing the following—all in Northampton: . . . October 24, Phoebe, Blue-headed Vireo, Nashville Warbler (latest ever).

***nasty,** *a.* Superior, first-class, excellent. *Slang.* — **1834** *Knickerb.* III. 37 *'Sling a nasty foot,'* means to dance exceedingly well. *Ib.*, *'She is a nasty looking gal,'* implies she is a splendid woman. **1912** MATHEWSON *Pitching* 68 Hoblitzell is a nasty hitter.

Natchez ˈnætʃɪz, *n.* [Orig. the Indian name (of unknown significance) of a town near the present city of Natchez, Mississippi.] A tribe of Indians formerly living on and near St. Catherine's Creek, in Mississippi. Also attrib.

1775 ADAIR *Indians* 86 In the year 1747, a Nachee warrior told me, that while one of their prophets was using his divine invocation for rain . . . he was killed with thunder on the spot. **1845** *Cherokee Advocate* (Tahlequah, Okla.) 24 April 4/3 The tradition has been widely recorded, that the dominion of the Natchez once extended even to the Wabash. **1895** G. KING *New Orleans* 75 The revolt of the Natchez Indians . . . threw the colony into the hitherto unexperienced troubles of an Indian war. **1938** *Southwestern Lore* June 13 The laws of the Natchez pemitted more than one wife, although they seldom had more than one or two.

b. Natchez Trace, a once popular thoroughfare from New Orleans to Natchez and on to Nashville, a total distance of about seven hundred miles.

1899 H. B. CUSHMAN *Hist. Indians* 478 This road was long known, and no doubt remembered by many at the present time by the name of 'Natchez Trace.' **1949** *Nat. Geog. Mag.* Feb. 181/2 Original builders of the Natchez Trace were buffaloes. . . . Several of these trails, when joined together by the Indians, led southwesterly from Nashville to the Mississippi.

***nation,** *n.*

1. A tribe of American Indians. See also **Five Nations, Six Nations.**

1650 *Md. Council Proc.* 260 The Ports adjoyning are very much pestered with great Concourse of Indians of several nations. **1722** COXE *Descr. Carolana* 49 Near the Bottom of the Bay . . . is the fair River of the Miamihas (so call'd because upon it lives Part of a Nation bearing the same Name). **1859** PUTNAM *Hist. Middle Tenn.* 583 These lines were run and completed . . . much to the satisfaction of the Indians of both nations. **1946** FOREMAN *Last Trek* 109 Here they were joined in a few days by the main body of the nation from Chicago.

b. (*cap.*) A particular region occupied by Indians, often with reference to the Indian Territory.

1725 in *Travels Amer. Col.* 98 The said Sharp . . . went to one of the Towns in the said [Cherokee] Nation. **1873** BEADLE *Undevel. West* 355 My first Sabbath in the 'Nation' [i.e., the Indian Territory] was bright and clear. **1923** J. H. COOK *On Old Frontier* 6 We saw plenty of Indians all the way through the Indian Territory, or 'Nation,' as it was called, but we had no trouble with them. **1949** *Sat. Ev. Post* 19 March 155/1 We were going down into the Nation, where the Indians were who traded for cur coon dogs.

attrib. **1884** *N.Y. Wkly. Tribune* 10 Oct. 5/4 Like an oasis in a desert, so Rob's fruit farm looked to me when I first saw it one noon day in summer, near the 'Nation' line.

2. The United States or its inhabitants.

c1792 in SEILHAMER *Amer. Theatre* III. (1888) 11 Too many Madisons in them [the Virginia towns] are found, Instead of fun, who study now the nation, And talk of politics and reformation. **1847** LOWELL *Biglow P.* 1 Ser. iv. 50 We're the original friends o' the nation, All the rest air a paltry an' base fabrication. **1948** *Chi. D. News* 20 Feb. 1/3 The speech was broadcast to the nation.

As the last term in **all, Cat, Catawba, Cherokee, Choctaw, Creek, Dakota, Indian, Mohawk, Nez Percé, Osage, palmetto, Sac, Seminole, Seneca, Small, Snake, tick, tobacco, Yankee nation.**

* **national,** *n.* Usu. *cap.*

1. *pl.* **a.** Members of the Hard-Shell faction of the Democratic party, so called because sectional differences were minimized by the faction. *Obs.* (Cf. * **Hard-Shell, 2.**) **b.** Members of the Greenback party *q.v.*

(a) **1844** J. C. CALHOUN in *Ann. Rep. Amer. Hist. Assoc.* (1899) II. 636 It was by the combined influence of N. York democrats and the Nationals or Whigs, that the oppressive Tariffs of 1828 and 1842 were imposed on us. **1857** *Lawrence* (Kans.) *Republican* 9 July 3 In some of the townships, too, there is a 'fair sprinkling' of 'nationals.' — (b) **1878** *Nation* 10 Oct. 221/1 Throughout the West this class [farmers] forms the largest portion of the Nationals. **1878** *Atlantic Mo.* Nov. 521 (*title*), The Nationals, Their Origin and Their Aims.

2. A soldier of the Union Army during the Civil War. *Obs.* Cf. * **national,** *a.* **6.**

1863 in MOORE *Rebellion Rec.* V. I. 38 A company of guerrillas . . . were captured by a body of Nationals belonging to Col. Boone's regiment.

* **national,** *a.*

1. Pertaining or belonging to a nation of Indians. *Obs.*

1754 *Mass. H.S. Coll.* 3 Ser. V. 31 [We] recommend to and expect it from you, for your own safety, to collect yourselves together, and dwell in your national castles. **1822** in MORSE *Rep. Indian Affairs* II. 169 The Cherokee Nation is governed by the acts of one National Council, held once a year by a national Committee, and members of Council. **1866** *Rep. Indian Affairs* 248 A national jail shall be built on the public grounds, upon which the councilhouse is now situated.

2. In the debate over the Constitution: Constituting a government which would eliminate the power of the separate states. *Obs.*

1788 MADISON *Federalist* xxxix, The Senate . . . will derive its powers from the States, as political and coequal societies; and these will be represented on the principle of equality in the Senate. . . . So far the government is *federal*, not *national*. **1824** in *Cong. Deb.* 25 Jan. (1830) 49/1 When the American colonies redeemed themselves from British bondage, and became so many independent nations, they proposed to form a national union. **1847** CALHOUN *Works* IV. 354 It is owing mainly to the States of Connecticut and New Jersey, that we have a federal instead of a national government.

3. Founded by or conducted under the auspices of the federal government.

1794 *Ann. 3d Congress* 1428 There shall be established, at each of the aforesaid arsenals, a national armory. **1840** *Niles' Reg.* 7 March 11/1 [A memorial from Mr. Henderson] asking for the establishment of a national hospital at Vicksburg. **1910** BOSTWICK *Amer. Pub. Library* 29 Dr. Putnam . . . has endeavored to make the institution [Library of Congress] in fact what it should be in name—the National Library.

4. Of persons: Concerned with the interests of the U.S. as a whole rather than those of a party, faction, or region.

1801 J. ADAMS *Works* IX. 585 Mr. Jefferson's administration . . . is too strongly infected with the spirit of party, to give much encouragement to men who are merely national. **1859** in W. LAWRENCE *A. A. Lawrence* 136, I am the son of Amos Lawrence, . . . who brought me up to be a 'national' man, as we understand that term.

5. In the names of political parties and factions (see quots.). Cf. **National Democratic Party, National Republican.**

1855 in HAMBLETON *H. A. Wise* 303 [The Know-Nothing party] professes now to be the only true National Conservative Union party. **1856** *Western Citizen* (Paris, Ky.) 22 Feb. 1/1 They were afraid that the National Americans [=Know Nothings], preferring a Democrat to a Black Republican for the Speakership, might secure the election of the Democratic candidate. **1876** *N.Y. Tribune* 18 May 1/1 Two National and five State Conventions were held yesterday, namely: Those of the National Greenback and Prohibition parties [etc.]. **1878** *Nation* 10 Oct. 221/1 The National party is a home product; it gathers up and mingles with itself many elements, but essentially it springs from our own economic difficulties. **1882** COOPER *Amer. Pol.* I. 196 The attempt to establish a third party in the Greenback, begot that to establish a National Prohibitory Party, which in 1880 ran James Black of Pennsylvania, as a candidate for the Presidency, and four years previous ran Neal Dow of Maine. **1884** *Boston Jrnl.* Aug., Seven regularly nominated tickets in the field . . . are the Democratic, Republican, . . . National Christian, Anti-Monopoly [etc.]. **1896** *Chi. Times-Herald* 25 July 3/4 Dr. Frank Powell, Mayor of La Crosse, Wis., rejoices in the distinction of having christened the new national bimetallic party. Several names were proposed at the meeting of silverites, and, after long debate, the name given above . . . was adopted. **1896** *National Silver Platform* in K. PORTER *National Party Platforms* 193 We, the national silver party, . . . hereby adopt the following declaration of principles. **1944** BURDICK *Farmers' Political Action N. Dakota* 129 The National Prohibition Party held its convention in Chicago on June 27 and 28.

6. During or with reference to the Civil War: Belonging to the Union. *Obs.*

1863 in MOORE *Rebellion Rec.* V. I. 52 One hundred and twenty-five rebels attacked seventy-five National troops at Ozark, Mo. **1893** *Nation* LVI. 85/2 The differences between National and Confederate writers have greatly diminished with the progress of time.

7. In special combs.: (1) **National Agreement,** the code of terms under which the major and the minor baseball leagues were organized on their present basis; (2) **bank,** see as a main entry; (3) **Banking Law,** the law enacted by Congress in 1863, under which the present banking system operates; (4) **banking system,** the framework of national banks under the National Banking Law; (5) **bird,** (*a*) the bald eagle, regarded as an American patriotic symbol, (*b*) *transf.* the turkey, because of its popularity for Thanksgiving and Christmas dinners; (6) **cemetery,** a cemetery created by Act of Congress chiefly for members of the military or naval forces of the U.S.; (7) **chairman,** the chairman of a national (party) committee; (8) **committee,** the "permanent committee" at the head of a national party chosen at each national convention for a period of four years; (9) **committeeman,** a member of the national committee of a political party; (10) * **convention,** a convention held by the delegates of a political party (now representing the states, territories, and possessions of the U.S.) to nominate candidates for President and Vice-President and to formulate party policy, cf. **Republican National Convention;** (11) **council,** see as a main entry; (12) **Dame,** a member of the National Society of the Colonial Dames of America; (13) **Day,** =**Independence Day;** (14) **Democratic party,** see as a main entry; (15) **forest,** =**forest reserve** (*a*), also attrib.; (16) **highway,** (*a*) a highway built by, or with the assistance of, the federal government, (*b*) a railroad, *rare;* (17) **League,** one of the two major leagues in American baseball, cf. **big league;** (18) **Leaguer,** a member or supporter of the National League; (19) **legislature,** Congress, cf. * **legislature,** *n.* **2;** (20) **monument,** a natural feature, as a mountain, canyon, etc., reserved by the federal government as public property; (21) **park,** see as a main entry; (22) **pike,** =**Cumberland road,** cf. **National Road 2, national turnpike;** (23) **platform,** a statement or a series of resolutions agreed upon by party delegates at a national convention as embodying the political principles for which the party stands; (24) **Republican Convention,** see as a main entry; (25) **Road,** see as a main entry; (26) **turnpike,** =**Cumberland road;** (27) **university,** a university projected, but never established, at Washington, D.C.; (28) **Youth Administration,** a government organization, orig. a part of the Works Progress Administration, established June 26, 1935, to aid persons between sixteen and twenty-five in obtaining work and to improve the educational, recreational and vocational opportunities of young people, usu. referred to as NYA.

(1) **1889** *Sporting Life* (Phila.) 29 May 2/5 The California League has made applicacion [*sic*] to enter the National Agreement. **1949** *Chi. Sun-Times* 10 Feb. 60/5 The suit . . . asked the court to declare the National Agreement, under which the game operated, illegal. — (3) **1883** *Cent. Mag.* July 398/1 A man's opinions on the protective tariff, or the national banking law, . . . were no test of his fitness to collect taxes. **1916** W. A. DU PUY *Uncle Sam* 141 The Department of

Justice is the prosecutor in cases of violations of the national banking law. — **(4) 1874** *Int. Review* March 217 The National Banking System has been an eminent success. **1900** *Cong. Rec.* 10 Jan. 736/1 The national banking system . . . should be abolished.

(5) (*a*) **1859** *Harper's Mag.* May 860/2 Those of you who know the habits of the national bird know full well that he never feeds upon carrion! **1894** ALDRICH *Two Bites* 63 The starry shield, supported by two crossed cannon cut out of tin and surmounted by the national bird in the same material . . . hung proudly over the transom. (*b*) **1904** *N.Y. Times* 25 Nov. 12 It may be that turkey was expensive this year, but if this was the fact there was no dearth of the National bird at the many feasts prepared. — **(6) 1866** *Statutes at Large* XIV. 310 To establish national cemeteries, and to purchase sites for the same . . . fifty thousand dollars [is appropriated]. **1949** *Southtown Economist* (Chi.) 25 Sep. 6/4 Dr. Donat F. Monaco . . . was buried September 15 in the national cemetery in Santa Fe. — **(7) 1904** *Forum* April 483 As national chairman he [Mark Hanna] conducted the campaign which carried McKinley to the White House. — **(8) 1848** *General Taylor's Two Faces* (Dem. Nat. Comm. 1848–52) 1 Published under authority of the National and Jackson Democratic Association Committee. **1914** *Cyclo. Amer. Govt.* I. 362 With the opening of the convention, the national committee is dissolved to give place to this supreme organ of the party by which is appointed a new national committee. — **(9) 1856** *Democratic Conv. Proc.* 72 It is intended to send the question of the selection of a National Committeeman to the next State Convention to be held in New York. **1949** *Dly. Ardmoreite* (Ardmore, Okla.) 8 Sep. 6/6 During the night, flunkies had typewritten the names of the national committeemen and committeewomen on slips of paper.

(10) 1834 *Indiana Democrat* 4 Jan., The Hoosier State like true democrats have taken the lead in appointing delegates to a National Convention. **1948** *Sat. Ev. Post* 10 July 19/1 The American constitution makes no provision for national conventions. — **(12) 1899** *N.Y. Jrnl.* 27 June 3/6 'You are a "National Dame," are you not?' asked Colonel Bartlett. — **(13) 1918** G. STUART *On Frontier* I. 248 We celebrated the national day by having a fine dinner with trout as the principal dish.

(15) 1905 *Forestry Bureau Bul.* 61. **1949** *L.A. Times* 4 June 4/5 The extra fire hazard . . . led to the U.S. Forest Service clamping the lid on all restricted National Forest areas in this region. — **(16)** (*a*) **1816** *Ann. 14th Congress* 2 Sess. 28 That the Secretary of this Department shall execute the orders of the President in relation to . . . The National Highways. **1900** *Cong. Rec.* 10 Jan. 736/1 The national highways should be open to the use of all on equal terms. (*b*) **1865** *Nation* I. 616/1 The National Highways. . . . The safety of travellers ought not to be trusted to the railroad companies. — **(17) 1877** (*title*), Constitution & By-laws National League. [**1943** *World Almanac* 680 The National League made its score in the eighth inning when Mickey Owen hit a home run off Alton Benton.] — **(18) 1944** *Chi. D News* 4 Oct. 29/2 'I was a Brown rooter all year,' said Gus, 'but I'm a National Leaguer.' **1949** *Sat. Ev. Post* 22 Oct. 112/1 'Big John' has well over 300 home runs to his credit—more than any other National Leaguer. — **(19) 1787** RANDOLPH in Elliot *Deb. Constitution* (1836) I. 144 Resolved, That a national executive be instituted, to be chosen by the national legislature. **1878** *Atlantic Mo.* Nov. 524/2 All classes should be represented in our national legislature in proportion to their numbers.

(20) 1909 *Nat. Geog. Mag.* Sep. 837/1 The principal value of the land as a national monument lies in the fact that the fantastic forms resulting from the rapid erosion of rock and soil make the spot one of exceptional beauty. **1938** THOMPSON *High Trails* 21 Generally a national monument is an object of historical or scientific interest worthy of national preservation, usually smaller in size, or scenery of national interest which still is not the supreme example of its type, or is not quite up to national park standards. — **(22) 1922** *World's Work* Dec. 215/1 The road is what was the old national pike, built nearly a century ago for ox-carts and Conestoga wagons. — **(23) 1856** *Democratic Conv. Proc.* 25 The Democratic party of the Union, standing on this national platform, will abide by . . . the Compromise measures. **1900** *Cong. Rec.* 10 Jan. 736/1 Both great political parties are no doubt getting ready in their next national platform to denounce the evil. *Ib.* 17 Jan. 904/2 It was a declaration in the national platform of the lack of power on our part to control our own affairs.

(26) 1817 *Ann. 14th Congress* 2 Sess. 465 To this we owed the benefits . . . of the great national turnpike leading from Fort Cumberland to Wheeling. **1822** WOODS *English Prairie* 52 From the north branch of the Potomac river, we passed a very hilly country, to a new road, called the National Turnpike. — **(27) 1790** in *W. & M. Coll. Quart.* 1 Ser. IX. 133, I observe that ye President . . . suggests ye good Policy of instituting a national University. **1816** *Niles' Reg.* X. 18/1 A bill for the establishment of a National University . . . is reported by the select committee of the house of Representatives. **1895** *N. Amer. Review* Feb. 210 A national university at Washington seems to be one of the most pressing of our public needs. — **(28) 1941** FERGUSSON *Southwest* 68 In 1939 the records of the National Youth Administration list fifty-three per cent of the state's population as 'Spanish-American.' **1943** MENEFEE *Assignment* 279 The National Youth Administration was likewise killed, although it was devoted entirely to giving vocational training to youth about to take jobs in war industry.

b. In combs. of obvious meaning or sufficiently explained in the quots.: (1) **national anniversary,** (2) **Colonization Society,** (3) **Covenant,** (4) **flag,** (5) **forest preserve,** (6) **game,** see as a main entry, (7) **government,** (8) **Grange,** cf. ***Grange,** (9) **Guard,** see as a main entry, (10) **holiday,** (11) **representative,** (12) **treasury.**

(1) 1840 *Niles' Reg.* 11 July 290/2 The national anniversary. The fourth of July just passed has been observed throughout the country as a general holiday. **1884** BLAINE *20 Years of Congress* I. 437 Two great states held their conventions [in 1862] on the National Anniversary. — **(2) 1893** JAMESON *Dict. U.S. Hist.* (1931) 106 *Colonization Society, The National.* An organization formed in 1816 at Princeton, N.J., its principal object being to encourage the emancipation of slaves by obtaining for them a place without the United States to which they might emigrate. — **(3) 1864** *Rio Abajo Press* 14 June 1/2 The American women are organizing a society, under the style of the *National Covenant*. . . . They are pledging themselves, for three years or during the war, not to purchase any foreign article when an American one can be substituted. — **(4) 1841** in *Pres. Mess. & P.* IV. 25 The national flag will be displayed. **1890** LANGFORD *Vigilante Days* (1912) 94 He procured a National flag, hired a drummer and fifer, and followed them.

(5) 1883 *Nation* 6 Sep. 201/1 A National Forest Preserve. The importance of forest preservation as a national measure has been widely discussed in the public press. **1905** *Forestry Bureau Bul.* No. 61, National Forest Preserve. A tract of land set apart from the public domain by proclamation of the President.—**(7) 1787** MADISON in *Sp. & Doc. Amer. Hist.* (1944) I. 61 He did not see the danger of the States being devoured by the National Govt. **1883** *Harper's Mag.* Nov. 936/1 Within the U.S. are four great [R.R.] routes all subsidized by the national government with grants of land, money, or both. — **(8) 1868** in COMMONS *Doc. Hist.* X. 79 The State Granges are in unity with the National Grange. **1946** HOLBROOK *Lost Men* 215 In 1867, along with Saunders and five others, Kelley organized the National Grange of the Patrons of Husbandry.

(10) 1866 MOORE *Women of War* 492 On the recurrence of the national holidays, as Thanksgiving and Independence, she was specially active in securing provisions. **1943** *World Almanac* 259 There are no 'National' holidays in the United States. Each State has jurisdiction over the holidays to be observed. These are designated either by legislative enactment or executive proclamation. The only National holiday ever proclaimed by Congress was when they ordered (April 30, 1869) that the one hundredth anniversary of the Constitution be observed as a National holiday. — **(11) 1811** *Agric. Museum* I. 244 The meeting of the national representatives in the fall of the year, affords an opportunity of receiving . . . whatever is rare or useful in our own extensive territory. — **(12) 1854** PIERCE in *Pres. Mess. & P.* V. 261 Applications for appropriations would have perverted the legislation of Congress, [and] exhausted the National Treasury. **1884** BLAINE *20 Years of Congress* I. 269 The seventh [section of an 1861 amendment] provided for the payment from the National Treasury for all fugitive slaves whose recapture is prevented by violence.

national bank.

1. In discussions and debate over the advisability of establishing a bank instituted by the federal government: A bank similar to the banks of sense **2.** below.

1790 MACLAY *Deb. Senate* 270 Yesterday, the Secretary's report on the subject of a national bank was handed to us, and I can readily find that a bank will be the consequence. **1841** TYLER in *Pres. Mess. & P.* IV. 63 The power of Congress to create a national bank to operate *per se* over the Union has been a question of dispute from the origin of the Government. **1856** *Democratic Conv. Proc.* 24 The Democratic party [declares]. . . . That Congress has no power to charter a national bank. **1856** *Western Citizen* (Paris, Ky.) 8 Feb. 2/1 The party . . . proposed to put down a National Bank, and did it.

2. The first bank of the U.S., chartered by Congress in 1791 for a period of twenty years. *Obs.*

1797 *Monthly Mag.* III. 199 Besides the said four funded stocks, a national bank is established at Philadephia. **1799** WELD *Travels* 41 As soon also as the seat of government is fixed there [in Washington, D.C.], the national bank . . . will be established at the same time.

b. The second bank of the U.S., chartered by Congress in 1816 and expiring by the limitation of its charter in 1836. *Obs.*

1837 JACKSON in *Pres. Mess. & P.* III. 301 The establishment of a national bank by Congress, with the privilege of issuing paper money receivable in the payment of the public dues, . . . drove from general circulation the constitutional currency and substituted one of paper in its place. **1842** *Whig Almanac 1843* 31/2 The National Bank had now been destroyed.

Hence **National Bankism.** *Obs.*

1842 *Gatherer & W. News-Scroll* (Cleveland, O.) 21 Jan. 3/2 Our friend Fairchild made a Waterloo charge along the entire ranks of ultraism, National Bankism, &c. &c.

3. Any of numerous commercial banks chartered under the federal government in accordance with the banking acts of 1863–64, empowered to receive, lend, and transmit money, and to issue currency notes; a building that houses such a bank.

1864 *Wkly. New Mexican* 3 June 1/4 The house ways and means committee will report a bill having adopted the amendment permitting states to tax the national banks. **1880** *Harper's Mag.* July 192/2 Instead of . . . long lines of canvas-topped wagons I saw . . . churches, and national banks. **1914** *Polit. Sci. Quart.* June 268 Membership [in the Federal Reserve system] is voluntary, and is open to state banks and trust companies as well as to national banks.

b. Attrib. with **circulation, examiner, note.**

1864 *N. Mex. Press* 2 Aug. 1/1 We have seen several National Bank notes of the denomination of ten dollars. **1882** *Nation* 23 Nov. 436/2 Before the end of 1883 the Government will . . . have paid off . . . some $30,000,000 held by the Treasury as security for national-bank circulation. **1932** GRAYSON *Leaders* 218 There was no system of supervision such as exists today, no controller of the currency, no national bank examiners. **1949** *Boston Globe* 26 June (Fiction Mag.) 2/1 The National bank examiner condemned this loan and declared the collateral worthless.

National Council. A congress of representatives of an Indian nation.

1792 PUTNAM in *Memoirs* 292 The War Club . . . belongs to the Charokees, a Ba[n]ditte of out Casts . . . not admited into the National Councils. **1820** in MORSE *Rep. Indian Affairs* (1822) II. 161 It is out of our power to see you, in any short time, on account of the National Council. **1942** DALE *Cow Country* 201 Upon Bushyhead's return to the Cherokee Nation he . . . called the Cherokee National Council to meet in special session.

National Democratic Party. (See quot. 1914.)

1896 (*title*), Proceedings of the Convention of the National Democratic Party, held at Indianapolis, Indiana, September 2 and 3, 1896. **1914** *Cyclo. Amer. Govt.* II. 85/1 The free silver element got control of the Democratic national convention at Chicago [in 1896], and nominated William J. Bryan on a free coinage platform. In September a conventon of gold Democrats . . . met at Indianapolis, took the name of National Democratic Party, and nominated John M. Palmer of Illinois and Simon B. Buckner of Kentucky for President and Vice-President. . . . With the passage of the gold standard act of March 14, 1900, the activity of the gold Democrats terminated. **1949** *So. Wkly.* 5 Oct. 3/2 In supporting the national Democratic Party, as at present constituted, they are giving aid and comfort to the enemies of the people of the South.

national game. (Also *cap.*) Baseball, esp. the game that evolved from the New York game *q.v.* played in accordance with rules adopted by the National Association of Base Ball Players.

1856 *Spirit of Times* 8 Nov. 165/2 Oh long may it flourish, our *National Game*—Here's a health, good old base ball to thee. **1867** *Ball Player's Chron.* 6 June 1/1 The game, as played in New York, . . . now began to attract general attention, and it was not long afterwards before the Massachusetts game became obsolete, and now we believe every such club has disbanded, or become an advocate of the National game. **1868** *N. Eng. Base-Ballist* 6 Aug. 1/2 By the foregoing it will be seen that it was rather up-hill work for the Pioneers in the National Game in New England to get it firmly established. **1945** *Chi. D. News* 4 Oct. 12/1 They are a credit to the national game and the great city they represent.

b. The game of poker. *Rare.*

1901 *Denver Republican* 26 Aug. 3/4 At the rear of the fan tan hall there is a poker room where celestial friends of the American national game may play both day and night.

National Guard. (See quot. 1918.) Also attrib.

1847 *Santa Fe Republican* 18 Dec. 3/1 Some National Guards that were at San Antonio had a small fight. **1857** *Harper's Mag.* Aug. 402/1 The National Guard, a military company, . . . were drawn up in front of the Hall. **1918** FARROW *Dict. Mil. Terms* 404 *National Guard.*—A body of militia, or a local military organization. In the United States, the regularly commissioned and enlisted militia of the various states, organized, armed and equipped as provided for the corresponding branches of the service in the Regular Army. **1949** *Minot* (N.D.) *D. News* 22 July 1/3 The National guard force of 300 is expected to stay several days longer.

Hence **National Guardsman.**

1916 *Outlook* 2 Aug. 773/2 (*heading*), From A National Guardsman. **1948** *Dly. Ardmoreite* (Ardmore, Okla.) 24 June 1/2 Nationa' guardsmen patrolled streets against looters after the business district was under water.

***Nationalism,** *n.* **1.** (See quot.) *Obs.* **2.** A form of socialism based on national control of all business; the ideal set forth by Edward Bellamy in his sociological novel *Looking Backward* (1888), and made the objective of a movement. *Obs.*

(1) 1846 WORCESTER 476/2 *Nationalism*, a national idiom or phrase. *Hamilton.* — **(2) 1889** *Nationalist* Sep. 180 This noble ship Nationalism will be freighted with the hopes of future millions. **1902** MARK TWAIN *Chr. Sci.* 762 (R.), To whom does Bellamy's 'Nationalism' appeal? Necessarily to the few: people who . . . are compassionate and troubled for the poor and hard-driven.

***Nationalist,** *n.* and *a.* **1.** *n.* An advocate of Nationalism. Also transf. **2.** *a.* Of or pertaining to the theory of Nationalism. Both *obs.*

(1) 1889 (*title*) The Nationalist. **1894** *Atlantic Mo.* Nov. 89 The work of Nationalists has hitherto been chiefly educational. — **(2) 1889** *Nationalist* Sep. 171 The growth of the Nationalist movement is so phenomenal that [etc.]. **1892** *N. Amer. Review* June 746 The first Nationalist club was organized in Boston by readers of 'Looking Backward' in 1888.

national park.

1. An area having exceptional interest or value because of its scenery, history, forests, etc., owned by the federal government and managed in the public interest. Also **national public park.** Cf. **Sequoia National Park.**

In June, 1864, Congress granted the Yosemite Valley to California on condition that the area should "be held for public use, resort, and recreation." This area, later included within Yosemite National Park provided for by Congress in 1890, was the first to which the term *national park* was applied as shown in the first group of examples. See A. Matthews, "The Word Park in the United States," in *Mass. Col. Soc. Pub.* VIII. 373–99.

[**1841** CATLIN *Letters & Notes* I. 262 What a beautiful and thrilling specimen for America to preserve and hold up to the view of her refined citizens and the world, in future ages! A *nation's Park*, containing man and beast, in all the wild and freshness of their nature's beauty!] **1868** J. D. WHITNEY *Yosemite Book* 22 The Yosemite Valley . . . has been made a National public park and placed under the charge of the State of California. **1946** *Chi. D. News* 19 Jan. 8/2 When America hits the vacation trail next summer the crowds in the national parks may be great enough to make even Old Faithful put on an off-schedule gush of amazement.

attrib. **1949** *Mazama* April 1/1 Its trails are among the finest in the national park system.

2. National Military Park, any one of several celebrated battlefields of the Civil War set aside for public commemorative purposes by the federal government.

1890 *Statutes at Large* XXVI. 333 An act to establish a national military park at the battlefield of Chickamauga. **1904** *Mass. Col. Soc. Pub.* VIII. 380 Though these are, in the Acts creating them, called sometimes National Parks and sometimes National Military Parks, the proper title would seem to be National Military Parks. There are four, as follows.

3. National Zoological Park, a tract of rough, picturesque land near Washington, D.C., set aside by Congress for preserving a representative collection of American animals.

1890 *Statutes at Large* XXVI. 78 The National Zoological Park is hereby placed under the directions of the regents of the Smithsonian institution. **1937** *Time* 4 Oct. 54/1 In 1925 William H. Mann, entomologist of the Department of Agriculture, was made director of Washington's National Zoological Park.

National Republican.

1. A member of the political party which in the campaigns of 1828 and 1832 supported John Quincy Adams and Henry Clay respectively for President. Also attrib.

After their defeat in 1832 the National Republicans joined with other elements to form the Whig party.

1828 *Address to Electors of Middlesex Co.* (Conn.), [Signed by] Committee on behalf of the National Republicans of the town of Middletown. **1831** J. Q. ADAMS *Memoirs* VIII. 437 [Henry Clay] was nominated by the National Republican Convention at Baltimore yesterday for the Presidency. **1884** BLAINE *20 Years of Congress* I. 106 The supporters of Adams called themselves National Republicans. **1949** *Social Studies* May 215/1 To the historian this spasm is not new: he has seen it gripping Federalists, National Republicans and Whigs, Southern slaveholding Democrats, and McKinley capitalists.

b. Hence **National Republicanism, National Republican party.**

1831 *American* (Harrodsburg, Ky.) 8 July 1/3 *Resolved*, That with such a candidate as Andrew Jackson, the Democratic Republican party, have nothing to fear from National Republicanism, 'Anti-masonry,' or any other combination. **1833** *Adv. Popular Rights* (Shelbyville, Ky.) 21 Sep. 2/5 His election by so large a majority is a triumph to the National Republican party. **1888** BRYCE *Amer. Commonw.* II. III. liii. 333 The National Republican, ultimately the Whig party, represented many of the views of the former Federalists.

2. *attrib.* Pertaining to the modern Republican party.

1872 (*title*), National Republican Grant and Wilson Campaign Song-Book. **1891** *Boston Journal* 25 Nov. 3/1 A National Republican Convention of delegated representatives of the Republican party will be held at the city of Minneapolis . . . for the purpose of nominating candidates for President and Vice President.

National Road.

1. = **national highway** (*a*).

1817 *Niles' Reg.* XII. 13/2 On the subject of national roads, the first that presents itself, and of primary importance, is a turnpike from Maine to Louisiana. **1858** W. P. SMITH *Railway Celebrations* 6 This Great Railroad is located nearly upon the line formerly traveled by the National Road, running between the Cities of Washington and Baltimore. **1946** *Newsweek* 6 May 9/2 National roads, planned for new Federal 40,000-mile system of interstate highways . . . will carry 20% of all motor traffic.

2. Esp. = **Cumberland road.** Now *hist.*

1822 WOODS *English Prairie* 53 This grand national road is intended to connect all the western country with the seat of government, as there is water communication from Cumberland to the city of Washington. **1831** WITHERS *Chron. Border Warfare* 59 The present National Road from Cumberland to Brownsville via Uniontown, differs in direction but little from Nemacolin's Path. **1948** JORDAN *National Road* 394 At no time in the National Road's long life of more than 140 years has it been busier.

***nations,** *n. pl.* As the last term in **Five, Seven, Six, Six United, United Nations.**

***native,** *a.* and *n.*

1. (*cap.*) A member of the Native American party. *Obs.*

1844 *St. Louis Reveille* 18 May 2/2 They poured in a sharp fire, and the Natives retired from the ground. **1848** *Campaign* (Wash., D.C.) 19 July 119/3 It is no use to deny that Gen. Taylor is not a Native. **1850** *Quincy* (Ill.) *Whig* 23 April 3/1.

2. In spec. combs.: (1) **Native American, Americanism,** see as main entries; (2) **party,** = **Native American party,** *obs.;* (3) **pony,** = **mustang,** also attrib., *obs.;* (4) **son,** a native of a certain place.

(2) **1844** in BOUCHER & BROOKS *Correspondence addressed to Calhoun* (1930) 257 Pause before you oppose the *Native party* though many of them are Whigs. — (3) **1873** ARNY *Items New Mex.* 61 We have . . . the wild native ponies of the country. **1883** *Gringo & Greaser* 1 Sep. 2/3 Races every day. Native pony and burro races. — (4) **1833** *Amer. R.R. Jrnl.* II. 510/2 Col. William Drayton . . . a native son of Carolina . . . left our shores. **1864** *Wkly. New Mexican* 25 Nov. 3 Lieut.-Colonel Chaves . . . is one of New Mexico's favorite native sons. **1949** *Sierra Club Bul.* March 12/2 The old saying that 'nothing is great or small except by comparison' is perhaps appreciated more by those of us who came from elsewhere than by native sons.

b. *To astonish the natives*, and variants, to shock or make a powerful impression on public opinion. *Humorous.*

1807 IRVING *Salmagundi* xii. 298 Unfortunate Straddle! may thy fate be a warning to all young gentlemen who come out from Birmingham to astonish the natives. **1848** *Campaign Flag* (Maysville, Ky.) 2 June 1/1 The vote he will receive in Kentucky will 'astonish the natives.' **1901** RYAN *Montana* 96 Much of her afternoon was spent there under that lady's surveillance, fashioning a party gown with which to astonish the natives. **1932** *K.C. Star* 17 Feb. 24 When you start to paralyze the natives it is just as well not to knock them too cold.

***Native American.**

1. *pl.* The members of the Native American party or the party itself. *Obs.* or *hist.* Cf. **Know-Nothing.**

1844 *Republican Sentinel* (Richmond, Va.) 13 July 3/5 The riot was caused by a branch of the Native Americans—'the very dregs of society, bent upon . . . the annihilation of the Roman Catholics.' **1856** *Western Citizen* (Paris, Ky.) 29 Feb. 3/4 You said you were a Democrat no longer, but were proud to say you were a native American. **1896** HASWELL *New York* 393 It was in this year [1842] that the evanescent political party, styled The Native Americans, came into existence. . . . All were pledged not to vote for any foreigner for office.

2. Native American party, a short-lived political party which arose about 1840, characterized chiefly by opposition to aliens, foreign-born citizens, and Roman Catholics. Now *hist.*

1839 *N.O. Picayune* 25 April 2/1 There is a party in New York called the Native American Party—few in numbers, but indomitable in resolution. **1848** *Campaign* (Wash., D.C.) 21 June 49/3 The Native American party was generally regarded as defunct. **1938** ASBURY *Sucker's Prog.* 363 Besides his interest in a meat stall, Poole owned a saloon, and was the leader of the rougher element of the Native American or Know Nothing Party.

3. *attrib.* or *adj.* Chiefly in the names of organizations formed by those opposed to aliens, foreign-born citizens, and Roman Catholics. *Obs.*

1835 *Niles' Reg.* 7 Nov. 165/1 Meantime the association of native American democrats assembled at the Howard House, and agreed upon the following ticket for *assembly*. **1841** W. KENNEDY *Texas* I. p. xlvi, Societies . . . for excluding foreign settlers in the States from the benefits of naturalization . . . have been organized in New Orleans and elsewhere, under the name of 'Native American Associations.' **1843** MARRYAT *M. Violet* xxxvii, The Yankee philosopher will to-morrow run for a seat in legislature; if he fails, he may turn a Methodist preacher, . . . a member of the 'Native American Society,' or a mason. **1884** BLAINE *20 Years of Congress* I. 205 In 1854 James Pollock was chosen governor by the sudden uprising and astounding development of the Native-American excitement.

4. *S.W.* A Spanish-speaking person born in America as contrasted with one born in Spain. Also attrib. or as adj.

1811 *Amer. Republic* (Frankfort, Ky.) 15 Feb. 3/3 The regular troops at San Antonio had received orders to march immediately to Saltee, in aid of the monarchists—it was expected that they would refuse to march, being mostly native Americans. **1890** *Las Voz del Pueblo* (Las Vegas, N.M.) 18 Oct. 4/1 Joe Lopez for sheriff is the favorite candidate with both the american and native-american elements of the county.

Native Americanism. Hostility towards all but native-born Protestant Americans, esp. as forming one of the basic principles of the Native American party. *Obs.*

1844 *Republican Sentinel* (Richmond, Va.) 20 July 2/3 We have always said that the spirit of 'Native Americanism,' so called, had its support in foreign principles. **1854** in HAMBLETON *H. A. Wise* 55 Native Americanism . . . is no recent thing in this country. It is a hoary and oft punished abomination of the Federal party. **1922** McCORMAC *J. K. Polk* 279 'Native Americanism' was said to have cost the Democrats votes in Pennsylvania.

Nativism ˈnetɪvˌɪzəm, *n.* Also **nativism.** A policy favoring native- as opposed to foreign-born citizens, esp. with reference to political movements. Now *hist.* Cf. **Native American party, political Nativism.**

1848 *Campaign Flag* (Maysville, Ky.) 14 July 1/4 Taylorism in the principal places where it has been supported is simply a resurrection of the rotting remains of Nativism. **1880** *Lib. Universal Knowl.* VII. 341 The [Hartford] convention's views on amending the federal constitution savored of that nativism that afterwards developed into a great but short-lived American party. **1949** *Hist. & Philos. Soc. Ohio Bul.* Jan. 20 During the middle of the last century nativism was very strong in parts of America, especially in the Ohio Valley.

Nativist ˈnetɪvɪst, *n.* One who believes in or advocates nativism. *Obs.*

1844 *St. Louis Reveille* 16 Nov. 2/2 The Whig party of New York . . . has united its fortunes with that of the Nativists. **1848** *Ill. Reveille* (Bloomington) 12 Oct. 3/1 All the Whigs admit that Taylor was first nominated by the Nativists.

attrib. **1848** *Campaign* (Wash., D.C.) 7 June 23/1 The nativist papers. . . indulged in remarks of the most vulgar and gross character in relation to Gen. Cass. **1864** NICHOLS *Amer. Life* II. 78 The nativist party, with its secret organization. **1894** *Forum* July 534 [The South] was full of nativist feeling in its best form.

nativistic ˌnetɪvˈɪstɪk, *a.* Of or pertaining to nativism. *Rare.* — **1880** *Nation* 22 April 311/1 The nativistic tendencies of the Whig party drove them [*sc.* German-Americans] almost to a man into the ranks of the Democracy.

***natural,** *a.* and *n.*

1. *n.* A person or thing that is natural or inevitable, or suited by nature for a particular purpose or role. *Slang.*

1925 WITWER *Roughly Speaking* 177 The fight was what promoters call a 'natural.' **1935** *Amer. Mercury* July 356/1 She was, in the vivid term which show business has borrowed from the rolling dice, a 'natural.' **1949** *Sat. Ev. Post* 22 Oct. 132/4 Technicolor was as much a natural for Disney as his cartoons were naturals for color.

2. *a.* Savage or wild. *Rare.*

1832 KENNEDY *Swallow Barn* II. 125 Ned Hazard's a pretty hard horse to ride, too; only look at his eye,—how natural it is!

3. In combs.: (1) **natural bridge,** see as a main entry; (2) **gas,** inflammable gas formed naturally in the earth and obtained for commercial purposes usu. by boring, also attrib.; (3) **road,** (see quots.), *obs.*

(2) **1845** SOL. SMITH *Theatr. Apprent.* 102 Many of the stores and shops in the village are lighted with natural gas! **1885** *Cent. Mag.* Jan. 466 Natural gas wells have been common in the oil country for years. **1945** SERVICE *Ploughman* 411 Rising about twenty feet into the air was a flaming jet of natural gas. — (3) **1824** BLANE *Excursion U. S.* 104 The road is a *natural* one, that is to say, it is a track left open and cleared, but which has never had a single cart load of gravel or stones thrown upon it. **1869** BREWER *Rocky Mt. Lett.* 12 The road is what is called here 'a natural road,' that is, the hand of man has done nothing except to build bridges across the streams.

natural bridge.

1. = * **floating bridge.** *Obs.*

1806 in *Ann. 9th Congress* 2 Sess. 1136 About fifty leagues above this natural bridge [on the Red R.], is the residence of the Cadeaux.

2. A natural arch formation suggestive of a bridge, esp. the one near Lexington, Va.

[**1775** BURNABY *Travels* 35 Sixty miles southward of Augusta courthouse, [there is] a natural arch, or bridge, joining two high moun-

Natural bridge (sense 2)

tains.] **1838** *Knickerb.* XII. 32, I am the only surviving witness of that most adventurous exploit of climbing the Natural Bridge in Virginia. **1949** *Dly. Oklahoman Mag.* (Okla. City) 9 Oct. 2/4 The state has four natural bridges.

* **naturalization,** *n.* **1. naturalization law,** a law prescribing the conditions and processes of naturalization. **2. naturalization papers,** *pl.* the papers or documents recording an application for naturalization or certifying completion of naturalization. Also transf.

(1) **1812** *Ann. 12th Congress* 1 Sess. II. 1571 The House resolved itself into a Committee of the Whole, on the bill supplementary to the naturalization laws. **1916** *Atlantic Mo.* Feb. 231/1 Most of the questions arising under the naturalization laws have had reference to the duty of the United States to extricate its newly made citizens from difficulties . . . in other countries. — (2) **1856** *Porter's Spirit of Times* 15 Nov. 181/2 There has come to light one case . . . of forging naturalization papers. **1945** *Sat. Review* 5 May 18/3 In spirit no less than background 'Liliom' has deserted Hungary and taken out its naturalization papers in America.

* **nature,** *n.*

1. all nature, "all creation," everybody, everything. *Colloq.*

1819 *Mass. Spy* 3 Nov.(Th.), Father and I have just returned from the balloon—all nature was there, and more too. **1862** LOWELL *Biglow Papers* 2 Ser. vi. 158 But I don't love your cat'logue style,—do you?—Ez ef to sell all Natur' by vendoo. **1878** STOWE in *Atlantic Mo.* Oct. 472/2 Cuff would prance round . . . and seem to think he . . . had the charge of *all natur'*.

b. *Like all nature,* "like the dickens." *Colloq.*

1824 *Woodstock* (Vt.) *Observer* 17 Feb., They said too 'twould shoot like *all nater,* 'Tis singlar what stories they tell. **1840** HOFFMAN *Greyslaer* III. 254 The poor critter would have been sucked under . . . and dragged off like all natur.

c. *To beat all nature,* to excel superlatively, to surpass "all creation." *Colloq.*

1825 NEAL *Bro. Jonathan* II. 93 Hurra for you—that beats all nater! **1852** H. C. WATSON *Nights in Blockhouse* 47, I know summut about redskins. This 'ere beats all natur. **1892** DUVAL *Young Explorers* 82 'Well, I declar, boys,' said he, 'ef this don't beat all natur.'

2. nature faker, one who falsifies or attempts to embellish nature. Also **nature faking.**

1908 HORNADAY *Camp Fires on Desert* 226 What a fine opportunity it offers for a nature-fakir's marvel! **1947** *Sports Afield* Dec. 6/3 It was apparent to me that the writer colored his material, particularly in regard to the nature faking episode. **1949** *Nat. Hist.* March 131/2 Many nature fakers had obtained free meals and fine cigars through the gullibility of newspaper reporters with space to fill.

Nauvoo nɔˈvu, *n.* [*Nauvoo,* Ill.]

1. Nauvoo fly, = **Mormon fly.** *Rare.*

1845 F. N. MOORE *Diary* (1945) 46, I heard one of the deck hands a little while ago cursing 'these damned Nauvoo flies.'

2. Nauvoo legion, a military force or militia organized by the Mormon community at Nauvoo, Ill. Now *hist.*

1841 *Times & Seasons* (Nauvoo, Ill.) 1 May 406/1 Previous to his death he held the offices of Quarter Master Sergeant in the Nauvoo Legion and Assessor for the city of Nauvoo. **1881** ROMSPERT *Western Echo* 346 General Joe Smith, and his brother Hiram, at the head of the Nauvoo legion, opposed the state militia which had been called out to enforce obedience to the law. **1947** *Time* 21 July 19/3 He [Joseph Smith] organized a Nauvoo Legion of 4,000 well-armed troops.

Navaho ˈnævəˌho, *n.* Also **Navajo.** [Amer. Sp. *Navajos, Navahos,* orig. *Apaches de Navahú,* or *Navajó,* so called from the pueblo *Navahú, Navajó,* "great fields," near where the Spaniards first found these Indians.]

1. An Indian of an important Athapascan tribe now occupying a large reservation in Arizona, New Mexico, and Utah; in full **Navaho Indian.** Also, *pl.,* the tribe of these Indians. Cf. **Johnny Navaho.**

[**1629** Z. SALMERON in *Archaeol. Inst. of Amer. Papers* (Amer. Ser.) IV. 294 (*footnote*), La nacion de los Indios Apaches de Nabajù.] **1780** in *N. Mex. Hist. Soc. Pub.* XXI. (1918), The causes which have contributed to the extermination of these pueblos . . . have been hunger and pestilence . . . to which may be added the war cruelly made upon them by the Utes and Navajos. **1808** PIKE *Sources Miss.* III. App. 9 The Nanahaws are situated to the north-west of Santa Fe . . . and are supposed to be 2000 warriors strong. **1822** J. FOWLER *Journal* 123 Ward and Duglass . . . state that the Spanierds have sent 700 men against the Nabeho Indeans. **1846** ROBINSON *Jrnl.* (1932) 40 A friendly Nabajo, named Sandeval, goes with us, as a guide to their country. **1949** *Time* 24 Oct. 87/1 Into the packed plaza three Navajos rode, chanting the ancient Riding Song of the tribe.

2. The area inhabited by the Navaho Indians. *Rare.*

1844 GREGG *Commerce of Prairies* I. 284 Of such character are the ruins of Pueblo Bonito, in the direction of Navajo, on the borders of the Cordilleras.

3. The language of the Navaho Indians.

1873 BEADLE *Undevel. West* 524 Nearly all the employes understood a little Navajo, but not enough to interpret. **1893** DONALDSON *Moqui Pueblo Indians* 65 Now and then a Moqui may speak a little English and some Navajo or Spanish or Mexican. **1948** *Salt Lake Tribune* 17 Dec. 16/5 Other tribal council members, speaking in Navajo, and through the use of an interpreter, agreed with Mr. Akeah.

4. *ellipt.* = **Navaho blanket.**

1909 WASON *Happy Hawkins* 26 The cook said I should roll up in the Navajos he'd brought. **1914** BOWER *Flying U Ranch* 12 His blanket was a scarlet Navajo, and his rope a rawhide lariat.

5. In combs. of obvious meaning: (1) **Navaho agency,** (2) **blanket,** (3) **country,** (4) **language,** (5) **reservation,** (6) **rug,** (7) **silver,** (8) **War.**

(1) **1945** *Chi. D. News* 6 Jan. 1/7 The incident was reported last night by James M. Stewart, general superintendent of the Navajo Agency. — (2) **1834** A. PIKE *Sketches* 99 An Indian girl with her Nabajo blanket, black, with a red border. **1941** *Harper's Mag.* Oct. 499/1 From the Indian country you may emerge with a Navajo blanket or two and a little silver and turquoise jewelry. — (3) **1847** *Santa Fe Republican* 17 Sep. 2/4 Maj. Walkers Battalion was to have left the Rio Del Norte . . . for the Navajoe country. **1944** JOHNSON *As I Dare* 317 The medicine dance was to begin after dark, and twilight lasts long in the Navajo country. — (4) **1944** JOHNSON *As I Dare* 327 The Navajo language has been of great use in communication, because the enemy has had no experts who could translate it.

(5) **1884** *N. Mex. Terr. Rep.* 86 Five companies are on the line of the A. & P. R. R., near the Navajo reservation on the south. — (6) **1944** JOHNSON *As I Dare* 305 Some of the small Navajo rugs with perfectly balanced designs upon them are made in the Indian vocational schools. — (7) **1941** FERGUSSON *Southwest* 199 He bought what he could, always selecting well-worked Navajo silver and blankets that were firmly woven and of harmonious design. **1944** JOHNSON *As I Dare* 288 Navajo silver would begin to include baby spoons and the designs on Indian woven rugs would begin to have a suspicious perfection of detail. — (8) **1863** *Rio Abajo Press* 11 Aug. 2/1 Two hundred and fifty more mounted volunteers are called for especially for the Navajo War, to serve in the First New Mexico.

b. Also (1) **Navaho ruby,** =**Arizona ruby;** (2) **sandstone,** a form of red sandstone found in New Mexico and Arizona; (3) **tea,** a species of alumroot, *Heuchera bracteata*, found in the Southwest.

(1) [**1861** NEWBERRY *Geol. Rep.* 93 Garnets and beryls of unusually fine quality are found in considerable abundance in the alluvial soil about Fort Defiance, and in the other portions of the Navajo country.] **1912** *Out West* March 216, I have constantly a very fine selection of Navajo silverware and jewelry, Navajo 'rubies' cut and uncut, peridotes and native turquois. — (2) **1934** WEBSTER. **1948** *Atlantic Mo.* Jan. 64/1 Follow one of these canyons far enough, and it usually ends either at a fall or in one of the echoing caves and chambers the Navajo sandstone is fond of forming. — (3) **1936** REICHARD *Navajo Shepherd & Weaver* 41 From the stems of the plant called 'Navajo tea' the pinkish tan may be obtained.

Also *Navaho bread, bridge, burro, children, fire dance, hogan, jewelry, loom, nation, slave*, etc.

* **naval,** *a.*

1. naval academy, a school for training men for naval service, esp. (*cap.*) the government school at Annapolis, Md. Also attrib.

1814 *Amer. State P.: Naval Affairs* I. 323, I would also respectfully suggest . . . the establishment of a naval academy. **1839** *Amer. R.R. Jrnl.* IX 139 Annapolis is . . . decidedly the best locality in the United States for the site of a Naval Academy. **1900** BENJAMIN *U.S. Naval Acad.* 368 Uniforms of the cadets . . . must be obtained from the Naval Academy storekeeper. **1949** *Sat. Ev. Post* 25 June 114/4 Many Negroes have written me, asking advice for entering the Naval Academy.

2. naval officer, a government official, now a member of the U.S. Treasury Department, on duty at a customhouse in a large port to estimate duties, countersign clearances, etc.

1732 *Cal. State P., Amer. & W. Indies* 215 Of which [nepotism] with respect to the Navall Officer's place, that of the Clerk of the Councill and the public Vendue Master, he hath given us very lately a specimen. **1739** *Boston Gaz.* 17 Dec., John Boydell . . was appointed . . . naval officer for the port of Boston. **1882** MCCABE *New York* 302 Offices . . . are used by the Collector of the Port, the Naval Officer, and the Surveyor of the Port. **1914** *Cyclo. Amer. Govt.* II. 499/1 In certain customs districts where a daily accounting with the Treasury Department is impracticable, a treasury official known as a naval officer acts concurrently with the collector in estimation of duties.

Navarino nɑvəˈrino, *n.* [*Navarino*, Greece, made famous by a battle there in 1827.] A bonnet of a style popular about 1845. In full **Navarino bonnet.** Also **Navarino scoop.** *Obs.* or *hist.*

1846 FARNHAM *Prairie Land* 101 A capacious sugar-loaf Navarino scoop which had once vied with the raven hair. *Ib.* 103 [The monkey] winked a little quicker when he faced the Navarino. **1863** TAYLOR *H. Thurston* 345 We wore Navarino bonnets then, and sleeves puffed out with bags of down. **1900** KING *When I Lived* (1937) 134 She wore on her head what was called in those days a 'Navarino' bonnet, with green bows half a yard high.

* **navel,** *n.* An orange having a small navel-like formation at its apex, usu. grown in California. In full **navel orange.** Also attrib.

1882 *Harper's Mag.* Dec. 58/2 He can go into his orchard and concern himself about his Navel or Brazilian varieties . . . without let or hindrance. **1888** LINDLEY *Calif. of South* 349 The navel orange possesses a thin skin, few or no seeds, tender pulp, and a high, winy flavor, which gives it precedence over all other varieties, budded or seedling, grown in Southern California. **1891** *Harper's Mag.* Jan. 170/1 The prices for fruit in the spring of 1890 [were] $1.60 per box for seedlings and $3 per box for navels. **1949** HERTRICH *Huntington Bot. Gardens* 9 By this time the navel orchard adjoining my home property fortunately had been abandoned and planted to alfalfa.

b. navel orange tree, a tree producing navel oranges.

1846 BROWNE *Trees Amer.* 58 Navel Golden-fruited Orange-tree. The author of the present work claims the honour of first introducing this variety [from Brazil] into the [U.S.]. **1900** E. J. WICKSON *Calif. Fruits* 355 (*caption*), Budded Navel Orange Tree, about Five Feet High.

nave wood tree. A tree having tough wood suitable for making naves for wheels. *Obs.* — **1685** *Springfield Rec.* II. 175 We marked . . . A Nave wood Tree O.O. in a Swamp or run of water. *Ib.* 179 In the Swamp [is] a Nave wood Tree marked, S P on the North side for Springfield.

* **navigate,** *v. intr.* To move, walk—used esp. of intoxicated persons. *Colloq.*

1846 *Spirit of Times* (N.Y.) 11 July 234/3 Well, by this time I began to think of navigating. **1904** *N.Y. Sun* 9 Aug. 10 She was so drunk that she could barely navigate. **1930** *Randolph Enterprise* (Elkins, W.Va.) 13 Feb. 1/1 The fellow was . . . hardly able to navigate as he was carrying a heavy load of Prohibition poison.

***navigation,** *n.* As the last term in **schooner, slack-water, steamboat navigation.**

* **navy,** *n.*

1. A pistol or revolver of a type used in the U.S. Navy.

The meaning of "navy" in the first quot. is not clear. It may refer to a sword but no other evidence for such a use is available. An early model of Colt's revolver was adopted as a sidearm in the Navy. Hence the sense here and navy pistol, revolver, six (-shooter) *qq.v.* in **3.** below. The explanation in quot. 1931 below is interesting but in error. Some early Colts did have a naval scene etched on the cylinder but the etching did not inspire this use.

1777 WAYNE in W. H. Smith *St. Clair P.* I. 388 Lieutenant Henry defended himself with great bravery . . . dangerously wounding two of the Indians with his navy. **1870** MARK TWAIN *Sk. New & Old* (1875) 140 (R.), She turned on that smirking Spanish fool like a wild cat, and out with a 'navy' and shot him dead in open court. **1931** WILLISON *Here They Dug Gold* 92 But early boom towns and mining camps generally prefer the Colt 'Navy' (.36), so named from a naval scene engraved round its barrel.

2. =**navy plug.**

1876 TRIPP *Student-Life* 399 Hawes had smoked 'navy' in it all the year of Sam's probation. **1891** SCOTT *Amer. Lawyers* 463 Another pull at the bottle, a few grains of quinine if it is 'ager day,' a 'chaw of navy' and the repast is finished.

3. In combs.: (1) * **navy agent,** a naval disbursing officer, a paymaster, *obs.;* (2) **bean,** a small white bean so called from its use in the Navy; (3) **Department,** see as a main entry; (4) **pistol,** =**navy revolver;** (5) **plug,** a strong, dark-colored plug tobacco, or a piece of this; (6) **Register,** an official list of officers and ships in the U.S. Navy; (7) **revolver,** a heavy, large-caliber revolver of a type used in the Navy, esp. an early model Colt's revolver adopted by the Navy as a sidearm; (8) **six (-shooter),** =prec.

(1) **1846** POLK *Diary* I. 293 Received notes . . . requesting me to withhold the Commission of Mr. Isaac H. Wright as Navy Agent of Boston. **1860** *36th Congress* 1 Sess. H. R. Rep. No. 621, 21 When articles are needed not embraced in a contract a requisition is made out by the master workman . . . and sent to the navy agent. — (2) **1856** KANE *Arctic Explor.* II. 94 Coffee . . . ; one part of the genuine berry to three of navy-beans. **1949** *Sat. Ev. Post* 22 Oct. 128/3 A baby under a year old sucked a navy bean into its lung, where the bean immediately swelled from moisture. — (4) **1849** E. CHRISTMAN in *One Man's Gold* (1930) 12, I have brought with me: One government rifle, one navy pistol, one small rifle pistol. **1948** *Popular Western* June 26/1 His had made a blurring movement toward the cedar-butted Navy pistol belted at his flank.

(5) **1869** ALDRICH *Bad Boy* (1870) 245 Between the beer and the soothing fragrance of the navy-plug, I fell into a pleasanter mood. **1945** MARSHALL *Santa Fe* 67 Through the dusty streets, into and out of the saloons and deadfalls, the tanned cowhands wandered, living according to legend, on navy plug and fortyrod, with a whirl at the tiger or monte for dessert. — (6) **1841** *S. Lit. Messenger* VII. 4/1 Statistics . . . that are furnished by the Navy Register will show [etc.]. **1949** *Sat. Ev. Post* 9 July 32/2 It's an old saw in the city that Norfolk is the mother-in-law of the Navy, with a boat hook in one hand, a Navy Register in the other, and Sister Sue standing by. — (7) *a***1861** WINTHROP *Canoe & Saddle* 26 This machine . . . is called a Six-shooter, an eight-inch navy revolver. **1944** KAHN *Cable Car Days* 45 Gold nuggets, faro, and navy revolvers . . . [were] involved in the intricate problems of the Bank of California. — (8) **1865** PIKE *Scout & Ranger* (1932) 27, I was advancing rapidly, with . . . my right [hand] on the stock of my 'Navy Six.' **1872** MARK TWAIN *Roughing It* 57 He might have to enforce it with a navy six-shooter. **1927** SANDBURG *Songbag* 272 It's now our outfit was complete—seven able-bodied men, With navy six and needle gun—our troubles did begin,

Navy Department. The department of the federal government charged with the control, supervision, and maintenance of the navy.

Immediately after the Revolution, United States naval affairs were administered by the War Department, but in 1798 the Department of the Navy was created.

1779 *Jrnls. Cont. Congress* XV. 1216 Congress took into consideration the report of the Marine Committee respecting the navy department. **1798** *Ann. 5th Congress* II. 1545 [Mr. Gallatin] did not think it necessary to establish a Navy Department. **1808** *Ann. 10th Congress* II. 1960 We had just navy enough . . . to give rise to the dignified style of 'the Navy Department,' which had dwindled down to a department of gunboats. **1943–4** *U.S. Govt. Manual* Winter 275 The Secretary of the Navy is head of the Navy Department.

***N. E.** An abbreviation of New England. Also attrib.

1645 *Plymouth Laws* 80 The Smyth to make a seale of two Roman letters namely N.E. to seale the measures besides the P. **1667** *Ib.* 153 The charge of the printing of the History of Gods dispensations towards N.E. **1824** *Commentator* (Frankfort, Ky.) 27 Nov. 3/1 The result in all the N.E. States, except Rhode Island, . . . is known. **1948** *Boston Post* 29 Aug. 1 (*heading*), Break in Heat Wave Due Today; Death Toll in N.E. Reaches 35.

Neapolitan ice cream. (See quots.) — [**1876** M. F. Henderson *Cooking* 309 Napolitaine Cream. . . . Vanilla, chocolate, and strawberry ice-creams are . . . filled in a mold the form of a brick in three smooth layers of equal size.] **1941** Farmer *Boston Cook Book* 580 Neapolitan Ice Cream. Pack two or three flavors of ice cream in layers in brick mold. One layer is usually lemon or orange ice. Freeze.

***near,** *a.* **1. near beer,** any beverage resembling beer. **2. near seal,** any fur treated and dyed to resemble seal, also attrib.

(1) 1909 *N.Y. Ev. Post* 23 Aug. 2 The refusal of the Cities Commission to prohibit the sale of imitation beer, commonly known as 'near beer.' **1941** Daniels *Tar Heels* 255 They had been drinking corn whisky and chasing it down with near beer — **(2) 1902** Lorimer *Lett. Merchant* 184 He leads the nag out into the middle of a ten-acre lot . . . and examines every hair of his hide, as if he expected to find it near-seal. **1908** K. McGaffey *Show-Girl* 119 All you ever had was a dirty handkerchief kimona, a Fluffy Ruffles skirt and a near-seal jacket.

Nebraska nəˈbræskə, *n.* [Name (said to be from an Indian expression *ni-bthaska* "river in the flatness," applied to the Platte river) of the former territory including the present state of Nebraska.] Attrib. with **bill, measure,** in the sense: Providing for the erection of the territory of Nebraska. Cf. **Kansas-Nebraska Bill.**

1854 *Maysville* (Ky.) *Eagle* 2 Nov. 1/2, I am in favor of living up to the laws as long as they are laws, whether it is the Fugitive Slave Law, the Nebraska Bill, or the Excise laws. **1854** *N.Y. Tribune* 27 Sep. 4/6 The 'Hards' support the Nebraska measure because it is infamous. **1858** Lincoln in Logan *Great Conspiracy* 58, I have always been quiet about it [abolition] until this new era of the introduction of the Nebraska Bill began.

b. Nebraska Democrat, a Democrat who favored the Kansas-Nebraska Bill. Also **Nebraska Democracy.** Both *obs.*

1855 *N.Y. Wkly. Tribune* 14 July 2/3 These men . . . are . . . nominating a Whig candidate against the Anti-Nebraska candidate for Governor of Maine, . . . with the sole object of electing the regular Nebraska Democrat candidate. *Ib.* 17 Nov. 2/1 The most numerous party in the new House will be the Nebraska Democracy, one hundred strong. **1856** *Charleston* (S.C.) *Mercury* 9 Jan. (*heading*), Nebraska Democracy at the North. **1856** *Ill. State Reg.* (Springfield) 5 June 4/1 They (the Nebraska democracy) are resolved on its extension.

c. Nebraska brick, (see quot.). *Obs.*

1888 *Harper's Mag.* July 235/1 A house built of squares of sod taken from the prairie—Nebraska or Kansas brick, as they are facetiously termed.

As the last term in **anti-Nebraska.**

Nebraskaism nəˈbræskəˌɪzəm, *n.* **1.** The principles underlying the Kansas-Nebraska Bill. *Obs.* **2.** A locution peculiar to Nebraska. *Rare.*

(1) 1856 *Iroquois Republican* (Middleport, Ill.) 15 May 2/5 The Peoria *Banner* has urged Gov. Kœrner through its columns to forsake Douglas and Nebraskaism. **1887** *Cent. Mag.* April 858/1 One or two . . . Whigs in central Illinois declared their adherence to Nebraskaism. — **(2) 1860** *Harper's Mag.* Jan. 282/2, 'I have seldom (if ever) met with a Nebraskaism,' says a Northwestern[er], 'in the [Editor's] Drawer.'

Nebraskan nəˈbræskən, *a.* and *n.*

1. Of or pertaining to Nebraska (see also quot. 1890).

1884 *N.Y. Wkly. Tribune* 2 April 10/4 The advantages which the Nebraskan Mennonites secure by *co-operative purchasing* of their implements, machinery, and supplies of all kinds, are manifestly . . . great. **1890** *Cent.* 3950/2 Nebraskan. . . . A native or an inhabitant of Nebraska. **1948** *Time* 26 April 23/2 Ohioans seemed as friendly to him as Nebraskans.

2. *Geol.* One of the divisions or stages in the interior of North America of the Pleistocene epoch.

1934 Webster. **1948** *Pacific Discovery* March–April 32/2 Four glacial stages are recognized in North America, from oldest to youngest, respectively: Nebraskan, Kansan, Illinoian, and Wisconsin.

Nebraskian nəˈbræskɪən, *n.* A native or citizen of Nebraska. Also transf. — **1858** *N.Y. Tribune* 9 Oct. 6/4 Nebraskians Off For Pikes Peak. **1860** *Mountaineer* (Salt Lake City) 5 May 145/2 The editor of the *Nebraskian* endorses the writer and his statement.

***neck,** *n.*

1. In horseracing, the length of a horse's neck.

1851 R. Glisan *Jrnl. Army Life* 64 On reaching the goal he was half a neck ahead. **1865** Mark Twain *Sk. New & Old* 32 She'd . . . always fetch up at the stand just about a neck ahead. **1949** *Cue* 30 April 10/2 Olympia . . . rallied very gamely and took the bitterly fought race by a neck.

2. In combs.: (1) **necklace poplar,** the cottonwood, *Populus balsamifera;* (2) **lace weed,** the white baneberry; (3) ***tie,** see as a main entry; (4) **twister,** a kind of spirituous drink, *slang, obs.;* (5) ***weed,** the purslane speedwell, *Veronica peregrina* (see also quot. 1833), so called because its flowers were reputed to cure scrofula; (6) **yoke,** a bar, usu. of wood, connecting two draft animals working abreast and supporting the end of the pole or tongue of the vehicle which they draw, see **singletree,** and cf. **sap neckyoke.**

(1) 1847 Wood *Botany* 507 P[*opulus*] *monilifera.* Necklace Poplar. . . . Near Troy, N.Y. . . . A tree 60–70 f[t] high. **1897** Sudworth *Arborescent Flora* 135 *Populus deltoides* . . . Yellow Cottonwood. . . . [Also called] Necklace Poplar (Tex., Colo.). — **(2) 1817–8** Eaton

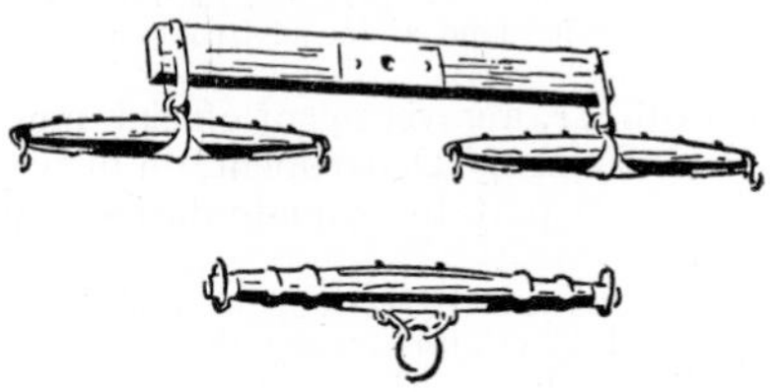

Neckyoke, doubletree (or evener) and singletrees

Botany (1822) 155 *Actaea alba,* necklace weed, white beads. . . . Berries white. **1821** *Mass. H.S. Coll.* 2 Ser. IX. 146. **1949** Palmer *Fieldbook Nat. Hist.* 193/2 Common names of white baneberry include necklaceweed, snakeroot, and white beads. — **(4) 1859** Cornwallis *New World* I. 300 Cold punch, gum ticklers, and neck twisters, drinks of Yankee concoction.

(5) 1833 Eaton *Botany* (ed. 6) 386 *Veronica agrestis,* field speedwell, neckweed. **1843** Torrey *Flora N.Y.* II. 42 Neck-weed. . . . Formerly considered a valuable remedy for scrophulous affections, but probably of little value. **1901** Mohr *Plant Life Ala.* 723. — **(6) 1868** Woodruff *Trotting Horse* 349 The neck-yoke came off the pole, and he got loose. **1919** Cady *Rhymes of Vt.* (1923) 103 You brace your feet and take the reins, The neckyoke bumps, the evener strains.

b. In various slang phrases: (1) *shot in the neck,* see ***shot,** *n.* and *a.;* (2) **neck of the woods,* a neighborhood or community; (3) *to get it in the neck,* to get the worst of it, to be hard hit.

(2) 1839 *Spirit of Times* 15 June 175/2 (We.), In this neck of the woods. **1947** *Chi. Sun* 20 Jan. 3/3 It will make no under-ice tests because they are 'not particularly worthwhile in that neck of the woods.' — **(3) 1887** *Courier-Journal* 20 Jan. 6/4 Dem dubs is goin' to git it in de neck in a minit. **1931** *Blue Valley Farmer* (Okla. City) 17 Dec. 1/7 The 'people' will get just what they have now, or 'get it in the neck.'

As the last term in **bottle, bull, crook, fiddle, goose, horse's, jerk, leather, little, long, red, ring, rough, rubber, short, swelled neck.**

***neck,** *v.*

1. *tr.* To cut the neck (i.e., the excrescence at the point where the lead was poured into the mold) off an old-fashioned round bullet for a muzzle-loading rifle. *Obs.* Cf. * **trim,** *v.* **1.**

[**1812** in KERCHEVAL *Hist. Valley Va.* 308 When you run your bullets, cut off the necks very close, and scrape them.] **1832** *Louisville Directory* 101 The women of the fort were constantly running bullets and necking them ready for the rifle.

2. To tie (cattle) neck to neck (see also quot. 1890).

1857 BRAMAN *Texas* 73 The usual practice of farmers, whenever they want work oxen, is to go to the prairie, and neck together, with ropes, as many pair of three and four year old steers as they desire. **1890** *Stock Grower & Farmer* 15 March 5/3 The method [of weaning calves] generally followed in a hilly country is as follows, and is known as 'necking.' You drive the calf off, four or five miles and tie it up short to a bush. **1931** DOBIE *Coronado's C.* 102 Every animal in the pen had been roped and led in necked to an old brindle ox.

3. *intr.* To indulge in amorous caresses. Usu. * **necking,** *n.*

1923–4 FOSTER *Larry* (1930) 26 Our main topic of discussion was 'necking.' **1926** *Amer. Mercury* Feb. 137/1 They are all against the theatre, dancing, necking, the cigarette, the lip stick and Sunday baseball. **1932** *Variety* 12 April 41/1, I didn't feel like necking, but I gave her a little kiss. **1949** *L.A. Times* 27 March 1/1 Coeds of John Muir College, in Pasadena, yesterday . . . cast a unanimous frown upon 'necking parties' in parked cars.

Hence **necker,** *n.*

1929 *Variety* 3 April 20/2 Champ necker and flame of the campus falls in love with a young and good looking professor.

* **necked,** *a.* **1. necked calf,** a calf being weaned by being tied up; a calf roped by the neck. **2. necked pine,** a variety of strawberry.

(**1**) **1890** *Stock Grower & Farmer* 15 March 5/3 If some passing puncher should hear the peculiar bawl that a 'necked' calf makes, he is dead sure to investigate. **1907** WHITE *Arizona Nights* 153 'No more necked calves,' they announced. — (**2**) **1851** CIST *Cincinnati* 295 Necked Pine—highest flavored. **1861** *Ill. Agric. Soc. Trans.* 469, I have a bed of Necked Pine so thickly matted that a mouse could not get through them.

* **necktie,** *n. attrib.* **necktie frolic, party, sociable,** a hanging. *Slang.*

1871 *Harper's Mag.* Nov. 949/2 Mr. Jim Clemenston, equine abductor, was on last Thursday morning, at ten sharp, made the victim of a neck-tie sociable. **1876** *Carson Valley News* (Genoa, Nev.) 21 June 2/4 It's hard to leave ye, old hills, but it's either the States or a necktie frolic for me. **1882** in *Nat. Geog. Mag.* LVI. 247 If Found within the Limits of this City after Ten O'Clock P.M. this Night, you will be Invited to attend a Grand Neck-tie Party. **1949** *Boston Globe* 17 July (Fiction Mag.) 11/3 If our gang knew what Bill and I know, there'd be a necktie party for you, son.

* **Ned,** *n.*

1. (See quot. and cf. **Old Ned.**) *Obs.*

1850 GARRARD *Wah-To-Yah* x. 140 Numerous were the curses showered on the 'Neds,' by the mountain men of our party. [Note:] Among many farmers, pork is familiarly called 'Ned,' and as pork forms a principal portion of the government rations, the United States employees were so termed, by the mountain men, in derision. *Ib.* xxi. 253 They were entitled every day to three-fourths of a pound of messpork or 'Ned.'

2. *To raise* (*promiscuous, merry*) *Ned,* to stir up trouble, to "raise Cain." *Slang.*

1848 LOWELL *Biglow P.* 1 Ser. v. 69 Your fact'ry gals . . . 'l go to work raisin' promiscoous Ned. **1870** in O. LOGAN *Before Footlights* 165 We are real smart girls . . . and can raise ned and keep folks A laughing. **1906** QUICK *Double Trouble* 223 You've been raising merry Ned, Florian, in your Brassfield capacity.

3. *By Ned!* a mild oath. *Colloq.*

1853 PAXTON *Yankee in Texas* 227 'By Ned,' says he, 'if it aint that owdacious critter of Miss Mash's.'

* **needle,** *n.*

1. =**cypress knee.** *Obs.*

1853 PAXTON *Yankee in Texas* 60 Around the foot of each tree are standing a number of those singular conical-shaped shoots, termed needles, resembling so many grave-stones.

2. a. needle grass, any one of several grasses, as the ant rice, *Aristida oligantha,* also attrib. **b. needle palmetto,** the blue palmetto, *Rhapidophyllum hystrix.*

(**a**) **1885** H. C. McCOOK *Tenants Old Farm* 341 A sort of grass known as ant-rice, or needle grass. **1944** BARBOUR *Eden* 124 Most characteristic feature of Florida is the needle-grass pond of the open piney-woods prairie. — (**b**) **1942** KENNEDY *Palmetto Country* 5 Another low-lying palmetto—variously called the dwarf, needle, porcupine, blue, or creeping palmetto—has an even wider range than the saw palmetto, extending from Florida to North Carolina and Texas.

As the last term in **Adam's, devil's darning, Eve's darning, Spanish needle.**

* **negative,** *v.*

1. *tr.* To reject (a person proposed for an office). Also *ppl.a.* used absolutely. *Obs.*

1706 SEWALL *Diary* II. 162 In stead of the Negativ'd were chosen B. Brown, 55. Ephr. Hunt, 42. **1720** *Ib.* III. 255 The govr. Consented to the Choice of the Councillours, having Negativ'd Col. Byfield and Dr. Clarke. **1876** BANCROFT *Hist. U.S.* IV. 6 Negativing six of the ablest 'friends of the people in the board.'

2. To veto (a bill or law).

1749 *Conn. Rec.* IX. 453 It would . . . invest the Governor . . . with a power to negative all acts that should be passed in our Assembly. **1804** *Guardian of Freedom* (Frankfort, Ky.) 29 Feb. 2/1 The question was taken on the resolution and negatived—ayes 13—noes 19. **1882** BANCROFT *Hist. U.S.* VI. III. 271 Madison put forth all his strength to show that a power of negativing the improper laws of the states is the most . . . certain means of preserving the harmony of the system.

* **Negro, nigger,** *n.* and *a.*

In informal use, esp. in the South, both *Negro* and *nigger* occur. In the treatment here no effort is made to distinguish between these two forms, the second of which is regarded as derogatory.

1. =**Negro English.** Also attrib. *Obs.*

1704 S. KNIGHT *Jrnl.* 38 You speak negro to him. I'le ask him. **1834** *Knickerb.* III. 445 And I would say too, that although *mighty smart,* and a *mighty smart chance, mighty big,* and *mighty little* was excellent 'nigger' dialect, yet it was not so refined, as an orator might use. **1884** *Amer. Philol. Soc. Trans.* XVI. App. 32 Such parasynetic forms as *sparrer-grass* for *asparagus* . . . are common enough in Negro.

2. A quality, custom, mannerism or the like, thought to be characteristic of Negroes. *Slang.*

1825 NEAL *Bro. Jonathan* I. 414 Cotch!—I reckon!—clear nigger that. **1853** PAXTON *Yankee in Texas* 61 Huntin' and fishin' on that day [Sunday] wer *clar* nigger, and went agin him. **1894** MARK TWAIN *P. Wilson* x, He found the 'nigger' in him involuntarily giving the road.

3. (See quot. 1875.) Cf. **Negro engine.**

1867 HOSMER *Trip to States by Way Yellowstone & Mo.* 58 The boat . . . struck the bar; they then began to work with the spars and nigger, and at two o'clock we got off. **1875** KNIGHT 1526/2 *Nigger,* . . . a steam-engine employed in hoisting; especially on shipboard and on the Western and Southern rivers. **1942** HEREFORD *Old Man River* 114 The other end of the rope was secured to the capstan, . . which was operated by a small engine called the 'nigger.'

4. a. A fault or defect in the insulating covering of an electrical conductor which may cause a short circuit. **b.** A steam ram or plunger used in a sawmill for turning or adjusting a log on the carriage. Both *colloq.*

(**a**) **1886** *Scientific Amer.* LIV 308/2 The consequence of neglect might be that what the workmen call 'a nigger' would get into the armature, and burn it so as to destroy its service. — (**b**) **1910** WHITE *Rules of Game* 32 When the car had flown back to its starting-point, the 'nigger' rose from obscurity to turn the log half-way round.

5. In miscellaneous combs.

The combs. into which this word has entered are extremely numerous. Many of them allude to slavery times and are now obsolete. No attempt is made here to include all of them. Some of the better-authenticated ones, as **Negro baby, business, dog, election, head, killer, meeting, minstrel, party, quarter, trader,** are given as main entries.

(1) **Negro bill,** a handbill advertising for a runaway slave; (2) **bounty,** a bounty paid to a Negro for enlisting in the armed services; (3) **bureau,** the Freedmen's Bureau; (4) **chaser,** a squiblike form of fireworks which when ignited zigzags over the ground, *colloq.;* (5) **consumption,** ?a type of tuberculosis; (6) **drunk,** extremely drunk; (7) **engine,** =**Negro 3;** (8) **equality,** social and political equality of Negroes with white people, also attrib.; (9) **luck,** unexampled or unexpected good luck; (10) **melodists,** =**Negro minstrels;** (11) **organ,** a periodical run by Negroes or presenting the point of view of Negroes; (12) **patch,** on a southern plantation, a patch or piece of land for growing crops for the use of Negroes; (13) **property,** property consisting of Negro slaves; (14) **question,** the social and political question or problem created by the existence of the Negro population in the U.S.; (15) **shooter,** a slingshot, *colloq.,* cf. **Negro-killer 3;** (16) **spiritual,** a religious song of folk character,

originating among American Negroes; (17) **state,** before the Civil War, a state in which Negro slavery was legal; (18) **talk,** irresponsible or exaggerated gossip emanating from Negroes; (19) * **toe,** (*a*) a variety of potato, (*b*) a Brazil nut; (20) **worshipper,** a disparaging term for a person who favored the abolition of slavery or was interested in the welfare of the Negro.

(1) 1894 M. TWAIN *Pudd'nhead Wilson* xviii. 19 (R.), He 'uz talkin' to de man en givin' him some bills—nigger-bills, I reckon, en I's de nigger. — **(2) 1780** JOS. JONES *Letters* 48 But the negro bounty cannot fail to procure men for the war under either scheme with the draught as the *dernier resort*. — **(3) 1867** *Columbia Press* (Umatilla, Ore.) 3 Aug. 2/2 [They hope to] requisition from the public treasury a *quantum sufficit* with which to cope with their brother tyrants of nigger bureau and bondocracy notoriety. — **(4) 1883** PECK *Bad Boy* 22, I had a lot of rockets and Roman candles, and six pin-wheels, and a lot of nigger chasers. **1921** MULFORD *Bar-20 Three* xvi. 217 Most likely they'll be nigger-chasers, th' way some folk'll be steppin' lively to get out of th' way.

(5) 1851 *De Bow's Review* XI. 212 Negro consumption is a disease almost unknown to medical men of the Northern states and Europe. — **(6) 1829** *Maysville Eagle* 4 Aug., I have never been right 'negro drunk.' — **(7) 1878** BEADLE *Western Wilds* 378 Then oaths, spars 'nigger-engine' and all the other available machinery were set in operation. **1882** *Harper's Mag.* Jan. 175/2 One of the 'nigger' engines is suddenly called into service to tighten a two-inch rope, or wind up a discarded cable. — **(8) 1856** *Ill. State Reg.* (Springfield) 26 June 3/3 The cry for negro equality is on their lips, and is *shrieked* from their fanatical hosts. **1905** N. DAVIS *Northerner* 52 You think I might be nice to Mr. Falls, negro equality and all? — **(9) 1851** GLISAN *Jrnl. Army Life* 90, I occasionally made him a little envious by my nigger-luck, as he is pleased to term it. **1947** CHALFANT *Gold, Guns, & Ghost Towns* 7 Mac told them their judgment was 'free nigger luck, that and nothing more.'

(10) 1851 LEWIS *Across Atlantic* 21 On the very day of my arrival at Boston, happening to ask what entertainment was going on in the town, I was told 'Negro Melodists.' — **(11) 1860** in J. DOY *Narr.* 126 The assertion that Doy, the nigger-stealer, was subjected to the indignities mentioned by the nigger-organ, is to our mind exceedingly doubtful. — **(12) 1856** DAVIS *Farm Bk.* 57 Run 3 plows. 1 in the negro patch cotton. *Ib.* 162 Worked out a part of the negro patch. — **(13) 1797** *Last Advice of C. Pettigrew to Sons* (Univ. N.C. MS), I became possessed of a negro property by my union with your mother. **1853** STOWE *Key* 181/2 Negro property is decidedly 'brisk' in this county [i.e., in Shelby Co., Ky.]. — **(14) 1832** *Cong. Deb.* 2 April 2348 [If] the South must be threatened with the negro question, and with having their throats cut if they attempted to resist, he would ask, on whose side was the bullying? **1906** *Outlook* 1 Dec. 844 (*caption*), The Negro Question Again. **1949** *Time* 31 Oct. 84/3 The South gradually transformed 'the Negro question' into a fanatical folk bias, coloring its segregated religion, its sex attitudes, its every moment in life.

(15) 1883 SWEET & KNOX *Through Texas* 339 Just about the time people have got used to tops buzzing about their ears, the 'nigger-shooter' mania breaks out. **1945** M. JAMES *Cherokee Strip* 4, I was fishing in my pocket for the nigger-shooter Mr. Howell had made me when I happened to look around, and there was Ad Poak coming over the rise in our pasture. — **(16) 1867** HIGGINSON in *Atlantic Mo.* June 685/1, I had for many years heard of this class of songs under the name of 'Negro Spirituals.' **1949** *Oregonian* (Portland) 10 Aug. 8/4 He found time to write books on his hobbies, on alligators and on Negro spirituals. — **(17) 1780** *Essex Inst. Coll.* XIII. 220 You did not carry home contemptible Ideas enough of the negro States or of this great Braggadocio. **1867** LOCKE *Swingin' Round* 49 Kentucky alone —the only nigger State in the North—wood hev bin helpless. — **(18) 1866** C. H. SMITH *Bill Arp* 105 All else was rumor and nigger talk. **1947** GRAHAM *There Was Once a Slave* 32 The white masters heard other whisperings too—vague, amusing 'nigger talk.' — **(19)** (*a*) **1853** *Mich. Agric. Soc. Trans.* V. 208 Some of the more approved [kinds of potatoes] are . . . the Niggertoe, the Meshannock, the Cumberland Kempt. (*b*) **1896** *D.N.* I. 421. **1947** PAUL *Linden* 337 There were special booths for sweet corn dipped in hot melted butter, . . . walnuts, chestnuts, butternuts, nigger-toes, almonds and castanas, sarsaparilla and root beer, grape juice, sweet cider, perry and lemonade.

(20) 1857 *Lawrence* (Kans.) *Republican* 9 July 2 There is not a 'border ruffian' or 'nigger worshipper' in Kansas who would not be put to flight by such a document. **1893** LELAND *Memoirs* 137, I saw countless friends or acquaintances . . . become all at once blatant 'nigger-worshippers,' abundant in proof that they had always had 'an indescribable horror of slavery.'

In similar combs. of obvious meaning or sufficiently explained in the quots.: (1) **Negro auction,** (2) **break-down,** (3) **camp meeting,** (4) **daytime,** (5) **English,** (6) **exodus,** (cf. **exoduster**), (7) **hoedown,** (8) **labor,** (9) **league,** (10) **Pinkster music,** (11) **show,** (12) **singing,** (13) **song,** (14) **stealing,** (15) **suffrage,** (16) **trot,** (17) **vote.**

(1) 1856 OLMSTED *Slave States* 31 This must not be taken as an indication that negro auctions are not of frequent occurrence. — **(2) 1899** HARTE *Hamlin's Mediation* 102 The dancing of the girl suggested a negro 'break-down' rather than any known sylvan measures. — **(3) 1851** *Knickerb.* XXXVII. 191 We wonder whether he ever attended a negro-camp-meeting at the South! — **(4) 1802** DAVIS *Travels* (1803) 385 Negur day-time . . . a cant term among the negroes for night; they being then at leisure.

(5) 1808 ASHE *Travels* 79 The husband . . . had lived long enough in Virginia to pick up some Negro-English. **1862** E. KIRKE *Among Pines* 132 Not to weary the reader with a long repetition of negro-English, I will tell in brief what I gleaned from an hour's conversation with the two blacks. — **(6) 1879** *Chi. Tribune* 4 May 4/2 Our editorial correspondent, writing from Vicksburg, concerning the negro exodus from the South, tells how strong is the desire and the purpose of the colored people to leave the Plantation States. **1906** in *Kans. Hist. Soc.* IX. 385 Their concerted movement to this state was there called 'the negro exodus' and, by many in Kansas, 'the negro invasion.' — **(7) 1865** in *Jrnl. So. Hist.* IX. (1943) 247 Evenings we are having a nigger hoedown as we do very often. — **(8) 1839** *Amer. R.R. Jrnl.* IX. 83 Negro labor is perfectly adapted to the construction of works of internal improvement. **1906** BELL *C. Lee* 243 Half the time this cheap negro labour . . . is drunk or striking. — **(9) 1868** in GUILD *Old Times* 375 The 'scalawags' of the South joined the 'carpet-bagger' of the North, became the head and center of negro leagues.

(10) *c***1824–38** G. FURMAN *Antiquities of L.I.* 266 The day [first Monday in June] has sunk lamentably low, and without any apparent reason; to ridicule *whistling*, it is called *Negro Pinckster Music*. — **(11) 1879** PECK *Peck's Fun* 37 (We.), There is a fortune in store for the nigger show that will . . . leave out a certain old joke. **1884** MARK TWAIN *H. Finn* xxvi. 261 They never see a holiday from year's end to year's end; never go to the circus, nor theater, nor nigger shows, nor nowheres. — **(12) 1844** J. COWELL *Thirty Years* II. 66 [Tom Blakeley] was the first to introduce negro singing on the American stage. — **(13) 1851** *Knickerb.* XXXVIII. 181 'E.P.,' whose portfolio appears especially rich in 'negro-songs,' sends us the following. **1922** *Amer. Folk-Lore* XXXV. 223 Swing Low, Sweet Chariot! . . . is one of the old and now exceedingly popular Negro songs. — **(14) 1819** *Niles' Reg.* XVI. 160/1 Sentence of death has been pronounced on a fellow in North Carolina, for negro stealing. **1862** E. KIRKE *Among Pines* 39 Why have you elected a president who approves of nigger-stealing?

(15) 1839 MARRYAT *Diary in Amer.* I. 151 About the year 1795 . . . the very point before us was ruled by the High Court of Errors and Appeals against the right of negro suffrage. **1949** *Ark. Hist. Quart.* Spring 11 The Democrats adopted resolutions opposing negro suffrage. — **(16) 1870** W. W. FOWLER *Ten Years in Wall Street* 195, I remember meeting him often in Broadway, making a bee-line for Wall Street, on that double-quick gait, known as the negro trot. — **(17) 1871** SOMERS *Southern States* 228 By dexterously 'fugling' the negro vote, [the governor] got himself advanced to this high position. **1949** *So. Wkly.* 19 Oct. 8/1 The current civil rights issue . . . was created by shrewd politicians in an effort to win the negro vote.

b. Designating things designed for the use of Negroes, esp. as slaves: (1) **Negro blanket,** (2) **boot,** (3) **cloth,** (4) **cotton,** (5) **gin,** (6) **hoe,** (7) **pipe,** (8) **rum,** (9) **school,** (10) **shirting,** (11) **shoe.**

(1) 1841 *N.O. Picayune* 3 March 3, 300 pair of Negro Blankets, in Store and for Sale. **1846** *Hunt's Merch. Mag.* XIV. 599 Tent cloth, heavy tarpaulin cloths, bed and negro blankets. — **(2) 1732** *S.C. Gazette* 1 April, He had on . . . a brown coat . . . and blue Negro Boots. — **(3) 1732** *S.C. Gazette* 17 June 4/1 (Th.), Just imported, white and blue Negro Cloth. **1760** *Ib.* 15 Nov. 3/1 A short new negro fellow . . . has on new white negro cloth jacket and breeches. **1872** POWERS *Afoot & Alone* 88 Their only garments, I judge, are kirtles of coarse negro-cloth, once almost white. — **(4) 1774** *N.C. Gazette* (New Bern) 2 Sep. 3/1 *Resolved*, That . . . we import no Article, directly or indirectly, from Great Britain, . . . viz. Artificers and Workmens Tools of all Sorts, Kendal or Negro Cotton. **1789** *Ib.* 29 Jan., He had on and carried with him a white negro cotton coat and breeches. **1818** *Norfolk Beacon* 19 Dec. 1/4 Negro Cottons. 10 Bales just received.

(5) 1890 BIFF HALL *Turnover Club* 211 And also into each glass went what is technically known as a 'jigger' of negro gin. — **(6) 1862** *Ill. Agric. Soc. Trans.* V. 507 There is no reason why we cannot compete with the bar-share plow, the nigger-hoes, and the unskillful labor of the Southern cotton States. — **(7) 1812** *N.Y. Ev. Post* 28 Sep. 3/3 Earthenware, &c. . . . Also, Landing from said Brig, 5 bales White Plains 48 boxes Negro Pipes. — **(8) 1842** in THOMPSON *M. Jones* (1872) 35 He seed lots of long-bearded chaps . . . drinking nigger rum and smokin yankee cigars. **1892** O'NEALL-CHAPMAN *Annals* 499 The women in the meantime drank rum, of that kind known as nigger rum, which they liked better than whiskey on account of its sweet taste. — **(9) 1740** W. SEWARD *Journal* 2, I am, moreover, to collect Subscriptions for a Negroe School in Pensilvania. **1833** in *Cent. Mag.* XXX. 786 The Deputy Sheriff . . . presented me with five indictments for a panegyric upon their virtuous and magnanimous actions, in relation to Miss Crandall's *nigger school* in Canterbury, [N.Y.]. **1948** *Duncan* (Okla.) *D. Banner* 1 July 10/1 The third one is a question of providing for Negro schools in some of the Oklahoma counties which find themselves cramped for funds.

(10) 1835 *S. Lit. Messenger* I. 260 The fabrics are heavy—negro shirtings 29 inches wide [etc.]. — **(11) 1755** in *Pub. Col. Soc.* XII. 97 By Doctr. Ross for 6 pr. Negro Shoes. **1852** *Fla. Plantation Rec.* 84, I saw Mr. Livingston the Man that [ma]kes your Negro Shoes.

c. In designations, often obs., of places set apart for or frequented by Negroes: (1) **Negro cellar,** a low dive frequented by Negroes, *rare;* (2) **corner,** a portion of a hall or church to which Negroes in attendance are restricted; (3) **crib,** =**Jim Crow car;** (4) **juke (joint),** a juke joint; (5) **kitchen,** the kitchen, as on a plantation, where food is prepared for Negro slaves; (6) **pen,** an inclosure or place of security for Negroes awaiting sale as slaves; (7) **street,** a road or a way leading to, or passing in front of, slave quarters; (8) **-ville,** a village of Negroes; (9) **yard,** =**Negro pen.**

(1) 1849 G. G. FOSTER *N.Y. in Slices* 28 The Five Point negro-cellar, with its tallow candle stuck in a bottle. — **(2) 1894** MARK TWAIN *P. Wilson* xxi, In the 'nigger corner' sat Chambers. — **(3) 1849** A. MACKAY *Western World* I. 102 'But where have you put him [a Negro]?' . . . 'Put him?—in the nigger crib, to be sure.' — **(4) 1936** *Scribner's Mag.* Dec. 27/2 Jim growed up mean and close-fisted and now he owns the Store and two nigger jooks and the whole mess of shanties. **1937** *Fla. Times-Union* (Jacksonville) 4 Nov., Before white folks started using the word, there were negro jook-joints as far back as I can remember.

(5) 1815 *Austin P.* I. (1924) 248 You will see that the Cook in the negro Kitchen keeps it in proper order. **1860** ABBOTT *South & North* 209 She will work . . . with no remuneration but such fare and dress as a scullion can find in a 'nigger kitchen.' — **(6) 1861** in STOWE *Key* 122/2 Suppose now, for a moment, that your daughter . . . was in these hot days incarcerated in a negro-pen. — **(7) 1865** in EASTERBY *S.C. Rice Plant.* (1945) 211, I have not been in my negro street nor spoken to a field hand since 1st March. — **(8) 1860** HELPER *Impending Crisis* 18 Like all other *niggervilles* in our disreputable part of the confederacy, the commercial emporium of South Carolina is sick and impoverished. — **(9) 1806** *Balance* V. 53/2, I am informed that there are several negro-yards in Savannah, where slaves imported into South Carolina are kept for sale. **1945** BOTKIN *My Burden* 158 They have big sandbars and planks fix round the nigger yards.

Also (1) **Negro cabin,** (2) **car,** (3) **gallery,** (4) **heaven,** (5) **house,** (6) **hut,** (7) **pew,** (8) **shanty.**

(1) 1790 BENTLEY *Diary* I. 180 There is . . . a group of Negro Cabins on the west side. **1906** BELL *C. Lee* 62 In her imagination the rows upon rows of negro cabins were rebuilt and whitewashed anew. — **(2) 1860** ABBOTT *South & North* 103 He was thrust into the negro-car, and sent out of the State. **1881** *Cent. Mag.* Nov. 126/2 The conductor came into the negro car to collect tickets. — **(3) 1844** UNCLE SAM *Peculiarities* II. 99 The 'nigger gallery'—the only part of an American theatre where men with the slightest tinge of African blood can be admitted. **1894** M. TWAIN *Those Extraordinary Twins* viii. 420 (R.), It usurped the place of pious thought in the 'nigger gallery.' — **(4) 1878** DALY in J. F. Daly *A. Daly* 249 There is a 'Nigger Heaven' (as the third tier is called in Troy) here, & as 'tis capacious I have been liberal with my pencilled passes. **1943** *Copper Camp* 153 The theater had a large skylight directly over the second balcony, or 'nigger heaven' as it was known to them.

(5) 1734 *S.C. Gazette* 19 Oct. 4/1 (*advt.*), To be Lett, A Plantation Scituate on Wampee Savannah, most of it being rich Savana land, . . . whereon is a large Barn, a dwelling house, and Negro houses. **1858** *Texas Almanac 1859* 85 He should see that . . . his negro-houses are made close and comfortable. — **(6) 1787** GRIEVE tr. Chastellux *Travels* II. 74 Not even a negro-hut was to be met with. **1864** NICHOLS *Amer. Life* I. 169 The tavern would take the lead, and all the little stores and negro huts could follow in its wake. — **(7) 1841** in W. J. & F. L. GARRISON *Life W. L. Garrison* III. 27 We recommend to abolitionists as the most consistent and effectual method of abolishing the 'negro pew' to take their seats in it, wherever it may be found, whether in a gentile synagogue, a railroad car, a steamboat, or a stage-coach. **1849** DAVIES *Amer. Scenes* 219 We . . . at once concluded that the section of pews at the end wall must be . . . the terrestrio-celestial elevation commonly called the 'Negro Pew.' — **(8) 1871** Goss *Soldier's Story* 18 The hospital camp at Savage's Station consisted of three hundred hospital tents and several negro shanties full of sick and wounded soldiers from the battle-fields.

d. Designating those having to do with Negroes, esp. as slaves: (1) **Negro breaker,** one who was especially severe in reducing Negro slaves to subjection, also transf.; (2) **catcher,** one who made a practice of catching runaway Negro slaves and returning them to their masters; (3) **hound,** a person who captured and returned fugitive slaves; (4) **monger,** a Negro trader; (5) **overseer,** a white man in charge of a group of slaves on a plantation; (6) **regulator,** one who aimed to regulate the conduct of Negroes in the South after the Civil War.

(1) 1845 F. DOUGLASS *Life* 57 All of this added weight to his reputation as a 'nigger-breaker.' **1899** CHESNUTT *Conjure Woman* 96 En dey ain' nebber be'n no nigger-breaker lack you roun' heah befo'. — **(2) 1853** STOWE *Key* 5/2 The trader, the kidnapper, the negro-catcher, the negro-whipper, and all the other . . . appendages of what is often called the 'divinely-instituted relation' of slavery. **1899** CHESNUTT *Wife of His Youth* 198 They got the notion somehow that Grandison belonged to a nigger-catcher. — **(3) 1862** *N.Y. Tribune* 9 May 12/5 It has been found by them that Schenk, Piatt, and the rest, are not negro-hounds. — **(4) 1741** *Georgia Col. Rec.* IV. 678 This exposes them to the Envy and Hatred of our Negro-Mongers.

(5) 1748 *Georgia Col. Rec.* VI. 215 The two Petitioners have for several Years past been Negro Overseers in South Carolina. — **(6) 1866** *Cong. Globe* App. 14 Nov. 33/3 Bands of 'guerrillas' and 'negro regulators' soon increased in numbers and audacity.

Also (1) **Negro dealer,** (2) **jockey,** (3) **speculator,** (4) **stealer,** (5) **teacher,** (6) **thief.**

(1) 1853 F. W. THOMAS *J. Randolph* 285 You know Robinson that nigger-dealer, who has the pen down town. — **(2) 1838** HALIBURTON *Clockmaker* 2 Ser. 32 A nigger-jockey, sir, says I, is a gentleman that trades in niggers,—buys them in one state, and sells them in another, where they arn't known. — **(3) 1812** in *Va. Hist. Mag.* XXXV. (1927) 285, I told him I was sorry . . . his wife . . . had a negro speculator for her husband. **1887** HARRIS *Free Joe* 3 To these young men the negro speculator . . . proceeded to address himself. — **(4) 1827** *Western Mo. Rev.* I 69 It will be the refuge of Negro-stealers and the Elysium of rogues. **1884** MARK TWAIN *H. Finn* xxxiii. 314 Only I couldn't believe it. Tom Sawyer a nigger-stealer!

(5) 1880 TOURGEE *Bricks* 163 A good many gentlemen called in to see the school . . . , merely desirous to see the pretty Yankee 'nigger teachers.' — **(6) 1853** SIMMS *Sword & Distaff* 499 Here's the box; it's got the pretickilar papers to convict him and to hang him, the villain, and the nigger thief, and murderer. **1877** JOHNSON *Anderson Co., Kans.* 24 Some came for political purposes— . . . some, to drive out the 'cursed Yankees,' whom they regarded as negro thieves.

e. Pertaining to political rule or government conducted or dominated by Negroes, usu. with reference to conditions in the South just after the Civil War, as **Negro domination, dynasty, government, legislation, rule, supremacy.**

1890 *Cong. Rec.* 2 June 5545/1 To rid themselves of what they are pleased to term 'negro domination,' [they] habitually count out the negro vote. — **1884** *Cent. Mag.* April 861/2 The methods which overturned the carpet-bag and negro dynasties find their justification . . . in the instinct of self-preservation. — **1877** BEARD *K.K.K. Sketches* 25 The governments in the South—State, district, and municipal—were negro governments. — **1885** *Mass. H.S. Proc.* 2 Ser. VI. 402 We visited several Southern cities . . . during the period of 'carpet-bag' government and negro legislation. — **1887** *Harper's Mag.* March 635/2 To be a Republican . . . was to be identified with the detested carpetbag government and with negro rule. — **1884** *Cent. Mag.* April 861/2 It was the period of negro supremacy—the reign of terror. **1949** *Ark. Hist. Quart.* Spring 11 They alleged that it paved the way for negro supremacy.

f. In the names of plants and animals: (1) **Negro bean,** (see quot.); (2) **bug,** a hemipterous insect, *Carimelaena pulicaria*, resembling the chinchbug, found esp. on blackberry and raspberry bushes; (3) **lice,** =**beggar lice.**

(1) 1894 *N. Amer. Rev.* Feb. 138 Our daily ration, which we received every day about noon, consisted of a little piece of cornbread, a morsel of rancid bacon, and six or seven spoonfuls of niggerbeans. — **(2) 1884** *Rep. Comm. Agric.* 390 The Flea-Like Negro-Bug. . . . The study of this species was undertaken with the object of breeding, and thereby settling the date of oviposition and hatching. — **(3) 1940** MENCKEN *Happy Days* 43 Sometimes a black-hearted boy would sneak into the adjacent brickyard, which was covered in large part with Jimpson weeds, plantains and other such vegetable outlaws, and return with a large ball of nigger-lice.

Also: (1) **Negro chub,** (2) **dick,** (3) **duck,** (4) **fish,** (5) **goose,** (6) **knocker,** (7) **pea,** (8) **weed.**

(1) 1884 GOODE *Fisheries* I. 618 The 'cut-lips,' 'Day chub,' or 'Nigger chub' is found in abundance only in the basin of the Susquehanna. It reaches a length of six or eight inches, and has no economic importance. — **(2) 1896** JORDAN & EVERMANN *Check-List Fishes* 265 Cut-lips; Nigger Chub; Nigger Dick. . . . Abundant in the basins of the Susquehanna, Hudson, Potomac, James, Roanoke, and Kanawha. — (3) **1876** *Fur, Fin, & Feather* Sep. 101/2 The gray-duck, shell-drake and teal . . . are obliged to tolerate in their society that . . . stupid, tough, shot-resisting thing, which is vulgarly called 'nigger duck.' — (4) **1888** GOODE *Amer. Fishes* 321 Next in importance . . . comes the Flat Fish, *Pseudopleuronectes Americanus*. . . . New York anglers call it the 'Nigger Fish.'

(5) **1917** *Birds of Amer.* I. 97/2 The Cormorants have many local names, such as 'Shag,' 'Lawyer,' and 'Nigger Goose.' **1947** *Nat. Geog. Mag.* Sep. 339/1 A large flight of cormorants, called there [No. Carolina] 'nigger geese,' passed close aboard. — (6) **1859** G. W. BAGBY *Writings* (1884) I. 258 (Th. Supp.), Another name for the nigger-knocker is hog-fish, and it is by far the ugliest tenant of the Virginia waters. Catfish are sweet and pretty compared to nigger-knockers. — (7) **1881** VAWTER *Prison Life* 51 In addition to this, we received about half a pint of cooked beans or peas. They were raised in the South to feed slaves, and were called the 'nigger peas,' but I think they are really a species of coarse black bean. — (8) **1894** *Amer. Folk-Lore* VII. 92 *Eupatorium purpureum*, nigger-weed, queen-of-the-meadow, Ind.

6. In colloq. phrases in which the spelling is usu. "nigger": **a.** *To let off a little nigger*, to act as a Negro supposedly would. *Rare.*

1882 *Yankee* May 175/1 You would swear from the words and sounds . . . that the fellow was going to tear somebody limb from limb. . . . No such thing . . . he is only letting off a little nigger.

b. *To work like a nigger*, to work very hard. *Colloq.*

1836 GILMAN *Recoll.* (1838) 189, I have toiled night and day, I've worked like a nigger, and more than a nigger. **1880** MARK TWAIN *Tramp Abroad* 40 He laid into his work like a nigger. **1939** *These Are Our Lives* 5 The next year I worked like a nigger and that fall John bought me a coat suit.

c. *A nigger in the fence*, =next.

1850 *Calif. Courier* (S.F.) 4 Sep. 2/6 The majority of the papers, however, think that there 'is a nigger in the fence' somewhere. [*Ib.* The *News* thinks it sees 'the nigger' in that corner.] **1876** *Silver City* (Ida.) *Avalanche* 11 Jan. 3/3 Some one 'has blundered,' or else there is a 'nigger in the fence' somewhere. **1933** CHELEY *Camping Out* 167 The fox can reason, too, and says to himself, 'What in thunder made that galoot set a trap as if it were a signpost? There's a nigger in that fence!

d. *A nigger in the woodpile*, a concealed or inconspicuous but highly important fact, factor, or "catch" in a situation, proposal, account, etc. Also in allusive use.

1852 in *Kans. Hist. Quart.* XI. (1942) 235 No 'nigger in the wood pile' here . . . ; white men are at the bottom of this speculation. **1911** W. WILSON in *Outlook* 11 Aug. 944 If you go through the schedules you will find some nigger in every wood pile. [**1948** *Time* 13 Dec. 81/2 Today's crop is obviously better educated and, if anything, up to a faster type of baseball. The culprit in the injury woodpile is the development of trick pitching.] **1949** *Chi. Tribune* 22 Sep. 24/3 Britons suspect there may be a joker in the dollar talks agreement. Enigma in the woodpile, perhaps?

As the last term in **Africa, buck, Congo, cornfield, cotton, dower, field, gone, hoe, house, Indian, Kentuck, new, plantation, white, white folks' Negro.**

∗**Negro baby. a.** (See quot.) *Obs.* **b.** (See quot.) **c.** A form of candy. *Slang.*

(**a**) **1871** DE VERE 117 Among the cant words produced by the late Civil War, nigger babies also became very popular; the term originated with the veterans serving under the Confederate General Hardee, who gave that name to the enormous projectiles thrown into the city of Charlestown by the Swamp Angel of General Gillmore, as his monster-gun in the swamps was ironically called. — (**b**) **1901** JEPSON *Flora of Western Middle Calif.* 129 S[*isyrinchium*] *bellum*. Blue-eyed grass. Nigger-babies. . . . Very common throughout California. Mar.–April. — (**c**) **1948** WESTON *Mother Lode* 94 Candies with birds and flowers in the centers, nigger-babies, gumdraps, an' lickorish whips.

Negro business. Business concerning Negroes, the acting of Negro roles on the stage, the business of trading in Negro slaves. *Obs.*

1853 STOWE *Key* 91/2 The justice introduces the business as follows:—Now, about this nigger business. **1869** DUMONT *Benedict's Cong. Songster* 9 Lew met with a hearty reception and concluded to adopt the 'negro business' as his profession. **1877** HABBERTON *Jericho Road* 150 That's better than we done when we was in the nigger business.

Negro dog. *S.* Before the Civil War, a dog trained to pursue and capture runaway slaves. Now *hist.*

1845 in STOWE *Key* 109/1 The undersigned having bought the entire pack of Negro Dogs (of the Hay and Allen stock), he now proposes to catch runaway negroes. **1892** J. C. HARRIS *On Plantation* 34 He says he gwine atter Bill Locke an' his nigger dogs. **1945** BOTKIN *My Burden* 122, I thunk I heared the nigger dogs and somebody on horseback.

Negrodom ˈnigrodəm, *n.* The area or territory in the U.S. in which Negroes were formerly held in bondage; Negroes collectively. *Obs.*

1847 *Cong. Globe* App. 13 Feb. 376/1 Our measures have given all that wide region to be the empire of negrodom. **1862** HAWTHORNE in Bridge *Personal Recoll.* (1893) 173, I ought to thank you for a shaded map of negrodom, which you sent me a little while ago. **1866** C. H. SMITH *Bill Arp* 24 That eventful period which you have fixed when . . . Niggerdom is to feel the power of your proclamation.

Negro election. (See quots.) *Obs.*

[**1866** CAULKINS *Hist. Norwich* 330 In former times, the ceremony of a mock election of a negro governor, created no little excitement in their ranks.] **1868** S. SMITH *Autobiography* 12 We chased all the niggers off the Common, as was usually done on occasions of gatherings, except on what was termed 'nigger 'lection,' which I don't know the meaning of to this day. I only know that on that day the colored people were permitted to remain unmolested on Boston Common. **1894** EARLE in A. G. Winslow *Diary* 118 (*footnote*), Boston had two election days. On Artillery Election the Ancient and Honorable Artillery had a dress parade. . . . The other day was called 'Nigger Lection,' because the blacks were permitted to throng the Common.

∗**Negrohead,** *n.* Also **niggerhead.**

1. A low grade of strong, dark-colored tobacco. In full **Negrohead tobacco.** Also attrib.

1809 IRVING *Hist. N.Y.* (1927) VI. ii. 311 He . . . thrust a prodigious quid of negro head tobacco into his left cheek. **1843** J. LUMSDEN *Amer. Mem.* 14 My next communication will probably contain full details of the methods adopted by the Virginian planters in the manufacturing of the nigger-head, ladies'-twist [etc.]. **1894** *Outing* XXIV. 355/1 These [cigarettes] are made of native grown tobacco or the rank cheap stuff called nigger-head twist. **1945** MENCKEN *Supp.* I. 528 In 1943 there was another [uproar] over the belated discovery that the American Tobacco Company was making a brand of tobacco called *Nigger Head*.

2. A stone or rock (see quot. 1886).

1847 HOWE *Ohio* 569 It was a saw mill, with a small pair of stones attached, made of boulders, or 'nigger heads,' as they are commonly called. **1886** *Smithsonian Inst. Rep.* II. 523 *Nigger head.* (1) The black concretionary nodules found in granite; (2) Any hard, dark, colored rock weathering out with rounded nodules or bowlders; (3) Slaty rock associated with sandstone. A quarryman's term. **1948** DICK *Dixie Frontier* 4 Bears rolled 'nigger head' stones over and ate the grubs and field mice.

attrib. and *transf.* **1854** *Pioneer* (S.F.) Feb. 100 After some pretty careful navigation among the . . . rocks and 'nigger-heads' that made off from the reef, . . . we at last effected a safe landing. **1936** MCKENNA *Black Range* 48 The hammers and war axes we took note of were nearly all made of a niggerhead rock not found in the vicinity.

3. (See quot. 1859.)

1859 BARTLETT 292 *Nigger Heads*, the tussocks or knotted masses of the roots of sedges and ferns projecting above the wet surface of a swamp. South. **1892** A. E. LEE *Hist. Columbus, Ohio* I. 274 Hummocks, called in the borough dialect 'nigger-heads,' formed by tufts of swamp grass. **1947** BROWN *Outdoors Unlimited* 314 The ptarmigan cackled in the manner of a Bronx cheer as it flew to a nearby nigger-head.

4. (See quot. 1871.) Also attrib. *Obs.*

1868 *N.Y. Herald* 6 July 3/2 The d——d radical party, with its niggerhead Congress. **1871** DE VERE 281 They were Democrats, and retorted upon violent Union men by calling them Niggerheads.

b. Hence **niggerheadism.** *Obs.*

1868 *N.Y. Herald* 7 July 6/2 It demanded . . . a final settlement of all the vexed questions of copperheadism and niggerheadism.

5. =**bisnaga.**

1877 HODGE *Arizona* 244 The kind [of cactus] commonly called the nigger head is round, of the size of a cabbage, and covered with large, crooked catlike thorns. **1879** WILLIAMS *Pacific Tourist* 292/2 The gigantic 'nigger-head' (*Echinocactus Cylindraceus*) lifts its bristling trunk sometimes four feet, and is three feet in diameter, covered with fish-hooks. **1940** JAEGER *Calif. Deserts* 181 Closely allied to this is the Mohavean niggerhead.

6. Any one of various plants (see quots.). *Colloq.*

1899 COULTER *Flora of Indiana* 984 R[udbeckia] hirta. Black-eyed Susan. Meadow Cone flower. Nigger-head. . . . Flowers from early June until the late frosts. **1902** *Out West* Oct. 452 He . . . told her the many aliases of *maguey*, . . . soapweed, 'niggerhead,' bear grass, Spanish dagger or bayonet. **1908** *Suburban Life* Aug. 68/1 In the East it is more commonly known as the ox-eyed daisy, while in the West it is frequently spoken of as the 'nigger-head.' **1931** CLUTE *Plants* 45 A number of composites with yellow rays and dark centers are commonly known as niggerheads, though the more polite term is black-eyed Susan. **1940** EARLY *N. Eng. Sampler* 317 Another remarkable weed is Echinacea (*Indian Head-root* or *Nigger-head*), a powerful drug, and an American cure-all for nearly three hundred years.

Negroidal nəˈgrɔɪdḷ, *a.* Like or resembling Negroes. *Obs.* — **1878** STANLEY *Dark Continent* I. 113 They were truly negroidal in hair and colour. **1881** CABLE *Mme. Delphine* 7 Comely Ethiopians culled out of the less negroidal types of the African live goods.

* **Negroism,** *n.* Also **niggerism.**

1. a. Endorsement of Negro slavery. **b.** Abolitionism. **c.** Domination by Negroes. **d.** The qualities or characteristics of Negroes.

(**a**) **1844** *St. Louis Reveille* 24 Nov. 2/4 Scrub and whitewash your spiritual niggerism, or you will forever rest in the valley of *Sheol!* **1862** *N.Y. Tribune* 14 April 8/4 Most of the common soldiers had been reared among negroes, had become infused with negroism, and knew nothing beyond it. — (**b**) **1847** *Cong. Globe* App. 323/2 He . . . thanked God that he voted against that Wilmot proviso. It smelt rank of negroism. **1856** *Ill. State Reg* (Springfield) 19 June 2/1 For every democrat who deserts to niggerism, one hundred old line whigs join the democracy against it. — (**c**) **1871** *Ku Klux Klan Rep.* VII. 608 [White people] would not submit to negroism in [Georgia]. — (**d**) **1900** *Cong. Rec.* 5 Feb. 1507/2 As a fresh manifestation of negroism, of what the negro's attitude is toward the white man, . . . its significance should not be allowed to escape us.

2. A word, expression, pronunciation, etc., characteristic of the speech of Negroes.

1859 BARTLETT viii, The term 'Americanism' . . . may then be said to include . . . Negroisms. **1878** BEADLE *Western Wilds* 19 This Hoosier language is the result of a union between the rude translations of 'Pennsylvania Dutch,' the negroisms of Kentucky and Virginia, and certain phrases native to the Ohio Valley. **1884** *Amer. Philol. Assoc. Trans.* XVI. App. p. xxxi, The wonderful figure-speech, specimens of which will be given later under the head of Negroisms.

Negro-killer, nigger-killer. 1. (See quot. 1916.) *Obs.* **2.** (See quot.) *Obs.* **3.** =**Negro shooter.** *Colloq.* **4.** (See quot.)

(**1**) **1855** DAVIS *Farm Bk.* 140 Planted out in rows 7 bushels of Spanish potatoes & in the bed 10 Spanish—5 Negro killers & 23 of Yams. **1916** MASSEY *Reminiscences* 22 Yams, Spanish, white and red (called 'nigger killers') potatoes were grown in abundance and put up in banks for winter use. — (**2**) **1856** OLMSTED *Slave States* 108 If a man does not provide well for his slaves, . . . he gets the name of a 'nigger killer.' — (**3**) **1940** WILSON *Wabash* 318 It is barefoot boys on country roads, with nigger-killers dangling from the pockets of their overalls and strings of 'yeller catfish' slung over their shoulders. — (**4**) **1944** CLARK *Pills* 130 This gun was popularly known to the trade as a 'nigger killer,' and it was said that it fired a standard short thirty-two caliber bullet sidewise.

Negroless ˈnigrolɪs, *a.* Not possessing Negro slaves. *Obs.* — **1859** *N.Y. Wkly. Tribune* 3 Sep. 5/3 The Democracy . . . want to furnish 'niggers for the niggerless,' but have a natural repugnance to 'lands for the landless.' **1866** RICHARDSON *Secret Service* 140 If you gentlemen who own negroes attempt to take the State of Missouri out of the Union, in about six months you will be the most—niggerless set of individuals that you ever heard of.

Negro meeting. 1. A meeting of Negroes for religious services. **2.** A meeting for a lecture or discussion concerning the slavery issue. Both *obs.*

(**1**) **1823** in MATHEWS *Memoirs* III. 350 The pranks that are played in the 'nigger meetings,' as they are called, are beyond belief—yelling, screeching, and groaning. **1863** E. KIRKE *Southern Friends* 111, I asked Preston if the old black led the services at the negro meetings. — (**2**) **1858** G. K. WILDER *Diary* 20 July (MS), We were 'at nigger meeting in the evening.'

Negro minstrel. One of a group of comedians, usu. white men in blackface, who give a performance consisting of Negro songs, dances, jokes, etc. Also any blackface comedian who uses Negro material.

1857 *Ladies' Repository* July 421/2 The negro minstrel may have a large audience. **1896** HASWELL *New York* 405 September [1843], the Chatham Theatre, in new hands, opened. A very notable attachment to the company was the 'Virginia Minstrels' . . . for this was the beginning of 'Negro minstrels.' **1948** MENCKEN *Supp.* II. 257 The Irishman and the German became standard types in American comedy, alongside the Negro minstrel introduced by Thomas D. Rice (1808–60) in the 30s.

attrib. **1889** MUNROE *Golden Days* 74 In one [gambling house] they found . . . a negro minstrel troupe. **1893** LELAND *Memoirs* 58 It is very commonly asserted that the first regular negro minstrel troupe appeared in 1842. This is quite an error. While I was at Mr. Greene's, in 1835, there came to Dedham [Mass.] a circus with as regularly-appointed a negro minstrel troupe of a dozen as I ever saw. **1948** *Ada* (Okla.) *Ev. News* 4 July 7/4 The Unit III group . . . gave a short negro-minstrel-type stunt, using padding and black-face, plus all the old clothes and old jokes they could put together.

b. Negro minstrelsy, the entertainment provided by Negro minstrels.

1855 *Western Citizen* (Paris, Ky.) 19 Oct. 3/2 Our town has been highly favored this week, with *negro minstrelsy*, as it is called, though to our notion, there was a good deal of 'white folks' about it. **1915** B. MATTHEWS in *Scribner's Mag.* June 754/1 Negro-minstrelsy is . . . absolutely native to these States.

Negro-ology ˌnigroˈɑlədʒɪ, *n.* Also **niggerology.** A pretended science dealing with Negroes. *Sarcastic. Obs.* — **1840** *Boston Transcript* 25 Jan. 2/4 (*heading*), Nigger-ology. **1859** *Mountaineer* (Salt Lake City) 17 Sep. 14/4 Judge Drummond, from Utah, is lecturing the New Englanders . . . on their sins, crafts, niggerology, murders, &c.

Negro party. 1. A political party of slaveholders. **2.** A political party sympathetic to the interests of Negroes. Both *obs.*

(**1**) **1857** *Lawrence* (Kans.) *Republican* 2 July 2 Although the number of Free State men, perhaps, treble the Nigger party, the election must be carried by the latter. **1860** HELPER *Impending Crisis* 169 The greatest good that could happen to this country would be the complete overthrow of the slave-driving democracy, *alias* the negro party. — (**2**) **1895** G. KING *New Orleans* 322 The carpet-bag and negro party . . . saw itself becoming hopelessly overmatched by the civil and social power organized against it. **1911** H. S. HARRISON *Queed* v. 55 He went bag and baggage to . . . the 'nigger party.'

Negrophilism nəˈgrɑfəlˌɪzəm, *n.* [* *Negrophile*, friend of Negroes, +*-ism*.] Excessive fondness for Negroes. *Obs.*

1846 *Cong. Globe* 18 May 838/1 (Th.), The gentleman from Ohio . . . the advocate of negro-philism. **1883** *Advance* 11 Oct., It is silly and unchristian to accuse him of 'Negrophilism,' simply because he stands up to plead for a race that has been oppressed and down trodden. **1904** *Nation* 11 Aug. 107/3 The President's comments should do good in the South, where the monstrous opinion has grown up that what it calls 'negrophilism' in the North regards rape by negroes with an almost apologistic toleration.

Negrophilist nəˈgrɑfəlɪst, *n.* A Negro-lover; one interested in Negroes. Usu. derogatory. *Obs.* — **1842** in S. LONGFELLOW *H. W. Longfellow* I. 449 When the Eastern negrophilists are prepared to pay a tax, they will have a right to dispose of the property of their Southern brethren. **1899** *Pop. Sci. Mo.* LV. 178 The most infatuated negrophilist would not stultify himself.

Negro quarter. The group of buildings occupied by the Negro slaves on a plantation. Often *pl.* Now *hist.*

1734 *N.Y. Gazette* 18–25 March 1/1 Coll. Thomas L——d keeps at some Miles distance from his dwelling House, Negro-quarters (as they are called). **1809** F. CUMING *Western Tour* 242 Alvis has a negro quarter, and nearly one hundred and fifty acres of land. **1819** THOMAS *Travels* 108 Negro quarters, which are shabby log buildings in the rear of the *great house*, were objects, however, not to be overlooked. **1913** EATON *Barn Doors & Byways* 167 The old foundation stones show that the house was once one hundred and ten feet long, with a gigantic kitchen and outstanding negro quarters. **1937** DORRIS *Old Cane Springs* 56 Furthermore, I would witness Christmas in the Negro quarters.

b. A Negro cabin. *Rare.*

1888 GRIGSBY *Smoked Yank* (1891) 60 We were guarded in a negro quarter or hut.

Negro trader. (See quot. 1897.)

1732 in *R.I. Hist. Soc. Coll.* XVI. 108 They kill'd several of the Negroes, and obliged . . . the rest to quit the Sloop, 13 of them getting into the Boat, & 9 into 2 Canoas with 4 Negro Traders then on board. **1818** *Nashville* (Tenn.) *Clarion* 10 Nov. 3/6 Mahone was once a waggoner, and is now believed to be a negro trader. **1897** TERHUNE *Old-field School* 24 'Negro traders,' whose business was to buy and sell slaves, were heartily despised by the very men who sold negroes to them to be shipped in droves to rice and sugar plantations in the far South. **1937** DORRIS *Old Cane Springs* 31 He had hoped Mr. Mullins wanted the Negroes for himself, and that he was not a 'regular nigger trader.'

* **neighborhood,** *n.*

1. neighborhood road, a road, maintained locally, which passes through or serves a rural neighborhood or community.

1843 CARLTON *New Purchase* I. 89 Notice here, a neighborhood road does not imply necessarily much proximity of neighbours. **1884** CABLE *Dr. Sevier* 395 The buggy was moving at a quiet jog along a 'neighborhood road.' **1903** *D.N.* II. 306.

2. neighborhood school, a school, usu. an elementary rural one, situated in, and serving the needs of, a neighborhood.

1842 *S. Lit. Messenger* VIII. 65/1 As this was what was called a 'neighborhood school,' the pupils necessarily came from a great distance. **1887** *Harper's Mag.* Feb. 353/2 There is a neighborhood school where English is taught.

3. *In the neighborhood of*, approximately, about. *Colloq.*

1854 *Fla. Plantation Rec.* 100, I have about in the neighborhood of 40 packed bales of Cotton. **1905** A. ADAMS *Outlet* 310 It was in the neighborhood of ninety miles across to the mouth of the Yellowstone. **1948** *Democrat* 19 Aug. 2/3 The . . . skyscraper . . . would cost 'in the neighborhood of 25 million dollars.'

* **Nelson,** *n.* [Edward W. *Nelson* (1855–1934), Amer. naturalist.] In the possessive in the names of birds: (1) **Nelson's oriole,** (see quot.); (2) **(sharp-tailed) finch,** = next; (3) **(sharp-tailed) sparrow,** (see quot.).

(1) **1917** *Birds of Amer.* II. 256 The Arizona Hooded Oriole, or Nelson's Oriole (*Icterus cucullatus nelsoni*) is similar to Sennett's Oriole, but paler and with its forehead entirely yellow. — (2) **1880** *Nuttall Ornith. Club Bul.* V. 32 Nelson's Sharp-Tailed Finch.—'Took a beautiful adult male, May 8, 1879; flushed him from a timothy meadow.' **1917** [see next.] — (3) **1887** RIDGWAY *Man. N. Amer. Birds* 413 *Ammodramus caudacutus nelsoni* . . . Nelson's Sparrow. **1917** *Birds of Amer.* III. 30 Nelson's Sparrow (*Passerherbulus nelsoni nelsoni*), also known as Nelson's Finch and as Nelson's Sharp-tailed Sparrow, is decidedly smaller than the Sharp-tailed Sparrow.

Nephite ˈnifaɪt, *n.* [Cf. *Neph*, an Egyptian divinity.] According to the *Book of Mormon*, a member of the nation found by Nephi, who with his father and brothers fled from Jerusalem to America about 600 B.C.

1830 *Book of Mormon* (1920) 108/2 Now the people which were not Lamanites were Nephites. . . . Those who are friendly to Nephi I shall call Nephites, or the people of Nephi. **1853** *Harper's Mag.* April 609/2 It was immediately revealed to the Prophet that . . . that chief was killed in the last great battle fought between Lamanites and Nephites. **1948** *Amer. Folk-Lore* Jan.–Mar. 26 'Translated beings'—John the Beloved and Three Nephites—have come to the aid of Latter-Day Saints on numerous occasions.

* **nerve,** *n.* **1. nerve root,** (see quots.). **2. nerve storm,** (see quot.).

(1) **1892** *Amer. Folk-Lore* V. 103 *Cypripedium acaule*, nerve-root. N.B. **1899** *Animal & Plant Lore* 115 The large lady's slipper is often called 'nerve-root' on account of its use as a nerve tonic. Western Massachusetts. **1949** [see ***Noah's ark**]. — (2) **1890** BILLINGS *Med. Dict.*, *Nerve-storms*, sudden attacks or paroxysms of neuroses or functional nervous disease.

* **nervine,** *n.* Any species of *Cypripedium*, supposed to be a tonic for nerves. — **1882** *Harper's Mag.* Feb. 435/2, I saw that she had been searching for nervine and sassafras.

* **nervy,** *a.* **1.** Having or requiring nerve or courage. **2.** Cheeky, bold, impudent. *Colloq.*

(1) **1884** *Lisbon* (Dakota) *Star* 5 Sep., The dealer was Miner Smoot, now in Denver, and a nervier man never lived. **1926** *N.Y. Times* 6 Oct. 16/1 He pitched to their strength and got away with it—the nerviest and most daring episode of the series. — (2) **1896** ADE *Artie* 75, I just received your nervy letter. **1948** *Pauls Valley* (Okla.) *D. Democrat* 2 May 4 Wouldn't it be rather nervy to ask her help?

neshaw nəˈʃɔ, *n.* [See quot. 1895.] (See quots.) In full **neshaw eel.** — **1839** STORER *Mass. Fishes* 158 *Muraena Argentea.* . . . The Silver Eel. . . . Its general color is silvery gray, darker upon its upper portion. . . . This species is taken in pots in October, when it leaves the ponds, and seldom at other times. At Holmes Hole, it is called 'Neshaw eel.' **1895** GERARD in *N.Y. Sun* 30 July, Neshaw, a local name in Massachusetts for a species of eel: from Narragansett 'neshau,' plural 'neshauog,' 'there are two,' probably referring to the fins of which there seem to be but two.

Nesselrode pudding. [Named for Count K. R. *Nesselrode* (1780–1862), Russian diplomat.] A frozen desert containing marrons and fruit.

1876 HENDERSON *Cooking* 312 Nesselrode Pudding. . . . Ingredients: Forty chestnuts, one pound of sugar, . . . one pint of cream, the yolks of twelve eggs [etc.]. **1941** FARMER *Boston Cook Book* 582 Nesselrode Pudding . . . 3 cups milk, 1 cup sugar . . . ¼ cup pineapple sirup, 1½ cups marrons canned in syrup [etc.]. [**1948** *Chi. D. News* 22 Oct. 45 I'll start it off with shrimp cocktail, then some porterhouse steak, some bourbon and nesselrode pie a la mode.]

* **nest,** *n.* As the last term in **bird's, fall bird's, hang, hornet's, hurrah's nest.**

* **nest,** *v. W. intr.* To become a nester *q.v.* — **1918** MULFORD *Man from Bar-20* xi. 114 Not satisfied with nestin' on a man's range, you had to start a little herd. **1936** BARNARD *Rider* 61 We cowpunchers had no use for the boomers. They came into our country, plowed up good grass, and started to nesting and working like the devil.

* **nester,** *n. W.* An opprobrious term for one seeking to settle down permanently as a homesteader, farmer, small rancher, etc., in a cattle-grazing region. — **1880** *Ft. Griffin* (Tex.) *Echo* 3 Jan., [A sheep man is] a tramp, an ingrate, a 'Nester,' and a liar. **1947** *Sierra Club Bul.* May 36 They did their best to keep the nester . . . out of the West and to terrorize or bankrupt him where he could not be kept out.

* **net,** *n.* As the last term in **brush, fly, fyke, gill, head, life, mosquito, pound, scap, scoop, scooping, stir, trap net.**

netop ˈnitap, *n. N. Eng.* [Algonquian; cf. Narragansett *netomp*, my friend.]

1. A friend; a companion, dear one. *Obs.*

1643 WILLIAMS *Key* (1866), *Netop Kunnatótemous.* Friend, I will aske you a Question. **1662** *New Haven Col. Rec.* 461 The Indian . . . shooke her . . . by ye hand, and asked her where her netop was. *c***1707** in G. SHELDON *Hist. Deerfield, Mass.* I. 362 She spake, saying, 'Netop, Netop, my master.' **1890** *N. & Q.* IV. 237 *Netop.* Fifty years ago, in New England, this word was not very uncommon among the older people. It meant a close friend, a chum, a companion. **1898** WESTCOTT *D. Harum* 289 'Mr. Harum and I are great "neetups," as he says.' . . . 'It means "cronies," I believe, in his dictionary.'

2. An Indian. *Obs.*

1704 S. KNIGHT *Journal* 38 You speak negro to him. . . . Hah! says Netop, now me stomany that. **1716** CHURCH *Philip's War* 19 Mr. Churches hands were fastned in the Netops hair. **1760** NILES *Indian Wars* I. 229 Mr. Wheelwright . . . should be such a netop's servant.

* **nettle,** *n.* As the last term in **bull, flowering, horse, sand horse, spurge, sting, wood nettle.**

nettle weed. A plant of the nettle family. — **1843** CARLTON *New Purchase* I. 159 [Settlers in Indiana] gathered a peculiar species of nettle, (called there nettleweed,) which they succeeded in dressing like flax. **1867** LACKLAND *Homespun* 18 Their blackened skeletons . . . overgrown with the nettleweeds and long grasses.

network ˈnɛtˌwɜk, *v.* [f. the noun.] *tr.* To cover (an area) with a network of railroad lines. — **1887** *Courier-Journal* 24 Jan. 8/1 It is only a question of time when railroads will net-work the Pan-handle. **1914** *Cyclo. Amer. Govt.* III. 139/1 Whole regions are networked, and one can go by trolley car from the Atlantic to the Middle West.

neutral ground. Also *cap.*

1. During the Revolution, an area in Westchester County, N.Y., lying between the British and the American lines. *Obs.* or *hist.*

1821 J. F. COOPER (*title*), The Spy; a Tale of the Neutral Ground. **1896** HASWELL *New York* 129 Captain H. L. Barnum wrote a volume entitled, 'The Spy Unmasked' . . . in which Birch was identified with Enoch Crosby, a resident of the present Putnam County, on the border of Westchester—the 'neutral ground' of the Revolution.

2. A zone between Spanish Texas and the U.S. declared neutral in 1806. Now *hist.*

1836 *Diplom. Corr. Texas* I. (1908) 83 The object of the concentration of forces at Jessup is to protect the frontier and the Neuteral [*sic*] Ground also to keep the Indians in check. **1856** YOAKUM *Hist. Texas* I. 133 Until the question of boundary between the two governments was settled, all the territory between the Sabine and the Arroyo Honda should be a *neutral ground*, not to be occupied by either party. *Ib.* 151 The territory . . . left as neutral ground by the agreement between Wilkinson and Herrera, had become the rallying point and refuge of a large number of desperate men. **1949** *N.O. Times-Picayune Mag.* 28 Aug. 16/2 On a June morning of that year [1812] a young, sober-faced lieutenant of the United States Army, named Augustus William Magee, rode alone into the Neutral Ground, an outlaw empire along the east side of the Sabine river.

3. (See quot. 1844.). *Obs.*

1844 *Knickerb.* XXIII. 775 The Government of the United States . . . have laid out between them [the Sioux and Sac and Fox Indians] a strip of country forty miles in width, denominated the 'Neutral Ground,' and on to which neither nation is permitted to extend their hunting excursions. **1858** WILKIE *Davenport* 187 He had ascended the Wabispinica River to the boundary line of the Neutral Grounds, early in September. [**1886** in *Ill. State Hist. Soc. Jrnl.* (1949) June 215/1, I have 640 acres of land in the State of texas and 160 in the newtral strip.]

* **Neutrals,** *n. pl.* (See quot. 1910.) Also **Neutral Nations.** — **1881** MORGAN *Houses Amer. Aborigines* 26 About 1651–'55 they [Iroquois] expelled their kindred tribes, the Eries, from the region between the Genesee River and Lake Erie, and shortly afterwards the Neutral Nations from the Niagara River. **1910** HODGE *Amer. Indians* II. 60 Neutrals. An important confederation of Iroquoian tribes living in the 17th century N. of L. Erie in Ontario, having four villages E. of Niagara r. on territory extending to the Genesee watershed. . . . They were called Neutrals by the French because they were neutral in the known wars between the Iroquois and the Hurons.

Nevada nəˈvædə, *n.* [The name (f. the Sierra *Nevada* Mts.) of a western state.] Used attrib. with **desert, land, nut pine, people, ringtail, settler, Territory.**

1860 *Mountaineer* (Salt Lake City) 14 Jan. 81/3 Now, therefore, I, Isaac Roop, Governor of the Provisional Territorial Government of Nevada Territory [etc.]. **1876** J. J. POWELL *Nevada* 15 [Mormon leaders issued] an edict, in 1855, recalling their Nevada settlers to Salt Lake. **1881** MARSHALL *Through Amer.* (1882) 248 Humboldt is rightly called an oasis in the desert for here we are in the middle of the Great Nevada Desert. **1897** SUDWORTH *Arborescent Flora* 18 *Pinus monophylla*. Single-leaf Piñon [is also called] Grey Pine (Nev.), Nevada Nut Pine (Cal.) **1901** *Independent* 18 April 888/1 Existing conditions are not the fault of the Nevada people. **1903** *Harper's Wkly.* 20 June 1029/2 Examples of what can be done with Nevada lands under sensible irrigation systems. **1948** *Ecological Monographs* April 171/2 Among the native mammals, carnivorous forms which could likely destroy either young or old tortoises are the desert bobcat, . . . and the Nevada ringtail.

Nevadan nə'vædn̩, *a.* and *n.* A native or resident of Nevada; of or pertaining to Nevada.

1878 *Gold Hill* (Nev.) *News* 15 March, Fred Hart's New Book, 'The Sazerac Lying Club,' is a veritable record of the sayings and doings of that peculiarly Nevadan club. **1910** *Morrison's Chi. Wkly.* 24 Nov. 33/1 In his thirty odd years of existence the man had absorbed his full share of the resourcefulness necessary to master the society of a Nevadan gambling camp. **1938** ASBURY *Sucker's Prog.* 323 The Cinch Room was an out-of-the-way annex to the billiard room of the Palace, and was established for the especial use of visiting Nevadans when the hotel was opened in 1875. **1947** *So. Sierran* Nov. 1/3 Incidentally, Nevadans built a very neat wide trail to the summit of their 11,910-foot peak.

Nevadian nə'vædɪən, *a.* Of or pertaining to the state of Nevada. — **1859** COOPER *Distribution Forests & Trees N. Amer.* 270 W partakes of the characters of those of Lower California and Arizona, and with the former may form a [floral] province to be called the Nevadian. **1877** M. TWAIN *Speeches* (1910) 1 (R.), I had just succeeded in stirring up a little Nevadian literary puddle myself.

* **new,** *a.*

1. Recently settled or available for settlement by white people.

1817 BRADBURY *Travels* 331 In the early settlements . . . of new country, its progress in improvements is slow. **1823** COOPER *Pioneers* viii, ['Patent'] was a term in common use throughout the *new* parts of the state. **1828** ——— *Notions* I. 341 The Americans call all that portion of their territory which has been settled since the revolution 'new.' If the state has been created since that period, it is a 'new state.' **1871** DE VERE 176 When the immigrant . . . must go to what is called *New Lands*, he has to be careful in his selection. **1880** *Cimarron* (N.M.) *News & Press* 15 April 2/4 Nelson W. Starbird, an enterprising young hackman, was driving along from the new to the old town.

2. In special combs.: (1) **new corn dance,** among American Indians, a ceremonial dance at the time of harvesting Indian corn, *obs.*, cf. **corn dance** (*a*), **green-corn dance;** (2) **issue,** designating a Negro regarded as offensively uppish in his new status after the Civil War, *slang, obs.;* (3) **rich,** *n.* and *a.* [tr. of F. *nouveaux riches*], (*a*) *n.* those who have recently become wealthy, (*b*) *a.* resembling the newly rich, showy, ostentatious; (4) **Settlers,** (see quot.), *obs.*

(1) *a***1820** in *Western Rev.* II. 161 There are a number of other Indian dances, such as the . . . Turkey dance, the new corn dance, the pipe dance. — (2) **1892** HARRIS *U. Remus & Friends* 266 The old man has fogy notions, especially in regard to colored people, and to some of the 'new issue,' as he calls them, he is known as 'a white-folks' nigger.' *Ib.* 340 He's des got enough er de new issue nigger in 'im fer ter sen' 'im fum de calaboose ter de chain-gang, en fum de chain-gang ter de gallus. — (3) (*a*) **1886** *Harper's Mag.* Oct. 795/2 The sons of the 'new rich' . . . are like men drunk with new wine. (*b*) **1923** BOWER *Parowan Bonanza* 157 You've never seen *me* look new-rich, have you, Bill? — (4) **1796** *Gaz. U.S.* 19 Nov. (*advt.*) (Th.), A new Ballet Dance, called the Back Countryman, or the New Settlers.

For **New Court party, New Deal, new departure, new Negro, new tenor,** * **New Year,** see as main entries.

b. Denoting land and regions: (1) **new-born land,** the homesteads held by those Indians of the Five Civilized Tribes born after 1906; (2) **ground,** see as a main entry; (3) **land,** land newly brought under cultivation, also attrib., cf. **new ground;** (4) * **Purchase,** any one of various large areas or tracts of land purchased by individuals or by a company from Indians or from the federal government for resale to settlers, *obs.*, cf. * **purchase;** (5) **settled,** *a.* newly occupied by settlers, *obs.*

(1) **1931** *Durant* (Okla.) *D. Democrat* 25 April 1/1 Restrictions on what is commonly known as 'new-born land,' of the Five Civilized Tribes will expire tomorrow. — (3) **1763** WASHINGTON *Writings* II. 196 The arm of Dismal, which we passed through to get to this new land (as it is called) is 3¼ miles measured. **1847** *De Bow's Review* IV. 235 The new land beds in the lower grounds are sixteen feet beds. **1881** *Rep. Indian Affairs* 31 The improvements . . . consist of the erection of houses, stables, fences, corrals, &c., and the breaking of new land. — (4) **1775** FITHIAN *Journal* II. 37, I met on the road, a tinker on the way to what is called the 'New Purchase.' **1852** REGAN *Emigrant's Guide* 219 The 'New Purchase,' as it was called, was to be open to the claims of settlers. **1947** *Amer. Sp.* XXII. 207 The journey of Mr. Thomas was undertaken with 'a view to explore the *Wabash Lands* in the *New Purchase*' in Western Indiana. — (5) **1718** *Mass. H. Rep. Jrnl.* II. 56 The House Request . . . that meet Persons be appointed . . . in the Eastern and new settled parts of the Province. **1797** F. BAILY *Tour* 307 All these new-settled places, and, in fact, almost all colonies, are filled with adventurers.

c. With reference to particular parts of the U.S. or their inhabitants: (1) **New Connecticut,** (*a*) =**Western Reserve,** *obs.*, (*b*) Vermont, *obs.;* (2) **Mexican,** *n.* and *a.*, (*a*) *n.* a native or resident of New Mexico, (*b*) *a.* of or pertaining to New Mexico; (3) * **South,** the South, with the activities, institutions, and spirit of its people reshaped in conformity with changes necessitated by the Civil War and Reconstruction, also transf.; (4) **Virginia,** the land west of the Alleghany Mountains that was formerly a part of Virginia and is now in West Virginia, *obs.*

(1) (*a*) **1837** W. JENKINS *Ohio Gaz.* 470 *Western Reserve*, oftentimes called New Connecticut, is situated in the northeast quarter of the state. **1841** *Hunt's Merch. Mag.* IV. 475 At the close of fifty years from its first settlement, New Connecticut, as the reserve used to be called, will equal Old Connecticut in population. (*b*) **1914** *Cyclo. Amer. Govt.* II. 529/2 A convention of the grants declared 'the inhabitants . . . in a state of nature . . . a free and independent state,' called New Connecticut, later Vermont (1777). — (2) (*a*) **1834** A. PIKE *Sketches* 170 Even the New Mexicans call him a great rascal. **1941** FERGUSSON *Southwest* 228 Few families are so completely urbanized as not to have a little ranch somewhere, and New Mexicans care for their own as long as they can. (*b*) **1834** A. PIKE *Sketches* 137 To an American, the first sight of these New Mexican villages is novel and singular. **1893** LUMMIS *Land of Poco Tiempo* 294 Twenty miles south of the New Mexican hamlet of Manzano, and the riddle of its ancient apple-trees, is the noble ruin of the pueblo of Abó. — (3) **1867** *Harper's Wkly.* 20 April 242/1 (*heading*), The New South. **1873** *Harper's Mag.* July 270/2 The result has been the development of a new South—one not exclusively and jealously agricultural, over which cotton is king, and rice and sugar sole vice-regents. **1948** *Seventeen* June 22/3 The townsfolk subsist on tattered memories of the Confederacy and the glory of the South that was; the Hubbards are the new South. — (4) **1755** EVANS *Analysis* 10 New Virginia. . . . So they call, for Distinction-sake, that Part of Virginia South East of the Ouasioto Mountains, and on the Branches of Green Briar, New River, and Holston River. **1804** *Fredericktown* (Md.) *Herald* 26 May 3/1 There is one particular, by which the lower and more Ancient part of the Dominion deeply affects both New Virginia and the Union at large. **1822** WOODS *English Prairie* 231 A man, who boarded a short time at my house, said, he was born in Old Virginia; that he removed, with his father, over the mountains into New Virginia.

For **New England, New English, New Hampshire, New Jersey, New Orleans, New York,** see as main entries.

d. Designating religious movements and denominations: (1) **New Divinity,** a system of Calvinistic theology originating with certain New England divines, esp. with Jonathan Edwards and his son, cf. **Edwardsism;** (2) **Haven,** *attrib.* designating the theological system of Taylorism *q.v.* (see quot. 1889); (3) **Light,** see as a main entry; (4) **measure,** *attrib.* denoting Presbyterians in accord with the teachings of the Rev. Charles Finney (1792–1875), *obs.;* (5) * **school,** see as a main entry; (6) * **Side,** =**New Light,** cf. **log college, new school 2.**

(1) **1883** SCHAFF *Religious Encycl.* II. 1634/2 [New England divines] anounced a few principles, which were called 'New-Light Divinity,' or 'New Divinity.' — (2) **1884** SCHAFF *Religious Encycl.* III. 2306/1 The 'New-Haven Theology' . . . was one of the most influential of the types of so-called 'New-School Divinity.' *Ib.*, The peculiarities of 'New Haven Divinity' as it existed in the generation among whom Dr. Taylor was a prominent leader [1822–58]. **1889** *Cent.* 1707/2 *New Haven Divinity*, a popular title for a phase of modified Calvinism, deriving its name from the residence of its chief founder, N. W. Taylor (1786–1858) of Yale Theological Seminary in New Haven, Connecticut. — (4) **1837** PECK *New Guide* 343 *Oberlin Institute* has been recently established in Lorrain County [Ohio], under the influence of 'new measure' Presbyterians.

(6) **1874** E. EGGLESTON *Circuit Rider* xvii. 153 Extremist measures against his more progressive 'new-side' brethren. **1936** *DAB* XVIII.

370/2 Thus the spirit of Tennent contributed greatly to strengthen the 'New Side' cause and helped to bring about the schism of 1741 in the Presbyterian Church.

Newark ˈn(j)uɚk, *n. attrib.* Produced or originated in or near Newark, New Jersey.

1817 W. COXE *Fruit Trees* 120 Newark King, or Hinchman Apple. This is a large, fair, and handsome apple; called the Newark King in East-Jersey. *Ib.* 133 Newark Pippin. Called the French Pippin in East-Jersey. **1870** TOMES *Decorum* 136 Never invite a plain-spoken person to dinner, for he will be sure to detect the Newark cider in your Champagne bottle. **1910** BOSTWICK *Amer. Pub. Library* 45 In the type of two-card [charging] system known as the 'Newark' system from its use in the free library at Newark, N.J., an additional record of the date is made on a flap attached to the inside of the book.

Newburg ˈn(j)ubɜg, *n.* [Origin obscure.]

1. A dish served with Newburg sauce.

1901 *Cosmopolitan* June 193/2 The cozy dormitory quarters give an added flavor to fudge, rarebits, newburgs and afternoon teas. **1946** HOWE *We Happy Few* 180 Then came lobster Newberg, heavy with cream and the sweet rich meat of the lobster.

2. Newburg sauce, a sauce for shellfish consisting of egg yolk, cream, and sherry or Madeira.

1908 LORIMER *J. Spurlock* 201 It was a fine sight to see the Major, skilfully blending crab-meat, fresh mushrooms, and oyster crabs in a delicious Newburgh sauce. **1941** F. M. FARMER *Boston Cook Book* 224 Newburg Sauce. 1 tablespoon butter, 1 tablespoon flour . . . 2 egg yolks, 2 tablespoons sherry [etc.].

New Court party. In Kentucky, a party which supported the creation of a new state supreme court when the old court opposed certain relief legislation. Cf. ∗**court party** (*b*).

[**1826** *Va. Herald* (Fredericksburg) 30 Aug. 3/1 There will be a majority in both branches against the re-organizing act of 1824, which brought the New Court into existence.] **1826** *Spirit of Seventy-Six* I. 14/1 The people declared at the polls at the last August election, . . . That the New Court party have not redeemed their promises. **1887** SCHURZ *Life Henry Clay* I. 203 The 'relief measures' came before the highest state court, which declared them unconstitutional; whereupon the court was abolished and a new one created, and this brought forth the 'old court' and the 'new court' parties in Kentucky.

New Deal. Also **new deal.**

1. A new arrangement for obviating disadvantages in an existing order or defects in a system of operations.

1834 in M. JAMES *Andrew Jackson* (1940) 671 A new bank and a New Deal. **1863** J. SHERMAN in *Sherman Lett.* (1894) 205 Charleston is not taken, the war is prolonged, and but little chance of its ending until we have a new deal. **1914** *Sat. Ev. Post* 31 Jan. 28/3 They were not patriotic or Republican enough to eliminate themselves and start a new deal.

b. New-Deal Convention, (see quot. and cf. **3. a.** below). *Obs.*

1876 *Chi. Tribune* 7 Aug. 1/6 On the 27th day of July what is known as 'The New-Deal Convention' was held. It declared itself the Republican party of the State of Arkansas, indorsed the national platform adopted at Cincinnati, and proclaimed that the party now administering the State affairs is without a platform or a financial or governmental policy or system.

2. The policies and principles of President Franklin D. Roosevelt (1882–1945) and his followers, or the program based on these principles. Also attrib.

1932 F. D. ROOSEVELT in *N.Y. Times* 3 July 1. 8/7, I pledge you—I pledge myself—to a new deal for the American people. **1948** *Chi. Maroon* 6 Feb. 3/4 Tugwell, . . . an early New Deal Brain-Truster, . . . is a sponsor of the Students for Wallace movement. **1949** *Business Week* 24 Sep. 88/2 One of the more successful of the New Deal experiments [was] the Home Owners Loan Corp.

Hence **New Dealish,** *a.*, **New Dealism,** *n.*

1936 *Rocky Mt. News* (Denver) 7 May 10/3 Two towers of progressive strength, more 'New Dealish' than most Democrats, will be lost to the administration in the next Congress. **1947** *Chi. Tribune* 23 July 12/7 The post office at Washington is able to find plenty of money to pay for the expensive engraving work required to produce the great variety of 'picture stamps' that have flooded the country since the event of New Dealism.

3. New Dealer, a. One who participated in the New-Deal Convention (see **1. b.** above). *Obs.* **b.** A believer in the policies and principles of President Franklin D. Roosevelt. Cf. **2.** above.

(**a**) **1876** *Chi. Tribune* 7 Aug. 1/6 The 'New-Dealers' appointed a committee to confer with the old State Central Committee at the 9th of August convention. — (**b**) **1934** *Amer. Mercury* June 246/2 The Unofficial Observer then plunges into a consideration of some fifty New Dealers who are helping the President make the country laugh. **1949** *Chi. D. News* 14 Nov. 12/2 [He] appears to be an old-time New Dealer.

new departure. The new regime in the South after the Civil War and Reconstruction; esp. (*cap.*) the policy, supported by the Democrats and the Liberal Republicans in the campaign of 1872, of regarding Reconstruction as completed and of granting universal amnesty. Also attrib.

1871 *Ku Klux Rep.* VIII. 425 The white people in our country, though they may accept what is known as the 'new departure,' are at heart unalterably opposed, in my opinion, to negro suffrage. **1871** *Harper's Mag.* Aug. 474/1 The following, [is] told by way of illustrating the significance of the 'new-departure' movement. **1872** J. SHERMAN in *Sherman Lett.* (1894) 335 There were five or six Republicans who . . . were inclined to support Cox as an Anti-Grant or new departure candidate. **1947** LUMPKIN *Southerner* 141 Back in Georgia Father had seen the post-Civil War shift from plantation-belt leaders to a new type entirely. These were called 'New Directionists,' or 'New Departure' Democrats.

New England.

1. That part of the U.S. lying east and north of the state of New York.

1616 SMITH *N. Eng.* 4 That part wee call *New England* is betwixt the degrees of 41. and 45. **1789** *Ann. 1st Congress* I. 215 What, then, ought to be the language of the people of New England on a proposal for taxing an article equally as useful to them as fruit is to the Southern States? **1870** *Scribner's Mo.* I. 143 New England is divided from the rest of the country. **1949** *Time* 31 Oct. 74/1 New England is the most highly industralized section of the country.

b. *New England of the West,* (see quot. 1871).

1850 E. S. SEYMOUR (*title*), Sketches of Minnesota, the New England of the West. **1871** DE VERE 660 Minnesota is known as the New England of the West, on account of the number of New England people to be found there. **1907** *Boston Transcript* 9 Nov.

2. Short for **New England rum.** Cf. **white face, white-faced New England.**

1827 J. HOWE *Journal* 12. I told him I would take some New England and molasses. *c***1887** in *Amer. Sp.* (1948) April 114/1 Not dreaming of invading Belfast, only to get their 'runlets' filled with 'New England.'

3. In combs.: (1) **New England boiled dinner,** a dinner consisting mainly of corned beef and vegetables cooked together; (2) **Confederation,** (see quot. 1889); (3) **dialect,** the speech characteristic of New Englanders; (4) **man,** (*a*) a man residing in New England, esp. one having the moral qualities usu. associated with Puritans, (*b*) a New England vessel; (5) **primer,** a primer schoolbook, probably compiled by Benjamin Harris, published in Boston about 1689, and frequently reprinted; (6) **rum,** (see quot. 1784); (7) **shilling,** a

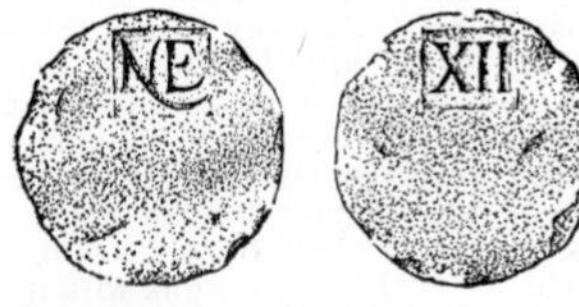

New England shilling, obverse and reverse

silver coin authorized in 1652 in Massachusetts with NE on the obverse and XII on the reverse; (8) **short o,** a vowel sound approximately that of the short u with rounded lips, used by some New Englanders in such words as *stone, home, only;* (9) **states,** *pl.* the northeastern states of the U.S.—New Hampshire, Vermont, Massachusetts, Rhode Island, Connecticut, and Maine; (10) **whiting,** (see quot.).

(**1**) **1939** WOLCOTT *Yankee Cook Bk.* xv, Corned beef was equally at hand for corned beef hash for the New England boiled dinner. **1947** BEROLZHEIMER *Regional Cookbook* 87 The New England boiled dinner may vary with the season and content of the vegetable bin. — (**2**) **1889** *Cent.* 481/1 New England Confederation. The union effected by the colonies of Massachusetts Bay, Plymouth, Connecticut and New Haven in 1643, suggested by the need of a common defense against the Dutch and the Indians. It was discontinued in 1684. **1943**

HICKS *Amer. Dem.* 21 As a result the New England Confederation, consisting of Massachusetts, Plymouth, Connecticut, and New Haven, was formed in 1643. — (3) **1788** HILTZHEIMER *Diary* (1893) 22 May 145 She spoke much in the New England dialect. — (4) (*a*) **1638** UNDERHILL *Newes from Amer.* (1837) 5 Let the clamor be quenched . . . that New England men usurp over their wives and keep them in servile subjection. **1789** MACLAY *Deb. Senate* 49 Lee led, Ellsworth seconded him, the New England men followed. **1845** COOPER *Chainbearer* xxix, The supercilious feeling of the New Englandman can very easily be traced to his origin in the mother country. (*b*) **1776** in *S. Lit. Messenger* XXVII. 326/2 A tender came last week to Hobbs' Hole and took a New England man, loaded with grain and flour, from the wharf.

(5) *c***1689** (*title*), The New-England Primer. **1780** *N.J. Archives* 2 Ser. IV. 630 New-England Primers To be sold by the Thousand or smaller Quantity at the Printing-Office, in Trenton. **1894** FORD *N. Eng. Primer* 38 No copy of this first edition of the New England Primer is known. — (6) **1709** BYRD *Secret Diary* (1941) 13 Parson Ware sent to me for a pint of canary, he being sick of the gripes with the New England rum. **1784** SMYTH *Tour* II. 30 New England takes off a great quantity of molasses raw, and from thence is distilled there, a very inferior ill-tasted spirit, named New England or Yankee Rum. **1930** WITTKE *Tambo & Bones* 96 A half dozen ruffians of the town . . . had imbibed too freely of New England rum. — (7) **1715** SEWALL *Diary* III. 56 Gave Mr. Short's daughter a New-England Shilling. — (8) **1934** WEBSTER. **1940** J. S. KENYON *Amer. Pron.* (ed. 8) 187 Several words with this 'New England short o' have found their way into the Middle West with New England emigrants, either in unrounded pronunciation, or at least what sounds to unaccustomed ears like A. — (9) **1787** CUTLER in *Life & Lett.* I. 195 [You are] acquainted with the institution of a Company in the New England States by the name of the Ohio Company. **1817** PAULDING *Lett. from South* I. 87 In Connecticut, and probably in nearly all the New-England states, . . . there has been little growth in numbers, since the western States became objects of attention. **1925** BRYAN *Memoirs* 218 In the New England States . . . the Grange . . . [demanded] the issuance of greenbacks by the Federal Government.

(10) **1884** GOODE *Fisheries* I. 240 The Silver Hake, or New England Whiting. *Merlucius Bilinearis*. . . . The Silver Hake commonly inhabits the middle depths of ocean. **1911** *Rep. Fisheries 1908* 316 Silver Hake (*Merluccius bilinearis*).—It is also called 'New England whiting.'

Also *New England cheese, Christian, currency, delegate, garden, ninepence, soldier, stagecoach, woods*, etc.

b. In the names of plants: (1) **New England aster,** a perennial aster having purplish flowers, common in the East; (2) **boxwood,** the flowering dogwood; (3) **daisy,** (see quot.), *rare;* (4) **mayflower,** (see quot.); (5) **mustard,** (see quot.), *rare;* (6) **pine,** a pine, *Pinus strobus*, found in the eastern part of the U.S. and valued for its soft, light wood; (7) **sedge,** (see quot.).

(1) **1814** BIGELOW *Florula Bostoniensis* 199 *Aster Novæ Angliæ*. New England Aster. . . . A tall, and very beautiful plant. Stem three feet high, brown, very hairy. **1931** CLUTE *Plants* 140 Several species of this tribe are called farewell-summer and the new England aster (*Aster Nova* [*sic*] *Angliae*), which lingers long in the fields and fence corners, is further distinguished as last-rose-of-summer. — (2) **1846** BROWNE *Trees Amer.* 350 *Cornus florida*, The Flowery Dogwood. . . . [Also called] New England Box-wood. . . . Flowers greenish-yellow and very large. — (3) **1674** JOSSELYN *Two Voyages* 80 *Umbilicus veneris*, or *New-England* daisie, it is good for hot humours. — (4) **1855** *Harvard Mag.* I. 232 Most admired of our spring flowers is the Ground Laurel, *Epigaea repens*, commonly called Trailing Arbutus, or New England Mayflower.

(5) **1672** JOSSELYN *N. Eng. Rarities* 54 A Plant like Knavers-Mustard, called New-England Mustard. — (6) **1785** MARSHALL *Amer. Grove* 101 New-England, or White Pine . . . is allowed to out top in growth most of our other trees. **1847** DARLINGTON *Weeds & Plants* 336 New England Pine . . . is also a most valuable tree,—furnishing an immense amount of lumber. — (7) **1843** TORREY *Flora N.Y.* II. 399 *Carex Novæ-Angliæ*. . . . New England Sedge. . . . Mount Marcy, Essex county, on the Adirondack river.

4. In derivatives: **a. New Englander,** a native or inhabitant of New England.

1638 *Mass. H.S. Coll.* 3 Ser. VI. 41 The New-Englanders, therefore, advanced the weal public all they could. **1775** JEFFERSON *Writings* IV. 244 The New-Englanders are fitting out light vessels of war. **1949** *Sat. Ev. Post* 29 Oct. 53/1 It is his conviction that New Englanders are about 95 per cent honest—though some of them are mighty slow on the draw.

b. New Englandish, *a.*, of or pertaining to New England. Hence **New Englandishness,** *n.*

1863 HAWTHORNE *Our Old Home* 25 A respectable-looking woman, . . . decidedly New-Englandish in figure and manners, came to my office. **1896** *Advance* 9 Jan. 51/1 There is a still more striking New Englandishness in the people themselves. **1948** *Dly. Ardmoreite* (Ardmore, Okla.) 4 July 3/5 The un-New Englandish name of Muench may become a power in this realm of Lowells, Cabots and Lodges.

c. New Englandism, see as a main entry.

d. New Englandly, *adv.*, in the manner of a New Englander. *Rare.*

*a***1886** DICKINSON *Further Poems* (1929) 60 Without the snow's tableau Winter were lie to me—Because I see New Englandly.

e. New Englandy, *a.*, suggestive of New England. *Rare.*

1861 TUCKERMAN in J. Hawthorne *N. Hawthorne & Wife* II. 275 For the book. . . . I claim little, but that it is New Englandy (I hope).

New Englandism.

1. A word or expression peculiar to New England.

1831 *Boston Transcript* 7 Sep. 2/3 Mr Pickering, however, thinks *hub* a New-Englandism only, but even if used through the country, the propriety of adopting it in writing might be questioned. **1835** *S. Lit. Messenger* I. 423 This is a New England-ism not confined to the vulgar. **1948** MENCKEN *Supp.* II. 198 Heffner . . . testifies that New Englandisms were common there in his boyhood.

2. The tone or culture characteristic of New England.

1858 H. W BEECHER *Life Thoughts* 27 New Englandism is but another name for Puritanism in the Independent sense. **1925** A. CARRICK *Collector's Luck* (1926) 165, I wonder, Reggie, if that is your latent New Englandism showing itself?

New Englandize, *v. tr.* To imbue with New England qualities. — **1883** T. SILLOWAY & L. POWERS *Cathedral Towns of England* 332 New-Englandize it [Ireland], and the Irish millennium would come. **1887** *Advance* 17 March 169/3 Be sure to watch with peculiar interest the development of this grand work of new-englandizing that Southeasternmost State of the Union [i.e., Florida].

New English.

1. *a.* Of or pertaining to New England.

1632 *Mass. H.S. Coll.* 4 Ser. VI. 184 Tis a ridle as yet to me whether you meane any Elder in these New English churches. **1725** T. SYMMES in Kidder *Exped. Lovewell* (1865) 38 This Action Merits a Room in the History of our New-English wars. **1870** LOWELL *Among My Books* 1 Ser. 234 All their unconscious training by eye and ear, were *New English* wholly.

2. *absol.* The people of New England. *Obs.*

1643 WILLIAMS *Key* (1866) 25 To that great Point of their [i.e., the Indians'] Conversion so much to bee longed for, and by all New-English so much pretended. **1647** ELIOT *Day-Breaking* 25 Cutting their Haire in a modest manner as the New-English generally doe.

new ground. Ground recently cleared for cultivation.

1624 SMITH *Gen. Hist. Va.* iv. 126 We haue ordinarily foure or fiue [barrels of produce an acre], but of new ground six, seuen, and eight. **1769** WASHINGTON *Diaries* I. 333 That piece of New Ground containing 14 Acres next the widow Sheridine's. **1949** *Southwest Rev.* Spring 192/1 It was the first day of February, the month that begins the year in the 'Deep South,' but no plows were in the field, no brush was burning in the 'new ground' around Jud's cabin.

attrib. **1771** *Md. Hist. Mag.* XIV. 134 Our new ground tob[acc]o Here has been Housed 3 or 4 days past. **1800** BOUCHER *Glossary* p. 1 *New-ground patch*: a piece of ground that has never been cultivated before. **1939** *These Are Our Lives* 11 Did you know that the best tobacco plants air raised on new ground land?

New Hampshire. [Name of one of the New England states.]

1. New Hampshire claimant, one of those who claimed land in what is now Vermont on the basis of titles granted by the royal governor of New Hampshire. *Obs.* Cf. **Green Mountain boy.**

1773 in *Hist. MSS Comm.* 14th Rep. App. X. (1895) 128 Regrets the failure of his expedient to settle the New Hampshire claimants. **1778** *Ib.* 15th Rep. App. VI. 396 Mr. Tryon's plan for restoring Peace in that quarter was by compensating the New Hampshire Claimants for their *actual* possessions out of the other Waste Lands of the Crown.

2. New Hampshire grant, a certificate issued by the royal governor of New Hampshire entitling the holder to a portion of land in the present state of Vermont. Also the land specified in such a certificate.

These grants were to land claimed by both New Hampshire and New York. The King of England, by an order in council on July 20, 1764, decided the controversy in favor of New York, but some settlers under the leadership of Ethan Allen maintained by force the legality of their New Hampshire titles.

1772 in *Hist. MSS Comm.* 14th Rep. App. X. (1895) 105 Mr. Hawley, who was among the first settlers under the faith of a New Hampshire grant. **1798** I. ALLEN *Hist. Vt.* 20 Some leading characters on the east side, by yielding up their New Hampshire Grants, had new or confirmation grants from New York on paying half fees. **1941** LEE *Stagecoach North* 6 The confusion all started in Connecticut years before when the New Hampshire grants were being parceled out in neat rectangles without reference to hills, dips, and bogs.

b. (*pl.*) The region in what is now Vermont affected by these grants (see quot. *a* 1817).

1772 in *Vt. Hist. Soc. Coll.* I. 6 The copy of the minutes of Council was read and also his Excellency's letter of compliance with the same, which diffused universal joy through the country of the New Hampshire Grants. *a***1817** DWIGHT *Travels* II. 113 Vermont was then regarded as a part of New-Hampshire; and in customary language was styled *the New Hampshire grants.* **1863** *Amer. Cyclo.* XVI. 73/2 The country west of the Connecticut was only known at that time [1760] by the name of 'New Hampshire Grants.' **1942** PEATTIE *Friendly Mts.* 65 So many people had taken advantage of Governor Wentworth's charters that the Green Mountain region had come to be known as the New Hampshire Grants.

New Jersey. [The name of one of the middle Atlantic states.] In combs.: (1) **New Jersey fir tree,** (see quot.); (2) **mosquito,** a mosquito found in New Jersey, reputed to be especially large and vicious; (3) **pine,** the scrub pine; (4) **tea,** =**American ceanothus,** used as a substitute for tea during the Revolution, also attrib., cf. **Jersey tea.**

(1) **1770** FORSTER tr. Kalm *Travels* 69 [Trees] which grow spontaneously in the woods which are nearest to Philadelphia [include] ... *Pinus tæda*, the New Jersey fir tree, on dry sandy heaths. — (2) **1897** *Cong. Rec.* 18 May 1137/2, I have never been in New Jersey, but I know the reputation of the New Jersey mosquito. — (3) **1832** BROWNE *Sylva* 234 New Jersey Pine. *Pinus Inops.* — (4) **1785** MARSHALL *Amer. Grove* 27 American Ceanothus, or New-Jersey Tea-tree, ... is a low shrub, growing common in most parts of North America. **1941** R. S. WALKER *Lookout* 59 The commonest shrub, perhaps, is New Jersey tea or redroot which grows profusely on the summit as well as on both sides of the mountain.

b. Also **New Jersey sands, sandstone.**

1870 *Rep. Comm. Agric. 1869* 410 Whatever may be said in ... depreciation of the productive value of 'New Jersey sands' [etc.]. **1882** MCCABE *New York* 313 The building is constructed of New Jersey sandstone.

* **New Light.**

1. A member of one of various American groups in sympathy with the revival of religious zeal. Usu. *pl.* with reference to such a group. Now *hist.*

It is in some instances impossible to ascertain which New Light group is referred to in the following quots., for the name was applied to various groups of seceders from the Presbyterian Church, joined by converts from other faiths. Among the American groups designated by this term were the followers of George Whitefield, whose New Side group seceded from the Philadelpha Synod in 1740; the Cumberland offshoot, which seceded in 1810 and eventually became the Cumberland Presbyterian Church; the Reformed Presbyterian Church, organized in 1833; and the Disciples of Christ. New Lights were characteristically nonconservative, freq. revivalist groups.

1743 HEMPSTEAD *Diary* 407 All come to settle the disorders that are subsisting among those called New Lights which follow Mr. Davenport. **1807** MCNEMAR *Ky. Revival* 29 These ... taught as an important truth, that the will of God, was made manifest to each individual ... by an inward light, which shone into the heart.—Hence they received the name of 'New-Lights.' **1856** CARTWRIGHT *Autobiog.* 219 Arianism was rife through all that country [Kentucky], although they called themselves 'Christians,' and were called by the world, New Lights, Marshallites, or Stoneites. **1871** EGGLESTON *Hoosier Schoolm.* 121, I don't know whether you're a Hardshell ... or a Campbellite, or a New Light. **1949** *Wm. & Mary Quart.* Jan. 43 The New Brunswick group, the 'new lights,' wished to give eloquence in preaching precedence over formal knowledge.

Hence **New Lightism,** the ideas and beliefs of the New Lights. *Obs.*

1755 *Essex Inst. Coll.* LII. 78 He seems a grave, close, heavy Man, not given to talk & deeply immerged in New Lightism. **1856** CARTWRIGHT *Autobiog.* 32 B. W. Stone stuck to his New Lightism.

2. =**crappie.** Cf. **Campbellite 2.**

1877 JORDAN in *Nat. Museum Bul.* No. 9, 21 *Pomoxys annularis.* ... Throughout Kentucky it is known as the 'New Light,' and sometimes as 'Campbellite.' **1885** J. S. KINGSLEY *Standard Nat. Hist.* III. 235 It is known as the crappie, new-light, Campbellite, and bachelor, and is an abundant fish in the Mississippi river. **1947** DALRYMPLE *Panfish* 84.

3. Attrib. in sense **1.** with **Baptist, divinity,** (see **New Divinity), exhorter, minister, order, preacher, stir.** All *obs.*

1765 J. BARTRAM *Diary* 9 Aug., Lodged at skinking mores A very religious house A new light baptist. — **1742** HEMPSTEAD *Diary* 402, 2 of them Newlight Exhorters begun their meeting. — **1744** EDWARDS *Works* (1834) I. p. cxviii/1 To attend the ministry of those that are called New Light ministers. — **1781** PETERS *Hist. Conn.* (1829) 139 A most thundering preacher of the new-light order. — **1784** SMYTH *Tour* I. 102 Here I ... had to defend myself against the formidable attacks of a new-light itinerant preacher. — **1810** in SWEET *Religion* 5 By the preaching of Mr. Whitefield thro' New England, a great work of God broke out in that country, distinguished by the name of the *New-Light-stir.* All who joined it were called *Newlights.*

b. Also transf. (see quots.). *Obs.*

1831 NANCY N. SCOTT *Mem. H. L. White* (1856) 249 A union of N. Light Federalists with Kentucky republicans ... cannot last. **1833** WYETH *Oregon* 25 What the *new-light* Doctrine of Phrenology calls the disposition bump of Inhabitiveness.

new Negro. A Negro slave newly brought from Africa. *Obs.*

[**1701** WOLLEY *Journal* (1902) 40 In *Barbados* new Negro's (i.e. such as cannot speak English) are bought for twelve or fourteen pounds a head.] **1732** *Cal. State P. Amer. & W. Indies* 55 Except proof were made that they were all new negroes and not been above 6 months in America. **1860** MORDECAI *Virginia* 350 The servants belonging to the old families in Virginia and especially those pertaining to domestic households, were as proud of their position as if the establishment was their own. I do not speak of the New Negroes, as the imported Africans were called, but of their descendants.

***newness,** *n.* **The Newness.** New England transcendentalism. *Obs.* — **1865** LOWELL *Writings* I. 363 There was a much nearer metaphysical relation ... between Carlyle and the Apostles of the Newness, as they were called in New England, than has commonly been supposed. **1889** *Cent. Mag.* XXXIX. 129/1 Next to Brook Farm, Concord was the chief resort of the disciples of the 'Newness.' Here lived Emerson, Thoreau, and Bronson Alcott.

New Orleans. [Name of a city in Louisiana.] In combs.: (1) **New Orleans boat,** (see quot. 1812), *obs.;* (2) **molasses,** molasses, comparatively light in color and high in sugar content, obtained as a by-product in the manufacture of sugar; (3) **moss,** the long moss, *Dendropogon usneoides;* (4) **sirup,** =**New Orleans molasses.**

(1) **1806** CRAMER *Navigator* 28 Kentucky and New Orleans' boats are generally to be had ready-made at the boat-yard of Sumrall and M'Collogh near the point. **1812** MELISH *Travels* II. 85 *Kentucky* and *New Orleans* boats are flats, with sides boarded like a house, about six or seven feet high, over which there is an arched roof. **1941** BALDWIN *Keelboat Age* 47 These craft, though they might vary very slightly in construction, were essentially alike whether they were called Kentucky or New Orleans boats for their intended destination. — (2) **1849** FOSTER *N.Y. in Slices* 82 The grocery-keeper ... buys a barrel of common New Orleans molasses at twenty-five cents per gallon, and retails it to his customers at sixpence the pint. **1885** *Buckeye Cookery* 99 In making ginger-bread ... always use New Orleans or Porto Rico molasses, and never syrups. — (3) **1877** BARTLETT 789 *New Orleans Moss,* ... a moss which hangs from the boughs of trees in Louisiana, giving to the landscape a weird-like appearance, ... is used in the South ... for mattresses, cushions, &c. — (4) **1898** *Kansas Star* 18 Dec. 5/2 New Orleans Syrup, per gal, 19¢.

b. New Orleanian, a native or inhabitant of New Orleans.

1948 *N.O. Times-Picayune Mag.* 5 Dec. 11/2 What should New Orleanians do about their protest? **1949** *Ib.* 10 April 5/2 Why were 344 New Orleanians fatally injured in motor vehicle accidents during the past six years?

* **Newport,** *n.* [Name of a city in Rhode Island.]

1. *attrib.* Characteristic of Newport, Rhode Island, as a fashionable resort. **2. reverse Newport,** a kind of ballroom dance. *Obs.*

(1) **1863** M. HARLAND *Husks* 187 It was the 'grand hop' night at the head-quarters of Newport fashion. **1894** BROWNELL *Newport* 14, I can fancy ... people who preferred a Jamestown barrack to a Newport cottage at the same price, maintaining that life was freer in Jamestown. **1924** VAN RENSSELAER *Social Ladder* 243 The seasoned member of the Newport colony enters into the cruel game of quashing the pride of the stranger with great glee. — (2) **1883** RITTENHOUSE *Maud* 179, I danced the reverse Newport with George Corliss for the first time and got it to perfection.

* **news,** *n.* In combs.: (1) **news agency,** see as a main entry; (2) **boat,** formerly a boat which met incoming vessels out at sea to obtain news of events abroad and

other information, *obs.;* (3) **bureau,** =**news agency 2;** (4) **butcher,** a vendor of periodicals, candy, fruit, and the like on railroad trains, cf. * **butcher,** *n.* **2;** (5) **company,** a firm acting as a wholesale dealer in newspapers and periodicals; (6) **coverage,** =**coverage 2;** (7) **depot,** a newsstand or shop at which newspapers are sold; (8) **editor,** an editor on a newspaper who edits local or foreign news or who has general charge of collecting and editing news; (9) **flash,** a brief news report; (10) * **gatherer,** a newspaper reporter; (11) **girl,** a girl who sells newspapers; (12) **hallow,** among American Indians, a shout to announce news, *obs.;* (13) **item,** an item of news; (14) **reel,** a reel of motion picture film devoted to news, also attrib.; (15) * **room,** a part of a newspaper office (see quot. 1923); (16) **schooner,** a schooner sent out to cruise at sea, for the purpose of intercepting packet ships and bringing back news, cf. **news boat;** (17) **service,** an agency or organization which supplies news to papers and other periodicals; (18) **stand,** a stand, usu. in the lobby of a large building or on a street corner, at which periodicals are sold, also attrib.; (19) **whoop,** =**news hallow,** *obs.*

(2) 1830 *Boston Transcript* 1 Sep. 2/2 The news-boat, T. H. Smith, belonging to the Associated Morning Papers, boarded the packet ship Caledonia, . . . 25 miles outside Sandy Hook, and before she was boarded by any other news-boat. *a***1882** WEED *Autobiog.* 56 The 'Courier' had no news boat. — **(3) 1873** *Harper's Mag.* July 234/1 The collection of information from a number of army correspondents stationed at different points made it necessary for the leading newspapers to have offices or 'news bureaus' at Washington. **1902** MACGOWAN *Last Word* 182 You look like the head of a news bureau. — **(4) 1894** *Dly. Ardmoreite* (Ardmore, Okla.) 1 Jan. 3/1 Ben R. Wheeler, an old time and popular news butcher on the Santa Fe . . . is in the city. **1947** BEEBE *Mixed Train Dly.* 85 The news butcher . . . still carries as stock in trade the immortal volume of senescent anecdotes, Thomas W. Jackson's *On a Slow Train Through Arkansas.*

(5) 1872 *Chi. Tribune* 9 Oct. 3/3 Newsmen will supply their counters from the Western News Company. **1884** *Tenth Census* VIII. I. 159 The American News Company . . . involved the consolidation of several of the largest newsdealing firms of New York City. — **(6) 1931** *Dly. News-Journal* (Murfreesboro, Tenn.) 21 April 5/5 Plans for intensified development of North American news coverage will be considered primarily. — **(7) 1873** *Winfield* (Kans.) *Courier* 15 May 3/2 Latest publications at Webb's news depot. **1877** HODGE *Arizona* 154 Tucson has . . . one news depot, . . . four feed and livery stables. — **(8) 1868** BAGBY *Old. Va. Gentleman* 190 Pollard he declared was 'the best news editor in the whole South.' — **(9) 1904** *Rochester Post Express* 12 Sep. 3 News Flashes from All Over. **1949** *Time* 3 Oct. 55/1 At 11:05, bells on U.P. and I.N.S. tickers in hundreds of newspapers signaled the big news flash.

(10) 1842 UNCLE SAM *Peculiarities* I. 27 We were here boarded by . . . the 'news gatherer' to the New York press. **1923** *Nation* 10 Oct. 369/2 It lacks that attribute of the exceptional which attracts the attention of the journalistic newsgatherer. — **(11) 1868** *Putnam's Mag.* I. 518/1 A few years ago, a news-girl was as rare a sight as a Dodo. **1870** *Scribner's Mo.* I. 124 Here is a little newsgirl . . . exclaiming lustily, 'Extra Commercial! Defeat of the French!' — **(12) 1765** TIMBERLAKE *Memoirs* 83 The News Hallow was given from the top of Tommotly townhouse. — **(13) 1844** *Knickerb.* XXIV. 179 News-items, matters of information; actual discoveries. **1949** *News-Reporter* (McMinnville, Ore.) 4 Aug. 6/2 There is nothing so scarce now as news items, unless it be harvest hands and money. — **(14) 1922** *Lit. Digest* 10 June 44/2 Let's have the news reel first. **1949** *St. Paul Pioneer Press* 19 June 11/3 Newsreel companies, too, must supply many theaters with the same print simultaneously.

(15) 1896 *Internat. Typog. Union Proc.* 29/1 The Daily Democrat changed hands the first of June, and after a conference with the new publishers, they put a union foreman in their newsroom the first week in July. **1923** G. C. BASTIAN *Editing Day's News* 9 Inside the News Room . . . [we find the] Managing Editor, . . . Makeup Editors . . . City Editor, . . . Telegraph Editor [etc.]. — **(16) 1831** *Boston Transcript* 14 Oct. 3/1 Our news schooner Second Edition has just come up and reports that she exchanged signals with our news schooner Third Edition, . . . but there was little prospect of her boarding the Hellespont until too late to furnish us with her intelligence this evening. **1873** *Harper's Mag.* March 590/2 One morning the *Courier and Enquirer* appeared with a postscript, announcing the arrival of their news schooner with the news by the Ajax, which had reached the offing the night before. — **(17) 1893** in PHILIPS *Making of Newspaper* 16 Certain excellent local newspapers . . . satisfied with the outside news-service of the press associations, pay for telegraph-tolls. — **(18) 1871** EGGLESTON *Hoosier Schoolm.* 77 You can buy trap-doors . . . dirt-cheap at the next newsstand. **1948** *This Week Mag.* 9 Oct. 26/3 Often, during the years, he paused at a newsstand. — **(19) 1775** ADAIR *Indians* 301 The others [*sc.* Indians] . . . told me . . . to be sure to call them, by sounding the news-whoop, as soon as he arrived at camp.

As the last term in **Boston, mung news.**

news agency. 1. A company that distributes periodicals, a news company. **2.** A company that supplies news to newspapers and other subscribers.

(1) 1873 F. HUDSON *Journalism* 521 News agencies . . . branched out and extended into colossal news companies as a . . . necessity of the age. **1887** *Postal Laws* 147 In admitting second-class publications sent from a news agency, postmasters will observe the following [rules]. — **(2) 1900** NELSON *A B C Wall St.* 154 *News agency.* Two companies, the New York News Bureau and Dow, Jones & Co,, supply Wall St. with news. Each uses a ticker service. **1925** BENEFIELD *Chicken-Wagon Family* 98 'Flimsy' is the thin mimeographed copy that comes in from news agencies that cover the city and suburbs.

* **new school.**

1. *attrib.* Designating those belonging to an advanced faction of a party or organization. *Obs.*

1806 FESSENDEN *Democracy Unveiled* I. 113 That were not justice in arrears, These New School folks would lack their ears. *Ib.* II. 35 Among our new-school rights and duties, There's no monopoly of beauties. **1816** *Emigrant's Guide* 17 Local politicians assume various appellations, such as New School and Old School Democrats, Snyderites, Clintonians, and many others, mostly derived from the name or principles of some popular demagogue.

2. (*cap.*) The less conservative element of the two factions into which the Presbyterian Church was divided from about 1825 to 1869. Also attrib. Now *hist.* Cf. **New Light, New Side.**

1837 in *Spirit XIX. Cent.* (1842) March 131 Our Presbytery had a meeting a few days ago, and some of the New School members were for putting irons upon me at once. **1837** W. JENKINS *Ohio Gaz.* 317 The public buildings consist of . . . two presbyterian churches, one of the old, and one of the new school. **1846** *Dollar Newspaper* (Phila.) 27 May 3/2 The General Assembly of the Presbyterian Church of the United States, (New School,) commenced its annual session in the Rev. Mr. Barnes' Church, on Thursday morning. **1884** SCHAFF *Religious Encycl.* III. 2306/1 The 'New-Haven Theology' . . . was one of the most influential of the types of so-called 'New School Divinity.'

Hence **New Schoolism.** *Obs.*

1838 in *Spirit XIX. Cent.* (1842) June 282 Perhaps my apprehensions are too much excited, being surrounded as I am with *New Schoolism* in all its forms, . . . and believing as I do, . . . it is the deadly enemy of our old Presbyterians.

b. New School Presbyterian, a member of the New School faction (cf. prec.). Also attrib. *Obs.*

1837 PECK *Gaz. Illinois* 72 The Illinois college at Jacksonville is [identified] with the 'New School' Presbyterians. **1857** *Quinland* I. 306 [The teacher] is a 'new-school' presbyterian minister, and prays from twenty to forty minutes every morning at the opening of the school. **1872** MCCLELLAN *Golden State* 406 The Old and New School Presbyterians have . . . 2,600 members and 3,500 Sunday-scholars.

3. *transf.* (See quot.)

1837 *S. Lit. Messenger* III. 107, I once read medicine . . . under a disciple of the 'new school' (vulgarly called steam doctors).

* **newspaper,** *n.* In combs.: (1) **newspaper clipping,** a portion, as an item of news, cut from a newspaper; (2) **English,** English of the type found in newspapers; (3) **exchange,** = * **exchange 2;** (4) **interviewer,** a newspaper reporter who interviews someone for a news story; (5) **item,** a bit of news in a newspaper; (6) **morgue,** =**morgue 2;** (7) **row,** in a city, a region in which newspaper offices are situated; (8) **stand,** =**newsstand.**

(1) 1838 *Diplom. Corr. Texas* I. 338 A newspaper clipping containing Van Buren's proclamation of the treaty. **1925** BRYAN *Memoirs* 273, I found a yellowed newspaper clipping with a date of 27 years ago. — **(2) 1888** *Harper's Mag.* May 962/2 The phrase 'newspaper English' has come to have a significance which is not flattering to newspapers. **1942** P. G. PERRIN *Writer's Guide & Index* 606 Good newspaper English is simply informal English applied to the daily recording of affairs. It is a style written to be read rapidly and by the eye—tricks of sound outside the headlines are out of place. — **(3) 1873** *Newton Kansan* 5 June 2/1 The Postmaster General has decided that the law forbids the free transmission of newspaper exchanges. — **(4) 1913** LA FOLLETTE *Autobiog.* 144 The letter impressed me as a precaution taken to forestall newspaper interviewers.

(5) 1850 D. G. MITCHELL *Lorgnette* x. 224 Merit is reckoned by the club-room babble, and the newspaper 'item.' — **(6) 1912** *Outing* Nov. 253/2 Did you ever try to buy a photograph of an important event ten years afterward? Usually the newspaper 'morgues' are your only hope. — **(7) 1872** *Chi. Tribune* 9 Oct. 1/5 Newspaper Row is filled to-night with a shifting multitude. **1887** *Courier-Journal* (Louisville) 17 Jan. 1/1 He can venture to tell a war story on Newspaper Row without having a chestnut bell rung on him. — **(8) 1893** POST *Harvard Stories* 31 At a newspaper-stand he bought all the picture papers.

As the last term in **agricultural, county, exchange, nullification newspaper.**

newspaporial ˌn(j)uzpeˈporɪəl, *a.* and *n.* [f. **newspaper*+*-orial*, poss. suggested by **editorial*.] **1.** *n.* A newspaper item. *Obs.* **2.** *a.* Of or pertaining to a newspaper.

(1) 1787 *Mass. Centinel* 18 July 4/1 (*caption*), English Newspaporials. **1882** *Jrnl. Education* 27 April 274/1 *Newspaporial*.—We have received the first three numbers of the Alabama Progress, a weekly educational paper. — **(2) 1794** *Columbian Centinel* 14 May 2/4 Newspaporial rule of three. **1881** *Kans. Hist. Coll.* II. 136 This correspondent was William A. Phillips, one of the ablest writers and hardest workers who ever did newspaporial labor in Kansas.

newspaporialist ˌn(j)uzpeˈporɪəlɪst, *n.* [f. prec.+ *-ist*.] A journalist. *Rare.* — **1871** *Vt. Hist. Gazetteer* II. 721/1 The Rev. Joshua Butts, . . . one of the Editors of the 'New York World,'—the popular newspaporialist.

newsy ˈn(j)uzɪ, *n.* A newsboy. *Colloq.* — **1904** *N.Y. Times* 16 July 7 He approached the 'newsy' and offered to buy a paper. **1916** C. SANDBURG *Chicago Poems* 42 The newsies are pitching pennies.

new tenor. (See quot. 1891.)

1738 *Duxbury Rec.* 262 Fifty pounds in bills of credit . . . of the new tenor, for one year's service in the work of the Ministry. **1744** *Boston News Letter* 8 Nov. 2/1 There shall be paid . . . any Person . . . who shall . . . go out and kill a male Indian . . . and produce his scalp, the sum of 100 Pounds in Bills of the New Tenor. **1891** *Cent.* 6233/1 *New tenor.* (*a*) In the financial history of Massachusetts and Rhode Island a form of paper currency of the public issues which began in 1737 in the former colony and in 1740 in the latter, and of which each bill bore a declaration that it should be equal in value to a stated amount of coined silver or of gold coin. (*b*) In Massachusetts, a new form of such currency, issued in accordance with an act of the year 1741 and subsequent years, and differing but slightly from that above described. **1895** *Pub. Col. Soc.* III. 9 They were known as old tenor, middle tenor, new tenor first, and new tenor second.

attrib. **1832** WILLIAMSON *Maine* II. 208 By act passed in March 1742, the new tenor bills were a tender, except in written contracts.

***Newtown,** *n.* [*Newtown*, L.I.]

1. Newtown pippin, the tree which bears the Newtown pippin or yellow Newtown apple. *Obs.*

1760 WASHINGTON *Diaries* I. 147 Grafted 10 of the New Town Pippin. **1785** *Ib.* II. 435 Received two New Town and 2 Golden Pippin trees.

b. A variety of highly prized yellow winter apple, also an apple of this variety.

1770 *Md. Hist. Mag.* XIII. 69 Things sent by the wagon 4 Barrills of Apples Russetins, Golden Pippins, Newtown Pippins & Parmains. **1840** *N.Y. Mirror* 4 April 327/2 Dealers in Newtonpippins and maple candy tell you . . . they can't afford their accommodations so low as they can be afforded in Chatham and Church streets. **1913** LONDON *Valley of Moon* 364 Every year he goes to England, and he takes a hundred carloads of yellow Newton pippins with him.

2. Newtown Spitzenburg, also **Newton Spitzemberg,** a Spitzenburg apple originally grown at Newtown, Long Island.

1817 W. COXE *Fruit Trees* 126 Newton Spitzemberg. This apple is in some parts of this State called the English, or Burlington Spitzemberg: it was brought from Newton on Long-Island. **1863** *Rep. Comm. Agric. 1862* 168 Newtown Spitzenberg. . . . A very hardy tree; good bearer; fruit of superior quality; keeps and bears transportation well.

Newtowner ˈn(j)uˌtaʊnɚ, *n.* =**Newtown pippin b.** *Obs.*—**1846** COOPER *Redskins* i, Their *poire beurée*, here at Paris, . . . will not compare with the New-towners we grow at Satanstoe.

***New Year.**

1. New Year cake, a cake prepared for New Year's Day. *Obs.*

1809 IRVING *Knickerb.* VII. vi, He was the first that imprinted new year cakes with the mysterious hieroglyphics of the Cock and Breeches. **1864** *Sacramento Union* 7 Jan. 5/2 Among the confectioner's greatest works, however, at this time, are the New Year's cakes.

2. New Year cooky, a cooky made for New Year festivities, esp. in Dutch communities. *Obs.*

1808 IRVING *Salmagundi* XX. 522 These notable cakes, hight new-year-cookies, . . . originally were impressed on one side with the burly countenance of the illustrious Rip. **1850** S. F. COOPER *Rural Hours* 433 Cake-jars are filling up . . . with raisined olecokes, with spicy, New Year cookies, all cakes belonging to the season. **1881** *Harper's Mag.* March 532/2, 'I want a dozen New-Year cookies,' she screamed.

3. New Year's address, (see quot.).

1830–45 FURMAN *Customs* 15 On the morning of . . . [New Year's Day] it is customary with the Carriers of the Newspapers to present their patrons with what is styled 'A New Year's Address,' being a number of lines of poetry on the opening of the New, and the closing of the old year, and in return expect and receive a douceur.

***New York.** [Name of an eastern state and its chief city.]

1. In combs., chiefly obs.: (1) **New York currency,** currency used in New York before the adoption of the Constitution of 1787 and current for some years afterward, cf. **New York money, shilling;** (2) **game,** the early form of baseball from which the modern game evolved, cf. **Massachusetts game;** (3) **Indians,** see as a main entry; (4) **money,** =**New York currency;** (5) **point,** a system of printing for the blind devised by Wm. B. Wait of the New York Institution for the Blind, and first published in 1868; (6) **price,** the price which a commodity will bring on the New York exchange; (7) **rules,** rules in accordance with which the New York game was played; (8) **shilling,** see as a main entry; (9) **state regency,** =**Albany regency;** (10) **Stock Exchange,** see as a main entry.

(1) 1756 ROGERS *Jrnls.* 14 According to the General's orders, my company was to consist of sixty privates, at 3s. New York currency *per* day. **1831** SLOCOMB *Amer. Calculator* 86 The dollar is reckoned in New York and N. Carolina 8s. od.=4/10 New York currency. — **(2) 1867** *Ball Players' Chron.* 6 June 1/1 Prominent among the admirers of the 'New York game' was Mr. John A. Lowell, of Boston, and if any one individual is entitled to the credit of fostering the national game in New England, Mr. Lowell is. **1909** *Collier's* 8 May 12/3 When, in the forties, the modern game, originating in New York, made its consequent advance, the boys called the old game the 'Boston game' or the 'Massachusetts game,' to distinguish it from the new-fangled 'New York game.' **1939** [see **Massachusetts game**]. — **(4) 1731** HEMPSTEAD *Diary* 232 In the Eve I put up into my portmantle . . . £58 in our bills of Cr. . . . [and] about 5 or £6 N york Mony.

(5) 1892 *Scribner's Mag.* Sep. 386/1 A fellow-pupil dictated to him Latin and Greek, and he printed the text in New York Point. **1914** *Cyclo. Amer. Govt.* I. 640 The 'New York point' was invented by Wait of the New York Institution for Blind. — **(6) 1872** TICE *Over Plains* 136, $2.04 cents per bushel . . . was about New York price for prime white wheat. — **(7) 1868** *N. Eng. Base-Ballist* 6 Aug. 1/1 In the fall of 1858 the first match under the 'New York' rules in New England was played on Boston Common between the Tri-Mountains and the Portland Club of Portland, Me. — **(9) 1839** *Maysville* (Ky.) *Eagle* 11 Dec. 2/5 His 'imperial guard,' the New York 'state regency' are discomfitted and dispersed.

b. In the names of animals, chiefly fishes, sufficiently defined in the quots., as (1) **New York bat,** (2) **black-fish,** (3) **count,** (4) **ermine,** (5) **flatfish,** (6) **gudgeon,** (7) **plaice,** (8) **rail,** (9) **shiner,** (10) **stickleback,** (11) **thrush,** (12) **warbler,** (13) **water thrush.**

(1) 1771 PENNANT *Synopsis* 367 New York Bat with a head shaped like that of a mouse, top of the nose a little bifid: ears short, broad, and rounded. **1842** *Nat. Hist. N.Y., Zoology* I. 6 The New-York Bat . . . is the most common species in our State. — **(2) 1818** *Amer. Mo. Mag.* II. 295 New-York Black-Fish. . . . The black-fish is one of the excellent edible fishes of the New-York market. — **(3) 1875** *Chi. Tribune* 1 Sep. 5/4 The luscious New York counts, and all the other choice varieties [of oysters], will be kept through the season. — **(4) 1842** *Nat. Hist. N.Y., Zoology* I. 36 The New-York Ermine. *Putorius Noveboracensis*. . . . [This animal destroys] hordes of mice.

(5) 1855 BAIRD in *Smithsonian Rep.* 349 The New York Flat-Fish. Winter Flounder. *Platessa plana*. — **(6) 1814** MITCHILL *Fishes N.Y.* 439 New York Gudgeon. *Esox flavulus*. . . . A pretty little fish. — **(7) 1842** *Nat. Hist. N.Y., Zoology* IV. 301 The New York Plaice . . . is considered as a delicate article of food. — **(8) 1844** *Nat. Hist. N.Y., Zoology* II. 263 The New-York Rail, *Ortygometra noveboracensis*, . . . is distributed through the United States in the interior to the Rocky mountains. — **(9) 1814** MITCHILL *Fishes N.Y.* 459 New York Shiner. *Cyprinus crysoleucus*. . . . Lives in the ponds. **1856** *Porter's Spirit of Times* 20 Dec. 253/2 [Pike-perch] can also be trolled for, successfully, with a frog, a New York shiner, or a minnow on spinning tackle.

(10) 1839 STORER *Mass. Fishes* 30 *Gasterosteus Noveboracensis*. The New York Stickleback. — **(11) 1839** PEABODY *Mass. Birds* 306 The New York Thrush, *Turdus Noveboracensis*. — **(12) 1917** *Birds of Amer.* III 154 New York Warbler. . . . By some observers, the song of this species is considered more musical than that of the Louisiana Water-Thrush. — (13) **1844** *Nat. Hist. N.Y., Zoology* II. 78 The New York Water Thrush. *Seiurus Noveboracensis*. . . . This musical little bird . . . is partial to the neighborhood of brooks, in search of insects.

c. In the names of plants and fruits, as (1) **New York fern,** (2) **Gloria Mundi,** (3) **shield fern,** (see quots.).

(1) **1943** SHIMER *Plant Names* 47 New York fern, Dryopteris noveboracensis. — (2) **1817** W. COXE *Fruit Trees* 117 Monstrous Pippin, or New-York Gloria Mundi. This apple originated on Long Island, state of New-York; it is of an uncommonly large size. — (3) **1843** TORREY *Flora N.Y.* II. 497 *Aspidium Noveboracense*. . . . New-York Shield-fern. Moist woods and thickets. **1901** MOHR *Plant Life Ala.* 316 *Dryopteris noveboracensis*. . . . New York Shield Fern. . . . Alleghenian and Carolinian areas.

d. Designating a **biscuit, cracker, cupcake,** such as were formerly popular in New York. *Obs.*

1714 SAMUEL SEWALL *Diary* II. 440, I had my New York Biscuit to eat, and a Bottle of Wine. **1846** W. G. STEWART *Altowan* I. 14 Their contents consisted of . . . the biscuit root, tasting exactly like a New York cracker newly baked. **1853** WEBSTER *Improved Housewife* 111 New York Cup Cakes.

2. In derivative expressions: (1) **New Yorkeress,** a female New Yorker; (2) **Yorkese,** a variety of English regarded as characteristic of the inhabitants of New York City, cf. **Bostonese 2;** (3) **Yorkish,** *a.* characteristic of New York; (4) **Yorkism,** a term in New Yorkese; (5) **Yorky,** =**New Yorkish.**

(1) **1871** HOWELLS *Wedding Journey* i. 10 The New-Yorkeress was stylish, undeniably effective. — (2) **1894** *Harper's Mag.* Oct. 695/1 'Cafe' . . . is New Yorkese for dram-shop. **1948** *Time* 13 Sep. 83/1 Wanted for radio series: one girl who speaks New Yorkese, has bad diction and careless enunciation. — (3) **1894** HOWELLS in *Harper's Mag.* May 822/2 The Nation was always more Bostonian than New-Yorkish by nature. — (4) **1832** *N.Y. Mirror* 12 May 359/2 The fashion of *moving* (is it not a wretched New-Yorkism?) has all my life given me a great annual disturbance.

(5) **1908** E. WHARTON *Hermit* 150 To be compared to her next! to be accused of being 'New Yorky'!

b. Esp. **New Yorker,** a native or inhabitant of New York.

1756 WASHINGTON *Writings* I. 315 The Jerseys and New Yorkers, I do not remember what it is they give [to their soldiers]. **1884** MATTHEWS & BUNNER *In Partnership* 127 'Are you a New Yorker, sir?' 'From the north of the State.' **1948** *N.Y. Star* 30 June 14/3 The Board of Transportation is appealing to New Yorkers to put up patiently with the confusion.

New York Indians. Indians of various tribes that formerly lived in the state of New York.

1827 *Spirit of Seventy-Six* (Frankfort, Ky.) 4 Oct. 2/4 The Menominie, Chippewa, Winnebago, and New York Indians, and a few of the Ottawas, were parties to it. **1894** ROBLEY *Bourbon Co., Kans.* 7 These various tribes of New York Indians, consisting of the remnants of the Senecas, Onondagas, Cayugas [etc.] . . . were called the 'Six Nations.' **1946** FOREMAN *Last Trek* 335 A number of these so-called New York Indians were living in Canada.

New-Yorkize n(j)uˈjɔrkaɪz, *v. tr.* To give (something or someone) the character or appearance of the institutions or people of New York City. *Colloq.*

1867 *Atlantic Mo.* March 342/2 What a reproach to Tammany, that a politician in far-off Chicago should have been the first to see the mode of New-Yorkizing the politics of the South! **1871** HOWELLS *Wedding Journey* i. 33 Broadway had filled her length with . . . that easily distinguishable class of lately New-Yorkized people from other places. **1942** LILLARD *Desert Challenge* 94 Will it, like much of Florida and some of southern California, be New Yorkized?

New York shilling. A shilling forming part of the New York currency *q.v. Obs.*

"At the time when the decimal system was adopted by the United States, the shilling or twentieth part of the pound in the currency of New England and Virginia was equal to one sixth of a dollar; in that of New York and North Carolina, to one eighth of a dollar" (*Cent. s.v. shilling*).

1834 *Knickerb.* III. 349 A levy was a coin; corresponding . . . to a New York shilling. **1836** CROCKETT *Exploits* 19 [The barkeeper] knew that a coon was as good a legal tender for a quart in the west, as a New York shilling, any day in the year. **1879** WILLIAMS *Pacific Tourist* 277/1 Carriages to any part of the city may be had for 'four bits'; the 'bit' being equivalent to the old New York shilling.

New York Stock Exchange. An organization of brokers in New York for buying and selling securities according to established rules; also the place where the trading is done. Also attrib.

The New York stock exchange is the oldest of its kind in the United States. On May 17, 1792, twenty-four brokers met on a spot across from 60 Wall St., and drew up a working agreement. Formal organization was effected in 1817.

[**1842** (*title*), Report of the Committee of the New York Stock and Exchange Board.] **1862** *Amer. Ann. Cyclo. 1861* 307/2 The highest, lowest, and average quotations for 1859, 1860, and 1861, at the New York Stock Exchange for the stocks most largely dealt in. **1900** NELSON *A B C Wall St.* 141 New York Stock Exchange seats command . . . $40,000. **1949** *Sat. Ev. Post* 29 Oct. 144/3, I was doing my yelling just then to a certain quotation clerk on the floor of the New York Stock Exchange.

* **next,** *a.* and *adv.*

1. Aware of things, "wise," esp. in phrases. *Slang.* Cf. * **get,** *v.* **7. i.**

1896 G. ADE *Artie* xvi. 146 I've been next, I'd tell you those. **1910** W. M RAINE *B. O'Connor* 225 Mrs. Mackenzie will put you next to the etiquette wrinkles when you are shy.

2. next man, anyone taken at random, the next comer. Usu. in comparative phrases introduced by *as.*

1857 *Lawrence* (Kans.) *Republican* 18 June 2 The Judge . . . will probably talk as long to a crowd without tiring them as the next man. **1902** S. G. FISHER *True Hist. Amer. Revol.* 146 We do not surrender our property to the next man who is an abler business manager. **1908** *N.Y. Ev. Post* 29 June 4 Mr. Bryan knows this as well as the next man.

Nez Percé. [F. "pierced nose," though there is no proof that the Nez Percé Indians practiced nose-piercing.] An Indian of the principal tribe of the Shahaptian family, discovered by Lewis and Clark in 1805 in what is now western Idaho. Also *pl.*, the tribe. Cf. **Pierced Nose.**

1832 in *Overland to Pacific* IV. (1934) 120 Here [hunters' rendezvous near Lewis River] we found about 120 Lodges of the Nez Perces and about 80 of the Flatheads. **1837** IRVING *Bonneville* I. 169 In another part of the field of action, a Nez Perce had crouched behind the trunk of a fallen tree and kept up a galling fire from covert. **1884** BARROWS *Oregon* 121 The Rev. Mr. Parker joined himself to the Nez Percés, and under their . . . protection, threaded his way to Walla Walla. **1947** DEVOTO *Across Wide Missouri* 97 He might have added Kanakas, Irish, Bannocks, Nez Perces, and Flatheads to the melting pot.

attrib. **1812** in *S. Dak. Hist. Coll.* IV. (1908) 157 The . . . Nez Perce nation have a tradition that the human race spring from this dog [prairie dog] and the beaver. **1832** *Ev. & Morning Star* (Independence, Mo.) Oct. 7/1 There were, of Capt. S's Fur company, Capt. Wythe's Oregon company, &c. about 250; of the Nepersee Indians, making a force of 300 against from 80 to 100 of the Black feet, Indians. **1884** BARROWS *Oregon* 121 [Whitman and Parker] met the Nez Percé Flat-Heads. **1949** *Pacific Discovery* May–June 16/1 According to some it is derived from the Nez Percé word meaning 'muddy water.'

N.G., *n.* and *a.* Abbreviation for "no go" or "no good." *Colloq.*

1839 *N.O. Picayune* 21 April 2/4 Though his grey-headed rival tried to win, it was n.g. (no go!) **1840** *St. Louis D. Pennant* 20 June (Th.), The bells, boys, and engines tried to get up a fire last night, but it was N.G. **1888** *Cin. W. Gazette* 22 Feb. (F.), Hill claims . . . that he will make the farmer sweat who have been asserting that his claim was N.G. **1928** *Amer. Mercury* Aug. 477/2 It's N.G.! Let's go!

Niagara naɪˈægərə, *n.* [Iroquoian. Name of a river and a famous waterfall between Lakes Erie and Ontario.]

1. In transferred uses (see quots.).

1843 STEPHENS *High Life N.Y.* II. 243 The winders were . . . kivered from top tu bottom with a hull Niagara of red silk. **1872** MARK TWAIN *Roughing It* 530 The flaming torrent . . . remains there [in the Hawaiian Islands] to-day all seamed, and frothed, and rippled, a petrified Niagara. **1912** COBB *Back Home* 321 Rivers of red pop had already flowed, Niagaras of lager beer and stick gin had been swallowed up. **1947** BEEBE *Mixed Train Dly.* 99 For two dollars we mounted to a bedroom whose Irish linen sheets, shaded bed lamps and Niagaras of hot water could have spelled luxury in New York.

b. (See quot.) *Obs.*

1865 SALA *Diary* II. 180 An elastic pipe must have passed through one of the 'Niagaras' or 'cataract curls'—the name given to the shower of true or false ringlets the ladies are in the habit of wearing at the back of their heads.

2. A kind of green grape descended from the Concord.

1884 *N.Y. Wkly. Tribune* 6 Feb. 10/2 Concord is still far in the lead, though Worden has many friends as the 'coming' black, and Niagara is being most largely tested among the whites. **1916** ALWOOD *Chemical Comp. Amer. Grapes* 6 [Grapes tested by government analysts include] Niagara, North Bass, Ohio. **1945** *Greeley* (Colo.) *D. Tribune* 15

March 10/8 Grapes: Concord, Fredonia, Wordon, Golden Muscat, Niagara, Portland are all hardy.

3. In special combs.: (1) **Niagara cane,** ?a walking cane obtained as a souvenir at Niagara Falls, *rare;* (2) **green,** bluish-green; (3) **gudgeon,** (see quot.); (4) **limestone,** a limestone formation occurring in the Upper Silurian in New York; (5) **shale,** (see quot. 1891); (6) **thyme,** (see quot.).

(1) **1891** WELCH *Recoll. 1830–40* 147 He wore a short, drab brown, sack coat, the prevailing fashion of those days, his hands stuck in his low coat pocket, his right hand holding a crooked neck Niagara cane, wrong end up, handle in the pocket. — (2) **1901** *World's Work* Aug. 1035/1 Running through the whole plan from the deeper barbaric primary colors to the delicate blue on the propylæa there greets you everywhere at intervals the Niagara green. — (3) **1842** *Nat. Hist. N.Y., Zoology* IV. 394 The Niagara Gudgeon. *Gobio cataractae*. . . . Body elongated and rounded. — (4) **1862** *Amer. Jrnl. Sci. & Arts* 2 Ser. XXXIII. 47 The regularly bedded layers present the usual lithological characteristics of the Niagara Limestone as it appears in Northern Illinois and Iowa. **1899** U.S. Geol. Surv. *Water Supp. Paper* No. 21, 14 At about 110 feet Lockport (often called Niagara) limestone is entered, which furnishes water containing sulphureted hydrogen.

(5) **1878** *Geol. Survey Ohio Rep.* III. 386 The Niagara shales here overlie the Clinton limestones. **1891** *Cent.* 5545/3 Niagara shale, a division of the Niagara group, especially interesting from its relation to the recession of Niagara Falls. It is there a shaly rock, and it underlies a more compact limestone, each division being at the present Falls about 80 feet thick. The shale wears away more rapidly than the limestone, which is thus undermined and breaks off in large fragments, greatly aiding the work of the water in causing the recession of the Falls. — (6) **1843** TORREY *Flora N.Y.* II. 67 *Micromeria glabella*. . . . Niagara Thyme. . . . On calcareous rocks, about the Falls of Niagara; Goat Island, and on Table Rock.

***nibbler,** *n.* The cunner, noted for nibbling the bait off hooks. *Colloq.* Cf. ***nipper 2,** and ***scamp.** — **1842** *Nat. Hist. N.Y., Zoology* IV. 173 The Bergall has various popular names: Nibbler, from its vexatious nibbling at the bait thrown out for other fishes [etc.]. **1859** BARTLETT 58 *Burgall, (Ctenolabrus ceruleus)*. . . . Other names are Nibbler, . . . and in New England, those of Blue Perch and Conner.

***Nicholas,** *n.* As the last term in **Saint, son of Saint Nicholas.**

Nicholite ˈnɪklˌaɪt, *n.* Also **Nicolite.** [Origin unknown.] A member of a religious sect in some respects resembling the Quakers. In full **Nicholite Quaker.** *Obs.*

1786 *Md. Journal* 21 Feb. (Th.), Not a Presbyterian, Baptist, Methodist, Dunker, Menonist, Nicolite nor even the peaceable old Quaker can now be prevailed with to contribute a single farthing towards the good design. **1804** DOW *Journal* (1814) 196 At night I lodged with one of the Nicholites, a kind of Quakers who do not feel free to wear coloured cloaths. *a***1870** CHIPMAN *Notes on Bartlett* 292 *Nicholites, Nicholite Quakers.* A sect in and about Delaware, about 1750–90.

***Nicholson,** *n.* [f. the name of the inventor.] (See quot. 1870.) Also **Nicholson-paved.** *Obs.*

1870 MACRAE *Americans* II. 172 In St. Louis I observed some streets floored with iron gratings, others macadamized, and others paved with wooden bricks laid on a floor of sanded planks, and cemented with asphalt. This is called the Nicholson pavement, and is found in New York, Chicago, and other cities as well as St. Louis. As long as it lasts, it is as safe, smooth, and noiseless a road as could be desired. **1881** *Harper's Mag.* April 711/1 Its broad, Nicholson-paved business streets are bounded . . . with warehouses. **1884** SWEET & KNOX *Through Texas* xxii. 301 'This,' said he, tapping with his cane one of the bowlders on the pavement, 'is none of your slippery asphalt or Nicholson.'

***nick,** *n.*[1] Crossbreeding in which a superior offspring results, or the animal secured in this way.

1889 WARFIELD *Cattle-Breed* 26 This thing of a 'nick,' or a successful cross, is as difficult as determining beforehand how much an animal will inherit from one or the other of its parents. **1897** *Outing* XXIX. 484/1 In time Star, a good one in the field, was bred to Druid, and Mr. Wells made a record with this nick. **1949** *Time* 1 Oct. 90/2 Actually, a breeder may run through hundreds of combinations before he hits a 'nick'—trade slang for a good hybrid.

nick nɪk, *n.*[2] Short for ***nickel 1.** *Colloq.* — **1857** *N.Y. Herald* 27 May 5/2 The bags containing the 'Nicks' were neat little canvass [*sic*] arrangements, each of which held five hundred [of the new coins]. **1865** SALA *Diary* II. 54 Two sticks of lollipops are to be had for two 'nicks.'

***nickel,** *n.*

1. Any one of various coins made in part of nickel, esp. a one-cent piece authorized in 1857 and discontinued in 1864. *Obs.* Cf. **three-cent,** *a.*, **nickel cent.**

1857 *N.Y. Herald* 27 May 4/6 'Nary red' will soon be an obsolete phrase among the 'boys,' and 'nary nickel' will take its place. **1863** *Chi. Tribune* 1 May 2/3 The heavy coinage of 'nickels' still continues, the number last week made at the mint in Philadelphia being 53,000. **1918** in *Pub. Col. Soc.* XX. 222 By 'nickels' are meant one-cent coins made of copper-nickel, first coined (of that material) . . . in 1858.

b. A five-cent piece made of three parts copper and one part nickel. Also fig.

1881 ROMSPERT *Western Echo* 233 My sales ran from seventy-five to one hundred and fifty dollars per day for several weeks. I shall leave the reader to *guess* at the *margins*, and only say that we did not *deal* in nickels. **1903** ALDRICH *Ponkapog P.* 120 Reaching out with some other man's hat for the stray nickel of your sympathy. **1949** *Nat. Geog. Mag.* Oct. 506/2 He had to import sacks of nickels and dimes.

2. In combs.: (1) **nickel bank,** a kind of gambling game in which nickels are used, *obs.;* (2) **cent,** = ***nickel 1,** *obs.;* (3) **-in-the-slot machine,** see as a main entry; (4) **novel,** a cheap, paper-covered, trashy novel, also attrib., cf. **dime novel;** (5) **nurser,** a tightwad, one who is stingy, *slang;* (6) **show,** a show to which a five-cent admission is charged, cf. next; (7) **theater,** =**nickelodeon 1.**

(1) **1888** *N.Y. World* May (Farmer), He started a nickel bank of his own, and won both fame and fortune as a gambler. — (2) **1863** G. HAMILTON *Gala-Days* 305, I shall by and by throw you a paltry nickel cent for your tropical dreams. **1872** *Harper's Mag.* Aug. 347/1 To make amends, he gave it a handful of nickel cents. — (4) **1896** SHINN *Story of Mine* 1 Pistols and bandits abound in a nickel-novel atmosphere. **1944** *Reader's Digest* July 71 A potbellied stove glowed in a corner and Harry, stretched on his back, read nickel novels all day and drank from an endless supply of beer bottles stored under the bed.

(5) **1924** *Cosmopolitan* Dec. 70/2 'A proper nickle-nurser, what I mean!' is Jerry Murphy's verdict. 'He is too stingy to harbor a doubt!' **1929** *Cent. Mag.* Autumn 64 'Bonehead,' 'nickel-nurser,' and flat-tire' are original tokens of his esteem for humanity. — (6) **1914** LOWRY *Himself* 165 Ragged and dirty children attending 'nickel shows' and buying quantities of cheap candy. — (7) **1912** BRECKINRIDGE & ABBOTT *Delinquent Child* 157 We have had . . . the excitement provided by the 'nickel theater.' **1914** *Collier's* 17 Jan. 4/3 There are too many nickel theatres around here.

As the last term in **five-cent, liberty head, plugged nickel.**

nickel-in-the-slot machine. A machine in which, by the insertion of a nickel in a slot, certain gears are, or may be, moved, thereby releasing gum, a bar of candy, etc. Also **nickel-in-the-slot scheme, nickel slot-machine.**

1889 *Tacoma* (Wash.) *News* 13 Dec. 3/5 The latest nickel-in-the-slot scheme is really a stroke of genius and is destined to revolutionize cheap literature in this country. **1893** *Harper's Mag.* March 494 [In Jacksonville] there were the same . . . nickel-in-the-slot machines [as in Asbury Park]. **1914** *Calif. Appellate Rep.* XXIII. 769 The statute under discussion relates only to gambling machines, and does not purport to make the business of manufacturing 'coin operating machines commonly known as nickel-in-the-slot machines' unlawful. **1947** *So. Sierran* Nov. 1/3 In fact, my $1.10 is sitting in a nickel slot-machine there.

nickelodeon ˌnɪklˈodɪən, *n.* [**nickel** (sense **1b.**)+ **odeon* (var. of **odeum*), a music hall.]

1. In the early days of motion pictures, a theater where a short picture, with or without singing, dancing, etc., could be seen for five cents. Now *hist.* Cf. **nicolet.**

1888 *Boston Transcript* 26 Nov. 5/7 Austin's Nickelodeon. . . . Open Day and Evening. Shows Hourly. **1908** *World To-day* Oct. 1053/1 There is no town of any size in the United States which does not contain at least one nickelodeon [moving-picture show]. **1949** *Business Week* 1 Oct. 6/3 He has been a success in the movie business since 1907, when he opened his first nickelodeon.

b. nickelodeon machine, ?=**mutoscope.**

1944 HOLTON *Yankees* 63 Needless to say Mother was completely enamored of them from the minute she looked into the top of the first little nickelodeon machine.

2. (See quot.)

1913 *Stand.* 1673/2 *Nickelodeon*, . . . a place of amusement generally charging no admission fee, containing various automatic machines, such as cinematographs, graphophones, etc., which may be used by patrons for a small charge.

3. A juke box.

1938 *Fla. Review* Spring 25/1 The requisites of a place entitling it to the name *jook* are . . . presence of the nickelodeon, and . . . of the dance-floor [etc.]. **1949** *Sat. Ev. Post* 15 Jan. 88/3 A nickelodeon at the end of the street emits a tinny piano tinkle.

*__nicker tree.__ *local.* = __Kentucky coffee tree.__ — __1785__ MARSHALL *Amer. Grove* 56 The Species with us, *Guilandina dioica,* Canadian dioiceous Bonduc, or Nickar Tree, . . . is said to grow plenty [in Kentucky], and is called the Coffee or Mahogany tree. __1890__ *N. & Q.* IV. 286 The name Nickar Tree is locally given in the United States to the Kentucky coffee tree.

__nicolet__ ˈnɪkəlɪt, *n.* (See quot. and cf. __nickelodeon.__) *Obs.* — __1914__ GRAU *Theatre of Science* 16 The 'Nicolet,' or five-cent store theatre, came into being.

__nievitas__ njeˈvitəs, *n. W.* [f. unrecorded meaning of dim. pl. of Sp. *nieve,* snow.] Any one of various California herbs of the genus *Cryptantha,* the small white flowers of which resemble forget-me-nots. — __1925__ JEPSON *Flowering Plants Calif.* 846 Cryptantha Lehm. Nievitas. __1932__ *Ariz. Agric. Exp. Sta. Bul.* 141, 25 They included such plants as alfilaria, . . . nievitas, bladderpod.

__niftiness__ ˈnɪftɪnɪs, *n.* The quality of being nifty, stylish, attractive. *Colloq.* — __1923__ WATTS *Luther Nichols* 27 His fixed purpose was to keep it so or to increase its niftiness.

__nifty__ ˈnɪftɪ, *a.* [Poss. f. **snifty,* having a pleasant smell.] Neat, stylish, smart.

__1865__ HARTE *Poems* (1871) 103 Here comes Rosey's new turn-out! Smart! You bet your life 'twas that! Nifty! (short for *magnificat*). __1928__ *Collier's* 10 Nov. 20/1 A guy who is a nifty dresser has class! __1948__ *Pauls Valley* (Okla.) *D. Democrat* 1 July 5/3 He batted a nifty .406 in 1941.

*__nig,__ *n.* __1.__ Short for **nigger. Slang.* __2.__ *All right on the nig,* holding views favorable to slavery. *Slang. Obs.* Cf. *__goose,__ *n.* __4. a.__

__(1) 1828__ RICE *Jim Crow* x, De Nigs in ole Virginny Be so black dey shine. __1840__ *N.O. Picayune* 20 Sep. 2/2 Two little nigs . . . had a most scientific set-to at the corner. __1905__ PRINGLE *Rice Planter* 160 Her manner is what the 'nigs' call 'stiff.' — __(2) 1856__ *Porter's Spirit of Times* 25 Oct. 132/3 The once all-absorbing 'goose question' has completely 'gin in,' and the only thing now necessary to know is, 'Is your man all right on the *nig?*'

__nig__ nɪg, *v. intr.* Short for **renege, v. Colloq.* — __1829__ *Mass. Spy* 10 June (Th.), If you hadn't a nig'd . . . you might have had better luck. __1859__ *Harper's Mag.* March 568/2 If you have got any trumps you had better play them and not undertake to nig any more!

*__nigger,__ *n.* See *__Negro.__

__nigger__ ˈnɪgɚ, *v.* [See note *s.v.* *__Negro.__]

__1.__ *tr.* (See quot.) *Obs.*

*c*__1824–38__ G. FURMAN *Antiquities L.I.* 228 The settlers who owned a few slaves employed them in this work; and hence, this process [grinding grain by samp mortar] was vulgarly called in that part of the State 'niggering corn.'

__2.__ To burn (a log) in two, or to burn off a piece or length of a log. Usu. with *off.* Also __niggering,__ *n. Colloq.*

Niggering a log (nigger, *v.* sense 2)

__1833__ S. SMITH *Life J. Downing* 22 He laid sticks across the large logs that were too heavy to move, and *niggered* them off with fire, and then roolled them up in piles and sot fire to 'em again. __1843__ CARLTON *New Purchase* I. 188 Niggering belongs mainly to very large timber, and pertains rather to the science of log-rolling than of preparing fuel. __1887__ J. KIRKLAND *Zury* 38 This [tree-trunk] he would measure off in about twenty-foot lengths, and at the end of each length he would build a fire, which . . would sever the log at that point, leaving it in lengths which could be hauled by a stout team over the snow to the place where they might be needed. This method of severing logs is called in the vernacular 'niggering them off,' whether because of its laziness, or of the blackness of the resulting heads. __1948__ DICK *Dixie Frontier* 126 Morning and evening dry limbs were laid in the widening gap until the log was burnt into length. After about a week the fires had done their work. This was called 'niggering off.'

__3.__ *To nigger it,* to live meagerly or barely. *Obs.*

__1857__ J. HYDE *Mormonism* 120 Many of the people express satisfaction in seeing these 'better-dressed fellers' obliged to 'nigger it' as well as themselves. __1878__ BEADLE *Western Wilds* 349 Was it not more of an honor to be the 'bishop's fourth' . . . than the 'slavey' of a poor mechanic, to 'nigger it on love and starvation?'

__4.__ *To nigger out,* (see quot.). *Obs.*

__1859__ BARTLETT 292 To *nigger out* land, signifies, in Southern phraseology, to exhaust land by the mode of tilling without fertilization pursued in the slave States.

__niggerish__ ˈnɪgərɪʃ, *a.* Like, or characteristic of, a Negro or Negroes. A derogatory term.

__1825__ NEAL *Bro. Jonathan* II. 67 Ye great niggerish lookin', wap-sided, haw. __1866__ *Atlantic Mo.* XVIII. 79/1 Aunt Judy's piety was in no respect the niggerish kind; when I say 'colored,' I mean one thing, respectfully; and when I say 'niggerish,' I mean another, disgustedly. __1948__ MENCKEN *Supp.* II. 124 Little effort seems to be made to conceal a way of speaking that sounds to many Northerners . . . somewhat niggerish.

*__night,__ *n.* In combs.: (1) __night accommodation,__ a night accommodation train, *obs.;* (2) __baseball,__ baseball played at night on fields illuminated by electric lights; (3) __city editor,__ on a big city newspaper, the editor in charge of the gathering and editing of local news at night, cf. __city editor;__ (4) __clerk,__ a clerk on night duty at a hotel receiving desk, also __night clerking;__ (5) *__club,__ = __night stick;__ (6) __editor,__ a newspaper editor who is on duty at night, on a morning newspaper, the editor of the final make-up; (7) __herd,__ *W.* the duty of keeping cattle herded at night, also *to ride night herd;* (8) __horse,__ *W.* a horse that is unusually sure-footed at night; (9) __key,__ a key for unlocking a night latch; (10) *__line,__ a line of night boats; (11) *__mare,__ *W.* (see quot. 1944); (12) __marshal,__ a town marshal who serves at night; (13) *__owl,__ *transf.* a person who is commonly up or abroad late at night; (14) __patrolman,__ a patrolman who serves at night; (15) __rider,__ see as a main entry; (16) __riding,__ the action of horsemen who ride at night to intimidate or terrorize, also attrib.; (17) __spot,__ a night club or similar place open to pleasure seekers at night, *colloq.;* (18) __stick,__ a stick or club carried by policemen at night, cf. *__billy, locust;__ (19) __wrangler,__ *W.* a wrangler who works at night.

__(1) 1881__ *Rep. Ala. R.R. Comm.* I. 53 [It was a] Night Accommodation. — __(2) 1910__ *Morrison's Chi. Wkly.* 1 Dec. 48/2 The future of night baseball is assured. __1949__ *L.A. Times* 6 June IV. 4/6 Night baseball may be as hot an issue as television when major league moguls put their heads together next winter. — __(3) 1892__ *Harper's Wkly.* 9 Jan. 42/4 The night city editor . . . has also had to send out reporters to look after matters brought to his attention after nightfall. __1916__ SEITZ *Training for Newsp. Trade* 63 The Night City Editor, checking up his schedule, asked for a report. — __(4) 1882__ SWEET & KNOX *Texas Siftings* 25 The night clerk is not so gorgeous or inclement as the day clerk. __1948__ *Good Housekeeping* Jan. 102/1 Night-clerking in third-rate hotels would not do for me. __1949__ *Sat. Ev. Post* 9 April 54/3, I suppose the night clerk saw you come in?

__(5) 1882__ MCCABE *New York* 383 The entire force on duty at the station dashed into the street, armed with their long night clubs. — __(6) 1920__ COOPER *Under Big Top* 40 The telegraph editor of the Kansas City Star looked up from his desk, toward the night editor. __1949__ *Time* 30 May 69/1 Stewart . . . had been night editor, sports editor and state editor of the Scripps-Howard *Press.* — __(7) 1884__ ALDRIDGE *Life on Ranch* 62 When on night-herd the men usually keep singing all the time as they ride round, that the cattle may know what is going on and not be suddenly startled by the sound or sight of a passing horseman. __1942__ DALE *Cow Country* 53 At two o'clock the last shift was awakened to come out to take over the task of riding night herd until daylight. — __(8) 1908__ *Sat. Ev. Post* 4 July 22/3 They made Blackie a night horse, for his sure-footedness was remarkable. __1942__ DALE *Cow Country* 51 Each man caught and saddled the mount he wanted, transferring his saddle from the 'night horse' staked near the wagon. — __(9) 1837__ NEAL *Charcoal Sk.* (1838) 136 The owner of the dog . . . took out his night-key, and walked up the steps. __1894__ WARNER *Golden House* i, In one of the noble houses . . . sat Edith Delancy . . . listening for the roll of wheels and the click of a night-key.

__(10) 1838__ *N.Y. Mirror* 21 April 343/2 The following boats constitute the night line. __1852__ *Hunt's Merch. Mag.* XXVI. 253 The passenger was entitled to be carried . . . by the night line. — __(11) 1929__ DOBIE *Vaquero* 99 His night horse, or, as he sometimes called this important animal his 'nightmare' . . . was generally the surest footed, the clearest sighted, and the most intelligent horse that a cowboy had in his string. **1944** ADAMS *W. Words* 105 Night mare A humorous name for the night horse, though it is never a mare. — **(12) 1915** YOUNG *Hard Knocks* 74 If you ever look my way while I am in Cheyenne, there will be a vacancy in this town for a night marshal. **1948** *Carthaginian* (Carthage, Miss.) 19 Aug. 1/7 Night Marshall H. H. Brooks, in making his rounds early Friday morning, noticed a late model Chrysler automobile . . . parked near the scene of the crime. — **(13)** *a***1846** *Quarter Race Ky.* 163 Do I know it, you no-souled, shad-bellied, squash-headed, old night-owl you! **1943** *Copper Camp* 81 As the word got around town of the endurance struggle under way in the hall, hundreds of night owls flocked to the scene. — **(14) 1884** *Colo. Springs Gazette* 11 Oct. 1/6 'Oh, Joe,' is a familiar cry from the old 'Vets,' and it keeps our night patrolmen from sleeping on their beats.

(16) 1875 *Chi. Tribune* 6 Nov. 3/6 To-night . . . there is to be a 'night riding' and shooting. It is not on the programme to do bodily harm to any person during these rides, but merely to arouse a degree of uneasiness in the darky's mind and cause him . . . not to go to the election. **1909** *Chambers's Jrnl.* Feb. 104/1 The first night-riding adventure . . . gave evidence of careful planning. — **(17) 1944** *Sat. Review* 23 Sep. 15/2 The thing which in the subway is called congestion is esteemed in the night spots as intimacy. **1948** *St. Paul Dispatch* 17 Sep. 25/2 They reported her visits to night spots and he won a divorce. — **(18) 1893** CRANE *Maggie* (1896) 98 The officer made a terrific advance, club in hand. One comprehensive sweep of the long night stick threw the ally to the floor. **1949** *Time* 14 Nov. 26/1 The police . . . charged into marchers and bystanders alike, swinging their nightsticks. — **(19) 1893** ROOSEVELT *Wilderness Hunter* 23 The night-wrangler was snatching an hour or two's sleep under one of the wagons. **1947** *Westerners' Brand Book* 52 Another boy was night-hawk or night-wrangler.

b. In the names of plants and animals: (1) ∗**night-caps,** *pl.* (see quot.); (2) **crawler,** any large angleworm; (3) **flutterer,** a term applied to an American moth belonging to any one of various species; (4) ∗**hawk,** see as a main entry; (5) **partridge,** =next; (6) **peck,** a local name for the American woodcock; (7) **willow-herb,** the evening primrose, *Oenothera biennis.*

(1) 1931 CLUTE *Plants* 60 Among other names that seem to be more fanciful than real are rabbit-bells for *Crotalaria rotundifolia* . . . and night caps for *Anemone nemorosa.* — **(2) 1924** *Collier's* 2 Feb. 3/1 He could stay up till 10 and hunt night crawlers in the garden with a lantern. **1949** *Esquire* March 88 Members of the Huck Finn school of fishing . . . have been looking for some way to enliven the almost impossibly sluggish night crawler. — **(3) 1784** J. BELKNAP *Hist. New Hampshire* II. 182 Insects . . . [include] Night flutterer *Sphinx.* Owl moth, many new species. Moth, or miller, *Phalæna.* **1832** WILLIAMSON *Maine* I. 172.

(5) 1888 TRUMBULL *Names of Birds* 153 At Pocomoke City (Worcester Co.), Md., and Eastville (Northampton Co.), Va., [the woodcock is called] Night Partridge. — **(6) 1888** TRUMBULL *Names of Birds* 153 The woodcock is known . . . in portions of North Carolina as the Night Peck. **1917** *Birds of Amer.* I. 225. — **(7) 1791** MUHLENBERG *Index Florae* 168 *Oenothera,* Night-willow herb. **1847** DARLINGTON *Weeds & Plants* 136 *Biennial Œnothera.* Evening Primrose. Night Willow-herb.

As the last term in **bank, bottle, Evacuation, ladies', over, patronage, Pope, pork, steamer, strawberry, white night.**

∗**nighthawk,** *n.*

1. Any one of various American goatsuckers of the genus *Chordeiles.* Occasionally confused with the whip-poorwill.

1778 CARVER *Travels* 466 The Night Hawk. This Bird is of the hawk species. **1812** WILSON *Ornithology* V. 65 Three species only, of this genus, are found within the United States; the Chuck-will's-widow, the Whip-poor-will, and the Night-hawk. **1913** EATON *Barn Doors & Byways* 119 The naturalists tell us that the night-hawks nest on top of the Manhattan skyscrapers **1948** *Sierra Club Bul.* March 11 Even after dark, the yap of a coyote, the zoom of a nighthawk, and the rustle made by a scampering mouse are all familiar sounds.

2. App. some kind of dish or vessel (poss. from a play upon ∗*nighthawk* and ∗*nightjar,* both names for the same bird). *Rare.*

1784 *Mass. Centinel* 10 July 3/3 Will be sold, by Public Vendue, . . . 3 doz. Dishes, 1 do., 6 Nighthawks, 2 doz. black Bowls, 4 do. large Porringers.

3. A cab which is operated at night. *Colloq.*

1855 *Monterey* (Calif.) *Sentinel* 4 Aug. 1/1 And don't you remember the Sundays, Bill Burns? Where the 'night hawks' and drivers would come. **1898** *Scribner's Mag.* XXIII. 443/2 Standing at the curb . . . are a few 'night hawks.'

4. (*cap.*) A member of a local unit of the Ku-Klux Klan who acts as a scout or courier.

1867 in LESTER & WILSON *Ku Klux Klan* 136 The officers of this . . . shall consist of . . . a Grand Cyclops of the Den and his two Night Hawks. **1884** *Cent. Mag.* July 405 The Grand Cyclops of the Den and his two Night Hawks. **1949** *Sat. Ev. Post* 22 Oct. 17/1 Cyclopes, Kludds, Kladds and Nighthawks are thumbing through the Kloran, the secret book of the Klan, studying the sonorous prayers and passwords.

5. =**night herder.**

1923 EVARTS *Tumbleweeds* 86 The night hawk hazed the remuda into a corral. **1939** ROLLINS *Gone Haywire* 61 Every two hours the night hawk who had completed his tour of duty would ride into camp and arouse his substitute. **1947** [See **night wrangler**].

transf. **1948** *Sierra Club Bul.* March 22 Ed Thistlethwaite . . . was our night hawk. It was to be his job . . . to get up and watch the dawn in the high and relatively high pasture lands to which the stock had been pushed, then to round them up and bring them down to work.

night herd, *v. W. tr.* To herd or have charge of cattle at night.

1903 A. ADAMS *Log Cowboy* ii. 11 Forrest night-herded them using five guards. **1944** ADAMS *W. Words* 105 Night herd To take charge of cattle on the bed-ground.

Hence **night herder, night herding.**

1908 *Sat. Ev. Post* 24 Oct. 10/1 On the edge of the band stood a long-eared, reddish, sleepy-eyed . . mule frequently used in night-herding. **1926** LORD *Frontier Dust* 132 Patrick Cullen, Esq. graduated as a night herder. **1942** DALE *Cow Country* 51 They then rode out to the herd, which was by this time up and grazing, in order to relieve the two men of the last night-herding shift and let them come in for breakfast.

∗**nightingale,** *n.* Any one of various American birds noted for their singing, as the cardinal and the white-throated sparrow.

1709 LAWSON *Carolina* 144 The Nightingales are different in Plumes from those in Europe. **1775** BURNABY *Travels* 17 In the woods [of Va.] there are . . . the mocking-bird, the red bird or nightingale [and] the blue-bird. **1804** CLARK in *Lewis & C. Exped.* I. (1904) 38 Passed a Small Creek . . . Which we named Nightingale Creek from a Bird of that discription which sang for us all last night. **1902** WHITE *Blazed Trail* 139 Down in the thicket, fine, clear, beautiful, . . . came the notes of the white-throat—the nightingale of the North.

b. nightingale sparrow, the song sparrow, *Melospiza melodia.*

1828 *Western Mo. Rev.* I. 520 Nightingale sparrow, *fringilla melodia,* a very diminutive sparrow, with plain plumage, but pours from its little throat a powerful song, like that of the nightingale.

c. *nightingale of Canada,* (see quot.). *Obs.* or *rare.*

1859 MACKAY *Tour* II. 267 The largest bull-frogs of the Old World. I was informed by a passenger that these were the 'veritable nightingales of Canada,' and that their croak sounded uncommonly like the words 'strong rum, strong rum.'

As the last term in **American, Swedish, Virginia, western nightingale.**

night rider.

1. A horseman who rides on sinister missions at night; esp. a member of a secret organization formed by southern white men just after the Civil War to overawe and keep in subjection the newly freed Negroes.

1879 *Cong. Rec.* 20 May 1480/2 There was much said . . . of kuklux, white leagues, and night-riders. . . . There are . . . no night-riders in the State of Louisiana. **1887** *Courier-Journal* 13 Feb. 9/3, I should like to have . . . anecdotes that would show the humor and give side-lights upon the character of that bold young night-rider. **1948** DICK *Dixie Frontier* 94 Patrols, called patterols by the slaves, were organized by the whites, and these night riders endeavored to enforce the regulations.

2. *pl.* or *collect.* A group of Kentucky tobacco-growers who (*c*1906–9) used violence in their efforts to perfect an association of tobacco producers.

1907 *Lit. Digest* 28 Dec. 976 The first appearance of the night riders was in November, 1906, when they destroyed some tobacco-barns and small factories in Todd County with a loss of about $10,000. **1909** *N.Y. Ev. Post* 15 April (Th.), The Presbyterian Church at Fredonia, Caldwell Co., Ky., was burned last night, and 'night-riders' are suspected. **1936** MILLER *Black Patch War* 18 The Night Rider burnt his warehouse and his purchase with it, and whipped him, and if he resisted, slew him.

3. =**night herder.**

1947 *Sierra Club Bul.* May 59 Back in the high country a night rider pushes the stock sometimes two or three miles from the frequently used meadow to grazing that is seldom touched.

nimble Will. A slender American grass, *Muhlenbergia schreberi,* which spreads rapidly in uncultivated fields and in the woods. — **1816** THOMAS *Travels Western Country* (1819) 168 In his field he pointed out to me a grass, of which I had heard much, known through all the western country by the name of *nimble Will.* **1894** COULTER *Bot. W. Texas* III. 523 Nimble Will.... Dry hills and woods, northern Texas and northward.

***Nimshi,** *n.* [Cf. *EDD Nimshie*, a flighty girl.] A fool, a silly person, a nitwit. *Colloq.* Cf. **Jehu Nimshi.** — **1848** BARTLETT 233 *Nimshi.* A foolish fellow, or one who habitually acts in a foolish manner. **1944** *N.Y. Herald Tribune Bk. Rev.* 24 Sep. 2/4 There were 'Nimshis'—which word describes the village nitwits, who were treated with tolerance and kindness, even when they barged into the front row of group photographs.

* **nine,** *a.* and *n.*

1. *Baseball.* The nine players making up a side or team.

1856 *Spirit of Times* 6 Dec. 229/1 A strong and safe striker, he gives great strength to the nine with whom he plays. **1869** *Terr. Enterprise* (Virginia, Nev.) 7 Oct. 3/1 The 'Muff' nine are expected to be in full force, and give the 'picked' nine a warming. **1948** *Herald-Press* (St. Joseph, Mich.) 14 Aug. 7/3 The local nine has averaged slightly over seven runs and 12 hits per game.

2. In combs.: (1) **ninebark,** see as a main entry; (2) **diamond,** a quilt pattern, also attrib.; (3) * **pence,** the Spanish real, having a value of about 12½ cents, or a coin of approximately its value, *obs.;* (4) **shooter,** a repeating rifle capable of firing nine shots without being reloaded, also **nine shooting,** *a., obs.;* (5) * **spotted,** *a.* designating a variety of ladybird the specimens of which have nine spots on the back.

(2) **1867** G. W. HARRIS *Sut Lovingood* 137 Irish chain, star ove Texas, sun-flower, nine dimunt... an' shell quilts. *Ib.* 144 Oh, my preshus nine dimunt quilt! — (3) **1828** *Yankee* 14 May 157/2 A *ninepence* in New-England... is a *shilling* in New York. **1892** A. E. LEE *Hist. Columbus, Ohio* I. 398 The coin in circulation at that time [*c*1821] was almost entirely Spanish, consisting of the silver dollar and its half, quarter, eighth and sixteenth, the last two being known as 'four pence-ha'penny' or 'fippeny bit,' and 'nine-pence' respectively. *Ib.*, The last two of these pieces being scarce, their place was supplied by cutting a quarter into two or four pieces, which passed for a 'nine-pence' or a 'fip' respectively and were known in popular parlance as 'sharp shins.' — (4) **1846** BRYANT *California* (1848) 166 Colonel Russell recollected that he had left his rifle at the camp—a 'nine-shooter.' *Ib.* 167 The result of the search for the 'nine-shooting' rifle was fruitless.

(5) **1861** *Ill. Agric. Soc. Trans.* IV. 347, I found numerous specimens of a nine-spotted lady-bird (*Coccinella novemnotata*, Herbst,) under dry cow-dung. **1867** *Amer. Naturalist* I. 278 The nine-spotted Lady Bug... is one of a large group of beetles, most beneficial from habit of feeding on the plant-lice.

b. *To get* (or *put*) *in the nineholes*, to get or put into a difficult situation. *Slang.*

1863 E. KIRKE *Southern Friends* 76 He owned har [the slave] till he got in the nineholes one day, and sold har ter the Gin'ral. **1877** *Cong. Rec.* 3 Nov. 230/1 We have put the gentleman in the 'nine-holes;' and there we intend to keep him. **1906** RIDLEY *Battles* 295 The only time he ever got Johnston apparently in 'a nine hole' was at Resaca, on May 15, 1864.

As the last term in **ball, baseball, college, field, freshman, home, long, scrub, seven-by-, three-twenty-, two-by-nine.**

ninebark ˈnaɪnˌbark, *n.* Any one of various white-flowered American shrubs of the genus *Physocarpus* with bark that separates readily into thin layers (see also quot. 1931).

1785 MARSHALL *Amer. Grove.* 146 Guelder Rose-leaved Spiraea, or Nine-Bark. This rises with many shrubby branching stalks... to the height of five or six feet. **1806** LEWIS in *L. & Clark Exped.* IV. (1905) 49 The seven bark or nine bark as it is called in the U' States is also common [near Ft. Clatsop]. **1860** CURTIS *Woody Plants N.C.* 104 Nine Bark... is found upon river banks in the western part of the State. **1931** CLUTE *Plants* 128 There were for instance, the nine-barks (*Hydrangea cinera* and *Physocarpus opulifolius*) which may be assumed to have nine times the efficiency of common barks. **1949** *Chi. Tribune* 25 Sep. III. E/5 Also the effective fall shrub, evergreen Euonymus japonica, the witch hazel, beautybush, privet, ninebark.

b. (See quot.)

1847 DARLINGTON *Weeds & Plants* 120 Opulus-leaved Spiræa.... A very showy ornamental species.... Sometimes called 'Nine-Bark Syringa.'

nineteenth hole. A convivial gathering place, such as a locker room, or club bar, where players congregate after playing golf. — **1921** MENCKEN *Amer. Language* 130 As a set-off to it—and to *nineteenth hole*, the one American contribution to the argot of golf, if *African golf* for craps be omitted—the English have an ecclesiastical vocabulary with which we are almost unacquainted. **1948** *Time* 19 Jan. 52/3 He dug into his pocket for $10,000 in prize money, played more for the fun of it than in the hope of beating anybody, and helped entertain on the 19th hole.

ninety-day gunboat. One of a number of heavily armed, quickly built screw gunboats added to the federal navy during the Civil War. *Obs.* — **1883** J. R. SOLEY *Blockade & Cruisers* 19 Some of them, within four months from the date of contract, were afloat, armed, and manned.... From their rapid construction, they were commonly known as the 'ninety-day gunboats.' **1886** *Harper's Mag.* June 7/1 The 'ninety-day gun-boats,' and the 'double-enders' were added to the navy list.

niño de la tierra. *S.W.* [Santamaría lists *niño, gillotalpa, grillo-topo, muereterriendo*, but not the term here given, as the name for this cricket.] =**sand cricket.** Cf. **Jerusalem cricket.** — **1925** BRYAN *Papago Country* 53 The 'niño de la tierra' (child of the earth), which has an evil reputation among the Mexicans, is a burrowing and wingless insect very like a grasshopper and as dangerous. **1947** *Desert Mag.* May 31/1 Baby-face or Niño de la tierra, child of the earth, is found near the Mexican border.

ninseng ˈnɪnsɛŋ, *n.* Also **ninsin.** An obsolete variant of "ginseng."

1748 CATESBY *Carolina* App. 16 *Aureliana Canadensis R.I. Lafiteau.* The Ginseng, or Ninsin, of the Chinese. An accurate description [of the plant]... gave light to the discovery of the same plant in Canada and Pensylvania. **1784** CUTLER in *Mem. Acad* I. 492 Ninsin. From the quality that grows in this country,... we have reason to hope it will become a valuable export. **1790** DEANE *N.-Eng. Farmer* 203/1 Panax, Ginseng, or Ninseng,... This plant is a native of our country, and is become a considerable article of commerce.

Nip nɪp, *n.* [f. *Nip*ponese.] A derogatory term for a Japanese. Also attrib. or as adj. *Colloq.* — **1942** *Time* 23 Feb. 52 Many is the chaplain, dodging dive-bombers, who has gotten up waving his fist at the unopposed Nip flyers. **1945** MENCKEN *Supp.* I. 609 The related *Nip*, from *Nipponese*, was reported in *American Speech* by Dwight L. Bolinger in April 1943.

nip and tuck. Also †**nip and chuck, tack.** A close approximation to equality in racing or other competition, neck and neck. Also attrib. *Colloq.*

1832 PAULDING *Westward Ho!* I. 172 There we were a rip [?misprint] *and* tuck, up one tree and down another. **1836** *Quarter Race Ky.* 16 It will be like the old bitch and the rabbit, nip and tack every jump. *a***1846** *Ib.* 123 Then we'd have it again, nip and chuck. **1869** *Putnam's Mag.* Jan. (De Vere), It was nip and tuck all along, who was to win her. **1890** SHIELDS *Big Game N. Amer.* 92 It was a nip-and-tuck race. **1949** *Oregonian* (Portland) 10 Aug. III. 1/5 The game was nip and tuck all the way.

b. Also as verb. *Rare.*

1897 WILKINS *Jerome* 239 By nippin' an' tuckin' an pinchin'.

Nipmuck ˈnɪpmʌk, *n.* [In Hodge said to be f. a native term, *Nipamaug*, "fresh-water fishing place."] *pl.* or *collect.* A tribe of Algonquian Indians formerly living in southern New England. Now *hist.*

1637 in *Mass. H. S. Coll.* 4 S. VI. 193 Your late message to the Neepmucks... hath wrought this effect. **1910** HODGE *Amer. Indians* II. 74/2 The Nashua dwelling farther N., are sometimes classed with the Nipmuc, but were rather a distinct body. **1945** WEBSTER *Town Meeting Country* 12 The Nipmucks to the north were less belligerent and, along with the Mohegans farther west, were dominated by the aggressive Pequots.

* **nipper,** *n.*

1. A thick band or mitten used by New England cod fishermen to protect their hands and wrists. *Colloq.*

1840 *Niles' Reg.* 15 Aug. 376/3 An article, neither mittens nor gloves, which he [Bay of Fundy fisherman] wears upon his hands, he calls *'nippers.'* **1884** *Nat. Museum Bul.* No. 27, 794 Fishermen's Nippers. Knit of woolen yarn and stuffed with woolen cloth. Gloucester, Mass.... Used on the hands of fishermen to enable them to grasp and hold a fishing-line better than they otherwise could do. **1897** KIPLING *Capt. Courageous* 56 A heavy blue jersey well darned at the elbows, a pair of nippers, and a sou'wester.

2. The cunner. *Colloq.* Cf. * **nibbler.**

1884 GOODE *Fisheries* I. 273 At Salem they are called 'Nippers,' and occasionally here and elsewhere 'Bait-stealers.' **1911** *Rep. Fisheries 1908* 308 Chogset (*Tautogolabrus adspersus*).—This fish... is also called... 'nippers.'

Nisei ˈnisɪ, *n.* [Jap., second generation.] An American-born Japanese, also as a *pl.*

1943 MENEFEE *Assignment* 191 The War Relocation Authority, after a delay of many months, finally began to release those Nisei, or American-born Japanese. **1948** *Newsweek* 30 Aug. 20/1 The 29-year-old Nisei claimed that she had taken a job with the Tokyo radio merely 'for the experience.' **1949** *Time* 20 June 25/2 He pushed the formation of the famed 442nd Combat Team, in which the Nisei in Italy gave distinguished proof of their loyalty to the U.S.

Nisqualli ˈnɪzˌkwɑlɪ, *n.* [App. a native name.] (See quot. 1910.) In full **Nisqualli Indians.** Also attrib.

1842 WILLIAMS *Tour to Ore.* 61 In the care of Dr. Richmond, on the other side of the Columbia, at the Puget Sound, among the Nisqually Indians. **1910** HODGE *Amer. Indians* II. 76/2 Nisqualli. A Salish tribe on and about the river of the same name flowing into the s. extension of Puget sd., Wash. **1940** SMITH *Puyallup-Nisqually* 24 He brings the line between the Puyallup and Nisqually west along the Nisqually River and cuts it sharply northward at a point just below the site of the second Nisqually village. **1948** *Nat. Hist.* April 190/3 The word may be a misspelling of the Nisqually-Puyallup Indian name for the big clam, 'gwe-duc.'

b. The language of these Indians.

1940 SMITH *Puyallup-Nisqually* 20 It has become usual to label the language as either Puyallup or Nisqually according to the river drainage on which the respective reservations were located.

nit nɪt, *n.* [Origin obscure. Poss f. G. *nichts.*] **1.** None, nothing. **2. nitwit,** a person of little intelligence. Both *colloq.*

(1) **1910** O. HENRY *Strictly Business* v. 66 'You fool. . . . Why did you do it?' 'The Stuff,' explained Thomas briefly. 'You know. But subsequently nit. Not a drop.' — (2) **1928** *Sat. Ev. Post* 4 Feb. 121/3 He's about the most complete nitwit I ever encountered—but useful . . . and harmless. **1948** *Chi. D. News* 18 Feb. 24/6 One's freedom of action to improve his lot . . . should not be challenged by any 'nitwit.'

* **nitre,** *n.* A precipitate of malic acid formed in making maple sirup.

1872 *Vt. Bd. Agric. Rep.* I. 219 The gritty sediment from maple syrup, commonly termed 'nitre.' **1882** *Ib.* VII. 65 The higher the [sugar maple] tree is tapped the more of nitre or malate of lime is found. **1949** *Highway Traveler* Feb. 39/1 Strainers . . . through which the hot syrup is passed to remove the 'nitre,' or 'sugar sand,' a fine gritty substance, before it is canned.

nitweed ˈnɪtˌwid, *n.* [?f. * *nit*, egg of a louse (f. its seed), + * *weed.* The minute scalelike leaves of the plant may have suggested the name.] = **pineweed.**

1817–8 EATON *Botany* (1822) 380 Nit-weed, false john's wort. . . . On the sandy plain west of Ball's spring, New Haven. **1843** TORREY *Flora N.Y.* I. 89 Ground Pine. Nitweed. Pine-weed. . . . Sandy fields and road-sides; common. June-August. **1907** LYONS *Plant Names* 414 Sarothra. . . . Orange-grass, Pine-weed, Bastard Gentian, Ground Pine, Nit-weed, False Johnswort.

nix nɪks, *n.* [G. *nix, nichts,* nothing. App. an Amer. borrowing.]

1. Nothing, none. *Slang.*

1855 *Golden Era* (S.F.) 15 April 1/3 You will soon be . . . a 'dried up' old bach., and in fact, 'good for nix.' **1870** *Virginia* (Nev.) *Terr. Enterprise* 27 Feb. 3/2 Nix.—No business in the criminal line came before Justice Ellis' Court yesterday. **1931** *K.C. Times* 6 Aug., That guy . . . started the 'brains he has nix' idea in cartoons.

b. Also with adverbial force as an expletive.

1909 CULLUM *Watchers* 24 'What are our chances?' 'Nix,' responded the scout decidedly. **1926** J. BLACK *You Can't Win* vi .67 'I'll go to the farmhouse. . . . and buy something.' 'Nix, nix,' said one; 'buy nothin'.' **1946** *Chi. D. News* 6 June (Comics) 43 Absolutely and positively nix!

2. (See quots.) Often *pl.* Cf. **nixie 1.**

1879 *Postal Laws & Reg.* 113 Misdirected second-class matter ('nixes'). **1883** *Postal Guide* 733 'Nixes' is a term used in the railway mail service to denote matter of domestic origin, chiefly of the first and second class, which is unmailable because addressed to places which are not post offices, or to States, etc., in which there is no such post office as that indicated in the address.

3. *nix cum arous,* there's nothing to it, nothing doing. *Colloq.*

1844 *Republican Sentinel* (Richmond, Va.) 27 July 1/1 Clay must rest contented; For he's 'nics cum arous' at the old White House. **1856** *Sacramento Union* 29 March 1/7 Our mouth watered for a whiff from the golden luxury, but it was 'Nix cum a rouse; nix for shtay, Mein Gott!' **1936** MENCKEN *Amer. Lang.* (ed. 4) 157 Whole phrases have gone through the same process, for example, *nix come erous* (from *nichts kommt heraus*).

4. *nix on,* enough of, have done with, no more of. *Colloq.*

1911 H. QUICK *Yellowstone N.* ii. 24 Nix on the Conversation game, said he. **1921** R. D. PAINE *Comr. Rolling Ocean* iv. 62 Camp Stuart at ten o'clock. Nix on that kid stuff.

nixie ˈnɪksɪ, *n.* and *adv.* [See **nix,** *n.*]

1. *n.* (See quot. 1949.) Also attrib. Cf. **nix,** *n.* **2.**

1901 *Cong. Rec.* 17 Jan. 1145/2 Mailing clerks, . . . directory, and nixie clerks . . . [shall receive] from $600 to not exceeding $1,400 per annum. **1929** *Lit. Digest* 5 Oct. 67/1 The similarity in appearance of the letters N.Y. and N. J. and Me. and Mo., . . . is responsible for many letters reaching the 'Nixie' division. **1949** *Amer. Sp.* April 136/1 Nixie. A piece of mail so damaged or illegible that it can go no farther in the mails.

2. *adv.* No indeed, nothing doing. *Colloq.*

1904 *Buffalo Express* 20 June 4 It is said that if China should adopt the German conscription rules she could put a force of 37,000,000 men in the field. Nixie. There isn't any field that would hold 37,000,000 men. **1914** G. ATHERTON *Perch of Devil* i. 108 They're all right to marry . . . but to sacrifice your life for, nixie.

* **no,** *adv.* and *a.*

1. In combs.: (1) **no-good,** an insignificant or worthless person, *slang;* (2) **-license,** denoting a community or town which votes that alcoholic beverages shall not be sold within its boundaries; (3) * **man's land,** see as a main entry; (4) **party man,** a man belonging to no political party, *obs.;* (5) **partyism,** the condition of being unaffiliated with any political party; (6) **-see-'em,** in Indian speech or in imitation of this, a minute biting fly or midge of the family Chironomidae, a punkie, *colloq.;* (7) **sir-ee,** *adv.* an emphatic form of "no," cf. the quots. *s.v.* **bob,** *interj.,* and see **yes sir-ee;** (8) **top,** a buggy having no top, in full **no-top buggy.**

(1) **1924** A. J. SMALL *Frozen Gold* i. 14 I'll learn you half-suckled no-goods what it means. — (2) **1880** *Amer. Punch* June 89/1 He says he had almost as soon travel through a temperance or no-license community as agent of a brewery. **1944** HOLTON *Yankees* 141 Massachusetts in the eighties operated under local option and Wellshaven was what was known as a no-license town. — (4) **1828** *Yankee* 16 July 230/3 Wo to the no-party-man, who is fed of both parties. **1861** NEWELL *Orpheus C. Kerr* I. 274 The abolitionists caused this terrible war, and it is our business, as no-party men, to finish it Constitutionally.

(5) **1848** *Campaign Flag* (Maysville, Ky.) 28 July 2/5 Nor can all the schemes of whiggery, the abominations of abolitionism, or the low intrigue of 'no-partyism' move her a single step. **1851** *Ore. Statesman* 5 Aug. 2/5 The truth is, that no-partyism is untenable. — (6) **1848** THOREAU *Maine Woods* 2 In the summer myriads of black flies, mosquitoes, and midges, or, as the Indians call them, 'no-see-ems,' make travelling in the woods almost impossible. **1914** *Outing* June 187/2 A No-seeum is a species of guerrilla gnat having two stingers in each foot and nine in the head. **1949** *Pacific Discovery* May–June 18/2 We regretted leaving everything except those diminutive torturers, the 'no-see-ums.' — (7) **1845** *Quincy* (Ill.) *Whig* 13 Dec. 1/5 Taint everybody that can put on the regimentalities, and look like old Mars, the god of war, with a decided touch of the Julius Junius Ceaze-her thrown in for effect. No, sir-ee! **1945** BOTKIN *My Burden* 190 No, siree, we put you out there to work, and you sure better work. — (8) **1827** *Harvard Reg.* Oct. 247 He who desires to be a big-Bug, rattling in a natty gig, No-top, or chaise, or tandem. **1860** *Charleston* (S.C.) *Mercury* 6 Nov. 1/7 (*advt.*), Top Buggies, No Top Buggies, and Concord Wagons. **1894** CHOPIN *Bayou Folk* 14 At Natchitoches . . . they found Pierre's no-top buggy awaiting them.

2. no-hit game, in baseball, a game in which a team fails to secure a hit. Also transf.

1913 *Lit. Digest* 5 July 35/1 He . . . was robbed of a no-hit game by a scratch single in the ninth inning. **1919** *Amer. Mag.* July 27/2 If you want to get the money and the girl, go to sleep and quit worrying; worry never pitched a no-hit game. **1922** *Dly. Press* (Ardmore, Okla.) 4 May 3/3 He helped hurl the Reds to a pennant, pitching a no-hit game among other things.

b. Also **no-hit no-run,** with reference to a game in which one side does not secure a hit or a run.

1947 *Chi. D. News* 11 July 23/4 In hurling the first no-hit, no-runs victory in the American League. . . . Black fanned five.

c. no-hitter, a no-hit game.

1938 *Dly. Ardmoreite* (Ardmore, Okla.) 13 April 8/4 Larry French pitched four no-hitters before coming up to the big leagues. **1949** *Oregonian* (Portland) 10 Aug. III. 4/2 He pitched a five-inning no-hitter against Hillsboro in his last previous start.

3. *No sabe* (or *savvy*), not to know or understand, generalized from the third person sing. of the Sp. *saber,* to know. *Slang.*

1850 *Calif. Courier* (S.F.) 25 Sep. 2/4 Altho' we *no sabe* Italian, 'we like the system,' as the boy said, and we can enjoy the singing. **1888** *Phoenix* (Ariz.) *Gaz.* 14 June 1/2 That some trickery is behind it we are all confident, but what it is we 'no sabe.' **1945** *Trinidad* (Colo.) *Chronicle-News* 1 June 2/6 Slain, who recently was commissioned in action, signaled to them to surrender. It was a case of 'no savvy.'

*** Noah's ark.** (See quots. 1890, 1898.)

1826 DARLINGTON *Florula Cestrica* 95 C[*ypripedium*] *pubescens*. . . . Noah's Ark. Yellow Mocasin [*sic*] flower. **1890** *Cent.* 4002/1 *Noah's ark*. . . . In *bot.*, the larger yellow lady's-slipper, *Cypripedium pubescens*. **1898** CREEVEY *Flowers of Field* 296 Stemless Lady's Slipper. Noah's Ark. Moccasin-flower. *Cypripedium acaule*. **1949** PALMER *Fieldbook Nat. Hist.* 148/2 It bears a number of common names such as Noah's ark, squirrel's shoes, camel's foot, nerveroot, old goose, Indian moccasin, and two lips.

*** noble,** *a.* In the names of trees, as **noble (silver) fir, laurel tree,** (see quots.).

1846 BROWNE *Trees* 411 *Laurus nobilis*, The Noble Laurel-tree. **1858** WARDER *Hedges & Evergreens* 257 Picea nobilis, Noble Silver Fir. . . . This majestic tree forms large forests in the northern part of California. **1885** ONDERDONK *Idaho* 31 The Noble Fir inhabits all our mountain ranges at an elevation of from 3,000 to 5,000 feet. **1949** COLLINGWOOD & BRUSH *Knowing Your Trees* 105 A cubic foot of noble fir wood when dry weighs twenty-eight pounds.

b. noble pine, =**pipsissewa.**

1892 *Amer. Folk-Lore* V. 100 *Chimaphila umbellata*, noble pine; bittersweet.

nocake ˈnokek, *n.* [Narraganset *nokehick*, "it is soft."] The meal of parched Indian corn, or food made from this. Cf. **hoecake.**

1634 WOOD *N. Eng. Prospect* 68 *Nocake* (as they [*sc.* Indians] call it) . . . is nothing but Indian Corne parched in the hot ashes; the ashes being sifted from it, it is afterward beaten to powder, and put into a long leather bag. **1764** HUTCHINSON *Hist. Mass.* I. 465 A small pouch of . . . Nuichicke, which is well enough translated Nocake, would support them several days in their travelling. **1832** DURFEE *Whatcheer* 25 In trays the nocake, and the joints of deer. **1948** *Sat. Review* 26 June 11/1 Aunt Luciny might play the part of a local witch with her ancient sagas, her herb remedies, and her baking of the Nocake.

attrib. *c***1880** HAZARD *Johnny-Cake P.* (1915) 58, I well remember the old no-cake mortar that used to stand in my grandfather's kitchen, upside down when not in use. . . . I think it would hold half a gallon of parched corn, or more.

*** nodding,** *a.* In the names of flowers of American genera or species, as **nodding cap, onion, pogonia, trillium,** (see quots.).

1814 BIGELOW *Florula Bostoniensis* 85 *Trillium cernuum*. Nodding Trillium. . . . In shady thickets. **1857** A. GRAY *First Lessons Bot.* (1866) 193 Nodding Trillium or Wake-Robin. **1907** LYONS *Plant Names* 366 P[ogonia] trianthophora. . . . Eastern U.S. Nodding Pogonia, Three-birds. **1933** SMALL *Southeastern Flora* 378 Nodding-caps. . . . Nodding-ettercap. Three-birds. **1939** *Nat. Geog. Mag.* Aug. 264/2 In middle-western hills and mountains the nodding onion (*A. cernuum*) is so named because of the pendent position of the blossoms, a lovely rose pink.

*** nodhead,** *n.* =**Jewett red.** *Obs.* — **1849** *N. Eng. Farmer* I. 54 The Nodhead . . . has done poorly with me as yet. **1859** ELLIOTT *Western Fruit Book* 149 Jewett's Red. . . . Nodhead. . . . Best adapted to strong clay soils North.

*** nog,** *n.* =**eggnog.** — **1851** A. O. HALL *Manhattaner* 10, I tremble to think of the juleps, and punches, and nogs, and soups. **1896** *Harper's Mag.* April 783/2 Mrs. Raker was holding a foaming glass to the sick man's lips. 'There; take another sup of the good nog,' she said.

nogal noˈgɑl, *n. S.W.* [Sp., walnut tree.] A walnut tree; a pecan tree.

1869 BROWNE *Adv. Apache Country* 262 We returned to our pleasant camping-place under the wide-spreading nogales, or walnut-trees, by the margin of the creek. **1892** *D.N.* I. 192 *Nogal:* properly the walnut tree, in Texas the pecan tree. . . . The hickory is called *nogal encarcelado*. **1904** WOOTON *Native Ornamental Plants N. Mex.* 20 The Walnut or Nogal (*Juglans rupestris*) is a native tree which deserves more attention in this region. **1913** ——— *Trees & Shrubs N. Mex.* 48 This family contains the well known walnut or *nogal*, the English walnut of commerce, the hickory nut, and the pecan.

*** noggin,** *n.* A person's head. *Colloq.*

1885 PHUDGE PHUMBLE *Greenhorn* 25 (We.), The full force of it against his noggin. **1893** M. A. OWEN *Voodoo Tales* 23 Lemme scratch dis hyeah ole noggin. **1942** WARNICK *Dialect Garrett Co, Md.* 11 Noggin', n., the head.

nolle ˈnɑlɪ, *n.* [L. *nolle* prosequi, to be unwilling to prosecute.] An acknowledgment or declaration of record by the plaintiff or his representative that a suit or indictment will be prosecuted no further. Also **nolle pros.** Cf. **non-pros.*

1871 EGGLESTON *Hoosier Schoolm.* 214, I now enter a *nolle* in his case . . . and I ask that this court adjourn. **1878** BEADLE *Western Wilds* 507 He had been indicted along with the others, and a *nolle* entered. **1895** *Denver Times* 5 March 1/3 John Doyle was dismissed on a nolle pros in both cases. **1948** *Chi. D. News* 7 May 16/1, I can't stop the state from taking a nolle prosse.

nolle ˈnɑlɪ, *v.* [See prec.] *tr.* To drop (a suit) by a nolle pros. Also **nol(le) pros.**

1845 HOOPER *Suggs* (1928) 97, I would '*nol pros.*' the case if I were you, and let this grief-stricken old man go home to his dying children. **1888** *Battle Creek Jrnl.* 7 March, The prosecution stated that it would be impossible to secure a conviction in either case, and he asked that they be nolled. **1895** *Chi. Times-Herald* 7 Nov. 7/1 Judge Seamon today nolled the indictments against Eugene V. Debs. **1948** *Lisle* (Ill.) *Eagle* 21 Oct. 1/5 Redmond points out that 74 of the 242 grand jury cases have either been stricken or Nolle Prossed on motion of the State's Attorney.

*** No Man's Land.**

1. A small island near Martha's Vineyard, Massachusetts. Also attrib.

1675 in C. E. BANKS *Hist. Martha's Vineyard* I. 35 That no man presume to land any goods anywhere at Marthas Vineyard, . . . Nomans Land, or Elizabeth Isles, unless at the places appointed. **1884** *Nat. Museum Bul.* No. 27 695 No Man's Land Fishing Boat. . . . The boats built from this model are employed in the shore fisheries about Vineyard Sound and No Man's Land.

2. The panhandle of Oklahoma.

Until 1890 this area, which had been ceded to the United States by Texas in 1845, was not assigned to any state or territory. It was proposed that it should form a separate territory of Cimarron.

1885 *Santa Fé Wkly. New Mexican* 16 July 3/2 Nearly 50,000 cattle . . . have been forcibly stopped and prevented from passing over the common trail . . . through the Indian country, the Cherokee strip and no man's land. **1896** *Cong. Rec.* 16 May 5338/2 From the Sabine to the Rio Grande, and from No Mans Land to the Gulf of Mexico he [W. H. Crain] was known to all. **1948** *Sooner Mag.* Nov. 22/1 No Man's Land, so called because Congress failed to assign the area to any administrative unit after the Compromise of 1850, has been the site of many struggles between Nature and Man.

3. (See quot.)

1892 WALSH *Lit. Curiosities* 806 *No Man's Land*. . . . Locally, the name is also given to a strip of territory on the boundary between Pennsylvania and Delaware. According to the official surveys, it seems to belong to Pennsylvania, but by habit and custom of the people to Delaware.

*** nominate,** *v. tr.* Of the President of the United States: To appoint (someone) to a particular office, subject to confirmation by the Senate.

1894 *Harper's Mag.* May 967/1 Senator Edward D. White was nominated by President Cleveland to be Associate Justice of the Supreme Court. **1900** *Cong. Rec.* 3 Jan. 633/2 Edward H. Banks . . . was nominated [to be collector of customs] and confirmed by the Senate . . . as Edward Banks. **1949** *Time* 31 Oct. 10/2 Last week the President . . . nominated two prominent Democratic job-hunters to $15,000-a-year jobs.

nominating convention. A party convention of delegates chosen to nominate candidates for political office.

1866 F. KIRKLAND *Bk. Anecdotes* 54 The following jaunty account is told of an interview with the Cabinet chiefs, just after the Baltimore Republican Nominating Convention. **1911** R. D. SAUNDERS *Col. Todhunter* iii. 43 This is the first time in the history of Mizzoorah that the Democrats nominate their candidate for governor at the polls, 'stead of in a nominatin' convention. **1946** ADAMS *Album Amer. Hist.* III. 90 With the Democratic Party divided within itself on the slave question, and with the new Republican Party opposing slavery, the nominating conventions of 1860 took place.

*** nomination,** *n.* (See quot. 1806.) *Obs.* Cf. **caucus nomination.** — **1806** WEBSTER 203/1 *Nomination*, . . . in Connecticut, a list of men selected by choice as candidates for council or congress. *a***1817** DWIGHT *Travels* I. 254 At the same time, and place, they vote, also, for twenty persons as a Nomination for the Council of the ensuing year.

*** non-,** *prefix.*

1. In combs.: (1) **noncommittal,** *n.* a refusal to commit oneself on a matter, *rare;* (2) **committal,** *a.* not committed on a particular issue, neither assenting or dissenting, neutral; (3) **committalism,** a policy or practice of being uncommitted on a particular question or in general; (4) **committally,** *adv.* in a noncommittal way; (5) **consumption,** a refusal to consume, as in the policy announced in 1774 by the American colonists of refusing to consume tea and other products imported from England or English possessions, also attrib.; (6) **exportation,** a lack, stoppage, or refusal of exportation, also attrib.; (7)

importation, intercourse, partisan, see as main entries; (8) **resident land,** land owned by someone who does not reside upon it or within the community where it is located; (9) **slaveholder,** one not an owner of Negro slaves, now *hist.;* (10) **slaveholding,** *a.* see as a main entry; (11) **treaties,** those Indian tribes not living on reservations in accordance with treaties with the U.S. Government; (12) **Volsteadian,** of liquor, not meeting the qualifications prescribed by the Volstead Act *q.v.*

(1) **1833** *Cong. Deb.* 30 Dec. 82 This message was a non-committal. The President does not announce clearly his own opinion. **1840** HALIBURTON *Clockmaker* 3 Ser. xii, Not lettin' on as if I know'd that he was there, for there is nothin' like a non-committal. — (2) **1829** ORNE *Lett. Columbus* 18 The non-committal system prevailed. **1843** *N. Englander* Oct. 523/2 The phrase, 'non-committal policy,' is used to signify a crafty concealment of one's opinions. **1949** *Western Polit. Quart.* March 95 The copper companies . . . were noncommittal, although favorable popular action on the bill doubtless was not unpleasing to them. — (3) **1838** *U.S. Mag.* I. 52 The Democratic party was determined to explore at least that portion of the plan of their opponents which involved a present non-committalism on the question of a National Bank. **1868** *Harper's Mag.* April 678/2 One of the party had been dwelling upon his non-committalism, and complaining that a 'plain answer to a plain question was never yet elicited from him.' — (4) **1885** HOWELLS *Silas Lapham* 148 'She's a pretty girl,' said Corey, non-committally. **1949** *Time* 10 Oct. 49/1 Papa muttered non-committally.

(5) **1774** J. ADAMS *Works* IX. 347, I believe we shall agree to non-importation, non-consumption, and non-exportation. **1774** *Jrnls. Cont. Congress* I. 53 A plan for carrying into effect, the non-importation, non-consumption, and non-exportation resolved on. *Ib.* 77 A non-consumption agreement . . . will be an effectual security for the observation of the non-importation. — (6) **1774** HUTCHINSON *Diary & Lett.* I. 323 They had agreed upon Non-Importation, Non-exportation, and Non-Consumption. **1774** *Jrnls. Cont. Congress* I. 76 We are of opinion, that a non-importation, non-consumption, and non-exportation agreement . . . will prove the most speedy, effectual, and peaceable measure. **1813** *Steele P.* II. 704 The senate declined acting on . . . the Licence and non-exportation Bills. — (8) **1839** CHAMBERLAIN *Ind. Gazetteer* 313 The large amount of non-resident lands has hitherto retarded improvements. **1881** *Mich. Gen. Statutes* I. 385 Such notice to owners of such non-resident lands, shall be served by posting up the same in three public places. — (9) *c***1841** in STOWE *Key* 149 The burden of this defence . . . is to fall upon the less wealthy class of our citizens, chiefly upon the non-slaveholder. **1880** TOURGEE *Bricks* 275 That struggle which the non-slaveholders fought . . . in the interest of the slaveholding aristocracy.

(11) **1885** ONDERDONK *Idaho* 15 Councils were held at Lapwai to apportion lands to the various chiefs of the Non-treaties. — (12) **1925** *N.Y. Times* 7 March 1/3 The third blow at the subterranean flow of non-Volsteadian liquids . . . was the preparation of instructions . . . for padlocking.

2. non-concur, *v. tr.*, to reject or refuse to agree to (a bill, passage, etc.). Also absol. Cf. ***concur,** *v.*

1703 SEWALL *Diary* II. 83 Bristol Business is Non-concurr'd by the Deputies. **1790** *Mass. Spy* 23 Dec. (Th.), The house then non-concurred that part of the message. **1823** TUDOR *Otis* 239 The Council non-concurred this resolve [from the House, Boston, 1766]. **1911** PERSONS *Mass. Labor Laws* 53 The House went on record as favorable to the resolution. The State nonconcurred.

b. Also with *in* and *with.* Usu. *intr.*

1855 *Chi. Times* 3 March 3/5 The House non-concurred with the Senate amendment appropriating $30,000 to purchase Camels for army use. **1862** *Cong. Globe* 9 July 3214/1, I hope the House will non-concur in that amendment of the Senate. **1907** *Springfield W. Republican* 20 June 1 The Senate has nonconcurred with the House amendments.

nondo ˈnɑndo, *n.* [Origin unknown.] The angelico, *Lingusticum canadense.* — **1791** W. BARTRAM *Travels* 45, I observed . . . the carminative angelica lucida. [Note:] Called nondo in Virginia: by the Creek and Cherokee traders, white root. **1889** *Cent.* 210/2 *Angelico,* . . . an umbelliferous plant of North America, . . . resembling the lovage. Also called *nondo.*

***none-so-pretty,** *n.* (See quots.) — **1892** *Amer. Folk-Lore* V. 93 *Silene Armeria* . . . none-so-pretty. Hatfield, Mass. **1931** CLUTE *Plants* 135 This term ['pretty Nancy' for *Silene armeria*], entirely meaningless as it stands, when turned about and straightened up a bit, is none other than none-so-pretty. A plant so weedy and aggressive as this scarcely deserves so poetical a name.

nonimportation ˌnɑnɪmporˈteʃən, *n. Hist.* The cessation of importing goods; a policy advocating such cessation.

1. Applied to the action taken by the American colonies in the Nonimportation Agreement *q.v.*

1768 in *Hist. MSS Comm.* 14th Rep. (1895) App. X. 76 Giving proceedings of merchants on non-importation and their two agreements of 1 Aug. 1768 and 17 Oct. 1769. **1775** in JOHNSTON *N. Hale* 153 Their Resources are many, and so large that the Americans' Nonimportation & exportation will be like the lightdust of the Ballanca.

2. Applied to the policy of the U.S. Government at the time of the Nonimportation Act *q.v.*

1809 *Steele P.* II. 617 Thus after running the destructive round of embargo—non-intercourse & non importation—we come back to the same place from which we started.

3. Nonimportation Act, a law passed by Congress on April 18, 1806, prohibiting the importation of specified articles from Great Britain, as a measure of reprisal for British violations of American commercial rights.

1811 *Salem Gazette* 29 Nov., The most odious measures of democracy in Congress, such as the Forcing Act, Non-importation Act, &c. have been prepared at midnight. **1812** *Niles' Reg.* III. 10/1 The non-importation act being still in force, must, in every respect, be carried into effect.

4. Nonimportation Agreement, (*a*) an agreement not to import British goods, made by merchants of colonial America in retaliation for the Townshend Acts (1767), (*b*) (see quot. 1889.).

(*a*) **1770** in *Pa. Mag.* VI. 118/2 A majority of your city have determined to break your Non-Importation Agrement. (*b*) **1774** in *Copley-Pelham Lett.* 276 [The] Committee Men, have now enter'd upon their department to put the Non Importation agreem't in force. **1889** *Cent.* 117/2 *Non-importation agreement,* an agreement made between the American colonies at Philadelphia, Oct. 20 1774, not to import anything from or manufactured in Great Britain or Ireland or the West Indies. This action was taken by way of retaliation for the passage by Parliament of certain acts for raising revenue in America.

5. Nonimportation Law, = Nonimportation Act.

1806 *State P.* (1819) VI. 255 The special message recommending a suspension of the non-importation law. **1811** *Niles' Reg.* I. 103/2 One of the first acts of Congress will be—to enforce the non-importation law.

nonintercourse nɑnˈɪntɚˌkɔrs, *n. Hist.*

1. The suspending of commercial relations; a policy advocating such suspension: **a.** Between the U.S. and Great Britain, or between the U.S. and both Great Britain and France.

1794 *Ann. 3d Congress* 566 Non-Intercourse with Great Britain. . . . On the motion of the 7th instant, [the House resolved] to prohibit all commercial intercourse between the citizens of the United States and the subjects of the King of Great Britain. **1809** JEFFERSON *Writings* XII. 265 We have substituted for it [the embargo] a non-intercourse with France and England and their dependencies, and a trade to all other places. **1813** S. MORSE in *N. Amer. Rev.* CXCVI. 123 The measures of the embargo, non-intercourse, and war I consider as just measures against this country [England]. **1948** *Chi. Tribune* 24 Oct. 24/3 The first Continental congress . . . created the Association to Enforce Nonintercourse with England.

b. Between the North and the South.

1851 in CLAIBORNE *Life Quitman* II. 122 Non-intercourse with abolition states . . . may also be recommended. **1859** in HARPER *S. B. Anthony* I. 184 Measures are in progress . . . to establish non-intercourse with you and to proscribe all articles of northern manufacture or origin, including New England teachers.

2. Nonintercourse Act, Law, a law suspending commercial intercourse between nations, esp. a retaliatory act or law passed by Congress in 1809, cutting off commercial relations with England and France and prohibiting British and French vessels from entering U.S. ports.

Since the 1809 quot. in the *OED* does not correspond to anything in the original French text, it may be reflecting American usage.

1800 JEFFERSON *Writings* XVIII. 216 The continuance of the non-intercourse law for another year, and the landing of our commissioners at Lisbon, have placed the opening of the French market . . . at such a distance that I thought it better to sell our tobacco at New York. **1832** JACKSON *Statesmanship in Writings* 236 The excise law in Pennsylvania, the embargo and nonintercourse law in the Eastern States, the carriage tax in Virginia, were all deemed unconstitutional. **1835** C. P. BRADLEY *I. Hill* 27 This, it is to be remembered, was immediately after the renewal of the nonintercourse act.

***nonpareil,** *n.* The painted bunting, *Passerina ciris,* of the southern and southwestern states.

[**1758** G. EDWARDS *Gleanings* I. 132 The Painted Finch . . . , more generally known to the curious in London by the name of Nonpareil and Mariposa.] **1811** WILSON *Ornithology* III. 68 Painted Bunting.

. . . This is one of the most numerous of the little summer birds of Lower Louisiana, where it is universally known . . . by the Americans [as] the *Nonpareil*. **1887** WARNER in *Harper's Mag*. Feb. 349/2 There [in La.] was the lively little nonpareil, which seemed to change its colour and is red and green and blue. **1917** *Birds of Amer*. III. 73.

∗**nonpartisan,** *a.*

1. Not partisan, free from political or party affiliation. Also absol.

1885 *Cent. Mag*. April 823 A citizens' ticket, largely non-partisan in character, was run for certain local offices. **1888** *Voice* 9 Feb., The non-partisans have for some time been making Mr. Johnson's position very uncomfortable for him. **1949** *Sat. Ev. Post* 22 Oct. 33/3 City elections are non-partisan and are briskly contested.

2. Nonpartisan League, a farmers' organization founded in North Dakota in 1915 to reform the system of marketing agricultural products and to sponsor state ownership and operation of public necessities.

1917 *New Republic* 3 Nov. 8/1 Many newspapers and public speakers are attacking the organization of northwestern farmers known as the Nonpartisan League. **1949** *Ward Co. Independent* (Minot, N.D.) 21 July 12/2 He also reminded labor that there would be no workmens compensation if it hadn't been for the Nonpartisan league.

Hence **Nonpartisan Leaguer.**

1922 *Outlook* 1 Nov. 368/1 He is backed by the more radical progressives and by the Non-Partisan Leaguers. **1923** *Collier's* 25 Aug. 5/1 Senator Brookhart of Iowa is an affinity of LaFollette, Shipstead, Johnson, and the Nonpartisan Leaguers of North Dakota.

non-slaveholding ˈnɑnˈslevˌholdɪŋ, *a.* **1.** Not believing in, practicing, or permitting slavery. **2. non-slaveholding state,** a state in which slavery was not legal.

(1) 1853 STOWE *Key* 208/2 Here we have the Presbyterian Church slave-holding and non-slaveholding, virtually formed into one great abolition society. **1865** in FLEMING *Hist. Reconstruction* I. 117 The outrages are mostly from non-slave holding whites against the negro, and from the negro upon the non-slaveholding whites. — **(2) 1819** *Ann. 15th Congress* 2 Sess. II. 1235 A line . . . shall divide the slave-holding from the non-slaveholding States. **1886** LOGAN *Great Conspiracy* 87 All 'open or covert attacks [on slavery] . . . ,' made either by the Non-Slave-holding States or their citizens.

noodlejees ˈnudl̩ˌjiz, *n. pl. Local.* [Dim. pl. of Du. *knoedel*, macaroni.] Noodles.

1848 BARTLETT 235 *Noodlejees*. (Dutch.) Wheat dough rolled thin and cut into strings like maccaroni. It is used for the same purpose. **1871** DE VERE 83 *Noodlejees*, an humble imitation of maccaroni and used like them for dumplings and in soup, retain in New York at least their old Dutch name, but are hardly known elsewhere. **1896** *D.N.* I. 383 *Noodeljees*, . . . 'noodles.' [N.J.]

∗**noon,** *n.*

1. big noon, (see quot.). Cf. **little noon,** *s.v.* ∗**little,** *a.*

1870 *Nation* 28 July 56/2 'Big noon' was the interval between the forenoon and afternoon sessions of the school. [In Pa.]

2. In combs.: (1) **noon basket,** a lunch basket; (2) **halt,** a halt in a journey for rest and refreshment at noon, also the place where such a halt is made; (3) **hour,** a period used for lunch and rest; (4) **house,** *N. Eng.* a house adjacent to a church for the convenience of those from a distance who wished to attend both morning and afternoon services, now *hist.;* (5) **mark,** see as a main entry; (6) **recess,** a school recess at noon.

(1) 1865 WHITNEY *Gayworthys* vi. 71 Don't you remember what we used to say at school, when we opened our noon-baskets? — **(2) 1843** FRÉMONT *Explor*. 15 At our noon halt, the men were exercised at a target. **1854** BARTLETT *Personal Narr*. II. 395 On our return we made a noon halt on the banks of the river. **a1918** G. STEWART *On Frontier* I. 115 John Dickey rode ahead from our noon halt to try to kill a sage hen. — **(3) 1889** *Charity Organisation Rev*. Aug. 341 He asked a few men to call every day at his noon hour at the place where he worked. **1902** WISTER *Virginian* xxx, Saving the noon hour, I had been in the saddle since six. — **(4) 1845** JUDD *Margaret* I. 110 Several elderly men and women went to what was called a 'Noon House,' a small building near the Schoolhouse, where they ate their dinner and had a prayer. **1891** EARLE *Sabbath* 102 There might have been seen a hundred years ago, by the side of many an old meeting-house in New England, a long, low, mean, stable-like building, with a rough stone chimney at one end. This was the 'noon-house,' or 'Sabba-day house,' or 'horse-hows,' as it was variously called. It was a place of refuge in the winter time, at the noon interval between the two services. **(6) 1871** EGGLESTON *Hoosier Schoolm*. 38 Then the master walked out . . . to spend the noon recess in the woods. **1903** FOX *Little Shepherd* xii, Georgie Forbes . . . brought out the terrible charge in the presence of a dozen school-children at noon-recess one day.

noon nun, *v. intr.* To spend the noon hour; to halt for rest and lunch at noon. Also with *it. Colloq.*

1805 LEWIS in *L. & Clark Exped*. II. (1904) 9 We nooned it just above the entrance of a large river. **1834** A. PIKE *Sketches* 66 We fell off from the prairie into a bottom of good land. . . . Here we nooned. **1919** WILSON *White Indian* 212 One day we were nooning on the big Sandy. **1932** *Frontier* Jan. 147/1 We'll make 'em think we're *noonin'* here, see, Kid?

∗**nooning,** *n.*

1. A period for rest and refreshment at the middle of the day.

1847 PARKMAN in *Knickerb*. XXX. 231 We stopped for a short nooning at the side of a pool of rain-water. **1904** MABIE *Backgrounds of Lit*. 186 There is time for luncheon and a quiet nooning for the horses. **1943** DEVOTO *Yr. of Decis*. 249 Nor was the scummy standing-water of the buffalo wallows any better for them when it was all they got to drink at nooning.

b. =**noon recess.**

1865 *Atlantic Mo*. Feb. 148/1 Two school girls—home for the nooning—are idling over a gateway. **1876** MARK TWAIN *Tom Sawyer* xviii. 157 She said she would look at pictures all through the nooning. **1882** *Harper's Mag*. Feb. 434/2 At nooning next day, too, the school-children were full of [stories].

c. *N. Eng.* The noon interval between morning and afternoon church services. Cf. **noon house.**

1865 WHITNEY *Gayworthys* 285 In the nooning Say joined herself to Blackmere again. *Ib*. 289 She reached the vestry just vacated by the Sunday School children, out now for their short 'nooning.' **1891** EARLE *Sabbath* 60 Not only could these men of authority keep the boys in order during meeting, but they also had full control during the nooning.

2. (See quot.)

1884 W. SHEPHERD *Prairie Exper*. 161 Through the heat of the day the sheep do not care to feed or to travel; if full they will lie down, seeking some shade, or drooping their heads under the shadow of each other's bodies: This is called nooning; it may begin as early as eight o'clock in the height of summer, and last till four or five in the evening.

3. In combs.: (1) **nooning place,** a place, usu. one having such natural advantages as water, grass, shade, etc., for a noon stop or halt in a journey; (2) **tree,** a tree in the shade of which one's nooning is spent.

(1) 1687 in *Amer. Sp*. XV. 290 At ye head of a bottom tending to ye aforesaid Nooning place. **1849** PARKMAN in *Knickerb*. XXXIII. 5 As we approached our nooning place we saw five or six buffalo. **1884** BOURKE *Snake Dance of Moquis* 77 A sorcerer [was] killed near this very nooning-place. — **(2) 1895** WIGGIN *Village Watch-Tower* 59 It was used as a 'nooning' tree by all the men at work in the surrounding fields.

b. Also **nooning hour, meal, sleep, spell, time.**

1863 WHITNEY *F. Gartney* xxiii, Luther Goodell . . . [got] into the way of straying up the field-path in his nooning hours. — **1865** ——— *Gayworthys* v, Baskets were opened and the simple nooning meal, that needed intervention of neither knife nor fork, was eaten. — **1890** PHILLIPS in C. Martyn *Wendell Phillips* 443 A picture of a dozen sailors, taking their nooning sleep. — **1867** LACKLAND *Homespun* 290 The workers . . . eat and drink their forenoon fill, not unmindful of the coming dinner and the nooning spell. — **1856** *Porter's Spirit of Times* 20 Sep. 39/1 'Twas noonin' time, an' thar was niggers enough roun' an' about that field to skear the deer to death.

noon mark. Formerly, in the absence of a timepiece, a mark made to indicate the position of a noon shadow; hence, noon. Now *hist.*

1854 B. J. TAYLOR *Jan. & June* 131 The sun has driven the shadows around under the west and north walls; it has reached the noon-mark on the threshold. **1880** COOKE in *Harper's Mag*. Sep. 585/2 Noon-mark was straightened out by the great gnomon of a tulip-tree on the turf dial where the shanty stood. **1889** ——— *Steadfast* 275 Goodness! 'tis most noon-mark and I haven't took a step towardst dinner. **1891** EARLE *Sabbath* 77 The time of the day was indicated to our forefathers in their homes by 'noon marks' on the floor or window-seats. **1948** *N. & Q.* Nov. 121/2, I should like to know whether . . . the term 'noon mark' was once common.

Nootka ˈnutkə, *n.* [*Nootka* Sound, harbor on Vancouver Island, British Columbia.]

1. Nootka cypress, an evergreen tree of the Pacific Coast, *Chamaecyparis nootkatensis*, valuable for its hard yellow wood. Also **Nootka Sound cypress.**

1892 APGAR *Trees Northern U.S.* 195 Nootka Sound Cypress. . . . Tree 100 ft. high in Alaska. **1897** SUDWORTH *Arborescent Flora* 79

Yellow Cedar. . . . [Also called] Nootka Cypress (Cal. lit.). Nootka Sound Cypress (cult. Eng.). *a***1915** MUIR *Travels Alaska* (1917) 39 The principal forest-trees are hemlock, spruce, and Nootka cypress.

2. Nootka fir, the Douglas fir, *Pseudotsuga taxifolia.*

1803 LAMBERT *Descr. Genus Pinus* 51 Nootka Fir. . . . A specimen . . . was discovered on the North-west coast of America [by Menzies.] **1813** MUHLENBERG *Cat. Plants* 89 *Pinus taxifolia*, Nootka fir.

3. Nootka hummingbird, (see quot. 1853).

1838 PARKER *Exploring Tour* 257 The Nootka humming bird has arrived, and is seen darting from bush to bush, feeding upon the opening flowers. **1853** SITGREAVES *Exped. Zuni & Colo. Rivers* 66 *Polytemus rufus*, Less.— The Nootka Humming Bird. . . . I found abundant in New Mexico.

4. Nootka rose, a wild rose, *Rosa nutkana*, common in the Pacific Northwest.

*c***1912** FRYE & RIGG *Northwest Flora* 221 R. nutkana Presl. (Nutka Rose). **1931** DAYTON *Western Browse Plants* 49 Nootka rose [is] . . . one of the commonest of the northwestern roses.

nopal noˈpal, *n.* [Sp. (<Nahuatl) in same sense. App. a new borrowing.] A cactus of the genus *Nopalea.* Also a prickly pear. Also attrib.

1823 JAMES *Exped.* II. 209 The nopals are considered characteristic of warm and dry climates. **1875** BOURKE *Journal* 30 May, A plant, plentiful in this country [along the South Cheyenne R.], called the nopal, or Tuna cactus, plate cactus, or Indian fig is employed with success to clarify water for drinking purposes. **1891** *Cent. Mag.* Jan. 386 More Nopal hedges were planted, and the old ones extended. **1949** *Time* 13 June 35/2 Their resentment grew when they learned that the Paseo would have a two-foot strip down the middle, planted to nopal and cactus.

nope nop, *adv.* [See note.] No. *Colloq.*

An orthographical representation of an emphatic form of *no*, the letter *p* orig. and often actually indicating nothing more than the closing of the lips. It has been regarded as an Americanism, but perhaps erroneously so. Cf. **yep.**

1888 *Chi. Tribune* (F.), 'I suppose you will be a literary man . . . when you grow up.' 'Nope,' said the little boy . . . , 'literary nuthin'!' **1923** BOWER *Parowan Bonanza* 14 'Nope, I'm a never-was,' Bill retorted shamelessly. **1948** *Parents' Mag.* March 122/2 Martha is apt to say 'Nope' to every request or suggestion I make.

* **Norman,** *n.* (See quot. 1908.) In full **Norman horse.**

1845 *Farmers' Cabinet* 15 March 261/2 The subscriber . . . will offer . . . his entire Stock of Norman Horses. . . . In a few words, they are the *Canada* Horse, on a larger scale, combining the form, activity and hardihood of that well known race, with greater size and strength. **1856** *Spirit of Times* 6 Dec. 228/1 There was 'Americans,' 'Black Hawks,' 'Hambletonians,' 'Bullocks,' 'Normans' and 'Rattlers'—all gathered to the show, and their owners claimed them all as trotters. **1908** BAILEY *Cyclo. Agric.* III. 481/1 The first importations of draft horses from France to America were almost universally called Normans. There was no apparent reason for the name, for none of these came from Normandy.

b. Also **Norman mare.**

1858 *Spirit of Times* 9 Jan. 299/2 On the whole, we have little doubt that fine, well-selected Canadian or Norman mares will prove to be the best mule mothers. **1876** *Harper's Wkly.* 4 Nov. 890/2 His colts by Kentucky and Norman mares were shown.

* **north,** *n.* and *a.*

1. (*cap.*) The population of the Northern States. Used esp. with reference to the sectional struggle between the North and the South.

1792 T. JEFFERSON in Padover *Jefferson* (1942) 203 (*footnote*), North & South will hang together, if they have you to hang on. **1855** PIERCE in *Pres. Mess. & P.* V. 344 [The] groundless allegation that the South has persistently asserted claims and obtained advantages in the practical administration of the General Government to the prejudice of the North. **1865** BOYD *In Camp & Prison* 460 With Mr. Johnson at the head of the Government of the North, who can foresee any thing save anarchy and dissolution? **1943** HICKS *Amer. Dem.* 366 Whatever the earlier sentiments of the North may have been, the reception of the news from Sumter made it clear that an overwhelming majority of the people in the free states were ready to fight to save the Union.

2. (*cap.*) The northern states, esp. those in which slavery never existed or did not long persist, i.e., those states bounded on the south by Maryland, the Ohio River, and Missouri.

1835 in MARTINEAU *Soc. Amer.* (1837) II. 132 Men of property and intelligence in the north. **1883** MARK TWAIN *Life on Miss.* 467 The very feature that keeps it [Mardi Gras] alive in the South—girly-girly romance—would kill it in the North or in London. **1949** *So. Wkly.* 5 Oct. 2/2 The labor leader criticized the alliance of 'reactionaries' from the North and Dixiecrats in Congress.

3. In combs.: (1) **North American,** an Indian of North America, also **North American Indian**(**s**); (2) **Americanism,** the political philosophy of those who agreed with John Tyler (1790–1862) in his views favoring the war with Mexico and the annexation of Texas, *obs.;* (3) **-bound,** bound for the north, going north; (4) **Carolina,** see as a main entry; (5) **Carolinian,** a native or inhabitant of North Carolina, also transf.; (6) **Dakotan,** a native or inhabitant of North Dakota; (7) * **-easter,** a waterproof cap or hat worn in stormy weather; (8) **-east rum,** =**New England rum;** (9) **-ender,** one living in the northern part of Boston, *obs.;* (10) * **man,** =**northern man;** (11) **Star State,** Minnesota; (12) * **west,** * **wester,** see as main entries; (13) **woods,** any one of several heavily timbered regions in the northern part of the U.S. or in Canada, also attrib.

(1) **1775** ADAIR *Indians* 197 Any English reader [of Spanish writers] . . . will not only find a wild portrait, but a striking resemblance and unity of the civil and martial customs, the religious rites, and traditions of the ancient Peruvians and Mexicans and the North Americans. **1825** NEAL *Bro. Jonathan* II. 1 The Man of America—the Original North American: . . . the 'Indian,' as he is called. **1837** *Diplom. Corr. Texas* I. (1908) 261 The prairie Indians are unskillful in the use of fire arms, who, without the guidance of N. American Indians, would be comparatively harmless. **1949** *Chi. Tribune* 8 Nov. I. 12/2 The very rich head of a business is vanishing as rapidly as the North American Indian. — (2) **1848** *Campaign Flag* (Maysville, Ky.) 24 March 1/5 In most of those States where North Americanism or Tylerism is favored . . . a disposition is evinced by opponents of the Mexican war to make capital out of the laurels which its principal hero has won in it. — (3) **1881** *Rep. Ala. R.R. Comm.* I. 58 While attending the North-bound freight train No. 24 as brakeman, I fell. **1949** *Dly. Ardmoreite* (Ardmore, Okla.) 25 Jan. 2/4 The Santa Fe lines reported that northbound trains were running up to 15 minutes late early today.

(5) **1780** LORD RAWDON in *Hist. MSS Comm.* 9th Rep. App. III. 11. (1910) 185 Hoping that the assistance of the North Carolinians might furnish a force for yet further efforts. **1873** *Winfield* (Kans.) *Courier* 17 July 1/5 The word 'galoot' does not mean us North Carolinians. **1949** *N.C. Hist. Rev.* April 218 One native North Carolinian is publishing in Atlanta ten trade journals ranging from jewelry to paper making. — (6) **1889** *N.Y. Semi-Wky. Tribune* 6 Dec. 13/4 The North Dakotans now had to draw for the remaining six-year term. **1949** *Ward Co. Independent* (Minot, N.D.) 21 July 5/1 Most North Dakotans welcome this information as they have been concerned over production questions. — (7) **1839** *Yale Lit. Mag.* III. 9 A large tarpaulin North Easter was the covering of my head. — (8) **1857** *Knickerb.* XLIX. 181 [They were] always doing everything in the fear of the Lord, even to selling north-east rum. — (9) **1868** S. SMITH *Autobiog.* 12 We were on the side of Bonaparte, you see—I mean we Boston boys, North-enders and South-enders.

(10) **1836** *S. Lit. Messenger* II. 111 The Southron . . . calls that a *Hare* which the North-man eats under the title of *Rabbit.* **1862** MOORE *Rebellion Rec.* V. 11. 281 No regiments calling themselves Mississippians are marching with the Northmen. — (11) **1909** *World To-day* Oct. 1108 The North Star State has been the scene of her greatest usefulness. Mrs. Potter commenced her educational work in Minneapolis. **1946** McWILLIAMS *So. Calif. Country* 173 Floats move through the streets of Long beach with such captions as 'Corn is King,' 'North Dakota: The Bread Basket of the Nation,' 'Minnesota: The North Star State.' — (13) **1881** *Harper's Mag.* May 867/1, I came out of the Adirondacks, or North Woods, free from cough, . . . with greater physical vigor than I had known for years. **1902** WHITE *Blazed Trail* 258 The old-fashioned, picturesque ice-road sleigh haul will last as long as north-woods lumbering. **1945** PEARSON *Country Flavor* 77 Isn't some hardy northwoodsman ready with a report?

North Carolina. [Name of one of the southeastern states.] In obs. combs.: (1) **North Carolina conch,** see **conch,** quot. 1870; (2) **regulator,** a regulator from North Carolina, see * **regulator 3;** (3) **rocker,** a large, long rocker used in placer mining; (4) **Yankee,** a nickname used locally for an industrious South Carolinian farmer newly arrived from North Carolina.

(2) **1769** *Boston Chron.* 6 Feb. 43/1 The North Carolina Regulators . . . drove a gang of villains back. — (3) **1851** WOODS *Gold Diggings* 187 In addition to the cradle, . . . the North Carolina rocker and the Long Tom are used to advantage upon the placers where the gold is very fine. — (4) **1933** HOLLANDER *Arme Blanken* 61 De boeren, die,

uit de omgeving van Washington en New Bern, N.C. afkomstig zich met gehuurde slaven in het Zuid Carolinische lage land op dezen tak van bestaan toelegden, hadden zich door hun vlijt en ondernemingslust plaatselijk den naam 'North Carolina Yankee's' verworven.

b. Also **North Carolina ague, company, convention, currency, emigration, money, senate.**

1834 C. A. DAVIS *Lett. J. Downing* 110 He shook like a North Carolina ague. — **1867** GOSS *Soldier's Story* 61 The Buffaloes, as the North Carolina companies were called, escaped in some cases by swimming the river. — **1826** BENTON *30 Years' View* (1854) I. 83/2 By the North Carolina convention, the same amendment was recommended. — **1796** *Receipt by J. Couch* 24 Feb. (Pettigrew P.), Received from Messrs John Ebenezer Pettigrue twenty pounds North Carolina currency it being for the first term of the present year [in U. of N. Car.]. — **1882** G. A. SALA *Amer. Revisited* I. 227 So perplexed and perturbed politicians all over the Union that the 'North Carolina Emigration' . . . formed the subject of a debate. — **1820** *Western Carolinian* 25 July, Corn—A cargo was sold on Saturday at 60 cents, payable in North-Carolina money. — **1868** *N.Y. Herald* 4 July 6/1 In the North Carolina Senate yesterday a resolution was introduced.

norther 'nɔrðɚ, *n.* [Poss. f. or suggested by Sp. *norte* in the same sense. See quots. under 1.] A furious cold wind from the north, esp. one blowing over Texas, the plains of the Southwest, or the Gulf of Mexico. Cf. **Texas, wet norther.**

(1) [**1776** tr. in HARRIS *Catholic Church in Utah* (1909) 182 Today we suffered much with the cold, because a 'norther' had been blowing all day. **1834** LATROBE *Rambler in Mexico* 14 '*El Norte!*' yelled the mate at my elbow, as a torrent of wind and spray swept over the deck.]

(2) **1820** DEWEES *Lett. from Texas* 17 A heavy storm of rain and sleet, together with a furious 'norther' overtook us. **1891** *Scribner's Mag.* X. 283 The weather along the Pacific highway has been uniformly pleasant, for northers are infrequent. **1949** *Kans. Hist. Quart.* Feb. 41 Here the first norther of the season struck, bringing heavy rains and bitter cold.

b. blue (Texas) norther, a particularly violent norther.

1871–3 *Texas Almanac* 98 There is evidently in these dry 'blue northers' (as they are called) a state of high electrical condition of the atmosphere. **1872** MORRELL *Flowers & Fruits* 234 A blue Texas norther whistled around my ears. **1947** *Trail Riders Bul.* Feb. 20/2 Ain't it been twenty b'low ever since that blue norther las' month?

∗**northern,** *a.* (Often *cap.*) In combs.: (1) **Northern Alliance,** (see quots. and cf. **Farmers' Alliance**); (2) **army, canoe,** see as main entries; (3) **colony,** a colony in the northern part of what is now the U.S., *obs.;* (4) **Conference,** one of the two conferences into which the Methodist Church divided over the question of slavery; (5) **copperheadism,** =**copperheadism;** (6) **democracy,** the northern wing or faction in the Democratic party; (7) **Democrat,** a Democrat of or from the North; (8) **doughface,** =**doughface 2,** *obs.;* (9) **Emigrant Aid Society,** an emigrant aid society existing in the North, *obs.;* (10) **Freesoil,** denoting one affiliated with or in sympathy with the Free-Soil party, *obs.;* (11) **made,** made in the northern states; (12) ∗**man,** a man living in or coming from the northern states; (13) **Methodist Church,** the Methodist Church in the North, cf. **Northern Conference** and see **Southern Methodism, Southern Methodist;** (14) **Presbyterian Church,** the Presbyterian Church in the North as distinguished from that in the South after the separation over slavery just before the Civil War; (15) **Republic,** the northern states during the Civil War, *rare;* (16) **rights,** designating one who championed the political rights of those in the North, *rare,* cf. **southern rights;** (17) **state,** (*a*) a state in the northern part of the U.S., esp. *pl.,* the states lying north of Mason and Dixon's line and the Ohio River, (*b*) *pl.,* the states north of the middle states, also the New England states.

(1) **1889** *N.Y. Semi-Wkly. Tribune* 10 Dec. 13/2 The Farmers' Convention . . . was devoted to . . . trying to smooth the way for a consolidation with the Northern Alliance. **1944** BURDICK *Farmers' Political Action N. Dak.* 33 The National Farmers' Alliance, which came to be known as the 'Northern Alliance,' was organized in Illinois in 1880. — (3) **1724** H. JONES *Virginia* 18 These . . . are the Indians that make Wars, and such Disturbance in the Northern and Southern Colonies. **1800** BOUCHER *Glossary* p. xlix, On the Continent, the Northern and Southern colonies are . . . called the *Northward* and *Southward.* — (4) **1853** STOWE *Key* 476 This Methodist Church subsequently broke into a Northern and Southern Conference. . . . The Northern Conference has still in its communion slave-holding Conferences and members.

(5) **1870** *Nation* 6 Jan. 4/1 The foul-mouthed organs of Northern Copperheadism. — (6) **1854** BENTON *30 Years' View* I. 10/1 [The Missouri question led to] a federal movement, . . . sweeping all the Northern democracy into its current. — (7) **1845** *Xenia* (O.) *Torch-Light* 23 Oct. 2/2 The Administration project of reduction of the tariff by the votes of the Northern Democrats. **1910** J. HART *Vigilante Girl* 293 These Chivs have been bullying us Northern Democrats long enough. **1949** *Pacific Spectator* Summer 257 The Northern Democrats . . . were committed to the policy of popular sovereignty — (8) **1844** in *Campaign Flag* (Maysville, Ky.) (1848) 23 June 3/6 The southern lion shook his mane, and the northern doughfaces crouched down at his feet. **1904** *N.Y. Ev. Post* 7 July 6 The same arguments are employed that Northern dough-faces used to be plied with in slavery days. — (9) **1867** DIXON *New Amer.* I. 21 A Northern Emigrant Aid Society was founded in Massachusetts.

(10) **1855** in HAMBLETON *H. A. Wise* 343 We shall endeavor to . . . make some extracts from it for the benefit of its Northern Freesoil readers. — (11) **1828** *Free Press* (Tarboro, N.C.) 24 Oct., I have a northern made Cotton Gin. **1865** *Atlantic Mo.* April 512/1 What, with those new Northern-made pantaloons on? — (12) **1803** J. DAVIS *Travels* 209 There was a perpetual conflict of opinions between these southern and northern men. **1929** ANDREWS *Scraps of Paper* 22 Every decent creature in it [*Uncle Tom's Cabin*] was a southerner—all the rascals . . . were northern men. — (13) **1855** *St. Louis Democrat* 21 April, We will suffer no person belonging to the *Northern* Methodist Church, to preach in Platte county after this date under penalty of tar and feathers for the first offense, and a hemp rope for the second. — (14) **1888** AUGHEY *Tupelo* 307 The question of reunion is before the general assemblies of both the northern and southern Presbyterian churches.

(15) **1865** BOYD *In Camp & Prison* 459, I saw how well he [Lincoln] governed the Northern Republic. — (16) **1855** *N.Y. Wkly. Tribune* 21 July 2/2 As the Northern Rights men of the present day, they [Federalists] were . . . denounced by their sectional opponents as a local and sectional party! — (17) (*a*) **1780** MADISON *Writings* I. (1900) 64 It appears from sundry accounts from the frontiers of New York and other Northern States, that the savages are making the most distressing incursions. **1857** *Rep. Comm. Patents 1856: Agric.* 63 In the Northern States, the migratory squirrel replaces the *Sciurus carolinensis,* of the South. (*b*) **1828** COOPER *Nations* I. 430 Religion . . . [is] inculcated . . . in all the northern and middle, and some of the southern states of America. **1852** EASTMAN *Aunt Phillis's Cabin* 260 In the Middle and Northern states free blacks are in a degraded condition.

b. In the names of animals: (1) **northern bald eagle,** (see quot.); (2) **moccasin,** (see quot.); (3) **phalarope,** a bird, *Lobipes lobatus,* of the family Phalaropodidae that breeds in northern Alaska and the far North; (4) **pike,** (see quot. 1856); (5) **rattlesnake,** (see quot.); (6) **shrike,** a shrike, *Lanius borealis,* found in the northern part of North America; (7) **swift,** the black swift; (8) **yellow-throat,** =**Maryland yellow-throat.**

(1) **1917** *Birds of Amer.* II. 81/2 In northwestern Alaska . . . and the Great Lakes occurs . . . the Northern Bald Eagle (*Haliæetus leucocephalus alascanus*). — (2) **1916** SETON *Woodcraft Man.* 320 The Copperhead . . . is the Highland, or Northern Moccasin or Pilot Snake, found from Massachusetts to Florida and west to Illinois and Texas. — (3) **1858** BAIRD *Birds Pacific R.R.* 706 Northern Phalarope . . . one of the handsomest and most graceful of the wading birds. **1944** *Mass. Audubon Soc. Bul.* Dec. 261 It proved to be a good birding day, with . . . a single Golden Plover, a Northern Phalarope, a Franklin's Gull [etc.]. — (4) **1856** *Spirit of Times* 1 Nov. 142/3 *Esox Boreus,* or the northern pike . . . ranks next to the muscalonge among our lake fishes. **1949** *Chi. Tribune* 23 Sep. III. 5/1 Will an Illinois fisherman fishing thru the ice for northern pike be likely to catch a pickerel?

(5) **1842** *Nat. Hist. N.Y., Zoology* III. 55 The Northern Rattlesnake. *Crotalus durissus.* — (6) **1857** *Rep. Comm. Patents 1856: Agric.* 86 One of the greatest enemies in this vicinity [n. Ill.] is the Northern shrike, or butcher-bird, (*Lanius borealis,*) the food of which consists almost wholly of arvicolae and a few white-footed prairie mice. **1945** *Mass. Audubon Soc. Bul.* Feb. 17 The Northern Shrike skimming this 'blasted heath' can be seen from December to March perched atop one of the tall red oaks of the bordering woods. — (7) **1858** BAIRD *Birds Pacific R.R.* 142 Northern Swift. . . . This remarkable swift was first indicated as North American by Dr. Kennerly, in the proceedings of the Philadelphia Academy. — (8) **1917** *Birds of Amer.* III. 159 Maryland Yellow-throat. . . . Other Names. . . . Northern Yellow-throat [etc.]. **1942** PEATTIE *Friendly Mts.* 196 From

the bushy swamp land to the northeast, the northern yellow-throat says: 'ricket-eer, ricket-eer.'

c. In the names of, or with reference to, plants: (1) **northern scrub pine,** (see quot.); (2) **Spy,** a variety of thin-skinned juicy winter apple, also an apple of this variety, in full **Northern Spy apple;** (3) **strawberry tree,** (see quot.); (4) **yellow-wood,** (see quot.).

(1) 1892 APGAR *Trees Northern U.S.* 178 Gray or Northern Scrub Pine . . . [is] a straggling shrub, sometimes a low tree, found wild in the extreme Northern States. — **(2) 1847** IVES *N. Eng. Fruit* 46 *Northern Spy.*—This new native fruit, originated near Rochester, N. York. It is a fine winter apple, and is one of the most popular fruits in New York. **1850** *N. Eng. Farmer* II. 404 Northern Spy Apple. We had hoped to be able to test the qualities of this apple ourselves. **1944** *Poetry Chap Book* Fall 14 And fragrant windrows of crisp Northern Spies Are scattered in the tumbled twisted sheaves. — **(3) 1813** MUHLENBERG *Cat. Plants* 44 *Arbutus Acadiensis,* Northern strawberry tree. — **(4) 1901** MOHR *Plant Life Ala.* 85 The Northern yellow wood (*Cladrastis tinctoria*) . . . reaches here its extreme southern station.

northern army. An army operating in the northern part of the U.S. Also, during the Civil War, the Union army.

1775 *Jrnls. Cont. Congress* III. 341 A committee will be appointed to procure as much hard money as will be necessary to be transmitted to the deputy pay master general in the northern army, to be used in Canada. **1814** *Niles' Reg.* VI. 37/2 General Harrison has received instructions from the war department, to return to the northern army. **1865** H. C. PHILLIPS *Hist. Sk. Paper Curr.* II. 43 The Northern Army still drained the congress of its hard money.

b. (See quots.) *Obs.*

1841 G. POWERS *Hist. Sk. Coos Co.* 105 An army of worms . . . began to appear the latter part of July, 1770, and continued their ravages until September. The inhabitants denominated them the 'Northern Army,' as they seemed to advance from the north or north west. *Ib.* 107 In ten days from the first appearing of the Northern Army, nothing remained of this corn but the bare stalks!

northern canoe. (See quots.) *Obs.*

[**1848** BALLANTYNE *Hudson Bay* (1890) 235 It was one of those called 'north canoes,' which are calculated to carry eight men as a crew, besides three passengers.] **1860** in *Narr. of Sam. Hancock* (1927) 163 What is termed a northern canoe is much larger and differently shaped from those made and used by the Indians south of the Straits of Fuca. **1867** ROTHROCK *Flora Alaska* 434 From it the celebrated 'northern canoes' are made. These canoes, 'dug' from a single trunk and afterwards steamed into shape, will often carry four tons.

* **Northerner,** *n.* A native or inhabitant of the northern states.

1831 in PECK *Guide* 60 You may see [in New Orleans] . . . much beautiful shrubbery, such for beauty and splendor and fragrance the Northerners have never seen. **1861** *Richmond* (Va.) *Examiner* 2 Dec. 2/2 The Northerners are destined to encounter much more in a Southern winter campaign than they dream of in their philosophy. **1945** *Chi. D. News* 1 Feb. 8/7 It's about time we long-suffering Northerners got it off our chest.

* **northward,** *a.* and *n.*

1. *n.* The northern colonies or states. Usu. *at* (or *from*) *the northward. Obs.*

1764 HABERSHAM *Letters* 20, I was lately at the Northward to visit two of my sons at New Jersey College. **1797** C. PETTIGREW *Lett. to J. Pettigrew* 8 Oct. (Univ. N.C. MS), If your Cousin . . . should be returned from the Northward, I shall probably see him. **1817** T. TROTTER *Lett.* 25 July (Pettigrew P.), I cannot get any Cast Iron from the northard.

2. *a.* Made in, or native to, the northern part of what is now the U.S. *Obs.*

1765 CROGHAN *Journal* 139 Southern Indians, who are always at war with the northward Indians. **1820** *Western Carolinian* 25 July, *Candles.* Northward, (mould Tallow) 18 *a* 20 cents. **1853** POYAS *Peep into Past* 114 It will be necessary to have a Northward man that's used to that business for an Overseer.

* **northwest,** *n.* and *a.*

1. (*cap.*) The region in the northwestern part of the U.S., or the region to the north and west of the settled or occupied portion of this country. Cf. **Pacific Northwest.**

As the frontier of the United States was pushed westward, the term *Northwest* progressively designated areas farther and farther from the Atlantic seaboard. The region north and west of the Ohio River was the first "Northwest" (see quot. 1789), but was usually designated as the *Northwestern Territory* or *Northwest Territory, qq.v.*

[**1789** *Ann. 1st Congress* I. 51 A message from the House of Representatives brought up a bill to provide for the government of the territory northwest of the river Ohio.] **1818** *Niles' Reg.* XIV. 208/2 From the north west we have unpleasant news anticipating hostilities with the Indians. **1856** *Democratic Conv. Proc.* 47 New Hampshire . . . went heartily for the champion of the North West [Douglas]. **1945** *Chi. Tribune* 16 Sep. IV. 10/2 The pioneer past is so close to the present in the northwest . . . that only one of the extracts in this collection was written before 1920.

2. In special combs.: (1) **Northwest (Company) blanket,** a type of blanket supplied by the Northwest Fur Company, *obs.;* (2) **fusee, fusil,** a light, cheap musket of a type supplied to Indians by the Northwest Fur Company, now *hist.*, cf. **Indian trader b, Northwestern gun;** (3) **gun,** =prec.; (4) **Territory,** =**Northwestern Territory,** also attrib.

(1) 1818 in M'KENNEY *Memoirs* I. (1846) App. 309 Northwest Company blankets . . . to measure six feet six inches long and five feet six inches wide; to weigh, per pair, eight pounds and a half. **1823** *Ib.* 297 How much should a three point Northwest blanket weigh, to be good? — **(2) 1826** *N. Amer. Rev.* Jan. 104 But that instrument [the rifle] is very seldom used by the Indians of the plains. . . . The bow and arrow are their most efficient weapons against the Buffalo, and the northwest fusils, as they are called, are the most common firearms. **1850** GARRARD *Wah-To-Yah* i. 16 The pursuer changed tack, only to be shot by one of the teamsters with a Nor'west fusil (Hudson Bay Company trade gun). *Ib.* ix. 119 A Purblo, *cached* behint a pile of dobies, shot him with a Nor'west fusee twice. **1947** DEVOTO *Across Wide Missouri* 64 What American firm makes guns like the Northwest fusees? — **(3) 1820** in *Wis. State H.S. Coll.* VII. 205 Trade . . . a Northwest cased gun, ten skins. — **(4) 1802** CUTLER in *Life & Corr.* II. 105 Spent [today] on N.W. Territory State Bill. It is a most palpable violation of the Constitution. **1857** BENTON *Exam. Dred Scott Case* 32 The new-born Congress . . . adopted . . . the famous ordinance of 1787, for the government of the North-West Territory. **1948** *Chi. Tribune* 17 Oct. (Grafic Mag.) 5/2 It demanded that most of the Northwest Territory, now the heartland of the United States, should be Indian territory under British guarantee.

* **northwester,** *n.*

1. An oilskin or waterproof coat worn chiefly by seafarers in rough weather. In full **northwester coat.**

1690 *Long Island Wills* (1897) 46 My Will is that my norwester Coat . . . may be given to Christopher Leaming. **1853** KANE *Grinnell Exped.* 296 A still more sentimental song sung in seal-skin breeks and a 'norwester.'

2. A man from the Pacific Northwest, or a tall tale regarded as characteristic of that region.

1836 IRVING *Astoria* I. 210 Now and then a chance party of 'Northwesters' appeared at Mackinaw from the rendezvous at fort William. **1884** MATTHEWS & BUNNER *In Partnership* 74, I told him two or three North-westers, just as well as I could in French, and then . . . he told me about the glass which broke when poison was poured into it.

3. (*cap.*) *pl.* The Northwest Fur Co.

1831 R. COX *Adv. Columbia River* II. 241 One partner, one clerk, and a few men belonging to the North-Westers were captured . . . by the Hudson's-Bay people. **1944** *Military Surgeon* Aug. 91/2 By 1810 it was clear that the Nor'westers were winning out in the strenuous competition of the fur trade.

* **northwestern,** *a.* Often *cap.*

1. *absol.* (See quot. and cf. * **northwester 1.**) *Obs.*

1701 C. WOLLEY *Jrnl. N.Y.* (1902) 28 The huge Lake of Canada, which lies to the northward of *New-York,* is supposed to be the most probable place for dispersing the cold Northwest-winds which alter the nature of this Climate, insomuch that a thick winter Coat there is commonly called a *Northwestern.*

2. Of or belonging to those regions situated northwest of the early European settlements in North America.

1789 *Ann. 1st Congress* I. 39 A report from the Secretary of War, on the negotiations of the Governor of the Western Territory with certain northern and northwestern Indians. **1807** *Ann. 10th Congress* 1 Sess. I. 16 Among our Indian neighbors in the Northwestern quarter, some fermentation was observed. **1859** *Harper's Mag.* Feb. 399/1 Constructing the railroad, he would choose a path which would be a continuation of the road that our great Northwestern emigration had hitherto followed.

3. In special combs.: (1) **Northwestern gun,** =**Northwest fusee, fusil;** (2) **iron,** a thong of rawhide used as rope in the Northwest, *obs.;* (3) **state,** a state in the northwestern part of the U.S., see note *s.v.* * **northwest;** (4) **Territory,** see as a main entry.

(1) 1859 *Cong. Globe* 16 Feb. 1069/1 The arms furnished to the Indians are what are called Northwestern guns. They are little popguns, with which nothing can be killed but the buffaloes. — **(2) 1910**

[see **shaganappi**]. — (3) **1835** INGRAHAM *South-West* I. 106 Produce of all kinds, brought from the 'Upper country,' (as the north western states are termed here). **1893** PAGE *Harper's Mag.* Dec. 22/2 [Virginians] are to be found in every Western and Northwestern State, where they begin as cowboys on ranches.

Northwestern Territory. The region, about 266,000 square miles in extent, east of the Mississippi River, north of the Ohio, west of Pennsylvania, and south of the Canadian border. Also attrib. Now *obs.* or *hist.*

The United States acquired this region from Great Britain at the close of the Revolution. New York, Virginia, Connecticut, and Massachusetts relinquished to the federal government their claims to parts of the region and in time the states of Ohio, Indiana, Michigan, Illinois, and Wisconsin were formed from it.

1796 in R. PUTNAM *Memoirs* 411 A vacancy [will be created] by this appointment on the judicial bench of the north western territory. **1798** *Ann. 5th Congress* I. 1045 A petition had been this morning presented . . . on the subject of the Northwestern Territory lands. **1857** in BENTON *Exam. Dred Scott Case* 34 The ordinance was intended for the government of the Northwestern Territory.

Norway pine. The red pine, *Pinus resinosa*, or its wood.

1829 GREENLEAF *Survey Maine* 110 Norway Pine is the common name in Maine, but improperly. **1942** HARLOW *Trees Eastern U.S.* 42 In any event, the name Norway pine has been used so long that the decision of the U.S. Forest Service to use the more logical name *red pine* met with severe criticism. **1948** *Milwaukee Jrnl.* 18 July 6/2 Anyone foolish enough to lay Norway pine to the weather is foolish enough to pay $100 per M.

* **Norwegian,** *a.* and *n.*

1. *n.* A fishing boat of a type used on the Great Lakes (see quot.). *Obs.*

1873 *Rep. Comm. Fisheries 1872–3* 9 At Milwaukee, for a time, the most of the boats were the sloop-rigged 'Norwegians,' afterwards abandoned, and the square stern adopted. *Ib.*, The 'Norwegian' is a huge, unwieldy thing, with flaring bows, great sheer, high sides, and is sloop-rigged. . . . She is only used by the Scandinavian fishermen.

2. Norwegian stove, tiller, (see quots.). *Obs.*

1875 KNIGHT 1534/1 Norwegian Stove . . . consists of a square wooden box lined with a soft, non-conducting substance. **1899** *Outing* XXX. 229/1 The 'Norwegian' tiller. . . . By this contrivance, instead of rudder lines or chains, a long stick is toggled to one end of the rudder yoke . . . so that the occupant thereof may grasp the stick and steer the craft from any part to which the steering stick may reach.

* **nose,** *n.* **1. nose paint,** intoxicating liquor. *Slang.* **2.** *nose for news*, an innate ability for ferreting out news. *Colloq.*

(1) **1881** HAYES *New Colo.* 158 We saw . . . a sign, in which the name which I have never encountered elsewhere was given to stimulating beverages. This sign was '*Nosepaint and Lunch.*' **1936** MCKENNA *Black Range* 90 When he got too much nosepaint he would take off his hat and his wig, to prove that he had been scalped by the Cheyenne Indians. — (2) **1893** in PHILIPS *Making of Newspaper* 54 Some managing editors are born with a 'nose for news.' **1894** SHUMAN *Steps into Journalism* 62 Among the most important of reportorial qualifications is that invaluable sixth sense called a 'nose for news.'

As the last term in **bloody, blue, bottle, buckwheat, bull, cold, hog, Pierced, sheep, shovel, star, white nose.**

* **notch,** *n. Chiefly E.* A narrow passageway or defile between mountains, or the narrowest part of such a passage. Also attrib.

1718 SEWALL *Diary* III. 195 Lodg'd . . . at Olcot's, about ½ way between the Notch of the Mountains and Hartford. **1823** WORCESTER *Geog. Dict.* II. 885/1 In the western part of these mountains there is a remarkable gap, called the *Notch.* **1906** CHURCHILL *Coniston* 2 Coniston Mountain, with its notch road that winds over the saddle behind the withers of it. **1925** in *Amer. Sp.* XV. 290/1 The railroad utilizes both notches, as does also a country road.

b. Also in place-names.

1784 BELKNAP *Papers* (1877) II. 182 About 11¼ arrived at the *Western Notch*, as it is called,—a narrow defile between the Mountains. **1945** *N.H. Troubadour* Jan. 10, I remember . . . driving up to Joe Dodge's . . . in Pinkham Notch.

As the last term in **Plymouth, top notch.**

***Notchers,** *n. pl.* (See quot.)—so called in allusion to the notches on their guns for those they had killed. *Slang. Obs.* cf. **top notcher.** — **1883** *Valencia Co.* (N.M.) *Vindicator* 15 Sep. 3/3 'Notchers' are men who wantonly take human life, apparently with the sole object of gaining reputation as desperadoes.

* **note,** *n.*

1. A thing worth noting, a surprise, a thing of great importance. *Colloq.*

1849 KINGSLEY *Diary* 32 This morning, the greatest note that has taken place yet come out. **1911** LINCOLN *Cap'n Warren's Wards* 157 Do you tell me that? That's a note, I must say.

2. In combs.: (1) **note broker,** a broker who handles promissory notes and, occasionally, bills of exchange; (2) **shaver,** one who makes a business of discounting notes, warrants, etc., a usurer, *slang*, cf. * **shaver;** (3) **shaving,** the practice of discounting notes at an excessive rate, also attrib., cf. **Wall Street note shaving.**

(1) **1870** W. W. FOWLER *10 Yrs. Wall St.* 226 This man, the casual observer would say, is an English Jew, who has gone into the business of a note broker. **1929** *Encycl. Brit.* IV. 233/1 Billbrokers are practically unknown in the United States; their general analogue is the note-broker. — (2) **1816** *Mass. Spy* 4 Sep. (Th.), We have too many note-shavers; too many gentlemen. **1911** SAUNDERS *Col. Todhunter* 113 Don't you forget that old Eph Tucker was a note-shaver long before he was a politician. — (3) **1828** *Yankee* I. 52/1 [By] the system of note-shaving that prevails here . . . the industrious and active are held in a state of bondage to the more wealthy and more lazy. **1862** *N. Amer. Rev.* July 113 This Wall-Street note-shaving life is a new field, a very peculiar field. **1911** SAUNDERS *Col. Todhunter* 113 He's got note-shavin' in his blood bigger 'n a mule.

As the last term in **accommodation, bank, buckwheat, California bank, century, change, Congress, consolidated, crop, dollar, facility, Federal Reserve, five-case, five-cent, fog, forwarding, fractional, gold, government, Illinois river, mash, merchant, Morris's, mush, national bank, patent, post, postal, relief, resurrection, sale, shape, shaped, Sherman, shop, state treasury, stock, tobacco, transfer, treasury, vendue, wildcat banknote.**

* **nothing,** *n.* **1.** In emphatic or exclamatory expressions, by no means, not at all. *Colloq.* **2.** *nothing to nobody*, beyond adequate description or setting forth. *Slang.*

(1) **1888** [see **nope**]. **1898** NICHOLAS *Idyl of Wabash* 175 'My account —nothing!' was her scornful ejaculation. **1923** WYATT *Invisible Gods* 66 'It is disloyal.' 'Disloyal nothing!' — (2) **1835** LONGSTREET *Ga. Scenes* 166 The way them women love punch is nothing to nobody! *a***1859** *N.Y. Spirit of Times* (B.), The way she would make Indian cakes, and the way I used to slick them over with molasses, was nothing to nobody.

Nothingarian ˌnʌθɪŋˈɛrɪən, *n.* One who subscribes to no particular religious faith or political party. Also not *cap.* *Obs.*

1776 in *Md. Hist. Mag.* IX. 66 He return'd [from Geneva] a strange jumble of Calvinism, Republicanism, & a deal of other isms, which in the Aggregate, make, what I have heard call'd, a Nothingarian both in Politics & Religion. **1845** LYELL *Second Visit* I. 139 A Nothingarian . . . was indifferent whether he attended a Baptist, Methodist, Presbyterian, or Congregationalist church, and was often equally inclined to contribute money liberally to any one or all of them. **1885** L. W. SPRING *Kansas* 70 Nineteen of the thirty-four reported themselves democrats, six registered as whigs, while independents, freesoilers, republicans, free-state men, and nothingarians found representatives among the remaining nine.

b. One who has no special occupation or interest. Also as adj. *Obs.*

1817 *Mass. Spy* 2 April (Th.), Office-hunters, brokers, clerks, staytape and buckram gentry, speculators, and nothingarians, crowd to the President's every Wednesday evening. **1889** *Open Court* 3 Jan. 1393 (*Cent.*), The blessed leisure of wealth was not to him the occasion of a nothingarian dilettantism, of idleness or selfish pursuits of vanity, pleasure or ambition.

***notice,** *n.* As the last term in **business, claim, stake notice.**

* **notion,** *n.*

1. *pl.* Small articles of trade, as tinware, clocks, combs, hairpins, ribbons, etc., such as were formerly sold by Yankee peddlers.

1796 *Aurora* (Phila.) 1 Feb. (Th.), Parentheses one within the other, like a nest of Boston boxes, commonly called notions. **1805** in *Jrnls. Lewis & Ordway* 199 We found Some little notions which Some Indian had hung up. **1886** *Harper's Mag.* July 174/2 People brought in . . . fancy shops for the sale of all manner of cheap and bizarre 'notions.' **1902** LORIMER *Lett. Merchant* 135, I was traveling out of Chicago for Hammer & Hawkins, wholesale dry-goods, gents' furnishings and notions. **1946** *Sears Cat.* (ed. 193) (Index), Notions.

b. *pl.* A miscellaneous assortment of various wares making up a cargo.

1805 SOUTHEY in *Ann. Rev.* III. 31 The Americans . . . , finding no longer a market there for their lumber cargoes, or notions, as they call them. **1815** *Niles' Reg.* VIII. 139/2 Nor does the lady, while sipping her tea, . . . dwell on the thought, whether it . . . was brought hither, via Salem, in a schooner with 'notions.' **1872** *Atlantic Mo.* April 398

Give a Yankee captain, in time of war, a schooner full of 'fish and notions,' a flag of truce to the enemy, and a free range of the seas.

2. In combs. of obvious meaning: (1) **notion counter,** (2) **house,** (3) **peddling crew,** (4) **seller,** (5) **stock,** (6) **store,** (7) **trade.**

(1) **1891** S. FISKE *Holiday Stories* (1900) 152, I went to the store . . . and recognised her . . . at the notion counter. **1907** *Scribner's Mag.* July 121 When the academic life palls I may be qualified to serve as manager of some small corner (say the notion counter) of a 'department store.' — (2) **1887** *Courier-Journal* 21 Jan. 7/2 The wholesale notion houses were pretty fully employed. — (3) **1809** IRVING *Knickerb.* IV. iii, He swore that he would have nothing more to do with such a squatting, bundling, . . . notion-peddling crew. — (4) **1839** *Chemung* (N.Y.) *Democrat* 17 April (Th.), A 'Notion seller' was offering Yankee clocks, &c.

(5) **1898** *K.C. Star* 18 Dec. 10/2 Greater attractions every day come to the Notions stocks. — (6) **1844** HOUSTOUN *Texas* (1845) 78 Outside a great many of the 'notion' stores, I saw just such figures hanging up. — (7) **1902** GHENT *Our Benev. Feudalism* 18 This tendency is pronounced in the notion trades and in the manufacture of women's ready-made wear.

As the last term in **Boston, Yankee notion.**

* **notional,** *a.* Full of notions or whims; overparticular or fastidious. *Colloq.*

1791 *Gaz. U.S.* 9 Feb. (Th.), If a man is a little odd in his ways, his friends say he is a notional creature, or full of notions. **1819** *Niles' Reg.* XVI. 224 A somewhat similar occurrence [took place] among the *notional folks* of Boston. **1904** *Hartford Courant* 1 July 10 The 'New York Evening Post,' fantastically notional about the use of English, announced last night that in a collision a surgeon had been 'painfully hurt.' **1949** *Boston Sun. Globe Mag.* 3 April 15/1 Don't you know Some people are notional just where they go So in Hell no Vermonters are found?

b. Inclined to think. *Rare.*

1823 COOPER *Pioneers* ix, I'm glad if the Judge is pleased; but I'm notional that you'll find the sa'ce overdone.

Nott stove. A trade-mark name for a stove designed to burn hard coal. *Obs.* — **1838** COOPER *Homeward Bound* xxxiv, Some New York cockney, who has wandered from the crackling heat of his Nott stove [etc.]. **1875** *Scribner's Mo.* Dec. 350/1 The good design and workmanship were inherited by the 'Nott' stoves, that superseded them [the Franklin stoves] on the coming in of anthracite.

Novanglian noˈvæŋglɪən, *a.* and *n.* Also **Novanglican.** [L. *Nova Anglia,* New England.] **1.** *n.* A native or inhabitant of New England. **2.** *a.* Of or pertaining to New England. Both *obs.*

(1) **1752** J. MACSPARRAN *Amer. Dissected* 31 The Novanglians in general, the Rhode-Islanders in particular, . . . have hit on the Art of enriching themselves by running in debt. **1813** J. ADAMS *Works* X. 49 You may find something upon correspondences, whig and tory, federal and democratic, Virginian and Novanglian, English and French. — (2) **1679** *N. Eng. Hist. Reg.* IV. 130 Nov-Anglian Heroes universall call, Did Constitute him major Generall. **1752** J. MACSPARRAN *Amer. Dissected* 31 The Novanglian clergy of our Church . . . have introduced a Custom [etc.]. **1862** TAYLOR *At Home & Abroad* 2 Ser. (1864) 339, I rather admire this stolid self-reliance and Novanglican assumption.

* **novel,** *n.* As the last term in **dime, international, nickel, purpose novel.**

* **novelty,** *a.* Designating theatrical groups employed or active in variety or vaudeville. — **1875** *Boston Transcript* 17 Aug. 1/7 Tony Pastor's Novelty Troupe . . . present . . . Sanford and Wilson in an Ethiopian sketch. **1887** *Courier-Journal* 31 Jan. 8/4 [The] proprietor and manager of the Andy Hughes American and European Novelty Company . . . was arrested. *Ib.* 6 Feb. 3/7 Comprising Twenty Frolicsome Queens of the Novelty World.

* **nowhere,** *adv. To be nowhere,* (see quot. 1859). *Colloq.* — **1859** BARTLETT 297 To be nowhere is to be at sea; to be utterly at a loss; to be ignorant. **1868** in DE VERE (1871), 620 When he began to ask me questions about surgery, I was just nowhere.

Noyesism ˈnɔɪzɪzəm, *n.* [f. John Humphrey *Noyes* (1811–86), founder of the Oneida community *q.v.*] Oneida communism *q.v.* Also **Noyesite,** =**Oneida Communist.** Both *obs.* — **1849** EASTMAN *Noyesism Unveiled* vii, Bible perfection and Noyesism are as diverse as light and darkness. *Ib.* 37 The witnesses in the case were all Noyesites except one or two who were formerly followers of him.

N.T. (See quot.) *Rare.* — **1879** TOURGEE *Fool's Errand* 46 One of the 'N.T.'s' became so full of the spirit of the occasion, that she kissed one of the colored boys who waited at the table. . . . ('NT' you know, is Southern euphemism for *Nigger Teacher.*)

* **nub,** *n.* **1.** = * **nubbin 1,** *rare.* **2.** The gist or crux of a matter, the point or moral of a story. *Colloq.*

(1) **1806** *Farmer's Almanac 1807* 17 March, It will not hurt oxen nor milch cows to give them once in a while a nub of corn or some potatoes. — (2) **1834** C. A. DAVIS *Lett. J. Downing* 210 That's pretty much the nub of the business. **1903** SHUMAN *Pract. Journalism* 61 The beginner cannot go far wrong if he gets the nub of the whole story into his first paragraph.

* **nubbin,** *n.*

1. A stunted or dwarfed ear of Indian corn.

1692 *Md. Hist. Mag.* XIII. 209 Jones saw him buy one beaver skin . . . for thirty ears and nubbins of corn. **1838** DRAKE *Tales* 150 A handfull of salt and a few nubbins of corn, were procured. **1891** *Outing* Nov. 108/1 Ef yore yeer measures full six inches ye're the lucky man, but ef it falls short o' that size its a nubbin an' don't count. **1948** *Nat. Geog. Mag.* Aug. 235/2 Nubbins of field corn featured our dinner.

attrib. **1854** DAVIS *Farm Bk.* 12 Made the fence from nubbin ridge to sulphur spring—168 panels.

transf. **1857** *Harper's Mag.* Feb. 399/2 They served me, at the 'American,' with a little hard *nubbin* of steak. **1888** KIRKLAND *McVeys* 59 There must always be a 'nubbin' of ground in one corner or in the middle, where short furrows come together and plague him. **1944** *Chi. D. News* 13 July 21/1 Have ready, for five or six portions, two nice pigs' feet, half a pound of tripe, half a dozen potatoes, an onion, a nubbin of garlic and a No. 1 can of tomatoes.

2. =**nub 2.** *Rare.*

1908 LORIMER *J. Spurlock* 127 That was the nubbin of my idea, suh.

As the last term in **cypress, peckerwood, vinegar nubbin.**

'nuf(f) sed. [Short for "enough (has been) said."] Fine, agreed, all right. *Colloq.* or *jocular.*

1841 *Spirit of Times* 30 Oct. 409/1 'N.S., nuf sed,' and up went *the soap.* **1892** DUVAL *Young Explorers* 151 'Nuf ced,' says Bill, 'you jess take care of your own har, and I'll see arter mine.' **1949** *Telephone Reg.* (McMinnville, Ore.) 4 Aug. 1/1 Maybe Greg should consult his dictionary a little more often when writing, rather than censoring [*sic*] others. 'Nuff said.

* **nullification,** *n. Hist.*

1. Action, based upon the doctrine of state sovereignty, taken by a state to abrogate within its limits the operation of a federal law, esp. the action taken by South Carolina with respect to the tariffs of 1829 and 1832. Now *hist.* Cf. **anti-nullification.**

The right of a state to nullify acts of Congress regarded by it as unconstitutional was affirmed in the Kentucky Resolutions *q.v.* of 1799. In 1828 South Carolina, in a set of resolutions, protested the unconstitutionality of the tariff, and accompanied the resolutions with Calhoun's "South Carolina Exposition," setting forth the theory of nullification. In 1832 a state convention in South Carolina passed an ordinance of nullification, which was rescinded in 1833.

1798 JEFFERSON *Writings* XVII. 386 Where powers are assumed which have not been delegated, a nullification of the act is the rightful remedy. **1830** *Mass. Spy* 27 Oct. (Th.), In Columbia (S.C.), the seat of Government, and the very focus of Nullification, two Nullifiers, and two anti-Nullifiers are chosen to the Assembly. **1886** LOGAN *Great Conspiracy* 464 Including within the scope of States Rights, the threats of Nullification, Disunion and Secession, . . . small wonder is it that, in those days [*c*1824–45], every fresh demand made by these political autocrats was tremblingly acceded to. **1945** ADAMS *Album Amer. Hist.* II. 245 Congress smoothed over the difficulty, and the right of nullification remained an unsettled issue.

Hence **nullificationize,** *v. Rare.*

1856 *Ill. State Reg.* (Springfield) 15 May 3/3 He argues that Mr. Calhoun, having nullificationized the democratic party proper, there was no other course left to the original white sheep . . . but to go into the black pen of abolitionism.

2. Nullification party, in South Carolina, the political party or faction composed of those who favored nullification of the high protective tariffs of 1828 and 1832. *Obs.*

1832 HONE *Diary* I. 70 These appointments prove the strength of the 'Nullification' party. **1846** MANSFIELD *Winfield Scott* 231 The name of the party of the majority was known as the nullification party, and that of the minority as the Union party.

3. In other combs. of obvious meaning, as **nullification candidate, law, newspaper, ordinance, tariff, test oath.**

1830 J. Q. ADAMS *Memoirs* VIII. 210 Mr. Calhoun will be the Nullification candidate. **1833** *Niles' Reg.* XLIV. 20/1 Mr. John C. West . . . has been required by governor Hayne to take the nullification test oath. **1857** BENTON *Exam. Dred Scott Case* 181 All the nullification newspapers opened for secession for that new cause. **1860** in LOGAN *Great Conspiracy* 112 We earnestly recommend the repeal of all Nullification laws. **1871** GROSVENOR *Protection* 230 The production has . . . increased little more . . . than it increased in eight years under the 'South Carolina nullification tariff.' **1949** MURRAY *This Our Land* 89 There were prominent men in South Carolina, however, who had openly condemned the Nullification Ordinance.

nullificator ˈnʌləfəˌketɚ, *n.* =**nullifier 1.** *Obs.* — **1830** *Mass. Spy* 27 Oct. (Th.), It is to be hoped that, if the Nullificators do move, it will be to Mexico, or beyond the Rocky Mountains. **1833** *Niles' Reg.* XLIV. 33/2 The 'nullificators' believe that they have obtained a glorious victory.

nullificatory ˌnʌləfəˈketərɪ, *a.* Of or pertaining to nullification or the Nullification party. *Obs.* — **1831** *Niles' Reg.* 8 Oct. 99/1 That which was wrong . . . in 'Hezekiah Niles,' is right in any English-agent or Englishman—and surely so in any nullificatory American who belongs to '*the* democratic party!' **1832** *Ib.* 29 Sep. 77/1 Nullificatory Articles.

nullifier ˈnʌləˌfaɪɚ, *n.*

1. An advocate of nullification *q.v.*, esp. with reference to the action of South Carolina in 1832. Now *hist.* Cf. **anti-nullifier.**

1830 *Mass. Spy* 7 July (Th.), This argument was considered by all the nullifiers as overwhelming. **1913** BASSETT *Short Hist. U.S.* 410 On February 1 [1833] the leading nullifiers met and decided to suspend the execution of the ordinance of nullification. **1948** *Reader's Digest* May 127/2 When the Nullifiers began to arm, Jackson at one time promised to march 200,000 troops into the rebellious state.

b. Great Nullifier, John C. Calhoun (1782–1850).

1850 *Quincy* (Ill.) *Whig* 12 Nov. 3/2, I speak of course of the Great Nullifier as of a historical character. **1882** H. VON HOLST *J. C. Calhoun* 104 Hundreds of eyes closely scrutinized the face of the 'great nullifier' as he took the oath to support the Constitution.

2. (See quot. 1859.) *Obs.*

1840 *N.O. Picayune* 20 Sep. 2/3 His understandings [shoes] could not be legitimately called boots, brogans or nullifiers. **1859** BARTLETT 298 *Nullifier* . . . was also applied to a sort of shoe, made like a decapitated boot, brought into fashion in the 'nullification' times.

* **nullify,** *v. tr.* Of a state or state authority: To refuse to enforce or uphold (a federal law). Also absol.

1798 JEFFERSON *Writings* XVII. 387 Every State has a natural right in cases not within the compact . . . to nullify of their own authority all assumptions of power by others within their limits. **1833** A. GREENE *Yankee among Nullifiers* 20 Why the case is perfectly clear: Nullify; I say nullify. **1877** *Harper's Mag.* March 595/2 The statesmen of South Carolina insisted upon the right of the State to nullify an unconstitutional act of Congress.

nully ˈnʌlɪ, *n.* =**nullifier 1.** *Colloq. Obs.* — **1832** *Boston Transcript* 31 Jan. 2/3 The Nullies made an attack upon their stronghold, carried off their voters, and thus gained the election. **1835** in E. J. HOOPER *Address Lit. Soc. Pittsborough,* The Gineral you know wants to keep a sharp look out upon them nullies in South Carolina.

* **number,** *n.*

1. *pl.* The series of ordinals and numerals used in giving the location of land that has been surveyed into ranges, townships, and sections. Cf. * **description.**

1852 REGAN *Emigrant's Guide* 65 The 'Numbers,' as they are called, ran thus:—'The North-east 40 of the South-east quarter of the 3d Section of Township 7 North, Range 1 East of the 4th principal Meridian, in the County of Fulton, and State of Illinois.' *Ib.* 294 When he goes to the Land Office, by giving the 'numbers' of the piece which he means to purchase, (which numbers he will obtain from some one living near the ground), he will be informed whether the ground is still open for sale, in which case he receives a deed at once.

2. *pl.* = * **policy 1.** Also attrib.

1897 ADE *Pink Marsh* 170 She tell Belle 'at she heah I like gin an' roll 'e bones an' play numbehs. **1949** BLANCHE *You Can't Win* 70 The 'numbers' racket is known by different names in various sections of the country—The Numbers, Policy, Clearing House, Butter and Eggs, and the Bug.

3. An item of information. *Slang.*

1903 A. H. LEWIS *Boss* 205 That's a nice number to hand a man!

4. number one, *a.*, of the finest quality, first-rate, also absol. *Colloq.* Cf. **A No. 1.**

1843 MARRYAT *M. Violet* xxviii, After having drained half-a-dozen cups of 'stiff, true, downright Yankee No. 1,' we all of us took our blankets. **1848** *Corr. R. W. Griswold* (1898) 242, I have some beautiful poems by me by Mrs. Barnes. . . . They are No. 1, full of passionate feeling and eminently worthy of a place. **1946** *Chi. D. News* 20 March 29 (*advt.*), No. 1 on the high school hat parade! your smooth spring bonnet from the millinery shop.

5. number six, a household remedy so designated, a kind of medicine.

1842 KIRKLAND *Forest Life* I. 71 We stick to thoroughwort,—balmony,—soot tea,—'number six,'—and the like. **1853** P. PAXTON *Yankee in Texas* 122 His old woman doctored me, and give me 'number six.' [**1902** *Sears Cat.* (ed. 112) 450 No. 6 Headache—Good for headache of any sort, fever, cold, nervousness, la grippe, etc.]

As the last term in **back, call, Dewey Decimal, federal number.**

* **numerous,** *a.* Superior, first-rate, preëminent. *Slang. Obs.* — **1841** *Spirit of Times* 27 March 43/3 (We.), In bar hunts *I am numerous.* **1860** HOLLAND *Miss Gilbert* 172 He sort o' stands round, and spreads, and lets off all the big talk he hears. Ain't he rather numerous, though? *Ib.*, 'It had occurred to me that he might be in a public position.' 'Well he does look numerous, that's a fact.'

* **nun,** *n.* **1. nun's eagle,** =**bald eagle. 2. nun's Holland,** a kind of fine Holland cloth. Also shortened to **nuns.** Both *obs.*

(1) **1842** DE SMET *Letters* (1843) 182 Amongst the most remarkable birds we distinguished the Nun's eagle, (so called by travellers on account of the color of its head, which is white, whilst the other parts of the body are black). — (2) **1745** in WATSON *Philadelphia* 179 nuns, bag and gulix. **1756** *Lett. to Washington* I. 362 Tandem & Nuns Hollands from 27/—to 52/—some of these exceeding fine.

* **nurse,** *n.* As the last term in **black, registered nurse.**

* **nut,** *n.* In combs.: (1) **nutcake,** chiefly *N. Eng.*, a doughnut or fried cake, cf. **Yankee nutcake;** (2) **candy,** candy containing nut meats; (3) * **cracker,** the cardinal grosbeak or Clark's crow *qq.v.*, cf. **Clark's nutcracker;** (4) **hatcher,** the nuthatch, *rare;* (5) **mill,** a mill for extracting the oil from castor beans, *obs.;* (6) **pick,** a small pick for removing nutmeats from nutshells; (7) **pine,** see as a main entry; (8) * **shell,** (see quot.), *obs.;* (9) **sundae,** a sundae served with nuts; (10) **wood,** see as a main entry.

(1) **1801** *Spirit Farmers' Mus.* 235 Heap the nutcakes, fried in butter. **1857** *Quinland* I. 36 The 'nut-cakes' are an institution of the country. Some call 'em 'dough-nuts,' and some 'fried cakes.' **1897** ROBINSON *Uncle Lisha's Outing* 253 'Come right in, all of you, an' have a fried cake an some cider.' . . . 'I wouldn't go ag'in a nut cake.' — (2) **1873** PHELPS *Trotty's Wedding* i, I'll get half a stick of nut-candy. — (3) **1688** HOLME *Armory* II. 242/2 The Virginian Nightingale . . . is called of some the Nut-craker, because it loves to feed on Kernells. **1874** COUES *Birds N.W.* 207 *Picicorvus Columbianus,* . . . American Nutcracker. **1944** *Nat. Geog. Mag.* June 690/1 We never see nutcrackers on the mountain-tops nor magpies in the valleys of eastern United States. — (4) **1862** *Ill. Agric. Soc. Trans.* V. 731 Even the Nuthatchers, are by many, indiscriminately called Sap-Suckers.

(5) **1831** PECK *Guide* 198 The beans are . . . put in a cylinder, and the screw, which is an immense one of wood, forces down a follower with great power. The screw is turned by a horse and a large lever, precisely similar to that of a cider mill, in New England, called a nut mill. — (6) **1890** BIFF HALL *Turnover Club* 173 They used to call themselves 'The Gigantic American Silver Show,' and gave away silver-plated nut-picks. **1931** *K.C. Times* 9 Dec. 20 His wife calls for an hour or so of his time in bruising fingers with a hammer and sticking them with a nut-pick. — (8) **1825** J. L. MOTLEY *Correspondence* (1898) I. 3 After that we [at Northampton, Mass.] went to ride in a nutshell, otherwise a monster of a carryall, with five seats in it; each seat holds five, so we had twenty-five in it. — (9) **1927** EUBANK *Horse & Buggy Days* 34 The girls then helped their mothers in the kitchen and learned the art of cooking . . . instead of building nut sundaes and drawing a salary with which to buy powder and paint. **1947** *Redbook* Aug. 91/1 Roger felt he needed something stronger than a nut sundae if he was going to think clearly.

As the last term in **bay, bitter, buckeye, buffalo, bull, butter, daddy, elk, European hazel, Gloucester, grass, ground, heart, hickory, hog, Illinois, king, kiskitomas, Madeira, Mississippi, mocker, pea, pecan, pig, pine, piñon, scaly-bark hickory, Springfield, tallow, tough nut.**

* **nuthatch,** *n.* As the last term in **red-bellied, white-bellied, white-breasted nuthatch.**

* **nutmeg,** *n.*

1. (*cap.*) Short for Nutmeg State *q.v.* Also a native or inhabitant of Connecticut.

1852 *Deseret News* (Salt Lake City) 17 April 1/1, I was sitting in the store of old Frank . . . when a real *nutmeg* came booming along, and in he comes with a heap of bundles in his fists. **1896** *Typographical Jrnl.* IX. 367 Down Among the Nutmegs. . . . The printers of Hartford are alive to their own interests. **1907** *Boston Transcript* 9 Nov., Popular names of the States: . . . New England of the West—Minnesota. Nutmeg or Wooden Nutmeg—Connecticut. [**1946** MCWILLIAMS *So. Calif. Country* 172 Those from Connecticut are 'nut-meggers.']

2. =**nutmeg tree.**

1856 *Mariposa* (Calif.) *Democrat* 5 Aug. 1/6 Here grows the oak, the fir, the hemlock, the nutmeg, the pine, . . . the arrow-wood, the elder, the cherry.

3. In combs.: (1) **nutmeg bread,** a kind of bread or cake flavored with nutmeg, *obs.;* (2) **hickory,** a hickory,

Carya myristicaeformis, chiefly southern, which bears a nut about the shape and size of a nutmeg, also **nutmeg hickory nut;** (3) **melon,** a muskmelon having a thin netted or reticulated rind suggestive of the surface of a nutmeg; (4) **schoolteacher,** a schoolteacher from Connecticut, *rare;* (5) **State,** a nickname for Connecticut, in allusion to the alleged practice of the natives of making nutmegs of wood and selling them as genuine; (6) ∗**tree,** the California nutmeg tree (the species referred to in the first quot. is not known); (7) **Yankee,** a native or inhabitant of Connecticut.

(1) **1777** in CRESSWELL *Journal* (1925) 235 We then got some wine, rum, Nutmeg Bread &c. to the amount of two Dollars more. — (2) **1810** MICHAUX *Arbres* I. 21 *J[uglans] myristicaformis*, . . . Nutmeg hickery nut . . . , nom donné par moi. **1901** MOHR *Plant Life Ala.* 101 The nutmeg hickory, when full grown, resembles the shagbark hickory in its pale, shreddy bark. — (3) [**1822** WOODS *Eng. Prairie* (1904) 307 There are many sorts of sweet melons. . . . I have only noticed musk, of a large size; and nutmeg, a smaller one.] **1843** *Farmers' Cabinet* 15 Sep. 68/2 [Premium:] For the best nutmeg melons, or variety thereof, not less than three in number [$]3. **1870** WARNER *Summer in Garden* xiv, The nutmeg-melons, having covered themselves with delicate lace-work, are now ready to leave the vine. **1941** *L.A.* Map. 265. — (4) **1866** C. H. SMITH *Bill Arp* 170 Fretman was a nutmeg skoolteacher who had gone round my naborhood with his skool artikles.

(5) **1857** *Harper's Mag.* Dec. 136/2 Let us repeat a story that comes fresh from the Nutmeg State. **1948** *Field & Stream* June 128/2 Nutmeg State sportsmen immediately set out on an anti-pollution program that may get results. — (6) **1836** HOLLEY *Texas* 88 Among the underwood are found . . . the delightful magnolia, the nutmeg tree [etc.]. **1894** *Amer. Folk-Lore* VII. 100 Torreya Californica, . . . nutmeg-tree, Cal. — (7) **1946** HODGINS *Mr. Blandings Builds Dream House* 20 He had expected him, also, to be taciturn, as befitted a Nutmeg Yankee.

As the last term in **bark, California, wooden, Yankee nutmeg.**

nut pine. Any one of various pines or species of pine, as *Pinus monophylla, P. edulis*, etc., indigenous to the southwestern and Rocky Mountain regions, that bear edible nuts. In full **nut pine tree.**

1845 FRÉMONT *Exped.* 221 A pine tree . . . which Dr. Torrey has described as a new species, under the name of *pinus monophyllus;* in popular language, it might be called the *nut pine.* **1850** KINGSLEY *Diary* 142 The evergreen oak and Nut Pine are all the varieties of trees or timber. **1896** SHINN *Story of Mine* 63 The nut-pine trees were soon cut down. **1949** COLLINGWOOD & BRUSH *Knowing Your Trees* 18/1 This is one of four nut pines of the Southwest.

nutria ˈnutrɪə, *n.* [Sp., otter.] A beaver or a beaver skin. *Obs.*

1820 *N.Y. Gazette* 24 Jan. 1/4 Nutra Skins, Buffalo Robes, by the bale. **1830** *Boston Transcript* 24 July 4/2, 10,000 Prime Neutras. **1860** *Alta California* (S.F.) 28 May 1/2 In 1831, Mr. Wolfskill, of Los Angeles, came in from New Mexico . . . under a license to trap *nutria* —a provincialism for 'beaver'—the proper word for which is castor.

nutshelly ˈnʌtˌʃɛlɪ, *a.* Condensed, brief, concise. *Rare.* — **1843** CARLTON *New Purchase* II. 171 So nut-shelly had all books and subjects become, that all could be even cracked and devoured in infant schools!

∗**Nuttall,** *n.* [Thomas *Nuttall* (1789–1859), Anglo-Amer. naturalist.] Used, chiefly in the possessive, in the names of birds, as **Nuttall's poorwill, sparrow, tern, whippoorwill, woodpecker,** (see quots.).

1839 AUDUBON *Ornith. Biog.* V. 335 Nuttall's Whip-Poor-Will. *Caprimulgus Nuttallii.* **1858** BAIRD *Birds Pacific R.R.* 93 *Picus Nuttalli* . . . Nuttall's Woodpecker. . . . Coast region of California. **1887** DENTON *Naturalist's Diary* (1949) 118 On the way home one day a man gave me a Nuttals poorwill. **1917** *Birds of Amer.* I. 54 Gull-billed Tern. *Gelochelidon nilotica.* . . . Other Names.—Marsh Tern; Egyptian Tern; Nuttall's Tern. *Ib.* III. 36/2 Nuttall's Sparrow [*Zonotrichia leucophrys nuttalli*] . . . has this uninterrupted stripe. **1921** HALL *Yosemite Nat. Park* 127 Some of its distinctive species of animals are . . . Nuttall Woodpecker, Mariposa Brush Rabbit [etc.].

b. Nuttall's dogwood, a species of dogwood, *Cornus nuttalli.*

1869 MUIR *First Summer in Sierra* (1911) 85 Nuttall's flowering dogwood makes a fine show when in bloom.

c. Nuttall's little hare, (see quot.).

1886 BANCROFT *Hist. Ore.* I. 85 A third new species is called Nuttall's little hare, *Lepus Nuttallii.*

∗**nutting,** *n.* A nutting party. Cf. **hickory nutting.** — **1852** FLEISCHMANN *Wegweiser* 162 Diese Einsammlung von Nüssen (Nutting, Nut-gathering, Nutting parties) bietet eine der Vergnugungen des Westens, oder eine Gelegenheit, wobei die Nachbarn in einer Gegend zusammenkommen. **1880** *Harper's Mag.* Dec. 89/2 The younger people had their berrying frolics, . . . nuttings, and the like.

nutwood ˈnʌtˌwud, *n.* Any one of various species of nut-bearing trees, as hickory, walnut, and the like. Also a tree or the wood of a tree of such a species. Also attrib.

[**1656** tr. VAN DER DONCK *New-Netherlands* in *N.Y. Hist. Soc. Col.* 2 Ser. I. 149 The nut-wood grows as tall as the oak . . . and is tough and hard. We now use it for . . . swivel trees and other farming purposes. It is also excellent firewood.] **1701** WOLLEY *Journal N.Y.* 75 [The Indians] had Needles of Wood, for which Nut-wood was esteemed best. **1775** FITHIAN *Journal* II. 76 These level bottoms, abound most in Walnut, Nut-wood, Locust &c. **1881** *Harper's Mag.* Feb. 357/1 Our [colonial] ancestors were content to dine from pewter plates . . . their few precious pieces of China being reserved for . . . display on the shelves of the . . . nut-wood parlor cupboards.

Nyack ˈnaɪæk, *n.* [f. a native word, *naiag*, point, corner.] The name of an Indian village (see quot. 1910), or the Indians occupying this. Also attrib. *Obs.*

[**1645** in RUTTENBER *Indian Tribes Hudson's R.* (1872) 118 The sachems . . . took upon them the responsibility for those of *Ouany* and its vicinity, viz: those of . . . *Marechhourick, Nyeck* and their neighbors [etc.].] **1844** *N.Y. Hist. Soc. Proc.* 107 There was also a band of Indians of the name of Naiack, who in 1645, were living below Red Hook, on Long Island. **1881** MORGAN *Houses Amer. Aborigines* 118 The Nyack house corresponds very closely with the last named. **1910** HODGE *Amer. Indians* II. 100/2 Nyack. . . . A former village, probably of the Unami division of the Delawares, on the w. bank of Hudson r. about the present Nyack, in Rockland co., N.Y. The tract was sold and the Indians were removed in 1652.

Nyantic naɪˈæntɪk, *n.* [Algonquian.] One of a tribe of Algonquian Indians formerly occupying the Connecticut coast from the Niantic River or inlet to the Connecticut River. Also attrib.

1647 in *Mass. H.S. Coll.* 4 Ser. VI. 346 It will be a mercy if a safe, and honorable peace may be settled . . . and a great addition to it, if the . . . Nyantick Indians bring in their wampum. *Ib.* 347 We desire . . . that you would send me to the Narraganset and Neyantick Sachems in the meane time. **1945** WEBSTER *Town Meeting Country* 11 The former were powerful and warlike, and held in subjection the Nyantics a little to the west and south.

O

∗**oak,** *n.* In combs.: (1) **oak grub,** an oak bush that sprouts from an oak root, also attrib.; (2) **leaf cigar,** allegedly a cigar made of oak leaves and sold by Yankee peddlers, *obs.*, cf. **live-oak penny-a-grab;** (3) **-leaf cluster,** in the U.S. Army, a bronze decoration representing a twig with four oak leaves and three acorns, awarded to holders of medals for valor, etc., as an indication that they have again distinguished themselves in the way indicated by the medal previously given; (4) **pruner,** a beetle, *Hypermallus villosus*, that lives on the pith of oak twigs; (5) **rail,** a rail of oak wood; (6) **shake,** a rough board or shingle split from oak wood; (7) **split,** a thin, narrow strip of white oak often used in bottoming chairs; (8) **tie,** a railroad crosstie made of oak.

(1) 1852 Ellet *Pioneer Women* 366 The bushes which sprang in a season from their roots, called 'oak grubs,' are difficult to remove from the soil. **1881** Nash *Two Yrs. Ore.* 44 The farmer who has a little capital and so can afford the first outlay, need not hesitate to clear this oak-grub land. — **(2) 1831** *Workingman's Gaz.* (Woodstock, Vt.) 15 Mar. 195/2 The Providence Patriot cautions the Boston grocers against wooden nutmegs and oak leaf cigars, from the land of steady habits. **1832** *Boston Transcript* 18 Feb. 1/1 Their deceptions of wooden nutmegs and wooden clocks, horn flints and oak leaf segars, have all been exposed. — **(3) 1918** in *Amer. Decorations, U.S. Army, 1862–1926* (1926) 516. **1949** *Sooner Mag.* June 23/3 He was posthumously awarded the Distinguished Service Cross for extraordinary heroism, the Air Medal, one Oak Leaf cluster and Purple Heart. — **(4) 1838** *Mass. Zool. Survey Rep.* 92 *Stenocorus putator*, or the oak-pruner, so named by Prof. Peck, inhabits the white and black oaks. **1899** D. Sharp *Insects* II. 286 *Elaphidion villosum* is called the oak-pruner in North America.

(5) 1846 Thorpe *Myst. Backwoods* 142 Seizing a large oak rail, we attempted to run it down [the alligator's] throat. — **(6) 1856** Ropes *6 Months in Kansas* 49 The cabin is made by . . . nailing 'oak shakes' outside, after the manner of clapboards. **1856** *Wkly. Oregonian* 27 Sep. (Th.), Oak shokes [*sic*], split out by hand, kivered the chamber floor. — **(7) 1932** W. Kelley *Inchin' Along* 23 And the battered white bed had been joined by three chairs, the bottoms of which were woven oak-splits. — **(8) 1880** *Cimarron News & Press* 8 April 1/5 Two lots of oak ties are rotted away.

b. Designating land, areas, regions, etc., upon which oak is the chief growth, as (1) **oak-and-hickory land,** (2) **barren,** (3) **flat,** (4) **hammock,** (5) **land,** (6) **opening,** (7) **prairie,** (8) **ridge,** (9) **shinnery,** (10) **swamp,** (11) **yard.**

(1) 1735 *Ga. Hist. Soc. Coll.* II. 49 It is about thirty miles from Charleston and the land is . . . very good, being most of it oak and hickory, which is counted the best for corn and peas. **1789** Morse *Amer. Geog.* 429 The high-lands commonly known by the name of oak and hiccory lands, constitute the fourth kind of soil [in S.C.]. [**1942** Nat. Pk. Service *Fading Trails* 256 Hunting is partly responsible for this, but removal of oak-hickory woods on uplands may have been an important factor.] — **(2) 1802** in *Pa. Mag. Hist.* XLVI. 28 The Country . . . from Easton to Hellers is excessively rocky poor & rough filled with Oak barrens & pines. **1890** *Cent.* 4120/1 Similar tracts [of scattered oak trees] in the more southern States, especially in Kentucky are called *barrens* and *oak-barrens*. — **(3) 1800** Hawkins *Sk. Creek Country* 29 Oak flats, red and post oak, willow leaved hickory . . . on its left side. **1885** *Outing* May 151 The trail into Hetch-Hetchy leaves the northernmost Yosemite road, known as the Oak Flat route, at Big Meadows. — **(4) 1766** J. Bartram *Diary* 10 Jan., At the south end of the oak-hammock runs eastward a large branch.

(5) 1666 *S.C. Hist. Soc. Coll.* V. 84 They were rather willing to paye a greater rent for what acres of oake land they should possess. **1765** Rogers *Acct. N. Amer.* 135 On the north [of N.C.], towards Virginia, are some oak-lands, like those of Virginia, on which they raise tobacco. **1849** Chamberlain *Ind. Gazetteer* 209 The oak land is more extensive than the beech. — **(6) 1833** in *Mich. Hist. Mag.* XVIII. 55 'Oak Openings' . . . a light sandy soil, poor, on which nothing but burr oak will grow. **1885** *N.H. Forestry Comm. Rep.* June 30 Originally a dense forest covered our state. There were no 'parks' as in the Rocky Mountain region, or 'oak openings' and grassy plains as in the valley of the Mississippi. **1940** Deam *Flora of Indiana* 16 The area has a great variety of habitats, ranging from lakes and rivers, bogs and marshes, dry sand and gravelly places, prairies, and remnants of prairies (oak openings) to the mesophytic forest. — **(7) 1818** Schoolcraft *Journal* 25 Instead of rich bottoms, we have a high oak-prairie. — **(8) 1789** Morse *Amer. Geog.* 247 On the banks of Lake Erie, are a few chesnut and oak ridges. *c***1835** Catlin *Indians* II. 46 We have . . . crossed oak ridges of several miles in breadth, with a sandy soil and scattering timber. — **(9) 1907** Cook *Border & Buffalo* (1938) 258 West of the pecan and oak shinnery ('cross-timber') belt, even on the eastern escarpment of the Llano Estacado, were thousands of beautiful cottonwood groves.

(10) 1702 in *Amer. Sp.* XV. 290/2 Westerly through ye oake Swamp to ye first line. **1862** *Ib.*, A move to intercept me from the direction of the white oak swamp. — **(11) 1835** Bird *Hawks* II. 52 His father . . . had suddenly checked his horse at the entrance of the little oak-yard.

As the last term in **ash, barren, Bartram's, basket, bastard, bear, blue, box, brash, bur, Charter, chestnut-leaved, chinquapin (scrub), cow, desert, duck, Durand, Emory's, English, goldcup, golden, golden-cup, gray, iron, jack, Jersey, Kellogg's, laurel, Lea's, live, live chestnut, lowland Spanish, maul, mountain, mountain chestnut, overcup (white), Pacific post, peach, pin, poison, poisoned, post, punk, red, ring, rock, rock chestnut, rocky, rough, ruffled, running, scarlet, scrub, scrubby, seaside scrub, shin, shingle, shingle willow, shrub, side, Spanish, spice, swamp, swamp chestnut, swamp post, swamp red, swamp Spanish, swamp white, tan-bark, Texas, turkey, valley, Valparaiso, water, wavy, white, willow, yellow oak.**

oakery ˈokərɪ, *n.* ?An inclosure where oaks are grown. *Rare.* Cf. **oak yard.** — **1836** Gilman *Recoll.* (1838) 213 Turning suddenly, he bounded over the fence into papa's oakery.

Oakley ˈoklɪ, *n.* =**Annie Oakley.** — **1945** *Chi. D. News* 28 Sep. 14/7 He liberally provides them with opening-night Oakleys to every play in town.

∗**oat,** *n.*

1. *pl.* (See quot.)

1804 in Gates *Fur Traders* (1933) 206 Richard brought a parcel of dried Meat, today, the Indians had not yet made any Oats. [Footnote:] Wild rice was ordinarily called 'oats' or 'wild oats' by the traders and voyageurs. It was gathered by Indian women in the late summer and was bartered by them for trade goods. Whenever it could be procured, 'oats' served as a staple article in the traders' diet.

2. oat chops, oats ground or chopped as food for stock. Cf. ∗**chop,** *n.* **2.**

1893 *Dly. Ardmoreite* (Ardmore, Okla.) 14 Dec. 1/4 Don't buy trash when you can get 100 pounds of fresh corn and oat chops for one dollar.

3. *To feel one's oats*, to feel frisky or lively, to feel "cocky," to enjoy a sense of importance. *Colloq.*

1831 *Boston Transcript* 22 Dec. 1/1 Whether the pony felt his oats, . . . He took a frightful canter. **1871** Pine *Beyond West* 225 Portland is yet young and simple-hearted—'feels its oats,' but its dignity more. **1947** *Hygeia* Nov. 939/1 A dynamic run-about met grandparents' eyes instead—boisterous, obstreperous, inclined to obstinacy, obviously feeling her oats.

As the last term in **horse-mane, sea, seaside, side, water, wild oats.**

oat ot, *v. tr.* To feed (a horse) with oats. Also absol. *Obs.*

1732 B. Lynde *Diary* (1880) 26 Next morning . . . dined at Hampton; . . . thence to Greenland, where oated, and for 2 horses and drink, 2s. **1778** Cutler in *Life & Corr.* I. 65 Oated and had my hair dressed. . . . After oating, we went on to Martin's two miles. **1855** Barnum *Life* 70 Old 'Bob' was duly oated and watered.

∗**oath,** *n. To take the oath*, (see quot.). *Humorous. Obs.* See also **amnesty, ironclad oath.** — **1882** E. A. Sala *Amer. Revisited* I. 68 'Taking the oath' meant, when you paid a visit to a friend's house accidentally finding a bottle of Bourbon whiskey and a pitcher of iced water in the recesses of a bookcase . . . and straight away swearing fealty to the Republic by 'liquoring up.'

oatmeal mush. Oatmeal cooked in water or milk, esp. when made from rolled oats; oatmeal porridge. — **1883** *Harper's Mag.* Aug. 465/1 You've been the means of starving me . . . on oatmeal mush.

obeah ˈobɪə, *n.* Often *cap.* [See note.]

This word is of African origin introduced here by slaves. Its root meaning appears to be "poison," though what appears to be the same word is used with varying significations in different parts of Africa. Santamaría relates it to an Egyptian word meaning "snake."

A form of religion formerly current among some of the Negroes in the South (see quot. 1872). Usu. attrib.

1763 GRAINGER *Sugar-Cane* IV. 370 (*footnote*), The Negro-conjurers, or Obia-men, as they are called, carry about them a staff, which is marked with frogs, snakes, &c. The Blacks imagine that its blow, if not mortal, will at least occasion long and troublesome disorders. **1846** *Dollar Newspaper* (Phila.) 8 July 2/1 His old negro nurse, who was an Obear woman, and therefore foretold events, . . . said this mark was an epaulette, and that he would be a great warrior. **1872** *Harper's Mag.* Mar. 558/1 Obeah is a kind of witchcraft, and is practiced by 'obeah men' by putting horse-hair, fowls' feet, fishes' bones, coney-skins, and other stuff into a pot, and burying the pot in the grounds or near the house of the person against whom the necromancy is to be employed. **1885** *Harper's Wkly.* 7 Nov. 727/1 Jean, in short, possessed the mysterious obi power, the existence of which has been recognized in most slave-holding communities. **1947** *Chi. Sun Book Week* 9 Feb. 16/5 And as a magnificent bonus on the very last night of your visit you are received into the sacred order of 'obi,' the almost extinct cult of the supernatural.

obedient plant. The dragonhead. — **1907** LYONS *Plant Names* 353 P[hysostegia] virginiana. . . . Canada and Eastern U.S. False Dragon-head, Obedient-plant, Lion's-heart. **1931** CLUTE *Plants* 61 The name of obedient plant, applied to *Physostegia Virginiana*, fairly suggests itself, for the blossoms may be pushed in any direction and will retain this pose for a long time.

O-be-joyful. Alcoholic liquor. *Slang.*

1830 *Greensborough* (N.C.) *Patriot* 4 Aug. 4/2 They didn't come to, till the old woman and her darter poured some o be joy full down their throates. **1884** HILL *Colo. Pioneers* 100 They joined in a little 'O-be-joyful,' to bind the bargain. **1914** *D.N.* IV. 77 *Oh-be-joyful.* Also *oh-be-rich-an'-happy.* Hard liquor.

Oberlinism ˈobɚlɪnˌɪzəm, *n.* [*Oberlin* College.] A doctrine of perfectionism formulated by C. G. Finney (1792–1875) and Asa Mahan (1800–1899), both of Oberlin College, Ohio. *Obs.* — **1843** CARLTON *New Purchase* II. 22 Would not more persons have been converted to Oberlinism, Finneyism, or Abolitionism?

Oberlinite ˈobɚlɪnˌaɪt, *n.* [See prec.] A believer in Oberlinism. *Obs.* — **1867** DIXON *New Amer.* II. 308 The Perfectionists, who declared that the world was already at an end, that the judgment had come down upon us, parted into Putneyites and Oberlinites.

obflisticate ɑbˈflɪstəˌket, *v.* [Humorous var. of **obfuscate, v.*] *tr.* To put out of the way; to deprive of luster. Also **obflisticated,** *a. Slang. Obs.*

1832 J. HALL *Legends of West* 38 These Mingoes . . . ought to be essentially, and particularly, and tee-totally obflisticated off of the face of the whole yearth. **1833** *Sk. D. Crockett* p. v, The still more delicate repast of a constant repetition of the terms '*bodyaciously*,' '*tetotaciously*,' '*obflisticated*,' &c. **1840** *Crockett Almanac* 10 He looked obflisticated.

obfusticated ɑbˈfʌstəˌketɪd, *a.* [See prec.] Overshadowed or eclipsed; bewildered. *Slang. Obs.*

1834 *Sun* (N.Y.) 5 June 2/3 The Colonel [i.e., Crockett], on the result becoming known swore 'he'd be te-to-natiously obfusticated if he would take the office on any condition.' *c***1844** R. H. COLLYER *Amer. Life* 4, I see, Doctor, you are a little obfusticated. **1871** *Republican Rev.* 6 May 1/2 [We] speak of things and events as we find them, without dealing in far fetched theories and other 'obfusticated' nonsense.

obione ˈobɪˌon, *n.* [Origin unknown.] A fleshy annual of the goosefoot family, common in desert regions in the West. — **1856** WHIPPLE *Explor. Ry. Route* I. 122 For camp-fires we depend upon twigs of obione, (greasewood), or the soft pulpy stalks of the yucca. **1892** COLVILLE *Death Valley Exped.* 181 The name was first printed under *Obione*, without description, in Emory's Report, 149 (1848).

obispo pine. [Sp., "bishop" and **pine.*] The bishop pine of California, *Pinus muricata.* — **1884** SARGENT *Rep. Forests* 200 *Pinus muricata.* . . . Obispo Pine. Bishop's Pine. **1897** SUDWORTH *Arborescent Flora* 28 California Swamp Pine. . . . Common names [include] . . . Anthony's Prickle-Cone Pine . . . Obispo Pine (Cal.).

***object,** *n.* In combs.: (1) **object chart,** a chart used in connection with object teaching; (2) **system,** =**object teaching;** (3) **teacher,** a teacher who practices object teaching; (4) **teaching,** (see quot. 1945).

(1) **1866** *Rep. Indian Affairs* 256 By the use of Wilson's object-charts, together with other expedients upon the plan of object teaching, these children are rapidly learning to speak the English language [etc.]. **1871** *Ib.* (1872) 306 A new and original series of 'object charts' gotten up expressly for the Indians of Oregon by myself. — (2) **1869** BRACE *New West* 75 The improvement which we have sought so much to bring before the public in New York . . . —the 'Object System'—has already been adopted here. **1878** *Harper's Mag.* March 604/2 This school is too large for strictly Kindergarten teaching; but the 'object system' . . . was the one adopted. — (3) **1872** BRACE *Dangerous Classes N.Y.* 193 We trust that no Primary School in New York will be without a well-trained 'Object-teacher.' — (4) **1860** H. BARNARD (*title*), Object teaching, and Oral Lessons on Social Science and Common Things. **1945** GOOD *Dict. Educ.* 409 Teaching, object: a method of elementary-school teaching derived from the work of Pestalozzi of Europe and introduced into the United States at the Westfield, Massachusetts, State Teachers' College in 1848 and at Oswego, New York, in 1861; based on the use and study of real objects, rather than textbooks, and characterized by oral instruction, careful planning of lessons, and the stimulation of observation and inquiry on the part of pupils.

oblong,** *n.* (See quot.) *Slang. Obs.* — *a1794** in C. MATHEWS *Writings* ii. 233 It was a common expression among the troops to call the bank bills *oblongs*. This was more especially the case at the gaming tables.

obscutely ɑbˈskjutlɪ, *adv.* [Fanciful formation.] (See quot.) *Colloq.* — **1859** BARTLETT 299 *Obscutely*, obliquely. A factitious word used in New England.

***observation,** *n.* In combs.: (1) **observation car,** a railroad car, usu. at the end of a train, designed to give passengers a better view of the scenery than is afforded by an ordinary coach, also one of the cars on an observation train; (2) **hive,** a beehive with glass sides permitting direct observation of the bees; (3) **locomotive,** a railroad locomotive especially designed for use in track inspection and pilot work; (4) **platform,** an open-air platform of an observation car; (5) **train,** a train run along a watercourse to allow passengers to watch a boat race, a train the coaches of which are specially constructed to afford passengers better than ordinary opportunities for viewing the scenery.

(1) **1872** *Harper's Mag.* May 876/1 You look out of the open 'observation car' as you sweep down from a height of 7000 feet. **1904** *N.Y. Ev. Post* 30 June 1 In the observation cars spectators were talking and laughing and waiting. **1948** *New Yorker* 25 Sep. 26/3 Directly ahead of us was the new streamliner's Lookout Lounge, or observation car. **1949** *Sat. Ev. Post* 5 Nov. 23/2 In the observation car, I take the end chair, and sit spellbound, watching the endlessly converging and dwindling rails. — (2) **1883** *Cent. Mag.* Oct. 815/2 On the outside wall of the cabin is fastened an observation hive, with glass sides. — (3) **1905** *Springfield W. Republican* 7 July 12 Edward J. Pitchetson and a pair of horses he was driving were instantly killed . . . by the Boston & Albany observation locomotive Berkshire. — (4) **1906** LYNDE *Quickening* 29 At the rear of the string of Pullmans was a private car, with a deep observation platform. **1916** DU PUY *Uncle Sam* 46 They came tumbling among the chairs of the observation platform.

(5) **1893** POST *Harvard Stories* 294 The 'gang' had got seats in the same car on the observation-train and were waiting for it to start. **1948** *Chi. D. News* 4 May 12/1 A new America unfolds to travelers on the two-story observation train, from their lofty point of vantage.

***observatory,** *n.*

1. A building in a prison yard from which a watch can be kept on prisoners. *Obs.*

1829 HALL *Travels* II. 346 In the centre of the yard [of the Philadelphia prison] is erected what is called an observatory.

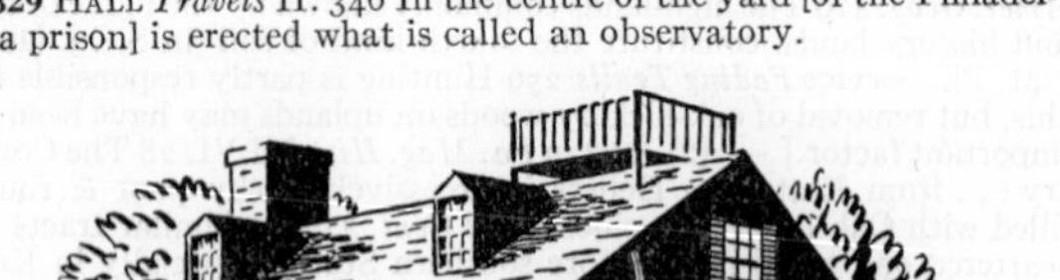

Observatory (sense 2), widow's walk, Captain's walk, or lookout (sense 1)

2. A cupola or railed-in deck or balcony on top of a house whence a wide view may be obtained. Also attrib.

1838 HAWTHORNE *Note-Books* I. 78 An old man . . . sits on a hill-top, or on the observatory of his house, and sees the sun's light. **1857** VAUX *Villas* 182 The observatory room is intended to be both useful and ornamental. *c***1870** BAGBY *Old Va. Gentleman* 297 The tops of houses, church steeples, the 'observatories,' . . . were alive with human beings. **1906** LYNDE *Quickening* 26 There were houses . . . hip-roofed, with a square balustered observatory on top.

3. (See quot.) *Obs.*

1870 MEDBERY *Men Wall St.* 314 This tendency [*c*1855] toward sharp and unscrupulous bear tactics was largely due to the presence of new men, known popularly as the 'Observatory,' who had come from the West with large accumulations of capital.

Ocala platform. [*Ocala*, Fla.] A political platform adopted by a Farmers' Alliance Convention in Ocala, Florida, in December, 1890. Now *hist.* — **1892** *Cong. Rec.* 28 May 4802/1 The Ocala platform [was] repudiated by the regular rock-ribbed Democrats. **1897** *Ib.* 26 March 357/1, I see that I have the attention of my friend from Kansas [Mr. Simpson], the great apostle of the Ocala platform.

occapee ˈɑkəpɪ, *n.* [Amer. Indian.] (See quots.) *Obs.* — **1816** in *Pub. Col. Soc. Mass.* XXIV. (1920–2) 202 [They] left them to drink their Occopy and to take the good of their bargain. **1830** *Boston Transcript* 14 Dec. 2/1 This diminution of the once powerful Mohegans, is to be ascribed, in part at least, to the Indian's well known love of *occapee*, or *strong water*.

* **occidental,** *a.* **1.** Belonging to the western United States. **2. occidental plane tree,** = **buttonwood 1.**

(1) 1846 *Knickerb.* XXVII. 471, 'I. L. of this vicinity,' writes an occidental correspondent, 'had carried the knife for a long time.' **1940** JAEGER *Calif. Deserts* 57 The occidental harvester (*P*[*ogonomyrmex*] *occidentalis*) is a large, reddish ant building conspicuous mounds of pebbles. — **(2) 1809** KENDALL *Travels* II. 28 Among the natural forest-trees, are the button-wood or occidental plane, the spruce-fir and the locust-tree. **1823** JAMES *Exped.* I. 21 The occidental plane tree is, perhaps, the grandest of the American forest trees.

occident ant. The western agricultural ant. — **1882** H. C. McCOOK (*title*), The honey ants of the Garden of the Gods and the occident ants of the American plains. **1884** *Amer. Naturalist* XVIII. 334 The occident ant (*Pogonomyrmex occidentalis*) was in Dakota confined to the bottom lands along the Missouri river.

occupation tax. 1. A tax levied upon persons or firms engaged in certain occupations. **2.** A tax for the Indians levied upon settlers who took up land in Indian territory.

(1) 1869 *Texas Constitution* 37 Occupation tax. . . . The Legislature shall have power to levy an income tax, and to tax all persons pursuing any occupation, trade or profession. **1888** BRYCE *Amer. Commonw.* II.II. xliii. 134 (*footnote*), License taxes or occupation taxes may be imposed . . . on grocery keepers, liquor dealers, insurance, vendors of patents [etc.]. — **(2) 1900** *Cong. Rec.* 2 Feb. 1458/2 The Five Civilized Tribes, with their great trust fund, with their great income from occupation tax, and especially from their income by way of royalties.

occupying claimant. (See quot.) Also attrib. *Obs.* — **1821** *Ann. 17th Congress* 1 Sess. I. 24 The Occupying Claimant Law [of Ky.] . . . the object of which was the settlement of conflicting land claims. **1859** BARTLETT 299 *Occupying claimant*, one who claims land by virtue of occupation of the same under the land systems of various States.

* **ocean,** *n.* In combs.: (1) **ocean-bound republic,** an expression of American aspiration for a republic extending from the Atlantic to the Pacific, *rare;* (2) **drive,** a road running close to the ocean; (3) **ferry,** (*a*) a sea lane for transoceanic steamers, (*b*) a transoceanic passenger boat; (4) **liner,** see * **liner,** *n.* **1;** (5) **spray,** see as a main entry.

(1) 1856 *Democratic Conv. Proc.* 57 It has ever been the dream of our statesmen, and an object dear to the hearts of our people to make America an ocean-bound republic. — **(2) 1886** I. D. HARDY *Oranges & Alligators* 127 Remarkable for its fine hotel accommodations, and for its celebrated 'ocean drive' along Amelia Island beach. — **(3)** (*a*) **1882** in McCABE *N.Y. by Sunlight & Gaslight* 361 In addition to these great ships that ply over the ocean ferry to Europe, there are lines to South and Central America. (*b*) **1885** *Lippincott's Mag.* Nov. 491/2 Fussy custom-house officers [get in the way of] . . . the newly-landed passengers from the ocean-ferries. **1892** *Cong. Rec.* App. 27 April 273/1 The ocean ferries ply unceasingly every day in the week between this country and Europe.

* **oceaner,** *n.* An ocean liner. *Rare.* — **1879** WHITMAN *Spec. Days* 136 Characteristic [of a] New York scene . . . [was] the proud, steady, noiseless cleaving of the grand oceaner down the bay.

oceanology ˌoʃənˈɑlədʒɪ, *n.* The science relating to the ocean; oceanography. — **1864** WEBSTER. **1896** *Smithsonian Rep.* 295 This brings us to the equally important question of oceanology, which should comprise a complete knowledge not only of the surface currents in the Arctic seas, but also surface and deep-sea temperatures [etc.].

ocean spray. A shrub, *Holodiscus discolor*, found in the western states. — **1906** PIPER *Flora Wash.* 330 Schizonotus discolor. . . . Ocean spray. **1940** *Ore. Guide* 20 In the spring and early summer . . . sweet syringa, ocean spray, and Douglas spirea form streamside thickets of riotous blossom.

ocelot ˈosəˌlɑt, *n.* [See note.] A large American spotted cat, *Felix pardalis*, of the Southwest.

The U.S. usage of this word is no doubt the result of a borrowing made from the Spanish in the Southwest. The *OED*, and subsequently other dictionaries, explain the term as derived f. Nahuatl *tlalocelotl*, the jaguar, the native name of the larger of two southwestern cats being thus conferred, in English, upon the smaller. Santamaría is prob. correct in suggesting that the Nahuatl term *ocelotl* designated the smaller cat.

[**1780** CLAVIGERO *Storia della Messico* II. 78 L' *Ocotochtli*, sare essere . . . della classe dei Gatti salvatachi.] **1809** KER *Travels* (1816) 243 An animal called ocstochly, a kind of wild cat, is remarkable, more for the fabulous account of it, than for any singular property with which it is endowed. **1867** *Amer. Naturalist* I. 286 Two other species of true long-tailed cats may possibly exist, particularly in the south-eastern portions [of Ariz.]. These are the Ocelot . . . and the Jaguar. **1942** Nat. Pk. Service *Fading Trails* 109 Then there are the ocelots, once known as far north and east as Louisiana.

ocherous ˈokərəs, *a.* [* *ocher* + *-ous*.] Of or like ocher, ochrous. — **1806** WEBSTER. **1885** *Cent. Mag.* XXX. 819 The red ocherous soil of their steep sides.

ocotillo ˌokəˈtijo, *n.* Also **ocotilla.** [Amer. Sp. *ocotillo* (dim. of *ocote* <Nahuatl), in same sense.] A cactus-like shrub, *Fouquieria splendens*, found in rocky desert regions of the Southwest. Also **ocotillo cactus.** Cf. **coachwhip 2, Jacob's staff.**

1856 *Wide West* (S.F.) Oct. 4/6 Aside from the grass, there is a shrub called the . . . *Ocetilla*. **1864** *Harper's Mag.* Nov. 697/2 Passing through some dense thickets of mesquit and ocochilla, the struggling family found themselves at the foot of a rocky bluff. **1948** *Nat. Hist.* April 181 The Ocotillo is frankly red, adding its flaming tips to every dry stick that looked dead a week or so ago.

* **October,** *n.* **1. October election,** an election held in October, cf. next. **2. October state,** a state which holds its general election in October instead of November. *Obs.*

(1) 1860 *N.Y. Tribune* 7 April 4/2 There is an ordeal to be passed prior to the decision of the Presidential contest, commonly known as the October Elections. **1949** *Ind. Mag. Hist.* March 13 The election of Abraham Lincoln in 1864 hinged to a large extent on the fact that the Union party was able to carry the October elections in Ohio, Indiana, and Pennsylvania. — **(2) 1885** *Cent. Mag.* Jan. 461 Skillful correspondents were sent out by the 'great dailies' to write up the preliminary struggles in 'the October States.' **1895** MYERS *Bosses & Boodle* 77 Until 1887, Ohio was an 'October' state. Under the first and second Constitutions, the election for state officers took place in October, while the Federal elections were held in November.

* **octopus,** *n. fig.* A powerful commercial organization, as a trust, having extended ramifications and influence. — **1878** in TARBELL *Hist. Standard Oil Co.* I. 182 One refiner after another . . . fell shivering with dislike into the embrace of this commercial octopus. **1901** NORRIS (*title*), The Octopus. **1950** *New Yorker* 4 Feb. 23/2 I've been indicted three times by this government. I've never been convicted. I'm supposed to be an octopus.

octoroon ˌɑktəˈrun, *n.* [f. *octo-* + *roon*, on the analogy of * *quadroon*.] A person of one-eighth Negro blood.

1860 in *Amer. Sp.* XXI. (1946) 237/2 [Artemus] Ward wrote an article 'The Octoroon' which appeared in the *Cleveland Plain Dealer* of April 21, 1860. **1887** *Harper's Mag.* Jan. 200/2 Her father was Spanish, her mother was an octoroon. **1911** G. D. JOHNSON *Bronze* 36 The Octoroon. One drop of midnight in the dawn of life's pulsating stream Marks her an alien.

* **odds,** *n. pl.* *To ask* (or *beg*) *no odds*, to seek no favor, to ask for no advantage.

1806 *Baltimore Ev. Post* 5 March 2/2 (Th.), No odds he begs Of any beast that walks upon four legs. **1836** *Quarter Race Ky.* (1846) 23, I ask no man any odds further than civility. **1894** *Cong. Rec.* 29 May 5447/1 Give us equitable laws and fair play, and South Dakota asks no odds of any State of the Union.

odometer oˈdɑmətɚ, *n.* [Prob. f. F. *odomètre*.] A device used on a wheel or wheeled vehicle for measuring distance traversed.

1791 JEFFERSON in *Harper's Mag.* LXX. 536/1 Pd. Leslie for an odometer 10 D[ollars]. **1885** CUSTER *Boots & Saddles* 127 Some officer wished to measure the distance of a days march, and having no odometer elected his wife to that office. **1948** *Utah Humanities Rev.* April 121 As finally constructed, the 'odometer' was small enough to be contained in a box eighteen inches long.

* **off,** *a.*, *adv.*, and *prep.*

1. *a.* Of a horse or athlete: Not up to his usual form. Also **off form,** *ellipt.* for *off in form*.

1846 *Spirit of Times* 18 April 91/1 He had endurance and speed enough to make a good race in any crowd, when 'all right,' but then, he [the horse] was liable to be oftener 'off' than otherwise. **1868** WOODRUFF *Trotting Horse* 300 It is assumed, not that the loser was 'off,' but that the winner is greatly superior. **1912** MATHEWSON *Pitching* 142 The Chicago pitchers were away off form in the series.

b. In combs.: (1) ***off color,** *a.* of questionable taste, risqué; (2) **market,** (see quot. 1870); (3) ***ox,** a stubborn, clumsy, unmanageable person, *colloq.;* (4) ***side,** the wrong or difficult side; (5) **year,** see as a main entry.

(1) 1875 HOLLAND *Sevenoaks* ix. 114 Everybody invited her, and yet everybody, without any definite reason, considered her a little 'off color.' **1932** *K.C. Times* 25 March 21 It seemed a bit strange for a minister to be so devoted a reader of such a (then) decidedly off-color publication. — **(2) 1870** MEDBERY *Men Wall St.* 137 An 'off' market, is where prices have fallen either in a week, a day, or even an afternoon. **1885** *Harper's Mag.* Nov. 842/1 He rejoices in an 'off' market when prices fall. **1900** NELSON *A B C Wall St.* 154. — **(3) 1848** LOWELL *Biglow P.* 1 Ser. 90 Ez to the answerin' o' questions, I'm an off ox at bein' druv. **1903** *D.N.* II. 352 off ox, n. One who is usually on the opposite side of a popular movement. — **(4) 1870** F. FERN *Ginger-Snaps* 299 The offside of a question has such an unconquerable attraction for him. **1901** JEWETT *Tory Lover* xii, There was some o' them fools that likes to be on the offside that went an' upheld him.

2. ***offset,** a mountain terrace.

1856 *Spirit of Times* 18 Oct. 106/3 Daguerrotyped upon the heart [are] . . . the hearth stone, garden, 'offsets,' orchard, green swells and hollows, mosses, old pines, and a thousand delicious memories that swarm before us now. **1873** BEADLE *Undevel. West* 284 We . . . now must make a wide detour to scale the cliff, or first offset, which frowns two thousand feet above us.

b. A stepwise or terraced excavation for extracting ore.

1872 *Vt. Bd. Agric. Rep.* I. 627 It consists in taking out the ore in successive offsets or stopes.

c. A fence built at right angles to a main fence.

1903 A. ADAMS *Log Cowboy* 54 The cattle . . . after following down the fence several miles had encountered an offset, and the angle had half the squad.

3. *prep.* In combs.: (1) **off-center,** out of alignment, "out of step"; (2) ***hand,** see as a main entry; (3) **islander,** a name given by Nantucketers to a person not born on Nantucket Island, Massachusetts.

(1) 1932 *K.C. Times* 30 May 12 This dear old country of ours can't be so terribly off center. — **(3) 1883** J. G. AUSTIN *(title)*, Nantucket Scrapes: being the experiences of an off-islander, in season and out of season, among a passing people. **1939** CHAMBERLAIN *Nantucket* 4 Artists and summer visitors have discovered its allure, and many fortunate 'off islanders' now live in old Nantucket houses.

As the last term in **bid, bite, block, blow, check, cut, force, jump-, lay, rake-, run, stand, stirring, sugaring, swear, throw, tip, turn, way off.**

***offense,** *n.* As the last term in **federal, penitentiary offense.**

***offer,** *v.* **1.** *intr.* To stand as a candidate for office. *Colloq.* **2.** *To offer one's vote,* to present oneself as a potential voter. *Obs.*

(1) 1803 *Steele P.* I. 405 The Gentlemen who prevailed upon me 'to offer' as they call it, consisted principally of the moderate men of both parties. **1835** LONGSTREET *Ga. Scenes* 234 Then lowering his voice to a confidential but distinctly audible tone, 'what you offering for?' continued he. — **(2) 1821** *Const. N.Y. of 10 Nov.* Art. II. § 1, And for the last year, a resident in the town or country, where he may offer his vote . . . shall be entitled to vote.

***offering,** *n.* **1.** Something offered for sale. **2. offering book,** a book in which a record is made of notes, bonds, etc., presented at a bank as a security or for discount. *Obs.*

(1) 1903 *Boston Ev. Transcript* 29 Aug., On Saturday next the Transcript will print an unusually attractive line of real estate offerings. — **(2) 1811** *Steele P.* II. 658 In short this is intended to furnish as a day book all the results which do not and cannot appear on the face of the offering book. **1858** J. S. GIBBONS *Banks of New-York* 29 No objection is made [to discounting someone's note], and the President scores opposite to it, on the Offering Book, the letter A—which means, *accepted.*

***offhand,** *a.* **1.** Of firing a gun: Without a rest or support; fired without a rest. Also as *adv.* **2. offhand ox,** the off ox. *Rare.*

(1) 1833 in *Amer. Sp.* XXIV. (1949) 150/2 Forty yards off-hand, or sixty yards with a rest, is the distance generally chosen for a shooting match. **1856** R. GLISAN *Jrnl. Army Life* (1874) 328, I surprised everybody by killing the duck at an off-hand shot. **1899** GREEN *Va. Word-Book.* 259 Off hand, *adv.* . . . From the hand; without the support of a rest. — **(2) 1845** F. DOUGLASS *Narrative* 58 He told me which was the in-hand ox, and which the off-hand one.

***office,** *n.*

1. A barroom, also a bar. *Facetious. Obs.*

1842 *Knickerb.* XX. 571 He ushered me into the bar-room—I beg pardon, into the office. **1855** HOLBROOK *Among Mail Bags* 62 We went up to what was then the bar, but in these temperance times would be called the 'office.'

2. The reception desk of a hotel.

1849 E. DAVIS *Amer. Scenes* 16 The waiter stared, and said he had none to take us to, except I would first go to the 'office' [the clerk's desk in a hotel]. **1863** RUSSELL *Diary* I. 16 At the 'office' of the hotel, as it is styled, there is a tray of blank cards and a big pencil, whereby the cardless man who is visiting is enabled to send you his name and title.

3. The business quarters of professional men, as dentists, lawyers, etc.

1856 FERGUSSON *America* 13 We . . . found him in his consulting-room, or 'office,' as physicians' and surgeons' consulting-rooms are always called in the States. **1864** NICHOLS *Amer. Life* I. 344 While in the office, as the American lawyer's chambers are called, a younger brother and partner told me they had a third brother. **1945** MENCKEN *Supp.* I. 503 An English lawyer, whether *barrister* or *solicitor,* never has an office, but always *chambers.*

b. The office of an executive in a college or school. Also transf.

1897 FLANDRAU *Harvard Episodes* 278 He would be upheld . . . if he gave Prescott an E. and brought the heavy hand of the Office down on him. **1902** G. M. MARTIN *Emmy Lou* 102 One day Miss Jenny was sent for. When one was sent for, one went to the office.

4. In combs.: (1) **office-beggar,** a person who asks to be appointed to a political office; (2) **building,** a building in which rooms are rented out as offices, also a building used as an office; (3) **chair,** a chair of a type usu. found in the office of a doctor, lawyer, etc.; (4) **force,** a group of workers in an office; (5) **name,** pen name; (6) **patient,** a patient who visits a physician at his office or consulting room; (7) **relation,** a relation existing by virtue of an office held, as by a minister or a teacher, *obs.*

(1) 1857 *Lawrence* (Kans.) *Republican* 2 July 2 How does it come that he can select no person for the office in Kansas but hungry office-beggars. **1882** *Nation* 9 Nov. 401/1 The abominable system which has converted our Government . . . into a mere machine for the use and the abuse of a horde of loaferish and hungry office-beggars — **(2) 1840** *Niles' Reg.* 23 May 182/1 The Free Trader office building has been crushed in and much shattered. **1913** *Outing* Jan. 479/1 In a Chicago office building devoted almost entirely to physicians' offices there is a group of doctors who, when they meet, seldom speak of anything except the woods. — **(3) 1901** MERWIN-WEBSTER *Calumet 'K'* xiii. 247 Bannon was sitting in the office chair with his feet on the draughting-table. **1910** *Sat. Ev. Post* 2 July 18/3 You have no idea what warlike sentiments I cautiously entertain in my office-chair. — **(4) 1900** SAVAGE *Midnight Passenger* 7 Certain gray-bearded bookkeepers, a couple of brisk stenographers [etc.] . . . were the office force besides the travelling manager. **1900** *Cong. Rec.* 17 Feb. 1903/2 A gentleman . . . has had an insufficient office force and has by reason of that fact been compelled to do more.

(5) 1928 *Sat. Ev. Post* 12 May 36/3 At least eight different writers . . . had been offering their comments under that name [=Richard Roe]—'office names' they are called in the profession. — **(6) 1897** STUART *Simpkinsville* 94 Even the doctors, . . . are wont to receive their 'office patients' in this comfortable fashion. — **(7) 1670** I. MATHER *Life R. Mather* 74 For some years after his accepting Office-Relation in Dorchester, he was in much Spiritual distress by reason of uncertainties concerning his own Eternal estate. **1742** in PEIRCE *Hist. Harvard* App. 86 [The] Overseers of Harvard College did . . . vote the removal of Mr. Nathan Prince (one of the Fellows and Tutors of said College) from all office-relation thereto.

As the last term in **accounting, agency, appointment, appointments, assay, business, central, employment, express, flag, forwarding, front, government, hotel, Hydrographic, Indian, intelligence, land, law, loan, log house, open, package, pension, post, presidential, rat, real-estate, signal, state, state land, ticket, tithing, war office.**

***office,** *v. intr.* To keep one's office or offices in a certain place. *Rare.* — **1891** *Nation* LIV. 303/2 An attorney officing in the same building.

***officer,** *n.* **1. officer bird,** the red-winged blackbird, *Agelaius phoeniceus.* **2. officer tree,** a saddletree designed for a cavalry officer. *Obs.* — **(1) 1902** CLAPIN 292 Officer-bird. A common name, especially in Canada and the Northern States, for the red-winged starling

(*Agelæus phœniceus.*) — (2) **1894** *Harper's Mag.* Feb. 350/1, I carefully adjusted my Whitman's officer-tree over a wealth of saddle blanketing.

As the last term in **accounting, county, depot, doughboy, executive, federal, general, health, land, line, loan, naval, probation, salary, special enforcement, stamp, steerage, truant officer.**

official family. The President's cabinet. — **1903** W.E. CURTIS *True A. Lincoln* 193 It was perfectly natural for the President to select a member of his official family from a State of such importance.

*__officiary,__ *n.* A body of officials. — **1888** *Voice* 5 April, It would be next to impossible . . . to get a city officiary in sympathy with the law. **1889** *Christian Union* 10 Jan., The virtual contract between officiary and pewholder.

off year. In politics, an election year in which a President is not elected. Also attrib.

1882 *Cong. Rec.* 14 Dec. 277/2 It is true this was in the off year, and not the Presidential year. **1906** *N.Y. Ev. Post* 5 Nov. 4 It would be contrary to all precedent if, in this off-year election, the party in power did not suffer a considerable diminution in its strength. **1949** *Time* 10 Oct. 24/3 He went on to lay down a proposition that would be heard again & again in the off-year election campaign.

b. A year when fruits, etc., are not so good as usual.

1898 WILKINS *People of Our Neighborhood* (1901) 105 All the orchards yielded . . . little fruit, for it was an unusually 'off year.'

O. F. M. An abbreviation of "Our First Men." *Obs.* — **1840** HALIBURTON *Clockmaker* 3 Ser. x, Jeremiah Sterling . . . is an O.F.M. as we call Our First Men among us. **1847** *Knickerb.* XXIX. 279 Here comes one of 'O.F.M.'

Ogallala ˌogəˈlɑlə, *n.* [Var. of Oglala *q.v.*, but as here used no doubt f. *Ogallala*, Neb., which is underlain by this formation.] *Geol.* A late Tertiary formation found in Nebraska and adjacent states. In full **Ogallala formation.**

1899 DARTON *Prelim. Rep. Geol. & Ground Waters Neb.* 734 Extending from Kansas and Colorado far into Nebraska there is a calcareous formation of late Tertiary age to which I wish to apply the distinctive name *Ogallala formation.* **1903** *Rep. State Geol. Neb.* I. 163 Just how far east one can trace the Ogallala is not safe to assert until the stratigraphy of the state can be studied more in detail. **1947** *Geol. Survey Kans. Bul.* 66, 24 The other principle mineral resources in Scott County are . . . the deposits of caliche near the top of the Ogallala formation.

Ogeechee lime. [*Ogeechee* River in Ga.] A southern species of tupelo, *Nyssa ogeche;* the acid fruit of a tree of this species. Also **Ogeechee tupelo.** Also attrib.

1785 MARSHALL *Amer. Grove* 97 The Ogeche Lime Tree. . . . The fruit is nearly oval, of a deep red colour of the size of a Damascene Plumb. **1821** NUTTALL *Travels Arkansa* 71 In this swamp, I also observed the *Nyssa aquatica, N. pubescens* (Ogechee lime, the fruit being prepared as a conserve). **1949** COLLINGWOOD & BRUSH *Knowing Your Trees* 251 Swamp (black) tupelo (*Nyssa sylvatica* variety *biflora*) and ogeechee tupelo (*Nyssa ogeche*) are of much less importance.

b. *pl.* The preserves made from the fruit of this tree.

1890 *Cent.* 3457/1 Its large acid fruit is made into a conserve called Ogeechee limes.

Oglala ogˈlɑlə, *n.* Also **Ogallallah, Oglalla.** [f. a native name or word said to mean "to scatter one's own."]

1. *pl.* =**Oglala Sioux.**

1838 PARKER *Exploring Tour* 63 They were Ogallallahs, headed by eight of their chiefs. **1847** PARKMAN in *Knickerb.* XXX. 484 Such a pipe among the Ogallallahs is valued at the price of a horse. **1867** *Harper's Wkly.* 5 Oct. 629/2 The Commission . . . on August 19 held a council on the steamer, at Fort Thompson, with the head chiefs of the Oglallas. **1898** KING *Warrior Gap* 30 He long had had influence with the Ogallallas. **1947** DEVOTO *Across Wide Missouri* 123 When Sublette & Campbell brought the Oglalas to the Platte in 1834 . . . a pressure began which by 1860 forced the Crows back as far as Powder River.

attrib. **1837** *Missionary Herald* XXXIII. 369/2 Came to the village of the Ogallallah Indians, consisting of more than two thousand persons. **1898** KING *Warrior Gap* 31 With him rode Baptiste, a half-breed Frenchman whose mother was an Ogallalla squaw. **1921** HEBERT *40 Yrs. Prospecting* 6 It was there that I saw Pawnee Killer, a big Ogalala Chief.

2. Oglala Sioux, the Indians making up the chief division of the Teton Sioux, found by Lewis and Clark on the Missouri River in the present South Dakota.

1857 *Spirit of Times* 21 Mar. 34/1 They proved to be a hunting-party of Ogallallah Sioux. **1879** WILLIAMS *Pacific Tourist* 47/1 Red Cloud is chief of the Ogalalla Sioux. **1947** DEVOTO *Across Wide Missouri* 191 Fort Laramie . . . would draw all the wandering trappers, . . . the Oglala Sioux, and finally the United States Army.

ogling glass. A monocle. *Humorous. Rare.* — **1843** *Knickerb.* XXII. 111 There he was promenading, . . . an ogling-glass lifted to his eye.

O-grab-me. [*Embargo* spelled backwards.] A facetious name applied to the embargo acts of 1807 and following years. Also attrib. Now *hist.*

1808 *Balance* 7 June 92 (Th.), As soon as O grab me! shall let go his end, I'll haste to relate the sweet tidings to you. **1810** LAMBERT *Travels* II. 506, I guess I shall soon be on the opposite side of the Line, in spite of their ograb-me laws. **1858** *S. Lit. Messenger* XXVII. 466/1 The war of 1812, and the famous 'O-Grab-Me,' as the wags of that day ana-grammatized the embargo measures of Mr. Madison.

Ohian oˈhaɪən, *n.* =**Ohioan.**

1819 in J. FLINT *Lett. from Amer.* 128 The Ohian is in many cases growing up to manhood. **1836** C. R. GILMAN *Life on Lakes* 54 (*footnote*), I use this word [Ohian] out of respect for Mr. Senator Ewing of Ohio, with whom, I believe, it originated. . . . He himself is the very man of all the world who should be called Buck Eye and not Ohian. **1944** *Chi. D. News* 29 June 1/3 Dewey said he had a long talk with the Ohian at breakfast.

Ohio oˈhaɪo, *n.* [Poss. f. Iroquois *Oheo*, "beautiful."] The name of a river, of a region, and of a state. In combs., now obs.: (1) **Ohio boat,** a flat-bottomed river boat used on the Ohio; (2) **boatman,** a boatman on the Ohio River; (3) **Company,** see as a main entry; (4) **fever,** a desire to move west to Ohio; (5) **grant,** a grant of land west of the Alleghany Mountains originally made over to the British Crown by the Six Nations in 1768, but purchased in 1773 by the Grand Ohio Company, a rival of the early Ohio Company; (6) **idea,** see as a main entry; (7) **land,** land held by the Ohio Company (sense **2.**); (8) **purchase,** =prec.

(1) **1852** STOWE *Uncle Tom* xii, A few days saw Haley, with his possessions, safely deposited on one of the Ohio boats. — (2) **1820** J. HALL *Lett. from West* 47 Eight or ten of those 'half horse and half alligator' gentry, commonly called Ohio boatmen. — (4) **1832** WILLIAMSON *Maine* II. 664 Another subject, already more essentially interesting to the prosperity of Maine, was the infatuating spirit of emigration to the western States—tauntingly denominated the 'Ohio fever.' **1835** *Knickerb.* V. 274 Such of them as some fifteen years since happened to reside in any part of New-England where what was called the 'Ohio fever' prevailed. **1904** in THWAITE *Travels* VIII. 57 (*footnote*), The 'Ohio fever' became a well known expression for this desire to move West.

(5) **1774** T. HUTCHINSON *Diary & Lett.* I. 185 He told me a final stop was put to the Ohio Grant. **1775** *Ib.* 421 The Tho. Walpole concerned in the Ohio Grant, I saw the first time. — (7) **1788** *Mass. Spy* 20 Nov. 3/4 Ohio Land. Two shares in the Ohio Company, containing 3000 acres, to be sold, or exchanged. — (8) **1788** *Mass. Spy* 3 April 2/4 Several families from the State of Massachusetts are already on their way to the Ohio purchase.

b. Used locally in the names of fishes, as **Ohio gold herring, gold shad, pike, redeye, salmon, shad, toter,** (see quots.).

1820 *Western Rev.* 54 Ohio Red-eye, *Aplocentrus calliops. Ib* 17 Ohio Goldshad. . . . Its vulgar names are Ohio Shad, Gold Shad, Green Herring, &c. *Ib.* 173 Ohio Gold Herring. *Notemigonus auratus.* . . . Not uncommon in the Ohio, Kentucky, Miami, &c. *Ib.* 362 Ohio Toter, *Hypentelium macropterum.* **1856** *Porter's Spirit of Times* 40/3 The Pike-perch, *Lucioperva americana*, variously known as the Glass-Eye, the Ohio Pike, the Yellow Pike, and possibly also, as the Ohio salmon. **1883** *Nat. Museum Bul.* No. 27, 455 *Clupea chrysochloris* . . . Ohio shad. **1902** *Rep. Comm. Fisheries* XXVII. 277 It at once became evident that the Ohio shad was an undescribed species.

c. In the names of things produced in Ohio, as **Ohio apple cider, flour, ham, paint, red, sandstone, whisky, wine.**

1832 *Louisville Pub. Advt.* 3 March, 350 barrels fresh Ohio Flour . . . for sale. **1835** HOFFMAN *Winter in West* I. 245 The frontiersman knocking the ashes from his tomahawk-pipe, passed me a flask of Ohio whiskey. **1852** TREMENHEERE *Notes* 159 We are now shipping 'Ohio red' [wheat] from Cleveland to New York at 65 to 67 cents the lowest prices we have known for some time. **1853** FOWLER *Home for All* 148 My material was composed of one part Blake's black Ohio paint, to six parts fine beach sand. **1855** BAXTER *America* 42 On the Atlantic seaboard, as well as in the Mississippian valley, American steamers occasionally race, when tarred-wood, lard-barrels, Ohio hams, or any other combustible material which may be at hand is thrown into the fires. **1864** *Ohio Agric. Rep.* XVIII. 25 A premium of $20 shall be offered for the best three samples of pure Ohio wine, made from the Catawba, Virginia Seedling or Delaware grape. **1865** *Chi. Tribune* 10 April 1 Pure Ohio Apple Cider . . . for sale. **1881** *Harper's Mag.* April 711/1 Lime stone . . . and gray Ohio sandstone are much used in construction.

d. In the names of fruits and plants, as **Ohio beauty, bluebell, ever-bearing raspberry, wallflower.**

1819 *Western Rev.* I. 93 The trees and plants peculiar to this region and giving a decided character to its vegetation: *Platanus occidentalis*, Sycamore or Button wood, *Hesperis pinnatifida*, Ohio Wall Flower [etc.]. **1842** KIRKLAND *Forest Life* II. 142 A beautiful perennial here [in Mich.] called the Ohio bluebell, a far larger plant than the one we know by that name. **1862** *Rep. Comm. Patents 1861: Agric.* 166 The Ohio ever-bearing raspberry is not the only one . . . to produce an autumnal crop of fruit; the same tendency is often observed in . . . [the] Black-cap. **1868** *Rep. Comm. Agric. 1867* 136 Ohio Beauty [a variety of cherry]. . . . Size, large; form, round, obtuse heart-shaped, sometimes nearly round.

Esp. **Ohio buckeye,** the common buckeye, *Aesculus glabra.*

1810 MICHAUX *Arbres* I. 38 Esculus ohioensis, *Ohio buck eye . . .'* nom donné par moi. **1832** BROWNE *Sylva* 227 We have denominated it Ohio Buckeye, because it is most abundant on the banks of this river. **1901** MOHR *Plant Life Ala.* 46 The characteristic trees [of Alabama include] . . . *Diospyros virginica* (persimmon), *Aesculus octandra* (Ohio buckeye) [etc.]. **1948** *Chi. Sun-Times* 20 April 32/2 The Ohio buckeye . . . is the first of all the big trees to burst forth with leaves.

Ohioan oˈhaɪəwən, *n.* A native or resident of Ohio.

1817 FORDHAM *Narr.* 165, I do not choose the risk of being insulted by any vulgar Ohioans. **1884** *N.Y. Wkly. Tribune* 13 Aug. 4/2 It was rather a matter of pride in Ohioans to send their sons there. **1949** *N. Eng. Quart.* June 207 Even more surprising, however, was the interest of the Ohioan, . . . William Henry Harrison.

b. Also **Ohiohian.** *Rare.*

1832 FERRALL *Ramble through U.S.* 68 Close by the granary, on which the young 'Ohiohians' and 'buck-eyes'—the lasses of Ohio are called 'buck-eyes'—seated themselves in pairs.

Ohio Company.

1. A land company controlled by Virginians, formed to colonize a tract of land south of the Ohio River granted to them by George II in 1749. *Obs.*

1748 in K. P. BAILEY *Ohio Company of Va.* 298 Petition of John Hanbury to the King on behalf of the Ohio Company, 1748. **1831** WITHERS *Chron. Border Warfare* 52 England gave to an association of gentlemen in Great Britain and Virginia, (under the title of the Ohio Company,) liberty to locate and hold in their own right, 600,000 acres of land within the country then claimed by both England and France.

2. A land company formed in 1786 for the purchase and colonization of a tract of land between the Ohio River and Lake Erie. *Obs.*

1787 CUTLER in *Life & Corr.* I. 204 Settled the principles on which I am to contract with Congress for lands on account of the Ohio Company. **1792** in *Ib.* I. 475 The Ohio Company . . . opened the sale of lands in the Western Territory by becoming the first purchasers of any considerable tract. **1876** *N. Amer. Review* April 256 No part of the state would suffer so much as Mr. Dane's own Essex District, where the shareholders of the Ohio Company chiefly resided.

Ohio idea. A scheme sponsored by Ohio Democrats between 1868 and 1876 whereby U.S. notes and bonds would be paid off with greenbacks. Also transf. *Obs.*

1880 in S. LEAVITT *Our Money Wars* (1894) 244 The defeat of Ewing will finally dispose of the Ohio Idea. **1881** *Cong. Rec.* 13 April 276/2 The Ohio idea is the absolute equality of all men before the law. **1886** POORE *Reminiscences* II. 349 Mrs. Hayes brought with her from her rural home what was known as 'the Ohio idea' of total abstinence from intoxicating drinks, and she enforced it at the White House.

Ohion oˈhaɪən, *n.* =**Ohioan.** *Rare.* — **1837** PECK *New Guide* 226 The shades of character will become blended, and the next generation will be Ohions, or to use their own native cognomen, Buckeyes.

Ohionian oˌhaɪˈonɪən, *n.* =**Ohioan.** *Rare.* — **1817** S. BROWN *Western Gazetteer* 148 Here [in New Orleans] in half an hour you can see . . . Kentuckians, Tennesseans, Ohionians, Pennsylvanians [etc.].

Ohiote oˈhaɪot, *n.* =**Ohioan.** *Rare.* — **1837** *N.Y. Mirror* 1 July 7/3 The Kentuckians and Ohiotes may praise the beauty of their women.

Oidonia ɔɪˈdonɪə, *n.* [Origin unknown.] (See quot.) *Rare.* — **1750** J. BIRKET *Cursory Remarks* 10 The wine most commonly Drunk here [in Portsmouth, N.H.] is from the Canaries & Western Islands—called Oidonia, tis of a pale collr. tasts harsh and is inclined to look thick.

* **oikology,** *n.* Also **oekology.** =**domestic science.** *Obs.*

1892 *Columbus* (O.) *Dispatch* 8 Dec., The latest Boston Science is oekology. **1896** *Advance* 23 Jan. 128/3 The chair of paidology and perhaps oikology will soon be founded in our universities. **1898** *Pop. Sci. Mo.* LII. 534 *Oikology* . . . includes also family life or homekeeping.

* **oil,** *n.*

1. Money. *Slang.*

1903 A. H. LEWIS *Boss* 121 The sooner we get th' oil, th' sooner we'll begin to light up.

2. In combs.: (1) * **oil-bearing,** *a.* of certain subterranean soils or rocks, or the region in which they are found, productive of mineral oil; (2) **belt,** a stretch of country yielding oil; (3) **Bowl,** the stadium at Rice Institute; (4) **business,** the business of producing and marketing petroleum; (5) **derrick,** a derrick over an oil well; (6) **exchange,** an exchange where petroleum securities are bought and sold; (7) **factory,** a factory where oil is extracted from animal or vegetable substances, esp. from whales and fish; (8) **house,** (*a*) a shed or a building where oil is extracted from whales or fish and stored, (*b*) a storehouse for storing oil; (9) **nut,** see as a main entry; (10) **sand,** a porous sand from which petroleum is obtained by drilling; (11) **well,** a well drilled for oil or petroleum, a well that produces oil, also attrib.

(**1**) **1863** *Jrnl. Franklin Inst.* April 271 The out-croppings of the limestone members of the Oil-Bearing Strata are quarried at points along the 'Philadelphia and Erie Railroad.' **1865** *3 Yrs. Among Working Classes* 197 The oil-bearing districts of the United States, although of vast value [etc.]. **1945** *Elk Mt. Pilot* (Crested Butte, Colo.) 19 July 4/6 The Weber oil bearing sandstone is encountered at depths of about 5700 to 5900 feet below surface in the Rangely district. — (**2**) **1865** *Harper's Mag.* April 563/2 The Canadian wells now flowing hundreds of barrels of oil are located on the borders of Lake Erie, far to the west of the so-called oil belt. **1894** *Cong. Rec.* 31 Jan. 1743/2 The great oil belt in this country commencing in New York, running through Pennsylvania, West Virginia, Ohio, and Kentucky, has its beginning in my district. — (**3**) **1944** *Chi. D. News* 8 Dec. 31/2 The station football team had received an official invitation to play in the Oil Bowl game at Houston. — (**4**) **1883** *Cent. Mag.* July 324/2 In the early days of the oil business, all wells were sunk in valleys. **1949** *Oil Marketer* 24 Oct. 7/1 Let us not forget that the Labor-Socialist government of Great Britain . . . is directly in the oil business.

(**5**) **1863** *Boston Herald* 16 Aug. 3/3 (Ernst), You see, in close proximity on every side, oil depots, oil refineries, oil derricks. **1948** *Ada* (Okla.) *Ev. News* 2 July 1/3 The work scheduled for Friday called for the shooting of scenes at the oil derrick. — (**6**) **1883** *Cent. Mag.* July 337/2 The oil exchanges at Bradford and Oil City are noisy and animated places. **1904** TARBELL *Hist. Standard Oil Co.* I. 95 The Oil Exchange passed votes of censure, and the Producers' Union turned them [oil brokers] out. — (**7**) **1841** *Niles' Reg.* 9 Oct. 96/1 The oil factory of the Staten Island Whaling company was burnt . . . with $30,000 worth of oil. **1914** STEELE *Storm* 81 I looked away at the dock and the oil-factory, black, desolate, dusty. — (**8**) (*a*) **1678** *N.H. Probate Rec.* I. 211, I doe give unto my Son . . . my storehouse, oyle house. (*b*) **1877** E. MARTIN *Hist. Great Riots* 108 The railroad buildings were destroyed as follows: Two round houses, . . . three or four oil houses.

(**10**) **1883** *Cent. Mag.* July 330/1 When the oil-sand is struck, the oil, mingled with gas, spurts up with great force. **1900** *Everybody's Mag.* July 78/2 There are several strata of this oil sand. **1945** *Elk Mt. Pilot* (Crested Butte, Colo.) 19 July 4/6 Early predictions that the deep oil sand at Rangeley would place the field in the category of 'major' fields are being confirmed almost daily. — (**11**) **1847** COLLINS *Kentucky* 249 The American Oil well is situated three miles above Burksville, on the bank of the Cumberland river. **1888** *Amer. Almanac* 275 Occupations of the People of the United States. . . . Oil-well operators and laborers, . . . Organ-makers. **1949** *Nat. Geog. Mag.* June 775/2 By flew . . . the oil wells of Oklahoma City.

b. In combs. in which the meaning is obvious or sufficiently explained in the quots.: (1) **oil boom,** (2) **bubble,** (3) **car,** (4) **company,** (5) **district,** (6) **drill,** (7) **fever,** (8) **field,** (9) **land,** (10) **lead,** (11) **prospector,** (12) **region,** (13) **share,** (14) **shark,** (15) **speculation,** (16) **spring,** (17) **stone,** (18) **stratum,** (19) **strike,** (20) **territory,** (21) **torpedo,** (22) **train,** (23) **wagon.**

(**1**) **1907** *St. Nicholas* June 718/1 Enterprise had been threatened with an 'oil boom.' **1949** *Dly. Oklahoman* (Okla. City) 16 Jan. 1/3 The conductor of the old train in the heydey of the Carter county oil boom . . . thought he was losing business if he didn't haul several corpses back to Ardmore. — (**2**) **1865** *Harper's Mag.* April 567/2 The entire oil regions . . . were consequently nearly deserted, and the then so-called 'oil bubble' exploded. — (**3**) **1876** INGRAM *Centennial Exp.* 336

The oil . . . was loaded by gravity upon oil cars. **1890** *Railways of Amer.* 146 It would require a separate article to give even a brief description of the different kinds of cars which are now used. . . . Mail-car, Milk-car, Oil-car. — **(4) 1865** *Harper's Mag.* April 565/1 The oil produced from the oil-springs . . . suggested the formation of an oil company in 1854. **1949** *Petroleum World* Sep. 28/1 The increasing number of 'farm-outs' of oil leases by major oil companies to smaller outfits is believed . . . to reflect a more careful attitude . . . on production outlays.

(5) 1862 *Scientific Amer.* 22 Feb. 122/1 This oil district [in Pa.] is peculiar in many respects. **1888** LINDLEY *Calif. of South* 339 Another oil-district was opened in the southern part of the county of Los Angeles in 1881. — **(6) 1867** *Rep. Comm. Patents 1865* II. 681 Oil drill, . . . a drilling apparatus which will remove broken and pulverized rock from the bore of a well, etc. — **(7) 1862** *Scientific Amer.* 22 Feb. 122/1 An 'oil fever' affected the community [in western Pa.]. **1890** *Harper's Mag.* Oct. 728/2 All the phenomena of the oil fever, which were repeated at so many centres of excitement, were here first inaugurated. — **(8) 1899** TARKINGTON *Gent. from Ind.* xviii, The 'Herald' boomed the oil-field. **1949** *Time* 21 Mar. 81/1 Oil field gumbo is a real test for a truck. — **(9) 1865** *Harper's Mag.* April 573/1 New oil lands have recently been discovered in Adams and Scioto counties. **1947** *Steamboat* (Colo.) *Pilot* 2 Jan. 2/6 Get an appraisal of the oil lands in that county.

Oil wagon *c*1900

(10) 1885 *Wkly. New Mexican Rev.* 16 April 3/5 An old Pennsylvania oil prospector had located a spring which bore every indication that the flow of water came from the vicinity of an oil lead. — **(11) 1910** *Sat. Ev. Post* 24 Sep. 73 Lured by the honey of high prices, the ant army of oil prospectors once more swarmed over the barren slopes. — **(12) 1862** *Prelim. Rep. 8th Census* 72 The Pennsylvania oil region . . . has thus far been the principal source [of petroleum]. **1868** J. D. WHITNEY *Life & Lett.* 265, I got them to make a topographical survey of the oil region. **1904** TARBELL *Hist. Standard Oil Co.* I. 3 A strip of Northwestern Pennsylvania, not over fifty miles long, [is] known the world over as the Oil Regions. — **(13) 1909** A. C. RICE *Mr. Opp* 269 What did you go and buy Widow Green's oil-shares back for? — **(14) 1883** *Nat. Museum Bul.* No. 27, 420 The oil shark is valued for the oil in its liver. **1896** JORDAN & EVERMANN *Check-List Fishes* 215 *Galeorhinus zyopterus*. . . . Oil Shark; Soup-fin Shark. Coast of southern California. **1949** *Fishes Western N. Atlantic* I. 72 This increase has resulted from the oil of one vitamin-rich species, the Soupfin or Oil Shark (*Galeorhinus galeus*).

(15) 1865 *Atlantic Mo.* XV. 392/2 In the beginning of the oil speculation . . . [many of the land owners] sold out at moderate prices to shrewd adventurers. — **(16) 1765** ROGERS *Acct. N. Amer.* 177 About 150 miles up this river [in N.Y.], are those remarkable springs, greatly esteemed by the Indians as a remedy for almost every disease; they are called the oil-springs. **1847** COLLINS *Kentucky* 540 A tar or American oil spring, from which tar or oil constantly flows, in considerable quantities. **1890** *Harper's Mag.* Oct. 724/1 Oil springs were known near the present town of Cuba [N.Y.]. — **(17) 1799** J. SMITH *Acct. Captivity* 38, I asked [him], what was the use of the beaver's stones, or glands, to them;—as the she beaver has two pair, which is commonly called the oil stones, and the bark stones? **1806** LEWIS in *L. & Clark Exped.* III. (1905) 319 The male beaver has six stones, two [of] which . . . resemble small bladders, contain a pure oil of a strong rank disagreeable smell, and not unlike train oil, these are called the oil stones. — **(18) 1883** *Cent. Mag.* July 324/1 The oil stratum lies on a level. — **(19) 1864** *Harper's Mag.* Dec. 59/2 It is certain that great oil-strikes are no longer looked for. **1949** *Ward Co. Independent* (Minot, N.D.) 21 July 1/1 Broker writes from Toronto and offers us a chance to get in on the big Redwater field oil strike in Alberta.

(20) 1865 *Chi. Tribune* 15 April 1 The subscriber has secured a very advantageous lease of oil territory adjoining a large oil well. **1898** WESTCOTT *D. Harum* 301 That section of country . . . wa'n't in the oil territory them days, or wa'n't known to be, anyway. — **(21) 1901** *Cosmopolitan* July 252/2 The oil torpedo was invented by Col. E. A. L. Roberts. . . . The first trial . . . was in the Ladies' Well, near Titusville, Pennsylvania, where on January 21, 1865, he dropped two torpedoes. — **(22) 1877** E. MARTIN *Hist. Great Riots* 143 The railroad authorities took the first opportunity to move an oil train which was standing near the depot. — **(23) 1945** *Life* 30 April 8 The oil wagon was used in the early 1900s to carry lubricating oil and kerosene for lamps, later carried gasoline for the horseless carriage. **1948** RITTENHOUSE *Vehicles* 76 Oil Wagon. This battered, workaday example of a tank-wagon indicates how oil was transported in early days. . . . Manufacturers . . . utilized any suitable, sturdy wagon gear and built the tank to fit the user's specifications.

Also *oil city, country, gusher, king, line, man, pipe, pool, state, stock, town*, etc.

For *to strike oil*, see ***strike**, *v.*

As the last term in **acorn, American, bear's, British, coal, cottonseed, Genesee, hammer, hickory, kerosene, mission, oleo, peanut, raccoon, rattlesnake, Seneca, Seneca Indian, soap, spring, sunflower oil.**

oildom ˈɔɪldəm, *n.* The world that is interested in the production and marketing of petroleum (see also quot. *c*1870). — ***c*1870** CHIPMAN *Notes on Bartlett* 301 *Oildom*. The Petrolean manufactures; the oil or petroleum part of Pa. **1904** TARBELL *Hist. Standard Oil Co.* I. 71 The rise [in freight rates] which had been threatening had come. . . . At the news all oildom rushed into the streets.

***oiled,** *a.* Inebriated. *Slang.* — **1737** *Pa. Gazette* 13 Jan. 2 He's Oil'd. **1924** P. MARKS *Plastic Age* 252 It was soon apparent that some of the couples had got at least half 'oiled' before the dance began.

***oiler,** *n.* **1.** A well that brings in oil, as opposed to one that brings in gas. **2.** A Mexican. *Slang.* Cf. **greaser.**

(1) 1890 *Columbus* (O.) *Dispatch* 24 May, The Ohio Oil Co. . . . drilled in an oiler . . . that will be the largest one in this field. **1950** *Dly. Ardmoreite* (Ardmore, Okla.) 17 Feb. 1/6 (*heading*,) Lone Grove Oiler Shows Good Signs. — **(2) 1907** S. E. WHITE *Arizona Nights* I. iv. 82 A few oilers livin' near had water holes in the foothills. *Ib.* III. ii. 282 We're livin' like a lot of Oilers.

oil nut.

1. The butternut or white walnut, *Juglans cinerea*. In full **oil nut tree.**

1694 *Topsfield Rec.* 86 From thence on a straight line to an oylenut tree which is Isaac Burtons tree marked. **1778** CARVER *Travels* 500 The Butter or Oilnut. . . . The tree grows in meadows, where the soil is rich and warm. **1829** GREENLEAF *Survey of Me.* 111 Juglans Cathartica.—(Oilnut, Butternut)—On rich alluvial lands—abounds on the Kenebeck. **1916** SETON *Woodcraft Man.* 275 White Walnut, Oil Nut, or Butternut (*Juglans cinerea*).

2. The buffalo nut, *Pyrularia pubera*.

1813 MUHLENBERG *Cat. Plants* 96 Oil nut, or Elk nut. **1933** SMALL *Southeastern Flora* 1250 P[yrularia] pubera . . . Buffalo-nut. Oil-nut. Mountain-coconut.

Ojibway oˈdʒɪbwe, *n.* [f. native terms *ojib*, to pucker up, and *ub-way*, to roast, i.e., to roast till puckered up, in allusion to the puckered seam on their moccasins. Cf. quot. 1825.] *pl.* The Chippewa Indians.

1700 in *Doc. Col. Hist. N.Y.* IV. 749 Upon the sides of [Lake Huron] . . . live severall Nations, vizt. the Christinos, the Ochipoy [etc.]. **1825** KEATING *Exped. St. Peter's River* II. 147 The term Chippewa, which is generally applied to this nation, is derived from that of O'chepe'wag, which . . . signifies plaited shoes, from the fashion of these Indians puckering their moccasins. **1885** *Minn. H.S. Coll.* V. 507 The Ojibways of Minnesota are on three reservations.

attrib. **1949** *Sat. Ev. Post* 22 Jan. 23/2 White men call it 'Indian Devil,' and the Ojibway name of Kween-go-ar-gay, 'the hard character,' has echoed in the native tongues from the polar islands to California.

b. The language of these Indians.

1835 HOFFMAN *Winter in West* II. 21 The Chippewa, or Ojibboai . . . is generally considered the *court language* of our northwestern tribes.

ojo ˈoho, *n. S.W.* [Sp. in same sense, lit. "an eye."] A spring. Often **ojo caliente,** hot spring.

1844 GREGG *Commerce of Prairies* I. 176 There are several warm springs (*ojos calientes*), whose waters are generally sulphurous and considered as highly efficaceous in the cure of rheumatisms and other chronic diseases. **1872** POWERS *Afoot & Alone* 143 West of the Pecos there begin to occur those peculiar desert springs, the Spanish ojos, the eyes which weep brackish tears. **1936** McKENNA *Black Range* 179 He told me that his people did not want to move from Ojo Caliente.

b. (See quot.) *Rare.*

1868 *Calif. Acad. Sci. Proc.* IV. 24 When the grave was opened, the lower section of an '*ojo*,' or earthen water jar, was found inverted over the skull.

O.K., *n.* Also **okay, okeh.** [See **O.K.,** *a.* and **O.K. Club.**]

1. A member of the O.K. Club. *Obs.*

1840 [see **K.O.**]. **1840** *N.Y. Dly. Express* 9 April 2/2 The Whig young men have a grand rally tomorrow night. On Friday, come the Indomitables—O.K.'s. **1840** *Boston Transcript* 15 April 2/1 When the Registry Law was first spoken of, the tail of the Democratic party, the roarers, buttenders, ringtails, O.K.'s, (flat burglary this latter title) and indomitables, talked strong about nullification and all that.

2. The symbol or watchcry of the O.K. Club. *Obs.* or *hist.*

1840 *N.Y. Dly. Express* 3 April 2/2 About 9 o'clock a procession from the 10th and other up town wards marched down Center Street headed by a banner inscribed 'O.K.' **1840** *Nat. Intelligencer* 7 Nov. 1/1 The Irish Locofocos in the 6th Ward [of N.Y.C.] have been parading the streets with shillelahs, swearing 'O.K.' &c. [**1947** *Sat. Review* 1 Nov. 47/3 Some time in the Forties the Democrats, twitted by the Whigs with illiteracy, adopted the 'OK' phrase thrown at them in scorn, and laughed it into general vogue.]

b. An alleged abbreviation of "Oll (all) Korrect." *Obs.* Cf. **O.K.,** *a.*, 2nd. quot. 1840.

1840 *Nat. Intelligencer* 7 April 1/2 The Locos translate 'O.K.' *oll korrect*, (Locofoco orthography, of which they are proud!) **1844** *Republican Sentinel* (Richmond, Va.) 28 Sep. 2/2 O.K. in the Whig vocabulary signifies *Oll Korrect*.

c. Used allusively and humorously (see quots.). *Obs.*

1840 *N.O. Picayune* 30 Sep. 2/4 O.K.—These initials, which in party parlance are understood to mean *All is correct*—viz. 'Oll Korrect'—are used now for *'Orful Katastrophe.'* **1841** *Cong. Globe* App. 5 Feb. 14 Jeremiah, of olden times, would be ashamed of his lamentations, were he here to hear the modern Whigs mourning over the distresses of the people, on account of a weak Treasury, O.K. Orful Kalamity.

3. An endorsement denoting approval.

[**1840** *Harrisburg* (Pa.) *Magician* 29 Aug. 3/1 What an ecstasy of delight coursed their veins . . . [after the Whig victories]. O. K. O. K. O. K. was the caption to the glorious news, in the *United States Gazette*.]. *c***1849** PAIGE *Dow's Sermons* I. 273 [Fortitude] infuses new life into his soul, while Hope adds an O.K. to his condition. **1946** *Science Digest* Aug. 30/1 These drugs are dangerous for some, no smart person will take them without first getting a physician's okay. **1950** *Tuscaloosa News* 27 Jan. 12/1 Okeh of Reds in China Urged.

O.K., *a.* Also **okay, okeh.**

1. "Oll (all) korrect," all right, satisfactory. *Colloq.*

This expression arose in New York City in the spring of 1840 during the progress of a bitter political campaign of that year. Evidence for this origin was well presented by A. W. Read in *The Saturday Review of Literature*, July 19, 1941, pp. 3 f. An excellent summary of the work done on O.K. is found in Mencken *Supp.* I. 269 ff. See also *Amer. Sp.* April 1941, 85 ff., and Dec. 1941, 246 ff. See **O.K. Club** below.

1840 *Atlas* 18 June 2 The band [of the Barre Whig Association] rode in a stage, which had a barrel of hard cider on the baggage rack, marked with large letters, 'O.K.'—oll korrect. **1840** *Atlas* 19 Aug. 2/4 These initials, according to Jack Downing, were first used by Gen. Jackson. 'Those papers, Amos [Kendall], are all correct. I marked them O.K.' (oll korrect). The Gen. was never good at spelling. **1856** *Town Talk* (S.F.) 28 June 2/4 Here is your dog; all O.K., only a little out of breath. **1873** E. S. PHELPS *Trotty's Wedding* xiii, So we had an O.K. time till we went to bed. **1944** *Chi. D. News* 17 Feb., Art up an alley is O.K., Deutsch finds, if you know how. **1950** *Age-Herald* (Birmingham, Ala.) 27 Jan. 1/4 Rep. Hobbs' Condition Reported Okeh.

b. In allusive and humorous uses (see quots.). *Obs.*

1841 *N.O. Picayune* 10 Jan. 2/4 I'm O.K.—off for the calaboose, and so is you. **1845** *St. Louis Reveille* 19 March 1/6 In settlin land as is kuvvered with water I got O.K. the wust possible name. I was out ove kabin out ove kredit out of ove korn out ove kash out ove Kumfort. **1852** *Lantern* (N.Y.) I. 254/1 Our Owl . . . is glad to assure the ladies that a custom, against which much absurd prejudice has hitherto prevailed, is all correct, or in common parlance, O.K.O.K. . . . The ladies have found out the true meaning of these mysterious capitals . . . is—Only Kissing.

O.K., *v.* Also **okay.** *tr.* To mark with the letters O.K., to approve. *Colloq.*

1888 *Missouri Republican* 25 Jan., Please O.K. and hurry return of my return. **1916** EATON *Idyl of Twin Fires* 244 Morrissy sold gravel to the town at 50 cents a load, from a gravel bed the town already owned, and, as selectman, O.K.'d his own bill! **1949** *Chesterton* (Ind.) *Tribune* 7 April 14/4 This was outlawed by the Taft-Hartley law but a new arrangement has been O.K.'d by the U.S. attorney general whereby the A.F. of M. may use this fund to pay its members to supply music free to worthy causes.

O.K., *adv.* All right. *Colloq.*

1841 *Miss. Free Trader* (Natchez) 25 Feb. 1/1 If they applaud and gently sigh 'O.K.' Twill cheer us more than gallons of Tokay! **1846** *Spirit of Times* (N.Y.) 11 July 232/1 That's it. O.K. Now I have got you. Go ahead. **1944** *Chi. D. News* 14 July 8/2 'Helen Ann! Let's pick flowers.' 'O.K.'

O.K. Club. A democratic club of New York City in 1840, so called in allusion to "Old Kinderhook," Martin Van Buren having been born at Kinderhook, N.Y. Now *hist.*

It was as a name for this club that O.K. was first used. Cf. "Kinderhook Club" in quot. 1840 *s.v.* **Kinderhook.**

1840 *New Era* (N.Y.) 23 March 3/2 The Democratic O.K. Club are hereby ordered to meet at the House of Jacob Colvin, 245 Grand street, on Tuesday evening, 24th inst. **1840** *American* (N.Y.) 28 March 2/3 This band of the *'Old Butt-Enders,'* reorganized under the new cognomen of *the O.K. club*, seemed to consider the invitation of the New Era as sufficient authority for violence and outrage. **1840** *Nat. Intelligencer* 7 April 1/2 Already the Locofocos have got out their banners and procession, and 'the Butt-enders' and 'Point-enders' are marching at night through our streets, led by the so-called 'O.K.' club, which is just now a cant phrase in Tammany. **1949** *New Yorker* 1 Oct. 64/2 The first meeting of the *O.K.* Club was held at the home of a member named Colvin, at 245 Grand Street, on Tuesday evening, March 24, 1840.

Okie ˈokɪ, *n.* [f. *Oklahoma.*] An itinerant Oklahoman, esp. a migratory worker. *Colloq.* — **1939** J. STEINBECK *Grapes of Wrath* 318 Okies—the owners hated them because the owners knew they were soft and the Okies strong, that they were fed and the Okies hungry. **1948** *Dly. Ardmoreite* (Ardmore, Okla.) 11 July 21/5 Sooners have less reason to be offended at being called 'Okies' than residents of other states have for their nicknames.

Okinagan ˌokɪˈnɑgən, *n.* Also **Oakinachen, Okanagan, Okanogan.** [A native term of unknown meaning.] "A name originally applied to the confluence of Similkameen and Okanogan rs., but extended first to include a small band and afterward to a large and important division of the Salishan family" (Hodge).

1849 ROSS *Adv. on Ore.* (1923) 311 The Oakinachens inhabit a very large tract of country. **1892** *Amer. Anthropologist* Jan. [Rev. Myron Eells gives etym. as meaning rendezvous.] **1910** HODGE *Amer. Indians* II. 114/2 In 1906 there were 527 Okinagan on Colville res., Wash., and 824 under the Kamloops-Okanagan agency, British Columbia.

Oklahoma ˌokləˈhomə, *n.* [Choctaw "red people." Name of a territory, later a state.]

1. A light, temporary hut or shanty, in allusion to such huts used in Oklahoma during the land rush of 1889. *Obs.* Cf. **eighty-niner.**

1889 *N.Y. Post* 21 Sep., A light fall of snow here [in Johnstown, Pa.] yesterday gave the people living in the Oklahomas a foretaste of what winter will be like in their shells.

2. *transf.* A large open space. *Humorous.* Cf. **Texas.**

1906 M. TWAIN *Speeches* 330 (R.), They placed Twitchell and me in a most colossal bedroom. There were six chairs in that Oklahoma.

3. In combs. of obvious meaning, as (1) **Oklahoma boom,** (2) **boomer,** (3) **colonist,** (4) **fever,** (5) **land,** (6) **pioneer,** (7) **run.**

(1) **1885** *Cent. Mag.* Aug. 603/2 An organized movement, known as 'the Oklahoma boom,' has been made to seize and colonize a larger body of the territorial lands. — (2) **1882** *Chi. Tribune* 28 Jan. 7/2 The petition . . . is regarded as an effort to make a little buncombe by the Oklahoma boomer. **1928** STANSBERY *Passing of 3D Ranch* 5 David L. Payne, the 'Oklahoma boomer,' had made such a hard fight for the opening of these lands for settlement, the United States government began negotiations for the purchase of the strip from the Cherokees. — (3) **1883** *Rep. Indian Affairs* p. xxiii, Notwithstanding his repeated expulsion from the Indian Territory, Payne and his party of 'Oklahoma Colonists' have twice during the present year made attempts at settlement in that country. — (4) **1891** O'BEIRNE *Leaders Ind. Territory* 98/1 Being struck, however, by the Oklahoma fever in 1889, he incautiously moved his herd to the promised land. (5) **1920** DALE in *Amer. Hist. Assoc. Rep.* (1925) 320 Little newspapers grew up near the border, established apparently for the . . . purpose of 'booming' the opening of Oklahoma lands to settlement. — (6) **1923** *Chronicles of Okla* I. 176 The old time Oklahoma pioneer had his vision. — (7) **1930** *Publishers' Wkly.* 8 Feb. 697 On April 22, 1889, this strip was opened up with the land rush known as the famous Oklahoma Run.

Oklahoman ˌokləˈhomən, *n.* A resident or native of Oklahoma.

[**1894** (*title*), Evening Oklahoman (Oklahoma City, Okla.)] **1901** *Outlook* 2 Feb. 280/1 Many of the old Oklahomans who are selling out expect to secure new homes at the opening. **1948** *Durant* (Okla.) *D.*

Democrat 4 July 2/5 Every Oklahoman appreciates an agency which seeks to protect our lives and property.

okra cotton. A variety of short-staple cotton. Also attrib. *Obs.* — **1840** *Niles' Reg.* 8 Aug. 368/1 Okra cotton. This species of cotton has now established amongst the planters of that part of Alabama where it was first discovered and most extensively cultivated, an undisputed superiority over all other varieties of the short staple. **1853** in J. A. TURNER *Cotton Planter's Man.* (1865) 126 Next, in the year 1837 or '38, the Twin or Okra cotton seed came up; seed sold at various prices, from $5 a quart to $160 per bushel.

olallie oˈlælɪ, *n.* [Chinook Jargon.] A berry, originally the salmonberry. Also (*cap.*) in place-names.

1855 ROSS *Fur Hunters* (1924) 100 His bark plate . . . [was] top-heavy with the most delicious *mélange* of bear's grease, dog's flesh, wappatoes, obellies, amutes, and a profusion of other viands. **1923** MEANY *Origin Wash. Geog. Names* 196 'Olallie' is the Chinook jargon word for berry. **1940** *Mt. Hood Guide* 20 Black bear . . . are often encountered . . . in the less frequented sections between Summit Meadows and Olallie Lakes.

* **old,** *a.*

1. In miscellaneous combs.: (1) * **old clothes,** everyday clothes; (2) **Congress,** the Congress under the Articles of Confederation; (3) **continental,** see as a main entry; (4) **cornfield school,** = **old field school,** *rare;* (5) **court party,** = **court party** (*b*); (6) **dirt,** in placer mining, dirt that has already been washed, *obs.;* (7) * **English,** *a.* of or pertaining to England, distinguished from New England, *obs.;* (8) * **field,** see as a main entry; (9) * **ground,** ground that has been some time in cultivation, as distinguished from new ground *q.v.;* (10) * **guard, Hunker,** see as main entries; (11) * **land,** land that is worn out or that has been in cultivation for a long time; (12) **money,** = **old tenor,** *obs.;* (13) **order Amish,** the most conservative element of the Amish; (14) **pay,** pay according to a previously current system of value, *rare,* cf. **old tenor;** (15) **river,** the former bed of a river which has cut itself a new channel; (16) **school,** see as a main entry; (17) * **soldier,** a cigar or cigarette butt, or quid of tobacco that has been chewed, *slang;* (18) **stand,** see * **stand,** *n.;* (19) **state line,** in West Tennessee, a line north of lat. 35° supposed until 1832 to be Tennessee's southern boundary, *obs.;* (20) **tenor,** see as a main entry; (21) **timey,** *a.* characteristic of old times; (22) * **town,** see as a main entry.

(1) 1788 MAY *Jrnl. & Lett.* 18 After breakfast met numbers of people going to meeting, in their old clothes, it being fast day. **1865** *Atlantic Mo.* XV. 73/1, I felt like some anxious mamma whose children . . . have accidentally appeared at dancing school in their old clothes. — **(2) 1789** in *Jrnl. Wm. Maclay* (1927) 22 Attended a joint committee on the papers of the old Congress. **1804** *Ann. 8th Congress* 1 Sess. 1062, I believe the Territorial government, as established by the ordinance of the Old Congress, the best adapted to the circumstances of the people of Louisiana. **1886** ALTON *Among Law-Makers* 119 The first Constitutional Congress of the United States assembled in the city of New York . . . pursuant to a resolution of the Old Congress of the Confederation [etc.]. — **(4) 1871** DE VERE 48 So-called self-made men are to this day fond of boasting that they never received any other education but in an old cornfield school.

(5) 1825 *New-Harmony* (Ind.) *Gaz.* 23 Nov. 71/3 The old court party ascertained that they had succeeded in electing a majority of the members of the next Legislature. **1901** Z. F. SMITH *Hist. Ky.* 51 The result [in 1835] was the triumph of the old-court party by a large majority. — **(6) 1851** *Alta Californian* 19 Aug., At Grizzley Bear bar they are engaged in washing 'old dirt,' that is, the dirt that was passed through the cradle last year. **1878** BEADLE *Western Wilds* 107 In places [we] pass hundreds of acres of 'old dirt,' which has been washed out and abandoned. — **(7) 1632** *Mass. H.S. Coll.* 4 Ser. VI. 184 Tis a ridle as yet to me whether you meane any Elder in these New English churches, or . . . old English. **1647** ELIOT *Day-breaking* 16 Now all see it [New-English ground] to bee scarce inferiour to Old-English tillage. — **(9) 1665** in W. S. PELLETREAU *Early L. I. Wills* (1897) 276, I doe give unto my son Anthony all my housing and land at the old ground and a fifty pound commonage. **1871** *Lawrence* (Kans.) *Republican Jrnl.* 21 March, As to pulverizing the soil, all 'old ground' in Kansas is apt to pulverize itself.

(11) 1715 in *Amer. Sp.* XV. 290/2 At the Corner of the said Jones's old land. **1871** *Rep. Indian Affairs* (1872) 230 It is my intention, during the coming season, to . . . summer-fallow as much of the old land as can be spared from cultivation. **1919** CADY *Rhymes of Vt.* (1923) 67, I learnt soon after I was born To never use 'old land' for corn. — **(12) 1780** *Va. State P.* I. 377 Fix my pay on the first footing of ten shillings old money, or fifty pounds of Tobacco pr: day. — **(13) 1923** ROSENBERGER *Pa. Germans* 125 And perhaps today more strict in enforcing the observance of those articles than are the Old Order Amish, are the Reformed Mennonites. **1945** *Amer. Sp.* April 85 The Old Order Amish of Lancaster County (and various other settlements in other states) are the important exception to the statement concerning trilingualism among the Pennsylvania Dutch. — **(14) 1687** SEWALL *Letter-book* I. 64 Having received your freight, viz: one ps of 8/8 a kentoll ould pay, if that be not [etc.].

(15) 1694 *Derby Rec.* 171 The Land which Thomas woster has Reserved . . . is bounded . . . west with the old River & East with the new River. **1787** in *Amer. Sp.* XV. 291/1 Beginning at the Roaring hole on the Old River. **1825** *Ib.*, To two sycamores at the mouth of the Old River. — **(17) 1834** CARUTHERS *Kentuckian* I. 12, I smokes the old sodgers what the gentlemen throws on the bar-room floor. *a***1877** in BARTLETT 438 Ladies who swab our sidewalks, . . . And . . . Haul off old soldiers lying there at rest. — **(19) 1862** in F. MOORE *Rebellion Rec.* V. II. 271 The same division . . . moved forward about two miles and a half, in the direction of Corinth, to the crossing of the 'Old State Line' with the 'Purdy and Farmington road.'

(21) 1850 A. J. DOWNING in *Horticulturist* V. 265 The terraced garden, too, is quaint and 'old-timey.' **1887** *Courier-Journal* 8 May 19/8 We are old-timey people, too. **1892** HARRIS *U. Remus & Friends* 151 We'll have a reg'lar ole-timey camp-meetin' gwine on here 'fo' you know it.

b. In similar expressions, often obs., of obvious meaning or sufficiently explained in the quots., as (1) **old charter bill,** (2) **country,** (3) **Defenders' Day,** (4) **Driver,** (5) **hickory,** *obs.,* cf. **Old Hickory** in **3.** below; (6) **home week,** (7) **-horse sale,** (8) **landmarkism,** (9) **ore.**

(1) 1895 in *Mass. Pub. Col. Soc.* III. (1900) 5 The final abandonment of the proposed bank . . . brought about the first emission of these notes. They were familiarly known as Colony or Old Charter Bills, and were put forth to pay the expenses of Phips's unfortunate expedition. — **(2) 1796** F. BAILY *Tour* 172 The scenery . . . [was] so very different from what we had been used to in the old country. **1902** CLAPIN 293 *Old Country*, At first, applied solely to England, but now meaning the Old World generally, and of course more especially Europe. **1947** *So. Sierran* March 4/2 They flew here from the old country. — **(3) 1903** *N.Y. Ev. Post* 12 Sep., To-day . . . is a holiday by legislative act. The day is known [in Md.] as Old Defenders' Day, in memory of the battle of North Point in 1814, in which the Maryland militia defeated an invading British army. — **(4) 1877** BARTLETT 437 *Old Driver*, euphemism for the devil. **1895** WIGGIN *Village Watch-Tower* 68 Pitts' relations or not, they're all wuss'n the Old Driver.

(5) 1858 VIELÉ *Following Drum* 225 [Scouts' shirts] are composed of a dark blue check material, warranted to last a week. . . . They are termed 'Old Hickories.' — **(6) 1904** *Boston Herald* 2 Aug. 6 In . . . Massachusetts this first week in August is being observed as Old Home Week, and preparations have been made for welcoming back . . . the visitors who return to their native, or earlier, home to renew acquaintance with former scenes and companions. **1922** H. L. FOSTER *Adv. Trop. Tramp* i. 8 Old Home Week in Hades! I could not resign then without being a quitter. — **(7) 1924** MCCONNELL *Frontier Law* 126 It was offered for sale at public auction . . . together with such other unclaimed freight as had accumulated since the last 'old-horse sale,' that being the name given to such sales. — **(8) 1898** B. F. RILEY *Hist. Baptists* 177 The principal features of 'Old Landmarkism' [*c*1850] were an insistence of Baptist apostolic succession; a declaration of the absolute necessity of properly authorized administrators of baptism [etc.]. — **(9) 1839** in *Mich. Agric. Soc. Trans.* VII. 368 The deposit [of ore] is mostly of inferior quality, being what is technically known as an old ore.

2. Used with reference to persons, often somewhat as a nickname, cf. **3.** below: (1) **old bach,** see **bach;** (2) **Christian,** ?an orthodox Christian as distinguished from a New Light, *rare;* (3) **coon,** see as a main entry; (4) **cornstalk,** an old ineffectual man, *rare;* (5) **girl,** one's wife, *jocular;* (6) **grad,** a former graduate; (7) **Harmonians,** the Rappists *q.v.* after the sale of their colony to Robert Owen in 1825, *obs.;* (8) * **lady,** (*a*) = **old girl,** *colloq.,* (*b*) *W.* a cook in a cow camp; (9) * **line,** denoting those in agreement with traditional doctrines and principles, conservative, used esp. of members of political parties; (10) **liner,** a member of the old guard *q.v.,* a conservative and dependable member of a party; (11) * **man, settler,** see as main entries; (12) **-side(d) Baptist,** = **Old School Baptist** *q.v., s.v.* **old school** as a main entry; (13) **timer,** a person who has been in a place or a position for a long time, an experienced person, also transf.; (14) **whale,** see ∗**whale;** (15) **Whig,** a member of the Whig party opposed to Henry Clay's leadership, a strict constructionist Whig.

(2) **1849** E. CHAMBERLAIN *Indiana Gaz.* 175 Presbyterians, Methodists, United Brethren, Christian, . . . Old Christian, (or New Light) and Baptists. — (4) **1823** COOPER *Pioneers* (1832) 242 What's that, old corn-stalk! you sapless stub!

(5) **1891** SLOAN *Fogy Days* 131 This avowment, I am aware, will detract a part of the glory, but I have still enough left to make me feel comfortable, and, besides, after the lapse of thirty-five brief years, have got the old girl to-boot. — (6) **1897** FLANDREAU *Harvard Episodes* 294 Why didn't you buck up with the old grads around the piano? **1912** NICHOLSON *Hoosier Chron.* 289 I'm getting to be an old grad myself, but those songs still give me a twinge. — (7) **1825** *New-Harmony* (Ind.) *Gaz.* 30 Nov. 78/1 The Old Harmonians, we believe, intended to commence the manufacture of silk. — (8) (*a*) **1871** EGGLESTON *Hoosier Schoolm.* xvii. 134 Here's the old lady and Shocky. **1884** NYE *Baled Hay* 88 It would harden me and the old lady. (*b*) **1892** *Outing* Feb. 359/1 The sight of the 'old lady,' . . . on a broncho loping up and down beside the cattle . . . is a striking contrast to the dignity he exhibits in the kneading of an ash cake or the broiling of a slice of 'sow belly.' — (9) **1856** *Cong. Globe* 9 Jan. 180 Have they offered us one of my colleagues, an old-line Whig? **1922** McCORMAC *J. K. Polk* 214 Old-line politicians such as Buchanan, Calhoun, Benton, and Blair were doing their utmost to ruin Polk's prospects. **1948** *Time* 13 Dec. 11/1 We 'Old Line Republicans' have said the same things for years.

(10) **1855** in HAMBLETON *H. A. Wise* 419 Endorsed thus by two 'old liners,' he was most cordially received. **1903** *N.Y. Ev. Post* 31 Oct. 5 The old-liners quietly backbite him for taking up a 'fanatic' like Johnson. — (12) **1847** POLK *Diary* III. 25 They were from several States of the Union, and belonged to . . . the old side-Baptists as they are sometimes called. **1858** *Harper's Mag.* May 853/1, I profess to be, what is vulgarly called, an 'old sided Baptist,' and have been for a number of years. **1862** in F. MOORE *Rebellion Rec.* V. II. 20 At the Cheesecoke Church, an antiquated building used by the 'Oldside Baptists,' erected in colonial times . . . the divisions parted. — (13) **1866** *New Princeton Rev.* V. 122 Most of us old timers . . . are poor now. **1894** *Outing* XXIV. 34/1 A cutter of some six to eight tons . . . , a regular old-timer, built in the days when the cod's head and mackerel tail model embodied the highest ideas of yacht architecture. **1949** *Chi. Tribune* 22 Oct. 10/3 Incidentally, the word 'know-how,' much in vogue these days is another old-timer long neglected by lexicografers.

(15) **1835** C. P. BRADLEY *I. Hill* 166 It is said the old Whigs are most averse to a reform. **1900** *Miss. Hist. Soc. Pub.* III. 78 A tabular view of the [Mississippi constitutional] convention [1868] . . . shows that it [included] . . . 2 Henry Clay Whigs, 4 Old Whigs.

b. In similar expressions, chiefly obs., of obvious meaning or sufficiently explained in the quots., as (1) **Old Baptist,** (2) **Comers,** (3) **countryman,** (4) **Hunker,** see as a main entry, (5) **issue,** (6) **Knickerbocker,** (7) **master,** (8) **Oregonian,** (9) **planters.**

(1) **1845** *Indiana Mag. Hist.* XXIII. 18, I see nothing awaiting the 'old Baptist' churches but utter annihilation. **1889** BUTLER *Recollections* 252 'Hardshell' Baptists . . . wish to be known as Old Baptists, or United Baptists. — (2) **1639** *Plymouth Laws* 67 The Court hath by mutuale assent & consent of all as well purchasers old comers as freemen enacted [etc.]. **1849** in *Mass. Col. Soc. Pub.* XVII. 363 These later pilgrims [i.e., those who came on the Anne and Little James] are reckoned with those who came in the Mayflower and Fortune, as the *Old Comers* or *Forefathers*. **1898** W. E GRIFFIS *Pilgrims in 3 Homes* 151 Those who reach New Plymouth in the Mayflower, Anne, and Little James were called the 'Old Comers,' or 'Forefathers.' — (3) **1828** PICKERING in *Amer. Quart. Rev.* IV. 211 Even the illiterate in our country will distinguish an Englishman by his pronunciation, and will designate him as an 'old countryman,' as we have often heard them do. **1848** BARTLETT 239 *Old countryman.* A native of England, Scotland, Ireland, or Wales. The term is never applied to persons from the Continent of Europe.

(5) **1879** TOURGEE *Fool's Errand* 87 The meeting was led . . . by a mulatto man named Robert, who was what is now called an 'old-issue free nigger.' **1899** CHESNUTT *Wife of His Youth* 214 Wright came of an 'old issue' free colored family, in which though the negro blood was present in an attenuated strain, a line of free ancestry could be traced beyond the Revolutionary War. — (6) **1882** McCABE *New York* 196 The descendants of the original Dutch settlers of New York . . . style themselves 'the Old Knickerbockers.' — (7) **1872** POWERS *Afoot & Alone* 61 Negroes everywhere . . . seemed to think they were not free unless they left the old master. — (8) **1882** *Harper's Mag.* Oct. 766/2 This unenterprising class of farmers, locally spoken of as 'the old Oregonians,' has declined in influence. — (9) **1624** *Va. House of Burgesses* 34 We, the old Planters, relieved them. **1871** DE VERE 165 In New England the first settlers were known as *planters*, and distinguished select families as *Old Planters*.

3. In nicknames of individuals: (1) **Old Abe,** (2) **Brains,** (3) **Buck,** (4) **Bullion,** (5) **Chapultepec,** (6) **Chippewa,** (7) **Commoner,** (8) **Fuss and Feathers,** (9) **Hickory,** (10) **Honest Abe,** (11) **Ironsides,** see **Old Ironsides c,** (12) **Mad Jackson,** (13) **Patroon,** (14) **Probabilities,** see as a main entry, (15) **Public Functionary,** (16) **Rail Mauler,** (17) **Roman,** (18) **Rough-and-Ready,** (19) **Thad,** (20) **Three Stars,** (21) **Tip,** (22) **Tippecanoe,** (23) **White Hat,** (24) **Zach, Zack.**

(1) **1860** *N.Y. Tribune* 26 May 1/6 Of course, 'Old Abe' was called out, and made an explanation of the matter. **1944** FAST *F. Road* 20 How come old Abe, he say to nigger man through the land, you is free? — (2) **1864** *Ore. State Jrnl.* 16 April 1/3 The General [i.e., Gen. Halleck] . . . enjoys the sobriquet of 'Old Brains.' — (3) **1846** *Quincy* (Ill.) *Whig* 10 Mar. 2/1 Drive Queen Vic from Canada, Up to the Russian line, For waiving old Buck's compromise, The line of forty-nine. **1861** *Charleston* (S.C.) *Mercury* 2 Feb. 4/5 Our stables are being rapidly filled, and in spite of Old Buck [James Buchanan] and his Major of Artillery, Fort Sumter and tight times, we anticipate some good racing. — (4) **1841** *Greene Co. Torchlight* (Xenia, O.) 19 Aug. 3/2 A Loco Foco at Washington, in counting up the 'jewels' of the Federal party, places Old Bullion, as he calls *him* of Missouri, at the head. **1892** WALSH *Lit. Curiosities* 841 *Old Bullion*, a sobriquet of Colonel Thomas Hart Benton (1782–1858), . . . given him for his persistent advocacy of a gold and silver currency. **1948** WESTON *Mother Lode* 16 General Frémont's father-in-law . . . was called 'Old Bullion' because he favored hard money.

(5) **1912** THORNTON II. 622 *Old Chapultepec.* General Winfield Scott (1786–1866). He won the battle of Chapultepec, Sept. 1847. — (6) **1852** *N.Y. Wkly. Tribune* 9 Oct. 4/2 Work with spirit and devotion, and the Third of November will behold Old Chippewa [Winfield Scott] the President elect of the United States. — (7) **1882** *Cent. Mag.* March 783/2 The 'Old Commoner' [Thaddeus Stevens] undoubtedly inaugurated this method. **1949** *Pa. Dutchman* 7 July 1/1 The writer was in the office of Thaddeus Stevens . . . and the 'Old Commoner' exclaimed [etc.]. — (8) **1852** *Scott Eagle* (Rising Sun, Ind.) 24 Oct. 4/4 Old 'Fuss and feathers'—Winfield Scott! The Chieftain's deeds proclaim. **1948** *Sat. Review* 31 Jan. 16/1 Much may be said . . . for the tactical address of Old Fuss and Feathers. — (9) **1815** *Reviewers Reviewed* 67 Nay, this kind of eloquence we find is equally as well understood by the Yankee fishermen of Stonington, as by the backwoodsmen of Kentucky and Tennessee, with old Hickory at their head. **1907** *Springfield W. Republican* 24 Oct. 8, I should not say that Old Hickory was faultless, but Andrew Jackson was as upright a patriot as ever any nation had. **1949** *Time* 21 March 56/3 Because of his toughness during the War of 1812, Andrew Jackson was nicknamed 'Old Hickory' by his soldiers.

(10) **1860** G. W. BUNGAY *Bobolink Minstrel* 62 Old 'Honest Abe' we will elect In a few days. **1949** *Lincoln Herald* June 24/2 Old Honest Abe had captured the hearts of his countrymen as no one else. — (12) **1858** WOODWARD *Reminiscences* 43 The big Warrior and others were in favor of giving Old Mad Jackson, as they called him, as much land as he wanted. — (13) **1881** *Harper's Mag.* March 538/2 The 'old Patroon' [Stephen Van Rensselaer] was a member of the Congress that elected John Quincy Adams President.

(15) **1867** *Harper's Wkly.* 18 May 311/3 Then your President was called the Old Public Functionary, and, if I am rightly informed, your present President had just sold out his tailor shop and was running for Alderman in his native State. **1914** *Cyclo. Amer. Govt.* I. 179 Buchanan was also nicknamed Old Public Functionary. — (16) **1860** *Boston Transcript* 23 May 2/2 The 'Old Rail Mauler' [Abraham Lincoln] takes like wildfire. — (17) **1832** *Cong. Deb.* 6 April 737 The 'old Roman' is known to his countrymen. **1846** F. WYSE *America* I. 87 To administer to the vanity, and appease the wounded pride of the 'old Roman,' as President Jackson was familiarly termed. — (18) **1846** *Cong. Globe* 24 May 865 Col. [Zachary] Taylor . . . had won for himself by his gallant conduct in the field the soubriquet of 'Old Rough and Ready.' **1948** *Time* 12 Jan. 90/3 Richard Taylor, son of Old Rough and Ready, surrendered the last of the Confederate armies east of the Mississippi. — (19) **1868** *Cong. Globe* 17 Dec. 131/1 With his own supporters . . . 'Old Thad' was a phrase of endearment; while even his foes spoke of him [Thaddeus Stevens] with pride as the 'great Commoner.'

(20) **1888** M. LANE in *America* 25 Oct. 15 *Old Three Stars*, General Ulysses Grant. — (21) **1836** *Wkly. Advertiser* (Russellville, Ky.) 21 Jan. 3/1 The manner in which Gen. Harrison, alias *Old Tip*, seems to be climbing towards the Presidential summit, engages a great deal of conversation here. **1947** DOWNEY *Lusty Forefathers* 245 All such souvenir articles, selling in vast quantities, spread the gospel for Old Tip. — (22) **1840** *Ill. State Reg.* (Springfield) 13 March 2/1 On it [banner] was inscribed 'Old Tippecanoe.' **1947** DOWNEY *Lusty Forefathers* 252 Were the Whigs trying to push Old Hickory off his pedestal with Old Tippecanoe? — (23) **1872** *Harper's Wkly.* 1 June 426/3 The Cincinnati candidate [Horace Greeley] is already . . . 'Old White Hat.' — (24) **1846** *Dollar Newspaper* (Phila.) 3 June 2/4 Old Zack [Gen. Zachary Taylor (1784–1850)], God bless him! has, through us,

on this day, planted his foot on this side of the river. **1847** *Sangamo Jrnl.* (Springfield, Ill.) 22 April 2/4 President Polk has hit upon a new scheme to prevent Old Zach from being President—that is, continue the war, and thus keep him in Mexico. **1880** *Cong. Rec.* 28 Jan. 584/1 The name of Zachariah Chandler, or 'Old Zach,' as he was more commonly called, was familiar in every household.

b. In nicknames of, or with reference to, states in the U.S.: (1) **Old Bay State,** (2) **Bourbon State,** cf. **Old Bourbon** in **4.** below, (3) **Dominion,** see as a main entry; (4) **Granite State,** (5) **Kentucky,** also **Old Kentuck, Old Kaintuck,** (6) **Line State,** (7) **Mother State,** (8) **North State** (i.e., North Carolina), (9) **South State,** (prob. South Carolina), *rare,* (10) **states,** (11) **United States,** (12) **Virginia,** see as a main entry; (13) **York.**

(1) **1838** *S. Lit. Messenger* IV. 164 Certain self-styled philanthropists of the good old Bay-State. **1947** PAUL *Linden* 326 The more absurd a law or a method of official procedure in Massachusetts appears to the liberals of the outside world, the more frantically will the leaders of the old Bay State rally around. — (2) **1898** *Chi. Times-Herald* 2 April 11/3 The ladies of the old Bourbon state [Missouri] seldom go into politics. — (4) **1900** C. WINCHESTER *W. Castle* i. 18 In the infinite mercy of God, a mighty revival visited that section of the 'Old Granite State' [New Hampshire].

(5) **1817** A. ROYALL *Lett. from Ala.* (1830) III. 9 It only exists in what is called old Kentucky, meaning that part of the state which extends from Mount Sterling to Danville, and which, I presume, was first settled. **1819** FAUX *Memorable Days* 190, I entered the city, the far-famed metropolis of old Kentuck. **1894** CHOPIN *Bayou Folk* 132 Ole Kaintuck. . . . Dat ain't no sech kentry as dis heah. **1946** WILSON *Fidelity* 3 Nearly every house had some antique furniture that had been brought in covered wagons from North Carolina or 'Old Kentucky,' our name for the part of the state [of Ky.] east of the Tennessee River. — (6) **1871** DE VERE 660 Maryland bears the proud title of *Old-Line State* from the *Old-Line* regiments which she contributed to the Continental Army in the War of the Revolution—the only state that had regular troops of 'the line.' **1947** *Dly. Racing Form* (Chi.) 6 Nov. 36/3 The Southern Maryland Agricultural Association . . . opens the final lap of racing in the Old Line State, Friday, November 14. — (7) **1866** F. KIRKLAND *Bk. Anecdotes* 142 Had R. M. T. Hunter's famous pronunciamento to the people of Virginia been accompanied with those last two lines, it . . . would have saved the 'old mother State' from plunging into a four years' war. — (8) **1839** *Spirit of Times* 27 July 247/3 (We.), On dits from the Old North State. **1884** BLAINE *20 Years of Congress* I. 90 Willie P. Mangum . . . represented the steadfast Union sentiment of the 'Old North State' Whigs. **1944** *Christian Cent.* 12 July 820/2 The Old North State has now done away with any discrimination in schoolteachers' pay on the basis of color. — (9) **1858** WOODWARD *Reminiscences* (1939) 130, I left the old South State.

(10) **1790** R. PUTNAM in *Memoirs* 237 The interest of the old States and theirs . . . is inconsistent with each other. *a***1861** WINTHROP *J. Brent* 14 He was an American horse—so they distinguish in California one brought from the old States. **1898** CANFIELD *Maid of Frontier* 29 He owed me a grudge back in the old states. — (11) *a***1865** BROWNE *Four Years in Secessia* 384 Wilkes is one of the strongest Union counties—probably the strongest—in North Carolina. The Rebels call it old United States, and declare it irrepressible. Deserters from the Southern service went about there with impunity. — (13) **1827** COOPER *Prairie* xxii, The time we worried it out together, among the red Hurons of the lakes, back in those rugged mountains of Old York!

c. With reference to areas within or adjacent to the present U.S.: (1) **Old Colony,** see as a main entry; (2) **Mexico,** Mexico, esp. as distinguished from New Mexico; (3) **South,** the southern states, esp. in allusion to these as they were before the Civil War; (4) **Thirteen,** the thirteen original colonies which combined to fight the Revolutionary War.

(2) **1863** *Rio Abajo Press* 28 April 1/3 Those whose business called them to Old Mexico were often obliged to camp out. **1890** *Stock Grower & Farmer* 11 Jan. 6/2 The sign riders cut the trail, going in the direction of Old Mexico. **1947** *Mazama* Oct. 4/1 All of you who are interested in Old Mexico . . . will be pleased to know that Mr. and Mrs. Roy K. Terry will give us an account of their recent trip into Mexico. — (3) **1873** *Harper's Mag.* July 271/1 Never in her most boastful days did the old South, under her cherished system of slave labor, produce better crops, or reap a richer remuneration for them. **1949** *Courier-Journal* (Louisville, Ky.) 3 Sep. 7/2 Mr. Tallant has poked more incisive fun at the modern Old South than anybody I know. — (4) **1845** *S. Lit. Messenger* XI. 584/2 Charleston . . . [was] the chief commercial city of the 'Old Thirteen.' **1904** *Hartford Courant* 30 Aug. 10 We want to see the Old Thirteen draw closer and closer together.

d. Designating various objects, often in expressions having the force of nicknames: (1) **Old Baldy, Betsy,** see **baldy,** * **betsy;** (2) **Cradle of Liberty,** Faneuil Hall in Boston, cf. *Cradle of Liberty;* (3) **Faithful,** a geyser in Yellowstone National Park which erupts about every sixty-seven minutes, also transf.; (4) **Glory,** the flag of the U.S.; (5) **Ironsides,** see as a main entry; (6) **Muddy,** the Missouri (also the Mississippi) River; (7) **Ned,** see as a main entry; (8) **Splitfoot,** the devil.

(2) **1830** *Boston Transcript* 31 Aug. 2/2 Last night the *great meeting* was gathered in the Old Cradle of Liberty, where every one met for a bit of child's play. — (3) **1870** *Helena* (Mont.) *D. Herald* 28 Sep., We classified and named some of them according to size. . . . Old Faithful, 7 by 8, irregular in shape, a solid column each hour 75 feet high. **1927** HALLIBURTON *Glorious Adv.* 212 Five times an hour with mechanical regularity the Old Faithful of volcanoes roared like a thousand angry lions. **1949** *Sat. Ev. Post* 4 June 36/2 The big sight, the most dependable of sight-seeing sights, [is] that accommodating geyser, Old Faithful. — (4) **1862** W. DRIVER in *Salem* (Mass.) *Reg.* 10 March, I carried my flag, 'Old Glory,' as we have been used to call it, to the Capitol, presented it to the Ohio 6th and hoisted it with my own hands on the Capitol. **1949** *Nat. Geog. Mag.* May 640/2 First to call it 'Old Glory,' probably as early as 1824, was William Driver, a sea captain living in Nashville, Tennessee, when Union forces took the city in 1862.

(6) **1944** *Reader's Digest* Oct. 37/1 'Old Muddy,' the Missouri River, was chiefly responsible for this flood. **1949** *N.O. Times-Picayune Mag.* 5 June 18/2 Old Muddy undergoes a metamorphosis after she leaves the river bed. — (8) **1863** I. KELSO *Stars & Bars* 212 Off he went as if old Splitfoot had been at his heels. **1867** LOWELL *Biglow P.* 2 Ser. 33 They go it like an Ericsson's ten-hoss-power coleric ingine, An' make Ole Split-Foot winch an' squirm, for all he's used to singein'.

4. In the names of liquors, usu. spirituous, and drinks, as (1) **Old Bourbon,** cf. * **Bourbon,** and see **b.** (2) above, (2) **Crow,** (3) **fashioned,** (4) **Monongahela,** cf. **Monongahela,** (5) **Nash,** (so called because made in Nash County, N.C.), (6) **orchard,** (7) **peach,** (cf. **peach brandy**), (8) **rye,** (9) **Tuscaloosa.**

(1) **1850** H. C. LEWIS *La. Swamp Dr.* 37, I would have sworn it was good old Bourbon whiskey. **1861** *Dly. Dispatch* (Richmond, Va.) 30 April 1/1 Yesterday, in drilling, three of the warriors 'fainted' and 'fell upon the field.' 'Tis rumored that 'Old Bourbon' had something to do with it. **1883** S. BONNER *Dialect Tales* 14, I assented, though dreading the villanous compound I should have to swallow under the name of 'old bourbon.' — (2) **1889** *Lisbon* (N.D.) *Star* 15 Feb. 3/1 The senator had a small flask of 'Old Crow' in his side pocket. **1940** BABER & WALKER *Longest Rope* 21 A quart or so of black coffee spiked with a good jolt of Old Crow, made a pretty fair brand of pain-killer. — (3) **1943** HALE *Between Dark & Daylight* 107 Tom Collinses, Martinis, and Old-Fashioneds so far. **1948** *Time* 19 Jan. 71/2 The whole thing sounds as old-fashioned as the pink lady, sniffed a San Francisco woman, ordering another old-fashioned. — (4) **1947** DEVOTO *Across Wide Missouri* 280 On the Glorious Fourth the officers drank 'a glass of good old Monongahela' to Old Hickory.

(5) **1833** *Amer. Turf Reg.* April 404 'Landlord, have you any *apple-jack?*' 'Yes; real old Nash.' — (6) **1810** *Farmer's Alm.* (Boston) Sep., Come, ye lovers of Old Orchard, let us take a walk into the fields. . . . O, this is a pleasant month not only to cider drinkers, but to all. **1851** *Knickerb.* XXXVII. 557 One of them . . . was quite importunate in his demands for 'old orchard.' — (7) **1845** HOOPER *Simon Suggs' Adv.* v, Thar's koniac and old peach and rectified, and lots I can't tell thar names. — (8) **1824** *Richmond Enquirer* 19 Oct. 1/1. **1835** INGRAHAM *South-West* II. 56 The painful effects of 'old rye' in the abstract upon the body. **1890** *Buckskin Mose* xvii, 243 He continued, lifting the Old Rye to his lips, 'here's long life to you.' **1949** *Pa. Dutchman* 16 June 1/3 They indulged excessively in 'Old Rye' and 'Monongahela.' — (9) **1835** HOFFMAN *Winter in West* I. 47 A venison steak and flask of old Tuscaloosa . . . gave cordiality to the meeting.

5. In the names of, or with reference to, games, dances, etc.: (1) **old army game,** (see quots.); (2) * **curiosity shop,** some kind of parlor game, *obs.;* (3) **Dan Tucker,** see as a main entry; (4) **family coach,** = * **stagecoach,** *obs.;* (5) **folks' concert,** (see quot.); (6) **sledge,** all-fours or seven-up; (7) **trimble toes,** (see quot.), *rare;* (8) **witch by the wayside,** a children's game; (9) **Zip Coon,** see **Zip Coon.**

(1) **1891** QUINN *Fools of Fortune* 275 Chuck-a-luck . . . is sometimes designated as 'the old army game,' for the reason that soldiers at the front were often wont to beguile the tedium of a bivouac by seeking relief from monotony in its charms. **1938** ASBURY *Sucker's Prog.* 32 One story is that it [stud poker] was devised by Union soldiers dur-

ing the Civil War, and for that reason became known as 'the old army game,' but the present author could find no mention of it in the various accounts of gambling in that period, nor do any of the old-time gamblers refer to it in their reminiscences. — (2) **1850** S. WARNER *Wide, Wide World* xxix, They played the Old Curiosity Shop; and Ellen thought Mr John's curiosities could not be matched. — (4) **1850** S. WARNER *Wide, Wide World* xxix, They played the Old Family Coach, . . . and Ellen laughed till she was tired; she was the coach door.

(5) **1899** *Essex Antiquarian* III. 73 Among the incidents that gave real enjoyment to our fathers few were more desired than the 'Old folks' concerts;' and their hearts would quicken at the remembrance of the evenings spent in singing over again the ancient songs. — (6) **1830** *Corrector* (Sag Harbor, N.Y.) 26 June 1/1 Lieutenant Poole . . . plays all cards From old sledge to ecarte. **1898** KING *Warrior Gap* 94 Papa, with one or two cronies, was playing 'old sledge' in the smoking compartment. — (7) *a***1846** *Quarter Race Ky.* 178 When my time came [in the dance], therefore, I . . . commenced 'the double shuffle,' . . . and finally finished off on 'old trimble toes'—a rare and difficult movement. — (8) **1881** *Harper's Mag.* Jan. 184/2 The young folks . . . played at 'prisoner's base' or 'old witch by the way-side.'

6. In the names of plants and animals: (1) **Old Billy,** =**old squaw;** (2) **Ephraim,** =***Ephraim,** also **old Eph;** (3) ***maid,** see as a main entry; (4) **Molly,** =next; (5) **squaw,** a common sea duck of the Northern Hemisphere, *Clangula hyemalis,* hence **old squawing,** hunting for ducks of this kind, *rare;* (6) **tick,** (see quot.), *rare;* (7) ***wife,** =**old squaw;** (8) **witch grass,** the common panic grass, *Panicum capillare;* (9) ***woman,** the beach wormwood; (10) **woman's smock,** (see quot.).

(1) **1917** *Birds of Amer.* I. 141 Old-Squaw. . . . Other Names. . . . Old Wife; Old Injin; . . . Old Molly; Old Billy. — (2) **1854** M. REID *Hunters' Feast* xxv. 221 Thur I saddled my mar, an' then rid back to git my gun, an' perhaps, to give old Eph'm a fresh taste o' lead. **1889** MUNROE *Golden Days* xiv. 152 Old Eph's dead enough. **1947** DEVOTO *Across Wide Missouri* 113 He fired a pistol into the thicket and then started throwing stones, to bring Old Ephraim out. — (4) **1841** *S. Lit. Messenger* VII. 220/1 An old molly has her nest in the inside. **1917** [see **Old Billy**].

(5) **1838** AUDUBON *Ornith. Biog.* IV. 105 They have various appellations, among others those of 'old wives' and 'old squaws.' **1860** in *Outing* (1913) March 688/2 Most everyone in town went old squawing to-day. **1945** *Mass. Audubon Soc. Bul.* Feb. 18 Just offshore are Cormorants, Scoters, Mergansers and the diving ducks: Golden-eye, Buffle-head, Old-squaw and American Eider. — (6) **1838** GOSSE *Letters* 220 The first season they are called Seed-ticks—the minute ones mentioned above; the next year they become Yearling-ticks; and the third, Old-ticks. — (7) **1634** WOOD *N. Eng. Prospect* (1865) 34 The Oldwives be a foule that never leave tatling day or night, something bigger than a Ducke. **1794** *Mass. H.S. Coll.* 1 Ser. III. 199 Sea fowl are plenty on the shores and in the bay; particularly the . . . sea duck, old wife, . . . widgeon, and peep. **1917** *Birds of Amer.* I. 141 Old-Squaw. . . . [Also called] Old Wife. — (8) **1847** DARLINGTON *Weeds & Plants* 403 Old-witch grass. . . . Sandy pastures, cultivated grounds; throughout the United States. **1894** COULTER *Bot. W. Texas* III. 508 Old witch grass. . . . Annual. . . . In cultivated land everywhere. — (9) **1931** CLUTE *Plants* 89 The plant called old man (*Artemisia abrotanum*) certainly has no connection with the devil and of course neither has the old woman (*Artemisia absinthium*).

(10) **1789** ANBUREY *Travels* II. 451 The leaves [of the tulip tree] grow in a very peculiar shape; from whence the tree has, in some places, the appellation of the old woman's smock.

Oldberg 'oldbɜg, *n.* Short for **Duchess of Oldenburg** *q.v., s.v.* ***Duchess.** *Obs.* — **1895** *Dept. Agric. Yrbk. 1894* 211 In this zone we enter the true agricultural part of our country, where apples (Oldberg, Baldwin, Greening . . .) attain their highest perfection.

Old Colony. Plymouth colony. Now *hist.*

1809 KENDALL *Travels* II. 36 To the south-east of Boston, distant about forty miles, is Plymouth, the oldest of the settlements in New England, and hence, in Boston, commonly known by the name of the *Old Colony.* **1831** *Boston Transcript* 31 Oct. 3/2 The roads are very good in all directions through the old Colony. **1914** A. MATTHEWS in *Mass. Col. Soc. Pub.* XVII. 362 This restriction, however, of the terms Pilgrims and Pilgrim Fathers exclusively to the Plymouth settlers is recognized at the present time only in the Old Colony itself.

attrib. **1769** in *Pub. Col. Soc.* XVII. 298 The Old Colony Club . . . met in commemmoration of the landing of their worthy ancestors in this place. **1770** *Ib.* 302 The Old Colony song with a number of others was sung, after which the company withdrew. **1798** *Columbian Centinel* 29 Dec. 3/1 The following toasts evinced that the spirit of the *Old Colony* patriots had been bequeathed to the inheritors of their soil. **1858** LONGFELLOW *Courtship M. Standish* I. 1 In the Old Colony days, in Plymouth the land of the Pilgrims [etc.].

old continental. 1. =**continental money. 2.** A former soldier of the Continental Army. Both *obs.*

(1) **1783** FRENEAU *Poems* (1861) 286 That damnable bubble the *old continental,* That took people in at this wonderful crisis. **1838** *U.S. Mag.* I. 13 This revival of the 'Old Continental,' by the present hard-money reform Administration, was indeed unexpected. — (2) **1807** IRVING *Salmagundi* xi, The great crowd of buzzards, puffers, and 'old continentals' of all parties, who throng to the polls, to persuade, to cheat, or to force the freeholders into the right way. **1945** *Yale Lit. Mag.* XI. 40 (Th.), The 'Old Continentals,' of which our grandfathers tell, would have been most arrant cowards in comparison with a regiment of our modern heroes.

old coon.

1. (See quot. 1877 and cf. **coon 2.**) *Colloq.*

1835 LONGSTREET *Ga. Scenes* 216 To be sure I will, my old coon—take it—take it, and welcome. **1877** BARTLETT 436 'He's an old coon,' is said of one who is very shrewd; often applied to a political manager.

2. A Whig. Also **old (Tip) coon,** =**Old Tip.** *Obs.* Cf. **coon 2. b.**

1840 *Chi. Tribune* 18 July 2/5 The log-cabin-hard-cider party seem on the wane, or the private beverage *alias* principle is getting too hard even for the old *coons.* **1842** *Spirit of Times* (Phila.) 5 May (Th.), 'The old Tip coon' is pictured flat on his back, in consequence of the Virginia elections. **1846** CORCORAN *Pickings* 190 'Why are you not a locofoco?' said we . . . 'I live too near the old coon (Harrison) for that.'

Old Dan Tucker.

1. The name of a tune or song, prob. of Negro origin. *Colloq.*

1844 *Edinburgh Jrnl.* I. 412 While I was at Boston, the Bunker's Hill monument was opened in great style by the President. . . . Before the carriage marched one of the volunteer bands, playing the negro tune of 'Get out the Way, old Dan Tucker.' . . . I found that it was a tune very much in favour with the worthy citizens. **1927** BENÉT *J. B.'s Body* 296 All the old barely-recorded chants that are the land and no one poet's or musician's, [as] 'Old Dan Tucker,' 'The Bell of Albany,' . . . and cruel Barbara Allen in her pride. **1947** *Sat. Review* 27 Sep. 12/2 The boy . . . joins in the singing of 'Sourwood Mountain' and 'Old Dan Tucker.'

2. (See quot. 1940.)

[**1930** WITTKE *Tambo & Bones* 180 Dan Emmett's 'Old Dan Tucker' won a permanent place in American song books and the song was widely used as a playparty game, and later revived for a barn dance.] **1940** *Square Dance* 211 Miss Tucker or Old Dan Tucker. This is a mixer in which the two step is the basic dance. One extra gent representing Old Dan Tucker, or an extra lady called Miss Tucker stands in the center of the floor. **1944** WILSON *Passing Inst.* 92 Some communities . . . allowed play-party games: 'Susie in the Ring,' 'Roxie Ann,' . . 'Old Dan Tucker.'

Old Dominion. The state of Virginia. Also attrib.

"Dominion" was used by English sovereigns in referring to the possessions in America. In the course of time Virginia was known as the Ancient Dominion *q.v.* then the Old Dominion (see A. Mathews in *Notes & Queries* 2 Ser. XII. 31).

1778 *Va. State P.* I. 311, I should not see the old Dominion this winter. **1861** *Vanity Fair* 25 May 246/2 We will wrap the flag of our fathers around the 'Pan Handle' of Virginia and upset the entire dish of Old Dominion Secession. **1905** *N.Y. Ev. Post* 16 May 7 The Old Dominion is unlikely to send anybody else until his [Lee's] statute has been received there. **1949** *Newsweek* 1 Aug. 15/1 This constituted outside interference' in the affairs of the Old Dominion.

b. In full **Old Dominion State.**

1883 *Harper's Mag.* Dec. 110/2, [I had] passed across the boundaries of the Old Dominion State. **1947** *Times-Herald* (Wash., D.C.) 9 May D-3/1 We boated on to two hundred of these silver perch, as they are familiarly known by the natives in the Old Dominion State.

oldermost 'oldɚ͵most, *a. W.* Oldest. *Obs.* — **1843** CARLTON *New Purchase* II. 70 Ain't that oldermost stranger a kinder sort a preacher? **1856** CARTWRIGHT *Autobiog.* (De Vere), Where is your oldermost child, said the man to the unfortunate father?

old field.

1. A field formerly cultivated or worn out, as in the cultivation of tobacco or cotton. Also **Indian old field.**

1635 in *Amer. Sp.* XV. 290/2 Northerly on Cugleyes ould field. **1761** *Descr. S.C.* 6 There are dispersed up and down the Country several large Indian old fields, which are lands that have been cleared by the Indians, and now remain just as they left them. **1905** *Forestry Bureau Bul.* No. 63, 5 This study has to do mainly with the life history of second-growth white pine on old fields and pastures in New England. **1949** COLLINGWOOD & BRUSH *Knowing Your Trees* 45 Pure stands of young Virginia pine frequently follow on old fields when agriculture is abandoned.

2. In combs.: (1) **old field birch,** any one of several birches, esp. the white birch; (2) **lark,** *S.* =**meadow lark;** (3) **parlor,** a retreat in an unused field, *rare;* (4)

pine, see as a main entry; (5) **preacher,** an old-fashioned rural preacher; (6) **school,** a school situated in an old field, esp. a rural elementary school, also attrib.; (7) **schoolmaster,** a schoolmaster in an old field school.

(1) **1810** MICHAUX *Arbres* I. 26 *White birch* [ou] *Old field birch,* (Bouleau des terreins secs.) **1832** BROWNE *Sylva Amer.* 123 In the state of Maine, . . . [the name] Old Field Birch is . . . employed to distinguish the white birch from the canoe birch. **1949** COLLINGWOOD & BRUSH *Knowing Your Trees* 175 This accounts for the tree quickly taking possession of burned-over, cutover and abandoned land, which has given it the name 'oldfield birch.' — (2) **1805** LEWIS in *L. & Clark Exped.* II. (1904) 180 There is a kind of larke here that much resembles the bird called the oldfield lark with a yellow brest and a black spot on the croop. **1811** WILSON *Ornithology* III. 22 Their general name is the Meadow Lark; among the Virginians they are usually called the Old Field Lark. **1917** *Birds of Amer.* II. 251. — (3) **1874** *Southern Mag.* XIV. 490 My old-field parlor is the only place in the world where I am free.

(5) **1904** T. E. WATSON *Bethany* 168 The tremendous emphasis with which the old field preacher uttered the words . . . I shall never forget. — (6) **1806** WEEMS *Washington* (1867) 12 The first place of education to which George was ever sent, was a little 'old field school.' **1862** BROWNLOW *Sketches* 225, I worked for wages long enough to enable me to acquire an 'old field-school English education.' **1948** DICK *Dixie Frontier* 172 Located at the edge of the forest, the schools were often called 'forest schools.' Others, located on worn-out cultivated areas, were called 'old field' schools. — (7) **1853** BALDWIN *Flush Times Ala.* 106 He had been an old-field schoolmaster.

b. Also in more occasional combs. of obvious meaning, as (1) **old field beach,** (2) **colt,** (3) **corn,** (4) **fence,** *attrib.,* (5) **ground,** (6) **growth,** (7) **land,** (8) **plum,** (9) **scrub,** (10) **tobacco,** (11) **trash.**

(1) **1741** *Brookhaven Rec.* 148 A certain piece of Thatch or thatch bed, lying between the little neck & the old field beach. — (2) **1835** *S. Lit. Messenger* I. 582, I could . . . only remember that every untrimmed old field colt was a regular descendant of Eclipse. **1946** NIXON *Va. Words.* — (3) **1829** COMMONS *Doc. Hist.* I. 240 Ploughs . . . started in old field corn. — (4) **1690** *Huntington Rec.* II. 70 A black oak by ye south cornar by a rock by ye ould feld fence side.

(5) **1772** *Md. Hist. Mag.* XIV. 278 Our Corn . . . is very good at all the Quarters, some of this old Field ground . . . Excepted. — (6) **1883** ZEIGLER & GROSSCUP *Alleghanies* 170 Smaller tracts are covered with what is known as old field growth—scrub oak and pines. — (7) **1883** ZEIGLER & GROSSCUP *Alleghanies* 175 It is not wise to select 'old field land,' with a view to raising it to a good state of cultivation. — (8) **1887** *Harper's Mag.* Sep. 588/2 She been goin' out between times, and getherin' old-field plums. — (9) **1834** CARUTHERS *Kentuckian* I. 12, I would bet my horse Talleyrand against an old field scrub that that fellow is a Yankee.

(10) **1771** *Md. Hist. Mag.* XIV. 128 Nothing but Rain is wanting to make the Oldfield tob[acc]o before the House very good. — (11) **1897** TERHUNE *Old-field School* 35 If she had carried what he named in his displeasure, 'old-field trash,' to 'the house,' she would have been detained there by the storm.

old field pine. Chiefly *S.* Any one of various pines, as the loblolly, sand, and yellow pines *qq.v.*

1797 HAWKINS *Letters* 89, The whole grown up with old field pine, some of them a foot and an half diameter. **1877** BARTLETT 363 *Loblolly Pine.* Sometimes called, in the Southern States, 'Old-field Pine,' and in Southern Virginia, 'White Pine.' **1894** COULTER *Bot. W. Texas* III. 554 *Pinus Taeda.* A tree 15 to 45 m. high. . . . Extending from the Gulf States to the valley of the Colorado. 'Loblolly pine.' 'Old-field pine.' **1949** COLLINGWOOD & BRUSH *Knowing Your Trees* 38/2 They grow best on exposed mineral soil such as abandoned agricultural land. Accordingly, the tree is called 'old field pine.'

* **old guard.** Also **Old Guard.**

1. *transf.* The conservative, dependable element in an organization, the old stand-bys. Also attrib.

1852 QUITMAN in Claiborne *Life Quitman* II. 164 What shall we of the strict state-rights school, what shall the 'Old Guard' do? **1881** *Chi. Tribune* 3 June 4/2 He is very differently situated now than when he was leading the 'Old Guard' in the Chicago Convention. **1949** *Chi. D. News* 26 March 6/4 Revolt of the Young Republican organization against the 'old guard' domination of the Illinois G.O.P. is reported gathering momentum.

Hence (1) **old guarder,** (2) **guardism,** (3) **guardist,** (4) **guardsman,** (5) **guardster.**

(1) **1946** *Chi. D. News* 6 April 6/2 [He was] an amiable, bumbling Old Guarder who had once been treasurer of the United States. **1948** *Ib.* 10 April 6/2 Crusty old-guarders of the Republican National Committee usually dismiss Stassen as a well intentioned young man who has a lot to learn about 'practical' politics. — (2) **1945** *Jefferson Co. Republican* (Jefferson, Colo.) 20 June 4/1 Jefferson County, politically, has long been considered one of the strongholds of Republican Old Guardism. **1947** *Harper's Mag.* Oct. 34/1 From the standpoint of a study of Old Guardism, however, the Athaeneum is Mecca itself. — (3) **1947** *Time* 25 Aug. 20/3 Old Guardists often try to link him with Wendell Willkie, who became a registered Republican less than a year before he became the party's nominee. — (4) **1948** *Sat. Ev. Post* 16 Oct. 49/2 Most of the Old Guardsmen in Congress are men of strong prejudices rather than deep principles.

(5) **1912** *Sat. Ev. Post* 27 July 4/1 The Old Guardsters were in the last ditch and they knew it.

2. (See quot.)

1900 *Cong. Rec.* 16 Feb. 1880/2 The regiments and the companies from Maryland . . . distinguished themselves throughout the Revolutionary war as . . . the Old Guard of the Continental forces.

Old Hunker.

1. *pl.* =**Hunker 1.** Also attrib.

1844 *Va. Free Press* 2 Jan. 2/2 The 'Chivalry' next tune their pipes for Annexation, but the 'Old Hunkers' of New York respond—'Not so fast.' **1850** P. HONE *Diary* II. 388 In this State the Democrats are all at swords' points; the Old-Hunkers say, Whigs rather than Barnburners. **1910** *Springfield W. Republican* 15 Dec. 2 This will shock republicans of the old hunker type, if any such exist in this time of political upheaval.

2. Old Hunkerism, =**Hunkerism.**

1844 in BOUCHER & BROOKS *Corr. addressed to Calhoun* (1930) 271 The slightest intimation to the public ear that *'Old Hunkerism'* is to prevail, and it is the death warrant of the Democracy. **1848** *Gem of Prairie* (Chi.) 25 Nov. 5/1 Were he to swing himself clear of 'Old Hunkerism,' and push out boldly into the current of reform, much . . . honor to himself, would be the result. **1906** *Springfield W. Republican* 6 Dec. 8 Thus does the president compromise in his advanced position with the old republican hunkerism.

Old Ironsides. The U.S. frigate "Constitution," launched in 1797.

1815 *Niles' Reg.* IX. Supp. 90/2 Old *Ironsides,* once more now rides, In search of English cruizers. **1900** *Cong. Rec.* 8 Feb. 1656/1 The frigate *Constitution,* better known as 'Old Ironsides,' is now moored to a wharf at the Boston Navy-Yard. **1948** *Chi. Tribune* 25 March 1. 24/7 In 1927 the navy had no one who could supervise the reconstruction of Old Ironsides and had to call in John Lord, a Maine shipbuilder.

transf. **1861** *Dly. Dispatch* (Richmond, Va.) 30 April 4/1 Virginia, Old Ironsides, is now boldly launched in the sea of war—her sails proudly flapping in the roar of the coming storm.

b. In the name of a club.

1841 *Louisville Journal* 31 May 2/2 The old Ironsides Club of Philadelphia has appointed a committee of its members to address Commodore Stewart, whom they have nominated for the Presidency.

c. (See quot. 1890.) *Obs.*

1856 *N.Y. Herald* 16 Jan. 3/1 A Broadside from Old Ironsides. Appeal from Commodore Stewart to Congress. **1890** *Cong. Rec.* 9 May 4383/1 Like the famous frigate Constitution, [Admiral Charles] Stewart received the appellation of 'Old Ironsides.'

* **old maid.**

1. The Indian mallow of the East Indies, *Abutilon theophrasti,* or a garden variety of zinnia, *Zinnia elegans.*

1839 *S. Lit. Messenger* V. 751/2 A particular spot in his garden was appropriated to the culture of old maids. **1880** *Scribner's Mo.* May 101/2 In my section an annoying weed is *Abutilon,* or velvet-leaf, also called 'old maid.' **1888** *Cent. Mag.* Oct. 896/1 The flower-garden overrun with . . . four-o'clocks, old-maids, and sunflowers.

2. old maid's breastpin, pink, (see quots.).

1892 *Amer. Folk-Lore* V. 92 *Saponaria officinalis,* old maid's pink. **1894** *Ib.* VII. 92 *Coreopsis,* sp., old maid's breastpin, Plymouth, O.

* **old man.**

1. A master, foreman, or overseer; the boss.

1837 *S. Lit. Messenger* III. 86, I say, darkie, the old man keeps good liquor, and plenty of belly timber, don't he? **1887** GEORGE *40 Yrs. on Rail* 167 All 'the boys' on the road will swear by their superintendents, and . . . they feel that if they can only lay it [a grievance] before the 'old man' it will be properly dealt with. **1949** HERTRICH *Huntington Bot. Gardens* 32, I declined to accept it, but suggested that he deduct this amount 'from the Old Man's bill.'

2. Any old man. Used as a substitute for "Old Mr. ———." Also fig. *Colloq.*

1843 CARLTON *New Purchase* I. 92 It ain't more nor a mile to oleman Sturgisses. **1910** W. M. RAINE *B. O'Connor* 30 When Old Man Trouble comes knocking at the door. **1910** O. HENRY *Strictly Business* 89 We punched cows together in Old Man Garcia's outfit. **1930** *Chi. D. Maroon* 28 Oct. 1/3 Old Man Stagg spoke a few words in commending . . . the students for their show of enthusiasm.

b. Old Man Eloquent, (see quot. 1900).

1846 *Quincy* (Ill.) *Whig* 3 March 2/3 We should suppose that the 'old man eloquent,' would pause in his career, and look about him.

1900 *Cong. Rec.* 25 Jan. 1208/1 John Quincy Adams, the 'Old Man Eloquent,' expressed very happily what we now . . . believe.

3. (See quot.)

1856 OLMSTED *Slave States* 207 'Well, now, old man,' said I, 'you go and cut me two cords to-day.' 'Oh, Marsa! two cords! Nobody couldn do dat.' *Ib.* (*footnote*), 'Old Man' is a common title of address to any middle-aged negro in Virginia, whose name is not known. 'Boy' and 'Old Man' may be applied to the same person.

4. A grizzly bear. *Colloq.*

1886 *Outing* IX. 108/1 You've got more sand than I thought you had to tackle the old man on the open plain.

5. Among the Indians, a wise man or seer.

1903 WHITE *Forest* 208 Certain individuals gain a remarkable . . . respect for wisdom, or hunting skill. . . . These men are the so-called 'old-men' often mentioned in Indian manifestoes.

6. a. Old Man of the Mountain, a natural formation on a mountainside having a fancied resemblance to the face of an old man (see also quot. 1871). **b. Old Man River,** the Mississippi River.

(a) 1871 *N.Y. Herald* 6 Sep. 6/6 It seems as if 'the Old Man of the Mountains' [i.e., Brigham Young] meant to fight every step of the federal government for the supremacy of Utah. **1939** PICKWELL *Deserts* 48/2 The devil's garden is well named: with boulders and 'barrels' and 'Old Men of the Mountain' it is a grotesque feature of the land of sun and wind and freakish rain. — **(b) 1933** *Lit. Digest* 12 Aug. 28/2 (*heading*), Who Owns Old Man River? **1949** *Nat. Hist.* Nov. 427/3 At last they have succeeded in vaulting the natural barriers between the Great Lakes and Old Man River.

7. In the names of plants: (1) **old man cactus,** a southwestern cactus, *Cephalocereus senilis*, the joints of which have long drooping hairs or whiskers, cf. **señita;** (2) **cholla,** =prec.; (3) ∗**-'s beard,** (*a*) =**fringe tree;** (*b*) the black gum, *Nyssa silvatica.*

(1) 1889 *Cent.* 899/2 Cereus. . . . The old-man cactus, *C. senilis*, is so called from the long gray hairs covering the top of the stem. **1948** *So. Sierran* May 5/2 The Organ Pipe and Senita (Old Man) Cacti are similar except the Senita has whiskers. — **(2) 1924** *Cent. Mag.* July 387/1 Among the chollas . . . [are] distinguished the 'old-man' cholla, silvery-haired with the sheaths of its dense covering of spines. — **(3)** (*a*) **1855** SIMMS *Forayers* 485 Don't forget the 'wake robbin,' and the 'old man's beard,' the leafy green look of the one, and the snow-white fringes of the other. **1941** R. S. WALKER *Lookout* 61 Fringe-tree, or Old Man's Beard, which is more often a shrub than it is a tree, builds snow-like spots in many places on the top of the mountain. (*b*) **1894** *Amer. Folk-Lore* VII. 90 *Nyssa sylvatica*, old man's beard, Lincolnton, N.C. **1949** *Nature Mag.* April 187/2 As the days shorten, fluffy old man's beard is white against the blue October sky.

Old Ned. (See quots.) *Colloq.* Cf. ∗**Ned.**

1833 J. E. ALEXANDER *Transatlantic Sk.* II. 83 A snow-white cloth was spread, on which were placed bacon, or 'Old Ned,' as it is called in Tennessee. **1869** *Overland Mo.* Aug. 129 Southern smoke-cured pork, in distinction from the Northern salted article, in allusion to the famous negro song, was termed '*Old Ned*,' from its sable appearance. **1936** *Amer. Sp.* XI. 316 Old Ned, n. Home-cured bacon. The term is used to mean *boar* in Taney county, Mo. **1949** *Amer. Folk-Lore* Jan.–Mar. 63 The devil was referred to as 'Old Ned' or 'Old Scratch.'

b. *To raise old Ned*, to raise Cain. *Colloq.* See ∗ **Cain.**

1859 *N.Y Wkly. Tribune* 10 Sep. 7/4 The accounts in The Tribune raise Old Ned. **1942** WARNICK *Dialect Garrett Co., Md.* 12 Raise old Ned, v. phr., to make a row (Slang).

Old Probabilities. (See quot. 1877.) *Colloq.* Cf. next.

1873 *Harper's Mag.* July 235/1 In an upper room of the Signal Service Bureau of the War Department 'Old Probabilities,' having studied the weather reports received from all sections of the country, is making up his prognostications for the morrow. **1877** BARTLETT 496 *Old Probabilities*, a term applied to the superintendent of the bureau at Washington, from which the weather reports are issued. **1888** *N.Y. Herald* 4 Nov. 8/4 As a rule Old Probabilities has been rather kindly disposed to both parties and has vouchsafed tolerable marching weather . . . [for both] republicans and democrats.

transf. **1873** *Cin. Commercial* 3 Mar. 3/2 The first indications of a breeze can be detected by any 'Old Probabilities' who hangs about the lobbies or occupies a seat in the Legislature, with as much certainty as the barometer indicates the coming storm. **1874** *Cong. Rec.* I. April 2679/1 A certain politician . . . seemed to have a political 'Old Probabilities' who foretold for him the political atmosphere.

Old Probs. (See quot. 1912 and cf. prec.) *Colloq.* — **1874** *Cin. Enquirer* 1 July 2/3. **1912** *Everybody's Mag.* Dec. (Almanac p. 3—Tu.), Cleveland Abbe ('Old Probs'), first man to make daily weather predictions, born, 1838.

∗ **old school.**

1. A faction of conservatives in the Democratic party, esp. such a group in Pennsylvania. Also attrib. *Obs.* Cf. **old school man** in **3.** (2) below.

1815 *Niles' Reg.* IX. 120/2 The federal and 'old school' democratic candidate for Congress, . . . has been elected. **1816** *Ib.* XI. 108 The highest federal vote in the city and county of Philadelphia was, 4449. . . . 'Old school' democrats, 2595. **1817** *Ib.* XII. 16 At the late election for state treasurer [of Pa.] the joint ballot of the legislature stood thus—for . . . James Brady, 'fed.' 20; James Whitehill, 'old-school,' 10. **1825** *Const. Advocate* (Frankfort, Ky.) 15 Dec. 4/4 The result of the last election . . . will be better understood as an overwhelming triumph of the regular nominated old school Democratic ticket. [**1830** *Mechanics' Press* (Utica, N.Y.) 10 July 279/1 He calls those composing the meeting in New York, 'Democratic Republicans,' and those which nominated him at Albany last week, 'Democrats of the Old School.']

2. Applied to or used of Old School Presbyterians. Cf. **3.** (3) below.

1837 in *Spirit XIX Cent.* (1842) Mar. 132 Doubtless you know what is going forward among the Old School. **1853** STOWE *Key* 211/1 The course of the Old-School Assembly after the separation, in relation to the subject of slavery may be best expressed by quoting one of their resolutions. **1857** *Richmond* (Va.) *D. Whig* 3 Sep. 2/3 But for the violation by an old School Presbytery, of the rule of discipline in regard to ministers under citation, he should never have terminated his affiliation with the Old School Church. **1900** *Cong. Rec.* 17 Jan. 916/2 The old hard-shell Presbyterian of the old school took occasion in his remarks . . . to say that the Lord had ordered everything.

Hence **Old Schoolism.** *Obs.*

1838 in *Spirit XIX Cent.* (1842) June 282 There is no form of *New Schoolism* . . . in this region . . . but what is the decided and implacable foe of Presbyterian *Old Schoolism.*

3. In special combs.: (1) **old school Baptist,** an extremely Calvinistic branch of the Baptist Church, dating from about 1835, cf. **Hard-shell Baptist;** (2) **man,** (see quot. 1818); (3) **Presbyterian,** (*a*) a conservative Presbyterian opposed to the views of the New School Presbyterians *q.v.*, (*b*) *a.* adhering to the views of such a Presbyterian.

(1) 1867 DIXON *New Amer.* II. 308 In a very short time this body was divided into Old School Baptists (called by their enemies Anti-effort Baptists), Sabbatarians [etc.]. **1949** *Pacific Northwest Quart.* April 124 In the period before the Civil War [they] generally preferred to be called Old School Baptists. — **(2) 1818** FEARON *Sketches* 139 The moderate democrats, [are] called by the several names of 'Independent Republicans,' 'Democrats of the Revolution,' and 'Old Schoolmen.' **1835** H. C. TODD *Notes* 34 The names of their political parties are *Patent Democrats, Old Schoolmen, Hartford Conventionalists* and *Blue-light Men.* — **(3)** (*a*) **1837** PECK *Gaz. Illinois* 72 McDonough College . . . is identified with the interests of the 'old school' Presbyterians. (*b*) **1847** H. HOWE *Ohio* 274 The first church, the old school Presbyterian, . . . was built about 1817. **1898** HARPER *S. B. Anthony* I. 218, I recommend that you form an acquaintance . . . with some well-settled Old-School-Presbyterian clergyman.

old settler, *n.*

1. One of the first or earliest settlers in a community.

1837 WM. F. GRAY *Diary* (1909) 224 Rude hospitality and unaffected kindness are the characteristics of the old settlers that I meet with. **1873** *Winfield* (Kans.) *Courier* 27 May 2/3 Mr. and Mrs. Kellogg . . . will long be remembered by the old settlers of Arkansas City, and Winfield.

2. A member of that part of the Cherokee Nation that settled west of the Mississippi before 1819. Also attrib.

1839 *26th Congress* 1 Sess. H.R. Ex. Doc. No. 129, 15 The President of the United States, and many of the principal men of the old settlers, do not recognise this as the settled government of the Cherokee Nation. **1860** in *Amer. Sp.* XXII. 204/1 These were known as the 'Old settler party,' or 'Western Cherokees.' **1900** *19th Ann. Rep. Bureau Amer. Ethnol.* 133 They were welcomed by their kindred, the 'Arkansas Cherokee'—hereafter to be known for distinction as the 'Old Settlers'—who held the country under previous treaties in 1828 and 1833.

old tenor. (See quot. 1895 and cf. **new tenor.**) Now *hist.* Cf. **Bay, Hampshire old tenor.**

1758 *Boston Rec.* 201 We enjoin you . . . That the funds be laid in Paper Bills of the Old Tenor, and not in Bills of the New Tenor. **1776** MCROBERT *Tour* 23 They have in New York two denominations of currency, *viz.* Old tenor, and lawful money. Old tenor is of very small value. **1895** in *Pub. Col. Soc.* III. 8 In 1737 there was a simultaneous issue in Massachusetts of two classes of Province Bills, one being identical in form with those which were already in circulation, while those of the other class stated that they were to be received on the basis of twenty shillings for three ounces of silver, troy weight. Bills of these forms were for a time thereafter distinguished under the titles of 'old tenor' and 'new tenor.' **1944** ADAMS *Album Amer. Hist.* I. 282 The previous currency had been called old tenor, and it had depreciated in value so much that a pound sterling was equivalent to eleven pounds old tenor.

old town.

1. A clearing or opening that was formerly the site of an Indian village. Usu. as a proper name.

[**1635** in *Amer. Sp.* XV. 291 Beginning on Wly. side of an old Indian Towne.] **1699** *Va. State P.* I. 65 The English intend to take up land and seat upon a place—called then old Town. **1707** *Va. Mag. Hist. & Biog.* V. 48 The Waynoak Indians . . . settled upon the South side of the Black Water Swamp, at a place now called the old town. **1843** HAYWARD *Gazetteer of Me.* 89 In later years, Indian Oldtown has become their village, and their principal place of residence. **1910** HODGE *Amer. Indians* II. 118 Oldtown. A village of the Penobscot on an island in Penobscot r., a few m. above Bangor, Me. It contained 410 inhabitants in 1898. **1947** [see **b.** below].

b. (See quot. 1947.)

1922 *Outing* March 249/1 *Alma*, a staunch Oldtown and flagship of our tiny fleet, was considered best bet for the first trial. [**1947** COFFIN *Yankee Coast* 163 The descendants of the Old Town Indians and the inheritors of their traditions have turned out, right up till our time, the lightest boat in the world, the canoe, of cedar and sheer poetry.]

2. In towns formerly Spanish or French: The old section of town as distinguished from the American-built section. *Obs.*

1855 in *So. Calif. Hist. Soc. Pub.* 16, 60 We next arrive at the part called Old Town by the americans and El Presidio by the Californians, this part is San Diego proper. **1883** *Cent. Mag.* June 230/1 However, the suburban lands [in New Orleans] were sold, old town and down-town property was sinking in value. **1885** *Wkly. New Mexican Rev.* 9 April 3/3 Albuquerque . . . has an old town like nearly all of the New Mexico cities.

Old Virginia.

1. Virginia, esp. the eastern portion of it. Also attrib.

1624 SMITH *Gen. Hist. Va.* A3 A Map of the old Virginia, with the figures of the Salvages. **1817** ROYALL *Letters from Ala.* (1830) 21 Foreigners often distinguish it [eastern and western Virginia] by the terms Old Virginia and New Virginia. **1894** MARK TWAIN *P. Wilson* xii, In Missouri a recognized superiority attached to any person who hailed from Old Virginia. **1948** DICK *Dixie Frontier* 88 The black people mourn for their 'Ole Virginny' homes and their loved ones.

b. Short for "Old Virginia tobacco." *Rare.*

1850 GARRARD *Wah-To-Yah* xiii. 169 We reclined on out-spread saddle blankets, . . . thoughtfully puffing 'Old Virginia,' from time-worn clay pipes.

c. Old Virginia breakdown, a kind of rollicking rustic dance.

1867 J. L. PEYTON *Adv. Grandfather* 170 Graceful minuets, Scotch reels or as they are sometimes called 'Old Virginia break downs,' were the order of the night.

2. Old Virginian, a Virginian of older times.

1800 TATHAM *Agric. & Comm.* 87 The inhabitants [of certain Spanish colonies] . . . partake . . . of the habits of that ancient order of happy and liberal people the *old Virginians.* **1893** PAGE in *Harper's Mag.* Dec. 10/2 [In Richmond] met, year after year, the old Virginians, . . . to enjoy the gay life of the capital of the Old Dominion.

* **oleo,** *n.* Short for next. Also attrib.

1888 *Pall Mall Gaz.* 26 Jan. 12/1 When the law [of Iowa] compelled the sale of 'oleo' for what it was . . . more has been realized from the summer make of butter. **1894** *N.Y. Wkly. Tribune* 14 March 1/3 We are going to give . . . the dairymen an even, fair chance with the 'oleo' men. **1913** *Industrial Worker* (Spokane) 4 Sep. 4/3 Every worker that . . . eats in cheap 'joints' knows what 'olio' is. **1949** *Amer. Butter & Cheese Rev.* Mar. 2/2 Oleo manufacturers do everything to dupe the consumer into thinking their product is butter.

* **oleomargarine,** *n.* Any one of various artificially prepared edible fats used as a substitute for butter. Also attrib.

1873 *Scientific Amer.* 18 Oct. 246 Description of the manufacture of artificial butter by the 'Oleomargarine Manufacturing Company.' *a***1877** *N.Y. Tribune* (B. 439), The [N.Y.] Governor having signed the act for the protection of buttermakers, all imitations of butter are hereafter to be sold only under the name of oleomargarine. **1948** *Democrat* 11 March 4/1 There have been federal statutes penalizing the sale of oleomargarine.

oleo oil. A yellow, buttery oil expressed from animal fats, and often used in making oleomargarine.

1882 *Missouri Rep.* LXXVII. 114 The proper butterfat is separated by a scientific process from the natural fat into oleo oil, which . . . is churned into butter. [**1884** *N.Y. Wkly. Tribune* 5 March 10/4 Many of the large western creameries use oleomargarine oil with which to adulterate and increase their 'butter' product.] **1906** E. H. RICHARDS *Food Materials* 58 Oleomargarine and butterine are prepared in a similar manner from oleo oil (beef fat) or neutral lard and milk by churning and salting and coloring to imitate butter.

* **olive,** *n.* As the last term in **Indian, mission, wild olive.**

* **olive,** *a.* In the names of birds: (1) **olive-back,** =next; (2) **-backed thrush,** a common thrush, *Hylocichla ustulata swainsoni*, having a back of olive-brown color; (3) **-sided flycatcher,** (see quot. 1839); (4) **-sided king-bird,** (see quot.).

(**1**) **1845** JUDD *Margaret* I. 148 The olive-backs trilled and chanted among the trees. **1945** *Mass. Audubon Soc. Bul.* March 43 Two Thrushes of annual interest to students are the migrant Olive-back and the Gray-cheek. — (**2**) **1844** *Nat. Hist. N.Y., Zoology* II. 74 The Olive-Backed Thrush is closely allied to the [hermit thrush]. **1946** STANWELL-FLETCHER *Driftwood Valley* 187 We spend the long bright evenings out on the lake, listening to the chorus of olive-backed thrushes. — (**3**) **1839** AUDUBON *Ornith. Biog.* V. 422 Olive-Sided Flycatcher, *Mus[c]icapa Cooperi*, . . . has never been observed in South Carolina, although I met with it in Georgia. **1948** *Pacific Discovery* March April 18/1 The oft-repeated song of the linnet and the unmistakable *McDeever!* of the olive-sided flycatcher are familiar sounds. — (**4**) **1844** *Nat. Hist. N.Y., Zoology* II. 118 The Olive-Sided King-Bird. *Tyrannus cooperi.* . . . This plain-colored species was discovered by William Cooper (from whom it derives its name) in 1829.

olla 'ɑlə, *n. S.W.* [Sp., pot. An Amer. borrowing.] A water pot or jar, of porous material, as earthenware or vegetable fiber.

1844 FARNHAM *Travels in Calif.* 367 The matrimonial alliance formed, the suitor presents his lady love with a jug, in their [i.e., Indian] language an *olo*, the acceptance of which denotes her consent.

An olla used with a head strap

1885 *Outing* Oct. 24/2 Opposite are two old crones filling 'ollas' of basket-work, rendered fully water-proof by a coating of either mesquite or pinon pitch. **1948** *Desert Mag.* Jan. 21/2 It must have been a big olla.

olykoek 'ɑlɪˌkuk, *n.* Chiefly *N.Y.* [Du. *oliekoek*, in same sense.] (See quot. 1947.)

1809 IRVING *Knickerb.* III. iii, The table . . . was always sure to boast an enormous dish of balls of sweetened dough, fried in hog's fat, and called dough nuts, or oly koeks. **1831** *N.Y. Mirror* 31 Dec. 204/3 They had neither prepared mince pies, nor oily cooks, nor crullers, nor any of the good things consecrated to St. Nicholas. **1947** BEROLZHEIMER *Regional Cookbook* 138 The doughnut originated in Holland where it was called 'olie koeken,' which means oil cakes. While the Pilgrims were in Holland on their trip to the New World, they learned to make doughnuts and brought this knowledge to Plymouth Rock as did the Dutch themselves later when they settled in New Amsterdam.

Omaha 'oməˌhɔ, *n.* [Osage name: "those going against the wind or current," "upstream people."] A member of a Siouan tribe of Indians in Nebraska. Also *pl.* or *collect.*, the tribe itself. Cf. **Maha.**

1823 LONG *Exped.* I. 166 As we were cutting up a log for fuel, one of the Omawhaws seeing a knot . . . requested us to cut it off for him. *c***1834** CATLIN *Indians* II. 6 A famous chief of the O-ma-haws, by the name of the Black Bird . . . requested them to take his body down the river. **1900** G. B. GRINNELL *Indian of To-Day* 12 He killed one more Omaha. **1949** *Nat. Geog. Mag.* Aug. 155/2 A few tribes, among them the Hidatsa, Mandan, Omaha, Pawnee, Ponca, and Iroquois, have been known to grow sweet corn.

attrib. **1839** *Boston W. Mag.* 12 Jan. 145/2 The Omaha village was one of the most beautiful that can be imagined. **1936** STREETER

Prairie Towns & Cattle Trails 190 He went with the Omaha Indians on a buffalo hunt. **1947** *Primitive Man* July 39 The Gros Ventres tribe . . . adopted the Grass dance, sometimes called the Omaha dance, as it spread rapidly over the northern plains in relatively recent times. **1949** *10 Story Western* May 39/1 He slew two of the enemy of eight Omaha Indian scouts and captured six of the eight horses.

Omahog ˈomə,hɔg, *n.* [*Omaha*+ * *hog.*] A native or inhabitant of Omaha, Nebraska.

1876 *Silver City* (Ida.) *Avalanche* 8 Feb. 2/2 A party of eight . . . Omahogs, or, in other words, citizens of Omaha, left Cheyenne Wednesday for the Black Hills. **1889** *Sporting Life* (Phila.) 3 July 1/5 (*heading*), The 'Omahogs' Closing In On the Leader—Great Work All Round. **1933** *Amer. Sp.* Dec. 80/2 Out-state newspapers often call the inhabitants of Omaha, Nebraska, *Omahogs.*

Omish ˈɑmɪʃ, *n.* Variant of **Amish.** Also attrib.

1844 RUPP *Relig. Denominations* 560 Omish or Amish, is a name which was, in the United States, given to a society of Mennonites. **1867** W. H. DIXON *New Amer.* II. 309 No sect escaped this rage for separation, for independence, for individuality; neither Unitarian, nor Omish, nor River Brethren. **1880** *Harper's Mag.* July 184/1 At the door some of the Omish women sat knitting in their tight snuff-colored gowns. *Ib.*, They stopped for the night at the pleasant little Omish village of West Union.

* **omnibus,** *a.* In combs.: (1) **omnibus bill,** (*a*) a legislative bill containing many dissimilar or unrelated items, (*b*) (*cap.*) the Compromise of 1850; (2) **sleigh,** a large sleigh used as a public conveyance, *obs.;* (3) **ticket,** a ticket admitting a number of persons, *rare.*

(1) (*a*) **1850** *Cong. Globe* App. 8 May 524/1, I am opposed to all omnibus bills. **1949** *Newsweek* 9 May 16/2 Purpose of the McGrath omnibus bill . . . is to get the President's program together in one package. (*b*) **1852** *N.Y. Wkly. Tribune* 20 March 1/2 There were numerous and powerful efforts made upon the celebrated Omnibus Bill. **1941** BUCKMASTER *Let My People Go* 176 The Omnibus Bill was passed, but the fight was carried up to the day the Fugitive Slave Law passed the Senate. — (2) **1839** *Spirit of Times* 28 Dec. 505/3 (We.), Omnibus-sleigh. **1860** *Boston Auditor's 48th Ann. Rep.* App. 323 City property [includes] . . . One Covered Omnibus Sleigh, One Box Top Sleigh. — (3) **1841** *Spirit of Times* 16 Oct. 385/3 (We.), Omnibus ticket. **1868** *Iowa Agric. Soc. Rep. 1867* 408 Some . . . tender hearted *friends* would take in their settlement and then proceed to some hole . . . in the fence and hand his 'omnibus ticket' to some other parent.

* **on,** *a.* **1.** Aware, possessing full knowledge or understanding. Cf. * **onto. 2.** Fashionable, in style. Both *Colloq.*

(1) **1885** *Santa Fe Wkly. New Mexican* 9 July 2/2 He hoped to sell the cavalry a large lot of supplies, but Major Van Horn was 'on.' **1910** TOMPKINS *Mothers & Fathers* 11 You would be so *on*, Bessie Trent. — (2) **1887** RITTENHOUSE *Maud* 403 He looked so good to my eyes standing there in his dark suit, . . . even the tie I preferred—a small dark one instead of the big flashy things that are 'on' now.

* **on,** *prep.*

1. a. Of a joke, laugh, or story: Against or at the expense of (someone). **b.** At the expense of, for (someone) to pay. Both *colloq.*

(**a**) **1866** *Harper's Mag.* July 271/2 There may be a joke about it; but if there is, it is on the Colonel, for he told me so. **1912** NICHOLSON *Hoosier Chron.* 205 It's one on Ed Thatcher, that's all! **1949** *Sat. Ev. Post* 5 Nov. 65/3 Old Doctor Winthrop, they say, when he entertained his classes with tales of Western exploration, used to tell that story on himself with a chuckle. — (**b**) **1871** *Republican Rev.* 29 July 2/3 After the first round they said it was 'on me.' **1949** *Summit Valley Times* (Argo, Ill.) 9 Nov. 8/1 Food and refreshments will be 'on the house' after 3 p.m. Nov. 13th.

2. Used in the sense of *in* or *upon* with reference to a train.

The *OED s.v. on, prep.* 1. d. says "With an enclosing carriage, *in* is used."

1886 *Cent. Mag.* XXXII. 471/2, I should go away on the first train. **1925** *Ladies' Home Jrnl.* Nov. 8/2 On the train he sat like one in a doze. [**1945** MENCKEN *Supp.* I. 490 An Englishman . . . does not get *on* a train or *aboard* it, but *in* it.]

3. In phrases: (1) *To be on it,* (*a*) to be skilled, ready for something, (*b*) (see quot. 1888), *slang;* (2) * *on time,* with reference to buying, to be paid for in instalments.

(1) (*a*) **1865** *Harper's Mag.* May 694/1 She's tolerable peert—the old 'oman is. Oh, she's on it, you bet. **1866** MARK TWAIN *Lett. Sandwich Isl.* (1938) 70 In San Francisco sometimes, if you offend a man, he proposes to take his coat off, and inquires, 'Are you on it?' **1881** A. A. HAYES *New Colo.* v. 77 You bet he could cook. He was just *on* it. (*b*) **1888** BARRERE-LELAND II. 97 This eccentric expression meant originally that a man was decidedly engaged in anything. It implied determination. 'I'm on it,' I understand it. It came into very general use about 1860. — (**2**) **1925** *Sat. Ev. Post* 10 Oct. 133/1 It's like peddling lots on time, instead of selling and developing acreage.

* **once,** *adv.* **1.** *once and again,* (see quot.). **2. once-over,** a quick examination or consideration of a person, plan, etc. *Slang.*

(**1**) **1859** BARTLETT, Once and again, occasionally, sometimes. A Southern phrase, equivalent to 'once in a while.' — (**2**) **1916** H. L. WILSON *Somewhere in Red Gap* v. 202, I got just about the once-over from every brute there, and that was all. **1949** *Sky Line Trail* Oct. 19/1 At the creek-bank he halted, giving me the once-over, then ambled unconcernedly away.

* **one,** *a.* and *n.*

1. A one-dollar bill.

1846 *Ill. State Reg.* 2 Oct. 2/6 Independent of the older issues, and such as are described in the Detectors, Ones, on the Banks of 'Broome county,' and 'Whitestown,' . . . have made their appearance. **1948** *Savings News* March 18/2 You see, my billfold had a $10 bill in it, not ten ones.

2. In combs.: (1) **one-and-a-half story house,** a house of one story with a low second story; (2) **arm,** see as a main entry; (3) **baser,** in baseball, a "single," or one-base hit; (4) **cent piece,** a coin worth one cent; (5) **dollar,** *attrib.* designating types of money having the value of one dollar; (6) * **eyed,** dishonest, *obs.;* (7) **eyed cat,** see **one old cat** as a main entry; (8) **gallus,** denoting anything small and insignificant, usu. attrib., *colloq.;* (9) * **horse,** see as a main entry; (10) **man power,** (see quot. 1892); (11) **night stand,** a small place where a traveling show stops for only one night, a one-night stop or show in such a town, also transf.; (12) **old cat,** see as a main entry; (13) **piece store,** (see quot.); (14) **price store,** a store in which goods are sold only at the marked price; (15) **term,** *attrib.* of or pertaining to a single term for the President of the U.S.; (16) **track,** *attrib.* denoting a mind regarded as narrow, capable of only a single train of thought, *colloq.;* (17) **-two-three,** see as a main entry.

(**1**) **1867** T. LACKLAND *Homespun* 66, We came near the . . . lane that led to the good man's little brown one-and-a-half story house. **1879** *Scribner's Mo.* June 260/1 Three hundred acres of moderately good ground, a neat one-and-a-half story house, with piazza. — (**3**) **1880** *Chi. Tribune* 12 May 8/5 Clapp . . . was brought in by Anson's one-baser. **1949** *L.A. Times* 13 March 25/8 Unser led off with a one-baser. — (**4**) **1873** *Statutes at Large* XVII. 427 The minor coins of the United States shall be a five-cent piece, a three-cent piece, and a one-cent piece. **1894** S. LEAVITT *Our Money Wars* 126 A pound of this metal [copper, tin, and zinc] coins 160 one-cent pieces.

(**5**) **1838** *N.Y. Advertiser & Exp.* 10 Jan. 3/4 He dwelt upon the One Dollar Bill Act. **1890** *Statutes at Large* XXVI. 485 From and after the passage of this act the coinage of the three-dollar gold piece, the one-dollar gold piece, and the three-cent nickel piece be, and the same is hereby, prohibited. **1946** *Reader's Digest* July 87/1 In a campus flower bed, through admissions of the prisoners, we found $5000 buried in one-dollar bills. — (**6**) **1833** *Sk. David Crockett* 24 In the slang of the backwoods, one swore that he would never be one-eyed. — (**8**) **1931** *K.C. Times* 25 Nov. 28 Driving 20-penny 'bachelor buttons' through the end of a one-gallus hand-me-down. **1945** MCATEE *Pheasant* 37 Neither are these birds benefited so much as the bob-white quail by the haphazard farming often described as 'one gallus.'

(**10**) **1848** POLK in *Pres. Mess. & P.* IV. 663 The Executive veto is a 'one-man power,' despotic in its character. **1892** W. S. WALSH *Literary Curiosities* 845 *One man power,* a term by which Americans personify a subject of their rooted jealousy, the government by, or great power lodged in, any single individual. **1925** BRYAN *Memoirs* 245 We want no one-man power. — (**11**) **1880** RANOUS *Diary of Daly Débutante* 189 This coming week . . . is to be what they call 'one-night stands.' **1917** KEPHART *Camping* I. 209 Water, wood, and good drainage may be all you need for a 'one-night stand.' **1948** *Chi. Tribune* 24 Jan. 1/2 The show . . . was to have finished the week here and then to have played one night stands thru central Ohio. — (**13**) **1882** G. A. SALA *Amer. Revisited* II. 13 Slop-shops, or 'one-piece stores' overflowing with guernseys, pea jackets, sou'-wester hats. — (**14**) **1850** in *Western Pa. Hist. Mag.* XXV. 132 Semi-Annual Sale of Dry Goods. At the One Price Store of A. A. Mason.

(**15**) **1845** *Cong. Globe* App. 13 Jan. 122/2 The North had been taunted with the fact that it never had had any but one-term presidents, democratic or federal. **1873** *Harper's Mag.* May 942/1 Belonging to the unfinished business [is] . . . the joint resolutions for the election of the President and Senators by the people, and for a one-term amendment to the Constitution. — (**16**) **1932** *K.C. Times* 5 May 20 The persons with the one-track mind are the ones who usually have the most collisions.

b. In the names of plants: (1) ***one berry,** (*a*) =**Indian turnip,** (*b*) =**checkerberry;** (2) **-seeded star cucumber,** (see quots.), cf. **single-seeded cucumber.**

(1) (*a*) **1877** BARTLETT 319 Jack-in-the-Pulpit. (*Arisæma triphyllum*). . . . In Connecticut, it is called *One-berry*. (*b*) **1892** *Amer. Folk-Lore* V. 100 *Gaultheria procumbens*, one-berry. — (2) **1847** DARLINGTON *Weeds & Plants* 141 *Sicyos angulatus*. . . . One-seeded star-cucumber. **1857** GRAY *Botany* 138 One-seeded Star-Cucumber. . . . Climbing annuals, with small whitish flowers. [**1901** MOHR *Plant Life Ala.* 748 *Sicyos angulatus*. One-seeded Bur Cucumber. . . . [Grows] Alleghenian to Louisianian area.]

c. *one catch all*, a children's outdoor game.

1876 J. BURROUGHS *Winter Sunshine* VIII. i. 210, I could not only walk upon the grass, but . . . play 'one catch all' with children, boys, dogs, or sheep upon it.

As the last term in **close, number, raw, sixteen-to-, twenty-one.**

one arm(ed).

1. one-armed bandit, a slot machine which upon occasion returns varying sums of money to the player who operates it by inserting a coin in a slot and pulling down on a lever (i.e., arm) of the machine. *Slang.*

[**1934** *Lit. Digest* 3 March 9/3 These slot machines are plain mechanical larceny.] **1940** *Amer. Mercury* Sep. 100/1 The machine that brought him from rags to riches was the notorious One Armed Bandit slot machine. **1949** *Newsweek* 21 Nov. (front cover), One-Armed Bandit: Annual Take $3,000,000,000.

Hence **one-armed banditry.**

1949 *Ill. State Reg.* 1 Feb. 4/1 There will be no compromise with one-armed banditry and commercialized vice.

2. one-arm lunch(room), a cheap restaurant in which the patrons do not eat at tables but in chairs provided with an armrest. *Slang.*

1912 NICHOLSON *Hoosier Chron.* 297 Everybody's saying 'Stop, Look, Listen!' . . . the white aprons in the one-arm lunch rooms say it now when you kick on the size of the buns. **1926** *New Masses* May 9/4 Countermen in the one-arm lunches yell '*coffee-and*' not so fiercely, they are mad tigers softened by May Day.

one-horse. *attrib.* Denoting a small farm upon which only a single horse is used. Often fig. with reference to anything small or inconsequential. *Colloq.*

1853 *Oregonian* (Portland) 19 Nov. 2/1 These *one-horse* meetings are got up by men whose capital consists in *brass*. [**1853** in WINTHER *Express* (1936) 86 The U.S. Mail Leaves Sacramento Daily for Marysville, Tehama, Red Bluffs, Cavertsburg, One Horse Town, Middletown, and Shasta.] **1860** *So. Cultivator* XVIII. 208, I am persuaded that you may notice the inquiries of a 'one horse' farmer, who only makes them to be benefitted. **1949** *N.Y. Times Bk. Review* 5 June 25/1 This group of poems . . . deal with the life on a one-horse, salt-water Maine farm.

Oneida oˈnaɪdə, *n.* [See note.]

"Anglicized compressed form of the common Iroquois term *tiionĕñʹiote*', 'there it it-rock has-set-up (continuative),' i.e. a rock that something set up and is still standing, referring to a large sienite bowlder near the site of one of their ancient villages" (Hodge).

1. An Indian of an Iroquoian tribe formerly dwelling in New York, but now found in Wisconsin and Canada as well. In the *pl.*, the tribe of such an Indian. Also attrib.

1666 *Mass. H.S. Coll.* 3 Ser. X. 63 Hereof the Mohawkes and the Oneiades have given assured notice; insomuch that he takes it for a truth. **1760** J. W. LYDEKKER *Faithful Mohawks* (1938) 102 Genl. Amherst being at the Oneida Lake on the preceeding Sunday went up as far as the Oneida town. **1840** COOPER *Pathfinder* i, There must be Oneidas or Tuscaroras near us, Arrowhead. **1907** *St. Nicholas* July 834/2 Joined by a couple of friendly Oneidas, they so frightened St. Leger's Indian allies that they decamped at once. **1948** *Green Bay* (Wis.) *Press-Gazette* 30 June 16/4 The pow-wows which will be staged at Oneida Sunday, as part of the first Oneida Indian homecoming in 120 years, are ritualistic and are not presented for entertainment.

2. Oneida Association, =**Oneida Community.** *Obs.*

1867 *Cin. Gazette* 24 May 1/4 We, the undersigned, acknowledge the above as the terms of our connection with the Oneida Association.

3. Oneida communism, a type of communism practiced by the Oneida Community. Also **Oneida Communist.** *Obs.* Cf. **Bible communism.**

1867 *N.Y. Tribune* 19 June 7/2 The Oneida Communists consider themselves to be the successors of the Apostles, to whom was promised the speedy second advent of Christ. **1876** *Galaxy* Dec. 817/1 Mr. Noyes . . . introduced this kind of discipline in the Bible class at Putney, Vermont, which was the root of the Oneida communism. **1900** ESTLAKE *Oneida Community* 103 The Oneida Communists demonstrated that conquest and captivity were no longer necessary to the evolution of civilisation.

4. Oneida Community, a community established by J. H. Noyes (1811–86) at Oneida, N.Y., in 1847–48, which practiced a type of communism of which a system of "complex marriage" and "mutual criticism" were prominent features. Cf. **Perfectionist, Bible Communist.**

1848 in G. W. NOYES *John Humphrey Noyes* 388 The original four-square nucleus of the Putney Community . . . will give tone to the Oneida Community. **1876** *Galaxy* Dec. 815/1 'Mutual criticism' in the Oneida Community . . . is the trial of any person by his social intimates. **1880** *Harper's Mag.* Jan. 192/2 It is but a few years since the Oneida Community gave up . . . the use of Graham bread as a staple and orthodox article of socialistic diet. **1930** *Amer. Mercury* Jan. 6/1 The most successful was, of course, John H. Noyes's Oneida Community.

attrib. **1947** *Chi. Sun* 18 Nov. 9/2 Tudor Plate by Oneida Community Silversmiths.

one old cat. A form of ball play in which the players batted one at a time until caught out, the catcher-out then batting.

This game was played variously according to the time and locality and the number of players participating. See quot. 1948 *s.v.* ***cat,** *n.* **3.** Along with town ball *q.v.* it was a precursor of baseball, but it continued to be played, usu. in rural communities, after that game became popular.

Variant names, as shown in the first group of quots., were used for the game.

(1) **1850** *Knickerb.* XXXV. 84 We never indulged in a game of chance of any sort in the world, save the 'baseball,' 'one' and 'two-hole cat,' and 'barn-ball' of our boyhood. **1915** *Amer. Mag.* Aug. 61/3 'Come into the yard and play one-a-cat,' he invited cheerily. '*Me* at the bat.' **1944** *Chi. D. News* 21 Nov. 19/1 Tony grabbed his glass like a kid choosin' up sides for one o' cat. **1946** *Greenville* (Ala.) *Adv.* 26 Sep., A game of 'One-eyed Cat' was resorted to. As few as three could play this game, and as many as five. **1948** *Dly. Ardmoreite* (Ardmore, Okla.) 6 July 8/4 'One-eyed cat' seems to have gone out of date with today's kids.

(2) **1865** *Harper's Mag.* April 607/2 On the very school-ground . . . are now visible the foot-marks of the same old games—'one old cat,' and 'two old cat.' **1909** *Collier's* 8 May 13/1 In the season of 1840–42, 'one-old-cat' became a fad. **1912** DREISER *Financier* 5 Frank . . . liked to play 'one old cat,' the new baseball game coming into vogue at that time. **1949** *Chi. D. News* 6 July 14/7 Juvenile pirates had their hang-outs and . . . one-old-cat and high-button-shoe football thrived.

***one-two-three.**

1. A ball game in which each player, after every out, changes his position until he earns the right to bat.

1867 CHADWICK *Base Ball Reference* 138 *One, Two, Three.*—Another preliminary practice game in which all the positions of the field are occupied alternately. **1891** *Amer. Folk-Lore* IV. 232 One, Two, Three! This game is similar to 'One o'Cat,' except that the players call out numbers, 'one, two, three, four,' etc. instead of the names of their positions. [**1909** *Collier's* 8 May 13/1 'Town' or 'round' ball was never played in or about New York; but the boys *did* play 'one-two-and-three-old-cat.']

2. (See quot. 1868.) Also attrib. with *order*.

1865 *Wilkes' Spirit of Times* 5 Aug. 381/1 The Mutuals gave them their second round O, by putting out their strikers in the one, two, three order. **1868** CHADWICK *Base Ball* 43 One, Two, Three . . . refers . . . to the order of going out, when the first three batsmen in an inning retire in succession. **1875** *Chi. Tribune* 24 Aug. 5/6 The White Stockings were retired in one, two, three order. **1926** *N.Y. Times* 11 Oct. 24/1 In the eighth the Yanks went out one-two-three.

***onion,** *n.* In combs.: (1) **onion fish,** (see quot.); (2) ***skin,** (see quot. 1890), also **onionskin ballot,** a ballot on thin or onionskin paper used for fraudulent purposes; (3) **snow,** (see quot.).

(1) **1884** GOODE *Fisheries* I. 244 The Grenadiers, or, as the fishermen frequently call them, on account of the size and shape of their eyes, 'Onion-fishes,' inhabit the deep parts of the ocean. — (2) **1879** *Cong. Rec.* App. 23 June 120/1 The term 'onion skin' or 'tissue ballots' had obtained a generic and well-defined meaning synonymous with stuffing the ballot-boxes.' **1890** *Cent.* 4113/1 *Onion-skin* . . . , a kind of paper; so called from its thinness, translucency, and finish, in which respects it resembles the skin of an onion. **1943** RODELL *Mystery Fiction* 198 Editors can ruin eyes and tempers on indistinct third carbons done on onion skin paper that is perfectly transparent. — (3) **1937** *Amer. Sp.* Oct. 238 'Onion snow' is one that falls after the onions are

planted. Generally it is a storm of short duration, coming after days of balmy spring weather.

As the last term in **bog, hog, prairie, Siwash, sweet, water, wild onion.**

Onondaga ˌɑnənˈdɔgə, *n.* [Iroquois *Ononta' gé*, a place-name meaning "on, or on top of, the hill."] An Indian of an important tribe formerly living in the present Onondaga County, New York; freq., in *pl.*, the tribe itself. Also attrib.

1684 *Mass. H.S. Coll.* 4 Ser. IX. 187, I haue perswaded all the considerable Indians, the Maquas, Sineques, Onondages, . . . to give up their lands. **1765** *Doc. Col. Hist. N.Y.* VII. 719 The Onondaga Speaker *Tyawarunt* spoke as follows. **1825** *New-Harmony* (Ind.) *Gaz.* 22 Oct. 29/1 The object of the Onondagas is to purchase our lands at Tonnewonta. **1945** *Reader's Digest.* Aug. 52 Iroquois and Onondagas in industrial centers are recognized as among the best structural steel workers in the world.

b. Onondaga limestone, *Geol.* limestone that is characteristic of the American Devonian period.

1899 ORTON *Rock Waters of Ohio* 680 The noblest fountain of Ohio . . . emerges directly from the Onondaga limestone.

c. Onondaga salt, salt obtained from Onondaga County, N.Y. *Obs.*

1843 *Niles' Reg.* 10 June 240/3 Onondaga salt . . . can now be delivered in New York for twenty-five cents the bushel of 56 pounds. **1849** *N. Eng. Farmer* I. 144, 1000 parts of Onondago coarse salt contain pure salt 991 parts.

***onto,** *prep. To be onto,* to have knowledge of, "to be wise to." *Slang.* — **1877** in ASBURY *Underworld of Chi.* opp. 80 (*caption*), And not be trying to put in so much style around the St. Mark's Hotel, for very near all of the boys are on to you. **1925** *Sat. Ev. Post* 26 June 56/2 Look here, I'm on to you. You want to interest me in the obsolete institution of marriage.

ontocycle ˈɑntəˌsaɪkl, *n.* [**onto-*, existing, + **cycle.*] *Biol.* The development that takes place in a cycle, earlier characteristics reappearing in the organism in its decline. — **1893** *Boston Soc. Nat. Hist. Proc.* 109 It is proposed to use in this way ontocycle or ontocyclon for the ontogeny, meaning the cycle of the individual. **1899** HYATT *Biol. Lectures* 134 (*Cent. Supp.*), The whole cycle of the ontogeny or ontocycle.

oolachon. See **eulachon.**

opeidoscope əˈpaɪdəˌskop, *n.* [Gk. *ops, opos*, voice, +*eidos* form, +*-scope.*] An instrument used for demonstrating and exhibiting the air vibrations caused by speaking and singing. *Obs.* — **1873** A. E. DOLBEAR in Prescott *Sp. Telephone* (1878) 262 While engaged in making a manometric flame capsule, I invented the opeidoscope.

* **open,** *n.* (See quot. 1846 and cf. **oak opening.**)

1846 W. G. STEWART *Altowan* I. 42 All openings of natural clearing are called 'opens' by the half-breeds of the Indian country. **1892** *Outing* Jan. 288/2 The elk were slowly trotting across an 'open' half a mile to the west. **1932** *D.N.* VI. 228 Like the word *prairie*, *desert* has gone out of everyday use; people say rather 'the open' or 'range' or use some special term.

* **open,** *a.*

1. Free from obstructions or restrictions, as (1) **open plains,** (2) **prairie,** (3) **range,** (4) **timber,** (5) **trail.**

(1) 1786 in *Amer. Sp.* XV. 291/1 On the N.E. side of the east Grove at two white oaks in the Open Plains. **1789** *Ib.*, To a white oak Standing in the open plains. — **(2) 1804** in *Wis. Hist. Coll.* XXII. (1916) 95 The hills or high Land is near the River . . . back of those hills is open prairie. **1887** I. R. *Lady's Ranche Life Mont.* 9 [We] struck off across the open prairie for the Great Divide. — **(3) 1890** *Stock Grower & Farmer* 15 March 6/3 The cow men of the open ranges will make money. **1947** *Dly. Ardmoreite* (Ardmore, Okla.) 27 July 7/4 This was open range with no fencing the first time he came to this Indian Territory. — **(4) 1884** *Cent. Mag.* Feb. 500/1 The ground in his front was, first, open timber. **1907** ANDREWS *Recoll.* 154 Two lines of our own cavalry [were] approaching us . . . through the open timber.

(5) 1901 WHITE *Westerners* 47 At Pierre he announced open trail.

2. Of an office or shop: Employing without discrimination both union and non-union workers. Cf. **closed shop.**

1896 *Typographical Jrnl.* IX. 445 Our next efforts were directed to the Morning Leader, also an 'open' office. **1901** *World's Work* July 914/2 The shop had previously been an 'open' one—that is, union and non-union men were employed without distinction. **1949** *Newsweek* 23 May 62/2 [He] proclaimed a crusade against the open-shop employers.

3. Of a town: Characterized by a lack of restrictions, or enforced restrictions, on drinking and gambling places and the like. Cf. * **wide open.**

1901 FLYNT *World of Graft* 11 The City Hall gang went into office on the promise that the town was to be open, an' they've kept it open. **1924** MCCONNELL *Frontier Law* 173 Idaho City was 'an open town,' in all the name implies. The doors of every palace of vice were thrown open. **1946** *Reader's Digest* July 96/2 Amarillo is the most open open-town in the country.

Hence **open town platform.**

1915 *Amer. Mag.* Sep. 51/2 On an 'open town' platform Gill was elected mayor in March, 1910.

4. In special combs.: (1) **open and shut,** quite simple or plain, prob. orig. from faro; (2) **board,** an association that transacts small dealings in options not permitted by the local stock exchange or board of trade; (3) **book,** (see quots.), *obs.;* (4) **branding,** the branding of cattle without the use of a chute; (5) **car,** a streetcar open on all sides for use in summer, especially by excursionists, also an automobile without any top; (6) **convention,** a political convention free from factional or "machine" domination; (7) **field run,** in football, a run through a broken field *q.v.;* (8) **gaited,** *a.* of a horse, having a gait, esp. in trotting, in which the hind feet overreach the outside limits of the front ones; (9) **house,** hospitality extended to visitors in general, as at a party when a number of guests are entertained; (10) * **kettle,** (see quot. 1892); (11) **primary,** a primary election in which all voters may participate without revealing their partly affiliations; (12) **rate,** a regular published railroad rate as distinguished from a special rate; (13) **season,** a season during which hunting and fishing, under prescribed conditions, are legal, cf. **closed season;** (14) **shelf,** (see quots. 1910, 1921); (15) **stove,** =**Franklin stove,** *obs.;* (16) **style,** (see quot.); (17) **top,** *attrib.* designating a vehicle the top of which is open, cf. **covered buggy.**

(1) 1841 *N.O. Picayune* 11 March 2/3 The contest between *Humming Bird* and *Maria Collier* was considered all but a 'dead open and shut game.' **1904** W. H. SMITH *Promoters* 162 It seems as if it was a dead open and shut that we've got to stay with 'em. **1946** GARDNER *D.A. Breaks Seal* 124 We had such an open-and-shut case against the man that Carr can't put up any fight. — **(2) 1870** MEDBERY *Men Wall St.* 15 The consolidation of the Government and the Open Boards with the old historic Stock Exchange. **1902** LORIMER *Lett. Merchant* 113 She's the daughter of old Job Dashkam, on the open Board. — **(3)** [**1868** *Nation* 2 July 5/2 The plan of keeping books open, in which any Republican can, at his leisure, inscribe his own name, and the name of the candidate of his choice, has been instituted for the caucus nominations, and been adopted.] **1902** MEYER *Nominating Systems* 73 The 'open book method' contains the germs of the direct vote system, and was tried at about the same time that direct primaries were first tried in Crawford county, Pennsylvania. — **(4) 1911** MULFORD *Bar-20 Days* 197 Chute-branding robbed them of the excitement . . . which they always took from open or corral branding.

(5) 1901 *World's Work* Aug. 1094 Cars are being made to fit every convenience, open cars for summer closed cars for winter . . . ; mail cars passenger cars, and cars with smoking compartments. **1910** J. A. MITCHELL *Dr. Thorne's Idea* 214 They took an open car. **1923** WATTS *L. Nichols* 228 He found . . . a comfortable open car not the latest model, a new runabout. — **(6) 1904** *N.Y. Ev. Post* 5 Sep. 1 The governor still asserts that the Republicans will have an 'open convention,' but the belief is general that he has decided to nominate Lieut-Gov. Higgins. — **(7) 1902** *Chi. Record-Herald* 28 Sep. III. 1/3 Open field runs were impossible, and all of Wisconsin's gains were made by straight bucks through the line. — **(8) 1872** *Vt. Bd. Agric. Rep.* I. 206 A good sized, rangy open-gaited and enduring horse of a good color. **1894** *Vt. Agric. Rep.* XIV. 97 His sire being Allen, his dam Lady Alice, . . . he is a pure open-gaited trotter. — **(9) 1861** *N.Y. Herald* 3 Jan. 4/1 The South Carolina Commissioners did not keep open house. **1934** WEBSTER. **1938** DOUTHITT *Romance & Dim Trails* 274 He keeps open house for all his friends and they are many. **1949** *Summit Valley Times* (Argo, Ill.) 9 Nov. 1/1 As it was 'open house' a large crowd was present.

(10) 1887 *Courier-Journal* 20 Jan. 7/3 Sugars—We quote . . . open kettle, $5\frac{3}{4}$ c, and granulated, $6\frac{3}{4}$ @ $6\frac{1}{2}$ c. **1892** *Mod. Lang. Notes* Nov. 393 *Open Kettle*—open pan in which the syrup is reduced until it begins to crystallize. . . . Also a trade name for sugar manufactured by this process. — **(11) 1934** WEBSTER. **1947** *Atlantic Mo.* July 21/2 Unfortunately they have very little to say in the election of their candidates, except on occasional splits in parties and in open-primary fights. — **(12) 1879** in TARBELL *Hist. Standard Oil Co.* I. 331 Do you know what the open rate, the published rate is to the seaboard by the barrel? **1904** TARBELL *Hist. Standard Oil Co.* I. 46 Mr. Alexander was to pay the open, or regular rate on oil. — **(13) 1896** *Outing* Sep. 596/2 The first day of September marks the beginning of the open season on pheasants, grouse, and quail in Oregon. **1948** *Chesterton* (Ind.) *Tribune* 28 Oct. 6/4 A brief open season on pheasants will enhance this autumn's pleasure for Hoosier sportsmen. — **(14) 1901** *World's Work* May 776/2 Just as in the case of the practical talents, a wide freedom to choose from the open shelves, discovers this boy to be strongly inspired by the feats of Kane. **1910** BOSTWICK *Amer. Pub. Library* 38 Practically all small and moderate sized American libraries are now 'open-shelf' which means that the user is allowed to go personally to the shelves and select his book. **1921** *Rural Organization* 144 Then the 'open shelf' plan was adopted, according to which books were selected at the central office to meet the need of the particular community to which they were to be sent.

(15) 1775 in *N.J. Archives* 1 Ser. XXXI. (1923) 144 Manufactured at Batsto Furnace, in West New-Jersey . . . open and close stoves of different sizes. **1788** FRANKLIN *Autobiog.* 370 [I] invented an open stove for the better warming of rooms. **1835** HOFFMAN *Winter in West* I. 28 A blazing fire of seasoned oak in a large open stove sputters and crackles before me. — **(16) 1903** *Churchman* 10 Oct. 447 The notes are of the open (or, as our English friends term it, minim or semi-breve) style. — **(17) 1771** *Conn. Rec.* XIII. 514 Every open chair and other open top riding wheel-carriage [shall be rated] three pounds. **1856** *Mich. Agric. Soc. Trans.* VII. 61 John Patton . . . [exhibited an] open top buggy.

***open,** *v.*

1. *tr.* To make (public land) available for entry and settlement.

1871 *Rep. Indian Affairs* (1872) 180 The influences at work to 'open' this lost home of the race are powerful, representing great and diversified interests. **1906** *Indian Laws & Tr.* III. 615 A nontransferable certificate . . . will entitle him [*sc.* the applicant for land] to go upon and examine the lands to be opened hereunder.

2. *To open the pot*, to place money in (a jack pot), thereby opening it for play.

1880 DICK *Amer. Hoyle* 202 The blind now deals, and any player in *his regular turn* may *open* or *break* the pot, provided he holds a pair of Jacks or better. **1949** *Sun. World-Herald Mag.* (Omaha) 24 April 2/1 The old man (Clarence) opened the pot with a dime.

***opener,** *n.* In poker, the person who begins the betting; also *pl.*, the cards, a pair of jacks or better, with which a person may open the jack pot.

1880 DICK *Amer. Hoyle* 203 After all the players who determine to go in have made good the bet of the player who opened the Jack Pot, . . . then the opener of the pot makes the first bet. **1909** WASON *Happy Hawkins* 114, I didn't hold openers. **1946** MOREHEAD & MOTT-SMITH *Penguin Hoyle* 122 If the opener cannot prove to the satisfaction of other players that he held openers, his hand is dead and cannot win the pot.

transf. **1902** *Out West* March 291, 'I got openers, this pot,' says he, tapping the rifle. **1948** MENJOU & MUSSELMAN *It Took 9 Tailors* 80 By the time the game was over I had lost $300 just in antes and openers.

As the last term in **bottle, can, eye-opener.**

***opening,** *n.*

1. A place in a swamp where it may be crossed. *Obs.*

1663 *Providence Rec.* V. 206 The place comonly Called the first opening of the great swampe. **1704** *Providence Rec.* IV. 178 On the south side of the place in the . . . great swampe which is Called the first opening.

2. An area in a forested region which is by nature treeless or only slightly timbered.

1798 C. WILLIAMSON *Descr. Genesee* iv, The openings, or large tracts of land, found frequently in this country free of timber, and showing great signs of having once been in a state of cultivation, are singularly curious. **1900** BRUNCKEN *N. Amer. Forests* 9 There were also light groves, called openings, in many places in the uplands. **1947** *Mich. Hist.* Sep. 269 Openings were tablelands usually studded with occasional oak trees.

3. A cleared field, or a site for a home or settlement. *Obs.*

1800 TATHAM *Tobacco* 6 Thus the planter is continually cutting down *new* ground, and every successive spring presents an additional field, or *opening* of tobacco. **1837** *Knickerb.* X. 491 Like thousands of others . . . he 'kept bachelor's hall,' until he had 'made an opening, and reared his rustic cot.'

4. The action by the federal government of throwing open for settlement land not previously available for settlers.

1889 in THOBURN *Oklahoma* (1916) II. 645 Owing to the press of other business upon Congress at the time the bill for the opening of the land was passed, there was no provision for territorial government made by Congress. **1914** *Sunset* April 767/1 At later drawings it was not unusual to dispose of a hundred thousand acres at an 'opening.' **1946** FOREMAN *Last Trek* 302 They had received allotments preceding the 'opening' of the Kiowa, Comanche, and Apache reservation.

As the last term in **clam, hickory, oak, timber, white oak opening.**

***opera,** *n.*

1. A small cigar, formerly popular with gentlemen attending the opera. In full **opera cigar.** *Obs.*

1857 *Lawrence* (Kans.) *Republican* 16 July 3 We do semi-occasionally puff an 'opera,' if we find one that suits. **1892** *Harper's Mag.* Feb. 486/2 I am also the man who introduced 'opera' cigars.

2. opera chair, a light folding chair for use in theaters and public halls.

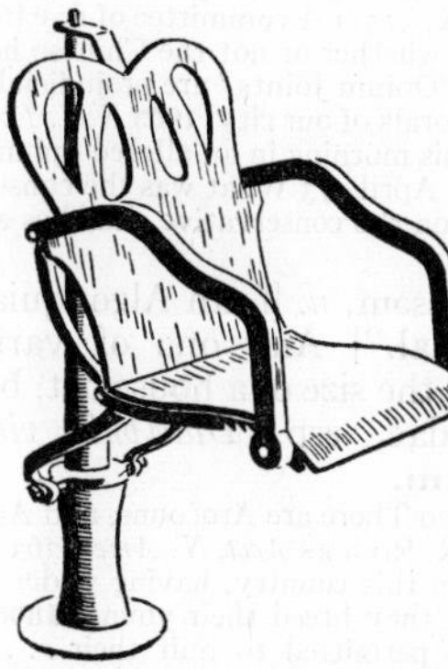

Opera chair of early (*c*1865) type

1872 *Chi. Tribune* 13 Oct. The parquet and dress circle are seated with opera chairs; the upper circles with sofas. **1895** *N.Y. Dramatic News* 6 July 3/4 Bargains in Opera Chairs.

3. opera pump, a woman's pump shoe with classic lines, usu. without trimming.

1931 *Durant* (Okla.) *D. Democrat* 31 Dec. 4/3 This opera pump of black kid has the new one-sided trim, consisting of an appliqued leaf of lizard stitched upon a background of pale green kid. **1935** *Montgomery Ward Cat.* (ed. 123) 105 Choice of four colors, three leathers and two heel heights in a classic Opera Pump you'll be proud to wear anywhere!

As the last term in **cork, Ethiopian, horse, light, soap opera.**

***operate,** *v. intr.* To follow a career of crime; to engage in political machinations. *Colloq.* — **1884** SWEET & KNOX *Through Texas* 16 This high-toned and honorable desperado 'operated' in one of the inland cities of Texas two years ago. **1901** W. A. WHITE in *McClure's Mag.* Dec. 147 Platt and Payn, operating with less than half a score of legislators, went down to Albany to take in the senatorial election.

operating company. A company that actually engages in some operation, as manufacturing, transportation, etc. — **1905** *McClure's Mag.* 349 By a complicated process of stock transfers, leases (for 999 years) and 'sales,' all among themselves, but through the medium of several underlying operating and holding companies, they managed [etc.].

***operation,** *n.* As the last term in **logging, prospect operation.**

***operative,** *n.* (See quot. 1905.) — **1905** *N.Y Press* 23 Oct. (*Cent. Supp.*), The word 'detective' became so offensive . . . that it was dropped by some successful [detective] agencies. The word chosen by the Pinkertons to take its place was 'operative.' **1927** SIRINGO *Riata* 153, I had pawned the pistol for twenty dollars . . . , and in its place I was carrying a small pistol belonging to another operative.

***operator,** *n.*

1. One who owns, or directs the operations of, a coal mine or other industrial plant or institution.

1838 *Niles' Reg.* 13 Oct. 112/2 Our trade . . . is brought nearly to a stand again, by a collision between the dealers, operators and boatmen, as regards the price of freight. **1851** CIST *Cincinnati* 170 The largest operators in this line [manufacturing alcohol], are Lowell Fletcher & Co. **1904** TARBELL *Hist. Standard Oil Co.* I. 27 He became interested in the oil business in 1862 . . . as an operator in West Virginia.

2. One who sends and receives telegraphic communications, or operates a typesetting machine, or handles telephone calls at a telephone switchboard.

1847 *De Bow's Review* IV. 138 Its receipt [was] acknowledged by the Montreal operator in 30 minutes. **1913** *Collier's* 20 Dec. 10/2 The operators of to-day have more comfort than their sisters of thirty years ago. **1948** *Lisle* (Ill.) *Advt.* 21 Oct. 6/5 Moreover, in many communities, including Downers Grove, we need more workers, particularly operators.

As the last term in **cotton, curbstone, dental, elevator, jitney, lobby, peckerwood, street, telegraph, telephone, wildcat operator.**

***opinion,** *n.* As the last term in **horseback, secesh opinion.**

* **opium,** *n.* **1. opium clipper,** a clipper ship engaged in transporting opium. *Obs.* **2. opium joint,** a low dive or resort frequented by those addicted to the use of opium. Also transf.

(1) **1853** *Hunt's Merch. Mag.* XXVIII. 264 From the transport of this drug by a few vessels named opium clippers, a few mercantile houses are also realizing magnificent profits. — (2) **1884** *Boston City Council Minutes* XIX. 375/1 A committee of five [to] be appointed to ascertain and report whether or not the Chinese headquarters, commonly known as the 'Opium Joints,' are prejudicial to the health and detrimental to the morals of our city. **1903** *N.Y. Ev. Post* 4 Sep., Four men were arrested this morning in an alleged opium joint. **1949** *N.Y. Times Bk. Review* 10 April 3/3 What was the consequence of . . the decades of attack upon the conservative churches as 'spiritual opium joints?'

opossum əˈpɑsəm, *n.* [f. an Algonquian word meaning "white animal."] Any one of various American marsupials about the size of a house cat, belonging to the family Didelphidae, esp. *Didelphis virginiana.* Also attrib. Cf. **possum.**

1610 *Estate of Va.* 29 There are Arocouns, and Apossouns, in shape like to pigges. **1765** R. Rogers *Acct. N. Amer.* 263 The Opposum is a remarkable animal in this country, having under its belly a bag or false belly, in which they breed their young. **1806** *Balance* V. 29/3 Many . . . should be permitted to quit their . . . hoes and spades, hog, hominy and opossum fat. **1877** Johnson *Anderson Co., Kans.* 138 Four of the braves had each nail kegs, covered with opossum skins. **1920** *Outing* April 59/3 The Blue Grass Farm Kennels of Berry, Ky., Offer for sale Setters and Pointers, . . . Coon and Opossum Hounds. **1949** *Sat. Ev. Post* 25 June 31/1 He reached down, gripped the nape of the trembling opossum and hoisted him gently to the platform.

b. *opossum up a gum tree,* =*possum up a gum tree. Obs.*

1816 Paulding *Letters from So.* (1817) 90 The batteaux-man fastened his boat to the stump of a tree, lighted his fire to broil his bacon, and began to sing that famous song of 'The opossum up the gum tree.' **1829** Boardman *Amer. & Americans* (1833) 209 It was impossible to view the former animal, with his long tail, without being reminded of the negro Hamlet's vocal episode, 'Opossum up a gum-tree.'

c. (See quots.) *Obs.*

1866 *Beadle's Mo.* July 58/2 A saying has become common among the people of North Carolina, that if a cat has nine lives, the opossum has nineteen.

As the last term in **Mexican, sapajou opossum.**

* **opposition,** *n.*

1. A public conveyance operating in opposition to one previously existing. *Obs.*

1830 *Balt. Gaz.* 7 Sep. 1/1 Opposition. The Baltimore, Washington and Georgetown *New Lines of Steel-Spring Coaches.* **1850** *Alta California* (S.F.) 3 Aug., The 'Opposition' has passed us during the shift but we catch it again. **1858** Stone *Old Put's Songster* 61 If they start an *opposition,* then eight out of every nine Will support the *imposition* of the combination line.

2. Also **opposition boat, ferry, line, stage.** *Obs.*

1849 *N.O. Picayune* 26 July 2/5 We found the steamers California and Mobile awaiting us, and although opposition boats, passengers were allowed to choose for themselves without any impertinence. **1858** *Alta California* (S.F.) 3 April 2/1 A correspondent . . . suggests a plan whereby an opposition line of steamers may be placed on the route between this port and New York, via Panama. **1858** *S.F. Bulletin* 19 April 1/1 An opposition ferry boat has been placed on the line between San Francisco and Contra Costa, which has had the beneficial effect of reducing the fare to twelve and a half cents. **1865** *Washoe* (Nev.) *Times* 29 July 3/1 Last week an opposition stage was put on between this place and Carson, running against the regular line of L. H. Dyer.

opticist ˈɑptəsɪst, *n.* One who is versed in optics. *Rare.* — **1884** *Pop. Sci. Mo.* XXIV. 814 The real cause . . . is now thoroughly understood by physiological opticists.

***option,** *n. Mining.* (See quot.) Cf. **county option.** — **1882** *Harper's Mag.* May 897/1 The large land-owners have adopted the policy of granting 'options'; that is, signing an agreement that if any person shall uncover a bed of ore on his land, the finder shall be entitled to a certain interest, generally one-third.

***optional** ˈɑpʃənl, *n.* An optional or elective course of study. — **1855** *Songs, Biennial Jubilee* (Yale), For optionals will come our way. **1857** *Yale Lit. Mag.* XXII. 291 (Th.), What was never known since the establishment of optionals, the number pursuing the study of Hebrew is nine.

***optional,** *a.* (See quot. 1856.) — **1856** Hall *College Words* (ed. 2) 340 During another portion of the course, he is allowed to select from certain branches those which he desires to follow. The latter are called *optional* studies. **1880** *Harper's Mag.* July 254/1 In the German universities the studies are all elective and optional.

optometrist ɑpˈtɑmətrɪst, *n.* [f. **optometry*+-*ist.*] One who is skilled in optometry. Also attrib. — **1904** *Optical Jrnl.* 23 June 69 (Cent. Supp.), One of the points to be thoroughly discussed will be the best name to give those who professionally test eyes for refractive errors. . . . In those States which have laws governing this line cf work the term used is 'Optometrist.' **1949** *Chi. D. News* 6 May 26/1 The optometry bill, for instance, would prevent any licensed optometrist from advertising his services.

Oquassa əˈkwæsə, *n.* [f. *Oquassa* Lake, Maine.] A small, somewhat slender lake trout, *Salvelinus oquassa,* found in Maine. In full **Oquassa trout.**

1884 *Nat. Museum Bul.* No. 27, 427 *Oquassa Trout; Blue-Black Trout.* Lakes in Western Maine. **1890** *Cent.* 4134/3 *Oquassa,* . . . the blue-backed trout. *Salmo oquassa.* (Rangeley Lake, Maine.) **1896** Jordan & Evermann *Check-List Fishes* 293.

O. R. An abbreviation for *ordered recorded. Obs.* — **1790** *Sumner Co.* (Tenn.) *Court Minutes* (MS) 27 Power of attorney from Alex Dever to Joseph McElurath is duly acknowledged & O.R. **1796** *Ib.* 105 Deed of conveyance . . . is duly proved by oath of Jno. Daveson and O.R.

***oral,** *n.* Short for *oral examination.* Freq. *pl.* — **1876** Tripp *Student-Life* 18 Do something splendid on the mathematics and the 'orals,' and I will wager any thing you will pass clear. **1939** G. Stewart (*title*), Doctor's Oral.

oralism ˈorəlˌɪzəm, *n.* The method by which deaf mutes are taught lip-reading. *Rare.* — **1883** *Amer. Ann. Deaf & Dumb* April 90 So far as oralism . . . is concerned.

* **orange,** *n.*[1] and *a.* In combs.: (1) **orange belt,** a region where oranges are extensively grown; (2) **-crowned warbler,** a small American warbler, *Vermivora celata;* (3) **dog,** the larva of the orange tree butterfly; (4) * **grass,** a North American weed, *Sarothra gentianoides,* having small yellow flowers and wiry stems; (5) **grove,** a grove of orange trees; (6) **orchard,** a grove of orange trees regularly planted and cultivated; (7) **ranch,** an extensive orange grove or orchard; (8) **root,** =**goldenseal;** (9) **sand,** (see quot.); (10) **State,** Florida.

(1) **1889** Davidson *Fla. of Today* 136 The *kumquat,* also, or *Citrus Japonica,* seems to have qualities that commend it to the attention of the culturists in the Orange Belt. **1945** Service *Ploughman* 227 From our house it was a bare twenty minutes' walk to the orange belt. — (2) **1825** Bonaparte *Ornithology* I. 45 During winter, the Orange-crowned Warbler is one of the most common birds in the neighborhood of St. Augustin, Florida. **1944** *Mass. Audubon Soc. Bul.* Dec. 261, I got 'kicks' out of seeing the following—all in Northampton . . . October 19, Orange-crowned Warbler. — (3) **1890** Ballard *Among Moths* 142 The common name in Florida for this caterpillar is 'the orange dog.' — (4) **1837** Darlington *Flora Cestrica* 324 Ground Pine. Nit-Weed. Orange-grass. **1882** E. K. Godfrey *Nantucket* 36 The orange grass with its fragrance now greeting us at every turn.

(5) **1766** J. Bartram *Journal* 56 [We] encamped at a great orange-grove. **1898** *Dept. Agric. Yrbk. 1897* 504 The velvet bean [is a widely grown forage crop] for Florida orange groves. **1945** Clarke *Pacific Crest Trailway* 115 Mt. San Antonio (Old Baldy) is especially beautiful in winter, rising a perfect pyramid of snow, 9,000 feet above orange groves and farms. — (6) **1872** *Harper's Mag.* May 881/1 You should drive to the Mission San Gabriel, where are the finest orange orchards. **1949** Hertrich *Huntington Bot. Gardens* 6 A small cottage . . . had been prepared for us in the midst of the orange orchard. — (7) **1910** *Out West* Feb. 155 'Look at these orange ranches!' orated the other comfortably. **1947** *Chi. Tribune* 16 Feb. (Grafic Mag.) 14/2 Lilli suggested that a Florida orange ranch would be more romantic and desirable. — (8) **1817–8** Eaton *Botany* (1822) 310 *Hydrastis canadensis,* orange root. **1857** Gray *Botany* 14. **1884** *Rep. Comm. Agric.* 132 Orange-root . . . is a perennial herb, seldom growing more than a foot high. — (9) **1870** *Rep. Comm. Agric.* 552 The surface geology of Mississippi is characterized by the presence, in almost every part of the State, of a drift formation, termed by Professor Higard 'The Orange Sand,' which, as its name indicates, is largely composed of yellow sands and sandstones.

(10) **1852** Cazneau *Eagle Pass* 74 Gopher John . . . was employed . . . by one of our gallant officers serving in Florida to guard a reservoir of the kind of turtle called *gophers,* in the 'Orange State.'

As the last term in **bitter, blood, Florida, kid-glove, mock, navel, Osage orange.**

* **Orange,** *n.*[2] In obs. combs.: (1) **Orange American,** (see quot.), cf. **Orange organization, Know-Nothing;** (2) **organization,** a name applied in Virginia to the Know-Nothing organization, which was bitterly opposed to Roman Catholics, cf. **Orange American;** (3) **riot,** an outbreak of violence in New York, July 12–14, 1871, between Protestant and Catholic Irishmen.

(1) **1855** in HAMBLETON *H. A. Wise* 223 My next point is, that the principles of the Orange Americans, that 'America shall be ruled by Americans,' that 'foreigners ought not to be eligible to office,' and 'that all public positions ought to be filled by natives of the soil,' are nothing more than revivals of the doctrines of Federalism, *British* Federalism of its worst type.—(2) **1855** in HAMBLETON *H. A. Wise* 221 Garbled extracts have been paraded before the people, without relation to the context, to give some color of authority to the designs of this resuscitated American, Orange, Protestant, Jesuit organization. — (3) **1872** BRACE *Dangerous Classes N.Y.* 30 No one doubted . . . during the Orange riot of 1871, the existence of 'dangerous classes' in New York. **1882** MCCABE *New York* 500 [The National Guard] have promptly and bravely responded to every call upon them . . . checking the Orange riots in 1871; and overawing the mob in the Railroad riots, in 1877.

* **oration,** *n.* As the last term in **Cincinnati, senior, stump oration.**

* **orator,** *n.* A student in college or high school selected to deliver a speech on a public occasion.

1737 *Harvard Rec.* II. 661 Voted, . . . that Mr Flynt Dr Wigglesworth & Mr Rogers be desired to appoint an Orator and Respondents among the Candidates for their Second degree. **1871** CUTTING *Student Life Amherst* 40 For the Exhibition, four orators are now chosen in each society from the Senior class. **1923** *Breeze* (Albion, Mich.) 24 Charles Rogers, Advertising Manager Breeze. Class orator.

As the last term in **alumnus, secession, silver, silver-tongued, stump orator.**

* **oratory,** *n.* As the last term in **buncombe, stump oratory.**

* **orchard,** *n.*

1. = **sugar orchard.**

1822 DWIGHT *Travels* III. 242 On our way we passed Mr. Wilbur's orchard, as it is here familiarly called: a handsome cluster of maples; from which in a single year he has made one thousand eight hundred pounds of sugar.

2. In combs.: (1) **orchard hangnest,** = **orchard oriole;** (2) **oriole,** an oriole, *Icterus spurius,* resembling the Baltimore oriole but slightly smaller and of duller plumage; (3) **people,** those engaged in the turpentine business, *rare;* (4) **starling,** = **orchard oriole;** (5) **turpentine,** turpentine obtained from a turpentine orchard *q.v.*, also attrib.

(1) **1844** *Nat. Hist. N.Y., Zoology* II. 140 The Orchard Oriole. *Icterus Spurius.* . . . Orchard Hangnest. **1917** *Birds of Amer.* II. 256 Orchard Oriole. . . . [Also called] Orchard Hang-nest. — (2) **1808** WILSON *Ornithology* I. 71 The Orchard Oriole . . . is no sneaking pilferer. **1945** *Nat. Geog. Mag.* June 734 *(heading)*, For a Pair of Orchard Orioles Spanish Moss Makes a Home. — (3) **1906** L. BELL *C. Lee* 249 In order to supply the demand, the orchard people are obliged each year to find two million acres of virgin forest for their operations. — (4) **1865** *Atlantic Mo.* XV. 516, I love his [the robin's] note and ways better even than those of the Orchard-Starling or the Baltimore Oriole. **1917** *Birds of Amer.* II. 256 Orchard Oriole. . . . [Also called] Orchard Starling.

(5) **1906** L. BELL *C. Lee* 197, I am going to sell the orchard turpentine rights of Guildford to get money for building. *Ib.* 247, I figure that between ten and twelve millions of dollars would corner the turpentine market and then put the price of orchard turpentine so high that it would practically be off the market.

As the last term in **crab, fruit, Indian, maple, maple sugar, old, orange, peach, pecan, persimmon, sap, sugar, turpentine orchard.**

orchestarion ˌɔrkəsˈterɪən, *n.* [*orchestra*+*-arion.*] A musical instrument, prob. one attempting to simulate the various instruments of an orchestra. *Obs.* Cf. **orchestrelle.** — **1872** in ODELL *Ann. N.Y. Stage* IX. 356 Robert Spice inventor and player on the Orchestarion.

* **orchestra,** *n.* A section of the auditorium of a theater, now usu. the forward part or all of the main floor. Also attrib.

1786 in G. O. SEILHAMER *Hist. Amer. Theatre* II. 206 *(footnote)*, The pit is very large and the theatrum and orchestra elegant and commodious. **1856** *Porter's Spirit of Times* 20 Dec. 262 Laura Keene's Theatre . . . Reserved Orchestra Seats, 75 cents. . . . Seats in orchestra stalls, $1 each. **1924** D. LAWRENCE *True Story W. Wilson* 117 A President . . . cannot sit in the orchestra or in the balcony.

orchestrelle ˌɔrkəsˈtrel, *n.* [**orchestra*+*-elle.*] A mechanical instrument intended to imitate the effect of an orchestra. Cf. **orchestarion.** — **1909** M. TWAIN *Death of Jean* 124 (R.), Paine began playing on the orchestrelle Schubert's 'Impromptu.'

* **orchis,** *n.* As the last term in **ragged, showy orchis.**

* **order,** *n.*

1. A portion or serving of food served in a public eating place. Cf. **short order.**

1906 O. HENRY *Four Million* 248 And all this while she [the waitress] would be performing astounding feats with orders of pork and beans, pot roasts [etc.]. **1926** in *Amer. Sp.* II. (1927) 414 'One order of split pea soup,' cries the customer.

2. In phrases: (1) *in order*, appropriate, suitable, befitting the occasion, *colloq.;* (2) *in short order*, see * **short.**

(1) *a***1861** WINTHROP *J. Brent* 85 If the gent has made a remark what teches you, apologies is in order. **1905** *N.Y. Times* 4 Sep., Good-byes were in order on the Erin last night.

b. In the names of organizations, as *Order of Cincinnati*, (cf. **Cincinnati 1.**), *Order of the Star-Spangled Banner.*

1789 in *Jrnl. of Wm. Maclay* (1927) 12 This spirit they developed in the Order of Cincinnati, where I trust it will spend itself in a harmless flame and soon become extinguished. **1894** C. STICKNEY *Know-Nothingism in R.I.* 4 In certain States we find promulgated orders and announcements of 'The Sons of '76,' and 'The Order of the Star-Spangled Banner.'

As the last term in **batting, Columbian, executive, express money, fraud, grocery, mail, New Light, short, side, standing, town order.**

See also **sailing, store, walking orders.**

* **order,** *v.*

1. *tr.* Used with ellipsis of *to be.*

1781 WITHERSPOON *Druid* No. 5 These things were ordered delivered to the army. **1873** J. H. BEADLE *Undevel. West* xi. 191 My bill was introduced by Senator Williams of Oregon, read by title, and ordered printed. **1907** MRS. HARRIS *Tents of Wickedness* II. iii. 144, I can order the horses brought round at ten o'clock.

2. *To order up*, in euchre, to ask an opponent who is dealing to take up the trump and discard.

1847 ROBB *Squatter Life* 129 His antagonist ordered the king up. **1899** CHAMPLIN & BOSTWICK *Cyclo. Games & Sports* (ed. 2) 298 If the player that orders up . . . fails to win three tricks he is euchred and his opponent scores two points.

* **ordinance,** *n.*

1. Ordinance of 1787, an Act of Congress of July 13, 1787, providing a system of government for the Northwest Territory.

[**1787** CUTLER in *Life & Corr.* I. 342 Was furnished with the ordinance establishing a government in the Western Federal Territory.] **1847** *Whig Almanac 1848* 33/2 The imperishable principle set forth in the ever-memorable Ordinance of 1787. **1857** *Congreg. Herald* (Chi.) 11 June 2/3 So Illinois, in spite of the ordinance of 1787, becomes a *Slave State*, by enslaving free citizens of the United States coming in from other States. **1948** *Pacific Spectator* Summer 255 Invoked in the discussion were the legal meaning and effect, as related to slavery, of . . . the Ordinance of 1787 for the government of the Northwest Territory, the Constitution . . . , the Missouri Compromise of 1820.

2. ordinance of secession, an enactment passed by a representative body in a seceding state signifying the intention of that state to withdraw from the Union. Now *hist.* Cf. **secession ordinance.**

1860 *Charleston* (S.C.) *Mercury* 22 Dec. 2/6 The Ordinance of Secession has been signed and ratified, and I pronounce the State of South Carolina an independent Commonwealth. **1948** *Chi. Tribune* 15 Feb. I. 24/3 South Carolina had passed its ordinance of secession on December 20 of the year just gone.

* **ore,** *n.* In combs.: (1) **ore car,** (*a*) a small car for hauling ore in a mine, (*b*) a railroad car designed to carry ore, also attrib.; (2) **chimney,** = * **chimney,** *n.* **2;** (3) **chute,** (*a*) a channel, shaft, or trough through which ore is conveyed from a higher to a lower level, (*b*) = * **chute,** *n.* **5;** (4) **house,** a house in which ore is stored; (5) **tipple,** a tipple *q.v.* for handling ore.

(1) (*a*) **1877** W. WRIGHT *Big Bonanza* 302 Our speed is probably not half that at which the cage is lowered when its only load is an empty ore-car. **1907** *St. Nicholas* Oct. 1145/1 We had to cross several tracks where small electric ore cars run to and from the smelter. (*b*) **1881** *Rep. Ala. R.R. Comm.* I. 64 Number of coal, stone or ore cars . . . 70.

1948 JOHNSTON *Gold Rush* 40/1 The ore-car tracks . . . are covered by long sheds. — **(2) 1882** *47th Congress* 1 Sess. H.R. Ex. Doc. No. 216, 195 The ore chimney is from 250 to 300 feet in length, and the ore is all taken out above the tunnel. **1896** SHINN *Story of Mine* 225 The general tendency of air currents in the Comstock is in the same direction as the slope of the ore chimneys. — **(3)** (*a*) **1868** *Terr. Enterprise* (Virginia, Nev.) 12 Jan. 3/1 He fell into an ore-chute, which led into a deep shaft. (*b*) **1896** SHINN *Story of Mine* 146 The rich ore chutes near the surface had been worked out. — **(4) 1876** POWELL *Nevada* 97 There are now at the ore-house and at the mills, 2,988,194-2000 tons, valued by assay at $478,080. **1910** J. HART *Vigilante Girl* 330 The rattle and roar of rock was heard . . . as it slid down the dump to the little stamp-mill and the ore-house below.

(5) 1947 BEEBE *Mixed Train Dly.* 286 The Trona, a mining road in the most desolate reaches of the Mojave Desert . . . only ventures out of the ore tipples to meet the Southern Pacific at Searles, California, in the darkest hours of early morning.

As the last term in **barrel, black, custom, gravel, mountain, mud, pay, sand, shipping, shot, velvet ore.**

Oregon ˈɔrɪgən, *n.* [This name of a western region and state app. resulted from a mapmaker's erroneous spelling of an early form of "Wisconsin" (River). See G. R. Stewart in *Amer. Sp.* April, 1944, 115 ff.]

1. In combs.: (1) **Oregon country,** =**Oregon territory;** (2) **fever,** the desire to settle in Oregon territory, now *hist.;* (3) **question,** a dispute, settled in 1846, over the boundary line between the U.S. and British territory in the Northwest; (4) **road,** =**Oregon trail,** *obs.;* (5) **territory,** the region west of the Rocky Mountains and between California and Alaska, now *hist.;* (6) **trail,** the old emigrant route (*c*1805–50) beginning at Independence, Missouri, and leading for about 2,000 miles through parts of Kansas, Nebraska, Wyoming, and Idaho, into the Oregon country; (7) **trailer,** one who followed the Oregon trail west.

(1) 1831 in *Overland to Pacific* IV. (1934) 106 Will see you . . . in regard to my application for a scituation in the first expedition to the Oregon Country. **1949** *Pacific Northwest Quart.* Jan. 3 Until the American missionaries entered the Oregon Country in the late 1830's, the area had been dominated by the fur-trading companies. — **(2) 1844** LEE & FROST *Oregon* vii. 88 Oregon is destined to be populated, even if the strange *'Oregon Fever'* which had been and is still raging in the United States, should subside. **1948** *Chi. Tribune* 8 Aug. 7/3 The 'Oregon fever' began to spread thru the Mississippi valley in 1841. — **(3) 1844** *Quincy* (Ill.) *Herald* 9 Feb. 3/2 The British minister at Washington has received instructions to negotiate relative to the Oregon question. **1944** ROSS *Westward* 58 In congressional debates on the Oregon Question, those senators who were opposed to admitting this wild country beyond the Rockies turned many a fearful and flowery phrase about cannibalism. — **(4) 1845** *Independence* (Mo.) *Express* 17 Nov. 1 They struck a small creek, kept their course still towards the south, and just at dark struck the *Oregon Road,* to the great joy of the party. **1849** in *Soc. Calif. Pion. Quart.* II. (1925) 97 There appeared to be a road that ran toward Lewis River that we supposed to be the Oregon Road.

(5) 1826 *Const. Advocate* (Frankfort, Ky.) 10 March 2/5 The wild sheep of the Rocky Mountains is indigenous in the Oregon territory. **1948** *Sat. Review* 15 May 30/1 The region included all of Washington, Idaho, and parts of Wyoming and Montana, but the Oregon territory was none the less a friendly land. — **(6) 1845** in *Wash. Hist. Quart.* I. 143 From where Oregon trail first strikes Platte to where we leave the south Fork is about 160 miles. **1949** *Life* 4 July 45/2 There they flung up trading outposts, like that at Fort Laramie on the Oregon Trail. — **(7) 1912** DAWSON *Pioneer Tales* 88 Here in such ideal surroundings we can picture campfires of the Oregon Trailers. **1949** *Sun. World-Herald Mag.* (Omaha) 3 April 18/3 Oregon Trailers of the 1850's often found Nebraska herbage so depleted by buffalo hordes that their plodding ox teams had to be fed hay and grain brought in the wagons.

b. In similar combs., chiefly occasional and obs., of obvious meaning, as (1) **Oregon Alps,** (2) **bacon,** (3) **bedstead,** (4) **boot,** (5) **boundary,** (6) **emigrant,** (7) **gold digger,** (8) **horse,** (9) **jargon,** (10) **mission,** (11) **mist,** (12) **wind.**

(1) 1844 LEE & FROST *Oregon* 209 Torrents, . . . from the Oregon Alps, dashed along to impede and prevent their progress. — **(2) 1872** POWERS *Afoot & Alone* 303 His flitch of Oregon bacon [was] gone. — **(3) 1851** *Ore. Spectator* 8 May 1/2 What is called an Oregon bedstead . . . consisted of two cross sticks run in between the logs of the houses; underneath the end of each was placed an upright stick by way of legs to the bed; length-wise on top thin boards were laid, and on top of this a good straw bed. — **(4) 1921** *D.N.* V. 109 Oregon boot, n. A device to hobble criminals in the open, somewhat like the ball and chain but less cumbersome. Said to have been devised in Oregon. **1924** G. C. HENDERSON *Keys to Crookdom* 94 He loaded the bandit down with an 'Oregon Boot,' a great heavy band of steel which was locked on to the ankle.

(5) 1845 *Whig Almanac 1846* 17 The clearest and best account we have seen of the Oregon Boundary controversy is given in the following article. — **(6) 1832** *Boston Transcript* 7 June 3/1 A meeting of Oregon emigrants will be holden in the Old Common Council Chamber, over the Supreme Court Room, School street, Boston, at 8 o'clock this evening, June 7th. — **(7) 1851** *Polly Peablossom* 110 'What, you hev never seen a live Grizzly?' exclaimed an old Oregon gold-digger. — **(8) 1889** *Cent. Mag.* Jan. 341/1 A strain of horses early imported into Montana from the West and known as the Oregon horse. — **(9) 1851** *32d Congress Spec. Sess.* Sen. Ex. Doc. No 4, 169 The agent communicated with one of them, familiar with the Tchinook language, or Oregon jargon, through Mr. Gibbs. **1910** HODGE *Amer. Indians* II. 146/2 Oregon jargon, Oregon trade language.

(10) 1850 HINES *Voyage* 95 At noon we arrived at . . . Chemekete, where the Oregon mission have commenced erecting mills. — **(11) 1864** *Ore. State Jrnl.* 24 Nov. 3/1 Last Thursday the regular 'Oregon mist' set in, and since then rain enough has fallen to atone for all the dry weather of the past six months. — **(12) 1913** W. C. BARNES *Western Grazing Grounds* 368 Unless one is using it [the diamond hitch] all the time and in constant practice one is apt to get mixed on it and end up with what is frequently called an 'Oregon wind.'

2. In the names of plants: (1) **Oregon alder,** the red alder, *Alnus rubra,* of the Pacific Coast; (2) **ash,** a western ash, *Fraxinus oregona,* valued for its hard, light wood; (3) **bearwood,** (see quot.); (4) **cedar,** a tall western cedar, *Chamaecyparis lawsoniana,* valued for its wood; (5) **corn,** (see quot.); (6) **crab apple,** a small tree, *Malus fusca,* having white flowers, found in western North America; (7) **fir,** (see quot.); (8) **grape,** a small evergreen shrub, *Mahonia aquifolia,* of the Pacific Coast, also the fruit of this; (9) **myrtle,** =**California laurel;** (10) **pea,** (see quot. 1855); (11) **pine,** the Douglas fir *q.v.,* or the wood of this; (12) **sunflower,** (see quot.); (13) **white fir,** (see quot.).

(1) 1874 GLISAN *Jrnl. Army Life* 480 Thus the Coast Range [of Oregon] . . . is covered with evergreen forests . . . intermixed at places with Oregon alder, balsam tree, . . . Oregon ash. **1949** COLLINGWOOD & BRUSH *Knowing Your Trees* 179 Red or Oregon alder is the most valuable and most plentiful of the few hardwoods of the Pacific slope. — **(2) 1869** *Amer. Naturalist* III. 407 Oregon Ash. . . . This first appears at the Dalles [Mont.]. **1949** COLLINGWOOD & BRUSH *Knowing Your Trees* 300/2 Oregon ash is the only timber ash of the Pacific region. — **(3) 1869** *Amer. Naturalist* III. 407 Oregon Bearwood (*Frangula Purshiana*). This species of Beechthorn occurs in both slopes of the Coeur d'Aleñe Mountains. — **(4) 1884** SARGENT *Rep. Forests* 179 Port Orford Cedar. Oregon Cedar. White Cedar.

(5) 1849 *N. Eng. Farmer* I. 368 Oregon corn . . . resembles the many-rowed corn of the south, excepting the ear is shorter. — **(6) 1884** SARGENT *Rep. Forests* 73 Oregon Crab Apple. . . . A small tree, sometimes 9 meters in height. — **(7) 1904** WOOTON *Native Ornamental Plants N. Mex.* 15 The Douglas Spruce or Oregon Fir (*Pseudotsuga taxifolia*) and the Bull Pine . . . would well repay the care necessary to getting them established. — **(8) 1851** *Ore. Statesman* 27 June 3/1 Oregon Grape, so called, is not a grape, but resembles the grape in size and appearance. **1949** *Jrnl. N.Y. Bot. Garden* July 153/1 In one bed is Oregon grape and beauty-berry, and against these are plantain-lilies. — **(9) 1934** WEBSTER. **1949** COLLINGWOOD & BRUSH *Knowing Your Trees* 243 'Oregon myrtle' supports a large number of roadside or home industries in southwestern Oregon, making ornamental woodwork, such as paper-weights, desk sets, trays, candlesticks, book-ends and the like.

(10) 1855 BROWNE in *Trans. Amer. Inst. N.Y.* 597 [The] Oregon pea . . . greatly resembles, if it is not identical with the oleaginous pea (*dolichos viridis*) lately introduced into France from China. **1856** *Rep. Comm. Patents 1855: Agric.* 259 The 'Oregon' pea was cultivated here [in Penna.]both in 1854 and 1855. — **(11) 1845** *N. Amer. Rev.* LX. 166 One of those gigantic Oregon Pines . . . whose prostrate trunk Douglas found to be two hundred and fifty feet in length. **1947** PEATTIE *Sierra Nevada* 148 Douglas fir . . . is known in the trade as Oregon pine. — **(12) 1845** WILKES *U.S. Explor. Exped.* IV. 434 The seed of the Balsamoriza (Oregon sunflower), is also used here, being pounded into a kind of meal. — **(13) 1897** SUDWORTH *Arborescent Flora* 54 *Great Silver Fir.* . . . Oregon White Fir (Cal.).

3. In the names of animals, chiefly birds, found in Oregon, as (1) **Oregon chickadee,** (2) **elk,** (3) **finch,** (4) **flying squirrel,** (5) **jay,** (6) **junco,** (7) **red squirrel,** (8) **robin,** (9) **(ruffed) grouse,** (10) **snowbird,** (11)

snowfinch, (12) towhee, (13) vesper sparrow, (14) wood rat.

(1) **1917** *Birds of Amer.* III. 211/2 The Oregon Chickadee (*Penthestes atricapillus occidentalis*) is smaller and darker than the eastern Chickadee. . . . It is found in the Pacific coast district from the Columbia River to British Columbia. **1949** KITCHIN *Birds Olympic Peninsula* 181 The Oregon chickadee is the western cousin of the black-capped chickadee of the east. — (2) **1867** *Beadle's Mo.* May 273/2 The 'wapiti,' Canadian stag, (*Cervus Canadensis*), or Oregon elk, attains a far greater size than any other species of North American deer. — (3) **1869** *Proc. Calif. Acad. Sci.* IV. 70 Pipilo Oregonus Bell, Oregon Finch. — (4) **1868** *Proc. Calif. Acad. Sci.* IV. 6 Pteromys Oregonus Bachman—Oregon Flying Squirrel.

(5) **1917** *Birds of Amer* II. 227 The Oregon Jay (*Perisoreus obscurus obscurus*) and his variant form, the Gray Jay . . . look like Canada Jays, with the wrong color of plumage. . . . Both are familiarly known as 'Camp Robbers.' **1949** KITCHIN *Birds Olympic Peninsula* 6 The Oregon jay feeds on beetles and larvae found in the festooned moss on fir branches. — (6) **1917** *Birds of Amer.* III. 47 Maybe the handsomest is the Oregon Junco (*Junco hyemalis oreganus*) with a black head and breast, sharply defined against a mahogany-brown back, white under parts, and pinkish-brown sides. **1948** *Pacific Discovery* Mar.–Apr. 15/2 A female Oregon junco scurried into a fuchsia bush at the southeast side of the Aquarium. — (7) **1873** MURPHY *Ore. Business Directory* 84 The Oregon red squirrel (*sciurus douglasii*) is found in all the mountains where nuts are plentiful. — (8) **1860** BAIRD in *Ives's Rep.* V. 5 *Turdus nævius*, Gm., Oregon robin. Colorado river. **1917** *Birds of Amer.* III. 240 The Varied Thrush, Alaska Robin, or Oregon Robin, as it is sometimes called, lives back in the mountains in the wilder sections where the timber is most dense. — (9) **1858** BAIRD *Birds Pacific R.R.* 631 Oregon Grouse. . . . Rocky mountains to Pacific coast of Oregon and Washington. **1917** *Birds of Amer.* II. 17 The four recognized races of this Grouse—the Ruffed Grouse . . . , the Canada Ruffed Grouse . . . , the Gray Ruffed Grouse . . . , and the Oregon Ruffed Grouse (Bonasa umbellus sabini)—extend the range of the species over much of the wooded regions of the United States and Canada. **1940** *Mt. Hood Guide* 19 Prominent but not numerous among the game birds is the Oregon ruffed grouse.

(10) **1852** BAIRD in Stansbury *Gt. Salt Lake* 316 [The] Oregon Snow-bird . . . occurs abundantly in Oregon and California. **1887** DENTON *Naturalist's Diary* (1949) 115 Have been here a week and have collected . . . Artic blue birds, Brewers blackbirds, Oregon snow birds, . . . and a water ouzel. — (11) **1837** *Phila. Acad. Nat. Sci. Jrnl.* VII. 188 [The] Oregon Snow-finch . . . is nearly related to the common snow-bird. **1886** BANCROFT *Hist. Ore.* I. 85 They were the chestnut-backed titmouse, *Parus rufescens*, [and] . . . Oregon snow-finch, *Fringilla Oregana.* — (12) **1891** *Cent.* 6406/3 *Oregon towhee*, a black, white, and chestnut towhee bunting, *Pipilo maculatus oregonus*, with spotted scapulars. **1917** *Birds of Amer.* III. 60 The group of Towhees, known as Spotted Towhees, and of which the Oregon Towhee is a member, are found in western United States and Mexico among the Chaparral. — (13) **1917** *Birds of Amer.* III. 24 Both of these forms are replaced in the Pacific coast district by the Oregon Vesper Sparrow (*Poœcetes gramineus affinis*). — (14) **1873** MURPHY *Ore. Business Directory* 85 The Oregon wood rat (*neotoma occidentalis*,) . . . is called by the Indians of Washington Territory, the *meskadah* or thief, owing to its kleptomanian propensities.

Oregonese ˌɔrɪgən'iz, *n.* An Oregonian, or Oregonians. *Obs.* — **1848** BRYANT *California* xv. 197, I think the Oregonese had a little the advantage of us in this respect. **1860** WHITMAN *Leaves of Grass* 35 One from Maine or Vermont, and a Carolinian and an Oregonese, shall be friends triune.

Oregonian ˌɔrɪ'gonɪən, *a.* and *n.*

1. *n.* A native or resident of Oregon. Cf. **old Oregonian.**

1845 *Phila. Public Ledger* 26 March 2/1 The Oregonians could govern themselves at home under the Federal Government as well as they could without it. **1865** STUART *Montana as It Is* 59 Oregonians are, however, better known by the name of 'Webfeet.' **1948** *Aurora* (Ill.) *Beacon-News* 7 Nov. 8/3 The Oregonians gave thumping approval at the polls to a $50 monthly old age pension plan.

b. An Indian of the Oregon region. *Obs.*

[**1890** GATSCHET *Klamath Indians* I. xcvii, The common belief of the Oregonians is that after death the soul travels the path traveled by the sun, which is the westward path.]

c. An emigrant bound for Oregon. Also transf.

1838 (*title*), Oregonian (Boston) [Organ of Ore. Provisional Emig. Soc., formed at Lynn, Mass., in Aug., 1838, to encourage emigration to Ore. Terr.] **1839** *Boston Wkly. Mag.* 27 April 271/3 We learn from the April number of the *Oregonian*, that it is contemplated to send out a company of emigrants to Oregon, to consist of not less than two hundred families. **1945** ADAMS *Album Amer. Hist.* II. 334 The Oregonians were interested in nothing short of Oregon.

d. *pl.* Cattle from Oregon. *Colloq.*

1910 BRONSON *Remin. Ranchman* 78 The dearest [were] the thick-loined, deep-quartered, dark red half-breed shorthorn Oregonians, descended from some of the best Missouri and Illinois strains, trailed by emigrants across the plains in the early 50s.

2. *a.* Of or pertaining to Oregon.

1873 BEADLE *Undevel. West* 762 There is a distinctly Oregonian look about all the natives and old residents. **1883** *Harper's Mag.* Nov. 943/2 Californian or Oregonian flour . . . can hardly surpass that of Utah. **1902** A. MACGOWAN *Last Word* 156 Washington . . . fell something short of the Barcan desert, or the Oregonian woods. **1928** *Amer. Mercury* Sep. 103/1 Lewis and Clark and the Astorians had made their Oregonian journeys.

Oregonly 'ɔrɪˌgənlɪ, *adv.* In the manner of an Oregonian. *Rare.* — *a***1861** WINTHROP *J. Brent* 243 Armstrong's opinion was only my own, expressed Oregonly.

orejano ˌore'hano, *n. S.W.* [Sp. in same sense.] (See quot. 1944.) — **1925** WILL JAMES *Drifting Cowboy* 70 I'd find myself all tangled up with a big two-year old 'orejana.' **1944** ADAMS *W. Words* 108 Orejano. . . . An unbranded and unmarked animal, the term being used principally in California, Oregon, and Nevada.

oreodon ə'riəˌdɑn, *n.* [f. Gk. *oros, oreos*, mountain, and *odous, odontos*, tooth] A genus of extinct four-toed ruminant mammal, about the size of a peccary, remains of which have been found in the western U.S. Also an animal of this genus. — **1851** *Phila. Acad. Nat. Sci. Proc.* V 238 Neither of these fossils Dr L[eidy] suspected belonged to Merycoidodon. . . . For the first he proposed the name of Oreodon. **1877** LE CONTE *Elem. Geology* (1879) 505 The Oreodon is another very remarkable animal, intermediate between the hog, the deer and the camel, which at this time inhabited the whole Continent from Nebraska to Oregon.

***organ**, *n.* As the last term in **bourbon, foot, hand, house, mouth, parlor, pipe, political organ.**

organ cactus. =**giant cactus.** Also **organ pipe cactus.**

1883 *Harper's Mag.* March 502/2 The enormous saguaras, the organ-cactus which . . . bristle over the landscape like masts or columns. **1908** HORNADAY *Camp Fires on Desert* 352 The mines are quite the northern limit of the organ-pipe cactus. **1947** *Time* 10 March 18/2 Afterwards, behind a Military Academy cavalry squadron, the two Presidents rode between rows of organ cacti and Mexican foot troops over the newly paved city streets to the great, tomb-like U.S. Embassy.

***organic**, *a.*

1. organic act, an act of Congress conferring the powers of government upon a territory. Cf. **enabling act.**

1850 E. S. SEYMOUR *Sk. Minn.* 277 The full term allowed by the organic act of the Territory. **1913** J. B. ELLIS *Lahoma* 211 Congress made them wait five months . . . before approving the Organic Act. **1949** *Pacific Northwest Quart.* Jan. 32 The spot to be located was the confluence as it existed at the time of Idaho's organic act, 10 years before.

transf. **1948** *Carpenter* April 7/1 Through the Organic Act the Department of Labor was established.

2. ***organic law,** the basic or fundamental law by virtue of which a government exists as such; also =prec.

1847 *Santa Fe Republican* 30 Oct. 2/1 This organic law provides for the appointment of various officers from Governor down. **1863** *Rio Abajo Press* 3 March 2/1 More than twelve years since Congress enacted our Organic Law; yet no steps are taken for its entering the Union as a State. **1900** *Cong. Rec.* 6 Feb. 1544/1 The fifteenth amendment . . . is a part of the organic law of this Republic.

***organization,** *n.* **1.** The body of officials, committee members, etc., that direct the affairs of a political party. **2.** Physical build or constitution. *Rare.*

(1) **1873** *Republic* I. 3 The Republican organization had become effete and corrupt. **1904** *Booklovers Mag.* Oct. 439 Editors are called in frequent consultation so as to be in close touch with the organization. — (2) **1890** LANGFORD *Vigilante Days* (1912) 456 She was of powerful organization, and having passed her life upon the borders, knew how to use the rifle.

***organize,** *v.*

1. *intr.* To effect or achieve an organization, esp. of political bodies; to elect a presiding officer, appoint committees, etc., preparatory to the orderly discharge of business.

1816 PICKERING 144 *To Organize*. . . . Used in speaking of political bodies. **1894** REED *Man. Parliamentary Law* 18 Those assemblies the membership of which can not be in dispute. . . can organize permanently at once. **1911** *N.Y. Ev. Post* 9 Jan. 3 The Legislature of New Jersey will organize to-morrow for the 135th time.

b. To unite in forming a labor or trade union.

1874 in C EVANS *Hist. United Mine Workers* I. 52 Organize secretly if you are not permitted to do so publicly, but do organize. **1921** J. R.

COMMONS *Trade Unionism* 563 Workers everywhere should insist upon their right to organize into trade-unions.

2. *tr.* To found or establish (unions or granges); to systematize (labor) or to form (laborers) into a union.

[**1832** *Cong. Deb.* 15 June 3575 A former Secretary of the Treasury . . . urged upon Congress . . . to imitate the Pacha, by 'organizing the whole labor of the country' in order to produce 'the greatest aggregate of national wealth.'] **1871** *Atlantic Mo.* May 557/1 The 'National Labor Union' was organized at Baltimore in 1866. **1872** *Chi. Tribune* 27 Dec. 4/2 Farmers' 'Granges,' or clubs, are being organized quite extensively in Illinois and Iowa. **1903** J. MITCHELL *Organized Labor* 431 Trade unionism in the United States is still in its infancy; American labor is still far from being organized. **1948** *News-Dispatch* (Michigan City, Ind.) 3 April 4/6 The CIO and AFL were beginning their Southern drives to organize both whites and Negroes.

transf. **1899** *Internat. Typog. Union Proc.* 112/1, I dispatched them organizing literature and letters, with a view to organizing their respective localities.

b. To prepare (a body of representatives or a political party) for proper functioning through the election of officers, committees, etc.

1840 *Niles' Reg.* 5 Dec. 218 Both houses [in S.C.] being organized the governor . . . transmitted his message on Tuesday the 24th. **1905** *McClure's Mag.* XXIV. 346 Brayton . . . 'organized' the Republican party; . . . he organized the General Assembly and ran it.

3. To set up or prescribe for (a county, territory, or territorial government) fundamental laws and regulations.

1851 FILLMORE in *Pres. Mess. & P.* V. 127 Some difficulties have occurred in organizing the Territorial governments of New Mexico and Utah. **1868** *Cong. Globe* 22 July 4344/2 When the Territory of Montana was organized . . . [I] gave it the name of Wyoming.

organized labor. Workingmen who are organized into labor unions. Also attrib.

1885 in C. EVANS *Hist. U. M. W.* I. 131 To organized labor . . . and to the generous and sympathetic public . . . we return our sincere and heartfelt thanks. **1924** WOLMAN *Growth of Amer. Trade Unions* 82 The number of wage earners . . . would not be considered by some a thoroughly fair base for measuring the achievement in size of an organized labor movement. **1948** *Time* 15 March 27/2 He thought of himself as the leader of all the people, not just of organized labor.

***organizer,** *n.* A member of a labor union whose duty it is to persuade other workmen to join a union. — **1874** in C. EVANS *Hist. U.M.W.* I. 60 One or more competent persons in each state embraced in the organization who shall be known as 'organizers,' and whose duties shall be to organize new lodges or branches. **1917** SINCLAIR *King Coal* 81 A letter which certified him to be Thomas Olson, an organiser for the United Mine-Workers.

* **original,** *a.* In combs.: (1) **original package saloon,** a saloon in which liquor is sold only in its original package in an attempt to evade state prohibition laws; (2) **settler,** =**first settler;** (3) **states,** the thirteen states united under the Articles of Confederation, and later under the federal Constitution; (4) **thirteen,** the thirteen American colonies that united to fight the Revolutionary War against Great Britain.

(1) **1906** in *Kans. Hist. Soc.* IX. 424 The liquor-dealers of Missouri proceeded at once to come into Kansas and set up 'original-package saloons' in every town. — (2) **1798** *Doc. Hist. N.Y. State* I. 675 Those who were received by the Original Settlers as 'accepted Inhabitants,' might have been born in America. — (3) **1802** *Ann. 7th Congress* 1 Sess. 1349 An act . . . for the admission of such State into the Union, on an equal footing with the original States. **1835** JACKSON in *Pres. Mess. & P.* III. 186 Such State should be admitted by its delegates into the Congress of the United States on an equal footing with the original States in all respects whatever. **1947** DOWNEY *Lusty Forefathers* 100 While the toasts drunk were to the Original States,which limited them to only thirteen, the evening was a grand one. — (4) **1855** *N.Y. Herald* 20 Dec. 1/4 Our boundaries have stretched from the 'original thirteen' westward, until the oceans wash our shores.

orignal əˈrɪnjəl, *n.* [Can. F. f. Basque *oregna,* stag.] The American moose or elk.

"Littré cites from Lescarbot, *Hist. de la Nouvelle France* (1615) xx, that the Basques landing on the American coasts gave to the American elk the name *orenac,* and that *orenac* in Basque meant 'stag' " (*OED*).

1698 TONTI *LaSalle's Last Discoveries* 5 It [La.] is stockt with all sorts of Beasts, as Bulls, *Orignacs,* Wolves, . . . Hares, Beavers, Otters. **1775** J. ANDERSON *Essays Relating to Agric.* 462 In North America they have a species of deer, called by the natives Orignial or Aurignial . . . probably the Moose-deer. **1781–2** JEFFERSON *Notes Va.* (1788) 57 (*footnote*), It were to be wished, that naturalists . . . would examine well the animals called there [in northern Amer.] by the names of grey and black moose, caribou, original [*sic*], and elk. **1895** COUES in *Exped. Z. M. Pike* I. 87 (*footnote*), There is no doubt about the meaning of these phrases; for *orignal, orignac, oriniac, orenac,* etc. are Basque forms of a name of the moose.

* **oriole,** *n.* Any one of various American birds of the family Icteridae, closely allied to the finches.

1782 LATHAM *Gen. Synopsis Birds* I. 417 Oriole. . . . These birds are inhabitants of America, except in a few instances. **1831** J. Q. ADAMS *Memoirs* VIII. 426 The oriole of Baltimore is the fiery hang-bird. **1947** *Sat. Review* 10 May 12/1 Even in an apartment there one is likely to see the flash of an oriole going past the kitchen window.

b. oriole basket, a form of go-cart, shaped somewhat like an oriole's nest, for small children.

1941 *Yankee* Dec. 39/2 One fascinating Oriole Basket costs only $1.

As the last term in **Audubon's, Baltimore, brown, Bullock's, golden, hooded, Nelson's, orchard, red-winged, Scott's oriole.**

Orleanese ˌɔrlɪənˈiz, *a.* Residing in New Orleans. *Rare.* — **1808** JEFFERSON *Writings* XII. 185 If the Orleanese Creoles would but contemplate these truths, they would cling to the American Union.

Orleanian ɔrˈlinɪən, *n.* A resident of New Orleans. Also, *obs.,* **Orleanois.**

1839 *N.O. Picayune* 9 April 2/1 'Go it, my red shirts' said one of the Orleanois. **1946** *N.O. Times-Picayune* 23 March 17/4 Orleanian Tells of Jap Tortures. **1948** *Highway Traveler* Dec. 18/1 Because Orleanians at one time depended upon the duel as a means of settling disputes, the extensive display of dueling pistols and swords on the second floor has special interest.

* **Orleans,** *n.*

1. New Orleans sugar. *Rare.*

1845 in BLAIR *Amer. Humor* (1937) 369 He gives Jim Smith, (the store-keeper over Bay's Mounting), *warnin* to fetch . . . sum 'Orleans' for sweetnin, or not to fetch himself; the . . . sugar has never failed to be thar yet.

2. Orleans boat, (see quot. 1817). Now *hist.*

1797 F. BAILY *Tour* 225 An Orleans boat (as it is here called) stopped at the town. **1817** FORDHAM *Narr. Travels* 79 These flat boats or Orleans boats as they are called in the Western Waters are from 12 to 25 feet wide, and from 30 to 90 feet long. **1941** BALDWIN *Keelboat Age* 47 Orleans boats were covered for their full length.

b. A Mississippi River steamboat bound for New Orleans.

1852 CASEY *Two Yrs.* 112 We could not help philosophising a little on . . . the emphatic uncertainty of the starting time of Orleans boats. **1884** MARK TWAIN *H. Finn* xxiv. 241 She's a big Orleans boat, and I was afeard she mightn't stop there.

3. Also (1) **Orleans college,** (2) **fever,** (3) **molasses,** (4) **territory,** (5) **theater.**

(1) **1895** KING *New Orleans* 293 Many a good story of the fathers . . . and elder brothers of the young gentlemen at the Orleans college. — (2) **1843** HALL *New Purchase* (1916) 193 Cure for Orleans [i.e., yellow] fever: two quarts of cold water, and cover up in bed. **1867** G. W. HARRIS *Sut Lovingood* 87 Gin em a rale Orleans fever in five minits. — (3) **1883** *Practical Housekeeping* 100 Ginger Cakes. One quart Orleans molasses, pint lard or butter [etc.]. — (4) **1806** in *Ann. 9th Congress* 2 Sess. 1137 Nature has marked with a distinguishing feature, the line established by Congress, between the Orleans and Louisiana Territories.

(5) **1895** KING *New Orleans* 293 The great lantern of the Orleans theatre.

orneriness ˈɔrnərɪnɪs, *n.* [f. **ornery* (var. of **ordinary*)+*-ness.*] The state of being ornery, meanness. *Colloq.*

1899 TARKINGTON *Gent. From Ind.* iv, Sometimes they . . . let loose their deviltries just for pure orneriness. **1927** JAMES *Cow Country* 229 The bronk's orneriness had come to the top, and that pony . . . begin to get sort of desperate and to looking for a way out. **1948** *Sat. Review* 5 June 15/2 There still seems some doubts as to whether the feud started from a row over a razorback hog, . . . or from the mere mixture of orneriness and mountain corn.

ornithoid ˈɔrnəˌθɔɪd, *a.* [Gk. *ornith-,* bird+*-oid.*] Resembling or approaching the structure found in birds. — **1858** HITCHCOCK *Ichnol. N. Eng.* 105, I attach the Typopus to the ornithoid Lizards. **1895** *Pop. Sci. Mo.* Sep. 693 Ornithoid lizards or batrachians.

oro ˈoro, *n. W.* [Sp. in same sense.] Gold, money. *Colloq.*

1850 *Placer Times* (Sacramento, Calif.) 2 Feb., It will thus be perceived that the *oro* is not confined to the Sierra Nevada. **1867** *Central City* (Colo.) *Times* 29 Oct. 4/1 The oro is plentiful in the above celebrated lode. **1929** DOBIE *Vaquero* 269 (Bentley), I plugged down $500 *puro oro* on the jack for an ace.

oroide ˈoroˌaɪd, *n.* [f. F. *or,* gold and Gk. *eidos,* form.] An alloy resembling gold. Also attrib. *Obs.* Cf. **goloid,** *n.*

1867 *N.Y. Tribune* 11 Dec. 7/8 Oroide case, a newly discovered composition, known only to ourselves, precisely like gold in appearance, as keeping its color as long as worn. **1876** *Avalanche* (Silver City, Ida.) 11 Jan. 3/2 The old man . . . [drew] forth an old Oroide watch. **1881** *Metal World* No. 6, 89 Oreide must not be confounded with oroide, which consists of 12 parts of caustic lime, 360 of sal-ammoniac, 600 of magnesia, 900 of tartar, 10,000 of copper, and 1,700 of zinc.

Oronoco ˌorəˈnoko, *n.* [f. the *Orinoco* River in South America.] A variety of strong-scented tobacco. In full **Oronoco tobacco.**

1660 *Va. State P.* I. 5 Two thousand five hundred pounds of good, sound, bright and large Arronoca Tobacco. **1682** in *Va. Hist. Mag.* I. 106 The Tob[acc]o I sent you . . . [consisted of] four hhds . . . sweet scented . . . the Residue were Orinoko. **1724** Jones *Present State* 40 There are two Sorts of Tobacco, viz. *Oroonoko* the stronger, and *Sweet-scented* the milder. **1775** *Amer. Husbandry* I. 225 The Oroonoko is principally in use in Chesepeak bay, . . . It is strong and hot; the principal markets for it are Germany and the North. **1896** P. A. Bruce *Econ. Hist. Va.* I. 436 Between the sweet-scented and the Oronoco, . . . there are several varieties.

transf. **1708** E. Cook *Sot-weed Factor* 18 Planters are usually call'd by the Name of *Oronooko*, from their Planting *Oronooko-Tobacco.*

orphans' court. [Prob. a translation of Du. *weeskamer*. Cf. Webster *s.v. orphan chamber.*] (See quot. 1914.) Also attrib.

1713 *Pa. Col. Rec.* II. 565 An act for Establishing Orphan's Courts. **1808** *Md. Laws* 87 The Proceedings of the Orphans' Court of Saint Mary's County. **1873** *Pa. Rep.* XIII. 121 An Orphans' Court sale is a judicial sale. **1914** *Cyclo. Govt.* I. 504 In New Jersey, Pennsylvania, Delaware and Maryland the probate of wills, the administration of decedents' estates and supervision of minor heirs is vested in orphans' courts. Their jurisdiction and powers are similar to those of probate courts in other states.

Ortley (pippin). A winter eating apple. *Obs.* — **1847** Ives *N. Eng. Fruit* 42 Ortley Pippin.—The size sometimes large, the form oblong; the skin, when ripe, a bright yellow. **1856** *Rep. Comm. Patents 1855: Agric.* 292 Winter apples [include] . . . Small Romanite, Ortley, or White Bellefleur, Baldwin.

* **ortolan,** *n.* The Carolina rail or the bobolink *qq.v.* Cf. **American ortolan.**

1836 Holley *Texas* 100 Ortolans, which form so celebrated a dish in Europe, are abundant in Texas. **1874** Coues *Birds N.W.* 538 *Porzana Carolina*, . . . Carolina Rail; Sora; 'Ortolan.' **1917** *Birds of Amer.* I. 207 Sora. *Porzana carolina*. . . . Other names. . . . Ortolan; Mud Hen.

Orukter Amphibolos. [Gk. *orukter*, digger, and *amphibolos*, thrown on both sides.] A self-propelled form of steam digger or dredge capable of going on land and water and able to dig or dredge on both sides of itself. Now *hist.*

1886 *Jrnl. Franklin Inst.* July 10 The Philadelphia Board of Health ordered of Evans, in 1804, a steam dredge . . . called the *Orukter Amphibolos* or Amphibious Digger. **1939** Clark *Railroads & Rivers* 51 By 1773, Oliver Evans began his experiments with the use of steam to propel both wagons and ships, although it was not until 1804 that he sent his *Oruktor Amphibolos* up the Schuylkill by means of paddle-wheels. **1941** *Sat. Ev. Post* 20 Dec. 40/4, I am sure a man as intelligent as your father would appreciate seeing the Orukter Amphibolos when he comes.

Osage oˈsedʒ, *n.* [f. tribal name *Wazhazhe*, war people.]

1. An Indian of the most important southern Siouan tribe west of the Mississippi River, first encountered by Europeans along the Osage River in Missouri. Also, often *pl.*, the tribe of such an Indian. Cf. **Little Osage.**

1698 tr. Hennepin *New Discovery* I. 141 Several Savages of the Nations of the Osages, Cikaga, and Akansa, came to see us. **1722** Coxe *Descr. Carolana* 16 The Yellow [River] is called the River of the Massorites, from a great Nation inhabiting in many Towns near its juncture with the River of the Ozages. **1842** *S. Lit. Messenger* VIII. 63/2, I found everything in possession of a party of ten or twelve Osages. **1947** *Prairie Schooner* Winter 403 Tribes are assembled Of Osage and Ponca.

b. The language of the Osage Indians.

1835 Irving *Tour on Prairies* (1850) 20 He spoke a jargon of mingled French, English, and Osage. **1945** Mathews *Talking* 87 She . . . said in Osage to the chief, 'I want to tell my son about the way we did things.'

2. Ellipt. for Osage orange *q.v.* as a main entry.

1884 *N.Y. Wkly. Tribune* 6 Aug. 13/2, I first fed osage, but being so tedious to gather I quit the hedge and went to the woods for mulberry.

3. In combs., chiefly obs.: (1) **Osage apple,** = **Osage orange;** (2) **buhr,** a form of silicious rock suitable for millstones; (3) **hedge,** a hedge made of Osage orange; (4) **hunting trail,** a trail between the Arkansas and Missouri rivers made by the Osage Indians; (5) **orange,** see as main entry; (6) **plant,** = **Osage orange;** (7) **prairie,** an extensive prairie region between the Arkansas and Missouri rivers formerly occupied by the Osage Indians; (8) **Reserve,** an area of about one and a half million acres in Oklahoma set apart by Congress in 1870 for the Osage Indians; (9) **thorn,** = **Osage orange.**

(1) **1804** Lewis in *L. & Clark Exped.* VI. (1904) 172 No appearance of the buds of the Osage apple. *Ib.* VII. 296. **1817** *Amer. Mo. Mag.* II. 57 Mr. Rafinesque read an interesting paper . . . on the Osage Apple. — (2) **1837** Wetmore *Gaz. Missouri* 73 An excellent substitute for the French buhr has been quarried in this country. . . . It is commonly called the Osage buhr. — (3) **1902** White *Blazed Trail* 102 An osage hedge and a board fence respectively bounded the side and back. **1930** Ferber *Cimarron* 42 She had planted the first young fruit trees, the vegetable and flower garden that now flourished in the encircling Osage hedge. — (4) **1843** Boone *Journal* (1917) 192 Followed until 2 o'clock the great Osage hunting trail.

(6) **1856** *Rep. Comm. Patents 1855: Agric.* 316 The Osage plant has, at all periods of its growth, a tap-root, longer and thicker than the top or stem. — (7) **1821** Nuttall *Travels Arkansa* 171 About eight miles from the Arkansa, commences the great Osage prairie, more than 60 miles in length. — (8) **1901** Duncan & Scott *Allen & Woodson Co., Kansas* 582 This strip began at the state line and ran westward beyond the surveys, while on the south it joined the Osage Reserve. — (9) **1869** *Rep. Comm. Agric. 1868* 251 Specimens of the single-row Osage thorn . . . had much the appearance of a line of brush with tops all outward.

b. In further combs. in which the meaning is obvious or made clear by the quots., as (1) **Osage agency,** (2) **buffalo dance,** (3) **camp,** (4) **children,** (5) **dance,** (6) **femme,** (7) **hunter,** (8) **Indian,** (9) **nation,** (10) **plum,** (11) **tongue,** (12) **trace,** (13) **tribe,** (14) **village.**

(1) **1945** Mathews *Talking* 2 This spot was . . . the last chance to get a shot at a deer on the trip from the Osage agency to the States. — (2) **1945** Mathews *Talking* 51 They might possibly have a ceremony more like the Osage buffalo dance. — (3) **1843** N. Boone *Journal* (1917) 200 The horses taken were picketed . . . so near the Osage camp that no more Pawnees would ever come there for them. — (4) **1822** *Missionary Herald* XVIII. 148 We are daily talking among ourselves about the way to obtain more of the Osage children.

(5) **1945** Mathews *Talking* 58, I have watched this dance every spring for years, and, as in the case of the Osage dances, I have never grown tired of it. — (6) **1808** Pike *Sources Miss.* 125 A Sac . . . was married to an Osage femme and spoke French *only*. — (7) **1835** Irving *Tour on Prairies* 48 Osage hunters had recently crossed the river on their way to the buffalo range. — (8) **1812** in *S. D. Hist. Coll.* IV. (1908) 151, I concluded they were Osage Indians. **1945** Mathews *Talking* 14, I had wasted some of the best years of my life . . . trying to make more comfortable the assimilation of the Osage Indian—and just horizon-gazing. — (9) **1804** Clark in *Lewis & C. Exped.* I. (1904) 36 They had letters from the man Mr. Choteau Sent to that part of the Osarge Nation settled on Arkansas River. **1818** *Wkly. Recorder* (Chillicothe, O.) 28 Aug. 19/1 Within a few months past they have made war upon the Osage nation.

(10) **1804** Clark in *Lewis & C. Exped.* I. (1904) 46 Wild plumb of a Superior . . . quality, Called the Osages Plumb Grows on a bush the hight of a Hasel. **1827** *Western Mo. Rev.* I. 323 Some of them, especially the yellow Osage plum, are among the most delicious fruits, we have ever tasted. — (11) **1812** in *S. D. Hist. Coll.* IV. (1908) 151 It was so dark I could not distinctly see my men, but heard the voice of one of them speaking to the Indians in the Osage tongue. — (12) **1818** Schoolcraft *Journal* 52 In pursuing up the valley of Swan Creek . . . we fell into the Osage trace, a horse path beaten by the Osages in their hunting excursions. — (13) **1906** *Indian Laws & Tr.* III. 253 All lands belonging to the Osage tribe of Indians . . . shall be divided among the members of said tribe. — (14) **1812** in *S. D. Hist. Coll.* IV. (1908) 150 On the 7th of October [1801], entered the Osage river . . . the 23rd . . . we have ascended within sixty miles of the Osage village. **1821** J. Fowler *Journal* 6 We set out early along the road leading to the Osage vilege.

c. *Osage band of Quapaw,* a group of Quapaw Indians who lived with the Osage 1876–93.

1946 Foreman *Last Trek* 314 They came to be known as the Osage band of Quapaw.

Osage orange. An American tree, *Maclura pomifera,* native to Arkansas and adjacent regions once occupied by the Osage Indians.

The wood of this tree was prized by the Indians for making bows, hence the French name bois d'arc *q.v.* and the American forms shown under **bodock.**

1817 BRADBURY *Travels* 160 (*footnote*), It bleeds an acrid milky juice when wounded, and is called by the hunters the Osage Orange. **1858** WARDER *Hedges & Evergreens* 202 The wood of the Osage Orange is nearly as hard as lignum vitae. **1848** *Ecological Monographs* April 205/2 Numerous hedges of osage orange are . . . fast disappearing as they are being cut for posts.

b. Osage orange hedge, a hedge formed of Osage orange trees or bushes. Cf. **Osage hedge.**

1855 *Chi. W. Times* 29 March 3/2 The introduction of the Osage orange hedges, as a substitute for fences on the Western prairies, . . . is becoming very general. **1896** *Typographical Jrnl.* IX. 51 Stone fences and osage orange hedges . . . inclose breeding establishments of fine stock on every road. **1941** FERGUSSON *Southwest* 157 Mrs. Hayden found a stately adobe house with water piped in, an osage orange hedge around an orchard.

c. Attrib. with **bush, hedgerow, seed, tree, wood.**

1846 BROWNE *Trees Amer.* 465 *Maclura aurantiaca*, The Osage Orange-Tree. **1855** *Chi. Times* 29 March 3/2 Over 3,000 bushels of Osage orange seeds was brought into the western market last year from Texas. **1859** MARCY *Prairie Trav.* 26 Wheels made of bois d'arc, or Osage-orange wood, are the best for the plains, as they shrink but little. **1892** ALLEN *Blue-Grass Region* 28 A pleasure it is, too, to come occasionally upon an Osage orange hedge-row. **1902** HARBEN *Abner Daniel* 282 It was a sequestered spot, well hidden from the rest of the road by an old hedge of Osage orange bushes.

* **Oscar,** *n.* [See note.] A small statuette, usu. gold, awarded annually since 1928 by the Academy of Motion Picture Arts and Sciences for the best performance, production, photography, and similar accomplishments of the year in motion pictures.

Said to have received this name from the remark of the secretary of the Academy upon seeing one of the statuettes, "He reminds me of my Uncle Oscar." See *Amer. N. & Q.* Oct. 1947, 105/1.

1936 *Time* 16 March 56/2 Awkward moments occurred at last week's ceremony when neither Director Ford nor Screenwriter Nichols appeared to claim their prizes—small gold statuettes which Hollywood calls 'Oscars.' **1949** *Chi. D. News* 25 March 1/5 She was handed the 'Oscar' for being the best actress of 1948.

b. *transf.* Any award for, or symbol of, excellence.

1941 *Time* (Air Exp. Ed.) 2 June 25/3 That these trials . . . did not keep [movie-] producer Gabriel Pascal from turning out a polished and distinguished product is a transcendent Oscar in the onetime cavalryman's lap. **1949** *Nat. Hist.* Nov. 417/3 If there are any 'Oscars' to be awarded in the world of animal acting, the vote of many naturalists will unhesitatingly go to the hognose snake, possum player extraordinary.

oscine ˈɑsɪn, *a.* [f. **Oscines*.] Of or pertaining to oscines or singing birds. — **1883** *Nation* 29 March 281 *Boot* . . . is used to denote the continuous front sheath of the tarsus of most oscine or singing birds, like the robin. **1885** *Library Mag.* Aug. 97 Those liquid bird-phrases . . . have been the same since first an oscine throat was filled with music.

osoberry ˈosoˌbɛrɪ, *n.* [Sp. *oso*, bear, +*berry*.] A western shrub, *Osmaronia cerasiformis*. — **1888** LINDLEY *Calif. of South* 331 We have . . . the white-blossomed 'Oso berry.' **1890** *Cent.* 4167/3 osoberry. . . . A shrub or small tree of western North America, *Nuttallia cerasiformis*. It has greenish-white flowers in racemes, blooming very early, followed by blue-black drupes with thin bitter pulp.

osophy ˈɑsəfɪ, *n.* [f. *phil*osophy*, *the*osophy*, etc.] A new or strange doctrine or theory. *Contemptuous.* — **1865** E. BURRITT *Walk to Land's End* (1868) 28 Hampton Court . . . is a parliament in which the idiosyncracies, *isms* and *osophies* of race and nation . . . are represented in a pleasant and instructive manner. **1897** *Advance* 28 Oct. 574/2 That man would be hard to please who could not find . . . some variety of doxy, or osophy, or ism, which would come within hailing distance of his theory of life and destiny.

Ostend manifesto. *Hist.* A statement issued in 1854 by the U.S. ministers to Spain, France, and Great Britain, meeting at Ostend, Belgium, recommending the purchase or, if Spain refused to sell, the seizure of Cuba by the U.S. Also **Ostend Circular.**

1856 in H. H. SMITH *Republican Nat. Conventions* (1896) 13 *Resolved*, That the highwayman's plea, that 'might makes right,' embodied in the Ostend Circular, was in every respect unworthy of American diplomacy. **1884** BLAINE *20 Years of Congress* I. 241 He was led by Mason and Soulé into the imprudence of signing the Ostend Manifesto. **1941** BUCKMASTER *Let My People Go* 237 The Ostend Manifesto was the answer.

osteopath ˈɑstɪəˌpæθ, *n.* [f. **osteopathy*.] One who practices osteopathy. — **1897** *Columbus* (O.) *Dispatch* 26 March, The [Iowa] house to-day passed the senate medical practice act, . . . driving out osteopaths . . . unless they pass examinations the same as physicians. **1948** *Look* 16 March 6/2 As an osteopath, I vigorously protest your story.

osteopathic ˌɑstɪəˈpæθɪk, *a.* Of or pertaining to osteopathy. — **1897** A. T. STILL *Autobiography* 114 During the winter of 1878 and 1879 . . . I treated partly by drugs, as in other days, but also gave Osteopathic treatments. **1948** *News-Palladium* (Benton Harbor, Mich.) 14 Aug. 2/7 My children were delivered by an osteopathic physician.

osteopathist ˌɑstɪˈɑpəθɪst, *n.* [f. **osteopathy*.] =**osteopath.** — **1905** *Independent* 16 Nov. 1142/2 The osteopathists claim to cure by manipulation of the spinal column.

***osteopathy,** *n.* A system of therapeutics based on the theory that structural derangement, esp. of the spinal column, is the principal cause of disease, and stressing the restoration of normal structure by manipulation. — **1891** A. T. STILL in *Kirksville* (Mo.) *Graphic* 16 Jan. 1/5 Its name [i.e., of 'the new science of health'] is and will be osteopathy. **1946** *This Week Mag.* 7 Sep. 18/3, I mentioned that osteopathy has been my cure-all during most of my tennis career.

Oswego ɑsˈwigo, *n.* [*Oswego* River, N.Y.]

1. Oswego (bass), the large-mouthed black bass.

1758 C. REA *Journal* (1881) 34 The Lake affords plenty of a Fish call'd Oswego Bass, also Perch, Roche, Trouts &c. **1897** *N.Y. Forest, Fish, & Game Comm. 2d Rep.* 176 There are two species of black bass, the small mouth, with the Latin name, . . . and the large mouth, . . . improperly called 'Oswego' bass. **1921** *Outing* June 108/2, I can't remember ever having caught one which really put up a battle, even a big Oswego.

2. Oswego bee balm, =**Oswego tea.**

1937 *Range Plant Handbook* W-134 Both spotted beebalm (*M. punctata*) and Oswego beebalm (*M. didyma*), also called Oswego tea, [yield] the valuable antiseptic drug, thymol.

3. Oswego system, a system of elementary school instruction based on the study of real objects rather than on textbooks. *Obs.* Cf. * **object system.**

1865 *Amer. Jrnl. Education* March 191, I shall confine myself mainly to some thoughts concerned with what is called in this country the 'Oswego System.' **1866** *Ib.* June 265 But what is the Oswego System?

4. Oswego tea, (see quots. and cf. **bee balm, Indian plume**).

1806 MCMAHON *Amer. Gardener's Cal.* 604 *Monarda dydima*. . . . Oswego-Tea. **1850** S. F. COOPER *Rural Hours* 117 Humming-birds . . . are partial to the bee larkspur also, with the wild bergamot or Oswego tea. **1947** *Nat. Geog. Mag.* July 62/1 Among the many useful plants they found . . . were two of this same Mint Family, Oswego Tea (*Monarda didyma*), and Wild Bergamot (*Monarda fistulosa*).

* **O.T.** An abbreviation for **old tenor.** *Obs.*

1768 *Boston Post-Boy* 20 June (Th.), John Spooner advertises 'Shot, £. 10 *Old Tenor* per Hundred. Wool Cards, £10 *O.T.* per Dozen. German Steel at 6s. 4d. *O.T.* per Pound. **1774** *Newport Mercury* 30 May (Th.), He might buy the tail of their flock at £.9 *O.T.* per head. . . . I put down for the deficient sheep and mare £.900 *O.T.* **1866** CAULKINS *Hist. Norwich* 294 After 1746, the fixed rate of O.T. currency was 45*s* to a dollar of N.T. 6*s*—that is, seven and one half to one.

* **Otaheite. 1. Otaheite cane,** sugar cane of a variety obtained from the island of Otaheite, now Tahiti. *Obs.* **2. Otaheite corn,** Indian corn, or a grain resembling this, obtained from Tahiti. *Obs.*

(1) **1812** *Niles' Reg.* II. 86/2 The former will have fifty acres in Otaheite cane this year. **1856** *Rep. Comm. Patents 1855: Agric.* 274 The 'Otaheite' cane originated in the Society Islands. — (2) **1805** in *Commun. to Mass. Soc. for Promoting Agric.* (1806) 26 A singular kind of grain, . . . Otaheite corn, . . . [was] distributed . . . to several gentlemen of this town [Boston], who raised it in their gardens. **1837** WILLIAMS *Florida* 111 The Guinea corn, Otaheite corn, and Millet, succeed very well.

otard oˈtɑrd, *n.* [Origin unknown.] ?A brand name for a kind of whisky. *Obs.* — **1856** *Harper's Mag.* Dec. 66/2 He . . . huddles a shirt, a case of dueling-pistols, and a bottle of 'Otard' into a small trunk. **1867** J. N. EDWARDS *Shelby* 514 Men offered tempting bribes in boxes of delightful *otard* and baskets of delicious champagne.

otary ˈotərɪ, *n.* [f. *otaria*, Latinizing of Gk. *ōtaros*, large-eared.] Any one of various eared seals. — **1847** WEBSTER 781/1 *Otary*, Eared seal; a name given to all those animals of the seal family which have external ears. **1880** J. ALLEN *N. Amer. Pinnipeds* 225 The largest species of the Otaries . . . are Hair Seals, while the smallest . . . are Fur Seals.

Hence **otarian,** *a.*, of or pertaining to eared seals; **otariid,** *n.*, a member of the family of eared seals. — **1880** J. ALLEN *N. Amer. Pinnipeds* 2 The walruses are really little more than thick, clumsy, obese forms of the Otarian type, with the canines enormously developed. . . . The walruses are merely elephantine Otariids.

Otoe ˈoto, *n.* ["From *Wat'lota* 'lechers' " (Hodge).] A member of a Siouan tribe of Indians; also *pl.*, the tribe. Also attrib.

1806 LEWIS in *L. & Clark Exped.* V. (1905) 20 We left the Ottoes on the river Platte. **1818** *Wkly. Recorder* (Chillicothe, O.) 28 Aug. 19/1 The Sioux, Ottoes, Mandans, &c. to the west, live more remote, and are less likely to receive immediate attention. **1835** J. T. IRVING *Ind. Sketches* I. 124 Our Otoe friend rode in front, accompanied by Major D——, the Indian agent. **1906** *Indian Laws & Tr.* III. 234 The Secretary of the Interior . . . [shall] pay, out of the funds of the Otoe and Missouri Indians, of Oklahoma Territory [etc.]. **1947** DEVOTO *Across Wide Missouri* 35 Our travelers were west of the Otos and Omahas, whom the river voyage passed.

otological ˌotəˈlɑdʒɪkl, *a.* Also **otologic.** [f. otology *q.v.*] Of or pertaining to otology.

1868 (*title*), Transactions Amer. Otological Association (New Bedford, Mass.) **1949** *Eye, Ear, Nose & Throat Mo.* Sep. 422/1 The late onset . . . is another characteristic feature of the otologic syndrome presented here. **1949** *Annals of Otology, Pharyngology & Laryngology* March 34 [The] individuals [were] referred to the University Clinics by physicians and otological specialists.

otologist oˈtɑlədʒɪst, *n.* [See next.] An ear specialist.

1874 ROOSA *Diseases of Ear* (ed. 2) 47 The high character of the work that has been done by American otologists. **1876** BARTHOLOW *Materia Medica* (1879) 549 Glycerine is used by otologists to soften cerumen. **1949** *Archives of Otolaryngology* Oct. 507 It is important that otologists be frank and honest with patients who have hearing losses.

otology oˈtɑlədʒɪ, *n.* [Gk. *oto-, ear, + *-logy.] The science of the ear and its diseases (see also quot. 1842).

1842 DUNGLISON *Medical Lexicon, Otology.* . . . The part of anatomy which treats of the ear. **1880** (*title*), American Journal of Otology, A Quarterly Journal of Physiological Acoustics. **1949** *Eye, Ear, Nose & Throat Mo.* Sep. 435/1 Clinical diagnosis in otology can rarely be made consistently on the basis of any one hearing test.

Otsego bass. A variety of whitefish, *Coregonus clupeiformis*, found in Otsego Lake, N.Y.

1822 DE WITT CLINTON in *Amer. Med. Philos. Reg.* III. 188 (*caption*), Account of the *Salmo otsego* or the Otsego basse. **1857** *Spirit of Times* 5 Dec. 209/2 The famous Otsego bass, of that lake, is a Corregonus. **1911** *Rep. Fisheries 1908* 318/1 The common whitefish . . . is known . . . also as 'Otsego bass' in the neighborhood of Otsego Lake, N.Y.

Ottawa ˈɑtəwə, *n.* [Can. F. *Otaua, Otawa*, from an Algonquian word meaning "trader."] An American Indian of a tribe found chiefly in Michigan and around the Great Lakes; also *pl.*, the tribe. Also *collect.*

1640 *Relations des Jésuites* (1858) 34/2 Au Sud . . . est vne Isle . . . habitée des Outouan. **1768** J. LEES *Journal* (1911) 39 The Ottawas . . . are a numerous Tribe, and are . . . chiefly on the North side of Lake Huron. *c***1836** CATLIN *Indians* II. 100 [The Potawatomis] have formerly been a part of the great tribe of Chippeways or Ot-ta-was. **1910** HODGE *Amer. Indians* II. 171/1 There were 197 Ottawa under the Seneca School, Okla. **1949** *Ill. State Hist. Soc. Jrnl.* June 147 The United Tribes of Potawatomi, Chippewas, and Ottawas were called together to sign away their lands

attrib. **1768** J. LEES *Journal* (1911) 39 The Ottawas . . . the Pous and Chipawas have almost the same language, and is called the Ottawa-Tongue. **1789** *Ann. 1st Congress* I. 42 The Wyandot, Delaware, Ottawa, Chippawa, Pottiwatima, and Sac nations . . . [inhabit] part of the country northwest of the Ohio. **1836** JACKSON in *Pres. Mess. & P.* III. 225 I transmit herewith . . . a treaty concluded with the Ottawa and Chippewa Indians. **1947** *Chi. Sun* 22 June 24/4 Many hundreds are expected to witness the native rituals in which honored Palefaces are taken into the Ottawa tribe.

b. The language of the Ottawa Indians.

1799 J. SMITH *Acct. Captivity* 37, I could not, at this time, talk Ottawa or Jibewa well. **1897** BLACKBIRD *Ottawa & Chippewa Indians* 81 Chicago is derived from she-gog-on, the locative case of the Ottawa word she-gog, meaning skunk.

***otter,** *n.* **1. otter breed,** the breed of the otter sheep. **2. otter sheep,** a variety of sheep having short, crooked legs resembling those of an otter. Both *obs.*

(1) **1811** D. HUMPHREY in *Phil. Trans.* CIII. 88 Hence proceeded a strongly marked variety in this species of animals, before unknown in the world. It has been called by the name of the Otter breed. — (2) **1809** KENDALL *Travels* I. 309 [In Conn.] some of the farmers are partial to a remarkable variety of sheep, which they call the otter-sheep. **1873** *Amer. Naturalist* VII. 742 The otter sheep . . . originated on the farm of Seth Wright, near Charles River, Mass. **1884** *Cent. Mag.* Feb. 516/1 There were also the Otter sheep, said to have originated on some island on our eastern coast.

Otterbein Methodist. A Methodist in sympathy with the religious views of Philip William Otterbein (1726–1813). *Rare.* Cf. **United Brethren.** — **1856** CARTWRIGHT *Autobiog.* 204 This gentleman was an *Otterbein Methodist.*

Ouija board. [F. *oui*, yes, + G. *ja*, yes, and * *board.*] A board bearing the trade-mark *Ouija* used with a planchette for spelling out mediumistic messages. Often not *cap.*

1895 RITTENHOUSE *Maud* 590 Once or twice he had referred to something a Ouija-board in Chicago had said, and how it had spelled my name in full. **1945** *Jefferson Co. Republican* (Golden, Colo.) 25 July 2/1 One had lost her mind from constant study of the ouija board. **1949** *U.S. Tobacco Jrnl.* 9 July 4/2 Taxation of cigarettes . . . has now reached such a stage of bewildering confusion as to defy an adding machine, a ouija board or a fortune teller.

***ounce,** *n.* Formerly used ellipt. in California for "ounce of gold dust," and to render Sp. *onza*, a gold coin worth approximately sixteen pesos. *Obs.*

In the first group of quots. the coin is prob. referred to. With reference to *onza*, this California use is the result of a new borrowing in the Southwest. In quot. 1853 the allusion is to one version of the story Twain made famous in his "The Celebrated Jumping Frog of Calaveras County."

(1) **1834** *Sun* (N.Y.) 6 June 3/2 The brig they offered to give me up if I would pay them fifty ounces in gold, which I shall not do. **1851** *Ore. Statesman* 2 Dec. 4/1 A bet of fifty 'ounces' ($850.) was instantly offered on the captain's proposition. **1853** *Sonora* (Calif.) *Herald* 11 June, I have two ounces and two double eagles, and all of them I bet on my toad. **1857** *S.F. Call* 26 March 1/2 Having shoulders strong and broad, he could make from twenty-five dollars to five ounces per day, and would not lose his time with Alcaldaism.

(2) **1849** *Pacific News* (S.F.) 25 Aug. 2/4 A friend of ours assured us that he had sold common scarlet blankets at from four, to ten ounces apiece. **1902** *Out West* Aug. 206 One of them said, . . . 'Well, my trunk's as big as his, and I guess I've got as much dust as he has,' so here came another ounce. **1947** CHALFANT *Gold, Guns, & Ghost Towns* 10 While provisions, such as were for sale at all, were by no means high at that particular time, an 'ounce' each appeared to be the standing price for every article in the tool line.

Our Lord's candle(stick). (See quot. 1915.)

1888 LINDLEY *Calif. of South* 330 When one sees 'Our Lord's Candlestick,' the stately *Yucca*, where He has placed it among the gray bowlders, the spiritual significance of the command is felt in its full force. **1915** ARMSTRONG & THORNBER *Western Wild Flowers* 40 Our Lord's Candle. Spanish Bayonet. *Yucca Whipplei.* White. Spring, summer. Cal., Ariz. . . . After they have blossomed, the tall, white stalks remain standing for some time, so that the hills look as if they had been planted with numbers of white wands. **1930** BONKER *Sage of Desert* 53 The flowers of our California variety, Yucca whipplei, one of the most beautiful of all Yuccas, are of a lovely golden hue, glowing in the bright sunlight like lighted candles before the altar, and known as 'Our Lord's Candle.' [**1948** *Nat. Hist.* April 180 The 'Candle of the Lord' sends up its triumphant banner to tell the desert traveler that spring has come.]

***out,** *adv.*, *prep.*, *a.*, and *n.*

1. *n.* In printing, an omission or something that is left out.

1784 FRANKLIN *Writings* IX. 263 [Your compositors'] *Forms* . . . are continually pester'd by the *Outs* and *Doubles*, that are not easy to be corrected. **1864** WEBSTER 926/3 *To make an out*, to omit something in setting up copy. **1906** M. TWAIN *Autobiog.* (1924) II. 281 (R.), He had left out a couple of words in a thin-spaced page of solid matter. . . . In the line in which the 'out' had been made.

2. Permission to go out. *Rare.*

1845 JUDD *Margaret* II. 198 She gave them [*sc.* pupils] their outs, rapped . . . on the window to call them in.

3. In baseball, the putting out of a player.

1860 in *Amer. Sp.* XXII. 204/1 Three 'outs' and one 'run.' **1945** MAXWELL *Folded Leaf* 75 The score was five to four, but there were three men on bases and no outs.

4. A flaw, defect, or blemish.

1885 PHELPS *Old Maids* II. 48 Sound as sense! Hadn't an out about him. **1901** *Scribner's Mag.* April 418/1 There were horses of every kind—except the right kind. Each one had his own peculiar 'out.' **1917** H. GARLAND *Son Border* 129 (Wentworth), Even hostling had its 'outs,' esp. in spring when the horses were shedding their hair.

5. A way out, a subterfuge or excuse. *Colloq.*

1926 J. BLACK *You Can't Win* 69 And if a copper grabs you you've got an out. You ain't exactly beggin'.

6. Used in substantival and adverbial combs.: (1) **outboundary,** one of the outermost boundaries; (2) **-camp,** a camp at some distance from the main or principal encampment; (3) **-doors,** see as a main entry; (4) ***fit,** see as a main entry; (5) ***house,** a privy; (6)

*law, see as a main entry; (7) *let, =Cherokee outlet; (8) *lier, one who lies out or camps in the forest as a bushwhacker or marauder, cf. **outlie,** *v.* in **8.** below; (9) ***line,** in fishing, a trout line, *obs.;* (10) **lying,** the action, or an instance, of remaining or living out in the forest as a scout, *obs.*, cf. ***outlying,** *a.;* (11) **oven,** (see quot. 1875); (12) **reach,** the act of reaching out; (13) ***rider,** *W.* a cowboy whose duty is to ride about a range in safeguarding his employer's interests; (14) ***riding,** *W.* (see quot. and cf. ***outride,** *v.*, in **8.** (13) below); (15) ***side,** ***-sider,** see as main entries; (16) **stock,** domestic livestock allowed to run at large on the range, *colloq.;* (17) **west,** a region west of older or earlier settled areas, also used adverbially and attrib., cf. **far west.**

(1) **1905** *Indian Laws & Tr.* III. 123 The same [is] to be reimbursed from the proceeds of the sale of said lands, for . . . the survey and marking of the outboundaries of the diminished reservation. **1906** *Ib.* 235 In full of all claims and demands of said Klamath and other Indians arising or growing out of the erroneous survey of the outboundaries of their reservation. — (2) **1844** *Knickerb.* XXIII. 116 The Sioux, . . . would not fail to attack, according to their custom, the out-camps.

(5) **1917** KEPHART *Camping* I. 210 If the well is near a stable or outhouse, or if dishwater is thrown near it, let it alone. **1944** JOHNSON *As I Dare* 285 Toilet facilities weighed heavily on the spirits of our young. The primitive outhouse was at least a hundred yards from the cabin, and a visit to it at night meant a long walk over a winding path through darkness relieved only by the brilliant stars. — (7) **1828** *Treaties U.S.A. & Indian Tribes* (1837) 424 The United States further guarantee to the Cherokee nation a perpetual outlet, west, and a free and unmolested use of all the country lying west of the western boundary of the above described limits. **1942** DALE *Cow Country* 190 There was abundant room for all in the Cherokee country proper, so the Outlet remained entirely unoccupied and almost untouched by the Cherokee people. **1945** MARSHALL *Santa Fe* 229 The Strip or Outlet was a rectangle about 150 miles long and sixty wide. — (8) **1812** MARSHALL *Kentucky* 226 Some out-lyers of the Chuckamoggas, committed depredations on the wilderness road, upon the travelling emigrants. **1854** SIMMS *Southward Ho!* 269 It is to hunt up these outlyers—to protect you from their annoyances, that I am here now. — (9) **1872** *Pa. Laws* 729 It shall not be lawful for any person or persons to take . . . any fish, by means of . . . outlines, night-lines swimmers or floating lines.

(10) **1827** COOPER *Prairie* xxii, Often have I talked the matter over with the Great Serpent of the Delawares, in the more peaceful hours of our out-lyings. **1840** ——— *Pathfinder* II. iii, I loved to think of my scoutings, and my marches, and out-lyings, and fights. — (11) **1875** KNIGHT 1583/1 The *out-oven* . . . is so called because built out of doors; not a *house*-oven. It has a domed chamber, is built of brick, and is heated by means of light wood or sticks burned inside. **1913** STRATTON-PORTER *Laddie* i, They went to bring wood for the cookstove, outoven, and big fireplace. — (12) **1870** WHITTIER *Poetical Works* (1895) 206/1 No proof beyond this yearning, This outreach of our hearts, we need. **1884** P. BROOKS *New Starts in Life* v. 80 What a different thing this life and this outreach toward man becomes. — (13) **1874** McCOY *Cattle* 348 [The] trail escapes the vigilant eye and Indian cunning and proficiency of the herdsman or outrider. **1939** ROLLINS *Gone Haywire* 230 Cowboys, patrolling as 'outriders' and 'line riders,' had always to keep an eye on them. — (14) **1926** BRANCH *Cowboy* 94 Groups of cowboys rode on inspection trips, 'outridings,' to locate the scattered groups of cattle, to note the condition of grass and water [etc.].

(16) **1852** *Fla. Plantation Rec.* 70 The Plough team is in Verry good work order also the out Stock is in good Living order. *Ib.* 78 The out stock look Verry well. — (17) **1835** HOFFMAN *Winter in West* II. 119 Old Kaintuck . . . whips all 'Out-West' in prettiness. **1848** *Corr. R. W. Griswold* (1898) 243 The 'out West Editor' would inform her, in due time, as to who he is. **1857** *Lawrence* (Kans.) *Republican* 4 June 2 But any one who has spent any time in farming 'out West,' will see that this is a mistake. **1887** GEORGE *40 Years on Rail* 62 New York State was considered 'out West' then.

b. Used in colonial times to form combs. now obs. or hist.: (1) **outdrift,** a passageway for cattle, an outlying pasture area [prob. f. Du. *uit-dryven*, which relates specifically to cattle]; (2) **garrison,** a garrison at an outpost or outfort; (3) ***land,** in a colonial town, land lying outside the inner bounds of the town jurisdiction; (4) **liver,** one who lives on the frontier or remote from others; (5) **lot,** in early times, a lot or piece of ground situated outside a town or other jurisdiction; (6) **party,** a military detachment that operates at a distance from the main body, as on the frontier; (7) **plantation,** a plantation outside the limits of a township or province; (8) **settlement,** a settlement on the frontier or in some other outlying region; (9) **settler,** one who lives on the frontier or in some other remote region; (10) ***town,** (*a*) in colonial times, a town on the frontier or away from a well-settled area, (*b*) *attrib.*, out of town, not included within the corporate limits of a town; (11) **townsman,** one who resides beyond the limits of a town; (12) **wharf,** a sea wall and wharf projected in 1673 and erected in Boston Harbor, to defend the town from attack by sea, and to encourage maritime trade.

(1) **1676** *Doc. Col. Hist. N.Y.* XII. 556 Capt. Cantwell took away ye privilege of ye Sayd way & outdrifft from ye widdow of ye Sayd Mr. Block. **1779** *N.J. Archives* 2 Ser. III. 71 This tract, besides the great advantage of out drift for cattle forever in the mountains adjacent, is exceedingly well watered. — (2) **1711** *N.C. Col Rec.* I. 826 Captain Brice detached from our out-garrisons fifty men. **1758** *Lett. to Washington* II. 291 Untill that time I do not see in what manner you can get in your Out Garrisons. — (3) **1645** *New Haven Col. Rec.* 198 All such who are admitted planters into howselotts freely, but have had noe outland formerly allotted to them, they shall each of them have 6 acres of upland to plant in. **1731** *R.I. Col. Rec.* IV. 442 An Act for erecting and incorporating the out-lands of the town of Providence, into three towns. **1875** TEMPLE & SHELDON *Hist. Northfield, Mass.* 219 [At] the first meeting of the town to act upon the apportionment of undivided lands, . . . it was voted to distribute the more desirable outlands to the inhabitants by choice. — (4) **1675** *Doc. Col. Hist. N.Y.* XII. 535 The Towne paying double to what the Outlivers. **1675** *Conn. Rec.* II. 268 That all out livers . . . doe take a speedy and effectuall course to get their women and children . . . to places of the most hopefull security.

(5) **1643** *New Haven Col. Rec.* 94 Mris Eldreds out lotts. **1774** in DURRETT *Louisville* 134 An out-lot of ten acres, contiguous to the town, shall be laid off for such as desire the same at an easy rent. **1886** Z. F. SMITH *Kentucky* 29 [They gave] to each man a half-acre lot and a ten-acre outlot. **1948** DICK *Dixie Frontier* 148 The area in and around one of these stations was plotted and each settler could hold one or more 'in lots' or building plots on the townsite and one or more 'out lots' or farming areas. — (6) **1756** ROGERS *Jrnls.* 18 A party of 220 French and Indians were preparing to invest the out-parties at Fort Edward. **1758** *Lett. to Washington* II. 275, I hope you will keep your Out Parties in a readiness to rendesvous on a short Notice. — (7) **1676** *R.I. Col. Rec.* II. 547 Your garrison is there setled to maintaine the interest of all our out plantations against their unlawful intrusions. **1765** ROGERS *Acct. N. Amer.* 112 The out-plantations upon this were deserted, their corn and cattle destroyed, great difficulties ensued to the colony. — (8) **1740** W. STEPHENS *Proc. Georgia* 621 Matters here and there among our Out-Settlements. **1782** CRÈVECOEUR *Letters* 81 [The] dialogue passed at an out-settlement, where I lately paid a visit. — (9) **1756** *Boston News-Letter* 15 April 2/1 Cruel and barbarous outrages [were committed by Indians] on the four Outsettlers of those Parts. **1824** MARSHALL *Kentucky* I. 196 Horses were stolen, and the out settlers Kept in fear, by skulking parties, who dared not attack any place of strength.

(10) (*a*) **1688** *Conn. Rec.* III. 438 I lately wrott you abt Watching and Warding in yor out townes. **1690** *Andros Tracts* II. 216 No suitable Provision was made for our out-Towns and Frontiers. (*b*) **1856** MACLEOD *F. Wood* 181 How far the out-town railroad lines, entering the city, are subject to municipal regulations, I am not at this time enabled to advise. — (11) **1714** *Topsfield Rec.* I. 182 If any out Townsmen shall Joyn with them, they shall pay to the ministers Rate as our Towns young men do. — (12) **1710** *Boston Rec.* 66 The proposalls . . . will be a means to have the Out wharves brought into good repaire. **1731** *Ib.* 25 The Wharf Latly Rebuilt . . . upon the Southerly End of the Out Wharf or Barricado . . . of Right belongs to the Town of Boston. **1880** WINSOR *Mem. Hist. Boston* I. 227 This 'out-wharf,' as it was sometimes called, . . . ran pretty nearly in the direction of the present Atlantic Avenue.

c. In baseball terms: (1) **outcurve,** a pitched ball that curves away from a right-handed batter, also attrib. and transf., cf. **incurve;** (2) **drop,** a drop ball which curves away from a right-handed batter, cf. ***drop,** *n.* **2;** (3) ***field,** see as a main entry; (4) **shoot,** =**outcurve.**

(1) **1881** *N.Y. Herald* 29 July 6/5 Reipslaugher, . . . not being used to the difficult delivery of Bond, found great difficulty in handling the in-shoots and out-curves. **1890** BIFF HALL *Turnover Club* 91 He professes to be a confirmed anarchist, and is always saying that he would delight in pitching an outcurve bomb at some bloated capitalist. **1909** *Collier's* 15 May 29/2 The outcurve, being a slow ball on account of its motion, is likely to take the same direction. — (2) **1893** *Harper's Wkly.* 8 July 657 Colby's best ball is his outdrop, which is very quick

and deceptive. **1912** C. MATHEWSON *Pitching* i. 19, I had what is known as the 'old round-house curve,' which is no more than a big, slow outdrop. — **(4) 1887** *Courier-Journal* 5 May 6/3 He has a queer drop and out-shoot on which McQuaid failed to give him strikes. **1903** BARBOUR *Weatherby's Inning* 230 Then followed an out-shoot and a drop, neither of which did Joe take to.

7. Used chiefly as an adv. to form combs. that are usu. adjectival: (1) **outdone,** nonplused, exhausted, disgusted, *colloq.;* (2) ***lying,** of persons, remaining or living in the forest for purposes of scouting or marauding; (3) **-of-state,** designating a person or thing coming from another state; (4) ***side,** see as a main entry; (5) **-state,** (see 2nd quot.); (6) ***ward,** designating one who lives on the frontier, *obs.*

(1) 1816 U. BROWN *Journal* I. 362 Now again we feel out done in finding it has left the Books & for what Cause we know not. **1929** A. ELLIS *Life* 70 Mamma was 'outdone' to think he would run them so hard. — **(2) 1755** *Lett. to Washington* I. 117 In our way Discover'd two outlying men one of which was taken. **1840** COOPER *Pathfinder* ii, I have come up the other [side of the river], in order to scout for the outlying rascals. — **(3) 1935** *Amer. Mercury* July 290/2, I was also faced with their prejudice against out-of-town and out-of-state teachers. **1948** *Herald-Press* (St. Joseph, Mich.) 14 Aug. 1/1 Many a speeding out-of-state motorist is of the opinion that the St. Joseph policemen are a lot of meanies.

(5) 1930 *Lincoln* (Neb.) *State Jrnl.* 12 Nov., Continuing he said: 'Ever think about out state people who buy 20 and 22 cent gas at home and then drive to Lincoln and fill their tanks at less than thirteen cents?' **1930** *Amer. Sp.* VI. 310 'Out-state' is a compound word not yet recognized by the dictionaries but frequently used by Nebraskans, Iowans, Coloradans, and Wyomingites. University students from these states reported two meanings: out in the state away from the main city, and out in the state away from the speaker's home. — **(6) 1713** *Va. State P.* I. 168 Foreign Indians . . [have] Killed and carryed off at least twenty of our outward Inhabitants and Tributary Indians. **1758** *Lett. to Washington* II. 313, I expect to hear of Some murder Committed by them when they Get to the outward Inhabitants.

8. Used to form verbs: (1) **outbat,** in baseball, to excel (opponents) in batting; (2) **Cherokee,** see **Cherokee,** *v.* **2;** (3) **Crockett,** to surpass David Crockett (1786–1836), the celebrated backwoodsman, *obs.;* (4) ***crop,** to excel (one) in making a crop, *rare;* (5) **field,** in baseball, to excel (opponents) in fielding; (6) ***fit,** to get or purchase an outfit; (7) **hit,** in baseball, to excel (opponents) in hitting; (8) ***law,** *W.* to allow (a horse) to run at large and become unmanageable, or to be spoiled in breaking; (9) ***lie,** to remain out in the forest or prairie as a scout or marauder; (10) **pitch,** in baseball, to excel (an opponent) in pitching; (11) **publish,** *N. Eng.* to publish in church for the last time the marriage banns of (a couple), *obs.;* (12) **rank,** (see quot. 1864 and cf. ***rank,** *v.* **1.**); (13) ***ride,** *W.* (see quot. 1874), also to ride the range, cf. ***outrider,** ***outriding** in **6.** above; (14) ***run,** to succeed better than another in a political race, *rare;* (15) **Yankee,** to outwit, surpass, get the better of (a person), as in trading, *colloq.*

(1) 1873 *Chi. Tribune* 4 June 1/7 The Mutuals outbatted their opponents, but the latter were much better fielders. **1886** *Outing* June 365/2 The Browns outbatted and outfielded the League nine, but the latter bunched their hits. — **(3) 1834** *Sun* (N.Y.) 3 April 2/3 Stop, stop, you out-Crockett Davy Crockett himself. — **(4) 1770** *Md. Hist. Mag.* XIII. 73 He assures me th[a]t . . . Rigges never outcropped Him.

(5) 1865 *Wilkes' Spirit of Times* 26 Aug. 411/3 They certainly outfielded the Atlantics. **1875** *Chi. Tribune* 17 Aug. 5/6 The Browns were outbatted and outfielded. — **(6) 1856** *3 Years on Kans. Border* 23 All the Mormon immigration would outfit there! **1923** BOWER *Parowan Bonanza* 8 One day in spring Bill Dale walked behind his burros into Goldfield and outfitted for a long trip. — **(7) 1930** *Dixon* (Ill.) *Ev. Telegraph* 26 Sep. 6/1. **1949** *Minot* (N.D.) *D. News* 22 July 8/8 Aberdeen out-hit and out-lasted St. Cloud, winning 11–9. — **(8) 1907** MULFORD *Bar-20* xx. 197 Yu has got about as much show catchin' one of them as a tenderfoot has of bustin' an outlawed cayuse. — **(9) 1826** COOPER *Mohicans* xviii, We are not about to start on a squirrel hunt, . . . but to outlie for days and nights, and to stretch across a wilderness. **1840** ——— *Pathfinder* ii, It is war-time, and no red-skin is outlying without using his senses.

(10) 1905 *Chi. D. News* 26 July 6/1 Duggleby outpitched Wicker up to the seventh inning. — **(11) 1719** SEWALL *Diary* III. 232, I was Out-published on the Thanksgiving-Day. **1727** *Canton* (Mass.) *Rec.* 22 The Names . . . haue been out published as the Law directs, By me Joseph Tucker town Clerk. — **(12) 1842** *Phila. Spirit of Times* 1 Sep. (Th.), It won't be long before he fills the place of some one of the drones and cakes who now outrank him. **1864** WEBSTER 928/1 *Out rank,* to take the precedence of, or be superior to, in rank; to rank. **1949** *Time* 12 Sep. 19/3 Older than his navigator and outranking him, he seemed to resent his pal's success. — **(13) 1874** MCCOY *Cattle* 345 He does not herd his cattle but designates certain bounds within which the employees permit the stock to range at will. This manner of holding stock is termed 'out riding' the country. **1907** MULFORD *Bar-20* 6 Skinny Thompson took his turn at outriding one morning after the season's round-up. — **(14) 1832** *Polit. Examiner* (Shelbyville, Ky.) 1 Sep. 1/5 Henry Clay, in his own state, can outrun any other man, be he friend or foe, by more than 5000 votes.

(15) 1846 MATHEWS *Writings* II. 308 (Th.), Let any Yankee take a journey south on a real good horse, and when he returns see if the beast he rides does not show he has been out yankeed. **1868** LOWELL *Writings* I. 350 Is it not that he out-Yankees us all? that his range includes us all?

9. In colloq. phrases: (1) *To have out, S.* to have (an indicated amount of cotton) picked from the field, *colloq.;* (2) *to be out for* (something), to be intent upon getting or achieving (a specified thing), also *to be out* (to do something); (3) *to get out from under,* see ***get,** *v.* **7. l.**

(1) 1854 *Fla. Plantation Rec.* 94, I suppose I have about 10 or 12 bales more out and will send a nother Load off on Satterday 2nd of Septr. — **(2) 1892** *Boston Jrnl.* 7 Aug. 4/3 The Bourbon Democrats are out for wildcat currency. **1901** MERWIN & WEBSTER *Calumet 'K'* 13 They're mostly out for results up at the office. Let's see the bill for it. **1901** WHITE *Westerners* 272 When they are out to have a good time, . . . they want somebody they can have their sort of fun with. **1932** GRAYSON *Leaders* 37 A band of Revolutionary soldiers . . . had not received their back pay, and were out to get it by any means.

As the last term in **average, back, bawl, beat, blow, break, call, caller-, camp, camper-, camping, chopping, clean, cut-, cutter-, cutting, drag, drop, fly, force, hand, hang, hide, hold, knock, lay, layer, look, pan, paper, peon, peter, pinch, pitch, put, ranked, run, sell, selling, setting, shut, smoking, spread, stand, straight, sweating, throw, tie, try, turn, turning, walk-, warning, wash, way, workout.**

outdoors aut'dorz, *adv.* and *n.*

1. *n.* A region, or the world, outside the limits of a dwelling.

1857 WILLIS *Convalescent* 121 The 'down party' . . . were enjoying the river from the uncommon out-doors of Mr. Grinnell's broad prairies. **1922** A. BROWN *Old Crow* 449 She stopped to breathe in the wood fragrances, coming now like a surprise. She had almost forgotten 'outdoors.' **1949** *Sky Line Trail* March 14/2 Trail Hikers, like all lovers of the outdoors, are by nature animal lovers as well.

2. *all outdoors,* the whole wide world; everybody. *Colloq.*

1846 *Quincy* (Ill.) *Whig* 17 Feb. 2/2, I was going to speak of the President's messige—Jimmy K's statement to all out-doors, and some parts of Ashey. **1862** LOWELL *Biglow P.* 2 Ser. i. 23 Ourn's the fust thru-by-daylight train, with all ou'doors for deepot. **1893** THANET *Stories* 209 It would have been enough for Esther's mother to know that anything was for my interests; it wouldn't have to help all outdoors, too!

b. In comparisons denoting something in the extreme. *Colloq.*

1830 S. SMITH *Life J. Downing* 64, I had a letter from him t'other day, as long as all out doors, in the Boston Advertiser. **1886** E. L. DORSEY *Midshipman Bob* I. ix. 87 There's a little Ass't-Paymaster here who is as airy as all out-doors.

Esp. *as big as all outdoors,* quite large, huge.

1825 NEAL *Brother Jonathan* I. 111 Stuffy feller (that bear) as ever you see'd; big as all out o' doors. **1918** RIDEOUT *Key of Fields* 296 That picture must be big as all outdoors. **1948** *Chi. Tribune* 28 March IV. 6/3 Its spirit is literally 'as big as all out-doors.'

3. *adv.* In the open air; out of doors.

1817 S. BROWN *Western Gazetteer* 113 The chimney is sure to be placed out doors. **1865** *Atlantic Mo.* XV. 110/2 Out-doors nothing but bare branches and shrouding snow. **1913** STRATTON-PORTER *Laddie* xiii, What you learn there [in school] doesn't amount to a hill of beans compared with what you can find out for yourself outdoors.

outer field. = ***outfield,** *n.* **1.** *Obs.*

1864 *Wilkes' Spirit of Times* 17 Dec. 244/3 The argument that players in the outer-field will not strive for bound-catches . . . is very weak, indeed. **1865** *N.Y. Herald* 11 July 5/4 The Empires batted well also, but their outer field was not as well attended to as it might have been. **1886** CHADWICK *Art of Pitching* 9 To hit at a ball so as to send it high to the outer-field.

* **outfield,** *n. Baseball.*

1. The part of the playing field beyond or outside the base lines. Cf. **infield.** Cf. **outer field.**

1868 CHADWICK *Base Ball* 73 The Irvingtons . . . took an out-fielder from his regular position, . . . and placed the substitute in the out-field. **1948** *Denison* (Tex.) *Herald* 2 July 12/3 Have you ever played the outfield?

2. The players, namely, the right, center, and left fielders, stationed in the outfield.

Quot. 1867 may belong under **1.** above.

1867 CHADWICK *Base Ball Reference* 138 The Out-Field—The out-fielders are the left, centre and right-field positions. **1897** *Outing* May 203/1 Rand and Burgess, with Lynch, . . . make up the outfield. **1948** *Dly. Ardmoreite* (Ardmore, Okla.) 30 March 6/4 If the Boston Braves win the pennant this year, they will do it without an outfield which is particularly strong defensively.

Hence **outfielder, outfielding.**

1860 in *Ball Players' Chron.* (1867) 12 Dec. 3/1 The out-fielding was only so-so. **1867** *Ball Players' Chron.* 20 June 3/2 The features of the match were the splendid out-fielding of Smith and Callaway the left fielders of the two nines [etc.]. *Ib.* 27 June 2/1 [This is] a very good style of batting to make bases on, when you see the out-fielders well out in the field, prepared for long, high balls. **1948** *Chi. Tribune* 3 April II. 1/6 An outfielder has more time for such side stepping.

* **outfit,** *n.*

1. The articles, equipment, etc., required by a minister or other governmental representative upon assuming duties in another country.

1787 JEFFERSON *Writings* VI. 238, I believe there is no instance of any nation sending a minister to reside anywhere without an outfit. **1814** *Columbian Centinel* 24 Dec. 2/3 The salary of a Plenipo. is 9000 dollars per year, and 9000 dollars outfit. **1849** *Whig Almanac 1850* 25/2 About $520,000 were voted to diplomatic agents, nearly $160,000 of which was for outfits.

2. The various parts of one's costume considered collectively, a costume.

1852 STOWE *Uncle Tom* v, Saying these words, she had tied and buttoned on the child's simple outfit. **1875** *Scribner's Mo.* Dec. 286/1 The comfortable dress for the mother or flannel outfit for the baby, can be sent under cover of a Christmas greeting. **1946** *Chi. D. News* 10 Aug. 12/3 Elaborate ceremonial outfits are fashioned by the women of the tribe.

3. Used colloquially in a variety of applications.

The wide use of this word, esp. in Western speech, is shown in the following groups of examples. Cf. **layout,** *n.*

1863 *Rio Abajo Press* 10 Feb. 2 There is a paper published at Albuquerque. . . . Why don't you send one as a sample of the outfit? **1867** MELINE *Santa Fe & Back* 74 This word 'outfit' is on duty night and day, without relief, from the Missouri River to California. To cross the plains, or go to the mountains, every one must get an outfit; and having outfitted, you become yourself an outfit. . . . The saddler who sold me my saddle assured me it was the best outfit he had furnished for some time. Bought a hat, and was told 'Well, Sir, I call that a good outfit.' **1869** MCCLURE *Rocky Mts.* 211 Everything is an 'outfit,' from a train on the plains to a pocket-knife. It is applied almost indiscriminately,—to a wife, a horse, a dog, a cat, or a row of pins. **1924** MULFORD *Rustlers' Valley* xi, You ain't believin' everythin' *this* outfit [i.e., person] tells you, are you?

a. A group of travelers, miners, hunters, soldiers, etc., associated in a common undertaking.

1869 S. BOWLES *Our New West* 163 With a mounted escort of about twenty gallant young miners . . . we made up a grand 'outfit.' **1902** WISTER *Virginian* 303 It's part of that outfit that's been hunting. **1923** VANCE *Baroque* 41 You'd have a grand time makin' me believe you wasn't in with this outfit clean over your ears. **1947** *Chi. Tribune* 6 July I. 3/1 Woehlke classified the Navajos as 'a marvelous outfit, always self-sufficient and self-supporting.'

b. A group of cowboys, together with the horses, teams, wagons, etc., used by them in range work, often preceded by the name of the cattle ranch to which the group is attached.

1876 WHILLDIN *Descr. W. Texas* 15 Twenty-five men are about as many as can work to an advantage in one gang, and for this number one large four-mule wagon, laden with provisions, camp equipage, a very little baggage, and about one hundred horses, make up 'the outfit.' **1890** *Stock Grower & Farmer* 15 March 6/3 John Donahue, range foreman for the G-bar outfit, came in on Monday. **1904** O. HENRY *Heart of West* 4 Me and you punched cows in the same outfit for years. **1947** *Denver Post* 2 March C. 3/6 Operators of small ranches might not be able to buy public grazing lands if this proposal becomes a law, while 'big outfits' would be.

c. A herd of cattle. Also horses.

1897 LEWIS *Wolfville* 226 When mixed cattle is in a bunch . . . an' you-all is ridin' through the outfit cuttin' out, y'ear-marks is what you goes by. **1897** *Outing* XXX. 480/2 They ain't cow-ponies any more, though, like the regular puncher's outfit used to be.

d. A group or combination of low individuals. *Contemptuous.*

1926 J. BLACK *You Can't Win* iv. 37, I was left on the bench with the two drunks. . . . The desk man pointed to us. 'What will I do with this outfit, Hayes?' **1931** *Randolph Enterprise* (Elkins, W.Va.) 4 March 4/2 The whole outfit acted like a lot of college boys after winning a big football game. **1946** STARRETT *Murder in Peking* 50 A little thing like a woman screaming wouldn't bother that outfit.

4. A supply, stock, a large number.

1901 GREENOUGH & KITTREDGE *Words & Their Ways* 1 The sum-total of our retrospect accounts for only the minutest fraction of our whole outfit of words and phrases. **1907** *St. Nicholas* May 641/1 If you do not happen to have enough newspapers on hand for the entire outfit of tepees and costumes, you can use a white muslin sheet for the wigwam. **1914** PALMER *Mountaineering & Explor. Selkirks* 86 These rodents . . . are likely, in the course of a few nights, to make away with not only food but also anything and everything else in one's outfit.

5. outfit store, a store selling supplies and equipment to woodsmen.

1880 *Bradstreet's* 11 Dec. 2/3 These firms own . . . 'outfit stores' for the many gangs of cutters who fell the timber.

As the last term in **bull, cow, floating, freight, horseback, pack, packadero, packing, traveling, wagon, wrecking outfit.**

* **outfitting,** *a.* **1. outfitting point,** a town or trading center where outfits are usually procured. **2. outfitting store,** a store where outfits may be procured. Cf. **outfit store.**

(1) **1848** BRYANT *California* i. 13 Independence, Mo., . . . has been for some years the principal outfitting point for the Santa Fé traders. **1864** *Rio Abajo Press* 5 April 4/3 Albuquerque is the Outfitting Point for persons from the East and North. — (2) **1927** SIRINGO *Riata* 43 Here there were two large outfitting stores, . . . also several saloons and dance-halls.

* **outing,** *n.* **1.** *pl.* Outing goods. See next. **2. outing cloth,** a light woolen, worsted, or mixture fabric used in garments for various kinds of outdoor sports. **3. outing flannel,** a soft, plain-woven cotton material, yarn-dyed or printed, napped on one or both sides.

(1) **1903** *Dockham's Textile Manufacture* 225 Outings, plaids, ginghams, etc. — (2) **1907** M. C. HARRIS *Tents of Wickedness* II. i. 120 Besides warm things . . . serges and outing cloths. **1930** *Randolph Enterprise* (Elkins, W.Va.) 2 Oct. (*advt.*), Outing Cloth .09½ Per Yd. Grey and Pink—Only 10 yards to a customer. — (3) **1890** (Advt. of Schairer & Millen, Ann Arbor, 1 March), 15 pieces New Stripe Outing Flannels, 15 cent quality, now 10 cents. **1909** *Cent. Supp.* 917/1 Outing flannel, a soft thin cotton material, made in imitation of flannel, with a short nap. **1914** E. STEWART *Lett. of Woman Homesteader* 74 One is a brown and red checked, and the other green with a white fleck in, both outing flannel.

* **outlaw,** *n.*

1. *W.* A horse that is incorrigibly vicious, either by temperament or because of brutal handling when being broken. Also attrib.

1885 ROE *Army Lett.* 337 Many a fine, spirited animal is ruined, made an 'outlaw' that no man can ride, just by the fiendish way in which they are first ridden. **1903** *Out West* Feb. 187 They'll take outlaws all right, but no broncos. **1927** SIRINGO *Riata* 140, I told him to trot out his outlaw horse. **1945** MATHEWS *Talking* 5, I remembered the colt, an iron-gray and a veritable outlaw that only a bolt of lightning had been able to subdue.

b. outlaw bronco, a bronco that is an outlaw.

1903 *Wide World Mag.* March 546 (*Cent. Supp.*), The whole Western country was scoured over for the wildest and most vicious 'outlaw' bronchos that could be found. **1949** *N.Y. Times Book Review* 13 March 22/4 His brother Billy was thrown by an outlaw bronco.

2. (See quot.)

1920 *Harvey's Wkly.* 17 April 5/2 The 'outlaw' railroad strikes . . . are unjustifiabfe. *Ib.* 19 June 11/1 No man who is a member of the union has a right to quit work unless the union bids him to quit. If he does he is an 'outlaw.'

Outogamis ˌutə'gæmɪz, *n.* [See quot. 1907.] One of the many names applied to the Fox tribe of Indians. *Obs.*

1667 *Relations des Jésuites* (1858) 21/1 Le pais des Outagami est du costé du Sud, vers le Lac des Illimouek. *Ib.* Vn iour entrant dans la Cabane d'vn Outagamy, ie trouuay son pére [etc.]. **1722** COXE *Descr. Carolana* 48 This is chiefly possess'd by the industrious and valiant Nation of the Outogamis. **1907** HODGE *Amer. Indians* I.

472/1 They [the Foxes] were known to the Chippewa and other Algonquian tribes as Utŭgamig, 'people of the other shore.'

∗**outrage,** *n.* One who is outrageous in conduct or appearance. *Colloq.* — **1869** MARK TWAIN *Innocents* 35 Who is that smooth-faced animated outrage yonder in the fine clothes? **1904** O. HENRY *Roads of Destiny* 351 This old medical outrage floated down to my shack when I sent for him.

outréness u'trenis, *n.* [F. *outré*, exaggerated, +*-ness*.] The state or quality of being *outré*, extravagant, or peculiar. *Obs.* — **1832** MOTLEY *Correspondence* I. 19 The University towns [in Germany] are the homes of 'outré-ness.' **1882** HAWTHORNE *Dr. Grimshawe* viii, A certain seemly beauty in him showed strikingly the . . . outréness of the rest of their lot.

∗**outside,** *n., a.,* and *adv.*

1. *n.* and *adv.* In Alaska, used with reference to the "states," or "back home." *Colloq.*

1902 MCKEE *Land of Nome* 198 Judge Noyes pulled up stakes and sailed for the 'outside' to prepare himself for his October ordeal before the Court of Appeals. **1945** SERVICE *Ploughman* 321 If I had been Outside it would have taken me five years to save a thousand dollars. **1949** *Nat. Hist.* Sep. 335/1 Juneau, Anchorage, Fairbanks, or Nome are very similar to any small town 'outside.'

2. In special combs.: (1) **outside board,** =**open board;** (2) **camp,** a camp for convicts at a distance from a state penitentiary or other prison; (3) **corner,** in baseball, the corner of the home plate furthest from the batter; (4) **Whig,** (see quot. and cf. ∗**outsider,** *n.* **1.**).

(1) 1870 MEDBERY *Men Wall St.* 305 The 'outside' Board was becoming a power. — **(2) 1880** in *Cent. Mag.* XXVII. 593/2 The most usual mode of punishment practiced at outside camps is by stocks. — **(3) 1912** MATHEWSON *Pitching* 159 A right-handed hitter will naturally push a curve over the outside corner of the plate toward right field. — **(4) 1913** A. C. COLE *Whig Party in So.* 321 Former Whigs [were] divided into Democrats, 'outside Whigs,' anti-Know Nothings, and Know Nothings.

b. In colloq. phrases: (1) *To get* (or *be*) *outside of* (something), to eat or drink (something), to have in one's stomach; (2) *to get outside a thing,* (see quot.).

(1) 1886 EBBUTT *Emigrant Life Kansas* 182 Directly he got outside of a few glasses of whisky, his manner was very different. **1890** SHIELDS *Big Game N. Amer.* 521 My wife said she knew, from his [*sc.* a raccoon's] full stomach and his sneaking look, that he was outside of her pet turkey. — **(2) 1889** FARMER 405/1 *To get outside a thing* is to understand it, or to use an expression very common in the West Indies, to get to the windward of it.

∗**outsider,** *n.*

1. One outside the ranks of a regular political party.

1844 in MARSH *Eng. Lang.* (1860) 274 [At the Baltimore convention of 1844, . . . a prominent member energetically protested against all interference with the business of the meeting by] outsiders. [The word, if not absolutely new, was at least new to most of those who read the proceedings . . . and it was now for the first time employed in a serious way.] **1853** *Oregonian* (Portland) 8 Oct. 2/1 It would seem that those who presume to *own* the democratic party have found out that they have not, and they seek this early to make a draw upon 'outsiders.' **1948** *Dly. Ardmoreite* (Ardmore, Okla.) 20 Jan. 10/1 Some of them expressed the belief that the convention delegates in recognition of this, may decide to nominate a political 'outsider' with vote-getting glamour.

2. (See quots.)

1848 W. ARMSTRONG *Stocks* 7 Outsiders are those of all ranks and classes who dabble in Stocks to a greater or less extent—they never buy or sell personally, but employ a Commission Broker for that purpose. **1888** *Economist* 27 Oct. 8/2 The insiders still hold the stocks and the outsiders refuse to come in to any considerable extent. **1934** in CRANES *Sins of N.Y.* (1947) 59 Drew had convinced his adversary that . . . they, as two mercenary captains, might win many fruitful victories at the cost of common enemies, the 'outsiders.'

3. An Indian assigned to, but not remaining within the limits of, a reservation. *Obs.*

1866 *Rep. Indian Affairs* 165 The only way he could properly feed the outsiders and obtain the requisite receipt from the chiefs of the bands properly under his charge.

4. (See quot. 1875.)

1875 KNIGHT 1582/1 *Out-sider.* (*Locksmithing.*) A pair of nippers with semi-tubular jaws, adapted to enter a keyhole and grasp the pin of a key, so as to turn it and unlock the door from the outside. **1896** *Columbus* (O.) *Dispatch* 15 Jan. 1/8 The burglary must have been well planned. Three of the doors . . . were opened by means of outsiders.

5. An outside passenger on a stage or bus.

1882 MCCABE *New York* 159 The number of 'outsiders' is carefully counted by 'spotters' or spies placed along the route.

∗**oven,** *n.*

1. *New Orleans.* An oval or ovenlike sepulcher or tomb in which the dead are buried above ground. Also attrib.

1851 WORTLEY *Travels* 126 The graves are also elevated. The dead are buried in sepulchral houses, which are termed here 'ovens.' These often contain three or four tiers. Those belonging to the wealthy are frequently very handsome, and built with marble walls. **1893** *Harper's Mag.* Feb. 374/1 The tombs are houses built upon the ground, and provided with cubby-hole or drawerlike compartments, to be sealed with a marble slab as each coffin is put in place. The term 'oven tombs' describes them well. **1921** *Chambers's Jrnl.* Aug. 511/1 There was no system in the arrangement of the 'ovens.'

2. ∗**oven bird,** the golden-crowned thrush, *Seiurus aurocapillus,* which builds an ovenlike or dome-shaped nest.

1841 THOREAU *Journal* 260 The oven-bird and plover are heard in the horizon. **1947** EDMINSTER *Ruffed Grouse* 35 The ovenbird and the hermit thrush sang to their mates.

As the last term in **bake, devil's, Dutch bake, mud, out oven.**

∗**over,** *adv., prep.,* and *a.*

1. *adv.* Until a later time or season.

1861 *Ill. Agric. Soc. Trans.* IV. 317 Old bugs live over, and produce eggs the following season. **1883** HAY *Bread-Winners* 172, I am so glad you resolved to stay over. **1898** NICHOLAS *Idyl of Wabash* 53 We don't want to winter them steers over.

2. *prep. Over one's signature,* with one's signature subscribed to what is written.

1806 *Spirit of Public Jrnls.* 96 (Th.), A writer over the signature of Zanga, is another buckram expression. Custom justifies, and therefore requires us to say, a writer under such a signature. **1826** *New-Harmony* (Ind.) *Gaz.* 22 March 207/2 A writer over the signature of 'A Farmer' . . . states that he has been completely successful . . . in saving his wheat [from weevils]. **1946** *Sunshine Mag.* April (In front cover), New preface over the author's own signature.

3. In combs.: (1) **over-and-over,** of or pertaining to top-sewing or overhanding; (2) ∗**cast,** in levying rates or taxes, an overestimate or excessive computation, *obs.;* (3) ∗**cloth,** in a straw-paper machine the blanket or endless apron conveying the paper to the press rolls; (4) **crop,** a crop that is excessively large; (5) **cup,** see as a main entry; (6) **cut,** (*a*) a short, direct way, as over a hill, (*b*) a cut from above; (7) **draw,** a rein passing over a horse's head, between the ears, to pull upward on the bit, in full **overdraw check;** (8) **glaze,** in ceramics, an additional glaze applied to a porcelain surface already glazed, also painting or decoration applied to glazed pottery, also attrib.; (9) ∗**haul,** a severe scolding or reprimand, *rare;* (10) **hill,** see as a main entry; (11) ∗**land,** see as a main entry; (12) ∗**look,** a height or elevation from which a view may be secured, or a view from such a place, also in place-names; (13) **mountain country,** land west of the Alleghany Mountains, *rare;* (14) ∗**night,** *attrib.* designating luggage slightly smaller than average, for use on short journeys; (15) **pass,** on a highway, a bridge or road, etc., that passes over a railway, canal or other road, cf. **underpass;** (16) **pitch,** (see quot. 1867); (17) ∗**plus,** superabundance, excess [cf. Du. *overschot,* in same sense]; (18) **plussage,** =prec.; (19) **slaugh,** see as a main entry; (20) ∗**throw,** (see quot. 1885); (21) ∗**yonder,** in the other world, in heaven, *colloq.*

(1) 1876 INGRAM *Centennial Exp.* 380 [The carpet machine was] intended to sew the breadths of carpets together by the 'over and over' stitch. **1898** HARPER *S. B. Anthony* I. 22 There is also a bed quilt the pieces sewed together with the fine 'over-and-over' stitch. **1916** in ADAMS *Pioneer Hist.* (1923) 353 The material was narrow, so there were two over-and-over seams, an abomination to any little girl. — **(2) 1771** *Conn. Rec.* XIII. 482 There was an over-cast made by the listers upon the grand levy of the year 1761, of the sum of £ 427 00. **1772** *Ib.* XIII. 579 Abatements for over-cast of the list . . . shall be made and certifyed by the listers. — **(3) 1888** *Scientific Amer.* 11 Aug. 81/1 It is highly requisite that the paper be well pressed and dried on the cylinders of the press and that the 'overcloth' be neither too dry nor too damp. — **(4) 1878** *Lumberman's Gaz.* 26 Jan., The fears entertained . . . that there would be a ruinous over-crop of logs . . . harvested this winter may be dismissed. **1879** *Harper's Mag.* July

198/2 Scarcely less dreaded by the peach-growers than a failure is an over-crop, when the superabundant fruit ripens too fast to be plucked. (6) (*a*) **1636** *Boston Rec.* 13 All the ground lying between the two brooks . . . and soe to the other end unto shortest overcut beyond the hill towards the north west. (*b*) **1883** *Harper's Mag.* Jan. 202/1 The axes were laid aside, and the spring-boards inserted in new mortises behind the tree, and a big two-handed saw [was] set at work to make the overcut. — (7) **1902** A. D. McFaul *Ike Glidden* 122 He was prancin' . . . until he got him hitched inter this new bitin' gear an' overdraw. **1905** *Springfield W. Republican* 8 Sep. 5 It is just as important that the abuse of the overdraw check should be corrected. — (8) **1880** *Harper's Mag.* Nov. 904/1 The over-glaze, that is, painting in mineral colors on either pottery or porcelain which has already received a fire glaze or enamel, so that the article is equally fit for use before as after decoration. **1881** *Ib.* May 835/1 It was unquestionably the most . . . satisfactory exhibit of amateur overglaze decoration made. **1884** *American* VII. 217 Enthusiastic amateurs have grappled with the pottery question, and the mysteries of 'overglaze' and 'underglaze' have engrossed [etc.]. — (9) **1797** J. Pettigrew *Lett.* 27 June (Univ. N.C. MS), The steward has provided very poorly untill lately, when the Trustees gave him a severe over-hall, and I believe threatened him severely.

(12) **1861** L. L. Noble *Voyage Icebergs* 37 Paths wound among rocky notches and grassy chasms, and led out to dizzy 'over-looks,' and 'short-offs.' **1884** *Lit. World* 23 Feb. 51/3 High overlooks upon the smiling valley. **1914** Palmer *Mountaineering & Explor. Selkirks* 122 Beyond the cleft, Beaver Overlook and the upper Beaver valley were imposingly in view. — (13) **1831** Withers *Chron. Border Warfare* 52 The English colonists early wanted the over-mountain country watered by the Ohio. — (14) **1935** *Montgomery Ward Cat.* (ed. 123) 582 Wards Finest—Tray Fitted Overnight Case. . . . About 12½ by 12½ by 6¼ in. **1949** *Boston Globe Mag.* 6 Nov. 2/5 Stanton hastily transferred a few things into his overnight bag.

(15) **1929** *Amer. City* Oct. 104/2 In certain cases where the construction of under- or over-passes cannot be avoided . . . my system simplifies them to an astonishing extent. **1949** *Courier-Journal* (Louisville, Ky.) 3 Sep. 1/5 If an overpass or underpass is built there, it could be extended out as far as perhaps Brooks and Broadway. — (16) **1862** *N.Y. Sun. Mercury* 13 July (Nichols). **1867** Chadwick *Base Ball Reference* 139 An Over-Pitch.—A ball pitched over the head of the catcher on which bases are made. **1868** ——— *Base Ball* 126 By an overpitch Fred got to his second. — (17) **1850** Taylor *Eldorado* (1862) 14 An idea of the splendid overplus of vegetable life within the tropics. **1888** *Economist* 3 Nov. 6/2 The available wheat supplies . . . have gone into consumption so rapidly as to change an overplus . . . into a deficiency. — (18) **1874** *Vt. Bd. Agric. Rep.* II. 636 When a full supply [of moisture] comes [from the roots], they open the portal and send out the overplussage.

(20) **1856** *Spirit of Times* 8 Nov. 165/1 Gessner [made] . . . three homes in succession, one of them being helped by an overthrow. **1885** Chadwick *Art of Pitching* 139 Any fielder throwing a ball out of reach of the player he is throwing to is said to be charged with an 'over throw.' **1949** *Telephone Reg.* (McMinnville, Ore.) 4 Aug. 1/2 There is no sliding and a player cannot run on overthrows. — (21) **1893** Mark Twain *P. Wilson* 238 (R.), Dey don't sell po' niggers down the river over yonder.

b. Designating cuts of various shapes made in the upper portion of the ear of domestic animals to indicate ownership, as (1) **over-bit,** (2) **keel,** *obs.*, (3) **slope.**

(1) **1887** *Scribner's Mag.* Oct. 508/2 Marks signifying ownership [of cattle] are called *over-bit, over-hack* [etc.]. **1946** *Democrat* 30 May 4/4 Strayed—One brindle cow, marked crop and overbit in each ear. — (2) **1677** *New Castle Court Rec.* 79 In each Eare a swallow forke and in the Right Eare an overkeel. **1693** *N.C. Col. Rec.* I. 388 Diana ffoster records her marke an undr keele and over keele on the right ear [etc.]. — (3) **1869** *Overland Mo.* Aug. 126, I had seen a brown-and-white-pied calf, with an overslope and a slit in the right, and a swallow-fork in the left. **1945** *Democrat* 20 Sep. 4/1 Weight above 800 pounds, marked overslope in left, crop and two splits in right.

c. In terms for wearing apparel: (1) **overalls,** see as a main entry; (2) **coat,** see as a main entry; (3) **shoe,** a rubber overshoe *q.v.* or a galosh, see also **arctic, India rubber overshoe;** (4) **skirt,** a skirt worn over another, esp. an outer or upper skirt usu. shorter than the dress skirt and draped; (5) **trousers,** trousers worn over one's usual trousers.

(3) **1851** Hall *Manhattaner* 51, I have worn out several umbrellas in my day; and overshoe-shod I have paddled the causeways of various cities. **1947** *Chi. D. News* 16 Dec. 22/3 She was last seen wearing . . . black suede shoes and brown overshoes. — (4) **1870** *Harper's Bazaar* 22 Oct. 675 Over-skirts are elaborate, and show great variety in design. **1891** Wilkins *N. Eng. Nun* 39 The waist and over-skirt were trimmed with black velvet ribbon.

(5) **1852** *Harper's Mag.* April 707/1 My duck over-trowsers . . . were beginning to be rather tender in certain places. **1894** *Scribner's Mag.* May 604/1 [The Rio Grande Mexican] must wear 'chap-parejos,' or over-trousers, of sheep- or goat-skin.

d. Designating persons: (1) ***Overcomers,** [cf. Rev. 2:7] a communistic religious sect founded in Chicago *c*1880, *obs.;* (2) ***lander,** one of those who went to the Far West in the days of the covered wagon; (3) ***man,** ?one holding a certain grade or rank in the police force, *obs.;* (4) ***seer,** see as a main entry.

(1) **1884** Schaff *Religious Encycl.* III. 1889/1 More recent developments of the same kind [as the Irvingites and the Millerites] may be instanced in the so-called 'Overcomers' of America. — (2) **1857** *Hutchings Mag.* March 398/1 Reader, if you have never been an *over-lander*, I will tell you a little about camp life. **1945** Adams *Album Amer. Hist.* II. 374 The overlanders went by many routes. — (3) **1885** *Encycl. Brit.* XIX. 341/2 The body of the force being termed 'patrol men,' with 'overmen' at stations and prisons.

5. Used to form verbs: (1) ***overbear,** of a fruit tree, to bear too much fruit; (2) **bill,** to "bill" or advertise to excess, *colloq.;* (3) ***crop,** *reflex.* (see quot. 1859), also transf., hence **cropping,** *n.*, excessive planting; (4) **cut,** in school, to absent oneself from (a class, lecture, or the like) in excess of the number of absences allowed; (5) **graze,** to graze (land) to excess; (6) **hand,** to oversew, to sew over and over; (7) **keel,** to mark (the ears of cattle) with an overkeel, *obs.;* (8) ***run,** in baseball, to run past or beyond (a base); (9) **slaugh,** see as a main entry.

(1) **1863** *Horticulturist* XVIII. 295/2 You can now point out every tree that was allowed to overbear. **1872** *Vt. Bd. Agric. Rep.* I. 118 The Bartlett and Louise Bonne de Jersey commence bearing young, and are inclined to over bear. — (2) **1890** J. Jefferson *Autobiog.* 229 My engagement in San Francisco was an unmistakable failure . . . I had been 'over-billed,' as it is technically termed. — (3) **1859** Bartlett 305 A planter or farmer is said to *overcrop* himself when he plants or 'seeds' more ground than he can attend to. **1866** C. H. Smith *Bill Arp* 27 General Hunter tried it your way and over-cropped himself. **1879** *Bradstreet's* 20 Dec. 2/2 The serious fault of our farmers is that of 'over-cropping.' **1881** *Uniontown* (Ala.) *Press* 8 Jan. 2/3 The failure of the crops in this section . . . was owing, in part at least, to over-cropping. — (4) **1929** *Chi. Tribune* 30 Jan. 1/4 The three women and seven of the men were expelled for overcutting classes.

(5) **1934** Webster. **1949** *Pacific Discovery* July–Aug. 2/1 In the South I have seen cattle tracks in overgrazed land become gullies ten feet deep. — (6) **1871** Burroughs *Wake-Robin* (1886) 155 The mouth [of the Baltimore oriole's nest] is hemmed or overhanded with horse-hair. **1897** *Advance* 8 April 452/2 All little maids in our grand-mother's day . . . [learned] the art of hemming and 'overhanding,' stitching and felling. — (7) **1647** *Md. Archives* IV. 310 One red heyfer Calfe . . . [with] both eares overkeeld. — (8) **1867** *Ball Players' Chron.* 14 Nov. 4/3 He fell over Murtha, who was in his way, and overran his base. **1948** *News-Palladium* (Benton Harbor, Mich.) 14 Aug. 6/3 Hazel, going down to second, overrun the base as Joe Mack rifled the ball to McCoy.

b. In participial formations: (1) **overalled,** clad in overalls; (2) **-flowed land,** land subject to overflow.

(1) **1908** *Smart Set* June 94/1 The familiar spectacle of half-grown boys and overalled and unshaven men. **1947** Brown *Outdoors Unlimited* 97 For a consideration—a package of gum for the family and a cigar for Farmer Griffith—one of the little overalled boys will bail out an old boat and even fetch a pole from the woodshed. — (2) **1814** Brackenridge *Views of La.* 160 There is certainly much sunken and overflowed land. **1942** Kennedy *Palmetto Country* 15 In 1850, when Congress deeded to the states all unsold swamp and overflowed lands within their boundaries, the grant to Florida was the largest ever made by the United States to any state.

As the last term in **brush, cross, cut, hang, haul, hold, lay, left, pass, picked, plant, pop, put, slop, stop, tumble, turn, turning, warmed, way over.**

overalls ˈovɚˌɔlz, *n. pl.* Also †**overall, overhalls, overhauls.** Trousers of strong cloth or leather worn by soldiers, hunters, and others engaged in outdoor work; in later use chiefly a garment worn by farmers, mechanics, factory workers, etc. Now usu. trousers with a bib and suspenders. Cf. **Mother Hubbard overalls.**

The first group of examples illustrates the variety of styles in overalls. They are worn either as outer garments or as a protection over one's usual clothes.

(1) **1845** Judd *Margaret* 358 He wore . . . a pair of overalls buttoning from the hip to the ankle. **1861** *Army Reg.* 488 *Canvas overalls for Engineer soldiers*—of white cotton; one garment to cover the whole of the body below the waist, the breast, the shoulders, and the arms.

1865 *Atlantic Mo.* XV. 61 Don insisted on my assuming . . . the leathern *chapareros* or overalls.

(2) 1776 *Jrnls. Cont. Congress* V. 855 A suit of cloaths shall be annually given each of the said officers and soldiers, to consist, . . . of two linen hunting shirts, two pair of overalls [etc.]. 1797 F. BAILEY *Tour* 342 Their clothes . . . consisted only of a pair of overhauls and a coarse hunting shirt. 1845 HOOPER *Suggs* (1928) 139 But Jim, son, get out from the fire!—you'll set your over-halls afire! 1946 *Chi. D. News* 22 Feb. 1/2 For clothing there are overalls for men, and print yard goods for women.

b. Also attrib. with **clothing, pants, pocket.**

1884 *Harper's Mag.* Aug. 402/2 A manufactory for canvas 'over-all' clothing. 1885 HOWELLS *Silas Lapham* iv, She was followed by the carpenter, with his rule sticking out of his overalls pocket. 1944 *Sears Cat.* (ed. 189) 432C Double Duty Overall Pants. . . . Made for tough service . . . double stitched with bright orange thread and then reinforced at nine points of strain with metal rivets that won't pull out.

overcoat ˈovɚˌkot, *n.* [Of obvious formation. Cf. Du. *overrok,* in same sense.] A large coat worn over one's regular clothing. Also attrib.

1807 IRVING *Salmagundi* xix. 507 Observing it to be dressed in a man's hat, a cloth overcoat, and spatterdashes, I framed my apology accordingly. 1856 CARTWRIGHT *Autobiog.* 201 My pistol . . . was in my overcoat pocket. 1893 *Harper's Mag.* Jan. 209/1 The last 'gen'lem' was a slender man, not quite forty years of age, who came in with his overcoat on. 1947 *Chi. D. News* 8 Jan. 37/2, I think I'll put on my overcoat and take the dog for a walk.

As the last term in **blanket, dust, pine, shingle-caped, wooden overcoat.**

overcup ˈovɚˌkʌp, *n.*

1. Short for next.

1817 BRADBURY *Travels* 288 Of the oak only, there are fourteen or fifteen species, of which the over cup (*Quercus macrocarpa*) affords the best timber. 1874 GLISAN *Jrnl. Army Life* 480 A few cotton-woods along the bottoms of the larger rivers; and overcup, pecan, sycamore, . . . and red elm, along the tributary streams.

2. overcup oak, any one of various trees, esp. *Quercus lyrata*, producing acorns deeply imbedded in their cups.

1804 DUNBAR *Life* 240 The margin of the river is clothed with such timber as generally grows on inundated lands, particularly a species of the whiteoak called vulgarly the overcup-oak. 1948 *Life* 5 April 57/1 The squat over-cup oaks of the South spread out to touch the northern red oaks.

3. overcup white oak, the mossy-cup oak, *Quercus macrocarpa.*

1795 MICHAUX *Journal* 15 June, Quercus glandulibus magnis, capsula includentibus, nommé *Overcup White Oak.* 1798 DUNBAR *Life* 93 Vegetable productions of the Swampy Grounds or such as are much exposed to the Annual Inundation. . . . Over cup White Oak. 1897 SUDWORTH *Arborescent Flora* 155 *Quercus macrocarpa. . . .* Overcup White Oak (Vt.).

overhill ˈovɚˌhɪl, *n.*

1. (*cap.*) *pl.* Apparently short for next. *Obs.*

1776 in *Amer. Sp.* XV. 291/2 The difficulty of marching from the valley Towns to the Overhills.

2. Overhill Cherokees, a division of the Cherokee Indians who lived among or west of the mountains in eastern Tennessee. Also attrib.

1763 *Ga. Gazette* 7 April 2/2 About the end of January, a Frenchman . . . arrived in the Overhill Cherokee towns from fort Assumption. 1784 JEFFERSON *Writings* III. 452 It would be to our interest to have an agency kept up with the Overhill Cherokees, and Martin the agent. [1883 ZEIGLER & GROSSCUP *Alleghanies* 16 The tribe [Cherokees] was distinguished by two great geographical divisions, the Ottari, signifying 'among the mountains,' and the Erati, signifying 'lowland.' Provincial historians have designated them as 'In the Valley' and 'Overhill' towns.] 1949 *N. Car. Hist. Review* Jan. 11 Eoneguski joined his forces with those of the Overhill Cherokee chief, Pathfinder.

3. *attrib.* Situated beyond the hills or involving those living there. *Obs.*

1816 WEEMS *Letters* III. 164, I am just arrived from my overhill excursion. 1895 WINSOR *Miss. Basin* 183 A Scotch baronet . . . was sent hither to prepare the way for a revival of this over-hill trade.

b. Esp. with reference to Indians. Cf. **2.** above.

1765 TIMBERLAKE *Memoirs* t.-p. Illustrated with an Accurate Map of their Over-hill Settlement. 1835 BIRD *Hawks* I. 83 From the time of the massacre of the over-hill Moravians . . . until the end of the year, Indians were ever prowling in the woods.

* **overland,** *a.* and *n.*

1. *n.* Short for overland stage or overland train *qq.v. Obs.*

1861 HAYES *Pioneer Notes* (1929) 256 Even with Overland and Pony and Telegraph, and what newspapers reach us by ocean lines, we are often greatly 'behind the times' in necessary information to form a correct opinion of the most important transactions. 1872 MARK TWAIN *Roughing It* 76 The place to keep a man 'huffy' was down on the southern Overland, among the Apaches. 1907 LONDON *Road* 5, I wanted to take the westbound overland that night.

2. *a.* Of or pertaining to a journey, communication, etc., across the great plains to or from the Far West.

1837 *S. Lit. Messenger* III. 61 In the course of this over-land journey, the most practicable line of communication would be explored. 1856 *Democratic Conv. Proc.* 27 The following is the resolution with respect to overland communication with the Pacific. 1890 LANGFORD *Vigilante Days* (1912) 122 The Northern Overland Expedition, as it was called, left St. Paul on the sixteenth of June, 1862. 1930 BANNING *Six Horses* 146 One bought 'overland hats,' 'overland boots,' 'overland coats,' 'overland ponies,' 'overland chickens,' 'overland eggs,' to the tune or blast of a real overland horn.

3. Of an individual or group: Engaged in, or having to do with, crossing the Great Plains.

1839 FARNHAM *Great Western Prairies* (1841) 11 It is the usual place of rendezvous and 'outfit' for the overland traders to Santa Fee. 1877 *Harper's Mag.* Dec. 85/1 The newspapers . . . gave me my first information of the sufferings of Mr. Fremont's overland party. 1907 ANDREWS *Recoll.* 94 The Sioux Indians . . . have repeatedly taken advantage of the weakness of the force stationed there, by trespassing on the property of overland emigrants.

4. In special combs.: (1) **overland coach,** a stagecoach operating across the western plains, esp. one used on the overland mail route, now *hist.;* (2) **mail,** see as a main entry; (3) * **route,** a route across North America from the Atlantic to the Pacific, esp. any one of the various routes between the Mississippi Valley region and California; (4) **stage,** a stagecoach operated on an overland route to the Far West, also attrib., now *hist.;* (5) **trade,** trade or commercial dealings carried on across the Great Plains of the West or Southwest; (6) **train,** a railroad train on a western overland route, also **overland passenger train.**

(1) 1860 *Alta California* (S.F.) 6 June 1/4 A ride in the overland coach across the country, is an era in a man's life. 1901 DUNCAN & SCOTT *Allen & Woodson Co., Kans.* 17 The little mule gave way to a two horse hack, then a jerky, or two horse stage, and finally an imposing Overland coach which, in its turn was succeeded by the passenger train. — (3) 1849 *Lady's Western Mag.* March 91/1 No matter—they are bound by the 'overland route.' 1884 HILL *Colo. Pioneers* 44, I was camping out with my freight trains down on the old overland route. 1948 CAUGHEY *Gold is Cornerstone* 96 Like the girl next door, the overland route appealed to midwesterners because it was near at hand. — (4) 1861 HAYES *Pioneer Notes* (1929) 253 By the Overland Stage arriving here on the 8th inst., I received your valued favor of the 12th ult. 1866 *Rep. Indian Affairs* 157 The overland stage line had just completed a survey for a new route. 1946 ADAMS *Album Amer. Hist.* III. 200 The Overland Stage still carried the passengers and the mail between the Missouri River and California.

(5) 1844 GREGG *Commerce of Prairies* I. 17 The overland trade between the United States and the northern provinces of Mexico, seems to have had no very definite origin. 1883 RITCH *Illust. N. Mex.* 25 The overland trade amounted . . . in 1876 to $2,108,000. — (6) 1889 CUSTER *Tenting on Plains* 357 The overland trains became an every-day sight to us. 1913 LONDON *Valley of Moon* 427 Now and again an overland passenger train rushed by in the distance.

b. Also **overland railroad, trail, wagon road.**

1862 KETTELL *Hist. Rebellion* I. 194 Frederick W. Lander . . . became superintendent of the overland wagon-road, in 1859 and 1860, to California. 1872 MCCLELLAN *Golden State* 412 The completion of the overland railroad brought . . . a great influx of professional thieves. 1947 *Steamboat* (Colo.) *Pilot* 2 Jan. 7/2 It was an important station on the overland trail.

overland mail.

1. Mail that is carried overland; an overland mail system or service. Also attrib.

1841 *Niles' Reg.* 6 Feb. 353/2 The news from China and India we have received by the overland mail. 1858 *Texas Almanac 1859* 28 Requesting the establishment by Congress of a weekly overland mail. 1865 *Ore. State Jrnl.* 16 Dec. 3/3 The above is a very important section of the overland mail route.

2. Esp. the mail or the mail service overland between St. Louis and San Francisco. Also attrib.

The carrying of the overland mail in the West was at first a private enterprise. In 1857 Congress authorized the establishment of a mail line to California. The semi-weekly carrying of mail by stage coach between St. Louis and San Francisco was begun in 1858. The service so performed was finally entirely superseded upon the completion of the transcontinental railroad in 1869. See LeRoy R. Hafen, *The Overland Mail* (1926).

1848 *Californian* (S.F.) 5 April 2/1 The Overland Mail for the States. **1870** F. H. LUDLOW *Heart of Continent* 10 The Overland Mail vehicle is of that description known as the Concord wagon. **1873** COZZENS *Marvellous Country* 85 An overland mail coach was occasionally attacked.

*** overseer,** *n.*

1. In a colonial town, an official chosen to have oversight of the general public business; a selectman. *Obs.*

1636 *Boston Rec.* 14 Not above one dwelling house shalbe built upon any one lott without the consent of the Townes overseers. **1638** *Springfield Rec.* II. 196 It was voted & concluded to have Six Select men Townesmen or Overseers.

2. Such an official chosen for a specific duty, as for the supervision and inspection of fences. *Obs.* Cf. **fence viewer.**

1633 *Dorchester Rec.* 4 If the overseers aforesayde do upon vewe find any pales of the feilds aforesayde defective [etc.]. **1640** *Boston Rec.* 56 Our brother Thomas Grubb and our brother Garrett Bworne are appoynted overseers of the fence at muddy river. **1668** *Cambridge Rec.* 176 Samuel Goffe, & Thomas Longhorne are appoynted overseers of the fences about the necke.

b. One having supervision of roads and highways, or charged with the upkeep of a particular road or section of road. *Obs.* Cf. **road overseer.**

1637 *Essex Inst. Coll.* IX. 67 There are appointed 3 men for overseers. **1704** *N.C. Col. Rec.* I. 607 Wm. Jackson presents George Gordon overseer of the High Wayes in his Room for the year Ensuing. **1733** *Md. Hist. Mag.* XV. 218 Charles Wells is appointed overseer of the roads . . . from the fording place of Davis's Run to Moale's Point.

c. =chimney viewer. *Obs.*

1654 *Rowley Rec.* I. 91 All thatched Chimnies in the towne shall be swept . . . and the overseers are reqvered to vew the day after. **1691** *Boston Rec.* 207 Ouerseers of Chimnies chosen.

d. A town official having supervision of the swine and sheep running at large. *Obs.*

1659 *Boston Rec.* II. 151 Richard Gridley is chosen overseer for the swine, and to levy two shillings, sixe pence by distress for every swine either unyoaked or unrung. **1681** *Cambridge Rec.* 257 The select men doe Alsoe appointd Abraham holman to bee ouerseer of the flocke. **1690** *Groton Rec.* 101 Ouer seeres of swine Jonathan Lawrenc Samll. Woods senr [etc.].

e. An official chosen to have oversight of fields and woodlands owned by a colonial town. *Obs.*

1667 *Charlestown Land Rec.* 164 Lift. Richard Sprague, William Dadie, Thomas Rand, and John Cutler, [were chosen] to ioyne with the overseers of the feild . . . to settle [etc.]. **1682** *Cambridge Rec.* 261 Chose this day . . . Samll. Chamne to be ouerseer ouer the hundred achers on the South side the riuer. **1697** *Providence Rec.* XI. 31 Joseph Whipple & Phillipp Tillinghast are Chosen Overseers . . . of all the Generall ffields.

f. A person having other special supervisory duties (see quots.). *Obs.*

1679 *Boston Rec.* 127 Overseers of Corders of Wood. **1681** *Ib.* 144 If the ouerseers of wood cordrs. finde any corders unfaithfull or defective [etc.]. **1682** *Plymouth Laws* 194 The Overseer of the Indians in each Towne shall . . . make Inquiry from time to time whoe of the said Indians have procured any English armes and seize the same. **1719** SEWALL *Diary* III. 234 Mr.Oliver in the name of the Overseers [of the meetinghouse] invites my Wife to sit in the Fore-Seat.

3. One of a number of officials chosen to have oversight of, or to manage, the affairs of a college, esp. Harvard.

1643 *N. Eng. First Fruits* (1896) 2 Over the Colledge are twelve Overseers chosen by the generall Court. **1723** in PIERCE *Hist. Harvard* 115 The memorial of the Overseers of Harvard College. **1832** WILLIAMSON *Maine* II. 563 Its government was committed to a board of 13 Trustees, including the President, and a supervisory body of 45 Overseers. **1946** *Sat. Review* 14 Sep. 5 Then he too retired, but was promptly elected to a seat on the Board of Harvard Overseers.

4. An officer in a Quaker group or society.

1832 WILLIAMSON *Maine* II. 699 Each society [of Quakers] has at least four Overseers, two males and two females.

5. The supervisor or manager of a ranch or cattle range.

1885 JACKSON *Zeph* iv, If he's going to be my overseer 'n' run that ranch, . . . he's just got to be my overseer 'n' nothin' else. **1907** LILLIBRIDGE *Trail* 154 The overseer did not seem surprised or offended.

6. overseer('s) house, a house for an overseer of Negro slaves. *Obs.*

1785 WASHINGTON *Writings* XII. 225 Sowed millet in eleven rows three feet apart, opposite to the overseer's house in the Neck. **1803** *Steele P.* I. 396, I have an Overseer with a few Hands, a good Overseer House. **1869** TOURGEE *Toinette* (1881) 22 You and Hulda shall have the overseer's house then.

As the last term in **buckra, Negro, road overseer.**

overslaugh ˈovəˌslɔ, *n.* [See note.] An obstruction, as a sand bar, shoal, or succession of islands, which hinders navigation, esp. in the Hudson River below Albany.

The currency of this term in the sense shown is prob. from a local use of the Du. *overslag*, a place on shore suitable for unloading goods from one ship into another or into a warehouse. Since the place on the Hudson where such transfers took place was at an obstacle to navigation, the word eventually assumed the new meaning.

1755 in *N. Eng. Hist. & Gen. Reg.* XVII. (1863) 349 The Vessele appeared down at the over Slaw or Shoals. **1776** C. CARROLL *Jrnl. Visit to Canada* (1845) 42 Having passed the overslaugh, had a distinct view of Albany. **1795** WINTERBOTHAM *Hist. View* II. 298 Ship navigation to Albany is interrupted by a number of islands, six or eight miles below the city, called the *Overslaugh.* **1901** STILLMAN *Autobiog. Journalist* I. 29 The 'overslough' or bar formed in the Hudson . . . prevented the steamers of greater draught from getting up to the wharf at Albany.

*** overslaugh,** *v.* **1.** *tr.* To pass over (someone) in favor of another, to ignore the rights and claims of (someone). **2.** To hinder, bar, thwart, overwhelm.

(1) 1846 *N.Y. Comm. Advt.* 21 Oct. (B.), It was found that public opinion would not be reconciled to overslaughing Taylor, and he was nominated. **1888** KIRKLAND *McVeys* 270 Now she would see whether or not she was to be overslaughed like dirt! — **(2) 1858** *Cong. Globe* 21 May 2293/2 Gentlemen on the other side of the House . . . hold their hands up in holy horror because the Private Calendar is to be overslaughed. **1903** *N.Y. Ev. Post* 28 Dec. 1 The spirit of commercialism will overslaugh every less practical consideration.

Owenism ˈo·ɪnˌɪzəm, *n.* The social and political philosophy of the Owenites. Now *hist.*

1830 *Mechanics' Press* (Utica, N.Y.) 19 June 254/2 What a precious compound of almost all that is unprincipled, is here presented:—Agrarianism, Owenism, . . . Antimasonry and Infidelity. **1905** LOCKWOOD *New Harmony Movement* 3 Owenism was the forerunner of Fourierism. **1949** *Indiana Hist.* June 175 The present study may be considered as a contribution to the understanding of the impact of Owenism.

Owenite ˈo·ɪnˌaɪt, *n.* An adherent of Robert Owen (1771–1858), a British communistic social reformer who was prominent in the experiment in practical communism at New Harmony, Indiana, after 1825. Cf. **New Harmony, New Harmonist, Rappists, Rappites.**

1826 *New-Harmony* (Ind.) *Gaz.* 25 Jan. 144/1 The Devil chuck'd. . . . To think what hellish transport he should feel, When all the howling Owenites were there. **1905** LOCKWOOD *New Harmony Movement* 5 The narrow type of religion which the Owenites so steadfastly opposed has in large measure disappeared. **1949** *Chi. Tribune* 9 Jan. 17/1 Communism in the midwest . . . was established in Indiana more than 100 years ago by New Harmony's social colonizers, the religious Harmonists of 1814, and the Owenites of 1825.

attrib. **1945** YOUNG *Angel in Forest* 270 Owenite converts sang their songs at every tavern and under the shadow of every church. **1949** *Chi. Tribune* 26 Nov. 10/3 However, it remained for one of the Owenite communists to come up, in 1826, with an amazing scheme whereby every place upon earth should arbitrarily be renamed.

*** owl,** *n.* In combs.: (1) **owl car,** a streetcar that runs late at night; (2) *** head,** a cheap revolver, so called from the device of an owl's head often used on the handle or stock, *colloq.*; (3) **line, =owl train;** (4) **-'s clover,** see as a main entry; (5) **train,** a train that begins its run late at night.

(1) 1889 FARMER 405/2 Owl-car, a tram-car plying late into the night. **1923** WATTS *L. Nichols* 218 Them old owl-cars don't run but once an hour. — **(2) 1944** CLARK *Pills* 130 Competing with the 'nigger killer' was the well-known Iver-Johnson 'owl head' which was a double-acting piece of unreliable rubber-stocked artillery. — **(3) 1866** *Cong. Globe* 26 March 1641 He is expected to take the owl-line, the midnight line, as it passes his house.

(5) 1856 *N.Y. Herald* 8 Jan. 1/2 The 'Owl Train,' due at Jersey City at five o'clock yesterday morning, did not arrive until afternoon. **1947**

L.A. Times 18 Jan. 1/1 (*heading*), 7 Killed and 86 Hurt in Wreck of Owl Train.

b. In various figurative expressions, esp. *like a boiled owl*, or variants of this (see quots.).

1831 H. J. FINN *Amer. Comic Annual* 106 Sly Cato hurried back, As solemn as an owl in black. **1831** S. SMITH *Life J. Downing* 125, I want to make them are chaps stare like an owl in a thunder shower. **1846** THORPE *Myst. Backwoods* 24 The way 'the dear creeters [the ladies] could pull music out of it [a piano] was a caution to hoarse owls.' **1857** *Harper's Mag.* Aug. 367/1, I felt, to use a certain figurative expression, 'like a boiled owl.' **1892** *Amer. Folk-Lore* V. 60 To feel like a stewed owl, or like a stewed monkey. More idiomatically, like a biled owl. **1906** O. HENRY *Trimmed Lamp* 33 Babbitt was in last night as full as a boiled owl.

As the last term in **barred, burrowing, cat, Columbian, elf, Florida screech, ground, Kirtland's, little, Mexican screech, mottled, night, prairie, pygmy, rain, red, saw-whet, screech, snow, spectral, squinch, swamp, Virginian(eared), white-fronted, whooping, Wilson's owl.**

owl's clover. Also **owl clover.** Any one of various Californian wild flowers of the genus *Orthocarpus.* Also with a defining term.

1898 A. M. DAVIDSON *Calif. Plants* 142 Another member of this family is the owl's-clover, or the painter's brush. **1915** ARMSTRONG & THORNBER *Western Wild Flowers* 498 Yellow Owl's Clover . . . often makes patches of bright color. **1937** *Range Plant Handbook* W-136 The owlclovers are widely distributed and occur in practically all parts of the West. **1948** *Chi. Tribune* 18 April VII. 9/1 In between patches are often found the purple-red owl clover, beds of the blue lupine, and the mariposa lilies.

***ox,** *n.* In obs. combs. designating vehicles, implements, etc., drawn or operated by an ox or by oxen, as (1) **ox jumper,** (2) **mill,** (3) **shovel,** (4) **sled,** (5) **sleigh,** (6) **train.**

(1) **1904** PRINGLE *Rice Planter* 71, I climbed into the ox jumper with the maid and told Marcus to drive home as quickly as possible. — (2) **1817** in *Ill. State Hist. Soc. Trans. 1910* 150 An inclined Wheel ox Saw Mill with two saws. **1837** PECK *Gaz. Illinois* 33 Ox mills on the inclined plane, and horse mills by draught, are common throughout . . . the state. — (3) **1823** *N. Eng. Farmer* II. 9 The most expeditious, effectual, and economical mode of making a drain would undoubtedly be to use oxen, and a scraper or ox-shovel, as it is sometimes called. — (4) **1842** in *Kans. Hist. Coll.* XIV. 755, I made also an oxsled. **1854** SHILLABER *Mrs. Partington* 20 Slides down-hill on the ox-sled runners, in winter, that the boys hauled up to the summit. **1904** WALLER *Wood-Carver* 82 Uncle Shim is driving the ox-sled down the Pent Road to Gilead.

(5) **1852** MOODIE *Roughing It* 9 We were descending a very steep hill, and encountered an ox-sleigh, which was crawling slowly up it in a contrary direction. — (6) **1849** in *Wagons West* (*c*1930) 120 We will now push off for good and any ox train that gets ahead of us will have to travele. **1892** in *S. Dak. Hist. Coll.* I. 75 The visitor . . . gazed with wonder upon the ox-train that conveyed the machinery for a stamp-mill.

b. In the names of plants: (1) **ox balm,** =**horse balm;** (2) ***heart,** a sweet cherry of any one of several varieties, also attrib.; (3) ***-eye,** see as a main entry.

(1) **1853** *Mich. Agric. Soc. Trans.* V. 130 The plants were very numerous, among which were oxbalm . . and marsh grass. **1931** CLUTE *Plants* 97 The bull daisy . . . , which is also called ox-eye daisy, is one of the largest and commonest of daisies, the ox-balm (*Collinsonia*) is merely a larger balm. — (2) **1852** *Knickerb.* XL. 190 From aloft ox-hearts and black-hearts nodded in the passing wind a kindly invitation. **1884** ROE *Nature's Story* 267 The moist sultriness of the Fourth finished the ox-heart cherries. **1903** ADE *In Babel* 189 The ox-heart tree which had blossomed so sturdily, showed not a cherry.

c. In miscellaneous combs.: (1) ***oxbow,** see as a main entry; (2) **chip,** a piece of dried cow dung, cf. **buffalo chip;** (3) **common,** land owned by a colonial town and set aside for pasturing oxen, *obs.;* (4) **express-man,** (see quot.), *obs.;* (5) **frame,** a frame or brake used in shoeing oxen, *obs.*, cf. quot. 1890 *s.v.* **ox-shoeing** below; (6) **proof,** of a fence, strong enough to bar oxen; (7) **runner,** a runner such as was used on an ox sled, *obs.;* (8) **shoe,** a flat piece of iron having five or six holes near the margin to receive as many nails in tacking it to the hoof of an ox to serve as a shoe; (9) **shoeing,** the process of putting shoes on oxen, also attrib.

(2) **1857** CHANDLESS *Visit Salt Lake* I. 122 Some one pitched on an old camping-place studded with 'ox-chips.' — (3) **1651** in G. W. CHASE *Hist. Haverhill, Mass.* 73 The ox-common . . . shall be for the use of them who live upon the east side of the mill brook. **1727** *N.H. Probate Rec.* II. 309, I give and Bequeath unto my son . . . my shear of marsh on the great ox Common. — (4) **1874** B. F. TAYLOR *World on Wheels* 43 You meet now and then a 'freighter,' as the ox-express-men of plain and prairie are called.

(5) **1844** *Knickerb.* XXIII. 155 An ox-frame standing by the door, and at one side a shed. — (6) **1886** S. W. MITCHELL *R. Blake* 21 'A hell-fence?' 'Yes, sir, that's what they call 'em here,—pig-tight, ox-proof, hoss-high, stumps upside down.' — (7) **1835** HOFFMAN *Winter in West* I. 246 Our sleigh, a low clumsy pine box on a pair of ox-runners, was soon after at the door. — (8) **1831** THOMAS B. HAZARD *Nailer Tom's Diary* (1930) 732/2 George Austing workt here makeing Ox Shoes. **1947** *Democrat* 3 July 4/4 We wonder how many of our readers have seen an ox shoe. One was added to the Democrat collection of curios last week. — (9) **1856** *Porter's Spirit of Times* 4 Oct. 71/3 Ox-shoeing. . . . We frequently find oxen, especially the large oxen, lamed by shoeing. **1890** LANGFORD *Vigilante Days* (1912) 226 We sat down upon an ox-shoeing frame, and talked over the whole matter.

d. *To drive the wrong ox*, to make a mistake. *Obs.*

1837 *Harvardiana* III. 237 They drove the wrong ox, when they sent me on this business.

As the last term in **beef, off, offhand, wild ox.** See also **Job's oxen.**

oxammite ɑksˈæmaɪt, *n.* [*oxalic*+*ammonium*+*ite.*] An oxalate of ammonium found in guano. — **1870** *Amer. Jrnl. Science* L. 274 Oxalate of Ammonia, which Professor Shepard names Oxammite. **1884** DANA *Mineralogy* (ed. 10) 433 *Oxammite.*—Ammonium oxalate . . . from the Guanape Islands.

***oxbow,** *n.*

1. (See quot. 1896.) Usu. in proper names.

1784 S. HOLLAND *Map of the Prov. of N.H.*, Gt Oxbow [Haverhill]. **1856** *Spirit of Times* 18 Oct. 106/3 The Ox-Bow lies on the New Hampshire side of the river. **1896** A. MATTHEWS in *Nation* 23 July 65 The term oxbow seems to have acquired in New England these two meanings: (1) the bend or reach of a river, and (2) the land enclosed, or partially enclosed, within such bend. . . . The oxbows of the Connecticut River are well known, the Great Oxbow at Newbury, Vt., and the Little Oxbow at Haverhill, N.H., having long been famous; and it is in that region that the term appears to have arisen. **1947** *Beaver* June 8/2 Starting up stream from South Nahanni, you have first some ten miles of slack water, where the river meanders silently round two oxbows.

attrib. **1867** RICHARDSON *Beyond Miss.* 63 It was the extreme point of an oxbow curve. **1875** TEMPLE & SHELDON *Hist. Northfield, Mass.* 12 The high plain here . . . turns the course of the Connecticut so that it makes an ox-bow bend. **1904** CHAMBERLAIN & SALISBURY *Geology* I. 181 If it [an abandoned channel curve] contains standing water and has the proper form, it is called an ox-bow lake. **1941** FERGUSSON *Southwest* 100 The North raged about the 'horseshoe' or 'ox-bow' route. But Mr. Butterfield bought a hundred Concord spring wagons and square-bodied coaches.

2. In special combs.: (1) **oxbow cut-off,** =**cut-off 1;** (2) **key,** a pin for preventing an oxbow from coming out of the yoke; (3) **stirrup,** a stirrup shaped like an oxbow.

(1) **1914** TARR *College Physiography* 150 The river flows temporarily along a straighter course at this point, giving rise to an ox-bow cut-off. — (2) **1882** *Rep. Indian Affairs* 480 Ox bow keys, 2 inch. — (3) **1907** S. E. WHITE *Arizona Nights* 5 Uncle Jim sat placidly on his white horse, his thin knees bent to the ox-bow stirrups, smoking.

***oxeye,** *n.*

1. Any plant of the genus *Heliopsis.*

1817–8 EATON *Botany* (1822) 302 *Heliopsis laevis*, ox-eye. . . . Tall resembling the sunflowers, for which it is often mistaken by botanists. **1939** *Nat. Geog. Mag.* Aug. 262/1 Oxeyes . . . are tall, leafy plants bearing numerous attractive bright-orange flower heads that come into bloom in late summer.

b. oxeye(d) daisy, (see quots.).

1817–8 EATON *Botany* (1822) 236 *Chrysanthemum leucanthemum*, ox-eyed daisy. . . . Fields. **1931** CLUTE *Plants* 97 The bull daisy (*Chrysanthemum leucanthemum*), which is also called ox-eye daisy, is one of the largest and commonest of daisies.

Also the black-eyed Susan *q.v.*

1894 *Amer. Folk-Lore* VII. 92 *Rudbeckia hirta*, . . . ox-eye daisy, somewhat general in Mass.

2. (See quots.)

1888 G. TRUMBULL *Names of Birds* 190 Black-Bellied Plover: Swiss Plover: Whistling Plover . . . Ox-Eye. **1917** *Birds of Amer.* I. 256 Black-bellied plover, *Squatarola squatarola*. Other names.—Black-breast; Black-breasted Plover; . . . Ox-eye; Four-toed Plover; Gump.

***oyster,** *n.*

1. =**oyster supper.** *Rare.*

*a***1738** BYRD *Secret Hist.* (1929) 37 In the Evening the Commissioners were invited to an Oyster and a Bowl by Mr Sam Smith a plain Man worth 2000 Pounds.

2. In combs.: (1) ***oyster bank,** =**oystershell bank,** *rare;* (2) ***boat,** app. a place where oysters are shucked or otherwise processed (see quot.); (3) **can,** (see quot. 1881); (4) **cannery,** a place where oysters are canned; (5) **commission,** (see quot.); (6) **field,** an oyster bed; (7) ***fish,** =**tautog;** (8) **law,** a law relating to the taking of oysters; (9) **packinghouse,** =**oyster cannery;** (10) **plantation,** a tract of submerged land upon which oysters are cultivated; (11) **planter,** the owner of an oyster plantation; (12) **police,** a police force established by Maryland and Virginia to enforce laws regarding oystering in those states, also attrib.; (13) **pond,** a pond in which oysters grow or are grown, also attrib.; (14) ***shell,** see as a main entry; (15) **weed,** the salsify.

(1) 1832 WILLIAMSON *Maine* II. 541 The Oyster banks in this town . . . consist of oyster shells from 12 to 15 feet in height. — **(2) 1890** *Cent.* 4219/2 oyster-boat . . . A large establishment or floating house, constructed on a raft, generally one story and sometimes two high. These houses are usually moored together, and kept in constant communication with the wharf by means of a swinging bridge, which rises and falls with the tide. They are usually about 15 yards long by 10 wide, and are divided into several compartments. — **(3) 1866** *Harper's Mag.* Oct. 636/1 The sutlers' shops had drifted . . . on to a shoal of oyster cans **1881** INGERSOLL *Oyster Industry* 246 *Oyster can.*—The tin receptacle, holding from one pint to four quarts, in which oysters are packed for shipment. These may be square, or round, and of various shapes. **1934** LOMAX *Amer. Ballads* 355, I cook my meals in an oyster can. — **(4) 1884** *Nat. Museum Bul.* No. 27, 1064 Oyster cannery.

(5) 1914 *Cyclo. Amer. Govt.* II. 595 Oyster Commissions. Commissions formed in a number of coastwise states for the control of the oyster and other shellfish industries. — **(6) 1888** *Amer. Anthropologist* I. No. 4. 297 The oysterfield . . . would supply a bounteous repast. **1948** *Amer. Sp.* XXIII. 297/2 The verb *shell* is also used in oystering, somewhat as in warfare, to mean applying shell to the oyster fields for the *spat* to grow on. — **(7) 1903** T. H. BEAN *Fishes N.Y.* 656 Naked Goby; Mud Creeper; Oysterfish. — **(8) 1880** *Bradstreet's* 16 Oct. 4/1 Mr. Richard H. Edmonds . . . concludes his admirable review . . . with a summary of the 'oyster laws' of Maryland and Virginia. — **(9) 1879** *Harper's Mag.* June 64/1 Along the water's edge . . . [are] the oyster packing houses.

(10) 1864 NICHOLS *Amer. Life* I. 270 Gentlemen living upon the rivers, sounds, and inlets in the vicinity of New York, have their oyster-plantations. **1879** *Bradstreet's* 3 Dec. 1/1 These lands are called oyster plantations. — **(11) 1859** *Huntington Rec.* III. 441 Resolved, that Tobias Dillon and Warren Lewis be appointed to serve notices on the oyster planters. **1879** *Bradstreet's* 3 Dec. 1/1 Some oyster planters now own many hundred acres. — **(12) 1870** *Md. Code: Supp.* 69 The commanding officer of the 'state oyster police force' is hereby charged with the enforcement of the provisions of this article [on fines]. *Ib.* 112 It shall be the duty of . . . the oyster police of the state . . . to examine the licenses of all boats or vessels engaged in taking or catching oysters. **1879** *Harper's Mag.* June 65/2 An oyster police was instituted by Virginia. — **(13) 1655** *Southold Rec.* I. 27 The above said ffower acres and a halfe of meadowe more or lesse in the Oysterpounds. **1658** *Ib.* 48 Which meadow was exchanged . . . for his Seller meadow at the Oysterponds. **1870** *Huntington Rec.* III. 592 Over and across the cove to the old oyster pond dam.

(15) 1716 in *Mass H.S. Coll.* 6 Ser. V. 328, I haue taken your oyster weed of late, and am much better for it.

b. Designating boats and implements used in taking or handling oysters, as (1) **oyster canoe,** (2) **pinkie,** (3) **pungy,** (4) **rake,** (5) **scow,** (6) **tongs.**

(1) 1883 *Nat. Museum Bul.* No. 27, 267 Model of a Chesapeake oyster-canoe. — **(2) 1883** *Nat. Museum Bul.* No. 27, 266 Shell-Fish Fishery. Vessels and Boats. . . . Model of an oyster pinkie. — **(3) 1882** *Cent. Mag.* July 352 The Baltimore clipper was the parent of several types of vessels. The famous oyster pungies of the Chesapeake are allied to it. **1904** *N.Y. Ev. Post* 25 March 7 The owner of an oyster pungy that lay at a dock when the fire began had the craft towed into the middle of the stream — **(4) 1705** *Providence Rec.* VI. 247 Oyster Rake 3 hammer and a hand Bill. **1784** THOMAS B. HAZARD *Nailer Tom's Diary* (1930) 64/1 Made four oaster Rake teeth for old James Congdon. **1884** *Nat. Museum Bul.* No. 27, 856 Oyster-rake or toothed dredge. Galvanized-iron frame; 12 teeth; net of iron-mesh.

(5) 1824 *Nantucket Inquirer* 26 Jan. (Th.), He wore a hat of the new oyster-scow cut, with a long piece of crape hanging to it. **1856** *Dollar Times* (Cin.) 11 Dec. 2/5 Our river boats are palaces of paint and gilding, but a leak from the bowsprit of an oyster-scow will sink one in fifteen minutes. — **(6) 1716** *Providence Rec.* VI. 161 To Iron Teeth for Oyster Tongs and Carpenters. **1866** *Dly. Richmond* (Va.) *Enquirer* 16 Feb. 3/1 It shall be lawful . . . to take oysters with any other instrument than common oyster tongs in the waters of Tangier and Pocomoke sounds. **1949** R. J. SIM *Pages from Past* 74 In oyster tongs the pin is thirty-two inches or more above the heads.

c. Designating places where oysters are served or sold, as (1) **oyster bar,** (2) **bay,** (3) **cellar,** (4) **house,** (5) **parlor,** (6) **rock,** (7) **room,** (8) **saloon,** (9) **shanty,** (10) **stand.**

(1) 1934 WEBSTER. **1947** DOWNEY *Lusty Forefathers* 186 New York City abounded in oyster bars. — **(2) 1891** *N. & Q.* VI. 17 Jan. 140 *Oyster Bay.*—In Philadelphia, many oyster saloons and eating houses where oysters are the leading item sold are called 'oyster bays,' at least on their sign boards. Occasionally, in the older part of the city, one comes upon the sign 'Oyster Rock.' **1940** MENCKEN *Happy Days* 132 He was a lout of fourteen whose father kept an oyster-bay in Frederick avenue. — **(3) 1830** WATSON *Philadelphia* 220 Oyster Cellars . . . did not at first include gentlemen among their visiters. **1938** WEYGANDT *Phila. Folk* 138 The oyster cellars of that day . . . are spoken of as institutions of dubious respectability. — **(4) 1834** NOTT *Novellettes* I. 94 He can escape from the empty pageant to the substantial and homely comforts of a beefsteak or oyster house. **1902** *Harper's Mag.* May 964/1 The most brilliant shop on the 'Avenoo' . . . was an oyster-house, and a very unusual, almost wonderful one of its kind. **1949** *Fishing Gaz.* Oct. 96/2 Hampton oyster houses are George T. Elliott, M. F. Quinn, and J. S. Daly and Son.

(5) 1875 *Chi. Tribune* 1 Sep. 5/5 Wilson's is decidedly the handsomest and most convenient oyster parlor in the city. **1930** FERBER *Cimarron* 77 They had supped on ham and eggs, fried potatoes, and muddy coffee in a place labeled Ice Cream and Oyster Parlor. **1948** WESTON *Mother Lode* 66 Downstairs Was Darling's Oyster Parlor.— **(6) 1891** [see **oyster bay**]. — **(7) 1883** *Cent. Mag.* Nov. 41/1 American life is invading the thoroughfare, . . . multiplying flashy saloons and cheap restaurants, cigar stores and oyster-rooms. *a***1889** W. D. O'CONNOR *Three Tales* 14 The street-floor of one of my houses in Hanover Street lets for an oyster-room. — **(8) 1833** *Knickerb.* I. 117 Certain fiery and bulbous excrescences [noses] to be seen about taverns and oyster-saloons. **1894** CABLE *J. March* xix, The two Rosemonters were about to walk past an open oyster saloon hard by the capitol. — **(9) 1844** *N.O. Picayune* 26 Feb. 14/5 We would suggest, to any enterprising proprietor of an oyster shanty, the idea of putting out a transparency . . . indicating . . . that '*Bivalvular testaceous edibles are here for disposal*'. **1903** H. HAPGOOD *Autobiog. of Thief* 66 In those days he 'hung out' in an oyster shanty.

(10) 1830 *Boston Transcript* 29 Sep. 2/4 The oyster stands in New Orleans have been leased for $6000, the same price as last year. **1851** A. O. HALL *Manhattaner* 7 Oyster stands, where dirty mouths and flickering tallow candles grinned ghostly satisfaction.

d. In the names of dishes prepared from oysters or in allusion to the use of oysters as food, as (1) **oyster cocktail,** (2) **cracker,** (3) **fritter,** (4) **gumbo,** (5) **loaf,** (6) **stew.**

(1) 1905 *Granville* (O.) *Centennial Cook Book* 121 [Recipe for:] Oyster Cocktail. **1949** *This Week Mag.* 30 April 20/2 George Otten likes his potato-pancake supper to start with oyster cocktail. — **(2) 1879** PECK *Peck's Fun* (1882) 90 (We.), A fist not bigger than an oyster cracker. **1890** *Cent.* 4219/2 *Oyster-cracker,* . . . a small kind of cracker or biscuit served with oysters. **1924** *Amer. Mercury* April 430/1 The custom that some Baptist churches have fallen into of oyster crackers and cubes of bakers' bread in the Lord's supper is to my mind unscriptural. — **(3)** *c***1852** SARAH J. HALE *New Book of Cookery* 308 *Oyster Fritters.*—Blanch some oysters in their own liquor. . . . Dip each in batter and fry them. **1946** *Sat. Ev. Post* 11 May 58/2 But they still go for Maryland oyster fritters, which they call 'flitters.' — **(4) 1823** G. A. MCCALL *Lett. from Frontiers* (1868) 94 The Doctor's eyes sparkled with a deeper blue as he seated himself and the oyster gombo . . . disappeared with prodigious celerity. **1941** F. M. FARMER *Boston Cook Book* 203 Oyster Gumbo 1 pint oysters, 4 cups Fish Stock . . . 1 cup cooked *or* canned okra, 2 cups tomatoes.

(5) 1893 *Harper's Mag.* Feb. 378/1 'Oyster loaves' . . . are among the queer edibles of [New Orleans]. **1941** F. M. FARMER *Boston Cook Book* 289 Oyster Loaf. Slice off top of small loaf of bread. Cut out center. . . . Fill with creamed oysters, put on top, and bake in moderately hot oven. — **(6) 1846** CORCORAN *Pickings* 128 Mrs. Smith was never known to have an oyster stew of an evening that she did not divide it with Mrs. Jones. **1949** *Pacific Spectator* Spring 224 We had oyster stew every Sunday in winter.

e. Designating social gatherings at which the eating of oysters is the chief attraction, as (1) **oyster banquet,** (2) **party,** (3) **roast,** (4) **supper.**

(1) 1897 *Ore. State Jrnl.* 10 April 5/2 After the meeting adjourned a number repaired to the Bonboniere where they were served to an oyster banquet. — **(2) 1861** *Vanity Fair* 9 Feb. 62/1 You'll have enough to do . . . when I give my oyster parties. — **(3) 1906** BELL *C. Lee* 326 Aunt Angie was to give an oyster roast on the shore. **1938** WEYGANDT *Phila. Folk* 145 When I was a child oyster roasts were common, indoors and out. — **(4) 1741** BENJAMIN LYNDE *Diary* 107

Oyster supper with all the Court. **1818** WEEMS *Drunkard's Looking Glass* 6 A posse of younkers, in Alexandria, . . . agreed to club for an oyster supper. **1949** *Mo. Hist. Rev.* April 215 Having been accustomed to boisterous corn-huskings and box-suppers at the country schoolhouse, he is uneasy at oyster suppers at the 'Opera House.'

f. In various figurative expressions.

1843 *Knickerb.* XXII. 83 Every place was shut as tight as an oyster. **1863** NORTON *Army Lett.* 139, I found Alf well, enjoying himself like an oyster in the mud. **1922** SANDBURG *Slabs of Sunburnt West* 6 You ain't got the sense God Gave an oyster.

As the last term in **box, bunch, Cincinnati, cocktail, coon, corn, cove, European, Kentucky, kitchen, mountain, prairie, raccoon, rock, Shrewsbury, soft, Spanish oyster.**

oyster ˈɔɪstɚ, *v.* [f. the noun.] *intr.* To take or gather oysters. — **1767** *Brookhaven Rec.* 186 The Trustees of the Town of Brookhaven shall have liberty . . . to grant liberty to the inhabitants of the town . . . to fish, oyster or clam anywhere within the bounds of the premises. **1896** *Voice* 13 Feb. 3/3 Being near the Gulf some would oyster and fish.

oystering ˈɔɪstərɪŋ, *n.* Taking, gathering, or raising oysters, esp. for commercial purposes. Cf. **oyster,** *v.*

1662 *Va. Statutes* (1823) II. 140 The poore Indians whome the seating of the English hath forced from their wonted conveniences of oystering. **1798** *Huntington Rec.* III. 195 No person or persons not being an Inhabitant or Inhabitants of this Town shall Practice Fouling Fishing Claming or Oystering in the Town of Huntington. **1881** *Rep. Indian Affairs* 169 These Indians have always made their living by oystering on the bay during the oyster season. **1948** *Amer. Sp.* XXIII. 297/2 The verb *shell* is also used in oystering.

* **oystershell,** *n.* In combs.: (1) **oystershell bank,** a pile or heap of oystershells; (2) **bark louse,** a scale insect, *Lepidosaphes ulmi,* very injurious to certain trees and plants; (3) **road,** =**shell road;** (4) **scale,** =**oystershell bark louse.**

(1) **1642** in *Amer. Sp.* XV. 292/1 East into the great creek from the Oystershell banck. **1731** *Ib.*, Beginning at the Oyster Shell Bank on the side of the Little Creek. — (2) **1868** *Rep. Comm. Agric. 1867* 73 The oyster shell bark louse or scale insect, *Aspidiotus conchiformis,* said to be exterminated by washing the tree with a mixture [etc.]. **1895** *Dept. Agric. Yrbk. 1894* 253 One form . . . for many years has been considered a true enemy of the oyster-shell bark louse of the apple. — (3) **1947** *Newsweek* 16 June 32/3 The island has 34 miles of oyster-shell roads, winding under great live-oak trees draped with Spanish moss. **1947** *Chi. Tribune* 21 Dec. (Grafic Mag.) 12/1 In time the RFD came through, and the oyster shell road followed. — (4) **1877** *Vt. Bd. Agric. Rep.* IV. 150 The insect is shorter and stouter than that of the oyster shell scale. **1924** DEAM *Shrubs of Indiana* 233 Some individuals of several species are attacked and even killed both in cultivation and in the wild state by the oyster-shell scale.

Ozark ˈozɑrk, *n.* [See last quots.] *pl.* A local band of Quapaw Indians, so called from their residence in the Ozark Mountain region of Missouri and Arkansas.

1819 NUTTALL *Travels Ark.* (1821) 81 The aborigines of this territory, now commonly called Arkansas or Quapaws and Osarks, do not at this time number more than about 200 warriors. [**1910** HODGE *Amer. Indians* II. 180/2 The spelling *Ozark* is an American rendering of the French *Aux Arcs,* intended to designate the early French post among the Arkansa (Quapaw) about the present Arkansas Post, Ark. **1946** *St. Louis Globe-Democrat* 9 June, Ozarks must have originated, not from the French term 'arc' or 'arque' with the sense of 'curve' or 'bend' or 'bow,' as has been so often maintained, but as an abbreviation of the great tribal name Arkansas. The French were in the habit of shortening the long Indian names by using only their first syllables. There are frequent references in their records to hunting or trading expeditions 'aux Kans,' or 'aux Os,' or 'aux Arcs,' meaning up into the territory of the Kansas, Osage, or Arkansas tribes. **1948** *Dallas Morn. News* 2 May II. 6/2 'Aux Arcs' means 'with bows,' and it referred to the Indian tribe native to that region.]

b. *attrib.* With reference to the region.

1831 PECK *Guide for Emigrants* II. 129 The Gasconade hills, improperly called the Ozark mountains. **1856** *Rep. Comm. Patents: Agric.* 308 The varieties referred to above are . . . the 'Ozark' seedling [etc.]. **1927** *Haldeman-Julius Quart.* Jan. 77/1, I have dwelt among the Ozark hill-billies up near the Missouri line.

Ozarker ˈozɑrkɚ, *n.* =**Ozarkian,** *n.* — **1943** *Nat. Geog. Mag.* May 596/1 'Are you an Ozarker?' I asked a friendly girl cashier.

Ozarkian ˈozɑrkɪən, *a.* and *n.*

1. *n.* A native of the Ozark Mountain region.

1945 *Chi. Tribune* 26 Aug. VII. 1/2 You can't beat these Ozarkians. **1949** *Ib.* 13 Nov. VII. 9/4 There's a saying that an Ozarkian's wealth is mostly dogs.

2. *a.* Of or pertaining to the Ozarks.

1931 *K.C. Times* 23 Oct., Ozarkian girls wouldn't know how to go about not keeping themselves kissable. **1947** BROWN *Outdoors Unlimited* 75 I've shot from Texas coastals and the Panhandle, around through Oklahoma and Ozarkian woods rims at bevies flushing like blackbirds from wintered reed beds.

P

Paas pɑs, *n. N.Y.* [Du. *Paasch*, in same sense. An Amer. borrowing.] Easter. Also attrib. *Obs.*

1809 Irving *Knickerb.* VII. i, Under his [Stuyvesant's] reign was first introduced the custom of cracking eggs at Paas or Easter. **1830** Cooper *Water Witch* I. i, Thou canst lighten thy heart in the Paus merrymakings. **1858** *N.Y. Tribune* 7 April 7/3 The St. Nicholas Society [will] on Easter Sunday celebrate the festival of Paas. **1859** Bartlett 307 *Paas Eggs.* Hard-boiled eggs cracked together by New York boys at the Easter season. They are often dyed of various colors in boiling.

b. Paas blummie, (see quots. and cf. **blummie**).

1859 Bartlett 307 *Paas Bloomachee*, i.e. Easter-flower. (*Narcissus pseudo-narcissus.*) Not the Pasque Flower of botanists, but the common Yellow Daffodil. **1921** H. Quick *Vandemark's Folly* 111 The hillsides were thick with the woolly possblummies in their furry spring coats protecting them against the frost and chill, showing purple-violet on the outside of a cup filled with golden stamens. [Note: Paasbloeme one suspects is the Rondout Valley origin of this term applied to a flower . . . the American pasqueflower.]

pac, see **pack.**

paccan. See **pecan.**

***pace,** *n.* In baseball, the speed of a pitcher's delivery. Also *dropping the pace, change of pace.*

1867 Chadwick *Base Ball Reference* 138 *Dropping the Pace.*—Sending in a slow ball suddenly after having pitched swiftly for some time. **1886** *Outing* June 365/1 But his pace is useless, as no one could stand the punishment involved in facing such a delivery behind the bat. **1948** *Dly. Ardmoreite* (Ardmore, Okla.) 19 April 6/1 About the fifth frame he began using his curve ball and change of pace.

As the last term in **planter's pace.**

***pacer,** *n.* As the last term in **Narragansett, square pacer.**

Pache ˈpætʃɪ, *n.* Also **'Pache.** Short for Apache *q.v. Colloq.*

1850 Garrard *Wah-To-Yah* xiii. 168 The Paches (Apaches) took my beaver. **1912** Raine *Brand Blotters* 282 Even in the daytime it would take a 'Pache, but at night—well, here's hoping the luck's good. **1948** *Sat. Ev. Post* 25 Dec. 11/3, I wonder who I'll see first—the messenger or the 'Pache.

pachysandra ˌpækəˈsændrə, *n.* [f. Gk. *pachys*, thick, and *-andra*, denoting this type of stamen.] The Allegheny Mountain spurge, *Pachysandra procumbens.* — **1934** Webster. **1941** R. S. Walker *Lookout* 52 Pachysandra, or mountain spurge blooms in March and April in the rich soil in Lookout Mountain woods.

***Pacific,** *n.* In combs.: (1) **Pacific canal,** the Panama Canal; (2) **Coast,** that part of North America, esp. of the U.S., that borders on the Pacific Ocean, also attrib.; (3) **coaster,** an inhabitant or native of the Pacific Coast; (4) **Confederacy,** a projected confederacy composed of the Pacific Coast states, *rare;* (5) **Confederation,** =prec., *obs.;* (6) **Empire,** that part of the U.S. adjacent to the Pacific Ocean, *obs.;* (7) **guano,** (see quot.), *obs.;* (8) **Northwest,** the northwestern part of the U.S.; (9) **Republic,** =**Pacific Confederacy;** (10) **seaboard,** =**Pacific Coast;** (11) **slope,** the region in North America, esp. that part in the U.S., lying west of the Continental Divide; (12) **sloper,** an inhabitant of the Pacific slope region; (13) **states,** *pl.* states in the Pacific slope region; (14) **time,** time as reckoned in the Pacific time belt or as prevailing on the 120th meridian west of Greenwich.

(1) **1900** *Cong. Rec.* 1 Feb. 1407/2 Build the Pacific canal . . . and you will make the Pacific slope the counterpart of our Atlantic seaboard. — (2) **1872** McClellan *Golden State* 523 The Pacific coast . . . contains an area equal to one-half of the whole territory of the Republic of America. **1917** *Birds of Amer.* III. 211/2 The Oregon Chickadee . . . is found in the Pacific coast district from the Columbia River to British Columbia. **1948** *Denison* (Tex.) *Herald* 2 July 12/2 The most valuable fish is the Pacific Coast salmon. — (3) **1883** *Harper's Mag.* Nov. 943/1 [The completion of the Union Central route has not] given the 'boost' to California that the 'Pacific coasters' so fondly dreamed of. **1893** M. Twain *Letters* (1917) II. xxxiii. 597 (R.), The men present were old gray Pacific-coasters. — (4) **1860** *Charleston* (S.C.) *Mercury* 8 Dec. 3/2 Already we hear of a Pacific Confederacy—of a Northwestern Confederacy—of a Southern Confederacy.

(5) **1847** *Dollar Newspaper* (Phila.) 13 Jan. 4/2 Certain individuals . . . are of the opinion that there ought to be established on the northwest coast of America, a new, independent Pacific Confederation, distinct and separate, though similar in its organization to the Atlantic Confederation of the United States. — (6) **1853** *S.F. Whig* 11 June 2/1 On it [platform] are inscribed . . . the honor and power of the Golden State, first born and heir apparent of the Pacific Empire. — (7) **1883** Smith *Geol. Survey Ala.* 118 'Pacific guano' is an artificial product made of a mixture of South Carolina phosphates, and the bodies and other refuse of fish. — (8) **1889** Union Pac. R.R. *Ore. & Wash.* 3 The resources and industries of the Pacific Northwest are so varied . . . as to not only suggest but enforce its consideration in sections. **1949** *Oregonian* (Portland) 10 Aug III. 5/1 Pacific northwest tourists are going down to the sea in greater numbers than ever before this summer. — (9) **1845** Sutter in *Hancock Eagle* (Nauvoo, Ill.) (1846) 10 April 1/7 With Oregon, a government and possibly 'Pacific Republic' might be created, with the most magnificent prospects. **1913** Goodwin *As I Remember Them* 114 There were thousands of men on the coast who were working to cause the secession of California, Oregon and Nevada, and to have them join the Southern confederacy or to organize an independent Pacific Republic. **1948** Caughey *Gold is Cornerstone* 244 Whenever Washington was lax or remiss, or whenever it verged on an unwanted interference, the Californians were apt to threaten a westward secession and the setting up of a Pacific Republic.

(10) **1838** *Knickerb.* June 556 Where the prairie stretches away, . . . shall sweep the long, hissing train of cars, crowded with passengers for the Pacific seaboard. — (11) **1845** Frémont *Exped.* 274 [We were] now about to turn the back upon the Pacific slope of our continent. **1948** *Pacific Discovery* Nov.–Dec. 16/2 Although it achieves its greatest size on the Pacific slope, its largest single 'pure' stand is that of the Kaibab National Forest in northern Arizona. — (12) **1876** *Benton Democrat* (Corvallis, Ore.) 18 Aug. 2/3 (*heading*), Pacific Slopers. **1883** *Harper's Mag.* March 648/1 'Well,' said the Pacific sloper, 'ef it's a private funeral, what do they call it a reception for?' — (13) **1820** Tudor *Lett. Eastern States* 57 When the future Pacific states come to be represented in congress . . . it may be difficult to get over this inconvenience. **1900** *Cong. Rec.* 16 Jan. 857/1 In the Pacific States, according to the same authority, 44 per cent of the national banks organized have failed. **1949** *L.A. Times* 6 Nov. 1/8 The overall increase for Pacific States is 5,251,000 or 53.9%. — (14) **1883** *N.Y. Herald* 18 Nov. 12/3 In the United States the standards will be known as the 'Eastern,' 'Central,' 'Mountain' and 'Pacific' times. **1949** *Chi. Tribune* 13 March 1. 3/4 The new railroad standard time established five time zones—one of the eastern provinces of Canada and four in the United States, called eastern, central, mountain and Pacific times.

b. Designating roads, railroads, mail, express, etc., crossing the continent to the Pacific Coast, as (1) **Pacific express,** (2) **mail,** (3) **railroad,** (4) **railway,** (5) **road.**

(1) **1856** *Porter's Spirit of Times* 11 Oct. 95/1 Pacific Express.—We are indebted to this prompt and vigilant establishment for early and full files of California papers. — (2) **1868** *N.Y. Herald* 2 July 6/1 The alleged Pacific Mail perjury case . . . was continued before the Supreme Court. — (3) **1838** *Knickerb.* June 556 The mammoth's bone and the bison's horn, buried for centuries, and long since turned to stone, will be bared to the day, by the laborers of the 'Atlantic and Pacific Rail-Road Company.' **1903** E. Johnson *Railway Transportation* 73 In the case of some of the Pacific railroads the charters were derived from the United States. **1949** *Iowa Jrnl. Hist.* Jan. 5 His scheme for a Pacific railroad must have contemplated a bridge over the Mississippi at some point. — (4) *c***1855** Robertson *Few Months* 113 The question of a Pacific Railway, has been in agitation in the States for some time.

(5) **1855** *N.Y. Tribune* 31 Dec. 1/2 This enterprise we shall probably live to see completed, even if we die before the Pacific Road is completed. **1896** *N.Y. Herald* 1 April 8/1 A joint sub-committee of the Pacific Railway Commissions of the Senate and House of Representatives has drawn up a bill to readjust the indebtedness of the Pacific roads to the government.

Also **Pacific type,** a type of locomotive having four pilot-truck wheels, six driving wheels and two trailing-truck wheels, used for pulling passenger trains in the West.

1928 STARR *100 Yrs. Amer. Railroading* 296 Of the famous type of to-day, we have the 'Decapod,' 2-10-0 type; the 'Atlantic,' 4-4-2 type, the latter figure standing for the number of wheels under the trailing truck; the 'Pacific,' 4-6-2 type [etc.].

c. In the names of plants and animals: (1) **Pacific diver,** the black-throated loon, *Gavia arctica;* (2) **fulmar,** any of various fulmars that nest on small islands near the shores of the North Pacific; (3) **post oak,** (see quot.); (4) **rattlesnake,** a rattlesnake, *Crotalus oreganus,* found on the Pacific slope; (5) **salmon,** (see quot. 1891); (6) **tomcod,** (see quot.); (7) **yew,** the short-leafed or western yew, *Taxus brevifolia.*

(1) **1874** COUES *Birds N.W.* 723 The Pacific Diver, as its name indicates, is confined to the West. — (2) **1839** AUDUBON *Ornith. Biog.* V. 331 Pacific Fulmar. *Procellaria Pacifica.* — (3) **1901** W. L. JEPSON *Flora of W. Middle Calif.* 142 *Q[uercus] Garryana.* Pacific Post Oak. . . . In the mountains or lower or middle elevations. — (4) **1921** *Outing* Aug. 217 In the West are found the prairie rattlesnake and the Pacific rattlesnake. **1948** *Pacific Discovery* Mar.–Apr. 10/2 In the high canyon dwelt a plentiful population of the Pacific rattlesnake.

(5) **1891** *Cent.* 5314/3 They form the genus *Oncorhynchus,* and are collectively called *Pacific salmon.* **1946** *Mazama* Dec. 33/2 The . . . streams . . . provide excellent habitat for many different kinds of anadromous fishes, among them the Pacific salmon, the aristocrat of all food fish. — (6) **1911** *Rep. Fisheries 1908* 317 Tomcod—The Pacific tomcod (M. proximus) is found from Monterey northward. . . . The name is also applied to the kingfish (Menticirrhus saxatilis) on the Connecticut coast. — (7) **1934** WEBSTER. **1940** *Mt. Hood Guide* 11 Pacific yew grows occasionally near streams and in moist places to timberline.

***pacifier,** *n.* A device, usu. of rubber and shaped like a nipple, for fretful babies to suck. — **1904** CRISSEY *Tattlings* 367, I put away my teething ring and baby 'pacifier' several years ago. **1940** SMITH *Puyallup-Nisqually* 182 The dried neck of the horse clam was tied to the baby's wrist and served both as a pacifier and teething ring.

pack pæk, *n.* Also **pac.** [Lenape *pacu,* a kind of shoe.] (See quot. 1875 and cf. **boot pack, shoe pack.**) Also attrib.

1875 KNIGHT 1590/1 *Pac; Pack.* A moccasin having a sole turned up and sewed to the upper. Though now made of leather of various kinds, the pac, as used by the Indians of the Six Nations, for instance, was made of hide boiled in tallow and wax; or of tawed hide subsequently stuffed with tallow or wax. **1922** *Outing* May 68/1 Footwear, pac boots 16 inches; rubber boots. **1944** *Sears Cat.* (ed. 189) 345 Leather top work Pac. . . . Not rationed. . . . If you wear size 6½ or 7 shoe, order size 6 pac.

***pack,** *v.*

1. *tr.* To carry or convey (goods, commodities, etc.), usu. on the back. Used of both persons and animals. Also fig.

1805 CLARK in *Lewis & C. Exped.* III. (1905) 181 Set all hands packing the loading over the portage which is below the grand shute. **1816** U. BROWN *Journal* II. 360, I let him know that I . . . meant to hire a horse of him to pack our provisions. **1902** LEWIS *Wolfville Nights* xi. 175 Gents, I dont pack the nerve! . . . an' I'm goin' to dig out. **1948** *So. Sierran* Feb. 1/3 Delos W. Colby, a man of stern perseverance, packed in household furniture on burro or mule back.

Hence ***packed,** *a.*

1852 in *Frontier* IX. (1929) 252, I saw the Indians have their dogs or wolves packed like mules. **1860** *Narr. of Samuel Hancock 1845–1860* (1927) 123 And they [Indians] appeared heavily packed and each carried a gun. [**1877** STANLEY *Rambles in Wonderland* 89 The *buccaro* drove in our horses, which were saddled and packed.]

b. To carry or stand the effects of (liquor). *Colloq.*

*a***1846** *Quarter Race Ky.* 103 The captain used to boast that he could pack a gallon without its setting him back any.

c. *intr.* or *absol.*

1889 Union Pac. R.R. *Ore. & Wash.* 15 An old pioneer packer, who for years packed through the country, [said] that his animals would keep in better condition on bunch grass alone than they would if fed on ordinary hay and grain.

d. To wear or carry as part of one's regular equipment; esp. to carry (a pistol). *Colloq.*

1890 LANGFORD *Vigilante Days* (1912) 436 No man that ever packed a star in this city can arrest me. **1949** *Milwaukie* (Ore.) *Rev.* 4 Aug. 4/4 It was a bit like shooting at a fellow who totes a 45 by a fellow who packs a 22.

e. *To pack sand,* to carry a heavy bag of sand as a punishment. *Obs.*

1864 *Placerville* (Calif.) *D. News* 25 Aug. **1884** HILL *Colo. Pioneers* 110 General Connor kept him for several days packing sand in his camp, and then ordered him out of town. [**1947** CHALFANT *Gold, Guns, & Ghost Towns* 67 A 50-pound sack of sand would be placed on a prisoner's back and with it he marched up and down the parade ground, with a soldier with a fixed bayonet to prod him if he lagged.]

2. *intr.* To cohere or settle into a compact or solid mass.

1844 in *Rep. Comm. Patents 1846* 34 [Cotton] does not pack and become hard. **1890–3** TABER *Stowe Notes* 8 The snow packs so rapidly that I can walk without much difficulty up and down the sides of boulders.

3. In combs., in some of which the first element is a noun: (1) **pack hitch,** =**diamond hitch;** (2) **horse man,** one in charge of pack horses; (3) **horse path,** a path or trace followed by pack horses; (4) ***man,** one engaged in transporting goods, usu. by pack animals, cf. ***packer 2;** (5) **outfit,** (*a*) such supplies or equipment as one can pack or carry, (*b*) a company of outfitters who conduct campers, fishermen, etc., into the mountains, using horses or burros; (6) **peddler,** one who sells from house to house various articles of merchandise, esp. dry goods, carried about in a pack; (7) **rat,** =**trade rat;** (8) **sack,** a sack for "packing" goods; (9) **trail,** a narrow trail suitable for pack animals; (10) **train,** a train of horses, mules, etc., loaded with packs; (11) **trip,** a trip made with pack animals, also **pack-tripping.**

(1) **1947** DEVOTO *Across Wide Missouri* 65 None of them had learned to throw a pack hitch. — (2) **1725** in *Travels Amer. Col.* 133 Issued to Capt Wm. Hatton . . . additional Instructions . . . forbiding his two Packhorse men to Trade. **1852** E. F. ELLET *Pioneer Women* 202 The other two teams went to an old tavern stand, well known to the early pack-horsemen and borderers of that region. **1935** ROLLINS *Discovery Ore. Trail* xci, His earliest employment was as a 'pack-horseman.' — (3) **1792** PUTNAM in *Memoirs* 288 There is now a pack horse path the whole distance which has ben much used by Indian war parties. **1842** *S. Lit. Messenger* VIII. 5/2 There was nothing but a packhorse path across the mountains. — (4) **1828** in *Kans. Hist. Quart.* V. 251, I & the two pack-men returned to the creek with six horses and all the baggage. **1894** WINSOR *Cartier to Frontenac* 326 There were suspicions that English packmen were following [the Indians].

(5) (*a*) **1912** *Out West* June 405 Get a pack outfit at El Tovar, and in the mystic mazes of the Coconino Forest, camp out, and travel daily until you can 'eat like a hired man, and sleep like a baby.' (*b*) **1947** *Sierra Club Bul.* May 96 Operating in the High Sierra region today, there are about 60 pack outfits. — (6) **1868** *Harper's Mag.* Aug. 348/2 Ten years ago a pack-peddler went through the town. **1944** WILSON *Passing Inst.* 70 We . . . married, and died in a small area, learning of the big outside world only through books and an occasional pack peddler or clock tinker who came in. — (7) **1885** ROOSEVELT *Hunting Trips* 13 These rats were christened pack rats, on account of their curious and inveterate habit of dragging off to their holes every object they can possibly move. **1949** *Nat. Hist.* Feb. 64/1 Lizards, rattlesnakes, and pack rats form the bulk of the island s terrestrial animal life. — (8) **1851** W. KELLY *Across Rocky Mts.* (1852) 117 We, the packers, were now busily employed making pack-sacks of a uniform size; and stowing and adjusting them. **1949** *Boston Globe* 15 May (Fiction Mag.) 1/1 The big man had stepped to the bar, . . . allowing the limp packsack to slip to the floor at his feet. — (9) **1843** in *Utah Hist. Quart.* II. (1929) 116 There is little grass in the mountains and the pack trail bad. **1949** *Boston Globe* 28 Aug. (Fiction Mag.) 9/2 Here at timberline the pack trail ended.

(10) **1853** in *Ore. Hist. Quart.* XLI. 354 Business seems to be reviving for here comes five pack trains from Oregon. **1949** *Sierra Club Bul.* July 4/2 Or you will go with a pack train and let a burro or a mule carry your supplies into places more distant than you can carry them yourself. — (11) **1931** DOBIE *Coronado's C.* 177 At any rate, he made a pack trip into the Big Bend from Muzquiz. **1948** *Sierra Club Bul.* Dec. 2/1 Our own feeling, based upon many months of knapsacking and pack-tripping in the Sierra, is that there is room in the Sierra for both the horse and the knapsacker.

b. Designating animals used in transporting goods, as (1) **pack burro,** (2) **dog,** (3) **mule,** [cf. Du. *pakmuil*], (4) **pony.**

(1) **1885** *Wkly. New Mexican Rev.* 23 April 4/4 He will . . . haul the product of their mines to Santa Fe on pack burros. **1948** *Sierra Club Bul.* March 38 At the end of the trip, however, he felt badly when we gave up our pack burros. — (2) **1844** *N.O. Picayune* 18 March 38/1 The only assistant they took with them was an Indian-trained pack

dog. **1946** STANWELL-FLETCHER *Driftwood Valley* 17 The pack dog, from the time he is big enough to travel, accompanies his master on every trip with his burden strapped on his back. — **(3)** [**1776** in HARRIS *Catholic Church in Utah* (1909) 128 We . . . entered a small mountain forest of pine trees in which we lost one of our pack mules.] **1892** DUVAL *Young Explorers* 90 We ascertained that all the animals had broken their ropes and gone off, except mine, Uncle Seth's and the pack mule. **1947** *Sierra Club Bul.* Nov. 1 To preserve a mountain area in its primitive state means a certain amount of restriction in its use, even by pack-mule campers. — **(4) 1870** KEIM *Sheridan's Troopers* 201 [The Indians] drive the herds and pack-ponies, or else on foot lead them. **1923** J. H. COOK *On Old Frontier* 98 We used pack ponies on the return trip.

* **package,** *n.* In combs.: (1) **package express,** a system or service for transmitting or forwarding packages, also attrib.; (2) **house,** ?a business house selling packaged liquor; (3) **man,** one engaged in hauling or transmitting packages, cf. **expressman 2;** (4) **office,** a railroad office where packages to be forwarded are accepted; (5) **paper,** strong, coarse paper used for wrapping packages; (6) **sale,** a sale of assorted goods in packages; (7) **service,** a service for forwarding or transmitting packages; (8) **steamer,** a steamer transporting packages; (9) **store,** a store in which only packaged liquor is sold; (10) **ticket,** a railroad ticket entitling the holder to a specified number of rides between certain points, a trip ticket, *obs.;* (11) **trade,** trade involving the sale of goods, esp. dry goods, in packages.

(1) 1840 *Boston Directory,* Harnden's New York package express. **1903** E. JOHNSON *Railway Transportation* 166 It is also argued that the Government could do the package-express business better than private companies can. — **(2) 1880** *Bradstreet's* 10 Jan. 2/2 General trade with package houses has been rather more active. — **(3) 1880** DELAND *J. Ward* 2 They were at the mercy of Phibbs, the package man, who brought their wares in his slow, creaking cart over the dusty turnpike from Mercer. — **(4) 1859** *Harper's Mag.* Sep. 504/1 More and more parcels [are] addressed to the 'package-office of the Harlem Railroad.'

(5) 1768 *R.I. Col. Rec.* VI. 548 One paper mill, at which is manufactured wrapping, package and other coarse paper. — **(6) 1821** *Ann. 16th Congress* 2 Sess. 1526 Package sales . . . by the assortments of merchandise they combine, excite most interest. — **(7) 1896** ERNST in *Bostonian Soc. Proc.* (1897) 25 Our word 'express,' denoting a systematic package service, has become a true Americanism. — **(8) 1944** NUTE *Lk. Superior* 287 The package steamers to and from the great port have become . . . a very important part of the city's life. — **(9) 1945** MARLOWE *Coaching Roads* 167 John Whipple kept an early 'package store,' having been licensed to sell not less than a quart at a time, none to be drunk on the premises.

(10) 1846 *Dly. Ev.Traveller* 15 Sep. 3/2 Package tickets will be taken on the special trains only. **1869** HALE *Sybaris* 119 They did not sell season tickets on the Great Northern; they sold package tickets. — **(11) 1887** *Courier-Journal* 21 Jan. 7/2 Staple cotton goods were more active in first hands and a fairly good package trade . . . was done by leading jobbers.

Packalet ˈpækəˌlɛt, *n.* [?Place or personal name.] (See quot.) *Obs.* — **1852** G. W. L. BICKLEY *History Tazewell Co., Va.* 104 The *Packalet* was introduced into Tazewell from Botetourt county, Va. Most of the fine grays, seen in our county, are of this stock. They are fine harness horses, and are not much inferior to others, if used under the saddle.

* **packer,** *n.*

1. One who engages in the business of preparing and marketing meat products. See * **packing 3,** and cf. Du. *pakker* and *haringpakker.*

1778 *Essex Inst. Coll.* XLIII.15 A scheme of some packers of Beef [was] this way; in the fall of the year they barrill'd it [etc.]. **1868** *Ill. Agric. Soc. Trans.* VI. 323 The live stock of the great North-West is . . . delivered into the hands of the Chicago packer. **1946** *Chi. D. News* 22 May 7/4 Packers under federal inspection killed 9,946 horses in April, highest of any month. **1949** *Fishing Gaz.* Oct. 92/1 Packers reported September, the first month of the oyster season, as being very good.

2. Chiefly *W.* One who transports goods by means of pack animals.

1788 CUTLER in *Life & Corr.* I. 402 Here we met a Packer with ten packhorses. **1885** *Wkly. New Mexican Rev.* 25 June 3/8 Tom Moore, the veteran packer who steered pack trains for Crook and Custer years ago up in the Sioux country, passed down the road Sunday with a complete packing outfit. **1947** *Sierra Club Bul.* May 21 The packers got up early, ate a hurried breakfast, ranged cursing after scattered animals, herded them into camp and saddled up.

b. A peddler or dealer who transports his goods on pack animals.

1804 *Md. Hist. Mag.* IV. 5 A tolerable track is beaten for us, however by a description of peddlars who pass by the name of 'packers.' **1850** N. KINGSLEY *Diary* 148 A load of provisions came in to night brought by packers to sell. **1911** J. F. WILSON *Land Claimers* 19 'Want any supplies today?' said the packer, coming forward.

c. A person who carries a pack.

1902 *Outing* Sep. 746/1 It is interesting to watch an old packer, long inured to the hardships of a life in the forests, as he lays out his pack and puts it together.

3. One skilled in arranging a pack on a pack animal.

1871 *Scribner's Mo.* II. 4 The dexterity with which a skilful packer will load and unload his horses is remarkable. **1923** BOWER *Parowan Bonanza* 111 Government men—but I didn't like the look of their packer.

As the last term in **beef, mule, pork, provision packer.**

* **packery,** *n.* = **pork packery.** Cf. **packing house.** — **1890** *Stock Grower & Farmer* 22 March 5/2 Then the party took in a Wichita hog killing and in Whittaker's big packery saw the fat porkers swing down to death. **1894** *Dly. Ardmoreite* (Ardmore, Okla.) 28 Feb. 2/1 The presence in the city of . . . representatives of the Fort Worth packery is of more than ordinary interest.

* **packet,** *n.* In combs.: (1) * **packet-boat,** a long, narrow boat or towboat of light draft designed esp. for carrying passengers and mail on canals, now *hist.;* (2) **line,** a number of packets or packet-boats under one management, operating regularly in series between certain places or ports; (3) **ship,** (*a*) an ocean-going vessel engaged in carrying mail, goods, and passengers, usu. sailing at stated intervals, (*b*) a passenger boat operating along the coast; (4) **steamer,** a steamboat, esp. one engaged in river traffic, operating as a packet.

(1)1822 in *Amer. Sp.* XXI. (1946) 306/2 The *packet-boats* are large and commodious, having every convenience to lodge and entertain from 25 to 45 or 50 passengers each. **1936** ASBURY *French Quarter* 75 On the Ohio the keelboat, also known as the packet-boat, reached dimensions that were truly Gargantuan. Many were more than a hundred feet long and twenty-five wide, with a passenger cabin aft and a huge cargo box forward. — **(2) 1839** *S. Lit. Messenger* V. 5/1 The packet line was a sort of hobby to Jeremiah Thompson. **1896** *Proc. of Bostonian Soc.* 24 The date of our first packet line is yet to be found, and will not be earlier, I think, than Queen Anne's time. The early packets on the New York and Philadelphia route were called 'stage-boats.' — **(3)** (*a*) **1782** MORRIS in Jay *Correspondence* II. 349 Joshua Barney . . . [is] now commanding the Packet Ship *General Washington.* **1880** CABLE *Grandissimes* 381 To ascend into the drawing-rooms seemed . . like going from the hold of one of those smart old packet-ships or his day [c1803] into the cabin. (*b*) **1883** *Harper's Mag.* Dec. 166/1 [We were] writing in the cabin of a packet-ship bound from New York to Charleston, South Carolina. — **(4) 1863** KETTELL *Hist. Rebellion* II. 463 These two vessels had been packet steamers, running to New York. **1883** EGGLESTON *Hoosier School-Boy* 115 The little packet-steamer was landing at the wharf.

As the last term in **canal, cotton, land, line packet.**

* **packet,** *v. intr.* (See quots.) *Obs.* Cf. **packeting,** *n.* — **1806** WEBSTER 213/2 *Packet,* to ply with a packet [i.e., coasting boat]. **1816** PICKERING 148 *To Packet.* 'To ply with a packet.' *Webst. Dict.* I have never known this verb used in *America;* nor is this signification given in the English dictionaries. It is probably a *local* use of the word.

packetarian ˌpækəˈtɛriən, *n.* A member of the crew of a packet. *Rare.* — **1882** *Harper's Mag.* July 281/1 The typical 'Jack' of the pre-propeller age—the 'packetarian,' and the able seaman of the clipper-ship fleet—has, however, utterly vanished.

packeting ˈpækɪtɪŋ, *n.* Transporting by means of packets. Also attrib. *Obs.* — **1813** *Boston D. Advt.* 9 March 3/4 Regular New York Packets. The subscribers respectfully inform the Publick that they continue the Packeting Business between Providence and New York. **1868** G. G. CHANNING *Recoll. Newport* 140 During the period of 'packeting,' it was no unusual thing . . . for the best sloops to reach Peck Slip, New York, in sixteen to seventeen hours.

* **packing,** *n.*

1. The wadding or "patching" used in a muzzle-loading gun. *Rare.*

1831 *N.Y. Tribune* 31 Dec. (Chipman), A piece of hickory shirting . . . was used for packing.

2. The transporting of goods by pack animals, or by individuals serving as carriers.

1843 *Amer. Pioneer* II. 162 Merchandise . . . was principally carried on pack horses until after 1788. Packing continued to be an important business in Kentucky until 1795. **1897** *Boston Ev. Globe* 4 Aug. 5/2 (Ernst), Prices for packing across the pass have risen to 25 and 27 cents per pound. **1948** *Hungry Horse News* (Columbia Falls, Mont.)

24 Sep. 8/1 Roy owns a valuable string of pack horses and does considerable packing for the forest service.

3. (See quot.) Cf. * **packer,** *n.* **1.**

1932 GRAYSON *Leaders* 393 The word 'packing' is sometimes misunderstood. Packing connotes slaughtering, the preparation of the slaughtered meat for the market, and then packing, shipment, and eventual distribution.

4. In combs.: (1) **packing center,** (see quot.); (2) **city,** a city in which packing is an important industry; (3) **company,** a company engaged in the packing business; (4) **establishment,** = **packing house;** (5) **house,** a house or establishment where meat and meat products are prepared for transportation and the market, now usu. a slaughtering house as well, also attrib., cf. **oyster packing house;** (6) **mule,** = **pack mule;** (7) **outfit,** = **pack train;** (8) **plant,** = **packing house;** (9) **room,** (*a*) the room in a ginhouse where ginned cotton is packed into bales, (*b*) a room in which articles or commodities of various kinds are prepared for shipment; (10) **screw,** a large screw of wood or metal used for exerting great pressure in packing or compressing various objects, as cotton, cf. **cotton press 1, cotton screw;** (11) **town,** a town in which packing is the main industry; (12) **yard,** a yard where fish or meat is packed for the market, *obs.*

(1) **1931** ADAMS & ALMACK *Hist.* 577 By 1880 the invention of the 'refrigerator' car, first tried in 1869, had completely changed the meat business of the United States, resulting in great packing centers from which meat was sent in all directions instead of being slaughtered for local use in each little community. — (2) **1890** *Stock Grower & Farmer* 8 Feb. 3/4 With the larger meat shops . . . dependent as they are on a central packing city for their supplies, . . . the cattle man's hopes will not be realized so soon. — (3) **1868** *Harper's Wkly.* 8 Aug. 509/4 The Portland Packing Company . . . [is] said to be the largest packing establishment in the world. **1946** *Prairie Farmer* 5 Jan. 16/2 The packing companies maintain that the present long work weeks provide sufficient take-home pay. — (4) **1844** *Lexington Observer* 2 Oct. 1/4 The Undersigned . . . has taken the Slaughtering and Packing Establishment.

(5) **1835** HOFFMAN *Winter in West* II. 115 One of the packing-houses, built of brick, and three stories high, is more than a hundred feet long, and proportionably wide. **1906** *Overland Mo.* Aug. 72/1 The packing house industry is one of the most completely standardized in existence. **1948** *Social Forces* Dec. 129/2 The packing houses plan for peak ham sales at Easter. — (6) **1826** in *Overland to Pacific* II. 159, I let him take the horse, on condition that he . . . furnish Capt. Brannin a first rate packing mule. — (7) **1885** *Wkly. New Mexican Rev.* 25 June 3/8 Tom Moore, the veteran packer . . . passed down the road Sunday afternoon with a complete packing outfit. — (8) **1931** *K.C. Star* 7 Sep., A Leavenworth man who formerly was part owner of a packing plant has filed suit. **1946** *Chi. D. News* 22 May 5/2 The 25 per cent increase in federally inspected plants, as reported by the OPA, has meant longer working hours for employees in packing plants and a return to work of thousands who had been laid off. — (9) (*a*) **1854** *Harper's Mag.* March 456/1 The 'packing-room' is the loft of the gin-house. (*b*) **1857** *Ib.* 443/1 We might now take a walk through the extensive cooperage and packing-rooms [of the fisheries]. **1892** *York Co. Hist. Rev.* 44 The shipping room, packing room, as well as the office, is on the 1st floor.

(10) **1803** *Mass. H.S. Coll.* 1 Ser. IX. 114 All these various operations, with a packing screw, are performed by water. **1884** HARRIS *Mingo* 259 He found that a wagon had been driven to his packing-screw. — (11) **1906** *World's Work* May 7508/2 Every possible opportunity is given for the men of Packingtown to drink. **1926** *Amer. Mercury* July 323/1 Not the trainyards, not the packing-town, . . . can take a jot from their pristine boorish sweetness. — (12) **1834** C. A. DAVIS *Lett. J. Downing* 24 Zekil is a knowin cretur; he keeps a packin-yard, and salts down more fish than any man in three counties round.

As the last term in **beef, hog, meat, pork packing.**

* **paddle,** *n.*

1. The distance traversed in a specified time by one paddling a canoe. *Colloq.*

1894 *Outing* XXIV. 187/1 There was fly-fishing to be had within a five-minutes paddle of our landing.

2. Denoting various things used as, or shaped more or less like, a paddle: **a.** A perforated, paddle-shaped ferule used in punishing Negro slaves; a blow from this. *Obs.*

1828 *Cherokee Phœnix* 10 April (B.), Should any negro be found vending spirituous liquors, without permission from his owner, such negro so offending shall receive fifteen cobbs or paddles for every such offence. **1859** J. REDPATH *Roving Editor* 59 'A paddle,' he rejoined, 'is a piece of board 'bout three fingers wide and half an inch deep wid holes in it.'

b. A small wooden instrument shaped like a boat paddle, used in working butter.

1876 *Vt. Bd. Agric. Rep.* III. 97 To smooth the top of butter, a wooden paddle, well prepared, should be used.

c. A battling stick used in washing clothes.

1884 CRADDOCK *Tenn. Mts.* 3 The garments, laid across a bench and beaten white with a wooden paddle, would flutter hilariously in the wind. **1886** *Amer. Philol. Assoc. Trans.* 36 *Battling-stick* is the name of the 'paddle or mallet' with which the clothes are battled.

d. A hornbook. *Rare.*

1886 Z. F. SMITH *Kentucky* 691 The smaller children were furnished with a paddle, which had their letters and a, b, c's printed upon it. When the paddle was finished, the children could then own a Dilworth speller.

3. paddlefish, a fish of the family Polyodontidae, esp. *Polyodon spathula,* found chiefly in the streams of the Mississippi Valley.

[**1686** tr. L'ESTRANGE *Conq. Florida* 121 We caught another sort of fish also, called Pexepalla, the Palat-fish; the head of it is covered with a kind of an elbow-hood, the upper point whereof is shaped like a Palet or Lingle.] **1807** JANSON *Stranger in Amer* 191 The paddle-fish . . . is four feet and four inches in length. The snout resembles in shape the paddle used by Indians in crossing rivers. **1908** *Cent. Mag.* July 457/1 In Louisiana it is known as billfish, billdom, and paddle-fish. **1948** *Sat. Review* 15 May 26/2 They were assailed by questions about the Paddlefish, the Brindled Stonecat, or the Tessellated Darter.

4. paddle tennis, a form of tennis played, chiefly by children, with wooden paddles and sponge rubber balls on a court about half the size of a regular tennis court. Also attrib.

1925 *Playground* March 710/1 He secured permission from Park Commissioner Francis B. Gallatin to mark several paddle tennis courts in Washington Square Park. **1944** MENKE *Encycl. Sports* 490 Frank P. Beal . . . originated Paddle Tennis in 1924 to provide children with a game that would teach them the rudiments of tennis.

b. platform paddle tennis, a form of paddle tennis for adults, played on a raised wooden platform, usu. covered.

1944 MENKE *Encycl. Sports* 491 In the end they came along with the game of Platform Paddle Tennis.

As the last term in **apple butter, basswood, bee, bucking paddle.**

* **paddle,** *v.*

1. *tr.* To propel (a canoe, boat, etc.) by means of a paddle; to transport (a person) in a canoe.

1738 THOMAS SMITH *Journals* (1821) 28, I paddled myself to N. Casco, dined at Mr. Noice's and visited several families there. **1784** BELKNAP *Jrnl. Tour to White Mts.* (1876) 20 Our horses swam after a canoe, in which we put our saddles and bags; an old woman paddled us over. **1841** COOPER *Deerslayer* xvi, I dares to say, the Delaware can paddle a canoe by himself. **1908** O. HENRY *Options* 73 I've paddled a canoe down Little Devil River. **1946** COLES *Fifth Man* 31 Little rowed parallel with the shore—I say rowed, though I understand you can only paddle those rubber dinghies.

b. *To paddle one's (own) canoe,* to get on or make one's way by individual effort. *Colloq.*

1828 J. HALL *Lett. from West* 261 The Lady of the Lake . . . 'paddled her own canoe' very dexterously. **1887** *Harper's Mag.* March 547/1 They couldn't see how he was to paddle his canoe all alone by himself. **1949** *Time* 4 July 25/2 They seem more interested in paddling their own canoes than shaping a strong third force that would be the best weapon against the communism they all hate.

2. To beat (a person) with, or as with, a paddle.

*a***1846** *Quarter Race Ky.* 89 (We.), I Paddled his 'tother end, with one of the pieces. **1904** *Hartford Courant* 23 June 8 A secret society of girls 'initiated' some neophytes by blindfolding them, . . . paddling them, and then rolling them down a steep hill. **1919** MRS. L. F. CODY *Mem. Buffalo Bill* 31, I had started from the porch to paddle every one of them [the children].

b. *To paddle the filling out of,* (see quots.). *Colloq.*

1883 HARRIS *Nights* (1911) 5 Dey des tuck'n tuck de cloze en lay um out on a bench, en ketch holt er de battlin'-stick en natally paddle de fillin' outen um. **1909** *D.N.* III. 355 Paddle. . . . To spank, whip. Also 'paddle the fillin(g) out of one,' to beat soundly.

* **paddling,** *n.* **1.** Beating, thrashing, or spanking with, or as with, a paddle; a beating. (Cf. **paddle,** *v.* **2.**) **2.**

Used attrib. with **boat** and **canoe**; Propelled by a paddle or by paddles.

(1) **1851** Hooper *Widow Rugby* 96 What a devil of a paddlin' the old woman gin him with the battlin'-stick. **1862** *N.Y. Tribune* 13 Jan. 4/4 All the starving, paddling, and pickling in the world will not insure good crops. . . . Let Bleeding Africa go. — (2) **1894** *Outing* XXIV. 422/1 A small fleet of paddling canoes and row-boats had gathered together. **1905** Pringle *Rice Planter* 144 She jumped into her paddling boat . . . [and] paddled herself across.

* **Paddy,** *n.* Also * **paddy.**

1. (See quot. 1818.) *Obs.*

1818 Fearon *Sketches* 369 In Washington, on last St. Patrick's day, according to custom, a figure was stuffed similar to our Guy Faux, and called Paddy. . . . In Philadelphia a gentleman informed me that there were numerous Paddies exhibited in the same style. **1823** *Niles' Reg.* XXIV. 72/1 A much respected old gentleman . . . every morning of the 17th March, was sure to find a 'Paddy' at his door—he took it into his house and proclaimed a feast in honor of the saint. **1843** *Knickerb.* XXII. 51 He may light upon a stuffed Paddy some six feet high.

2. *local.* The ruddy duck, *Erismatura jamaicensis.* Also * **paddy-whack.**

1895 Ridgway *Ornith. Illinois* II. I. 185 Ruddy Duck . . . [is called] Hickory-head, Greaser, Paddy, Noddy, Paddy-whack, [etc.]. **1917** *Birds of Amer.* I. 152 Other names [of the ruddy duck are] . . . Paddy-whack; Stub-and-twist; . . . Dinky; Dinkey; Paddy.

3. paddy wagon, = **Black Maria.**

1942 Berrey & Van den Bark *Amer. Thesaurus Slang* 448. **1948** *Aurora* (Ill.) *Beacon-News* 7 Nov. 9/2 Police who attempted to enforce city segregation rules met with a torrent of jeers, and several tennis players who sat down on the courts had to be carried to paddy wagons.

As the last term in **dumb, steam paddy.**

padgo, see **patgo.**

* **padlock,** *v.* Used in combs. having to do with the closing by an injunction, state law, or administrative order, of a shop, storeroom, tavern, theater, etc., as a means of enforcing a law, esp. of a law against a liquor nuisance, prostitution, indecent exhibitions, etc., as (1) **padlock court,** (2) **injunction,** (3) **judge,** (4) **law.**

(1) **1925** *Lit. Digest* April 55/1 All such cases will be transferred from the Admiralty Court to the padlock court. — (2) **1928** *Lit. Digest* 12 May 12/2 The padlock injunction procedure will henceforth be used to the fullest possible extent throughout the United States. — (3) **1925** *N.Y. Times* 9 March 1/8 By April 1 I expect to have one padlock Judge sitting continuously to hear nothing but padlock cases and to issue padlock orders. — (4) **1925** *N.Y. Times* 9 March 1/8 He had been urging incessantly the policy of proceeding under the padlock law. **1928** *Observer* 26 Feb. 18/3 The New York police had banned the play and shut up the theatre under the 'Padlock Law.'

Also **padlocking court, judge.**

1925 *N.Y. Times* 6 March 6/5 A padlocking court operates without a jury. *Ib.* 7 March 1/3 A padlocking court with a padlocking Judge to sit during the Summer drying up New York was the plan announced yesterday.

padre ˈpɑdrɪ, *n. S.W.* [Sp. in same sense. An Amer. borrowing.] A priest or monk.

1792 in *Wash. Hist. Quart.* V. 306 There are besides in the establishment two more Pilots, a Padre (or Priest) and a Surgeon. **1827** in *Ashley-Smith Explor.* (1918) 216 Still at the Mission of San Gabriel . . . the men commenced work again this morning for the old Padre. **1949** *L.A. Times* 8 May III. 6/6 In this sense the padres of this mission greet you with a hearty welcome.

b. Used as a title.

1854 Bartlett *Personal Narr.* II. 320 Padre Pacheco and another gentleman dined with me today. **1871** *Republican Rev.* 15 July 2/2 If we are not mistaken, Padre Gallegos presided at one of the largest and most enthusiastic of their meetings. **1949** *L.A. Times* 20 May 2/5 She used to tell little Angelina stories of a man she had known—a warm, personal friend named Padre Junipero Serra.

Paducah pəˈd(j)ukə, *n.* [f. Siouan name, *Padouca* (?contraction of *Penateka,* honey-eaters).] *pl.* (See quot. 1885 and cf. **Comanche.**)

[*a*1726 L'Isle *Atlas Nouveau* (Carte de la Louisiane et du Cours du Mississipi), Pays des Apaches et des Padoucas.] **1770** Pittman *Present State* 40 The Arcansas or Quapas Indians . . . bring in very frequently young prisoners and horses from the Cadodaquias, Paneise, Podoquias, &c. **1819** *Wkly. Recorder* (Chillicothe, O.) 12 March 245/3 The main body of this people [are] generally denominated Padoucas, and White Padoucas. **1885** J. S. Kingsley *Stand. Nat. Hist.* VI. 188 The Comanchee tribe is one of the most important in North America. In the older works they figure as the Paducahs, the name applied to them by the Osage. **1942** Stegner *Mormon C.* 150 Others affirmed that somewhere in Kentucky there was a tribe known as the Paducas who spoke Welsh and were whiter than other Indians.

attrib. **1818** *Lynchburg* (Va.) *Press* 7 Aug. 2/6 Some time ago this sanguinary tribe took a Pado woman prisoner.

* **page,** *n.* A messenger or an errand boy serving a legislative body. Also attrib.

1840 *Boston Transcript* 18 Feb. 2/1 A page took them to the Clerk—the Clerk handed them to the Speaker. **1910** C. Harris *Eve's Husband* 118 Occasionally . . . [an influential citizen] got his little boy appointed as a 'page' in the hall of Representatives. **1949** *Time* 27 June 61/1 The Capitol Page School . . . is attended by the House's 49 page boys, the Senate's 21, the Supreme Court's four, and a few more Capitol-employed boys.

As the last term in **comic, first, front, House, riding, sport(s) page.**

* **page,** *v. tr.* (See quot. 1904.) Also * **paging,** *n.*—**1904** *N.Y. Sun* 21 Aug. 5 A bell boy is called. 'Here, page Mr. Smith, Room 186,' the clerk will say. The process of 'paging' Mr. Smith consists of calling out his name in the dining and other public rooms of the hotel. **1932** *K.C. Star* 21 Jan. 22 She was found without paging at a hotel the other night.

paho ˈpɑho, *n.* Also **baho.** [Hopi *pȃho.*] (See quot. 1910 and cf. **prayer stick.**)

1883 in Donaldson *Moqui Pueblo Indians* (1893) 70, I tried to buy a bahoo of one of these attendants, but he declined to sell it, saying that if he did his stomach would burst open. **1893** Donaldson *Moqui Pueblo Indians* 71 The day before these singular final ceremonies the men of the antelope order prepare many little prayer sticks, called ba-hoos. **1910** Hodge *Amer. Indians* II. 304/2 The idea of feeding the gods is expressed by one form of the Hopi prayer stick, the *paho,* 'water prayer,' to which a small packet of sacred meal is tied.

paid fire department. A fire department the members of which are regularly employed and paid. Cf. **volunteer fire company, department.** — **1858** Holmes *Autocrat* vi. 145 Boston . . . , considering its paid fire department, . . . has some right to look down on the mob of cities. **1889** M. Twain *Conn. Yankee* xxx. 382, I was . . . training some horses and building some steam fire engines, with an eye to a paid fire department, by and by.

paid-up plan. (See quot.) — **1873** M. Twain *Gilded Age* xlviii. 435 (R.), What the insurance companies call the 'endowment,' or the 'paid-up' plan, by which a policy is secured after a certain time without further payment.

* **pail,** *n.* As the last term in **dinner, filing, lunch, Shaker pail.**

Paincourt pænˈkɔr, *n.* (See quots.)

1787 Jefferson *Notes on Va.* (1803) 12 Six miles above the mouth it [Mo. River] is brought within the compass of a quarter of a mile's width: yet the Spanish merchants at Pancore, or St. Louis, say they go two thousand miles up it. **1838** Flagg *Far West* I. 119 For many years St. Louis was called *'Pain Court,'* from the scarcity of provisions, which circumstance at one time almost induced the settlers to abandon the design. **1946** *St. Louis Globe-Democrat* 23 June, The mocking nickname 'Paincourt,' i.e., 'short of bread,' used in French days, suggests that it [St. Louis] was often afflicted by a shortage of flour.

pain-killer. Any one of various medicines or remedies for abolishing or relieving pain.

1853 *La Crosse Democrat* 7 June 2/4 Ayer's Cherry Pectoral, Perry Davis' Pain Killer. **1886** Ebbutt *Emigrant Life* 119 We kept a bottle of 'Pain-killer' in the house . . . for medicinal purposes. **1947** Chalfant *Gold, Guns, & Ghost Towns* 44 He had cured colic in his horses with a certain brand of pain killer.

* **paint,** *n.*

1. Short for **paint horse.**

1848 Bartlett 243 Paint. In some of the Southern States, a horse or other animal which is spotted, is called a *paint.* **1870** Duval *Big Foot Wallace* 125 If that fellow hadn't been a sort of pet of captain's, I wouldn't have shot him off that wall-eyed 'paint' of his'n! **1947** *Dly. Oklahoman* (Okla. City) 5 Nov. 1/1 (*heading*), Claremore Saddles Old Paint For Birthday of Will Rogers.

b. The color of such a horse.

1866 *Wilkes' Spirit of Times* 28 April 130/3 Our Mexican vaqueras have a specific word, Spanish or Indian or 'patois,' for every shade of color, for every variety of 'paint,' and for every peculiarity of form.

2. In combs.: (1) * **paintbrush,** see as a main entry; (2) **clay,** clay used in making paint; (3) **horse,** *W.* a piebald horse or one of conspicuous coloration, cf. **pinto;** (4) **king,** one who has made a fortune in paints, or in the paint business; (5) **pony,** = **paint horse;** (6) * **pot,** (see quot. 1940); (7) **store,** a store which specializes in selling paints.

(2) **1882** *Econ. Geol. Illinois* II. 55 There is a local deposit of paint clays underlying the true northern drift. — (3) **1856** *Harper's Mag.* Nov. 756/1 The color of the American wild horse is generally chestnut; but hundreds are often seen which are known as 'calico' or 'paint

horses' from their many colors. **1949** *10 Story Western* May 25/2 He knew it was Julian Eads in the lead by the flashy paint horse. — (4) **1884** HOWELLS *Silas Lapham* 244 She might be expected at least to endure the paint-king and his family.

(5) **1892** DUVAL *Young Explorers* 71 A Mexican lad mounted on a paint (piebald) pony, with a spear in his hand, cantered off a couple of hundred yards, and laid the spear flat on the ground. — (6) [**1878** *Rep. Supt. Yellowstone Nat. Pk.* 8 Various paint pools, fossil forests, and other places of interest were discovered.] **1880** MCELRATH *Yellowstone Valley* 111 Midway between them is 'Hell's Half Acre,' appropriately decorated with the 'Devil's Paint Pots.' **1940** *Places to See in Wyo.* v/1 Sometimes the water and steam mixes with soft substance near the surface; the outlet then is a paint-pot or mud volcano in which the thick mud boils or appears to boil and bubble. — (7) **1840** *Niles' Reg.* 11 April 96/2 Dennis Spurrier, paint store.

As the last term in **nose, Ohio, war paint.**

∗**paint,** *v. To paint the town red,* to go on a riotous or reckless spree. *Colloq.*

1884 *Boston Jrnl.* 13 Sep., A 'spectrophotometric study of pigments,' by Professor Nicolls, is recommended to young men who intend to 'paint the town red.' **1921** PAINE *Comr. Rolling Ocean* 108 He thinks it's smart to paint the town red. **1948** *Aurora* (Ill.) *Beacon-News* 7 Nov. (Comics) 5 Every time you work late at the hospital, your wife skips out to paint the town red.

∗**paintbrush,** *n.* Any one of various plants of the genus *Castilleja* having bright-colored bracts. Cf. **devil's, Diana's, Flora's, Indian paintbrush,** ∗**painted cup.** — **1915** ARMSTRONG & THORNBER *Western Wild Flowers* 472 Paint Brush. *Castilleja miniata.* Red. Summer. Northwest. This is a very handsome kind, from one to four feet tall, with a smooth stem, and smooth leaves. **1947** *Mazama* Dec. 23/2 Each meadow produced exactly the right shade of paintbrush, or pedicularis, or aster or lupine, to blend with the other varieties growing in that particular area.

∗**painted,** *a.*

1. Designating horses, mules, and ponies that have been painted or appear to have been painted.

1866 SHANKS *Recollections* 274 'Oh,' answered Granger, 'you can't fool me with "painted mules."' (Granger had been a quarter-master, and in his early days had frequently been imposed upon by traders in repaired condemned animals.) **1927** RUSSELL *Trails* 177 Uncle Sam pulls him down off a high-headed, painted buffalo horse. *Ib.* 124 He starts ridin' 'round on a painted pony.

2. In the names of plants and animals: (1) **painted beauty,** (see quot. 1909); (2) **bunting,** (*a*) =**nonpareil,** (*b*) Smith's longspur, *Calcarius pictus,* also **painted lark bunting;** (3) ∗**cup,** =∗**paintbrush,** also with defining term; (4) **finch,** =**nonpareil;** (5) **goose,** =**emperor goose;** (6) **salamander,** a salamander characterized by bright-colored markings; (7) **tortoise,** a brilliantly marked turtle or terrapin, *Chrysemys picta,* found in ponds and in slow streams throughout the U.S., also **painted turtle;** (8) **trillium,** a showy perennial herb, *Trillium undulatum,* especially common in New England.

(1) **1901** DICKERSON *Moths & Butterflies* 79 A butterfly that is distinctly American, and that is found throughout the United States except, perhaps, in some mountainous districts, is the Painted Beauty. **1909** *Cent. Supp.* 928/2 painted-beauty. . . . A handsome American nymphalid butterfly, *Vanessa huntera,* occurring in lower Canada and over most of the United States. — (2) (*a*) **1811** WILSON *Ornithology* III. 68 Painted Bunting. . . . This is one of the most numerous of the little summer birds of Lower Louisiana. **1945** MATHEWS *Talking* 12 Miracles like the . . . first V of Canada geese, the visit of a painted bunting [etc.]. (*b*) **1874** COUES *Birds N.W.* 121 *Plectrophanes Pictus.* Painted Lark Bunting. **1890** *Cent.* 4234/1 *Painted bunting,* . . . a very common longspur of western and northwestern America, of many variegated colors. — (3) **1821** NUTTALL *Travels Arkansa* 143, I was pleased to see the Painted Cup of the eastern states. **1857** GRAY *Botany* 294 C[*astilleja*] *septentrionalis.* (Mountain Painted-Cup.) . . . Alpine region of the White Mountains, New Hampshire, and Green Mountains, Vermont. **1903** AUSTIN *Land of Little Rain* 221 The willows do better; painted-cup, cypripedium, and the hollow stalks of span-broad white umbels, find a footing among their stems. — (4) *c***1730** CATESBY *Carolina* I. 44 *Fringilla tricolor.* The Painted Finch. . . . They breed in Carolina and affect much to make their nests in Orange-Trees. **1831** AUDUBON *Ornith. Biog.* I. 279 Few vessels leave the port of New Orleans during the summer months, without taking some Painted Finches. **1917** *Birds of Amer.* III. 73 Painted Bunting, *Passerina criis.* . . . [Also called] Painted Finch.

(5) **1872** COUES *Key N. Amer. Birds* 283 Painted Goose. Emperor Goose. Wavy bluish-gray, with lavender or lilack tinting. **1917** *Birds of Amer.* I. 163 Painted Goose. . . . This is the 'least known and the most beautiful' of all the wild geese which make their summer home in the Far North. — (6) **1839** STORER *Mass. Reptiles* 251 *Salamandra picta.* . . . The painted Salamander. **1869** *Amer. Naturalist* III. 158 Our common *Desmognathus fuscus,* or Painted Salamander, was observed by me in Maine. **1947** BISHOP *Handbook of Salamanders* 300 Painted Salamander. *Ensatina eschscholtzii picta.* — (7) **1839** STORER *Mass. Reptiles* 208 *Emys picta.* . . . The painted Tortoise. **1842** *Nat. Hist. N.Y., Zoology* III. 12 The Painted Tortoise. . . . For the variety and beauty of its markings, this is unquestionably the handsomest of our fresh-water species. **1949** *Life* 11 April 81 A painted turtle cranes its neck in the spring sun. — (8) **1855** *Harvard Mag.* I. 236 The Painted Trillium (*pictum*) is by far the most delicate of the species. **1943** PEATTIE *Great Smokies* 277 The dark-centered erect white trillium, and the painted trillium . . . are plentiful enough in their favored habitats.

b. Painted Desert, a region in north central Arizona along the Little Colorado River, famous for the colors of its rocks and sands.

1861 NEWBERRY *Geol. Rep.* 76 The peculiar physical aspect and geological structure of the Painted Desert prevail over a wide belt of country bordering the Little Colorado on the east. **1949** *Nat. Geog. Mag.* June 738/2 We were to know how similar to Arizona's Painted Desert were these round hillocks, splashed with paint.

c. Painted Rock, a rock formation exhibiting a variety of colors.

1825 KEATING *Exped. St. Peter's River* I. 274 The Painted Rock . . . seizes more powerfully upon the imagination of the trading voyager on our western streams, than the finest natural features of their splendid scenery. **1878** CONKLIN *Arizona* 201 Among the finest of these are the 'Painted Rocks.'

painter ˈpentɚ, *n.*

1. Variant of ∗*panther. Colloq.*

[**1764** REUTER *Wachau* 577 *Painter,* or *Panther,* has the color of a Deer.] **1802** DAVIS *Travels* (1803) 382 My master . . . said that I ought to live among *painters* and wolves, and sold me to a *Georgia* man for two hundred dollars. **1946** *Reader's Digest* March 136/1 When my mother insisted that I say 'panther' for 'painter,' . . . my feeling was that Mr. Howell knew better.

b. Attrib. with **blanket, kitten, meat, trap, yell.**

1840 HOFFMAN *Greyslaer* II. 255 By the everlasting hokey, if he hasn't got one foot in a painter trap. **1848** RUXTON in *Blackw. Mag.* LXIV. 140 'Painter meat can't "shine" with this,' says a hunter. **1850**

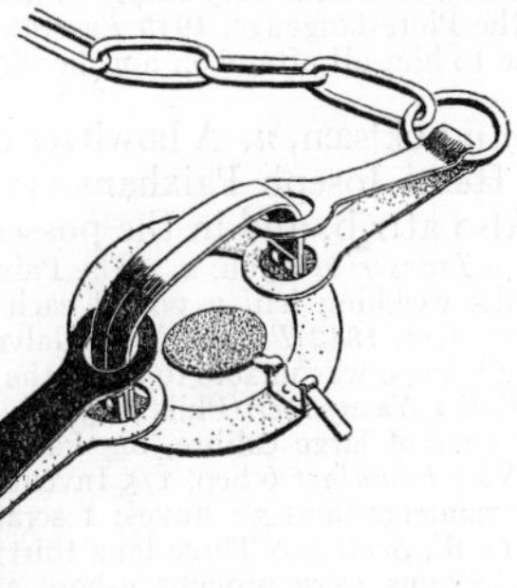

"Painter" trap or bear trap

LEWIS *La. Swamp Doctor* 170 Don't you want some bar-meat or painter blanket? *Ib.* 171 Please, Mr. Bar-Grave, cotch me a young bar or a painter kitten. **1867** HARRIS *Sut Lovingood* 54 Sum ove the wimmin fotch a painter yell.

2. In figurative expressions.

1845 KIRKLAND *Western Clearings* 124 When I saw she was coming to life, I ran like a painter. **1846** *Quarter Race Ky.* 85 Don't holler so! you are no worse nor a painter. **1849** *Knickerb.* XXXIII. 171 If you should see me now, you would grin like a 'painter.'

∗**painter's brush.** =∗**paintbrush.** Cf. **scarlet painter's brush.** — **1868** BOWLES *Colorado* (1869) 61 The painter's brush, as familiarly called here, is . . . something like the soldier's pompon in form, . . . in every shade of red from deepest crimson to pale pink, and again in straw colors from almost white to deep lemon. **1910** MRS. H. WARD *Canadian Born* x. 206 Anderson had brought her to a wild garden of incredible beauty. . . . Painter's brush, harebell, speedwell, golden-brown gaillardias.

∗**painting,** *n.* As the last term in **fire, sand painting.**

paisano paɪˈsɑno, *n. S.W.* [Sp. in sense **1**, Amer. Sp. in sense **2.**]

1. A fellow countryman, a rustic, peasant, or country fellow.

1844 KENDALL *Narr. Santa Fé Exped.* II. 230 [He] invariably called me his paisano, or country man. **1893** LUMMIS *Land of Poco Tiempo* 88

Every one was out, but they were no longer the friendly paisanos we had known. **1941** FERGUSSON *Southwest* 246 The Spanish clustered in towns. They fought Indians only when they had to, to assure safety and security. Security was what the paisano wanted.

2. (See quot. 1858.)

1844 GREGG *Commerce of Prairies* I. 195 There is to be found in Chihuahua and other southern districts a very beautiful bird called *paisano* (literally 'countryman'), which, when domesticated, performs all the offices of a cat in ridding the dwelling-houses of mice and other vermin. **1858** BAIRD *Birds Pacific R.R.* 73 [*Geococcyx*] is represented in the United States by a single species known as the Paisano, Chapparal [*sic*] Cock, or sometimes Road Runner, on account of its frequenting public highways. **1944** ADAMS *W. Words* 112 Paisano. . . . A road runner, a chaparral bird.

Paiute paɪˈjut, *n.* [Origin obscure. Poss. f. *pah* (water) and *Ute*, water Ute, or f. *pai* (true) and *Ute*, true Ute.] *pl.* or *collect.* (See quot. 1910.)

[**1776** in W. R. HARRIS *Catholic Church in Utah* (1909) 227 Because all those whom we met spoke the Yuta language, the same as do the Payutas farther west, we called all the people I have spoken of Yutas Cobardes (Coward Utes).] **1827** J. SMITH in Carew *Hist. Pasadena* (1930) I. 136 Passing down this river some distance, I fell in with a nation of Indians who call themselves Pah Utches. **1910** HODGE *Amer. Indians* II. 186/2 Paiute. A term involved in great confusion. In common usage it has been applied at one time or another to most of the Shoshonean tribes of w. Utah, N. Arizona, S. Idaho, E. Oregon, Nevada, and E. and S. California. **1947** B. HAILE *Prayer Stick Cutting* 43 Neckbands . . . should be of otter or beaver skin obtained from the . . . Paiutes.

attrib. **1845** FRÉMONT *Exped.* 260 They rarely carried home horses, on account of the difficulty . . . of guarding them afterward from the Pa-utah Indians, who inhabit the Sierra, at the head of the *Rio Virgen*, (river of the Virgin). **1938** LEFT HANDED *Son of Old Man Hat* 11 A Paiute girl came to our place. **1949** *Nat. Hist.* June 268/1 Major Powell . . . named it Tapeats Creek after a Paiute Indian in his employ.

b. The language of these Indians. Also **Paiute language, tongue.**

1853 BREWERTON *With Kit Carson* (1930) 84 This disturbance was finally quieted by Kit's replying in the Pau-Eutaw tongue. **1870** *Terr. Enterprise* (Virginia, Nev.) 22 March 3/1 The little Piute boys . . . play at marbles. It sounds very funny to hear their 'knuckle down,' uttered in the Piute language. **1915** *Everybody's Mag.* Oct. 461/2, I talked Piute to him all afternoon and he didn't understand a word of it.

Paixhan pɛkˈsæn, *n.* A howitzer cannon of a type devised by Henri Joseph Paixhans (1783–1854), a French general. Also attrib. and in the possessive. Now *hist.*

1832 *Boston Transcript* 2 Jan. 2/2 The Paixhan's cannon . . . sends 160 iron balls weighing half a pound each to a distance of from 3,000 to 4,000 feet. **1842** *Texas Times* (Galveston) 14 Dec. 3/2 The steamer Guadaloupe was unable to reach the shore with her Paixhan shot. **1846** *Dollar Newspaper* (Phila.) 15 July 2/2 She will also carry out twenty guns of large calibre, big Paixhans or Bomfords. **1861** *Richmond* (Va.) *Examiner* 6 Sep. 1/5 Inventory of munitions . . . 19 sponges, 17 rammers, and 32 staves; 1 scraper for 8-inch paixhan. **1937** ELLIOTT *W. Scott* 459 Three long thirty-twos and three eight-inch Paixhain guns were brought ashore and set up, with back-breaking labor.

* **palace,** *n.*

1. (*cap.*) = **Governor's mansion.** *Obs.*

1752 in G. O. SEILHAMER *Hist. Amer. Theatre* (1888) I. 42 The Emperor of the Cherokee nation with his Empress and their son . . . were received at the Palace by his Honour the Governor.

2. (*cap.*) The official residence of the President of the U.S. *Obs.*

1792 in *Columbia Hist. Soc. Rec.* XVI. (1913) 130 The President . . . with the Commissioners examined the several plans for the Capitol and the Palace. **1833** *Md. Hist. Mag.* XIII. 280 There are other lions in the city [Washington, D.C.]—especially the 'roaring Lion' up in the Palace as they call the President's House here.

b. Palace troops, the supporters of President Jefferson's administration. *Obs.*

1809 QUINCY in E. Quincy *Life J. Quincy* 174 The result [of the voting] was astonishing to Campbell and the leaders of the Palace troops.

c. Palace in the Wilderness, (see quot.). *Obs.*

1872 *Harper's Mag.* Dec. 42 The books . . . were assigned a room in the 'Palace in the Wilderness,' as the unfinished Capitol was then derisively styled by those who preferred New York or Philadelphia as the seat of government.

3. *S.W.* = **palacio**—prob. a translation of that word.

1803 PIKE *Sources Miss.* 212 The public square is in the centre of the town; on the north side of which is situated the *palace* (as the[y] term it) or government house, with the quarters for guards, &c. **1855** *Santa Fe Gazette* 8 Dec., The legislative Assembly of the Territory of New Mexico convened in the Palace, in Santa Fe, on Monday. **1885** *Wkly. New Mexican Rev.* 22 Jan. 4/6 The old palace, the only palace known as such in the land, was seared with age before Europeans ascended the Allegheny mountains. **1949** *Time* 5 Sep. 11/1 There in the warm nights around the Palace of the Governors, the city [of Santa Fe, N.M.] was holding its 237-year-old fiesta, to celebrate the reconquest of the Indians by the Spanish.

4. = **palace car.**

1877 HALE *G. T. T.* 220 A belated baggage agent came into the palace for orders. **1877** *Harper's Mag.* March 580/2 Up to the Yellow Springs platform came two unusual palaces, especially engaged.

5. Used attrib. to designate any one of various conveyances fitted out with superior accommodations, as (1) **palace car,** cf. **Pullman palace car,** (2) **coach,** (3) **day car,** (4) **drawing room,** (5) **sleeping car,** (6) **steamer,** (7) **stock car,** (8) **train.** Now *obs.* or *hist.*

(1) **1868** *Dispatch & Vanguard* (S.F.) 28 March 1/1, I enjoyed the equivocal luxury of traveling in a 'palace' or 'sleeping car.' **1947** BEEBE *Mixed Train Dly.* 136 During the 'nineties voyagers on the grand tour of Colorado filled to capacity the diminutive sleeping and Palace cars on the Rio Grande Southern for trips 'around the circle.' — (2) **1880** INGHAM *Digging Gold* 19 To cross the continent . . . is, with the aid of the palace-coach and sleeper, but the pleasure-trip of a week. **1943** HOWARD *Montana* 81 Fritz's admiring friends . . . boarded his 'palace coach' with its staterooms, library, bar, observation and dining cars, and kitchen. — (3) **1870** RAE *Westward by Rail* 50 This company build and run their own elegant sleeping coaches and palace day cars, and have no worn out rails to run over. — (4) **1881** MARSHALL *Through Amer.* (1882) 63 Such a car is not unfrequently termed a 'palace drawing-room *and* sleeping-car,' and not inappropriately, for the internal fittings, the gildings, and the paintings, are of the highest order in point of elegance and taste.

(5) **1867** HOSMER *Trip to States by Way Yellowstone & Mo.* 80 We got a good 'square meal' at this place, and took a palace sleeping-car. **1947** *Reader's Digest* July 120/2 The roomette is much better than the standard accommodations of George M. Pullman's Pioneer Palace Sleeping Car. — (6) **1844** *Knickerb.* XXIV. 192 Pleasant was the fishing-excursion . . . on board the matchless palace-steamer Knickerbocker. **1890** *Montreal W. Gaz.* 24 July 7/6 The palace steamer St. Lawrence collided with a Canadian steam yacht. — (7) **1874** MCCOY *Cattle* 423 [They] are now having constructed a large number of cars that are known as the 'Palace Stock Cars.' They are cars made longer than the usual stock cars now in use; and are so built that each animal is provided with a stall in which it can lay down. **1889** *Gleaner* (Gallup, N.M.) 11 March 1/3 A train of thirty palace stock cars passed through Trinidad on the Santa Fe on the afternoon of the 4th inst. Each car . . . is fitted up with ventilators, has twelve drinking troughs . . . rests on springs, and has air-brakes. — (8) **1874** B. F. TAYLOR *World on Wheels* 162 The wounded lay . . . packed away in the box-cars. But you heard less complaint than is made any day on a palace-train.

b. palace hotel, a hotel affording superior accommodations.

1884 *Cent. Mag.* March 643/1 It [Washington, D.C.] has no elevated railroads, no palace hotels, no mammoth elevators, no great commercial establishments. **1889** M. TWAIN *Conn. Yankee* xxxviii. 488 (R.), A Republican simplicity . . . has invented and exported to the Old World . . . the palace hotel, with its multifarious conveniences, comforts, shows, and luxuries.

As the last term in **dry-goods, eating, floating, gin, ice, Imperial, rum, silver palace.**

palacio pəˈlɑsɪo, *n. S.W.* [Sp., palace.] The official residence of a state governor. — **1844** GREGG *Commerce of Prairies* I. 203 These bricks are called *adobes*, and every edifice, from the church to the *palacio*, is constructed of the same stuff. **1885** *Wkly. New Mexican Rev.* 18 June 4/1 There he created a palacio.

palatial car. A palace car. *Rare.* — **1873** M. TWAIN & WARNER *Gilded Age* xxix. 267 (R.), As the down noon express was leaving H—— yesterday a lady . . . attempted to force herself into the already full palatial car.

* **Palatine,** *n.*

See A. Matthews, "The word palatine in America" in *Mass. Col. Soc. Pub.* VIII. (1902–4), 203–224.

1. The title of the senior proprietor of the Carolina colony; also the holder of this title. *Obs.*

1669 *Fundamental Const. Carolina* i, The eldest of the Lords Proprietors shall be Palatine; and upon the decease of the Palatine, the eldest of the seven surviving proprietors shall always succeed him. **1726** *S.C. Hist. Coll.* II. 144 (The Governor) represented the Palatine, and the others the rest of the Lords Proprietors. **1903** in *Mass. Col. Soc. Pub.* VIII. (1906) 209 In Carolina the term Palatine was for over half a century in use as the title of a person. Nowhere else in this country do we meet with that exact title.

2. In obs. combs.: (1) **Palatine fever,** (see quot.)—so called because of the large number of immigrants from the Palatinate; (2) **light,** a mysterious light occasionally seen during the nineteenth century off Block Island, R.I., thought by the superstitious to be connected with the loss by shipwreck or murder of the passengers of a Palatine vessel; (3) **-'s court,** a court made up of the palatine and proprietors of the Carolina colony, *obs.*

(1) **1901** O. KUHNS *German & Swiss Settlements* 71 Later in the [eighteenth] century when speculation had taken possession of ocean transportation, sickness was so unfailing a concomitant of the journey that ship-fever was generally known in Philadelphia as 'Palatine fever.' — (2) **1811** in *Mass. Col. Soc. Pub.* VIII. 218 (*title*), Meteoric Appearance Called the Palatine Light. **1903** *Ib.* 224 These stories of the Palatine Light . . . are of course curious rather than important. — (3) **1669** *Fundamental Const. Carolina* xxviii, Ye Palatine's court, consisting of the palatine and the other seven proprietors. **1694** *N.C. Col. Rec.* I. 401 Ordered that . . . ye other [be] reteined to longr Time or be delivered by the Palatines Court.

***palaver,** *n.* The terminology associated with a particular trade or profession, jargon. *Rare.* — **1909** M. TWAIN *Is Shakspeare Dead?* vii. 74 (R.), I have been a quartz miner . . . and know all the palaver of that business.

***pale,** *a.* In special combs.: (1) **pale disease,** a disease affecting sheep, *obs.;* (2) ***face,** see as a main entry; (3) **laurel,** (see quot.); (4) **-leaf hickory,** (see quot.); (5) **sucker,** (see quot.).

(1) **1870** *Rep. Comm. Agric. 1869* 42 In Ohio several reports of death from 'pale disease' are received. — (3) **a1862** THOREAU *Maine Woods* 311 Shrubs and small trees in swamps: . . . *Kalmia glauca* (pale laurel), . . . *Prunus Pennsylvanica* [etc]. — (4) **1901** MOHR *Plant Life Ala.* 91 Pignut hickory and pale-leaf hickory (*Hicoria villosa*), a tree of medium size, lately distinguished.

(5) **1842** *Nat. Hist. N.Y., Zoology* IV. 200 The Pale Sucker, *Catostomus pallidus,* . . . is a common species, and is taken about the beginning of April.

***paleface,** *n.*

1. A white man as distinguished from an Indian. A term usu. employed by Indians or in imitation of them.

1823 MCCALL *Lett. from Frontiers* (1868) 72 An Indian chief . . . thus accosted him,—'Ah, *Paleface!* what brings you here? you seem to take pleasure in saying rude impertinencies.' **1868** WHYMPER *Alaska* 36 It is very rare to find those who are the better for intercourse with the 'pale faces.' **1948** *Chi. D. News* 18 March 20/7 Income tax is a devilish invention of the paleface, brothers.

attrib. **1841** COOPER *Deerslayer* xi, 'This is the paleface law,' resumed the chief. **1850** GLISAN *Jrnl. Army Life* 18 The right and wrong of these cruel encounters will . . . [rest at] one time with the red man—at another with his pale-face brother. **a1861** WINTHROP *Canoe & Saddle* 240 He had even condescended to take lessons in cookery from the pale-face squaws of the Willamette. **1899** CUSHMAN *Hist. Indians* 464 The young warrior resolved in the coming future to make the pale-face maiden his wife. **1949** *Sat. Ev. Post* 2 July 29/1 Those [Indians] who had been exposed to college did sleep in the cabins on paleface beds.

Hence ***pale-faced,** *a.*, white, white-skinned.

1832 DURFEE *Works* (1849) 68 Confounding pale-face friends with warring foes. **1881** *Rep. Indian Affairs* 113 They compare favorably with their pale-faced brothers. **1902** *Atlantic Mo.* Dec. 803/2 The pale-faced missionary and the hoodooed aborigine are both God's creatures.

2. Whisky. *Slang. Obs.* Cf. ***bald face 2.**

1846 *Spirit of Times* (N.Y.) 11 July 234/3 Provided well with bread, meat, and a bottle of pale-face, which were stowed away in a pair of leather saddle bags.

3. (*cap.*) (See quots.)

1868 *Nashville* (Tenn.) *Union & Dispatch* 8 March, Another mysterious order, it would seem, has been organized in this city—the Pale Faces. **1872** *42d Cong. H. Rep.* 2 Sess. Rep. 22, I. 6 Some called them Pale Faces, some called them Ku-Klux. I believe they went under two names. **1939** HORN *Invisible Empire* 348 By December, 1869, the Pale Faces had grown so strong that they had a paper of their own in Nashville known as 'The Pale Face.'

***palisades,** *n. pl.* (Orig. *cap.*) A line of bold precipitous cliffs along the western bank of the Hudson River north of Fort Lee, N.J. Also a similar formation elsewhere.

1827 BEAUFOY *Tour* 41 The curious natural barrier called the 'Palisades,' . . . forms its western bank for seven or eight leagues. **1907** WHITE *Arizona Nights* 20 The cliffs and palisades near at hand showed dimly behind the falling rain. **1948** *Chi. Tribune* 20 June VII. 13/5 Often it slides along the base of steep cliffs which will remind you of the Hudson's palisades.

***palisadoes,** *n. pl.* =prec. *Obs.* — **1821** STANSBURY *Pedestrian Tour* (1822) 18 Elevated eight hundred and fifty-two feet above the surface of the Hudson, we trace the winding of that spacious river, from the Pallisadoes, to the middle of the Highlands, through which it passes. **1840** *Penny Cyclo.* XVI. 179/2 From Tappan to a distance of about 8 miles from the town of New York, the Palisadoes, as they are called, extend along the river.

***pallbearer,** *n.* At a funeral, one of those who carry the coffin.

The precise function of the pallbearers in the first quots. is not clear.

1727 COMER *Diary* (1893) 32 [She] exchanged this world for a better . . . , and I was chosen a pall bearer. **1828** MCCABE *New York* 232 The best of kid gloves must be furnished to the pall bearers. **1949** *Lubbock* (Tex.) *Morn. Avalanche* 23 Feb. II. 4/7 He said he got all his exercise by being pallbearer for his friends who did exercise.

***palm,** *n.*

1. The hemlock. *Obs.*

1625 MORRELL *N. Eng.* 15 All ore that Maine the Vernant trees abound. . . . The Hasel, Palme, and hundred more are there. **1791** LONG *Voyages* 44 [Near Lake Superior] the palm, birch, ash, spruce, and cedar grow large.

b. =**Joshua palm.**

1879 WILLIAMS *Pacific Tourist* 289/1 It is palm-like, and often called a 'palm' and 'cactus,' but *it is neither.*

2. In combs.: (1) **Palm Beach,** [f. *Palm Beach,* Fla.], a light fabric of cotton and wool or mohair bearing the trade-mark name *Palm Beach,* also attrib.; (2) **garden,** a place decorated with potted palms where meals and other refreshments are served; (3) **grill,** =prec.; (4) **leaf,** see as a main entry; (5) **warbler,** the American warbler, *Dendroica palmarum,* or the subspecies, *D. p. hypochrysea.*

(1) **1922** H. L. FOSTER *Adv. Trop. Tramp* 1, I had just applied for a job as stoker, but a Palm Beach suit, a Panama hat, and a cane did not seem to be convincing costume on the figure of an applicant for the position. **1949** *N.O. Times-Picayune Mag.* 3 April 11 Slacks for champions tailored of Palm Beach get the votes of golf's greats. — (2) **1900** GEORGE ADE *More Fables in Slang* 164 They dined at a Palm-Garden that had Padding under the Table-Cloth and a Hungarian Orchestra in the Corner. — (3) **1920** WILSON *Red Gap* 377 At this he looks around at the crowded tables in this palm grill.

(5) **1828** BONAPARTE *Ornithology* II. 12 The Palm Warbler, *Sylvia Palmarum,* . . . is found during winter in Florida . . . and in other parts of the territory wherever the orange-tree is cultivated. **1949** *Chi. Tribune* 14 Sep. 1/4 Bird students have identified more than a dozen varieties there this fall, including the rare golden winged, the black and white, the myrtle, magnolia, redstart, palm, black throated green, Tennessee, and water thrush.

As the last term in **fan-leaf, heart-of-, royal, Washington, yucca palm.**

palma 'palmə, *n. S.W.* [Sp. in same sense.] Any one of various American palms, or a plant or tree resembling this.

1838 TEXIAN *Mexico v. Texas* 64 At the foot of a large palma . . . the stranger assisted by the villagers began to dig. **1872** POWERS *Afoot & Alone* 138 It is only the palmas, in their grimly sleepless vigils . . . [on] the Staked Plain. **1919** C. G RAHT *Romance of Davis Mountains* 287 Palma. An aloe . . . well known in the Southwest as the 'Spanish Dagger.'

***palmetto,** *n.*

1. The palmetto as a state or party emblem or badge in South Carolina. Cf. **3. b.** below.

[**1778** in *N. & Q.* 3 Ser. VIII. (1865) 279 The device for the Great Seal of South Carolina:—A palmetto tree, supported by twelve spears . . . and at the foot of the palmetto an English oak fallen.] **1833** *Polit. Examiner* (Shelbyville, Ky.) 4 May 1/2 Taking the flag from the hands of the aid, he shook open the folds, and displayed the arms of the state, and Carolina's palmetto, and large gold letters engraved upon it—'*Liberty, it must be preserved.*' **1847** *Whig Almanac 1848* 23/1 Lieut. Col. Dickinson . . . was bearing the Palmetto proudly amid the storm.

b. (*cap.*) A South Carolinian.

1860 *Charleston* (S.C.) *Mercury* 13 Dec. 3/2 [Salutation:] Brother Palmettos.

2. Short for palmetto fan or palmetto hat *qq.v.*

1852 STOWE *Uncle Tom* xxx, Mr. Skeggs, with his palmetto on, . . . walks around to put farewell touches on his wares. **1944** CLARK *Pills* 219 Bearing little kinship to the wide-brimmed planter's hats and derbies were the cheap palmettos. **1949** *Sky Line Trail* March 18/1 Toleration, bring yourself to attention and apply that palmetto!

3. In combs.: (1) **palmetto brush,** a coarse scrubbing brush made from the fibrous roots of the scrub palmetto; (2) **bush,** a young or dwarfed plant of some species of southern palmetto; (3) **cabbage,** =**cabbage palmetto;** (4) **country,** the region in the southeastern part of the U.S. where palmetto prevails; (5) **fan,** =**palm leaf fan;** (6) **fly flap,** a device made of palmetto branches for driving away flies; (7) **ground,** ground where palmetto is the prevailing growth; (8) **hat,** =**palm-leaf hat;** (9) **juice,** a liquid obtained from the esculent portions of the palmetto; (10) ***royal,** the Spanish dagger, *Yucca gloriosa;* (11) **scrub,** the saw palmetto, *Serenoa serrulata;* (12) **swamp,** a swamp in which palmetto is the prevailing growth.

(1) **1913** *Country Life* Nov. 94/3 For the making of palmetto brushes the problem is to remove the pith without destroying the fibres. — (2) **1784** HUTCHINS *Hist. Narrative La. & W. Fla.* 34 The whole is . . . covered with thick wood, Palmetto bushes, &c. **1812** *Niles' Reg.* III. 237/1 Many more must have been slain, but were hid from our view by the thick and high Palmetto bushes. **1901** *Scribner's Mag.* April 433/1 Narrow grooves have been worn in the hillsides, divided one from the other by . . . pyramids of earth and clay, crested with the stunted stems and roots of palmetto bushes. — (3) **1802** DRAYTON *S. Carolina* 6 Their soil is of very sandy nature; producing . . . palmetto cabbage, palmetto royal, silk grass. — (4) **1942** KENNEDY *Palmetto Country* 24 The Palmetto Country rests upon what is geologically known as the Floridian Plateau, which compared to the rest of the continent, is a mere infant of some forty-five million years.

(5) **1865** *Nation* I. 240 A negro man-servant waited at the table, over which presided the landlady, with a palmetto fan in her hand. **1948** *Time* 5 July 34/3 It was the delegates who gave the convention most of its strawberry festival flavor—a homy mixture of galluses, shirtsleeves, palmetto fans, odd hats and lax faces. — (6) **1830** *Pensacola* (Fla.) *Gaz.* 14 Aug. 2/1 My informant on landing was met by the Light House man, who was keeping up an incessant motion with a palmetto fly flap in each hand—'mosquitoes appear to be bad, sir'—said he. — (7) **1744** MOORE *Voy. Georgia* 124 The Indians were prevailed upon to return to the Palmetto ground. — (8) **1747** *N.J. Archives* XII. 364 The woman . . . [wore] blue worsted stockings, palmeta hat, scarlet red cloak [etc.]. **1889** *Cent. Mag.* Feb. 516/2 Before the end of the month all the women in St. Martinville were wearing palmetto hats. — (9) **1845** GREEN *Texian Exped.* 152 Several were left on the road exhausted for the want of water and here they commenced unfortunately, the use of the palmetto juice as a substitute.

(10) **1741** *S.C. Hist. Soc.* IV. 43 This Fort . . . [had] a Ditch without on all sides, Lined round with Prickly Palmetto Royal. **1786** WASHINGTON *Diaries* III. 34 Sowed . . . all the seed I had of the palmetto royal. **1813** MUHLENBERG *Cat. Plants* 35 *Yucca gloriosa*. Broad-leaved (palmetto royal) Car. — (11) **1880** *Scribner's Mo.* July 423/2 The palmetto scrub rustled, the shambling feet shuffled away. **1905** N. DAVIS *Northerner* 292 Before him was a stretch of dazzling sand, the feathery green of palmetto scrub and the blue waters seen through a burning mist. — (12) **1853** P. PAXTON *Yankee in Texas* 56 The '*marais*' or slough, . . . according to my friend Joe's account, changed into a 'branch:' then after running through a cypress brake or two, ultimately assumed the form of a palmetto swamp.

b. In expressions, now chiefly obs., alluding to the palmetto as the emblem of South Carolina, and sometimes with esp. reference to the nullification episode in that state's history, as (1) **palmetto banner,** (2) **button,** (3) **Chivalry,** (4) **City,** (5) **cockade,** (6) **flag,** (7) **Guard,** (8) **man,** (9) **people,** (10) **republic,** (11) **speech,** (12) **State,** (13) ***tree.**

(1) **1850** in CLAIBORNE *Life Quitman* II. 38 May I hope that Mississippi will . . . allow the Palmetto banner the privilege of a place in her ranks. — (2) **1833** *Md. Hist. Mag.* XIII. 356, I saw the Nullification badge very frequently in S.C. that is the blue cockade and the small palmetto batton [*sic*]. **1846** MANSFIELD *Winfield Scott* 24 The palmetto cockade and the palmetto buttons distinguished the *nullifiers* from the *Unionists*. — (3) **1857** *Herald of Freedom* (Lawrence, Kans.) 24 Jan. 1/8 Occasionally, some nomad secessionist may have illumined its columns, in not inelegant phrase, concerning the gentility and mettle of the renowned Palmetto Chivalry. — (4) **1857** *Harper's Mag.* June 1/1 Our artist has possessed himself of the Palmetto City—Charleston, South Carolina. **1860** *Charleston* (S.C.) *Mercury* 15 Dec. 3/5 We arrived in the Palmetto City without anything occurring to mar the pleasure of . . . the most delightful trip.

(5) **1846** MANSFIELD *Winfield Scott* 248 Sullivan's Island . . . was daily visited by respectable citizens, . . . most of whom wore the palmetto cockade. — (6) **1860** *Charleston* (S.C.) *Mercury* 15 Nov. 2/4 The Minute Men of Norfolk, Va., have written to this city for the pattern of the Palmetto flag. **1894** *Harper's Mag.* May 946/2 The streets [of Charleston, S.C.] bloomed with palmetto flags, and with a great variety of mottoes. — (7) **1854** MRS. C. A. MOWATT *Autobiog. Actress* 248, I was solicited to deliver an address to the Charleston Volunteers, in commemoration of their departure for Mexico. I think they were styled the Palmetto Guard. — (8) **1861** *Vanity Fair* April 201/1 The bold Palmetto men, Sumter stormed. — (9) **1861** *Dly. Dispatch* (Richmond, Va.) 30 April 2/3 The gallant Palmetto people . . . have come to aid Virginia in the defence of her soil.

(10) **1860** *Charleston* (S.C.) *Mercury* 25 Dec. 4/5 A salute of one hundred guns was immediately fired in honor of the Palmetto Republic. — (11) **1840** *Niles' Reg.* 4 April 77/2 Mr. Everett said he had yielded the floor to explanation, not for a palmetto speech. — (12) **1843** *Knickerb.* XXI. 222 The merry days of good old Christmas are still observed in the Palmetto State. **1948** *Sat. Ev. Post* 10 July 12/3 Although Palmetto State folks may have hesitated to brag the first year, they're safe now. — (13) [**1778** in *N. & Q.* 3 Ser. VIII. (1865) 279 The device for the Great Seal of South Carolina:—A palmetto tree, supported by twelve spears . . . and at the foot of the palmetto an English oak fallen.] **1865** G. HAMILTON *Skirmishes* 172 If he is concocting . . . rebellion, can he not go on just as blithely under the Stars and Stripes as under the Palmetto-tree?

c. In expressions indicative of the use of palmetto in building, as (1) **palmetto cabin,** (2) **house,** (3) **hut,** (4) **shanty,** (5) **thatched.**

(1) **1820** *Amer. Naturalist* III. 458 With a palmetto cabin, plenty of oysters, game and fish, he lives a free and easy life. — (2) **1741** *S.C. Hist. Soc.* IV. 42 [The army] came to Some Palmetto Houses, where they Halted about one Hour. — (3) [*c*1730 CATESBY *Carolina* I. 69 A man . . . builds a hut with Palmetto-Leaves, for the shelter of himself and family while they stay.] **1739** W. STEPHENS *Proc. Georgia* I. 480, I found them well covered from bad Weather by a strong Palmetto Hut. **1880** G. W. CABLE *Grandissimes* iv. 22 Among the squaws . . . was one who had in her own palmetto hut an empty cradle, scarcely cold. — (4) **1947** *Chi. Tribune* 21 Dec. (Grafic Mag.) 12/2 He and Hilda prefer to live in his palmetto shanty during the trapping season.

(5) **1888** CABLE *Bonaventure* 86 On a bank of this bayou . . . [stood] the palmetto-thatched fishing and hunting lodge. **1895** G. KING *New Orleans* 34 There is absolutely no seeing of Bienville's group of palmetto thatched huts by the yellow currents of the Mississippi.

As the last term in **bayonet, blue, cabbage, great, needle, saw, silktop, silver, silvertop, sword palmetto.**

palmilla pɑlˈmijə, *n. S.W.* [Sp. in Amer. Sp. sense shown here.] Any one of various plants, esp. an agave, whose bulbs or roots are used for soap. Cf. **amole.**

1844 GREGG *Commerce of Prairies* I. 160 Among the wild productions of New Mexico is the *palmilla*—a species of palmetto . . . , whose roots . . . , when bruised, form a saponaceous pulp called *amole*, much used by the natives for washing clothes. **1851** M. REID *Scalp Hunters* 125, I could only see the long bayonets of the picturesque *palmillas*. **1937** NICHOL *Natural Vegetation Ariz.* 199 Scattered over the mesa land and sometimes approaching the density of a forest the picturesque palmillo (*Yucca elata*) occurs with occasional cholla . . . and bisnaga.

***palm leaf.**

1. A summer hat made of the leaves of the fan palm or saw palmetto. In full **palm-leaf hat.**

1820 *Boston D. Advt.* 18 May 2/6 (Ernst). **1835** H. C. TODD *Notes* 59 The best beaver hats, and in large quantities, are made at Reading, Massachusetts, wherein, and New England generally, two million Palm leaf hats are manufactured. **1927** BENÉT *J. B.'s Body* 317 He . . . can whip five Yanks with a palmleaf hat.

2. A fan made of a leaf of the fan palm. In full **palm-leaf fan.**

1832 *Boston Transcript* 18 June 3/1 Palm Leaf Fans. One case just received and for sale very low. **1852** *Knickerb.* XXXIX. 153 Fans, of all sorts and sizes, were in constant use, from nine-penny palm-leafs to two-shilling paper-spreads. **1912** NICHOLSON *Hoosier Chron.* 163 He fanned himself in a desultory fashion with a palm leaf. **1948** *Sat. Ev. Post* 10 July 71/2 He puttered about in baggy trousers, white vest and ruffled alpaca coat, waving his palm-leaf fan.

Palo Alto hat. (See quot. 1935.)

1849 HOLMES *Nux Post coenatica* iii. 10 He wore a Palo Alto hat. **1850** HAWTHORNE *Note-books* II. 163 Glazed caps and Palo Alto hats were much worn. **1856** *Harper's Mag.* Oct. 594/1 The sub-Indian agent . . . was a man . . . with black curling hair, reaching, beneath a slouched Palo Alto hat, down to his shoulders. **1935** BUCKBEE *Saga of Old Tuolumne* 121 Piled on the sidewalk were rubber boots known as 'Wellingtons,' slickers, elk-skin leggings and hats called 'Palo Alto' —broad-brimmed affairs, distinct style evolved, of course, for the gold-rush trade. In after years, an old miner, glancing at one of John B. Stetson's world-famous 'Boss-of-the-Plains' hats, remarked that it was mighty like his own rusty 'paly-altie lid.'

palo amarillo. *S.W.* [Sp. in Amer. Sp. senses shown here.] (See quots.)

1846 ABERT *Exam. N. Mex.* 77 We saw . . . also, a 'mahonia,' the leaves of which are very much like the holly; this the Mexicans call 'palomereo.' **1931** DAYTON *Western Browse Plants* 36 Hollygrape is commonly known by a number of other names, such as Oregon grape, hollyleaf barberry, mahonia, and palo amarillo. *Ib.* 55 Chamiso . . . has reddish bark on the older stems and yellowish green on the younger twigs. . . . Mexicans sometimes call it palo amarillo.

palo blanco. *S.W.* [Amer. Sp. in same sense.] A western hackberry, *Celtis reticulata*, the bark of which is of a light color. — **1901** VAN DYKE *Desert* 147 All the common growths like the sage, the mesquite, the palo fierro, and the palo blanco, are blossom bearers. **1938** CALKINS *Native & Exotic Plants* 52 Palo Blanco or White Bark Hackberry . . . furnishes shade along many of the dry washes.

palodura ˌpɑloˈdurə, *n. S.W.* [Amer. Sp. *palo duro*, in same sense.] =prec. — **1907** COOK *Border & Buffalo* (1938) 91 There was a thicket of stunted hackberry and palodura, hard poles of chinawood, close to where the old campfire had been.

palo fierro or **hierro.** (See quot. 1931.)

1894 *Amer. Anthrop.* July 293 During the rest of the year the Indians draw there, . . . gathering the fruit of the catclaw, mesquite beans, and the bean of the *palo fiero.* **1931** DAYTON *Western Browse Plants* 86 Tesota (Olneya tesota) is variously known as arbol (or palo) de hierro, and desert (Mexican, or Sonora) ironwood. **1949** *Desert Mag.* June 22/2 The great washes along the highway were crowded with palo verde trees and ironwood, or *palo fierro.*

attrib. **1912** LUMHOLTZ *New Trails* 224 All the mules, donkeys, and horses gathered at once around a lone but very large palo fiero tree to eat its dark green juicy leaves.

palomilla ˌpɑloˈmijə, *n. S.W.* [Sp. in same sense.] (See quots.)— **1941** FERGUSSON *Southwest* 326 Queen Isabella sent to Mexico, palomillos; or pintos, which later Texans called 'paint horses.' **1944** ADAMS *W. Words* 111 Palomilla. . . . A milk-white or cream colored horse with a white mane and tail.

palomino ˌpæloˈmino, *n.* [Sp. in unrecorded Amer. Sp. sense shown here. Cf. prec.] (See quot. 1932.) Also attrib.

1914 *Sunset* May 995/1 A Palomino stallion with arching neck and muscle-ridged barrel led the dozen brown and mottled mares of his seraglio up a silent hillside. **1932** BENTLEY *Sp. Terms* 176 Palomino. . . . A term commonly used in the Southwest and California to describe a horse of a silver yellow color. Such a horse often is given no other name but is known as the *palomino. Palominos* are favorites with Western riders and are supposed to be intelligent and enduring. **1939** ROLLINS *Gone Haywire* 128 He pointed to a small *palomina* (cream-colored) horse which was tethered in the foreground. **1949** *Esquire* March 29/1 They'll reserve a golden palomino horse for you—all yours for the length of your stay.

palooka pəˈlukə, *n.* [Origin unknown. See quot. 1948.] An inferior prizefighter, a ham, a boob, a lout. *Slang.*

1925 WITWER *Roughly Speaking* 287 Ben will make 'at palooka's pan over for you in any style you wish, Reverend Jephtha. **1933** *Amer. Sp.* Oct. 37/2 He still looks plenty good enough to take the English palooka. **1948** MENCKEN *Supp.* II. 768 Palooka. . . . Probably borrowed from the race-track, where it signifies a sorry nag. It may be related to the synonymous *palouser*, which may be derived from the name of the *Palouse* Indians of the Northwest. Holt . . . suggests that it may come from the Spanish *peluca*, a term of reproof.

Palouse pəˈlus, *n.* Also **Paloose, Paloas, Pelouse,** etc. [See note.] *pl.* and *collect.* (See quot. 1910.) Also **Palouse Indians.**

"For a grassy expanse the French have the word *pelouse;* and, a century ago, when French-Canadian voyageurs of the fur companies beheld in springtime the wild tumult of bunchgrass hills north of Snake River, they called it the *Pelouse* country—the grass lands." (Meany, *Origin Wash. Geog. Names* (1923) 207).

1838 PARKER *Exploring Tour* 283 Here we found a village of Paloose Indians who are a band of the Nez Percés. **1849** in *31st Cong.* 1 Sess. Sen. Ex. Doc. 52 (1850) 171 The *Paloas* Indians inhabit a section of country north of the Cayuse tribe, and number about 300. **1855** *N.Y. Wkly. Tribune* 2 June 1/2 The Yakimas, Clikitats, . . . and the Palouse . . . will be assembled at the same time and place. **1912** MANRING *Conquest of Couer d'Alenes* 81 A considerable number of Palouses had gathered in the vicinity of Red Wolf's crossing.

b. Palouse horse, (see quot. and cf. **appaloosa**).

1947 DEVOTO *Across Wide Missouri* 77 The Nez Perces had learned selective breeding . . . and had developed a distinctive stock called the Pelouse horse, the 'Appaloosa' of a later date.

palouser pəˈluzɚ, *n.* [f. *Palouse* region.] (See quots.) *Colloq.*

1918 *D.N.* V. 27 *palouser.* . . . A lantern made by attaching a bale, horizontally, to an empty can and by inserting a candle through a hole in the side. [Northwest.] **1923** *Outing* March 257/3, I found a bright new lard pail left by some former camper, and made a palouse (pronounced paloose), an Indian invention of inestimable value in camp. **1948** MENCKEN *Supp.* II. 233 [In Washington] *palouser* [signifies] a greenhorn, a home-made lantern, or a sunset.

palo verde. *S.W.* [Amer. Sp. in same sense.] A leguminous plant of the genus *Cercidium*, or of the closely related genus *Parkinsonia.* Cf. **lluvia de oro, retama.**

1854 BARTLETT *Personal Narr.* II. 188 The vegetation consisted of mezquit and palo verde. **1912** *Out West* May 300 A small squad had been sent in search of 'Indian signs,' right in among the clumps of palo verde and mesquite. **1947** *So. Sierran* May 4/2 The flaming red of the Ocotillo and the bright lemon yellow of the Palo Verde were outstanding.

attrib. **1860** *Proc. Calif. Acad. Sci.* II. (1863) 129 In the eastern part of the *Papagoria*, the country is . . . covered with a low growth of *mesquite* and *palo verde* brush.

palpitating bosom. =**patent heaver.** *Obs.* — **1876** in GUILD *Old Times* (1878) 385 If I do not entertain the ladies about gypsies, mice, rats, redingotes, polonaise, pinbacks, false calves, and palpitating bosoms, they will be dissatisfied.

palpitator ˈpælpəˌtetɚ, *n.* =prec. *Obs.* — **1868** POMEROY *Nonsense* (1870) 36 (We.), I had her curls, her frizzle, her rats, her waterfall! I had her spiral palpitators, her bird's-nest, her veils. **1891** S. M. WELCH *Recoll. 1830–40* 116 They did not shew those forced good forms which the tailor dressed American girl now exhibits; no pads, no stays, no palpitators, no bustles, no French heels.

palto ˈpɑlto, *n. S.W.* [Amer. Sp. *paltó*, in same sense.] An overcoat. *Rare.* — **1848** E. BRYANT *California* xvi. 213 He pointed with much meaning and earnestness to my coarse palto, as being an excellent protection against the chills of the morning.

Pamunkey pəˈmʌŋkɪ, *n.* [f. a native expression meaning "sloping hill," "rising upland."] Indians making up the leading tribe of the Powhatan confederacy of Virginian Algonquian tribes, now on a reservation in a bend of the Pamunkey River in King William County, Va. Also an Indian of this tribe. In full **Pamunkey Indian.**

[*c***1612** STRACHEY *Hist. Travel Va.* (1849) 62 Upon Panunky or the Prince's River. **1624** SMITH *Gen. Hist. Va.* (1907) 164 Within two or three dayes we arrived at Pamaunkee.] **1624** JONES *Virginia* 5 A *Pomunkee* . . . is as fierce and frightful as any *Amorite.* **1894** POLLARD *Pamunkey Indians of Va.* 10 This tract was secured to the Pamunkey Indians by the colonial assembly, and they are restrained from alienating the same. *Ib.*, No one who visits the Pamunkey could fail to notice their race pride. **1910** HODGE *Amer. Indians* II. 198/2 In 1722, when the Pamunkey last appear in a public treaty, they were said to number only about 200. . . . They live chiefly by fishing, with some small farming, and have entirely lost their language and original characteristics.

* **pan,** *n.*

1. = * **fire pan.** *Obs.*

1845 W. T. THOMPSON *Chron. Pineville* 162 His pan [was] upon one shoulder and his musket on the other.

2. In placer mining, a shallow circular metal vessel used in washing gold from gravel, etc.; also the contents of such a pan, a panful.

1849 *Alta California* (S.F.) 20 June 2/3 Scores of dispirited looking objects are wandering up and down the Arroyo to-day, with their pans and picks upon their shoulders. **1897** LEONARD *Gold Fields Klondike* 28 It may be well to state that a 'pan' of dirt is two miners' shovels, and that in ordinary placer mining a claim is considered quite good when it yields from ten to fifteen cents to the pan. **1947** PERRY *Cities of Amer.* 167 One man had washed eight hundred dollars' worth out of a single pan of gravel.

3. The broad posterior part of a whale's lower jawbone.

1883 *Nat. Museum Bul.* No. 27, 293 These cases contain the 'pans' (posterior portions of the jaw-bone of the sperm-whale). **1887** GOODE *Fisheries* V. 232 (*footnote*), Canes made full length from the ivory of the 'pan' of the sperm whale.

4. In combs.: (1) * **pancake,** (*a*) a tortilla, *rare*, cf. **buckwheat pancake, clam pancake,** (*b*) a cap or hat shaped like a pancake, also **pancake hat,** *obs.;* (2) **cake cactus,** (see quot.); (3) **dowdy,** see as a main entry; (4) **fish,** a fish of such size and quality as to be suitable for frying in a pan, also attrib., cf. Du. *pan(ne) visch;* (5) **fisherman,** a fisherman who catches panfish, also **panfishing;** (6) * **handle, handler,** see as main entries; (7) **jerker,** (see quot.), *slang, obs.;* (8) **pie,** =**pandowdy.**

(1) (*a*) **1872** POWERS *Afoot & Alone* 201 Mexicans . . . [live] on pancakes, beans and red pepper. (*b*) **1875** NADAL *Impressions of London Social Life* 143 The cap [pictured in McGuffey's Second Reader] was peculiar, though about the year '56 we had something like it called

the 'Pancake.' **1931** *K.C. Times* 17 Sep., Women are going wild over the pancake hat. — (2) **1940** JAEGER *Calif. Deserts* 179 The remarkable pancake cactus (*O. chlorotica*) has great, flat, orbicular joints 'like pancakes' (3 to 8 inches in diameter), light green in color. — (4) **1805** ORDWAY in *Jrnls. Lewis & O.* 272 [We] made a fish drag of willows and caught 520 fine pan fish. **1856** *Spirit of Times* 20 Sep. 43/2 Sucker landed three dogfish, one old black gar, [and] seven panfish. **1949** *St. Paul Pioneer Press* 19 June 1/8 This year Otto's acres are jam-packed with the pan fish bait.

(5) **1934** *Nat. Geog. Mag.* LXV. 604 Persons who love simple panfishing, with an old-fashioned reed pole, find here their heart's content. **1947** DALRYMPLE *Panfish* 33 We might note here that the White Perch, fished in his restricted ranges by numerous Panfishermen, is really not a Perch at all, except in common name. — (7) **1878** PINKERTON *Strikers* 55 The 'pan-jerkers'—All that large class of loafers who subsist by rendering some slight service about restaurants. — (8) **1805** *Pocumtuc Housewife* (1906) 25. **1862** G. HAMILTON *Country Living* 70 No pan-pie with hot brown bread on Sunday morning. **1882** *Maine Bd. Agric. Rep.* XXVI. 403 You have all heard of the pan-dowdy, or pan-pie, the pride of our grandmothers.

b. In terms relating to mining in the West: (1) **pan amalgamation,** separating gold and silver from ore by a process which involves grinding in a panlike iron vessel; (2) **amalgamator,** an apparatus used in pan amalgamation; (3) **charge,** the contents of a pan amalgamator; (4) **mill,** a pan amalgamator; (5) **miner,** one who mines gold with a miner's pan or rocker; (6) **tailings,** *pl.* the refuse material resulting from panning auriferous soil; (7) **test,** a test made with a pan to determine the amount of gold ore in soil; (8) **washing,** the washing of auriferous soil in a gold pan, also an instance of such a washing; (9) **working,** =**pan washing.**

(1) **1871** RAYMOND *3d Rep. Mines* 392 The Washoe Pan Amalgamation. — (2) **1871** RAYMOND *3d Rep. Mines* 429 The first building contains . . . Dodge's pan-amalgamator and settler. — (3) **1882** *47th Congress* 1 Sess. H.R. Ex. Doc. No. 216, 651 The pan-charge is drawn into the settlers and thinned down. — (4) **1888** *Chi. Inter-Ocean* 8 March, On their way to inspect the California pan mill.

(5) **1880** INGHAM *Digging Gold* 69 The gold [was] too evenly distributed through them to pay the ordinary pan miner to wash it.— (6) **1896** SHINN *Story of Mine* 88 The term 'tailings' as here used includes all the ore residues, or waste, whether slimes, pan tailings, or concentrates. — (7) **1901** WHITE *Westerners* 208 He showed them . . . hanging walls, country rock, pan tests. — (8) **1874** RAYMOND *6th Rep. Mines* 21 These tailings . . . will yield, under pan-washing, a fair prospect, and very often a notable quantity of gold. **1889** Union Pac. R.R. *Ore. & Wash.* 66 Pan washings in small gulches, and primitive arastras . . . merely discover—they do not develop [resources]. — (9) **1876** DODGE *Black Hills* 109 No man can make more than the barest wages by pan-working a single claim in the Black Hills.

As the last term in **bascule, bed, dead, dish, fire, fry, gold, hard, mush, prospecting, rifle, samp, sap, sauce, see-saw, shut, silky, tilt, tin, torch, wash, Wheeler pan.**

* **pan,** *v.*

1. *intr.* Of gravel or soil: To produce gold. Hence, *fig.*, to pay.

1848 DANA *Mineralogy* 317 Gravel or soil . . . is said to *pan well* or *pan poorly* according to the result. **1882** BAILLIE-GROHMAN *Camps in Rockies* 19 Out here them tony chin music don't pan worth a cent.

2. *tr.* To wash (auriferous soil) in a miner's pan.

1863 in *Mont. Hist. Soc. Contrib.* III. (1900) 137, I panned the pan of dirt and it was a good prospect. **1923** BOWER *Parowan Bonanza* 33 Rock so rich that he could break it up by hand and pan it in the spring. **1949** *Nat. Geog. Mag.* Oct. 511 He set out to pan stream-bed gravel for yellow treasure.

b. Also absol.

1850 KINGSLEY *Diary* 123 About 200 Indians & squaws came down and began to pan all around us. **1880** NYE *B. Nye & Boomerang* 163 The long-haired man gets a gold-pan and doubles himself up over the ditch and begins to pan. **1949** *World-Herald Mag.* (Omaha) 3 July 8/1 He found 10 thousand prospectors digging in the hills and panning along the creeks.

3. To wash (gold) from auriferous soil by means of a pan.

1883 RITCH *Illust. N. Mex.* 88 Gold can be panned from the sands of any of the streams and arroyas running down from the mountains.

4. *transf.* To capture.

1887 GOODE *Fisheries* V. 477 The crew 'panned' about 10,000 seals, but did not succeed in putting them on board.

5. To criticize severely. *Colloq.*

1922 *Collier's* 21 Jan. 4/2 The sport writers panned Knockout Pierce. **1948** *Capital-Democrat* (Tishomingo, Okla.) 17 June 2/2 Being a newspaperman who has been razzed often himself, he couldn't resist the temptation to pan us about a pied line and the word held which came out 'hell.'

6. *To pan* (something) *off on*, to palm off on. *Rare.*

1884 *Gringo & Greaser* 15 Feb. 2/3 The dirty lie he was trying to pan off on the public for the truth.

7. *To pan out*, to wash (auriferous earth, etc.) in a gold pan.

1839 *Amer. R.R. Jrnl.* VIII. 99 Old machines are invariably burnt up, and the ashes 'panned out' for the fine gold that has lodged in the joints of the wood. **1852** CLAPPE *Lett. from Calif.* 212 Of course they immediately prospect it, which is accomplished by panning out a few basinfuls of the soil.

transf. **1879** *Harper's Mag.* Sep. 510 The population, like the dirt, was slowly panned out. **1890** LANGFORD *Vigilante Days* (1912) 189, I have panned that fellow out and couldn't get a color.

b. To obtain (gold) by washing ore in a miner's pan; hence, *fig.*, to produce (anything).

1851 WOODS *Gold Diggings* 54 It [the gold] is then drawn off into a pan through holes at the bottom of the cradle, and 'panned out,' or washed, in the same way as in prospecting. **1873** *Newton Kansan* 16 Jan. 2/1 [Franklin's father's] business failed to 'pan out' enough profit. **1927** SANDBURG *Songbag* 108 We'll come back again When we've panned out our pile.

c. Of a mine or mineral-bearing soil: To produce gold or minerals.

1872 *Kansas Mag.* I. 558/2 No amount of scientific effort could make it [the dirt] 'pan out' better. **1878** BEADLE *Western Wilds* 41 The diggins begun to pan out rich.

d. Of any enterprise, person, or thing: To yield results, to turn out, prove to be useful or successful.

1868 WHYMPER *Alaska* 282 'It panned out well' means that 'it gave good returns.' **1871** HAY *Pike County Ballads* 13, I don't pan out on the prophets And free-will and that sort of thing. **1885** *Wkly. New Mexican Rev.* 15 Jan. 2/5 Taylor informed the doctor that he had lost his hat in the Rio Chiquito and desired another, but this wouldn't 'pan out' with Dr. Alexander. **1890** *Stock Grower & Farmer* 15 Feb. 6/2 This delightful winter is about to pan out too dry for stock. **1946** *Reader's Digest* March 145/1 As the tobacco crop hadn't panned out, no front addition or stairway had been built. **1949** *Sat. Ev. Post* 2 April 118/2 About a quarter of these tips result in stories—the rest simply don't pan out.

8. *To pan up*, to pay up. *Rare.*

1880 *Amer. Punch* Jan. 3/1 Those whose subscriptions run out with the January number, are politely notified to 'pan up.'

* **Panama,** *n.*

1. Panama Canal, the canal across the Isthmus of Panama.

American interest in this canal was greatly increased by the acquisition of California. Decisive action for its construction, however, was not taken until 1903–4. The canal was ready for use in 1914.

[**1839** *Boston W. Mag.* 3 Aug. 379/1 At the Isthmus of Panama, where several attempts have been made to lay the plan of the said canal, the whole breadth of the country, from one sea to the other, is not more than 21 miles.] **1880** *Nation* 5 Feb. 90 The United States government and the Panama Canal. **1889** *Atlantic Mo.* March 350/1 It is as reasonable to maintain that the Panama Canal is to constitute part of the coast-line of Mexico as of that of the United States. **1914** *Yale Review* July 708 The Panama Canal is about to open a new highway between the Atlantic and the Pacific. **1949** *N.O. Times-Picayune Mag.* 20 Nov. 26/2 Remember that in 1899 the great Panama canal was still a dream.

2. Panama fever, either yellow fever or malaria contracted in the Panama region.

1850 TYSON *Diary in Calif.* 29 The so-called *Panama fever* rarely occurs, unless previous disease has wasted the powers. **1940** RIESENBERG *Golden Gate* 109 Complaints charged that the frequent burials at sea resulted from improper care of those who had contracted 'Panama fever' or 'yellow fever.'

Pan-America. North, Central, and South America.

1901 *Everybody's Mag.* Oct. 412/2 Pan-America is the home of the entire family of Cacti. **1948** *Chi. Tribune* 30 March 1. 1/6 (*heading*), 21 Pan-America Nations Open Parley Today.

b. =**Pan-American 2.** *Obs.*

1901 *Cosmopolitan* Sep. 484/2 Pan-America is the fundamental novelty at Buffalo.

Pan-American ˈpænəˈmɛrəkən, *a.* and *n.* [Gk. *pan-*, all, + * *American.*]

1. *n.* A delegate to a Pan-American congress; one interested in Pan-American affairs.

1890 *Ann Arbor Reg.* 3 March 6 The Pan-Americans. . . . The delegates to the International American conference are beginning to talk about final adjournment. **1891** *Harper's Mag.* June 3/2 Our own ignorance . . . respecting our South-American neighbors, despite even the Pan-Americans [is culpable]. **1948** *Dly. Ardmoreite* (Ardmore, Okla.) 23 April 8/1 (*heading*), Pan Americans Hit Communism.

2. *ellipt.* The exposition at Buffalo. *Rare.* Cf. **Pan-America b.**

1901 *Cosmopolitan* Sep. 458/2 Criticism of the esthetic attractions of the Pan-American is invidious for the reason that Chicago has given us so stern a standard of comparison. **1901** *Scranton* (Pa.) *Tribune* 3 Oct. 1/6 (*heading*), Pennsylvania Day at the Pan-American.

3. *a.* Of or pertaining to North, Central, and South America as a whole.

1889 *N.Y. Ev. Post* 27 Sep. 4/3 European Opinion on the Pan-American Congress. **1907** *Amer. Pol. Sci. Rev.* Feb. 192 The American governments to appoint . . . a permanent commission on Pan-American affairs.

Hence **Pan-Americanism,** the idea or advocacy of a political union composed of all the states in the western hemisphere.

1901 *World's Work* Oct. 1325/2 If our future relations with the Latin-American countries . . . should take this salutary course the sentimental idea of Pan-Americanism will be no longer a dream, but an accomplished fact. **1948** *Chi. Tribune* 6 July I. 1/1 Pan-Americanism means equality of all nations and sympathetic co-operation among all nations.

Panamint ˈpænəˌmɪnt, *n.* [App. native name.] (See quot. 1910.) Also **Panamint Indians.**

1893 *N. Amer. Fauna* VII. 174 It is much prized by the Panamint Indians as an article of food. **1903** James *Indian Basketry* 85 The Panamint Indian women of Death Valley, California, make their baskets of the year-old shoots of aromatic sumac. **1910** Hodge *Amer. Indians* II. 199/1 Panamint. A Shoshonean division formerly occupying a considerable area in and around Panamint valley, s.e. Cal., and extending s. in scattered rancherias toward Mohave r. **1933** Chalfant *Story of Inyo* 37 Malarango, chief of the Panamint (or Coso) Indians, had attained the ripe old age of (supposed) ninety years.

Panamite, see **Pennamite.**

panatela ˌpænəˈtɛlə, *n.* [Sp. *panetela*, in same sense.] A cigar of a characteristic shape and size. — **1908** *Sat. Ev. Post* 5 Dec. 41/4 If the shape of my Panatela doesn't appeal to you I have others that will. **1949** *Tobacco Jobber* Aug. 22/2 Stetson Cigar, 5c Panetelas, . . . had entering upon the most extensive national advertising campaign in its history.

panbore ˈpænˌbor, *n.* [?Du. *panboor* in same sense.] A trepan, a tool for perforating the skull in trepanning. *Rare.* — **1646** *Essex Probate Rec.* I. 49, 1 little hack-hamer, 2 pan bores & galloes.

***Pandora's box.** Some now indefinable medical device. *Rare.* — **1721** *N.-Eng. Courant* 7–14 Aug. 1/1 That they [inoculators] be compleatly armed with Incision-Lancet, Pandora's-Box, Nut-Shell and Fillet.

pandowdy pænˈdaudɪ, *n.* [See note.] A dessert of apples prepared in various ways. Cf. **apple dowdy, apple pandowdy.**

Pandowdy is usu. a deep-dish apple pie, freq. one sweetened with molasses. The crust may be of pastry, biscuit dough, or cake dough. Sometimes it is steamed, sometimes baked. The name is also applied to brown betty. See *Ling. Atlas*, Map 292, for further discussion and for other names for pandowdy.

The origin of the term is obscure. *EDD* lists an obs. *pandoulde*, custard, from Somerset. Also cf. *EDD*'s *dowl*, a verb meaning to knead or mix dough in a hurry, and *dowler*, a cake or a dumpling made in a hurry.

?**1805** *Pocumtuc Housewife* (1897) 25 (Ernst). **1830** S. Smith *Life J. Downing* 101 You dont know how queer it looks to see . . . politics and pan-dowdy . . . jumbled up together. **1893** Leland *Memoirs* I. 74 Pan-dowdy—a kind of coarse and broken up apple-pie. **1895** Coffin *Daughters of Revolution* 55 Pandowdy was a compote of apples, with several layers of pastry, made from rye meal, baked in a deep earthen dish and eaten with milk. **1947** Berolzheimer *Regional Cookbook* 142 Both the Pandowdy and Cob Pie are served by cutting out squares of the biscuit, turning the squares upside down on the crust, adding butter, and covering with the apple mixture, then with thick unbeaten cream.

b. (See quot.) *Obs.*

[**1856** Hall *College Words* (ed. 2) 342 The band [Pandowdy, noise-making band of Bowdoin] corresponds to the *Calliathump* [*sic*] of Yale.]

***panel,** *n.* In combs.: (1) **panel-crib,** a prostitute's room with a secret entrance whereby a thieving accomplice can enter, a house containing such rooms; (2) **fence,** a fence made of rails laid in panels, cf. **staked and ridered fence;** (3) **game,** the trick or game of stealing by means of the panel-crib; (4) **house,** =**panel crib;** (5) **thief,** a thief who works the panel game on his victim.

(1) **1848** Judson *Mysteries N.Y.* I. 14 We will leave her to seek a victim for her panel-crib, for she has long been an active panel-thief. **1892** Walsh *Literary Curiosities* 854 The lair of a panel-thief is called indiscriminately a panel-house, panel-crib, or panel-den. — (2) **1800** Tatham *Tobacco* 10 The *worm* or *pannel* fence, *originally of Virginia*, consists of malled rails. **1858** Warder *Hedges & Evergreens* 113 A half-acre lot, with a seven-foot panel-fence on one side and a hedge on the other. — (3) **1857** *Spirit of Times* 5 Dec. 213/3 Females are employed as decoy-ducks to induce the yokels from the rural districts into places of *un*questionable character, where they are sure to be plundered of their money by the panel-game. **1910** J. Hart *Vigilante Girl* 309 When the required deviltry is a little too raw—such as poisoning, or the panel-game—then big wigs like Bell or Tower hire thugs. — (4) **1848** Judson *Mysteries N.Y.* II. 44 This is a panel house and I have led a bad, bad life for many a year. **1892** [see **panel crib**]. **1930** Terrett *Only Saps Work* 55 Others were pickpockets, or loft thieves, or house-burglars, or panel-house sneak-thieves.

(5) **1844** *Quincy* (Ill.) *Herald* 23 Aug. 3/1 Alexander Hoag, a notorious panel thief, . . . escaped from prison last night. **1882** McCabe *New York* 488 If discovered, the panel thief endeavors to disable the victim. **1947** *True* Nov. 69/1 The two lawyers had in addition the business of every free-lance safecracker, forger, arsonist . . . bucket-shop proprietor, and panel thief whose business was worth having.

***panhandle,** *n.*

1. A narrow strip of land extending out from, and forming part of, a state. Often as a proper name. Cf. **Texas Panhandle.**

1856 *Spirit of Times* 8 Nov. 159/1 He was from old Virginny—from what, he said, they called the *Pan-handle.* **1862** *Cong. Globe* 11 Feb. 754/3, I want to compare the district of Mr. Segar with the Wheeling district. One is called the pan-handle of the East, and the other the pan-handle of the West. **1919** Lewis *Free Air* 207 She had driven through the panhandle of Idaho into Washington. **1949** *Lubbock* (Tex.) *Morn. Avalanche* 23 Feb. II. 1/1 The arrowheads and spear-heads are from many historical points in the Panhandle.

b. (See quot.) *Obs.*

1907 *Boston Transcript* 9 Nov., A list of the popular names of the States. . . . Panhandle—West Virginia.

c. Also attrib. with **beat, country, county, solon, town.**

1851 J. J. Hooper *Widow Rugby's Husband* 121, 'I want his hide . . . ,' said a fellow from Pan-Handle Beat. **1881** Romspert *Western Echo* 146, I saw four Indians, who, from their dress, I recognized to be *Kiawas*, from the pan-handle country. **1894** *McClure's Mag.* III. 112/1 Its domain, including portions of nine Panhandle counties as big as small States, was taken by the company in payment for the Texas Capitol building. **1899** C. Graham *Ipanê* 178 Like . . . some Pan Handle town during the progress of a bar-room fight. **1902** O. Henry *Roads of Destiny* 256 The Panhandle solon winds his muffler above his well-buttoned overcoat.

2. (*cap.*) A nickname given to a railroad running across the panhandle of West Virginia.

1868 Flint *Railroads of U.S.* 125 The Pennsylvania Railroad Company has recently purchased the Pan-Handle, or Steubenville Railroad, extending from Pittsburg to Newark in Ohio. **1915** *Chi. D. News Almanac 1916* 632 Pittsburgh, Cincinnati, Chicago & St. Louis (Pan Handle).

b. Attrib. with **engine, flyer, road.**

1875 Sipes *Pa. R.R.* 18 The Pittsburg and Steubenville Railroad . . . is commonly called the 'Pan-handle road,' from the fact that it runs through the strip of Western Virginia wedged in between the State of Pennsylvania and the Ohio river. **1877** E. Martin *Hist. Great Riots* 78 This work was done by Pan-Handle engines. **1903** *N.Y. Times* 11 Dec. 3, 15 injured and one dead resulted from the wrecking of the east-bound Panhandle flyer this evening.

3. Panhandle State, (see quot.).

1894 *N.Y. Wkly. Tribune* 7 March 4/3 West Virginia [is] . . . nicknamed the Panhandle State.

4. The act of borrowing money. *Slang.*

1900 G. Ade *More Fables in Slang* 142 Waiting on the Door-Step to give him the Sign of Distress and work the fraternal Pan-Handle on him.

panhandle ˈpænˌhændl, *v.* [Poss. f. panhandler *q.v.*] *intr.* To beg, esp. on the street. Also *tr.* and transf. *Slang.*

1904 G. H. Lorimer *Old Gorgon Graham* 53 A lot of men . . . who wouldn't think of asking for money, will panhandle both sides of a street for favors. **1944** *Nat. Geog. Mag.* June 210 Pl. xiv, Eastern Brown Pelicans haunting St. Petersburg, Florida, wharves have become so fat and lazy that they seem to prefer 'panhandling' for fish rather than diving and catching their own. **1949** *Chi. D. News* 13 Aug. 1/1 Men in Skid Row are quick to panhandle each other.

Also **panhandling,** *n.* and *a.*

1906 *Charities* 17 Feb. 695/2 This has been an open winter for panhandling. **1949** *Sat. Ev. Post* 7 May 25/2 The 'tame' panhandling park bear is far more perilous and much more liable to attack than his wild brother.

panhandler ˈpæn,hændlɚ, *n.* [App. f. **pan*+ **handler.*]

1. A beggar. Also transf. *Slang.*

1899 ADE *Doc' Horne* 255 He had 'sized' the hustler for a 'panhandler' from the very start. **1913** *Sat. Ev. Post* 1 Nov. 7/3 [The ship] became a sort of maritime panhandler, haunting strange ports, thankful for small favors and bartering her self-respect for a pittance. **1949** *Chi. Tribune* 20 Feb. I. 7/2 The tramp is a panhandler, working only when forced to do so.

2. (Usu. *cap.*) One who lives in a panhandle, sense **1.**

1941 FERGUSSON *Southwest* 335, I talked all this over with a native-born Panhandler. **1949** *10 Story Western* May 28/2 He remembered how it was down there in the Panhandle—how the Panhandlers hated these Rio Valley floaters as no Idaho man could.

panic session. The first session of the Twenty-third Congress, so called because of the financial distress which prevailed at the time. *Obs.* — **1842** *So. Quart. Rev.* I. 88 The sudden and violent contraction of 1833 . . . produced the scenes of what is usually termed the 'panic session.' **1854** BENTON *30 Years' View* I. 369/2 On the second day of December, 1833, commenced the first session of the Twenty-third Congress, commonly called the Panic session.

Panisee ˈpænə,si, *n.* [Amer. Indian.] An Indian medicine man. *Obs.* — **1624** WINSLOW *Good Newes* 41 This caused one Pecksnot who was a *Pinese*, being a man of a notable spirit to come to Hobbamock. **1844** WHITTIER *Poetical Works* 27/1 For that chief had magic skill, And a Panisee's dark will, Over powers of good and ill.

***panning,** *n.*

1. The action of washing auriferous dirt in a pan; an instance of this. Also with *out.* Cf. **gold panning.**

1839 *Amer. R.R. Jrnl.* VIII. 99 This operation is continued until all the sand is removed, and nothing but the gold left. It is called 'panning out.' **1848** DANA *Mineralogy* 317 The operation of hand washing is called in Virginia *panning.* **1876** *Grass Valley* (Calif.) *Union* 19 Sep. 3/3 Not a single panning has been made but shows plenty of gold. **1908** E. S. MEADE *Story of Gold* 39 A small amount of gold is still taken out by the simple process of panning.

attrib. **1850** KINGSLEY *Diary* 122 Stoped down to day and made a panning trough to pour quicksilver from the riffler into. **1880** INGHAM *Digging Gold* 54 The Panning Process, consists of a tin or sheet-iron pan [etc.]. **1882** *47th Congress* 1 Sess. H.R. Ex. Doc. No. 216, 568 F. A. Huntington of San Francisco, manufactures this rocking and panning amalgamator for saving fine gold and floured mercury.

2. Severe criticism. *Colloq.* Cf. ***pan,** *v.* **5.**

1852 *Marysville* (Calif.) *Herald* 7 Aug. 1/5 We apprehend that the candidates will undergo a system of panning, tomming and sluicing too thorough to pass current, if they should prove light or worthless. **1949** *Time* 7 March 58/3 The campus paper even set itself to a brisk panning.

panoche pəˈnotʃɪ, *n.* Also **panocha, penuche.** [Sp. *panocha,* in the Amer. Sp. sense shown in **1.**]

1. Raw or crude sugar.

1847 *Californian* (Monterey) 10 April 3/2 The cargo consists of 180 bales (about 26,000 lbs.) of Mexican Sugar; 30 Packages Panoche and one Bale of Zarapies. **1879** WILLIAMS *Pacific Tourist* 300/2 The ordinary brown sugar (panoche) of the Mexicans is also obtained from this plant. **1936** MCKENNA *Black Range* 52 With ten pounds of jerky, a cone of *penoche,* or pressed brown sugar, and a serape, or gray blanket, a Mexican is fitted for a trip of several hundred miles through the mountains.

attrib. **1930** *Sunset* Dec. 30/2 At lower left are seen fondant-dipped and penoche-dipped figs and prunes.

2. A kind of brown-sugar candy. Cf. **fruit panoche.**

1871 *Rep. Indian Affairs* (1872) 359, I doubt the good policy of issuing bread, and at times candy (panoche,) to the pupils. **1949** *Ariz. Quart.* Autumn 255 He made the most luscious panocha and rich syrups, which he sold to the public.

attrib. **1949** *Chi. Tribune* 28 Sep. II. 2/2 Our recipe for Butterscotch Cake, and Penuche Icing, is printed on the recipe folder inside Softasilk packages.

pansaje pɑnˈsɑhe, *n. Texas.* [App. f. Sp. *panza,* belly, +*aje.*] (See quot. 1902.) *Obs.*—**1893** *Galveston News* 11 Feb. (Th.), A pansaje where all could refresh the inner man. **1902** CLAPIN 300 *Pansage.* In Texas, a feast or 'barbecue' for men exclusively, in which the 'pauza' [*sic*], or body of the animal is barbecued.

***pantaloonery,** *n.* "The particular description of fabrics from which pantaloons are made" (B. '59). *Obs.* — **1857** *Seaboard Towns* (Ernst), A good stock of cloths, pantaloonery, vestings &c.

panther ledge. (See quot.) *Obs.* — **1842** *Nat. Hist. N.Y., Zoology* I. 48 The Panther . . . prefers for its usual retreat, ledges of rocks inaccessible to man, which are known familiarly to the hunters under the name of *panther ledges.*

pantie ˈpæntɪ, *n.* [Dim. of **pants.*] A pair of drawers or small trousers. Usu. **panties.**

1845 *Knickerb.* XXVI. 433 If your panties weren't sheeted home at the bottom, you'd out-jump a monkey. **1848** BURTON *Waggeries* 19, I hadn't on nothin' . . only a blue cotting shirt and sail-cloth pantys. **1945** MACDONALD *Egg & I* 18 A little boy named Waldo wet his panties while we were standing in front of the class for reading. **1949** *Dly. Ardmoreite* (Ardmore, Okla.) 23 Feb. 2 A new low price on a good well-made pantie in this popular long wearing fabric.

transf. **1909** *Sat. Ev. Post* 24 April 15/3 New York and Pennsylvania would be inhabited by cow-persons in décolleté leather panties. **1949** *Ib.* 26 March 35/2 Large bottles in woven straw panties stood on the checked table top.

***pants,** *n. pl.* As the last term in **California, copperas, ice cream, overall, sack, store pants.**

***pap,** *n.* Political patronage; revenue from public office. Also in combs. See also **cider pap.**

1841 *Cong. Globe* App. 29 Jan. 300/2 The very new States are nursed from their chrysalis territorial condition into existence upon Federal pap from the Executive spoon. **1863** *Rio Abajo Press* 17 Feb. 2/2 Our good-for-nothing, Government pap-sucking goslings. **1894** *Voice* 6 Sep., The Prohibition Party is the only party that is not controlled by public pap-seeking politicians and the debauching power of the saloon.

papabot ,pɑpəˈbot, *n. local.* [F. Poss. f. the bird's alarm note.] (See quots. 1917, 1931.)

1838 AUDUBON *Ornith. Biog.* IV. 24 In the neighbourhood of New Orleans, where it [the Bartram sandpiper] is called the 'Papabote,' it usually arrives in great bands in the spring. **1917** *Birds of Amer.* I. 247 Upland Plover. *Bartramia longicauda.* . . . [Also called] Prairie Snipe; Papabotte; Quaily. **1931** READ *La.-French* 55 As a table bird the upland plover is much prized; it was formerly served in the New Orleans restaurants, appearing on the menu as *Papabotte à la Créole* (*Français-Créole*), *Papabotte Grillé,* 'broiled papabotte,' and *Papabotte Rôti,* 'roast papabotte.' **1949** *N.O. Times-Picayune Mag.* 27 Nov. 16 Some call this 'upland' variety the Papabotte, from sound of his call.

Papago ˈpɑpəgo, *n.* [See quot. 1949.] An Indian of a Piman tribe formerly dwelling south and southeast of the Gila River, Arizona. Also *collect.* and *pl.*, the tribe of such an Indian.

1839 FORBES *Hist. Calif.* 162 On the River Gila . . . Papaga, 4000. **1911** WRIGHT *Winning Barbara Worth* 101 She pointed to a smoky, copper-colored Papago in a green headcloth and decorated shirt. **1949** ALICE JOSEPH *Desert People* 3 The Indians who live in this desert country are known to white people as the Papago. The name probably comes from that given them by their neighbors (as heard and recorded by the Spaniards): *pavi coatam,* 'the Bean-eating People,' or *pavi au'autam,* 'the Bean People,' from the tepary bean which was a staple food item.

attrib. **1878** HINTON *Arizona* 227 South and west of these lie the old Papago villages and wells. **1910** HODGE *Amer. Indians* II. 200/2 Like the Pima, the Papago women are expert basket makers. **1936** *Univ. Ariz. Gen. Bul.* 3, 118 These caterpillars feed on a spreading four-o'clock or on the Papago spinach on the desert. **1941** FERGUSSON *Southwest* 116 What happened to the early Hohokam people is still in dispute. Some archaeologists believe they were the ancestors of the modern Pima and Papago folk who still live in brush shelters on the desert.

Esp. **Papago Indian.**

1864 *Harper's Mag.* Dec. 25/1 The Papago Indians also do good service by . . . killing the hostile savages who infest the country. **1902** NEWELL *Irrigation* 45 The Papago Indians of the Southwest, living by crude methods of agriculture, have learned how to make use of the erratic water supply. **1948** *Ariz. Republic* (Phoenix) 3 March 11/3 Papago Indian representatives today made a personal plea . . . for a hard-surfaced highway across their reservation from Sells to San Xavier.

b. The language of these Indians.

1912 LUMHOLTZ *New Trails* 185 Hydrophobia is called in Papago *nótakik,* derived from *nótak,* crazy, mad. **1942** CASTETTER & BELL *Pima & Papago Agric.* 141 He, too, had some knowledge of the calendar and also spoke Papago.

Papagueria ,pɑpəgəˈriə, *n.* [Amer. Sp. *Papaguería,* given by Santamaría as a collect. term for the Papago Indians.] The country inhabited by the Papago Indians. Also **Papagueria country.**

1860 *Proc. Calif. Acad. Sci.* II. (1863) 136 It is situated in the center of a large plain, forming part of the *Papagoria.* **1878** HINTON *Hand-Book Ariz.* 365 They formerly lived in the Papagueria country. **1946** UNDERHILL *Papago Indian Religion* 11 They emerged at the eastern extreme of Papagueria and marched to the west, driving the former inhabitants either north or south.

***papaw,** *n.*[1] Also **pawpaw.**

1. Any one of various North American trees or shrubs of the genus *Asimina*, esp. *A. triloba*. Cf. **Asimina.**

1709 LAWSON *Carolina* 105 The Papau is not a large Tree. **1785** WASHINGTON *Diaries* II. 347 Planted my Cedars, all my Papaw, and two Honey locust Trees in my Shrubberies. **1875** *Amer. Naturalist* IX. 390 The pawpaw, persimmon and pecan are found more or less abundantly over the southern two-thirds [of Illinois]. **1941** R. S. WALKER *Lookout* 61 In the same locality one finds a dwarf papaw standing from two to four feet high, bearing edible fruit.

b. The wood or bark of the papaw tree.

1773 D. JONES *Jrnl. Visits Indians* (1865) 47 The wood is called paupaw, it is very light, and bears a kind of fruit in shape resembling a cucumber, but too luscious to some stomachs. **1886** *Harper's Mag.* June 58/2 Traces are made of hickory or papaw, as also are bed-cords.

2. The oblong, edible, yellowish fruit of the American papaw tree. Cf. ***custard apple, Kansas banana, Missouri banana.**

1792 IMLAY *Western Territory* 211 Papaw. This fruit . . . is in shape more like a seed cucumber than any thing else. **1826** FLINT *Recoll.* 328 Of wild fruits, there are the pawpaw, the persimon, the Chickasaw plum, and the pine woods grape. **1944** DUNCAN *M. Graham* 33 In season there was wild fruit, free for the seeking—wild grapes, pawpaws, persimmons, wild crab apples, and plums—and sweeter nuts than were ever bought over a counter.

3. (*cap.*) (See quot. 1885.)

1864 *Cong. Globe* 9 March 1017/3 They even accuse us radicals of speaking disparagingly of the militia of Missouri. It is false . . . except so far as relates to what are called Paw-Paws. **1885** *Mag. Amer. Hist.* March 297/2 *Paw-Paws.*—Equivalent to 'Bushwhackers' . . . current in Missouri. The paw-paw is a wild fruit of the genus *Asimina*, on which the bushwhackers are supposed to subsist.

4. In combs. in which the meaning is obvious or is made clear by the quots.: (1) **papaw bark,** (2) **brandy,** (3) **bush,** (4) **grove,** (5) **patch,** (6) **shrub,** (7) **smile,** (8) **thicket,** (9) **tree,** (10) **whistle,** (11) **wood.**

(1) 1891 THANET *Otto the Knight* 248 He and another guard . . . tied Looney to a gum-tree by strips of pawpaw bark like the niggers make reins out of. — **(2) 1867** DEVOE *Market Ass't* 384 Having met at the house of a friend where there was some paw-paw brandy, the distiller remarked that [etc.]. — **(3) 1785** WASHINGTON *Diaries* II. 444 Sent to Mr. Digges for Papaw Bushes to replace the dead ones in my Shrubberies. **1841** *S. Lit. Messenger* VII. 533/2 A grove of scrubby pawpaw bushes. **1944** *Chi. Tribune* 6 Aug. VII. 1/5 Great pawpaw bushes, with leaves iridescent in their green loveliness. — **(4) 1837** PECK *Gaz. Illinois* 234 One of its (south Fork's) heads is near the Paupau grove.

(5) 1883 EGGLESTON *Hoosier School-Boy* 64 Bob Holliday . . . took his place among the pigeon-slayers in the paw-paw patch. **1927** SANDBURG *Songbag* 161 'Way Down in the PawPaw Patch,' and 'All Chaw Hay on the Corner,' were play-party songs in early times in Indiana. — **(6) 1827** *Western Mo. Rev.* I. 255 A pawpaw shrub, hanging full of fruits, . . . is to us one of the richest spectacles. — **(7) 1852** *S. Lit. Messenger* XVIII. 680/2 To add to the charms of his delivery, he wore a poppaw smile, a sort of sickly-sweet expression on his countenance. — **(8) 1855** *Ore. W. Times* 12 May (Th.), So out we goes to the paw-paw thicket, and pealed [*sic*] a right peart chance o' bark. **1912** NICHOLSON *Hoosier Chron.* 7 The paw-paw thicket where fruit for the gods lures farm boys on frosty mornings in golden autumn. — **(9) 1733** BYRD *Journey to Eden* (1901) 314 We also saw in this place abundance of papa trees, the wood whereof the Indians make very dry on purpose to rub fire out of it. **1888** CRADDOCK *Despot* 9 A locust was shrilling from a pawpaw tree.

(10) 1872 EGGLESTON *End of World* 77 As for papaw whistles, why, I say Jericho wouldn't a-tumbled for no such music. — **(11) 1773** in *Cincinnati Misc.* I. 265 Wednesday 6th, . . . spent some time in fitting poles of pawpawwood, which is very plenty here and very light, so that it is used chiefly for canoe poles.

papaw 'pɒpɔ, *n.*[2] Also **pawpaw.** [Origin unknown.]

1. One of the shells used as a counter in a game of chance. See next. *Obs.*

1728 *Boston Rec.* 224 No Person or Persons what soever [shall] Presume to play . . . with Shells, or Papaws or any thing of that nature.

2. (See quots.) *Obs.* Cf. **prop,** *n.*[1]

1764 T. HUTCHINSON *Hist. Mass.* (1936) I. 395 They [Indians around Mass. Bay] took five small pieces of bone, flatter than a die and longer, black on the one side and white on the other, these they put into a small wooden tray or platter, and giving it a stroke on the ground the bones all flew into the air. . . . According as the bones happened to be more or less of one colour, so they won or lost. . . .The Negroes in Guinea have a game of the same sort, which they call paw-paw. **c1817** in *N. & Q.* VI. (1946) 138 Who blew up the ship? Nigger, why for? 'Cause he couldn't go to 'lection An shake paw-paw. **a1915** in *Pub. Col. Soc.* XVIII. (1917) 61 The game of Paw-paw, or props, was played with four small shells, known to naturalists as the *Cyproea Moneta*, and was one of the gambling games much practiced by the boys of Boston.

***pape,** *n.* (See quots. and cf. ***pope.**)

1831 AUDUBON *Ornith. Biog.* I. 281 Some persons give the name of *Nonpareil* to this species, [Painted Finch] but it is more commonly known by that of *Pape*, which, in fact, is a general appellation given by the inhabitants of Louisiana to all the smaller species of thick billed birds. **1905** BAIRD *Hist. N. Amer. Birds* II. 89 Nonpareil: Painted Bunting. . . . One of the most numerous summer birds of Lower Louisiana . . . was universally known among the French inhabitants as *Le Pape*. **1931** READ *La.-French* 55 *Pape*, generally used by itself, but sometimes followed by the adjective *rouge, doux, doré*, or *vert*, has become the common word in Louisiana for the Nonpareil or Painted Bunting.

***paper,** *n.*

1. A ballot made of paper. *Obs.* Cf. **paper vote.**

1643 *Plymouth Laws* 74 In every Towne there [shall] be three or foure men chosen by writing their names in papers as the majestrates are chosen to rate all the Inhabitants. **1660** *Springfield Rec.* I. 267 And ye Moderator shall always be chosen by Papers.

2. (See quot. 1938.)

1842 *S. Lit. Messenger* VIII. 412/1, I found myself . . . around a table in a corner, and the 'papers' in motion. **1894** MASKELYNE *Sharps & Flats* 43 In America . . . one may still find 'saloons' which are stocked entirely with this kind of 'paper' as the cards are called. **1938** ASBURY *Sucker's Prog.* 37 In the early days of Poker the marked cards used by sharpers were prepared beforehand by the gamblers themselves, and were known as 'paper;' or were marked during the process of the game with the finger nail or a needle point embedded in a ring.

b. *To play the papers*, to gamble. *Obs.*

1859 D. W. C. PETERS *Life & Adv. of Kit Carson* 354 Poor Kit was in a bad way one hour before we parted. The fact is, you know, he'd bin playin' the papers (meaning gamblin) and had lost everything.

3. In combs.: (1) **paper baler,** a machine for compressing and baling wastepaper; (2) **birch,** an American birch, *Betula papyrifera*, the white bark of which is used for making baskets, canoes, etc., cf. **canoe birch;** (3) **bread,** =**piki,** *rare;* (4) **carrier,** a person who delivers newspapers; (5) **car-wheel,** a car wheel made of compressed paper; (6) **currency,** paper money issued by a government, or negotiable bank notes used as money; (7) **dollar,** a piece of paper money of the value of one dollar; (8) **farmer,** a person who has theories about farming and farm problems, but no practical experience, cf. **book farmer;** (9) **fog,** depreciated paper money such as post notes, *slang, obs.*, cf. ***fog,** ***n.* 1;** (10) **folder,** an instrument for folding paper, a paper knife; (11) **gum disease,** a form of consumption found among Negroes, so called because the mucous membrane lining the mouth is, in the early stages of the disease, pale and white, *obs.;* (12) **hornet,** =**paper wasp;** (13) **leg,** (see quot.); (14) **-making wasp,** =**paper wasp;** (15) **-money colony,** a colony that issued paper money, *obs.;* (16) **rind,** an orange with a thin skin, also attrib.; (17) **route,** a route along which a carrier regularly delivers papers; (18) **sack,** a paper bag; (19) **shell,** see as a main entry; (20) **stock,** raw material from which paper is made, also attrib.; (21) **title,** a title or claim to land based upon a document of some kind, *obs.;* (22) **tobacco,** ?tobacco for use in making a kind of cigarette, *rare;* (23) **vote,** a written vote, *obs.;* (24) **wasp,** any wasp, as a yellow jacket, that makes a nest of paperlike material.

(1) 1909 *Buckeye Informer* IX. 209 The Little Giant paper Baler is a daisy. It is just what we needed to take care of scrap paper. — **(2) 1810** MICHAUX *Arbres* I. 25 *Paper birch* (Bouleau à papier). **1832** BROWNE *Sylva* 121 This tree . . . is known to the Americans . . . [as] Paper Birch. **1949** *L.A. Times* 5 June (Home Mag.) 34/2 The white birch . . . [is] very similar to the lovely paper birch of our Northeastern States. — **(3) 1882** *Harper's Mag.* June 78/1 Rolls of the peculiar 'paper bread' were given to us. — **(4) 1797** in *Amer. Sp.* XXI. (1946) 118/1 He informs them that his engagements as paper carrier are nearly discharged, and begs them to discharge to him their engagements as paper takers. **1855** COOKE *Ellie* 22 In all their occupations, as newsboys, paper-carriers, errand runners, . . . Beau Sam or Sam Beau . . . was easily the chief and leader.

(5) 1885 *Harper's Mag.* Feb. 455/1 The Allen Paper Car-wheel Company claims a capacity of fifteen thousand paper car-wheels a year. — (6) **1723** *Amer. W. Mercury* 7 Nov. 2/2 The natural Situation of these Counties and the Practice of our Neighbours, has laid us [of Penna.] under the necessity of coming into a Paper Currency. **1807** A. Bancroft *Life Washington* (1808) 218 The depreciation of the paper currency had reduced the pay of the American officers to a pittance. **1900** *Cong. Rec.* 4 Jan. 653/1 With the habits of our people and their preference for the use of paper currency wherever possible instead of gold and silver coinage [etc.]. — (7) **1778** *N.H. Hist. Soc. Coll.* IX. 108, I have been for Some time receiving old Silver Debts paid numerically in paper Dollars which for some time past has been but a quarter & now not more than one fifth of their true value. **1870** M. H. Smith *20 Years Wall St.* 423 The common necessaries of life were exorbitantly high, and a paper dollar was worth only thirty-six cents in coin. **1949** *Nat. Geog. Mag.* Oct. 507/1 Air base payrolls introduced paper dollars just before the war. — (8) **1873** *Winfield* (Kans.) *Courier* 22 May 2/2 The 'Grange' organizations and 'paper farmer's club' are good enough in their way. — (9) **1813** *Columbian Centinel* 7 April 2/2 His next resort [to obtain cash] must be *Paper Fog.* **1816** *Niles' Reg.* X. 216/1 It is asserted that the treasury of the United States has nearly two millions of *paper fog* in its vaults, at this moment.

(10) **1781** *Salem Gazette* 3 July, Isaac Greenwood . . . [makes] Paper-Folders, Sand-Boxes, Bannisters for Stair-cases. **1871** Stowe *Pink & White Tyranny* 98 Lillie took a paper-folder, and cut the leaf out quite neatly. **1884** Cable *Dr. Sevier* xxxi, Picking up his paper-folder and shaking it argumentatively. — (11) **1851** *De Bow's Review* XI. 212 Some overseers call it the paper-gum disease. — (12) **1870** *Amer. Naturalist* III. 52 The Paper Hornet (*Vespa maculata*) often enters my nucleus hives, when I am rearing Italian queen bees. **1943** Peattie *Great Smokies* 287 Paper hornets drone about the old deserted cabins. — (13) **1900** Spurr *Yukon Diggings* 18 He pronounced the last word [gentleman] with such a peculiar intonation that I felt sure he used it as synonymous with 'tenderfeet' or 'paper-legs' or other terms by which Alaskans designate greenhorns. — (14) **1867** *Amer. Naturalist* I. 140 The odor that arises from the Tarantula killer when she uses her sting . . . resembles the odor of the paper-making wasp (Vespa), only much stronger.

(15) **1738** *Virginia Gaz.* 4–11 Aug., A caution to the Paper-Money Colonies. **1739** W. Douglass *Discourse Currencies* 19 We see . . . in our Paper Money Colonies, the Currencies have incredibly depreciated from Sterling. — (16) **1882** *Harper's Mag.* Dec. 58/2 He can go into his orchard and concern himself about . . . his paper-rind St. Michaels. **1891** *Ib.* Jan. 180/1 But there are many excellent varieties—[of oranges] . . . the paper rind [etc.]. — (17) **1868** *Figaro* (S.F.) 23 July 2/1 A Paper Route—One of the best on the most substantial city daily. **1943** *Copper Camp* 146 There were paper routes galore, as the camp supported four newspapers. — (18) **1944** *Chi. D. News* 14 July 9/2 She carried a thermos jug of coffee and a couple of sandwiches in a paper sack to eat on the bus.

(20) **1875** Knight, *Paper-stock Bleacher*, . . . for expressing the bleaching material from paper stock, without having recourse to the draining vat. . . . *Paper-stock Washer*, a machine for cleansing shredded rags preparatory to pulping. **1888** *Amer. Almanac* 276 Occupations of the People of the United States. . . . Traders in paper & paper stock. — (21) **1794** *Ann. 4th Cong.* 2 Sess. 2803 The decisions of the State courts . . . discountenanced improvement titles, and gave the preference to paper titles. **1845** *Ill. Rev. Statutes* 104 Every person in the actual possession of lands or tenements . . . shall be held and adjudged to be the legal owner . . . to the extent and according to the purport of his or her paper title. — (22) **1817** *Conn. Courant* LIII. 10 June 4/5 (*advt.*), For Sale. . . . Junk and paper Tobacco. — (23) **1692** *Boston Rec.* 210 Ouerseers of the poore Chosen by papor Votes. **1706** *Ib.* 38 Voted that One Collector be chosen . . . by a Paper Vote. — (24) **1854** H. H. Riley *Puddleford* 216 The 'paper-wasp' was gathering wild cotton and flax. **1898** Deland *Old Chester Tales* 181 A gray ball showed that the paper-wasps liked the crumbling shelter.

b. Used in expressions, chiefly obs., to designate things that exist merely on paper and hence are nonexistent or ineffectual, as (1) **paper blockade,** a blockade that is proclaimed but not made effective by force; (2) **boom,** a boom promoted by schemes and plans that exist only on paper; (3) **city,** a projected or promoted town or city that is never built; (4) **mine,** a mine existing only on paper; (5) **town,** =**paper city,** also attrib.

(1) **1803** *Ann. 7th Congress* 2 Sess. 129 Paper blockades were substituted for actual ones, and the staple commodities of our country lay perishing in our store-houses. **1862** Kettell *Hist. Rebellion* I. 124 [Jefferson Davis] denounced the proclamation of the United States in relation to Southern ports, as a mere paper blockade. — (2) **1887** *Courier-Journal* 8 Jan. 4/4 [The article] was a general description of how paper booms are worked by sharpers upon fools. — (3) **1847** *Hunt's Merch. Mag.* XIV. 517 In 1835–6, years so remarkable for speculations in 'paper cities' and 'corner lots,' fortunately but little influence was experienced from the prevailing mania here. **1878** Beadle *Western Wilds* 365 The Pacific Railroad was pushing westward, and paper cities were springing up along its way. — (4) **1853** *Hunt's Merch. Mag.* XXVIII. 315 Moneyed men are no longer found ready to invest their wealth in paper mines.

(5) **1819** Evans *Pedestrious Tour* 228 On this river too is General Simcoe's paper town called London. **1889** Davidson *Fla. of Today* 226 The paper-town shark is one of the most recent evolutions. **1948** Dick *Dixie Frontier* 151 Many towns . . . never got beyond the stage of 'paper towns.'

c. In obs. combs. with reference to the use of paper money, as (1) **paper aristocracy,** (2) **bank,** (3) **basis,** (4) **lie,** (5) **man,** (6) **manufacturer,** (7) **pay.**

(1) **1838** *N.Y. Advt. & Exp.* 11 April 3/1 The cry . . . of the Loco Focos in this City is, 'Rag Barons—no paper aristocracy . . . Andrew Jackson and Thomas Humbug Benton.' — (2) *c*1720 *Mass. Bay Currency Tracts* 380 A paper bank can't be as good as the bank of England or Holland til paper is as good as Silver. — (3) **1900** *Cong. Rec.* 18 Jan. 944/2 The people of the United States will be upon a paper basis in part at least, and that will be paper issued by the banks. — (4) **1876** *Scribner's Mo.* Jan. 432/2 The good sense of the people and the good faith of the people will have a voice, and the 'paper lie' will go into everlasting disgrace.

(5) **1794** J. Taylor *Enquiry into Principles* 25 When paper men get into Congress, or members are metamorphosed into paper men after they get there, it is obvious that they will be influenced by their personal private interest, producing them an immense profit in cash, rather than the public good. — (6) **1820** J. Flint *Lett. from Amer.* 193 Many of the paper manufacturers were obliged to suspend specie payments. — (7) **1691** C. Mather in *Mass. Bay Currency Tracts* 17 If neither Silver can be had, nor Corn brought in without loss both to the Government and People, what remains but Accounts, Bills, or such like Paper-pay?

As the last term in **Abolition, accommodation, administration, basswood, bonnet, bucktail, building, campaign, cattle, collar, comic, Confederate, cornstalk, county, curtain, dictionary, exchange, fiber-faced, funny, hardware, interchange, live, mail order, municipality, package, penny, picture, post-office, press, scratch, sheathing, state, steamer, tar, test, thumb, title, wall, western paper.**

***paper,** *v. To paper out,* to keep (cold) out by the use of paper. *Rare.* — **1855** Ropes *6 Mo. in Kans.* 87 We must paper out the cold wind.

***papering,** *n.* **1.** Wall paper. **2. papering system,** the practice of securing an audience for a theatrical performance, etc., by issuing free tickets. *Obs.*

(1) **1883** *Harper's Mag.* Feb. 365/1 This room remains in its original state, with the exception of the papering. **1893** S. Hale *Letters* 282, [I] came home with brooms, . . . bread, dishtowels and papering for Fullum's room. — (2) **1895** *N.Y. Dramatic News* 26 Oct. 5/3 The 'papering' system has been indulged in too freely in some quarters.

***papers,** *n. pl.* As the last term in **A.B., close, first, free, naturalization, protection, second, walking papers.**

papershell ˈpepɚˌʃɛl, *n.* **1.** (See quots.) **2.** A kind of firecracker. *Obs.* **3.** A thin-shelled pecan. In full **paper-shell pecan.**

(1) **1884** Goode *Nat. Hist. Aquat. Anim.* 776 The terms 'Soft Crab,' 'Paper-shell,' and 'Buckler' denote the different stages of consistency of the shell. **1911** *Rep. Fisheries 1908* 309/1 While growing a new shell, [edible crabs are cal l] 'soft-shell,' 'paper-shell,' 'buckler,' and 'hard-shell.' — (2) **1889** *Cent. Mag.* April 832/2 In the two hours' interval was a display of . . . crackers, serpents, paper-shells. — (3) **1912** *Bur. Plant Industry Bul.* No. 251, 46 With reference to the pecan, the term 'papershell' has been extended in its application until it is now practically without significance. **1912** *Outing* Oct. 377/1 The only difference between the so-called 'paper-shell' pecan and the fruit from wild trees of the forest is that the former has been grown on a budded or grafted tree, the scions being from a named variety. **1945** *N. Eng. Homestead* 27 Oct. 20/2 Paper shell pecan in Shell 50¢ per pound.

papoon pæˈpun, *n.* [Prob. f. some form of **papoose.**] (See quots.) *Obs.* Cf. **sweet corn 2.**

1822 *N. Eng. Farmer* 7 Sep. 48/1 A gentleman [Capt. Richard Bagnal] of this place [Plymouth, Mass.] . . . on his return, after the expedition, brought some ears of that [i.e., sweet] corn. . . . There [on the Susquehannah R.] called the *Papoon corn* probably from its tenderness and sweetness made the *food* of *children.* **1848** C. L. Fleischmann *Nordamerikanische Landwirth* 115 Early Sweet-Corn, oder Early Sugar-Corn . . . auch wohl Papoon-Corn (Melonenkorn) genannt . . . frisch und gedorrt dienen sie zur Bereitung mehrer schmackhaften Speisen. **1884** *Vt. Agric. Rep.* VIII. 278 A few ears . . . were brought to Plymouth [1779] from the region of the Susquehanna river, and [it] was described as having a white shriveled grain when ripe, with a red cob, and called 'pa-poon corn.' But not till within a few years . . . has it been generally cultivated for culinary purposes.

papoose pæ'pus, *n.* [Algonquian in sense **1.**]

1. An Indian baby or young child.

1634 WOOD *N. Eng. Prospect* (1865) 108 This little Pappouse travells about with his bare footed mother to paddle in the Icie Clammbankes. **1711** *N.H. Prov. P.* III. 477 (*footnote*), Voted, That for . . . every minor or Papoose [slain], fifteen pounds be payd out of the Treasury. **1846** *Knickerb.* XXVII. 211 Squaws, papooses, men and missionaries were there to partake of their dinner. **1949** *Chi. D. News* 23 Sep. 1/3 Papoose Born At Fair in Doc's Absence.

transf. **1851** *Cin. D. Commercial* 27 Oct. 1/6 They were highly delighted when they saw the fire-horse's brother (another steamboat) *with a papoose* (the yawl) hitched to her tail, ascending the river.

b. Any child. *Jocular.*

1871 *Republican Rev.* 16 Sep. 1/4 White squaws and papooses are the best to commence practising on. **1945** *Chi. D. News* 12 July 12/1 Braves, squaws and papooses of the Illini, arise!

2. =**blue cohosh.** *Obs.* Cf. **papoose root.**

1830 *Huntingdon* (Pa.) *Courier* 15 Sep. 4/5 American Remedies Wanted . . . Squaw or Poppoose, (Caulophyllum Tholictroides.)

3. In combs.: (1) **papoose basket,** a basket-like cradle or receptacle for a papoose; (2) **board,** a board to which a papoose may be strapped so that it can be carried about; (3) **coat,** ?a garment worn by a papoose, *obs.;* (4) **fashion,** in the fashion or manner of a papoose; (5)

Papoose board

frame, (see quot.); (6) **question,** a childish question, *obs.;* (7) **root,** =**blue cohosh,** or a medicine made from this.

(1) **1902** *Out West* March 273 As with nearly all Western Indians, the Pomo infant was wrapped in swaddling clothes and tightly laced in a pappoose basket. **1939** SUMMERHAYS *Vanished Ariz.* 117 They brought me some finely woven baskets and a beautiful papoose-basket or cradle, such as they carry their own babies in. — (2) [**1858** VIELE *Following Drum* 204 They had with them several little copper-colored papooses strapped down . . . to a shingle.] *a***1918** G. STUART *On Frontier* II. 49 The infants are strapped to a papoose board and this board hung over the pommel of the mother's saddle. **1942** WEYGANDT *Plenty of Penna.* 37 There are objects of folk art, too, that appeal: baskets of sweet grass and carriers of birch bark, . . . papoose boards and snow-shoes. — (3) **1633** *N.H. Doc. & Rec.* I. 74, 5 papoose cootes. — (4) **1839** TOWNSEND *Narrative* 196 Several of these women have little children tied to their backs, sewed up papoose fashion, only the head being seen. **1946** *Chi. D. News* 23 March 2/2 Mothers give a hitch to their infants, slung papoose-fashion on their backs, and off they go.

(5) **1902** *Amer. Folk-Lore* 252 Also *pappoose* frame, 'a term in use to designate certain Indian cradles.' — (6) **1648** SHEPARD *Clear Sun-Shine* 14 He was soon snib'd by the other Indians, calling it a Papoose question. — (7) **1815** DRAKE *Cincinnati* 85 Poppoos root. **1843** TORREY *Flora N.Y.* I. 33 *Leontice thalictroides* . . . Blue Cohosh. Pappoose-root. . . . The root of this plant is in some repute as a diuretic and bitter. **1943** PEATTIE *Great Smokies* 190 The old wives of the mountains today are not averse to . . . giving their teething children a little papooseroot.

papoose pæ'pus, *v.* [f. the noun.] *tr.* To confine or bind like a papoose. *Rare.* — *a***1861** WINTHROP *Canoe & Saddle* 204 This fashionable martyr was being papoosed in a tight-swathing wicker-work case.

pappy-fish. =**harvest fish.**

1896 JORDAN & EVERMANN *Check-List Fishes* 351 Harvest-fish; Pappy-fish. South Atlantic Coast of United States. **1897** *N.Y. Forest, Fish & Game Comm.* 2d Rep. 239 *Rhombus paru.* . . . Harvest-Fish—Pappy-fish. A summer visitor in Gravesend Bay and sometimes rare, but formerly abundant. **1903** T. H. BEAN *Fishes N.Y.* 456.

par pɑr, *n.* [Du. *paard,* in the sense shown here.] (See quot. 1940.) — **1891** H. C. BUNNER *Zadoc Pine* 41 Occasionally one of them [the children] would recognize a home-returning father, and, without pausing in the merry round of Spanish Fly, or Par, would give his parent the hail of equality, 'H'lo, Pa.' **1940** MENCKEN *Happy Days* 143 Along with my brother Charlie I was watching and admiring some older boys playing at par, which was the Baltimore name for leap-frog.

* **parade,** *n.* As the last term in **dress, shirt-tail parade.**

parade ground. An extent of open level ground, usu. within or adjacent to a fort, where soldiers are accustomed to parade.

1724 in TEMPLE & SHELDON *Hist. Northfield, Mass.* 200 The soldiers will be safe, even if the enemy get within the parade ground. **1902** ALDRICH *Sea Turn* 295 He flung back the flap and looked down upon the parade-ground with its radiating white-walled streets.

attrib. and *transf.* **1863** GAIL HAMILTON *Gala-Days* 174 Besides abundance of food and parade ground, these happy fowls have a very agreeable prospect. **1866** MRS. WHITNEY *L. Goldthwaite* vi, Clothes-lines like a parade-ground of telegraphs. **1892** *Harper's Mag.* Dec. 137 Both dismounted at the parade-ground gate.

* **parakeet,** *n.* =**Carolina parrot.** — **1709** LAWSON *Carolina* 142 The Parrakeetos are of a green Colour, and Orange-Coloured half way their Head. **1858** BAIRD *Birds Pacific R.R.* 67 *Conurus Carolinensis.* . . . Parakeet; Carolina Parrot. . . . Southern and southwestern States, as far west as the Missouri.

parara pə'rɛrə, *n.* Also **pararee.** Variants of prairie *q.v.*

1789 MORSE *Amer. Geog.* 463 A parara . . . is an extensive, rich plain without trees, and covered with grass. **1816** U. BROWN *Journal* II. 148 If those Pararees was in Pennsylvania or Maryland I should Call them Abominable Swamps with high rough grass. **1858** *Harper's Mag.* March 439/2 At nightfall you see parties of emigrants making their way in slow lines across the rolling prairie (or 'parara,' as the borderers like to call it).

parasitic jaeger. A species of jaeger, *Stercorarius parasiticus.* — **1887** RIDGWAY *Man. N. Amer. Birds* 22. **1917** *Birds of Amer.* I. 36 The Parasitic Jaeger is a robber and lives largely on what it can take by force from its smaller brethren.

* **parched,** *a.*

1. parched corn, Indian corn roasted for use as food.

1622 MOURT *Relation* 46 At this towne of *Massasoyts* . . . wee . . . bought about a handfull of Meale of their parched Corne. **1807** GASS *Journal* 132 After eating a few grains of parched corn, we set out at 8 o'clock. **1901** WASHINGTON *Up From Slavery* 10 Parched corn was used for coffee, and a kind of black molasses was used instead of sugar. **1945** *Chi. Tribune* 29 Jan. 6/3 For emergency ration, he carried a bag of parched corn.

b. (*cap.*) (See quot. 1800.) *Obs.*

1800 BOUCHER *Glossary* p. l. *Ebo-Nan,* and *Parch'd Corn;* two favourite tunes, or jigs, among the negroes are so called. **1819** *Ky. Almanac 1820* 30, I wished them to play parch'd corn.

c. Hominy or popcorn. *Obs.*

1828 COBBETT *Treatise on Corn* §20 The parched corn talked of here, means that which is called homany, in Virginia and the Carolinas. **1850** S. F. COOPER *Rural Hours* 388 Besides these different ways of cooking the maize, we should not forget parched or 'popped' corn, in which the children delight so much. **1876** HALE *P. Nolan's Friends* xi, Travelers of to-day, solicited in palace cars to buy sugared parched-corn, do not know, perhaps, that this is the food of pioneers in front of Apaches.

d. parched corn flour, =**parched meal.**

1712 in *Va. Hist. Mag.* VI. 50, I ordered the Indians to get parched corn flouer ready in order to return as soon as my horses come. **1820** *Amer. Antiq. Soc. Trans.* I. 283 The knapsack is an old blanket, and contains some parched corn flour, jerked meat, and leather.

e. parched corn men, followers of Wm. H. Harrison (1773–1841), in allusion to their alleged hardihood. *Obs.*

1840 NORTON *Tipp. Songs* (1888) 63 'Parch'd corn' men can't stand it much longer.

2. parched meal, meal made by pounding parched or roasted Indian corn in a mortar. *Obs.*

1643 R. WILLIAMS *Key* (1866) 39 *Nókehick.* Parch'd meal which is a readie very wholesome food, which they eat with a little water, hot or cold. **1805** LEWIS in *Ann. 9th Congress* 2 Sess. 1039 [We] have thus been enabled to reserve the parched meal, portable soup, and a considerable proportion of pork and flour. [**1846** BRYANT *California* (1848)

372 My servant obtained, with some difficulty, from the Indians at the rancho, a pint cup of *pinole*, or parched corn-meal.]

parching corn. =**popcorn.** *Obs* — **1845** *Knickerb.* XXV. 199 Over head hung bunches of parching-corn. **1948** C. L. FLEISCHMANN *Nordamerikanische Landwirth* 115 Pop-Corn, oder Parching-Corn.

∗**parchment,** *n.*

1. The dried hide of an animal, as an elk or buffalo. In full **parchment hide.** *Obs.*

1805 LEWIS in *L. & Clark Exped.* III. (1905) 12 Roots of three different kinds . . . were foalded in as many parchment hides of buffaloe. **1823** JAMES *Exped.* III. 50 These traders offered various articles . . . in exchange for horses and mules, bison-robes, and parchment or parfleche.

b. *In the parchment*, said of a hide in a dried, undressed condition to distinguish it from a green or a dressed hide.

*c*1785 S. PEARS *Narrative* (MS) 4 [Except] one elk skin in the parchment . . . we had not anything to live on. **1805** LEWIS in *Ann. 9th Congress* 2 Sess. 1043 Deer and elk tallow, elk skins dressed and in parchment.

2. A diploma received upon graduation from college; an official certificate.

1851 *Knickerb.* XXXVIII. 93 [The boy] had just obtained his 'parchment' from an eastern college. **1856** CARTWRIGHT *Autobiog.* 59 This permit to exhort was all the license I ever received from the Church to preach until I received my parchment of ordination. **1896** MOE *Hist. Harvard* 73 Three of these lusty young feed-casters were not given their parchments for *thirty-two years.*

3. In obs. combs.: (1) **parchment money,** a form of paper money printed on parchment; (2) **moose,** dried moose hide, cf. ∗**parchment 1;** (3) **proprietor,** in those parts of the U.S. formerly held by Spain, one who holds or owns land by virtue of an old Spanish grant; (4) **right,** a right granted by or contained in an official document.

(1) **1723** *N.-Eng. Courant* 3 June 2/1 On Tuesday last a Woman try'd at our Superior Court for counterfeiting the Parchment Money of this Province, was brought in guilty. **1727** COMER *Diary* (1893) 25 This month in Boston the authorities made parchment money, i.e. a penny two pence, and 3 pence. — (2) **1775** in *Pub. Champlain Soc.* XXI. 190 Mr Forbersher himself ware so destresst that he eat all the Parchment Moose &c and many of his Furs and even a few garden seeds which he proposed to have sown the following Spring he also eat to Satisfy hunger. — (3) **1870** *Republican Rev.* 22 Oct. 2/1 Some lineal (?) descendant of a defunct parchment proprietor, draws forth his Spanish Grant and imperatively demands an immediate possession. — (4) **1791** *Ann. 1st Congress* II. 1915 The deviation from charters, and the infringement of parchment rights . . . had been made on different principles from those now mentioned.

pard pɑrd, *n.* Short for **pardner.** *Slang.*

1850 A. T. JACKSON *Forty-Niner* (1920) 18 It makes a lot of difference having a pard with you. **1888** *Austin* (Tex.) *Statesman* 1 Nov. 3/9 Actually, pard, I took you for a cross between a mad bull and a New York dude. **1947** *Trail Riders Bul.* Feb. 20/1 Wal, Sluefoot Jones—that's my pard . . . gits the job, 'long with me.

pardner ˈpɑrdnɚ, *n.* Also **pardener.** [Var. of ∗*partner.*] A close associate, partner or chum.

1795 DEARBORN *Columbian Grammar* 137 Improprieties, commonly called Vulgarisms, . . . [include] Pardener for Partner. **1855** *N.Y. Herald* 3 Dec. 5/3 Then mourn not for yer pardner's death. **1949** *Sat. Ev. Post* 21 May 69/2 So long, pardner.

Hence **pardnership.**

1862 LOWELL *Biglow P.* 2 Ser. iii. 99 Thet is, to hev the pardnership under th' ole name continner. **1897** Chi. Record *Klondike* 91 Congeniality and implicit confidence are the basis of a 'pardnership.'

parental school. A school for delinquent or, sometimes, defective children. — **1905** *Atlantic Mo.* Dec. 754 Her son, becoming more unmanageable by his teachers, was threatened with the parental school. **1910** *Harper's Wkly.* 18 June 13/3 The Parental School is provided for the same class of boys who are now sent to the present truant-schools.

Parent-Teacher Association. A local organization for social and educational purposes, composed of teachers and parents of elementary and high-school pupils, and functioning in connection with a school.

1915 CHURCHILL (*title*), Parent-teacher Associations in the Rural and Village Schools of Oregon. **1916** *Ann. Amer. Acad.* Sep. 141 The Parent-Teacher Association has passed its experimental stage. **1946** *Chi. D. News* 20 Feb. 14/4 The Parent-Teacher Association is by all odds the organization best able to clean up the Chicago schools.

Often **P.-T.A.** Also attrib.

1925 *K.C. Star* 4 Feb. 11/1. **1945** *Suburban List* 8 Feb. 17/2 Founders Day was observed Monday evening at the local PTA meeting held at Union school. **1947** *Democrat* 6 Nov. 1/1 It is proposed to organize a County Council of the P.-T.A.

parfleche ˈpɑrfleʃ, *n.* [f. Can. F. in same sense, app. f. F. *parer*, to parry, and *flèche*, arrow, from its use sometimes as a shield.] A hide, usu. of buffalo, that has been haired and dried; an article, as a robe, made of this. Also attrib.

1844 FRÉMONT *Exped.* 237 Some of us had the misfortune to wear moccasins with parfleche soles, so slippery that we could not keep our feet. **1882** R. I. DODGE *Our Wild Indians* 254 (*footnote*), Among almost all the Plains tribes, the thing made of it is also 'parfleche.' **1947** DEVOTO *Across Wide Mo.* 434 To the trapper 'parfleche' meant 'rawhide,' the stuff itself, not objects made of it.

Parfleche used by Plains Indians

b. A box or envelope of rawhide for storing dried meat and, occasionally, for carrying clothing and other things.

1910 HODGE *Amer. Indians* II. 203/1 Parfleche. . . . The ordinary skin box of the Plains and Rocky mtn. tribes, made of stiff-dressed rawhide from which the hair has been removed. It is usually of rectangular shape, varying from 2 by 3 ft in size for the largest boxes.

∗**parietal,** *n.* **1.** A demerit or deduction affecting a student's standing made by a parietal board or committee. **2.** A member of a parietal board or committee in a college. Both *obs.*

(1) **1836** *Harvardiana* III. 44 What is't ye do? Beware the parietals! **1851** HALL *College Words* 223 The deductions made by the Parietal Committee are also called *Parietals.* — (2) **1851** HALL *College Words* 223 The members of the [parietal] committee are called, in common parlance, *Parietals.*

∗**parietal,** *a.* Resident within the walls or buildings of a college; of or pertaining to the discipline administered by an officer or committee residing on a college campus.

1836 *Harvardiana* III. 98 Had I forgotten, alas! the stern parietal monitions? **1851** HALL *College Words* 223 At Harvard College the officers resident within the College walls constitute a permanent standing committee, called the Parietal Committee. They have particular cognizance of all tardiness at prayers and Sabbath services, and of all offences against good order and decorum. **1893** *Nation* 5 Jan. 16/1 One might call it, in college phrase, a style of parietal admonition.

∗**paring,** *n.* =**apple paring.** In full **paring bee.** *Colloq.* Cf. **apple bee.**

1845 *Lowell Offering* V. 269 When we were about to have a paring bee we sent our invitations a day or two previous. **1887** *Cent. Mag.* Dec. 331/1 There was nothin' wuth declarin', 'Cept I'd kissed her onct or twice, At a huskin' or a parin'. **1933** ANDREWS *Community Industries Shakers* 205 'Paring bees' were held several times a week in the fall.

∗**parish,** *n.*

1. In some southern states, formerly a district or subdivision of a county serving as the ultimate political unit in local government.

In the South, as well as in New England, this term was originally ecclesiastical, but it quickly took on a political aspect which gained precedence and has persisted in Louisiana, where the parish corresponds to the county in other states.

1641 in NEILL *Virginia Carolorum* 165 Resolved, That the county of Upper Norfolk be divided into three distinct parishes. **1705** BEVERLEY *Virginia* IV. 9 Besides this Division into Counties, and Parishes, there are two other Sub-divisions. **1829** SHERWOOD *Gaz. Georgia* (ed. 2) 12 The separate sections of the settled parts of the State were denominated Parishes . . . ; *now* they were called counties. **1891** *Harper's Mag.* June 111/2 The Virginians preserved the parish, but its boundary lines were often coterminous with those of the county, while in more than one instance a parish included more than a single county. **1900** *Cong. Rec.* 5 Feb. 1498/1 The subdivisions of my State instead of being called counties are called parishes.

2. (See quots. 1828 and 1875.)

1828 WEBSTER *s.v. Society* 7 In *Connecticut*, a number of families united and incorporated for the purpose of supporting public worship, is called an *ecclesiastical society*. . . . In Massachusetts, such an incorporated society is usually called a *parish*, though consisting of persons only, without regard to territory. **1875** IERSON ed. Lamson *Church First 3 Cents*. VII. ii. 308 The term 'parish' is applied in America to congregations, considered as the minister's 'cure of souls' without the reference to local limits with which in England it is associated. **1891** WILKINS *N. Eng. Nun* 119 This poor parish had no settled preacher.

3. In combs.: (1) **parish country,** a region where parishes prevail, *obs.;* (2) **court,** *La.* a court having certain jurisdiction within a parish; (3) **judge,** (see quot. 1826), *obs.;* (4) **levy,** a levy made by a parish, sense **1,** *obs.;* (5) **library,** a library serving a parish; (6) **prison,** a prison serving a parish, sense **1.**

(1) **1853** SIMMS *Sword & Distaff* 58 They had just passed an ancient Clubhouse, such as may be found, to this day, throughout the parish country of South Carolina. — (2) **1834** BAIRD *Valley Mississippi* 273 The Parish Courts [in La.] hold a regular session in each parish on the first Monday in every month. **1853** STOWE *Key* 74/1 The parish court [in La.] decreed that she should recover 1200 dollars. — (3) **1826** FLINT *Recoll.* 350 The 'parish judge' . . . decides probate affairs, and holds a parish court, which takes cognizance of a great variety of causes. **1851** HALL *Manhattaner* 95 Forgetful of the . . . duties of Parish Judge (a historical office now) . . . , [he] is drinking the liquid notes. — (4) **1713** *N.C. Col. Rec.* II. 37 All Friends that do suffer. . . . Either for not bearing arms or Refusing to pay Parish Levies . . . [should] keep a true act. of the sum they suffer.

(5) **1854** THOREAU *Walden* 119 Let the village . . . not stop short at a pedagogue, a parson, a sexton, a parish library, and three selectmen, because our pilgrim forefathers got through a cold winter once on a bleak rock with these. **1910** BOSTWICK *Amer. Pub. Library* 5 Church or parish libraries [were] established in many of the colonies. — (6) **1891** *Atlantic Mo.* June 805/1 The convicts in the chain gang in the New Orleans Parish prison and the Birmingham mines.

As the last term in **banner, close, poll parish.**

∗**park,** *n.* [Senses **2, 3,** and **4,** pertaining as they do to the West, are app. the results of Amer. borrowings f. French.]

1. An area resembling an artificial park or pleasure ground occurring naturally in a forest or unsettled region. Also in place-names.

1643 in *Amer. Sp.* XV. 292/1 That parcell of land at Dunn Park, whereof lyeth on the south side of Dunn Creeke, and Parke on the North. **1686** *Ib.*, Three thousand acres of Land . . . on both sydes a great runne and commonly called and known by the name of Beverley Parke and adjoining on the one part thereof to Buttons Rainge. **1834** CLAY in Benton *30 Years' View* I. 418/1 It was a most beautiful country [near Lexington, Ky.]—all the lands in it, not in a state of cultivation, was in parks (natural meadows).

attrib. **1876** DODGE *Black Hills* 66 The country is covered with pine timber, in which are many irregular 'park' openings. **1918** VISHER *So. Dakota* 44 The more open 'park area,' developed on the schist, slate, and igneous rock, has many broad valleys lower than the limestone plateau.

2. An inclosed place into which buffalo, elk, etc., are lured or driven for slaughter. *Obs.*

*c***1797** in MASSON *Bourgeois* 279 The chief of the park thinks that if he were to eat any of this meat thus killed, it would be out of his power to make buffaloes enter his park ever after; so he must have meat killed in the open field for his own use. **1805** LEWIS in *L. & Clark Exped.* I. (1904) 313 There was a park which they had formed of timber and brush, for the purpose of taking the cabrie or antelope. **1839** LEONARD *Adventures* (1904) 224 After travelling a short distance we arrived at a large pen, enclosing about three-fourths of an acre, which they call a park or correll.

3. The narrow piece of land within the oxbow bend of a river.

1808 PIKE *Sources Miss.* (1895) II. 380 Passed the *Park*, which is ten miles round, and not more than three quarters of a mile across. **1895** COUES in *Ib.* 381 (*footnote*), Near the N.E. corner of St. Clair Co. and the S.E. corner of Henry Co. [Missouri]. The Park is a narrow, somewhat rectangular loop of the Osage, including some bold bluffs in its bight.

4. In the Rocky Mts., esp. in Colorado and Wyoming, a valley shut in by high hills or mountains.

For a full discussion of the word in this sense see A. Matthews in *Mass. Col. Soc. Pub.* VIII. 373 ff.

1839 in *Ore. Hist. Soc. Quart.* XIV. 263 At noon we entered a very large valley, called *the Park*, at the entrance of which we crossed the North Fork of the River Platte. **1872** TICE *Across Plains* 183 The Indian name for these parks signified 'cow-lodge' or 'bull-pen' on account of the immense herds of buffalo with which they abounded. The Canadian French trappers, the first intruders into these mountain recesses, for the same reason called them '*parcs*,' which in French signifies an enclosed pasture. **1943** DEVOTO *Yr. of Decision* 64 [Telling] what scalps had been taken along the Yellowstone, who counted *coup* in Middle Park.

attrib. **1878** HINTON *Arizona* 48 The park system is found chiefly in that portion of the Rocky Mountains enclosed by a part of Wyoming and the whole of Eastern Colorado. **1947** *Canadian Alpine Jrnl.* June 102 This offered an easy way up and west to a beautiful park area near timberline.

5. Short for **ball park.**

1867 *Chi. Times* 25 July 5/2 These cars connect with the stock-yards dummy, which runs to within a short distance of the park. **1917** MATHEWSON *Sec. Base Sloan* 217 Which way is the park from here, please?

6. =**parking,** *n.* **3.**

1900 *Cong. Rec.* 17 Feb. 1894/1 There are hundreds of little parks at the intersection of streets.

7. In special combs.: (1) **park bencher,** an idler who sits in a park; (2) **loafer,** =prec.; (3) **ranger,** a ranger who patrols a park; (4) **way,** see as a main entry.

(1) **1909** O. HENRY *Options* 260 When I was twenty feet away the park-bencher called to me. — (2) **1861** *Vanity Fair* 13 April 173/1 A brutal looking young park-loafer . . . 'shied' a stone . . . at the superior biped with wings. — (3) **1941** FERGUSSON *Southwest* 144 In 1933 they were all brought under uniform control, and park rangers now assiduously police almost two million acres of land. **1949** *Sat. Ev. Post* 12 March 30/1 The more-or-less established trails I covered in the line of duty, as a park ranger, and the high-altitude climbing was extracurricular.

As the last term in **ball, baseball, city, double, driving, game, grazing, motor, mountain, national, National Military, National Zoölogical, Sequoia National, state park.**

∗**park,** *v. tr.* To put, set, or draw up in a particular place and leave temporarily (a wagon, train, automobile, etc.).

1864 BILLINGS in F. H. Garrison *John S. Billings* 95 The trains are parked along the edge of the river. **1867** RICHARDSON *Beyond Miss.* 79 And at night the wagons are parked in a circle. **1900** *Cong. Rec.* 2 Feb. 1445/1 No part of said street . . . shall be used for depot purposes, or railroad yard, or for the purpose of switching, shifting, or parking cars. **1948** *Democrat* 1 Jan. 4/2 Drivers now can park or back into alleys or up to loading platforms with much greater ease.

transf. **1915** YOUNG *Hard Knocks* 182 He offered me ten dollars per day . . . if I would go, and help park this wood—meaning by that, to haul it from side hills to where they could get at it with ox teams to transport it to the post. **1945** *Sky Line Trail* Feb. 9/2 There are deep pockets in a parka into which you could park a sandwich, extra sweater, suntan oil, cigarettes or what-have-you. **1949** *Desplaines Valley News* (Summit, Ill.) 6 May 10/1 [She] suggests that the community provide a nursery for mothers who find it difficult to park tiny children when shopping, at work, or otherwise engaged in activities of the home.

parka ˈparkə, *n.* [Of Eskimo origin. Cf. Aleut. Esk. *parka*, outside garment made of skin.] A long shirt or jacket made originally of skins, now of wool, heavy drill, or the like, with a hood. Also transf.

1868 WHYMPER *Alaska* 144 The men had very naturally a strong desire to obtain skin clothing for winter use. . . . This was generally known as the 'Parka mania' (from *parka*, Russian for skin shirt or coat). **1902** LONDON *Daughter of Snows* 168 He . . . took in the priests and choir-boys in their surplices,—*parkas*, he called 'em. **1948** *Sierra Club Bul.* March 6 Hands disappeared into gloves and parkas blossomed out in full force.

b. A pointed hood.

1944 *Sears Cat.* (ed. 189) 231 Pixie Parka—Furry looking brushed fabric (55% rayon, 45% cotton) with cunning peaked top, chin ties. One size, fits 3 to 6 years. **1949** *This Week Mag.* 17 Sep. 15/4 When it spoke through layers of fur and parka I recognized the voice.

Parker House roll. A soft roll made by folding one half of a round of bread dough over the other. — **1883** *Practical Housekeeping* 41 Parker House Rolls. . . . To mold, cut with cake-cutter; put a little melted butter on one-half and lap nearly over on the other half. **1949** *Chi. Tribune* 28 Oct. 5/1 The guests were served mashed potatoes, and gravy, . . . Parker House rolls, apple pie with cheese, coffee, and milk.

Parkerism ˈparkɚˌɪzəm, *n.* The theological teachings of Theodore Parker (1810–60). *Obs.* — **1850** B. ALCOTT *Journals* 227 Groton Conventions, . . . Parkerism, Conversations, and Emerson—these were significant aspects of the time.

∗**parking,** *n.*

1. The setting of a house well back from the front line of a building lot.

1884 *Cent. Mag.* March 649/2 In Washington, however, the streets were wide enough to permit this without sacrificing any private property, and the system of 'parking' thus became the rule, and not the exception.

2. An area, usu. turfed and planted with trees, in front of, or immediately adjacent to, a building.

1885 E. INGLE *Local Inst. Va.* 109 Spaces were left [in Williamsburg, Va.] for a market place, court-house green and parking for the palace. **1918** *Idaho Agric. Exp. Sta. Bul.* 105, 46 If necessary to place the poles in the parking they should be set next the walks and painted green.

3. In Washington, D.C., an open space, beautified with grass, flowers, etc., from which several streets radiate. Cf. **park,** *n.* **6.**

1900 *Cong. Rec.* 17 Feb. 1895/1 The little plats of ground at the intersection of streets which are generally denominated 'parkings.'

4. *attrib.* Designating areas where automobiles may be parked, as (1) **parking ground,** (2) **lot,** (3) **space.**

(1) **1944** *Chi. Tribune* IV, Highest parking ground east of the Rockies is this area on Clingman's Dome in Great Smoky Mountain park. — (2) **1924** H. CROY *R.F.D. No. 3* 172 Some of the people still lingered under the arc light, with its summer collection of bugs still in it, waiting for the two to come from the parking lot. **1949** *Lubbock* (Tex.) *Morn. Avalanche* 23 Feb. II. 10/1 Bids will be asked for laying pavement over the Tech parking lots. — (3) **1924** *Collier's* 5 Jan. 17/2 Secretary Mellon has asked permission to move the Washington Monument so as to get more parking space.

b. parking meter, a mechanical device, installed near a parking space and operated by means of an inserted coin, which keeps tab on the length of time a car is parked near it.

1936 *Dly. Oklahoman* (Okla. City) 4 Nov. 12/3 (*caption*), Patent Claims Are Granted On Gumm's Parking Meters. **1949** *Chi. D. News* 11 Aug. 3/4 A runaway horse and wagon collided with a parking meter.

c. parking ticket, a ticket or summons to court given by a policeman to a motorist who has violated a parking regulation.

1947 *Denver Post* 2 March A. 1/2 Parking tickets no longer could be fixed. **1949** *Time* 18 April 40/3 He tried to turn down a parking ticket by claiming congressional immunity.

Parkman('s) wren. [f. George *Parkman* (1791–1849), Boston physician.] (See quot. 1917.) — **1839** AUDUBON *Ornith. Biog.* V. 310 Parkman's Wren. *Troglodytes Parkmanii* . . . I have named it after my . . . friend, George Parkman. **1917** *Birds of Amer.* III. 194/2 The Western House Wren, or Parkman Wren (*Troglodytes aëdon parkmani*), as he is called.

parkway ˈpɑrkˌwe, *n.*

1. (See quot. 1898.) Also attrib.

1887 *Visit to States* xxix. 378 This broad parkway has a magnificent drive on either side of a central walk for pedestrians. **1898** *19th Cent.* April 585 'Park-ways,' to connect the great outlying woodlands . . . with the Metropolitan Parks of Boston and the surrounding townships. These park-ways are broad boulevards with margins of grass, wood, and river. **1938** *L.A. Times* 5 Aug. 10/3 The Arroyo Seco Parkway . . . will be centered by a six-foot parkway division strip.

2. A strip of land, usu. turfed and planted with trees, beside a street, etc. Cf. **parking,** *n.* **2.**

1903 *N.Y. Times* 16 Aug., He must tear up the parkway again, rebuild it with proper earth, and plant in it trees that will give shade. **1948** *Dly. Ardmoreite* (Ardmore, Okla.) 2 May 13/1 He is also putting in the sprinkler system on the parkway.

parlay ˈpɑrlɪ, *v.* Also **parlee.** [F. f. It. *paroli.*] *tr.* To wager (money) on a horse race, cards, etc., and to continue to wager the original stake plus the winnings on subsequent races, hands, etc. Also absol. and transf.

1828 *Richmond Whig* 20 Feb. 1/3 (Th.), As well, sir, might you ask the adventurer at Faro, who paralees (I believe, sir, that most of us are old enough to remember the term, although I trust that with the practice it is quite obsolete), who paralees I say [etc.]. **1892** QUINN *Fools of Fortune* 194 Almost all [faro] bankers will allow a player to 'parlee,' as the percentage is largely in favor of the bank. **1895** *How to Make Money on Small Cap.* 63 Were he, however, to what is termed 'parley' his money—that is to say, if . . . he put his $5 on his choice on the first race, and, if the horse should win, put all the winnings and his original $5 on the next race, and so on. **1949** *Sat. Ev. Post* 25 June 32 H. J. Heinz . . . parlayed a pickle into one of the most valuable family heirlooms in America.

***parlor,** *n.* In combs.: (1) **parlor car,** see as a main entry; (2) **girl,** a maid who takes care of the parlor, the table, and the door; (3) **grand,** short for "parlor grand piano"; (4) ***house,** an expensive type of brothel provided with a parlor; (5) **match,** a friction match containing little or no sulphur; (6) **melodeon,** =next; (7) **organ,** a musical instrument having metal reeds acted upon by currents of air set in motion by a bellows, and controlled from a keyboard like that of a piano, also transf.; (8) **set,** a set or suite of matched furniture suitable for a parlor; (9) **stove,** a stove suitable for use in a parlor; (10) **suit,** =**parlor set.**

(2) **1863** A. D. WHITNEY *F. Gartney* iii, The parlor-girl made her appearance with her mop and tub of hot water to wash up the silver and china. **1880** HOWELLS *Woman's Reason* xviii, I've never seen distinctions in society so awful as the distinction between shop-girls and parlor-girls. — (3) **1856** *Porter's Spirit of Times* 8 Nov. 168/2 Chickering's Pianos at the Boston Fair—carried away the palm of excellence, as by far the best instruments exhibited, whether Grand, Semi-Grand, or Parlor Grand. **1883** WILDER *Sister Ridnour* 168 Mrs. Kendrick has a new 'parlor grand' that is perfectly magnificent. — (4) **1872** CRAPSEY *Nether Side N.Y.* 142 For some years past a most deplorable change has been going on which has had the effect of great-

Parlor organ (*c*1884)

ly decreasing the number of parlor houses, while houses of assignation have multiplied in the same ratio. **1947** CRANE *Sins of N.Y.* 273 Until a few years ago New York had some of the fanciest parlor houses in the U.S.

(5) **1898** *K.C. Star* 20 Dec. 9/2, 12 boxes Parlor Matches . . . 5¢. **1927** *Scribner's Mag.* March 326/2 There is only one good match—that is the big, soft-nosed parlor-match that will light on anything. — (6) **1909** O. HENRY *Roads of Destiny* vii. 107 The natives were panning out enough from the beach sands to buy all the rum, red calico, and parlour melodeons in all the world. — (7) **1845** in *Cincinnati Misc.* I. 179 'I was on a visit to Vermont a few weeks since,' said he, 'and intended to buy a parlor Organ.' **1943** POWELL *Home Again* 96 There was an ordinary parlor organ, but on the days in which Old Lady McCan, . . . attended services, the organ in the Baptist Church could not be used. — (8) **1873** *Winfield* (Kans.) *Courier* 24 July 2/3 Better to use the old cane-seated chairs . . . than to tremble at the bills sent him from the upholsters for the most elegant parlor set ever made. **1920** HOWELLS *Vacation of Kelwyns*, There was a parlor set of black walnut. — (9) **1825** *Vt. Aurora* (Vergennes) 25 Aug. 4/3 He has on hand, a complete assortment of . . . Parlor, Shop, and Cooking Stoves.

(10) **1875** *Chi. Tribune* 21 Nov. 1/4 Parlor Suits. It will pay you to compare prices before buying. **1892** *York Co. Hist. Rev.* 99 In the furniture department are all kinds of cabinet ware, bedroom and parlor suits.

As the last term in **beauty, bridge, hotel, ice cream, ladies', old field, oyster, refreshment, shoe, shoe-shining parlor.**

parlor car. A railroad passenger car equipped with superior accommodations, as individual chairs, sofas, etc., and for riding on which an extra fare is now usu. charged (see quot. 1895).

1868 H. M. FLINT *Railroads of U.S.* 406 We left Albany . . . in a Pullman's saloon parlor car. **1895** WAIT *Car-Builder's Dict.*, The names *parlor-car, drawing-room car* and *chair-car* are all used somewhat indiscriminately, but *chair-car* ordinarily refers to a parlor-car with adjustable or reclining chairs, for riding in which no extra fare is charged. **1946** *Harper's Mag.* Jan. 38/2, I . . . spent a whole day in the lounge half of a combination diner and parlor car.

attrib. **1892** HOWELLS *Quality of Mercy* 89 Impossible to identify parlor-car passengers. **1903** E. JOHNSON *Railway Transportation* 146 The profits . . . from the parlor- and sleeping-car traffic are really smaller than those obtained from the day coach service. **1949** *Sat. Ev. Post* 30 April 106/2 Otto has a hard time getting a seat in the parlor car on No. 11 when he goes home for a rest from his wheel-house duties.

b. parlor cattle car, a cattle car of a superior type.

1881 *Chi. Times* 30 April, The first parlor cattle-car left to-night for New York.

Parmachenee Belle. [f. *Parmachenee* Lake, Me.] A type of artificial trout fly used by anglers.

1890 *Outing* Aug. 87/2 Seasonable Trout Flies . . . Moosehead and Rangeley Lakes. Par-machenee Belle—Body, yellow; remainder red and white mixed. **1923** *Ib.* Feb. 224/2 On streams where such flies as Royal Coachman, Silver Doctor, and Parmacheene Belle are takers in the daytime, after nightfall the angler must resort to opposites, indiscriminates. **1948** *Chi. Tribune* 20 June II. 7/1 Now it's a realistic hypocrisy revolution in trout flies, with some anglers saying phooey to the old time attractor flies like the Royal Coachman, Parmachene Belle and other similar patterns.

* **parole,** *n.*

1. ?A certificate given an Indian chief by a government representative in token of his being regarded as the legal head of his tribe. *Obs.*

1804 CLARK in *Lewis & C. Exped.* I. (1904) 129 To the Grand Chief we gave a Flag and the parole (certificate). **1806** in E. H. CRISWELL *Lewis and Clark* (1940) 61/2, I just informed the chiefs that I had merely assembled them to deliver the parole of the general and present the marks of distinction.

2. In combs.: (1) **parole board,** a board in charge of paroling prisoners; (2) **camp,** any one of several camps established by the federal government for northern soldiers who had been captured and paroled by the Confederacy but who were not yet regularly exchanged, *obs.;* (3) **officer,** an officer concerned with the oversight of paroled prisoners; (4) **system,** (see quot.).

(1) [**1908** *Charities* 26 Sep. 730/2 Clearly the Board of Parole is acting adversely to its own rule.] **1916** *N.Y. Times Mag.* 9 Jan. 19 There will be weekly meetings . . . of the Parole Board. **1949** *N.O. Times-Picayune Mag.* 13 Nov. 24/3 A five-man parole board in Washington considers many factors before granting a request for parole. — **(2)** **1867** Goss *Soldier's Story* 53 Three months followed in the parole camp, where I regained strength. **1892** *Cong. Rec.* 18 March 2220/1 It was necessary for this man to get a pass from this parole camp when he left? — **(3)** **1907** *Charities* 24 Aug. 609/2 Three parole officers and one parole matron have been added to the police department. **1949** *N.O. Times-Picayune Mag.* 13 Nov. 23/2 He became chief probation and parole officer for the federal court. — **(4)** **1900** *Cong. Rec.* 1130/2 We have in that State what is known as the parole system. Prisoners are put out on their good behavior.

* **parole,** *v. tr.* To release conditionally (a prisoner—freq. one who has served part of his sentence in a penal institution).

1790 D. FANNING *Narrative* 32, I then parolled the prisoners, except 30, which I sent to Wilmington. **1865** BOUDRYE *Fifth N.Y. Cavalry* 269 We are going to be paroled when these rolls are finished. **1948** *Chi. D. News* 27 Feb. 1/6 Another of those parolled . . . put up $5,000 as a fee.

* **paroled,** *a.* Placed on parole.

1865 BOUDRYE *Fifth N.Y. Cavalry* 196 It is remarkable how readily paroled Rebel soldiers affiliate with us. **1908** *Independent* 16 Jan. 146/2 Of his one thousand and seven or eight hundred paroled men, up to this evening, seventy-seven have fallen. **1925** *Scribner's Mag.* Oct. 410/1 A large proportion of paroled prisoners have been reclaimed from their evil ways by this judicious system.

parolee pəˌroˈli, *n.* One who is paroled. — **1936** M. PURVIS *Amer. Agent* 182 A study of the individual prisoner . . . would be beneficial . . . particularly when he becomes a parolee. **1949** *Welfare Bul.* March 7/1 It will enable the Department to serve parolees more fully.

* **parquet,** *n.* Also **parquette.** The main floor of a theater, or that part of it extending back from the orchestra as far as the parquet circle *q.v.* Also attrib.

1835 INGRAHAM *South-West* I. 221 The pit or parquette, as it is here termed, which is considered the most eligible and fashionable part of the house. **1842** *Chi. American* 18 Aug., Parquet tickets 50 cents. **1917** McCUTCHEON *Green Fancy* 343 Parquet $217.50, dress circle $105.

b. parquet circle, that part of the main floor of a theater beneath the galleries.

1854 in E. THOMPKINS *Boston Theatre* (1908) 15 Persons who purchase Tickets . . . for either the Parquette, Parquette Circle, Balcony [etc.]. **1896** BIRKMIRE *Planning of Amer. Theatres* 62 The parquette circle . . . is arranged in steps.

* **parrot,** *n.* As the last term in **Illinois, thick-billed parrot.**

* **Parrott,** *n.* [Robert Parker *Parrott* (1804–77), Amer. inventor.] A muzzle-loading, cast-iron, rifled gun having the breech reinforced with a band of wrought iron. In full **Parrott gun.**

1862 HALSEY *New Union Song Bk.* 49 At Pulaski they could not see How our Parrotts pecked their ramparts. **1862** NORTON *Army Lett.* 72 A little way on the other side a battery of Parrott guns. **1865** BOUDRYE *Fifth N.Y. Cavalry* 33 Our company and company E were ordered to cover the parrot gun battery. **1901** CHURCHILL *Crisis* 422 His cap is fanned off by the blast of a Parrott six feet above his head. **1945** MARLOWE *Coaching Roads* 18 He [Treadwell] invented . . . the gun long known as the Parrott gun (Parrott, he claimed, having appropriated his ideas).

Also **Parrott rifle.**

1935 HILL *Sea Dogs of Sixties* 171 She had two wounded, one by a sniper's ball, the other by the bursting of the Parrott rifle.

* **parsley,** *n.*

1. parsley haw, a small tree, *Crataegus apiifolia,* found in the southern states. Cf. next.

1884 SARGENT *Rep. Forests* 81. **1897** SUDWORTH *Arborescent Flora* 232 *Cratægus apiifolia.* . . . Parsley Haw (N.C., Ala., Fla., Miss., La.). . . . Parsley-leaved Haw (S.C.).

2. parsley-leaved, *a.* In the names of plants, etc.: Having leaves similar to sprigs of parsley.

1785 MARSHALL *Amer. Grove* 166 *Vitis laciniosa.* Canadian Parsley-leaved Vine. . . . The leaves are cut into many slender segments, somewhat in the manner of a Parsley-leaf. **1813** MUHLENBERG *Cat. Plants* 49 *Crataegus apiifolia,* Parsley-leaved hawthorn. Car. Cherok. **1860** CURTIS *Woody Plants N.C.* 83 Parsley-leaved Haw. . . . The fruit is red and about 1/4 inch long. **1892** APGAR *Trees Northern U.S.* 105 *Crataegus apiifolia.* (Parsley-leaved Thorn.) . . . Virginia and south, in moist woods. **1941** R. S. WALKER *Lookout* 64 Of the ornamental trees, the parsley-leaved thorn makes a splendid contribution to the mountain with its handsome foliage.

* **parson,** *n.* (See quot.) Cf. **Maryland, tipsy parson.** — **1816** in G. SHAW *Gen. Zool.* IX. 407 [The indigo bunting] is called in Carolina the Parson.

* **part,** *n.* "The parting of the hair" (*Cent.*). — **1871** M. TWAIN *Sk. New & Old* (1875) 260 (R.), He brushed his hair with elaborate care, accomplishing an accurate part behind. **1895** *Cent. Mag.* Aug. 489/1 His straight, smooth hair, with its definite part.

* **parterre,** *n.* A section in a theater beneath the galleries. Also = next.

1836 T. POWER *Impr. of Amer.* (ed. 2) I. 92 A narrower selvage round the vast area of our parterre. **1883** *Harper's Mag.* Nov. 884/1 Over this [the half-tier] in succession, are the parterre, the first and second tiers, and then the balcony and the gallery.

b. parterre box, in a theater, a box located beneath the balcony.

1896 BIRKMIRE *Planning of Amer. Theatres* 5 The hangings between the *parterre* boxes and the nineteen of the *grand* tier [of the Metropolitan Opera House] are of a maroon tint.

partialism ˈparʃəlˌɪzəm, *n.* A religious view that does not take into account all the facts bearing upon a subject. *Obs.* — **1872** BEECHER *Yale Lectures on Preaching* I. 26 Your mode of presenting the truth will be imperfect. Your partialisms are full of danger. **1897** *Advance* 2 Dec. 779/3 The Gospel also is in danger . . . from partialism, because men do not fully realize what Christ is in his three offices of prophet, priest, and king.

partialist ˈparʃəlɪst, *n.* One who holds a partial theory or is inclined toward partialism. Also **partialistic,** *a. Obs.* — **1844** EMERSON *Nominalist & Realist* Ess. 2 Ser., Very fitly, therefore, I assert, that every man is a partialist. **1896** GLADDEN in *Ohio Ch. Hist. Soc. P.* VII. 141 The whole partialistic scheme of a rulership which is for a portion of mankind and against the rest.

* **particular,** *a.* Used as an intensive, esp. in *to give* (someone) *particular hell, jesse, lightning, saltpeter. Slang.* Cf. also * **Moses,** *n.* **3.**

1846 *Spirit of Times* 6 June 176/2 Our boys did give them *'most particular Jesse,'* and that is all I have time to tell you about the battle. **1847** J. S. ROBB *Squatter Life* 31 [To an editor.] Don't forget to gin the town below particular saltpetre. **1861** *Oregon Argus* 19 Jan. (Th.), The overseer charged the driver to give him particular hell. **1871** *Harper's Mag.* Oct. 690/1 Ef Pat Role, or any other consarned Irishman, kicks up a muss 'bout these yer diggings, he'll kotch partic'lar lightnin'.

***particularist,** *n.* An adherent of the policy of States' rights; one who favors strict construction. Also attrib. or as adj. *Obs.*

1876 *N. Amer. Rev.* Oct. 338 During the administration of Washington the particularist tendencies were mostly quiet. **1885** *Mag. Amer. Hist.* March 297/1 *Particularists.*—A wing of the post-revolutionary Whigs. . . . They were also known later on as 'Anti-Federals.' **1913** A. C. COLE *Whig Party* 8 Jackson had led many to believe that he was decidedly friendly to the particularist cause.

partida pɑr'tidə, *n. S.W.* [Sp., a group, a band.] A party, band; also a drove of cattle.

c1892 *D.N.* I. 192 Partida: a drove of cattle. This word answers to the common American words 'a lot,' 'a heap,' etc. speaking of an indefinite quantity. **1929** DOBIE *Vaquero* 66 (Bentley), Mustang Gray . . . rounded up a partida of Cortina bandits.

b. Also **partidario,** (see quot.).

1941 FERGUSSON *Southwest* 177 He (the partidario) farms out ewes to a herder, who agrees to return the same number, . . . after a term, usually of five years. The partidario pays all expenses, even taxes, and, of course, takes all the risk of flood and drought, blizzard, disease, or other losses.

parting line. A boundary line between two properties. *Obs.* — **1699** *Boston Rec.* 233 The way shall [run] . . . to the gate in the parting line between Mr. Winthrops land and Major Townsends farm. *Ib.*, [The way is] to run . . . through the gate in the parting line between John Tuttle & Jonathon Tuttle.

partisan 'pɑrtəzn̩, *n.* [F. in same sense. An Amer. borrowing.] The leader of an Indian war party; also the chief, or one in charge, of a band of trappers. Also attrib. *Obs.*

1761 NILES *Indian Wars* II. 565 Monsieur Longville . . . was a famous partisan or partner with [the Indians]. **1827** COOPER *Prairie* xx, What tribe or nation has not felt the blows of the Dachotahs? Mahtoree is their partisan. **1861** *Harper's Mag.* March 451/1 Captain Dalrell, who had won great renown as a partisan warrior with Putnam, proposed . . . a night surprise of Pontiac's encampment.

partition fence. A fence serving to divide the property of two landowners. Also **partitional fence.**

1639 *Dedham Rec.* 51 That may both be a Partition fence in the same, as also may serve for a course unto a water mill. **1858** *Boston Rec.* II. 145 All partitional fences . . . shall be ordered by the select men. **1870** *Rep. Comm. Agric. 1869* 395 Partition fences must be proof against sheep.

***partner,** *n.* As the last term in **change, general, side, silent, special partner.**

partnership fence. A fence owned commonly or jointly by neighbors. — **1845** *Indiana Senate Jrnl.* 20 Sess. 335 A bill to provide for the dissolving of partnership fences.

***partridge,** *n.*

1. *S.* The bobwhite, *Colinus virginianus.*

1587 HAKLUYT tr. Laudonnière *Notable Historie* 6ʳ As we passed throw these woods we saw . . . Partridges gray and redde, little different from ours, but chiefly in bignesse. **1612** SMITH *Virginia* I. 15 Partridges there are little bigger than our Quailes, wilde Turkies are as bigge as our tame. **1709** LAWSON *Carolina* 67 The woods [were] stor'd every where, with . . . great Store of Partridges, Cranes, and Conies. **1856** *Spirit of Times* 6 Sep. 9/1 Far to the Southward, Quail, or as they are there called, Partridge, are now ready. **1938** MATSCHAT *Suwannee River* 208 Quail, commonly called partridges throughout the South, are very shy and timid.

2. The ruffed grouse, *Bonasa umbellus.*

1630 HIGGINSON *N.-Eng.* 15 And [I] my selfe . . . sprung a Partridge so bigge that through the heauinesse of his Body could fly but a little way. **1701** WOLLEY *Journal N.Y.* 40 They have great store of wild-fowl, as Turkys, Heath-hens, Quails, Partridges, Pigeons. **1856** GOODRICH *Recoll.* I. 98 The *partridge* of New England is the *pheasant* of the South, and the *ruffed grouse* of the naturalists. **1947** *Collier's* 29 March 92/2 If in New England a person mentions 'partridge,' they have in mind the ruffed grouse.

3. In combs.: (1) **partridgeberry,** see as a main entry; (2) **bush,** (see quot.); (3) **hawk,** =**goshawk;** (4) ***pea,** a sensitive pea of the genus *Chamaecrista,* esp. *C. fasciculata;* (5) **plant,** the wintergreen, *Gaultheria procumbens;* (6) **plum,** =**partridgeberry 2;** (7) **run,** a run, dash, or dance step suggestive of the quick running away of a partridge, *obs.;* (8) **trap,** a trap in which partridges are taken; (9) **vine,** =**partridge plant.**

(2) **1843** *Amer. Pioneer* II. 125 The vivid green leaves and bright scarlet berries of the 'Partridge bush,' or 'Checkerberry.'. — (3) **1895** *Dept. Agric. Yrbk. 1894* 231 From the persistency with which this species hunts the ruffed grouse in many of the Northern States, it has received the name 'partridge hawk.' **1917** *Birds of Amer.* II. 68 Goshawk. *Astur atricapillus atricapillus.* . . . [Also called] Blue Darter; Partridge Hawk; Dove Hawk. — (4) **1787** *Amer. Museum* II. 451/2 The eastern shore bean . . . has been mistaken, by some, for the common tare or partridge-pea. **1873** *Harper's Mag.* April 751/1 The partridge-pea, with its crimson hood, Is scattered about like drops of blood. **1949** *Mo. Bot. Garden Bul.* Feb. 51 Partridge pea . . . is perhaps one of the most valuable of our quail-food plants. (5) **1850** S. F. COOPER *Rural Hours* 105 Violets . . . grow there, with . . . squaw-vine, partridge-plant, pipsissiwa. **1894** *Amer. Folk-Lore* VII. 93 *Gaultheria procumbens,* partridge-plant, N.Y. — (6) **c1876** H. B. STOWE *First Christmas* 121 Little Love gathered stores of bright checker berries and partridge plums. — (7) **1807** IRVING *Salmagundi* xvii. 460 [Rigadoon] gave a short partridge run, and with mighty vigor and swiftness did bolt over the walls with a somerset. **1825** PAULDING *J. Bull in Amer.* 113 Several . . . were seen cutting pigeon wings and taking the partridge run with all the alacrity imaginable. — (8) **1832** KENNEDY *Swallow Barn* II. 223 The model by which boys build partridge-traps. **1858** *S. Lit. Messenger* XXVI. 254/2 Like the figger 4 trigger to a imments partrich trap. — (9) **1880** *Harper's Mag.* Nov. 864/1 Here are soft beds of rich green moss studded with scarlet berries of wintergreen and partridge vine. **1907** *N.Y. Ev. Post* (s.-w. ed.) 6 May 5 In the basket was one growing plant with moss and a bit of partridge vine.

As the last term in **American, birch, black, crested, Gambel, mountain, night, plumed, savanna, scaled, spruce, swamp, tufted, valley, Virginia, Virginian partridge.**

partridgeberry 'pɑrtrɪdʒ,berɪ, *n.*

1. A trailing plant, *Mitchella repens,* common throughout the eastern U.S. Also the wintergreen, *Gaultheria procumbens.* Cf. **checkerberry.**

1714 *Phil. Trans.* XXIX. 63 Another Plant, . . . Partridge-berries, excellent in curing the Dropsy; a Decoction of the Leaves being drank several days as a Tea. **1784** CUTLER in *Mem. Amer. Acad.* I. 410 *Mitchella.* . . . Partridgeberry. The stems trailing. . . . Blossoms white. In thick woods and swamps. **1814** BIGELOW *Florula Bostoniensis* 101 *Gaultheria procumbens.* Partridge berry. . . . A plant universally known for its pleasant aromatic flavour. **1948** *Green Bay* (Wis.) *Press-Gazette* 30 June 2/2 We hoped to find twinflowers and partridge-berries to record in moving pictures.

2. The fruit of such a plant.

1810 in WILSON *Ornithology* III. 109 A favourite article of their diet is the heath-hen plum, or partridge-berry. **1905** WIGGIN *Rose* 112 Partridge-berries glowed red under their glossy leaves.

3. partridgeberry vine, the partridgeberry, *Mitchella repens.*

1868 BEECHER *Norwood* 91 Here the little queen took on airs, and sent her Ethiop . . . [for] some partridge-berry vines from the edge of the wood. **1910** EATON *Barn Doors & Byways* 245 We have come upon ferns still flaunting through the snow and partridge berry vines scratched up into sight by some hungry bird.

***party,** *n.* In combs.: (1) **party boss,** one who has a position of authority and influence in a political party; (2) **bummer,** a person who lives by political chicanery; (3) **collar,** *fig.* a symbol of subjection to a political party, *colloq.;* (4) **convention,** a convention held for the purpose of making party nominations; (5) **line,** see as a main entry; (6) **machine,** anything, as an office, that serves the interests of a political party organization; (7) **machinery,** the leaders, advisers, committees, etc., engaged in carrying on the work of a political party; (8) **manager,** =**party boss;** (9) **platform,** a formal statement of the principles and policies of a political party; (10) **plunder,** (see quot.); (11) **question,** a question or subject upon which political parties differ as a matter of party policy; (12) **regularity,** the practice or custom of faithfully supporting one's party, cf. ***regular,** *a.;* (13) **ticket,** (*a*) a list of candidates for office put forward or indorsed by the leaders or representatives of a political party, (*b*) a printed ballot containing such a list; (14) **vote,** (*a*) a vote, as in Congress, along strict party lines, (*b*) the collective vote polled by a political party; (15) **whip,** the pressure exerted by a party upon its members in a legislature, also the person who exercises this pressure.

(1) **1927** *Scribner's Mag.* March 269/1 No judge would risk offending the alderman and party-boss of a large pivotal ward. **1948** *Chi. Tribune* 20 June IV. 4/4 He accepted his first nominations and won his first congressional elections as the gift of party bosses. — (2) **1888** BRYCE *Amer. Commonw.* II. III. lxiv, Certain salaries and fees in local

offices are kept notoriously high, so that the incumbent may freely 'bleed' for party use, or what is the same thing, for the use of party 'bummers.' — (3) **1906** M. Twain *What Is Man?* (1917) iv. 44 (R.), In America if you know which party collar a voter wears you know what his associations are. — (4) **1881** *Nation* XXXIII. 4 The slipshod method in which the Vice-President is commonly chosen by party conventions.

(6) **1891** Thanet *Otto the Knight* 266 He can't be trusted to run the office as a party machine, and Milton Bedford can! — (7) **1829** Orne *Lett. Columbus* 71 (Ernst), Gen. Jackson was also less embarrassed by party machinery than any other candidate ever was. **1913** La Follette *Autobiog.* 53, I knew nothing about the underlying forces which at that time controlled and in large measure still control, party machinery. — (8) **1881** *Bradstreet's* IV. 305 The voters of Kings county have usually been relied upon by party managers. **1911** H. S. Harrison *Queed* xxiii. 291 The party managers, always respectful to an angry electorate, thereupon announce [etc.]. — (9) **1848** Lowell *Biglow P.* 1 Ser. viii. 111 It gives a Party Platform, tu, jest level with the mind Of . . . honest folks thet mean to go it blind. **1946** *Reader's Digest* May 34/1 Party platforms are usually a mass of compromises and evasions.

(10) **1870** *Nation* 24 Feb. 113/2 Nor do we see how those who hold that the nomination to places in the public service is party 'plunder,' or 'spoils,' can well object to this. — (11) **1803** *Ann. 7th Congress* 2 Sess. 337 This ought not to be made a party question. **1830** in Benton *30 Years' View* I. 165/2 The extent of the jurisdiction of Georgia, and the policy of removing the Cherokees and other Indians to the west of the Mississippi, have become party questions. — (12) **1902** E. C. Meyer *Nominating Systems* 17 The notion of party regularity had grown upon the people. **1913** *Boston Herald* 18 July 8/2 (Ernst), I would preserve my party regularity, no matter what else I did. — (13) (*a*) **1843** *Niles' Reg.* 176/3 The party ticket nominated at Tammany Hall was generally voted and was generally successful. **1913** La Follette *Autobiog.* 233 These old machine leaders thus came to the support of the party ticket in 1900. (*b*) **1886** *Cent. Mag.* Nov. 77/1 Before election day, many thousands of complete sets of the party ticket are printed, folded, and put together, or, as it is called, 'bunched.' — (14) (*a*) **1846** *Whig. Almanac 1847* 10/2 It has been re-enacted in substance by the present Congress, by a strict party vote. **1868** *Ore. State Jrnl.* 25 July 2/4 The bill was passed by a strict party vote. (*b*) **1904** *Brooklyn Eagle* 9 June 4 One unable to hold his straight party vote in his own city would be a calamity.

(15) **1880** *Scribner's Mo.* Oct. 908/2 The vigorous cracking of the party whip is a pretty sure sign that corruption has crept into the management. **1900** *Cong. Rec.* 8 Feb. 1641/1 Every vote that can be obtained by the party whip, by threats, and by cajolery will be obtained to pass the bill.

b. Designating clothing suitable for wearing to a social gathering, as (1) **party dress,** (2) **fixings,** (3) **gown,** (4) **rig.**

(1) **1875** Stowe *We & Neighbors* 38 What are you going to do about the girls' party dresses? **1923** Watts *L. Nichols* 257 That's a party-dress, isn't it? — (2) **1944** *Vogue* July 136 Party Fixings are fluffy matters intended to display expense and multiplicity of ingredients and vulgar ingenuity in decoration. — (3) **1899** Tarkington *Gentleman from Ind.* xvii, It was a Rouen 'party-gown' wherewith she chose to abash poor John Harkless. **1904** Lovett *R. Gresham* 65 The girls wore . . . faded party gowns. — (4) **1865** Stowe in *Atlantic Mo.* July 105/2 Holloa, Bess! is that your party-rig? **1881** Rittenhouse *Maud* 24 Here I sit in party-rig waiting for Elmer.

c. Also (1) **party call,** a social call made on a hostess who has recently entertained one; (2) **wire,** a party line (sense **2.**).

(1) **1910** Tompkins *Mothers & Fathers* 144 They only came twice, and those were party calls. — (2) **1920** Lewis *Main Street* 189 Did you hear me putting one over on these goats that are always rubbering in on party-wires?

As the last term in **abolition, administration, American, bank, basket, berry, box, bucktail, calico, calumet, candy, chowder, citizen, Clay, country, court, Creole, dance, dancing, Dark Lantern, Democratic, donation, donkey, dove, Dutch, Equal Rights, Federal, fishing, Free Democratic, Free Soil, French, gander, Granger, Grasshopper, Greenback, hemp, husking, ice, ice cream, Jackson, Johnson, Know-Nothing, labor, lap, law and order, leap year, Liberal Republican, Liberty, Locofoco, lower, lumbering, lynching, mail, maple sugar, marooning, meat, minority, National Democratic, National Republican, Native, Native American, necktie, Negro, New Court, no-, nullification, Old Court, out, oyster, People's, Personal Liberty, petting, place, play, Populist, pound, prohibition, prohibitory, proslavery, prospecting, radical, ranging, relief, Republican, roosting, rum, rush, scalping, sectional, Seward, sheepshearing, shower, sitting-up, spoils, stag, starvation, State Rights, steamboat cotillion, strawberry, sugar, surprise, tacky, thimble, third, toleration, trading, trapping, treaty, union, upper, waffle, war, watermelon, Whig, white man's, Wistar party.**

party line.

1. The officially adopted policies of a political party. Also transf.

1834 Benton *30 Years' View* I. 431/2 Look at the vote in the Senate upon the adoption of the resolution, also as clearly defined by a party line as any party question can ever be expected to be. **1906** *World's Work* Oct. 8135/2 What Federation heads are counting on is the growing willingness of voters to break the regular party lines. **1947** *Chi. Tribune* 2 Nov. 13/1 Reece charged . . . that the call represented a yielding by the President to the 'party line' of our 'most vociferous radical groups.' **1949** *Sat. Ev. Post* 5 March 127/1 Her mother hated it, and Dotty was a girl who followed her mother's party line.

attrib. **1948** *Dly. Ardmoreite* (Ardmore, Okla.) 2 May 5/4 On party-line votes, this will give the democrats guarantee of a two-thirds majority.

Hence **party liner.**

1949 *Va. Quart. Review* Winter 44 For the past eleven years he has allied himself with, and never broken on any significant issue from, the 'party-liners.'

2. A telephone circuit serving more than one subscriber. Also attrib.

1902 *Encycl. Brit.* XXXIII. 237/2 A number of subscribers can be placed upon a single circuit or 'party line.' **1947** *Chi. D. News* 14 Oct. 10/2 When a party-line phone is rung, all the others can now be kept silent. **1948** *Chi. Sun-Times* 7 Sep. 47/1, I was talking on a country party-line telephone from a farm in Pennsylvania the other day

parula (warbler). [Dim. f. L. *parus,* titmouse.] A small American warbler, *Compsothlypis americana,* having a brownish-yellow patch on the back.

1887 Ridgway *Man. N. Amer. Birds* 491 Eastern United States and Canada, breeding throughout. . . . *C. americana.* Parula Warbler. **1917** *Birds of Amer.* III. 123 The Parula Warbler has been called the Blue Yellowback, but the name 'Parula,' . . . was given it because of the Chickadee-like habit of searching for its food. *Ib.,* If one watches long enough he is pretty sure to see the Parula hanging from a limb. **1942** Peattie *Friendly Mts.* 206 In a small opening at the end of the bog . . . the rapid 'zee-e-e-e-e-ip' of the parula warbler is heard.

parvenuess ˈpɑrvəˌn(j)uˑɪs, *n.* [*∗parvenu,* masc. +*ess.*] A female parvenu. *Rare.* — *a***1910** O. Henry *Rolling Stones* iii. 58 As proud and satisfied as a prince that's abjured a two-hundred-dollar crown for a million-dollar parvenuess.

pasa ˈpɑsə, *n. S.W.* [Sp. in same sense.] (See quot.) — **1844** Gregg *Commerce of Prairies* II. 135 The grapes, carefully dried in the shade, make excellent *pasas* or raisins, of which large quantities are annually prepared for market.

Pasanien pəˈseniən, *n.* [El *Paso,* Texas.] A native or resident of El Paso, Texas. *Rare.* — **1866** *Wkly. New Mexican* 9 March 2/2 Juarez has made another draft upon the purses of the Pasaniens.

pasear ˌpɑsɪˈɑr, *n. W.* and *S.W.* [Sp. inf., to walk, go, used as a noun.] A trip or excursion. Also transf.

[**1840** R. H. Dana *Two Yrs.* xxviii. (1869) 258 He was going to *pasear* with our captain a little.] **1847** *Calif. Star* (S.F.) 24 July 2/3 All hands were busy making preparations for their trip to the States. . . . I am told this *pasear* over the mountains, will cost the Commodore [Stockton] five thousand dollars. **1908** *Sat. Ev. Post* 24 Oct. 6/3 Get a cayuse and I'll take that *pasear* with you. **1948** *Popular Western* June 16/2 Yuh're takin' a little *pasear* to the penitentiary in Walla Walla.

attrib. **1914** *Sunset* July 64/1 It was pasear madness that made despairing feet give way to auto tires—it is the undiminishing nature of pasear joys that is stretching the eighteen-million-dollar highway through the state.

paseo pɑˈseo, *n. W.* [Sp., a walk.] A walk or ride for pleasure.

1840 R. H. Dana *Two Yrs.* xxii. (1869) 181 The theme of . . . conversation . . . in our afternoon's *paseo* upon the beach. **1848** *Calif. Star* (S.F.) 8 Jan. 3/1 A party of us mounted for a *pasea,* and such sports as we might pick up by the way. **1902** *Out West* Dec. 683 Such bosoming of motherly hills, knee-deep with winter wild flowers, as you may have unrolled to you in an afternoon's *paseo* from the metropolis, for ten or fifteen cents carfare each way.

pashofa pəˈʃofə, *n.* Also **Pashofah.** [Prob. f. a native word or words.] **1.** A kind of stew made from fresh pork and hominy. **2. Pashofah dance,** (see quots.).

(1) **1930** *Durant* (Okla.) *D. Democrat* 22 Oct., More than 1200 Indians and a number of white guests converged on the campus where dozens of pots of pashofa and tom fulla had been prepared by famous Indian women cooks. — (2) **1891** O'Beirne *Indian Territory* I. (Insert A) p. x, The Chickasaw full-bloods, however, are more superstitious than their neighbors. Witch doctors and Pashofah dances being still popular in some localities. [*Ib.,* The dance of the 'Pasho-

fah' which is believed to be a certain cure in many stages of disease, is carried on in front of the patient.]

*pass, *n.*[1] As the last term in **cattle, forward, labor, over, trip, underpass.**

pass pas, *n.*[2] *S.W.* [?Sp. *pasa*, raisin.] *attrib.* Designating wine or whisky made from grapes. *Obs.*

1840 *N.O. Picayune* 6 Sep. 2/4 The wild American youths . . . were highly excited with pass whiskey, which they had been drinking at some fandango. **1844** GREGG *Commerce of Prairies* II. 77 The inhabitants [of the El Paso valley] manufacture [from grapes] a very pleasant wine, somewhat resembling Malaga. A species of *aguardiente* (brandy) is also distilled from the same fruit. . . . These liquors are known among Americans as 'Pass wine' and 'Pass whiskey.' **1854** BARTLETT *Personal Narr.* I. 186 Brandy, or *aguardiente*, is also made from the grape. It is of a light color, and is known in New Mexico as 'Pass Whiskey.'

***pass,** *v.*

1. a. *tr.* Of the catcher in baseball: To fail to catch a pitched ball. Cf. **passed ball. b.** *intr.* (See quot.)

(a) 1867 *Ball Players' Chron.* 4 July 1/2 Walters forced Buckley to pass balls, Martin securing his run by these errors. — **(b) 1889** *Amer. Folk-Lore* II. 155 In New England the ordinary term used to express the throwing and catching of a ball by two or more persons is *pass.* 'Let's go out and *pass*.'

2. Of a light-complexioned Negro: To act as a white person and to be regarded as such.

1933 MADISON GRANT *Conquest of Continent* 269 This enables some of these light Negroes to 'pass' as Whites. **1948** *Time* 16 Feb. 25/1 Possibly as many as 5,000,000 people with 'a determinable part' of Negro blood are now 'passing' as whites.

3. *tr.* In baseball, to permit (a batter) to reach first base on balls, or as a result of being hit by a pitched ball. Cf. ***walk,** *v.* **1.**

1900 *Chi. Times-Herald* 9 May 4/2 McFarland walked and Brodie stepped in front of a slow one and was passed to first. **1912** MATHEWSON *Pitching* 102 In the ninth he passed a couple of men, and a hit tied the score. *Ib.* 304 Once I started to pass 'Hans' Wagner in a pinch to take a chance on the next batter. **1928** *Dly. Ardmoreite* (Ardmore, Okla.) 25 March 12/4 They didn't want to pass me to get a crack at Gehrig.

4. With adverbs: (1) *To pass in*, to die, cf. ***check,** *n.*[2] **3. b;** (2) *to pass up*, to disregard or decline, to fail to take advantage of. Both *colloq.*

(1) 1904 *N.Y. Ev. Jrnl.* 5 May 2, 'I may die,' he told friends, 'and I want to breathe American air again before I pass in.' — **(2) 1896** G. ADE *Artie* xii. 112 Well I guess I'll pass up the whole thing. **1930** *Randolph Enterprise* (Elkins, W.Va.) 2 Oct. 4/2 Republicans . . . try to console themselves . . . in passing up a man of the people like Neely.

5. In combs. in some of which the first element is a noun: (1) **pass ball,** the action of throwing a ball back and forth; (2) ***book,** a book kept by a soldier or sailor in which articles of clothing, etc., are checked off as issued to him by the storekeeper or supply officer; (3) **monte,** ?three-card monte, *obs.;* (4) ***over,** a narrow passage or way through a mountainous country or across a mountain, *obs.;* (5) **shooting,** (see quot.); (6) **system,** the system of giving passes over railroad lines; (7) ***-way,** = ***passover.**

(1) 1871 L. H. BAGG *At Yale* 317 Pass ball was considerably practiced in the gymnasium yard, and to some extent on the college or city green. — **(2) 1880** LAMPHERE *U.S. Govt.* 181/2 [Cadets] will supply themselves with . . . 1 pass-book. **1907** *Naval Acad. Reg.* 75 After the requisitions are served, they shall be entered in the pass books of the midshipmen, by the storekeeper. — **(3) 1866** *Wkly. New Mexican* 21 July 1/4 They immediately staked their little all, if not their whole kit, at a licensed table of pass monte. — **(4) 1839** LEONARD *Adventures* (1904) 230 [We] continued all day without any interruption, and in the evening encamped at the foot of the passover.

(5) 1877 C. HALLOCK *Sportsman's Gaz.* 204 Another method is pass shooting; that is, standing . . . in belts of woods, over which the birds fly when travelling in their afternoon flights to the roosting and feeding grounds. — **(6) 1873** *Newton Kansan* 3 July 2/1 J. Edgar Thompson . . . thinks the effort of the railways to abrogate the pass system will prove a failure. **1903** E. JOHNSON *Railway Transportation* 154 There is, moreover, evidence of a growing moral sense in the public mind against the pass system. — **(7) 1889** *Harper's Mag.* June 66/1 We stood in the passway, amid the deepening shadows of the twilight.

b. In phrases: (1) *To pass the buck*, see ***buck,** *n.*[1] **6.** (2); (2) *to pass a dividend*, to omit or fail to pay a dividend; (3) *to pass in one's checks, chips*, see ***check,** *n.*[2] **3. b.** and ***chip,** *n.* **4. b.** (3); (4) *to pass meeting*, (see quot.), *obs.*

(2) 1870 MEDBERY *Men Wall St.* 137 To 'pass' a dividend. . . . A dividend is said to be passed when the directors vote against declaring it. **1895** E. CARROLL *Principles Finance* 295 *To pass a dividend*, to fail to make an expected dividend. **1903** *Forum* Oct. 209 Concerns which not only passed dividends but went bankrupt. — **(4) 1850–8** O'NEALL-CHAPMAN *Annals* 32 A pair of young people about to marry are said to pass meeting by their purpose being announced at one monthly meeting, when a committee is appointed to inquire if there be any objections.

***passage,** *n.* **1. passage car,** =**passenger car. 2. passage wagon,** (see quot. 1774). Both *obs.*

(1) 1833 *Advocate of Popular Rights* (Shelbyville, Ky.) 26 Oct. 2/6 The locomotive had 5 freight and 2 passage cars attached. **1848** *Hunt's Merch. Mag.* XVIII. 540 The property of the company consists of . . . 55 eight-wheeled passage cars. — **(2) 1774** J. ADAMS *Diary* Wks. II. 357 [Near Phila.] we saw two or three passage wagons, a vehicle with four wheels, contrived to carry many passengers and much baggage. **1860** GREELEY *Overland Journey* 106 The express-line . . . has run out some thirty passage wagons from Leavenworth.

As the last term in **deck passage.**

Passamaquoddy ˌpæsəməˈkwadɪ, *n.* [Said to be a native name meaning "plenty of pollack," a codlike marine fish plentiful on the coast.] (See quot. 1910.) Also attrib.

1842 *Wasp* (Nauvoo, Ill.) 3 Sep. 3/1 Our Passamaquoddy Indians are divided into two political parties, between which a good deal of acrimonious feeling exists. **1857** *Spirit of Times* 11 July 292/2 Much interest was felt in the birch canoe race, between some Indians of the Passamaquoddy, Penobscot and Micmac tribes. **1910** HODGE *Amer. Indians* II. 207/2 Passamaquoddy. . . . A small tribe belonging to the Abnaki confederacy. . . . They formerly occupied all the region about Passamaquoddy bay and on St Croix r. and Schoodic lake, on the boundary between Maine and New Brunswick.

passed ball. (See quot. 1867.)

1861 *N.Y. Sun. Mercury* 10 Aug. (E. J. Nichols). **1867** CHADWICK *Base Ball Reference* 139 A passed ball is one muffed by the catcher on which a base is run. **1880** *S. F. Globe* 12 July 1/5 Irwin . . . took second on a passed ball. **1949** *News-Herald* (Marshfield, Wis.) 19 July 9/4 The runner went to third on a passed ball and stayed there as English walked.

***passenger,** *n.* In combs.: (1) ***passenger agent,** a railroad agent who sells tickets to passengers; (2) **car,** see as a main entry; (3) **depot,** a station where railroad

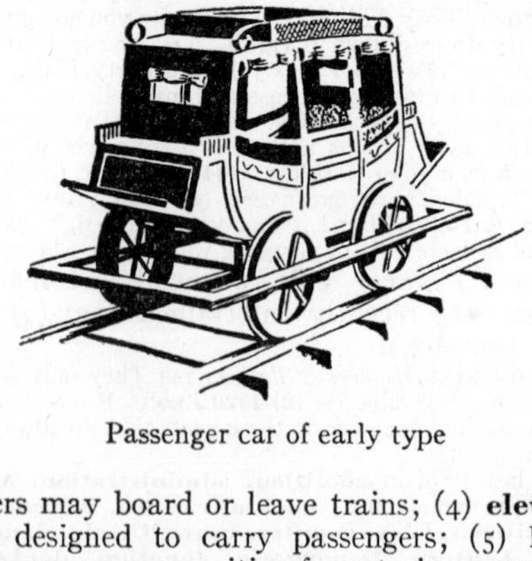

Passenger car of early type

passengers may board or leave trains; (4) **elevator,** an elevator designed to carry passengers; (5) **house,** a shelter for passengers waiting for a train, *rare;* (6) **mile,** (see quots.); (7) **pigeon,** see as a main entry.

(1) 1890 BIFF HALL *Turnover Club* 108 He was traveling through the South at the time, and the accommodating passenger agents down in that country made his bosses read [etc.]. **1944** *Santa Fe Time Table* 12 Nov. 63 Huntington Park, Calif. . . . F. L. Weeks, Passenger Agent. — **(3) 1849** [see **freight depot**]. **1882** PANGBORN *Picturesque B. & O.* 46 The fashion in the Monumental City being to term passenger-depots 'stations,' prefixing the name of the street they are located upon. — **(4) 1886** *Standard Guide of Washington* 205 The building . . . is furnished with passenger-elevator, steam-heating, deposit-vaults, speaking tubes. **1919** MORLEY *Haunted Bookshop* (1921) 87 Maybe he had no right to be riding in the passenger elevator.

(5) 1839 *Amer. R.R. Jrnl.* VIII. 169 Passenger houses in Dedham and Canton. — **(6) 1934** *Recent Sociol. Trends* 169 (*footnote*), 'Passenger-miles' (the number of passengers carried one mile). **1945** *Tracks*

June 34/1 Passenger-miles—a passenger-mile represents one passenger transported one mile.

b. *To wake (up) the wrong passenger* (and variants), to wake or call a passenger other than the one requesting such service; usu. fig., to misjudge an adversary or the person with whom one has to deal. *Colloq.*

1839 *N.O. Picayune* 25 April 2/4 Treat it otherwise and you 'wake up the wrong passenger.' **1862** E. KIRKE *Among Pines* 53 Extending his hand to me, he said: 'I see, sir, I've woke up the wrong passenger.' **1886** POORE *Reminiscences* I. 38 The large brass door knockers were vigorously plied, and sometimes quite a commotion was caused by 'waking up the wrong passenger.'

As the last term in **deck, local, season, through, way passenger.**

passenger car.

1. A railroad car for carrying passengers.

1832 *Amer. R.R. Jrnl.* I. 305/3 Arrived, 9 passenger cars with 71 passengers. **1924** *Railway Rev.* 16 Feb. 294/1 Window sills and arm rests in all-steel passenger cars are generally made of wood. **1949** *Chi. Tribune* 17 Nov. III. 4/6 They represent, road officials said, a radical departure from conventional passenger car design.

b. passenger car house, a train shed for coaches.

1847 *Hunt's Merch. Mag.* XVI. 211 Attached to this station, are also . . . two wood and water stations . . . a brass foundry, passenger car house, passenger rooms, offices &c.

2. An automobile for carrying persons. Also attrib.

1948 *Herald-Press* (St. Joseph, Mich.) 14 Aug. 5/1 But for these shutdowns the week's passenger car output would have been close to 90,000. **1948** *News-Palladium* (Benton Harbor, Mich.) 14 Aug. 12/4 Passenger car production held almost steady this week despite a growing parts and material scarcity.

passenger pigeon. A wild pigeon, *Ectopistes migratorius,* once common throughout North America, but now extinct.

1802 BINGLEY *Anim. Biog.* (1813) II. 225 Passenger Pigeons visit, in enormous flocks, the different parts of North America. **1857** *Rep. Comm. Patents 1856: Agric.* 148 The passenger pigeon, or wild pigeon, . . . is very rarely met with except in communities of millions or billions. **1917** *Birds of Amer.* II. 44 The last passenger pigeon. She died in the Cincinnati Zoological Park in 1914. **1947** *Democrat* 27 March 4/3 The passenger pigeons, once here by the millions, are gone never to return.

passhico ˈpæʃɪko, *n.* [Of native origin.] = **camass.** Also the bread prepared from the camass root. Also attrib. *Obs.*

1805 LEWIS in *Lewis & Clark Exped.* (1905) III. 78 Those people gave us a Small piece of Buffalow meat, Some dried Salmon beries & roots in different States, Some round and much like an onion which they call Pas she co (quamash. the Bread or Cake is called Pas-shi-co) Sweet, of this they make bread & Supe. *Ib.* 107 We Purchd. Dried cherries Pashequar root and Pashequar marsh [mash] or bread. **1806** LEWIS in *Ib.* IV. 3 When prepared for uce by the same process before discribed of the white bulb or *pashshequo quawmash*, it becomes black, and is more shugary than any f[r]uit or root that I have met with in uce among the natives.

* **paster,** *n.*

1. (See quot. 1885.) *Obs.* Cf. * **sticker,** *n.* **1.**

1870 *Cong. Globe* 13 April 2659/3 There were ten tickets . . . which were scratched and had pasters with the name of Caleb N. Taylor. **1885** *Mag. Amer. Hist.* March 297/2 Narrow slips of paper gummed on the back and bearing printed names of candidates . . . are distributed by local political leaders prior to or during an election, so that voters may readily re-arrange ballots to suit their own individual preferences. Pasters . . . reduce 'scratching' . . . to a system. **1906** *N.Y. Ev. Post* 5 Nov. 7 The ballots to be used to-morrow must bear pasters with McMillan's name on them.

2. A slip of paper which is pasted over some part of a printed bill, circular, or the like.

1882 *Nation* 6 July 7/2 The Erie and Central Railroads have made the attempt to rid themselves of all liabilities . . . by putting a 'paster' on their bills of lading. **1906** *World's Work* May 7511/1 You may read upon its label that it has been 'U.S. Government Inspected.' The paster on the box from which it came assures us again of that fact.

pastor pɑsˈtɔr, *n. S.W.* [Sp. in same sense. An Amer. borrowing.] A sheep-herder.

1849 *31st Congress* 1 Sess. Sen. Ex. Doc. No. 64, 132 The flock [of sheep] was under Mexican and not Navajo control, and, from my conversation with the pastor, became assured that our apprehensions were groundless. **1879** in THOS. HUGHES *G.T.T.* (1884) 20 Two young Americans . . . were murdered by their 'pastors' for plunder. **1906** ADAMS *Cattle Brands* 20 Here I found a flock of sheep and a pastore. **1941** FERGUSSON *Southwest* 177 The pastor, shepherd, was at everybody's beck and call. But he had the constant companionship of his dog, and no finer beast was ever known than a well-trained sheep-dog.

* **pastorate,** *n.* A parsonage. — **1929** M. HOLLAND *Industrial Explorers* 187 He brought down parental wrath by filling the pastorate with horrible odors on the afternoon that his mother was serving tea to the Ladies' Aid.

pastorium pæsˈtorɪəm, *n. S.* [Based on L. *pastorius*, belonging to a pastor.] A Baptist parsonage. — **1934** WEBSTER. **1948** *Democrat* 7 Oct. 1/4 A contract for the construction of a new pastorium by the Baptist Church of Jackson, was awarded . . . to the lowest bidder.

* **pasture,** *n.*

1. (See quots.) Also attrib.

1884 GOODE *Fisheries* I. 201 There are also certain local schools of fish which have names of their own; for instance, . . . the 'Pasture School' of Cape Ann. **1890** *Cent.* 4323/1 *Pasture*, . . . one of the compartments of a deepwater weir . . . ; that part of the weir which the fish first enter. **1895** *Stand.* 1290/3 *Pasture*, . . . an inshore spawning-ground for codfish.

2. In special combs.: (1) **pasture bird,** (see quot.); (2) **lot,** a plot of land used as a pasture; (3) * **man,** a cattleman who leases grazing land, *rare;* (4) **range,** an expanse of open country suitable for grazing stock; (5) **rose,** a rose, *Rosa virginiana*, or its flower, of the eastern states.

(1) **1888** TRUMBULL *Names of Birds* 195 American Golden Plover. . . . To the old people of West Barnstable [Mass.], Pasture-Bird. — (2) **1693** *Norwalk Hist. Rec.* 85 To Elnathan Hanford for his part and portion out of his father's estate . . . : To pasture lott [£]18. **1873** *Winfield* (Kans.) *Courier* 7 Aug. 1/5 Many farmers who live in the creek bottoms have open pasture lots fenced with a stock or open post and rail fence. **1902** MCFAUL *Ike Glidden* 111 Chase Yourself up 'crost the pasture lot. — (3) **1895** *Cong. Rec.* 15 Jan. 997/2 The first names of the pasture men that I see upon my list are [etc.]. — (4) **1860** GREELEY *Overland Journey* 325 A broad expanse of dried-up pasture range . . . [shows] the protracted fierceness of the summer drought. **1881** ROMSPERT *Western Echo* 170 The home ranch is located upon some good, rich pasture-range, and by a good water.

(5) **1934** WEBSTER. **1949** *Mo. Bot. Garden Bul.* Feb. 52 The genus Rosa [is] represented at the Arboretum by the Prairie Rose (*Rosa setigera*), and the Pasture Rose (*R. carolina*).

As the last term in **bee, berry, big, bush, cow, English, goose, huckleberry, mesquite, stone, timber, wood pasture.**

* **pasture,** *v. intr.* Of bees, to gather honey *upon* a certain place. *Rare.* — **1880** *Harper's Mag.* Oct. 777/2 One of our modern apiaries, with its bees pasturing upon acres of carefully cultivated honey plants.

* **pat,** *v. intr.* To beat time for dancing by clapping the hands, tapping the feet, etc. Also * **patting,** *n.*, **patting song.** Cf. **Juba.**

1850 in *Annals of Iowa* 3 Ser. IX. (1910) 467, I heard some good fiddling and thought . . . of sweet home and the merry ones that, no doubt, at that time were 'patting it down' to some old favorite air. **1851** *De Bow's Review* X. 625 Charley's fiddle is always accompanied with Ihurod on the triangle, and Sam to 'pat.' **1869** *Atlantic Mo.* July 74/2, I was made to dance 'Juba' to the time which the comedian himself gave me by means of his two hands and one foot, and which is technically called 'patting.' **1892** HARRIS *U. Remus & Friends* 197 This song is sung with what Uncle Remus would call the 'knee racket;' that is to say, it is a 'patting' song.

* **patch,** *n.*

1. = **ball patch.** Now *hist.*

1799 WELD *Travels* 67 The grease and the bits of rag, which are called patches, are carried in a little box. **1837** WETMORE *Gaz. Missouri* 48 While the men were firing, the women made it their business to cast balls and cut patches, so as to keep up the defence. **1946** *Chi. D. News* 6 Feb. 25/4 Patches, in which the bullets are seated, usually are made from a wax-treated piece of linen, or, in a few instances, waxed paper.

2. (See quots.)

1877 E. MARTIN *Hist. Great Riots* 460 The whole population of the coal regions living in cities, towns and small settlements, are often called 'patches.' **1947** *Theology Today* July 205 The imprint of isolation is more firmly fixed in the miner's soul by the hardships which he shares in common with the rest of the miners in the camp or 'patch.'

3. (See quots.)

*c***1900** KING *When I Lived* (1937) 185 By the side of the bed was placed a high-backed so-called easy chair . . . covered with a gay colored chintz ('patch' it was called then). **1927** *Old-Time N. Eng.* April 158 The counterpane was never quilted and seventy-five years ago was frequently made of 'patch,' a cotton fabric with glazed printed design, and usually matched the bed-hangings.

4. In combs., chiefly obs.: (1) * **patch box,** a receptacle in the stock of a muzzle-loading rifle for patches (sense **1.**); (2) **head (coot),** also **patch polled coot,** *local*, the surf scoter, *Melanitta perspicillata;* (3) **leather,** leather, usu. dressed fawn skin, for making patches (sense **1.**); (4) **quilt,** a patchwork quilt, also fig.

(1) **1855** HOLBROOK *Among Mail Bags* 231 A post-office clerk . . . had crammed the stolen notes into the 'patch-box' of the rifle. — (2) **1888** TRUMBULL *Names of Birds* 103 Surf Ducks. In Maine, . . . Patch-Head; in Massachusetts . . . and at Stonington, Conn., Patch-Polled Coot. **1917** *Birds of Amer.* I. 151 Surf Scoter. . . . Other Names. . . . Patch-head; Patch-head Coot. — (3) **1807** GASS *Journal* 13 March, Each man has also a sufficient quantity of patch-leather. — (4) **1850** LEWIS *La. Swamp Dr.* 95 Untying the scrap-bag of memory, she proceeded to make a patch-quilt for me, of a case that resembled the one we were ministering to. **1881** *Harper's Mag.* March 528/2 The patch-quilt was a most marvelous affair. **1925** *Frontier* May 26 He drew the faded patch-quilt over his head.

As the last term in **bean, berry, brier, brush, bullet, corn, cotton, cucumber, four, fruit, garden, huckleberry, Indian corn, Negro, papaw, pea, peanut, plant, potato, strawberry, sweet potato, timber, tobacco, tomato, truck, turnip, watermelon, wood, yellow patch.**

* **patch,** *v. tr.* To fit a patch about (a rifle ball). Cf. * **patch,** *n.* **1.**

1843 CARLTON *New Purchase* II. 255 Therefore, we at last ventured on *patchin* the balls separately. *a***1846** *Quarter Race Ky.* 138 The bar . . . was hunting about for me, when, just as I was patching my ball, he again saw me. **1877** HALLOCK *Sportsman's Gazetteer* 545 If the bullet is the right size and properly patched, the patch will not be torn in putting the cartridge into the chamber.

* **patching,** *n.*

1. Material for rifle patches.

1835 LONGSTREET *Ga. Scenes* 286 [He] drew out his patching, found the most even part of it [etc.]. **1887** *Harper's Mag.* June 61/1 In the bullet-pouch were carried . . . the cotton 'patching' . . . and the precious extra flints.

2. *To smell the patching*, to be close to and threatened by danger. *Colloq.*

1834 CROCKETT *Tour* 208 Which finally made the federal party smell the patching that drove them from the field in April.

3. *Not a patching to*, in no way comparable to. *Colloq.*

Cf. *OED not a patch (up)on. EDD* has also *not a patch to.*

1851 *Polly Peablossom* 52 All the sailors an' French parrots in Orleans ain't a patchin' to him. **1921** GREER-PETRIE *Angeline at Seelbach* 2 The Phoenix Hotel . . . aint a-patchin' to Miss Seelback's place. **1944** *D.N.* Nov. 25 *patchin', not a patchin' to:* n. No comparison with. 'Your dog *ain't a patchin'* ter mine.'

* **patchwork,** *n.* As the last term in **crazy, log cabin patchwork.**

* **pate,** *n.* As the last term in **bald, woolly pate.**

* **patent,** *a.* and *n.*

1. The territory or land conferred by a land patent or grant.

1631 *Mass. Bay Rec.* I. 88 Noe person w[ha]tsoeuer shall trauell out of this pattent, eithr. by sea or land, without leaue from the Governr, Deputy Governr, or some other Assistant. **1789** *Smithtown Rec.* 179 The line between the two Patents to be the middle of said road. **1845** COOPER *Chainbearer* xxv, This is Mooseridge Patent, and Washington, late Charlotte County.

2. In combs.: (1) **patent agent,** (see quot. 1859); (2) **column,** a column of stereotyped material in a newspaper, cf. **boiler plate;** (3) **Democrat,** a radical member of the old Democratic Republican party, *obs.;* (4) **flour,** superior flour made from the finest part of the endosperm of the wheat by a milling process patented *c*1880; (5) **gentry,** patent men, *obs.;* (6) **heaver,** (see quot. and cf. **palpitating bosom, palpitator**); (7) **insides,** *pl.* sheets of proper size, printed on one side with miscellaneous matter and sold to editors of small newspapers who fill up the blank sides, cf. **patent outsides;** (8) **land,** =**patented land,** *obs.;* (9) **lawyer,** a lawyer whose specialty is patent law; (10) **leather,** see as a main entry; (11) **line,** a boundary line of an area or district held by patent, *obs.;* (12) **lock,** a swindling device, cf. **patent safe,** *obs.;* (13) **man,** a professional swindler, *obs.;* (14) **note,** =**buckwheat note,** now *hist.;* (15) **outsides,** =**patent insides;** (16) **safe,** attrib. and comb. with reference to a small pocket safe used in a trick to swindle a "sucker" out of his money, *obs.*

(1) **1859** BARTLETT 310 *Patent Agent*, one who procures patents for inventors. **1886** J. A. PORTER *New Stand. Guide of Washington* 110 Business Houses of Washington, D.C. [include] . . . claim agents, collecting agents, patent agents. — (2) **1944** CLARK *Pills* 241 Literary men of a base, but exceedingly clever, stripe popularized it by filling the 'patent' columns of the local papers with advertisements and testimonials of the most seductive nature. — (3) **1818** FEARON *Sketches* 139 The political parties [in Phila.] at present range I believe as follows: 1st. The violent democrats called 'Patent Democrats.' 2nd. The moderate democrats [etc.]. **1835** H. C. TODD *Notes* 34 The names of their political parties are Patent Democrats, Old Schoolmen, Hartford Conventionalists, and Bluelight Men. — (4) **1886** *Cent. Mag.* May 46/2 For three years the patent flour, as it was called, sold at the uniform price of ten dollars a barrel at the mill. *c***1940** SNYDER *Through Silken Sieve* 33 Patent flour is the more refined portion of the wheat meal from which all or a portion of the clears have been removed.

(5) **1851** GREEN *Twelve Days* 198 He illustrated the frauds which the '*patent gentry*' have over those who play depending on their own judgment. — (6) **1938** *Reader's Digest* Aug. 61 Plumpness was then [1860's and 70's] the main desideratum, and an expansive bosom was obtained by a rubber device called a 'patent heaver.' — (7) **1882** RITTENHOUSE *Maud* 103 The funny places in all the old patent-insides of newspapers talk about the sweet girl graduate. **1931** *Sat. Ev. Post* 28 Feb. 129/2 Some publishers bought patent insides, which were the interior pages of the newspaper ready printed for use. — (8) **1732** in *Amer. Sp.* XX. (1945) 274 Much the least part of the patent lands are actually held at 3s. 4d. — (9) **1886** POORE *Reminiscences* II. 27 The defense was conducted by Edwin M. Stanton, previously known at Washington as a patent lawyer. **1920** LEWIS *Main Street* 157 A few years ago I was talking to a patent lawyer from Chicago. **1949** *Time* 5 Dec. 25/2 Jackson was dissenting sharply from a Supreme Court ruling last week, disbarring an aged patent lawyer from practice before the U.S. Patent Office because he had submitted a ghostwritten article as evidence.

(11) **1675** *Dedham Rec.* V. 31 [We] marked it [the line] to the patint line whear we did set vp a stake. **1685** *Plymouth Laws* 295 Plimouth, Duxbury, Scituate [etc.] . . . together with all such places and Villages, that do or may lye between the said Towns and the Patent Line [shall] be a County. — (12) **1873** BEADLE *Undevel. West* 141 A score of 'smart Alecks' relieved of their surplus cash by betting on the . . . 'patent lock,' . . . and other beautiful uncertainties. — (13) **1850** GREEN *Twelve Days* 197 Mr. Green, for the purpose of showing the overwhelming advantages which a professed gambler or '*patent*' man has over all others . . . illustrated his skill by playing a game or two. — (14) *c***1832** in JACKSON *White Spirituals* 47 [It has] a page in defense of shape-notes, which Funk called 'patent' or 'character' notes; and a metrical index. **1895** HOWELL *Recollections* 143 As it was very difficult to fix these syllables to the right notes, the books were printed in what they called patent notes. **1930** *Musical Quart.* Oct. 397 The 'Fasola Folk,' those who still apply the Elizabethan names to the notes of songs made in pre-Revolutionary America and sing them with the help of the 132-year-old 'patent notes,' still number from about 30,000 to 50,000 souls.

(15) **1871** *Lancaster Intelligencer* 3 April (DeVere), The editor who surrenders control of one-half of his paper to some manufacturer of *patent-outsides*, may make a slight reduction in his current expenses, but in the end he will lose both money and influence. **1890** *Boston Jrnl.* 7 March 4/5 He was running his patent outsides for country newspapers. — (16) **1855** *Scientific Amer.* 11 Aug. 381/3 The sharpers who practice the 'patent safe game' are keen fellows, and try to maintain an appearance the very reverse of rogues. **1857** *N.Y. Herald* 1 Sep. (B.), Was Gen. Scott, by a sort of patent safe or Peter Funk operation, diddled out of his ten thousand? **1858** *N.Y. Tribune* 3 Nov., A flashy looking man with a black moustache, who is probably a patent safe operator. **1883** BUEL *Metrop. Life Unveiled* 145 The 'patent safe' and 'pocket-book dropping' games were once very popular and successful.

b. Also in the names of manufactured articles for which a patent has been issued: (1) **patent corn sheller,** cf. * **sheller,** *n.* **1;** (2) **hay scales;** (3) **pill.**

(1) **1895** JEWETT *Nancy* 138 When he died he'd failed all up, owing to that patent cornsheller he'd put everything into. — (2) **1848** THOREAU *Maine Woods* 15 It looked like the balance-box of a patent hay-scales. — (3) **1851** GREEN *Twelve Days* 155 These agents are among us in different capacities, some taking subscriptions for literary works, some with patent rights, some as patent pill pedlars, &c., &c. **1908** PHILLIPS *Old Wives* 87 As for health, she decided that the patent-pill advertisements were right, that her trouble was altogether nerves.

c. In phrases: (1) *Commissioner of Patents*, the government official in charge of the patent office; (2) *patent applied for*, a phrase sometimes put on an article to protect its use or manufacture while the issuance of the patent is pending, also *patent pending.*

(1) **1836** *Statutes at Large* V. 117 There shall be established and attached to the Department of State, an office to be denominated the Patent Office; the chief officer of which shall be called the Commissioner of Patents. **1903** *Cong. Directory* (58th Cong., Extra. Sess.)

251 The Commissioner of Patents . . . is by statute made the tribunal of last resort in the Patent Office. — (2) **1894** *Boston Ev. Transcript* 5 March 5/7 Elmer E. Vance's Marvellous Realistic Comedy Drama. 'Patent Applied For.' **1925** *Sat. Ev. Post* 18 July 129 Warner Auto-Polish. . . . Patent applied for. **1949** *L.A. Times* 22 May II. 32/1 Licensed by the University of Illinois Foundation. United States Patent Pending.

As the last term in **land, trust patent.**

***patent,** *v.*

1. *tr.* To obtain a patent right to (land or a mining claim).

1675 *Va. State P.* I. 8 Major Lawrence Smith . . . did patent foure thousand six hundred acres of land. **1815** DRAKE *Cincinnati* 51 The following is the course pursued in locating and patenting these lands. **1874** RAYMOND *6th Rep. Mines* 519 Several lodes . . . may be patented in common. **1947** CHALFANT *Gold, Guns, & Ghost Towns* 159 That mine and the Gettysburg, crossing it, are reported to have been the first mines patented in Nevada.

2. To grant (land) by a patent.

1789 MORSE *Amer. Geog.* 261 They patented away to their particular favorites a very great proportion of the whole province. **1831** PECK *Guide* 319 The Military Bounty Tract . . . was set apart by Congress and patented for soldiers who served in the last war.

patented land. Any land the title to which exists through a patent. *Obs.*

1711 BYRD *Secret Diary* (1941) 400, I ordered that every week two troops should range at the head of the river and if they found any Indians on patented land to take away their guns. **1774** *Pa. Gazette* 14 Dec. Supp. 2/3 To be sold . . . One tract of patented land. . . . **1796** *Ann. 4th Congress* 2 Sess. 2691 The revenues of this State [N.C.] are derived from taxes on . . . all patented lands, except lots in towns [etc.].

***patentee,** *n.* One to whom a grant of land has been made through a patent (see also quot. 1677). *Obs.*

1640 *Mass. H.S. Coll.* 4 Ser. VI. 58 The Bishop caused a Quo Warranto to be sued forth in the King's Bench against our Patentees. **1677** HUBBARD *Narrative* I. 4 In the year 1630, more of the Persons interested in said Patent (thence commonly called Patentees) . . . transported themselves and their Families into said *Massachusets.* **1798** I. ALLEN *Hist. Vermont* 15 The patentees or possessors after ten years were to pay ninepence sterling per annum . . . as quit-rent to his Majesty. **1827** DRAKE & MANSFIELD *Cincinnati* 26 The original patentee . . . sold a part of his interest in this ground.

patenteed ˌpætn̩ˈtid, *a.* Provided with letters patent to land. *Rare.* — **1775** ADAIR *Indians* 144 (*footnote*), Since the patenteed race of Daublers set foot in their land they [*sc.* Indians] have gradually become worse every year.

patent leather.

1. A leather having a hard, smooth, glossy surface freq. made by applying to it several coats of oil varnish.

1829 *Amer. Advertiser* (Phila.) 29 July 1/2 Just received, an extensive assortment of Japanned Patent Leather, of superior quality. **1852** MORFIT *Tanning & Currying* (1853) 453 Glazed or Varnished Leather . . . known in commerce as *patent leather* is very largely used for dress boots and shoes. **1944** *Sears Cat.* (ed. 189) 313 Perfect dress-up shoes in shiny patent leather.

2. *pl.* Short for "patent leather shoes" or "patent leather boots." Cf. next.

1849 FOSTER *N.Y. in Slices* 64 Our young gentlemen . . . thus preserve their patent-leathers. **1895** RITTENHOUSE *Maud* 587, I know his beautiful patent-leathers must have suffered. **1910** TOMPKINS *Mothers & Fathers* 356 [He was] humbly removing the overshoes that covered Mr. Hammond's patent leathers.

3. *attrib.* Designating footwear made of patent leather, as (1) **patent leather boots,** (2) **gaiters,** (3) **shoes,** (4) **slippers.**

(1) **1847** ROBB *Squatter Life* 181 (We.), Out swung a large *flag,* with the names of 'Jones, importer, manufacturer, and patent leather boot and shoe *artiste.*' **1850** MATHEWS *Moneypenny* 8 Patent-leather boots in a perfect state of polish. — (2) **1867** HARRIS *Sut Lovingood* 142 One red-comb'd, long-spurr'd, dominecker feller, frum town, . . . [wore] patent leather gaiters. — (3) **1854** RICHARDS *V. Life* (1912) 43 Grandfather took us down street to be measured for some new patten leather shoes at Mr Ambler's. — (4) **1945** MACDONALD *Egg & I* 18 Creaking down the street through the dry snow to dancing school, our black patent leather slippers in a flowered bag, our breath white in front of us.

b. In more occasional combs., as **patent leather bag, brim,** etc.

1842 in *Uniform of the Militia* (Montpelier, Vt.) (1843) 64 Cap—black beaver . . . black patent leather peak. **1898** *K.C. Star* 18 Dec. 15/3 Mr. Zangwill . . . wears a white-crowned yachting cap, with a patent-feather brim. **1914** D. W. ROBERTS *Rangers* 11 When 'patent-leather civilization' overtook them they were ill at ease. **1919** LEWIS *Free Air* 59 He inspected the slope-topped, patent-leather motoring trunk on the rack at the rear of the Gomez-Dep. **1948** *Range Riders Western* May 25/2 One of them . . . carried a glistening patent-leather bag in his hand.

patgo ˈpɑtgo, *n. S.* Also **padgo.** [La. F. *pategau,* in same sense. See note.] (See quots.)

"*Pategau,* which is used in the parish of Pointe Coupée, owes its *t* to popular substitution of Fr. *patte,* 'paw,' 'foot' (of a bird), for *pape.* Cf. Fr. *patte-d'oie,* 'goosefoot' " (Read, *Louisiana-French* (1931) 56).

1827 WILLIAMS *West Florida* 78–9 Patgoes are a kind of introduction to a dance. A wooden bird is fixed on a pole, and carried through the city by some slave. . . . A time and place is then set apart for the fair patrons of the patgoe to assemble, who are usually attended by their beaux. . . . The patgoe is shot at; and the fortunate marksman, who first succeeds in killing it, is proclaimed king. **1848** *S. Lit. Messenger* XIV. 482/1 The padgo was already in position. **1888** CABLE *Bonaventure* 68 For 'Thanase there was . . . the *papegaie,* or, as he called it, *pad-go*—the shooting-match.

***path,** *n.*

1. The warpath. *Rare.*

1841 COOPER *Deerslayer* xii, The dignity of a warrior on his first path, and the gravity of the circumstances in which they were placed, . . . [made] levity out of season.

2. pathfinder, one who discovers a way; an explorer. Also fig.

This word was app. coined by Cooper. The English adopted it from the title of his well-known novel. Cf. Du. *padvinder, padverkenner.*

1840 COOPER (*title*), The Pathfinder. **1857** GLADSTONE *Englishman in Kansas* 112 Full of cool courage and determination as the Western pathfinder is. **1904** H. W. MABIE *Backgrounds of Literature* 223 Whitman was a pathfinder, and his joy in the great new world of human experience that he explored no one would take from him. **1920** BOK *Americanization* 167 It is difficult to believe . . . that the 'Ladies' Home Journal' was a path-finder.

b. (*cap.*) Esp. applied to John C. Frémont (1813–90). Also *Pathfinder of the West.*

1850 *Living Age* XXVI. 207/2 The feet of three men have pressed the slopes of the Rocky Mountains: . . . Humboldt . . . ; Audubon . . . ; and Fremont, the pathfinder of empire. **1879** WILLIAMS *Pacific Tourist* 97/1 To the north you can see the snowy heads of the Wind River Mountains, with the peak named after Fremont, the gallant Path-finder of the West. **1947** PEATTIE *Sierra Nevada* 58 The famous Pathfinder came from the east as a military leader of government expeditions ostensibly organized for the innocent purpose of geographical explorations to the Pacific.

c. = **pathmaster.** *Jocular. Obs.*

1858 *N.Y. Tribune* 4 Dec. 3 [Philip C. Schuyler] is now repudiated by the Republican party all over Kansas, and couldn't be elected 'Pathfinder' in his own town.

d. A publication giving routes and other items of interest to travelers. *Rare.*

1901 MERWIN & WEBSTER *Calumet 'K'* 28 Bannon . . . took a railroad 'Pathfinder' from his grip.

3. pathmaster, an official in charge of keeping up roads and paths. Cf. **road overseer.**

Cf. Du. *padmeester* in the same sense, used locally in N. Holland.

1842 KIRKLAND *Forest Life* I. 230 So it is with regard to roads. The consultation about them, the choice of commissioner and of pathmasters, . . . certainly tend to improve the faculties of those concerned. **1880** C. W. BUTTERFIELD *Hist. Dane Co., Wis.* 933 The first Pathmaster in town was Mahlen Hasbrock. Then the road district included the entire town. **1923** ADAMS *Pioneer Hist.* 109 Randolph Whipple said he came here in 1837 and soon after was elected pathmaster.

As the last term in **beaver, carry, carrying, cattle, cow, deer, heel, hog, Indian, logging, mule, packhorse, portage, race, ridge, scout, shoestring, sleigh, trading, wagon, war, warrior's path.**

pat hand. In draw poker, a hand that is played without drawing more cards. Cf. *to stand pat, s.v.* ***stand,** *v.* — **1868** *How Gamblers Win* 51 When quick work is to be made with a victim, 'pat hands,' in other words, hands which fall complete, as flushes, fulls, or four of a kind are given out. **1891** QUINN *Fools of Fortune* 216 A bold player will sometimes decline to draw any cards, and pretend to have a 'pat' hand, and play it as such when he has none.

pathy ˈpæθɪ, *n.* [f. **-pathy* in many medical terms as **allopathy,* *homeo*pathy,* *hydro*pathy.*] A school or method of medical practice or treatment. *Humor.* or *contempt.* — **1855** M. THOMPSON *Doesticks* 64 All the 'pathies' and 'isms' of medical Empiricism, . . . have all received from the wise ones of the nineteenth century belief and credence. **1897** *Amer. Pediatric Soc. Trans.* 6 A few works on household medicine, certain pathies, and manuals for nurses . . . were considered unworthy of mention.

patio ˈpɑtɪo, ˈpætɪo, *n.* [Sp. in sense **1.**]

1. An inner court or garden open to the sky, usu. within, or connected with, a building.

[**1827** LONGFELLOW in S. Longfellow *H. W. Longfellow* I. 128 The streetdoor opens into a short passage through which you pass into the court,—in Spanish, the *patio.*] **1846** A. ROBINSON *Life in Calif.* 16 We rode into the 'patio,' or court-yard, where a servant took the horses. **1947** *Chi. Maroon* 25 July 2/1 Tables will be set up in the patio with free cokes, and a faculty member or new student from each state will be on hand to welcome new students.

attrib. **1934** WHITE *Folded Hills* 20 Most houses of the better class had the customary *patio* fountain with its surrounding of vines and shrubs and flowers. **1947** *Nat. Geog. Mag.* July 14/2 Californians have every reason to be proud of their patio gardens.

2. (See quot. 1881.)

1856 *Hutchings' Mag.* Sep. 104/1 The ore deposited on the *patio*, another set of laborers engage in separating the large lumps and reducing them to the size of common paving stones. **1881** RAYMOND *Mining Gloss., Patio,* the yard where the ores are cleaned and assorted; also, the amalgamation floor, or the Spanish process itself of amalgamating silver ores on an open floor.

b. patio process, in mining, a process of amalgamating silver ore by spreading it on an open floor for treatment.

1860 *Proc. Calif. Acad. Sci.* II. (1863) 133 No experiments have been made in working this ore by the *patio* or Spanish-American amalgamation process. **1878** HINTON *Arizona* 205 Refractory amalgamation ores . . . [require] to be roasted before reduction . . . in the *patio*, the barrel, and the salt process. **1910** SANTLEBEN *Texas Pioneer* 28 The ore was worked . . . by *patio*, or cold amalgamation process.

***patriarch,** *n.* In the Mormon Church, one esp. empowered to invoke and pronounce blessings within a prescribed jurisdiction. — **1843** H. CASWALL *Prophet of 19th Cent.* 12 And to old Joseph Smith was assigned the somewhat undefined position of 'Patriarch.'

***patriot,** *n.*

1. patriot army, the American army of the Revolution.

1783 WASHINGTON *Writings* VIII. (1835) 568 The character of those, who have persevered through every extremity . . . being immortalized by the illustrious appellation of the *patriot army.* **1881** *Harper's Mag.* Jan. 189/1 A worthy Friend, Joseph Tatnall, . . . alone dared to grind corn for the famishing patriot army.

b. (See quot.) *Obs.*

1841 J. STURGE *Visit to U.S. in 1841* (1842) 112 One of my fellow-passengers had been a soldier in the so-called 'patriot' army which enlisted against Santa Anna, in the revolt of Texas.

2. Patriots' Day, April 19, a legal holiday celebrated in Maine and Massachusetts since 1894, as the anniversary of the battle of Lexington in 1775.

1894 *Boston Transcript* 18 April 8/4 Lowell mill agents, having heard the indignant protest against the running of machinery in the mills Patriots' Day, have decided to reconsider their action. **1948** *Dly. Ardmoreite* (Ardmore, Okla.) 18 April 14/7 They are down to play a second game in the afternoon, since it's Patriot's day in Boston.

***patrol,** *n.* In combs.: (1) **patrol box,** a signal box used by a patrolman; (2) **district,** a district in a city constituting the beat of a policeman or policemen; (3) **judge,** a judge who moves to different parts of a race track to see that no rules of the race are broken; (4) **law,** before the Civil War, a law in some southern states providing for the patrolling of Negro quarters, *obs.*, cf. **patroller, patrol system;** (5) **man,** a man, as a soldier or policeman, who patrols, cf. **highway, night, state patrolman;** (6) **system,** *S.* the system which involved the patrolling of Negro quarters, *obs.;* (7) **wagon,** a police wagon used to carry prisoners or a squad of policemen; (8) **watch,** watchmen who patrol a district or place.

(**1**) **1894** STEAD *If Christ Came to Chicago* 266 The nearest patrolman who sees it [a fire] hastens to his patrol-box and sends in a fire alarm. — (**2**) **1882** MCCABE *New York* 371 The city was divided into separate patrol districts. — (**3**) **1839** *Spirit of Times* 15 June 177/1 (We.) The patrole judges. **1868** WOODRUFF *Trotting Horse* xxix. 243 Sending out patrol judges, they started them for another heat. — (**4**) **1858** DOUGLAS in Logan *Great Conspiracy* 70 If the People of a Territory want Slavery, they will encourage it by passing affirmatory laws and the necessary police regulations, patrol laws and Slave Code.

(**5**) **1867** CRAWFORD *Mosby* 330 [They] captured five patrolmen, from whom, by the exercise of strength, awkwardness, and a mixture of deception, they succeeded in obtaining the countersign. **1947** *Sierra Club* (So. Calif. Chap.) *Sched.* 126, 12 It is doubly important that the Ski Mountaineers have some well trained patrolmen in our ski areas each week-end and to have proper first aid equipment to care for and evacuate the injured. — (**6**) **1880** TOURGEE *Invisible Empire* xii, The old 'patrol' system of the ante-bellum days and a devout belief in its necessity was also one of the active causes of the rapid spread of the Klan. — (**7**) **1887** *Courier-Journal* 22 Jan. 3/5 The patrol wagon, filled with officers, was driven to the place at a breakneck speed. **1947** *Chi. Tribune* 16 Nov. I. 4/3 Shoplifters claim that the indignation and shame of being ushered into the patrol wagon is the worst punishment they can suffer. — (**8**) **1810** *Boston Selectmen* 426 Return of the patrole watch read. **1821** *Ib.* 227 The subject of granting permission for private patrole watches, was committed to the Chairman.

As the last term in **fire, highway patrol.**

***patroller,** *n. S.* Also **pateroller, patter-roller,** etc. (See quot. 1901.) Now *hist.*

1867 HARRIS *Sut Lovingood* 166 The pat-rollers mite cum in an' spile hit wif thar durn'd foolishness. **1901** B. T. WASHINGTON *Up from Slavery* 77 The 'patrollers' were bands of white men . . . organized largely for the purpose of regulating the conduct of the slaves at night in such matters as preventing the slaves from going from one plantation to another without passes, and for preventing them from holding any kind of meetings without permission and without the presence at these meetings of at least one white man. **1948** *Sat. Ev. Post* 23 Oct. 100/4 The 'patterollers' . . . were on the lookout for any Negro who might be abroad at night without a passport.

b. Used in, or with reference to, a formerly popular song about patrollers. Now *hist.*

1862 in HARRIS *U. Remus & Friends* (1892) 196 He sing en he play—oh, gals, go 'way! Whar de patter-roller never kin see. **1880** ——— *U. Remus* (1884) 41 Run, nigger, run; patter-roller ketch you—Run, nigger, run; hit's almos' day. **1927** BENÉT *J. B.'s Body* 40 He's friends with de ha'nts and steel won't touch him But the paterollers is sure to cotch him.

***patron,** *n.* [See note.]

In sense **1.** the word is pronounced [paˈtron] and is an Amer. borrowing from French. McDermott includes it in his *Glossary.* Sense **2.** is an extension in meaning of the English word, while sense **3.** (also pronounced as in **1.**) is the result of a borrowing from Spanish.

1. Among voyageurs and fur traders, the master or steersman of a boat. Now *hist.*

1814 BRACKENRIDGE *Views La.* 206 The *patron* came to inform Mr. Lisa, they were begging him for a biscuit. **1817** BRADBURY *Travels* 192 Her crew consisted of five French Creoles, four of whom were oarsmen, and the fifth steered the boat, he is called the *patron.* **1849** T. T. JOHNSON *Sights Gold Region* 12 The Creoles . . . were generally the patrones or captains, and owners of the boats. **1941** DORSEY *Master of Miss.* 14 The crew put up glib arguments to stop here, but the newest *patron* on the rivers knew better—boat-hands being what they were.

2. (See quot. 1851.) *Obs.*

1818 *N. Amer. Rev.* March 427 To provide additional security [against extravagance], the following law, requiring the appointment of a patron, has been passed. **1851** HALL *College Words* 225 At some of the colleges in the United States, the patron is appointed to take charge of the funds, and to regulate the expenses, of students who reside at a distance.

3. *S.W.* (See quot. 1932.)

1859 T. R. WARREN *Dust & Foam* 154 (Bentley), The fifth, the patron or captain, was arrayed in a broad-brimmed hat, in possession of which he considered himself dressed. **1895** REMINGTON *Pony Tracks* 58 You can only go there if Don Gilberto, the *patron* of the hacienda . . . will take you in the ranch coach. **1932** BENTLEY *Sp. Terms* 178 Patron. . . . Master; chief; head supervisor. The nearest equivalent to the Spanish *patron*, as used in the Southwest, is the English word 'boss.' **1949** *Pacific Discovery* May–June 13/1 The average *hacendado* or *patrón*, enjoying low taxes and practically 'free labor,' can make satisfactory profits without modern agricultural implements.

***patronage,** *n.* As the last term in **executive, state patronage.**

patronage night. A night designated by a theater for the attendance of its regular patrons. *Rare.* — **1870** M. H. SMITH *20 Years Wall St.* 395 Grace Church in the season, the opera on a patronage night, . . . cannot boast of a more fashionably or elegantly attired company.

patroon pəˈtrun, *n.* [Du. in same sense.]

1. A proprietor of one of the tracts of land granted by the old Dutch government of New York and New Jersey. Now *hist.*

Such tracts, having 16 miles of seacoast or Hudson River frontage or a combination of the two, were granted members of the Dutch West India Company who settled fifty colonists. Patroons finally lost manorial privileges *c*1850.

1744 A. HAMILTON *Itin.* (1907) 74 Jeremiah Ranslaer . . . is dignified here with the title of Patroon. **1839** *Maysville* (Ky.) *Eagle* 11 Dec. 2/4 The tenants of the old Patroon . . . refuse to pay this rent any longer now that the patroon is dead. **1868** LOSSING *Hudson* 120 The

Patroon was invested with power to administer civil and criminal justice. **1944** JOHNSON *As I Dare* 247 There was in that old New York a comfortable acceptance of class distinction, born of the old world, and of the Dutch patroons, and of other inherited attitudes.

transf. **1838** *S. Lit. Messenger* IV. 305 They are addressed to a gentleman well known and highly appreciated in the annals of White Sulfur, the grand master of ceremonies for years on festive occasions, and by prescription the Patroon of the establishment. **1947** ROBINSON *Great Snow* 104 How's the Dutchess County patroon weathering the storm?

attrib. **1787** in G. O. SEILHAMER *Hist. Amer. Theatre* (1888) II. 228 Went to England to see the world and rub off a little of the patroon rust. **1797** JEFFERSON *Writings* IX. 403 With the English influence in the lower, and the Patroon influence in the upper part of your State, I presume little is to be hoped. **1859** PHILLIPS *Speeches* (1863) 287 Your Barnburners said, 'Patroon titles are unrighteous.' **1904** *Baltimore Amer.* 5 Oct. 8 Now that New Yorkers can ride a mile a minute in their nice new sewer, they had better get rid of their horsecar relics of the old patroon days.

2. patroon land, land belonging to a patroon's manor. *Obs.*

1758 in A. TOMLINSON *Military Jrnls.* 13 Marched into the Pateroon Lands to Landlord Lovejoys. **1885** A. JOHNSTON *Hist. U.S.* 245 Most of the 'patroon lands' were then [*c*1844] gradually sold to the tenants.

patroonry pə'trunrɪ, *n.* A system of landownership based on manorial rights. *Obs.* — **1858** *N.Y. Tribune* 30 Jan. 5/3 Another Blow at Patroonry.—The land-holders of Rensselaer county . . . had a meeting at West Sandlake on the 27th.

patroonship pə'trunʃɪp, *n.* A landed estate owned and governed by a patroon. *Obs.* — **1848** IRVING *Knickerb.* (rev. ed.) II. ix, The good Oloffe indulged in magnificent dreams of foreign conquest and great patroonships in the wilderness. **1884** *Mag. Amer. Hist.* Jan. 11 His estate would be constituted a manor, or in Dutch parlance a patroonship, with privileges similar to those of a baron in England.

***pattern,** *n.* A quantity of material sufficient for a garment.

1695 SEWALL *Letter-Book* I. 152 Send my wife a Pattern of Silk for a gown. **1782** *Essex Inst. Coll.* XXXVIII. 54 A Patton for two Pare of overalls and two Westcoats—and a patton of White Ribed Stuf for a Wescoat & Briches. **1806** LEWIS in *L. & Clark Exped.* IV. (1905) 186 One beaver skin, or two of those of the Raccoon or tiger catt forms the pattern of the robe. **1876** in GUILD *Old Times* (1878) 403 Six yards was a big pattern for a gown when I was courting.

As the last term in **clamshell, Concord, cotton, double log, dress, log cabin pattern.**

patter-roller, see ***patroller.**

Patton stock. (See quot. 1893.) *Obs.* — **1876** *Ill. Dept. Agric. Trans.* XIII. 322 Some grades of the 'Patton' stock are said to have been found in Madison. **1893** G. W. CURTIS *Horses, Cattle* 158 In 1797 some of these [shorthorn] cattle were taken across the line [from Va.] to Kentucky by a Mr. Patton, soon becoming quite well-known as the 'Patton Stock' [Durhams].

***patty,** *n.* **1. pattypan,** a scalloped summer squash. In full **pattypan squash.** Cf. **simlin. 2. patty shell,** a case made of puff paste in which creamed meats and vegetables and the like are served.

(1) **1907** *Suburban Life* April 237 We put in four egg-plants, two hills of crookneck squash and two hills of pattypan squash. **1926** *Ladies' Home Jrnl.* Nov. 149/3 Best known is the Patty Pan, or Cymling. — (2) **1909** FARMER *Boston Cook Book* 462 Patty Shells. Roll puff paste one-quarter inch thick. . . . Brush over with cold water. **1935** MITCHELL *America* 221 One Eastern restaurant advertised a dish called 'Chicken à la King en Pattie shell.'

paugie 'pɔgɪ, *n.* Also **paugy.** [f. the second element of scuppaug *q.v.*] The scup or porgy, *Stenotomus versicolor.* Also attrib.

1840 *N.Y. Mirror* 5 Sep. 87/2 Perhaps we may all of us live to see a Paulding paugy boat. **1848** BARTLETT 258 It is singular that one half the aboriginal name, *scup,* should be retained for this fish in Rhode Island, and the other half, *paug,* changed into *paugie* or *porgy,* in New York. **1911** *Rep. Fisheries 1908* 315/2 Scup (*Stenotomus chrysops*). . . . Common local names are 'scuppaug,' 'paugy,' 'porgy,' 'pogy' [etc.].

pauhagen pɔ'hegən, *n.* [f. an Algonquian term of obscure significance.] =**menhaden.** — *a***1838** in *Mass. Zool. Survey Rep.* 48 There are nearly three hundred and twelve thousand *pohegans* used for bait—and nearly as many thrown away, and strewed on the land for manure. **1910** HODGE *Amer. Indians* II. 212/1 Pauhagen. One of the New England names of the menhaden, or mossbunker. . . . Other spellings are paughaden, poghaden, pauhaugen.

Paul Bunyan. In folklore, a celebrated mythical lumberjack who performed amazing feats of lumbering in the Northwest. Also **Paul Bunyan-like.**

1924 *Frontier* Nov. 18 The winter that Paul Bunyan had the contract to log off Eastern Montana was an exceptionally bad one. **1946** R. PEATTIE *Pac. Coast Ranges* 279 Gone, too, is the bunkhouse where loggers made their own entertainment, gambling for tobacco or telling Paul Bunyan yarns. **1947** *So. Sierran* Nov. 3/2 There are pine, fir and spruce forests, wildflower meadows (with Paul Bunyan-like larkspurs seven feet high!) oak woods, . . . colorful cliffs, and deserts.

Paul Jones. A kind of dance combining square dancing and ball room dancing in which partners are changed, often used to acquaint people with one another. — **1920** *Atlantic Mo.* July 89/1 The whole sprightly, smiling, hand-clasping population seems engaged in one vast 'Paul Jones'—all hands round and swing together to the right, with no one sitting aloof in the corner, refusing to join the dance. **1948** *So. Sierran* Feb. 2/2 Both lost their voices helping to mix things up (in a nice way!) in two 'Paul Jones.'

***pause,** see **pose.**

***pavement,** *n.* **1.** A natural formation of flat stones, usu. across the bed of a stream. Freq. *pavement of rocks.* **2.** In mining, the stones lining the bottom of a sluice; stone riffle blocks.

(1) **1747–8** WASHINGTON in *Amer. Sp.* XV. 293 A certain Tract of waste & ungranted Land . . . beg: at a hickory & Walnut against a Pavement of Rocks. **1770** —— *Diaries* I. 424 The pavement of Rocks are only to be seen at low Water. **1918** A. W. GILES *Country about Camp Lee, Va.* 24 The water descends by a series of cascades and rapids between granite walls and over an uneven granite pavement. — (2) **1880** INGHAM *Digging Gold* 77 Great care is taken to wash any particles of sand or dirt that might contain fine gold from the blocks of pavement before their removal.

As the last term in **Belgian, block, Nicholson, Russ, shilling pavement.**

***pavilion,** *n.* **1.** (See quot. 1820. Cf. *OED* ***pavilion,** 7, 7 b.) **2. pavilion gauze,** (see quot.). Both *obs.*

(1) **1820** *N. Amer. Review* X. 116 The Board [at the Univ. of Va.] next proceeded to consider a plan of university buildings. They recommend *pavilions,* to contain each a lecture-room and from two to four apartments, for a professor and his family; and that these pavilions should be united by a range of *dormitories,* sufficient each for the accommodation of two students only. **1828** in MRS. M. B. SMITH *40 Yrs. Washington Soc.* (1906) 224 On two other sides running from north to south are the Pavillions, or Professor's houses, at about 60 or 70 feet apart, connected by terraces. [At U. of Virginia.] — (2) **1858** in EASTERBY *S.C. Rice Plant.* (1945) 350 It amounts in Money to upwards of $130, and in Sugar, Molasses, Flour, Coffee, Handkerchiefs, Aprons, Homespun and Calico, Pavilion Gause (Musquito Nets) . . . to the am't of $110 more.

As the last term in **bathing, board pavilion.**

Pawnee pɔ'ni, *n.* [App. f. *pariki,* horn, with reference to their method of hairdressing in which the forelock when dressed somewhat resembled a horn. Cf. **Arikara.**]

1. *pl.* or *collect.* A Caddoan confederacy or nation of Plains Indians formerly living chiefly in the valley of the Platte River in Nebraska.

See also **grand Pawnee** and **great Pawnee.** For foreign variants of earlier date see Hodge, *Amer. Indians, s.v.*

1770 PITTMAN *Present State* 40 The Arcansas or Quapas Indians . . . bring in very frequently young prisoners and horses from the Cadodaquias, Paneise, Podoquias, &c. of which they dispose to the best advantage. **1778** CARVER *Travels* 118 This is the road they [Indians] take when their war parties make their excursions upon the Pawnees. **1841** WILLIAMS *Tour to Ore.* (1921) 31 The Caws (or Kauzas) told me that the Pawnees were a bad nation, and that they had a battle with them. **1925** TILGHMAN *Dugout* 13 The Pawnees were late going south that year. **1949** *Nat. Geog. Mag.* Aug. 155/2 A few tribes, among them the Hidatsa, Mandan, Omaha, Pawnee, Ponca, and Iroquois, have been known to grow sweet corn.

b. The language used by these Indians.

1806 PIKE *Sources Miss.* II. App. 48, I asked . . . [for] a Tetau prisoner who spoke Pawnee, to serve as an interpreter. **1821** FOWLER *Journal* 55 Mr. Roy—He Spoke Some Pane and (in) that language our Councils Ware Held.

c. (See quot.) *Obs.*

1846 ST. JOHN *Lake Superior Country* 11 Again, there have been persons hanging about the office at Copper Harbour, with pockets full of Permits for persons never in the country, and never intending to be there, who came to be known by the name of '*Pawnees,*' from their putting their paws upon the shoulder, and 'a word in your ear' to every explorer who had really made examination, the moment he arrived.

2. An Indian of the Pawnee nation. In full **Pawnee Indian.**

1808 PIKE *Sources Miss.* 140 The Tetaus had recently killed six Pawnees. **1840** BIRD *Robin Day* 8, I had done a good act, and like the young Pawnee Indian, . . . I did not know it. **1889** G. B. GRINNELL *Pawnee Hero Stories* 246 The Pawnee who was disguised as a wolf could trot up close to the village of his enemy. **1946** FOREMAN *Last Trek* 242 The Sioux made two more raids, killing a Pawnee each time.

3. In combs., chiefly obs.: (1) **Pawnee country,** a region occupied by the Pawnee Indians; (2) **horse,** a horse owned or once owned by the Pawnees; (3) **hunting grounds,** the hunting grounds resorted to by the Pawnee Indians; (4) **Loups,** the Skidi, an Indian tribe of the Pawnee confederacy, also attrib., cf. **Wolf Pawnee;** (5) **macaroni,** (see quot.); (6) **Mohas,** =**Pawnee Loups;** (7) **Pict,** [F. *Pani Piqué,* tattooed Pawnees], a member of a confederacy of Indians closely related to the Pawnees, also *pl.*, this confederacy, also attrib.; (8) **Republic,** (see quot. 1946), also the Indians comprising this group; (9) **Republicans,** *pl.* a tribe of Pawnees who once lived on the Republican River, cf. **Republican Pawnee;** (10) **Ricaree,** =**Arikara;** (11) **Rock,** (see quot.); (12) **whistle,** a whistle of warning or announcement characteristic of the Pawnee Indians, *obs.*

(1) 1835 IRVING *Tour on Prairies* 103 We were in the Pawnee country. **1847** RUXTON *Adv. Rocky Mts.* (1848) 277 We were now in the outskirt of the Pawnee and Comanche country. — **(2) 1779** [see **Chickasaw horse**]. **1835** IRVING *Tour on Prairies* 189 A fine Pawnee horse that had his ears slit and saddle-marks on his back. — **(3) 1835** IRVING *Tour on Prairies* 58 The Osages . . . had represented to him the perils that would attend him on an expedition to the Pawnee hunting grounds. — **(4) 1805** in *Ann. 9th Congress* 2 Sess. 1046 Panias Loups, (or wolves.) . . . These are also a branch of the Panias proper. **1823** JAMES *Exped.* II. 165 The camp had been occupied by a war party of Skeeree or Pawnee Loup Indians. **1856** BECKWOURTH *Life* (1931) 25 Six or seven Indians of the Pawnee Loup band came into our camp.

(5) 1894 ROBLEY *Bourbon Co., Kans.* 38 They had nothing to eat but jerked buffalo and Pawnee macarroni [*sic*]. This latter was a very succulent dish much sought after by the Pawnee Indians. It was made from the small entrails of antelope and fish-worms. — **(6) 1843** N. BOONE *Jrnl.* (1917) 187 Whether this was caused by a fear that we'd frighten off the buffalo, or not, they kept up a continual alarm of Pawnee Mohas. — **(7) 1805** in *Ann. 9th Congress* 2 Sess. 1075 Pania Piqûe. . . . [Also] called Paunee Piqûe. **1823** JAMES *Exped.* II. 282 We supposed it to be the road leading from the Pawnee Piqua village on Red river to Santa Fé. **1856** BECKWOURTH *Life* (1931) 13 The Pawnee Pics or Tattoed Pawnees. **1916** THORBURN *Hist. Okla.* I. 124 The confusion of the two tribes was doubtless due to the French traders and trappers, who called the Wichitas 'Pawnee Piques,' i.e. Tattooed Pawnees, hence the corrupted American term, Pawnee Pict. — **(8) 1917** WILL & HYDE *Corn Among Indians* 145 The Pawnee Republics had only enough corn to thicken their soup. **1946** FOREMAN *Last Trek* 237 He found the Pawnee Indians living in four towns in an association that the government officials called the 'Pawnee Republic.' — **(9) 1805** in *Ann. 9th Congress* 2 Sess. 1045 Panias proper and Panias Republicans live in the same village. **1808** PIKE *Sources Miss.* II. App. 14 On the La Platte, reside the grand Pawnee village, and the Pawnee loups on one of its branches, with whom the Pawnee republicans are at war.

(10) 1819 NUTTALL *Travels Ark.* (1821) 81 Another kindled a fire near one of the tombs, probably for the purpose of sacrificing food, as I have seen practised by the Pawnee-Rikasrees of the Missouri. — **(11) 1848** ROBINSON *Santa Fe Exped.* (1932) 11, 15 miles west of Walnut Creek [near the Arkansas R.] stands the famous Pawnee Rock, near which a hard battle was once fought between 3000 Pawnees and 60 traders. — **(12) 1844** GREGG *Commerce of Prairies* I. 309 The 'Pawnee whistle' . . . at once made known the character of our visitors.

Also *Pawnee chief, fort, hunter, nation, scout, squaw, tribe, village, warrior, woman,* etc.

As the last term in **grand, Great, Republican, Wolf Pawnee.**

pawpaw, see **papaw.**

Paxton boys. [f. *Paxton,* Pa.] A band of Pennsylvania frontiersmen, headed by Lazarus Shaw, which became a political force after the massacre of the Conestoga Indians in 1763. Now *hist.*

1764 (*title*), The Paxton Boys. **1811** GRAYDON *Memoirs* (1846) 46 The unpunished . . . massacre of certain Indians at Lancaster . . . had so encouraged their murderers, who called themselves Paxton boys, that they threatened to perpetrate the like enormity upon a number of other Indians. **1831** WITHERS *Chron. Border Warfare* 79 The Paxton boys twice assembled in the neighborhood of the city, for the purpose of assaulting the barracks and murdering the Indians. **1833** WATSON *Hist. Tales of Phila.* 66 [The Indians] were . . . massacred . . . at mid-day by an armed band of ruffians, calling themselves the 'Paxtang boys.' **1949** *Pa. Mag. Hist.* Jan. 76.

* **pay,** *n.*

1. An article or articles used as a medium of payment. *Obs.* Cf. **country pay, current pay.**

1659 *Mass. H.S. Coll.* 4 Ser. VII. 233 There was only found 10 sheepe-wethers fitt to kill . . . [and] I sould [them] to the neighbors for other pay, excepting the skins & woole which ar kept. **1704** S. KNIGHT *Journal* 42 *Pay* is Grain, Pork, Beef, &c. at the prices sett by the General Court that Year. **1767** *Essex Inst. Coll.* XLVIII. 75 If you should purchase light pay, then proceed for Turks island.

2. A remunerative yield of metal in a stratum or vein. Also **big pay.**

1862 in *Pacific. N.W. Quart.* XXXIV. 51 We . . . worked off the top dirt down to the *pay.* **1880** G. INGHAM *Digging Gold* i. 41 The great richness of the gold-fields . . . enabled some lucky miners to make rich strikes and proportionately 'big pay.' **1904** E. ROBINS *Magnetic North* II. 148 Mining up here's an awful gamble. . . . No real 'pay' outside of this little gulch.

3. In combs., in some of which the first element is verbal: (1) **pay audience,** an audience made up of people who have paid an admission fee; (2) **car,** a railroad car carrying pay for employees, and from which payment is made; (3) **check,** a check given in payment of wages; (4) **department,** a department or branch of service, as in the U.S. Army, having to do with the paying out of money; (5) **envelope,** an envelope containing a person's wages; (6) **foot,** a mining foot (see * **foot,** *n.* **2.**) on a pay claim; (7) * **-master,** see as a main entry; (8) **school,** a school in which tuition is paid by the patrons, a private school, also attrib.; (9) **station,** a place where telephones, equipped with devices for receiving payment of toll, are available for public use, also a telephone in such a place.

(1) 1934 *DAB* XIII. 373 He gave illustrated lectures to pay audiences. — **(2) 1867** *Comm. & Fin. Chron.* 22 June 791 Also one pay car. **1948** *Dly. Ardmoreite* (Ardmore, Okla.) 20 May 16/5 They all had to report to the pay car for their money. — **(3) 1909** O. HENRY *Roads of Destiny* 360 Joe Wheeler signs the voucher for his pay-check. **1943** MENEFEE *Assignment* 104 The average paycheck here is only $28 a week. — **(4) 1816** *Ann. 14th Congress* 2 Sess. 27 The same observation applies to the pay departments. **1876** INGRAM *Centennial Exp.* 747 At the beginning of the war he accepted a position in the pay department of the United States Treasury in Washington.

(5) 1901 *Scribner's Mag.* XXIX. 401/1 A young machinist stepped quickly up to the window, received his yellow pay envelope with a brisk thanks. **1949** *Time* 4 Dec. 21/1 The sight of smoking factory stacks and the feel of cash in the weekly pay envelope had been habit forming. — **(6) 1869** J. R. BROWNE *Adv. Apache Country* 294 Is she on the Wild-Cat or Legitimate? How many pay feet does she offer? — **(8) 1856** MACLEOD *F. Wood* 191 The cost to us in taxation is not one fifth the usual expense for an ordinary pay-school education. **1883** *Rep. Indian Affairs* 90 In addition to the above there are a number of 'pay schools.' — **(9) 1923** WATTS *L. Nichols* 209 [He] rushed off to the nearest telephone pay station to call up the Grace house. **1948** *Time* 21 June 2 When you drop a nickel in a pay station and dial a call . . . as many as 1000 telephone relays go into action.

b. Designating or alluding to natural formations in which metals, esp. gold, occur in paying quantities, as (1) **pay chimney,** (2) **claim,** (3) **creek,** (4) **dirt, gravel,** see as main entries, (5) **ledge,** (6) **lode,** (in fig. context), (7) **ore,** (also fig.), (8) **quartz,** (9) **rock,** (also fig.), (10) **shoot,** (11) **streak,** (also fig.), (12) **vein.**

(1) 1876 RAYMOND *8th Rep. Mines* 107 The gold is . . . evenly distributed through the pay chimneys. — **(2) 1902** WILSON *Spenders* 338 All the pay-claims have been located, I guess. — **(3) 1911** ROLT-WHEELER *Boy with Census* 289, I came back another way, in order to take in a little group of houses on a small pay-creek.

(5) 1880 INGHAM *Digging Gold* 284 The nearness of the pay-ledges to the surface of the ground [gives the mines of the Black Hills an advantage]. — **(6) 1945** *Reader's Digest* Jan. 53/1 What is going to happen to scores of communities swollen by war orders when the pay lode runs out? — **(7) 1876** POWELL *Nevada* 109 In December, 1870, the largest body of pay-ore ever found on the Comstock Lode, up to that time, was discovered in this mine. **1942** LILLARD *Desert Challenge* 83 The inhibited middle class of other states are pay-ore [for 'wide-open' Nevada]. — **(8) 1901** WHITE *Westerners* 211 Lots of that is pay quartz. — **(9) 1862** in M. TWAIN *Letters* 64 (R.), We'll have a mill-site, water-power, and pay-rock, all handy. **1869** BRACE *New West* 247 'The first thing for a man,' he said, 'is to live true to his convictions; if he doesn't do that, he had better sell out; *there's no pay-rock in him!*' **1947** CHALFANT *Gold, Guns, & Ghost Towns* 141

Thompson and Ramsay prospected over the same ground . . . and struck some pay rock that was almost the pure stuff.

(10) 1876 RAYMOND *8th Rep. Mines* 107 The first pay shoot is 150 feet . . . in length along the vein. — (11) 1856 *S.F. Bulletin* 11 Oct. 1/1 These lucky miners worked one, two, and even three years, to reach the pay streak. 1890 RYAN *Told in Hills* 93 Stickin' to that old trail was a pay streak—hey? 1949 *Nat. Geog. Mag.* Oct. 507/1, I never found the pay streak. — (12) 1875 *Chi. Tribune* 30 Aug. 8/4 The Mountain Lion lode . . . [has] a pay vein that will compare favorably with the leading mines of Boulder County.

As the last term in **beaver, corn, country, current, fore, longevity, merchantable, old, paper, provision, rate, silver, store pay.**

***pay,** *v.*

1. In various colloq. phrases: **a.** *To pay in trade,* (see quot. 1820).

1820 FLINT *Lett. from Amer.* 201 Employers are also in the habit of deceiving their workmen, by telling them that it is not convenient to pay wages in money, and that they run accounts with the storekeeper, the tailor, and the shoemaker, and that from them they may have all the necessaries they want very cheap. The workman who consents to this mode of payment, procures orders from the employer . . . and is charged a higher price for the goods than the employer actually pays for them. This is called *paying in trade.* 1948 DICK *Dixie Frontier* 118 'Paying in trade' . . . often worked to the disadvantage of the workman.

b. *What is to pay?* what is the matter? what is wrong?

For this and next, see *EDD old Nick to play* (*s.v. play*) in similar sense.

1845 S. SMITH *Jack Downing's Letters* 33 (We.), Thinks I, what's to pay now. 1882 THAYER *From Log-Cabin* 164 'What, then, is to pay?' urged his mother earnestly. 1908 FREEMAN *Shoulders of Atlas* 80 'What is to pay now?' said she.

c. *Something is to pay,* something is wrong.

1877 *Harper's Mag.* Jan. 295/1 He gathered an idea . . . that 'somethin' wuz to pay,' as he expressed it to himself. 1896 WILKINS *Madelon* 102 Somethin's to pay—that girl acted queer.

d. *To pay the fiddler,* see ***fiddler,** *n.* **3.**

2. Esp. *pay-as-you-go,* pay or discharge obligations as they are incurred. Usu. attrib.

1840 *Farmer's Cabinet* 15 May 319/1 Pay as you go . . . is the truest economy. 1874 CARTER *Comm. Rollingpin* 97 'Pay as you go' might have been a good maxim for our forefathers, but the fashion now is to get passes if possible. 1880 *Bradstreet's* 23 Jan. 8/1 The city . . . has gone on the pay-as-you-go principle. 1949 *Sat. Ev. Post* 5 March 34/1 Now, thanks to the pay-as-you-go policy, there are many who find they owe the government nothing, and millions find themselves in the pleasant role of creditors.

pay dirt. Dirt or soil containing a mineral, as gold, in sufficient quantities to justify mining. Cf. ***dirt,** *n.* **1.**

1856 *Spirit of Times* 6 Sep. 13/1 On the Merced the miners are doing well, many getting out pay-dirt in their drifts that will pay big. 1897 LEONARD *Gold Fields Klondike* 28 Those who had claims sunk shafts which revealed 'pay dirt' at a few feet below the surface and became richer as the lower ground was reached. 1948 WESTON *Mother Lode* 44 A party of prospectors hit pay dirt there in the autumn of 1848.

b. Also *fig.* and *transf.*, esp. in the phrase *to strike pay dirt. Colloq.*

1873 *Vt. Bd. Agric. Rep.* II. 167 'Science' has paid me on the farm, and I am still working that placer, finding 'pay dirt' all the way, though not down to the 'bed-rock' yet. 1884 *Cent. Mag.* Nov. 60 [He] lives East in a style that proves that he has lots of pay dirt somewhere. 1903 *Nation* 1 Oct. 266 The German archaeological expedition to Babylon has now struck 'pay dirt,' and has unearthed a mass of cuneiform tablets. 1945 *Chi. D. News* 1 Aug. 1/3 Treasury investigators are striking pay dirt in their drive against tax evasion. 1949 *Amer. Photography* March 145/1 At Calgary, Canada, we cut into another fine streak of camera pay dirt in the annual stampede and roundup held there in the first week in July.

pay gravel. Gravel containing a mineral, as gold, in such quantities as to justify mining.

1871 HARTE *Poems* 30, O, why did papa strike pay gravel In drifting on Poverty Flat? 1899 —— *Mr. Jack Hamlin's Mediation* 99 Hardly a cartload of 'pay-gravel' ever arrived safely at its destination. 1948 JOHNSTON *Gold Rush* 32/1 A prospector climbed the brush fence, sank a shaft through the soil, and struck 'pay gravel.'

fig. 1884 MATTHEWS & BUNNER *In Partnership* 63 It appears the young woman had refused to have anything to do with him for a long period; but he seems to have struck pay gravel about two days before my arrival.

paying teller. In a bank, one who cashes checks or pays out money on other collection items.

1840 *Spirit of Times* 9 May 113/3 (We.), He stepped up to the paying teller. 1895 CARROLL *Principles Finance* 118 *Paying teller.* The paying teller is often called the 'first teller.' His duties are perhaps more exacting than those of any other officer of the bank. He is generally the custodian of the cash, and is personally responsible for the same. 1902 BELL *Hope Loring* 59 Once the paying-teller . . . asked one of them the reason.

***paymaster,** *n.*

1. *paymaster general, a. An officer in the U.S. Army in charge of paying the officers and men. *Obs.* **b.** (See quot.)

(a) 1775 *Jrnls. Cont. Congress* II. 94 There [shall] be a pay master general, and a deputy under him, for the army in a separate department. 1861 *Army Reg.* 346 The Paymaster-General shall keep in his office such record as may be necessary. — (b) 1881 *Naval Encycl.* 638 *Paymaster-general.*—The chief of Bureau of Provisions and Clothing, . . . styled paymaster-general, . . . is appointed by the President from among the senior paymasters [of the Pay Corps of the U.S. Navy].

2. paymaster's car, a railroad car used by the official who pays the employees. Cf. **pay car.**

1867 *Comm. & Fin. Chron.* 8 June 726 The equipment of the road consists of . . . the following cars: 87 passenger, 7 sleeping, . . . 2 paymaster's. 1868 *Ib.* VI. 521/1 These cars are described as follows—passenger (night 4, first class 32, and second class 3) . . . paymaster 2, . . . box stock 47, rack stock 36.

***payment,** *n.* As the last term in **corn, Indian, time, tobacco payment.**

payment ground. The place where annuity goods are delivered to Indians. *Rare.* — 1866 *Rep. Indian Affairs* 250 It shall be unlawful for any person to bring any kind of drinks, except coffee, on or near the payment ground.

***pea,** *n.*

1. = **sight pea.** *Rare.*

1838 GOSSE *Letters* 131 Some mark the barrel with a line of chalk to aid the sight in the darkness; others neglect this, and seem to know the position of the 'pea' by instinct.

2. = **pea coal.**

1880 *Bradstreet's* 2 Oct. 5/4 The sizes used are 'lump,' 'steamboat,' 'broken,' and 'pea.' 1949 *Black Diamond* 26 Feb. 54/3 For the better grades of Central Pennsylvania and Northern West Virginia coals, prices range as follows: . . . nut and pea, $3.50–$4.50.

3. In combs.: (1) **pea blower,** a small toy blowgun in which small peas are used, cf. **bean shooter;** (2) ***brush,** brush on which pea vines are trained; (3) **country,** a country or region where peas abound; (4) **patch,** see as a main entry; (5) **rifle,** a small-bore rifle shooting a bullet about the size of a pea, *obs.;* (6) **thresher,** a machine for removing peas from the pod and vine.

(1) 1821 IRVING in P. M. Irving *Life W. Irving* II. (1862) 59 The three eldest boys kept the house in misery for two or three days by pea-blowers. — (2) 1852 *Knickerb.* XL. 378 Justice Hawkins [was] sitting upon a decayed stump in front of the hotel, with a pea-brush alongside of him. 1941 *Yankee* Dec. 8/3 Was unable to sell his dearly bought mulberry trees for $1 per hundred to be used for pea-brush. — (3) 1853 SIMMS *Sword & Distaff* (1854) 191, I kin find as many partridges, or doves, to shoot, in a pea country, as any man can pint a gun at.

(5) 1856 *Spirit of Times* 18 Oct. 113/1 Squirrels . . . may still be barked with the pea-rifle by marksmen. — (6) 1944 CLARK *Pills* 288 Most remarkable of all the revolutionary implements which began to appear in stock were reapers and binders, hay bailers, pea threshers and transplanting machines.

b. In the names of birds, insects, and plants: (1) ***peabird,** (see quots.); (2) ***bug,** = **pea weevil;** (3) **fly,** = **pea weevil;** (4) **locust,** the Kentucky coffee tree; (5) **nut, vine,** see as main entries; (6) **weevil,** an indigenous North American weevil, *Mylabris pisorum,* that destroys peas by eating out their interiors.

(1) 1872 *Amer. Naturalist* VI. 397 The black-headed grosbeak is . . . well known as the 'Pea-bird,' from its fondness for green peas. 1917 *Birds of Amer.* II. 258 Baltimore Oriole. *Icterus galbula.* . . . [Also called] Fire-bird; Pea-bird; Hammock-bird. — (2) 1786 *Columbian* Sep. 38 [For] the best information, founded on actual experience, for preventing damage to crops by insects; especially the wheat-fly, the pea-bug, and the corn chinch-bug or fly,—a gold medal. 1876 *Field & Forest* II. 55 The larvae . . . eat their way in, in the same manner as *Bruchus pisi* or the 'pea-bug.' — (3) 1789 in *Mem. Phila. Soc. for Promoting Agric.* I. (1808) 317 The pea fly, *Bruckus pisi,* is a small beetle of that kind which we call wevel, but is more than twice their size, of an ovate form and brownish colour. — (4) 1820 *Amer. Farmer*

I. 398/1, I send you a pod of the 'Coffee Nut Tree,' sometimes called *pea locust.*

(6) 1841 HARRIS *Insects Injur. Veget.* (1862) 62 This little insect, ... the ... pea-weevil, ... is better known in America by the incorrect name of pea-bug. **1925** HERRICK *Man. Injurious Insects* 355 The Pea Weevil. ... From New York southward it is probably the most serious enemy of the garden pea.

c. In expressions sufficiently defined in the quots., as (1) **pea coal,** (2) **dropper,** (3) **lay,** (4) **line,** (5) **pie,** (6) **viner.**

(1) 1877 BARTLETT 454 *Pea-Coal,* the smallest-sized coal of commerce, ... obtained from sifting the larger sizes. — **(2) 1876** KNIGHT 1643/2 *Pea-dropper,* ... an implement for planting pease in hills. — **(3) 1850** *Rep. Comm. Patents 1849: Agric.* 401 After this mass of vine has been turned under, you have a 'pea-lay,' over which sow a bushel and a half of wheat per acre. — **(4) 1940** CUMMINGS *Amer. & His Food* 57 During this decade the ... Railroad, cutting through the 'Pea Shore' region of New Jersey, ... ran a special express train of one or two cars, known as the 'Pea Line,' to pick up perishable produce.

(5) 1890 MCALLISTER *Society* 97 'What is pea pie?' I asked. 'Cow peas and bacon,' was the answer. — **(6) 1943** CROW *Amer. Customer* 179 The pea viner is perhaps the most marvelous of them all. Vines fresh from the field are fed into the robot which hulls the peas, grades them as to size, and sends them on their way to the cooker.

d. In figurative phrases.

1871 STOWE *Sam Lawson* 44 Lawyer Dean he flew around like a parched pea on a shovel. **1902** HARBEN *A. Daniel* 206, [I] come as nigh as peas hittin' 'er in the jaw.

As the last term in **Albany, asparagus, beach, black-eyed, butterfly, cabbage, California, chaparral, Chickasaw, coffee, cornfield, cow, English, fodder, gentleman's, goober, ground, Indian, Japan, Magotty Bay, milk, miraculous, Negro, Oregon, partridge, posy, prairie, red, sensitive, sight, Slate River, speckled, stock, turkey, whippoorwill, wild pea.**

Peabody ˈpibʊdɪ, ˈpibədɪ, *n.* [Echoic.] **1.** =next. **2. Peabody bird,** the white-throated sparrow, *Zonotrichia albicollis.* Cf. **Sam Peabody.**

(1) 1917 EATON *Green Trails* 16 All day long in this pasture the Peabodies, or white-throated sparrows, sing their flutelike call. **1941** SETON *Trail of Artist-Naturalist* 217 From among these, in a drier spot, sprang the Peabody's mate. — **(2) 1864** E. A. SAMUELS *Rep. U.S. Comm. Agric.* (1865) 422 White-Throated Sparrow—Peabody Bird—Wheat Bird. ... This beautiful sparrow arrives in Massachusetts by the first week in April. **1897** CHAPMAN *Bird-Life* 188 Later, you will hear the sweet, plaintive notes that give to this bird the name Peabody-bird. **1941** SETON *Trail of Artist-Naturalist* 224 My sweet singer of the tamaracks, ... the night singer of the Assiniboine, was neither more nor less than the white-throated sparrow, the Peabody bird of New England, the nightingale of the farther north.

* **peace,** *n.* In combs.: (1) **peace belt,** a belt of wampum used among North American Indians as a symbol of peace, *obs.;* (2) **dance,** an Indian dance celebrating peace, *obs.;* (3) **Democrat,** *hist.* during the Civil War, a member of the Democratic party in the North who opposed the war and urged the substitution of peaceful measures, *obs.*, cf. **copperhead,** *n.* **2;** (4) * **maker,** a justice of the peace, *obs.;* (5) **measures,** *pl.* measures adopted by Congress in the Compromise of 1850; (6) **party,** a group of those who in times of national stress favor peace; (7) **pipe,** a ceremonial tobacco pipe, usu. having a long stem and adorned with feathers, used among North American Indians as a peace symbol, also fig.; (8) * **policy,** *hist.* the present Indian policy inaugurated by President Grant in 1869, providing for a board of ten commissioners to serve without compensation in regulating Indian affairs; (9) **Society,** a society or organization which advocates peaceful adjustments of national differences which might lead to war, also in the names of particular groups of this kind; (10) **song,** see quot.), cf. **peace dance,** *obs.;* (11) **talk,** a talk or conference with or among Indians in the interests of peace.

(1) 1758 *N.J. Archives* XX. 297 Peace was solemnly ratified by a large peace belt. **1798** HAWKINS *Letters* 312, I have received ... from the northern nations and southern tribes a broad peace belt. **1828** BERNHARD *Reise* II. 128 Unter den Curiositäten waren die bedeutendsten zwei *canoes* ... ein *peace belt,* oder Friedensschärpe, die aus einer weissen, von Glasperlen gestickten Leibbinde besteht, zwei Hande breit. — **(2) 1793** in *Mich. Hist. Coll.* XVII. 618 The Indians were about twenty in number. ... Round and round they danced ... the war dance, the peace dance, the scalping dance, &c. **1851** in SCHOOLCRAFT *Indian Tribes* (1853) III. 173 In the evening we were entertained with a grand peace-dance. — **(3) 1864** *Ore. State Jrnl.* 16 July 1/4 The Peace Democrats or conservative fellows, as they call themselves, insisting upon the Union as it was, are thus rebuked by their Southern friends in the Richmond Whig. **1886** LOGAN *Great Conspiracy* 557 Many of these leaders ... addressed the great gathering ... of nearly one hundred thousand Vallandigham-Anti-War Peace-Democrats, at Springfield, Illinois. **1946** HENDRICK *Lincoln's War Cabinet* 401 The 'Peace Democrats' had nominated this most remorseless of Copperheads on a platform calling for the immediate end of the war. — **(4) 1683** *Pa. Col. Rec.* I. 66 The Question was asked in Councill whether Peace Makers should sitt once a month.

(5) 1850 *Harper's Mag.* Dec. 122/1 We recorded at the proper time, the passage by Congress of the several measures generally known as the 'peace measures' of the session. — **(6) 1813** *National Intelligencer* (Wash., D.C.) 9 Nov. 1/4 One of the most curious geniuses among the whole of the Eastern peace party ... is William Jones, Esq. the Governor of Rhode Island. **1846** *Quincy* (Ill.) *Whig* 17 Feb. 2/5 The peace party in the Senate consists of all the whig force. **1861** *Richmond* (Va.) *Examiner* 6 Sep. 2/4 A convention of sympathy with the peace party assembled at the Court-House yesterday afternoon. — **(7) 1760** CROGHAN *Journal* 105 Brother to Confirm what we have said to you I give you this Peace Pipe. **1896** BRUCE *Econ. Hist. Virginia* I. 164 Among the most valuable treasures of each town was the peace-pipe. **1948** *Chi. D. News* 28 April 44/2 The nation's scientists whose chief tool is the microscope will meet at the Stevens Hotel June 10–12 to smoke the peace pipe. — **(8) 1871** *Rep. Indian Affairs* (1872) 68 There are more than one-half of all the roving Apaches ... reaping the benefit of the 'peace policy.' **1910** HODGE *Amer. Indians* II. 219/1 For nearly 40 years the Board of Indian Commissioners has cooperated with the Government, favoring such legislation and administration in Indian affairs as by peaceful methods should put an end to Indian discontent, make impossible Indian wars, and fit the great body of Indians to be received into the ranks of American citizens. ... A strong element of popular support [has been given] to this Peace Policy. — **(9) 1815** in N. WORCESTER *Friend of Peace* I. v. 38 The name of this society shall be The Massachusetts Peace Society. **1841** *Niles' Reg.* LIX. 330/3 The following memorials and petitions were presented and appropriately referred: By Mr. Clay, from the American peace society, asking that [etc.]. **1861** *Richmond* (Va.) *Examiner* 19 Dec. 3/4 The Peace Society recently discovered in Arkansas turns out to be a great farce.

(10) 1775 in CRESSWELL *Journal* (1925) 115 Saluted them with a Volley, which the Indian Warriors returned, then proceeded to the Council house, dancing, beating the drum, and singing the Peace Song, all the way. — **(11) 1789** *Steele P.* I. 51, I only mean to hold a peace talk. **1800** HAWKINS *Sk. Creek Country* 72 Peace talks are always addressed to the cabin of the Mic-co. **1852** REYNOLDS *Hist. Illinois* 165 All the 'peace talks' ever presented to the red men, could not have kept them in peace.

* **peach,** *n.*

1. =**peach brandy.**

1809 WEEMS *Marion* (1833) 77 Suppose you take a glass of peach. **1847** FIELD *Drama in Pokerville* 25 Mr. Major Slope, ... having been out to get a little 'peach,' had returned just at the climax.

2. A pretty or charming girl. *Slang.*

1865 *Prairie Chicken* (Tilton, Ill.) 1 June 3/2 What is the propriety of calling a pretty girl .. 'peaches,' etc.? **1896** ADE *Artie* 5 Don't it kill you dead to see a swell girl—you know, a regular peach—holdin' on to some freak with side whiskers and thinkin' she's got a good thing? **1949** *Sun. World-Herald Mag.* (Omaha) 1 May 2/1 The new recipe for making a peach cordial: Buy her a drink.

b. Anything regarded as superior or extraordinary. *Slang.*

*c***1870** B. HARTE *How Are You, Sanitary* i, Phrases such as camps may teach. ... Such as 'Bully!' 'Them's the peach!' **1913** LONDON *Valley of Moon* 65, I've got a temper, a peach of a temper. **1928** L. NORTH *Parasites* 20 'That's a peach of a car,' said she.

3. In combs.: (1) **peach blow,** (*a*) the color of a peach bloom or an object having this color, also attrib., (*b*) a potato having a pinkish tinge about the eyes, or the variety which produces this, in full **peachblow potato;** (2) **borer,** =**peach tree borer;** (3) * **bud,** (see quot. and cf. **peach land, peach soil**), *obs.;* (4) **bug,** (see quot.); (5) **curl,** a leaf curl affecting the peach tree, also **peach leaf-curl;** (6) **cut,** a social gathering where peaches are cut and prepared for preserving, *obs.;* (7) **land,** see as a main entry; (8) **oak,** the willow oak; (9) **orchard,** see as a main entry; (10) **pit,** the pit or seed of a peach, also attrib.; (11) **scale,** a scale insect that attacks peach trees; (12) **soil,** soil upon which wild peach is the native growth; (13) * **tree,** see as a main entry; (14)

wagon, a light, open wagon, esp. adapted for carrying crated peaches, *obs.;* (15) **worm,** a worm or caterpillar injurious to peach trees; (16) **yellows,** a destructive disease of the peach tree which turns its leaves a characteristic pale-yellow color.

(1) (*a*) **1829** T. FLINT *G. Mason* 32 The Red Bud in a thousand places was one compact tuft of peach-blow flowers. **1904** O. HENRY *Four Million* 208 Her eyes were dreamily bright, her cheeks genuine peachblow. (*b*) *a***1849** EMMONS *Agric. N.Y.* II. 45 Peach-Blow Potato. . . . It is a good bearer, and is common in the winter in the Albany market. **1855** *N.Y. Herald* 15 Dec. 6/3 There is a variety known as the 'peach blow,' which is also a hardy potato. **1884** *Rep. Comm. Agric.* 416 The Colorado Potato-beetle . . . appeared in greater numbers than it has done since 1881, attacking the 'Peach-blows' chiefly. — **(2) 1850** *N. Eng. Farmer* II. 222 Among those matters of interest . . . , the 'peach-borer,' its ravages, and remedy, have occupied a prominent place. — **(3) 1869** *Overland Mo.* III. 130 Texas is notable for the number of its soils. In Montgomery County there is what they call a 'peach-bud.' — **(4) 1854** EMMONS *Agric. N.Y.* V. 262 (Index), Peachbug, 79, 80. [*Ib.* 79–80 *Cetonia inda. Scarabaeus indus.* . . . They are charged . . . [with feeding] upon the ripening fruits: particularly do they select the best peaches.]

(5) 1888 *Amer. Naturalist* XXII. 738 *T[aphrina] deformans* Tul., causing the 'peach curl' of the leaves of the peach tree. **1904** *Westm. Gaz.* 6 Oct. 10/2 A fungus disease called peach leaf-curl . . . does injury to the extent of £600,000 annually in the United States. **1948** *L.A. Times* 8 Aug. (Home Mag.) 29/2 Your specimens are infected with mildew fungus disease and peach leaf curl. — **(6) 1877** BARTLETT 36 The terms apple-cut and peach-cut are also common. — **(8) 1835** J. MARTIN *Gaz. Va.* 209 Peach oak (so called from the resemblance of its leaves to that of the peach tree). **1897** SUDWORTH *Arborescent Flora* 177 *Quercus phellos* Linn. Willow Oak. . . . Common Names . . . Peach Oak (N.J., Del., Ohio).

(10) 1841 G. BUSH *Anastasis* (B.), You put an apple-seed or a peach-pit into the ground and it springs up into the form of a miniature tree. **1947** *Democrat* 14 Aug. 5/5 In California, peach pit fuel is on the market. — **(11) 1895** *Dept. Agric. Yrbk. 1894* 265 The New Peach Scale. . . . In the District of Columbia the insect is found only upon peach. — **(12) 1858** *Texas Almanac 1859* 76 The three soils mentioned above, namely, stiff black, peach, and cane-soils, are the principal soils in this portion of the country. — **(14) 1879** *Harper's Mag.* July 194/1 At every station . . . one sees those peculiar vehicles . . . known as peach wagons, square, cumbersome, and roomy, unloading their luscious contents.

(15) 1814 *Cramer's Almanac 1815* (Pittsburgh) 55 (*heading*), Remedy For The Peach Worm. **1856** *Rep. Comm. Patents 1855: Agric.* 299 The ravages of the peach-worm have proved more extensive than usual. — **(16) 1889** *Rep. Secy. Agric.* 22 Special attention has been given . . . to *peach yellows* in Maryland, Delaware, and other States. **1897** *Boston Jrnl.* 11 March 7/6 Does the cultivation of the peach in this State depend upon the control of peach yellows by legislation?

b. In the names of foods, drinks, etc., prepared from or involving peaches: (1) **peach and honey,** ?a drink made from peaches and honey, cf. **peach brandy;** (2) **beer,** beer made from peaches, *obs.*, cf. **peachy,** *n.;* (3) **brandy,** a spirituous liquor made from the juice of peaches; (4) **bread,** (see quot. and cf. **peach leather**), *obs.;* (5) **butter,** a thick sauce made of stewed peaches; (6) **cobbler,** a cobbler in which peaches are used; (7) **leather,** (see quot. 1877); (8) **loaf,** (see quot. and cf. **peach bread**), *obs.;* (9) **Melba,** a dessert consisting of preserved peaches, vanilla ice cream, and fruit sauce; (10) **pickle,** a peach preserved in vinegar and sugar and, usu., spiced; (11) **sauce,** a sauce made of peaches, cf. **Shaker peach sauce;** (12) **water,** a flavoring extract made from peach leaves.

(1) 1821 QUITMAN in Claiborne *Life Quitman* I. 69 He invited me to 'peach and honey'—something I had never tasted before. **1861** NEWELL *Orpheus C. Kerr* I. 212 [The South Carolina gentleman] clears a mighty track of everything that bears the shape of . . . brandy-sour, peach-and-honey, irrepressible cocktail [etc.]. — **(2) 1656** WILLIAMS in *R.I. Hist. Soc. Pub.* ns. VIII. 144 The Scot within named hath bene taken up, drowned . . . in going ouer in his Canow, having drunck too much Peach bear. — **(3) 1711** BYRD *Secret Diary* (1941) 403 After drinking two drams of peach brandy we returned to Mrs. Randolph's. **1887** HARRIS *Free Joe* 3 He was a Virginian, he declared; and, to prove the statement, he referred all the festively inclined young men . . . to a barrel of peach-brandy in one of his covered waggons. **1949** *Hist. & Philos. Soc. Ohio Bul.* 86 Peach brandy was manufactured at Gallipolis and shipped to Kentucky. — **(4) 1709** LAWSON *Carolina* 17 We found great Store of . . . barbacu'd Peaches, and Peach-Bread; which Peaches being made into a Quiddony, and so made up into Loves like Barley-Cakes.

(5) 1869 *Atlantic Mo.* Oct. 483/1 Sometimes peach-butter is made, with cider, molasses or sugar. **1935** H. L. DAVIS *Honey in Horn* 12 For sweets there were tomato preserves, peach butter, wild black-cap jam [etc.]. — **(6) 1859** BARTLETT 90 Cobbler . . . a sort of pie, baked in a pot lined with dough of great thickness, upon which the fruit is placed; according to the fruit, it is an apple or a peach cobbler. Western. **1947** *Reader's Digest* April 130/2 You could smell a peach cobbler all through dinner. — **(7) 1877** BARTLETT 454 Peach-Leather, Peaches boiled, rolled out, and dried in the sun. **1943** *Amer. Weekly* (N.Y.) 25 July 21 Mrs. Sayre's recipe for peach leather was as follows: Take a peck of ripe peaches . . . press them through a coarse sieve. . . . Add brown sugar, cook . . . spread on plates. . . . Set in the sun every day until thoroughly dried so that the paste may be rolled up like leather. — **(8) 1709** LAWSON *Carolina* 49, I bought, for 2 or 3 Flints, a large Peach-Loaf, made up with a pleasant sort of Seed. — **(9) 1926** *Ladies' Home Jrnl.* Nov. 176/3 For years chefs in great hotels have concluded their most important banquets with Peach Melba. **1948** *Sat. Ev. Post* 16 Oct. 22/1 There were cocktails, four kinds of wine, champagne, indestructible squab chickens, peach Melba, and . . . brandy.

(10) 1827 MRS. HALL *Letters* 165 One of the best pickles I ever ate is peach pickle. **1864** *Hist. North-Western Soldiers' Fair* 139 [Donations include] 1 keg peach pickles. — **(11) 1879** BISHOP *4 Months in Sneak-Box* 34 Bread and butter, with Shakers' peach-sauce . . . contributed to furnish a most satisfactory meal. — **(12) 1867** DIXON *New Amer.* II. 101 The ladies at Mt. Lebanon . . . make rose-water, cherry-water, peach-water. **1879** A. D. WHITNEY *Just How* 78 Half a teaspoonful of peach-water or essence of bitter almonds.

As the last term in **clingstone, desert, Indian, Jersey, vinegar, wild peach.**

peacherino ˌpitʃəˈrino, *n.* = ∗**peach,** *n.* **2.** *Slang.*

[**1900** *Kans. Gazetteer* 690 As a hero you forever take [R. P. Hobson] the 'peacherino' yam.] **1908** G. H. LORIMER *J. Spurlock* iv. 71, I went up in the air like an old wife happening by the office and discovering her husband dictating to a new blonde peacherino instead of old reliable. **1928** *Chambers's Jrnl.* Feb. 98/2 Though Captain Reginald saw little of her except at meals, he realised that here indeed was a 'peacherino.'

peach land.

1. *S.W.* Land upon which wild peach is a native growth.

1831 HOLLEY *Texas* (1833) 37 [Brazoria] is not located in a prairie . . . ; but upon a wooded elevation of peach-land.

b. *peach and cane land,* (see quots. and cf. **peach soil**).

1831 HOLLEY *Texas* (1833) 51 When a colonist wishes to describe his land as first rate, he says it is all peach and cane land. **1834** *Visit to Texas* vii. 71 The soil . . . passes for the best kind of land, especially when the wild peach tree is found growing upon it, when it is called peach and cane land.

2. Land suitable for growing peaches.

1868 *Mich. Agric. Rep.* VII. 432 Mr. Stocking . . . thought the high bluffs along the western shore were the best peach lands.

peach orchard.

1. An orchard of peach trees.

1676 GLOVER *Va.* in *Phil. Trans.* XI. 628 Here are likewise great *Peach-Orchards,* which bear such an infinite quantity of Peaches, that at some Plantations they beat down to the Hoggs fourty bushels in a year. **1758** *Va. State P.* I. 257 We overtook them at a peach orchard. **1849** *31st Congress* 1 Sess. Sen. Ex. Doc. No. 64, 103, I noticed the ordinary Navajo hut, (a conical lodge,) and close by it a peach orchard. **1906** LYNDE *Quickening* 19 It was goin' to . . . run right smack thoo' you-uns' peach orchard. **1949** *Democrat* 27 May 1/6 A hillside with suitable soil is the ideal place for a peach orchard.

2. peach orchard coal, a superior variety or grade of coal. *Obs.*

1830 *Providence D. Advt.* 14 Aug. 1/5 The *North American Coal Company,* are daily receiving large quantities of their superior *Peach Orchard* or *Centerville Coal.* **1874** COLLINS *Kentucky* I. 210 The Peach Orchard coal, the cannel coal, and the block coal . . . are among the finest in the world.

∗**peach tree.** In combs.: (1) **peach tree borer,** the larva of a moth injurious to peach trees, esp. that of the clearwing moth, *Sanninoidea exitiosa;* (2) **tea,** an infusion made from the twigs of a peach tree and water; (3) **yellows,** = **peach yellows.**

(1) 1850 *N. Eng. Farmer* II. 74 Captain George Pierce . . . said that the peach-tree borer would stand scalding-hot water. **1892** KELLOGG *Kansas Insects* 91 Peach-Tree Borer. (*Ægeria exitiosa.*) . . . The pest is an American insect, unknown on the peach trees of other countries. — **(2) 1941** M. L. SMITH *God's Country* 65 She went to the kitchen and made some peach tree tea out of some peach tree twigs.

— (3) **1854** Emmons *Agric. N.Y.* V. 262 (Index), Peachtree yellows, 113.

peachy ˈpitʃɪ, *n.* [f. ∗*peach*, ?on the pattern of *perry*, pear cider.] ?A beverage resembling cider made from the fermented juice of peaches. *Rare.* — **1781** Peters *Hist. Conn.* 245 They make peachy and perry; grape, cherry, and currant wines.

pea coat. =**pea jacket.** — **1790** *Pa. Packet* 4 Jan. 2/2 There are now lodged in the said Office . . . 1 pea coat; . . . 1 coatee [etc.]. **1862** Harte *Luck of Roaring Camp* 222, I borrow a pea-coat of one of the crew, and . . . am doubtfully permitted to pass into one of the boats.

Pea coat or pea jacket

peag pig, *n.* =**wampumpeag.** Cf. **mowhackees, peak, roanoke, wampum.**

1648 *Conn. Rec.* I. 179 No peage, white or black, [shall] bee paid or receiued, but what is strung . . . sutably, and not small and great, vncomely and disorderly mixt. **1658** *Portsmouth Rec.* 84 Eleven shillings after the Rate of Eight white peages per peny. **1677** Hubbard *Narrative* I. p. ix, He cast off first his Blanket, then his Silver-lac'd Coat . . . , and Belt of Peag. **1697** Sewall *Diary* III. 399 Wenoquaspouish . . . gave him a string of Peag.

b. Attrib. with **armlet, belt.**

1676 I. Mather *King Philip's War* (1862) 146 The English . . . struck down several Indians, one of which had on a great Peag Belt. **1820** Eastburn & Sands *Yamoyden* 12 Their peäg belts are girt for fight. **1820** *Ib.* 24 Collar beneath and gorget shone, The peag armlets and the zone.

pea jacket. [App. f. Du. *pij-jakker* in same sense. Bense suggests a north Frisian form *pijekkat* as a possible source.] A double-breasted jacket of heavy woolen material, freq. worn by sailors. Cf. **sea pea jacket.**

1721 *Amer. Wkly. Mercury* 23–30 March 2/2 Cloathed with a double-breasted Pee-Jacket. **1830** *Mechanics' Press* (Utica, N.Y.) 19 June 256/3 A weather beaten New England skipper, in a pea jacket, stumped him by exclaiming, 'Darned if I don't bet you!' **1949** *Time* 3 Jan. 16/3 He wore only winter underwear under his pea jacket.

b. Also **P jacket.**

1889 *Outing* May 123/2 The coat should be a roundabout or 'P' jacket in shape.

peak pik, *n.* =**peag.** Now *hist.*

1638 *Md. Council Proc.* I. 73 Entred by Capt. Henry fflute . . . 7 fathome of peake. **1709** Lawson *Carolina* 194 The general and current Species of all the Indians . . . is that which we call Peak, and Roanoak; but Peak more especially. **1738** Byrd *Dividing Line* (1901) 34 That species of conque shell which the Indian peak is made of. **1944** Footner *Rivers of East. Shore* 137 For currency, the Nanticokes used 'roanoke' and 'peake,' sometimes called 'wampum-peake,' two kinds of shell. . . . Peake, white in color, was made of cockleshell.

peaker ˈpikɚ, *n.* **1.** (*cap.*) Short for **Pike's Peaker.** *Obs.* **2.** (See quot. 1905.)

(1) **1861** *Knickerb.* Aug. 121 Though but a few months in the country, he is as good a Peaker as the next man. **1872** *Kans. Mag.* Jan. 45 The flats or bottom lands, extending from the city southward, were white with the tents of the 'Peakers.' — (2) **1905** *Forestry Bureau Bul.* No. 61, 43 *Peaker.* 1. A load of logs narrowing sharply toward the top, and thus shaped like an inverted V. . . . 2. The top log of a load. **1926** Rickaby *Ballads* 97 His peakers rise above the clouds.

∗**Peale.** [Titian Ramsey *Peale* (1799–1885), Amer. naturalist.] In possessive in names of birds: (1) **Peale's egret,** (see quot.); (2) **Peale's falcon,** (see quot.).

(1) **1860** Baird *Birds N. Amer.* 661 *Demiegretta pealii,* Peale's egret, . . . [is found on the] seacoast of South Florida. — (2) **1887** Ridgway *Man. N. Amer. Birds* 248 [From the] Aleutian Islands, west to Commander Islands, and south along Pacific coast to Oregon [we find] . . . Peale's Falcon. **1917** *Birds of Amer.* II. 89 Peale's Falcon (*Falco peregrinus pealei*) is a duskier slate above than the Duck Hawk.

peanut ˈpiˌnʌt, *n.* [∗*pea*+ ∗*nut.*]

1. The small edible nut of any one of several herbs of the genus *Arachis,* esp. *A. hypogaea;* any one of these herbs. Cf. **goober, groundnut 2, ground pea 1.**

1807 Irving *Salmagundi* xii. 301 Young seniors go down to the flag-staff to buy pea-nuts and beer. **1834** *Sun* (N.Y.) 2 April 2/3 The pit at the Bowery was usually filled with a set of pea-nut-eating geniuses. **1837** Williams *Florida* 112 The pea nut produces a large crop. **1949** *Chi. Sun-Times* 5 Jan. 72/2 In Massachusetts it's against the law to eat peanuts in church.

b. (See quot.) *Rare.*

1794 Wansey *Excursion to U.S.* (1798) 250, I brought from the United States with me . . . of nuts, hiccory and chinquopin, or pea nut.

c. (See quots.) *Colloq.* and *slang.*

1866 *Washoe* (Nev.) *Eastern Slope* 21 July 2/1 What kind of consistency is it—you fellows sing peanuts to the President once elected, and throw off onto him in this way before the next? **1893** *Harper's Mag.* May 947/2 The farm land yields, in local parlance, 'everything from peanuts to persimmons.'

2. Someone or something paltry, trifling, contemptible, usu. attrib. *Slang.* Cf. **peanut politics.**

1836 Dunlap *Mem. Water Drinker* (1837) II. 25 They were your peanut fellows, I suppose. **1854** *Cong. Globe* 19 May 1230/3, I know them—a set of peanut agitators and Peter Funk philanthropists. **1892** *Cong. Rec.* 18 June 5394/2 This country is not a peanut institution; it is a great country. **1910** McCutcheon *Rose in Ring* 203, I suppose that peanut aristocrat friend of yours has told you it ain't swell or proper to wear tights. **1947** *Newsweek* 22 Dec. 18/1 Pauley estimated that altogether they involved less than $1,000,000—just 'peanuts in the whole scheme of things.'

3. In special combs.: (1) **peanut bar,** a candy bar made mostly of roasted peanuts; (2) **boy,** a boy who sells peanuts; (3) **brittle,** a brittle candy containing roasted peanuts; (4) **bum,** a college "jollification" at which peanuts are eaten, *obs.*, cf. **bum,** ***n.* 1;** (5) **butcher,** a butcher (sense **2.**) who sells peanuts; (6) **butter,** see as a main entry; (7) **candy,** candy having roasted peanuts in it, also fig. **peanut-and-molasses-candy,** attrib.; (8) **cart,** a stand on wheels at which peanuts are roasted and sold; (9) **chocolate,** a sweetened drink made of pounded parched peanuts over which boiled milk is poured; (10) **digger,** (see quot. 1876); (11) **gallery,** the last or uppermost gallery in a theater, cf. **Negro heaven;** (12) **machine,** a machine for harvesting peanuts; (13) **oil,** a yellow oil expressed from peanuts which is used in soaps, in oleomargarine, as a salad oil, etc., also attrib.; (14) **politics,** petty politics, political action inspired by mean or narrow motives, *slang,* cf. **2.** above; (15) **roaster,** a contrivance for roasting peanuts; (16) **stand,** a station, booth, or movable stand where roasted peanuts are sold.

(1) **1894** *Life* 10 May 312/1 When I got there the angels forced my mouth open with a peanut bar. **1947** Baskins *Dr. Has Baby* 80 A good Sunday afternoon for me . . . is a solid two-feature bill, a couple of shorts, a travelogue, a color comedy, and a chocolate peanut bar or two. — (2) **1857** *Spirit of Times* 5 Sep. 12/1 At length the mare reached the quarter pole, where a little pea-nut boy had stationed himself. **1873** M. Twain *Gilded Age* xxxvi. 333 (R.), In the cars, you know, the peanut-boy always reassures you with his eye, and hands you out a book of murders if you are fond of theology. — (3) **1903** *N.Y. Ev. Post* 2 Oct. 7 It is impossible for one man to prescribe that all records [of great eating] henceforth shall be measured in peanut brittle, or veal cutlets, or canned corn. **1945** Maxwell *Folded Leaf* 16 He . . . saw . . . Bea Crowley and Sylvia Farrell, who were trying to make a brown-and-white fox terrier sit up and beg for peanut brittle. — (4) **1871** Bagg *At Yale* 70 [At] a 'peanut-bum' . . . a sack containing one or two bushels of peanuts is emptied upon the floor, and an indiscriminate scramble is made for them.

(5) **1903** *Cin. Enquirer* 3 Jan. 11/5 You know, all the men who sell are butchers. There are the peanut butcher, the ticket butcher, the candy butcher, and the sandwich butcher. **1913** *Sunset* Sep. 518/2 The peanut butcher had brought a table at the request of a sad-faced man with a nose that turned under. — (7) **1856** Stowe *Dred* I. 51 Danc-

ing, flirting, writing love-letters, and all other enormities down to eating pea-nut candy. **1885** PORTER *Incidents & Anecdotes Civil War* 201 There was a large assembly of persons of the genuine peanut-and-molasses-candy stripe. **1901** MATTHEWS *Notes on Speech-Making* 53 Some postprandial addresses are so thin in theme, and so thick with jokes, that they resemble the peanut candy where you can not see the candy for the peanuts. — **(8) 1919** CADY *Rhymes of Vt.* (1923) 122 The barber leaves his door ajar, The peanut cart is steaming. — **(9) 1904** STERLING *Belle* 224 We were glad to drink potato coffee and peanut chocolate.

(10) 1876 KNIGHT 1644/1 *Peanut-digger*, a kind of plow with trailing branches, which raises from the soil the vines with the nuts attached, and leaves them . . . to be afterward gathered and picked by hand or by . . . [a] peanut-picker. **1946** *Chi. Sun* 25 Dec. 8/3 Mechanical peanut and potato diggers soon may be in large scale use. — **(11) 1893** POST *Harvard Stories* 108 (We.), I believe on the strength of my promise he bought a seat in the peanut gallery. **1945** *New Yorker* 5 May 15/1 We were sitting in the peanut gallery of the Opera House. — **(12) 1939** *These Are Our Lives* 66 We own our own team, two mules, our wagon and plows; Mr. Makepeace pays the fertilizer bill, but the expenses of the peanut machine and labor has to come out of us. — **(13) 1900** SADTLER *Handbk. Industr. Org. Chemistry* (ed. 3) 50 Arachis oil (peanut oil, erdnuss oil). . . . The best qualities . . . are used for table oil and the inferior grades for soap-making. **1911** LEWIS *Apaches N.Y.* 132 He trimmed the peanut-oil lamp. **1943** MENEFEE *Assignment* 245 Uncle Sam had called for extensive peanut plantings, . . . to step up production of peanut oil. — **(14) 1887** *N.Y. Mail & Exp.* 27 May (F.), If the Governor would consent not to play pea-nut politics. **1909** *N.Y. Ev. Post* 4 Feb. (Th.), They used to talk about 'peanut politics' at Albany, but a peanut is too large and respectable an object to yield a comparison for yesterday's action of the State Senate.

(15) 1902 *Sears Cat.* (ed. 112) 589/3 The Boss Peanut and Coffee Roaster is the only successful roaster on the market. **1939** *These Are Our Lives* 283 [He] drew out a gallon at a time as needed for his peanut roaster. — **(16) 1864** PASTOR *Combination Songster* 66 A blackguard by the name of McCarty . . . was book-keeper to a peanut-stand, And sold apples by the dozen. **1947** *Time* 27 Jan. 58/2 He was always dabbling shrewdly in dry cleaning stores and peanut stands.

Also *peanut business, crop, man, patch, peddler, planting, vendor,* etc.

As the last term in **hog, running, Spanish, wild peanut.**

peanut 'pi,nʌt, *v. tr.* To make small or insignificant. *Rare.* Cf. **peanut,** *n.* **2.** — **1884** *Cong. Rec.* 24 April 3356/1 The chairman of the Committee on Appropriations proposes to cut down, to cheese-pare, to peanut this whole business, so that if we should get into a war we will not be able to compete with any foreign nation.

peanut butter. A paste or spread made from ground roasted peanuts to which seasoning, etc., has been added.

1903 *Harper's Bazaar* Oct. 981 Two [sandwiches] of wholewheat bread with peanut butter. **1935** MITCHELL *America* 211 If you are stupid enough to ask for sandwiches with your afternoon tea you will get a tremendous triangle with a wobbly upper deck . . . or even pea-nut butter. **1948** *Mazama* Dec. 6/1 Peanut butter flew thick, and cries for more bread and 'Where's another knife?' were heard.

b. Also (1) **peanut butter cooky,** (2) **peanut butter sandwich.**

(1) 1941 FARMER *Boston Cook Book* 674 Peanut Butter Cookies. ½ cup butter, ½ cup peanut butter [etc.]. **1941** *Dly. Oklahoman* (Okla. City) 7 Oct., Peanut butter cookies are rich and crunchy, delicious to eat and fun to make. — **(2) 1927** HALLIBURTON *Glorious Adventure* 331 We never even got to our stuffed eggs and peanut-butter sandwiches. **1948** *Savings News* Jan. 11/1 I'll be eating a peanut butter sandwich for lunch every day this month.

pea patch.

1. (*cap.*) (See quot. 1818.)

1778 in SERLE *Journal* 311 The Eagle unmoored & came down to the Pea-Patch below Newcastle; but the Wind falling scanty, she was obliged to anchor. **1818** *Niles' Reg.* XIV. 15/1 Capt. Babcock, of the U.S. engineers, is advertising for a large quantity of lumber, to be used in the contemplated fortification of the Pea Patch, a marshy island in the Delaware river, below New Castle. **1833** E. T. COKE *Subaltern's Furlough* i, We . . . arrived abreast of Fort Delaware, or the 'Pea Patch,' built upon a low reedy island, which divides the river in two channels.

2. A patch or comparatively small area planted in peas.

1834 *Knickerb.* III. 35 Didn't I turn that pied heifer of yourn into my pea patch? **1941** STUART *Men of Mts.* 120 Tear off the damn Dingus silk shirts . . . for to make skeery-crows out'n for the pea patch!

* **pear,** *n.*

1. *S.W.* Short for prickly pear *q.v.* Also attrib.

1905 *Bur. Plant Industry Bul.* 74, 20 It is universally recognized throughout the pear region of southwestern Texas that the plant has a decided tendency to increase the flow of milk. **1911** THORNBER *Native Cacti as Emergency Forage Plants* 481 Three men with teams and wagons are needed to haul the pear to the machine, and a fourth man with team and wagon to haul the chopped material away. **1932** HARRY WILLIAMS *Legends* 254 Then there is the story of . . . the aged Mexican pearchopper. **1949** *Sun. World-Herald Mag.* (Omaha) 1 May 10/4 By 1925 the pear covered something like 60 million acres, including some of the best land.

2. In special combs.: (1) **pear blight,** see as a main entry; (2) **burner,** a machine for singeing off the spines of cacti that are to be used as cattle feed; (3) **butter,** a thick sauce of pears stewed down, usu. in their own juice; (4) **cactus,** =**prickly pear;** (5) **haw,** the blackthorn, *Crataegus tomentosa*, also **pear hawthorn.**

(2) 1905 *Bur. Plant Industry Bul.* 74, 20 After a day or two of feeding the sound of the pear burners . . . brings the whole herd to the spot immediately. **1911** WOOTON *Cacti in N. Mex.* 20 By using the 'pear burners' the standing plants may be singed in the pasture, just enough for the day's feed, and the cows left to gather it. — **(3) 1872** *Harper's Mag.* May 808/1 Then came the inevitable sauces and sweetenings. Apple-butter, pear-butter, plum-butter, and wild-grape-butter—this latter the most piquant of all the mountain sauces used with meats or on hot bread-and-butter. — **(4) 1929** A. ELLIS *Life* 10 My mother would gather pear cactus, and split it carefully, throwing it into the water.

(5) 1884 SARGENT *Rep. Forests* 79 Black Thorn. Pear Haw. **1892** APGAR *Trees Northern U.S.* 106 Black or Pear Hawthorn; . . . wild in western New York, west and south. **1897** SUDWORTH *Arborescent Flora* 230 *Cratægus tomentosa*. Black Haw. . . . [Also called] Pear Haw (Miss., Ohio).

As the last term in **bell, button, cabbage, choke, fall butter, June, pound, prickly, Saint Michael's, seckel, sugar, wild pear.**

pear blight. 1. A fire blight destructive to pear trees. **2. pear blight beetle,** a beetle, as *Anisandrus pyri*, the larvae of which are injurious to pear trees.

(1) 1854 EMMONS *Agric. N.Y.* V. 165 Atmospheric Blight . . . proves itself to be independent of the cause that sometimes produces the pear blight. **1856** *Mich. Agric. Soc. Trans.* VII. 714 The pear blight, too, is as yet unknown among us, but is steadily marching to the west. — **(2) 1854** EMMONS *Agric. N.Y.* V. 113 *Scolytus* (*Tomicus*) *pyri*. . . . Pear-blight Beetle. . . . This insect has been highly injurious to the pear tree in New-England. [**1881** OMEROD *Man. Injur. Insects* (1890) 330 In America this species of beetle, . . . known . . . under the name of *Xyleborus pyri*, popularly known as 'Pear Blight' is . . . injurious to both Pear and Apple.]

* **pearl,** *n.* In combs.: (1) **pearl bean,** (see quot. 1855); (2) **millet,** a cereal grass, *Pennisetum glaucum*, also a kind of sorghum.

(1) 1855 BROWNE in *Trans. Amer. Inst. N.Y.* 596 Pearl bean, without strings, from Germany, a fine variety, used as 'snaps' when green, or in a dried state when shelled. **1860** DISHER *Cowells in Amer.* (1934) 98 Vegetables . . . Pearl Beans. — **(2) 1896** BEAL *Grasses N. Amer.* I 187 *P*[*ennisetum*] *typhoideum*. Pearl, Indian, African, Cat-tails, or Horse Millet. **1901** MOHR *Plant Life Ala.* 135 Various kinds of sorghum, known as durrha or kafir corn, millo maize, and pearl millet.

As the last term in **bastard, dust, Wabash pearl.**

pearly everlasting. An American herb of the thistle family, *Anaphalis margaritacea*. — **1857** GRAY *Botany* 229 *Antennaria margaritacea*. Pearly Everlasting. **1872** *Vt. Bd. Agric. Rep.* I. 281 Pearly everlasting, a perennial, occupies the knolls of cool, hill pastures.

* **peat,** *n.* **1. peat meadow,** a meadow or level area in which peat occurs. **2. peat swamp,** a swamp in which peat abounds; also as a proper name.

(1) 1836 *Niles' Reg.* 17 Sep. 48/2 A peat meadow . . . in Salem, on the old Boston road, has been burning. **1883** *Cent. Mag.* Sep. 650/1 In Eastham, large stumps may be discovered nearly a mile from land, and ancient peat-meadows now lie under water. — **(2) 1839** BUEL *Farmer's Companion* 70 The inert, insoluble matter of peat-swamps is rendered soluble and enriching, by . . . manure. **1884** ROE *Nature's Story* We make the most of our peat swamps, fallen leaves and rubbish in general. **1929** E. N. DANENBERG *Romance Norwalk* (Conn.) 13 This swamp should not be confused with Peat Swamp,—so called because at one time early Norwalkers used to gather peat for their fires in its oozy depths, and which is between Norwalk and Westport.

pea time.

1. *fig.* The time proper or fitting for certain actions or attitudes. *Colloq. Obs.*

1862 LOWELL *Biglow P.* 2 Ser. 11 Ther' 's ollers chaps a-hangin' 'roun' that can't see pea-time's past.

2. *The last of pea time(s)*, the end of the time when

peas are in season; hence, *fig.*, the last stage, or a trying or difficult time or period. *Colloq.*

1834 CARUTHERS *Kentuckian* I. 190 [He] whines it out to us like an old woman in the last of pea-time. **1893** M. A. OWEN *Voodoo Tales* 199 'Deed my gyarden am a-lookin' mighty bad. Hit look mo' lak de las' o' pea-time den de fust o' truck-time. **1904** E. ROBINS *Magnetic North* I. 63 Things looked pretty much like the last of pea time.

b. Used of persons in comparisons.

1888 CRADDOCK *Broomsedge Cove* 174 Ye oughter git some air an' light, Marcelly; ye look like the las' o' pea-time. **1911** SAUNDERS *Col. Todhunter* 108 'What on earth's the matter, Bill?' he asked. 'You look like the last of pea-times.'

peavey ˈpivɪ, *n.* [Usu. said to be named from Joseph *Peavey*, its inventor, but see note below.] (See quot. 1905.) Cf. **driving pike.**

"According to Mr. J. C. French, of Roulette, to the writer, May, 1925, it [the peavey] was devised by John Peavey, a blacksmith at Bolivar, Allegheny Co., N.Y., about 1872" (*Old-Time New England*, July 1925, 28).

*c*1870 in E. C. BECK *Songs of Mich. Lumberjacks* (1931) 49 With jam pikes and with peaveys These brave men nobly go. **1905** *Forestry Bureau. Bul.* No. 61, 43 A stout lever 5 to 7 feet long, fitted at the larger end with a metal socket and pike and a curved steel hook which works on a bolt; used in handling logs, especially in driving. A peavy differs from a cant hook in having a pike instead of a toe ring and lip at the end. **1949** *Boston Globe* 14 Aug. (Fiction Mag.) 8/1 In every ounce of his close-built body there was sinewy strength from early and constant familiarity with the axe, the cross-cut saw, the peavey, cant-hook, paddle and pike.

attrib. **1902** WHITE *Blazed Trail* 270 A peavey-hook it is my pride. **1947** *Sat. Ev. Post* 8 March 58/2 The peavey handle bent in an arc, and suddenly straightened as the log was twisted free.

pea vine.

1. A clambering plant, somewhat like some species of the cultivated pea, found as a native growth in various parts of the U.S.

1675 *Pa. Mag.* VI. 89 You have Grass as high as a man's Knees, . . . interlac'd with Pea-Vines, and other Weeds that Cattel much delight in. **1796** in IMLAY *Western Territory* (ed. 3) 518 In the state of Tenasee cattle at present support themselves among the reeds, pea-vines, rye-grass, and clover. **1892** J. L. ALLEN *Blue-Grass Region* 14 [The forest], together with cane-brakes and pea-vines, covered the face of the country.

attrib. **1870** *Amer. Naturalist* IV. 30 The meadows are bounded . . . by the Pea-vine mountains (so-called from the frequency with which the lupines or wild peas are met with on its sides). **1880** TOURGEE *Bricks* 61 Richards . . . came from up North somewhere about 1790, when everybody thought this pea-vine country was a sort of new Garden of Eden.

2. The vines of some species of cultivated pea.

1766 BARTRAM *Journal* 25 The last frost killed the . . . pea-vines, sun-flowers [etc.]. **1928** BRADFORD *Ol' Man Adam* 184 Git yo' haid outn dem pea vines, Judy.

b. pea vine hay, pea vines cured as hay.

1860 *So. Cultivator* XVIII. 211 A little corn with Pea Vine Hay will keep them fat. **1932** W. KELLEY *Inchin' Along* 55 Everybody knows there is nothing a mule likes better than pea-vine hay with the peas left on.

pecan pɪˈkɑn, *n.* [Algonquian *pakan*, any hard-shelled nut.]

1. A species of hickory, *Carya illinoensis*, or a tree of this species.

Early writers not infrequently regarded this tree as a species of the walnut, *Juglans*. Also called Illinois nut, Mississippi nut, *qq.v.*

[**1772** ULLOA *Noticias Americanas* 116 La una de estas llaman *Pacanos*, que es un genero de *Nogál* de mas corpulencia que ellos, pero en madera y hoja muy semejante.] **1773** in HUTCHINS *Va., Penn., Md., & N. C.* 52 The timber, Bois Connu, or Paccan, Maple, Ash, Button Wood. **1802** ELLICOTT *Journal* 284 Peccan, (*Juglans illinoinensis*,) . . . is met with as high as the Wabash. **1892** DUVAL *Young Explorers* 188 Many groves of Pecan, elm and oak trees dotted its surface, giving it the appearance of ornamented grounds. **1948** *Dly. Ardmoreite* (Ardmore, Okla.) 21 July 7/3 Stately old elms vie with the pecans and crape myrtle.

b. Lumber of the pecan tree.

1948 *Home Helper* (Oak Park, Ill.) Dec. 8/1 Nowadays, most hardwood floors are of oak, maple, beech, birch or pecan.

2. The richly-flavored nut of this tree. Cf. **pecan nut.**

1822 WOODS *English Prairie* 228 Pecan is a sort of walnut, said to be the finest nut in this country. **1876** *Forest & Stream* 13 July 376/2 Spending a few days at Concho, gathering pecans, visiting the fine springs at Kickapoo [etc.]. **1945** *Silverton* (Colo.) *Standard* 23 Feb. 3/2 I've had luscious apples from Washington state, pecans from Mississippi.

3. In combs.: (1) **pecan cigar case-bearer,** the larva of a moth, *Coleophora caryaefoliella;* (2) **hickory,** = **pecan 1,** *obs.;* (3) **nut,** see as a main entry; (4) **pie,** a soft, one-crust pie containing pecans.

(1) **1923** FORBES *Lepidoptera N.Y.* 211 In economic literature it is referred to as the 'hickory cigar case-bearer' or the 'pecan cigar case-bearer.' — (2) [**1785** MARSHALL *Amer. Grove* 69 Pecan or Illinois Hickery.] **1847** DARLINGTON *Weeds & Plants* 304 *C*[*arya*] *olivæformis*. . . . Olive-shaped Carya. Pecan Hickory. Pecan nut. — (4) **1941** FARMER *Boston Cook Book* 611 Pecan Pie. 3 eggs, 1 cup light corn sirup . . . 1 cup pecans, broken in pieces [etc.]. **1947** *This Week Mag.* 18 July 20/5 Every famous greenhouse, nursery and garden . . . fetches out the juleps, the fried chicken and pecan pies.

b. Also in combs. of obvious meaning: (1) **pecan gathering,** (2) **orchard,** (3) **shell,** (4) **sheller,** (5) **tree.**

(1) **1902** O. HENRY *Roads of Destiny* 153 Those brigands might justly have been taken for a little party of peaceable rustics assembled for a fish-fry or pecan gathering. — (2) **1939** *These Are Our Lives* 104 He saw some little boys in the pecan orchard stealing nuts and turned the Ford off the road and went tearing across the field to the orchard. **1949** *Plant Physiology* Jan. 17 Leaf samples for chemical studies were taken from four trees in each of four . . . blocks in a pecan orchard near Albany, Georgia. — (3) **1883** SWEET & KNOX *Through Texas* 270 And about pecan-shells. It is said that when they are hard, the winter is going to be cold. — (4) **1943** MENEFEE *Assignment* 185 In 1938 the Mexican pecan shellers were working for about 5 cents an hour in this pecan-shelling capital of the world.

(5) **1834** A. PIKE *Sketches* 70 About noon, we saw the first pecan tree which had greeted us. **1949** *N.O. Times-Picayune Mag.* 27 Nov. 59/4 Her husband manages plantation's 400 acres of pecan trees.

As the last term in **bastard, bitter, paper shell, wild pecan.**

pecan nut.

1. = **pecan 2.**

1778 CARVER *Travels* 501 The Pecannut is somewhat of the walnut kind, but rather smaller than a walnut, being about the size of a middling acorn. **1877** HABBERTON *Jericho Road* xiii. 125 At one time he gathered pecan nuts.

2. = **pecan 1.** In full **pecan nut tree.** Also attrib.

1778 CARVER *Travels* 500 The Hazelnut, the Beechnut, the Pecannut, the Chesnut, the Hickory. **1821** NUTTALL *Travels Arkansa* 214 The Pecannerie, now the most considerable settlement in the territory, except Arkansas, derived its name from the Pecan nut-trees (*Carya olivaeformis*), with which its forests abound. **1949** *Okla. Cotton Grower* 15 May 3/6 Watch carefully to see when to apply spray to control pecan nut case-bearer.

3. pecan nut hickory, = **pecan hickory.** *Obs.*

1820 GILLELAND *Ohio & Miss. Pilot* 256 *C. olivæformis* (pecan nut hickory) Abundant in the rich forests of Illinois and the Missouri state.

pechita ˈpetʃɪtə, *n. S.W.* [Prob. dim. f. Amer. Sp. *beche* (<Zapotecan word), used of various leguminous plants.] (See quots.)

1878 HINTON *Handbook Ariz.* 346 The fruit, which is a kind of bean, and called by the natives pechita, is a splendid feed for cattle, hogs, and horses. **1912** LUMHOLTZ *New Trails* 331 They had their season on chia and used to come as far as Quitobaquita and Santo Domingo to gather mezquite beans (called by the Mexicans *pechita*) and eat sahuaro and pitahaya. **1925** BRYAN *Papago Country* 27 Mortars in solid rock, called 'béchete' or 'péchita' holes, are found near all watering places and testify to the activity of these people. *Ib.* 42 These beans were a staple food of the Papago Indians, and their mortars, called 'béchete holes,' can be found in many localities.

*peck, *v. tr.* (See quot.) *Colloq.* — **1835** LONGSTREET *Ga. Scenes* 77 It was a common custom of those days with boys, to dye and peck eggs on Easter Sunday, and for a few days afterwards. . . . Our 'young operatives' sallied forth to stake the whole proceeds of their '*domestic industry*' upon a peck. Egg was struck against egg, point to point, and the egg which was broken was given up as lost to the owner of the one which came whole from the shock.

pecker (mill). (See quots.) Now *hist.* — **1802** DRAYTON *S. Carolina* 121 Three kinds of rice mills, called *pecker*, *cog*, and *water* mills, are used in this state. The first is the most simple; and, probably, that which was first in use. It is so called, from the pestle's striking somewhat in the manner of a wood pecker, when pecking a tree. **1949** MURRAY *This Our Land* 41 After being thrashed by flail or whipped off, the rice was milled and dressed wholly by hand or by a crude machine called a 'pecker.'

peckerwood ˈpɛkɚˌwud, *n.* [Inversion of **woodpecker.*]

1. A woodpecker. Also in a proper name.

1835 in *Dly. Home* (Talladega, Ala.) 28 Feb. (1910) 2/2 From the mouth of Peckerwood creek . . . Henry G. Woodward [is road supervisor]. **1859** BARTLETT 314 Peckerwood, western for Woodpecker. **1909** F. CALHOUN *Miss Minerva* 140 A big, red-headed peckerwood. **1947** BROWN *Outdoors Unlimited* 76 Sitting there watching the jays and peckerwoods and listening to the distant shrillings of a hawk, I thought Lucius looked tougher than a pine-knot.

2. A poor white.

1938 J. DANIELS *Southerner Discovers South* 172–8 (Wentworth), The gentlemen & the Negroes are afraid . . . of the rednecks, the peckerwoods. . . . Will Percy . . . found an old starving peckerwood in Greenville & he set him up in a little stand to sell papers. **1949** *Time* 7 March 28/1 Like his daddy, the late, loud Gene, who purposefully played the peckerwood, Hummon stood for . . . perpetuating in office the Talmadge dynasty, its heirs and assigns.

3. In combs.: (1) **peckerwood mill,** *S.* a small portable sawmill, *colloq.;* (2) **nubbin,** a very small nubbin of corn suitable only for woodpeckers, *rare;* (3) **operator,** an operator of a peckerwood mill; (4) **sawmill,** = **peckerwood mill.**

(1) 1943 *Democrat* 1 July 2/2 The peckerwood mills are almost as rare in Clarke as the ivory-billed woodpecker. — **(2) 1866** C. H. SMITH *Bill Arp* 95 If it didn't rain any more and the entire crop was prudently gathered he might make a peck to the acre of peckerwood nubbins. — **(3) 1946** *Newsweek* 15 April 68/1 Conditions encourage not the efficient, experienced producers but the peckerwood (Southern expression for woodpecker) operators. — **(4) 1945** *News-Age Herald* (Birmingham) 23 Sep. two-B/6 It jumped from Walter's first little 'peckerwood' sawmill to a substantial wholesale lumber business. **1946** *Newsweek* 15 April 68/1 Operators of fly-by-night 'peckerwood' sawmills are busy in the backwoods supplying the black market with lumber.

Peckhamite ˈpɛkəmaɪt, *n.* [For J. S. *Peckham*, an Amer. chemist.] (See quot. 1890.) — **1881** *Pop. Sci. Mo.* XVIII. 861 Professor J. Lawrence Smith has found a new meteoric mineral in the analysis of the great meteorite which fell in Emmett County, Iowa, in May, 1879, and has named it Peckhamite. **1890** *Cent.* 4348/2 peckhamite. . . . A silicate of iron and magnesium found in rounded nodules in the meteorite of Estherville, Emmett county, Iowa. It is intermediate between enstatite and chrysolite in composition.

pecky ˈpɛkɪ, *a.* [f. * *peck*, a stroke.] "Decayed in such a manner that holes or pockets are formed: applied especially by lumbermen to cypress timber" (*Cent. Supp.*).

1848 DICKESON & BROWN *Rep. on Cypress Timber of Miss. & La.* 8 That species of decay to which it [the cypress] is most liable, shows itself in partial and detached spots at greater and less distances, but often in very close proximity to each other. . . . Timber affected in this way is denominated by raftsmen Pecky. **1876** *Gwilt's Arch. Gloss. s.v.*, Pecky, timber in which the first symptoms of decay appear. An American term.

b. pecky cypress, the wood from a pecky cypress tree.

1942 KENNEDY *Palmetto Country* 8 Worm-eaten 'Pecky' cypress was once used only for fencing and stakes. . . . Pecky cypress is never less than one hundred years old (the borers do not attack younger trees).

Pecos ˈpekəs, *n.* A tribe of Indians who occupied Pecos, a large town southeast of Santa Fe, from *c*1300 to 1838. Usu. attrib. with reference to the town.

1846 ABERT *Exam. N. Mex.* 39 The old church . . . was erected under the direction of the Jesuits, who founded schools there, and who labored much to reclaim the Pecos Indians from their superstitions. **1910** HODGE *Amer. Indians* II. 220/2 In prehistoric times the Pecos people occupied numerous pueblos. . . . The Pecos declare that they came into their valley from the S.E. **1947** MARTIN *Indians* 71 This trade decreased as the Pecos people produced more and more of their own pottery.

pecos ˈpekəs, *v.* [f. *Pecos* River.] *tr.* (See quot 1944.) *Slang.* — **1929** DOBIE *Vaquero* 293 To 'pecos' a man one shot him and rolled his body into the river—the one river that drained an empire. **1944** ADAMS *W. Words* 113 Pecos. . . . To shoot a man and roll his body into the river.

pectoral sandpiper. A small sandpiper, *Pisobia melanotos.*

1828 BONAPARTE *Synopsis* 318 The Pectoral Sandpiper . . . inhabits throughout the United States and West Indies. **1883** *Nat. Museum Bul.* No. 27, 149 *Actodromas maculata.* Pectoral Sandpiper. **1948** *Sat. Ev. Post* 16 Oct. 54/4 He is an expert on the feeding habits of the pectoral sandpiper.

* **peculiar,** *a.* and *n.*

1. *n. N. Eng.* A district or piece of land neither constituting, nor belonging to, a town or township; also the owner or occupant of such land. *Obs.*

1720 *Conn. Rec.* VI. 210 Mr. John Read, who dwells between Fairfield and Danbury, [shall] be likewise annually listed, as a peculiar to Danbury. **1739** *Ib.* VIII. 230 This Assembly being informed that a certain piece of land in the county of Windham . . . is not in any town but still remains a peculiar, . . . Be it enacted . . . That the said tract of land be annexed to the town of Voluntown. **1779** *Vt. State P.* (1823) 297. **1809** KENDALL *Travels* I. 17 Precincts or peculiars are in some cases ordered to be rated at or in certain towns, and in such cases are rated and governed by the town.

2. peculiar institution, the institution of slavery. Now *hist.*

1842 BUCKINGHAM *Slave States* I. 216 Slavery is usually called here 'our peculiar institution.' **1856** *S. Lit. Messenger* XXII. 243/1 There is a certain class of minds who see in every effort of the kind, some imaginary thrust at the 'peculiar institution.' **1904** *Nation* 12 May 375 Men . . . having no vital interest in the 'peculiar institution,' had Confederate pressure, not State loyalty, to draw them from their homes. **1949** *Social Studies* May 216/1 Its Southern leaders used the party machinery for the purpose of defending the South's 'peculiar institution.'

transf. **1855** *Yale Lit. Mag.* XX. 278 (Th.), Yankees do have a weakness for patent medicine. It is one of their peculiar institutions. **1857** E. STONE *Life J. Howland* 282 Judge Branch . . . welcomed the guests to all the enjoyments of a Rhode Island 'peculiar institution' [i.e., a clambake].

b. *pl.* Negro slaves. *Obs.*

1860 *Charleston* (S.C.) *Mercury* 11 Dec. 1/5, I met . . . the 'peculiar institutions' carrying lightwood up the back steps and sweeping the gravel walks. **1861** *Dly. Richmond* (Va.) *Enquirer* 20 July 3/2 Several 'peculiar institutions' were ordered to be punished for various offences.

c. Also **peculiar domestic institution,** an expanded form of "peculiar institution." *Obs.*

*c***1852** in FARMER 413/2 The dangers which at present threaten the peculiar domestic institutions of the South. **1885** *Mag. Amer. Hist.* March 297/2 *Peculiar institution.*—In full 'the *peculiar* domestic *institution* of the South'—meaning negro slavery.

d. Mormon polygamy. *Obs.*

1852 *N.Y. Wkly. Tribune* 23 Oct 6/6 We spent a week among the Mormons, had a very fair opportunity of forming an opinion of them and their (peculiar) institution. **1853** *Harper's Mag.* April 621/1 Pratt, the great expounder of their [Mormon] doctrines, boldly advocates this practice, at the same time explaining the various guards which they profess are thrown around the 'peculiar institution' to prevent immoral results. **1888** *Ogden* (Utah) *Union* 11 June 1/3 The Cleveland Convention . . . finished its labors and adjourned without saying anything mean, or otherwise, about the 'peculiar institution' of the Sagebrush Democrats of Utah.

* **peddler,** *n.* **1.** *Essence of the peddler*, the odorous secretion of a skunk. *Rare.* Cf. **essence peddler. 2. peddler's wagon,** a wagon or cart in which a peddler carries his goods.

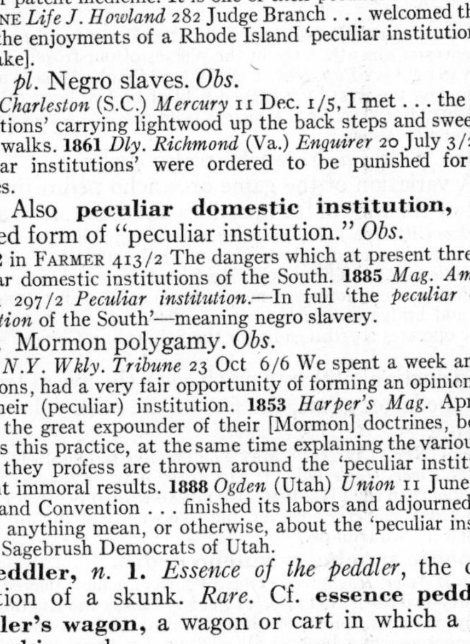

Peddler's wagon or trading wagon

(1) 1858 *Harper's Mag.* Sep. 567/1 Like most Methodist ministers, he had but one good suit of clothes, and those completely saturated with essence of the peddler. — **(2) 1836** in *Jrnl. So. Hist.* I. 370 A Yankee who has a store at Cahaba which supplies a number of Pedlars Wagons, told me that one of his wagons was going to Selma. **1887** GEORGE *40 Yrs. on Rail* 153 He had the finest peddler's wagon I ever saw.

As the last term in **book, clock, Connecticut, dope, essence, fruit, gospeling, liquor, pack, pocket, ticket, tin, tree, Yankee peddler.**

* **peddling,** *n.* As the last term in **tin, whisky peddling.**

pedicure ˈpɛdəˌkjʊr, *n.* [F. *pédicure.*] (See quot. 1890.)

1848 R. DUNGLISON *Med. Lex.* 635/2 *Pedicure,* Chiropodist. **1889** *Science* XIV. 308/1 Dentists, pedicures, trained nurses, and veterinarians. **1890** *Cent.* 4354/3 *Pedicure.* . . . 1. The cure or care of the feet. . . . 2. One whose business is the surgical care of the feet.

pedicure ˈpɛdəˌkjʊr, *v.* [f. prec.] *tr.* To treat (the feet) by removing corns, bunions, etc. Hence **pedicuring, pedicurist.**

1894 *Mute's Chron.* (Columbus, O.) 5 May, Two hot footbaths a week and a little pedicuring will remove the cause of much discomfort. **1894** *Columbus Dispatch* 25 Dec. 4/3 The art of pedicurist is very greatly in demand among society women of New York. **1896** *Ib.* 6 March 4/4 One's lower extremities are pedicured without cost. **1902** *Boston Globe* 21 Sep. 47/3 Every woman should learn the scientific care of her own feet, or the art of pedicuring.

pedigree ˈpɛdəˌgri, *v.* [f. the noun.] *To pedigree away,* to get rid of or lose (a feature or quality) by keeping stock pure. *Rare.* — **1901–2** *Rep. Kans. State Bd. Agric.* 5 (*Cent. Supp.*), Necessity demanded that in Short-horn line breeding an Outcross was essential, that the milk should not be pedigreed away.

pedregal ˌpedreˈgɑl, *n. W.* [Sp., a stony place.] (See quot. 1932.)

1853 Kane *Grinnell Exped.* 289, I am struck more and more with the evidences of gigantic force in the phases of our frozen *pedragal.* **1881** Bryant & Gay *Pop. Hist. U.S.* IV. 378 [Santa Anna's] position was flanked on the west by a rugged field of broken lava, called the Pedregal. **1932** Bentley *Sp. Terms* 178 pedregal. . . . A rocky section of country; a lava flow.

pedro ˈpedro, *n.* [f. sancho pedro *q.v.*]

1. A variation of the game of sancho pedro in which sancho, or the nine of trumps, does not count. Also attrib.

1876 *Silver City* (Ida.) *Avalanche* 15 March 2/3 Whist, pedro, pool, solo-sixty, etc., seem to be flourishing pastimes. **1929** R. S. & H. M. Lynd *Middletown* 281 The growing rigidity of the social system today is centering parties more and more upon cards, pedro among the workers and bridge among the others. **1947** *Sat. Ev. Post* 17 May 102/3 He operates a pedro game for the Sabine and Chinese shrimpers.

2. In auction pitch and cinch *qq.v.*, the five of trumps. Also in the latter game, the five of the same color as the trump suit.

1874 *Reno* (Nev.) *Crescent* 8 May 2/3 The five of trumps is 'pedro.' **1880** Dick *Amer. Hoyle* (ed. 13) 210 Pedro may be taken with any trump higher than the Five. **1946** Morehead & Mott-Smith *Penguin Hoyle* 59 Many players, however, bid five when holding any pedro, with as few as two trumps.

b. pedro sancho, =**sancho pedro.**

1880 Dick *Amer. Hoyle* (ed. 13) 210 Pedro Sancho is played with a pack of fifty-two cards. **1944** *Pocket Book of Games* 199 Auction Pitch has many variants. Most of them—Pedro, Pedro Sancho, Dom Pedro, Snoozer—have been swallowed up by their own ultimate creation, Cinch.

As the last term in **Don, double, sancho pedro.**

peedoodles piˈdudlz, *n. pl.* [App. fanciful.] =**buck fever.** *Rare.* — **1835** Longstreet *Georgia Scenes* 211 'The stranger's got the peedoodles,' said a fourth, with humorous gravity.

***peekaboo,** *n. attrib.* Designating garments of eyelet-embroidered material, or of other decorative effect involving small holes. Also transf.

1906 *Springfield W. Republican* 10 May 13 In San Francisco there is no winter suit and summer suit. The same medium-weight garment is worn the year round and the peek-a-boo waist is unknown. **1908** Yeslah *Tenderfoot S. Calif.* 14 All I had in that blamed trunk of mine was some peek-a-boo underwear and drop stitched stockings. **1948** *Ariz. Republic* (Phoenix) 1 March 14/2 Mela Armstrong modeled . . . the black cocktail dress featuring a peek a-boo bodice and open back of the bodice.

***peel,** *v.* **1.** *To peel it,* (see quot.). *Slang. Obs.* **2.** *To keep one's eye peeled,* see ***eye,** *n.* **b.** (3). — (1) **1859** Bartlett 314 *To Peel it,* to run at full speed. 'Come, boys; peel it now, or you'll be late.'

peeled stick convention. A mass meeting in Cleveland, Ohio, before the Civil War. *Rare.* — **1880** *Cong. Rec.* 19 March 1708/2 Did they not meet in Cleveland in the 'peeled stick' convention, all armed and ready to resist the authority of the United States?

***peeler,** *n.* Also ***pealer.**

1. Anything of an exceptional nature, as a violent storm. *Slang.*

1823 Cooper *Pioneers* xv, It's a peeler without, I can tell you, good woman. **1845** Kirkland *Western Clearings* 74 We're goin' straight to a bee-tree. . . . It's a real peeler, I tell ye! **1861** *Entertaining Things* I. 197 The gale . . . was a steady hard blow, what sailors call a peeler.

b. A person of extraordinary qualities; an active or energetic person. *Slang.*

1833 S. Smith *Major Downing* 218 Them are Pennsylvany chaps are real pealers for electing folks when they take hold. **1869** Stowe *Oldtown Folks* 117 She was spoken of with applause under such titles as 'a staver,' 'a pealer,' 'a roarer to work.' **1882** Thayer *From Log-Cabin* 198 He's a peeler for work too; ain't afraid to dirty himself.

2. (See quot.) *Obs.*

1881 *Cong. Rec.* 3 May 447/1 The peelers . . . are that part of the Va. debt not yet funded. They are selling today at about thirty-eight cents in the dollar.

3. *W.* A cowboy or bronc peeler *qq.v.* Also a teamster or driver. *Slang.*

1902 *Out West* June 623 The 7TX peelers is all in on this play, . . . and the 10 EC outfit will want a hand too. **1914** Bower *Flying U Ranch* 7 This is Mr. Mig-u-ell Rapponi, boys—a peeler straight from the Golden Gate. **1943** L. V. Hamner *Short Grass* 163 The driver, or 'peeler,' rode the wheel horse and guided the whole team with one line.

As the last term in **apple, elm peeler.**

***peep,** *n.*

1. Any of various sandpipers, esp. the least sandpiper. Also the Carolina rail.

1794 *Mass. H.S. Coll.* 1 Ser. III. 199 Sea fowl are plenty on the shores and in the bay; particularly the gannet, . . . widgeon, and peep. **1898** N. Brooks *Boys of Fairport* 208 Blackie . . . was over on the ma'ash with Sam Perkins, shooting peeps. **1920** Lincoln *Mr. Pratt* 211 Blessed if he didn't come back with a dozen peep and ringnecks. **1940** Gabrielson & Jewett *Birds Ore.* 262 Like other small sandpipers, these little 'peeps' are consummate masters of the art of synchronized motion.

2. *as drunk* (or *tight*) *as a peep,* (see quot. 1864). *Colloq.*

1855 *Knickerb.* XLV. 429 If drunk as a peep, he 'lays down.' **1864** Sala in *Dly. Telegraph* 27 July, [The] New England mind . . . has long since endorsed the locution 'as tight as a peep,' to express an utter state of tipsification.

As the last term in **bird, sand peep.**

***peep,** *v.*

1. peep-eye, the child's game of peekaboo.

1887 *Harper's Mag.* Dec. 79/1 He made futile efforts to play 'peep-eye' with anybody jovially disposed in the crowd.

2. peepstone, the magic spectacles with which Joseph Smith allegedly read the inscribed golden plates containing the *Book of Mormon.* Usu. *pl.*

1842 Kidder *Mormonism* 64 From this time, neither spectacles nor 'peep-stones' were used in order to obtain a revelation. **1882** Buel *Metropolitan Life Unveiled* 346 He followed the calling of a well-digger, and it was while engaged in this employment that he found what was afterward called his 'peep-stone.' **1940** *Reader's Digest* April 144/2 Her voice was scornful. 'You're the man [Joseph Smith] who looks into peepstones!'

b. Any stone supposed to have magical properties.

1870 Beadle *Utah* 22 He began to 'divine' the locality of things which had been stolen, by means of a 'peep-stone' placed in his hat, and by the same means to point out where hidden treasures lay. **1948** *Amer. Folk-Lore* Jan.–Mar. 29 Dreams, promptings of the spirit, and peep-stones have all combined to make the reticent girl give in to the proposals of a polygamous suitor.

***peeper,** *n.* Any of certain frogs, esp. of the family Hylidae, that make peeping noises; usu. the small tree frog, *Hyla crucifer.*

1857 Hammond *Northern Scenes* 30 All is still now, save the piping notes of the little peeper along the shore. **1889** Ellwanger *Garden's Story* 19 The chorus of the *Hylodes,* or peepers, . . . that piercing treble . . . that nothing—even the katydid—can equal in strident intensity. **1949** *N.Y. Times Mag.* 20 March 15/2 The robin sometimes gets ahead of the season. The peeper never does. This small, brown toad, being cold-blooded, partakes of the temperature of its environment.

***peerless,** *a.* An epithet often applied to W. J. Bryan (1860–1925). — **1900** *Cong. Rec.* 4 Jan. 652/2 Self-seeking politicians, timorous souls, may fall away from us, but the paramount issue and the peerless candidate will remain. **1925** *K.C. Times* 27 July 7/2 The interim between this period [1904] and the next presidential election of 1908 was occupied by Mr. Bryan, now known by many of his followers as 'The Peerless Leader.'

peetweet ˈpitwit, *n.* [Echoic.] (See quot. 1917.)

1839 Peabody *Mass. Birds* 370 From its note, it is called the Peetweet, which is its familiar name. **1858** Thoreau *Maine Woods* 135 A company of peetweets were twittering and teetering about over the carcass of a moose. **1917** *Birds of Amer.* I. 249 Spotted Sandpiper. *Actitis macularia.* . . . Also called Peep; Peetweet.

***peg,** *n.*

1. A prong or tine fastened to a pole or string, used for harpooning turtles.

[c1735 CATESBY *Carolina* II. 39/1 Turtle are most commonly taken at the Bahama-Islands . . . by striking them with a small Iron Peg of two Inches long, this Peg is put in a Socket at the End of a staff 12 Feet long.] **1827** G. A. McCALL *Lett. from Frontiers* (1868) 178 The Colonel had directed Maximo to bring with him his turtle-sein, his 'peg' and all other appliances for hunting the green turtle. **1881** INGERSOLL *Oyster Industry* 244 In Florida the turtle-grains have only one prong and one barb (half a barb) when anything but a 'peg' is used.

2. In baseball, a throw, esp. a smart, hard one.

1922 *Dly. Press* (Ardmore, Okla.) 2 May 2/2 The latter crossed safely when White dropped Fuller's peg from home. **1948** *Miami* (Okla.) *D. News-Record* 4 July 4/4 A bad peg in the ninth spoiled his effort and he suffered his second setback of the year.

As the last term in **shoe, shucking peg.**

***peg,** *v.* **1.** *tr.* To hang up (tobacco) by means of pegs. **2.** To hook (a mat or rug). — (1) **1850** *Rep. Comm. Patents: Agric.* 321 '*Pegging*' tobacco is the neatest and best mode [of putting away tobacco]. . . . Pegs are driven in [the stalk] with a mallet, in a slanting direction, so as to hook on the sticks in the house. . . . [The tobacco is then] pulled up in the house, and there hung upon the sticks. — (2) **1898** *Boston Transcript* 16 April 14/5 To peg means [to crochet], . . . but is oftener used in relation to mats made of rags or yarn drawn through bagging—burlap.

***pegging awl.** (See quot.) — **1875** *Fur, Fin & Feather* (ed. 3) 119 The smaller species of loon I have heard variously called the spike-bill, the cape-race, . . . the gun-greaser, the pegging-all [*sic*], etc.

pekan ˈpɛkən, *n.* [Can. F., f. Algonquian.] The fisher or black cat, *Martes pennanti.* Also **pekan weasel.** Cf. ***fisher,** *n.* **1.**

[a1716 PERROT *Mémoire des Sauvages de l'Amérique* (1864) 56 Et que dans les chasses éloignées, où ils ont costume d'aller, il y a des ours, des cerfs, des biches, des chevreuils, . . . quelques peccans et des loutres.] **1796** MORSE *Amer. Geog.* I. 200 Fisher. In Canada he is called Pekan. **1804** CLARK in *Lewis & C. Exped.* I. (1904) 132 [The Sioux] furnish Beaver, . . . Pekon, (*pichou*) Bear & Dear Skins. **1838** *Mass. Zool. Survey Rep.* 24 *Mustela Canadensis*, Pekan Weasel or Fisher Weasel. . . . It is very troublesome on sable lines by robbing the traps of the sable. **1917** *Mammals of Amer.* 117/1 The largest of all the Martens is an animal . . . variously designated as the 'Pekan,' 'Fisher,' . . . and 'Black Cat.' **1947** CAHALANE *Mammals* 179 The fisher has many other names, equally inappropriate: fisher cat, black cat, Pennant's cat (after the Welsh naturalist), fisher marten, and pekan.

pelado peˈlado, *n.* *S.W.* [Sp. in Amer. Sp. sense shown here.] A penniless, ignorant person, one of a low social class; usu. as a term of contempt for a Mexican peon. Also attrib.

1847 RUXTON *Adv. Rocky Mts.* (1848) 207, I again packed my mules, . . . under a fusilade of very hard names from the pelados. **1863** *Rio Abajo Press* 5 May 2/2 Our enterprising men expect to make double the price, and when making their calculations they do so more like a Pelado buying sugar by the picayune's worth than men who understand business economy. **1926** MRS. O. L. SHIPMAN *Taming Big Bend* 85 He . . . called them Protestants, pelados, and thieves. **1948** CHAPLIN *Wobbly* 110 Sleeping *pelados* would be huddled around our doorstep when we returned home at night.

pele fish. = **paddle fish.** *Obs.* — **1609** HAKLUYT *Va. Richly Valued* 100 There was another fish [in the Miss R.] called a pele fish: it had a snout of a cubit long, and at the end of the vpper lip it was made like a peele. **1821** NUTTALL *Jrnl.* 326 There was another which they called the Pele-fish, destitute of scales, and with the upperjaw extended in front a foot in length, in the form of a peel or spatula.

***pelican,** *n.*

1. Pelican flag, the flag of Louisiana.

1860 *Charleston* (S.C.) *Mercury* 25 Dec. 4/5 The Pelican flag of Louisiana was unfurled in the streets, amid tremendous cheering . . . The Pelican flag consists of a red star upon a white field, with the ancient Louisiana emblem of a Pelican feeding her young. **1865** RICHARDSON *Secret Service* 40 There were Pelican flags, and Lone Star flags, and devices, unlike anything in the heavens above.

2. Pelican State, a nickname for Louisiana.

1859 *Harper's Mag.* May 853/2 A well-known writer in the Pelican State writes us a good thing from one of his little folks. **1934** SHANKLE *State Names* 119 The name, the *Pelican State* was given to Louisiana from the fact that this bird is so frequently seen along the streams . . . which fact caused it to be chosen as the emblem in the state coat of arms. **1949** *N.O. Times-Picayune Mag.* 27 Nov. 53/2 Now Mississippi has nosed out the Pelican State.

As the last term in **brown, rough-billed, white, wood pelican.**

pelon, see **pilon.**

pelon dog. [Sp. in Amer. Sp. combination *perro pelón* in sense shown here.] The Mexican hairless dog. — **1882** SWEET & KNOX *Texas Siftings* 61 The pelon dog is found in Austin . . . and in *tamales.* **1902** CLAPIN 304 *Peon dog* [*sic*], in Texas, a name sometimes given to the hairless Mexican Dog.

***pelter,** *n.*

1. (See quot. 1902.) *Colloq.*

Senses **1.** and **2.** may be from different sources. An old or worthless horse may be so called because it is paltry. *Pelter,* meaning a paltry or peddling person is marked *obs.* in the *OED* and in Webster.

1856 *Knickerb.* XLVIII. 314 When his earthly tenement yields his soul no shelter, May it animate the corpse of an ancient pelter. **1874** *Billings' Farmer's Allminax* 18 Porky Billings . . . alwuss had on hand an old flag-tailed pelter, with a glass eye, tew trade with ennyboddy. **1896** ADE *Artie* 4 It's like hitchin' up a four-time winner 'longside of a pelter. **1902** CLAPIN 303 Pelter, in parts of New England, an old, worn-out horse.

2. A fast horse, one that pelts or goes swiftly. *Colloq.*

1901 *Munsey's Mag.* XXIV. 484/1 It ain't the first time the pelter's carried double.

peltrist ˈpeltrɪst, *n.* A dealer in peltry. *Obs.* — **1830** *Cong. Deb.* 10 May 932/1 The peltrist, with his knotted strings of account for furs. **1877** BARTLETT 791 *Peltrist,* a seller of finished peltries; a vendor of manufactured furs.

pembina pɛmˈbinə, *n.* [Can. F. f. Cree *nipin,* summer, and *minam,* whortleberries.]

1. The bush or high cranberry, or the fruit of this.

1824 KEATING *Narrative* (1825) II. 48 Of the plants observed in this neigbourhood [*sic*], besides the Pembina, we can only mention the common hop and the raspberry-bush. [Near Pembina, N.D.] **1877** BARTLETT 457 *Pembina,* the fruit of the *Viburnum edule,* which Michaux and Gray regard as a variety of the *V. opulus,* or Cranberry Tree of Maine. **1931** CLUTE *Plants* 23 Another aboriginal word still in use for an edible wild fruit is pembina, which seems to be the Indian equivalent for a species of viburnum (*V. Americanum*) whose acid drupes relished by both Indians and whites, render the English name of highbush cranberry significant.

b. (*cap.*) (See quot.) *Obs.*

1876 *Ventura Free Press* (San Buenaventura, Calif.) 8 Jan. 2/2 The proposal to form a new Territory, to be called Pembina, out of the northern portion of Dakota, is an old matter.

2. Pembina buggy, cart, [prob. f. *Pembina* (now Cavalier), earliest trading post (1797–98) in North Dakota], (see quots.). *Humorous. Obs.* Cf. **Red River cart.**

1859 in *Pac. N.W. Quart.* XXXI. 293 We number 20 persons and have 27 horses & mules, 7 Pembina Carts, very broad wheels, no tire & no iron on them. **1860** *Harper's Mag.* Oct. 587/2 'Pembina buggy' is the honorary title which they [homemade carts] receive from those who despair of otherwise making jolts endurable.

pemmican ˈpɛməkən, *n.* Also **pemitigon.** [Cree *pimikkân,* f. *pimiy,* grease.] Among the Indians and frontiersmen, a form of prepared buffalo flesh or venison (see quot. 1824). Cf. **summer, winter pemmican.**

In modern usage the term refers, usu., a to mixture of raisins, coconut, dates, figs, peanuts or pecans, etc., ground up and compressed, forming a food of high energy value.

1791 in *Pub. Champlain Soc.* XXI. 425 One Canoe had been and returned loaded with Pimmecon while we were away. **1824** KEATING *Narrative* I. 447 (*footnote*), Pemmican is the meat of the buffalo, . . . cut into thin slices, which are jerked in the sun or smoke . . . ; it is then dried before the fire until it becomes crisp, after which it is [pounded]; . . . it is mixed up with an equal weight of buffalo grease, or marrow fat poured on when hot and liquid. . . . Sometimes, in order to give it a pleasant taste, it is mixed with a sort of wild cherry, which is pounded and introduced, stone and all. **1868** WHYMPER *Alaska* 203 Dall purchased about 250 lbs. of dried deer and moose meat and fat, and also a kind of native pemmican. **1946** *Mazama* Dec. 31/2 Our lunch that evening consisted of pea soup, pemmican, peach nuggets and tea.

transf. and *attrib.* **1906** M. TWAIN *Howells* 230 (R.), Where does he get [in his literary style] its pemmican quality of compression? **1944** *Military Surgeon* Aug. 91/1 From the point of view of the fur trader, explorer, aviator and soldier, the pemmican process is more important than canning.

b. Pemmican War, the struggle for supremacy between the Northwest Fur Company and the Hudson's Bay Company.

1944 *Military Surgeon* Aug. 91/1 This Indian food invention did not impinge strongly upon the consciousness of Europe, or indeed of Europeans in North America, until the Pemmican War of 1812–21.

***pen,** *n.*[1]

1. (See quot. 1820.) *Obs.*

1820 FLINT *Lett. from Amer.* 236 The little inclosure [at a camp meeting in the woods] . . . is by the religious called *Altar,* and some scoffers are wicked enough to call it *Pen.* **1843** CARLTON *New Purchase* 158 A stout fellow lying on the straw in the pen . . . kicking and pummeling away as if scuffling with a sturdy antagonist.

2. The inclosure made by the walls of a log cabin. *Obs.* Cf. **double penned cabin.**

1846 *Xenia* (O.) *Torch-Light* 23 July 4/1 The rude, long pen, was the whole house. **1850** LEWIS *La. Swamp Doctor* 147 The house consisted of a double log cabin, of small dimensions, a passage, the full depth of the house, running between the 'pens.'

3. =**bull pen 1. b.** *Obs.*

1845 SIMMS *Wigwam & Cabin* 2 Ser. 93 The 'pen' in which I was to be kept secure . . . is one well known to the less civilized regions of the country. . . . It is technically a 'bull pen,' and consists of huge logs, roughly put together, crossing at right angles, forming a hollow square,—the logs too massy to be removed, and the structure too high to be climbed. **1866** GOSS *Soldier's Story* 144 Every batch of prisoners sent into the 'pen' were accompanied by a spy in U.S. blue.

4. An inclosure for Negro slaves about to be sold. *Obs.*

1852 STOWE *Uncle Tom* xvii, You mean to . . . put my boy like a calf in a trader's pen. **1859** *First Impr. of New World* 242 'The pen' had yesterday been cleared out, with the exception of one woman with her six little children.

5. ∗**penstock,** see as a main entry.

6. **pen trap,** a trap consisting of a pen into which something can be enticed or driven.

1884 *Nat. Museum Bul.* No. 27, 1017 Pen Traps. Pocket Traps. Fishslide or Trap. . . . Made of wooden slats set in a sloping frame, with box at upper end. **1902** WHITE *Conjuror's House* ii, Then a little movement brought the scene flashing before her—the white snow, . . . the little square pen-trap.

As the last term in **branding, bull, corn, cotton, cow, Georgia, goose, hog, horse, Indian, log, moose, Negro, penitent's, pig, prison, rail, shuck, slave, stock, turkey, wolf pen.**

pen pɛn, *n.*[2] Short for ∗**penitentiary.** *Colloq.*

1884 CRADDOCK *Tenn. Mts.* 68 He b'lieved the Pen could claim it ez convict labor. **1889** *Provo* (Utah) *Amer.* 28 March 1/4 What John got was eighteen months in the pen. **1948** *Range Riders Western* May 29/1, I don't like to see a young fellow like you come right out of the pen and start right out workin' for another stretch either.

penalty envelope. A postage-free envelope for use in the transaction of government business, so called because of the statement on the envelope: "Penalty for private use to avoid payment of postage. . . ."

1879 *Postal Laws* § 147 Requisitions for . . . official penalty-envelopes are required to be made upon printed forms. **1893** CUSHING *Story of P.O.* 196 Postmasters are not authorized to make use of the penalty envelope in ordering copies of the *Postal Guide* for the public. **1917** J. A. MOSS *Officer's Manual* 272 Official letters are mailed in penalty envelopes.

∗**pence,** *n.* As the last term in **five, four, nine, seven, sixpence.**

∗**pencil,** *n.* In combs.: (1) **pencil pusher,** one who works with a pencil, an office clerk, *slang;* (2) **sharpener,** a device for sharpening lead or slate pencils; (3) **tablet,** a pad of paper, usu. of a low quality, which may be used for writing in pencil but not in ink.

(1) 1890 *Stock Grower & Farmer* 28 June 3/4 The pencil pusher gazed reverently after him. — **(2) 1860** *Rep. Comm. Patents 1859* I. 258 Improved Eraser and Pencil Sharpener. **1947** *Sat. Review* 30 Aug. 31/2 The automatic pencil-sharpener is gathering dust in a corner, too. — **(3) 1936** *Sears Cat.* (ed. 173) 728 Ruled Pencil Tablet. 8×10 in. 75 sheets (150 pages) . . . 2 for 8¢. **1944** CLARK *Pills* 45 Across the way there was an assortment of school-books, pencil tablets, . . . and epsom salts.

As the last term in **gold, ink, soapstone pencil.**

Pend d'Oreilles ˈpɛndɔˈrel, *n. pl.* (See quot. 1907.) Also attrib.

1837 IRVING *Capt. Bonneville's Adv.* 191 They made no halt until they reached an encampment of the Pends Oreilles, or Hanging-ears. **1885** ONDERDONK *Idaho* 134 With the Pend d'Oreilles, when reduced to severe straits, it is not uncommon to bury the very old and very young alive. **1907** HODGE *Amer. Indians* I. 646/2 Kalispel (popularly known as Pend d'Oreilles, 'ear drops'). A Salish tribe around the lake and along the river of the same name of the N. part of Idaho and N.E. Washington. **1948** *Ore. Hist. Mag.* March 54 Pend Oreille Lake is from the Pend d'Oreille Indian tribe, and derived from the French by a shortening of the words 'pendent d'oreille,' meaning ear pendent or ear ring.

Pendletonian ˌpendlˈtonɪən, *a.* Supporting the Democratic and State rights leader of Ohio, George Hunt Pendleton (1825–89). *Rare.* — **1868** *N.Y. Herald* 3 July 4/2 They are of the Pendletonian stripe, greenback and States rights men.

penelopize pəˈnɛləpaɪz, *v.* [*Penelope* of Homer's *Odyssey.*] *intr.* To spin out a task endlessly. *Obs.* — **1841** BENTON in *Cong. Globe* App. 14 June 43/2 Diplomacy was still drawing out its lengthened thread—still weaving its long and dilatory web—still Penelopizing. **1853** MOTLEY in Holmes *Life J. Motley* 72 There is nothing for it but to penelopize, pull to pieces, and stitch away again.

peneplain ˈpinəˌplen, *n.* [L. *paene,* nearly, + ∗*plain.*] (See quot. 1894.)

1894 *Nation* 9 Aug. 99/2 A lowland of moderate relief close to sea level—a *peneplain,* as I should term it. **1900** *Pop. Sci. Mo.* March 552 Such a peneplain is characteristic of old topography. **1936** CRONEIS & KRUMBEIN *Down to Earth* 218 The lower set of sediments must have been deposited, then folded, and finally eroded to a peneplain.

Hence **peneplanation,** *n.*

1943 PEATTIE *Great Smokies* 317 During the long slow process of peneplanation, all but those rocks most resistant to chemical and physical atmospheric attack were very deeply weathered.

penicaso ˌpɛnəˈkæso, *n.* [Origin uncertain.] A kind of fabric. *Obs.* — **1733** *S.C. Gazette* 4 Aug., Just Imported . . . platillas and clouting diaper. . . . penicasoes, ell wide chittaes [etc.].

Peninsula State. A nickname for Florida. — **1886** *Chi. W. News* 29 April 4/3 Florida is the Peninsula state and its people are Fly-Up-the-Creeks, both for obvious reasons. **1949** *Sun. World-Herald Mag.* (Omaha) 10 April 18/1 More people traveled to the Peninsula State this season than ever before.

∗**penitent,** *n.* **1.** One of the Penitentes. *Obs.* **2. penitents' pen,** = ∗**pen,** *n.* **1.** Now *hist.*

(1) 1844 GREGG *Commerce of Prairies* I. 259 As the lash was pointed only with a tuft of intwisted sea-grass, its application merely served to keep open the wounds upon the penitent's back. **1885** BAYLOR *On Both Sides* 176 Then followed a discussion of the Quakers, . . . the Mormons, the Penitents of New Mexico. — **(2) 1832** FERRALL *Ramble* 71 A little in advance before the booths was erected a platform for the performing preacher, and at the foot of this, inclosed by forms, was a species of sanctuary, called 'the penitents' pen.' **1948** DICK *Dixie Frontier* 199 At the foot of the stand was a straw-floored enclosure about thirty feet square, known as 'the altar' or 'penitent's pen.'

Penitentes ˌpɛnɪˈtɛntɪz, *n. pl.* [Sp.] Members of a religious order of flagellants among certain Spanish-American natives of New Mexico and southern Colorado who practice self-castigation, esp. during Holy Week.

1838 TEXIAN *Mexico vs. Texas* 79 [The procession] is rendered shocking and repulsive by *penitentes,* who walk at the head of the *cortege,* naked from the waist upwards, and bare-legged. **1900** *Independent* 26 April 1008/1 This inversion of sensation is the basis for the extraordinary mania which shows itself . . . among those sects who call themselves Flagellantes and Penitentes. **1949** *Nat. Geog. Mag.* Dec. 824/1 Penitentes are a living counterpart of the santos.

attrib. **1881** CHASE *Editor's Run in N. Mex.* 114 At the lower end of the habitations [in the Cimarron] we found the Penitente church, a mud house.

∗**penitentiary,** *n.* A state or federal prison, as opposed to a reformatory. Cf. **state penitentiary.**

1812 *Niles' Reg.* I. 351/2 The legislature of Georgia have appropriated $10,000 towards erecting a penitentiary. **1872** BRACE *Dangerous Classes N.Y.* 35 In the Eastern Penitentiary of Pennsylvania . . . from one-fourth to one-third of the inmates are foreigners. **1948** *Chi. D. News* 3 March 22/7 They require the trial or dismissal of cases pending against defendants already in the penitentiary.

attrib. **1814** *Niles' Reg.* VI. 250/1 The penitentiary establishment is an honor to mankind. **1819** *Mass. Resolves* 1 June 33 The penitentiary system can be so improved, as to accomplish more effectually than corporal punishment, the prevention of crimes. **1838** CLAY *Speeches* (1842) 343 Its author better deserved a penitentiary punishment than those against whom it is directed. *c***1870** BAGBY *Old Va. Gentleman* 291 The State Guard . . . watched over the penitentiary convicts employed in grading the walks. **1911** VANCE *Cynthia* 195 Either you will carry out your undertaking with Mr. Rhode, or I'll devote my fortune to seeing that you spend the balance of your days behind penitentiary bars.

b. penitentiary offense, an offense that is punishable by imprisonment in a penitentiary.

1855 *Chi. Times* 29 Jan. 2/2 Laws making it a penitentiary offence for the planters to *ask,* or the merchant to *make,* such pecuniary advancements. **1883** MARK TWAIN *Life on Miss.* 223 There was a United States law making it a penitentiary offense to strike . . . a pilot. **1941** FERGUSSON *Southwest* 347 Having or selling liquor on an Indian reservation is a penitentiary offense.

Pennacook ˈpɛnəˌkuk, *n.* [Thought to be f. an Abnaki word meaning "at the bottom of the hill or highland."] (See quot. 1910.) Also attrib. *Obs.*

1831 *Boston Transcript* 21 March 3/2 The Penacook Indians . . . used to predict the weather from the movement of the morning fog, which usually passed off in a direction towards the sea or towards the mountains. **1880** *Harper's Mag.* May 818/1 Toward the close of the seventeenth century, the tribe became a mixed race of Mohicans, Delawares, Pemacooks [etc.]. **1910** HODGE *Amer. Indians* II. 225/1 Pennacook. . . . A confederacy of Algonquian tribes that occupied the basin of Merrimac r., and the adjacent region in New Hampshire, N.E. Massachusetts, and the extreme S. part of Maine.

Pennamite ˈpɛnəmaɪt, *n.* Also **Panamite.** A nickname for a Pennsylvanian. Cf. **Pennite.**

1784 *Mass. Centinel* 19 May 2/1 John the Pennamitte . . . presented Joseph the ferryman with precious stones, and oil-olive. **1835** TODD *Notes* 23 Pennsylvanians are also called *Panamites*, and a justice denominated *squire.* **1896** LEONARD *Cent. of Congregationalism in Ohio* 40 The number of Pennamites [Presbyterians from Pennsylvania] and Pilgrims [Congregationalists from New England] might be nearly equal.

***pennant,** *n.* A flag or banner awarded as the symbol of a championship in some sport, esp. baseball; also, *fig.*, the championship thus won.

1880 N. BROOKS *Fairport Nine* 188 Billy Hetherington . . . was entrusted with the championship pennant. **1893** *Outing* Sep. 458/2 The Hopkins Academy carried away the pennant in '91. **1946** *Sat. Ev. Post* 3 Aug. 20/1 Now I know the Red Sox will win the pennant—anything can happen now.

attrib. **1886** *Outing* Aug. 572/2 Questions by the dozen came in . . . in regard to the probable issue of the pennant races in the professional arena. **1915** *Lit. Digest* 21 Aug. 360/3 The New York Giants . . . are not often far from the pennant class. **1948** *Ada* (Okla.) *Ev. News* 4 July 9/2 The Boston Braves today opened up a four-game lead in the National League pennant race.

Pennite ˈpɛnaɪt, *n.* =**Pennamite.** — **1872** *Harper's Mag.* Jan. 318/1 Below will be found a careful compilation of the various nicknames given to the States and people of this republic: . . . Pennsylvania, Pennites, and Leatherheads.

***pennock,** *n.* A variety of apple. *Obs.* — **1817** W. COXE *Fruit Trees* 145 Pennock. A very large, fair, red apple, much admired as an early winter fruit. **1847** IVES *N.-Eng. Fruit* 42 *Pennocks.*—This is a large apple; the form round, rather oblong; the skin a dull red. **1949** *Amer. Forests* Sep. 20/1 Dilworth's Apple and Pennock's Apple.

Pennsylvania ˌpɛnslˈvenjə, *n.* [See note.] A middle Atlantic colony and state.

"My country was confirmed to me . . . by the name of Pennsylvania; a name the King would give it in honour of my father. . . . I proposed . . . *Sylvania*, and they added *Penn* to it" (1681 Penn in Janney *Life W. Penn* 165).

1. Short for **Pennsylvania currency.** *Obs.*

1790 *Jrnl. Wm. Maclay* (1927) 324, I owe him four shillings and sixpence, Pennsylvania.

2. Used attrib. or as an adj. in combs., chiefly obs.: (1) **Pennsylvania ark,** =**Pennsylvania wagon;** (2) **Blue,** (see quot.); (3) **Bucktail,** see quots. *s.v.* ***bucktail,** *n.* **2;** (4) **corn,** a variety of corn; (5) **Cossacks,** see ***Cossack,** *n.* **2;** (6) **crude,** an oil produced in Pennsylvania and adjacent regions; (7) **currency,** currency issued by Pennsylvania before 1789; (8) **Dutch,** see as a main entry; (9) **fireplace,** see ***fireplace,** *n.* **2;** (10) **German,** see as a main entry; (11) **horse,** a heavy horse suitable for drawing a Pennsylvania wagon; (12) **hurricane,** (see quot.); (13) **mile,** a very long mile, as one over the early cut-up roads of the Pennsylvania oil regions; (14) **money,** =**Pennsylvania currency;** (15) **oil region,** a region in Pennsylvania where petroleum was first secured commercially in the U.S.; (16) **road wagon,** =**Pennsylvania wagon;** (17) **type oil,** oil having the characteristics of Pennsylvania crude; (18) **wagon,** a strong wagon, such as a Conestoga, made in Pennsylvania; (19) **wagoner,** the driver of a Pennsylvania wagon.

(1) **1891** WELCH *Recoll. 1830–40* 135 Almost any day from April to October, might have been seen passing . . . a dozen in line of Pennsylvania Arks (wagons) or 'Prairie Schooners,' so called from their rising stem and stern, with great canvas covers, sustained by curved top hoops. — (2) **1838** *Mass. Agric. Survey 1st Rep.* 34 The Chenango [potato], sometimes called the Mercer, or Pennsylvania Blue. — (4) **1739** *Georgia Col. Rec.* III. 429 We all were disappointed by long sickness, and planting the yellow Pensilvania Corn. **1838** *Mass. Agric. Survey 1st Rep.* 24 The stover of the Pennsylvania corn, which is a gourd-seed variety would probably yield from a third to a half more than ours in weight.

(6) **1913** *Outing* Jan. 423/1 Pennsylvania crude yields twenty per cent of sixty specific gravity gasoline and fourteen per cent of sixty-five specific gravity. — (7) **1775** *Jrnls. Cont. Congress* III. 279 A quantity of silver and gold, not exceeding 20,000 pensylv. curry . . . for the use of the army in Canada. **1780** *Va. State P.* I. 370 He shall be paid for shot twenty five pounds pr. ton Pensylvania currency. **1831** SLOCOMB *Amer. Calculator* 86 The dollar is reckoned in . . . New Jersey, Pennsylvania, . . . 7s. 6d. = 3/8 Pennsylvania currency.

(11) **1826** FLINT *Recoll.* 10 He rode a huge Pennsylvania horse. — (12) **1827** J. BERNARD *Retrosp.* 250 A 'Pennsylvany hurricane,' like a 'Caroliny swamper,' was indeed, a common term, nearer home, for a sublime Munchausenism—vulgarly speaking, a long lie. — (13) **1863** *Boston Sun. Herald* 16 Aug. 3/3 (Ernst), If you take any of them [i.e., roads], and travel as far as you can in a day, it will be a Pennsylvania mile. — (14) **1771** FRANKLIN *Autobiog.* 286 Therefore I immediately agreed on the terms of fifty pounds a year, Pennsylvania money. **1787** CUTLER in *Life & Corr.* I. 248 Bill, 6 *s.*, 6 *d.*, Pennsylvania money.

(15) **1862** *Prelim. Rep. 8th Census* 72 The Pennsylvania oil region . . . has thus far been the principal source [of petroleum]. **1888** *Chautauquan* Feb. 271/1 An oil well can be drilled . . . in less than one-tenth of the time that was required when the Pennsylvania oil regions were first explored. — (16) **1845** SOL. SMITH *Theatr. Apprent.* 136 The baggage was sent in a large Pennsylvania road wagon. — (17) **1945** *Elk Mt. Pilot* (Crested Butte, Colo.) 19 July 4/6 Long known for its production of crude Pennsylvania type oil from shallow depth, the Rangely district has [etc.]. — (18) **1810** M. DWIGHT *Journey to Ohio* 39 This line is the shape of a Pennsylvania waggon. **1891** WELCH *Recoll. 1830–40* 66 Enormous arks of the so-called 'Pennsylvania wagons,' driven with four to ten horses. — (19) **1810** M. DWIGHT *Journey to Ohio* 29 Among my list of cast offs, I would rank Dutchmen, a Pensylvania waggoner, ditto gentlemen—for their profanity.

b. Also (1) **Pennsylvania bituminous coal,** (2) **blue grass,** (3) **cowboy,** (4) **delegation,** (5) **line,** (6) **market.**

(1) **1840** *Niles' Reg.* 25 April 128/3 Pennsylvania bituminous coal. Supplies of this coal . . . are expected in this market in a few days. — (2) **1884** *Cent. Mag.* Jan. 444/2 Large droves of Carolina cattle were driven through Virginia to fatten on Pennsylvania blue grass, before going to the Philadelphia market. — (3) **1943** MENEFEE *Assignment* 7, I heard one Bridgeport Scandinavian deliver a long diatribe against the 'Pennsylvania cowboys' from Scranton and other depressed areas. — (4) **1789** MACLAY *Deb. Senate* 11, I mentioned a favorable disposition in some of the Maryland gentlemen to be in unison with the Pennsylvania delegation.

(5) **1833** KERCHEVAL *History* 191 They had again protested at the Pennsylvania line, against being taken out of the state. — (6) **1913** J. W. SULLIVAN *Markets for the People* 104 The Pennsylvania markets usually get along with a single market-master, assisted by a laborer or two on market days.

c. In the names of plants: (1) **Pennsylvania dwarf mountain maple,** (2) **fir tree,** (3) **mountain laurel,** (4) **saxifrage,** (5) **swamp rose,** (6) **wild oat,** (7) **wind flower.**

(1) **1785** MARSHALL *Amer. Grove* 2 *Acer pennsylvanicum.* Pennsylvania Dwarf Mountain Maple. — (2) **1770** FORSTER tr. *Kalm's Travels* 69 Pennsylvania Fir Tree (*Pinus Amer.*) — (3) **1785** MARSHALL *Amer. Grove* 127 Pennsylvania Mountain Laurel (*Rhododendrum maximum*). — (4) **1847** DARLINGTON *Weeds & Plants* 143 Pennsylvania Saxifrage. Tall Saxifrage. . . . Swampy meadows and low ground.

(5) **1795** WINTERBOTHAM *Hist. View* III. 392 Pennsylvania swamp rose. — (6) **1843** TORREY *Flora N.Y.* II. 452 *Avena Pennsylvanica.* . . . Pennsylvania Wild-oat. . . . Wet meadows: rare. — (7) **1869** FULLER *Flower Gatherers* 28 [The anemone] blooms later, in May and June, and is called the 'Pennsylvania Wind Flower.'

d. *Pennsylvania of the West,* (see quot.).

1894 *N.Y. Wkly. Tribune* 7 March 4/3 Missouri, from the Indian name for the river, meaning 'muddy water'; sobriquet, the Pennsylvania of the West.

Pennsylvania Dutch.

1. *collect.* The descendants of seventeenth- and eighteenth-century immigrants to southeastern Pennsylvania from southern Germany and Switzerland.

As used in this expression, "Dutch" is a rendering of "Deutsch," meaning German. The expression "Pennsylvania Dutch" has become securely established but "Pennsylvania German" is a more accurate expression, "Dutch" being, in this case erroneously, associated with Holland.

1868 BEECHER *Norwood* 468 Them Pennsylvania Dutch think more of their horses than they do of themselves. **1910** *Harper's Mag.* Aug. 473/1 Those strange people, the Pennsylvania Dutch, . . . after well two hundred years, have kept themselves alien amidst the other Americans. **1949** *Pa. Dutchman* 21 July 1/5 The average tourist thinks of the Pennsylvania Dutch as being only those who are dressed in the Amish costume.

attrib. **1882** P. E. GIBBONS *'Pennsylvania Dutch'* 401 A 'Pennsylvania Dutch' remedy for whooping-cough. **1895** ROBLEY *Bourbon Co., Kans.* 155 Mr. Miller was from Pennsylvania, of the old 'Pennsylvania Dutch' stock, and was a most excellent man and citizen. **1910** *Harper's Mag.* Aug. 474/1 We do not know how the Pennsylvania Dutch ideal of rural life was evolved.

b. The traits or characteristics of the Pennsylvania Dutch.

1863 *Puget Sound Herald* (Steilacoom, Wash.) 12 Dec. 1/7 Thar ain't no Pennsylvieanny Dutch about me.

c. Pennsylvania Dutchland, the region occupied by the Pennsylvania Dutch. *Colloq.*

1942 WEYGANDT *Plenty of Penna.* 21 The gospel of good food that was so generally preached in Pennsylvania Dutchland . . . has been carried even to the uttermost corners of the state. **1949** *Pa. Dutchman* 16 June 1/5 In the larger regions of Pennsylvania Dutchland (that is, in all of the Dutch counties *other than* Lancaster County) we do not have anything uniquely unique to offer.

d. Pennsylvania Dutchman, =Pennsylvania German 1.

1855 *N.Y. Wkly. Tribune* 21 April 3/6 The first and oldest portion of them are the Pennsylvania Dutchmen, whose ancestors came to this country as early as 1683. **1947** *Sat. Ev. Post* 8 March 76/4 Almost his first stop was at the . . . home of Samuel H. Kress, a Pennsylvania Dutchman.

2. The Palatinate dialect of High German, with English intermixed, spoken by Pennsylvania Germans. Also transf.

1856 *Spirit of Times* 4 Oct. 71/1 But *revenons a mouton*, which, in plain Pennsylvania Dutch means how Fogie Antique caught—no, didn't catch—catfish. **1882** P. E. GIBBONS *'Pennsylvania Dutch'* 381 The 'Pennsylvania Dutch,' which is spoken over a large portion of our own State, . . . seems to be nearly homogeneous. **1942** WEYGANDT *Plenty of Penna.* 174 She was equally at sea when he tried her in Pennsylvania Dutch.

Pennsylvania German.

1. A descendant of immigrants from South Germany and Switzerland who settled in southeastern Pennsylvania in the seventeenth and eighteenth centuries.

1869 *Nation* 30 Dec. 584/1 Divine service among the Pennsylvania Germans is held in High German. **1924** M. B. LAMBERT *Pa. German* ix, If a Pennsylvania-German were to go to the Pfalz today and speak only Pennsylvania-German in his intercourse with the natives, . . . he would find it difficult to persuade them that he had not been born and reared in the Pfalz. **1945** *Amer. Sp.* April 98 As for the other Pennsylvania Germans, their chance of maintaining a threefold language culture began to fade out with the passing of the common school law in 1834.

2. =Pennsylvania Dutch 2.

1869 *Nation* 30 Dec. 583/2 The Pennsylvania German is a South German dialect, . . . more or less interspersed with Germanized English words. **1924** [see **1.** above].

Hence **Pennsylvania Germanism,** a term typical of this speech.

1948 MENCKEN *Supp.* II. 156 The former is a common Pennsylvania Germanism.

Pennsylvanian ˌpɛnslˈvenjən, *a.* and *n.*

1. *n.* A citizen or resident of Pennsylvania.

1698 THOMAS *West-New-Jersey* 17 Trades-Men, whose Wages are upon the same Foot with the Pensilvanians. **1782** CRÈVECOEUR *Letters* 58 Europeans . . . become, in the course of a few generations, not only Americans in general, but either Pennsylvanians, Virginians, or provincials, under some other name. **1804** *Fredericktown* (Md.) *Herald* 14 April 3/4 The enlightened Pennsylvanians and Jerseymen of Congress, clamoured loudly against this policy. **1945** *Md. Conservationist* 7/2 The Potomac River . . . is very heavily fished by Washingtonians and approximately 4000 West Virginians and Virginians as well as Pennsylvanians.

b. *pl.* In the Revolutionary War, a regiment mustered in Pennsylvania.

1776 *Battle of Brooklyn* I. i, Know, then, that the Marylanders, the Pennsylvanians, and the rife [*sic*] regiments, are mostly composed of *Europeans*.

2. *a.* Residing in, belonging in, or characteristic of Pennsylvania.

1698 THOMAS *West-New-Jersey* 2 They (as the Pensilvanian Indians) observe the New Moons with great Devotion. **1744** B. FRANKLIN (*title*), An Account of the New Invented Pennsylvanian Fire-Places; . . . With Directions for Putting Them Up. **1827** J. BERNARD *Retrosp.* 183 Like Pennsylvanian 'bundlers,' they passed the night in innocent conversation. **1853** BUNN *Old Eng. & N. Eng.* I. 167 Mr. Nicholas Biddle . . . issued the notorious Pennsylvanian bonds.

b. In the names of various plants characteristic of Pennsylvania.

1785 MARSHALL *Amer. Grove* 127 *Rhodendrum maximum.* Pennsylvanian Mountain Laurel. This grows to the height of about six or eight feet. **1814** BIGELOW *Florula Bostoniensis* 107 *Saxifraga Pennsylvanica.* Pennsylvanian Saxifrage. . . . A tall, green plant, of little beauty, growing in meadows. **1843** TORREY *Flora N.Y.* I. 15 *Ranunculus Pennsylvanicus.* Pennsylvanian Crowfoot. . . . Banks of rivers, in damp soils, chiefly on the Hudson River and in the northern counties.

c. *Geol.* Of or pertaining to one of the periods of the Paleozoic era.

1916 *Proc. Iowa Acad. Sci.* XXIII. 166 The presence of this basin . . . also explains the belted arrangement of the outcrops of the Pennsylvanian formations. **1949** *Photogrammetric Engineering* June 239 The uplands are underlain by the more resistant rocks of Lower Pennsylvanian . . . and Precambrian age.

*** penny,** *n.*

1. The U.S. one-cent piece.

"There is a bad habit, west of New England, of calling a cent a penny" (B. '77).

1831 *Boston Transcript* 17 March 1/1 'They are all pennies,' says he; 'nothin but pennies.' He meant cents, but they call em pennies in New York. **1910** *Sunset* March 333/2 More than two generations have passed since the little penny of the 'Indian Head' was first introduced. **1949** *Southtown Economist* (Chi.) 25 Sep. 8/1 Those pennies, nickels, dimes, yes even more, that we throw away could be given to help those people less fortunate than ourselves.

2. Used in combs. to designate an article or an amount of something costing one cent: (1) **penny daily,** (2) **dip,** (3) **goods,** (4) **grab,** (5) **paper,** (6) **roll,** (7) **whistle.**

(1) **1834** *Sun* (N.Y.) 25 June 2/1 The proprietors of the mammoth sheets . . . are about to reduce their subscription price to $8, in consequence of the inroads which the penny dailies are making upon them. **1840** GARRISON in W. J. & F. L. Garrison *Life W. L. Garrison* II. 418 Leavitt has started a penny daily, to advocate the third-party project. — (2) **1861** *Vanity Fair* 2 March 98/1 Mr. McCrowder . . found himself lying on the floor of a small and unknown room, at once lighted and perfumed by a penny dip. — (3) **1892** *York Co. Hist. Rev.* 32 They manufacture all kinds of stick candy and make a prominent specialty of penny goods. — (4) **1857** UNDERHILL & THOMPSON *Elephant Club* 72 You will, under no circumstances, buy and smoke a 'penny grab.'

(5) **1839** BRIGGS *H. Franco* II. 2 Three or four cartmen . . . were seated on their car tails, each of them studying a penny paper. **1894** FORD *P. Stirling* 297 The third [headline], printed in an insignificant little penny paper, never read and almost unknown by reading people. — (6) **1851** *Harper's Mag.* Jan. 151/4 The baker gave him the three penny rolls. — (7) **1869** J. R. BROWNE *Adv. Apache Country* 59 Red, white, green, and gray blankets [for the Indians] . . . and penny whistles for the small fry.

3. In special combs.: (1) **penny ante,** a poker game in which the ante is limited to a penny, also fig., and attrib.; (2) **-in-the-slot machine,** (see quot.); (3) **pitching,** a game in which the contestants try to pitch a penny on or close to a mark; (4) **poker, =penny ante,** also attrib.; (5) **post,** mailman, *obs.*; (6) **savings bank,** a savings bank that accepts deposits of as little as a penny; (7) **tree, =hop tree,** cf. **wafer ash.**

(1) **1855** M. THOMPSON *Doesticks* 259 Napoleon spends most of his time playing penny 'ante' with the three Graces. **1946** *Negro Digest* Aug. 48/1 Compared to the man Bilbo, 63-year-old John Rankin is strictly penny ante and colorless. **1949** *Boston Globe Mag.* 25 Sep. 9/5 Somebody started a penny-ante poker game. — (2) **1901** *World's Work* Aug. 1057/2 The mutoscope . . . has become known as a penny-in-the-slot machine for diversion, rather than for serious purposes. — (3) **1871** BAGG *At Yale* 534 Perhaps to the list of student amusements should be added the games of . . . leap-frog, . . . penny-pitching [etc.]. — (4) **1849** FOSTER *N.Y. in Slices* 29 We came upon the penny poker dens of the thieves and negroes. **1861** *Harper's Mag.* May 862/1 Cooney was in the habit of spending his evenings at a game of 'penny-poker,' the stakes being generally confined to small amounts.

(5) **1855** HOLBROOK *Among Mail Bags* 103 At about the same time, I consulted one of the Brooklyn penny-posts, whose beat took in Pat's residence. **1868** HAWTHORNE *Notebooks* I. 26 Fame! Some very humble persons in a town may be said to possess it,—as the penny-post, the town-crier. — (6) **1891** *Atlantic Mo.* June 814/2 A penny savings bank, chartered under state law, was organized at Chattanooga about ten months ago. — (7) **1931** CLUTE *Plants* 61 The wafer

ash (*Ptelea trifoliata*) is not an ash, but the fuits [*sic*] are like wafers and may suggest other objects, as the name penny-tree clearly shows.

As the last term in **half, pitch, ten, Washington penny.**

* **pennyroyal,** *n.*

1. A native American mint of the genus *Hedeoma*, esp. *H. pulegioides.*

1630 HIGGINSON *New-England* 9 Diuers excellent Pot-herbs grow abundantly among the Grasse, as . . . Penyroyall, Wintersauerie, Sorrel [etc.]. **1795** WINTERBOTHAM *Hist. View* III. 398 Among the native and uncultivated plants of New-England, the following have been employed for medicinal purposes: . . . Horsemint, spearmint, watermint, and Pennyroyal. **1832** CHILD *Frugal Housewife* 115 Some make a decoction of indigo-weed, and other of pennyroyal, and bathe horses with it, to defend them from insects. **1931** CLUTE *Plants* 144 Practically the only pennyroyal we know of in America is a little plant of the mint family (*Hedeoma pulegioides*) which inhabits dry hillsides and makes its presence known, when trod upon, by a strong aromatic odor.

b. =**pennyroyal tea.**

1809 IRVING *Knickerb.* VII. x, A whole army of old women . . . were bent upon driving the enemy out of his bowels . . . with catnip and penny royal. **1854** S. SMITH *Down East* 103, I give her sage, . . . and cammermile, and pennyryal, and motherwort, and balm. **1903** WHITE *Forest* 106 [Each] heralds the particular merits of his own fly-dope. [There are] eager advocates of the advantages of . . . pennyroyal.

c. *Oil of pennyroyal*, a commercial oil prepared from American pennyroyal and used as a mosquito repellent.

1815 *Niles' Reg.* IX. 94/2 Oils, of mint, sassafras, worm and penyroyal [*sic*] and castor, . . . are to be found in our druggists' shops. **1897** *Outing* XXX. 377/1 As good a mixture as I know of [for an insectifuge] contains: Three ounces pine-tar, one ounce oil of pennyroyal, and two ounces castor oil.

2. One of various other plants, as a species of mountain mint.

1784 CUTLER in *Mem. Acad.* I. 463 *Trichostema*. . . . Wild Lavender. Great Pennyroyal. . . . In old fields. **1806** CLARK in *Lewis & C. Exped.* V. (1905) 110, I observe here . . . water penerial [pennyroyal], elder, coalts foot [etc.]. **1894** *Amer. Folk-Lore* VII. 96 *Pycnanthemum lanceolatum*, . . . pennyroyal, Minn.

3. =**pennyroyal hymn.** *Obs.*

1905 *Methodist Rev.* LXXXVII. 704 The attitude to take toward the sort of tune . . . variously denominated, 'gospel song,' 'spiritual song,' 'pennyroyal,' has cost the Commission a good deal of vexation of spirit.

4. Used attrib. or as an adj. (see quot. 1902 and cf. next). *Obs.*

1864 *Ohio Agric. Rep.* XVIII. 21 If the gentleman has any Pennyroyal cattle I hope to see them at the Fair. **1902** CLAPIN 304 *Pennyroyal*, in the West, used adjectively to describe inferior stock. 'A pennyroyal steer or bull.'

b. (See quots. 1927, 1928.)

1892 *Chi. Tribune* 20 July 4/6 Abraham Lincoln, Jefferson Davis, . . . and Adlai E. Stevenson all came from what is locally known as the 'Pennyrile deestrict' of Kentucky. [**1927** *Mt. Life* (Berea, Ky.) Jan. 1/1 One of the lovers of Kentucky said to me that the State is divided into three parts. To the east we have the Mountains. Moving westward we come to the Blue Grass. Following the setting sun we come to the 'Pennyrile.'] **1928** *Ib.* Oct. 11/1 Sculptured into the surface of Kentucky like a nail-studded horseshoe open to the north, the 'Knobs' belt surrounds the Blue Grass region and separates it from the Pennyroyal (Pennsylvanian) plateau.

c. pennyroyal hymn, (see quot. 1850). *Obs.*

1850 JUDD *R. Edney* 274 He sang one, popularly known as a pennyroyal hymn,—a measure that combines unction and vivacity. **1895** WIGGIN *Village Watch-Tower* 115 It was pennyrial hymns she used to sing mostly.

d. pennyroyal pasture, a pasture seeded with pennyroyal.

1847 *Knickerb.* XXX. 562 They didn't help me any more than it would to turn a colt into a penny-royal pasture.

e. pennyroyal tea, a tea made from the leaves of the American pennyroyal.

1841 *Knickerb.* XVII. 391 A little penner'yal tea would be good for Burks. **1847** B. F. TAYLOR *World on Wheels* 99 They give penny-royal tea to bring out the measles. **1894** R. E. ROBINSON *Danvis Folks* 5 It would be a good thing for her tu take a leetle pennyr'yal tea. **1948** *Hoosier Folklore* March 6 Pennyroyal tea is a sure cure for cold if the ailing one drinks the tea hot and stays indoors for a day or so.

As the last term in **bastard, false, western pennyroyal.**

Penobscot pə'nɑbˌskɑt, *n.* [f. a native term of debated significance. See Hodge.] An Indian of a tribe formerly occupying the country on both sides of the Penobscot River and Bay. Also, *pl.*, the tribe of such an Indian. Usu. attrib.

1779 S. LOVELL *Jrnl. Penobscot Exped.* (1881) 97 We are visited by some Penobscot Indians who are determined to proceed with us. **1831** *Boston Transcript* 7 Oct. 1/2 Last week, a wretched and destitute Penobscot Indian was seen traversing our streets. **1893** *Chi. Tribune* 3 July 1/3 The Penobscot tribe of Indians is represented now by ten members from Old Town, Maine. **1942** Nat. Pk. Service *Fading Trails* 50 Many an aged Penobscot . . . still wistfully awaits the day when the . . . peculiar 'click-lick' of caribou's feet will resound once more in the frosty air of the morning. **1947** COFFIN *Yankee Coast* 225 When the first Europeans came blowing by, the Maine coast was the home of the Abenakis, tall Algonkian Indian race—Sokokis, Anasaguntícooks or Androscoggins, Canibas or Kennebecs, Wawennocks or Penobscots.

* **pension,** *n.* In combs.: (1) **pension agent,** one who acts as an agent for another in securing a pension; (2) **attorney,** a lawyer specializing in pension laws; (3) **bill,** a legislative bill authorizing the payment of a pension to designated persons, also **private pension bill;** (4) **bureau,** =**pension office;** (5) **grab,** a pension bill designed to give generous pensions; (6) **grabber,** (*a*) one who is quick to claim a pension right, (*b*) a congressman who votes for more and bigger pensions; (7) **office,** a federal office that administers the pensions granted by the government; (8) **shark,** =**pension agent.**

(1) **1848** *Whig Almanac 1849* 28/2 There are 43 Pension Agents, who charge $2 on every $100 they pay out. **1902** HANDSAKER in *Pioneer Life* 38 There was no necessity to employ a pension agent ('sharks,' they were called). — (2) **1898** *K.C. Star* 18 Dec. 5/3 Assistant Secretary Webster Davis . . . is urged by all who fancy that his extremely liberal pension views would be put in practice, to the delight of the pension attorneys and with an immediate increase of the pension vote. — (3) **1868** *N.Y. Herald* 10 July 6/1 In the evening session a long list of private pension bills was passed. **1887** *Courier-Journal* 6 Feb. 1/7 The United States Senate . . . ground out sixty-six more pension bills. *Ib.* 7 Feb. 4/4 He has recently signed a Mexican 'service' pension bill. — (4) **1900** *Cong. Rec.* 8 Jan. 676/2 The other amendment urged by the Grand Army . . . is that in estimating disabilities the Pension Bureau shall aggregate minor disabilities so as to give a soldier under that act a pensionable status.

(5) **1888** *Nation* 2 Feb. 84/1 It is impossible to imagine Gov. Hill vetoing the pension grab or issuing the tariff-reform message. — (6) (*a*) **1887** *Courier-Journal* 10 Feb. 4/5 It is not so hard a fate, after all, that keeps the Confederate soldier from appearing as a pension grabber. (*b*) **1900** *Cong. Rec.* 16 Feb. 1886/2, I hope it will do some good in stopping the greyhound speed which some of you pension grabbers want to make in giving pensions to soldiers. — (7) **1778** *Jrnls. Cont. Congress* X. 19 *Resolved*, . . . That a Pension Office be forthwith opened, and kept in the Place where Congress shall from Time to Time hold its Session. **1898** *K.C. Star* 21 Dec. 3/4 A new section was inserted, making the chief of the record and pension office a brigadier general. — (8) **1900** *Cong. Rec.* 19 Jan. 1004/1 Of the money awarded to the soldiers . . . over two-thirds, or one-half, went to the pension sharks of Washington.

As the last term in **invalid, service pension.**

Penstemon 'pɛnstɪmən, *n.* [See note.] A genus of herbs, chiefly American, of the family Scrophulariaceae; also (not *cap.*) a plant of this genus.

This plant or plant genus was named by John Mitchell, a botanist in Va., in 1741 in a Latin treatise he wrote in that year. Later botanists changed the spelling to "pentstemon" (Gk. *pente*, five, +*stēmōn*, thread, taken as meaning stamen). See quot. 1942.

1741 J. MITCHELL in *Acta Physico-Medica* VIII. 214 (Appendix) Penstemon. **1832** *Boston Transcript* 30 June 2/1 We noticed many fine specimens of herbaceous plants. Among them were . . . pentstemon, lysimachia numularia. **1915** ARMSTRONG & THORNBER *Western Wild Flowers* 478 There are a great many kinds of Pentstemon and some of our handsomest and most conspicuous western flowers are included among them. **1942** *Stand. Plant Names* 471/2 Penstemon (*Pentstemon*). . . . The original spelling of the scientific name, Penstemon, has only recently been adopted by botanists.

* **penstock,** *n.* Any one of various structures or contrivances (see 1st group of quots.), used to contain water or to direct or convey it to a desired place. Also attrib.

(1) **1799** *Amer. Philos. Soc.* IV. 349 Let ABCD Fig. 1 represent a large cistern or penstock, and MKLN an orifice made in one of its sides. **1828** WEBSTER *Penstock*, a narrow or confined place formed by a frame of timber planked or boarded, for holding or conducting the water of a mill-pond to a wheel, and furnished with a flood gate which may be shut or opened at pleasure. **1851** CIST *Cincinnati* 103 Here the first fire-plug,—a wooden pent-stock [*sic*] was placed. **1864** WEBSTER 966/2 *Pen-stock*, . . . the barrel of a wooden pump. **1894**

Pop. Sci. Mo. LXV. 613 A penstock . . . is a great tube, usually . . . of boiler plate, . . . conveying water under head into the wheel-case in which the turbine revolves.

(2) **1846** EMMONS *Agric. N.Y.* I. 265 The penstock water of the city [of Albany] contains, of Soluble matter, per gallon, 4.64; Organic matter, 8.00. **1886** *Leslie's Mo.* XXI. 745/1 A never-failing penstock offers refreshment to thirsty beasts. **1898** HARPER *S. B. Anthony* I. 7 In the other end were the sink and the 'penstock' which brought water from a clear, cold spring high up in the mountain. **1901** *World's Work* Aug. 1053/2 The imprisoned waters of the mighty penstock were released. **1948** *Sierra Club Bul.* May 3/1 The two forks and a portion of the Kings below their junction would be diverted through 44.5 miles of covered conduits, tunnels, and penstocks.

* **Pentecostal,** *a.*

1. Designating any one of various religious organizations stressing, in general, sanctification, baptism with the Holy Spirit, and divine healing. Also denoting a building in which members of such a sect worship.

1928 *Amer. Mercury* Oct. 184/2 The Pentecostal Nazarenes have largely duplicated the Methodist system of government by district conferences. **1932** MEAD *Changing Culture* 108 Most of the poor whites go to the Pentecostal Church. **1949** *Gladewater* (Tex.) *Times-Tribune* 31 July II. 1/2 The wedding ceremony will be performed at the Faith Tabernacle Pentecostal Church.

2. Pentecostal Holiness Church, (see quot. 1947 and cf. * **Holiness**).

1947 *Yearbook of Amer. Churches* 68 Pentecostal Holiness Church This body grew out of the holiness movement in the South and the Middle West from 1895 to 1900. It is premillenial in belief and encourages glossolalia. **1948** *Dly. Ardmoreite* (Ardmore, Okla.) 30 May 8/3 The funeral services will be conducted in the Pentecostal Holiness church Saturday afternoon.

* **penthouse,** *n.* An apartment or house built on the roof of a tall building. — **1921** *Country Life* April 65/1 Two of the elevators were designed to run to the roof, where a pent-house . . . was being built. **1947** *True* Nov. 8 Our building is twenty-one stories high with a penthouse on top.

pent-way ˈpɛntˌwe, *n.* (See quot.). — **1877** BARTLETT 458 Pent-Way. A road, not public, and generally kept closed. A few such ways remain in New England.

penuche, see **panoche.**

Penutian pəˈnutɪən, *a.* Of or pertaining to a linguistic family of Indians found in northern California. — **1934** WEBSTER. **1947** DEVOTO *Across Wide Missouri* 11 These Indians . . . belonged to what ethnologists call the Penutian family.

peon ˈpiən, *n. S.W.* [Sp. *peón*, a common laborer.]

1. A person held in serfdom by a landlord or creditor. Also a common laborer.

The early use of *peon* in India is presumably borrowed from Portuguese and French, and has no connection with the American borrowing from Spanish.

1826 DEWEES *Lett. from Texas* 56 The Peons, or lower class, are a sort of slaves, who are employed by the aristocracy. **1882** CHASE *Editor's Run in N. Mex.* 107 Maxwell's force . . . [consisted] of two or three whites, a few Mexicans in his service, and a few peons, or Mexican young men bought and owned, according to a custom then [1856] prevailing in the Territory. **1945** MARSHALL *Santa Fe* 9 In 1850 New Mexico came into the Union as a free soil territory—and went on buying and selling slaves as of old, calling them *peons* and *peonas*.

b. (See quot.) *Obs.*

1851 *S.F. Picayune* 12 Nov. 2/3 One of the justices of the peace gave permission to the Indians to dance the *peon*, a favorite dance of theirs, and went himself with six Californians to prevent any disturbance.

2. Also attrib. (see quots.).

1847 HENRY *Campaign Sk.* 134 This 'peone' system is fully equal to our slavery. **1852** CAZNEAU *Eagle Pass* 10 It is here on this border that we must meet and blight, by the scorching fire of public opinion, the threatening iniquity of peon servitude. **1856** *Wide West* (S.F.) Oct. 4/7 These laborers are worked under the Mexican *peon system* deprived of its harshest features. **1880** *Las Vegas* (N. Mex.) *Eureka* Jan. 4/4 What would the average Mexican greaser or peon family say to be invited to sit at some of our Kansas farmers' tables? **1926** *Sat. Ev Post* 13 March 5/2 'Peon lovers' is the homely old-timers' phrase for Americans who do it from choice.

peon ˈpiən, *v. S.W.* [f. noun.] *tr.* To reduce (one) to the status of a peon. Also *to peon out*, to hire out. *Colloq.* — **1895** REMINGTON *Pony Tracks* 92 The Mexican punchers . . . are mostly *peoned*, or in hopeless debt to their *patrons*. **1912** HOUGH *Story of Cowboy* 218 The honest cowboys . . . were referred to as being 'peoned out' to their employers.

peonage ˈpiənɪdʒ, *n.* A form of servitude involving the holding of peons or dependents for service, esp. in payment of debts.

1849 *31st Congress* 1 Sess. Sen. Ex. Doc. No. 64, 49 From this cause, and the miserable system of 'peonage' that prevails, the products of agriculture are barely sufficient to support the inhabitants [north of El Paso]. **1893** LUMMIS *Land of Poco Tiempo* 20 Peonage in disguise is still effective in New Mexico. **1906** *Nation* 10 May 579/2 The Mexican institution of peonage which the Federal statutes had long ago made a crime in order to keep it out of Arizona and New Mexico. **1949** *Chi. Tribune* 10 Sep. 1. 12/4 The department is considering a possible further charge of peonage against the Browns.

attrib. **1903** *Nation* 3 Dec. 436/3 More peonage revelations in various portions of the South must be opening the eyes of those editors who criticised us last spring for believing that the Alabama cases were other than sporadic and unparalleled happenings. **1906** *Ib.* 10 May 579/2 The transplanted peonage system, this 'new slavery,' like all such elaborate systems of crime or oppression was not a sudden invention, but a growth.

peonism ˈpiənˌɪzəm, *n.* =prec. *Obs.* — **1850** D. WEBSTER *Works* V. 351, I understand that *peonism*, a sort of penal servitude, exists [in Calif.]. **1857** DAVIS *El Gringo* 231 Another peculiar feature of New Mexico is the system of domestic servitude called peonism, that has existed, and still exists, in all the Spanish American colonies.

* **peony,** *n.* A tea made from the peony. *Obs.* — **1886** *Outing* Dec. 229/2 Among her other remedies were anise seed, peony and chamomile.

* **people,** *n.*

1. People of the North, a group of reputedly brave hunters and warriors (descended from Canadians, English, Scots, and various Indian tribes) representing the remains of Lord Selkirk's colony and the Hudson's Bay Company. *Obs.*

1841 NICOLLET *Report* 49 The Metis call themselves 'free people' (*gens libres;*) but by their neighbors they are designated as '*Metis of the Red river,*' '*the Red-river People,*' '*the People of the North.*'

2. People's party, a political party thought of as including or representing everybody; esp. as the official designation of the Populist party *q.v.* Also attrib. Now *hist.*

1811 *Niles' Reg.* I. 9/2, I will attach myself, as an editor, to no party but the People's Party, whose wish is '*peace, liberty and safety.*' **1880** *Cimarron News & Press* 26 Aug. 2/2 The convention of the People's Party met at the Court House . . . last Saturday. **1900** *Cong. Rec.* 25 Jan. 1169/1 A statement . . . entitled 'A reply to the People's Party Handbook.' **1946** HOLBROOK *Lost Men* 275 Donnelly re-entered politics and quickly became the leading figure, as well as the dominant one, in the new People's Party, whose members were called Populists.

3. People's Union ticket, at the beginning of the Civil War, a local ticket or list of candidates pledged to support the government despite politics as distinguished from those supporting the government as partisans.

1861 *Dly. Dispatch* (Richmond, Va.) 31 May 3/2 The only tickets in the field are known as the People's Union ticket and the Republican Union ticket.

As the last term in **bird, brown, buckra, dugout, fasola, fork, frontier, orchard, Pilgrim, plain, sales, union, western, Worm People.**

Peoria pɪˈorɪə, *n.* [Explained in Hodge as derived, through F., from a native word, *Piwarea*, "he comes carrying a pack on his back," a personal name.] *pl.* or *collect.* One of the principal tribes of the Illinois confederacy of Indians.

1770 PITTMAN *Present State* 51 The principal Indian nations in this country are, the Cascasquias, Kaoquias, Mitchimamias, and Peoryas. **1826** *Va. Herald* (Fredericksburg) 4 Nov. 2/4 A treaty of peace, amity, and friendship, was concluded . . . between the Delaware nation and their confederates, the Shawnees, Kickapoos, Pinkashaws, Weas, Peorias, and Senecas. **1949** *Chi. Tribune* 20 Feb. (Grafic Mag.) 14/4 The subtribes making up the confederation were the Kaskaskia, Peoria, Tamaroa . . . , and others.

pep pɛp, *n.* [f. * *pep*per.] Brisk energy, vigor, "go." Also attrib. *Slang.* Cf. * **pepper,** *n.* **2.**

[**1857** *S.F. Call* 3 April 1/1 Enter: *K. N. Head,* (prominent pep. dealer.)] **1912** *Collier's* 13 April 19/1 'Sure, the good old pep,' interposed Callahan. **1935** WEEKLEY *Something About Words* 65 Few words have been more welcome in England than *pep*, for *pepper*, recorded in American for 1915, but usually printed in inverted commas in England until the last few years. **1949** *Nat. Hist.* Sep. 314/3 Fears that Old Faithful may be 'losing its pep' are entirely unjustified.

b. pep demonstration, meeting, rally, smoker, a meeting held before an athletic event, esp. a football game, to stir up enthusiasm.

1915 in *Sooner Mag.* (1947) Nov. 14/1 The pep demonstration held the night before the game was a striking event. **1924** FOSTER *Larry*

(1930) 36 We went to the big rally and pep smoker held every year by the alumni before the Pitt game. **1931** *K.C. Star* 6 Oct., An impromptu 'pep' meeting was held on a downtown street corner. **1945** *Boulder* (Colo.) *D. Camera* 24 Nov. 4/2 Speaking at a pep rally. . . . Dr. Allen told his audience . . . other schools are spending money for players.

c. pep talk, a speech or talk designed to instil interest, confidence, or enthusiasm in those present.

1939 GILBERT *Forty Yrs.* 67 He was impulsive and highly emotional and a pep talk of any sort always got him. **1949** *News-Reporter* (McMinnville, Ore.) 4 Aug. 8/6 With pep talks and some 'horse play,' they ably advertised their annual event.

pep pɛp, *v.* [f. the noun.] *To pep up,* to put life, energy, spirit into (a person or thing). *Colloq.*

1925 H. L. FOSTER *Trop. Tramp. Tourists* 56 'Just leave them to me,' said the Social Manager. 'I'll get them started, and all pepped up, and the rest will be easy.' **1931** *K.C. Times* 30 Sep., Maybe all this sad world needs to pep up business, is more mirrors. **1949** *Time* 14 March 91/1 Retailers . . . now thought that the easier credit would pep up sales.

* **pepper,** *n.*

1. = **pepper tree.**

1893 SANBORN *S. Calif.* 116 There are several handsome avenues shaded with peppers. **1897** *Outing* March 582/1 The peppers throve and the magnolias didn't.

2. = **pep,** *n.*

[**1847** LONGFELLOW in *Life* (1891) II. 85 The paper on 'Nine new Poets,' by the editor, is full of pepper.] **1912** *Collier's* 13 April 19/1 'I'm not sure but spirit is more important.' 'The pepper,' said Bill Dorgan. **1913** *Amer. Mag.* Aug. 40/1 Some of the writers watching me in the spring accused me of loafing and of having lost my 'pepper.'

3. In combs.: (1) * **pepper-and-salt,** (see quots.); (2) **box,** see as a main entry; (3) * **bush,** (*a*) the privet andromeda, *Xolisma ligustrina,* (*b*) = **sweet pepper (bush);** (4) **mint candy,** see as a main entry; (5) * **pot,** see as a main entry; (6) **root,** the crinkleroot, *Dentaria diphylla,* or any other species of Dentaria; (7) **tea,** a tea-like medicinal preparation containing a liberal amount of pepper; (8) * **tree,** an evergreen tree or shrub, *Schinus molle,* found in the warmer portions of the U.S.; (9) * **wood (tree),** = **California laurel.**

(1) **1861** WOOD *Botany* 384 *Erigenia,* Pepper-and-Salt. **1890** *Cent.* 4384/1 *Pepper-and-salt,* the plant harbinger-of-spring: so named from the mixture of white petals and dark stamens. **1931** CLUTE *Plants* 139 Among the first plants of the earlier season, is a little species of the parsley family, whose umbels of tiny pin-dotted flowers give it the name of pepper-and-salt (*Erigenia bulbosa*). Its more appropriate name, however, is harbinger-of-spring. — (3) (*a*) **1784** CUTLER in *Mem. Amer. Acad.* I. 443 *Andromeda.* . . . White Pepperbush. . . . Common in swamps. **1860** CURTIS *Woody Plants N.C.* 96 Pepper-Bush. (*A[ndromeda] ligustrina.*)—This occurs in all the Districts. (*b*) **1869** FULLER *Flower Gatherers* 231 Father calls it a 'Pepper-bush.'

(6) **1814** PURSH *Flora Amer.* II. 439 *Dentaria diphylla.* . . . The roots of this plant . . . are used by the natives instead of mustard; in the mountains it is generally known by the name of Pepper-root. **1857** GRAY *Botany* 31 Toothwort. Pepper-root. . . . Rootstocks of a pleasant pungent taste. **1901** MOHR *Plant Life Ala.* 525. — (7) **1841** *S. Lit. Messenger* VII. 38/1 The pepper-tea done me heap of good. **1905** LINCOLN *Partners* 23 'Pepper tea' was a new prescription for the boy, and he watched . . . while Miss Tempy turned some milk into a bowl, flooded it with boiling water, added a spoonful of sugar, and vigorously shook the pepper box over the mess. **1925** TILGHMAN *Dugout* 33 They poured the tobacco into the barrel; strained the pepper tea and added it. — (8) **1857** HAYES *Pioneer Notes* (1929) 183 When I was at San Bernardino last, I obtained two small fir trees and two pepper trees. **1949** HERTRICH *Huntington Bot. Gardens* 4 When the widening of Huntington Drive was necessary, it was a great misfortune to have to eliminate all of these pepper trees. — (9) **1934** WEBSTER. **1947** CHALFANT *Gold, Guns, & Ghost Towns* 25 It was a small flat-topped point . . . with a few nice trees standing together, among them a beautiful pepperwood—spice wood, we called it. **1949** *Nat. Hist.* March 130/2 Under a pepperwood tree they did find a pile of glass flakings.

* **pepperbox,** *n.* A revolver of an early type having five or six barrels revolving upon a central axis. Also attrib. Now *hist.* Cf. * **coffee mill.**

1850 [see **Allen**]. **1861** *Richmond* (Va.) *Examiner* 7 Dec. 3/2 The pistol is one of the old-fashioned pepper-box sort—self cocking, and, by parties used to handling such arms, is regarded as dangerous at either end. **1901** CHURCHILL *Crisis* 280 Out of his coat pocket hung the curved butt of a big pepper-box revolver. **1948** *Chi. Tribune* 7 March I. 38/5 When gold was discovered in California a favorite weapon of the rugged 'forty-niners' was the pepper-box.

Also **pepperbox pistol.**

1920 SAWYER *Our Rifles* 65 The rifle was made about 1855, when pepper-box pistols were in everyday use. **1949** *Lubbock* (Tex.) *Morn. Avalanche* 23 Feb. II. 1/1 Among the rare pistols an 1850 double-barreled dueling pistol [and] an 1860 'pepperbox' pistol which has six barrels.

* **pepperidge,** *n.*

1. The black or sour gum, *Nyssa sylvatica;* also a tree of this species. Also attrib.

1743 HEMPSTEAD *Diary* 406 Wee Sawed of a pr Peperage wheels for my Stone Cart. **1810** MICHAUX *Arbres* I. 30 *Peperidge,* fréquemment usitée par les Hollandois du New Jersey. **1826** COOPER *Mohicans* vi, He tendered . . . the venison in a trencher, really carved from the knot of the pepperage. **1857** *Spirit of Times* 5 Dec. 217/3 The blood-dyed piperidge leaf, Will shine as brightly as the flowers. **1916** SETON *Woodcraft Man.* 294 Sour Gum, Black Gum, Pepperidge, or Tupelo (*Nyssa sylvatica*) A forest tree up to 110 feet high; in wet lands.

Pepperbox or coffee mill

2. The pepper vine of the southern states.

1901 MOHR *Plant Life Ala.* 611 Woody climbers. . . . Pepperidge . . . [is] frequent, on bushes, or ascending high trees.

3. pepperidge tree, = **1.** above.

1689 *Huntington Rec.* II. 56 A piperage tree marked faceing eastward and south ward. **1772** *Southampton Rec.* III. 272 A peperidge tree, originally marked . . . now . . . stands two rods and three feet to the northward of Capt. Stephens fence. **1929** SHELTON *Salt-box House* ix. 67 A certain tract of land beginning at the highway near my present house . . . to a pepperidge tree.

peppermint candy. Candy, usu. in small striped sticks, flavored with peppermint.

1843 *Knickerb.* XXII. 46 Her red lips contrast with her white skin as do red stripes with the white in Stewart's peppermint candy. **1916** WILSON *Somewhere* 355 He's having a high old time with a sack of peppermint candy and a copy of the *Scientific American.* **1949** *Sat. Ev. Post* 19 March 157/2 It's to buy things with: striped peppermint candy, and fire crackers and balloons.

Also **peppermint-candy-striped dress, peppermint stick.**

1948 *Sat. Ev. Post* 23 Oct. 29/1 She paused before a shop window of flaxen-pigtailed mannikins, wearing peppermint-candy-striped dresses. **1949** *Lisle* (Ill.) *Eagle* 31 March 3/3 From the mathematical standpoint, he says he has tried all the angles—from roulette to hunting the red centered piece of candy that would entitle him to a free peppermint stick.

* **pepperpot,** *n.* (See quot. 1890.) Cf. **Philadelphia pepperpot.**

*a*1790 MACPHERSON *Memoirs* 205 'And what have you got for dinner, Quashiba (said my uncle)?'—'Me have got peppa pot, Massa.' **1832** *Boston Transcript* 23 Jan. 1/1 O! then farewell, hot pepperpot, Since I, alas! may taste thee not. **1890** *Cent.* 4384/2 *Pepper-pot.* . . . Tripe shredded and stewed, to the liquor of which small balls of dough are added, together with a high seasoning of pepper. (Pennsylvania.) **1946** HIBBEN *Cookery* 35 Lay in Dumplings for Pepperpot and cook as directed.

peppy 'pɛpɪ, *a.* [f. **pep,** *n.*] Full of pep, energetic, lively. *Colloq.* — **1926** *Contemp. Rev.* June 720 The 'peppy' American girl expects to be given a drink by her companion at a party. **1948** *Mazama* Dec. 9/1 Now more clearly came the peppy voice, accompanied by an occasional soft giggle in the background—'and a one, two, three, and right *turn!*'

Pequot 'pikwɑt, *n.* [App. a contraction of *paquatanog,* destroyers.] An Indian of a warlike Algonquian tribe at one time holding sway over most of southern New England; also *pl.,* the tribe.

1631 *N.H. Hist. Soc. Coll.* IV. 226 Wee heare their numbers exceed any but the Pecoates and the Narragansets. **1637** *Conn. Rec.* I. 10 To parle w[i]th the bay aboute o[u]r settinge downe in the Pequoitt Countrey. **1714** SEWALL *Diary* III. 12 Commissioners met to give Govr. Saltonstall an Opportunity to vindicate himself relating to the Pequot and Mohegan Indians. **1848** HOLMES *Poetical Works* (1895) 30/1 He heard the Pequot's ringing whoop. **1945** WEBSTER *Town Meeting Country* 11 The Pequots were probably the bravest and most ferocious of all the New England tribes.

b. The language of the Pequot Indians.

1848 LOWELL *Biglow P.* I Ser. p. xiii, Colds in the head . . . Transformed the helpless Hebrew thrice a week To guttural Pequot or resounding Greek.

***perambulator,** *n.* One who performs a perambulation for establishing or preserving the boundaries of a town. *Obs.* — **1667** *Muddy R. & Brookline Rec.* 39 Mr. John Hull . . . [and] Peter Aspinwall are chosen perambulators for the bounds between Muddy River and Roxbury. **1708** SEWALL *Diary* II. 222 So took leave of the perambulators.

percent pə'sɛnt, *v.* [f. the noun.] *Educ. tr.* To rate or evaluate (a student or examination) in terms of per cent. *Obs.* — **1883** *Student* 286 When students are found obtaining help of others they are not percented at all. **1883** *Cin. Bd. of Educ. Rep.* No. 53, 71 As in Physics so in United States History, there is no percented written examination.

***percentage,** *n.* Advantage or profit. *Slang.* — **1911** *Chi. D. News* 2 March 6/6 Johnny Coulon is unable to see the percentage in taking on Frankie Conley for another pummelling in the adjacent future. **1949** *So. Wkly.* 29 June 2/1 There is no 'percentage' in training with Republicans, not for Southerners, in any event.

***perch,** *n.* As the last term in **black, blue, bride, bridge, buffalo, chinquapin, golden-eyes, gray, ground, log, pirate, pond, raccoon, red, ring, Sacramento, salt-water, sea, silver, strawberry, sun, surf, trout, white, widow's, yellow perch.**

percosan pə'kosn̩, *n.* Variant of **pocosin.** Also attrib. *Obs.*

1709 LAWSON *Carolina* 9 As we row'd up the [Santee] River, we found the Land . . . scarce any Thing but Swamp and Percoarson, affording vast Ciprus-Trees. **1737** BRICKELL *N. Carolina* 12 There are likewise Perkosons and Swamps, which are good Pasturage for Cattle. **1859** G. W. PERRY *Turpentine Farming* 9 Every kind of turf should be turned over, such as low bush huckleberry, gallberry, percosan bush.

percussion table. (See quot. 1876.) *Obs.* — **1876** KNIGHT 1666/1 *Percussion-table.* . . . A form of ore-separating apparatus consisting of a slightly sloping table on which stamped ore or metalliferous sand is placed to be sorted by gravity. A stream of water is directed over the ore, and the table is subjected to the concussion at intervals. **1876** RAYMOND *8th Rep. Mines* 310 This apparatus presents features which have been superseded in the best modern percussion-tables.

***per diem.** An amount or allowance of so much money a day, usu. with reference to members of Congress or of state legislatures. In full **per diem allowance.**

1809 *Ann. 10th Congress* 2 Sess. 350 Officers of the United States . . . have received . . . the per diem allowance fixed by law. **1812** *Niles' Reg.* I. 361/2 The *per diem* of the members have been raised to *four* dollars. **1903** HART *Actual Govt.* 131 Many of the constituencies limit the length of session to 40 or 60 days, and it is very common to cut off the per diem at the expiration of the specified time. **1949** *Lisle* (Ill.) *Eagle* 31 March 15/2 This per diem includes supervisors who are residents of the county seat while the board of supervisors is in regular session or engaged in committee work.

perfecting press. (See quot. 1876.)

1858 *Printer* I. 95 This wonderful achievement . . . the perfecting press. **1876** KNIGHT 1666/2 *Perfecting-press,* . . . one in which the paper is printed on both sides during one passage through the machine. **1929** E. W. HOWE *Plain People* 139 Long after we had a three-story building of our own, perfecting press and type-setting machines.

Perfectionism pə'fɛkʃən,ɪzəm, *n.* The system or doctrine of religious perfection taught by the Oneida communists. Now *hist.* Cf. **Noyesism.**

1837 *Advocate of Moral Reform* 15 Dec., To those who are . . . ignorant of the name and nature of Perfectionism we fear we shall hardly be able to make ourselves intelligible. **1849** EASTMAN *Noyesism Unveiled* 15 We thought it should hereafter be known by the more appropriate name of *Noyesism,* in preference to *Perfectionism.* **1937** NOYES *My Father's House* 5 He spent his time and much of his fortune traveling about the country preaching 'Perfectionism.'

***Perfectionist,** *n.* A member of a communistic religious sect founded by John Humphrey Noyes (1811–86), at Oneida, N.Y. Now *hist.* Cf. **Bible communist, Christian Perfectionist, Oneida community, Perfectionism, stirpiculture.**

1834 (*magazine title*), The Perfectionist. **1867** DIXON *New Amer.* II. 208 Perfectionists . . . profess to base their theory of family life on the New Testament, most of all on the teachings of St. Paul. **1875** *N. Amer. Rev.* CXX. 227 The success that he ascribes to the Shakers, the Perfectionists, and the rest. **1900** ESTLAKE *Oneida Community* 81 The communists were at first called Perfectionists because they professed to be a people who had been saved from sinning. **1937** NOYES *My Father's House* 7 The little band of Perfectionists lived together as one family.

perfecto pə'fɛkto, *n.* [Sp., perfect.] A cigar that is unusually large in the middle and small at both ends. Often *cap.*

1895 WILLIAMS *Princeton Stories* 57 Bring some Perfectos, Jackson—please pardon me, I forgot entirely that you smoked. **1918** VACHELL *Some Happenings* iii. 32 She examined the Perfectos critically and selected one. **1948** *Herald-Press* (St. Joseph, Mich.) 14 Aug. 5/3 Don't chew the cigar or talk with a perfecto clamped in the mouth.

***performer,** *n.* As the last term in **bone, leg, minstrel, specialty performer.**

***periodicals,** *n. pl.* Recurring drinking bouts or sprees. *Slang.* — *a*1897 *N.Y. Times* (Barrère & Leland), Are you in the book business? . . . Ma and pa were talking last night about your having your little periodicals. **1902** H. L. WILSON *Spenders* x. 107 They telegraphed the Butte National to wire his description, and the answer was 'tall and drunk.' Well, son, his periodicals wa'n't all.

As the last term in **agricultural, college periodical.**

Perique pə'rik, *n.* [La. F., see quot. 1931.] A tobacco of strong flavor and tough fiber raised in Louisiana. In full **Perique tobacco.**

1882 *Cong. Rec.* 6 April 2642/2 Perique tobacco may be sold by the manufacturer or producer . . . in the form of carottes . . . without the payment of tax. **1885** CUSTER *Boots & Saddles* 84 The officers gave this chief tobacco—Perique I think it is called. **1931** READ *La.-French* 57 *Perique* is said to have been the popular pseudonym of Pierre Chenet, an Acadian who first produced this variety of tobacco. **1949** *Tobacco* 7 April 15/1 Perique is the only tobacco steeped in its own juice, and has a mildly fermented smell, like wine.

Perkinism 'pɜkɪn,ɪzəm, *n.* (See 1st quot. and cf. **tractor 1.**) Also **Perkinist.** Now *hist.*

1842 O. W. HOLMES *Medical Essays* (1892) IX. 15 Metallic Tractors, invented by one Dr. Perkins, an American, and formerly enjoying great repute for the cure of various diseases. . . . For more than thirty years this great discovery . . . has been sleeping undisturbed in the grave of oblivion. . . . Very few know anything of its history, and hardly even the title which in its palmy days it bore of Perkinism. *Ib.* 19 One Dr. Fuller, . . . himself a Perkinist, thus expressed his opinion. **1949** GORDON *Æsculapius Comes to Colonies* 228 A patent was obtained; doctors and philosophers greatly approved, and professors of three American universities said they believed in Perkinism.

Perkins tractor, see **tractor 1.**

***permit,** *n.* A fee paid by an Indian for permission to do a particular thing. Also in combs. *Obs.* — **1891** O'BEIRNE *Leaders Ind. Territory* 101/2 He pays permits for twenty-five renters. *Ib.* 155/2 He became Permit Collector, and still holds that position.

permit pə'mɪt, *n.* [f. Amer. Sp. *palometa* (> **palmet* > **parmit* > *permit*), in sense **1.**]

1. (See quot. 1948.)

1884 GOODE *Fisheries* I. 329 The African Pompano—*Trachynotus goreensis.* . . . In the Gulf of Mexico it is not unusual, being known at Key West as the 'Permit.' **1948** W. A. READ in *Language* XXIV. 256 *Palometa* has been corrupted to *permit* in the popular designation of the great pompano (*Trachinotus goodei*), the round pompano (*T. falcatus*), and the African pompano (*T. goreensis*), this last species being not uncommon in the Gulf of Mexico.

2. *Permit of Indian River, Indian River permit,* the round pompano, *Trachinotus falcatus.*

1896 JORDAN & EVERMANN *Check-List Fishes* 348 *Trachinotus falcatus.* . . . Round Pampano; Palometa; Permit of Indian River. East coast of United States, Cape Cod to Florida. **1911** *Rep. Fisheries 1908* 314/1 Other species [of pompano] found on our eastern coast are the 'old-wife' . . . ; the 'round pompano,' or 'Indian River permit;' the 'permit' or 'great pompano.'

***Perry,** *n. attrib.* Denoting objects named for Captain O. H. Perry (1785–1819), after his victory on Lake Erie. *Obs.* — **1813** *Col. Centinel* 1 Dec. 4/1 A young lady of this city, in remarking on the present rage for *Perry* shoes, *Perry* mantles, etc. observed, that if it continued, she must also be in the mode, and should, she believed, begin by wearing a *Perry*-wig. **1814** *Aurora* 2/1 The ladies are generally mounting *cockades* on Perry hats. This is at once a handsome compliment to the gallant commodore, and a powerful stimulus to all military gentlemen.

persimmon pə'sɪmən, *n.* [Of Algonquian origin. Cf. Cree *pasiminan,* dried fruit.]

1. The edible plumlike fruit of the persimmon tree.

1612 SMITH *Virginia* I. 12 The fruit like medlers; they call Putchamins, they cast vppon hurdles on a mat, & preserue them as Pruines. **1670** DENTON *Brief Descr. N.Y.* (1845) 3 The Fruits natural to the Island are Mulberries, Posimons, . . . Huckelberries. **1785** BELKNAP in Cutler *Life & Corr.* II. 235, I inclose you the seeds of the Persimmon, a fruit natural to Pennsylvania, and the Pomegranite of Carolina. **1898** DUNBAR *Folks from Dixie* 77 Ike was happy, for the frost had turned the persimmons. **1948** *Democrat* 23 Sep. 4/3 In latitudes further north the persimmon usually awaits the first frost to become edible.

2. The tree bearing this fruit.

1635 *Rel. of Maryland* 18 Also there are divers sorts of Fruit-trees, as Mulberries, Persimons, with severall other kinds of Plummes, and Vines, in great aboundance. **1709** LAWSON *Carolina* 102 Persimmon is a Tree, that agrees with all Lands and Soils. **1901** MOHR *Plant Life Ala.* 68 Shrubby hawthorns, . . . persimmon, and black gum . . . [were] entangled with the tough vines of bamboo briers. **1949** *Yrbk. Agric.* 568/2 Food supplies may be depleted by the heavy cutting of species like beech, dogwood, sassafras, and persimmon.

3. In combs.: (1) **persimmon beer,** *S.* a beer made from persimmons; (2) **bread,** a kind of bread made from persimmon pulp, cf. quot. 1817; (3) **skin,** a light-complexioned Negro.

(1) **1737** BRICKELL *N.Carolina* 38 The following are made in the Country, *viz.* Cyder, Persimon-Beer, made of the Fruit of that Tree [etc.]. *c***1898** CHRISTIAN *Days* 17 Our wine was made of dew-berries, and as a substitute for whiskey, we made corn and persimmon beer. **1944** ADAMS *Album Amer. Hist.* I. 17 Persimmon beer . . . was sometimes substituted for more palatable drinks if these were not obtainable. — (2) [**1684** in READ *La.-French* 103 An early reference to the food prepared from persimmons by Indian women is made by Henry de Tonti, who speaks, on November 14, 1684, of 'des pastes d'un certain fruit qu'ils appellent *Paquimina*, lequel est fort bon.' **1817** J. BRADBURY *Travels* 37 A wooden bowl was now handed round, containing square pieces of cake, in taste resembling gingerbread. On enquiry I found it was made of the pulp of the persimon, mixed with pounded corn. This bread they call stanica.] **1892** HARRIS *Plantation* 122 There was persimmon bread; what could be more toothsome than that?— (3) **1927** BENÉT *J. B.'s Body* 150 Grievin' yaller gals always does all right. Next time I'se gwine to git me a coal-black gal. I'se tired of persimmon-skins.

b. In other combs. in which the meaning is obvious or sufficiently explained in the quots.: (1) **persimmon bark,** (2) **bush,** (3) **grove,** (4) **grub,** (5) **orchard,** (6) **pond,** (7) **sapling,** (8) **seed,** (9) **time,** (10) **tree,** (11) **wilt.**

(1) **1865** KELLOGG *Rebel Prisons* 324 One of the principal remedies for diarrhea was prepared from oak, sweet gum, and persimmon bark. — (2) **1786** WASHINGTON *Diaries* II. 102 A parcel of small Persimon bushes. *c***1845** W. T. PORTER *Big Bear Arkansas* 132 They circled about among the switch-cane and priscimmon bushes a long time. **1944** WILSON *Passing Inst.* 177 Many an upland field not good for cultivation formerly had its flock of sheep, browsing among the sassafras and persimmon bushes. — (3) **1830** DEWEES *Letters* (1852) 127 We came across a beautiful persimmon grove, which looked to us as though there were a large quantity of persimmons to be found in it. — (4) **1788** WASHINGTON *Diaries* III. 336 The Women . . . were employed in taking up the Persimmon grubs in No. 7.

(5) **1863** *Rep. Comm. Agric.* 64 Pleasant prairies and old fields abounding in peach and persimmon orchards and wild orange groves. — (6) **1626** in *Amer. Sp.* XV. 294/2 Extending Southerly . . . towards the pursimond ponds. **1642–3** *Ib.*, Down to Newport News with the families of Skowen's damms and Persimon Ponds. — (7) **1887** *Cent. Mag.* March 662/2 The woods on the right gave place to . . . persimmon saplings, blackberry bushes, and rampant weeds. — (8) *c***1898** CHRISTIAN *Days* 21 We made very good and mighty pretty buttons of persimmon seed, boiling them first to make them soft enough to pierce for eyes; these were too large for the children's clothes. **1949** *Nat. Hist.* May 221/2 During the Civil War . . . Confederate soldiers boiled persimmon seeds as a substitute for coffee. — (9) **1832** KENNEDY *Swallow Barn* II. 164 *'Possums* in general were not to be followed till persimmon time.

(10) **1737** WESLEY *Journal* I. 402 In the moistest part of this land [in Ga.] some persimmon-trees grow (which bear a sort of yellow, clear, luscious plum). **1883** *Harper's Mag.* Sep. 645/1 Climb the persimmon tree and git yer breakfast. **1949** *Sat. Ev. Post* 25 June 79/3 He remembered seeing him in the persimmon tree near the corn patch. — (11) **1941** R. S. WALKER *Lookout* 66 A few years ago, a disease known as the persimmon wilt appeared in middle Tennessee, later spreading to other states.

c. In various colloq. phrases.

Expressions such as the typical examples here given were formerly exploited as established features of frontier vernacular.

(1) *A huckleberry to a* (or *one's*) *persimmon,* nothing in comparison with something; (2) *to be a huckleberry over* or *above* (someone's) *persimmon,* to be beyond someone's capacity, to outrank one; (3) *to be a jump above* (someone's) *tallest persimmons,* to be beyond someone's immediate comprehension or understanding; (4) *to bring down the persimmon,* to win the prize; (5) *the longest pole knocks the persimmon,* and variants, the best man wins; (6) *to rake up* (or *walk off with*) *the persimmon(s),* to pocket the winnings, to get the prize.

(1) **1832** PAULDING *Westward Ho!* I. 80 If the horn gets broadside to the current, I wouldn't risk a huckleberry to a persimmon that we don't every soul get treed, and sink to the bottom. **1856** SIMMS *Eutaw* 553 My larning . . . ain't a huckleberry to your persimmon.— (2) [**1833** *Advocate* (Shelbyville, Ky.) 14 Sep 3/5 You can come huckelberry over my persimmon to-day.] **1834** CROCKETT *Narr. Life* 70 But to do this, and write the warrants too, was at least a huckleberry over my persimmon. **1885** D. D. PORTER *Incidents Civil War* 204 'I am the fleet-surgeon of the Mississippi squadron!' . . . 'I'm a huckleberry above that persimmon, 'cause I'm the chief cook.' — (3) **1845** *Knickerb.* XXV. 425 Wall now, that are's a jump above my tallest persimmons. — (4) **1857** *Porter's Spirit of Times* 3 Jan. 294/2 The lad that goes a sparking on a spanking horse of his own, is the one that 'brings down the persimmon!'

(5) **1863** RUSSELL *Diary* II. 62 Let both parties meet where there will be no interruption at the scalping business, and the longest pole will knock the persimmon. **1893** *Cong. Rec.* 25 Aug. 904/1, I would in the language that is popular on the banks of the Mississippi River where I reside, 'let the longest pole knock the persimmon.' **1948** DICK *Dixie Frontier* 314 When one suitor was successful to the disappointment of several others, the experience was summed up thus: 'The tallest pole takes the persimmon!' — (6) **1857** *S.F. Call* 3 April 4/2 He will deal himself four aces and his opponent four queens, so that your honor will perceive he must 'rake the persimmons.' **1871** DE VERE 50 To rake up the persimmons is a frequent term for 'pocketing the stakes.' **1888** *Walla Walla* (Wash.) *Union* 20 Oct. 3/2 The elevator company walked off with the persimmon.

As the last term in **black, Japan, Mexican, mustang, Texas persimmon.**

persimmony pəˈsɪmənɪ, *a.* Miserly, closefisted. *Rare.* — **1837** J. C. NEAL *Charcoal Sk.* (1838) 65 These Timpkinses . . . won't lend me any money, because I can't pay, and they're persimmony and sour about cash concerns.

*** personal,** *n.*

1. In a newspaper or other periodical, an item about a person, esp. an advertisement of a highly personal nature. Also attrib. *Colloq.*

1864 in STERLING *Belle* (1904) 238 I inclose you a 'personal' from Brother Clement, published in yesterday's *Enquirer.* **1892** M. TWAIN *Amer. Claimant* iii. 33 (R.), Put a personal in the *Baltimore Sun.* **1948** *Chi. D. News* 30 Aug. 19/3 German newspapers have 'personal' columns filled with advertisements for mates.

2. Personal Liberty party, a political party in New York and Pennsylvania in 1887 which opposed legislation aimed against saloons and the liquor traffic.

1887 *N.Y. Tribune* 12 Oct. 2 The alliance of the Democratic party and of the Personal Liberty party, to pass a law to open the liquor stores from 2 P.M. until midnight on Sunday, is alarming the clergymen of the State. **1887** *Public Opinion* 29 Oct. 58/1 The Personal Liberty party believe that they ought to be able to spend their Sundays as they see fit.

peskily ˈpɛskɪlɪ, *adv.* In a pesky or vexatious manner. *Colloq.*

1834 C. A. DAVIS *Lett. J. Downing* 139 The Post Office accounts was the next bother; and that puzzled all on us peskily. **1835–7** HALIBURTON *Clockmaker* 1 Ser. xxi. 188 When he seed that, he grew most peskily ryled. **1877** *Atlantic Mo.* July 77/2 It does rile him peskily.

peso ˈpeso, *n. S.W.* [Sp., a coin. An Amer. borrowing.] =**Mexican dollar.** Also, jocularly, an American dollar.

1840 *N.O. Picayune* 18 Sep. 2/5 I'll give a heap of *paysos* for Santa Fe just for your sakes. **1907** WHITE *Arizona Nights* 255 'Here Tony,' said he with a slight laugh, 'here's a peso.' **1947** *Newsweek* 24 Feb. 52/3 But there was no record that the 940,000 pesos had ever been deposited

*** pet,** *n.*

1. pet bank, (see quot. 1914). *Obs.*

1834 C. A. DAVIS *Lett. J. Downing* 353 Mr. Van Buren . . . didn't say nothin about hard money in the place [of bank bills]. . . . The *safety fund* banks and the *pet* banks couldn't drink that toast no how. **1852** GOUGE *Fiscal Hist. Texas* p. vii, Does the deep experience of the evils we have suffered under both a national bank and a league of 'pet banks' incline us to separate bank and State? **1914** *Cyclo. Amer. Govt.* II. 674/2 *Pet Banks.* Term derisively applied by the opponents of President Jackson to the state banks which Amos Kendall and Secretary Taney selected in 1833 in which to place the government deposits, in place of the Second United States Bank.

2. * pet lamb, a. =**Fire Zouave. b.** (See quot.) Both *obs.*

(a) **1861** *N.Y. Tribune* 18 July 3/4 A Pet Lamb Astonishes the Secessionists.—The Richmond papers tell of a Fire Zouave who was caught and taken to Fairfax. — **(b) 1892** M. A. Jackson *Gen. Jackson* 224 The malcontents left their posts . . . and taunted 'Jackson's pet lambs,' as they called the Stonewall Brigade.

petaca pe'takə, *n.* [Amer. Sp. (<Nahuatl *petlacalli*) in same sense.] A receptacle, as a box or bag. — **1885** *Outing* Oct. 55/1 From some dark corner of the mess-bags, or petacas, he unearthed a handful of dried apples.

* **peter,** *v. intr.* To fail, become exhausted, or give out. In full *to peter out.* Also **petered,** *a. Colloq.*

1846 *Quincy* (Ill.) *Whig* 6 Jan. 1/4 When my mineral petered why they all Petered *me.* If so be I gets a lead, why I'm Mr. Tiff again. **1854** H. H. Riley *Puddleford* 84 He 'hoped this 'spectable meeting war n't going to Peter-out.' **1869** *Overland Mo.* III. 127 After a long desert journey the oxen become much 'petered.' **1949** *Ward Co. Independent* (Minot, N.D.) 21 July 5/5 From the Ward county border west the crops peter out fast.

Peter bird. (See quot. 1949.) — **1925** W. D. Funkhouser *Wild Life in Ky.* 297 Often locally called the 'Peter-Bird' because of its incessant, high-pitched, oft-repeated call of 'peter, peter, peter, peter,' generally followed by a hoarse 'de-de-de-de.' **1949** *Chi. Tribune* 25 Feb. 1. 18/3 Signs of Spring . . . Feb. 1—Peter bird (tufted titmouse) singing (Cantigny woods).

* **Peterborough,** *n.* Also **Peterboro.** A birchbark canoe of a type made at Peterborough, Ontario. Also attrib.

1895 *Outing* XXVI. 465/1 It is true canoeing, too, when the artist Seavey, the genial Hiawatha of the A. C. A., packs his big, open Peterboro full of tents and camp duffle, raises his little terra-cotta colored sail, and glides off Indian fashion. **1897** *Outing* XXX. 540/2 I've got a bran-new Peterboro in the boat-house. **1949** *Webster's Geog. Dict.* 875/1 Peterborough. . . . Seat of a provincial normal school. Home of the 'Rice Lake' or 'Peterborough' birch-bark canoe.

Peter Funk. A swindler, a by-bidder at an auction. Also attrib.

1834 Greene *Perils of Pearl St.* 51 Peter Funk . . . is the very imp of deception; . . . his name is sometimes used figuratively to signify any thing which is employed for the purpose of deception. **1845** *Quincy* (Ill.) *Whig* 4 Nov. 2/4 A green-*looking* youth . . . strayed into one of the Peter Funk auctions on Broadway. **1889** *Portland* (Ore.) *Intelligencer* 21 Feb. 3/4 When he returned at 2 o'clock the same night he had $64 in cash and 27 peter funk watches to show for the large sum he had started out with. **1938** Asbury *Sucker's Prog.* 182 These latter gentry, commonly called Peter Funks, were themselves a source of great annoyance.

b. Peter Funkism, trickery, the practice of swindling.

1849 G. G. Foster *N.Y. in Slices* 34 You may find the red flag of Peter Funkism flying in Pearl-street and other 'heavy' quarters, where it is generally supposed that transactions are *bona fide* and dealers responsible. **1853** *Hunt's Merch. Mag.* XXVIII. 649 The *Commercial Register* . . . under the title of '*Peter Funkism in New York*,' relates what it denominates 'a trick in the clothing trade.'

petitionee pə,tɪʃə'ni, *n.* The person against whom a petition is made. *Obs.* — **1764** *Conn. Rec.* XII. 262 The said Wheeler refused . . . to give the petitioner any further day of payment thereon, unless the petitioner would . . . execute notes of hand to the petitionee for the whole added together. **1767** *Ib.* 618 Under the circumstances the petitioner ought not in equity to be holden to answer the same to the petitionee.

peto 'pito, *n.* [Echoic.] (See quot. 1890.) Cf. **Peter bird.**

1832 Thos. Nuttall *Manual Ornith. U.S. Land Birds* 236. **1890** *Cent.* 4426/3 peto. . . . The tufted titmouse of the United States, *Parus* or *Lophophanes bicolor.* [**1897** *Ann. Rep. Indiana Dept. Geol.* 1135 The Tufted Titmouse frequents all kinds of woodland. . . . Their loud whistle sounds *peto, peto, peto, peto.*]

* **petrel,** *n.* As the last term in **Kaeding's, least, Wilson's petrel.**

* **petrified,** *a.*

1. petrified forest, a region where the organic substance in logs, stumps, etc., has been changed to mineral matter.

1830 *Ill. Mo.* Oct. 31 The earth's surface is literally covered with stumps, roots and limbs of petrified trees; presenting the appearance of a 'Petrified Forest,' broken and thrown down by some powerful convulsion of nature. **1882** Wylie *Yellowstone Nat. Pk.* 70 About four miles from the Bridge, is the Petrified Forest or, more truthfully, the petrified trees that give rise to the name 'Petrified Forest.' **1949** *Rocks & Minerals* March–April 125/2 Some petrified forests were along this route that we could have investigated.

2. petrified wasp('s) nest, a madreporite or fossil coral (see quot. 1824).

1814 *Amer. Mineral. Jrnl.* I. 4 The marine production, commonly called 'petrified wasp's nest,' or 'honeycomb.' **1818** *Amer. Jrnl. Science* I. 385 These fossils are known by the name of petrified wasp-nests, from the resemblance they bear to the nests of those insects. **1824** Blane *Excursion U.S.* 116 In one part [of the rapids near Louisville, Ky.], there is a large reef of coral and madreporite, which latter substance, from its singular appearance, the people call 'petrified wasps' nests.'

petrolatum ,pɛtrə'letəm, *n.* [* *petrol*+*atum,* as in *acetatum, sulphatum.*] A tasteless, odorless pharmaceutical substance consisting essentially of the refined residue resulting from the distillation of petroleum.

1887 *Scientific Amer.* 7 May 293/3 With a silk handkerchief apply petrolatum evenly. **1890** Webster 1073/2 *Petrolatum* is the official name for the purified product. *Cosmoline* and *vaseline* are commercial names for substances essentially the same, but differing slightly in appearance and consistency or fusibility. **1944** *Sears Cat.* (ed. 189) 877A/4 Plain Petrolatum. . . . Clear, odorless. Use on cows' teats to resist chapping.

petrolization ,pɛtrələ'zeʃən, *n.* [f. * *petrolize, v.*+ * *-ation.*] The process of covering the surface of stagnant water with a film of petroleum. *Rare.* — **1901** L. O. Howard *Mosquitoes* 193 The petrolization of mosquito-breeding pools is one of the most important measures to be taken in the warfare against mosquitoes.

* **petrolize,** *v. tr.* (See quot. 1901.) Also absol. — **1901** L. O. Howard *Mosquitoes* 193 To the Italians we are indebted for a useful expression, which we might just as well adopt, namely to 'petrolize,' meaning to treat waters with kerosene. **1903** *Boston Transcript* 28 April 9/2 All the breeding places [of the mosquito] treated last year will again be petrolized this year.

* **petticoat,** *n.*

1. (See quot.)

1890 *Cent.* 4429/3 Petticoat . . . a garment worn by fishermen . . . made of oilcloth or coarse canvas, very wide and descending to the calf of the leg, generally with an insertion for each leg, but sometimes like a woman's petticoat.

2. In combs.: (1) **petticoat barvel,** =prec.; (2) **pipe,** see as a main entry; (3) **trousers,** (*a*) wide, baggy trousers, *obs.,* (*b*) = * **petticoat.**

(1) **1884** *Nat. Museum Bul.* No. 27, 796 *Petticoat barvell.* 'A very useful garment to fishermen, better serving the purpose of pants in warm weather, by permitting the free circulation of air around the body of wearer.' — (3) (*a*) **1753** *N.J. Archives* XIX. 291 He took with him . . . two Pair of Petticoat Trowsers. **1761** *Ib.* XX. 597 An English servant lad . . . [had] long petticoat trowsers, much worn. (*b*) **a1870** Chipman *Notes on Bartlett* 318 *Petticoat-trowsers,* trowsers, very short but of great width, worn by fishermen.—Essex Co., Mass. **1881** *Harper's Mag.* Jan. 190/1 One day two sailors, dressed in petticoat trousers, . . . arrested the attention of a young girl.

petticoat pipe. (See quots.)

1864 Webster 977/3 *Petticoat pipe,* . . . one of a series of short, conical pipes, in a smoke-box, to equalize the draught. **1876** Knight 1676/2 *Petticoat-pipe,* . . . a pipe (*a*) in the chimney (*b*) of a locomotive, which comes down over the exhaust-nozzle (*c*), and conducts the escaping steam and the smoke and sparks which follow the induced current into the arrester *d.* **1888** *Scientific Amer.* LIX. 369 Most of our engines are still run with a diamond stack and short smoke-box, with the petticoat-pipe for leading the steam into the stack.

* **petting,** *n.* Hugging, kissing, and fondling, esp. by young couples. Also attrib.

1928 J. P. McEvoy *Show Girl* 11 They have no time to perfect their petting technique. **1931** F. L. Allen *Only Yesterday* v. 90 They were said . . . in darkened rooms or in parked cars to engage in the unspeakable practice of petting and necking. **1949** *Chi. Tribune* 24 June 3/4 The Midway is a wonderful place for petting but what can the university do about it?

b. petting party, (see quot. 1925).

1924 *Collier's* 9 Feb. 16/2, I don't know what's the matter with girls nowadays. . . . Even petting parties seem too slow for 'em. **1925** Krapp *Eng. Lang. in Amer.* I. 117 Who will know a generation hence that a snugglepup is a young man who attends petting parties, and that a petting party is a party devoted to hugging? **1947** *Chi. Tribune* 11 Dec. 3/6 Parents of some 300 high school students who staged a mass drinking and petting party . . . have been questioned by the police.

* **petty morel.** The American spikenard, *Aralia racemosa.* Also attrib.

1778 Carver *Travels* 511 *Spikenard,* vulgarly called in the colonies Petty-Morrell, . . . appears to be exactly the same as the Asiatick spikenard. **1832** Child *Frugal Housewife* 28 Petty morrel-root, and horse-radish, well steeped in cider, are excellent for jaundice. **1892** *Amer. Folk-Lore* V. 97 *Aralia racemosa,* Indian root; life of man; petty morrell. N.H.

peverly 'pɛvəlɪ, *n.* [Echoic, see quot. 1885.] = **Peabody bird.** — **1814** *Mass. H.S. Coll.* 2 Ser. III. 101 Among the birds that are found here [Lancaster, N.H.] are the . . . martin . . . *peverly.* **1885** in *Birds* *of Amer.* (1917) III. 39 A bird spoke up out of the wood and said, 'Sow wheat, Peverly, Peverly, Peverly!' . . . Ever since then this little feathered oracle has been known as the Peverly bird.

* **pew,** *n.* As the last term in **body, Negro, town pew.**

pewee ˈpiwi, *n.* Also **pewit.** [Echoic.] Any one of various small birds, as the chewink, or any of various small flycatchers, as the phoebe bird.

1796 MORSE *Univ. Geog.* I. 210 Towhe Bird, Pewee, Cheeweeh. *Fringilla erythrophthalma.* **1878** DENTON *Naturalist's Diary* (1949) 5 The birds were flying around and looked much like our pewee of Massachusetts. **1939** LINCOLN *Migration* 92 In the case of the Pewee . . . such descents are merely preliminary to the regular latitudinal migratory flights.

b. pewee flycatcher, the phoebe bird, *Sayornis phoebe.*

1810 WILSON *Ornithology* II. 78 [The] Pewit Flycatcher, *Muscicapa Nunciola,* . . . I overtook . . . in the low swampy woods of North and South Carolina. They were feeding on smilax berries. **1823** JAMES *Exped.* I. 263 *Muscicapa fusca*—Pewee fly-catcher, Wilson. **1917** *Birds of Amer.* II. 203 Wood Pewee. *Myiochanes virens.* . . . [Also called] Pewee Flycatcher.

As the last term in **bridge, short-legged, small, western black, wood pewee.**

peyote peˈjotɪ, *n.* [Amer. Sp. (<Nahuatl), in sense **1.**]

1. A cactus, esp. *Lophophora williamsi.* Cf. **mescal,** *n.* **1.**

[**1754** ORTEGA *Apostolicos Afanes de la Compañia de Jesus* 18 Porque los mas con el peyote y vino, que bebian estavan incapazes de valerse de sus piernas, para mantenerse en pie [etc.].] **1892** *D.N.* I. 193 Peyote: a plant of the cactus family, sometimes called 'dry whiskey,' as it is said to produce intoxication when chewed (*Mamillaria fissurata,* Engelm., or *Anhalonium fissuratum,* Lemaire). Probably of Mexican origin. [Tex.] **1896** *Therapeutic Gaz.* 15 Jan. 7/2 The local Mexican name upon the Rio Grande is *peyote* or *pellote,* from the old Aztec name *peyotl.* **1945** MATHEWS *Talking* 81 At same time he couldn't hardly see nothin' 'count too much peyote.

2. (See quots. and cf. **pinole,** which may be the term intended.) *Rare.*

1849 AUDUBON *Western Jrnl.* 186 Out of these acorns the Indians make their 'payote,' a kind of paste, which they dry, and then put into water in flakes, no doubt to allow the acrid matter to escape. *Ib.* 213 The food of these Indians is chiefly the 'payote' made from the acorns into a kind of gruel.

3. In combs.: (1) **peyote button,** =**mescal button;** (2) **cult,** =**peyotism,** also **Peyote church;** (3) **disk,** =**mescal button.**

(1) **1930** *Durant* (Okla.) *D. Democrat* 15 Oct. 2/5 The religion based on the curious effects of eating the peyote button, or dried top of spineless cactus, is now the study. **1947** *Chi. D. News* 22 Aug. 1/3 Revert said it was possible that the girls were drugged with the peyotl button, a narcotic weed known as the 'sacred mushroom of the Aztecs.' — (2) **1932** MATHEWS *Wah-Kon-Tah* 330 To one side was the conical Peyote Church. **1935** *Durant* (Okla.) *D. Democrat* 15 Oct. 2/5 Indians Favor Peyote Cult. **1941** FERGUSSON *Southwest* 288 Recently Taos Indians have journeyed over into Oklahoma and brought back the peyote cult, which has caused great political upheavals. — (3) **1930** FERBER *Cimarron* (Bentley), Her quick eye had leaped to the table where lay the round peyote disk or mescal button which is the hashish of the Indian.

Peyotism peˈjotɪzəm, *n.* [f. prec.] A religion based on the curious physical and psychological effects of eating the peyote button. Also **Peyotist.** — **1934** PETRULLO *Diabolic Root* v, The Peyotists are suspicious of any white man who appears in their midst and asks questions or in other ways demonstrates his interest in the religion. **1945** MATHEWS *Talking* 83 It is still a prayer to Wah-Kon-Tah of the old religion, notwithstanding the symbols of Peyotism with which they adorn themselves.

pfeffernuss ˈpfɛfɚˌnʊs, *n.* [G.] A small, nutlike spiced cake. — **1934** WEBSTER. **1938** HARK *Hex Marks Spot* 187 Then, there are *pfeffernüsse* (pepper-nuts)—my aunt used to make the best I've ever eaten.

P. G. Abbreviation for *public gaol* (see quot.). *Obs.* — **1748** *Va. Statutes at Large* V. 554 The said keeper shall cause a strong iron collar, with the letters P.G. stamped thereon, to be put on the neck of every runaway.

Phacelia fəˈsilɪə, *n.* [Gk. *phakelos,* bundle, with ref. to its fasciculate flowers.] A genus of American plants of the waterleaf family. Also (not *cap.*) a plant of this genus. Also attrib.

1817–8 EATON *Botany* (1822) 386 *Phacelia bipinnatifida,* phacelia. **1898** A. M. DAVIDSON *Calif. Plants* 119 There are many kinds of Phacelias; the flowers vary much in size and in color and form, but they always grow in clusters that last a long time. **1903** AUSTIN *Land of Little Rain* 145 Larkspur in the *coleogyne,* and for every spinosa the purpling coils of phacelia. **1947** *Canadian Alpine Jrnl.* June 17 From the pass, which bears no name, and which we later called 'Phacelia' Pass, on account of large numbers of the flower, *Phacelia sericea,* found there, the landscape was hidden from our view.

* **phaeton,** *n.* A two-seated, open automobile. — **1908** *Internat. Motor Cyclo.* 367/1 *Phaeton.*—An open carriage, frequently provided with a top and a single seat (for two) for the owner, and, generally, a servant's seat fixed at the rear and entered from both sides. **1922** *Automotive Industries* XLVII. 759/1 In the 1906 Handbook [of the Association of Licensed Automobile Manufacturers], Packard, Walters and Stevens-Duryea used the name 'phaeton.'

* **phalarope,** *n.* As the last term in **northern, summer, Wilson's phalarope.**

* **Pharisees,** *n. pl.* **1.** The Liberal Republicans and Democrats who in 1872 nominated Horace Greeley (1811–72) for President. **2.** The Republican bolters of 1884. Cf. **mugwump.** Both *obs.*

(1) **1872** *Cin. Times & Chron.* 3 July 2/2 The battle had scarcely opened before I saw that Greeley's Pharisees and Tweed's followers had bargained. — (2) **1884** *N.Y. Ev. Post* 20 June (*Cent.*), We have yet to see a Blaine organ which speaks of the Independent Republicans otherwise than as Pharisees, hypocrites, dudes, mugwumps, transcendentalists, or something of that sort. **1888** *N. & Q.* I. 184 On the nomination of James G. Blaine for the Presidency (June 6th, 1884), a strong opposition developed itself among disaffected Republicans calling themselves 'Independents.' . . . They were called 'dudes,' 'Pharisees,' etc.

Ph.B. [Abbrev. of L. *Philosophiae Baccalaureus.*] Bachelor of Philosophy, used for, or in connection with, an academic degree.

1883 *Cent. Mag.* May 158/1 They gave me a diploma which . . . didn't have a lot of letters after my name like his—A.B. or Ph.B. or whatever they are. **1903** *Univ. Chicago Pres. Rep. 1892–1902* 112 Students in Commerce and Administration receive the Ph.B. degree. **1942** *Gen. Cat., U. of Wis.* 54 The general rule governing election of studies outside the College of Letters and Science is that students in any of the B.A. or Ph.B. courses are allowed to elect a maximum of 20 credits in other colleges and schools of the University under conditions specified below.

Ph.D. [Abbrev. of L. *Philosophiae Doctor.*]

According to the evidence at present available, *Ph.D.* was known in British academic circles before it made its appearance in Amer. use, but app. British holders of the degree secured it from Germany. It was prob. from Germany that the practice of granting such degrees came to be an established procedure in American education, and the use of *Ph.D.* appears to have a German rather than a British background. The term as first used here, just as in England, had reference to Germany, but later to American institutions. Yale was app. the first American school to grant such a degree. See ***doctor,** *n.* **4,** and the first chapter in Ernest V. Hollis, *Toward Improving Ph.D. Programs.*

1. A Doctor of Philosophy.

1869 *Atlantic Mo.* Jan. 89/2 His cousin, the Ph.D. from Göttingen, cannot help despising a people who do not grow loud and red over Aryans and Turanians. **1911** HARRISON *Queed* 218 There were only three Ph.D.'s among them. **1949** *Sat. Ev. Post* 2 April 26/3 They are all addressed as 'Mister,' apparently on the theory that a Ph.D. is a dead scholar.

2. The academic degree granting a person the status of a Doctor of Philosophy. Also transf.

1903 W. JAMES *Memories & Studies* 331 A Ph.D. in philosophy would prove little . . . as to one's ability to teach literature. **1925** *Scribner's Mag.* Oct. 2/2 He awards Barnum a Ph.D. in humbugology. **1949** *N.O. Times-Picayune Mag.* 20 Nov. 2/3 He is now working on his Ph.D.

* **pheasant,** *n.*

1. The ruffed grouse, *Bonasa umbellus.*

1625 MORRELL *New England* 15 The Fowles that in those Bayes and Harbours feede . . . Are Swans and Geese, Herne, Phesants, Duck & Crane. **1698** THOMAS *Pensilvania* 13 There are an Infinite Number of Sea and Land Fowl, of most sorts, *viz.* . . . Turkies, . . . Pheasants, Partridges, [etc.]. **1834** *Indiana Mag. Hist.* XV. 255 The thick woods are well stocked with game such as deer, turkeys, foxes, rabbits or pheasants as they are called here. **1917** *Birds of Amer.* II. 34 The Ruffed Grouse (called 'Partridges' in most of the northern States) . . . is popularly but quite inaccurately called 'Pheasant' in the southern, and also in some of the northern States, notably Ohio and Pennsylvania.

2. Any of several other American grouse (see quots.). Cf. **Montana pheasant.**

1805 LEWIS in *L. & Clark Exped.* II. (1904) 295 As I passed these mountains I saw a flock of the black or dark brown phesants [Richardson's grouse]: . . . this bird is fully a third larger than the common phesant of the Atlantic States. **1808** Pike *Sources Miss.* 168 Some distance up we found buffalo, higher still the new species of deer and pheasants [dusky grouse]. **1850** Houstoun *Hesperos* I. 245 Another bird which our driver called a pheasant, but which, on making inquiry, we discovered to be a fowl possessed of much rarer qualities—namely, the *prairie hen.*

3. pheasant chicken, app. some breed or variety of the common domestic chicken. *Rare.*

1854 *Pa. Agric. Rep.* 205 E. Culbertson, for best pair Pheasant chickens.

Phi Beta. *ellipt.* =next. Used attrib. — **1845** C. T. Brooks *Poem* 11 Him no dread honors wait— . . . no Phi Beta days! **1883** *Harper's Mag.* Sep. 636/1 The Phi Beta address of Mr. Adams was but another voice of the spirit [etc.].

Phi Beta Kappa. An honorary Greek-letter society, orig. a secret society founded at William and Mary College in 1776, having chapters in many American colleges.

1776 in *Wm. & Mary Coll. Quart.* IV. 214 A list of Members who have been Initiated into the S. P. *alias* ΦBK Society. **1831** *N.Y. Mirror* 3 Sep. 71/2 Chancellor Kent will deliver an oration before the Phi Beta Kappa Society, at the annual commencement of Yale College. **1912** Nicholson *Hoosier Chron.* 278 Sylvia . . . just walked through everything and would be chosen for the Phi Beta Kappa. **1949** *Newsweek* 5 Dec. 54/2 Selby won a Phi Beta Kappa key at Northwestern.

***Philadelphia,** *n.* [A city in Pennsylvania founded and named by Wm. Penn in 1682.] In combs.: (1) **Philadelphia flour,** a bolted flour manufactured in Philadelphia, *obs.;* (2) **greenlet,** =**Philadelphia vireo;** (3) **ice cream,** an ice cream made without eggs from flavored cream; (4) **pepper pot,** a highly seasoned soup containing tripe and vegetables, in full **Philadelphia pepper pot soup;** (5) **porter,** a malt liquor made in Philadelphia, *obs.;* (6) **vireo,** a vireo, *Vireo philadelphicus,* found in the eastern states.

(1) **1723** *N.-Eng. Courant* 4 Feb. 2/2 The best new Philadelphia Town-boulted Flower, to be sold by Mr. William Clark. **1761** in H. M. Brooks *Gleanings* 26 Choice new Raisins by the Cask, Philadelphia Flour and Bar Iron per Quality. — (2) **1892** Torrey *Foot-Path Way* 11 At last we had before us the rare and long desired Philadelphia greenlet. **1917** *Birds of Amer.* III. 104 Philadelphia Vireo. *Vireosylva philadelphica.* . . . Other Names—Philadelphia Greenlet; Brotherly-love Vireo. — (3) **1846** Beecher *Domestic Receipt-Book* 167 Philadelphia Ice Cream. **1941** Farmer *Boston Cook Book* 556 Philadelphia Ice Cream has no added thickening. — (4) **1930** Williamson *Amer. Hotel* 217 A long list could be made of American culinary creations. It would include such concoctions as . . . Philadelphia pepper-pot, succotash. **1944** *Chi. D. News* 1 March 21/1 And so he essayed this dinner: Philadelphia pepper pot soup, potted beef in the Portuguese manner, caraway potatoes in the Dutch manner. **1947** Sessions *Cities of Amer.* 105 A lot of the things the city sells are things that it made famous, such as . . . its hearty tripe soup called Philadelphia pepper pot.

(5) **1844** Uncle Sam *Peculiarities* I. 43 Philadelphia Porter, Saratoga Springwater [etc.]. **1845** J. W. Norris *Chi. Directory* 98 The bar will be furnished with the best of Liquors, such as . . . London Brown Stout, Scotch Ale, Philadelphia Porter. — (6) **1869** *Amer. Naturalist* III. 504 The Philadelphia Vireo . . . was first described . . . from a specimen taken near Philadelphia, in 1851. **1949** *Jrnl. N.Y. Bot. Garden* June 134 Migrants reported on only a single occasion are the northern shrike, . . . Philadelphia vireo, . . . and the dovekie.

b. In less frequent, usu. obs., combs. of obvious meaning or sufficiently explained in the quots., as (1) **Philadelphia beer,** (2) **brick,** (3) **butter,** (4) **butter pear,** (5) **centennial,** (6) **cricket,** (7) **democrat,** (8) **fire stove,** (9) **ham,** (10) **iron,** (11) **money,** (12) **pilot boat,** (13) **raspberry,** (14) **snap,** (15) **system.**

(1) **1834** Nott *Novellettes* I. 10 He drank a pint of Philadelphia beer. — (2) **1807** *Indep. Chronicle* 21 Sep. 3/2 The Subscriber has been a considerable expense for several years past in the improvement of Face Bricks . . . superior to the Philadelphia Bricks, both for appearance and for turning water. **1909** *Cent. Supp.* 164/2 *Philadelphia brick,* a fine quality of hard smooth-faced brick of a deep red color. — (3) **1758** *Newport Mercury* 26 Dec. 3/2 Choice Flour, Ship Bread and Philadelphia Butter by the Firkin. — (4) **1844** *Farmers' Cabinet* 15 Aug. 29/1 The Philadelphia Butter Pear is said to be the same as the Virgalieu, or White Doyenné.

(5) **1885** *Cent. Mag.* May 7/1 The Philadelphia Centennial, . . . three years in preparation, . . . was strongly supported by the United States Government. — (6) **1894** *Harper's Mag.* June 17/2 In Philadelphia cricket the prize is a place on the eleven which is to uphold the honor of the town against an opposing English or Australian team of players. — (7) **1868** *N.Y. Herald* 30 July 6/5 A Philadelphia democrat . . . offers the following. — (8) **1759** *Newport Mercury* 20 Nov. 4/3 A Handsome Philadelphia Fire Stove, to be sold by Peter Bours. — (9) **1844** M. C. Houston *Texas* (1845) 84 The buffalo tongues are very praiseworthy, and so are the Philadelphia hams, which they assert . . . 'whip the Westphalia by a long chalk.'

(10) **1790** *Columbian Centinel* 18 Sep. 8/4 Joseph Blake . . . [sells] Philadelphia Iron, English Goods, &c. — (11) **1723** *Amer. Wkly. Mercury* 22–29 Aug. 2/2 William Bradford of New-York takes Philadelphia Paper Money, upon Reasonable Terms. — (12) **1813** *Salem Gaz.* 22 Oct. 3/2 Last evening arrived, the tandem Philadelphia pilot boat jocular term for a freight wagon . . . from a three weeks cruise in Rhode-Island and Connecticut. — (13) **1874** *Dept. Agric. Rep. 1873* 389 The Philadelphia raspberry was regarded as the best berry for profit. — (14) **1937** Mitchell *Horse & Buggy Age* 68 The snappers on the cheap whips were not made separately, but were all of a piece with the plaiting. . . . They were known as Boston snaps, while the others—the loose snappers—were called Philadelphia snaps.

(15) **1842** Buckingham *E. & W. States* II. 306 The system of discipline pursued here, is that which is called the Auburn, or Silent System, in contradistinction to the Philadelphia, or Solitary System.

Philadelphia lawyer. A shrewd lawyer, one well versed in the fine points of law and in legal technicalities and trickery. Usu. in phrases.

Quot. 1788, supplied by A. W. Read, indicates that this expression arose in England. It is included here because of its much greater vogue in this country in modern times than in England. It may have been inspired by the long, skilful, and highly successful maneuvering and negotiating abroad of Benjamin Franklin, the great Philadelphian, in behalf of his native city and state and the American cause in general.

1788 Let. from Citizen of Amer. to his Corresp. in Philadelphia in *Universal Asylum & Columbian Mag.* April II. 182 They have a proverb here [in London], which I do not know how to account for;—in speaking of a difficult point, they say, *it would puzzle a Philadelphia lawyer.* **1803** *Balance* 15 Nov. 363/1 It would (to use a Yankee phrase) *puzzle a dozen Philadelphia lawyers,* to unriddle the conduct of the democrats. **1861** *Crisis* (Columbus, O.) 26 Dec. 4/1 The Judge refers to the manner of passing important laws in Congress and so mixing them up that any one less gifted than 'a Philadelphia lawyer' could never find them. **1947** *Dly. Times* (Chi.) 28 Nov. 14/3 The new violation ticket will be in quadruplicate, and traffic officials say it takes a 'Philadelphia lawyer' to fix it.

***Philadelphian,** *a.* and *n.*

1. *n.* A native or resident of Philadelphia, Pennsylvania.

1744 A. Hamilton *Itinerarium* (1907) 164, I dined with Mr. Fletcher in the company of two Philadelphians. **1817** Paulding *Lett. from South* I. 90 When the Philadelphian is hard pushed, he boasts of his squares and his wide streets, his beef and his butter. **1947** *Harper's Mag.* Sep. 200/2 The Proper Bostonian is a very well-defined type—more so . . . than the Proper Baltimorean, the Proper Philadelphian, or the Proper person of any other city.

b. The speech of Philadelphians. *Rare.*

1870 *Nation* 4 Aug. 73/1 'It don't signify' is pure Philadelphian.

2. *a.* Of or pertaining to Philadelphia.

1775 *Sh. View of Ld. High Admiral's Jurisdiction* 35 A Philadelphian ship might be tried with a fairer chance of condemnation at Halifax. **1855** H. A. Murray *Lands of Slave & Free* I. 360 The only peculiarity in the Philadelphian mint is a frame-work for counting the number of pieces coined. **1856** MacLeod *F. Wood* 31 So Benjamin Wood went on driving his trade in fish with his Philadelphian brethren.

***philanders,** *n. pl.* (See quot.) *Obs.* — **1828** *Yankee* 3 Sep. 288/1 *Philanders.* . . . When they play this, they all take hold of hands. excepting one who is seated in a chair in the middle of the room; round this one they all march in a circle, . . . singing the while, 'Come Philanders, . . . choose your true love now or never, and be sure you choose no other.' The person seated in a chair, if a boy, chooses a girl from the circle [etc.].

Philippine cane. A species of sugar cane. *Obs.* — **1834** R. Baird *Valley Mississippi* XXIV. 304 The Philippine or ribband cane is rapidly supplanting this species of cane.

philopena ˌfɪlə'pinə, *n.* [App. f. Du. or F. *philippine,* in same senses.]

1. (See quot. 1848.)

1839 Briggs *H. Franco* II. 143 There would be [at the party] . . . scandal by the wholesale, besides sugar kisses, and philippinas. **1848** Bartlett 138 There is a custom common in the Northern States at dinner or evening parties when almonds or other nuts are eaten, to reserve such as are double or contain two kernels, which are called *fillipeens.* If found by a lady, she gives one of the kernels to a gentleman, when both eat their respective kernels. When the parties again meet, each strives to be the first to exclaim, *Fillipeen!* for by so doing he or she is entitled to a present from the other. **1861** *Remin. Loco-*

motive Engineer 21, I, too, sat down, and liked to have made myself sick eating philopenas. **1917** RICHARDSON *R. Mahony* III. v. 213 She had won a pair of gloves in a philippine with Mr. Urquhart.

b. *transf.* A twin. *Rare.*

1894 M. TWAIN *Pudd'nhead Wilson* xi. 557 (R.), 'Boys, I move that he keeps still and lets this human philopena snip you out a speech.' **1894** —— *Those Extr. Twins* i. 323 (R.), 'Ugh,' it was awful—just the mere look of that phillipene!'

c. French philopena, (see quot.).

1908–9 *D.N.* III. 357 *philopena,* n. A variation of the regular game is called *French philopena,* in which one of the participants eats a bit of candy or a kernel of a nut from the other's mouth [East Alabama].

2. A forfeit incurred in this game. Also attrib.

1857 GUNN *N.Y. Boarding-Houses* 139 We remembering her rashly volunteering a $100 wedding-dress . . . in order to get off from paying a forfeit philopoena. **1864** *Md. Hist. Mag.* XXI. 299 He said he was trying to get something to give us for philippena. **1893** *Harper's Mag.* March 609/1 She put on her ring again, using the philopena circlet as a guard.

* **phlegm,** *n.* In humorous or slang combs.: (1) **phlegm cutter,** a drink of whisky or other liquor; (2) **disperser,** =prec.; (3) **splitter,** (see quot.). All *obs.*

(1) **1806** *Balance* 13 May 146/3, I have heard of a jarum, of phlegm-cutter and fog driver. **1810** LAMBERT *Travels* (1813) II. 299 A *phlegm-cutter* is a double dose just before breakfast. **1849** A. MACKAY *Western World* II. 67 He alternated pretty frequently between the julep, the cobbler, the phlegm-cutter, and the gin-sling. — (2) **1818** FEARON *Sketches* 252 Drinking . . . is effected by individuals taking their solitary 'eye-openers,' 'toddy,' and 'phlegm dispersers.' — (3) **1848** *Calif. Star* (S.F.) 3 June 4/1 At the first grogshop Billy took what he called an 'eye-opener,' made of gin and bitters, then a 'phlegm-splitter' of rum and water, and lastly a 'nor-wester' of raw whiskey.

phoebe ˈfibɪ, *n.* [In **1.** in imitation of the bird's note; in **2.** in allusion to * *Phoebe,* a girl's name.]

1. Any of several flycatchers of the genus *Sayornis,* esp. *S. phoebe* of the eastern part of the U.S. Cf. **western phoebe.**

1700 *Essex Inst. Col.* VIII. 216 Heard a Phebe and other birds sing. **1839** IRVING in *Knickerb.* XIII. 434 The Pewit, or Pe-wee, or Phoebe-bird . . . is called by each of these names. **1948** *Pacific Discovery* March–April 16/1 Occasionally the phoebe . . . appears at the window corner to snatch a struggling insect from the web of the golden orb weaver.

2. Phoebe lamp, (see quot.).

1935 *Col. of Conn.* 15 Phoebe lamps: . . . These were similar to Betty lamps in shape. . . . Some had double wicks from a nose on either side.

Phoenix City. The city of Chicago, so called because of its recovery after the fire of 1871. *Obs.* — [**1877** *Chi. Times* 5 Aug., Reports . . . seem to indicate that ancient Sodom and Gomorrah have pheonixed themselves somewhere in the neighborhood.] **1887** GEORGE *40 Years on Rail* 206 Chicago bears to-day the title of the 'Phoenix City.'

phone fon, *n.* [f. * telephone *q.v.*]

1. The earphone or headphone of a telephone. *Obs.*

1884 *Sci. Amer.* 19 July 43/2, I made a telephone as shown in the *Scientific American,* Supplement, No. 142. The phones are made of ebony, and are perfect. **1887** *Denver Graphic* 29 Jan. 7/3 Dakota keeps her ear at the 'phone but she can only make out an excited Congressional mumbling at the Washington end.

2. Short for * **telephone.**

1886 *Calif. Maverick* (S.F.) 13 Feb. 1/3 To him I related the famous fiend's new invention—this 'phone that could talk in foreign languages. **1908** *Sat. Ev. Post* 4 July 8/3, I got my husband on the 'phone right quick. **1949** *Chi. Tribune* 9 Dec. III. 7, I hear the phone ringin'.
attrib. **1924** WITWER *Roughly Speaking* (1925) 5, I captured first, second and third prize in a beauty contest just before retiring from public life to enter the phone service. **1927** JAMES *Cow Country* 199 He came back in the hotel and went in the phone-booth and then he proceeded to call them up, one after another. **1947** *This Week Mag.* 18 July 10/3 But the next night, in my hotel, I looked you up in the phone book.

* **phonograph,** *n.* A machine that reproduces sounds mechanically recorded on a cylinder or disk of metal or wax or other substance; esp. such a machine patented by Thomas A. Edison in 1877. Also fig.

1877 *Scientific Amer.* 17 Nov. 304 Whoever may speak into the mouth-piece of the phonograph. **1893** *Scribner's Mag.* June 695/1 These words, which have just run off the phonograph of my memory, were spoken a quarter of a century ago. **1912** *Ladies' Home Jrnl.* March 35/3 With the Edison Phonograph you get the latest hits of Broadway's musical productions, while they are hits. **1946** WILSON *Fidelity* 127 Later our postmaster-druggist owned a phonograph.
attrib. **1879** G. B. PRESCOTT *Speaking Telephone* 305 Having provided thus for the durability of the phonograph plate, it will be very easy [etc.]. **1902** LORIMER *Lett. Merchant* 214 The phonograph records of a fellow's character are lined in his face. **1949** *Reader's Digest* Dec. 139/1 Sixteen million American phonograph owners are bewildered and unhappy.

* **phonographic,** *a.* Of or pertaining to a phonograph *q.v.*

1878 T. A. EDISON in *N. Amer. Rev.* CXXVI. 532 They are required to do no more by the phonographic method. **1890** *Boston Transcript* 3 Feb. 2/5 A phonographic toy is an Edison toy that seems like a parody of nature. **1913** *Munsey's Mag.* March 957/1 In order to get some idea of the difficulties that lay in the way of complete synchronization, . . . let us see just how the ordinary phonographic record is made.

phony ˈfonɪ, *a.* and *n.* [See note.]

No doubt f. **fawney* (<Irish), a finger-ring, used in the vocabulary of thieves of a gilt brass ring used in the *fawney rig.* See *OED s.v. Fawney.*

1. *n.* A fake or pretender. *Slang.*

1941 S. V. BENÉT *Listen to People* (1942) 485 We'll stick by . . . the Greek who runs the Greek's . . . the stuffed shirts, the 'yes but' men and the handsome phonies. **1949** *Chi. Tribune* 17 Sep. III. 18/3 You're nothin' but a phoney!

2. *a.* Counterfeit, not genuine. *Colloq.*

1900 ADE *More Fables* 138 'Overlook all the Phoney Acting by the Little Lady, Bud,' said the Fireman to the Advance Agent. **1909** *Sat. Ev. Post* 6 March 38/2, I . . . gave the sucker my name and address (both phony of course) and promised to send two hundred dollars as soon as I got home. **1949** *Chi. Tribune* 7 Oct. 12 Stop moaning about that phony blonde and her phonier lawsuit.

* **photo,** *n.* **1. photo finish,** in racing, a finish so close that a photograph or picture is required to decide the winner. Also attrib. *Colloq.* **2. photo play,** a motion picture.

(1) **1944** HALSEY *Best Friends* 167, I would come in for a photo finish with the Dust Bowl. **1949** *L.A. Times* 9 April II. 5/3 Lorenzo Del Riccio, inventor of a photo-finish camera used in horse racing, . . . yesterday was assured the right to compete with his licensed user, Photo Chart, Inc. — (2) **1912** *Everybody's Mag.* Oct. 505/2 History, too, is made alive again, . . . by the clever photo-plays that dramatize the hard, dry facts into living stories. **1921** *19th Cent.* April 661 A photo-play is seen by scores of millions of persons throughout the globe.

* **photograph,** *n.* **1. photograph gallery,** a photographer's studio. **2. photograph stone, tree,** a stone upon which there is a dendrite, a representation resembling a shrub or tree.

(1) **1858** F. J. COOK *Letters* (1946) 19 Sep. 46, I . . . visited . . . Brady's celebrated photograph gallery. **1949** *Chi. Tribune* 18 Sep. 27/4 Andrew Burgess . . . bought and operated Brady's national photograf gallery in Washington. — (2) **1872** TICE *Over Plains* 130 The proprietor called my attention to some stones used for flagging the pavement, which he said were 'photograph stones.' I found several large slabs fringed around with images of miniature trees and forests. *Ib.* 131 We commenced splitting the slabs, and wherever there was an indication of a seam, we always found the 'photograph tree' and sometimes a picture representing a forest.

photographic gallery. = **photograph gallery.**

1866 *Ore. State Jrnl.* 30 June 4/4 Ellsworth and Cardwell, Proprietors Cardwell Photographic Gallery, 89 First Street, Portland. **1877** HODGE *Arizona* 149 There are . . . two tin shops, . . . one harness shop, one photographic gallery [etc.]. **1949** *Sun. World-Herald Mag.* (Omaha) 22 May 5/1 Solomon D. spent the next winter teaching school . . . and earned money enough to put up the county's first photographic gallery.

photophone ˈfotəˌfon, *n.* [f. * *photo-* + * *-phone.*] An instrument which, by means of a beam of light, transmits spoken words to a distance. *Obs.* — **1880** A. GRAHAM BELL in *Jrnl. Franklin Inst.* CX. 246 We have named the apparatus for the production and reproduction of sound in this way 'The Photophone,' because an ordinary beam of light contains the rays which are operative. **1889** PREECE & MAIER *Telephone* 104 Bell and Sumner Tainter have constructed an apparatus, to which they gave the name of 'photophone,' which enabled them to reproduce words at a distance by the aid of luminous rays.

* **phrasing,** *n.* (See quot. 1851.) *Obs.* — **1835** TODD *Student's Manual* 115 Should you allow yourself to think of going into the recitation-room, and there trust to 'skinning,' as it is called in some colleges, or 'phrasing,' as in others, or 'mouthing it,' as in others. **1851** HALL *College Words* 228 *Phrasing,* reciting by, or giving the

words or phraseology of the book, without understanding their meaning.

phrenology frɛˈnɑlədʒɪ, *n.* [Gk. *phreno-*, mind, + *-logy.*] A study of the mind based upon the assumption that the mental faculties and traits of a human being are manifested in the shape of his skull.

1805 in B. RUSH *Sixteen Introductory Lectures* (1811) 271 Very different is the state of phrenology, if I may be allowed to coin a word, to designate the science of the mind. **1832** *Amer. R.R. Jrnl.* I. 517/3 This famous Lecturer on Phrenology, and a disciple of the late Dr. Gall, arrived here on Saturday. **1870** M. H. SMITH *20 Yrs. Wall St.* 295 Slim, spare, with a head and face that defy phrenology and Lavater to read, he has had uniform success. **1881** *Smithsonian Inst. Rep.* (1883) 499 To all these studies we have given the name of Comparative Psychology or Phrenology.

physical education. (See quot. 1945.) Also attrib.

1858 *So. Cultivator* XVI. 32/1 The subject of physical education is beginning to attract attention. **1945** CARTER V. GOOD *Dict. of Education* 298/1 physical education: the program of instruction and participation in big-muscle activities designed to promote desirable physical development, motor skills, attitudes, and habits of conduct. **1949** *Democrat* 4 Aug. 3/5 Ground was broken for a new physical education and community center.

physic dance. Among certain American Indians, a ceremonial dance in the spring during which a medicine, as the black drink *q.v.*, is prepared and taken. *Obs.* — **1765** TIMBERLAKE *Memoirs* 77 There was to be a physic-dance at night [among the Cherokee Indians]. **1819** *Niles' Reg.* XVI. Supp. 101/1 The physic dance was very much in use formerly [by the Cherokee Indians].

***physician,** *n.* As the last term in **county, eclectic, Indian, school physician.**

Physician General. Formerly a rating for a physician serving with the army, or a physician holding this rate. *Obs.* — **1775** in *Amer. Sp.* XX. (1945) 274 It has been suggested that the College be converted into a hospital and Dr. Clossy Physician General to the American army. **1777** *Jrnls. Cont. Congress* VII. 162 There [shall] be a physician and Surgeon General with the main army.

Piankashaw paɪˈæŋkəˌʃɔ, *n.* ["Possibly connected with *Päyangitchaki*, 'those who separate' " (Hodge).] An Indian of a tribe related to the Miamis, originally settled in the Middle West; in *pl.*, the tribe. Also attrib.

1757 *Doc. Col. Hist. N.Y.* VII. 268 There came several of the Chiefs of the Wawioughtanes and Pianguisha Nations. **1810** *Amer. Republic* (Frankfort, Ky.) 17 Aug. 1/5 The old Piankashaw chief, Groble came . . . and asked his permission to retire over the Mississippi. **1883** *Hist. White Co., Ill.* 293 It was learned that three Indians of the Pe-anke-shaw tribe had been skulking about the settlement. **1949** *West Va. Hist.* Jan. 102 Two days later a treaty with the Piankashaws confirmed the treaties made with the Kaskaskias and Delawares.

Piankatank paɪˈæŋkəˌtæŋk, *n.* [App. a native name.] (See quot. 1910.) Also attrib. — **1910** HODGE *Amer. Indians* II. 241/1 Piankatank. A tribe of the Powhatan confederacy on Piankatank r., Va. They numbered about 200 in 1608. **1946** *Nat. Geog. Mag.* Jan. 56/1 When the Piankatank tribe defied his authority, Powhatan made a surprise night attack.

***piano,** *n.* As the last term in **horse, jitney, player, steam piano.**

Pianola ˌpiəˈnolə, *n.* Also **pianola.** [Said to have been coined by Edwin S. Votey, who in 1896 invented the device to which it refers.] A trade-mark name for a form of player piano. Also attrib.

1899 *Boston Transcript* 3 June 12/7 The Pianola may be seen any day at the warerooms. **1915** *Chi. D. News Almanac 1916* 615/2 The Coe music collection . . . [contains] 560 pianola rolls. **1948** *Chi. Maroon* 6 Feb. 4/3 Apart from these pianos there exist a number of pianolas in so-called practice rooms.

* **piazza,** *n.* A veranda or porch. Cf. **hotel piazza.**

The transition from the British to the American sense is indicated in the following example (see A. Matthews "Piazza" in *Nation* 1 June 416):—**1699** *Va. Statutes at L.* (1823) 421 The two parts of the building shall be joined by a cross gallery of thirty foot long, and fifteen foot wide each way, . . . raised upon piazzas, and built as high as the other parts of the building.

1724 JONES *Virginia* 26 It is a lofty Pile of Brick Building adorn'd with a *Cupola*. . . . There is a spacious *Piazza* on the *West* Side, from one Wing to the other. **1809** WILSON *Prose* I. 162 Many of the buildings [in Charleston, S.C.] have two, three, and four ranges of piazzas, one above another, with a great deal of gingerbread work about them. **1949** *L.A. Times* 13 Nov. (Home Mag.) 8/3 Maybe you called it the piazza or veranda.

attrib. and *comb.* **1835** INGRAHAM *South-West* I. 197 A little piazza-girted cottage . . . stood on the banks of the river. **1906** J. A. HARRISON *George Washington* 198 The piazza politician, sipping his toddy, spreading his legs, and discussing constitutional questions on the spacious verandahs of open-air Virginia.

b. piazza chair, a chair suitable for use on a piazza.

1876 A. D. WHITNEY *Sights & Insights* I. 8 There were settees, and regular piazza chairs. **1903** BURNHAM *Jewel* 324 Mr. Evringham took the doll from her arms, and . . . deposited it in a piazza chair.

***piazzaed,** *a.* Of a house: Provided with a piazza. *Colloq.* — **1838** COOPER *Home as Found* ix, Still its inns were of respectable size, well piazzaed, to use a word of our own invention, and quite enough frequented. **1891** WILKINS *N. Eng. Nun* 191 In the distance she could see the Tenney house—white-painted and piazzaed, a village mansion.

pic pɪk, *n.* Short for picayune *q.v. Obs.* — **1838** GOSSE *Letters* 103 The negroes ferried me over the romantic river, for which I paid a 'pic' (i.e. a picayune, the sixteenth of a dollar, or half a 'bit'), the smallest silver coin current. **1855** M. THOMPSON *Doesticks* 202 A stranger must disburse an avalanche of 'bits,' 'pics,' and 'levys,' before he can get even a plate of cold victuals.

picacho pɪˈkætʃo, *n. S.W.* [Sp., peak, summit.] (See quots.)

1857 in MOWRY *Ariz. & Sonora* (1864) 188 Between Tucson and the Gila . . . is a well-known *picacho*, at the base of which water is often found in pools. **1861** NEWBERRY *Geol. Rep.* 53 [There are] floods of lava . . . doubtless of common origin with those which surround the Picacho. **1906** *Out West* Feb. 103 The Picacho [is] a huge, splintered, battle-ax-shaped peak of red sandstone, that was a landmark from Tucson to the Sonoran border. **1948** *So. Sierran* Jan. 3/1 Our first climb, on Saturday, was to Picacho on the California side of the river.

picaillon ˌpɪkəlˈjon, *n.* [F., a small copper coin in Savoy.] = **picayune 1.** *Obs.*

1832 PAULDING *Westward Ho!* I. 124 And then he put his hand in his pocket, and gave her a *pickalion*. **1841** *Knickerb.* XVII. 49 Haven't made a single picaillon since the Belshazzur stove her bottom. **1842** tr. SEALSFIELD *Life in New World* 106 Now not give a piccalu for it.

picaneau ˈpɪkəˌno, *n.* (See quot. 1941.) *Obs.* — **1773** in T. HUTCHINS *Topog. Descr. Va.* (1778) 57 In the lake [Illinois] is great plenty of fish, and in particular Sturgeon, and Picannau. **1941** MCDERMOTT *Glossary* 116 picaneau. . . . A name given by the French on the Mississippi to the gar, duckbill gar, jack or gar fish (*lepisosteus platostomus*).

picaro ˈpɪkəˌro, *n. S.W.* [Sp. *picaro*, rogue, knave. An Amer. borrowing.] A rogue, vagabond. *Obs.* — **1834** A. PIKE *Prose Sk. & Poems* 99 What little silver I have . . . is better bestowed in my big chests than in the pockets of that picaro. **1844** G. W. KENDALL *Santa Fe Exped.* II. i. 28 Ochoa . . . expressed the greatest abhorrence of Lalezar and his herd of ladrones and picaros as he called them

picaroon ˌpɪkəˈrun, *n.* [Origin obscure. Cf. MF. *piqueron*, spur.] (See quot. 1905.) Cf. **pick handspike, pick pole.**

Picaroon, pick handspike, or pick pole

1837 *N. Amer. Review* April 354 The rafters . . . [make] use of a picaroon, or pole with a spike in the end of it, which is repeatedly and unmercifully driven into the boards, taking out perhaps a piece at each time. **1850** JUDD *R. Edney* 42 Richard, armed with a picaroon, descended the slip, some thirty feet, to the basin, where the logs lay in the water ready to be drawn in. *Ib.* 220 The Boy made his picaroon fast to his boat with a rope. **1905** *Forestry Bureau Bul.* No. 61, 43 *Picaroon*, a piked pole fitted with a curved hook, used in holding boats to jams in driving, and for pulling logs from brush and eddies out into the current.

picayune ˌpɪkɪˈjun, *n.* and *a.* [F. *picaillon.*]

1. *n. S.* A coin of small value, as a five-cent piece or bit. Often as a symbol of something of very slight value. Cf. **fip(p)enny bit,** * **fourpence.**

1805 *Amer. Pioneer* II. 228 One can't buy any thing [at New Orleans] for less than a six cent piece, called a *picayune*. **1835** AUDUBON *Ornith. Biog.* III. 160 Not a 'pecayon' would they receive in return. **1948** *Reader's Digest* Dec. 148/1 Don't care a picayune how you waste that boy's time, do you?

transf. **1903** *Scribner's Mag.* April 508 The very fathers of our country were a pack of jealous picayunes, who bickered while the army starved.

2. *a.* =next.

1813 *Cramer's Alman. 1814* (Pittsburgh) 60 The incessant hum of the blabbering (coloured) market women, seated on the ground, . . . by the side of their picharoon (six cent) piles of vegetables. **1892** *Chi. Tribune* 7 April 4/1 The picayune Democratic majority in the House has taken $300,000 off the appropriations for Indian education. **1947** PEATTIE *Sierra Nevada* 39 It is a mountain-top wilderness little affected by the picayune busy-ness of human activities.

picayunish ˌpɪkɪ'junɪʃ, *a.* Of little value, paltry, contemptible. Hence **picayunishness,** *n.*

1855 OLIPHANT *Minnesota* 283 She belongs to that darned picayunish old 'coon, Jim Mason, and he'll run her till she sinks, or busts up, and then God help the crowd. **1887** *Springfield W. Republican* 14 Oct., A sad picayuneishness that allows [etc.]. **1948** *Time* 1 Nov. 24/3, I don't have time to pay much attention to little picayunish things.

piccaninny, see **pickaninny.**

***pick,** *n.* As the last term in **ice, nut, tooth, Washoe pick.**

***pick,** *v.*

1. *tr.* To harvest (cotton) by plucking it from the open bolls.

1823 *Baptist Mag.* IV. 181, I helped to . . . plant, hoe, pick, gin and pack the cotton with my own hands. **1917** J. F. DUGGAR *Southern Field Crops* 361 In some localities considerable cotton is picked in December. **1949** *Charleston* (S.C.) *News & Courier* 6 Feb. D. 7 All the people I saw that day picking cotton . . . were negroes.

b. To free (cotton) of its seed, to gin. *Obs.* Cf. **pickage, pickery, picking.**

1807 JANSON *Stranger in Amer.* 370 Private families gin their cotton by the hand, which is called *picking*, and this work is set apart for the evening. **1834** in BASSETT *So. Plant.* 73 The runinge geares that is hear I cant under take to pick a crop with them. **1876** in GUILD *Old Times* (1878) 395 The matrons picked, and quilted, and talked and gave the men 'hankins.'

2. To remove (ears of corn) from the stalks. Cf. ***break,** *v.* **12. b.** (1).

1833 SILLIMAN *Man. Sugar Cane* 13 Indian corn . . . is picked early in autumn. **1907** *Office of Exper. Sta. Bul.* No. 173, 34 The average man picks 59 bushels of corn per day. **1949** *Chi. D. News* 18 Feb. 4/2, I have picked corn this fall and I also have worked on the section.

3. To pluck (the strings of) or play (a banjo or mandolin).

1848 *New Negro Forget-me-not Songster* 39, I pick upon de Banjo string, Wid de double back action spring. **1894** *U. of Chi. Wkly.* 18 Oct. 7/2 The Misses Ellet, Coolidge, . . . and Wooley will pick the mandolin. **1931** WILLISON *Here They Dug Gold* 236 The banjo player has difficulty picking his strings. **1950** *Dly. Ardmoreite* 14 Feb. 1/5 Sam, the eldest, picked a banjo and sang.

4. To remove (stones) from farm land. Also **picking,** *n.*

1850 *N. Eng. Farmer* II. 164 Sometimes the number of stones is so great, and the size so small, that the labor of 'picking,' . . . is either neglected, or but imperfectly done. **1868** GREELEY *Autobiog.* 39 Picking stones is a never-ending labor on one of those rocky New England farms. **1949** *Sat. Ev. Post* 12 March 68/3 Picking rocks was hateful to me, as there was always a new crop every time we plowed the ground.

5. (See quot.)

1881 INGERSOLL *Oyster Industry* 246 *Pick.*—To gather wild oysters for seed from the muddy shores at low tide. (Georgia.)

6. *Logging.* To free or start (a log jam) by releasing key logs. Cf. **pick handspike, pick pole.**

1905 WIGGIN *Rose* 4 The boys will be picking the side jams today, and I'm going down to work on the logs.

7. *To pick a brand,* (see quot. and cf. **picked brand**).

1909 A. B. PAINE *Captain Bill McDonald* 98 At their leisure they 'picked the brand' which is the range idiom for picking the hair from around the brand with a pocket-knife, so the brand may be seen.

8. In combs.: (1) **pick handspike, =picaroon;** (2) **pole, =picaroon;** (3) **room,** a room for picked but as yet unginned cotton.

(1) **1870** MCCLUNG *Minnesota* 148 With no other instrument than a 'pick hand-spike,' seven or eight feet long, [they] cross deep, wide, and rapid streams, standing on a single log. — (2) **1837** *N. Amer. Review* April 353 The persons who undertake it [breaking a jam] must go on to the mass of logs, work some out with their pickpoles, cut some to pieces, attach ropes to others to be hauled out by the hands on shore. **1905** WIGGIN *Rose* 4 If you come along, bring your own pick-pole. — (3) **1854** DAVIS *Farm Bk.* 105 Cleaned out the pick room to put cotton in. **1916** MASSEY *Reminiscences* 213 We slept one night in a ginhouse and 'pickroom' during a very heavy rainfall.

b. In colloq. phrases: (1) *To pick a* (or *one's*) *flint,* to roughen or renew the edge or surface of a gunflint that comes in contact with the lid of the "pan," hence, *fig.*, to get ready, prepare for a new effort; (2) **to pick up,* (*a*) to detect (a person) in a mistake, to show up, (*b*) to tidy up, put in order, (*c*) (see quot.), cf. **picked up.**

(1) **1833** FLINT *D. Boone* 79 Boone, picking the flint of his rifle, . . . took aim at the panther. **1871** *Northern Vindicator* (Estherville, Iowa) 8 July, The Blizzards [a baseball club] should pick their flints and try again. — (2) (*a*) **1846** SOL. SMITH *Theatr. Apprent.* 149 The bystanders . . . were crowding around the table in great numbers to see the fun—all considering me most undoubtedly 'picked up.' **1881** PIERSON *In the Brush* 44 He had to 'stand treat' all around among his companions, for being thus, in the vernacular of the country, 'picked up' by the preacher. (*b*) **1861** *Ill. Agric. Soc. Trans.* IV. 204 We did not find 'things picked up in it'—no air of comfort about it. **1889** FARMER 419/1 *To pick up a room,* is a New England phrase for putting it in order. (*c*) **1944** HOLTON *Yankees* 241 Aunt Melvenia or Mother, according to which house it was, would strip off the dried fish from the skin and pull it into small pieces. This was known as 'picking up' the fish.

***pickage,** *n.* The charge for "picking" or ginning cotton. *Obs.* Cf. ***pick,** *v.* **1. b.** — **1849** *De Bow's Review* VII. 486 It goes to pay warehouse charges, freight, insurance . . . weighages, *pickages,* pressage.

pickaninny 'pɪkəˌnɪnɪ, *n.* [See note.] A Negro child.

This word is the result of an attempt by African slaves to pronounce some such word as Pg. *pequenino,* little, small, a boy, or the Sp. *pequeño niño.* The earliest evidence for the word in English is from the West Indies but it may have passed from Pg. into African use in Guinea. Slaves no doubt introduced it into the U.S. See *OED s.v. piccaninny,* and an article by A. Matthews in the source of quot. 1653 below.

[**1653** in *N. & Q.* 10 Ser. IV. (1905) 129/1 Some women [in Barbados], whose pickaninnies are three yeares old, will, as they worke at weeding . . . suffer the hee Pickaninnie, to sit astride upon their backs.] *c***1770** BOUCHER *Glossary* xlix, A Pickaninny; a male infant: probably from the Spanish picade nino, pequeno nino. **1868** *Putnam's Mag.* I. 713 The result of the examination was, that I gave the pickaninny a sharp lecture on the sin of running away, and sent her back to live with her present employers. **1948** *Chi. Defender* 23 Oct. 7/3, I thought it was okay to call a little colored kid a pickaninny or report the answers of Joe Louis and Satchel Paige in Negro dialect.

attrib. **1871** MARK TWAIN *Screamers* 132 Old Mann used to own and command a pickaninny, bull-headed, mud-turtle-shaped craft of a schooner. **1873** C. GORDON *Boarding-School Days* 242 You black piccaninny debbil, I learns you p'liteness. **1903** R. BEDFORD *True Eyes* 321 By pickaninny daylight the mounted men were in motion.

***picked,** *a.* In combs.: (1) **picked brand,** *W.* (see quots. and cf. ***pick,** *v.* **7.**); (2) **over,** *a.* remaining after the best has been removed; (3) **up,** *a.* (*a*) *N. Eng.* designating a dinner warmed over from a previous meal, cf. **to pick up* (*c*), and ***pickup,** *n.* **1,** (*b*) brought together by chance, makeshift, *colloq.*, cf. ***pickup,** *n.* **1.**

(1) **1894** *McClure's Mag.* III. 113/2 A 'picked' brand . . . is accomplished by simply picking out tufts of hair . . . in the lines of the desired figure. **1944** ADAMS *W. Words* 114/2 picked brand Accomplished by picking out tufts of hair in the lines desired by the aid of a jackknife. It is seldom done except by dishonest men until they can get the animal out of the country, as it is only a temporary marking. — (2) **1839** *Cong. Globe* App. 2 Jan. 47/2 All the emigrants went on to the new lands, where they could get first choices at $1.25 per acre, because they could not give that sum for picked-over lands in the old counties. **1886** N. SHEPPARD *Before an Audience* 124 Audiences in England outside of the Established Church . . . have a picked-over appearance. The church takes the cream, the chapel the milk of society. — (3) (*a*) **1771** J. ADAMS *Diary* Wks. II. 275 We had a picked up dinner. **1867** LACKLAND *Homespun* 126 A sort of 'picked-up' dinner is set before them. **1941** *L.A.* Map. 313. (*b*) **1835** *Capt. Nath. Wyeth Jrnl.* 235 This is a picked up lot and I have great fears they will committ robbery and desertion.

***picker,** *n.*

1. A laborer or a machine that picks cotton in the fields.

1759 in COMMONS *Doc. Hist.* I. 115, [I] will suggest the propriety of sending a few trustworthy hands ahead of the regular pickers to gather from the early opening. **1891** THANET *Otto the Knight* 325 A far-away song [was] floating up from the cotton-fields filled with pickers. **1949** *Time* 28 Feb. 91/1 Seated at the controls of the big mechanical picker, he's like a man with a thousand hands, picking fabulous quantities of cotton in a single day with speed and ease.

b. A machine for gathering or picking corn. Cf. ***corn,** *n.* **4.** (17).

1946 *Harper's Mag.* Oct. 308/1 Today a giant mechanical picker goes out at dawn and brings in twelve hundred bushels before dark.

2. (See quot.)

1800 TATHAM *Tobacco* 82 The *pickers* are the first gradation of subordinate officers under the rank of inspectors.

3. (See quot. and cf. **crevicing.**)

1851 *Alta Californian* 18 Nov., 'The Pickers' is the generic name, given a year or two ago, to a class of miners in Mariposa, who, being too lazy, or not having time to sink holes themselves, would go about with a sheath knife and pan and earn their livelihood by picking among the rocks.

As the last term in **banjo, bone, copper, corn, cotton, peanut, rifle, squirrel picker.**

∗**pickerel,** *n.* In combs.: (1) **pickerel flower,** =**pickerel weed;** (2) **frog,** a frog, *Rana palustris,* found in eastern North America; (3) **State,** South Dakota, a nickname; (4) ∗**weed,** any one of various American aquatic herbs or species of herbs of the genus *Pontederia.*

(1) **1842** HAWTHORNE *Notebooks* (1932) 155 The blue spires and broad green leaves of the pickerel-flower . . . contrast and harmonize so well with the white lilies. **1867** EMERSON *May-Day* 44 Through gold-moth-haunted beds of pickerel-flowers. — (2) **1839** STORER *Mass. Reptiles* 238 The Pickerel Frog . . . is as frequently . . . met with about the margins of fresh water brooks and ponds, as in any other situations. **1906** M. C. DICKERSON *Frog Book* 189 The brook and the fields and meadows near make the home of the Pickerel Frogs. **1949** *Amer. Photography* Sep. 581/3 The pickerel frog is found throughout the eastern part of the country north to Hudson's Bay. — (3) **1899** *Mo. So. Dakotan* I. 182, I have noticed Senator Pettigrew referred to as the 'statesman from the Pickeral [*sic*] state.' — (4) **1784** CUTLER in *Amer. Acad. Mem.* I. 433 *Pontederia* . . . Pickerel-weed. Blue Spike. Blossoms blue. Common on the borders of ponds and rivers. July. **1880** *Harper's Mag.* June 70 The frog pond with lush growth of arrow leaves and pickerel weed. **1944** HOLTON *Yankees* 147 Pink lady's slippers grew in abundance among the rosy needles, and thence through a pasture along the pond shore, smelling of pickerel weed, and so to the familiar swamp again.

As the last term in **chain, yellow pickerel.**

∗**Pickering,** *n.* [Charles *Pickering* (1805–78), Amer. physician.] A small tree toad, *Hyla crucifer.* In full **Pickering frog, Pickering's hyla.**

1901 *Everybody's Mag.* April 382/2 At this time one may collect the tadpoles of pickerings and the common hyla or tree-toad. **1913** EATON *Barn Doors & Byways* 280 In the swamp the Pickering frogs were singing shrilly—*phee, phee, phee*—far above the limits of the human voice. **1949** *Amer. Photography* Sep. 581/1 The spring peeper, or Pickering's hyla is found very commonly from New Brunswick to Manitoba and south to Florida, Mississippi, Louisiana, Arkansas and Kansas.

Pickeronian ˌpɪkəˈronɪən, *n.* A political follower of Timothy Pickering (1745–1829). Also attrib. or as adj. — **1800** *Aurora* (Phila.) 16 May (Th.), The three parties are now known by the designation of the Republicans, the Adamites, the Pickeronians. *Ib.* 19 May (Th.), The Pickeronian columns either led or directed every odious measure which has been brought forward. **1809** *Ann. 10th Congress* 2 Sess. 1065 No Administration, even if composed of Adamites, Pickeronians, Jeffersonians, and Madisonians . . . could uphold this navy system in time of peace.

Pickeroon ˌpɪkəˈrun, *n.* =prec. *Obs.* — **1800** *Aurora* (Phila.) 3 Sep. (Th.), The bloody and remorseless character of the Hamiltonians and Pickeroons. **1808** *Essex* (Mass.) *Reg.* 2 April (Th.), Let the Lacoites, the Kitites, the Pickeroons, the Refugees, the Tories, the British, and the whole Federal fry that follows them, be convinced [etc.].

pickery ˈpɪkərɪ, *n.* =**cotton pickery.** *Obs.* — **1851** *De Bow's Review* XI. 693 One of these presses may be seen at the Pickery in New Orleans.

∗**picket,** *n.*

1. A portion of a tree trunk set upright in the ground to form part of a stockade or barrier, esp. as a defense against hostile Indians. *Obs.*

1785 DENNY *Journal* 59 All hands set to work chopping, clearing &c., and preparing timber for block-houses and pickets. **1807** GASS *Journal* 42 The pickets are 13½ feet above ground. **1843** HAWKS *D. Boone* 57 The fort consisted of several cabins, surrounded by pickets ten feet high, planted firmly in the ground.

b. The stockade formed by such timbers.

1833 CATLIN *Indians* I. 81 The piquet is composed of timbers . . . eighteen feet high, set firmly in the ground at sufficient distances from each other to admit of guns and other missiles to be fired between them. **1838** INGRAHAM *Burton* I. 219 In advance . . . , about two hundred yards, stood a blockhouse protected by a picket.

2. A thin, narrow strip of wood used as a lath or as a paling for a fence.

1853 FOWLER *Home for All* 109 All the outside walls or inclosing to be of pickets or strips of common refuse stuff, about four inches wide. **1871** EGGLESTON *Hoosier Schoolm.* 92 Miss Martha Hawkins, . . . leaning over the palings—pickets she called them—of the garden fence, talking to the master. **1897** BRODHEAD *Bound in Shallows* 102 The pickets of the Morrows' fence struck white upon the road-side shadows.

3. A rifle bullet of .451″ diameter having a conoidal front and a hemispherical base.

The Col. Pickett of quot. 1904 has not been identified.

1858 DEANE *Hist. & Sc. Fire-arms* 263 A form of conical projectile used and called a 'picket' in the United States, and also used in several of the German states. [**1868** *Rep. to Govt. U.S. on Munitions War* 14 (Boxer ammunition), The bullet has a picket of wood running through its centre half-way from the apex of the cone towards the base. *Ib.* 16 The bullet, as in the Boxer, has the wooden picket through half its longer axis, and the clay plug in the base for expansion. **1904** E. S. FARROW *Amer. Small Arms* 56 This bullet was made for Col. Pickett, the well-known grizzly bear killer. It is for patching with paper. The mould has extra long bearing for core-peg. *Ib.* 63 This is the famous Col Pickett's .45–325 patched, express bullet.]

4. In combs.: (1) **picket header,** a machine for shaping the heads of pickets (sense **2.**); (2) **pin,** *W.* (*a*) a pin or stake to be driven into the ground in tethering a horse, also fig., (*b*) any one of various small ground squirrels of the genus *Citellus,* so called in allusion to their appearance when sitting erect as they often do, also **picket-pin gopher;** (3) **rope,** *W.* a rope used in picketing a horse or mule, also attrib.; (4) **wire,** ?a wire fence, *obs.*

(1) **1883** *Harper's Mag.* Jan. 208/2 To them [*sc.* mills] are attached planers, shingle machines, picket headers, and so on. — (2) (*a*) **1847**

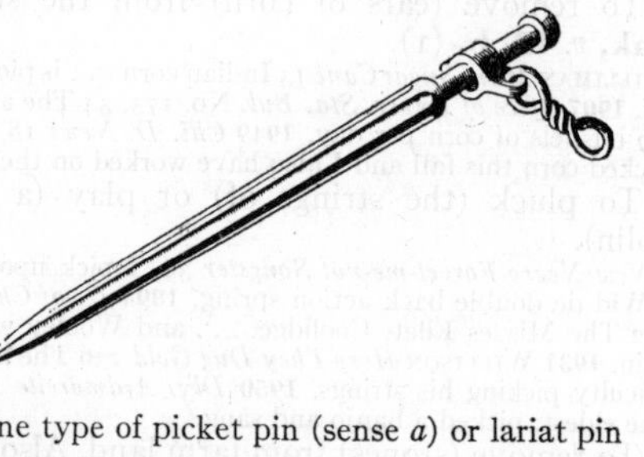

One type of picket pin (sense *a*) or lariat pin

RUXTON *Adv. Rocky Mts.* (1848) 211 The half-frozen animals, standing over their picket-pins and collapsed with cold. **1897** LEWIS *Wolfville* 26 The fact's done pulled its picket-pin an' strayed from my recollections. (*b*) **1936** *Univ. Ariz. Gen. Bul.* 3, 79 Last of the ground squirrels to be mentioned are the small ones . . . variously known over the West as spermophiles, picket-pin gophers, or simply ground squirrels. **1947** CAHALANE *Mammals* 342 They spend a great deal of their time sitting straight up on their haunches, their backs and necks as straight as ramrods. For this reason they are often called 'picket pins.' — (3) **1834** in *N. Mex. Hist. Rev.* II. (1927) 298 The Acting Asst. Qr Master will have prepared a suitable number of wooden posts for the support of the Picket rope. **1874** G. C. EGGLESTON *Rebel's Recoll.* 37 One young gentleman . . . [found] himself assigned to a picket rope post, where his only duty was to guard the horses. **1946** *Sierra Club Bul.* Dec. 4 We had carried with us all of our pack and picket ropes that could be spared. — (4) **1860** OLMSTEAD *Back Country* 280 Half the streets tolerably good pastures, . . . the best gardens in a setting of picket wire. [**1929** DOBIE *Vaquero* 161 My route now turned up the stream known to early-day Spaniards as Rio de las Animas; to the French as the Purgatoire; and to the Mountain Men and American bull-whackers as the Picketwire.]

b. Designating inclosures, structures, etc., made of pickets (sense **1.** or **2.**), as (1) **picket corral,** (2) **fence,** (3) **fort,** (4) **gate,** (5) **house,** (6) **hut,** (7) **lane,** (8) **paling,** (9) **shack,** (10) **stockade,** (11) **work,** (12) **yard.**

(1) *a***1918** G. STUART *On Frontier* II. 127 They have a picket corral of box elder logs . . . where they corral their horses every night. — (2) **1800** *Boston Carpenters' Rules* 32 (Ernst), Plain picket open fence. **1949** *News-Herald* (Marshfield, Wis.) 19 July 3/4 Did you ever try to build a picket fence? — (3) **1775** *Mass. H.S. Coll.* 2 Ser. II. 230 This fort consists of two large block-houses, and a large barrack, which is

enclosed with a picket fort. **1827** McKENNEY *Tour to Lakes* 141 The old fort . . . was only a *picket*-fort, and on the water's edge. **1846** —— *Memoirs* I. 127 The old picket fort standing on the plain. — **(4) 1857** TOMES *Americans in Japan* 317 The streets of Hakodadi . . . are subdivided into various wards by means of picket-gates, which cross from side to side, and are closed after dark. **1874** *Vt. Bd. Agric. Rep.* II. 515, I have also fitted in one end of the bay a comfortable room for my hens, . . . using picket gates to each of the stairways to prevent them from coming up into the upper part of the barn.

(5) 1863 *Rio Abajo Press* 20 Jan. 3/2 A certain lot situated in the town of Mesilla, . . . and on which is erected a picket house. **1884** ALDRIDGE *Life on Ranch* 171 Beyond that was a picket-house, where the men slept, one room of which was fitted up as a blacksmith's forge, and another used as a saddle-room and storehouse for corn. **1943** L. V. HAMNER *Short Grass* 6 Along the creeks, picket houses of slender poles, set in a trench, with mud daubed between the pickets, were used. — **(6) 1844** GREGG *Commerce of Prairies* I. 206 Wood buildings of any kind or shape are utterly unknown in the north of Mexico, with the exception of an occasional picket-hut in some of the ranchos and mining places. — **(7) 1902** *Conjuror's House* 38 The great trading-house attracted his attention, with its narrow picket lane leading to the door. — **(8) 1857** *Atlantic Mo.* I. 97/1 It is a square area of two acres in extent, inclosed by a mossy picket paling. — **(9) 1927** SIRINGO *Riata* 80 At midnight our crowd ushered in the new year of 1881, in front of our picket shack.

(10) 1860 CLAIBORNE *Sam. Dale* 110 Fort Wayne—a mere picket stockade, garrisoned by only one company—resisted for several days a combined attack led by Tecumseh. — **(11) 1804** CLARK in *Lewis & C. Exped.* I. (1904) 208 The [Mandan] Village . . . containes houses in a kind of Picket work. **1842** *Amer. Pioneer* I. 236 This horn-work, as well as the fort itself, was a mere stockade or picket work. — **(12) 1845** *Big Bear Ark.* 60 'Twarnt but a little squar picket yard.

c. *on picket*, engaged in service as a sentry, also *from picket. Colloq.*

1775 in JOHNSTON *N. Hale* 158 Your being on Picquet is a sufficient excuse that you wrote no more. **1861** NORTON *Army Lett.* 34, I have just returned from picket. **1899** *Mo. So. Dakotan* I. 159 An accidental discharge of a gun one night in the hands of a man on picket. **1944** PENNELL *Rome Hanks* 41 You're on picket, aren't you?

***picketing,** *n.* A stockade or palisade made of pickets (sense **1.**). *Obs.*

1755 *N.H. Hist. Soc. Coll.* V. 254 Seven men . . . [were] getting a few poles to complete the new picketing of the fort. **1813** *Niles' Reg.* IV. 12/2 An order was given to retreat within the picqueting. **1860** CLAIBORNE *Sam. Dale* 25 These forts were merely a number of log cabins built around a small square, . . . the whole surrounded by a rough picketing.

***picking,** *n.* In combs., usu. obs., relating chiefly to removing the seed from, or harvesting, cotton, as (1) **picking bee,** (2) **day,** (3) **frolic,** (4) **time.**

(1) 1828 CHARLES GREEN (unpublished letter), Mother went to a picking Bee to pick wool the week Before She Deseased. **1943** MENEFEE *Assignment* 48 In 1943 the townspeople were prepared to turn out for a picking-bee lasting most of the season, if necessary, to save the crop. — **(2) 1880** *Bradstreet's* 13 Oct. 3/2 From 25 to 30 picking days have been lost. — **(3) 1807** JANSON *Stranger in Amer.* 370 Private families gin their cotton by the hand. . . . Sometimes they invite their acquaintances to what they call 'a picking frolic,' at which, after the visitors have duly performed their task, they are regaled with a supper, and the evening concludes with a reel or country dance. — **(4) 1835** INGRAHAM *South-West* II. 285 'Picking time' . . . continues where full crops are made until the first of December. **1949** MURRAY *This Our Land* 87 Picking time begins about August 20.

As the last term in **corn, cotton, easy, wool picking.**

pickleworm ˈpɪkl̩ˌwɜm, *n.* The larva of a moth, *Diaphania nitidalis*, of the family Pyralididae (see quot.). — **1870** *Amer. Naturalist* IV. 614 A new pest to the cucumber in the West, the Pickle worm, . . . is a caterpillar which bores into the cucumbers when large enough to pickle, and it is occasionally found in pickles.

***pickup,** *n.* and *a.*

1. (See quot. 1848.) Also **pickup dinner.** *Colloq.*

1848 BARTLETT 249 A *pick-up*, or a *pick-up* dinner, is a dinner made up of such fragments of cold meats as remain from former meals. The word is common in the Northern States. **1934** CARMER *Stars Fell* 94 A ham and a chicken and a roast are served with . . . beaten biscuit and corn bread, a salad and a watermelon, for just a 'pick-up potluck dinner.' **1948** *Chi. Tribune* 11 July (Grafic Mag.) 18/1 The only pick-ups I like are out of the icebox around midnight. Scram!

b. Anything, as a bargain, obtained as chance offers. *Colloq.*

1930 *San Antonio* (Texas) *Light* 31 Jan. 14/7 (*advt.*), A real pickup for someone: 50 feet on Broadway. . . . An exceptional site. **1930** *Publishers' Wkly.* 19 April 2111 Should traveler's discounts be allowed on *pickups?*

2. A nugget of gold picked by hand. *Rare.*

1905 REX BEACH *Pardners* i. (1912) 29 By Christmas we had a streak uncovered that was all gold. She was coarse, and we averaged six ounces a day in pick-ups.

3. A relatively small, light automobile truck for light hauling. In full **pickup truck.** Also **pickup body,** a small, detachable body for use on various types of light trucks.

1932 *K.C. Times* 21 Jan. 22 There was a delivery car with a pick-up body on it in King City, Monday. **1944** *Democrat* 29 June 1/4 This includes all operators of trucks and pickups whose gasoline rations are not controlled through the local War Price and Ration Board. **1948** *So. Sierran* April 4/1 The work will be made lighter if someone will provide the use of a pick-up truck for removing the dirt.

***picnic,** *n.* A small piece of shoulder bacon cut somewhat in the shape of a ham. In full **picnic ham.**

1910 L. D. HALL *Market Classes of Meat*, Picnics or Calas (formerly termed California hams) are cut 2-½ ribs wide. . . . They . . . are sold almost entirely as sweet-pickled, smoked and boiled meats. **1944** *Chi. D. News* 13 July 21/2 A picnic ham may be boned, rolled and tied before roasting to make carving easier. **1949** *New Harmony* (Ind.) *Times* 5 Aug. 6/2 Smoked Picnics, 3 to 5 lb. average lb. 45 c.

As the last term in **basket, stag picnic.**

***picture,** *n.*

1. *pl.* Playing cards. *Slang. Obs.*

1853 SIMMS *Sword & Distaff* (1854) 275, I hev' the pictars in my own hand. **1855** —— *Forayers* 506 Flirting the cars at 'old sledge' from well-thumbed and greasy packs of 'pictures.'

2. In combs.: (1) **picture bride,** a woman, esp. a Japanese, admitted to this country on a sponsor's proving by a photograph that she is his fiancée; (2) **paper,** a newspaper or similar publication consisting wholly or chiefly of pictures, also **pictured paper,** *obs.*; (3) **show,** a showing or exhibition of pictures, a motion picture show; (4) **store,** a store at which pictures are sold.

(1) 1913 *Sunset* July, Fifty-two per cent of the Japanese arrivals by ship at the port of San Francisco are women—'picture brides.' **1920** *Pacific Review* Dec. 355 'Picture brides' have been brought in and upon their arrival set to work on the farm. — **(2) 1852** *Lantern* (N.Y.) II. 154/1 Folks here are tired of the jabber of your great city papers. . . . Truth is, we want pictured papers—we've enough home made gammon in our own. **1867** *Harper's Mag.* 2 Feb. 80/1 I'm sure, Dear, the Picture Papers can not make Frights of us now! **1907** *St. Nicholas* June 678/1 The little knicknack shop around the corner [sells] picture papers, spruce gum, needles and Malaga raisins. — **(3) 1881** CARLETON *Farm Festivals* 69 'Twas a picture-show, a lecture, and a sermon — all united. **1925** *Scribner's Mag.* Oct. 430/1 There's young people and parties, and a picture-show every night. — **(4) 1856** *Spirit of Times* 15 Nov. 174/3 She requests an interview at W. & S.'s picture store, in the city. **1884** *Cent. Mag.* Oct. 874/2, I went to see the landscapes at Radfield's picture-store.

b. In slang phrases: (1) *Consarn* (*blast, drat,* etc.) *your* (or *his*) *picture*, damn him, you; (2) *to spoil one's picture*, to mutilate one's face, as in fighting; (3) *to be high up in the pictures, to be in the picture*, to be highly successful or of importance; (4) *to break into pictures*, to become a motion picture worker, esp. as an actor or actress, cf. ***break,** *v.* **12. b.** (9).

(1) 1825 J. NEAL *Bro. Jonathan* 387 Young Bob's dad—consarn his pictur! **1843** *Yale Lit. Mag.* IX. 79 Is that the way the Britishers larnt ye to treat a gal, blast your infarnal pictur! **1875** WINANS *Reminiscences* 63 Consarn yer picter, young feller—see what you've done. **1904** HOLLEY *Samantha at St. Louis Exposition* 164 Whoa! back up! Dum your dum picter! Whoa I say! **1926** *Mt. Life* (Berea, Ky.) 8/2 A member might say 'doggon,' 'dadburn' or 'blame my picture,' but if he used stronger expletives . . . it might mean excommunication at the next meeting. — **(2) 1835** *Vade Mecum* (Phila.) 14 Feb. 3/1 If I ketch him—burn his skin—I'll spile his pickter. **1846** DURIVAGE *Stray Subjects* 167 Ef I could only come across that ere Vermonter which I was took in by, if I wouldn't spile his picter, bust my boots and gallowses! **1847** ROBB *Squatter Life* 137, I jest swar a bible oath, I'd spile his pictur' so he couldn't enjoy campmeetin' much. — **(3) 1851** *Polly Peablossom* 147 He was gettin' too high up in the pictures enny how. **1902** C. MORRIS *Stage Confidences* 202 Oh, well, I feel that I am in the picture, when I wear black during Lent. — **(4) 1925** *Motion Picture* Oct. 54/1 She played the good fairy when I was trying to break into pictures. **1948** MENJOU & MUSSELMAN *It Took 9 Tailors* 76 While there, I would try to break into pictures in Hollywood.

As the last term in **cigarette, clock picture.**

pictured rocks. Rocks upon which quaint designs have been produced by weathering, usu. applied as a proper name to sandstone cliffs about 300 feet high in

Alger County, Michigan, along the shore of Lake Superior.

1820 in NUTE *Lk. Superior* (1944) 73 It is only 12 miles from LaGrand Sable to the Pictured Rocks, one of natures works of grandeur and sublimity. . . . They are called the pictured rocks from the circumstance of their being variegated with the veins of different kinds of ore running through, and colouring the surface. **1857** CHANDLESS *Visit Salt Lake* 121 Travelling . . . over steep ridges, beside pictured rocks (on the right hand, never on the left). **1902** HULBERT *Forest Neighbors* 158 From Lake Huron to the Pictured Rocks. **1946** NEWTON *P. Bunyan* 180 They came out on the shore of Lake Superior, on the high plateau of the Pictured Rocks.

pided ˈpaɪdɪd, *a.* [Var. of **pied.*] Parti-colored, marked with different colors in patches or blotches. *Colloq.*

1757 *S.C. Gazette* Supp. 23 June, A black and white pided cow . . . a red and white pided heifer. **1845** HOOPER *Simon Sugg's Adv.* 144 The old feller looked as pided as a rattle-snaik. **1930** RAINE & BARNES *Cattle* 300, I just saw the old piedied steer we lost out of the herd last fall.

***pie,** *n.*

1. *fig.* Political patronage, graft. *Slang.*

1879 *Dly. Telegraph* (Lond.) 26 Dec., Men may come and men may go; the Grant 'Boom' may be succeeded by the Sherman 'Boom;' but Pie goes on for ever. **1916** *N.Y. Times* 12 May, Take your tribute but buy national defense with it, don't waste it in 'pork' and 'pie' and Populist lunacies!

Hence **pie counter, pie hunter.**

1898 *K.C. Star* 20 Dec. 5/1 Early arrivals talked of abolishing unnecessary offices and reducing the number of appointments. This smoked out the pie-hunters of both parties. **1903** *N.Y. Times* 15 Dec. 3 When his constituents asked him why he could not secure more routes [for postal free delivery] the only reply he could make was that he could not get up to the 'pie counter.'

2. *fig.* Something quite easy, a treat, a cinch, also *easy as pie. Slang.*

1889 *Outing* Nov. 150/2, I thought it would just be pie for me to buy him, and take him through the 'bushes.' **1905** N. DAVIS *Northerner* 93 It will be just . . . pie for them, won't it? **1948** *Chi. Tribune* 27 June II. 27/3 'Sure,' said Sam. 'Easy as pie.'

3. In special combs. and derivatives: (1) **pie à la mode,** pie served with ice cream on it; (2) **belt,** (see quot.); (3) **biter,** see as a main entry; (4) **buggy,** *W.* a ranch wagon sent to town for supplies, *facetious, obs.;* (5) **card,** a meal ticket; (6) **-eyed,** *a.* drunk, *slang;* (7) **fork,** a fork for use in eating pie; (8) **knife,** a knife used in serving pies; (9) **social,** =next; (10) **supper,** a social gathering at which the supper consists of pies made and sold, usu. for some charitable purpose; (11) **wagon,** (*a*) (see quots.), (*b*) a roadside diner or vehicular lunch stand, *slang.*

One form of pie wagon

(1) **1929** *Ladies' Home Jrnl.* April 96/3 Apple pie à la mode—there's a real man's dessert! **1947** *So. Sierran* Nov. 1/2 A delicious dinner of roast beef and apple pie a la mode was made doubly enjoyable by the spirited community singing . . . and the distribution of a surprising number of door prizes. — (2) **1939** WOLCOTT *Yankee Cook Book* 126 New England, as everyone knows, is supposed to be the Pie Belt and when a Down-Easter thinks of pie he sets the buckle forward a notch. — (4) **1890** *Stock Grower & Farmer* 28 June 3/4 Why I have seen half a hundred 'pie buggies' standing on our streets in one day, waiting for a chance to get up to a grocery to load up with swine bosom, flour, canned goods, etc. — (5) **1908** DAVENPORT *Butte Beneath X-Ray* 56 Say, Andy, you've just got to jar loose with five bucks for my pie card is so full of holes it looks like a piece of mosquito bar. — (6) **1909** S. E. WHITE *Rules of Game* I. 102 'Oh, he's in town. . . .' 'Drunk, eh?' 'Spifflicated, pie-eyed, loaded, soshed.' **1924** *T.P.'s & Cassell's Wkly.* 6 Sep. 631/1 He is partial to a 'shot of gin,' and on occasion will drink till he is 'pie-eyed.' — (7) **1887** C. B. GEORGE *40 Yrs. on Rail* ix. 187 An exquisite set of pie forks, of English make, and valued at seventy-five dollars. — (8) **1875** STOWE *We & Neighbors* 474 Of course the reader knows that there were the usual amount of berry-spoons, and pie-knives, and crumb-scrapers. — (9) **1929** *Randolph Enterprise* (Elkins, W.Va.) 14 March 1/5 There will be a pie social at the Ivy Hill School House. . . . The proceeds will go for the benefit of the school. **1947** *Steamboat* (Colo.) *Pilot* 30 Jan. 4/2 There will be a pie social at the Pleasant View school house.

(10) **1931** *Durant* (Okla.) *D. Democrat* 5 Feb. 1/1 A pie supper and candidate meeting will be held at the east ward school house. **1948** *Dly. Oklahoman* (Okla. City) 31 Oct. D. 6/1 They sent the price of pie skyrocketing at a pie supper to raise money for horns and drums. — (11) (*a*) **1929** HOSTETTER & BEESLEY *It's a Racket* 234 Pie Wagon—police patrol wagon. **1944** ADAMS *W. Words* 115 pie wagon A trailer used behind the chuck wagon. (*b*) **1939** *These Are Our Lives* 235 From the cheap radio above the counter, where Gus the owner of the pie wagon leaned chewing on a match stick, the pant and grunt of a Negro singer came through a hammering beat of orchestration.

b. In the names of plants: (1) **pie marker,** (see quot.); (2) **melon,** a melon used for pies, *obs.;* (3) **plant,** see as a main entry; (4) **print,** =**pie marker;** (5) **rhubarb,** =**pieplant 1;** (6) **squash,** a squash suitable for making pies.

(1) **1899** *Animal & Plant Lore* 120 *Abutilon Avicennae* is called 'butter-print,' 'pie-print,' and 'pie-marker,' because its pods are used to stamp butter or pie crust. Ohio, Illinois, Iowa, and Missouri. — (2) **1859** *Trans. Mich. Agric. Soc.* X. (1860) 623 Best pie melon, H. J. Young . . . $0.50. — (4) **1899** [see **pie marker**].

(5) **1817–8** EATON *Botany* (1822) 442 *Rheum tataricum,* pie rhubarb. **1857** GRAY *Botany* 378 *Rheum Rhaponticum* is the Pie Rhubarb, so commonly cultivated for the sake of its fleshy and acid esculent leaf-stalks. — (6) **1886** *Colo. Springs Republican* 21 Oct. 1/2 It reports the gift of forty pie squash.

4. In colloq. phrases: (1) *To cut a pie,* to meddle in a matter; (2) *as short as piecrust,* impatient, testy, snappish; (3) *as nice* (or *good*) *as pie,* very nice or agreeable; (4) *to have enough pie,* to be done for, used up.

(1) **1843** HALIBURTON *Attaché* Ser. xi, By gosh, Aunty, . . . you had better not cut that pie: you will find it rather sour in the apple sarse, and tough in the paste. — (2) *c*1849 PAIGE *Dow's Sermons* I. 287, I feel as short as pie-crust. I mean to put it to all the women in creation, in the hardest kind of style. **1851** NORTHALL *Curtain* 174 None of them will speak to you, or if they do, they are as short as pie-crust. — (3) **1847** PAIGE *Dow's Sermons* I. 21 (Th.), Let her alone and in five minutes the storm will be over, and she as good as pie again. **1917** MCCUTCHEON *Green Fancy* 275 He is as nice as pie this afternoon. — (4) **1866** MARK TWAIN *Lett. Sandwich Isl.* 77 In the sorrowful expression of its deserted halls . . . and its decayed magnificence, it seems to proclaim, in the homely phrase of California, that it has 'got enough pie.'

As the last term in **chicken, cream, custard, Eskimo, family, fruit, grasshopper, huckleberry, jack, lemon, Marlborough, meat, pan, pea, pecan, pot, pumpkin, sand, scuppernong, shoofly, smoky, squash, sweet potato, vinegar, Washington pie.**

pie-biter ˈpaɪˌbaɪtɚ, *n.* One who is fond of pie; an adept at biting through pies. Also transf. *Slang.*

1868 *Terr. Enterprise* (Virginia, Nev.) 2 April 3/1 Through these same [April fool] doughnuts many a lunch-eater and pie-biter came to grief. **1890** LANGFORD *Vigilante Days* (1912) 308 [Hilderman] was the original of the story of 'The Great American Pie-biter.' This feat of spreading his jaws so as to bite through seven of Kustar's dried-apple pies, had been frequently performed by him. **1902** WISTER *Virginian* ix, You're a plumb pie-biter. **1938** DOUTHITT *Romance & Dim Trails* 106 [He was] better known over the northwest and in camp life as Pie Biter, because he was very fond of pie.

***piece,** *n.*[1]

1. An article or item of baggage.

1890 *Railways of Amer.* 253 The cases in which pieces go astray are astonishingly rare. **1914** STEELE *Storm* 274 The man on the steps had taken up his luggage, but now he put the two pieces down again.

2. In combs.: (1) **piece bag,** a little bag for small pieces or odds and ends of cloth; (2) **box,** =prec.; (3) ***work,** designating a bedquilt made up of small pieces of cloth sewed together.

(1) **1869** ALCOTT *Little Women* II. 11 So rich a supply of dusters, holders, and piece-bags. **1900** DIX *Deacon Bradbury* 251 Mr. Bradbury

. . . sought his wife, who was upstairs sorting over her piece-bag. — (2) **1898** M. DELAND *Old Chester Tales* 272 It has been lying there in my piece-box for six years. — (3) **1842** KIRKLAND *Forest Life* I. 90 No gorgeous piece-work bed-quilts exhibiting stars of all magnitudes and moons in all quarters.

b. In colloq. and fig. phrases: (1) *To speak a piece*, in school, to recite or repeat a memorized piece of prose or poetry before one's schoolmates as an exercise in elocution, also *to speak one's piece*, to unburden oneself of one's opinions or views; (2) *to be cut off the same piece of goods*, to be of the same kind.

(1) **1865** BROWNE *A. Ward; His Travels* 128, I have spoken my Piece about the Ariel. **1890** *Harper's Mag.* Dec. 139/2 Don't you want to hear me speak my piece? **1902** O. HENRY *Heart of West* 167, I spoke my piece, explaining how the Brazilian diamonds and the fire kindler were laying up sufficient treasure to guarantee the happiness of two. **1949** *No. Dak. Hist.* Jan. 23 He didn't like recitations, and would rather hunt rabbits, than speak pieces. — (2) **1905** WIGGIN *Rose* 41 He wa'n't cut off the same piece o' goods as the other Watermans.

As the last term in **bail, bed, bosom, breech, burned, cat, fifty-cent, five-cent, five-center, forty-acre, hand, horse, Mexico, middle, mourning, one-cent, sight, string, twenty-cent piece.**

piece pis, *n.*[2] [f. voyageur F. *pièce*, in the sense shown here.] (See quots.) *Obs.* or *hist.*

1809 A. HENRY *Travels* 15 The freight of a canoe . . . consists in sixty *pieces*, or packages, of merchandize, of the weight of from ninety to a hundred pounds each. **1944** *Military Surgeon* Aug. 90/1 The standard bag of the middle plains, which came to be known as a *piece* of pemmican, was about the size of our usual pillow cases. A *piece* was reckoned at 90 pounds although in practice the bags ranged over and under that weight. **1949** *World-Herald Mag.* (Omaha) 19 June 5/2 In the north, 80 pounds is considered a 'piece.' . . . In the days of the early fur traders that was considered a proper load of skins for a man.

b. (See quot.) *Obs.*

1847 LANMAN *Summer in Wild.* 106 By one piece they [i.e., Indian medicine men] mean a blanket, a pair of leggings, a knife, a gun, or any other useful article.

***piece,** *v. tr.* To make (a quilt) by sewing together small pieces or scraps. — **1884** WILKINS in *Harper's Mag.* July 304/2 They won't . . . hev to piece quilts fur a livin'. **1938** *Cattleman* May 12/3 She devoted much of her time to knitting and piecing quilts.

Portion of a pieced quilt

***pied,** *a.* In combs.: (1) **pied-bill dabchick,** =next; (2) **-billed grebe,** the American dabchick, *Podilymbus podiceps;* (3) **corn,** corn the grains of which are of various colors, *rare;* (4) **duck,** a black duck, *Camptorhynchus labradorius*, with white head and markings, now extinct, cf. **sand shoal duck.**

(1) **1731** CATESBY *Carolina* I. 91 The Pied-Bill Dopchick. . . . These Birds frequent fresh water-ponds in many of the inhabited parts of Carolina. **1828** BONAPARTE *Synopsis* 418 The Pied-bill Dobchick, *Podiceps carolinensis*, . . . inhabits the whole continent of America. — (2) **1839** PEABODY *Mass. Birds* 377 The Pied-Billed Grebe, or Dobchick, *Podiceps Carolinensis*, comes to us from the north early in autumn. **1917** *Birds of Amer.* I. 8 The Pied-billed Grebe . . . is a more accomplished swimmer than any duck of which I have knowledge. **1949** *Nat. Hist.* March 134 The Pied-billed Grebe's habit of drawing a 'blanket' over its nest makes it an interesting study in bird behavior. — (3) **1887** *Courier-Journal* 27 Jan. 7/7 Pied or Mixed Corn. First premium, T. J. Tichenor. — (4) **1637** MORTON *New Canaan* 68 Ducks there are of three kindes, pide Ducks, gray Ducks, and black Ducks in great abundance. **1875** *Fur, Fin, & Feather* (ed. 3) 119 Of the various fowl called vulgarly coot, are the pied-duck, . . the surf-duck . . . and the American scoter.

***Piedmont,** *n.* An upland region immediately east of the Blue Ridge and Appalachian mountains and extending from New York to Alabama. Usu. attrib. or as adj.

1755 in *Amer. Sp.* XXI. (1946) 118/1 Between the South Mountain and the hither Chain of the Endless Mountains . . . is the most considerable Quantity of valuable Land that the English are possest of; and runs through New-Jersey, Pennsilvania, Mariland and Virginia. It has yet obtained no general Name, but may properly be called *Piemont*, from its Situation. **1855** *S. Lit. Messenger* XXI. 672/2 The next breadth of country, known in several of the States as the Piedmont district, was more salubrious in its atmosphere. **1927** in *Amer. Sp.* XV. 295/1 A contour line through the falls of these rivers marks the boundary between Tidewater Virginia and that region which rolling upward to the foothills of the Appalachians is today known as the Piedmont Plateau. **1949** *Highway Traveler* Feb. 33/1 The State Garden Club and affiliated clubs will have on display gardens from the sunny southeast through the coastal plain and piedmont plateau.

Hence **Piedmonter,** an inhabitant of this region.

1941 DANIELS *Tar Heels* 337 Like the Piedmonters', their contempt is for their own cousins.

Piegan ˈpigən, *n.* [f. native name *Pikuni*, in allusion to their badly dressed robes.] One of the tribes of the Blackfoot confederacy, or an Indian of such a tribe.

1790 UMFREVILLE *Present State of Hudson's Bay* 200 The Black-foot, Paegan, and Blood Indians. These Indians, though divided into three tribes, are all one nation, speak the same language, and have the same customs. **1868** *N.Y. Herald* 29 July 5/2 The Gros-Ventres have agreed . . . to keep peace with the whites and all the Indian tribes save the Pagons and Blackfeet. **1910** HODGE *Amer. Indians* II. 246/2 In 1858 the Piegan in the United States were estimated to number 3,700. **1949** *Nat. Hist.* May 195/2 The Blackfoot Confederacy includes, beside the Blood, the South and North Piegans and the Northern Blackfoot tribes.

Also **Piegan Indian.**

1938 THOMPSON *High Trails* 104 It is called Roes Basin, a corruption of Rose Basin, the name Grinnell bestowed in honor of his hunting companion, Charles Rose, a half-breed Piegan Indian. **1948** *Time* 5 July 31/1 Said a 72-year-old Piegan Indian in Alberta last week: '. . . Leave us alone.'

pieplant ˈpaɪˌplænt, *n.*

1. The garden rhubarb, *Rheum rhaponticum*, the tender esculent leafstalks of which are used in making pies.

1847 WEBSTER 825/2 *Pie-plant, Pie-rhubarb*, the garden rhubarb, used as a substitute for apples in making pies. **1930** FERBER *Cimarron* 44 Mother Bridget was in the Mission vegetable garden, superintending the cutting of great rosy stalks of late pie plant. **1949** *Hobbies* Sep. 114/2 With all their new-found modus-operendis they do not hold a candle to Grandma's pie plant.

transf. and *attrib.* **1870** MARK TWAIN *Screamers* 58 (R.), You are the loser by this rupture, not me, Pie-plant. **1884** NYE *Baled Hay* 207 Afterward pulverize and spread over the pie plant bed. **1908** DAVENPORT *Butte Beneath X-Ray* 17 The conversation finally drifted upon the subject of Butte's favorite dessert—cream pie, mince pie, pieplant pie.

2. A preparation of rhubarb, esp. one that can be spread like butter. In full **pieplant butter.**

1855 *Amer. Inst. N.Y. Trans.* 401 The following list of the prices of the preserved fruits. . . . Pie-plant, in square glass bottles, holding over 2 lbs. weight, [cost] $5.00 [per dozen bottles]. **1885** *Buckeye Cookery* 251 *Pie-plant Butter* . . . is a nice preserve, and children should be encouraged to eat it during the winter.

***Pierce,** *n. attrib.* Of or pertaining to a democratic faction made up of those in accord with the political views of Franklin Pierce (1804–69), 14th President of the U.S. (1853–57). *Obs.*

1855 *N.Y. Wkly. Tribune* 17 March 4/1 Our dispatches from New-Hampshire proclaim the triumphant success of the combined forces of the Whigs, Free-Soilers, Know-Nothings, and Anti-Nebraska Democrats, over the Pierce Nebraska party of that State. **1855** HAMBLETON *H. A. Wise* 240 N. P. Banks, Jr., is triumphantly re-elected from the seventh district against the combined opposition of the Pierce democracy and the whigs. **1901** CHURCHILL *Crisis* 9 He . . . was a Pierce Democrat, who looked with complacency on the extension of slavery.

Pierced Nose. =**Nez Percé.** Also attrib.

1805 CLARK in *Lewis & C. Exped.* III. (1905) 78 They call themselves the *Cho pun-nish* or *Pierced noses.* **1837** IRVING *Bonneville* I. 183 A Pierced-nose chief, named Blue John by the whites. **1855** KIP *Diary of Indian Council* 11 The Nez Perces, or pierced-nose Indians, received their name from the early traders.

* **pig,** *n.*

1. = * **whaleback.** In full **pigboat.** Now *hist.*

1898 *N. Amer. Rev.* June 723 Whalebacks, or 'pigs,' as the lake sailors call them. **1949** *Sat. Ev. Post* 16 April 162/2 Called whalebacks, they had pointed prows and rounded sides, and quickly earned the name 'pigboat' from sailors.

2. In special combs.: (1) **pig and whistle,** (see quots.), *obs.;* (2) **bank,** a small savings bank in the form of a little pig; (3) **box (boat),** app. a boat of a boxlike shape, *obs.;* (4) * **club,** an organization of young people, usu. farm boys, interested in learning the best methods of pig raising; (5) **corral,** a pigpen, *rare;* (6) **drover,** =**hog drover,** *obs.;* (7) **fish,** any one of various fishes which have some characteristic suggestive of a pig; (8) **iron baron,** a man of wealth dominant in the pig iron industry; (9) * **nut,** see as a main entry; (10) * **pen,** (*a*) (see quot.), *obs.,* (*b*) *W.* a form of brand, *obs.;* (11) **-'sfoot corner,** (see quot.), *obs.;* (12) * **skin,** a football, *colloq.;* (13) **tight,** *a.* of a fence, secure against pigs' getting through it, cf. **bull strong;** (14) **wick,** any one of various small grebes, *colloq.* [the source and significance of this name are not clear].

(1) 1839 *Spirit of Times* 26 Oct. 397/3 (We.), He has since taken . . . three coblers and two pig and whistles. **1846** CORCORAN *Pickings* 75 A 'pig and whistle' is the only reg'lar eye-opener. — **(2) 1909** *Sat. Ev. Post* 13 March 35/2 The girl bought a china pig savings-bank, and the couple began dropping spare change into it. **1948** *Chi. Tribune* 12 Dec. (Comics) 11 Look at the funny pig bank—and the swell A-B-C books to color. — **(3) 1856** *Spirit of Times* 6 Dec. 226/1 Allow your bay-man to fill the bottom of the pig-box . . . with lots of *wet* salt hay. *Ib.*, The gentleman . . . greatly prefers his well-cushioned armchair . . . to a pig-box boat. — **(4) 1924** CROY *R.F.D. No. 3* 53 They were members of 'pig clubs' [and] went to stock-judging shows.

(5) 1913 CATHER *O Pioneers!* 46 Her eyes went back to the sorghum patch south of the barn, where she was planning to make her new pig corral. — **(6) 1845** F. DOUGLASS *Narrative* 28 It was almost a sufficient motive, not only to make me take off what would be called by pig drovers the mange, but the skin itself. — **(7) 1807** *Mass. H.S. Coll.* 2 Ser. III. 56 The pig-fish is of the size and form of a sculpion, but with a head not so large and bony. **1842** *Nat. Hist. N.Y., Zoology* IV. 52 The Common Bull-Head, *Cottus virginianus*, . . . is known under the various popular names of Sculpin, . . . Sea Robin, Bull-head, Sea Toad, and Pig Fish. **1937** PEARSON *Adv. in Bird Protection* 333 They are mullet, pig fish, pin fish and cravalle. — **(8) 1887** *Courier-Journal* 15 Feb. 2/2 Col. Colyar, . . . the original Pigiron Baron who advocates Mr. Randall's Republican views in the volunteer State, laughs with ghoulish glee.

(10) (*a*) **1872** *Harper's Mag.* April 690/2 A one-story wooden structure attached to a Tavern of only tolerable repute . . . became the rallying-place of the [Tammany] tribes. This [room], by reason of its general unsightliness, was denominated by Tammany's political adversaries the 'Pig-Pen.' (*b*) **1890** *Stock Grower & Farmer* 15 March 6/2 On all the horses recovered their hot brand was changed to a 'Pig Pen.' — **(11) 1913** GOODWIN *As I Remember Them* 38 Passing an open stand on the corner—it would be called a 'buffet' nowadays; it was called 'pigsfoot corner' then—Fairfax stopped at the counter and ordered a cup of hot coffee and a sandwich. — **(12) 1894** *U. of Chi. Wkly.* 11 Oct. 8/2 Roby put the pigskin over the line. **1948** *Redbook Mag.* April 66/3 The pigskin was fumbled, subsequently, but the referee ruled 'momentary possession.' — **(13) 1859** [see **bull strong**]. **1935** *Ada* (O.) *Herald* 1 Nov., The specifications for a good stake-and-rider line, or road-side fence were that it should be 'pig tight, horse high and bull strong.' — **(14) 1877** BARTLETT 464 Pigwick. A Small species of duck, very numerous in the coves and rivers of the eastern shore of Maryland. It has remarkably red eyes, feeds on fish, keeps near the shore, and is a great diver.

b. In colloq. phrases: (1) *Pigs in clover,* (*a*) a symbol of complete contentment, (*b*) a parlor game the object of which is to roll marbles into special holes in a board by tilting it; (2) *in less than a pig's whistle,* (see quot.), [cf. * *pig's whisper* in *OED* in the same sense]; (3) *as common as pig tracks,* quite common or ordinary.

(1) (*a*) **1813** *Boston-Gazette* 7 Jan. (Th.), Canadians! Then in droves come over, And live henceforth like pigs in clover. (*b*) **1895** WILLIAMS *Princeton Stories* 203 With an expression on his face which reminds you of when 'Pigs in Clover' was the rage, [he] darts across the room. — **(2) 1859** BARTLETT 320 'I'll do so in less than a pig's whistle,' that is 'in less than no time.' — **(3) 1944** *Reader's Digest* Dec. 17/1 Why, the girl was 'Frog Hollow trash,' 'as common as pig tracks!'

As the last term in **blind, river, slough, striped, whistle pig.**

* **pigeon,** *n.*

1. =**passenger pigeon.**

1612 SMITH *Virginia* I. 15 In winter there are great plenty of Swans, . . . Oxeies, Parrats, and Pigeons. **1709** LAWSON *Carolina* 44 You may find . . . Indian Towns . . . that have more than 10 0 Gallons of Pigeons Oil, or Fat; they using it with Pulse. **1782** CRÈVECOEUR *Lett.* 37 We have twice a year the pleasure of catching pigeons, whose numbers are sometimes so astonishing as to obscure the sun in their flight. **1917** *Birds of Amer.* II. 45/1 A most remarkable attribute of the Pigeon was its disregard of the presence of human beings in its roosting and nesting places.

b. Also *pigeon of passage. Obs.*

c1729 CATESBY *Carolina* I. 23 *Palumbus migratorius.* The Pigeon of Passage. . . . Of these there come in Winter to Virginia and Carolina, from the North, incredible numbers. **1781–2** JEFFERSON *Notes Va.* (1788) 74 *Columba migratoria.* . . . Pigeon of Passage. Pigeon. **1789** MORSE *Amer. Geog.* 60 American Birds . . . enumerated [include] . . . Water Pelican, Pigeon of passage, White crowned pigeon.

2. In combs.: (1) **pigeon distance,** the distance at which passenger pigeons were usu. shot, *obs.;* (2) * **diver,** the little auk, *Alle alle;* (3) **falcon,** (see quot. 1917); (4) **guillemot,** a guillemot of the Pacific Coast, *Cepphus columba;* (5) * **house,** *La.* (see quot.), *obs.;* (6) **hunt,** a hunt for passenger pigeons, *obs.;* (7) **nesting,** (see quot.), *obs.;* (8) **paradis,** *local* (see quot.); (9) **ranch,** an extensive farm where pigeons are raised, *rare;* (10) **roost,** see as a main entry; (11) **season,** in a particular region, a time when there were great flocks of passenger pigeons about, *obs.;* (12) **stand,** a place where hunters lay in wait to destroy passenger pigeons, *obs.;* (13) **stool,** a support for a pigeon used as a decoy in taking pigeons in nets, *obs.;* (14) * **tail,** the pintail duck, *Dafila acuta;* (15) **-tailed coat,** a coat having a tail shaped like a pigeon's tail; (16) **tremex,** a horntail, *Tremex columba;* (17) * **wing,** see as a main entry; (18) **woodpecker,** =**flicker.**

(1) 1840 SIMMS *Border Beagles* II. 299 The school-master, . . . though a Yankee, was able to ride and shoot and had done execution more than once at pigeon-distance. — **(2) 1839** PEABODY *Mass. Birds* 400 The Little Guillemot, *Uria alle*, sometimes called the Little Auk or Pigeon Diver, . . . are not regular visitants, but occasional, solitary wanderers. **1844** *Nat. Hist. N.Y., Zoology* II. 281 This little *Sea Dove, Sea Pigeon, Greenland Dove, Pigeon-diver*, or *Ice-bird*, is but rarely seen on our coast. — **(3) 1880** *Cimarron News & Press* 23 Dec. 1/5 Of the falcons we have the lanier, peregrine, pigeon, Richardson's and rusty-crowned falcon or sparrow hawk. **1917** *Birds of Amer.* II. 89 Pigeon Hawk. *Falco columbarius columbarius.* . . . [Also called] Pigeon Falcon. — **(4) 1883** *Nat. Museum Bul.* No. 27, 180 *Uria columba.* . . . Pigeon Guillemot. . . . North Pacific (both sides), breeding south to California. **1917** *Birds of Amer.* I. 24/1 Mr. Dawson says that the Pigeon Guillemot is 'unquestionably the most characteristic water-bird of the Puget Sound region.'

(5) 1849 E. DAVIS *Amer. Scenes* 90 The basement was of brick, . . . and the upper part was of wood, terminating in a pigeon house. . . . It was a place of punishment and torture for the oppressed slave. . . . Such buildings are very common, and generally pass under the euphemistic name of 'pigeon-houses.' — **(6) 1827** *Harvard Reg.* 38, I was solicited one morning to go with him on a pigeon-hunt. **1856** GOODRICH *Recoll.* I. 100, I can recollect no sports of my youth [*c*1800] which equaled in excitement our pigeon hunts, generally taking place in September and October. — **(7) 1869** *Mich. Laws* I. 213 No person . . . [shall] destroy any wild pigeon or pigeons . . . where they are gathered in bodies for the purpose of brooding their young, known as pigeon-nestings. — **(8) 1936** ARTHUR *Old New Orleans* 58 *Pigeon paradis*, cooked with raisins and wine, truly a dish deserving a heavenly name. — **(9) 1901** *Denver Republican* 19 Aug. 8/3 The pigeon ranch at Los Angeles is the only one of its kind in the world.

(11) 1897 MARK TWAIN *Autobiog.* (1924) I. 114, I remember the pigeon seasons, when the birds would come in millions and cover the trees. — **(12) 1844** *Knickerb.* XXIV. 28 There too is a pigeon stand, built for murderous purposes; and there too is the booth of pine branches erected to conceal the sportsman. — **(13) 1867** DE VOE *Market Ass't* 173 A pigeon-stool is then driven in the ground near the 'floor,' but so as not to be covered when the 'net' is sprung. — **(14) 1848** HERBERT *Field Sports* (1852) I. 128 *Anas Acuta.* . . . The Winter Duck, Sprigtail, Pigeontail, *vulgo.* **1917** *Birds of Amer.* I. 128.

(15) **1889** *Harper's Mag.* Aug. 386/1 [Wearing] a pigeon-tailed coat, . . . he sat gravely and sturdily down amid his peers. **1901** CHURCHILL *Crisis* 202 He ran to his room to don for Virginia that glorious but useless full dress,—the high bearskin hat, the red pigeon-tailed coat. — **(16) 1879** *Scribner's Mo.* Aug. 502/2 The pigeon-tremex, — *Tremex columba* . . . ,—and a great pest it is, too. **1891** *Cent.* 6457/3 *Tremex columba* is a large and handsome North American horntail, the larva of which bores the trunks of shade-trees, particularly the maple, and is known as the *pigeon-tremex*. — **(18) 1844** *Nat. Hist. N.Y., Zoology* II. 192 This species . . . is called Highhole, Yucker, Flicker, Wake-up and Pigeon Woodpecker . . . in this State. **1917** *Birds of Amer.* II. 163 Flicker. *Colaptes auratus auratus.* . . . [Also called] Clape; Pigeon Woodpecker; Yellow-hammer.

b. In the names of plants: (1) **pigeon berry,** any one of various small fruits or the plants or trees producing these, as the pokeweed, bristly sarsaparilla, serviceberry, blue dogwood; (2) **berry bush,** any bush that produces pigeon berries; (3) **cherry,** the pin cherry, *Prunus pennsylvanica;* (4) **grass,** (*a*) the yellow foxtail, *Setaria lutescens*, or the European green foxtail, *S. viridis*, (*b*) the crab grass, *Digitaria sanguinalis;* (5) **plum,** any of the tropical sea grapes of the genus *Coccolobis*, esp. *C. laurifolia*, also attrib.; (6) **weed,** the angelica tree *q.v.*, or a field weed, *Lithospermum arvense;* (7) ∗**wood,** the porkwood, *Torrubia obtusata*.

(1) **1775** BURNABY *Travels* 11 Tobacco and Indian corn are the original produce of the country; likewise the pigeon-berry and rattle-snake root. *a***1870** CHIPMAN *Notes on Bartlett* 310 Partridge-Berry . . . in at least some parts of N.E., is contradistinguished by the name of *Pigeon Berry*. **1937** *Range Plant Handbook* B127 This evergreen, olive-like shrub . . . is variously known as coffeeberry, pigeonberry, yerba-del-oso, and cascara sagrada. — **(2) 1784** CUTLER in *Amer. Acad. Mem.* I. 411 *Cissus*. . . . Pigeon-Berry Bush. Pigeons feed on the berries which has been the occasion of its trivial name. **1832** WILLIAMSON *Maine* I. 115 The *pigeon-berry bush* is as tall as that of a blackberry, bears an abundance of small purple berries, the chief food of pigeons. — **(3) 1850** *N. Eng. Farmer* II. 160/1 The small, red, wild cherry, often called the pigeon cherry, . . . very much resembles some of our cultivated varieties. — **(4)** (*a*) **1838** *Mass. Agric. Survey* 1st Rep. 128 There were several patches of black or pigeon grass when the dyke was built. **1901** MOHR *Plant Life Ala.* 358. (*b*) **1894** *Amer. Folk-Lore* VII. 104 *Panicum sanguinale*, pigeon-grass, Hopkinton, Iowa. **(5) 1743** CATESBY *Carolina* II. 94 Pigeon-Plum . . . . In December the Fruit is ripe, and is the Food of Pigeons and many wild Animals. **1775** *Mass. H.S. Coll.* 2 Ser. II. 287, I had nothing to assist Nature with, but a Tea of Piggen plumb Roots, and Spruce. **1897** SUDWORTH *Arborescent Flora* 192 *Coccolobis laurifolia*. . . . Pigeon Plum. — **(6) 1784** CUTLER in *Amer. Acad. Mem.* I. 431 *Aralia*. . . . Shot Bush. Pigeon Weed. Blossoms white. Berries black. Common in new plantations. **1850** JOHNSTON *Notes* I. 305 Richer clover also had come up on another drained spot, and less of the pigeon-weed, as it is here called, with which this clay land is infested. **1889** VASEY *Agric. Grasses* 103 Pigeon-Weed . . . grows chiefly in cultivated grounds. — **(7) 1884** SARGENT *Rep. Forests* 117 *Pisonia obtusata*. . . . Pigeon Wood. . . . Wood heavy, rather soft, weak, coarse-grained. **1897** SUDWORTH *Arborescent Flora* 192.

c. *drop-the-pigeon*, see ∗**drop,** *v.* **4. c.** (1).

As the last term in **Carolina, clay, flyer, migrant passenger, migratory passenger, passenger, prairie, sea, stool, wild pigeon.**

pigeoneer ˌpɪdʒəˈnɪr, *n.* [f. ∗*pigeon* + ∗*-eer*.] (See quot.) — **1918** *Boston Ev. Rec.* 11 Jan. 9/2 A pigeoneer is an expert handler of homing pigeons.

pigeon roost. An extensive area, sometimes as much as 100,000 acres, where passenger pigeons roosted and nested. Also as a place-name. *Obs.*

[**1634** WOOD *N. Eng. Prospect* (1898) 30 Many of them [i.e., passenger pigeons] build amongst the Pine-trees, thirty miles to the North-east of our plantations; joyning nest to nest, and tree to tree by their nests, so that the Sunne never sees the ground in that place, from whence the Indians fetch whole loades of them.] **1808** PIKE *Sources Miss.* 104 At some islands about 10 miles above Salt river . . . there were pigeon roosts, and in about fifteen minutes my men had knocked on the head and brought on board 298. **1899** CUSHMAN *Hist. Indians* 387, I first heard a sermon by Mr. Bell at the Pigeon roost about twelve years ago. **1923** *Arrow Points* 5 Jan. 18 This locality might have been a pigeon roost in the days when hordes of wild pigeons passed this way en route to feeding grounds south of here.
transf. **1861** STOWE in *Independent* 21 Nov. 1/1 A whole pigeon-roost of yet undreamed-of fancies.

∗**pigeonwing,** *n.* **1.** A fancy step executed by jumping up and striking the legs together, often *to cut a pigeon-wing*. Also the music for such a dance. Cf. **buck and wing. 2.** (See quot.) *Obs.*

(1) **1807** IRVING *Salmagundi* vii, No pigeon-wing disturbs your *contredanse*. *Ib.* i, He never cut a pigeon-wing in his life. **1873** *Kalama* (Wash.) *Beacon* 26 April 1/2 Frank is going around on crutches, and will not likely attempt the 'pigeon-wing' for three or four weeks. **1947** PAUL *Linden* 50 He had . . . a Chickering grand piano on which he played, with amazing dexterity, all the reels, jigs, pigeon-wings, moriscos, sarabands, . . . and cancans known to the Old World taverns . . . or to the surging American frontiers. — **(2) 1872** *Atlantic Mo.* Feb. 165 The miller spreads or reefs his sails, like a sailor,—reducing them in a high wind to a mere 'pigeon-wing' as it is called, two or three feet in length.

pigeonwing ˈpɪdʒənˌwɪŋ, *v. tr.* and *intr.* To teach (a person) to dance the pigeonwing; to go in the manner of one executing the pigeonwing. *Obs.*

1826 COOPER *Mohicans* xxi, The toes are squared, as though one of the French dancers had been in, pigeon-winging his tribe. **1839** POE *Works* (1902) III. 255 The rascal . . . pigeon-winged himself right up into the belfry of the House of the Town Council. **1877** BEARD *KKK Sketches* 59 The boss straggler, having eluded the individual on two sticks by pigeon-winging it through a hole in the roof, rolled upon the green sward beneath.

∗**pigmy,** see ∗**pygmy.**

∗**pignut,** *n.*

1. The broom hickory, *Carya glabra*, or a related species; also the nut of such a tree. Also attrib.

1666 *Warwick* (R.I.) *Rec.* 404 Upon a straight lyne from ye pond to a pignut tree standing upon a hill. **1705** BEVERLEY *Virginia* II. 16 There are also several Sorts of Hickories, call'd Pig-nuts, some of which have as thin a Shell as the best French Walnuts. **1785** MARSHALL *Amer. Grove* 68 *Juglans alba minima*. White, or Pig-nut Hickery. This generally grows pretty large, sometimes to the height of eighty feet or more. **1949** *Pacific Spectator* Spring 224 We went up a little hill with hickory nut and pignut trees on it amidst the laurel bushes.

2. a. A now unidentifiable nut or tuber. *Rare.* **b.** The jojoba, a shrub or small tree found in the Southwest.

(a) 1847 RUXTON *Adv. Rocky Mts.* (1848) 258 A large grizzly bear [was] . . . searching for yampa-roots or pig-nuts. — **(b) 1897** *Amer. Folk-Lore* X. 143 *Simmondsia Californica*, pig-nut, Arizona.

∗**pike,** *n.*[1] As the last term in **bony, buffalo bony, driving, Dutch, federation, glass-eyed, grass, ground, jack, land, Missouri, mud, Ohio, rattlesnake, Sacramento, shun, silver, wall-eyed, yellow pike.**

Pike paɪk, *n.*[2] [See quots.]

1. Originally on the Pacific Coast, a man from Pike County, Missouri, later as a highly derogatory term (see quot. 1946).

In the first group of quots. the region from which the Pikes came is definitely indicated.

(1) [**1852** *Placer Times* (Sacramento) 5 Feb. 2/5 Some 'honest hombres' from 'Pike,' in the Gallery of the American Theatre last evening, . . . were quite at a loss to decide whether the scene represented a *big coffee mill or a quartz machine*.] **1854** *Pioneer* (S.F.) April 252 'Pike' is a genius. He is wrapped up body and soul, in the State of Missouri. Pike, O! Pike, it is my name, Missourer is my nation, Pike County is my dwelling place, And Pike is my salvation! **1860** *N. Californian* (Union) 22 Feb. 1/6 A 'Pike' in the California dialect, is a native of Missouri, Arkansas, Northern Texas, or Southern Illinois. **1948** *Sat. Ev. Post* 14 Aug. 21/1 There was a migration [to Calif.] from Missouri and neighboring states about the turn of the century, known as 'The Pikes.'

(2) [**1847** *Calif. Star* (S.F.) 18 Sep. 2/3, I hope our friend B——, has given you an account of a most delightful trip we had a short time since . . . the summit of the Sierra Nevada, a new pass through those mountains, the 'Pikies,' and so on.] **1855** *Varieties* (S.F.) 25 July 1/1 In the course of a short ramble yesterday . . . we fell in with a couple clear grit 'Pikes.' **1880** *Harper's Mag.* Sep. 535/1 Nothing could be falser than the sketches which . . . confound these uncouth but decent people with the Pikes or swaggering thieves and ruffians of the West. **1946** *St. Louis Globe-Democrat* 17 Nov., The term 'Pike' or 'piker,' in the sense of a worthless, lazy, good-for-nothing person arose first in California in the days of the Forty-Niners.

2. Used attrib. and in derivative expressions, usu. with reference to the language of the Pikes. *Obs.*

1861 *Humorist* (S.F.) 26 Oct 5/1 He was 'sittin on de rail,' . . . talking politics profound, when along came a specimen from Pikedom, that *we* would have mistaken for Jim Porter, the Kentucky Giant. **1866** *Chi. Tribune* 25 Dec., *To climb down* to anything is Western or Pike-Californian (Pike itself being derivated slang); . . . an act which involves all the energy and danger of climbing without its ambition or hopefulness. **1879** HOWELLS *Lady of Aroostook* 319 He hears around him the vigorous and imaginative locutions of the Pike language, in which, like the late Canon Kingsley, he finds a Scandinavian hugeness. **1948** MENCKEN *Supp.* II. 126 The Pike county dialect of the Mississippi was only a transient phenomenon.

b. Also predicatively, in the sense: Of the nature of a Pike or of Pikes. *Rare.*

1863 *Harper's Mag.* June 25/2 Society in San José is decidedly 'Pike' in its character.

3. a. Pike countian, a person from Pike County, Mo. **b. Pike County man,** =prec. Both *obs.*

(a) 1863 MASSETT *Drifting About* 243 These 'Pike countyans' are a most extraordinary looking set of people. *Ib.* 244 Your 'Pike' countyian is not very communicative, and is apt to look upon everything and everybody with suspicion. — **(b) 1853** WINTHROP *Letters* 28 June, Rough enough, too, are some of these 'Pike County' men, as they say,—real backwoodsmen who have fallen into pleasant places. **1869** J. R. BROWNE *Adv. Apache Country* 334 'Are you going back to the States?' said I to a Pike County man, with a wagon-load of wife and children.

*** Pike,** *n.*[3] [Zebulon Montgomery *Pike* (1779–1813), Amer. brigadier gen. and explorer.] Used in the possessive in various expressions: (1) **Pike's Peaker,** one who went out in 1859 to the Pikes Peak area in search of gold; (2) **Peak (gold) fever,** feverish excitement inspired by the discovery of gold in Colorado in 1858–59; (3) **Peak or bust!,** a phrase originating from the efforts of gold seekers to reach the Pikes Peak area about 1859; (4) **Pikes,** the name given a regiment of Gen. Pike's soldiers in the War of 1812 who were armed with muskets and with pikes instead of bayonets. All *obs.* or *hist.*

(1) 1859 *Alta California* 17 Aug. (Th.), Gentile and Mormon, bull whacker and Pike's Peaker, all seem to mingle freely. **1889** BANCROFT *Ariz. & N. Mex.* 697 The 'Pike's Peakers' had proved more than a match for the 'Texan rangers.' **1941** FRITZ *Colorado* 106 The disappointed Pike's Peakers threatened him with violence. — **(2) 1872** TICE *Over Plains* 201 When the 'Pike's Peak fever' broke out, gold hunters . . . flocked to this supposed Eldorado. **1877** JOHNSON *Anderson Co., Kans.* 270 In the spring of 1859 the inhabitants of the town . . . caught the 'Pike's Peak' gold fever, and the town was abandoned. **1891** O'BEIRNE *Leaders Ind. Territory* 68/2 When the Pike's Peak fever was at its height young Doyle started for the gold fields of Colorado and remained there about twelve months. — **(3) 1879** WILLIAMS *Pacific Tourist* 23/1 At the time of the opening of the Pike's Peak excitement in gold diggings, two pioneers made themselves conspicuous by painting in large letters on the side of their wagon cover: *'Pike's Peak or Bust.'* **1948** *Atlantic Mo.* Feb. 31/2 You said 'Pike's Peak or bust!' when you made up your mind to do something. — **(4) 1889** *N. & Q.* III. 102 Pike's Pikes.—What does this expression mean? . . . It was a kind of punning or canting allusion to Pike's name that prompted the arming of this regiment of 'Pike's pikes' in the manner indicated.

*** pike,** *n.*[4] An amusement district (see quots.). Usu. *cap.*

1903 *Cin. Enquirer* 1 May 6/5 And have you heard the news so rare? It's just the kind you like: The Midway at St. Looy's Fair They're going to call The Pike. **1912** *Out West* June 411/1 If you are somewhat blase and desire unique diversion there is the Pike with its varied amusements. **1948** *Pacific Discovery* Sep.–Oct. 15/1 On the pike at Long Beach one day he was watching one of the several snake shows.

*__pike,__ *v. piked up,* graded up. *Rare.* — **1872** HUNTINGTON *Road Master's Ass't* 60 How often do we see a piece of track at the foot of a steep grade, on a high embankment, *piked up* as far as possible.

pike pole. A long pole, usu. one provided with a spike and hook at one end, used as a lever in raising weights, or in driving and floating logs. Cf. **driving pike.**

1830 *Palladium* (Toronto) 29 Aug. 244/1 How delightful to rise early in the foggy morning and devote the livelong day to punching alligator-gars in the belly with a pike-pole! **1877** *Scribner's Mo.* Dec. 149 The running and rafting implements, pike-poles, etc., are made ready. **1949** *Chi. D. News* 17 Sep. 1/7 Firemen worked with pike pole and shovel in the wreckage.

piker ˈpaɪkɚ, *n.* [See note.]

From various sources. In sense **1.** derived from **Pike,** *n.*[2] **1.** The source of the term in sense **2.** is not clear. It may be a different word. Because of the lateness of the Amer. evidence it is not likely that the word in this sense is a continuation of the use of **piker*, a robber, thief, 1301–1549 in *OED.* Sense **3.** of course refers to the fish. For sense **4.** cf. **Pike,** *n.*[2] **1.**

1. (*cap.*) *W.* A person from Missouri, esp. one from Pike County. Cf. **Pike,** *n.*[2]

1860 *Marysville* (Calif.) *Appeal* 30 March 3/1 Pillbox said they were there for the benefit of the 'Pikers,' that they might learn to read. **1907** CONNELLEY *Doniphan's Exped.* 9 Mr. Moore says that in California in the early days Missourians were called 'Pikers' indiscriminately and generally. **1934** RAMSAY *Mo. Place-Names* 62 Its [Pike County, Mo.] size doubtless accounted for the fact that Westerners usually thought of newcomers as natives of Pike County and called them 'Pikers.' **1948** A. K. WILLIAMS *Gold Rush Days* 33 The rest of the train called these people from Pike County Missouri 'Pikers,' and afterwards this word was applied to anyone who would not help in an undertaking or who would quit or leave a friend in distress.

2. A vagrant, a gambler with small means (see also quot. 1898).

1872 CRAPSEY *Nether Side N.Y.* 98 A 'piker' is a tolerated collapse who makes a stray bet when he can borrow a 'check.' **1876** HEARN *Amer. Miscellany* (1924) I. 183 There was . . . Dan Booker, the withered old 'piker' who used to wander about the levee bent crescent-wise with age, and finally died in the Workhouse, serving out a sentence of vagrancy. **1898** *N.Y. Journal* 12 Aug. 1/7 (Ernst), For all that he afterward became a real estate king, John Pettit started in as a 'piker.' That's what the downtown brokers call a man who speculates with a few hundreds at a time instead of with thousands. The term is often heard on the track, too, and in gambling rooms.

3. One who fishes for pike. *Rare.*

1892 *Outing* July 303/2 Once when returning after an unsuccessful day of fishing, I met an old 'piker.' *Ib.* 304/2 An old 'piker' volunteered to guide me and initiate me into the secrets of his art.

4. An incompetent person, poor sport, "cheap skate." *Slang.*

1898 *Boston Sun. Globe* 15 May 36/4 There are two kinds of salesmen, the 'pikers,' who grind away all the time, and the men who bunch their hits, to use a baseballism. **1945** SERVICE *Ploughman* 195 My companion immediately produced the coin and not wishing to seem a piker, I followed suit.

attrib. and *transf.* **1946** *Chi. D. News* 22 Nov. 20/2 The next crash will make 1929 look like a piker. **1947** *Sat. Ev. Post* 15 March 111/3 It is natural that I should have gone far beyond the sort of piker activities which characterize the average soldier.

pikery ˈpɪkərɪ, *n.* A cathartic powder, hiera picra. *Rare.* — **1878** STOWE *Poganuc People* 158 He'll put it through; he won't go back on his tracks, but it's pikery and wormwood to him.

Pike's tern. [f. Nicholas *Pike* (1818–1905), an Amer. naturalist.] (See quots.)

1869 *Proc. Calif. Acad. Sci.* IV. 69 Sterna Pikei, Lawr., Pike's Tern. **1917** *Birds of Amer.* I. 62/1 Arctic Tern Sterna paradisæa *Brünnich* . . . Other Names.—Common Tern; Sea Swallow; . . . Portland Tern; Pike's Tern. [**1928** *Condor* Sep.–Oct., 292 The ornithologist is interested in Pike not merely from the circumstances that a Tern from Monterey, now known to have been an Arctic Tern, was named *Sterna pikei,* but on account of his other activities. . . . He introduced the English Sparrow into America and received the first birds in Brooklyn, New York, in 1850 and 1852.]

piki ˈpikɪ, *n.* [Hopi Indian.] (See the later quots.) Cf. **hoecake.**

1859 T. H. HASKELL *MS Diary* in Brigham Young Univ. Lib. 16 Nov., He spent the day trading for peak, dried peaches, &c. *Ib.* 27 Nov., We feasted with old Thur on peak, hominy, beef soup, sweet mush and red pepper. **1893** DONALDSON *Moqui Pueblo Indians* 72 Piki, or corn bread of many colors, is plentiful, and the evidences of a feast are on every hand. **1922** CURTIS *N. Amer. Indian* 43 The commonest food derived from corn is *piki*, a paper-thin bread baked on a smoothly polished stone moderately heated by a fire beneath it. **1948** *Southwestern Jrnl. Anthrop.* Winter 376 Corn, flour, breadstuffs—especially piki (wafer bread)—melons, chili, and dried fruit were most sought after.

attrib. **1936** STEPHEN *Hopi Jrnl.* II. 1197 The men quarry out and roughly dress the *piki* stone to required dimensions, but the women finish and smooth it by rubbing. **1938** *Southwestern Lore* June 7 Tortillas and tamales, of Mexican provenience, are festal foods among the Tarahumara, while pici-bread is not known. **1949** *Desert Mag.* June 24/3 Piki bread is made by the Hopi Indians.

Pikish ˈpaɪkɪʃ, *a.* Characteristic of a Pike. *Obs.* Cf. **Pike,** *n.*[2] **1.** — **1848** *Dly. Morn. Herald* (Maysville, Ky.) 27 Dec. 2/1 The idea of producing alarm by announcing that the Cholera was in New Orleans, is peculiarly *Pikish.* **1869** J. R. BROWNE *Adv. Apache Country* 40 If 'George' was a little verdant and rude of speech, he . . . was by no means destitute of a dry, Pikeish sort of wit that occasionally and at very remote intervals burst upon us like a bomb-shell.

*** pile,** *n.*

1. One's fortune, a sum or amount of money, usu. large. *Slang.*

1741 *Poor Richard's Almanac* April, Rash mortal, ere you take a wife, Contrive your pile to last for life. **1841** *N.O. Picayune* 10 Dec. 2/2 Betting was quite brisk, and quite a 'pile' changed hands on the occasion. **1938** ASBURY *Sucker's Prog.* 317 A half-tipsy miner had just come from the diggings with a handsome pile.

2. In slang phrases: *To bet* (or *drop, go, make, stake*) *one's pile.*

For *to size (someone's) pile*, see ***size, *v.* 2.**

1839 *N.O. Picayune* 29 March 2/2 Friends of the Lubber, becoming excited at the unexpected termination of the first heat, were willing to go a 'small pile' somewhere in the neighborhood of even. **1850** SAWYER *Way Sketches* 119 Quite a large number of persons have 'made their piles' in this region. **1856** *Spirit of Times* 6 Sep. 4/1 Let us when we recognize 'true grit' and 'game' always bet our pile on it. **1891** *Appeal-Avalanche* (Memphis) 26 April 5/7 He dropped his pile on the races yesterday afternoon. **1944** JOHNSON *As I Dare* 5 Here lies Peter Roleum. He staked his pile and got no ile.

As the last term in **ash, brush, corn, cross, grub, hash, trap, woodpile.**

*** pile,** *v.*

1. *intr.* Used with adverbs or prepositions: To climb or get *in, off, over,* etc., a vehicle, obstacle, etc. *Colloq.*

1841 L. B. SWAN *Journal* (1904) 30 Brooks brought up his lumber wagon (near Niles, Mich.) and we all 'piled in.' **1866** F. KIRKLAND *Bk. Anecdotes* 333/2 Three Johnnies came 'piling' over the works into the Federal lines. **1919** WILSON *Ma Pettengill* 138 In comes the special [train], the officials pile off. **1947** *So. Sierran* Dec. 3/3 So after breakfast they pile into cars laden with grub and sleeping bags, . . . bound for some old ghost town in the desert.

b. *fig.* To attack, jump *onto. Slang.*

1894 *Outing* XXIV. 417/1 The dog . . . [will] never 'pile onto' any more bears. **1906** SINCLAIR *Jungle* 183 Like as not a dozen [policemen] would pile on to him at once, and pound his face into a pulp.

2. a. *To pile up the agony,* to prolong the climax or effect of something to a point where it becomes painful. **b.** *To pile it on,* to give all the unpleasant details, to exaggerate, to attack with every weapon at one's command. Both *colloq.* or *slang.*

(a) 1839 MARRYAT *Diary Amer.* 1 Ser. II. 39, I must not omit a specimen of American criticism . . . 'I do think he piled the agony up a little too high in that last scene [of a play].' **1875** STOWE *We & Neighbors* 219 They think there is no way but to 'pile up the agony,' to intensify the sense of danger and responsibility. — **(b) 1852** *Los Angeles Star* 3 April 1/5 The wags observed that Caleb was getting exceedingly uneasy, and 'piled it on.' **1947** *N.Y. Times* 12 Oct .v. 2/3 After that the only question in the minds of the partisan Fordham crowd was just how heavily the visitors would pile it on.

pileated woodpecker. A red-crested and white-marked black woodpecker, *Ceophloeus pileatus,* found in heavily forested areas. Cf. **black woodcock.**

[**1782** LATHAM *Gen. Synops. Birds* I. 554 Pileated Woodpecker.] **1811** WILSON *Ornithology* IV. 24 The Pileated Woodpecker is suspected of sometimes tasting the Indian corn; the Ivory-billed never. **1893** *Scribner's Mag.* June 760/2 Such purely forest birds as the pileated and ivory-billed woodpeckers. **1948** *Dly. Ardmoreite* (Ardmore, Okla.) 23 July 11/5 The ivory-billed woodpecker is fast becoming extinct in the United States, while the pileated woodpecker is close on its heels.

***pile-driver,** *n.* (See quot. and cf. **stake driver.**) — **1857** HAMMOND *No. Scenes* 177 [A bird] known in these parts [N.Y. State] as the 'Pile-driver' . . . is about the homeliest creature in these woods. It is a small grey heron.

*** Pilgrim,** *n.* Also ***pilgrim.**

1. An early settler of Massachusetts or of Plymouth and Massachusetts jointly, a firstcomer to New England.

A. Matthews in *Mass. Col. Soc. Pub.* XVII. (1914) 293–391 has shown that *pilgrim* was applied to "the early Massachusetts settlers . . . a century and a half before the word was specifically applied to the Plymouth settlers." See note under **Pilgrim Father.**

1702 C. MATHER *Magnalia* (1853) I. 68 These Ministers came over to Salem in the summer of the year 1629. . . . The passage of these our pilgrims was attended with many smiles of Heaven upon them. **1820** G. SPRING *Tribute to N.-Eng.* (1821) 27 The Pilgrims of New-England were men who had pity on the heathen. **1893** *Harper's Mag.* April 706/1 Immigration from New England was comparatively trivial in numbers. . . . It is the ideas of the Pilgrims and not their descendants that have had dominion in the young commonwealth [Kansas]. **1914** *Mass. Col. Soc. Pub.* XVII. 361 Hence by about 1800 the terms Pilgrims and Pilgrim Fathers, which had then become well established, meant any early settlers of either of the two colonies which in 1692 were united under the Province of the Massachusetts Bay. And such use of the term continued for many years—indeed, still continues.

b. A settler of any other early colony or town. *Obs.*

1660 in *Mass. Col. Soc. Pub.* XVII. 366 [New Haven colony] bounds extended neare unto Cold Spring, beyond Pilgrims Harbour. **1794** *Ib.* 369 Toasts on the occasion, *viz.* . . . The Pilgrims in Concord. **1872** J. G. WHITTIER (*title*), The Pennsylvania Pilgrim [i.e., Francis D. Pastorius].

2. A settler of Plymouth colony, esp. one of those who founded the colony in 1620.

1798 *Columbian Centinel* 29 Dec. 2/4 'The Heirs of the Pilgrims' Celebrated on Saturday Dec. 22, the 177th Anniversary of the landing of their Forefathers at Plymouth Rock. **1841** A. YOUNG *Chron. Pilgrim Fathers* 88 The term Pilgrims belongs exclusively to the Plymouth colonists. **1948** *Life* 13 Sep. 36/1 Do we even give sober thanks in the manner of the Pilgrims? We do not.

3. Locally applied as a title to persons celebrating Forefathers' Day. Sometimes used sarcastically. *Obs.*

1798 *Columbian Centinel* 29 Dec. 2/4 Gen. Lincoln presided . . . at the board of the 'Pilgrims,' which was amply and characteristically furnished with every species of wild food. **1804** in *Mass. Col. Soc. Pub.* XVII. 344 A great number of well-fed, well-dressed Pilgrims, who had never endured penance beyond a drunken head-ache, were walking about with some impatience.

b. One of the persons celebrating the 200th anniversary of the founding of Jamestown, Va. (1607). *Obs.*

1807 in *S. Lit. Messenger* XXIV. 307/2 The sacred soil was saluted by the shouts of the *Pilgrims.* **1857** *Ib.* 311/2 On the 15th [of May, 1807], the pilgrims repaired to Williamsburg to participate . . . in the festivities held in honor of the Declaration of Independence.

4. (See quots.) *Obs.*

1821 NUTTALL *Trav. Arkansa* 226 Not far from this place near the mouth of the Arkansas River, a few days ago were encamped, the miserable remnant of what are called the Pilgrims, a band of fanatics, originally about 60 in number. They commenced their pilgrimage from the borders of Canada, and wandered about with their wives and children through the vast wilderness of the western states, like vagabonds, without ever fixing upon any residence. **1890** *N. & Q.* V. 257, I have by me a very brief account of a sect of fanatics called 'Pilgrims,' who about 1817 settled at Pilgrim island in the Mississippi river, thirty miles below New Madrid, Mo. The sect is said to have originated in Canada, Vermont and New York State. They were finally robbed of their money and broken up, their prophet with a few followers settling at or near Arkansas Post.

5. A newcomer into the West, a tenderfoot.

1841 W. L. MCCALLA *Adv. In Texas* 46 After such an address from a citizen of that calumniated country Texas to a shattered old pilgrim, I took the liberty of withdrawing to another apartment. **1864** *Rio Abajo Press* 21 June 2/1 A large number of Pilgrimes are camped ten miles from here on the *Gallo.* They are en route for the Arizona Mines. **1890** LANGFORD *Vigilante Days* (1912) 116 Some of the companies were composed entirely of 'pilgrims,' a designation given by mountain people to newcomers from the States. **1943** HOWARD *Montana* 139 They were for the most part 'pilgrims' who remained and were 'made into hands.'

6. *W.* (See quot. 1887.) Also attrib.

1885 *Rep. Indian Affairs* 120 This, we think, is a very fair crop of calves considering the fact that the cattle were what is called 'pilgrim' cattle (cattle for the States that had never passed through a winter before without being housed and fed). **1887** *Scribner's Mag.* II. 508/1 'Pilgrim' and 'tenderfoot' were formerly applied almost exclusively to newly imported cattle. **1942** DALE *Cow Country* 194 They mingled with 'drift cattle' from Kansas or with the trail herds of 'pilgrim cattle' from Texas.

7. In special combs.: (1) **Pilgrim Church,** (see quot. 1897); (2) **City,** (see quot.); (3) **Father,** see as a main entry; (4) ***shell,** a kind of sea shell, *obs.,* cf. **cradle shell;** (5) **Society,** (*a*) a society at Concord, Mass., in honor of the first settlers of that place, *obs.,* (*b*) a society organized in 1820 in honor of the founders of the Plymouth colony.

(1) 1806 A. HOLMES *Discourse* (Dec. 22) 10 The pilgrim church first settled at Amsterdam; but, after a few years' residence in that city, it removed to Leyden. **1897** ARBER *Story of Pilgrim Fathers* 355 Membership in the Pilgrim Church was the first qualification: intended, or actual, emigration to New England was the second. *Ib.* 357 We also speak of the Pilgrim Church: meaning by that the Scrooby Congregation in their migrations to Amsterdam and Leyden. — **(2) 1856** *Western Citizen* (Paris, Ky.) 11 Jan. 1/5 Boston with all her faults, belittling as they are, is still the Pilgrim City and the pride of Massachusetts. — **(4) 1882** E. K. GODFREY *Nantucket* 34 Besides the 'pilgrim' shells, so numerous that we almost overlook their beauty [etc.].

(5) (*a*) **1793** in *Mass. Col. Soc. Pub.* XVII. 369 At the Anniversary Meeting of the Pilgrim Society in Concord, . . . they spent the evening in grateful and Christian conviviality. **1914** *Mass. Col. Soc. Pub.* XVII. 370 It is interesting to find . . . a Pilgrim Society at Concord thirty years before a similarly-named society was formed at Plymouth. (*b*) [**1807** *Columbian Centinel* 7 Jan. 2/3 The writer would propose, that an association be formed, to be denominated the *Pilgrim*

Society. The number of members to consist of 101, corresponding with the numbers of the first settlers.] **1819** *Mass. General Laws* II. 518 An Act to incorporate the Pilgrim Society. **1834** *Sun* (N.Y.) 22 July 3/1 The inhabitants of the town of Plymouth . . . recently voted to transfer the remainder of the charge to the Pilgrim Society.

b. Also (1) **Pilgrim anniversary,** (2) **bark,** (3) **festival,** (4) **forefathers,** (5) **founders,** (6) **mothers,** (7) **people,** (8) **Puritan,** (9) **Rock,** (10) **-'s day,** (11) **stock,** (12) **story.**

(1) **1817** *Columbian Centinel* 27 Dec. 2/3 The Pilgrim Anniversary was celebrated at Plymouth, on Monday last. — (2) **1857** WHITTIER *Poetical Works* 314/2 Come these from Plymouth's Pilgrim bark? — (3) **1842** *Juliet* (Ill.) *Courier* 2 Feb. 2/6 Among the toasts given at the recent pilgrim festival in New York celebrating the landing of the pilgrims. — (4) **1866** MARK TWAIN *Lett. Sandwich Isl.* 117 A band of stern, . . . old Puritan knights . . . full of that fervent zeal and resistless determination inherited from their Pilgrim forefathers. **1947** *Sat. Ev. Post* 15 March 151/2 The Pilgrim forefathers were clapped into dungeons before sailing for the New World.

(5) **1830** J. F. WATSON (*title*), Annals of Philadelphia, . . . from the Days of the Pilgrim Founders. — (6) **1836** in QUINCY *Hist. Harvard* II. 697 The name of Priscilla Mullins carries us back to our Pilgrim *Mothers.* — (7) **1654** JOHNSON *Wonder-w. Prov.* 61 Those who were in place of civill Government . . . begun to think of a place of more safety in the eyes of Man, then the two frontire Towns of Charles Towne, and Boston were for the habitation of such as the Lord had prepared to Governe this Pilgrim People. **1914** *Mass. Col. Soc. Pub.* XVII. 370 It is interesting to find the early Massachusetts settlers called a Pilgrim people . . . a century and a half before the . . . Plymouth settlers. — (8) **1848** L. CASS *Address* (Dec. 22) 33 The Pilgrim Puritans . . . raised an altar in the western wilderness, and died around it. — (9) **1849** WHITTIER *Poetical Works* 372/1 For well she keeps her ancient stock, The stubborn strength of Pilgrim Rock.

(10) **1856** *Spirit of Times* (N.Y.) 27 Dec. 272/2 Pilgrim's Day.—Our New England cousins celebrated their great anniversary of St. Jonathan's day by a dinner and banquet. — (11) **1862** LOWELL *Biglow P.* 2 Ser. vi. 155 Our Pilgrim stock wuz pithed with hardihood. — (12) **1943** *Life* 20 Dec. 11 In presenting the Pilgrim story and relating it to present-day America *Life* gave us an editorial . . . worthy of being read from any pulpit in the land.

As the last term in **bone, Plymouth pilgrim.** See also *Sons of the Pilgrims.*

Pilgrim Father.

1. One of those who founded the Plymouth colony in 1620. Usu. *pl.*

"This restriction, however, of the terms Pilgrims and Pilgrim Fathers exclusively to the Plymouth settlers is recognized at the present time only in the Old Colony itself" (1914 A. Matthews in *Mass. Col. Soc. Pub.* XVII. 362).

1799 *Columbian Centinel* 25 Dec. 3 Hail Pilgrim Fathers of our race, With grateful hearts your toils we trace. **1876** CROFUTT *Transcontinental Tourist* 157 What American man, woman or child, does not feel a heart-throb of exultation as they think of the glorious achievements of Progress since the landing of the Pilgrim Fathers, on stanch old Plymouth Rock! **1908** O. HENRY *Options* 89 One brother . . . came in the *Mayflower* and became a Pilgrim Father. **1949** *Oak Leaves* (Oak Park, Ill.) 24 Nov. 3/1 The Pilgrim Fathers were mindful of that same great truth.

2. In transf. and allusive uses (see quots.).

1824 HODGSON *Lett. from N. Amer.* II. 11, I am surprised by the proofs which are presented to me of the learning of the 'Pilgrim Fathers,' as they call the first settlers. **1842** in *Mass. Col. Soc. Pub.* XVII. 371 Thus much for the public career of this great Indian benefactor to the Pilgrim Fathers of Connecticut. **1880** CABLE *Grandissimes* 27 The pilgrim fathers of the Mississippi Delta with Gallic recklessness were taking wives. **1906** in *Mass. Col. Soc. Pub.* XVII. 372 The early efforts of Josh Billings and Artemus Ward, the Pilgrim Fathers of Phonetics, . . . were not taken seriously.

* **pill,** *n.* In combs.: (1) **pill bag,** a bag in which a doctor carries medicines and instruments; (2) **bottle,** a cannon, *rare;* (3) **bug,** any wood louse of the family Armadillididae which rolls itself into a ball when disturbed.

(1) **1852** *Knickerb.* XL. 470 After procuring his degree, he had not the wherewithal to buy him pill-bags. **1931** DOBIE *Coronado's C.* 43 James had been educated to medicine in Kentucky, their native state, and riding with his 'pill bags' over the far-stretched hills of the Colorado River satisfied his ambition. — (2) **1861** *N.Y. Tribune* 12 July 6/4 We almost vowed that the champagne made as much noise as the reports of Uncle Sam's 'pill-bottles.' — (3) **1843** *Nat. Hist. N.Y., Zoology* VI. 52 *Armadillo Pillularis* . . . is known under the name of Pill-bug, from its form, in a contracted state, completely resembling a pill. **1902** JORDAN & HEATH *Animal Forms* 105 There remain the groups of the pill- or sow-bugs (Isopods) and the sand-fleas.

As the last term in **blue, patent pill.**

* **pillar,** *n.*

1. The old Spanish dollar, so called from the Pillars of Hercules shown on the reverse. Usu. attrib. *Obs.*

1683 *Conn. Rec.* III. 119 All peices of eight, Mexicoe, pillor and Civil peices shall pass at six shillings apeice. **1686** SEWALL *Letter-Book* I. 30 Shipped by Saml. Sewall on the two Brothers . . . 39½ oz. Mexico and Pillar. **1741** *N.J. Archives* 1 Ser. VI. 118 Pillar pieces of eight, seventeen penny weight twelve grains, four shillings and six pence three farthings.

2. pillar cactus, = **saguaro.**

1860 *So. Enterprise* (Thomasville, Ga.) 2 May 1/5 The only thing that grows with any luxuriance is the pillar cactus.

pillo ˈpijo, *n. S.W.* [Sp.] A rascal. *Obs.* — **1845** GREEN *Texian Exped.* 234 This fellow also told us he had been in the United States, and knew the difference between a gentleman and a pillo.

* **pillow,** *n.*

1. A boxing glove. *Slang.*

1894 *Outing* XXIV. 443/1 Piled on a little table were four as dirty and badly-stained 'pillows' as I had ever set eyes on.

2. A game so called. *Colloq.*

1897 R. M. STUART *Simpkinsville* i. 35 'Spinning the plate,' 'dumb-crambo,' 'pillow,' 'how, when and where,' were the innocent games that composed the simple diversions of the evening. **1902** PIDGIN *Q. A. Sawyer* 239 After this game others followed in quick succession. There were 'Pillow,' 'Roll the Cover,' 'Button, Button, Who's Got the Button?' 'Copenhagen,' and finally 'Post Office.'

3. pillow sham, (see quot. 1879). Also attrib.

1879 WEBSTER 1573/1 *Pillow-sham,* a covering, usually of embroidered linen, laid over the pillow of a bed when it is not in use. **1926** *Chi. Tribune* 11 Sep. 2/2 Then there was the pillowsham holder. **1947** *Chr. Sci. Monitor* 15 Jan. 6/5 And pillow shams! Like the splasher, they were painstakingly worked in red outline.

As the last term in **prairie pillow.**

pilon piˈlon, *n. S.W.* [Sp. *pilón,* in Amer. Sp. sense shown here.] (See quot. 1883.) Also **pelon.** Cf. **lagniappe.**

1883 SWEET & KNOX *Though Texas* 348 *Pelon,* was nothing more nor less than any little trifle thrown in,—a kind of voluntary commission to the customer. **1896** *Amer. Folk-Lore* IX. 97 The custom of pelon as it exists along the Rio Grande is analogous to that of l'agniappe in Louisiana. **1939** *Amer. Sp.* April 96 The Rio Grande valley, to the south, uses the Mexican *pilon.*

piloncí piˈlonsɪ, *n. S.W.* Variant of next. *Obs.* — **1845** GREEN *Texian Exped.* 264 Our cook brings us in . . . two and a half pounds of brown sugar, 'piloncí.' **1847** HENRY *Campaign Sk.* 267 The juice [of sugar cane] when sufficiently boiled is run into molds in the shape of truncated cones. In this shape, wrapped around with strips of cane from which the juice is expressed, it is exposed for sale, and called piloncí.

piloncillo ˌpilonˈsijo, *n. S.W.* [Sp. dim. of *pilón,* in Amer. Sp. sense shown here.] (See quots.) *Obs.*

1844 GREGG *Commerce of Prairies* I. 173 When short of means they often support themselves upon only a *real* each per day, their usual food consisting of bread and a kind of coarse cake-sugar *piloncillo* to which is sometimes added a little crude ranchero cheese. **1898** CANFIELD *Maid of Frontier* 207 'Peloncillo,' crude brown sugar, in a stick as big as Pancho's plump leg. **1926** *Cent. Mag.* Nov. 26/2 Peloncillo, a brown sugar from Mexico, almond-bar, and special chocolate might appear.

transf. **1864** MOWRY *Ariz. & Sonora* 27 The whole region between the Rio Grande and the Santa Cruz is broken with conical-shaped hills and mountains, called by the Mexicans *peloncillos.*

* **pilot,** *n.*

1. A guide over a land route.

1672 in *Pub. Col. Soc.* XVIII. 189 In a Short Trauil After wee mett with ye Riuor Hosick wch wee Set or corse for by Direction of or Indian Pilate, and ther at nigh an howre before Son sett we dismounted. **1755** *Lett. to Washington* I. 117 Returned having went 35 miles by Computation of our Pilot. **1842** M. CRAWFORD *Journal* 19 We should have traviled on but we was afraid of being in the night without water, this is the difficulty of traviling without a Pilot.

b. A railroad conductor. *Rare.*

1842 BUCKINGHAM *Slave States* I. 188 Keeping up the maritime phraseology, by which the conductor is called 'the pilot,' and the sound of 'all aboard' announces that . . . all the passengers are in the cars.

c. A mule that works in the lead, in full **pilot mule.** *Obs.*

1887 CUSTER *Tenting on Plains* 352 [In driving a prairie schooner] a small hickory stick, about five feet long, called the jockey-stick, not unlike a rake-handle, is stretched between a pilot and his mate. *Ib.,* A broad piece of leather . . . divides over the shoulders of the lead or pilot mule.

d. (See quot.)

1926 Rickaby *Ballads* 236 *Pilot.* A man in charge of a fleet of rafts. He is, of course, a skilled riverman and thoroughly familiar, not only with the river on which he is rafting, but also with rivers and their ways generally.

2. = **pilot snake** (*a*).

1782 Crèvecoeur *Letters* 236 The most dangerous one is the pilot or copperhead. **1860** *Harper's Mag.* April 584/1 They had been cautioned against getting into the swamps, as the deadly rattlesnake, and still more fatal 'pilot,' were frequently found in those localities. **1946** *Atlanta Jrnl. Mag.* 3 March 8/2 People were afeared of rattlers and pilets, or copperheads, especially when they were quiled up.

3. The cowcatcher on a locomotive. *Colloq.*

1846 Wyse *America* I. 396 There is usually a 'pilot,' made of stout frame work, placed in front of the leading engine, to which it is attached. **1904** O. Henry *Roads of Destiny* 235 The train with the tiny Stars and Stripes fluttering from the engine pilot arrived. **1947** *Chi. D. News* 21 April 1/1 When the I.T.R. train, bound for Granite City with 48 passengers, struck the pile debris flew up and dented the pilot and cab.

b. (See quot.)

1914 *D.N.* IV. 111 *pilot*, n. One of the low front wheels of a locomotive. 'When the *pilots* strike a cow, they generally jump the track.' Also *pilot wheel.* [Kansas.]

4. The black-bellied plover.

1888 Trumbull *Names of Birds* 192 On the coast of Virginia . . . the name of Pilot has been given, as it is always seen leading the large flights of birds which the rising tides drive from the shoals and oyster rocks. **1917** *Birds of Amer.* I. 256 Black-bellied Plover *Squatarola squatarola*. . . . [Also called] Whistling Field Plover; Pilot, May Cock.

5. = **bunko steerer.** *Slang.*

1892 *Brighton* (Utah) *Rec.* 30 April 1/1 Yesterday McMullen's friend received a letter from McMullen in which the writer said he had been 'steered' to Omaha by a 'pilot.'

6. In special combs.: (1) **pilot biscuit,** (see quot. and cf. next and **pilot cracker**); (2) **bread,** a kind of ship's biscuit, a pilot cracker; (3) **cloth,** a kind of coarse blue cloth used for overcoats and sailors' garments; (4) **cracker,** = **pilot biscuit;** (5) **farmer,** one who alternately farms and serves as a river pilot, *rare;* (6) * **fish,** see **Menominee whitefish,** quot. 1903; (7) **house,** (*a*) a house on land in which a pilot lives or stays while waiting for incoming or outgoing boats, (*b*) a structure forward on the upper deck of a ship, esp. of a steam vessel, that shelters the steering gear and helmsman; (8) **snake,** (*a*) = **copperhead 1,** (*b*) the pine snake of the Atlantic Coast, *Pituophis melanoleucus*, (*c*) a harmless blacksnake, *Elaphe obsoleta*, (*d*) (see quot.); (9) **weed,** the rosinweed, *Silphium laciniatum* (see also quot. 1885).

(1) **1944** *Chi. D. News* 11 Oct. 25/1 The pilot biscuit—great flat round crackers that may be purchased at the grocer's—were toasted and lightly spread with butter. — (2) **1788** *Md. Jrnl.* 7 March (Th.), The subscriber has just begun to bake Ship, Pilot, and Cag Bread. **1894** *Outing* XXIV. 252/2 He quickly wrapped up some pilot-bread and . . . tied the package under the balloon. — (3) **1840** *Knickerb.* XV. 140 His winter clothing is usually a peet jecket and trowsers, of strong pilot cloth. **1889** Brayley *Boston Fire Dept.* 193 Coats of pilot-cloth were then made which proved entirely satisfactory. — (4) **1880** *Harper's Mag.* Jan. 224/2 Rhene . . . watches the pilot crackers shovelled out, two to each boy.

(5) **1883** Mark Twain *Life on Miss.* 486 (R.), The pilot-farmer disappears from the river annually about the breaking of spring, and is seen no more until frost. — (7) (*a*) **1812** Stoddard *Sk. Louisiana* 160 On the south side of the east pass, about three miles from the bar, is the pilot house. **1827** Williams *W. Florida* 18 A small fort and pilot house formerly stood near the west end of the island. (*b*) **1846** *Quarter Race Ky.* 127 He placed his hand upon a small brass knob at the back of the pilot house. **1914** Steele *Storm* 148 Crimson sat in the doorway of his pilot-house. — (8) (*a*) **1789** *Amer. Philos. Soc.* III. p. xx, [The Poor-Robin's-plantain is] said to frustrate the bite both of the rattle snake, and of his supposed precursor the pilote-snake. **1916** Seton *Woodcraft Man.* 320 The Copperhead . . . is the Highland, or Northern Moccasin or Pilot Snake, found from Massachusetts to Florida and west to Illinois and Texas. (*b*) **1853** in Marcy *Explor. Red River* (1854) 211 The names of Bull, Pine, and Pilot snake, are commonly given to different species of [*Pituophis*]. (*c*) **1890** *Cent.* 4491/3 *Pilot-snake*, a harmless snake of the United States, *Coluber obsoletus*. **1898** *Smithsonian Rep.* 846 *Coluber obsoletus obsoletus, Say.* . . . This species is found over the entire Eastern district of the United States. It is gentle in its disposition and sluggish in its movements. . . . This is the 'pilot snake' of the Allegheny mountaineers. **1949** *Scientific Mo.* Jan. 54/2 The pilot blacksnake, also called the mountain blacksnake, is frequently confused with the common blacksnake. (*d*) **1892** *Smithsonian Rep.* 832 The fox snake appears to be moderately common in some localities. It is often known as the 'pilot snake.' — (9) **1847** Emory *Military Reconn.* 11 On the uplands . . . occasionally is found the wild tea . . . and pilot weed. **1885** *Girl's Own Paper* Jan. 171/1 The compass plant—variously known, also, as the pilot weed, polar plant, and turpentine weed—is a vigorous perennial.

As the last term in **lightning, river pilot.**

* **pilot,** *v.*

1. *tr.* To guide (a person or party) over land or about a place.

1649 J. Eliot in *Lancaster* (Mass.) *Rec.* 16, I therefore hired a hardy man of Nashaway . . . to mark trees so that he may Pilot me thither in the spring. **1788** Washington *Diaries* III. 361 We set off, pilotted by Mr. Hough thro' by Roads. **1841** Gurney *Journey* 173 The farmer, his wife, and little boy, 'piloted' us to Boston. **1903** *N.Y. Times Sat. Rev.* 26 Sep. 665 Designed first of all for the visitor or the Gothamite piloting friends about the city.

2. To put (a bill) *through* a legislative assembly.

1889 *K.C. Times & Star* 20 May, Representative Garnett cheerfully says he has piloted most of his bills through. **1929** *Randolph Enterprise* (Elkins, W.Va.) 21 March 1/4 The bill . . . piloted . . . thru the House by Representative Karl Kyle.

Pima ˈpima, *n.* [See note.] *collect.* and *pl.* "As popularly known, the name of a division of the Piman family living in the valleys of the Gila and Salt in s. Arizona. Formerly the term was employed to include also the Nevome, or Pimas Bajos" (Hodge).

Said to be from a native word meaning "no" incorrectly understood and applied by missionaries. The term prob. was brought into American use from Spanish.

[**1775** Font *Diary* (1913) 16 Muy de mañana se despacharon unos Yndios, â dor aviso de nuestra venida â los Pimas del rio Gila.] **1864** *Harper's Mag.* Dec. 23/2 It was gratifying . . . to know that the Pimos were rapidly becoming a civilized people. **1942** Castetter & Bell *Pima & Papago Agric.* 130 Unlike Mohave, the Pima, and especially Papago, could not afford to destroy all their property and goods on the occasion of death in the family.

attrib. **1850** *Calif. Courier* (S.F.) 3 July 2/3 From the Pecos river in Texas to the Pimos villages on the Gila, roving bands of Apaches are hovering around the emigrants, stealing their animals. **1878** Hinton *Arizona* 231 South of the Pimo reservation one hundred miles, is the Papago reservation. **1931** *Frontier* Nov. 42/2 A big Pima buck tried to sell him a cord of mesquite stovewood. **1947** *Chi. Tribune* 22 June (Grafic Mag.) 18/5 Ira Hayes, a Pima Indian, was one of the immortal six marines who raised the American flag on the summit of Mount Suribachi in Iwo Jima.

b. (See quot.)

1936 *Sears Cat.* (ed. 173) 469 Pima is the finest of all American cotton.

Also **Piman,** *n.* and *a.*

1942 Castetter & Bell *Pima & Papago Agric.* 1 The Pimans, a name applied to the whole group of Pima-Papago in both Mexico and the United States, anciently extended in irregular distribution from southern Sonora to the Gila River. *Ib.* 5 The second main Piman division . . . occupied the slopes of the watershed which extends irregularly westward from Huachuca Mountain to Nogales.

* **pimp,** *v. intr.* (See quot. 1851.) *Obs.* — **1819** Peirce *Rebelliad* (1842) 33 Did I not promise those who fish'd And pimp'd most any part they wish'd! **1851** Hall *College Words* 231 *Pimp*, to do little, mean actions for the purpose of gaining favor with a superior, as, in college, with an instructor.

* **pin,** *n.*

1. An ornamental badge or brooch adopted as a symbol or emblem of a fraternity, society, etc.

1871 Bagg *At Yale* 144 Its original badge was a rectangular gold plate, about the size and shape of the present Beta Xi pin. **1893** Post *Harvard Stories* 216 Freddy . . . asked me one day why Sheffield wore that funny little pin all the time. **1910** J. Hart *Vigilante Girl* 19 My dear fellow, you may cast aside your Eastern frigidity in fact, I will call it your Cambridge frigidity, for I see you wear a Harvard pin.

2. (*cap.*) *pl.* Members of a belligerent secret society founded about 1856 by full-blooded Cherokee Indians who were bitterly hostile both toward the civilizing procedure of the U.S. Government and toward white people and those of mixed blood who, in general, approved the governmental policies. Also **Pin Society.** *Obs.*

1863 *Rep. Ind. Affairs* 215 The enmity existing between the 'pins' and half-breeds will end in murder. **1866** in *Cong. Globe* 15 Jan. (1873) 617/3 The 'Katoowha society' had its signs, grips, and passwords; its members at one time wore a pin as a badge of membership and identity; and this becoming known, furnished an appropriate name for the mysterious organization by which it will ever be known, 'The Pin society.' **1873** *Ib.*, There has been for the last seventeen years in the [Cherokee] nation a secret society called the 'Pins.' . . . The Pin Society . . . was organized five years before the war. [**1932** J. B. BARRY *Texas Ranger* 175 These Indians were known as 'Pin Indians,' that is, all the Indians who were on the side of the Union.]

3. In special combs.: (1) **pinback,** some now unidentifiable article of feminine attire, *obs.;* (2) **ball,** (*a*) a soft ball serving as a pincushion, (*b*) **pinball sight,** (see quot.); (3) **check,** *attrib.* denoting a fabric having small pinhead-like dots or checks in it, cf. ***pin-stripe;** (4) **fish,** (*a*) the sailor's-choice, *Lagodon rhomboides,* (*b*) a small sparoid fish, *Diplodus holbrooki;* (5) **flat,** (see quot.), *obs.;* (6) ***head,** (*a*) a small minnow, (*b*) a dull, stupid person, *colloq.,* (*c*) **pinhead sight,** see **pinball** (*b*); (7) **headed,** *a.* denoting one who is a pinhead, *slang;* (8) **hook,** (*a*) a fishhook made of a bent pin, also attrib., (*b*) **pinhook lawyer,** a mean, pettifogging lawyer, *colloq.;* (9) **pool,** any one of several games of pool or billiards in which wooden pins are used; (10) ***tail,** (*a*) *W.* the sharp-tailed grouse, *Pedioecetes phasianellus,* (*b*) the ruddy duck, cf. **spike pintail;** (11) **tailed grouse,** =**pintail** (*a*); (12) ***wheel,** (see quots.).

(1) **1875** *Chi. Tribune* 23 Nov. 7/3 She . . . made as much show of dress as her limited means would allow, even her 'pinback' being formed in the most taking style. **1876** in GUILD *Old Times* (1878) 387 There were no pinbacks then [*c*1840]; no redingotes, prunellas, nor bustles. — (2) (*a*) **1803** BOWNE *Life* 176/2 We went to a room where they keep their work for sale,—pocket-books, pin balls [etc.]. **1895** A. BROWN *Meadow-Grass* 211 Them pinballs my neighbor, Mis' Dyer, made with her own hands. (*b*) **1883** KNIGHT *Supp.* 682/1 *Pin-ball Sight,* (*Rifle*) another name for the *bead-sight:* called also pin-head sight. — (3) **1942** RAWLINGS *C. Creek* 139 He wore one blue mail-order shirt . . . and one pair of blue pincheck pants until they dropped from his unlaundered body. — (4) (*a*) **1878** *Nat. Museum Proc.* 378 *Logodon rhomboides.*—Robin; Pin-fish. Excessively abundant everywhere in the harbor [Beaufort]. **1911** *Rep. Fisheries 1908* 315/1 Sailor's Choice. . . It is also called 'robin,' 'pinfish,' 'salt-water bream,' [etc.]. **1949** *Fishes Western N. Atlantic* I. 373 Mackerel, menhaden (*Brevoortia*) and pinfish (*Lagodon*) are included in its known diet. (*b*) **1884** GOODE *Fisheries* I. 386 The Pin-fish . . . is abundant at Charleston and about Beaufort, North Carolina.

(5) **1878** N. H. BISHOP *Voyage of Paper Canoe* 25 Down the current [of the St. Lawrence] floated 'pin-flats,' a curious scow-like boat, which carries a square sail. — (6) (*a*) **1845** JUDD *Margaret* I. 18 Minnows and pinheads were flashing and skirting through the clear, bright stream. (*b*) **1896** ADE *Artie* 168 There's just as many pin-heads on State Street as you'll find anywhere out in the woods. **1924** DAWES in *Glasgow Herald* 14 Jan. 9 There are too many 'pinheads' throwing mud. — (7) **1908** MULFORD *Orphan* ix. 106 And the pin-headed wart went and blabbed the whole thing. — (8) (*a*) **1840** *S. Lit. Messenger* VI. 386/2 Ellen used to fish there for minnoes with a pin-hook. *c***1866** BAGBY *Old Va. Gentleman* 48 [He must] fish for minnows with a pin-hook, and carry his worms in a cymling. **1897** *Outing* Aug. 439 With the shiner and young perch, [the sunfish] ranks among the first victims of pin-hook wiles. (*b*) **1834** CROCKETT *Life* 207 In this hunt every . . . little pin-hook lawyer was engaged. — (9) **1864** DICK *Amer. Hoyle* (1866) 428 The game of Pin Pool is played with two white balls and one red, together with five small wooden pins. **1899** ADE *Fables in Slang* 16 The Local Editor of the Evening Paper was playing Pin-Pool with the Superintendent of the Trolley Line.

(10) (*a*) **1894** CRANE in *Outing* XXIV. 385/2 We found the pin-tails more frequently on the sides of hills, about the coolies in the rolling prairie. **1948** *Green Bay* (Wis.) *Press-Gazette* 12 July 15/8 The population of pintails is a 20 per cent increase over last year. (*b*) **1917** *Birds of Amer.* I. 152 Ruddy Duck . . . [Also called] Pintail. **1948** *Nat. Hist.* April 175/1 The next morning several dozen nervous pintails settled on the zoo pond. — (11) **1827** D. DOUGLAS *Journal* (1914) 74 On the plains I killed several curlews, and in the woods a number, both male and female, of *Tetrao phasianellus,* the Pin-tailed Grouse. **1880** FARRAR *Five Years Minn.* 158 In the woods the tree-partridge, here called the pheasant, and the pin-tailed grouse abound. — (12) **1885** *Harper's Mag.* Jan. 275/2 The hides next pass into a queer-looking contrivance known as a 'pin-wheel,' a stout circular wooden box, in which they are churned about in warmish water, dropping upon stout wooden pins attached to the circumference.

b. In the names of plants: (1) **pin-birch,** =**gray birch,** (2) **cherry,** (see quot. 1897); (3) **clover,** =**alfilaria;** (4) **cushion cactus,** (see quots.); (5) **grass,** =**alfilaria;** (6) **oak,** see as a main entry; (7) **weed,** any herb of the genus *Lechea.*

(1) **1894** *Amer. Folk-Lore* VII. 98 *Betula populifolia* . . . pin-birch, Penobscot Co., Me. — (2) **1884** SARGENT *Rep. Forests* 66 Pin Cherry. . . . The small acid fruit used domestically and by herbalists in the preparation of cough mixtures, etc. **1897** SUDWORTH *Arborescent Flora* 240 *Prunus pennsylvanica.* . . . Wild Red Cherry. . . . Pin Cherry (N.H., Vt., N.Y., Mich., Ohio, Iowa, N. Dak.). **1948** *Green Bay* (Wis.) *Press-Gazette* 13 July 11/4 There were numerous clumps of pin and choke cherry. — (3) **1884** W. MILLER *Dict. Names of Plants* 106/2 Pin-grass, or Pin-clover, of California: *Erodium cicutarium.* **1925** JEPSON *Flowering Plants Calif.* 592 The term filaree, a contraction of the Spanish Alfilerilla, is, like the names Pin Clover or Pin Grass, indifferently applied to either this species or to no. 5. [E. moschatum]. — (4) **1918** VISHER *So. Dakota* 89 The small milkweed (Asclepias pumila), the pincushion cactus (Mammilaria vivipara), and Parosela aurea are rather numerous. **1949** HERTRICH *Huntington Bot. Gardens* 22 Mammillaria compressa [is] commonly known as pincushion cactus.

(5) **1847** *Californian* (S.F.) 10 July 3/1 Quality of Pasture—Bunch Grass; Clover; Wild Oats and Pin Grass, in all abundance. **1949** PALMER *Fieldbook Nat. Hist.* 241/3 Common names include wild musk, pin clover, pin grass, pinweed, and heron's-bill, mostly based on character of fruit. — (7) **1814** BIGELOW *Florula Bostoniensis* 29 Lechea minor Small Pin weed. . . . Flowers minute. **1893** TORREY *Foot-Path Way* 72 Acres and acres of horseweed, pinweed, stone clover, poverty grass, . . . and bearberry!

c. *To stick pins into* (a person), to provoke to action, stir up, annoy. *Colloq.*

1903 LEWIS *Boss* 184 This aint meant to stick pins into you.

As the last term in **badge, battle, bosom, breast, bridle, clothes, crown, fraternity, hair, husking, king, liberty, picket, school, stake, stick, ten pin.**

pinacate ˌpinəˈkɑtɪ, *n.* [Amer. Sp. (<Nahuatl) in same sense.] Any one of various wingless beetles of the genus *Eleodes* found in dry regions in the West. Also **pinacate beetle.**

1924 *Cent. Mag.* July 389/1 Usually, however, you would see the *corredor del camino* catching lizards or picking up black pinacate beetles. **1935** BARNES *Ariz. Place Names* 333 Pinacate Lava Flow and Valley [are] . . . named for the beetle found here called Pinacate by the Mexicans. **1936** *Univ. Ariz. Gen. Bul.* 3, 115 Probably the best known beetle of the state is the Pinacate or the beetle that stands on its head.

***pincers,** *n. pl.* Tongs for handling ice. *Rare.* — **1890** *Harper's Mag.* April 746/1 [Lucilla] saw a burly ice-man, his iron pincers dangling from his hand.

***pinch,** *n.*

1. *W.* The place at which a mineral vein or bed becomes markedly thin. See also **clay pinch.**

1873 BEADLE *Undevel. West* 333 All the strange terms in mining parlance: 'true lodes, fissure-veins, pinches.' **1878** ——— *Western Wilds* 486 Next, perhaps, he finds the vein widening . . . ; again he encounters a 'pinch' or 'cap,' and hope almost dies out ere he gets through it.

2. *W.* (See quots.)

1849 *Maysville* (Ky.) *Herald* 8 Jan. 2/2 The price of a glass of whiskey, in the gold region of California, is a pinch of gold dust—so that the amount the seller receives depends upon his capacity to take a big pinch. **1907** *Sunset Mag.* Dec. 159 Next day the place opened as a saloon, with a full outfit of liquors which were sold at one dollar or a pinch of gold dust a drink. **1948** A. K. WILLIAMS *Gold Rush Days* 26 About the smallest medium of exchange was a 'pinch' and this was all the gold a person could pick up between their thumb and first finger.

3. pinch batter, in baseball, a player who goes in to bat in the place of another, usu. in a "pinch" or emergency. *Rare.* Cf. **pinch hitter.**

1928 *Chi. Tribune* 5 Oct. 26/1 The pinch batter exercised rare judgment and drew a pass.

***pinch,** *v.*

1. *W. intr.* Of a vein of ore: To become narrow or thin (see also quot. 1877).

1869 MCCLURE *Rocky Mts.* 267 They know that it [the lead] may cap, or pinch, or play out entirely. **1877** W. WRIGHT *Big Bonanza* 164 The miners are never discouraged so long as they find a good width of quartz. . . . What they do not like, however, is to find the walls coming together—'pinching,' as they call it. The coming together of the walls pinches out or cuts off the vein. **1880** *Harper's Mag.* Feb. 395/1 Ore is harder and more expensive to work, and the veins 'pinch' (or contract to very small dimensions).

2. pinch bug, any one of various stag beetles, esp. *Lucanus dama.*

1856 MARK TWAIN in *Iowa Jrnl. of Hist.* XXVII. 423 A tenor and bass duet by thirty-two thousand locusts and ninety-seven thousand pinch bugs was sung. **1876** Mark Twain *Tom Sawyer* v. 57 It was a large black beetle with formidable jaws—a 'pinch-bug,' he called it.

3. a. *To pinch out* or *down*, of a vein or mineral, to run out, to end. Also transf. **b.** *to pinch in*, to encroach *on* or *upon* so as to confine or restrict.

(**a**) **1869** *Overland Mo.* III. 283 The Russian River Valley 'pinches out' at Cloverdale. **1931** Willison *Here They Dug Gold* 70 Almost all veins begin to taper off and many 'pinch out' entirely. **1945** *Newsweek* 9 April 45/1 He watched his control of the Idaho Maryland Mines Corp. pinch down to the vanishing point. **1947** Chalfant *Gold, Guns, & Ghost Towns* 78 High-grade veins were followed as they pinched down, even to half-inch seams which were profitably 'spooned out.' — (**b**) **1873** Beadle *Undevel. West* 346 Winter 'pinched in' on mining operations in Utah. *Ib.* 754 The spurs of the Sierras put out westward toward the Coast Range, and, in mining parlance, 'pinch in' upon the plain.

pinch-hit ˈpɪntʃˌhɪt, *v. Baseball. intr.* To bat in the place of another, usu. in a "pinch" or emergency. Also transf.

1931 *K.C. Star* 17 Dec. 24 John Neilson gave the talk, . . . but I thought they were just using him to pinch-hit for Bo McMillin. **1948** *Capital-Democrat* (Tishomingo, Okla.) 17 June 5/5 Duggan Smith, pinch hitting for W. C. Whiteley, had sent a high drive out to center. **1949** *Lubbock* (Tex.) *Morn. Avalanche* 23 Feb. II. 4/6 In his absence, he has called upon three good friends, also authors of daily columns, to pinch hit for him and give his readers a 'change of pace.'

Hence **pinch-hitter, pinch-hitting.**

1912 *Lit. Digest* 10 Aug. 238/2 Things did not run very smoothly the famous 'Cub' pinch hitter himself tells us. **1947** *L.A. Times* 6 Oct. 11/7 Brown, the former U.C.L.A. diamond star, kept up his red-hot pinch hitting when he singled for Phillips in the third and scored DiMaggio. **1949** *Newsweek* 5 Dec. 54/2 Taking over the column as a vacation pinch hitter, he was given it permanently when its regular conductor returned.

pinching bug. =**pinch bug** (see also quot. 1890).

1850 Garrard *Wah-To-Yah* 226 Then Noah was so hurried to git the yelaphants, pinchin' bugs, an sich varmint aboard [etc.]. **1890** *Cent.* 4495/1 *Pinching-bug*, the dobson or hellgrammite. Western Pennsylvania. **1948** *Chi. Tribune* 30 May (Comics) 2 The Policeman agreed to try the plan and presently the Cowboy produced the pinching bug.

pinder ˈpɪndɚ, *n.* Also **pindar.** *S.* [Kongo *mpinda*, in same sense.] The peanut or goober. Also attrib.

[**1707** Sloane *Jamaica* I. p. lxxiii, I was assured that the Negroes feed on Pindals or Indian Earth-nuts, a sort of pea or bean producing its pods under ground.] **1848** *Rep. Comm. Patents 1847* 190 The ground pea of the south, or . . . the gouber or pindar pea, is highly recommended in the Tallahassee Floridian. **1907** *Suburban Life* May 263/2 Other common names are pindar, goober, ground-nut, ground-pea and monkey-nut. **1948** Mathews *Southernisms* 111 In colloquial speech we call peanuts *pinders, goobers*, and *ground peas.*

pindle ˈpɪndl, *v.* [App. a back-formation from **pindling.**] *intr.* To pine or languish. *Colloq.* — **1893** *Voodoo Tales* 13 Ef yo' don't tell de bees 'bout all de bornin's an' weddin's an' fun'als dey gwinter (going to) cl'ar out air else sorter pindle (pine) an' die. **1931** in Wentworth, Poor Cora pindled along for a year . . . afore she died.

pindling ˈpɪndlɪŋ, *a.* [f. **pine, v.* Cf. **dwindling*, f. **dwine, v.*] Sick, puny, trifling. *Colloq.*

1861 Stowe *Pearl Orr's Isl.* I. 25 [The baby is] such a pindling little thing. **1890** Wiggin *Timothy's Quest* 115 Mis' Pennell's got a new girl to help round the house,—one o' them pindlin' light-complected Smith girls. **1930** H. Zink *City Bosses* 7 The elder Kelly ran a pindling grocery store.

***pine,** *n.*

1. (*cap.*) *pl.* A region covered with pines, esp. an extensive area in New Jersey extending from Lakewood to Cape May County.

1856 *Spirit of Times* 6 Sep. 9/1 Except a few on the barrens . . . and in the Pines of New Jersey, there are none within reach of our city sportsmen. **1892** *Outing* July 303/1 That part of South Jersey called the 'Pines' or 'Pine Barrens' is wild and lonesome. **1949** *Sat. Ev. Post* 12 March 17/1 [These towns] surround and pepper the wilderness of the Pines, a lost region under a veil of rutted trails as intricate as a cobweb.

2. In combs.: (1) **pine almond,** the seed of a pine; (2) ***apple,** see as a main entry; (3) **bur,** the cone or fruit of the pine tree; (4) **drops,** a stout, purplish-brown plant, *Pterospora andromedea*, found in stiff clay soil on the roots of pine trees, cf. **Albany beechdrops;** (5) **gum,** crude turpentine from a pine; (6) **knot,** see as a main entry; (7) **lander,** one who lives in pinelands; (8) **land looker,** =**timber cruiser;** (9) **mast,** the seeds collectively of pine trees; (10) ***nut,** the seed of various low-growing pines, as the piñon, found in the western and southwestern parts of the U.S.; (11) **quill,** =**pine spill;** (12) **rock,** app. a steep-sided hill which exposes considerable rock and supports a growth of pine trees, *obs.;* (13) **rust blister,** a fungoid disease which kills white pines and other five-needled pines, also called blister rust, and white-pine blister rust; (14) **sap,** any one of various herbs of the genus *Hypopitys*, esp. *H. lanuginosa*, false beechdrops, also attrib., cf. **beech-drops;** (15) **settlement,** a settlement in a region covered with pines; (16) **spill,** *local*, a pine needle, cf. **pine quill;** (17) **State,** a nickname for Georgia, *obs.;* (18) **straw,** pine needles, esp. dried ones, also attrib.; (19) **tag,** a pine needle; (20) **tassel,** =prec.; (21) **top,** cheap whisky in making which pine tags are allegedly used; (22) ***tree,** see as a main entry; (23) **weed,** (*a*) orange grass, *Sarothra gentianoides*, (*b*) corn spurry, *Spergula arvensis;* (24) **wood,** see as a main entry.

(**1**) **1842** Thoreau *Journal* I. 338, I need not think of the pine almond or the acorn and sapling when I meet the fallen pine or oak, more than of the generations of pines and oaks which have fed the young tree. — (**3**) **1800** Hawkins *Sk. Creek Country* 77 They collect old corn cobs and pine burs. **1899** Green *Va. Word-Book* 276 *Pine-burr*, the cone of the pine-tree. — (**4**) **1857** Gray *Botany* 261 *Pterospora.* Pine-drops . . . *P. Andromedea.*—Hard clay soil, parasitic on the roots apparently of pines, from Vermont, Peekskill and Albany, N.Y., and N. Pennsylvania northward and westward: rare. **1899** Going *Flowers* 260 In July pine-roots give a home and a maintenance to some curious parasitic plants—'pine-drops,' 'pine-sap,' and 'Indian-pipe' or 'ghost-flower.'

(**5**) **1855** Simms *Forayers* 434 A leetle pine-gum plaister on that head of yourn will stop up the sore places. **1921** *Frontier* May 5 The Sheep Eaters lived in tepees made of cedar thatched with moss and cemented by pine gum. — (**7**) **1839** Kemble *Residence in Ga.* 75 He gave me a lively and curious description of the Yeomanry of Georgia, more properly termed pine-landers. **1922** Kephart *So. Highlanders* 433 As the plantations expanded, these freedmen were pushed further and further back upon more and more sterile soil. They became 'pine-landers' or 'piney-woods-people,' 'sand-hillers,' 'knob-people,' 'corn-crackers,' or 'crackers.' — (**8**) **1892** *Outing* Jan. 280/1 The letter was signed: 'John Scales, pine land looker and estimator.' — (**9**) **1879** *Diseases of Swine* 214 Some old stock-raisers say that this disease [thumps] is always worse after a heavy pine mast, which my own experience confirms.

(**10**) [**1776** in *Catholic Church in Utah* (1909) 157 Three Yuta women and a child . . . gave us some . . . cherries, limes and pine nuts.] **1845** Frémont *Exped.* 222 A party of twelve Indians came down from the mountains to trade pine nuts, of which each one carried a little bag. These seemed now to be the staple of the country. **1947** *Sierra Club Bul.* March 4/1 It is far too late now to advocate . . . a return . . . to the Indian's custom of living on the income of natural resources, the replenishable deer, acorns, pine nuts and grasshoppers. — (**11**) **1873** Miller *Amongst Modocs* 180 On that side where only grass has grown and pine quills fallen, . . . the ground is often broken. — (**12**) **1644** *New Haven Col. Rec.* I. 142 The land towards Mr. Goodyears farme and the plaine by the pine rock may be viewed. **1654** *Ib.* 206 The plaine by the pine rocke. **1843** Margaret Fuller *Summer on Lakes* 171 The sugar loaf rock is a fragment in the same kind as the pine rock we saw in Illinois. — (**13**) **1928** *Sat. Ev. Post* 10 March 69/2 [It will] blight this lovely coast the way the pine-rust blister is blighting our splendid pines. — (**14**) **1837** Darlington *Flora Cestrica* 267 Pine sap. False Beech drops. **1901** Mohr *Plant Life Ala.* 652 Monotropaceae. Pinesap Family. . . . *Hypopitys hypopitys* . . . Pinesap. **1943** Peattie *Great Smokies* 172 To those who have never seen them, trillium and blood-root and pinesaps are unimaginable plants.

(**15**) **1836** Gilman *Recoll.* (1838) 51 Our summers were usually passed at Springland, a pine settlement. — (**16**) **1901** *Harper's Mag.* Dec. 45/2, I ain't goin' to have . . . [honey] full o' dry bark an' pine spills, dead bees, an' all them sorts o' trollick. — (**17**) **1846** *Warrock's Alm. 1847* 22 Georgia, Pine [State]. — (**18**) **1832** Kennedy *Swallow Barn* I. 295 The ground was strewed with a thick coat of pine-straw. **1884** Cable *Dr. Sevier* lvii, Mary Richling . . . still had on the pine-straw hat. **1939** *These Are Our Lives* 51 The pen was grounded with pine straw as was the shelter. — (**19**) **1851** *S. Lit. Messenger* XVII. 226/2 We made a [bonfire] of dead boughs and 'pine-tags.' **1899** Green *Va. Word-Book* 276 *Pine-tag*, the needle or leaf of the pine-tree.

(**20**) **1858** Willis *Convalescent* 393 The wilderness [is] covered thick with a compost of pine-tassels and dead leaves. — (**21**) **1858** *S. Lit. Messenger* XXVII. 463/2 A rough, but hearty frolic, characteristic of the time and place, with . . . profusion of 'pine-top' succeeded. **1931**

Amer. Sp. VII. 50 The 'drinks' are 'pine-top,' 'white mule,' [etc.]. — **(23)** (*a*) **1814** BIGELOW *Florula Bostoniensis* 73 *Sarothra gentianoides* Pine weed. . . . A small, erect, branching plant. (*b*) **1891** *Amer. Folk-Lore* IV. 148 *Spergula arvensis* was very fittingly named *Pine Weed.*

b. In the names of birds: (1) **pine bullfinch,** =**pine grosbeak;** (2) **creeper,** =**pine warbler;** (3) **creeping warbler,**=**pine warbler;** (4) ***finch,** a small North American bird, *Spinus pinus*, also known as **pine linnet, pine siskin;** (5) **grosbeak,** a large grosbeak, *Pinicola enucleator*, about nine inches long and of a general red or reddish color, found in coniferous forests of northeastern North America; (6) **grouse,** the dusky grouse, *Dendragapus obscurus*, of the Rocky Mountain region; (7) **hen,** =prec.; (8) **jay,** (see quot.); (9) **linnet,** =**pine finch;** (10) **siskin,** =**pine finch;** (11) **swamp warbler,** the black-throated blue warbler, *Dendroica caerulescens;* (12) **warbler,** a small insectivorous migratory bird, *Dendroica pinus* or *vigorsi*, inhabiting pine woods throughout eastern North America.

(1) 1828 BONAPARTE *Ornithology* III. 17 The female Pine Bullfinch is eight and a half inches long. **1917** *Birds of Amer.* III. 3 Pine Grosbeak. Pinicola enucleator leucura. . . . [Also called] Pine Bullfinch. — **(2)** *c***1730** CATESBY *Carolina* I. 61 *Parus Americanus lutescens.* The Pine-creeper. . . . They creep about Trees; particularly the Pine- and Fir-trees; from which they peck Insects, and feed on them. **1917** *Birds of Amer.* III. 148 Pine Warbler. *Dendroica vigorsi.* . . . [Also called] Pine-creeping Warbler; Pine Creeper. — **(3) 1811** WILSON *Ornithology* III. 25 [The] Pine-Creeping Warbler . . . inhabits the pine woods of the Southern states, where it is resident. **1917** [see **pine creeper**]. — **(4) 1810** WILSON *Ornithology* II. 133 [The] Pine Finch . . . seeks the seeds of the black alder, on the borders of swamps, creeks and rivulets. **1917** *Birds of Amer.* III. 16 Pine Siskin. . . . [Also called] Pine Finch; Pine Linnet; American Siskin.

(5) 1772 *Phil. Trans.* LXII. 402 [The] Pine Grosbeak . . . visits the Hudson's Bay settlements in May, on its way to the north, and is not observed to return. **1890** *Atlantic Mo.* Aug. 255/2 [I] saw with perfect distinctness . . . two pine grosbeaks in bright male costume,—birds I had never seen before except in winter. **1942** RICH *We Took to Woods* (1948) 239, I saw a pine grosbeak in a little poplar tree. — **(6) 1851** in SCHOOLCRAFT *Indian Tribes* (1853) III. 112 The pine grouse, and quail, geese, ducks, and cranes, abound in their proper season. **1917** *Birds of Amer.* II. 12 Dusky Grouse. *Dendragapus obscurus obscurus.* . . . [Also called] Blue Grouse; Pine Grouse; Pine Hen [etc.]. —**(7) 1883** *Harper's Mag.* Oct. 711/1 A strapping young fellow with a gun in his hand came up to me and asked if I would like to have a shot at a 'pine hen.' **1917** [see **pine grouse**]. — **(8) 1917** *Birds of Amer.* II. 219 Steller's Jay, *Cyanocitta stelleri stelleri.* . . . [Also called] Mountain Jay; Pine Jay; Conifer Jay. — **(9) 1874** COUES *Birds N.Y.* 115 Pine Linnet. . . . The erratic movements of this species . . . render it difficult to define its limits with precision. **1941** SETON *Trail of Artist-Naturalist* 151, I was out every fine day, and nearly always got or saw something—crows, juncos, shrikes, pine linnets, chickadees.

(10) 1887 RIDGWAY *Man. N. Amer. Birds* 400 Northern North America, breeding from northern United States northward, and south in Rocky Mountains; south, in winter, to Gulf States and Mexico. . . . Pine Siskin. **1947** *Chi. Tribune* 28 Dec. VI. 1/1 They checked in a number of long eared sawwhet, and screech owls, some pine siskins, which were found munching on birch cones and pods, . . . and the cross-bill. — **(11) 1812** WILSON *Ornithology* V. 100 The Pine-swamp Warbler is four inches and a quarter long, and seven inches and a quarter in extent. — **(12) 1917** *Birds of Amer.* III. 149/1 The Pine Warbler is a well-named bird, because its nesting sites are always in pine trees.

c. In the names of other animals: (1) **pine borer,** any one of various insect larvae that bore into pine trees; (2) **horn snake,** (see quot. and cf. **horn snake**), *obs.;* (3) **lizard,** the fence lizard *q.v.*, found in the warmer parts of the U.S.; (4) **mouse,** a reddish-brown vole, *Microtus pinetorum*, about four inches long, found often in pine barrens; (5) **snake,** any one of various harmless snakes of the genus *Pituophis*, esp. *P. melanoleucus*, commonly found in pine woods in the Atlantic Coast region, also *attrib.;* (6) **squirrel,** a squirrel found in coniferous forests, esp. *Sciurus hudsonicus*, the common American red squirrel, cf. **chickaree;** (7) **weevil,** any one of various weevils injurious to pine trees.

(1) 1862 *Rep. Comm. Patents 1861: Agric.* 614 The larvae [*sic*] of this insect is evidently a pine-borer, for I have found it about saw-mills. **1884** *Rep. Comm. Agric.* 379 The Common Longicorn Pine-Borer . . . is destructive to the white pine. — **(2) 1808** T. ASHE *Travels* xxviii. 243 We called the following [snakes] to our recollection:—ribbon snake, pine-horn or bull snake, with a spear in his tail. — **(3) 1842** *Nat. Hist. N.Y., Zoology* III. 33 From its abundance in pine forests, [the brown swift] has obtained the name of Pine Lizard. **1895** *Outing* XXVI. 34/2 A pine lizard ran up the trunk of a cedar tree. — **(4) 1851** AUDUBON *Quadrupeds N. Amer.* III. 216 *Arvicola Pinetorum.* . . . Leconte's Pine-Mouse. . . . This species bears some resemblance to Wilson's Meadow Mouse. **1945** MCATEE *John & Joe* 16 There are in the east, groundhogs, chipmunks, pine mice, meadow voles, and Geomys gophers.

(5) 1791 W. BARTRAM *Travels* 276 The pine or bull snake is very large, and inoffensive with respect to mankind. **1895** *Outing* XXVI. 39/2 A pine snake, bloated and glistening, wriggles across the road. **1941** LYON *Hills* 192 Inside that bird nest was a small piece of discarded pine snakeskin, the original bands still faintly visible. — **(6) 1805–9** HENRY *Camp. Quebec* 44 The sterility of the country had afforded us no game. . . . Nothing in short but the diver and a red pine squirrel, which was too small and quick to be killed by a bullet. **1857** *Rep. Comm. Patents 1856: Agric.* 67 This pretty and active little animal is well known through the Northern States, under the names of 'Red-Squirrel,' 'Chickaree,' 'Pine Squirrel,' and, sometimes, 'Mountain Squirrel.' **1949** *Reader's Digest* May 122/1 On a hunting trip in central Oregon I happened to see a pine squirrel caching his winter food supply. — **(7) 1862** *Rep. Comm. Patents 1861: Agric.* 605 *Hylobius pales* and *Hylurgus Terebrans*, also infesting the pine, now [in April] abound. **1868** *Amer. Naturalist* II. 165 Another Pine-weevil (*Hylobius pales*, Fig. 4) also abounds in May.

d. Denoting things made from, or consisting of, a pine, pines, or pine products, as (1) **pine canoe,** (2) **corner,** cf. ***corner,** *n.* **1,** (3) **fence,** (4) **hotel,** (5) **house,** (6) **lumber,** (7) **overcoat,** (8) **pole cabin,** (9) **raft,** (10) **rail,** (11) **shack,** (12) **shingle,** (13) **slab,** (14) **snag,** (15) **stump.**

(1) 1775 CRESSWELL *Journal* (1925) 85 Got a large pine canoe out of some drift wood with great labour. — **(2) 1799** *Herald of Freedom* (Edenton, N.C.) 27 March, Beginning at a pine corner of his own survey. — **(3) 1870** EMERSON *Soc. & Solitude* vi. 132 Draw a pine fence about them and for fifty years they mature for the owner their delicious fruit. **1882** PECK *Sunshine* 134 We filled the stove about half full of pine fence. — **(4) 1909** O. HENRY *Options* 275 In the village I found a pine hotel called the Bay View House.

(5) 1891 O'BEIRNE *Leaders Ind. Territory* 218/1 He owns several pine houses, and a stock ranch and a range which are scarcely equaled in that portion of the country. — **(6) 1803** *Ann. 8th Congress* 2 Sess. 1506 The country on the east side of Lake Pontchartrain . . . would, however, afford abundant supplies of pitch, tar, and pine lumber. **1890** LANGFORD *Vigilante Days* (1912) 499 In three days our craft was completed. She was as stanch as pine lumber and nails could make her. — **(7) 1896** *Cong. Rec.* 20 Jan. 796/2 The bill provides that the Committee shall . . . get as cheap a coffin as it can bargain for . . . perhaps what they call in the army a pine overcoat. — **(8) 1864** *Harper's Mag.* June 123/2 He would have seen the two 'camped out' together in the same tent or pine-pole cabin. — **(9) 1883** MARK TWAIN *Life Miss.* iii. 41 He took a berth on a Pittsburgh coal-flat, or on a pine raft.

(10) 1862 *Harper's Mag.* March 491/1 You can get your friends to look on the pine rail fences inclosing corn-fields any where south of New Jersey. — **(11) 1930** FERBER *Cimarron* 209 They flocked from miles to hear him, and the crude pine shack that was the courtroom would be packed to suffocation. — **(12) 1820** *Detroit Gazette* 16 June 2/2 The Subscriber . . . has on hand . . . 150,000 Pine Shingles. **1876** MARK TWAIN *Tom Sawyer* x. 95 He picked up a clean pine shingle . . . and painfully scrawled these lines. — **(13) 1666** *East-Hampton Rec.* I. 248 A Pine slab by the well with my lath bench. **1881** *Chi. Times* 16 April, About everybody who keeps house in Chicago has paid $7 per cord for pine slabs for kindling-wood. *c***1908** CANTON *Frontier Trails* 95 We built breastworks at the ranch building from heavy pine slabs. — **(14) 1885** M. THOMPSON *By Ways & Bird Notes* 24, I ken mek er bee-line to that air ole pine snag.

(15) 1659 *Watertown Rec.* I. I. 65 Abram Brownes Land . . . begins ten rod from Rich. Bloyse his lott, & soe apon a straite line to a pine stump. **1894** *Home Missionary* Oct. 328 This pine-stump land . . . is proving to be the best potato land in the world. *Ib.* 329 Another of these pine-stump country churches granted twenty-three letters last year to members who have gone into the cities.

e. Denoting places or areas upon which pines are the prevailing growth, as (1) **pine barren,** see as a main entry, (2) **bluff,** (3) **commons,** (4) **flats,** (5) **flatwoods,** (6) **hill country,** (7) **knob,** (8) **land,** (9) **lick,** (10) **lot,** (11) **plain,** (12) **ridge,** (13) **savanna,** (14) **swamp.**

(2) 1766 J. BARTRAM *Journal* 41 We rowed . . . by some oak and pine-bluffs. **1938** MATSCHAT *Suwannee River* 219 They crossed a pine bluff. — **(3) 1815** *Mass. H.S. Coll.* 2 Ser. IV. 290 The pine commons of Wareham, Sandwich, and Plymouth, are very extensive and contiguous, affording a wide range for sheep. — **(4) 1807** IRVING *Salma-*

gundi xvi. 421 Some . . . enjoy the varied and romantic scenery of burnt trees, . . . pine flats [etc.]. **1866** W. REID *After the War* 416 Between New Orleans and Jackson, one saw little to admire in the pine flats that lined the railroad for nearly its whole length. **1949** *Amer. Sp.* April 112/1 Pine Flats, *n. pl.* Level woodlands, covered chiefly with yellow pine. [Marlboro Co., S.C.]

(**5**) **1942** KENNEDY *Palmetto Country* 4 Shrub-like saw palmetto underlies the pine flatwoods from Florida northward into South Carolina and westward to Louisiana. — (**6**) **1857** STROTHER *Virginia* 203 He was the acknowledged cock of the walk, and *preux chevalier* of the pine-hill country. — (**7**) **1841** GREGG *Diary & Lett.* (1941) I. 76 Of all the growths of Arkansas there is probably now [*sic*] more universal than sassafras—it is to be found almost everywhere . . . amongst the pineknobs and walnut and hackberry groves, nay, everywhere in the timber. — (**8**) *c*1660 *Lancaster Rec.* 271 Thare is another peice of upland . . . which buts northerly upon Common Land Sum part pine Land partly oak Land. **1776** ROMANS *Concise Hist.* 15, I shall treat of them by the names of pine land, Hammock land, savannah, swamps, marshes, and bay, or cypress galls. **1948** *Sat. Ev. Post* 4 Sep. 30/1 There was a stillness here in the flat lonesome pinelands. — (**9**) **1781** in *Amer. Sp.* XV. 280/2 At the foot of the nobs About a Mile No. Wt. from the pine Lick.

(**10**) **1840** *Knickerb.* XVI. 206 These [land-lookers] met you at every turn, ready to furnish 'water-power,' 'pine-lots,' . . . or any thing else, at a moment's notice. **1905** *Forestry Bureau Bul.* No. 63, 16 This map is not designed to show the merchantable pine lots in New England. — (**11**) **1665** *Lancaster Rec.* 79 A slipe of medow ground Runing through the most part of a great pine plaine. **1860** GREELEY *Overland Journey* 111 The surrounding prairies—sterile as 'pine plains' are apt to be. **1935** *Ecological Monog.* Jan. 66 Southern New England, except the mountains, was . . . covered with oak-hickory and oak-chestnut on the uplands, while the sandy, so-called 'Pine plains' were pitch pine. — (**12**) **1788** SCHÖPF *Reise* II. 242 Den höhern und trocknern Theil dieser Fläche nehmen die unermesslichen Fohrenwaldungen ein; die daher dry Pine ridges oder Pine Barrens genannt werden. **1802** ELLICOTT *Journal* 184 On one of the pine ridges I saw a few stones. **1949** *Pacific Discovery* Jan.–Feb. 5/1 Each saddle in a pine ridge or pass through the rimrock was in my boyish imagination a new route to be explored for the first time by a white man. — (**13**) **1735** *Ga. Hist. Soc. Coll.* II. 43 We rode about two miles farther, where we came to a large pine savannah. **1791** W. BARTRAM *Travels* 208 The cattle which only feed and range in the high forests and Pine savannas are clear of this disorder. — (**14**) **1635** *Cambridge Prop. Rec.* 6 The pine Swamp on the north east. **1862** NORTON *Army Lett.* 62 We are bivouacked in a pine swamp.

f. Designating streams flowing through or situated in pine forests, as **pine bayou, brook, creek, river.**

1647 *New Haven Col. Rec.* 314 Wm. Andrewes propowned that . . . [he] might have a neck of land . . . beyond the pine river. **1652** *Ib.* 105 All the land from that wch is commonly called the pine brooke by the English. **1800** HAWKINS *Sk. Creek Country* 22 There are several pine creeks on this side. **1821** *Amer. Jrnl. Science* III. 41 A little above the pine bayou . . . there is a large quantity of blind coal.

As the last term in **Apache, apple, balsam, bastard, bird's-nest, bishop, black, blister, board, Boston, box, bristlecone, broom, buckwheat, bull, cat, cattail, cedar, cork, cornstalk, Cuban, Del Mar, Digger, Douglas, elastic, fat, festoon, foothills yellow, foxtail, frankincense, Georgia, gigantic, ginger, gray, ground, hard, heavy-wooded, hemlock, hickory, jack, Jeffrey, Jersey, joint, knobcone, Labrador, loblolly, lodgepole, longleaf, longleaf yellow, long-leafed, longschat, mast, masting, meadow, Montana black, Monterey, necked, New England, New Jersey, noble, northern scrub, nut, Obispo, old field, Oregon, piñon, pitch, pond, ponderosa, poor, poverty, prince's, pumpkin, red, ridge pole, rock, rosemary, sand, sap, sapling, savanna, scrub, scrubby, short-leaf, short-leaved, short-leaved yellow, short straw, Sierra, slash, smooth-barked, Southern, Southern spruce, split, spruce, sugar, swamp, switchtail, table-mountain, tamarack, timber, torch, trailing, turpentine, twisted, Virginia, Virginian, water, white, white-bark(ed), yellow pine.**

* **pineapple,** *n.*

1. A hand grenade or bomb. *Slang.*

1929 HOSTETTER & BEESLEY *It's a Racket* 25 Tossers of bombs took orders for 'pineapples,' then 'went into production,' and finally placed them for explosion. **1944** *Common Ground* Summer 9 Used to be a small-arms plant: bullets for the huntin' crowd, police cartridges, and pineapples for gangsters.

2. In combs.: (1) **pineapple bush,** the strawberry shrub; (2) **cactus,** (see quot.); (3) **cheese,** a cheese molded in the shape of a pineapple and suspended in netting to give the surface a reticulated appearance; (4) **squash,** (see quot.).

(**1**) **1881** *Harper's Mag.* April 744/1 There were [on Lost Island, La.] . . . pine-apple bushes bursting with blossoms; stiff magnolias half hiding their haughty flowers. — (**2**) **1947** *So. Sierran* May 4/2 And last, rare and very beautiful, the Mohave Fishhook or Pineapple Cactus, Echinocactus Polyancistrus, with clustered iridescent magenta-pink blossoms, [was] seen in considerable number. — (**3**) **1830** *Buffalo* (N.Y.) *Republican* 4 Sep. 2/3 (*advt.*), Fresh Groceries . . . Pine Apple cheese, very fine. **1893** HOWELLS *Coast of Bohemia* 204 Pine-apple cheese was Philistine. — (**4**) **1890** *Amer. Naturalist* XXIV. 732 The *Pine Apple* squash . . . was introduced in 1884. . . . It is a winter squash, creamy white when harvested, of a deep yellow at the later period.

pine barren. Chiefly *S.*

1. A tract of poor sandy or peaty land upon which pine is the prevailing growth. Also transf.

1731 in *Pa. Gazette* 29 April–6 May 1/2 At our first setting out we had a sandy Pine Barren to walk in, which was covered pretty thick with large Pine Trees. **1830** PAULDING *Chron. Gotham* 26 Mr. Puddingham . . . had so over-cultivated a thin-soiled intellect, that he . . . turned it into a pine-barren. **1948** MENCKEN *Supp.* II. 196 The extension of Piedmont speech eastward is blocked by the so-called pine barrens.

attrib. **1743** CATESBY *Carolina* II. p. iv, The third and worst kind of Land is the Pine barren Land, the name implying its character. **1837** WILLIAMS *Terr. of Florida* 89 Pine barren swamps . . . are natural basins, containing the waters of the surrounding country. **1843** CARLTON *New Purchase* VI. 36 Our heroes closed their profane exhibition, by consigning . . . all the Carolinas and the whole pine barren world to the swearer's own diabolical father. **1901** MOHR *Plant Life Ala.* 116 Pine-barren flats and Hydrophytic plant associations.

2. In the names of plants and animals, as (1) **pine barren beauty,** (2) **scorpion,** (3) **sundrop,** (4) **terrapin,** (see quots.).

(**1**) **1884** W. MILLER *Dict. Names of Plants* 106/2 Pine-barren Beauty, *Pyxidanthera barbulata.* — (**2**) **1782** CRÈVECOEUR *Letters* 236 The southern provinces are the countries where nature has formed the greatest variety of . . . scorpions, from the smallest size, up to the *pine barren,* the largest species known here. — (**3**) **1901** MOHR *Plant Life Ala.* 638 *Kneiffia linearis.* . . . Pine-barren Sundrops. . . . Southern Virginia along the coast to Florida, west to Louisiana. — (**4**) **1884** GOODE *Fisheries* I. 158 The Carolina Box Turtle [*Cistudo carolina*]. . . . In the Southern States it is known as the 'Pine-barren Terrapin.'

pine knot.

1. A knot of pine wood. Also attrib.

1670 *Plymouth Rec.* 119 There shalbe noe pine knot picked. **1808** BARKER *Indian Princess* III. i, [She] lit me with her pine-knot torch to bedward. **1830** *Mass. Spy* 26 May (Th.), At night parties collect by pine-knot fire, and play cards for the earnings of the day. **1945** BOTKIN *My Burden* 62 When the boys would start to the quarters from the field, they would get a turn of lider [lightwood] knots. I 'specks you knows 'em as pine knots.

2. In transf. and fig. senses, usu. having reference to the toughness, hardness, etc., of such knots.

1812 PAULDING *J. Bull & Bro. Jonathan* 5 Jonathan, though as hard as a pine-knot . . . could bear it no longer. **1856** MACLEOD *F. Wood* 48 The human pine-knot John C. Calhoun. **1876** WARNER *Gold of Chickaree* 360 Relaxation! . . . When you know as well as I do, that you are a pine knot for endurance. **1885** *Cent. Mag.* March 680 Have you got anything like a good mellow iron wedge, or a fried pine-knot in your pocket? **1904** STRATTON-PORTER *Freckles* 95 He was as tough as a pine-knot and as agile as a panther.

pinenet 'paɪnˌnet, *n.* Variant of epinette *q.v.* (sense **1.**). *Obs.* — **1810** PIKE *Sources Miss.* App. I. 55 The banks of the river to the Meadow river, have generally either been timbered by the pine, pinenett, . . . or the aspen tree. **1820** GILLELAND *Ohio & Miss. Pilot* 146 The swamps are timbered with pinenet, sap-pine, and hemlock.

* **Piners,** *n. pl.* (See quot. 1894 and cf. * **pine,** *n.* **1.**)

1894 *D.N.* I. 332 Piners: those who live in the Jersey pines,—the 'ridge' sections (eastern and southern) of the state. **1894** *Harper's Mag.* Aug. 337/1 The term 'piners' is synonymous with the term 'poor whites' in the South. **1948** MENCKEN *Supp.* II. 180 There must be rich material in the dialect of the so-called *Pineys* or *Piners* in the central and southern counties.

* **pinery,** *n.* A pine forest, esp. as the scene of lumbering activities. Also attrib.

1822 *Mass. Spy* 30 Jan. (Th.), [We] found a continued pinery for about a mile. **1926** *Amer. Sp.* II. 100/2 The lumberjacks have found anthologists who appreciate better than did the singers themselves the charm of the pinery songs. **1948** *Green Bay* (Wis.) *Press-Gazette* 12 July 15/6 Son Henry was working in the Green Bay pineries when the call for volunteers came.

* **pine tree.** In combs.: (1) **pine-tree beetle,** = **pine borer;** (2) **cod,** (see quot.); (3) **flag,** any one of various New England colonial flags using the pine tree as an emblem, esp. such a flag for use at sea provided for by

the Massachusetts council in April 1776, now *obs.* or *hist.;* (4) **rattlesnake,** ?= **timber rattlesnake;** (5) **State,** Maine, a nickname, hence **Pine Tree Stater.**

(1) **1854** Emmons *Agric. N.Y.* V. 262 (Index), Pine-tree beetles, 82, 83 [etc.]. — (2) **1884** Goode *Fisheries* I. 201 In Southeastern Maine the name 'Pine-tree Cod' is also in use [as a name for the cod]. — (3) **1896** *Peterson Mag.* ns. VI. 288/2 These vessels all sailed under the pine-tree flag. This flag was of white bunting, on which was painted a green pine-tree, and upon the reverse the motto: 'Appeal to Heaven.' **1947** Coffin *Yankee Coast* 194 Then it was English again; then the Continental Congress's pine-tree flag flew over it; . . . then, finally, the Stars-and-Stripes. [**1949** *Lisle* (Ill.) *Eagle* 31 March 3/5 Such a flag, with a pine tree design added thereto, was carried at the Battle of Bunker Hill.] — (4) **1887** Custer *Tenting on Plains* 139 The most venomous of snakes, called the pine-tree rattlesnake.

(5) **1860** *Harper's Mag.* March 454/2 The 'Pine-tree State,' like a Yankee clock with wooden works, would cease to run without its *main-spring* [i.e., the lumber industry]. **1946** Holbrook *Lost Men* 248 He worked so ably that by 1846 he had got the Pine Tree Staters to vote a prohibition law. **1948** *Democrat* 12 Feb. 1/6 The Pine Tree State Maine's motto is 'I guide.' Its state bird is the chicadee and its flower the pine cone and tassel.

b. Used in expressions referring to a currency issued by the Massachusetts colony in 1652; esp. **pine-tree shilling,** a crude silver coin about the size of a half-dollar having on one side a representation of a pine tree as an emblem.

Pine-tree shilling

1830 *Boston Transcript* 17 Dec. 2/1 (*heading*), Pine Tree Shilling. **1840** *Ib.* 27 March 2/3 A lad found . . . a 'Pine Tree' three pence—one of the first silver coins issued in the Colonies. **1849** *Hunt's Merch. Mag.* XX. 200 The device of a pine tree upon one side of the shilling has given to the entire series the general designation of 'the pine tree coinage.' **1864** Webster *Pine-tree money*, money coined in Massachusetts in the seventeenth century, and so called from its bearing a figure resembling a pine-tree. **1934** *Univ. Wis. Studies Soc. Sci.* XX. 236 The pinetree shilling, compared with the English shilling, was a debased coin, since £129 in Massachusetts minted money had the silver content of £100 sterling.

pine wood.

1. A forest of pine trees. Usu. *pl.*

1694 *Mass. H.S. Coll.* 4 Ser. I. 105 Our whole company came to Greenbush, a place so called from those pine-wooods [*sic*]. **1826** Flint *Recoll.* 263 In dry and hilly pine woods, far from streams and stagnant waters, it [i.e., Spanish moss] almost wholly disappears. **1850** Drake *Treatise* 60 Such are the celebrated *Pine Woods*, to the protecting influence of which the people of New Orleans and Mobile commit themselves for safety, in yellow fever seasons; expecting to enjoy an equal immunity from intermittents and remittents. **1939** R. T. Peterson *Wings at Dusk* 13 Whenever I see one Flushing befoh me Histing his flag, like a buck in de pine-wood [etc.].

attrib. **1688** in *Phil. Trans.* XVII. 945 That which is called Pine-wood Land. **1805** *Ann. 9th Congress* 2 Sess. 1093 The house is on a point of a high pine woods bluff. **1872** McClellan *Golden State* 204 These hogs . . . are somewhat like the North Carolina pine-woods hogs. **1894** Torrey *Fla. Sketch-Book* 6 One of the three novelties which I knew were to be found in the pine lands . . . [was] the pine-wood sparrow.

b. pine-wood knot, = **pine knot 1.**

1836 Simms *Mellichampe* 423 The heavy pine-wood knot was lifted above the head of the tory.

2. pine-wood(s) grape, the turkey grape, *Vitis lincecumi*, of the southeastern U.S.

1826 Flint *Recoll.* 255 They are common through the pine-woods of Louisiana, and known by the name of the pine-woods grape. **1862** *Rep. Comm. Patents 1861: Agric.* 485 'Post-oak grape,' 'Pine-wood grape,' *Vitis Linsecomii*, (new species.) . . . Grows in eastern and middle Texas and western Louisiana. **1923** *Stand. Plant Names* 526/1.

pingue ˈpɪŋgwe, *n.* Also **pinguay.** [Sp. *pingüe*, fat.] **1.** (See quot.) **2. pingue weed,** a perennial herb, *Hymenoxys floribunda*, found in the Southwest, from which an inferior kind of rubber has been produced.

(1) **1909** *Springfield W. Republican* 24 June 14 The disease known as 'pingue,' which for several years has been disastrous on the sheep ranches of the Southwest. It is supposed to afflict sheep as a consequence of their eating the leaves or the roots of the so-called rubber plant. — (2) **1906** *Indian Laws & Tr.* III. 166 The Secretary of the Interior is hereby authorized and directed, and empowered . . . to lease an experimental farm on which to plant, and grow the plant known as pinguay weed, or similar rubber producing plant.

***pinion,** see **piñon.**

***pink,** *a.* In combs.: (1) **Pink Beds,** (see quot.), *obs.;* (2) **curlew,** the scarlet ibis, *Guara rubra*, or the roseate spoonbill, *Ajaia ajaja;* (3) ***eye,** (*a*) a contagious form of conjunctivitis characterized by the pinkish color of the eyeball, (*b*) = **redeye,** *slang;* (4) **lemonade,** lemonade that has been colored pink, usu. sold at circuses and fairs; (5) **root,** the root of an herb of the genus *Spigelia*, esp. *S. marilandica*, used as a vermifuge, also the plant or species of plant producing this, cf. **Carolina pinkroot;** (6) **saucer,** (see quots.); (7) **tea,** a gay or frivolous social gathering attended largely by women, also transf. and as a verb.

(1) **1883** Zeigler & Grosscup *Alleghanies* 187 What is locally known as the Pink Beds, in the northwestern part of Transylvania, a dense forest plateau, is an absolute wilderness in which a lost traveller might wander for days before finding his way to a settlement. — (2) **1858** Baird *Birds Pacific R.R.* 683 *Ibis Rubra.* . . . Red or Scarlet Ibis; Pink Curlew. . . . Mr. Audubon saw it but once, when a flock of three passed high over his head in Louisiana. **1917** *Birds of Amer.* I. 175/1 Formerly the Spoonbills, or 'Pink Curlews,' as the Florida hunters know them, were extensively shot and feathers shipped to Jacksonville. — (3) (*a*) **1855** *Amer. Inst. N.Y. Trans.* 359 An opthalmic disease, called the pink eye, . . . attacks horses from the country, and injures their sale. **1945** *Somerset News* 22 March 4/2 Mrs Oscar Benson, who has been ill for several days with pink eye, returned to her classroom at the Elementary School on Monday. (*b*) **1941** Seton *Trail of Artist-Naturalist* 365 After a coupla mugs of pinkeye, nothin' would suit him but he wants to play the game. — (4) **1890** *Outing* March 474/1 These were followed by sardines, and the whole washed down by numerous cocktails of pink lemonade. **1949** *Oregonian* (Portland) 10 Aug. 16/5 There'll be popcorn, pink lemonade and prizes galore for the picnickers.

(5) **1764** *Ann. Reg. 1763* 54/1 Produce of South Carolina. . . . Pinkroot, 1 cask. **1802** Drayton *S. Carolina* 63 Pink root, or Indian Pink. (Spigelia Marilandica). . . . [It] has become a profitable article of trade with the Cherokee Indians . . . and is used in worm cases, with much success. **1942** Nat. Pk. Service *Fading Trails* 173 The prairie plant locally known as 'pink-root' is a favorite item, together with grasshoppers, lizards, and other small animal life. — (6) **1864** Webster 989/2 *Pink-saucer*, a small saucer, the inner surface of which is covered with a pink coloring matter, used in giving color to small articles. **1888** *N.Y. World* 22 July (F.), Flesh tights . . . are colored with what we call pink saucer in the profession, a kind of stuff you buy at the druggists. — (7) **1887** *Harper's Mag.* Jan. 204/1 A Protestant good cause is to be furthered by a bazar or a 'pink tea.' **1900** *Land of Sunshine* Aug. 152 Markham [is] . . . pink-teaing on thin flattery, instead of Doing Something—ach! **1945** *Boulder* (Colo.) *D. Camera* 2 Nov. 7/4 Yes, the war was no pink tea.

b. pink and blue shower, an occasion upon which the friends of an expectant mother assemble, bringing presents of baby things. Cf. ***shower,** *n.* **2.**

1945 *Roundup* (Mont.) *R. Tribune* 22 Feb. 5/3 A pink and blue shower was given in honor of Mrs. Lawrence Sealey.

As the last term in **bunch, Carolina, chimney, election, fire, grass, Indian, moss, prairie, strawberry, swamp, wild pink.**

***Pinkerton,** *n.* [Allan *Pinkerton* (1819–84), organizer of a detective bureau in Chicago in 1850.] A member of a Pinkerton detective agency, a private detective or law enforcement officer. Usu. *pl.*

1884 Peck *Peck's Boss Book* (1892) 72 (We.), I am no Pinkerton. **1889** Salmons *Burlington Strike* 387 The switchmen found out that their company was not desired by the Pinkertons. **1912** Whitlock *Fall Guy* 3 The country banks were nearly all protected by the Pinkertons. **1949** *Chi. D. News* 4 May 14/7 There were Pinkertons fighting pitched and bloody battles with Carnegie Steel strikers.

attrib. **1873** *Harper's Mag.* Oct. 720/2 The entire establishment is denominated 'Pinkerton's National Detective Agency.' **1906** C. D. Wright *Battles of Labor* 131 The immediate occasion of the fighting was the approach of a body of Pinkerton detectives. **1947** *Chi. Tribune* 2 Nov. (Grafic Mag.) 28/1 Capt. Herbert S. Mosher, head of the criminal investigation department, took charge of the Pinkerton phases of the investigation.

Hence **Pinkertonian, Pinkertonianism.** *Obs.*

1892 *Chi. Tribune* 9 July 12/3 The strikers commit acts of violence simply because they hate and despise the Pinkertonians. *Ib.* 18 July 4/3 They wanted to arm themselves in order to fight 'Pinkertonianism.'

Pinkertonism ˈpɪŋkɚtn̩ˌɪzəm, *n.* The policy of employing private police.

1891 *Voice* 26 Feb. (Th. MS), You can't make men moral by law and Pinkertonism. **1915** SIRINGO (*title*), Two Evil Issues, Pinkertonism and Anarchism, by a Cowboy Detective Who Knows, as He Spent Twenty-Two Years in the Inner Circle of Pinkerton's National Detective Agency. **1948** *Pacific Northwest Quart.* Oct. 295 Washington Populists . . . adopted a state platform . . . which . . . demanded . . . the prohibition of 'Pinkertonism.'

pinkie ˈpɪŋkɪ, *n.* [See note.] A vessel having a high, narrow-pointed stern, used in the cod and coast fisheries. *Obs.* or *hist.* Cf. **oyster pinkie.**

Prob. f. a popular Du. diminutive *pinkie* for *pinkje* in the sense shown here. From the earliness of its appearance and its use by fishermen, it may not have originated here.

Pinkie

1685 in NOBLE *Records* I. 283 Vriah Cleomen's . . . was Indicted by the name of uryah cleoments . . . yt lately Came from England in the Pynche Adventure, John Balston master. **1842** BUCKINGHAM *E. & W. States* I. 107 Vessels collectively he [Bay of Fundy fisherman] calls *craft*, and subdivides them into *Pinkies, Pogies, Jiggers,* &c. **1891** COOKE *Huckleberries* 234 I'd ruther sail a pinky round Pint Judy pint in a sou'easter. **1948** *Sat. Ev. Post* 9 Oct. 140/3 In addition to the Morgan and Conrad, several smaller craft have been acquired, including the pinkie Regina M.

Pinkster ˈpɪŋkstɚ, *n.* [Du.] In regions of early Dutch influence, Whitsunday or Whitsuntide. Also attrib. Now *hist.*

See the source of quot. 1946 for an account of the observance of this holiday in America.

1797 W. DUNLAP *Diary* I. (1931) 65 The settlements along the river are dutch, it is the holiday they call pinkster & every public house is crowded with merry makers. **1821** COOPER *Spy* xxix, Upon my word, you'd pass well at a pinkster frolic. **1896** EARLE *Col. Days N.Y.* 196 There was one old-time holiday beloved of New Yorkers whose name is now almost forgotten,—Pinkster Day. **1946** *N. & Q.* June 35/2, I prefer to consider Pinkster only in those places where it could be said to have enjoyed a stronghold—the New York City and Albany areas.

b. In the names of flowers that bloom about Whitsuntide, esp. the wild honeysuckle, *Azalea nudiflora.*

1743 CLAYTON *Flora Virginica* 21 *Azalea* . . . Pinkterbloem. **1867** DE VOE *Market Ass't* 379 There is . . . [a] peculiar-looking fruit, which, some forty years ago, became known to me, and, in fact, to many boys of my acquaintance, as the *May-apple*. However, afterwards, I found it generally known as *pinkster-apple*, and *hog-apple*. **1881** *Harper's Mag.* March 526/1 [The Pinkster king] and his followers were covered with Pinkster *blummies*—the wild azalea, or swamp apple. **1946** *N. & Q.* Aug. 80/2 It should be noted that the pinkster flower (*Azalea nudiflora*) is widely known as wild honeysuckle.

c. (See quot.)

1895 *D.N.* I. 392 *Pinxter*, Easter. [Used by] negroes in N.Y.

pinnated grouse. The prairie chicken, *Tympanuchus cupido americanus*, or the heath hen.

1812 WILSON *Ornithology* VI. 45 In those open plains called the barrens of Kentucky, the Pinnated Grous was seen in great numbers. **1856** *Spirit of Times* (N.Y.) 6 Sep. 9/1 The Pinnated Grouse, the noblest of American game birds, is in perfection both for shooting and for board. **1917** *Birds of Amer.* II. 24 Prairie Chicken. . . . [Also called] Pinnated Grouse.

pinning blanket. A blanket suitable for pinning around a baby. — **1895** WIGGIN *Village Watch-Tower* 113, I wish to the land the moths had eat the pinning-blanket. **1906** LYNDE *Quickening* 24 So now we see to what high calling Thomas Jefferson's mother purposed devoting him while yet he was a helpless monad in pinning-blankets.

pin oak. Any one of various American oaks, orig. *Quercus palustris* of the eastern states, but later used, often locally, of oaks somewhat resembling this or confused with it.

1813 MUHLENBERG *Cat. Plants* 87 Swamp or Pin Oak. **1847** COYNER *Lost Trappers* 23 The young trapper was relieved by the arrival of two of the company, one of whom climbed a pin-oak tree, that stood in the edge of the brush. **1949** *Mo. Bot. Garden Bul.* April 92 Pin oak (*Quercus palustris*) . . . [is] a very good tree for city planting.

pinochle ˈpiˌnʌkl̩, *n.* [Origin unknown.] A card game resembling bezique but played with two packs from which all cards below the nines are left out. Also attrib.

1864 DICK *Amer. Hoyle* (1866) 137 Bezique . . . is known among our German brethren as *Peanukle*. **1931** *K.C. Times* 31 Dec. 16 The Times reports Pleasant Hills' champion pinochle player couldn't spell pinochle to save his neck. **1949** *Reader's Digest* Dec. 101/2 Pinochle is your passion and I don't want it should take my place in your life.

Hence **pinochler,** one who plays pinochle. *Rare.*

1894 *Harper's Mag.* LXXXIX. 698/1 'Come, now young fellows,' he said to the Pinochlers.

pinole piˈnolɪ, *n.* *S.W.* [Amer. Sp. (<Nahuatl *pinolli*) in same sense.] A food prepared from seeds of various plants roasted and ground and mixed with other ingredients (see quot. 1853).

1844 GREGG *Commerce of Prairies* I. 159 This [mesquite] pod, which, like that of the honey-locust, encloses a glutinous substance, the Apaches and other tribes of Indians grind into flour to make their favorite *pinole*. **1853** BREWERTON *With Kit Carson* (1930) 46 Penole is made by parching Indian corn; then grinding it, and mixing with cinnamon and sugar. **1894** *Outing* Feb. 355/1 Tortillas of pinol are far better than the best hoecakes of the Southern States. **1942** CASTETTER & BELL *Pima & Papago Agric.* 38 In 1862 they sold the War Department more than one million pounds of wheat, as well as pinole, chickens, green peas, green corn, pumpkins and melons.

piñon ˈpɪnjən, *n.* Also **pinion.** *S.W.* [Sp. *piñón*, pine seed or nut; in Amer. Sp. applied to various trees and shrubs.]

1. Any of several low-growing pines of the West producing edible nutlike seeds, as *Pinus parryana, P. cembroides*, and *P. edulis.* Cf. **single-leaf piñon.**

1831 PATTIE *Personal Narr.* 43 A nut of the shape and size of a bean . . . grows on a tree resembling the pine, called by the Spanish, pinion. **1846** ABERT *Exam. N. Mex.* 19 The banks were composed of high, rugged sandstone rocks, covered with a dense growth of cedar and pinyon. **1903** AUSTIN *Land of Little Rain* 12 One finds spreading growth of pinon, juniper . . . lilac and sage. **1948** *Pacific Discovery* Nov.-Dec. 18/1 The piñons of the arid uplands and mesa lands supplied the 'pine-nuts' so valuable as food to many Southwestern Indian tribes.

attrib. **1846** MAGOFFIN *Down Santa Fe Trail* 76 Took a walk this P.M. through the pinon woods adjacent, &c. **1902** *Everybody's Mag.* Jan. 37/1 When the ochre has changed to a red powder, pinon-gum is added and stirred constantly until it carbonizes and forms with the ochre a black powder. **1948** *Reader's Digest* Jan. 70/1 Anywhere in America has its particular hearth perfume—piñon smoke in Santa Fe.

b. The wood of such a tree.

1881 CHASE *Editor's Run in N. Mex.* 206 The common fuel is pinon, the best fire-place wood in the world, full of pitch, and burns like a pine knot. **1942** STEGNER *Mormon C.* 341 There he built a pyre of cedar, piñon and juniper four feet high.

2. A nutlike seed produced by a tree of this kind. In full **piñon (pine) nut.**

1846 ABERT *Exam. N. Mex.* 32 The markets have . . . great quantities of . . . 'uvas' or grapes, and 'pinones,' nuts of the pine tree. **1864** *Rio Abajo Press* 9 Feb. 3/1 Two women [Navajoes] . . . had been ten days travelling, during which time their food was cedarberries and piñon nuts. **1947** *Desert Mag.* Dec. 33/1 High prices are being paid for pinyon pine nuts this year.

3. In special combs.: (1) **piñon jay,** a bluish western corvine bird, *Cyanocephalus cyanocephalus,* that feeds on piñon nuts, cf. **blue crow;** (2) **mouse,** the large-eared deer mouse, *Peromyscus truei truei;* (3) **pine,** = **piñon 1;** (4) **tree,** = **piñon 1.**

(1) **1887** DENTON *Naturalist's Diary* (1949) 115 We started off for the piñon hills after the piñon jays. **1941** FERGUSSON *Southwest* 121 The Mesa Verde National Park . . . is a high plateau where . . . piñon-jays scream, and fluffy-tailed squirrels scold heatedly. — (2) **1885** HAVARD *Flora W. & S. Texas* 408 True's Pinon mouse differs then from the common white-footed mouse, *Hesperomys leucopus,* in the fact that it chooses a different character of the country where it is found, as its home; in its more robust form; in its extraordinary large ears. — (3) **1854** BARTLETT *Personal Narr.* I. 235 Several pines, among them the *Pinus edulis,* or piñon pine. **1948** *Sierra Club* (So. Calif. Chap) *Sched.* 127, 67 It is about 3,000 feet high with many pinon pines and desert wild flowers all around. — (4) **1839** LEONARD *Adventures* (1904) 157 Its top is covered with the pinone tree. **1941** FERGUSSON *Southwest* 325 Junipers and piñon trees on the slopes give way to cottonwood and hackberry noisy with birds along the creek.

pinto ˈpɪnto, *a.* and *n. S.W.* [Sp., spotted (lit. "painted").]

1. *n.* A spotted or piebald horse.

1860 *Marysville* (Calif.) *Appeal* 9 Feb. 3/1 The struggle . . . ended in the success of the black horse, which came out some twenty-five feet in advance of the 'Pinto.' **1890** *Stock Grower & Farmer* 26 July 6/3 We had an old pinto that was the worst bluffer that I ever saw. **1949** *Sat. Ev. Post* 16 April 26/1 Wagons moved slower than pintos, and the new country was no easier than the last.

2. *a.* Of a horse: Piebald, spotted.

1867 HARTE *Condensed Novels* 259 Concepcion . . . was reported to have chased the devil in the shape of a fleet pinto colt all the way from San Luis Obispo to San Francisco. **1907** WHITE *Arizona Nights* 321 Goodrich sets him behind them little pinto cavallos he has. **1947** *Nat. Geog. Mag.* June 745/2 Suddenly the arena master spurs his pinto pony and dashes up the line of vehicles.

transf. **1945** *Everybody's Digest* Aug. 85 He's havin' his forehoofs roached and rasped by a pink and white pinto filly.

3. pinto bean, a mottled variety of the kidney bean. [Cf. *pinto,* in Amer. Sp. in same sense.]

1916 BOWER *Phantom Herd* 46 A girl gave me a handful of pinto beans. **1949** *This Week Mag.* 5 March 28/2 The pinto bean is a stranger on the easterner's table.

pinwheel ˈpɪnˌhwil, *v. tr.* In tanning, to subject (a hide) to the action of the pinwheel. — **1885** *Harper's Mag.* Jan. 276/2 Grains and splits together are again 'pin-wheeled,' preparatory to one final soaking in strong bark liquor, the parting salute of the tan-yard.

* **piny,** *a.* Also * **piney.**

1. Of land: Overgrown (at one time) with pines, lacking in fertility, poor. *Obs.*

1709 LAWSON *Carolina* 74 Not but that there has been Sixty-six Increase for one measure sown in Piny-Land, which we account the meanest Sort. **1782** CRÈVECOEUR *Letters* 146, I am at a loss to conceive on what the inhabitants [of Nantucket] live, . . . their piny lands being the most ungrateful soil in the world. **1789** WASHINGTON *Diaries* IV. 48 Good and bad lands—cultivated and in woods—some high and barren, and others low, wet and piney. **1879** TOURGEE *Fool's Errand* 334 It's like Northern farming in a piney old-field,—looks well enough, but don't pay.

2. piny woods, *S.* a region of pine woods (see also quot. 1909). More often **piney woods.** *Colloq.*

1800 HAWKINS *Sk. Creek Country* 29 Broken piny woods and reedy branches on its right side. **1887** HARRIS in *Cent. Mag.* XXXIV. 543/2 I tested the piney woods of Georgia thoroughly years ago. **1909** *D.N.* III. 357 *piney-woods,* n. The common expression for *backwoods.* [East Alabama.] **1947** *Newsweek* 1 Sep. 19/2 The rednecks were the poverty-stricken white tenant farmers and sharecroppers who lived in the piney woods and barren red-clay hills behind the Delta.

3. In various combs., usu. with derogatory implications, as **piny wood(s) county, fight, Georgian, rooter, tory.**

1809 WEEMS *Marion* (1833) 127 Had this savage spirit appeared among a few poor British *cadets,* or *piney wood* tories it would not have been so lamentable. **1835** LONGSTREET *Ga. Scenes* 128 He could not be reconciled until he fretted himself into a pretty little *piney*-woods fight, in which he got whipt. **1903** STILES *Four Years* 296 He used to wear a red zouave fez that ill-befitted the peculiar, sallow-pallid complexion of the piny-woods Georgian. **1938** MATSCHAT *Suwannee River* 42 Legend would have the vicious wild hogs, or 'piney woods rooters,' of the swamp region as the offspring of De Soto's original thirteen sows, many times removed. **1949** *Time* 7 March 28/2 The unit-voting system makes it possible for Hummon's beloved piney-woods counties to outvote their city neighbors.

Also *piny woods district, frolic, gentry, planter, region, settler,* etc.

b. piny woods tacky, a scrub pony, a "poor white." *Colloq.*

1846 *Spirit of Times* (N.Y.) 11 July 234/3 Mac mounted a piney-woods-tacky (named Rasum) and hied him off to Charleston. **1888** *Cent. Mag.* XXXVI. 799/2 If Mr. Catlett will come to Georgia and go among the 'po' whites' and 'piney-wood tackeys,' he will hear the terms 'we-uns' and 'you-uns' in every-day use.

* **pioneer,** *n.*

1. One who goes into a new country to settle, a frontiersman. Cf. **Mexican, Oklahoma pioneer.**

*a***1817** DWIGHT *Travels* II. 459 A considerable part of those, who *begin* the cultivation of the wilderness, may be denominated *foresters,* or *Pioneers.* **1860** HANCOCK *Five Years* 243 A life for which none but the hardiest of the native 'pioneers' and frontiers men are fitted. **1949** *N. Dak. Hist.* Jan. 5 The days of the pioneer and homesteader are gone.

attrib. **1842** H. MANN *Oration* (4 July) 35 Our pioneer settlers would not have abandoned their homes for the western wilderness. **1913** LONDON *Valley of Moon* 95 She remembered from her childhood the talk by the pioneer women of the courtesy and attendance of the caballeros of the Spanish California days. **1949** *St. Paul Pioneer Press* 19 June 1/4 This veteran's wife of 1949 has plenty in common with the pioneer woman of 1849 who stayed at her husband's side while he blazed new trails.

2. In special combs.: (1) **Pioneer Day,** (*a*) a legal holiday in Utah, July 24, commemorating the arrival of the Mormons at Salt Lake City in 1847, also attrib., (*b*) **Idaho Pioneer Day,** a holiday in Idaho, June 15, commemorating Great Britain's relinquishment of the Oregon country in 1846, (*c*) in the West, a fun festival, embellished with mock kangaroo courts, rodeos, etc.; (2) **(-s') Society,** a society whose members are the pioneers of a given community.

(1) (*a*) **1886** *Boston Jrnl.* 7 Aug. 2/4 The 'pioneer day' in Salt Lake, which celebrates the entrance of the Mormons to the valley, was rather gloomy this year. **1942** STEGNER *Mormon C.* 234 They help promote Pioneer Day pageants in honor of the first settlers in the valley. (*b*) **1911** *Idaho State Jrnl.* 3 Feb. 120 An Act . . . adding Idaho Pioneer Day as a holiday. (*c*) **1945** *Gunnison* (Colo.) *Courier* 26 July 1/1 Hereford and Horse Shows and Pioneer Day contributing to the growing fame of the Gunnison event. — (2) **1869** DANA *Two Years* (new ed.) 439, I have already been invited to deliver the anniversary oration before the Pioneer Society, to celebrate the settlement of San Francisco. **1884** *Ore. State Jrnl.* 7 June 5/4 The members of the Lane County Pioneers' Society met here last Thursday and held their first annual re-union. **1945** *Gunnison* (Colo.) *Courier* 26 July 1/5 He is a member of the Pioneer Society, and found time to visit with old friends.

b. Also **pioneerdom, pioneerish, pioneerism.** *Rare.*

1873 *Porcupine* 13 Sep. 379/2 A . . . Californian, who had arrived . . . from the States, close on to the age of pioneerdom. **1900** *Kans. Hist. Coll.* VI. 211 Men like General Lane and Judge Thacher could not be expected to affiliate with each other any more than culture could be expected to exist together with pioneerism, however heroic or magnetic. **1902** WHITLOCK *13th District* 153 'That is more than agricultural, or pioneerish,' said Emily, 'that's actually savage.'

* **pioneer,** *v.*

1. *tr.* To take or lead (a person or persons) into new country. *Obs.*

1838 *Yale Lit. Mag.* III. 86 You find him [the Conn. emigrant] pioneering our population along the western prairies. **1882** *American* V. 87 Björn Anderson pioneered these newcomers to the Western States.

b. To make (one's way), to occupy or open up (a place or way) as a pioneer.

1848 *Knickerb.* XVIII. 152 He rented it [an old Dutch house] out to a numerous family that had just pioneered its way from Cape Cod. **1885** *Cent. Mag.* Sep. 739/1 Miners had pioneered the way some distance down the river in search of gold. **1943** GABRIELSON *W. Refuges* 3 Our fathers who pioneered this land accomplished much for which they should be praised.

2. *intr.* To go into unsettled regions as a pioneer. Also transf.

1945 *Roundup* (Mont.) *R. Tribune* 22 Feb. 5/2 Wm. Meyersick, was the native son of parents who pioneered on upper Cottonwood creek near Lewistown. **1949** *Lincoln Co. News* (Oceanlake, Ore.) 4

Aug. 3/1 A Lincoln county farmer has recently done a little pioneering in the production of better forage.

Pious Fund. *Hist.* A large sum of money collected by the Jesuits in the seventeenth century and later for missionary work among the Indians of the Californias. Also attrib.

After 1848 Mexico refused to pay any part of the income from this fund to beneficiaries in upper California. The case was brought by the U.S. before the Hague Tribunal which in 1902 decided it in favor of the U.S., this being the first case to be tried before the Permanent Court of Arbitration of the Hague.

1847 SIMPSON *Overland Journey* 169 In addition to their annual stipends of four hundred dollars each, the monks possessed in Mexico a considerable property in lands and money, composed of donations and bequests, and known as the 'Pious Fund of California.' **1902** *Out West* Oct. 466 John T. Doyle [is] dean of the California bar, hero of the historic 'Pious Fund' litigation now arbitrating between the United States and Mexico. **1929** WILBUR *Juan Maria de Salvatierra* 31 This is the famous Pious Fund, still extant, which was founded to support Jesuit missions [in California].

*__pipe,__ *n.*

1. =**pipe of peace.**

1751 GIST *Journals* 50 Four Indians, two from each Tribe (who had been sent before to bring the long Pipe) . . . came in. **1848** COOPER *Oak Openings* II. 9 The smoker passing the pipe to his neighbor as soon as he had inhaled a few puffs. **1944** ROSS *Westward* 97 Then there would follow the pipe, and friendliness.

2. The distance a traveler goes while smoking a pipe of tobacco. Among voyageurs the time or the distance covered between rest periods when a smoke was taken. *Obs.*

The uses shown here reflect foreign influences. Irving's use suggests Du. *pijp*, used locally as a measure of time and distance. See *WNT s.v. pijp*, p. 1716, and Berghaus *s.v. blaffen*, 149/1. The use among voyageurs is a similar extension of F. *pipe*. The time and the distance denoted by a pipe varied greatly among the voyageurs. See McDermott, *s.v. pipe*.

1800 in FRIEDERICI (1947) 506/2 A pipe, in the most general acceptation of the word, seemed to be about three quarters of an English mile. **1809** IRVING *Hist. N.Y.* (1927) III. vii. 172 Such extraordinary speed did he make, that he arrived at Fort Amsterdam in less than a month, though the distance was full two hundred pipes, or about 120 miles. **1825** KEATING *Exped. St. Peter's River* II. 86 Voyagers compute distances on the water by *pipes*, which are the intervals between the times they cease to paddle in order to smoke their pipe. **1847** LANMAN *Summer in Wild.* 142 Having paddled about three pipes, (about eighteen miles,) we generally landed upon a pleasant sandbar. *Ib.*, A 'pipe,' I should here remark, is what a sporting gentleman might call a *heat* of six miles. **1902** CLAPIN 309 In the languages of the old French 'voyageurs,' a *pipe* meant two leagues, i.e. the time of smoking a pipe.

3. A pipedream; something regarded as easy, a "cinch." *Slang.*

1902 CLAPIN 309 Pipe, . . . in newspaper parlance, an assignment which a reporter knows will fail. **1908** O. HENRY *Options* 170 He had a pipe that the first inhabitants of America arrived here on stilts. **1912** LONDON *Smoke Bellew* 107 'A system to beat a bankin' game ain't possible.' 'But I'm showing you this one. It's a pipe.'

4. In combs.: (1) **pipe dance,** an Indian ceremonial dance in which the pipe of peace plays a conspicuous part, a calumet dance, cf. *pipe of peace dance;* (2) **Franklin,** =**Franklin stove,** *obs.;* (3) ***layer,** one who manipulates an election by bringing floaters to vote in a particular way, an intriguing politician; (4) **laying,** the action or practice of manipulating an election, esp. by bringing in floaters, *slang,* now *hist.;* (5) **line,** a line of pipe, usu. extending across country, for the conveyance of oil, gas, or water, also attrib. and transf.; (6) **of friendship,** =**pipe of peace;** (7) **of peace,** see as a main entry; (8) **organ,** an organ in which the tone is produced from pipes, as distinguished from a reed organ; (9) ***stem,** a thin leg, *humorous;* (10) **stem wood,** (see quots.); (11) **stone,** a soft stone or red clay, so named because the Indians carved tobacco pipes from it, also attrib.; (12) **tomahawk,** a tomahawk with a hollow handle, the head serving as a pipe bowl; (13) **vine,** the Dutchman's-pipe, *Aristolochia macrophylla*, or a related species; (14) **weed dynasty,** the succession of Presidents from Virginia starting with George Washington, so called in allusion to Virginia as a tobacco-producing state.

(1) **1778** CARVER *Travels* 268 The Indians have several kinds of dances . . . as the Pipe or Calumate Dance, the War Dance, the Marriage Dance, and the Dance of the Sacrifice. **1832** CATLIN *Indians* I. 55 One of these scenes . . . appeared to me to be peculiar to this tribe [the Assiniboins], and exceedingly picturesque in its effect; which was described to me as the *pipe-dance*. **1945** ADAMS *Album Amer. Hist.* II. 233 The Indians put on a pipe dance; presents were distributed. — (2) **1797** *N.Y. State Soc. Arts* I. 388 [The close-stove method] can claim . . . but a trifling preference to the Pipe-Franklin. — (3) **1840** *Richmond Inquirer* Nov. (Th.), The profuse use of gold, corruption of the franchise by pipelayers and yarn spinners . . . have conspired to elect W. H. Harrison. **1896** HASWELL *New York* 379 The Democratic papers dwelt upon the act and termed the perpetrators 'pipe-layers'; which term was for a long while applied to them and to the party, and is still in current use to denote concealed and indirect methods of political or other action. — (4) **1841** *Cong. Globe* App. 26 Jan. 120/1 Others say that fraud, double voting, pipe laying, transfer of voters from one point to another, Hessians conducted by police officers and agents from city to city,—that these have done much to carry the election. **1911** GOUVERNEUR *As I Remember* 12 'Pipe laying' was an organized scheme for controlling votes, and derived its name from certain political manipulations connected with the introduction to Croton water in New York City.

(5) **1879** TARBELL *Hist. Standard Oil Co.* I. 354 The pipe lines owned and controlled by the parties hereto have a joint capacity for transportation. **1879** *Appletons' Ann. Cyclo. 1878* 618/1 A bill passed both Houses of the [N.Y.] Legislature to provide for the incorporation of pipe-line companies, and was sent to the Governor. **1948** *Sheep Breeder* Dec. 19/3 Sometimes the price of meat in the pipelines of distribution goes up—a fact that gives rise to claims that we are speculating. — (6) **1765** J. BARTRAM *Diary* 18 Nov., Ye governour & superintendent otherwise called ye beloved man shaked hands with them all but before ye delivery of ye medals, smoked in ye pipe of friendship. — (8) **1885** *Wkly. New Mexican Rev.* 9 April 4/2 The Easter offering which goes toward the purchase of a new pipe-organ amounted to $150. **1907** *St. Nicholas* Oct. 1120/1 The wedding party arrived at the church, and the new pipe organ for the first time gave forth the strains of the wedding march. — (9) **1883** EGGLESTON *Hoosier School-Boy* 33 Little Columbus Risdale picked himself up on his pipe stems and took his place at the end of this row.

(10) **1791** W. BARTRAM *Travels* 24, I observed, growing on the banks of this sequestered river . . . the great evergreen *Andromeda* of Florida, called Pipe-Stem Wood, to which I gave the name of Andromeda formosissima, as it far exceeds in beauty every one of this family. **1813** MUHLENBERG *Cat. Plants N. Amer.* 43 Pipestem wood, *Andromeda acuminata*. — (11) **1804–5** LEWIS in *L. & Clark Exped.* VI. (1905) 44 The third is called *red pipe stone river.* **1869** *Amer. Naturalist* II. 648 At Sioux Falls . . . a layer of Pipestone occurs intercalated with the quartzite. **1948** *Chi. Tribune* 22 Feb. IV. 6/3 He has something to say about horse-thieves, about the Sioux, the pipe-stone quarry, . . . about eagles and grasshoppers. — (12) **1757** *Lett. to Washington* II. 129 Wm. Grymes 2 lbs. Butter & a pipe Tomahawk. **1902** *Amer. Folk-Lore* 263 There is also a pipe-*tomahawk* much in vogue with the early traders to the west. — (13) **1847** DARLINGTON *Weeds & Plants* 268 The Pipe Vine or Dutchman's Pipe, is a native of the West and South. **1886** *Cent. Mag.* May 237/2 Professor Gray's modest house, where wistaria, forsythia, and pipe-vine intertwine their varying greenery. — (14) **1816** FIDFADDY *Adv. Uncle Sam* 21 Being the *third* of the pipeweed dynasty, he [Madison] determined to be at least the second in the philosophic regime of the family.

5. *To lay pipe(s), fig.* to bring in as voters persons not legally qualified as such, to lay a foundation for political preferment or office.

1848 BARTLETT 251 To lay pipe means to bring up voters not legally qualified. **1862** *Fraser's Mag.* July 28 To charge him, in the technical language of his party, with 'pulling wires,' and 'laying pipes' for the Presidency. [**1893** *Home Missionary* Oct. 305 The Irish . . . who began by laying our water-pipes . . . now lay a different kind of pipe, and make our city government.]

For *to hit the pipe*, see ***hit,** *v.* **3. d.**

As the last term in **cob, corncob, drive, Dutchman's, friend, hair, hatchet, horn, Indian, leader, log, medicine, mud, peace, petticoat, Powhatan, scape, Sioux, stand, stove, T.D., tobacco, tomahawk, war pipe.**

*__pipe,__ *v.*

1. *intr.* To smoke a pipe. *Rare.*

1846 MCKENNY *Memoirs* I. 71 These hardy adventurous fellows never rose from their paddles, nor stopped except to '*pipe.*'

2. *Mining. tr.* To wash (dirt) away by means of a jet of water from a pipe; to supply (a claim) with water for this purpose. *Obs.*

1878 BEADLE *Western Wilds* 149 Worked-out mines . . . [with] all the soil 'piped' away in search of the 'pay dirt.' **1882** *47th Congress* 1 Sess. H.R. Ex. Doc. No. 216, 629 Some of the smaller claims are not piped more than one hundred to one hundred and fifty days per year. At the large mines piping goes on night and day.

3. To put down a system of pipes in (a town) for the conveyance of water or gas, to convey (water, gas, etc.) by means of a pipe or pipe line. Also fig.

1884 *Boston Jrnl.* Jan., A special town meeting . . . to hear the report of the committee with reference to piping the town. **1889** *Whitby* (Eng.) *Gazette* 27 Sep. 3/2 A large Philadelphia syndicate has secured the gas rights in Indiana . . . and will pipe the natural gas to Chicago. **1904** CRISSEY *Tattling* 334, I used to . . . lie awake nights trying to pipe lines of influence into the working department of the White House. **1906** BELL *C. Lee* 243 My engineer found them ladling out the crude turpentine by hand, when you know it ought to be piped.

4. *To pipe down*, (see quot. 1900). Usu. imper. *Slang.*

1900 *D.N.* II. 49 pipe down, *v. phr. i.* To stop talking. [U.S. Naval Academy.] **1932** *K.C. Star* 30 March 22 'Pipe down,' replied the husband. 'What do you expect for a $10 paint job, grand opera?'

pipe-lay, *v. Polit. intr.* To take measures preparatory to securing some desired action or event. *Slang. Obs.* Cf. **pipelayer, pipelaying.** — **1848** *Campaign Flag* (Maysville, Ky.) 14 April 3/6 He was *pipe-layed* out of his election last year. **1888** *S.F. Wkly. Examiner* 22 March (F.), There are not a few who are pipe-laying and marshalling forces for the fray when the conventions meet.

pipe of peace. Among Indians, a ceremonial pipe, often decorated, smoked at a council meeting or as a sign of amity and peace. Also fig.

[*c***1691** in *La. Hist. Coll.* I. (1846) 172 This was the first place where we saw the calumet, or pipe of peace. . . . This nation is called Cahaynohoua.] **1705** BEVERLEY *Virginia* III. 20 They take a Pipe much larger and bigger than the common Tobacco Pipe, expressly made for that purpose . . . they call them the Pipes of Peace. **1872** MARK TWAIN *Roughing It* 173 While smoking the pipe of peace after breakfast we watched the sentinel peaks put on the glory of the sun. **1946** *Life* 27 May 36 (*caption*), 'Smoking' The Pipe of Peace.

b. *pipe of peace dance*, = **pipe dance.** *Obs.*

1841 CATLIN *Indians* II. 242 Their warriors and braves . . . dance. around in a circle . . . in the '*pipe of peace dance.*'

Piper's thickset. A variety of wheat. *Rare.* — **1856** *Rep. Comm. Patents 1855: Agric.* 182 'Piper's Thickset,' a coarse red wheat, with thick clustered ears, a stiff straw, and very prolific, but liable to mildew.

* **piping,** *n.* **1.** A method of mining that employs a powerful jet of water directed by a pipe or hose. *Obs.* **2. piping plover,** a small, pale plover, *Charadrius meloda*, chiefly of the Atlantic Coast.

(1) **1873** BEADLE *Undevel. West* 267 Lastly was introduced 'piping,' and complete hydraulic mining. **1881** RAYMOND *Mining Gloss.* — (2) **1828** BONAPARTE *Synopsis* 296 Ringed Plover . . . and Piping Plover. . . . Common all along the eastern sea coast of North America. **1917** *Birds of Amer.* I. 264/1 Truly a bird of the beach-sand is the Piping Plover.

***pipit,** *n.* As the last term in **sky, Sprague's pipit.**

***pippin,** *n.* As the last term in **Albemarle, Bullock's, fall, Holland, Jersey, Kerry, Maryland, Newtown, New York, Ortley, red-town pippin.**

***pippins,** *n. pl.* (See quot.) *Colloq.* — **1891** *Amer. Folk-Lore* IV. 149 *Gaultheria procumbens* seems to have an almost endless variety of epithets. . . . Young people at Gilsum [Mass.] . . . now call the young shoots *Pippins.*

pipsissewa pɪp'sɪsɪˌwɔ, *n.* [See note.] Any plant of the genus *Chimaphila*, as prince's pine, *C. corymbosa*, or a medicinal preparation made from this. Also **pipsissewa tea.**

"This is a word of Cree (Algonk.) origin, . . . *pisisiwayoo.* It means 'he reduces it to small particles.' . . . This name is apparently a corruption of a word meaning, 'he makes liquid hot,' alluding to this Indian's use of hot infusions of the plant in order to induce profuse perspiration in the treatment of typhus" (W. R. Gerard in *Garden & Forest* IX. (1896) 292).

1789 in *Amer. Philos. Soc. Trans.* III. xvii, An infusion of the plant Pyrola *maculata* has been frequently used for some years in Pennsylvania, under the name of *pipsiseva.* **1818** *Mass. Spy* 25 Feb. (Th.), [On the Schuylkill, the Indians] procured the herb called by them Phipsissiway, in great plenty. . . . I informed him that we had given Phipsissiway tea, very strong, and as hot as he could drink. **1941** SETON *Trail of Artist-Naturalist* 121, I drank pipsissewa tea from time to time, but fear it had little virtue.

Piqua 'pɪkˌwɔ, *n.* [See quot. 1910.] *pl.* or *collect.* Indians making up one of the main divisions of the Shawnee, or the division which they compose. Also attrib.

1805 HARRIS *Tour* III. 111 At the Pickawee towns, above seventy miles higher, it is not above thirty yards wide, but is passable for loaded boats fifty miles higher. **1910** HODGE *Amer. Indians* II. 260/2 Piqua (contr. of *Bi-co-we-tha*, of indefinite meaning, but referring to ashes). One of the five principal divisions of the Shawnee. Their villages at different periods were Pequea, in Pennsylvania; Lick Town, on Scioto r. in Pickaway co., Ohio. etc. **1945** KENNY *West Va. Place Names* 28 Pickaway suggests the part played by Monroe County soldiers against the Ohio Picquas.

* **pirate,** *n.* **1.** * **pirate fish,** a gar pike, *Lepisosteus osseus. Obs.* **2. pirate perch,** a perchlike fish, *Aphredoderus sayanus*, found in sluggish streams.

(1) **1771** TAYLOR *Voyage* 89 One of the people told us, that in this lake [Champlain] is found the surprising *Pirate-fish*, called by the *Indians* Chaourasou. It is much like a pike; but cover'd with such scales as no sword can penetrate. — (2) **1870** *Amer. Naturalist* IV. 107 Pirate Perch (*Aphrodedurus* [*sic*] *Sayanus*). . . . The adult fish, measuring five inches in length, has been seen frequently to swallow one of its own kind measuring an inch. **1883** *Nat. Museum Bul.* No. 27, 468 Pirate Perch. The United States from New York southward; west to and throughout the Mississippi Valley. **1903** T. H. BEAN *Fishes N.Y.* 354.

As the last term in **land, river, timber pirate.**

Piscataway pɪs'kætəˌwe, *n.* [f. a native place- or personal name of uncertain meaning.] A former Indian village (see quot. 1910), or, *pl.*, the Indians occupying this.

1837 BOZMAN *Hist. Md.* II. 290 It is entitled, 'an act for the defense of providence,' and appears to have been made for the purpose of enabling the governor 'to settle a garrison at Piscattoway.' **1910** HODGE *Amer. Indians* II. 262 Piscataway. A former Conoy village situated on Piscataway cr., in Prince George co., Md., the residence of the Conoy chief at the time of the English occupancy of Maryland in 1634. **1945** KENNY *West Va. Place Names* 8 The second [name] suggests an early residence of the Conoys, and perhaps the Piscataways.

pisco 'pisko, *n.* Aguardiente *q.v.*, or a similar liquor—so called from Pisco, Peru, where it was originally made. Also attrib.

1849 in *Amer. Sp.* XXIV. (1949) 266/1 On our way he pointed out the guard-house . . . the distillery house, where the famous pisco is made. **1873** *Ib.*, The company all together, we propose a taste of fragrant *pisco* (Peruvian white brandy). **1940** RIESENBERG *Golden Gate* 209 These were the tolerant days when famous Pisco Punch was being served at the Bank Exchange on Montgomery Street by its inventor, Duncan Nichol. . . . 'Two of 'em and you hug a wildcat,' people said of the potent Pisco.

pishamin 'pɪʃəmɪn, *n.* [See note.] Poss. a variant of persimmon *q.v.* (see quot. 1890).

This word is puzzling. According to the 1890 quot. below, it is a Negro variant of persimmon and was taken to Africa from this country by those who went as colonists to Liberia. The term may possibly be from an Indian source. Cf. the quots. given under **plaquemine.** Bartram's spellings were at times fantastic, and it is not certain now what plant he had in mind when he used the word. It is app. obs.

1766 J. BARTRAM *Diary* 14 Jan., The lower rich ground produceth gledistia, pishamins, cephalanthus. **1890** *Cent.* 4510/3 *pishamin.* . . . Same as *persimmon.*—*Sweet* and sour pishamin, in Sierra Leone, two climbing shrubs, *Carpodinus dulcis* and *C. acida*, of the *Apocynaceæ*, bearing edible fruits resembling the persimmon: so called by colonists from the southern United States.

piskun 'pɪskʌn, *n.* Also **pishkun.** [See note.] A pound or corral, often making use of a V shaped barrier terminating at the top of a cliff, into which Indians, esp. the Blackfeet, lured or drove buffalo to slaughter them. Cf. **surround,** *n.*

This term is said to be from the language of the Blackfeet Indians and to mean "deep-blood-kettle." Mathew Cocking (see quot. 1949 below), a Hudson's Bay Company trader, described such a pound he saw in Saskatchewan in 1772. See John C. Ewers in *Jrnl. Wash. Academy of Sciences* XXXIX. (1949) 355–60.

[**1805** LEWIS in *L. & Clark Exped.* (1904–5) II. I. 94 Today we passed on the Star'd side the remains of a vast many mangled carcasses of Buffalow which had been driven over a precipice 120 feet by the Indians & perished.] **1892** *Scribner's Mag.* Sep. 281 In the later days of the *piskŭn*, the man who brought the buffalo went to them on horseback, riding a white horse. **1943** HOWARD *Montana* 23 Often buffalo were driven over cliffs, the 'buffalo runs' or 'pishkuns' under which Montanans still find rich hoards of arrowheads and other Indian implements. **1949** *Jrnl. Wash. Acad. Sci.* XXXIX. 360/1 We can date the last bison drive of the Blackfoot at about the year 1872. This was a full century after Mathew Cocking's first description of the use of the piskun by Indians of the northwestern plains.

pismo clam. A clam, *Tivela stultorum*, found on the southwest coast of North America — so called from Pismo Beach, Calif. —

1934 WEBSTER. **1949** *Nat. Hist.* June 252/1 Five minutes of barefoot beach scratching had uncovered half a sack of four-inch Pismo clams.

pistareen ˌpɪstərˈin, *n.* [Prob. f. an unrecorded diminutive **pesetarín>pestarín>pistareen*, evolved by non-Spanish speakers from the Sp. *peseta*.] A small Spanish coin, the old peseta, once current in the American colonies and the early republic; the value of this coin. *Obs.*

1744 *Pa. Gazette* 15 Nov. 3/3 He counterfeits Pisterines, and had in his Pocket, when he deserted, Pieces of hammer'd Copper, and a Phial of Quick-Silver. **1773** FITHIAN *Journal* I. 72 A Bit is a pisterene bisected; or an English six pence, & passes here for seven pence Half-penny. **1831** *N.Y. Mirror* 22 Oct. 122/2 When I left the house I was nine dollars and a pistareen better off than when I went in. **1891** WELCH *Recoll. 1830-40* 168 The common silver coin known as Pistareen . . . was worth sixteen and two-thirds cents.

b. half (a) pistareen, the Spanish real, or one part of a bisected pistareen, a short bit. *Obs.*

1765 *Mass. Gazette* 26 Sep. (Th.), Several persons have been committed to Goal for uttering Counterfeit Dollars, Quarter of Dollars, and half Pistareens. **1828** *Yankee* 14 May 157/2 A ninepence in New England, Virginia, and some other parts of our confederacy, for aught I know, is a shilling in New-York, and a 'leven-penny-bit in Pennsylvania; and a half-pistareen is about a 6th part less everywhere.

c. head pistareen, an old Spanish peseta with the image of a head stamped on it. *Obs.*

1829 *Mass. Spy* 29 July (Th.), The head pistareens are worth 20 cents.

d. Attrib. in the same sense as picayune *q.v.* and possibly inspired by this. *Obs.*

1860 EMERSON *Conduct of Life* 4 Now and then, an amiable parson . . . believes in a pistareen-Providence, which, whenever the good man wants a dinner, makes that somebody shall knock at his door, and leave a half-dollar. **1862** *N.Y. Observer* 12 June 192/1 Breeders of the best imported stock will not, and ought not, to sell at the prices offered by our *pistareen* farmers.

* **pistol,** *n.*

1. A pocket pistol or flask. *Humorous.*

1821 STANSBURY *Pedestrian Tour* (1822) 111, I sat within this hermit-like cave, and dined upon the contents of the 'case and pistol' with which every true pedestrian should be provided. **1889** *Bellevue* (Ida.) *Press* 31 Aug. 3/5 Lambert . . . came out with a pocket flask of whiskey—commonly called a 'pistol'—in his hand.

2. In combs.: (1) **pistol gallery,** a place having facilities for target practice with pistols; (2) **pocket,** =**hip pocket;** (3) * **-shot,** one accustomed to shooting a pistol; (4) **toter,** one who carries a pistol, usu. concealed, *colloq.;* (5) **toting,** carrying a pistol, usu. in a concealed or illegal manner, also attrib.

(1) **1841** *Spirit of Times* 15 Sep. 346/1 (We.), Hudson's Sparring Rooms and Pistol Gallery. **1910** J. HART *Vigilante Girl* 292 When you're in a pistol-gallery you're shooting at a mark. — (2) **1865** *Boston Jrnl.* 22 May 4/4 In her pistol pocket handy, Just like a thoughtful man, she had a prudent little flask of brandy. **1939** ABBOTT-SMITH *We Pointed* 7 The old-time saddle eat both ways, the horse's back and the cowboy's pistol pocket. — (3) **1856** *Porter's Spirit of Times* 15 Nov. 177/2 This will be a match of unusual interest, both parties being acknowledged as among the very best pistol-shots in the country. **1873** MILLER *Amongst Modocs* 303 The officer and Hirst—both . . . famous pistol-shots—leapt the ditches and came darting over. — (4) **1911** *Boston Herald* 14 Oct. 6/4 The New York law has the drop on pistol toters. **1948** *This Week Mag.* 9 Oct. 22/2 An untrained pistol-toter usually shoots himself in the leg the first time out.

(5) **1907** *Springfield W. Republican* 13 May 6 The Texas legislature has taken action toward breaking up the pistol-toting habit. **1943** POWELL *Home Again* 146 It was during that period when Judge Sheffield had become fanatical on the subject of 'pistol-toting.'

As the last term in **belt, buffalo, cap, Derringer, revolving, rifle pistol.**

pistolship ˈpɪstəlˌʃɪp, *n.* The art of using a pistol. *Rare.* — **1895** WISTER *Harper's Mag.* March 537/2 The Governor, on setting foot in Idaho, had begun to study pistolship.

* **pit,** *n.*[1]

1. An exchange, or part of the floor of an exchange, set aside for transactions in a particular commodity, as wheat or oats.

1886 *Harper's Mag.* July 192/1 Back of the 'Pit' is the Call Room. **1902** NORRIS (*title*), The Pit.

2. In combs.: (1) **pit boss,** one in charge of a coal pit; (2) **-coal indigo,** pit coal allegedly sold as indigo by Yankee peddlers, *obs.;* (3) **man,** (see quot. 1876), in full **pitman rod;** (4) **trader,** one who has dealings in a pit (sense **1.**).

(1) **1917** SINCLAIR *King Coal* 110 The pit-boss rose from his chair and knocked the ashes from his pipe. — (2) **1826** FLINT *Recoll.* 32 Fine stories about Yankee tricks . . . and wooden nutmegs, and pit-coal indigo, and gin made by putting pine-tops in the whiskey. **1827** *Western Mo. Rev.* I. 85 The tin wagon, pit-coal-indigo, wooden nutmeg, and wooden clock missionaries find the harvest beginning to fall short. — (3) **1813** *Niles Reg.* IV. 111/2, I apply the power by means of a connecting rod or rods (or pitman, as it is called when applied in saw-mills). **1876** KNIGHT 1720/1 *Pitman.* . . . The rod which connects a rotary with a reciprocating object, as that which couples a crank with a saw-gate, or a steam-piston with its crank-shaft. So called from the lower man of a pair who worked in a pit at the lower end of the saw. **1919** CADY *Rhymes of Vt.* (1923) 186 The pitman rod

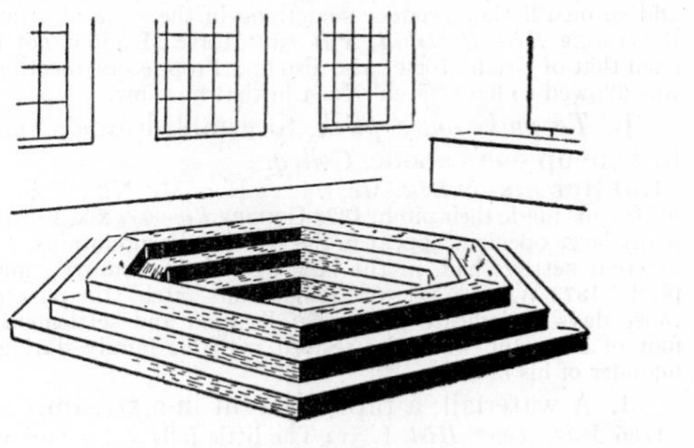

Pit in an exchange

[would] act quaint and queer. — (4) **1905** *Denver Republican* 6 Sep. 10/2 Pit traders and commission houses were the principal sellers.

As the last term in **bone, coal, corn, cyclone, gold, pork, provision, salt, slab, storm, sturgeon, test, trading, wheat, wolf pit.**

pit pɪt, *n.*[2] [Du. in same sense.] The hard stone or seed of a fruit. Cf. **peach pit.**

1848 BARTLETT 252 *Pit.* (Dutch, *pit*, a kernel,) The kernel or nut of fruit; as, a cherry-*pit.* **1873** W. MATTHEWS *Getting On in World* 26 One man may suck an orange and be choked by a pit, another swallow a penknife and live. **1949** *L.A. Times Home Mag.* 11 Dec. 25/2 Cut prunes from pits into small pieces.

pita ˈpitə, *n. S.W.* [Sp. in same sense.] Fiber obtained from various plants, esp. those of the genus *Agave*, and used chiefly for cordage. Also the plant supplying such a fiber, or a rope made of it. Also attrib.

1759 tr. VENEGAS *Nat. Hist. Calif.* I. 44 One species of them called pita, supplies the Indians with thread for making their nets and other uses. *Ib.* 78 They . . . take with them . . . a pita net, in which they put their fruit and seeds. **1844** GREGG *Commerce of Prairies* 88 (Bentley), There is one species whose fibres, known in the country as *pita* are nearly as fine as dressed hemp. **1852** CAZNEAU *Eagle Pass* 56 A coarse bag, made of woven grass or the all-useful *pita* of the country, and sometimes a box as well as a bag, . . . is what you will find in a Camanche camp. **1932** BENTLEY *Sp. Terms* 182 The *pita* fiber when twisted into a rope makes a very strong and hard cord known as a *pita* or a *maguey* .It is the most commonly used lassoing cord of the vaqueros and cowboys in the Southwest.

pitahaya ˌpitəˈhajə, *n. S.W.* [Amer. Sp. in same sense.] Any one of various cacti, esp. the giant cactus, or its edible fruit.

1759 tr. VENEGAS *Nat. Hist. of Calif.* I. 43 And as the pitahaya is very juicy, it is chiefly found in a dry soil. **1847** *23rd Congress* 1 Sess. Sen. Ex. Doc. No. 7, 158 It [a cactus plant] is called in California pitahaya, but it appears that the Mexicans call by that name all large columnar cacti, the fruit of which is edible. **1901** VAN DYKE *Desert* 146 In summer, . . . the cholla, the ocatillo, the pitahaya come along with pink or gold or red or blue flowers. **1942** CASTETTER & BELL *Pima & Papago Agric.* 59 Pitajaya or pitaya here refers to the fruit of either or both *Carnegiea gigantea* and *Lemaireocereus Thurberi;* sahuaro invariably refers to *Carnegiea gigantea.*

attrib. **1925** BRYAN *Papago Country* 46 The pitahaya dulce or organ-pipe cactus (*Cereus thurberi*) consists of a clump of columns, each 3 to 4 inches in diameter and 3 to 8 feet high.

* **pitch,** *n.*[1]

1. The portion or tip of land extending farthest into the fork of a stream. *Obs.*

1694 in *Amer. Sp.* 295/1 At a small naked pine Standing on the pitch of a point that makes the mouth of Quanticott creek on the North side of the Creek. **1764** *Ib.*, A certain tract of waste and ungranted Land . . . in the pitch of the fork of Opakon & Mill Creek. **1770** WASHINGTON *Diaries* I. 410 The Fort is built in the point between the River Alligany and Monongahela, but not so near the pitch of it as Fort Duquesne stood.

2. A piece of ground selected by a settler or allotted to him, usu. for a house or farm. Now *obs.* or *hist.*

1699 *Derby Rec.* 207 The laying out of John Pringles pitch upon the good hill. **1703** *Waterbury Prop. Rec.* 224 To relinquish his pich at the upper end of woster swamp. **1809** GRAY *Letters* 275 As we approached the American boundary, we found a few settlements, what the Americans call a *pitch.* They cut down some trees, make a log-house, sow some corn; next year they cut down more trees, and sow more corn, and so on till they produce something in the style of a farm. **1888** BITTINGER *Hist. Haverhill, N.H.* 56 'Morse Meadow' got its name from that of Uriah Morse, who also at a Proprietors' meeting in 1763 was allowed to have 'pitch' No. 1 in that meadow.

b. *To make one's pitch*, to establish one's residence, to take up one's abode. *Colloq.*

1764 HUTCHINSON *Hist. Mass.* I. 22 Here Mr. Nowell and some of his friends made their pitch. **1823** COOPER *Pioneers* xix, Elizabeth saw many large openings appear in the sides of the mountains, . . . where different settlers had, in the language of the country, 'made their pitch.' **1873** WRIGHT *Sk.* 368 He made his 'pitch' (the phrase used in those days to indicate permanent location and settlement) at the foot of Ant Hill, where he resided with his family during the remainder of his life.

3. A waterfall; a rapid descent in a stream.

1786 *Mag. Amer. Hist.* I. 312 The little falls . . . is now very perceivable as the water is very low—only one small pitch. **1839** HOLMES *Explor. Aroostook River* 12 The first pitch of water is near the mouth of Bowling Brook. **1871** RAYMOND *3d Rep. Mines* 201 At Shoshone City there is a cataract 100 feet high, and four miles below another, the Great Shoshone Falls, 210 feet in height, with several violent pitches, in the river immediately above them.

4. The game of all fours or seven-up. Cf. **auction pitch.**

1860 GEO. T. CLARK *Diary* (MS) 10 Had a game of pitch in our tent today. **1874** *Northern Vindicator* (Estherville, Iowa) 7 March, He can find good quarters with a jolly crowd who know how to play 'pitch.' **1947** *Chi. Tribune* 19 Oct. VII. 1/1 The fire engine house has been the scene of a game of pitch every night for 52 years.

5. In colloq. or slang phrases: (1) *To slink one's pitch*, to get off one's high horse, to become very humble; (2) *to take the pitch out of*, *W.* to subdue a cow pony by allowing it to exhaust itself in bucking under conditions favorable to the rider.

(1) **1853** J. G. BALDWIN *Flush Times Ala.* 26 Many a witness . . . 'slunk his pitch mightily' when old Kasm put him through on the cross-examination. — (2) **1907** WHITE *Arizona Nights* 94 In a cow boy's 'string' of from six to ten animals the boss assigns him two or three broncos to break in to the cow business. Therefore, each morning we could observe a half dozen or so men gingerly leading wicked looking little animals out to the sand 'to take the pitch out of them.'

* **pitch,** *n.*[2] In combs.: (1) **pitch knot,** a pine knot; (2) **pine,** see as a main entry; (3) **wood,** resinous wood obtained from pitch pine.

(1) **1792** BELKNAP *Hist. New-Hampshire* III. 90 A lighted pitch-knot is placed on the outside of a canoe, which not only attracts the fish, but gives the fishermen direction where to strike. **1850** WATSON *Camp-Fires Revol.* 157 We must have some more pitch-knots on the fire. — (3) **1825** NEAL *Bro. Jonathan* I. 292 The pitch wood was lighted and set in the fireplace. **1828** SHERBURNE *Memoirs* ix. 193 We then lost our course, but obtaining an abundance of excellent pitch-wood, we made our way by conjecture.

* **pitch,** *v.*

1. *S. tr.* To plan for, plant (a crop). *Colloq.*

1688 JOHN CLAYTON in *Phil. Trans.* XVII. 980 The Gentlewoman where I lived, was a very Acute Ingenious Lady; who one day Discoursing the Overseer of her Servants, about pitching the ensuing Year's Crop [etc.]. **1772** *Md. Hist. Mag.* XIV. 273 We have pitched above 9 tenths of our Crop. **1841** FOOTE *Texas & Texans* II. 380 The planter commences pitching his crops—beginning with corn in the fore part of February. **1944** *D.N.* Nov. 48 *pitch a crop:* phr. To plant a crop. S.Va., w.N.C.

2. *intr.* Of a roof or floor: To slope downwards.

1771 *Copley-Pelham Lett.* 137, I should have the Roof to pitch from under the Arkitraves of the Chamber Windows. **1858** *Ill. Agric. Soc. Trans.* III. 538 The roof may pitch both ways, or shed at the ends. **1897** F. C. MOORE *How to Build a Home* 94 The floor shall pitch from building to the front of piazza $\frac{1}{4}$ inch to every foot of width.

3. *Baseball. tr.* To deliver or throw (the ball) to the batter; to play as a pitcher in (a game). Often absol. Cf. **pitched ball.**

1845 in *Appletons' Ann. Cyclo. 1885* 77/2 The ball must be pitched and not thrown to the bat. **1868** CHADWICK *Base Ball* 60 When he [the pitcher] makes a motion to pitch and does not do so, or steps outside his ground in pitching, he makes a balk. **1890** W. CARLETON *City Legends* 37 Will you pitch or catch? **1949** *Newsweek* 18 April 82/2 He picked rookie Gene Bearden to pitch the game.

4. *W.* (See quots. and cf. * **pitching,** *n.* **2.**)

1883 SWEET & KNOX *Through Texas* 68 The majority of Texas ponies buck, or pitch as it is sometimes termed. **1900** GARLAND *Eagle's Heart* 98 A horse that reared and leaped to fling its rider was said to 'pitch.' **1949** *Sat. Ev. Post* 9 April 43/1 The sorrel didn't pitch when I first hit the saddle.

5. In combs.: (1) **Pitchfork steer,** ?a steer so called from his brand, *obs.;* (2) **grifter,** (see quot.); (3) * **hole,** a hole or other defect in a road; (4) **man,** one who sells small articles on the street, at fairs, carnivals, etc., also **pitchwoman** in transf. sense, *colloq.;* (5) **out,** in baseball, a pitching of the ball wide of the home plate so as to give the catcher a good opportunity to cut a runner off at a base.

(1) **1890** *Stock Grower & Farmer* 2 Aug. 4/3 The 'Pitchfork' steers sold here last week at $24. They were fat. — (2) **1911** *Cosmopolitan* Jan. 231 'Slum fakers' and 'pitch grifters,' or sellers of canes, whips, and horns, and workers of small fortune-telling and gambling devices, were making the welkin rasp with their grating voices. — (3) **1874** *Vt. Bd. Agric. Rep.* II. 659 The highways leading to our larger villages, . . . are frequently so full of pitchholes or 'cahoos' as to render them totally unfit for travel. **1890** *Harper's Mag.* Oct. 657/2 The highway was frequently interrupted by 'pitch holes.' — (4) **1934** WEBSTER. **1948** *Chi. Tribune* 25 Jan. (Grafic Mag.) 17/1 For several seasons she went buzzing ahead of the New York company with her enthusiastic pitchwoman spiels. **1949** *Time* 19 Dec. 34/3 They are all journalistic racketeers—I mean pitchmen.

(5) **1912** C. MATHEWSON *Pitching* vii. 157 If a catcher can get a pitchout on a hit and run sign he upsets the other team greatly.

b. In phrases relating or alluding to baseball: (1) *To pitch for* (a team), to play on (a team) in the capacity of a pitcher, also transf.; (2) *to pitch a curve*, to throw a baseball so that it curves; (3) *to be in there pitching*, to be putting forth one's best efforts, *colloq.*

(1) **1885** *Wkly. New Mexican Rev.* 21 May 3/6 A base ballist, who pitched for the Emmets of Chicago last season has been employed to play with the Albuquerque Browns. **1949** *Time* 14 March 22/1 Johnson stayed in there, ready to pitch for the party when he was called from the bench. — (2) **1909** CALHOUN *Miss Minerva* 46, I can knock a home-run an' pitch a curve an' ketch a fly. — (3) **1943** *Sat. Ev. Post* 26 June 75/3 Everybody on the system is in there pitching, trying to save a locomotive or piece of locomotive. **1947** *Chi. D. News* 24 Jan. 1/6 Whenever I feel I can help I'll be in there pitching.

pitched ball. *Baseball.* A ball thrown by the pitcher to the batter.

1856 *Spirit of Times* 22 Nov. 197/2 The striker should also be compelled to run . . . when three fair pitched balls had been given him. **1912** MATHEWSON *Pitching* 14 Big League ball-players recognize only two kinds of pitched balls—the curve and the straight one. **1948** *Houston* (Tex.) *Post* 14 June 4/1 Bollweg was hit by a pitched ball in the seventh.

* **pitcher,** *n.*

1. In baseball, the player who throws the ball to the batters. Also attrib.

1845 in *Appletons' Ann. Cyclo.* XXV. 77/2 A runner can not be put out in making one base when a balk is made by the pitcher. **1907** *St. Nicholas* June 720/2 Raising his hands high above his head and twisting himself up in the most approved pitcher style, he tightened his grasp on the ball and let drive. **1948** *Chi. D. News* 4 June 36/8 Claude Passeau's job with the Cubs is to tutor young pitchers throughout the Chicago farm system.

2. *W.* A horse that pitches or bucks.

1892 DUVAL *Young Explorers* 57 He had a Roman nose, white eyes and protuberant stomach, and was a most expert 'pitcher' whenever he wanted to get rid of his rider. **1939** ROLLINS *Gone Haywire* 259 He's th' doggonedest meanest pitcher I's ever seen that warn't an intentional killer.

3. In the possessive in special combs. relating to baseball: (1) **pitcher's base,** the pitcher's box, *obs.;* (2) **battle,** a contest for supremacy between rival pitchers in a game; (3) **box,** the station occupied by the pitcher in pitching; (4) **game,** a game which exhibits little but the rival skills of the pitchers; (5) **mound,** the pitcher's box; (6) **plate,** (see quot.); (7) **point,** (see quots.), *obs.;* (8) **square,** the pitcher's box; (9) **station,** the pitcher's box.

(1) **1867** *Ball Players' Chron.* 27 June 5/4 For seventy-five yearly subscriptions we will give: One sett of best bases, one dozen regulation base balls, one National score book, striker's and pitcher's bases, and one pair foul ball flags. — (2) **1891** *Appeal-Avalanche* (Memphis) 26 April 5/3 It was a pitchers' battle. — (3) **1887** *Courier-Journal* 27 May 2/4 Terry finished the game in the pitcher's box. **1949** *Time* 5 Sep. 40/2 He can reach an outside pitch and send it lining into left field, or rifle it through the pitcher's box. — (4) **1886** CHADWICK *Art of Pitching* 51 The monotonous and uninteresting 'pitcher's games' prevailed to a greater extent than previously known in the history of the game.

(5) **1914** *Collier's* 31 Jan. 6/3 Bury me under the pitcher's mound at the ball bark. — (6) **1916** [see ***plate,** *n.* **1**]. — (7) **1857** *Spirit of Times* 28 Feb. 420/3 The home base and pitcher's point [are] to be each marked by a flat circular iron plate, painted or enamelled white. **1868** CHADWICK *Base Ball* 50 There are also two other plates of less size than the home base, which are called the 'pitcher's points.' — (8) **1887** *Courier-Journal* 30 Jan. 10/3 The space of ground covered by the pitcher's square has been reduced. — (9) **1880** N. BROOKS *Fairport Nine* xiv. 183 Jake Coombs, at pitcher's station, satirically said that the captain of the Fairports had not got his sea-legs on yet.

As the last term in **change, cream, devil's cream, forefathers', ice, wash pitcher.**

***pitcher plant.** Any one of various plants of the American genera *Sarracenia* and *Darlingtonia,* having leaves suggestive of a pitcher; esp. the sidesaddle flower, *S. purpurea,* of the northeastern states. Cf. **California pitcher plant.**

1857 GRAY *Lessons Botany* 179 Dr. Sarrazin of Quebec . . . was one of the first to send our common Pitcher-plant to the botanists of Europe. **1944** NUTE *Lk. Superior* 322 Late June and early July find the swamps full of magnificent pitcher plants, sundews and orchids in bloom. **1949** *Nat. Hist.* June 281/1 The leaves of the common pitcher plant are also pitfalls for ground-inhabiting insects.

attrib. **1869** FULLER *Flower Gatherers* 185 It belongs to the rare Pitcher-plant family, and I am very glad we have one for examination. **1949** *Nat. Hist.* Oct. 382/2 The Pitcher Plant Spider spins a web across the throat of the leaf and catches insects as they slide toward the depths of the trap.

b. pitcher-plant mosquito, (see quot. 1913).

1913 *Geog. Soc. Chicago Bul.* 5, 193 The pitcher-plant mosquito (*Wyeomyia smithii*) is known to breed in the leaves of pitcher-plants only. **1949** *Nat. Hist.* Oct. 382/3 Wrigglers of the Pitcher Plant Mosquito are found only in the water collected in pitcher plant leaves.

***pitching,** *n.*

1. *Baseball.* The action of throwing the ball to the batter. Also attrib.

1858 *N.Y. Tribune* 18 Aug. 7/3 The pitching was good on both sides. **1896** CHADWICK *Spalding's Base B. Guide* 2 A new form of pitching tables are included in the records of the pitching of 1895. **1949** *Dallas Morn. News* 9 May II. 7/2 Brown's pitching duels, with Christy Mathewson, another diamond immortal, were famous.

2. (See quot. 1865.) Also attrib.

1865 in PIKE *Scout & Ranger* (1932) 70, I had scarcely touched his back, when he began that species of rearing and plunging, known in Texas as 'pitching,' in California as 'spiking,' and in this country as 'bucking.' **1889** *Cent. Mag.* Jan. 335/1 A Texas pony does not break his legs or fall over backwards in the 'pitching' process as does the 'cayuse' of the North-west. **1948** *Sat. Review* 28 Aug. 37/1 Bucky Durant calmly rolled a cigarette as he sat atop the pitching bronc.

As the last term in **dollar, penny pitching.**

pitch pine.

1. Any one of various North American pitch-yielding pines, as *Pinus rigida, P. palustris,* etc. Also a tree of such a species or the wood of such a tree. Cf. **Georgia (pitch) pine.**

1676 *Essex Inst. Coll.* LVI. 306, 4½ acres of land . . . bounded by a pitch pine, small heap of rocks [etc.]. **1771** *Copley-Pelham Lett.* 138 The floor of the Peazas except that next the kitchen should be Pitch Pine. **1806** *Ann. 9th Congress* 2 Sess. 1115 The short-leaved, or pitch pine . . . is always found upon arid lands. **1949** R. J. SIM *Pages from Past* 97 The bottom is of Jersey pitch pine.

attrib. **1684** *Manchester Rec.* 17 A pich pine tree marked with 4 marks. **1736** *Boston Rec.* 150 Add to the South East Side Ten foot To be Built of square Pitch Pine Timber. **1824** *Mass. Spy* 15 Dec. (Th.), [He snatched] a pitch pine knot blazing from the fire. **1870** WHITTIER *Poetical Works* (1894) 99/2 Would the saints And the white angels dance and laugh to see him Burn like a pitch-pine torch?

2. Denoting a *barren* or *plain* where pitch pine prevails.

1734 *N.H. Probate Rec.* II. 508, I also give unto my sd. son . . . the one half of my Thirty Acres of Land Lying between Black-Water Bridge, and the Pitch-Pine Plains. **1807** *Ann. 10th Congress* 1 Sess. I. 671 The circumjacent country was a low pitch-pine barren. **1832** WILLIAMSON *Maine* II. 136 They left [their packs] . . . in a pitch-pine plain, where the trees were thin, and the brakes at that time of the year small.

Pittsburgh ˈpɪtsbɜg, *n.* [For Wm. *Pitt* (1708–78), Eng. statesman.] In combs.: (1) **Pittsburgh coal,** coal mined at Pittsburgh, Pa.; (2) **stogy,** a stogy *q.v.* made at Pittsburgh; (3) **wagon,** a heavy freight wagon used in traffic between Pittsburgh and eastern cities. All *obs.*

(1) **1851** HALL *Manhattaner* 49 And you have never seen a fire hugged until you behold a violet lipped Creole before a blazing grate of Pittsburg coal. — (2) **1909** *Sat. Ev. Post* 13 March 16/2 During business hours he also smoked Pittsburgh stogies constantly, when he wasn't chewing them. **1923** [see **poker-faced**]. — (3) **1826** FLINT *Recoll.* 8 We passed hundreds of Pittsburg waggons, in the crossing. **1832** PAULDING *Westward Ho!* I. 66 Occasionally they encountered one of those 'land carracks' called Pittsburg wagons.

Pittsburgher ˈpɪtsˌbɜgə, *n.* A native or resident of Pittsburgh, Pa.

1835 HOFFMAN *Winter in West* I. 71 The Pittsburgers . . . are more bent upon increasing their 'fathers' store than on beautifying the favoured spot in which they dwell. **1880** *Harper's Mag.* Dec. 52 The care-worn Pittsburgher flees when his daily duties end, glad to escape for the time the all-pervading soot and smoke. **1949** *Highway Traveler* Feb. 27/2 Chances are, if you are a Pittsburgher visiting in another city, the first person you talk to will say, 'So you're from the smoky city.'

Pitt team. One of the freight teams formerly engaged in transporting goods over the Cumberland Road to Pittsburgh. Now *hist.*

1913 *Proc. Pa.-Ger. Soc.* XXII. 106 Why stranger, many a time I stood right here on this spot and counted over fifty 'Pitt teams' in a string pass me both ways, one right after another. 'Pitt teams' were six-horse teams. **1930** OMWAKE *Conestoga Teams* 85 On the new road broad-wheeled wagons, such as were known by the name of Conestogas, Turnpike Schooners, or Pitt Teams, were supposed to carry thirty barrels of flour or three tons.

piut pjut, *n.* [Imitative.] (See quot.) — **1808** WILSON *Ornithology* I. 53 The Gold-winged woodpecker . . . has numerous provincial appellations in the different states . . . such as . . . 'Hittock,' 'Yucker,' 'Piut,' 'Flicker.'

pivotal state. (See quot. 1914.)

1884 *Cent. Mag.* Nov. 125 The 'pivotal States' . . . sometimes make the nomination turn upon considerations of the lowest kind. **1914** *Cyclo. Amer. Govt.* II. 695/1 A doubtful state whose electoral vote is so large that it may determine the choice of a President is a 'pivotal state.' **1948** *Fargo* (N.D.) *Forum* 28 Sep. 4/2 Wallace is expected to get considerable votes in the pivotal states of New York and California.

pivot tooth. (See quot. 1875.)

1842 in KOCH *Hist. Dent. Surgery* I. 269 In 1811 after I came to the United States I saw a pivot tooth which had been set by Dr. Kuhn, of Lancaster, Pennsylvania. **1875** KNIGHT 1722/1 *Pivot-tooth* . . . an artificial crown attached to the root of a natural tooth by a dowel-pin of wood or metal occupying the nerve-canal. **1909** KOCH *Hist. Dent. Surgery* I. 258 Many pivot teeth were removed at the patient's will for the purpose of cleansing.

pixilated ˈpɪksəˌletɪd, *a.* [See note.] Led astray as if by pixies, confused, bewildered. Also intoxicated. *Colloq.*

The *OED* has *Pixy-led, Pixy-leading,* and the *EDD* has *Pixy-led, -laid, -laden,* meaning led astray or bewildered. The form here, first reported from Marblehead, Mass., may, therefore, not have originated in this country.

1848 in *Amer. Sp.* XVI. (1941) 79/2 You'll never find on any trip That he'll be pix-e-lated. **1886** BYNNER *Agnes Surriage* 56 'We'll be pixilated 'n' driven on to th' rocks an ye don't wake up.' **1891** *Amer. Folk-Lore* IV. 159 Words from the dialect of Marblehead. . . . Pixielated. Confused, bewildered. **1938** *Our Army* Feb. 9/1 To make a bad matter pixilated, Glumbo is on guard and can't ride herd on the ex-farmer. **1949** *Chi. Tribune* 22 Oct. 10/3 Our American variant 'pixilated,' with the generalized meaning of eccentric, confused, crazy or intoxicated, has long been familiar in Essex county, Mass.

***place,** *n.*

1. In a college class, the position occupied by a student with reference to his classmates in a system of "placing" students. *Obs.* Cf. ***place,** *v.* **1.**

1727 in *Mass. Col. Soc. Pub.* XVI. 554 Howlet should be admitted to his Degree, but be degraded to ye lowest place in ye Class; and yt Saltonstall's Degradation shall be abated in measure, yt is to say, he shall take his place between Stephens & Parker in ye Class, & that that [*sic*] they shall take these places in their Class whenever they appear together, & particularly this day. **1743** *Ib.* 736 That whereas Waldoe a Senior Sophister has petition'd, that he may be rais'd to an higher Place in his Class, said Petition was maturely consider'd & voted, unanimously, that it be dismiss'd. **1925** *Mass. Col. Soc. Pub.* XV. 82 A common form of punishment was to degrade a student a certain number of places in his class.

2. Also (1) **place congregation,** (see quot.), *obs.;* (2) **hit,** in baseball, a hit in a desired direction or to a particular place in the field, also **place hitting,** cf. ***place,** *v.* **3.**

(1) **1844** Rupp *Relig. Denominations* 414 Each individual colony, called the *place congregation*, is independent in its individual concerns. — (2) **1896** Chadwick *Spalding's Base B. Guide* 75 There is no plainer rule known to scientific batting in base ball than that technically termed '*facing for position*,' a point of play which is the fundamental rule governing the '*place hit*' in batting, which hit is the very acme of scientific play at the bat. *Ib.* 76 It is necessary, under such circumstances, for the batsman to avail himself of '*place* hitting.'

As the last term in **bald, bar, boarding, boiling, burying, canoe, carriage, carrying, chimney, dropping off, dumping, fire, firing, fishing, frontier, home, hoorah, jumping-off, landing, licking, line, loafing, nooning, riding, rolling, roosting, scratching, stamping, tight, wooding place.**

***place,** *v.*

1. *Educ. tr.* (See quot. 1925.)

This method of ranking students with reference to their classmates, and of arranging their names in a corresponding manner on class lists prevailed at Harvard from 1642 to 1769. See A. Matthews in *Mass. Col. Soc. Pub.* XXV. 420–27.

1718 in T. Clap *Hist. Yale-College* 28 Their Names should be inserted in the Class, as they were at first placed. **1763** in *Mass. Col. Soc. Pub.* XV. 115 Josephus Kidder. Mr & Mr John Lowthrop to be placed in the Catalogue as we may find them graduated in their own Colleges. **1831** P. Wingate in Peirce *Hist. Harvard Univ.* (1833) 311 Much dissatisfaction was often excited by placing the classes (and I believe all the other Colleges had the same practice). **1925** *Mass. Col. Soc. Pub.* XV. 82 Down to 1769 the members of each class, at some time during their Freshman year, were 'placed' in an order of precedence corresponding to the social position of their fathers, and a common form of punishment was to degrade a student a certain number of places in his class. This principle was applied for the last time in June, 1769, in the case of the Class which had entered in 1768 and was to graduate in 1772.

2. To recall or determine who or what (a person or thing) is; to identify. *Colloq.*

1855 *Knickerb.* XLV. 194 Who *is* our friend who writes us the following? . . . And [are] 'K. Y.' his initials? If yea, we can't 'place' him. **1890** *Harper's Mag.* July 291/2 He had no memory of having ever heard it before. . . . For a while he could not place it.

3. Of a batter in baseball: To hit (a ball) in such a way as to send it to any chosen part of the field. Cf. **place hit, place hitting.**

1880 *Brooklyn D. Eagle* 22 Aug. (E. J. Nichols). **1886** Chadwick *Art of Batting* 33 The highest degree of skill in scientific batting is reached when the batsman can 'place a ball'—in any part of the field he chooses.

placer ˈplæsɚ, *n. W.* [Sp. in sense **1.**]

1. A deposit of sand, gravel, detritus, etc., in which gold occurs in minute particles; a place where such sand, gravel, etc., is washed for gold. Also transf.

1842 *Niles' Reg.* 8 Oct. 96/1 They have at last discovered gold [in Calif.]. . . . Those who are acquainted with these 'placeres,' as they call them, (for it is not a mine), say it will grow richer, and may lead to a mine. **1851** *S.F. Picayune* 1 Oct. 2/2 Those who have given their attention to the cultivation of the soil . . . have found, in the abundant and luxuriant crops they raised, more prolific and richer 'placers' than any they might have discovered in the mountains. **1912** London *Smoke Bellew* 311 The source of Klondike placers found at last. **1948** Johnston *Gold Rush* 11/1 Their search was rewarded by further discoveries of rich placers.

b. Used of land in which valuable minerals occur. *Obs.*

1880 Ingham *Digging Gold* 234 In Leadville, Colorado, it was declared—the land being placer—that as it was 'valuable for minerals,' it was not subject to entry as a town site.

2. In combs., chiefly obs.: (1) **placer camp,** a camp of placer miners; (2) **claim,** a mining claim located on a placer deposit; (3) **digging,** (*a*) *pl.*, a place at which placer mining is or may be carried on, (*b*) the action of mining by placer methods; (4) **district,** a region where placers occur; (5) **dredge,** a dredge used in placer mining; (6) **field,** an area where placers occur; (7) **gold,** see as a main entry; (8) **ground,** ground where gold can be obtained by placer mining; (9) **mine,** see as a main entry; (10) **miner,** one who mines gold by placer methods; (11) **mining,** the separating, by means of washing, either in a gold pan or by hydraulic means, of particles of gold from the deposits or formations in which they occur; (12) **prospect,** an indication that placer mining will be profitable.

(1) **1890** Langford *Vigilante Days* (1912) 69 Few . . . of the great number of placer camps in the Rocky Mountains . . . survive beyond the third year of their existence. **1948** Weston *Mother Lode* 94 Jenny Lind . . . was a rich placer camp even in 'forty-nine. — (2) **1869** *Overland Mo.* III. 42 It is like taking out 'big pay' from a placer claim. **1910** J. Hart *Vigilante Girl* 329 To stop work on a placer claim constituted abandonment. — (3) (*a*) **1850** *Calif. Courier* (S.F.) 3 Dec. 2/3 The placer diggings are highly productive. *a***1918** G. Stuart *On Frontier* I. 86 Went to 'Mad Ox Canyon,' to look for placer diggings. **1948** Johnston *Gold Rush* 51/2 One of the richest placer diggings was located on East Weaver Creek. (*b*) **1856** *Harper's Mag.* June 117/2 The old system of *placer* digging has ceased to exist. **1890** Harte *Waif of Plains* 116 Ye'll hev to get rid of them ther fixins if yer goin' in for *placer* diggin'! — (4) **1897** Leonard *Gold Fields Klondike* 85 Outside of the Yukon region there are seven other placer districts.

(5) **1947** *Steamboat* (Colo.) *Pilot* 30 Jan. 2/8 They had been dismantling the old placer dredge in Way's gulch. — (6) **1899** U.S. Geol. Surv. *Water Supp. Paper* 23, 12 Along the northern end of the range some promising placer fields have been discovered. **1906** *Out West* Feb. 124 The gold of the newly-discovered placer fields had much to do with his choice. — (8) **1872** C. King *Mountaineering in Sierra Nev.* 288 In failing gold-industry, and the gradual abandonment of placer-ground to Chinamen, there is abundant pathos. **1891** *Scribner's Mag.* Dec. 766/2 There is not . . . a hydraulic mine in New Mexico, despite the enormous areas of placer-ground.

(10) **1853** *S.F. Journal* 28 July 4/4 The placer miners are doing well; in many places very well. **1947** *Field & Stream* June 30/3 Quite a few men are to be found going over gravel bars that were turned over many, many times by placer miners in years gone by. — (11) **1856** *Porter's Spirit of Times* 2 Nov. 194/2 The success of those engaged in placer mining generally, is said to be extraordinarily good. **1949** *L.A. Times* 11 July 21/2 Placer mining will be conducted with power shovels. — (12) **1897** Leonard *Gold Fields Klondike* 69 The placer prospects continue to be more and more encouraging and extraordinary.

Also *placer bed, deposit, discovery, operations, period, rush, tool, washer, working*(*s*), etc.

As the last term in **coyote, gold, surface placer.**

placer ˈplæsɚ, *v. tr.* To mine (gold) by washing auriferous sand, gravel, etc. Also transf. — **1868** *Harper's Wkly.* 22 Aug. 541/3 [The salt mine] was placered among the States, different pots being designated by the names of the States for whose use they were set. **1901** *Out West* Jan. 116 Gold . . . dust and nuggets were being 'placered' in Los Angeles county more than a decade before Marshall's 'discovery' of California gold on Sutter Creek.

placer gold. Gold occurring in more or less coarse grains or flakes and obtainable by washing the sand, gravel, etc., in which it is found. Also in combs.

1848 *Californian* (S.F.) 29 May 1/2 Those who find it necessary to have the correct standard can be accommodated by the subscriber, who will take Placera Gold in payment. **1872** *Harper's Mag.* Dec. 22 This is 'sluicing,' a variety of placer gold digging or gulch mining. **1902** McKee *Land of Nome* 1 The rich placer-gold deposits were discovered by a small party of prospectors in the late autumn of 1898. **1948** A. K. Williams *Gold Rush Days* 51 Quartz mining had come into prominence in California and it was taking the people by storm, just the same as the placer gold had a few years before.

placer mine. A mine from which a mineral, esp. gold, in particles or flakes, may be obtained by washing the sand, gravel, etc.

1848 Bryant *California* App. 473 From all that I can learn as to similar deposits of gold elsewhere, I believe these [in upper Calif.] to be the richest *placer* mines in the world. **1948** Johnston *Gold Rush* 2/2

The placer mines yielded such fabulous returns that true stories of their richness had the semblance of the wildest fiction.

b. Also as a verb, *tr.* To subject (a region) to mining by the placer method. Also *intr.*, to carry on placer mining.

1865 BAXLEY *What I Saw* 419 This entire mountain . . . was once *placer-mined* over its entire surface. **1890** *Stock Grower & Farmer* 19 July 4/4 A man who came to Arizona, . . . lived on brown beans and placer-mined on Hassayampa creek. **1944** *Life* 20 Nov. 11/2 She now is the wife of Johnny Matson, a prospector, who placer-mines for gold up the Seventy Mile River.

placeta plɑˈsitə, *n. S.W.* [Sp. in same sense.] A small square or garden, usu. adjacent to a residence or other building. Cf. **plazita.**

1847 MAGOFFIN *Down Santa Fé Trail* 211 Her house is large, . . . and the placita quite pretty, for she takes pride in raising choice fruit trees. **1867** MELINE *2000 Miles on Horseback* 152 The portal, or main entrance, opens upon an interior square, (*patio* or *placita*), around which is a gallery. **1941** FERGUSSON *Southwest* 251 A house might start with one room or several, but as families grew, so did houses, putting out wings which might in time come together to make a patio, or placita, as it is called in New Mexico.

***plague,** *n.* As the last term in **American, Chocorua, cold, grasshopper, white plague.**

plague of the back. (See quots.) *Obs.* — **1672** JOSSELYN *N. Eng. Rarities* 3 Cold . . . many times strikes the Inhabitants both English and Indian with that sad Disease called there the Plague of the Back, but with us Empiema. **1698** in *Phil. Trans.* XX. 167, I made the same Remark you do, about the *Plague of the Back*, that it is greatly distant from an *Empyeme.* I have tasted it more than once personally, it seems more of a *Collick*, yet is undoubtedly a *Nervous Dolour.* The Country People have learned of the *Indians* to steep *Castoreum* in *Rum*, and so cure it.

* **plain,** *n.*

1. *pl.* Extensive regions of level or rolling treeless country, prairies.

1755 L. EVANS *Anal. Map Colonies* 13 The rest have retired beyond the woodless Plains over the Mississippi. **1806** *Ann. 9th Congress* 2 Sess. 1110 The immense plains known to exist in America, may owe their origin to this custom [of burning grass in the fall or winter]. **1925** TILGHMAN *Dugout* 1 Far scattered over the rolling Western plains . . . the old dugouts tell their story of the past. **1947** *Reader's Digest* Oct. 78/1 Black blizzards roared across the Plains, devastating crops.

attrib. **1867** RICHARDSON *Beyond Miss.* 79 Plains-travel and frontier life are peculiarly severe upon women and oxen. **1877** R. I. DODGE *Hunting Grounds* v. 63 'Old Bridger,' the most thorough and justly celebrated of all plains guides. *Ib.* 67 Another plains malady . . . is called 'moon-blind.' **1946** *Chi. D. News* 3 June 28/2 Today, the Plains States are no longer treeless prairies.

2. In the pl. in special combs.: (1) **plains country,** the prairie region of the central and western U.S., cf. **plain country** in **b.** below; (2) **craft,** a knowledge of, and skill in making use of, the nature lore of the plains; (3) **Indian,** an Indian of one of the tribes that formerly occupied the prairie region of the U.S., freq. *pl.*, these tribes collectively; (4) **land,** a prairie region; (5) **man,** a man accustomed to life on the plains; (6) **marl,** (see quot.); (7) **people,** those who live on the plains; (8) **rifle,** (see quots.); (9) **tribe,** a tribe of Indians living on the western plains; (10) **wagon,** a wagon used on the western plains, cf. **plain wagon** in **b.** below.

(1) **1885** *Cent. Mag.* June 230/2 The three hundred weary miles of treeless and barren-looking plains country. **1923** J. H. COOK *On Old Frontier* 61 Hundreds of bands of mustangs [were] ranging western Texas and the Plains country. — (2) **1898** KING *Warrior Gap* 38 That green youngster up there in front hasn't learned the first principles of plainscraft yet. **1902** T. ROOSEVELT in *Deer Family* 55 Such hunting, though great fun, does not imply any particular skill either in horsemanship, marksmanship, or plainscraft. — (3) **1852** in *Mich. Hist. Mag.* IX. 397 Though the plains Indians frequently go unpunished, that is no reason why our Indians here should be butchered. **1913** LONDON *Valley of Moon* 438 A lithograph . . . of a Plains Indian, in paint and feathers. **1949** *Sky Line Trail* Oct. 12/2 Some bands of Plains Indians are known to have travelled 2,000 miles on raids. — (4) **1893** *Harper's Mag.* May 944/1 One-third of the State is plains land, and two-thirds are cut up by mountains.

(5) **1870** KEIM *Sheridan's Troopers* 66 [A good horse for hunting buffalo] is a treasure in the esteem of a plainsman. **1949** *Sun. World-Herald Mag.* (Omaha) 13 Feb. 16/3 He was a dashing plainsman and crack shot whose exploits formed the basis for the Diamond Dick stories. — (6) **1905** *Forestry Bureau Bul.* No. 66, 9 The greater proportion of the uplands in western Kansas and Nebraska is covered by deposits of very fine sand . . . and silt . . . known geologically as 'plains marl' and 'loess.' — (7) **1905** *Nation* 5 Jan. LXXX. 11/1 As a plains people they [the Pawnee] were largely dependent upon the chase. — (8) **1920** SAWYER *Our Rifles* 50 At first the gunsmith merely did 'shorten her up a bit.' The result still was a Kentucky, but a slightly abbreviated one. The next step was towards greater handiness by lessening the weight forward . . . by tapering the barrel and mounting it with a half-stock. Such a rifle was really the first Plains rifle. **1948** *Chi. Tribune* 7 March 1. 38/4 When the Daniel Boones reached the plains they needed a shorter, heavier barreled gun, and the plains rifle developed, about the same time that the flintlock gave way to percussion lock. — (9) **1870** KEIM *Sheridan's Troopers* (1885) 29 The Plains Tribes have, as yet, presented no prominent warriors in the character of leaders. **1949** *Nat. Geog. Mag.* Oct. 473/1 What the buffalo was to the Plains tribes the caribou is to the Indians of the far north.

(10) **1906** *Out West* Jan. 50 It was a 'plains wagon,' a later follower of the old Conestoga, loaded from seat to end-gate with household goods.

b. Also, sometimes, in the sing., as (1) **plain country,** (2) **fox,** (3) **land,** (4) **people,** see as a main entry, (5) **wagon.**

(1) **1792** IMLAY *Western Territory* 52 The plain country . . . is considered as little better than barren land. — (2) **1842** *Nat. Hist. N.Y., Zoology* 1. 46 This species [i.e., the gray fox] is more common in the southern counties than farther north. On Long Island it is very abundant, and is there frequently known under the name of the *Plain* or *Grass Fox.* — (3) **1875** TEMPLE & SHELDON *Hist. Northfield, Mass.* 64 Plain lands . . . were then reckoned nearly worthless.

(5) **1852** in *Wash. Hist. Quart.* XV. 127 A Noon repairing plain wagon.

As the last term in **bottom, brush, burnt, camass, caribou, delta, fever-and-ague, grass, grease(wood), great, Great American, mesquite, pine, ragged, sage, sagebrush, salt, staked, walnut plain.**

plain people.

1. a. (See quot.) *Obs.* **b.** (See quot.)

(**a**) **1871** DE VERE 281 It is said that the freedmen, in the first glow of their rights, proposed to call the Whites *Plain People*, in return for the term *Colored People*, by which they were designated themselves. — (**b**) **1900** *Cong. Rec.* 5 Feb. 1525/1 We appeal to the unofficial masses, . . . the great body of our citizenship, whom Abraham Lincoln affectionately denominated 'the plain people.'

2. The Amish, Mennonites, and Dunkards, so called from the plainness of their dress and style of living. Often *cap.*

1904 H. R. MARTIN *Tillie* 113 But can't you see the inconsistentness of the plain people? **1929** *Sat. Ev. Post* 23 March 165/1 You found it in your heart for to join the Plain People, didn't you, Carlie? **1948** *Chi. Tribune* 25 Jan. IV. 5/4 The Plain People, as they are known, won't use automobiles or tractors, have no telephones, plumbing or political parties.

plaisance pləˈzɑns, *n. local.* [See quot. 1919.] A pleasure ground, usu. *cap.* with reference to an area on the south side of Chicago, esp. that between Jackson and Washington Parks. Cf. * **midway,** *n.* **1.**

1871 Olmsted, Vaux & Co. *Plan of the South Park, Chi.* 24 We shall term the first 'open,' and shall apply the old word 'Plaisance' to such as is intended to be enclosed with a high fence and used only by day. **1919** CAROLINE KIRKLAND *Chi. Yesterdays* 188 Paul Cornell, while a Park Commissioner, brought *Plaisance* home with him from Paris. I cannot find the exact meaning for the word, but it may be roughly defined as 'a place of pleasure.' **1937** *Fortune* XVI. Dec. 143/1 Along the south edge of the campus [of the University of Chicago] runs the Midway, a wide green plaisance where Little Egypt once danced the hootchy-kootchy for the raucous World's Fair crowds of 1893.

***plan,** *n.* As the last term in **American, Baltimore, California, city manager, consolidated school, crawfish, Dalton, European, instalment, manual labor, Mississippi, presidential, traveling, Washington plan.**

* **planer,** *n.* = **planing machine.** Also attrib.

1864 WEBSTER 995/1 *Planer-head*, . . . the slide-rest of a planing-machine, or planer. **1874** *Vt. Bd. Agric. Rep.* II. 745 This stock is . . . [taken] to the planer, a moving bed which passes under a stationary knife at the head. **1904** *McClure's Mag.* Feb. 372 The employers finally proposed discharging their planer-men one at a time, substituting stone-cutters gradually.

planer tree. [I. J. *Planer* (1743–89), Ger. botanist.] A small tree, *Planera aquatica*, resembling the elm, found in wet places in the southern states.

1810 MICHAUX *Arbres* I. 39 Planer tree, nom de la personne à laquelle cette espèce a été consacrée. **1832** BROWNE *Sylva* 246 The planer tree is of the second order, and is rarely more than 35 or 40 feet high. **1901** MOHR *Plant Life Ala.* 46 Planer tree (*Planera aquatica*)

. . . and green ash (*Fraxinus lanceolata*) are frequent inhabitants of the forest-clad swamps. **1930** MATTOON *Forest Trees Okla.* 62 The water elm or planer tree is found on low wet flood plains of the larger streams of the eastern part of the State.

planilla pləˈnijə, *n.* W. [Dim. of Sp. *plana*, a level ground. Cf. *planilla* in Amer. Sp. in the sense of a large flat pan or tray for washing metals.] A cleaning floor at a mining station. — **1876** RAYMOND *8th Rep. Mines* 5 Sheds over planillas at Day tunnel and Deep Gulch tunnel. *Ib.* 7 A much larger quantity of waste vein-matter . . . has to be examined and passed over the planillas or cleaning-floors.

∗**planing,** *n.*

1. planing machine, a machine for planing and truing up planks.

1805 *Amer. State P. Misc.* II. 130 Planing machine for sawing bellows boards, &c. **1875** KNIGHT 1729/1 The cylinder planing-machine . . . is now the usual machine.

2. planing mill, a mill or plant in which lumber is dressed and finished by being passed through planers, edgers, molding machines, etc. Also attrib.

1844 *Knickerb.* XXIV. 184 The uplifted arm of Labor . . . meets his eye everywhere, in the . . . planing mill. **1888** *Amer. Almanac* 275 Occupations of the People of the United States. . . . Salt-makers. . . . Saw & planing mill operatives. **1947** *Downtown Shopping News* (Chi.) 18 Aug. 11/4 The first planing mill in America was set up in Philadelphia about 100 years ago.

∗**plank,** *n.* and *a.*

1. One of the declarations or statements of principles in the platform of a political party or other organization.

1848 *Boston Courier* 28 Sep. 2/2 Another plank in the platform is, no Cass or other plank to be added. **1925** BRYAN *Memoirs* 108, I explain elsewhere the origin of the most prominent plank in the platform. **1948** *Chi. D. News* 24 June 16/2 Federal aid for education produced a meaningless plank.

2. In combs.: (1) **plank fence,** a fence made of planks; (2) **fencing,** =prec.; (3) **road,** see as a main

One form of plank fence

entry; (4) **shanty,** a shanty made of planks; (5) **sidewalk,** =**board sidewalk;** (6) **walk,** a walk made of planks or boards, cf. **boardwalk.**

(1) **1841** *Spirit of Times* 2 Jan. 523/1 (We.), Plank fence. **1850** *Western Jrnl.* III. 339 A plank fence round a forty acre lot, five feet tall. **1892** ALLEN *Blue-Grass Region* 28 Some [limestone fences] being torn down and superseded by plank fences or post-and-rail fences.— (2) **1880** MARK TWAIN *Tramp Abroad* 386 Every few hundred yards, one came across a panel or so of plank fencing. **1885** *Rep. Indian Affairs* 167 We have . . . 2 miles of plank fencing. — (4) **1867** RICHARDSON *Beyond Miss.* 29 A few pleasant white warehouses . . . and unpainted plank shanties were erected.

(5) **1855** *Chi. W. Times* 9 Aug. 1 The workmen were removing the plank sidewalk. **1910** J. HART *Vigilante Girl* 327 Bursts of burlesque sympathy came from the bystanders on the weed-grown plank sidewalks. — (6) **1820** *Boston Selectmen* 145 An application from the proprietors of St. Paul's Church for a portion of the street was committed to the Chairman, granting liberty on condition they . . . lay a plank walk. **1915** G. M. WHITE *Rose o' Paradise* 105 As they reached the plank walk, the boy lagged back.

b. *To have the plank,* to have the floor. *Facetious* and *rare.* Cf. ∗**floor,** *n.* **b.**

1832 KENNEDY *Swallow Barn* I. 185 'Silence,' said Ned, 'Mr. Walker has the plank; we can only hear one at a time!'

As the last term in **basswood, bucket, early-morning, gang, gold, gold standard, grub, money, runner, stage, States' rights, tariff, trust plank.**

∗**plank,** *v.*

1. *tr.* To produce or put up (money) readily, also with *down, out. Colloq.*

1824 *Nantucket Inquirer* 19 April (Th.), His guardy was sent for, and he planked the cash. **1894** MARK TWAIN *P. Wilson* ix, In de fust place, you gits fifty dollahs a month; you's gwine to han' over half of it to yo' ma. Plank it out! **1947** *Reader's Digest* Aug. 118 Kyle planked down $2000 won in Army poker games.

2. To broil, or bake, and serve (esp. fish) on a plank or board.

1877 HOWELLS *Out of Question* 134, I suppose you plank horn-pout, here. **1906** PRINGLE *Rice Planter* 298 The hope of getting a shad fresh from the river and having it planked.

∗**planked,** *a.* Of meat, esp. fish: Cooked and served on a piece of plank.

1855 *Baltimore Sun* 30 April (B.), Did you ever eat a planked shad? **1928** *Collier's* 29 Dec. 22/1 She didn't realize how easily planked steaks and seats on the aisle could become a habit. **1946** HIBBEN *Cookery* 69 Proceed, then, to season and cook it exactly as in the foregoing directions for Planked Shad.

b. planked eagle, (see quot.). *Facetious.*

1902 MARK TWAIN *Belated Passport* (1928) 190 (R.), The trademark of the richest and freest and mightiest republic of all the ages: the pine disk, with the planked eagle spread upon it, his head and shoulders among the stars, and his claws full of out-of-date war material.

plank road. A road made of planks placed transversely on longitudinal supporting timbers.

1848 *Mich. Gen. Statutes* I. (1882) 914 All corporations hereafter created for the purpose of constructing plank roads, shall be subject to the provisions hereinafter contained. **1923** ADAMS *Pioneer Hist.* 179 We turn east . . . and we are on the Plank Road proper. **1943** WOOD *W. Reed* 7 Even the plank road was submerged in sticky red gumbo, stirred up by days of rain and renewed military operations.

attrib. **1847** *Hunt's Merch. Mag.* XVI. 368 The plank road system originated in Canada, in 1835. **1881** *Mich. Gen. Statutes* I. (1882) 402 The commissioner of highways of each township . . . [shall] see that all plank or gravel road companies . . . maintain their roads in . . . good and safe condition. **1948** *Democrat* 8 Sep. 8/3 The first organization formed in the state [of Ala.] for constructing plank roads was The Canebrake Plank Road Company which projected a road from Demopolis to Uniontown in 1848.

b. plank-roader, (see quot.). *Obs.*

1861 *Remin. Locomotive Engineer* 102 These engines were very large . . . being up on seven feet wheels. From the circumstance of their being planked between the spokes of their 'drivers,' that is, having a piece of plank set between the spokes, the 'boys' used to call them the 'plank-roaders.'

Plan of Union. An agreement adopted by the American Presbyterian and Congregational churches early in the nineteenth century, permitting their members in the Middle West to unite. Also **Plan of Unionism.** *Obs.*

1808 in SWEET *Religion on Amer. Frontier* II. 469 It was voted unanimously, that this body acceed to the plan of union with the Presbyterian church in the United States. **1856** W. S. KENNEDY *Plan of Union* 144 The last half century has . . . developed a new type or modification of ecclesiasticism . . . which we may call co-operative Presbyterianism, Plan of Unionism, or Presbyterialized Congregationalism. *Ib.* 152 The missionary, with the Plan of Union in his hand and the love of God in his heart.

planometer pləˈnɑmətɚ, *n.* (See quot. 1864.) — **1864** WEBSTER 995/2 *Planometer,* . . . a plane, hard surface, used as a standard gauge for plane surfaces. **1876** KNIGHT 1726/2 Plane-surfaces are produced by the planing-machine, by the file, and by grinding, using an abradant. For the purpose of verifying their accuracy, the *planometer* was devised by Whitworth.

∗**plant,** *n.* In combs.: (1) **plant bed,** a bed of well pulverized rich soil in which plants, esp. of tobacco, are grown preparatory to transplanting; (2) **bug,** any one of various bugs that infest plants and suck their juices, also attrib.; (3) ∗**cane,** sugar cane grown from planted seed or germs, as distinguished from ratoon or stubble cane, also cane for planting a new crop; (4) **patch,** a small fertile area of well pulverized soil in which plants, esp. of tobacco, are grown, usu. for transplanting.

(1) **1833** *Niles' Reg.* XLIV. 411/1 He is clearing new grounds; preparing and burning plant-beds. **1904** GLASGOW *Deliverance* 486 If the rain had come a week later the tobacco would have been ruined. I've just been taking it up out of the plant-bed. **1907** *St. Nicholas* May 651/1 A 'running' board was put around the base and a plant bed about a foot wide made within this. — (2) **1856** *Rep. Comm. Patents 1855: Agric.* 93 There are several insects of the 'plant-bug' species found both upon the young and the old bolls. **1892** KELLOGG *Kansas Insects* 80 Tarnished plant bug (*Lygus lineolaris*). . . . The blossoms

of apple trees are a favorite feeding ground of this pest. — (3) **1827** COMMONS *Doc. Hist.* I. 214 Most of the plant cane, and also stubbles of Creole cane in new land mark the row. **1853** *Harper's Mag.* VII. 757 The 'growing crop' in Louisiana consists of three kinds of cane: the first is technically called 'plant cane' and is that which springs directly from the 'seed cane.' **1892** *Mod. Lang. Notes* Nov. 393 *Seed cane*—the seed or plant cane. — (4) **1760** WASHINGTON *Diaries* I. 126 Visited my Quarters and saw a plant patch burnt at the Mill. **1775** in RAUCK *Boonesborough* 177, [I] am just going to our little plant patches in hopes the greens will bear cropping. **1819** *Amer. Farmer* I. 204, I have a plantpatch, an old standing one, on a branch which we have always been able to water in the night or morning.

As the last term in **air, basket, beefsteak, cardinal, centennial, century, chocolate, coffee, compass, corpse, cow, drilling, fan, fever, fountain, frog, frost, gravel, gum, ice, inch, lead, loco, milk, milk sick, moccasin, obedient, Osage, oyster, packing, partridge, pie, pitcher, poke, polar, red ink, resurrection, rolling, rosin, sailor, silk, snow, soap, tea, unicorn, vanilla, vinegar, Virginia, Whig, white man's plant.**

* **plant,** *v.*

1. *tr.* To bury (a deceased person). *Slang.*

1855 *Harper's Mag.* Dec. 37/1 [The yellow fever] don't take the acclimated nor the 'old uns;' . . . but let it catch hold of a crowd of 'Johnny come latelys,' and it plants them at once. **1898** CANFIELD *Maid of Frontier* 186 They planted Chisolm in the little cemetery. **1939** ROLLINS *Gone Haywire* 22 Us fellers, admirin' 'im like we did, wanted to plant 'im in a dignified way.

2. To introduce or deposit (fish) in a pond or stream; to deposit (oysters, oyster shells, etc.) in artificial beds. Cf. * **planting,** *n.* **1.**

1871 *Pa. Laws* 276 Fishes planted and retained in private ponds shall be at the disposal of their owners. **1880** *Bradstreet's* XXVI. 6/1 The oystermen used to . . . plant them on staked territory. **1945** *Jefferson Co. Republican* (Golden, Colo.) 2 May 1/5 Clear Creek, in the Golden region, is on our schedule for planting trout this year.

3. With prepositions and adverbs: (1) *To plant in,* to plant with; (2) *to plant over,* to plant again, replant; (3) *to plant to,* to plant with.

(1) **1866** *Rep. Indian Affairs* 85 And 764 acres under cultivation and sown in wheat, oats, and timothy, or planted in potatoes and other vegetables. — (2) **1867** *Rep. Iowa Agric. Soc.* (1868) 450 Of those who did plant before the rains the majority had to plant over. — (3) **1900** *Year-bk. U.S. Dept. Agric.* 461 Around this central oasis cluster a dozen smaller ones, all planted to the same palms. **1949** *Reader's Digest* Aug. 129/1 With 19,000 acres planted to cotton this year, he is one of the dozen biggest cotton producers in the United States.

***plantain,** *n.* As the last term in **English, mud, poor Robin's, rattlesnake, snake, toad, white plantain.**

* **plantation,** *n.*

1. A homestead, farm, or estate.

As a rule, in New England and the North, plantations were moderate in size, and were worked by their owners, with or without hired help. In the South plantations often embraced hundreds or thousands of acres, and were devoted to raising tobacco, cotton, rice, and sugar cane, largely by slave labor.

1645 *New Haven Col. Rec.* 200 Noe planter, inhabitant or sojourner within or belonging to this towne . . . [shall] purchase any plantation or land . . . of any Indian. **1783** STOKES *View* 1 Plantation in the Sugar and Rice Colonies, denotes a piece, or tract of land, which is either granted to, or purchased by, a person to cultivate for his own use. But in the Northern British Colonies, where the produce is similar to that of England, the lands they cultivate are more frequently called Farms, than Plantations; as they informed me, when I was at New York. **1842** BUCKINGHAM *Slave States* II. 155 The master of the house, Mr. Taylor, was not yet returned from 'the plantation,' as all farms are called here [in Ga.]. **1944** *Chi. Tribune* 10 Dec. (Grafic Mag.) 3 Daisy Williams, the only daughter of the owners of Sweet Briar plantation.

2. An Indian village or settlement. *Obs.*

1646 EBENEZER HAZARD *Hist. Coll.* II. (1794) 64 If any Sagamore, or plantacon of Indians . . . hide, protect . . . or further the escape of any such offender or offenders, the English will require satisfaccon of such Indian Sagamore or Indian plantacons. **1682** M. RAWLINSON *Narr. Captivity* 13 There was, as I said, about six miles from us, a smal Plantation of Indians. **1709** LAWSON *Carolina* 77 For this Plant [purslane] is never met withal in the Indian plantations, and is, therefore, suppos'd to proceed from Cow-Dung, which beast they keep not.

3. (See quots.)

1809 KENDALL *Travels* III. 173 *Location* is a modern term, for a tract of land, of which the limits are defined, and the property conveyed to a purchaser. The same thing was formerly called a *plantation.* **1891** *N. & Q.* VI. 264 When the Maine township becomes settled, it receives a name, and organizes a local 'plantation' government of a simple kind and with limited powers. . . . There are, however, some named plantations which have gone back in population and now have no local government. **1914** *Cyclo. Amer. Govt.* II. 387/2 The term plantation used by the earliest settlers in many of the colonies meant originally 'settlement' but long ago ceased to be used except in Maine where it still designates a political subdivision inferior to town. **1945** *Nat. Geog. Mag.* Sep. 289 Some of the islands are 'plantations.' This term goes back to colonial times, but means in Maine today a minor civil division or unit of local government having the status between that of an organized township and an incorporated town.

4. (See quot. 1881.) Cf. **oyster plantation.**

1881 INGERSOLL *Oyster Industry* 246 *Plantation.*—Cultivated areas of oyster-bottom. A common and legal term in the state of Delaware. **1891** W. K. BROOKS *Oyster* 127 Before the bottom was laid out in private plantations, there were very few persons living there.

5. In combs., usu. obs., of obvious meaning, relating or alluding to southern plantations, as (1) **plantation account-book,** (2) **bell,** (3) **bitters,** (4) **book,** (5) **cart,** (6) **darkey,** (7) **dog,** (8) **fly,** (9) **frolic,** (10) **gate,** (11) **horse,** (12) **manners,** (13) **melody,** (14) **Negro,** (15) **press,** (16) **road,** (17) **school,** (18) **shoes,** (19) **shot-gun,** (20) **sick nurse,** (21) **slave,** (22) **song,** (23) **store,** (24) **style,** (25) **system,** (26) **wagon.**

(1) **1888** CABLE in *Cent. Mag.* Nov. 112/1 They were only nine in all—old, yellow, ragged, torn, leaves of a plantation account-book. — (2) **1840** *N.O. Picayune* 18 Aug. 2/6 The subscribers . . . offer for sale . . . Plantation Bells. **1887** *Cent. Mag.* Nov. 112/2 Now the tones of the big plantation-bell are heard. . . . All the gangs stop work, and people and animals go trooping to the quarters for dinner. — (3) **1867** DIXON *New Amer.* II. 96 These people say, they want no Cherokee medicines, no plantation bitters, no Bourbon cocktails. **1944** CLARK *Pills* 222 Three years after the Civil War the manufacturers of Plantation Bitters boasted that below the Potomac they were selling five million dollars' worth of their product each year. — (4) **1902** G. C. EGGLESTON *D. South* 58 Why, I keep the plantation book, you know.

(5) **1840** *N.O. Picayune* 28 July 1/5 Light Jersey Wagons; Drays; Plantation and City Carts. — (6) **1865** PIKE *Scout & Ranger* (1932) 146 No other musician can render the piece on the violin or banjo like an Arkansas plantation darkey. — (7) **1839** *S. Lit. Messenger* V. 377/1 Tommy King . . . followed by several lean, plantation dogs, brought up the rear. **1853** STOWE *Key* 186/1 The leaders of the community . . . keep this blind furious monster of the *mob,* very much as an overseer keeps plantation-dogs, as creatures to be set on to any man or thing whom they may choose to have put down. — (8) **1862** *Harper's Mag.* Nov. 736/1 Here [in the middle and southern states] is another agent of Nature, the *Musca plantarium*—'Plantation Fly.' — (9) **1884** HARRIS *Mingo* 234 His voice was the loudest at the corn-shucking, his foot was the nimblest at the plantation frolics.

(10) **1892** HARRIS *Plantation* 19 To the lonely lad it seemed a long journey to Mr. Snelson's—through wide plantation gates. — (11) **1790** FANNING *Narrative* 64, 12 plantation Horses, three unbroke . . . [£]96.00. — (12) **1857** W. R. ALGER *Genius & Posture of Amer.* 6 This slaveholder [James M. Mason] has grossly insulted our Congressional delegation . . . , carrying his insults so far . . . that our distinguished Senator . . . was forced openly to rebuke his 'plantation manners.' **1897** *Cong. Rec.* 31 March 548/2 When I was a boy, . . . I used to read a great deal about what the early Republicans called 'plantation manners.' — (13) **1881** *Harper's Mag.* May 818/2 The plantation melodies and minstrel ballads have won popularity wherever the English language is spoken. **1893** *Ib.* April 802/1 Used to singing 'spirituals' and plantation melodies, they carried into the rendition of the cantata the simplicity and the primitive pathos of their musical natures. — (14) **1771** *Md. Hist. Mag.* XIV. 135 My People . . . do not live so well as our House negroes, But full as well as any Plantation negroes. **1880** E. JAMES *Negro Minstrels' Guide* 4 Short crop, or plantation negro wigs, $12 per dozen. **1911** SAUNDERS *Col. Todhunter* 3 His speech . . . was a blend of the softly blurred speech of the Southerner, some of which is frankly borrowed from the liquid vernacular of the plantation negro.

(15) **1847** *De Bow's Review* III. 18 Great improvements in plantation presses have been introduced. — (16) **1884** CRADDOCK *Where Battle Was Fought* 120 She and Marcia . . . started for an afternoon walk along the quiet plantation road. — (17) **1865** in FLEMING *Hist. Reconstruction* II. 174 It cannot be expected that a man or woman whose only school training heretofore has been that of the plantation-school . . . should show the same quickness. — (18) **1869** TOURGEE *Toinette* (1881) 266 Then she thought of her heavy plantation shoes. — (19) **1832** in COMMONS *Doc. Hist.* I. 129, I leave my plantation shot-gun with you.

(20) **1905** PRINGLE *Rice Planter* 145 This is an old time plantation sick nurse, who, though very old, flies to relieve the sick with enthusiasm. — (21) **1853** STOWE *Key* 16/2 Douglass . . . was a plantation slave in a proud old family. **1900** *Cong. Rec.* 31 Jan. 1367/1 The registrar may require every applicant for registration to prove his age. . . . A white man 50 years of age would find it exceedingly

difficult to make this proof, . . . as would also the old plantation slave. — **(22) 1855** *Putnam's Mo.* Jan. 72/2 Upon his ears there fell the echo of a new plantation song. **1884** *Cent. Mag.* March 681/1 The negro-minstrel . . . sang and jumped Jim Crow, alternating this *chanson de geste* with 'Clar de Kitchen' and other genuine plantation songs. — **(23) 1891** THANET *Otto the Knight* 160 You can see the plantation-store and mill. **1937** CALDWELL *Their Faces* 12 The plantation store carries in stock staple groceries and clothing. — **(24) 1856** OLMSTED *Slave States* 545 They were generally neatly dressed, . . . but in a distinctly plantation or slave style. **1943** *Chi. Tribune* 23 May VII. 7/1 Thousands . . . have eaten plantation style chicken.

(25) 1884 *Cent. Mag.* April 859/2 Because of this, no immediate and general breaking up of the plantation system occurred in the South in 1865. — **(26) 1795** *Pittsburgh Gaz.* 11 July 1/2 For Sale, On reasonable terms for Cash, Whiskey, or Flour, a good Plantation Waggon. **1841** CIST *Cincinnati* (*advt.*), Every description of plantation wagons, ox carts [etc.].

Also *plantation dress, hand, hymn, life, servant, tool, whip,* etc.

b. Plantation State, a nickname for Rhode Island, in allusion to its orig. title of "State of Rhode Island & Providence Plantations."

1846 *Warrock's Almanac 1847* 22 Rhode Island, Plantation State.

As the last term in **cane, cotton, dwelling, frontier, huckleberry, Indian, indigo, lumber, manor, morus, out, oyster, rice, slave-rearing, tobacco plantation.**

* **planter,** *n.*

1. A farmer, owner, or proprietor of an agricultural holding or estate.

The word in this sense is chiefly southern. It was first used (see group 1 of the quotations) of the usu. wealthy slaveholders of Virginia and Maryland whose chief crop was tobacco. The word in its wider use (group 2) retained its connotation of wealth, being regularly applied to the rich plantation-owners of the South, but (group 3) was sometimes applied to small proprietors.

(1) **1619** *Va. House of Burgesses* 11 Provided first that the Cape Marchant do accept of the Tobacco of all and everie the Planters here in Virginia. **c1790** HADFIELD *Diary* 4 The long-legged Virginian planters as tall as maypoles, as ill-shaped as the branches of an oak, would, without ceremony, help themselves to any bowl of a stranger's toddy (which is rum and water with sugar) and make no apology. **1837** *S. Lit. Messenger* III. 86 It may suit my neighbor . . . to have one of them high-headed Roanoke planters to come here.

(2) **1682** ASH *Carolina* 7 [From the peach] the Planters compose a pleasant refreshing Liquor. **1800** TATHAM *Agric. & Commerce* 46 The cultivator who follows the ancient track of his ancestors, is called a *planter;* he who sows wheat, and waters meadows, is a *farmer.* **1817** S. BROWN *Western Gazetteer* 150 The yearly income of many of the planters, amounts to 20,000 dollars. **1907** ANDREWS *Recoll.* (1928) 74 The fact that during the Civil War they remained peacefully toiling at the homes of the planters, so many of whom were absent, shows the kind relations that existed between master and slave. **1949** *Time* 5 Dec. 40/3 Slavery was still a respected institution and a gentleman planter could work his lands in peace and dignity.

(3) **1732** *S.C. Gazette* 97/1 Certain ill-minded Persons, having industriously endeavoured to persuade the poorer sort of Planters, that this Law was calculated for their Oppression and Ruin. **1823** JAMES *Exped.* I. 71 The solitary planter, who has chosen his place remote from the habitation of any other family, has sometimes . . . a hand-mill. **1870** *Scribner's Mo.* I. 157 It is, however, somewhat difficult for the Florida farmers, or planters, . . . to get their potatoes to market. **1949** *Dly. Ardmoreite* (Ardmore, Okla.) 23 Feb. 3/5 His farm was called a plantation and he was a planter.

b. planter's pace, (see quot.). *Obs.*

1688 in FORCE *Tracts* III. No. 12, 35 Yet they ride pretty sharply, a Planter's Pace is a Proverb, which is a good sharp hand-Gallop.

2. An uprooted tree or tree trunk so planted or fixed in the channel of a river as to be a menace to navigation. Now *hist.*

1790 FORMAN *Journey* (1888) 44 We discovered that we were fast upon a planter—that is, the body of a tree firmly embedded in the river bottom. **1806** CRAMER *Navigator* 18 Planters are large bodies of trees firmly fixed by their roots in the bottom of the river, in a perpendicular manner, and appearing no more than about a foot above the surface of the river in a middling state. **1846** MCKENNEY *Memoirs* I. 152 Planters are trees, also; and, like sawyers, are also firm set at bottom, but are either too short to be seen above water, or have been . . . broken off. **1941** DORSEY *Master of Miss.* 25 Enormous and deeply embedded 'planters' stretched their stout limbs under water, threatening to rake unwary craft.

3. An agricultural implement for planting seeds.

1850 *Rep. Comm. Patents 1849* 151 Having thus fully described my improved grain and seed planter. **1873** *Ill. Dept. Agric. Trans.* X. 248 Mr. Smith said the clubs would meet this combination by a loaning of planters to each other. **1949** *Lubbock* (Tex.) *Morn. Avalanche* 23 Feb. 11. 6/4 For Sale: . . . 3 row tool bar lister, 2 row planter, 2 row cultivator.

As the last term in **chestnut, corn, cotton, cottonseed, hand, indigo, oyster, rice, seed, small, sorghum, southern, tobacco, Virginia planter.**

* **planting,** *n.*

1. The placing of shellfish in artificial beds.

1870 R. H. DAVIS in *Scribner's Mo.* I. 58/1 He went on for a while, calculating silently how many oysters would be needed for planting next week. **1884** *Nat. Museum Bul.* No. 26, 222 The only other branch of the industry not yet alluded to, is 'planting.' **1949** *Fishing Gaz.* Aug. 80/3 The clams were seeded over 15 acres in the Maquoit Middle Bay section to make the first time that shellfish planting has been done in this country from a plane.

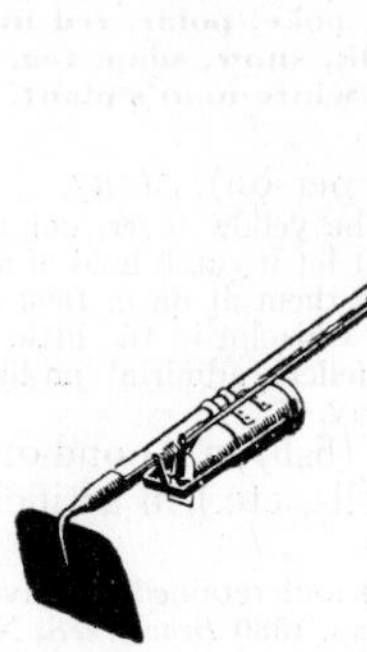

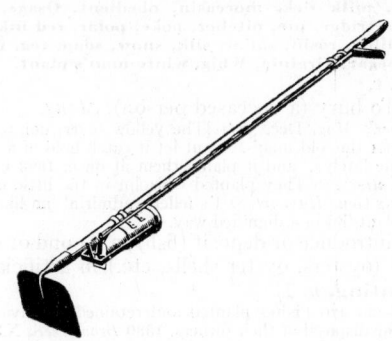

Early (*c*1856) type of planter (sense 3)

2. In combs.: (1) **planting aristocracy,** the wealthy slave-owning class in the South before the Civil War, *obs.;* (2) **field,** in colonial times, a field in which crops were planted, as distinguished from one for hay or pasture; (3) **interest,** a plantation, or the planting aristocracy *q.v.*, *obs.;* (4) **lot,** a lot or small tract of land suitable for producing crops, *obs.;* (5) **right,** the legal right or permission granted to or by an Indian to plant or cultivate a particular area or piece of ground, *obs.;* (6) **state,** a state in which agriculture is the chief occupation.

(1) 1856 OLMSTED *Slave States* 272 From the beginning the planting aristocracy had merely been living on its capital. — **(2) 1636** *Cambridge Prop. Rec.* 330 Whosoeuer findes eyther horse [,] Cow, ox, goate, or Any other beast, in Any of the planting feildes . . . shall haue six pence a peice for bringing them out. **1684** *Providence Rec.* XVII. 30 On ye westerne part of John Scott his planting ffield a litle up the streame. — **(3) 1836** GILMAN *Recoll.* (1838) xiii. 90 Papa was visiting his planting interest on Edisto. **1843** in TURNER *Cotton* (1865) 60, I stated the grand object which this system of improved culture proposes to accomplish for the planting interest of the country. — (4) **1640** *N.H. Prov. Papers* I. 138 None shall fell any oke timber . . . , except it be upon their planting lott. **1676** *Essex Inst. Coll.* LVI. 301 Henry Brown . . . conveyed to John Bayly . . . part of one end of my planting lott butting upon meadow of sd. Bayly.

(5) 1700 *Brookhaven Rec.* 92 This planting Rite shall Descende to them & there children for Ever. **1762** *Huntington Rec.* II. 450 [We] do fully & absolutely give . . . unto them the said trustees . . . all the Soyl Right Planting and Hunting right and all the remainder. — **(6) 1835** *Jamestown* (N.Y.) *Jrnl.* 7 Jan. 2/4 The great agricultural staples of the planting states are produced by a species of labor peculiar to those states.

plaquemine ˈplækəˌmin, *n.* (See quots.) Cf. **pishamin.**

[**1684** in READ *La.-French* 103 An early reference to the food prepared from persimmons by Indian women is made by Henry de Tonti, who speaks, on November 14, 1684, of 'des pastes d'un certain fruit qu'ils appellent *Paquimina,* lequel est fort bon.' **1885** in MELLICK *Story Old Farm* (1889) 165, I have tried in vain in the best English gazeteers to find Pluckamin. I think it may be a corruption of *Puckamin,* which, I believe, though I cannot be sure, was a dialect form of the Algonquian, *Putchamin,* corrupted by our ancestors to persimmon, the fruit of that name.] **1931** READ *La.-French* 103 Plaquemine, *f.* The fruit of the persimmon tree is called *plaquemine;* the tree itself, *le plaqueminier,* a word which ends in the familiar suffix *-ier. Plaquemine* came into Louisiana-French, through the Mobilian dialect, from Illinois *piakimin,* 'persimmon.' The names for the persimmon tree and its fruits are known to all the French inhabitants of Louisiana. [**1944** H. T. KANE *Deep Delta Country* 201

A 'Plaquemines [i.e., the name of a La. parish] count' meant a piece of bold manipulation.]

∗**plaster,** *n.* **1. plasterbill,** *Mass.* the surf scoter, *Melanitta perspicillata,* so called from the adult male's having a large round spot suggestive of a patch of court plaster on the basal half of the bill. **2. plaster sick,** of land, impaired in fertility from the excessive use upon it of plaster of Paris. *Rare.*

(1) **1888** TRUMBULL *Names of Birds* 103 Surf Scoter: Surf Duck: Black Duck. . . . At Chatham, [called] Plaster-Bill. **1917** *Birds of Amer.* I. 151 Surf Scoter. *Oeidemia perspicillata.* . . . [Also called] Pictured-bill; Plaster-bill; Morocco-jaw [etc.]. — (2) **1839** *Mass. Agric. Survey 2d Rep.* 42 He says he knows nothing of land become, as it is termed, plaster-sick.

As the last term in **land, shinplaster.**

∗**plaster,** *v. tr.* To treat (a crop) with plaster of Paris. Also **plastered,** *a.* — **1814** J. TAYLOR *Arator* 155 [Bird-foot clover] among the plastered wheat will be three or four fold more luxuriant, than among the adjoining unplastered. **1860** T. D. PRICE *Diary* (MS) 11 June, Finished plastering corn, put 2 barrels of plaster on the corn.

∗**plat,** *n.* An extent of level, open country, mesa land. *Obs.* Cf. **town plat.** — **1814** BRACKENRIDGE *Views La.* 107 There are many fine tracts, and extensive platts. **1878** BEADLE *Western Wilds* 65 Westward a more fertile plat rose even to the foot of the Huaquetories.

∗**plate,** *n.*

1. *Baseball.* (See quot. 1916.) Cf. **home plate.**

[**1857** *Spirit of Times* 28 Feb. 420/3 The home base and pitcher's point to be each marked by a flat circular iron plate, painted or enamelled white.] **1867** *Ball Players' Chron.* 5 Sep. 5/1 Thorne . . . pitched slow, 'drop' balls, many of which struck outside of 'the plate.' **1916** BANCROFT *Handbook* 82 Plate. A small surface of rubber, metal or stone which marks the fourth or home base, called also the home plate. There is also a similar plate marking the pitcher's box, called the pitcher's plate. **1949** *Telephone Reg.* (McMinnville, Ore.) 4 Aug. 2/1 Big Lee Reeder collected a pair of triples in four times at the plate.

2. *pl.* = ∗**golden plates.** *Obs.* or *hist.*

1844 HUNT *Hist. Mormon War* 13 Instead of looking at the 'reformed Egyptian characters' upon the plates, the Prophet was forced to resort to the old 'peep-stone,' which he had previously used in money-digging. **1882** BUEL *Metropolitan Life Unveiled* 348 He was also told that certain plates of gold, whereon was written the history of America before Christ, were lying buried in the hill Cumorah.

3. In combs.: (1) **plate boy,** a high cupboard in which plate for table use is kept, *obs.;* (2) **house,** a restaurant characterized by the speed with which the customers were served, *obs.;* (3) **matter,** syndicated reading matter supplied to newspapers on stereotype plates, also attrib.; (4) **shy,** (see quot.).

(1) **1899** *Boston Globe* 17 Sep. 33/2 Jacobean plate boys, with shelves rising nearly to the ceiling, are being especially built. — (2) **1829** HALL *Travels* I. 31 On the 21st of May, I accompanied two gentlemen, about three o'clock to a curious place called the Plate House, in the very centre of the business part of the busy town of New York. **1837** *Bentley's Misc.* I. 125 Leandish, that has the plate-house at Hoboken. — (3) **1887** W. REID *Westminster Rev.* Oct. 862 This plate-matter became at once so popular with country publishers that new features were from time to time introduced. . . . Today one of these 'plate-matter' manufacturing firms has branch offices and foundries in New York, Boston [etc.]. **1907** GIVEN *Making a Newspaper* 230 Plate matter is a boon to the country editor. — (4) **1912** C. MATHEWSON *Pitching* iv. 90 For a long time, 'Josh' Devore, the Giant's left-fielder was 'plate shy' with left-handers—that is, he stepped away.

b. *spin the plate,* = *break the pope's (man's) neck q.v., s.v.* ∗**break,** *v.* **12. b.** (2). *Colloq.*

1892 LUMMIS *Tramp Across Continent* 185 But 'the mill' and 'the bullet' and 'spinning the plate' and a hundred other diversions as childish and as childishly enjoyable fully entertained us. **1942** PHILIPS *Big Spring* 186 Parties were given by people at home where we played old-fashioned games like Spin the Plate [etc.].

As the last term in **auto, bake, barrel, base, belt, boiler, breast, copper, home, phonograph, running, tie plate.** Also ∗**gold,** ∗**golden plates.**

∗**platform,** *n.*

1. *fig.* A set of principles issued officially by a political party. Also the document embodying these principles.

The first political platform is said to have been that of the National Republicans, adopted in Washington, May, 1832. See Edward Stanwood, *History of the Presidency* (1884), 155–8. App. "platform" in this fig. sense is rare before *c*1848. The chief inspiration for this application was the use of the word in the sense of a material platform from which speakers address audiences. Cf. ∗**plank,** *n.* and *a.* **1.**

[**1803** *Mass. Spy* 27 April (Th.), The platform of Federalism.] **1844** *Address Dem. State Conv. Va.* 3 Feb. in *Niles' Reg.* LXV. 408/1 These are our doctrines—this the broad platform on which we stand. Here is our confession of faith . . . old as the constitution—old as the days of our fathers. **1868** ROSE *Great Country* 333 Apart from these little inelegances of speech, there are certain forms of expression which are awkward and unmeaning, such as calling the declaration set forth by a candidate for office, or by any party, as to principles &c., 'a platform.' **1949** *Time* 5 Dec. 91/3 That party which would promise farmers the largest bonus out of the Treasury would garner many votes not obtainable on . . . an honest, sound platform.

attrib. **1860** *Harper's Mag.* June 114/1 A 'Platform Committee,' consisting of one member from each State, was appointed.

b. Also *platform of principles. Obs.*

1848 *Niles' Reg.* LXXIV. 8/1 The letter of General Taylor . . . seems to be adopted by the Whigs of the country, as containing their platform of principles. **1887** *N.Y. Ev. Post* 20 Aug. (*Cent.*), A man does not bolt his party, but the candidate or candidates his party has put up. Sometimes, though less properly, he is said to bolt the platform of principles it has enunciated.

c. A set of principles representing a single person's views.

1848 D. WEBSTER *Writings & Speeches* (1903) XIII. 367, I think he [Zachary Taylor] has made as good a platform for himself as other people, elsewhere, have made for themselves. **1903** O. HENRY *Roads of Destiny* 166 He leaned on the desk and declared his platform to the clerk.

2. In a railroad car, the separate floor space at the end, affording a means of entrance and exit; the corresponding part of a streetcar. Also attrib.

1849 *Hunt's Merch. Mag.* XXI. 683 They are not allowed, under any circumstances, to stand on the platforms of the cars. **1905** *N.Y. Ev. Post* 27 Sep. 3 Baron Komura waved good-bye to New York this morning from the rear platform of the Montreal Express. **1944** KAHN *Cable Car Days* 60 The line operated for several years without earning enough to pay platform wages.

3. In special combs.: (1) **platform balance,** = **platform scale;** (2) **car,** a railroad freight car without either a top or sides, a flatcar; (3) **dance,** a dance on a roofless

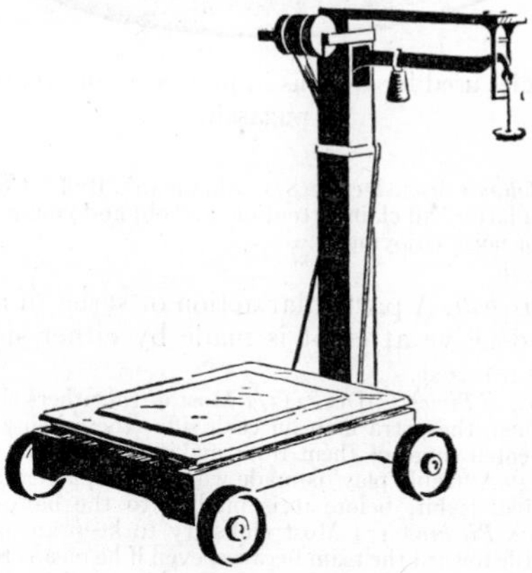

Platform scales

platform erected in the woods or forest, *obs.;* (4) **paddle tennis,** see ∗**paddle,** *n.* **4. b;** (5) **scale(s),** a weighing machine having a platform for whatever is to be weighed, used esp. for heavy objects weighing up to about 1,000 lbs.

(1) **1811** *Boston Selectmen* 14 Dearborn's patent platform balance [for weighing hay, etc.]. **1860** HOLMES *E. Venner* iii, The master weighed himself at the grocer's on a platform-balance, some ten days after he began keeping the school. — (2) **1843** E. H. DERBY *Two Months Abroad* 20/1 Diligences and private carriages are . , . transferred to platform cars, and at Rouen again placed on wheels, and put 'en route' for Havre. **1878** BEADLE *Western Wilds* 52 He only had to take his store to pieces, ship it on a platform car to the next city, and set up again. — (3) **1891** C. ROBERTS *Adrift Amer.* 9 There is a kind of amusement in the backwoods known as a platform dance.

(5) **1834** *Amer. R.R. Jrnl.* III. 726/1 [To] E. & J. Fairbanks [for] a Concentrated Platform Scale—a diploma [was awarded]. **1876** KNIGHT III. 2049/2 Platform-scales were probably in use in England in 1796, one being patented in that year by Salmon. **1947** PAUL *Lin-*

den 84 Spring balances were used for meat, platform scales for sacks of meal.

As the last term in **Baltimore, Buffalo, Cambridge, Chicago, depot, gold standard, Lincoln, minor, national, observation, Ocala, party, revolving, Saybrook, State rights, Tennessee platform.**

***platform,** *v. intr.* To work *for* the inclusion of something in a political platform. *Rare.* — **1859** LINCOLN *Works* (1894) I. 535 The point of danger is the temptation in different localities to 'platform' for something that will be popular just there.

***platoon,** *n.* A body *of* policemen, a police squad. — **1876** INGRAM *Centennial Exp.* 614 After these [policemen] came double platoons of men. **1903** *Atlantic Mo.* Sep. 295 She looks out of the window and sees the platoon of policemen on a run to quell a riot.

Platte Purchase. A triangular tract of almost two million acres of land, bounded on the west by the Missouri River north of Kansas City and included, since 1837, in the state of Missouri, purchased from the Indians in 1836 by the federal government.

1850 GARRARD *Wah-To-Yah* xxiii. 277 Andrew . . . was from the Platte Purchase in Missouri. **1894** ROBLEY *Bourbon Co., Kans.* 4 This territory between the due north line and the Missouri river was known as the 'Platte Purchase.' **1947** *Dly. Oklahoman* (Okla. City) 21 Sep. 5-D/1 The Platte purchase . . . covered 2,000,000 acres in northwestern Missouri.

***platter,** *n.* **1.** = ***bowl,** *n.* **1.** *Obs.* Cf. **la platte. 2.** *twirl the platter,* =*spin the plate,* see ***break,** *v.* **12. b.** (2).

(1) **1778** [see ***bowl,** *n.* **1**]. **1833** CATLIN *Indians* I. 88 Groups of Indians are engaged in games of the 'moccasin' or the 'platter.' —

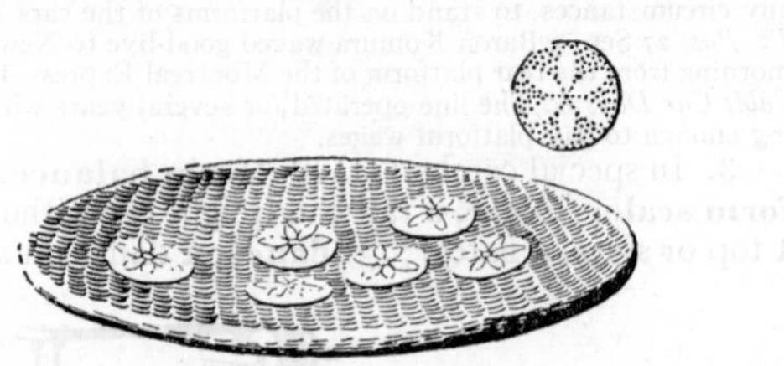

Articles used by Indians in platter, la platte, bowl, or pugasaing

(2) **1868** *Ballou's Mag.* Dec. 518/1 'Blindman's Buff,' 'Copenhagen,' 'Twirl the Platter,' all claim attention, and old and young continue in the scene of noisy enjoyment.

***play,** *n.*

1. *Baseball.* A particular action or series of actions in which a decisive attempt is made by either side to advance its interest.

1856 *Spirit of Times* 13 Dec. 245/1 Most of the others showed good play, although the extra man on each side (there being ten in the field) prevented some of them from making runs. **1868** CHADWICK *Base Ball* 46 A 'treble play' is made when three players are put out after the ball is hit, before it is pitched to the bat again. **1912** MATHEWSON *Pitching* 174 Most clubs try to keep an umpire from feeling hostile toward the team because, even if he means to see a play right, he is likely to call a close one against his enemies, not intending to be dishonest.

2. In noun and adjective combs., in some of which the first element is verbal: (1) **playboy,** a sporty fellow, usu. or ostensibly wealthy, devoted to frivolous pleasure-seeking, *slang;* (2) **broker,** an agent who serves as an intermediary between dramatists and managers or actors; (3) **-by-play,** *a.* denoting a running commentary on a game; (4) **carpenter, doctor,** one who rewrites or revises plays to make them more suitable for the stage; (5) ***house,** a miniature house in which children may play, see **b.** below; (6) **party** (see quots.); (7) **room,** a room in which children may play, also such a room for both children and adults; (8) **song,** a song used in a play or game; (9) **spell,** a time or period allotted to play.

(1) **1926** *N.Y. Times* 11 Oct. 24/2 The playboy of baseball might have heard his name go ringing down the corridors of baseball as a man who won a series game with a home run. **1949** *Sat. Ev. Post* 5 March 115/1 She had had a quarrel with a playboy. — (2) **1910** *N.Y. Dramatic Mirror* 12 March 9/4 Practically all of the new playwrights have been discovered by play-brokers. **1925** *Scribner's Mag.* Sep. 283/2 The great Delando . . . lifted his keen glance to the play-broker who sat opposite him. — (3) **1931** F. L. ALLEN *Only Yesterday* viii. 207 Thousands more sat in warm living-rooms to hear the play-by-play story over the radio. — (4) **1925** WITWER *Roughly Speaking* 224 Song writers, scenario concocters, play carpenters . . . have clicked off fortunes by declaring the female sex to be poison. **1928** *Observer* 10 June 6/4 Shakespeare . . . knew all, and more than all, about the technique of play-writing that is known by the most efficient 'play-doctor' in Broadway, New York.

(5) **1857** M. J. HOLMES *Meadow-Brook* xxv, At a short distance from the house was a tall cypress . . . where now was a play-house. **1907** *St. Nicholas* May 651/1 In the center of this little yard was a play-house. — (6) **1902** *D.N.* II. 241 play-party, n. A party at which old-fashioned games are played [s. Ill.]. **1944** *Ib.* Nov. 25 play-party: *n.* A party where dancing games are played to the singing of the participants. This is to get around the church's ban on dancing. **1946** WILSON *Fidelity* 105 Play-parties were and are very little different from square dances. — (7) **1838** *Knickerb.* XI. 12 One Saturday afternoon when seated with two or three other children in my little play-room. **1949** *Chi. Tribune* 11 Dec. (Grafic Mag.) 16/4 Lotta room here in the basement for a pingpong table . . . washing machine . . . playroom . . . den. — (8) **1898** HARRIS *Tales* 19 The negroes made the night melodious with their play-songs, and everything combined to make the occasion a memorable one, especially to the young people. — (9) **1845** JUDD *Margaret* II. 186 And her own play-spell comes, if, indeed, her whole life were not a play-spell. **1878** STOWE *Poganuc People* 209 Even household disciplinarians recognized a reasonably well-behaved child's right to a Saturday afternoon play-spell.

b. *To upset one's playhouse,* to bring one's plans to naught. *Colloq.*

1939 *These Are Our Lives* 120 But if the tenants did become land-owners it certainly would upset my playhouse and that of others like me.

As the last term in **block, double, force, forced, force-out, gun, photo, team, triple, wild play.**

***play,** *v.*

1. *tr.* To gamble on or at (cards, races, etc.).

1858 PETERS *Kit Carson* 354 The fact is . . . he'd bin playin' the papers (meaning gambling) and had lost everything. **1907** *Collier's* 6 April 15/2, I asked him whether he could play the stock market in the office of A without a 'lookout' or a 'case-keeper' (precautions obtaining in a first-class faro game). **1916** *Chi. Tribune* 3 Oct. 1/6 (*heading*), Six Lists of Where to Play the Ponies Given to Judge Landis. **1948** *Ib.* 13 March 6/4 Monty disclosed that he had quit playing the horses and poker because he was now a life insurance salesman and knew the odds were against gamblers winning a fortune.

2. To act as if (a person) belonged to a designated class; to take (a person) *for. Slang.*

1869 MARK TWAIN *Innocents* 294 Playing us for Chinamen because we were strangers and trying to learn! **1876** *Stanislaus Co. W. News* (Modesto, Calif.) 30 June 1/4 The Austin Indians played him for a sucker. **1892** CRANE *Maggie* (1896) 60, I wonder if I've been played for a duffer.

3. *intr.* To pretend or make believe as a basis of play.

1861 STOWE *Pearl Orr's Isl.* I. 147, I played their nest was a city, and I spoiled it. **1890** *St. Nicholas* Oct. 1007 We played that we were gypsies. **1949** *N.O. Times-Picayune* 27 Nov. (Comics) 2 Let's run home and play cowboys.

4. *quasi-tr.* To impose (something) on, to play (a trick), cheat, palm *off. Slang.* Cf. *to play off* in **5. b.** (3) below.

1871 HARTE *Luck of Roaring Camp* 11 It's playing it pretty low down on this yer baby to ring in fun on him that he ain't going to understand. **1890** —— *Heritage of Dedlow Marsh* 100 The folks you trust is playing it on ye. **1896** SHINN *Story of Mine* 249 You can't play it off any longer.

b. *To play on* (someone), to trick. *Rare.*

1878 *Scribner's Mo.* XV. 812/1 Ye went back on her, and shook her, and played on her, and gave her away—dead away!

5. In colloq. or slang phrases: (1) *To play the advantage over,* (see quot.), *obs.;* (2) (*a*) *to play to* (or *in*) *hard luck,* to have a hard time of it, (*b*) *to play big luck,* to have good fortune; (3) *to play smash with,* to smash up, crush, overwhelm, also fig.; (4) *to play a town,* to perform a play in a town; (5) *to play favorites,* to show special favor or partiality; (6) *to play sharp on,* to deceive by being sharp.

(1) **1839** MARRYAT *Diary in Amer.* II. 235 The gamblers on the Mississippi used a very refined phrase for 'cheating'—'playing the advantages over him.' — (2) (*a*) **1885** *Santa Fé Wkly. New Mexican* 9 July 3/6 These young people have been 'playing to hard luck' in the southwest. **1895** *N.Y. Dramatic News* 6 July 4/2 A certain old friend . . . was in that undesirable position that we call 'playing in hard

luck.' (*b*) **1914** Bower *Flying U Ranch* 158 You're playing big luck, if you only had sense enough to know it. — (**3**) **1887** *Courier-Journal* 17 Jan. 1/7 (*caption*), Plays Smash With a Passenger Train on the Fitchburg Railroad. **1902** Harben *A. Daniel* 43 You young bloods are a-goin' to play smash with the gals' hearts to-night. — (**4**) **1896** *N.Y. Dramatic News* 29 Aug. 11/3 A troup of barnstormers . . . are playing the smaller towns in this vicinity.

(**5**) **1902** Wilson *Spenders* 201, I mustn't 'play favourites,' as those slangy nephews of mine put it. **1905** Beach *Pardners* i. 31 Not wishing to play any favourites, I'd picked up a basket of tomatoes, a gunny-sack of pineapples, and a peck of green plums. — (**6**) **1863** Norton *Army Lett.* 186 In testing my eyes . . . the doctor held up something and asked me what it was, I had played sharp on him by taking an inventory of the articles on the table.

For *to play hob, horse, possum*, see the nouns.

b. With adverbs and adjectives: (1) *To play alone*, (see quot. 1864), also *to play it alone*, in fig. use; (2) *to play even*, to avoid financial loss or disaster; (3) **to play off*, (*a*) to go away from one's customary place, to act indifferent, or wily, to impose on by feigning sickness, (*b*) in a game or contest, to break a tie by continuing play; (4) *to play pat*, (see quot.); (5) **to play up*, to make much of.

(**1**) **1864** Dick *Amer. Hoyle* (1866) 62 *Play Alone.*—To play a hand without one's partner. **1873** *Winfield* (Kans.) *Courier* 24 July 3/1 The horses attached to [the] hack which runs between this place and Wellington, one day last week concluded to 'play it alone.' — (**2**) **1877** W. Wright *Big Bonanza* 427 The 'honest miner' . . . will sometimes resort to 'ways that are dark' in order to 'play even.' — (**3**) (*a*) **1836** Howard *Stewart* 140, I stay mostly in the neighbourhood of Commerce at present, and sometimes work, to prevent being suspected. I play off occasionally. **1863** Norton *Army Lett.* 135 If I did want one [a discharge], I fancy. . . . I could play off on the doctors and get it. **1945** Botkin *My Burden* 72 Howsomever, it was hard sometimes to get her to believe you sick when you tell her that you was, and she would think you just playing off from work. (*b*) **1880** *Chi. Inter-Ocean* 7 June 6/2 The tie game of yesterday was played-off to-day, the Chicago's winning a victory over the home team. **1901** *Munsey's Mag.* Jan. 570/1 We're going to play off for the Wolcott cup. — (**4**) **1887** Keller *Draw Poker* 11 *Playing Pat*, playing an original hand without drawing cards. A favorite device of bluffers.

(**5**) **1926** *Publishers' Wkly.* 22 May 1687/1 Let us play up the habits, the appearances, the likes and dislikes, let us sell authors to our public. **1930** *Ib.* 8 Feb. 706/2 He plays up the fact that there is smart reading just as there are smart clothes.

c. *Play ball!* in baseball, the call of the umpire to begin play.

1867 *Ball Players' Chron.* 8 Aug. 1/2 At 2.20 P.M. the Nationals were sent to the bat, and 'Play ball!' was the cry of the umpire. **1948** *Dly. Ardmoreite* (Ardmore, Okla.) 19 April 6/6 The cry 'play ball' will sound at Washington, Boston and Cincinnati with 125,000 fans expected to witness the proceedings.

For *to play ball with* see ***ball**, *n.*[1] **3. e.**

playa 'plɑjə, *n. S.W.* [Sp., a beach, strand.] A broad, level place that accumulates water after a rain, but is at other times dry, a dry lake. Cf. **mud playa.**

1854 Bartlett *Personal Narr.* I. 246 The playas . . . seemed to have an extent of twenty-five or thirty miles. **1873** *Las Cruces* (N.M.) *Borderer* 6 Jan. 1/4 We have . . . descended . . . into and along the great plain north of the preat *Playa de los Pimas.* **1892** Bourke *On Border with Crook* 129 Down in the plains or deserts, called in the Spanish idiom 'playas' or 'beaches' there were quite large herds of antelope. **1945** Marshall *Santa Fe* 188 In the *playas*—saucerlike depressions in the desert—were beds of glistening salt and gypsum.

attrib. **1900** *Amer. Geog. Soc.* XXXII. 39 Playa Lake: A shallow, storm-water lake. When dried it forms a playa. Local in Southwest.

b. Used as a proper name or in such names in the sense of a beach.

1855 in *So. Calif. Hist. Soc. Pub.* XVI. 59 La Playa (the beach) is that part of the city nearest the mouth of the harbor. **1948** *Chi. Tribune* 21 March 1. 6/4 Just north of the plant is the site of a proposed Playa del Rey yacht harbor with a capacity of 9,000 pleasure craft.

***played**, *a.* Exhausted, worn out, passé. *Colloq.*

1872 *Republican Rev.* 16 March 2/4 The days of forked sticks for plows is about played, if farmers here want to come up to the age in which we live. **1883** Mark Twain *Life on Miss.* xliii, That's all played now. **1897** *Outing* XXIX. 421/2 He's about played.

***player**, *n.* As the last term in **ball, banjo, base, bone, home, poker, policy, team player.**

player piano. A piano designed to be played by a mechanism known as a piano player.

[**1901** *Everybody's Mag.* Oct. 490/1 In the section devoted to musical instruments one can hear hourly concerts by mechanical piano-players.] **1908** *Sat. Ev. Post* 14 Nov. 20 Many player pianos are deficient in one vital point—they do not give *human expression* to the music, no matter how skilfully you manipulate them. **1949** *10 Story Western* May 44/2 He backed heavily against the player piano, and the jar set the machine off into a burst of loud, tinny music.

plaza 'plæzə, *n. S.W.* [Sp., an Amer. borrowing.]

1. A public square or market place; an open place connected with a fort, mine, etc.

1836 Latrobe *Rambler in Mexico* 79 Our party entered [Zacualtipan]; wheeling . . . across the Plaza, with ringing spurs and jingling arms. **1885** *Wkly. New Mexican Rev.* 8 Jan. 2/5 The old palace . . . is in the center of the town, and opposite the plaza. **1948** Weston *Mother Lode* 74 Like so many camps of the Southern Mines section, it was built around a plaza.

Also **plaza publica** in same sense. *Obs.*

1844 Gregg *Commerce of Prairies* I. 111 On driving through the streets [of Santa Fé] and the *plaza publica*, everyone strives to outvie his comrades.

2. A place of residence, a pueblo. *Obs.*

1846 Hughes *Diary* 75 Returned from the Grazing Ground to Galisteo and lodged in a Rico's plaza. **1885** *Wkly. New Mexican Rev.* 22 Jan. 4/6 Living Indians of to-day variously tell of a tradition that one of the pueblos or plazas of Santa Fe was known as 'Poga' or 'Apoga.'

plazita plɑ'sitə, *n. S.W.* Diminutive of **plaza.**

1863 *Rio Abajo Press* 28 April, He called Jose the majordomo to the plazita. **1880** *Harper's Mag.* April 678/1 This is the 'little square,' or *plazita*, and around it the house is built in the form of a quadrangle. **1890** *Outing* Aug. 354/1 Towers followed Violante into the tiny *placita* at the rear.

pleasant spoken. Agreeable in conversation. *Colloq.* — **1873** M. Twain & Warner *Gilded Age* 187 (R.), Senator Dilworthy was . . . a pleasant-spoken man, a popular man with the people. **1896** *Peterson Mag.* Jan. 97/1 He is very pleasant-spoken, and invited me to come and spend the night with him.

pleasurable carriage. =**pleasure carriage.** *Obs.* — **1802** *Ann. 7th Congress* 2 Sess. 1238 The committee respectfully submit the following bill, to repeal the laws laying duties on . . . pleasurable carriages. **1806** *Phila. Ordinances* (1812) 200 The following articles . . . are hereby made taxable . . . gigs, riding chairs, chaises, and other pleasurable carriages.

***pleasure**, *n.* In combs.: (1) **pleasure car**, a railroad coach used for pleasure trips; (2) **carriage**, a carriage used for pleasure; (3) **ground**, (see quot.); (4) **sleigh**, a sleigh used for pleasure; (5) **wagon**, a light wagon used for pleasure rather than for business.

(**1**) **1833** *Amer. R.R. Jrnl.* II. 481/3 A pleasure car has been flying between this town and the river. **1949** Murray *This Our Land* 93 The engine hauled two 'pleasure cars,' and a small carriage on which was mounted a field piece loaned by Major Belton for the occasion. — (**2**) **1794** Priest *Travels* (1802) 31 There are 806 two and four wheeled machines entered at the office, and pay duty, as *pleasure carriages.* **1877** *Harper's Mag.* March 518/1 A pleasure carriage, the first ever brought into Litchfield Hill, Conn. . . . was in use as late as 1812. **1905** Valentine *H. Sandwith* 19 She was accused of having persuaded Mr. Sandwith in acquiring the mundane 'pleasure carriage' they were now riding in. — (**3**) **1846** *Porter's Spirit of Times* 11 July 234/1 Since the legislative Solons of Massachusetts have prohibited trotting and racing, the Courses have taken the name of 'pleasure grounds.' — (**4**) **1774** in Crèvecoeur *Sk. 18th-Cent. Amer.* (1925) 146 The pleasure-sleigh . . . can easily carry six persons. **1856** *Mich. Agric. Soc. Trans.* VII. 59 Davis, Austin & Co., Jackson, [exhibited a] pleasure sleigh.

(**5**) **1827** Beaufoy *Tour* 18 At Hoboken, a number of gigs, horses, and neat light vehicles, called pleasure-wagons, are always kept for hire. **1866** A. D. Whitney *L. Goldthwaite* xv. How impertinent we are, rushing at the tremendousness of Washington in the way we do; scaling it in little pleasure-wagons, and never taking in the thought of it at all!

***pleb**, *n.* A member of the freshman class at college orig. and usu. a freshman at West Point. Cf. next.

1852 *Knickerb.* XXXIX. 171 The new cadets or 'plebs,' having been in the battalion but a few days, were not well enough disciplined to be detailed for guard. **1883** *Harper's Mag.* Nov. 908/1 At West Point, no matter how stooped the entering pleb, he is soon taught to carry himself as erect as any man in America. **1913** LaFollette *Autobiog.* 12, I was one of the greenest of all the 'plebs' [at Wis. U.]—a boy right from the farm.

***plebe**, *n.*

1. A member of the freshman class at West Point or at Annapolis.

1833 *Mil. & Naval Mag. of U.S.* II. (1834) Oct. 85 My drill master [at West Point], a young stripling, told me I was not so '*gross*' as most other pleibs, the name of all new cadets. **1860** in *Amer. Hist. Rev.*

XXXIII. 601 In most of our tents the cadets and plebes live together, 2 cadets, and 2 plebes to wait on them generally. **1948** MENJOU & MUSSELMAN *It Took 9 Tailors* 26 New arrivals are called plebes and a plebe is the dirt beneath an upperclassman's shoes; but to add insult to injury, a plebe has to clean and polish the shoes while he is being stepped on.

attrib. **1834** in *Mil. & Naval Mag. of U.S.* III. 281, I was reckoned, already, as one of a class of cadets [at West Point]. To be sure, it was the 'plebe class;' but what of this? **1860** in *Amer. Hist. Rev.* XXXIII. 605 They say mine is the only plebe coat which fits. **1947** *Newsweek* 6 Oct. 78/2 The 'plebe' system which gives upper classmen authority over newcomer midshipmen filled Smith with revulsion.

b. plebeskin, civilian dress. *Slang.*

1888 *N.Y. World* 22 July (F.), The fourth class entered camp on Monday, but are still wearing their plebeskins.

2. (See quot. 1890.) Also attrib.

1890 CUSTER *Following Guidon* 213 These youths [graduates from West Point] were called 'tads' and 'plebes.' **1899** T. HALL *Tales* 19 Ten to one the 'plebe' lieutenant is able to cut in ahead of the troops they are pursuing.

* **pledge,** *n. College.* A student who has been accepted for membership in a fraternity or sorority but who has not been formally initiated.

1901 *U. of Chi. Wkly.* 1 Aug. 1087/1 Still if the Kappas are as bad as you say—you say they lifted two pledges last year. **1945** MAXWELL *Folded Leaf* 52 Shortly after seven o'clock the pledges appeared, one at a time, in the hotel lobby. **1949** *Reader's Digest* Aug. 71/1 The chapter might . . . keep Tom as a sort of permanent pledge.

transf. and *attrib.* **1930** *Randolph Enterprise* (Elkins, W.Va.) 18 Dec. 1/1 [They] . . . have been announced as two of five pledges chosen by the University Dramatic club at Morgantown. **1944** *Chi. D. News* 28 Oct. 1 After the incident, Soik turned in his pledge pin. **1947** *Loyola News* (Chi.) 6 Nov. 10/2 The men are those selected from prospective candidates who attended the fraternity's Pledge Smoker last Friday night. **1949** *Time* 21 March 47/2 As a finale to Brown's pledge week, fraternity men had made the rounds of chapter houses to 'congratulate' each other.

* **pledge,** *v. College. tr.* To prevail upon (a student) to promise to join a sorority, fraternity, etc. Also *intr.*, to make such a promise.

1871 BAGG *At Yale* 62 They are very attentive to his wants and do not leave him until he is 'pledged.' **1887** *Lippincott's Mag.* Nov. 741 If as the result of several such interviews he is approved, he is asked to 'pledge,' that is promise to join the society. **1901** *Munsey's Mag.* Feb. 734/2 The time and manner of pledging members to the fraternities vary with different colleges. **1949** *Reader's Digest* Aug. 69/1 The rushing season, during which freshmen are pledged to the various houses, was in full swing.

* **pleurisy,** *n.* **1.** (See quot.) *Obs.* **2. pleurisy root,** the butterfly weed, *Asclepias tuberosa*, or its root.

(1) **1775** ROMANS *Nat. Hist. Fla.* 249 In Georgia i saw one or two instances of a disorder among blacks, to which the people give the odd name of the pleurisy of the temple, of the forehead, of the eye, and so on; i am told they have a pleurisy for every part of the head. — (2) [**1764** *N.C. Morav. Rec.* II. (1925) 569 Milkweed or Pleurisy Root prefers stony ground; has leaves like an Orange tree, and a brown stem. It grows about one foot high, and at the top has one or more bunches of pretty, white, little flowers.] **1781–2** JEFFERSON *Notes. Va.* (1788) 36 [Medicinal] native plants. Senna. . . . Pleurisy root. Asclepias decumbens. **1932** HARVEY *Wild Flowers* 55 Butterfly Weed or Pleurisy Root . . . bears brilliant orange flowers, arranged in flat, terminal clusters.

plew plu, *n.* =**plus.** Now *hist.* Cf. **beaver plew.**

1848 RUXTON *Life Far West* v, Beaver fetching as high a price as five and six dollars a 'plew.' **1851** HOWE *Hist. Coll. Great West* 303 The 'beaver' is purchased at from two to eight dollars per pound; the Hudson's Bay Company alone buying it by the pluie or 'plew,' that is, the whole skin, giving a certain price for skins, whether of old beaver or kittens. **1947** DEVOTO *Across Wide Missouri* 158 The free trapper had to prepare his plews himself unless he had a wife or there was a village of Indians at hand where he could hire a squaw.

pliers man. (See quot.) *Obs.* — **1897** HOUGH *Story of Cowboy* 207 Of later times the faithful cowboy who worked on a fenced ranch is sometimes called contemptuously a 'pliers man' by the rustlers who have no fences of their own.

P.L.L. (See quot.) *Obs.* — **1870** MACRAE *Americans* II. 261 A vast and secret organization, only vaguely known to the public by the cabalistic letters 'P.L.L.' variously interpreted 'Personal Liberty League,' and 'Public Liquor League,' was understood to have expended hundreds of thousands of dollars in undermining the Republican position, and to have pledged 40,000 electors to vote the Democratic ticket and get the grog-shops opened.

***plot,** *n.* As the last term in **A. B., bean, house, town plot.**

***plover,** *n.* As the last term in **bull, bullhead, bullheaded, chattering, chicken, field, killdeer, mountain, piping, prairie, rock, semipalmated, snowy, upland, Wilson's, yellow plover.**

* **plow,** *n.* Also * **plough.**

1. *transf.* A plowman with his plow and plow animal(s). *Obs.*

1760 [see **pointing**]. **1776** ROWE *Diary* 309 This morning Mr. Hammonds Plough began to Plough up the Pasture. **1786** WASHINGTON *Diaries* III. 87 The Plows at Muddy hole (where 3 were at Work) had finished the East cut of Corn. **1787** *Ib.* 158, I set them to filling up gullies where the plows were at work.

2. Any one of various thin iron or steel implements, cast or made in one piece, of various sizes and shapes, readily attachable (and detachable) to the "foot" of a plow stock (*q.v.*) by means of a heavy bolt, usu. called a "heel bolt." Cf. **plow point.**

Dictionaries have not recognized this sense, which is app. chiefly *S.*, but they define "plow" as denoting the entire implement, consisting essentially of a beam, handles, "foot," and plowshare. Different kinds of plows in the sense in which the term is used here are the bull-tongue, buzzard wing, scooter, shovel, sweep, turn(ing) plow, and twister *qq.v.*

1827 *Western Mo. Rev.* I. 82 The cotton . . . is thinned carefully, and plows, in the form of scrapers, are used, as the technical phrase is, to scrape it out. **1872** *Vt. Bd. Agric. Rep.* I. 225 Passing from these inventions of the long ago, we come to the first cast iron plow made in America. This plow, all that is left of it, is in the museum; the whole casting is in one piece, comprising sole, standard, mouldboard and share. **1883** SMITH *Geol. Survey Ala.* 544 As a rule, the bed or ridge is opened with a narrow plow (scooter or bull-tongue).

3. In combs.: (1) **plow bird,** the yellow-breasted chat, *Icteria virens, colloq.;* (2) **car,** before the development of modern dump cars, a flatcar for hauling gravel, earth, etc., having guides along the sides and a sheet-steel apron between the cars to permit the use in unloading of a plowlike implement, similar to a snowplow, carried on the last car of a train, and drawn forward in unloading by a cable on a drum operated by the engine, *obs.;* (3) **gang,** a group of Negro slaves who work together in plowing, *obs.;* (4) **hand,** a Negro slave working as a plowman, *obs.;* (5) **point,** (see quot. 1875) [in quots 1856, 1944 the meaning may be that of **2.** above]; (6) **stock,** see as a main entry.

(1) **1898** FOX *Kentuckians* 105 'There are mountain birds up here, too'—a polyglot chat was chuckling. 'Hear that? My father used to call that the "plough-bird."' — (2) **1898** HAMBLEN *Gen'l Manager's Story* 284 Inside of a week he had a steam shovel at work in the gravel pit, and plough cars on the road. — (3) **1860** OLMSTED *Back Country* 47 There was also a driver of the hoe-gang who did not labor personally, a foreman of the plow-gang. — (4) **1840** in COMMONS *Doc. Hist.* I. 335, I am frequently compelled to work them in three separate classes, . . . plow hands, hoe hands, the full grown & small hands. **1892** HARRIS *U. Remus* 60 The little boy was going through the negro quarters yelling at the top of his voice, repeating the refrain of a nonsense song he had heard the plough-hands sing.

(5) **1856** *Fla. Plant. Rec.* 478 Paid Mr. Lem Jones 50 cts. on account of '54 [1854] maid by J. Evans for 2 Plow points. **1875** KNIGHT 1748/1 Plow-point. A detachable share at the extreme front end of the plow-body, forming an apex to the junction of the mold-board, sole, and land-side. **1944** CLARK *Pills* 207 As often as farmers bought commercial fertilizers, plowlines, backbands and plow points in the spring they purchased spring supplies of 'stripes' for shirts.

As the last term in **barrel, barring, bog, breaking, breaking-up, brush, buggy, buzzard, cary, chill, clipper, contour, corn, dagon, disk, ditching, double, double moldboard, double shovel, duck bill, Empire, fluke, gang, gopher, grasshopper, hauling, hilling, ice, Jacob's, Michigan double, prairie, railroad, railway, reclamation, scouring, seed, seeding, shovel, sidehill, snow, sod, Spanish, stirring, stubble, turn, walking plow.**

***plow,** *v. To plow around, fig.* To get around or circumvent, to circulate among or associate with. *Colloq.* — **1888** SHERIDAN *Memoirs* I. 463 General Grant had 'ploughed around' the difficulties of the situation. **1888** BRYCE *Amer. Commonw.* II. III. lxx. 557 The more skilful leaders begin (as it is expressed) to 'plough around' among the delegations of the newer . . . States.

plow stock.

1. *Chiefly S.* The wooden or iron frame consisting of a strong beam, handles, and "foot" to which a plow (sense **2.**) is attached. Cf. **shovel plow stock.**

1786 WASHINGTON *Diaries* III. 5, [I] directed them to get me . . . scantling for Plow stocks. **1865** *Ore. State Jrnl.* 28 Oct. 4/2 Plow

Stocks etc., made to order, on short notice. **1944** CLARK *Pills* 276 Center and rear passageways were blocked with piles of iron plows, rolls of plowlines, plow stocks, . . . and axes.

2. The draft animals used in plowing.

1868 *Rep. Comm. Agric. 1867* 419, I fed the plough stock. **1889** *Rep. Secy. Agric.* 259 Consumption of corn in the cotton States is always less in proportion at this date, because [of] . . . the necessity of general and late feeding of 'plow stock.'

*plug, *n.*

1. Short for **plug hat.** Also attrib. *Colloq.*

1852 *Lantern* (N.Y.) I. 200/1 The Maine-iacs aforesaid have been in the habit of conveying such material [i.e., 'bricks'] to their homes, secreted on their persons, generally in that article of their dress denominated the hat, castor, or 'plug.' **1878** HART *Sazerac Lying Club* 226 'Where's your plug, John?' inquired our devil, addressing himself to the Indian and pointing at his head. **1904** O. HENRY *Roads of Destiny* 223 He wore a high, well-kept silk hat—known as a 'plug' in Elmville.

2. Short for **plug horse.** Also, rarely, **plugamore,** *Colloq.*

The use of the Du. *plug* in approx. this same sense is interesting and possibly significant. The word is similarly used in New Zealand and Australia. See the *OED.*

1860 O. H. OLDROYD *Lincoln's Campaign* (1896) 171 There's an old plow 'hoss' whose name is 'Dug,' . . . He's short and thick and a regular 'plug.' **1898** WESTCOTT *D. Harum* xxv, But as fur's that old plugamore of a hoss was concerned, I got it both ways. **1919** CADY *Rhymes of Vt.* (1923) 85 The nod or wink or shoulder-shrug That sold the fambly pung or plug. **1948** *Chi. Tribune* 12 Dec. (Grafic Mag.) 5/5 He was a hopeless plug and never ran in the money.

b. An ineffectual, unskilled, or inconsequential person. Also attrib.

1863 in BILLINGS *Hardtack* 72 Next came General Meade, a slow old plug, For he let them get away at Gettysburg. **1920** LEWIS *Main Street* 308 You figure I'm just a plug general practitioner. **1948** *Redbook* March 48/2 You—you broken reed! You doormat! Old steady, unimaginative, dumb *plug!*

3. In misc. uses: **a.** (See quot. 1909.) **b.** In angling, a cylindrical casting bait. **c.** (See quot.) **d.** A good word or bit of advertising.

(a) 1909 *Cent. Supp.* 1022/2 plug. . . . A book that does not sell at all. (Booksellers' slang.) **1930** *Publishers' Wkly.* 15 March 1456/1 The so-called plugs are weeded out . . . making room for new titles. — **(b) 1932** *K.C. Times* 13 May 22 There is some balm for the fellow who thinks he is paying too much for his plugs, flies and other equipment. **1949** *Esquire* March 91 The plug caster must learn to make the wooden minnow live if he hopes to dupe a musky, for muskies are fond of animated lures. — **(c) 1940** MENCKEN *Happy Days* 249 A plug was a cigar so overstuffed with filler that sucking wind through it would probably be unfeasible. — **(d) 1929** *Variety* 10 July 1/5 The island's hotels, the glass-bottom boats through which one views the natural aquariums, the various tours and all the rest are Wrigley owned. Everything gets a Wrigley plug, for the benefit of his gum. **1947** *Sat. Review* 10 May 32/3 He is . . . putting in a plug for Lake Tahoe as a resort.

4. In combs.: (1) **plug cut,** a form of plug tobacco; (2) **hat,** a man's hat having a tall cylindrical crown, earlier fire plug hat *q.v.*, also attrib.; (3) **hatted,** *a.* provided with or wearing a plug hat; (4) **horse,** an old broken-down horse, *colloq.*, see note to **2.** above; (5) **muss,** a free-for-all brawl or row, *obs.;* (6) **press,** a press used in making plug tobacco; (7) **puller,** ?a railroad engineer, *slang;* (8) **tile,** =**plug hat;** (9) **tobacco,** tobacco pressed into flat rectangular cakes; (10) **-ugly,** see as a main entry.

(1) 1896 *Internat. Typog. Union Proc.* 55/1, 5 lbs. Seal plug cut, $2.90. **1920** LINCOLN *Mr. Pratt* 197 What's hasheesh? Plug cut or cigars? — **(2) 1863** in *Three Yrs. Among Working Classes U.S.* (1865) 223 Fancy a ragged man . . . with a gun, a knapsack, a butcher's knife and a plug hat. **1881** BUEL *Border Outlaws* 170 They were only after the 'plug hat' crowd. **1949** *World-Herald* (Omaha) 15 May F. 1/5 The greenbacks picture a cigar-smoking fat man in a plug hat saying 'In Tax Exemption We Trust.' — **(3) 1881** ROMSPERT *Western Echo* 235 Finding that they were plug-hatted, nickel-plated fellows, with lots of *conceit,* we concluded to have some fun. **1947** BEEBE *Mixed Train Dly.* 250 For twenty years no other event more startling than the arrival of the stately plug-hatted Senator from Montana marked the annals of the U.V. — **(4) 1887** *Courier-Journal* 4 Feb. 3/5 Wanted—40 plug horses and mares at Lum Simon's Stables. **1946** *Reader's Digest* March 153/2 One day Mr. Howell returned from Enid driving two respectable plug horses.

(5) 1857 *Knickerb.* L. 584 The exceeding utility of a hot poker—*properly applied*—In quelling a riot or 'plug-muss.' **1861** MOORE *Rebellion Rec.* I. III. 81 [His] massive under-jaw and breadth of neck indicated him 'some in a plug muss.' — **(6) 1944** CLARK *Pills* 147 It would seem that every farmer with a stock of raw tobacco, . . . and a homemade plug press introduced some romantically named product to the nation's chewers. — **(7) 1898** *McClure's Mag.* X. 366 He read the riot act . . . in a manner that the oldest 'plug-puller' on the road had never heard equalled. — **(8) 1883** MARK TWAIN *Life on Miss.* 570 (R.), Kid gloves, plug tile, hair parted behind. — **(9) 1814** *Ann. 17th Congress* 2 Sess. 1218 Plug tobacco manufactured at Columbia, one shilling and three pence per pound. **1948** JOHNSTON *Gold Rush* 43/1 Here paused the relentless hand of progress, sparing . . . the old-timers with their plug tobacco and legendary 'yarns.'

As the last term in **cut, navy, spark, spear-head plug.**

*plug, *v.*

1. *tr.* To debase (a coin) by removing a portion of the metal and filling the cavity with an inferior substance. Usu. ***plugged,** *a.*, ***plugging,** *n.*

1694 *Mass. H.S. Coll.* 4 Ser. I. 106 If a piece of eight be plugged, it will not pass. **1797** *Ann. 5th Congress* 2 Sess. I. 718 They knew the silver coin circulated by tale, the gold by weight; the value of the latter had actually diminished by various means, such as sweating, plugging, clipping, &c. **1890** BIFF HALL *Turnover Club* 207 And the first speaker wilted at once, and paid the price of his folly with a plugged quarter. **1909** O. HENRY *Options* (1916) 245 Mr. Hinkle told me you'd never taken in a lead silver dollar or a plugged one.

b. plugged nickel, peso, used as a symbol of nothing, not a red cent. *Slang.*

1923 MULFORD *Black Buttes* 265 He says . . . he'll see us both in hell before he'll pay a plugged peso. **1947** *Chi. Sun* 20 Jan. 8/4 If it's true that 'silence is golden,' some of us gals wouldn't have so much as a plugged nickel to our names!

2. In playing ball, to tag out an opponent by hitting him with the ball. *Colloq.*

1856 *Spirit of Times* 27 Dec. 276/3 If an adversary gets hold of the ball before he (the striker) has made two steps, he *must* 'plug' the batsman before he reaches his first base.

3. To remove a small plug from (a melon) to see if it is ripe.

1876 *Sutter Banner* (Yuba City, Calif.) 3 Aug. 1/6 Let me plug 'em to find a ripe one? **1883** PECK *Bad Boy* 49 He came over after some cantelopes for breakfast, and plugged a couple to see if they were ripe. **1948** *Chi. Tribune* 25 June II. 3/3 The safest and best way to tell quality is to 'plug' the melon.

transf. **1881** *Chi. Times* 12 March, The final inspection and plugging, in order to ascertain the sound condition of each bale [of cotton], can take place at any time subsequent.

4. To anticipate or block (a person); to thwart (a plan). *Slang.*

1880 *Scribner's Mo.* Aug. 492/2 One fisherman 'plugs' another when he puts out from shore and casts in ahead of him. **1896** ADE *Artie* 110, I wouldn't like to start in and plug his game.

5. *intr.* To strive hard to obtain, usu. with *for* or *away. Colloq.*

1900 G. ADE *More Fables in Slang* (1902) 44 And get up every Morning ready to Plug for a Renaissance of their Early love. **1908** K. MCGAFFEY *Show-Girl* 109 Is it considered au fait for a bride-about-to-be to do a little plugging for wedding presents this early in the game? **1948** *Herald-Press* (St. Joseph, Mich.) 14 Aug. 4/5 He'll keep plugging away until he catches that one.

6. Of a log jam: To become stuck or impeded.

1902 WHITE *Blazed Trail* 338 Several times the jam started, but always 'plugged' before the motion had become irresistible.

***plugger,** *n.* **1.** = ***capper. 2.** A faithful and persistent booster. Both *slang.*

(1) 1891 QUINN *Fools of Fortune* 239 Regular dealers are employed and usually four of five 'pluggers' (by which term are designated men who play for the house and with money belonging to the proprietors). — **(2) 1921** *Cleveland Enterprise* 4 June 1/3 Everybody out here is a booster and plugger for one common purpose.

plug-ugly 'plʌgˌʌglɪ, *n.* [Origin unknown.] A tough or roughneck, orig. a member of a city gang of rowdies active in such places as Baltimore, New York, and Philadelphia. *Slang.*

1856 *Butte Rec.* (Oroville, Calif.) 29 Nov. 3/7 The . . . Plug Uglies . . . went to Philadelphia on election day, . . . to fight off and whip the democracy from the polls. **1892** CRANE *Maggie* (1896) 121 And she goes off that with plug-ugly who looks as if he had been hit in the face with a coin die. **1948** *Sat. Review* 3 April 31/2 He was always concerned about the welfare of his employees, yet he hired a small army of plug-uglies to repress the slightest stirring of unionism among them.

attrib. **1861** *Ill. Agric. Soc. Trans.* IV. 278 The De Soto 'Plug Ugly' Continentals, failed to make their appearance on the grounds as per agreement. **1863** BROWNE *Four Yrs. in Secessia* (1865) 298 During the reign of General Winder and his Baltimore plug-ugly Detectives, the grossest abuses were practiced. **1875** *Chi. Tribune* 4 Nov. 2/1 The Baltimore *American* has an unanswerable showing of facts of the plug-ugly element for which it was once noted.

b. An ardent proslavery advocate in the Kansas struggle of 1854–58. Also attrib. *Obs.*

1857 *Lawrence* (Kans.) *Republican* 16 July 2 The usurpers—or, as Vaughn of the Leavenworth Times significantly terms them, the '*plug uglies.*' *Ib.* 30 July 2 Only a pitiful minority of the actual voters of Kansas, cast their votes for delegates to the plug ugly convention, soon to assemble at Lecompton.

c. In derivatives, as **plug-uglydom, plug-uglyism.** *Obs.*

*a***1861** WINTHROP *Open Air* 232 If the rural population did not give us a bastard imitation of Lexington and Concord, . . . all Pluguglydom would treat us *à la* Plugugly somewhere near the junction of the Annapolis and Baltimore and Washington Railroad. **1865** BROWNE *Four Yrs. in Secessia* 272 If justice were meted out to Major Turner, he would be executed summarily, and . . . the Prison Inspector . . . formerly a Baltimore blackguard, and aspirant for the honors of Plug-uglyism . . . would share his fate.

d. Plug-Uglymore, a nickname for Baltimore. *Obs.*

1861 *N.Y. Tribune* 15 July 6/4 Indeed, the number of slaves there [in Baltimore] held can scarcely be regarded as involving so much wealth as the piratic slave-trade, in which Plug-Uglymore is known to bear her part most gallantly.

***plum,** *n.*

1. A state or federal office obtained as a result of political "pull." *Slang.* Cf. **political plum.**

1887 *Courier-Journal* (Louisville) 13 Jan. 3/4 Senator Beck gets the credit for most of the Federal appointments in Mason county. . . . The boys enjoying the plums will support anybody who is for him and them. **1911** *N.Y. Ev. Post* 3 Jan. 8 The 'plum' is a luscious fruit in the shape of an office under the State government, which many people are on the lookout to secure. **1949** *Chi. Tribune* 30 Nov. 21/1 (*heading*), Democrats Get $17.68 Per Day Census Plums.

2. In combs.: (1) **plum-bread,** (see quot.), *obs.;* (2) **butter,** a thick sauce made of plums stewed down in their own juice; (3) **cot,** (see quots.); (4) **leather,** (see quot. and cf. **apple leather, peach leather**); (5) **muss,** [f. **plum*+Du. *moes*, pap, porridge] (see quot.), *obs.;* (6) **puddinger,** a whaling boat used in short voyages in the north Atlantic Ocean, also a member of the crew of such a boat, *slang;* (7) ***tree,** *fig.* the source of political offices, jobs, etc., cf. ***plum,** *n.* **1.** above.

(1) **1709** LAWSON *Carolina* 104 The *Indians* get many Bushels [of hurts, huckleberries or blues] and dry them on Mats, whereof they make Plum-Bread, and many other eatables. — (2) **1872** *Harper's Mag.* May 808/1 Then came the inevitable sauces and sweetenings. Apple-butter, pear-butter, plum-butter, and wild-grape-butter—this latter the most piquant of all the mountain sauces used with meats or on hot bread-and-butter. — (3) **1901** *World's Work* Sep. 1213/1, I was skeptical as to the existence of the 'plum-cot,' or the cross between the plum and apricot. **1942** *Stand. Plant Names* 262/2 Plumcot. Prunus armenica × P. salicina. — (4) **1943** L. V. HAMNER *Short Grass & Longhorns* 58 They made plum leather. . . . She cooked the plums, pressed them through a homemade colander . . . spread the pulp out in sheets and dried it.

(5) **1877** BARTLETT 475 Plum-Muss. Plums boiled, mashed together, and dried in the form of a sheet. — (6) **1851** MELVILLE *Moby Dick* 95 After listening to these plum-puddingers till nearly eleven o'clock, I went up stairs to go to bed. **1874** C. M. SCAMMON *Marine Mammals* 241 Provincetown has ever been foremost with her numerous fleet of plum-puddingers, . . . which are small vessels employed on short voyages in the Atlantic Ocean. — (7) **1904** *Newark Ev. News* 27 June 6 It is pretty tough to shut the statesmen off from one of the biggest branches of the plum tree in this summary fashion.

As the last term in **barren, beach, buffalo, bunch, Canada, Cherokee, Chickasaw, cliff, creek, date, goose, gopher, ground, Guiana, heath hen, hog, horse, ivory, Japan, June, old field, Osage, partridge, pigeon, political, prairie, sand, sugar, yellow plum.**

***plumb,** *v.* and *adv.* **1.** (See quot. 1844.) *Obs.* **2. plumb center,** centrally, absolutely in the center. *Colloq.*

(1) **1844** HOUSTOUN *Yacht Voy. Texas* II. 205 Plumbing the track, the Texan term for tracing a road, is, at all times, a slow and tedious operation. **1850** ——— *Hesperos* II. 141 He was well aware that the vague and indistinct track which (in prairie language) he had been *plumbing*, led somewhere in the direction of the hostelry. — (2) **1848** RUXTON *Life Far West* i, He made it throw plum-center. **1851** M. REID *Scalp Hunters* xx. Most of them [*sc.* Delawares] can hit 'plumb centre' with any of their mountain associates. **1886** *Outing* Nov. 104/2 So down I jumps an' gin her [the bear] one through the brisket, plumb-center fust shot.

plumbeous vireo. A regional variety of the blue-headed vireo, a bird of this variety.

1872 COUES *Key to Birds* 122 Plumbeous Vireo. Leaden-gray, rather brighter & more ashy on the crown. **1878** ——— *Birds Colo. Valley* 519 My suspicions that they were not the Plumbeous Vireos had at first been aroused by hearing the song. **1917** *Birds of Amer.* III. 108/2 The Plumbeous Vireo . . . of the southern Rocky Mountain Region . . . breeds from northern Nevada, northern Utah, northeastern Wyoming and southwestern South Dakota south through Arizona and southwestern Texas to the mountains of Mexico.

***plume,** *n.* In combs.: (1) **plume grass,** (see quot. 1861); (2) **lock,** (see quot.), *rare;* (3) **stick,** (see quot.), *rare.*

(1) **1861** WOOD *Botany* 807 *Erianthus,* Plume Grass. . . . Stout, erect grasses, remarkable for their large woolly or silky, tawny panicles. **1901** MOHR *Plant Life Ala.* 334. — (2) **1891** *Harper's Mag.* Dec. 36/2 The larger ones were already wearing the Blackfoot plume-lock, or tuft of hair tied and trained to stand erect above the forehead. — (3) **1882** *N.Y. Tribune* 5 March, The plume-stick [among the Zuñis] is a mere twig, a little larger in circumference than a lead-pencil, having bound to one end a duck's feather. *Ib.*, The prayers . . . were addressed directly to the plume-sticks, which were placed one by one in the bottom of the hole, the feathers standing upright. . . . The sticks were then reverently covered up.

As the last term in **Apache, soldier's plume.**

***plumed,** *a.*

1. Plumed Knight, (see quots.).

1876 INGERSOLL in *Republican Nat. Conv. Proc.* 74 Like a plumed knight, James G. Blaine marched down the halls of the American congress. **1888** M. LANE in *America* 1 Nov. 15 *Plumed Knight.*—A name conferred upon the Hon. James G. Blaine at the National Republican Convention at Cincinnati, in 1876, by the Hon. Robert G. Ingersoll. **1949** *Newsweek* 19 May 60/2 She married a son of James G. Blaine, the Republicans' 'Plumed Knight.'

b. *pl.* The followers of James G. Blaine (1830–93). *Obs.*

1884 *N.Y. Wkly. Tribune* 16 July 4/1 The announcement . . . was received with another outburst of applause in which the Plumed Knights of his district took a rousing lead.

2. plumed partridge, quail, =mountain quail.

1839 AUDUBON *Ornith. Biog.* V. 226 Plumed Partridge. *Perdix Plumifera.* . . . This bird inhabits the dense woods along the tributary streams of the Columbia River. **1874** HITTELL *Resources Calif.* 402 The plumed quail . . . is a partridge, ten inches long, very plump in body, handsome in color, majestic in its bearing, and graceful in motion. **1903** AUSTIN *Land of Little Rain* 171 If you had ever owned one of Seyavi's golden russet cooking bowls with the pattern of plumed quail, you would understand all this without saying anything.

plumosa plu'mosə, *n. S.W.* [Prob. f. Sp. *plata plumosa*, feathery silver.] Silver that occurs in feathery flakes. *Obs.* — **1854** *Pioneer* (S.F.) Jan. 32 The ores are generally 'Plomosa,' of from 8 to 16 per cent pure silver. **1879** VIVIAN *Wanderings in Western Land* 355, I saw specimens of ore from this neighbourhood [Calif.], showing a considerable quantity of this 'plumosa,' which in appearance resembles thin layers of zinc blende.

***plump,** *adv. To vote plump,* ?to vote directly or without qualification. *Rare.* — **1776** in J. ADAMS *Works* III. 55 Our delegates in Congress, on the first of July, will vote plump [on the question of Amer. independence].

***plunder,** *n.*

1. Baggage, personal effects, household goods, etc.

The locale of our earliest evidence does not bear out the idea that this term comes from German or Dutch. See R. M. Stone, *Studien über den deutschen Einfluss auf das amerikanische Englisch* (1934), *s.v.*

1805 LEWIS in *L. & Clark Exped.* II. (1904) 220, I dispatched Sergt. Ordway with 4 Canoes and 8 men to take up a load of baggage as far as Capt. Clark's camp and return for the remainder of our plunder. **1839** *N.O. Picayune* 23 April 2/4 A Kentuckian started from some point in his native state, with a flat boat richly laden with corn, apples, chickens and other up-country '*plunder*' for this city. **1892** C. ROBINSON *Kansas Conflict* 28 On leaving St. Louis the boat was well filled with passengers and their 'plunder.' **1948** DICK *Dixie Frontier* 113 Mules and a hardy tough breed of Indian and Spanish horse . . . were used to carry the money and 'plunder.'

attrib. **1846** MAGOFFIN *Down Santa Fé Trail* 2, [I] received two or three visits—next I arranged my trunk 'plunder-basket.'

2. plunderbund, a group engaged in exploiting the public. *Colloq.*

1914 *Voice of People* (N.O.) 8 Jan. 1/1 The whole force of the Texan plunderbund . . . are howling at the heels of the dauntless army of workers. **1949** *Chi. Tribune* 2 Sep. 12/6 Hello, suckers who voted for the continuation of chaos and corruption and the plunderbund last November.

plunge bath. A bath taken by plunging into the water. — **1848** THOREAU *Maine Woods* 68 The continual bathing of our bodies in mountain water, alternate foot, sitz, douche, and plunge baths, made this walk exceedingly refreshing. **1897** *Voice* 3 June 7/2 [A woman] who never fails to do her exercises before a big plunge bath, is sure to have smaller bills with the doctors.

*** plunger,** *n.* A small boat or yacht.

1860 *North-west* (Port Townsend, Wash.) 12 July 3/1 The following craft were entered for the stakes:—Sloop H. L. Tibbals, Port Townsend; . . . plunger Venus, built at Esquimault, and the plunger Star of the South, also of Esquimault. **1892** *Outing* March 467/1 Yachting on the Pacific coast dates from about 1869, . . . though a few small plungers and sloops had long been owned on the bay. **1900** HARTE *Treasure of Redwoods* 109, I've got him safe on that 'plunger' down at the wharf.

As the last term in **horse, Wall Street plunger.**

***plunk,** *n.* A dollar. *Slang.* — **1891** J. MAITLAND *Dict.* **1901** *Everybody's Mag.* Oct. 433/1 He'd heard twelve plunks or so would pay for the Midway show. **1920** LEWIS *Main Street* 200 I'm letting the days drown in worship of 'a good deal, ten plunks more per acre.'

***plunk,** *v. tr.* To shoot. *Colloq.* — **1891** *Outing* Nov. 138/2, I would plunk the big gobbler I could distinguish from where I lay. **1916** WILSON *Somewhere* 120 Darned if he didn't up with this here air gun . . . and plunk me with a buckshot it carried.

*** plural,** *a.* Of or pertaining to polygamy as formerly practiced by Mormons.

1894 *Cong. Rec.* 23 Jan. (1900) 1103/1 Former polygamists . . . are utterly neglecting their former plural wives and children of those wives. **1900** *Ib.* 20 Jan. 1013/1 His status as a polygamist, unlawfully cohabiting with plural wives, affording constitutional grounds for expulsion. **1922** *Nation* 28 June 768/1 Celestial marriages have taken the place of plural marriages. **1948** *Newsweek* 12 Jan. 38/2 Once a basic tenet of the Mormon Church, the doctrine of plural marriage was formally abandoned in 1890.

*** plurality,** *n.*

1. The total number of votes obtained by the leading candidate in an election; in exact usage, such a total if no candidate receives a majority.

In quot. 1789, since it is possible for a single candidate to secure more than half the votes, *plurality* necessarily includes the concept of *majority.*

1789 *Ann. 1st Congress* 1 Sess. I. 21 All committees shall be appointed by ballot, and a plurality of votes shall make a choice. **1804** *Mass. Spy* 18 Jan. (Th.), In several states, many great offices are filled, and even the chief magistracy, by various methods of election. The public will is sometimes expressed by pluralities instead of majorities. **1898** *N.Y. Tribune* 10 Nov. 1/4 In New-Jersey, owing to the bold and palpable ballot-box stuffing and other frauds . . . the apparent plurality of Foster M. Voorhees, Republican candidate for Governor, has greatly decreased. **1948** *Chi. D. News* 24 Feb. 1/6 The . . . primary resulted in a 120,000 plurality for Long over three other candidates. But that was not the clear majority necessary for election.

attrib. **1851** *Harper's Mag.* July 276/1 Among the measures passed was . . . the Plurality Act, in accordance with which members of Congress at the second trial . . . are elected by a plurality of votes.

2. In an election wherein there are more than two candidates: The excess of votes obtained by the leading candidate over an opponent, esp. over his nearest competitor.

1860 *Boston Transcript* 7 Nov. 2/3 In Massachusetts . . . Lincoln's clear majority 42,371, Lincoln's plurality over Douglas 70,460, Lincoln's plurality over Bell 82,450. **1894** *Harper's Mag.* Jan. 318/1 In Massachusetts, F. T. Greenhalge, Republican, was elected Governor by a plurality of 30,000. **1949** *So. Wkly.* 19 Nov. 5/1 Any candidate for President receiving a plurality of only one vote in the State over his nearest opponent receives also the entire 47 electoral votes of New York.

plurisyllable ˈplʊrəˌsɪləbl̩, *n.* (See quot.). — **1924** J. S. KENYON *Amer. Pronunciation* 30 (*footnote*), A Monosyllable is a word of one syllable; a Plurisyllable is a word of more than one syllable.

plus plu, *n.* [Can. F. *plu, plus,* in same sense. Cf. McDermott *s.v. plus.*] Formerly in the fur trade a large, first-class beaver skin adopted as a unit of value. Now *obs.* or *hist.* Cf. **plew.**

1801 in GATES *Fur Traders* 163 On my telling him to give three Plus &. that I should let him have strong Rum he complied. **1807** DUNBAR *Travels* 51 Each skin has a conventional value. What they call a *plu,* is equal in value to a dollar. Thus, two goat-skins make a *plu,* an otter's skin two *plu.* **1813** LUTTIG *Jrnl.* 125 They shewed us a Horn which they made which holds 40 Loads of Powder, instead of giving 20 Load for a Plus. **1842** BUCKINGHAM *E. & W. States* III. viii. 389 In 1784, at the post of the Pic, a bear was estimated at one plus, an otter, three martins, a lynx, fifteen muskrats, respectively, one plus. A buffalo robe two plus. A keg of mixed rum, thirty plus.

plute plut, *n.* Short for "plutocrat." *Slang.*

1910 *Sat. Ev. Post* 17 Sep. 27/3 When it is necessary Sanders can fulminate against plutocracy and its associated and predacious plutes in a most approved manner. **1923** E. F. WYATT *Invis. Gods* II. iv. 65 Paul's a plute and a snob . . . a kind of a cad—proud of using people. **1932** *Randolph Enterprise* (Elkins, W.Va.) 18 Feb. 5/2 You'll hear the plutes cry out, The 'Yellow Peril' is Japan.

Plymothean ˌplɪməˈθiən, *n.* A native or inhabitant of Plymouth, Mass.

1631 *N.H. Hist. Soc. Coll.* IV. 228 [The Englishmen] who survived were rescued by those of Plymouth out of the hands of Chicka Talbott and his Indians, who . . . intended to have destroyed them and the Plymotheans also. **1702** C. MATHER *Magnalia* (1853) I. 55 [Squanto had been] brought back by one Mr. Dermer, about half a year before our honest Plymotheans were cast upon this continent. **1914** in *Pub. Col. Soc.* XVII. 360 For twelve years (1769–1780) the celebrations at Plymouth were purely local, the speakers and participants being either Plymotheans or from the neighboring towns in the Old Colony.

Also **Plymothean Fathers,** the Pilgrim Fathers.

1806 A. HOLMES *Discourse* 32 The summary of the religious tenets of the Plymothean Fathers, inserted in this discourse, was collected from their writings.

*** Plymouth,** *n.*

1. Plymouth pilgrim, (*a*) = *** Pilgrim 2,** (*b*) *pl.* during the Civil War a derisive name used in the South for northern soldiers.

(*a*) **1805** *Independent Chron.* 3 Jan. 2/4 The Plymouth pilgrims have carefully confined their approbation of John Adams to his private character. — (*b*) **1865** KELLOGG *Rebel Prisons* 51 Great crowds of people thronged the street corners to stare at the 'Plymouth Pilgrims,' as the city papers sarcastically called us. *Ib.* 61 The balance of the Plymouth pilgrims came in, including the remainder of our regiment.

2. In other expressions relating to the first colonists at Plymouth, Mass., as **Plymouth explorers, Fathers.** For **Plymouth Rock,** see as a main entry.

1830 *Collegian* 231 My rickety arm-chair, which the old lady . . . affirmed to have come over from England with the Plymouth Fathers. **1903** C. F. ADAMS *3 Episodes Mass. Hist.* I. 20 These islands the Plymouth explorers reported had been 'cleared from end to end.'

Plymouth Rock.

1. A granite boulder in Plymouth Harbor, Mass., where the Pilgrims are said to have landed in 1620.

1837 MARTINEAU *Society* I. 134 The other festival . . . was the celebration of Forefathers' Day;—of the landing of the Pilgrims on Plymouth Rock. **1900** *Cong. Rec.* 15 Feb. 1842/2 Their ancestors landed with the Pilgrim fathers at Plymouth Rock. **1949** *Hobbies* Nov. 147/1 Thanksgiving . . . makes us think of the Pilgrims, their landing at Plymouth Rock in 1620, and all the other historic facts connected with this great historic event.

Hence **Plymouth Rocky,** *a.* designating one having marked Puritanical traits, or one who is inordinately proud of being a descendant of the Plymouth settlers. *Rare.*

1868 *Harper's Mag.* Sep. 574/1 A gentleman with a tendency to brokerage . . . is known among personal friends to be one of the Plymouth Rockiest of Puritans.

2. An American chicken or breed of chickens, the best-known variety of which is characterized by long yellow legs and evenly barred feathers.

1849 *N. Eng. Farmer* I. 386 *Plymouth Rock.*—This is a new variety, recently formed at Plymouth. **1882** *Harper's Mag.* Sep. 489/1 Here Plymouth Rocks and well-fed Brahamas cackled, oblivious to all things terrestrial but themselves. **1945** *N. Eng. Homestead* 27 Oct. 16/2 He was showing White Face Black Spanish chickens and Columbian Plymouth Rocks before World War I.

pocan ˈpokən, *n.* = **poke,** *n.*[2] **1.** Also attrib.

1866 LINDLEY & MOORE *Treas. Botany* 885/2 The Pocan, or Virginian Poke or Pokeweed, is a branching herbaceous plant, with a smooth green or sometimes purplish stem. **1877** BARTLETT 478 Poke Berry. The berry of the Phytolacca, from which a rich purple juice is extracted, and used as a dye. Also called Pigeon-berry and *Pocan.* **1931** CLUTE *Plants* 24 No such doubt exists regarding the derivation of poke-weed (*Phytolacca decandra*). . . . This plant is certainly the pocan of the Indians and the pocan-bush of the whites.

*pocket, *n.*

1. An area or nook adjoining a larger tract. Also a cove or valley among mountains.

[**1745** *N.H. Probate Rec.* III. 293, I also give to my said Son Samuel the Marsh called the Little Pocket & all the flat facing or Lying Against the Same.] **1860** *Harper's Mag.* Oct. 604/1 On Saturday afternoon we brought up in a 'pocket' near the Lac de Gros Butte, where we were protected on two sides by water, and on one side by an impassable marsh. **1934** VINES *Green Thicket World* 65 They rode a few miles down the Big River's way and drew up at a pocket.

b. (See quot.)

1862 *Congregationalist* 30 May (Chipman), The General Association of Indiana met . . . at Francisco, Gibson Co., in the 'Pocket,' that part of the State lying south of the Ohio and Mississippi Railway.

2. (See quot.) *Obs.*

1842 *Amer. Pioneer* I. 419 'Pockets' for inclosing letters are of modern mention. (Pockets are envelopes prepared and franked.)

3. A bag or sack into which cotton is placed as it is picked. *Colloq.*

1881 *Harper's Mag.* Oct. 728/1 There is not a process to which the lint is submitted after it is thrown from the negro's 'pocket' that does not act directly on the quality of the cloth that is finally produced.

4. A receptacle of strong paper pasted inside the cover of a library book to hold the charging cards.

1887 *Library Notes* March 282 The Acme Pocket . . . is made of strong manila, cut with a peculiar die so that the cards can be put in and taken out with the greatest rapidity, and yet are firmly held. **1910** BOSTWICK *Amer. Pub. Library* 45 When the book is on the shelf the book card is kept in it, in a pocket provided for the purpose. **1947** *Staff Lookout* (Denver Pub. Lib.) Winter 7/1 A date slip, pasted on the outer and bottom edge, was placed on the fly leaf to serve as a pocket.

5. In combs.: (1) ***pocketbook,** see as a main entry; (2) **boom,** (see quot.); (3) **canyon,** =**box canyon;** (4) **claim,** *W.* a place where gold occurs in pockets or small cavities, cf. **pocket diggings;** (5) **cutter,** a pickpocket who cuts the pockets of his victims; (6) **diggings,** (see quot.), *obs.;* (7) **field,** an oil field in which a pocket or pool of oil is tapped; (8) **gopher,** an American burrowing rodent of the family Geomyidae, having fur-lined cheek pouches opening outside the mouth; (9) **hatchet,** a hatchet carried in a leather pocket or holster; (10) **hunter,** *W.* one who seeks for gold occurring in pockets; (11) **knife assayer,** *W.* (see quot.), *obs.;* (12) **lightning conductor,** a pistol, *obs.;* (13) **miner,** *W.* =**pocket hunter;** (14) **mining,** mining that specializes in exploiting deposits of gold in pockets; (15) **mouse,** any one of various burrowing rodents of the genus *Perognathus,* found in the western U.S. and so called from their external cheek pouches; (16) **peddler,** (see quot.), *obs.;* (17) **scales,** spring scales suitable for carrying in the pocket; (18) **veto,** (see quot. 1888).

(2) 1905 *Forestry Bureau Bul.* No. 61, 43 *Pocket boom,* a boom in which logs are held after they are sorted. — **(3) 1907** COOK *Border & Buffalo* (1938) 262 The place they selected was a pocket-cañon just south of the mouth of Thompson's Cañon. — **(4) 1865** MARK TWAIN *Notebook* (1935) i. 6 (R.), Went out to the 'pocket' claim.

(5) 1885 *Milnor* (Dak.) *Teller* 5 June 2/3 Deck hands on the steamer Mary Morton were being robbed by pocket-cutters among the roustabouts. — **(6) 1877** BARTLETT 476 *Pocket diggings,* a term used by gold-miners to denote hollow places where gold is concentrated as in a pocket. — **(7) 1883** *Cent. Mag.* July 327/1 About ten miles from the clearing lay the little oil town of Clarendon, . . . a pocket-field, as the oil men call it, developed about ten years ago. — **(8) 1873** EGGLESTON *Myst. Metrop.* 37 She would . . . explain how the pocket-gophers built their mounds. **1948** *Democrat* 19 Aug. 2/4 Pocket gophers are second only to ground squirrels in total damage to the agriculture of California. — **(9) 1917** KEPHART *Camping* I. 269 Of course you have . . . either a pocket hatchet or a big bowie-knife.

(10) 1947 *Field & Stream* June 30/3 Now and then a 'pocket-hunter' (a different breed than the placer miner) will find a place in the hills containing perhaps a few hundred dollars in gold. — **(11)** *c***1938** WILLIAMS *MS* 332 One very common way [of testing gold-bearing ore] is by testing with a pocket knife and they frequently call those who are familiar with this way of testing ores, 'Pocket knife assayers.' — **(12) 1867** *Prescott* (Ariz.) *Gaz.* 31 July 3/1 They were armed with shot-guns, revolvers and pocket 'lightning' conductors, and were otherwise well 'heeled.' — **(13) 1909** MARK TWAIN *Is Shakespeare Dead?* 75 (R.), I have been a 'pocket' miner—a sort of gold mining not findable in any but one little spot in the world, so far as I know. I know how to find the compact little nest of yellow metal reposing in its secret home under the ground. **1902** LONDON *Daughter of Snows* 207 The pocket-miner's eyes sparkled. — **(14) 1872** MARK TWAIN *Roughing It* 436 In that one little corner of California is found a species of mining . . . called 'pocket mining.'

(15) 1884 *Cassell's Nat. Hist.* III. 124 These animals [Saccomyidæ] . . . by American writers . . . are called 'Pocket Mice.' **1947** *So. Sierran* March 3/3 This mouse is about one inch longer than the Pocket Mouse, its tail being half its total length. — **(16) 1892** *Nation* 28 July 66/1 The liquor traffic is now largely conducted by men called pocket-peddlers—men who stand on the street corners with a bottle in one pocket and a glass in the other, and will sell you a drink in a doorway or a horse-shed. — **(17) 1876** *Wide Awake* 145/1 'He's a beauty,' said Cousin Jack, producing his pocket-scales and tape measure. **1886** *Outing* May 161/2 Out pocket-scales now! Is it a three or four or five-pound trout? — **(18) 1884** LABOR *Cyclo. Polit. Science* III. 1065/2 This potent executive weapon, angrily called a 'pocket veto' at the time, was first employed by Jackson at the close of the summer of 1829–30. **1888** BRYCE *Amer. Commonw.* I. I. vi. 74 (*footnote*), If Congress adjourns within the ten days allowed the President for returning the bill, it is lost. His retaining it under these circumstances at the end of a session is popularly called a 'pocket veto.' **1949** *N.Y. Times Bk. Rev.* 5 June 27/1 The natural clearance of action with various interested agencies may include the right of pocket veto.

As the last term in **breast, hip, log, overall, pistol, saddle, shoe, way pocket(s).** For *pocket full of rocks,* see ***rock,** *n.*

*pocket, *v.*

1. *Polit. tr.* Of the President or a state governor: To defeat (a bill) passed in the closing days of a legislative session by retaining it unsigned. Also *to pocket veto.* Cf. **pocket veto.**

1848 *Cong. Globe* 24 Jan. 225/1 This House saw a President of the United States very coolly pocket a bill. **1927** T. C. PEASE *U.S.* 471 The measure passed House and Senate, but Lincoln pocketed it. **1948** *Sierra Club Bul.* Feb. 12/1 In 1944, H.R. 2241, introduced by Congressman Barrett, was passed by both houses but was pocket-vetoed by the President.

2. *Mining. intr.* Of a vein of ore: To spread out or expand into a pocket.

1873 BEADLE *Undevel. West* 336 A vein . . . 'pinching' and 'pocketing' alternately towards the interior. **1883** ——— *Western Wilds* 563 [The vein] may 'pocket' suddenly in a chamber the size of a keg, barrel or hogshead.

3. To become puckered or bagged. *Rare.*

1873 A. D. WHITNEY *Other Girls* xxv, That carpet . . . hadn't begun to pocket yet.

4. *tr.* To supply (a book) with a pocket for holding library cards. Cf. ***pocket,** *n.* **4.**

1887 *Library Notes* March 282 Among the things 'to be done' to each book [is] 'pocketing.' . . . The Acme Pocket . . . is made of strong manila, cut with a peculiar die so that the cards can be put in and taken out with the greatest rapidity, and yet are firmly held.

*pocketbook, *n.*

1. A purse.

1816 *Niles' Reg.* X. 216/1 Two methodist preachers were lately robbed of their pocket-books, containing very considerable sums in bank notes. **1925** BRYAN *Memoirs* 44 Noticing father's pocketbook upon the bureau, it occurred to some one of us . . . to count the money. **1949** *Chi. D. News* 10 May 1/3 Police found $269 in cash in old pocketbooks distributed about the scrupulously clean house.

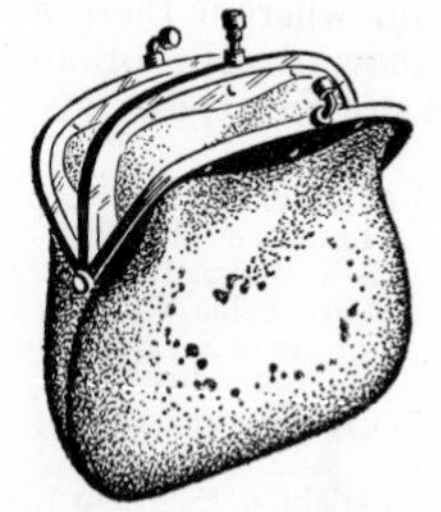

One form of pocketbook

transf. **1885** *La Cuisine Creole* 134 When it [the dough] is risen it is ready to form into shapes, called pocket-books.

fig. and *attrib.* **1894** H. H. FURNESS *Address* 4 Our ideal Provost must know the exact location in every rich man's body of the pocket-book nerve. **1924** BEARD *American Govt.* 258 The laws go deep into the pocketbooks of citizens. **1947** *Time* 15 Sep. 87/3 The New Look could be acquired with comparatively little pain to either torsos or pocketbooks.

2. pocketbook drop, dropper, a means of swindling; a thief who drops a pocketbook containing counterfeit money as a lure.

1845 *N.Y. Herald* 7 May 2/2 The writer in the American Review . . . enumerates the potential agencies to which . . . Mr. Polk owes his election [as] . . . 'pocket-book droppers,' 'brothel-owners and bullies' [etc.]. **1892** WALSH *Lit. Curiosities* 457 Originally the word ['heeler'] had no political significance, but was applied to an accomplice of the pocket-book dropper. **1896** HASWELL *New York* 446 In a file of an old newspaper, I noticed the case of one having been duped by a swindle at that time [*c*1847] and for some years after known as the 'pocket-book drop,' then a favorite trick.

pockety ˈpɑkɪtɪ, *a.* **1.** Of an ore vein: Characterized by pockets. **2.** Of the nature of a secluded hollow.

(1) 1870 RAYMOND *3d Rep. Mines* 220 The mineral veins found in the lime formations are '*pockety*' and of uncertain development. **1942** LILLARD *Desert Challenge* 180 Men digging an outdoor toilet in Tonopah uncovered a 'pockety pay shoot' of rich ore. — **(2) 1893** *Columbus* (O.) *Dispatch* 18 May, A tiny, pockety vale whose surface is almost level on either side to the edge of noble bluffs.

poco ˈpoko, *n.* and *adv.* [See note.]

1. *n.* An old clothes-man. *Student slang. Obs.*

Webster derives this from Italian and Spanish *poco*, little, not much. In sense **1.** it may be a fanciful contraction of "poor clothes-man." In sense **2.** it is clearly from the Sp.

1876 G. H. TRIPP *Student-Life* 287 Everybody knew it in a few hours,—professors and tutors . . . the 'goodies' and 'pocos.' **1881** W. H. HILLS *Students' Songs* (1885) 33 A poco lived on Brighton Street.

2. *a.* and *adv. W.* (See quot. 1932.)

1846–7 MAGOFFIN *Down Santa Fe Trail* (1926) 81 Accompanied by Jane who rather doubted my ability to ascend at first, . . . it was poco poco, and when I had gotten to a great rock [etc.]. **1888** *Outing* Oct. 67/2 The trip to the Fort might wait. *Mañana. Poco tiempo.* After a while. **1932** BENTLEY *Sp. Terms* 184 *Poco* is often used in connection with such words as *tiempo, malo* or *frio.* It is commonly used by Americans in the border territory.

pocosin pəˈkosn̩, *n.* Also **pocoson, pocosen, poquoson,** etc. ["The name is from Renape *pákwesen*, a verbal adjective meaning 'it (the land) is in a slightly watered condition'" (Hodge).] An area of low ground or swamp, miry in summer, and covered with shallow water in winter. Cf. **black, blind pocosin.**

See *Amer. Anthropologist* Jan. 1899, ns. I. 162–70, and *Reader's Digest* Feb. 1934, 6 ff., for discussions of this word and the places designated by it. See also R. M. Harper in *Bul. Torrey Bot. Club* 41 (1914) 209–20.

1643 in *Amer. Sp.* XV. 296 Nigh unto a reedy Swampe or Poquoson. **1713** *N.C. Col. Rec.* II. 69 John Burkett took up and surveyed . . . a certaine parcell of Land . . . beginning at a Gume by ye side of a great Swamp . . . [running] to ye pocosson [etc.]. **1893** *Outing* Jan. 271/1 The drive is one of the large pocosons so common in the lower pine country. **1944** *Sat. Ev. Post* 9 Sep. 13/1 The Indians called these queer round swamps pocosins. The white hunters and woodsmen, differentiating them sharply from the more typical swamps of irregular shape along the creeks and rivers, called them bays, . . . perhaps because the bay tree or shrub abounds in them.

attrib. **1691** in *Amer. Sp.* XV. 296/2 To a small red oake by ye side of ye said pocoson swamp. **1720** *Ib.*, So Down ye Pocoson branch to William Evans his line. **1811** *Mass. Spy* 23 Jan. (Th.), A considerable extent of that kind of flat, wet pine lands, which is known in N. Carolina by the name of poccooson lands. **1883** SMITH *Geol. Survey Ala.* 522 East of Troy, . . . in the 'Pocoson' region, the valleys, which have the luxuriant growth and appearance of swamps, are surrounded on three sides by ridges of snow-white sand. **1949** *Highway Traveler* Feb. 33/1 First blossoms appear in January in the coastal pocosin country with flowering of camellias and azaleas at Orton and Airlie Gardens.

b. In proper names.

1631 in *Amer. Sp.* XV. 296/2 A river called the Pocoson river. **1763** WASHINGTON *Writings* I. 194 From Suffolk to Pocoson Swamp is reckoned about 6 miles. **1836** W. B. ROGERS *Rep. Geol. Reconnoissance Va.* 23 At Pocosin, a flat swampy country, which is often inundated by the tides, this deposite is uniformly met with by digging a few feet below the surface.

* **pod,** *n.* [See note.]

Sense **1.** has been explained as showing an extension in use of "pod" meaning a seed vessel of a long form, from the practice of certain birds, whales, seals, etc., of following each other in line suggesting peas in a pod. See S. B. Liljegren in *Anglia Beibl.* XXXI. (1920) 67–9. The *OED* has later British evidence for the term. Sense **2.** may be of a different word, but the article above cited mentions "pod team" as one in which the draft animals work tandem. But cf. *EDD* "pod" meaning the body of a cart. In **3.** "pod" appears to be from various sources.

1. A flock of birds, a small herd or school of whales or seals.

1832 D. WEBSTER *Private Corr.* I. 526 We saw several small pods of coots go by. **1851** MELVILLE *Moby Dick* 487 Well, one day we lowered for a pod of four or five whales. **1949** *Chi. D. News* 12 Nov. (Comics) 4/3 A pod of seals scramble from the Arctic Sea onto a shelf of ice.

2. (See quot. and cf. **pod sleigh.**)

1915 DUNBAR *Hist. Travel in Amer.* I. 49 American colonial sleds were generally called either pungs or pods, though the Canadian cariole was also used.

3. In combs.: (1) **pod auger,** see as a main entry; (2) **man,** one accustomed to "pod" seals, i.e., to drive them into a "pod" or bunch for the purpose of clubbing them; (3) **sleigh,** (see quot. and cf. **2.** above), *colloq.;* (4) **team,** (see note above), also, app. by confusion, **pog team.**

(2) 1842 *Spirit of Times* (Phila.) 6 July (Th.), The ruffians—fishermen, oystermen, and 'podmen' who fought at Gloucester Point. — **(3) 1942** RAWSON *N.H. Borns a Town* 227 Many a long pod sleigh went ringing along to the jingle of its sleighbells, well laden with frozen hides and hogs or whatever the farm or mill or shop had to send 'off.' — **(4) 1853** *Turnover* 36 (Th.), You see Hookem wanted to hire Zeb's horse to put into a pod team with the Marston's sorrel. **1932** *Old Times N. Eng.* Jan. 140/2 The Wilson Tavern . . . was a stopping place for the market wagons or 'pog teams' that were passing through from towns further north.

As the last term in **fringe, milkweed, rattle, sickle pod.**

pod auger. An auger having an almost straight channel or groove, so called from the resemblance of its tapered boring cylinder to a seed pod.

Pod auger

1833 *Niles' Reg.* XLIV. 403/1 The new twist gimblet is almost as much superior to the old English gimblet, as the screw auger is to the old pod auger. *c*1887 in *Amer. Sp.* (1948) April 114/2 Before 1800 almost all of the boring was done with Pod augurs. **1947** *Newsweek* 16 June 55/2 In 1849, a new syndicate, using a pod auger (like an oil drill), brought up three gold links . . . from a hard object struck at 108 feet.

transf. and *attrib.* **1878** *Cong. Rec.* 15 Feb. 1123/1 A law has been worked through—and I say 'worked through' in the highest pod-auger sense that you can express by it. *c***1887** in *Amer. Sp.* (1948) April 114/2 Old times before the invention of machinery are sometimes referred to as 'Pod Augur' days.

Podunk ˈpodʌŋk, *n.* [f. Mohegan or Mass. dial. of Algonquian, app. meaning "a neck or corner of land." See quot. 1910 in **2.** below.]

1. Orig. an Indian place-name used in Connecticut and Massachusetts (see quots.), later applied in derision to any small or insignificant place. Also attrib.

1666 *Doc. Col. Hist. N.Y.* III. 121 Yesterday there was a party of the Mowhawkes at Podunck (a place between this town [Hartford, Conn.] and Windsor.) **1793** P. WHITNEY *County of Worcester, Mass.* 77 There is one large pond . . . called by the Indians Quaboag Pond; but now more generally denominated Podunk Pond, from a tract of meadow adjoining, which the Indians call Podunk. **1841** *N.O. Picayune* 15 Jan. 4/1, I was born'd and got my brot't'n up in that ere house; but my native place is down in Podunk. **1865** NORTON *Army Lett.* 277, I presume that just about this time of day you are sitting in one of the slips in that 'Podunk' or 'Chachunk' (what do you call it?) 'meetin' house.' **1901** *Harper's Wkly.* 7 Sep., He might just as well have been John Smith of Podunk Centre. **1949** *Democrat* 13 Jan. 2/4 Residents of Podunk [Mass.] have determined to let the world know that there really is such a community.

2. *pl.* or *collect.* (See quot. 1910.)

1842 STONE *Uncas & Miantonomoh* 31 The Podunks resided upon the lands now comprised in the town of East Hartford. **1859** *N.Y. Wkly. Tribune* 8 Oct. 3/1 The Numkatunks, Quinnipiacs, Podunks, and Quinnebogs, were present from New-Haven and vicinity. **1910** HODGE *Amer. Indians* II. 271/1 Podunk. A band or small tribe on Podunk r., in Hartford co., Conn., closely related to the Poquonnoc. Their principal village, also called Podunk, was at the mouth of that river. **1935** *Col. of Conn.* 1 A few years previously in 1631 the chief of one of the Indian tribes in the Connecticut Valley, the Podunks, had journeyed to the Massachusetts and Plymouth Colonies to invite them to see the fertile Connecticut Valley.

podunker 'podʌŋkɚ, *n.* [Echoic.] A frog. *Rare.* — **1857** HAMMOND *No. Scenes* 30 There, hear that venerable podunker off to the right, with his deep bass.

poffertje pə'fertjə, *n.* [Du. in same sense.] A small, light puffcake. Also attrib. *Obs.* — **1890** *Cent. Mag.* Nov. 49 Beside her . . . sat Jan Wisenkerke watching a buxom darky in a scarlet turban frying poffertjes. *Ib.*, The kitchen walls were covered with . . . waffle-irons, poffertje pans.

pogamoggan ˌpɑgə'mɑgən, *n.* (See quots. 1805 and 1910.)

1805 LEWIS in *L. & Clark Exped.* III. (1905) 20 The Poggâmoggon is an instrument with a handle of wood covered with dressed leather about the size of a whip handle and 22 inches long; a round stone of 2 pounds weight is also covered with leather and strongly united to the leather of the handle by a throng of 2 inches long; a loop of leather united to the handle passes arond the wrist. a very heavy blow may be given with this instrument. **1885** ONDERDONK *Idaho* 136 Their characteristic weapon is the *poggamoggan.* **1893** *Outing* Oct. 10/1 Originally, no doubt, each action meant something, as the stealthy approach, . . . the hurling of the tomahawk or pogamoggan, and so on. **1910** HODGE *Amer. Indians* III. 271/2 Pogamoggan. A club, cudgel, war-club: from Chippewa *pägämâgan* or *pûgûmagan* (according to dialect), meaning, literally, '(what is) used for striking.'

pogonip 'pɑgəˌnɪp, *n. W.* [A Shoshonean term, said to mean "white death."] A heavy fog in which fine particles of snow seem to be flying, occurring in mountain country, esp. in Nevada, in winter, and obscuring the sun, sometimes for days.

1865 STUART *Montana as It Is* 29 [Snake Indian words] Fog—Pagin-up. **1879** HART *Sazerac Lying Club* 16 He observed what he at first supposed to be a huge bank of dark clouds descend over the valley . . . a phenomenon . . . termed by the Shoshone Indians 'Pogonip.' **1931** *Durant* (Okla.) *D. Democrat* 11 March 2/5 The United States Weather Bureau is going to make an investigation of 'pogonip,' that mysterious and dreaded frosted fog that Nevada Indians fear so much. **1949** *Exciting Western* May 71/2 The snow was very thin along that trail, and under it was the ice of the pogonip.

transf. **1870** *Terr. Enterprise* (Virginia, Nev.) 14 Sep. 3/1 They all want to . . . see . . . the elephant, the tiger, the whangdoodle, the pogonip and the roaring cowmunga.

b. In full **pogonip fog.**

1892 *Scientific Amer.* LXVI. 240/3 The pogonip fog is peculiar to elevated altitudes in the Nevada Sierras. **1949** *Exciting Western* May 70/1 Had Stiber ever come through a *pogonip* fog in this country?

pogy 'pogɪ, *n.* [Origin obscure. Poss. a contraction of Algonquian *pauhaugen*, or a variant of paugie or porgy *qq.v.*]

1. The menhaden (see also quot. 1884).

1858 *Maine Agric. Rep.* II. 69 The fish known as menhaden, and often called along shore 'hard-heads' and 'poggies,' . . . after being boiled, are pressed . . . to extract an oil. **1884** GOODE *Fisheries* I. 276 On the coast of Oregon the large species [of the surf-fish family] (especially *Damalichthys argyrosomus*) are called 'Pogy' or 'Porgee,' in allusion to their undoubted resemblance to the scup or porgee of the East. *Ib.* 386 In New England it [*Stenotomus versicolor*] is generally called 'Scup,' while about New York the second syllable of the abbreviated Indian name has been lengthened into 'Paugy' or 'Porgy.' . . . Another Indian word, 'poghaden,' a corrupted form of the Abnaki name for the menhaden, . . . has been changed to 'pogy' and 'porgy,' thus leading to much confusion. *Ib.* 445 At Beaufort, North Carolina, . . . [the moonfish] is called the 'Porgee' or 'Pogy.' **1913** LONDON *Valley of Moon* 235 An' we used to go out on the Rock Wall an' catch pogies an' rock cod.

attrib. **1880** *Harper's Mag.* Aug. 347/1 The 'pogy' business was the catching of porgies and menhaden for their oil. *Ib.* 349/1 Broken yawls and dories, spars, a cast-off 'pogy'-press, unhooped tubs and barrels—had been piled upon an old wharf. **1914** W. D. STEELE *Storm* 247 The po'gie-men got one up to St. Peters.

b. (See quot.) *Obs.*

1840 *Niles' Reg.* 15 Aug. 376/3 Chebacco boats and small schooners are known to him [the Bay of Fundy fisherman] as 'pinkies,' 'pogics' [*sic*], and 'jiggers.'

2. pogy chum, = **chum,** *n.* **2.**

1858 *Maine Agric. Rep. 1857* 69 What remains after extracting the oil, is called 'poggy chum,' and sells at twenty cents per barrel. **1864** *Ann. Rep. Agric. Maine* 42 About all I know of marine manures is this: Rock weed, muscle bed and pogy chum will make grass grow.

pohano po'hɑno, *n.* (See quot.) *Rare.* — **1672** JOSSELYN *N. Eng. Rarities* 20 The Maccarib, Caribo, or Pohano, [is] a kind of Deer, as big as a Stag, round hooved.

poigan 'pɔɪgən, *n.* [?f. an Indian word.] App. some form of Indian dance. *Obs.* or *rare.* — **1807** *Staunton* (Va.) *Eagle* 28 Aug. 2/3 You are no more to dance the *Wabano*, nor the *Poigan*, or *pipe dance.* **1809** KENDALL *Travels* II. 293 The *poigan, poagan,* pipe or calumet-dance is a dance introduced from among Indians of the south.

Poinsettia pɔɪn'sɛtɪə, *n.* [Joel R. *Poinsett* (1779–1851), Amer. minister to Mexico where he discovered the plant in 1828.] A genus of tropical, alternate-leaved plants of the spurge family; (not *cap.*) a plant of this genus.

1836 in *New Philos. Jrnl.* (Edinburgh) April 412 Poinsettia pulcherrima. . . . By whom this truly splendid plant was communicated to Willdenow's Herbarium, I am not informed, but it was again discovered by Mr. Poinsette in Mexico, and sent by him to Charleston in 1828, and afterward to Mr. Buist of Philadelphia. **1868** GRAY *Field Botany* 294 *Euphorbia pulcherrima*, or Poinsettia, of Mexico. **1948** *Home Helper* (Oak Park, Ill.) Dec. 18/3 The poinsettia is a sensitive plant which will drop its leaves when conditions of soil moisture or temperature displease it.

* **point,** *n.*[1]

1. The tapering end of a forest or woodland that reaches down into a prairie or surrounding treeless country.

1637 in *Amer. Sp.* XV. 297/2 Easterly butting out with a point of wood. **1683** *Oyster Bay Rec.* I. 174 A sartaine neck or poynt of wood land. **1741** *Ga. Hist. Soc. Coll.* II. 252 A point of woods . . . stretches itself out towards the south-east. **1836** J. HALL *Statistics of West* 83 The forest has pushed long capes or points into the prairie.

b. Esp. *point of timber.*

1831 M. A. HOLLEY *Texas* (1833) vi. 62 The intervening country is clothed with a thick and luxuriant growth of grass . . . with occasional points and islands of timber, as the wooded projections and scattered clumps of trees are called. **1856** CARTWRIGHT *Autobiog.* 328 We rode two miles, and the point of timber was plain in view.

2. A lightning rod, or one of the tapering projections on this. *Obs.*

1766 *Essex. Inst. Coll.* LII. 275 A new Meeting-House building . . . was struck with Lightning; it had Points and a Conductor as far as the Bellfree. **1870** MARK TWAIN *Sk. New & Old* 22, I told him to put up eight 'points,' and put them all on the roof, and use the best quality of rod.

3. A short black strip woven into a Mackinaw blanket to indicate its weight or size. Cf. **point blanket.**

In an advertising brochure issued by the manufacturers of these blankets in 1943 the following occurs: " 'Points' were originally distinctive marks woven in the blanket by the makers to designate size. A letter of 1780 from the Company's Governor at Albany Fort, Hudson Bay, stated that 'the points are known to every Indian as the price paid for the blanket, as 2 points, 2 beaver, 3 points, 3 beaver,' etc."

1818 MCKENNEY *Memoirs* I. 309 Northwest Company blankets—so called—three points, to measure six feet six inches long. **1921** *Outing* Nov. 82/1 Hudson Bay blankets run as follows: Three point, 60×72 inches, double, weight, 8¼ lbs.; 3½ point, 63×81 inches, double, weight, 10 lbs.; 4 point, 72×90 inches, double, weight, 12 lbs. 'Points' refer to the markings on the blankets and indicate their size. **1947** *Sports Afield* Dec. 86/1 Back in 1779 the number of 'Points' on a Hudson's Bay Blanket indicated the number of beaver skins it was worth.

4. (*cap.*) Short for "West Point" *q.v.*

1828 COOPER *Notions* I. 274 To these relics of a former age, must be added the actual and flourishing establishment at the 'Point,' which comprises a village of academic buildings, barracks, and other adjuncts. **1922** *Frontier* Nov. 14 Ada's father had been C.O. when we were in the Point, and nearly every member of the class had been at one time or another in love with her.

5. *Baseball.* (See quot. 1868.) Hence *in the points*, in excellent form. *Obs.*

1867 *Chi. Times* 25 July 5/3 He throws to the bases with accuracy and plays well all the points belonging to a pitcher. **1868** CHADWICK *Base Ball* 13 An attentive study of the rules of the game, and of those special applications of them known as 'points.' **1917** MATHEW-

SON *Sec. Base Sloan* 126 He never failed of a hit save when Pattern was in the points.

6. *Stock market.* A theory, rumor, or fact upon which a speculation may be based. Hence the phrase *to deal on points.*

1870 MEDBERY *Men Wall St.* 83 The first element in speculation is the 'point.' If the operator has a good 'point,' he has a 'sure thing.' **1870** M. H. SMITH *20 Yrs. Wall St.* 556 These rumors are called points, and men who buy and sell, in consequence of them, are said to 'deal on points.' **1875** DALY *Big Bonanza* (1884) 21 When a man gives another man a point, sir, why he naturally expects [some money]. **1892** WALSH *Lit. Curiosities* 910.

b. A hint, tip, or pointer. *Colloq.*

1877 HARTE *Story of Mine* (1896) 324 One of those officials come up to this yer ranch . . . to get points about diamond-making. **1892** *Nation* 6 Oct. 263/2 A clever young man easily makes the mistake of supposing that he could have given Solomon points about women.

7. In some educational institutions, a unit of academic credit.

1903 *N.Y. Times* 29 Aug., For university credit, each 30 hours course counts one point, and laboratory work at the rate of 60 hours to one point.

8. A locality or place.

1903 *N.Y. Ev. Post* 19 Aug., The number here is now estimated at 21,000 persons from Eastern points, with fully 35,000 persons in addition from California. **1926** *Publishers' Wkly.* 18 Dec. 2256 The business must be going to distant points—New York, Chicago, etc.

9. *W.* The head or van of a herd. Cf. **10. b.** (2) below.

*a***1918** G. STUART *On Frontier* (1925) 189 The horse herd and mess wagon pulled out and then the herd started, with two cowpunchers in the lead or 'point.' **1949** *10 Story Western* May 38/2 They had reached the point of the herd, and the horse was trying to bend them!

10. In combs.: (1) **point blanket,** a blanket having "points" (see **3.** above) woven into it, also **half point blanket;** (2) **-ender,** a member of a political faction in the Democratic party in N.Y. *c*1840, *obs.;* (3) **flow,** (see quots.), *obs.;* (4) **man,** *W.* (see quot. 1903); (5) **-no-point,** something that seems to have a point, but really has none, also attrib.; (6) **shooting,** ?shooting from a particular place or point, *obs.*

(1) **1797** HAWKINS *Letters* 347, 2 2½ point blankets, $2.25 . . . $4.50. **1822** MORSE *Rep. Indian Affairs* I. 55 A half point blanket is sold for four skins. **1947** DEVOTO *Across Wide Missouri* 32 The Company is sending . . . thirty-five pairs of one-point Mackinaw blankets.— (2) **1840** *Nat. Intelligencer* 7 April 1/2 Already the Locofocos have got out their banners and procession, and 'the Butt-enders' and 'Point-enders' are marching at night through our streets. — (3) **1856** OLMSTED *Slave States* 473 The subsequent culture [of rice] is the same as I have described, after the second or 'point' flow, in the first plan. **1859** *Harper's Mag.* Nov. 727/2 The ground [is] kept dry until the young plants appear. . . . At this period the water is a second time spread over the field in what is called the point flow. — (4) **1903** A. ADAMS *Log of Cowboy* 28 Two riders, known as point men, rode out and well back from the lead cattle, and by riding forward and closing in as occasion required, directed the course of the herd. **1939** ROLLINS *Gone Haywire* 166 The foremost man in each file was a so-called point man or point rider.

(5) **1869** *Cong. Globe* 1 April 432/3 It may be . . . that we decline to accept the 'point-no-point' policy of the party whom the gentleman from New York [Mr. Wood] in part represents here. **1878** *Cong. Rec.* 17 April 2606/1 The resolution is . . . mere *brutum fulmen.* It sails for point-no-point, and it reaches no point. — (6) **1874** LONG *Wild-Fowl* 71 For point-shooting, shooting from a blind on shore, or in the edge of the willows from a boat, a few hints may be welcome. **1876** *Fur, Fin & Feather* Sep. 90/2 Towards noon we prepared to move out into the clear water onto a bog, there get some point shooting.

b. In phrases: (1) *point of fork(s),* the place at which two streams flow together, *obs.;* (2) *to ride (at) point, W.* (see quot. 1941 and cf. **9.** above).

(1) **1784** WASHINGTON *Diaries* II. 302 The Line which divides the Commonwealths of Virginia and Pensylvania crosses both these Rivers about two miles up each from the point of fork. **1789** ANBUREY *Travels* II. 405, I was detained . . . on account of the overflowing of the river, at what is termed the Point of Forks, where James River divides. — (2) **1916** BOWER *Phantom Herd* 245 You see a herd drifting before a storm, . . . with your pal riding point. **1941** FERGUSSON *Southwest* 32 Experienced men rode 'at point' to direct the lead steers and to set the pace.

For other phrases see under **1. b, 5.** and **6.** above.

As the last term in **bird, blue, division, five, Folsom, New York, outfitting, pitcher's, plow, shipping, trading, way point.** See also **West Point.**

point pɔɪnt, *n.*[2] [f. Voyageur F. *pointe,* in same sense.] (See quots. 1941, 1947.) Now *hist.*

1808 PIKE *Sources Miss.* 58 We made twenty eight points in the river; broad, good bottom, and of the usual timber. [**1941** McDERMOTT *Glossary* 123 pointe, n. f. . . . This curious word is obviously a contribution of the *voyageur* who measured distance on the river by the bends of the stream as indicated by the points or arms protruding, but it was used apparently for *wooded* points only.] **1947** *St. Louis Globe-Democrat* 26 Jan., The important Eleven Points River in Oregon County has an old name that has aroused much speculation but little certainty. . . . The real explanation, I believe, lies in a special meaning that once attached to the French word 'pointe,' used by the old voyageurs in measuring distance by the bends in a river.

b. *points and bends,* (see quots.).

1826 FLINT *Recoll.* 258 It is the entire uniformity of the meanders of the rivers, called in the phrase of the country, 'points and bends.' **1850** HOUSTOUN *Hesperos* II. 47 The uniformity of the 'points and bends,' as they are called in the country [along the Mississippi], is very remarkable. The deepest channel is *in* the 'bend,' and also the strongest force of the current.

***point,** *v.* **1.** *intr.* To direct one's course, to set out in an indicated direction. *Colloq.* **2.** *W. tr.* To cause the head of a herd to turn in a desired direction.

(1) 1876 MARK TWAIN *Tom Sawyer* 89 (R.), Now they're stuck. Can't find it. Here they come again. Now they're hot. Cold again. Hot again. Red hot! They're p'inted right, this time. **1889** —— *Conn. Yankee* 264 (R.), 'I am but now come from the Valley of Holiness, please you sir.' 'I am pointed for that place myself.' — (2) **1903** ADAMS *Log Cowboy* 43 Priest sent Officer to the left and myself to the right, to point in the leaders. **1947** PRICE *Trails I Rode* 184 One time we were pointing a herd, Bill on one side and I on the other.

Pointed Hearts. The Coeur d'Alêne Indians of northern Idaho. *Obs.* Cf. **Coeur d'Alêne.** — **1831** COX *Adv. on Columbia R.* II. 150 The Pointed Hearts, or as the Canadians call them, Hearts of Awls, are a small tribe inhabiting the shores of a lake 50 miles east of Spokane House. **1849** [see **Coeur d'Alêne**].

***pointer,** *n.*

1. A sign indicating a trail or road. *Obs.*

1793 BENTLEY *Diary* II. 48 There is a pointer in the Road to direct the passenger to the right in the way to Dartmouth College. **1816** U. BROWN *Journal* II. 233 There was an old rotten tree Laying there with pointers marked by some person or other.

2. An inferior hog of a poor or worthless breed, prob. so called from its long, pointed snout. *Obs.*

1852 *Mich. Agric. Soc. Trans.* III. 184 One good grade sow, and two pointers. **1868** *Iowa State Agric. Soc. Rep. 1867* 423 A few pointers who never die, or cease to breed, can be found.

3. An ox that works at the head of a team. *Rare.*

1866 in *Neb. Hist. Mag.* XIII. (1932) 149 After awhile I get my last pointer yoked, drive the whole team around and hitch it on the wagon tongue, and am ready to pull out.

4. *W.* =**point man.**

1869 *Overland Mo.* III. 126 On the march the mighty herd sometimes strings out miles in length, and then it has 'pointers,' who ride abreast of the head of the column. **1908** *Pacific Mo.* March 324/2 The pointer is the herdsman who rides at the head of a straggling herd of cattle on the march, a sort of Cowboy John the Baptist. **1943** L. V. HAMNER *Short Grass* 50 Two men, his best, were put near the front of the line . . . these were the pointers.

5. In the navy, a gun pointer.

1904 *Scientific Amer.* 18 June 475 The turrets are trained by one man, the trainer; and each gun is pointed by another man, the pointer, who fires the gun.

As the last term in **blue, Five, West Pointer.**

***pointing,** *n.* The action of putting a point on a plowshare. *Colloq.* — **1760** WASHINGTON *Diaries* I. 148 Cook Jack . . . went to plowing in the 12 Acre Field, . . . as did the other plow, abt. 5 oclock after Pointing. **1822** *Murphey P.* I. 278 The Farmers calculate upon making Crops with the same ploughs, without Pointing.

***poison,** *n., a.,* and *adv.*

1. *n.* Strong alcoholic drink. *Jocular.*

1805 RED JACKET in *Freemason's Mag.* (Phila.) II. 388 We gave them corn and meat; they gave us poison in return. [note:] Alluding it is supposed to ardent spirits. **1876** MILLER *First Fam'lies* 128 A true Californian of Sierras . . . heads straight up to the bar, . . . hoists his Poison, throws back his head, and then falls back wiping his mouth. **1886** *Chi. Graphic News* 10 April 83/3 He can now imbibe his favored 'poison' in many situations where it were otherwise unseemly.

attrib. **1877** *Billings' Farmer's Allminax* 15 Desaitful, and dang'rous kritter, . . . And besides a pizon hitter. **1883** MARK TWAIN *Life on Miss.* xxii, The multitudes of poison-swilling Irishmen had departed.

1907 WHITE *Arizona Nights* 136, I went with him to his little old poison factory [i.e., saloon].

b. In jocular or slang phrases: *Name* (or *nominate*) *your poison*, indicate what drink you would like.

1876 *Carson Valley News* (Genoa, Nev.) 2 June 2/2 Nominate your poison, gents; it's my treat. 1949 *L.A. Times* 3 April 25/2 Step up, gents, and name your poison.

2. *adv.* Very, extremely. *Slang.*

1840 HOFFMAN *Greyslaer* I. 61 The night was pison cold, I tell ye. 1884 MARK TWAIN *H. Finn* xxvii, The funeral sermon was very good, but pison long and tiresome. 1894 ——— *P. Wilson* xiv, You's got to be pison good, en let him see it.

3. In combs.: (1) **poison arrow,** an arrow that has poison on its point; (2) **ash,** any one of various plants of the genus *Toxicodendron*, as poison ivy, poison sumac *qq.v.;* (3) ∗**berry,** the sheep laurel, *Kalmia angustifolia*, or the China tree; (4) **berry tree,** (see quot.); (5) **camass,** the death camass of the western states; (6) **darnel,** the bearded darnel, *Lolium temulentum*, an annual grass; (7) **dogwood,** =**poison sumac;** (8) **elder,** =**poison sumac;** (9) **field,** =**poisoned field,** *obs.;* (10) **flag,** (see quot. 1909); (11) **hemlock,** the common hemlock, *Conium maculatum;* (12) **ivy,** see as a main entry; (13) **oak,** =**poison sumac,** also any bushlike poison ivy, esp. the species of the Pacific Coast and the Southeast; (14) **sumac,** a swamp-growing American sumac, *Toxicodendron vernix*, syn. *Rhus vernix*, *R. venenata*, poisonous to the touch, having pinnate leaves and greenish-white berries; (15) ∗**tree,** =prec.; (16) **vine,** =**poison ivy,** esp. *Toxicodendron radicans*, cf. **cow poison vine;** (17) **wood,** (*a*) =**poison sumac,** also attrib., (*b*) the bumwood, *Metopium linnaei*, of southern Florida, (*c*) the crabwood, *Gymnanthes lucida.*

(1) 1872 MCCLELLAN *Golden State* 605 In such dread do the people hold the poison-arrow, scalping-knife, and tomahawk of these 'red devils.' — (2) 1763 W. LEWIS *Comm. Phil.-Technicum* 330 Mr. Catesby, in his history of Carolina, describes one, called there the poison-ash. 1855 DAVIS *Farm Bk.* 141 Sunday a warm day—I was laid by handling the poison ash. 1949 PALMER *Fieldbook Nat. Hist.* 250/3 Poison sumac is also known as thunderwood, poisonwood, swamp dogwood, poison dogwood, poison ash, poison tree, poison elder, and swamp sumac. — (3) 1672 JOSSELYN *N. Eng. Rarities* 49 Spurge Lawrel, called here Poyson berry, it kills the English Cattle if they chance to feed upon it, expecially Calves. — (4) 1803 J. DAVIS *Travels* 79 The mocking-bird . . . was warbling, close to my window, from a tree called by some the Pride of India, and by others the Poison-berry Tree.

(5) 1940 SMITH *Puyallup-Nisqually* 91 The bulbs of the poison kamas, which looks like the ordinary kamas but has yellow flowers, were eaten raw when they first began to sprout. — (6) 1889 VASEY *Agric. Grasses* 75 Lolium temulentum (Poison Darnel). . . . The seeds have long enjoyed a reputation of being poisonous to stock, and also to mankind when mixed in large quantity with the wheat or rye used in the making of bread. 1901 MOHR *Plant Life Ala.* 388 Poison Darnel. . . . Introduced with grain and sparingly naturalized in . . . Oregon, California, and Eastern United States. — (7) 1814 BIGELOW *Florula Bostoniensis* 72 *Rhus vernix.* Poison dogwood. Swamp Sumach. . . . Grows in bunches in wet swamps. — (8) 1817–8 EATON *Botany* (1822) 428 *Rhus vernix*, poison sumach, poison elder . . . Berries green, at length whitish. . . . Very poisonous. . . . Damp. 1949 [see **poison ash**]. — (9) 1694 in *Amer. Sp.* XV. 298/1 To a black oak in a poyson field. 1728 *Ib.*, To two red oaks in a poyson old field. 1757 in *Amer. Sp.* XV. 298/1 By a red oak saplin in a poyson field on a level.

(10) 1840 DEWEY *Mass. Flowering Plants* 194 *Iris versicolor.* Blue or Poison Flag. Common on wet grounds, and about sluggish water. 1909 WEBSTER 1665 *Poison flag*, any of several blue-flowered American irises, as *I. versicolor.* — (11) 1817–8 EATON *Botany* (1822) 247 *Conium maculatum*, poison hemlock. Stem very branching. 1931 CLUTE *Plants* 116. — (13) 1743 CLAYTON *Flora Virginica* 33 *Rhus*, . . . Poison-Oak. 1869 MUIR *First Summer in Sierra* (1911) 34 Poison oak or poison ivy (*Rhus diversiloba*), both as a bush and a scrambler up trees and rocks, is common throughout the foothill region. 1949 *L.A. Times* 26 May 2/2 The girl's shoes were found in the steep arroyo bank in a clump of poison oak. — (14) 1820 GILLELAND *Ohio* R. *pumilum* (poison sumach). 1949 [see **poison ash**].

(15) 1756 KALM *Resa* II. 211 Poyson-tree, d. ä. det forgifftiga trä, kallades af Ängelsmän och Svänskar en art af *Rhus.* 1785 MARSHALL *Amer. Grove* 130 *Toxicodendron.* The Poison Tree. 1949 [see **poison ash**]. — (16) 1709 LAWSON *Carolina* 101 The Poison Vine is so called, because it colours the Hands of those who handle it. What the Effects of it may be, I cannot relate. 1798 DUNBAR *Life* 97 We have a Vine called the poison vine, from a property it possesses of affecting some persons passing near it, by causing an inflammation of the face resembing an Erysiplas. Other persons may handle this vine with impunity. 1860 CURTIS *Woody Plants N.C.* 118 Poison Vine. (*Rhus radicans.*)—Now considered by Botanists as only a variety of *Poison Oak.* — (17) (*a*) 1721 DUDLEY in *Phil. Trans.* XXXI. 145 The Poyson-Wood-Tree grows only in Swamps, or low wet Grounds, and . . . is by some called the *Swamp Sumach.* 1897 SUDWORTH *Arborescent Flora* 276 *Rhus vernix.* . . . Poisonwood (Tenn.). (*b*) 1884 SARGENT *Rep. Forests* 54 Poison Wood. Coral Sumach. . . . Bum Wood. Hog Plum. 1897 SUDWORTH *Arborescent Flora* 274 *Rhus metopium.* . . . Poisonwoood (Fla.). (*c*) 1884 SARGENT *Rep. Forests* 121 *Sebastiana lucida.* . . . Crab Wood. Poison Wood. 1897 SUDWORTH *Arborescent Flora* 271 *Gymnanthes lucida.* . . . Crabwood (Fla.). Poisonwood (Fla.).

As the last term in **beaver, buckeye, bug, crow, dew, fish, fly, forage, milk, sheep, snake poison.**

∗**poisoned,** *a.* In combs.: (1) **poisoned field,** app. a tract of land the soil of which is regarded as having been rendered sterile and unfit for cultivation, an Indian old field, *obs.*, cf. **poison field;** (2) **oak,** =**poison oak,** *rare;* (3) **stone,** ?=**mad stone,** *rare.*

(1) 1724 JONES *Virginia* 35 The whole Country is a perfect Forest, except where . . . have been formerly Indian Towns, and poisoned Fields and Meadows, where the Timber has been burnt down in Fire-Hunting or otherwise. 1733 in *Amer. Sp.* XV. 298 On the poison'd or Indian Fields lying on both sides the path leading from the fork of James River to Buckingham. 1748 WASHINGTON *Jrnl. of Journey over Mts.* 27 To 2 Red Oaks and W: Oak in a Poyson'd field by a Road. — (2) 1807 in *S. Lit. Messenger* XXIV. 309/1 In vain did a brawny wreath of the poisoned oak . . . grasp the trembling marbles, for the purpose of averting their fall. — (3) 1878 GUILD *Old Times* 50 Every known remedy was applied, including the various snake roots and the poisoned stone.

poison ivy. Any one of several vinelike sumacs, poisonous to the touch, having trifoliate leaves, greenish flowers, and white berries. Also attrib.

[1624 J. SMITH *Virginia* V. 170 The poysoned weed is much in shape like our English Ivy.] 1784 CUTLER *Amer. Acad. Mem.* I. 422 *Hedera.* . . . Poison Ivy. . . . It produces the same kind of inflammations and eruptions . . . as the poison wood tree. 1869 *Rep. Comm. Agric. 1868* 204 The Poison ivy (*Rhus toxicodendron*) is sometimes mistaken for the Virginia creeper, but they can be easily distinguished by the leaf. 1949 *Sat. Ev. Post* 5 March 89/3 Her brother, who was with her, had climbed a tree covered with a poison-ivy vine.

b. (See quot.)

1897 SUDWORTH *Arborescent Flora* 315 *Kalmia latifolia.* . . . Poison Ivy (Tenn , Ala.).

∗**poisonous,** *a.*

1. In the names of plants and trees (see quots.).

1737 BRICKELL *N. Carolina* 95 The Poysonous Vine, so called, by reason it colours the Hands of those that handle it, of a yellowish Colour. 1770 FORSTER tr. Kalm *Travels* I. 68 *Rhus vernix* the poisonous Sumach, in wet places. [Catalog of trees near Phila.] 1846 BROWNE *Trees Amer.* 186 *Rhus venenata*, The Poisonous Rhus. 1847 WOOD *Botany* 620 *L[olium] Temulentum. Poisonous Darnel.* . . . Remarkably distinguished from all other grasses by its poisonous seeds. N. Eng. to Penn. July.

2. poisonous elder, =**poison elder.**

1778 CARVER *Travels* 507 The Alder or *Elder*, termed the poisonous elder, nearly resembles the other sorts in its leaves and branches, but it grows much straiter, and is only found in swamps and moist soils. 1836 EDWARD *Hist. Texas* 66 [He took the names of the shrubs] which he could designate, as . . . the Dwarf Elder, the Poisonous Elder [etc.].

pokahickory ˌpokəˈhɪkərɪ, *n.* Also **pohickory.** [Algonquian *pawcohiccora*, a cluster word designating a food prepared by the Indians from pounded nuts and water.] (See quots.) Cf. **hickory.** — *c*1618 STRACHEY *Virginia* 99 A woman goddesse . . . whoe hath . . . at all tymes ready drest greene vskathomen and pokahickory, (which is greene corne brused and boyled, and walnutts beaten small, then washed). 1896 BRUCE *Econ. Hist. Va.* I. 167 The aborigines gathered a great abundance of hickory nuts, and placing them in mortars into which water had been poured, pounded shell and kernel until a milky liquor, known as pohickory, had been made.

poke pok, *n.*[1] [Var. of **uppowoc.**] The tobacco plant or some other plant used for smoking; the cured leaves of such a plant. *Obs.*

1634 *Rel. Beginnings of Md.* 20 After this, was brought before them a great Bagg, filled with a large Tobacco-pipe and Poake, which is the word they vse for Our *Tobacco.* 1797 *Mass. H.S. Coll.* 1 Ser. V. 57 He then wishing to smoke a pipe, ransacked the island for tobacco; but, finding none, filled his pipe with *poke*, a weed which the Indians sometimes used as its substitute. 1860 TUCKERMAN ed. Josselyn *N.*

Eng. Rarities 191 (*footnote*), The species intended by Josselyn [referred to by him as 'Live-for-ever, a kind of cud-weed'] is our everlasting. . . . The dried herb [was] used by the fishermen instead of tobacco, and no doubt called by them *poke*.

poke pok, *n.*[2] [Virginian *puccoon*, a name used by the Indians for various plants employed in dyeing.]

1. =**pokeweed.** Cf. **Indian poke, Virginia poke,** and see **polk,** *n.*[2] **2.** (2). Cf. **pocan.**

1708 Byrd in *W. & M. Coll. Quart.* 2 Ser. I. 190 We call the plant here [in Virginia] Poke, it bears a purple berry. **1789** *Amer. Philos. Soc.* III. p. xix, *Poke*, has of late given promising experiments in the cure of cancers. **1882** *Cent. Mag.* May 153/2 Mr. Robinson recommends a score or more of American plants as suitable for English woods and hedge-rows. . . . The plants and flowers named are poke, golden-rod [etc.]. **1945** *Chi. Tribune* 13 May vii. 1/3 Opal had found the first tightly curled leaves of poke, the best known of all Ozark greens.

b. The American or swamp hellebore, *Veratrum viride.*

1847 Wood *Botany* 557 *V. viride*. . . . Poke. White Hellebore. . . . Root large, fleshy, with numerous long fibres. . . . The root is emetic and stimulant, but poisonous, and should be used with caution.

2. In combs.: (1) **pokeberry,** see as a main entry; (2) **bush,** =**pokeweed,** *obs.;* (3) **greens,** the leaves of young pokeweed used as food, cf. **poke salad, sallet;** (4) **juice,** the juice of pokeberries; (5) **milkweed,** (see quots.); (6) **patch,** a tract overgrown by pokeweeds, *rare;* (7) **plant,** =**pokeweed;** (8) **root,** see as a main entry; (9) **salad, sallet,** (see quots.); (10) **stalk,** the stalk of a pokeweed, used as a political symbol in the presidential campaign of 1844 by those supporting James K. Polk (1795–1849), the Democratic candidate, *obs.*, cf. **polk stalk** (*a*); (11) **weed,** a coarse perennial herb, *Phytolacca americana*, whose roots and dark-purple berries are emetic and purgative, also attrib.

(**2**) **1733** Byrd *Journey to Eden* (1901) 289 At our first Landing we were so hampered with Brambles, Vines and Poke Bushes, that our Horses could hardly force their way thro' them. **1865** *Atlantic Mo.* Feb. 172/2 He told us it was a poke-bush. — (**3**) **1848** *Knickerb.* XXXI. 222 The southern negro will dance after eating his poke-greens and bacon. **1941** Daniels *Tar Heels* 262 Backbone and greens (or 'sallet' which includes turnip, mustard, and poke greens but apparently no collard greens) are not only a choice food of the poor but almost a cult among some of the well-to-do. — (**4**) **1868** *Putnam's Mag.* I. 225 'What! Do you tax peanuts?' said they. 'O, yes,' said I . . . 'peanuts . . . poke-juice, . . . skimmerton pans, . . . bell-pulls, laggers, loafers, and fillibusters.'

(**5**) **1891** *Cent.* 4588/3 poke-milkweed. . . . An American plant, *Asclepias phytolaccoides*, with some resemblance to pokeweed. **1902** *Amer. Folk-Lore* 254 After poke is named the '*poke* milkweed' (*Asclepias phytolaccoides*), also called '*poke*-leaved milkweed' and '*poke*-leaved silkweed.' — (**6**) **1858** *Spirit of Times* 2 Jan. 274/3 Gloster 'hid' the dogs in the brake, beyond which was an extensive poke-patch, where the bears 'lived.' — (**7**) **1789** Anburey *Travels* (1791) II. 375 Vegetables not being over abundant in these back woods at any time . . . we adopt the custom of the inhabitants who gather the leaves of the poke-plant, just as they shoot above the ground and are tender and soft. **1945** *Chi. Tribune* 28 Oct. vii. 1/7 Along the wooded trail, poke plants growing head high have taken on minstrel show colors. — (**9**) [**1789** see **poke plant.**] **1880** Harris *U. Remus* (1884) 197, I got mustard, en poke salid, en lam's quarter in dat baskit. **1946** *Atlanta Jrnl. Mag.* 3 March 9/2 The young leaves of the polk plant make poke sallet.

(**10**) **1844** *St. Louis Reveille* 9 June 2/1 When a Polk procession shall come to march through the streets, with a tall poke stalk, as their standard, and a gaunt poke fluttering on its top, what a tremendous enthusiasm they will create! — (**11**) **1751** *Gent. Mag.* July 306/2 The Phytolacca . . . [is] known to almost every one in America, by the name of pokeweed. **1880** Allan-Olney *New Virginians* I. 53 They had stained it pink with poke-weed berries. **1945** *N. Eng. Homestead* 13 Oct. 6/4 Pokeweed, huckle and blueberries, wild roses, bittersweet and hazelnut bushes are also appreciated.

∗**poke,** *n.*[3]

1. The skunk cabbage, *Symplocarpus foetidus* (see quot. 1830).

1778 Carver *Travels* 518 Skunk Cabbage or Poke is an herb that grows in moist and swampy places. The leaves of it are about a foot long, and six inches broad, nearly oval, but rather pointed. The roots are composed of great numbers of fibres, a lotion of which is made use of by the people in the colonies for the cure of itch. There issues a strong musky smell from this herb. **1830** Rafinesque *Medical Flora U.S.* II. 251 Poke as applied to the *Symplocarpus foetidus* was given the plant on account of its most conspicuous feature in early spring—its poke (bag-) like spattle. The name as applied to *Veratrum viride* is due to the frequent confusion of the plant with the *Symplocarpus* with which it grows in company and which it slightly resembles in its early stages.

2. Short for **shitepoke.** Cf. **mud poke, skouk.**

1794 Morse *Amer. Geog.* 165 Green Bittern. Poke. Skouk. *Ardea virescens.* **1844** *Nat. Hist. N.Y., Zoology* ii. 224 The Poke, Chalk-line, Fly-up-the-creek, or Schyte Poke as he was called by our Dutch progenitors, is a southern species. **1920** *Outing* May 75/1 'Poke' (little green herons) were more numerous than humans.

3. A bag or bladder blown up to serve as a buoy in whaling.

1883 *Nat. Museum Bul.* No. 27, 304 When the whale ceases its progressive motions the poke or buoy appears on the surface and the line is regained. **1887** Goode *Fisheries* v. 270 When the 'pokes' are used, the officer gives the order to 'Blow up! Blow up!'

∗**poke,** *n.*[4]

1. A device put on the necks of cattle, horses, etc., to keep them from breaking through or jumping over fences. Also ∗**poker.** Cf. **poke,** *v.*, and see **cow poke, goose poke.**

1805 T. B. Hazard *Nailer Tom's Diary* (1930) 260/2 Put Poker on one of my oxen. **1809** Kendall *Travels* II. 198 A hog . . . by some mischance had turned his poke, so that his throat was squeezed into

Poke or poker on a cow

one of the acuter angles. **1828** Webster, *Poke* In *New England*, a machine to prevent unruly beasts from leaping fences, consisting of yoke with a pole inserted, pointing forward. **1880** *Scribner's Mo.* Feb. 511/2 A chapter might be written of fence breakers and leapers; . . . of horses who, in spite of pokes, take fences like trained steeple-chasers. **1949** R. J. Sim *Pages from Past* 105 Such a rig is known as a 'poke.' It is put on the neck of a critter with fence-jumping inclinations.

2. a. Some form of game now unknown. *Obs.* **b. poke-hooked,** *a.* (see quot. 1883).

(**a**) **1824** *Nantucket Inquirer* 12 Jan. (Th.), No person shall play Foot-ball or Poke, Stick-ball or Swinger, within the compact part of the town of Nantucket. — (**b**) **1883** *Cent. Mag.* April 902/1 [Many] sea-fish, and many river-fish, swallow the hook, and are caught . . . because it is fastened in their stomachs. In the Gloucester fisherman's language of today, a fish so captured is called 'poke-hooked.' **1897** Kipling *Captains Courageous* 78 Help us here, Harve. It's a big un. Poke-hooked, too.

poke pok, *v.* [Related to ∗**poke,** *n.*[4]] *tr.* To put a poke on (an animal). Also **poked,** *a. Obs.*

1786 *East-Hampton Rec.* IV. 256 To order the owners of all such cows or horses, to yoke, poke or fetter them. **1828** Webster, To poke an ox. *New England.* **1850** *Knickerb.* XXXV. 24 Upon two 'poked' colts, which we caught and bridled with beech withes, [we] descended to the shore of the Horicon.

pokeberry ˈpokˌbɛrɪ, *n.*

1. The dark purple berry of the pokeweed, or the plant itself.

1774 Fithian *Journal* I. 269 To Day Harry boil'd up a Compound of Poke-Berries, Vinegar, Sugar &c to make red Ink. **1839** in *Mich. Agric. Soc. Trans.* VII. 414 *Phytolacca decandra.* Poke berry. **1900** *Everybody's Mag.* Dec. 498/1 The juice of the poke-berry, boiled with alum, made crimson. **1947** *Chi. Tribune* 2 Nov. vii. 13/2 Along the drives, one sees some wild grapes, foxgrapes (just out of reach), pokeberries, and persimmons.

b. *pl.* In allusion to James K. Polk (1795–1849) when he was a candidate for President in 1844. Now *hist.* Cf. **poke stalk.**

1844 *Republican Sentinel* (Richmond, Va.) 20 July 4/1 Their Coon is dosed to death with *Polk berries.* **1948** *Dly. Ardmoreite* (Ardmore, Okla.) 28 June 2/4 Ox drivers in Tennessee who favored Clay, covered the horns of their oxen with clay while the Polk boys gathered poke berries and stained the horns of their oxen.

2. Attrib. with **ink, juice, rum, stain.**

1834 CARUTHERS *Kentuckian* II. 215 His face looks like it was boiled in poke-berry juice and indigo. *c***1845** *Big Bear Ark.* 103 Who made Pokebery stains in dimons and squares and circles and harts and so on at quiltins for me? **1889** COOKE *Steadfast* 76 Old Isaac . . . had come in . . . after a dole of poke-berry rum for his rheumatism. **1940** WILSON *Wabash* 3 He knows how to make pokeberry ink and where to find the best pawpaws, butternuts, and sassafras root. **1948** DICK *Dixie Frontier* 218 A simpler remedy was one composed of part poke-berry juice and three parts whisky

pokelogan ˈpokˌlogən, *n.* Also **pokeloken.** *local.* [Poss. f. *peceláygan,* "a stopping place," in the Malecite dial. of Algonquian. See Hodge.] (See quots.) Cf. **logan.**

"The term *pokeloken* is . . . commonly pronounced *popelogan* by the lumbermen of Maine" (De Vere *MS Notes* (*c*1873) 20).

1848 THOREAU *Maine Woods* 51 We passed what McCauslin called a pokelogan, an Indian term for what the drivers might have reason to call a poke-logs-in, an inlet that leads nowhere. **1855** HALIBURTON *Nature & Hum. Nature* II. 404 A poke-loken is a marshy place or stagnant pool connected with a river. **1858** THOREAU *Maine Woods* 100 [The moose tracks] were particularly numerous where there was a small bay, or *pokelogan,* as it is called, bordered by a strip of meadow. **1895** GERARD in *N.Y. Sun* 30 July, Pokeloken, a word used by hunters and lumbermen in Maine and New Brunswick to denote a marshy place or stagnant pool extending into the land from a stream or lake. **1905** *Forestry Bureau Bul.* No. 61, 43 *Pokelogan,* a bay or pocket into which logs may float off during a drive. (N[orth] W[oods], L[ake] S[tates Forest].)

pokemoke ˈpokəˌmok, *n.* [Origin unknown.] (See quot. 1942.) *Slang.* — **1862** POOLE *Double-Quick Songster* 46 Oh, when my love he went away, those words to me he spoke, Be true to me, don't drink too much, nor play in the pokemoke. **1942** BERREY & VAN DEN BARK 457 Poke-a-moke, a swindling activity in which a swindler 'finds' a purse or lets a victim 'find' it, and returns it to the 'owner,' a confederate, who gives them a tip on a good investment as a reward.

poker ˈpokɚ, *n.* [F. *poque,* in same sense. See Asbury *Sucker's Progress,* 20 ff.]

1. Any of several varieties of a card game in which each player, at a single stage or successive stages in the dealing, meets or calls the highest bet or raise at the table, raises the bet, or withdraws from the betting.

1834 HILDRETH *Dragoon Campaigns* (1836) 128 The M—— lost some cool hundreds last night at poker, in camp, and is to meet some brother officers at Rodger's to night. **1865** *Gold Hill* (Nev.) *News* 29 April 2/2 Soldiers are sometimes induced to invest in a game called '*pocaire*' in sunny France, but known to the vulgar on the Mississippi and elsewhere as 'draw.' **1894** *Life* 9 Aug. 90/1 Poker: A pastime invented to demonstrate the truth of the natural law concerning a certain class of people and their money. **1949** *N.Y. Times Mag.* 3 July 23/2 He would be a good man to go hunting with, a good man to play poker with.

attrib. **1844** COWELL *Thirty Years* 94 He was, apparently, quietly shuffling and cutting the poker-deck for his own amusement. **1908** DAVENPORT *Butte Beneath X-Ray* 35 It dawned upon him that he didn't know how to play the game and he ceased to be a poker fiend.

2. In special combs.: (1) **poker chip,** a chip or counter used in playing poker; (2) **dice,** dice marked with the ace, king, queen, jack, ten, and nine instead of the usual spots, also a game played with five of such dice with rules taken from the game of poker, also attrib.; (3) **face,** see as a main entry; (4) **-faced,** *a.* having a poker face.

(1) **1879** *Cimarron News & Press* 20 Nov. 4/3 The toughest thing we have heard about any candidate for office in this section is that he got his poker chips cashed after he 'experienced religion.' **1944** *Vogue* 1 Oct. 178 Army men on every front, Navy men on every sea, ask for . . . hard candy (the lemon and lime jaw-crushers are good travellers), . . . all sorts of Chance apparatus (dice, poker chips, cards). — (2) **1874** *Macomb* (Ill.) *Eagle* 23 Nov. 1/5 'Now, gentlemen,' said she, 'we will throw poker dice.' **1948** *Coronet* April 36/1 You can always find a drugstore selling punchboard chances or a cigar store with a poker-dice game. **1949** *Time* 19 Dec. 21/3 The rules of play are like those of plain poker dice except for two special conditions. — (4) **1923** *Nation* 18 July 61 The picture of that poker-faced gentleman placidly smoking a Pittsburg stogie. **1949** *Time* 12 Sep. 20/1 The poker-faced fellow was putting up a terrific fight.

b. Designating persons who play poker or are skilled in this game, as **poker clergy, player, sharp.**

1907 MARK TWAIN *Autobiog.* 569 (R.), He 'held the age,' as the poker-clergy say. — **1844** COWELL *Thirty Years* 94 The cabin was entirely cleared . . . with the exception of one of the poker players. **1892** *Brighton* (Utah) *Rec.* 19 March 1/5 A good poker player may win a pot on a pair of deuces. — **1861** STONE *Pacific Song Book* 39 The poker sharps begin to pout . . . I played all night and cleaned them out.

c. Denoting places of low resort where poker is played, as **poker flat** (also transf.), **joint, room.**

1869 HARTE (*title*), The Outcasts of Poker Flat. **1938** ASBURY *Sucker's Prog.* 427 There were a dozen grades of Poker Flats, which the New York *Mercury* in 1886 described as 'the newest racket in gambling.' **1948** *Atlantic Mo.* March 60/1 The college had to spend over $200,000 given by alumni and friends for 'Poker Flats,' a little apartment building that can house twelve faculty families. — **1911** CHASE *Yosemite Trails* 267 They cleaned him out like a tenderfoot in a 'Frisco poker-joint. **1912** *Out West* Jan. 85/1 I'd supposed you'd left most of it at a poker joint by this time. — **1888** *Austin* (Tex.) *Statesman* 1 Nov. 6/6 Judge Noonan's decision will probably have the effect of closing all poker rooms in the city.

As the last term in **bean, blind, draw, Indian, penny, stick, straight, stud, twenty-card, twenty-deck, whisky poker.**

poker ˈpokɚ, *v. intr.* and *tr.* To play poker, to win from (one) at poker. *Colloq.* or *slang.* — **1844** *N.O. Picayune* 26 Feb. 9/2 They had left off 'bragging' and 'pokering.' **1949** *10 Story Western* May 23/1 He'd get a man drunk and poker him out of his money.

poker face. A face or facial expression that reveals nothing of what is in one's mind. *Colloq.* Cf. **dead pan.**

[**1873** LAWRENCE *Silverland* 111 Speech goes for nothing; for Poker-language is not only always parliamentary, but intended expressly to mislead and mystify: therefore, skill in physiognomy is most valuable, though even this must frequently be liable to err.] **1885** *Encycl. Brit.* (ed. 9) XIX. 283/2 A good *poker face* is essential; the countenance should not betray the nature of the hand. **1945** GARDNER *Golddigger's Purse* 115 Suppose back of that poker face of hers is a shrewd, calculating mind that isn't missing a bet.

Also, rarely, as a verb.

1925 WITWER *Roughly Speaking* 243 His teeth clicked and he gave me a long, thoughtful look, but I poker-faced him and went on plugging my [switch-] board.

pokerish ˈpokərɪʃ, *a.* [f. *poker, a hobgoblin, devil.] **1.** Of a thing or place: Having a ghostly or unearthly appearance, dreadful. **2.** Of a person: Affected with a fear of something ghostly or unearthly. **3.** Of a situation: Enigmatic. Cf. **poker face.**

(1) **1827** *Mass. Spy* 21 Nov. (Th.), A patriarchal ram, who would fight anything but a pokerish looking ducking gun. **1888** WARNER *On Horseback* 93 At one uncommonly pokerish place, where the wet rock sloped into a bog, the rider . . . thought it prudent to dismount. — (2) **1831** *Georgian* (Savannah) 22 Jan. 2/5 (Th. Supp.), She looked plaguy pokerish at me. **1891** ELLIS *Check 2134,* 96, I feel pokerish tonight. — (3) **1948** *Sat. Ev. Post* 3 July 31/1 It appeared to me to be distinctly 'pokerish.' He gave no sign that would show how his mind was working.

pokerishness ˈpokərɪʃnɪs, *n.* The quality of unearthliness. *Rare.* — **1845** N. P. WILLIS *N.Y. Ev. Mirror* 29 Jan. 4/1 ['The Raven, is] unsurpassed in English poetry for subtle conception, masterly . . . versification, and consistent sustaining of imaginative lift and 'pokerishness.'

pokerist ˈpokərɪst, *n.* A poker player. *Rare.* — **1873** *Winfield* (Kans.) *Courier* 15, 1/4 Probably Missouri and Arkansas can produce more leading pokerists than most Western or Southern States.

pokeroot ˈpokˌrut, *n.* The American hellebore, or the pokeweed. Also the root of either of these plants.

1687 CLAYTON *Va.* in *Phil. Trans.* XLI. 150 Poake-root, i.e. *Solanum bacciferum,* a strong Purge, and by most deemed Poison. **1784** CUTLER in *Amer. Acad. Mem.* I. 492 *Veratrum.* . . . White Helebore. Poke-root. Indian Poke. Common wet meadows and swamps. June. **1891** *Memphis Appeal-Avalanche* 23 April 8/1 For Rheumatism, Malaria and Syphilis, P.P.P. (Prickly Ash, Poke Root and Potassium) is the best known remedy. **1905** VALENTINE *H. Sandwith* 65, I'm sure I'd never trust him after he nearly poisoned you all, mistaking poke-root for burdock.

b. A medicinal preparation from the root of such a plant.

1883 HARRIS *Nights* (1911) 84 Yer I is, gwin on eighty year, en I aint tuck none er dat ar docter truck yit, ceppin' it's dish yer flas' er poke-root w'at ole Miss Favers fix up fer de stiffness in my j'ints.

Polack ˈpolæk, *n.* Also **Polock.** [See note.] A person of Polish stock, an immigrant from Poland. *Colloq.*

Since the latest evidence for this word in the *OED* is dated 1657, the term may have been formed anew here.

1900 *Cong. Rec.* 7 Feb. 1625/2, I have some Polacks in my district, and . . . the blood of Pulaski, the brave Pole who fell at Savannah in the defense of American liberty, has never been avenged. **1913** *Industrial Worker* (Spokane) 12 June 4/2 The Polock, the Jew, the Irish, the Negro, stood together like a stone wall. **1948** MENCKEN

Supp. II. 75 In the case of *Polack* American usage has perhaps been influenced by German example.

∗**Poland,** *n.* **1.** Short for next. **2. Poland China,** an American breed of hogs, similar to the Berkshires, also attrib. **3. Poland topknot,** a variety of the Poland breed of chickens, also attrib.

(1) **1895** *Bur. Animal Industry Circ.* No. 4, 3 A few instances of disease among my 'improved breeds,' Poland, Chester Whites, Durocs, and Yorkshires. — (2) **1879** *Diseases of Swine* 178 Cholera in Kansas and Nebraska seems to attack preferably the Berkshire, and the Berkshire crossed by the Poland-China. **1901** Washington *Up From Slavery* 265 Few things are more satisfactory to me than a high-grade Berkshire or Poland China pig. **1949** *Hoard's Dairyman* 25 Nov. 848/3 Included are horses, a pony, dogs, and a Poland China hog. — (3) **1846** *Spirit of Times* 16 May 141/2 The Poland Top-Knot fowls are highly recommended as layers. **1849** *N. Eng. Farmer* I. 309 The Poland Top Knots seldom sit, and are excellent for those who keep hens expressly for eggs.

As the last term in **golden-spangled Poland.**

Polanisia ˌpoləˈnɪʒɪə, *n.* [f. *poly-*+*aniso-*+*-ia* "many dissimilarities," in allusion to the many differences of the stamens from those of the related genus *Cleome.*] A large genus of herbs of the caper family. Also the clammy weed, *P. graveolens.* — **1843** Torrey *Flora N.Y.* I. 67 *Polanisia graveolens.* Heavy-scented Polanisia.... Gravelly banks of rivers and lakes.... June–August. **1933** Small *Southeastern Flora* 576 Polanisia ... Clammy-weed. Spider-rose. Worm-weed.

∗**polar,** *n.* **1. polar plant,** =**compass plant. 2. polar wave,** a wave of cold weather. *Rare.*

(1) **1842** *Farmers' Cabinet* 15 Nov. 111/2 At mid-day, the plane of the Polar plant passes through the sun, and thus it shuns the light. **1851** M. Reid *Scalp Hunters* xxxv, We were traversing the region of the 'polar plant,' the planes of whose leaves, at almost every step, pointed out our meridian. — (2) **1888** *St. Paul Globe* 22 Jan., Another polar wave struck [Chippewa Falls, Wis.].... This morning spirit thermometers indicated from 62 to 65 deg. below.

∗**pole,** *n.*

1. A fishing rod. Cf. **fishing pole.**

1782 Thomas B. Hazard *Nailer Tom's Diary* (1930) 32/1 Robert gave me a pole for Greans to ketch Fish. **1832** *N.H. Hist. Soc. Coll.* III. 84 A pole from 12 to 20 feet, with a line about the same length, is provided with a hook of three fourths of an inch bow. **1948** *Alva* (Okla.) *Review-Courier* 2 July 2/6 If you go out there and fish with a rod or pole you will probably come away disappointed.

2. In horse racing, the goal posts or the posts marking off distances along a track.

1836 *Quarter Race Ky.* (1846) 20 Crump wheeled his horse round before reaching the poles. **1898** *K.C. Star* 18 Dec. 3/1 Andes ... took up the pace and led to the half mile pole. **1947** *Dly. Racing Form* (Chi.) 3 Nov. B/1 Slowly that black muzzle began to creep ahead and he started to draw out ... in the last furlong, at about the sixteenth pole.

b. *To have* (or *take, draw*) *the pole,* to have, etc., the inside track. Also fig.

1852 Bristed *Upper Ten Th.* 229 (*footnote*), A horse that has the pole, means that he has drawn the place nearest the inside boundary-fence of the track. **1860** *N.Y. Tribune* 16 June 1/2 Patchen drew the pole, and had the outside. **1868** Woodruff *Trotting Horse* 207, I was forced to let them take the pole in the turn. **1902** McFaul *Ike Glidden* 198 Drawing the pole was a position evidently in favor of the colt.

3. *Lumbering.* (See quot. 1905.)

1900 Bruncken *N. Amer. Forests* 97 Today he goes over the same lands and takes what he left thirty years ago, this time down to the 'pole' of eight inches and less in diameter. **1905** *Forestry Bureau Bul.* No. 61, 17 *Pole,* a tree from 4 to 12 inches in diameter breast-high.... A *small pole* is a tree from 4 to 8 inches in diameter breast-high. Syn: low pole. A *large pole* is a tree from 8 to 12 inches in diameter breast high. Syn: high pole.

4. In combs.: (1) **pole bean,** any one of various climbing beans, also attrib.; (2) **boat,** see as a main entry; (3) **hat,** ?a top hat, *rare;* (4) **horse,** a horse harnessed alongside the pole or tongue of a vehicle, as distinguished from a leader; (5) **line,** a line of telephone or telegraph poles; (6) **locomotive,** a locomotive for use on a pole railroad, *obs.;* (7) **pulling,** an Indian ceremony celebrating the taking down of the scaffold upon which a corpse had been exposed for a time, *obs.;* (8) **railroad,** a railroad for logging purposes upon which poles are used for rails; (9) **raising,** a ceremony in which a liberty pole is raised, *obs.;* (10) **road,** =**pole railroad,** *obs.;* (11) **trail,** (see quot. 1902); (12) **wagon,** a circus wagon for carrying tent poles.

(1) **1770** *Boston Gaz.* 12 March 4/3 (*advt.*), Broad Winsor, broad White Pole, dwarf yellow and dwarf speckled Beans, with a general Assortment of Garden Seeds. **1830** *N.Y. Constellation* 11 Sep. 3/2 They are an early pole bean, do not run very high, and are very prolific. **1941** Stuart *Men of Mts.* 192 We drove down past Shelton's polebean patch. — (3) **1862** *Harper's Mag.* Dec. 100/2 If we'd a coon-skin cap, ... we was dressed up sure. We hadn't no occasion then for gloves, pole-hats, nor broadcloth. — (4) **1823** Cooper *Pioneers* iv, The leaders were of gray, and the pole-horses of a jet black. **1889** *Harper's Mag.* June 160/2 The leaders sprang upward and onward ..., the pole-horses simultaneously crashing backward and downward.

(5) **1906** *Indian Laws & Tr.* III. 179 The right to locate ... pole-lines, and conduits ... [shall] be allotted in severalty to any individual Indian [etc.]. **1947** *This Week Mag.* 15 March 22/3 Around 1930, a pole line was completed across a desolate stretch between Denver and Lamar. — (6) **1887** *Harper's Mag.* March 638/2 He finds in Richmond a 'pole locomotive,' made to run on logs laid end to end. — (7) **1824** Hodgson *Letters from N. Amer.* I. 216 At the celebrated ceremony of the 'pole-pulling,' the family connexions assemble from a great distance. **1878** Guild *Old Times* 105 When the days of mourning had passed and the time had arrived for taking down the scaffold and consigning the bones to their final resting place, mirth and jollity succeeded. It was called a pole-pulling, and was a gala day with the Indians. — (8) **1878** *Lumberman's Gaz.* 6 April, They use on these pole railroads trucks with iron wheels. — (9) **1878** Beadle *Western Wilds* 38 The Whigs had a pole-raisin' along o' the election o' old Zach Taylor.

(10) **1878** *Lumberman's Gaz.* 6 April, These pole roads can be laid in the 'branch roads' direct to the skidways. **1893** *Scribner's Mag.* June 708/2 'Pole-roads' are built, where cars with wheels with concave faces run on poles instead of rails. — (11) **1902** White *Blazed Trail* 277 For when the snows are deep and snowshoes not the property of every man who cares to journey, the old-fashioned 'pole-trail' comes into use. It is merely a series of horses built of timber across which thick Norway logs are laid. **1908** —— *Riverman* 36 The trail led through the brush across ... a pole trail above a marsh to camp. — (12) **1920** Cooper *Under Big Top* 134 All eight of them, with the pole-wagon clattering along behind, ran away also.

b. In combs., chiefly obs., denoting structures made of poles, as (1) **pole bridge,** (2) **cabin,** (3) **fence,** (4) **house,** (5) **shack,** (6) **shanty,** (7) **wigwam.**

(1) **1809** Asbury *Journal* III. 311 O! the rocks, roots, pole bridges, and mosquitoes. **1860** Greeley *Overland Journey* 204 [We followed the Weber R.] some four or five miles to the shaky pole-bridge. **1943** *Copper Camp* 139 Across the copper water ditch from the mines, toes slipped on the insecurity of a rickety single-pole bridge. — (2) **1790** Asbury *Journal* II. 75 Jesus is not always in our dwellings; and when he is not, a pole cabin is not very agreeable. **1897** W. E. Barton *Hero in Homespun* 7 [They] began life in a pole cabin, at first unchinked. — (3) **1754** Hempstead *Diary* 628 In the aftern[oon] I was setting up Pole fence next the highway over Long bridge. **1870** *Rep. Comm. Agric. 1869* 399 Pole fence must be four and a half feet high, ... and when the stakes are placed seven feet apart there must not be less than six horizontal poles well secured to the stakes. **1942** Stegner *Mormon C.* 5 They grinned at each other over the pole fence. — (4) **1796** Asbury *Journal* II. 292 At a pole-house [in S.C.] I talked a while on 1 Chron. vii, 14, and administered the sacrament. **1873** Beadle *Undevel. West* 88 The streets were eight inches deep in white dust as I entered the city of canvas tents and pole-houses.

Pole fence

(5) **1940** Stuart *Trees of Heaven* 167 It don't make no difference to me nohow fer I could live in a pole shack with a dirt floor. — (6) **1881** Rompsert *Western Echo* 48 Every ten or fifteen miles there is a pole shanty and *picket* corral built upon the river-side among the trees. **1893** *Outing* May 135/2 Near by are some old shacks, or pole shanties, in which the Indians along the Columbia River place their

dead. — (7) [**1637** MORTON *New Canaan* I. iv, The Natives of New England . . . gather Poles in the woodes and put the great ends of them in the grounde, placinge them in forme of a circle or circumference, and bendinge the Toppes of them in forme of an Arch, they bind them together with the Barke of Walnut trees, which is wondrous tuffe, so that they make the same round in the Topp.] **1864** *Harper's Mag.* June 115/1 Their houses are often the pole wigwams of the Indian, shaped like a sugar loaf, with merely a hole at the top to let the smoke out and the rain in.

c. *To pole cure,* to cure tobacco by hanging it on poles.
1899 *Soils Div.* (Dept. Agric.) *Rep.* No. 62, 30 The present method of manipulating these tobaccos after they are pole cured is quite different from what it was years ago.

As the last term in **apple, ash, butting, cane, carajo, clothes, dead, dog, fish, float, gee, hickory, hitching, hoop, hoop-and-, ladder, liberty, lodge, medicine, pick, pike, push, pushing, rib, ridge, scalp, set, setting, shad, spike, stack, swing, tad, tally, telephone, ten-foot, tote, trolley, war, weight, well, whisky pole.**

* **pole,** *v.*

1. a. *tr.* To finish off (a rail fence) by laying a pole from one pair of crossed stakes to another. **b.** To provide (beans) with poles upon which to climb. Both *obs.*
(a) 1662 *Portsmouth Rec.* 116 All out fences . . . being sufishently staked and pould. — **(b) 1783** SAMUEL DEANE *Diary* (1849) 354 Polled the beans. **1806** R. B. THOMAS *Farmer's Almanack for 1807* 26 June/2 Attend to your corn. Pole beans. Salt cattle.

2. *tr.* To propel (a boat or other craft) by using a pole long enough to touch bottom; to transport (merchandise) in this manner. Cf. * **poling,** *n.*
1769 RICHARD SMITH *Four Great Rivers* (1906) 75 We stopt to make Oars for our Canoe having poled it all the Way from Cookoose with a little Help from a Paddle. **1848** E. BENNETT *Mike Fink* 13/2 Dick Weatherhead's legs . . . [are] long enough to pole a boat up the Massassip, in a high stage o' water. **1865** BROWNE *A. Ward; His Travels* 14 There was a wharf, but the enterprising Mexican peasantry, who subsist by poling merchandise ashore in dug-outs, indignantly tore it up. **1948** DICK *Dixie Frontier* 119 On this the boatmen walked as they poled the boat upstream.

b. *absol.* To navigate by poling a boat. Also *to pole off,* to shove off with poles.
1831 R. COX *Adv. Columbia R.* 249 After pushing off, we poled away with might and main. **1873** BEADLE *Undevel. West* 703 The boat usually stuck fast for a while, till the hands could 'pole off,' when she would back out. **1949** *Sat. Ev. Post* 15 Jan. 16/1 The only people they'd seen were the watermen, . . . poling silently with their slow rhythm by the shallow margins where the soft crabs lived under the shore grass and seaweed.

transf. To go slouching along slowly. *Colloq.*
1892 HARRIS *Plantation* 111, I des put out, I did, an' I went a polin' home, an' it make me feel mighty good when I got dar. **1900** JEWETT in *Atlantic Mo.* Aug. 162, I saw Cap'n Lorenzo polin' back up the road all alone.

c. To move a craft through (water) by means of a pole.
1862 HARTE *Luck of Roaring Camp* 230 We still fought our way forward, resting and rowing by turns, and oftener 'poling' the shallower surface.

d. *reflex.* To throw (oneself) over something by means of a pole. *Rare.*
1839 KIRKLAND *New Home* (1840) 15 The ditch on each side was filled with water and quite too wide to jump over. . . . He 'poled' himself over the ditch in a moment.

3. *intr.* (See quot. 1851.) *Obs.* Cf. **poler,** *n.* **1.**
1851 HALL *College Words* 233 *Pole.* At Princeton and Union Colleges, to study hard, e.g. to pole out the lesson. **1895** WILLIAMS *Princeton Stories* 39 Others dissipate merely to the extent of cutting chapel twice in succession or pretending that they have not poled all night for an examination. **1915** POOLE *Harbor* 54 At first I honestly tried to 'pole,' to find whether, after all, I couldn't break through the hard dry crust of books and lectures down into what I called 'the real stuff.'

pole boat. A boat propelled by poling. Also attrib.
1827 COMMONS *Doc. Hist.* I. 285, I saw three large pole boats loaded with bales of cotton. **1881** *Cong. Rec.* 26 Feb. 2151/1 Here is a stream navigable for a pole-boat. *c***1945** HOPKINS *Okefenokee* 53 One Jesse Aldridge had made many poleboat loads of Okefenokee moonshine at this place.

Also **pole-boating,** *n. Rare.*
1837 SHERWOOD *Gaz. Georgia* (ed. 3) 193 A revolution in the mode and manner of transshipping goods must take place. The slow, tedious and expensive process of pole-boating will be exploded.

* **polecat,** *n.*

1. A skunk of the genus *Mephitis.* Also any of various animals allied to the skunk, of the genera *Spilogale* and *Conepatus.* Also attrib. Cf. **wood pussy.**
1688 CLAYTON *Va.* in *Phil. Trans.* XVIII. 124 There are [in Virginia] several sorts of Wild Cats, and Poll-Cats. **1799** J. SMITH *Acct. Captivity* 11 [The Indians] gave me a . . . polecat skin pouch, which . . . contained tobacco, killegenico, or dry sumach leaves, which they mix with their tobacco. **1805** LEWIS in *L. & Clark Exped.* III. (1905) 4 Some of the dressey young men orniment the tops of their mockersons with the skins of pole-cats. **1888** *Ipswich* (Mass.) *Chron.* 15 Sep. 2/4 In most parts of the Southwest a skunk is called a polecat. **1917** *Mammals of Amer.* 132/1 The Skunk . . . is known in different localities by special names, such as 'wood-pussy,' 'essence-peddler,' and 'pole-cat.' **1948** *Time* 13 Dec. 29/1 He hunted wildcat, bobcat, polecat, foxes, coons, possums and rabbits.

2. In special combs.: (1) **polecat coffee,** ?coffee of an inferior kind, *rare;* (2) **dance,** a form of Indian dance, esp. among the Creeks, *obs.;* (3) **root,** =**polecat weed,** *rare;* (4) **shot,** shot of a size suitable for shooting polecats, *obs.;* (5) **tree,** (see quot.); (6) **weed,** the skunk cabbage, *Symplocarpus foetidus,* cf. **poke,** *n.*[3]; (7) **wood,** see **polecat tree.**
(1) 1830 *Lancaster* (O.) *Eagle* 1 May 2/1 They have on hand 1500 lbs. Polecat Coffee 1000 lbs. Rio do. — **(2) 1772** *Travels Amer. Col.* 532 The women . . . came into the Square and danced round the fire, the pole Cat dance. **1837** *S. Lit. Messenger* III. 391/1, I was informed that this was called by the Indians the *Pole Cat Dance* though our friends were disposed to distinguish it by the more agreeable . . . name of the *Shell Dance.* — **(3) 1761** KALM *Resa* III. 47 De Svenske kallade henne *Björnrotter* eller *Björnblad;* men ängelsmännerna *Polecat-rot* [tr. 1770: polecat root]. — **(4)** *a***1861** WINTHROP *Canoe & Saddle* 27 Behold, also, this other double-barrelled piece of artillery, loaded . . . with polecat-shot, in case we should see one of these black and white objects skulking along shore.
(5) 1897 SUDWORTH *Arborescent Flora* 298 *Rhamnus caroliniana* . . . Indian Cherry. . . . [Also called] Polecat-tree (Tex.) Polecat wood (Ark.). — **(6) 1743** CLAYTON *Flora Virginica* 186 Calla aquatilis odore alii vehemente prædita, radice repente, vulgo Pole Cadweed [ed. 1762: Pole-Cat-weed]. **1844** DUNGLISON *Med. Lex.*, Polecat weed, *Dracontium fœtidum.*

Pol. Econ. Among college students, an abbreviation for "Political Economy." — **1893** POST *Harvard Stories* 12, I have not been tutoring you in Pol. Econ. **1904** LOVETT *R. Gresham* 73, I've got to take on a coach to make up my Pol. Econ. from last year.

poleo poˈleo, *n. S.W.* [Sp., pennyroyal, but in Amer. Sp. applied to various other plants.] Blue curls, *Trichostema lanceolatum.* Cf. **bastard pennyroyal, turpentine weed.** — **1872** POWERS *Afoot & Alone* 277 The vast mustard plains . . . stretch from Los Angeles to the sea. . . . In places this wide waste is of a dusty or coffee-green, with the little poleos. **1939** GARNER *Windows in Old Adobe* 134 The sheltered *corredor* along the north side of the house was crowded with growing things . . . rue and costmary, *poleo* and marjoram.

poler ˈpolɚ, *n.* **1.** (See quots. and cf. * **pole,** *v.* **3.**) **2.** One who propels a boat by means of a pole. Cf. * **pole,** *v.* **2.**
(1) 1851 HALL *College Words* 234 As a boat is impelled with *poles* so is the student by *poling,* and it is perhaps from this analogy that the word *poler* is applied. **1915** POOLE *Harbor* 54 More pitiful still were the 'polers,' the chaps who were working for high marks. — **(2) 1893** *Outing* June 201/1 The best polers I ever chanced to see were a father and son, guides of the government reservation on the Cascapedia River. **1895** *Ib.* Oct. 71/1 A pole is attached to the bow of the lighter; the other end is held by a bare-footed negro, who walks along [the towpath]. . . . There are generally two polers to each lighter.

* **police,** *n.*

1. A policeman. *Colloq.*
1839 *Chi. American* 5 Sep., There is a police in attendance . . . in the theatre. **1856** MARK TWAIN *Adv. Snodgrass* 8 He was a police. **1942** BRANSON *Pricking Thumb* 29 'I'm the police,' he said.

2. The cleaning of a camp, the condition of a camp with respect to cleanliness. Cf. * **police,** *v.*
1893 *Outing* May 158/1 The police of the camp was found to be excellent. **1894** *Ib.* July 312/2 The camp was at all times in good police.

3. In combs.: (1) **police blotter,** = * **blotter,** *n.* **1,** also attrib.; (2) **board,** a board of police commissioners; (3) **captain,** one having the rank of captain in a police force; (4) **commissioner,** an officer or a member of a commission, appointed by the state or, usu., by the municipality, who determines or helps to determine the policy and conduct of the police department; (5) **jury,** (see quot. 1890); (6) **-jury ward,** (see quot.); (7) **power,** the power of government to regulate its police affairs, esp. to advance the public welfare through restraint and compulsion exercised over private rights, the power to limit civil liberties; (8) **reporter,** a newspaper reporter who covers the police department; (9) **surgeon,** a surgeon connected with a police department.

(1) 1900 *Everybody's Mag.* Nov. 460/2 The man has one of the longest police-blotter records in the country. **1947** *Chi. D. News* 1 Aug. 7/3 The police blotter reveals only part of the story of sex obscenities. — **(2) 1856** MacLeod *F. Wood* 208 The whole Police Board was elected at the late election. —**(3) 1894** Ford *P. Stirling* 356 After a consultation with the police captain, the companies were told off, and filing out of the various doors, they began work. **1932** *Atlantic Mo.* CXLIX. 542 When the leaders gave the command to march, the mounted police captain swung his men across the formation. — **(4) 1857** *Harper's Mag.* Aug. 401/2 The Police Commissioners were busy in organizing their force in the various wards of the city. **1911** *Masses* Feb. 12/1 The police commissioner glanced over the letter once again.

(5) 1840 *N.O. Picayune* 22 Aug. 2/1 Will our friends . . . tell us what is meant in their city by the police jury? **1890** *Cent.* 4592/3 *Police jury*, . . . the local authority in each parish (corresponding nearly to the board of supervisors of each county in many other States), invested with the exercise of ordinary police powers within the limits of the parish, such as prescribing regulations for ways, fences, cattle, taverns, drains, quarantine, support of the poor. **1914** *Cyclo. Amer. Govt.* II. 705/2. — **(6) 1891** *Cent.* 6821/2 Police-jury ward, in Louisiana, the chief subdivision of the parish. — **(7) 1827** *Supreme Ct. Rep.* XXV. 442 The power to direct the removal of gunpowder is a branch of the police power, which unquestionably remains . . . with the states. **1895** *N.Y. Dramatic News* 23 Nov. 3/2 That tribunal . . . decided that the legislature in passing the law had acted within the 'police powers' of the state. **1914** *Cyclo. Amer. Govt.* II. 706/1 Congress is using the commerce power to accomplish the same objects which the state pursues through the police power. — **(8) 1834** *Sun* (N.Y.) 23 July 2/3 Your police reporter be one dam liar. **1949** *Newsweek* 14 Nov. 63/1 He was a 20-year-old, $25-a-week Sacramento Union Police reporter. — **(9) 1868** *N.Y. Herald* 2 July 8/3 Dr. Waterman, police surgeon, was called and dressed the wounds. **1895** *Denver Times* 5 March 5/4 Police Surgeon Wheeler sewed up a big gash in his head.

As the last term in **fire, harbor, Indian, kitchen, oyster, state, vigilance police.**

* **police,** *v. tr.* To clean up (a camp). Also * **policing,** *n.* Cf. * **police,** *n.* **2.**

1862 Trollope *N. Amer.* II. vii. 192 Of the camps . . . 44 per cent. [were] fairly clean and well policed. **1865** *Atlantic Mo.* March 289/1 The sickening, pestilential odor of a huge camp without sewerage or system of policing, made the air a horror. **1908** *Pacific Mo.* Feb. 209/2 Their camps are like those of an army, their tents in rough rows and well policed. **1946** Newton *P. Bunyan* 62 Napoleon policed the camp area in a gentlemanly way.

* **policy,** *n.*

1. A game in which the players bet upon the occurrence of a number or a series of numbers to be drawn in a lottery or otherwise determined. Also attrib. Cf. * **number,** *n.* **2.**

1830 *Baltimore Amer.* 26 Aug. 3/2 *To Adventurers and the Public*, Policy Certificates, *in the greatest variety*, Whole And Shares, Constantly For Sale. **1862** Poole *Double-Quick Songster* 38 He used to play in the policy, and often made a hit, For he got the lucky numbers from a moke in Thomas Street. **1949** *Newsweek* 8 Aug. 20/1 Policy—the numbers game—is a form of lottery. It has been called 'the poor man's Monte Carlo.'

b. In special combs. of obvious meaning, as **policy dealer, player, shop, slip.**

1865 *Three Yrs. Among Working Classes U.S.* 263 Notorious baggage smashers, bounty jumpers . . . gamblers, fancy men, policy dealers, loafers [etc.]. **1875** *Chi. Tribune* 21 Nov. 13/1 The policy-dealers hide themselves in out of the way places, but their haunts must be known to the police. — **1847** C. White (*title*), The Policy Players. An Ethiopian Sketch. **1901** Harrigan *Mulligans* 65 A policy player's chances are a hundred to one against him. — **1858** in *Amer. Sp.* XII. 116/1 The propinquity of the 'lottery agency' and the '*policy-shop*,' just round the corner. **1914** Keate *Destruction Mephisto's Web* 84 The Chinese and Mexican Lotteries, and in some cities Policy Shops, are now about the only ones in operation. — **1890** *Cent.* 4593/2 *Policy slip*, . . . the ticket given on a stake of money at a policy-shop. **1948** *Chi. D. News* 12 Jan. 1/2 Italian lottery ring was smashed . . . with the seizure of a printing plant and 250,000 policy slips.

Also *policy baron, gambling, king, office, officer, ring,* etc.

2. policyholder, a person to whom an insurance policy has been issued.

1851 Cist *Cincinnati* 98 Penn Mutual Life Insurance Co. of Philadelphia. . . . All the profits divided among the policy holders every year. **1911** *Okla. Session Laws* 3 Legisl. 203 He is satisfied that they are worth one hundred thousand dollars ($100,000), and that the deposit is made with him by the company for the protection of all his policy-holders.

As the last term in **border state, canal, Chinese, endowment, floating, peace, shotgun, state policy.**

policy ˈpɑləsɪ, *v.* [f. the noun.] *tr.* (See quot.) *Obs.* — **1877** Bartlett 479 To *policy* is to bet on certain numbers coming out in the lottery drawings. A person can take any of the numbers in the scheme and *policy* them.

* **poling,** *n.* The action of propelling a boat with poles. — **1814** Brackenridge *Views La.* 205 The water is generally too deep to admit of poling. **1845** *Knickerb.* XXV. 193 The current being remarkably swift, the voyagers in keels and barges had to ascend the river bank in advance of their vessels, which were then drawn by ropes through the swift current, that would not admit of the ordinary means of 'poling' against the stream.

polio ˈpolɪo, *n.* Poliomyelitis. Also one who has had this disease. *Colloq.*

1931 *Survey* 15 Oct. 93/1 (*heading*), Panic and Polio. *Ib.* 15 Nov. 202/3 The Puzzle of Polio. **1934** *Ladies' Home Jrnl.* Feb. 107/1 Health departments of cities and states poured out money to buy serum from recovered polios to try to cure already sick babies by shooting that serum into their spines. **1949** *New Harmony* (Ind.) *Times* 5 Aug. 1/5 The Town of New Harmony was doused very efficiently last Thursday afternoon by a spraying plane . . . as a precautionary measure against polio.

attrib. **1934** *Ladies' Home Jrnl.* Feb. 10/1 How did the polio fighter—a hulking hundred and seventy-five pounds, and six feet in his socks—come to catch it? **1949** *News-Herald* (Marshfield, Wis.) 19 July 9/3 The polio scare is believed to be the reason [attendance has fallen off].

Polish-American ˈpolɪʃəˈmɛrəkən, *n.* and *a.* **1.** *n.* The language used by Americans of Polish ancestry. **2.** *a.* Of or pertaining to Americans of Polish ancestry.

(1) 1936 Mencken *Amer. Language* 674 Every Polish housewife in Baltimore, for instance, buys *oszczechy* in season—and whether you hear the word spoken or see it written you are surprised to learn that it is the English oyster adopted into Polish-American. — **(2)** *Ib.* 673 The Polish-American journalists are rather more careful than most. **1949** *Dziennik Związkowy* (Chi.) 19 Nov. 6/1 Athletic friends of State Senator Peter J. Miller . . . are planning a banquet in honor of the Polish American public official sometime in February.

* **political,** *a.* In combs.: (1) **political bargain,** (see quot.); (2) **bee,** an inspiration for some kind of political action, *colloq.;* (3) **boss,** one holding a dominant position in political affairs, also **political bossism;** (4) **capital,** anything which affords political advantage, often in phrases; (5) **convention,** = * **convention 2;** (6) **dead beat,** an unscrupulous politician, *slang;* (7) **fence,** the standing, reputation, chances, etc., which a politician has; (8) **general,** (see quot.), *rare;* (9) **gravy,** favors obtained by political means, *slang,* cf. * **gravy,** *n.* **3;** (10) **ground hog,** a wary politician, *rare;* (11) **machine,** = * **machine,** *n.* **2;** (12) **nativism,** nativism in political matters, *obs.;* (13) **organ,** a periodical which supplies news of special interest to members of a particular political party; (14) **plum,** = * **plum,** *n.* **1,** *slang;* (15) **pork,** = * **pork,** *n.* **1,** *slang;* (16) **pull,** power or ability to get things done in politics, political influence, cf. * **pull,** *n.;* (17) **ring,** = * **ring,** *n.* **1.**

(1) 1914 *Cyclo. Amer. Govt.* II. 710/2 *Political Bargain*, an agreement, usually corrupt, between contending political factions or individuals by which support is given a measure or candidate in return for a like favor. — **(2) 1931** *K.C. Times* 3 Oct., Many a man has gotten a political bee in his bonnet that has turned out practically as disastrously. — **(3) 1893** *Dly. Ardmoreite* (Ardmore, Okla.) 12 Nov. 2/2 Machine methods in this state and political bossism in Brooklyn have been repudiated by the people. **1912** *Out West* June 401 Are you interested . . . in the way people are defrauded, and bunkoed, and swindled, and played with by the political bosses? **1949** *Time* 7 March 28/1 As an up-to-the-minute 1949 model of the old Southern political boss, Hummon had shown a marked talent for exploiting credulity, prejudice and ignorance. — **(4) 1842** H. Mann *Boston Oration* 4 July 78 In common and expressive phrase, this is called 'making political capital' out of a thing. **1889** Farmer 429 Incidents which tell in a man's favor constitute part of the political capital of his supporters.

(5) **1881** *Harper's Mag.* Jan. 307/1 A young village statesman sneered at a man who attended a political convention . . . and brought his own cigars. **1912** NICHOLSON *Hoosier Chron.* 362 She wanted this Garrison girl to see a political convention. — (6) **1868** *N.Y. Herald* 4 July 4/6 Perhaps there are not a few political deadbeats here looking after the Democratic Convention. Oh, no! — (7) **1900** *Cong. Rec.* 5 Feb. 1522/1 The gentleman from Missouri has been running with the McKinley Administration until his political fences have got into very bad order. **1949** *Ill. State Hist. Soc. Jrnl.* Sep. 293 He had to repair his political fences in the South and West. — (8) **1868** *Ore. State Jrnl.* 1 Aug. 2/1 Blair is known as . . . a 'political general,' who held two offices, Major general in the Army and member of Congress, and drew pay for both at the same time. — (9) **1945** *Somerset News* 22 March 1/3 Perhaps some of the Shore weeklies which live on O'Conor-Tawes political gravy and large ads from Jewish concerns will bat out loud and vigorous editorials of protest.

(10) **1893** [see **ground hog 1.**]. — (11) **1838** *N.Y. Advt. & Exp.* 21 March 3/5 Mr. Benton's prominent head to-day was to prove that the United States Bank was a great political machine, and as such exerted great political influence. **1949** *Chi. Tribune* 2 Sep. 12/6 We asked for it when we voted into the Presidency a product of a crooked political machine. — (12) **1844** *Quincy* (Ill.) *Herald* 22 Nov. 2/6 He is a plain, honest man, . . . disclaiming any connection with the Whig party and *Political Nativeism.* — (13) **1879** *Bradstreet's* 29 Oct. 4/3 Bradstreet's is not a political organ, but is solely a business journal for business men. — (14) **1945** *Somerset News* 22 March 1/1 At least one young lawyer who need not look to either Democratic faction or to the Republicans for political plums in order to keep himself alive. **1949** *Sun. World-Herald Mag.* (Omaha) 22 May 5/2 Postoffices of that day were not juicy political plums.

(15) **1947** *Chi. Tribune* 21 June 8/1 We referred to this noble, eleemosynary project as pure political pork, which is just what it is. — (16) **1887** *Harper's Mag.* March 497 Political 'pulls' have lost much of their ancient power. **1948** *Sat. Ev. Post* 11 Sep. 113/3, I think it was a job she got through political pull. — (17) **1892** DALY *Test Case* (1893) 21 We're not so far behind the times as you think. We have a political ring and a boss.

* **politician,** *n.* The white-eyed vireo, *Vireo griseus* (see first quots.).

1804–14 WILSON *Amer. Ornithology* II. 166 This bird builds a very neat little nest . . . of . . . bits of rotten wood, . . . pieces of paper, commonly newspapers, an article most always found about its nest, so that some of my friends have given it the name of the *Politician.* **1844** *Nat. Hist. N.Y., Zoology* II. 122 The White-Eyed Greenlet. *Vireo noveboracensis.* . . . From its habit of using bits of newspapers in the construction of its nest, Wilson says that it is sometimes called the Politician; intending thereby a sly allusion to feathering its nest by the use of even the commonest materials. **1917** *Birds of Amer.* III. 109 White-eyed Vireo. . . . Other names.—White-eyed Greenlet; Politician.

As the last term in **crossroads, fence, gopher, machine, practical, scrub, small potato, ward politician.**

* **politics,** *n. To play politics,* to engage in any activity for purely political purposes, to use means not always dignified and honorable in order to gain advantage. — **1907** *Springfield W. Republican* 13 May 6 Mr. Balfour has seized the opportunity [of the Colonial Conference] to play politics, and has apparently come out squarely in favor of trade preference. **1911** *N.Y. Ev. Post* 17 March 4 The people of the country as a whole are tired of seeing political parties trying to 'play politics.'

As the last term in **machine, peanut, practical, safe, spoils, State's rights, ward politics.**

* **Polk,** *n.*[1] [James K. *Polk* (1795–1849), 11th President of the U.S.]

1. Polk game, a political maneuver regarded as typical of Polk and his supporters. *Obs.*

1852 *Fredericksburg* (Va.) *News* 18 June 2/4 Another Polk game. . . . That game wont do, to play twice. The charm is off.

2. Used in obs. derivatives with reference to Polk and his followers: **a. Polk-at, Polecat. b. Polkery. c. Polkism. d. Polkite. e. Polkocracy.**

(a) **1844** *Republican Sentinel* (Richmond, Va.) 31 Aug. 3/2 From the braggadocio of the Federalist newspapers . . . one would be very naturally led to believe that . . . the Democratic party was a mere faction of unprincipled 'Loco Foco' 'Polk-ats.' *Ib.* 21 Sep. 3/3 The President of the Coon Club . . . stated that the name of *Democrat* was too good for the Polk Party, and that they ought to be called the *Polecats.* — (b) **1844** *N.Y. Morning Courier* 3 Dec. 2/2 The students of the University of Virginia . . . had a bonfire in glorification of Polkery, on Friday night. *Ib.,* As soon as Polkery speaks out and avows itself. **1847** *Sangamo Jrnl.* (Springfield, Ill.) 22 April 2/4 Polkery would soon go into a state of essence and would scarcely be found. — (c) **1844** *Lexington* (Ky.) *Observer* 2 Oct. 3/5 Van Burenism not Polkism. . . . Dr. Fairchild . . . is the second of the 'Democratic' electors of this State in 1840, who honorably refused to be sold to Polk. — (d) **1852** *Knickerb.* XXXIX. 281 A friend of mine heard an enthusiastic *Polkite* holding forth in a grocery, concerning Clay and the Tariff. — (e) **1845** *Xenia* (O.) *Torch-Light* 23 Oct. 2/3 Whig majority on joint ballot, 22! Last year the Whig majority was 16. So goes Polkocracy. *Ib.* 2/6 The township, . . . which has heretofore been locofoco, this year gives a Whig majority. What a *licking* for Polkocracy.

3. Polk corn, a variety of corn, prob. named for James K. Polk. *Obs.*

1856 *Rep. Comm. Patents: Agric.* 170 For ten years past, I have planted the 'Polk' corn, which constantly improves.

polk pok, *n.*[2] [Variant of **poke,** *n.*[2]]

1. =poke, *n.*[2] **1,** or the green shoots of this used for food. *Colloq.*

1861 TALLACK *Friendly Sk.* 66 The tall spikes of the abundant red 'iron weed,' the 'polk,' the yellow mulleins . . . render the varied forms of the landscape still more interesting. **1932** *K.C. Times* 19 May 18 If someone would start canning the old-fashioned barnyard greens, composed of polk, slick dock, wild lettuce, etc., they would have something to talk about.

2. In combs.: (1) **polk stalk,** (*a*) (*cap.*) **=poke stalk,** *obs.,* (*b*) a gun, *colloq.;* (2) **weed,** (see quot. and cf. **poke,** *n.*[3] **1**).

(1) (*a*) **1844** *Republican Sentinel* (Richmond, Va.) 22 June 1/2 These animals begin to venture out a little of nights, since the Baltimore Convention, but are slyer by a long sight than foxes, and are ready to 'make tracks' upon the slightest brandishing of a *Polk* stalk. (*b*) **1945** WALLACE *Barington* 19 Papa's still got that damned old polk stalk. — (2) **1892** *Amer. Folk-Lore* V. 104 *Symplocarpus foetidus,* Polk-weed.

* **polka,** *n.*

1. (See quot.) *Obs.*

1883 *Cent. Mag.* July 378/1 He looped [to the end of the leader], for a stretcher or tail-fly, what is known, technically, as the 'polka,' with scarlet body, red hackle, brown and white tail, and wings of the spotted feathers of the guinea-fowl.

2. In combs.: (1) **polka dot,** see as a main entry; (2) **spot,** a polka dot, *rare;* (3) **troops,** Mexican troops who fought under or alongside the "Polkos" (i.e., aristocrats, from their frequenting dance salons where the polka was then fashionable) in an uprising against president Gómez Farias in 1847, *obs.,* see Santamaría *s.v. Polkos.*

(2) **1891** S. W. WELCH *Recoll. 1830–40* 183 The Spittalfields [handkerchiefs] were dark wine color with splashes of what are called polka spots in lighter color. — (3) **1847** *Santa Fe Republican* 18 Dec. 3/1 Yesterday some National Guards that were at San Antonio had a small fight and the battalions of Hidalgo and Victoria (*Polka troops—gentlemen soldiers*)—ran like cowards.

polka dot. One of many round dots used for pattern in certain textile fabrics. Also transf.

1884 BOURKE *Snake-Dance Moquis* 119 Covered with white spots which . . . resolved themselves into white arrow-heads and polka-dots, the latter arranged longitudinally, two and two. **1885** CRADDOCK *Prophet* xv. 274 Should some chemical process obliterate for a time a leopard's spots, consider the satisfaction of a creature to find himself once more restored to his natural polka-dots. **1949** *Chi. D. News* 1 June 20/2 A sartorial revolution . . . will succeed in overthrowing the reactionary reign of the polka-dot before we even know it.

Also attrib., sometimes in transf. and fig. senses.

1883 NYE *Baled Hay* 238 A . . . youth, wearing a dessert-spoon hat and polka-dot socks. **1928** *Collier's* 18 Aug. 29/1 It was not even the perfection of his tiny dark polka-dot mustache. **1947** ROBINSON *Great Snow* 13 He wore a turndown collar, polka-dot bow tie, starched cuffs with stiff-shanked cuff links of intaglio and gold. **1949** *L.A. Times* 20 April 1/5 Gov. Sid McMath today authorized a call for the National Guard as the polka-dot series of Northern Arkansas forest fires swept toward the more populous Northeastern Arkansas area.

Also **polka-dotted,** *a.,* ornamented with polka dots.

1908 DAVENPORT *Butte Beneath X-Ray* 9 Miss P—— received her guests in a lovely polka dotted frock of mouseline de soie. **1928** F. N. HART *Bellamy Trial* i. 3 He wore a shabby tweed suit, a polka-dotted tie.

* **poll,** *n.*

1. *pl.* A place at which votes are cast in an election.

1802 *Ann. 7th Congress.* 1 Sess. 1377 The polls shall be kept open from eight o'clock in the morning till seven o'clock in the evening. **1911** *Okla. Session Laws* 3 Legisl. 213 The polls shall be open at seven o'clock A.M. and closed at six o'clock P.M. **1949** *Lincoln Co. News* (Oceanlake, Ore.) 4 Aug. 1/2 The polls will open at 8 a.m. and remain open until 8 p.m.

2. a. poll list, a list of those eligible to vote. **b. poll parish,** a group of persons formally associated for ecclesiastical purposes, without regard to definite territorial limits (see quot. 1792), so called in distinction from "territorial parish." *Obs.*

(a) **1824** *Ann. 18th Congress* 1 Sess. 947 It is by law imperatively made the duty of inspectors to destroy such double ballots as, on a comparison with the poll lists, . . . clearly appear to be fraudulent. **1877** *Mich. Gen. Statutes* I. (1882) 148 It shall be the duty of the inspectors of election of each voting precinct, to cause to be numbered in figures, and in numerical order, the name of every person entered upon the poll lists required by law to be kept at such election. — (b) **1792** *Mass. H.S. Coll.* 1 Ser. I. 115 These [parishes] have no distinct territories, both meeting houses being in the central or compact part of the town. They are called poll parishes; each inhabitant having a right by law to belong to which parish he pleases; only signifying his choice, by leaving his name for that purpose with the town clerk. **1821** *Ib.* 2 Ser. X. 32 An unhappy controversy arose between him and Noah Sprague, Esq. which terminated in the erection of a poll parish.

***polliwog,** *n.* (See quot. 1854.) Also attrib. *Obs.* — **1854** A. M. MURRAY *Lett. from U.S.* (1856) I. 197 Party terms, . . . such as Adamantines, Hard-shells, Soft-shells, Loco-focos, Rick-burners, and Pollywogs, . . . have originated in casual expressions made use of by public speakers which have happened to hit the fancy of the hearers, so that they became cant terms. **1864** SALA in *Dly. Telegraph* 27 Sep., 'The slimy machinations of the pollywog politicians have usurped the government of our city,' said Poer.

Pollyanna ˌpɑlɪˈænə, *n.* A highly optimistic, good-humored girl, so called in allusion to the heroine of stories by Mrs. John Lyman Porter (1868–1920). Also transf. and attrib.

1921 *Collier's* 11 June 11/1, I should not like to hold stock in a company with Pollyanna as president. **1929** *Variety* 10 April 23/2 He wrings the jury's heart and makes a dribbling Pollyanna out of a hard-boiled New York judge. **1948** *Chi. Tribune* 8 Aug. (Comics) 8 Jack is such a sap that he's taken in by all of Jato's phony, goody-goody, Pollyanna act.

Also **Pollyannaish,** *a.*

1923 *Grey Towers* 277, I wrote a paper for English 198 and the reader put on the outside, 'All right but Polly-Annaish.' **1948** *Time* 6 Dec. 90/2 Mildly Saroyanesque throughout and a trifle Pollyannaish at the end, in its best scenes *The Silver Whistle* is genuinely funny.

***Polyphemus,** *n.* (See quot. 1890.)

[**1775** CRAMER *Papillons Exotiques des Trois Parties du Monde* I. 8/1 *Polyphemus.* . . . Haare woonplaats is in *Niew-Jork* et *Jamaika.*] **1890** *Cent.* 4607/1 polyphemus . . . (*cap.*) . . . the vernacular name of one of the largest American silkworms or silkworm-moths, *Telea polyphemus.* The caterpillar feeds on many different native trees, as oak, walnut, hickory, willow, elm, maple, poplar, etc. **1901** DICKERSON *Moths & Butterflies* 170 The Polyphemus is hardy, is native, and feeds on our native oaks and elms. **1949** *Nat. Hist.* June 274/3 Like the may-fly and the great silk moths (Polyphemus, Cecropia, and Luna), the fish fly . . . lives but a short time.

Also **Polyphemus moth.**

1893 BALLARD *Among Moths & Butterflies* 39 More than six months he slept in his cocoon; and now in April, 1871, he is a handsome Polyphemus moth. **1949** *Nat. Hist.* Feb. 81/1 The Polyphemus moth gets its name from the large 'eye' in each lower wing, because in classical mythology Polyphemus was one of the one-eyed Cyclops.

b. Polyphemus cocoon, the cocoon of this moth.

1914 *Country Life* May 57/2 In December four polyphemus cocoons were discovered on a small maple tree within a block of my house. **1949** *Nat. Hist.* Feb. 79/2 Polyphemus cocoons especially need moisture to ensure perfect insects.

***pomace,** *n.* In local uses. **1.** (See quots. and cf. **bagasse.**) **2.** =**castor pomace. 3.** Refuse that is skimmed off in making scuppernong wine.

(1) **1877** RUEDE *Sod-House Days* 152 He was very much amused to hear the folks [at the cane mill] talk about 'them molasses' and being told to 'take away them pummies' (pomace—crushed cane). **1943** POWELL *Home Again* 94 We did not call them bagasse as they do in Louisiana, but called them 'pummies' (pomace). — (2) **1896** *Dept. Agric. Yrbk. 1895* 192 Castor-oil plants have been cultivated to some extent in the United States for over twenty years. . . . The pomace is considered valuable for fertilizing purposes. — (3) **1942** RAWLINGS *C. Creek* 223 Now some folks, when that time comes, skim off the pummies.

Pomo ˈpomo, *n.* [See 2nd quot.] *collect.* or *pl.* A group of Indians of north central California noted for their basketry.

1872 *Overland Mo.* April 328/1 In the great family of Pomos on Russian River, who have many dialects, and a name for each—as Ballo Ki Pomos, Cahto Pomos, etc. [**1872** *Ib.* Dec. 498/2 Pomo, . . . though it signifies 'people,' originally, I think, meant 'earth,' being manifestly related to the Wintoon *pum* or *paum,* which denotes 'earth.'] **1902** *Out West* Jan. 11 In basketry the Pomos found an outlet for the highest conceptions of art that their race was capable of. **1910** HODGE *Amer. Indians* II. 277/1 The Pomo were the most southerly stock on the coast not brought under the mission influence of the Franciscans.

attrib. **1933** HARRINGTON *Gypsum Cave, Nev.* 87 The Pomo 'tee-weave' is somewhat similar. **1936** REICHARD *Navajo Shepherd & Weaver* 149 To demonstrate his skill, . . . a Pomo Indian basket-maker fashions a basket so small it must be kept in a tiny bottle.

Pomona wine. (See quot. 1814.) *Obs.* — **1788** *Mass. Centinel* 18 Oct. 40/2 The drink with this should be beer, cyder, pomona wine, milk and water, or simple water. **1814** *Henderson's N.C. Almanack* 14 *Pomona Wine* is made by adding to new cider strained or scummed in the above manner, about one 5th or 6th of good spirits and keeping it until old and ripe.

***pompadour,** *n.* A style of combing the hair straight back from the forehead without a part; hair combed in this way. Also as an adverb.

1895 *Wkly. Examiner* (S.F.) 19 Sep. 1/7 Henry Jacob has a pompadour and a profile not unlike Durrant's. **1905** *Westminster Gaz.* 7 Nov. 12/1 Because Congressman Roberts has been so successful a campaigner and still had his hair cut pompadour, it does not follow that General Bartlett can win with his hair cut banged. **1947** *Chi. D. News* 13 Nov. 33/3 This is attached with an elastic under the pompadour, and artfully disguises a three-inch haircut.

attrib. **1944** *Sears Cat.* (ed. 189) 559 Have the newest hair style with pompadour rolls that transform your whole appearance.

pompano ˈpɑmpəˌno, *n.* Also **pampano.** [Sp. *pámpano,* vine tendril, in Amer. Sp. applied to various fishes, prob. because of their color.] A fish of the genus *Trachinus* found along the Atlantic and Gulf coasts of the U.S.; esp. the Carolina pompano, highly prized as a food fish.

1840 *N.O. Picayune* 1 Sep. 2/1 There was a tall dinner party at the New Brighton Hotel, Pass Christian, on Sunday. Pompanos were plentiful, and sparkling hock flew about. **1911** *Rep. Fisheries 1908* 313–4 Pompano, or Pampano (*Trachinotus carolinus*).—An excellent food fish, found on the Atlantic coast from Cape Cod to the Gulf, being very common on the Florida coasts. . . . Other species found on our eastern coast are the 'old-wife,' or 'gaff-topsail pompano;' the 'round pompano,' or 'Indian River permit;' the 'permit' or 'great pompano,' which is frequently not distinguished from the 'common pompano' (*T. carolinus*) by the fishermen. **1947** DALRYMPLE *Panfish* 264 A four-pound Pompano, or a small Blue, will give you some bad moments on light tackle.

attrib. **1851** HALL *Manhattaner* 161 We forgot our military sighings in the discussion . . . of the momentous question whether it was orthodox to eat rum-omelette with 'pompano'-fish. **1881** INGERSOLL *Oyster Industry* 247 *Pompano-Shells.*—Mollusks of the genus *Donax.* (Florida gulf.) Eaten by the pompano.

b. California pompano, the poppy fish, *Palometa simillima,* of the Pacific Coast.

1896 JORDAN & EVERMANN *Check-List Fishes* 351 California Pompano. Pacific Coast of United States, Puget Sound to San Diego. **1911** *Rep. Fisheries 1908* 314/1.

pompion ˈpɑmpɪən, *n.* [Amer. Sp. *pompón,* in sense **1.** The spelling "pompui" in the first quot. below is puzzling. It may reflect the feeling that the word was French.]

1. The pompon, a gray, edible fish, *Anisotremus surinamensis,* found in Florida and Louisiana.

1799 A. ELLICOTT in *Life & Lett.* 186 A great abundance and variety of fish may be taken: such as . . . pompui. **1849** G. G. FOSTER *N.Y. in Slices* 42 From the plump and rosy Salmon of Portland, to the piquant Pompion of Pensacola and the Green Turtle of the Keys, every species of substantial and rare Fish can be found in the Markets of New York.

2. pompion berry, (see quots.).

1833 EATON *Botany* (ed. 6) 86 *Celtis occidentalis,* nettletree, pompion berry. **1859** BARTLETT 331 *Pompion Berry,* another name for the fruit of *Celtis occidentalis.*

pom-pom-pullaway. [App. of fanciful origin.] A children's game somewhat resembling a tug of war. Also the signal to start in other games. — **1921** *Collier's* 8 Jan. 17 (*heading*), Pom-Pom Pull-away. **1945** M. JAMES *Cherokee Strip* 48 During the dinner hour when there were so few of us on the school ground I learned to take part in a few games: tag; hide-and-seek; prisoner's base; pom-pom-pull-away.

Ponca ˈpɑŋkə, *n.* [Native name of unknown meaning.] An Indian of a tribe belonging to the Dhegiha group of the Siouan family; also, *pl.*, the tribe. Also collect. and attrib.

1819 Nuttall *Travels Ark.* (1821) 82 Their language scarcely differs from that of the Osage, Kanzas, Mahas, and Poncas of the Missouri. **1867** *Harper's Wkly.* 5 Oct. 629/2 Our illustrations are representations of this Council, a Village of the Santees, and portraits of Chiefs of the Poncas and Santee tribes. **1930** Ferber *Cimarron* 142 Ranged along the rear of the tent were the Indians. Osages, Poncas, Cherokees, Creeks. **1949** *Nat. Geog. Mag.* Aug. 155/2 A few tribes, among them the Hidatsa, Mandan, Omaha, Pawnee, Ponca, and Iroquois, have been known to grow sweet corn.

attrib. **1812** in Stella M. Drumm *Luttig Journal* (1920) 49 Made Island of Bonhomme and Ponca Country. **1825** in *19th Cong.* 1 Sess. House Doc. 117 (1826) 6 Arrived at the Poncar village . . . a council was held, and a Treaty concluded with the Poncar Tribe of Indians. **1858** *Spirit of Times* 27 Feb. 405/2 A delegation, considerably scared, came up from Neobrarah City, . . . with serious complaints against the Ponca Indians. **1949** *L.A. Times* 17 May iv. 2/8 McDonald is the son of the late Buffalo Chief of the Ponca tribe and is a member of the Ponca tribal council.

b. (See quot.)

1946 Foreman *Last Trek* 255 Formerly known as the 'Poncas of Dakota,' they became in 1882 the 'Poncas of Nebraska' when the boundary line between the states was established on the forty-third parallel.

c. The language of these Indians.

1889 *Amer. Anthrop.* Jan. 56 In Dakota there are seven model prefixes, and in Ponka there are nine.

poncho ˈpɑntʃo, *n.* [Amer. Sp. in same sense. An Amer. borrowing.] A piece of heavy cloth or a blanket having a slit in the center to permit its use as a cloak or raincoat. Cf. **India rubber poncho, manga, Mexican poncho.**

1826 F. B. Head *Journey* (1827) 19 In sleeping out at night I have found my poncho (or rug) nearly wet through with the dew. **1897** *Outing* XXX. 284/1 For active service . . . the two regiments would need to be supplied with . . . rubber blankets or 'ponchos,' which can be used as a garment or blanket. **1949** *Nat. Geog. Mag.* Aug. 219/1 He carried food, spare clothing, and a poncho.

* **pond,** *n.* In combs.: (1) **pond fresh(et),** (see quots. 1863, 1947); (2) **hole,** a comparatively small but deep pond; (3) **man,** (see quot.); (4) **manure,** muck obtained from a pond for use as fertilizer.

(1) **1863** *Hunt's Merch. Mag.* XLVIII. 186 A Pond Freshet is a temporary rise of water in the creek, for the purpose of running out logs, rafts, boats, etc. **1865** *Atlantic Mo.* XV. 398/2 Last May, for instance, occurred a pond-fresh, long to be remembered on Oil Creek, when the stream rose with such furious rapidity that the loaded boats became unmanageable. **1947** *Time* 10 March 55 'Pond freshets,' (artificial floods) were operated in Oil Creek [Pa.], before pipe lines were laid, to float boats to market loaded with oil in barrels and bulk. Sawmill dams were opened, often twice a week, causing a quick rise in the stream. Waiting boatmen then cast off and went whirling down Oil Creek in their frail craft, watched by excited crowds. — (2) **1784** *Amer. Acad. Mem.* I. 409 *Cephalanthus.* . . . Globe-Flower Shrub. Pond Dogwood. Button Bush. . . . Common in watery swamps and pond-holes. **1872** Holmes *Poet* 94 Some of these little stagnant pond-holes are a good deal deeper than you think. — (3) **1905** *Forestry Bureau Bul.* No. 61, 43 *Pond man,* one who collects logs in the mill pond and floats them to the gangway. — (4) **1847** in Commons *Doc. Hist.* I. 195 Getting out pond manure.

b. In the names of plants: (1) **pond apple,** (see quot.); (2) **bush,** (*a*) =**pond spice** (*b*), (*b*) =**pond spice** (*a*); (3) **buttonwood,** (see quot.); (4) **cypress,** (see quot.); (5) **dogwood,** (see quots.); (6) **lily,** a water lily, esp. the yellow water lily or spatterdock, *Nuphar advenum;* (7) **-lily begonia,** the shell begonia, *Begonia conchaefolia;* (8) **moss,** any one of various water mosses of the genus *Fontinalis;* (9) **pine,** a pine, *Pinus serotina,* found in sandy, swampy regions in the southern states; (10) **spice,** (*a*) a shrub, *Litsea geniculata,* found in ponds in the pine barrens from Virginia to Florida, cf. **pondbush** (*b*), (*b*) the spicebush, *Benzoin aestivale,* or a related species, cf. **pondbush** (*a*).

(1) **1884** Sargent *Rep. Forests* 23 *Anona laurifolia.* . . . Pond apple. . . . Common and reaching its greatest development within the United States on the low islands and shores of the Everglades in the neighborhood of bay Biscayne. — (2) (*a*) **1859** Hillhouse tr. Michaux *Sylva* II. 118 [The red bay] is seen . . . round the ponds covered with the *Laurus aestivalis,* (Pond-bush). (*b*) **1860** Curtis *Woody Plants N.C.* 92 Pond Bush. (*Tetranthera geniculata,* Nees.)—Occupies small ponds in the Lower District, giving a gray smoky aspect to these localities. — (3) **1894** *Amer. Folk-Lore* VII. 90 *Cephalanthus occidentalis,* pond buttonwood, crouper-bush. Ferrisburgh, Vt. *Ib.* 103 *Agropyrum glaucum,* . . . slough-grass, pond-grass, Colorado blue-grass, blue-grass, S.W. Neb. — (4) **1909** *Cent. Supp.* 335/2 Pond-cypress, a subspecies of the bald cypress, *Taxodium distichum imbricarium,* regarded by some as a distinct species, growing in or around ponds, swamps, and shallow streams, from the Dismal Swamp to Florida and Alabama.

(5) **1784** [see **pond hole**]. **1813** Muhlenberg *Cat. Plants* 15 *Cephalanthus occidentalis,* Pond dogwood. **1833** Eaton *Botany* (ed. 6) 87 *Cephalanthus occidentalis,* button bush, pond dog-wood. . . Swamps. — (6) **1748** Eliot *Field-Husbandry* i. 5 A natural Pond . . . over grown with Pond Lillies. **1947** Paul *Linden* 367 On the Linden ponds, frogs' eggs, turtles, pond lilies with flat leaves, not shaped like plates, or hearts or anything else in nature: shaped like leaves. — (7) **1892** *Amer. Folk-Lore.* V. 96 *Begonia Warscewiczii,* pond-lily begonia. Cambridge, Mass. — (8) **1874** Long *Wild-Fowl* 204 [They] live chiefly upon acorns, pond-moss . . . and insects. **1875** *Fur, Fin & Feather* (ed. 3) 117 Widgeon . . . feed more by night than day, chiefly upon pond-moss, the blades, roots, and seeds of various water-grasses, insects, &c. — (9) **1810** Michaux *Arbres* I. 17 *Pond pine* (Pin des mares), nom donné par moi à cette espèce, qui n'en a aucun dans les Etats méridionaux. **1832** Browne *Sylva* 241 The Pond Pine frequently recurs in the maritime parts of the Southern States. **1949** Collingwood & Brush *Knowing Your Trees* 42 Pond pine bears such local names as marsh pine, bay pine, and pocoson pine.

(10) (*a*) **1857** Gray *Botany* 380 *T[etranthera] geniculata.* (Pond Spice.) . . . Swamps, Virginia and southward. April. (*b*) **1901** Mohr *Plant Life Ala.* 519 *Benzoin.* . . . Pond Spice. . . . Eastern North America, 2 [species]. *Benzoin benzoin.* . . . Spicewood. Feverbush. . . . *Benzoin melissaefolium.*

c. In the names of animals: (1) * **pondfish,** any one of various small sunfishes of the family Centrarchidae, see also **black-eared pondfish;** (2) **frog,** any of various frogs found in or near ponds, *obs.;* (3) **perch,** =**fresh-water sunfish.**

(1) **1842** *Nat. Hist. N.Y., Zoology* iv. 31 The Common Pond Fish. *Pomotis vulgaris.* . . . This beautiful little fish has derived one of its popular names, viz. Sun-fish, from the glittering colors it displays while basking in the sun. **1903** T. H. Bean *Fishes N.Y.* 484 The common sunfish, or sunny, pumpkin seed, bream, tobacco box, and pondfish is one of the best known fishes of the United States. — (2) **1672** Josselyn *N. Eng. Rarities* 38 The Indians will tell you, that up in the Country there are Pond Frogs as big as a Child of a year old. **1832** Williamson *Maine* I. 169 Of the Frog kind are six species:—1. the Toad; 2. the pond Frog; 3. the speckled Frog; 4. the tree Toad; 5. the bull Frog; and 6. the green Frog. — (3) **1765** Rowe *Diary* 82 We caught at least ten dozn. of Pond Perch. **1839** Storer *Mass. Fishes* 11 *P[omotis] vulgaris.* Fresh water Sun Fish. Pond Perch. . . . Though seldom brought to market, it is considered by many, an excellent edible fish.

As the last term in **beaver, big, brick, buffalo, bush, cow, cypress, false, grass, ice, mill, mustang, oyster, persimmon, prairie, roosting, saleratus, wash pond.**

ponderosa ˌpɑndəˈrosə, *n.* [L. *ponderosus,* heavy.] The bull pine *q.v.* In full **ponderosa pine.** Also attrib.

1878 Hinton *Arizona* 292 *Ponderosa* reaches a height of 70 feet; some firs are higher. **1937** *Range Plant Handbook* B-44 Deerbrush is most commonly found in the ponderosa pine and mixed conifer belts. **1949** *Democrat* 2 June 3/1 Ponderosa Pine. Ponderosa wood is light in color, varying from creamy white to straw.

pondy ˈpɑndɪ, *a.* Abounding in ponds, marshy, swampy.

1686 *Springfield Rec.* II. 266 The Revd. Mr. Pelatiah Glover desires . . . thirty or forty acres of wet Pondy Land at poor brooke. **1770** Washington *Diaries* I. 427 The Kanhawa . . . in many places very rich; in others somewhat wet and pondy. **1805** Clark in *Lewis & C. Exped.* III. (1905) 236 A low pondey Countrey, maney places open with small ponds.

pone pon, *n. S.* ["The word is from Powhatan *äpân* 'something baked,' from *äpen* 'she bakes' " (Hodge). See the first group of quots.]

1. Corn bread baked in large, flat, oval cakes shaped by hand. Also such a loaf or patty of bread.

(1) **1612** Smith *Virginia* I. 17 Eating the broth with the bread which they call Ponap. *c***1612** Strachey *Hist. Trav. Va.* (1849) 73 They . . . receave the flower in a platter of wood, which, blending into flatt, broad cakes, . . . they call appones, which covering with ashes till they be baked, . . . and then washing them in faire water, then let them dry with their own heate, or ells boyle them with water, eating the broath with the bread, which they call ponepopi. **1797** *Mass. H.S. Coll.* V. 55 When the maize was in its milky state, they used to prepare a delicious food, composed of that and some other ingredients, which they called *appoon.*

(2) **1634** *Rel. Beginnings of Md.* 17 Their ordinary diet is Poane and Omine, both made of Corne, to which they adde at times, Fish, Fowle, and Venison. **1711** BYRD *Secret Diary* (1941) 308 The boatwright was affronted that I gave him pone instead of English bread for breakfast. **1796** *Latrobe Journal* 16 The same cask also contains cherries, a few biscuits, and pones of Indian and wheat bread. **1823** DODDRIDGE *Backwoodsman & Dandy* 43 In them days we had but little bread besides jonny-cake and pone. **1908** *Sunset* July 236/1 His lunch consisted of a few bottles of jam, a 'pone' of bread, and about a peck of shrimps. **1949** *Amer. Sp.* April 110/1 Indian Bread, *n.* Corn bread prepared in pones.

b. A lump or swelling. *Colloq.*

1895 in WENTWORTH 467 He's got a pone in his side. **1913** KEPHART *So. Highlanders* 224 Old Uncle Bobby Tuttle's got a pone come up on his side; looks like he mought drap off, him bein' weak and right narvish and sick with a head-swimmin'.

2. pone bread, corn bread in the form of oval hand-shaped pones or loaves.

1785 *Md. Hist. Mag.* II. 258, I procured some milk and excellent pone bread from a hut. **1879** *Scribner's Mo.* June 223/1 Now that the wagons were up and 'pone' bread and beef stews had re-appeared in the menu, the Foot Cavalry, feeling its keep, waxed fat and kicked. **1937** DORRIS *Old Cane Springs* 78 Then pone bread, light bread, and biscuits were brought in.

As the last term in **ash, corn, Indian, potato, sweet potato pone.**

ponhaws 'pɑnhɔs, *n.* Also **pawnhaus, ponhoss.** [f. a word used in the Rhine Palatinate for various foods made of scraps or leftovers chopped fine. See Lambert *Dict. Pa.-German s.v. pannhas.*] =**scrapple.**

1869 *Atlantic Mo.* Oct. 483/1 Some make *pawn-haus* from the liquor in which the pudding was boiled; adding thereto corn-meal. **1882** GIBBONS *Pa. Dutch* 423 Mr. W. liked the fried *pawn-haus* although he found it rather rich. **1943** *Chi. D. News* 8 Sep. 25 Originally, Ponhaws or scrapple was made from the head of the freshly killed porker, but good, fresh, lean pork of any cut may be used. **1949** *Amer. Sp.* April 112/1 Ponhoss, *n.* A kind of scrapple. [Newberry Co., S.C.; DeKalb Co., Ga.]

poñil po'njil, *n. S.W.* [Amer. Sp. in same sense.] =**Apache plume.** — **1904** WOOTON *Native Ornamental Plants N. Mex.* 27 Associated with the desert willow is a rosaceous plant sometimes called Ponel by the Mexicans, (its botanical name is *Fallugia paradoxa*), which would be tolerably valuable in cultivation. **1931** DAYTON *Western Browse Plants* 50 Apache plume (*Fallugia paradoxa*), also known as fallugie and ponil attains a height of about 7 feet.

* **pony,** *n.*

1. A translation of a Latin or Greek text used by students to avoid study, any translation or key so used. Also transf. *Colloq.*

1827 *Harvard Reg.* Sep. 194 I'll tell you what I mean to do. Leave off my lazy habits . . . and stick to the law, Tom, without a *Poney.* **1850** *Yale Banger* 2 Dec., The tutors with ponies, their lessons were learning. **1869** TOURGEE *Toinette* (1881) 290 It became one of my tasks to learn and repeat her lessons to her until she partly understood them. She used to boast of me among her companions as her 'pony.' **1949** J. B. HERRICK *Memories* 25, I didn't play poker or use a pony in Latin or Greek.

attrib. **1860** *Songs of Yale* 45 We could keep a pony leaf In the bottom of the mug.

2. Something small of its kind: **a.** A small glass of beer; a small glass for other drinks.

1849 G. G. FOSTER *N.Y. in Slices* 81 The game is kept up, mollified now and then by a choice swig at the 'poney.' **1899** BREEN *Thirty Years* 234 After swallowing a second 'pony,' amid cheers and exclamations of 'Isn't he a daisy?' **1943** *Harper's Mag.* Dec. 44/2 Dr. Stuker rapidly downed two ponies of brandy.

attrib. **1885** *Santa Fe Wkly. New Mexican* 30 July 4/2 It's the exclusive pony-glass dealers who harvest the nickles these warm days. *a***1910** O. HENRY *Rolling Stones* xv. 231 Del Delano drank a pony beer.

b. A small ballet dancer. Also attrib. *Theat. slang.*

1908 K. MCGAFFEY *Show-Girl* 118, I went into the pony ballet of a LaSalle Theatre show—can you see me as a pony? **1948** *Sat. Ev. Post* 3 July 63/2 In the chorus of ponies—the smallest sized dancers—there was a pert redhead named Gracie Barrett.

c. A book or issue of a magazine of esp. small size. Also attrib.

1946 *New Yorker* 28 Dec. 15/1 The small type was calculated to destroy what might be left of a soldier's vision; nevertheless, the pony was hungrily read—sometimes by a dozen or more people. *Ib.*, This is the last issue that will be reproduced in a pony edition and sent overseas to the services. **1948** *Time* 8 March 56/2 November 1942—Time's first 'pony edition'—a miniature magazine for overseas distribution, mostly to U.S. armed forces.

3. Short for **pony express.**

1860 *No. Californian* (Arcata) 25 April 2/4 A procession was formed to escort the Pony from the boat to the express office. **1869** *Territorial Enterprise* (Virginia, Nev.) 8 Aug. 3/2 At Sutton avenue, last evening, the buck-board was about 200 yards ahead of the pony.

4. In special combs.: (1) **pony engine,** (see quot. 1864); (2) **express,** see as a main entry; (3) **grass,** (see quot. 1909); (4) **lodge,** *W.* ?an Indian lodge or station where Indians grazed their ponies, *obs.;* (5) **penner,** (see quot.), *obs.;* (6) **post,** =**pony express;** (7) **purse,** (see quot. 1859), *obs.;* (8) **report,** (see quots.); (9) **rider,** a pony-express rider; (10) **truck,** on locomotives of certain types, a two-wheeled truck under the front end; (11) **turning plow,** a light draft breaking plow.

(1) **1864** WEBSTER 1012/1 *Pony engine*, a locomotive used for switching cars from one track to another. [U.S.] **1877** MCCABE *Hist. Great Riots* 344 All was quiet there on the 23d, only an occasional pony engine being allowed to move along the track. — (3) **1883** ALLEN *New Farm Book* 112 (*footnote*), The pony grass may perhaps be mentioned as one of the principal of the winter grasses in that region [near Green Bay]. **1909** WEBSTER, pony grass. A perennial grass (*Calamagrostis stricta*) of the northern United States. — (4) **1876** CROFUTT *Trans-Continental Tourist* 157 The Indians, with their squaws, papooses, and 'pony lodges,' turn their despairing faces.

(5) **1878** BISHOP *Voyage Paper Canoe* 137 They hold at Chincoteague [Va.] an annual fair, to which all the 'pony-penners' . . . bring their surplus animals [marsh-tackies] to sell. — (6) **1893** CUSHING *Story of P.O.* 420 Before railroads led to every part of the country the only communication was by pony post. — (7) **1859** BARTLETT 332 *Pony-purse*, a subscription collected upon the spot, or from a few persons. **1865** *Harper's Mag.* Aug. 322/2 A pony purse was made up among the members to buy candles. — (8) **1877** *Harper's Mag.* Dec. 57/1 Condensed abstracts, known as 'pony' reports, are made and forwarded to smaller towns. **1909** *Census Bul.* 216 28 June 67 (*Cent. Supp.*), Besides the full reports delivered to large papers are the 'pony' reports—condensations of the full reports, sold at a cheaper rate. — (9) **1887** W. WRIGHT *Big Bonanza* 118 A Pony rider . . . reported that the Piute Indians . . . had murdered two or three men. **1913** G. D. BRADLEY *Story of Pony Express* 58 The saddle-bag used by the pony rider for carrying mail was called a *mochila*.

(10) **1883** KNIGHT *Supp.* 613/2 [The Mogul locomotive] is made in several sizes, but with the typical three pairs of connected drivers and a swinging pony truck in front. — (11) **1944** CLARK *Pills* 283 The 'buster' and 'pony' turning plows were made fairly efficient implements.

As the last term in **black, calico, California, cayuse, Cherokee, cow, creole, cutting, French, Indian, marsh, mustang, native, pack, paint, prairie, sand-hill, Sioux, Spanish, squaw, Texas pony.**

pony 'poni, *v.*

1. *tr.* and *intr.* Of a student: To use a pony in preparing or reciting a lesson; to prepare (a lesson) with the aid of a pony. *Slang.*

1847 in HAMMOND *Remembrance of Amherst* (1946) 153 (We.), The others are ponying most unmercifully. **1852** *Yale Tomahawk* May, We learn that they do not poney their lessons. **1853** *Songs of Yale* 23 If you poney he will see. **1908** DAVENPORT *Butte Beneath X-Ray* 134 It were a hundred times better to teach the average boy how to build a fence, . . . dress a beef or re-sole a pair of shoes than to read Euripides or 'pony' his way through three or four years of Latin.

b. To tutor (a student). *Rare.*

1865 *Harper's Mag.* July 213/2 A classmate, whom . . . I had ponied through term after term of Latin, Greek, and mathematics.

2. *To pony up*, to pay or hand over a specified amount. *Slang.*

1824 *Atlantic Mag.* I. 343 (F. and H.), Every man . . . vociferously swore that he had ponied up his 'quarter.' **1910** MCCUTCHEON *Rose in Ring* 190, I reckon you'll pony up the five thousand, won't you? **1949** *Chi. Tribune* 21 Sep. 26/1 Secretary of Agriculture Brannan has impatiently ordered congress to . . . pony up 7 million dollars.

transf. **1908** DAVENPORT *Butte Beneath X-Ray* 164 Remembering he had not been into confessional for sometime he starts in to see Father M—— and pony up for his past misdeeds.

pony express.

1. A rapid postal and express system employing relays of ponies, esp. the system operated 1860–62 from St. Joseph, Mo., to Sacramento, Calif. Now *hist.*

1847 *N.Y. Wkly. Tribune* 18 Dec. 4/5 By our Pony Express from the South, we have intelligence from New Orleans to the afternoon of the 2d. **1849** in ADAMS *Pioneer Hist.* (1923) 154 Accordingly we established a private 'pony express' on our own hook between Mason and Jackson. **1860** *S.F. National* 19 March 2/3 Pony Express. . . .

The Central Overland Pony Express Co. will start their Letter Express from San Francisco to New York and intermediate points, on Tuesday, the 3rd day of April next. **1948** *Democrat* 8 January 6/2 The Pony Express . . . first charged $5 for each letter.

2. Attrib. with **line, rider, route, service, stable.**
1869 J. R. BROWNE *Adv. Apache Country* 481 In May, 1862, William Talcott, an employe in the Pony Express service, went to look for his ponies in the nearest ranges of mountains. **1880** *Scribner's Mo.* July 456/1 Both offices established pony-express lines to the principal camps in the mountains. **1890** LANGFORD *Vigilante Days* (1912) 29 Tracy & Co., of Lewiston, had a pony express route from that town to Salmon River. **1893** MAJORS *70 Years on Frontier* 180 'Pony Bob' was employed by Wells, Fargo & Co., as a pony express rider, in the prosecution of their transportation business. **1948** *Chi. D. News* 26 Aug. 4/1 St. Joseph, Mo. . . . The original Pony Express stable was put up for sale for $442.32 but no one bid on it.

pooch putʃ, *n.* [?f. **pouch.*] **1.** A dog, esp. an inferior one. **2.** (See quot.) Both *slang.*
(1) 1927 *Collier's* 3 Dec. 32/4 Therefore, at home, the trick pooch got all the attention, eating at the table with the family. **1949** *Chi. Tribune* 18 Dec. 23/1 He can spot a stray pooch a mile off. — **(2) 1939** ROLLINS *Gone Haywire* 137 The only feasible menu, in addition to gallons of coffee, seemed at the moment to be beans, 'sow belly' (bacon), 'pooch' (a stew of canned tomatoes, sugar and bread) [etc.].

pook puk, *n. W.* [App. a native Indian word.] (See quots.) *Obs.* Cf. **allocochick, peag, wampum.**
1856 WHIPPLE *Indian Tribes* 52 Of numerous articles not figured in the plates, a few may be noticed here: . . . Several strings of 'pook'—consisting of bits of thin white shells, broken into pieces . . . and drilled in the centre. **1858** *Harper's Mag.* Sep. 464/1 These shell beads, which they [Mojave Indians] call 'pook,' are their substitute for money, and the wealth of an individual is estimated by the 'pook' cash he possesses. *Ib.* 464/2 Among the Cuchans, in 1852, a foot of 'pook' was equal in value to a horse.

***pool,** *n.*[1] (See quot.) — **1883** *Cent. Mag.* July 323/1 When once a new '*pool*,' or belt of [oil-]producing territory is found, the wells multiply rapidly. **1946** *Dly. Ardmoreite* (Ardmore, Okla.) 15 Dec. 27/2 In the Lone Grove pool there are four drilling wells, all nearing the completion stage.

***pool,** *n.*[2]

1. The collective amount wagered on a horse race or other contest. Also attrib.
1868 *N.Y. Herald* 3 July 10/1 Let us take a glance at the pool stand before the races begin. **1887** *Advance* 13 Oct. 641/1 Why is it claimed by the advocates of horse-racing that 'books' and 'pools' are essential to its maintenance? **1907** WHITE *Arizona Nights* 236 We had pools on the results, gave odds, made books, and kept records.

2. A fund made up of contributions by several speculators united for sharing profits and losses. Also the group of speculators so united.
1870 MEDBERY *Men Wall St.* 137 *Pool.* The stock and money contributed by a clique to carry through a corner. **1885** *Harper's Mag.* Nov. 842/2 Some relief is afforded by a 'let up,' or the withdrawal from the market of the 'clique,' or 'pool,' or combination of operators that cornered him. **1910** *N.Y. Ev. Post* 31 Jan. (Th.), I told him I thought we could cancel all the Alaska claims; that a lot of prominent people had formed a pool, and that the evidence would prove it.

3. A combination entered into by previously competing business men or companies, esp. railroads, to avoid injurious competition and to control prices and rates.
1875 *Chi. Tribune* 2 Nov. 7/1 The great pool or combination of the roads leading from this city to the East is now in working order, the agreement for a division of earnings having been signed by all the roads, except the Erie and Chicago Line. **1905** *McClure's Mag.* 42 With business men everywhere forming pools, . . . there was money in it for the state that would . . . give a licence.
attrib. **1875** *Chi. Tribune* 8 Dec. 12/5 There are about as many more which send their coal to the company's yards, . . . which are known to the trade as 'pool' collieries. **1881** *Chi. Times* 4 June, The company will now compete with the other pool lines leading eastward. **1884** *N.Y. Wkly. Tribune* 26 March 2/4 The third pool operators recently secured a reduction of ¼ cent per bushel below the price paid by the operators of the first and second pools.

b. A group of locomotive engineers available for duty. Also attrib.
1945 *Dly. Sentinel* (Grand Junction, Colo.) 27 Nov. 6/1 The east end engineers' pool was increased one turn Monday. . . . Relieving him in his freight pool turn is Engineer Frank Olson.

4. In special combs.: (1) **pool box,** in horse racing, a box into which the wagers on a certain horse are placed, cf. **1.** above; (2) **gambling,** gambling in which the wagers are pooled, those participating sharing proportionately in the gains and losses, also attrib.; (3) **hall,** =**poolroom,** also attrib.; (4) **joint,** a poolroom of a low type; (5) **room,** see as a main entry; (6) **seller,** one who sells chances in a betting pool, *obs.;* (7) **selling,** the selling of chances or shares in a betting pool, *obs.*
(1) 1887 *Courier-Journal* 1 May 13/5, I feel worse about such a race than when I have a lot of my own money in the pool-box. **1902** MCFAUL *Ike Glidden* 171 The vehement cheers of those about the pool box seemed more deafening as the race progressed. — **(2) 1882** MCCABE *New York* 548 The great evil of 'pool' gambling is that it encourages young men and boys to enter into the combinations. **1886** CHADWICK *Art of Pitching* 7 The professional exemplars of the game were a few of them under the influence of the pool-gambling element. *Ib.*, They prohibited pool-gambling on all professional association club grounds. — **(3) 1928** *Collier's* 29 Dec. 43/2 He entered a pool-hall speak-easy. **1944** PENNELL *Rome Hanks* 63, I heard a young pool-hall lounger standing idly in Pawnee street refer to him as Old Man Beckham. — **(4) 1930** H. ZINK *City Bosses in U.S.* 137 Money paid by saloons, gambling and pool joints, and houses of the underworld.
(6) 1887 *Advance* 13 Oct. 6/1 No less than 15 poolsellers were in the grand stand. **1892** *Pall Mall Gaz.* 4 May 5/1 The New York police have steadfastly resisted the efforts of enterprizing 'pool-sellers' to make betting on horse racing as easy for women as for men. — **(7) 1869** J. H. BROWNE *Great Metropolis* 573 Pool selling is managed in this way. **1893** *Chi. Tribune* 20 April 4/1 The Senate today by a decisive vote referred to the Committee on Judiciary three bills on the question of pool-selling and bookmaking.
As the last term in **blind, discretionary, pin, railroad, salmon, whisky pool.**

pool pul, *v.* [f. **pool,** *n.*[2]] *tr.* To place (resources) in a common fund or stock. Also fig. Cf. **pooling,** *n.*
1872 *Chi. Tribune* 8 Dec., The receipts were to be 'pooled.' **1884** *Harper's Mag.* March 573/2 Small writers who pooled their wits to make a great one. **1943** MENEFEE *Assignment* 31 Local manufacturers pooled their resources in order to get and to fill war orders.

pooling 'pulɪŋ, *n.* Entering into a pool or combine to avoid competition and to control rates, usu. of railroads. Also attrib.
1884 *American* VII. 229 A pooling combination to regulate prices. **1887** *1st Rep. Interstate Commerce Comm.* 34 When the pooling system was put in force by the Trunk Line Association. **1905** *McClure's Mag.* 47 The several companies broke faith; they gave rates or cut prices, so that between the law and the mutual distrust of trustees, pooling-trusts broke up.

poolist 'pulɪst, *n.* A member of a pool. Cf. ***pool,** *n.*[2] **3.** *Obs.* or *rare.* — **1870** H. W. FOWLER *Ten Yrs. in Wall Street* 329 The very frankness with which the combination talk of their plan, leads the bears to suppose that there is nothing in it, for who would suspect a poolist of frankness.

poolroom 'pul͵rum, *n.* A room in which pool is played, or in which bets on races, prize fights, etc., are placed. Also attrib.
1875 *Chi. Tribune* 12 Aug. 7/4 Fox's Pool Room. . . . Pools sold at 11 A.M. sharp. **1895** J. L. FORD *Lit. Shop* 150 For three hours I sat with my two Israelitish friends—a pool-room keeper and a dime-museum keeper respectively—and talked. **1924** *Scribner's Mag.* Dec. 636/2 It is far better . . . to have young men and boys working in the gymnasium . . . than to have them loafing on the street corners, or in the poolrooms. **1949** *Nat. Bottlers' Gaz.* Oct. 77/1 Thirty years ago, bowling was in the questionable company of the poolroom, and most alleys were dingy basement adjuncts of saloons.

pooquaw 'pukwɔ, *n.* [See quot. 1902.] =**quahog.**
1643 R. WILLIAMS in *R.I. Hist. Soc. Coll.* (1827) V. 104 Poquaûhock, Obs: This the English call Hens, a little thick shell fish which the Indians wade deep and dive for. **1807** *Mass. H.S. Coll.* 2 Ser. III. 58 The poquau is found in Old Town Harbour, at Cape Poge, and in Menemsha pond: great quantities are exported. **1902** *Amer. Folk-Lore* XV. 254 *Pooquaw.* A Nantucket name for the round clam (hard clam), known in other parts of New England as *quahog.* The word, *poogwaw*, as the earlier form *pequaock* shows, is a corruption of the Indian word revealed in the Narragansett *poquau hock*, Massachusetts *poquahoc.* The Indian term signifies literally 'tight *or* tightly closed shell,' from *poquau*, 'thick,' *hock*, 'that which covers.' **1910** HODGE *Amer. Indians* II. 332/2 The last half of the word [*quahog*] has survived in English, while in Nantucket the first part has come down as *pooquaw.*

***poor,** *a.*

1. Sick, unwell, "poorly." *Colloq. Obs.*
1758 in A. TOMLINSON *Military Jrnls.* 15 Corperal Carpenter was taken poor. *Ib.* 25 This day at knight Leiut. Smith came back & very poor he was the rest of the guard returned well. **1758** S. THOMPSON *Diary* (1896) 12 Our men are very poor, and we scarce could get men for work or for guard.

2. In combs.: (1) **poor buckra,** see as a main entry; (2) **bull,** a piece of tough meat from an old bull buffalo, *slang, obs.*, cf. **poor doe;** (3) **do,** (see quots.); (4) **doe,** (see quot. 1845), *obs.;* (5) **farm,** a farm maintained at public expense for the care of the poor, cf. **county poor farm;** (6) **folksy,** *a. S.* (see quot. 1859), *colloq.*, cf. **poor white folksy;** (7) *** **man,** see as a main entry; (8) **master,** one having charge of administering public relief for the poor; (9) **trash,** =**poor white trash,** also transf.; (10) **valley,** (see quot. 1925), also attrib.; (11) **white,** see as a main entry; (12) **will,** a bird of the western states and Mexico, *Phalaenoptilus nuttalli,* resembling the whippoorwill, but lacking one stressed syllable of its note, cf. **dusky, frosted poorwill.**

(2) **1848** RUXTON in *Blackw. Mag.* LXIV. 303 'Poor bull' it was in all conscience: the labour of chewing a mouthful of the 'tender loin' was equal to a hard day's hunt. — (3) **1909** *Pioneer Days Southwest* 253 When we had hogmeat we would fry a few pieces, take the grease and crumble corn bread in it, putting in water and salt, and we had a pot of soup called 'poor doo.' **1913** KEPHART *So. Highlanders* 292 The old Germans taught their Scotch and English neighbors the merits of scrapple, but here it is known as poor-do. — (4) **1845** KENDALL *Santa Fe Expedition* I. 36, [I learned that] among the Texan hunters the term 'poor doe' is applied, regardless of gender, to any deer that may happen to be lean. **1892** DUVAL *Young Explorers* 98 Even rattlesnake ain't as bad as it looks, and their fat is fust rate to fry poor doe in.

(5) **1852** GUNNISON *Mormons* 145 A Poor Farm of forty acres is in the centre, controlled by the bishops. **1949** *Chi. Tribune* 2 Dec. 20/7 It use to be a disgrace to go to the 'poor farm' and be cared for by the rest of society. — (6) **1859** BARTLETT 332 *Poor Folksy.* Like, or after the fashion of, poor people. **1904** GLASGOW *Deliverance* 358, I don't see what you want to traipse around with that little poor-folksy yaller dog for. — (8) **1873** *Harper's Mag.* April 799/2 The 'prisoner' said he would prefer to pay the fine; and . . . he walked over to the poor-master of the town and paid the ten dollars. **1894** ROBINSON *Danvis Folks* 291 Jake's goin' tu see the s'lec'men, er the poormaster. — (9) **1863** E. KIRKE *Southern Friends* 55 The poor trash who scratched a bare subsistence from a sorry patch of beans and collards. **1867** L. BAKER *U.S. Secret Service* 207 There was the lean, lank, sallow, dirty, hang-dog specimen of the 'poor trash' of the South. **1949** *Painter & Decorator* Oct. 33/1 *All* trades are guided and guarded by law and inspection except painters and decorators. They are the 'poor trash' of the building trades!

(10) **1792** in *Amer. Sp.* XV. 299/1 Beginning on the South Side of the poor Valley nobs. **1925** *Va. Geol. Survey Bul.* No. 25, 13 The Devonian black shale is noted for the poor quality of its soil and the valleys carved in it are almost universally known throughout the middle and southern Appalachians as 'poor valleys.' — (12) **1878** *Nat. Museum Proc.* I. 427 *'Antrostomus' nuttali.*—Poor-will. **1887** ROOSEVELT in *Cent. Mag.* March 664/2 At nightfall the poor-wills begin to utter their boding call from the wooded ravines . . . ; not 'whip-poor-will,' as in the East, but with two syllables only. **1949** *Pacific Discovery* Jan.–Feb. 12/1 In the same manner we hunted raccoons, owls, and poorwills.

b. In the names of plants: (1) **poor pine,** (see quot.); (2) **-Robin's plantain,** any of various herbs used for medicinal purposes, as the rattlesnake weed, *Hieracium venosum;* (3) **toe,** (see quot.), *colloq.*

(1) **1897** SUDWORTH *Arborescent Flora* 29 *Pinus echinata.* Shortleaf Pine. . . . Poor Pine (Fla.). . . . *Pinus glabra.* Spruce Pine. . . . Poor Pine (Fla.). — (2) **1778** CARVER *Travels* 517 *Poor Robin's Plantain* is of the same species as the last [the rattlesnake plantain], but more diminutive in every respect; it receives its name from its size, and the poor land on which it grows. **1791** *Amer. Philos. Soc.* III. 115 *Hieracium Kalmii* (*Rattle-Snake-Plantain, Poor-Robin's Plantain*). — (3) **1889** VASEY *Agric. Grasses* 103 *Richardsonia scabra* (Mexican Clover; Spanish Clover; Florida Clover; Water Parsley; Bell-Fountain; Poor Toe; Pigeon-weed, etc.)

As the last term in **cattle, land, spring poor.**

poor buckra. (See quot. 1856.) Now *hist.*

1855 SIMMS *Forayers* 182 Benny Bowlegs had but small esteem for the class whom he described as 'poor buckrah.' **1856** *Dollar Times* (Cin.) 11 Dec. 1/7 'Poor buckrah,' 'poor white trash,' or 'white trash,' are the terms by which the negro designates them, and 'poor' means a great deal in this connection. It includes not simply pecuniary poverty, but ignorance, boorishness, and general social degradation. The southern negro never applies the term poor to any one who has the manners and breeding of a gentleman, however light his purse. **1949** *State* (Raleigh, N.C.) 24/3 Sometimes they would have a falling-out, and the white children would say 'nigger, nigger, nigger,' and the colored ones would say 'po' buckra, 'po' buckra.'

poor joe. Also †**poor job, Job.** [See note.] A local name for the great blue heron.

Turner finds this term in use among the Gullahs and cites its occurrence in Vai (Liberia and Sierra Leone) as a name for the heron. It was app. introduced here by African slaves.

1736 MOORE *Voyage Ga.* (1744) 57 [There are] Numbers of the Heron Kind of different Species and Colours some small ones of the most beautiful White which are called Poor Jobs, from their being generally very lean. **1850** E. P. BURKE *Reminisc. Ga.* 138 Many large birds live in the marshes [in Georgia] by digging worms and snails. The largest of these are the gannet and 'poor job.' . . . The poor job is a good deal larger and as white as snow. **1943** GABRIELSON *W. Refuges* 117 A 'poor Joe,' as goes the local designation for the angular, awkward, great blue heron, flaps away with dangling legs.

*** **poor man.** [In the possessive.]

1. In the popular names of foods and plants (see quots.).

1787 in T. E. DEVOE *Market Book* 181 As I have travelled thro' all the States, I will furnish the *Bill of Fare: . . . Georgia,* a poor-man's pudding with a glass of water. **1855** DAVIS *Farm Bk.* 188 First next the ditch are the Harper peas to a peach tree and then come the gray crowder or poor mans pea. **1868** G. G. CHANNING *Recoll. Newport* 25, I was fed entirely upon bread and milk, and whitepot, pronounced *whitpot.* This last was strictly a Rhode-Island dish, and sometimes called the 'poor man's custard.' **1883** SMITH *Geol. Survey Ala.* 521 The Florida clover, or 'poor man's trouble,' is the greatest pest in the way of a weed. **1899** *Animal & Plant Lore* 118 *Pteris aquilina,* the bracken fern, is called [in Ala.] 'poor man's soap,' because its root stocks will make a lather with water.

2. *W.* Of or pertaining to mining enterprises that may be developed mainly by the work of the owner without very much capital, as (1) **poor man's camp,** (2) **diggings,** (3) **mine.** Chiefly *obs.*

(1) **1880** *Harper's Mag.* Feb. 393/2 So easily handled are these new-fangled ores that this is pre-eminently the 'poor man's camp.' **1891** Union Pac. R.R. *Utah* (4th ed.) 41 This ore, through leaching, would be found at some depth from the surface, and for this reason it is not a poor man's camp. — (2) **1875** *Chi. Tribune* 14 Oct. 7/3 If it did pay, it would be what is called poor man's diggings, for it was no place where capital could be successfully employed. **1876** DODGE *Black Hills* 109 It has passed into a proverb that 'placer' mining is the poor man's diggings, while 'quartz' mining is only for the rich. — (3) **1897** LEONARD *Gold Fields Klondike* 85 Every man is now looking for a 'poor man's mine' which requires only strength, understanding and perseverance to yield either a modest or a large fortune.

poor white.

1. An ignorant, shiftless, poverty-stricken southern white. Usu. collect. or pl.

"In discriminating southern speech, it was not used to include all white persons who were poor. . . . The 'poor-whites' were those who were both poor and conspicuously lacking in the common social virtues and especially fell short of the standard in certain economic qualities" (W. T. Couch, ed., *Culture in the South* 414). Cf. **clay eater, cracker, dirt eater, mean white.**

1819 FAUX *Memorable Days* 118 The poor white, or white poor, in Maryland, . . . scarcely ever work. **1886** EBBUTT *Emigrant Life* 120 He was an emigrant from Tennessee, a 'poor white,' a man that the niggers looked down upon, almost too proud to work, but too poor to do without. **1948** *Atlantic Mo.* Nov. 62/2 The 'poor white,' the 'red-neck,' the 'peckerwood,' are not alone the victims of the War Between the States.

attrib. **1836** PAULDING *Slavery in U.S.* 205 The slave of a gentleman universally considers himself a superior being to 'poor white folks.' **1880** *Scribner's Mo.* June 293/1 Her parents were of the 'poor white' class and lived in some remote Virginian wild.

2. poor white folksy, of or pertaining to poor white people or to poor white trash *q.v.* Also absol. Cf. **folksy.**

1864 *Harper's Mag.* Aug. 412/2, I wouldn't do my hair in a three strand braid on no account; it is too poor-white-folksy for me. **1868** *Putnam's Mag.* June 704 That wretched caste commonly spoken of as the 'mean whites,' the 'poor white folksy.' **1902** G. C. EGGLESTON *D. South* 240 An' a mighty poor white folksey breakfas' he'll git too.

3. poor white trash, the poor whites of the South. Also attrib.

1833 KEMBLE *Journal* II. 112 The slaves themselves entertain the very highest contempt for white servants, whom they designate as 'poor white trash.' **1903** J. RALPH *Making of Journalist* 130 [The people in southern Ind.] were pure Anglo-Saxons, but were of the 'poor white trash' order. **1947** *Christian Cent.* 20 Aug. 999/1 Let us have a poll tax everywhere and make it high enough really to prevent the 'pore white trash' from voting.

transf. **1946** PEASE *Sequestered Vales* 99 Were it not for this it would quickly revert to a medley of inferior grasses . . . or of poor white trash like cudweed.

Hence **poor colored trash,** *rare.*

1882 Buel *Metropolitan Life Unveiled* 598 She confessed that her companionship was not among the Creoles, whom she regarded as 'poor colored trash.'

pop pɑp, *n.*[1] A short and familiar form of **papa.*

1838 in *S.W. Hist. Quart.* XXX. (1926) 147 Sent my packet . . . to pop in the post office in N Orleans. **1892** Duval *Young Explorers* 195 Run right down to the 'tater patch, and tell pop there's a gentleman here wants to see him. **1948** *Denison* (Tex.) *Herald* 1 July 1/3 Butch . . . was vacationing with his pop at the popular National Park Service Lake Texoma resort.

b. Any elderly man.

1889 *Sporting Life* (Phila.) 29 May 2/6 'Pop' Chadwick is among those who are opposed to the wire. **1947** *Dly. Oklahoman* (Okla. City) 28 Dec. 5/8 'Pop,' as he is known in this area, will use the 'fancy' cane to help guide his sightless way during his strolls along Shamrock streets.

***pop,** *n.*[2] A peanut that has no nut or fruit in it and hence bursts readily with a slight "pop" when pressed. *Colloq.*

1869 *Rep. Comm. Agric. 1868* 221 [The pods] turn out to be nothing more than what is popularly called 'pops.' **1906** Pringle *Rice Planter* 388, I would feel very proud of the yield [of peanuts] if there were not so many 'pops' in them. *Ib.*, Last year from ten acres he sold thirteen hundred bushels of prime peanuts, entirely exempt from 'pops,' and worth three dollars per bushel.

As the last term in **egg, May, soda pop.**

***pop,** *v.*

1. *tr.* To heat or roast (popcorn) till it bursts with a "pop."

1850 *Quincy* (Ill.) *Whig* 12 Nov. 4/1 One barrel of rice corn will make 32 barrels after popping. **1857** *Spirit of Times* 25 April 119/1 Little Kate was popping corn over the grate. **1949** *Sat. Ev. Post* 21 May 36/1 Last year American farmers grew some 300,000,000 pounds of popcorn. This, when popped, is enough to fill 2,400,000,000 ten-cent bags.

2. In baseball, to hit (a ball) so that it rises high in the air but does not go far from the batter and is easily caught. Also absol. *Colloq.*

1867 *Ball Players' Chron.* 6 June 2/3 On Hunniwell popping one up which fell into Sumner's hands, Smith had to retire, a double play putting both out. **1912** Mathewson *Pitching* 204 Then Doyle popped up a weak foul behind the catcher. **1947** *L.A. Times* 3 Oct. II. 1/7 Johnson swung and popped up to end the inning.

b. *To pop* (*out*) *to* (*one*), of a batter: To get put out by knocking a fly ball that is caught by an opposing player.

1931 *K.C. Times* 19 Oct., Hallahan replaced Grimes on the mound for the Cardinals and then Bishop popped out to 'Pepper' Martin. **1948** *Chi. Tribune* 7 March II. 1/4 Lupien popped to Johnson.

3. In combs.: (1) **popcorn,** see as a main entry; (2) **eye,** a bulging or prominent eye; (3) **-eyed,** *a.* having popeyes, open-eyed with expectation, wonder, etc.; (4) **fly,** in baseball (see quot. 1887); (5) **-gun bill,** a contemptuous term applied orig. to a number of tariff bills each of which reduced the tariff on a single commodity, *obs.;* (6) **-gun elder,** a variety of elder frequently used in making popguns; (7) **-gun wood,** =prec.; (8) **over,** a puff made of thin flour batter rich in eggs and cooked quickly to insure lightness and puffiness; (9) **robin,** (see quot.), *obs.;* (10) **sicle,** a confection frozen on a small stick which serves as a handle for use when partaking of it, also attrib.; (11) **skull,** =**busthead,** *slang;* (12) **squirt,** (see quot. 1877), *colloq.*

(2) **1828** Royall *Black Book* II. 377 But the lawyer of lawyers is his partner, . . . a shrimp in size, a sallow complexion, small face, and little blue pop eye, with a great deal of white. *c***1895** Norris *Vandover* (1914) 35 Besides Turner herself there was Henrietta Vance, a stout, pretty girl, with pop eyes and a little nose. — (3) **1824** Royall *Lett. from Ala.* 176 The first countenance I caught was Senator Foot, of Connecticut—a handsome middle-sized black pop-eyed Yankee. **1932** *K.C. Star* 26 May 22 The young lady quickly typed for her with neatness and dispatch . . . while we looked on pop-eyed. — (4) **1887** *Outing* May 101/2 Probably the most peculiar effect which the axial rotation of a ball has upon its flight may be noticed by a close observer in the behavior of the so-called 'pop-flies,' balls which shoot upwards in the air [when hit by the batter]. **1949** *News-Herald* (Marshfield, Wis.) 16 July 9/4 Nowitzke came up with the outstanding fielding gem of the game in the second inning, racing into short center to make a glove-handed stab of Bauer's pop fly.

(5) **1894** *Cong. Rec.* App. August 13 1202/1, I propose to speak . . . of these 'four' pop-gun bills which are . . . to be fired from this House into the country to try to give some sugarcoating to the action of the House . . . on the general tariff bill. — (6) **1906** *Out West* March 176 The little shrubby popgun elder of the East is supplanted here by a tree twelve to twenty inches in diameter. — (7) **1861** *Harper's Mag.* Aug. 363/2 'Sambuca' . . . was quite too learned a name, however, for the Bakertown [Conn.] boys. Their own plain elder or pop-gun wood suited their tastes better. — (8) **1876** M. F. Henderson *Cooking* 71 Breakfast Puffs, or Pop-overs . . . may be baked in roll-pans. **1945** *Suburban List* 8 Feb. 11/2 Maple syrup is a 'natural' for griddle cakes, waffles, popovers and hot biscuits. — (9) **1830** J. F. Watson *Philadelphia* 168 In the country, morning and evening repasts were generally made of milk, having bread boiled therein, or else thickened with pop-robbins,—things made up of flour and eggs into a batter, and so dropt in with the boiling milk.

(10) **1931** *K.C. Times* 17 Aug., That [job] of gathering up the popsickle sticks over the country. **1941** S. V. Benét *Listen to People* (1942) 471 The usual crowd . . . kidding the local cop and eating popsicles. — (11) **1867** G. W. Harris *Sut Lovingood* 222 [He] tuck hissef a buckload ove popskull. **1945** *New Yorker* 4 Aug. 44/1 The prices are enormous—$200 for a bottle of popskull schnapps. — (12) **1848** N. Ames *Childe Harvard* 92, I will . . . meet thee, and thou shalt take 'Pop-squirts,' and fight with me on 'Cambridge Lake!' **1877** Bartlett 484 *Pop-Squirt,* an insignificant, but pretentious fellow.

popcorn ˈpɑpˌkɔrn, *n.*

1. A variety of small-eared corn, *Zea mays everta,* the mature grains of which pop open when subjected to dry heat; the kernels of such corn. Also attrib. Cf. **parching corn,** ***rice corn.**

1819 Faux *Mem. Days* 302, I crossed the Big Wabash . . . at La Valette's ferry, where is beautiful land, fine young orchards, and two lonely families of naked-legged French settlers, from whom I received two curious ears of poss [*sic*] corn. **1850** *Quincy* (Ill.) *Whig* 12 Nov. 4/1 Pop corn is dependent for its peculiar powers . . . upon the quantity of oil which its whole contains. **1891** *Scribner's Mag.* Dec. 770/1 A representative from every Spanish family in New Mexico joined the annual *conducta* . . . his burros laden with . . . coffee, pop-corn-meal and dried meat. **1948** *Durant* (Okla.) *D. Democrat* 4 July 5/3 The purpose of our visit was to see a field of popcorn which had been used in an experiment with fertilizer.

2. =**popped corn.**

1860 *Marysville* (Calif.) *Appeal* 6 April 4/1 Corn is good to fatten hogs, and I know of no good reason why 'pop-corn' should not lard a man. **1946** *Harper's Mag.* Oct. 311/1 So important has become the sale of popcorn in movie theaters that the Fox Midwest Amusement Corporation, in Kansas City, has about four thousand acres in popcorn.

attrib. and *transf.* **1855** M. Thompson *Doesticks* 257 [He] had just pawned his coat and a spare shirt to get money to set himself up in business again, as a pop-corn merchant. **1945** *Reader's Digest* Aug. 28 If I am buying popcorn at a popcorn wagon [etc.]. **1949** *Amer. Milk Rev.* May 10 Some folks call it 'Popcorn,' others call it 'Buckshot,' still others call it 'Pot' or 'Cup' or 'Dry,' but no matter what the label it's all Cottage Cheese.

3. In special combs.: (1) **popcorn ball,** a confection consisting of popped corn made to cohere by the use of sirup; (2) **candy,** ?=prec.; (3) **flower,** a plant or flower of the genus *Plagiobothrys,* so called in allusion to its white flowers; (4) **machine,** a machine, usu. on wheels, for popping popcorn; (5) **man,** a vendor of popped corn; (6) **party,** a social gathering for popping and eating popcorn; (7) **stand,** a place where popped corn is sold; (8) **string,** kernels of popped corn threaded and used as an ornament.

(1) **1875** *Chi. Tribune* 21 Nov. 2/6 Each one had grown tired of jaw-breakers and popcorn balls. **1947** *Downtown Shopping News* (Chi.) 2 Jan. 16/3 Pop corn balls are the delight of every child. — (2) **1904** O. Henry *Heart of West* 278 The old woman has got some popcorn candy and rag dolls. **1946** Wilson *Fidelity* 87 Popcorn candy made in this way is like a new kind of nut or fruit. — (3) **1902** *Out West* May 512, I love . . . February's shower Of 'shooting-stars' minute; Flakes of the white and yellow 'popcorn-flower.' **1932** *Ariz. Agric. Exp. Sta. Bul.* 141, 25 They included such plants as alfilaria, . . . combseed popcorn flowers, . . . bladderpod. — (4) **1918** *Sat. Ev. Post* 24 Aug. 46/1 We brought out the Butter-Kist pop corn machine and made the pop corn business a vital part of retail stores of all descriptions. **1947** *So. Sierran* July 4/2 It was all of the popcorn machines at Coney Island gathered in convention going full blast but altogether invisible.

(5) **1855** M. Thompson *Doesticks* 78 A company . . . composed entirely of . . . stage-drivers, candy-peddlers, pop-corn men. **1944** Holton *Yankees* 110 The popcorn man and the balloon vendor did a rushing business, too. — (6) **1907** *St. Nicholas* May 615/1 The idea had come to them . . . to invite them up some evening for a popcorn

party. **1948** *Dly. Ardmoreite* (Ardmore, Okla.) 15 Jan. 5/3 Examples she gave of family recreation included: Talent nights, . . . candy pulls and popcorn parties. — **(7) 1876** INGRAM *Centennial Exp.* 758 The total amount realized from concession contracts . . . is over $290,000, divided as follows . . . ; the soda water venders, $20,000 . . . proprietors of the pop-corn stands, $8,000 [etc.]. **1945** *Las Animas* (Colo.) *Leader* 25 July 2/1 Waddell had the Athletics goofy by buying a mockingbird owned by the proprietor of a popcorn and peanut stand. — **(8) 1946** *Time* 23 Dec. 13/2 The Walkers had a Christmas tree and hoped to festoon it with popcorn strings—if they could find some popcorn. **1949** *Cleveland Plaindealer* 11 Dec. (Pict. Mag.) 24 The cookies combine just as well with colored lights, popcorn strings or the usual miscellany of tinsel, snow and Christmas balls.

* **Pope,** *n.*

1. *La.* The painted bunting.

1763 in *Amer. Sp.* XX. (1945) 49 The *Pope* is a bird that has a red and black plumage. **1890** *Cent.* 4620/3 *Pope*, . . . The painted finch, or nonpareil. . . . (Louisiana.) **1945** *Amer. Sp.* Feb. 49 *Pope*. . . . The English-speaking people of New Orleans call the bird 'pop.'

b. The nighthawk, *Chordeiles minor*, mistaken for the whippoorwill. *Rare.*

1781 PETERS *Hist. Conn.* (1829) 194 The whipperwill . . . is also called the pope, by reason of its . . . bawling out *Pope!*

2. Short for some such expression as "Pope Day (or Night) celebration." Also attrib. *Obs.*

1769 *Boston Chron.* 6–9 Nov. 361/2 Description of the Pope, 1769. **1772** *Boston Gaz.* 3 Feb. 3/2 The ingenuity of some of those nocturnal Sley-frolickers, had added the Drum and Conk-shell, or Pope-horn, to their own natural, noisy, abilities.

3. A nickname for the Rev. Timothy Dwight (1752–1817), president of Yale College (1795–1817). *Obs.*

1800 *Aurora* (Phila.) 12 Sep. (Th.), Dr. Dwight, the President of Yale College, [is] universally called the Pope. . . . Theodore Dwight, brother of the Pope, is a candidate for Congress. *Ib.* 16 Dec. (Th.), Long Allen and the Pope of Connecticut.

4. a. Pope Day, the fifth of November, celebrated as the anniversary of the Gunpowder Plot. **b. Pope Night,** the night of the fifth of November, celebrated orig. as the anniversary of the Gunpowder Plot. Both *obs.* Cf. **Pork Night.**

It seems unlikely that these terms originated here, but no British evidence is available for them. See *Pub. Col. Soc. Mass.* XII. (March, 1909) 288–95.

(a) 1769 ROWE *Diary* 194 Nov. 6. Monday—The People have behaved Well, being Pope Day. **1821** *Columbian Centinel* 10 Nov. 1/4 Monday last. Nov. 5th, being 'Pope Day,' brought to my recollection scenes of former days. **1823** TUDOR *Life J. Otis* 25 A custom of English origin, prevailed in Boston [*a*1774], and occasionally in other seaports of Massachusetts, of celebrating the fifth of November, the day of the well known Gunpowder plot, which was called *Pope day*.

(b) 1773 ROWE *Diary* 254 Very quiet for a Pope Night. **1842** *Lowell Offering* II. 111 But the little boys of Amesbury and Salisbury, have a celebration, which, so far as I know, is peculiar to themselves. It is the observance of Pope Night, or the Fifth of November, by bonfires upon the hills, shoutings, and all such demonstrations of rejoicing. **1907** *Nation* 24 Oct. 376 Until very recently, at least, the boys of Portsmouth, N.H., have celebrated Pope Night, without knowing or caring much about Guy Fawkes and the Gunpowder Plot.

* **poplar,** *n.*

1. The American tulip tree, *Liriodendron tulipifera*, or its wood.

1709 LAWSON *Carolina* 93 The Tulip Trees . . . are, by the Planters, call'd Poplar, as nearest approaching that Wood in Grain. **1868** GRAY *Field Botany* 42 L[*iriodendron*] *Tulipifera*. A tall, very handsome tree, in rich soil, commonest W[est], where it, or the light and soft lumber (much used in cabinet-work), is called White-wood, and even poplar. **1888** WARNER *On Horseback* 91 It was a poplar, or tulip.

2. In combs.: (1) **poplar birch,** (see quots.); (2) **borer,** =**poplar tree borer;** (3) **canoe,** a dugout canoe made from the trunk of a poplar tree, *obs.;* (4) **leaved-birch,** the American gray birch; (5) **spring,** a spring near a prominent poplar tree, *colloq.;* (6) **swamp,** a swamp in which there are many poplars; (7) **tree borer,** the larva of a beetle, *Saperda calcarata*, injurious to poplars; (8) **worm,** the larva of any one of various insects injurious to poplar trees.

(1) 1817–8 EATON *Botany* (1822) 203 *Betula populifolia*, white birch, poplar birch. 30 to 40 feet high. **1945** PEARSON *Country Flavor* 52 In various localities they [gray birches] are called poverty birch, poplar birch, paper birch, or old-field birch. — **(2) 1884** *Rep. Comm. Agric.* 383 The Poplar-Borer . . . has been destructive to poplar trees on the shores of Casco Bay. — **(3) 1775** ADAIR *Indians* 395 The enemy now and then passed the river in their light poplar canoes. **1893** LELAND *Memoirs* I. 55 An occasional Maryland dug-out or poplar canoe. — **(4) 1813** MUHLENBERG *Cat. Plants* 88 *Betula populifolia*, Poplar-leaved birch. **1821** NUTTALL *Travels Arkansa* 178 In places near the margin of the river, [was] the poplar-leaved birch. **1897** SUDWORTH *Arborescent Flora* 139.

(5) 1904 E. GLASGOW *Deliverance* 432 He left the house presently and strolled slowly down to meet Maria by the poplar spring. — **(6)** [**1687** *Waterbury Prop. Rec.* 207 Ye lo land up among ye hills in a kind of a popple swamp. **1718** *Providence Rec.* XVI. 48 A small piece of meadow Lieing att a Place Called Popple swamp.] **1754** *Georgia Col. Rec.* VI. 433 [He] prayed for three hundred and forty Acres of Land, situated on the West end of Lands laid out for James New on Poplar Swamp. — **(7) 1854** EMMONS *Agric. N.Y.* V. 262 (*index*), Poplartree borer, 121, 133. [*Ib.* 121 The larvae of the *Saperda calcarata* infest lombardy poplars.] — **(8) 1806** *Balance* V. 228/2 The scratch from a cat poisoned by the poplar worm was equally pernicious. **1807** IRVING *Salmagundi* xiii. 327 Last year the poplar worm made its appearance.

As the last term in **American black, balsam, Carolina, flowering, hickory, necklace, silver, sweet, tulip, yellow poplar.**

Poplocracy pɑˈplɑkrəsɪ, *n.* Also **popocracy.** [Cf. **Popocrat**] The policies of the Populist party; popular rule. *Obs.* — **1895** *Voice* 18 July 5/3 Our fight will be for poplocracy, popular rule. **1896** *Boston Jrnl.* 24 Oct. 7/3 He is ready to support Popocracy.

Popocrat ˈpɑpəˌkræt, *n.* [*Pop*ulist+Dem*ocrat*.] A Populist. *Obs.* — **1896** *Chi. Tribune* 4 Aug. 1/1 The first returns are always in favor of the Popocrats. **1898** *Cong. Rec.* 31 Jan. 1308/2 A man is a very mean man who would try to steal a piece of five minutes, and none but a Popocrat would do it.

Popocratic ˌpɑpəˈkrætɪk, *a.* Also **Poplocratic.** [Cf. prec.] Pertaining to the Populist party. *Obs.*

1895 *Voice* 18 July 5/3, I think no more significant name could be found than the Poplocratic Party. **1896** *Chi. Tribune* 4 Aug. 1/1 Incomplete returns . . . indicate Popocratic gains. **1904** *Omaha Bee* 16 Aug. 4 If it is so important that the people of Nebraska move cautiously in the selection of their chief executive this year, why did not the popocratic conventions discover the fact before?

popped corn. Popcorn that has been popped by heating.

1850 JOHNSTON *Notes* I. 151 *Popped corn* is a novelty which the European travelling towards the west will, in this maize-growing region, probably meet with for the first time. **1947** *Downtown Shopping News* (Chi.) 2 Jan. 16/2 This popped corn and cranberries were then threaded on long strings to festoon the Christmas tree.

b. Also in phrase (see quot.).

1843 *Yale Lit. Mag.* VIII. 141 [He] danced about the apartment like a parcel of popped corn in a frying-pan.

* **popper,** *n.*

1. A form of firecracker.

1841 *S. Lit. Messenger* VII. 219/2 Firing poppers in the drawing-room. **1844** W. T. THOMPSON *Major Jones's Courtship* (1872) 167 Every body tuck Crismus, specially the niggers, and sich other carryins on—sich dancin and singin, and shootin poppers and sky-rackets, you never did see.

2. (See quot. 1876.)

1876 *Knight* 1764/2 *Popper*, a domestic implement for popping corn. It is usually a wire basket, which is held over the fire and shaken or

One form of popper (sense 2) or corn popper

revolved so as to keep the corn moving. **1913** EMERSON *R. Fielding at Snow Camp* 98 There was a basket of popcorn and several 'poppers' and the crowd of young folk were soon shelling corn and popping it. **1949** *Sat. Ev. Post* 21 May 36/2 It operates popcorn machines on a concession basis . . . and turns out home poppers for the kitchen trade.

3. The snapper of a whiplash. *Colloq.*

1876 CROFUTT *Trans-continental Tourist* 42 How often the sharp ring of the 'popper' aroused the timid hare or graceful antelope? **1877** RUEDE *Sod-House Days* 80 The lash is about $1\frac{1}{2}$ inches thick at the handle, and tapers to the popper, and a good hand will make them crack like a pistol.

As the last term in **brush, corn, silk popper.**

***popping,** *n.* and *a.* **1. popping corn,** =**popcorn 1.** **2. popping cracker,** =**popper 1.** *Obs.*

(1) **1850** S. F. COOPER *Rural Hours* 388 Acres of 'popping corn' are now raised near the large towns, expressly for this purpose; the varieties called rice-corn, and Egyptian corn, are used, the last kind being a native of this country, like the others. **1949** *Wholesale Grocery News* April 49/2 Reynolds' Original Hybrid Yellow is Tops in Popping Corn. — (2) **1894** CABLE *J. Marsh* xviii, He uz jis a-brouzin' round the campus sawt o' like a hobble hawss, fum de sprain he got de night he drap de poppin' crackers.

popple bark. The bark of the poplar tree, used in tonics. *Colloq.* — **1891** GARLAND *Main-travelled Roads* (1922) 292 When they's anything the matter with me, I take a lunkin' ol' swig of popple-bark and bourbon. **1903** W. J. LONG *Beasts of Field* 120 The beaver eats only bark—the white inner layer of 'popple' bark is his chief dainty.

***poppy,** *n.* As the last term in **Buddy, bush, celandine, matilija, Mexican prickly, prickly, thistle, tree poppy.**

poppycock ˈpɑpɪˌkɑk, *n.* [Du. *pappekak,* lit. "soft dung."] Nonsense, foolish talk, bosh. Also attrib. *Colloq.*

1865 BROWNE *A. Ward; His Travels* 35 You won't be able to find such another pack of poppycock gabblers as the present Congress of the United States. **1902** PIDGIN *Q. A. Sawyer* 152 'Oh, that was all poppycock,' said Hiram. 'He said that just to get even with you, when you were telling about your grandfathers and grandmothers.' **1949** *Newsweek* 21 Nov. 93/1 The story verges on sheer poppycock.

poppy mallow. Any one of various American plants of the genus *Callirrhoë* having poppylike flowers. — **1870** *Amer. Naturalist* III. 162 The Poppy-mallow (*Malva Papaver*) . . . forms one of the most brilliant figures in the prairie carpet [in Kans.]. **1939** *Nat. Geog. Mag.* Aug. 229/1 Callirhoe . . . the musical Greek name of the poppy mallow . . . , is the same as that borne by a nymph of the sea.

Pops pɑps, *n. pl.* Short for Populists. *Slang.*

1894 *Dly. Ardmoreite* (Ardmore, Okla.) 20 Jan. 3/1 Poor 'pops.' Their doom is just ahead. **1896** *Chi. Times-Herald* 27 July 6/1 He is a broad young man . . . and the pops' platform contains 'isms' enough even to suit him. **1910** *Sat. Ev. Post* 16 July 31/3 The Democrats gained control of the Senate in the 90s by combining with the Populists and giving the Pops patronage and good committee assignments.

***popular,** *a.*

1. a. (See quot. 1867.) **b.** (See quot.) Both *obs.*

(a) **1848** LOWELL *Biglow P.* 1 Ser. i. 13 He see a cruetin Sarjunt a struttin round as popler as a hen with 1 chicking. **1867** *Ib.* 2 Ser. p. lviii, A few phrases not in Mr. Bartlett's book which I have heard [include] . . . *Popular:* conceited. — (b) **1884** *Sat. Review* 8 Nov. 590/2 [In] an out-of-the-way New York restaurant, . . . a young citizen observed, 'I don't call this very popular pie.' They have come to take popular quite gravely and sincerely as a synonym for good.

2. popular sovereignty, sovereignty vested in the people as a whole.

A phrase applied specifically before the Civil War to the doctrine that Congress should allow the people of the territories and states to regulate their own domestic matters, particularly slavery.

1848 *Whig Almanac 1849* 4/2 If you decide that we have not governed faithfully . . . , you prove yourself an enemy of Popular Sovereignty. **1858** DOUGLAS in Logan *Great Conspiracy* 72 Let us maintain the great principles of Popular Sovereignty, of State rights and of the Federal Union as the Constitution has made it. **1948** *Pacific Spectator* Summer 256 Popular sovereignty could work only one way —to promote the spread of slavery.

3. popular vote, the vote of the entire electorate as distinguished from the electoral vote (sense **2.**).

1840 *Politician's Reg.* 4 All the States but South Carolina choose their Electors by a popular vote. **1893** *Harper's Mag.* April 803/1 Complete returns from the election gave the following result of the popular vote. **1949** *Western Polit. Quart.* March 89 With seventy-one electoral votes and approximately 6,342,000 popular votes cast in the 1948 election, this area is receiving more attention from the national party organizations than ever before.

***populate,** *v. intr.* To become populous. *Obs.*

1796 MORSE *Amer. Geog.* I. 556 Its [Lancaster's] trade is already great, and must increase, in proportion as the surrounding country populates. **1802** *Ann. 7th Congress* 2 Sess. 93 They have, I admit, attempted to show . . . that our empire is large, that it is populating fast. **1831** WITHERS *Chron. Border Warfare* 290 Lots were given away by lottery to intending actual settlers . . . and in a few months, Judge Symmes was able to write that 'it populates considerably.'

***population,** *n.* As the last term in **federal, floating population.**

Populism ˈpɑpjəˌlɪzəm, *n.* The principles and policy of the Populist party. Now *hist.*

1893 *Forum* Oct. 244 The doctrinal basis of Populism is socialism. **1910** *Sat. Ev. Post* 3 Sep. 26/3 The insurgency of 1910 is merely a passing recrudescence of the populism of 1892. **1949** *Miss. Valley Hist. Rev.* March 585 As an enthusiast for Populism . . . he helped to contribute to the victory of the People's party in Colorado.

Populist ˈpɑpjəlɪst, *n.* [L. *populus,* people, +*-ist.*]

1. A member of the Populist party. Now *hist.*

1892 *Chi. Tribune* 8 July 4/5 The calamity platform adopted by the Populists at Omaha might invite a limited measure of support in a droughty season or a grasshopper year. **1903** *Forum* Jan. 327 As soon as hard times come again, we shall have the Populist with his wail of woe. He may not flourish under the same name—he was a Greenbacker before. **1948** *Chi. D. News* 4 May 12/1 Imagine the old Populists . . . trying to cover up their political affiliations.

attrib. **1893** *Chi. Tribune* 26 April 10/6 The rank and file of the 'kickers' who made up the Populist vote are not for a third party. **1910** *Sat. Ev. Post* 3 Sep. 26/3 The Populist platform described the gold standard as a 'vast conspiracy against mankind.' **1949** D. O. MCGOVNEY *Amer. Suffrage* 111 In the early nineties the Populist movement had threatened the same.

2. Populist party, the popular designation for the People's party *q.v.*, organized in 1891 to champion the interests of workers in general and the agrarian classes in particular against the moneyed interests of the country. Now *hist.*

1893 *Nation* 19 Jan. 43/2 The situation results from the rise of the Populist party. **1906** in *Kans. Hist. Soc.* IX. 425 The Populist party was in truth the outgrowth of the Farmers' Alliance, which, originating in the South, soon spread throughout the country, absorbing and assimilating the state Granges and similar organizations. **1916** *N.Y. Times* 22 Nov. 9/2 [Nebraska] was said to be the last State in which the Populist Party existed.

populistic ˌpɑpjəˈlɪstɪk, *a.* Of or pertaining to the Populist party. — **1894** *Advance* 4 Oct., It was Mr. Bryan & his populistic ideas which were the bone of contention. **1904** *Booklovers Mag.* Jan. 4 In 1900 the Populistic support showed signs of ebbing in the face of better agricultural conditions.

Populite ˈpɑpjəˌlaɪt, *n.* A Populist. Also attrib. Now *hist.*

1892 *Chi. Tribune* 7 July 12/6 The Populites ought to have put a rainmaker on the tail of their ticket and to have adopted a platform of 'money and weather to order.' **1898** *Cong. Rec.* 8 Feb. 1553/1 Mr. Kolb . . . has been the head and shoulders of the Populite party of Alabama since its organization. **1935** CASON *90°* 73 Their enemies termed them Populists (or, more commonly, *Populites*).

Populization ˌpɑpjələˈzeʃən, *n.* Placing under the control of Populist doctrines. *Rare.* — **1897** *Nation* 25 Nov. 413/2 After the Populist victory in the State election last fall, the leaders of the party made it plain that the Populization of the [state] college would be carried still further.

porcelain ˈporslɪn, *n.* [F. *porcelaine.*] (See quots.) *Obs.*

1705 HARRIS *Navigantium atque itinerantium* II. 906/2 Then we delivered our Presents, consisting of Axes, Knives, a great Collar of white and blew Porcelain, with some Gowns. **1709** LAWSON *Carolina* 191 The Hair of their [the Indians'] Heads is made into a long Roll like a Horses Tail, and bound round with Ronoak or Porcelain, which is a sort of Beads they make of Conk-Shells. **1911** BLAIR *Indian Tribes Upper Miss. Valley* I. 152 'Porcelain' was the Canadian-French term for the shell, glass, or porcelain beads used as money and ornaments by the Indians—the 'wampum' of English writers.

porcelaintype ˈporslɪnˌtaɪp, *n.* (See quot. 1938.) — **1869** MARK TWAIN *Letters* (1917) I. 160, I have bundled up Livy's picture, and will try and recollect to mail it tomorrow. It is a porcelaintype. **1938** RAMSAY *Mark Twain* 175 Porcelaintype. . . . This variety of photograph, produced on a sensitized porcelain plate or 'opal' glass, was formerly popular and is still occasionally made, but is now known in the trade simply as a 'porcelain' or an 'opal.' It was often retinted by hand.

***porch,** *n.* A veranda.

1832 KENNEDY *Swallow Barn* II. 41 Hafen Blok was regaling his circle of auditors in the porch at Swallow Barn. **1916** S. ANDERSON *Windy McPherson's Son* 30 When the evening papers were distributed he hurried home to sit on the porch before the house. **1948** MENJOU & MUSSELMAN *It Took 9 Tailors* 19 It was a big frame house with a wide porch.

attrib. **1835** BIRD *Hawks* I. 37 The coach . . . stopped at the porch-step. **1916** WILSON *Somewhere* 183 Them riding pants fixed her good in the minds of our lady porch-knockers. **1948** *Democrat* 22 April 1/7 Porch and Lawn Chairs, Swings, Gliders and Metal Tables.

b. porch climber, a second-story thief. *Slang.*

1900 G. ADE *More Fables* 218 [They] supposed him to be a Retired Porch-Climber.

As the last term in **back, carriage, house, shed, side, storm, sun porch.**

***porcupine,** *n.*

1. Any rodent of the family Erethizontidae, having long, sharp spines loosely attached to the skin. Cf. **Canada porcupine.**

1634 Wood *N. Eng. Prospect* 22 The Porcupine is a small thing not much unlike a Hedgehog. **1743** Catesby *Carolina* II. xxx, These Porcupines are natives of New England, and the more Northern parts of America, and are sometimes, tho' rarely, found as far South as Virginia. **1809** A. Henry *Travels* 146 (*footnote*), The animal, which, in America, is called the porcupine, is a hedge hog, or urchin. **1949** *Canadian Alpine Jrnl.* May 53 At dusk, a porcupine made the mistake of wandering into camp, allowing us to add variety to the diet.

attrib. **1665** *Narragansett Hist. Reg.* III. 71 [They sent] a porcupine bagg for a present to the Queene. **1775** Cresswell *Journal* 116 Went over the River and bought a Porcupine Skin of an Indian. **1939** White *One Man's Meat* 128, I learn that $42.50 was paid out in porcupine bounties, and $13.88 to a typist. **1942** Kennedy *Palmetto Country* 5 Another low-lying palmetto—variously called the dwarf, needle, porcupine, blue, or creeping palmetto—has an even wider range than the saw palmetto.

b. porcupine brandy, (see quot.). *Obs.*

1855 *Golden Era* (S.F.) 29 April 1/7 Did you ever go on . . . a nine days spree on porcupine brandy—stuff that they sell for a short *bit* a glass, and from which you receive a long *bite* in return?

2. porcupine grass, a tall grass, *Stipa spartea*, found chiefly in the West, the flowering glume of which has long, strong awns.

1857 Gray *Botany* 549 Porcupine Grass. . . . Plains and prairies, from Illinois and N. Michigan northwestward. **1941** Seton *Trail of Artist-Naturalist* 226 His thick stockings were most inviting targets for the noted spear-grass or porcupine-grass of the Plains.

3. porcupine-quill work, among Indians, beadlike ornamental work made of porcupine quills.

1819 P. Wakefield *Excursions in N. Amer.* 285 Their porcupine-quill work is elegant. **1850** Garrard *Wah-To-Yah* (1927) vii. 87 Their robes, leggins, and skin dresses, glittered with beads and porcupine quillwork. **1949** *Sat. Ev. Post* 16 April 158/3 Only rarely can they find a Chippewa squaw who is still turning out porcupine-quill work.

porgy 'pɔrgɪ, *n.* [Origin not clear. It may be related to **paugie,** but cf. Sp. *pargo*, a fish name.] Any one of various marine fishes, esp. any one of the various North American species of sea bream of the family Sparidae.

1775 Romans *Nat. Hist. Florida* App. p. xix, A little to the north hereof is a small reef . . . where vast quantities of groopers, snappers, amber-fish, porgys, margate-fish, rock-fish, yellow-tails, Jew-fish, &c. may be taken. **1849** D. Webster *Private Corp.* II. 337 [I] caught some fish, namely, tautog and skippog, the same, I suppose as are called 'Porgee' in New York. **1949** *Fishing Gaz.* Sep. 90/1 Porgies and Virginia croakers have been coming in.

Attrib., esp. with reference to boats used in porgy fishing.

1879 *U.S. Comm. Fish & Fisheries* V. 141 Mr. Wasson gave an interesting account of the use of 'porgy chum' as a food for sheep and poultry. **1880** *Harper's Mag.* Sep. 510/1 Among the rest are two of the singular 'porgy steamers' turned to mackereling. **1906** *N.Y. Ev. Post* (Sat. Supp.) 18 Aug. 1 The 'porgy' boats, dirty, snub-nosed, and half the time unfit to be afloat on anything bigger than a pond are far removed in standing from their fellows. **1914** Steele *Storm* 191 For the first time that season the porgie fleet moved in around Long Point.

b. porgy hunting, (see quot.). *Slang.*

1904 *Scribner's Mag.* May 548 When we cruise about, hooking on to any job we can catch, and at any price we can get for it, that's porgy hunting.

As the last term in **flannel-mouthed, goat's-head, grass, sheepshead porgy.**

* **pork,** *n.*

1. *Polit.* Federal money granted for local improvements on a political patronage basis. *Colloq.*

1879 *Cong. Rec.* 28 Feb. 2131/1 St. Louis is going to have some of the 'pork' indirectly; but it will not do any good. **1916** *N.Y. Times* May 12 The militia plan has appealed to some of the nation's thrifty legislators as a fair substitute for 'pork.' **1949** *News-Herald* (Marshfield, Wis.) 19 July 4/3 That difference of more than $54,000,000 includes a lot of pork for individual Senators.

2. In combs.: (1) **pork barrel,** see as a main entry; (2) **bill,** (see quots. and cf. **pork barrel bill**); (3) **business,** the business of curing and marketing pork; (4) **chopping,** cutting up pork in the process of curing it, *obs.;* (5) **City,** Cincinnati, Ohio, a nickname, cf. **Porkopolis;** (6) **crop,** the quantity of pork packed in a year, *rare;* (7) **dodger,** pork prepared as food in the form of balls or dodgers; (8) **eater,** (see quots.), now *hist.;* (9) **fish,** a name used locally for any one of various American fish of the family Haemulidae, cf. **grunt,** * **hogfish;** (10) **ham,** (see quot.), *obs.;* (11) **house,** a business house that deals in pork; (12) **king,** a person of great wealth derived from raising hogs or dealing in pork; (13) **merchant,** a merchant who deals in pork; (14) **Night,** (see quot. and cf. **Pope Night**); (15) **packer,** one engaged in the business of preparing and marketing pork; (16) **packery,** a place where pork and related products are prepared for market; (17) **packing,** the business of dressing, curing, and marketing pork, also attrib.; (18) **pit,** the part of the stock exchange devoted to trading in pork; (19) **raiser,** one who raises hogs for the market, cf. **cattle raiser;** (20) **season,** formerly the season, in winter, when pork could be cured, *obs.;* (21) **tenderloin,** tenderloin obtained from a hog; (22) **wood,** (see quot. 1884).

(2) **1901** *Cong. Rec.* 2 March 3527/1 This bill [the river and harbor bill] has become known in the most remote corners of the United States . . . as the pork bill of Congress. [**1943** DeVoto *Yr. of Decis.* 288 On the third he vetoed the seasonal pork, the rivers and harbors bill.] — (3) **1838** Ellsworth *Valley of Wabash* 42 The pork business, in its various branches, has furnished the commencement and completion of many splendid fortunes. **1848** *Rep. Comm. Patents 1847* 549 In consequence of the rapid development of the pork business in western states . . . we have, in another place estimated the number of swine in the United States at 35,000,000. — (4) **1850** S. Warner *Wide, Wide World* xxv, Miss Fortune had no idea of having pork-chopping or apple-paring done there.

(5) **1847** Robb *Squatter Life* 19 A streak of *fat* was waiting for his arrival in the pork city. **1855** M. Thompson *Doesticks* 309 Being in the vicinity of the Pork city (where they have a ham on the top of the tallest church spire in the place, pointing with the knuckle end to Heaven,) I had an opportunity to visit a large wine-cellar. — (6) **1872** *Dly. Morning Chron.* (Wash.) 2 May 2/2 The pork crop of 71–'2 is more abundant in quantity and finer in quality than that of any previous year. — (7) **1844** M. C. Houston *Texas* (1845) 223 Our fare was not bad of its kind, there being 'pork dodgers' and 'dough doings,' (corn bread) chicken fixings and sausages. — (8) **1801** A. Mackenzie *Voyages* 33 Part of whom proceeded from thence to Rainy Lake, as will be hereafter explained, and are called Pork eaters, or Goers and Comers. **1857** *Jrnl. Rev. Peter Jacobs* 72 All *pork eaters* from Canada do not know how to make it. **1944** Nute *Lake Superior* 44 Those who came from Montreal were 'pork-eaters' in voyageurs' parlance. — (9) *c*1733 Catesby *Carolina* II. 4 The Pork Fish . . . is broad and short, and somewhat flat. . . . The Bahamians esteem this a good Fish. **1888** Goode *Amer. Fishes* 81 The Norfolk Hog-fish, *Pomodasys fulvomaculatus*, . . . is the . . . 'Porkfish' and 'Whiting' at Key West. **1911** *Rep. Fisheries 1908* 310/2 *Grunt.*—The name of several small *Hæmulidæ* quite common off the south Atlantic and Gulf coasts, and sometimes found on the California coast. Different species are known as . . . 'sargo,' 'pork-fish,' etc. *Ib.* 314/1 Porkfish (*Anisotremus virginicus*).

(10) **1774** in *Amer. Hist. Rev.* VI. (1900) 84 For Dinner smoack'd bacon or what we cal pork ham. — (11) **1836** in *Jrnl. So. Hist.* I. (1935) 350 It is a pity that such a beautiful City as Cincinnatti should be so polluted by '*Pork.*' Walk through the City & you see at every step '*Pork House*'—'*Pork House.*' **1890** Howells *Boy's Town* 36 Cooper-shops, where the barrels were made, alternated with the pork-houses. — (12) **1893** M. Howe *Honor* 155 Gwendolin O'Shaunessey, the daughter of old O'Shaunessey the Western pork-king. — (13) **1838** *N.Y. Advt. & Exp.* 7 Feb. 3/3 Cincinnati has always enjoyed a high reputation for the superior quality of the pork, lard and bacon cured by her 'Pork Merchants.' **1872** *Harper's Mag.* Feb. 369/1 A pork merchant . . . received him kindly, being used to deal with hog-drovers. — (14) **1909** *Pub. Col. Soc.* XII. 291 Perhaps the one place where it [i.e., Pope Night] lingered longest is in the old town of Portsmouth, New Hampshire . . . the performance has changed to the blowing of horns and the carrying about of pumpkin lanterns by boys, none of whom know the origin of the celebration, and even the name has been changed to Pork Night.

(15) **1838** *N.Y. Advt. & Exp.* 7 Feb. 3/3 It is due to that enterprising class of citizens, the pork packers, that the error should be corrected. **1949** *Boston Globe* 26 June (Fiction Mag.) 2/1 These corporations were principally distillers, manufacturers of tobacco, and especially, beef and pork packers. — (16) **1856** *Sacramento Union* 24 March 4/1, I 'spose it was made by some of them Cincinnati Germans, in imitation of the squealin' at a pork packery. **1880** *Lib. Universal Knowl.* X. 447 Broom factories, pork packeries, soap-works are found in Nebraska. — (17) **1851** Cist *Cincinnati* 228 Pork and Beef Packing. **1854** *Maysville* (Ky.) *Eagle* 14 Nov. 2/2 This and the old, well-known and popular pork-packing house of Messrs. Coons & Dobbins . . . are the only establishments of the kind here. **1902** Lorimer *Lett. Merchant* 143 You've got to eat hog, think hog, dream hog—in short go the whole hog if you're going to win out in the pork-packing business. — (18) **1887** *Courier-Journal* 3 Feb. 7/4 The brokers who stick to the pork pit day in and day out the year round. — (19) **1839**

Indiana H. Rep. Jrnl. 23 Sess. 231 The scarcity of [salt] . . . is likely to prove so mischievous to the interests of our pork raisers and dealers. **1880** INGHAM *Digging Gold* 203 Is this the *honor* of Western pork-raisers?

(**20**) **1854** BUSCH *Wanderungen* I. 247 Wer weniger als hundert Stück besitzt, uberlässt sie, wenn die *Pork-Season* beginnt. — (**21**) **1917** McCUTCHEON *Green Fancy* 22 'Ham and eggs, pork tenderloin, country sausage, rump steak and spring chicken,' said Mr. Bacon. — (**22**) **1884** SARGENT *Rep. Forests* 117 *Pisonia obtusata*. . . . Pigeon Wood. Beef Wood. Cork Wood. Pork Wood. **1897** SUDWORTH *Arborescent Flora*.

b. In the names of dishes in which pork and some other food are cooked or served together, as (1) **pork and beans,** (2) **cabbage,** (3) **greens,** (4) **molasses,** (5) **potato balls.**

(**1**) **1775** J. ANDREWS *Letters* 95 Pork and beans one day, and beans and pork another and fish when we can catch it. **1891** SALA in *Times* (London) 22 Feb. 2/3 Then I heard of the contemplated establishment of a London American club, the scheme of which seemed to comprise unlimited cocktails, . . . pork and beans, soft-shell crabs [etc.]. **1948** *Dly. Ardmoreite* (Ardmore, Okla.) 12 May 1/3 My wife can't buy pork and beans with sympathy. — (**2**) **1704** S. KNIGHT *Journal* 15 Shee serv'd in a dish of Pork and Cabage. **1775** in *Mass. Hist. Soc. Proc.* 2 Ser. IX. (1894) 59 When I came home I had a hearty dinner of pork and cabbage. **1919** DENTON *Naturalist's Diary* (1949) 198 It was a splendid dinner consisting of slices of fried ham, boiled pork and cabbage, creamed potatoes, corn bread. — (**3**) **1868** W. BAKER *New Timothy* (1870) 193 An' you don't love pork an' greens? **1887** M. E. WILKINS *Humble Romance* 244 If we could hev some cabbage, or some pork and greens, how the light would stream in. — (**4**) **1843** *Quincy* (Ill.) *Herald* 3 Feb. 1/1 Pork and molasses for those that like it; and lick your own fingers. **1859** GRATTAN *Civilized Amer.* I. 64 Probably the most fearful is when it [pig's meat] is eaten with treacle, by way of sauce, and then playfully called pork and 'lasses (molasses).

(**5**) **1846** BEECHER *Domestic Receipt Book* 290 *Pork and Potato Balls*. Take one-third chopped pork or ham, either raw or cooked, and two-thirds of cold cooked potatoes chopped fine. Mix them up with egg, *a little* salt and pepper, and then make into balls and fry, or merely cook in a skillet.

As the last term in **barrel, clear, mess, political pork.**

pork barrel.

1. A barrel in which pork is kept.

1801 R. B. THOMAS *Farmer's Almanack for 1802* 1–3 May/2 *Better spare at the brim, than at the bottom*, is an old proverb, and should teach us to mind our pork and cider barrels. **1842** *Juliet* (Ill.) *Courier* 2 Feb. 3/1 Farmers can be accommodated with a very good Pork Barrel in exchange for Oats Butter or Wheat. **1866** *Cent. Mag.* Sep. 787/2 When the pork-barrel was empty they *shot* [a hog]. **1945** NEWTON *Paul Bunyan* 158 It was as big around as a pork barrel.

2. *Polit.* A governmental appropriation or bill which supplies funds for local improvements designed to ingratiate congressmen with their constituents. Also transf. *Colloq.*

1913 *Standard Dict.* 1932/3. **1916** *N.Y. Ev. Post* 12 May, The River and Harbor bill is the pork barrel par excellence, and the rivers and harbors are manipulated by Federal machinery and not by State machinery. **1949** *Time* 30 May 12/2 The pork barrel rumbled merrily about the Senate chamber, flattening out economic forces before it.

attrib. **1916** *N.Y. Times* May 12 This bill is a 'pork barrel' proposition. **1916** *Chi. Tribune* 8 Oct. II. 2/1 Even the 'pork barrel' patriots deemed it the better part of valor not to press it before election. **1947** *Denver Post* 2 March A. 1/2 From a pork barrel affair city government in Dallas became a business venture.

b. pork barrel bill, a legislative bill designed to secure an appropriation of government funds to be expended in such a way as to ingratiate the sponsors of the bill with a particular group of voters.

1913 LA FOLLETTE *Autobiog.* 60 It was on the so-called 'pork-barrel' bill for river and harbor appropriations. **1950** *Reader's Digest* Jan. 96/2 The Army Civil Functions appropriation bill—once known as the Rivers and Harbors bill and still called the 'pork barrel' bill—this year provided for 275 projects.

Porkopolis pɔr'kɑpəlɪs, *n.* **1.** Cincinnati, Ohio, a nickname. Now *hist.* **2.** Chicago, Ill., a nickname.

(**1**) **1844** *Spirit of Times* (Phila.) 27 Sep. (Th.), Parson Miller has not entirely succeeded in regenerating the morals of *Porkopolis* yet. **1946** ADAMS *Album Amer. Hist.* III. 215 'Porkopolis' Cincinnati, Ohio, still maintained first place in the pork packing industry. — (**2**) **1869** L. SIMONIN *Grand-Ouest* 11 Chicago . . . fait concurrence à Cincinnati, et lui dispute le surnom de *Porcopolis*, ou la ville des porcs. **1908** LORIMER *J. Spurlock* 23, I was determined that, so long as I was in Porkopolis, I should do as the porkers did.

Porkopolitan ˌpɔrkə'pɑlətn̩, *a.* and *n.* One who lives in Cincinnati. Of or pertaining to that city. *Obs.* — **1860** *Charleston* (S.C.) *Mercury* 27 Nov. 4/2 (*heading*), Porkopolitan Wit. **1898** *N.Y. Tribune* 28 May 5/2 The Porkopolitans won as they pleased.

porky 'pɔrkɪ, *n.* Short for porcupine *q.v. Colloq.*

1902 W. HULBERT *Forest Neighbors* (1903) 146 We found the Porky asleep in the sunshine. **1921** *Outing* July 148/3 A well fed, rotund porcupine blocked the trail ahead, noted with customary porky indifference our approach, and amiably waddled off to one side. **1949** *Sky Line Trail* Oct. 18/2 That night, at Pipestone Flats, a pesky porky supped at my camp, satisfying its salt-craving by dining heartily upon my sweat-saturated hatchet handle.

***porpoise,** *n.* As the last term in **harbor, skunk porpoise.**

***porridge,** *n.* Slush or ice, snow, etc. Also attrib. *Colloq.*

1700 SEWALL *Diary* II. 26 Because of the Porrige of snow, Bearers . . . rid to the grave. **1870** *Scribner's Mo.* I. 154 While the engineers were floundering in the porridge at the west end, they wisely resolved to . . . sink a shaft to grade. **1880** *Scribner's Mag.* Jan. 331/2 The water was full of porridge-ice.

As the last term in **acorn, bean, Indian, pumpkin, samp, sap porridge.**

***port,** *n.* As the last term in **lake, lumber, lumbering, prairie port.**

portaal pə'tɔl, *n.* (See quot. 1848.) *Obs.* — [**1769** SMITH *Tour* 65 You first enter an inclosed Shed or Portus which serves as a Wood house or Ketchin and then the Body of the Edifice.] **1848** BARTLETT 258 Portaal. (Dutch) A portal, lobby. Used by people of Dutch descent, in New Jersey and New York, for a small passage or entry of a house, and pronounced *pit-âll*.

***portage,** *n.*

1. The carrying or transporting of canoes, goods, etc., overland from one stretch or body of navigable water to another, usu. around rapids, falls, etc.

1759 *New Amer. Mag.* Aug. 577 The portage by land is both fatiguing and dangerous. **1846** G. WARBURTON *Hochelaga* 102 This branch is interrupted in its course by numerous rapids and cataracts, to such an extent as to preclude the possibility of ever navigating it without frequent 'portages.' **1921** *Outing* Feb. 212/3 A portage . . . would bring us to the shores of another lake. **1948** *Nat. Geog. Mag.* Aug. 214/2 The first of our nine portages was simple.

b. *To make a portage*, to carry or transport canoes, goods, etc., over a carrying place.

1698 tr. HENNEPIN *New Discovery* I. 74 [We] brought up our Bark to the great Rock of Niagara, . . . where we were oblig'd to make our Portage; that is, to carry over-land our Canow's and Provisions, and other Things, above the great Fall of the River, which interrupts the Navigation. **1755** EVANS *Anal. Map Colonies* 18 You are obliged to make a Portage up three pretty sharp Hills about eight Miles. **1897** *Outing* XXX. 583/2 We camped at night, made our portages, and traveled rapidly.

2. A land route or passageway along which canoes and goods are carried around obstructions in a stream or between navigable bodies of water. Also a place where such a route begins or ends.

1698 tr. HENNEPIN *New Discovery* I. 75 The Portage was two Leagues long. **1755** EVANS *Anal. Map Colonies* 23 From Bohemia, where large Flats or small Shallops can come, there is a Portage of eight Miles to Cantwell's Bridge. **1804** *Md. Hist. Mag.* IV. 14 After riding eight miles we came to the place called the Portage, on Little River, a navigable water of the Wabash. **1903** WHITE *Forest* 6, I once met an outfit in the North Woods, plodding diligently across portage. **1949** *Prairie Club Bul.* March 6 You will see the . . . old Chicago Portage where the early voyagers portaged from Mud Lake and Lake Michigan to the Desplaines and Mississippi Rivers.

attrib. **1845** FRÉMONT *Exped.* 194 The portage-ground was occupied by emigrant families. **1887** TOURGEE *Button's Inn* 8 To have cut a wagon-road along the old portage route . . . would have required the services . . . of at least a thousand axemen. **1894** WINSOR *Cartier to Frontenac* 258 The party began to carry the material . . . along the portage track for twelve miles.

3. In special combs.: (1) **portage collar,** (see quot. and cf. **tumpline**), *obs.;* (2) **path,** a path along which boats and goods are portaged; (3) **railroad,** a railroad connecting navigable waters; (4) **road,** a road over which boats and goods are portaged; (5) **summit,** the highest point of a portage on a canal, *rare*.

(**1**) **1853** BOND *Minnesota* 240 Voyageurs . . . use the 'portage-collar,' which is a strap passing around the forehead, attached at each end to the burden . . . to be carried, which is also partly supported upon the back. — (**2**) **1812** MELISH *Travels* II. 259 Hitherto I had seen nothing but *log houses* since I left Canton. . . . [I] was advised to go by the portage path. **1843** *Amer. Pioneer* II. 24 Its eastern limit was defined to be the course of the Cuyahoga, the Muskingum, and the old portage path. — (3) **1836** P. H. NICKLIN *Peregrination* xiv, The Portage Rail Road across the Allegheny mountain, . . . will also claim a portion of our epistolary labours. **1883** *Harper's Mag.* Nov. 739/2 The Oregon Railway and Navigation Company had acquired . . . some short portage railroads. — (4) **1817** S. BROWN *Western Gaz.* 262 In wet seasons the portage road is very bad. **1864** *Harper's Mag.* Nov. 740/2 We knew that from the head of the rapids a portage road . . . descended to a cluster of rude houses.

(5) **1832** *Amer. R.R. Jrnl.* I. 196/1, I have the honor to . . . report on the reconnaissance . . . from Hudson river to the portage summit of the Ohio canal.

As the last term in **rail, wagon portage.**

portage ˈportɪdʒ, *v.* [f. the noun.] *tr.* To carry (boats, goods, etc.) over a portage, to avoid (falls or rapids) by making a portage. Also **portaging,** *n.*

1836 in *Minn. Hist. Bul.* IV. (1922) 381 Made three miles, and encamped fatigued enough after our first day's Portaging. **1871** HUYSHE *Red River Exped.* 104 (*footnote*), Boats, provisions, &c. &c., have to be 'portaged' or carried over this break [in the navigation]. **1896** *Harper's Mag.* June 118/1 All the chutes of these big rivers have to be portaged. **1925** HEMING *Living Forest* 136 We started to portage our outfit over the point. **1949** *N.O. Times-Picayune Mag.* 4 Dec. 30/3 We were compelled to portage our canoes and heavy equipment on our heads over rocky trails.

portal pɔrˈtɑl, *n. S.W.* [Sp. in same sense. An Amer. borrowing.] An arcade.

1844 GREGG *Commerce of Prairies* I. 144 The only attempt at anything like architectural compactness and precision, consists in . . . buildings, whose fronts are shaded with a fringe of *portales* or *corredores.* **1892** LUMMIS *Tramp Across Continent* 153 Outside, in the long *portal,* was enough blue, and red, and white corn to feed an army of horses. **1948** *Southwestern Rev.* Summer 245/2 What are now empty mule stalls then used to be *portals* of a convent.

* **porter,** *n.*[1]

1. One who assists in carrying the coffin at a funeral. *Obs.*

1702 *Boston Rec.* 25 It is being proposed . . . that there be a Moderation in the . . . wages of Porters for carrying the corps. **1780** *Essex Inst. Coll.* XV. 69 Elisabeth ye Daughter of Captn. Benja[min] West buryed with porters and paull holders. **1882** MCCABE *New York* 233 Porters to carry the coffin from the house to the hearse are paid $1.50 each.

2. In certain railroad cars, esp. Pullmans, an attendant who waits upon passengers, makes up berths, etc. Cf. **Pullman porter.**

1877 ROE *Army Lett.* 164 The porter in our car caught Hal, but Ryan told him to let the dog go. **1891** *Appeal-Avalanche* (Memphis) 27 April 1/1 The colored porter on the chair car of the passenger train yesterday evening lost his balance and fell off the train. **1949** *Sat. Ev. Post* 21 May 132/4 The Pullman Company maintains a dormitory in Miami where the layover porters can obtain a free bed.

* **Porter,** *n.*[2] (See first quot.) A variety of apple; also the tree on which it is grown. In full **Porter apple.**

1847 IVES *N. Eng. Fruit* 39 *Porter.*—Originated on the farm of the Rev. Samuel Porter, in Sherburne, Mass. The fruit is sometimes large, the shape oblong. **1870** *Rep. Comm. Agric. 1869* 521 J. F. C. Hyde . . . [recommends] the Gravenstein and Pumpkin Sweeting for baking, and Porter for fall. **1887** WILKINS *Humble Romance* 238 On the right of the garden were two old appletrees, a Baldwin and a Porter.

* **porterhouse,** *n.*

1. Short for next.

1854 *Harper's Mag.* Jan. 269/2 Will you have it rare or well-done? Shall it be a porter-house? **1913** LONDON *Valley of Moon* 410 Good things all the way up from juicy porterhouse and the kind of coffee Mrs. Hall makes.

2. porterhouse steak, a choice beefsteak cut from the loin next to the sirloin, allegedly so called because this kind of steak was made popular about 1814 by Martin Morrison, a N.Y. porterhouse keeper. Cf. **family, ward porterhouse.**

1841 MATHEWS *Writings* 206/2, I guess I'll take a small porterhouse steak without the bone. **1948** *Time* 21 June 26/3 In New York City last week the average for porterhouse steak was $1.03 a pound.

***portfolio,** *n.* A position in the cabinet of the President of the U.S. — **1884** BLAINE *20 Years of Congress* I. 40 Robert J. Walker . . . [was] already indicated for the portfolio of the Treasury in the new administration. **1925** BRYAN *Memoirs* 408 Secretary Bryan . . . resigned his portfolio rather than sign the second note to Germany.

* **Portland,** *n.* [App. in allusion to *Portland,* Me.]

1. A cutter or light sleigh designed for two passengers. In full **Portland sleigh.**

1893 *Outing* Feb. 369/1 Then I ran as if the fiend were on my track, for a four-minute bay roadster and a dainty Portland were behind. **1902** *Sears Cat.* (ed. 112) 379/2 As our cutter department is a part of our large Kalamazoo vehicle factory . . . we can sell a high grade Portland with a good, substantial top as described below. **1922** CADY *Rhymes* (1926) 32 Our Portland sleigh will always stay Inside my mind and body.

2. a. Portland Fancy, a kind of dance. **b. Portland tern,** the long-tailed or arctic tern, *Sterna paradisaea.*

(a) **1898** WISTER *Lin McLean* 13 Do yu' know the Portland Fancy? **1904** LOVETT *R. Gresham* 63 Below, the couples . . . were circling the hall in the rapidly weaving figures of the Portland Fancy. — (b) **1874** COUES *Birds N.W.* 691 *Sterna Portlandica.* Portland Tern. . . . The subject of the present article differs materially from any other Tern I have seen. **1917** *Birds of Amer.* I. 62 Arctic Tern. *Sterna paradisæa.* . . . [Also called] Short-footed Tern; Portland Tern; Pike's Tern.

Portlander ˈportləndɚ, *n.* A native or inhabitant of Portland, Me., or Portland, Ore.

1855 *N.Y. Wkly. Herald* 21 April 2/6 The Portlanders had just tried stringent enforcement of the Prohibitory Law. **1940** *Mt. Hood Guide* xii, Portlanders have a sort of reverence for their mountain. **1946** *Oregonian* (Portland) 10 July 1/1 Just so Portlanders would not get too downhearted, he predicted 'fair and warmer' for Wednesday. **1949** *Ib.* 10 Aug. III. 1/5 The Portlanders remained in front all the way thereafter, but never by more than a run or two.

portledge ˈportlɪdʒ, *n.* [App. f. **portage,* in same sense, poss. through confusion with **privilege,* sometimes similarly used.]

1. Orig. the freight or cargo furnished by a sailor taking part in a common venture; later, a mariner's wages. Also attrib. *Obs.*

1636 *Maine Doc. Hist.* III. 97 There are 6 of them men which . . . would nott take them vnlesse Mr. Winter would giue them bills for the last yeares Portledge. **1639** *Ib.* 185 Eduard Trebie . . . Creditor for his ½ share for his portledge monye.

2. portledge bill, a list of the names of the crew of a ship with an indication of the amount owed each for wages, allowances, etc. *Obs.*

1668 *Mass. Bay Rec.* IV. II. 390 The masters . . . shall make cleere agreem[en]ts wth. their marriners & officers for their wages, & those agreements enter into a booke, . . . a copy whereof the master, as a portlege bill, shall leaue wth. their owners. **1775** *Mass. Archives* CCVI. 94 To the am[ount] of Mens wages as per Portledg Bill 56. 17. 11½.

Port Orford cedar. [*Port Orford,* Oregon.] A large and valuable evergreen tree, *Chamaecyparis lawsoniana,* found in western North America. Also **Port Orford cypress.**

1873 MURPHY *Ore. Business Directory* 98 The Port Orford cypress (*cupressis lawsoniana*), grows luxuriantly west of the Coast Range, along the shores of the Pacific. **1884** SARGENT *Rep. Forests* 8 The change from the northern to southern forest is marked by the . . . Port Orford Cedar (*Chamæcyparis Lawsonia*). **1946** *Mazama* Dec. 69/1 Port Orford cedar on the other hand is probably doing the best of the conifers.

b. The wood of this tree.

1948 *Chi. Purchasor* March 23/2 Port Orford cedar is a white, or very pale, yellow wood, with a rather sour, cedar-like odor.

posada poˈsɑdə, *n. S.W.* [Sp. in same sense. An Amer. borrowing.] An inn.

[**1828** W. IRVING in *Life & Lett.* (1864) II. 285 The squalid miseries of the Spanish posados.] **1833** HOFFMAN *Winter in West* (1835) 93 Like our sturdy Pennsylvanian, they always help their fellow-travellers of the caravanserai, or posada, before attending to themselves. **1846** ABERT *Exam. N. Mex.* 33 We got our saddles and saddle blankets, and endeavored to form them into a bed on the earthen floor of our luxurious 'posada.' **1891** HARTE *Tam Tassajara* II. 102 (Bentley), There were some Mexicans lounging about the posada.

pose poz, *n.* [Voyageur F., from *poser,* to deposit.] (See quots.) Now *hist.*

1784–1812 THOMPSON *Narrative* (1916) 294 A Rest, or Pose, is the distance the cargo of a canoe is carried from place to place and then rest [as on portages]. **1858** *Spirit of Times* 30 Jan. 338/1 In crossing a long portage, they do not go through the whole distance with one load, but divide it into 'poses,' or rests; and carry in succession each load to the first 'pose,' and then carry them to the second one, and so on, so that they can rest in walking back for the loads. **1941** MCDERMOTT *Glossary* 126 The average length of a *pose* was about one-third of a mile. The *voyageurs,* having progressed so far, deposited their loads and returned for more; when the canoe and all the load had been moved to this point, the *voyageurs* struck out immediately for the next *pose.*

Also **pause.** *Obs.*

1846 St. John *Lake Superior Country* 46 He then goes and sets another, to which the packs left at the first pause are brought, and thus the portage is marked by pauses. **1851** Howe *Hist. Coll. Great West* 159 When the porterage is of much length, they [voyageurs] divide it into *pauses*, or distances traveled without stopping to rest. These average about a third of a mile.

posish pəˈzɪʃ, *n.* Abbrev. of "position." *Colloq.* — **1862** Norton *Army Lett.* 113 Snorting their impatience to 'get into posish,' came the Monitor, the Galena and others. **1901** Flynt *World of Graft* 199, I'd give 'em exactly what they asked for, or t'row up the posish.

positionist pəˈzɪʃənɪst, *n.* A posture master, a professional acrobat. *Obs.* — **1843** Odell *Annals N.Y. Stage* V. 61 [On October 2nd, the popular and ubiquitous T. G. Booth joined (the circus), as well as Jenkins, Edwards, and Hamlin,] the astonishing positionist.

possau pəˈsaʊ, *n.* [App. native word.] = **black drink.** *Obs.* — **1800** Hawkins *Sk. Creek Country* 76 While they are dancing, the possau is brewed. This is a powerful emetic. *Ib.* 79 The youth, during this initiation, . . . drinks the possau.

***possessed,** *a.* Very eager (to do something). *Colloq.* For **all possessed** see ***all 3.** — **1886** *Harper's Mag.* Sep. 582/2 He was possessed to get a cattle ranch out to Colorado.

possession house. A house or hut built *c*1772 to bolster a land claim in the disputed territory of the New Hampshire Grants *q.v.* *Obs.* — **1772** *Doc. Hist. N.Y. State* IV. 803 [Certain people of Bennington] are artfully endeavoring to support a Claim to the intermediate Territory, under the Weak pretence of Hutts hastily Built on small Spotts of Ground which they Term possession Houses.

***possible,** *a.* Used as an interjection (see quots.). *Colloq.* — **1835** Todd *Notes* 8 O my! with possible! [are] universal interjections [in America]. **1844** Uncle Sam *Peculiarities* I. 118 Mr. Pogue.—You knew Mr. Bompard? . . . He is in disgrace with his honour, Judge Murphy. Mr. Shippensburg.—Possible!—How so?

possibles ˈpɑsəbḷz, *n. pl.* [Sp. *posibles*, wealth, means. An Amer. borrowing and not a continuation of the slang use shown in the *OED*.] One's belongings or accouterments. *Colloq.* Cf. next.

1841 Farnham *Travels* 55/1 The loss of their [i.e., the horses'] services in transporting their traps and furs, and 'possibles,' (clothing, cooking utensils, &c.,) was severely felt. **1886** *Outing* Dec. 198/2 Dick had a big tepé, . . . not ter speak uv a considerable lot of possibles ter make things comfortable. **1947** Brown *Outdoors Unlimited* 296 Some of those 'Possibles' are a lot older than the rucksack.

possible sack. *W.* [See prec.] A bag in which camping provisions and personal belongings are carried. *Obs.* — **1846** W. G. Webb *Altowan* I. 142 Auguste . . . , by dint of much search in his possible-sack, found a piece of tobacco. **1889** *Outing* May 124/1 It is a good thing to have a bag twelve by eighteen inches for a 'possible' sack.

possum ˈpɑsəm, *n.* [See **opossum.**]

1. = **opossum.**

1613 Whitaker *Good Newes Va.* 41 The female possown . . . will let forth her young out of her bellie, and take them vp into her bellie againe. **1735** *Ga. Hist. Soc. Coll.* II. 60 A possum . . . is very like a little pig. **1838** Drake *Tales Queen City* 151 A fierce little junior . . . had often signalized himself on the banks of Licking river, as the 'real thing,' in hunting 'coons' and 'holeing possums.' **1948** *Sat. Review* 29 May 4/2 The possum broke out of his cage.

b. As an article of food.

[**1670** D. Denton *Brief Descr. N.Y.* 7 They eat likewise Polecats, Skunks, Racoon, Possum, Turtles, and the like.] **1834** *Sun* (N.Y.) 9 April 3/2 Ye git de good roast goose, and dare ye git de nice bak'd possum—gravy all run down. **1948** *Dly. Ardmoreite* (Ardmore, Okla.) 25 Nov. 7/5 No turnip greens, no hog jowls, and we're fresh out of roast possum!

Also *possum and tater*, and variants. *Colloq.*

1891 Sloan *Fogy Days* 43 In home yard, on rude table laid, [is] 'Possum and 'tater. **1917** *Mammals of Amer.* 297/2 Baked 'Possum and Sweet Potato are the joy of the Southern darky. **1949** *N.M. Quart. Rev.* Spring 91 'Possum and sweet potatoes, the pride of the Sunday table, were rarities after Jefferson's death.

2. *transf.* A paltry fellow, one who dissembles or is crafty. *Colloq.*

1833 in *Amer. Sp.* VIII. (1933) 75 A 'Possum. The western phrase for a paltry fellow—a coward. **1846** *Ib.* XXII. 204/2 That fellow fou't beautiful; if he's a specimen of the Choctaws that live in these parts, they are screamers; the infernal sarpents! the d——d possums! **1891** *Harper's Mag.* Dec. 49/2 I'm a 'possum for adapting myself to any odd hollows.

b. Deception or deceit. *Rare.*

1843 Carleton *New Purchase* II. 201 Tim Scratch know'd better not to come! He's not sick no how—it's all possum!

c. (See quot.)

1938 Matschat *Suwannee River* 28 A harmless spreading adder, locally called the 'possum,' puts on . . . a ferocious appearance when disturbed. . . . But call possum's bluff, and it flops over and plays dead.

3. In colloq. combs. of obvious meaning or sufficiently explained in the quots., as (1) **possum belly,** (2) **catcher,** (3) **dog,** (4) **fat,** (5) **fat and hominy,** (6) **hair,** (7) **hound,** (8) **hunt,** (9) **hunting,** (10) **sign,** (11) **supper,** (12) **toddy.**

(**1**) **1939** Rollins *Gone Haywire* 66 There was a sufficient supply of firewood in the 'cooney' or 'possum belly' (a baggy, dried cowhide fastened horizontally beneath the wagon box and used for carrying a reserve of fuel). **1948** *Sat. Ev. Post* 25 Dec. 69/3 As a matter of fact, a caboose has something like that, too—the 'possum's belly,' a long storage space beneath the car for holding tools and heavy equipment. — (**2**) **1855** Willis *Convalescent* 73 On our way through the woods, my 'possum-catcher stepped off to take a look at his steel-trap set at a hole in a rock. — (**3**) *a***1846** *Quarter Race Ky.* (1854) 90 (We.), Oh, my stars and possum dogs. **1916** Massey *Reminiscences* 27 Another kind of night-hunting of which I was very fond was for possums and coons. . . . A good possum dog was a great treasure. — (**4**) **1800** in Warfel *N. Webster* 292 Massa Webser plese put sum Hommany and sum Good Possum fat and sum two tree good Banjoe in your new what-you-call-um Book for your fellow Cytzen Cuffee. **1892** Duval *Young Explorers* 122 Cudjo . . . gave it as his deliberate opinion 'that Mass Seth's yearlin' fixins was better'n 'possum fat and sweet mertaters' [*sic*].

(**5**) **1824** Blane *Excursion U.S.* 134 'Possum fat and hommony' is a favourite dish with Western and Southern negroes. **1856** C. White *Oh, Hush!* 7 I'd gib you everything dat's nice, . . . Dar's possum fat an' hominy. **1930** Wittke *Tambo & Bones* 169 Suppose, frinstance, dat yoa eat yoa full ob possum fat an' hominy. — (**6**) **1709** Lawson *Carolina* 188 The Indian Womens Work is . . . to make Mats, Baskets, Girdles of Possum-Hair, and such-like. — (**7**) **1900** *Cong. Rec.* 11 Jan. 784/1 A 'possum hound or dog is a very trusty and tried friend of the colored person. **1941** Stuart *Men of Mts.* 345 We see men with foxhounds, possum hounds, shotguns and pistols tradin' under the beech trees. — (**8**) **1841** *Spirit of Times* 17 July 235/1 (We.), A 'possum Hunt. **1949** *Nat. Hist.* May 223/1 According to song and story, most 'possum hunts end at the foot of a 'simmon tree. — (**9**) **1840** *S. Lit. Messinger* VI. 784/1 He is fond of possum, rabbit, and coon-hunting. **1948** *Sat. Review* 28 Aug. 12/3 Chism is savoring the pure pleasure of possum hunting, now that autumn has come with its frosty and luminous nights.

(**10**) **1903** Fox *Little Shepherd* xxi, 'Possum signs were plentiful. — (**11**) **1884** Harris *Mingo* 6 Many who read this will remember the "possum suppers' which it was Mingo's delight to prepare for these young men. — (**12**) **1888** *Cent. Mag.* XXXVI. 766/1 A favorite small beer in those sections where the persimmon-trees flourished best was made of the fruit of that tree, and was called in the vernacular of at least one part of the Confederacy "possum toddy.'

b. In the names of plants and trees: (1) **possum berry,** (see quot.), cf. **possum haw** (*a*); (2) **grape,** = **frost grape;** (3) **haw,** (*a*) a withe rod, *Viburnum nudum,* (*b*) the swamp holly, *Ilex decidua;* (4) **oak,** the water oak, *Quercus nigra;* (5) **wood,** = **persimmon 2.**

(**1**) **1894** *Amer. Folk-Lore* VII. 90 *Viburnum nudum*, possum-berry, Ocean Springs, Miss. — (**2**) **1936** Kroll *Share-cropper* 109, I got some wild possum grapes for her, but the grapes were very sour. **1949** *Amer. Photography* April 244/3 It is also called possum grape, and is found, more or less commonly, from North Carolina to Nebraska and south to Florida and Texas. — (**3**) (*a*) **1860** Curtis *Woody Plants N.C.* 90 Possum haw. . . . The fruit is a deep blue. (*b*) **1898** Sudworth *Forest Trees U.S.* 89 Ilex decidua Walt. Deciduous Holly. . . . Names in use.—Holly (Tex., Ark., Mo.); Bearberry (Miss.); Possum Haw (Fla.). **1942** Tehon *Native Ill. Shrubs* 162 The Possumhaw is an upright shrub, or less often a small tree, with gray bark made warty by corky lenticels. — (**4**) **1884** Sargent *Rep. Forests* 152 *Quercus aquatica.* . . . Water Oak. Duck Oak. Possum Oak.

(**5**) **1897** Sudworth *Arborescent Flora* 321 *Diospyros virginiana.* . . . Possumwood (Fla.). **1910–2** *Trans. Tex. Acad. Sci.* (1913) 86 The term 'Possum Wood' is not current here, but the fact is well known among negroes that 'possums are fat in Nov. when 'simmons are ripe.

c. In colloq. phrases: (1) *To play possum,* = **possum,** *v.;* (2) *possum up a gum tree,* (see quots.), *obs.;* (3) *to come the possum over,* to deceive; (4) *to grin like a possum,* to assume an expression suggestive of that of a possum.

(**1**) [**1779** Anburey *Travels* (1923) II. 227 This method of feigning death is what preserves [the opossum] . . . from the mountain cat, and other carnivorous animals.] **1822** *Notices E. Fla.* 40 (Th. Supp.), After being severely wounded, they have been known to lie for several hours as if dead. . . . Hence the expression of 'playing possum' is common among the inhabitants, being applied to those who act with cunning and duplicity. **1949** *Time* 5 Sep. 13/1 By last week, in the Senate investigation of Washington five-percenters, it became plain that John had been playing possum the whole time. — (**2**) **1831** Peck *Guide*

156 The very woods and hills shake with the negro song of 'possum up a gum-tree.' **1840** HALIBURTON *Clockmaker* 3 Ser. xxi, Many's the time I have danced 'Possum up a gum tree' at a quiltin' frolic or huskin' party. **1848** G. E. ELLIS *Let.* (Bartlett MS), 'Possum up a gum tree' [is used] at the South & West, for *opossum.* — (3) **1862** E. KIRBY *Among Pines* 189 He seems well enough, sir; I believe he's coming the possum over mother. — (4) **1939** *These Are Our Lives* 252, I can go to sleep grinning like a 'possum.

b. possum hunt, *v. intr.* To hunt for possums. *Colloq.*

1900 *Cong. Rec.* 11 Jan. 784/1, I used to 'possum hunt.

possum 'pɑsəm, *v.* [f. the noun.] *intr.* and *tr.* To feign death, to dissemble, pretend. *Colloq.*

1832 FLINT *Geog. Mississippi Valley* (ed. 2) I. 67 In the common parlance of the country, any one, who counterfeits sickness . . . is said to be 'possuming' [ed. 1828 oppossuming]. **1853** BALDWIN *Flush Times Ala.* 150 All this time I was possuming sleep . . . as innocent as a lamb. **1894** CABLE *J. March* xxii, A dim shape . . . vanished before he could add, 'He was possuming!'

possuming 'pɑsəmɪŋ, *n.* **1.** (See quot.) **2.** Hunting possums. Both *colloq.* — (1) **1846** LEVINGE *Echoes from Backwoods* II. 32 'Possuming is become an idiom; a term signifying any one who is humbugging or deceiving.—(2) **1869** *Routledge's Every Boy's Annual* 607 To go out with him on a 'possuming expedition.

∗**post,** *n.* [See note.]

The *OED* lists no fewer than ten ∗*post*'s (in addition to ∗*post-* the prefix) and Webster has six. Since none of these terms originated in the U.S., and in the interests of simplicity of treatment, no attempt is here made to differentiate between the various ∗*post*'s (including the prefix) that are involved in the senses and combs. below.

1. An establishment or settlement, esp. one for trade, in a sparsely settled area; a trading post.

1796 HAWKINS *Letters* 15, I believe a small post might be kept to advantage. **1818** DARBY *Emigrant's Guide* 4 Like all other establishments made in America, the first settlements of Louisiana were detached, and known by the term of 'posts.' **1905** COLE *Early Oregon* 9 Near the site of the post of the Hudson Bay Company . . . was Elkton. **1940** *Places to See in Wyo.* xxi/1 In 1834, Robert Campbell and William L. Sublette who had been trapping in the Rocky Mountains then for some years, decided to build a post a mile and a half above the confluence of the Laramie and the North Platte.

attrib. **1871** *Republican Rev.* 1 April 2/1 Indians stole Levinsky's buggy horses from the Post trader's corral. **1881** *Rep. Indian Affairs* 83 Books had been opened at the post-trading store for some time for the entry of claims. **1890** *Harper's Mag.* Oct. 654/1 The post factor, Mr. Rankin, was sick in bed, and the Indians were on a spree. **1946** STANWELL-FLETCHER *Driftwood Valley* 13 The post managers of the H.B.C. . . . always seem to be remarkably capable men and wonderfully hospitable hosts.

2. (See quot. 1891.)

1867 CRAWFORD *Mosby* 138 All the post were soon the other side of the Hazel in a safe place. **1891** *Cent.* 4639/1 post. . . . The occupants, collectively, of a military station; a garrison.

b. A local chapter of a veterans' organization, esp. of the G.A.R. and the American Legion.

1868 in *Nat. Memorial Day 1869* (G.A.R.) 7 Posts and comrades will in their own way arrange such fitting services and testimonials of respect as circumstances may permit. **1886** *San Jose* (Calif.) *Mercury* June 1/2 The Posts in Santa Clara county have members from every army corps and every State that adhered to the Union. **1949** *Minot* (N.D.) *D. News* 22 July 3/3 He is a past commander of Grand Forks post No. 6 of the American Legion.

attrib. **1903** ADE *In Babel* 251 You ought to heard old Cap Nesbit the other night after post-meetin'.

3. In combs.: (1) **post auger,** an instrument for boring post holes; (2) **ax,** (see quot. 1927), *obs.;* (3)

One type of post auger

∗**bellum,** *a.* after the Civil War; (4) **bill,** "a waybill of letters mailed by a postmaster" (W. '34); (5) **cedar,** (*a*) an incense cedar, *Libocedrus decurrens,* (*b*) the white cedar, *Chamaecyparis thyoides;* (6) **croaker,** =∗**Lafayette 1;** (7) **driver,** (*a*) an implement for driving posts into the ground, (*b*) =**stake driver;** (8) **graduate,** see as a main entry; (9) **guide,** *Conn.* a post serving as a guide to travelers, a guidepost, *obs.*, cf. **mile post;** (10) **note, oak, office,** see as main entries; (11) **rider,** one who rides post, either as a private or as a post-office employee; (12) ∗**stage,** a stagecoach, *obs.;* (13) **stamp,** a piece of postage currency *q.v.*, *obs.;* (14) **township,** a town or township in which a post-office is established,

Post axes

obs.; (15) **village,** a village with an independent post office.

(1) **1819** *Plough Boy* I. 123 Hoxie's patent post auger for digging post holes. **1901** MERWIN & WEBSTER *Calumet 'K'* 269 A swarm of men with spades, post augers, picks, and shovels had invaded the C. & S.C. right-of-way. — (2) **1812** in *Old Time N. Eng.* XVII. (1927) 188 The name 'Post Axe,' appears in a manuscript of sale, dated 1812. **1927** *Old Time N. Eng.* April 191/1 The mortising axe or post axe . . . a conspicuously long-and-narrow-bitted, short-handled instrument, employed for cutting mortise holes, by hacking out the tongue between auger borings made for the purpose. — (3) **1874** *Southern Mag.* XIV. 37 It [Atlanta] looks so little like a *post-bellum* town. **1944** CLARK *Pills* 29 Like their post-bellum successors they [i.e., stores] were found at the crossroads at central points in the more populous and older communities, and along the rivers. — (4) **1792** *Ann. 2nd Congress* 62 The deputy postmasters . . . [shall] answer to him, for all by or way letters, and shall specify the same . . . in the post bill. **1855** HOLBROOK *Among Mail Bags* 375 As the post-bill was missing, the Hartford post master expressed the opinion that the letter had very probably fallen into the hands of the mail robber.

(5) (*a*) **1884** SARGENT *Rep. Forests* 176 *Libocedrus decurrens.* . . . White Cedar. Bastard Cedar. Post Cedar. Incense Cedar. **1897** SUDWORTH *Arborescent Flora* 64 *Libocedrus decurrens.* . . . Post Cedar (Cal., Nev., Idaho). (*b*) **1897** SUDWORTH *Arborescent Flora* 77 *Chamœcyparis thyoides.* . . . Post Cedar (Del.). — (6) **1896** JORDAN & EVERMANN *Checklist Fishes* 399 *Leiostomus Xanthurus.* . . . Spot; Goody; Post-croaker; Oldwife; Lafayette. — (7) (*a*) **1857** *Rep. Comm. Patents 1856* I. 128 Sampson, Junium M. Post-driver Mar. 25, 1856. (*b*) **1888** *Harper's Mag.* Sep. 509/1 The call of the caribou . . . is a hoarse pumping sound, very much of the character emitted by that species of bittern called by some a 'post-driver,' or 'stake-driver,' only vastly louder. — (9) **1796** *Comm. Acts & Laws* 344 The Selectmen in the several Towns . . . [shall] erect, and keep up Post Guides . . . [indicating] the principal Road, or Roads, from the Towns wherein they are erected, to the Town . . . adjoining. **1839** *Conn. Statute Laws* 637 Any person or persons [who] shall pull down, break, or deface any mile-stone, post-guide, or other monument for the direction of travellers . . . shall pay . . . treble damages.

(11) **1705** *Boston News-Letter* 19 Nov. 2/2 Whoever can give any true Intelligence of her to . . . the Post-Rider . . . shall be sufficiently Rewarded. **1888** *Experiences of Forty-Niner* 28 He proved to be the mail post-rider from Santa Fé. — (12) **1738** *Va. Gazette* 28 April, Alexander Spotswood, Esq.; . . . lately formed a new Regulation for carrying on the several Post-Stages with greater Expedition and Certainty than hitherto. **1771** *Essex Inst. Coll.* XI. 39 Benj. Hart . . . now drives the post stage lately improved by John Noble. — (13) **1857** *Spirit of Times* 18 April 102/3 He will send you the balance, on receipt of ten red-headed post stamps, solely to pay postage. **1863** *Merch. Mag.* Feb. 133 It is no doubt the case, if the government paper money was discredited like post stamps or the shinplasters of individuals and corporations, a severe pressure would result in a moment. — (14) **1837** W. JENKINS *Ohio Gaz.* 55 *Alexander,* a post township on

the south line of Athens county. *Ib.* 85 *Boardman*, a flourishing post township of Trumbull county. **1842** *Popular Encycl.* V. 304/1 *Onondaga;* a post-township and capital of Onondaga county, New York. (**15**) **1827** SHERWOOD *Gazetteer of Georgia* p. v, Post Village. **1874** ALDRICH *P. Palfrey* vi, The letter . . . was dated at an obscure little post-village with a savage name somewhere on the frontiers of Montana.

4. In various phrases designating different kinds of fences.

[**1658** *Boston Rec.* 145 All outside fences aboutt pastures or cornfeilds shall bee substantially fenced, either with five rayles, or posts and pales, or sufficient stone walls, or other wise.] **1858** WARDER *Hedges & Evergreens* 107 We must raise timber for post-and-bar fence or depend upon the pines and cedars of distant regions. **1861** *Ill. Agric. Soc. Trans.* IV. 202, 509 acres, inclosed in a model manner with a substantial post and board fence. **1861** in LOGAN *Great Conspiracy* 295 They found a post-and-log fence across the Winchester turnpike. **1871** BAGG *At Yale* 145 The building . . . stands back a rod or more from the street, being separated from it by a post-and-chain fence.

b. Esp. *post and rail (fence)* and variants, a relatively straight fence in which rails are placed between posts.

1641 *New Haven Col. Rec.* 54 Fencing wth . . . strong and substantiall posts and rales . . . nott above 18d. **1786** WASHINGTON *Diaries* III. 30 [Spaded] a piece of ground No. West of the green House, adjoining thereto, the garden Wall, and Post and rail fencing

Post and rail fence

lately erected as yards for my stud horses. **1843** *Farmers' Cabinet* 15 Jan. 184/1 The expense . . . would not exceed the expense of preparing and setting up a panel of post-and-rail fence. **1886** ROOSEVELT in *Cent. Mag.* July 338/1 It is impossible to come up at full speed and 'fly' a high post-and-rails, in the way a hedge, brook, or low fence can be gone at. **1945** *Reader's Digest* Dec. 122/1 Going off the road into a post-and-rail fence can put you beyond worrying about other injuries.

As the last term in **ball, bar, base, bridle, cedar, chair, clothes, constitutional, corner, cross, forked, foul, frontier, grave, hitching, horse, lamp, locust, mile, penny, pony, powder, stage, telegraph, telephone, tie, trading, war, well, whistling, wintering post.**

* **post,** *v.*[1] *tr.* To protect (land) from trespass by prescribed legal means. Usu. * **posted,** *a.*

1907 *Springfield W. Republican* 22 Aug. 6 The ranch was eventually reached, after opening and closing several gates, all marked 'Posted.' **1910** *Ib.* 24 Nov. 10 Farmers have posted their land in all directions and are expressing dissatisfaction at the slaughter of deer. **1945** MCATEE *Pheasant* 31 There are many controlled shooting areas and much posted land.

* **post,** *v.*[2] *tr.* To inform (a person or oneself) on some subject. Usu. passive, and occas. with *up*. *Colloq.*

[**1846** *Dollar Newspaper* (Phila.) 22 July 3/4 Presuming you wish to keep your Ledger *posted up*, I drop you a line to tell you something of matters and things.] **1891** SLOAN *Fogy Days* 136, I was posted and asked the old lady how old she was when she married. **1923** MULFORD *Black Buttes* 33 If he goes to town, an' there's anythin' you can find out about him, you might learn all you can. . . . Post the boys about him, anyhow. **1947** COFFIN *Yankee Coast* 321 They are well posted on news and history, on law and industry.

absol. **1902** *Kans. State Hist. Soc. Trans.* VII. 427, I thought you would like something fresh to read and post up on what is going on in the country.

* **postage,** *n.*

1. Postage stamps. *Colloq.*

1862 NORTON *Army Lett.* 130 Paper, ink, pen and postage is forthcoming.

2. In combs.: (1) **postage currency,** =**postal currency,** also **postage-stamp currency,** now *hist.;* (2) **-due stamp,** a postage stamp affixed to a piece of mail to indicate the amount in which the postage is deficient; (3) * **stamp,** an ungummed stamp used as currency during the Civil War, *obs.* or *hist.*

(**1**) **1862** *Boston Transcript* 22 July 2/4 The Postage Stamp Currency. . . . The demand already is immense. **1862** *Washington Republican* 6 Sep. 2/1 The Assistant Treasurer is . . . using his best endeavors to procure . . . the 'Postage Currency,' in order to relieve the whole community from the embarrassment consequent upon the scarcity of 'silver change.' **1946** ADAMS *Album Amer. Hist.* III. 135 The Treasury, without Congressional authorization, issued 'Postage Currency,' which supplied the need for small change. — (**2**) **1893** CUSHING *Story of P.O.* 425 The postage due stamps . . . used . . . by postmasters or clerks only . . . are supposed never to come into possession of the public. — (**3**) **1862** *Boston Transcript* 18 July 2/2 Postage Stamps as a Legal Tender. It is said that the Treasury Department will issue a large quantity of stamps for general circulation. . . . They will be printed on thick paper without gum. **1949** *Hobbies* Oct. 132/2 With the advent of the Civil War, shortages brought us the strange encased postage stamps, postal currency, and fractional paper money.

As the last term in **first-class postage.**

* **postal,** *n.*

1. Short for **postal card.**

1871 W. DRYSDALE *Lett.* (*OED*), I have already, by postal, . . . acknowledged receipt of your late favour. **1920** HOWELLS *Vacation of Kelwyns* 208 'Just drop a postal,' the husband said.

2. Short for postal car *q.v.*

1891 *Rep. Postmaster-Gen.* 583, 2 daily lines of 50-foot postals superseding 2 lines of 40-foot.

3. In combs.: (1) **postal car,** a railway mail car fitted up with boxes and other conveniences for assorting and distributing mail en route, cf. **railway postal car;** (2) **card,** a post card with a postage stamp printed upon it, issued by the Post Office Department, also a somewhat similar card privately issued and admitted to the mail when properly stamped; (3) **clerk,** a railway mail clerk, cf. **railway postal clerk;** (4) **currency,** a paper currency authorized July 17, 1862, the notes of which bore the facsimiles of postage stamps, *obs.* [issued to take the place of actual postage stamps which had been used instead of coins, and superseded by the fractional currency *q.v.*, authorized in 1863]; (5) **note,** a money order bearing the name of the payee.

(**1**) **1868** *N.Y. Herald* 17 July 5/6 A postal car is attached . . . to the express trains from New York to Buffalo. **1903** E. JOHNSON *Railway Transportation* 176 The postal cars now being put into service are models of the builder's art. — (**2**) **1872** *Statutes at Large* XVII. 304 The Postmaster-General . . . [is] authorized and directed to furnish and issue to the public, with postage-stamps impressed upon them, 'postal cards,' manufactured of good stiff paper. **1916** WILSON *Somewhere* 345, I wanted to send a postal card to the North American Cleaning and Dye Works. **1950** *Chi. Tribune* 9 Jan. II. 1/2 Handwriting experts at county fairs gave exhibitions of writing the Twenty-third Psalm and the Lord's prayer on a postal card. — (**3**) **1872** *Statutes at Large* XVII. 310 Every route-agent, postal clerk, or other carrier of the mail shall receive any mail-matter presented to him, if properly prepaid by stamps. **1949** *Gladewater* (Tex.) *Times-Tribune* 31 July II. 6/8 Miss Iva Tucker attended a postal clerks convention in Dallas. — (**4**) **1862** *Washington Republican* 15 Aug. 2/3 The five and twenty-five cents stamps are printed on yellow bank note paper, and the tens and fifties on white paper. Their technical denomination is 'postal currency.' **1894** LEAVITT *Our Money Wars* 203 Postal Currency Gone [in 1876]. **1906** MARK TWAIN *Lett. to Sec. of Treasury* 229 (R.), 25 and 50 cent postal currency.

(**5**) **1882** *Nation* 27 July 64/1 A bill providing for the issue of postal notes for sums not exceeding five dollars was passed in the House on Friday. **1893** CUSHING *Story of P.O.* 213 A postal note may be drawn for any amount less than $5. **1949** *Chi. Tribune* 11 Dec. IV. 15/1 Collectors who wish first day cancelations of this stamp may send self-addressed envelopes . . . to the postmaster at Saratoga Springs with a postal note or money order remittance to cover the cost of the stamps.

poster 'postɚ, *n.* [f. *goal*post.*] In football, a drop kick or place kick in which the ball touches the goalposts. *Obs.* — **1876** P. H. DAVIS *Football* 462 Whether it touch such cross-bar or the posts it is called a poster and is not a goal.

postgraduate post'grædʒuɪt, *a.* and *n.*

1. *n.* A person taking a course of study or reading after graduation. Also transf.

1890 *Cent.* 4641/3 *Postgraduate*, . . . a graduate; one studying after graduation. **1900** *Cong. Rec.* 19 Feb. 1917/1 Now, the Senator is a senior, a post-graduate of great distinction of the academy of which he is now a member. **1904** WALLER *Wood Carver* 178 Marking out the work for the post-graduates . . . has filled my time.

2. *a.* Pertaining to advanced study carried on after graduation.

1858 *N.Y. Tribune* 12 Nov. 5/5 Prof. Francis Lieber gave yesterday . . . a lecture introductory to a series on the History of Commerce forming a portion of the Post-Graduate Course of Columbia College. **1921** *Ladies' Home Jrnl.* Jan 16/3, I go . . . after studying at Cornell and taking a post-graduate course in Columbia. **1949** *Chi. D. News* 4 Oct. 1/4 He took postgraduate work at Harvard.

postilion basque. (See quot. 1890.) — **1871** *Scribner's Mo.* II. 209 Bodices are pointed in front and lengthened into postillion basques behind. **1890** *Cent.* 4642/3 *Postilion-basque,* a woman's basque having its skirt cut at the back into short square tabs or coat-tails, after the fashion of a postilion's coat.

***posting,** *n.* Putting down fence posts. *Rare.* — **1788** WASHINGTON *Diaries* III. 321 In the Neck, the Posting, Railing and ditching was compleated this Morning up to the Gate.

post note. A promissory note payable to order at a specified future date, as distinguished from a note payable to bearer on demand. Now *hist.*

Issued by banks and other financial institutions before the Civil War as a circulating medium and especially "resorted to by many banks during the great commercial revulsions in 1836–7" (B. '48).

1791 JEFFERSON in *Harper's Mag.* LXX. 534/2 Rec'd. from bank a post note . . . for 116 2/3 D. **1852** GOUGE *Fiscal Hist. Texas* 32 Nearly a page of the Journal [is] devoted to a report and resolution of the Committee of Finance on a branch post-note of the United States Bank. **1912** DREISER *Financier* 20 Steemberger . . . used to come to the elder Cowperwood's bank . . . with . . . post-notes of the United States Bank in denominations of one thousand, five thousand, and ten thousand dollars.

post oak.

1. One of various species of oak the wood of which is suitable for posts; a tree of any of these species.

Applied chiefly to the iron oak, *Quercus stellata,* of the eastern states, and the swamp post oak, *Q. lyrata,* of the South.

[**1764** REUTER *Wachau* 559 Post Oak.] **1775** ROMANS *Nat. Hist. Fla.* 18 The principal however are the following: . . . Virginian white oak. . . . Dwarf white oak, or post oak. **1852** MARCY *Explor. Red River* (1854) 6 The country adjoining is high, rolling prairie, interspersed here and there with groves of post-oak, and presents to the eye a most pleasing appearance. **1945** BOTKIN *My Burden* 263 They found the body of a white man hanging to a post oak.

2. In combs.: (1) **post-oak flat(woods),** a flat stretch of land covered with post oaks; (2) **grape,** the summer grape, *Vitis aestivalis.*

(1) **1884** GREGG *Commerce of Prairies* II. 193 Some of the uplands, . . . known usually as 'post-oak flats,' . . . seem to be based upon quick-sand. **1883** SMITH *Geol. Survey Ala.* 294 Uplands and so-called wooded prairies or post-oak flatwoods. **1903** O. HENRY *Four Million* 58 Joe Larrabee came out of the post-oak flats of the Middle West. — (2) **1845** F. B. PAGE *Prairiedom* 83 The post-oak grape . . . grows abundantly on the high-lands bordering on the western rivers [in Texas]. **1891** COULTER *Bot. W. Texas* 1. 62 Summer grape. . . . Abounding in the sandy post-oak woods of eastern Texas it is called 'post-oak grape' or 'sand-grape.'

b. Also **post-oak glade, land, prairie, ridge, woods.**

1836 WM. N. WYATT *Travel Diary* (1930) 22 Rode over some poor barrens and post oak glades. — **1800** HAWKINS *Sk. Creek Country* 20 Between these rivers, there is some good post and black oak land. — **1868** *Rep. Comm. Agric. 1867* 61 In Lowndes county, Alabama, . . . great havoc was committed . . . in the post oak prairie lands. — **1836** EDWARD *Hist. Texas* 46 They are protected . . . by . . . post-oak ridges. **1940** DEAM *Flora Indiana* 528 Indian-physic . . . grows in dry soil and is usually found on the crests and slopes of chestnut oak and post oak ridges. — **1819** SCHOOLCRAFT *Mo. Lead Mines* 37 The wild turkey is still very common . . . during the heat of the day in the open post oak woods. **1892** DUVAL *Young Explorers* 14 About noon we came to a small stream by a strip of post oak woods.

* **post office.**

1. A kind of kissing game.

The meaning of the term in quot. 1851 is not clear.

1851 GREEN *Twelve Days* 157 Then, again, how often have the professors of Christianity violated all moral principles in the . . . game of Post-office, where we find stationed some beautiful sister as post mistress, whose duty it is to write the names of those from whom she thinks she can secure the postage. **1855** *Quincy* (Calif.) *Prospector* 31 March 2/1 We are astonished to see men and women who are looked upon as samples for the rising generation, join in such childish plays as . . . 'Post office,' &c. **1949** *Sat. Ev. Post* 12 March 60/3 After a time this palled and they played Post Office.

2. A place or town with a post office.

1860 GREELEY *Overland Journey* 39 Our next post-office above Jones's was Hickory Grove. **1872** TICE *Over Plains* 122 A short distance southeast of Middle Boulder Post-office, rich lodes have been discovered.

3. In combs.: (1) **post-office address,** the name or address of a place to which mail will be delivered by the post office; (2) **box,** one of many pigeonholes in a post office, in which private mail is placed, to be either asked for or taken out by the renter of the box; (3) **car,** =**postal car;** (4) **corner,** a small village containing a post office; (5) **Department,** the department of the U.S. Government charged with handling the mails; (6) **paper,** ?post paper, a half sheet of which folded forms the ordinary letter paper, *obs.*

(1) **1861** *Army Reg.* 373 Post-office address for October, Fort Jay. **1901** *Chi. Tribune* 16 Feb., Give postoffice address in full, including county and State. — (2) **1836** *N.Y. Mirror* 9 July 11/2 Applications through Post-Office Box, five hundred and fifty-nine. **1861** *Chi. Tribune* 26 May 1/9 Best of references given. P.O. Box 776. **1945** *Sat. Review* 6 Oct. 22/3 These letters all come from a post office box, with no other identification save the name. — (3) **1857** *Mich. Gen. Statutes* I. (1882) 869 The prices shall . . . be . . . a fair compensation for their post-office car. **1903** E. JOHNSON *Railway Transportation* 180 The additional pay received by the railroads that supply and haul full-sized railway post-office cars is as follows. — (4) **1891** *Outing* Nov. 96/1 Scattered through the great northern wilderness of California are 'post-office corners' and small towns that nestle in bends of rivers or in fertile mountain valleys.

(5) **1782** *Jrnls. Cont. Congress* XXIII. 672 If any postmaster, post-rider, or other person employed in the Post Office Department, shall be guilty of a breach of the said oath . . . [he] shall forfeit and pay three hundred dollars. **1943–4** *U.S. Gov't. Man.* Winter 270 Responsibility rests upon the Post Office Department to prevent, to the extent possible, the use of mails to interfere with the War Program. — (6) **1842** *Cultivator* IX. 160 If young men . . . who lack wherewithal to amuse themselves . . . would procure a few quires of paper, (that called 'post-office paper' is suitable,) and stitch them neatly together and commence saving *scraps* from the newspapers . . . they would . . . gather a large bundle of Odds and Ends.

b. Preceded by identifying words: **branch post office,** a branch of a main city post office, providing services connected with the mails; **distributing p.o.,** a post office set up for the distribution of local mail; **inferior p.o.,** in colonial times, one of the provincial post offices; **private p.o.,** a privately controlled place or organization for handling private mails, as that of a company; **volunteer p.o.,** a post office run by volunteer help.

1871 BAGG *At Yale* 213 A branch post-office was connected with the Bookstore, the 'boxes' whereof were rented for a dollar each, or one half the price of those in the general office. — **1819** E. DANA *Geog. Sk.* 78 The distributing post-office is kept here. — **1711** *Boston News-Letter* 16–23 April 2/2 The Inferiour Post-Offices in this Province of the Massachusetts-Bay, New-Hampshire, Rhode-Island and Connecticut will also take in Letters to go by the said Pacquet. — **1848** *Whig Almanac 1849* 47/2 Private post-offices, as in New York, ought not to be required, with a surplus cent levied on each letter. — **1860** GREELEY *Overland Journey* 125 A volunteer post-office is just established, to which an express-office will soon attach itself.

As the last term in **railway post office.**

***posy,** *n.* In obs. combs.: (1) **posy ball, dance,** (see quot.); (2) **pea,** (see quot.); (3) **watcher,** (see quot.).

(1) **1837** WILLIAMS *Florida* 116 The Posey Dance, of St. Augustine is introduced in a different manner. *Ib.,* The lady selects from her visitors, some happy beau, . . . and presents him with a boquet [*sic*]. . . . If he accepts . . . , he is king of the ball, which shortly after succeeds, and the posey lass becomes queen, as a matter of course. The posey ball is a mixed assembly. — (2) **1893** *Amer. Folk-Lore* VI. 140 *Lathyrus odoratus,* posy peas. Franconia, N.H. — (3) **1843** *Cong. Globe* 29 Dec. 81/3 Mr. Wright presented a petition from James Wilson, the keeper of the gate at the Capitol (commonly called the posey-watcher).

* **pot,** *n.*

1. (See quot. 1891.)

1856 BAGBY *Old Va. Gentleman* 228 He has no great faith in 'cases,' but believes in betting on three cards at a time, and has a special hankering for 'the pot.' **1891** QUINN *Fools of Fortune* 194 In the [faro] 'lay-out' . . . the ace, deuce, queen and king are called the big square; the deuce, tray, queen and jack the second square, and so on; the six, seven and eight are called the pot.

2. The circular bowl or crib of a pound net.

1865 *Mich. Laws* 717 The size of the meshes of all the pot of said nets, shall not be less than two and a half inches in extension.

3. In combs.: (1) **potashery,** (see quot. 1882), *obs.;* (2) **cheese,** (see quots. 1859, 1935, and cf. Du. *potkaas,* a kind of cheese kept or prepared in pots); (3) **closet,** a closet where pots are kept; (4) * **hook,** (see quot.), *obs.;* (5) **hound,** a dog of a nondescript or mongrel breed, *colloq.,* cf. **pot licker** (*b*); (6) * **house,** designating a politician of a cheap, contemptible kind, *slang;* (7) **lead,** [Du. *potlood*], (see quot. 1890), cf. **pot lead,** *v.;* (8) **licker,** (*a*) a low, contemptible fellow, *slang, obs.,* (*b*) =**pot hound,** also attrib.; (9) * **metal,** (*a*) designating work shoes made of hard, coarse black leather, (*b*) used in allusion to metallic currency, both *obs.;* (10) **-pie,** a pie made with meat, now usu. a baked dish of diced meat and vegetables with a top crust of pastry, also a fricassee of meat and dumplings, cf. **apple, clam pot-pie;** (11) **rack,** the cry of a guinea fowl, hence **potracking;** (12) * **walloper,** (see quot. 1859), also transf.

(1) **1846** G. WARBURTON *Hochelaga* I. 263 Potasheries, tanneries, breweries, iron-works, paper-works, and others. **1882** THAYER *From Log-Cabin* 150 A pot-ashery was an establishment containing vats for leeching ashes, and large kettles for boiling the lye. — (2) **1812** PAULDING *J. Bull & Bro. Jonathan* 115 Tell me, thou heart of cork, . . . and brain of pot cheese. **1859** BARTLETT 420 *Smear-case,* . . . a preparation of milk; . . . otherwise called Cottage-Cheese. In New York it is called Pot-cheese. **1935** *Col. of Conn.* 12 Pot cheese, Dutch cheese, and bonnyclabber were the same. These were generally sweetened with maple sugar. — (3) **1867** *Harper's Mag.* Dec. 64/2 It [*sc.* the oil] is on the third shelf, right-hand side of the pot-closet. **1890** S. HALE *Letters* 245 This morning arrived the dusky band . . . who will . . . finish the *odds* and *ends* of cleaning, the bottom of the pot closet and the top of the front door. — (4) **1749** ROBERT GOODBY *Life of Bampfylde-Moore Carew* (1788) 80 He ordered Mr Carew on shore, taking him to a blacksmith, whom he ordered to make a heavy iron collar for him, which in Maryland they call a pot-hook, and is usually put about the necks of the runaway slaves.

(5) **1903** A. ADAMS *Log Cowboy* 238 Common old pot hounds and everyday yellow dogs have gone out of style entirely. **1929** DOBIE *Vaquero* 100 We all had colds and coughs till it was like a bunch of Texas pot hounds baying a 'possum when we tried to sleep. — (6) **1809** IRVING *Knickerb.* IV. vi, [He was] distracted by petitions of 'numerous and respectable meetings,' consisting of some half dozen scurvy pot-house politicians. **1873** MILLER *Amongst Modocs* 105 A pot-house politician should represent us at the court of St. James's, if such an Indian is to be taken as a representative of his race. — (7) **1890** *Cent.* 4652/3 *Pot-lead,* . . . black-lead or graphite: as, a *pot-lead* crucible. (The word is now used chiefly of graphite in stove-polish applied to the hulls of racing-yachts below the water-line to diminish the friction of the water by giving a smooth surface.) **1894** *Outing* XXIV. 194/1, [I used] very fine sandpaper and pot lead till my boat's bottom was beautifully burnished. — (8) (*a*) **1830** ROYALL *Southern Tour* I. 78 This was said like a man, and never came into the heads of pot-lickers and scrubs. (*b*) **1932** RANDOLPH *Ozark Mt.* 223 Jethro was splitting wood as I rode into his little clearing, heralded by the clamor of a great number of pot-licker dogs. **1947** *Democrat* 30 Oct. 4/3 A hound is a hound, regardless of whether he is July, Red Bone, Walker, potlicker or just plain hush-puppy. — (9) (*a*) **1845** *Knickerb.* XXVI. 415 The butcher's apprentice . . . wears 'pot-metal brogans.' **1853** P. PAXTON *Yankee in Texas* 25 He had . . . divested his feet of a heavy pair of 'pot metal' boots, and invested them in two old, worn-out, slip-shod brogans. (*b*) **1930** BOUCHER & BROOKS *Corr. Addressed to Calhoun* 317 (*footnote*), Tod and the Democrats stood for 'hard money' and Tod was dubbed 'Pot-Metal' Tod by his opponent.

(10) *a*1792 MONETTE *Miss. Valley* (1848) II. 8 The standard dinner dish at log-rollings, house-raisings, and harvest days, was a large pot-pie. **1858** STONE *Golden Songster* 50 Oh, don't you remember . . . the pot-pies we made of the squirrels and quail? **1940** MENCKEN *Happy Days* 59 The Rennert also offered an oyster pot-pie that had its points, but the late Jeff Davis, manager of the hotel (and the last public virtuoso of Maryland cookery), once confessed to me that its flavor was really due to a sly use of garlic. — (11) **1840** *S. Lit. Messenger* VI. 386/2 The guinea-fowls make a great racket, with their pot-rack. **1883** HARRIS *Nights Uncle Remus* (1911) 193 The squawking and *pot-racking* went on at such a rate that the geese awoke. **1886** *Pop. Sci. Mo.* XXVIII. 640 That the dusting of chickens, cackling of geese, and the 'pot-racking' of Guinea-hens have not given rise to an elaborate series of weather proverbs is, I think, surprising. — (12) **1859** BARTLETT 335 Pot-Walloper. A scullion. **1913** LONDON *Valley of Moon* III. vii, Is he not the Cave-Bear Pot-Walloper and Gridironer, the most fearsome, and, next to me, the most exalted of all the Abalone Eaters?

b. In colloq. phrases: (1) *To be pot and can in,* to be of one mind with respect to, *obs.* [cf. Du *pot en pan met iemand zijn,* in the same sense]; (2) *top of the pot,* a place of preeminence, something of superior excellence; (3) *to put the big pot in the little one,* and variant [cf. F. *mettre les petits plats dans les grands,* in the same sense], to do something in a most elaborate manner; (4) *to have one's name in the pot,* (see quot.).

(1) **1789** *Amer. Museum* V. 297/2, I suppose we shall be pot and can in the general conviction, that the kingdom cannot be supported by keeping clear consciences. — (2) **1840** HALIBURTON *Clockm.* Ser. III. ix. 112 Indeed, among our ministers he is actilly at the top of the pot. He is quite 'a case,' I do assure you. **1843** *Amer. Pioneer* II. 454 Linen shirts, especially seven hundred, was counted the very top of the pot, and he who wore an eight hundred linen shirt was counted a dandy. — (3) **1893** *Outing* Sep. 473/1 She announced her intention of putting 'de big pot in de little one—dish-rag and all,' which means great things. **1948** *Dly. Ardmoreite* (Ardmore, Okla.) 27 July 6/1 The town is very happy over its birthday and proposes, as the old saying has it, to put the big pot in the middle or something to make an occasion of the day. — (4) **1946** *Atlanta Jrnl. Mag.* 3 March 9/2 When one wants to be counted in on a deal he has his name in the pot.

As the last term in **apple butter, batter, bean, boiling, buckwheat, cow, cream, dinner, dye, fish, hominy, jack, mush, paint, pepper, shell, skilly, stick, stink pot.**

* **potato,** *n.* In combs.: (1) **potato bake,** an occasion when friends and neighbors come together and bake and eat potatoes; (2) **ball,** (*a*) the small round berry or seed ball of the potato plant, (*b*) a ball or croquette of mashed potatoes; (3) **bank,** *S.* a cone-shaped heap of sweet potatoes suitably covered with bark, straw, earth, etc.; (4) **beetle,** the Colorado beetle, *Leptinotarsa decemlineata,* which destroys the leaves of the Irish potato, also attrib.; (5) **bug,** (*a*) =**potato fly,** (*b*) =**potato beetle,** cf. **Colorado potato bug;** (6) **chip,** a thin slice of raw potato fried in deep fat; (7) **chowder,** chowder in which potatoes are used; (8) **clay,** a substance used by the Hopi Indians in making pigments; (9) **coffee,** a coffee substitute made of potatoes chopped up and roasted [the meaning of the term in the first quots. is not clear]; (10) **digger,** an implement, now horse-drawn, for digging and gathering potatoes, cf. **digger;** (11) **fly,** any one of various soft-bodied beetles of the family Meloidae which are injurious to potatoes, cf. **potato beetle, potato bug;** (12) **gospel,** (see quot.), *rare;* (13) **gun,** (see quot. 1909); (14) **heap,** a conical heap or pile of potatoes protected against the weather by a covering of straw or earth, cf. **potato bank;** (15) **hill,** =prec., also transf.; (16) **hole,** (see quot. 1940); (17) **hook,** an agricultural implement with bent tines for digging potatoes; (18) **house,** a house for storing potatoes; (19) **patch,** a comparatively small

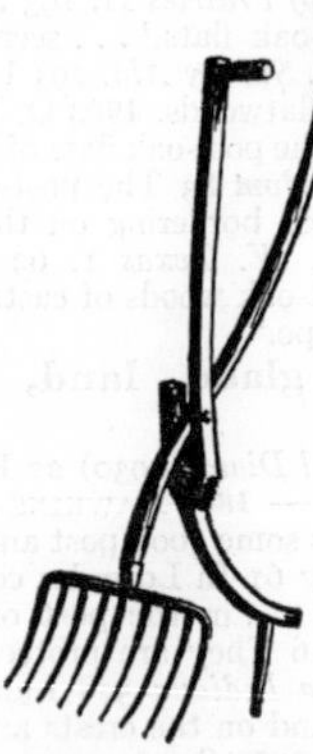

Potato digger of early (*c*1856) type

field or area in which potatoes are planted; (20) **pone,** bread in the form of pones, made of potatoes; (21) **slip,** *S.* a young sweet potato plant suitable for setting out; (22) **vine,** the foliage of the potato plant, used esp. of the sweet potato; (23) **whisky,** whisky made of potatoes, *obs.;* (24) **worm,** the larva of a sphinx or hawk moth injurious to potatoes, also attrib.

(1) **1889** *Pueblo* (Colo.) *Review & Standard* 7 Nov. 3/2 The Potato Bake at Monument . . . will positively . . . take place tomorrow. **1948** *Prairie Club Bul.* May 9 An added attraction will be a potato bake. — (2) (*a*) **1823** T. B. HAZARD *Nailer Tom's Diary* (1930) 596/1 Planted a Potatoe Ball. **1887** *Vt. Bd. Agric. Rep.* IV. 33 Nature can make potato balls, but she couldn't make the Early Rose. (*b*) **1850** MARY RANDOLPH *Va. Housewife* 99 Potato Balls. Mix mashed potatoes with the yelk of an egg, roll them into balls, flour them [etc.]. **1887** I. ALDEN *Little Fishers* xi, Mrs. Decker . . . was serving three lovely fish and a bowl of potato balls for 'Decker' and herself. — (3) **1854** DAVIS *Farm Bk.* 117 George . . . put dirt on the potato Banks. — (4) **1868** *Amer. Naturalist* III. 129 The New Potato-beetle . . . made its appearance in the immediate neighborhood of Washington, D.C. **1882** G. A. SALA *Amer. Revisited* II. 173 The nightshade family is represented by the Potato-Beetle weed (*Solanum rostratum*). **1946** *March of Progress* Feb. 173 Among the latter are the potato and cucumber beetles.

(5) (*a*) **1799** E. DRINKER *Journal* (1889) 347 They call them here . . . the Potato-Bug, being numerous on the potato tops. **1907** BAILEY *Cyclo. Amer. Agric.* II. 524/1 The old-fashioned potato-bug or blister-beetle (*Epicauta vittala*) is combated in the same way as the Colorado potato-beetle. It is now rarely seen. (*b*) **1890** *Cent.* 4649/1. **1949** *N.Y. Times Bk. Review* 5 June 14/2 It was settled that I should receive 1 cent per hundred for picking potato bugs. — (6) **1878** *Amer. Home Cook Book* 67 Put around potato chips prepared as follows. **1948** *Pauls Valley* (Okla.) *D. Democrat* 4 July 3/2 Grocery stores reported a heavy sale on such picnic items as potato chips and sandwich bread. — (7) **1882** GODFREY *Nantucket* 64 To be sure, the Nantucketers make what they call a 'potato chowder'; but then a potato chowder without fish or clams . . . [is] a flat and insipid dish. — (8) **1902** *Rep. Smithsonian Inst. 1900* 469 Some of the talc-like substance, called potato-clay . . . is then produced, and the operator puts a piece about the size of a walnut in his mouth. — (9) **1815** in KITTREDGE *Old Farmer* (1904) 184 Potato coffee.—From a Philadelphia Paper. **1825** T. B. HAZARD *Nailer Tom's Diary* (1930) 642/1 Edward Carr dug Potato Coffee. **1904** STERLING *A Belle* 224 [In the South during the Civil War] tea and coffee proved to be our greatest lack, and . . . we were glad to drink potato coffee and peanut chocolate.

(10) **1845** *Quincy* (Ill.) *Whig* 18 Dec. 2/5 A new potatoe digger was recently exhibited in operation at Salem, West Jersey. **1945** *Hardin* (Mont.) *Tribune-Herald* 15 Feb. 2/4, I will sell at public auction to the highest bidder the following property: . . . 1 corn cultivator, 1 sulky plow, 1 potato digger. — (11) **1806** in KITTREDGE *Old Farmer* (1904) 186 The potatoe fly, or bug, appears about the first of July. **1854** EMMONS *Agric. N.Y.* V. 96 *Cantharidae.* . . . They are at times abundant upon potato vines, whence they have acquired the name of potato fly, particularly the Epicauta vittala. — (12) **1883** BURROUGHS in *Cent. Mag.* Aug. 531/1 Your rose-colored philanthropies, your potato gospels (vegetarianism) . . . and the like. — (13) **1869** MARK TWAIN *Innocents Abroad* 540 (R.), Out comes a little potato-gun of a revolver. **1909** *Cent. Supp.* 1046/1 potato-gun. . . . A special form of powder-gun for dusting potato-plants with an insecticide. — (14) **1858** *Texas Almanac 1859* 85 He should carefully examine his potato-heaps, and know that every thing has been done to secure this crop from decay. **1886** *Cong. Rec.* 10 June 5749/1 Instances are related in which potato heaps covered with earth and left out during winter have been entered by the gophers and the tubers carried off.

(15) **1821** NUTTALL *Travels Arkansa* 148 To the west continued a proximate chain of piney hills, with remarkable serrated summits, known by the familiar name of the Potatoe hills. **1845** *Big Bear Ark.* 22 Them ar 'Indian mounds' ar tater hills. **1888** *Harper's Mag.* April 705/1 When Jones watched his potato hill, his smoke-house was sure to be entered. — (16) *c*1775 BOUCHER *Glossary* p. 1, All the 'moodies I For Mollsey, in my 'tatoe-hole, put by. **1839** *Knickerb.* XIII. 305 Under a part of the floor, was a small excavation in the earth, which the host called his potato-hole, since, being near the fire, it served in winter to keep his potatoes from freezing. **1940** WRIGHT *Pioneer Life* 248 Potato Hole—A hole dug several feet deep in the ground in which potatoes or turnips were kept during the winter. The vegetables were covered with loose earth several inches deep to keep the frost away from them. — (17) **1856** *Mich. Agric. Soc. Trans.* VII. 53 D. O. & W. S. Penfield . . . [exhibited] six Partridge's potatoe hooks. **1874** *Vt. Bd. Agric. Rep.* II. 551 Then with axes, potato hooks, and bog hoes, the turf was all peeled off — (18) **1791** W. BARTRAM *Travels* 192 The lowest or ground part is a potatoe house. **1920** *3d Nat. Country Life Conf. Proc.* 155 Potato houses . . . are isolated and located with special reference to the good of the products involved. — (19) **1794** ELIZABETH DRINKER *Journal* (1889) 229 John brought in a Mole he found in a potato patch that he was laying out. **1913** LONDON *Valley of Moon* 404 Hall put Billy to work on the potato patch—a matter of three acres which the poet farmed erratically. **1948** *Dly. Ardmoreite* (Ardmore, Okla.) 5 May 5/1 With great pride he shows her potato patch and tomatoes and beans and onions to his friends.

(20) **1839** *S. Lit. Messenger* V. 377/1 Master Billy taking a piece of potato pone daintily between his fingers . . . [said] 'This *patetta poon* is exceeding fine.' **1942** KENNEDY *Palmetto Country* 26 They all lived off potato pone made from the sawdust. — (21) **1855** DAVIS *Farm Bk.* 190 The hands set out potatoe slips about 20 rows. — (22) **1777** FITHIAN *Journal* I. 257, I took a Walk thro' the Pumpkin & Potato Vines. **1854** DAVIS *Farm Bk.* 116 Cut Some potatoe vines for hey. **1945** EASTERBY *S.C. Rice Plantation* 23 (*footnote*), In Peedee parlance 'three white frosts make a black frost'; that means that all the potato vines and other delicate plants had been killed so completely that the leaves were black. — (23) **1817** *Yankee Traveller* 75 Wrangle . . . drove a lucrative trade in the sale of potatoe whisky, and adulterated New-England rum. — (24) **1850** S. F. COOPER *Rural Hours* 202 The common green potato, or tobacco-worm, is said to become a moth of this kind. **1879** *Scribner's Mo.* July 395/1 You would be surprised to see the tongue of the potato-worm sphinx, when it is uncoiled. **1939** *L.A.* Map 236.

b. In colloq. phrases: (1) *To set up and skin a tater,* to dine, *obs.;* (2) *that's the tater,* that's a fact, *obs.;* (3) *to tell* (something) *to the potatoes,* an expression of disbelief, *obs.;* (4) *to hold one's potato,* to wait, be patient, cf. ***horse,** *n.* **8.** (2).

(1) **1829** *Maysville* (Ky.) *Eagle* 17 Nov., Perhaps stranger, you'll set up and skin a 'tater? — (2) **1835** LONGSTREET *Ga. Scenes* 234 They'll go for you to the hilt, against creation, tit or no tit, that's the tatur. — (3) **1856** SIMMS *Charlemont* 321 Would you, indeed? Tell that to the potatoes. Don't I know better. — (4) **1892** *Cong. Rec.* 27 Jan. 600/1 Now let me beg of the gentleman to hold his potato.

As the last term in **biscuit, blue, bog, burr, Carolina, carter, country, cranberry, duck, early purple, English, hog, hot, Indian, La Plata, Mercer, merino, prairie, purple, rusticoat, round, Saratoga, sea, Shaker, slip, small, Spanish, swamp, swan, sweet, tule, white, wild potato.** Also in *pl.*, **French fried potatoes.**

Potawatomi ˌpɑtəˈwɑtəmɪ, *n.* [App. f. *Potawatamiñk,* people of the place of the fire.] An Indian of an Algonquian tribe first encountered by Europeans on the islands of Green Bay, Wis. Often *pl.* with reference to the tribe. Cf. **citizen, prairie Potawatomi.**

[**1640** *Relation des Jésuites* (1858) 35/1 Es enuirons de cette nation sont les Nadvesiv, les Assinipour, les Eriniouaj, . . . et les Pouutouatami.] **1698** tr. HENNEPIN *New Discovery* 74 We sent afterwards three Men to buy Provisions in the Village with the *Calumet* or Pipe of Peace, which the Poutouatami's of the Island had given us. **1722** COXE *Descr. Carolana* 48 The Nations who dwell on this River, are Outogamis, Malominis . . . Sacky, and the Poutouatomis before-mentioned. **1807** *Ann. 10th Congress* 1 Sess. 575 All hopes of the speedy recovery of their prisoners from the hands of the Pattawatamies . . . [are] at an end. **1868** *N.Y. Herald* 31 July 5/4 The Senate . . . ratified treaties with the Potawatamies. **1949** *Jrnl. Ill. State Hist. Soc.* June 147 The United Tribes of Potawatomi, Chippewas, and Ottawas were called together to sign away their lands.

attrib. **1789** *Ann. 1st Congress* I. 41 The treaties of Fort Harmar, . . . with the sachems and warriors of the Wyandot, Delaware, Ottawa, Chippawa, Pattiwatima, and Sac nations, . . . appear to have been negotiated . . . so as to unite the interests of the United States with the justice due the said Indian nations. **1808** *Ann. 12th Congress.* 1 Sess. II. 1857 A young man from the Delaware towns came to inform me that a Pottawatomie Indian had arrived at the towns. **1900** *Cong. Rec.* 5 Feb. 1503/1, I ask unanimous consent for the immediate consideration of the bill . . . for the relief of John Anderson, a Pottawatomie Indian, and his adult children.

potlatch ˈpɑtlætʃ, *n. N.W.* [Chinook *patshatl,* a gift, giving.] An occasion upon which gifts are distributed; a festival on such an occasion. Cf. **cultus potlatch.**

*a*1861 WINTHROP *Canoe & Saddle* 57 [The Klickatat Indians] expressed the friendliest sentiments, perhaps with a view to a liberal 'potlatch' of trinkets. **1870** *Cong. Globe* 2 March 1647/2 (Th. Supp.), Let me say that I have been to distributions of annuities; they are called 'potlashes' in my country; and I have seen blankets torn into quarters and distributed. I have seen bolts of red calico torn, and a yard given to every grown squaw, and half a yard to every papoose. **1884** *S.F. Chron.* Sep., A potlatch is . . . a sort of grand reunion and general gathering, lasting sometimes for weeks. **1948** *Amer. Folk-Lore* Jan.–Mar. 7 A potlatch in that culture is predominantly a social and not a religious occasion.

transf. and *attrib.* **1845** WILKES *U.S. Explor. Exped.* IV. 310 After the bargain was completed, and the price agreed upon, under the form of 'potlatch' or 'gift,' the equivalent was always to be again treated for, and thus the price of the article or service was often very much enhanced. **1930** HAEBERLIN & GUNTHER *Puget Sound Indians* 17 Every village as far as possible had a potlatch house.

potlatch ˈpɑtlætʃ, *v. N.W.* [f. Chinook.] *tr.* To give. Also **potlatching,** *n.*

1847 PALMER *Journal* 150 *Pot-latch* Give. **1898** *Land of Sunshine* April 219 In case the sentence is carried out they will be compelled to 'potlatch' a very large amount. **1915** *Nat. & Science on Pac. Coast* 195 Potlatching has been bitterly opposed by missionaries and officials in charge of Indian affairs, who object to the practice as a sinful waste.

pot lead, *v. tr.* (See quot. 1890.) Also **pot-leaded,** *a.* — **1890** *Cent.* 4652/3 *Pot-lead,* . . . to coat with pot-lead: as, to *pot-lead* a yacht. **1894** *Outing* XXIV. 72/1 The racing shell, used only three times, its bottom pot-leaded, is brought out.

Potomac marble. (See quot.) *Obs.* — **1841** BUCKINGHAM *America* I. xvi. 303 This corridor is separated from the body of the Senate chamber, by a colonnade of very beautiful pillars, formed of a highly variegated and richly coloured breccia, found on the banks of the Potomac, and called, from this, Potomac marble.

potrero poˈtrɛro, *n. S.W.* [Sp., pasture land.] A pasture or meadow. Also in place-names and attrib.

1848 SUTTER *MS Diary* 7 Mar., 6 Men have been sent from the Race, on acct. having no tools, employed them to get the small potrero repaired. **1854** *Calif. Chronicle* (S.F.) 16 May 4/5 Their claim . . . covers the lands adjoining and beyond Mission creek, and known as the 'Potrero.' **1886** VAN DYKE *So. Calif.* 106 When, in the heat of day, one comes to some little *potrero* where pine-clad hills inclose a soft green meadow, . . . then this bird makes a strange, sweet feeling in the wanderer's heart. **1923** SAUNDERS *So. Sierras Calif.* 105 Ahead in the sun lay the Devil's *Potrero*—a verdant, wild-flowery bowl rimmed around with mountains. **1948** *Petroleum World* April 30/1 The sands at Newhall Potrero are too easily mudded off to permit the use of heavy mud while drilling through the productive interval.

b. (See quots.)

1872 BOURKE *Journal* 3 Dec., Hills break away in potreros. **1890** *Arch. Inst. Amer. P.* IV. 158 These cliffs appear like pillars, or gigantic posts, hence their Spanish name 'Potreros.' **1941** FERGUSSON *Southwest* 354 A potrero is a narrow ridge between canyons, and a saddle is a sag between peaks.

potro ˈpotro, *n. S.W.* [Sp. in same sense.] (See quots.) — **1929** DOBIE *Vaquero* 8 A rancher told me that if I would break seven wild potros (young horses) he would let me have my pick of the seven. **1944** ADAMS *W. Words* 118/1 potros. . . . Young horses, up to the time when they change their milk teeth, or about four and one-half years of age; colts, fillies.

***potter,** *v. intr.* (See quot. *a*1870.) Also **pottering time,** (see quot.). *Colloq. Obs.* — **1791** BENTLEY *Diary* I. 254 After *pottering time* is over, which is running upon the broken ice without falling into the water & requires great activity, comes on *marble time.* ***a*1870** CHIPMAN *Notes on Bartlett* 335 *Potter.* To tread upon ice floating, or to leap from one to another piece of it floating, or to walk upon loose spars floating upon water.—Eastern coast of Massachusetts.

Potter Baptist. (See quot.) *Obs.* — **1836** COX *Baptists* 463 Some small churches in the vicinity of Providence, who advocate it [*sc.* open communion], have acquired the designation of 'Potter Baptists,' from a minister of that name.

***pouch,** *n.* A mail or express bag. Also attrib.

1833 *Niles' Reg.* XLIV. 337/2 The letter mail bag, or 'Pouch,' was missed between New Brunswick (N.J.) and New York. **1874** PINKERTON *Expressman & Detective* 207, [I will get] you to have a key made similar to a pouch-key. **1887** *Postal Laws* 408 The postmaster is at once provided with the necessary pouches, locks, keys, pouch bills, and labels. **1903** *Chi. Chronicle* 11 April 1/4 This is the second theft . . . , two pouches having been stolen on the night of March 13.

As the last term in **mail, medicine, shot, through pouch.**

pouched rat. A pocket gopher or a kangaroo rat.

1826 J. GODMAN *Nat. Hist.* II. 90 The Pouched-Rat. *Pseudostoma Bursarium;* Say . . . [Vulgarly called Salamandars; Pouched Rat; Sand-Rat; etc.] *Ib.* 91 In Florida, Georgia, etc., and the plains adjacent to the Missouri, the pouched-rat is to be found in great numbers. **1844** FARNHAM *Travels in Calif.* 388 The Pouched Rat, and the . . . Small Marmot, are curious little creatures. **1874** COUES *Birds N.W.* 366 In the stomachs of those [buzzards] examined I found the remains of burrowing pouched-rats (*Thomomys fulvus*).

pouderie ˈpudərɪ, *n. W.* [Voyageur F.] (See quot. *c*1760.) *Obs.* — [***c*1760** in MCDERMOTT *Miss. Valley Fr.* (1941) 126 What pleases me most is, that we see no rain; and after a certain period of snow and *poudrerie* (it is thus that they call a fine snow that sifts in everywhere) the air is pure and clear.] **1851** HOWE *Hist. Coll. Great West* 341 We forced the ascent in spite of the driving *pouderie*, crossed the crest, descended a little, and encamped.

***pound,** *n.*

1. *W.* An inclosure in which buffalo are trapped. *Obs.*

1871 S. BROWN *Western Gazetteer* 199 A small party is sent out to decoy the animals into the pound. **1876** ALLEN *Amer. Bisons* 472 The rushing of a herd over a precipice or into a pound prepared especially to entrap them.

2. Short for **pound net.**

1870 *Amer. Naturalist* IV. 403 These fish being caught in gill-nets and 'pounds,' are generally taken from the water some hours after being actually entrapped. **1911** *Rep. Fisheries 1908* 311/2 [The horseshoe crab] is caught by hand and in pounds and weirs. **1935** LINCOLN *Cape Cod Yesterdays* 146 He is in the 'pound,' and the pound of a weir is, to a fish, the condemned cell.

3. In combs.: (1) **pound boat,** a flat-bottomed, centerboard boat used in the pound fisheries of the Great Lakes; (2) **net,** a net arranged to serve as a trap in taking fish, also attrib. and **pound netter;** (3) **party,** a social gathering at which each one in attendance brings a pound of something to be donated or used on the occasion (orig. and often as in quot. 1877), cf. ***pound,** *v.* **2;** (4) **pear,** (see quot. 1899), *obs.;* (5) **sweet,** =next; (6) **sweeting,** a variety of apple, also attrib.

(1) **1884** *Nat. Mus. Bul.* No. 27, 700 Lake Erie pound boat. . . . Their peculiar construction enables them to carry large quantities of fish in shallow water and to lift the bowl of the pounds without upsetting. — (2) **1856** *Mich. Gen. Statutes* I. (1882) 577 The penalties of this section shall not apply or work injury to persons who are the present owners of the pound or trap nets. **1904** *Newark Ev. News* 13 June 6 The charges against the pound net fishermen are that by using nets of too small mesh they destroy tons upon tons of young food fishes. **1949** *Fishing Gaz.* 15 Dec. 106/2 Several good catches of whitefish, however, were recently made by pound netters in this lake. — (3) **1877** BARTLETT 487 Pound-Party. An assemblage, usually the parishioners of a country clergyman whose salary is inadequate to his support, which on an evening agreed upon meets at his house, carrying tea, coffee, and other articles of necessity put up in pound packages, as contributions to him. **1942** RAWLINGS *C. Creek* 40 But how was I to have known this and that the Townsends' invitation to a pound party was not a social gesture. — (4) **1899** VANDERBILT *Flatbush* 279 The last of the crop [of pears] was gathered in October or November; this late variety was called the 'pound pear,' from its great size. They ripened in the house after being gathered, but were used chiefly for sweetmeats. **1949** *Hist. & Philos. Soc. Ohio Bul.* April 85 Francis McCormick had several hundred apple trees, besides 'Pound pears and Sickle Pears.'

(5) **1859** F. R. ELLIOTT *Western Fruit Book* 102 Pumpkin Sweet. Pound Sweet, Lyman's Pumpkin Sweet [etc.]. . . . An old Connecticut fruit, valued for baking. **1923** *Stand. Plant Names* 539/1. — (6) **1853** *Knickerb.* XLII. 172 A wood-pecker . . . was drumming away upon a decayed limb of the old 'pound-sweeting' apple tree. **1895** A. BROWN *Meadow-Grass* 211 There were great pound sweetings, full of the pride of mere bigness.

As the last term in **buffalo, dog, fish, log pound.**

***pound,** *v.* **1.** *tr.* To walk upon, to tramp (a sidewalk, etc.). *Slang.* **2.** To aid (a minister) with a pound party.

(1) **1909** O. HENRY *Options* (1916) 30 I'm pounding the asphalt for another job. **1923** L. J. VANCE *Baroque* vi. 33, I won't get sent back to pound sidewalks for what I'm pulling off tonight. — (2) **1931** *Durant* (Okla.) *D. Democrat* 12 March 4/3 (*caption*), Caney Pastor Pounded.

poundable ˈpaʊndəbl̩, *a.* Of livestock: Subject to being placed in a pound. *Obs.*

1657 *Hempstead Rec.* I. 26 All yonge Cattell . . . that shall bee found in the filld ore hard after the abovesaid day shall bee poundabell by aney that will pound them. **1660** *Ib.* 91 Hooges to bee poundable. **1687** *East-Hampton Rec.* II. 207 All swine that goe in the Towne or Limits thereof unyoaked are poundable by any parson that shall soe find them.

***poundcake,** *n.* As the last term in **Indian, molasses poundcake.**

***pounding,** *n.*

1. The occasion of a pound party in behalf of a minister. *Colloq.*

1939 HARRIS *Purslane* 140 It was Miss Cole, the school teacher, who first suggested a pounding at Sunday school the next Sunday. **1947** *Gainesville* (Fla.) *Sun* 22 July 3/5 Methodist Church members had a pounding for Rev. Leo King and his wife Friday night.

2. a. pounding barrel, a barrel in which clothes are pounded in washing them. **b. pounding mill,** a powder mill, or a stamping mill, or one for cleaning rice.

(a) **1853** *Mich. Agric. Soc. Trans.* IV. 87 One pounding barrel, for clothes. **1894** ROBINSON *Danvis Folks* 176, I don't see . . . haow father ever got holt o' his boots when I'd hid 'em in the paoundin' berril. — (b) **1789** MORSE *Amer. Geog.* 369 They might avail themselves of a good situation on a creek, for a pounding mill. **1815** *Niles' Reg.* VIII. 291/1 The pounding mill belonging to the great establishment of the Messrs. Duponts, . . . was accidentally blown up. **1905** PRINGLE *Rice*

Planter 142 The cows and pigs are fed on the flour a gray substance that comes from the grain as the chaff is removed in the pounding mill.

*pout, *n.* As the last term in **bull, horn, horned, mud pout.**

pouty ˈpaʊtɪ, *a.* Inclined to pout, peevish. *Colloq.*

1863 G. Hamilton *Gala-Days* 221 They never were tired when anything was to be done, or . . . peevish, or pouty, or 'offish.' **1897** Brodhead *Bound in Shallows* 99, I had acted kind of pouty that night. **1912** Wason *Friar Tuck* 77 With a pouty look on his face, Tank sez: 'It's time we fixed up an' moved out into the dark.'

***poverty,** *n.* In combs.: (1) **poverty birch,** (see quots.); (2) **grass,** any one of various grasses, as *Aristida dichotoma,* that grow in poor, sandy soil; (3) **pine,** ?a dwarf pine growing in poor soil, *rare;* (4) ***weed,** (*a*) =**rabbit tobacco,** (*b*) the heath aster, *Aster ericoides.*

(1) 1897 Sudworth *Arborescent Flora* 139 White Birch. . . . Common Names. . . . Old Field Birch. Poverty Birch (Me.). **1945** Pearson *Country Flavor* 52 In various localities they [gray birches] are called poverty birch, poplar birch, paper birch, or old-field birch. — **(2) 1832** *Boston Transcript* 30 April 2/3 Fields, before perhaps never turned with a plough, and long given up to barrenness and poverty-grass, are now broken up in readiness to receive the grain. **1864** Thoreau *Cape Cod* 20 A moss-like plant, *Hudsonia tomentosa* . . . called 'poverty-grass,' because it grew where nothing else would. **1947** Bump *Ruffed Grouse* 226 When this occurs open areas revert to 'poverty grass,' weeds and moss. — **(3) 1880** Tourgee *Bricks* 94 His rider's feet just . . . [brushed] the low 'poverty-pines' which grew by the roadside. — **(4)** (*a*) **1876** Hobbs *Bot. Hand-Book* 92 Poverty weed, Life everlasting, Gnaphalium polycephalum. **1907** Lyons *Plant Names* 212 G[naphalium] obtusifolium L. (G. polycephalum Mich.) Canada to Florida and west to Texas and Manitoba. Life-everlasting, . . . Poverty-weed, Rabbit Tobacco. (*b*) **1943** Peattie *Great Smokies* 168 The next year ragweed and heather aster, appropriately called poverty-weed in some places, take over.

***powder,** *n.* In combs.: (1) **powder charger,** = ***charger;** (2) **gourd,** a gourd used by hunters as a container for powder; (3) **money,** tax money for the purchase of gunpowder for common defense, *obs.;* (4) **post,** (*a*) the powdery, worm-eaten wood resulting from the activities of a certain beetle, also attrib. and **powder-posted,** *a.,* (*b*) designating a beetle of the family Lyctidae the larvae of which feed in very dry wood; (5) **rate,** in colonial times a rate or assessment levied for providing gunpowder for common defense, *obs.*

(1) 1868 *Putnam's Mag.* May 592/2 [An alligator's] hollow tooth makes a good powder charger. — **(2) 1775** in Pusey *Road to Ky.* (1921) 42 My hors . . . threw Down the Saddel Bags & Broke three of our powder goards. **1845** Hooper *Simon Suggs' Adv.* 201, I finds the big powder gourd they all kept their powder in. **1945** Botkin *My Burden* 31, I git the pin loose and jerk the door open so quick and hard I knock the powder gourd down what was hanging over it. — **(3) 1715** *Mass. H. Rep. Jrnl.* I. 8 All Ships or other Vessels that Load or Unload at the Port of Kittery . . . [shall] Pay the Duties of Impost and Powder Money according to Law. **1721** *Ib.* III. 208 The former Impositions of Powder Money, double Light Money, and double Duties on Wine. — **(4)** (*a*) **1790** Deane *N. Eng. Farmer* 151/1 The smaller kind [of timber worm] eats only the sappy part of the wood, turning it to what is vulgarly called *powder-post.* **1863** Mitchell *My Farm* 83 A wild, sweeping, gallant blaze . . . wrapped old powder-post timbers in its roar. **1888** Jewett *King of Folly Island* 125 The j'ints is all powder-posted. (*b*) **1934** Webster. **1941** *Chi. D. News* 7 Feb. 21 These are undoubtedly powderpost beetles.

(5) 1651 *Watertown Rec.* I. I. 22 The two Constables . . . gaue an acompt of the powder rate of the last yeare. **1681** *Springfield Rec.* II. 147 Voted by ye Town to ffree David ffrow ffrom a powder Rate & all other Town Rates.

As the last term in **baking, cocktail, cypress, giant, heave, Hercules, mammoth, prayer, soda, washing powder.** Also in *pl.,* **Saratoga powders.**

powder burn, *v. tr.* To burn (an object) with the hot gases that issue from a firearm when discharged. — **1846** W. G. Stewart *Altowan* I. 125 That he might powder-burn the bear by the nearness of the shot. **1853** *S. Lit. Messenger* XIX. 463/1, I got in pursuit with another officer . . . determined this time to powder-burn my game.

***power,** *n.*

1. Religious enthusiasm or frenzy. *Obs.*

[*c***1845** *A True Picture* 57 An individual started from his seat, exclaiming. . . . 'I feel it,' meaning what is commonly termed among them the power of God.] **1862** *Harper's Mag.* Dec. 101 These exercises had been prolonged nearly an hour when several of the seekers were taken with 'the power.' **1923** J. H. Cook *On Old Frontier* 231 A great revivalist of the shouting Methodist school, who could soon have great numbers of blind followers under the influence of 'the power.'

2. power line, a line of cables over which electrical power is transmitted.

1913 London *Valley of Moon* III. xiv, Everywhere was manifest the 'new' farming—great irrigation ditches, dug and being dug, the land threaded by power-lines from the mountains. **1949** *News-Herald* (Marshfield, Wis.) 19 July 4/1 This was the point of view of Democrats in the House who fought, and successfully, to keep the power lines in the Interior bill.

3. power press, a printing press driven by mechanical power.

1841 Cist *Cincinnati* (*advt.*), They have in their Printing establishment . . . five Power Presses. **1871** Ringwalt *Amer. Encycl. Printing* 172/1 *Fly,*—an invention for taking off or delivering the sheets from a power-press.

As the last term in **implied, one-man, police, slave, treaty-making, veto, war-making power.** Also **enumerated powers.**

Powhatan ˌpaʊəˈtæn, *n.* [See quot. 1927 in **2.** below.]

1. *collect* or *pl.* (See quot. 1910.) In full **Powhatan Indians.**

1800 Jefferson *Notes* 96 Of these the *Powhatans,* the *Mannahoacs,* and *Monacans,* were the most powerful. **1881** Morgan *Houses Amer. Aborigines* 34 The Long House was not peculiar to the Iroquois, but used by many other tribes, as the Powhattan Indians of Virginia, the Nyacks of Long Island, and other tribes. **1910** Hodge *Amer. Indians* II. 302/2 Powhatan. The tribe which gave name to the Powhatan confederacy. Its territory was in what is now Henrico co., Va., and the tribe numbered about 150 in 1608.

attrib. **1800** Jefferson *Notes* 99 The older ones among them preserve their language in a small degree, which are the last vestiges on earth, as far as we know of the Powhatan language. **1946** *Nat. Geog. Mag.* Jan. 54/1 The Powhatan confederacy of Tidewater Virginia consisted of Algonquian-speaking tribes.

b. Powhatan pipe, ?a tobacco pipe thought to be of the type used by the Powhatan Indians. *Obs.*

1866 Cooke *Surry* 61 On the table lay pipes of every form, . . . and the plain but excellent Powhatan pipe of Virginia. **1869** Tourgee *Toinette* (1881) 221 Geoffrey . . . was fairly settled to a smoke with one of the old man's genuine 'Powhatan' pipes.

2. (See quot.)

1927 Read *La. Place-Names* 55 *Powhatan* is derived from Algonquian *pow'waw* or *po'wah,* 'priest,' 'sorcerer,' or 'medicine-man,' and *-atan,* 'Hill,' 'mountain.' Compare the etymology of *powwow. Powhatan* signifies the 'hill of the medicine-man.' It was on a hill, then, that Powhatan, who was himself the chief sorcerer or medicine-man, conducted his mysterious rites. [**1947** *Reader's Digest* April 92/2 The Powhatan was temporizing until he could form a confederacy to sweep the palefaces into the sea.]

powwow ˈpaʊwaʊ, *n.* [See note.]

This term is derived from the word used by the Indians for the medicine man, the root meaning of which was "he dreams," i.e., he derives his art from his dreams. Cf. quot. 1927 *s.v.* **Powhatan 2.** The spellings are numerous: *powow, powah, powaw, pouwau, powwaas, powwas, powwah.* Since *c*1850 *powwow* has increasingly prevailed.

1. An Indian medicine man, priest, wizard or magician. Now *hist.*

1624 Winslow *Good Newes* 22 The actor of this fact was a *Powah,* one of special note amongst them. **1764** Hutchinson *Hist. Mass.* I, 473 Upon him [God] they had their first dependence for recovery from sickness, but if he failed them they applied to their powows. **1850** Hawthorne *Scarlet Letter* xxii. Many a church-member saw I, walking behind the music, that has danced in the same measure with me, when Somebody was fiddler, and, it might be, an Indian powwow or a Lapland wizard changing hands with us! **1907** *Springfield W. Republican* 21 March 13 There were among them [the Indians of New England] men and women whom they called powaws. These were a combination of conjurer and physician, and were held in profound respect. **1949** *N. Eng. Quart.* June 247 The idea that the name Noman was derived from Tequenonum, an Edgartown pawwaw, is equally mythological.

attrib. **1843** Whittier *Writings* VII. 257 Without were 'dogs and sorcerers,' . . . Powah wizards, and 'the foul fiend.' **1938** Hark *Hex Marks Spot* 49 He told me about a pow-wow doctor who lives not far from here.

2. A noisy conjuring or ceremonial rite held or performed by Indians; a council or conference of Indians.

1625 in Friederici (1947) 484/2 And sodainely cryed '*Bowh, waugh,*' . . . In the time of their *Pauose.* **1648** Shephard *Clear Sunshine* 18 [The Indians] have utterly forsaken all their *Powwaws,* and given over that diabolicall exercise, being convinced that it is quite contrary to praying unto God. **1788** May *Jrnl. & Lett.* 94 The Indians made one of their hellish pow-wows, which lasted till the hour of rising. **1890** Custer *Following Guidon* 46 We find it is impossible to hurry the Indians much, they have so many powwows and ceremonies before determining upon any important action. **1948** *Green Bay* (Wis.) *Press-Gazette* 30 June 16/5 At 1:30 the initial pow-wow with the ritualistic dances will be presented by the Mohawks.

transf. The healing art, magic or witchcraft. Also attrib.

1855 J. G. HOHMAN (*title*), Pow-Wow; or, Long Lost Friend. A Collection of Mysterious and Invaluable Arts and Remedies for Men as well as Animals. **1856** KANE *Arctic Explor.* II. 126 My skill in pow-wow had given me a sort of correlative rank among [the Esquimaux angekoks]. **1901** *Scribner's Mag.* Nov. 525 The 'powwow-doctors' [among the Dunkers] still repeat over many bedsides the mysterious formulas. **1948** *Democrat* 8 Jan. 7/7 A witch doctor rattled tin cans . . . to break a powwow curse.

b. Any assembly, meeting, or gathering, esp. one thought of as noisy and demonstrative. *Colloq.*

1812 *Salem Gazette* 5 June 3/3 The Warriors of the Democratic Tribe will hold a powow at Agawam on Tuesday next. **1870** *Terr. Enterprise* (Virginia, Nev.) 18 Jan. 3/2 In the Chinese quarter of the city there was a grand pow wow. **1947** *Chi. Tribune* 18 Oct. 10/7 I've heard of a judge who freed all defendants who bought tickets to a political pow-wow.

c. (See quot. 1871.) *Obs.*

[**1852–3** *Burlesque Catalogue* (Yale) 35 The students are forbidden to occupy the State-House steps on the evening of Presentation day, since the Faculty design hereafter to have a Powwow there, as on the last.] **1871** BAGG *At Yale* 275 About the year 1850, the custom arose among the Freshmen of celebrating their accession to sophomoric dignity by a performance called a 'Pow-wow,' upon the night of Presentation Day. It was held upon the State House steps, and consisted of burlesque speeches, songs and poems.

powwow ˈpaʊwaʊ, *v.* [See prec.]

1. *intr.* Of Indians: To act as a conjuror, to engage in a powwow. Now *hist.*

1646 *Mass. Bay Rec.* III. 98 No Indian shall at any time pawwaw or p[er]forme outward wor[shi]pp to their falce gods. **1751** J. BARTRAM *Observations* 32 Here was a place where the Indians had been a pawawing. **1788** DENNY *Journal* 129 Several days pass over. Indians powwowing. **1835** LATROBE *Rambler N. Amer.* II. 204 Companies of old warriors might be seen sitting smoking under every bush; arguing, palavering, or 'pow-wowing.' **1947** *Dly. Oklahoman* (Okla. City) 21 Sep. 5–D/2 McKenney saw an Indian far off in the west who wore a peculiar costume, and who appeared to be pow-wowing.

b. *transf.* To counsel, deliberate, converse, esp. in a noisy or vehement manner. *Colloq.*

1818 *Mass. Spy* 9 Sep. (Th.), The Indian fashion (unknown in England) of powowing and huzzaing in approbation of toasts, is generally unwelcome to a majority of those who are engaged in it. **1884** MARK TWAIN *H. Finn* iii. We would go to the cave and powwow over what we had done. **1911** SAUNDERS *Col. Todhunter* 189 Me and him ain't had a chance to pow-wow together for four or five years.

2. *tr.* To make (a person) the object of a powwow.

*c***1705** in FORCE *Tracts* I. No. 8, 9 Capt. Brent (a papist) coming thither on a visit, and seeing his little prisoner thus languishing said 'perhaps he is pawewawd i.e. bewitched.' **1856** KANE *Arctic Explor.* II. 116, I gave him a piece of red flannel, and powwowed him. **1872** *Newton Kansan* 17 Oct. 1/4 The noble savages were willing to be feted and whiskeyed and pow-wowed.

powwower ˈpaʊˌwaʊɚ, *n.* =**powwow,** *n.* **1.** Also transf.

1646 *Mass. Col. Rec.* III. 98 Ye p[ro]curer [shall be fined] five pounds, ye pawwawer five pounds. **1774** D. JONES *Journal* (1865) 79 This apparel is also used by their pou-wouers in their attempts of healing the sick. **1882** GIBBONS *Pa. Dutch* (ed. 3) 402 In Lehigh, I remember a few years ago to have seen the names of two persons put down as *powwowers*. **1938** HARK *Hex Marks Spot* 140 Again the pow-wower walked back and forth across the strings, and for some time thereafter the rubbing and the walking alternated.

powwowing ˈpaʊˌwaʊɪŋ, *n.* The action on the part of an Indian, or of Indians, of performing or taking part in a powwow. Also transf.

1642 LECHFORD *Plain Dealing* 117 They will have their times of Powaheing, which they will, of late, have called Prayers, according to the English word. **1764** HUTCHINSON *Hist. Mass.* I. 475 (*footnote*), Their sweatings in their hot houses was a more rational remedy than the powwowing. **1871** *Rep. Indian Affairs* (1872) 582 The potency seems to be in the blowing and 'pow-wow-ing.' **1905** LINCOLN *Partners* 8, I cal'late there must have been some high old pow-wowin' in the old house. **1938** HARK *Hex Marks Spot* 52 Pow-wowing is a hidden but by no means secret art among the people of Pennsylvania.

b. powwowing days, (see quots.). *Obs.*

1824 DODDRIDGE *Notes* 64 We commonly had an open spell of weather during the latter part of February, denominated by [some] 'Pawwawing days,' and by others 'Weather breeders.' **1851** HOWE *Hist. Coll. Great West* 168 Toward the latter part of February, we commonly had a fine spell of open warm weather, during which the snow melted away. This was denominated the '*pawwawing days*'—from the supposition that the Indians were then holding their war councils.

pozo ˈposo, *n. S.W.* [Sp., a well.] A well or spring.

1854 BARTLETT *Personal Narr.* II. 465 (*footnote*), *Noria* is properly a wheel or engine for drawing water from a well; the term is also applied to wells where wheels are so employed, to distinguish them from *pozos*, or common wells. **1877** BARTLETT 489 *Pozo.* (Span.) A spring or well. A word in use on the frontier of Mexico. **1912** LUMHOLTZ *New Trails* 263 Other pozos were twenty feet in diameter, with a deposit two feet deep. **1932** BENTLEY 185 *Pozo* is restricted in written use to descriptive or other writings dealing with Spanish American territory in the Southwest and elsewhere. In spoken English in the Southwest its use is not uncommon among those who know Spanish well.

b. Also in place-names.

1925 BRYAN *Papago Country* 118 Walls Well, Bates Well, and Coyote Water are American place names; Agua Caliente and Pozo Redondo record the travel and settlement of the Spanish.

pozzoli poˈzolɪ, *n. W.* [Amer. Sp. *pozole* (<Nahuatl), a dish of boiled meat and corn.] (See quot.) *Obs.* — **1850** in *Amer. Sp.* XXIV. (1949) 266/1 We landed, hauled up our boat, and found two tall, naked Indians, engaged in cooling their evening meal of *pozzoli*, or boiled corn.

***practical,** *a.* In combs.: (1) **practical politician,** one engaged in the actual problems of politics, esp. of controlling votes, working for a party, etc., freq. depreciative; (2) **politics,** politics involving actual work in a party, or attempts at actual control of an election; (3) **printer,** a printer who has had practical experience.

(1) **1812** *Ann. 12th Congress* 1 Sess. 2210 There were two circumstances, inherent in this system of coercing Great Britain by commercial restrictions, which ought to have made practical politicians very doubtful of its result. **1890** HOWELLS *Shadow of Dream* I. i, He was a 'practical' politician; he adhered to his party in all its measures. — (2) **1868** BANCROFT in Howe *Life & Letters G. Bancroft* II. 185 These are the considerations that led me to the views that have governed my life in questions of practical politics. **1904** A. FRENCH *Barrier* 163 Any campaign which they [*sc.* reformers] conduct would be the usual formal and ineffectual protest against 'practical politics.' — (3) **1839** *Indiana H. Rep. Jrnl.* 23d Sess. 553 In the opinion of Messrs. Douglass Maguire and D. V. Culley, practical printers, the time allowed Douglass & Noel to complete the public printing was insufficient. **1874** *Internat. Typog. Union Proc.* 88 A practical printer is one who has had the four years' experience. **1892** *York Co. Hist. Rev.* 74 Charles H. Sprenkel, Justice of the Peace and Practical Printer.

***practice,** *n.* In combs.: (1) **practice game,** a game played for practice, usu. before a formally scheduled game; (2) **ship,** a ship used at the Naval Academy in giving the cadets practical instruction in seamanship.

(1) **1885** *Wkly. New Mexican Rev.* 9 April 3/3 The clubs of Santa Fe, Las Vegas, Raton and Socorro have already had practice games. — (2) *a***1861** WINTHROP *Open Air* 227 There they found the Naval Academy in danger of attack, and Old Ironsides—serving as a practice-ship for the future midshipmen—also exposed. **1898** *How to Gain Admission to Annapolis* 8 About the fifth of June each year, the members of the first, third and fourth classes embark on the Academy practice ship.

***practiser,** *n.* (See quot.) *Obs.* — **1900** A. ALLEN *P. Brooks* I. 290 There were other similar [mission] stations in the vicinity, where [seminary] students officiated by reading service and extempore preaching. . . . The common name given to them was *practisers*, with the emphasis on the second syllable.

***practitioner,** *n.* In Christian Science, an authorized or recognized healer.

1883 EDDY in *Christian Science Jrnl.* I. 3 The most of our practitioners have plenty to do and many more are needed. **1915** DREISER *Genius* 710 Angela had somehow concluded . . . that Christian Science, as demonstrated by its practitioners, might help her through this crisis, though she had no real faith in it. **1946** *Christian Science Jrnl.* LXIV. (Dec.) 616 We called on a practitioner to learn what this Science was.

***Praeses,** *n.* A college president. *Obs.* — **1836** *Harvardiana* III. 98 Did not the Praeses, himself, most kindly and oft reprimand me? **1851** HOLMES *Poetical Works* (1895) 114/1 The good old Præses cries, . . . 'You have passed, and are classed With the *Boys of '29.*'

***pragmatism,** *n. Philos.* An American philosophical movement initiated by C. S. Peirce (1839–1914) and William James (1842–1910), characteristic doctrines of which are that the practical consequences of a conception are the expression of its whole meaning, and that the object of thinking is to develop general principles of conduct.

"As late as 1893, when I might have procured the insertion of the word pragmatism in the *Century Dictionary*, it did not seem to me that its vogue was sufficient to warrant that step" (1903 Peirce *Lectures on Pragmatism* V. 13). Peirce later adopted the word *pragmaticism* to distinguish his particular philosophy from other forms of pragmatism: "So, then, the writer, finding his bantling 'pragmatism' so promoted, . . . begs to announce the birth of the word 'pragmaticism,' which is ugly enough to be safe from kidnappers" (1905 Peirce in *Monist* XV. 165 f.).

1898 W. JAMES *Philos. Conceptions & Pract. Results* 5 The principle of practicalism or pragmatism, as he [C. S. Peirce] called it, when I first heard him enunciate it at Cambridge [Mass.] in the early '70s, is the clue . . . by following which . . . we may keep our feet upon the proper trail. *Ib.* 6 Our conception of these effects, then, is for us the whole of our conception of the object, so far as that conception has positive significance at all. This is the principle of Peirce, the principle of pragmatism. **1910** *Morrison's Chi. Wkly.* 1 Dec. 22/1 'Pragmatism' has become a feature of the Sunday supplement and the popular magazines, and a sweet morsel in the mouth of the undergraduate. **1948** *Chi. D. News* 18 Dec. 6/3 Marxian dialectic . . . is vastly inferior to American pragmatism as a means of approaching the truth.

Hence ***pragmatist,** one who accepts this philosophy.

1903 *Hibbert Jrnl.* March 578 A contemporaneous review of an American pragmatist. **1907** *Chi. Times* 8 Feb. 178 The pragmatist takes religion as he finds it, a working life; . . . he studies the Christian life, and considers that the best way to study it is to live it; . . . he is content to leave many things unexplained. **1949** *Newsweek* 23 May 90/2 Emerson began his rise to fame as the first outstanding American philosopher, the pragmatist who made possible William James and John Dewey.

prairie ˈprɛrɪ, ˈprerɪ, *n.* [F., a meadow.]

The word has been variously spelled, as *perarie, priory, prer-ie, peraira, perara,* etc.

1. A level or rolling area of land, destitute of trees and usu. covered with grass.

The word has been, and still is, applied variously. See the quots.

[**1770** PITTMAN *Present State* 45 La Prairie De Roches is about seventeen miles from Cascasquias.] **1773** in HUTCHINS *Va., Pa., Md., & N.C.* 55 The Prairies (Meadows) extend further from the [Illinois] river. **1792** *Amer. Philos. Soc.* III. 219 Some of these *Prairies* are high lands, surrounded by an extensive timbered country, in many places much lower than the clear lands. **1832** CATLIN *Indians* I. 24 The buffalo . . . roams over the vast prairies. **1947** *Reader's Digest* Oct. 148/1 The prairies are all right. The mountains are all right.

b. With specifying words. Cf. **door, trembling prairie,** and for **chocolate prairie** see ***chocolate 1,** quot. 1869.

1817 FORDHAM *Narr. Travels* 202 We then travelled . . . through part of the Long Prairie . . . ; and the *English Prairie*, with all its swelling hills, . . . opened at once upon our sight. **1826** in PECK *Guide* (1831) 209 The Big Prairie in Missouri, between Cape Girardeau and New Madrid, is . . . perhaps more properly barren land. **1946** G. HUTTON *Midwest at Noon* 6 The climate was milder than it was farther north in the lowland prairie.

c. In a quasi-adj. and generic sense equivalent to "prairie land."

1805 in THOBURN *Stand. Hist. Okla.* I. 32 We found the country all prairie, except small copses of wood, cedar, cotton and musketo. **1901** DUNCAN & SCOTT *Allen & Woodson Co., Kans.* 580 About six per cent of the original surface of the county was covered with forest and the remainder was prairie. **1944** *Amer. Scholar* Summer 331 Prairie everywhere owes its character to the most abundant and important grasses.

d. In transf. uses (see quots.). Also attrib.

1915 MUIR *Travels Alaska* (1917) 300 The nearly level glacier stretched indefinitely away in the gray cloudy sky, a prairie of ice. **1934** *Nat. Geog. Mag.* LXV. 599 For generations swamp hunters [in the Okefenokee] have pushed over these prairie waters. **1942** RAWLINGS *C. Creek* 51 We use the word 'prairie' in a special sense. We have no open plains, but around most of the larger lakes are wet flat areas thick with water grasses, and these we call our prairies. They are more nearly marshes, yet we save the word 'marsh' for the deep mucky edges of lake and river, dense with coontail and lily pads.

2. In special combs. and derivatives: (1) **prairie bitters,** (see quot.), *obs.;* (2) **breaker,** =**prairie plow;** (3) **breaking,** the breaking of prairie soil in bringing it into cultivation; (4) **butter,** (see quot.), *obs.;* (5) **chips,** buffalo chips *q.v., obs.;* (6) **coal,** =prec.; (7) **cocktail,** (see quot.); (8) **cottage,** a type of residence esp. designed for the western plains; (9) **dew,** whisky, *slang, obs.;* (10) **-dom,** the region of western prairies, *obs.;* (11) **feathers,** (see quot.), *obs.;* (12) **fire,** a fire that sweeps over a grassy prairie, also attrib.; (13) **forestry,** forestry designed to grow trees in a prairie region; (14) **fuel,** (see quot.), *obs.;* (15) **hay,** hay made from prairie grass; (16) **itch,** (see quot.), *obs.;* (17) **law,** usage followed on the prairies, *obs.;* (18) **life,** life as it is led on the western prairies, also attrib.; (19) **loo,** (see quot.), *obs.;* (20) **match,** app. a match esp. suitable for use on the prairies, *obs.;* (21) **-ology,** the ability to make one's way on the prairies, *rare;* (22) **oyster,** =**prairie cocktail,** *obs.;* (23) **pillow,** ?a pillow stuffed with prairie grass, *obs.;* (24)

Type of prairie cottage popular *c*1848

plow, (see quot. 1876); (25) **renovator,** (see quot.), *obs.;* (26) **twister,** (see quot.).

(**1**) **1848** BARTLETT 260 *Prairie-bitters*, a beverage common among the hunters and mountaineers. It is made with a pint of water and a quarter of a gill of buffalo-gall, and is considered an excellent medicine. — (**2**) **1867** DIXON *New Amer.* I. 44 When the ground is . . . cut by the prairie breaker, the rosin-weed disappears. **1902** *Sears Cat.* (ed. 112) 476/3 Our Prairie Breaker combines many desirable qualities. — (**3**) **1846** in *Minn. Farmers' Diaries* (1939) 69 Made arrangements with him about Prairie Breaking. **1886** EBBUTT *Emigrant Life Kans.* 45 Will Hopkins . . . used to do a good deal of prairie-breaking, having a twenty-four inch plough and six yoke of oxen. — (**4**) **1884** SHEPHERD *Prairie Exp.* 221 One mixture is so strange that it must be mentioned. . . . It has many names; the most harmless is, perhaps, prairie butter. When the meat is fried, if any grease remain in the pan, add flour and water, stir, and mix thoroughly till you produce a frothy batter; spread this on your bread, and, if of my taste—leave it. It is less troublesome to make than butter.

(**5**) **1843** W. A. FERRIS *Life in Rocky Mts.* (1940) 28 The 'prairie chips' . . . were so saturated with water that they could not be coaxed to burn. **1897** HOUGH *Story of Cowboy* 179 Some of the boys kicked together enough of the abundant prairie chips—the only fuel within sixty miles of that point. — (**6**) **1939** C. L. DOUGLAS *Cattle Kings* 324 He could not bring himself to relish food cooked with 'prairie coal.' **1948** *Southwestern Rev.* Summer 238/1 When the permanent settlers and their families came, this 'prairie coal' became the standard fuel. — (**7**) **1890** *Cent.* 4668/1 prairie-cocktail. . . . A raw egg, peppered and salted, and drunk in vinegar or spirits. Also called *prairie-oyster*. [Western U.S.] — (**8**) **1838** ELLSWORTH *Valley of Wabash* 52 At considerable expense of time and labor, we have prepared a plan . . . of a house or 'Prairie cottage' for the western settler. — (**9**) **1846** BURNHAM *Stray Subjects* 81 Jest fetch on your 'prary dew' for the hull lot, and d—— the expense.

(**10**) **1845** (*title*), Prairiedom: Rambles & Scrambles in Texas or New Estrémadura. **1866** *Ill. Agric. Soc. Trans.* VI. 285 The day is coming rapidly which is to usher in general planting of them [i.e., hardy varieties of evergreens] over all prairiedom. — (**11**) **1901** ROOT *Overland Stage* 338 They slept from year to year on ticks filled with hay—they called it 'prairie feathers.' — (**12**) **1824** in *Ind. Hist. Soc. Pub.* IV. 82 We then rode on to the prairie and rode twice through the prairie fire, which, owing to there being no wind, moved very slowly. **1884** ALDRIDGE *Life on Ranch* 54 Prairie fires do annually a considerable amount of damage in the Western States, by burning a large amount of winter range. **1948** *Dly. Ardmoreite* (Ardmore, Okla.) 6 May 1/2 The newspaper and radio were flooded with calls for information about the storm rumor as it spread with prairie fire speed over town. — (**13**) **1890** *Stock Grower & Farmer* 8 Feb. 5/1, I regard the thorough fining of the soil before planting as one of the very important steps in prairie forestry. — (**14**) **1847** JOHN T. HUGHES *Doniphan's Expedition* 21/1 This 'prairie fuel' (buffalo chips) . . . is a tolerable substitute for wood, in dry weather, but is worse than useless in wet weather.

(15) c1835 in *Wis. State H.S. Coll.* XV. (1900) 283 Here I fed myself, but could get nothing but Prairie hay & pumpkins for my horse. **1949** *Dly. Oklahoman* (Okla. City) 13 Feb. D. 4/4 More than 2,500 tons of the prairie hay used in the recent haylift operations to save icebound livestock in the western states were supplied by hay growers around Vinita, Okla. — **(16) 1877** BARTLETT 489 *Prairie-Itch*, a cutaneous eruption caused by the friction of the fine red dust of prairie countries in summer. — **(17) 1827** COOPER *Prairie* vii, It is the usage of their people, and what may be called the prairie law. — **(18) 1843** FRÉMONT *Explor. Rocky Mts.* 9, I have collected . . . twenty-one men, principally Creole and Canadian *voyageurs*, who had become familiar with prairie life in the service of the fur companies in the Indian country. **1886** *Cent. Mag.* May 238/2 He was doubtless the original of Dr. Battius, the naturalist of one of Cooper's prairie-life novels. — **(19) 1835** HOFFMAN *Winter in West* I. 221, I was contented to wrap myself as closely as possible in my buffalo robe, and join him in a game of *prairie loo*. . . . The game consists merely in betting upon the number of wild animals seen by either party towards the side of the vehicle on which he is riding, a wolf or deer counting ten, and a grouse one. The game is a hundred.

(20) 1865 PIKE *Scout & Ranger* (1932) 53, I drew a box of prairie matches from my pocket, — **(21) 1869** *Repub. D. Jrnl.* (Lawrence, Kans.) 25 May, To experienced plainsmen and frontiersmen, skilled in woodcraft and prairie-ology. — **(22) 1890** [see **prairie-cocktail**]. **1905** BELASCO *Girl of Golden West* 1 Mix me a prairie oyster. . . . Crack the egg—I'll stand [the cost]. — **(23) 1840** *Crockett Almanac* 20 She got her living by making Prairie pillows. — **(24) 1839** in *Cultivator* VII. 33/1 It may be amusing to eastern readers, to hear a description of a 'prairie plow.' Fancy, then, a plow share weighing 125 lbs., the beam fourteen feet long, attached to a pair of cart wheels, to the tongue of which are hitched from three to seven yoke of oxen. **1876** KNIGHT 1782/1 *Prairie-plow*, a large plow supported in front on wheels, and adapted to pare and overturn a very broad but shallow furrow-slice.

(25) 1883 KNIGHT *Supp.* 717/2 *Prairie Renovator*, . . . an implement with tearing harrow teeth, drawn over the surface of grass land to loosen the roots and the soil, dislodge moss, uproot weeds, and break up the matted vegetation. — **(26) 1902** W. M. DAVIS *Elem. Phys. Geog.* ii. 67 Violent local storms . . . are often called cyclones, or prairie twisters, in the Mississippi valley, but the name tornado is to be preferred.

b. Designating places or regions in prairie country: (1) **prairie city,** a city in a prairie region; (2) **claim,** an area of public land claimed or subject to claim by a settler, *obs.*; (3) **country,** country consisting of prairies or a prairie; (4) **farm,** a farm established on prairie land; (5) **land,** (*a*) land made up of prairies or a prairie, meadow land, (*b*) a region of prairies, a prairie-like expanse; (6) **ocean,** the western prairies; (7) **port,** a place well located for trade in a prairie region; (8) **region,** (*a*) a region of prairie land, (*b*) esp. the black belt region of central Alabama; (9) **state,** (*a*) (*cap.*) a nickname applied to Illinois and to North Dakota, (*b*) *pl.* those states in the prairie region of the West.

(1) 1857 UNDERHILL & THOMPSON *Elephant Club* 99 The car had just left the flourishing prairie city of Scraggsville. **1944** LANKS *Alaska* 3 Though it's a prairie city, Edmonton is not flat. — **(2) 1836** in *Wis. Hist. Mag.* XIX. 450, I mentioned I think . . . that I had sold the prairie claim that I had near this place. **1857** *Lawrence* (Kans.) *Republican* 4 June 2 Many untaken prairie claims are yet inviting the emigrant hither. — **(3) 1806** *Ann. 9th Congress* 2 Sess. 1136 The quality of the land is supposed superior to that on the Red river, until it ascends to the prairie country, where the lands on both rivers are probably similar. **1907** LILLIBRIDGE *Trail* 152 The darkness that precedes morning has the prairie country in its grip. **1946** ADAMS *Album Amer. Hist.* III. 261 Hay Burning Stoves were useful in this prairie country. — **(4) 1838** ELLSWORTH *Valley of Wabash* 49 A late and lamented brother of the writer . . . had just finished a prairie farm containing 800 acres. **1886** P. G. EBBUTT *Emigrant Life Kans.* 198, I don't think Anderson had enough energy in him to start a prairie farm for himself.

(5) (*a*) **1807** GASS *Journal* 145 Back from the river the tops of the hills, to a great distance are prairie land. **1894** GARLAND in *Harper's Mag.* June 144/1 Toward noon they left the sunny prairie land of northern Illinois and southern Wisconsin. (*b*) **1862** *Rep. Comm. Patents 1861: Agric.* 548 Of the cultivated animals of prairie-land, . . . it will be hard to find distinguishing traits. **1869** STOWE *Oldtown Folks* The children travelled onward along the winding course of the river, through a prairie-land of wild-flowers. — **(6) 1844** GREGG *Commerce of Prairies* I. 311 On our passage this time across the 'prairie ocean' which lay before us . . . there was now a plain wagon trail. **1855** BOYNTON *Journey through Kans.* 159 The whole party found themselves '*becalmed*' on the prairie-ocean. **1939** VESTAL *Old Santa Fe Trail* 4 In the old days, travellers themselves spoke habitually of 'making port,' urged Congress to enact navigation laws for the 'prairie ocean.' — **(7) 1848** RUXTON in *Blackw. Mag.* LXIV. 21 Independence may be termed the 'prairie port' of the western country. **1862** *Harper's Mag.* Sep. 447/2 As Independence is the eastern, so may the Mora be considered the western prairie port of the great Santa Fé trail. — **(8)** (*a*) **1826** T. FLINT *Recoll.* 166 Those [mounds] on the Ohio are covered with very large trees. But in the prairie regions . . . they are covered with tall grass. **1873** *Newton Kansan* 13 Feb. 2/4 We cannot compute the value it would add to the prairie region. (*b*) **1883** SMITH *Geol. Survey Ala.* 304 Putting Chambers and Lee together with the counties which constitute the *Prairie region*, we have the nucleus of the Central cotton belt. **1901** MOHR *Plant Life Ala.* 99 The term 'prairie region,' applied to this plain, refers . . . to the black, calcareous, highly fertile soil of these uplands. — **(9)** (*a*) **1842** *People's Adv.* (Carrollton, Ill.) 6 Aug. 4/5 *Glorious News!!* Federal Coon Whiggery extinct in the Prairie State! **1900** *Harper's Wkly.* 8 Sep. 853/3 A large number of Dunkers (German Baptists) from Indiana and Pennsylvania have settled in communities in the Prairie State [i.e., North Dakota]. **1949** J. MONAGHAN *This is Ill.* 138 The nation began to hum the wonders of the Prairie State. (*b*) **1852** STOWE *Uncle Tom* xlv, Brave and generous men of New York, farmers of rich and joyous Ohio, and ye of the wide prairie states, answer, is this a thing for you to protect and countenance? **1949** *Kans. Hist. Quart.* Feb. 39 The area between the western boundaries of the prairie states and the Rocky Mountains was designated as the Kansas and Nebraska territories in 1854.

c. Designating Indians and others living in or associated with prairie regions, as (1) **prairie Apache,** (2) **band,** (3) **burner,** (4) **dandy,** (5) **hunter,** (6) **Indian,** (7) **man,** (8) **Potawatomi,** (9) **tribe.**

(1) 1917 WILL & HYDE *Corn Among Indians* 45 South and west of the river were the Crows, Cheyennes, and Arapahoes, and, in earlier times, the Kiowas, Prairie-Apaches, and Comanches. — **(2) 1946** FOREMAN *Last Trek* 38 The western contingent became known as the 'Prairie band,' while the others were denominated the 'Vermilion band' from their residence on the river of that name. — **(3) 1884** ALDRIDGE *Life on Ranch* 80 The gentle reader would no doubt like to hear how we threw our lariats on him, and dragged him to the nearest tree, there suspending him by the neck, as a warning to all future prairie-burners. — **(4) 1851** in *Neb. Hist. Pub.* XX. 237 The Prairie Dandy [Indian], after his manner, displays quite as much sense and taste as his city prototype.

(5) 1841 *S. Lit. Messenger* VII. 56/2 The author has conversed with a number of our prairy hunters, and Texan adventurers. **1847** PARKMAN in *Knickerb.* XXX. 289 He differs as much from the genuine 'mountain-man,' the wild prairie hunter, as a Canadian voyageur. — **(6) 1829** *Va. Herald* (Fredericksburg) 28 Feb. 3/3 These prairie Indians doubtless intend making war on the white inhabitants of this frontier, which is greatly exposed. **1874** GLISAN *Jrnl. Army Life* 463 These men are never so happy as when . . . in pursuit of a band of fleeing, horse-thieving, prairie Indians. — **(7) 1857** in *Ann. Wyoming* XI. (1939) 87 Mr. Ward . . . is an experienced Prairie man. **1863** *Ladies' Repository* Aug. 486/2 He said the prairie man's name was Job Smith. — **(8) 1946** FOREMAN *Last Trek* 36 The 'Prairie Pottawatomi,' or Illinois band of that tribe, were living on the Illinois River. **1949** *Midland Naturalist* Sep. 470 Those who occupied the present Chicago site were the Prairie Potawatomi. — **(9) 1846** SAGE *Scenes Rocky Mts.* ix, The mode of marriage prevalent among the mountain and prairie tribes would seem rather strange. **1887** *Scribner's Mag.* II. 505/2 The local prejudice against the prairie tribes . . . has probably discouraged any attempts to perpetuate Indian appellations.

d. Designating vehicles used, or suitable for use, in prairie regions, as (1) **prairie car,** (2) **cart,** (3) **clipper,** (4) **engine,** (5) **schooner,** (6) **ship,** (7) **wagon.**

(1) 1846 *De Bow's Review* II. 109 A prairie car has been patented. — **(2) 1843** JAMES L. SCOTT *Journal* 84 Two men came along, moving to Iowa, with an ox-team and a prairie cart. For fellies and tyre, they had the half of a hickory sapling bent around the ends of the spokes, which formed the wheels. — **(3) 1870** KEIM *Sheridan's Troopers* 49 The coaches or 'prairie clippers,' as they are called by the denizens of the country, pitched and jolted. **1939** VESTAL *Old Santa Fe Trail* 5 He proposed to build—with their backing—a fleet of large prairie clippers to carry cargo to the cussed Spaniards. — **(4) 1945** MARSHALL *Santa Fe* 281 Over a twisting track near Needles, Fred Jackson took the 1010, a big, high-wheeled prairie engine, around the curves at sixty-five miles an hour. [**1947** BEEBE *Mixed Train Dly.* 12 No. 5. a Baldwin-built Prairie-type engine, was the only one in running order at Foley at the moment.]

(5) 1841 ELIZA R. STEELE *Summer Journey* 134 So much is this appearance acknowledged by the country people that they call the stage coach, a prairie schooner. **1949** *Chi. D. News* 17 May 6/4 The 'prairie schooner,' one of 30 originals . . . arrives here by Air Force plane Tuesday. — **(6) 1851** M. REID *Scalp Hunters* iii, I do not remember a more striking picture than to see the long caravan of waggons, the 'prairie ships,' deployed over the plain. — **(7) 1855** in *N.Y. Herald* (1856) 9 Jan. 2/1 The vehicle, which, like most ambulances, or prairie wagons,' as they call them here, proved rather airy. **1867** DIXON *New Amer.* I. 37 Our big Concord coach has been exchanged for a light prairie waggon, smaller in size, frailer in build, without a door, with very bad springs, and with canvas blinds for windows. **1948** *Chi. D. News* 10 April 6/2, I have an idea that too much of the squirrel rifle and prairie wagon tradition still runs in the bloodstream of most Americans to permit them [etc.].

3. In the names of, or in allusion to, animals: (1) **prairie alligator,** (see quot.); (2) **beef,** (see quot.); (3) **buffalo,** (see quot.), *obs.;* (4) **cattle,** (*a*) cattle living on the prairies, (*b*) buffaloes, both *obs.;* (5) **chipmunk,** (see quot.); (6) **cricket,** ?=**Mormon cricket,** *obs.;* (7) **dog,** see as a main entry; (8) **down,** a breed or variety of sheep, *obs.;* (9) **eel,** a jocose term for a prairie rattlesnake, *obs.;* (10) **fly,** (see quot. 1890); (11) **fox,** the kit fox; (12) **gopher,** a ground squirrel of the genus *Citellus;* (13) **ground squirrel,** =**prairie dog;** (14) **hare,** (*a*) the varying hare, *Lepus americanus,* (*b*) the white-tailed jack rabbit, *L. townsendi;* (15) **horsefly,** a horsefly common on the plains; (16) **lawyer,** (see quot.), *obs.;* (17) **marmot,** =**prairie dog;** (18) **marmot squirrel,** =prec.; (19) **mole,** the Canada pocket gopher, *Thomomys talpoides;* (20) **mouse,** (see quot.); (21) **rabbit,** a western jack rabbit; (22) **rat,** ?=**prairie dog,** *obs.;* (23) **rattler,** short for next; (24) **rattlesnake,** (see quot. 1890); (25) **rooter,** a hog of a nondescript breed; (26) **shark,** =prec.; (27) **snake,** a snake often found in prairie regions; (28) **squirrel,** (*a*) =**prairie dog,** (*b*) any of various spermophiles of the western prairies, as *Citellus tridecemlineatus;* (29) **turtle,** a tortoise, *rare;* (30) **wolf,** a coyote.

(1) 1894 *Harper's Mag.* Feb. 456/1 The form [of walking stick] common over the greater part of the United States, . . . [called in some states] 'prairie alligators,' our *Diapheromera ferata* . . . may be compared to an animated straw. — **(2) 1844** GREGG *Commerce of Prairies* I. 54 The excitement that the first sight of these 'prairie beeves' [buffaloes] occasions . . . beggars all description. — **(3) 1806** LEWIS in *L. & Clark Exped.* V. (1905) 80 A speceis of Lizzard called by the French engages prarie buffaloe are native of these plains as well as of those of the Missouri. I have called them the horned Lizzard. — **(4)** (*a*) **1836** *Knickerb.* VIII. 287 There is not a more stirring sight than that of driving a herd of the prairie cattle over the river. (*b*) **1844** GREGG *Commerce of Prairies* I. 97 While in the midst of the buffalo range, travellers usually take the precaution of laying up a supply of beef for exigencies in the absence of 'prairie cattle.'

(5) 1888 *Ipswich* (Mass.) *Chron.* 15 Sep. 2/4 In some parts of the country . . . a gopher . . . [is] a striped squirrel or prairie chipmunk. — **(6) 1860** M. REID *Odd People* 341 [The Yamparico] finds a resource, however, in the prairie cricket, an insect . . . of the *gryllus* tribe. — **(8) 1836** J. HALL *Statistics of West* 149 The prairie down, bearing a strong similarity to the celebrated breed of 'south downs,' in England . . . should be kept exclusively upon high ground and pine herbage. — **(9) 1868** *Harper's Mag.* Feb. 299/2 It was . . . his duty to secure all the prairie eels that might come within reach.

(10) 1818 in *R.I. Hist.* I. (1942) 129 The Prairie fly is about the size of a honey bee and about the colour with green heads and there is another kind that keeps in the Woods very large. **1890** *Cent.* 4668/2 prairie-fly. . . . One of various species of flies of the family *Tabanidæ* which attack cattle. [Western U.S.] — **(11) 1839** MARRYAT *Diary in Amer.* I. 206 [In list of fur obtained every year by American Fur Co.] Prairie Fox . . . 5000. **1875** BURROUGHS *Winter Sunshine* 108 The prairie fox, the cross fox, and the black or silver-grey fox, seem only varieties of the red fox. — **(12) 1875** *Amer. Naturalist* IX. 148, I elect to write about the prairie gopher—as I shall call that particular species known in the book as *Spermophilus Richardsoni* . . . for several reasons. **1907** LILLIBRIDGE *Trail* 15 The longitudinal stripes of a prairie gopher or on the back of a bobwhite. — **(13) 1844** GREGG *Commerce of Prairies* II. 228 It was denominated the 'barking squirrel,' the 'prairie ground-squirrel,' etc., by early explorers. — **(14)** (*a*) **1840** EMMONS *Mass. Quadrupeds* 58 *Lepus Virginianus.* Harlan. Prairie Hare. . . . This species is common throughout the New England States, and is known generally as the White Rabbit. (*b*) **1868** *Amer. Naturalist* II. 536 Prairie Hare (*Lepus Townsendii*). This hare is common east of the Rocky Mountains. **1917** *Mammals of Amer.* 280/1 Although called the Prairie Hare, this species is found also on mountain slopes.

(15) 1835 in *Overland to Pacific* VI. (1936) 98 The prairie horse-fly is very annoying. Its bite is like the thrust of the point of the lance. When brushed off the blood immediately starts out. — **(16) 1860** GREELEY *Overland Journey* 93 It is impossible for a stranger to the prairies to realize the impudence of these prairie-lawyers [gray wolves]. — **(17) 1826** GODMAN *Nat. Hist.* II. 114 The Prairie Marmot. *Arctomys Ludovicianus.* . . . Commonly called Prairie-dog. **1888** *Ipswich* (Mass.) *Chron.* 15 Sep. 2/4 Usually a country that is inhabited by prairie dogs, or more properly by prairie marmots, has a dry, thin atmosphere. — **(18) 1872** TICE *Over Plains* 253 *Cynomys* literally means Dog-Mouse, or Dog-rat. . . . Those who have not fancied the latter, have proposed to call him the Prairie Marmot Squirrel. — **(19) 1808** PIKE *Sources Miss.* 31, [I] caught a curious little animal on the prairie, which my Frenchman termed a *prairie mole,* but it is very different from the mole of the States.

(20) 1868 *Amer. Naturalist* II. 534 Prairie Mouse (*Hesperomys Sonoriensis*). This widely spread Mouse is common at Fort Benton [Mont.]. — **(21) 1846** in *S.W. Hist. Ser.* III. (1935) 176 A fire broke out in the brush . . . alarming the prairie rabbits, almost the only tenants that we saw of this poor and barren country. — **(22) 1846** *Spirit of Times* (N.Y.) 11 July 229/1 Couldn't kill a prairie rat on the whole route to save us from starvation. — **(23) 1878** BEADLE *Western Wilds* 133 The only dangerous snakes are the little prairie rattlers, seldom over two feet long. **1948** *Chi. Tribune* 30 May (roto.) 14 A prairie rattler coils to strike; its prey is a rabbit. — **(24) 1817** S. BROWN *Western Gaz.* 31 The only venomous serpents, are the common and prairie rattlesnake, and copper-heads. **1890** *Cent.* 4668/3 *Prairie-rattlesnake,* . . . one of several different rattlesnakes inhabiting the prairies, as the massauga, *Sistrurus catenatus,* and especially *Crotalus confluentus.* **1948** *Nat. Hist.* April 187/1 An extensive campaign was waged against the prairie rattlesnake.

(25) 1872 *Ill. Dept. Agric. Trans.* IX. 204 The old fashioned 'prairie rooter and elm peeler' are banished from the county. — **(26)** *a***1885** in *Cent. Mag.* XXXII. 787/2 'Prairie-sharks' and 'razor-backs' were the local names for them. — **(27) 1843** FRÉMONT *Explor. Rocky Mts.* 12 A large prairie-snake . . . was occupied in eating young birds. **1846** ABERT *Exam. N. Mex.* 14 [Cheyenne language] prairie snake sa sa nit tan. — **(28)** (*a*) **1808** PIKE *Sources Miss.* 155 We returned and on our way, killed some prairie squirrels, or wishtonwishes. **1857** *Rep. Comm. Patents 1856: Agric.* 81 The famous 'Prairie Dog,' or 'Prairie Squirrel,' exists in great abundance on the plains west of the Missouri River. (*b*) *Ib.* 73 These are with great propriety called 'Prairie Squirrels,' for their true home is on the prairie. **1859** BARTLETT 181 *Ground squirrel,* a name sometimes erroneously given to the striped and spotted prairie squirrel. **1900** *Out West* Sep.–Oct. 218 His cousin, the gopher, has real pockets on the outside of his cheek, . . . but this prairie squirrel simply distends his cheeks. — **(29) 1846** DE SMET *Ore. Missions* (1847) 241 In every one of their old encampments we observed great quantities of prairie-turtle shells, a proof of their being numerous and serving as food for the savages.

(30) 1804 CLARK in *Lewis & C. Exped.* I. (1904) 108 A Prarie Wolf came near the bank and Barked at us this evening. **1898** CANFIELD *Maid of Frontier* 39 The long howl of the prairie wolf rose on the air and hung tremulant. **1948** *Dly. Ardmoreite* (Ardmore, Okla.) 18 April 14/7 There are practically only two distinct kinds of wolves in America—the large gray timber wolf and the coyote or prairie wolf.

Also (1) **prairie horse,** (2) **nag,** (3) **pony,** (4) **team.**

(1) 1843 in *Miss. Val. Hist. Rev.* XII. 89 Mounting their prairie horses they disdained not the escort of his company to Western Missouri. **1860** HOLMES *E. Venner* xxiii, The prairie horse knew the trick of the cord. — **(2)** *a***1861** WINTHROP *Canoe & Saddle* 50, I could not ride the leagues, . . . barebacking the bonyness of prairie nags. — **(3) 1837** IRVING *Bonneville* I. 69 [They] are generally well mounted on . . . short, stout horses, similar to the prairie ponies. — **(4) 1836** in *Annals of Iowa* 3 Ser. XXIII. 141, I have had a notion of buying one half of a prairie team as breaking is very dear. **1847** ROBB *Squatter Life* 42 You look . . . tired as a prairie team, arter a hard day's ploughin'.

b. In the names of birds: (1) **prairie bird,** (*a*) generically, any bird that lives on the prairie, (*b*) (see quots.); (2) **bobolink,** (see quot.); (3) **chick,** a young prairie chicken; (4) **chicken,** see as a main entry; (5) **cock,** the male sage cock or grouse; (6) **crane,** the sandhill crane, *Grus canadensis tabida;* (7) **dove,** ?=**golden plover,** *rare;* (8) **falcon,** (see quot. 1874); (9) **finch,** (see quot.); (10) **fowl,** (*a*) =**prairie chicken,** (*b*) (see quot.); (11) **grouse,** =**prairie chicken;** (12) **hawk,** a hawk that lives on the prairies, as the sparrow hawk, *Falco sparverius;* (13) **hen,** a prairie chicken or a clapper rail; (14) **horned lark,** (see quot.); (15) **lark,** (*a*) =prec., (*b*) Sprague's pipit, *Anthus spraguei;* (16) **marsh wren,** (see quot.); (17) **owl,** (*a*) the burrowing owl, *Speotyto cunicularia hypogaea,* (*b*) (see quot.); (18) **pigeon, plover,** see as main entries; (19) **reedbird,** =**lark bunting;** (20) **runner,** prob. the road runner *q.v., rare;* (21) **sharp-tailed grouse,** (see quot.); (22) **skylark,** (see quot.); (23) **snipe,** =**golden plover;** (24) **titlark,** the common titlark, *Anthus spenoletta rubescens;* (25) **turkey,** =**sage grouse;** (26) **warbler,** a small warbler, *Dendroica discolor,* chiefly of the eastern part of the country.

(1) (*a*) **1805** CLARK in *Lewis & C. Exped.* II. (1904) 184 An emence number of Prairie burds now sitting of two kinds. **1873** *Amer. Naturalist* VII. 197 (*caption*), The Prairie Birds of Southern Illinois. (*b*) **1917** *Birds of Amer.* I. 257 Golden Plover. *Charadrius dominicus dominicus.* . . . [Also called] Prairie-bird. *Ib.* II. 212 Horned Lark. *Otocoris alpestris alpestris.* . . . [Also called] Prairie Bird. *Ib.* III. 76/1 The name White-winged Prairiebird [for the lark bunting] . . . seems to avoid confusion with . . . the Lark Sparrow. — (**2**) **1917** *Birds of Amer.* III. 76 Lark Bunting. *Calamospiza melanocorys.* . . . [Also called] Prairie Bobolink. — (**3**) **1878** RUEDE *Sod-House Days* 230 Graybill has over 100 chicks, and the other day he caught seven prairie chicks just hatched and put them under a hen he has in the house, with the hope of taming them.

(**5**) **1805** CLARK in *Lewis & C. Exped.* III. (1905) 123 Send out Hunters to shute the Prairie Cock a large fowl which I have only Seen on this river. **1900** GARLAND *Eagle's Heart* 107 A belated prairie cock began to boom. — (**6**) **1844** *Yale Lit. Mag.* IX. 328 The snow storm had changed into a driving sleet. At intervals was heard . . . the discordant croak of the prairie crane, evidently enjoying highly the rage of the elements. **1863** in *N.D. Hist. Quart.* II. (1928) 249 Camped at night at Platte River, shot one prairie crane and whistler on wing. — (**7**) **1849** PARKMAN *Oregon Trail* (1944) 111 And three eggs which he found in the nest of a prairie-dove. — (**8**) **1874** COUES *Birds N.W.* 339 *Falco Mexicanus* var. *Polyagrus* (Cass.) Coues. American Lanier or Prairie Falcon . . . attacks and overpowers the great hares of the West. **1940** JAEGER *Calif. Deserts* 102 Of the birds of prey, the spirited prairie falcon seems most typical of the desert. — (**9**) **1839** AUDUBON *Ornith. Biog.* V. 19 [The] Prairie Finch, *Fringilla Bicolor,* . . . inhabits a portion of the Platte country, in large flocks.

(**10**) (*a*) **1804** CLARK in *Lewis & C. Exped.* VI. (1905) 121 The Prairie Fowl common to the Illinois are found as high up as the River Jacque. **1893** ROOSEVELT *Wilderness Hunter* 92 When making long wagon trips over the great plains, antelope often offer the only source of meat supply, save for occasional water fowl, sage fowl, and prairie fowl—the sharp-tailed prairie fowl, be it understood. (*b*) **1866** *N.J. Laws* 681 No person shall . . . kill, or take, or destroy any pinnated grouse, commonly called prairie fowl. — (**11**) **1852** TREMENHEERE *Notes* 274 For common shooting, there is . . . also prairie grouse in abundance. **1917** *Birds of Amer.* II. 24/1 The Prairie Grouse weighs about two pounds and its flesh is tender, juicy, and delicious. — (**12**) **1817** FORDHAM *Narr. Travels* 143 Saw some prairie hawks, blue bodies, ash coloured belly and wings, tipped with black. **1907** LILLIBRIDGE *Trail* 259 Answering, coercing, swift as the swoop of a prairie hawk, as a human being in abandon, the man's arms were about her. — (**13**) **1804** *Lewis & Clark Exped.* I. (1904) 181 Capt Lewis. . . . Saw great numbers of Prarie hens. **1932** *Smithsonian Institution Bul.* 257 The prairie hen is highly insectivorous from May to October inclusive. — (**14**) **1887** RIDGWAY *Man. N. Amer. Birds* 348 Upper Mississippi Valley and region of the Great Lakes . . . *O[tocoris] alpestris praticola.* Prairie Horned Lark. **1948** *Ecological Monographs* April 206/1 The eastern meadow lark . . . and the prairie horned lark are the most common.

(**15**) (*a*) **1805** *Lewis & Clark Exped.* VI. (1905) 187 The Prarie lark, bald Eagle, & the large plover have returned. **1806** *Ib.* V. (1905) 176 The dove the black woodpecker . . . the prairie lark, . . . are found in this valley. (*b*) **1885** *Encycl. Brit.* (ed. 9) XIX. 112/2 In North America [pipits] are represented by only two species—*Neocorys spraguii,* the Prairie-Lark of the north-western plains, and *Anthus ludovicianus,* the American Titlark. — (**16**) **1917** *Birds of Amer.* III. 198/2 On the Great Plains and prairie districts, . . . [the long-billed marsh wren] is known as the Prairie Marsh Wren. — (**17**) (*a*) **1846** SAGE *Scenes Rocky Mts.* xii, The prairie-owl and rattlesnake maintain friendly relations with [prairie dogs]. **1907** LILLIBRIDGE *Trail* 13 He would have watched the movement of a coyote or a prairie owl, for the simple reason that it was the only visible object endowed with life. (*b*) **1917** *Birds of Amer.* II. 101 Short-eared Owl. *Asio flammeus.* . . . Other Names.—Marsh Owl; Swamp Owl; Prairie Owl. — (**19**) **1851** *Proc. Acad. Nat. Sci.* V. 218 Calamospiza bicolor. Prairie Reedbird.

(**20**) **1888** *Pittsburg Despatch* (F.), Man has a friend in the Prairie Runner, which is the name of a bird whose mission in life is to supervise the centipede census. — (**21**) **1887** RIDGWAY *Man. N. Amer. Birds* 204 Great Plains of United States . . . *P[ediocœtes] phasianellus campestris.* Prairie Sharp-tailed Grouse. — (**22**) **1917** *Birds of Amer.* III. 171/1 Sprague's Pipit [*Anthus spraguei*], called the Missouri Skylark, or sometimes the Prairie Skylark. — (**23**) **1851** WM. KELLY *Across Rocky Mts.* (1852) 66, I shot a brace of prairie snipe. **1890** *Cent.* 4668/3. **1917** *Birds of Amer.* I. 247 Upland Plover. *Bartramia longicauda.* . . . [Also called] Prairie Snipe. — (**24**) **1831** AUDUBON *Ornith. Biog.* I. 408 The notes of the Prairie Titlark are clear and sharp, consisting of a number of *tweets,* the last greatly prolonged. **1917** *Birds of Amer.* III. 169.

(**25**) **1828** BONAPARTE *Ornithology* III. 55 There existed in the interior of America a very large species of Grous, called by the hunters of the west the Prairie Turkey. — (**26**) **1811** WILSON *Ornithology* III. 87 [The] Prairie Warbler . . . I first discovered in that singular tract of country in Kentucky, commonly called the Barrens. **1945** *Mass. Audubon Soc.* Jan. 266 The nearest to a chromatic scale among the bird songs we hear is given by the prairie warbler.

4. In the names of plants: (1) **prairie bean,** (*a*) the Metcalfe bean, *Phaseolus metcalfei, obs.,* (*b*) a leguminous plant of the genus *Thermopsis,* esp. *T. montana;* (2) **burdock,** =**prairie dock;** (3) **clover,** any species of the genus *Petalostemon,* a plant of this genus; (4) **daisy,** the common daisy, *Chrysanthemum leucanthemum;* (5) **dock,** the dock rosinweed, *Silphium terebinthinaceum;* (6) **epinette,** a now unidentifiable plant, *obs.;* (7) **fennel,** =**biscuit root;** (8) **flower,** (*a*) a flower that grows wild on the prairies, (*b*) (*cap.*) Abraham Lincoln, a nickname; (9) **gourd,** a gourd or gourdlike plant that grows on the prairie; (10) **grass,** any one of various grasses found growing wild on the prairies of the West; (11) **indigo,** (see quots.); (12) **innocence,** prob. *Collinsia verna,* found in the central states; (13) **June grass,** (see quot.); (14) **lily,** see as a main entry; (15) **moneywort,** (see quot.); (16) **onion,** any of numerous species of *Allium,* esp. *A. stellatum,* common throughout the plains region; (17) **pea,** (*a*) a plant of the genus *Geoprumnon,* one of the buffalo beans, (*b*) (see quot.); (18) **phlox,** a perennial herb, *Phlox pilosa,* having pink, purple, or white flowers; (19) **pink,** (see quot. 1932); (20) **plum,** a Chickasaw plum, *Prunus angustifolia,* or a related species, also attrib.; (21) **potato,** (see quot. 1917); (22) **rose,** see as a main entry; (23) **sage,** a sagebrush, prob. *Artemisia tridentata;* (24) **smoke,** (see quot.); (25) **tea,** (see quot.); (26) **thistle,** a thistle, *Carduus undulatus,* found in prairie regions; (27) **tomato,** =**ground cherry;** (28) **turnip,** see as a main entry; (29) **willow,** (see quots.).

(**1**) (*a*) **1805** LEWIS in *L. & Clark Exped.* II. (1904) 29 The Indians of the Missouri make great use of this cherry, . . . mashing the seed boiling them with roots or meat, or with the prarie beans and white apple. **1885** HAVARD *Flora W. & S. Texas* 501 *Phaseolus retusus* (Prairie Bean.) Common on prairies west of the Pecos. (*b*) **1932** RYDBERG *Flora Plains & Prairies* 454 Thermopsis R. Br. Yellow Pea, Golden Pea, Prairie Bean. **1938** THOMPSON *High Trails* 85 Later in the season the prairie exhibits carpets of wild geranium, wild onion, lupine, prairie bean, wild rose, . . . and many others. — (**2**) **1847** WOOD *Botany* 336 *S[ilphium] Terebinthinaceum.* Prairie Burdock. . . . Prairies, Western, and Southern states. — (**3**) **1857** GRAY *Botany* 95 *Petalostemon,* Prairie Clover. . . . Chiefly perennial herbs, . . . [with] small flowers. **1939** *Nat. Geog. Mag.* Aug. 247/2 Prairie clovers may be white, pink, purple, or violet. **1947** *Iowa Acad. Sci. Proc.* LIV. 29 The conspicuous plants are: . . . rattlesnake master (*Eryngium yuccafolia*), red and white prairie clovers (*Petalostemon purpureum*) and *P. candidum.* — (**4**) **1856** *N.Y. Herald* 21 Jan. 3/5 In the first division, for example, we had the laurel tulip, narcissus, . . . prairie daisy, honeysuckle. **1941** SETON *Trail of Artist-Naturalist* 187 Then follow, these processionaires, . . . the avens, the prairie daisies, the yarrow, the harebell, the vetch, and lilies like a flame.

(**5**) **1839** in *Mich. Agric. Soc. Trans.* VII. 419 *Silphium terebinthinaceum.* Prairie dock. **1949** *Chi. Tribune* 14 Oct. 12/4 You can see the tall, brown stalks of the prairie dock standing erect but devoid of their bright yellow flowers. — (**6**) **1841** DE SMET *Letters* (1843) 110 Beyond it grows a medicinal plant, bearing a yellow flower with five petals, called the prairie epinette. — (**7**) **1939** *Nat. Geog. Mag.* Aug. 219/2 First to peep forth are the tiny primroses and whitlows, followed soon . . . by prairie fennel. **1938** *Range Plant Handbook* W55 Biscuitroots . . . are also known locally as hogfennel, prairiefennel, whiskbroom-parsley, wildcarrot, wildparsley, and by the generic name, *Cogswellia.* — (**8**) (*a*) **1836** J. HALL *Statistics of West* 56 The prairie-flower displays its diversified hues. **1894** *Harper's Mag.* Aug. 422/1 To be sure there were patches of orange prairie flowers all about. [**1922** WILSON *Merton of Movies* 69 Ain't I the little prairie flower, getting wilder every hour?] (*b*) **1861** *Vanity Fair* 23 Feb. 90/1 Mr. Lincoln . . . was called out at the next station and received applause and shouts of 'Hail to the Prairie Flower!' **1862** BROWNE *A. Ward: His Book* 181 One man from Ohio . . . mistook me for Old Abe and addrest me as 'The Pra-hayrie Flower of the West!' — (**9**) **1847** EMORY *Military Reconn.* 405 We also have the prairie gourd, (*cucumis perennis*) that is abundant also from Bent's fort to Santa Fé. **1865** in *So. Calif. Hist. Soc. Pub.* XVI. 57 In the San Joachin valley we noticed many plants common to the prairies, such as the prairie gourd.

(**10**) **1812** *Conn. Courant* 24 Nov. 2/3 [They] were one night in danger, in consequence of the Indian setting the prairie grass on fire.

1877 RUEDE *Sod House Days* 62 My shoes have a hole in them and ought to be mended. The prairie grass is hard on them. **1949** *Prairie Schooner* Spring 28 It is the same sage and prairie grass; the hills are the same lonely, clay hills. — **(11) 1846** EMORY *Military Reconn.* 399 The other [plant] is what our men call prairie indigo, (*baptisia leucantha*). **1933** SMALL *Southeastern Flora* 678 B[aptisia] leucantha. . . . White wild-indigo. Prairie-indigo. — **(12) 1869** FULLER *Flower Gatherers* 90 Another species, called *Prairie Innocence*, has very branching stems, and flowers of pink or rosy whiteness. — **(13) 1913** BARNES *Western Grazing Grounds* 64 The principal grasses are the bunch grasses of the wheat-grass group . . . , prairie June grass (*Koeleria cristata*) and blue joints.

(15) 1869 FULLER *Flower Gatherers* 247 One of the Lysimachias of the west is called *Prairie Money-wort.* — **(16) 1822** WOODS *English Prairie* (1904) 222 Prairie onions are common in moist situations. — **(17)** (*a*) **1848** BRYANT *California* ii. 28, I observed, also, a plant producing a fruit of the size of the walnut, called the prairie-pea. . . . In a raw state, it [the fruit] is eaten by travellers on the plains to quench thirst. **1943** DEVOTO *Yr. of Decis.* 155 They . . . made spiced pickles of the 'prairie peas' and experimented with probably edible roots. (*b*) **1869** *Amer. Naturalist* III. 162 One of the earliest flowers [of the Kansas plains] is the Prairie-pea (*Astragalus Mexicanus*). — **(18) 1934** WEBSTER. **1944** *Amer. Scholar* Summer 334 The bright pink or purple of the prairie phlox, the white masses of New Jersey tea, and the buffalo bean . . . were all familiar sights to the pioneers of the Midwest. — **(19)** *a***1885** in *Cent. Mag.* XXXII. 787/1 In July and August it [the Iowa prairie] is pink with the 'prairie pink,' dotted with scarlet lilies. **1932** RYDBERG *Flora Plains & Prairies* 890 Lygodesmia. D. Don. Wild Asparagus, Skeleton-weed, Prairie Pink.

(20) 1814 BRACKENRIDGE *Views La.* 62 Amongst the species of plums in Louisiana . . . there is none more interesting than the prairie plum, (*prunus chickasa*) which literally covers tracts of ground. **1850** PHILIP ST. GEORGE COOKE *Scenes & Adventures* (1857) 250 Having pretty thoroughly exhausted the prairie plum crop . . . they were now prone to the land of pork and beans. **1949** *World-Herald Mag.* (Omaha) 3 July 2/1 Fuel was one of the toughest problems. The Poole family tried prairie plum bush, seldom thicker than a man's thumb. — **(21) 1823** BELTRAMI *Pilgrimage* (1828) II. 321 We devoured whatever they gave us, and everything appeared to me delicious, even some roots which they call prairie-potatoes, and which I had before thought detestable. **1917** KEPHART *Camping* II. 379 *Potato, Prairie.* Prairie turnip. Indian or Missouri Breadroot. The *pomme blanche* of the voyageurs. *Psoralea Esculenta.* . . . Often sliced and dried by the Indians for winter use. Palatable in any form. — **(23) 1843** FRÉMONT *Explor. Rocky Mts.* 14 The *artemisia*, absinthe, or prairie sage, as it is variously called. **1944** *Amer. Scholar* Summer 335 Pleasing variety is added to the wealth of autumnal colors by the . . . gray color of the prairie sage. — **(24) 1893** *Amer. Folk-Lore* VI. 136 *Anemone patens*, var. *Nuttalliana*, . . . gosling, prairie smoke, crocus. Minnesota.

(25) 1894 *Amer. Folk-Lore* VII. 98 *Croton monanthogynus*, . . . prairie tea, common from the Gila to the Rio Grande. — **(26) 1920** *Mont. Extension Service Bul.* 45, 101 Prairie thistle (and also bull thistle) is readily destroyed by tillage and is, therefore, of little importance in cultivated fields. — **(27) 1837** IRVING *Bonneville* I. 40 They had to eke out their scanty fare with . . . the Indian potato, the wild onion, and the prairie tomato. — **(29) 1891** *Cent.* 6929/1 Prairie willow, a grayish shrub, *Salix humilis*, related to the sage-willow, growing 3 to 8 feet high, common on dry plains, etc., in the United States. **1901** MOHR *Plant Life Ala.* 466 *Salix humilis.* . . . Prairie Willow. . . . In the barrens, flat gravelly ground.

5. Designating various natural features of the prairies, esp. with respect to soil and topography, as (1) **prairie belt,** (2) **bluff,** (3) **bottom,** (4) **branch,** (5) **canebrake,** (6) **drain,** (7) **drift,** (8) **formation,** (9) **gumbo,** (10) **hill,** (11) **island,** (12) **knob,** (13) **marsh,** (14) **mesa,** (15) **mountain,** (16) **mud,** (17) **pond,** (18) **ravine,** (19) **ridge,** (20) **sod,** (21) **soil,** (22) **uplands.**

(1) 1883 SMITH *Geol. Survey Ala.* 265 North of the Prairie belt the Gravelly Pine Hills have great resemblance to this division. — **(2) 1936** EDWARD *Hist. Texas* 30 Matagorda . . . [is] laid out on a prairie bluff. **1841** CATLIN *Indians* I. 66 We launched off one fine morning, taking our leave of . . . the beautiful green fields, hills, and dales, and prairie bluffs, that encompass the enchanting shores of the Yellow Stone. — **(3) 1823** JAMES *Exped.* I. 123 Our party encamped . . . in a narrow, but beautiful and level prairie bottom. **1868** *Iowa State Agric. Soc. Rep. 1867* 139 On strong prairie-bottom it [the Rio Grande bearded wheat] is liable to get down. — **(4) 1869** *Republican D. Jrnl.* (Lawrence, Kans.) 7 March, Even the prairie branches on which there are no trees or bushes always afford sufficient stock water.

(5) 1831 HOLLEY *Texas* (1833) 118 Corn is obtained in the prairie cane-brakes. — **(6) 1857** BRAMAN *Texas* 40 [The Old Caney River in Colo.] is very little else, above tide-water, than a large prairie drain. — **(7) 1862** *Ill. Agric. Soc. Trans.* V. 203 The soil is a whitish prairie drift, similar to the land in the basin of Egypt. — **(8) 1886** WINCHELL *Walks & Talks* 280 The prairie formation is a stratified deposit of fine clay, sand, and alluvial matter. — **(9) 1919** LEWIS *Free Air* 4 The car shot into a morass of prairie gumbo—which is mud mixed with tar, fly-paper, fish glue, and well-chewed, chocolate-covered caramels. When cattle get into gumbo, the farmers send for the stump-dynamite and try blasting.

(10) 1807 GASS *Journal* 29 We went on about a mile to high prairie hills on the north side of the river. **1839** LEONARD *Adventures* (1904) 251 The country is generally composed of prairie hills, covered with excellent grass. — **(11) 1807** GASS *Journal* 246 We went down the [Mo.] river [in N.D.] upwards of 70 miles to day, and encamped on a prairie island. — **(12) 1808** PIKE *Sources Miss.* 18 Hills, or rather prairie knobs [were] on both sides. — **(13) 1942** Nat. Pk. Service *Fading Trails* 164 According to the exact usage of botanical terms, we should call the Everglades a fresh-water marsh rather than use the somewhat fanciful term 'prairie-marsh.' **1947** *Chi. Tribune* 7 Dec. I. 1/8 Everglades National park [is] a 454,000 acre expanse of mangrove trees, prairie marshes, and innumerable lakes and streams. — **(14) 1852** MARCY *Explor. Red River* (1854) 104 In addition to the physical similitude between the deserts of Arabia, the steppes of Central Asia, and the prairie mesas of our own country, a very striking resemblance is also observed in the habits and customs of the respective inhabitants.

(15) 1853 in *So. Hist. Ser.* VII. (1938) 374 Prairie mountains, or detached elevations, seldom so linked together as to deserve to be called a chain of mountains. — **(16) 1891** WELCH *Recoll. 1830–40* 148 After a tedious, dismal, back-aching journey from Wisconsin Territory, . . . through prairie mud, . . . [we] reached [Detroit]. — **(17) 1844** in *Calif. Hist. Soc. Quart.* IV. (1925) 325 The Prairie ponds [near Grand Island, Neb.] are well stored with wild ducks. — **(18) 1828** in *Mo. Hist. Rev.* VIII. 187 One of the party discovered a spring, the water of which bubbled through white sands, at the head of a prairie ravine. — **(19) 1843** FRÉMONT *Explor. Rocky Mts.* 16 The road led across a high and level prairie ridge.

(20) 1838 in JOHN PLUMBE *Sketches* (1839) 31 The Delegates . . . have no doubt but prairie sod, well turned over and planted with corn in season, will produce 35 bushels to the acre . . . and 20 bushels of wheat. **1927** BENÉT *J. B.'s Body* 17 The tomahawk is buried in prairie-sod. — **(21) 1817** S. BROWN *Western Gaz.* 66 The common field near the town contains nearly 5000 acres, of excellent prairie soil. **1876** *Ill. Dept. Agric. Trans.* XIII. 288 The prairie soils are usually darker, more crude, coarser and wetter than the woodland. — **(22) 1851** M. REID *Scalp Hunters* xxxv, A life spent beneath the blue heaven of the prairie-uplands and the mountain 'parks,' had made astronomers of these reckless rovers. **1892** *S. Dak. Hist. Coll.* I. 62 The prairie uplands must be settled along the railways.

As the last term in **bald, black, border, bottom, camass, door, dry, fire, flat, Grand, grass, great, grub, high, hogbed, hogwallow, limestone, looking-glass, marsh, mesquite, mound, oak, open, Osage, piny woods, post-oak, ridge, river, rolling, sage, salt, sand, shaking, shell, soda, stake, sunken, swamp, timber, trembling, upland, water, weed, western, wet, woods prairie.**

prairie chicken.

1. Any one of three species of grouse native to prairie country, or a bird of such a species.

The species are: *Tympanuchus cupido americanus*, of the Mississippi valley, ranging from Manitoba to Texas, but now disappearing (cf. **heath hen, pinnated grouse, prairie hen**); *T. pallidicinctus*, of western Texas, sometimes called the **lesser prairie chicken;** and the sharp-tailed grouse, *Pedioecetes phasianellus*, of the West, the prairie chicken of the Northwest.

[**1691** tr. in *S.W. Hist. Quart.* XXX. (1927) 211 There are many deer, prairie chickens, and wild ducks; but these are to be had only in the winter time.] **1839** F. A. WISLIZENUS *Rocky Mountains* (1912) 31 No large game as yet. A few prairie chickens was all that we shot. **1899** GARLAND *Prairie Folks* 19 But the sun burst up from the plain, the prairie-chickens took up their mighty chorus on the hills. **1949** *N. Dak. Hist.* Jan. 14 The 'coo' of the prairie chicken and the twittering of the meadowlark greet us announcing the beginning of another day.

b. One of these birds used as food.

1840 *N.O. Picayune* 13 Sep. 2/2 The travelling public will find . . . a fine table covered with white fish . . . and prairie chickens. **1851** M. REID *Scalp Hunters* ii, I need not describe a dinner at the Planters', with its venison steaks, its buffalo tongues, its 'prairie chicken.'

2. (See quot. and cf. note to **1.** above.)

1917 *Birds of Amer.* II. 26 The Lesser Prairie Chicken . . . occurs on the Great Plains, from Kansas south to west-central Texas; its plumage is similar to that of the Prairie Chicken but paler. *Ib.* 27 Sharp-tailed Grouse. *Pediœcetes phasianellus phasianellus.* . . . [Also called] Prairie Chicken of the Northwest; Northern Sharp-tailed Grouse.

prairied ˈprerɪd, *a.* Abounding in prairies. *Obs.* — **1849** WHITTIER *Poetical Works* (1894) 371/2 The South-land boasts its teeming cane, The prairied West its heavy grain. **1859** *Ib.* 219/2 In sunny South and prairied West Are exiled hearts remembering still, . . . The homes of Haverhill.

prairie dog.

1. A burrowing rodent of the genus *Cynomys*, found on the Great Plains and in the Rocky Mountain region.

The prairie dogs are of several species, the common one being *C. ludovicianus.*

1774 in PEYTON *Adv. Grandfather* (1867) 121 One of the singular and interesting sights on my route was the villages of the Prairie dogs. **1882** *Smithsonian Rep.* 1173 Prairie dogs (*Cynomys ludovicianus*) seem to have a most intense dread of rattlesnakes (*Crotalus confluentus*).... Where does one find a prairie-dog town but that it is teeming with snakes. **1947** *Chi. D. News* 20 March 14/3 [They] make my book resemble a head of lettuce that has been gnawed by a pack of prairie dogs.

b. With specifying words.

1867 *Amer. Naturalist* I. 362 The short-tailed Prairie Dog (*C*[*ynomys*] *Gunnisonii*)... is distinguished from the other by its smaller size [etc.]. **1917** *Mammals of Amer.* 202/2 Gunnison Prairie Dog.—... Darker in color; tail tipped with white. New Mexico and Colorado to Arizona. *Ib.* 205/2 Wherever White-tailed Prairie Dogs live in the neighborhood of cultivated ground they are very injurious to green crops.

c. (*cap.*) (See quot.) *Obs.*

1845 *St. Louis Reveille* 14 May 2/4 The inhabitants of... North West Territory [are called] Prairie Dogs.

2. In combs. of obvious meaning, as (1) **prairie-dog brown,** *rare,* (2) **city,** (3) **country,** (4) **hillock,** (5) **hole,** (6) **hunter,** (7) **rabbit,** (8) **town,** (9) **village.**

(1) **1902** WISTER *Virginian* xvi, There is a brown skunk down in Arkansaw. Kind of prairie-dog brown. — (2) **1850** in *Annals of Iowa* 3 Ser. IX. (1910) 459 This day we saw the first prairie dog city. — (3) **1873** BEADLE *Undevel. West* 82 We next entered 'Dog-town,' eastern border of the prairie-dog country. — (4) **1850** GARRARD *Wah-To-Yah* x. 138 The animals sank up to the fetlocks in the loamy bottom soil,... or shyed around the prairie dog hillocks.

(5) **1871** *Overland Mo.* VI. 559/2 The herdsmen gallop to and fro, or their horses break into a prairie-dog hole, and the riders go over their heads. **1913** CATHER *O Pioneers!* 20 The next summer one of his plow horses broke its leg in a prairie-dog hole and had to be shot. — (6) **1885** *Amer. Naturalist* XIX. 922 The long lost black-footed ferret, or prairie dog-hunter, of Western Kansas, whose rediscovery was recorded a few years since by Dr. Coues. — (7) **1917** *Mammals of Amer.* 289/1 The Long-eared or Arizona Cottontails make use of Prairie Dog holes to such an extent that the ranchmen call them 'Prairie-dog Rabbits.' — (8) **1843** N. BOONE *Journal* (1917) 204 Passed great quantities of Prairie dog towns. **1948** *Dly. Oklahoman* (Okla. City) 16 May E. 16/4 One of the state's largest prairie dog towns is in this area. — (9) **1823** JAMES *Exped.* II. 142 We passed a number of prairie dog villages... along the [Platte] river. **1890** CUSTER *Following Guidon* 206 [He] made his tortuous way through the prairie-dog village.

prairie lily. A plant of the lily family growing on the prairies. Also applied to non-liliaceous plants (see quots.).

1907 LYONS *Plant Names* 520 Mentzelia laevicaulis... Golden Prairie-lily. **1918** VISHER *So. Dakota* 82 Abundant Monocotyledons, other than the grasses, are wild onion and prairie lilies. **1947** *Iowa Acad. Sci. Proc.* LIV. 29 Phlox, pasque flower,... spiderwort, prairie lilies, prairie smoke, and paint brush, may yet be seen in fragmentary grassland patches.

prairie pigeon.

1. The upland plover, *Bartramia longicauda.*

1874 COUES *Birds N.W.* 503 In most parts of the West, between the Mississippi and the Rocky mountains, this Tattler, commonly known as the 'Prairie Pigeon,' is exceedingly abundant during the migrations.

2. (See quots.)

1902 *Everybody's Mag.* May 496/1 Among all birds I do not know of a more beautiful species than the Franklin's Rosy Gull.... The settlers call them 'prairie pigeons.' **1917** *Birds of Amer.* I. 51 The farmer... calls them 'Prairie Pigeons,' a pretty and appropriate title, though in reality they are Franklin's Gulls. *Ib.* 254 Eskimo Curlew.... [Also called] Prairie Pigeon. *Ib.* 257 Golden Plover.... [Also called] Prairie-bird; Prairie Pigeon. **1949** *Amer. Photography* June 382/2 In the west the Eskimo curlew flights so resembled those of the passenger pigeon that they were called 'prairie pigeons.'

prairie plover. The mountain plover, *Eupoda montana.* Also used of other birds (see quots.).

1851 WM. KELLY *Across Rocky Mts.* (1852) 68 A stand of prairie plover most opportunely made their appearances as we pulled up. **1888** TRUMBULL *Names of Birds* 173 *Bartramia longicauda....* In Southern Wisconsin... in 1851 this bird... was known as the Prairie Plover, and also as the Prairie Snipe. **1890** *Cent.* 4668/2 The American golden plover, *Charadrius dominicus.* Also called *prairie-plover* and *prairie-snipe.* **1941** SETON *Trail of Artist-Naturalist* 299 The white-tailed longspurs, the prairie plover, were all gone, wholly routed by the plough.

prairie rose. Specifically, *Rosa setigera*, a climbing wild rose having large deep-pink flowers when first expanded. Also loosely applied to *R. arkansana* and other shrubby species of plains regions.

1822 WOODS *English Prairie* 218 But the prairie-roses, balm, here called bergamot, and sassafras-wood... have all powerful scents. **1886** in M. D. WOODWARD *Checkered Yrs.* (1937) 131 The prairie roses have begun to creep out from the grass. **1909** SCHNEIDER *Woody Plants Pike's Peak* 144 Occasionally the prairie rose (*Rosa arkansana*) occurs in very restricted patches. **1946** THOMPSON *Amer. Daughter* 36 We gazed with awe upon the prairie rose, a delicate pink flower growing close to the ground, whose thorny stem belied its tender beauty.

prairie turnip. The prairie potato, *Psoralea esculenta*, or the edible root of this.

1814 BRACKENRIDGE *Views La.* 249 The prairie turnip, is a root very common in the prairies, with something of the taste of the turnip, but more dry; this they eat dried and pounded, made into gruel. **1832** CATLIN *Indians* I. 56 The 'Pomme Blanche,' or prairie turnip, ... is found in great quantities in these northern prairies, and furnishes the Indians with an abundant and nourishing food. **1941** McCOWAN *Naturalist* 246 The Crees and Blackfeet were glad to make a meal from the edible root of the Prairie Turnip.

prairillon prɛˈrɪlən, *n.* [f. Amer. F., a diminutive of *prairie.*] A little prairie or meadow. Now *hist.*

1823 in READ *La.-French* (1931) 179 A tract of land situated in the Little Prairie of the Woods—or in the *Prairiellon de la Prairie des Bois*, as the name is given in the *American State Papers*, III (1823), 525, ed. Green. **1843** FRÉMONT *Explor. Rocky Mts.* 64 We were posted in a grove of beech,... with a narrow prairillon on the inner side. **1846** SAGE *Scenes Rocky Mts.* xxiii, The less elevated parts of these mountains are frequently covered with groves of small timber and openings of grass suitable for pasturage, while intermingled with them are occasional valleys and *prairillons* of diminutive space, favorable to the growth of grain and vegetables. **1931** READ *La.-French* 178 The earliest reference that I have found to the prairie is in the corrupted spelling Priarillon, recorded on a Spanish survey of 1797.

* **praise,** *n. attrib.* Designating persons, places, etc., associated with the praise or worship of God. *Colloq.*

1866 CARPENTER *At White House* 209 Their place of worship was a large building which they called 'the praise house;' and the leader of the meeting, a venerable black man, was known as 'the praise man.' **1869** HIGGINSON *Army Life* 20 The little old church or 'praise-house,' [is] now used for commissary purposes. **1879** WEBSTER *Supp.* 1574/1 *Praise-meeting,* a meeting for praise; a religious meeting, in which the time is mainly occupied by singing. [*U.S.*]

praline ˈpralin, *n.* [F., an Amer. borrowing.] A sugar and nut candy. Also attrib.

1809 A. HENRY *Travels* 265, I left our fort on Beaver Lake... provided with dried meat, frozen fish, and a small quantity of praline, made of roasted maize, rendered palatable with sugar. **1899** in RANKIN *K. Chopin* (1932) 274 They played at a small table on which were a shaded lamp, a few magazines and a dish of *pralines.* **1949** *N.O. Times-Picayune Mag.* 6 Nov. 6/3 This 'praline woman' was to Loyola what the hot tamale, oyster, and ice cream men were to LSU.

prarow ˈprero, *n.* =**brarow.** *Obs.* — **1807** GASS *Journal* 51 Captain Clarke and one of the men went to hunt and killed a deer and a prarow. **1812** J. CUTLER *Topog. Descr. Ohio* 168 A species of badger, called prarow, inhabits these plains.

* **prate,** *v. intr.* Of passenger pigeons: To utter a characteristic cry or note. *To prate for,* to lure (pigeons) by imitating this note. Also * **prating,** *n.* Now *hist.*

1853 in F. H. ALLEN *Thoreau's Bird-Lore* (1925) 112 He... *prated* for them; they came near and then flew away. **1854** *Ib.* 114 Their *prating*... is like a sharp creak. **1945** *Auk* Jan. 136 Many and many a time... have I heard my father *prate* for pigeons. Father was born and brought up in Westford, Mass.... Wild pigeon prating consisted of voice delivered through tightly approximated lips, with a buzz or vibration of those lips, in two somewhat prolonged, high-pitched monotones.

* **prayer,** *n.* In combs. now obs.: (1) **prayer circle,** a group of persons who pray together; (2) **cure,** cure or healing brought about by prayer; (3) **lodge,** =**medicine lodge;** (4) **meal,** meal used by Indians in religious rites; (5) **powder,** (see quot.); (6) **ring,** =**prayer circle;** (7) **stick,** (see quot. 1910), cf. **paho.**

(1) **1880** DEMING *Adirondack Stories* 25 As a preliminary to the sermon, a prayer-circle was formed. — (2) **1877** PHELPS *Story of Avis* 390 Should he try Colorado, the South,... Spiritualism, or the prayer-cure? **1888** *Pittsburg Dispatch* 29 July (F.), There is also a doctor of mystic philosophy from Boston, who advertises a course of

instruction on faith cure, [and] prayer cure. — (3) **1925** TILGHMAN *Dugout* 22 The medicine men of the Cheyennes had built prayer lodges and were industriously making medicine. — (4) **1882** *Cent. Mag.* Aug. 527/2 [The Indians] prayed aloud, each scattering a pinch of their prayer-meal, composed of corn-meal with an admixture of finely ground precious sea-shells, which they always carried with them in little bags.

(5) **1825** NEAL *Bro. Jonathan* I. 4 A silver bullet—a leaf o' the Bible, for wadding—and a charge of 'prayer-powder'—powder, over every 365 grains of which, the Lord's prayer has been said. — (6) **1846** *Knickerb.* XXVIII. 305 When a 'prayer ring' was to be formed, he announced it at the close of a sermon. — (7) **1865** TYLOR *Early Hist. Mankind* 89, I do not know whether any of these curious prayer-sticks are now to be seen. **1894** *Nation* 13 Sep. 204/1 The prayer-sticks . . . are sent by a special courier, on the second day of the celebration, to the fanes of the rain-gods. **1910** HODGE *Amer. Indians* II. 304/1 *Prayer sticks*, sticks to which feathers are attached, used as ceremonial supplicatory offerings. **1947** B. HAILE *Prayer Stick Cutting* 49 Gray Man mentions many more prayersticks than White Singer does and presents numerous details about them.

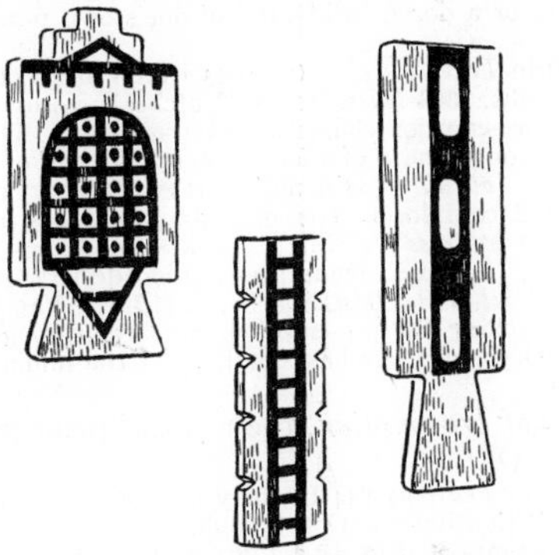

Prayer sticks such as the Pueblo Indians used

∗**praying,** *a.* In combs. now obs. or hist.: (1) **praying band,** =**prayer circle;** (2) **circle,** =prec.; (3) **Indian,** see as a main entry; (4) **man,** a man accustomed to pray, *colloq.;* (5) **town,** a town or village composed of praying Indians.

(1) **1883** *Cent. Mag.* Sep. 788/2 The Woman's Christian Temperance Union is the lineal descendant of the Woman's Crusade of 1874, whose first 'praying band' was led from the Presbyterian Church of Hillsboro' by Mrs. Thompson. **1900** WINCHESTER *W. Castle* 44 He had seen [him] years before, . . . conducting a revival meeting with a praying-band, of which he was leader. — (2) **1850** FOOTE *Sk. Virginia* 414 They began to hold praying circles, as they were called, in different parts of the congregation. — (4) **1845** *Indiana Mag. Hist.* XXIII. 40, I had been a praying man for some time.

(5) **1670** ELIOT *Brief Narr.* 7 Both of them [were] to take care of the new Praying-Town beyond them. **1674** *Mass. H.S. Coll.* 1 Ser I. (1806) 163 They killed but one or two of them [i.e., praying Indians], about one praying town, called Wamesit. *Ib.*, They were at some other praying towns of Indians.

praying Indian. An Indian converted to Christianity. Also attrib. Often *pl.* and *cap.* Now *hist.*

1652 in *Tears of Repentance* (1653) B2, 5 There was a storm . . . but when I came to this end I found a calm, the Praying Indians were all well, they arose in the morning, Prayed to God, and went about their business. **1674** in *Mass. H.S. Coll.* 1 Ser. I. (1806) 194 Letters of the same import are intended to be given to the teachers of the other new praying Indian towns. **1764** HUTCHINSON *Hist. Mass.* I. 285 The war was hurried on by a piece of revenge, which Philip caused to be taken upon John Sausmann, a praying Indian. **1945** WEBSTER *Town Meeting Country* 42 The white magistrates bring justice and peace to the Praying Indians.

∗**preacher,** *n.*

1. (See quot.) *Rare.*

1829 ROYALL *Pennsylvania* II. 38 You scarcely go a mile in Pennsylvania but you see a *Preacher*—as signboards are called. They point out the road, but never travel it.

2. a. preacher life, life spent in preaching. *Rare.* **b. preachers' stand,** (see quot.).

(**a**) **1870** STEPHENS *Married in Haste* 101 How much of the old preacher life must cling about you. — (**b**) *a***1870** CHIPMAN *Notes on Bartlett* 339 *Preachers' Stand.* A pulpit in a church; a platform for a preacher at 'Camp Meetings.' The latter use occasioned the former, among certain people.—Southern and Western usage; but occasional, in N[ew] E[ngland].

c. In phrases: (1) *preacher in charge,* in the Methodist Church, a preacher who has charge of a particular station or circuit; (2) *preacher-in-the-pulpit,* (see quot. 1884); (3) *preacher of the day,* a preacher who has charge of the services on a particular day.

Preachers' stand of portable type

(**1**) **1871** EGGLESTON *Hoosier Schoolm.* 220 The good minister . . . in Methodist parlance was called 'the preacher-in-charge of Lewisburg Station.' — (**2**) **1884** MILLER *Plant-names, Orchis spectabilis,* Preacher-in-the-pulpit, Showy Orchis of N. America. **1905** W. H. GIBSON *Our Native Orchids* 20 The white sepals unite in an arch bending over the Anther cells in such a way as to give the name 'Preacher in the Pulpit' to the orchid. — (**3**) *a***1817** DWIGHT *Travels* I. 268 At this entertainment the Preacher of the Day, and his successor, are present.

As the last term in **barn, camp, circuit, Indian, junior, kill, New Light, old field, schoolhouse, senior, Yankee preacher.**

∗**preaching,** *n.* In combs.: (1) **preaching ground,** the area or grounds, as at a camp meeting, where public religious services are held; (2) **stand,** =**preachers' stand.**

(**1**) **1820** FLINT *Lett. from Amer.* 232 This new arrangement made a striking change in the camp, the bustle being removed from the centre and distributed along the outskirts of the preaching ground. **1856** STOWE *Dred* I. 318 Before departing to the preaching ground, he had arranged a slow fire. — (**2**) **1856** STOWE *Dred* I. 326 The assembly poured in and arranged themselves before the preaching stand. **1860** *Harper's Mag.* Dec. 83/1 The preaching-stand . . . [was] neither cleaner nor more ornamental than the rest of the church.

b. (See quot.) *Obs.*

1853 P. PAXTON *Yankee in Texas* 116 To the latter [a Southerner], drawing his comparison from his idolized rifle, a thing is *'as sure as shooting,'* while to the former [a Yankee], more pious or more hypocritical, it is *'as sartin as preachin'.'*

As the last term in **gospel, stated preaching.**

∗**precinct,** *n.*

1. *N. Eng.* An area or region under the spiritual care of a minister or clergyman. Also attrib. *Obs.*

1708 *Braintree Rec.* 70 It was then voted that there should be two distinct precincts or societies, in this Town for ye more regular & convenient upholding of ye worship of God. **1717** *Canton* (Mass.) *Rec.* (1896) 4 It was voted . . . that ye sd Precinct Congregation would proceed to ordain mr Josiph morse. **1793** *Mass. H.S. Coll.* 1 Ser. III. 1 In this town is one whole Congregational precinct, where the Rev. Joseph Barker is settled as minister.

2. (See quot. *a*1870.)

1713 SEWALL *Diary* II. 405 Ipswich Hamlet petitions the Genl. Court to give them the Powers of a Precinct. **1716** *Mass. H. Rep. Jrnl.* I. 89 Praying that . . . they may be vested with the Powers and Priviledges of a Precinct. **1722** *Ib.* III. 184 Voted That the——Day of April, be Appointed a Day of Fasting and Prayer . . . throughout the several Towns and Precincts of this Province. *a***1870** CHIPMAN *Notes on Bartlett, Precinct,* . . . a town whose corporate rights did not include sending deputies to the Col[onial] legislature.—Mass., before 1776.

attrib. **1718** *Mass. H. Rep. Jrnl.* II. 101 A Draught of the Settlement of the Precinct Line between *Ipswich & Chebacco.* **1731** in *Cal. State P.,*

Amer. & W. Indies (1732) 32 Six Acts of the Massachusetts Bay 1731 . . . making more effectual provision for the calling of precinct or parish meetings.

3. An election district.

The use in quot. 1833 is unusual.

1833 *Sk. D. Crockett* 150 The store happened to be a precinct for holding elections. **1877** JOHNSON *Anderson Co., Kans.* 78 On the canvass of the vote the probate judge threw out all the returns except the Shannon precinct. **1925** BRYAN *Memoirs* 85 The precinct in which our country home near Lincoln was located. **1948** *Shelby* (Mont.) *Promoter* 16 Sep. 1/4 Anyone that has moved since the last election should have the move recorded so that they can vote in the proper precinct.

attrib. **1884** *Boston Jrnl.* 15 Sep., Precinct election officers need not necessarily vote in the precinct in which they are appointed. **1890** *Cong. Rec.* 3 June 5565/2 No man can be appointed [in Ala.] to hold a precinct election unless he is known to be a 'lightning man,' a ballot-box stuffer, a false counter. **1911** *Okla. Session Laws* 3 Legisl. 78 The precinct board of canvassers, shall canvass the vote. *Ib.* 227 The precinct election board shall be chosen for a term of four years. **1949** *Chi. Tribune* 1 Sep. 18/2 His political bosses tried to fire him because he wouldn't hire their precinct workers.

4. One of the districts into which a city is divided to facilitate the work of the police. Also attrib.

1864 *N.Y. Herald* 4 April, The body was removed to the Fourth precinct station house. **1884** *N.Y. Wkly. Tribune* 12 March 7/4 Williams is a stranger to the police of the Twenty-ninth Precinct. **1902** ALDRICH *Sea Turn* 198 The keys were at the precinct station. **1949** *Sat. Ev. Post* 9 April 24/1 The precinct men had gone. So had the homicide squad, except for Joe.

5. In special combs.: (1) **precinct captain,** one who looks after the interests of a political party in an election precinct; (2) **court,** a court in a political subdivision of a town, township, or county, *obs.;* (3) **house,** a house serving as the headquarters of an election precinct, also attrib.

(1) 1941 HAYAKAWA *Language* 225 They may fail to tell us . . . what precinct captains and ward heelers do. **1948** *New Yorker* 25 Sep. 26/1 An old trick is for the precinct captain to burn a little hole in the voting-machine. — **(2) 1704** *N.C. Col. Rec.* I. 605 Ordered that the Marshall bring forth the body of Tho: Evans to the next pr[e]cinct Court to answer the comp[lain]t. **1715** *Ib.* II. 206 Said land shall be appraised by four honest men . . . appointed by the Precinct Court. — **(3) 1863** MOORE *Rebellion Rec.* V. I. 77 The Mayor of Philadelphia . . . called upon all able-bodied men to assemble next morning at the precinct-houses of the election districts. **1890** T. HALL *Tales* 171 He did very well to copy off the entries in a precinct house register . . . , but that was about all he could do.

As the last term in **election, road, voting precinct.**

* **predicate,** *v. tr.* To found, affirm, base, etc. (an action, decision, etc.) *on* or *upon* some particular basis or data.

1766 CLAP *Hist. Yale Coll.* 21 The Trustees . . . [passed] another Vote predicated upon sundry former ones, wherein they finally settled that College at New-Haven. **1839** in E. L. PIERCE *Mem. & Lett. C. Sumner* II. 105 This [opinion] . . . is predicated upon my confidence in his ability. **1888** CLEVELAND in *Daily News* (London) 10 Sep. 5/4 The reform we seek to inaugurate is predicated upon the utmost care for established industries and enterprises.

pre-empt prɪˈempt, *v. tr.* To secure (public land) by pre-emption. Also absol.

1850 LEWIS *La. Swamp Doctor* 87 A few hours' ride from town was one of these islands, 'pre-empted' by a man named Spiffle. **1867** RICHARDSON *Beyond Miss.* 138 Land is plenty and everybody preëmpts. **1900** GOODLANDER *Fort Scott* 14 If you wanted to pre-empt the land you had to build a house or a shanty . . . and live there off and on for six months before you could use your pre-emption right. **1948** A. K. WILLIAMS *Gold Rush Days* 7, I preempted 160 acres for which I paid the government $16.00 an acre.

b. To obtain (a mining claim) by pre-emption. *Obs.*

1876 HARTE in *Scribner's Mo.* Jan. 373/2 Any other man but me couldn't hev bin sich a fool as to preëpmt sich a claim fur gold. **1877** JOHNSON *Anderson Co., Kans.* 59 He jumped the claim . . . and pre-empted it in the spring of 1856.

c. *transf.* To take as if by pre-emption.

1855 OLIPHANT *Minnesota* 162 Wal, I guess, if you can find a corner that's not pre-empted, you may spread your shavings there [for a bed]. **1908** O. HENRY *Strictly Business* 179 Clearly, that spot in the moral vineyard was pre-empted. **1948** JOHNSTON *Gold Rush* 42/2 Motor cars preëmpt space once occupied by stage and freight wagons.

pre-emptible prɪˈemptəbl, *a.* Of land: Available for purchase and settlement by pre-emptors. *Obs.* — **1857** *Lawrence* (Kans.) *Republican* 28 May 4 Any lands owned by government, not military or Indian reserves, are preemptible, whether surveyed or not. **1886** *N. Amer. Rev.* Jan. 54 As preemptible land recedes farther into the West, . . . it becomes more surely impossible for the man without means to establish himself.

* **pre-emption,** *n.*

1. The act of acquiring, or the right to acquire, public lands upon fulfilling conditions made by the government. Also transf.

1747 *Baltimore Rec.* 21 Mr. Alexander Lawson applied also to enter his Preemption of making out Ground into the water. **1797** *Pittsburgh Gaz.* 23 Sep. 2/4 The principal object to be obtained, is a relinquishment of the Indian title to the lands in Massachusetts preemption. **1855** HOLBROOK *Among Mail Bags* 288 His chair was appropriated by a fatigued neighbor, who 'squatted' on the vacant territory, regardless of 'pre-emption' or pre-session. **1901** DUNCAN & SCOTT *Allen & Woodson Co., Kans.* 582 Finding that the Indians would not settle on the Reserve, the Government, in 1860, had all of these lands offered for sale and opened to pre-emption.

Also of a mining claim.

1864 *Rocky Mt. News* (Denver) 3 Aug. 3/2 Particularly is this so when . . . one is passing over territory made magically sacred by containing six or a dozen 'wild cats' of one's own purchase or pre-emption!

attrib. **1780** in *Travels Amer. Col.* 643 Received a Letter and Preemption Warrant. **1804** *Miss. Herald* (Natchez) 10 July 4/1 Those of you who are pre-emption claimants must swear. . . . That you were 21 years of age or the head of a family on the 3rd day of March 1803. **1839** THOREAU *Journal* I. 98 A mere surveyor's report or clause in a preëmption bill contains matter of quite extraneous interest. **1880** *Cimarron News & Press* 11 March 3/4 Manuel Munis, of Madison, Colfax county, N.M., . . . made pre-emption declaratory statement 492. **1949** *Jrnl. Ill. State. Hist. Soc.* Sep. 292 Little Van had salvaged his plan by backing the pre-emption measures through which the bona fide settler could purchase his land at the minimum price of $1.25 per acre.

b. *right of pre-emption,* the right of prior purchase of public land. *Obs.*

1790 *Kentucky Petitions* 154 In the year 1786 he . . . aplied for his Right of preemtion but the Court would not admit of his proving his Right of preimtion. **1816** *Ann. 14th Congress* 2 Sess. 373 The right of pre-emption in the purchase of public lands in said Territory may be extended. **1864** *Wkly. New Mexican* 27 May 2/4 The right of pre-emption under the homestead act of May 20, 1862.

2. A piece of land obtained or to be obtained by pre-emption. *Obs.*

1844 *Filson Club Hist. Quart.* IX. 235 Each of these two men . . . had a pre-emption of 1400 acres. **1887** *Harper's Mag.* June 69/2 The 'claims' and 'pre-emptions' were marked to await the time when the owner could safely take possession.

3. In special combs., now obs. or hist.: (1) **pre-emption certificate,** a certificate issued to one who has secured a pre-emption right; (2) **claim,** a claim to public land made in accordance with pre-emption laws, the land embraced in such a claim, also transf.; (3) **company,** (see quot.); (4) **land,** (see quot.); (5) **law,** any one of various federal laws giving the first right in securing public land to actual occupants complying with certain prescribed conditions; (6) **right,** see as a main entry; (7) **settler,** a settler or occupant of public land having a pre-emption right.

(1) 1780 in *Travels Amer. Col.* 642 My pre-emption certificates [were sent down] by James Brown. **1812** *Ann. 12th Congress* 1 Sess. II. 2352 Citizens . . . whose lands have not been . . . claimed in right of donation or pre-emption certificates . . . [are] confirmed in their respective claims. — **(2) 1783** in *Travels Amer. Col.* 671 Depositions proving Joh. Ross assignment of a Settlement and preemption claim to 1400 acres of land. **1868** HANKINS *Dakota Land* 450 Let me beg of you not to set up a pre-emption claim to a double *vis-a-vis* seat for the exclusive convenience of your particular traps. **1900** DRANNAN *Plains & Mts.* 576 She asked if I had not told him to stay on the pre-emption claim that night. — **(3) 1838** GURNEY *Jrnl. & Lett.* II. 131 Another circumstance which gave me a similar impression was the combination of a large company, called the 'Pre-emption company,' to deprive the Indians of the Seneca Nation, in New York, of their reserved lands. — **(4)** *c***1826** STANLEY *Jrnl.* 240 We paid a visit to an old Squatter, who had settled here on what is called pre-emption land: That is, land which has never been put up to sale, and to which consequently he has no title; but for which, when put up by Congress, he had the first choice of paying the moderate sum demanded, without valuing his improvements.

(5) 1837 VAN BUREN in *Pres. Mess. & P.* III. 389 The limitations and restrictions to guard against abuses in the execution of a pre-emption law will necessarily attract the careful attention of Congress

1890 *Stock Grower & Farmer* 25 Jan. 7/1 Thus secure the disposition of this vast area of public lands to actual settlers under our homestead and pre-emption laws. — (7) **1858** *Texas Almanac 1859* 24 This act extends to preemption settlers or their assigns the time to return their field-notes to the Land Office for patent. **1907** ANDREWS *Recoll.* 130 Preëmption settlers from various counties had conflicting claims before the land office.

pre-emptioner prɪˈɛmpʃənɚ, *n.* =**pre-emptor.** Also transf. *Obs.* Cf. **swamp pre-emptioner.**

1838 *Cong. Globe* App. 142 Suppose a pre-emptioner was to go there and say, Mr. President, this house is too large for you; I am an industrious cultivator, one of the bone-and-sinew men, and claim a pre-emption to part of this house. **1841** *Knickerb.* XVII. 278 They amused themselves by calling the exclusives 'squatters,' 'preëmptioners,' etc. **1872** TICE *Over Plains* 80 The plain is dotted with new shanties of the homesteaders and pre-emptioners.

pre-emptionist prɪˈɛmpʃənɪst, *n.* =**pre-emptor.** *Obs.* — **1850** LEWIS *La. Swamp Doctor* 24 Such is the character of the pioneers and pre-emptionists of the swamp. **1878** *Rev. Statutes* 415 (*margin*), Oath of pre-emptionist, where filed, penalty.

pre-emption right. The right given an occupant to secure public land by compliance with pre-emption laws.

1784 FILSON *Kentucke* 37 The Settlement and pre-emption rights arise from occupation. **1824** DODDRIDGE *Notes* 99 Building a cabin and raising a crop of grain, however small, of any kind, entitled the occupant to four hundred acres of land, and a preemption right to one thousand acres more adjoining. **1948** DICK *Dixie Frontier* 67 As a result there had grown up in colonial days a custom of allowing pre-emption rights to squatters.

attrib. **1930** HENRY *Conquer. Plains* 180 Preemption Right laws followed, under which a citizen could buy a quarter section at generally from one dollar and a quarter to two dollars an acre and was not required to settle on it.

Also with reference to mineral land.

1855 GLISAN *Jrnl. Army Life* 225 This only refers to pre-emption right, that is, the title to mineral land conferred by virtue of having first 'squatted on it.'

b. (See quots.) *Obs.*

1792 IMLAY *Western Territory* 13 Virginia gave farther rewards and encouragements at this time to the first settlers, for the perils they had undergone in the establishment of their settlement, of a tract of 1000 acres, called a pre-emption right, to be laid off adjoining to the settlement of 400 acres, the grantee paying only office fees for the same. **1823** NUTTALL *Journal* 115 The preemption rights, as they are called, are a certain species of reward or indemnification for injuries sustained in the late war.

* **pre-emptive,** *a.* Of or pertaining to the pre-emption of public land.

1795 *Ann. 3d Congress.* 2 Sess. 1154 The State had a right more positive than the pre-emptive one, to lands actually occupied and defended by hostile tribes of Indians. **1875** YOUNG *Hist. Chautauqua Co., N.Y.* 66 Robert Morris became seized of the preemptive title to all the lands in the state west of the eastern boundary of the Holland Purchase. **1944** MAU *Development Cent. & West. N.Y.* 68 Enterprising men quickly sensed the opportunity of making substantial profits by purchasing the pre-ëmptive rights of Massachusetts.

pre-emptor prɪˈɛmptɚ, *n.* One who secures public land in accordance with pre-emption laws.

1846 WORCESTER 557/1 *Pre-emptor*, one who practises pre-emption. **1870** *Colo. Gazetteer* 250 After the lapse of six months or more, many of these sham preemptors will be successful in 'proving up' their bogus claims at the land office. **1943** HOLT *Carver* 48 Mr. Steeley, being county commissioner, had a house a degree better than the new pre-emptors.

prefect ˈprifɛkt, *n. S.W.* [Sp. *prefecto*, an Amer. borrowing.] A magistrate, ruler, or governor.

1846 *Jrnl. Major Philip Barbour* (1936) 19 He then informed General La Vega that he had a communication for the Prefect of the District. **1850** *31st Congress* 1 Sess. Sen. Ex. Doc. No. 76, 4 Prefects and alcaldes [in N.M.] impose fines and incarcerate, without the intervention of a jury. **1888** J. J. WEBB *Adventures* 192 He claimed four mules as stolen property, and we were notified to take them before the prefect's court for trial.

* **preferred,** *a.*

1. *absol.* Short for next.

1892 *Chi. Tribune* 9 July 11/1 Subscribers will secure a bonus in Common Stock of 50 per cent of the amount of their subscription to the Preferred. **1949** *Ill. Agric. Assoc. Rec.* Oct. 11/2 The class 'A' preferred was to be sold to individuals.

2. preferred stock, stock which has priority over common stock in assignment of dividends and in distribution of assets. Also attrib.

1850 *Mass. Acts & Resolves* 375 The Connecticut River Railroad Company are hereby authorized to issue . . . preferred stock. **1919** BABSON *Bonds & Stocks* 172 An effort is then made only to ascertain . . . the amount remaining for dividends on the Preferred and Common stocks. **1923** *Collier's* 18 Aug. 21/2 Mr. Simmons . . . thanked the boys for their applause for the preferred-stock idea. **1947** *Newsweek* 7 July 66/2 Corporations have been acquiring new creditors and preferred-stock holders whose interest and dividends are a fixed and continuing charge in bad years as well as good.

prehaps prɪˈhæps, *adv.* A jocular variant of **perhaps.* — **1836** *Quarter Race Ky.* (1846) 24, I thought I'd make a rise on chuck-a-luck, but you *prehaps* never saw such a run of luck. **1856** DERBY *Phoenixiana* 125 You hear . . . the pleasant screak of the victim Whose been shot prehaps in his gizzard.

prelat preˈlɑ, *n.* [F. *prélart*, in the same sense.] A tarpaulin used over a boat to protect cargo in bad weather. *Obs.* or *hist.* — **1876** HALE *P. Nolan's Friends* i, A long tarpaulin, called the prélat, was stretched over the whole length of the boat. **1941** MCDERMOTT *Glossary* 128.

prêle prɛl, *n. W.* [F. in same sense.] A plant or species of plant of the genus *Equisetum*, found on the western prairies.

1843 FRÉMONT *Explor. Rocky Mts.* 46, I encamped on a spot which afforded good grass and *prêle* (*equisetum*) for our animals. **1846** SAGE *Scenes Rocky Mts.* viii, An abundance of prelée [*sic*] and rushes afforded fine pasturage to our animals. **1852** STANSBURY *Gt. Salt Lake* 27 The grass is generally very abundant, and prêle (the common scouring-rush) is found in great plenty.

* **premier,** *n.* The Secretary of State in the President's cabinet.

1855 *N. Y. Herald* 22 Nov. 4/4 The casting vote between the Premier and the Kitchen is subject to the caprices and vacillations of the President, whose official position makes him supreme over both the acts of the premier and the counsels of the Kitchen. **1878** *Harper's Mag.* March 490/2 The diplomatic anteroom, where foreign dignitaries await audience with the Premier, is handsome in its appointments. **1905** *Washington Post* 21 March 4 Elihu Root . . . is ideally equipped for the duties of the Department of State, but it is considered unlikely that he could be induced to return to the Cabinet even as premier.

Hence * **premiership.**

1928 H. MINOR *Story Dem. Party* 69 Madison had cabinet troubles, too. Monroe accepted the premiership in March, 1811.

* **premium,** *n.*

1. Public land given as a reward for military service or to encourage timber culture in the West. *Obs.*

"Any person who shall plant, protect, and keep in a healthy, growing condition for ten years forty acres of timber . . . on any quarter-section of any of the public lands of the United States shall be entitled to a patent for the whole of said quarter-section at the expiration of said ten years on making proof of such fact" (1873 *Statutes at Large* XVII. 605–6).

1836 *Diplom. Corr. Texas* I. (1908) 56 The pay and rations of the United States with a premium of six hundred and forty acres, will induce just as many to come. **1885** *Cent. Mag.* XXIX. 794/2 Nearly one-fifth of this vast area [the western plains] was 'entered' in 1882, which shows the growing influence of the princely premiums offered by Congress and by many of the Western States to encourage tree-planting.

2. premium land, in Texas under Mexican rule, land granted to certain impresarios as a reward for fulfilling contracts concerning the colonization of the impresario grants. *Obs.*

1838 C. NEWELL *Revol. Texas* 186 [These grants] consisted . . . in a claim . . . to a certain amount of premium land. *Ib.* 187 If they had introduced ninety-nine families, and not the hundredth, they were entitled to no proportion of premium land whatever.

prep prɛp, *n.* [Abbrev. of **pre*paratory.]

1. A student in a preparatory school. Also attrib.

1890 *Cent.* 4695/1 *Prep*, a student who is taking a preparatory course of study; especially, one who is preparing for college. (College slang, U.S.) **1947** *Sat. Ev. Post* 15 March 23/3 Unless you get written credits for two years of high school, I can't nominate you for the prep class. **1948** *Chi. D. News* 6 Dec. 23/4 (*caption*), 2 Preps Die In Oregon Bush Crash.

2. prep school, a preparatory school. Also attrib.

1895 WILLIAMS *Princeton Stories* 128 After awhile he found himself walking with the freshman way out toward the Prep. school. **1903** *Chi. Record-Herald* 7 June III. 1/1 A crowd of nearly 4,000 university, 'prep' school and grammar school rooters cheered from the bleachers. **1949** *Woodlawn Booster* (Chi.) 14 Sep. 1/5 In 1903 . . . Hyde Park traveled to Brooklyn to meet the Brooklyn Poly for the Prep school championship of the country.

* **preparatory,** *a.* In combs.: (1) **preparatory department,** in a school, a department which prepares students for collegiate work; (2) **lecture,** a lecture for those who are to be confirmed in church, *obs.*

(1) **1848** *Ind. Gen. Assoc. Doc. 1848–9* II. 279 Connected with the Institution is a flourishing Grammar School, which serves the double purpose of a Normal School and a Preparatory Department. **1881** *Ore. State Jrnl.* 8 Jan. 5/3 The preparatory department numbers between sixty and seventy pupils. — (2) **1854** RICHARDS *Village Life* (1912) 51 She said instead we could wear our new black silk basks and go with her to Preparatory lecture, so we did, but when we got there we found that Mr Daggett was out of town so there was no meeting.

prerevolutionary ˈpriːrɛvlˈuʃən,ɛrɪ, *a.* Belonging to the time before the American Revolutionary War (1775–83). — **1868** BEECHER *Norwood* 328 Planted in 1646, it was more than a hundred years old when the pre-revolutionary excitements were taking place in Boston. **1874** ALDRICH *P. Palfrey* x, Since the hanging of a witch or two in the pre-revolutionary days, the office of sheriff there has been virtually a sinecure.

* **prerogative court.** A probate court. *Obs.*, except in New Jersey.

1711 *Conn. Rec.* V. 283 Mary Wakeman, an orphan, has made application to this Assembly for liberty to appeal from an act or sentence of the prerogative court in the county of Fairfield. **1793** *N.J. Rep.* (1901) 180 The Orphans' Court is . . . a court partaking of the powers of a chancery and prerogative jurisdiction, instituted by law to remedy and supply the defects in the powers of the Prerogative Court, with regard to the accountability of executors, administrators, and guardians. **1917** *N.J. Equity Rep.* LXXXVIII. 263 An appeal was taken to the prerogative court.

Presbygational ,prɛzbəˈgeʃənl, *a.* [*Presbyterian + *Congregational.] Characterized by features of both Presbyterian and Congregational methods of church government, with specific reference to the Plan of Union (1801–52) of these two denominations. *Obs.* — **1895** R. E. THOMPSON *Hist. Presb. Churches* 72 This 'Presbygational' system, as it afterward was nicknamed, . . . had respect especially to the settlement of western New York from New England. *Ib.* 183 The Presbyterians . . . [urged] these Presbygational churches to become thoroughly Presbyterian.

Presbygationalism ,prɛzbəˈgeʃənl,ɪzəm, *n.* [See prec.] The combination of features of both Presbyterian and Congregational methods of Church government, as in the Plan of Union (1801–52). — **1892** *Advance* 10 Nov. 927/3 It was recommended that their [Congregational] churches be associated with presbytery. . . . The result was Presbygationalism, a composite creature, symbolic of little else than the folly of its progenitor. **1893** *Ib.* 30 March 249 An ecclesiasticism wherein delegates duly elected by vote of the local churches are required to sit with a teaching eldership that are not thus delegated, and to share ecclesiastical power with them, is Presbygationalism.

* **Presbyterian,** *n.* **1. Presbyterian billiards,** (see quot.). **2.** *cold* (or *cool*) *as Presbyterian charity,* quite cold. Both *colloq.* and *obs.*

(1) **1873** *Winfield* (Kans.) *Courier* 31 July 1/7 That transcendently interesting amusement commonly called croquet, but vulgarly signified 'Presbyterian billiards.' — (2) *a***1836** CROCKETT *Tour* (Bartlett), Well, Colonel, the river is pretty considerable for a run; but the water is as cool as Presbyterian charity. **1859** BARTLETT 91 *Cold as Presbyterian Charity.* I know not the origin of this saying, and am not aware that there is less charity in this sect than in any other.

As the last term in **Cumberland, New School, Old School Presbyterian.**

* **present,** *a.* (See quots.) *Colloq.* — **1848** BARTLETT 261 *Present,* put on the back of letters to persons residing in the place where the letter is written. Peculiar to the United States. The Spanish equivalent *presente* is also used in Central America. **1905** *D.N.* III. 16 *Present,* adj. The word is put on the envelope of letters to persons residing in the town where the letters are written, and which are not sent through the post.

* **preservatory,** *n.* A place or apparatus for preserving meat, vegetables, etc., by keeping them cool. *Obs.* — **1853** FOWLER *Home for All* 116 My ice-house consists of *two stories*—the upper one for ice, the lower, a room kept cool by the ice and its drippings, a preservatory for keeping fruit, butter, eggs, fresh meat, fish, bacon, pies, etc. **1876** KNIGHT 1783/2 *Preservatory,* an apparatus for preserving substances to be used as foods.

* **preserve,** *n.* As the last term in **fish, forest, national forest, state preserve.**

* **presidency,** *n.*

1. (Usu. *cap.*) The office or position of President of the U.S.

*a***1800** TWINING *Visit* (1894) 136 General Washington . . . remained there till 1789, when the general voice of his country called him from his pastoral pursuits to the Presidency of the Government. **1896** *Chi. Tribune* 9 July 1/3 William Jennings Bryan is more than a dark horse candidate for the Presidency. **1948** *Time* 10 May 21/1 Harry Truman's nomination for the presidency was apparently in the bag.

b. The office of the presiding officer or president of the U.S. Senate. *Obs.* Cf. * **president 4.**

1804 CUSHING in Cutler *Life & Corr.* II. 176 Can they submit to the degradation of the presidency of a man [Aaron Burr] lying under the legal imputation of murder?

2. *Mormon Church.* A council, consisting of a president (*q.v.* sense **6.**) and two counselors, that exercises jurisdiction in spiritual or temporal matters throughout the entire church (see next) or throughout a stake (*q.v.* sense **2**).

1838 in HUNT *Hist. Mormon War* (1844) 213 He observed to the people, that they must obey the presidency, and if the presidency led them astray, they might destroy them. *a***1853** in GARDNER *Faiths of World* II. 492/2 The hierarchy of the Mormon church has many grades of offices and gifts. The first is the presidency of three persons. **1944** *Utah Hist. Quart.* Jan.–Apr. 26 The presidency of the St. George Stake wrote to Wilford Woodruff, then president of the Church, asking for additional help.

b. First Presidency, the highest council of this kind, consisting of the head of the hierarchy of the church and two counselors, and having jurisdiction over the entire church.

1841 *Times & Seasons* (Nauvoo, Ill.) May 413/1 The Chairman then read a resolution . . . in which the first Presidency of the Church, and others are commanded to make a solemn proclamation to the Kings of the earth. **1905** *Out West* Sep. 244 Each Bishop, I will remark, has two Counselors to assist him, these three forming a Bishopric; and the President over the entire Church also has two Counselors, they with him constituting the First Presidency.

3. The office held by the president of a railroad, labor union, etc. Cf. * **president 3.**

1853 *Knickerb.* XLII. 104 Benjamin Loder, Esq., has retired from the presidency of the New York and Erie Rail-road. **1901** MERWIN & WEBSTER *Calumet 'K'* 63, I had ambitions to be promoted to the presidency [of the railroad], but it didn't seem very likely. **1949** *Time* 26 Dec. 55/1 At 53, like manna in the wilderness, came an offer of the presidency of the College of New Jersey.

* **president,** *n.*

1. The highest or ruling officer in an American colony or "province." *Obs.*

1608 SMITH *Works* (1910) 6 The Counsell was sworn, and the President elected [at Jamestown], . . . where was made choice for our scituation. **1681** *Maine Doc. Hist.* IV. 401 The majestrates haue elected & Appointed the Honored Thomas Danforth Esqr our present Deputy Gouernor to be President of the Province of Maine for the yeare ensuing. **1705** BEVERLEY *Virginia* IV. 201 The first Constitution of Government appointed by them, was by a President and Council, which Council was nominated by the Corporation, . . . and the President annually chosen by the People. **1731** *Cal. State P. Amer. & W. Indies* (1732) 1, Representation of the President, Council and General Assembly of New York to the King. Sep. 15, 1731.

b. The executive head or governor of a state government. *Obs.*

The use of *president* in these early examples, and the election procedure indicated in them, are reflections of the fact that chief executives of the colonies had been called "presidents" (cf. sense **1.**) and had been elected by councils. By 1800 *president* had yielded place, in popular use, to *governor* (*q.v.* sense **2.**). Cf. **first magistrate.**

1776 *Del. Constitution* § 7 A President or Chief Magistrate shall be chosen by joint ballot of both Houses. **1780** *Va. State P.* I. 371 When the Governors or Presidents of two or more States act in the field together, he who has been longest in office shall take rank of all other Governors or presidents. *a***1817** DWIGHT *Travels* II. 154 Bartlett derived its name from his Excellency Josiah Bartlett, some years since President of [N.H.].

2. (*cap.*) The chairman or presiding officer at the meetings of the Continental Congress, in full *President of Congress. Obs.*

1774 *Hist. MSS Commission* 14th Rep. App. X. (1895) 232 Copy of a Letter from General Gage, to the Honble Payton Randolph, Esqr President of the American Continental Congress sitting at Philadelphia. **1776** A. ADAMS *Familiar Lett.* 149 The mansion-house of your President [John Hancock] is safe, and the furniture unhurt. **1783** in HILDEBURN *Cent. of Printing* II. 409 Proclamation. By His Excellency Elias Boudinot, Esquire, President of the United States in Congress Assembled. **1828** COOPER *Notions* I. 102 There is no such officer now known to the country as a 'President of Congress.'

b. (*cap.*) Hence, the highest executive officer of the U.S. Government. Also as a title.

1787 *Constitution* ii. § 4 The President, Vice-President, and all civil Officers of the United States shall be removed from office on Impeachment for, and conviction of Treason. **1808** *Ann. 10th Congress* 1 Sess. I. 335 The President of the United States is Commander-in-chief of the Army and Navy. **1855** PIERCE in *Pres. Mess. & P.* V. 312 These long continued efforts had brought upon the Government . . . such indignities as to induce President Adams . . . to speak of it in terms of the highest indignation. **1949** *Chi. D. News* 23 April 6/1 Johnson 'talked turkey' to the President.

c. The highest executive of the Republic of Texas. *Obs.*

1836 *Diplom. Corr. Texas* I. (1908) 144 Remember me to the President and Cabinet. **1846** POLK *Diary* I. 309 At 6 O'Clock this evening Gen'l Samuel Houston, late President of Texas and now a Senator in Congress, called.

d. (See quot.) *Rare.*

1859 *N.Y. Wkly. Tribune* 8 Oct. 3/3 John Ross, the President or head chief of the Cherokees, lives at Taleguah, the capital of the nation.

e. The chief executive officer of the Confederate States of America. Also as a title. Now *hist.*

1861 *Charleston* (S.C.) *Mercury* 7 Feb. 2/6 The State Conventions all expect to elect the President and Vice President of the Confederacy as well as the Representatives to the Congress. **1866** F. KIRKLAND *Bk. Anecdotes* 114/2 Some of the Sixth Missouri Cavalry visited the former residence of 'President' Davis. **1948** *N.O. Times-Picayune Mag.* 26 Dec. 5 There was nothing cheering about the prospects of a Yuletide in the Richmond White House of President and Mrs. Davis, but they still improvised 'the trimmin's' for the Confederacy's last Christmas.

3. The chief executive officer of a business or industrial company, as a bank, railroad, etc.

1781 *Jrnls. Cont. Congress* XXI. 1188 It is hereby ordained, . . . that those who are . . . subscribers to the said bank be . . . a corporation and body politic to all intents and purposes, by name and stile of 'the President, Directors, and Company of the Bank of North America.' **1909** *Nation* 11 March 251 One is a little irritated to learn that President, meaning the chairman of a business concern, is branded as an Americanism [in the *OED*]. **1946** *Chi. D. News* 20 Dec. 4/3 He is a past president of the Chicago Traffic Club. **1949** *L.A. Times* 12 July 13/7 H. D. Ivey, president of the Citizens National Trust & Savings Bank . . . , yesterday completed his twentieth year as president of Citizens National.

4. The officer, normally the Vice-President of the U.S., who presides at the meetings of the U.S. Senate. In full *president of the Senate.*

1787 *Constitution* i. § 3 The Vice President of the United States shall be President of the Senate, but shall have no vote. **1789** *Annals 1st Congress* I. 17 The Senate proceeded, by ballot, to the choice of a President, for the sole purpose of opening and counting the votes for President of the United States. John Langdon was elected. **1900** *Cong. Rec.* 22 Feb. 2062/2 Mr. President, yesterday I gave notice to the Senate that to-day, at the completion of the reading of the Farewell Address, . . . I would [speak].

5. In some states, the chief officer of a village or town (see quot. 1914).

1830 *Mechanics' Press* (Utica, N.Y.) 6 Feb. 103/3 The President of Brooklyn has offered a reward of a hundred dollars for the apprehension of the villain who has escaped. **1844** *Indiana Senate Jrnl.* 29 Sess. 211 A bill for the relief of the president and trustees of the town of Greencastle. **1914** *Cyclo. Amer. Govt.* III. 47/2 *Presidents of Villages,* the official title of the chief officer of a village in New York, Vermont, Michigan, Illinois, Wisconsin, and Minnesota. More often the title mayor is used. **1949** *Chi. Tribune* 29 Dec. II. 1/6 Vows He'll Keep Steger Fully Fire Protected. Many Are Applying, President [of Village] Says.

6. The chief executive official of the Church of Jesus Christ of Latter-day Saints, or a subordinate official with similar powers and responsibilities. Cf. ***presidency 2.**

1841 *Times & Seasons* (Nauvoo, Ill.) May 413/1 The president then addressed the conference and congregation on the duties of the elders, and on the different orders of the priesthood. **1876** *Ogden* (Utah) *Freeman* 9 Dec. 2/5 All the presidents, high priests, apostles, seventies, bishops, elders . . . are requested to meet at the tabernacle. **1949** *Sat. Ev. Post* 12 Feb. 32/1 On one of his western tours . . . Phineas Barnum, the circus impresario, . . . was enthusiastically entertained by another great showman—Brigham Young, all-powerful president of the Church of Jesus Christ of Latter-day Saints.

7. One of the chief officers of The First Church of Christ, Scientist, in Boston, Mass., and of some branch churches.

1895 M. B. EDDY in *Church Manual* 17 The President of this Church shall hold his Office one year only, and is eligible to this office once in three years. **1924** *Christian Science Jrnl.* July 203 He is a member of Third Church of Christ, Scientist, Los Angeles, where he has served as President.

8. (Usu. *cap.*) In combs.: (1) **president-elect,** one who has been elected president, esp. of the U.S., but has not taken office; (2) **general,** a president who outranks or is superior to all minor presidents in a system, society, or federation; (3) **judge,** (see quot. 1914 and cf. **presiding judge**); (4) **maker,** one who inspires or directs the political maneuvering attendant upon the nomination and election of a President of the U.S.; (5) **making,** the choosing of a President, the political machinations culminating in the election of a President of the U.S., also attrib.; (6) **pro tem,** a senator, usu. a party leader chosen to serve as presiding officer of the Senate in the absence of the Vice-President; (7) **-'s biscuit,** (see quot.), *obs.;* (8) **-'s family,** the cabinet of the President of the U.S., also **President's official family;** (9) **-'s house,** the official residence of the President of the U.S., the White House; (10) **-'s levee,** a reception given by the President of the U.S.; (11) **-'s March,** a march composed in honor of the President of the U.S.; (12) **-'s message,** (*a*) (*cap.*) an address or communication delivered before, or sent to, Congress by the President of the U.S., (*b*) a communication from the president of the Republic of Texas to the Texas congress, *obs.*

(1) **1825** in M. BAYARD SMITH *Forty Yrs. Washington Soc.* (1906) 187 The succeeding day, Thursday, citizens and strangers crowded to pay their respects, not only to the President-elect, but to Mr. Crawford and Genl. Jackson. **1861** *Charleston* (S.C.) *Mercury* 22 Jan. 2/7 What a delicious bit of B'hoyism to come from a president elect at a time like this! **1949** *Sky Line Trail* Oct. 3/1 First to congratulate the president-elect was E. P. Holmes, retiring president. — (2) **1754** *Mass. H.S. Coll.* 3 Ser. V. 70 [It is proposed] that the said general government be administered by a President-General, to be appointed and supported by the crown. **1809** J. ADAMS *Works* IX. 620 At the meeting of the Cincinnati at New York, . . . they choose Hamilton their President-General. **1858** BANCROFT *Hist. U.S.* VII. 140 Galloway, of Pennsylvania, . . . proposed for the government of the colonies a president-general, to be appointed by the king. — (3) **1833** *Ind. Mag. Hist.* XXII. 64 Hon. Gustavus A. Everts, president judge [of the Circuit Court of Elkhart Co., Ind.]. **1849** CHAMBERLAIN *Ind. Gazetteer* 65 The President Judges are chosen by the Legislature, and the Associate and Probate Judges by the people. **1914** BOUVIER *Law Dict.* 2676/2 *President Judge,* a title sometimes given to the presiding judge. It . . . is now used in the courts of common pleas in Pennsylvania. So in the old Virginia court of appeals. — (4) **1859** L. WILMER *Press Gang* 216 Mr. Forney, president-maker and editor of the Philadelphia *Press,* is already on his side. **1948** *Time* 5 July 21/1 John L. Lewis . . . used to fancy himself as a President-maker and still does as a President-breaker.

(5) **1830** *Argus W. Amer.* (Frankfort, Ky.) 1 Sep. 2/3 This new mode of President making invented by Mr. Clay, whatever may be its results, excites some curiosity. **1897** *Chi. Record* 8 March 4/2 The question of 'availability' is always a prominent one in president making. — (6) **1850** *31st Congress* 1 Sess. Sen. Ex. Doc. No. 64, 3 [To] Hon. Wm. R. King, President pro tem. of the Senate. **1907** C. C. ANDREWS *Recoll.* (1928) 126 Mr. Bright said he never felt at home in speaking in the Senate, though he felt entirely self-possessed in stating questions, etc., in the chair as president pro-tem. — (7) **1833** APPLETON in S. Hale *Life T. G. Appleton* 121 The refreshments [at a London party] were simple to plainness; . . . the cake what we call 'President's Biscuit.' — (8) **1790** MACLAY *Deb. Senate* 193 As I came out from the Hall, all the President's family were there—Humphreys, Jackson, Nelson, etc., etc. **1905** *Independent* 2 March 470/1 There will be but one change in the President's official family,—that of Postmaster-General. — (9) **1792** HILTZHEIMER *Diary* (1893) 10 April 174 The Governor, Mr. Wills, Mr. Gurney, Rakestraw, Williams and myself went to the corner of Market and Ninth Streets, to select the site for the President's house and at the same time to notify the tenants to move immediately. **1881** *Harper's Mag.* March 544/2 From the park east of the Capitol to the President's House . . . there is a long stretch of government land. **1945** ADAMS *Album Amer. Hist.* II. 235 The President's House was a lonely abode for the Hero of New Orleans.

(10) **1832** DUNLAP *Hist. Amer. Theatre* 89 To Humphreys has been ascribed some of that anti-republican etiquette which attended the president's levees. — (11) **1801** in M. BAYARD SMITH *Forty Yrs. Washington Soc.* (1930) 30 Who in due military form saluted the President, accompanied by the President's March played by an excel-

lent band attached to the corps. — **(12)** (*a*) **1810** in P. H. MUSSER *James N. Barker* (1929) 36 The President's Message will at last produce nothing. **1915** *Amer. Rev. of Reviews* Jan. 13/2 The President's Message. . . . Mr. Wilson appeared in person on the Second day of the session, and delivered his message to Congress. (*b*) **1840** *N.O. Picayune* 18 Nov. 2/4 The President's Message to the Texian Congress of 1840–41, was delivered in 'manuscript.'

As the last term in **bank, caucus, college, cowboy, ex-, railroad, rump, vice-, war President.**

presidente ˌprɛzəˈdɛntɪ, *n. S.W.* [Sp.] The chief executive officer of a village or town (see also quot. 1939).

1863 D. FERGUSSON *Rep. to Congress* 2 (Bentley), The 'presidente' of the municipality . . . has set about repairing and changing the road in the vicinity. **1923** WALLACE SMITH *Little Tigress* 166 (Bentley), But the white-whiskered presidente changed that. **1939** ROLLINS *Gone Haywire* 12 When he used ranching terms, he was more apt to employ words common on the Southern border, for example . . . *caporal* or *presidente* in substitution for 'old man' (ranch owner).

∗**presidential,** *a.* In combs. relating chiefly to the President of the U.S. or to the office of the President: (1) **presidential boom,** an increase of interest in, or enthusiasm for, a candidate for President; (2) **campaign,** a political campaign leading up to, and culminating in, the election of a President of the U.S.; (3) **canvass,** =prec.; (4) **chair,** the office of President of the U.S.; (5) **contest,** the contest for the Presidency of the U.S.; (6) **convention,** a convention held by a political party for nominating candidates for President and Vice-President of the U.S.; (7) **count,** the official count of presidential electoral votes, made by the Senate; (8) **election,** a quadrennial election in which a President and Vice-President of the U.S., or, more exactly, presidential electors, are chosen by popular vote; (9) **elector,** =∗**elector;** (10) **electoral vote,** the vote which a candidate for President of the U.S. receives in the electoral college; (11) **fever,** (see quot. 1914); (12) **governor,** during or immediately after the Civil War, a governor appointed by President Lincoln or President Johnson for one of the southern states, *obs.;* (13) **mansion,** =**President's house,** also transf.; (14) **message,** =**President's Message** (*a*); (15) **office,** (*a*) the office or position of a President of the U.S., (*b*) (see quot.); (16) **plan,** the plan of Presidents Lincoln and Johnson for restoring the southern states to statehood in the Union after the Civil War; (17) **term,** the period of four years for which a President of the U.S. is elected; (18) **timber,** a person or persons regarded as suitable for the Presidency of the U.S.; (19) **year,** (*a*) a year spent in the office of president, (*b*) a year in which a presidential election occurs.

(1) 1887 *Courier-Journal* 11 Jan. 4/5 Now Don Cameron's dawning Presidential boom is the thing. **1892** *Chi. Tribune* 4 April 4/6 Holman's presidential boom may be likened to a gob of dough that hasn't a bit of yeast within a thousand miles of it. — **(2) 1835** C. P. BRADLEY *Isaac Hill* 60 He finally thought the time had arrived for taking an active part in the presidential campaign. **1945** *Sat. Review* 24 Feb. 9/1 We may expect to be informed all over again in the next Presidential campaign that the Roosevelt policies were spawned in the diseased brains of crackpot professors. — **(3) 1841** *Spirit of Times* 24 July 250/2 (We.), During the Presidential canvass he stated [etc.]. **1900** *Cong. Rec.* 26 Jan. 1234/2, I saw much of him at the national headquarters of the committee which managed Mr. Blaine's Presidential canvass. — **(4) 1792** HAMILTON *Works* VIII. 261 Mr. Jefferson aimed with ardent desire at the Presidential chair. **1848** *Literary Amer.* 25 Nov. 356/3 If 'Harry of the West' had reached the Presidential chair, the road would doubtless have been completed. **1900** *Cong. Rec.* 31 Jan. 1341/1 There was a Jackson in the Presidential chair to take that bank by the throat and compel it to go into liquidation.

(5) 1846 *Hancock Eagle* (Nauvoo, Ill.) 10 April 1/3 The Presidential contest of '44 was drawing to a close, and the 'returns' from respective States began coming in. — **(6) 1872** *Atlantic Mo.* May 640 The time for the Presidential convention draws near. **1949** *New Yorker* 9 July 54/3 The journalistic pieces . . . include . . . a Presidential convention story. — **(7) 1877** *Harper's Mag.* Dec. 148/1 Scenes of tumult . . . signalized the closing hours of our last Congress in the endeavor to prevent the consummation of the Presidential count. — **(8) 1801** in M. BAYARD SMITH *Forty Yrs. of Washington Soc.* (1906) 21 A great and preponderating majority in the Presidential election decided the relative strength of parties. **1944** *Reader's Digest* Oct. 45/2 America must hold a presidential election. — **(9) 1789** HILTZHEIMER *Diary* (1893) 7 Jan. 148 Went to the State House and voted for ten Presidential Electors, who are to meet next month in Reading. **1820** *Niles' Reg.* XVIII. 432/1 We lately noticed an alleged defect in the law of this state, as to the election of presidential electors. **1949** D. O. McGOVNEY *Amer. Suffrage* 34 We call them 'presidential electors' for short, although they vote for vice president as well as for president.

(10) 1945 *Newsweek* 15 Jan. 32/3 A resolution providing for the counting of Presidential electoral votes on Saturday was adopted. — **(11) 1882** *Cent. Mag.* Jan. 435/1 This honor comes to me unsought. I have never had the presidential fever. **1914** *Cyclo. Amer. Govt.* III. 47/1 *Presidential Fever*, a phrase used to denote the eager desire for, and ambition to gain, the presidency of the United States, prevalent among prominent political leaders and 'favorite sons' in the several states. — **(12) 1866** in FLEMING *Hist. Reconstruction* I. 195 Then came the appointment of Presidential Governors, an anomaly heretofore unknown in a Government composed of states which were once supposed to possess some at least of the attributes of sovereignty. — **(13) 1829** *Va. Herald* (Fredericksburg) 11 March 2/1 When the President retired, the procession was re-formed, and he was conducted to the Presidential Mansion. **1949** *Sat. Ev. Post* 15 Oct. 143/1 Dr. Wallace Sterling, the new president of the university, spent a morning in work clothes moving into the presidential mansion recently. — **(14) 1839** *S. Lit. Messenger* V. 752/2 Our bachelor . . . was poring over one of those long presidential messages. **1859** WILMER *Press Gang* 193 Martin Van Buren, in one of his Presidential messages, proposed to make embezzlement of the public money a felony punishable by confinement in the State's Prison. **1950** *Chi. Tribune* 5 Jan. 1/1 Democratic senators and house leaders visited the White House yesterday and with Mr. Truman went over the state of the Union, budget, and other Presidential messages to be delivered to congress.

(15) (*a*) **1798** WASHINGTON *Writings* XIV. 24 From the want of the list, which I left in the Presidential office, . . . it would be hazardous . . . to give a decided opinion. **1838** *Speeches D. Barnard* 102 In which he took occasion to set forth, very fully his notions in regard to the powers and duties of the presidential office. (*b*) **1882** *Nation* 2 Nov. 370/2, 1,951 of these [post] offices are filled by appointment of the President, and are known as Presidential offices, and the remainder—44,280—are filled by appointment of the Postmaster-General. — **(16) 1879** TOURGEE *Fool's Errand* 49 The plan . . . was what has since been known as the 'presidential plan.' — **(17) 1813** in S. K. PADOVER *Jefferson* (1942) 356 On this principle I prefer the Presidential term of four years, to that of seven years. **1839** *26th Congress* 1 Sess. Sen. Doc. No. 2, 15 Losses appear to have occurred from defaults among officers in every 'administration' or presidential term. — **(18) 1892** *Chi. Tribune* 4 April 4/5 Senator Cullom of Illinois is better Presidential timber than was generally supposed. **1947** *Steamboat* (Colo.) *Pilot* 2 Jan. 1/5 Eugene D. Millikin is regarded as presidential timber by all of the Republican political big shots. — **(19)** (*a*) **1785** R. H. LEE in J. Adams *Works* IX. 544 My presidential year [in Congress] being ended, I had left New York for this place. **1877** in W. S. TYLER *Hist. Amherst Coll.* 207 The class that graduates tomorrow carries with it the memory of your first presidential year [at Amherst]. (*b*) **1876** *Scribner's Mo.* Jan. 432/2 It is 'Presidential year,' and the great question concerning the currency is to be settled. **1944** *Chi. D. News* 21 March 10/1 'Roll Out the Barrel' was not a political ditty, but politicians always try to roll it out in presidential years.

Also *presidential candidate, character, favorite, game, levee, party, picnic, possibility, problem, ticket, vacancy*, etc.

∗**presiding,** *a.*

1. presiding elder, in the Methodist Church, a minister who has supervision over the churches and preachers in a certain district. Now *hist.*

[**1800** in W. W. SWEET *Religion on Amer. Frontier* IV. (1946) 221, I believe some of the people in one place endeavoured to set the President Elder against me, which they accomplished.] **1807** in *Va. Hist. Mag.* XXXIV. (1926) 134 Camp meeting, and the presiding elder, Father Meade, and several other preachers. **1831** PECK *Guide* 258 There are three districts, over each of which is a presiding Elder. **1944** JOHNSON *As I Dare* 199, I stood between factions in the church, and sometimes interviewed presiding elders about the next pastoral assignment.

2. presiding judge, =**president judge.** *Obs.*

1802 *Ann. 7th Congress* 1 Sess. 117 The constant changing of presiding judges . . . hung up the business. **1869** TOURGEE *Toinette* (1881) 245 Geoffrey's counsel . . . called the attention of His Honor, the Presiding Judge of the Court, to the fact that [etc.].

presidio prɪˈsɪdɪˌo, *n. S.W.* [Sp., a garrison or fort.] A fort or post where soldiers, usu. fewer than 50, lived with their families and cultivated the land about them.

These posts were Spanish institutions designed to protect frontiers against aggression and to safeguard the missions.

1763 tr. DU PRATZ *Hist. of Louisiana* (1758) I. 11 On his route [he] met with no nation, till he came to the *Presidio*, or fortress of *St. John Baptist*, on the *Rio* (River) *del Norte*, in *New Mexico.* **1808** SHALER *Journal* (1935) 60 The whole country [California] is divided into six military districts, called *presidios*, or garrisons. **1831** BEECHEY *Voyage* II. 85 The village and presidio of Monterey are situated upon a plain between the anchorage and a range of hills covered with woods of pine and oak. [**1947** *Sooner Mag.* Nov. 7/1 His next assignment is as deputy commander at the Presidio in California.]

attrib. **1840** DANA *Two Years* xviii, 160 A bull was expected down from the country, to be baited in the presidio square. **1898** ATHERTON *Californians* 204 At one of the Presidio hops she spent the evening . . . in a boat on the bay with an officer who was as accomplished a flirt as herself.

* **press,** *n.* In combs.: (1) **press agent,** orig. an agent in charge of advertising for a theater, in later use, one who secures publicity for a person, business, enterprise, etc.; (2) **agentry,** publicity, advertising, *colloq.;* (3) **association,** an organization for collecting news and supplying it to newspapers, cf. **Associated Press;** (4) **board,** an ironing board, *obs.;* (5) **box,** (*a*) a booth or stall for the convenience of newspaper reporters covering a meeting, contest, etc., (*b*) in an old-fashioned cotton press, the large boxlike receptacle into which the lint was placed for packing into bales; (6) **boy,** a boy who assists a pressman in a printing establishment; (7) **clipping bureau,** =**clipping bureau;** (8) **club,** an organization made up of those engaged in printing, publishing, or writing; (9) **congress,** a congress or convention of representatives of the press; (10) * **gang,** (*a*) representatives of newspapers, as editors and reporters, (*b*) newspapers collectively, *contemptuous* and *rare;* (11) * **man,** one who operates a press in a cotton gin; (12) * **paper,** heavy paper or pasteboard used in binding books; (13) **report,** a report or news item given to, or appearing in, the press or newspapers.

(**1**) **1894** *Standard Dict.* 1408/2. **1896** *Outlook* 19 Dec. 1132/2 It has been a favorite device of the Spanish 'press agents' to report Maceo's death. **1949** *Chi. Tribune* 9 Dec. 18/3 This was the first time that a press agent had hit on a truthful first page story in a month of Sundays. — (**2**) **1920** *Outing* March 249/3 This latter affair sounds like a combined burst of spread-eagle patriotism and Scotch press-agentry. **1947** *Chr. Sci. Monitor* 20 Dec. 13/7 P. T. Barnum, the celebrated circus magnate, was the leading advocate of press-agentry and ballyhoo in his day. — (**3**) **1877** *Harper's Mag.* Dec. 58/2 The American Press Association is an organization similar to the Associated Press. **1917** SINCLAIR *King Coal* 212 We limit the amount of news the Western press association can suppress. **1948** *Senior Scholastic* 15 March 10/1 In the United States, there are three major press associations, each privately owned and controlled. — (**4**) **1849** G. G. FOSTER *N.Y. in Slices* 14 The press-board has been placed across the back corner of the shop. **1896** J. C. HARRIS *Sister Jane* 17 I've got this pressboard on my lap, or I'd fetch it myself.

(**5**) (*a*) **1889** *Sporting Life* (Phila.) 10 July 5/5 The upper stand . . . will contain the seats for ladies and their escorts and the private boxes, not forgetting the press box. **1947** *Chr. Sci. Monitor* 5 June 11/1 The press box has always been forbidden territory to the average sports fan. (*b*) **1948** DICK *Dixie Frontier* 253 The seeds were taken out in the lint house and carried in baskets to the press box. — (**6**) **1890** *Cent.* 3560/3 *Machine-boy*. . . . In the United States known as *feeder* or *press-boy*. — (**7**) **1903** *Christendom* April ii. (*advt.*), United States Press Clipping Bureau. **1949** *Chi. Tribune* 5 July II. 1/2 Catherine Sickles came to the Consolidated Press Clipping bureau when she was a little girl. — (**8**) **1896** *Peterson Mag.* ns. VI. 311/1 The Pittsburgh Women's Press Club made a wise choice in selecting for a secretary Miss Marie de Sayles Coyle. **1931** *K.C. Times* 5 Sep., Rock Port Press Club Found. — (**9**) **1894** SHUMAN *Steps into Journalism* 17 Joe Howard, a New York writer, . . . was one of the speakers at the World's Fair Press Congress in Chicago.

(**10**) (*a*) **1840** *Spirit of Times* 11 Jan. 535/1 (We.), In compliment to the 'Press gang' . . . [they] were invited to occupy seats over the Judge's stand. **1887** *Courier-Journal* 20 Jan. 1/7 Sam Morse, of the Chicago *Times*, announced that he had perfected an arrangement by which the press gang could get into the hall of the House. (*b*) **1859** L. WILMER (*title*), Our Press Gang; or, a Complete Exposition of the Corruptions and Crimes of the American Newspapers. — (**11**) **1851** *De Bow's Review* XI. 693 The press . . . will, no doubt, effect a great revolution in making the planters their own press-men, thus obviating the expense of repressure in the commercial cities. **1869** *Overland Mo.* III. 10 The pressmen and ginners, too, like the fields, have been snowed upon. — (**12**) **1760** *Boston Gazette* 16 June, Ink Horns, . . . writing and press paper, . . . knitting needles. **1791** *Ann. 2d Congress* 1000 [Manufactures include] Pasteboards, fullers or presspapers, paperhangings. — (**13**) **1868** *N.Y. Herald* 10 July 4/2 Another Question of Privilege—The Press Reports. **1899** *N.Y. Journal* 10 Aug. 14/4 How can they, with all press reports censored as they are?

As the last term in **Associated, beater, bogus, card, collar, Columbian, cotton, cotton baling, cylinder, drill, drop, free, hay, Mormon hay, mud, perfecting, plantation, plug, power, rolling, screw, steam cotton, Washington, web, web perfecting press.** Also **beggars' presses.**

* **pressure,** *n.* In combs.: (1) **pressure cooker,** an airtight cooking vessel in which food can be cooked by steam under pressure; (2) **group,** a group organized to exert pressure, esp. of a political nature.

(**1**) **1921** *Ladies' Home Jrnl.* March 117 The National Steam Pressure Aluminum Cooker. **1949** *This Week Mag.* 5 March 28/3 That was Cora's way until she met Mrs. Shaffer's new pressure cooker. — (**2**) [**1906** *World's Work* Oct. 8135/2 They expect in this way to bring enough pressure to bear on Congress to make it give heed to their demands as the spokesmen of a large proportion of organized labor.] **1939** WEBSTER (*New Words*). **1949** *Desplaines Valley News* (Summit, Ill.) 28 Oct. 4/1 Illinois state representatives . . . are harassed by pressure groups.

* **pretty,** *a.* **1. pretty-by-night,** (see quot. 1931). *Colloq.* **2. pretty-prettyness,** the quality of being merely pretty, slightly *contemptuous.*

(**1**) **1872** EGGLESTON *End of World* 169 She planted some pretty-by-nights in an old cracked blue-and-white tea-pot. **1931** CLUTE *Plants* 135 This, however, is not the case with the four-o'clock (*Mirabilis jalapa*) which bears the name of pretty-by-night and lives up to it. — (**2**) **1926** LUCAS MALET *Dogs of Want* i, The coquettish little Cities of the Plain . . . and their cheap pretty-prettiness of countless hotels. **1931** *Observer* 6 Sep., The revulsions into Sunday School pretty-prettiness are equally enterprising.

pretzel ˈprɛtsḷ, *n.* [G. *Prezel, Brezel,* in same sense.] A kind of brittle salted bread or German biscuit, often made in the form of a knot or ring. Also attrib.

[*c***1824–38** G. FURMAN *Antiquities L.I.* 261 Our honest, good-natured Dutch ancestors . . . were satisfied with the *Oly Cookes, Pretzies,* [etc.].] **1888** *San Juan Prospector* (Del Norte, Colo.) 15 May 1/4 No German-American dictionary contains the word 'pretzel,' 'bretzle,' or 'bretsel.' . . . A bretzle is such a curious piece of delicatessen; such a horny, salty, hard-shelled, twisted jaw-breaker that they want to know all about them. **1949** *St. Paul Pioneer Press* 19 June, Industrial progress has come to the rescue of pretzel-benders.

b. pretzel jag, (see quot.).

1944 *N. & Q.* IV 55 Pretzel Jag: An affliction . . . suffered by persons sensitive to table salt, . . . often assumed by the victims to be the effect of the beer itself.

preventorium ˌprivenˈtorɪəm, *n.* An institution in which persons, esp. children, threatened with tuberculosis are treated in an effort to prevent the development of the disease. — **1909** *Boston Ev. Transcript* 10 Nov. (*heading*), To Fight Tuberculosis New York Will Have $700,000 Preventorium. **1947** *Chi. Tribune* 11 Dec. 3/7 Twenty girls between the ages of 6 and 14 marched to safety yesterday when fire destroyed their dormitory at the Ridge Farm Preventorium.

* **preview,** *n.* A previous view or survey. Esp. an exhibition of a motion picture to a select group before its release to the public. Also attrib.

1882 F. RUSSELL in *Chi. Advance* 13 April 227 At the beginning of each quarter a pre-view of the lessons should be given to the Sabbath schools. **1899** *Lutheran* (Phila.) 6 April 321 The consecutive lessons . . . may furnish both review and preview as essential features. **1924** WITWER *Roughly Speaking* 34 The following day there was a special preview of 'Her Husband's Wife.' **1949** *Dly. Ardmoreite* (Ardmore, Okla.) 4 Dec. 1/8 This 18 minute sound movie . . . was screened for the membership at a preview showing.

* **previous,** *a.* and *adv.*

1. Hastily, precipitously. *Too previous,* too hasty, premature. *Colloq.*

1883 PECK *Bad Boy* 85 When I saw Pa feeling under the bed for a bed slat I got upstairs pretty previous now. **1890** *Boston Jrnl.* 21 June 2/2 The grumbling in this matter has been too previous. **1900** HALE *Letters* 356 Carla Atkinson is coming here to lunch with me, . . . but I'm too previous, and she won't be here for half an hour.

2. previous question, in a deliberative body, the question of whether the immediate pending question or questions shall be voted on at once with little or no further debate.

In the U.S. the previous question is now used as a device to limit debate and bring the immediate question to a vote. In England it is used to postpone action on the main question.

1739 *Boston Rec.* 220 A previous Question was put . . . .Voted in the Affirmative. **1840** *Boston Transcript* 19 March 2/3 The previous question was called for and sustained. **1896** *Internat. Typog. Union Proc.* 2/1 Upon the previous question being ordered, [they] were unanimously adopted by a rising vote.

* **previousness,** *n.* The state of being previous, improper haste. *Colloq.*

1884 *Boston Jrnl.* 4 March 2/1 (*caption*), A Case of Previousness. **1885** *Ib.* 16 April 2/1 Mr. Peck seems to be the victim of his own over-confidence and indiscreet previousness. **1892** *Law Times* XCIII. 413/1 His previousness, however, is not always effective.

Prex prɛks, *n.* [Fanciful from * *President.*] A students' term for a college president. *Slang.*

1828 *Yankee* I. 232/1 Our Prex says this:—You surely miss [etc.]. **1871** BAGG *At Yale* 655 The students, among themselves, rarely mention his name unless preceded with the title 'Prex,' which is oftener used alone to designate him. **1906** *N.Y. Ev. Post* 11 June 6 If the various unpopular 'Prexes' would study the grounds of their unpopularity, they would find it in the quasi-servile position they have forced upon many of their faculty.

Prexy ˈprɛksɪ, *n.* =prec. *Slang.*

1871 BAGG *At Yale* 655 The title 'Prex' . . . is oftener used alone to designate him [the president] among the Seniors, the modified form of 'Prexy' is somewhat in vogue, in familiar talk. **1949** *Birmingham-Southern College Bul.* June 1/3 Dr. P. J. James New Athens College Prexy.

transf. **1945** *Chi. Sun.* 7 Dec. 34/1 (*caption*), Hulbert Takes Over As [Golf] Association Prexy. **1949** *Hobbies* Nov. 125/3 Many [philatelists] for years have wanted 'Old Glory' in color on a stamp and continuing in each issue (like the Prexies) of each series for current use.

* **price,** *n.* In combs.: (1) **price catalogue,** a catalogue that lists the prices of certain goods; (2) **tag,** a tag marked with a price and attached to a commodity for sale.

(1) **1861** *Chi. Tribune* 26 May 1/9 Illustrated price Catalogues of Pianos and Melodeons sent free of charge. — (2) **1881** *Harper's Mag.* Sep. 587/1 He . . . busied his hands nervously in untying a little green price tag from the handle of the umbrella. **1932** *K.C. Times* 9 March 18 It would be fine . . . if the buttons on things we buy were fastened on as tight as the price tags.

As the last term in **beaver, Bunker Hill, close, Congress, curb, cut, government, money, New York price.**

Price Raid. [Sterling *Price* (1809–67), Confederate general who raided in Kansas in Oct., 1864.] In combs. now obs. or hist.: (1) **Price Raid claim,** one of the claims for pay made by volunteers who had taken part in resisting the Price Raid, also **Price Raid commission,** a commission appointed to inquire into the validity of the Price Raid claims; (2) **Price Raid scrip,** scrip issued by the Kansas government, and redeemed in part by Congress in 1872, to satisfy the Price Raid claims.

(1) **1869** in D. W. WILDER *Annals of Kans.* (1886) 510 The State of Kansas has . . . assumed Price Raid claims to the amount of half a million, . . . which ought to be paid by the General Government. *Ib.* 458 These forged or fabricated claims purport to have been sworn to before the Secretary of the Price Raid Commission. — (2) **1872** in D. W. WILDER *Annals of Kans.* (1886) 565 There have been audited claims for which the scrip commonly known as the Price Raid Scrip has been issued or ordered to be issued. **1873** *Winfield* (Kans.) *Courier* 11 Jan. 3/4 Price raid scrip wanted.

* **prick,** *n.* A pricker or priming wire for keeping open the touch-hole of an old-time musket. *Obs.*—**1859** *Kans. State Hist. Soc. Trans.* V. 581 Ordnance stores this day turned over to Samuel Medary, . . . 100 cap pouches and pricks, worn.

* **prick,** *v.* **1.** *tr.* To prod (powder) into a touchhole with a pricker. **2.** To pierce or cut the tail of (a horse) in such a way as to cause him to carry the tail high. **3.** (See quot.) All *obs.*

(1) **1775** *Mass. H.S. Coll.* 2 Ser. II. 292, I order'd my men . . . to prick dry Powder into the Touchholes. — (2) **1868** WOODRUFF *Trotting Horse* 228 It was the fashion to have horses pricked and docked. — (3) **1862** *Army Lett.* 89, I've been in the service over a year now and I've never been 'pricked' (marked absent without leave).

* **prickly,** *a.* In combs.: (1) **prickly ash,** a prickly shrub or small tree of the genus *Zanthoxylum;* (2) **beaver,** (see quot.); (3) **gooseberry,** the wild gooseberry, *Grossularia cynosbati;* (4) **heat,** (see quots.); (5) **pear,** see as a main entry; (6) **phlox,** the California gilia, *G. californica,* a shrubby plant with showy pink flowers common in chaparral regions; (7) **poppy,** any plant of the genus *Argemone,* esp. the Mexican (prickly) poppy *q.v.;* (8) **ray,** a species of skate, *Raja eglanteria.*

(1) **1709** LAWSON *Carolina* 101 Prickly-Ash grows up like a Pole; of which the Indians and English make Poles to set their Canoes along in Shoal-Water. **1821** NUTTALL *Jrnl.* 110, I saw here a prickly ash (*Zanthoxylion Clava Herculis*), the size of an ordinary ash, but the same species as that of the southern states, and the bark proving equally efficacious for allaying the tooth-ache. **1941** R. S. WALKER *Lookout* 61 Prickly-ash, or tooth-ache tree grows in certain favored spots, and the hop-tree is occasionally found at both the north end and south end of Lookout. — (2) **1845** DE SMET *Ore. Missions* (1847) 155 The American porcupine, the *Hystrix dorsata,* is called by modern Zoologists, the *Prickly Beaver.* — (3) **1795** WINTERBOTHAM *Hist. View* III. 393 Prickly gooseberry, *Ribes cynosbati.* **1833** EATON *Botany* (ed. 6) 305 Prickly gooseberry. . . . Berries prickly, dark brown, . . . Catskill Mt. **1860** CURTIS *Woody Plants N.C.* 84 Prickly gooseberry. . . . Distinguished from the others by its prickly fruit, which is brownish when ripe, and eatable. — (4) **1736** WESLEY *Works* I. (1829) 36, I found she had only the prickly heat, a sort of rash, very common here [Savannah, Ga.] in summer. **1859** BARTLETT 342 *Prickly Heat,* a cutaneous eruption or rash which appears during the excessive heat of summer. **1945** TOBIAS *Essentials Dermatology* 436 Prickly heat is an inflammatory condition characterized by an eruption of discrete, pimple-sized papules and papulo-vesicles having an erythematous halo.

(6) **1902** *Out West* May 512, I love . . . Even the wild color-clash When 'Indian pinks' plunge after 'prickly phlox' Flirting her damask hem. **1948** *L.A. Times* 5 Dec. (Home Mag.) 23/3 Well has it been called the prickly phlox, for its woody stems are covered with little leaves, sharp and spiny and rich green in tone. — (7) **1836** EATON *Botany* (ed. 7) 168 *Argemone mexicana,* prickly poppy. . . Platte River. **1942** LILLARD *Desert Challenge* 166 They nettled their fingers picking the prickly white poppy that grows along the roadside. — (8) **1842** *Nat. Hist. N.Y., Zoology* IV. 368 The Prickly Ray. . . . I have never seen but the single specimen . . . found on the shore of Staten Island, Richmond county.

prickly pear. The pear-shaped fruit of any flat-jointed cactus of the genus *Opuntia,* or a cactus of this genus. Also attrib.

1618 STRACHEY *Virginia* 119 Here is a cherry-redd fruict both within and without . . . which wee call the prickle peare. **1739** *Ga. Hist. Soc. Coll.* I. 188 The islands in Georgia are full of the prickly pear shrubs which feed flies. **1846** in CLAIBORNE *Life Quitman* I. 286 There were still the same stunted chapparal, disagreeable prickly-pear bushes. **1893** ROOSEVELT *Wilderness Hunter* 256 Mixed among them were prickly pears, standing as high as our heads on horseback. **1949** *Sun. World-Herald* Mag. 1 May 10/4 They found several parasites were fond of prickly pear.

Also **prickly-pear cactus.**

1857 GRAY *Lessons Botany* 96 We discern the stem . . . in the flattened joints of the Prickly-Pear Cactus. **1923** J. H. COOK *On Old Frontier* 29 The cattle seemed to be very fond of the prickly-pear cactus, and would eat them in spite of thorns. **1949** *Nat. Hist.* Feb. 88/2 Prickly pear cactus and spiny horned toad are common on the same arid lands.

* **pride,** *n.* In combs. and phrases: (1) *Pride of China,* =next; (2) *of India,* the China tree, *Melia azedarach,* in full *Pride of India Tree;* (3) *of Ohio,* (see quot.); (4) *of the West,* Cincinnati, Ohio, a nickname; (5) **-weed,** the horseweed, *Leptilon canadense.*

(1) **1785** WASHINGTON *Diaries* II. 383 Next 3 rows of the Seed of the Pride of China. **1901** MOHR *Plant Life Ala.* 588 Pride of China. Bead Tree. . . . Of some value for lumber. **1949** *Hist. & Philos. Soc. Ohio Bul.* April 71 A tall conical envelope of straw . . . protected the Pride of China, a tree brought from New Orleans. — (2) **1803** J. DAVIS *Travels* 79 The mocking-bird . . . was warbling, close to my window, from a tree called by some the Pride of *India,* and by others the Poison-berry Tree. **1829** B. HALL *Forty Etchings* No. XXI, In this Sketch the Pride of India tree will be observed growing before the house. **1893** *Harper's Mag.* April 756/2 This causeway broadened into a sandy street under huge pride-of-India trees, whose branches met overhead. **1949** SPRUNT & CHAMBERLAIN *S.C. Bird Life* 487 The Redstart . . . may be often found feeding about the abundant Pride of India or 'umbrella' trees near Negro cabins and settlements. — (3) **1861** WOOD *Botany* 503 *Dodecatheon.* . . . Pride of Ohio. . . . *D. Meadia.* . . . A singularly elegant herb, on prairies, dry or rocky soils, Penn. to Ind., Ill., Wisc. and throughout the Western states. — (4) **1835** HOFFMAN *Winter in West* II. 120, I could not but admit that the amphitheatre of green hills opposite me did really shut in 'The Pride of the West.'

(5) **1817–8** EATON *Botany* (1822) 373 *Erigeron canadense,* fleabane, pride-weed. . . . Powdered leaves useful in stopping blood. **1821** *Mass. H.S. Coll.* 2 Ser. IX. 150 *Erigeron canadense,* Pride-weed. **1845** LINCOLN *Botany* App. 101/2.

As the last term in **American, prince's, Venus('s) pride.**

prie-dieu ˈpriˌdju, *n.* [F.] (See quots. and cf. **Carolina wren.**) — **1883** *Harper's Wkly.* 3 March, The *prie-dieu*—'pray god'—utters its soprano note; water-hens and plovers call across the marsh. **1918** ARTHUR *Birds of La.* 72 Carolina Wren. . . . La p'tite wren; Ben-à-riz; Prier-Dieu.

*__priest,__ *n.* As the last term in **abolition, high, Indian, Shaker priest.**

priestly ˈpristlɪ, *n.* [Prob. f. a personal name.] A variety of apple tree or its fruit. *Obs.* — **1806** *Balance* V. 140/1 Plant the largest growing trees, such as priestly's on the north side. **1818** *Amer. Mo. Mag.* II. 428/2 Table Apples [include] . . . Priestly, November.

primarian praɪˈmɛrɪən, *n. Educ.* A pupil in a primary school. *Rare.* — **1883** *Education* July 637 It is . . . important for a primarian to develop a keen perception of relations in respect to the words of his reader.

*__primary,__ *n.*

1. =**primary meeting.**

*a***1861** WINTHROP *Open Air* 147, I accepted the office of Orator of the Day at our primary. **1882** *Nation* 28 Sep. 256/1 The decision of the question, who should be the Republican candidate for the Governorship . . . was in the hands of the politicians who 'fix' and 'run' primaries. **1912** NICHOLSON *Hoosier Chron.* 326 He had personally led the fight in the Fraser County primaries and had vanquished Bassett!

2. Short for next.

The rules under which such primaries are held vary; e.g., in the closed primary the voter must be a member of the party whose ticket he votes; in an open primary such membership is not necessary.

1901 *Outlook* 2 March 477/2 The recent trial of direct primaries in Minneapolis, Minn., has forced every one to recognize that disinterested citizens will attend primaries . . . if they are allowed to vote directly for candidates. **1949** *Lubbock* (Tex.) *Morn. Avalanche* 23 Feb. I. 6/6 In the primary Gettys polled 170 votes to Campbell's 136.

3. direct primary, a preliminary election in which the people vote for the nomination of party candidates; the method or system of such an election. Also attrib.

1900 *Outlook* 8 Sep. 91/2 The important political news last week was all connected . . . with the issue of direct primaries. **1913** *N.Y. Times* 11 Nov. 7/1 The matter of direct primaries as an issue was revived to-day when Gov. Glynn told Senate Leader Wagner . . . that the Legislature ought to pass a genuine direct primaries bill. **1945** *Chi. D. News* 22 March 10/4 We have had so many experiences that justify this statement, notably the direct primary law which was to cure all the evils of the old system.

4. Attrib. in senses **1.** and **2.** with **campaign, convention, law, system.**

1900 *Cong. Rec.* 22 Jan. 1036/2 The nomination of the primary convention settles the whole business. *Ib.* 31 Jan. 1369/1 It was in a Democratic primary campaign. **1902** MEYER *Nominating Systems* 19 The primary . . . is summoned by the local party managing committee or some other prescribed authority . . . under statutory law, where caucus or primary laws have been enacted. **1913** *Forum* July 53 The remedy for all the evils of every known primary system is direct elections.

5. In special combs.: (1) **primary assembly,** =**primary meeting;** (2) **caucus,** =prec.; (3) **court,** a court of first jurisdiction; (4) **day,** the day on which a primary election is held; (5) **ditch,** *W.* in a system of irrigation, a ditch leading directly out of the main canal or water supply; (6) **election,** (*a*) an election at a primary meeting, a caucus election, (*b*) an election by a direct primary, also attrib.; (7) **meeting,** a meeting in a precinct, county, or other election district, at which voters belonging to the same political party take the first steps towards the nomination of party candidates, as by the selection of delegates to a convention, a caucus for choosing candidates.

(1) **1801** *Spirit Farmers' Mus.* 61 The Editor of the Gazette of the United States . . . notices the 'Primary Assemblies' of our towns. **1884** *Cent. Mag.* Nov. 127 The primary assemblies which appoint the delegates to the nominating conventions notoriously embrace but a small part of the voters of a party. — (2) **1821** *Mass. Spy* 11 April (Th.), And this was all the hocus-pocus of a primary caucus. **1902** MEYER *Nominating Systems* 7 A new institution, the 'representative caucus,' [was] composed of delegates selected in primary caucuses held in case of cities in the wards, and in case of counties in the townships. — (3) **1880** *Harper's Mag.* Sep. 647/2 In one of these primary courts in that state [S.C.] . . . a case was on trial. — (4) **1911** *Morrison's Chi. Wkly.* 23 Feb. 9/2 The people of Chicago must go to the polls on primary day and do their choosing wisely. **1948** *Sat. Ev. Post* 11 Sep. 144/4 The tested political machines of her opponents . . . were ready for the practical professional job of getting the voters to the polls on primary day, June twenty-first.

(5) **1890** *Stock Grower & Farmer* 22 Feb. 8/2 The company undertakes to construct the primary ditches from the canals to the highest point on the line of each section. — (6) (*a*) **1835** C. P. BRADLEY *Isaac Hill* 54 The freemen of the State were called upon to give, at their primary elections, an expression of their opinion. **1895** *Cent. Mag.* Oct. 831/1 In a primary election held in Louisville . . . some voters in one district were openly paid as much as seventy-five dollars each. (*b*) **1901** *Amer. Rev. of Reviews* Oct. 465/1 The Minnesota primary election law, passed by the State Legislature during the session of 1899 . . . was extended . . . so as to make the nominations of candidates for all except State offices matters of direct popular choice. **1911** *Okla. Session Laws* 3 Legisl. 231 The secretary of the State Election Board shall . . . certify to the auditor of the state all the necessary expenses incurred in conducting . . . primary elections. — (7) **1829** *Niles' Reg.* XXXVI. 363/2 The battle is in reality fought in the primary meetings, and not on the day appointed by law for the election. **1885** *Cent. Mag.* April 825 Nine out of ten of our wealthy and educated men . . . are really ignorant of the nature of a caucus, or a primary meeting, and never attend either.

As the last term in **run-off, sub primary.**

prime praɪm, *v.* [App. f. the adj.] *tr.* To cut off the best parts of the carcass of (an animal). *Rare.* — **1738** BYRD *Dividing Line* (1901) 199 We only prim'd the Deer, being unwilling to be encumbered with their whole Carcasses.

*__primer,__ *n.* A drink (see quot.). *Colloq.* — **1862** *Harper's Mag.* 312/1 Notwithstanding the refreshment of a dozen on the half shell at Washington Market, and a primer, . . . which primer was simply a gill of Bourbon straight.

primer class. A class of small children studying the primer. — **1902** G. M. MARTIN *Emmy Lou* 3 Neither did she know any of the seventy other little boys and girls making the Primer Class.

*__priming,__ *n.*

1. *fig.* and *allusive.* A small or trivial thing, a small part. *Colloq.* or *slang.*

1833 J. HALL *Harpe's Head* 88 You aint no part of a priming to me. **1854** BULLARD *Now-a-Days* 11 He's wall enuf, but he hain't a primin' to Bob Sykes.

2. *collect.* and *pl.* The tobacco leaves pulled off the growing plants.

1899 M. L. FLOYD *Cultivation of Cigar-Leaf Tobacco* 14 The first priming, which means the first four leaves taken from the stalk, also the last priming, which means the last four or six leaves taken from the top of the stalk, are kept separate. **1904** GLASGOW *Deliverance* 166 The very primings ought to be as good as some top leaves.

*__primitive,__ *a.*

1. primitive area, a large area in a national forest set aside for preserving the natural conditions which it exhibits.

1934 WEBSTER. **1936** *Collier's* 9 May 84/2 When you go into a primitive area you're on your own—just as much as Kit Carson or Jim Bridger or Lewis and Clark were a century or more ago. **1947** *So. Sierran* July 1/1 The boundaries of the San Gorgonio Primitive Area will remain practically undisturbed.

2. Primitive Baptist, a Hard-Shell or Old School Baptist. Also attrib.

1851 *Polly Peablossom* 143 Brethren Crump and Noel were both members of the Primitive Baptist Church. **1901** *Harper's Mag.* Dec. 99, I am ashamed of being a Primitive Baptist! **1948** *Dly. Ardmoreite* (Ardmore, Okla.) 15 July 14/1 The Washita Valley Primitive Baptist association will meet at the Primitive Baptist church here, July 22.

*__prince,__ *n.*

1. A wealthy businessman or industrialist. Cf. **rubber prince.**

1841 BUCKINGHAM *America* III. 427 Capitalists and merchants [of Boston] . . . are here called 'princes.' **1884** *Cent. Mag.* Sep. 796 At a shady end of the veranda, are seen the railroad king, . . . the bonanza mine owner, the Texas rancher, and the Pennsylvania iron prince

2. In combs.: (1) **Prince Albert,** (*a*) a long, double-breasted frock coat for men, in full **Prince Albert coat,** (*b*) a variety of potato, *obs.* [these designations were no doubt given in allusion to Prince Albert, afterwards King Edward VII, who visited the U.S. in 1860]; (2) **Alberted,** *a.* attired in a Prince Albert coat, *rare;* (3) **-'s pine,** (*a*) the pipsissewa *q.v.*, (*b*) (see quot.); (4) **-'s piny,** ?=prec., sense (*a*), *colloq.;* (5) **-'s pride,** (see quot.), *obs.*

(1) (*a*) **1884** RITTENHOUSE *Maud* 270, I ran out and ushered Mr. Lyons in, gotten up to kill in his Prince Albert coat. **1947** *Sat. Ev. Post* 22 Feb. 140/4 He sat with the skirts of his greasy Prince Albert draped across his pendulous abdomen. (*b*) **1867** DE VOE *Market Ass't* 342 Among the best varieties [of potatoes] are the Carters, kidneys (black and white), mercers, buckeyes, peach-blows, Prince Alberts, Western reds [etc.]. — (2) **1906** *Out West* May 431 When 'God made man after His own image,' it was a far-seeing job. As we look at ourselves, indeed—barbered, Prince-Alberted, led-by-the-nose of convention—it is become a little hard to trace the family likeness. — (3)

(*a*) **1817–8** EATON *Botany* (1822) 236 *Chimaphila umbellata*, prince's pine, bitter wintergreen. . . . Both species are tonics and diuretics. **1938** THOMPSON *High Trails* 86 Where woods are thickest prince's pine and pink pyrola are common. (*b*) **1884** SARGENT *Rep. Forests* 201 *Pinus Banksiana*. . . . Gray Pine. Scrub Pine. Prince's Pine. — (**4**) **1858** COOKE in *Atlantic Mo.* March 526/2 [We were] always out in the woods between schools, huntin' checker-berries, and young winter-greens, and prince's piney. **1861** *Harper's Mag.* Oct. 652/1 [She] hung the shelf above the chimney with bundles of . . . sweet fern, sweet-cicely, prince's piny, sassafras root [etc.].

(**5**) **1859** BARTLETT 323 *Pipsissewa*, . . . a popular domestic remedy, much used by the Indians and now of the U.S. Pharmacopœia. Also called Prince's Pride and Wintergreen.

b. In the names of various apples and berries, possibly from a personal surname.

1817 W. COXE *Fruit Trees* 101 Princes Harvest . . . is a very fine apple for stewing when green, and when ripe is a very pleasant eating apple. *Ib.* 109 Fall, or Holland Pippin . . . appears to be the same with Princes large Pippin of New-York. **1862** *Rep. Comm. Patents 1861: Agric.* 198 *Prince's Scarlet Climax*. . . . Bright scarlet, fine flavor, very productive, a splendid market berry.

princess tree. (See quots.)

1933 SMALL *Southeastern Flora* 1186 P. tomentosa . . . Princess-tree. Karri-tree. **1941** R. S. WALKER *Lookout* 64 Among these [trees from China], perhaps, the most conspicuous is the princess tree, or Paulownia, which was introduced into America many years ago. The tree was named for the daughter of Czar Paul I, Anna Paulowna of Russia. **1949** COLLINGWOOD & BRUSH *Knowing Your Trees* 307/1 The name 'princess tree' is also applied to this species.

* **principal,** *a.* and *n.*

1. *n.* The head, or one of the heads, of a primary or secondary school. Cf. **assistant principal.**

1833 in *Cent. Mag.* XXX. 780/1, I am, sir, . . . permitted to be the Principal of the Canterbury, (Conn.) Female Boarding School. **1851** CIST *Cincinnati* 55 Each of the school districts, occupying a School Building, has a Male Principal and a Female Principal. **1902** TOMPKINS *Hist. Rec. Rockland Co., N.Y.* 314 On April 19, 1858, Mr. L. Wilson became principal of the school. **1949** *Lubbock* (Tex.) *Morn. Avalanche* 23 Feb. 1. 10/6 Price was named to the position of principal of the new school to be placed in operation in northeast Lubbock.

2. principal chief, =**head chief.**

1795 *Pittsburgh Gaz.* 5 Dec. 3/1 The Cherokee chiefs, together with the Little Turkey, and the other principal chiefs of the Cherokees accompanied the Governor, to the garrison. **1810** *Amer. Republic* (Frankfort, Ky.) 17 Aug. 2/1 Whilst these measures were progressing a principal Potawatimic chief arrived. **1831** *American* (Harrodsburg, Ky.) 11 March 1/1 Principal Chief authorized to order the apprehension of Intruders, and to deliver them over to the United States, or . . . to expel or punish them or not, as they please. **1949** *Nat. Hist.* May 195/2 He is one of a number of so-called Minor Chiefs of the Blood Tribe, the Principal Chief being Chief Shot-Both-Sides.

3. principal meridian, in U.S. Government surveys, one of the true geographical meridians established under the authority of the Surveyor General of the U.S. for use as a reference line in subdividing public lands in a particular region. Cf. **second principal meridian.**

1831 PECK *Guide* 294 The town is laid out in fractional sections, thirteen or fourteen, in township 5 north, in range 10, west of the third principal meridian. **1909** *Indian Laws & Tr.* III. 417 Range forty-three west of the sixth principal meridian. **1949** *Downers Grove* (Ill.) *Rep.* 31 March 15/6 The Southeast Quarter of Section 6, Township 38 North, Range 11, East of the Third Principle Meridian, . . . in Du Page County, Illinois.

principe ˈprɪnsəˌpe, *n.* [?Sp. *príncipe*, prince.] A kind of cigar. *Obs.*

1838 *Yale Lit. Mag.* III. 268 And I am here . . . ! for the last time at liberty here unquestionably *ex fumo dare lucem*, as my principe might say. *a***1846** *Quarter Race Ky.* 168 After a good substantial supper, I lit a 'York County Principe,' (the like of which sell in these regions [Penna.] at the rate of four for a penny.) **1869** J. R. BROWNE *Adv. Apache Country* 350 Posters . . . displaying to the public eye the prodigious assortments of Regalias, Principes, Cheroots, etc., . . . to be had within the limits of their cigar and tobacco emporium.

* **Principle,** *n.* In Christian Science, a synonym for God. Also **divine Principle.**

1883 M. B. EDDY in *Christian Science Jrnl.* 2 June 2 God is no longer a mystery to the Christian Scientist, but a divine Principle. **1898** S. J. HANNA in *Progress* June 640 God is the Principle of the Universe and man—of all that really is. **1914** *N. Eng. Mag.* April 57 Convinced that this healing was not a miracle, but the operation of divine Principle, she [Mrs. Eddy] searched the Scriptures for the explanation of that Principle.

* **print,** *n.* As the last term in **butter, job, moccasin, pie print.**

* **printer,** *n.* As the last term in **practical, public, senate, state printer.**

printing telegraph. (See quot. 1890.)

1847 *Rep. Comm. Patents 1846* 351, I therefore characterize my invention as the first recording or printing telegraph by means of electro-magnetism. **1860** PRESCOTT *Telegraph* 402 The printing telegraph . . . was proposed in September, 1837. **1890** *Cent.* 4733/3 *Printing-telegraph*, . . . any form of automatic self-recording telegraph, as the 'ticker' of a stock-reporting telegraph.

print shop. A printing office or printery. — **1921** *Amer. Printer* 5 Nov. (*heading*), Visit to an old Oxford printshop. **1948** *Capital-Democrat* (Tishomingo, Okla.) 17 June 2/2 She's wise in the ways of the printshop and won't come by on Thursdays when the folder's going.

* **prison,** *n.* In combs.: (1) **prison lot,** a lot of land on which a prison is built; (2) **pen,** in the Civil War, a pen-like prison. Both *obs.*

(**1**) **1678** *Conn. Hist. Soc. Coll.* VI. 184 A piece of the land in the prisson Lott. **1795** in CHALKLEY *Scotch-Irish Settlement Va.* I. 404 Two orders of the Augusta Court, March, 1788, granting to Hum-[phreys] to build an *Elaboratory* on the prison lot [etc.]. — (**2**) **1865** WHITMAN *Spec. Days* 79 Blackest and loathsomest of all, the dead and living burial-pits, the prison-pens of Andersonville. **1888** GRIGSBY *Smoked Yank* 16 Perhaps some old soldier . . . may let it lead him back to the old camp ground, or prison pen.

As the last term in **log, log house, parish, sheriff's, state prison.**

prisoner's dance. Among Indians, a dance celebrating the capture of a prisoner or prisoners. *Obs.* — **1791** J. LONG *Voyages* 35 The dances among the Indians [include] . . . 7. The prisoner's dance.

prissy ˈprɪsɪ, *a.* [?f. *prim* and *sissy*.] Prim, sissified. *Colloq.* — **1931** *K.C. Times* 30 Dec. 16 When we were a small boy we thought there couldn't be anything more aggravating than a prissy little girl. **1949** *Chi. Tribune* 15 Dec. 24/5 Vulgar people cry 'Hooray!' But prissy persons squawk.

* **private,** *a.* and *n.*

1. (See quot. 1851.) *College slang. Obs.* Cf. * **public,** *a.* and *n.* **2.**

1848 *Oration before H[arvard] L[odge] I.O.O.F.* (Hall), Reckon on the fingers of your mind the reprimands, deductions, parietals, and privates in store for you. **1851** HALL *College Words* 245 At Harvard College, one of the milder punishments is what is called *private admonition*, by which a deduction of thirty-two marks is made from the rank of the offender. . . . Often abbreviated into *private*.

2. In combs.: (1) **private bill(s) day,** (see quot. 1914); (2) **boardinghouse,** =**private entertainment,** *obs.*; (3) **car,** a railroad car fitted up for occupancy by a single person or party, also attrib.; (4) **entertainment,** a private home where travelers were taken in and lodged for pay, so called to avoid the tax on inns and public houses, *obs.*, cf. * **home 1;** (5) **land claim,** (*a*) a claim of a private individual to land allegedly subject to the federal land laws, (*b*) *Committee on Private Land Claims*, a Congressional committee authorized to investigate such claims; (6) **pension bill,** see **pension bill;** (7) **post office,** see **post office 3. b.**

(**1**) **1881** *Harper's Mag.* March 552/1 At almost any moment except in the 'morning hour' and on 'private bill day,' an exciting and masterly discussion may begin. **1914** *Cyclo. Amer. Govt.* III. 65/2 Private-bills day in the federal House of Representatives is the day regularly set apart for the consideration of private business—especially of claims against the government, and pension bills. This day is Friday in every week, but may be devoted to other business by a majority vote of the House. — (**2**) **1841** BUCKINGHAM *America* I. 21 We took up our quarters [in N.Y. City] at the adjoining house, which was what is called a private boarding-house. — (**3**) **1832** *Amer. R.R. Jrnl.* I. 495/3 Parties of twenty or more persons can be accommodated . . . with a private car. **1917** SINCLAIR *King Coal* 258 He took others of his private-car friends and introduced them to his North Valley friends. — (**4**) **1788** SCHÖPF *Reise* II. 53 Wir brachten eine Nacht auf einer Plantage [in Va.] zu, wo man nach der hiesigen Gewohnheit, und unter dem Titel von Private Entertainment, Reisende gegen Bezahlung beherberget, ohne Wirthshaus zu halten. **1839** C. A. MURRAY *Travels* I. 95 The owners and occupants of land (being generally two or three miles apart) are most of them tavern-keepers, or, as it is there [in western Va.] termed, they keep 'private entertainment.' **1897** *Outing* XXX. 65/2 This time we had come up from Richmond through the Peninsula, . . . sometimes taking pot-luck at typical 'private entertainments.'

(**5**) (*a*) **1891** *Statutes at Large* XXVI. 854 An act to establish a court of private land claims, and to provide for the settlement of private land claims in certain States and Territories. (*b*) **1868** *N.Y. Herald* 2 July 3/4 Mr. Orth . . . from the Committee on Private Land Claims, reported the Senate bill. **1880** *Cimarron News & Press* 11 March 1/7 The McGarraghan claim is once more being argued before the committee on private land claims.

As the last term in **buck, high private.**

***privateer,** *n.* A free-lance soldier. *Obs.* — **1676** I. MATHER *K. Philip's War* (1862) 58 Hearing many profane oaths among some of our Souldiers (namely those Privateers, who were also Volunteers). **1677** HUBBARD *Narrative* I. 18 Our Horseman with the whole Body of the Privateers ... ran violently down upon them over the said Bridg.

privateersman ˌpraɪvəˈtɪrzmən, *n.* An officer or seaman of a privateer. Also transf. *Obs.*

1779 *Narragansett Hist. Reg.* I. 40 The privateersmen took the fish boats. **1862** MOORE *Rebellion Rec.* V. II. 184, I was to endeavor to effect the release of our officers held as hostages by the rebels, by delivering their privateersmen within their lines on parole. **1885** *Cent. Mag.* Nov. 65/1 In and out among the craft of heavier burden shuffled the small, tough bronchos. Their riders ... were the doughty privateers-men, returning with a convoy of pack-animals.

***privet,** *n.* "In the southern United States, a small oleaceous tree of wet grounds, *Forestiera acuminata*" (*Cent.*). — **1884** SARGENT *Rep. Forests* 112 *Forestiera acuminata*.... Privet.... Borders of swamps and streams, in low, wet soil.

* **privilege,** *n.*

1. The land occupied by one in exercising his rights to a particular property. Also in place-names. *Obs.*

1700 *Md. Hist. Mag.* XX. 287 Benjors Priviledge. **1882** GODFREY *Nantucket* 92 Every fractional part of a common or privilege was noted.

2. = **water privilege.** Cf. **mill privilege.**

[**1827** BEAUFOY *Tour* 71 It owes its rapid increase and importance to ... the great water power—or, as the inhabitants term it, 'privilege of water'—of the river which passes through it.] **1835** *Knickerb.* April 272 There was also a great business done at a tilt-hammer forge, over a fine 'privilege,' where 'the sweet waters meet.' **1865** *Maine Bd. Agric. Rep.* X. 138 Bond Brook ... furnishes an excellent privilege for considerable machinery.

3. *Stock market.* (See quot 1890.)

1870 MEDBERY *Men Wall St.* 101 'Privileges' approach very nearly to the nature of a bet. Privileges are either *puts* or *calls.* **1890** *Cent.* 4738/3 *Privilege*, ... a speculative contract covering a 'put' or a 'call,' or both a put and a call (that is, a 'straddle').

4. *privilege of the floor*, (see quot. 1859).

1859 MACKAY *Tour* II. 10 The speakers of both the upper and lower house [in Va.] did me the honour of admitting me to what is called 'the privilege of the floor.' I had thus an opportunity of listening to the debates, and of observing the easy, decorous, and expeditious manner in which the public business is transacted. **1902** MARK TWAIN *Does the Race of Man Love a Lord?* 443 (R.), The ex-Congressman clings piteously to the one little shred that is left of his departed distinction—the 'privilege of the floor.'

As the last term in **hotel, hydraulic, mill, water, watering privilege.** Also *pl.*, **wintering privileges.**

* **prize,** *v. S. tr.* To compress (cured tobacco) into a hogshead or other container.

1724 JONES *Virginia* 40 [They] by Degrees *prize* or press it with proper Engines into great Hogsheads. **1863** *Ill. Agric. Soc. Trans.* V. 669 Tobacco of this description should be ... prized lightly in the casks so as to admit of a free and open leaf. **1902** *Farmers' Bul.* No. 60, 17 The leaves ... are tied into hands and bulked down for a short time, after which they are 'prized' into hogsheads.

Hence * **prizing,** *n. Obs.*

1793 *Md. Hist. Mag.* VI. 214 Tobacco underwent a repacking and priseing preparatory to shipping. **1820** *Amer. Farmer* I. 395 We must defer to another number some remarks on *prizing*, and the manufacturing of chewing tobacco. **1864** *Maine Agric. Soc. Returns 1863* 164 In prizing, the different qualities should not be mixed.

* **pro-,** *prefix.* Used in expressions alluding to attitudes in or toward the North and the South engendered by the slavery issue, as **pro-rebel, slave, slaver, slaverite, southern.** Cf. **pro-slavery.**

1856 in L. W. SPRING *Kansas* (1885) 48, I tell you I'm pro-slave. **1858** *N.Y. Tribune* 29 Dec. 6/4 The Pro-Slavers all went home without any action. **1866** F. KIRKLAND *Bk. Anecdotes* 65/1 Some one was discussing the character of a pro-Southern clergyman—a time-serving Washington domine. **1868** *Ore. State Jrnl.* 31 Oct. 1/3 The pro-rebel Democracy have chimed in. **1923** COBB *Kansas* 15 You visit the historic place ... where old John Brown turned right around and eliminated a few pro-slaverites.

***probabilities,** *n. pl.* Weather forecasts. Cf. **Old Probabilities.** — **1886** *Pop. Sci. Mo.* Aug. 546 The official publications embrace the 'probabilities' and the so-called 'weather-maps.'

* **probate,** *n.* In combs.: (1) **probate court,** a court having jurisdiction of probate and administration; (2) **judge,** the judge who presides over a probate court, cf. *Judge of probate;* (3) **of wills,** an officer who probates wills.

(1) **1726** *Mass. H.S. Coll.* 6 Ser. V. 426, I never gave any inventory into the Probate Court at Boston. **1864** *Wkly. New Mexican* 17 June 2/2 This certificate ... he must deliver to the clerk of the Probate Court for the county in which the marriage was celebrated. **1949** *N.O. Times-Picayune Mag.* 25 Dec. 12/3 Clerk Inge of the probate court of Adams county, Miss., knew nothing of the 'white ant' back in 1849. — (2) *c***1844** *Indiana Mag. Hist.* XXII. 379 In the summer of 1823 the offic[e] of Probate Judge became vacant. **1946** *Democrat* 9 May 1/5, I wish to thank everyone who so loyally supported me in the race for Probate Judge. — (3) **1863** J. PARTON *Butler in New Orleans* (1864) 213 Major Strong ... found at Biloxi a probate of wills, who was also a justice of the peace, to whom he committed the child.

* **probation,** *n.*

1. *Law.* A system of control and tutelage under court supervision provided in some cases for convicted defendants, usu. young persons or first offenders in misdemeanor cases, who are not imprisoned but released on suspended sentences. Also the status of such a defendant.

1878 *Mass. Acts & Resolves* 147 The mayor of the city of Boston shall appoint, annually ... a suitable person ... to recommend ... the placing on probation of such persons as may reasonably be expected to be reformed without punishment. **1914** *Cyclo. Amer. Govt.* III. 63/1 Although adult probation has made great progress, it has not kept pace with juvenile probation. **1949** *Time* 5 Dec. 26/2 They asked Washington's District Court to reduce their sentences and let them go free on probation.

attrib. **1908** (*title*), First Report of the State Probation Commission [of N.Y.]. **1908** *N.Y. State Probation Comm. Rep. 1907* 10 Hon. Dennis McCarthy ... [was appointed] a member of the State Probation Commission.

b. The status of a student who has been given a limited time within which to improve his conduct or scholastic standing or be dismissed, usu. *to put on probation.*

1897 FLANDRAU *Harvard Episodes* 235 The next day the Office put Billy 'on probation.' **1948** *Chi. Maroon* 7 May 4/4 Zarichny had then been placed on 'stricter probation' ... for 'inviting students to his room for discussion of political ideologies.'

Also transf. and attrib.

1930 *Chi. D. Maroon* 7 Oct. 4/4 Seven Ohio State university fraternities have been on the probation list of Dean Joseph A. Park since June 1. **1949** *Chi. Tribune* 16 Dec. 1/2 The university placed the Sigma Phi Epsilon chapter here, and all of its individual members, on probation for the remainder of the academic year.

2. probation officer, an officer of a municipal criminal court appointed to assist in the exercise of its probationary functions.

1880 *Mass. Acts. & Resolves* 87 The aldermen of any city, except the city of Boston, ... may establish the office of probation officer. **1908** *Charities* 26 Sep. 731/2 Boys on probation or parole might reside there under the immediate supervision of a probation or parole officer. **1949** *St. Paul Pioneer Press* 19 June 9/1 Probation officers are seeking other 'big brothers' to carry on the good work during the summer.

* **probationer,** *n.*

1. One who has joined a church on a probationary basis and is not yet a full member.

1856 CARTWRIGHT *Autobiog.* 39 There were in the entire bounds of the Western Conference, of members, probationers, colored and all, two thousand, four hundred and eighty-four. **1867** DIXON *New Amer.* II. 132 The [Shaker] family at North House contains two orders of members (1) Probationers, (2) Covenanters. **1871** EGGLESTON *Duffels* 169, I believe he became a 'probationer,' but his creed was never quite settled enough for him to accept 'full membership.'

2. A convicted delinquent responsible to the convicting court and under the supervision of a probation officer.

1907 in *N.Y. State Probation Comm. Rep.* (1908) 78 Whenever a probationer is reported to the judge as having violated the terms of his probation the judge uses his discretion as to the subsequent disposition of the case. **1908** *Charities* 26 Sep. 731/2 Such houses already exist in some cities, for probationers. **1949** *N.O. Times-Picayune Mag.* 13 Nov. 23/4 Usually probationers are first offenders with good, clean records behind them.

probationist proˈbeʃənɪst, *n.* **1.** A candidate for church membership. **2.** One who believes in the doctrine of future probation. — (1) **1885** *Congregationalist* (*Cent.*), What portion of the probationists uniting with the M[ethodist] E[piscopal] church become full members? — (2) **1898** *Advance* 5 May 601/1, I am satisfied the probationists among us are an extremely small minority.

* **probe,** *n.* An investigation, usu. by a legislative body, in an effort to discover evidences of law violation.

1903 *Christendom* 9 May 151/1 Few words are commoner in newspaper headlines than 'probe,' which is newspaper English for an investigation of alleged abuses. **1922** *Dly. Press* (Ardmore, Okla.) 3 May 1/5 Launch Probe to Bare War Frauds: Harding Takes Hand. **1948** *Chelsea* (Mass.) *Rec.* 30 Nov. 8/7 A number of attorneys were disbarred as an outgrowth of that probe.

* **probe,** *v. tr.* To carry out or conduct an investigation, esp. into the management of (an organization). Also absol.

1884 *N.Y. Wkly. Tribune* 12 March 1/2 The Senate Committee did not probe the Public Works Department in vain. **1922** *Dly. Press* (Ardmore, Okla.) 2 May 1/7 To Probe Abduction of Pastor. **1948** *Time* 11 Oct. 64/2 The St. Louis *Post-Dispatch* admonishes cubs, with good reason, that *probe* is to be 'generally reserved for surgeons,' and is not a synonym for *investigate.*

Hence **prober,** *n.*

1949 *Chi. Tribune* 23 Sep. 23/1 (*heading*), Prober Blames High Food Cost On Middleman.

proc prɑk, *n.* Short for proclamation money *q.v. Obs.*

1755 J. Murray *Letters* (1901) 78 The Money I get since the Presidents Currency came out is all proc. **1806** Weems *Letters* II. 335 Can I remit silver, or North Carolina Proc? **1860** Mordecai *Va.* 279 This money was called *proc.* (i.e., proclamation money,) and was issued on bits of thick paper, about the size of a playing card, and for various sums, from sixpence up to forty shillings.

b. Also **proc money.** *Obs.*

1773 *Cape Fear* (N.C.) *Mercury* 29 Dec. 1/2 A reward of 100£ currency or 25£ proc money will be paid on a conviction of the offenders, and delivery of the slaves to John Ancrum Esq. **1896** H. White *Money & Banking* 16 Six shillings was considered by the home government a fair average of the colonial valuations of the Spanish dollar. This valuation came to be known by the term proclamation money, or proc. money.

* **process,** *n.* **1.** *W. attrib.* Designating persons having, or professing to have, superior and secret methods for extracting precious metal from ore. *Obs.* **2. process kettle,** a kettle used in processing meats, vegetables, etc., for preserving them.

(1) **1876** Raymond *8th Rep. Mines* 3 The process-owner is [interested], because it may enlarge the field of his operations. **1877** W. Wright *Big Bonanza* 139 'Process-peddlers,' with little vials of chemicals in their vest pockets, went from mill to mill to show what they could do and would do, provided they received from $5,000 to $20,000 for their secret. — (2) **1883** *Nat. Museum Bul.* No. 27, 222 The 'process kettle' or 'tub' . . . is then closed . . . and the oysters again steamed. **1892** *York County Hist. Rev.* 59/2 [They] make a specialty of . . . tools of every description, pump, 'process kettle' for canners [etc.].

As the last term in **patio, sluice, trustee, Washoe process.**

* **processioner,** *n. S.* One appointed to examine and renew the landmarks of a precinct or area (see also quot. 1890).

1731 *Bristol* (Va.) *Vestry Bk.* 59 Order'd that George Tucker be Prosessioner in the Stead of Robert Tucker jun[io]r who is Lame and cannott Officiate as prosessioner. **1795** in Summers *Ann. S.W. Va.* 463 The said Processioners to examine their business the first day of February next. **1890** *Cent.* 4747/2 *Processioner,* a county officer in North Carolina and Tennessee charged with the duty of surveying lands at the request of an occupant claiming to be owner.

prock prɑk, *n.* [Of fanciful origin.] A fabulous quadruped having two short legs opposite two long ones, so as to be able to browse on mountain sides. *Obs.* Cf. **sidehill gouger.** — **1840** *N.O. Picayune* 8 Sep. 2/1 Koch, the proprietor [of a St. Louis Museum], . . . first discovered the prock. **1896** *Advance* 4 June 823/1 That fabulous 'prock,' an animal whose two right legs were only half the length of the left legs.

* **proclamation,** *n.* **1.** Short for proclamation money, *q.v.* as a main entry. *Obs.* **2.** *Proclamation of Emancipation,* = **Emancipation Proclamation.**

(1) **1751** *N.J. Archives* XIX. 110 Lands pay already 2s. 6d. Proclamation, for every 100 Acres. — (2) **1862** Lincoln in Logan *Great Conspiracy* 435 What good would a Proclamation of Emancipation from me do? **1900** *Cong. Rec.* 15 Jan. 806/2 [Lincoln's] greatest title is that of the Emancipator, earned by issuing . . . the proclamation of emancipation.

As the last term in **amnesty, Buncombe proclamation.**

Proclamation money. Colonial money valued according to a standard for use in American colonies prescribed by Queen Anne in a proclamation in 1704, in which the Spanish dollar of 17½ dwt. was rated at six shillings. Also a form of paper currency issued in some of the states during or soon after the Revolutionary War. *Obs.* or *hist.*

1716 *N.J. Archives* 1 Ser. IV. 271 Annuall payment . . . must not be paid in bills but in current silver money of the easterne divesion, or proclamation money. **1775** in *Amer. Sp.* XX. (1945) 274 Resolution to collect Proclamation money to meet expenses incurred by delegates to the Continental Congress. **1778** *N.C. State Rec.* XIII. 375 According to law valued said negro James at eighty pounds Procklamation Money. **1860** [see **proc**]. **1942** Rawson *N.H. Borns a Town* 29 Proclamation money was to be paid annually.

proctor's freshman, see ***freshman,** *n.* **1.**

***prod,** *n. On the prod,* angry, on a rampage. *Colloq.* — **1903** A. Adams *Log Cowboy* ix, When he [a man] came near enough to us, we could see that he was angry and on the prod. *Ib.* xi, Several steers showed fight, and when released went on the prod for the first thing in sight. **1947** DeVoto *Across Wide Missouri* 26 Not only the Arikaras but the Blackfeet were on the prod.

* **produce,** *n.* In combs.: (1) **produce merchant,** a merchant who deals in country produce *q.v.;* (2) **store,** (see quot.).

(1) **1841** Cist *Cincinnati* (*advt.*), Produce, Forwarding, and Commission Merchants. **1870** H. M. Smith *20 Years Wall St.* 398 The oysterbeds yield a supply as certainly as the farm of the produce merchant. **1944** Clark *Pills* 23 With the capital from the sale of cotton he bought more cotton, chickens, eggs, hides and everything else that could possibly be sold to produce merchants in Mobile. — (2) **1865** Sala *Diary* II. 47 For rent, a 'Produce' store. 'Produce' means greengrocery, just as 'Feed' means corn-chandlery.

***producer,** *n.* One who has general charge of the production of motion pictures. Cf. ***angel,** *n.* **2.** — **1918** V. O. Freeburg *Photoplay Making* 272 The producer read the scenario and handed it back with the remark that it was very well written. **1948** *Good Housekeeping* Jan. 44, I also had fallen arches from tramping to producers' offices, chilblains from the reception I got there.

prof prɑf, *n.* (Also *cap.*) An abbreviation of professor, orig. used by students. *Slang.*

1838 *Yale Lit. Mag.* III. 144 For Proffs and Tutors too, Who steer our big canoe, Prepare their lays. **1932** *New Yorker* 14 May 19/2 Well, and what are you doing, Prof? **1950** *Chi. Tribune* 3 Jan. IV. 1/2 A comely co-ed Gets by . . . 'Cause her profs believe in 'passing fancies.'

professional school. A school in which students are prepared for a profession. — **1881** *Harper's Mag.* March 628/1 Degrees shall yet be lawful certificates of proficiency to be accepted at their 'face value' by professional schools. **1914** *Cyclo. Amer. Govt.* III. 635/2 The Division of Higher Education [of the Bureau of Educ.] has charge of the statistics . . . regarding universities, colleges, technological schools, normal schools, and professional schools.

* **professor,** *n.*

1. In jocular or grandiose use, applied to a person assumed or claiming to be learned, experienced, or skilled in some vocation or profession (see quots.).

1774 in Hildeburn *Cent. of Printing* II. 182 Catalogue of New and Old Books, to be sold by Auction, by Robert Pell, Bookseller, and Professor Book-Auctioneering. **1859** Bartlett 343 Professor. . . . The application of the word to dancing-masters, conjurers, banjoplayers, etc., has been called an Americanism. **1870** Macrae *Americans* II. 334 The title of 'Professor' is often absurdly employed in the States. Tailors are sometimes called professors. I observed that a barber in Chicago was advertising himself as a professor of haircutting. A corn-cutter called himself a professor of corns and bunions. Another man with a patent called himself a professor of soap. **1944** Ross *Westward* 130 The occupant of the lowest rung of the social ladder was the piano-player, known always as 'the professor.'

2. *Professor of Dust and Ashes,* (see quot. 1851). *Obs.*

1847 Wells & Davis *Sk. Williams Coll.* 77 Was interrupted a moment just now, by the entrance of Mr. C——, the gentleman who makes the beds, sweeps, takes up the ashes, and supports the dignity of the title, 'Professor of dust and ashes.' **1851** Hall *College Words* 247 *Professor of Dust and Ashes,* a title sometimes jocosely given by students to the person who has the care of their rooms.

As the last term in **alumni, assistant, career, full, head professor.**

* **progressive,** *a.* and *n.*

1. A member of a political group holding views which they regard as more enlightened and advanced than those of their opponents, esp. (*cap.*) a member of a political party organized in 1912 by the supporters, chiefly Republicans, of Theodore Roosevelt, and favoring, among other things, direct primaries and female suffrage.

1846 *Quincy* (Ill.) *Whig* 19 March 2/4 Thereupon a series of questions and tart replies took place, which shows that the most amiable feelings do not exist among the 'progressives' at Washington. **1914** *Cyclo. Amer. Govt.* III. 76/2 The defeat of their candidate in the Convention, the progressives attributed to fraudulent decisions of the Republican National Committee. **1948** *Time* 12 Jan. 13/1 The Progressives temporarily displaced the Democrats as the second party in eleven Western states.

Also **Progressive movement, party, Republican, ticket.**

1914 *Cyclo. Amer. Govt.* III. 76/1 Formation of the Progressive Party.—Among the leading, though unofficial, heads of the progressive movement, was Theodore Roosevelt. **1931** *Army & Navy Jrnl.* 26 Dec. 385/4 Sponsorship of this movement by Senator Lafollette, a Progressive Republican, places the measure in a particularly strategic position. **1948** *Chi. Tribune* 4 Jan. I. 4/3 William Howard Taft, a Republican, was President, but incurred the enmity of his predecessor, Theodore Roosevelt, who launched the Bull Moose or Progressive movement. *Ib.*, The elder LaFollette got the 13 electoral votes of his home state of Wisconsin when he ran for President on the Progressive ticket in 1924.

2. Progressive Quakers, (see quot. 1804 and cf. **Hicksite**).

1855 *N.Y. Wkly. Tribune* 28 April 4/6 The proverbial hospitality of the Progressive Quakers of Chester County is proffered to strangers who may wish to attend these meetings. **1904** *Old Dartmouth Hist. Coll.* No. 8, 16/2 These Hicksites are called Progressive Quakers.

Also **Progressive Friends.** *Obs.*

1855 *N.Y. Wkly. Tribune* 28 April 4/6 The Pennsylvania Yearly Meeting of Progressive Friends . . . is to convene near Kennett-square, Chester Co., on Sunday, May 20. *Ib.* 9 June 3/5 The Third Yearly Meeting of the religious society of Progressive Friends adjourned *sine die* last evening.

* **Progressivism,** *n.* The political philosophy of the Progressive party, esp. of the Wisconsin portion of it led by Robert M. LaFollette, an independent candidate for the Presidency in 1924.

1923 *Collier's* 25 Aug. 24 We are in for another wave of progressivism or populism or greenbackery—or whatever you call it. **1944** *Newsweek* 24 July 46/2 His progressivism dates back to his Western managership of Teddy Roosevelt's Bull Moose campaign. **1949** *Southwest Rev.* Spring 148/1 The strongest third party movement in recent American history, LaFollette Progressivism, was native to Wisconsin.

* **prohibition,** *n.*

1. The prohibiting by law of the manufacture and sale of spirituous liquors for general use, now often with reference to national prohibition (1920–33) under the Volstead Act. Cf. **anti-prohibition.**

1851 *Amer. Temp. Union. Ann. Rep.* 27 The State of Vermont has struggled arduously to arrive at the summit level of entire prohibition. **1925** Bryan *Memoirs* 186 His views on the initiative and referendum and prohibition had not altered. **1949** *Newsweek* 21 Nov. 28/1 He was one of the biggest mobsters that Prohibition spawned.

2. In combs.: (1) **prohibition agent,** a federal officer charged with the enforcement of the Volstead Act; (2) **amendment,** (*a*) an amendment to a state constitution prohibiting the manufacture and sale of spirituous liquors for common use, (*b*) the Eighteenth Amendment (1919) to the Constitution of the U.S., prohibiting the manufacture, sale, and transportation of spirituous liquors, except for certain specified purposes; (3) **candidate,** a candidate for political office indorsed or sponsored by the Prohibition party; (4) **law,** a law prohibiting the manufacture and sale of intoxicating liquors for general use; (5) **party,** a political party having as its fundamental principle opposition to the manufacture and sale of intoxicating liquors; (6) **state,** a state in which the sale of liquor for general use is prohibited.

(1) **1929** *Chi. Tribune* 12 Feb. 5/5 Prohibition agents were not as gentle as they might have been when they rushed about searching the guests. **1946** *Chi. D. News* 21 Nov. 16/1 In the twenties the great white father often showed up in the guise of a prohibition agent. — (2) (*a*) **1883** *Harper's Mag.* Dec. 162/1 The prohibition amendment was defeated [in Ohio]. **1886** *Ib.* June 157/1 The Prohibition amendment was carried [in R.I.] by a decisive majority. (*b*) **1917** *Nation* 9 Aug. 138/2 Some wild things are said about last week's vote in the Senate in favor of a prohibition amendment of the Constitution. **1949** *Chi. Tribune* 20 Dec. 20/3 The connection of 'McCoy' with liquor goes back much earlier than the prohibition amendment. — (3) **1877** *Harper's Mag.* Dec. 146/1 The monograph of Hon. Robert C. Pitman, . . . Prohibition candidate for Governor of [Mass.] . . . possesses a value to the student of sociology. **1909** G. F. Parker *G. Cleveland* 71 In addition, something over 300,000 votes had been cast for the Prohibition and the Greenback candidates. — (4) **1884** *N.Y. Wkly. Tribune* 20 Aug. 7/1 The platform . . . means specifically that the prohibition law shall be enforced. **1949** *Dly. Oklahoman* (Okla. City) 13 Feb. D. 2/2 A petition will be circulated calling for repeal of the state's liquor prohibition law.

(5) 1869 in D. L. Colvin *Prohibition in U.S.* 73 We adopt the name of the National Prohibition Party, as expressive of our primary object. **1948** *Time* 12 Jan. 13/1 The Prohibition Party has nominated a candidate for President ever since its formation in 1869. — (6) **1892** *Outing* Dec. 209/1 They have no beer here: North and South Dakota are prohibition states. **1949** *Time* 10 Oct. 27/3 The state's church-going United Drys . . . were fiercely proud of living in a prohibition state.

Also *prohibition convention, enforcement, friend, meeting, news, official, paper, policy, system,* etc.

* **prohibitionist,** *n.* One who favors the legislative prohibition of the manufacture and sale of spirituous liquors, a member of the Prohibition party. Also attrib. Cf. **anti-prohibitionist.**

1854 (*title*), The Prohibitionist [a monthly journal in the state of New York]. **1892** W. S. Walsh *Lit. Curiosities* 922 Since 1872 the Prohibitionists have entered the field of national politics. **1946** *Life* 27 May 80 (*caption*), Prohibitionist drives are aimed at drying up individual states through local option and referendums.

* **prohibitory,** *a.* In combs.: (1) **prohibitory law,** = **prohibition law,** in full **prohibitory liquor law;** (2) **party,** = **Prohibition party.**

(1) **1854** *La Crosse Democrat* 11 April 2/2 Gov. Seymore, of New York, vetoes the Prohibitory Liquor Law. **1889** P. Butler *Recollections* 25 Those who have watched the progress of the temperance reform in Iowa have noticed that, while the prohibitory law is enforced almost throughout the State [of Iowa], there are yet exceptions. — (2) **1882** Cooper *Amer. Pol.* I. 196 The Prohibitory Party, however, never accomplished anything by separate political action.

* **project,** *v. S. intr.* To experiment, trifle, play tricks with; to saunter, meander, loiter *around.* Also **projecting,** *n. Colloq.*

1820 J. Hall *Lett. from West* 290 A man who goes into the woods . . . has a . . . great deal of *projecking* to do, as well as hard work. **1887** *Courier-Journal* 1 Feb. 1/1 Mr. Oakley is a dangerous man to 'projec' with. **1906** Lynde *Quickening* 135 Don't you know you oughtn't to go projecting around in the woods all alone?

prom prɑm, *n.* = * **promenade 2.** Also attrib. *Colloq.* Cf. **junior, senior prom.**

1894 *Outing* XXIV. 68/2 For two days . . . in January the room is crowded with 'Prom' girls and their escorts. **1912** Nicholson *Hoosier Chron.* 187, I went up there once to see a girl I had met at a Prom. **1947** *Downtown Shopping News* (Chi.) 20 Jan. 15/1 I'm picking my 'corsage' for my prom date! **1949** *Harvard Alumni Bul.* 9 July 778/1 The spread became a senior class affair with all the disadvantages of a 'prom.'

* **promenade,** *n.*

1. = **promenade deck.**

1826 McKenny *Tour to Lakes* (1827) 27 Then comes, and over all, *the grand promenade*, with an awning, when the sun or rain requires it, over the whole. **1845** *Knickerb.* XXV. 61 On the upper deck the engineers and sailors, ladies, emigrants and gentlemen, sat side by side upon the single seat which ran all round the promenade. **1873** Howells *Chance Acquaintance* i, On the forward promenade of the Saguenay boat . . . Miss Kitty Ellison sat.

2. A ball or dance given by college students, usu. of a particular class, orig. **promenade concert.** Cf. **junior prom.**

1864 *Harper's Mag.* Sep. 501/1 The Promenade concert . . . has lately become a signal feature of the week. **1871** Bagg *At Yale* 664 The Junior Promenade Concert is not a very ancient affair. **1905** *N.Y. Herald* 22 Jan. 10 Yale men assumed the rôle of host . . . for the vanguard of the fair guests invited to the Junior Promenade, the gayest event of the college year.

3. promenade deck, an upper deck of a vessel where passengers are accustomed to promenade.

1829 *Amer. Traveller* 14 Sep. (Ernst), The engraving above exhibits what may emphatically be called a Land Barge . . . with a Cabin, Births, etc. below . . . [with] a promenade deck, awning, seats, etc. above. **1911** Vance *Cynthia* 148 They paused by the after rail of the promenade deck.

Promethea prəˈmiθɪə, *n.* [L. *Promēthea*, fem. of *Prometheus.*] **1.** Short for next. **2. Promethea moth,** the Prometheus moth.

(1) **1890** *Cent.* 4767/1 prometheus. . . . Also *promethea, promethia.* **1912** *Country Life* 15 June 32/2 Cynthia and Promethea have smaller leaf-encased cocoons. **1949** *Nat. Hist.* Feb. 80/2 The Cecropia and Promethea have their wings wrapped around their bodies and bear little resemblance to the beautiful insects they will be an hour later. — (2) **1901** DICKERSON *Moths & Butterflies* 119 Late in fall and winter we may find brown cocoons containing the chrysalides of the Promethea moth swinging from the branches of the wild cherry, the sassafras, . . . and the ash. **1949** *Amer. Photography* March 166/2, I have made the same type of series showing the life history of the polyphemus and promethea moths.

***Prometheus,** *n.* **1.** A name given by Coues to the Blackburnian warbler *q.v.*, in allusion to the flame color of its breast. **2.** (See quot. 1890.)

(1) **1884** COUES *Key N. Amer. Birds* (ed. 2) 302 *D[endrœca blackburniae]* . . . Blackburn's Warbler. Prometheus. . . . Chin, throat, and fore breast, intense orange or flame-color. — (2) [**1775** CRAMER *Papillons Exotiques des Trois Parties du Monde.* I. 118/1 *Promothea.*] **1890** *Cent.* 4767/1 prometheus. . . . The popular name and also the technical specific name of a large silk-spinning moth, *Attacus prometheus*, or *Telea* or *Callosamia promethea.*

***promote,** *v.* **1.** *Educ. tr.* To advance (a pupil) from one class or grade to another. **2.** To further the sale of (an article) by advertising, to encourage the use of (something).

(1) **1876** *Scribner's Mo.* Feb. 584/1 Their mother holds them back; will not let them be 'promoted,' or dragged through at high-pressure speed from class to class. **1902** *Forum* June 471 Because of the manner of grading and promoting, the graded school tends to keep all the children of each grade in intellectual lock-step. — (2) **1930** *Publishers' Wkly.* 31 May 2732/2 The books all to be individualized in appearance and fully promoted. **1949** *Nat. Bottlers' Gaz.* Oct. 77/1 Alley owners have been active in promoting the use of their lanes by youngsters and women during the morning and afternoon period.

***promotion,** *n.* Encouraging the sale of an article by advertising.

1926 *Amer. Mercury* Feb. 165/2 One plastic surgeon . . . has for several years employed a publicity representative who is charged with . . . the promotion of publicity. **1928** *Publishers' Wkly.* 26 May 2169 Promotion cannot be done without waste. . . . But the idea back of the new mergers is the idea of outlets, of promotion, of selling more goods. **1950** *Calif. Citrograph* Jan. 91/2, I spent the next 12 years in food and produce sale promotion and advertising.

***prong,** *n.*

1. A branch or fork of a stream, swamp, road, etc. *Colloq.*

1725 in *Amer. Sp.* XV. 300 To a Gum on the south side of the north prong of the Spring Swamp. **1784** WASHINGTON *Diaries* II. 311 Carpenters Creek, a branch of Jackson's, which is the principal prong of James River. **1929** DOBIE *Vaquero* 273 It is cut through by many canyons, or prongs. **1945** *Chi. Tribune* 13 May VII. 1/1 One is the south prong of Jack's Fork, the other is a fussy protesting creek.

2. In combs.: (1) **prongbuck,** a male pronghorned antelope; (2) **doe,** the female of the pronghorned antelope; (3) **horn,** short for next; (4) **horn(ed) antelope,** a deerlike ruminant, *Antilocapra americana*, found on the western prairies and popularly called an antelope.

(1) **1834** *Penny Cyclo.* II. 71/2 The prongbuck inhabits all the western parts of North America from the 53° of north latitude to the plains of Mexico and California. — (2) **1890** *Cent.* 4771/1 The prongdoe regularly drops twins. — (3) **1826** GODMAN *Amer. Nat. Hist.* II. 324 The prong-horn . . . is usually called a goat by the Canadians. **1917** *Mammals of Amer.* 35/1 The American Pronghorn, known also as the 'Prongbuck,' 'Pronghorned Antelope,' or, simply, 'Antelope,' has the distinction of being the sole representative of a family. **1946** *Mazama* Dec. 33/2 Antelope or pronghorn have the distinction of being the sole representative of a family classification. — (4) *a***1815** ORD *N. Amer. Zoology* (1894) 308 The Prong-Horned Antelope is found in great numbers on the plains and the high-lands of the Missouri. **1826** GODMAN *Amer. Nat. Hist.* II. 131 He describes the . . . Prong-horn Antelope. **1948** *Nat. Hist.* Dec. 436/2 The first chapter deals with the pre-historic history of the pronghorn antelope.

pronto ˈprɑnto, *adv.* [Sp. in same sense.] At once, promptly. *Colloq.*

1850 GARRARD *Wah-To-Yah* xi. 146 Me be off *pronto.* **1911** WRIGHT *Winning Barbara Worth* 96 All we have to do with it is to push for Rubio City pronto and cash our pay checks. **1949** *Milwaukie* (Ore.) *Review* 28 July 1/5 Tickets for Sunday's double-header are going like hot cakes. Better get yours pronto.

pronunciamento prəˌnʌnsɪəˈmɛnto, *n. S.W.* [Sp. *pronunciamiento*, an Amer. borrowing.] A proclamation or manifesto.

1836 *Diplom. Corr. Texas* I. (1908) 121 Pronunciamentos are taking place, in favor of Federalism . . . without any molestation from the government. **1875** *Scribner's Mo.* July 275/1 The 'Emperor Norton,' a harmless creature who firmly believes that he is the legitimate sovereign of the United States and Mexico; issues frequent pronunciamentos. **1932** BENTLEY *Sp. Terms* 187.

***proof,** *n.* and *a.* As the last term in **Baltimore, bomb, bottle, final, fire, fly, fool, fourth, mosquito, mouse, ox proof.**

proofread ˈprufˌrid, *v. tr.* To read and correct (printers' proofs or matter to be printed). — **1934** WEBSTER. **1947** *Mazama* June 3/2 When we proof-read the copy we felt tempted to go.

proofreader ˈprufˌridɚ, *n.* One whose profession is reading printers' proof for detecting and indicating errors.

1832 *Boston Transcript* 10 May 2/1 We will wager our quill that he or his proof-reader, if he is so fortunate as to have one, is a presbyterian. **1883** *Harper's Mag.* Feb. 469/2 A new proof-reader seemed to be needed. **1907** *Dly. Chron.* (London) 4 April 6/6 Thomas Bailey Aldrich . . . entered literature as a 'proof-reader.' This is the American equivalent of our 'corrector to the Press' or 'printer's reader.' **1949** *Chi. D. News* 4 May 14/7 In another row was a proof reader from a Chicago newspaper.

prop prɑp, *n.*[1] [Origin unknown.] A shell used in a game of chance. Also (*pl.*) the game itself (see quot. 1938). Now *hist.* Cf. **papaw,** *n.*[2]

1833 SNELLING *Exposé of Gaming in N. Eng.* 11 [We] threw the *props* upon the table. **1861** *Humorist* (S.F.) 30 Nov. 5/3 Great preparations are being made for *subterranean* 'Props,' *Faro* and *Monte* games, and the parties suppose a bar and a shrewd 'capper' or two, will *take in* the 'greenies,' and *keep out* the police. **1938** ASBURY *Sucker's Prog.* 47 More often, however, it is known as Props. This game was played with small oblong sea shells, the tops of which were sliced off. The hollows were then filled with red sealing-wax, and the player bet that he could throw the shells so that an odd or even number of red spots would show.

attrib. **1833** SNELLING *Exposé of Gaming* 10 The prop table was covered with green baize, was about ten feet long, and was framed with rough ash or hickory, the bark on. *Ib.* 26 They keep the prop box and roulette table alternately. **1868** *How Gamblers Win* 97 It is said that there is not a prop-house in the city of New York.

prop prɑp, *n.*[2] Chiefly *La.* [f. F. *propre*, used in La. in the sense shown here.] A settling or precipitation tank or kettle, usu. the third in a series of such receptacles, usu. five, in which sugar-cane juice is treated in sugar-making. *Obs.* Cf. ***battery 2, flambeau.** — **1862** *Rep. Comm. Patents: Agric.* 303 The juice is run off into a subsiding or precipitating tank, which I shall name the 'prop;' from prop, the juice, after subsiding, is run into the 'strike,' or battery. **1887** *Cent. Mag.* Nov. 116/1 In the course of the boiling [the sirup] is ladled successively into . . . 'the prop' or 'proy,' 'the flambeau,' 'the sirop,' and 'the battery.'

prop prɑp, *n.*[3] Short for next. *Obs.* — **1875** *Chi. Tribune* 9 Sep. 7/1 The prop Alleghany, with her machinery disabled, is anchored at the clay Banks, Lake Erie.

***propeller,** *n.*

1. A steamboat, esp. one for lake service, driven by a screw propeller. Also attrib. and in appositive use. *Obs.* Cf. **steam propeller.**

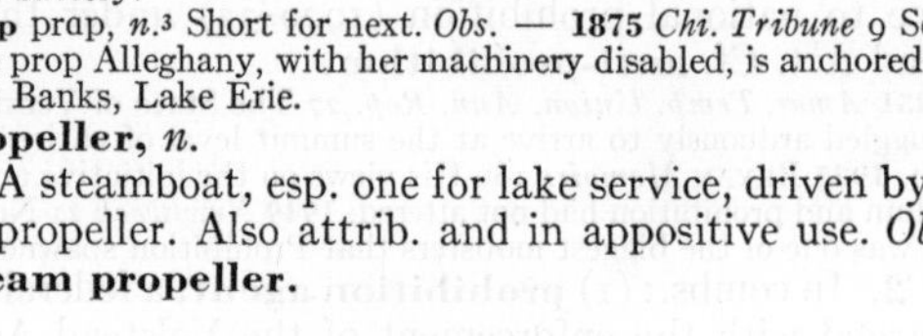

Propeller (sense 1) or steam propeller of an early type

1843 *Hunt's Merch. Mag.* VIII. 574 The building of the propeller Hercules is the commencement of a new era in lake navigation. **1848** *Ib.* XVIII. 664 The steamboat and propeller proprietors on the lakes have entered into an arrangement. **1894** *Harper's Mag.* Jan. 318/2 The propeller *Dean Richmond*, with a crew of eighteen men, sank in Lake Erie October 15th.

2. (See quots.)

1875 KNIGHT 1488/2 One other mode of draft is to be noticed, and that is the *propeller*, in which the cutting apparatus [of the mower] is ahead of the horses, which push the implement before them. **1883** KNIGHT *Supp.* 724/2 *Propeller*, . . . a kind of trolling bait, having oblique wings which cause it to rotate in the water. **1905** *Hartford Courant* 2 Feb. 1 [In] the big propellers—the fire engines that furnish their own power— . . . the power is applied to the rear wheels.

*__property,__ *n.* As the last term in **bonanza, intangible, Negro, slave property.**

*__prophet,__ *n.*

1. Among American Indians, a religious leader, freq. one who advocated return to uncorrupted ancestral customs and beliefs. Now *hist.*

For a discussion of the prophet's role and an enumeration of the principal ones, see Hodge *s.v.*

1800 HAWKINS *Sk. Creek Country* 84 This last town has taken the war club, and dance the prophets dances, and are used as spies on the war party. **1810** *Ann. 12th Congress* 1 Sess. II. 1858 An agent from the British arrived at the Prophet's town . . . to urge the Prophet to unite as many tribes as he could against the United States. **1896** *Bureau Amer. Ethnol. 14th Rep.* 764 When Tävibo, the prophet of Mason valley, died, about 1870, he left a son named Wovoka. **1949** *West Va. Hist.* Jan. 103 The object of Tecumseh and the Prophet was to form a combination of all northeastern and southwestern tribes.

2. A term applied to Joseph Smith, founder of the Mormon Church, and to subsequent leaders and high priests in the organization. Also as a title.

1834 *Sun* (N.Y.) 26 July 2/1 It appears, however, that their prophet, Smith, was somewhat intimidated by the force that had assembled to oppose them. **1838** *Test* (Rushville, Ill.) 12 Dec. 3/5 A portion of the Latter Day Saints, headed by the prophet Joe, have formed themselves into a society to pillage and plunder. **1892** GUNTER *Miss Dividends* 121 'The prophet up there,' he nods his head in the direction of Brigham Young's private residence, 'and some of the other leaders of the Church are beginning to be afraid of Tranyon.' **1900** *Cong. Rec.* 24 Jan. 1129/2 A sworn complaint charging Prophet Snow with adultery with his ninth wife was made. **1947** *Chi. Tribune* 16 July 24/3 It was at Montrose in 1842 where the church's martyred prophet, Joseph Smith, declared the Mormons would 'become a mighty people in the midst of the Rocky Mountains.'

As the last term in **Stuffed, Veiled Prophet.**

*__proposition,__ *n.* A matter requiring attention, something to be dealt with. Also used of persons and usu. preceded by a modifying term. *Colloq.* Cf. **border state proposition.**

1877 BURDETTE *Rise of Mustache* 258 For a long time the good lady held out stoutly against the chicken proposition. **1893** *Scribner's Mag.* June 756/1 'Aren't you ashamed to tell me this?' 'Of course I am, but that isn't the proposition just now.' *a*1904 S. E. WHITE *Blazed Trail* viii. 146 I'm a pretty rank proposition, myself. **1932** BECK *Wonderland* 124 Government is no longer the simple proposition it was in the days of Andrew Jackson. **1950** *Boston Globe Mag.* 1 Jan. 4/4 It's a proposition that might pay off pretty good.

proposition ˌprɑpəˈzɪʃən, *v. tr.* To propose something to (a person), to ask (one) *for* something. *Slang.* — **1927** *Collier's* 24 Dec. 36/4 He propositioned her to use his lodge at Big Bear [Lake] for her party. **1949** *Chi. Tribune* 10 Dec. 12/5 Count that day gained in which A sofomore sonny Won't proposition pop For movie money!

proprietarian prəˌpraɪəˈtɛrɪən, *n.* **1.** ?An advocate or supporter of proprietary government for the North American colonies. **2.** A stickler for propriety. Both *obs.* — **(1) 1776** J. ADAMS *Wks.* (1854) IX. 411 The quakers and proprietarians together have little weight. — **(2) 1866** HOWELLS *Venetian Life* xx, The *Conversazioni* of the rigid proprietarians where people sit down to a kind of hopeless whist . . . and say nothing.

*__proprietary,__ *n.* and *a.*

1. *n.* The owner, or one of the owners, by royal grant, of any one of various American colonies. Also **lord proprietary.** Now *hist.*

1637 *Md. Archives* I. 23 Insolencies, mutinies and contempts against the Lord Proprietary and the government of this place. **1683** *Pa. Col. Rec.* I. 57 Wm. Penn, proprietary and Governer of Pensilvania. **1757** FRANKLIN *Writings* III. 372 No part of these monies was ever paid by the *proprietaries* or ever raised on their estates. **1854** BANCROFT *Hist. U.S.* I. 243 Some other rights were conferred on the proprietary—the . . . power of creating manors and courts baron.

2. *a.* Of or pertaining to a proprietor or owner of an American colony. Now *hist.*

1704 PENN in *Gt. Brit. Hist. MSS Comm. 15th Rep.* App. IV. 79 How much better the Colonies thrive in proprietary hands than under the immediate government of the crown. **1789** MORSE *Amer. Geog.* 97 The second [type of government in the Amer. colonies] was a proprietary government, in which the proprietor of the province was governor. **1914** *Cyclo. Amer. Govt.* I. 315/2 The charters of the British colonies in America are usually divided into three groups; corporation, proprietary, and royal.

proprietor prəˈpraɪətɚ, *n.*

"Anomalously formed and substituted in 17th c. for the etymological word *Proprietary*. . . . App. first used of the 'proprietors' of the North American Colonies" (*OED*).

1. =**proprietary,** *n.* Also **lord proprietor.** *Obs.*

1637 *Md. Archives* IV. 4 To answere the severall crimes of sedition, pyracie and murther w[hi]ch shalbe on the Lord Proprietors behalfe. **1737** in SCHARF *Hist. Maryland* I. 401 Commissioners were appointed by the Lord Baltimore and the Proprietors of Pennsylvania. **1851** DIXON *W. Penn* (1872) 291 The latter now his heir, and, as it seemed, the future lord proprietor of Pennsylvania.

2. One of a group of landowners acting together in certain regulatory or governmental capacities in a colonial town. Now *hist.*

1645 *Mass. Col. Rec.* II. 115 A committee [is] appointed to lay out ye way through Roxberry . . . , & to judge what is meete satisfaction to ye propriet[o]rs. **1753** *Brookhaven Rec.* 168 That peice or parsel of land called the Gore peice of land . . . shall belong to the propriators of the town of brookhaven. **1819** MCMURTRIE *Sk. Louisville* 166 The town [New Albany, Ind.] was laid out by the Messrs. Scribners who were the proprietors in 1814. **1949** *Jrnl. Ill. State Hist. Soc.* Sep. 318 The great fence was managed by officers called 'syndics' elected at assemblies of the proprietors.

b. Used of Indians. *Obs.*

1664 *Brookhaven Rec.* 12 Massetewse and Sunke squaw, Native proprieters and owners of all the lands. **1689** *Huntington Rec.* II. 48 Wee the above named Indians beeing the sole and true proprietors of the premises . . . doe putt the said samuell cetcham in the Lawfull and Pecable possession of the said Island.

As the last term in **parchment, store proprietor.**

prorate ˈproret, *n.* A part determined by prorating. — **1904** F. LYNDE *Grafters* vii. 92 A hundred thousand is a pot of money. I take it for granted the Western Pacific will stand its pro-rate?

prorate proˈret, ˈproˌret, *v.*

1. *tr.* To allot or divide (fares, dividends, business, etc.) proportionately. Hence **prorating,** *n.*

1860 *Cong. Globe* 21 Dec. 180/1 The amendment . . . requires this company to prorate passenger fare with all railroad companies or lines which terminate either at Alexandria, Washington or Baltimore. **1911** WEBNER *Factory Costs* 212 On the other hand, there is no possible way of entirely avoiding a prorating or averaging of expense. **1923** BLAISDELL *Fed. Trade Comm.* 298 If the group has sufficient control over its constituents to control and prorate production it may lengthen its period of control without establishing monopoly prices.

2. *intr.* or *absol.* To make an agreement or arrangement based proportionately on a given rate, *with* another company.

1867 *Chi. Times* 21 March 4/1 The Hannibal and St. Jo road . . . is bound to 'pro-rate' with any and all roads coming to Hannibal. **1906** *N.Y. Ev. Post* 17 May 2 The New England roads ought to pro-rate, but refuse to do so.

prosecuting attorney. An attorney chosen or designated by a state or county to conduct the prosecution in court proceedings, usu. involving cases of a criminal nature.

1838 *Indiana H. Rep. Jrnl.* 23 Sess. 42 John W. Payne . . . was . . . declared duly elected Prosecuting Attorney of the second Judicial Circuit of the State of Indiana. **1912** NICHOLSON *Hoosier Chron.* 180 The Republican prosecuting attorney of Ranger County joined with the local bank in certifying to Miles's probity. **1949** *Boston Globe Mag.* 25 Dec. 2/2 The prosecuting attorney was a huge man, loved and respected by everyone.

proslavery proˈslev(ə)rɪ, *a.*

1. Favoring Negro slavery, or its continuance.

1839 *Corr. R. W. Griswold* (1898) 24 Their delinquent, office-seeking pro-slavery brethren of this benighted region [central N.Y.]. **1855** in HAMBLETON *H. A. Wise* 305 The party is accused of being pro-slavery. **1906** *N.Y. Ev. Post* 24 March, The Rev. Ambrose Converse, a Northern man with Southern principles, made his pro-slavery Philadelphia *Christian Observer* so 'coppery' during the civil war that Seward suppressed it. **1949** J. MONAGHAN *This is Ill.* 64 He swore lifelong vengeance against proslavery men.

b. *absol.* Advocacy of Negro slavery.

1862 *Cong. Globe* 12 May 2067/2 The ultraism and madness of pro-slavery in the border States.

2. In derivatives now obs. or hist. **a. proslaverish,** *a.* favoring slavery. **b. proslaveryism,** the forces and principles favoring or upholding slavery, cf. **Free-Soilism. c. proslaveryite,** one who favored slavery. See also *__pro-,__ *prefix.*

(**a**) **1856** S. Robinson *Kansas* 115 The governor, with very pro-slaverish leanings, replied [etc.]. — (**b**) **1855** *N.Y. Tribune* 14 April 5/2 After the votes were counted, Pro-Slaveryism built bonfires in our streets in rejoicings for a 'Democratic victory.' **1885** L. W. Spring *Kansas* 26 The border experienced a boisterous revival of pro-slaveryism. **1905** Hume *Abolitionists* 159 The issue between Pro-Slaveryism and Anti-Slaveryism came up. — (**c**) **1860** *Charleston* (S.C.) *Mercury* 24 Nov. 2/7 Rumors from Kansas say that large bodies of pro-slaveryites and free-soilers had assembled in the northern part of the Territory. **1862** *Crisis* (Columbus, O.) 23 Jan. 1/4 The Abolitionists of old England sowed the seed, the Abolitionists of New England plowed it, and the Pro-Slaveryites of the South put the sickel [*sic*] to reap the infernal crop.

3. proslavery party, a party or faction interested in upholding or extending slavery, esp. the group opposed to the Free-Soilers in the Kansas struggle (1854–58). Now *hist.*

1855 *Kickapoo City* (Kans.) *Pioneer* 31 Oct., The pro-slavery party of this Territory will meet you with open arms and a hearty welcome. **1894** Robley *Bourbon Co., Kans.* 50 The migratory hordes of the Pro-slavery party had, under the faint pretense of 'election,' taken possession of the Territory. **1948** *Chi. Tribune* 11 July (Grafic Mag.) 2/3 The town of Lawrence, Kan., was raided by a pro-slavery party.

* **prospect,** *n.*

1. A spot or location giving indications of the presence of minerals. Cf. **5.** below and see **placer prospect.**

1832 *Ill. Mo. Mag.* May 368 This is a pretty good prospect—this looks well, to be sure—a right smart chance of metal, I declare! **1873** *Cottonwood Observer* (Alta, Utah) 16 July 2/2 New prospects are being developed every day. **1901** White *Westerners* 208 He led them . . . from prospect to prospect, from shaft to shaft. **1949** *World Petroleum* Feb. 50/2 Actual acquisition of promising prospects and their subsequent development will be carried on . . . by the parent companies.

2. (See quot. 1872.) Cf. **5.** below.

1850 *S.F. Picayune* 11 Sep. 2/4 The bed of the river, from the 'prospects' which have been made, indicate that if the stream is turned by the canal, the fortunes of those interested are by no means questionable. **1854** *Wide West* (S.F.) 1 Oct. 1/8 The prospects may be perhaps a cent to the pan, . . . and if a party should attempt to 'tom' it he could not make fifty cents per day. **1872** Mark Twain *Roughing It* 443 A '*prospect*' is what one finds in the first panful of dirt—and its value determines whether it is a good or a bad prospect.

3. (See quot.) *Obs.*

1890 Blaikie *Summer Suns in Far West* 39 At one place [in Colo.] you change into what is called a 'prospect' or open carriage, in order to have a better view of the wonderful scenery.

4. A prospective customer. Also attrib. *Colloq.*

1922 Sinclair Lewis *Babbitt* iii. § 3 The fortnightly form-letter, to be mimeographed and sent out to a thousand 'prospects.' **1947** *Sat. Ev. Post* 8 March 58/2 I'll get you the New York customer and prospect lists. **1948** *Best's Insurance News* 1 March 39/1 There is no natural thrill in acquiring a new prospect such as we feel when closing a sale.

5. In combs. (senses **1.** and **2.**) of obvious meaning, as (1) **prospect camp,** (2) **holder,** (3) **hole,** (4) **operations,** (5) **shaft,** (6) **work.**

(1) **1894** *Harper's Mag.* Jan. 323/2 Nothing but bad whiskey can 'rile' the humor of a prospect camp. — (2) **1885** *Santa Fé Wkly. New Mexican* 31 Dec. 4/3 Every prospect holder in the district feels that he is banking his time and money on a 'sure thing.' — (3) **1855** *Golden Era* (S.F.) 7 Sep., *Thy house* . . . does not mean a low, ill-shaped, smoky cabin, surrounded with 'prospect holes,' piles of dirt and sundry nuisances. **1945** MacDonald *Egg & I* 20 In the spring Gammy took us for walks in the hills and we were careful not to fall in 'prospect holes.' — (4) **1876** Raymond *8th Rep. Mines* 196 Hence our prospect-operations for the past year have been confined exclusively to the western portion.

(5) **1876** Raymond *8th Rep. Mines* 56 As determined by the prospect-shafts, the channel falls toward this end on a steep grade. **1936** McKenna *Black Range* 185 The ten-foot hole was a prospect shaft that he had sunk near the placers on the Animas River. — (6) **1882** *47th Congress* 1 Sess. H.R. Ex. Doc. No. 216, 290 Prospect work is all that has thus far been done.

* **prospect,** *v.*

1. *Mining. intr.* To explore or search in a particular region for gold or silver deposits.

1841 *N.O. Picayune* 4 Feb. 1/6 There are now a large number of persons *prospecting* upon the hills in the rear of Dubuque. **1850** Audubon *Western Jrnl.* 201 We tried to 'prospect' for ourselves, and we lost three days. **1916** Thoburn *Stand. Hist. Okla.* I. 21 The Wichita Mountains were again visited in 1650, . . . the object being to prospect for gold, and silver. **1949** *Sky Line Trail* Oct. 23/2 Kin yo tell me why Dave Martin went ober de udder side ob de mountain to go prospectin for spec'mens?

transf. **1867** Crawford *Mosby* 296 Mountjoy, who was ahead some distance *prospecting*, came back and reported the enemy advancing. **1884** *N. Eng. Hist. & Gen. Reg.* XXXVIII. 340 Wherever I have prospected in the records [in Eng.], . . . I have found indications of [genealogical material of] great richness. **1949** *New Yorker* 9 July 57/1 There is wonderful stuff in it [a book], for which you will have to prospect and dig.

2. Of a mine or pay dirt: To yield, promise, turn out *well* (or in some stated manner) upon actual test. Also *tr.*

1851 Kingsley *Diary* 167 They say it does not prospect verry well. **1867** *Wkly. New Mexican* 23 Feb. 1/3 [A pan of] black dirt, . . . prospected sixteen colors. **1882** *47th Congress* 1 Sess. H.R. Ex. Doc. No. 216, 77 The Hunter mine . . . is prospecting well.

3. *tr.* To work through or examine (a place, region, etc.) in an effort to find if it affords precious minerals.

1851 Clappe *Lett. from Calif.* 92 There is a deep pit in front of our cabin, and another at the side of it, though they are not worked, as when 'prospected,' they did not 'yield the color.' **1858** *N.Y. Tribune* 20 Sep. 7/2 [He] left Cherry Creek, near Pike's Peak, on the 27th of July, having satisfactorily 'prospected' a rich gold region. **1876** *Pioche* (Nev.) *D. Jrnl.* 26 April 1/6, I the undersigned, have done work to hold and prospect the claim known as the 'Montgomery mine,' located in Ely Mining District, Lincoln county, State of Nevada. **1927** Russell *Trails* 10 Once I had a notion of walkin' in an' prospectin' the place, but there's somethin' ghostly about it an' I change my mind. **1949** *Sat. Ev. Post* 5 March 68/4 The next practical dreamer to fall under the spell of the Trona basin was Clinton E. Dolbear, an engineer and promoter who prospected the lake in 1906.

transf. **1865** Mark Twain *Sk.* (1926) 159 You can get that book and prospect her. **1889** ——— *Conn. Yankee* 132 These donkeys didn't prospect these liars for details.

b. To examine carefully (a small amount of earth or gravel) to see how rich it is in gold or silver.

1857 *Miners' Own Book* 24 In order to test the quality of the rock being crushed, the contents of the blanket are frequently washed into a *batea*, or broad Mexican bowl, and prospected. **1864** in *N. Mex. Hist. Rev.* (1949) April 115 Prospected three pans of dirt and pegged out at 10 O cloc. no color here.

prospecting ˈprɑspɛktɪŋ, *n.* Searching for places where gold or silver may be profitably mined.

1850 Colton *3 Years Calif.* 292 Half their time is consumed in what they call prospecting; that is, looking up new deposits [of gold]. **1892** *Harper's Mag.* Dec. 140 Prospecting means hunting gold, and is the fourth and greatest of the learned professions. **1949** *Nat. Geog. Mag.* Oct. 507/1 Into about 95 days . . . must be crammed all the prospecting, mining, farming, and much of the other commercial activity.

b. In combs., as **prospecting camp, diggings, horn, pan, party, shaft, trip.**

1848 *N.Y. Lit. World* 3 June (B.), Two or three men with a bucket, a rope, a pick-axe, and a portable windlass. . . . This . . . is a prospecting party. **1849** *Pres. Mess. Congress* II. 457 It is obvious that the shallow pits now sunk on the vein [of copper] . . . can only be regarded . . . as mere superficial explorations, or 'prospecting diggings,' as they are called in the west. **1869** *Overland Mo.* March 279/1 Over one of the hoisting shafts there is a large wooden bucket with a rope and rude windlass such as you might see on the prospecting shaft of the poorest miner. **1872** McClellan *Golden State* 124 Ten million dollars in gold had been extracted from the mines, . . . the rocker, shovel, prospecting pan, and crevice-knife, being the only machinery employed. **1880** *Cimarron News & Press* 22 July 2/2 New Mexico ought to become one vast prospecting camp for the next five years. **1896** Shinn *Story of Mine* 46 His return to pick, pan, and prospecting horn, his death under the cloud of partial insanity . . . are among the dramatic elements of this strange life history. **1948** Johnston *Gold Rush* 52/2 A number of miners disappeared while on prospecting trips, leaving no trace of their fate.

Also *prospecting company, days, drift, drill, mill, pit, tool, tour, work,* etc.

* **prospectively,** *adv.* In a prospecting manner. *Rare.* — **1830** *Courtland* (Ala.) *Herald* 20 Aug. 2/5 A company starts from Carroll county this day to explore the upper middle . . . of Alabama, striking prospectively about the mouth of the Kiamulga river.

prospector ˈprɑspɛktɚ, *n.* One who explores a region for gold or silver deposits, or for oil.

1846 St. John *Lake Superior Country* 75 From what I have seen of the mines and veins, I am of opinion it will be found worth thinking upon by all '*explorers*,' and '*prospectors*.' **1903** Austin *Land of Little Rain* 70 But prospectors and Indians get a kind of a weather shell that remains on the body until death. **1950** *Reader's Digest* Jan. 124/1 Many an early prospector staked his wildcat test strictly by hunch.

transf. **1889** Davidson *Fla. of Today* 226 The tourist and prospector for a home in Florida goes on his tour of inspection.

b. prospector's hitch, (see quot.).

1913 *Outing* Jan. 428/2 The crosstree hitch . . . is a hitch very generally used by prospectors, and for this reason is known in some localities as the 'prospector's hitch.'

As the last term in **coal, land, railroad prospector.**

***protean,** *a.* Of drama: Presenting one actor in different roles. Also absol. (see quot. 1890). — **1890** *Cent.* 4792/2 Protean. . . . An actor who plays a number of parts in one piece. [Theatrical slang.] **1892** *Chi. Tribune* 4 Aug., The academy is not so rich in Shakespearean scenery as in . . . appurtenances of the protean drama.

***protection,** *n.* In combs.: (1) **protection forest,** (see quot.); (2) **money,** money paid by a law violator to grafting law enforcement officers for the privilege of being unmolested in an illegal pursuit; (3) **papers,** (see quot.), *obs.*

(1) **1905** *Forestry Bureau Bul.* 61 Protection forest. A forest whose chief value is to regulate stream flow, to prevent erosion, holding shifting sand, or exert other indirect beneficial effect. — (2) **1923** *Nation* 24 Oct. 449 The men that help unload get $1 a case, and the revenue officers $2 protection money. **1938** ASBURY *Sucker's Prog.* 433 Kelly was often in the bad graces of the police; he resented the necessity of paying protection money, and never did so except under compulsion. — (3) *c***1855** ROBERTSON *Few Mos.* 177 At the Custom Houses, therefore, it is customary to grant 'protection papers' to any of the sailors, on the representation of the owners of the ships, that they have been five years in the country.

As the last term in **anti-, Cape Cod protection.**

***protector,** *n.* As the last term in **check, chest, head, spark protector.**

***Protestant,** *n.* In combs.: (1) **Protestant Episcopal,** designating the Anglican Church in the U.S., or a bishop of that church; (2) **Episcopalian,** a member of the Protestant Episcopal Church; (3) **Episcopalism,** the doctrines and polity of the Protestant Episcopal Church; (4) **Methodist,** designating the Methodist Protestant Church, also a member of that church, cf. **Methodist Protestant.**

(1) **1780** in W. S. PERRY *Hist. Amer. Episcopal Ch.* II. 21 On the motion of the Secretary it was proposed that the Church known in the province as Protestant be called 'the Protestant-Episcopal Church,' and it was so adopted. **1894** *Harper's Mag.* March 642/2 Obituary. . . . Theodore B. Lyman, Protestant Episcopal Bishop of North Carolina, aged seventy-eight years. **1944** PENNELL *Rome Hanks* 6 He had a pension from the Protestant Episcopal Church. — (2) **1814** in J. ADAMS *Works* X. 87 The opposition consisted chiefly of the Friends or Quakers, the Menonists, the Protestant Episcopalians. — (3) **1836** *S. Lit. Messenger* II. 282 In regard to Protestant Episcopalism in America it may be safely said that . . . there were no written memorials extant. — (4) **1844** RUPP *Relig. Denominations* 424 Some of the preachers and people . . . thought it best to unite with a body of seceders from the Methodist Episcopal Church, who held a convention in Baltimore, and took the name of Protestant Methodist Church. **1846** *Indiana Mag. Hist.* XXIII. 320, I believe the Protestant Methodists are trying to resuscitate their church in the town.

***prothonotary,** *n.* **1.** =**county clerk.** *Obs.* **2.** Short for next. **3. prothonotary warbler,** a handsome southern orange- or golden-colored warbler, *Protonotaria citrea*, frequenting regions near streams and swamps.

(1) **1776** J. ADAMS *Familiar Lett.* 216 Mr. Francis Hopkinson, . . . it seems, is . . . a son of a prothonotary of this county. *a***1821** BIDDLE *Autobiog.* 195 There were a number of applicants for the office of Prothonotary for the county of Dauphin. — (2) **1811** WILSON *Ornithology* III. 72 The Blue-winged Yellow Warbler . . . greatly resembles this in its general appearance; but the bill of the Prothonotary is rather stouter, and the yellow much deeper. — (3) **1790** LATHAM *Index Ornithologicus* II. 542 Prothonotary Warbler . . . Habitat in *Louisiana.* **1874** COUES *Birds N.W.* 47 Prothonotary Warbler. . . . This species was noticed by neither Expedition; it only reaches the lowermost Missouri. **1948** *Time* 30 Aug. 14/2 Did you ever see a prothonotary warbler?

protocol ˈprotəˌkɑl, *n. S.W.* [Sp. *protocolo*, in same sense. An Amer. borrowing.] (See quot.) — **1890** *Cent.* 4797/2 *Protocol*, . . . in the parts of the United States acquired from Mexico, the original record of the transfer of land.

protracted meeting. A series of religious services held during the morning, afternoon, and evening for a number of days.

1834 *Biblical Repertory* VI. 337 This circumstance [i.e., the fewness of ministers] suggested the idea of *protracted* meetings that the ministers might have the opportunity of meeting people at one time and one place. **1835** *Sentinel & Star in West* (Philomath, Ind.) 13 June 19/3 We have had a protracted meeting at Howard, which lasted sixteen days. **1889** P. BUTLER *Recollections* 211 This protracted meeting resulted in a great ingathering. **1948** *Chi. Tribune* 21 Nov. VII. 1/7 Loafers' Glory . . . acquired that name years ago when a protracted meeting was held in the little log schoolhouse.

***prove,** *v.* Usu. with *up.*

1. *Mining. tr.* To test or try out (a vein).

1848 *Hunt's Merch. Mag.* XVIII. 285 Some of them [Indian diggings], 'proved up' by the whites, have turned out very valuable. **1853** *Harper's Mag.* March 444/1 Copper mining is however in its infancy, and all that has yet been done is hardly more . . . than may be expressed by the phrase, common among miners, of 'proving up' the veins.

2. To complete the pre-emption process on (public land or a homestead), to validate (a title) or substantiate (a claim) to government land by complying with the regulations for securing it by pre-emption.

1850 E. S. SEYMOUR *Sk. of Minn.* 209 No attempt has been made 'to prove' the land in this vicinity. **1883** *Gringo & Greaser* 1 Sep. 1/1 They should be rigidly required to prove up their titles within a given time. **1946** *Reader's Digest* Jan. 110/1 If he continued to live on it and develop it for five years he could 'prove' his claim and acquire full title. **1950** *Ib.* Jan. 85/2 In 1912, while proving up a homestead near Holly, Colo., Frakes joined the Methodist Church.

b. *intr.* To complete the requirements for securing public land.

1857 *Lawrence* (Kans.) *Republican* 28 May 2 A man buying a claim with a house already on it, must himself erect one before he can prove up and take the duplicate for his land. **1911** J. F. WILSON *Land Claimers* 140 He's going to prove up in April.

c. *To prove up on*, to make good one's claim to something.

1878 BEADLE *Western Wilds* 43 My wife proved up on her Cherokee blood. **1945** *Chi. Tribune* 2 Sep. (Grafic Mag.) 5/1 There were some out-and-out cheaters, and while some of them were detected and prevented from proving up on their claims, others profited richly by their devices.

***province,** *n.*

1. The Louisiana Territory. *Obs.*

1857 BENTON *Exam. Dred Scott Case* 87 [The vote] was given on the principle of total exclusion of slavery from the whole province of Louisiana. **1880** CABLE *Grandissimes* 362, I know that Congress has divided the province into two territories. **1888** ——— in *Cent. Mag.* Dec. 254/1 Agents of the Revolution had come from France and so 'contaminated,' as he says, 'the greater part of the province.'

2. (*cap.*) One of the districts or divisions of the Invisible Empire or Ku-Klux Klan.

1867 *41st Congress* 2 Sess. H.R. Misc. Doc. No. 53, 315 The officers [of the Ku-Klux Klan] . . . shall consist of . . . a Grand Giant of the Province. **1877** BEARD *K.K.K. Sketches* 74 The Grand Division, or Empire, was subdivided into Realms, Provinces, and Dens. *Ib.*, The ruler of a Province was termed a Grand Giant. **1934** *Kourier* Aug. 37/2 Aliens from several parts of Province five were given the K-Uno Degree.

3. In combs.: (1) **province bill,** a paper bill or note issued by the government of the province of Massachusetts Bay, now *obs.* or *hist.*; (2) **Lands,** see as a main entry; (3) **line,** the boundary between the U.S. and Canada, *obs.*; (4) **tax,** a tax levied on property within an American province or colony, *obs.*

(1) **1711** *Essex Inst. Coll.* IV. 186/2 Fifty pounds in Province Bills. *a***1756** *Mass. H.S. Coll.* 2 Ser. IV. 99 Some time about the year 1703, upon the occasion of the Indian War, came forth 'Province Bills,' which we call Paper Money. **1895** *Pub. Col. Soc.* III. 7 The £50,000 in Province Bills for loans of 1714 were followed by a similar issue of £100,000 in 1716, to be loaned for ten years. — (3) **1798** I. ALLEN *Hist. Vermont* 67 Some Green Mountain Boys, undertook to carry those gentlemen over the province line, to some settlements in Lower Canada. **1809** KENDALL *Travels* III. 277 The bay itself . . . is intersected by what is called the *province-line* . . . , which is the southern boundary of Lower Canada. — (4) **1703** *Boston Rec.* 34 Agreed that the Select men . . . do this weeke take ye Lists of the Polls, . . . in order to ye Apportioning the Province Tax. **1774** *Manchester Rec.* II. 147 Voted that the select-men be a Committee: forthwith to Hire the province Tax for the year 1774.

Province Lands. Lands belonging to a province (see also quot. 1947). Also attrib.

1755 in *Amer. Sp.* XX. (1945) 274 Respecting the distressed circumstances of the people in the Province Lands, &c. **1914** W. D. STEELE *Storm* 106 Then there was a draught of beach-plums from a hill to the south, and after that the Province Land Pines shut in, straight, man-planted rows. **1947** *Amer. Sp.* XXII. 264 Sir St. Vincent Troubridge cites *Province Lands.* . . . I assume that the present-day use of the term (the greater part of the town of Provincetown, owned by the Commonwealth of Massachusetts and free to the use of any citizen whose use does not interfere with a use already in operation) is already in some dictionaries.

***provincial,** *a.* and *n.*

1. *n.* A soldier of one of the British provinces which later became the U.S. Now *obs.* or *hist.*

1756 *Lett. to Washington* I. 205 Nor will I ever Serve in the provincialls below the Rank I bear. **1775** CUTLER in *Life & Corr.* I. 49 We obtained an exact account of the number of Provincials that were killed and wounded. **1852** REYNOLDS *Hist. Illinois* 46 General Braddock landed [with] . . . 2,000 men, regulars and provincials.

2. *a.* Of or pertaining to one of the former British colonies in what is now the U.S. *Obs.* or *hist.*

1683 *Pa. Col. Rec.* I. 72 Consideration arising whether ye Govrs. three Voyces should stand in Prov[incia]ll Councill as by ye ould Charter. **1689** *Ib.* 253 Possession . . . had been formerly given to ye said Woollaston, persuant to a Decretall order of ye Provinll Judges. **1757** *General Orders* 39 The Men Belonging to ye Provensial reg[imen]ts who are Appointed to Do ye Duty of Rangers are to Be Emmediately Supplyed with Leather Shot Bags. **1776** *Amer. Hist. Rev.* I. 308 A Letter from Owen Jones Provincial Treasurer here to a County Treasurer was read.

3. In special obs. combs.: (1) **provincial congress,** a legislative assembly in one of the British provinces which later formed the U.S.; (2) **court,** a court in one of the British provinces that later became the U.S.; (3) **troops,** troops belonging to, or recruited from, the American provinces.

(1) 1774 CUTLER in *Life & Corr.* I. 47 Thanksgiving appointed by the Provincial Congress, and not by the Governor. **1823** THACHER *Military Jrnl.* 20 Our Provincial Congress have addressed the several towns of the colony. **1949** MURRAY *This Our Land* 19 The Provincial Congress had elected him Lieutenant-Governor. — **(2) 1669** *Md. Archives* II. 172 The Matter . . . is only examinable & punishable by the honourable Justices of the Provincial Court. **1732** FRANKLIN *Poor Richard's Almanac 1733* 22 Provincial Courts in Maryland. — **(3) 1747** *Georgia Col. Rec.* VI. 187 The Provincial or Extra Troops [have] been lately discharged. **1775** JEFFERSON *Writings* I. (1892) 460 Washington set out from here on Friday last as generalissimo of all the provincial troops in North America.

***provision,** *n.* In combs.: (1) **provision car,** a railway car especially adapted for carrying provisions; (2) **crop,** *S.* a food crop; (3) **land,** land suited for growing food crops; (4) **packer,** = ***packer 1;** (5) **pay,** pay in provisions, *obs.;* (6) **pit,** the part of an exchange devoted to trading in provisions; (7) **state,** (see quot.); (8) **store,** a store in which provisions, esp. for domestic animals, are sold; (9) **train,** *W.* a train of wagons carrying provisions.

(1) 1865 FLEMING *Hist. Reconstruction* I. 18 There remained fit for use . . . 1 baggage car, 1 provision car, 2 stock and 2 flat cars. — **(2) 1838** in EASTERBY *S.C. Rice Plant.* (1945) 254 The weather is now fine the Provision crop is sorry it is so through out the neighbourhood. **1858** *Ib.* 346 Her duties are selected on the upland, or in the cultivation of the provision crops. — **(3) 1825** in COMMONS *Doc. Hist.* I. 252 This tract contains . . . excellent cotton and provision land. — **(4) 1871** GROSVENOR *Protection* 259 The attempt to shut it [i.e., salt from the W. Indies] out is simply an endeavor to deny to our provision-packers the benefit of that tropical sunlight.

(5) 1683 *East-Hampton Rec.* II. 131 Agreed . . . with mr. peter Benson to teach school the Next yeare . . . and for his Wages hee is to be payd the some of thirty five pound in probision pay. **1692** SEWALL *Letter-Book* I. 7 Some of the Provision-Pay was Wheat, which I sold, for Indian Corn; being inform'd 't would greatly gratify the poor. — **(6) 1887** *Courier-Journal* 3 Feb. 7/4 Within a very few minutes after the opening the crowd in the provision pit increased. **1902** LORIMER *Lett. Merchant* 178 Four or five years ago little Jim Jackson had the bears in the provision pit hibernating. — **(7) 1872** *Cong. Globe* 8 March 1527/1 [In 1778, the people of Conn.] produced flour, grain, and other commissary supplies, . . . [securing] to the State the honorable distinction of being called 'the provision State.' — **(8) 1796** *Boston Directory* 245 Fletcher Jonathan, provision store Torry's wharf, house Middle street. **1881** *Ore. State Jrnl.* 1 Jan. 8/2 Callison & Osburn is prepared to furnish . . . everything usually kept in a first class Grocery and Provision Store. — **(9) 1850** GARRARD *Wah-To-Yah* v. 75 He was in charge of a Provision train. **1896** *Harper's Mag.* April 764/1 Blücher . . . found that he had captured . . . all the enemy's hospital outfit, his field-smithies, and his provision-train.

***provisional,** *a.* and *n.*

1. *n. Philately.* A postage stamp issued for temporary use, as those brought out in the South before the Confederate Government stamps were available.

1886 *Stamp Collector* (Chi.) July 14 Such rare provisionals as the Memphis 5-cent envelope, the 5-cent Mobile . . . attracted much attention. **1929** DIETZ *Postal Service of Confed. States* 40 Postmaster J. H. Francis, of Marion, Va., claims to have used the first Confederate Provisional.

2. *a.* In combs.: (1) **provisional army,** an army raised for temporary service, as in an emergency; (2) **government,** a temporary government, esp. one established by Congress in a territory prior to its becoming a state; (3) ***governor,** a governor appointed by the President of the U.S. for one of the southern states during the Reconstruction period after the Civil War, *obs.*

(1) 1797 *Ann. 5th Congress* I. 16 So much of the President's Speech as relates to . . . making arrangements for forming a provisional army, [shall] be referred to Messrs. Tracy, Sedgwich . . . and Vining. *Ib.* 239 Provision [shall] be made by law, for empowering the President to raise a provisional army. **1861** LEE in M. A. Jackson *Gen. Jackson* 166, I have the pleasure of sending you a commission of brigadier-general in the Provisional Army. — **(2) 1803** CUTLER in *Life & Corr.* II. 148 Look at the power given to the President by the provisional government of Louisiana. **1852** GOUGE *Fiscal Hist. Texas* 25 The chief reliance of the Provisional Government was . . . on loans. **1880** TOURGEE *Bricks* 175 The period of actual reconstruction had passed, and independent, self-regulating States had taken the place of Military Districts and Provisional Governments. — **(3)** [**1864** in FLEMING *Hist. Reconstruction* I. 120 The provisional governor shall canvass such returns and declare the person having the highest number of votes elected.] **1900** *Cong. Rec.* 25 Jan. 1171/2 Will the Senator tell me who was the provisional governor appointed by President Johnson? **1907** ANDREWS *Recoll.* 153 The President had appointed provisional-governors for some other southern states.

provisioner prəˈvɪʒənɚ, *n.* One who supplies or deals in provisions.

1866 HOWELLS *Venetian Life* 102 Among other provisioners who come to your house in Venice, are those ancient *contadine,* who bring fresh milk in bottles carefully packed in baskets filled with straw. **1887** *Council Bluffs Herald* 17 Jan., Every article of staple and fancy goods in the provisioner's line. **1894** *Cosmopolitan* XVII. 58 The display was on either side of the provisioner's door.

***Proviso,** *n.* = **Wilmot Proviso.** *Obs.* — [**1846** POLK *Diary* II. 76 Had there been time, there is but little doubt the Senate would have struck out the slavery proviso & that the House would have concurred.] **1848** *Whig Almanac 1849* 8/2 Long ere this, however, the Proviso or Free Soil question had become a potent element in the feud which divided the party in New York.

***provo,** *n.* = next. *Obs.*

1777 CRESSWELL *Jrnl.* (1925) 227 If I did not choose to return to Virginia with Lieutenant Noland I would be put in the provo immediately. **1779** *N.J. Archives* 2 Ser. III. 226 Two of them made their escape, and the other two are safely lodged in the provo of the continental troops. **1832** DUNLAP *Hist. Amer. Theatre* 43 The Jail, then called the provo, where American prisoners suffered for asserting the rights of their country, scowled on the east.

***provost,** *n.*

1. (See quot. 1890.) Cf. ******provost cell.*

1780 *Heath P.* III. 112 He has flung into the provost many of our friends. **1890** *Cent.* 4807/2 *Provost,* . . . a temporary prison in which the military police confine prisoners until they are disposed of.

2. In some colleges and universities, an officer of high rank charged with various executive or administrative duties.

1835 *Knickerb.* V. 137 It was thought expedient to divide the duties and powers of the President between that officer and another, to be called the *Provost.* **1922** *Who's Who in Amer.* XII. 702/2 Claxton, Philander Priestley, univ. provost; . . . provost Univ. of Ala. since 1921. **1946** *Harvard Univ. President's Rept.* 15 By recent action of the two governing boards, the Statutes of the University have been amended to provide for a Provost of the University.

3. In combs.: (1) **provost guard,** a detail of soldiers appointed to perform police duties, the quarters occupied by such a detail; (2) **marshal,** the chief police officer in some of the American colonies, *obs.*

(1) 1778 *Jrnls. Cont. Congress* X. 74 About thirty [officers] . . . have been confined in the provost guard and in the most loathsome gaols. **1862** MOORE *Rebellion Rec.* V. II. 151 Major Fisher . . . was left in Corinth with a provost-guard, to prevent pillage and protect the public stores. **1883** SWEET & KNOX *Through Texas* 595 We may be caught by the provost-guard, and put in the bull-pen. — **(2) 1619** *Va. House of Burgesses* 9 If any private person be found culpable . . . [of drunkenness, he is] to lye in bottes 12 houres in the House of the Provost

Marshall. **1773** in *Hist. MSS Comm.* 14th Rep. App. X. (1895) 182 Recommends his father-in-law John Row, who has been for many years Sheriff of Maryland, for the appointment of Provost Marshal of East Florida.

prowl car. A police patrol car. — **1939** WEBSTER (*New Words*). **1948** *Chi. Tribune* 20 June (Comics) 5 We have every prowl car in all towns and cities within a 200 mile radius looking for your wife and daughter!

prox praks, *n. Conn.* and *R.I.* [Short for * *proxy.*]

1. A vote cast by a deputy or substitute. In full **prox vote.** Cf. * **proxy 1.**

1669 *R.I. Col. Rec.* II. 242 Mr. Peleg Sanford and Mr. John Coggeshall are to assist for the opening of the proxes. **1689** *R.I. Col. Rec.* III. 333 Capt'n Nathaniel Coddington, Capt'n Robert Carr, are appointed to open the prox votes on the day of Election. **1843** *R.I. Hist. Soc. Coll.* V. 64 Such of the colony as could not attend the General Assembly, had the right to send their votes for these officers by some other persons; hence the origin of the terms prox, and proxy votes, as applied to the present mode of voting for state officers in Rhode Island.

2. (See quots.)

1816 PICKERING 157 The abbreviation *Prox* is also used in *Rhode Island,* for the *Ticket;* (as it is called elsewhere) that is, the *List* of Candidates at Elections. **1885** *Mag. Amer. Hist.* March 298/1 *Prox* or *proxy.*—Formerly used in Rhode Island and Connecticut to denote an election at which voting by proxy was allowed under certain conditions. *Ib.* 406 The word *prox* or *proxy* is still used in Rhode Island, not to designate an election where proxies are used—the practice being abandoned—but to describe the printed ballots themselves.

prox praks, *v.* [f. the noun.] *intr.* To vote by means of a prox. *Obs.* — **1758** *Narragansett Hist. Reg.* IV. 39 There is some of the frinds of Smithfield that has not yet proxed for Governor.

* **proxy,** *n.*

1. (See quot. 1816.)

1660 *Conn. Rec.* I. 346 The remote Plantations that use to send Proxies at the Election by their Deputies. **1816** PICKERING 156 This use of the term *proxies* [for written votes or ballots] is not known, I believe, in any of the States, except *Rhode Island,* and *Connecticut.* It is also used sometimes as equivalent to *election,* or *election-day.* **1885** [see **prox,** *n.* **2**]. **1947** *Christian Cent.* 20 Aug. 998/2 The vote was 20 to 0 with three proxies being voted by the chairman.

2. Among Mormons, one who substitutes for another; esp. one who takes the place, in a marriage, of a dead husband or wife to whom the other party in the marriage is regarded as actually united in wedlock. Also attrib.

1882 WAITE *Adv. Far West* 89, I must raise up seed for my dead brother and you must be sealed to your husband while I act as proxy. *Ib.* 123 Another case illustrating the Proxy doctrine as it is called came to my knowledge a few days ago. *Ib.* 215 *Proxy Women.* This is a common term in Utah, and signifies that a woman is married to one man for 'time,' and sealed to another for eternity.

* **prudential,** *n.*

1. *pl. N. Eng.* =**prudential affairs.** Also transf.

1646 *Mass. Bay Rec.* II. 180 Every township, or such as are deputed to order the prudentialls thereof, shall have power to present to the Quarter Court all idle and unprofitable persons. **1774** in F. CHASE *Hist. Dartmouth Coll.* I. 263 Agreed with Frederick Ernest . . . to take the care of the kitchen, and inspect and conduct the prudentials of it. **1891** CHASE *Ib.* 565 The condition of the College in its prudentials was such as might well have led any one to hesitate to take the helm.

2. In combs.: (1) **prudential affairs,** *N. Eng.* the business and administrative affairs of a colonial town requiring the exercise of prudence and discretion in their management; (2) **committee,** an advisory committee; (3) * **man,** *N. Eng.* a man selected with others to have charge of the prudential affairs of a colonial town.

(1) **1644** *Springfield Rec.* I. 175 Power to order in all the prudential affaires of the Towne. **1738** *R.I. Col Rec.* IV. 547 The prudential affairs of the said town. — (2) **1822** *Missionary Herald* XVIII. 1 American Board of Commissioners for Foreign Missions. Report of the Prudential Committee. **1910** *N.Y. Ev. Post* 26 Nov. Supp. 10 During his . . . 25 years as member of the prudential committee, he has missed but one meeting. — (3) **1647** *Ipswich Rec.* 7 Feb., There was chosen for the prudentiall men for this year, Major Denison, John Tuttle [etc.]. **1685** *N.H. Prov. Papers* I. (1867) 48 About one thousand acres . . . were divided and parcelled out by the servants of Capt. Mason and others, the select, or prudential men (of the town of Portsmouth), as they were called.

* **prunellas,** *n. pl.* Shoes made of prunella.

1833 *Sk. D. Crockett* 147 With forms not screwed into fashion's mould, nor feet encumbered with light prunellas, they trip the fairy dance. **1891** F. H. SMITH in *Cent. Mag.* March 735 He had changed his shoes, his white stockings now being incased in low prunellas tied with a fresh ribbon. **1914** E. STEWART *Lett. Woman Homesteader* 38 Little Mandy, . . . I am afraid, was a selfish little beast since she had to have her prunellas when all the rest of the 'young uns' had to wear shoes that old Uncle Buck made out of rawhide.

psorosis səˈrosɪs, *n.* [f. * *psora,* the itch, +*-osis.*] (See quot. 1909.)

1896 *U.S. Dept. Agric., Div. Veget. Physiol. & Pathol. Bul.* No. 8, 30 Psorosis, a disease known in Florida as 'tears' or 'gum disease,' is often confounded with foot rot, but is unquestionably quite distinct. . . . Psorosis does not kill the bark entirely. **1909** *Cent. Supp.* 1080/2 psorosis . . . A disease which affects orange-trees, causing injury to the bark, accompanied by a flow of gum. **1949** *Calif. Citrograph* Dec. 55 Lemon & Orange Trees for Spring Delivery . . . on Sweet and Tangelo Root Psorosis Free Valencia Trees.

psychographist saɪˈkagrəfɪst, *n.* [f. **psychograph*+*-ist.*] A person who obtains "spirit writings." — **1904** *K.C. Times* 12 July (*Cent. Supp.*), Of fifteen clairvoyants . . . , and 'psychographists' whom I have called upon . . . the majority have informed me that clergymen are their best customers.

P.-T.A., see **Parent-Teacher Association.**

***ptarmigan,** *n.* As the last term in **white-tailed, willow ptarmigan.**

Puants pjuˈants, *n. pl.* [See note.] The Winnebago Indians. *Obs.*

The origin of this name is not altogether clear. From the variant spellings given in Hodge II. 961/2 it seems likely that the French found these Indians with a name which it was easy for them to convert into their word *Puants,* i.e., stinkers. Cf. **Stinkards.**

1722 COXE *Descr. Carolana* 19 Miles from the Land Carriage, into the great Bay of the *Pouteouotamis,* or the *Puans,* which joyns, on the North-West, with the great Lake of the *Alinouecks.* [**1750** *Arch. Canadian Govt. Ser. B* XXVI. 1 Que s'ils vouloient luy donner des preuves de la Soumission, . . . il faloit qu'ils dis-continuassuit d'aller en party sur les Sioux, Sakis, puants, et Renards.] **1852** *Dakota Tawaxitku Kin* 1 Jan. 4/2 Champlain . . . learned of the existence of Gáston Rapins, (Sault St. Marie,) Grand Lac, (Superior,) and the nation of Puans, (Winnebagos,) living upon a Bay, (Green Bay). **1949** *Jrnl. Ill. State Hist. Soc.* June 196 A party of Puants ('Stinkers' —from Wisconsin) rashly attempted to kidnap Clark from his quarters on the second night.

* **public,** *a.* and *n.*

1. *n.* (See quot. 1823.) *Obs.* or *hist.*

1788 in FORD *N. Webster* I. 225 January 15. At a heelkicking at Mr. Houletts Public. **1823** I. HOLMES *Account* 341 These publics are generally weekly assemblies by dancing-masters, free for all his scholars and their parents, and nearly so for all females. **1896** HASWELL *New York* 107 John Charraud, an émigré, or, more properly, a refugee, from the island of Hayti after the revolution there, opened a dancing-school at 47 Murray Street; he subsequently gave his 'publics' at the City Hotel.

2. An admonition or rebuke given in public. *College slang. Obs.* Cf. * **private 1.**

1837 *Knickerb.* IX. 244, I was reported to the government . . . and received a 'public.' **1876** TRIPP *Student-Life* 133 If we make a noise . . . we shall get publics, if nothing worse.

3. In combs.: (1) * **public bill,** a government note issued by a public bank, *obs.;* (2) **continental thanksgiving,** a day appointed by Congress for giving thanks, *obs.;* (3) **crib,** the U.S. Treasury or the spoils of public office; (4) **day,** see as a main entry; (5) **dinner,** a well advertised dinner in honor of some distinguished person; (6) **domain,** land belonging to a state or, more commonly, to the general government, public lands; (7) **employment office,** an employment office or bureau; (8) **enemy,** see as a main entry; (9) **entertainment,** a regularly licensed inn, tavern, or public house as distinguished from a private entertainment *q.v.;* (10) **hydrant,** (see quot. 1850), *obs.;* (11) **land,** see as a main entry; (12) **letter,** a letter concerned with public matters, *obs.;* (13) **printer,** a printer officially designated to print government documents, forms, etc.; (14) **school,** see as a main entry; (15) **service corporation,** a corporation that operates a public utility; (16) **square,** a square or rectangular area in a town used as a park, market place, etc., a plaza; (17) **telephone,** a telephone in a public place for the use of the public upon payment of a small charge; (18) **town meeting,** =**town meeting,** *obs.;* (19) **vendue,** * **work,** see as main entries.

(1) **1714** *Mass. Bay Currency Tracts* 105 We have had Twelve Years Experience already of Publick Bills, with great Honour, Safety, and Success. **1720** *Ib.* 336 Let now the Publick Bills of Credit be thus Supported, which They ought to be. — (2) **1780** STILES *Diary* II. 485 December. . . . 7. This day is public Continental Thanksgiving recommended by Congress & authorised in each State by their respective Legislatures. — (3) **1853** *La Crosse Democrat* 8 Nov. 1/5 [The delegates have] no other view . . . than to get one elected who will . . . give them a key to the public crib. **1904** BISHOP *Polit. Drama* 124 The early appearance of the 'public crib' as a synonym for the spoils of office is a point of some interest.

(5) **1784** in *Md. Hist. Mag.* XXXI. 206 Dr. Wetherspoon arrived here [Edinburgh] a few days ago, when a Public Dinner was given him by a number of American friends—The toasts were sent to press for publication, but were refused a place in the paper. **1890** HOWELLS *Boy's Town* 117 There was going to be an oration and a Public dinner, and they were already setting the tables under the locust trees. **1944** PENNELL *Rome Hanks* 140 Mr. Theron began to talk . . . of the custom, in America, of shying plates at the waiters at public dinners. — (6) **1832** in *Whig Almanac 1844* 38/1 Within a few years . . . restless men have thrown before the public their visionary plans for squandering the public domain. **1909** *Indian Laws & Tr.* III. 389 The Secretary of Interior . . . is authorized to allot any Indian on the public domain who has not heretofore received an allotment, . . . eighty acres of agricultural [land]. **1949** *Sat. Ev. Post* 2 April 125/1 Proof of the titles to three quarters of the land in the United States—once the public domain—is in the Archives. — (7) **1891** *Ohio Bur. Labor Statistics 14th Rep.* 14 The superintendents of the 'Free Public Employment Offices' are required by law to report to this Bureau. — (9) **1788** SCHÖPF *Reise* II. 53 Der Vortheil des Unterschieds zwischen Private und Public Entertainment ist auf des Seite der Landleute. **1833** KERCHEVAL *History* xlvi, He had married a wealthy widow who kept a large house of public entertainm't unto which resorted those of the best quality and such others as business called to that town.

(10) **1833** *Amer. R.R. Jrnl.* II. 510/1 (*caption*), Public Hydrants. **1850** *Banker's Mag.* IV. 834 No public hydrants, for the gratuitous supply of water for domestic uses, are provided. **1876** KNIGHT 2415/1 [Street-sprinklers] are usually filled from the public hydrant or fire-plug. — (12) **1775** *Warren-Adams Lett.* I. 56 You will collect from the publick Letter by this Express our Sentiments with regard to the necessity of assuming civil Government constantly increasing upon us. **1848** *Santa Fe Republican* 15 Jan. 4/1 After marching three miles we met Kit Carson direct on express from California with a mail of public letters for Washington. — (13) **1835** J. HALL *Sk. of West.* II. 193 The State treasurer, auditor, attorney general, and public printer, are, under the constitution, elected by the general assembly. **1900** *Cong. Rec.* 18 Jan. 953/2 The Report on Agriculture . . . was retained by the Public Printer for nine months and one day.

(15) **1908** STEVENS *Liberators* 187 The public service corporation had dictated the nomination of the entire Republican State and Legislative ticket. **1912** NICHOLSON *Hoosier Chron.* 79 This capable firm was retained by most of the public service corporations. — (16) **1786** in DURRETT *Louisville* 174 [Lots] 224, 225, 226, Public Square. **1860** *Lexington* (Ill.) *W. Globe* 26 April 3/1 That mammoth show . . . has left an appointment to meet the people of Lexington on the 7th day of May, 1860, on the Public Square. **1944** PENNELL *Rome Hanks* 75 Everyone within the eye of the lens had struck an attitude as if he were a statue in a public square of his home town. — (17) **1893** *McClure's Mag.* I. 394/2 There were even days when the Joneses questioned whether they were not running a public telephone, so often did the bell ring. — (18) **1639** *Watertown Rec.* I. 1. 5 If any of ye Freemen be absent from any Publick Towne meeting . . . , he shall forfett for every time 2*s.* 6*d.*

b. Designating various types of schools provided at public expense and managed by public authority for the use of a community. Cf. **public school** as a main entry.

1710 *Boston Rec.* 73 [A town committee] now propose to Erect a Brick Building . . . to be let out for the Support of a Publick writeing School in the Town. **1715** *Ib.* 113 Real Estate for the use of the Publick Lattin School. **1775** BURNABY *Travels* 70 In each county throughout this province [Md.], there is a public free-school. **1832** WILLIAMSON *Maine* II. 537 It was insisted by the eastern people, that a public Seminary planted among them would enlarge and spread the benefits of education. **1911** *Amer. Phys. Ed. Rev.* XVI. 390 The department of physical training in a public high school exists primarily for the promotion of health . . . among the mass of students.

As the last term in **John Q., traveling public.**

public day.

1. A day employed in public business. Also a day when the public may participate in, witness, or be heard in some activity.

1722 FRANKLIN *Writings* II. 20 An honest Neighbour . . . [was] in Town some time since on a publick Day. **1797** BOWNE *Life* 12, I go to Boston every public day. **1866** F. KIRKLAND *Bk. Anecdotes* 644/1 Once, on what was called 'a public day'—when Mr. Lincoln received all applicants in their turn—the first thing he saw [etc.].

2. A commencement day in college.

1829 *Va. Lit. Museum* 95 *Public Day.*—On Saturday last, the 18th, instant, the following exercises took place in the Rotunda [at the Univ. of Va.], in the presence of the Rector and Visiters and a numerous assemblage of the public. **1851** HALL *College Words* 249 *Public day*, in the University of Virginia, the day on which the certificates and diplomas are awarded to the successful candidates. **1901** *Harper's Mag.* Dec. 205/1 Tim and his wife used to go to school public days to see him.

public enemy. A person who is a menace to the public. Also **public enemy number 1.** Also transf.

1934 WEBSTER. **1939** *Chi. D. News* 10 April 3 (*caption*), Frank J. Loesch, former president of the Chicago Crime Commission and the man who added 'public enemy' to the nation's vernacular, as he appeared on his 87th birthday yesterday. **1941** *Dly. Oklahoman* (Okla. City) 2 Oct., Overcooking is Public Enemy No. 1 in the vegetable kingdom. **1949** *Nat. Hist.* Sep. 325/1 Clothes moths are generally considered to be Public Enemy No. 1 by the American housewife.

* **publicity,** *n. attrib.* Designating persons and agencies for securing publicity.

1907 LINCOLN *Old Home House* 37 You two can be proprietors and treasurers if you want to. But active manager and publicity man—that's yours cheerily, Peter Theodosius Brown! **1907** UPTON SINCLAIR *Indust. Republic* 142 He had an army of experts to help him . . . skilful lobbyists, newspapers and publicity bureaus. **1911** J. C. LINCOLN *Cap'n Warren's Wards* xi. 180 He and his friends needed a representative on the press—a publicity agent, so to speak. **1928** *Publishers' Wkly.* 16 June 2439 Many 'publicity men' admit frankly that their intention is to sell the author to the public.

public land.

1. Land owned by the public, most commonly by the national government. Often *pl.*

1789 *Ann. 1st. Congress* I. 61 These troops were raised . . . to prevent all intrusions on the public lands. **1832** CLAY *Speeches* (1842) 220 There is public land enough to found an empire. **1900** *Cong. Rec.* 17 Feb. 1903/1 The surveyor-general of the State writes me that there are more inquiries for public land than there have been for years. **1947** *Trail & Timberline* June 93/1 Western Conservationists have won a skirmish and lost a battle for public lands in the present Congress of the United States.

attrib. **1846** *Niles' Reg.* 11 July 304/2 Public Land Bill. The debate in the house of representatives on the graduation bill, terminated at 2 o'clock yesterday. **1854** BENTON *30 Years View* I. 11/2 Among these was the great and prominent class of the public land purchasers. *Ib.* 12/2 Many members of Congress were among the public land debtors. **1900** *Cong. Rec.* 10 Jan. 754/1 A bill (H. R. 5763) to extend the public-land laws to the district of Alaska.

2. public-land state, a state containing public land belonging to the federal government.

1900 *Cong. Rec.* 4 Jan. 648/1 The bill . . . declaring the character of the accounts between the United States and the several public-land States. **1910** PINCHOT *Fight for Conservation* 93 We are facing in the public-land States west of the Mississippi the great question whether the Western people are to be predominately a people of tenants . . . or freeholders and free men.

* **public school.**

1. A free elementary or secondary school maintained by taxation or by funds accruing from public lands, and usu. managed by the local government. Also a building housing such a school.

In England *public school* usu. refers to an endowed school, such as Rugby and Charterhouse. See *OED*.

1636 *Harvard Rec.* I. 171 The Court voted for the erecting a publick Schooll or Colledge in Cambridge. **1785** *Jrnls. Cont. Congress* XXVIII. 378 There shall be reserved the lot N 16, of every township, for the maintenance of public schools, within the said township. **1835** ABBOTT *N. Eng.* 25 The town is divided into several school districts, in each of which there is a public school during the winter months. **1949** *Sat. Ev. Post* 23 April 26/1 As kids we had gone to the same public school.

attrib. **1830** *Williams's N.Y. Ann. Reg.* 194 Extracts from the Report of the Committee, appointed by the Trustees of the Public School Society, February 1829. **1838** *Speeches of D. Barnard* 124 Which would go into the hands of the commissioners of common schools as public school moneys for distribution among the districts. **1857** *Mass. Acts & Resolves* 712 The sum expended for *building and repairing* public school-houses during the past year, reached . . . $588,214. **1870** O. LOGAN *Before Footlights* 274 A procession in the West would not be complete without the presence of the inevitable public school children. **1920** HOWELLS *Vacation of Kelwyns* 115 [She brought] out what was best in the twenty-five or thirty children . . . answering from their regulation public-school desks.

2. public school land, land set aside by the public land laws for public schools. See quot. 1785 in **1.** above.

1900 *Cong. Rec.* 31 Jan. 1353/2 We are leasing not only our public school lands, but our public domain. **1944** DUNCAN *M. Graham* 161 And there was a clause favoring the speedier sale of public school lands.

public vendue. A vendue *q.v.*, often with *at* or *by*. Also attrib.

1678 *N.J. Archives* (1880) I. 196 Desiring it may be sold at a public vendue for the payment of his just debts. **1705** *Boston News-Letter* 23 April 2/2 On Tuesday the 15th of May next will be Exposed to Sale by Publick Vendue . . . one quarter part of a Farm. **1710** *S.C. Statutes* II. 348 The person herein after appointed publick vendue master, or his deputy. **1851** A. CARY *Clovernook* 231 Bills posted in front of the Clovernook Hotel, . . . stating, in large printed letters, that there 'would be sold at public vendue, . . . all the following property.'

* **public work.** An architectural or engineering structure or improvement, as a canal, park, building, etc., done by the government at public expense and for the welfare of the public. Usu. *pl.*

1676 in NEILL *Virginia Carolorum* 361 For haveing upon specious pretences of publique works raised great unjust taxes [etc.]. **1777** *N.H. Comm. Safety Rec.* 69, £4-5-6 for working & finding Tools . . . , on the publick works at New Castle. **1818** *N. Amer. Rev.* VIII. 11 Upon an application of the citizens of Petersburg [Va.], the Board of Public Works directed their Engineer to make a survey. **1850** GLISAN *Jrnl. Army Life* 29 The most important public work in the vicinity is the United States Navy Yard. **1903** E. JOHNSON *Railway Transportation* 16 The opening of the Erie Canal roused Pennsylvania to action, and in 1826 she began her system of 'public works,' the main feature of which was a composite rail and water route. **1932** *Army & Navy Jrnl.* 30 April 837/1 Title V of the bill sets up a Public Works Administration.

* **publishment,** *n.* The action of making public the banns or the names of persons intending marriage. *Obs.* or *hist.*

1692 *Mass. Province Laws* I. 61 The fee to be paid for every marriage shall be three shillings, and for publishment and certificate thereof, one shilling. **1788** *Mayflower Descendant* XI. 41 Levi Young Entred his Intentions of Marriage with Molly Godfrey Both of Chatham in order for Publishment. **1898** *Hist. Northampton, Mass.* I. 104 The publishment, when not posted, is . . . supposed to have been made by announcement.

puccoon pəˈkun, *n.* [f. Algonquian. "According to Trumbull and Gerard the word is from, or from the same root as, the name for blood" (Hodge).] Any one of various plants, or their roots, prized by the Indians for their yielding red or yellow pigment. Also the pigment itself. Also attrib. Cf. ***bloodroot, Sanguinaria.**

1612 SMITH *Virginia* 13 Pocones is a small roote that groweth in the mountaines, which being dryed and beate in powder turneth red; and this they vse for swellings, aches, annointing their ioints, painting their heads and garments. *c***1618** STRACHEY *Virginia* 64 Their heads and shoulders they paint oftennest, and those red, with the root pochone. *Ib.* 192 Poughkone, the red paint or die. **1775** CRESSWELL *Journal* 72 Clark . . . showed me a root that the Indians call pocoon, good for the bite of a Rattle Snake. **1824** DODDRIDGE *Notes* 148 Indian physic, or bowman root, a species of epicacuanha was frequently used for a vomit and sometimes the pocoon or blood root. **1948** *Life* 5 April 59/1 In the left foreground grow purplish wild phlox and verbena alongside orange puccoon.

b. Also **puccoon root.**

1709 LAWSON *Carolina* 172 For want of this Root, they sometimes use Pecoon-Root, which is of a Crimson Colour, but it is apt to die the Hair of an ugly Hue. *c***1866** BAGBY *Old Va. Gentleman* 60 An exceedingly strange whim . . . accompanied by preposterous vagaries about the virtues of puccoon-root, 'jimson' weed, white oak bark. **1893** *Amer. Folk-Lore* VI. 137 *Sanguinaria Canadensis,* puccoon, Banner Elk, N.C.; puccoon root, Anderson, Ind. **1949** *Sat. Ev. Post* 16 April 143/1 Recollection of his recent capers in the sun caused the boy suddenly to blush like a puccoon root.

As the last term in **Canadian, red, yellow puccoon.**

* **pucker,** *n.* In colloq. or slang combs. and derivative expressions, usu. obs.: (1) **pucker brush, bush,** (see quot. 1897); (2) **mouth,** the summer flounder, *Paralichthys dentatus;* (3) **-stoppled,** *a.* flouted, treated with contempt, embarrassed; (4) **struck,** fond of finery.

(1) 1897 SUDWORTH *Arborescent Flora* 117 *Myrica cerifera.* Wax Myrtle. . . . Puckerbush (Fla.). **1901** *Rhodora* June 159 We found after struggling through the 'pucker-brush' which formed an almost impassible barrier before it, . . . that it was a most interesting place. — **(2) 1884** GOODE *Fisheries* I. 178 In Rhode Island the names Brail and Puckermouth are used. — **(3) 1838** *N.Y. Mirror* 23 June 411/1 Says he, I don't be licked by a woman no how; well says she I don't be pucker-stoppled in that way, I can tell ye. — **(4) 1901** SARAH R. M. GREENE *Flood-tide* xxxiii. 296, I hope as the years go by your tastes 'll git a little more pucker-struck: the's sech a thing as not bein' pucker-struck enough.

* **puckery,** *a.* Of fruit or other food: That makes the mouth pucker.

1834 S. SMITH *Major Downing* 47, I guess he'll find the apple-sauce full as puckery when he gets down into it. **1916** PORTER *David* 274 You know what she is—sour as a lemon an' puckery as a chokecherry.

b. puckery hickory, (see quot.). *Obs.*

1724 JONES *Virginia* 145 Such [dealers] have often doubly cheated the Government; first by running Tobacco, or entering all light Hogsheads at Importation, which in their Language is called *Hickory-puckery;* and then again by getting a Debenture for Tobacco that has been run, or entering all heavy Hogsheads for Exportation, which they term *Puckery-hickory.*

* **pudding,** *n.* **1.** (See quot. 1860.) **2.** *To turn a pudding,* of a kite: To turn down and upward. Both *obs.*

(1) 1840 NEAL *Beedle's Sleigh Ride* 13 His cravat had a pudding in it. **1860** MORDECAI *Virginia* 185 Those who could afford neither the valet, nor so extensive an investment of muslin, resorted to a substitute for its bulk, in what was called a pudding, or . . . a pad, which formed the foundation on which the cravat was built. **1868** G. G. CHANNING *Recoll. Newport* 241 The collar of the shirt . . . was inclosed by what was called either a cravat or stock or neckcloth or 'pudding.' — **(2) 1844** *Knickerb.* XXIV. 260 There is one which has just 'turned a pudding' twenty times.

As the last term in **bread, corn, corporation, cottage, cranberry, float, fried, hasty, huckleberry, Indian, Marlborough, meal, Nesselrode, pumpkin, punk, sawdust, stir, sweet potato, tipsy pudding.**

pudjicky ˈpʌdʒɪkɪ, *a.* [Origin obscure.] Fussy, sensitive. *Colloq.*

1866 A. D. WHITNEY *L. Goldthwaite* iii, She's dreadfully *pudjicky,* Emma Jane is; she won't have anything without it's exactly right. **1891** *Amer. Folk-Lore* IV. March 71 *Pudgicky,* similar to preceding [*pernickety*], but with a notion of being cross and fretful. . . . *Cambridge, Mass.* **1911** *D.N.* III. 546 *Pudjiky, putchy,* . . . sullen, or pettish. 'Mary's acting a little pudjiky today.' [Neb.]

pueblano pweˈblano, *n. S.W.* [Sp., see quot. 1942.] One who lives in a pueblo, a villager. In quot. 1849, those living in San Jose, Calif. — **1849** *Alta California* (S.F.) 28 Dec. 1/3 The Pueblanos are much frightened at the proposal of changing the capital. [**1942** SANTAMARÍA *Diccionario* 528/2 Puebleño, Pueblero. Gentilicios comunes y corrientes en la literatura y en la conversación amerindohispana, por lugareño o habitante de un pueblo.]

pueblo ˈpwɛblo, *n.* [This Sp. word meaning village was used, in the *pl.*, to refer to the Pueblo Indians. See **2.** below.]

1. An Indian village made up of several separate adobe or stone buildings, or a large, many-storied, terraced building serving to house the members of the whole community. Also attrib. Cf. **purbelo.**

1808 SHALER *Journal* (1935) 62 Santa Cruz, near Point Ano Nuevo, and a *pueblo* of the same name in its neighbourhood, from the northern frontier of the juris[dic]tion of Monterrey [Calif.]. **1836** EDWARD *Hist. Texas* 162 When the Alcaldes or the citizens of the *pueblo* are plaintiffs or defendants, the conciliation shall be had . . . before the first Corregidor. **1867** LATHAM *Black & White* 173 Over all the territory of Mexico the Indians are the cultivators of the land, living by themselves in villages, 'pueblos,' selling their labour in advance to the large proprietors. **1950** *L.A. Times* Midwinter 3 Jan. 7/2 The story of how Los Angeles rose from a sleepy pueblo to become the giant of the West . . . is one of the most extraordinary in American history.

2. (*cap.*) An Indian belonging to a tribe that lives in one of these villages or buildings, usu. *pl.*, with reference to the tribe.

1834 A. PIKE *Sketches* 141 These Pueblos, (a word which signifies tribes—of Indians) are in fact, all handsome, athletic men. **1870** *Republican Rev.* 21 May 2/3 The Utes are known to be the best Indians in the Territory—always, of course, excepting the Pueblos. **1893** T. C. DONALDSON *Moqui Pueblo Indians* 10 The beautiful legend of the Pueblo looking from the roof of his house for the coming of Montezuma.

In full **Pueblo Indian.**

1844 GREGG *Commerce of Prairies* I. 132 Two thousand of the insurgent mob, including the Pueblo Indians, pitched their camp in the suburbs of the capital [Santa Fe]. **1949** *Nat. Geog. Mag.* Dec. 783/2 Long-haired Pueblo Indians wrapped in cotton blankets exchange stare for stare with visiting easterners.

attrib. **1849** *31st Congress* 1 Sess. Sen. Ex. Doc. No. 64, 63, I notice here [at Jemez], on the outskirts of the village, the usual accompaniments of Mexican and pueblo towns. **1882** *Harper's Mag.* June 80/1 The hard earthen floor of the room was covered with Navajo and Pueblo blankets. **1906** H. Quick *Double Trouble* 25 A glimpse of an interior hung with Navajo blankets, Pueblo pottery. **1941** Fergusson *Southwest* 275 The New Museum borrowed features of the pueblo missions especially the twin towers of Acoma.

b. Used in archaeology with reference to periods when, it is thought, the building of pueblos prevailed.

1934 Morris *Digging in Southwest* 56 The period following Basket Maker III has been labeled Pueblo I. **1937** *Southwestern Lore* Dec. 55 Use of the reducing atmosphere in firing pottery, therefore, is a fundamental cultural trait of the Pueblo culture, a culture that seems to have resulted from an early contact of the Basket Maker and Mogollon cultures. **1946** *Science Digest* Aug. 34/1 Men and women too had lived in the cave long before Pueblo times. **1949** *Travel* Dec. 8/1 The great common denominator of the Pueblo Period was survival by natural defenses.

3. In derivatives as **puebloan, puebloism.**

1855 *Golden Era* (S.F.) 14 Jan. 1/6 San Francisco has abounded with gambling ever since her days of primitive *Pueblo-ism.* **1933** Harrington *Gypsum Cave, Nev.* 20 The upper layer contained . . . such artifacts as fiber strings, . . . occasional pieces of Puebloan pottery, and selenite pendants in varying stages of completion. **1937** *Southwestern Lore* Sep. 30 A few dish-like vessels, and one plaque were also found, which are definitely not Puebloan but are Hohokam. **1940** Jaeger *Calif. Deserts* 125 These turquoise deposits are scattered over a considerable area, yet the Puebloans seem to have found them all, for modern prospectors say they have never found an unworked outcropping.

***puff adder.** =**hog-nosed snake.** — **1882** *Amer. Naturalist* XVI. 566 Twice afterward I noticed this strange habit of the puff adders. **1949** *Nat. Hist.* Nov. 415/2 This formidable behavior has . . . earned it a reputation for being aggressive and highly poisonous, as well as the sinister names 'puff adder,' 'hissing viper,' and 'spread head.'

* **puffer,** *n.*

1. Any one of several fishes of the family Tetraodontidae, esp. the globefish, *Sphoeroides maculatus,* of the Atlantic Coast.

1814 Mitchell *Fishes N.Y.* 473 Puffer. . . . He is called in some places, *toad-fish,* because his back is mottled with yellow and dark. **1911** *Rep. Fisheries 1908* 317/1 Swell-fish (*Tetraodontidæ*).—The different species are known as 'globe-fishes,' 'puffers,' 'swell-toad,' etc.

2. (See quot. 1884.)

1864 Webster 1059/1. **1884** Goode *Fisheries* I. 170 The Porcupine Fishes—Diodontidæ. Swell Fishes and Puffers.—There are four species of this family inhabiting the Atlantic coast, and two on the coast of California.

3. =**harbor porpoise.**

1884 Goode *Fisheries* I. 14 On the Atlantic coast occurs most abundantly the little Harbor Porpoise *Phocaena brachycion* Cope, known to the fishermen as 'Puffer,' 'Snuffer' [etc.]. **1911** *Rep. Fisheries 1908* 314/1 Porpoise (*Phocœna communis*).—A cetacean found on the north Atlantic and north Pacific coasts, ascending rivers. It is known as 'harbor porpoise,' 'herring-hog,' 'puffer' [etc.].

puffing grubby. A sculpin (see quot. 1884). — **1884** Goode *Fisheries* I. 258 On our Atlantic coast are found several species of . . . [the Cottidae], generally known by the name 'Sculpin,' and also by such titles as 'Grubby,' 'Puffing-grubby,' 'Daddy Sculpin' [etc.]. **1911** *Rep. Fisheries 1908* 315/1.

pugasaing ˈpʌgəˌsɔ·ɪŋ, *n.* [App. an Indian term.] = ***bowl,** *n.* **1.** *Obs.* — **1848** Schoolcraft *Indians* 188 Pugasaing; or, the game of the bowl . . . is the principal game of hazard among the northern tribes. *Ib.* 189 The term pugasaing denotes this act of throwing. It is the participial form of the verb.

pug brandy. [Cf. s.w. Eng. dial. **pug,* "apple pulp."] A low grade of brandy, supposedly made from the refuse of a cider press. *Obs.* — **1857** *Harper's Mag.* Nov. 859/1 He was addicted to the use of the low wines of the distilleries, bald-face whisky, pug brandy, hard cider, etc.

puim pwɪm, *n.* [f. the native term for the game.] (See quots.) *Obs.* — **1634** Wood *N. Eng. Prospect* 85 The Indians . . . have two sorts of games, one called *Puim,* the other *Hubbub,* not much unlike Cards and Dice, being no other than Lotterie. **1764** T. Hutchinson *Hist. Mass.* I. 470 They had two principal games of chance, one they called puim, this was much the same with a game Charlevoix mentions among the Miamis, which he calls jeu des pailles, or the game of straws.

* **puke,** *n.*

1. (*cap.*) A Missourian. A nickname.

The reason for this application of the term is not known. Cf. Irish *puke,* "a poor puny unhealthy-looking person" (P. W. Joyce, *English As We Speak It,* 308).

1835 A. Parker *Trip to Texas* 87 The inhabitants . . . of Michigan are called *wolverines;* . . . of Missouri, *pukes,* &c. **1893** *Chi. Tribune* 26 April 6/4, I have noticed . . . a great many learned and owl-like explanations of why Illinoisans are called 'Suckers' and Missourians 'Pukes.' **1948** *Dly. Ardmoreite* (Ardmore, Okla.) 11 July 21/5 Missourians have rejoiced in the name of 'Pukes' and Illinoisians as 'Suckers.'

Hence **Pukedom,** Missouri. Also attrib. *Obs.*

1853 *Alta California* (S.F.) 7 May 2/2 The steamers from the Ohio have just commenced bringing round their quotas, to add to the general outpouring from the States around our own Pukedom homestead. **1856** Brewerton *War in Kans.* 367 A week ago, one hundred well-armed men could have stormed our town, but our condition was not known in 'Pukedom.'

b. A ruffian or obnoxious person. *Contemptuous.*

1847 Robb *Squatter Life* 152 Captain and all hands are a set of cowardly *pukes!* **1867** Devens *Pictorial Bk.* 159 I'll show you how I parole such pukes as you are. **1943** DeVoto *Yr. of Decision* 310 They had become resentful of croakers, called him a Puke, and moved on.

2. pukeweed, (see quot.). *Colloq.*

1848 Dunglison *Med. Lexicon* 510/1 *Lobelia Inflata,* Indian Tobacco, Wild Tobacco, Puke Weed [etc.].

* **Pulaski,** *n.* A tool that may be used as an ax or as a mattock, so called from its designer, E. C. Pulaski, a forest ranger, who *c*1910–20 perfected such an implement for the use of rangers and forest fire fighters. Also attrib.

1924 *Frontier* Nov. 20, I saw Paul, his back bowed, his Pulaski swingin' like a flail, an' his breath comin' in short gasps. **1946** *Trail & Timberline* June 91/1 Planting hoes, grub hoes, and Pulaski hoes had been provided by the rangers as well as planting bags and burlap in which trees were covered and protected from the sun. **1948** *Highway Traveler* Aug. 37/1 Besides technical information on fighting fire with chemicals, or with axe and pulaski, smoke-jumpers are taught to bail out from a specially-constructed tower.

pulchritudinous ˌpʌlkrəˈt(j)udn̩əs, *a.* [f. L. *pulchritudo,* beauty, +*-inous.*] Beautiful, fine, morally excellent.

1912 L. J. Vance *Destroying Angel* xv. 217, I love my love with a P because he's Perfectly Pulchritudinous and Possesses the Power of Pleasing. **1925** *Times* (London) 13 Dec. 11/6 In an American paper . . . the Yarmouth councillors were described as 'pulchritudinous.' **1949** *Chi. Tribune* 21 Feb. I. 28/5 By us the hippopotamus. . . . Is never counted pulchritudinous.

Pulitzer Prize. Any one of various annual prizes in arts and letters established by Joseph Pulitzer (1847–1911), an American (Hungarian born) author and publisher. Also attrib.

1918 *N.Y. Times* 3 June 9/7 The annual Pulitzer Prize of $1,000 for the best play written and produced by an American playwright in 1917 . . . [has] been awarded to Jesse Lynch Williams for his comedy, 'Why Marry?' **1921** *New Republic* 22 June 114/2 The University is not bound to distribute the Pulitzer Prizes according to any particular method of award. **1947** *Newsweek* 12 June 63/3 The Pulitzer Prize committee demonstrated its concern for things Russian in its journalistic awards for 1946.

Also **Pulitzer.**

1950 *Time* 23 Jan. 38/3 In 1941, Herblock drew the cartoon for N.E.A. that won him a Pulitzer.

* **pull,** *n.* Influence susceptible of being used for one's advantage. *Colloq.* or *slang.*

1887 *N.Y. Herald* 21 Feb. 3/3 He can't be put in jail because he has a pull. **1911** Wright *Winning Barbara Worth* 25 'Tis a good healthy pull he must have to be seperatin' us from thim San Felipe police. **1948** *Chi. Tribune* 21 Nov. 20/7 Thus far I have not been able to find out just what 'has it' means, unless it means 'pull.'

As the last term in **candy, chicken, gander, political, taffy-pull.**

* **pull,** *v.*

1. *S. tr.* To break the ears of (corn) from the stalks in harvesting.

1805 Parkinson *Tour* 384 To pulling the corn. **1854** Davis *Farm Bk.* 114 Finished puling & hauling the reed brake corn. **1949** *Southwestern Hist. Quart.* Oct. 153 A Negro boy named Smith was sent to pull corn.

2. *S.* (See quot. 1882.)

1843 in Thompson *M. Jones* (1872) 161 I've had more than usual to tend to about the plantation, pullin fodder and pickin out a little. **1882** *Cent. Mag.* XXIV. 873 The first work toward gathering the corn crop in Georgia is to strip the stalks of their blades, *i.e.,* 'pull the fodder,' which is done in August or September. **1948** Dick *Dixie Frontier* 100 This was known as pulling fodder.

3. To drawl. *Rare.*

1857 MARK TWAIN in Paine *Biog.* (1912) I. 118 (R.), 'What makes you pull your words that way?' . . . 'You'll have to ask my mother . . . she pulls hers, too.'

4. To draw (a gun). Also absol.

1883 MARK TWAIN *Life on Miss.* xxvi, When they happened to meet, they pulled and begun. **1903** *N.Y. Sun* 2 Dec. 3 (*headline*), He Thought Simms Was Going To Pull A Gun. **1949** *Oak Leaves* (Oak Park, Ill.) 24 Nov. 7/2 Both pulled guns on him and commanded that he drive to the Forest Preserves in Lyons.

5. In special colloq. and slang senses: **a.** *tr.* To stretch or draw (candy) until it is ready to set. Cf. **candy pull(ing). b.** To "fix" (a race). **c.** To play (a trick), to commit (a crime). **d.** *intr.* Of a log jam: To break. **e.** Of an advertisement: To secure results.

(a) 1842 in THOMPSON *M. Jones* (1872) 79 'Oh, come in, child, and set a while with the galls—they's pullin lasses candy in the parlor. **1893** *Harper's Mag.* Feb. 442 He pulled the candy with glee, but also with eager industry, covering platter after platter with his braided sticks. — **(b) 1902** WISTER *Virginian* xxxv, 'This race will not be pulled,' said McLean. — **(c) 1916** WILSON *Somewhere* 353 But Pete had pulled this too often before when in difficulties. **1948** *Ariz. Republic* (Phoenix) 29 Feb. I. 8/1 Rumor has it that a gang of 'toughs' will . . . pull one of the slickest holdups since Billy the Kid terrorized the Southwest. — **(d) 1902** WHITE *Blazed Trail* 329 When the logs began to cave under them . . . the foreman set the example of hunting safety. 'She "pulls," boys,' he yelled. — **(e) 1914** S. H. ADAMS *Clarion* 33 Talk about ads. that pull! It pulled like a mule-team and a traction engine and a fifty-cent painless dentist all in one.

b. In colloq. phrases: (1) *To pull it*, to run away; (2) *to pull for*, to favor, aid, encourage; (3) **to pull out*, to withdraw *from* an undertaking, to leave, depart, proceed; (4) **to pull up*, short for *to pull up stakes*, see ***stake,** *n.* **4. a;** (5) *to pull a boner*, see ***boner.**

(1) 1804 FESSENDEN *Orig. Poems* (1806) 79 And then she flew straight out of sight, As fast as she could pull it. — **(2) 1903** *Forum* Oct. 311 Such committees are exposed to all kinds of influence— . . . all pulling for this or that applicant. **1949** *Nat. Geog. Mag.* Sep. 321/1 I'm usually pulling for the Indians instead of the cowboys. — **(3) 1884** *Missouri Republican* 24 Feb. (Farmer), He knows that if he keeps his money in the . . . business . . . he will lose it all, and so he has pulled out. **1887** F. FRANCIS *Saddle & Mocassin* viii. 146 For a minute or two they stood looking at one another, and then Doc 'pulled out.' **1891** C. ROBERTS *Adrift Amer.* 18 The train that was to take me on . . . was nearly ready to 'pull out,' as the phrase goes in America. **1907** LONDON *Road* 194 While there, we met McAvoy, Fish, Scotty, and Davy, who had also pulled out from the Army. — **(4) 1931** *K.C. Times* 1 Dec. 20 When a man becomes decidedly dissatisfied with his wife, he's pretty sure to pull up and leave her.

6. In noun combs.: (1) ***pull back,** (see quot.); (2) **boat,** (*a*) a boat propelled by pulling a rope, *rare* [cf. Du. *trekschuit*], (*b*) (see quot.); (3) **bone,** the wishbone of a chicken, also **pully bone.**

(1) 1905 *Forestry Bureau Bul.* No. 61, 39 *Haul back*, a small wire rope, traveling between the donkey engine and a pulley set near the logs to be dragged, used to return the cable. (P[acific] C[oast] F[orest].) . . . [Also called] back line, pull back, trip line. — **(2)** (*a*) **1883** *Harper's Mag.* 172/2 It is a treat to see a powerful young Dutchwoman handle a rope on a pull-boat. (*b*) **1903** *Sci. Amer.* 17 Oct. 276/3 In the cypress swamps of Louisiana there are employed what are known as pull-boats, an evolution from the plan of placing a hoisting engine upon a scow and snaking the logs out of the swamp. . . . The endless-rope pull-boat engines have 44-inch winding drums. — **(3)** *a***1906** O. HENRY *Trimmed Lamp* 136 In her mind she could hear the girls shrieking over a pullbone. **1939** HARRIS *Purslane* 148 The girls scrambled over the pulley-bone of the turkey. **1949** *Amer. Sp.* XXIV. 288 Directions for canning chickens without bones tell how to remove the *pully bone* from the breast meat.

pulldoo ˈpʊldu, *n. local.* [F. *poule d'eau*, "water hen."] The American coot. — **1859** BARTLETT 347 *Pull-doo*, a small black duck found in the bays and inlets of the Gulf of Mexico. **1917** *Birds of Amer.* I. 214.

pulled wool. Wool taken from the skin of a dead sheep. — **1832** *Niles' Reg.* 29 Sep. 67/1 There continues a good demand for fleece and pulled wool. **1890** *Stock Grower & Farmer* 5 April 5/1 At Boston pulled wools are quiet.

***puller,** *n.* As the last term in **bell, gander, grub, plug, stump, wire puller.**

puller-in, *n.* (See quot. 1942.) *Slang.* — **1895** J. L. FORD *Lit. Shop* ix. (1896) 132 The Jewish old-clothing quarter that lies close to the Five Points is near by. The 'pullers-in,' as the sidewalk salesmen are termed in the vernacular of the trade, transact business with a ferocity that can be best likened to that of Siberian wolves. **1942** BERREY & VAN DEN BARK *Amer. Thesaurus Slang* 542 puller-in, . . . one who tries to induce passers-by to come into a store.

pullikins ˈpʊləkɪnz, *n. pl.* [f. **pull, v.*+**-kins*, dim.] Pincers, forceps. Also fig. *Colloq.*

1845 *Big Bear Ark.* 171 He sings out for the pinchers—swore they were his favorite insterments—always used 'em—beat pullicans to h——! **1860** MORDECAI *Virginia* 272 As a preacher he drew the fangs of Satan with his spiritual pullikins. **1949** *Amer. Sp.* April 112/1 Pullikins, *n. pl.* Tweezers for pulling teeth. [Baldwin Co., Ga.]

***pulling,** *n.* **1. pulling-bone,** (see quot. 1877 and cf. **pullbone**). **2. pulling-hook,** a hook on which taffy is pulled.

(1) 1877 BARTLETT 502 *Pulling-Bone*, the common name in Maryland, Virginia, &c., for the yoke-like breast-bone of chickens, by pulling which till it breaks children and young ladies settle which will be the first married. **1939** *L.A.* Map 215. — **(2) 1886** *Harper's Mag.* June 93/2 The paste [for candy] then goes to the 'pulling-hooks,' where for five or six minutes it is pulled and twisted and repulled and retwisted.

As the last term in **flax, gander, goose, gun, molasses candy, pole, sorghum, wire, wool pulling.**

***Pullman,** *n.* [George M. *Pullman* (1831–97), the designer.]

1. A railroad passenger car, esp. a sleeping car, built by the Pullman Company. Cf. **horse-power Pullman.**

1870 *R.R. Gazette* 2 April 3/2 Six new Pullman's—four commissary and two sleeping cars—are now receiving 'lightning' finishing strokes in the paint shop. **1892** LUMMIS *Tramp Across Continent* 1 Railroads and Pullmans were invented to help us hurry through life and miss most of the pleasure of it. **1946** *Chi. D. News* 7 March 10/2 Is somebody trying to couple a Pullman to the gravy train?

attrib. **1870** *R.R. Gazette* 2 April 3/1 Two of the new Pullman coaches . . arrived Thursday. **1906** LYNDE *Quickening* 178 He had engaged Pullman reservations for six persons to New York. **1948** *N.M. Quart. Rev.* Winter 432 There were cancelled pullman reservations for the next day.

b. In the possessive: The Pullman Company's. *Obs.*

1868 H. M. FLINT *Railroads of U.S.* 406 We left Albany . . . in a Pullman's saloon parlor car. **1872** TICE *Over Plains* 7 Back into one of Pullman's sleeping cars, I was soon stowed away in one of its ample berths. **1879** VIVIAN *Wanderings Western Land* 92 A night in a Pullman's 'sleeper,' and the morning found us far on the way to Toronto.

2. In special combs.: (1) **Pullman conductor,** a railroad conductor in charge of a Pullman train; (2) **porter,** a porter who works on a Pullman car; (3) **train,** a railroad train made up of Pullman cars.

(1) 1887 *Courier-Journal* 6 Feb. 4/1 The body of Pullman Conductor Burgess was one of the first taken out. **1947** *Chi. Sun Book Week* 13 July 2/2 The Pullman conductor on tomorrow's noon train has been given your transportation. — **(2) 1890** *Harper's Mag.* Jan. 327/1 Samson is a former Pullman porter, and a most efficient servitor. **1947** *Chi. D. News* 28 Feb. 1/2, I remember the Pullman Porter. He was a real hero. — **(3) 1905** RICE *Sandy* 129 When the Pullman train came into the Clayton station, he was leaning against a truck in a pose of studied indifference. **1945** *Chi. D. News* 4 April 19/4 Her description of how she helped deliver a baby on a Pullman train . . . would tear at anyone's heartstrings.

b. Designating various types of railroad passenger cars built by the Pullman Company, as (1) **Pullman car,** (2) **colonist sleeping car,** (3) **hotel car,** (4) **palace car,** (5) **parlor,** (6) **roomette,** (7) **sleeper,** (also transf.), (8) **sleeping car.**

(1) 1867 *Comm. & Fin. Chron.* V. 347/2 These Pullman cars . . . are quite as strong and serviceable as they are elegant and luxurious. **1949** J. MONAGHAN *This is Ill.* 144 The American Railway Union refused to handle Pullman cars. — **(2) 1889** Union Pac. R.R. *Ore. & Wash.* 80 A Pullman colonist sleeping car line is now in operation between Portland . . . and Kansas City. — **(3) 1875** *Chi. Tribune* 11 Sep. 1/7 Pullman hotel cars are also run on the western part of the road. **1940** *Quiz* [Quest. 382] The trip from Boston to San Francisco consumed eight days [in 1870], and was made in Pullman 'hotel cars,' then the newest thing in railroading. — **(4) 1870** *Republican Rev.* 6 Aug. 1/2 The road [from Kansas to Denver] now carries four of the Pullman Palace Cars. **1940** EARLY *N. Eng. Sampler* 320 His stint accomplished, Mr. McAllister took a Pullman Palace car to New York, and had dinner at the Union Club.

(5) 1868 BOWLES *Colorado* (1869) 11 In your Pullman parlor, . . . the journey to San Francisco may be made with . . . comfort and luxury, unequaled hitherto. — **(6) 1941** SKINNER *Soap Behind Ears* 67 The rooms in the newer of what are known as the 'leading' hotels are often of dimensions akin to those of a Pullman roomette. — **(7) 1875** *Chi. Tribune* 11 Sep. 3/2 Every item of wood, iron, or upholstery which enters into the make-up . . . of a Pullman sleeper is Selected with Skilled Care. **1929** J. PARKER *Old Army* 195 We traveled in Pullman sleepers as far as Chicago. **1949** *Sat. Ev. Post* 15 Oct. 115/3

You, too, will want the Pullman Sleeper because it is, first of all, such a good-looking deeply cushioned sofa. . . . Yet, when extra sleeping space is needed, you will have a restful, full-size bed, *as easily as pulling out a drawer*. — (8) **1907** *St. Nicholas* July 771/2 This route ain't as popular as if it had Pullman sleeping cars. **1940** *Quiz* [Quest. 407] Mr. Pullman regarded the converted passenger coaches merely as experiments, and at Chicago in 1864 he began building the first real Pullman sleeping car . . . Pullman's first sleeper . . . cost $20,178.

* **pulp,** *n.* A magazine printed on cheap paper made of woodpulp and usu. containing matter of a cheap, sensational nature.

[**1931** *Sat. Ev. Post* 7 March 60/4 The downfall of the old dime novel was started by the cheap movies; it was completed by the newsprint, or pulp paper, magazine.] **1931** *Frontier* Nov. 82/1 Even should he fail to publish in the big magazines, and never graduate from the 'pulps,' he can rise to as much as ten cents a word.

In full **pulp magazine.**

1931 *Frontier* Nov. 83/1 We need some outlets for the work, with pay, of young and enthusiastic writers; something to keep them away from the 'pulp' and 'slick paper' magazines. **1947** *Chi. Sun* 18 Nov. 43/4 In obscure books and pulp magazines, those pseudo-scientific scriveners peeked into the future. **1948** *Sat. Ev. Post* 3 July 27/1 He was the living proof that there may be something in the pulp-magazine ads which show pictures of knotty-muscled supermen.

pulperia ˌpulpəˈriə, *n. S.W.* [Amer. Sp. *pulpería* in same sense.] A grocery and liquor store. *Obs.*

1825 Paulding *Journal Cruise* (1831) 9 There were but two rooms in it, one of which was occupied as a granary and bed-room, and the other as a pulparia. **1827** Head *Journey* 159 It is a pulperia (shop), and is filled with peons drinking. **1869** Dana *Two Years* (new ed.) 451 Tom Wrightington, who kept the rival pulperia, fell from his horse when drunk.

* **pulpit,** *n.* **1.** A raised platform from which a machine can be observed and controlled. **2. pulpit rock,** a rock having the appearance of a pulpit.

(1) **1880** *Harper's Mag.* Dec. 62 Another shout, and the boy touches another lever in the gallery of levers, irreverently termed the 'pulpit.' **1903** *Electrical World* 26 Dec. 1051/2 The operator of the hoisting motor stands in a pulpit above the floor. — (2) **1841** Barber & Howe *Hist. Coll. N.Y. State* 201 One mile west of the village [Oxbow], is a rock called 'pulpit rock.' **1888** *Harper's Mag.* June 41/1 Its side ravines have fantastic pulpit rocks and pinnacles.

pulque ˈpulkɪ, *n. S.W.* [Amer. Sp. (f. a native word) in the same sense. An Amer. borrowing.] A fermented drink made from various species of *Agave*, esp. *A. atrovirens*.

[**1529** in J. de Paredes *Recopilacion de Leyes de los Reynos* (1681), Usan los Indios de la Nueva España de una bebida, llamada pulque, que desilan los magueyes.] **1796** Morse *Univ. Geog.* I. 729 (*footnote*), *Pulque* is the usual wine or beer of the Mexicans, made of the fermented juice of the Maguei. **1829** *Western Mo. Rev.* May 658 The Maguey, is a plant, that grows in many parts spontaneously, and from which they derive a liquor, called *pulk*, which is much used in large cities. **1949** *Nat. Hist.* Nov. 385/1 They plague the fleshy leaves of the several species of maguey (*Agave* spp.), an ever-present source of Mexico's popular and potent alcoholic beverages: pulque, mescal, and tequila.

attrib. **1894** *Outing* Jan. 303/2 The pulque shops have signs, such as 'The Devil,' and 'The Little Hell.'

b. (See quot.) *Rare.*

1873 Arny *Items regarding N. Mex.* 22 A species of the maguey plant grows in the Caballo Mountains . . . from which a sweet wholesome and palatable food as well as drink is made by the Mexicans and Indians. . . . The food is called 'Pulque' and the liquor 'Mescal.'

pulqueria ˌpulkəˈriə, *n. S.W.* [Amer. Sp. *pulquería* in same sense.] A place where pulque is sold.

1847 Ruxton *Mexico* 43 (Bentley), After leaving the pulqueria we visited . . . the dens. **1894** *Outing* Jan. 302/2 Here are stalls for the sale of cheap refreshments, and more *pulquerias*. **1934** S. E. White *Folded Hills* 375 He can play his guitar and entertain the drunkards in the *pulquerias*.

pulse-warmer. (See quot. 1942.) *Colloq.* — **1876** Bourke *Journal* 1 March, 'Pulse-warmers' about 6 inches long will preserve the wrists. **1942** Warnick *Dialect Garrett Co., Md.* 12 Pulse-warmer, n., knitted covering for the wrist.

pulu ˈpulu, *n.* [Hawaiian.]

1. A soft cottony chaff obtained in the Hawaiian Islands from the leaf stalks of various tree ferns of the genus *Cibotium*.

1858 *S.F. Bulletin* 21 May 2/6 Pulu! Pulu! Pulu! For sale at the Rochester Bedding Store. **1865** *Eastern Slope* (Washoe, Nev.) 30 Dec. 2/4 When thoroughly cleaned and pulped, it is . . . superior to pulu, inasmuch as it does not form into hard lumps.

2. A fern from which this substance is obtained. In full **pulu fern.** Also **pulu tree.**

1860 *No. Californian* (Arcata) 27 June 1/4 The pulu tree is a species of Fern . . . growing to a height of from fifteen to twenty-five feet. **1861** in *Amer. Sp.* XXII. (1946) 150 As to the *other* fruits and flowers of the country, there ain't any, except 'Pulu' or 'Tuler,' or whatever they call it,—a species of unpoetical willow that grows on the banks of the Carson. **1888** *Proc. Calif. Acad. Sci.* 12 As accidentally introduced alive, I may refer to the specimen of *Athoraphorus* found in a bale of the 'Pulu' fern brought from the Sandwich Islands for mattress making.

* **pump,** *n.* In combs.: (1) **pump log,** a log suitably bored or hollowed out for making a pump or a water pipe, now *hist.*, cf. **water log;** (2) **thunder,** (see quot.), *colloq.;*

Pump log, water log, or log pipe

(3) **tree,** ?a hollow tree suitable for a pump log (see also quot. 1928).

(1) **1816** *N. Amer. Rev.* III. 429 The mill for grinding apples . . . is an overshot, and is fed by a pump log. **1879** Stockton *Rudder Grange* 197 He looked like he'd been drawn through a pump-log. **1937** Lincoln *Wilmington Del.* 207 The committee reported that it would require eight hundred and thirty-five feet of pump-logs. — (2) **1891** *Cent.* 5891/1 *stake-driver*. . . . The American bittern. . . . Also *pile-driver, pump-thunder, thunder-pumper.* — (3) **1871** Burroughs *Wake-Robin* (1886) 11 One sees them [i.e., bluebirds] hovering with a saucy, inquiring air about barns and out-buildings, . . . inspecting knot-holes and pump-trees. **1928** *Old Time N. Eng.* Jan. 128/1 Edward Haycock, . . . with the pump auger . . . bores sixteen-foot white oak logs end-wise for wooden 'pump-trees,' at Fountainville, Bucks County, Pa.

As the last term in **China, irrigation, tea, thunder pump.** See also **opera pump.**

pumpage ˈpʌmpɪdʒ, *n.* The total amount or quantity pumped.

1881 *Scientific Amer.* XLIV. 361 The pumpage for last year amounted to 21,120,792,786 gallons. **1930** *Randolph Enterprise* (Elkins, W.Va.) 11 Dec. 1/6 The monthly report . . . was also presented showing a total pumpage of 19,460,000 gallons of water. **1949** *Chi. Tribune* 22 Dec. 2/1 That is more than $2\frac{1}{2}$ times last year's average daily pumpage of the Chicago water department—971.8 million gallons.

pumpernickel ˈpʌmpɚˌnɪkl, *n.* [G.] A form of dark, heavy bread, slightly sour, made of unbolted rye.

The *OED* records this word as early as 1756 in allusion to its use in Germany. The term app. never caught on in British use. Its Amer. currency is no doubt the result of an independent borrowing.

1839 Longfellow *Hyperion* ii, The devil take you, and your Westphalian ham, and pumpernickel! **1940** Hatcher *Buckeye Country* 300 If you stop at the local eating place and dance hall you may be refreshed with beer, gooseliver, and pumpernickel all made in the village. **1945** *Reader's Digest* May 50/1 Little bakeries . . . consistently produce delicious hard-crust white bread, honest black pumpernickel . . . and magnificent sour rye.

***pumping,** *n.* (See quot. 1887.) — **1875** *Chi. Tribune* 8 Dec. 3/2 They thought of a hand-car, and then shudderingly considered the job of pumping 200 miles. **1887** M. Roberts *Western Avernus* 241 A hand-car coming along . . . with some section hands working it along by means of the lever, 'pumping,' as it is commonly called.

* **pumpkin,** *n.*

1. A chump or dolt. *Colloq.* Cf. **pumpkin head** (*b*).

1768 in Buckingham *Newspaper Lit.* I. 148 Come shake your dull noddles, ye Pumpkins, and bawl. **1788** *Mass. Convention* (1856) 303 If a southern man heard it, he would call us pumpkins. **1855** Oliphant *Minnesota* 271 It's clar to me . . . that you've been residing among the Punkins in the Yankee States, and have not been long enough in our country to comprehend the gen-i-us of our institutions. **1927** Benét *J. B.'s Body* 61 Seward and Chase'll do for my pair of pumpkins.

2. A person of consequence or importance. *Colloq.*

1848 Lanman *Alleghany Mts.* (1849) 128 The contest consisted in their efforts to excel each other in complimenting their friend, and the climax of the argument seemed to be that Mr. Clingman was not *'some pumpkins'* but 'Pumpkins.' **1899** T. HALL *Tales* 14 The other two are troops of the Eleventh that think themselves particular pumpkins.

b. Esp. **some pumpkin(s).**

1846 *Spirit of Times* 18 April 91/2 Tom is 'some punkins.' **1909** O. HENRY *Roads of Destiny* 210 He was some pumpkin both in politics and colour. **1947** *N.Y. Times* 12 Oct. v. 2/6 Hornsby also thinks Hornsby was some pumpkins as a hitter.

Also of things.

1846 *Spirit of Times* 25 April 97/1 The skins, Indian relics, etc. are 'some punkins' and no mistake. **1869** BARNUM *Struggles & Triumphs* 569 You had better not wager too much on your fast horse, for you know mine is some pumpkins.

3. The orange color of a ripe pumpkin. *Rare.*

1850 LEWIS *La. Swamp Doctor* 73 He described the awful effects it [*sc.* ague] had upon our gals, developing their spleens, and bringing the punkin to their blessed faces.

4. *local.* (See quot.)

1897 KIPLING *Captains Courageous* iv. 120 Stripping the sea-cucumbers that they called pumpkins.

5. In combs.: (1) **pumpkin bread,** see as a main entry; (2) **butter,** a preserve or thick sauce made by boiling down pumpkins; (3) **head,** (*a*) (see quots.), (*b*) a stupid fellow, a dolt, *colloq.;* (4) **hood,** a snugly fitting hood or helmet of a shape suggestive of a pumpkin, *obs.*, cf. **muskmelon bonnet;** (5) **johnnycake,** johnnycake made of meal and pumpkin; (6) **pie,** see as a main entry; (7) **pine,** the white pine, *Pinus strobus*, of the eastern U.S., or a tree of this variety; (8) **porridge,** a porridge made of pumpkin, *obs.;* (9) **pudding,** a pudding made of boiled pumpkin; (10) ∗**seed,** see as a main entry; (11) **tavern,** ?a small or insignificant tavern, *rare;* (12) **vine,** (*a*) the coarse, decumbent vine of *Cucurbita pepo*, which bears pumpkins, (*b*) designating a kind of toy flute made from a pumpkin vine.

(2) 1853 in *Ore. Hist. Quart.* XLI. 365, I commenced making pumkin buter this morning. **1893** M. A. OWEN *Voodoo Tales* 6 The place of the vegetables was taken by . . . little jars of a villainous sweet compound of pumpkin stewed with watermelon-juice and known to all as 'punkin-butter.' — **(3)** (*a*) **1781** PETERS *Hist. Conn.* 195 Newhaven is celebrated for having given the name of *pumpkin-heads* to all the New-Englanders. It originated from the Blue Laws, which enjoin every male to have his hair cut round by a cap. When caps were not to be had, they substituted the hard shell of a pumpkin. **1944** ADAMS *Album Amer. Hist.* I. 120 A pumpkin shell was placed over the head and the hair was trimmed around the rim of the shell. From this custom came the name 'pumpkin head.' (*b*) **1848** IRVING *Knickerb.* IV. xi, Beside each pumpkin-head peered the end of a rusty musket. **1918** LINCOLN *Shavings* 232 Can't make a man out of a punkinhead. — **(4) 1863** A. D. WHITNEY *F. Gartney* xv, Aunt Faith, in her pumpkin hood and Rob Roy cloak. **1899** A. BROWN *Tiverton Tales* 239 The sled was empty, save for a rocking-chair where sat an enormous woman enveloped in shawls, her broad face surrounded by a pumpkin hood.

(5) 1915 T. B. HAZARD *Jonny-Cake P.* 51 But, oh, them pumpkin jonny-cakes. — **(7) 1809** KENDALL *Travels* III. 145 Of the white pine, the lumberers distinguish two varieties, one of which they call *punkin pine* . . . on account of the softness and fine grain of the wood. **1947** PAUL *Linden* 187 The solid old flooring of pumpkin pine, strewn with sawdust, rumbled and clicked beneath the tread of seamen's boots. — **(8) 1657** *East-Hampton Rec.* I. 120 Mrs. Gardiner spoke to Mary & Arther about pomkin porrage. **1699** E. WARD *Trip N. Eng.* 9 Pumpkin Porrage being as much in esteem with New-England saints, as Jelly Broth with Old-England Sinners. — **(9) 1805** *Indep. Chronicle* 26 Dec. 3/1 Clams and oysters, succatouch and pumpkin puddings, turkies, ducks [etc.]. **1840** A. M. MAXWELL *Run through U.S.* I. 81 My opposite neighbour to-day at dinner urged me to make an experiment on some 'real, genu*ine*, Yankee, New England, pumpkin pudding.'

(11) 1832 *Boston Transcript* 23 April 1/1 'Here,' said my droll companion, 'we shall find small potatoes, or I lose my guess, for I never had any great opinion of these pumpkin taverns.' — **(12)** (*a*) **1765** J. BARTRAM *Diary* (Remarks), It [frost] killed ye pumkin vines & many of ye leaves of ye carolina peas but did not hurt ye tomatis. **1913** EATON *Barn Doors & Byways* 210 The leaves of the pumpkin vines are drooping round their stems. (*b*) **1882** BEARD *Handy Book* 163 The pumpkin-vine flute, like the corn-stalk fiddle, will amuse small boys.

b. Also **pumpkin griddle cake, molasses, sauce.**

1704 S. KNIGHT *Journal* 67 That night Lodgd at Stonington and had Roast Beef and pumpkin sause for supper. **c1880** HAZARD *Jonny-Cake P.* (1915) 51 Then again, in the olden time, we used to have . . . the nice little round pumpkin griddle-cakes. **1893** M. A. OWEN *Voodoo Tales* 147 Hit time for punkin-sass an' roast 'possum. **1923** ADAMS *Pioneer Hist.* 358 Pumpkin molasses was their usual sweetening.

c. In fig. and exclamatory expressions. *Colloq.*

c1845 *Big Bear Ark.* 16 They were real *know-nothings*, green as a pumpkin-vine—could'nt, in farming, I'll bet, raise a crop of turnips. **1847** ROBB *Squatter Life* 82 Your head is swelled as big as a *pumpkin!* **1892** HARRIS *U. Remus & Friends* 147 Den I'm a punkin ahead er yo' 'simmon, is I? **1906** FITZGERALD *Sam Steele's Adv.* 237 We're rich, nevvy—rich as punkins!

As the last term in **basswood, sugar, wild pumpkin.**

pumpkin bread. Bread made of pumpkin and corn meal.

[**1704** S. KNIGHT *Journal* 47 But the Pumpkin and Indian mixt Bred had such an Aspect, and the Bare-legg'd Punch so awkerd or rather Awfull a sound, that we left both.] **1819** *Western Rev.* I. 185 Pumpkin bread and cakes are as much used in the interior of Kentucky, as pumpkin pies in New-England. **1909** *Pioneer Days Southwest* 252 We would stew our pumpkins till done and put it in meal and salt it . . . work it up into a dough making it into small thin cakes called pumpkin bread. **1944** DUNCAN *M. Graham*, She had to grind dried pumpkin to make flour for pumpkin bread because the cornmeal was out.

pumpkin pie. Pie made of pumpkin.

1654 JOHNSON *Wonder-w. Prov.* 174 This poor Wilderness hath . . . plenty of wine and sugar, . . . and quince tarts instead of their former Pumpkin Pies. **1843** P. HONE *Diary* II. 203, I came away, . . . as good a Yankee as ever ate pumpkin pie on Thanksgiving Day. **1949** *Chi. Tribune* 16 Dec. III. 7/4 Add a finishing touch to pumpkin pie with a ginger cream topping.

b. (See quot.)

1891 A. M. EARLE *Sabbath* 110 Women . . . ate and exchanged doughnuts, slices of rusk, or pieces of 'pumpkin and Indian mixt' pie.

∗**pumpkin seed.**

1. Any one of various small, flat, fresh-water sunfishes, esp. *Eupomotis gibbosus*. Also the butterfish, *Poronotus triacanthus*.

1814 *Mass. H.S. Coll.* 2 Ser. III. 102 There are, however, various kinds of smaller fish, viz. . . . bill fish; pumpkin seed, or flat fish, &c. **1881** STODDARD *E. Hardery* 203 Job Gorham can't show anythin' but eels and pumpkin-seeds and bullheads for his pond. **1911** *Rep. Fisheries 1908* 314/1 *Pumpkin-seed.*—A name applied to the sunfish (*Eupomotis gibbosus*) of the brooks of New York and New England, and to the butterfish (*Poronotus triacanthus*) in Connecticut. **1949** *Pacific Spectator* Spring 230 Horn pout, . . . yellow perch, punkin seeds, and shiners could be caught by anybody.

2. a. (See quot.) **b.** ?Designating extremely poor, thin cattle. *Obs.* **c.** (See quot. 1921.)

(a) 1884 J. A. HENSHALL *Camping in Fla.* 15 There are the 'skimming-dish,' the 'pumpkin-seed' and the 'flat-iron' models, all half round yacht built boats. — **(b) 1890** *Stock Grower & Farmer* 12 July 3/3 These men have been buying the 'pumpkin seed' cattle of Minnesota and Wisconsin, and selling them to feeders. — **(c) 1921** *Outing* Dec. 105/2 By far the most popular snowshoe is the pumpkin-seed type. . . . The shape is that of a pumpkin seed with a tail attached. **1922** *Ib.* April 331/1, I used 'Indian Runner,' 'Canadian,' 'Pumpkin Seed' and on trails the 'Bear paw,' but never for all purposes or any purpose have I ever used a shoe that compares with the Alaskan.

∗**punch,** *n.* Energy, vigor, "go." *Slang.* — **1911** E. FERBER *Dawn O'Hara* xvii. 254 It lacks that peculiar and convincing quality poetically known as the punch. **1921** R. D. PAINE *Comr. Rolling Ocean* i. 7 Dad is the kindest, finest man that ever lived, but he lacks the punch.

As the last term in **bell, biscuit, egg-and-milk, gong, kidney, rock, rum, worm punch.**

∗**punch,** *v.*

1. *W. tr.* To drive (cattle) as if by prodding them on; to work on a ranch as a cowboy.

1890 *Stock Grower & Farmer* 21 June 4/1 J. O. Phillips . . . will be initiated into the business of punching cattle. **1923** BOWER *Parowan Bonanza* 276 In that case . . . you'd still be punchin' cows for your dad, most likely. **1944** JOHNSON *As I Dare* 337, I come out here from Ioway when I was a kid, to punch cattle.

2. a. punch board, a gambling device consisting of a board having a number of holes in it one of which when punched yields a lucky number, name, etc., which entitles the player to a prize. Also attrib. **b. punch ticket,** a ticket, as on a railroad, which when used is punched by the proper employee and returned to the purchaser to be used again.

(a) 1931 *Outlook* 12 Aug. 459/2 The punch-board racket is a polite business. **1949** *Democrat* 15 Dec. 4/1 We would like to amend his paragraph to include punch boards. — **(b) 1887** GEORGE *40 Yrs. on*

Rail 227 Many cases have been reported where in punch-tickets the bits of pasteboard punched out have been saved and carefully glued in the old places. **1890** *Harper's Mag.* May 908/1 A person . . . who by many punch-tickets builds up the fortunes of the stockholders.

punche ˈpʌntʃɪ, *n. S.W.* [App. a native word.] A plant, prob. *Nicotiana attenuata*, or a form of tobacco obtained from this by the Indians of the Southwest.

1834 A. PIKE *Sketches* 43 They had been there to trade hard bread, blankets, punche, beads, &c., for buffalo robes, bear skins, and horses. **1844** GREGG *Commerce of Prairies* I. 156 Universal as the use of tobacco is among these people, there is very little of it grown, and that chiefly of a light and weak species, called by the natives *punche*, which is also indigenous, and still to be met with growing wild in some places. **1893** DONALDSON *Moqui Pueblo Indians* 65 No. 7 is named from the 'bunchi,' or native tobacco, cultivated by all the pueblos of New Mexico and Arizona. **1941** *Amer. Sp.* Oct. 181 *Punche*, a poor kind of tobacco used by Indians and found in trade among the Mexicans and Americans.

***puncheon,** *n.*

1. A thick, heavy piece of rough timber, usu. split from a log and having at least one hewed surface. Also in generic sense.

1725 in *Travels Amer. Col.* 150 [We] went to Old Estotoe a large Town and very well ffortifyed all round with Punchins and also ditched on the Outside with the sd Punchins. **1791** in JILLSON *Dark & Bloody Ground* 109 It is kept covered from the weather by a deer skin and some pieces of puncheon. **1843** OLIVER *Eight Months* 236 Trees are split up into what are termed puncheons, of three or four inches in thickness, which are laid down on the sleepers. **1946** RICHTER *Fields* 164 The puncheons had holes for seat legs.

attrib. **1754** *Lett. to Washington* I. 48, I have erected a puntion Fort. **1776** DUNBAR *Life* 23 We have also begun the making of Staves, of which there are already made 13 hundred of white oak Puncheon Staves—A Hired Man is employed in building Negro houses. **1842** *Amer. Pioneer* I. 139 During a slight lull in the gale, . . . he got up from the hold and threw overboard all the puncheon shooks and about fifty barrels of flour, to lighten her. **1886** Z. F. SMITH *Kentucky* 39 We have the tradition of the border school-house or rude logs and puncheon seats on the dirt floor.

b. Also (1) **puncheon door,** (2) **floor.**

(1) 1827 *Western Mo. Rev.* I. 447 [There] was a log pen, roofed, ten feet square, with three wooden windows, and a white washed puncheon door. **1886** Z. F. SMITH *Kentucky* 150 The outlet was a puncheon door with a bar to secure it. — **(2) 1791** in JILLSON *Dark & Bloody Ground* 111 Puncheon floors are all right as long as it is cold enough to let them be covered with furs. **1949** *Southwestern Hist. Quart.* Oct. 114 A number of cabins were reported to have puncheon floors.

***puncher,** *n. W.* A cowboy or cowpuncher. Also in appositive use.

1870 *Terr. Enterprise* (Virginia, Nev.) 17 Aug. 3/1 All the time the punchers are flying from ox to ox, plying their sticks right and left. **1897** *Outing* XXX. 164/2 Cautiously picking his way . . . appeared the picturesque figure of an old 'puncher' friend from Colorado. **1949** *Pacific Discovery* July–Aug. 1/1 Two biologists, sent to the Pribilofs to study fur seals, unexpectedly found themselves 'punchers' in a 'reindeer Roundup' on St. Paul.

As the last term in **bull, cattle, cow, dog, dude, mule puncher.**

***punching,** *n.* As the last term in **bull, cow, punching.**

pung pʌŋ, *n.* Chiefly *N. Eng.* [Short for **tom pung.**] A form of bob sleigh, usu. drawn by one horse. Cf. **gopher 1. b.**

1825 COOPER *L. Lincoln* xxv, He was in the act of seating himself in the pung. **1901** *Scribner's Mag.* April 503/1 This old pung'll do to carry home fish in a pinch. **1949** *Sat. Ev. Post* 12 March 60/4 A man drove into the yard in an old pung.

attrib. **1835** *Knickerb.* VI. 564, I remember a pung-ride one evening to an inn. **1858** *Ib.* LII. 539 Two young 'Suckers' . . . jumped into a one-horse pung wagon.

As the last term in **double, Dutch, tom pung.**

punger gourd. Origin and meaning obscure (see note). Now *hist.*

Turner, p. 149, records among Gullah personal names [pɒŋgɒ], fatness. Poss. **punger gourd =fat gourd.**

1884 *Tenn. Code* 526 The following property shall be exempt from execution, seizure or attachment— . . . Heads of Families. . . . Two gourds, two punger gourds, One carpet [etc.]. **1944** W. BLAIR *Tall Tale Amer.* 66 The punger gourd, the biggest of the lot, held four or five gallons.

punging ˈpʌŋɪŋ, *n.* Jumping on and off a moving pung; hitching a sled to, or stealing a ride on, a pung. *Colloq.* — **1892** HOWELLS *Quality of Mercy* 101 He started up the street at a gait which was little short of a run, and which exposed him to the ridicule of such little boys as observed his haste, in their intervals of punging. **1913** *Outing* Feb. 538 All other winter sports might fail us or grow stale, but pungin', real pungin', on the heel of the runner of a real pung, remained till the February thaw, at least, and often long into March.

pungle ˈpʌŋgl̩, *v.* Orig. *S.W.* [Sp. *póngale* (f. *poner*), out with it, let's have it.] *tr.* and *intr.* To contribute, pay, hand over (money). Also transf. *Colloq.*

1854 *Pioneer* (S.F.) April 237 [To] the last war . . . we are indebted . . . for an additional slice of territory and its consequent classical influence upon our language, by the entry of such precious words and phrases, as 'hombre,' 'vamose the ranch,' 'pungle,' *et id omne genus.* **1867** *Terr. Enterprise* (Virginia, Nev.) 23 Feb. 3/3 All night the clouds pungled their fleecy treasures. **1884** MARK TWAIN *H. Finn* v, I'll make him pungle, too, or I'll know the reason why. **1910** *Sat. Ev. Post* 8 Oct. 4/3 You fellows down here can pungle if you want to, but that frijole-flavored stew doesn't get a cent from me!

Usu. with *down.*

1851 *Calif. State Jrnl.* (San Jose) 26 March 3/3 The initiated regard the bet as 'open and shut,' and they 'pungle down' their purse, which finds its way into the hands of an interested party as stake holder. **1857** *S.F. Call* 6 Jan. 2/2 '*Pungale* down, gentlemen; come, *pungale*,' as the vingt-et-un lady used to say.

pungy ˈpʌŋgɪ, *n.* Also **pungo.** [Origin obscure, but cf. **bungo.**] "A small boat like a sharpey. [Massachusetts]" (*Cent.*). Cf. **oyster pungy.**

1854 SIMMS *Southward Ho!* iii. 28 Their most innocent name is 'pungo'—a sort of schooner, hailing mostly from Manhattan and Massachusetts. **1880** G. A. TOWNSEND *Tales Chesapeake* 29 They launched the pungy, not alone. **1893** *Outing* XXII. 150/2 Craft of all kinds, from the stately merchantman to the pungy loaded with fruit from the 'Eastern sho',' dotted the bay.

***punish,** *v. Baseball. tr.* (See quots.)

1867 *Ball Players' Chron.* 6 June 2/1 Some excellent batting was now shown, Hunniwell's pitching being punished in style. **1868** CHADWICK *Base Ball* 44 The pitcher is said to be 'punished' when the batsmen find no difficulty in hitting away the balls he delivers to them. **1886** — *Art of Pitching* 58 The pitcher is 'punished' when the balls he pitches to the bat are easily hit to the field in such a manner as to prevent them from being fielded in time to put either the batsman or base-runners out.

***punishment,** *n.* A fine imposed upon a student for violation of college rules. Also attrib. *Obs.* — **1686** *Harvard Rec.* 260 The Steward . . . [shall] be accountable . . . to the College Treasurer for all Study rents, Detriments, Punishments, Gallery Money [etc.]. **1738** *Ib.* II. 680 (in margin), Butler & Steward allow'd 20/ per year for making up &c the punishment Bills.

***punk,** *n.* and *a.* [See note.]

The idea that this word is of Amer. Indian origin app. stems from a suggestion to that effect in the *OED* (1909) *s.v.* Previous to that time dictionaries related the word to **spunk.* The *EDD* records *punk*, touchwood, as occurring in the n. country and Shropshire. The Delaware Indian *punk* means primarily ashes (cf. also however quots. *c*1618 below and 1895 *s.v.* punkie). For "rotten wood" the Delawares used an entirely different word, *wipiechkeu.* If the older view of the origin of this word is correct, sense **1.** is not an Americanism.

1. *n.* Touchwood, spunk.

[*c*1618 STRACHEY *Virginia* 74 Some of them, more thriftye then cleanly, doe burne the coare of the eare to powder, which they call pungnough, mingling that in their meale, but yt never tasted well in bread or broath.] **1687** CLAYTON *Virginia* 149 As the East-Indians use Moxa, so these burn with Punk, which is the inward Part of the Excrescence or Exuberance of an Oak. **1705** BEVERLEY *Virginia* III. 49 Or else they take Punck, (which is a Sort of a soft Touchwood, cut out of the knots of Oak or Hiccory Trees, but the Hiccory affords the best,) this they shape like a Cone, . . . and apply the Basis of it to the parts affected. **1827** *Western Mo. Rev.* I. 443 In digging into this mound, there were found two pieces of rotten wood, vulgarly called punk,—the one weighing three pounds, and the other five. **1925** HEMING *Living Forest* 36 Into it he poured a little dry, powdery punk, and laid the nest down beside his fire-board.

b. *transf.* (See quots.) *Slang.*

1886 *Amer. Philol. Assoc.* XVII. 41 *Punk*, at least in a certain Virginia college, is used as the name of a box of good things from home. **1891** *Contemporary Rev.* Aug. 255 Bread [in America] is called punk. **1917** J. A. MOSS *Officers' Man.* 485 *Punk*—light bread.

2. A slow-burning preparation sold in long pencil-like pieces and used chiefly in igniting fireworks.

1869 ALDRICH *Bad Boy* 92 Here and there were tables at which could be purchased the smaller sort of fireworks, such as pin-wheels, serpents, double-headers, and punk warranted not to go out. **1907** LONDON *Road* 92 It would last for hours, and my cell-mate called it a 'punk.'

b. A cigarette. *Slang. Obs.* Cf. **punk cigar.**

1889 *Oregonian* (Portland) 15 Dec. 9/3 They told the merchant that the 'punks' were for an older brother.

3. A form of incense.

1870 in De Vere 157 A Chinese lady of rank in San Francisco walks attended by three maids of honor, bearing lighted sticks of punk highly perfumed. **1890** *Boston Jrnl.* 10 May 5/8 The burning of innumerable sticks of bamboo punk, which sent forth a faint, sickening odor. **1914** E. Stewart *Lett. of Woman Homesteader* 150 Before it, suspended by a wire from the rafters, was a cow's horn in which a piece of punk was burning, just as the incense is kept burning in churches.

4. (See quot. 1932.) *Slang.*

Punk in the sense of a harlot is recorded in the *OED* as early as 1596. Its origin in this sense is not clear. That the term as used here developed from the earlier sense of a prostitute appears unlikely. It is rather to be associated with the adjective as shown in **5. b.** below.

1932 *Lit. Digest* 1 Oct. 24/1 Punks, in the jargon of the underworld, . . . 'ain't criminals, they're just punks—small-time lawbreakers.' **1949** *Chi. Tribune* 10 Dec. 10 This punk must have robbed a bank or got paid off for settin' a forest fire!

5. *a.* Of timber: Decayed, rotten.

1902 S. E. White *Blazed Trail* ii. 18 Supplies ran low unexpectedly; trees turned out 'punk.' *Ib.* 128 Thorough smoking in the fumes of punk maple would obviate this. *a***1904** — *Blazed Trail Stories* iii. 49, I cull every log, big or little, punk or sound, that ain't sawed square.

b. Of a person or thing: Of poor quality, worthless. *Slang.*

1896 G. Ade *Artie* iii. 23 And this crowd up there was purty-y-y punk. **1901** *U. of Chi. Wkly.* 1 Aug. 1088 He . . . had it impressed upon him that the Pi Gams were 'punk.' **1919** Morley *Haunted Bookshop* (1921) 45 We have to stock the new stuff, a large proportion of which is punk. **1949** *L.A. Times* 21 May 6 This jail has about as punk, if not the punkest grub I ever packed away.

6. In combs.: (1) **punk cigar,** ?a piece of punk used as a cigar, *obs.;* (2) **oak,** the water oak, *Quercus nigra;* (3) **pudding,** (see quot.), *colloq.* [from the bird's note]; (4) **wood,** =**punk 1.**

(1) **1891** *Outing* Dec. 181/2 We found him at last squatting on the grass in rear of the sutler's store, contentedly puffing a 'punk' cigar. — (2) **1884** Sargent *Rep. Forests* 152 *Quercus aquatica*. . . . Possum Oak. Punk Oak. . . . Probably not used except as fuel. **1897** Sudworth *Arborescent Flora* 175 Common names [of the water oak include] . . . Duck Oak, Possum Oak, Punk Oak. — (3) **1877** Bartlett 651 Stake-driver, the bittern, so called from its booming. Adirondacks. The same bird is also called punk-pudding. — (4) **1883** *Harper's Mag.* Feb. 427/2 She opened a flint-and-tinder box and struck a spark into the punk-wood. **1903** White *Forest* 180 Sometimes a faint rounded shell . . . swelled above the level, to crumble to punkwood at the lightest touch of our feet.

punkie 'pʌŋkɪ, *n.* [See quot. 1895. The dim. ending suggests that the term passed through Dutch on its way into English.] Any one of various minute biting flies or midges of the family Chironomidae, esp. those of the genus *Culicoides.* Cf. **brulot, burning fly, no-see-'em.**

1769 R. Smith *Tour* (1906) 42 We begin to be teazed with Muscetoes and little Gnats called here [n.w. New York] Punkies. **1840** *Knickerb.* Sep. 270 Of all the tortures of this nature, that inflicted by the *gnat* (sand-flies, punkies, brulos, for they bear all these appellations,) is the least endurable. **1895** Gerard in *N.Y. Sun* 30 July, Punkey, punky, the sand fly, a minute insect well known to sportsmen and camping parties. Powhatan 'pungu,' Delaware 'pungus,' from 'pung' dust, 'ashes,' 'fine powder.' The insect is named from its minute size. **1933** Cheley *Camping Out* 423 The 'punkeys' and 'midgets' can outstrip them [mosquitoes] for ferocity and the painful character of the wound which they inflict.

attrib. **1909** *Country Life* June 158/3 Miscellaneous duffle included . . . 'punky-dope' cholera mixture, witch hazel.

punky 'pʌŋkɪ, *a.* [f. ***punk,** *n.*] Of wood: Partially decayed, resembling punk. Also fig.

1872 Huntington *Road-Master's Ass't* 117 A bridge may . . . have a small knot partially decayed, or 'punky,' as it is termed. **1904** *N.Y. Times* 5 May 8 Written by another man Mr. Austin would doubtless find these verses as amusing as the rest of us do, . . . would appreciate their punky pretentiousness. **1926** Rickaby *Ballads* 63 Were you punky, were you hollow, You had been a lucky fellow.

***pup,** *n.*

1. =**prairie dog.** *Obs.*

1851 Howe *Hist. Coll. Great West* 66 Rattlesnakes . . . rattling an angry note of warning if, in its play, a thoughtless pup approaches too near. **1853** in Brewerton *With Kit Carson* (1930) 271, I am inclined to believe that the younger pups sometimes find the presence of these 'boarders' [i.e., snakes] a very *killing* sort of nuisance.

2. *W.* (See quots.)

1898 W. B. Haskell *2 Yrs. in Klondike* 253 Every creek has its pups, and if any of them become of considerable importance they may have pups also. **1899** *Harper's Wkly.* 8 April 341/1 None of the side gulches—or 'pups' as they were called—were favored by the stampeders. **1904** E. Robins *Magnetic North* II. 137 Little creek; call 'em pups here.

3. pup tent, =**shelter tent.**

1863 in *Ohio Arch. & Hist. Quart.* XXXVIII. 651 About 10 A.M. we . . . pitched our pup-tents. **1949** *Sky Line Trail* Oct. 19/1 Boldly, they'd enter my pup tent and nuzzle in my pack, seeking civilized grub.

As the last term in **barking, blue, hound, red, yellow pup.**

Pup tent

pupelo pju'pilo, *n. N. Eng.* [Origin unknown.] Cider brandy *q.v.* — **1806** *Salem Reg.* 7 April (Th.), Do you not deny to the poor labourer the common refreshment of a little toddy, and stint him with a glass of pupelo? **1885** Eggleston in *Cent. Mag.* April 884/2 Cider they reenforced by distilling it into 'pupelo,' or brandy.

***puppy,** *n.* **1.** A coin of small value. *Obs.* **2. puppy love,** sentimental and transitory affection between a boy and a girl. *Colloq.*

(1) **1800** *Columbian Centinel* 1 Feb. 2/4 If tugging a man's cloak costs '*damn'd puppy*' how much will writing an insolent letter to the President of the United States, come to? **1846** Cooper *Redskins* xxx, The debtors of the deceased can meet his obligations with a coin technically called 'puppies.' — (2) **1834** Caruthers *Kentuckian* I. 175 Oh! it is nothing more than puppy love! **1948** *Chi. Tribune* 24 Feb. III. 1/2, I doubt if there's such a thing as puppy love.

As the last term in **ground, hush, mud, water puppy.**

purbelo 'pɜblo, *n.* Also **purbulo, purblo.** Variants of **pueblo.** Also attrib.

1846 Robins in *Santa Fe Exped.* (1923) 41 On the 21st day of September, 1846, we . . . camped at St. Domingo, a Purbelo village on the Rio del Norte. **1847** Coyner *Lost Trappers* 171 The governor . . ordered a Captain Viscarro with sixty men, ten of whom were brave Purbulo Indians, living near Santa Fe, to conduct these exiles. **1850** Garrard *Wah-To-Yah* xix. 212 Them Purblos have *cached* our cavyard, I spect.

***purchase,** *n.* A tract of land acquired by a colony, a private person or company, a state, or the central government, either directly from the Indians or from some agency that has extinguished Indian claims. Freq. in place-names.

1670 *Derby Rec.* 308 A parcel of Land . . . bounded with a littel brooke and with English purches on ye south side. **1725** *Huntington Rec.* II. 354 It was voated and agreed to make a new division in the old purchass between the Cold Spring and Cow harbour. **1813** *Ann. 12th Congress* 2 Sess. 930 Thence . . . to the western boundary of the Osage purchase. **1894** *Harper's Mag.* April 676/2 The bride . . . is well known and much admired, not only in the Purchase, but in this city. **1927** *Mt. Life* (Berea, Ky.) Jan. 1/1 Indeed, the traveler, following the westward urge, may go further and reach the Purchase.

b. (See quot.)

1909 Webster 1737/2 *Purchase,* . . . in New Hampshire, an unorganized minor territorial division consisting of land which was originally laid off and sold by the State to an individual or individuals.

As the last term in **Holland, Indian, Louisiana, new, Ohio, Platte, Sioux, Susquehannah, walking purchase.**

purchased court. (See quot. 1887.) *Obs.*

1653 *So. Records* I. 93 At a purchased cort, the said action of Slander entered per Tho. Vale plf against Sam. Dayton defendant, [was] tryed by 12 men. **1654** *Ib.* 97 An action of Battery entered per Thomas Burnet plf against Iohn Cooper defendt to bee tryed at a purchased cort April 2d next being the next third day of the week. **1887** *Records E.-Hampton* I. 4 The term 'purchased court,' or purchasing a court, occurring in these records simply means that the court was held at an extra occasion and the fees of the court were paid by a litigant and were simply a compensation for the time of the court.

purchasing agent. An agent authorized to purchase something for his principal. — **1823** in McKenny *Memoirs* I. 302, I supplanted none of . . . the purchasing agents, in our cities, by others of my own selecting. **1906** Lynde *Quickening* 212 We have to monkey with the purchasing agent of a corporation.

* **pure,** *a.* and *adv.* In combs.: (1) **pure-blood,** see as a main entry; (2) **blooded,** *a.* =next; (3) **bred,** *a.* having blood of only one strain, also absol.; (4) **food,** designating enactments, persons, etc., connected with regulating the purity of canned or compounded foods; (5) **quill,** the real thing, *slang.*, cf. **simon-pure.**

(2) **1821** in Morse *Rep. Indian Affairs* II. 69 The number of pure blooded Indians is extremely small, say fifty or sixty, and is rapidly decreasing. **1903** *Kans. State Bd. Agric. Bienn. Rep.* XIII. 63 A quarter of a billion acres of grass, nurturing 10,000,000 head of cattle, . . . [can] be doubled in value in a single decade, if only pure-blooded sires are used in all the cow herds. **1949** *Time* 5 Dec. 116/2 He claimed he could distinguish between octoroons, quadroons and pure-blooded Africans by his sense of smell. — (3) **1869** *Rep. Comm. Agric. 1868* 10 Specimens of pure-bred domestic fowls. **1894** *Vt. Agric. Rep.* XIV. 105 A pure bred . . . is an animal eligible to record in the pedigree register of its breed. **1949** *Hoard's Dairyman* 10 Nov. 795/1 Grade and pure-bred cattle are both tested in dairy herd improvement association work. — (4) **1894** *Jrnl. Franklin Inst.* April 267 Senator Paddock, of Nebraska, . . . after years of futile struggle, succeeded in having the Senate pass what is known as the Pure Food Bill. **1911** *Outlook* 13 May 48/1 Many pure-food experts . . . desired that the use of benzoate in foods should be forbidden altogether. **1913** *Collier's* 16 Aug. 24 Idaho [is] a pure food state. **1947** *Chi. Tribune* 2 Nov. IV. 4/2 He was one of the great fraternity of medicine men who went up and down the land, prior to the pure food and drug act.

(5) **1888** *Detroit Free Press* Aug. (F.), When religun is religun, an' it's the pure quill an' no water in it, there's never one of us but kin take it in large doses.

pureblood ˈpjʊrˌblʌd, *a.* and *n.*

1. *n.* An Indian of unmixed descent.

1882 *Harper's Mag.* May 895/1 The half and quarter breeds, though a mongrel race, seem to have . . . greater powers of resistance than the pure-bloods. **1889** *Cong. Rec.* 9 Feb. 1714/1 Out of the pure-bloods I suppose it would be almost impossible to find a single man qualified . . . to perform the duties of a juryman. **1947** *Amer. Sp.* April 81 Distinguish this type . . . from 'pure' bloods of one of the three principal racial stocks.

2. A pure-bred animal.

1894 *Vt. Agric. Rep.* XIV. 166, I do not wish to speak as a specialist, although having bred pure bloods for almost thirty years. **1903** *Kans. State Bd. Agric. Bienn. Rep.* XIII. 63 Likewise fifty per cent. can be added to the value if pure-bloods only are used in the northern half of this territory.

3. *a.* =**pure-blooded.**

1859 *Mich. Agric. Trans.* X. 355 All the theory in the world . . . cannot convince our people that the Durham cattle will keep as easy . . . as the pure blood, elegantly-constructed sprightly Devon. **1888** *Vt. Agric. Rep.* X. 49 Why don't you get some pure blood Holsteins?

* **purgatory,** *n. N. Eng.* (See quots. 1888, 1902.) Also as a place-name.

1766 Cutler in *Life & Corr.* I. 12 Hunted in Purgatory with Mr. Dean and Mr. Penniman [for botanical specimens] this afternoon, but found nothing. **1888** Whitney *Names & Places* 160 Along the coast of New England, and in the interior, narrow ravines with nearly perpendicular walls are called 'purgatories,' **1902** A. Matthews *Purgatory River* 1 (*footnote*), There are in New England several small brooks to which the name of Purgatory is given, either because they drain swamps, or flow through or near rock chasms which are called Purgatories.

b. (See quot. 1831.) Also attrib. *Obs.*

1831 Peck *Guide* 308 In the low prairies near the Wabash, are swamps, called by the people *purgatories*, which are almost impassable in the wet season. **1834** ——— *Gaz. Illinois* 172 The eastern part of Allison's Prairie, towards the Wabash, contains some wet land and purgatory swamps.

purgery ˈpɜdʒərɪ, *n.* [F. *purgerie.*] (See quot. 1876.) — **1848** *Hunt's Merch. Mag.* XVIII. 337 The sugar is . . . carried to the *purgery*, a large building. **1876** Knight 1836/1 *Purgery*, the portion of a sugar-house where the sugar from the coolers is . . . allowed to drain off its molasses.

purging house. =prec. — **1848** *De Bow's Review* VI. 358 Two large purging houses, built of stone and wood. **1862** *Rep. Comm. Patents 1861: Agric.* 310 Better attention to the cultivation and seasons favorable to the maturation of the cane, . . . together with the well-arranged purging-houses, . . . [will] result in a fair yield.

Puritan Fathers. Those Puritans who settled in New England, esp. at Plymouth, early in the seventeenth century.

1806 in Thacher *Hist. Plymouth* (1832) 232 December 22.—This is the 186th anniversary of the first landing of our puritan fathers. **1831** *Boston Transcript* 10 Sep. 1/1 They talk of the Puritan Fathers of New England as the only models of human excellence—as the *ultima thule* of human wisdom. **1870** R. C. Winthrop *Oration on Landing of Pilgrims* 39, I rejoice, too, that the Puritan Fathers of Massachusetts, who followed them [i.e., the Pilgrim Fathers] to these shores ten years afterwards, . . . were, if not technically and professedly, yet to all intents and purposes, Separatists, also. **1894** Leavitt *Our Money Wars* 15 The Boston Puritan Fathers got . . . a share of the buccaneering plunder.

puro ˈpuro, *n. S.W.* [Sp. in same sense.] A cigar. *Obs.* — **1844** Gregg *Commerce of Prairies* I. 243 The puro or cigarro is seen in the mouths of all. **1880** *Cimarron News & Press* 18 March 3/1 He promises to send us some *puros* when he gets down into Sonora, if he can do so without the duty coming too high.

purp pɜp, *n.* Humorous variant of * *pup.*

1865 *Gold Hill* (Nev.) *News* 8 May, Yesterday morning some twenty carcasses of dead purps testified to the efficacy of the sanitary drug. **1876** *Wkly. Comanche* (Tex.) *Chief* 22 June 3/1 Which one tied the pan to the purp's tail? **1947** *So. Sierran* Dec. 2/3 First couple to climb 100 peaks together, also the purp!

* **purple,** *a.*

1. In the names of plants: (1) **purple bladderwort,** an aquatic herb, *Vesiculina purpurea*, common in ponds in the eastern states; (2) **buckeye,** (see quot. 1909); (3) **cane,** (*a*) a variety of raspberry, (*b*) a variety of sugar cane, the mature stalks of which are purple or purplish in color; (4) **coneflower,** a plant, *Echinacea purpurea*, of the thistle family; (5) **haw,** the bluewood, a small tree or shrub, *Condalia obovata*, often forming dense chaparral or thickets in Texas and westward; (6) **potato,** a now unidentifiable kind of potato, *obs.*, cf. **early purple potato;** (7) **sand grass,** (see quot.).

(1) **1843** Torrey *Flora N.Y.* II. 20 *Utricularia purpurea.* Purple Bladderwort. . . . It is common in the neighboring parts of New-Jersey. — (2) **1897** Sudworth *Arborescent Flora* 294 *Æsculus octandra hybrida.* . . . Purple Buckeye. **1909** *Cent. Supp.* 171/2 *Purple or purplish buckeye*, a variety (*hybrida*) of the yellow buckeye, which has purplish or pink flowers. — (3) (*a*) **1862** *Rep. Comm. Patents 1861: Agric.* 167 The *Purple Cane*, or American Red Cane, . . . [is] a very valuable variety of raspberry. **1871** *Ill. Agric. Soc. Trans.* VIII. 173 The varieties in common use are Purple-cane, a very prolific, light-purple, soft berry, valuable for family use only, . . . Doolittle Black-cap [etc.]. (*b*) **1897** W. C. Stubbs *Sugar Cane* 79 The purple cane is conspicuous for its increased powers of germination and multiplication. **1917** *Dept. Agric. Bul.* No. 486, 6 Cases are also reported of plain Louisiana Purple cane throwing off sports of striped cane. — (4) **1928** Bailey *Cyclo. Horticulture* 1087 Echinacea . . . Purple Cone-Flower. **1939** *Nat. Geog. Mag.* Aug. 220/2 Striking contrast is provided by some of the most brilliant flowers of the prairie notably . . . the purple coneflower, the butterfly milkweed, . . . and the prickly pears.

(5) **1806** Lewis in *L. & Clark Exped.* IV. (1905) 274 Near the river we find the Cottonwood, . . . the purple haw, . . . and whiteburry honeysuckle. — (6) **1775** Romans *Nat. Hist. Florida* 123 *Purple potatoe*, having that colour throughout except a very little of the heart. **1790** S. Deane *N.-Eng. Farmer* 224/2. — (7) **1901** Mohr *Plant Life Ala.* 129 The grasses [along the shores of Mobile and Perdido bays] are: . . . *Cenchrus megacephalus* (sand bur), *Sieglingia purpurea* (purple sand grass).

2. In the names of birds: (1) **purple finch,** an American finch, *Carpodacus purpureus;* (2) **gallinule,** a gallinule, *Ionornis martinica*, of the southern states; (3) **grackle,** (see quot. 1916), cf. **maize thief b;** (4) **jackdaw,** see **jackdaw;** (5) **martin,** a large North American swallow, *Progne subis;* (6) **-throat humming bird,** the black-chinned hummingbird, *Archilochus alexandri*, of California.

(1) *c*1730 Catesby *Carolina* I. 41 The Purple Finch. . . . They feed on the berries of the Juniper. **1949** *Dly. Oklahoman Mag.* (Okla. City) 4 Dec. 16/5 Mingling with the common hordes are occasional small flocks of purple finches and pine siskins. — (2) **1813** Wilson *Ornithology* IX. 71 The Purple Gallinule [was seen] in a thick swamp, a short distance from Savannah, Georgia. **1944** *Nat. Geog. Mag.* June 694/1 And then there were Purple Gallinules, decked out in brilliant purple, green, sky-blue, red, and yellow. — (3) **1782** Latham *Gen. Syn. Birds* I. II. 462 Purple Grakle. . . . This inhabits Carolina. **1916** Seton *Woodcraft Man.* 315 Purple Grackle or Crow Blackbird (*Quiscalus quiscala*). . . . When flying it holds its long tail with the edge raised like a boat, hence 'boat tail.' **1949** *Sat. Ev. Post* 15 Oct.

112/3 Her soft fine hair straggling loosely under the remodeled hat on which a purple grackle had expired and was forever embalmed.

(5) **1743** CATESBY *Carolina* II. p. xxxvi, Land-Birds which breed and abide in Carolina in the Summer, and retire in Winter: . . . The yellow Titmouse. The purple Martin. The humming Bird. **1939** LINCOLN *Migration* 55 The Purple Martin is an early migrant. — (6) **1869** *Amer. Naturalist* III. 188 On returning in June I found here [in Cal.] the Purple-throat Humming Bird.

3. In miscellaneous combs.: (1) **Purple Heart,** see as a main entry; (2) **quartz,** (see quot.); (3) **shore crab,** (see quot.); (4) **veil,** the egg-mass of the angler, *Lophius piscatorius.*

(2) **1896** *Cosmopolitan* XX. 450 The fluor-spar is locally known as 'purple quartz.' — (3) **1883** *Nat. Museum Bul.* No. 27, 112 Six species of Crabs are regarded as edible on the Pacific coast . . . [including the] Purple Shore Crab (*H[eterographus] nudus*). — (4) **1905** *Nat. Geog. Mag.* July 337/1 Off the New England coast a curious object is often found floating on the water, somewhat resembling a lady's veil . . . of a violet or purple color. The fishermen allude to it generally as the 'purple veil.' . . . On examining the substance with a magnifying glass . . . it was obvious that the purple veil, as a whole, was the egg-mass of a fish.

Purple Heart. (See quot. 1782.)

[**1782** WASHINGTON *Writings* (1938) XXIV. 488 The General, ever desirous to cherish virtuous ambition in his soldiers, as well as to foster and encourage every species of military merit, directs that whenever any singularly meritorious action is performed, the author of it shall be permitted to wear over his facings over the left breast, the figure of a heart in purple cloth, or silk, edged with narrow lace or binding.] **1932** *Army & Navy Jrnl.* 27 Feb. 602/4 Awards of the Purple Heart for acts or service performed prior to Feb. 22, 1932, will be confined to the following persons. **1950** *Chi. Tribune* 5 Jan. 3/4 He was awarded the Purple Heart for battle wounds.

b. *Order of the Purple Heart,* an organization composed of those to whom the Purple Heart has been awarded, the institution of such awards.

1932 *Army & Navy Jrnl.* 27 Feb. 602/3 Subsequent to the Revolution the Order of the Purple Heart seems to have fallen into disuse and no further awards were made. **1949** *Chi. D. News* 16 Nov. 18/6 Fourteen chapters of the Military Order of the Purple Heart are sponsoring a benefit show and dance.

purpose novel. A novel written for the purpose of discussing or exposing some social or economic problem. — **1893** *Forum* Jan. 594 The purpose-novel is an odious attempt to lecture people who hate lectures, to preach at people who prefer their own church, and to teach people who think they know enough already. **1894** *Harper's Mag.* Oct. 797/1 There is an analogy to this feeling in the present reaction against the domestic, the pathological, and the 'purpose' novels.

* **purse,** *n. attrib.*

1. Designating boats and various devices used in connection with purse seines.

1879 *Rep. Comm. Fisheries* V. 126 The captain of the gang is in charge of the 'purse-boat.' **1884** *Nat. Museum Bul.* No. 27, 1000 Davit-iron. . . . Used in Cape Ann seine-boats. The purse-blocks hook into it. *Ib.* 1001 Seine purse-ring. . . . Made of brass, with roller, to prevent chafing of purse-line. **1889** K. MUNROE *Dorymates* 40 Through these [rings] ran a second stout line, known as the 'purse-rope.' **1890** *Cent.* 4860/1 Purse-ring, a metal ring attached to the bride-rope on the foot of a purse-seine, for the pursing-line to run through.

2. In other combs.: (1) **pursenet fish,** a name suggested by John Winthrop (1606–76) for the basket fish or sea spider, *obs.;* (2) **seine,** a seine that may be drawn into the form of a purse or bag; (3) **seiner,** (see quot. 1890).

(1) **1671** in *Phil. Trans.* VI. 2223 Until a fitter English name be found for it, why may it not be called . . . a Basket-Fish, or a Net Fish, or a Purs-net Fish? — (2) **1870** *Amer. Naturalist* IV. 515 Purse-seines are used to the best advantage in capturing [mackerel]. **1911** *Rep. Fisheries 1908* 312/1 [Mackerel] are caught in purse seines, pounds, weirs, gill nets, etc., and with hook and line. — (3) **1890** *Cent.* 4860/1 *Purse-seiner,* a vessel employed in the menhaden or the mackerel purse-seine fishery. **1949** *This Week Mag.* 15 Oct. 7/1 If we were getting ahead, buying more boats and a purse seiner . . . it wouldn't be so bad.

As the last term in **pony, sea purse.**

***purse,** *v. tr.* To draw the mouth of (a purse seine) together. — **1880** *Harper's Mag.* Sep. 510/1 The two ends are brought together, and the net pursed up. **1889** MUNROE *Dorymates* 40 Hauling on this rope and 'pursing' the seine is the hardest part of the entire job.

purslane speedwell. An annual herb, *Veronica peregrina,* of North America. — **1817–8** EATON *Botany* (1822) 508 *Veronica peregrina,* purslane-speedwell. **1898** CREEVEY *Flowers of Field* 250 Neckweed. Purslane Speedwell. . . . A common weed throughout the United States.

* **push,** *v.* In combs.: (1) **push ball,** a game in which members of opposing teams try to push a large ball to opposite goals, the ball used in this game, also attrib. and fig.; (2) **button,** a button which, when pressed, serves as a control for one device or another, as to close or open an electric circuit, also attrib.; (3) **car,** a railroad handcar (see also quot. 1890); (4) **over,** one easily defeated or overcome, *slang;* (5) **pole,** a pole used in pushing a boat forward, also **pushing pole,** cf. **setting pole.**

(1) **1896** MOE *Hist. Harvard* 62 The Faculty . . . stuck to the Freshmen—since the upper three classes were on the other side of the push-ball. **1898** *Encycl. Sport* II. 168/2 Pushball was developed . . . into an organized game about the year 1895 by the Newton Athletic Club near Boston. **1905** *Brooklyn Eagle* 20 Feb. 16 A feature of the relay meet will be the pushball game, between teams of 20 men each. — (2) **1878** G. B. PRESCOTT *Speaking Telephone* 376 The push button or key used in short circuits serves to close the latter in a very simple manner. **1911** VANCE *Cynthia* 207 He stopped by the push-button for the annunciator in the main saloon. **1948** *New Republic* 29 Nov. 15/3 The vision of the clean, fast, economical, impersonal push-button war grows dim. — (3) **1884** NYE *Baled Hay* 225 A section-crew . . . riding down that mountain on a push-car. **1890** *Cent.* 4862/3 *Push-car,* . . . a car used at a ferry-slip to connect an engine with a train on a ferry-boat. (U.S.) — (4) **1906** *Outing* Jan. 461/2 To me it looks like a push-over. **1948** *Chi. Tribune* 14 March 1. 1/1 The delegation . . . includes colonial-minded Anglophiles; one world college professors who bundled with Browder and were pushovers for communist front organizations during the war.

(5) *a***1811** HENRY *Camp. Quebec* 195 The pushing-pole was of the same kind of materials [ash or birch], . . . and if iron could be had was shod at the but-end. **1884** A. M. MAYER in *Sport in Amer. Woods* II. 751 Boats . . . with a broad stern in which was a roomy seat for the pusher to stand on while he plied his 'gaff.' This was the name given to the pushing-pole. **1938** MATSCHAT *Suwannee River* 52 'Ye an' me hain't lost,' Freeman Carter told the push-pole in his hand, 'we is jest misplaced.'

***pusher,** *n.* (See quot. 1909.) Cf. **horse, pencil pusher.** — **1909** *Cent. Supp.* 1088/3 *pusher.* . . . In *railroading,* an assisting locomotive placed behind a train to aid the train-engine in surmounting a steep grade. The use of a pusher over a short incline makes it possible to handle heavy trains with single engines over long levels above and below the incline. **1947** BEEBE *Mixed Train Dly.* 74 A train is made up on the Heights, usually with a road engine and pusher.

***puss,** *n.* **1. puss-paw,** =**pussy's toes. 2. pusstail,** (see quot.). — (1) **1945** *Sky Line Trail* June 6/1 Nestled, however, near scattered rocks, heliotrope, puss-paw and occasionally avalanche lilies, are found. — (2) **1890** *Cent.* 4863/2 *Pusstail,* a common grass of the genus *Setaria:* so called on account of the bristly cylindrical spikes. More often called *foxtail.*

pus(s)ley 'pʌslɪ, *n.* A common colloq. variant of * *purslane.* Also attrib.

1833 A. GREENE *Life D. Duckworth* II. 71 All their writin is like pussly and witch-grass—you never can know where to find it. **1919** CADY *Rhymes of Vt.* (1923) 224, I don't desire no city chap, . . . To write a piece for me that tells. . . . That eels are fond of pusly greens. **1949** *This Week Mag.* 9 April 28/2 A few weeks later he'd spy the milder-flavored narrow dock and other edible weeds, the 'pussly,' the dandelions [etc.].

b. *meaner than pusley,* and variants, quite mean. *Colloq.*

1858 *Salem* (Ill.) *Adv.* 3 Feb. 1/4 The whole tribe on 'em is meaner than pusley. **1907** FREEMAN *By Light of Soul* 399 He treated her as mean as pusley.

* **pussy,** *n.* In the names of plants: (1) **pussy('s) paws,** a California plant, *Calyptridium umbellatum;* (2) **-'s toes,** (see quot. 1892), also **pussytoe;** (3) **willow,** (*a*) any willow having large silky catkins, as *Salix discolor,* (*b*) a silky fabric, also **pussy willow taffeta.**

(1) **1909** WEBSTER. **1915** ARMSTRONG & THORNBER *Western Wild Flowers* 124 The flower-clusters are like pink cushions, so the pretty little name of Pussy-paws is appropriate. **1947** PEATTIE *Sierra Nevada* 126 Pussypaws has now a mossy look, its stems are red and its flowers dark. — (2) **1892** *Amer. Folk-Lore* V. 98 *Antennaria plantaginifolia,* . . . pussy's toes. Worcester, Mass. **1949** *Chi. Tribune* 9 Jan. VI. 5/7 In early summer, one may see blue, white, and yellow violets, . . . pussy-toes, salt and pepper, poppies. — (3) (*a*) **1869** J. G. FULLER *Flower Gatherers* 52 The aments appear before the leaves, and are covered with hairs so soft and silken that children often call them Pussy-Willows. **1949** *Lisle* (Ill.) *Eagle* 31 March 5/4 The spring motif decoration of jonquils and pussy willows . . . gave a gay and festive setting. (*b*) **1919** MORLEY *Haunted Bookshop* 155 'A lining of pussy-

willow taffeta and an embroidered slip-on,' she was saying. **1920** *Montanan* May 26 For girls, a simple little sport-costume of silk tricolette or pussy-willow taffeta . . . will be quite all right this season.

As the last term in **wood pussy.**

pussyfoot ˈpusɪˌfut, *v.*

1. *intr.* To tread softly in the manner of a cat, to proceed cautiously or slyly. *Colloq.*

This use was inspired by or associated with the nickname, "Pussyfoot," given to Wm. E. Johnson (b. 1862) in allusion to his catlike policies in pursuing lawbreakers in the Indian Territory. He later became a noted advocate of prohibition.

1903 *Atlanta Const.* 20 March 3 Vice-President Charles Warren Fairbanks is pussy-footing it around Washington. **1949** *Time* 9 May 25/2 The ones who pussy-footed, side-stepped, straddled, carried water on both shoulders and compromised were left at home.

2. Also: **a. pussyfooted,** *adv.* **b. pussyfooter,** *n.* **c. pussyfooting,** *a.*

(**a**) **1893** *Scribner's Mag.* Nov. 653 Men who were beginning to walk pussy-footed and shy at shadows. — (**b**) **1927** *Sat. Ev. Post* 24 Dec. 9/1 A good politician is a natural-born pussy-footer. **1946** HOLBROOK *Lost Men* 160 The appeasers and pussyfooters of 1850 also provided that any territories that might come into the Union later could do so with or without slavery. — (**c**) **1928** *Collier's* 29 Dec. 38/1 The wrappings which . . . the pussy-footing politicians impose upon a candidate. **1949** *Time* 9 May 24/1 Pussyfooting Tom Connally thought Acheson went 'a little too far,' in his answer.

∗**put,** *v.*

1. *intr.* To extend. *Obs.*

1822 J. FOWLER *Journal* 102 Heare the mountain Puts a Cross the Plain to the River Delmort about 6 miles to our right. **1853** McCONNEL *Western Char.* 137 Upon some point of timber which puts a mile or two within the plain . . . the 'squatter' cleaves out, and renders habitable, a home for himself.

2. In colloq. noun combs.: (1) **put in,** turn or place to speak, affair; (2) **put out,** (*a*) annoyance, inconvenience, (*b*) in baseball, the act of retiring or putting out a player.

(**1**) **1853** MARK TWAIN *Hannibal Jrnl.* 25 May, Never speak when it's not your 'put-in.' **1902** HARBEN *A. Daniel* 301 This ain't no put-in o' mine, gracious knows! — (**2**) (*a*) **1833** NEAL *Down-Easters* I. 83, I shouldn't think twould be any put-out to you to take somebody else. **1843** STEPHENS *High Life N.Y.* II. 32 Don't be oneasy about the trouble, it won't be no put out to Captin Doolittle. (*b*) **1885** *Calif. Athlete* (S.F.) 19 Dec. 5/1 He assisted yesterday in fourteen put outs. **1949** *St. Paul Pioneer Press* 12 Aug. 15/5 Behr also sparkled at his first base position, accounting for 16 putouts.

3. In verbal combs., usu. colloq.: (1) ∗**put back,** to demote or turn back (a pupil); (2) **down,** (*a*) to cure or preserve (meat, etc.) for future use, also **putting down,** *n.*, (*b*) to build or construct by laying down; (3) **from,** of a stream, to make or flow from; (4) ∗**in,** (*a*) of a stream, to come or flow in, (*b*) to deliver (logs) at a mill or landing; (5) ∗**into,** of a stream or ravine, to flow, empty, lead into; (6) **out,** (*a*) to stretch away, extend, (*b*) to cause or permit (a horse) to show his best speed, (*c*) to spend, hand out (money) freely; (7) ∗**over,** to do something effectively, make a success of, cf. **b.** (15) below; (8) ∗**up,** (*a*) to extend or lead up from, (*b*) to make or restore (a rail fence) by laying the rails in place, (*c*) to stake, deposit, provide (money), (*d*) to build, fashion, construct, (*e*) to put in jail, (*f*) to size up, estimate, "figure out."

(**1**) **1887** PERRY *Flock of Girls* 78, I don't want to lose anything, and have to be put back when school begins. — (**2**) (*a*) **1843** *Knickerb.* XXI. 436 Daniel Gilbert's property . . . *cut up* very handsomely, (to borrow the common figure upon such occasions, derived from the putting down of pork for the winter). **1881** JEWETT *Country By-Ways* 40 He's put down a kag of excellent beef. **1889** COOKE *Steadfast* 229 Who'll put down my pork and beef as Almiry did? (*b*) **1887** *Courier-Journal* 2 Feb. 3/6 For furnishing the material and putting down new footway crossings in the Eastern and Western districts of the city. — (**3**) **1773** FITHIAN *Journal* I. 56 From his house we see the Potowmack, and a fine River putting from it. — (**4**) (*a*) **1809** CUMING *Western Tour* 97 The creek . . . puts in from the Virginia side. **1903** A. ADAMS *Log of Cowboy* 347 The trail on leaving the river led up Many Berries, one of the tributaries of the Yellowstone putting in from the north side. (*b*) **1902** WHITE *Blazed Trail* 96 We contracted last fall . . . to put in five million feet of our timber. *Ib.* 99 Besides you still own the million and a half which, if you do not care to put them in yourself, you can sell for something in the skids. **1905** *Forestry Bureau Bul.* No. 61, 44.

(**5**) **1807** GASS *Journal* 172 A small river . . . puts into a large bay on the south side of the Columbia. **1903** A. ADAMS *Log of Cowboy* 362 Our pilot led us up the divide . . . , weaving in and out around the heads of creeks putting into either river. — (**6**) (*a*) **1755** *N.J. Archives* XIX. 532 To be sold. . . . A Plantation . . . about three Quarters of a Mile from a good Landing that puts out of said River. **1840** HOFFMAN *Greyslaer* I. 116 A ledge of bald rock to the left yonder . . . puts out from the ridge. **1878** BEADLE *Western Wilds* 311 Commenced the ascent of the Buckskin, a low range of partially-wooded hills, putting out across the plateau nearly to the Colorado. (*b*) **1868** G. A. McCALL *Lett. from Frontiers* 345 After a mile's gentle trot, I '*put him out*,' and he went as steadily as ever. (*c*) **1884** *Boston Jrnl.* 13 Sep., 'McKinley would be elected,' says an Ohio correspondent, 'if the opposing candidate did not have a rich father-in-law, who will put out money freely.' — (**7**) **1914** GRAU *Theatre of Science* 127 The superb text of the spoken play was not 'put over' concretely in the visualization. **1932** GRAYSON *Leaders* 371 It was finally put over, however. **1949** *Chi. Tribune* 4 Dec. II. 6/5 There will be a lot of scheming aimed at putting over trades. — (**8**) (*a*) **1847** HOWE *Hist. Coll. Ohio* 539 They came to a deep ravine, putting up from the river in a southerly direction. (*b*) **1860** CLAIBORNE *Life of Dale* 27 We were preparing to dismount, when some one cried out that the fence had been put up again. (*c*) **1857** *Spirit of Times* 3 Jan. 292/3 The friends of the grey never lost faith in his winning sure, but were a little shy about putting up their 'dough.' **1911** LINCOLN *Cap'n Warren's Wards* 237 You're putting up for it, and I ought to be much obliged. (*d*) **1866** *Ill. Agric. Soc. Trans.* VI. 79 These plows are put up in a substantial manner. **1912** NICHOLSON *Hoosier Chron.* 219 Sylvia was as well 'put up' as any of the girls. (*e*) **1872** BRACE *Dangerous Classes N.Y.* 289 He kept himself drunk for three weeks, and smashed a number of policemen, and was 'put up.' **1901** HARBEN *Westerfelt* 289 'Ef I was you-uns,' she called back from the door, 'I'd have 'er put up!' (*f*) **1880** MARK TWAIN *Tramp Abroad* 192 Say, didn't I put you up right? . . . I spotted you for my kind the minute I heard your clack. **1895** *Cent. Mag.* Sep. 674/2 'What is to be will be.' That's about the way I put it up.

b. In colloq. and slang phrases: (1) ∗*To put it (in)to* (someone), to get the better of (someone), to chastise, berate; (2) *to put the joke* (or *laugh*) *(up)on* (someone), to get off a joke (or laugh) at the expense of someone; (3) *to put up or shut up*, to make good, produce proof, etc., or cease talking, to come out openly or stop objecting; (4) *to be hard put up for*, to be hard put to it for, *rare;* (5) *to put the law on* (someone), to bring legal action against someone; (6) *to put oneself into* (something), to devote oneself wholeheartedly to (something); (7) *to put* (someone) *onto* (something), to acquaint (someone) with little-known facts about (something), *to put* (someone) *on*, to inform (someone); (8) *to put it all over* (someone) to excel or beat (someone) decisively; (9) *to put it there*, to shake hands expressive of full agreement or accord; (10) *to put up a fight*, to champion something with great boldness, to struggle for; (11) *to put it up to* (someone), to place the responsibility and desirability for action squarely upon (someone); (12) *to put* (someone) *wise*, to inform (someone); (13) *to put* (something) *on the ball*, of a baseball pitcher, to pitch with all his skill and strength; (14) *to put the run on*, to get the better of, drive (someone) off; (15) *to put* (something) *over on* (someone), to deceive, trick.

(**1**) **1835** LONGSTREET *Ga. Scenes* 29 Dod drot my soul if he's put it to daddy as bad as he thinks he has. **1875** STOWE *We & Neighbors* 100 You ought to hear me expound the commandments, and put it into them about stealing and lying. — (**2**) **1853** HAWTHORNE *Works* (1883) IV. 289 Cadmus suspected . . . that he was putting a joke upon him. **1902** LORIMER *Lett. Merchant* 271 It was a month after that before Bud could go down Main Street without some man . . . reaching out and fetching him a clip on the ear for having come back and put the laugh on him. — (**3**) **1878** HART *Sazerac Lying Club* 167 'P. U. or S. U.' means put up or shut up, doesn't it? **1947** *Time* 27 Jan. 17/3 The time has come when we shall have to put up or shut up. — (**4**) **1879** TOURGEE *Fool's Errand* 29 [They] was mighty hard put up for excuses.

(**5**) **1888** STOCKTON *Dusantes* 104 If he dares to open a package of mine, I'll put the law on him! — (**6**) **1889** *Cent. Mag.* March 778/2 She had put herself into it for all she was worth. — (**7**) **1895** *N.Y. Dramatic News* 12 Oct. 5/3 Mr. Jack is always a newspaper man's friend, and only too pleased to put one on 'to a good thing' in the shape of news. **1904** W. H. SMITH *Promoters* 308 I'll put you on, and tell you all about it when you get here. — (**8**) **1899** G. ADE *Fables in Slang* (1902) 163 There was one boy who could put it all over the other members. **1920** LEWIS *Main Street* 281 Wasn't it true that

American aviators put it all over them Frenchmen? — (9) **1903** R. BEDFORD *True Eyes* 344 'You're my mate; put it there!' He held out his hand and Lawler gripped it. **1909** F. CALHOUN *Miss Minerva* 112 'Put it there, partner,' and the fascinating stranger held out a grimy paw.

(10) **1903** *N.Y. Sun* 2 Dec. 7 Mrs. Vanderbilt is a woman of spirit, and the first to put up a fight against the iron-clad rule of the Board. **1904** *Chi. Tribune* 22 June 6 If they put up a fight against Roosevelt they would be beaten. — (11) **1908** *Atlantic Mo.* Nov. 582 What are we to do? Let us put it all up to the governor or president. **1932** TARBELL *O. D. Young* 239 It was this putting up to a youth the final responsibility of his education . . . to which the public so quickly answered. — (12) **1910** E. S. FIELD *Sapphire Bracelet* 38 'Didn't the clerk at the hotel put you wise to me?' demanded Mr. Warner. **1922** PARRISH *Case & Girl* 330 Finally I ran across a kid who put me wise. — (13) **1912** C. MATHEWSON *Pitching* x. 214 He will come into camp, and the first day out put every thing he has on the ball to show the manager 'he's got something.' — (14) **1914** BOWER *Flying U Ranch* 188, I wouldn't be hopeful of putting the run on this Dunk person by telling him ghost stories.

(15) **1916** H. L. WILSON *Somewhere in Red Gap* i. 19 Funny, the way the little man tried to put it over on us, letting on he was just puzzled —not really bothered, as he plainly was. **1924** W. M. RAINE *Troubled Waters* xix. 209 What are you trying to put over on me? Why don't you go to Mack and ask him?

***putty,** *n.* In combs.: (1) **putty blower,** a blowtube for shooting pellets of putty or other small objects; (2) **head,** a soft-headed, stupid person [cf. *EDD putty-brain* in similar sense]; (3) **root,** an American orchid, *Aplectrum hyemale*, producing a corm filled with a glutinous matter that may be used as a cement.

(1) **1861** NEWELL *Orpheus C. Kerr* I. 156 [The muskets] are inferior to the putty-blowers of our innocent childhood. **1897** *Outing* April 60/1, [I] thought of barn-yard cleaning in a wet-spring, and ejected the morsel as a pellet leaveth the putty-blower. — (2) **1856** M. J. HOLMES *L. Rivers* 370 He got so engaged about the darned 'liquor law,' and the putty-heads that made it, that he'd no idee 'twas so late. **1864** TROWBRIDGE *Cudjo's Cave* 399 We must fight it through, or go back, like that putty-head Deslow. **1892** *Amer. Folk-Lore* V. 145 *Putty-head.*—A term of reproach. Soft head, stupid. — (3) **1817–8** EATON *Botany* (1822) 250 *Corallorhiza hyemalis*, adam and eve, putty root. . . . A cement resembling putty may be made of the root. **1858** R. HOGG *Veg. Kingdom* 779 The tubers of *Aplectrum hyemale* are so viscid that they are called *Putty-root* in the United States, and are used for cementing broken earthenware.

putz pʌts, *n. local.* [G. (<*putzen* to adorn) in the Pa.-G. sense shown here.] A Christmas decoration including an improvised stable or cave housing the Christ child in a manger, with Mary and Joseph, and usu. the shepherds, the wise men, heavenly hosts, and various other representations, a crèche.

1926 *Ladies' Home Jrnl.* Dec. 82/2 The putz is simply the pictured story of the Nativity, built near or at the base of the Christmas tree. **1938** HARK *Hex Marks Spot* 186 You see, everybody's curious to see what kind of putz everybody else has this year, so they go around visiting. **1949** *L.A. Times Home Mag.* 11 Dec. 10/2 His original thought was to reproduce the 'putz' or 'yard' reminiscent of his childhood in Southeastern Pennsylvania.

Puyallup puˈjæləp, *n.* [f. an Indian word of unknown meaning.] *pl.* An important Salish tribe of Indians in western Washington, now on Puyallup reservation in that state. Also attrib.

1892 BOSTON TILLICUM *Puyallup Indians* 16 No, he wasn't a Puyallup Indian. **1896** *Columbus* (O.) *Dispatch* 1 Dec. 14 He . . . draws lessons from the freedom and enjoyment of the Puyallup reservation Indians, which he thinks results from their freedom. **1903** JAMES *Indian Basketry* 53 These [tribes] are the Miskuwallis, Puyullaps, Squaxin and Muckleshoots. **1940** SMITH *Puyallup-Nisqually* xi, The Puyallup have long been thought of as a salt water and river people in distinction to the horse owning Nisqually.

***pygmy,** *n.* In combs.: (1) **pygmy owl,** any one of various owls of the genus *Glaucidium*, esp. *G. gnoma;* (2) **rattlesnake,** any one of several small rattlesnakes of the genus *Sistrurus*, cf. **massasauga, prairie rattlesnake;** (3) **weed,** a low, tufted annual, *Tillaestrum aquaticum*, found along the Atlantic Coast.

(1) **1858** BAIRD *Birds Pacific R.R.* 62 *Glaucidium Gnoma.* . . . The Pigmy Owl. . . . The smallest owl known to inhabit North America. **1917** *Birds of Amer.* II. 119/1 Dr. Coues gave the Pygmy Owl an excellent character. — (2) **1921** *Outing* Aug. 217/1 The pygmy rattlesnake (known also as the hog-nosed rattlesnake) is found in the Southeastern States. **1944** *Mass. Audubon Soc. Bul.* Dec. 262 Poisonous snakes found in the region . . . are . . . massasauga, pigmy, diamond-back, banded, and canebrake rattlesnakes. [**1949** *Democrat* 22 Sep. 1/2 The small rattlesnake is one of the pigmy rattlers commonly called ground snakes in this locality [Clark Co. Ala.]. — (3) **1817–8** EATON *Botany* (1822) 487 *Tillaea ascendens*, pigmy weed. Very minute. **1901** MOHR *Plant Life Ala.* 533 Pigmy-weed. . . . Southeastern Massachusetts to Maryland and southeastern Pennsylvania.

***pyramid,** *n.* and *v.* **1.** *n.* In football, a wedge formation of players to advance the ball. **2.** *v. tr.* On the stock exchange, to increase (the amount of one's holding) by selling at favorable times and using all the proceeds to purchase more stock. Cf. **parlay,** *v.*

(1) **1899** A. H. QUINN *Pa. Stories* 25 It was Penn's ball. The pyramid started with the cheers of ten thousand back of it. — (2) **1902** G. H. LORIMER *Lett. Self-Made Merchant* v. 64 He'd invent a scheme for speculation in wheat and go on pyramiding his purchases till he'd made the best that Cheops did look like a five-cent plate of ice-cream. **1927** P. MARKS *Lord of Himself* 23 He pyramided his winnings and piled gold on gold and finally saw himself a millionaire three times over.

Pyrex ˈpaɪrɛks, *n.* [A trade-mark name coined from **pie* and **-ex.*] Glass that is especially resistant to heat, chemicals, and electricity; utensils made of this. Also attrib.

1917 *Ladies' Home Jrnl.* May 92/1 All women today welcome enthusiastically Pyrex. **1921** *Ib.* Feb. 80/1 Pyrex does not chip, discolor, nor wear out. **1940** EILMANN *Medicolegal & Indust. Toxicology* 19 Transfer this distillate to a 500 c.c. Pyrex flask. **1949** *Highway Traveler* Feb. 14/2 The casting of the 200-inch pyrex mirror at Corning, N.Y., and its shipment to the West Coast . . . received national attention.

pyxie ˈpɪksɪ, *n.* [f. genus name *Pyxi*danthera (in allusion to the lidlike opening of the anthers).] (See quot. 1882.) — **1882** *Harper's Mag.* June 65 The delicate pyxie (*Pyxidanthera barbulata*), a little prostrate trailing evergreen, forming dense tufts or masses, . . . is strictly a pine-barren plant, and its locality is confined to New Jersey and the Carolinas. **1892** *Amer. Folk-Lore* V. 100 *Pyxidanthera barbulata*, pyxie moss. N.J.

Q

qua-bird ˈkwɑˌbɝd, *n.* [f. its cry.] (See quot. 1917.) Cf. ∗**quawk.**

1791 W. BARTRAM *Travels* (1793, ed. 3) 291 A[rdea] clamator, corpore subcæruleo; the quaw bird, or frogcatcher. **1834** NUTTALL *Water Birds* II. 56 About the middle of October, the Qua birds begin to retire from this part of Massachusetts, toward their southern winter quarters. **1917** *Birds of Amer.* I. 194 Black-crowned Night Heron. *Nycticorax nycticorax nævius.* . . . [Also called] American Night Heron; Qua-bird; Quawk.

quack kwæk, *n.* [Variant of ∗*quick.*]

1. Short for next.

1839 BUEL *Farmer's Companion* 144 To clean the ground of the roots of foul plants, as dock, quack, etc. **1909** *N.Y. Ev. Post* (s.-w. ed.) 11 March 5 In conquering the quack he did the one thing that could have enabled him to get a crop from that unfertilized soil. **1948** JACOBS *We Chose Country* 189 The big garden across the road, where we fought quack instead of weeds, really established us.

2. quack grass, the European couch grass, *Agropyron repens,* naturalized throughout the U.S. Cf. ∗**quake grass.**

1817–8 EATON *Botany* (1822) 494 *Triticum repens,* wheat-grass, couch-grass, quack-grass. . . . Very troublesome in fertile soil, and useful in barren sand. **1884** VASEY *Agric. Grasses* 108 Quack grass. . . . There has been a good deal of discussion relative to this grass, some pronouncing it one of the vilest of weeds. **1949** *This Week Mag.* 17 Sep. 2/2 That means the quackgrass and the sassafras is getting the best of him.

quackawarry ˈkwækəˌwɑrɪ, *n.* [Imitative.] =**qua-bird.** *Rare.* — **1808** MRS. GRANT *Memoirs* II. 324 Quackawarry is the Indian name of a bird, which flies about in the night, making a noise similar to the sound of its name.

∗**quadrangle,** *n.* (See quot. 1909.)

1903 *Science* 7 Aug. 187 (*Cent.*), The Philadelphia Special folio, embracing four fifteen-minute quadrangles. **1909** *Cent. Supp.* 1094/1 quadrangle. . . . A region measuring 15′ lat. by 15′ long. (or 30′ lat. by 30′ long., or 1° lat. by 1° long., according to the density of the population) as shown on an atlas sheet of the United States Geological Survey. **1916** *Iowa Acad. Sci. Proc.* XXIII. 127 Work by the writer in the Richland Center quadrangle, Wisconsin, seems to have established plains at two distinct levels. **1948** *So. Sierran* Feb. 2/3 Cuyama Peak—5,800 feet (Cuyama Peak Quadrangle—Army Engineers' Map).

∗**quadroon,** *n.* **1. quadroon (fancy) ball,** formerly in New Orleans, a ball attended by part-Negro women and white men, often to enable the latter to choose mistresses. Now *hist.* **2. quadroon Choctaw,** a Choctaw Indian of mixed blood. *Obs.*

(1) **1805** *Amer. Pioneer* II. 236 The colored women have . . . their weekly balls, (called quartroon balls) at which none but white gentlemen attend. **1888** DALY *Lottery of Love* 18, A brace of my men . . . were jugged for kicking up a rumpus at a quadroon fancy-ball. **1948** *Chi. Tribune* 8 Feb. (Grafic Mag.) 18/3 Most notorious of the carnival affairs, was the Quadroon ball, given by the young men of the town for their mistresses and friends. — (2) **1891** O'BEIRNE *Leaders Indian Terr.* 68/1 Mr. Lowery's father was a white man and his mother a quadroon Choctaw.

∗**quadruplex,** *a. Electric Telegraph.* Designating or pertaining to a system, invented by Edison in 1874, by which four messages, two in each direction, may be sent simultaneously over one wire.

1875 KNIGHT 1842/1 Quadruplex Telegraph. **1878** HART *Sazerac Lying Club* 92 The Western Union Telegraph Company are now using the quadruplex system on the Virginian and Salt Lake circuit, by means of which four messages may be sent simultaneously over a single wire. **1899** *N.Y. Tribune* 22 Oct. (Supp.) 15/3 One of Edison's greatest inventions is the quadruplex system of telegraphy.

quager ˈkwɑgɚ, *n.* [Origin unknown. Poss. an Africanism. Cf. *kwa* (Twi, Gold Coast), sound of scratching, in Turner 119, and cf. **quaqua.**] App. the gopher, *Gopherus polyphemus,* of the southern states. *Obs.* — **1831** ROYALL *Southern Tour* II. 102 [Near Augusta, Ga.,] there are a few larger heaps of earth . . . in the shape (or nearly) of a grave, said to be made by a kind of tarapin, Quagers, or some such name.

quaggery ˈkwægərɪ, *n.* [f. ∗*quag*+∗*-ery.*] A bog or marsh. *Rare.* — **1843** CARLTON *New Purchase* xlvi. 117 Two rods above and one below, the quaggery required a pole to touch its bottom some fifteen feet long.

quahog ˈkwɔhɔg, *n.* Also †**quogue, quahaug, cohog,** etc. [Algonquian. Cf. Pequot *p'quaughhaug,* hard clam.] The round or hard clam, *Venus mercenaria,* of the Atlantic Coast. Cf. **pooquaw.**

1753 *Southampton Rec.* III. 6 The Trustees shall have the care of the fishery of Quogue to dispose of it as they shall think fit. **1871** DE VERE 29 The more costly beads came from the largest shells of the Quahaugh or Cohog, a welk, known in the Middle and Southern States as the Round Clam, and belonging to the genus *Venus mercenaria,* which is so called on account of their being used as currency. **1949** R. J. SIM *Pages from Past* 66 The quahog, or hardshell clam, is deservedly the most famous of all.

attrib. **1788** CUTLER in *Life & Corr.* (1888) I. 416 Went into the water; found a great number of clam cohog shells. **1815** *Mass. H.S. Coll.* 2 Ser. IV. 289 The quahaug clam is common, and the oyster is taken in two or more places. **1883** GOODE *Fishery Industries U.S.* 45 The Clam and Quahaug Fishery. **1947** COFFIN *Yankee Coast* 180 Those islands over there are white-sided because they are pure quahaug shells piled up through a thousand years of Indian feasting.

transf. **1790** WALLCUT *Jrnl.* in *Mass. H.S. Proc.* 1 Ser. XVII. 190 The doctor informs me of plenty of mussels and quahogs up the Muskingum and Wolf Creek. **1914** LINCOLN *Kent Knowles* 450 We're all quahaugs . . . That's the trouble with all the folks of all the nations; they stay in their shells and they don't try to know and understand their neighbors.

quahog ˈkwɔhɔg, *v. intr.* To dig or take quahogs.

1913 *D.N.* IV. 56 Been *cohoggin'* every day since Tuesday. **1935** LINCOLN *Cape Cod Yesterdays* 53 If you are a professional—if you 'go quahauging' regularly, to earn a living—you do work hard indeed. **1949** KATHLEEN KNIGHT *Bass Derby Murder* 122, I was down to the pond quahoggin', all afternoon.

Hence **quahogger,** *n.*

1935 LINCOLN *Cape Cod Yesterdays* 55 The Bay is seldom very rough, land is not far distant, and the deep quahauger knows how to handle a boat.

∗**quail,** *n.*

1. Any one of several small game birds of the family Odontophoridae.

In the northern and eastern states, the bobwhite or American partridge of the genus *Colinus,* esp. *C. virginianus,* is the commonest quail; in the West and Southwest, the most common species are the California quail of the Pacific Coast, the Massena quail of Arizona, the plumed partridge or mountain quail of the Pacific Coast, the blue quail of the Southwest, etc. (*qq.v.*). Besides these latter, the bobwhite has been introduced into the Rocky Mountain and Pacific Coast areas.

1625 MORRELL *N. Eng.* 15 All, along the Maine: The Turtle, Eagle, Partridge, and the Quaile. **1701** WOLLEY *Journal N.Y.* 40 They have great store of wild-fowl, as Turkys, Heath-hens, Quails, Partridges, Pigeons. **1869** J. R. BROWNE *Adv. Apache Country* 76 Quail were very abundant as we drew near our first camping-place on the Gila. **1947** *Democrat* 27 Feb. 2/2 There is outspoken discontent among sportsmen . . . regarding the scarcity of quail this season.

attrib. **1856** *Porter's Spirit of Times* 22 Nov. 193/1 It is not long since that we replied, to a query where good quail shooting can be had, within three hundred miles of our city: 'No where!' *Ib.* 27 Dec. 269/1 'Don' is as good a quail dog as man ever shot over. **1865** MARK TWAIN *Sk. New & Old* 34 He got the frog out and prized his mouth open and took a teaspoon and filled him full of quail shot. **1897** *Outing* April 94/2 Ever since last quail-time I have been casting rather dubious glances at a certain old gun. **1933** ROCKFELLOW *Log Ariz. Trail Blazer* 21, I had filled his side with quail-shot as we learned later.

2. With specifying terms.

1849 *31st Congress* 1 Sess. Sen. Ex. Doc. No. 64, 52 Four different kinds of quails were killed: the common quail; the tufted quail, slightly ash-colored [etc.]. **1917** *Birds of Amer.* II. 10 [Also called] Fool Hen; Black Quail.

3. A girl, a co-ed. *Student slang.*

1859 *Yale Lit. Mag.* XXIV. 291 (Th.), The freshman heareth of 'Quails,' he dresseth himself in fine linen, he seeketh to flirt with ye 'quails,' but they know him not. **1909** *N.Y. Ev. Post* 11 March (Th.), The 'quails' have been barred at Wesleyan—'quails' is the Middletown University's name for her 'co-eds.' **1947** *Time* 6 Oct. 68/1 A less active sport is 'piping the flock,' when Cal males watch Cal 'quails' preening in the sun on the steps of Wheeler Hall.

4. In special combs.: (1) **quail brush,** (see quots.); (2) **tracks,** (*a*) poor handwriting, *colloq.*, (*b*) **quail track corn,** an unidentifiable kind or variety of corn, *obs.;* (3) **trap,** a trap for catching quail.

(1) **1925** JEPSON *Flowering Plants Calif.* 327 A[triplex] lentiformis (Torr.) quail brush. **1931** DAYTON *Western Browse Plants* 31 Big saltbush (*A. lentiformis*), sometimes called quailbrush, is perhaps the largest of our native saltbushes. — (2) (*a*) **1842** *Yale Lit. Mag.* VIII. 96, I can't always decipher *quail tracks.* **1855** HOLBROOK *Among Mail Bags* 404 The most skilful interpreters of the species of chirography known as 'quail tracks,' are often taxed to their utmost capacity. (*b*) **1855** *Mich. Agric. Soc. Trans.* VI. 495 One acre of quail track corn; planted on muck land. — (3) **1790** T. B. HAZARD *Nailer Tom's Diary* (1930) 117/1 Snow. went to meeting. at Night made quail Trap. **1933** SPIER *Yuman Tribes* 72 A quail trap . . . was a basket-like contrivance of arrowweed propped on a split stick and baited with seed.

b. In the names of birds: (1) **quail dove,** (2) **hawk,** (3) **head,** (4) **sparrow,** (see quots.).

(1) **1891** *Cent.* 4889/1 *quail-dove.* . . . An American pigeon of the genus *Starnœnas. S. cyanocephalus* is the blue-headed quail-dove, found in the West Indies and Florida. **1895** *Dept. Agric. Yrbk. 1894* 211 Among the birds [in southern Fla.] may be mentioned the white-crowned pigeon, Zenaida dove, quail doves [etc.]. — (2) **1917** *Birds of Amer.* II. 67 *Accipiter cooperi.* . . . [Also called] Quail Hawk. — (3) **1844** *Nat. Hist. N.Y., Zoology* II. 164 The Quail-Head. *Ammodramus Caudacutus.* . . . It is found in salt marshes where it breeds. — (4) **1917** *Birds of Amer.* III. 26 Grasshopper Sparrow. . . . *Ammodramus savannarum australis.* . . . [Also called] Quail Sparrow.

As the last term in **American, Arizona, blue, California, Cincinnati, desert, fool, Gambel's, helmet, marsh, Massena, Mearns's, Mexican, Montezuma, mountain, plumed, Rio Grande, scaled, sea, shell, snow, swamp, top knot, valley, Virginia quail.**

***quake grass.** =**quack grass.** *Obs.* — **1840** DEWEY *Mass. Flowering Plants* 250 *Triticum repens.* Quake, or Quack, or Couch Grass. Sometimes from its resemblance to wheat, it is called Wheat-Grass.

quakenasp ˈkwekɪnˌæsp, *n.* =**quaking asp.** Also attrib. — **1822** J. FOWLER *Journal* 143 The timber on the mountains Heare is Pitch Pine Spruce Pine Hemlock and quakenasp the latter of which there are vast quantityes. **1905** *N.Y. Ev. Post* 2 Sep., I have seen quakenasp groves on the summer range, where you could walk miles and miles through these bluebells.

* **quaker,** *n.* Also * **Quaker.**

1. Short for **Quaker gun.** *Obs.*

1830 N. AMES *Mariner's Sk.* 7 Our six iron six-pounders and six *quakers,* (wooden guns,), were, like the millenial lion and lamb, lying down together in the hold. **1862** *N.Y. Tribune* 13 March 5/5 The fancied impregnability of the position turns out to be a sham. . . . Some of our soldiers cried when they found that 'quakers' were mounted on the Rebel breastworks.

2. (*cap.*) A guessing game played with coins.

1907 MARK TWAIN *Chapters from Autobiog.* 473 (R.), They wanted me to play the game of 'Quaker' with them.

3. In combs.: (1) **Quaker Agent,** (see quot.), *obs.;* (2) ***bonnet,** (see quots.); (3) **City,** (*a*) Philadelphia, Pa., a nickname, (*b*) (see quot.), *obs.;* (4) **fip,** a kiss, *obs.;* (5) **gun,** a dummy gun, so called because of the doctrine of nonresistance held by the Quakers, *obs.;* (6) **gunboat,** a sham gunboat, *obs.;* (7) **ladies,** the small pale-blue flowers of the bluet, *Houstonia caerulea;* (8) **poet,** (see quots.).

(1) **1904** D. H. BIGGERS *From Cattle Range* (1944) 8 Through some influence a great many Quakers were appointed. . . . Indian agents, hence . . . the term 'Quaker Agents' was applied [*c*1869] to Indian agents in general. — (2) **1898** BRITTON & BROWN *Illust. Flora* III. 212 *Houstonia coerulea.* Bluets. . . . Called also Quaker Ladies, Quaker bonnets, Venus' Pride. **1915** ARMSTRONG & THORNBER *Western Wild Flowers* 252 Quaker Bonnets. *Lupinus laxiflorus.* . . . This is very common in Utah, handsome and conspicuous. — (3) (*a*) **1836** T. POWER *Impressions of Amer.* i. 51 It was night before we gained the Quaker city. **1948** *Lawton* (Okla.) *Constitution* 4 July 10/2 Don't criticize the Republicans for their behavior in the Quaker City. (*b*) **1859** *Ladies' Repository* Jan. 51/2 Richmond, Indiana, is the 'Quaker City of the West,' as it is one of the principal settlements of Friends. — (4) **1846** *Quincy* (Ill.) *Whig* 28 Feb. 2/2 However happy he might have been to pay the *Quaker fip,* . . . he was mortified at her seeming want of modesty in demanding it in the presence of so many witnesses.

(5) **1809** *Ann. 10th Congress* 2 Sess. 1367 Our vessels bound to England will, if they make any show of resistance, do it by *Quaker* guns. **1888** DORSEY *Midshipman Bob* 88 'He's like a Quaker gun,' said Haxall—'piles of appearance, but no damage done.' — (6) **1864** *Nat. Almanac* (Phila.) 76/2 (Ernst), A quaker gunboat made of logs, with funnels of pork barrels. — (7) **1871** *Scribner's Mo.* II. 102 Tenderest of all in yonder woods, where hepatica, and May blossoms, and Quaker ladies twinkle into life. **1947** *Chi. Tribune* 29 June VII. 1/8 Everything from shy Quaker Ladies to sought after . . . golden coreopsis, . . . blooms with utter abandon. — (8) **1864** *Ladies' Repository* Sep. 538/1 But we were intending to give a sketch of our Quaker Poet [i.e., Whittier]. **1912** *Out West* April 260/2 Much of the peace, good will and sterling sturdiness of these substantial citizens have become a part of life and upbuilding of the town which takes its name from Whittier, the Quaker Poet.

b. Quakerdelphia, jocose for Philadelphia. *Obs.*

1846 *Dollar Newspaper* (Phila.) 21 Jan. 2/1 Our neighbor city of Gotham, like Quakerdelphia, occasionally deals in abuse of public charities.

As the last term in **dancing, fighting, gay, hickory, Hicksite, Keithian, Nicholite, Progressive, Shaking, Singing, Whig Quaker.** See also **Free Quakers.**

* **quaking,** *a.* In combs.: (1) **quaking asp,** any of several species of aspen, esp. the American aspen, *Populus tremuloides,* a tree, or its wood, of one of these species; (2) **aspen,** =prec.; (3) * **grass,** (see quot.).

(1) **1825** in DALE *Ashley-Smith Explor.* (1918) 152 This range of mountains is . . . closely timbered with pine, cedar, quaking-asp, and a dwarfish growth of oak. **1906** *Out West* Feb. 117 The quaking asp . . . finishes with an exquisite satin lustre and pearly tones in its pure white wood. **1916** SETON *Woodcraft Man.* 272 Quaking Asp, Quiver Leaf, Aspen Poplar, or Popple (*Populus tremuloides*). — (2) **1843** in *Utah Hist. Quart.* II. (1929) 115 A little quaking aspen on the creeks, and pine on the mountains. **1947** *True* Nov. 110/3 Me and four soldiers chased them through heavy pine and quaking aspen. — (3) **1889** VASEY *Agric. Grasses* 109 Rattlesnake Grass; Fall Quaking Grass. . . . Cattle are fond of it, both green and when made into hay.

* **qualify,** *v. tr. passive.* To be sworn in.

[**1723** *Pa. Statutes* III. 382 Every such brewer . . . shall be qualified by oath . . . that he or she will not . . . use any of the said ingredients.] **1795** *Pittsburgh Gaz.* 26 Dec. 2/2 Mr. Hillhouse appeared, was qualified, and took his seat. **1867** *Cong. Globe* App. 16 Feb. 165/3 He said he had come to file his bond and be qualified. **1909** *Lafollette's Mag.* 9 Jan. 6/1 Our Primary Election law provides that an elector seeking office . . . if elected, 'will qualify as such officer,' implying, of course, that he will also serve.

quamash ˈkwɑmæʃ, *n.* Variant of **camass.** Also attrib.

1806 LEWIS in *L. & Clark Exped.* V. (1905) 170 Immediately above the springs on the creek there is a handsome little quamas plain of about 10 acres. **1839** TOWNSEND *Narrative* 124 Captain W. . . . finally bought of them a small quantity of dried salmon, and a little fermented kamas or *quamash* root. **1896** *Garden & Forest* IX. 253/1 *Camass.* . . . Variants: Camas, Cammas, Quamash, and Quamish.

quandy ˈkwɑndɪ, *n. N. Eng.* [Origin obscure. Webster suggests Algonquian.] The old squaw duck. — **1875** *Fur, Fin & Feather* (ed. 3) 119 Along the coast of New England it [i.e., the long-tailed duck] is generally called the quondy. **1888** G. TRUMBULL *Names of Birds* 89 Two other odd names met with among old New England gunners are Scoldenore, at Portsmouth, N.H., and Quandy, at North Scituate and Plymouth, Mass.

quantiers ˌkɑntɪˈe, *n. pl. La.* [f. F. *quartiers,* flaps (see 1st quot.).] (See quots.)

[**1758** LE PAGE DU PRATZ *Hist. Louisiane* II. 195 Ils joignent autour de pied comme un chausson qui auroit la couture par-dessus; la peau est coupée trois doigts plus longue que le pied; . . . mais les quartiers sont de huit à neuf pouces de haut.] **1887** *Harper's Mag.* March 611/1 The negroes . . . protected their feet with what they called *quantiers,* made in this way. **1895** G. KING *New Orleans* 335 Their shoes, called 'quantiers,' were pieces of raw-hide, cut so as to lace comfortably over foot and ankle.

Quapaw ˈkwɔpɔ, *n.* [f. native name *Ugákhpa,* downstream people.] A Sioux Indian of a southwestern tribe. Also (*pl.*) the tribe of such an Indian. Cf. **Osage 3. c.**

[**1723** BARCIA *Ensaya Cronologico* II. 279/2 Que vivian en vna Casa grande, y que conocian mui bien à los Indios de Capa, y otres cosas.] **1772** in *Travels Amer. Col.* 520 The Quarpas . . . or Arkansaws (a small nation on the west side of Mississippi). **1821** NUTTALL *Travels Arkansa* 223 In the spring and autumn the Quapaws have a custom of making a contribution dance. **1900** *Cong. Rec.* 1 Feb. 1420/2 The Quapaws have had their lands completely allotted to them. **1946**

FOREMAN *Last Trek* 163 There was also a village of two hundred and fifty Quapaw.

attrib. **1770** PITTMAN *Present State* 40 The Arcansas or Quapas Indians live three leagues above the fort, on the side of the river. **1845** *St. Louis Reveille* 18 March 1/6 The Quapaw chief replied that if this was their excuse for avoiding a regular 'stand up fight,' he would obviate it by dividing his power with them. **1879** *K.C. Times* 4 May 1/4 There are, also, 286 sections of land set apart for the Quapaw reservation. **1947** *Dly. Oklahoman* (Okla. City) 21 Sep. 1-D/3 No more pathetic chapter would be there than the story of the Quapaw Indians, once owners of vast lands south of the Arkansas.

quaqua ˈkwɔkwɔ, *n.* [Origin unknown. Cf. **quager.**] (See quot.) *Obs.* — **1784** SMYTH *Tour* I. 46 Keeping time and cadence most exactly, with the music of a banjor (a large hollow instrument with three strings), and a quaqua (somewhat resembling a drum).

* **quarantine,** *n.* In combs.: (1) **quarantine ground,** an area in which ships, livestock, etc., are quarantined; (2) * **law,** a law quarantining livestock; (3) **line,** = **fever line.**

(1) **1808** *Ann. 10th Congress* 1 Sess. 1753 The ship arrived at the quarantine ground, near the harbor of Boston. **1942** DALE *Cow Country* 203 Wide strips were left for trails across the Outlet and lands were also set aside for quarantine grounds. — (2) **1885** *Wkly. New Mexican Rev.* 29 Jan. 2/2 The quarantine law . . . if rightly enforced, will keep out diseased cattle. **1916** THOBURN *Stand. Hist. Okla.* II. 702 Important measures which passed both houses of the Fourth Legislative Assembly . . . were the following: A comprehensive banking law; a general election law; . . . and a general live stock quarantine law. — (3) **1890** *Stock Grower & Farmer* 19 April 4/2 Thousands of cattle are going daily into the Creek, Chickasaw and Choctaw country from points in Texas below the quarantine line. **1948** *Southwestern Hist. Quart.* Oct. 156 Cunningham's report was not followed when the quarantine line was established in 1890, but it served as a working basis for future use.

* **quarantine,** *v. tr.* To isolate (a disease), to protect (a place) by restricting access to it. Also * **quarantined.**

1879 *Diseases of Swine* 163, I desired to make an effort to quarantine the disease and confine it to his herd. **1890** *Stock Grower & Farmer* 24 May 7/3 The state [of Neb.] is strictly quarantined against all cattle from Texas. **1950** *Calif. Citrograph* Jan. 99/1 Shipment of host fruit into other quarantined areas would be possible only on condition that they be subjected to treatment that would destroy 100% of the flies.

* **quarry,** *n.* (See quots. and cf. **cedar quarry.**) *Obs.* — **1856** OLMSTED *Journey Seaboard Slave States* 152 The principal stock [in the Dismal Swamp], now worked into shingles, is obtained from beneath the surface—old trunks that have been preserved by the wetness of the soil. . . . The quarry is giving out, however.

quartee kwɑrˈti, *n. La.* = **quartillo.** Usu. attrib.

1839 *N.O. Picayune* 6 Feb. 2/2 He vas vell known in all the quartee shops and cabarets round the market. **1886** *Boston Herald* 18 July, If the purchaser demands quartee (2½ cents' worth) rice, and quartee beans, two lagniappes are given. **1949** *N.O. Times-Picayune Mag.* 11 Sep. 12/3 Quartée red beans, quartée rice, Little piece of salt meat to make it taste nice.

quartel, see **cuartel.**

* **quarter,** *n.*

1. *N. Eng.* A particular section, tract, or district regarded as a unit of settlement; the settlers on such an area. Also attrib. *Obs.*

1640 *New Haven Col. Rec.* 42 Every one of the 5 quarters whose proportion of meadow is under 8 acres, shall have itt in the iland in the east riuer. **1649** *Ib.* 478 Mr. Crane complained of Samuel Whitehead for leaving open ther quarter gate. **1702** *Derby Rec.* 338 The first quarter is from an heap off stones between his barn & my house eastward. **1761** in C. O. PARMENTER *Hist. Pelham, Mass.* 225 Voted that Each quarter Build their own Scole Houses.

2. = **Negro quarter.** Freq. *pl.* Now *hist.*

1724 JONES *Virginia* 36 The Negroes live in small Cottages called Quarters. *c***1845** *Big Bear Ark.* 128 Tell the niggers in the kitchen to holler to the niggers in the quarter to holler back agin to the kitchen, for hell has *surely* broken loose! **1916** THOBURN *Stand. Hist. Okla.* I. 261 'The quarters' . . . formed a picturesque feature of the old time plantation life. **1947** LUMPKIN *Southerner* 32 When . . . Dennis was sent for by the overseer or by Grandfather, or when Jerry told him he must report him, he would simply vanish from the quarters.

3. A quarterly exhibition in a school. *Obs.* Cf. * **quarter days** in **9.** below.

1782 in S. BALDWIN *Simeon Baldwin* 103 Heard our Pupils rehearse a Tragedy preparing for Quarter.

4. A fourth of a dollar. In full *quarter of a dollar.*

[**1704** *Boston News-Letter* 11 Dec. 2/1 Old Rix Dollars of the Empire . . . [Value] 4 [s.] 6 [d.]. . . . All Halves, Quarters and lesser Pieces are to Pass in Proportion to the above Rates.] **1783** *Md. Gazette* 5 Sep. 3/3 Price half a dollar to grown people, and a quarter to children. **1789** *Ann. 1st Congress* I. 228 A gallon of molasses is worth a quarter of a dollar before it is distilled. **1845** *St. Louis Reveille* 1 Jan. (Supp.) 1/2 Dimes shall jingle, Quarters ring, and halves shall mingle. **1949** *Nat. Geog. Mag.* Oct. 506/2 Any coin smaller than a quarter was a rarity.

attrib. **1876** MILLER *First Fam'lies* 227 This last adventure wore him down to about the condition of an old quarter-coin. **1886** STAPLETON *Major's Christmas* 35 When I want a five-cent meal, I goes to a five-cent concern; simularly when I goes to a quarter house, I calkerlate to pay the cash.

b. (See quot.) *Obs.*

1857 *Spirit of Times* 24 Jan. 341/1 All persons receiving or collecting money in behalf of the city . . . take the Spanish coins known as quarters . . . only in the rates prescribed in the bill recently passed by Congress, namely—the quarter at 20 cents [etc.].

5. = **quarter section.**

1804 *Fredericktown* (Md.) *Herald* 19 May 3/3 By Shell's place and Hobbs's mill on Linganore to a gate-post at the going into F. Dorsey's old quarter, thence east to the fourth branch of Linganore. **1890** *Stock Grower & Farmer* 21 June 8/2 The southeastern quarter of section eight [8] township seven [7] north, range twenty-eight [28] east, containing 160 acres. **1946** *Reader's Digest* March 151/2 Papa dismounted and set his stake on what proved to be the Southeast Quarter of Section 17.

6. Short for **quarter ticket.** *Obs.*

1805 *N.-Eng. Palladium* (Boston) 1 Jan. 2/5 Warranted undrawn Tickets and Quarters, for sale at Gilbert & Dean's truly fortunate Lottery-Office. **1929** *Pub. Col. Soc. Mass.* XXVII. 178 The practice of selling 'halves,' 'quarters' and 'eighths' originated in the lottery offices and prevailed in most of the lotteries including the Harvard College Lottery of 1806.

7. A fourth of a mile, a quarter-mile race. Cf. **9. b.**

In English use only with *mile* expressed, as *a quarter of a mile, a mile and a quarter.*

1827 COOPER *Prairie* iv, His camp is but a short quarter from us. **1878** BEADLE *Western Wilds* 31 It was weeks before I could walk a quarter. **1899** A. H. QUINN *Pa. Stories* 196 I've run the quarter for three years and won a first and second in it, as you know.

8. In football, a quarterback *q.v.* Also the position played by this man.

1887 *Outing* Oct. 70/1 In a scrimmage he places it on the ground, and at a signal from his quarter, snaps the ball back by a downward and backward pressure with his foot. **1899** QUINN *Pa. Stories* 27 Then Frank was sent in to quarter to run the team. **1909** *Dly. Maroon* (Chi.) 8 Oct. 1/5 Cunningham at quarter will doubtless astonish many Maroon men by his accurate passing.

9. In special combs.: (1) **quarterback,** in football, a backfield player, formerly stationed directly behind the center to receive the ball and pass it to a runner, also attrib., cf. **8.** above, and see **scrub quarterback;** (2) **bill,** a bill or account rendered a student at the end of a quarter; (3) **blood,** one who is one-quarter Indian, also attrib. and **quarter-blooded,** cf. **fullblood,** *n.* **1,** * **half-blood 2;** (4) **breed,** the offspring of a half-breed and a white person, a quarter-blood, also attrib.; (5) **court,** a court sitting quarterly, as a court of quarter sessions, now *hist.;* (6) **days,** (see quot. and cf. **3.** above), *obs.;* (7) **dollar,** a silver coin having one-fourth the value of a dollar; (8) **eagle,** a gold coin worth $2.50, or one-fourth of an eagle; (9) **hand,** *S.* (see quot.), *obs.;* (10) **master captain,** an officer in the U.S. Army with the rank of captain having duties similar to those of a quartermaster; (11) **meeting,** a meeting held approximately every three months, esp. in certain religious denominations, as among the Methodists and Quakers; (12) **pitch,** of a roof, an amount of slope equal to one-fourth the length of the roof, *colloq.;* (13) **post,** see as a main entry; (14) **sawing,** (see quot.); (15) **section,** a tract of land containing 160 acres and forming one-fourth of a section, cf. **5.** above; (16) * **session,** (see quot.); (17) **stake,** a stake set up at the corner of a quarter section of land, cf. **corner post;** (18) **ticket,** one-fourth part or share of a lottery ticket, *obs.,* cf. **6.** above; (19) **township,** one-fourth of a township; (20) **tree,** ?a tree helping to mark off a quarter of a surveyed tract, *obs.,* cf. **quarter post;** (21) **yearly,** *adv.* once in a quarter of a year, quarterly, *obs.*

(1) **1879** in P. H. DAVIS *Football* (1911) 468 The man who first receives the ball from the snap-back shall be called the quarter-back.

1947 *Chi. Sun* 4 Nov. 22/3 He has more poise, passing and all-round generalship than any quarterback playing this year. **1949** *Desplaines Valley News* (Summit, Ill.) 28 Oct. 7/3 They plowed over from the one foot line on a quarterback sneak. — **(2) 1660** *Harvard Coll. Rec.* I. 193 Dammages [done by students to College property] . . . shall be duly payd in their Quarter Bills to the Steward of the Colledge. **1734** in PEIRCE *Hist. Harvard* App. 126 Every scholar, in the first quarter-bill made up after his admission, shall be charged six shillings to the use of the College for Gallery money. **1790** *Harvard Laws* 6 The parents . . . [shall] give bond . . . in the sum of two hundred ounces of silver, to pay their several quarter-bills. — **(3) 1834** *Sun* (N.Y.) 23 Oct. 2/3 The watch returns were crowded with the names of . . . fifteen men, from every shade of color from the blackest Ethiopean, to the quarter blooded mulatto. **1845** *Knickerb.* XXV. 236 Of this description was a quarter-blood, of great beauty. **1930** FERBER *Cimarron* 340 And now every full blood, half blood, or quarter blood Osage was put on the Indian Roll, and every name on the Indian Roll was entitled to a Head Right. — **(4) 1827** MCKENNEY *Tour to Lakes* 387 Three were full blood, the remainder half breeds, and quarter breeds. **1880** *Harper's Mag.* Dec. 35/1 Douglas was soon to marry . . . a French quarter-breed girl. **1942** RICH *We Took to Woods* (1948) 38 That fellow there . . . was my quarter-breed guide.

(5) 1622 in W. M. WEST *Source Book Amer. Hist.* (1913) 76 At a great and generall Quarter Courte held for Virginia in the Afternoone the 22 of May 1622. **1680** *N.H. Hist. Soc. Coll.* VIII. 41 You are hereby required to summon Wilmot Oliver to appear tomorrow . . . at the quarter court to be held at Dover. **1933** *Pub. Col. Soc.* XXIX. xvii, The Suffolk County Court was one of the inferior quarterly courts (as distinct from the 'Greate Quarter Courts,' which meant the Court of Assistants) which were established by the Great and General Court at the session of March 3, 1635/36. — **(6) 1860** in L. P. BROCKETT *Our Country's Wealth* (1882) 870/1 At the close of the winter schools we had what we used to call our *Quarter-days*, when the schools came together in the meeting-house, with a large congregation of parents and friends. The public exercises were reading, spelling, and speaking single pieces, and dialogues. — **(7) 1794** *Amer. Calendar* 59 Silver Coins: . . . Quarter Dollars. Dismes. Half Dismes. **1873** *Rev. Statutes* (1878) 696 The silver coins of the United States shall be a trade-dollar, a half-dollar, or fifty-cent piece, a quarter-dollar [etc.]. — **(8) 1792** *Ann. 2d Congress* 71 Quarter eagles; each to be of the value of two dollars and a half dollar. **1887** *Courier-Journal* 17 Feb. 2/5 The banking-firm of Zimmerman & Forshay . . . received yesterday . . . $10,000 in quarter eagles. **1948** Numismatic Gallery *Cat. U.S. Gold Coins* 8 No quarter eagles were minted in 1799, 1800 or 1801. — **(9) 1856** OLMSTED *Slave States* 433 The field-hands are all divided into four classes, according to their physical capacities. The children beginning as 'quarter-hands' . . . [finally become] 'full hands.'

(10) 1907 *N.Y. Ev. Post* (s.-w.) 13 May 6 The person enjoying the title of quartermaster captain (a rank that causes our British cousins to smile). — **(11) 1639** *Portsmouth Rec.* 7 At a quarter Meeting ye first Thursd 1639 Nicholas Browne doth dismisse himself [etc.]. **1799** in W. W. SWEET *Religion on Amer. Frontier* IV. (1946) 219 Brother Burk . . . wrote to me informing me of the state of the circuit and desired me to prepare to take it at Quarter-meeting. — **(12) 1842** KIRKLAND *Forest Life* II. 79 It took a full hour to make our principal architect acknowledge that water would run off a roof which sloped at any less than 'quarter-pitch.' — **(14) 1898** S. B. GREEN *Forestry in Minn.* 299 Quarter-sawing. . . . The log is first quartered and then sawed into boards, cutting them alternately from each face of the quarter of the log.

(15) 1804 *Statutes at Large* II. 281 Public lands of the United States, the sale of which is authorized by law, may . . . be purchased . . . in entire sections, in half sections, or in quarter sections. **1885** *Santa Fé Wkly. New Mexican* 1 Oct. 1/2 The great railroad companies have appraised and sold their land grants, fixing a price on every quarter-section. **1949** *Ward Co. Independent* (Minot, N.D.) 21 July 1/1 He has three quarter-sections leased and plans to drill there. — **(16) 1914** *Cyclo. Amer. Govt.* I. 504/2 In Pennsylvania the sessions of the local courts of original jurisdiction for the trial of criminal cases, the creation of local districts and the granting of liquor licenses are called quarter sessions. — **(17) 1845** MRS. KIRKLAND *Western Clearings* 2 Section and quarter-stakes, eighties and forties, and fractions, are plain enough when one is habituated to them. — **(18) 1790** *Columbian Centinel* 9 Oct. 31/2 Whole and quarter Tickets in the Monthly State Lottery, may be had of David West. **1845** SOL. SMITH *Theatr. Apprent.* 85, I went to a lottery-office with a quarter ticket I had purchased. — **(19) 1832** WILLIAMSON *Maine* II. 572 In 1798, the residue was offered for sale in quarter townships at a dollar by the acre.

(20) 1651 in *Amer. Sp.* XV. 153/1 To a Nother quarter tree on the barrons. — **(21) 1791** *Ann. 1st Congress* 2012 The interest of the debt should be paid quarter-yearly. **1861** *Army Reg.* 154 Every officer having public money to account for, and failing to render his account thereof quarter-yearly, . . . will be promptly dismissed.

b. In combs. of obvious meaning referring to the racing of horses over a quarter of a mile distance (cf. 7. above), as (1) **quarter-horse,** (2) **match,** (3) **nag,** (4) **pole,** (5) **race,** (6) **racing,** (7) **stretch,** (8) **tackey,** (9) **track.**

(1) 1834 *Sun* (N.Y.) 24 May 1/3 Well, where is your quarter horse? **1893** ROOSEVELT *Wilderness Hunter* 45 The frightened deer . . . sped off across the grassy slopes like a quarter horse. **1949** *L.A. Times* 22 May v. 11/2 The other [was] a prize-winning registered Palomino quarter-horse, named Carmen. — **(2) 1845** HOOPER *Suggs* (1928) 13 He stole . . . his father's plough-horses to enter them in 'quarter' matches at the same place. — **(3) 1834** *Sun* (N.Y.) 24 May 1/3 So you must be after the quarter nag. Jim, fetch up Lazy Sam, will you? **1834** BRACKENRIDGE *Recollections* 225 Cunning is the wisdom of fools; but it is only a quarter nag. **1892** DUVAL *Young Explorers* 210, I lit out fur de house faster'n a quarter nag. — **(4) 1868** WOODRUFF *Trotting Horse* 259 At the quarter-pole she had recovered her stroke. **1894** *Outing* XXIV. 142/2 Held his place until the quarter-pole was reached.

(5) 1792 TOULMIN *Descr. Kentucky* 12 His time is employed in quarter-races, cock-fights. **1835** LONGSTREET *Ga. Scenes* 24 Away went Bullet, as if in a quarter race, with all his beauties spread in handsome style. **1889** *Harper's Mag.* Aug. 386/2 [They] had foot-races for themselves, and quarter-races for their horses. — **(6) 1784** SMYTH *Tour* I. 22 In the southern part of the colony, and in North Carolina, they are much attached to *quarter-racing*. **1892** ALLEN *Blue-Grass Region* 130 From the first, there had stood out among the Kentuckians broad exhibitions of exuberant animal vigor . . .—foot-racing for the men, and quarter-racing for the horses. — **(7) 1827** *Spirit of Seventy-Six* (Frankfort, Ky.) 7 June 2/5 Finally, entering the quarter stretch, his snout was seen a little in advance of Charlotte's, and he passed the Judges' stand less than a length ahead. **c1875** BAGBY *Old Va. Gentleman* 306 He run a quarter-stretch down the low-grounds of the base. — **(8) 1851** *Polly Peablossom* 174 It'll be 'the old quarter tackey word.' — **(9) 1884** *Cent. Mag.* Nov. 118 There was a quarter-track . . . if he chose to enjoy the pleasures of horse-racing.

As the last term in **fifth, French, German, Indian, log house, Negro, silver, slave, Spanish quarter(s).**

*** quarterly,** *a.* and *n.*

1. *n.* A Sunday-school book or pamphlet containing lessons for one quarter of the year.

1919 CUNNINGHAM *Chronicle* 88 When they went below she picked up a Quarterly and glanced at the title of the lesson. **1939** *These Are Our Lives* 158 'Get your book,' I said, and Kate went over to the little walnut table, got her quarterly, and handed it to me.

2. *M.E. Church.* **Quarterly Conference,** orig. **quarterly meeting conference,** (see quot. 1844).

1844 RUPP *Relig. Denominations* 448 A *quarterly meeting conference* is composed of all the travelling and local preachers, exhorters, stewards, and leaders, belonging to any particular circuit or station. **1919** CUNNINGHAM *Chronicle* 302 He answered, referring to the final Quarterly Conference where the question of his return to the Paxton charge should be decided. **1949** *West Va. Hist.* Jan. 119 There was a Quarterly Conference held at the Benjamin Webb preaching appointment on July 6, 7, 1805, according to the Rev. John W. Reger's papers.

quarter post. *Surveying.* A post or marker set up at a corner of a quarter section of land. Also attrib.

1849 *31st Congress* 1 Sess. H.R. Ex. Doc. No. 5, II. 508 After descending the precipice, the descent was gradual till we came to the quarter-post which is in a cedar swamp. **1881** *Mich. Gen. Statutes* I. 210 The surveyor as above employed shall sink into the earth at all section and quarter-post corners from the surface to a depth of at least three feet, a column of broken brick. **1947** *Mich. Hist.* June 186 I'll run compass lines across sections from quarter post to quarter post until I know that my compass work is all right.

quartette table. A nest of four small tables, or a table belonging to such a nest. *Obs.* — **1856** COZZENS *Sparrowgrass P.* 89 In one door-way stood a tray of delicate confections, upon two slender quartette tables. **1857** *Harper's Mag.* March 453/1 On this quartette-table we will lay the portfolio.

quartillo kwarˈtijo, *n. S.W.* [Sp. *cuartillo.*] The fourth part of a real.

1844 KENDALL *Narr. Santa Fé Exped.* II. 190 A galopina, or kitchen girl, . . . soon explained the business of the holy brother by dropping a quartillo into the box. **1878** BEADLE *Western Wilds* 190 Even the boys took their first lesson by pitching for *quartillas*. **1945** MARSHALL *Santa Fe* 25 Everyone gambled, even the little Mexican children, playing with three-cent coins called *quartillas*.

*** quartz,** *n.*

1. *Mining.* A quartz vein, or ore obtained from this, containing deposits of gold or, sometimes, silver.

[**1852** *Deseret News* (Salt Lake City) 24 Jan. 4/1 I've seen a right smart chance of hills, As full as they could hold, Of . . . *quartz* and *quartz* of gold.] **1878** DENNIS in Morris *Pub. Service Alaska* (1879) Rich veins of quartz have been found and are now being tested. **1912**

WHEELER *Selkirk Mts.* 142 South, is a rich mountainous country where galena and free milling quartz are mined. **1948** A. K. WILLIAMS *Gold Rush Days* 56, I continued mining around the Mother Lode country, sometimes I would find some rich quartz, work it awhile and when I had taken out all that laid on the surface, would move on.

2. In combs.: (1) **quartz battery,** a stamp, or series of stamps, for crushing quartz ore; (2) **camp,** a camp of quartz miners; (3) **claim,** a mining claim where valuable mineral-bearing quartz occurs or is thought to occur; (4) **crusher,** a machine for crushing or pulverizing quartz; (5) **gold,** (see quot.); (6) **lead,** a lode or vein of mineral-bearing quartz; (7) **mill,** a machine for pulverizing quartz, a stamp mill; (8) **mine,** a mine from which gold or silver is obtained by quartz mining; (9) **miner,** a miner who does quartz mining; (10) **mining,** (see quot. 1890), also attrib.

(1) **1869** J. R. BROWNE *Adv. Apache Country* 346 Quartz-batteries are battering; hammers are hammering. **1942** LILLARD *Desert Challenge* 207 Quartz batteries stomped on ore. — (2) **1910** *Haines* (Alaska) *Pioneer Press* 18 March 2/3 For Conrad City, located in the heart of the newly discovered and fabulously rich quartz camp of the Windy Arm District, take our daily trains to Caribou. — (3) **1851** *S.F. Picayune* 27 Nov. 2/2 Finally, they were discovered at work, and they then resolved to apportion the land in quartz claims. **1884** *Cent. Mag.* Oct. 843/2 Locating a quartz claim on a mountainside . . . is not a short cut to wealth. — (4) **1852** *Mt. Echo* (Downieville, Calif.) 25 Dec. 2/2 Before many months, Patcool's quartz crusher will be in operation, under the direction of a Downieville company. **1892** *Harper's Mag.* Dec. 140 The Rocky Mountain method of prospecting is by means of the gold-pan or the quartz-crusher.

(5) **1874** RAYMOND *6th Rep. Mines* 317 The gold found in it . . . is largely 'quartz gold,' that is, not rounded and water-worn, but irregular and frequently twisted in form, usually very bright, and always of fine quality, as is the gold of the quartz-veins. **1936** MCKENNA *Black Range* 272 The Knight brothers discovered the rich quartz gold of Grass Valley, California. — (6) **1851** *S.F. Picayune* 19 Sep. 2/5 A party of five from Nevada, while prospecting upon the South Fork of the North Fork of the Yuba river, struck upon a quartz lead. **1927** SIRINGO *Riata & Spurs* 79 Finally, by the light of the lantern, the quartz lead about three feet wide was discovered. — (7) **1851** *S.F. Picayune* 4 Nov. 2/2 We would earnestly recommend the managers of quartz mills, in other parts of the country, to give this method a trial. **1947** *So. Sierran* Dec. 2/2 In every direction there were signs of miners' diggings, and here and there the ruins of a quartz mill. — (8) **1851** *Ore. Statesman* 9 Sep. 2/2 The yield is said to be greater than that of the richest quartz mines of California. **1891** *Cent. Mag.* Feb. 533/2 This auriferous region [in Calif. has] . . . the most productive quartz mines. — (9) **1852** *S.F. Herald* 5 Oct. 1/5 (*heading*), To Capitalists and Quartz Miners. **1859** *S.F. Bulletin* 5 May 1/2 At Kern river, the quartz miners are mostly awaiting the result of certain extensive experiments now being made by a mineralogist.

(10) **1851** *San Jose* (Calif.) *State Jrnl.* 19 March 3/3 Recent letters from Grass Valley speak in the most flattering terms with regard to the Quartz mining operations in that quarter. **1890** *Cent.* 4900/1 In California and other gold-mining regions mining in the solid rock is commonly called *quartz-mining*, in contradistinction to *placer* and *hydraulic mining*. **1948** WESTON *Mother Lode* 16 All that remains today of this once important center of quartz mining . . . are a few mounds of crumbling adobe.

b. Also **quartz crushing machine, diggings, interests, nugget, prospecting, rock.**

1850 *Calif. Courier* 23 Nov. 2/4 We learn that as [*sic*] quartz crushing machine has been shipped direct for thi[s] port on the steamship Constitution. — **1851** *Ore. Statesman* 9 Sep. 2/2 Late intelligence from the mines reports the discovery of rich quartz diggings between Shasta and Scott's River. — **1858** *S.F. Bulletin* 21 May 3/2 Goodman, Diltz & Co. . . . have contributed much to the improvement of quartz machinery and the development of quartz interests in this country. — **1862** *Ib.* 22 Sep. 1/2 A quartz nugget was taken from Major Downie's claim worth $104. — **1877** RAYMOND *Statistics Mines & Mining* 220 This action gave an impetus to quartz-prospecting. — **1850** *Calif. Courier* 11 July 2/2 The old associations and home affections do not fade away, though in a distant land we stand upon 'gold pavements' and 'quartz rock.' **1852** *N.Y. Wkly. Tribune* 10 April 1/5 The discovery of Quartz rock at Grass Valley is not a recent event.

c. *quartz on the brain,* =**gold fever.** *Obs.*

1865 STUART *Montana As It Is* 8 Some of them are suffering from a severe attack of an epidemic known as 'quartz on the brain,' which is now raging furiously all over Montana.

As the last term in **bull, gold, pay, purple, rotten quartz.**

* **quawk,** *n.* =**qua-bird.** *Colloq.*

1844 *Nat. Hist. N.Y., Zoology* II. 227 The Black-crowned Night Heron, or Quawk, . . . derives its popular name from the deep guttural cry. **1895** CHAPMAN *Handbook Birds* (1904) 137 Occasionally they [i.e., black-crowned night herons] utter a loud, hoarse *quawk*, the origin of their common name. **1926** BENT *Life Hist. N. Amer. Marsh Birds* 197 The familiar night heron or 'quawk' is one of the best known and most widely distributed of our herons.

quayotto kwaˈjɔto, *n. S.W.* [Amer. Sp. *cuayote* (<Nahuatl), a plant of the genus *Gonolobus.*] =**galleta.** — **1878** HINTON *Arizona* 254 The hill and mountain sides, far up to the pine and cedar belt, are covered with the bunch grass,—quayotto or black grama.

quebrada keˈbradə, *n. S.W.* [Sp. in same sense.] (See quot. 1890.) Cf. **barranca.**

*a***1861** WINTHROP *J. Brent* 211 We took breakneck leaps across dry quebradas in the clay. **1890** *Cent.* 4903/1 *Quebrada*, . . . a gorge; a ravine; a defile: a word occasionally used by writers in English on Mexican and South American physical geography, and by the Spanish Americans themselves, with about the same meaning as *barranca*. **1894** *Outing* Feb. 357/1, I knew a little tree that bridged a deep *quebrada*. **1949** *Américas* Sep. 17 The men wore rags and undoubtedly lived in one-room shanties in the quebradas along with their families of six or eight.

* **queen,** *n.*

1. An Indian woman having the rank of a chief in her tribe.

1675 *Conn. Rec.* II. 403 They say the Indyans are scattered; the two sachems Suikquens, Nononanto, & ye Queene beeing neere ye Nipmug Country. **1822** MORSE *Rep. Indian Affairs* I. 31 A woman of this tribe (the Nottoways), about sixty years old, named Edie Turner, is its present reigning Queen. [**1949** *Sat. Ev. Post* 2 April 126/4 A woman in California wrote recently that she was made queen of the Cherokee tribe in 1930.]

2. *New Orleans.* A girl or woman selected by the king of a ball to share with him the honors of a king's ball. *Obs.* Cf. * **king,** *n.* **2.**

1844 *N.O. Picayune* 19 Feb. 1/3 The bawl cum on, and wus opened as usual by the kings and thar queens. **1856** *Sacramento Age* 20 Oct. 3/1 These balls were reigned over by four kings and four queens, who reigned for one night only, and then appointed their successors.

3. A pretty or attractive girl or woman who in a contest of some kind has been adjudged the most beautiful. *Slang.*

1908 DAVENPORT *Butte Beneath X-Ray* 341 The winner will be advised at once and within a week thereafter I will set forth on my pilgrimage to pay my respects to the Queen of Beauty, Montana's fairest flower. **1947** *Chi. Tribune* 21 June 2/5 Sixteen assorted 'queens' of such things as spring, sports, tomatoland, sauer kraut, and others in Michigan and northern Indiana cities arrived here yesterday morning. **1949** *Ill. Agric. Assoc. Rec.* Oct. 13/3 Illinois had queens of all sorts this summer from corn to sauerkraut.

4. In combs.: (1) **Queen Anne musket,** =**queen's arm;** (2) **Anne's lace,** (see quots.); (3) **City,** see as a main entry; (4) **Elizabeth's bone,** the cramp bone or patella of a sheep, *obs.;* (5) **fish,** (see quot. 1911); (6) **full,** a poker hand consisting of three queens and a pair; (7) **of floods,** the Mississippi River; (8) * **of the meadow,** =**joe-pye weed;** (9) **of the prairie,** a tall perennial American herb, *Filipendula rubra,* found in meadows and prairies; (10) **-'s arm,** a musket of a type originally used by British soldiers in the time of Queen Anne (1702–14), *obs.;* (11) **-'s delight,** a herbaceous plant, *Stillingia sylvatica,* of the southern states; (12) **-'s lace,** =**Queen Anne's lace;** (13) **snake,** (see quot. 1909); (14) **town,** (see quot.), *rare.*

(1) **1775** in JAMES HALL *Sk. of West* (1835) II. 263 We struck whilst the iron was hot, fixed Mr. Cooke off with a good Queen Anne musket, plenty of ammunition [etc.]. **1873** BAILEY *Life in Danbury* 127 It will kick a mule out of countenance inside of three seconds, and even put a blush on a Queen Anne musket. — (2) **1913** EATON *Barn Doors & Byways* 273 [The] wild carrot bears a dainty, flat-topped white bloom sometimes as large as a saucer, and a long bed of them will often appear like a strip of delicate embroidery along the wayside, making their more aristocratic title of Queen Anne's lace entirely applicable. **1949** *Courier-Journal* 3 Sep. 6/4 Queen Anne's Lace (Daucus carota) is a biennial weed of the umbellifera family and is the uncultivated form of the garden carrot. — (4) **1846** *Knickerb.* XXVII. 17 From the Pope's Eye, to Queen Elizabeth's bone, each preferable and available slice . . . was apparent to his practised eye.

(5) **1884** GOODE *Fisheries* I. 380 This species is known as 'King-fish' or 'Queen fish.' **1911** *Rep. Fisheries 1908* 314/1 Queen-fish (*Seriphus politus*).—A small food fish of excellent quality found on the Pacific coast south of Tomales Bay. It is also called 'kingfish.' — (6) **1878** HART *Sazerac Lying Club* 229 She became involved in a game of

Indian poker with Horned-Toad Sunday, in which she lost her gorgeous attire on a queen-full. **1923** MULFORD *Black Buttes* 109 Slattery's queen-full won. — **(7) 1832** *Polit. Examiner* (Shelbyville, Ky.) 25 Aug. 1/5 From a vast uncultivated territory, covered with a dense forest—broken only by the luxuriant prairie—the Queen of Floods, and her noble tributaries, . . . the west within a few years, has become a mighty populous portion of the Union. — **(8) 1892** *Amer. Folk-Lore* V. 98 *Eupatorium purpureum*, Queen of the meadow. Worcester Co., Mass. **1949** *Jrnl. N.Y. Bot. Garden* July 153/1 The third bed . . . has a beautiful stand of maiden-hair fern and queen-of-the-meadow. — **(9) 1852** NOLL *Flora Penna.* 100 S[piræa] lobata, Murr. *Queen of the Prairie.* **1898** CREEVEY *Flowers of Field* 146 Queen-of-the-prairie. . . . A stately, beautiful plant adorning the meadows and prairies south and west of Pennsylvania. **1947** *Mich. Hist.* Sep. 272 Other rare specimens of prairie flora are reported by the same authority, including queen-of-the-prairie, a beautiful member of the rose family.

(10) [**1710** *N.H. Prov. Papers* II. 612 All Volunteers in the service . . . Shall bear the Queens Arms & enjoy them for their own for ever of her Majesties Royal Gift.] **1716** *Providence Rec.* VI. (1894) 188 To a gun one of ye Queenes arms 01–04–00. **1829** *Mass. Spy* 20 May (Th.), One of the party returned the salute with an old queen's arm. **1898** N. BROOKS *Boys of Fairport* 196 Ned Martin carried the heavy 'Queen's arm' that had belonged to his grandfather, who fought at Bunker Hill and Concord. — **(11) 1868** GRAY *Field Botany* 295 *Stillingia sylvatica*, Queen's Delight. Dry soil from Virginia S[outh]. **1927** BENÉT *J. B's Body* 217 The red is pokeberry-juice, the gray is green myrtle, The deep black is queen's delight. — **(12) 1907** FREEMAN *By Light of Soul* 52 She walked slowly between the fields, which were white and gold with queen's-lace and golden-rod. **1947** BEEBE *Mixed Train Dly.* 88 This freight train, carrying its passengers in the caboose and wading pleasantly through springtime Arkansas meadows brave with daisies and queen's lace, is the Graysonia, Nashville and Ashdown's morning redball. — **(13) 1902** *Smithsonian Rep. 1900* 104/2 Specimen of Queen snake, *Natrix leberis*, from Great Falls, Md. **1909** *Cent. Supp.* 1098/2 *Queen snake*, a water-snake, *Natrix leberis*, of the central and eastern United States. — **(14) 1886** *Tascosa* (Tex.) *Pioneer* 12 June, To Tascosa and to Oldham, the queen town and the banner county, The Pioneer this morning dedicates its future years of labor.

b. *Queen of the West*, *Queen of the Pacific*, (see quots. and cf. **Queen City 2.**).

1835 HOFFMAN *Winter in West* I. 130 It is in vain for thriving Pittsburg or flourishing Louisville . . . to dispute with Cincinnati her title of 'Queen of the West.' **1835** A. PARKER *Trip to Texas* 76 St. Louis will . . . remain in all time to come, the . . . 'Queen of the West.' **1879** VIVIAN *Wanderings Western Land* 102 This young 'Queen of the West' [Chicago] is said now to interfere somewhat seriously in many markets with old-established New York. — **1851** *S.F. Picayune* 19 Sep. 2/4 Some person, gifted with a sufficient amount of patience, may undertake to compile the history of San Francisco . . . the Queen of the Pacific.

c. *To a* (or *the*) *queen's taste*, thoroughly, completely. *Colloq.*

1902 HARBEN *Abner Daniel* xxxiii. 279 You worked 'im to a queen's taste—as fine as split milk. **1911** R. D. SAUNDERS *Col. Todhunter* ix. 126 They've got you finished off to the queen's taste.

As the last term in **beauty, cattle, Kentucky, voodoo queen.**

Queen City.

1. Cincinnati, Ohio. A nickname.

1838 B. DRAKE (*title*), Tales and Sketches from the Queen City. **1896** *N.Y. Dramatic News* 18 July 15/1 This has been a gala week for the Queen City. **1949** *Hist. & Philos. Soc. Ohio Bul.* April 99 That enthusiastic booster for the 'Queen City,' Dr. Daniel Drake, . . . was the founder and promoter of both organizations.

2. In the nicknames of cities: (1) *Queen City of the* (*Upper*) *Lakes*, Chicago, Ill., Cleveland, Ohio, or Buffalo, N.Y.; (2) *of the Plains*, Denver, Colo.; (3) *of the West*, Cincinnati, Ohio.

(1) 1839 *Dly. Chi. American* 13 April 2/1 Is it not for the pride and interest of the Queen City of the Upper Lakes to sustain it? **1844** *Gem of Prairies* (Chi.) 13 June 3/2 Just as midnight was giving up to the 'small wee hours,' we arrived in the haven of the Queen City of the Lakes. **1846** *N.Y. Tribune* 6 July 1/6 You would be astonished, agreeably so, to visit Queen City of the Lakes, and note its rising importance. **1855** BAXTER *America* 241 Then take Buffalo, well deserving its appellation, 'the Queen City of the Lakes.' — **(2) 1870** *Colo. Gazetteer* 40 Denver, the principal city and capital of Colorado—the Queen City of the Plains—is the county seat of Arapahoe county. **1943** *Colo. Mag.* Jan. 15 The Queen City of the Plains started in 1878. — **(3) 1867** *Ball Players' Chron.* 18 July 1/4 At Columbus they had been joined by a committee of the Cincinnati Clubs, who escorted them to the Queen City of the West. **1947** PERRY *Cities of Amer.* 148 In her younger days, when Longfellow called her the 'Queen City of the West,' he was not indulging in mere polite flattery.

b. Also in more occasional nicknames sufficiently explained in the quots., as (1) *Queen City of the Mississippi*, (2) *of the Mississippi Valley*, (3) *of the Prairie*, (4) *of the East*, (5) *of Iowa*, (6) *of the Hills*, (7) *of the Western World*, (8) *of the Rio Grande*, (9) *of the Mountains*, (10) *of Vermont*, (11) *of Montana.*

(1) 1843 MARRYAT *M. Violet* xli, St. Louis has been described by so many travellers, that it is quite useless to mention anything about this 'queen city of the Mississippi.' — **(2) 1845** *St. Louis Reveille* 19 Jan. 1/6 *Saint Louis:* The Queen City of the Mississippi Valley. — **(3) 1848** in *Chi. Tribune* (1948) 25 July 20/5, I have risen early this morning to resume my pen and I must devote this page to my impressions of [Chicago] the 'Queen City of the Prairie.' — **(4) 1857** *Spirit of Times* 11 April 86/1 Ere long its bows rippled the smooth bosom of the stream off the wharves of the 'Queen City of the East' [i.e., Portland, Me.].

(5) 1858 WILKIE *Davenport* 214 Davenport to-day, in size and beauty, stands peerless among rivals,—the 'Queen City' of Iowa. — **(6) 1863** *Houston* (Tex.) *Tri-Wkly. News* 7 Jan. 2/4 When the conflict is over . . . the Queen City of the hills [Houston, Tex.] will stand a living monument to Southern patriotism and valor. — **(7) 1871** *N.Y. Herald* 14 Oct. 4/3 Gone for a time is the Queen City of the Western World [Chicago], her dominance passed to others. — **(8) 1880** *Albuquerque* (N.Mex.) *Review* 24 April 2/1 The day was born that was to be the day of all days for Albuquerque, the Queen City of the Rio Grande. — **(9) 1890** BALLOU *New Eldorado* 58 Helena, the interesting capital of Montana, . . . is called the 'Queen City of the Mountains.'

(10) 1892 *Vt. Agric. Rep.* XII. 120 Burlington, the 'queen city' of Vermont, offers inducements to people of various tastes. — **(11) 1893** *Outing* March 446/2, I headed for Helena, the 'Queen City' of Montana, which lay forty-five miles to the west.

quelite keˈlite, *n. S.W.* [Amer. Sp. (<Nahuatl) in same sense.] Any one of various plants used as pot herbs, esp. lambs' quarters, purslane, and the Rocky Mountain bee weed. — **1911** *Ann. Rep. Smithsonian Inst.* 458 The leaves and young shoots we cook as 'greens' . . . are known by the Spanish name of quelite. **1912** LUMHOLTZ *New Trails* 130 Quelite, inexpensive and easy to cultivate, should be accepted by civilized households.

querida kɛˈridə, *n. S.W.* [Sp. in same sense.] Darling, sweetheart. — **1834** A. PIKE *Sketches* 105 Querida, when the turtle dove is attacked by the hawk . . . , she has been known to take refuge in the bosom of man. **1925** BURNS *Saga of Billy the Kid* 85 In every placeta in the Pecos some little senorita was proud to be known as his querida.

∗ **querl**, *n.* [Cf. *EDD quirl*, a shiver, tremor. No doubt related to *EDD squirl*, Sc., an ornamental twist or tail in writing.] (See quot. 1879.)

1853 B. F. TAYLOR *Jan. & June* 23 [The grapevine's] aspirations were soon manifested in the display of divers mermaidish-looking ringlets, with two or three dainty 'quirls' therein. **1879** WEBSTER *Supp.* 1575/2 *Querl* . . . a coil; a twirl; as the *querl* of hair on the fore leg of a blooded horse. **1889** COOKE *Steadfast* 162 A hundred resolute little quirls above the low forehead.

∗**question**, *n.* As the last term in **abolition, Alabama, bank, goose, grass, liquor, Missouri, Negro, Oregon, papoose, party, previous, race, salt, silver, slave, slavery, southern, tariff, Texas question.**

∗ **quick**, *a.*

1. *absol.* Short for ∗ *quicksilver. Obs.*

1882 *47th Congress* 1 Sess. H.R. Ex. Doc. No. 216, 651 As fast as it collects the 'quick' passes by an inverted siphon to the strainers.

2. In combs.: (1) **quick lunch**, a lunch that can be served and eaten quickly, also attrib.; (2) ∗ **silver**, designating a *machine* or *feeder* employed in utilizing quicksilver in mining operations; (3) **-silver weed**, the early meadow rue, *Thalictrum dioicum;* (4) ∗ **water**, (see quot. 1905).

(1) 1903 *N.Y. Ev. Post* 24 Sep. 8 The quick lunch man a few blocks away from the grocery store. **1920** *Chi. Tribune* 10 Nov. 8/3 The first sign of 'crumbling' on the part of the British empire that we have observed is the welcome extended to the 'quick lunch.' — **(2) 1850** *Calif. Courier* 27 July 1/2 Quicksilver machines have been used there, and some of them were profitable where it was easy digging. **1882** *Rep. H. Rep. Prec. Met. U.S.* 507 A quicksilver feeder has been devised for feeding mercury to gold mills. — **(3) 1893** *Amer. Folk-Lore* VI. 136 *Thalictrum dioicum*, quicksilver weed. Penobscot Co., Me. — **(4)** *a***1862** THOREAU *Maine Woods* 276 The Indian navigator naturally distinguishes by a name those parts of a stream where he has encountered quick water and forks. **1905** *Forestry Bureau Bul.* No. 61, 44 *Quickwater*, that part of a stream which has fall enough to create a decided current.

quickhatch ˈkwɪkhætʃ, *n.* [f. Algonquian. Cf. Cree *kĭkkwâhakes*, used as the name of the animal because it was hard to hit.] The wolverine.

1743 CATESBY *Nat. Hist.* II. xxx, The Quickhatch . . . inhabits the very Northern Parts of *America* and has not been observed by any Author, or known in *Europe* till the year 1737, one was sent to Sir *Hans Sloane* from *Hudson's Bay.* **1789** MORSE *Amer. Geog.* 55 Beasts of different *genus* from any known in the old world [include] . . . the Opossum, the Racoon, the Quickhatch. **1855** in SCHMIDT *Briefe* 146 Die gefrässige *Wolverene* (Gulo luscus), auch Quickhatch und Hudsonsbai-Bär genannt, lebt an der atlantischen Küste bis zu sehr hohen Breiten hinauf.

* **quid,** *n.* [Abbrev. of * **tertium quid.**] (*cap.*) *pl.* (See quot. 1914.) Now *hist.*

1805 JEFFERSON *Writings* (1830) IV. 45 That I have avowed . . . any predilection for those called the third party, or Quids, is . . . false. **1818** FEARON *Sketches* 139 The political parties [in Pa. include] at present . . . no party men, called 'Quids.' **1914** *Cyclo. Amer. Govt.* III. 128/1 The Quids were the John Randolph . . . men, opposed to Jefferson and Madison. They formed the first 'third party' in the United States. Randolph claimed that his were the Republican principles of 1798, and that Jefferson and Madison had departed from them. **1920** *Collier's* 14 Feb. 18/2 The acrid Randolph . . . is the only person that history identifies conspicuously with the 'Quids.'

attrib. **1817** *N.Y. Herald* 7 May 3/1 The federal assembly ticket for Columbia county has also succeeded, . . . owing to a great number of the federals joining with the democrats in supporting a quid ticket.

b. Hence **quiddical,** *a.*, **Quiddism,** *n.*, **Quidtown,** *n. Obs.*

1805 *Natchez* (Miss.) *Messenger* 1 July 2/3 Some who have from the *frog pond* [?Boston] strided, To be by Quids at Quidtown [?Washington] guided. **1805** *N.-Eng. Palladium* (Boston) 23 July 2/3 The editor of the *Ægis* . . . denied the truth of the charge of '*Quiddism*,' alledged against him in the *Palladium.* **1807** *Staunton* (Va.) *Eagle* 28 Aug. 4/1 When the time for the trial of *Aaron*, the emperor of the sect of *quids*, or the quiddical emperor, drew nigh, the man whose face was like unto scarlet, journeyed towards the city of Richmond.

quien sabe. *S.W.* [Sp. *¿quien sabe?*] Who knows? Also attrib. *Colloq.*

1846 ABERT *Exam. N. Mex.* 51 To all our other questions with regard to this ancient town, we received the usual Mexican reply of 'quien sabe.' **1864** *Weekly New Mexican* 23 Dec. 2/4 We cannot trust an answer in the common vernacular to which we are accustomed, and must reply in all the Spanish we are master of, *quien sabe.* **1949** *Southwest. Rev.* Summer 235/1 One yarn thrown in as a sort of *quien sabe?* item suggests an even more unpalatable morsel.

Quileute ˈkɪljut, *n.* [App. the native name.] (See quot. 1910.) Also the language of these Indians.

1856 in *H.R. Ex. Doc. 37* 34th Cong. 3 Sess. 102 Many of the Kuinae-alts, and Kuille-pates were on a visit to this tribe. **1908** *Pacific Mo.* Feb. 131/1 It was the wine of adventure . . . which tempted the young Quileutes of a by-gone generation to sack Cake Island. **1910** HODGE *Amer. Indians* II. 340/2 Quileute. A Chimakuan tribe, now the only representative of the linguistic stock, whose main seat is at Lapush, at the mouth of Quillayute r., about 35 m. s. of C. Flattery, w. coast of Washington. **1948** *Amer. Folk-Lore* Oct.–Dec. 414 Only the Salish languages and the Quilieute of Cape Flattery have structural similarities to Wakashan.

* **quill,** *n.*

1. Some now unidentifiable part of a gun. *Obs.*

1770 PATTEN *Diary* 248, I got 2 quils for Esqr underwoods Gun from john Gillmor. **1775** *Ib.* 343 Shed forged a Guard and some Rods for pining on the Quills and Stock on the Gun and I attended a Meeting of the town.

2. *pl.* Money. *Slang. Obs.*

1855 in HAMBLETON *H. A. Wise* 426 [Uncle Sam] and his wife [Miss Know-Nothing] . . . married each other for money, at first, or for 'quills' as they say.

3. *pl. S.* A simple musical instrument made of pieces of reed or cane of different length and size. Also attrib.

1883 HARRIS *Nights* (1911) 69 Uncle Remus declared that Brother Rabbit could perform upon the quills, an accomplishment to which none of the other animals could lay claim. **1886** *Cent. Mag.* Feb. 521/2 But to show how far the art of playing the 'quills' could be carried . . . see this 'quill tune' . . . from a gentleman who heard it in Alabama.

4. In special combs.: (1) **quillback,** (see quots.); (2) **pig,** (see quot. 1917); (3) **-tail coot,** (see quots.); (4) **wheel,** in spinning, a wheel for winding thread upon quills or spools, also as verb (see quot. 1851); (5) **wood,** ?elder or sumac used for quills in spinning, *obs.;* (6) **wort,** (see quot. and cf. **joe-pye weed**).

(1) **1882** JORDAN & GILBERT *Syn. Fishes N. Amer.* 119 *Carpiodes cyprinus.* . . . Quillback; Spear-fish; Sail-fish; Skimback. **1911** *Rep. Fisheries 1908* 314/1 *Quillback.*—A sucker (*Ictiobus velifer*) found abundantly in the Mississippi Valley. — (2) **1885** *Harper's Mag.* July 225/2 The cabin was . . . tenanted only by an interesting family of what the guides quaintly call 'quill pigs.' **1917** *Mammals of Amer.* 217/1 Anyone who has traveled in the woods of the northern United States is familiar with the Porcupine, or Quill Pig. — (3) **1888** TRUMBULL *Names of Birds* 112 Ruddy Duck of Wilson 1814. . . . At Tuckerton N.J., [called] Quill-tail coot. **1917** *Birds of Amer.* I. 152 Ruddy Duck. *Erismatura jamaicensis.* . . . [Also called] Bumblebee Coot; Quill-tailed Coot; Heavy-tailed Coot. — (4) **1851** HALL *College Words* 251 At the Wesleyan University 'when a student . . . "knocks under" or yields a point, he says he *quillwheels*, that is he acknowledges he is wrong.' **1881** ALCOTT *New Conn.* (1886) 113 The 'rolls' were spun into threads, then run upon spools by the 'quill wheel and blades,' and thus made ready for the shuttle.

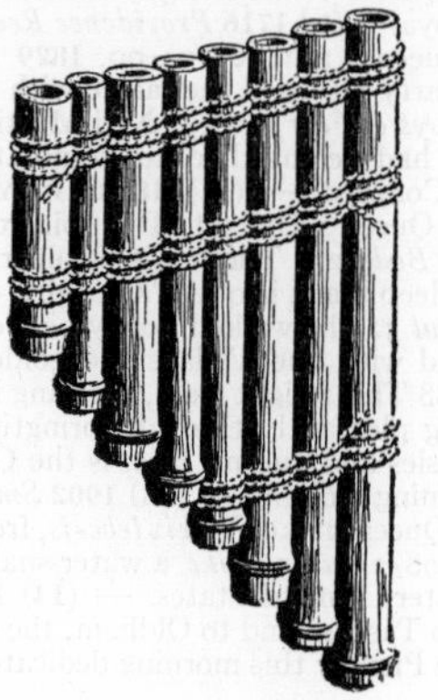

Quills (sense 3)

(5) **1806** LEWIS in *L. & Clark Exped.* IV. (1905) 59 There is a shrub which grows commonly in this neighbourhood which is precisely the same with that in Virginia sometimes called the quill-wood. — (6) **1894** *Amer. Folk-Lore* VII. 92 *Eupatorium purpureum*, . . . quill wort, Indian gravel root, West Va.

As the last term in **Dutch, elder, head, pine, pure, turkey call quill.** See also * **hedgehog's quills.**

* **quill,** *v.* [Prob. f. the quick movements involved in quilling or winding thread or yarn on a quill.] *intr.* (See quot. 1942.) *Colloq.* — **1869** *Overland Mo.* III. 127 A trig, smirk, little horse . . . often has to 'june,' or 'quill,' or 'get up and quill.' **1942** WARNICK *Dialect Garrett Co., Md.* 12 Quillin', v., going at a rapid pace.

* **quilt,** *n.* **1.** An article of apparel worn by women. **2. quilt sitting,** = **quilting bee.** Both *obs.*

(1) **1774** FITHIAN *Journal* I. 184 She appears to Day in a Chintz cotton Gown with an elegant blue Stamp, a Sky-Blue silk Quilt, spotted Apron. *Ib.* 185 [Miss Hale] is drest in a white Holland Gown, cotton Diaper Quilt very fine, a Lawn apron. **1778** *Holyoke Diaries* 99 Bought a Blue Sarsnet quilt. — (2) **1831** *Boston Transcript* 29 Sep. 2/2 We shall have Horticultural Whist Parties next; and who knows but a Horticultural Quilt-sitting may bring together all the old maids of the last half century?

As the last term in **crazy, flag, log cabin, patch, sunflower, tumbler quilt.**

* **quilt,** *v.* **1.** *intr.* To make a quilt or quilts. **2.** *tr.* To secure or fix (a needle) in needlework by taking incompleted quilting or running stitches.

(1) **1838** *U.S. Mag.* I. 342 She could knit, spin, weave, and quilt. **1934** VINES *Green Thicket World* 95 She could quilt better. — (2) **1908** FREEMAN *Shoulders of Atlas* 236 As she spoke, she quilted her needle into her work and tossed it on a table.

* **quilting,** *n.* In combs. designating a gathering of the women of a neighborhood to engage in quilting, as (1) **quilting bee,** (2) **frolic,** (3) **match,** (4) **party.** Cf. **bed quilting.**

(1) **1832** GOODRICH *System of Univ. Geog.* 107 The females also have similar meetings called 'quilting bees,' when many assemble to work for one, in padding or *quilting* bed coverings or *comforters.* **1907** *St. Nicholas* Oct. 1145/2 Grandmother . . . often rode five and ten miles to visit her distant friends, attending quilting bees and corn-huskings. **1948** *Minneapolis Star* 17 Sep. 31/1 (*caption*), Old Fashioned Quilting Bee. — (2) **1819** NOAH *She Would Be a Soldier* I. i, I'm the boy for a

race, for an apple-paring or quilting frolic. **1868** LOSSING *Hudson* 349 The old Dutch house . . . [was] the very dwelling wherein occurred Katrina Van Tassel's memorable quilting frolic. — **(3) 1818** WEEMS *Drunkard's Looking Glass* 4 He does not trouble his head about asking the Fool where he has been, whether at a Funeral, or a Wedding . . . or a Quilting-match. **1881** ALCOTT *New Conn.* 137 The Wolcott Dialect. . . . Quilting match. — **(4) 1833** SMITH *Life & Writings Downing* 151 (We.), A few others . . . wouldn't invite poor Mrs. No-tea to their husking and quilting parties. **1907** *St. Nicholas* 1044/2 She had gone, with her grandmother whom she was visiting, to a quilting-party. **1948** *Minneapolis Star* 17 Sep. 31/1 Nobody sees Nellie home when the women of Halvarson Bowers post 187, VFW auxiliary, have a quilting party.

Quinaielt kwɪˈnʌlt, *n.* [App. the native name.] (See quot. 1910.) Also attrib.

1856 in *H.R. Ex. Doc. 37* 34th Cong. 3 Sess. 21 Only the Quinnoyaths agreed to sign the treaty of Olympia. **1889** *Amer. Anthro.* Oct. 331 A Quinaielt Indian once professed to have obtained a feather of one of these birds. **1903** JAMES *Indian Basketry* 191 A Quinaielt basket bore a certain design, a favorite pattern in the tribe, but not the slightest clue to its meaning could be obtained. **1910** HODGE *Amer. Indians* II. 342/2 Quinaielt. A Salish tribe on Quinaielt r., Wash., and along the coast between the Quileute and the Quiatso on the N. . . . In 1909 they numbered 156, under the Puyallup school superintendency. **1933** CHELEY *Camping Out* 4 The Quinaielt Indians of the far Northwest used a drill which tapers at each end.

quince drink. (See quots.) *Obs.*

1666 *Md. Archives* II. 149 Quince drink thirty per gallon. **1676** GLOVER *Va.* in *Phil. Trans.* XI. 628 Here are also great stores of Quinces, which are larger and fairer than those of England, and not so harsh in taste; of the juice of these [quinces] they also make Quince-drink. **1709** LAWSON *Carolina* 109 Of this Fruit, they make a Wine, or Liquor, which they call Quince-Drink, and which I approve of beyond any Drink which that Country affords. . . . The Quince-Drink most commonly purges those that first drink it.

Quincy granite. Granite quarried in Quincy, Mass.

1835–7 HALIBURTON *Clockmaker* (1937) 150 (We.), I thought that are Quincy granite was so amazin strong all natur wouldn't break it. **1857** VAUX *Villas* 63 A range of stores, called Commercial Block . . . is now erected in Quincy granite on Commercial Wharf, Boston. **1882** MCCABE *New York* 236 Quincy granite is extensively used.

* **quinine,** *n.* **1. quinine bush,** (see quot. 1909). **2.** * **quinine tree,** (see quots.).

(1) 1909 *Cent. Supp.* 1100/1 quinine-bush. . . . The bear-brush, *Garrya Fremontii:* so called because its leaves served pioneers in the place of quinine. **1934** *N. Mex. Agric. Exp. Station Press Bul.* 713, 1 This shrub has many common names, among them being chaparral, coffee-berry, fever bush, gray-leaf dogwood, and quinine bush. — **(2) 1897** SUDWORTH *Arborescent Flora* 267 *Ptelea trifoliata.* Hoptree. . . . [Also called] Quinine-tree (Mich.). **1931** CLUTE *Plants* 122 Among other plants reputed to be a cure for malaria were . . . the ague-bark or quinine tree (*Ptelea trifoliata*). The latter, however, is not the species from which true quinine is obtained.

quinnat ˈkwɪnæt, *n.* [f. *t'kwinnat,* the name of this fish in the Salishan dialects of the Columbia R. region.]

1. =next.

[**1806** LEWIS in *L. & Clark Exped.* IV. (1905) 284 We arrived at the entrance of Quinnette creek which we ascended a short distance.] **1829** J. RICHARDSON *Fauna Bor.-Amer.* 219 This salmon . . . is known by the name of quinnat. **1911** *Rep. Fisheries 1908* 315/1 The California salmon, . . . or quinnat (*O*[*ncorhynchus*] *tschawytscha*), is found from Monterey to Alaska. **1948** *Pacific Discovery* July–Aug. 26/2 When referring to 'salmon' we will mean the true salmon (also known as quinnat, chinook or king) which invariably dies after spawning.

2. quinnat salmon, a commercially important salmon, *Oncorhynchus tschawytscha,* weighing about twenty-two pounds, found on the upper Pacific Coast. Cf. **king salmon.**

1874 HITTELL *Resources Calif.* 407 The most important fish of California is the quinnat salmon. **1881** *Amer. Naturalist* XV. 183 The quinnat salmon, from its great size and abundance is more valuable than all other fishes on our Pacific coast together. **1922** *Outing* Nov. 95/2 Three years ago, the Department of Fisheries planted quinnat salmon in Lake Ontario.

***quint,** *n.* A bicycle for five riders. *Obs.* — **1896** *Boston M. Journal* 26 June 3/7 The quint made its first appearance on Memorial Day.

quirt kwɜt, *n.* Orig. *S.W.* [Sp. *cuarta,* in the Amer. Sp. sense shown here.] A whip, usu. consisting of leather thongs attached to a stock about a foot long, used by horseback riders.

1845 *Amer. Rev.* Feb. 127/2 The 'quirt,' with its long heavy lash of knotted raw-hide [was] in his hand. **1889** *Denver Press* 9 Aug. 3/1 The quirts flew through the air with every gallop. **1949** *Boston Sun. Globe* 1 May (Fiction Mag.) 3/2 Now point that plug towards San Pedro and give it a cut with your quirt.

quirt kwɜt, *v. tr.* To strike (a horse) with a quirt. Also **quirting,** *n.*

1888 ROOSEVELT in *Cent. Mag.* April 854/2 A first-class rider will sit throughout it all without moving from the saddle, quirting his horse all the time. **1921** *Outing* May 82 He quirted his animal on the withers—movie style, I suppose. **1932** BENTLEY *Sp. Terms* 131 From the noun has come the verb to *quirt* and the Anglicized *quirting* used in such a phrase as 'He gave the animal a sound quirting.'

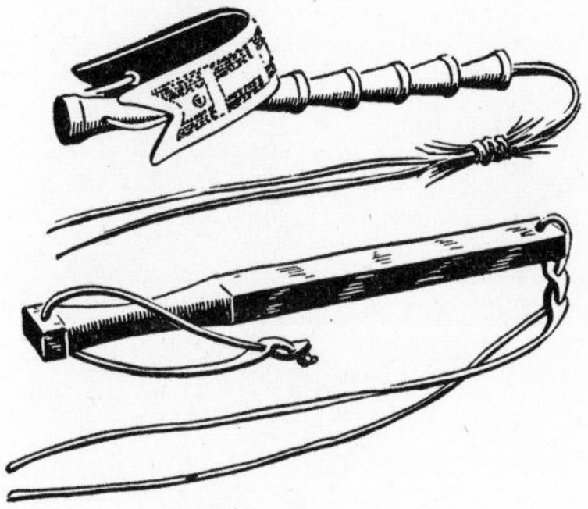

Typical quirts (Crow and Cheyenne)

***quit,** *v. To quit off,* to cease, stop. *Colloq.* — **1874** EGGLESTON *Circuit Rider* 249 That's what every body thought . . . until you quit off going with her so suddenly. **1894** *Advance* 1 March, I don't see how you ever made up your mind to quit off [from study].

***quite,** *adv. quite a few,* (see quot. 1909). *Colloq.* — **1883** *Harper's Mag.* Oct. 706/1 There's quite a few about among the rocks. **1909** *D.N.* III. 415 *quite a few, n. phr.* A considerable number. [Aroostook, Me.]

* **quitter,** *n.* That which, or one who, quits or shirks.

1881 *Standard* (London) 7 Sep. 5/2 They may perhaps have a right to the term 'quitter,' to stigmatise an animal that will not make a fight. **1887** *Columbus Dispatch* 31 May, The mighty pressure gives confidence that the [gas] well will not be a quitter. **1921** PAINE *Comr. Rolling Ocean* 5 The college can call me a quitter if it wants to. **1949** *Sat. Ev. Post* 15 Oct. 141/3 It's been worn by great battlers in every sport, but never by a quitter or dirty player.

quiz kwɪz, *n.* [f. * *quiz, v.*] An oral or written examination. Also attrib.

1867 *Atlantic Mo.* Oct. 468/2, I attended the quizzes, as they call them, pretty closely. **1915** CAMPBELL *Proving Virginia* 226 The black-robed Seniors assembled . . . to perform the last holy rites over their antique manuscripts, quiz papers, precious testimonials of midnight toil. **1949** *Time* 18 April 8/3 This measures the student's present proficiency and not his past success in cramming for quizzes.

b. quiz game, a questions-and-answers game.

1945 *E. Jefferson Sentinel* (Edgewater, Colo.) 26 July 5/4 Mrs. Critchfield, chairman and hostess, then conducted three quiz games.

quoddy ˈkwɑdɪ, *n.* and *a. local.* [Indian term for the pollack. Cf. *Passamaquoddy,* f. a term meaning "plenty of pollack."] **1. quoddy boat,** (see quot. 1884). **2. quoddy salmon,** the pollack, *Pollachius virens.*

(1) 1884 *Nat. Museum Bul.* No. 27, 694 The Quoddy boat is sloop-rigged, and is largely employed in the herring and other shore fisheries in Passamaquoddy Bay and vicinity. It is celebrated for speed and seaworthiness. **1910** HODGE *Amer. Indians* II. 347/2 The truncated form *Quoddy* appears also in place nomenclature. There are also 'quoddy boats' in this region. — **(2) 1884** GOODE *Fisheries* I. 230 At Eastport these fish are often called 'Quoddy Salmon.'

* **quorum,** *n.* **1.** In the Mormon Church, an organized group of men who are in the same grade of priesthood, as (*a*) *quorum of the Seventies,* (*b*) *quorum of the Twelve.* **2. quorum court,** ?a court of justices of the peace sitting together. *Obs.*

(1) (*a*) **1841** *Times & Seasons* (Nauvoo, Ill.) 16 Aug. 514/1 The Saints are informed that the quorum of the Seventies have withdrawn their fellowship from Elder Jesse Turpin, until he make satisfaction, to said quorum for his conduct. [**1862** *N. Amer. Review* July 223 The

'Seventies' are separated into quorums of seventy members in each, of which there were, in 1855, thirty-nine.] (*b*) **1842** *Times & Seasons* 1 Dec. 31/1 Elder W. Richards, of the Quorum of the Twelve, was unanimously called to the chair. **1905** *Out West* Sep. 249 Choosing two counselors, he re-organized the First Presidency, filled the vacancies thus occasioned in the quorum of the Twelve, and otherwise set the Church in order. **1949** *Miss. Valley Hist. Rev.* March 630 The first printing in Missouri was an eight-page epistle published by the Quorum of the Twelve Apostles of the Church at Winter Quarters, Omaha Nation, in December, 1847. — (**2**) **1847** *Hunt's Merch. Mag.* XVII. 378 The Quorum Court [in Tenn.] sits the first Monday of every month.

quota ˈkwotə, *v. tr.* To impose in accordance with a quota. Also **quotaing,** *n. Obs.*

1784 E. GERRY in *N. Eng. Hist. & Gen. Reg.* XLIX. 431 Their places should be speedily supplied by Troops to be *required* & quotied on the several States by Congress. **1786** JEFFERSON *Writings* (1905) V. 367 A convention might be formed between Portugal, Naples and the United States, by which the burthen of the war might be quota-ed on them, according to their respective wealth. **1798** *Ib.* VII. (1896) 267 They shall be free hereafter to tax houses separately, as by an indirect tax. This is to avoid the quotaing of which they cannot bear the idea.

R

***R,** *n.* A brand used on a slave (see quot.). *Rare.* — **a1861** in BUCKMASTER *Let My People Go* (1941) 5 For riding or going about in the night, or riding horses in the daytime without leave, a slave may be whipped, cropped, or branded in the cheek with the letter R.

***rabbit,** *n.* In combs.: (1) **rabbit berry,** = **buffalo berry,** also **rabbit's berry;** (2) **bush,** a western shrub, *Chrysothamnus graveolens*, or a related species, used as a retreat by jack rabbits, also **rabbit brush;** (3) **egg,** an Easter egg; (4) **fever,** = **tularemia,** also **rabbit's fever;** (5) ***fish,** (*a*) the smooth puffer, *Lagocephalus laevigatus*, having teeth resembling those of a rabbit, (*b*) the spotted balloonfish, *Cyclichthys schoepfi;* (6) ***foot,** see as a main entry; (7) **hawk,** the red-tailed hawk, *Buteo borealis;* (8) **moth,** a flannel moth, *Megalopyge opercularis*, the larva of which feeds on the orange and other trees in the south Atlantic states; (9) **mouth (sucker),** = **cutlips** (*b*); (10) **round-up,** *W.* the hunting and driving together for extermination of the jack rabbits of a given area; (11) **tobacco,** the balsamweed, *Gnaphalium obtusifolium;* (12) **vein,** (see quot.); (13) ***weed,** a woody plant with small yellow flowers, *Gutierrezia sarothrae*, of the Middle West and Southwest.

(1) **1804** *Lewis & Clark Exped.* VII. (1905) 52 We found Some red berreys which they call Rabbit berrys. **1839** *Knickerb.* XIII. 432 We found, on the west bank, a kind of large whortleberry, called *wabosimin*, or rabbits'-berry, by the Odjibwas. **1892** APGAR *Trees Northern U.S.* 132 *Shepherdia argentea.* (Buffalo-berry. Rabbit-berry.) . . . A small handsome tree, 5 to 20 ft. high, wild in the Rocky Mountains, and sometimes cultivated east. — (2) **1852** STANSBURY *Gt. Salt Lake* 235 The only vegetation today has been a little dwarf artemisia, grease-bush, rabbit-bush, . . . and an occasional dwarf cedar on the bluffs. **1927** CATHER *Death Comes* 95 The sandy soil of the plain . . . was splotched with masses of blooming rabbit brush—that olive-coloured plant that grows in high waves like a tossing sea, at this season covered with a thatch of bloom, yellow as gorse, or orange like marigolds. **1949** *Amer. Cattle Producer* April 12/1 The soil was heavier and had poorer drainage as was indicated by the presence of big rabbitbrush and greasewood. — (3) **1868** *Terr. Enterprise* (Virginia, Nev.) 11 April 3/1 To-morrow is Easter Sunday when all the children will be on the lookout for rabbit eggs. — (4) **1940** EILMANN *Medico-legal & Indust. Toxicology* 308 Tularemia, . . . also known as 'Rabbit's Fever,' . . . frequently comes under the 'Compensation Act' as infection often occurs from the handling or dressing of diseased rabbits. **1949** *Chi. Sun-Times* 4 June 9/1 Cook County's first case of rabbit fever in 1949 is also one of the strangest.

(5) (*a*) **1842** *Nat. Hist. N.Y., Zoology* IV. 330 The Lineated Puffer . . . is called Rabbit-fish, according to Schoepfi, on account of the whiteness of its flesh. **1897** *N.Y. Forest, Fish, & Game Comm.* 2 Rep. 224 Rabbit-Fish; Smooth Puffer. — Occasionally taken in the fall in Gravesend Bay. (*b*) **1883** *Nat. Museum Bul.* No. 27, 428 *Chilomycterus geometricus.* . . . Spiny Box-fish; Rabbit-fish; Swell Toad. East coast of the United States from Southern Massachusetts to Texas. — (7) **1851** *De Bow's Review* XI. 54, 1st, *Rabbit hawk.* **1903** O. HENRY in *McClure's Mag.* Dec. 144/1, [I] noticed a rabbit-hawk sitting on a dead limb in a water-elm. — **(8) 1890** *Cent.* 4924/3 *Rabbit-moth* . . . : so called from its soft furry appearance and rabbit-like coloration. — **(9) 1882** *Nat. Museum Bul.* No. 26, 144 Hare-lip Sucker. . . . Rabbit-mouth Sucker. **1911** *Rep. Fisheries 1908* 317 The different species [of sucker] are known as . . . 'rabbit-mouth,' 'harelip,' 'split-mouth,' 'red horse' [etc.].

(10) 1887 *Lisbon* (Dak.) *Star* 23 Dec. 7/1 A California Rabbit Roundup. **1911** *N.Y. Ev. Post* 21 Dec. 7/2 Twelve hundred jack rabbits . . . were bagged in a big rabbit round-up of the sort now popular in western Kansas, where the 'jacks' have been causing much trouble for farmers. — **(11) 1880** HARRIS *U. Remus* (1884) 66 'Den he drawd de rockin'-cheer in front er de fier he did, en tuck a big chaw terbarker.' 'Tobacco, Uncle Remus?' asked the little boy, incredulously. 'Rabbit terbarker, honey. . . .' **1949** *Amer. Sp.* April 110/1 Rabbit tobacco (a species of weed often rolled into homemade cigarettes, especially by boys trying to learn to smoke). — **(12) 1856** FERGUSSON *America* 195 Along the tunnel, about half-way between the second and third vein there is a bed of coal, called [in a Pa. mine] the 'rabbit-vein,' very productive of this gas. — **(13) 1884** *Harper's Mag.* Sep. 502/2 The prairies—middle lands, . . . covered with sorry bunch-grass and sad rabbit-weed—were neglected. **1902** *Everybody's Mag.* Jan. 36/2 There is a yellow-green dye that is used occasionally; it is made from the flowering tops of the rabbit-weed.

As the last term in **antelope, blacktail, black-tailed, brush, dead, graveyard, gray, jack, jackass, marsh, mule, prairie, prairiedog, rock, sage, snowshoe, swamp, water, white rabbit.**

***rabbit-foot.** Also ***rabbit's-foot.**

1. A clover, *Trifolium arvense*, having soft, furry flower heads. In full **rabbit-foot clover.**

1817–8 EATON *Botany* (1822) 491 Rabbit-foot, field clover. . . . Grows in dry pastures or barren fields. **1889** *Cent.* 1060/1 Other species, mostly weeds of little value, are the yellow or hop clover, . . . the stone, hare's-foot, or rabbit-foot clover [etc.].

2. The foot of a rabbit carried as a charm or good-luck token. Also *to work a rabbit's-foot on* (someone), to steal a march on, get the better of. *Colloq.*

1876 HEARN *Amer. Miscellany* (1924) I. 185 After the girl told that [ghost] story, Banjo Jim seldom passed along the Row at night without a rabbit's foot in the breast pocket of his woolen shirt. **1902** HARBEN *A. Daniel* 309 Pole worked the rabbit-foot on them back there. **1948** *Salt Lake Tribune* 17 Dec. 34/6 A dimestore rabbit's foot paid off with one of 1948's biggest football surprises and landed his team in the Delta bowl.

transf. **1922** *Sunset* Dec. 10/2 Presently the word went round that I was a 'rabbit's foot'—a bringer of good luck—and the gamblers began to give me money to place for them.

racacha ˈrɑkəˌtʃɑ, *n.* [La. F. (<Sp.) See Read 146 ff.] (See quots.) — **1841** *S. Lit. Messenger* VII. 77/2 [From the Creole's moccasins] there projected an enormous pair of spurs, (racafacs) the rowels some six inches long. **1931** W. A. READ *La.-French* 146 *Racacha* is used along the Gulf Coast and in the city of New Orleans as the name of the Bur-Grass or Hedgehog Grass. . . . *Racacha* has found its way into English, and is used in the sense of 'sand-spur' as far west as Texas. . . . The original meaning of *racacha* in Louisiana must have been *sand-bur*, whence was developed that of spur, owing to the fancied resemblance between a bur and a horseman's spur.

raccoon ræˈkun, *n.* Also **†rackoon, †arocoun,** etc. [Of Algonquian origin. Cf. Virginian *ärä'kun*, scraper, scratcher, prob. in allusion to the creature's scratching for crabs, etc., along streams and shores.]

1. A grayish brown, furry animal, *Procyon lotor*, common throughout North America. Cf. **fisher raccoon.**

1608 SMITH *Works* (1910) 23 The Empereur *Powhatan*, each weeke once or twice, sent me many presents of Deare, bread, *Raugroughcuns.* **1610** *Estate of Virginia* (1844) 13 There are Arocouns, and Apossouns, in shape like to pigges. **1799** J. SMITH *Acc't of Remark. Occurrences* (1870) 82 It is a received opinion among the Indians that the snakes and racoons are transmutable; and that a great many of the snakes turn racoons every fall, and racoons snakes every spring. **1882** *Vt. Agric. Rep.* VII. 69 He believes the racoon and the skunk are beneficial to the farmers. **1949** *Nat. Hist.* Oct. 383/1 About 7 p.m. a young female raccoon came to the cookhouse porch.

b. The flesh of this used as food.

[**1632** MORTON *N. Eng. Canaan* (Force Tracts II.) 54 The Racowne is a beast as bigg, full out, as a Foxe, with a Bushtayle. His Flesh excellent foode. **1843** *Amer. Pioneer* II. 424 Bacon was made [in Ill. or Ohio] of salted and smoked raccoons.] **1937** COFFIN *Kennebec* 230 Baked raccoon is no poor man's meat.

c. *transf.* A member of the New Jersey militia in the American Revolution. *Obs.*

1779 *N.J. Archives* 2 Ser. III. 703 Each *devoted racoon* [is] to receive down forty *soft* or *paper* dollars.

d. Short for **raccoon skin.**

1815 LUTTIG *Jrnl.* 130 Raccoon from your country will not bring 62½c in Kentucky, it is only those from the Illinois, one of which is worth two of yours.

2. In combs.: (1) **raccoon berry,** (see quot.); (2) **bridge,** (see quot. 1791), *obs.*, cf. **Indian bridge;** (3)

dog, (see quot.); (4) **fox,** =**cacomistle;** (5) **grape,** =**coon grape;** (6) **oyster,** =**coon oyster,** also attrib.; (7) **perch,** (see quots.); (8) **skin,** the skin of the raccoon, often used for garments, etc., also attrib.; (9) **swamp,** a swamp in which raccoons are abundant.

(1) **1867** DE VOE *Market Ass't* 379 Mandrake, May-apple, raccoonberry, or wild lemon.—This fruit is a stranger in our markets, and only occasionally found among our citizens; and, no doubt, if it was esteemed at all, it would be cultivated and become more plentiful. — (2) **1791** W. BARTRAM *Travels* 445 We were obliged to carry every article of our effects, and this by no other bridge than a sapling felled across it, which is called a raccoon bridge. **1793** CAMPBELL *Travels* 220 Crossing a deep swamp, ourselves on Racoon bridges. — (3) **1902** *Amer. Folk-Lore* 256 From the *raccoon* have been named the following: Raccoon-dog (*Canis procyonoides*) of Japan and northern China [etc.]. — (4) **1859** COOPER & SUCKLEY *Nat. Hist. Washington Terr.* 114 The ring-tailed bassaris, often called raccoon fox, is common in California, where the people tame it. **1917** *Mammals of Amer.* 108 Ring-tailed Cat. . . . [Also called] Mountain Cat, Raccoon Fox.

(5) **1834** AUDUBON *Ornith Biog.* II. 80 The Racoon Grape is characterized by . . . the small size of the bluish-black fruit. — (6) **1835** AUDUBON *Ornith. Biog.* III. 181 Oysters on what are called in the Southern States and the Floridas 'Racoon oyster beds.' **1885** *Harper's Mag.* Jan. 219/1 When the mangrove grows on the outer edge of the water-line, and drops its aerial roots, . . . the spat of the raccoon oyster finds a lodgement. — (7) **1896** JORDAN & EVERMANN *Check-List Fishes* 357 *Perca flavescens*. . . . Yellow Perch, American Perch; Ringed Perch; Raccoon Perch. Fresh waters of the eastern United States. **1947** DALRYMPLE *Panfish* 211 Dark, vertical body markings . . . have caused the Yellow Perch to be called Ringed Perch, Raccoon Perch, Zebra Perch, etc. — (8) **1624** SMITH *Gen. Hist. Va.* III. 48 He sat covered with a great robe, made of *Rarowcun* skinnes. **1643** WILLIAMS *Key* (1866) 144 *Mohĕwonck*, a Rakoone-skin coat. **1839** *S. Lit. Messenger* V. 99/1 His father . . . had suffered him to raise pocket money . . . by selling hare-skins and rackoon-skins. **1903** FOX *Little Shepherd* i, A small raccoon-skin haversack hung from one of the prongs. — (9) **1667** *Oyster Bay Rec.* I. 81 The S[ai]d bounds [begin] from Raccoon Swamp. **1764** in *Amer. Sp.* XV. 156/2 To a Pine near where the mouth of the blue marsh Branch makes into Rackoon swamp.

b. Designating articles of apparel made of raccoon skins or fur.

1649 *Conn. Rec.* I. 497 An Inventory of the Estate of Mr. William Whiting: . . . 2 Racoone coats, 1 Wolf skin coate [etc.]. **1743** *N.J. Archives* XII. 181 A new Rachoon Hat. **1840** *Knickerb.* XVI. 163 He then made me a rakish raccoon-cap, with a flaunting tail to it. **1947** *Sports Afield* Dec. 30 The day of the raccoon coat is over, but the coon still has need of brains to keep his skin. **1949** *N.O. Times-Picayune Mag.* 6 Nov. 6/2 He grew up well before the raccoon-coat and hip-flask age.

c. Also (1) **raccoon fat,** (2) **fur,** (3) **hunt,** (4) **hunter,** (5) **hunting,** (6) **oil.**

(1) **1832** *Louisville Directory* 98 [The ground-wheat flour] was shortened with racoon fat. — (2) **1779** *N.J. Archives* 2 Ser. III. 170 An apprentice lad . . . [is] supposed to have taken out of his master's hatter's shop . . . about half a pound of raccoon furr cut off the skins. — (3) **1824** in *Ind. Hist. Soc. Pub.* IV. 69 We proposed a racoon hunt, which is always at night, but for lack of dogs we gave it up. **1858** VIELÉ *Following Drum* 82 [They] recounted . . . an exciting raccoon hunt. — (4) **1944** *Democrat* 28 Sep. 1/3 Rabbit and raccoon hunters may start out in quest of these animals.

(5) **1774** in *Pa. Mag. Hist.* XLIV. 200, I was out Rackoon Hunting the other Night with 10 or 11 more. **1809** A. HENRY *Travels* 131 Racoon-hunting was my more particular and daily employ. — (6) **1690** in *Pub. Col. Soc.* XIV. 151 Little or none, but Rakoons oile for aches.

raccoon ræˈkun, *v. intr.* To hunt raccoons. *Rare.* — **1834** C. A. DAVIS *Lett. J. Downing* 265 The Gineral . . . tell'd a plaguy long story about his goin out once with a gang of his niggers a rakoonin. *Ib.* 267 It would a gone all round the country that I know'd nothin about rakoonin.

***race,** *n.*[1]

1. *Polit.* A competition or contest for public office.

1855 I. C. PRAY *Mem. J. G. Bennett* 288 He had been the first to start many of them upon the ground for a successful political race. **1912** COBB *Back Home* 279 See if there ain't . . . something definite . . . on the race for state senator!

b. *To make the race,* to undertake a candidacy for public office (see also quot. 1881).

1881 PIERSON *In the Brush* 132 To 'make the race' was to secure an election. **1903** *N.Y. Ev. Post* 17 Sep. 1 Mr. Cutting ran up stairs to tell Dr. Gould . . . that Mr. Grout would make the race. **1949** *Dallas Morn. News* 1 May 1/7 He might perhaps consider making the Senate race.

2. In combs.: (1) **race-about,** a small racing boat; (2) **path,** (*a*) a race track, (*b*) (see quot.), *obs.;* (3) **way,** (*a*) a mill race, (*b*) a channel or passageway.

(1) **1901** *Boston Transcript* 1 Feb. 6/5 The Knockabout Association of Boston . . . offers a cup to be known as the 'Inter-city Cup for race-abouts.' **1905** *St. Nicholas* Aug. 865 There were . . . pennants for the raceabouts and half-raters. — (2) (*a*) **1737** JOHN BRICKELL *North-Carolina* 39 Horse-Racing they are fond of, for which they have Race-Paths, near each Town, and in many parts of the Country. Those Paths, seldom exceed a Quarter of a Mile in length, and only two Horses start at a time, each Horse has his peculiar path, which if he quits and runs into the other, looses the Race. **1847** HOWE *Ohio* 555 There was the very race-path still existing. (*b*) **1828** *Western Mo. Rev.* I. 512 The 'Devil's' race paths, tea table, oven, etc., are places of difficult or hazardous navigation, that frequently occur. — (3) (*a*) **1828** in S. JENKINS *Story of Bronx* (1912) 199 Fourteen mill sites, each fifty by one hundred feet were mapped out along the raceways. **1904** *N.Y. Ev. Post* 8 June 2 Several men were assaulted, and some were thrown into the raceway. (*b*) **1875** KNIGHT 1355/2 In the lay [of the power loom] . . . is a raceway for the shuttle. **1898** *Inland Printer* Nov. 178/1 This machine will select the type, place them in a raceway and move them along until a line is set up.

As the last term in **anybody's, Cape, fall, match, scrub, steamboat race.**

***race,** *n.*[2] Used in numerous expressions relating to actions, problems, etc., arising from social tensions between white people and Negroes, as (1) **race conflict,** (2) **consciousness,** (3) **feeling,** (4) **issue,** (5) **line,** (6) **prejudice,** (7) **problem,** (8) **question,** (9) **riot,** (10) **war.**

(1) **1880** TOURGEE *Invisible Empire* xii, Any one who asked the support of colored men as against a Democratic nominee was precipitating a race-conflict. — (2) **1905** *N.Y. Ev. Post* 11 Oct. 4 If the white race are permeated with race consciousness, there is no danger of amalgamation. — (3) **1904** PAGE in *McClure's Mag.* March 549/2 [With] race-feeling growing, . . . it is time that all sensible men should endeavor . . . [to] look at the subject frankly. — (4) *c***1875** in J. S. REYNOLDS *Reconstruction in S.C.* 304 The government is wholly composed of negroes elected on the race issue, asserted even against white Republicans.

(5) **1891** *Cong. Rec.* App. 17 Jan. 101/1 At Marion, Ind., . . . when the Democrats were attempting to have a rally, . . . they were attacked by the colored people, the race line being distinctly drawn by that race. — (6) **1899** CHESNUTT *Wife of His Youth* 7, I have no race prejudice, . . . but we people of mixed blood are ground between the upper and the nether millstone. **1948** *Sat. Review* 27 March 26 The only people without race prejudice are now in the first and second grades. — (7) **1891** *Cong. Rec.* 16 Jan. 1431/1 If they would allow us to proceed it would be but a short time until what is called 'the race problem,' in my opinion, would settle itself. **1949** *Chi. Tribune* 28 Dec. 1/1 City Tackles Race Problem: Here Is Story! — (8) **1889** *Boston Jrnl.* 26 Dec. 2/4 The Wilmington, N.C., Star (Dem.) thinks that time only can solve the race-question in the South. — (9) **1890** *Our Day* May 406 Race Riots in the South. **1950** *Time* 2 Jan. 57/1 In 1917, 39 Negroes and eight whites were killed in a three-day race riot.

(10) **1897** *Chi. Tribune* 28 July 3/7 Race riot in the jail. . . . This gave the negroes an excellent chance to start a 'race' war.

b. race suicide, the gradual disappearance of a race, esp. through the voluntary failure of its members to produce offspring in sufficient numbers. Also transf.

1901 *Amer. Acad. Pol. Sci. Ann.* July 88 The American farm hand, mechanic and operative might wither away before the heavy influx of a prolific race from the Orient. . . . For a case like this I can find no words so apt as 'race suicide.' **1927** WEBSTER. **1949** *L.A. Times* 15 June 2/7 It wouldn't be surprising if the lunar inhabitants had learned to make atomic bombs thousands of years ago and used them to commit race suicide.

***racer,** *n.*

1. The common blacksnake, *Coluber constrictor*, or a related species. Also attrib. and **blue, green racer.**

1823 JAMES *Exped.* I. 267 *Columber constrictor*—Racer. **1898** *Smithsonian Rep.* 794 The *Zamenis constrictor* is the 'black snake' of the East and the 'blue' and 'green racer' of the West. **1946** STUART *Plum Grove Hills* 85 They slid to the foot of the mountain like racer snakes before a new-ground fire.

2. A poor or thin fish.

1832 WILLIAMSON *Maine* I. 159 [The salmon] then stay till the next May, when they return with their young to the sea; these are 'the racers' so called. **1911** *Rep. Fisheries 1908* 314/1 *Racer.*—A shad that has spawned and is lean and worthless.

3. An automobile designed for great speed.

1903 *Outing* Sep. 713/1 American manufacturers will be making better racers before next year's contest. **1916** WILSON *Somewhere*

289 Once she'd tramped on the gas of a ninety-horsepower racer and socked him against a stone wall at a turn some fool had made in the road. **1925** *Sat. Ev. Post* 19 Sep. 52/2 There was no body on the racer, as we know bodies today—nothing but a flat bed, as near as I can describe it.

As the last term in **black, blue, horse, scrub racer.**

rachel ˈretʃl̩, *n.* [f. *Rachel*, name for a girl.] (See quot.) *Obs.* — **1840** in RABB *Tour* (1920) 48, I observed [in Indiana] . . . Miss Hunter engaged in a species of handiwork which, I learned, upon inquiry, was a 'rachel,' a convenient sort of head-gear made of soft yarn, very elastic and partaking of the various natures of cap, bonnet, and hood.

∗**racing,** *n.* As the last term in **harness, scrub racing.**

∗ **rack,** *n.*[1]

1. In a river, a framework to obstruct the passage of fish. *Obs.*

1735 *Pa. Col. Rec.* IV. 24 Racks are a much greater Obstruction to Navigation than Wears.

2. = **horse rack.**

1827 *Mass. Spy* 24 Oct. (Th.), I reckon in futur you'll hitch your creter to the rack afore Patty Pott's door. **1843** CARLTON *New Purchase* II. 211 One dozen horses [were] at Carlton's rack.

3. (See quots.)

1843 CARLTON *New Purchase* I. 5 The stages of that day wore no boots. In place of that leather convenience, was a cross-barred ornament projecting in the rear to receive the baggage or at least half of it. This receptacle was called the 'Rack.' **1903** *Nation* 6 Aug. 115/2 Another Americanism we miss under Racks, the technical name for the side plankings or buffers of our ferry slips. **1905** *N.Y. Ev. Post* 20 Dec. 1 Three of the Lackawanna 'racks,' as the arrangements of piles to fit the ferryboats are called, were left intact.

4. In colloq. combs.: (1) **rackabone,** a lean person or animal [app. short for *rack of bones q.v.* in same sense]; (2) **heap,** a mass of rubbish, also transf.

(1) **1854** M. J. HOLMES *Tempest & Sunshine* 59 Turn that old rackerbone of yourn straight round, and turn down that ar street. **1900** *Cong. Rec.* App. 6 March 117/2 A Western farmer had a college-bred son who went off preaching. . . . He came back with an old rackabone. — (2) **1857** T. H. GLADSTONE *Englishman in Kans.* 280 He was escorted some distance down the river by several of our citizens, who, seeing him pass several rack-heaps in quite a skilful manner, bade him adieu and returned to Atchison. **1883** MARK TWAIN *Life on Miss.* xxiii, There was only one boat advertised. . . . She was a venerable rack-heap. **1889** P. BUTLER *Recollections* 72 There were in the river heaps of drift-wood, called 'rack-heaps,' dangerous places into which the water rushed with great violence.

b. In colloq. phrases: (1) *rack of bones,* a skeleton (of a fish), hence a thin or skeleton-like person or animal [a variant of *EDD ragabones* (*s.v. rag sb.*[1] 6), the skeleton of a fish or animal]; (2) *to stand up to the rack,* and variants, to accept one's duty or fortune without complaining.

(1) **1804** ORDWAY in *Jrnls. Lewis & O.* 128 We Saw the rack of Bones of a verry large fish. **1856** G. D. BREWERTON *War in Kans.* 314 Indeed she was to all appearances but a mere rack of bones, over whose unpicturesque outline nature had condescended to draw an angular wrinkling of skin. **1949** *Sat. Ev. Post* 2 April 97/2 Mount that rack o' bones you call a horse and ride in front o' me. — (2) **1834** CROCKETT *Narr. Life* 61, I was determined to stand up to my rack, fodder or no fodder. **1842** *Juliet* (Ill.) *Courier* 2 Feb. 4/4 Come up to the rack today, and bring the fodder with you. **1890** *Stock Grower & Farmer* 12 July 4/2 For several years cattlemen have been severe losers but most of them have stood pluckily to the rack. **1903** BROWN *How to Beat Game* 74 It keeps about two-thirds of them constantly financiering in order to 'come up to the rack.'

As the last term in **baggage, basket, bridle, cane, dry-goods, fish, hay, hitch, hitching, horse, pot, shingle, shuck, storm rack.**

rack ræk, *n.*[2] [Du. *rak,* in sense shown here.] (See quots.) *Obs.* — **1832** J. F. WATSON *Hist. Tales N.Y.* 27 The 'Racks,' so called, along the Hudson river, were Dutch names for Reaches. Thus, Martelaers rack meant the Martyr's reach or struggling place; Lange rack was Longreach; and Klauver rack, clover reach, &c. **1930** HALE in *Amer. Sp.* V. 164 *Rack.* . . . The Dutch navigators divided the Hudson into *racks* or *reaches.* The former word remains in Claverack, but the word *reach* does not appear in place names [i.e. in eastern New York].

racker ˈrækɚ, *n.* A horse that moves with a racking gait.

1829 *Sporting Mag.* XXIII. 266 The racker comes to us from our North Western territory. **1840** MARRYAT *Diary* 3 The Americans are very fond of fast trotting horses; I do not refer to rackers, as they term horses that trot before and gallop behind. **1902** MCFAUL *Ike Glidden* 108 Lickety got ter puffn' up his ole hoss, soze you'd a thought it was the Millbridge Racker.

∗ **racket,** *n.*[1] Also **racquette, racquet.**

1. A snowshoe consisting of a light wooden frame and a network of cords.

[**1613** PURCHAS *Pilgrimage* VIII. iv. 630 Their Dogges . . . haue rackets tyed vnder their feet, the better, to runne on the snow.] **1677** HUBBARD *Narrative* II. 27 It was not possible for any to have travelled that Way, unless they carried Rackets under their Feet, wherewith to walk upon the Top of the Snow. **1704** *N.H. Prov. Papers* II. 419 They have upwards of 30 pr. of Snow Shoes and Racketts already made. **1897** *Outing* XXIX. 362/1 When the racquette is fastened the heel and toe are free. **1949** *Boston Globe* 14 Aug. (Fiction Mag.) 2/2 This mysterious stranger . . . put on racquets like any bushman and disappeared.

attrib. **1780** E. PARKMAN *Diary* 199, I was drawn by a number of Rackettmen, in a very handsome Sleigh. *Ib.* 207 Another snowstorm . . . covers ye Rackett Tracks and fills ye Roads again. **1942** PEATTIE *Friendly Mts.* 292 French Canadians in the United States have nearly a hundred local 'racquette' clubs scattered throughout New England and New York.

2. a. A similar shoe for walking over marshy ground. **b.** (See quot.)

(**a**) **1846** DE SMET *Ore. Missions* (1847) 193 The savages travel over these marshy places in *Rackets.* — (**b**) **1864** WEBSTER 1080/2 *Racket,* . . . a broad wooden shoe or patten for a horse, to enable him to step on marshy or soft ground.

3. A kind of dance employing the slide and the shift or change. Also attrib. and with defining term. *Obs.* Cf. ∗**racketing,** *n.*

1881 RITTENHOUSE *Maud* 30 Do you dance the raquet? **1885** DODWORTH *Dancing* 51 Racket Waltz (One-Slide Racket in Waltz Time). *Ib.* 52 Changes are made . . . by alternating the one-slide racket with the three-slide.

∗**racket,** *n.*[2] As the last term in **ghost, grab racket.**

racketeer ˌrækɪˈtɪr, *n.* [f. ∗*racket, n.*[2]+*-eer.*] One who carries on a racket, esp. a member of a gang or association of criminals who practice extortion, intimidation, etc. *Slang.*

1928 *Amer. Mercury* Aug. 475/2 Joey . . . had quit as a racketeer, and lived on the proceeds of his highly questionable home brew. **1949** *Dly. Ardmoreite* (Ardmore, Okla.) 4 Dec. 5/1 A decline in black market operations . . . has brought racketeers into counterfeiting.

b. Also as a verb. Hence **racketeering,** *n.*

1928 *Time* 30 Jan. 11/2 In 36 years in Chicago I have never been held up, robbed, or racketeered. **1928** *Dly. Express* (London) 14 Sep. 1/4 'Racketeering' is the new word that has been coined in America to describe the big business of organised crime. **1929** HOSTETTER & BEESLEY *It's a Racket* 79 Maxie for years had been racketeering the Jews and Jewish merchants of Chicago. **1949** *Sat. Ev. Post* 4 June 22/3 Four police squads assigned to the water front were merged under one command to coordinate the drive on racketeering in the harbor.

∗**racketing,** *n.* The performance of the dance known as the racket. *Obs.* Cf. ∗**racket,** *n.*[1] **3.** — **1882** RITTENHOUSE *Maud* 127 Mr. Menager must needs add his share to praise my grace in raqueting.

racket store. (See quots. 1905, 1916.) *Colloq.*

1894 *Dly. Ardmoreite* (Ardmore, Okla.) 30 April 1 (*advt.*), The Racket Store. **1905** *D.N.* III. 91 *racket* (*store*), n. Bazar. 'There are two *rackets* in Springdale.' 'I bought it at the big *racket store.*' Universal [n.w. Ark.]. **1916** *Ib.* IV. 341 Racket store, n. A five and ten cent store. W. Res., Kan., La. **1924** CROY *R.F.D. No. 3* 89 It was a 'kitchen shower.' The glittering array was piled high, like a special sale in a racket store—dishpans, saucepans, pie pans . . . and so on.

∗ **Rad,** *n.* = ∗ **radical 2.**

1867 *Harper's Wkly.* 14 Sep. 590/2 He [President Johnson] handled a favorite bat, which he called his 'Policy,' and with which he had given a 'daisy cutter' to many a ball pitched by him by the Rads. **1871** *Harper's Mag.* XLIII. 319/1 When the elective franchise for the nigger was presented, A plan to have them vote by the Rads was invented. **1898** PAGE *Red Rock* 411 He was abusing Leech and Still and pretty much all the Rads.

radar ˈredɑr, *n.* [See note.]

This term is derived from *ra*dio *d*etecting *a*nd *r*anging. It arose in the U.S. Army to distinguish the American device from a similar locator developed by the British and called by them a *radiolocator.*

A device for ascertaining, by means of properly focused radio waves, the distance, altitude, and direction of motion of an object out of sight or hearing. Also attrib.

1941–2 *Gen. Marshall's Rep. to Sec'y of War,* Process of building up ground service forces and supplies (mechanics, ordnance and radio technicians, signal personnel, radar warning detachments [etc.]). **1943** *N.Y. Herald Tribune* 12 Dec. (Book Sect.) 6 Mr. Shenton defines pleasant nouns such as . . . recent entries like radar and photogrammetry. **1950** *L.A. Times* 3 Jan. II. 1/2 The radar truck, trailer and power generator are stationed on the edge of the landing field.

***radiator,** *n.* A fixture through which steam or hot water from a central heating plant circulates in order to warm a room. Cf. **steam radiator.**

1851 CIST *Cincinnati* 213 By the introduction of evaporatory radiators and registers, the air is kept moist. **1906** *N.Y. Ev. Post* 29 Dec. Sat. Supp. 1 There are still thousands who stay by their own firesides—or radiators—on that day. **1948** *Savings News* March 4/1 Go inside and you find no radiators, no registers, no hot air vents.

b. The container or a part of the container for the water used in a cooling system, esp. of an automobile. Also attrib.

1900 *Sci. Amer. Supp.* 25 Aug. 20617/3 The present water circulating plan . . . has . . . the defect of complicating the mechanism by the addition of tanks, radiators and pumps. **1931** CALDWELL *Amer. Earth* 87 Git some water for the radiator, Jake. **1949** SPRUNT & CHAMBERLAIN *S.C. Bird Life* 489 City sparrows have learned that the radiator grills of motor cars often provide insects for the taking.

***radical,** *a.* and *n.*

1. *pl.* (See quot. 1847.) Also attrib. *Obs.*

1847 *Semi-Wkly. News* (Fredericksburgh, Va.) 21 Oct. 2/2 The Barnburners are the progressives, the radicals. **1848** *N.Y. Wkly. Tribune* 26 Feb. 4/2 You have received accounts of the organization, officers, &c, of the Radical Convention which assembled in this city to-day.

2. During, and for a short time after, the Civil War, a member of a group in the North who favored extreme measures against the South, as abolition of slavery, confiscation of property, etc. Now *hist.*

1862 NORTON *Army Lett.* 129, I suppose the radicals have got enough of Burnside now. **1870** *Republican Rev.* 31 Sep. 3/1 The Governor's . . . record as a radical of the advanced school, running back to the organization of the Republican party, has not been marred by any action of his in this Territory. **1949** *Lincoln Herald* June 24/1 The radicals were determined to prevent his renomination.

b. Of or pertaining to this group.

1868 *N.Y. Herald* 4 July 5/2 The radical candidate for Governor . . . hurries back to Vicksburg. *Ib.*, The snug little sum of $37,321.40 has already been paid to four radical papers. **1874** COLLINS *Kentucky* I. 217, 7 Radical negroes at 2 A.M. called out of his house one who voted the Democratic ticket, and Kukluxed him by shooting him with bird-shot. **1883** *Cent. Mag.* Oct. 957/2 'A Radical Abolitionist' . . . puts a false interpretation on the language used by Chief-Justice Taney in the Dred Scott Case.

3. Radical Democracy, any one of various political groups or factions, esp. the Barnburners and the Free-Soilers, not disposed to go along with those in the party whom they regarded as too conservative. *Obs.*

1847 *Semi-Wkly. News* (Fredericksburgh, Va.) 21 Oct. 2/2 The Barnburners with their 'Radical democracy' can never long govern this great State. **1848** *N.Y. Wkly. Tribune* 5 Aug. 3/3 The *Ann Arbor Free Democrat*, organ of the Radical Democracy of Michigan, . . . has hauled down the Cass and Butler flag, and raised that of Van Buren and Free Soil. **1880** *Dly. Inter-Ocean* (Chi.) 3 June 9/5 On the 4th of July, 1864, a convention, under the name of 'the Radical Democracy,' met at Cleveland, Ohio, and nominated John C. Fremont for President.

4. Radical party, (see quot. 1914).

1863 *Atlanta Intelligencer* 13 Nov. 1/1 The opponents of the radical party, their opponents—their enemies, as he described them—must get out of the State. **1876** *S.F. Dly. Examiner* 10 Oct. 2/1 The real issue with the Radicals is to divert public attention from the unexemplified corruption of the Radical party during the past eight years. **1914** *Cyclo. Amer. Govt.* III. 131/1 Radical Party. A name sometimes given to the Republican party especially soon after the Civil War, and, while often applied generally to the whole party by its opponents, more commonly applicable to the extreme element and its leaders in determined opposition to the policy and acts of President Johnson.

5. Radical Republican, a member of the Republican party who favored drastic measures against the South at the close of the Civil War.

1865 *Atlanta D. Intelligencer* 1 Oct. 3/1 The radical Republicans are now proposing a compromise on the negro-suffrage question. **1900** *Cong. Rec.* 14 Feb. 1799/2 An election law . . . put the election machinery into the hands of three unequivocal radical Republicans appointed in each county. **1949** *Fla. Hist. Quart.* Jan. 219 The Radical Republicans had nominated Harrison Reed . . . for the governorship.

b. Hence **Radical Republicanism.** *Obs.*

1867 *Fredericksburg* (Va.) *News* 2 July 2/2 All these funds are employed in . . . paying the expenses of propagandists of varied complexions to preach the doctrines of Radical republicanism in the cities and on the plantations of the South. **1868** *Ore. State Jrnl.* 24 Oct. 1/6 Your example is of rare value as a contribution to the assailed cause of Radical Republicanism.

***radicalism,** *n.* The political principles of the radicals of Civil War days. Now *hist.*

1865 *Nation* I. 66 The particular aversion of the Golden Circle was radicalism of every sort, and hence no lodges were erected in South Carolina or Massachusetts. **1874** in FLEMING *Hist. Reconstruction* II. 152 If that body [Congress] and the President show a disposition to . . . maintain Radicalism in Louisiana, then Wells, Anderson & Co. will, no doubt, rule accordingly. **1949** *Ark. Hist. Quart.* Spring 74 The Brooks-Baxter War was the final struggle of Radicalism to maintain its power in Arkansas.

***radio,** *n.* [See note.]

"The term 'Radio' was suggested as the mark of wireless telegrams under the Radio Convention drawn up in Berlin in 1906 (see *Internat. Radiotelegr. Convention Service Reg.* x. 34), and adopted as this by the U.S. Congress in 1912" (*OED Supp.*).

Wireless telegraphy, a message sent by wireless telegraphy, or a set for receiving such messages. Also attrib.

1912 *Act of Congress* in *Year-bk. Wireless Telegr.* 96 The radio operator . . . must furnish to the inspector evidence that he is 'skilled in the use of the apparatus.' **1921** *Sci. Amer.* 2 July 5/1 As a boy of fifteen, Armstrong became interested in radio and erected a radio station at his home. **1925** H. L. FOSTER *Trop. Tramp Tourists* 97 It fairly shrieked with . . . jazz from radios. **1950** *Chi. Tribune* 17 Jan. 14/5 We just turn on the radio.

radiotrician ˌredɪəˈtrɪʃən, *n.* [*radio*+*electrician*, a trade-mark word.] An expert in radio mechanics. — **1929** *Cin. Enquirer* 5 Oct. 21/2 (*heading*), Become a Radiotrician. **1945** MENCKEN *Supp.* I. 573 *Radiotrician*, perhaps suggested by *electrician* rather than by *mortician*, was adopted by the radio repairmen in the late 1920s.

***radish,** *n. attrib.* Designating insects injurious to radishes. Cf. **cabbage radish.**

1854 EMMONS *Agric. N.Y.* V. 262 (*index*), Radish-bug, 135. [*Ib.* 135 *Halticides.* Genus *Haltica.* . . . They feed upon the leaves of vegetables.] **1873** *Amer. Naturalist* VII. 242 The cabbage web moth . . . is noticed; also the radish weevil. **1891** *Cent.* 4935/2 *Radish-fly*, . . . an American dipterous insect, *Anthomyia raphani*, injurious to the radish.

***raft,** *n.*

1. A dense flock of waterfowl. Also **raft fowl.** Cf. **raft duck.**

1709 LAWSON *Carolina* 150 Raft-Fowl includes all the sorts of small Ducks and Teal, that go in Rafts along the Shoar. **1872** *Fur, Fin & Feather* (ed. 2) 26 These great collections [of ducks] are termed rafts. **1949** SPRUNT & CHAMBERLAIN *S.C. Bird Life* 135 The Greater Scaup . . . congregates there in large flocks or 'rafts,' as they are called.

2. A mass of driftwood in a river, impeding or obstructing navigation.

1772 B. ROMANS in P. L. Phillips *Notes B. Romans* 122, I Could not Proceed any farther not being provided with any Tools, to Clear the River, of the Rafts a little higher up. **1844** *La Grange* (Tex.) *Intelligencer* 13 June, From the known indefatigable character of that gentleman, the public may rest assured that the Raft will be removed at the earliest period. **1949** *Southwestern Hist. Quart.* April 411 The first recorded description of the raft of the Colorado River was in 1690.

b. Esp. with reference to a large obstruction in the Red River between Oklahoma and Texas. Now *hist.*

1825 *Austin P.* II. (1924) 1077 This has opened the Eyes of Govt. Relative to the Raft in Red River and measures are about to be taken to open it. **1878** *Cong. Rec.* 16 Jan. 370/2, I am told that trees have been found growing from the vegetable mold, which had formed upon that raft. **1941** DORSEY *Master of Miss.* 173 By good daylight, the *Archimedes* was steaming head-on into the Raft.

3. In special combs.: (1) **raft bridge,** (see quot.), *obs.;* (2) **duck,** (*a*) the scaup duck, *Nyroca marila*, or a related species, (*b*) the redhead, *Nyroca americana*, also **red-headed raft duck.**

(1) **1862** in MOORE *Rebellion Rec.* V. II. 478 Over this stream there is a floating or raft-bridge. — (2) (*a*) **1824** LATHAM *Gen. Hist. Birds* X. 302 [The] Scaup Duck . . . is known in Georgia, and called by some the Raft Duck. **1856** *Spirit of Times* 13 Dec. 242/2 Of ducks, the most numerous, at this season, are the scaups, *Fuligula Marila*, known on Long Island and the Jersey shores as 'broad bill,' on the Delaware as 'blue bill,' on the Chesapeake as the 'black head,' and in Virginia as the 'raft duck.' **1917** *Birds of Amer.* I. 135. (*b*) **1888** TRUMBULL *Names of Birds* 51 *Aythya americana.* . . . From Pamlico Sound to South Carolina commonly known as the Red-Headed Raft Duck. **1917** *Birds of Amer.* I. 131.

As the last term in **Indian, log, lumber, pine, timber, tule raft.**

*** raft,** *v.*[1] **1.** *tr.* To cross (a stream) by means of a raft. **2.** *intr.* To use a raft, travel on a raft. **3.** * *To raft off,* to begin a voyage on a raft, to push *off* on a raft. All *colloq.*

(1) **1765** ROGERS *Journals* 177 The river St. Francis . . . is very still water and may be easily rafted where you cross it. **1845** FRÉMONT *Exped.* 251 We had expected to raft the river. — (2) **1741** *N. Eng. Hist. & Gen. Reg.* XXXIII. 330 We met with great difficulty in passing that River, first attempting to wade . . . , then tried to Raft but it was so shallow in some places we could not use it. **1753** WASHINGTON *Diaries* I. 57 Sent our Horses a little way up French Creek to raft over and encamp. — (3) **1841** COOPER *Deerslayer* vi, These foxes will be rafting off to storm your castle. *Ib.* viii, Vagabonds will have to swim for it, or raft off, to come near this place.

raft ræft, *v.*[2] [f. **raft,* *n.*, multitude.] *intr.* To go, associate *with. Colloq. Rare.* — **1888** DELAND *J. Ward* 173 He hadn't no trade learned, neither,—just rafted with men as bad as him.

*** rafter,** *n.* **1.** (See quot.) **2. rafter level,** a homemade level of wooden strips or laths. *Obs.*

(1) **1889** *Cent.* 825/3 *Carline,* . . . a transverse iron or wooden bar placed across the top of a railroad-car from side to side to support the roof-boards. Sometimes called a *rafter.* — (2) **1786** WASHINGTON *Diaries* III. 106 After doing this, and levelling part of the ground (with a Rafter level). . . . I intended to have run a course or two of Fencing. **1834** J. F. BURKE *Brit. Husbandry* I. 534 In America, where it is much used for ascertaining the declination of land, it is called a rafter-level.

*** rag,** *n.*

1. *pl.* Paper money, esp. depreciated bank notes. *Obs.*

The *OED* shows "rag" used of money 1590–*a*1700, but the use shown here is prob. a new and independent development.

1782 J. TRUMBULL *M'Fingal* 97 O'er heaps of rags, he waves his wand, All turn to gold at his command. **1830** *Mechanics' Press* (Utica, N.Y.) 10 April 171/3 Over $100,000 of these *rags* have been palmed upon the community. **1868** in GUILD *Old Times* (1878) 375 The United States have $350,000,000 of these bonds deposited to enable private individuals to bank and issue the 'rags' as currency of the country, not drawing six per cent., the lawful interest, but more generally from twenty to twenty-five per cent. on the issues, while the government pays to these banks the gold interest on these bonds.

attrib. **1817** PAULDING *Lett. from South* II. 122 This comfortable dog palmed upon us a bank-note of some distant Rag-Manufactory. **1818** *Niles' Reg.* 29 Aug. 3/2 However, we see in the newspaper; that the cashier of a 'full bred' *rag shop* in the western country, lately stabbed and killed a respectable citizen seeking the payment of debts due to him. **1840** *Liberator* (Boston) 21 Aug. 134/2 Stop your ears against the din of 'hard cider and log cabins,' hard currency and rag currency. **1870** M. H. SMITH *20 Years Wall St.* 366 They denounced the certificates as rag capital, and would have nothing to do with the investment.

b. In obs. combs.: (1) ***rag baby,** *transf.* a symbol used by Thomas Nast, and perhaps other cartoonists, for inflation brought on by the issuance of paper currency; (2) **bank,** a bank that issued or dealt in paper money; (3) **baron,** a financial magnate dealing in paper money.

(1) **1875** *Chi. Tribune* 16 Oct. 6/4 The 'rag-baby' will yet show remarkable signs of life in Pennsylvania, in Indiana, and in all the Southern States. **1879** *Cin. Commercial* 13 Feb. 4/1 If the Democrats could succeed in nominating Grant for the Republicans, and the Republicans could impose Tilden on the Democrats, there might arise a good time for a third party, provided the Rag Baby was not put in the lead. — (2) **1818** *Niles' Reg.* 30 May 227/1 The title of the bank shall be—'the rag-bank of the universe.' **1831** *American* (Harrodsburg, Ky.) 8 July 2/2 We would be glad to know if Mr. Harlan and Mitchel prefer *two* rag Banks to one of *Gold* and *Silver.* — (3) **1818** *Niles' Reg.* XIV. 226/1 The name of a *Jew* and 'rag-*baron*' is synonimous. **1855** *Chi. Times* 8 March 2/1 He advocates . . . treating the hostility of the 'rag barons' with the contempt it deserves.

c. In derivatives: **rag-monger,** =**rag baron; ragocrat,** an advocate of rag money or a banker who issued it. Both *obs.*

1818 *Niles' Reg.* 26 Sep. 65/1 If it were otherwise, an *illicit* rag monger, who gave *all* his good money in exchange for counterfeit paper, knowing it to be such, might plead in excuse for passing such paper, that it afforded him the means of subsistence! — **1838** *N.Y. Advt. & Exp.* 18 April 3/1 The Government of this country has . . . called them [the merchants and the banks] all sorts of 'Rag Barons,' 'Ragocrats' and 'Aristocrats,' and the like. **1842** H. W. BEESON *Speech* 9 July 12/2 (Th. S.), 'Pauper labor' indeed—and we have now, thanks to the ragocrats, got some of that blessing here.

2. A piece of music in ragtime. Cf. **3.** (12) below.

1914 *World's Work* Feb. 445/1 Next you hear the Portland Band and The Round-Up Band in the bleachers occupying the moments with well rendered 'rags' and martial airs. **1948** *Dly. Oklahoman* (Okla. City) 31 Oct. D. 18/1 If record buyers can stand just one more 'Twelfth Street Rag,' it should be by the concert pianist, Liberace.

3. In special combs.: (1) **rag carpet,** a carpet made of rags, esp. one made by weaving the rags together; (2) **carpeted,** *a.* covered or furnished with a rag carpet; (3) **carpeting,** carpeting woven or otherwise made of rags; (4) **chewing,** the action of chewing the rag, *slang,* see **b.** below; (5) **city,** in the West in the days of the gold rush, a town in which the people lived chiefly in tents or flimsy houses made largely of cloth; (6) **house,** *W.* a house made chiefly of cloth, *obs.;* (7) **lamp,** a lamp consisting of a rag lying in a bath of oil or lard, *obs.;* (8) **rug,** a rug made of rag strips tied or sewn together, sometimes having a warp of heavy cotton; (9) **shag,** (see quot. 1909), *colloq.;* (10) **shanty,** *W.* =**rag house;** (11) **store,** ?a dry-goods store, *rare;* (12) **time,** music characterized by frequent syncopation, as in many Negro melodies, with a regularly accented accompaniment, also attrib.; (13) ***weed,** a hardy weed of grayish-green color, belonging to the genus *Ambrosia,* cf. **sand ragweed;** (14) **wick,** a rag used as a wick, cf. **rag lamp.**

(1) **1823** *N.Y. Mirror* 9 Aug. 10/1 The floor was covered with rich Venetian carpeting, carefully preserved from wear by sundry pieces of household manufacture, denominated rag-carpet. **1944** WILSON *Passing Inst.* 9 On the floor was the best rag carpet owned by the family. — (2) **1845** KIRKLAND *Western Clearings* 185, I led the young gentleman through the shop into the rag-carpeted sitting-room of Mrs. Larkins. **1889** *Cent. Mag.* Jan. 410/2 The fire . . . flung strange shadows over the rag-carpeted floor. — (3) **1813** *Niles' Reg.* III. 329/1 Articles manufactured by Mrs. Webster, . . . a laudable example of female industry, and economy [include] 22 yards of bottle green and black cloth, . . . 24 do. rag carpeting. **1887** I. ALDEN *Little Fishers* ix, Her hands had been busy over long seams of rag carpeting. — (4) **1885** *Santa Fé Weekly New Mexican* 1 Oct. 1/3 After a few minutes rag-chawing a verdict of 'came to his death from unknown causes,' is promptly rendered.

(5) **1851** in *Pioneer* (S.F.) (1854) Jan. 43 He started for Bidwell's Bar, a rag city about thirty-five miles from Marysville. *a***1916** WEBSTER *Gold Seekers of '49* (1917) 123 Sacramento City at this time was built principally of cloth houses and tents. . . . It was generally known as the 'Rag City.' — (6) **1890** CUSTER *Following Guidon* 220, I envied that [a dugout] for the wind would not toy with his habitation . . . as it did our 'rag houses.' — (7) **1889** MARK TWAIN *Conn. Yankee* xlii. 531 He had re-instituted the ancient rag-lamp. — (8) **1920** LEWIS *Main Street* 131 Her neat black shoes firm on a rag-rug, . . . Mrs. Warren listened without comment. **1948** *Chi. D. News* 27 Aug. 10/4 The display includes braided, hook and rag rugs, spreads, fancy table cloths, doilies and knitted wear. — (9) **1887** *Conn. Courant* 7 July (*Cent.*), While the Ragshags were marching, . . . [he] caught his foot in his ragged garment and fell. **1909** WEBSTER 1764/4 *Ragshag,* . . . a ragged person, esp. a masquerader.

(10) **1851** L. CLAPPE *Lett. from Calif.* 94 The first artificial elegance which attracts your vision is a large rag shanty, roofed, however, with a rude kind of shingles. — (11) **1869** MARK TWAIN *Innocents Abroad* xvi. 157 (R.), Filthy dens on first floors, with rag stores in them. — (12) **1897** ADE *Pink Marsh* 159 He told of his belief that the angels in heaven played 'ragtime' music. **1905** *Denver Republican* 6 Sep. 4/4 This part of the crowd failed to respond to ragtime, Sousa, or even the masters. **1947** PAUL *Linden* 331 The first ragtime song I remember was restrained, indeed, in its syncopation, and was inspired by the advent, or increased popularity, of the telephone. — (13) **1790** DEANE *N.-Eng. Farmer* 176/1 The milk of cows in summer is sometimes made very bitter by their feeding on rag-weed. **1948** *Democrat* 23 Sep. 7/2 Ragweed is responsible for about 80 per cent of hay fever discomfort. — (14) *a***1918** G. STUART *On Frontier* 31 A tin lamp holding about a quart of lard with a rag wick in its spout which, when lighted, would cast a strong light for several yards.

b. *To chew the rag,* to talk, argue, to talk at length. Hence **rag chewing.** *Slang.*

1901 *McClure's Mag.* April 576/2 There are a few soreheads . . . who chew the rag about corruption an' the way the town's run. **1939** *These Are Our Lives* 561 They can have more fun settin' there chewin' the rag.

As the last term in **bank, boiled, chalk, dish, gland, medicine, rebel, rug, sugar, wash rag(s).**

*** rag,** *v.* **1.** *tr.* and *intr.* To dance, or play (tunes), in ragtime. **2.** *To rag out,* to dress up. Both *slang.*

(1) **1917** *Lit. Digest* 25 Aug. 28/2 Jazz bands take popular tunes and rag them to death to make jazz. **1919** *Lit. Digest* 26 April 28/1 While society once 'ragged,' they now 'jazz.' — (2) **1865** BROWNE *A. Ward; His Travels* 180 Don't make fun of our clothes. . . . We ain't goin' to *rag out* till we git to Nevady! **1894** HOYT *Texas Steer* (1925) II.

20 Speaking of clothes, don't you think me and ma are ragged out pretty well for folks right off a ranch?

∗**ragged,** *a.* In combs.: (1) **ragged edge,** the verge, *colloq.;* (2) **island,** ?an island having an irregular shore line, *obs.*, cf. **ragged plain;** (3) **orchis,** (see quot. 1909); (4) **plain,** (see quot.), *obs.*

(1) **1878** BEADLE *Western Wilds* 91 He is constantly in trouble, and sometimes on the ragged edge of starvation. **1911** LINCOLN *Cap. Warren's Wards* 254 The Dunns are dangerously close to the ragged edge. — (2) **1639** in *Amer. Sp.* XV. 381/1 Lying towards the head of a bay behind the ragged islands. **1642** *Ib.*, Lying before the ragged Islands commonly known by the name of the Long ponds. — (3) **1814** BIGELOW *Florula Bostoniensis* 206 *Orchis psycodes.* Ragged Orchis. . . . This is our common species. **1909** *Cent. Supp.* 905/1 *Ragged orchis, Blephariglottis lacera*, of the eastern United States, with greenish-yellow flowers, the lip deeply fringed or lacerate. — (4) **1634** in *Pub. Col. Soc.* III. 186 Certain rivers stopping the fire from coming to clear that place of the country, hath made it unuseful and troublesome to travel through, insomuch, that it is called 'ragged plain,' because it tears and rents the cloaths of them that pass.

∗**ragging,** *n.* (See quot.) — **1890** *Cent.* 4939/1 *Ragging*, . . . a method of fishing for the striped-bass, etc., in which a red rag is used as a fly.

rah rɑ, *interj.* Short for *hurrah* (see also quot. 1877). Usu. reduplicative and attrib. Also **rah-rahing,** *a.*, and **rah-rahism,** *n.*

1872 *Harper's Mag.* Jan. 319/1 The other [battery] flashed in the pan, and a few voices piped, 'Rah for Seymour!' **1877** BARTLETT 792 *'Rah! 'rah! 'rah!* The formula for a cheer by the students of Harvard College, Cambridge. **1892** *Outing* Oct. 37/1 He no longer felt stage-fright surrounded by the 'rah-'rahing mob.' **1930** *Chi. D. Maroon* 9 Dec. 4/1 Students engage in rah-rahism because it gives them a certain simple amount of enjoyment. **1949** *N.O. Times-Picayune Mag.* 6 Nov. 5/4 Loyola missed out on most of the headaches and some of the raucous 'rah, rah' fun of the era.

b. rah-rah boy, a college student.

1924 *Public Opinion* 15 Feb. 152/1 Whether we liked it or not, college and life are better mixers than they were when father was a rah-rah boy and wore those comedy clothes.

∗**raid,** *n.* As the last term in **Missouri, Price raid.**

∗**raider,** *n.* (See quot. 1866.) *Slang. Obs.* — **1866** GOSS *Soldier's Story* 102 Where a thief [at Andersonville prison] had the boldness to steal in open daylight, and by a dash, grab and run, to get off with his booty, he was termed a 'raider,' which was considered one grade above the sneaking 'flanker.' **1894** MARK TWAIN *Pudd'nhead Wilson* xiii. 776 (R.), It's perfectly plain that the thief took advantage of the reception . . . to raid the vacant houses undisturbed. . . . It's the same old raider.

∗**rail,** *n.*

In **railbird** (*a*) and in some of the expressions cited at the conclusion of this entry, "rail" alludes to a bird and hence is not the same word as that shown in the other combs. and expressions given.

1. In misc. combs.: (1) **railbed,** the roadbed of a railroad, *rare;* (2) **bird,** (*a*) the Carolina rail, *Porzana carolina*, (*b*) a spectator who, as it were, perches on a rail, also one who secretly estimates the speed of race horses in their private trials, *slang*, cf. ∗**clocker;** (3) **car,** a railroad coach, also attrib.; (4) **cut,** a portion of a log cut off to be split into fence rails, the length of this, approx. ten or twelve feet; (5) **fence,** see as a main entry; (6) **length,** the length of a fence rail, about ten feet; (7) **mauling,** splitting fence rails; (8) **pen,** a pen made of fence rails; (9) **portage,** a portage where a railroad is used; (10) **road,** see as a main entry; (11) **sickness,** illness from riding on a train; (12) **splitter,** see as a main entry; (13) **splitting,** the action of splitting rails, also attrib.; (14) **stuff,** =**rail timber,** *colloq.;* (15) **tie,** a crosstie; (16) **timber,** timber suitable for splitting into fence rails; (17) **tree,** a tree suitable for splitting into fence rails.

(1) **1880** MARK TWAIN *Tramp Abroad* 306 The railbed was as steep as a roof. — (2) (*a*) **1808** ASHE *Travels* 160 [Among the birds described by Catesby is] Soree. Rail-bird. *Rallus Virginianus.* **1865** *Atlantic Mo.* XV. 95 Gunners congregated in numbers dangerous to themselves, shooting rail and reed-birds. (*b*) **1892** *Columbus* (O.) *Dispatch* 24 Nov., The 'rail birds,' that is, those who are clinging to the pine boards forming the press box, began to shout, 'Left, right, left, right.' **1944** *Chi. D. News* 4 Aug. 24/1 The Homewood rail birds, captivated by her unusually lengthy strides, decided to measure her prints. **1949** *Chi. D. News* 7 May 1 (*legend*), Olympia, the Railbirds' Choice, Struts His Stuff. — (3) **1834** *Knickerb.* III. 112 My time sped again at the rate of rail-car travel. **1839** *Holyoke Diaries* 183 Went to Boston in the rail Car first time. **1946** *Life* 27 May 6/2 He pointed to the rail-car shortage of the 1945 marketing season. — (4) **1774** PATTEN *Diary* 328 Jamey and Bob and I went and cut 4 Rail cuts on Matthew Littles lott between and little meadow and split 2 of them allmost they made 35 rails. **1880** *Scribner's Mo.* Feb. 503/2 The pole fence was laid after the same fashion of a rail fence, only the poles were longer than rail-cuts.

(6) **1650** *Rowley Rec.* 61 Number 1 to Mr. Carlton; thirty rail Lengths. **1935** *Ada* (Ohio) *Herald* 1 Nov., Cutting it into about three rail lengths . . . was no child's play. — (7) **1867** in *Amer. Sp.* XXII. 204/2 Jis' go at hit like hit wer a job ove rail-maulin'. — (8) **1842** *Cultivator* IX. 160 Buckwheat may be thrashed upon just such a rail pen, covered over with rails, much better than upon the ground. **1948** DICK *Dixie Frontier* 98 The cattle and horses either ran in the forest or were kept in a rail pen. — (9) **1882** *Harper's Mag.* Dec. 4/1 Another stretch of river reaches to the Dalles, the second cataract, passed by a rail portage fifteen miles long.

(11) **1905** *Scientific Amer.* 478 'Rail-sickness' may claim its victims. — (13) **1826** FLINT *Recoll.* 34, I find I am chartered on a rail-splitting Yankee. **1887** J. KIRKLAND *Zury* 21 Gluts are wooden wedges used in rail-splitting. — (14) **1774** PATTEN *Diary* 328, I got leave of Matthew Little to cut Rail stuff on his land that we began to cut on and the boys cutt one or 2 cuts more.

(15) **1854** J. R. BARTLETT *Personal Narr.* II. 574 In the valley of the Santa Cruz, between Tubac and Santa Cruz, are very considerable forests of mezquit, the best material for rail-ties that can be found. — (16) **1662** *Portsmouth Rec.* 386 He is to presarve all the Rayle timbar. **1791** PATTEN *Diary* 91, I cutt Rail timber on the highway at the west end of Benjn Smiths land and I got 3¾ Quarts of Rum from John Bell. **1878** GUILD *Old Times* 117 The first was interrogated very closely as to the cutting of some rail-timber and its value. — (17) **1676** *Jamaica* (L.I.) *Rec.* I. 182 They are to have Liberty to take any timber . . . in our commons exsept Clappborde trees and Rayle trees under eightene inches.

2. In phrases: (1) *To split rails*, to make fence rails by splitting rail timber; (2) *to ride a rail*, (see quot.), *obs.;* (3) *to ride* (someone) *on a rail*, to punish (someone) by placing him astride a rail and carrying him about as an object of derision, *colloq.;* (4) *to beat the devil and carry a rail*, to beat most decisively—from the rural custom sometimes followed of having a superior contestant in a foot race carry a rail as a handicap; (5) *to hunt the top rail*, to flee most precipitately, as over a high rail fence, *colloq.*

(1) **1714** HEMPSTEAD *Diary* 38, I was at home al day spliting Railes & holing Posts. **1820** *Niles' Reg.* XVIII. 256/1 At 97 he went into the woods and split 100 chesnut rails in less than a day. **1907** *St. Nicholas* Oct. 1078/1 You never split a rail in your life. [**1945** *This Week Mag.* 15 Sep. 2/3 True, there are no longer rails to split or woodboxes to keep full.] — (2) **1836** T. POWER *Impressions* I. 299 Here I enjoyed my first lesson in what is familiarly termed riding a rail. . . . The term is derived from a fence-rail being occasionally used to supply the place of a broken thoro'-brace, by which all these stages are hung. — (3) **1837** HAWTHORNE *Twice-Told Tales* (1879) I. 126 The millmen . . . [hesitated whether to] ride him on a rail, or refresh him with an ablution at the town-pump. **1949** *Sat. Ev. Post* 2 July 67/1, I feel . . . somewhat like the man who was being ridden out of town on a rail. — (4) **1872** *Dly. Gaz.* (Little Rock, Ark.) 25 Aug., For a sample of honesty this beats the devil and carries a rail.

(5) **1912** BOWER *Flying U.* 203 It's hunt the top rail, and do it quick, when old Weary straightens out his lips like that.

As the last term in **ail, bottom, Carolina, cedar, chestnut, clapper, draw, edge, English, fence, fencing, guard, H, hitch, hitching, horse, king, loafer, New York, oak, pine, single, slip, snake, sora, split, strap, T, third, tie, Virginia, X rail.**

∗**rail,** *v. tr.* To lay (a railroad track) with rails. — **1888** *Harper's Mag.* June 125/2 One hundred and fifty miles of new road graded last year, which was to receive its rails this spring, will not be railed.

rail fence.

1. A fence made of wooden rails, usu. constructed in zigzag fashion, but sometimes straight with posts at the joints.

Rail fences differ considerably in structure. See *L. A.* Map 117 for the different names and different types of such fences. See also **stake and rider(ed) fence, ten-rail fence.**

1649 *Charlestown Land Rec.* 110, I doe sell . . . five Akers of planting Land . . . [bounded] on the North by the ould raile fence. **1761** *Boston Selectmen* 161 Mr. Cushing is desired to repair the Rail Fence round the Common. **1880** *Scribner's Mo.* Feb. 503/2 The pole fence was laid after the same fashion of a rail fence, only the poles were longer than rail-cuts. **1949** *Chi. D. News* 9 Aug. 6/2 Floyd and Joe find themselves straddling a rail fence.

b. crooked rail fence, = **worm fence.**
1831 J. FOWLER *Tour New York* 79 The usual description of fences are *worm*, or crooked rail fences. **1856** *Rep. Comm. Patents 1855: Agric.* 20 Formerly, cattle were kept here through the winter with very little protection except a crooked rail fence.

c. rail and stake fence, a stake and ridered fence.
1869 *Rep. Comm. Agric. 1868* 258 This form of thorn fence is similar to the old time 'herring-bone' rail and stake fence.

2. A fence of the post-and-rail type having a designated number of rails, as **five, four, six rail fence.**
[**1640** in SHURTLEFF *Log Cabin* (1939) 119 Fencing with 5 railes, substantiall posts, good railes, well wrought, sett vp and rammed, that pigs, swine, goates and other cattel may be kept out.] **1669** *Groton Rec.* 28 We order that all the out side fences about all corn-feilds orchards and gardens in towne shalbe a sufficient five Rail fence. **1829** *Yankee* April 120/2 Saw three bipeds in gowns jump over a 'four rail fence' without touching—conjectured they had practised the Italian gymnastics. **1945** *Chi. Tribune* 12 Aug. VII. 1/3 Then she . . . climbs a six-rail fence, walks thru a watermelon patch, a cornfield, and a patch of weeds, opens a stock gate, and is on the highway.

As the last term in **Virginia, worm, zigzag rail fence.**

rail-ride ˈrelˌraɪd, *v. tr.* To ride (a person) on a rail. Also **rail-riding,** *n.* — **1861** *N.Y. Tribune* 22 Oct. 4/6 A dozen scamps . . . will be hired by the well-supplied Aristocrat to tar-and-feather, rail-ride, shoot or stab or hang, the poor Man with One Nigger. **1902** CLAPIN 328 *Rail-riding*, a savage punishment, which consists . . . in placing the culprit upon the sharp edge of a rail, to be carried through the streets.

*** railroad,** *n.*

1. (See quots.) *Obs.* Cf. **corduroy road.**
1835 ABDY *Journal* III. 65 The road was hilly and bad; great part of it being what is vulgarly called 'corduroy,' or 'bang-up,' or 'railroad.' The term alludes to the planks or rails, which are placed transversely; so that the road presents the appearance of [corduroy]. **1852** CASEY *Two Yrs.* 164 The worst kind of stage-road is what is called a rail-road, viz., a number of logs laid parallel across a swamp, or bottom, over which the drive is a succession of jolt, jolt, jolt, and would most certainly be a good prescription to a dyspeptic patient, or one affected with ennui.

2. a. A kind of liquor. **b.** A railroad train. **c.** A college cheer, presumably one that imitates the sound of a railroad locomotive. All *obs.*
(**a**) **1835** *Vade Mecum* (Phila.) 8 Aug. 3/6 The pair were well acquainted with that species of liquor now styled 'Railroad,' and vended at three cents a glass. **1857** *Santa Barbara* (Calif.) *Gaz.* 29 Jan. 4/3 The drinks ain't no good here—there ain't no variety in them, neither; no white-nose, apple-jack, stone-wall, chain-lightning, railroad, hailstorm. — (**b**) **1856** MARK TWAIN *Adv. Snodgrass* 26 Drat my buttons, if I wasn't astonished at the way that rail road was a gittin over the ground. — (**c**) **1902** BELL *Hope Loring* 170 'Now a railroad for Poe,' cried Hope, when the first [cheer] had ceased.

3. In combs.: (1) **railroad car,** one of the coaches or carriages of a railroad train; (2) **chain,** railroads so connected as to make possible continuous travel between given points, *rare*, cf. *** chain,** *n.* **2;** (3) **City,** (see quot.), *obs.;* (4) **connection,** communication by rail, railroad facilities; (5) **crossing,** a place where a railroad and a highway cross each other; (6) **crosstie,** = **crosstie;** (7) **cut,** (see quot. 1940); (8) **depot,** = *** depot,** *n.* **1;** (9) **eating house,** a restaurant at a railroad station; (10) **euchre,** (see **euchre,** *n.* **1. c,** quot. 1889); (11) **fever,** great enthusiasm for the construction of railroads; (12) **fire,** a fire caused by a railway locomotive; (13) **grade,** a graded portion of a railroad track; (14) **grant,** a land grant made to a railroad; (15) **iron,** iron rails, iron for rails, cf. **T railroad iron;** (16) **land,** public land given to railroads to help finance their construction, also attrib.; (17) **limits,** (see quot.), *obs.;* (18) **monitor,** a 32-pound rifled gun mounted on an armored railroad car, and used by the Confederates at the battle of Savage's station, *obs.;* (19) **plow,** = **railway plow;** (20) **pool,** a combination of several railroads for their mutual advantage; (21) **rope,** rope of a kind used on railroads; (22) **tie,** a crosstie; (23) **time,** (*a*) fast time, (*b*) the system of time used by a railroad.

(**1**) **1830** *Mechanics' Press* (Utica, N.Y.) 17 April 183/3 The prizes are to be awarded mostly in silver medals; and are offered on the following subjects: Iron castings, . . . Steam Carriages, Rail Road Car, Canal Boat. **1946** *Life* 27 May 6/2 Marshall . . . reported the need for 50 railroad cars immediately. — (**2**) **1837** *Richmond* (Va.) *Enquirer* 7 Feb. 3/3 The Rail-road chain will soon be complete from the interior of North Carolina almost to Boston. — (**3**) **1839** *Ladies' Repository* Jan. 51/2 Indianapolis is the 'Railroad City,' from the number of railroads centering at that point. — (**4**) **1865** KELLOGG *Rebel Prisons* 47 [Tarboro, N.C.] is in railroad connection with the South by a short branch road. **1884** *Gringo & Greaser* 15 Jan. 1/1 The 'Democrat Pictorial Annual for 1884' . . . has a map showing Albuquerque's railroad connections, present and prospective.

(**5**) **1834** *Sun* (N.Y.) 31 Oct. 3/1 The Directors of the Boston and Providence rail road have caused large sign boards to be placed at each crossing, over the highway, with a conspicuous notice upon it in these words: *Rail Road Crossing:—Look out for the Engine.* **1882** LATHROP *Echo of Passion* xiii, It was a solemn group that wound up the highway from the railroad crossing, coming back. — (**6**) **1946** WILSON *Fidelity* 16 A tie-hack, I might say by way of explanation, was a professional maker of railroad crossties. — (**7**) **1862** F. MOORE *Rebellion Rec.* V. II. 403 On Friday morning we held the ridge, in front of which runs an incomplete railroad-cut. **1940** *Quiz* [Quest. 13] What is a railroad cut? When the right-of-way of a railroad is cut through

Railroad cut

a hill, knoll or slope to provide a roadway, the excavation is called a cut. — (**8**) **1836** J. HANCOCK *Merchant's Guide Boston* 63 (Ernst). **1945** *Chi. Tribune* 3 June VII. 1/5 At the railroad depot the water was just ready to go into the door. — (**9**) **1873** *Newton Kansan* 5 June 3/2 Wm. Pierce is having the old age Saloon entirely remodeled for a railroad eating house. **1902** O. HENRY *Roads of Destiny* 186 [The passengers] slouched limberly over to the railroad eating-house.

(**11**) **1852** *Ore. Statesman* 20 Jan. 1/6 The people up country are likewise agitated with the railroad fever. **1880** *Bradstreet's* 15 Sep. 8/1 A railroad fever is pervading various portions of the state. — (**12**) **1892** *Vt. Agric. Rep.* XII. 122 The railroad fires have been most destructive in this County, having burned over thousands of acres. — (**13**) **1894** ROBLEY *Bourbon Co., Kans.* 14 The pike, or grade, like a railroad grade, was constructed across all river and creek bottoms. — (**14**) **1857** *Lawrence Republican* 4 June 4 There is . . . the question of Railroad grants made by Congress to all the new States but one. **1946** PARTRIDGE & BETTMANN *As We Were* 77 Kansas—a State richly endowed by railroad grants welcomed the new settlers.

(**15**) **1827** SHERWOOD *Gaz. Georgia* 40 Hollow ware is made in abundance, and some railroad iron. **1887** *Courier-Journal* 3 Feb. 3/3 Eight young men . . . were set at work unloading railroad iron from the steamer Lake Winnipeg. — (**16**) **1872** *Newton Kansan* 17 Oct. 3/3 Mr. Wm. B. Blake . . . having purchased railroad land east of town, is about building a fine residence thereon. **1890** *Stock Grower & Farmer* 8 March 5/3 The intervening sections of the Atlantic & Pacific railroad land grant [in Ariz.] are owned by the cattle men and are not fenced. **1908** *Pacific Mo.* Jan. 6/1 The people on the railroad lands began to want deeds. [**1947** *Mich. Hist.* June 187 This timber was also on railroad grant land.] — (**17**) **1873** *Harper's Mag.* Nov. 913/1 The policy of the government in holding its own lands within what are called 'railroad limits'—that is to say, within twenty miles on each side of the railroad—for settlement under the pre-emption and homestead laws . . . prevents land monopoly in this region. — (**18**) **1885** *Cent. Mag.* July 460/1 General Lee's famous railroad monitor was approaching. — (**19**) **1854** *Pa. Agric. Rep.* 425 R. Hall, for railroad plow and boy's plow.

(**20**) **1886** A. T. HADLEY *Railroad Transportation* 91 The earliest railroad pools were probably developed in New England, but they were on a small scale. — (**21**) **1833** *Amer. R.R. Jrnl.* II. 207/3 Townsend and Durfee, of Palmyra, *Manufacturers of Railroad Rope* . . . offer to supply Rope. — (**22**) **1856** WHIPPLE *Explor. Ry. Route* I. 79 *Douglass spruce*, which is also abundant upon the sides of the mountains, would afford a better material for railroad ties. **1945** *Reader's Digest* Jan. 53/2 He made 334 railroad ties and sold them. — (**23**) (*a*) **1864** CATE *Two Soldiers* 41, I obtained another horse and we made railroad time until we reached Big Creek. (*b*) **1880** *Cimarron News & Press* 22 July 3/1 Local time is 55 minutes slower than railroad time. **1946** WILSON *Fidelity* 42 He said that Fidelity kept sun time rather than railroad time because it was nearer the sun.

b. Designating persons and groups of persons having to do with railroads: (1) **railroad brakeman,** =**brakeman;** (2) **commission,** a group of men in a state charged with the duty of regulating and controlling common carriers, esp. railroads, in the public interest; (3) **commissioner,** a member of a railroad commission; (4) **conductor,** =***conductor 3;** (5) **grader,** one who works at grading a railroad; (6) **king,** a leader in the railroad industry; (7) **lawyer,** a lawyer employed by a railroad to safeguard and further its interests; (8) **lobby,** a lobby maintained by a railroad to promote legislation in its favor, also **railroad lobbyist;** (9) **magnate,** a wealthy railroad-owner or operator; (10) **man,** a railroader, a man well disposed toward a railroad or toward the construction of railroads; (11) **president,** the president of a railroad company; (12) **prospector,** one who is exploring the possibilities for a railroad; (13) **ring,** a group of persons who manipulate the affairs of a railroad for their own interests; (14) **senator,** a member of the U.S. Senate who works for the interests of railroads; (15) **tycoon,** =**railroad magnate.**

(1) 1898 *K.C. Star* 18 Dec. 2/3 Grant Meade became a railroad brakeman. — **(2) 1887** *Doc. & Sp. in Amer. Hist.* (1943) III. 162 Investigate any complaint forwarded by the railroad commissioner or railroad commission of any State or Territory. **1914** *Cyclo. Amer. Govt.* III. 109/1 At the beginning of the twentieth century, nearly every state in the United States had a railroad commission. — **(3) 1845** *Mass. Acts & Resolves* 582 The Governor . . . shall appoint . . . five persons, who shall, together, constitute 'the Board of Railroad Commissioners.' **1946** HOLBROOK *Lost Men* 262 He was made railroad commissioner of Iowa. — **(4) 1842** *Liberator* (Boston) 21 Jan. 10/1, I care not in what garb you may appear—whether it is the habit of a preacher of the gospel, or with the kingly power of a rail-road conductor, or in any other garb—you are emphatically a child of the devil.

(5) 1945 MARSHALL *Santa Fe* 10 Dan Blush, the contractor, was offering $1.75 a day for railroad graders. — **(6) 1868** *Comm. & Fin. Chron.* VI. 295/1 Two railroad kings . . . have entered the lists. **1904** TARBELL *Hist. Standard Oil Co.* I. 93 The acquiescence of the 'railroad kings' . . . was followed by an unwilling promise to break the contracts with the company. — **(7) 1890** DAVIS *Gallegher* 6 Richard F. Burrbank was one of the most prominent of New York's railroad lawyers. **1946** FOREMAN *Last Trek* 234 The oft-recurring handiwork of the railroad lawyer in these Indian treaties is obvious to the reader. — **(8) 1888** *Boston Globe* 5 Feb. 1/3 If any 'railroad lobbyist' cast reflections on his character he would wipe out the whole kit and caboodle of them. **1913** LA FOLLETTE *Autobiog.* 124 The railroad lobby outside and the railroad members inside would have prevented any action. — **(9) 1885** CRAWFORD *Amer. Politician* 174 Great railroad magnates . . . found in him a character and intelligence precisely suited to their ends. **1890** *Boston Jrnl.* 9 Jan. 2/1 This control may place [great power] in the hands of railroad magnates should they take an interest in deciding the political fortunes of the State.

(10) 1863 G. HAMILTON *Gala-Days* 70 The railroad-men at Saratoga tell you that you can go straight from there to the foot of Lake George. **1870** RAE *Westward by Rail* 191 Throughout the state of California the scheme [of putting through a railroad] became so popular, that to be a 'railroad man' was one of the best claims wherewith to secure the votes of electors. **1949** *S.F. News* 14 March 14/1 Nearly 400,000 miners and 50,000 railroad men on coal-hauling lines face two weeks without work because John L. Lewis has shut down the coal mines east of the Mississippi. — **(11) 1892** MARK TWAIN *Amer. Claimant* xiv. 149 (R.), A lawyer, doctor, editor, author, tinker, loafer, railroad president, saint. **1949** *Chi. D. News* 9 Aug. 10/5 His chance of becoming an American railroad president is probably about one in ten million. — **(12) 1894** CABLE *J. March* xx, Two or three Northern capitalists—railroad prospectors—were on the following Friday, at the Swanee Hotel. — **(13) 1870** *Nation* 12 May 296/2 The performance may be considered the greatest raid ever yet made by a railroad Ring on a State Government. — **(14) 1837** *Nation* 10 March 199/1 [Mr. Blodgett] is in one sense a 'railroad man.' . . . But it is said that he will not be a 'railroad Senator.'

(15) 1947 BEEBE *Mixed Train Dly.* 133 The angry voices of farmers and their elected legislators at first irritated and then terrified the railroad tycoons in Denver.

As the last term in **belt, cable, dog's tail, double, electric, elevated, horse, land grant, lateral, logging, Pacific, pole, portage, ship, street, subterranean, trunk, underground railroad.**

***railroad,** *v.*

1. *intr.* To travel by rail, usu. with *it.*

1858 *Harper's Mag.* Dec. 1/2 Railroading it through northern Georgia . . . they arrived at Montgomery. **1908** O. HENRY *Options* 171 From Washington we railroaded it to New Orleans. [**1945** *Tracks* June 31/1 *Rail it,* like its pleasant parallel *go it,* has gone where the whangdoodle mourneth for her firstborn.]

2. To work on a railroad.

1877 BARTLETT 512 *To railroad,* to be a conductor on a railroad. Pennsylvania. **1898** HAMBLEN *Gen. Manager's Story* 22, I had never railroaded in any capacity before. **1949** *L.A. Times* 26 April 20/1 Railroading? We *are* railroading, mister. We made the railroads what they are.

3. *tr.* To send (a person) to a place of punishment or to an institution with immoderate speed and often by means of manufactured or false evidence.

1877 *N.Y. Herald* 9 March 8/4 'Railroaded!' Joe Coburn Takes the Cars for His Ten Years' Home [i.e., Sing Sing]. **1911** *Masses* Jan. 9/1 Any man that becomes obnoxious to the power of wealth or that criticises an administration can be railroaded to jail on any trumped-up charge. **1949** *Chi. Tribune* 29 Dec. 11/1 Every year thousands of our old people, though perfectly sane, are railroaded to state mental institutions.

transf. **1948** *Time* 25 Oct. 28/2 But the Western powers, who wanted to avoid any suspicion of railroading the small nations, politely agreed to answer.

4. To send or carry *into, out,* or *through* in a high-handed manner, to dispatch with undue speed or fraud.

1889 *Boston Jrnl.* 25 Jan. 2/2 The Supreme and Superior Judges in Connecticut . . . are paid only a moderate salary, and are railroaded out of office at the age of seventy. **1900** *Cong. Rec.* 24 Jan. 1129/1 They railroaded their State [Utah] into this Union. **1923** WYATT *Invis. Gods* 176 Herman C. Riley . . . railroaded the infamous anti-civil-service act through the State legislature. **1948** *P.C.C. Chronicle* (Pasadena, Calif.) 7 May 2/5 Gray . . . was unable to railroad the measure through the council.

5. To transport by railroad.

1891 ELLIS *Check* 2134 263 They were 'railroaded' thither. **1893** C. S. LELAND *Memoirs* 69 We were marched and railroaded back to Philadelphia. **1909** *Sat. Ev. Post* 15 May 10/3 The keynote of railroading a circus is simply this: minimum distance combined with maximum population.

railroader ˈrelˌrodɚ, *n.* A person working in some capacity on or with a railroad.

1856 *Iroquois Republican* (Middleport, Ill.) 8 May 3/2 The recent outbreak at Cincinnati was originated by a scuffle between young Walker, a railroader, and Cochran, a rail ripper. **1927** SIRINGO *Riata* 97 Shots could be heard downtown, fired by hilarious cowboys and railroaders. **1945** *Tracks* June 39/1 He praised the railroaders for their achievements in the Sixth War Loan campaign.

***railroading,** *n.* **1.** Traveling by rail. **2.** The action of building or operating a railroad. **3.** The action of rushing something through, also attrib. Cf. ***railroad,** *v.* **3.** and **4.**

(1) 1855 LOWELL *Letters* I. 224, I hoped also to have a quiet Sunday . . . after a week's railroading. **1880** *Harper's Mag.* Aug. 485 [She had] about a hundred miles more of railroading to be done. — **(2) 1870** in TARBELL *Hist. Standard Oil Co.* I. 78 The South Improvement Company . . . may seize upon the lands of other parties for railroading. **1949** *Business Week* 1 Oct. 62/2 Railroading is a service business. — **(3) 1884** *American* VIII. 104 A conviction was secured in an hour or two. . . . The 'railroading' feature . . . produces a painful feeling. **1949** *Chi. Tribune* 29 Dec. 11/2 Of course not all the old people in our mental institutions are victims of railroading.

rail-splitter ˈrelˌsplɪtɚ, *n.* One who splits rails, often in allusion to Abraham Lincoln and his supporters. Cf. **Illinois rail-splitter.**

1860 *Cong. Globe* App. 19 June 462/2 They call him 'Uncle Abe,' 'Old Abe,' 'Honest Old Abe,' 'The old rail-splitter,' 'The flat-boatman,' &c. **1860** *Charleston* (S.C.) *Mercury* 20 Dec. 4/2 The latter was to catch the 'free speech' portion of the community, and the former the 'sleekish' element of the railsplitters; and the game was well played. **1935** *Ada* (Ohio) *Herald* 1 Nov., But the day and generation of railsplitters is behind us. **1949** J. MONAGHAN *This is Ill.* 76 The Lincoln-Douglas Debates gave the Rail Splitter a national reputation.

b. *Rail-splitter of the West,* Abraham Lincoln, a nickname.

1860 *Charleston* (S.C.) *Mercury* 29 Nov. 1/3 That you will quail before the lank Rail-splitter of the West,—I *cannot believe it.*

***railway**, *n.*

1. (See quots.) *Obs.*

*a***1870** CHIPMAN *Notes on Bartlett* 353 *Railway* is, in the U.S., applied to a 'marine railway.' **1899** *Boston Transcript* 28 Jan. 14/1 In Massachusetts the steam lines are legally designated 'railroads' while 'railways' refers to the lines operated by animal or electric power.

2. In combs.: (1) **railway car,** =**railroad car;** (2) **conductor,** = ***conductor 3;** (3) **depot,** = ***depot 1;** (4) **grading,** the work involved in making a railroad roadbed; (5) **king,** =**railroad king;** (6) **magnate,** =**railroad magnate;** (7) **mail clerk,** a clerk in a railway post office; (8) **plow,** (see quot.); (9) **postal car,** a railway car serving as a railway post office: (10) **postal clerk,** a clerk in the railway mail service of the U.S. Post Office; (11) **post office,** a post office in a mail car, also attrib.; (12) **snowplow,** a plowlike contrivance for removing snow from the roadbed of a railroad.

(1) 1828 *Cong. Deb.* 9 April 2249 The rail way car at Charleston, South Carolina, . . . weighs upwards of one ton. **1894** *Harper's Mag.* July 316/1 Railway cars for transporting the army were appropriated at Omaha. — **(2) 1883** *Cent. Mag.* Aug. 574/1 Azalea . . . [had] found a stout and bald-headed railway conductor, whose adoration made amends for his lack of romance. — **(3) 1863** MOORE *Rebellion Rec.* V. I. 60 At Richmond, La., they destroyed the railway dépôt, together with its contents. — **(4) 1881** MARK TWAIN *Tramp Abroad* 155 The heavy work in . . . the new railway gradings is done mainly by Italians.

(5) 1847 E. D. BANCROFT *Lett. from England* 113 We both went to a concert at Mr. Hudson's, the great railway 'king,' who had just made an immense fortune from railway stocks. **1904** TARBELL *Hist. Standard Oil Co.* I. 73 Mr. Archbold . . . and his colleagues had gone to the railway kings to remonstrate. — **(6) 1874** *Southern Mag.* XIV. 128 Mr. Horace F. Clark [was] second only to his father-in-law, Commodore Vanderbilt, as a railway magnate. **1891** *Denver D. News* 27 Dec., Last year President Mears sent each of the railway magnates of the country a pass over his road, engraved on a plate of silver. — **(7) 1900** *Cong. Rec.* 3 Jan. 638/1 Mr. Sewell presented a petition of sundry railway mail clerks of Asbury Park, N.J. — **(8) 1883** KNIGHT *Supp.* 741/2 *Railway Plow* 1. A plow attached to a car or locomotive and used in excavating or ditching alongside the track. . . . 2. A snow plow. — **(9) 1881** *Rep. Ala. R.R. Comm.* I. 64 Number of railway postal cars . . . 1. **1910** PRESCOTT *Early Day Railroading* 231 The C. & N.W. Ry. . . . built the first Railway Postal Car for the use of the mail service.

(10) 1887 *Courier-Journal* 6 Feb. 16/6 Many seek appointment under the impression that the position of railway postal clerk is a 'soft snap.' **1924** *Railway Post Office* June 7/3 The average salary of railway postal clerks for 1923 was $2,107. — **(11) 1874** *Rep. Postmaster-General* 209 Each railway post-office clerk . . . is required to attach to each package of letters he makes up a facing or label. **1903** E. JOHNSON *Railway Transportation* 173 Sometimes the railway post-offices occupy an entire car . . . and sometimes they occupy a part of a car, usually the baggage-car, in which an apartment is fitted up as a post-office. — **(12) 1867** *Harper's Wkly.* 26 Jan. 49/4 The late heavy snow-storm of December 28, . . . has brought into requisition the lately-invented railway snow-plow.

As the last term in **electric, elevated, ferry, freight, horse, inclined, log, logging, marine, Pacific, rope, scenic, ship, street, subterranean, suspension, trunk railway.**

***rain**, *n.* In combs.: (1) **rain barrel,** a barrel in which rain water from the eaves of a house is caught; (2) **belt,** (*a*) a belt or region subject to rain, (*b*) **rain belt theory,** the theory that sufficient rainfall would come in the arid regions in the West as soon as agricultural operations were begun; (3) **belter,** (see quot. 1909); (4) ***bird,** (see quot.); (5) ***bow,** see as a main entry; (6) **check,** a check or ticket issued to a spectator at an outdoor performance, to be used on a subsequent occasion if the performance is stopped by rain, also transf.; (7) **coat,** a waterproof coat worn as a protection against rain [cf. Du. *regenrok*]; (8) **crow,** the yellow-billed cuckoo, *Coccyzus americanus*, also the black-billed cuckoo, *C. erythrophthalmus*, so called because they are especially clamorous before a rain; (9) **dog,** (see quot.); (10) **frog,** a tree frog or spring peeper, whose cry is especially frequent during a rain; (11) **owl,** (see quot.); (12) **table,** (see quot.); (13) **water barrel,** =**rain barrel;** (14) **water fish,** (see quot.).

(1) 1884 CRADDOCK *Tenn. Mts.* 17 The ash-hopper was visible close in the rear; the rain-barrel affiliated with the damp wall. **1948** DICK *Dixie Frontier* 300 When coopers established their shops, rain barrels were placed at one or two corners. — **(2)** (*a*) **1878** HINTON *Arizona* 201 The Santa Cruz [Valley], up to Tubac, marks the western limit of a notable rain-belt. **1894** *Cong. Rec.* 11 Aug. 8434/2 In the rain belts of the East the vegetation comes up in the spring. **1913** *Chi. Record-Herald* 21 March 12/4 The cubs still are in the rain belt and still feasting on an indoor diet. (*b*) **1890** in HENRY *Conquer. Plains* (1930) 332 If the 'rain-belt' theory were correct, these countries [i.e., Spain, France and Italy] would long ago have had sufficient precipitation for successful agriculture. — **(3) 1902** NEWELL *Irrigation* 367 As the rain-belters marched triumphantly westward, they found that their movements were facilitated by companies formed to place loans and take mortgages on real estate. **1909** *Cent. Supp.* 1110/1 rainbelter. . . . A farmer, in the western part of the United States, who settles on the semi-arid plains during a wet season, relying upon a continuance of sufficient rainfall. — **(4) 1819** THOMAS *Travels* 161 The *meadow lark*, the *kildee*, and the *land plover* inhabit the prairies. The last has been called the *rain bird*, from its notes being more frequently heard in the calm that precedes changes of the atmosphere.

(6) 1890 (rain check issued by Detroit Base Ball Assoc.), Raincheck. In case rain interrupts game of this date before 3 innings are played, this Check will admit Bearer to Grounds for next League Game only. **1945** *New Yorker* 9 June 16/2 The idea . . . was for an actual raincheck, to be handed to those jaunty types who say they will take a raincheck when declining an invitation. **1949** *Sat. Ev. Post* 22 Jan. 100/2 Her performance so impressed the Russian team that she received an invitation to show her stuff at Moscow; the notice given was so short, however, that Fanny asked for a rain check. — **(7) 1830** WATSON *Philadelphia* App. 52 As a defence from rain, the men wore 'rain coats,' and the women 'camblets.' **1944** CLARK *Pills* 220 Almost as formal as the fancy 'boiled shirts' were the raincoats or mackintoshes. — **(8) 1806** LEWIS in *L. & Clark Exped.* V. (1905) 205, I saw both yesterday and today the Cookkoo or as it is sometimes called the *rain craw*. **1864** *Richmond* (Va.) *Examiner* 11 June 1/2 At the sound of cannon from the 'front,' these hags croak like 'rain crows' before a storm. **1947** *Democrat* 2 Oct. 4/2 From time to time a raincrow or a cardinal will make a raid on the worms. — **(9) 1872** MARK TWAIN *Roughing It* 513 What the sailors call 'rain-dogs'—little patches of rainbow—are often seen drifting about the heavens.

(10) 1827 MCKENNEY *Tour to Lakes* 158 We found the few people who live near its mouth, . . . [with] rain frogs on the logs of their huts to sing them to repose. **1942** RAWLINGS *C. Creek* 145 They appear in June, full-fledged, and do not seem to change their size all summer. Martha calls them the rain-frogs. They are inch-long, animated pieces of pale green enamel. — **(11) 1917** *Birds of Amer.* II. 103 Barred Owl. *Strix varia varia*. . . . Other Names.—Hoot Owl; Rain Owl; Wood Owl [etc.]. — **(12) 1873** RAYMOND *Silver & Gold* 30 Rain table for Sacramento, . . . arranged according to the seasons, showing the amount in inches of each month, during twenty-three years, and for each rainy season; also the mean . . . annual amount of rain. — **(13) 1869** *Rep. Comm. Agric. 1868* 317 Musquitoes . . . may be seen by thousands in old rain-water barrels. **1944** FAST *F. Road* 6 Jeff came in with kindling, his head dripping wet from the rain-water barrel. — **(14) 1897** *N.Y. Forest, Fish & Game Comm. 2d Rep.* 232 *Lucania parva*. . . . Rainwater-Fish.—This killifish is abundant in Peconic, Shinnecock and Great South Bays.

***rain**, *v.* In phrases.

1. *To know enough to go in when it rains*, and variants, to be at least ordinarily intelligent. Often in negative contexts. *Colloq.*

1855 WITCHER *Widow Bedott P.* (1881) 36 (We.), He was a *saftly* feller—dident scarsely know enough to go in when it rained. **1857** *Knickerb.* XLIX. 95 When it commences to rain, the celerity with which he 'comes in' would do credit to maturer years. **1906** *Springfield W. Republican* 12 July 2 Every citizen of Vermont who is capable of going in when it rains ought to understand [etc.]. **1923** WYATT *Invis. Gods* 19 Hetherington Marshfield . . . [doesn't] know enough to go in when it rains!

2. *To rain out*, in the passive (*a*) of a crop: to be ruined by too much rain, (*b*) of an outdoor game or event: to be halted by rain.

(*a*) **1944** CLARK *Pills* 88 Behind him at home was a cotton crop which had been rained out. (*b*) **1928** *Chi. Tribune* 18 June 27/7 (*heading*), Sox, Boston Series Final Is Rained Out. **1948** *Lawton* (Okla.) *Constitution* 4 July 12/2 The Giants gained a half game over the McAlester Rockets, who were rained out last night. **1949** *News-Herald* (Marshfield, Wis.) 19 July 9/2 The Pittsburgh–New York game was rained out and re-scheduled to make a double-header today.

***rainbow**, *n.*

1. Short for rainbow trout *q.v.*

1922 *Outing* March 246/1 There are Dolly Varden and rainbow in the Kings Rivers. **1950** *L.A. Times* 1 Jan. II. 12/2 Limits of rainbow from 8 to 12 inches long are being taken from the inland waterway near Nelson's Landing.

2. In combs.: (1) **rainbow cactus,** a cactus, *Echinocereus rigidissimus,* of the Southwest, having red and white spines; (2) **chaser,** a visionary, one who strives for impossible or impracticable things, also **rainbow chasing,** *colloq.;* (3) **darter,** the blue johnny or soldier fish, *Oligocephalus caeruleus,* of the Mississippi Valley, or a related fish; (4) **fish,** =prec.; (5) **snake,** the hoop snake or horn snake *qq.v.;* (6) **trout,** a trout, *Salmo irideus,* native to the coastwise mountain streams of California or a species, *S. shasta,* closely related to this.

(1) **1893** *Garden & Forest* 11 Oct. 429/2 One [booth] sells the 'Rainbow Cactus,' which is a good species of Echinocactus. **1930** BREAZEALE *Color Schemes of Cacti* 14 A flower of the rainbow cactus, *Echinocactus rigidissimus,* about three-fourths natural size. — (2) **1892** *Courier-Journal* 1 Oct. 1/8 The rainbow chasers of the Administration are not idle these days. **1904** *N.Y. Ev. Post* 1 Sep. 7 Early in the campaign he had told his associates that it was of no use to go rainbow chasing after Massachusetts, Wisconsin, or Illinois. **1908** *Hampton's New Broadway Mag.* Nov. 599/1 We had no business whatever to go rainbow chasing. — (3) **1882** *Nat. Museum Bul.* No. 16, 514 *Poecilichthys.* . . . Rainbow Darters. *Ib.* 517, P. coeruleus. . . . Blue Darter; Rainbow Darter; Soldier-fish. **1903** T. H. BEAN *Fishes N.Y.* 518 The blue darter, blue Johnny, rainbow darter, or soldier fish, is found in the Ohio valley and in some parts of the Mississippi valley. — (4) **1888** GOODE *Amer. Fishes* 205 In this limpid pool were many gorgeously-colored species, the angel-fish, the parrot-fish, the rainbow-fish. **1890** *Cent.* 4934/2 *Rainbow-fish,* . . . the blue darter.

(5) **1907** DITMARS *Reptile Book* 266 The Rainbow Snake lives in swamp and timbered areas, and along the borders of streams, where it burrows into the damp soil. **1949** *N.O. Times-Picayune Mag.* 23 Oct. 2/2 Mrs. Rainbow Snake laid herself a passel of nice white eggs, top, and 15 of them hatched, below. — (6) **1882** *Nat. Museum Bul.* No. 16, 312 S[almo] irideus.—California Brook Trout; Rainbow Trout. **1950** *L.A. Times* 22 Jan. VI. 7/1 Arizona and Nevada Fish and Game authorities have planted 250,000 rainbow trout in the lake waters.

Raines Law. [John Raines (1840–1909), Amer. lawyer and politician.] Used attrib. with reference to a law passed in 1896 in New York State, restricting Sunday liquor sales to hotels: **a. Raines (Law) hotel,** a saloon provided with rooms in order to comply with the law, often used as a place of assignation. **b. Raines Law sandwich,** a sandwich served with liquor in order to meet the legal requirement that liquor should be served only with food. *Obs.*

(a) **1896** *N.Y. Dramatic News* 11 July 3 Even the hardened court interpreter fled trembling to the nearest Raines hotel. **1901** FLYNT *World of Graft* 154 There's the Raines law hotel people for one. **1911** *Jrnl. Criminal Law & Criminology* Jan. 834 'The Committee of Fourteen' was organized in 1905 for the suppression of 'Raines Law Hotels' and their attendant abuses in New York City. — (b) **1904** *N.Y. Times* 9 May 5 The various saloons along Surf Avenue where Police Capt. Dooley killed the Raines Law sandwich last season.

***raise,** *n.*

1. An increase in wages or pay.

For a criticism of this use see *Amer. Sp.* for Aug. 1931, 407–10. **1898** *Scribner's Mag.* Oct. 489/1 A. J. Packer . . . had begun to ponder doubts of his wisdom in agreeing to the second 'raise.' **1923** WATTS *L. Nichols* 76 Luther himself . . . could not get up the courage to touch Schulte for a raise. **1949** *Sat. Ev. Post* 2 April 121/2 They figured it was good experience for me, and that the extra dough would keep me from hitting them for a raise.

2. *To make a raise,* to secure money or something else of value or importance. *Colloq.* or *slang.*

1837 NEAL *Charcoal Sk.* (1838) 96, I made a raise of a horse and saw. **1878** BEADLE *Western Wilds* 41 At last I made a little raise . . . and concluded to come home. **1900** HANDSAKER in *Pioneer Life* 35 The two brothers 'made quite a raise' in the California mines soon after their discovery.

***raise,** *v.*

1. *tr.* To form or appoint (a committee). *Obs.*

1711 *Boston Rec.* 80 The Summe of Thirteen hundred pounds . . . [shall be] Layd out in Some Real Estate for the use of the Publick Lattin School, . . . by Such other Committee as the Town may hereafter raise . . . for that Service. **1823** *Boston School Com. Minutes* 8 Nov., The Committee raised . . . to consider the state of the E. Cl. School, reported by their Chairman.

2. (See quot.) *Obs.*

1775 BURNABY *Travels* 151 When the trees are fallen, they yoke seventy or eighty pair of oxen, and drag them along the snow. It is exceedingly difficult to put them first in motion, which they call raising them.

3. To surmount or gain the top of (a hill or slope). *Colloq.*

1804 ORDWAY in *Jrnls. of Lewis & O.* 168 We raised a Steep bank back of this bottom. **1869** MARK TWAIN *Innocents Abroad* 387, I 'raised the hill' and stood in Odessa for the first time. **1872**—— *Roughing It* 287 As I 'raised the hill' overlooking the town, it lacked fifteen minutes of twelve. **1934** BARROWS *Ubet* 280 Every time I would raise a ridge, I expected to see him; for the signs were fresh.

4. To falsify the value of (a check, note, etc.) by changing the sum specified in it to a larger amount.

1856 *Ill. State Reg.* (Springfield) 15 May 3/3 Raised notes can be easily detected by carefully examining the denomination and die work. **1872** *Laramie* (Wyo.) *Independent* 2 Feb. 3/2 We learn by telegraph, of the arrest of three persons who have recently done an extensive business of 'raising' checks. **1905** *N.Y. Ev. Post* 9 June 6 A few days ago a check 'raised' with extraordinary skill made its appearance in a police court. **1950** *Nature Mag.* March 168/3 One form of monetary forgery is the attempt to raise a bill . . . by altering the numerals.

For *To raise Cain,* (one's) *hair, the hatchet, Ned, the roof, a stake, the yell,* see the nouns.

***raised,** *a.* As the last term in **cane, house raised.**

***raiser,** *n.* One who participates in a raising bee. *Obs.* — **1705** SEWALL *Diary* II. 139 Drove a Pin in the Ministers House which I found Raising; bolted on the Raisers out of Bishop's Lane before I was aware. **1854** THOREAU *Walden* 49 No man was ever more honoured in the character of his raisers than I.

As the second term in **check, club, cotton, hair, pork, sob, stock raiser.**

***raising,** *n.*

1. =next.

[**1672** in ROADS *Hist. Marblehead* (1880) 26 Paid for rum and charges about fish with wine at raising the Lentoo at the Meeting House . . . 2 s. 6 d.] **1758** in J. F. HAGEMAN *Hist. Princeton* (1879) I. 12 Princeton first named at the raising of the first house built there by James Leonard, A.D. 1724. **1877** *Harper's Mag.* May 821/2 Husking bees, quiltings, and raisings are yet the enthusiastic occasions of tremendous labor and equal fun. **1947** DOWNEY *Lusty Forefathers* 106 Most of the meeting-houses, houses, and barns in New England would never have gone up if it had not been for good folk gathering from all over the countryside for the raising.

attrib. **1779** E. PARKMAN *Diary* 162 In Northboro [I] was compelled to go into Deacon Paul Newton's to raising Supper. **1786** HILTZHEIMER *Diary* (1893) 7 April 83 Afterward went to a raising frolic at Robert Erwin's. **1790** *Ib.* 31 July 162 Was present at the raising dinner of the high house on the north side of Market Street, . . . belonging to Henry Seckel. **1929** SHELTON *Salt-box House* ix. 63 There was feasting, with . . . 'raising-cake' and other appropriate viands.

2. raising bee, a house-raising by friends and neighbors who assemble at the invitation of one of their number, and usu. enjoy a social evening at the close of their labors. *Obs.*

1833 SHIRREFF *Tour* (1835) 159 While at Brantford, we observed a raising bee, that is, raising the frame of a house by a collection of people. **1852** REGAN *Emigrant's Guide* 309 These 'raising bees,' as they are called, have the salutary effect of bringing the people together, for the cultivation of friendly feelings, and as large numbers turn out, the work is light to each. **1887** KIRKLAND *Zury* 13 When the 'raising bee' took place, the refreshments . . . had to be cooked by Selina.

As the last term in **barn, beef, cabin, cotton, face, flag, fruit, log, log cabin, mule, pole, stock raising.**

***rake,** *n.* =**rake-off,** *n. Slang.* — **1899** BREEN *Thirty Years* 265 There were so many persons of political importance looking after this fund, for the purpose of getting what was termed a 'rake' out of it, that [etc.].

As the last term in **ash, buck, bull, cranberry, hand, loafer, muck, oyster, scratch, sweep, under, vine rake.**

***rake,** *v.*

1. a. rake-down, a social gathering, a "shindig." *Obs.* **b. rake-off,** an unearned share or profit, an amount, etc., usu. obtained illegally. Both *slang.*

(a) **1850** in *Annals of Iowa* 3 Ser. IX. 450 We had a 'rake down' there that evening, Adam White presiding as fiddler. — (b) **1891** QUINN *Fools of Fortune* 188 This percentage is technically known as the 'rake-off,' and insures the proprietors of the establishment a handsome royalty on all winnings. **1950** *Time* 2 Jan. 52/2 Are you a man of business or a philanthropic distributor of rake-offs?

2. In slang phrases, esp. *to rake down, in,* to be very successful, to take one's winnings in gambling.

1839 *Spirit of Times* 13 July 223/3 (We.), If he has anything like as good a horse as the balance, he is certain to *rake down the corn.* **1845** SOL. SMITH *Theatr. Apprent.* 151 With one hand he gracefully turned over four Kings and a Jack, and with the other tremblingly 'raked down' the pile of bank notes, gold and silver. **1851** *Oquawka* (Ill.) *Spectator* 22 Oct. 1/4 Then, of course, they 'dropped the gate' upon them and 'raked in the pile.' **1926** O. L. SHIPMAN *Taming Big Bend* 128 He was sitting at a poker table about to rake in a jackpot he had won. **1949** *Boston Globe Sun. Mag.* 22 May 7/2 Each time he raked home a pot he patted the old shoe and crowed a little.

*__raker__, *n.* As the last term in **muck, self-raker.**

*__rally__, *n.* A political mass meeting for arousing enthusiasm for a particular candidate or cause. Also transf.

1840 *Niles' Reg.* LIX. 20/2 *Rally of the democracy of Niagara.* . . . More voters were brought together, than upon any previous occasion in Niagara county! **1920** *3rd Nat. Country Life Conf. Proc.* 48 Funds for the school are obtained through rallies held in the churches on the fifth Sunday. **1947** *Harper's Mag.* March 232/1 When they attended Montana political rallies, Mrs. Wheeler knitted with calm absorption.

*__ram__, *n.* **1. ram beaver,** ?a hat in the style of a beaver but made of wool. Poss. a hat made of **roram,** *q.v. Obs.* **2.** *__ram's head,__ a species of moccasin flower, *Cypripedium arietinum,* having a flower the shape of which suggests a ram's head.

(1) **1809** IRVING *Knickerb.* VI. vii, The biting steel clove through the stubborn ram-beaver. **1853** *Knickerb.* XLII. 650 The rain, descending on Tom's ancient 'ram-beaver,' and drenching that 'helm to storm impermeable,' . . . had no power to disturb Tom's good-nature. — (2) **1843** TORREY *Flora N Y.* II. 288 Cypripedium arietinum. . . . Ram's-head. . . . Near Oneida lake. **1907** *St. Nicholas* Aug. 939/1 Only by rare good fortune will the ram's-head . . . reward our search.

As the last term in **mountain, rebel ram.**

ramada rəˈmædə, *n. S.W.* [Sp. in same sense.] An arbor or arborlike structure.

1869 HAYES *Pioneer Notes* (1929) 289, I paid them a dollar for my bath, at the rustic bathing establishment they have constructed, consisting of two goods' boxes sunk in the ground, sheltered by a *ramada.* **1911** WRIGHT *Winning Barbara Worth* 201 Every evening under the ramada Barbara sat with her father, often alone. **1949** *Desert Mag.* April 24/1 In a brush ramada the Navajo women weave their blankets while the older children tend the sheep.

*__Ramage__, *n.* [Adam *Ramage* (1770–1850), a Philadelphia printer.] *attrib.* Designating a printing-press, or some part of this, designed by Ramage.

1827 *Hallowell* (Me.) *Gaz.* 21 June 4/3 For Sale, a small font of Brevier, nearly new; also a Printing Press with a new Ramage Screw. **1830** *Boston Transcript* 31 Aug. 4/4 For Sale . . . 1 New Ramage Press, in good order. **1874** B. F. TAYLOR *World on Wheels* I. iii. 24 The cargoes of those boats . . . was something wonderful . . . plows, axes and Bibles; teachers, preachers and Ramage presses. **1923** YOUNG *Founding Utah* 349 The old Ramage press had a lever which the printer pulled in the printing of each page. **1949** *Miss. Valley Hist. Rev.* March 634 It was . . . printed on a small wrought-iron Ramage press.

Rambo ˈræmbo, *n.* Also **rambo.** [Prob. f. *Rambour* (Rambures, a village near Amiens), the name of a variety of apple.] A variety of apple, or an apple of this variety. Also attrib.

[**1817** W. COXE *Fruit Trees* 104 Rambour D'ete, or Summer Rambour. . . . This fruit is also called the Rambour franc: it was imported into the United States from the garden of St. Cloud.] *Ib.* 116 Rambo, or Romanite. This apple is much cultivated in Delaware, Pennsylvania, and New Jersey. **1906** *N.Y. Ev. Post* 5 May, There were still the meetings of an evening . . . beneath the rambo apple tree. **1942** WEYGANDT *Plenty of Penna.* 64 The Rambo apple is not generally raised nowadays.

rambunctious ræmˈbʌŋkʃəs, *a.* [*EDD,* Vol. VI, attributes *rambunkshus* to Ireland. Irish emigrants may have brought it to this country.] Fierce, wild, uncontrolled, rampageous. *Slang.*

1830 *Boston Transcript* 1 Sep. 3/1 If they are 'rumbunctious' at the prospect, they will be 'riproarious' when they get a taste, for a 'copious acquaintance' with Vinegar. **1900** NICHOLSON *Hoosiers* 54 The word *rambunctious,* reported from New York State as expressing impudence and forwardness, cannot be peculiar to that region, for it is used in Indiana in identically the same sense. **1949** *Travel* Dec. 3/2 It is pleasant to find traces, however slight, of that rambunctious delight in grotesque exaggeration which has been a characteristic part of American humor since frontier days.

*__ramrod__, *n.* A boss; one in charge, as the superintendent of a ranch. Also as a verb. *Slang.*

1880 NYE *B. Nye & Boomerang* 60 John Humpfner, the ram-rod of the New York House, feared that the explosion might break the large French plate glass windows of his palatial hotel. **1948** *Popular Western* June 15/2 This is Tex Grant, the star-toter who ramrods this burg. **1950** *Boston Globe Mag.* 8 Jan. 2/1 Mason swore he's a-ramroddin' the outfit and we'll do business with him, if we ever do any business.

ramsquaddle ˈræmˌskwɑdl, *v.* [Fanciful coinage.] *tr.* To overcome, to "use up (a person) bodaciously." *Slang. Obs.* — **1830** *Vt. Statesman* (Castleton) 1 Sep. 1/2 *The persecutors of Henry Clay:* They ought to be ramsquaddled and chewed up by a ring-tailed roarer. **1830** *N.Y. Constellation* 11 Sep. 2/5 May I be tetotally twisted if I cant ram-squaddle two like you.

ramus ˈreməs, *n.* [f. *ignor*amus* by metanalysis.] An ignoramus. *Slang. Obs.* — **1839** *Knickerb.* XIII. 450 The ignorant ramus! **1855** *Harper's Mag.* Aug. 290/2 The people are sich ignorant ramusses.

rance sniffle. *local.* (See quot.) *Obs.* — **1869** *Overland Mo.* III. 131 'Rance sniffle' is a strange combination of words to express a mean and dastardly piece of malignity. I have never heard it outside of Georgia.

ranch ræntʃ, *n. S.W.* and *W.* [f. **rancho.**]

1. A village, private house, a tavern, a ranch house.

This word has been used with so many shades of meaning that it is not always easy to distinguish between this and the following senses.

1808 PIKE *Sources Miss.* 254 When we arrived at the Ranche, we soon had out a number of boys, who brought in the horse. **1858** GOVE *Letters* 130 Last night the wind commenced blowing and all day . . . it has blown terrifically, harder than ever. Several tents have blown down, and I thought at one time my ranch would go under. **1877** RUEDE *Sod-House Days* 48 Had to build a chimney and fireplace before I could make dinner, and when I had made it it consisted of one dish of mush. The ranch got full of smoke, too, but I did not care much because the door and window being opposite, the place was cleared in a short time. **1889** F. BUTLER *Recollections* 229 We saw how the people had been murdered, the trains plundered and the ranches burned along our route. **1904** in *Kans. Hist. Soc.* IX. 10 We followed the Santa Fe trail west . . . to a little wayside trading-house south of the big bend of the Smoky Hill, called a ranch, as all such places on the plains were then called.

2. A small cultivated farm or country place; also an extensive establishment for grazing cattle, sheep, etc., often with a prefixed term.

1831 PATTIE *Personal Narr.* 221 [At] a ranch. . . . I procured a horse for three dollars. **1888** *Cent. Mag.* Jan. 412/1 There are [in Mont.] hay ranches, grain ranches, milk ranches, horse ranches, cattle ranches, and chicken ranches. **1908** JOHNSON *Pacific Coast* 86 Any farm or country house with land attached, even if there is no more than a garden patch, is a 'ranch,' in California. **1948** *So. Sierran* Feb. 1/3 One of the Angeles National Forest's most enchanting landmarks [is] the Colby Ranch in Upper Big Tujunga Canyon.

3. In combs.: (1) **ranch brand,** the brand put upon cattle to show to what ranch they belong; (2) **butter,** butter produced on a ranch; (3) **egg,** *W.* a fresh egg; (4) **house,** a house belonging to a ranch, the living quarters of a rancher, cf. **adobe ranch house;** (5) **man,** a man who owns or works on a ranch, esp. a cattle ranch.

(1) **1874** McCOY *Cattle* 7 He then decides what his 'ranch brand' and ear marks shall be. — (2) **1876** *Belmont* (Nev.) *Courier* 9 June 3/4 Ranch butter (a choice sort), for sale at Emerson's. **1880** *Cimarron News & Press* 26 Aug. 3/1 Fresh Ranch Butter at Porter's. — (3) **1908** *Sunset* Dec. 792/2 If you were working with ranch eggs, store eggs or yard eggs, it might be different. **1943** HOWARD *Montana* 144 Ranch eggs at this time cost a dollar a dozen. — (4) **1862** *Harper's Mag.* June 14/1, I rode on about five miles further, where I reached a small ranch-house. **1949** *L.A Times Home Mag.* 11 Dec. 20/3 They fell heir to the Santa Margarita ranch house.

(5) **1856** *Spirit of Times* 4 Oct. 75/1 The dusty, rusty, rough-clad, huge-pawed creatures, known as ranch-men, will not this season, as in former ones, be compelled to force their grain, &c., upon buyers, at the price their generous souls may see fit to pay. **1949** *Dly. Ardmoreite* (Ardmore, Okla.) 4 Dec. 10/1 The ranchmen are piling up hay in strategic places to feed stock if the severe cold comes again.

Also *ranch chicken, country, cow, cowboy, foreman, girl, hand, home, life, outfit, owner, people, road, style, woman,* etc.

As the last term in **bee, breeding, bull, cattle, chicken, cow, dairy, dry, dude, fox, fruit, goat, grain, grape, grub, hay, hog, home, hop, horse, Indian, milk, mountain, orange, pigeon, road, sheep, stage, stock, whisky, wood ranch.**

ranch ræntʃ, *v.* [f. the noun.]

1. *intr.* To operate a ranch, to farm. Also quasi-*tr.*

1872 MARK TWAIN *Roughing It* 242 He had been farming (or ranching, as the more customary term is) in Washoe District. **1890** *Internat. Ann., Anthony's Photogr. Bul.* III. 32 Any enterprising young tourist . . . can find plenty of work and fun among the jolly fellows who 'ranch it' in the West. **1949** *L.A. Times* 5 June 14/7 The park includes nearly 70,000 acres of Western North Dakota badlands where Roosevelt ranched as a youth.

2. *tr.* To put (an animal) on a ranch.

1873 Beadle *Undevel. West* 663 Six hundred miles . . . had worn out my horse, and on the 16th instant I 'ranched him' twenty miles south of Beaver. **1890** Langford *Vigilante Days* (1912) 481 In pursuance of that agreement, he immediately branded and ranched [the ponies].

Also **ranched,** *a.* of furs: Produced on a ranch.

1947 *Sports Afield* Dec. 80/1 We offer a special marketing service on Silver Fox, Mink, and other Ranched Furs.

rancher ˈræntʃɚ, *n. W.* [Prob. f. the noun or verb, but cf. **ranchero.**]

1. A person who owns or operates a stock ranch. Also, rarely, a cowboy.

1836 Field *Three Yrs. in Tex.* 24 At his approach he was met by two hundred Mexican Ranchiers and Indians. **1866** *Rep. Indian Affairs* 189 Teamsters, packers, herders, ranchers, and miners all over the country have become exasperated. **1949** *This Week Mag.* 28 May 11/2 He sold out his business an' turned rancher only about 25 years ago.

2. A farmer.

1884 W. Shepherd *Prairie Exper.* 125 If stock-owners are in power, they say to the small rancher, 'Fence your fields.' **1890** *Stock Grower & Farmer* 11 Jan. 6/3 The majority of ranchers, however, neglect the fruit trees.

As the last term in **cattle, grain, irrigation, stock rancher.**

ranchera ræn'tʃerə, *n. W.* [Sp. in Amer. Sp. sense shown here.] A countrywoman, a farm woman. *Obs.* — **1838** Texian *Mexico v. Texas* 302, I did not think . . . that she was more than a common ranchera. **1884** *Advance* 14 Aug., So fearful are the dainty creatures of being considered rancheras or countrywomen.

rancheria ˌræntʃəˈriə, *n. S.W.* [Sp. *ranchería*, in similar sense. An Amer. borrowing.] An Indian village (see also quot. 1841). Cf. **Indian rancheria, summer rancheria.**

1759 tr. Venegas *Nat. Hist. Calif.* I. 76 The houses of the Californians make no better appearance than their habits. Those of every rancheria are only wretched huts, near the few waters found in the country. **1790** W. Reveley *Exped. to No. Calif.* 16 Towards the mountains they saw a town, or *Rancheria*, of the *Indians*, which appeared to be composed of branches of trees, and huts in pyramidal form, covered with earth. **1841** W. Kennedy *Texas* II. 42 *Rancho*, and *Rancheria*, are used in Spanish America to signify a labourer's house, or a collection of peasants' huts, from one and upwards. Be the number great or small, if there be not a church, the aggregate is called *Rancheria*. **1899** *Land of Sunshine* April 233 The Captain of the rancheria (who is elected yearly by his fellows) opened the fiesta with an address. **1948** Johnston *Gold Rush* 52/2 A large force . . . set out for a *rancheria* located in Hayfork Valley.

attrib. **1846** Bryant *What I Saw in Calif.* (1848) 345 [His speech] is a mixture, in about equal parts, of German, English, French, Spanish, and *rancheria* Indian, a compounded polyglot or linguistic *pi.* **1857** *Rep. Explorations Pacific R.R.* (War Dept.) VI. III. 92 *Elymus arenarius* . . . grows in all parts of California where there are deserted Indian lodges, and is, therefore, called . . . 'rancheria grass.'

ranchero ræn'tʃero, *n. W.* [Sp. in Amer. Sp. sense shown here.] One who owns, operates, or works on a stock ranch. Also attrib.

1827 Dewees *Lett. from Texas* 66 A few wealthy rancheros dwell in the country, who own vast herds of stock, of all kinds. **1846** in Doubleday *Jrnl. Maj. P. Barbour* (1936) 168 The enemy whose line was formed on a curve parallel to the woods in his rear—as follows—Ranchero cavalry on his right [etc.]. **1934** White *Folded Hills* 271 They were an easy-going people of the old *ranchero* breed. **1949** Gann *Tread of Longhorns* 13 Many a peaceful ranchero and his family learned the sorrowful and baleful meaning of that blood-curdling yell.

b. A ranch (see also quot. 1887).

1887 *Scribner's Mag.* II. 509 *Ranchero* is the steward of the mess; it is used in New Mexico, and less frequently elsewhere. **1913** London *Valley of Moon* 293 South of that you'll find government land mixed up with forest reserves and Mexican rancheros.

ranching ˈræntʃɪŋ, *n. W.* Operating a ranch, esp. a cattle ranch, working on a ranch. Also attrib.

1863 in *Frontier & Midland* XVII. (1936) 288/1 A ranch is properly a grazing farm and the term 'ranching' sometimes means farming but is generally applied in this country [Idaho] to taking care of stock. It is not at all safe to allow cattle to run on account of the Indians. **1873** Beadle *Undevel. West* 267 'Ranching' came next and all this industry is not lost. **1949** *Amer. Cattle Producer* April 4/2 We have had one of the worst winters . . . in all my ranching experience.

As the last term in **bee, cattle, stock ranching.**

ranchito ræn'tʃito, *n. W.* [Dim. of **rancho.**] A small ranch or farm.

1850 Garrard *Wah-To-Yah* xvii. 208 To the Ranchito is something less than a mile. **1906** Adams *Cattle Brands* 92 He had sent to a near-by ranchito for a man who had at least the reputation of being quite a hunter. **1949** *Boston Sun. Globe Mag.* 3 April 2/4 Its only inhabitants [were] an occasional Tejano family living in a small ranchita with a few cows, chickens and goats.

rancho ˈræntʃo, *n. W.* [Sp. in Amer. Sp. sense of a small farm.] =**ranch** in senses **1.** and **2.** Cf. **Indian rancho.**

1808 Pike *Sources Miss.* 260 Marched early and at nine o'clock arrived at a Rancho. **1863** Massett *Drifting About* 131 A man would buy a tract of land or a 'rancho' for perhaps $1000 or so. **1910** J. Hart *Vigilante Girl* 179 Occasionally a raid would be made on a great rancho, . . . and a herd of horses stolen. **1950** *L.A. Times* Midwinter 3 Jan. 21/1 There were houses and little ranchos scattered all around what is now the sprawled-out city.

***Randall,** *n. attrib.* Designating the followers of Congressman S. J. Randall (1828–90), an advocate, in the Democratic party, of the protective tariff. — **1887** *Courier-Journal* 6 Feb. 2/1 Below is the tariff correspondence between the tariff reformers on one side and the Randall men . . . on the other. **1900** *Cong. Rec.* 31 Jan. 1365/2, I was a Randall Democrat.

Randallite ˈrændəlˌaɪt, *n.* **1.** A follower of S. J. Randall. *Obs.* Cf. ***Randall,** *n.* **2.** (See quot.) Both *obs.* — **(1) 1887** *Courier-Journal* 6 Feb. 2/1 Speaker Carlisle's Efforts to Arrive At an Understanding With the Randallites. — **(2) 1890** *Cent.* 4953/3 *Randallite.* (After Benjamin *Randall* (1749–1808), founder of the body of Free-will Baptists at New Durham, New Hampshire, in 1780.) A Freewill Baptist. (Rare.)

***random,** *n. Surveying.* A line run at random from which to start a survey. In full **random line.**

1743 *N.J. Archives* 1 Ser. VI. 155 You are to chain eastward . . . untill the Point come to have the same bearing as the course which by your best judgment you conceive you ought to run for the random line. *Ib.* 159 You may then come back to the place where your random cutt Delaware & in your comeing you may compute the course of the true line. **1787** Ellicott in Mathews *Life A. Ellicott* 64 We prepared to proceed down the River to a proper place for correcting the random line by astronomical observations.

***range,** *n.*

1. An area of uncultivated ground or wild country over which domestic or wild animals range for food, now esp. a cattle range.

1626 in *Amer. Sp.* XV. 381/1, 300,000 acres of land, which will feed such nombers of people, with plentifull range for Cattle. **1775** Rauck *Boonesborough* 179 Buffaloe had abandoned their range & were gone into other parts. **1880** *Cimarron News & Press* 19 Feb. 3/2 Mr. Porter has a valuable range enclosed in 28 miles of wire fence. **1949** *Amer. Cattle Producer* April 11/1 Not only is such range poor today but it will be poor for years to come.

b. A row of lots, usu. fronting a river or other body of water. Now *hist.*

1681 *Conn. Probate Rec.* I. 325 On halfe of my great Lott in the westermost Rang of Lotts. **1684** *Jamaica* (L.I.) *Rec.* I. 291 The proportion that did belong to Mr. Bryan Newtons lot [was] . . . ye 20th lot among ye rang of small lots that front to ye River. **1715** *Boston Rec.* 57 This List contains an accompt of the first Range of Lotts. **1947** *Harper's Mag.* July 82/1 It's difficult because it consists largely of re-locating the old lines of original lots and ranges run by pioneers with crude compasses.

c. An area or territory patrolled by rangers. *Obs.*

1692 *Va. State P.* I. 38 Hoping yor Honrs will considr our duty was the harder, and that our Ranges being bad and Stony, are forst to be att ye charge of Shewing [our horses].

d. An area ranged over by an Indian tribe. *Obs.*

1843 Frémont *Explor. Rocky Mts.* 15 We were now in the range of the Pawnees. **1849** *31st Congress* 1 Sess. Sen. Ex. Doc. No. 64, 175 As we are now coming into the vicinity of the Comanche 'range,' I have given orders for cartridges to be issued to the command.

2. In the public land survey, a row of townships lying between two meridians six miles apart, the rows being numbered in order from east to west from the principal meridian.

For a discussion of the origin of this system of surveying land see F. C. Hicks, ed., *A Topographical Description* . . . by T. Hutchins, Cleveland, 1904, pp. 37 ff.

1785 *Jrnls. Cont. Congress* XXVIII. 376 The geographer shall designate the townships . . . by numbers progressively from south to north; always beginning each range with number one. **1825** *New-Harmony* (Ind.) *Gazette* 15 Oct. 23/3, I have levied on the fractional section No. 39, in township 4, south of range 14. **1949** *Democrat* 5 May 8/6 All being in Township 9 North, Range 3 East.

3. *Mining.* (See quots.)

1866 *Harper's Mag.* 689/1 In the best mining grounds the veins run in an east and west, north and south direction, approximately. These are termed 'ranges,' whether applied to a mine or a district. **1919** A. H. Fay *Glossary of Mining* 556 In the Lake Superior region, a term applied to a deposit of iron ore and the associated rocks. . . . Now the term simply means deposits of iron ore, which are known as 'ranges,' even if the ground where they occur be low swamps.

4. In combs. often in allusion to cattle ranges or the West: (1) **range bear,** = *ranger **3;** (2) **boss,** the boss of an outfit rounding up cattle on a range; (3) **cattle,** cattle raised or fed on a range, also attrib.; (4) **delivery,** (see quot. 1884 and cf. **book count**); (5) **fire,** a fire that devastates a range; (6) **herding,** herding cattle on a particular range; (7) **horse,** (see quot. 1859); (8) **line,** (*a*) (see quot. and cf. **2.** above), (*b*) the boundary line of a cattle range; (9) **rider,** a cowman who rides the range; (10) **state,** a state in which there are large cattle ranges; (11) **war,** disturbances, often involving armed encounters, arising from conflicting claims to a cattle range; (12) **way,** a way for taking cattle to and from a range.

(1) **1893** Roosevelt *Wilderness Hunter* 265 They insist on . . . others with names known only in certain localities, such as the range bear, the roach-back, and the smut-face. **1897** Hough *Story of Cowboy* 230 In a few instances the cowboy has ridden alongside and with his six-shooter killed the grizzly, cinnamon, or 'range bear.' — (2) **1893** Chittenden *Ranch Verses* 94 The range boss's outfit rides in through the herd Cutting out and inspecting. **1948** *Range Riders Western* May 17/2 He could ride and rope to the satisfaction of the most critical range boss. — (3) **1885** *Wkly. New Mexican Rev.* 9 April 3/3 The cattle are . . . one of the best bunches of range cattle in New Mexico. **1948** *Ariz. Republic* (Phoenix) 29 Feb. 1. 1/1 Approximately 100,000 range cattle are moving out of drought-browned sections of California to forage areas of Montana, Idaho, . . . and Nevada. — (4) **1884** Aldridge *Life on Ranch* 171 He offered to sell 'on range delivery.' This . . . means that the cattle are not counted out to the buyer, but the books of the ranch are shown, containing the number of cattle bought and sold, and calves branded. **1903** *Out West* Feb. 190 If I was to go 'way off somewheres and buy a lot more cattle, range delivery, from some one I knew didn't own them, first whipping him for claiming to own 'em— . . . why that would be just like our war.

(5) **1945** *Jefferson Co. Republican* (Golden, Colo.) 25 July 1/3 Everyone knows what forest and range fires mean. [**1949** *L.A. Times* 4 June 7/6 A range grass fire which swept 2500 acres was brought under control today by 100 firemen.] — (6) **1884** Aldridge *Life on Ranch* 65 The object of this system of 'range herding,' as it is called, is to save the cattle as much as possible from being driven about or interfered with. — (7) **1859** Marcy *Prairie Traveler* iv, For prairie service, horses which have been raised exclusively upon grass, . . . or 'range horses,' as they are called in the West, are decidedly the best. **1944** Johnson *As I Dare* 283 They were just the same sort of bony, unpedigreed little range horses that I had known in Mexico. — (8) (*a*) **1817** *Niles' Reg.* XII. 97/2 The north and south lines dividing the townships are called *range* lines. **1949** *Surveying & Mapping* Jan.–Mar. 31/2 From east to west the townships were divided by range lines, also 6 miles apart. (*b*) **1945** Mathews *Talking* 226 The peace of my ridge is not a peace but a series of range-line skirmishes. — (9) **1890** *Stock Grower & Farmer* 28 June 3/4 A few years more will see all the last of the range rider. **1942** Dale *Cow Country* 115 That there were bad men and worthless men among the range riders cannot be denied.

(10) **1927** James *Cow Country* 15 It's come to a point, in the range States along the Rockies, where the horse has accumulated till he's in the way. — (11) **1912** Mulford *Buck Peters* 16 He learned of the things that had occurred since he had left; of the bitter range-war. **1949** *10 Story Western* May 29/2 He was a Litchfield man and he wouldn't interfere in a range war of Litchfield's. — (12) **1685** *Charleston Land Rec.* 196 [The lot is bounded] South Eastrly by the range way two pole broad. **1707** *Cambridge Prop. Rec.* 236 We stated a way . . . from ye Range way Near said Lawrences house to ye Range way where sd ffasset dwells.

Also *range animal, beef, branding, broadhorn, bull, cattleman, cook, country, county, cow, foreman, man, manager, pony, privilege, riding, rights, rule, sheep, stealing, steer, stock,* etc.

b. In phrases: (1) *On the range,* of animals, living on a range away from an owner; (2) *to be at range,* to be turned loose on a range; (3) *to take the range,* to depart, *obs.;* (4) *to go* (or *be helped*) *over the range,* to die or be killed; (5) *to ride (the) range,* to look for or after stock on a range; (6) *to run on the same range, transf.* to associate, grow up together.

(1) **1831** Peck *Guide* 171 Thousands of hogs are raised without any expense, except a few breeders to start with, and a little attention in hunting them on the range, and keeping them tame. **1925** Tilghman *Dugout* 78 Most of his stock had been out on the range and escaped the Indians. — (2) **1832** Watson *Hist. Tales N.Y.* 84 All horses at range are ordered to be branded. — (3) **1834** Simms *Guy Rivers* 452 The Sooner you 'take the range' the better. — (4) **1887** *Scribner's Mag.* II. 508/1 'To go over the range' is to die, as any reader of Bret Harte's frontier stories knows. **1901** Ryan *Montana* 6 There must have been some reason for the suspicion that she helped him 'over the range,' as they say out here.

(5) **1883** in *Frontier* X. (1930) 257/2 Mrs. Puett . . . is riding the range now seeing to her horses. **1946** *This Week Mag.* 16 Feb. 9/1 She rode the range from the time she was big enough to hoist herself into a saddle. — (6) **1904** O. Henry *Heart of West* 4 We been runnin' on the same range, and ridin' the same trails since we was boys.

As the last term in **bee, breeding, cattle, close, coast, cook, cooking, cow, fall, free, gas, gold, grass, gravel, grazing, hog, home, horse, hunting, Indian, open, pasture, sagebrush, sheep, spring, stock, summer, turkey, vendue, winter, wood range.**

*__range,__ *v.*

1. *intr.* Of cattle: To forage on a range.

1746 *Georgia Col. Rec.* VI. 155 All Cattle belonging to Ebenezer that he found ranging with those of the Trust should be drove up together. **1885** *Cent. Mag.* April 841 The snow lies on them too deeply in winter for cattle to range, as in Montana, all the year through. **1930** *Denver Post* 22 June II. 9/3 Those cattle were branded with a beer mug brand and ranged around Freeze Out mountain.

2. *tr.* To allow (cattle) to graze over an area. Also fig.

1857 Olmsted *Journey through Texas* 184 They ranged their cattle over as much of the adjoining prairie as they chose. **1909** Wason *Happy Hawkins* 197, I got nine hundred dollars I wish you'd range out with the rest o' my herd.

*__ranger,__ *n.*

1. A member of a body of armed men, usu. mounted, employed to range over an area for its protection; a person employed to protect the western frontier against the Indians.

1670 *Mass. H.S. Coll.* 1 Ser. VI. 211, [I] saw one of captain Willet's rangers coming on post on horseback. **1776** *Jrnls. Cont. Congress* V. 606 The regiment of rangers, now in the pay of . . . South Carolina [shall] be placed upon continental establishment. **1812** *Niles' Reg.* II. 119/2 The several companies of rangers, authorised to be raised by a late act of congress for the protection of our north-western frontier against the Indians, are already in active service. **1912** Raine *Brand Blotters* 250 This graceless scamp . . . was not the lieutenant of rangers. **1948** Dick *Dixie Frontier* 264 From the seventeenth century on, paid soldiers known as Rangers had served on the fringes of the frontier.

attrib. **1835** Whittier *Poetical Works* (1894) 504/1 The Indian points his hand To where across the echoing glen Sweep Harmon's dreaded ranger-band. **1857** *Harper's Mag.* 644/1 Let the *Ranger* system, then, be adopted in place of the old discipline—a system in which each man, acting in concert with his fellows, yet fights on his own. **1889** Mark Twain *Conn. Yankee* xxxix. 499 (R.), My horse . . . was a beauty, glossy as silk, and naked as he was when he was born, except for bridle and ranger-saddle.

b. With the name of the government employing the ranger.

1833 S. Smith *Major Downing* 191 They are the likeliest company [of soldiers] I've seen since I went with my Tennessee rangers to New Orleans. *c***1835** Catlin *Indians* II. 71 Another demand, . . . was for the restoration of an United States ranger, . . . who had been captured. **1840** Dana *Two Years* xxviii. 311 There was but one man in the only house here, and him I shall always remember as a good specimen of a California ranger. **1861** *Chi. Tribune* 26 May 1/2 Capt. Frank Bennett, Illinois Rangers, . . . offered himself. **1867** *Wkly. New Mexican* 4 May 2/2 The Arizona rangers . . . were on the road from Santa Cruz to the mine when they were attacked.

c. Short for **Texas ranger.**

1896 *Harper's Mag.* XCIV. 66/2 To have been a Ranger is a badge of distinction in Texas to this day. **1948** *Popular Western* June 12/2 That was a little quick draw insurance which Grant hadn't practiced since he was a rookie Ranger in Henchley's company down on the Pecos.

2. An officer employed to protect an area against, or to take charge of, strays.

1744 *Pa. Gaz.* 15 Nov. 3/3 Any Person or Persons, who have lost one or more of the following Strays, by applying to William Hartley, of Charles Town, Chief-Ranger for Chester County, . . . proving in their Lawful Property, . . . may be informed where to find them. **1828** *Cherokee Phenix* (New Echota, Ga.) 27 March 1/2 The ranger shall be entitled to one dollar for every horse so posted; and it shall further be the duty of the ranger, to endeavor to place in good hands, all work horses for keeping on account of their labor, or otherwise. **1891** O'Beirne *Leaders Ind. Territory* 44/2 He is now a candidate for Ranger of Blue county. **1949** *Tenn. Hist. Quart.* March 32 Law required that any freeholder 'taking up' a stray animal on his land should report it to the ranger or justice within ten days.

3. (See quot.) In full **ranger bear.**

1868 *Amer. Naturalist* I. 657, I had at one time two tamed [black bears, *Ursus americanus*]. . . . One was what is called the 'Ranger' Bear. . . . The other was what is called a 'Hog Bear,' and was shorter-legged and blacker. So I am sure the Hog Bear and Ranger are of one species.

4. A cow allowed to feed on a range.

1885 *Wkly. New Mexican Rev.* 7 May 3/6 Benjamin McLean, . . . now a heavy cattle raiser in Socorro county, with 28,000 head of rangers there, is stopping at the Las Vegas springs. **1903** *Kans. State Bd. Agric. Rep. 1901–2* 15 The best rangers I ever saw on the Chicago market were high-grade Short-horns from Montana.

5. A cattleman who ranges cattle.

1890 *Stock Grower & Farmer* 11 Jan. 4/2 The quarantine forced our people to market our stock direct in the stock yards and taught us that it was more profitable . . . than to sell our yearlings to the northwestern rangers.

6. Attrib. in the sense of forest ranger, park ranger *qq.v.*

1913 *Collier's* 6 Dec. 10/2 She is responsible for the immediate discovery and report of every fire in the ranger district overlooked by her station. **1947** *Sierra Club Bul.* May 89 Basic law which governs the use of park facilities made it impossible for us to rent ranger cabins. **1948** *Hungry Horse News* (Columbia Falls, Mont.) 17 Sep. 1/4 The planting from the fish and wildlife hatchery at Creston is in cooperation with the Big Creek ranger station of Flathead national forest.

As the last term in **buffalo, bush, buttermilk, district, forest, Georgia, Grant, Moccasin, mossbacked, mounted, park, rifle, Southern, swamp, Texas, United, Virginia, wood ranger(s).**

ranginess ˈrendʒɪnɪs, *n.* The quality of being rangy. *Colloq.* — **1872** *Vt. Bd. Agric. Rep.* I. 213 A cross of a 900 or 1000 lb. mare with a 1100 or 1200 lb. horse, with bone, ranginess and endurance, is not too violent a cross.

***ranging,** *a.* In combs.: (1) **ranging bear,** =**ranger,** *n.* **3;** (2) **company,** a military company of rangers; (3) **party,** a party or company made up of rangers, a party that ranges; (4) **timber,** timber suitable for use as cross timbers in the construction of a house or ship. All *obs.*

(1) **1796** Morse *Univ. Geog.* I. 196 The Ranging Bear . . . is carnivorous. — (2) **1756** Washington in *Lett. to Washington* II. 3 (*footnote*), I promised . . . that a regular force may be established in lieu of the militia and ranging companies. **1836** Edward *Hist. Texas* 99 Let a ranging company or companies be organized in military form and order.—(3) **1758** *Essex Inst. Coll.* XVIII. 115 The other two [companies were] . . . left for Ranging Parties. **1836** Crockett *Exploits* 121 [He] headed a ranging party. — (4) **1682** *Dorchester Rec.* 265 The same day was granted to Philip Withington liberty to get Rangeng timber for a dwelling house in the Commons. **1786** Patten *Diary* 517, I took a stick of Ranging timber of Robt to the mouth of the brook. **1816** *Mass. H.S. Coll.* 2 Ser. VII. 114 Abington and its vicinity formerly afforded large supplies of square and ranging timber.

***rangy,** *a.* **a.** Of a place: Commodious, permitting range. **b.** (See quot.) **c.** Of a horse's gait: Adapted to ranging. **d.** Of a person or animal: Long of leg and arm, angular.

(a) **1880** Lanier *Poems* (1884) 5 Breathe it free, By rangy marsh, in lone sea-liberty. **1883** C. Hallock *Sportsman's Gaz.* 452 The Toronto (Canada) Hunt Club has . . . a large rangy shed for the horses. — (b) **1890** *Cent.* 4956/1 *Rangy*, . . . sometimes applied to a roving person, as a lad who wanders from home, or who has a predilection for a roving life, as that of a sailor. (U.S.) — (c) **1891** *Harper's Mag.* July 206/2 He cannot . . . sit close without pounding to the long rangy trot of a big thorough-bred. — (d) **1899** Ade *Doc' Horne* 42 He was considerably over six feet tall, raw boned, and rangy. **1946** Halliday & Noble *Whys & Hows Cooking* 242 The ideal beef animal . . . has . . . less bone and more flesh, . . . than has the angular type, sometimes designated as 'rangy.' **1949** *Time* 10 Oct. 90/2 Medium height (5 ft. 10½ in.) and rangy, Henry is a 34-year-old copy of his father.

***rank,** *v.*

1. *Mil. tr.* To outrank, to have precedence over (another) by virtue of superiority in rank. Cf. **outrank,** *v.* Also transf.

1812 in P. H. Musser *Jas. N. Barker* (1929) 57 Col. Scott and Lt. Elliott both declared no one should go to rank me. **1841** *S. Lit. Messenger* VII. 766/1, I have Mr. Sanford under my command—I *rank* him. **1904** *Delineator* Dec. 933 The Secretary of State ranks all the other members of the Cabinet.

b. *To rank out*, to deprive (someone) of something by virtue of having superiority over him in rank. Also **ranked out,** *a.*

1872 Roe *Army Lett.* 66 Faye has been turned out of quarters—'ranked out,' as it is spoken of in the Army. **1917** J. A. Moss *Officers' Man.* 485 *Ranked-out*, to be compelled to vacate by a senior, as 'to be ranked-out of quarters.'

2. (See quot. 1905.)

1859 T. D. Price *Diary* (MS) 25 Dec., Drew some firewood on sled to rank in shed. **1905** *Forestry Bureau Bul.* No. 61, 44 *Rank*, to haul and pile regularly, as, to rank bark or cord wood.

***ranking,** *a.* Leading, foremost, superior in rank.

1862 *Yale Lit. Mag.* XXIX. 80 (Th.), His ranking officers were both gone. **1912** Haskin *Amer. Govt.* 11 The literary merit of McKinley's messages improved after John Hay became his ranking adviser. **1931** *Publishers' Wkly.* 20 June 2849/1 The publishing industry of this country . . . now takes a ranking place in the economic structure.

rank list. *Educ.* A list showing the comparative standing of students on the basis of scholarship. — **1876** Tripp *Student-Life* 129 It helps a man to be good at some one thing, either a splendid oar, or in the Nine, or the Glee Club, or the Pierian, or a good gymnast. It is a hundred times better than the rank-list. *Ib.* 270 The rank-list came out at last. **1884** R. Grant *Average Man* 22 If Woodbury Stoughton only chose to work, he could have any place on the rank-list.

ranstead ˈrænstɛd, *n.* Also **ramsted.** [See quot. 1830.] The common toadflax. In full **ranstead weed.**

1790 Muhlenberg *Flora* 173 Linaria, Ransted. **1830** Watson *Philadelphia* 642 The Ranstead weed . . . came first from Wales, being sent as a garden flower for Mr. Ranstead of Philadelphia, an upholsterer and a Welshman. **1857** Gray *Botany* 284 Toad-Flax. Butter-and-eggs. Ramsted. . . . A showy but pernicious weed.

rantankerosity ˌræntæŋkəˈrɑsɪtɪ, *n.* The state of being rantankerous. *Colloq. Obs.* — **1860** *Marysville* (Calif.) *Appeal* 20 March 2/2 The 'peeps' worked themselves up into a high strung rantankerosity of jollification.

rantankerous rænˈtæŋkərəs, *a.* [App. f. **cantankerous.*] Cantankerous, perverse, quarrelsome. *Colloq.*

1832 Paulding *Westward Ho!* I. 180 Not he, the rantanckerous squatter. **1898** Harris *Tales of Home Folks* 48 They never had such a rantankerous nigger to deal with. **1905** *N.Y. Ev. Post* 24 Nov. 6/5 M. William S. Manning of Albany is responsible for the creation of a strange new slang hybrid, at any rate. 'Rantankerous' is a happy combination of 'rambunctious' and 'cantankerous,' however inappropriate it is applied to the Albany author.

rantum-scootum ˈræntəmˈskutəm, *a.* [Var. of **rantum-scantum.*] Harum-scarum, disorderly. *Rare.* — **1885** *Harper's Mag.* 3 March 614/1 He's a deal sight more serious-minded than most of the rantum-scootum boys.

***rap,** *n.*[1] A rebuke, blame, a prison sentence, often in such phrases as *to get* (*beat, take*) *the rap*. *Slang.*

The *OED* records **rap*, *v.* (1733——) in the slang sense of to swear (a thing) against a person, to perjure oneself. There may be a connection between the verb in this sense and the sense of *rap* here shown.

1777 *Amer. Pioneer* II. 17 The post master general . . . has lately had a rap, which I hope will have a good effect. **1865** *Atlantic Mo.* March 297/2 He who has the bad taste to meddle with the caprices of believers . . . gets the rap and the orders of dismissal. **1928** *Amer. Mercury* Aug. 482/1 I'd at least beat *that* rap. **1949** *Sat. Ev. Post* 2 July 19/1 He carried the banner and took the rap for Roosevelt in the Senate for many years.

Rap ræp, *n.*[2] Short for **Rapaho,** or **Arapaho.** *Colloq. Obs.* — **1886** *Outing* Nov. 104/1 Sing'lar I never struck the Shoshone trail; they must 'a' crossed the mountains by 'nother pass, but Raps nor Sioux, thar war none.

***rap,** *v. tr.* To criticise, condemn. *Slang.* Cf. ***rap,** *n.*[1]

1906 *N.Y. Ev. Post* 23 Nov. 5 Football was sharply rapped and rowing was highly praised. **1926** J. Kerney *Pol. Educ. Woodrow Wilson* 105 In screamer headlines the conference was rapped as a secret and reprehensible thing. **1949** *Chi. D. News* 22 Sep. 5 (*caption*), Trial Delays Rapped by Judge.

Rapaho ˈræpəˌho, *n.* Short for **Arapaho.** *Colloq.*

1848 Ruxton *Life Far West* i, Maybe you'll get 'roped' (lasso'd) by a Rapaho. **1857** *Spirit of Times* 21 March 57/1 Buffler aint runnin' now, and a starved Rapaho wouldn't be no-ways back'ard about makin' a raise of our mules and packs, you may depend. **1886** *Outing* Nov. 104/1 Every fall, about this time, the Sioux or Rapahoes visits one 'nother, and generally pass near here.

***rapid,** *a.* and *n.* [In **1.** poss. influenced by F. *rapide, rapides.*]

1. *n.* A place in a river where the water descends rapidly but without waterfalls or cascades, usu. *pl.*

1765 CROGHAN *Journal* 136 What is called the Fall here, is no more than rapids. 1802 ELLICOTT *Journal* 19 The rapids are occasioned by the water falling from one horizontal stratum of limestone, to another. 1848 THOREAU *Maine Woods* 25 Just above McCauslin's, there is a rocky rapid, where logs jam in the spring. 1949 *Nat. Hist.* June 269/1 Nearing its juncture with the Colorado, the incline increases rapidly, and the stream hurdles over a rough course of low terraces and boiling rapids.

b. rapids piece, (see quot.).

1926 RICKABY *Ballads* 236 *Rapids piece.* A section of a raft. So called because when approaching a dangerous rapids the raft was divided for easier handling in the passage.

2. rapid transit, local passenger transportation, sometimes restricted to modes of transportation faster than those operating in street traffic. Also attrib.

1882 MCCABE *New York* 67 Rapid transit, too, now so fully developed, will . . . keep the present population resident in their own city. 1894 *N.Y. Wkly. Tribune* 7 March 12/1 The people of the Potrero and of South San Francisco will soon have rapid transit to the heart of the city. 1914 *Cyclo. Amer. Govt.* III. 151/1 Rapid transit facilities [can] be introduced . . . either by the construction of elevated or subway . . . lines, or a combination of elevated and subway lines. 1949 *L.A. Times* 1 April II. 8/4 We feel rapid transit is so urgent that we deemed it necessary to overlook some defects in the legislation you propose.

rapist 'repɪst, *n.* [f. the verb.] One guilty of rape. Also transf.

1889 *Columbus* (O.) *Dispatch* 13 June, Two horse thieves and a rapist were sentenced. 1948 *Washington Post* 5 Dec. 24M/3 Sex squad detectives and park police yesterday pressed their search for a rapist believed to have assaulted a 14-year-old girl. 1949 *Time* 19 Dec. 23/3 We follow a system which amounts to rape of the land. We are no careful husbandmen—not husbands but rapists.

∗**rapper,** *n.* One who allegedly secures communications from the spirits of the dead, who announce their presence by raps or knocks. *Obs.* Cf. **spirit rapper, rapping.** — 1851 *Calif. Christian Adv.* (S.F.) 24 Dec. 1/2 This lovely spot has become the seat of the delusive magic of modern 'Rappers.' 1875 *Chi. Tribune* 1 Oct. 7/3 Something of a sensation was excited by the appearance . . . of Margaret Fox Kane, one of the original rappers of Rochester a quarter of a century ago.

Rappist 'ræpɪst, *n.* A member of a communistic religious society founded by George (i.e., Johann Georg) Rapp (1757–1847); a Harmonist. Now *hist.* Cf. **Economist.**

1845 *Essays on Chr. Union* 372 The following are the principal religious sects in America . . . : The Protestant Episcopal Church, . . . the Rappists, Shakers, Mormons, . . . and other small sects and parties. 1884 SCHAFF *Religious Encycl.* III. The Rappists emigrated to Economy, seventeen miles northwest of Pittsburg. 1903 *Encycl. Americana* VIII. *s.v. Harmonists*, also called Rappists and Economists, . . . emigrated to America, settling in the Connoquenessing Valley, where the Harmony Society was established.

Rappite 'ræpaɪt, *n.* = prec. Now *hist.*

1832 FERRALL *Ramble* 92 The Rappites had been in possession of the place [New Harmony, Ind.] for six years. 1864 NICHOLS *Amer. Life* II. 29 The Rappites . . . founded large communities and gathered wealth by industry. 1949 *Indiana Hist.* June 184 The Rappites, after their return to Pennsylvania, maintained active trade relations with Louisville.

attrib. 1852 *N.Y. Wkly. Tribune* 17 April 1/3 The plaintiff was Joshua Nachtrieb and the defendants the Trustees and Elders of the Rappite Society of Communists established at Economy. 1905 LOCKWOOD *New Harmony Movement* 35 The Rappite organization long since ceased to be a community and became a closed corporation administered for the benefit of a dwindling membership. 1947 *Tenn. Hist. Quart.* Dec. 294 The Rappite colony had been very successful in its financial operations.

∗**rareripe,** *a.* and *n.*

1. An early-ripening variety of peach, a peach of such a variety. In full **rareripe peach.**

1722 *N.-Eng. Courant* 3 Sep. 2/1 Having in his Garden a plentiful Crop of Rare-Ripes, he agreed with an Ethiopian Market-Man . . . to bring him an Horse-load of them to Town. 1819 *Ky. Alman. 1820* (Lexington) 26, I was presented with a fine rare ripe peach. 1884 *N.Y. Wkly. Tribune* 20 Feb. 11/1 Rare-ripes [are] red-fleshed, and yellow-fleshed, but red at the stone.

transf. 1861 HOLMES *E. Venner* vi, *Rosa Milburn.* Sixteen. Brunette, with a rare ripe flush in her cheeks. 1890 LOWELL *Biglow P.* 2 Ser. Intro. 239 President Lincoln said of a precocious boy that he was a *rareripe*.

2. rareripe corn, a variety of Indian corn that matures more rapidly than do other varieties. *Obs.*

1786 WASHINGTON *Diaries* III. 145 The Eastern rare-ripe Corn . . . had yielded . . . unproductively both at Muddy hole and in the Neck. 1799——*Writings* XIV. 231 All that part . . . is to be planted with rare-ripe corn. 1835 J. MARTIN *Descr. Virginia* 59 In the year 1619 two crops of rare-ripe corn were made.

∗**raring,** *a.* Madly eager, full of desire *to go*, etc. *Slang.* — 1909 E. BANKS *Myst. Fran. Farrington* 49 They made me raring, tearing mad to look at 'em. 1923 F. N. HART *Bellamy Trial* i. 10 Both sides are rarin' to go, and they are not liable to touch their peremptory challenges [of jurymen].

rasher 'ræʃɚ, *n.* [App. f. local Pg. *rasciera*, a kind of fish.] A rockfish, *Rosicola miniatus*, found off the coast of California. — 1889 *Nat. Museum Proc.* III. 146 The following species of 'rock-fish' were obtained by us in Monterey Bay. The names used by the fishermen . . . [include]: Meron, Tom-cod, Jack-fish, . . . Rasher. 1896 JORDAN & EVERMANN *Check-List Fishes* 429.

∗**raspberry,** *n.* As the last term in **black, leafy, mountain, Ohio ever-bearing, Philadelphia, red, rose-flowering raspberry.**

raspberry shrub. (See quot. 1945.)

1832 CHILD *Frugal Housewife* 82 Raspberry shrub mixed with water is a pure, delicious drink in summer. 1886 WARNER *Their Pilgrimage* xi, Mr. Glow and King and Forbes, sipping their raspberry shrub in a retired corner of the bar-room, were interested spectators of the scene. 1945 *This Week Mag.* 30 June 13/1 Raspberry Shrub 4 quarts raspberries 1 quart cider vinegar Sugar Clean and pick over berries. Cover with vinegar and let stand four days. Strain. To each cup of juice add one cup of sugar. Boil 15 minutes and bottle when cold.

raster 'ræstɚ, *n.* Short for **arrastre.** *Obs.* — 1851 *S.F. Herald* 28 July 2/3 Rastra, or track mills, (as simple contrivances for amalgamating,) are now being made, each of which will crush and amalgamate forty-five hundred pounds of the quartz per day. 1885 *Wkly. New Mexican Rev.* 2 April 3/4 Messrs. Probst and Gonzales will construct an old style Mexican 'raster,' crushing the ore with heavy boulders and horse power.

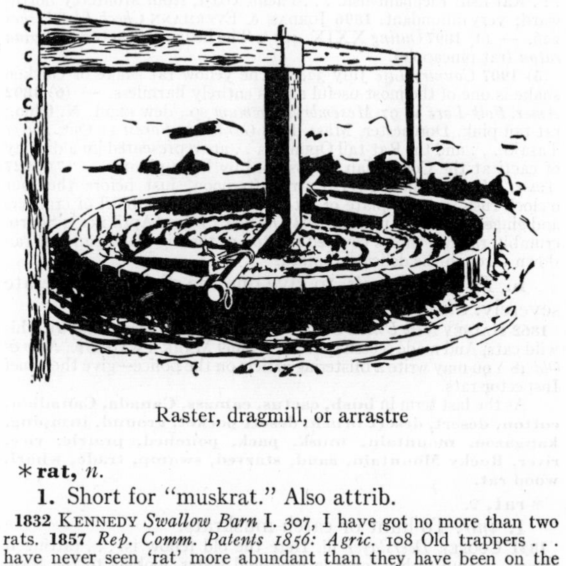

Raster, dragmill, or arrastre

∗**rat,** *n.*

1. Short for "muskrat." Also attrib.

1832 KENNEDY *Swallow Barn* I. 307, I have got no more than two rats. 1857 *Rep. Comm. Patents 1856: Agric.* 108 Old trappers . . . have never seen 'rat' more abundant than they have been on the prairies of Northern Illinois. 1926 *Rep. La. Dept. Conservation 1924–26* 108 The leasing company takes no percentage of the catch. It believes in leaving it to the trapper or 'rat rancher' to sell his own winter's take without let or hindrance.

b. rat house, a dome-shaped structure of rushes and mud in which muskrats live.

1921 *Outing* Oct. 26/3 The next year on inspecting the 'rat houses I discovered they were extraordinarily high but did not appear to have very thick walls. 1949 R. J. SIM *Pages from Past* 57 This would be an aid in penetrating a rat house more easily.

2. (*cap.*) A nickname for a member of a certain religious sect in Indiana *c*1824. *Obs.*

1843 CARLTON *New Purchase* II. 88 When rumour declared we intended to elect a man nominally a Rat, . . . the wrath was roused of the people, religious, and irreligious, of all other sects. *Ib.* 89 The people . . . [were determined] to keep out a Rat.

3. (See quot.)

1850 LEWIS *La. Swamp Doctor* 113 There were four or five brother 'Rats' besides myself residing in the hospital, all candidates for graduation, and all desirous of obtaining sufficient medical lore.

4. A pad of a shape somewhat like that of a rat, used in certain styles of women's coiffure. Cf. * **mouse,** *n.* **1.**

1863 A. D. WHITNEY *F. Gartney* xi, The luminous tresses . . . rippled . . . after a style of their own that in these later days Fashion and Art have striven hopelessly to achieve with crimping-pins and—'*rats!*' **1909** *Dly. Maroon* (Chi.) 6 Oct. 3/3 No rats, puffs, transformations, switches, curls or bangs may be worn by Barnard college Freshmen. **1946** T. JONES *Skinny Angel* 96 She had long teeth and darting, brown eyes in a long face framed in oily gray hair strained tidily over a half-moon of rat.

5. *pl.* Used as an interjection to express incredulity. *Slang.*

1890 *Road* (Denver, Colo.) 24 May 1/1 Much is being said concerning Teller's loyalty to silver. Rats! **1920** LEWIS *Main Street* 446 Sam Clark interrupted, 'Rats, they never even thought about making love.'

6. In special combs.: (1) **rat-and-tan,** designating a terrier, app. one of a common sort, *rare;* (2) **biscuit,** a form of rat poison; (3) **fish,** a fish of the genus *Chimaera*, esp. *C. colliei* of the Pacific Coast; (4) **pineapple,** a thorny tropical plant, *Bromelia pinquin*, often used for hedges; (5) **snake,** (see quot. and cf. **chicken snake**); (6) * **tail,** in plant names (see quots.); (7) **trap cheese,** a common yellow cheese often used in baiting rat traps.

(1) **1876** *Vt. Bd. Agric. Rep.* III. 130 [It] is about as sensible as to expect a mastiff to spring from the loins of a rat-and-tan terrier. — (2) **1907** *Collier's* 30 March 12/2 Did Mr. Scranton scatter about a schoolroom or playground, where children might find and eat it, rat-biscuit, he would presumably be arrested. **1931** *K.C. Star* 26 Oct., It was suggested to him by the clerk that he buy rat biscuits instead. — (3) **1882** *Nat. Museum Bul.* No. 16, 54 *Chimæra*. . . . Rat-fishes. . . . Mostly of the northern seas; not valued for food. *Ib.* 55 *C. coliæi*. . . . Rat-fish; Elephant-fish. . . . Pacific coast, from Monterey northward; very abundant. **1896** JORDAN & EVERMANN *Check-List Fishes* 226. — (4) **1897** *Outing* XXIX. 425/1 The hedges of cactus and *pina raton* (rat pineapple).

(5) **1907** *Country Life* July 328/3 The yellow rat snake or chicken snake is one of the most useful and is entirely harmless. — (6) **1892** *Amer. Folk-Lore* V. 97 *Mesembryanthemum* sp., dew plant. N. Ohio.; rat-tail pink. Dorchester, Mass. **1893** *Garden & Forest* 11 Oct. 429/1 Tasajo . . . and the Rat-tail Opuntia . . . are represented [in a display of cacti at the Columbian Exposition] by large plants. — (7) **1927** *Amer. Mercury* Jan. 28/1 Every afternoon, just before the four o'clock rush, a small plate of rat-trap cheese and a bowl of crackers and gingersnaps were put out. **1947** *Reader's Digest* April 131/1 Sharp, crumbly rattrap cheese covered the top of the big black pan and ran down through the delicate custard.

b. *To give one rats*, to give one the dickens, to berate severely. *Slang.*

1862 HALSEY *New Union Song Book* 49 He gave them rats, with his wild cats, And made secesh quite sick. **1869** MARK TWAIN *Sk., New & Old* 48 You may write a blistering article on the police—give the Chief Inspector rats.

As the last term in **bush, cactus, camass, Canada, Canadian, cotton, desert, desert brush, desert pocket, ground, jumping, kangaroo, mountain, musk, pack, pouched, prairie, rice, river, Rocky Mountain, sand, starved, swamp, trade, wharf, wood rat.**

* **rat,** *v.*

1. *intr.* To hunt or catch muskrats.

1841 COOPER *Deerslayer* iii, Here the old fellow is! . . . ratting it away . . . ; up to his knees in mud and water, looking to the traps and the bait. **1950** *Dly. Ardmoreite* (Ardmore, Okla.) 14 Feb. 4/5, I think I'll stop 'ratting after this year. Man, it is pretty hard to trample the marshes all day long.

2. *tr.* To denounce (a newspaper or printing office) as employing rat or scab labor; to relegate (a printer or compositor) to the status of a rat. *Slang.*

1851 *Ore. Statesman* 7 Oct. 2/6 We have confidence enough in the [printing] craft to believe that no member would *rat* it. **1874** *Internat. Typog. Union Proc.* 22 Attempt to force non-Union printers upon Union printers. Result: Unfavorable. Office 'ratted.' **1898** *Ib.* 60/1 Mr. Hotchkiss, who had refused to obey the call of the committee . . . , was ratted.

Hence **ratting,** *a.* and *n.*

1851 *Ore. Statesman* 30 Sep. 2/5 The Spectator 'family' have finally been successful in their ratting attempts, and are now employing Printers at rates twenty-five per cent less than those paid [here]. **1948** *Antioch Review* Spring 52 If their records are clear of 'ratting' or strikebreaking and they are technically competent, they seldom have any difficulty in joining.

b. To get out (a paper) with rat labor.

1896 *Internat. Typog. Union Proc.* 28/1 The proprietor . . . was asked to discharge the compositor, which he refused to do, saying he would rat the paper first.

c. *To rat on*, to betray, tell on (someone). *Slang.*

1947 *Atlantic* Oct. 60/1, I hoped they'd get tired soon and put me back into the cell because I didn't want to rat on the fellow who'd given me that blueprint. **1948** *Sat. Ev. Post* 4 Sep. 91/1 If he remains one of the boys, he will be accused of ratting on his own kind when it becomes necessary to crack the whip.

3. To dress (a person's) hair with a rat.

1866 A. D. WHITNEY *Goldthwaite* x, Next morning, at breakfast, Sin Saxon was as beautifully ruffled, ratted, and crimped . . . as ever.

* **rate,** *n.* In combs.: (1) **rate bill,** a bill for school tuition pro-rated among the patrons according to the number of pupils each sends, *obs.;* (2) **card,** (see quot.); (3) **cutting,** the lowering of freight rates by a railroad; (4) **maker,** one who makes or sets rates, formerly a person selected to assess the rates or taxes in a town or colony; (5) **pay,** money collected, or to be collected, as rates or taxes, *obs.;* (6) **war,** a struggle or competition over rates, esp. railroad rates.

(1) **1838** *Speeches of D. Barnard* 51 And provides for the payment of any deficiency . . . by a rate-bill against those who furnish children to be instructed. **1923** ADAMS *Pioneer Hist.* 295 They had in those early days a rate bill, so much a pupil, and it was no great sum either. — (2) **1905** E. E. CALKINS & R. HOLDEN *Art of Advertising* 352 A rate-card is a card or printed sheet giving the advertising rates in a given publication. — (3) **1888** *Economist* 10 Nov. 8/3 One of the leading bear influences has been the old evil of rate-cutting by the railroad companies. **1949** *Chi. Tribune* 28 Dec. 1/3 There was some rate cutting last year, but it was not as conspicuous as now. — (4) **1660** *Mass. H.S. Coll.* 4 Ser. VII. 249 The rate makers think it is just that 18*li.* for a mans head should pay as many pence as 18*li.* for a horse. **1682** *Derby Rec.* 130 The Town have chosen Sar Johnson mr. John Hubbel & Abel Gun listers & rate makers. **1716** *Conn. Hist. Soc. Coll.* VI. 321 Voted that the Listers and Ratemakers distribute the New Law book in this Town. **1903** E JOHNSON *Railway Transportation* 285 The producers and carriers . . . are trying to get the trade of the markets reached by the rate-makers' road.

(5) **1680** *Boston Rec.* 137 Allowed to James Euerall & his Daughtr Manninge 20ᵈ. in rate pay in consideration of theire houses beinge burnt. **1686** *Ib.* 84 Ye Sume of Sixtye pounds . . . [is] to be p[ai]d as rate pay. — (6) **1893** *Chi. Tribune* 28 April 16/1 Horns Still Locked. The Santa Fe and Rio Grande Keep Up Rate War. **1903** E. JOHNSON *Railway Transportation* 218 In 1869 a 'rate war' carried the rates for a time to 25 cents a hundred [pounds] for all classes.

b. In phrases: (1) *As sure as rates*, very surely or certainly; (2) *to cut rates*, to reduce freight rates.

(1) **1815** HUMPHREYS *Yankey* 55 The man is . . . horn mad, as sure as rates. **1854** S. SMITH *Down East* 238 But you'll kill that mare, colonel, as sure as rates. — (2) **1872** *Chi. Tribune* 20 Nov. 4/4 Agents, soliciting freights, when not allowed to 'cut rates,' have connived at this underselling. **1884** *Cong. Rec.* 10 Dec. 164/1 If one road cuts the rates, it will get the freight.

As the last term in **country, county, cow, cut, first, graveyard, Indian, open, powder, pro-, school, state, through, Turk's rate(s).**

* **rate,** *v. tr.* To carry or convey at a fixed rate. — **1881** *Chi. Times* 12 March, Large quantities of freight have been rated through to New York by this and other lines.

ratherish ˈræðərɪʃ, *adv.* In a slight degree, somewhat, rather. *Colloq.* — **1846** H. N. MOORE *Fitzgerald & Hopkins* 30 For my part, I became ratherish confused, and rather sheepishly got up from Nancy's lap. **1887** *Library Mag.* 12 Feb. 422 Mr. Lang has a ratherish good opinion [of Longfellow's poems].

rathskeller ˈrɑtsˌkɛlɚ, *n.* [G., an eating and drinking place in a city hall, usu. in the cellar.] A beer saloon or a restaurant, usu. below street level.

1900 ADE *More Fables* 159 Mr. Byrd . . . happened to be in a Rathskeller not far away. **1903** *Current Lit.* April 495/2 The first rathskeller was established in New York in 1863 by Fred. Hollander **1928** *Amer. Mercury* Oct. 175/2 It's called the rathskeller. **1947** BEEBE *Mixed Train Dly.* 291 You go downstairs through the cocktail lounge and through the men's bar and through the rathskeller.

ratification meeting. A public meeting to signify approval of a political action or proceeding, as the nomination of a party candidate. — **1848** *Campaign* (Wash., D.C.) 21 June 64/2 A great democratic ratification meeting was held at New Orleans on the night of the 8th June. **1904** *N.Y. Ev. Post* 23 June 2 The first Roosevelt ratification meeting of the campaign will be held this evening, when the Republican Club of the 31st Assembly District will endorse the nominees of the Chicago convention.

***ratoon,** *n.* A portion of a stalk of sugar cane suitable for planting, a sugar-cane stump. Also **ratoon cane.**

1827 *Western Mo. Rev.* I. 82 It is propagated by cuttings or slips of the cane stalk, called rattoons. **1862** *N.Y. Wkly. Tribune* 22 March 6/2 From seven acres of 'ratoon cane' 21 hhds. of sugar were made in January, 1849. **1890** *Cong. Rec.* 9 May 4387/1 Sugar-cane is propagated from cuts called 'rattoons.'

rattinet ˌrætɪˈnɛt, *n.* (See quot. 1890.) — **1812** *Niles' Reg.* II. 9/1 Much of it [i.e., wool] . . . may be wrought into *worsted* stuffs, such as shalloons, rattinets, durants. **1890** *Cent.* 4973/3 rattinet, . . . a woolen stuff thinner than ratteen.

***rattle,** *n.*

1. The jointed organ at the end of a rattlesnake's tail, or one of the articulated parts of which this is composed. Usu. *pl.*, and often, though erroneously, regarded as an accurate indication of the snake's age.

1624 Smith *Gen. Hist. Va.* 30 Those Rattels are somewhat like the chape of a Rapier but lesse, which they take from a taile of a snake. **1674** Josselyn *Two Voyages* 27 [The rattlesnake] had a rattle which is nothing but a hollow shelly business joynted. **1733** Byrd *Journey to Eden* (1901) 293 We kill'd two very large Rattle-snakes, one of 15 and the other of 12 Rattles. **1815** *Niles' Reg.* IX. 152/1 A rattlesnake in the Alleghany mountains . . . had twenty-nine rattles, and must, therefore, have been thirty-two years old. **1948** *Great Falls* (Mont.) *Tribune* 18 Sep. 4/4 She saw a coiled rattlesnake, ran to a shed, found an ax, chopped off the snake's head and removed 14 rattles from its tail.

transf. and *attrib.* **1855** Simms *Forayers* 317 He is . . . a liquid serpent, who will glide into the porches of your dwelling, and coil himself in a corner, yet sound no rattle. **1869** J. R. Browne *Adv. Apache Country* 394, I inquired if these vicious reptiles, of which I had heard so much in Aurora, were of the rattle or copperhead species.

b. The sound made by these when shaken or vibrated.

1851 Glisan *Jrnl. Army Life* 70 My Comanche horse will jump ten feet at the sudden rattle of one of these reptiles.

2. *pl.* A popular name for croup. *Obs.*

1744 Hempstead *Diary* 434 A Child . . . died of the Rattles or Throat Destemper. **1806** W. Pettigrew *Lett.* 26 Nov. (Univ. N.C. MS), He was then taken very bad with the rattels.

3. A mild expletive. *Rare.*

1787 Tyler *Contrast* v. i, But what the rattle makes you look so tarnation glum? *Ib.* ii, What the rattle ails you?

4. *pl.* (See quot. 1888.) *Colloq.* Cf. ***rattle,** *v.* **2.**

1888 *Cosmopolitan* Oct. 452/2 The younger players are not infrequently attacked by what in base-ball vernacular is known as 'the rattles,' a complaint much akin to what sportsmen call the 'buck-fever,' and actors 'stage fright.' **1893** *Chi. Tribune* 28 April 7/3 The Pittsburgs had a bad case of 'rattles' and were not in it from the start.

5. In combs., some of which are based on the verb: (1) **rattle-and-snap,** (see quot.), *obs.;* (2) ***box,** (*a*) any one of various species of *Crotalaria*, esp. *C. sagittalis*, the seeds of which rattle in the pod when ripe, (*b*) the silver-bell tree, *Halesia carolina*, (*c*) the bladder campion, *Silene latifolia*, (*d*) the rattles of the rattlesnake, *rare;* (3) **pod,** =**rattlebox** (*a*); (4) **ran,** (see quot. 1867); (5) **snake,** see as a main entry; (6) **tailsnake,** a rattlesnake, *rare;* (7) **-te-bang,** a discordant rattling, banging noise, also as adv. and adj., *colloq.;* (8) ***weed,** (*a*) the bugbane, *Cimicifuga racemosa* (see also quot. 1931), (*b*) **rattleweed juice,** =**bug juice,** *obs.*

(1) ?**1849** S. C. Upham *Notes on Voyage to Calif.* (1878) 225 The *roulette, keno, rattle-and-snap* and other small-fry gamblers pay less [rental] amounts. — **(2)** (*a*) **1817–8** Eaton *Botany* (1822) 255 *Crotalaria sagittalis*, rattle-box. **1943** Holt *Carver* 199 He would caution stockmen against the rattlebox (*Crotalaria*). (*b*) **1884** Sargent *Rep. Forests* 106 Rattlebox. Snow-drop tree. . . . Reaching its greatest development in the southern Alleghany mountains. **1897** Sudworth *Arborescent Flora* 323 Silverbell-tree. . . . Rattlebox (Tex.). (*c*) **1893** *Amer. Folk-Lore* VI. 138 *Silene cucubalus*, rattle-box. Berkshire Co., Mass. (*d*) **1913** Stratton-Porter *Laddie* i, The only things to be careful about were a little, shiny, slender snake, . . . and a big thick one with . . . a whole rattlebox on its tail. — **(3)** **1898** A. M. Davidson *Calif. Plants* 133 There are the 'rattle-pods,' so common in sandy soil; this plant is called loco weed by the stockmen, and is believed to loco horses. **1929** Dobie *Vaquero* 9 To make sure that the firecrackers exploded in a strategic spot we cut siene (rattle pod) switches, split the ends, and inserted the firecrackers in the split. — **(4)** **1867** De Voe *Market Ass't* 57 The plate-piece (in Boston called *rattle-ran*) is commonly used for corned or salted beef, and the best for pressing. **1941** Farmer *Boston Cook Book* 314 The fancy brisket commands a higher price and may easily be told from the rattleran by the selvage on the lower side and the absence of bones.

(6) **1867** Cozzens *Sayings* 106 An Enormous Rattletail Snake—a regular whopper. — **(7)** **1824** *Old Colony Memorial* (Plymouth) 6 March (Th.), [He said] as how they had ten thousand rattletraps, and kept up a tarnation sort of rattlety bang. **1872** *Newton Kansan* 29 Aug. 4/2 The bells should be of the noisy, rattle-te-bang kind. **1889** *Boston Jrnl.* 16 Jan. 2/3 Rattletybang, crash, came a whole assortment of bottles, flasks and cigar boxes. — **(8)** (*a*) **1791** *Amer. Philos. Soc.* III. 114 *Actæa racemosa* (American Bane-berry, Black Snake-root, Rattle-weed.) **1893** *Amer. Folk-Lore* VI. 136 *Cimicifuga racemosa*, rattle-weed. Banner Elk, N.C. **1931** Clute *Plants* 110 *Crotalaria sagittalis*, with pods that rattle attractively is frequently known as rattle-box or rattle-weed. (*b*) **1876** *San Bernardino* (Calif.) *D. Times* 2 June 3/2 Marshal Wall worries the votaries of rattleweed juice so, that they don't indulge very liberally.

As the last term in **bull, horse, rattlesnake rattle(s).**

***rattle,** *v.*

1. *intr.* Of a rattlesnake: To produce a noise by vibrating the rattles.

1776 in *Jrnl. of Nicholas Cresswell* (1925) 145, I have seen some [rattlesnakes] with ten of them [rattles], they generally rattle at your approach and are easily avoided. **1823** Doddridge *Logan* ii. ii, The large snake rattles, and bites. **1888** Roosevelt in *Cent. Mag.* June 201/1 One or two [rattlesnakes] coiled and rattled menacingly as I stepped near.

2. *tr.* To confuse, embarrass, or disconcert (a person). *Colloq.* Cf. ***rattle,** *n.* **4.**

1869 J. R. Browne *Adv. Apache Country* 282, I think he was slightly rattled by the formidable appearance of our escort. **1927** Russell *Trails* 21 By this time these savages are so rattled that the snappin' of a twig would turn the whole band back.

rattled snake. A rattlesnake. *Rare.* — **1748** Washington *Writings* I. 6 This day see a Rattled snake, ye first we had seen in all our journey.

***rattler,** *n.*

1. A rattlesnake. *Colloq.*

1827 Cooper *Prairie* xxxiii, It would be no easy matter to judge of the temper of the rattler by considering the fashions of the moose. **1914** Bower *Flying U Ranch* 132 Say, they hang together like bull snakes and rattlers, don't they? **1948** *Duncan* (Okla.) *D. Banner* 2 July 7/8 Those who can get up enough courage to bite into the fried rattler say it tastes like chicken.

2. A train, esp. a fast one (see also quot. 1945). *Slang.*

1900 Flynt *Notes Itin. Policeman* 178 Hustle, Cigarette, there's our rattler. **1945** *Tracks* June 29/2 *Battle-wagon* for coal wagon, *rattler* for freight car.

As the last term in **diamond, ground, king, Lone Star, prairie, throat, tiger, timber rattler.**

rattlesnake ˈrætḷˌsnek, *n.*

1. Any one of various American pit vipers of the family Crotalidae having a tail terminating in a rattle.

There are two genera, *Sistrurus* and *Crotalus*, and many species, all being confined to America. Rattlesnakes vary in size from the small ground rattlesnake or massasauga to the diamond-back, which sometimes attains a length of eight feet.

1630 Higginson *N.-Eng.* 12 There are some Serpents called Rattle Snakes, that haue Rattles in their Tayles. **1705** *Boston News-Letter* 18 June 2/2, 4 of our English Prisoners at Mont-Real . . . were so put to it for Provisions by the way, that they were forced to eat Rattle Snakes. **1807** Gass *Journal* 113 A rattle-snake came among our canoes in the water. **1949** *Democrat* 22 Sep. 1/2 They had killed a rattlesnake the week before with 17 rattles.

transf. **1862** E. McDermott *Pop. Guide Internat. Exhib.* 185 [At] an American bar . . . visitors may indulge in 'juleps,' . . . 'cobblers,' 'rattlesnakes,' 'gum ticklers' [etc.]. **1867** *Wkly. New Mexican* 2 March 2/1 [The] copperhead principle . . . hissed encouragement, in the North during the rebellion, to the less degraded rattlesnake of secession. **1944** Stafford *Boston Adv.* 337 The Baron, a handsome, well-tailored man in his thirties, a cosmopolitan and sycophant of wealthy women was, as someone said, a 'rattlesnake' at cards.

b. *S.* A variety of watermelon, so called from the markings on its rind.

1855 Davis *Farm Bk.* 152 This day has been spent in planting small patch crops—Watermelons—Muskmelons—Squashes cucumbers—Rows 1 to 8 Rattlesnake . . . 9 to 13 Ice Rind. **1883** *Chi. Tribune* 1 July 2/2 The melons are the rattlesnake or Augusta variety, and are the finest melons grown. **1942** Castetter & Bell *Pima & Papago Agric.* 119 Varieties which do well at the Coöperative Field Station are Klondike, . . . Tom Watson, Stone Mountain and Georgia Rattlesnake.

2. In combs.: (1) **rattlesnake bee,** (see quot.), *rare;* (2) **colonel,** a title conferred in derision upon anyone who had killed a rattlesnake, in jocular or contemptuous allusion to the fondness of Americans for military titles [see A. Matthews in *N. Eng. Quarterly* X. (1937) 341–45], *obs.;* (3) **den,** (see quot. 1898); (4) **flag,** any one of several flags having a rattlesnake as a device and usu. the motto "Don't Tread On Me," used by the colonies at the outbreak of the Revolution; (5) **killer,** the road runner *q.v.;* (6) **money,** paper money having on it the device of a rattlesnake, *obs.;* (7) **pike,** (see quot.); (8) **pilot,** =**copperhead 1;** (9) **-'s cousin,** =prec.; (10) **serum,** a serum used in cases of rattlesnake bite; (11) **-'s mate,** =**copperhead 1;** (12) **State,** South Carolina, a nickname, *obs.*

(1) **1940** H. BRADLEY *Such Was Saratoga* 46 Across the lake the Arnolds had only recently invited all hands to a 'Rattlesnake Bee' whereby the venomous reptiles which long had infested that neighborhood were summarily excised by fire and lethal weapons. — (2) [**1744** A. HAMILTON *Itinerarium* (1907) 97 Had it been a rattlesnake I should have been entitled to a colonel's commission for it is a common saying here that a man has no title to that dignity until he has killed a rattlesnake.] **1755** in *N. Eng. Quart.* X. (1937) 341 (*footnote*), At 10 we came to the River and waited 6 Hours before we could ferry over at 8 at Night we halted at a Rattle snake Colonels named Crisop. *Ib.* 344 Ferried over the River [Potomac] into *Maryland* . . . there lives Colonel Cressop, a Rattle Snake, Colonel, and a D——d Rascal. — (3) **1834** *S. Lit. Messenger* I. 98 To the reputed wonders of rattlesnake dens . . . we cannot testify. **1898** *Smithsonian Rep.* 1189 Where these snakes are numerous, they are inclined to gather in considerable numbers in caverns in rocks and similar places in order to undergo their winter sleep. Such places form the rattlesnake dens about which we hear occasionally. — (4) **1895** *Stand.* a689 (plate), Rattlesnake Flag of the Revolution. **1925** T. H. CUMMINGS *First Flag* 3 Some of the southern colonies used a rattlesnake flag with the motto 'Don't tread on me.'

(5) **1877** HODGE *Arizona* 224 There is also a small bird, no larger than the wren, which is called the rattlesnake-killer. — (6) **1803** *Ann. 7th Congress* 2 Sess. 246 We never ought to lose sight of an old Revolutionary motto, on our *rattlesnake money,* 'United we stand, divided we fall.' **1804** *Ann. 8th Congress* 2 Sess. 1595 They were at liberty to pay in paper at that time current in Georgia, (except what was called rattlesnake money.) — (7) **1947** DALRYMPLE *Panfish* 220 Colloquially, the Sauger is also your old friend the Sand Pike, or Gray Pike, or Ground Pike, or Rattlesnake Pike, or Pickerel, or Pickering, or—of all things—Horse-fish! — (8) **1934** WEBSTER. **1948** *Democrat* 4 Nov. 1/3 [He] reported killing a rattlesnake pilot, or copperhead moccasin, which had been partaking of a strange diet. — (9) **1819** *Niles' Reg.* XVII. 44/2 'A rattlesnake's mate, or cousin' was lately killed at Wilton, R.I.

(10) **1945** *Greeley* (Colo.) *D. Tribune* 4 Aug. 1/6 Late Friday night police were assisting in an effort to locate rattlesnake serum. — (11) **1818** *Amer. Jrnl. Science* I. 84 *Syctalus Cupreus,* or Copper-head Snake, . . . [is known] in New-England, by the names of *rattlesnake's mate* and *red adder.* **1907** *Ann. Rep. N.J. State Museum* 188 Copper Head Snake. . . . Deaf Adder. Rattlesnake's Mate. — (12) **1861** *N.Y. Tribune* 16 Nov. (Chipman), The recent magnificent exploit [at Beaufort, S.C.] on the coast of the Rattlesnake State.

b. In the names of plants: (1) **rattlesnake fern,** a species of grape fern, *Botrychium virginianum,* having sporangia resembling the rattles of a rattlesnake; (2) **grass** a handsome stout species of American grass, *Glyceria canadensis,* the spikelets of which suggest the rattles of the rattlesnake; (3) **herb,** the baneberry; (4) **leaf,** (see quot.); (5) **master,** any one of various plants reputed to cure the bite of a rattlesnake, often the button snakeroots of the southeastern states, also **rattlesnake's master,** cf. **yucca-leaved rattlesnake master;** (6) **plantain,** any of various orchids of the genus *Goodyera,* the coloration of whose leaves suggests that of a rattlesnake; (7) **root,** see as a main entry; (8) **violet,** (see quot.); (9) **weed,** any one of various plants reputedly efficacious in the treatment of rattlesnake bites, or associated with the rattlesnake in some other way.

(1) **1814** PURSH *Flora Amer.* II. 656 *Botrychium virginicum.* . . . It is known by the name of Rattle Snake Fern. **1931** CLUTE *Plants* 109 The spore-cases of one of our ferns are borne in spikes that so strongly suggest the rattles of the rattlesnake that it is commonly known as the rattlesnake fern. — (2) **1814** BIGELOW *Florula Bostoniensis* 25 *Briza Canadensis.* Rattlesnake grass. . . . A large grass found in meadows and readily recognized by its swelling spikelets. **1843** TORREY *Flora N.Y.* II. 466. **1878** KILLEBREW *Tenn. Grasses* 2 *Glyceria Canadensis,* Rattlesnake Grass, . . . resembles quaking grass very much. — (3) **1736** FRANKLIN *Poor Richard's Almanac 1737* 3 (*caption*), Rattle-Snake Herb. **1763** in *Amer. Sp.* XX. (1945) 49 The *Rattle-snake-herb* has a bulbous root, like that of a tuberose, but twice as large. The leaves of both have the same shape and the same colour, and on the under side have some flame-coloured spots. — (4) **1817–8** EATON *Botany* (1822) 294 *Goodyera pubescens,* rattle-snake leaf, scrophula-weed.

(5) **1806** *Farmer's Calendar* (Utica, N.Y.) D4[r] Notwithstanding a free use of sweet oil, plantane, hoarhound, *prenanthet alba,* called here rattlesnake's master, &c. the swelling and pain progressed. **1897–8** *Bur. Amer. Ethnol. Rep.* I. 426 The campion (*Silene stellata*), locally known as 'rattlesnake's master.' **1943** PEATTIE *Great Smokies* 189 Thus a little orchid, the rattlesnake plantain, with net-veined leaves, looks enough like a snakeskin to suggest that it may be a 'rattlesnake-master' or cure for snake bites. — (6) **1778** CARVER *Travels* 482 Remedies . . . Providence has bounteously supplied, by causing the Rattle Snake Plaintain, an approved antidote to the poison of this creature, to grow in great profusion where-ever they are to be met with. **1897** ROBINSON *Uncle Lisha's Outing* 32 Tangles of hobble bush sprawled over the russet carpet of hemlock leaves, gayly flecked with variegated rattlesnake plantain. **1943** [see prec.] — (8) **1818** *Amer. Jrnl. Science* I. 15 May 368 Rattlesnake violet (*Viola primulifolia*) in full flower. — (9) [**1760** J. LEE *Intro. Botany* App. 324 Rattlesnake Weed, *Eryngium.*] **1846** EMORY *Military Reconn.* 387 The prairies were covered with tall stalks of the rattlesnake weed, (*rudebeckia purpurea.*) **1885** *Outing* Nov. 180/1 A pretty thing sends a creeping feeling down our backs, because it is rattlesnake weed. **1936** REICHARD *Navajo Shepherd & Weaver* 45 A yellow-green commonly seen is made by brewing the leaves and stems of one of the goldenrods (Bigelovia) called by some Whites 'tall rattlesnake weed,' by others 'sneezeweed.'

c. Designating places where rattlesnakes abound. Cf. **rattlesnake den.**

1666 *Lancaster Rec.* 301 Northardly it is bounded by pine Land and sum Rocky Called Ratel Snake hill. **1724** SEWALL *Letter-Book* II. 172 The Head-Line . . . [runs] from Rattlesnake Rock to Philips's Brook. **1725** *Suffield Doc. Hist.* 326 We also laid out a Highway of three Rods wide beginning att the gravilley hill att the North End of a Rattlesnake plain. **1844** *Knickerb.* XXIV. 188, I found myself in the centre of a large rattle snake patch.

d. Also (sometimes in the possessive) (1) **rattlesnake grease,** (2) **oil,** (3) **rattles.**

(1) [**1764** *N.C. Morav. Rec.* II. (1925) 582 Rattlesnake fat melted . . . [is] used as a salve for pain in the limbs.] **1856** A. CARY *Married* 232 He bound both her feet up in rattlesnake grease. **1893** M. A. OWEN *Voodoo Tales* 105 Yo' kin brag on rattlesnake grease . . . twell yo' tongues is all wo' ter frazzles. — (2) **1738** BYRD *Dividing Line* (1901) 181 Nothing will do this [ease gout pain] more Suddenly than Rattle-snake's Oyl. **1847** RUXTON *Adv. Rocky Mts.* (1848) 203 An old crone was busy decocting simples. . . . She asked me to taste it, giving it the name of aciete de vivoras—rattlesnake-oil. . . . It was not really viper-oil, but was so called. **1948** *Vt. Quart.* July 119 The earliest doctors were 'Indian Doctors' who depended upon rattlesnake oil for all their cures. — (3) **1899** H.B. CUSHMAN *Hist. Indiana* 583 The wampum was made of strong, dressed buckskin adorned with various things, points of buck horns, rattlesnake rattles [etc.]. **1920** THOMAS *Ky. Superstitions* 10 To hasten child-delivery, beat a rattlesnake's rattles fine and give the powder to the one that is in labor. . . . Blue Grass.

As the last term in **banded, bastard, black, diamond, diamond back, dumb, ground, horned, northern, Pacific, pine-tree, prairie, pygmy, tiger, water, wood rattlesnake.**

rattlesnake root. Any one of various plants regarded as efficacious in cases of rattlesnake bite. Cf. **fern snakeroot, Seneca rattlesnake root.**

1682 ASH *Carolina* 11 They have three sorts of the Rattle-Snake Root which I have seen; the Comous or Hairy, the Smooth, the Nodous, or Knotted Root: All which are lactiferous, or yielding a Milkie Juice. **1792** POPE *Tour S. & W.* 97 Rattle-Snake Root, . . . from its strong aromatic Smell, the Rattle-Snake will never approach, and [it] is accordingly used by the Indians to banish that and other Serpents from their Lodgments. **1806** *Mass. Spy* 30 April (Th.), *Seneca,* or *rattle snake root:* . . . has been celebrated as a specific in the cure of croup. **1941** R. S. WALKER *Lookout* 48 Among the wild plants once employed as antidotes for the bites of poisonous reptiles are . . . Samson snakeroot, . . . Virginia snakeroot, button snakeroot, and rattlesnake-root.

***rave,** *n.* A sidepiece of a wagon-body frame or of a sleigh (see also quot. 1905). Also attrib.

1847 *Rep. Comm. Patents 1846* 81 The raves are carried in front in such a form as to furnish a frame for the dash-board. **1886** *Scientific Amer.* 27 Feb. 130/2 The rave bolts [in a bobsleigh] extend upward from the runners in front and rear of the knees. **1905** *Forestry Bureau Bul.* No. 61, 44 *Rave,* a piece of iron or wood which secures the beam to the runners of a logging sled. (N[orth] W[oods], L[ake] S[tates Forest].)

***raven,** *n.* As the last term in **sea, white-necked raven.**

***raw,** *a.* and *n.*

1. *W.* An untrained pony. Also **raw one.** *Colloq.*

1895 *Outing* XXVI. 389/2 The animals are mostly from the Texan and New Mexican mustang herds. They pay for a 'raw' on an average fifty dollars. *Ib.* 476/2 The way to circumvent fancy prices is to buy a 'raw' and make him over into a 'trained.' **1944** ADAMS *W. Words* 124/2 raw one The cowboy often uses this term in speaking of a green bronc.

2. Of land: Not cleared or opened for cultivation.

1883 SWEET & KNOX *Through Texas* 282 [He] came to Atascoso County, Texas, and bought a piece of raw land [etc.]. **1901** DUNCAN & SCOTT *Allen & Woodson Co., Kans.* 199 He moved into a board shanty on practically a raw piece of land.

3. In combs.: (1) **rawheel,** (see quot.), *rare;* (2) ***hide,** see as a main entry; (3) **salad,** (see quot.), *obs.;* (4) **trotter,** (see quot.), *obs.*

(1) **1849** in *Amer. Sp.* XXI. (1946) 227/2 We saw a man in Sacramento when we were on our way here, who was a tenderfoot, or rawheel, or whatever you call 'em, who struck a pocket of gold. — (3) **1781** WITHERSPOON *Druid P.* 25 *Raw salad* is used in the South for *salad.* N.B. There is no salad boiled. — (4) **1843** MARRYAT *M. Violet* 272 When the traveller is a 'raw trotter' or a 'green one' (Arkansas' denomination for a stranger), the host employs all his cunning to ascertain if his guest has any money.

***rawhide,** *n.*

1. A whip made of rawhide.

1829 *Mass. Spy* 16 Sep. (Th.), She took down a raw hide, and kept the whip moving. **1896** HARRIS *Sister Jane* 273 The rawhide descended with a swishing sound. **1941** STUART *Men of Mts.* 345 The men are . . . spurrin 'em and usin the rawhides.

2. *pl.* Shoes made of rawhide.

1887 *Scribner's Mag.* II. 512/1 Over a pair of stiff, straight boots—jacks, Bluchers, or raw-hides—an Indian is complacently and outrageously exultant.

3. (See quot.)

1939 ABBOTT-SMITH *We Pointed* 161 Rawhides. Derisive Northern name for Texas cowhands. It referred to the Texans' habit of mending whatever broke down or fell apart on the trail, from a bridle to a wagon tongue, by tying it up with strips of rawhide.

4. In combs.: (1) **rawhide artist,** a cowboy who is skilled in the use of the branding iron; (2) **State,** Texas, a nickname; (3) **Texan,** an exceptionally rough, tough person from Texas, *obs.*

(1) **1894** *Harper's Mag.* Feb. 356/1 A rawhide artist paints HF in the sizzling flesh. — (2) **1869** *Overland Mo.* Aug. 130/2 The Rawhide State particularly excels in that fusty savagery of idioms peculiar to the swaggering drawcansirs of the South-west. — (3) **1883** SWEET & KNOX *Through Texas* 18, I'm just pining away for a fight. I'm a rawhide Texan, I am.

b. Also in expressions denoting or referring to things made of, or provided with, rawhide, as (1) **rawhide**

Rawhide boat, buffalo boat, or bull boat

boat, (2) **-bottom(ed) chair,** (3) **hinge,** (4) **lariat,** (5) **parfleche,** (6) **reata,** (7) **rope,** (8) **snake whip.**

(1) **1847** JOHN D. LEE *Journals* (1938) 101 Pres. B. Young said that he would build the rawhide boat, decided that Pres. (B. Y.) superintend building of the boat. — (2) **1850** LEWIS *La. Swamp Doctor* 149 On a raw-hide-bottomed chair, I sat in that log cabin. **1898** CANFIELD *Maid of Frontier* 18 The rawhide-bottomed chairs slightly marked the dirt-floor. **1947** *Harper's Mag.* Dec. 498/1 He just set there in the old rawhide-bottom chair by the cookstove. — (3) **1898** CANFIELD *Maid of Frontier* 204 The door, made of heavy planks, hung to rawhide hinges. — (4) **1850** GARRARD *Wah-To-Yah* xvii. 198 He borrowed our rawhide lariats.

(5) **1917** WILL & HYDE *Corn Among Indians* 133 After a certain amount had been stored in the lodge in dressed skin bags and rawhide parfleches, the remainder of the harvest . . . was stored in caches. — (6) **1872** MCCLELLAN *Golden State* 346 With the raw-hide reata stretched from the captured animal to the pummel of the saddle, [the horse will] lead the most refractory animal at will. **1949** GANN *Tread of Longhorns* 37 Following the hair rope, the rawhide *reata* was evolved. — (7) **1841** FOOTE *Texas* II. 384 [A] lariat [is] a platted raw-hide rope. **1948** *Dly. Ardmoreite* (Ardmore, Okla.) 30 March 4 Yore rawhide rope will bust in twenty pieces in a minute! — (8) **1932** W. KELLEY *Inchin' Along* 211 The ox drivers . . . popped their seven-foot rawhide snake whips.

rawhide ˈrɔˌhaɪd, *v. tr.* To whip (a person) or to drive (horses) with, or as with, a rawhide whip. *Colloq.*

1858 *Spirit of Times* 6 Feb. 356/3 One of our citizens was rawhided in the street, and in the presence of numerous spectators, by a Mr. Huntington. **1883** MARK TWAIN *Life on Miss.* iii. 61 (R.), Some raftsmen would rawhide you until you were black and blue. **1949** *Sat. Ev. Post* 7 May 103/1 Joe went along as packer, rawhiding a string of bony horses up into the brownie country and cooking for the party.

Hence **rawhider,** =**bullwhacker 1.** *Slang.*

1908 *Pacific Mo.* Feb. 155, I was first, as old rawhiders all confessed.

b. (See quot.)

1947 BAILEY *River of No Return* 179 In the winter it [mail] was transported by sled, on horses wearing snowshoes, or raw-hided—wrapped in a buffalo hide and pulled by horse or man power.

rawhiding ˈrɔˌhaɪdɪŋ, *n.* **1.** A severe beating with a rawhide whip. Also transf. **2.** (See quot.)

(1) **1848** *Knickerb.* XVIII. 519 The editor, it was predicted, would catch a rawhiding before sun-set. **1948** *Time* 2 Feb. 10/3 Truman stormed into Congress and gave Alexander Fell Whitney, co-leader of the strike, one of the savagest verbal rawhidings ever dealt a private citizen by a President of the U.S. — (2) **1890** *Columbus* (O.) *Dispatch* 1 July, Those Big Four yardmen . . . do more 'rawhiding' than the men in . . . any other yards. 'Rawhiding' means that they have very hard work to perform.

***ray,** *n.* As the last term in **clear-nosed, cow-nose(d), hedgehog, prickly, sting ray.**

rayon ˈreɑn, *n.* and *a.* [f. ******ray,* beam, light, +*-on.*] A glossy silklike textile thread or yarn, produced chemically from cellulose, or a fabric made of such thread. Also attrib.

1924 *Drapers' Rec.* 14 June 685/2 'Glos' having been killed by ridicule, the National Retail Dry Goods Association of America has made another effort to produce a suitable name for artificial silk. This time their choice has fallen on 'rayon.' **1931** *Chi. Tribune* 18 Jan. II. 8/1 Rayon yarns were being bought steadily by knitters and weavers. **1947** *Democrat* 26 June 3/2 Summer cottons and rayons may be wonderfully freshened by using plain gelatin.

***razor,** *n.*

1. (See quot. 1848.) *Slang. Obs.*

1848 *Yale Lit. Mag.* XIII. 283 (Th.), A pun, in the elegant College dialect, is called a razor, while an attempt at a pun is called a sick razor. **1849** *Gallinipper* Dec. (Hall), All armed with squibs, stale jokes, dull razors, puns.

2. In combs.: (1) **razor clam,** one of various mollusks of the family Solenidae, esp. *Ensis directus,* having a long, narrow shell; (2) **handle,** =prec.

(1) **1882** SIMMONDS *Dict. Useful Animals, Razor fish,* in America *Solen ensis* is called the razor clam. **1935** LINCOLN *Cape Cod Yesterdays* 48 The dictionary . . . even mentions the 'razor clam' among them. — (2) **1835** AUDUBON *Ornith. Biog.* III. 182, I have seen it [i.e., the Oyster-Catcher] . . . take up a 'razor-handle' or solen, and lash it against the sands until the shell was broken and the contents swallowed.

b. Also ***razor back, razor-back buffalo, razor-back clam** (cf. **razor clam**), **razor-back sucker,** (see quots.).

1886 *Nat. Museum Proc.* VIII. 13 *Ictiobus urus,* Agassiz. Razor-back Buffalo. **1888** GOODE *Amer. Fishes* 69 [The Strawberry Perch] is also called 'Bar-fish,' 'Razor Back.' **1896** JORDAN & EVERMANN *Check-List Fishes* 241 *Xyrauchen cypho.* Razor-back Sucker; Hump-backed Sucker. **1948** *Trailways Mag.* Fall 27/1 Any and all fall frequent victim to a variety of baits ranging from spile worms and razorback clams to live smelt and bone jigs.

c. *Blue as a razor,* quite blue. *Colloq.*

c1849 PAIGE *Dow's Sermons* I. 52 [The violet] is always blue—'blue as a razor'—though never intoxicated, except seemingly with delight.

As the last term in **Indian, safety razor.**

razz ræz, *n.* **1.** Short for next. **2. razzberry,** [sp. variant of **raspberry*], a sound, sign, etc., expressive of dislike, derision, disapproval. Both *slang.*

(1) **1921** *Collier's* 15 Jan. 20/1 The mob gave him the razz. **1926** N. V. LINDSAY *Going-to-the-Stars* 52 Let us think of the Irish flute in the morn, . . . And forget our jazzes and our razzes and our hates. — (2) **1918** in *Liberty* 11 Aug. (1928) 9/2 The razzberry was deafening, and he had an omelet hung on his ear. **1948** *Dly. Ardmoreite* (Ardmore, Okla.) 27 May 8/3 Here in the home of the Bronx jeer it usually is rewarded with a noisy razberry.

razz ræz, *v.* [f. the noun.] *tr.* To hiss, deride. Also **razzing,** *n. Slang.*

1924 P. MARKS *Plastic Age* 52 The fellows razzed the life out of me. *Ib.* 60, I dont mind the razzing myself, . . . but I don't like the things they said to poor little Wilkins. **1944** JOHNSON *As I Dare* 225 In his early days he had to face a good deal of razzing because the world so generally believed that he was the original of Little Lord Fauntleroy. **1948** *Great Falls* (Mont.) *Tribune* 27 Sep. 14 Boy, would the kids razz you!

razzle-dazzle ˈræzl̩ˌdæzl̩, *n.* A term of fanciful origin to convey the idea of rapid and confused motion, bewilderment, confusion, riotous jollity, intoxication, etc. Also attrib. and as verb. *Slang.*

1889 *Gallup* (N.M.) *Gleaner* 18 March 4/2 A Kansas paper . . . recently told of a 'regular old razoooper, who, having got a skate on, indulged in a glorious razzle-dazzle.' **1889** *Road* (Denver, Colo.) 28 Dec. 5/1 Clint Butterfield incloses us a razzle-dazzle card of some kind that has a very neat little design of a nightmare etched in blood red and India ink. **1890** GUNTER *Miss Nobody* xv. (*heading*), Little Gussie's Razzle Dazzle. *Ib.* xiv, I'm going to razzle-dazzle the boys . . . with my great lightning change act. **1891** *Truth* (Louisville) 19 July 8/1 It razzle-dazzles into the prices with all of its teeth sharpened, and whatever price stands in the way comes out of the engagement cut in two. **1950** *Time* 2 Jan. 44/1 Lady Bullfighter Conchita Cintron declared that she would give up the razzle-dazzle of the ring for the tranquillity of marriage.

***reach,** *n.* A well sweep. *Colloq.* — **1887** FREDERIC *Seth's Brother's Wife* 144 The fences had been rebuilt, the farm yard cleaned up and sodded, the old well-curb and reach removed.

***reader,** *n.* **1.** One accustomed or trained to read or recite in public. **2.** One of the two members elected to conduct the services of a Christian Science church or society.

(1) **1869** MARK TWAIN *Innocents* 92 The 'Reader' . . . rose up and read the same old Declaration of Independence. **1915** J. R. SCOTT *Technic of Speaking Voice* 591 To the speaker, and much more to the reader, bearing takes precedence of gesture. — (2) **1895** EDDY in *Church Man.* 18 The readers must devote a suitable portion of their time to preparation for reading the Sunday lesson. **1949** *Chi. D. News* 7 March 12/2 In every Christian Science church, . . . a man and a woman are elected from the membership to serve three-year terms as Readers.

As the last term in **brand, first, proof, second, small potato reader.**

***reading,** *n.* As the last term in **dumb, sight, water reading.**

***readjuster,** *n.* A member of a political party in Virginia (1878–83) which sought legislative readjustment of the state debt. Now *hist.* — **1879** *Nation* 13 Nov. 317 Further news from Virginia indicates that the Repudiators, or Readjusters, as they call themselves, have elected a majority of the General Assembly. **1914** *Cyclo. Amer. Govt.* I. 572/2 In Virginia [in 1880] there were two tickets, those of the 'regulars' and the 'readjusters.'

***readmission,** *n.* The restoration of one of the seceding southern states to its place in the federal union after the Civil War. *Obs.* — **1864** *Ore. State Jrnl.* 24 Dec. 3/1 A resolution was offered providing for the re-admission of Louisiana into the Union. **1865** C. SCHURZ in *39th Congress* 1 Sess. Sen. Ex. Doc. No. 2, 44 The only manner in which, in my opinion, the southern people can be induced to grant to the freedman some measure of self-protecting power in the form of suffrage, is to make it a condition precedent to 'readmission.'

***ready,** *a.* and *n.*

1. *n.* The state of being ready or prepared. *Colloq.*

[**1855** in *Amer. Sp.* XII. 115/2 The music got '*good ready*' for a fair start, and at the word 'go' they went.] **1878** B. F. TAYLOR *Between Gates* 71 A time hardly long enough for a century plant to get a good ready for blossoming. **1897** LEWIS *Wolfville* 2 So we begins to draw in our belts an' get a big ready.

2. a. ready bell, a signal for a steamboat to start. **b. ready print,** =**boiler plate.**

(a) **1894** MARK TWAIN *Pudd'nhead Wilson* xviii. 18 (R.), In about an hour I heard de ready-bell, en den de racket begin. — (b) **1930** FERBER *Cimarron* 161 Sabra . . . was selecting fascinating facts from the stock of ready-print brought with them from Wichita, fresh supplies of which they would receive spasmodically by mail or express via the Katy or the Santa Fe. **1935** *Amer. Mercury* Aug. 474/1 The average weekly consists mainly of four pages of 'home print' material and four pages of 'ready print.'

***real estate.**

1. (See quot.) *Obs.*

1857 BENTON *Exam. Dred Scott Case* 19 In some States, as in Virginia, and others, slaves are only chattels: in others, as in Kentucky and Louisiana, they are real estate.

2. In combs.: (1) **real-estate ad,** an advertisement of real estate for sale; (2) **agency,** an agency or company that deals in real estate; (3) **bank,** ?a bank that issues currency notes secured by real estate, *obs.;* (4) **boom,** a period when transactions in real estate are numerous and prices are high; (5) **office,** the office of a real-estate company.

(1) **1916** EATON *Idyl of Twin Fires* 9, I sought for a copy of the *Transcript,* and ran over the real estate ads. — (2) **1849** *Pacific News* (S.F.) 6 Dec. (Supp.) 2/5 Stockton Forwarding, Commission And Real Estate Agency. **1866** *Elevator* (S.F.) 26 Oct. 1/1 (*advt.*), Real Estate Agency. P. A. Bell, Real Estate Agent. — (3) **1838** in J. STURGE *Visit to U.S.* (1842) xcvi, Among the amendments proposed, was one by Major Anthony, that the signature of the President of the Real Estate Bank should be attached to the certificate of the wolf scalp. **1843** *Niles' Reg.* 4 March 5 Real estate bank. . . . A committee of the legislature of Arkansas have reported the facts connected with the management of this institution. — (4) **1887** *Courier-Journal* 3 May 4/3 The leading dailies are publishing stunning accounts of the real-estate boom. **1950** *L.A. Times* Midwinter 3 Jan. 8/1 Major real estate booms started here as early as 1892.

(5) **1879** STOCKTON *Rudder Grange* i, Euphemia sometimes went with me on my expeditions to real estate offices. **1947** *Chi. D. News* 24 Jan. 3/4 The Pea Jacket Bandit, a pimply youth of about 22, netted $250 today in a holdup of a real estate office.

Also *real-estate business, development, fraud, lottery, matter, transaction,* etc.

b. Designating persons having to do with real estate, as (1) **real-estate agent,** (2) **broker,** (3) **dealer,** (4) **editor,** (5) **jobber,** (6) **speculator.**

(1) **1850** SAWYER *Way Sketches* 114 The cities appear on maps suspended from the offices of 'real-estate agents,' as large and as well as New York or London. **1908** O. HENRY *Options* 5 He was a man about the size of a real-estate agent. — (2) **1849** *Pacific News* (S.F.) 8 Dec. (Supp.) 1/1 Auction and Commission Merchants and Real Estate Brokers. **1884** HOWELLS *Silas Lapham* v, It seems to me that it is about time for you to open out as a real-estate broker. — (3) **1861** *Phila. Press* 7 Feb. 1/7 Real-estate dealers state that transactions are fewer, and of less magnitude, than have been known at any time in many years. **1903** *Chi. Chronicle* 11 April 1 For many years he was one of the prominent real estate dealers of Chicago. — (4) **1907** GIVEN *Making Newspaper* 27 Under the managing editor are . . . the financial, sporting, real estate, and society editors, and the editor of the Sunday supplements.

(5) **1854** *Pioneer* (S.F.) Jan. 34 Let capitalists and real estate jobbers look to this subject. — (6) **1873** *Harper's Mag.* Feb. 473/2 Samuel N. Pike, the well-known real estate speculator, died in New York City. **1880** *Ib.* Sep. 562 This region. . . was seized upon by real-estate speculators.

Also *real-estate man, owner, promoter,* etc.

***realize,** *v. tr.* To pass through or have actual experience of. *Obs.* — **1776** A. ADAMS *Familiar Letters* 138 To-night we shall realize a more terrible scene still. **1791** WASHINGTON *Writings* XII. 62, [I hope] that you may find it [i.e., national happiness] in your nation, and realize it yourself.

realizing sense. A sense of actuality, reality, or familiarity.

1806 VAILL in I. Parsons *Mem. J. Vaill* 95, I have . . . a fixed and realizing sense of the truths contained in the word of God. **1862** QUINT *Potomac & Rapidan* (1864) 86 When a 'realizing sense' of the behavior needed in Massachusetts was obtained, the change was decidedly comfortable. **1898** H. HARLAND *Comedies & Errors* 87 (*Cent.*), Since he had no 'realizing sense' of men, how could he hold men?

***Realm,** *n.* In the Ku-Klux Klan, a district or state under the authority of a Grand Dragon.

1868 in *Cent. Mag.* XXVIII. 409/1 By order of the G. D., Realm No. 1. **1924** *Imperial Night-Hawk* 10 Sep. 6 The district meeting of the Ku Klux Klan held recently at Twin Lakes, Realm of Iowa, was a huge success. **1934** *Kourier* July 46/1 It is a fiery cross, made by a Klansman of Philadelphia, Realm of Pennsylvania.

realtor ˈriəltə, *n.* A real-estate agent, esp. one who is a member or affiliated member of the National Association of Real Estate Boards.

1922 SINCLAIR LEWIS *Babbitt* xiii. 157 We ought to insist that folks call us 'realtors' and not 'real-estate men.' Sounds more like a reg'lar profession. 1926 *Amer. Mercury* Feb. 244/1 The term *realtor* was coined by Charles M. Chadbourn of Minneapolis, and by him presented to the Minneapolis Real Estate Board, which in turn conveyed it to the National Association of Real Estate Boards. 1949 *Downers Grove* (Ill.) *Rep.* 31 March 9/4 Seventy-five realtors and their guests attended the regular monthly meeting of the Du Page Board of Realtors.

reaping frolic. A social gathering of neighbors to assist one of their number in harvesting. *Obs.* — 1774 CRESSWELL *Journal* 26 What they call a reaping frolic . . . is a Harvest Feast. 1833 MARTINEAU *Illust. Polit. Econ.* VIII. I. 18 They meant to have a reaping frolic when the corn should be ripe.

***rear,** *a.* and *v.* **1. rear crew,** the men who work at the rear of a log drive. **2. rear-horse,** (see quots.). Cf. ***devil 4.** (4).

(1) 1893 *Scribner's Mag.* June 715/1 Behind them follows the 'rear crew,' the name indicating the work they do. — (2) 1869 *Rep. Comm. Agric. 1868* 308 The *Mantes* or 'rear-horses' prey upon other insects. 1900 *Everybody's Mag.* July 21 Most people are acquainted with the praying mantis—otherwise known as the 'rearhorse.'

reb rɛb, *n.* (Often *cap.*) =**rebel 1.** Cf. **Johnny Reb.**

1862 NORTON *Army Lett.* 128 The mud will prevent the rebs from moving north. 1927 BENÉT *J. B.'s Body* 181 'Hello, Charley,' he said, 'Where you been?' . . . 'Out hearing the Rebs,' he said. 1947 *Sierra Club Bul.* May 80 The stars and stripes, the flag of our now united country raised in honor of our visit, and I, an old battle-scarred and weather-worn Reb.

***Rebekah,** *n.* A member of the organization known as the Daughters of Rebekah. Also **Rebekah degree, lodge.** Cf. ***Daughters** (2).

1913 *Chi. Record-Herald* 16 March v. 6/5 The staff of Maple Leaf Rebekah Lodge, No. 369, will confer the Rebekah degree on a large class of candidates. 1930 *Randolph Enterprise* (Elkins, W.Va.) 16 Jan. 5/4 They sure have a fine bunch of Odd Fellows and Rebekahs down there. 1949 *Milwaukie* (Ore.) *Review* 28 July 6/3 Mrs. Wanda Million and Mrs. Esther Lineagar were initiated into the Milwaukie Rebekah lodge at last week's meeting in the city hall.

***rebel,** *n.* (Also *cap.*)

1. One who espoused the cause of the South during the Civil War. Now *hist.*

1861 *Alexandria* (Va.) *Gazette* 27 April 4/2 The New York Courier & Enquirer is more belligerent and savage against the 'rebels!' than ever. 1892 TRUMBULL *Knightly Soldier* 280 The rebels have a few sharpshooters with Whitworth rifles. 1944 PENNELL *Rome Hanks* 53 I'll see you don't get hurt except at the hands of the Rebels—that I can't help.

b. *pl.* The Southern Confederacy. *Obs.*

1863 *Cincinnati Gaz.* 5 Feb. 3/2 What the Rebels Hope of Northern Copperheads. 1864 *Wkly. New Mexican* 3 June 1/4 The Rebels are reported to have ordered an entire fleet from French builders. 1865 *Atlantic Mo.* March 285/2 The Rebels keep their best generals for their Home Guard.

2. In combs. and derivatives: (1) **rebel brigadier,** (see quot. 1914); (2) ***-dom,** the Confederate States during the Civil War, *obs.;* (3) **-ess,** (see quot.), *obs.;* (4) **gray,** the gray cloth used in making uniforms for southern soldiers during the Civil War, also attrib.; (5) **-ism,** the spirit, practice, or polity of the southerners during the Civil War, *obs.;* (6) **state,** one of the states that composed the Confederate States of America; (7) **yell,** a characteristic yell uttered by southern soldiers, usu. when going into action, during the Civil War, also transf.

(1) 1878 *N. Amer. Rev.* CXXVI. 93 Unlike the 'rebel brigadiers,' his presence is not a rock of offense to the loyal mind. 1914 *Cyclo. Amer. Govt.* III. 156/2 *Rebel brigadiers,* an epithet of contempt applied by the radical Republicans in Congress about 1874 to Congressmen from the southern states because a larger portion of the Representatives had been officers in the Confederate army. — (2) 1862 GRAY *Letters* 480 As to Rebeldom, there is now hardly any State that we have not got some foothold in. 1887 BILLINGS *Hardtack* 280 Afterwards [soldiers] went by thousands into other sections of Rebeldom. — (3) 1863 *Rocky Mt. News* (Denver) 29 Jan. (Th.), A new word appears in the newspapers, which had not been thought of by Lindly [*sic*] Murray when he wrote his grammar. We refer to the word 'rebeless,' a female rebel. — (4) 1866 GREGG *Life in Army* 172 If they had been dressed in rebel gray, . . . no doubt they would have met with a warm welcome. 1895 *Cent. Mag.* May 18/1 He stripped off his rebel-gray jacket.

(5) 1862 *Constitution* (Middletown, Conn.) 26 March (Chipman), There is a good deal of rebelism in the *Old Bailie.* 1867 *Cong. Globe* 10 Dec. 103/3 The action of Congress can have no other effect than to embarrass the work of reconstruction, . . . to feed the spirit of rebelism and incite insubordination. — (6) 1861 in E. COWELL *Diary* 352 The rebel States have made proffers to purchase vessels in England and other European countries. 1944 FAST *F. Road* 167 It was not essentially a problem of reconstruction, not even a problem of readmission of the rebel states into the Union. — (7) [1866 GOSS *Soldier's Story* 19 Then the whole majestic mass of rebels, with their peculiar yell, in marked contrast with the three distinct cheers of our men, sprang forward upon the plain.] 1868 *Ore. State Jrnl.* 26 Sep. 2/5 It was the 'old rebel yell.' 1908 MCGAFFEY *Show-Girl* 228 [We] turned loose a Rebel yell for help and pretty soon along comes a tugboat. 1948 *Dly. Ardmoreite* (Ardmore, Okla.) 15 July 1/8 The 20-minute-show Dixieland put on for Russell had a hard time getting started, but was more liberally sprinkled with rebel yells.

b. Also (1) **rebel army,** (2) **bushwhacker,** (3) **cabinet,** (4) **chief,** (5) **conch,** (6) **Confederacy,** (7) **rag,** (8) **ram,** (9) **stars and bars.**

(1) 1861 MCCLELLAN in *Own Story* 91 How did you learn that Buckner and Smith have joined the rebel army? — (2) 1869 in FLEMING *Hist. Reconstruction* II. 40 One of Governor Clayton's agents is a rebel bushwhacker whom I captured and tried by a drum-head court-martial in 1864. — (3) 1884 *Cent. Mag.* April 826/1 These newspapers . . . would be in the hands of the rebel Cabinet next morning. — (4) 1868 *N.Y. Herald* 2 July 4/3 The old gentleman waxed warm in his eulogy of the rebel chief [R. E. Lee].

(5) 1861 *N.Y. Tribune* 27 Nov., A Negro on this Key [Key West, Fla.] . . . is a more successful cultivator of the soil than all the rebel conchs together. — (6) 1861 *Richmond* (Va.) *D. Dispatch* 31 July 2/3, I would like nothing better than to take Richmond—now that it has become disgraced by becoming the Capital of the rebel Confederacy. — (7) 1862 NORTON *Army Lett.* 64 Our color guard . . . planted the flag of the Eighty-third on the fortification so long disgraced by the rebel rag. — (8) 1864 *Wkly. New Mexican* 10 June 2/4 The honor of destroying the rebel ram Arkansas belongs to [Commodore Wm. D. Porter]. — (9) 1945 *Chi. D. News* 28 April 2/3 (*heading*), Rebel Stars and Bars Flies Over Okinawa.

As the last term in **Anglo, cotton, pro-, reconstructed, unreconstructed rebel.**

***rebellion,** *n.* As the last term in **Dorr('s), Great, Mormon, slave-holders', whisky rebellion.**

rebellionist rɪˈbɛljənɪst, *n.* An advocate of the southern cause during the Civil War. *Obs.* — 1862 *N.Y. Tribune* 19 June 4/6 A very large vote was polled [in Wilmington]. In this city, it reached to 1,434, which is only 80 votes less than the rebellionists polled in the whole county a week ago.

rebozo reˈboso, *n. S.W.* and *W.* [Sp., or Amer. Sp. in about the same sense. See Santamaría.] A shawl or long scarf worn over the head and shoulders by Spanish-American women.

1829 PATTIE *Narrative* (1839) 285 The Indian women were all clad in blue petticoats, a cotton *camisas,* with bosom and sleeves ruffled; then thrown gracefully over a blue and white *revoza* or scarf, all of their own manufacture. 1847 *Dollar Newspaper* (Phila.) 20 Jan. 4/2 The costly *ribosa* of the beautiful and refined Senorita is frequently in contact with the blanket of the coarse and brutish Ranchero. 1909 M. AUSTIN *Lost Borders* 167 Marguerita leaned her fat arms on the table, wrapped in her blue reboza. 1948 *Time* 3 May 34/3 The stylish people think a *rebozo* is the badge of a housemaid.

rebulk riˈbʌlk, *v. tr.* To bulk (tobacco) again in curing it. *Colloq.* Cf. ***bulk,** *v.* — 1925 *New-Harmony* (Ind.) *Gaz.* 28 Dec. 107/2 Should it be not much heated it will be sufficient to unbulk it in one place and rebulk it in another simultaneously—in about three weeks from its first bulking the tobacco will be ready for packing into hhds.

rebunch riˈbʌntʃ, *v. tr.* and *absol.* To arrange or form into new groups or bunches. Also **rebunching,** *n.* — 1881 *Harper's Mag.* Oct. 723 A sure though gradual rebunching of the small farms into large estates. 1888 BRYCE *Amer. Commonw.* II. III. lxvi. 500 They can destroy, rebunch, fail to distribute, and what not as they please.

recede riˈsid, *v. tr.* To cede back or give up again to a former owner. — 1771 in F. CHASE *Hist. Dartmouth Coll.* I. 435 The lands on the west side Connecticut river might be receded back to New Hampshire. 1805 M. CUTLER in *Life & Corr.* II. 185 The first step was to re-cede Alexandria to Virginia.

***receipt,** *v.* **1.** *tr.* To give written acknowledgment of having received (money, etc.). **2.** *intr.* To give a receipt *for* money, etc.

(1) 1787 CUTLER in *Life & Corr.* I. 376, [I] have delivered him one hundred and ten dollars . . . , which he has receipted to me as received on the account of the Ohio Company. 1798 I. ALLEN *Hist. Vermont* 233 In a short time forty prisoners were returned. . . . Major Fay, as Commissary of prisoners, receipted them. — (2) 1832 *23d Cong.* 1 Sess. Sen. Doc. No. 512, II. 829 [Stock] will be delivered . . . to an issuing officer, . . . who will receipt therefor. 1913 LONDON

Valley of Moon 503 These two assistants had ... been receipted for by the local deputy sheriff.

receiptor rɪˈsitɚ, *n. Law.* A person who gives a receipt for property committed or bailed to him by the attaching officer.

1814 *Mass. Supreme Ct. Rep.* XI. 319 The receiptors are precluded, by their own act, from calling in question the validity of the attachment. **1872** BOUVIER *Law Dict.* (ed. 14) II. 418/2 *Receiptor.* In Massachusetts. A name given to the person who, on a trustee process being issued and goods attached, becomes surety to the sheriff to have them forthcoming on demand. **1914** *Ib.* (ed. 8, Rawle) III. 2824/2 The officer taking the goods often, instead of retaining them in his own manual control delivers them to some third person, termed the 'receiptor,' who gives his receipt for them.

receivability rɪˌsivəˈbɪlətɪ, *n.* Acceptability, esp. with reference to bills or notes. — **1813** JEFFERSON *Writings* XIII. 276 These bills would make their way ... by their receivability for customs and taxes. **1834** *Cong. Deb.* 2 Jan. 128 The receivability of the notes of the bank, in payment of all public dues, gave [the U.S.] another interest in the circulation and general management of the institution.

* **receiver,** *n.*

1. (See quot. 1793.) *Obs.*

1705 *Va. State P.* I. 98 The inconveniency of ignorant or negligent Receivers [will be] entirely removed. **1793** *Md. Hist. Mag.* VI. 214 Tobacco did not [*c*1750] undergo a public inspection as now—men skilled in that article were employed by the merchants (and who were called receivers) to view, weigh and give receipts to the planters.

2. In a government land office, an official who receives the money for land that is sold.

1834 JACKSON in *Pres. Mess. & P.* III. 51 Upon his report ... of the proceedings in the register's and receiver's offices at Indianapolis I deemed it proper to remove both of those officers. **1873** EGGLESTON *Myst. Metrop.* 96 The lawyer ... was brother-in-law to the receiver of the land-office. **1907** *Indian Laws & Tr.* III. 275 The amount at which ... water rights shall be sold shall ... be paid to the receiver of the local land office.

3. The part of a telephone that is placed to the ear in receiving a message.

[**1877** *Nature* XVI. 403/2 The apparatus at each end ... becomes alternately transmitter and receiver, first being put to the mouth to receive sounds, and then to the ear to impart them.] **1888** BELLAMY *Looking Backward* 69 With the receiver at your ear, I am quite sure you will be able to snap your fingers at all sorts of uncanny feelings if they trouble you again. **1949** *Sun. World-Herald Mag.* (Omaha) 10 April 2/1 You reach for the receiver, usually without much hope that it is a wrong number.

* **receiving,** *n.* or *a.* **1.** * **receiving house,** (*a*) (see quot.), *obs.*, (*b*) (see quot. 1900). **2. receiving vault,** a place in a cemetery where the bodies of the dead are placed temporarily before final interment.

(1) (*a*) **1854** in W. E. CONNELLEY *Kansas* 343 It is recommended that, at such points as the Directors [of the Emigrant Aid Society] select for places of settlement, they shall at once construct a boarding house, or receiving house, in which 300 persons may receive temporary accommodation on their arrival. (*b*) **1900** NELSON *A B C Wall St.* 157 *Receiving houses,* houses which make a business of receiving and selling cash grain. **1901** MERWIN & WEBSTER *Calumet 'K'* 288 Farmers were driving their wheat-laden wagons to the hundreds of local receiving houses. — (2) **1872** *Amer. Naturalist* March 160 In excavating the 'receiving vault' of the Riverview Cemetery, ... 'a bushel basket full of axes' were found. **1898** ATHERTON *Californians* 348 The house—it was like entering the receiving vault on Lone Mountain.

reception rɪˈsɛpʃən, *v.* **1.** *passive.* To be received at a reception. **2.** *intr.* To attend receptions. *Colloq.* — (1) **1887** *New Orleans States* 8 May 6/2 Celebrities of one kind or another ... have been teaed and receptioned to their own and everybody else's satisfaction. — (2) **1889** LOWELL *Letters* II. 407 Here I am busy dining and receptioning again.

reception committee. A committee that formally welcomes a person or persons. — **1851** NORTHALL *Curtain* 89 We believe Mr. Marks consulted some members of the reception-committee. **1898** *K.C. Star* 19 Dec. 1/5 The reception committee entered the car.

* **recess,** *n.*

1. An eating place or restaurant. *Obs.*

1844 *Akron Buzzard* 25 June 4/3 He is now prepared to furnish, Soda, and Ice Cream, at the Akron Recess. **1891** WELCH *Recoll. 1830–40* 337 The town had an abundance of 'Restaurants,' 'Recesses' and 'Coffee Houses,' as they were variously called.

2. A period of cessation from school work during which pupils play games, eat lunches, etc. Cf. **little, noon recess.**

1851 QUENTIN *Reisebilder* II. 58 Um 12 Uhr verliess ich mit den Kindern die Schule. Sie haben eine Pause (Recess) von einer Stunde. **1880** ROLLINS *N. Eng. Bygones* 176, I see them now, leaping at recess past the gap in the wall. **1949** *Sat. Ev. Post* 12 March 56/2 He used to follow his mistress to school, and we boys played with him at recess to our mutual satisfaction.

attrib. **1869** STOWE *Oldtown Folks* 431 At recess-time she strolled out with me into the pine woods back of the school-house. **1902** G. M. MARTIN *Emmy Lou* 60 The recess-bell rang. **1946** WILSON *Fidelity* 84 A half dozen biscuits soaked in it ought to keep starvation away until recess time.

b. big recess, the period between the morning and afternoon sessions of school when pupils eat lunch. Cf. **big noon,** *s.v.* * **noon.**

1902 L. BELL *Hope Loring* 19 It was 'big recess,' as the children called it. **1903** FOX *Little Shepherd* iii, At noon—'big recess'— Melissa gave Chad some cornbread and bacon.

recharter ˌriˈtʃɑrtɚ, *n.* The renewal of a charter, esp. with reference to the second Bank of the U.S. *Obs.* — **1832** *Cong. Deb.* 9 Jan. 1515 The president and directors of the United States' Bank have petitioned for a recharter of that institution. **1853** *Harper's Mag.* Jan. 261/2 The Governor's Message recommends the re-charter of all private banks, under proper restrictions.

recharter ˌriˈtʃɑrtɚ, *v. tr.* To charter again, esp. to renew the charter of the Bank of the U.S. Also **rechartering,** *n. Obs.* — **1831** *Cong. Deb.* 13 Dec. 1431 The vote ... will be far from disclosing the actual opinions of members in regard to rechartering the bank. **1884** *19th Cent.* Dec. 1005 The Vice-President ... was found to be opposed to the rechartering of a United States Bank.

* **recitation,** *n.* In a school, the action of answering questions on a prepared lesson or exercise; the occasion or class period when this is done.

1770 FITHIAN *Journal* I. 8 At nine the Bell rings for Recitation. **1837** PECK *New Guide* 353 Two able professors ... hear recitations and deliver lectures. **1904** *Churchman* 6 Aug. 237 The recitations [at W. Point] are not merely occasional or scattered questions, but a demonstration of principle at the blackboard, or a solution of problems. **1949** *No. Dak. Hist.* Jan. 23 We had a school entertainment at the school, with recitations and dialogues.

attrib. **1827** *Harvard Reg.* Sep. 202 We hurry to the Chapel, and then crowd to the recitation room. **1834** PECK *Gaz. Illinois* 88 Lebanon Seminary has a commodious chapel, or recitation hall. **1855** *Knickerb.* XLV. 14, I resided ... within hearing of the recitation-bell. **1864** *Harper's Mag.* Sep. 456/2, I saw my little sister with a timid, half-frightened manner moving to the recitation bench. **1882** M. HARLAND *Eve's Daughters* 210 Or recitation-hour is upon you, and you have neither lesson, nor book.

recitationist ˌrɛsəˈteʃənɪst, *n.* One who delivers a reading or recitation. — **1885** STEDMAN in *Cent. Mag.* Feb. 512/1 The youth ... has heard this last of the recitationists deliver one of his poems. **1887** *Ohio State Jrnl.* (Columbus) 24 June, She is a clear, graceful recitationist.

* **recite,** *v.*

1. *tr.* To reply to questions about (a lesson, etc.) or repeat (a poem or other assignment) in a school recitation.

1743 *Holyoke Diaries* 35 Wee Recited Tully's offices. **1823** B. A. GOULD *Syst. Educ. Free Schools Boston* 22 The boys come into school in the morning, prepared to recite a given portion. **1903** WIGGIN *Rebecca* 54 [She] recited ... grammar after school hours to Miss Dearborn alone. **1948** *Sat. Ev. Post* 23 Oct. 122/3 Yes, I've memorized today's poem, but I don't find it worth reciting.

2. *intr.* To answer a question in a school recitation, to repeat a lesson. Also **reciting,** *n.*

1759 *Essex Inst. Coll.* XLIX. 6 Finished reciting, the Dr. gave us good advice. **1815** *Niles' Reg.* IX. 18/1 Those not immediately engaged in reciting ... remain in their own chambers. **1904** *Churchman* 6 Aug. 237 Each cadet [at W. Point] must be prepared to recite every day upon all the subjects of study upon which he is engaged.

* **reclamation,** *n.* In combs.: (1) **reclamation engineer,** an engineer engaged in reclaiming the arid or alkali lands in the West; (2) **plow,** (see quot.), *obs.;* (3) **Service,** a bureau in the Department of the Interior that has charge of improving desert lands in the West.

(1) **1919** HOUGH *Sagebrusher* 250 The camp of the reclamation engineers and construction men lay upon a bench or plateau. — (2) **1883** KNIGHT *Supp.* 745/2 *Reclamation Plow,* a plow for breaking new land. — (3) **1906** *Out West* Feb. 84 The work of the Reclamation Service is greater than the mere watering of certain acres of land. **1947** CLELAND *Calif. in Our Time* 172 The Reclamation Service next filed on four million miners' inches of the 'unappropriated' waters of the Colorado.

* **reclining,** *n. attrib.* Designating a *chair* or *seat* so constructed that one may recline in it.

1865 *Atlantic Mo.* Jan. 37/1 Mrs. Blake was sitting in her reclining-chair as Miss Pix entered. **1903** WIGGIN *Rebecca* 139 The premiums . . . were three—a book-case, a plush reclining chair, and a banquet lamp. **1943** MENEFEE *Assignment* 117 She boarded the eastbound bus at Mattoon, . . . and settled her ample proportions into the reclining seat next to me.

b. reclining-chair car, a railroad coach equipped with reclining chairs.

1890 H. PALMER *Stories Base Ball Field* 223 Free Reclining Chair Cars between Chicago and Omaha.

***recognize,** *v.*

1. *Law.* **a.** *tr.* To bind over by a recognizance. **b.** *intr.* To enter into a recognizance. *Obs.*

(**a**) **1699** *Pa. Col. Rec.* I. 563 The said Edward Robinson recognized himself in 300 £. **1809** TYLER *Vt. Rep.* I. 148 Mallery was recognised by Justice Seaton to appear in this court. **1898** PAGE *Red Rock* 561 He had had her recognized to appear. — (**b**) **1754** *Md. Archives* I. 507 Two of them [=offenders] . . . have recognized for their appearance at the next Assizes. **1783** in PARMENTER *Hist. Pelham Mass.* 250 Samuel Sampson as principal in behalf of said John recognizes to the Commonwealth in the sum of fifty pounds with sureties.

2. *tr.* To acknowledge (a person) as having a right to be heard on the floor of an assembly.

1888 BRYCE *Amer. Commonw.* I. I. xiii. 187 A recent Speaker . . . [was] universally condemned because he had usually 'recognized' (*i.e.* called on in debate) his own friends only. **1923** H. M. ROBERT *Parliamentary Law* 570 A member is said to have 'obtained the floor' when he has risen and addressed the chair . . . and has been 'recognized' by the chair.

***reconstruct,** *v.*

1. *tr.* After the Civil War, to re-establish (the South and its different state governments) in conformity with the reconstruction program of the North. Also ***reconstructed,** *a.*

1865 C. SCHURZ in Hart *Amer. Hist. Contemporaries* IV. 452 The people are willing to reconstruct their State Governments. **1867** EMERSON *Works* XI. (1904) 352 The aim of the hour was to reconstruct the South; but first the North had to be reconstructed. **1898** DUNBAR *Folks from Dixie* 191, I thought that I was reconstructed, but I'm not. **1900** *Cong. Rec.* 25 Jan. 1172/1 Negro suffrage was brought upon the South solely by reason of the rejection, by the reconstructed South, of the fourteenth amendment to the Constitution.

transf. **1886** in B. DAVIS *Geronimo* (1929) 199 He [an Indian] is thoroughly reconstructed [by a term in prison]. **1904** *N.Y. Times* 13 June 2 Aguinaldo gives evidence of having been thoroughly 'reconstructed.' **1922** HEBARD *Bozeman Trail* II. 192 Red Cloud died, as he lived, declared Captain Cook—an Indian who never pretended to be reconstructed.

b. reconstructed rebel, a southerner forced to accept the reconstruction program for the South.

1870 LOWELL *Among My Books* 141 They all came in, like reconstructed rebels. **1886** in SLOAN *Fogy Days* (1891) 164 Though a reconstructed rebel, I do not feel that I committed treason.

c. reconstructed state, a southern state restored to the Union after the Civil War in accordance with the program of Congress.

1868 *N.Y. Herald* 4 July 5/2 The Mississippi delegation will at least insist on leaving the nomination to the delegations from the reconstructed States. *a***1880** in TOURGEE *Invisible Empire* iv, The report of the committee of the Tennessee Legislature tells the results in . . . the then (1864–68) only Reconstructed State.

***reconstructing,** *a.* Of or pertaining to the remaking of southern institutions after the Civil War in accordance with the plan of Congress. Also as a noun.

1865 *Nation* I. 386 The Reconstructing State Convention of Alabama has pronounced against the repudiation of the war debt of the state. **1866** LOWELL *Biglow P.* 2 Ser. xi. 244 We've gut an awful row to hoe In this 'ere job o' reconstructin'. **1879** BISHOP *4 Months in Sneak-Box* 280 His business was managed and the county funds handled by a white politician of the 'reconstructing' element then in power.

***reconstruction,** *n.*

1. The reorganization of the government of the U.S. *Rare.*

1861 *Cin. Commercial* 28 Jan. 2/3 The project of Re-construction is one by which the expression of the popular will in the election of the 6th of November, is to be revolutionized out of existence, and the Northern States to be converted into the subjugated provinces of King Cotton. *Ib.*, The capacity for the re-construction of the Government does not exist among us.

2. The reorganization and restoration of the seceding states of the South to the Union, the remodeling of the governments of the southern states in accordance with the program of Congress.

1863 *Savannah Repub.* in *Boston Sun. Herald* 23 Aug. 3/7 He who advocates reconstruction advocates submission, and he knows it; but he thinks the word reconstruction less objectionable than submission. **1879** TOURGEE *Fool's Errand* 49 This was in the primary period of what has since become memorable as the era of 'reconstruction.' **1949** *N.Y. Times Mag.* 20 March 65/2 The town has been severely tested in the past by yellow fever, floods, . . . reconstruction and five-cent cotton.

attrib. **1866** *Ore. State Jrnl.* 3 March 1/5 Congress has had a reconstruction committee of fifteen members. **1873** *Newton Kansan* 15 May 4/2 It still desired the overthrow of the reconstruction laws. **1904** *N.Y. Ev. Post* 12 May 7 Ever since the period of chaos known as the Reconstruction era, the negro has been the under dog in Southern Republicanism. **1949** *N.O. Times-Picayune Mag.* 11 Dec. 42/3 In Reconstruction days, after slaves became free men, they had to fend for themselves for the most part.

b. reconstruction act, bill, an act of Congress, esp. (*cap.*) one of 1867, setting forth the procedure and the conditions for the readmission of southern states into the Union. *Obs.* or *hist.*

1867 in HARRELL *Brooks & Baxter War* 37/1 After a most careful and most thorough consideration of the *Reconstruction Act* itself, . . . we regard reconstruction under that act as an impossibility. **1867** *Fredericksburg* (Va.) *News* 12 July 2/2 The new Reconstruction bill . . . sets aside the Southern State Governments, and puts them under complete subjection to the military authority. **1868** *Democratic Conv. Proc.* 60 We regard the reconstruction acts, so called of Congress, as . . . an usurpation.

reconstructionary ˌrikənˈstrʌkʃənˌɛrɪ, *a.* Of or pertaining to the reconstruction of the South after the Civil War. *Obs.* — **1879** TOURGEE *Fool's Errand* xxxix. 290 To overawe and suppress the Union, Federal, or Reconstructionary element of the South, was of itself an undertaking of no difficulty whatever to the trained leaders of that section.

reconstructionist ˌrikənˈstrʌkʃənɪst, *n.*

1. A southerner who advocated reorganizing the southern social system so as to avoid beginning and continuing civil strife. Also **reconstructionist party.** *Obs.*

1861 in CHESNUT *Diary* (1906) 15 Now we may be sure the bridge is broken. And yet in the Alabama Convention they say Reconstructionists abound and are busy. **1864** THROOP *Future* 119 The act of secession extinguished the Union party as soon as it was adopted, except as a *reconstructionist* party, in which form it continued, though much enfeebled, to exist till after hostilities commenced. **1866** W. REID *After the War* 404 There were 'reconstructionists' who believed, from the day of the defeat at Gettysburg, that Southern independence was hopeless.

2. One who, after the Civil War, participated in, or was friendly toward, the reconstruction of the South in accordance with the plans of Congress. Now *hist.*

1888 HARRIS in *Harper's Mag.* April 703/2 The Republican 'reconstructionists' . . . barred the way. **1944** FAST *F. Road* 93 Concurrent with that, those of us who can enter politics, not as an opposition, but as men who wish to work with the reconstructionists.

***record,** *n.*

1. The sum of what one has done, the leading acts or achievements in the life of a person or a political party.

1856 *Greeley on Lincoln* (1893) 133 A candidate must have a slim record in these times. **1922** J. F. RHODES *McKinley & Roosevelt Administrations* 292 Roosevelt . . . dilated on the 'Record of the Republican party.' **1950** *Chi. Tribune* 17 Jan. III. 1/1 When a politician tells you to look at the record, be sure you look at both sides.

b. A criminal record.

1901 *Land of Sunshine* April 234 In that crowded hall were many men with 'records.' **1949** *L.A. Times* 16 May 13/1 His record dated back to 1937 and included seven different types of crime including attempted murder and shoplifting.

2. (*cap.*) Short for **Congressional Record.**

1873 *Cong. Rec.* 21 March 135/1 No Senator now has a complete file of the *Record*. **1900** *Ib.* 10 Jan. 730/2 Why can not that be printed in the *Record?*

3. A grooved cylinder or disk which, when properly used on a phonograph or dictaphone, reproduces sounds. Also attrib.

1896 *Critic* 21 Nov. 322/2 A man who uses a gramophone . . . talks into his machine and hands the records to his typewriter. **1908** *Sat. Ev. Post* 29 Aug. 25/3 There's no end of fun in making your own records. . . . This can be done in your own home with the Edison Phonograph and with Edison Record Blanks. **1946** WILSON *Fidelity*

107 The postmaster entertained us with numerous records on his graphophone.

4. *To put* (oneself, a vote, etc.) *on record,* to make a definite declaration of one's attitude or opinion. Also *to go on record.*

1900 *Cong. Rec.* 11 Jan. 785/1, I would be perfectly contented if Senators would put their vote on record. **1905** *Springfield W. Republican* 20 Oct. 1 The American association of bankers last week put itself on record as favoring government subsidies. **1930** *Publishers' Wkly.* 1 Feb. 567 He asked the jury to free the defendant, and thus go on record as opposing the tactics of Mr. Yarrow and his organization. *Ib.* 570 Alfred McIntyre . . . has already gone on record in favor of 'fewer and better books.'

As the last term in **family, phonograph, war record.**

* **recorder,** *n.*

1. An official of a county or court whose duties consist of recording wills, deeds, etc. Cf. **county recorder.**

1816 U. Brown *Journal* II. 228 Col Pindal now writes to the recorder of Deeds at Richmond. **1948** *Shelby* (Mont.) *Promoter* 16 Sep. 1/4 There were 3,400 registered voters for the primary in July and M. P. Lyon, clerk and recorder said yesterday, that an additional 126 had registered during the past few weeks.

b. In mining camps in the West, a person selected to keep a record of each man's claim. Now *hist.*

1852 *N.Y. Wkly. Tribune* 9 Oct. 7/5, I. Wilcox is the Recorder of the hill diggings, and Dr. Hardgrave of the ravines. **1947** Chalfant *Gold, Guns, & Ghost Towns* 59 Claim jumping was greatly restricted by the unusual practice of the Recorder in refusing to record any claim until he had personally visited the ground and satisfied himself that it was correctly staked.

2. A municipal judge having criminal or magisterial jurisdiction. Also **recorder's court.**

1846 Corcoran *Pickings* 34 'You are charged with disturbing the peace,' said the Recorder. **1880** *N.O. Picayune* Oct., There were two charges made against him in the Recorder's Court. **1883** Sweet & Knox *Through Texas* 355 He is brought before the recorder to answer to the following high crimes and misdemeanors.

As the last term in **county, general, vote recorder.**

* **recording,** *a.* **1. recording bell,** (see quot.). **2. recording telegraph,** (see quot. 1876).

(1) 1895 Wait *Car-Builder's Dict.* 104 Recording-bell (street-cars). A bell attached to a bell-punch or other instrument on which the conductor records the fares collected, to indicate that fact to the passengers. — **(2) 1860** Prescott *Telegraph* 73 In 1837, Prof. S. F. B. Morse made known . . . his recording telegraph which justly retains his name. **1876** Knight 1902/1 *Recording-telegraph,* a telegraph provided with an apparatus which leaves a record of the message transmitted.

* **red,** *n.*

1. *pl.* Red men, Indians. *Colloq.*

1804 C. B. Brown tr. Volney *View* 351 A body might have been formed capable of defending itself both against whites and reds, the savage on the one hand, and the land jobber on the other. **1881** *Cimarron News & Press* 17 Feb. 2/2 It is high time that the reds receive some punishment on account of their various misdeeds. **1927** Siringo *Riata* 137 Then one of the reds pulled his gun and shot a deer dead.

2. = **red cent.** *Colloq.*

1849 *Alta California* (S.F.) 12 July 1/5 Silver is not Plenty on the Pharaoh and his host's Tables, and any body can sea it, and bet a red on any card he chuses. **1936** McKenna *Black Range* 267 Many who came into Frisco had not a dad-blasted red left to their name.

3. *In the red,* (*a*) (see quots.), (*b*) in debt. Also *out of the red,* out of debt. *Colloq.* or *slang.*

(*a*) **1838** Gosse *Letters* 266 Deer-hunting has now commenced. . . . The animal is now said to be 'in the grey,' as in the summer he is 'in the red.' **1877** Caton *Antelope & Deer of Amer.* (1881) 149 Frontiersmen and hunters . . . say the deer is in the *red* or the *blue,* as it may be in the summer or the winter coat. (*b*) **1929** Witwer *Yes Man's Land* 248 The big Broadway picture cathedrals ain't where the producers get their epics out of the red. **1948** *Mazama* June 1/1 Rigid enforcement of economies in running expenses will lift the club's balance sheet out of the red where it now is.

As the last term in **Dago, Jersey, Jewett, Kentucky, Rhode Island red.**

* **red,** *a.*

The combinations in which this word occurs are very numerous. Many are given in the following groups. Others may be found as main entries.

1. In combs. that refer to American Indians: (1) **red brethren** (or **brothers**), (2) **children,** (3) **devils,** (4) **man,** [see A. Matthews in *Pub. Col. Soc. Mass.* VIII. 149–50, cf. **4.** (9) below], (5) **skin.**

(1) 1808 Pike *Sources Miss.* 122, I was obliged to convince my red brethren that . . . I would not suffer them to plunder my men. **1864** *Wkly. New Mexican* 9 Dec. 1/3 Horses and cattle [were] carried off by the *peaceable* red brethren. **1878** Conklin *Arizona* 21, I had intended if I kept my health—and whiskey—intact, to finally bestow it upon some of my red brothers, the Arizona Indians. — **(2) 1801** Hawkins *Letters* 379 Your father is desirous that his red children would consent to establish houses of entertainment and ferries on these roads. **1866** *Rep. Indian Affairs* 298 Now, this is the principal desire of your red children. — **(3) 1834** Caruthers *Kentuckian* I. 24 If a man should stand addlin his brains about the right and wrong of the thing, the red devils would just knock them out to settle the matter. **1946** Richter *Fields* 21 Jary used to tell of the little girl in Pennsylvany who ran from the corn patch when she seen the red devils coming. — **(4) 1725** *Miss. Prov. Arch.* II. (1929) 486 There were three men in a cave, one white, one red and one black. . . . The red man who is the Indian, for they call themselves in their language 'Red Men,' went out of the cave second. **1868** *Winnemucca* (Nev.) *Argent* 30 July 3/3 At the snuff of the iron horse, the noble red man can but scornfully [k]nit his brow, or quietly 'grin and bear it.' **1949** *Chi. D. News* 30 Jan. 10/5 He says the red men are denied their civil rights.

(5) 1699 in H. E. Smith *Colonial Days* (1900) 49 Ye firste Meetinge House was solid mayde to withstande ye wicked onsaults of ye Red Skins. **1868** Whymper *Alaska* vii, Perhaps in no other part of America can the 'redskin' be seen to greater perfection. **1947** *Dly. Ardmoreite* (Ardmore, Okla.) 13 Aug. 13/7 Many redskin youths will continue to follow the rites practiced before the white man reached the southwest.

b. Red Paint Indians, Men, People, (see quot. 1947).

1917 Moorehead *Stone Ornaments Amer. Indian* 53 Oval forms occasionally found in the Red Paint People's graves in Maine are much weathered and appear very old. **1947** Coffin *Yankee Coast* 225 Before the dawn and the Dawn People, there were the Red Paint Men. . . . They have been gone so long now that not even the teeth of them are left, only the red paint, color of life, they smeared their bodies with. **1949** Denton *Naturalist's Diary* 3 They went to Maine to open the graves of the Red Paint Indians for remains and relics.

Also *red American, face, flesh, friend, hunter, Indian, Negro, people, race, savage, sister, warrior,* etc.

2. In the names of, or with reference to, trees and shrubs: (1) **red Astrachan,** a red or reddish summer apple; (2) **bay,** a lauraceous tree, *Persea borbonia,* of the southern states, also attrib., cf. **alligator pear, avocado pear;** (3) **beech,** a popular designation for the American beech, *Fagus grandifolia;* (4) * **berry,** any one of several American plants, esp. the red baneberry, *Actaea rubra,* producing bright-red berries; (5) **birch,** the river birch, *Betula nigra,* cf. **broom birch;** (6) **buckeye,** the southern species of buckeye, *Aesculus pavia,* smaller than that found further north; (7) **bud,** any one of various American trees or species of trees of the genus *Cercis,* esp. *C. canadensis,* of the interior and southern U.S., also the buds of such a tree used as a salad or garnish; (8) **cypress,** = **bald cypress,** also attrib.; (9) **elder,** the red-berried elder, also the cranberry tree *q.v.;* (10) * **fir,** the Douglas fir, also any one of various true firs of the western U.S.; (11) **flowering maple,** = **red maple;** (12) **hickory,** the mockernut hickory, or the pignut, *Carya glabra;* (13) **larch,** the American larch or tamarack, *Larix laricina,* also **red American larch;** (14) **locust,** the common American locust, *Robinia pseudoacacia;* (15) **maple,** any one of various American maples, as *Acer rubrum,* having crimson flowers, cf. **red-flowering maple;** (16) **mulberry,** an American tree, *Morus rubra,* bearing reddish fruit, also attrib.; (17) **osier,** (*a*) the silky cornel, *Cornus amomum,* (*b*) another variety of dogwood, *C. stolonifera,* in full **red osier dogwood;** (18) **raspberry,** the American raspberry, *Rubus strigosus,* or its fruit; (19) **rod,** the red osier (*a*) or a similar plant, also **red-rod cornus;** (20) **root,** the American ceanothus, or any of various other American plants, as bloodroot, green amaranth, and climbing bittersweet; (21) **russet,** any of various reddish apples, in full **red russet apple;** (22) * **shank(s),** a species of chamiso *q.v.;* (23) **spruce,** a species of spruce, *Picea rubra,* found in the eastern states, usu. in swamps.

(1) **1847** IVES *N. Eng. Fruit* 36 *Red Astracan.*—This beautiful apple is of medium size, of a round and rather flat form. **1948** *Newsweek* 30 Aug. 32/1 The best and most popular American apples are descended from Russian apple trees—Borominka, Titovka, Red Astrakhan, Alma Ata—imported into the United States a hundred years ago. — (2) *c*1730 CATESBY *Carolina* I. 63 The Red Bay. . . . The wood is fine grain'd, and of excellent use for Cabinets, &c. **1744** MOORE *Voy. Georgia* 116 To the South, is a little wood of red bay trees. **1901** MOHR *Plant Life Ala.* 96 The sweet illicium . . . and red bay (*Persea carolina*) are here met with. — (3) **1637** MORTON *New Canaan* II. ii, Beech there is of two sorts, redd and white. **1894** *Amer. Folk-Lore* VII. 99 *Fagus sylvatica,* white beech, red beech, N.Y. — (4) **1785** WASHINGTON *Diaries* II. 338, I discovered . . . the red berry of the Swamp. **1916** BAILEY *Cyclo. Horticulture* V. 2924/2 [*Rhamnus*] *crocea.* Redberry. Evergreen shrub to 3 ft., with rigid often spinescent branches. . . . Calif.

(5) **1785** MARSHALL *Amer. Grove* 19 *Betula lenta.* Red Birch. This grows to a pretty large size. **1850** S. F. COOPER *Rural Hours* 385 The *red birch,* also a tree of the largest size, is the kind used for brooms. **1949** COLLINGWOOD & BRUSH *Knowing Your Trees* 172 River birch is also called red birch, blue birch, and black birch. — (6) **1860** CURTIS *Woody Plants N.C.* 48 Red Buckeye. . . . The root of this species is sometimes used as a substitute for soap in washing woollen cloths. **1941** R. S. WALKER *Lookout* 61 Red buckeye grows in moist situations at the foot of the mountain. — (7) **1705** BEVERLEY *Virginia* IV. 56 [The people of Va.] dish up [roots, herbs, etc.] various ways, and find them very delicious Sauce to their Meats; . . . such are the Red-buds, Sassafras-Flowers, Cymnels, Melons and Potatoes. **1709** LAWSON *Carolina* 100 The Red-Bud-Tree bears a purple Lark-Heel. **1949** *Democrat* 17 Feb. 4/1 The red bud, the yellow jessamine and other of the early spring flowers have been blooming for two weeks or more. — (8) **1860** CURTIS *Woody Plants N.C.* 29 The *Red Cypress* has its heart of a reddish tint, is preferable to the others for timber, and cannot be split. **1883** SMITH *Geol. Survey Ala.* 292 *Taxodium distichum,* [is] the variety yielding the red cypress lumber. **1884** SARGENT *Rep. Forests* 184. — (9) **1794** S. WILLIAMS *Nat. Hist. Vt.* 69 Vegetables . . . applied to medicinal purposes [include] . . . Red Elder. **1821** *Mass. H.S. Coll.* 2 Ser. IX. 155 Plants . . . indigenous in the township of Middlebury [Vt. include] . . . *Sambucus pubescens,* Red elder. [**1832** WILLIAMSON *Maine* I. 107 The elder is of two species, the black and red.]

(10) **1844** LEE & FROST *Ten Years Oregon* 81 The red fir constitutes the greater part of the timber of the country, which is a very inferior quality of timber, being of no more value than our hemlock. **1949** COLLINGWOOD & BRUSH *Knowing Your Trees* 106 In close stands the trunks of red fir are clear of branches from sixty to eighty feet. — (11) *c*1730 CATESBY *Carolina* I. 64 The Red flowering Maple. These Trees grows to a considerable height; but their trunks are not often very large. **1832** BROWNE *Sylva* 107 The wood of the red-flowering maple is applicable to interesting uses. — (12) **1709** LAWSON *Carolina* 99 There is another sort, which we call red Hiccory . . . ; of which Walking-Sticks, Mortars, Pestrils, and several other fine Turnery-wares are made. **1897** SUDWORTH *Arborescent Flora* 114 Mockernut (Hickory). . . . [Also called] Red Hickory (Fla.). *Ib.* 115 Pignut (Hickory). . . . [Also called] Red Hickory (Del.). — (13) **1785** MARSHALL *Amer. Grove* 103 *Pinus-Larix rubra.* Red American Larch-Tree. **1897** SUDWORTH *Arborescent Flora* 32 Tamarack. . . . [Also called] Red Larch (Mich.). — (14) **1810** MICHAUX *Arbres* I. 38 Locust . . . *Red Locust* (Acacia rouge). **1832** BROWNE *Sylva* 298 From this variety in the color of the wood . . . are derived the names of Red, Green and White Locust.

(15) **1770** FORSTER tr. Kalm *Travels* I. 167 The red Maple, or *Acer rubrum,* is plentiful in these places [near Chester, Pa.]. **1919** STURTEVANT *Notes on Edible Plants* 21 *A*[*cer*] *rubrum.* Red Maple. Swamp Maple. . . . In Maine, sugar is often made from the sap. **1949** *Jrnl. Mammalogy* Aug. 227 The most numerous trees are hemlock, . . . red maple, . . . and white ash. — (16) **1717** *Petiveriana* III. 12/1 Common red Mulberry. Is very sweet and one of our earliest Fruit, next the Strawberry. **1743** CATESBY *Carolina* II. p. xxi, The Red Mulberry-Tree . . . is the only native mulberry of Carolina and Virginia. **1942** HARLOW *Trees Eastern U.S.* 179 Red mulberry is a relatively rare tree not often cut for lumber. — (17) (*a*) **1817–8** EATON *Botany* (1822) 252 *Cornus sericea,* red osier. . . . Properties similar to the *florida.* (*b*) *a*1862 THOREAU *Maine Woods* 174 There grew . . . *Cornus stolonifera,* or red osier, whose bark, the Indian said, was good to smoke. *Ib.* 314 *Cornus stolonifera* (red-osier dogwood), prevailing shrub on shore of West Branch. **1946** STANWELL-FLETCHER *Driftwood Valley* 112 The moose browsed on young twigs of willow and red-osier dogwood. — (18) **1802** in *Mass. Hist. Soc. Proc.* 1 Ser. XVII. 216 The second crop was then full grown, as were also red raspberries. **1879** *Scribner's Mo.* May 14/2 But when the red raspberry blooms, the fountains of plenty are unsealed indeed. — (19) **1785** MARSHALL *Amer. Grove* 36 *Cornus sanguinea.* American Red-rod cornus. . . . The bark of the young shoots is very smooth, and of a beautiful dark red colour. **1843** TORREY *Flora N.Y.* I. 290 *Cornus Sericea.* Swamp Dogwood, Red-rod. . . . Margin of swamps and banks of streams.

(20) **1709** LAWSON *Carolina* 78 The Red-Root whose Leaf is like Spear-mint, is for . . . sore Mouths. **1857** P. ST. G. COOKE *Scenes & Adventures* 234 Here is . . . the 'red-root;' it makes a good tea; soldiers all over the Far West know and use it. **1941** R. S. WALKER *Lookout* 59 The commonest shrub, perhaps, is New Jersey tea or red-root which grows profusely on the summit as well as on both sides of the mountain. — (21) **1817** W. COXE *Fruit Trees* 123 Golden Pearmain. Called in New-York and East-Jersey, the Ruckmans, or Dutch Pearmain; and in other places the Red Russet. **1849** *N. Eng. Farmer* I. 31/2 *Red Russet* apples . . . seem to be intermediate between the Baldwin and Roxbury Russet. — (22) **1902** *Out West* May 515 [This is] doubtless the small tree known in this region as 'red-shank.' **1931** DAYTON *Western Browse Plants* 53 Chamiso . . . is almost everywhere regarded as a pest, but it is possible that it and its congener, redshanks, sometimes called yerba del pasmo or ribbon-wood (*A. sparsifolium*), may have medicial properties. — (23) **1810** MICHAUX *Arbres* I. 18 Abies nigra . . . *Black* or *Double spruce,* nom . . . dans les Etats du nord. *Red spruce,* dans les mêmes contrées. **1943** PEATTIE *Great Smokies* 157 Thus it is with the red spruce, for instance, that crowns only our highest peaks.

b. In the names of herbaceous plants: (1) **red baneberry,** either of two perennial herbs of the genus *Actaea;* (2) **chaff,** a variety of wheat, usu. attrib., *obs.;* (3) **cob,** a variety of corn the cob of which is red; (4) **cohosh,** see **cohosh;** (5) **columbine,** the columbine, *Aquilegia canadensis;* (6) **lily,** any one of various American red-flowered lilies, as the wood lily, *Lilium philadelphicum;* (7) **maize,** a variety of corn the kernels of which are red; (8) **pea,** a common field pea having red seeds; (9) **trillium,** a wake-robin of the genus *Trillium,* having red or dark purple flowers; (10) * **weed,** (*a*) = **pokeweed,** (*b*) field sorrel; (11) **windflower,** an anemone having red or reddish flowers.

(1) **1814** BIGELOW *Flora Bostoniensis* 129 *Actaea rubra,* Red Bane berries . . . grows in swamps and dark woods. May. June. **1940** DEAM *Flora Indiana* 457 Red Baneberry . . . is very local in a few of our northern counties. — (2) **1804** J. ROBERTS *Pa. Farmer* 103 Of the early yellow, and red chaff, from one to one and a half [bushels are sufficient]. **1855** BROWNE in *Amer. Inst. N.Y. Trans. 1854* 590 Red-chaff white wheat, from England . . . is rather tender and probably would not succeed as a fall wheat, north of Virginia. — (3) **1868** *Iowa State Agric. Soc. Rep. 1867* 166 The yellow dent and a reddish red-cob variety . . . are mostly esteemed. **1894** *Vt. Agric. Rep.* XIV. 36 Fodder grown from a later variety of western or southern red cob corn, [was] often cut before it was ripe.

(5) **1640** PARKINSON *Theater of Plants* 1367 One [columbine] out of Virginia with a single flower, which Master John Tradescant brought from thence is *Aquilegia Virginiana flore rubescente præcox.* The early red Columbine of Virginia. **1840** DEWEY *Mass. Flowering Plants* 22 Red Columbine . . . inhabits dry woods and fields, and rocky situations. Canada to Virginia. **1912** NICHOLSON *Hoosier Chron.* 124 She found red and yellow columbines tucked away in odd corners. — (6) **1672** JOSSELYN *N. Eng. Rarities* 42 Red Lillies grow all over the Country innumerably amongst the small Bushes. **1872** TICE *Over Plains* 96, I here found a splendid red lily, as large as a cup, (*Lillium Philadelphicum*). — (7) **1899** CUSHMAN *Hist. Indians* 22 One branch of the Omahas asserted that their founder arose out of the water, bearing in his hand an ear of red maize. — (8) [?**1740** *Importance of Jamaica* 34 Besides the *English* Peas, there is the black-eye Pea, red Pea, Bonnavest-Pea.] **1805** PARKINSON *Tour* 352 He showed me some of the red peas so much famed in America. **1819** *Plough Boy* I. 130 Permit me to recommend to the notice of the farmers of your vicinity, the culture of the common red pea (cow peas). — (9) **1934** WEBSTER. **1945** *Chi. Tribune* 5 April 10/2 We found the first red trillium in the center woodlot April 3, about 20 days before they normally blossom.

(10) (*a*) [**1624** SMITH *Gen. Hist. Va.* V. 170 [In the Bermudas] is also frequently growing a certaine tall Plant, whose stalke being all ouer couered with a red rinde, is thereupon termed the red weed.] **1667** *Phil. Trans.* II. 796 There grows a Berry (by report) both in the Bermudas and New England, call'd the Summer-Island-Redweed, which Berry is as red as the Prickle-Peare. (*b*) **1894** *Amer. Folk-Lore* VII. 97 *Rumex acetosella,* red sorrel, red weed, West Va. — (11) **1861** WOOD *Botany* 203 *A*[*nemone*] *multifida.* Red wind-flower. . . . Rocks, northern Vt. and N.Y., W. to Lake Superior; rare. **1869** FULLER *Flower Gatherers* 28 Another species, the Red Wind Flower, has reddish purple blossoms.

c. In more occasional or colloquial plant names sufficiently defined in the quots.: (1) **red bark cypress,** (2) **cotton grass,** (3) **-cup moss,** (4) **elm,** (5) **grape,** (6) **grass,** (7) * **heart,** (8) **-heart hickory,** (9) **-ink plant,** (10) **puccoon,** (11) * **ribbon,** cf. 4. (13) below, (12)

Romanite, (13) **-root willow,** (14) **sorrel,** (15) **straw wheat,** (16) **sweet(ing),** (17) **-town pippin.**

(1) **1897** SUDWORTH *Arborescent Flora* 76 *Cupressus guadalupensis.* . . . Arizona Cypress. . . . [Also called] Red-bark Cypress (Ariz.) Arizona Red-bark Cypress (*C. Arizonica*) (Cal. lit.). — (2) **1814** BIGELOW *Florula Bostoniensis* 16 *Eriophorum Cyperinum,* Red cotton grass. . . . A common and very tall meadow grass. . . . Spikelets . . . covered with dull reddish wool. **1840** DEWEY *Mass. Flowering Plants* 259 Red Cotton-Grass . . . [is] common in swamps and pools, and in rich muddy bottoms and banks. — (3) **1892** *Amer. Folk-Lore* V. 105 105 *Cladonia bellidiflora* (a common lichen), red-cup moss. General in N.E. — (4) **1789** in *Amer. Museum* VII. (1798) 6/1 In many parts of the state of New-York, grows a tree called by the inhabitants 'red-elm.' It is undoubtedly a species of ulmus. **1916** SETON *Woodcraft Man.* 285 Slippery Elm, Moose, or Red Elm (*Ulmus fulva*). Smaller than White Elm, maximum height about 70 feet. Wood dark, reddish, hard, close, tough, strong. . . . Its leaves are *larger* and *rougher* than those of the . . . [White Elm]. **1949** COLLINGWOOD & BRUSH *Knowing Your Trees* 231 Other common names are red elm, red-wooded elm, rock elm and Indian elm.

(5) **1884** ROE *Nature's Story* 356 The earlier red grapes, including the Delaware, Brighton, and Agawam, not only furnished the table abundantly, but also a large surplus for market. — (6) **1838** *Mass. Agric. Survey* 1st Rep. 18 Red grass or Fox grass. — (7) **1937** *Range Plant Handbook* B39 The branches of a number of species, such as whitethorn (*C. cordulatus*) and redheart, or spiny myrtle (*C. spinosus*), end in spines. **1949** *Nature Mag.* Nov. 423/1 Several blue-flowered and lilac-flowered *Ceanothus* enter chaparral, and among them is redheart, *C. spinosus.* — (8) **1897** SUDWORTH *Arborescent Flora* 113 *Hicoria ovata.* . . . Shagbark (Hickory). . . . [Also called] Redheart Hickory (Miss.). — (9) **1866** LINDLEY & MOORE *Treas. Botany* 885/2 Its dark purplish berries . . . contain a purplish-red juice somewhat resembling red ink, and hence it is sometimes called the Red-ink Plant. **1893** DANA *Wild Flowers* 92 Pokeweed. Garget. . . . The berries serve as food for the birds. . . . From their dark juice arose the name of 'red-ink plant,' which is common in some places.

(10) **1843** TORREY *Flora. N.Y.* I. 73 Red Puccoon . . . is in considerable repute for its emetic, cathartic, and expectorant qualities. — (11) **1833** SILLIMAN *Man. Sugar Cane* 13 The kind of Cane planted is Red Ribbon. **1856** *Rep. Comm. Patents: Agric.* 273 The varieties of cane which have hitherto been most cultivated in Louisiana are the 'Striped-blue Ribbon,' . . . 'Red Ribbon,' or 'Violet.' — (12) **1849** THOMAS *Amer. Fruit Culturist* 164 Carthouse. . . . Red Romanite, of Ohio. . . . Much cultivated in Ohio valley and sold at New-Orleans. — (13) **1817–8** EATON *Botany* (1822) 443 *Salix discolor,* red-root willow, basket willow. — (14) **1894** *Amer. Folk-Lore* VII. 97 *Rumex acetosella,* red sorrel, red weed, West Va.

(15) **1768** WASHINGTON *Diaries* I. 274 The Red Straw Wheat had but very little or no appearance of head. — (16) **1742** HEMPSTEAD *Diary* 391 They are Sprouts taken up at the Root of our Red Sweeting. **1817** W. COXE *Fruit Trees* 169 Red Sweet. A very valuable cider apple, cultivated in East Jersey. — (17) **1785** JEFFERSON *Writings* (Bergh) XIX. 19 They have no apples here to compare with our Red-town pippin.

3. In the names of animals: (1) **red adder,** =**copperhead 1;** (2) **-backed salamander,** a common salamander, *Plethodon cinereus,* found in eastern North America; (3) **bat,** a common species of American bat, *Nycteris borealis,* of a red or reddish color; (4) **bug,** (*a*) a reddish, six-legged, microscopic mite or chigger, *Trombicula irritans,* (*b*) the cotton stainer, *Dysdercus suturellus,* also **red cotton bug,** cf. **cotton red bug;** (5) ***deer,** the common Virginia or white-tailed American deer, *Odocoileus virginianus,* so called from its appearance in its summer coat; (6) **fox,** the common fox, *Vulpes fulva,* of North America, also attrib.; (7) **grain beetle,** a grain beetle, *Cathartus gemellatus,* of a reddish color; (8) **-legged grasshopper, locust,** a widely distributed locust, *Melanoplus femur-rubrum,* ?also the Rocky Mountain locust, *M. spretus,* a migrating species extremely destructive to vegetation; (9) **lynx,** =**bay lynx;** (10) **mite,** the red spider; (11) **moose,** prob. a young moose when it is of a reddish brown color, *rare;* (12) **scale,** a scale insect, *Chrysomphalus aonidum* or *C. aurantii,* esp. injurious to citrus fruit trees; (13) **snake,** any one of various snakes having red markings, esp. a harmless snake of the family Colubridae; (14) **squirrel,** a small North American squirrel, *Sciurus hudsonicus,* many varieties of which are widely distributed throughout the U.S.; (15) **wolf,** a wolf of a predominantly tawny color, *Canis niger niger,* or one of its subspecies, found from Illinois to Texas and Florida.

(1) **1818** *Amer. Jrnl. Science* I. 84 *Scytalus Cupreus,* or Copper-head Snake, . . . [is known] in New-England, by the names of *rattlesnake's mate* and *red adder.* **1859** BARTLETT 99 [The copperhead] has various other popular names, as Copper-belly, Red Viper, Red adder. — (2) **1839** STORER *Mass. Reptiles* 245 *S[alamandra] erythronota.* Green. The red-backed Salamander. . . . The motions of this species are very agile. **1945** *Mass. Audubon Soc. Bul.* March 57 Two-lined and Red-backed Salamanders and added new Wood and Tree Frogs to our store. — (3) **1812** WILSON *Ornithology* VI. pl. 150 Red Bat. **1884** J. S. KINGSLEY *Stand. Nat. Hist.* V. 167 The *Atalapha noveboracensis,* or Red Bat, is perhaps the most common of the Eastern American Bats. — (4) (*a*) **1827** WILLIAMS *West Florida* 29 Red bugs are numerous, especially in mossy woods. **1944** BARBOUR *Eden* 97 John's plaintive musings over the discomfort of redbugs . . . were a constant delight. (*b*) **1837** WILLIAMS *Florida* 71 Red Cotton Bug, . . . an insect that pierces the capsule of the cotton, enters the seed and deposits its egg. **1856** *Rep. Comm. Patents 1855: Agric.* 104 The 'redbugs,' . . . 'cotton-stainers,' generally make their appearance about August, or late in July.

(5) [?**1607** PERCY in Smith *Works* (1910) p. lxix, There is also great store of Deere both Red and Fallow.] **1709** LAWSON *Carolina* 123 Some take him [*sc.* the elk] for the red Deer of America; but he is not. **1885** *Wkly. New Mexican Rev.* 18 June 4/6 [Near Santa Fe] wild turkeys are common; also the black-tailed and red deer. — (6) [**1637** MORTON *New Canaan* 79 The Foxes are of two colours; the one redd, the other gray.] **1778** *Essex Inst. Coll.* LXIX. 109 Sold . . . 38 red fox skins, at 23s. **1917** *Mammals of Amer.* 72/2 The Red Fox mates in February or early in March. **1949** *Chi. Tribune* 29 Dec. 8/2 They had seen two other red foxes, but the animals were too far away and their shots missed. — (7) **1895** *Dept. Agric. Yrbk. 1894* 290 An insect of some importance in the South is the square-necked or red grain beetle. — (8) **1867** *Amer. Naturalist* July 271 The Red-legged Grasshopper . . . has been for several years immensely destructive in the far West, especially Kansas. **1868** *Rep. Comm. Agric. 1867* 66 These insects destroy the red-legged locusts. **1925** HERRICK *Man. Injurious Insects* 328 The red-legged grasshopper . . . injures corn, oats, rye, timothy, blue grass, and soy beans. — (9) [**1875** *Smithsonian Misc. Coll.* XIII. I. 65 [Among] species of the Nearctic realm which occur in the Mexican region . . . the red lynx and raccoon are examples.] **1917** *Mammals of Amer.* 157.

(10) **1894** *Vt. Agric. Rep.* XIV. 176 A little kerosene on the roosts will destroy the red mites that are so troublesome. — (11) **1858** THOREAU *Maine Woods* 141 He had the horns of what he called 'the black moose that goes in low lands.' . . . The 'red moose' was another kind. — (12) **1884** *N.Y. Wkly. Tribune* 30 Jan. 10/4 A fruit committee in San Diego, Cal., recommended against the 'red scale and cottony cushion scale.' **1950** *Calif. Citrograph* Jan. 102/4 January and February are usually preferred months for the fumigation of oranges . . . for red scale control. — (13) **1688** CLAYTON *Va.* in *Phil. Trans.* XVIII. 134 There is another sort of deadly Snake, called the Red Snake. **1744** MOORE *Voy. Georgia* I. 120 Besides the rattle-snake . . . there are also many others, as the black, the red, and the chicken snake. **1842** *Nat. Hist. N.Y., Zoology* III. 49 The Red Snake . . . is a beautiful little serpent, found under stones and logs. — (14) [**1637** MORTON *New Canaan* 81 There are Squirils of three sorts, very different in shape and condition; one . . . is red, and hee haunts our houses and will rob us of our corne.] **1682** ASH *Carolina* 22 There are . . . the Red, the Grey, the Fox and Black Squirrels. **1949** *Nat. Hist.* Nov. 403/1 They will interbreed with gray squirrels but not with the larger fox or red squirrel.

(15) **1942** ALLEN *Extinct & Vanishing Mammals* 229 The typical form of red wolf was slightly the smallest of the three races and the most southwestern, with a range extending from central Texas southwestward to the Mexican tableland. **1949** *Minot* (N.D.) *D. News* 22 July 7/2 The red wolf has recently been exterminated in the American southeast.

b. In similar names sufficiently defined in the quots.: (1) **red bead snake,** (2) **hare,** (3) **hog,** (4) **louse,** (5) **mole,** (6) **racer,** (7) **sand rat,** (8) **scorpaena,** (9) **-thighed locust,** (10) **weevil,** (11) **worm.**

(1) **1802** G. SHAW *Gen. Zool.* III. II. 502 Red Bead Snake, *Coluber Guttatus.* . . . A native of Carolina. — (2) **1879** GOODE in *Smithsonian Misc. Coll.* XXIII. IV. 19 *Lepus Americanus,* var. *Washingtonii.*—Red Hare.—West of Rocky Mountains from Columbia River into British Columbia. — (3) **1893** *Nat. Duroc-Jersey Rec.* I. 17 The origin of the 'red hog' known today as the Duroc-Jerseys, cannot be positively traced. . . . In some of the counties of New York . . . they were called Red Rocks. — (4) **1864** *Ohio Agric. Rep.* XVIII. 143 Late oats were injured by a red insect, called by farmers 'red lice.'

(5) **1781** PENNANT *Hist. Quadrupeds* II. 487 Red Mole. . . . *Talpa rubra Americana.* — (6) **1886** VAN DYKE *So. Calif.* 155 The 'red racer' is a long, lithe snake of brilliant color, with a black head, and wonderful speed. **1949** *L.A. Times* 22 June III. 16/4 Found locally are blue racers, gopher snakes, red racers, California boa, California king, and garter snakes. — (7) **1867** *Amer. Naturalist* I. 394 Only the Red

Sand-rat (*T*[*homomys*] *fulvus*) is at all common [in Ariz.]. — **(8) 1818** MITCHILL in *Amer. Mo. Mag.* II, 245 Red Scorpoena.—*Scorpoena rufa*, with a more ruddy colour of the skin. — **(9) 1884** J. S. KINGSLEY *Stand. Nat. Hist.* II. 194 *Caloptenus femur-rubrum*, the Red-thighed Locust, is found throughout North America.

(10) 1855 *Amer. Inst. N.Y. Trans. 1854* 282 The insect that has destroyed so much wheat in Western New-York and Pennsylvania and Northern Ohio this season, . . . is called the 'red weevil.' — **(11) 1705** BEVERLY *Hist. Virginia* IV. xix. (1722) 267 Seed-Tick and Red-Worms are small Insects, that annoy the People by Day, as Musketaes and Chinches do by Night.

c. In the names of fishes and crabs: (1) ***red bass,** the red drum, *Sciaenops ocellata*, common along the Atlantic Coast; (2) **breast,** the red-breasted bream, *Lepomis auritus*, cf. **e.** (2) below; (3) ***crab,** (see quot. 1884); (4) ***dace,** the shiner or redfin, *Luxilus cornutus;* (5) **drum,** the branded drum, *Sciaenops ocellata*, an important food fish of the Atlantic Coast; (6) ***fish,** any one of various American fishes of a red or reddish color or having red markings, as the channel bass, *Sciaenops ocellata*, the blueback salmon, *Oncorhynchus nerka*, etc.; (7) **grouper,** a grouper, *Epinephelus morio*, common along the Gulf Coast and the Atlantic Coast south of Virginia; (8) ***horse,** any one of various American suckers of the family Catostomidae, also the red drum, cf. **4.** (5) below; (9) **minnow,** any one of various cyprinoid fishes, as *Lythrurus cyanocephalus*, of the rivers of the central states; (10) ***mouth,** any one of various red-mouthed fishes of the genus *Haemulon*, also attrib.; (11) **perch,** (*a*) the white perch, *Morone americana*, (*b*) the rosefish, *Sebastes marinus*, (*c*) = ***garibaldi;** (12) **roncador,** the black croaker, *Rhinoscion saturnus;* (13) **salmon,** the bluebacked salmon; (14) **snapper,** an important food fish, *Lutianus campechinus*, found on the Atlantic and Gulf coasts; (15) **-spotted trout,** (*a*) the brook trout, *Salvelinus fontinalis*, (*b*) = ***Dolly Varden;** (16) ***tail,** the horny head, *Nocomis kentuckiensis;* (17) **throat trout,** the cutthroat trout; (18) **trout,** the namaycush, or a similar trout.

(1) 1842 *Nat. Hist. N.Y., Zoology* IV. 75 At Charleston, it [i.e., the branded corvina] is called Bass, Sea Bass, and Red Bass. **1879** KILBOURNE & GOODE *Game Fishes U.S.* 37/1 In the Carolinas, Florida, and the Gulf, we meet the name 'Bass,' and its variations, 'Spotted Bass,' 'Red Bass,' [etc.]. — **(2) 1888** GOODE *Amer. Fishes* 66 In Pennsylvania it is called 'Sun-Perch,' . . . elsewhere it is the 'Red Breast.' — **(3) 1883** *Nat. Museum Bul.* No. 27, 112 The Red and Rock Crabs are most abundant on the rocky shores of the northern side of the Golden Gate, where but little fishing is done. **1884** GOODE *Fisheries* I. 771 The Red Crab—*Cancer productus*. This is a very common species in the Bay of San Francisco. — **(4) 1842** *Nat. Hist. N.Y., Zoology* IV. 208 The Red-fin. *Leuciscus cornutus*. . . . Associated with the Brook Trout. It has the various popular names of Red-fin, Red Dace, and Rough-head. **1911** *Rep. Fisheries 1908* 309/2 *Dace*, a common name applied to different species of the *Cyprinidæ* family, generally modified by some descriptive prefix, as 'horned dace,' 'red dace,' etc.

(5) 1709 LAWSON *Carolina* 156 Black Drums are a thicker-made fish than the Red Drum, shap'd like a fat pig. **1911** *Rep. Fisheries 1908* 314 Red Drum.—The redfish (Sciaenops ocellatus). Also known as 'channel-bass.' — **(6) 1763** tr. DUPRATZ *Hist. Louisiana* II. 26 This Gulf abounds with delicious fish; as . . . red fish, cod, sturgeon, ringed thornback, and many other sorts. **1834** *S. Lit. Messenger* I. 121/2 The waters too, furnished their finny . . . treasures,—the red fish, buffalo [etc.]. **1949** *Fishing Gaz.* 15 Dec. 72/1 Redfish averaged 5 cents per pound during that November month. — **(7) 1842** *Nat. Hist. N.Y., Zoology* IV. 21 This beautiful fish . . . is called by the fishermen, Groper and Red Groper. **1911** [see **red-bellied snapper** *s.v.* ***red-bellied** as a main entry]. — **(8) 1796** HAWKINS *Letters* 38 This is the most valuable creek known here for . . . trout, perch, rock, red horse. **1819** THOMAS *Travels* 212 The *red horse* is also of the *sucker* kind. It is large and bony, weighing from five to fifteen pounds. **1944** *Chi. D. News* 17 July 21/1 Red-horse, shovel-bills, and other strangely named creatures of the river. — **(9) 1820** *Western Rev.* II. 242 *Rutilus ruber* . . . is said to live in the small streams which fall into the Elkhorn and Kentucky. . . . It is commonly called Red-minny. **1890** *Cent.* 3778/2 Among these [cyprinoids] may be mentioned the red minnows of the genus *Chrosomus*, as *C. erythrogaster*.

(10) 1842 *Nat. Hist. N.Y., Zoology* IV. 89 The Speckled Red-Mouth, *Hemulon fulvo-maculatum*, . . . is a very savory food. **1883** *Nat. Museum Bul.* No. 27, 477 *Ictiobus bubalus*. . . . Red-mouth Buffalo-fish. Mississippi Valley. **1884** GOODE *Fisheries* I. 398 [From] the brilliant red color of the inside of the mouth and throat, from which they have sometimes been called Red Mouths, or Flannel Mouths. *Ib.*, The Red-mouth Grunt, *Diabasis aurolineatus*, is probably the Flannel-mouthed Porgy. — **(11)** (*a*) **1769** in RICHARD SMITH *Tour Four Great Rivers* (1906) 45 Other Fish common in the Lake & other Waters, according to Information are . . . Red Perch, Catfish. **1819** WARDEN *Statistical Acct. U.S.* I. 431 The following fishes are found in the Lakes Champlain [etc.] . . . red-perch, white-perch [etc.]. (*b*) **1871** *Amer. Naturalist* V. 400 The common *Sebastes*, or 'Red Perch' at Eastport, feeds upon the same species. **1911** *Rep. Fisheries 1908* 313/1. (*c*) **1884** GOODE *Fisheries* I. 276 The names 'Gold-fish' and 'Red Perch' are also used, . . . referring to its brilliant orange colorations. — **(12) 1882** *Nat. Museum Bul.* No. 16, 572 *Sciæna saturna*, . . . Red Roncador. **1911** *Rep. Fisheries 1908* 314/2. — **(13) 1881** MCLEAN *Cape Cod Folks* 137 [He] related anecdotes redolent of 'red salmon.' **1945** *Md. Conservationist* 8/1 There are five species of Pacific salmon: . . . the sockeye, also known as blue-back and red salmon. — **(14) 1775** ROMANS *Nat. Hist. Fla.* App. 52 The fish caught here . . . are such as . . . red, grey and black snappers. **1879** *Harper's Mag.* Dec. 26/1 The next dish was baked red snapper. **1949** *Lincoln Co. News* (Oceanlake, Ore.) 4 Aug. 1/2 The crab net should be baited with a good sized hunk of carrion—almost anything from a dead crow to a filleted red snapper carcass will do.

(15) (*a*) **1842** *Nat. Hist. N.Y., Zoology* IV. 235 Red Spotted Trout. . . . Those from running streams are better flavored than the pond trout. (*b*) **1884** GOODE *Fisheries* I. 504 The Dolly Varden Trout—*Salvelinus Malma* . . . is known in the mountains as 'Lake Trout,' 'Bull Trout,' 'Speckled Trout,' and 'Red-spotted Trout.' — **(16) 1820** *Western Rev.* I. 238 Kentuckian Shiner. . . . Vulgar names, Indian Chub, Red tail, Shiner, &c. — **(17) 1897** *N.Y. Forest, Fish & Game Comm. 2d Rep.* 223 *Salmo mykiss*. . . . Black-Spotted Trout; Red-Throat Trout. — **(18) 1766** ROWE *Diary* 94, [I] caught a fine Red Trout. **1903** T. H. BEAN *N.Y.* 267 The lake trout has received many names, among which are . . . lunge, red trout, gray trout, and black salmon.

d. In other fish names sufficiently defined in the quots.: (1) **red cusk,** (2) **fallfish,** (3) **fin,** (4) **side, -sided minnow.**

(1) 1884 GOODE *Fisheries* I. 244 A single species is known in California, the so-called Red Cusk, *Brosmophycis marginatus*. **1891** *Cent.* 5018/2 red-cusk. . . . A brotuloid fish, *Dinematichthys* or *Brosmophycis marginatus*, of the coast of California, of a pale-reddish color. — **(2) 1909** *Cent. Supp.* 459/3 Red fall-fish, a small minnow, *Notropis rubricroceus*, found about waterfalls in tributaries of the Tennessee and Savannah rivers. — **(3) 1818** *Amer. Mo. Mag.* II. 324/2 Red Fin, or Rough-head, *Cyprinus cornutus*. . . . Called by some, rough headed dace. **1911** *Rep. Fisheries 1908* 316/1 *Shiner*, a common name applied to the redfin (*Notropis cornutus*) from New England to Kansas and Alabama. **1948** *Iowa State Coll. Jrnl. Science* Oct. 83 The spotfin shiner is confined in the county to the Des Moines river drainage, and a species closely related to it, the redfin . . . is limited to the Skunk River drainage system. — **(4) 1873** *Mich. Gen. Statutes* I. (1882) 581 Nothing in this act shall be construed as prohibiting . . . any person from catching mullet, suckers, red-sides, wall-eyed pike, or sturgeon. **1883** *Nat. Museum Bul.* No. 27, 487 *Squalius elongatus*. . . . Red-sided Shiner; Red-sided Minnow. . . . Western Pennsylvania; Ohio Valley; Great Lakes; Upper Mississippi Valley.

e. In the names of birds: (1) **red-backed sandpiper,** the dunlin, *Pelidna alpina sakhalina;* (2) **breast,** the robin redbreast *q.v.*, cf. **3. c.** (2) above; (3) **-cockaded woodpecker,** a woodpecker, *Dryobates borealis*, of the pine woods of the southern states; (4) **crossbill,** the common crossbill, *Loxia curvirostra pusilla;* (5) **curlew,** (*a*) =**pink curlew** (*a*), (*b*) the great marbled godwit, *Limosa fedoa;* (6) **mocking (bird),** the brown thrasher; (7) **owl,** =**red screech owl;** (8) **poll warbler,** =**palm warbler,** cf. **yellow redpoll;** (9) **screech owl,** the screech owl, *Otus asio*, in its reddish-brown phase of coloration; (10) **-shafted flicker,** =next; (11) **-shafted woodpecker,** a western flicker, *Colaptes cafer collaris*, related to the golden-winged woodpecker; (12) ***start,** a warbler, *Setophaga ruticilla*, found in the eastern states; (13) ***tail,** =**red-tailed hawk,** also **redtail hawk,** cf. **3. c.** (16); (14) ***wing,** (*a*) any one of various birds of the genus *Agelaius*, esp. the red-winged blackbird, (*b*) (see quot.).

(1) 1813 [see **redback** (as a main entry) **1**]. **1911** FORBUSH *Hist. Game Birds Mass.* 284 The Red-backed Sandpiper feeds largely on worms, crustaceans, and insects. **1940** GABRIELSON & JEWETT *Birds Ore.* 263 The handsome Red-backed Sandpiper is a common migrant on the coast. — **(2) 1795** *Bickerstaff Alm. 1796* (Norwich, Conn.) Bv,

Yet the red breast chirrups cheary, While the mittened lass attends. **1917** *Birds of Amer.* I. 231 Knot. *Tringa canutus.* . . . [Also called] Beach Robin; Red-breast; Buff-breast. **1949** *Chi. Tribune* 24 Sep. 10/3 A small puddle on Oakwood av. was crowded, Coney Island fashion, with 20 or 30 redbreasts splashing merrily away; others lined up four deep, awaiting their turns. — **(3) 1810** WILSON *Ornithology* II. 103 Red-cockaded Woodpecker. *Picus Querulus.* This new species I first discovered in . . . North Carolina. **1917** *Birds of America* II. 144/2 Of the total food of the Red-cockaded Woodpecker over four-fifths is insects. — **(4) 1867** *Amer. Naturalist* I. 44 The Common or Red Crossbill . . . is of desultory habits. **1917** *Birds of Amer.* III. 10/2 The White-winged Crossbill . . . seems to be somewhat less common than the Red Crossbill. **1947** *Iowa Acad. Sci. Proc.* LIV. 380 A small flock of Red Crossbills were observed on various dates from March 4–11, 1945.

(5) *(a)* **1731** CATESBY *Carolina* I. 84 *Numenius ruber.* The Red Curlew. . . . These Birds frequent the Coast of the Bahama Islands, and other parts of America between the Tropicks. *(b)* **1813** WILSON *Ornithology* VII. 30 Our gunners call it [i.e., the godwit] the Straight-billed Curlew, and sometimes the Red Curlew. **1844** *Nat. Hist. N.Y., Zoology* II. 253 [*Limosa fedoa*] is generally called the Marlin, and less frequently Red Curlew. **1917** *Birds of Amer.* I. 241. — **(6) 1688** CLAYTON *Va.* in *Phil. Trans.* XVII. 995 The Red Mocking . . . sings very well, but has not so soft a Note as the gray Mocking Bird. — **(7)** [**1785** PENNANT *Arctic Zool.* II. 231.] **1812** WILSON *Ornithology* V. 83 [The] Red Owl . . . [is] well known by its common name, the Little Screech Owl. **1884** BURROUGHS in *Cent. Mag.* Dec. 218 A winter neighbor of mine in whom I am interested . . . is a little red owl whose retreat is in the heart of an old apple-tree. — **(8) 1844** *Nat. Hist. N.Y., Zoology* II. 89 The Red-Poll Warbler, . . . although very abundant in the Southern States from November to April, . . . has seldom been noticed in this State. — **(9) 1883** *Cent. Mag.* Sep. 681/2 The nests were probably plundered at night, and doubtless by the little red screech-owl.

(10) 1846 ABERT *Exam. N. Mex.* 21 To-day I again saw the red shafted flickers, and endeavored to get a shot at them. **1942** CASTETTER & BELL *Pima & Papago Agric.* 214 This dried tobacco might be stored in real bird nests kept in the house, but often in a cavity made by the red-shafted flicker . . . in a sahuaro tree. — **(11) 1831** WILSON *Ornithology* IV. 245 Red-Shafted Woodpecker. *Colaptes Mexicanus.* **1917** *Birds of Amer.* II. 165/1 West of the Mississippi . . . [we find] the Red-shafted Woodpecker (*Colaptes cafer collaris*). — **(12)** *c***1730** CATESBY *Carolina* I. 67 The Red-Start. . . . These Birds frequent the shady Woods of Virginia. **1949** SPRUNT & CHAMBERLAIN *So. Carolina Bird Life* 386 The Redstart is a summer resident in the Piedmont. — **(13) 1812** WILSON *Ornithology* VI. 75 Early next morning the unfortunate Red-tail was found a prisoner. **1894** *Outing* XXIII. 406/1 The red-tail hawk has his story of a cold wintry day. **1949** KITCHIN *Birds Olympic Peninsula* 65 The red-tail is a common hawk on the Peninsula. — **(14)** *(a)* **1778** CARVER *Travels* 474 The second sort [of blackbird] is the red wing, which is rather smaller than the first species. **1947** *Chi. Tribune* 2 Sep. 7/3 The grackles and redwings also are having a high old time these days roaming around the country. *(b)* **1917** *Birds of Amer.* I. 118 Gadwall. *Chaulelasmus streperus.* . . . [Also called] Redwing.

f. In other bird names sufficiently defined in the quots.: (1) **red grassbird,** (2) **hawk,** (3) **mavis,** (4) **-naped sapsucker,** (5) **neck,** cf. **4. b.** (10) below, (6) **thrush,** (7) **-vented thrush.**

(1) 1844 *Nat. Hist. N.Y., Zoology* II. 165 The Swamp Finch, *Ammodramus Palustris,* . . . is often called the Red Grass-bird in this State. — **(2) 1917** *Birds of Amer.* II. 71 Red-tailed Hawk. *Buteo borealis borealis.* . . . Other Names.—Red Hawk; Hen Hawk [etc.]. — **(3) 1854** THOREAU *Walden* 171 Near at hand, upon the topmost spray of a birch, sings the brown-thrasher—or red mavis, as some love to call him—all the morning. **1917** *Birds of Amer.* III. 179. — **(4) 1917** *Birds of Amer.* II. 150 The Yellow-bellied Sapsucker and its western variant, the Red-naped Sapsucker (*Sphyrapicus varius nuchalis*), are the most migratory of all the Woodpeckers.

(5) 1847 *Sangamo Jrnl.* (Springfield, Ill.) 22 April 1/4 The 'Canvass back' and 'Red neck,' started up in fields on all sides. **1872** *Wisconsin Laws* 186 No person shall catch, kill or otherwise destroy . . . any 'mallard or red neck' duck. **1888** TRUMBULL *Names of Birds* 47 In the neighborhood of Philadelphia hunters were in the habit of supplying the market with this duck [the canvasback], under the name of 'Red-head,' or 'Red-neck.' — **(6) 1789** MORSE *Amer. Geog.* 60 American Birds [which] have been enumerated [include the] Yellow Rump, Towhe Bird, Red Thrush. **1917** *Birds of Amer.* III. 179 Brown Thrasher. *Toxostoma rufum.* . . . [Also called] Red Thrush. — **(7) 1873** *Amer. Naturalist* VII. 328 Next comes the Red-vented, or Crissal Thrush (*H[arporhynchus] crissalis*); also inhabiting the Colorado and Gila valleys.

4. In miscellaneous combs.: (1) **red beds,** *W. Geol.* reddish strata of sedimentary deposits, also attrib.; (2) **boy,** a dollar, esp. a gold one, *slang, obs.;* (3) * **cap,** a porter who assists with hand luggage at a railroad station; (4) * **cow,** a theatrical benefit, *obs.;* (5) * **horse,** a nickname for a Kentuckian, *obs.,* cf. **3. c.** (8) above; (6) **hot,** a hot dog or frankfurter, *slang;* (7) **ibis,** a form of red artificial fly used in fishing; (8) * **light,** used in allusion to prostitution, esp. with reference to a district where brothels abound; (9) * **man,** *(a) pl.* a company or gang of criminals that operated in West Virginia about 1870, *obs.,* *(b)* (*cap.*) a member of the Improved Order of Red Men, a fraternal and benevolent society organized in 1834 in Baltimore; (10) **money,** paper money issued in 1780 by Maryland, *obs.;* (11) **Republican,** one who holds radically republican views and favors violent means for obtaining political reform, also attrib. or as adj.; (12) **Republicanism,** the principles and policy of red Republicans, *obs.;* (13) * **ribbon,** used in allusion to those opposing prohibition, *obs.,* cf. **white ribbon, white-ribboner** and see **2. c.** (11) above; (14) **schoolhouse,** a schoolhouse painted red, regarded as a symbol of the free public school system of the U.S., often **little red schoolhouse;** (15) **shirts,** *(a)* a name for Yankee troops in the Maine–New Brunswick boundary dispute, *obs.,* *(b)* the political supporters of Gen. Wade Hampton (1818–1902) in his candidacy for the governorship of South Carolina in 1876, now *hist.*

(1) 1888 *Encycl. Brit.* (ed. 9) XXIII. 202/2 West of this [in Texas] . . . is the gypsum country, consisting of the so called 'red beds' of the western United States. **1905** *Forestry Bureau Bul.* No. 65, 7 The Red Beds Belt is named from the geological formation prevailing in western Oklahoma and the eastern part of the Texas 'Pan Handle.' — **(2) 1849** *One Man's Gold* (Jrnl. of Enos Christman) (1930) 96 I hope you may always have plenty of 'red boys.' — **(3) 1919** LEWIS *Free Air* 245 A factory illuminated by arc-lamps,—the baggage—the porter . . . red caps. **1950** *Calif. Citrograph* Jan. 132/3 It began to look as if he would miss his train, even with the help of two redcaps. — **(4) 1839** *N.O. Picayune* 5 April 2/2 Their bill is a very attractive one, and we sincerely trust there will be 'plenty of customers to the red cow.'

(5) 1835 HOFFMAN *Winter in West* I. 177 The spokesman was evidently a 'red-horse' from Kentucky. *c***1845** PAULDING *Amer. Comedies* (1847) 192 We've got some o' most all kinds: . . . Linsey-woolseys, Red-horses, Mud-heads. — **(6) 1896** *Chi. Tribune* 29 June 12/1 The residents . . . do not like the odor of fried chicken and 'red-hots' wafted into their windows. **1915** *Chi. Herald* 3 Dec. 13/2 The brewery project was as unsubstantial as the froth blown off the coldest one in town by a longshoreman holding a redhot in his left hand. — **(7) 1899** VAN DYKE *Fisherman's Luck* 27 H.E. G——, fishing with a small trout-rod, a poor, short line, and an ancient red ibis of the common kind, rose and hooked a lordly salmon. — **(8) 1900** *Boston Transcript* 4 Dec. 14/3 The disorderly houses in the 'red-light' district were all closed last night. **1945** SERVICE *Ploughman* 326 Vice seemed to me a more vital subject for poetry than virtue, more colourful, more dramatic, so I specialized in the Red Light atmosphere. — **(9)** *(a)* **1893** CUSHING *Story of P. O.* 354 There was . . . an organization in West Virginia called 'Red Men' who were banded together for certain purposes known only to themselves. *(b)* **1913** *Chi. Record-Herald* 16 March V. 6/6 Invitations have been extended to visiting Red Men and others not affiliated with any of the tribes.

(10) 1779 *Md. Hist. Mag.* II. 344 It is Projected to Give our Red Money a Value by making it a Tender in all Payments. **1782** *Md. Jrnl.* 31 Dec. (Th.), The House is against taking either black or red Money in Payment for taxes. — **(11) 1852** STOWE *Uncle Tom* xxiii, That's one of your red republican humbugs, Augustine! **1900** *Cong. Rec.* 7 Feb. 1616/1 The candidates and supporters of the Democratic party were held up before the people as a gang of socialists, red republicans, anarchists, and nihilists. — **(12) 1815** E. P. WHIPPLE *Oration* 4 July 29 We are proposing all those intricate problems which red republicanism so swiftly solves. **1858** *N.Y. Tribune* 11 Jan. 2/5 When Mr. Bigler was in Kansas last summer, he was the known, open and enthusiastic advocate of what some hereabout call Red Republicanism. — **(13) 1879** MARK TWAIN *Letters* (1917) I. xix. 355 (R.), He couched his lance and ran a bold tilt against total abstinence and the Red Ribbon fanatics. — **(14) 1862** BROWNE *A. Ward: His Book* 71 A C of upturned faces in the Red Skool House. **1901** *World's Work* June 868/1 If we turn to 'the little red schoolhouse' of the rural districts, the sanitary condition is often still worse. **1947** *Chr. Sci. Monitor* 1 March 6/1 The little red schoolhouse is too small for 1947.

(15) *(a)* **1839** *N.O. Picayune* 16 March 2/5 The Yankee troops engaged in the Maine fuss are called *'red shirts.'* *(b)* **1945** A. B. WILLIAMS (*title*), Hampton and His Red Shirts South Carolina's Deliverance in 1876. **1949** *Chi. Tribune* IV. 23 Oct. 2/2 With his famous 'red shirts,' he crowded the 'carpet-bagger' Chamberlain aside.

b. In combs., often occasional, of obvious meaning or sufficiently defined in the quots.: (1) ***red brick,** (2) **cent,** (3) **coatism,** (4) ***flannel (hash),** (5) **(ham) gravy,** cf. **redeye gravy,** (6) **lemonade,** (7) **lion,** (8) **liquor,** (9) **monkeys,** (10) **necks,** cf. **3. f.** (5) above, (11) **nose,** (12) **pup,** (13) **rise,** (14) **rover,** (15) ***stone,** (16) **Strings,** (17) **tapey,** (18) **tapist.**

(1) **1905** O. HENRY *Four Million* 141 The restaurant was next door to the old red brick in which she hall-roomed. — (2) **1839** J. S. JONES *People's Lawyer* I. i, It would not have cost you a red cent. **1949** *Boston Globe* 19 June (Fiction Mag.) 5/1 I don't owe you a red cent. — (3) **1841** *Southron* (Nashville, Tenn.) May 172/2, I call it downright roguery—it is British aristocracy sir—real redcoatism. — (4) **1923** *Nation* 26 Dec. 732/1 Salt codfish . . . boiled with beets and served with pork scraps (cubes of salt pork fried brown), it is considered delectable. If any is left over, it can be chopped fine and 'het up' for breakfast as 'red flannel hash.' **1947** COFFIN *Yankee Coast* 275 Here are . . . modern chopping-trays, century-old ones, hieroglyphed with many hashes, red-flannel and codfish.

(5) **1939** HARRIS *Purslane* 302 We like them for breakfast with red ham gravy. **1949** *Sat. Ev. Post* 2 July 68/3 The ladies were in the kitchen, cooking up some of that fine Kentucky country ham and red gravy. — (6) **1902** *Everybody's Mag.* Jan. 71/2 They stand about in picturesque groups, chewing tobacco, . . . drinking red lemonade. — (7) **1853** B. F. TAYLOR *Jan. & June* 154 Here a game of goal is going on, and here, a game of 'red lion.' **1891** *Amer. Folk-Lore* IV. 225 Red Lion. The players 'count out' to see who shall be 'Red Lion,' who must retreat to his den. — (8) **1922** KEPHART *So. Highlanders* 137 A slick-faced dude from Knoxville . . . told me once that all good red-liquor was aged. **1946** *St. Louis Globe-Democrat* 20 Oct., Long before 1849, the river boatmen along Loutre Slough had such names as . . . Gunboat, a name for a saloon; and Gore, for the red liquor that was there consumed. — (9) **1850** LEWIS *La. Swamp Doctor* 118 In one of the upper apartments was a private patient, labouring under the disease indifferently known as the blue-devils, red-monkeys, seeing injuns, or man-with-the-poker.

(10) (*a*) **1830** ROYALL *Southern Tour* I. 148 This may be ascribed to the *Red Necks*, a name bestowed upon the Presbyterians in Fayetteville [N.C.]. (*b*) **1929** A. ELLIS *Life* 202 George starts to complain that it was run by a bunch of 'red necks.' **1947** *Newsweek* 1 Sep. 19/2 The rednecks were the poverty-stricken white tenant farmers and sharecroppers who lived in the piney woods and barren red-clay hills behind the Delta. — (11) **1934** LOMAX *Amer. Ballads* 169 Whoop—ee! Drink that rot gut, drink that red nose. — (12) *c*1844 R. H. COLLYER *Amer. Life* 14, I have heard of a litter of dogs being sold and paid for by a litter of cats. This is no worse than some Banks in New York State known as 'red-back,' or 'red-dog' which were only redeemed by another known as 'red-pup,' one being about as valuable as the other. — (13) **1888** *Encycl. Brit.* (ed. 9) XXIII. 203/1 These freshets, laden with the rich red loam of the plains, usually reach the lower inhabited sections of the State [of Texas] in periods of drought, and are termed 'red rises.' — (14) **1891** *Amer. Folk-Lore* IV. 224 Red Rover. The boy who is 'it' is called the 'Red Rover,' and stands in the middle of the street, while the others form a line on the pavement on one side.

(15) **1808** CUMING *Western Tour* 473 The term '*Redstone*' was also applied in New Jersey in 1790 to the above mentioned western counties of Pennsylvania. **1816** U. BROWN *Journal* I. 283 This day was heretofore appointed by the Masons . . . to walk in procession in the Town of Union which afforded an Opertunity to see many of the redstone farmers. — (16) **1871** *Ku Klux Klan Rep.* II. 363 [In 1868] the republican party had three secret organizations in operation in the State [N.C.], the Union League, the Heroes of America, and the Red Strings. **1879** TOURGEE *Fool's Errand* 108 You mean the 'Red Strings' I suppose. — (17) **1889** *Columbus* (O.) *Dispatch* 21 Jan., Whether the newspaper reports are extravagant, or the official reports are too red-tapy or timid, . . . it is hard to say. **1890** *Stock Grower & Farmer* 17 May 3/2 The money would be acceptable but the methods too red-tapey and slow. — (18) **1853** *S.F. Herald* 16 Jan. 2/4 The plan . . . is a humbug idea of some red tapist or cheapening Congressman.

red ash.

1. An American tree, *Fraxinus pennsylvanica*, having a strong, durable brown wood. Cf. **green ash.**

1784 CUTLER in *Mem. Acad.* I. 492 *Fraxinus*. . . . The White Ash. The Red Ash. The Black Ash. The Prickley Ash. **1862** BROWNE *Sylva* 159 The red ash is a beautiful tree, rising perpendicularly to the height of 60 feet. **1892** APGAR *Trees Northern U.S.* 123 Red Ash . . . [is] a smaller and more slender tree than the White Ash. **1942** HARLOW *Trees Eastern U.S.* 269 Red ash is a swamp or stream-bank tree whose bark is similar to that of white ash.

2. A variety of coal which when burned produces ashes of a reddish color. Also attrib.

1857 GUNN *N.Y. Boarding Houses* 60 Her coal merchant demurs about bringing a ton of Red Ash or Peach Orchard—until paid. **1874** RAYMOND *6th Rep. Mines* 507 Mr. Franklin B. Gowen . . . determined to make this large body of land available for the production of coal, the upper or red-ash veins having been worked out. **1907** *St. Nicholas* May 669/1 The coal is the red ash, burns very freely and gives plenty of heat.

redback ˈrɛdˌbæk, *n.*

1. =**red-backed sandpiper.**

1813 WILSON *Ornithology* VII. 25 Red-backed Sandpiper: *Tringa alpina;* . . . inhabits both the old and new continents, being known . . . in the United States, along the shores of New Jersey, by that [i.e., the name] of the Red-back. **1917** *Birds of Amer.* I. 237.

2. A red dog bank or a note issued by such a bank. Now *hist.* Cf. **red dog** as a main entry.

1840 *Chi. Tribune* 18 July 2/5 The red back Banks now furnish almost our only currency. **1842** *Wasp* (Nauvoo, Ill.) 2 July 1/4 The notes of the *Farmers' Bank of Amsterdam* (red-back) are no longer redeemed at their agency in Albany. **1850** *Quincy* (Ill.) *Whig* 3 Dec. 2/3 If the people of the south part of the State are opposed to it, they can refuse the bills, and still luxuriate in . . . Ohio red backs and Indiana shin-plasters. **1948** *Southwestern Hist. Quart.* Jan. 297 When the red backs first made their appearance they were valued per dollar at only 37½ cents specie.

b. One of the treasury notes issued by the republic of Texas in 1838. *Obs.*

1852 GOUGE *Fiscal Hist. Texas* 106 This deprived the holders of 'red backs' of even a promise to pay interest on their demands. **1889** H. H. BANCROFT *Works* XVI. 345 [The exchequer bills] soon suffered the same fate as the treasury notes, or red-backs as they were called from the color of the paper.

***red-bellied,** *a.* In combs.: (1) **red-bellied nuthatch,** the small Canada nuthatch, *Sitta canadensis*, the under parts of which are reddish-brown in color; (2) **snapper,** =**red grouper;** (3) **snipe,** the long-billed dowitcher, *Limnodromus griseus scolopaceus*, in summer plumage; (4) **woodpecker,** a red-headed woodpecker, *Centurus carolinus*, having under parts of a red or reddish color.

(1) [**1808** WILSON *Ornithology* I. 43 Red-bellied, black-capt nuthatch. *Sitta varia.*] **1839** PEABODY *Mass. Birds* 339 The Red-bellied Nuthatch . . . holds by its feet to the bark and sleeps, head downwards. **1917** *Birds of Amer.* III. 203. — (2) **1879** *Smithsonian Inst. Coll.* XXIII. IV. 49 *Epinephelus morio*, . . . Red-bellied Snapper. . . . Southern Atlantic States. **1911** *Rep. Fisheries 1908* 316/2 The red grouper (*Ephinephelus morio*) is called . . . 'red-bellied snapper' in Florida. — (3) **1883** *Nat. Museum Bul.* No. 27, 148 *Macrorhamphus griseus scolopaceus* (Say). Red-bellied Snipe; Greater Gray-back. **1917** *Birds of Amer.* I. 230/2 The Long-billed Dowitcher is known locally as . . . the Red-bellied Snipe. — (4) *c*1728 CATESBY *Carolina* I. 19 The Red-bellied Wood-pecker. . . . The belly near the vent . . . is stained with red. **1844** *Nat. Hist. N.Y., Zoology* II. 189 The Red Bellied Woodpecker . . . comes to us from the South in the spring, and advances as far north as Canada. **1917** *Birds of Amer.* II. 161/2 The Red-bellied Woodpecker . . . evinces a decided taste for fruit. **1949** HADLEY *Indiana Birds* 49/1 Of all our native woodpeckers none is handsomer or of more striking appearance than the red-bellied.

b. In miscellaneous names (see quots.).

1709 LAWSON *Carolina* 126 Red-bellied Land-Snakes [are found in Carolina]. **1842** *Nat. Hist. N.Y., Zoology* III. 16 The Red-bellied Terrapin. *Emys rubriventris* . . . is one of the largest of the genus. *Ib.* IV. 236 [In] the Red-bellied Trout, *Salmo erythrogaster*, . . . not only the colors externally are extremely vivid, but the flesh is of a bright red approaching carmine. **1846** AUDUBON & BACHMAN *Viviparous Quad. N. Amer.* I. 292 *Sciurus Ferruginiventris* . . . Red-Bellied Squirrel. . . . Several specimens were received from California. **1917** *Birds of Amer.* II. 75/1 The entire under parts of the Red-bellied Hawk (*Buteo lineatus elegans*) are sometimes rich dark reddish. **1920** COPPER *Under Big Top* 44 That would be a red-bellied bream.

***redbelly,** *n.*

1. a. A fish, as the long-eared sunfish, *Xenotis megalotis*, having a salmon-colored belly. **b.** The red-bellied terrapin, *Pseudemys rubriventris*.

(**a**) **1791** W. BARTRAM *Travels* 14 We presently took some fish, one kind of which is very beautiful; they call it the red-belly. **1820** *Western Rev.* II. 49 A fine species, called Red-belly, Black-ears, Black-tail Sunfish, &c. . . . lives in the Kentucky, Licking, and Sandy rivers, &c. — (**b**) **1877** BARTLETT 699 The most celebrated [terrapin] is the diamond-back; there are also the *yellow-bellies, red-bellies, loger-heads, snuff-boxes*, etc.

2. a. redbelly chub, shiner, the red-bellied dace, *Chrosomus erythrogaster*. **b. redbelly squirrel,** a fox squirrel, *Sciurus niger rufiventer*, of the Mississippi Valley.

(**a**) **1820** *Western Rev.* II. 237 Redbelly Shiner. *Luxilus erythrogaster*. . . . A very distinct and insulated species. . . . It is called Red belly

Chub. — (b) **1826** GODMAN *Nat. Hist.* II. 141 The Red-Belly Squirrel. . . . Its general colour is dark grayish brown above, with a bright yellowish red beneath.

* **redbird,** *n.* Any one of various small American birds of red or partially red plumage, esp. the cardinal or the summer tanager. Cf. **summer, Virginia, Virginian redbird.**

1670 DENTON *Brief Descr. N.Y.* 6 There is also the red Bird, with divers sorts of singing birds. **1709** LAWSON *Carolina* 144 The Red-Birds (whose Cock is all over of a rich Scarlet Feather, with a tufted Crown on his Head, of the same Colour) are the Bigness of a Bunting-Lark. **1867** LATHAM *Black & White* 186 The green peas . . . are devoured before the gardener can pick them, by the 'red bird,' the bright red cardinals. **1949** *Democrat* 27 May 4/3 The first birds to sound off in the morning before dawn seem to be the red birds.

* **red-breasted,** *a.* In combs.: (1) **red-breasted sandpiper,** (*a*) the American knot, *Calidris canutus rufus,* (*b*) the dunlin; (2) **sapsucker,** = * **red-breasted woodpecker;** (3) **snipe,** the dowitcher, *Limnodromus griseus;* (4) **thrush,** the common American robin; (5) * **woodpecker,** the red-breasted sapsucker, *Sphyrapicus varius ruber,* of the California region.

(1) (*a*) **1813** WILSON *Ornithology* VII. 43 Red-breasted Sandpiper . . . [is a] prettily marked species. **1917** *Birds of Amer.* I. 231 Knot. *Tringa canutus.* . . . Also called Red Sandpiper; Red-breasted Sandpiper; Red-breasted Plover. (*b*) **1874** COUES *Birds N.W.* 489 *Tringa Alpina* var. *Americana.* American Dunlin; Black-bellied or Red-breasted Sandpiper. — (2) **1917** *Birds of Amer.* II. 151 Although the Red-breasted Sapsucker nests throughout our Oregon woods, I do not find his home very often. **1948** *Pacific Discovery* March–April 17/1 In winter the red-breasted sapsucker, flashing red and black, flies across the court. — (3) **1813** WILSON *Ornithology* VII. 45 The Red-breasted Snipe arrives on the sea coast of New Jersey early in April. **1917** *Birds of Amer.* I. 229 Dowitcher. *Macrohamphus griseus griseus.* . . . [Also called] Red-breasted Snipe (summer). — (4) **1785** PENNANT *Arctic Zool.* II. 335 Red-breasted [Thrush]. **1823** JAMES *Exped. Rocky Mts.* I. 263 *Turdus migratorius*—Red-breasted thrush.

(5) **1839** AUDUBON *Ornith. Biog.* V. 179 [The] Red-breasted woodpecker, *Picus Ruber,* . . . has most of the habits of the common Red-headed Species. **1879** *Nat. Museum Proc.* I. 429 [The] Red-breasted Woodpecker . . . is a rather rare winter sojourner at Marysville and Murphy's.

red cane. a. =**purple cane** (*b*). **b.** =**purple cane** (*a*). — (**a**) **1856** *Rep. Comm. Patents 1855: Agric.* 274 In general, the Red cane is said to yield less juice than the Red-striped. — (**b**) **1862** *Rep. Comm. Patents Agric. 1861* 167 The Purple Cane, or American Red Cane, . . . is however, no Black-cap.

red cedar.

1. Any one of various species of American trees of the genus *Juniperus,* esp. *J. virginiana;* also the western red cedar, *Thuja plicata,* and the incense cedar, *Libocedrus decurrens.* Also a tree, or its wood, of one of these species. Cf. **western red cedar.**

[**1682** *S.C. Hist. Coll.* II. 28 This Country hath the Oak . . . and divers sorts of lasting Timber that England hath not; as Cedar white and red, Cypress, Locust, Bay.] **1737** JOHN BRICKELL *North-Carolina* (1911) 63 The *Red Cedar* is encompassed with a vast number of Branches, which grow gradually lesser and shorter, as they approach the top of the Tree, so that it grows exactly in the Form of a Pyramid. **1782** *Phila. Ordinances* (1812) 49 The said grate or grates shall be fixed in a frame of stone, or good red cedar. **1817** *N. Amer. Rev.* V. 316 The stump of a red cedar stood near the shore. **1901** MOHR *Plant Life Ala.* 81 On these rugged grounds [in the Tenn. R. valley region] the red cedar . . . predominates. *Ib.* 133 On these shell banks [on the Gulf coast] the West Indian red cedar (*Juniperus barbadensis*) is frequently found in full perfection. **1949** COLLINGWOOD & BRUSH *Knowing Your Trees* 136 Of the eleven species native to the United States, red cedar is the most widely distributed and most important.

2. Attrib. with *bucket, chest, post, timber, tree.*

1742 *Harvard Rec.* II. 716 His Acco[unt] of Red Cedar Posts amounting to Thirty two pounds 10/ [shall] be allow'd. **1785** MARSHALL *Amer. Grove* 70 *Juniperus virginiana.* Red Cedar-Tree. . . . The berries are smaller than those of the Juniper. **1797** *Ann. 4th Congress* 2 Sess. 2113 It would be expedient . . . to secure some of the lands in South Carolina and Georgia, well clothed with live oak and red cedar timber for the purpose of building ships of war. **1846** *Catholic Herald* (Phila.) 30 Aug. 272/4 Red or white cedar chess for housekeepers to preserve clothing, made to order. **1851** *Knickerb.* XXXVII. 377 The country-bred traveller . . . inhales the odor of the red-cedar buckets.

* **red cherry. 1.** An American wild cherry, esp. *Prunus pennsylvanica.* Also attrib. **2.** The fruit of this tree or shrub.

(1) [**1717** *Petiveriana* III. 12/1 Red-Cherry. A large Tree in the Woods.] **1737** JOHN BRICKELL *North-Carolina* 77 The *Red Cherry* Tree, is very scarce, and rarely to be met with. **1900** BRUNCKEN *N. Amer. Forests* 117 The little red cherry shrub known as *Prunus pennsylvanica* is called fire cherry in Wisconsin, and probably elsewhere because it is always found on burnt tracts. — (2) **1848** ROBINSON *Santa Fe Exped.* (1932) 8 On the banks of the creek we found an abundance of red cherries growing on small bushes. *a***1862** THOREAU *Maine Woods* 284 The Indian . . . sometime also ate the northern wild red cherries . . . but they were scarcely edible.

* **redding,** *n.* A mixture of water and red clay or ochre used to redden the hearth and sides of a fireplace. — **1866** A. D. WHITNEY *L. Goldthwaite* x, The brick hearth and jambs [were] aglow with fresh 'redding.'

* **reddish,** *a.* **1. reddish egret,** a heron of the southern states and Central America, *Dichromanassa rufescens.* **2. reddish violet,** (see quot.).

(1) **1785** PENNANT *Arctic Zool.* II. 447 Reddish Egret. . . . Inhabits Louisiana. **1835** AUDUBON *Ornith. Biog.* III. 411 The Reddish Egret is a constant resident on the Florida Keys. **1944** *Nat. Geog. Mag.* June 308 The Reddish Egret, like the Little Blue Heron, has a white phase, showing no color in the plumage. Tip of beak and feet are dark. — (2) **1856** *Rep. Comm. Patents 1855: Agric.* 273 The *Red-striped* [sugar] cane, which was originally brought from the Dutch colony of Java, and the *Violet* or *Reddish-violet,* which is only a variation from the former, . . . will generally prosper . . . [in] the Southern States.

red dog.

1. (See quot. 1886.) Also attrib. *Obs.* or *hist.*

1838 *N.Y. Advt. & Exp.* 21 April 1/4 Aptly enough are these banks called 'Wild Cat' and 'Red Dog.' **1862** *N.Y. Tribune* 14 June 4/2 We have suffered from red-dog bankers and one-horse brokers for the last twenty years. **1886** *Mag. Western Hist.* III. 202/2 The banks toppled to the earth. . . . They were known universally under the name of 'wild-cats.' The most worthless were styled 'red-dog.'

2. A bill or note issued to serve as money by a wildcat or red-dog bank. Also attrib. *Obs.* or *hist.*

1838 J. T. SMITH *Jrnl.* 30 The terms Wild Cat & Red Dog are given [in Michigan] to monies whose credit is going or gone. **1912** *Lit. Digest* 5 Oct. 548 National banks [were created] . . . after the era of wildcat and red-dog private-banknote currency.

3. (See quot.)

1893 *Cong. Rec.* App. 4 Jan. 313/1 Some of the very lowest grades of flour, the flour which is called in common parlance 'red dog,' which is very little better than offal, sometimes goes abroad without any particular brand.

red ear. An ear of a red variety of corn, traditionally prized at corn huskings as entitling its finder to kiss the girls present.

'**1714** S. SEWALL *Diary* 8 April II. (1879) 434 Jonas Aosoe, saith that he took up the Govr Dungan's Terms, brought a Red-Ear of Indian Corn to Mr. Thomas Mayhew to signify it. **1793** BARLOW *Hasty Pudding* III. 19 For each red ear a gen'ral kiss he gains. **1844** *Lowell Offering* IV. 63 The red ear was industriously sought, as its happy finder was allowed the privilege of saluting each fair girl in the room. **1948** *Chi. Tribune* 24 Oct. 36/3 The ultimate aim of the corn husking was the same as ever—the discovery of a red ear.

Hence **red-ear kiss.**

1828 *Yankee* Sep. 288/1 As for their delightful good old fashioned wheel-barrow kisses, I think, they are all of a piece with red-ear kisses, field-beds and bundling.

* **redemption,** *n.* The restoration of political control in the South to white people by the overthrow of the carpetbag regime. *Obs.* — **1880** TOURGEE *Bricks* 380 All over the county, the process of 'redemption' was being carried on. **1884** *Cent. Mag.* April 862/1 Since the political 'redemption' of 1872–6, these methods have been wholly unnecessary.

* **redemptioner,** *n.* (See quot. 1815.) Now *hist.*

1771 *Md. Hist. Mag.* XIII. 174 Try, if & Redemptioner, to get Him on the terms agreed to by Robert, if an Indented servant get Him on the best terms you can. **1815** DWIGHT *Remarks on Rev. of Inchiquin's Lett.* 86 Your next topic of scandal is the state of those, whom you call Redemptioners; persons, who, wishing to come to America, and not having sufficient property to pay their passage, agree with the captain of the ship to become bound, as servants, for such a period of time as that their service will amount to the sum, which they have engaged to pay. **1893** EGGLESTON *Duffels* 57 Why did I leave my father's house to take you, a poor redemptioner just out of your time? **1938** HARK *Hex Marks Spot* 131 There, according to the custom, the redemptioner bound himself in writing to serve his master for a certain term of years.

* **redemptionist,** *n.* **a.** =prec. *Rare.* **b.** One who advocates the redemption of paper money in metallic currency. — (**a**) **1862** T. F. DEVOE *Market Book* 97 At a later period, many such persons were known as 'Redemptionists;' that is, they had power to redeem their persons by paying certain sums of money instead of labor or service.

— (b) 1876 *White Pine* (Nev.) *News* 22 July 2/1 That Act is no longer the *sine qua non* of the redemptionists of either party, and is therefore a stumbling block removed from both the 'hards' and the 'softs.'

redeye, *n.

1. Whisky of very poor quality. In full **redeye whisky.** *Slang.* Cf. **Ohio redeye.**

1819 QUITMAN in Claiborne *Life Quitman* I. 42 Whiting and I had to treat to 'red-eye,' or 'rot-gut,' as whiskey is here [Ky.] called. **1872** *Cong. Globe* 28 May 3969/3 (Th.), Take what we call in Kentucky red-eye whisky, and the best Bourbon, . . . and the tax is the same on each. **1949** *10 Story Western* May 40/2 It was a Saturday night and the raw redeye was hot in the bellies of the men packed along the bar.

2. Any one of various American fishes, esp. the rock bass.

1820 RAFINESQUE *Ichthyologia Ohiensis* 31 Red-Eye. *Aplocentrus.* . . . Ohio Red-Eye. *Aplocentrus calliops.* . . . A beautiful fish from eight to twelve inches long. **1857** *Spirit of Times* 21 March 38/2 The craw-fish . . . is found to be sometimes an excellent bait . . . for the angler who is pursuing . . . the rock-bass, or the *'red-eye,'* to use the nomenclature of Kentucky. **1903** T. H. BEAN *Fishes N.Y.* 477 The blue-spotted sunfish, also known as the green sunfish and redeye, occurs from the Great Lakes region . . . south to Mexico.

3. A watchful eye. *Slang. Obs.*

1833 J. HALL *Harpe's Head* 90 Keep a red eye out, boys,—that chap is not too good to steal.

4. early China redeye, a variety of bean. *Obs.*

1859 *Ill. Agric. Soc. Trans.* III. 503 The early China red-eye is very early and prolific.

5. a. =**red-eyed vireo. b.** (See quot.)

(a) *a*1862 THOREAU *Maine Woods* 172 The birds sang quite as in our woods,—the red-eye, red-start, veery, wood-pewee, etc. — (b) **1917** *Birds of Amer.* I. 261 Semipalmated Plover. *Ægialitis semipalmata.* . . . [Also called] Ring Plover; Red-eye; Beach-bird.

6. (See quot.) *Obs.*

*a*1870 CHIPMAN *Notes on Bartlett, Red-eye,* . . . a copperhead.

7. redeye gravy, *S.* unthickened gravy made by adding water to the grease from fried lean meat, esp. ham. *Jocular.* Cf. **red (ham) gravy** *s.v.* ***red,** *a.* **4. b.** (5).

1947 *Reader's Digest* April 130/1 Pinky brown slices of cured ham that almost floated in red-eye gravy. **1949** *Newsweek* 11 July 6/2 Truman had . . . 'good Missouri hams, red-eye gravy, and hominy grits.'

***red-eyed,** *a.* In combs.: (1) **red-eyed cowbird,** (see quot. 1889); (2) **flycatcher** =**red-eyed vireo;** (3) **greenlet,** =**red-eyed vireo;** (4) **towhee,** the chewink; (5) **vireo,** the little hangnest, *Vireo olivaceus.*

(1) **1917** *Birds of Amer.* II. 246 Red-eyed Cowbird. Tangavius aeneus involucratus *Lesson. Ib.*, The Red-eyed Cowbird is a handsomer bird than that feathered wretch, the Cowbird. — (2) *c*1730 CATESBY *Carolina* I. 54 *Muscicapa oculis rubris.* The red-ey'd Flycatcher. . . . These breed in Carolina, and retire Southward in Winter. **1871** BURROUGHS *Wake-Robin* (1886) 57, I hear all along the line of the forest the incessant warble of the red-eyed fly-catcher. **1900** HIGGINSON *Outdoor Studies* 144 The Red-eyed Flycatcher, heard even more constantly, is less generally identified by name — (3) **1844** *Nat. Hist. N.Y., Zoology* II. 124 The Red-Eyed Greenlet. *Vireo olivaceus.* . . . A common species. Migrates south from this State in the beginning of October. — (4) **1917** *Birds of Amer.* III. 58. **1939** *Nat. Geog. Mag.* March 353 The one species found east of the Mississippi River is the well-known red-eyed towhee.

(5) **1839** AUDUBON *Ornith. Biog.* V. 430, I found the nest of the Red-eyed Vireo nearly finished. **1949** *Dly. Oklahoman Mag.* (Okla. City) 4 Dec. 16/2 We found more junco nests than any other species except the red-eyed vireo.

red gum. 1. (See quot. 1916.) Also attrib. **2.** (See quot.) *Obs.*

(1) **1839** *S. Lit. Messenger* V. 113/2 Dislodge the rackoon from its lofty hole in the red-gum tree. **1916** SETON *Woodcraft Man.* 288 Sweet Gum, Star-Leaved, or Red Gum, Bilsted, Alligator Tree, or Liquidambar (*Liquidambar Styraciflua*) A tall tree up to 150 feet high of low, moist woods, remarkable for the corky ridges on its bark, and the unsplitable nature of its weak, warping, perishable timber. **1942** HARLOW *Trees Eastern U.S.* 193 Now that veneered furniture has so largely replaced solid pieces, redgum wood has come into prominence. — (2) **1849** *Rep. Comm. Patents: Agric.* (1850) 393 The first uredo I shall mention is known familiarly to the farmer as rust, red-rag, red-robin, red-gum, and comes out in yellow orange blotches on the stem.

red haw. 1. The fruit of any one of various American trees of the genus *Crataegus*, esp. *C. coccinea*, or a tree producing such fruit. **2.** (See quot.)

(1) **1717** *Petiveriana* III. 12/1 Red Haw. Of an agreeable Taste, and four times as big as ours in Europe. **1787** *Amer. Acad. Mem.* II. I. 159 Black Haw, four inches diameter, and producing good fruit. Red Haw. **1893** *Amer. Folk-Lore* VI. 141 *Cratægus coccinea*, var. *mollis*, red haw. Gen. in Central States. **1944** DUNCAN *M. Graham* 237 He talked of red haws, wood violets, May apples, lady-slippers, and dogwood—in a land that had no shade. — (2) **1910–12** *Trans. Tex. Acad. Sci.* (1913) 80 *Ilex decidua* Walt. Called a 'Red Haw' here; also Yaupon.

redhead, *n.

1. An American duck or species of duck, *Nyroca americana*, allied to the canvasback.

1709 LAWSON *Carolina* 150 Red Heads . . . are very sweet food, and plentiful in our Rivers and Creeks. **1917** *Birds of Amer.* I. 131/1 In the Redhead we have the counterpart of the Canvas-back. **1947** BEROLZHEIMER *Regional Cookbook* 98 Canvasback, redhead, black ducks and mallards are the best-tasting of the wild ducks as they are broad-billed, grass-eating birds.

2. A common American woodpecker, *Melanerpes erythrocephalus*, having a red head, and white and black plumage elsewhere.

[**1764** REUTER *Wachau* 579 *Red Heads* . . . do much harm to the corn.] **1831** AUDUBON *Ornith. Biog.* I. 145 As soon as the Red-heads have begun to Visit a Cherry or Apple tree, a pole is placed along the trunk of the tree. **1947** *Iowa Acad. Sci. Proc.* LIV. 377 This honey must support a large number of bees throughout the winter, which may in turn account for the winter colony of Redheads, numbering as high as twenty in some winter seasons.

In full **red-headed woodpecker.**

*c*1728 CATESBY *Carolina* I. 20 The Red-headed Wood-pecker . . . is the only one of the Wood-peckers that may be termed domestick. **1884** *Cent. Mag.* Dec. 222/2 A red-headed woodpecker . . . drums upon a lightning-rod on his neighbour's house.

3. *W.* See quot. 1857 and cf. **blue head** *s.v.* ***blue,** *a.* **4. d.** (3). *Obs.*

*a*1846 *Quarter Race Ky.* 92 They, with their furniture, and the remains of a forty-two gallon 'red-head,' came down Deer Creek. **1857** *Spirit of Times* 15 Aug. 371/2 It has been well said, that at the present day, every 'red head,' a peculiar name for Western whiskey barrels, contains at least twenty fights.

redirect ˌridəˈrɛkt, *a.* (See quot. 1889.) Also absol.

1889 *Cent.* 2048/2 The steps in the examination of a witness are the . . . direct examination by the party calling him, and the cross-examination by the opposite party; after which may follow a reëxamination or redirect examination by the former [etc.]. **1909** E. L. BANKS *Mystery F. Farrington* 324 If the British attorney has finished his cross-examination, I will begin my re-direct. **1944** *Chi. D. News* 22 Dec. 6/2 She will return for redirect questioning under the guidance of her own attorney.

redistrict riˈdɪstrɪkt, *v. tr.* To divide anew (a town or state) into districts, usu. for the apportionment of representation. Also **redistricting,** *n.*

1850 in PARMENTER *Hist. Pelham, Mass.* 198 Thomas Buffum, Monroe Eaton, Olney Cook [constitute] a committee to redistrict the town. **1890** *N.Y. Wkly. Tribune* 22 Oct. 12/3 Democratic rascalities in redistricting and in voting and counting will not prevent but will hasten and insure the passage of a bill to secure fair Congressional elections in future. **1921** *Rural Organization* 121 The appended map of Filmore County, Nebraska, shows a proposed redistricting of schools. **1949** *Ill. State Reg.* (Springfield) 1 Feb. 6/4 States throughout the nation are eyeing the Illinois plan for redistricting schools which has proved to be a tax saver as well as a more efficient means of educating youths.

***red legs.** (See quot. 1885.) *Obs.*

1869 *Republican D. Jrnl.* (Lawrence, Kans.) 11 July, Colonel Hays of Johnson County, one of the bravest and best of the gallant soldiers, who lost a leg in the service of his country, had two horses stolen by Hoyt's 'Red Legs.' **1885** L. W. SPRING *Kansas* 285 Early in the struggle [the Civil War in U.S.] an organization appeared known as 'Red-legs,' from the fact that its members affected red morocco leggings. It was a loose-jointed association, with members shifting between twenty-five and fifty, dedicated originally to the vocation of horse-stealing, but flexible enough to include rascalities of every description. At intervals the gang would dash into Missouri, seize horses and cattle, . . . and repair with their booty to Lawrence. **1902** *Kans. Hist Coll.* VII. 576 It . . . was in retaliation for outrages committed in western Missouri by 'red legs,' from Lawrence.

red oak.

1. An American oak, *Quercus borealis*, or any one of various related species; also a tree, or its wood, of such a species. Cf. **water red oak.**

1633 *Plymouth Rec.* I. 64 Lott layeth on the easterly side of the fourth lott and att the south end bounded with a Rid oake stake.

1634 WOOD *N. Eng. Prospect* 16 Of Oakes there be three kindes, the red Oake, white, and black. **1655** *Relation of Md.* 22 The timber of these parts is very good . . . ; the white Oake is good for Pipe-staves, the red Oake for wainescot. **1754** *S.C. Gaz.* 5 Feb. 3/2 Choice land at *Beach Hill*, for rice indico and corn, well timber'd with pine and cypress, red and white oak. **1814** PURSH *Flora* II. 631 Quercus falcata. . . . A very large tree, commonly called Spanish Oak. In the southern states it is known by the name of Red Oak. **1947** COFFIN *Yankee Coast* 163 It is boned with Maine red oak and fleshed with knotless Maine white pine.

2. red oak bark, the bark of a red oak, often used in tanning.

1901 H. ROBERTSON *Inlander* 310, I des gwine down to de branch to git me some red-oak bark. **1945** BOTKIN *My Burden* 63 The way they tanned it was to take red oak bark and put it in vats made something like troughs that held water.

red pine. Any one of various American pines, as the Norway pine, Georgia pine, and Douglas fir, having reddish bark.

1809 KENDALL *Travels* III. 145, I have referred the sapling of the lumberers to the yellow, red or Norway pine. **1832** BROWNE *Sylva* 229 This invaluable tree is known . . . in the Northern States, [as] Southern Pine and Red Pine. **1845** FRÉMONT *Exped.* 233 The red pine . . . is here [in the Rocky Mts.] the principal tree. **1850** ALLEN *10 Yrs. Ore.* 408 The white pine is frequent; and the red pine (*pinus colorado* of the Mexicans) which constitutes the beautiful forest along the banks of the Sierra Nevada to the northward, is here the principal tree. **1949** COLLINGWOOD & BRUSH *Knowing Your Trees* 24 The straight clean trunk and reddish brown bark of the red pine is a familiar feature of the forest stands of the Northeast.

attrib. **1852** EASTMAN *Aunt Phillis's Cabin* 52 He was up stairs in a red pine crib, sound asleep with his thumb in his mouth.

Red River. *attrib.* Designating people and objects found in or coming from the vicinity of the Red River in northeast Texas or the Red River of the North.

1841 NICOLLET *Report* 49 The Metis call themselves 'free people,' (*gens libres;*) but by their neighbors they are designated as '*Metis of the Red river,*' '*the Red-river People,*' '*the People of the North.*' **1849** E. SMITH *Journey through Texas* 23 The cotton thus produced ranks in the New Orleans market as 'Red River' cotton, and is a fine and long staple. **1871** *Rep. Indian Affairs* (1872) 255 Nearly all these persons came into St. Cloud with one of the 'Red River trains,' a long procession of carts that comes annually laden with furs, from the Northwest and the British possessions. **1885** M. D. WOODWARD in *Checkered Yrs.* (1937) 99 Many are having red River fever as well as Red River itch. **1894** EGGLESTON in *Harper's Mag.* Feb. 467/1 The young man in the white blanket coat asked if we would like a Red River turtle.

b. Esp. **Red River cart,** a crude homemade cart having wheels sawed from a tree trunk, so called in allusion to the Red River of the North. Cf. **Pembina buggy, cart.**

[**1801** A. HENRY *Journal* Sep., Men now go again for meat with small low carts, the wheels of which are of one solid piece sawed from the ends of trees whose diameter is three feet. These carriages we find are more convenient and advantageous than to load our horses on their backs, and the country being so smoothe and level we can make use of them to go in all directions.] **1905** WHEELER *Selkirk Range* 155 In places, as many as twelve or fourteen ruts, made by the endless succession of Red river carts . . . used by the early freighters, may be seen side by side, worn in the black alluvial mould. **1920** TRINKA *Out Where West Begins* 30 A line of Red River carts running to St. Paul was established. **1947** BURDICK *Life on Red River of N.* 37 The squeaking of the ungreased Red River carts could be heard for miles.

red rock.

1. A rock that is red, esp. a sandstone of the Triassic period. Also attrib.

1888 *Harper's Mag.* June 43/1 This is the 'red rock region,' the district of the Gypsum Hills. **1898** PAGE *Red Rock* 583 Hiram Still had one night seen the 'Indian Killer' standing by the red-rock. **1950** *L.A. Times* 22 Jan. VI. 1/1 One of the most interesting desert tours within easy distance from Los Angeles is to Willow Springs and Red Rock Canyon.

2. In the names of various fishes and crabs (see quots.).

1883 *Nat. Museum Bul.* No. 27, A large 'Red Rock Crab' (*Echidnoceros setimanus*), living about the Farallone Islands, off San Francisco, is occasionally brought to the markets of that city as a curiosity. *Ib.* 493 *Acipenser rubicundus.* . . . Rock Sturgeon; Red Sturgeon, Mississippi Valley; Great Lakes, and northward. **1884** GOODE *Fisheries* I. 265 Orange Rock-Fish (*Sebastichthys pinniger*) . . . is usually called simply 'Red Rock-Cod,' or 'Red Rock-fish.' **1896** JORDAN & EVERMANN *Check-List Fishes* 434 *Hexagrammos asper.* . . . Red Rock-trout. Alaska to Monterey. **1911** *Rep. Fisheries 1908* 314/2 The red-fish (*Sebastodes melanops*) . . . is also known as 'red cod,' 'red rock-fish,' etc.

red-shouldered, *a.* In combs.: (1) **red-shouldered blackbird,** the red-winged blackbird, or a related species; (2) **buzzard,** =next; (3) **hawk,** a common hawk, *Buteo lineatus*, of eastern North America; (4) **heron,** the great blue heron; (5) **marsh blackbird,** = **red-winged blackbird,** *obs.*

(1) **1858** BAIRD *Birds Pacific R.R.* 529 *Agelaius Gubernator* . . . , Red-shouldered Blackbird. . . . Pacific Coast of the United States. Colorado River? **1917** *Birds of Amer.* II. 248 Red-winged Blackbird. *Agelaius phoeniceus phoeniceus.* . . . [Also called] Red-shouldered Starling; Red-shouldered Blackbird. — (2) **1844** *Nat. Hist. N.Y., Zoology* II. 10 The Red-Shouldered Buzzard, or Winter Hawk, . . . lays four or five bluish eggs. **1917** *Birds of Amer.* II. 74. — (3) **1812** WILSON *Ornithology* VI. 86 [The] Red-shouldered Hawk . . . preys on Larks, Sandpipers and the small Ringed Plover. [**1945** *Mass. Audubon Soc. Bul.* March 39 There are some pairs of nesting Red-shoulders, Sharp-shins or Broad-wings.] — (4) **1785** LATHAM *Gen. Synopsis Birds* III. 85 Red-Shouldered H[eron]. *Ardea Hudsonias.* . . . By some supposed to be the *female* of the last [Great H.]. **1917** *Birds of Amer.* I. 184 Great Blue Heron. *Ardea herodias herodias.* . . . [Also called] Red-shouldered Heron.

(5) **1857** *Rep. Comm. Patents 1856: Agric.* 128 The red-winged starling, or red-shouldered marsh blackbird . . . is dispersed over the whole of the United States, the fur countries, the great Western plains, the Rocky Mountains [etc.]. **1874** COUES *Birds of Northwest* 187 The Red-shouldered Marsh Blackbird is of common occurrence in all suitable places throughout the Missouri region.

red stick.

1. One of the sticks, painted red, used about 1812 by the Indian chief Tecumseh (?1768–1813) as the magic symbol of his war party. Also transf. *Obs.*

1819 *Niles' Reg.* XVI. *Supp.* 102/2 [Tecumseh] carried with him a red stick, to which he attached certain mystical properties, and the acceptance of which was considered as the joining of his party; from hence the name red stick applied to all Indians hostile to the United States. **1854** *S. Lit. Messenger* XX. 400 The red sticks were lifted by the Catawbas against the Shawnese.

2. Orig. an Indian who accepted one of Tecumseh's red sticks and thus joined his war party; later any Indian warrior. Also attrib.

1817 *Niles' Reg.* XIII. 296/1 The number of hostile Indians, including the 'Red-Sticks' and Seminoles, [is estimated] at more than two thousand. **1845** SIMMS *Wigwam & Cabin* 1 Ser. 121 He had proved his skill and courage in several expeditions against the Chowannee red sticks. **1846** MCKENNEY *Memoirs* I. 164 The sticks he [Tecumseh] distributed on that occasion being painted red, secured for those who agreed to co-operate with him, the title of 'Red-sticks.'

3. Attrib. with **class, dancing, party, tribe.**

1817 *State P.* (1819) XII. 339 From below where the Red Stick class reside. *Ib.*, I have heard . . . that the Red Stick party have commenced their Red Stick dancings again. **1817** *Niles' Reg.* XII. 336/1 Never one of them has been known to join the red stick party. **1938** MATSCHAT *Suwannee River* 40 His mother belonged to the Red Sticks Tribe, a branch of the Creek Indians.

***red-tailed,** *a.* In combs.: (1) **red-tailed black hawk,** a western variety, *Buteo borealis calurus*, of the red-tailed hawk, or a hawk of this variety; (2) **buzzard,** =next; (3) **hawk,** a common hen hawk of the U.S., esp. *Buteo borealis*, found in the East.

(1) **1858** BAIRD *Birds Pacific R.R.* 22 Red-tailed Black Hawk. . . . To a casual observer this bird would present somewhat the appearance of the black hawk of the United States. **1869** *Amer. Naturalist* III. 184 Two fine specimens of the Red-tailed Black Hawk . . . would not allow of a very near approach. — (2) **1839** AUDUBON *Synopsis Birds* 6 *Buteo borealis.* Red-tailed Buzzard. **1887** C. C. ABBOTT *Waste-Land Wanderings* ii. 35 The only one of them that is prone to cry out while circling overhead is the red-tailed buzzard or hen-hawk. — (3) **1805** CLARK in *Lewis & C. Exped.* III. (1905) 257 Large red tailed Hawks, ravens & crows in abundance. **1945** MATHEWS *Talking* 4, I had come back to the very spot where I had lain as a boy, watching the circling of the red-tailed hawks.

***redtop,** *n.*

1. Any one of various pasture grasses, as bluejoint, *Calamagrostis canadensis.*

1792 MUHLENBERG in *Life & Corr. Cutler* II. 293 What is Bird-grass, Red-top, Wire-grass, Dog's grass? **1891** WILKINS *Humble Romance* 92 The whole yard . . . [was] covered with a tall waving crop of red-top. **1935** H. L. DAVIS *Honey in Horn* 1 Outside . . . was a ten-mile stretch of creek-meadow with wild vetch and redtop and velvet-grass reaching clear to the black-green fir timber of the mountains.

2. Herd's grass, *Agrostis stolonifera major* (see quot. 1937). Cf. **finetop.**

1818 J. TAYLOR *Arator* 204 A large meadow in bottom land, of a grass called red top or herd's grass, was cut in dry weather. **1901** MOHR *Plant Life Ala.* 370. **1937** *Range Plant Handbook* G8 It seems preferable to use redtop, as a generic name for most of the native range species of *Agrostis.*

3. In combs.: (1) **redtop clover,** red clover; (2) **grass,** any one of various pasture grasses naturalized in the U.S., as herd's grass, *Agrostis stolonifera major;* (3) **hay,** hay obtained from redtop grass, also transf.

(1) **1879** *Scribner's Mo.* Dec. 248/1 If the cultivator can wait for the . . red-top clover he will find it far better. **1886** ROE in *Harper's Mag.* July 247/1 They began with red-top clover. — (2) **1790** DEANE *N.-Eng. Farmer* 115/1 The red top grass is so natural to every soil in this country, that all our old fields. . . are full of it. **1870** *Rep. Comm. Agric. 1869* 88 *Agrostis vulgaris* (red-top grass) and *Agrostis alba* (white-top grass or white bent) are well known valuable meadow grasses. — (3) **1872** EGGLESTON *End of World* 65 When a man comes to Clark township, . . . a cultivating a crap of red-top hay onto his upper lip, and a-lettin' on to be a singin'-master, I suspicions him. **1884** *Rep. Comm. Agric.* 233 The ergot of the red-top hay in Missouri and Illinois produced identical effects with that in the wild rye of Kansas.

reduction works. 1. A place where ores are reduced or smelted, a smeltery. **2.** (See quot.)

(1) **1865** *Harper's Mag.* Feb. 285/2 Down in a beautiful little valley . . . stand the reduction works . . . and peon quarters of the Mowry Silver Mines. **1883** RITCH *Illust. N. Mex.* 35 A few reduction works, smelters and stamp mills have been erected and are in operation in nearly every county of the Territory. — (2) **1894** GOULD *Dict. Medicine* 1244/1 *Reduction-works,* a cremating establishment for disposing of the filth and refuse matter of a city.

***red-winged,** *a.*

1. red-winged blackbird, the red-winged starling or marsh blackbird, *Agelaius phoeniceus.*

[**1633** *Declaration of Lord Baltimore's Plantation* 26 There are Owsels and Black-birds with red shoulders.] **1797** WILLIAM DUNLAP *Diary* I. (1931) 68 Cross over to my Orchard [in Amboy, N.Y.] . . . Kill 5 snipe, 3 red wing'd black birds, 2 Larks and a Bittern. **1811** WILSON *Ornithology* IV. 37 Red-winged Starlings . . . are known by various names in the different states of the union; such as . . . Red-winged Blackbird, Corn or Maize Thief, Starling, &c. **1903** AUSTIN *Land of Little Rain* 241 It must be a happy mystery. So you would think to hear the redwinged blackbirds proclaim it clear March mornings. [**1948** JACOBS *We Chose Country* 161 The male redwing blackbirds . . . always arrive a week before the females.]

b. In other names for this bird, as (*a*) **red-winged icterus,** (*b*) **maize thief,** (*c*) **oriole,** (*d*) **starling.**

(*a*) **1839** AUDUBON *Ornith. Biog.* V. 3 Their habits are similar to those of the Red-winged Icterus. (*b*) **1794** *Amer. Philos. Soc.* IV. 108 This ingenious gentleman was induced to suppose, from the peculiar melancholy cry of a red-winged-maize-thief, that a snake was at no great distance. (*c*) **1785** PENNANT *Arctic Zool.* II. 256 The Red-winged Orioles build their nests in bushes. **1844** *Nat. Hist. N.Y., Zoology* II. 141 The Red-Winged Oriole . . . is regarded by the farmer with great aversion. **1917** *Birds of Amer.* II. 248. (*d*) *c*1728 CATESBY *Carolina* I. 13 The red wing'd Starling. . . . They are the boldest and most destructive Birds in the Country. **1881** *Amer. Naturalist* XV. 393 The Red-winged Starlings generally leave this region [in Iowa] before we have any severely cold weather.

2. red-winged sea robin, (see quot.).

1897 *N.Y. Forest, Fish, & Game Comm. 2d Rep.* 245 *Prionotus strigatus.* . . . Red-Winged Sea Robin.—Makes its appearance later than *P. carolinus.*

***redwood,** *n.*

1. A red willow. *Obs.*

1778 CARVER *Travels* 31 About all the great lakes, is found a kind of willow, termed by the French, bois rouge, in English red wood. **1819** WARDEN *Statistical Acct. U.S.* III. 97 In the lower parts are found oak, elm, . . . red-wood sumach.

2. An unusually large and valuable California and Oregon tree, or species of tree, *Sequoia sempervirens,* or building material obtained from such a tree. Also attrib. Cf. **Sequoia redwood.**

Cf. Sp. *palo colorado,* used by de Anza and others in California many years before the coming of Americans.

1832 LEONARD *Narrative* (1904) 180 In the last two days travelling we have found some trees of the Red-wood species, incredibly large—some of which would measure from 16 to 18 fathom round the trunk at the height of a man's head from the ground. **1847** *Calif. Star* (S.F.) 4 Dec. 2/1 The 'nut brown' of red wood lumber is not sufficiently fanciful for San Francisco. **1851** *Calif. Courier* (S.F.) 16 Jan. 2/2 Eighteen houses are ready and many being built, most of them of red wood, which grows in abundance in this neighborhood. **1905** ATHERTON *Travelling Thirds* 162 The wonders of a Californian mountain-forest—of redwood and pine, mandroño and oak. **1950** *L.A. Times* Midwinter 3 Jan. 63/1 The monumental redwoods, thousands of years old, stand with silent splendor in the snow.

transf. **1878** B. F. TAYLOR *Between Gates* 289 The young pioneers are the young redwoods of mankind.

3. In expressions (sense **2.**) of obvious meaning, as **redwood belt, canyon, cutting, Empire, grove, mountains, shanty.**

1848 FOSTER *Guide* 32 Before the gold fever came on, there were said to be about 200 deserters in the 'Redwood Cuttings' of Upper California from the squadron. **1879** HOWELLS *Lady of Aroostook* 66 'Now, if you were taking some nice girl with you!' . . . 'To those wilds? To a redwood shanty in California, or a turf hovel in Colorado?' **1882** *Nation* 19 Oct 326/3 The Sierra forests [are] the only forests in California, outside of the redwood belt, of more than local importance. **1886** *San Jose* (Calif.) *Mercury* June 3/1 A mill site is sought as near the redwood groves as the . . . ground will permit the building of a wagon road. **1913** LONDON *Valley of Moon* 293 There's some fine redwood canyons, with good patches of farming ground that run right down to the ocean. *Ib.* 314 We'll collect . . . somewhere down in them redwood mountains south of Monterey. **1949** *Highway Traveler* Feb. 20 The Redwood Empire, from San Francisco north into Oregon, is such a land.

Also *redwood board, country, hotel, picket, plank, rail, shingle, tree, wall,* etc.

b. redwood sorrel, (see quot.).

1915 ARMSTRONG & THORNBER *Western Wild Flowers* 272 Redwood Sorrel. *Oxalis Oregana.* White, pink. Spring, Cal., Oreg., Wash. **1949** HOWELL *Marin Flora* 7 It includes the redwood sorrel (*Oxalis oregona*).

Ree ri, *n.* **1.** Short for **Arikara.** Also attrib. **2. Ree corn,** (see quot. 1881).

(1) **1812** in STELLA M. DRUMM *Luttig Journal* (1920) 84 In the afternoon 4 Rees arrived to give us Notice that their Corn was gathered and ready for trade. **1871** in *N. Dak. Hist. Quart.* X. (1943) 9 We were eight in all . . . a teamster—a Ree Indian for guide and myself. **1883** SHIELDS *Rustlings in Rockies* 128 They told us that a roving band of Chippewas had invaded the Rees reservation a few days ago, and stolen several ponies. — (2) **1881** *Rep. Indian Affairs* 36 Yield of crops raised by Indians from 580 acres, . . . estimated: Ree corn (a small early variety), 345 acres, 3,500 bushels. **1917** WILL & HYDE *Corn Among Indians* 24 Ree corn, talked of by all the tribes, had been officialy distributed on many of the reservations.

***reed,** *n.* In combs.: (1) **reed bird,** the bobolink, esp. in its fall plumage, cf. **prairie reedbird;** (2) **brake,** =**canebrake,** also attrib.; (3) **cane,** (see quot. 1818).

(1) **1795** PRIEST *Travels* 90 [Among a] wonderful variety of small birds . . . , the *reed-bird,* or american ortolan, justly holds the first place. **1859** *Pa. Laws* 640 It shall be unlawful for any person or persons to shoot, kill, trap or destroy rail birds or reed birds. **1947** PAUL *Linden* 366 The bobolink, among all the reed birds, had an undeserved lack of popularity with the New England boys. — (2) **1850** DRAKE *Treatise* 197 Sluggish wet-weather streams, with marshy borders, having . . . a considerable growth of small cane;—hence they are called 'switch-cane marshes' and 'reed-brakes.' **1854** DAVIS *Farm Bk.* 46 Planted the Dean cotton on the left side of the reed brake Bridge. **1948** *Carthaginian* (Carthage, Miss.) 19 Aug. 4/4 Total of 190 acres, 70 acres of good reedbrake corn land and 70 acres of cotton land. — (3) **1817** S. BROWN *Western Gazeteer* 78 The Reed Cane . . . grows south of the ridge of hills. **1818** DARBY *Emigrant's Guide* 77 There are two very distinct species of the arundo, or large reed cane, growing in southern Louisiana; the *arundo gigantea,* and the *arundo aquatica.* **1833** FLINT *D. Boone* 151 Each is prepared with a bundle of long, dry, reed cane, or other poles, to which are attached splinters of burning pine.

As the last term in **Indian, sand, winter reed.**

reedy ˈridɪ, *n.* **1.** =**reedbird. 2. reedy swamp,** a swamp overgrown with reeds. Both *colloq.*

(1) **1856** *Porter's Spirit of Times* 11 Oct. 90/3 Niggers ain't fit to shoot reedies. *Ib.* The small boy . . . volunteers some information about a 'ree-ee-dy' that he just saw. — (2) **1635** in *Amer. Sp.* XV. 382/2 Beginning at a little valley butting upon a Reedy Swamp. **1638** *Ib.*, Beginning North upon a reedy Swamp.

***reefer,** *n.* **1.** (See quot.) **2.** (See quot. 1943.) **3.** A marijuana cigarette. Also attrib. *Slang.*

(1) **1881** INGERSOLL *Oyster Industry* 247 *Reefer,* a natural reef-growing or untransplanted oyster. (Mobile to Texas.) — (2) **1943** *Sat. Ev. Post* 26 June 73/3 Pacific Coast perishables roll east in reefers—refrigerator cars. **1949** *Fishing Gaz.* Oct. 64 Rex Silver Reefer combines high speed with positive forced air refrigeration for

Express Agency's perishable traffic. — (3) **1946** *Chi. D. News* 21 Dec. 3/7 The girl told of various 'reefer flats' where marijuana was sold. **1949** *Jrnl. N.Y. Bot. Garden* Aug. 185/2 The smoking of marihuana (reefers) produces no general results which would seem to warrant the present stringent and punitive laws regarding its possession and use.

* **reel,** *n.*

1. On a reaping machine, a rotatory contrivance with horizontal bars at the ends of the radial arms, by which the grain is pressed toward the cutters.

1876 Knight 1890/2 The machine . . . had a reel with twelve vanes to press grain toward the cutter. **1899** *Sat. Ev. Post* 10 June 795 The platform conceived by Cyrus H. McCormick for receiving the cut grain deposited thereon by the reel, . . . remains the same in principle today.

2. Orig. a series of photographs suitably mounted (see quot. 1901) for use in a mutoscope *q.v.;* in later and current use a length of motion-picture film rolled on a large spool or wheel.

1901 *Everybody's Mag.* Aug. 230/2 Ordinary photographs are printed from the negative film and mounted on cards arranged in due sequence and mounted on a central spool, from nine hundred to twenty-seven hundred pictures to a 'reel,' as it is called. **1915** *Chi. Herald* 1 Nov. 8/5 'The Sentimental Lady' is five reels of whipped cream lightness and frothy texture. **1949** *N.O. Times-Picayune Mag.* 24 April 23/2 It's just the first reel and the boy and girl are fighting already.

Hence **reeler,** with a specifying term, to indicate the approximate length of a motion picture.

1916 *Chi. Herald* 17 Feb. 3/4 Essanay will make an international release of the eight-reeler. **1922** Wilson *Merton of Movies* 89, I got another two reeler to pull off after this one.

As the last term in **clock, four-handed, Kentucky, six, six-handed Virginia, stop, Virginia, York reel.**

re-eligibility riˌɛlədʒəˈbɪlətɪ, *n.* Eligibility for reelection to office.

1785 Madison *Writings* II. 174 For neither branch [of the Legislature] does it seem necessary or proper to prohibit an indefinite re-eligibility. **1788** Jefferson *Writings* VI. 426 There is another strong feature in the new Constitution, which I . . . strongly dislike. That is, the perpetual re-eligibility of the President. **1888** Bryce *Amer. Commonw.* II. ii. xlix. 103 Some States limit his [the governor's] re-eligibility.

re-emit ˌri·əˈmɪt, *v. tr.* To emit again, esp. to reissue (bank bills and notes).

1739 W. Douglass *Discourse Currencies* 10 The Province of Massachusetts-Bay . . . have since A. 1702 emitted and re-emitted Bills of publick Credit. **1759** Franklin *Works* (1840) III. 203 The trustees of the loan office might reëmit the same sums. **1884** *American* VIII. 311 The notes are not held, when redeemed, but re-emitted.

***re-export,** *n.* A commodity exported after being imported, the amount of such a commodity. — **1761** Glen *Descr. S. Car.* 48 The Exports of South Carolina Produce are inserted in one Account, and the Re-exports of imported Commodities and Manufactures in another. **1874** Raymond *6th Rep. Mines* 524 Tabular statement of imports, exports, and re-exports of gold and silver coin and bullion from 1867 to 1873, inclusive.

* **refectory,** *n.* A grogshop, also "an eating-house, restaurant" (B. '59).

1834 *Sun* (N.Y.) 28 July 2/2 They pitched upon the basement story of the house No. 28 Park Row, kept as a first rate refectory by Mr. Nathaniel N. Sanborn. **1852** *Harper's Mag.* Sep. 488/2, I was at Lawson's Refectory last night. **1919** Morley *Haunted Bookshop* (1921) 153 A few doors from the bookshop was . . . one of those pleasant refectories where the diner buys his food at the counter and eats it sitting in a flat-armed chair.

***reference,** *n. Surveying.* An observation of position in terms of longitude and latitude or some known point. — **1804** Clark in *Lewis & C. Exped.* I. (1904) 139 After this I will put the Course Destance & refferences of each day first and remks. after. **1816** U. Brown *Journal* ii. 231 The reference he must take, was to go back to the Large Poplar at the beginning & start fair.

* **referendum,** *n.* The practice or principle of submitting a legislative act to a vote of the people or members of an organization.

1870 *Mass. Statistics Labor Rep.* I. 358 We want the referendum. **1911** *Okla. Session Laws* 3 Legisl. 236 When a citizen, or citizens, desire to circulate a petition . . . invoking a referendum upon legislative enactments, such citizen or citizens shall [etc.]. **1948** *Chi. D. News* 18 Dec. 6/4 He got the measure submitted to a referendum and it won.

* **reflector,** *n.* A contrivance for baking by reflected heat, as from a campfire. Also attrib.

1839 Kirkland *New Home* 262 Will he find fault with the clay-built oven, or even the tin 'reflector?' **1853** McConnel *Western Char.* 268 The housewife . . . would have thrown a 'Yankee reflector' over the fence. **1885** *Cent. Mag.* 838 The biscuits were baked in the tin reflector oven. **1947** *So. Sierran* Nov. 3/1 Our packs had now increased to nearly sixty pounds because of the extra food and equipment such as an axe, reflector oven, reserve fishing tackle, and a few little geological specimens.

reflunk riˈflʌŋk, *v. intr.* (See quot.) *Slang.* — **1829** *Va. Lit. Museum* 30 Dec. 460 To reflunk, 'to retreat, to back out.'

* **reform,** *n.* **1. reform club,** a club organized to promote temperance. Also attrib. **2. reform school,** "a school for the confinement, instruction, and reformation

Reflector or biscuit baker

of juvenile offenders, and of young persons of idle, vicious, and vagrant habits" (B. '59).

(1) **1877** *Mich. Gen. Statutes* I. (1882) 154 Reform club temperance societies may be incorporated in pursuance of the provisions of this act. **1882** Rittenhouse *Maud* 124 Then the Reform Club was organized, Mr Dietrich signed the pledge and now all is well with them.— (2) **1887** *Mass. Acts & Resolves* 405 There shall be established, in the town of Westborough, . . . a school, for the . . . reformation of juvenile offenders, to be called the State Reform School. **1949** *Ward Co. Independent* (Minot, N.D.) 21 July 1/8 Three of the four Minot boys . . . were finally incarcerated in the reform school until they are 21.

As the last term in **Civil Service, labor, land reform.**

* **Reformer,** *n.* **1.** (See quot.) **2.** A Campbellite. Now *hist.*

(1) **1831** Peck *Guide* 258 The Reformers, or Methodist Protestant church, have several societies and preachers in the State [of Ill.]. — (2) **1834** Peck *Gaz. Illinois* 91 The Cambellites, or 'Reformers,' as they usually term themselves, have several large, and a number of smaller societies. **1871** Eggleston *Hoosier Schoolm.* xii. 101 Squire Hawkins . . . had become a member of the 'Reformers' . . . who now call themselves 'Disciples,' but whom the profane will persist in calling 'Campbellites.' **1931** Sweet *Religion* 26 Between 1829 and 1832, something like 10,000 Kentucky Baptists withdrew to form the Disciples Church. Besides the Campbell followers, who were known as *Reformers* [etc.].

As the last term in **Baptist, labor, revenue reformer.**

* **refreshment,** *n.* In combs.: (1) **refreshment bar,** (see quot.); (2) **car,** a dining car; (3) **parlor** (see quot.). All *obs.*

(1) **1868** Rose *Great Country* 255 There was what is called a refreshment bar, at which no alcoholic drinks were to be obtained, as we were still under the dread rule of the Maine Liquor Laws. — (2) **1868** Bowles *Colorado* (1869) 9 The Atlantic states provide on none of their railways as yet so elegant and ease-giving carriages as the saloon and sleeping and refreshment cars that are offered to travelers on the long routes of the West. **1891** *Ohio Falls Exp.* (Louisville) 11 July 5/2 Refreshment Cars will be attached to the Excursion Train. — (3) **1908** White *Riverman* 60 They supported row upon row of saloons, . . . refreshment 'parlours,' where drinks were served.

refrigerating car. =**refrigerator car.** — **1869** *Rep. Comm. Patents 1868* I. 774/2 The Refrigerating Car . . . has a plurality of metallic chambers for the respective reception of 'way' and 'through' freight. **1886** *Harper's Mag.* July 205/2 Packing-houses transfer their edible remains to boxes, barrels, and refrigerating cars.

* **refrigerator,** *n.*

1. A box or boxlike receptacle used for maintaining, by the use of ice or by a system of refrigeration, a temperature sufficiently low to preserve perishable foods. Cf. **gas refrigerator.**

In R. O. Cummings, *The American and His Food* (1941 ed.) 36, Thomas Moore, a Md. farmer, is credited with the invention of this household convenience. Early in the 19th century British travelers (see quots. 1834, 1848 below) regarded the contrivance as of American origin.

1803 THOMAS MOORE (*title*) An Essay on the Most Eligible Construction of Ice-Houses, Also, a Description of the Newly Invented Machine Called the Refrigerator. **1834** FERGUSSON *Pract. Notes* 211, I was curious to know how they contrived to preserve untainted their fish, butcher-meat, &c. in such weather as the present, and Mr Gadsby [in Washington, D.C.] very civilly took me down to his larder in the basement and showed me what he called a *refrigerator.* **1848** MAURY *Englishwoman* 215 Their washing-machines, refrigerators, rocking chairs, . . . are admirable. [Re some 'Yankee Notions' found in a London shop.] **1891** *Memphis Appeal-Avalanche* 26 April 3/2 We have everything from a 5c can opener to a $25 refrigerator. **1949** *Chesterton* (Ind.) *Tribune* 7 April 11 Come in and see these handsome, quality-built refrigerators that bring new beauty, new convenience, and new economy to your kitchen.

transf. and *attrib.* **1883** HAY *Bread-Winners* 237 Have our prisoners taken down to the Refrigerator and turned over to the ordinary police. **1948** *Aurora* (Ill.) *Beacon-News* 7 Nov. 2/4 In slicing refrigerator cookies for baking, use a thin bladed, very sharp knife.

b. Also attrib. in the sense of refrigerator car. Cf. **3.** below.

1881 *Chi. Times* 4 June, American refrigerator beef sold at London and Liverpool to-day at 5½ d. **1945** BAKER *Party Line* 15 Stretched alongside the tracks are . . . long runways, supported on high scaffoldings, from which refrigerator freights are iced.

2. Short for next.

1868 *Comm. & Fin. Chron.* VI. 215/2 There are now 613 Blue Cars in the line, including twenty 'Refrigerators.'

3. refrigerator car, a railway car in which a low temperature can be maintained for transporting perishable commodities, esp. meat.

1868 *Rep. Comm. Patents 1867* II. 1386/2 Refrigerator Car. . . . The air from the upper part of the car passes down through the ice chamber. **1950** *Calif. Citrograph* Jan. 100/4 A new method of using hot water to remove ice from refrigerator cars . . . has been announced.

* **refugee,** *n.*

1. A loyalist during the Revolutionary War who sought refuge under the protection of the British crown. *Obs.*

1778 T. HUTCHINSON *Diary & Lett.* II. 218 [Penobscot] is to be erected into a new Province, and to be given to the Refugees, upon the same quitrents as the N. Hampshire and other Grantees. **1783** *Va. Gazette* 20 Dec. 2/1 If none but refugees of good characters are to be sent to Halifax, those of bad characters ought to be sent to *Hell-infact*, which will nearly include the whole. **1888** LOWELL *Lit. & Polit. Addresses* 203 Most of the refugees who, during or after the Revolutionary War, went to England . . . found themselves out of place.

attrib. **1780** *Heath P.* III. 32 Colonel Delancy was with the refugee horse. **1823** THATCHER *Military Jrnl.* 183 A captain of Colonel Delany's battalion of refugee troops, with about one hundred American royal regulars, was posted near a river.

b. A marauding Tory, esp. of New York State, fighting in guerrilla bands during the Revolutionary War. *Obs.*

1780 J. ANDRE (*title*), The Cow-Chace, In Three Cantos, Published on Occasion of the Rebel General Wayne's Attack of the Refugees' Block-House On Hudson's River. **1821** COOPER *Spy* xviii, The Cowboys were sometimes called Refugees.

2. A Canadian or Nova Scotian who came to help the U.S. during the Revolutionary War. *Obs.*

1785 *Jrnls. Cont. Congress* XXIV. 268 There are now serving in the Regiment . . . officers and men chiefly Refugees from Canada. **1796** *Ann. 4th Congress* 2 Sess. 1728 A tract of land . . . [shall] be immediately appropriated to compensate the refugees from the British provinces of Canada and Nova Scotia.

b. Used attrib. with reference to claims or tracts for refugees. *Obs.*

1812 *Niles' Reg.* II. 13/2 The speaker laid before the house . . . [a letter] on the subject of the refugee claims. **1812** MELISH *Travels* II. 222 A stripe of land about three miles broad, and 42 miles long . . . was appropriated to the relief of such as had to abandon their settlements in the time of the war, and take refuge in other places, and is thence called *refugee land.* **1837** W. JENKINS *Ohio Gaz.* 371 *Refugee tract*, . . . a narrow strip of country, 4½ miles broad from north to south, and extending eastwardly from the Scioto river, 48 miles.

3. During the Civil War, a person who left his home in order to seek refuge or to aid the other side. Also attrib.

1864 CUMMING *Hospital Life* (1866) 146/2 His two daughters were with him, and were keeping house in *two* rooms, refugee style. **1865** *Statutes at Large* XIII. 508 The Secretary of War may direct such issues of provisions, clothing and fuel, as he may deem needful for the . . . supply of destitute and suffering refugees and freedmen and their wives and children. **1888** GRIGSBY *Smoked Yank* (1891) 236 General Hazen asked me to take charge of the refugee train that was assigned to his division. **1896** *Cong. Rec.* App. 25 April 299/1 These 'Home Guards' [in e. Tenn.] piloted the Union refugees northward from the whole Southern country . . . up through the mountains into Kentucky, where they organized into regiments under the flag of the Union.

4. refugee bean, a now unidentifiable bean or variety of bean. *Obs.*

1859 *Ill. Agric. Soc. Trans.* III. 503 The refugee bean (long, dark clouded,) has the same characteristics.

* **refugee,** *v. tr.* and *intr.* To cause (a person) to become a refugee; to seek or to take refuge.

1806 HAWKINS *Letters* 429 It will be some time before the Creek young will get rid of the remains of that alloy which debased the agents and refugeed their associates. **1864** CUMMING *Hospital Life* (1866) 157/2 Many of the citizens of Mobile . . . had *refugeed* from fear of an attack. **1904** R. E. LEE *Recoll. Gen. Lee* 270 In the early years of the struggle, my mother and sisters, when 'refugeeing,' had boarded . . . at his home. *c***1943** *Flags of Five Nations* 6 Here refugeed French nobility fleeing the guillotine, and San Domingan planters escaping massacre at the hands of their slaves.

Hence * **refugeed,** *a.*

1874 COLLINS *Kentucky* I. 162 [There have been] about 1,200 deaths, within the year past, among the negroes refugeed at Camp Nelson.

refuse (public) land. A piece of comparatively undesirable public land either taken up last by settlers or left altogether unclaimed. *Obs.* — **1832** CLAY *Speeches* 225 This pretension may be . . . to graduate the public lands to reduce the price, and to cede the 'refuse lands' (a term which I believe originated with him [i.e., Benton]) to the States within which they lie. **1845** *Indiana Senate Jrnl.* 29 Sess. 541 A joint resolution on the subject of the refuse public lands in Indiana.

regal moth. A large, handsome moth, *Citheronia regalis*, the larva of which is known as the hickory horned devil *q.v.* Also **regal walnut moth.** See also **royal walnut moth, walnut moth.**

1854 EMMONS *Agric. N.Y.* V. 238 *Ceratocampa regalis.* . . . Regal Walnut-moth. . . . It feeds on the walnut. **1887** DENTON *Naturalist's Diary* (1949) 121, I have . . . caught eight sphinx moths, and many others, one like the regal walnut moth. **1912** *Country Life* 1 Aug. 38 The blue horned hickory devil which turns into the Regal moth.

regardless rɪˈgardlɪs, *adv.* Ellipt. for "regardless of cost, labor, consequences," etc., in spite of all. *Colloq.*

1872 MARK TWAIN *Roughing It* 334 We are going to get the thing [*sc.* funeral] up regardless, you know. **1896** *Advance* 30 July 150 Miss Bond got herself up regardless, and came in resplendent in ruby velvet and white swansdown. **1911** QUICK *Yellowstone Nights* 289 We got . . . messages from him to rush S.F. 41144 to its passage, regardless.

* **regency,** *n.* =**Albany regency.** Also attrib. Now *hist.* Cf. **State Regency.**

1824 *Niles' Reg.* 4 Sep. 3/1 These great states . . . will add a *moral force* . . . that will forbid their being the *tail-pieces* of any 'junto,' or 'regency' that can ever be got up. **1830** *Albany Jrnl.* 10 Sep. 1/2 The Regency folks in Greene county go the hog. **1859** *N.Y. Herald* 2 Sep. 4/4 Having slaughtered him and cut him up the Regency offer his carcass for sale as they would a round or a shoulder of beef. *a***1882** WEED *Autobiog.* 121 Of the eight senators elected, six were Clintonians, and two Regency men.

* **regenerator,** *n.* (See quot.) *Obs.* — **1871** *Harper's Mag.* Sep. 603 General Connor . . . and others who sided with him, in attempting to bring about a harmony between the people of Utah, and the institutions of the republic, were stigmatized by the church party as 'The Regenerators.'

* **regent,** *n.*

1. A member of a board governing a single state university or college, or supervising all the state schools, or other special educational institutions.

1813 *Niles' Reg.* V. 79/2 The regents of the university, expressly endeavored to effect this important object. **1890** *Stock Grower & Farmer* 6 Sep. 3/1 The Board of Regents of the Agricultural College of New Mexico have issued invitations to the ceremonies of laying the corner stone of the college edifice. **1947** *Sat. Ev. Post* 15 March 161/1 Perhaps you'll be able to take Regents' tests.

b. A member of the governing board of the Smithsonian Institution.

1846 POLK *Diary* (1929) 146, I rode out in my carriage to meet the regents of the Smithsonian Institute on the public grounds. **1906** *N.Y. Ev. Post* 1 Dec. 1 The regents of the Smithsonian Institution assemble for their annual meeting next Tuesday.

2. In Harvard University, a disciplinary officer.

1814 *Harvard Laws* 7 The Regent and Proctors, shall reside in the College. **1902** CORBIN *Amer. at Oxford* 275 A Regent has among other duties a general charge of the rooms the fellows live in, and usually makes each room and its occupant a yearly visit.

3. (*cap.*) *pl.* The members of the Albany regency. *Obs.*

1838 *N.Y. Advt. & Exp.* 6 Jan. 4/2 The Regents' skill, the Regents' power, Have vanished in a single hour.

regidor ˌrehiˈdor, *n. S.W.* [Sp., in same sense.] A magistrate of a city, a governor or prefect.

1834 A. PIKE *Sketches* 170 The Regidor, or Assistant Alcalde, Miguel Sena, has only perjured himself three times. **1895** G. KING *New Orleans* 115 Instead of a superior council, there was a cabildo, with regidores, alcaldes [etc.]. **1934** *So. Calif. Hist. Soc. Pub.* 16, 142 He was *regidor* of Los Angeles in 1838–39.

***region,** *n.* As the last term in **cane, cotton, fruit, gold, grasshopper, lumber, oil, prairie, Rocky Mountain, salt, sand hill, stock, turpentine, wave, wiry grass region.**

***register,** *n.*[1] **1.** (See quot.) **2.** *register of deeds*, an official who registers or records deeds. Cf. **county register.**

(1) **1851** HALL *College Words* 257 *Register*, in Union College, an officer whose duties are similar to those enumerated under Registrar. — (2) **1735** *Boston Rec.* 129 The Town will proceed to the Choice of a . . . Register of Deeds for the County of Suffolk. **1913** *Indian Laws & Tr.* III. 573 Copies [of a roll of the Chippewa Indians] may be made and filed for record with the registers of deeds of the various counties.

***register,** *n.*[2]

1. A book in which guests at a hotel, inn, etc., register their names.

1834 *Sun* (N.Y.) 7 June 4/1 They found the name of 'J. Thompson' on the register of the City Hotel. **1902** HARBEN *A. Daniel* 151 Wilson is at the hotel. I saw his name on the register this morning. **1949** *St. Paul Pioneer Press* 19 June 20/5 Her husband, John, didn't even wait to sign the register in their honeymoon hotel.

2. A contrivance over an opening in the wall or floor of a room, by means of which the flow of heated air from a furnace can be regulated; also the opening through which the air passes.

1847 *Rep. Comm. Patents 1846* 30 The openings from these furnaces, in the floors or walls of apartments are usually covered with a kind of revolving valve, called the register. **1906** FREEMAN *By Light of Soul* 309 He found his mother warming herself by the sitting-room register. **1947** *Woodlawn Booster* (Chi.) 20 Aug. 8/2 Candy should be kept in a cool, dry place away from hot radiators and warm air registers.

As the last term in **alarm, army, cash, heat, hotel, Navy, social, time, water register.**

***register,** *v.*

1. *intr.* To record one's name, address, etc., on the register of a hotel.

1848 *Literary Amer.* 14 Oct. 237/1 Sixty miles down the Monongahela brought us to *Pittsburgh*, and about half past 7 P.M., I was registered at the 'Monongahela House.' **1912** CROLY *M. A. Hanna* 459 Whenever prominent men registered at the hotel, Mr. Hanna managed to meet them. **1947** BASKINS *Dr. Has Baby* 180 'Isn't this something?' I stage-whispered to John, as we registered.

transf. **1947** *Nat. Geog. Mag.* Feb. 223 (*caption*), J. M. Bryant's name is one of thousands 'registered' by visitors.

2. *tr.* To enrol (a student) in a school, or in various study and recitation classes. Also *intr.*

1894 *Univ. Chi. Reg.* 166/2 The student must register for each quarter. **1925** F. B. O'REAR *Duties of Registrar* 154 Forms [are] presented for use in admitting students, in registering them for work, and providing course cards. **1947** *Democrat* 30 Jan. 1/4 (*heading*), 39 From Clarke Register At Auburn.

***registered,** *a.* In combs.: (1) **registered bond,** a bond issued with the name of the holder written on the bond and recorded in a register; (2) **debt,** a part of the national debt which, after the Assumption Act, was registered with the treasury but not funded by bonds; (3) **nurse,** a trained nurse who has passed a state board examination for registration in that state.

(1) **1861** *Statutes at Large* XII. 259 The Secretary of the Treasury . . . is authorized to issue coupon bonds, or registered bonds, or treasury notes. **1914** *Cyclo. Amer. Govt.* I. 142/2 The holder of a registered bond cannot suffer loss if the security be stolen. — (2) **1794** *Ann. 3d Congress* 26 A statement of the Domestic Debt of the United States . . . 2d. The Registered Debt. — (3) **1934** WEBSTER. **1949** *Reader's Digest* June 91/1 They passed with flying colors the examinations for registered nurse.

registering punch. "An instrument used by railroad conductors, with which they are required to cut from a card the amount of fares they receive" (B. '77).

***registrar,** *n.* A college or university official who keeps the records of students' enrolments and grades.

1813 *Niles' Reg.* V. 80/1 John W. Francis, M.D. *Registrar.* **1851** HALL *College Words* 257 At Harvard College, the Corporation appoints one of the Faculty to the office of *Registrar.* **1940** *Univ. of Ill. Bul.* 9 George Philip Tuttle, B.S., Registrar.

***registration,** *n.* Enrolment in a college or university. Also attrib. — **1897** *Univ.* (Chi.) *Rec.* I. 199, June, Tuesday. . . . Matriculation and Registration of Incoming Students. **1940** *Univ. of Ill. Bulletin* 101 Former students who enter after the registration days in either semester pay a late registration fee.

registry law. A law concerned with the registration of voters. — **1839** MARRYAT *Diary in Amer.* II. 227 The Lofo-foco party resist every proposition for a registry law. **1865** *Ore. State Jrnl.* 23 Dec. 2/5 S.B. No. 1, the registry law, was indefinitely postponed.

regrade riˈgred, *v.* **1.** *tr.* To grade (a road) again. **2.** To regroup the students of (a class).

(1) **1826** *Cong. Deb.* 18 Nov. 1572 (Ernst), The road . . . is to be regraded. **1884** *Cent. Mag.* March 648/2 The city was torn up from one end to the other, and regraded. — (2) **1887** *Conv. Amer. Instructors of Deaf Proc.* 141 You may start out . . . with a class well graded, and before you have been at work three months you will find that you ought to regrade.

***regular,** *n.* A party member who faithfully stands by his party, a standpatter. Cf. **United States regular.**

1840 *Maysville* (Ky.) *Eagle* 3 June 3/2 The friends of a certain individual . . . are now circulating, a *Prospectus* for the purpose of ascertaining how many 'Regulars' may be depended upon as certain. **1904** *Indianapolis News* 27 July 6 The new chairman is a regular of the regulars. He is a Democrat, whether his party is for gold or for silver. **1914** *Cyclo. Amer. Govt.* I. 111 The 'hards' were New York Democrats, the name 'hard' being applied to the regulars by the opposing faction. **1950** *Time* 16 Jan. 18/3 Douglas made up his mind to go after the governorship, an idea that struck horror into the ranks of the regulars.

b. (*cap.*) *pl.* (See quots.) *Obs.* or *hist.*

1752 in *N.J. Archives* XIX. 225 We hear from *Elizabeth-Town*, that an odd Sect of People have lately appeared there, who go under the Denomination of Regulars. **1931** SWEET *Religion* 44 The origin of the terms Separate and Regular came from the Great Awakening in New England. The Separates were those who were particularly revivalistic and separated from the churches which did not support the revival, thus they became known as *Separates.* Those who did not thus separate were known as *Regulars.*

***regular,** *a.*

1. Of a candidate for office: Nominated or supported by the officially constituted organization of a party.

1827 *Hallowell* (Me.) *Gaz.* 20 June 3/1 If they vote for such a one solely because he is the 'regular candidate' as the cant phrase is, . . . let them take the consequences. **1887** *Boston Dem. City Com.* Bylaw 12 (Ernst), A regular Democratic nominee.

b. Of a nomination or ticket: Made or chosen by the officially constituted party, esp. in a party convention.

1829 in COMMONS *Doc. Hist.* V. 156 Men who have long passed current as genuine and faithful . . . have aspired to break down the Regular nominations of the Democratic party. **1902** MEYER *Nominating Systems* 17 [The people] were drilled into a blind acceptance of 'regular nominations.'

c. Of a person or a vote: Supporting the established or official party organization, opposed to the insurgents.

1846 MACKENZIE *Van Buren* 182 He is a regular Democrat; was health officer in Philadelphia when he wrote the above letter. **1904** *Booklovers Mag.* Jan. 8 In the last two presidential contests he has been 'regular,' having voted for Bryan.

d. Of a political party or organization: Recognized as the authorized party or organization.

1864 *Ore. State Jrnl.* 16 April 2/5 He and O'Meara run [*sic*] on the same ticket, in opposition to the 'regular Democratic party.' **1949** *Dziennik Związkowy* (Chi.) 19 Nov. 6/2 The annual Fall Festival sponsored by the 35th Ward Regular Republican Organization . . . will be held Tuesday evening.

2. In special combs.: (1) **regular Baptist,** (see quot. 1847), *obs.* or *hist.;* (2) **session,** a session of Congress or of a state legislature that convenes at a time specified by law; (3) **two-forty,** (see quot.), *obs.;* (4) **way,** (see quot. 1900).

(1) **1847** L. Collins *Kentucky* 110 This revival had the happy effect of bringing about a union between the *Regular* and *Separate* Baptists. **1849** Chamberlain *Ind. Gazetteer* 71 The Regular Baptists are numerous. **1941** Stuart *Men of Mts.* 331. — (2) **1837** *Diplom. Corr. Texas* (1908) I. 264 There was no intention to bring up the subject of Texas and the question of its annexation, until the regular session which commences . . . on the first Monday in December. **1912** Nicholson *Hoosier Chron.* 534 It was Morton Bassett's legislature . . . brought back to the capital to do those things which it had left undone at the regular session. — (3) **1867** Latham *Black & White* 158 Two minutes and forty seconds is the least time in which a match horse is expected to do his mile, and 'a regular 2.40' is a slang phrase expressive of anything 'fast' all through the States. — (4) **1857** *Merchants' Mag.* July 136 Very often in the report of stock sales, the letters r.w. are attached to certain operations. This 'regular way' means the delivery of the stock sold the next day. **1900** Nelson *A B C Wall St.* 157 *Regular, or regular way*, the term of sale employed when the delivery is to be made at or before 2–15 P.M. on the day succeeding that of the making of the contract.

***regular**, *adv.* (See quots. and cf. **regular way.**) — **1865** *Harper's Mag.* April 616/2 People who have plenty of money buy for cash or 'regular'—which means that the stock will be delivered and paid for next day. **1870** Medbery *Men Wall St.* 50 Where the seller . . . hopes to get a better price, or cannot make a delivery of stock until next day, he sells *Regular*.

***regulating**, *a.* Of persons or groups of persons: Belonging to an association of regulators (senses **2.** and **3.** below). *Obs.*

1768 *Boston Chron.* 8 Aug. 315/1 The reforming or regulating people will not suffer process civil or criminal, to be executed, but where, and against whom they think proper. **1808** in Beadle *Undevel. West* 410 Should the accused person or persons raise up with arms in his or their hands, . . . in opposition to the regulating company [etc.]. **1828** J. Hall *Lett. from West* 291 The citizens formed themselves into a '*regulating company*,' a kind of holy brotherhood, whose duty was to purge the community of its unruly members.

***regulation**, *n.* The mode or practice of policing or governing a society through regulators. Also attrib. Cf. **army, Jim Crow regulation(s).**

[**1768** *N.C. Col. Rec.* VII. 700 Regulators' Advertisement. . . . We are determined to have the Officers of this county under a better and honester regulation than they have been for some time past.] **1837** *S. Lit. Messenger* III. 648 The outrages of the borderers—the frontier law of 'regulation' or 'lynching' which is common to new countries all over the world, are ascribed to slavery. **1867** A. Gregg *Hist. Old Cheraws* 130 Such, however, was not the history of the Regulation Movement on the Pedee.

***regulator**, *n.*

1. In Philadelphia, a surveyor who laid out the lines for house foundations, streets, etc. *Obs.*

1721 *Phila. Ordinances* (1812) 12 No person or persons . . . [shall] lay the foundation of any building, before they have applied themselves to the surveyors or regulators. **1782** *Ib.* 48 Regulators . . . [may] enter into or upon any lot or land . . . , and survey and measure the same.

2. A member of any one of various bands or volunteer committees, formed ostensibly to preserve order, prevent crime, etc., but actually, in many cases, to commit violence and illegal acts. Cf. **Negro regulator.**

1753 in *N.J. Archives* XIX. 326 These young Persons do stile, or are stiled, Regulators; and so they are with Propriety; for they have regulated my dear Husband, and the rest of the bad Ones hereabouts. **1808** in Beadle *Undevel. West* 410 The blood of him or them shall not be required of any of the persons belonging to the regulators from the clan the person so killed belonged to. **1859** *Harper's Mag.* July 255/2 From *Arizona* we have intelligence of outrages by organized bands of ruffians, who, under the name of Regulators, attempted to expel the Mexican inhabitants from Sonorita Valley. **1949** Gann *Tread of Longhorns* 125 The individual killings did not stop the theft of cattle, and the Regulators adopted a more drastic and bloodthirsty policy.

attrib. **1845** *Amer. Whig. Rev.* I. 124/1 Hinch, the Regulator Captain [in Shelby Co., Texas], had always been the unrivalled hero of such occasions. **1865** Pike *Scout & Ranger* (1932) 128 He had taken a prominent part . . . in the Moderator and Regulator struggle in 1836–8.

3. In the back country of the Carolinas, a member of various illegal or extralegal organizations: **a.** In South Carolina formed (*c*1767–69) to purge the region of horse thieves and other criminals. Now *hist.* Cf. **lynch,** *n.*

1767 in A. Gregg *Hist. Old Cheraws* 136 Those licentious spirits that have so lately appeared in the distant parts of the Province [of S.C.], . . . assuming the name of Regulators, have . . . illegally tried, condemned, and punished many persons. **1768** *Boston Post Boy* 22 Aug. 2/1 Charles-Town, South-Carolina, . . . July 25. . . . The last Accounts from the Back Settlements, say, that the People called the Regulators were to have a Meeting at Lynche's Creek. **1802** Drayton *S. Carolina* 196 Regulators . . . , rather than travel all the way to Charleston, for the purpose of carrying on prosecutions in the courts of law, inflicted summary punishment on all trespassers on their persons, or properties. [**1948** Dick *Dixie Frontier* 233 Thus came into being the Regulator or other extralegal organization, which appeared in every section.]

b. In North Carolina formed (*c*1768–71) to resist official oppression. Now *hist.*

1768 *N.C. Col. Rec.* VII. 731 At a general meeting of the regulators on April 30th it was laid before us an Appointment of the Officers. **1784** Smyth *Tour* I. 228 The Regulators of North Carolina were, and still are among the worthiest, steadiest, and most respectable friends to British government and real constitutional freedom. **1943** Peattie *Great Smokies* 52 The Regulators may have been a rash lot, little more than a mob; but they really fired some of the opening shots in the American Revolution.

attrib. **1770** *N.C. Col. Rec.* VII. 848 John Wilcox fell in with us as we left ye Regelater Camp.

***rein**, *n.* As the last term in **hitch, hitching, jerk rein.**

***rein**, *v.* [The origin of this use, known only from the examples given, is puzzling. Did Washington write **hein*, or **hain?* (See *OED* and *EDD*.) Cf. Du. *reinen*, to fence off.] *tr.* To protect (a field) from stock. *Obs.* — **1799** Washington *Writings* XIV. 230 This field, after the rye has been eaten off by the sheep, is to be reined from stock of all kinds. *Ib.* 231 The other part . . . is to be equally well enclosed, and reined up from stock.

reina ˈreɪnə, *n.* [Sp., queen.] A rockfish, *Hispaniscus elongatus*, of the California coast. — **1884** Goode *Fisheries* I. 266 This species is known as 'Reina' (Queen) at Monterey. It is a small fish . . . and lives in deep water. **1911** *Rep. Fisheries 1908* 314/2.

reinsman ˈrenzmən, *n.* A person skilled in handling reins, a driver. Also fig. Cf. **driver's seat.**

1855 in *Voice* 8 Feb. (1894), 30,000 . . . deeming themselves as skilful reinsmen as those selected by the Boards of Excise, have assumed the driver's seat. **1870** M. H. Smith *20 Yrs. Wall St.* 263 His driver, an imported Englishman, is said to be the best reinsman in America. **1930** Banning *Six Horses* 361 A reinsman was a master driver who, by virtue of his exceptional skill, was able to drive each span of his complement wholly independent of the other.

***relax**, *n.* Diarrhea. *Colloq. Obs.* — **1805** *Lewis & Clark Exped.* VII. (1905) 164 Several of the men Sick with the relax. **1832** Wyeth *Journal* 155 Our men troubled with the relax.

***relay**, *n.* **1. relay house,** (see quot. 1890). **2. relay station,** a station where horses are changed on a stage or courier route. Both *obs.*

(1) **1831** *Boston Transcript* 19 March 2/3 Mr. W. will make trips at any time during the day, to such points on the road as far as the rely-house [*sic*], as parties may desire. **1890** *Railways of Amer.* 230 The term Relay House, the name of a well-known station, originated in the fact that the horses [on a horse railroad] were changed at that place. — (2) **1870** Keim *Sheridan's Troopers* 49 The nearest settlement was Pond City, quite an extravagant appellation for a relay station. *a***1918** G. Stuart *On Frontier* I. 150 There were relay stations along the route, where two minutes were allowed to change horses and mail. **1927** Walgamott *Remin. Early Days* II. 14 These stations were called relay or swing stations and were built to house twelve head of standing horses and provide living quarters for a Stalk [*sic*] Tender and herder.

***release**, *n.* The releasing for publication, broadcast, or showing, of reports, news items, or motion pictures. Also that which is released.

1907 *N.Y. Ev. Post* (s.-w. ed.) 15 July 4 The report was given to the press associations . . . labelled 'confidential,' with a fixed date for 'release,' before which no part of it was to be used. **1932** Beck *Wonderland* 77 Not being able to reach the American mothers through the press, some of these bureaus have taken to the air, in the form of radio releases. **1949** *St. Paul Pioneer Press* 19 June 11/3 Busiest year on record for total releases is 1921 when American moviegoers had their choice of 854 different features.

***release**, *v. tr.* To permit the publication, broadcasting, etc., of a report, news items, etc. — **1904** *N.Y. Times* 25 July 5 Chairman Cannon's speech and President Roosevelt's response are completed. The latter is in the hands of the press associations, and will be released Wednesday afternoon. **1932** Beck *Wonderland* 77 During the years 1923 to 1929, this Bureau released to the press of the country, over a thousand items similar to those just described.

***relief**, *n.*

1. relief note, a note issued by the state of Pennsylvania in 1841 to pay interest on the public debt, etc.

bearing a promise to be received for all obligations due the state. *Obs.*

1842 *Spirit of Times* 15 Feb. (Th.), I've had five breezes, seven blow-outs, nine shindies, and a dozen ructions on this $1 Relief note. **1894** LEAVITT *Our Money Wars* 77 Pennsylvania, in this crisis, issued $3,100,000 of what was called 'Relief Notes.'

2. relief party, (see quot. 1893). *Obs.*

1825 *New-Harmony* (Ind.) *Gaz.* 1 Oct. 7/2 The long continued and bitter contest between the Relief and Anti-relief parties in Kentucky, has resulted in the complete success of the latter. **1840** *Maysville* (Ky.) *Eagle* 15 July 3/1 Gen. Meredith was followed by William Worthington, Esq., a gentleman who in his palmy days, was the 'brag' speaker of the old Relief party of Kentucky. **1893** JAMESON *Dict. U.S. Hist.* (1931) 22 Anti-Relief Party, a political party in Kentucky opposing the relief of delinquent debtors and consequently the so-called Relief Party. This party was defeated by the Relief Party in the Gubernatorial contest of 1824, but regained control two years later.

As the last term in **farm, special relief.**

***religion,** *n. To experience religion*, see ***experience,** *v.*

***religious,** *a.* **1.** *W.* Of a horse: Having no vicious traits. **2. religious boat,** (see quot.). Both *obs.* — (1) **1869** *Overland Mo.* III. 127 It is amusing to hear one ask of another, when about to purchase a horse: 'Is he religious?' — (2) **1835** REED & MATHESON *Visit* I. 183 The steamer . . . is what is called a religious boat. There are Bibles strewed in the men's cabin, and a subscription-box for the Episcopal Tract Society.

***relinquishment,** *n.* A tract of abandoned or relinquished land. — **1886** *Cong. Rec.* 28 June 6238/1 Nearly every land agent . . . advertises as a prominent feature of his business 'Relinquishments for sale.' **1897** *Outing* XXIX. 570/2 He had . . . bought a relinquishment up the river.

reloan riˈlon, *n.* An act involving the loan of the same money a second time. — **1790** *Ann. 1st Congress* 2021 The United States . . . [will provide for] all such part of the debts of the respective States, . . . [as shall] be subscribed towards a loan to the United States, upon the principle of either of the plans which shall have been adopted by them for the reloan of their present debt. **1802** *Ann. 7th Congress* 1 Sess. 1171 The bill before us authorizes a reloan of the whole Dutch debt. *Ib.* 1172, I will therefore move so to amend the bill as to make all the reloans reimbursable before 1809.

relocatable riˈloketəbl̩, *a.* Subject to being relocated. — **1872** MARK TWAIN *Roughing It* xli. 290 (R.), At midnight the ledge would be relocatable.

relocate riˈloket, *v.*

1. *intr.* To move and resettle. Also *tr.* Cf. **locate,** *v.* **1.**

1841 WEBSTER II. 457/2. **1851** CIST *Cincinnati* 143 [This] determined the company to re-locate on higher ground. **1866** *Rep. Indian Affairs* 76 If the Indians could be removed to some remote place equally fertile, and there relocated, it would no doubt be to their advantage. **1894** *Advance* 31 May, The congregation is preparing to re-locate in the north part of the city.

2. *W. Mining. tr.* To ascertain again the location of a mineral deposit.

1874 RAYMOND *6th Rep. Mines* 517 They formed a code of laws, relocated the various outcrops, went to work in earnest and developed the mines. **1948** JOHNSTON *Gold Rush* 31/1 One day, underground workers brought the unwelcome news that the gold-bearing vein had faulted, and considerable drifting would be required to relocate it.

b. To jump (a mining claim) that another has already located. Cf. **locate,** *v.* **2. c.**

1885 *Weekly New Mexican Rev.* 16 April 3/5 [They] proceeded without ceremony to re-locate, jump, take possession and hold the same [oil claim] by force of arms. **1902** MCKEE *Land of Nome* 107 The main assets of this company consisted of . . . claims which, having already been taken or 'located,' had been 'jumped' or 'relocated' by certain individuals on some of the pretexts suggested by the looseness of our mining laws.

3. To change the location of (a section of railroad).

1908 *Pacific Mo.* Feb. 204/2 The section east of here . . . has been practically all relocated, in places the new track being miles away from the original location.

***relocation,** *n.* The action or fact of locating again. Also attrib.

1873 *Ill. Dept. Agric. Trans.* X. 371 The court shall appoint three viewers to examine and make the necessary re-location. **1901** WHITE *Claim Jumpers* (1916) 232 Under the terms of a relocation, we can use the old stakes and 'discovery.' **1948** *Sierra Club Bul.* Dec. 5/1 A general relocation of the road was thereupon planned, including a higher crossing of Yosemite Creek.

b. relocation center, a place to which, when the U.S. entered World War II, those on the West Coast who were born in Japan or were of Japanese descent were removed by the government in what was then felt to be the public interest.

1943 MENEFEE *Assignment* 68 Hearst reporters got anti-Japanese statements from Mayor Fletcher Bowron and other prominent figures in Los Angeles and played up the Dies Committee's 'exposures' of the relocation centers. **1949** Calif. Acad. Sci. *News Letter* April 3 After the indignity of wartime relocation centers, he was engaged in 1947 as preparator in paleontology at the California Institute of Technology.

relocator riˈloketɚ, *n.* One who relocates. — **1902** MCKEE *Land of Nome* 206 It frequently happens that a number of relocators assemble at the same spot, watches in hand, near midnight of a December 31, prepared to drive down their stakes at the first moment of the new year.

***Remington,** *n.* A gun of a type devised by Philo Remington (1816–89), an American inventor, or by the Remington Arms Co. Usu. attrib.

1871 W. W. GREENE *Modern Breech-Loaders* 192 The Remington Rifle. This rifle was tried at Wimbledon, as long ago as 1866. . . . It has been extensively used in America, France, Denmark, and Austria, and also by the papal troops. **1873** *Rep. Chief of Ordnance* 88 The Board proceeded to test for rapidity of fire . . . Remington No. 86. **1890** *Cent.* 5175/2 *Remington rifle*, an arm extensively used in the armies of the United States, France, Denmark, [etc.]. . . . The gun has been officially adopted by the United States Navy Department. **1949** *Lubbock* (Tex.) *Morn. Avalanche* 23 Feb. II. 1/1 Among the rare pistols are an 1850 double-barreled dueling pistol . . . and a five-shot Remington pistol.

remittance man. (See quot. 1944.) — **1924** BECHDOLT *Tales* 114 There were . . . that breed of English younger sons who became known throughout the West as remittance-men. **1944** ADAMS *W. Words* 125/1 remittance man Usually socially outcast members of the nobility of England who came west to relieve their families of further embarrassment. They were called this because they depended for existence upon the remittance of money from their families overseas.

remonetization riˌmʌnətɪˈzeʃən, *n.* The restoration of a metal, esp. silver, to its former use as legal tender.

1876 *44th Congress* 2 Sess. Sen. Rep. No. 703, 90 It is not a particular silver coin, the remonetization of which is demanded, but it is the metal silver. **1900** *Cong. Rec.* 10 Feb. 1692/2 Now is the very time to renew . . . the movement toward the remonetization of silver to which we Republicans have so often pledged ourselves. **1925** BRYAN *Memoirs* 113 Many prominent Republicans were on record as in favor of remonetization.

remonetize riˈmʌnəˌtaɪz, *v. tr.* To restore (silver) to its former use as legal tender. — **1877** *N.Y. Tribune* 16 Nov. (B.), You bankers had better accept my bill to remonetize silver. **1882** ALDENHAM *Bimetallic Controversy* 225 If Germany to-morrow were to remonetise silver, with the same rapidity it would come up again.

remonta rəˈmontə, *n. S.W.* [Sp., remounts for a cavalry unit.] (See quots.)

1842 in *Calif. Hist. Soc. Quart.* XIX. (1940) 209 I was much interested in the lively scene of a *remonta*, when at a designated place, the *remudadero*, a *manada* of thirty to forty horses, led by a mare with a bell, is driven into a *corral*. The desired saddle-horses are then caught with a lasso. **1887** *Scribner's Mag.* II. 512 You will not see these extraordinary foot-coverings if he is whipping up a . . . *remontha* (bunch of saddle-horses). **1902** CLAPIN 334 *Remonta*, . . . a Spanish word in use on the plains of the South-West, to signify a group of saddle-horses.

removalist rɪˈmuvl̩ist, *n.* One in favor of a removal, as of a state capital, to another place. *Rare.* — **1835** *Ashtabula* (Ohio) *Sentinel* 19 Sep. 3/2 Samuel Butler, Esq. has been nominated by the removalists . . . for representative.

remuda rəˈmudə, *n. S.W.* [f. Sp. in the Amer. Sp. sense of a spare horse or remount.] A group of saddle horses kept to supply remounts. Also **remudadero,** a place where such horses are kept.

1842 [see **remonta**]. **1892** *D.N.* I. 251 *Remudo* or *remuda:* a 'bunch' of horses, about a score. Usually applied to geldings only. [Texas.] **1948** *Sat. Ev. Post* 10 July 84/2 I had Pat, Montana, Dixie and Maverick in my *remuda.*

***rendezvous,** *v.* **a.** *tr.* To meet (a person), to arrange (an appointment). **b.** *W.* To bring together cattle from over a wide area. Both *obs.*

(a) **1841** COOPER *Deerslayer* v, I've come on this lake, Master Hutter, to rende'vous a fri'nd. *Ib.* viii, The Delaware and I rendezvous'd an app'intment, to meet this evening at sunset on the rendezvous-rock at the foot of this very lake. — **(b)** **1872** *Newton Kansan* 26 Sep. 2/4 Thirty thousand head of cattle are rendezvoused in Coffeyville.

***rendition,** *n.*

1. The action of rendering a judgment or verdict.

1802 *Ann. 7th Congress* 1 Sess. 173 You might see one judge beginning a cause . . . and a different one entirely making the rendition of judgment. **1858** *Baltimore Sun* 17 Aug. (B.), On the rendition of the verdict, the large audience present manifested enthusiastic approbation. **1906** *Indian Laws & Tr.* III. 240 Upon the rendition of such judgment . . . the Secretary of the Interior is hereby directed [etc.].

2. The action or performance of a dramatic or musical piece.

1877 Furness ed. *Hamlet* I. p. xiv, In their rendition of *Hamlet* by the Messrs Devrient, . . . the First Quarto has been proved by them to be more effective than the Second. **1897** Howells *Open-eyed Conspiracy* xi, Nothing could be more false than the motives and emotions of the drama as the author imagined them, but . . . their rendition by these sincere souls was yet more artificial.

renewal system. A system of pruning vines by which the superfluous canes are cut away above the lowest buds of the cane. *Obs.* — **1862** *Rep. Comm. Patents 1861: Agric.* 474 This is what we call the 'renewal' system, and we consider it preferable to the 'spur' system. **1874** *Vt. Bd. Agric. Rep.* II. 279 That method called the renewal system is the best for this climate.

***renovator,** *n.* As the last term in **feather, prairie renovator.**

Rensselaerite ˈrɛnslərˌaɪt, *n.* [Stephen Van *Rensselaer* (1765–1839), governor of N.Y.] A soft, fine, and compact variety of talc. — **1837** *N.Y. Nat. Hist. Survey* 1st Rep. 2nd Geol. Dist. 153, I propose to call it *Hemi-Prismatic Tabular* Spar. The trivial name I have conferred upon it, is *Rensselaerite,* in honor of the Hon. Stephen Van Rensselaer. **1862** Dana *Manual of Geol.* 81 *Rensselaerite* is a kind of soapstone of compact texture, and either gray, whitish, greenish, brownish, or even black, color.

***rent,** *n.*

1. rent agent, a real-estate agent who looks after the renting of property.

1891 *Harper's Mag.* June 60/2 David Berry became used to the surly calls of the rent agent. **1916** Du Puy *Uncle Sam* 122 It is a very small thing to send a man to a rent agent for a key to inspect lodgings.

2. *rent corn, Indian corn given or accepted as rent.

1863 in Rothert *Muhlenberg Co.* 276 My rent corn dispose of as soon as you can for the best price you can get.

3. *for rent,* to be rented.

1879 Stockton *Rudder Grange* i, There were none advertised for rent. **1904** *Charlotte Observer* 27 May 4 For Rent . . . First class dwelling, No. 907 Elizabeth Avenue. **1949** *Clearing-Stickney* (Ill.) *Bul.* 28 Oct. 8/5 Room for rent in priv[ate] home.

As the last term in **anti-, box, dead, store rent.**

***rent,** *v.*

1. *intr.* To secure the use of a place by paying rent.

1671 in Neill *Virginia Carolorum* 335 We suppose . . . that there is in Virginia above forty thousand persons . . . [of whom some] have come into settle and rent. **1911** Ovington *Half a Man* 44 [Negroes were] unable to rent in neighbourhoods suitable for respectable men and women.

2. To be let out at rent. Also as an infinitive noun used attributively.

1861 *Chi. Tribune* 26 May 1/8 To Rent—Very Low—Two Floors. **1865** *Ib.* 15 April 1 House To Rent, And Furniture For Sale. **1904** *N.Y. Ev. Post* 18 June 2 The blossoming of 'To rent' signs on Broadway graphically shows the real situation.

b. To be let *for* a designated amount.

1784 Washington *Diaries* II. 292 The Plantation on which Mr. Simpson lives rented well—viz. for 500 Bushels of Wheat. **1805** *N.-Eng. Palladium* (Boston) 26 July 3/3 Two convenient Tenaments, for small families, that will rent at 12 pr. cent of what they will be sold for. **1947** *Chi. D. News* 25 Feb. 1/4 (*caption*), 4-Room Apartment To Rent for $120.

rental library. A library where a charge is made for lending books. — **1928** *Publishers' Wkly.* 14 July 169 His basement bookstore . . . is now the home of an unusually successful rental library. **1946** *Red Book* (Chi.) Sep. 709/2 Install Good Rental Libraries & Keep Them That Way.

***rep,** *n.* In colloq. or slang use, short for: **a.** (*cap.*) Republican.

1817 *Niles' Reg.* XII. 16/2 The joint ballot of the legislature stood thus—for Wm. Findlay, 'rep.' 82. **1948** *Sat. Ev. Post* 23 Oct. 152/1 We hated to see him get into that argument out West over whether the Reps. or the Dems. had spent more money on land reclamation.

b. Representative. In modern use, a cowboy sent as the representative of his ranch to a roundup, rodeo, etc., hence a "top hand."

1848 *Oquawka* (Ill.) *Spectator* 8 Nov. 2/4 We are much pleased with the position friend Sanders has taken, and hope that he will continue in the good cause until the 'Reps' of all 'Egypt' will have a true knowledge of the wishes of the people. **1905** *N.Y. Ev. Post* 28 Jan., We come face to face with six cowboys. They are the 'top hands' or 'reps' of a big cattle ranch. **1947** Price *Trails I Rode* 43 One time there was a rep from the 7 U K who came to our outfit.

reparationist rɛpəˈreʃənɪst, *n.* An abolitionist who believed that reparation should be made to the slaves (see quot. 1859). *Obs.* — **1859** J. Redpath *Roving Editor* p. vi, I am an Abolitionist—and something more. I am in favor, not only of *abolishing* the Curse, but of making *reparation* for the Crime. Not an Abolitionist only, but a Reparationist. The negroes, I hold, have not merely the inalienable right to be free, but the legal right of compensation for their hitherto unrequited services to the South. **1860** —— *Life J. Brown* 220 John Brown was not merely an emancipationist, but a reparationist.

***repeat,** *v.*

1. and repeat, to run again a course already traversed. Also transf.

1819 *Va. Herald* (Fredericksburg) 19 May 4/5 Second day two miles and repeat, free for all ages, for an elegant Patent lever watch, warranted to be worth $200. **1856** *Spirit of Times* 20 Dec. 259/3 'Four mile heats' is the English term, not 'four miles and repeat,' an Americanism. **1903** A. Adams *Log of Cowboy* 131 A race horse can't beat an ox on a hundred miles and repeat to a freight wagon.

2. *intr.* To vote more than once in a single election. Cf. ***repeating,** *n.*

1882 *Golden* (N.M.) *Retort* 28 July 1/1 If the population 'repeats' as fast on a count as did the voters at the polls . . . Las Vegas would number about 6000. **1888** Bryce *Amer. Commonw.* II. iii. lxiv. 469 Vagabonds . . . are ready to stuff ballot-boxes, to buy votes, to 'repeat,' etc.

***repeater,** *n.*

1. A firearm capable of firing a number of shots without being reloaded.

1838 in *Alton* (Ill.) *Spectator* (1839) 3 Jan. 1/1 Also, Repeaters which may be discharged eighteen times without reloading. **1908** *Pacific Mo.* Jan. 2/1 Jack Hayes had equipped the Texas Rangers with the

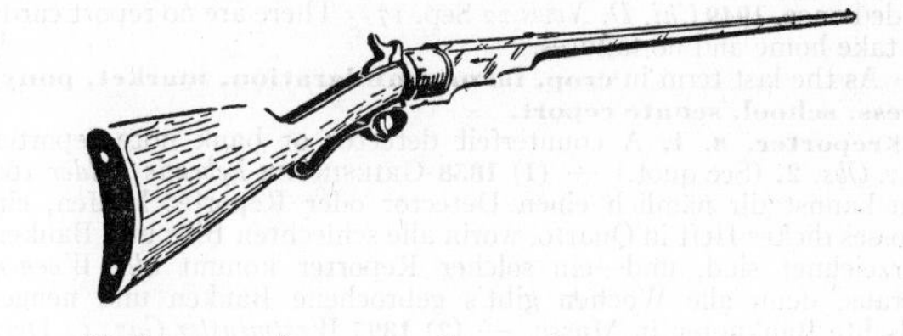

Early type of repeater (sense 1), revolving rifle, or five-shooting rifle

lesser gun and in a running fight had stampeded the Indians with this new repeater. **1941** Seton *Trail of Artist-Naturalist* 271 White men carry a repeater, and fire many shots.

2. *Telegraphy.* (See quot. 1860.)

1860 Prescott *Telegraph* 93 A repeater is an apparatus designed for the purpose of duplicating from one electric circuit to another the breaks and completions received from the transmitting station, for the purpose of renewing power lost by the escape of the electric fluid into the earth through bad insulation. **1876** Knight 1917/2 The apparatus on the right-hand side of the repeater therefore remains quiet while the rest is working.

3. *Politics.* One who votes, or attempts to vote, more than once in an election.

1861 Newell *Orpheus C. Kerr* I. 244 This morning . . . I discovered six Repeaters among my men. Each of them voted six times last election day. **1884** *Cheyenne* (Wyo.) *Sun* 3 Nov. 1/2 Twenty five men, charged with being repeaters, were arrested here this morning. **1946** *Aurora* (Ill.) *Beacon-News* 15 Sep. 2/1 The Red Sox, under Jimmy Collins, . . . bounced back like an election repeater.

4. (See quot.)

1869 *Harper's Mag.* Oct. 756/1 'Repeaters' or 'rounders'—for the terms are synonymous—are those who are known to make the rounds of all the station-houses.

5. A criminal repeatedly committed to prison.

1884 *Fortn. Rev.* March 389 A repeater before he was of age; a rounder, bruiser, and shoulder hitter. **1924** G. C. Henderson *Keys to Crookdom* 5 These repeaters are observed to have certain very definite characteristics. **1949** *Sat. Ev. Post* 23 April 17/1 He became what the FBI calls a recidivist, or repeater.

b. Also attrib. and transf.

1947 *Christian Cent.* 5 Feb. 184/3 The fact that some of the [venereal] cases were repeaters somewhat lowers the total number of men involved. **1947** *Chi. Tribune* 1 Nov. 11/4 His release was secured by court order after the legislature changed the so-called 'repeater' act, leaving the sentence to the discretion of the judge.

6. One who repeats an athletic feat.

1895 *Outing* XXVI. 456/2 He is a 'repeater' of the first rank, such performances as winning two three-mile races in the same day . . . seeming easy for him.

7. An item which proves popular on the market. *Colloq.*

1921 *Collier's* 19 Nov. 13/2 Merchants are getting $7.50 for them, and as a shoe it's a repeater.

*__repeating,__ *n.* The action or practice of voting more than once in an election. Also attrib. — **1870** *Nation* 26 May 327/1 Mr. Sherman contrived to make it [the bill] also a means of preserving the purity of the ballot-box against white 'repeating,' false registering, false voting, and other approved Democratic machinery. **1903** Hapgood *Autobiog. of Thief* 173 He was sent to Sing Sing for his repeating methods at election.

* **repeating,** *a.* **1.** Of firearms: Capable of firing several shots without being reloaded. **2. repeating race,** a race run to a certain point and repeated over the same course.

(1) **1824** Blane *Excursion U.S.* 47, I saw there several of the celebrated 'repeating swivels.' **1843** Doggett *Railway & Steamship Guide* 22 The above is a true representation of the Colt's Patent Repeating Pistol. **1949** Gann *Tread of Longhorns* 26 The greatest contribution to long distance shooting . . . was made when Oliver Winchester came out with his repeating rifle. — (2) **1868** Woodruff *Trotting Horse* 60 It is not the fast-trotting that will do the mischief, but the amount of work needful to put the youngster in fix for a repeating race.

replant rɪˈplænt, *n.* A plant that is set out to replace another. — **1855** *Fla. Plantation Rec.* 133, I find that the replant is hard to live in cons quence of the hot Son and rain. **1868** *Ill. Agric. Trans.* VII. 172 The Gophers . . . will continue to take the re-plants year after year.

***report,** *n.* A statement furnished parents and guardians of the progress made by a pupil in school, now often made on a suitably printed card. Hence **report card.** — **1897** Terhune *Old-field School* 112 The report [c1840] was written upon an oblong piece of foolscap, folded once. **1949** *Chi. D. News* 22 Sep. 17/3 There are no report cards to take home and no failures.

As the last term in **crop, farm, immigration, market, pony, press, school, senate report.**

***reporter,** *n.* **1.** A counterfeit detector or bank note reporter *qq.v. Obs.* **2.** (See quot.) — (1) **1858** Griesinger *Lebende Bilder* 166 Du kannst dir nämlich einen Detector oder Reporter kaufen, ein grosses dickes Heft in Quarto, worin alle schlechten Bills und Banken verzeichnet sind, und—ein solcher Reporter kommt *alle Wochen* heraus, denn alle Wochen gibt's gebrochene Banken und neugefälschte Banknoten in Masse. — (2) **1895** *Westminster Gaz.* 12 Dec. 7/2 When a point was obtained, and the birds were fairly located, . . . the dog took his master right back to where the covey still lay crouched. . . . Such animals are called 'reporters.'

As the last term in **bank, court, market, police, sob, social, sports reporter.**

reporterize rɪˈportəˌraɪz, *v. tr.* To subject to the influence of reporters. Also **reporterized,** *a.* — **1888** *Harper's Mag.* July 314/2 Our reporterized press is often truculently reckless of privacy and decency. **1892** Howells *Quality of Mercy* 152 The Events had been in the management of a journalist, . . . a certain Bartley Hubbard, who had risen from the ranks of the reporters, and who had thoroughly reporterized it in the worst sense.

reportorial ˌrepɚˈtorɪəl, *a.* Characteristic of, pertaining to, or consisting of reporters.

1858 *82d Anniv. of Amer. Indep.* (Boston) 6 As far as reportorial observation could extend, the best possible temper prevailed. **1896** *Houston* (Tex.) *D. Post* 16 Feb., The man I licked up town is the last one of the editorial and reportorial staff of my newspaper that I have treated in the same manner. **1950** *Chi. Tribune* 1 Jan. 1/3 Devine consented to having pictures taken but stopped any reportorial quizzing when his client said he hated 'to contribute to the edification of morons.'

reportorially ˌrepɚˈtorɪəlɪ, *adv.* In the capacity or manner of a reporter. — **1862** *N.Y. Tribune* 22 April (Chipman), At headquarters this morning—I mean those of Gen. Heintzelman, to which I am reportorially attached—I found things quiet enough. **1901** *Pop. Sci. Mo.* Feb. 382 The newspaper must keep pegging away at it [*sc.* the weather], editorially and 'reportorially.'

repose rɪˈpoz, *n.* [f. F. *poser*, to deposit. See **pose,** ***rest,** *n.* **1.**] (See quot.) *Obs.* — **1853** Bond *Minnesota* 240 The voyageur often finds 'a repose,' that is, something to place his burden upon while he rests, every three miles in crossing a portage.

* **representative,** *n.*

1. A member of a colonial assembly or, later, of a state or territorial representative body, esp. the lower house.

1635 *Essex Inst. Coll* IV. 93/1 By the towne representative, 22nd of the 12th moneth. **1776** *N.Y. Prov. Cong. Jrnls.* I. 519/1 The style or title of this House . . . shall be '*the Convention of the Representatives of the State of New-York*' **1809** Kendall *Travels* I. 27 The deputies are now frequently denominated representatives. They were anciently called committeemen. **1949** *Democrat* 24 Feb. 15 Hon. J. F. Gillis, well known citizen and representative from Clarke in the state legislature, observed his 83rd birthday Monday.

2. A person representing a congressional district or a state at large in the lower house of Congress. Also as a title.

1787 *Constitution* i. §2 No person shall be a representative who shall not . . . be an inhabitant of that state in which he shall be chosen. **1898** *K.C. Star* 18 Dec. 4/1 Interest was added to the discussion . . . by an amendment offered by Representative Little. **1949** *Chi. D. News* 22 April 20/7 The most formidable opponent is likely to be Representative Carl Vinson of Georgia.

b. representative-at-large, (see quot. 1914).

[**1914** *Cyclo. Amer. Govt.* I. 383/1 Since 1842 it has been the law that in case of an increase in the representation of a state, its additional member or members shall be elected at large and the former number elected by the old districts until the legislature shall have redistricted the state.] **1944** *Chi. D. News* 15 Dec. 18/2 Ham Fish sounded off, and then Stephen A. Day, representative-at-large of Illinois.

3. In combs.: (1) **representative district,** a district which elects a representative to a state legislature; (2) **government,** a government based upon a system through which the people govern through their chosen representatives; (3) **hall,** the chamber of the lower house of a legislative body, also *hall of representatives;* (4) **recruit,** (see quot.), *obs.;* (5) **-s' chamber,** =**representative hall.**

(1) **1846** *Mich. Gen. Statutes* I. (1882) 138 If such county shall be divided into two or more senatorial or representative districts, the inspectors of election [etc.]. **1931** *Survey* 1 Oct. 37/1 Representative districts were carved out, for the purpose of selecting legislators and congressmen. — (2) **1798** *Ann. 5th Congress* 1132 Ought we to conclude that . . . the representative government of the United States will be destroyed by the Representatives themselves? **1913** La Follette *Autobiog.* 129 Payne and his associates stood for the destruction of representative government. — (3) **1817** S. Brown *Western Gazetteer* 98 The hall of representatives [is] on the second [floor of the state house]. **1865** Richardson *Secret Service* 81 The Mississippi State House . . . is a faded, sober edifice of the style in vogue fifty years ago, with the representative hall at one end, the senate chamber at the other. **1873** *Newton Kansan* 27 Feb. 2/1 A resolution was passed excluding Dr. Rohrbacher of Sumner county from representative hall. — (4) **1865** Sala *Diary* II. 50 If a gentleman be exempted by age or incapacitated by physical causes from being draughted, he may still pay the debt of devotion to the Republic by purchasing a 'Representative Recruit,' and sending him to Riker's Island.

(5) **1789** *Ann. 1st Congress* 207 The oath should be administered to the President in the outer gallery adjoining the Senate Chamber, [rather] than in the Representatives' Chamber. **1823** Tudor *Life J. Otis* 435 He found the door of the representatives chamber locked.

As the last term in **collar, national, state representative.** Also **House of Representatives.**

represa rəˈpresə, *n. S.W.* [Sp. in same sense.] A dam for impounding water in a dry region.

1894 *Amer. Anthrop.* July 293 They plant crops . . . which they irrigate by means of water drawn from natural and artificial dams (*charcos* and *represos* respectively). **1925** Bryan *Papago Country* 257 Represos are commonly built in adobe flats, and frequently only the borrow pit, from which earth was taken to make the dam, holds water. **1942** Castetter & Bell *Pima & Papago Agric.* 43 At times small earthen dams or *represas* were constructed, usually in adobe flats, to impound flood waters for household purposes.

attrib. **1908** Hornaday *Camp Fires on Desert* 180 If the pools are dry, the nearest water will be in the Represa Tanks, twenty-five miles away in an air line on the Camino del Diablo.

reprize rɪˈpraɪz, *v. S. tr.* To prize *q.v.* (tobacco) again. — **1758** *Lett. to Washington* II. 323, 3 hhd . . . was to light & I Carried Tobco. from mudy hole and reprizd. & maid one heavier. **1898** *Treasury Decisions Customs* II. 799 Dealers in leaf tobacco are permitted to break original packages received by them, and rehandle, assort, and reprize the same.

* **Republic,** *n.* Also **republic.** The United States.

1789 *Hist. of Congress* (1834) 150 Concessions have been made from political motives, which, we conceive, may endanger the republic. **1848** *Commercial* (Wilmington, N.C.) 28 Nov. 2/2 (Th. Supp.), Mr. Jefferson styled those who contended for the veto power in the early days of the Republic, Monocrats. **1900** *Cong. Rec.* 20 Feb. 1996/1 The very scheme of government involved in itself . . . expansion of the protection of the Constitution over all parts of the domain of the Republic.

b. The independent state of Texas between 1836 and 1845. In full **Republic of Texas.** *Obs.*

1836 in GOUGE *Fiscal Hist. Texas* 57 An act to establish a General Land-Office for the Republic of Texas. **1892** DUVAL *Early Times Tex.* 20 Whilst at this place our company was formally mustered into service of the embryo Republic of Texas.

As the last term in **American, great, Lone Star, ocean bound, Pacific, palmetto, Pawnee, United Republic.**

***Republican,** *a.* and *n.* Also **republican.**

1. *n.* A member of a Pennsylvania political party opposed to the Constitutionalists *q.v.* Now *hist.* Cf. **Republican party 1, Republican society.**

1782 J. ADAMS *Diary* Works III. 353 Vaughan has a brother in Philadelphia, who has written him a long letter about the Constitutionalists and the Republicans. *a***1821** BIDDLE *Autobiog.* 195, I found Council nearly divided between what were then called Republicans and Constitutionalists. **1949** *Pa. Hist.* April 128 In 1800 . . . the Republicans overthrew the Federalists and took control in Pennsylvania.

b. A member of the early Republican party, a Democratic-Republican. Now *hist.*

1799 WASHINGTON *Writings* XIV. 181 (*footnote*), We are sure there will be none on the part of the *Republicans*, as they have very erroneously called themselves. **1809** KENDALL *Travels* III. 3 By the exclusive assumption of the name *republican*, the assuming party designs to throw, upon the other, the stigma, . . . of a fondness for regal government. **1830** *Mechanics' Press* (Utica, N.Y.) 19 June 254/1 It's a mockery of what we once knew as the Republican Party, to call the present Tammany leaders . . . by the name of Republicans. **1948** *Chi. Tribune* 29 Feb. I. 24/5 The republicans prevailed in the main, and were finally triumphant upon the adoption of the Bill of Rights.

transf. **1832** FERRALL *Ramble* 88 The stumps . . . and 'republicans,' (projecting roots of trees, so called from the stubborn tenacity with which they adhere to the ground) . . . rendered the difficulties of traversing this forest [great].

c. A member of a group having attachment to the U.S. who formed a temporary government at Baton Rouge after the expulsion of the Spaniards from the region west of the Perdido River. Now *hist.*

1811 *Amer. Republic* (Frankfort, Ky.) 4 Jan. 2/4 The president has ordered Governor Claiborne to take possession of the country, lately recovered from the nominal possession of the Spaniards west of the Perdido, and held by the Republicans, *who have sued to be admitted into the American union.* **1949** *N.O. Times-Picayune Mag.* 28 Aug. 17/1 Around these outlaws Magee mobilized his 'Republican Army of the North.' *Ib.* 17/2 At the Trinity 80 of the Republicans were captured.

d. (*cap.*) A member of the modern Republican party organized in 1854–56.

[**1854** A. E. BOVAY in Curtis *Republican Party* (1904) I. 177 Urge them [the opponents of the Kansas-Nebraska Bill] to forget previous political names and organizations, and to band together under the name I suggested to you at Lovejoy's Hotel in 1852, I mean the name 'Republican.'] **1858** *Harper's Mag.* May 832/2, 92 are Republicans, 22 Democrats, and 6 Americans. **1949** *Chi. D. News* 2 Aug. 12/2 The last Republican they were able to elect President was a Californian.

2. (See quot. 1813 and cf. **Republican Pawnee.**) *Obs.*

1807 DUNBAR *Travels* 52 The Great Panis . . . were at war with the nation called Republicans. **1813** STUART *Narratives* 238 A band of Panees also reside on the Fork of it,—they are upwards of 600 in number, occupied some years ago the same town with the grand Panees on the Platte, and on account of their revolt from their chief have since been known by the name of Republicans, which title is also given to that branch of the Kanzes river where their village stands. **1818** *Lynchburg* (Va.) *Press* 7 Aug. 2/6 There are three bands or tribes of Pawnees; *Republican, Loup*, and *Big step*, residing a few leagues apart.

3. *a.* Used in the predicate, usu. with reference to the modern Republican party.

1836 *S. Lit. Messenger* II. 284 Virginia was republican. **1872** *Newton Kansan* 22 Aug. 2/1 [We] shall be known and found genuinely Republican. **1884** *N.Y. Wkly. Tribune* 13 Aug. 1/3 Louisiana is Republican under such circumstances. **1945** *Sat. Review* 24 Feb. 7/1 For well over a half a century the newspapers of the United States have been heavily Republican.

4. In combs.: (1) **Republican convention,** a meeting of the leaders and representatives of the Republican party, also short for **Republican National Convention;** (2) **dog,** (see quot.), *obs.;* (3) **Methodist,** one of a group of Methodists who withdrew from the Methodist Episcopal Church in 1792 and after 1794 became known as Christians; (4) **National Committee,** the chief executive agency of the Republican party, consisting usu. of two delegates from each state chosen by the National Convention; (5) **National Convention,** a convention of delegates of the Republican party selected in the various states and assembled to nominate candidates for President and Vice-President and to draw up a party platform; (6) **party,** see as a main entry; (7) **Pawnee,** see as a main entry; (8) **Society,** a society of Pennsylvania Republicans, see **Republican party 1,** *obs.;* (9) **state,** a state that normally supports the Republican ticket, also **Republican State Committee,** a committee that looks after the interest of the Republican party within a state; (10) **swallow,** the cliff swallow, *Petrochelidon albifrons*, which lives in large flocks.

(1) 1812 *Boston Selectmen* 51 A committee from the Republican Convention of the County of Suffolk. **1944** *Reader's Digest* Oct. 72/2 A few days before the Republican convention the boss of a tough West Side ward in Chicago called on Frain in his office in the Chicago stadium. — **(2) 1821** *Amer. Jrnl. Science* III. 27 There are also [on the north side of the Arkansas], it is said, prairie dogs, called by some republican dogs, on account of their living in large families.— **(3) 1844** RUPP *Relig. Denominations* 167 At first they took the name of 'Republican Methodists,' but at a subsequent conference resolved to be known as Christians only. **1919** *Census: Religious Bodies 1916* II. 448/2 James O'Kelley, of Virginia, with a considerable body of sympathizers, withdrew . . . and organized the 'Republican Methodists,' who later joined with others in . . . the 'Christian Church.' — **(4) 1860** *Republican Convention Proc.* 1 Hon. Edwin D. Morgan, of New York chairman of the Republican National Committee, called the Convention to order. **1949** *Sooner Mag.* May 7/1 He has served several terms as Republican national Committeeman from Oklahoma. **(5) 1856** *Western Citizen* (Paris, Ky.) 18 April 3/3 Officers and Delegates to the Republican National Convention, were appointed. **1948** *Chi. Tribune* 25 March I. 6/1 A two day deadlock . . . started the rivalry between Pool, a delegate to the last two Republican national conventions, and Daily, a circuit judge since 1927. — **(8) 1779** HILTZHEIMER *Diary* (1893) 22 Feb. 38 In the evening met the Republican Society at Duffy's Tavern, 32 members present. **1804** *Guardian of Liberty* (Frankfort, Ky.) 14 July 2/2 A number of gentlemen under the name of the Republican Society prepared a Barbecue. — **(9) 1855** *N.Y. Wkly. Tribune* 14 July 1/5 The Republican State Committee . . . met at Albany on the 4th inst. **1857** BENTON *Exam. Dred Scott Case* 36 The only limitation upon its power was . . . in the obligation to dispose of the soil, to populate it, and to build up future Republican States upon it. **1925** BRYAN *Memoirs* 74 The state of Nebraska was a Republican state.

(10) 1824 AUDUBON in *Ann. Lyceum of N.Y.* I. 164 In the spring of 1815, I saw a few of these birds for the first time at Henderson. . . . I drew up at the time a description under the name of *H. republicana, Republican swallow*, in allusion to their mode of association for the purposes of building and rearing their young. **1917** *Birds of Amer.* III. 84 Cliff Swallow. . . . [Also called] Republican Swallow.

b. In miscellaneous combs. of obvious meaning referring to the modern Republican party, as (1) **Republican boss,** (2) **campaign book,** (3) **caucus.**

(1) 1888 *Voice* 9 Aug., The Barney Rourke Association, a social organization named after that gin-miller and Republican 'boss.' — **(2) 1904** *Omaha Bee* 16 Aug. 4 The republican campaign book stands upon . . . a record of promises made good. — **(3) 1884** *Boston Jrnl.* 14 Aug., The Republican caucuses in Boston will be held on the evening of Wednesday, the 27th inst. **1945** WEBSTER *Town Meeting Country* 205 He may stay away from the Republican caucus or town meeting.

Also *Republican candidate, club, committee, concern, county committee, county convention, daily, elephant, journal, leader, majority, nominee, paper, primary, senator, state convention, ticket, vote,* etc.

As the last term in **anti-, black, Democratic, federal, federo-, Independent, Jeffersonian, Liberal, National, Pawnee, radical, red, silver, union, white republican.**

***Republicanism,** *n.* The principles and policies of the earlier Democratic-Republican party; later, those of the present Republican party.

1801 CUTLER in *Life & Corr.* II. 44 Jefferson's speech though a mixed medley of Jacobinism, Republicanism, and Federalism . . . is extremely smooth. **1855** *N.Y. Herald* 19 Nov. 8/3 But republicanism is put in the background as a political power by the demonstration of strength made by the Know Nothings in this State. **1900** *Cong. Rec.* 22 Jan. 1035/1 The colored race casts a solid vote for the cause of Republicanism. **1949** *Chi. D. News* 2 Aug. 12/2 The group repeatedly affirmed its faith in traditional Republicanism.

b. A term or expression characteristic of the people of a republic, esp. of the U.S. *Rare.*

1868 HAWTHORNE *Our Old House* 47 He used to come and sit or stand by my fireside, . . . [with] kindly endurance of the many rough republicanisms wherewith I assailed him.

As the last term in **black, Independent, radical, red Republicanism.**

∗**Republicanize,** *v.* **1.** *tr.* To make (a country) republican in character. **2.** To secure (a state or region) for the Republican party.

(1) **1867** HELPER *Nojoque* 405 Sooner or later, Mexico, and all other parts of the vast continent of which it is a section, must be Americanized—Republicanized, Caucasianized, Protestantized. — (2) **1871** *Cin. Commercial* 29 Aug. 4/2 The fact is that before Kentucky can be Republicanized, it must be educated. **1948** *N.W. Ohio Quart.* Summer 147 With a two-thirds majority in both halls of Congress, the Republicans proceeded to put into effect its plan to Republicanize the South.

Republican party.

1. In Pennsylvania, from about 1780 to 1800, a political party advocating changes in the state constitution. *Obs.* Cf. ∗**Republican 1,** and **Republican Society.**

1788 *Pa. Gaz.* 9 Jan. 3/2 It is the duty of the antifoederalists, in a particular manner in Pennsylvania, to learn wisdom from the conduct of the republican party.

2. The Democratic-Republican party. *Obs.* Cf. ∗**Democratic,** *a.* **2.** (8).

1800 MONROE in Benton *30 Years' View* I. 354/1 The fair prospect of the republican party may be overcast. **1825** *Constitutional Adv.* (Frankfort, Ky.) 15 Dec. 4/4 The result of the last election, as regards the politics of the State, is considered a complete victory of the old Republican party over the new Republican party. **1847** POLK *Diary* (1929) 187 He had been in favour of Mr. Crawford as the nominee in the caucus of the Republican party.

3. The modern national political party organized in 1854–56 to oppose the extension of slavery, later advocating a liberal interpretation of the Constitution, protective tariffs, etc.

1856 *N.Y. Herald* 19 Nov. 8/3 The new republican party has quickly finished its career in the State. **1949** *Chi. D. News* 2 Aug. 12/2 The Republican party . . . must campaign to convince organized labor that it can have a fair deal. **1950** *Time* 2 Jan. 2/2 The principle of the Republican Party itself was archaic and had been archaic for years.

As the last term in **Liberal, National Republican party.**

Republican Pawnee. (See quot. 1907.)

1813 STUART *Narratives* 240 The Republican Panees generally bring out the same quantity and kind as their relations the Big village of the Platte. **1838** PARKER *Exploring Tour* 50 On the third, [we] passed the village of the Tapage and Republican Pawnee Indians. **1907** HODGE *Amer. Indians* I. 707 Kitkehahki. . . . One of the tribes of the Pawnee confederacy . . . sometimes called Republican Pawnee, as their villages were at one time on Republican r. **1946** FOREMAN *Last Trek* 182 This treaty was signed by representatives of the . . . Republican Pawnee.

repudiated state. A state that has repudiated its debts. *Obs.* — **1847** SHELBURN *Tourist's Guide* 257 A banker . . . asked me if I thought those repudiated States would ever be willing or able to meet the demands on them.

repudiationist rɪˌpjudɪˈeʃənɪst, *n.* One who repudiates, or advocates repudiation of, some responsibility, esp. state debts. — **1862** *N.Y. Tribune* 21 Jan. (Chipman), Jeff. Davis was first known in public life as a Repudiationist. **1896** *Columbus* (O.) *Dispatch* 7 Oct. 4 Every day the repudiation of the repudiationists becomes more certain.

request envelope. An envelope bearing a request that it be returned to the sender if unclaimed in a designated number of days. Cf. **special request envelope.**

[**1855** BÜCHELE *Land und Volk* 267 Inländische Briefe, auf welchen die worte stehen: to be preserved (aufzubewahren), trifft dieses Schicksal [i.e., of being opened in the dead letter office, and if possible, returned to the writer] nicht, sondern sie bleiben liegen, bis der Absender sie verlangt.] **1865** *Rep. Postmaster-General* 8 To encourage the purchase of *request envelopes*, the law should be changed so as to allow the return of such letters to the writers free of postage. **1893** *Cong. Rec.* 18 Feb. 1802/1 You have allowed . . . the right of the Postmaster-General to have printed upon the request envelope, 'if not called for' within any number of days fixed, 'return to——.'

∗**Rescinder,** *n.* One of the seventeen members of the Massachusetts House of Representatives who in 1768, in compliance with the demands of the royal governor, voted to rescind a previous vote to send a circular letter to the legislatures of the various provinces acquainting them with the state of affairs with Great Britain. *Obs.* — **1768** in *Pub. Col. Soc.* XXV. 49 On brave Rescinders! to yon yawning cell, Seventeen such miscreants, sure will startle Hell. *a***1827** *Ib.* 48 The seventeen members were branded with the name of Rescinders, & were held up to view in a contemptuous manner.

rescue grass. [App. a perversion of ∗*fescue grass.*] A brome grass, *Bromus unioloides*, cultivated in the southern states for forage and hay. — **1884** VASEY *Agric. Grasses* 106 *Bromus unioloides* . . . is said to have been introduced into Georgia by General Iverson, of Columbus, and by him called rescue grass. **1901** MOHR *Plant Life Ala.* 827.

∗**reservation,** *n.*

1. A tract of land set aside by agreement between the government and an Indian tribe, reserved for the exclusive use and occupancy of the Indians. Also the Indians on such a tract of land.

Some states had set aside reservations before the U.S. Government was given power to make treaties with the Indians.

1789 *Ann. 1st Congress* I. 41 The reservation, in the treaty with the Six Nations, . . . is within the territory of the State of New York, and ought to be so explained as to render it conformable to the Constitution of the United States. **1792** *Mass. H.S. Coll.* 1 Ser. I. 285 The Indians are settled on all the reservations made by this state [N.Y.]. **1825** *Statutes at Large* VII. 245 From the lands above ceded to the United States, there shall be made the following reservations, of one mile square, for each of the half breeds of the Kanzas nation. **1871** *Rep. Indian Affairs* (1872) 283 The interests of the reservation were rapidly declining. **1949** *N.O. Times-Picayune Mag.* 4 Dec. 8/3 He looked easily like the best fed redskin on the reservation.

attrib. **1861** *Harper's Mag.* Aug. 308/1 In 1853 laws were passed for the establishment of a reservation system in California. **1866** *Weekly New Mexican* 8 June 2/1 Don Esteban Coruna . . . was killed by the reservation Navajos. **1877** *Rep. Indian Affairs* 40 The following are the productions of the reservation farm and garden. **1893** G. W. CURTIS *Horses, Cattle* 96 [We have made] careful, continued observation of the ponies belonging to the various 'Reservation' tribes. **1947** *Christian Cent.* 13 Aug. 981/1 It declares that the reservation system, with its continuing segregation, 'tends to perpetuate a way of living that has proved neither constructive nor satisfying to the Indian.'

Esp. **reservation Indian.**

1866 *Rep. Indian Affairs* 100 The reservation Indian is under the protection of the general government. **1923** *Montanan* May 7 Having had some little experience with reservation Indians . . . I approached and gave the sign-talk gesture and its verbal equivalent, 'How?' **1946** FOREMAN *Last Trek* 260 Eighty of them came to their agency and enrolled with the reservation Indians.

b. With the name of an Indian tribe.

1796 *Mass. H.S. Coll.* 1 Ser. V. 21 In the district comprehended between the Oneida reservation, and the Mohawk river, . . . there were, in 1785, but two families. **1876** RAYMOND *8th Rep. Mines* 324 The Uncompahgre district includes all lands drained by the Uncompahgre and its tributaries as far north as the Ute reservation. **1944** JOHNSON *As I Dare* 306 We . . . had as our table companions the government agent from the Ute reservation and his school-teacher wife.

c. *To leave* (or *be off*) *the reservation*, to go outside the limits of a reservation, also transf.

1871 *Republican Rev.* 25 Feb. 1/4 The Apaches of La Canada . . . have left the reservation. **1885** *Wkly. New Mexican Rev.* 5 Feb. 4/7 The Navajoes in New Mexico are reported to be off their reservation and depredating among the cattle. **1900** ADE *More Fables* 37 He bribed the Hired Girl to tell him Everything that happened while he was off the Reservation. **1936** MCKENNA *Black Range* 65 It might have been Apaches. We heard a few days ago that a bunch has left the reservation. **1949** *Sat. Ev. Post* 2 July 67/1 Truman's sweeping demand for civil-rights legislation . . . stampeded the Southerners right off the reservation.

2. A tract of land set apart for some other use, the action or fact of reserving such land.

1792 *Ann. 2d Congress* 1036 The claims covered by the first reservation are—1st. The bounties in land given by the said state of North Carolina in their Continental line. **1859** BARTLETT 361 Reservation, a tract of the public land reserved or set aside for some public use, as for schools.

3. An engagement of seats, rooms, etc., in advance of their use. Often *to make* (or *procure*) *a reservation*, to reserve something for use at a designated time.

1906 LYNDE *Quickening* 118 That sleeping-car reservation for Thomas Corden—have you secured it? **1925** *Scribners' Mag.* July 32/1 Ward-Belmont [School] for girls. . . . Reservations for 1925–26 should be made as soon as possible to insure entrance. **1949** *Sky Line Trail* March 14/2 It is most important that hikers procure their hotel reservations well in advance.

As the last term in Connecticut, Flathead, forest, government, Indian, military, Navaho, salt, school, state reservation.

∗**reserve,** *n.*

1. An alternate commissioner or deputy of a New England colony in the councils of the New England Confederation. In full **reserve commissioner.** *Obs.*

1648 *Mass. Bay Rec.* III. 121 At a generall Court of Election, held at Boston, . . . there was chosen . . . Tho[mas] Dudley, . . . Reserue Commission[e]r. **1652** *Mass. Bay Rec.* IV. I. 77 Att a Gennerall Courte of Elecctjons, held at Boston, . . . Mr. Simon Bradstreete, Capt. Wm. Hawthorne, were chosen Commissioners. . . . Jno. Endecot, Esq. . . . Rich. Bellingham, Esq., Reserves. **1665** *Conn. Rec.* II. 18 Mr. Mathew Allyn [was chosen] a reserue.

2. In place-names, a place reserved for the future use or occupancy of an individual. *Obs.*

1700 *Md. Hist. Mag.* XX. 283 Olivers Reserve. *Ib.* 286 Richardsons Reserve.

3. (*cap.*) =**Western Reserve.**

1817 S. BROWN *Western Gazetteer* 323 Mill-stones, grind-stones, and whet-stones, are made in several parts of the Reserve. **1847** HOWE *Hist. Coll. Ohio* 188 The hardships and privations of the early settlers of the Reserve, are well described in the annexed article. **1949** *Chi. Tribune* 18 Sep. IV. 15/1 By 1817, the westward trek into the Reserve had turned into 'one of the largest and most homogeneous mass migrations in American History.'

4. A district or area reserved by Indians, in treaties with white people, for their own use; an individual Indian's reserved land. *Obs.*

1805 *Statutes at Large* VII. 98 The Mingoes . . . [reserve] also a tract of five thousand one hundred and twenty acres. . . . The latter reserve to be subject to the same laws [etc.]. **1845** HOOPER *Simon Sugg's Adv.* vi, He had brought with him to be 'certified' . . . an Indian woman whose 'reserve' was an excellent one.

5. =**reservation 1.** (see also quot. 1866).

1857 GIHON *Geary & Kansas* 20 The balance of his [Delaware Indian] reserve is now covered with squatters. **1866** *Rep. Indian Affairs* 105 He reports several temporary reserves or farms, upon which small numbers of Indians have been collected. **1881** *Ib.* 7 The mesa known as Menlo Park. . . . is the northeastern part of the reserve. *attrib.* **1865** PIKE *Scout & Ranger* (1932) 20 One faction . . . ascribed the murder to the Reserve Indians of Texas. *Ib.* 33 We saw no Indian signs until we got within three miles of the Reserve-line on the east. *Ib.* 47 A little further along was a pass, given . . . to a Reserve Comanche of an unpronounceable name.

6. Any piece of land set aside for a special purpose.

1807 JEFFERSON *Writings* XVI. 422 We therefore met the chiefs . . . and agreed on a general boundary which was to divide their lands from those of the whites, making only some particular reserves, for the establishment of trade and intercourse with them. **1850** GLISAN *Jrnl. Army Life* 19 In view of more easily controlling the sale of contraband articles to . . . the soldiers occupying military reserves in the Indian country, the government has found [etc.]. **1912** *Out West* March 161/1 This remedy is being locally applied right here in the San Gabriel Mountains in the Angelus Reserve by the United States government, with Mr. R. H. Charlton as Chief Forester.

7. (See quot.) *Obs.*

1838 in AUDUBON *Ornith. Biog.* IV. 150 The pond is artificial, and such as in this country [S. Carolina] is called a 'Reserve.' It . . . is intended to preserve water sufficient, when needed, to irrigate and overflow the rice.

8. In special combs.: (1) **reserve bank,** one of the twelve banks created by the federal government for the deposit of reserves by member banks; (2) **city,** any of certain cities in which national banks are required to keep certain minimum reserves against demand and time deposits; (3) **section,** =**reserved section.**

(1) **1913** *Statutes at Large* XXXVIII. I. 251 The term 'member bank' shall be held to mean any national bank, state bank, or bank or trust company which has become a member of one of the reserve banks created by this Act. **1947** *Dly. Ardmoreite* (Ardmore, Okla.) 13 Aug. 10/1 American Airlines handled about $153,000,000 in this manner for the reserve banks of the district it serves. — (2) **1900** *Cong. Rec.* 15 Feb. 1832/2 Ordinarily the country banks deposit their reserves and deposits in the reserve cities, which in turn deposit them in New York. **1913** *Statutes at Large* XXXVIII. I. 262 The Federal Reserve Board shall be authorized: . . . To add to the number of cities classified as reserve and central reserve cities. — (3) **1848** *Indiana Gen. Ass. Doc. 1848–9* II. 285 The amount of principal and interest remaining due and unpaid, for seminary lots on reserve sections around the University buildings is . . . in Monroe county $3,699.00.

As the last term in **forest, gold, Indian, Miami, Osage, school, Western Reserve.**

***reserve,** *v. tr.* To put (an Indian) on a reservation. *Colloq.* Cf. ***reserved 1. c.** — **1870** *Republican Rev.* 21 May 3/1 If they [the Utes] must be 'reserved' let their reservation be where they are most contented to stay.

***reserved,** *a.*

1. a. Of land: Kept free of settlement. **b.** Of public land: Retained unsold for some public use. **c.** Of an Indian: Put on a reservation.

(a) **1764** *N.H. Hist. Soc. Coll.* IX. 145 Maj[o]r How . . . came to advise about settling upon ye Lds. reserved Land. — (b) **1832** WILLIAMSON *Maine* II. 679 The '*reserved lands*' . . . were principally lots reserved for the future disposition of government, in the grants of townships; including probably parts of the nine Indian townships on the Penobscot river. **1890** *Statutes at Large* XXVI. 651 Certain sections of California are hereby reserved . . . , and set apart as reserved forest lands. — (c) **1864** *N. Mex. Press* 13 Sep. 1/3 Granting that actual depredators were unreserved Navajoes, it is evident that the reserved ones became accessories after the fact.

2. reserved section, (see quot. 1817 and cf. **sixteenth section**).

1804 PUTNAM in *Memoirs* 441 The printing . . . was Blanks for Leasing the reserved sections. **1817** M. BIRKBECK *Notes on Journey* 161 In the sale of public lands, there is a regulation, which I have before mentioned, that the sixteenth section, which is nearly the centre of every township, shall not be sold. It is called the reserved section; and is, accordingly, reserved for public uses in that township for the support of the poor, and for purposes of education.

reservee ˌrɛzɝˈvi, *n.* An Indian residing on a reservation. *Rare.* — **1835** *Indian Laws & Tr.* II. 445 And all such reservees as were obliged by the laws of the State in which their reservations were situated, to abandon the same . . . shall be deemed to have a just claim.

***resident,** *n.*

1. (See quots.) *Obs.*

1851 HALL *College Words* 258 In the United States, graduates who are desirous of pursuing their studies in the place where a college is situated . . . can do so in the capacity of *residents* or *resident graduates.* **1859** BARTLETT 361 *Resident Graduate,* graduates of colleges who are desirous of pursuing their studies at a college, without joining any of its departments. They may attend the public lectures . . . , and enjoy the use of its library.

2. resident fellow, (see quots. 1851, 1925). *Obs.*

1722 in *Pub. Col. Soc.* XVI. 466 That the Vacancy in the Corporation by the decease of the Rev[d] M[r] Ioseph Stevens of Charlestown be fill'd up by the Election of a Resid[t] Fellow in his Stead. **1851** HALL *College Words* 122 At Harvard College, the tutors were formerly called *resident fellows.* **1925** in *Pub. Col. Soc.* XV. lxiii, In time there arose the designations 'non-resident Fellows' and 'resident Fellows,' the distinction being that resident Fellows were the young appointees actually engaged in teaching—that is, Tutors.

resin weed. =**rosinweed.** Also **resin grass.** Cf. **compass plant.** — **1852** MACKINNON *Atlantic Sk.* I. 268, I found that he had spoken the truth, and that the resin grass, or weed, had peculiar leaves which always grew in the same direction. **1856** FERGUSSON *America* 372 The most prominent plant is the resin-weed. It has a palmated leaf, and grows to a considerable height. . . . It exudes a resin, and is aromatic to the taste.

***resolute,** *v. intr.* To make or pass a resolution or resolutions. — **1860** *Savannah Republican* 13 March (De Vere), When you have done resoluting, you will only have lost your time. **1900** *Cong. Rec.* 17 Feb. 1901/2 They resolute, . . . and he bears the resolutions down and has read them to the House.

***resolution,** *n.* As the last term in **Expunging, joint, Kentucky, secesh, Virginia Resolution(s).**

***resolve,** *n.* As the last term in **Boston, enrolled, Mecklenberg, Suffolk Resolve(s).**

***resort,** *n.* A disorderly house or other place of questionable repute. See also **seaside, summer resort.**

[**1868** M. H. SMITH *Sunshine & Shadow* 432 One or two houses up town . . . became so notorious as resorts of the abandoned, that they were compelled to close.] **1884** *N.Y. Herald* 31 Oct. 6/1 Kuntz keeps a well known resort at No. 115 Chatham street. **1888** *Nation* 9 Aug. 102/2 Tompkins . . . [enticed] a school-girl of thirteen . . . to 'a resort' out side the city.

***respirator,** *n.* (See quot.) Cf. **iron lung.** — **1931** *Science Supp.* 27 Nov. 10/1 The respirator is a machine which was designed to replace manual methods of artificial respiration in cases in which the procedure must be carried out for long periods such as days or weeks.

respirometer ˌrɛspəˈrɑmətɚ, *n.* **1.** (See quot.) **2.** A measuring instrument used in studying respiration. — (1) **1883** KNIGHT *Supp.* 753/1 *Respirometer,* the name adopted by Mr. Fleuss for his diver's apparatus for supplying air to a person beneath the surface of the water. — (2) **1890** *Cent.* 5111/1.

***respond,** *v.* **1.** *tr.* To answer, discharge, or satisfy, as by payment. **2.** *intr.* (See quot.) Both *obs.*

(1) **1677** *Mass. Ct. of Assistants Rec.* I. 117 Wm. Long . . . was Attached and bound ouer in one hundred twenty & sixe pounds to respond the decree & Judgment of this Court. **1680** *Ib.* 171 The Secretary . . . shall require of the plaintiffe tenn pounds in money as Caution to respond the charges of sajd Court. — (2) **1828** WEBSTER, Respond, . . . to be answerable; to be liable to make payment; as, the defendant is held to respond in damages.

*__responsibility,__ *n.* (See quot.) — **1890** *Cent.* 5112/1 *Responsibility*, . . . ability to answer in payment; means of paying contracts.

*__rest,__ *n.* **1.** (See quot. and cf. **pose** and **repose.**) *Obs.* **2.** The action of resting a title. — **(1) 1784–1812** THOMPSON *Narrative* (1916) 294 A Rest, or Pose, is the distance the cargo of a canoe is carried from place to place and then rest [as on portages]. — **(2) 1888** *Economist* 20 Oct. 2/1 This rest of the title is backed by a Policy of this Company.

*__rest,__ *v.*

1. *Law. intr.* To end voluntarily the introduction of evidence.

1867 *Harper's Mag.* July 266/1 The plaintiff had been nonsuited for a reason which was apparent—he had rested too soon—stopped short in his proof. **1906** *Harper's Mo.* Nov. 837 On the 9th of April, the prosecution having rested, Judge Curtis opened for the defence.

b. *tr.* To allow (a case) to stand as presented, without the adducing of further evidence, to cease producing evidence in support of (a case).

1905 MITCHELL *Constance Trescot* 183 All the evidence for the plaintiffs was before the court, and Greyhurst sat down, stating that the plaintiff rested the case. **1950** *Chi. Tribune* 23 Jan. 1/8 Defense attorneys . . . elected to rest their case without calling a single witness in behalf of their clients.

c. To allow (a title to real estate) to stand without further or repeated searching of records.

1888 *Economist* 20 Oct. 2/1 Title Guarantee and Trust Co. . . . A title once examined and guaranteed is *rested* by this Company.

2. To hang up (a hat or coat). *Colloq.*

1897 LEWIS *Wolfville* 70 The old lady . . . asked me to rest my hat the second I'm in the door. **1912** COBB *Back Home* 229 Judge Priest . . . made him rest his hat and overcoat . . . and sit down.

3. *To rest up*, to regain strength by resting. Also **resting up.**

1895 MARK TWAIN *Joan of Arc* viii. 458 (R.), He could not rest up from his fatigue when he got worn out. *a*__1918__ G. STUART *On Frontier* II. 192 There was never any such thing as 'resting up' or 'laying over'; the herd was kept moving forward all the time. **1922** Z. GREY *To Last Man* 284 Get rifle and ammunition, bake bread, and rest up before taking again the trail of the rustlers.

restaurant ˈrɛstərənt, *n.* [F. in same sense.] A public dining room; an establishment in which meals are sold to the public. Also attrib. Cf. **restaurat, restorator.**

[**1827** COOPER *Prairie* xix, Those delicious and unrivalled viands . . . are unequalled by anything that is served . . . at the most renowned of the Parisian *restaurants*.] **1836** *N.Y. Mirror* 30 July 39/3 The Boston place is called the Albion; and consists of chambers for repose, with a 'restaurant' for refection. **1873** *Newton Kansan* 20 Feb. 3/2 Mr. Critchfield . . . has taken possession of Col. Irving's old restaurant stand. **1950** *Chi. Tribune* 9 Jan. 25/1 My father wants me to take over his restaurant when he gets old.

b. restaurant car, (see quot. 1876). Cf. **diner, dining car.**

1876 KNIGHT 1923/2 *Restaurant-car*, one adapted for affording meals to passengers on board while traveling. **1890** *Railways of Amer.* 146 It would require a separate article to give even a brief description of the different kinds of cars which are now used . . . Refrigerator-car, Restaurant-car, Sleeping-car.

As the last term in **horse, lager beer restaurant.**

restauranter ˈrɛstəˌrantɚ, *n.* One who owns or operates a restaurant. Cf. **restorator.** — **1887** *Ohio State Jrnl.* 20 July, The headquarters of Mr. Kiesewetter are at Diebold's, an opulent restauranter and general purveyor to the wants of delegates. **1888** *Chi. Inter-Ocean* 7 March 4/5 A leading restauranter in New York has figured the average time of three thousand business men at their downtown luncheon is eight minutes.

restaurat ˈrɛstəˌrat, *n.* Obsolete variant of **restaurant.** — **1833** *Niles' Reg.* XLIV. 178/1 A coffee room or *restaurat* will be established on the Third street front of the building. **1863** RUSSELL *Diary* I. 331 A village of restaurants or 'restaurats,' as they are called here, and of bathing boxes has grown up.

Restitutionist ˌrɛstəˈt(j)uʃənɪst, *n.* (See quot. 1858.) Also **Restitutionism,** *n. Obs.*

1773 BOUCHER *View of Causes Amer. Revol.* 261 (*footnote*), Those who, during their connexion with Great Britain, were contented to be called Dissenters or Independents, are now pretty generally become either Universal Restitutionists, Arians or Socinians. **1858** *N.Y. Tribune* 12 Feb. 3/2 *The Worcester* (Mass.) *Transcript* gives the following account of the *ism* called 'Restitutionism,' which has lately sprung up in Worcester and some other places: 'The Restitutionists believe that what man lost in the fall is now beginning to be restored, and that the germ now confined to their own small number, is yet to bud and flourish till it cover the earth. They are all Restitutionists in one sense—they believe that everything is to come back to its original form and purity.'

restorationism ˌrɛstəˈreʃənˌɪzəm, *n.* The belief that all men will at some time be restored to a state of happiness in the future life. — **1834** J. N. BROWN *Encycl. Relig. Knowl.* 1019/1 The Independent Messenger . . . is devoted to the cause of Restorationism. **1884** SCHAFF *Relig. Encycl.* III. 1972/1 It is to be feared that belief in restorationism and annihilationism is increasing within orthodox communions.

restorationist ˌrɛstəˈreʃənɪst, *n.* One who believes in restorationism, esp. a member of a sect formed by a group seceding from the Universalist denomination in 1831 and affirming a doctrine of limited future punishment.

1834 J. N. BROWN *Encycl. Relig. Knowl.* 1018/2 Though the Restorationists, as a separate sect, have arisen within a few years, their sentiments are by no means new. **1878** *N. Amer. Rev.* March 357 Now and then a purgatorial restorationist . . . is especially offensive for his use of these literal pictures of horror. **1892** *Critic* Oct. 177/2 He is a restorationist and this optimistic view . . . imparts a certain tinge to his handling of all themes.

restorator ˈrɛstəˌretɚ, *n.* A restaurant-keeper. Also a restaurant. *Obs.*

1796 *Boston Directory* 261 Julien——, restorator, Milk street. **1877** BARTLETT 793 *Restorator*, the keeper of a restaurant, or house of refreshment. **1896** in *Bostonian Soc. Proc.* 26 It was an immigrant . . . who introduced here the word 'restorator,' on July 12, 1793, which remains as a sporadic folk-word, while society patronizes restaurants.

restrictionist rɪˈstrɪkʃənɪst, *n.* **a.** An opponent of the extension of slavery. *Obs.* or *hist.* **b.** One favoring the policy of protection of industry. **c.** One who favors legislation restricting sales of liquor.

(a) 1820 *Niles' Reg.* XVIII. 258/2 We undertake to say that there is not a single *confessed* restrictionist elected throughout the whole territory. **1857** BENTON *Exam. Dred Scott Case* 87 Some of the most strenuous of the restrictionists had begun . . . to hold the language of conciliation. — **(b) 1830** *Cong. Deb.* 5 May 893/2 We refer to England, that country which the restrictionists visit with such unmeasured abuse. **1832** *Ib.* 31 May 3226 Restrictionists, who call the people 'operatives,' ought to say subject instead of citizen. — **(c) 1887** *Voice* 9 June 4 The restrictionists say, they wish to cut down the number of saloons by one-half.

restrictive covenant. *Real Estate.* A covenant or agreement entered into by property owners in a particular community, usu. in a city, restricting the free use of land, as for residential purposes only, or restricting occupancy to members of one race or social group.

1934 WEBSTER. **1946** THOMPSON *Amer. Daughter* 257, I moved into the apartment in violation of the restrictive covenant. **1949** *Reader's Digest* May 126/1 Restrictive covenants created Little Tokyos.

rest room. A room in a public building, business establishment, etc., affording conveniences, esp. toilet facilities, for those desirous of rest and comfort.

1900 *Outlook* 6 Oct. 296 Rest-Rooms for Farmers' Wives. **1913** *Collier's Mag.* 20 Dec. 10/2 We did not have any rest rooms then. **1949** *Lubbock* (Tex.) *Morn. Avalanche* 23 Feb. I. 11/7 While the carnivorous rodent was being chased about the darkened theater, it fled into the rest room.

resubmissionist ˌrisəbˈmɪʃənɪst, *n.* One who favors submitting to a second popular vote a prohibition amendment already in force. — **1884** *N.Y. Wkly. Tribune* 27 Aug. 7/3 The Conference Committee recommended that the Re-Submissionists be granted a place on the Democratic State ticket. **1890** *Public Opinion* 20 Sep. 547 The political alliance between the Resubmissionists and Democrats in Kansas places the 'straight-out' Prohibitionists in a peculiar position.

*__result,__ *v. tr.* To make a decision *that*, etc. *Obs.*—**1812** N. WORCESTER *Bible News* (ed. 2) 176 (Pickering), According to Dr. Milner, the Council of Nice resulted, in opposition to the view of Arius, that the Son was peculiarly of the Father. **1816** PICKERING 164 Some of our writers on ecclesiastical affairs constantly use this verb, . . . thus: 'The Council resulted that the parties should do certain things.'

resumptionist rɪˈzʌmpʃənɪst, *n.* An advocate of the resumption of specie payments. *Obs.* — **1875** *Chi. Tribune* 14 Oct. 1/6 The schemes of the contractionists, bullionists, and resumptionists, had been interfered with. **1878** *Cong. Rec.* 26 Jan. 598/1 We are resumptionists. We deny . . . that there is [in the West] one particle of the spirit of repudiation.

resurface riˈsɝfɪs, *v. tr.* To supply (a pavement or road) with a new surface. Also **resurfacing,** *n.*

1894 *Columbus* (O.) *Dispatch* 15 Sep., The resurfacing of the pavement about the Court House has progressed far enough to give the Judges some idea [etc.]. **1901** *Dept. Agric. Yrbk. 1900* 352 The road was resurfaced with limestone. **1943** *Democrat* 1 July 2/1 Work of resurfacing the section . . . is nearing completion.

*__resurrection,__ *n.* In combs.: (1) **resurrection fern,** the gray polypody, *Polypodium polypodioides*, found on rocks and tree trunks in the southern states; (2) **note,** a bank note of the second Bank of the U.S. (1816–36) which was issued again by the successor of the bank, the Bank of the U.S. of Pennsylvania, *colloq., obs.;* (3) **plant,** any one of several plants, as club mosses, of the genus *Selaginella*, which, dried, reëxpand if wetted; (4) **robe,** a garment worn by a Millerite, in expectation of the second coming of Christ, *obs.*

(1) **1909** *Cent. Supp.* 467/1. **1938** MATSCHAT *Suwannee River* 219 Brilliant green resurrection ferns grew all over the leaning trunks. — (2) **1838** *Cong. Globe* App. 12 Feb. 80/1 (*caption*), Resurrection Notes. *Ib.* 23 April 305/3 A large proportion of these resurrection notes, as they have been aptly called, which have been issued and reissued by order of the new bank, are of the denomination of five dollars. — (3) **1870** MASTERS *Henfrey's Bot.* 413 One or two of the species [of Selaginellae] roll up their fronds when dry, and unfold them again when placed in water, owing to the rapid absorption of the fluid, whence they have been called Resurrection plants. **1893** G. D. LESLIE *Lett. Marco* xviii. 119 'A resurrection plant' . . . some sort of large lichen or spleenwort from Colorado. — (4) **1843** *Niles' Reg.* 4 March 16/3 Some of the devotees, attired in their resurrection robes, were actually nearly frozen to death waiting in a bleak, exposed situation out of doors, the awful consummation of all things.

*__resuscitator,__ *n.* An oxygen inhalator. — **1945** *Gunnison* (Colo.) *New-Champion* 22 Nov. 8/6 The Gunnison stockmen voted $25 for the resuscitator. **1947** *Steamboat* (Colo.) *Pilot* 16 Jan. 3/3 The resuscitator purchased by public subscription for the Cortez fire department paid off in big dividends last week.

retail store. A store in which commodities are sold in small quantities directly to the consumer.

1785 MADISON *Writings* II. 162 Retail Stores are spreading all over the country. **1838** A. BELL *Men & Things* (1862) 198 In Philadelphia there are, consequently, a prodigious number of storing warehouses; of retail 'stores' there are . . . very few. **1882** MCCABE *New York* 267 Third avenue . . . is devoted to small retail stores. **1948** *U.S. Investor* 29 Dec. 1/1 Only to a lesser degree is this true of retail stores of the type operated by Sears Roebuck and Montgomery Ward.

*__retainer,__ *n.* (See quots.) — **1811** *Tenn. Rep.* II. 167 A retainer to the camp must be a person who, from his situation and nature of his employment, has a right to be at the camp, and within the line of sentinels. **1890** *Cent.* 5120/1 *Retainer*, . . . a sutler, camp-follower, or any person serving with an army who, though not enlisted, is subject to orders according to the rules and articles of war.

retake ˈritek, *n.* In motion pictures, another photographing or photograph of a particular scene. Also as a verb. *Colloq.*

1918 HOMER CROY *How Motion Pictures Are Made* v. 126 Directly on finishing the scene it is filmed again, the second exposure being called a 'retake.' **1922** WILSON *Merton of Movies* 167, I certainly hate to get out and wait in wet clothes while Sig Rosenblatt is thinking about a retake. **1929** WITWER *Yes Man's Land* 304 This here's no quickie and I can't retake all that stuff and still do business.

retama rəˈtɑmə, *n. S.W.* [Sp. in Amer. Sp. sense shown here.] =**palo verde.**

1891 COULTER *Botany West Tex.* 94 P. aculeata . . . [is] often cultivated for ornament and known as 'retama.' **1909** MACKENSEN *Trees & Shrubs San Antonio* 25 The retama is very elegant and is often planted for ornament. **1949** *Chi. Tribune* 20 Feb. 30/3 Cedar and mesquite alone are costing Texas ranchers 115 million dollars a year. Add the sage and cactus, . . . blackjack oak, retama and prickly pear and the toll is terrific.

retiracy rɪˈtaɪrəsɪ, *n.*

1. Retirement, seclusion.

1829 *Va. Lit. Museum* 30 Dec. 460 *Retiracy*, 'solitude' *Western States.* **1859** *La Crosse D. Union* 11 Nov. 2/3 [The writing of a political history] is begun . . . amid the retiracy which is so favorable to its accomplishment. **1873** WALLACE *Fair God* 162 He left the house, and once more sought the retiracy of the gardens. **1894** *Confederate Veteran* Dec. 373/1 Uncle Dan Emmett . . . is to-day quietly spending the evening of his life in the retiracy of a humble home in the outskirts of Mt. Vernon, O.

2. (See quot. 1848.) *Obs.*

1848 BARTLETT 274 *Retiracy*, sufficiency; competency. It is said, in New England, of a person who has retired from business with a fortune, that he has a retiracy; i.e. a sufficient fortune to retire with. **1860** *New Haven Palladium* (De Vere), When Mr. Watson found he had a sufficient retiracy, he gave up his lucrative business, and devoted himself to horticultural pursuits.

3. The act of retiring or state of being in retirement from a court room.

1864 *Harper's Mag.* April 711/2 After a few minutes retiracy the jury returned into court.

*__retire,__ *v.*

1. *intr.* and *tr.* In baseball, to leave the home plate upon being put out; to put out (a player or side).

1867 *Ball Players' Chron.* 6 June 2/1 His run, however, was the only one scored, as the next three strikers retired in succession. **1874** *Chi. Inter-Ocean* 6 July 9/1 Cuthbert then sent a long fly to left field, and retired when it landed in Hall's hands. **1917** MATHEWSON *Second Base Sloan* 180 The first batsman was retired on an easy toss from Chase to Jim. **1949** *News-Herald* (Marshfield, Wis.) 19 July 9/4 Nowitzke gobbled up Bauer's grounder and threw him out to retire the side.

2. *tr.* To withdraw or take (a thing) away from its usual place or the performance of its customary function.

1883 *Lisbon* (Dak.) *Star* 12 Oct., Eighteen packet boats have been retired by several of the packet lines . . . , owing to the low stage of water. **1888** *Amer. Humorist* (London) 2 June 5/2 Mr. Bonner retired him [a horse] from the track!

retorter rɪˈtɔrtɚ, *n.* One who retorts metals. — **1876** RAYMOND *8th Rep. Mines* 415, 2 amalgamators, 2 retorters and boiler-men.

*__return,__ *n.* and *v.* **1.** *n. To go behind the returns,* (see quot. 1914). **2.** *and return,* and back again.

(1) **1877** *Electoral Commission Proc.* 934 Much has been said here by those opposed to us about 'going behind the returns,' and the terrible consequences of such an act. **1914** *Cyclo. Amer. Govt.* III. 211/1 *Returns, Can't Go Behind The,* a phrase indicating the demands of the Republican party, adopted by the electoral commission Feb. 7, 1877, in the Hayes-Tilden disputed election case, that the commission was not competent to investigate the eligibility of the list of electors submitted by the state authorities. — (2) **1887** GEORGE *40 Yrs. on Rail* 88 The train . . . ran from Waukegan to Chicago and return every day.

As the last term in **candle box, schedule return(s).**

returning board. In some states, a board composed of those appointed to determine officially the results of popular elections. Also attrib.

1874 *43d Congress* 2 Sess. H.R. Rep. No. 101, 6 This conviction among them has been strengthened by the acts of the Kellogg legislature abolishing existing courts and judges, . . . by continuing the returning board with absolute power over the returns of elections. **1878** DALY in J. F. Daly *A. Daly* 254 Excitement is at fever heat about the Returning Board trials. **1886** Z. F. SMITH *Kentucky* 812 Even by the count of the celebrated *returning-board* expedient, Tilden's popular majority was 157,394. **1893** *McClure's Mag.* I. 383/1 'The Potter Committee' [was] appointed to investigate the operations of the returning boards in the South.

*__re-union,__ *n.* The restoration of the South, after its secession, to its former place in the Union. *Rare.* — **1863** *Rio Abajo Press* 4 Aug. 2/2 This is an important point for us 'Mudsills' to consider in view of 're-union' upon the basis of 'compromise.'

revamp riˈvæmp, *v. tr.* To reconstruct, repair, patch up again.

1850 MITCHELL *Lorgnette* I. 141 Even the soberer subjects of History, he told me, must be re-vamped in some tasty way. **1932** *K.C. Times* 5 April 18 If this depression keeps on . . . he is going to have his heels revamped or something. **1949** *Chi. Tribune* 22 Oct. 10/3 Revamped, the story appeared in the 'Eastern Slope,' Washoe, Nev., Dec. 23, 1865.

Revengeless Christians. (See quot.) *Obs.* — **1796** MORSE *Univ. Geog.* I. 283 [The Mennonists] call themselves the Harmless Christians, Revengeless Christians, and Weaponless Christians.

*__revenue,__ *n.*

1. =**revenuer.** *Colloq.*

1883 ZEIGLER & GROSSCUP *Alleghanies* 257 My pards mout tak' ye fer a revenoo, an' let a hole thro' ye. **1907** H. B. WRIGHT *Shepherd of Hills* 69 He's just some revenue.

2. In combs.: (1) **revenue agent,** (see quot. 1864); (2) **bill,** a congressional bill providing for the raising of revenue; (3) **-cutter service, marine,** (see quot.); (4) **reformer,** one interested in reforming or changing the revenue laws; (5) **tariff,** a tariff designed primarily to secure revenue as distinguished from a protective tariff.

(1) **1864** *Statutes at Large* XIII. 224 Revenue agents . . . [shall] aid in the prevention, detection, and punishment of frauds upon the internal revenue. **1943** *Chi. D. News* 24 Dec. 6/1 We would hate to be a revenue agent with that gal up in the cove. — (2) **1794** *Ann. 3d Congress* 697 Revenue Bill. . . . Laying additional duties on goods, wares, and merchandise, imported into the United States. **1842** in MACLEOD *F. Wood* 95 The discussion of the revenue bill of last session, and motion of reference of the tariff portion of the President's message this session, have convinced me [etc.]. — (3) **1890** *Cent.*

5134/3 *Revenue marine*, or *revenue-cutter service*, a corps organized in 1790 . . . for the purpose of guarding the coast and estuaries of the United States for the protection of the customs revenue. — (4) **1870** *Nation* 19 May 311/1 The high protectionists are not sorry, while the revenue reformers are. **1887** *Courier-Journal* 2 Feb. 1/3 The Speaker will consult with the leading revenue reformers of the House tomorrow.

(5) **1820** *Ann. 16th Congress* 1 Sess. 1966 They enacted . . . a revenue tariff, without the least regard to the situation of the country. **1887** *Courier-Journal* 19 Feb. 4/1 They are the identical arguments which the Courier-Journal has been pounding into the understanding of the people in its fight for a revenue tariff.

As the last term in **internal revenue.**

revenuer ˈrɛvəˌn(j)uɚ, *n.* A term used by moonshiners for a revenue agent enforcing the laws against illicit distilling. *Colloq.*

1880 *Dly. Inter-Ocean* (Chi.) 1 June 12/1 His wife and daughter discharged their conjugal and filial duty by . . . watching from their home for the approach of the 'Revenyors.' **1895** CRADDOCK *Mystery Witch-Face Mt.* 15 The 'revenuers' . . . never rode alone. **1949** *Américas* Aug. 10/1 The 'revenoo-ers' slowed the production of illegal whiskey.

∗**reverend,** *a.* Also ∗**reverent.**

1. (See quot. 1936.) *Colloq.*

1837 WETMORE *Gaz. Missouri* 336 'Muster courage to take . . . a tablespoonful, three times a day.'—'Jist reverend, without water, doctor?' **1837** SHERWOOD *Gaz. Georgia* (ed. 3) 71 *Reverent*, for strong; *reverent whisky, i.e.* not diluted. **1888** CRADDOCK *Despot* 467, I thunk the reverend stuff would fetch ye. **1936** *Amer. Sp.* XI. 317/1 Reverend, adj. Pure, full strength, undiluted. 'Do you want this here castor oil *reverend*, or shall I mix some sody-pop in it?' Ozark Mts.

2. reverend set, (see quots.). *Obs.*

1826 GLINT *Recoll.* 15 A firm push of the iron-pointed pole on a fixed log, is termed a 'reverend' set. **1832** PAULDING *Westward Ho!* I. 83 They placed their shoulders against the long poles, one end of which was loaded with iron, and making what was called a 'reverend set,' walked steadily to the stern of the broad-horn, propelling her forward at the same time.

∗**reverse,** *a.* **1. reverse English,** (see quot. 1909 and cf. ∗**English,** *a.* and *n.* **1.**). **2. reverse Newport,** see ∗**Newport.** — (1) **1909** *Cent. Supp.* 427/1 Reverse English, in billiards, a stroke which twists the cue-ball on the side opposite to the direction in which it should go after taking the first cushion. **1949** *Sat. Ev. Post* 25 June 30/3 He had a vicious chop shot that landed just over the net, with reverse English, and bounced back on his side.

reviewing stand. A temporary structure from which a parade or procession may be reviewed or seen to advantage. — **1897** *Boston Jrnl.* 15 Jan. 6/5 The local chapter . . . [suggested] a reform in . . . the erection of reviewing-stands for spectators on the occasion of processions on the next inauguration day. **1947** *Newsweek* 3 March 40/2 Past the governor's reviewing stand . . . moved bands mounted on trucks advertising Coca-Cola.

∗**revival,** *n.*

1. A series of evangelistic meetings for awaking religious enthusiasm.

The earliest evidence for this use is American. In the first half of the 19th century British travelers regarded the term and the institution as American. See quot. 1832. The original form of the expression may have been that shown in **b.** below.

1799 in YOUNG *Jessamine Co., Ky.* 197, I have written several others to assist in holding the revival. **1832** MRS. TROLLOPE *Domestic Manners* I. 105 They preach and pray all day, and often for a considerable portion of the night in various churches and chapels. . . . This is called a Revival. **1948** *Capital-Democrat* (Tishomingo, Okla.) 24 June 6/1 The revival is now underway and will probably continue through next Sunday.

b. *revival of religion*, a period of renewed interest in and devotion to religion.

1702 C. MATHER *Magnalia* I. 71/2 There was a notable Revival of Religion among them. *a*1817 DWIGHT *Travels* II. 277 Four considerable revivals of Religion have taken place in Somers during his Ministry. **1874** COLLINS *Kentucky* I. 25 The 'Great Revival' of religion begins in the Green river country.

2. Revival man, =**Stoneite.** *Obs.* Cf. **New Light.**

1847 DAVIDSON *Presbyterian Ch. in Ky.* 167 The clergy and people became divided into two distinct parties—the Orthodox and the New Lights—one assuming the honorable style of '*Revival Men*,' and affecting superior sanctity and zeal, and stigmatizing the other unjustly as '*Anti-Revival Men.*' *Ib.* 190 A division into two clearly defined parties was the inevitable result. To these parties were given by the former [i.e., the enthusiastic party], the names of *Revival* and *Anti-Revival* men.

As the last term in **great, tin-pan revival.**

revocal rɪˈvokl̩, *n.* Revocation. *Rare.* — **1862** *N.Y. Tribune* 9 June (Chipman), The President's revocal of General Hunter's proclamation was well received at Port Royal.

∗**Revolution,** *n.* Short for Revolutionary War *q.v.*

1789 *Ann. 1st Congress* 150 He recollected that, before the Revolution, very little was imported. **1840** *Louisville Pub. Adv.* 2 July 2/4 The spirit of the Revolution arose, and the Federal party was crushed by the election of Mr. Jefferson. **1943** MENEFEE *Assignment* 29 Continental Square, in the center of town, is named after the Continental Congress that met there in the darkest days of the Revolution.

b. Also attrib., esp. **Revolution War.** *Obs.*

1789 *Jrnl. Wm. Maclay* (1927) 114 He has been characterized to me as a stanch Revolution man and genuine Whig. **1795** *Mass. H.S. Coll.* 1 Ser. IV. 203 During the revolution-war, the publick opinion was . . . strongly in favour of the abolition of slavery. **1801** JEFFERSON *Writings* X. 226 All these petitions were depending . . . when the Revolution War broke out.

c. The Texan war of independence from Mexico; the American Civil War. *Obs.* Cf. ∗**revolutionist,** *n.*

1857 OLMSTED *Journey Through Texas* 234 Families who came here before the Revolution. **1861** E. COLWELL *Diary* 248 But to turn from all our insignificant affairs 'The Revolution' is stalking through this vast country with rapid strides.

As the last term in **Bear Revolution.**

∗**Revolutionary,** *a.*

1. Of or pertaining to the Revolutionary War, or those who fought in it.

1798 *Ann. 5th Congress* 1337 He regretted to see so different a spirit animating our citizens now, from that which animated them in our Revolutionary struggle. **1834** *Sun* (N.Y.) 18 June 2/2 The remnant of revolutionary heroes that yet remain will be invited as guests. **1931** *Sat. Ev. Post* 4 July 75/4 Nearly all of them were of Revolutionary stock. **1946** *This Week Mag.* 16 Feb. 28/2 Now his favorite foods are prepared in this Revolutionary home.

b. Revolutionary tea, (see quot.).

1944 *Herb Magic* 7 Labrador Tea—Also known as Revolutionary Tea—a quite different flavor . . . 'somewhat like Oriental Tea.'

2. Revolutionary War, the war for independence carried on by the American colonists against Great Britain (1775–83). Also attrib.

1800 HAWKINS *Sk. Creek Country* 26 These Indians were very friendly to the United States, during the revolutionary war. **1844** RUPP *Relig. Denominations* 54 During the revolutionary war many of our churches were scattered by the male members being engaged with the army. **1907** *St. Nicholas* Sep. 1054/1 Jane McCrea . . . was killed by Indians during the Revolutionary War period.

∗**revolutioner,** *n.* One who took part in the Revolutionary War. *Colloq. Obs.*

1822 *Niles' Reg.* 20 July 322/2 Mr. R. [is] an old revolutioner. **1835** CROCKETT *Tour* 52 General Morton is a revolutioner, and an officer in the society of old soldiers called the 'Cincinnati Society.' **1872** *Harper's Wkly.* 25 May 411/4 An old 'Revolutioner' says that of all the solemn hours he ever saw, that occupied in going home one dark night . . . was the most solemn.

∗**revolutionist,** *n.* One in sympathy with the South during the Civil War. *Obs.* — **1861** in W. LAWRENCE *A. A. Lawrence* 171 Massachusetts troops fired on in Baltimore. Washington barely saved from the revolutionists. **1865** RICHARDSON *Secret Service* 17 Early in 1861, I felt a strong desire . . . [to learn] what the Revolutionists wanted, what they hoped and what they feared.

∗**revolver,** *n.* A pistol in which a number of barrels, or, more usually, a cylinder suitable for separate charges or

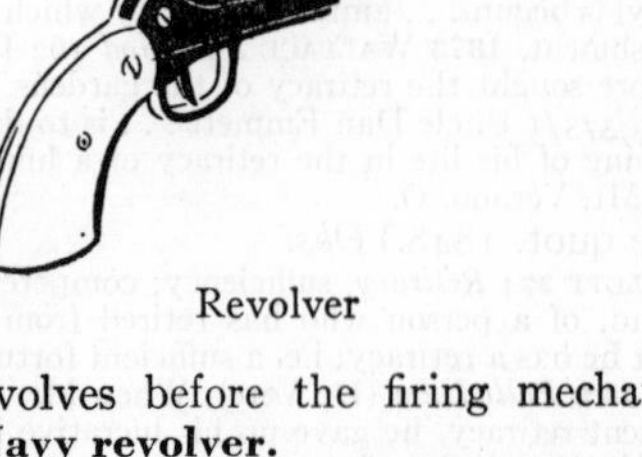

Revolver

cartridges, revolves before the firing mechanism. Cf. **California, Navy revolver.**

1835 COLT in *Abridgm. Patent Specifications, Fire-Arms* (1859) 84. **1920** HOWELLS *Vacation of Kelwyns* 35 He suddenly realized with a neuralgic poignancy that his revolver was meant to kill a man. **1949**

Columbus (O.) *Sun. Dispatch* 16 Oct. c. 2/5 The man then took a revolver from the wounded officer.

attrib. **a1861** WINTHROP *J. Brent* 208 They were close to us, within easy revolver shot. **1872** POWERS *Afoot & Alone* 129, I saw a youth . . . strap his spelling-book to his revolver belt. **1890** *Stock Grower & Farmer* 21 June 3/2 The arrest and punishment of a few of the revolver packers would make the practice unpopular.

* **revolving,** *a.* In combs.: (1) **revolving chair,** = **swivel chair;** (2) **cookstove,** (see quot.); (3) **door,** a storm door or weather door, usu. in a kind of cylindrical vestibule, having two or four sections that revolve on a central upright axis [in the 1939 ref. Theophilus Van Kannel of Philadelphia is said to have invented such a door *c*1889]; (4) **fund,** a special fund appropriated by the government for financing public business enterprises, so called because funds paid out or loaned are expected to return to the fund to be used again in a similar manner; (5) **pistol,** = * **revolver,** *obs.*, cf. **Colt's revolving pistol;** (6) **platform,** a railroad turntable, *obs.;*

Revolving platform

(7) **rifle,** a repeating rifle having a cylinder containing chambers for separate charges or cartridges that are brought in succession before the firing mechanism.

(1) **1911** E. FERBER *Dawn O'Hara* xii. 170 The big man seated in the revolving chair up in front. **1943** *Life* 3 May 4 You state that Jefferson wrote the Declaration of Independence on the revolving chair which he invented. — (2) **1931** *Old-Time N. Eng.* Oct. 82/1 In 1832, Henry Stanley of Poultney, Vt., invented a stove with a rotary low-down top which was popular for many years. It was called a 'Revolving Cook Stove' and different parts of the circular top could be turned so as to rest immediately over the fire box. — (3) **1931** *K.C. Times* 21 Nov. 26 They have put their revolving doors up again in the city. [**1939** *Chi. D. News* 11 Feb. (Mag.) 13.] **1949** *Reader's Digest* Aug. 140 The little man paid for the picture . . . and walked briskly through the revolving door. — (4) **1932** *Atlantic Mo.* CL. 223, I had not thought of conducting a mission; nor do I maintain a revolving fund for deserving aspirants. **1932** *Durant* (Okla.) *D. Democrat* 4 Feb. 2/4 The farm board's revolving fund is rapidly becoming a dissolving fund.

(5) **1847** PARKMAN in *Knickerb.* XXX. 24 The other jerked a little revolving pistol out of his pocket. **1923** *Outing* Jan. 171/3 First called 'revolving pistol,' it was shortened to revolver. — (6) **1833** *Amer. R.R. Jrnl.* II. 533/2 A revolving platform is generally placed in the centre of the turn out. **1834** *Ib.* III. 271/1 (*advt.*), Railroad Turnouts, Revolving Platforms and Sidelings. — (7) **1848** in *Minn. Hist.* XVII. (1936) 299 After breaking a very fine revolving rifle . . . they gave him some buffalo meat and told him to go. **1865** TROWBRIDGE *Three Scouts* 363 General Stanley . . . [was] giving them exercise and practice with their new revolving rifles. [**1948** *Chi. Tribune* 7 March I. 38/6 The society's collection includes several Colt revolving chambered percussion rifles.]

re-wood riˈwʊd, *v. tr.* To plant (land) again with trees; to repair (a bridge) with new wooden parts. — **1886** *N.Y. Tribune* (s.-w. ed.) 24 Dec. (*Cent.*), Rewooding the high lands where the streams take rise. **1908** *Indian Laws & Tr.* III. 333 For the purpose of rewooding and repiling the present old bridge, . . . the sum of twelve thousand dollars.

rewrite man. (See quots.)

1901 *Munsey's Mag.* Nov. 222/1 Much of the copy that reaches the big newspaper offices is passed over to the 'rewrite man.' **1902** CLAPIN 335 Rewrite man. In newspaper parlance, an experienced reporter who has the gift of unerringly seeing what is valuable in a story, and rewriting it into terse and picturesque style, so that it stands out. This is a development of the last two years. **1949** *Sat. Ev. Post* 2 April 122/2 The rewrite man must be able to take the bare factual bones of any type of story and clothe them in reasonably colorful prose.

Also **rewrite desk, story.**

1912 G. M. HYDE *Newspaper Reporting* 125 The terms 'rewrite story' and 'follow-up or follow, story,' are names which newspaper men apply to the rehashed or revised versions of other news stories. **1935** *Amer. Mercury* July 379/2, I have yet to discover an instance of real literary talent being brought to the surface by back-breaking chores on the rewrite desk. **1950** *World-Herald Mag.* (Omaha) 8 Jan. 8/3 Life on the rewrite desk used to have one paralyzing disadvantage.

R.F.D. Abbreviation of **rural free delivery.** Often attrib.

1916 H. L. WILSON *Somewhere in Red Gap* ix. 361 These here poor R.F.D. stage drivers had to do the extra hauling for nothing. **1946** WILSON *Fidelity* 198 The rural postoffice has practically disappeared because of the R.F.D. **1947** ROBINSON *Great Snow* 67 The R.F.D. mailman also delivered the *Times*, which he wanted for further news of the storm.

* **rheumatism,** *n.*

1. rheumatism root, (*a*) the twinleaf, *Jeffersonia diphylla,* which grows wild in the eastern states, (*b*) the wild yam, *Dioscorea paniculata.*

(*a*) **1843** TORREY *Flora N.Y.* I. 34 *Jeffersonia diphylla.* Twin-leaf Rheumatism-root. . . . [The root] is sometimes employed as a remedy in chronic rheumatism. **1898** CREEVEY *Flowers of Field* 308 Twin-leaf. Rheumatism-root. . . . A plant of low growth, not uncommon in the woods of western New York, southward and westward. (*b*) **1887** BENTLEY *Man. Botany* 706 The rhizome of *D*[*ioscorea*] *villosa,* the Wild Yam of the United States, is regarded as a valuable remedy in Virginia in rheumatism, and is hence commonly known as 'rheumatism root.'

2. rheumatism weed, (*a*) any one of various evergreen herbs, as the pipsissewa *q.v.*, (*b*) (see quot.).

(*a*) **1784** *Amer. Acad. Mem.* I. 444 Rheumatism-Weed . . . abounds near White-Mountains. **1872** *Atlantic Mo.* June 748/2 The umbelled pyrola, or rheumatism-weed, . . . and the roots of the yellow dock, were favorite ingredients [for a 'diet drink' of herbs]. (*b*) **1894** *Amer. Folk-Lore* VII. 94 *Apocynum androsæmifolium,* rheumatism-weed, West Va.

* **Rhexia,** *n.* A genus of plants of the family Melastomaceae, or any plant of this genus. — **1833** WHITTIER *Poetical Works* (1894) 262/1 The rhexias dark, and cassia tall. **1887** BURROUGHS in *Cent. Mag.* July 327 Parts of New England have already a midsummer flower nearly as brilliant and probably far less aggressive and noxious, in meadow beauty, or rhexia.

Rhode Island. *attrib.*

1. Designating things pertaining to or characteristic of Rhode Island.

1790 *Jrnl. Wm. Maclay* (1927) 252 When we came in we found them [the Senate] on the Rhode Island resolves. **1872** *Atlantic Mo.* April 399 It required twenty-five hundred pounds in Rhode Island paper to buy one golden guinea. **1886** POORE *Reminisc.* I. 384 She could make a regal Cape Cod chowder, or roast a Rhode Island turkey. **1894** *Amer. Folk-Lore* VII. 91 *Chrysanthemum leucanthemum,* Kellup weed, Rhode Island clover, Montpelier, Vt. **1941** *L.A.* Map 286.

2. Rhode Island Red, a breed of single- or rose-combed domestic fowls valued for meat and eggs and characterized by long, heavy bodies, yellow legs and brownish-red plumage.

1902 *Outing* April 64/2 In like manner the Rhode Island Red has originated in this country. A certain Mr. William Tripp, then of Little Compton, in the State of Rhode Island, bought from a neighbor, a Mr. Sisson, a rose-combed Brown Leghorn cockerel to cross upon his flock of buff Malay hens. . . . The object Mr. Tripp had in mind was to increase the productivity of his flock, not to produce a new breed. **1931** CALDWELL *Amer. Earth* 76 We lived on a small farm and had . . . a flock of Rhode Island Red chickens. **1949** *Chi. Tribune* 26 Sep. 1/3 A pen of 13 Rhode Island Red hens . . . has won the 38th annual Storrs egg laying test just completed at the University of Connecticut.

Also **Rhode Island White,** (see quots.).

1926 *U.S. Dept. Agric. Farmers' Bul. 1506,* 9 The Rhode Island White of which the rose comb is the only variety, is identical with the Rose-Comb Rhode Island Red, except that the plumage should be pure white, free from any tint of brassiness. **1949** HUTT *Genetics of Fowl* 16 It is true that colors usually distinguish varieties, but color is the sole difference between the Rhode Island Whites and Rhode Island Reds, which have thus far been classed as two distinct breeds.

3. In special combs. and derivatives; (1) **Rhode Island bent,** a variety of lawn grass, *Agrostis capillaris;* (2) **Rhode Islander,** a native or inhabitant of Rhode Island, also transf.; (3) **Rhode Island greening,** a variety of green or greenish apple, also a tree producing this apple.

(1) **1790** DEANE *N.-Eng. Farmer* 123/1 The Rhode Island bent, as it is called, or red top grass, will do with less drying than some other grasses. **1899** *Dept. Agric. Yrbk. 1898* 494 Creeping bent (*Agrostis stolonifera*) and Rhode Island bent (*A. canina*) are much prized for lawns.—(2) **1665** RICHARD SMITH, JR. *Letter* (1937) 80 We are here att Naragansett much abused by Rode Jlanders. *a***1817** DWIGHT *Travels* II. 37 Free born Rhode-Islanders ought never to submit to be priest-ridden. **1871** *N.Y. Herald* 28 July 6/1 It was a regular old fashioned Rhode Islander of a clam bake. **1948** *Nat. Geog. Mag.* Aug. 137/2 When Rhode Islanders say they are going 'down city' or 'to the city,' they mean Providence. — (3) **1817** W. COXE *Fruit Trees* 129 Jersey, or Rhode-Island Greening. Sometimes called the Burlington Greening. **1884** ROE *Nature's Story* 400 Those umbrella-shaped trees are Rhode Island greenings. **1949** *Chi. Tribune* 6 Oct. 12/3 There are a third more . . . Golden Delicious and Wealthy; nearly two and a half times more Stayman and Baldwin, and about twice as many R. I. Greening, Northern Spy and Ben Davis apples.

***rhododendron,** *n.* As the last term in **Catawba, Lapland rhododendron.**

Rhodora roˈdorə, *n.* [L., name of a plant.] A flowering plant or shrub, *Rhodora canadensis,* found chiefly in New England.

1839 EMERSON *Poems* (1867) 37, I found the fresh Rhodora in the woods. **1869** FULLER *Flower Gatherers* 59 The Azaleas, or Swamp Honeysuckles, are beautiful cousins of the Rhodora. *a***1886** DICKINSON *Works* (1924) 82 The crocus stirs her lids, Rhodora's cheek is crimson.

Rhody ˈrodɪ, *n.* =**Little Rhody.** *Obs.* — **1856** *Repub. Campaign Songster* 34 So stand, dear Rhody, never fear, Though small you be, you're spunky. **1862** HALSEY *New Union Song Book* 68 And in the van the stalwart men From Rhody's sea-beat side.

***Rialto,** *n.* (See quot. 1916.) — **1888** *N.Y. Herald* 29 July 8/5, I would like to say a few words . . . in behalf of the *habitues* of the Rialto, unfortunately known as 'hamfatters.' **1916** F. RIDER *New York City* 53 The theatre life of New York is comprised within the fairly narrow area of Broadway and the adjacent side streets, from 40th to 50th st.—a stretch popularly known as the 'Rialto.' **1929** ZORBAUGH *Gold Coast & Slum* 10 Clark street is the Rialto of the slum.

riata riˈætə, *n.* Also **reata.** *W.* [Sp. *reata,* in the Amer. Sp. sense shown here.] A rope, esp. one of leather or rawhide, a lariat. Cf. **hair, rawhide lariat.**

1846 *Californian* (Monterey) 12 Sep. 1/1 A riata (rope) was made fast to the broken bone and the jaw dragged out. **1924** BECHDOLT *Tales* 103 They had failed to take into account . . . a skill with the reata. **1949** GANN *Tread of Longhorns* 37 These reatas were so popular that many men clung to them as late as the 1920's.

b. *To coil up one's riata,* to die. *Rare.*

1871 *Overland Mo.* March 285/2, I'm a-coilin' up my *riata,* Jim.

c. *Knights of the Riata,* cowboys. *Jocose.*

1889 *Oregonian* (Portland) 4 Oct. 5/1 The tournament . . . promises to develop some exciting contests between the visiting 'Cow Punchers' and the Oregon 'Knights of the Riatta.'

***ribbed,** *a.* **ribbed boiler, mussel, road** (cf. **corduroy road**), (see quots.). See also **rock ribbed.**

1833 FIDLER *Observations* 122 Such roads are denominated by the native, 'ribbed or corduroy roads,' an appellation not ill chosen. **1883** KNIGHT *Supp.* 756/2 *Ribbed Boiler,* one with corrugations or projecting ribs to add to the surface exposed to the fire. Used for greenhouse boilers. **1883** *Nat. Museum Bul.* No. 27, 236 *Modiola plicatula,* . . . known as the Ribbed-mussel, is found from Georgia to Casco Bay, Maine.

***ribbon,** *n.*

1. =**ribbon cane.** Also with a designating term. Cf. ***red,** *a.* **2. c.** (11).

1837 WILLIAMS *Florida* 106 Three kinds of cane are planted in the Territory, the creole, otaheita, and ribon. **1856** *Rep. Comm. Patents: Agric.* 273 The varieties of cane which have hitherto been most cultivated in Louisiana are the 'Striped-blue Ribbon;' the 'Green Ribbon' [etc.].

2. a. A long, narrow strip of cloth especially prepared and inked for use on stamping devices and typewriters. **b.** A narrow strip of paper used on a stock ticker, a ticker tape.

(a) 1876 KNIGHT 1936/2 Ribbons for hand-stamps are tapes saturated with an oily pigment. **1918** OWEN *Typewriting Speed* 140 Work in a law office calls for the use of *black* ribbons on your machine. **1949** *Canadian Alpine Jrnl.* May 72 An ordinary typewriter provides a very good medium . . . with a clean black ribbon. — **(b) 1882** MCCABE *New York* 338 The offers and bids . . . are noted on the long ribbons of the thousands of 'tickers.'

3. A narrow band or streak of different color in slates.

1898 *19th Rep. Geol. Survey* VI. 257 The normal product of roofing slates is called No. 1 stock, and this is entirely free from ribbons.

4. In combs.: (1) **ribbon arrangement,** (see quot.), *obs.;* (2) **cane,** a variety of sugar cane the stalks of which when mature are marked with red or purplish longitudinal stripes, also **ribbon plant cane,** and attrib.; (3) **counter,** in a store, a counter at which ribbon is sold; (4) **hog,** (see quot.), *rare;* (5) **snake,** an American garter snake, *Thamnophis saurita.*

(1) **1910** BOSTWICK *Amer. Pub. Library* 167 In some open-shelf libraries a so-called 'ribbon' arrangement of fiction has been adopted, in which the fiction is placed on one shelf around the room, with non-fiction classes above and below it. — (2) **1827** in COMMONS *Doc. Hist.* I. 215 Some ribbon plant cane have suckered on the 9th. **1833** SILLIMAN *Man. Sugar Cane* 10 The Ribbon Cane . . . appears to be a hybrid between the Violet and the Otaheitan varieties. **1929** L. F. CARR *Amer. Challenged* 252 Some extra-fine ribbon-cane molasses. **1945** *Democrat* 29 March 4/2 Seed Cane—800 stalks old fashioned ribbon cane. — (3) **1907** *St. Nicholas* Oct. 1107/2 He was standing at the ribbon-counter. **1916** W. A. DU PUY *Uncle Sam* 22 'Mr. Summer Boarder,' said the curly-haired Dowling, 'it is back to the ribbon counter for you.' — (4) **1924** CROY *R.F.D. No. 3* 133 His ambition was to raise 'ribbon hogs'—hogs which would be awarded the prize at the local stock show.

(5) **1736** CATESBY *Carolina* II. 50 *Anguis gracilis fuscus.* The Ribbon-Snake. This is a slender Snake. **1827** WILLIAMS *W. Florida* 29 The garter, riband, green, chequered, and glass snakes, make up the account of this species, in West Florida. **1904** PRINGLE *Rice Planter* 105 There was a small ribbon snake, a foot long and one inch round!

b. *To a ribbon,* to perfection. *Colloq.*

1841 COOPER *Deerslayer* i, Now that's Judith's character to a ribbon!

As the last term in **red, striped blue, white ribbon.**

rib pole. One of the poles or timbers on which the boards covering a log cabin were laid. *Obs.* — **1837** *S. Lit. Messenger* III. 82 The roofs of loose boards laid on long rib-poles betokened an abundance of timber. **1870** NOWLAND *Indianapolis* 50 Suspended by a rope (fastened to the rib-pole above), hung a thing that looked something in shape like the bow of a base viol.

Ricaree ˈrɪkəˌri, *n.* =**Arikara.** Also attrib.

1817 in *Mo. Hist. Soc. Col.* III. (1940) 383 The Ricarees and the Mandans the Gros-ventres and the Assiniboins find themselves near the establishment of Lord Selkirk. **1828** *Central Watchtower* (Harrodsburg, Ky.) 1 March 1/3 It is remarkable, that a party of the Rickaree Indians, . . . in their late attack on a party of the Missouri Fur Company, . . . were armed, as General Ashley tells us, with 'London Fuzils.' **1868** HENRY A. BOLLER *Among Indians* 33 The Riccarees were savage-looking Indians, and more sullen and insolent than any we had yet met.

***rice,** *n.*

1. =**wild rice.**

1778 CARVER *Travels* 523 [The Indians place] their canoes close to the bunches of rice, in such position as to receive the grain when it falls. **1820** in *Wis. Hist. Coll.* VII. 199 The Indians around Sandy Lake, in the month of September, repair to Rice Lake to gather their rice. **1876** *Ib.* 266 Madam [an Indian woman] with the pole, forces the canoe slowly into the standing rice. **1950** *Chi. Tribune* 18 March 10/3 New rice will stir in the lake's dark bed And one more spring be born.

2. In combs.: (1) **rice barrel,** a barrel for rice; (2) **bird,** (*a*) any one of various small birds that frequent rice fields, esp. the bobolink, (*b*) (*cap.*) a nickname for an inhabitant of a rice region, esp. a South Carolinian; (3) **bunting,** =**bobolink;** (4) **coal,** *local,* anthracite coal sufficiently small to pass through $\frac{1}{4}$ in. round mesh; (5) ***corn,** a variety of Indian corn having grains somewhat resembling rice; (6) **cut-grass,** a marsh grass, *Leersia oryzoides,* having grains resembling rice grains, also **rice-like cut-grass;** (7) **mill,** a mill for removing the husk from rough rice; (8) **plantation,** a plantation devoted to the cultivation of rice; (9) **planter,** (*a*) the owner of a rice plantation, (*b*) (see quot.); (10) **rat,** (see quot. 1891); (11) **shell,** (see quot.); (12) **swamp,** a low swampy area, covered usu. or periodically with water, on which rice is or can be grown; (13) **thrasher,** a machine for thrashing rice.

(1) *c***1728** CATESBY *Carolina* I. 38 Of the Saplings, or young trees are made the best Hoops for Tobacco, Rice, and Tar Barrels. **1853** SIMMS *Sword & Distaff* (1854) 277 He rolled over a pile of rice barrels. — **(2)** (*a*) *c***1728** CATESBY *Carolina* I. 14 The Rice-Bird . . . [is] esteemed in Carolina the greatest delicacy of all other Birds. **1949** *Sat. Ev. Post* 30 April 43/2 Her gustatory experiences have included beaver, buffalo, muskrat . . . , horse meat and tiny ricebirds spitted whole and eaten in a single mouthful. (*b*) **1777** *Md. Journal* 9 Dec. (Th.), Next comes in Sir H——y Cl——ton, . . . And swore he'd make the rice-birds think on. **1869** *Overland Mo.* III. 128 For a very obvious reason, the South Carolinians are called 'Rice-birds.' — **(3)** **1783** LATHAM *Gen. Synopsis Birds* II. 188 Rice B[unting], *Emberiza oryzivora.* **1857** *Rep. Comm. Patents 1856: Agric.* 127 The 'Meadow Bird,' in Louisiana, the 'Reed Bird,' in Pennsylvania, the 'Rice-Bunting,' in the Carolinas, and the 'Bob-o-link,' in New York, and thence eastward, are all the same. — **(4)** **1934** WEBSTER. **1949** *Retail Coalman* Oct. 19/2 Effective October 1, Old Company's anthracite prices become $12.50 per ton for egg, stove and chestnut; $10.00 for pea; $7.25 for buckwheat; $6.25 for rice; and $4.65 for barley.

(5) **1849** EMMONS *Agric. N.Y.* II. 265 Rice corn . . . is used principally for popping. **1851** J. F. W. JOHNSTON *Notes N. Amer.* I. 152 In some the horny part is large, as in the varieties known by the names of brown, Canada, rice, and pop corns. **1938** DAMON *Grandma* 168 It must be 'rice' corn: the sharp spikes made shelling painful, but the flavor was esteemed better. — **(6)** **1857** GRAY *Botany* 540 Rice Cutgrass. . . . Wet places; common. [**1901** MOHR *Plant Life Ala.* 363 *Homalocenchrus oryzoides.* . . . Rice-like cutgrass . . . [grows] all over the State.] **1948** *Iowa State Coll. Jrnl. Science* Oct. 106 *Leersia* (rice cutgrass), *Glyceria* (mann grass), and *Ranunculus* (crowfoot) . . . are typical of the wet-meadow stage. — **(7)** **1775** SCHAW *Jrnl. of a Lady of Quality* (1923) 148 We stayed all the forenoon with him, saw his rice mills, his indigo works and timber mills [in N. Car.]. **1888** BILLINGS *Hardtack* 406 The [signal] station was built on the top of a rice-mill. **1905** JOHNSON *Highways* 275 Into this mortar or 'rice mill' the rice was put, and then was crushed with a wooden pestle. — **(8)** **1732** in *Amer. Sp.* XX. (1945) 274 It is well judged to admit, that only the Tobacco and Rice Plantations require negroes of all the Northern Colonies. **1843** *Knickerb.* XXI. 223 On the rice plantations however it is not so. **1947** *Chr. Sci. Monitor* 24 Jan. 5/6 Brookgreen, which combines parts of four old rice plantations along the Waccamaw River, was dedicated in 1932. — **(9)** (*a*) **1766** in *Amer. Sp.* XX. (1945) 274 Resolution of rice planters. **1856** OLMSTED *Slave States* 409, I left town yesterday . . . with a letter in my pocket to Mr. X., a rice-planter. **1949** MURRAY *This Our Land* 74 With favorable prices, and slave labor comparatively cheap, quite a few rice planters piled up large fortunes. (*b*) **1876** KNIGHT 1938/1 *Rice-planter*, . . . an implement for sowing rice.

(10) **1891** *Cent.* 5166/3 Rice-field mouse, an American sigmodont murine rodent, the rice-rat, *Hesperomys (Oryzomys) palustris*, abounding in the rice-fields of the southern United States. **1947** HANDLEY & PATTON *Wild Mammals of Va.* 50 In the salt and brackish marshes along the bays and rivers of the eastern portion of the State the rice rat is a common species. — **(11)** **1838** AUDUBON *Ornith. Biog.* IV. 33 Those beautiful shells [in Florida], which, on account of their resemblance to grains of rice, are commonly named rice-shells. — **(12)** **1731** in *Pa. Gaz.* 29 April–6 May 2/2 These Rice Swamps are flat low Grounds, by the Sides of Rivers or Runs. **1884** F. Y. HEDLEY *Marching through Ga.* (1890) 325 The only route was a narrow causeway built up through the rice swamp. — **(13)** **1848** *De Bow's Review* VI. 133 Rice Thrashers [are shown].

b. In other combs. pertaining to wild rice, as (1) **rice bed,** (2) **eater,** (3) **lake,** (see quots.).

(1) **1852** MOODIE *Roughing It* 94 There's a big buck feeding on the rice-bed near the island. — **(2)** **1839** C. F. HOFFMAN *Wild Scenes* I. 138 Some, from the fairness of her complexion, insisted that she must belong to the Rice-eaters (Menomonés), or White Indians of the north, who dwell near the country of the Long-knives. — **(3)** **1820** in *Wis. Hist. Coll.* VII. 199 The Indians around Sandy Lake, in the month of September, repair to Rice Lake to gather their rice. **1856** *Spirit of Times* 13 Sep. 25/1 Its migration extends so far north as to Hudson's Bay, where, and in the innumerable rice lakes of the northwest, are its principal breeding places.

c. Designating foods prepared chiefly of rice, as (1) **rice battercake,** (2) **custard,** (3) **waffle.**

(1) **1868** BAKER *New Timothy* (1870) 40 Now Miss Loo had eaten almost nothing since dinner, and there were rice batter-cakes for supper. — **(2)** **1828** MRS. BASIL HALL *Aristocratic Journey* (1931) 221 A most admirable dinner . . . boiled turkey, roast chicken, asparagus, pease, potatoes, rice custard, and sweetmeats all admirably dressed and nicely served. **1846** *Knickerb.* XXVII. 552 A composition of butter, rice, and milk, dignified with the name of 'rice-custard.' — **(3)** **1845** SIMMS *Wigwam & Cabin* 2 Ser. 99 We had enjoyed all the warm comforts of hot rice-waffles, journey-cake, and glowing biscuit. **1887** *Cent. Mag.* Nov. 16/2 Little darkies . . . [were] supporting plates of hot batter-cakes, muffins, Sally Lunns, rice waffles.

As the last term in **ant, Canada, Carolina, clammy, covered, creole, Indian, mountain, Tennessee, upland, water, wild rice.**

ricer 'raɪsɚ, *n.* A small press in which cooked potatoes, fruits, etc., are forced through perforations of the diameter, approximately, of a grain of rice. — **1896** *Columbus* (O.) *Dispatch* 21 Nov. 11 Cook one quart of blanched chestnuts in boiling stock till tender, press them through a ricer [etc.]. **1936** *Sears Cat.* 655/1 Potato Ricer Removable heavy retinned seamless bowl . . . 26c.

* **rich,** *a.*

1. richroot, the root of some now unidentifiable plant. *Obs.*

1698 *Phil. Trans.* XX. 403 Mr. Fisher, a Friend of mine, brought me this Root from Potoxen River in Maryland, and he tells me, they there call it, Rich-Root, and use it as a specifick against the Scurvy.

2. richweed, any one of various American plants, as the bugbane, *Cimicifuga racemosa*, horse balm, *Collinsonia canadensis*, and the white snakeroot, *Eupatorium urticaefolium.*

1762 CLAYTON *Flora Virginia* 79 *Actæa racemis longissimis.* . . . *Nostratibus* Rich-weed & *aliquibus* Black-Snake-root. **1804** CLARK in *Lewis & C. Exped.* I. (1904) 79 In those small Praries or Glades I saw wild Timothy, lambs-quarter, Cuckle burs, & rich weed. **1859** BARTLETT 452 *Stone-Root*, (*Collinsonia Canadensis*,) a plant used in medicine. . . . It is also called Rich Weed. **1894** *Amer. Folk-Lore* VII. 92 *Eupatorium ageratoides*, richweed. Banner Elk, N.C.

For *to strike it rich* see ***strike,** *v.*

Richardson ground squirrel. A spermophile, *Citellus richardsoni*, found from Minnesota to Montana and Nevada, so named for Sir John Richardson, who first collected specimens in 1822. — **1938** THOMPSON *High Trails* 83 The Richardson ground squirrel, a brownish gray, is common all over the prairie. **1941** SETON *Trail of Artist-Naturalist* 189 The Richardson or yellow ground squirrel . . . nests in colonies like those of the prairie dog.

Rickettsia rɪ'kɛtsɪə, *n.* [f. H. T. *Ricketts* (1871–1910) Amer. pathologist.] A genus of bacteria-like organisms which cause certain diseases, as Rocky Mountain spotted fever; also (not *cap.*) an organism of this genus.

1921 *Jrnl. Amer. Med. Assoc.* 17 Dec. 1968/1 The same Rickettsia-like bodies were isolated from the blood, brain and kidneys of guinea-pigs suffering from the experimental disease induced by this Polish virus. **1948** *Hygeia* Jan. 19/1 The laboratory reported they had found rickettsia in the blood of one of the patients. **1949** *Time* 7 Nov. 75/1 Like Chloromycetin, it deals with many of the rickettsias.

Hence **rickettsial,** *a.*

1949 *Time* 14 March 99/1 Aureomycin has been successful against many rickettsial and virus-like diseases: Q-fever, rickettsial pox, parrot fever, typhus fever.

rickey 'rɪkɪ, *n.* [Said to be f. a personal name.] A drink consisting of the juice of a lime pressed into spirituous liquor to which carbonated water has been added. Cf. **gin rickey, Scotch rickey.** — **1911** *Chi. D. News* 16 Sep. 28/2 Bertrand soon knew the difference between a Rickey and a Sour. **1945** MENCKEN *Supp.* I. 254 The addition of sugar converts a *rickey* into a Tom Collins.

rickrack 'rɪkˌræk, *n.*[1] [Reduplication of **rack*, to stretch.] A kind of trimming made of serpentine braid. Also attrib.

1884 RITTENHOUSE *Maud* 326 Splendid sempstress—clothes nearly all done—Rickrack and featheredge on the moon. **1910** C. HARRIS *Eve's Husband* 279 Poor Adam had lived for years with a wife who wore rick-rack braid on her petticoats because it was durable. **1944** CLARK *Pills* 200 Lace and rickrack were in constant demand.

rickrack 'rɪkˌræk, *n.*[2] [Echoic.] The rhythmic noise of oars in the oarlocks. *Rare.* — **1888** DORSEY *Midshipman Bob* 193 He had never heard such sweet music in his life as the 'rick-rack, rick-rack' of the oars in the thole-pins.

ricos 'rikoz, *n. pl. S.W.* [Sp. in same sense.] Those of wealth, the rich.

1874 J. WEBB *Memoirs* 43 The Pinos and Ortizes were considered the 'ricos' and those most respectable leaders in society and political influence. **1865** *Wkly. New Mexican* 3 Feb. 2/2 These Indians were Navajoes, and of the *ricos.* **1949** MCWILLIAMS *No. from Mexico* 75 By comparison with the *pobres*, the *ricos* made the transition to American rule with comparative ease.

riddle land. (See quot.) *Obs.* — **1818** T. PICKERING in *Mass. Spy* 14 Oct., And what is riddle land? That which is of so open and loose a texture as to let the rain falling on it pass through it.

***ride,** *n.* As the last term in **black, boat, buckboard, buggy, cradle, fire, hay, joy, out, rail, sleigh, sleighing, straw ride.**

* **ride,** *v.* [In sense **1.** f. Du. *rijden*, regularly so used.]

1. *tr.* To convey or haul in a cart or other vehicle. *Obs.*

1687 in MUNSELL *Annals of Albany* II. 97 It is very requisite that there be fyre-wood rid to ye indian houses. **1692** *Ib.* 121 Ye sheriffe

. . . is required to see each trader ride a load of wood to the said house. **1778** *Mass. H.S. Coll.* 2 Ser. II. 443 Recd. two Waggoners to Ride wood. **1848** BARTLETT 276, I heard a witness in a court-room testify that he had '*rode* some hogs from the wharf to the store,' by which he meant that he carried a load of dead hogs on his cart. **1867** DE VOE *Market Ass't* 420, I have known instances where young *calves* have been taken from the *cow* in the morning, rode some fifteen or twenty miles through a hot sun to the market-boats or railroad station.

2. (See quot.) *Slang. Obs.*

1851 HALL *College Words* 162 Hobbies are used by some students in translating Latin, Greek, and other languages, who from this reason are said to ride, in contradistinction to others who learn their lessons by study, who are said to *dig* or *grub*.

3. (See quot.)

1893 ROOSEVELT *Wilderness Hunter* 216 If the tree is too tall it [*sc.* the moose] 'rides' it, that is straddles the slender trunk with its fore legs, pushing it over and walking up it until the desired branches are within reach.

4. In phrases: (1) *To ride (the) fence*, etc., (*a*) in the West, to ride regularly along the fence around a cattle ranch to inspect and keep it in order, cf. ***fence, *n.* 3.** (14), (*b*) to fail to take a positive stand on a matter, cf. ***fence, *n.* 2. b.** (3); (2) *to ride a state*, to canvass or cover a state in the interests of a political candidate or campaign; (3) *to ride (on) trail, W.* (see quot. 1882); (4) *to ride a line, W.* to ride a prescribed boundary to prevent cattle from straying beyond it; (5) **to ride the waves*, (see quot.); (6) *to ride a log*, (see quot.); (7) *to ride mail*, to carry the mail; (8) *to ride one's luck*, to trust to one's luck, *slang;* (9) *to ride herd (on)*, see ***herd, *n.* b.** (3); (10) *to ride a saw*, in using a crosscut saw with another, to bear down on the saw on the going away or thrusting stroke, *colloq.;* (11) *to ride* (someone) *a bug hunting*, to take to task severely, *colloq.;* (12) *to ride (on) a rail*, see ***rail, *n.***

(1) (*a*) **1881** CHASE *Editor's Run in N. Mex.* 49 Mr. Chase . . . has general supervision, with a boss on each ranch, to attend to all details, such as hiring the necessary help to 'ride the fences.' **1949** *This Week Mag.* 9 April 19/2 He roped and branded an' rode fence lines. (*b*) **1948** *Capital-Democrat* (Tishomingo, Okla.) 3 June 6/6, I am not going to ride the fence on any issue. — (2) **1882** *Narragansett Hist. Reg.* I. 292 He was a strong 'Governor Fenner man,' and rode the State in his behalf. — (3) **1882** BAILLIE-GROHMAN *Camps in Rockies* 347 The process of driving cattle is called 'riding on trail,' one of the most laborious and dreary undertakings imaginable. **1902** WISTER *Virginian* ix, All spring he had ridden trail, worked at ditches during summer. [**1947** *Newsweek* 21 April 61/1 A lone cowboy, riding a trail along the edge of an arroyo . . . came upon a mass of huge bones.] — (4) **1888** ROOSEVELT in *Cent. Mag.* March 669/1 Even for those who do not have to look up stray horses, and who are not forced to ride the line . . . there is apt to be some hardship. **1942** DALE *Cow Country* 117 In its larger aspects it included driving trail herds, joining in the roundup, branding calves or beef animals, and 'riding a line.'

(5) **1897** *Outing* XXX. 134/2 We had that most delightful experience which some ingenious wheelman has called 'riding the waves.' The fine dirt road . . . led over a succession of short hills, the down slopes of which were steep enough to carry one up the next ascent. — (6) **1905** *Forestry Bureau Bul.* No. 61, 44 *Ride a log, to*, to stand on a floating log. — (7) **1910** RAINE *B. O'Connor* 14 He was riding mail between Aravaipa and Mesa. — (8) **1907** LONDON *Road* 218 He was riding his luck, and with each pass the total stake doubled.

(10) **1924** SHEPHERD *P. Bunyan* 103 He didn't care who pulled the other end, and he didn't care if they'd ride the saw, he said, if they felt like it, but what he didn't want was for 'em to drag their feet—he drawed the line on that. — (11) **1934** VINES *Green Thicket World* 138 Greenberry did something that might have made Naomi ask God to ride him a bug hunting.

***rider,** *n.*

1. One who carries news, dispatches, letters, etc., over a given route. *Obs.*

1738 *Va. Gazette* 28 April, Riders are engag'd so conveniently, that no Post-Horse is to cross Potowmak or Susquehanna. **1788** FRANKLIN *Autobiog.* 352, I was satisfy'd without retaliating his refusal, while postmaster, to permit my papers being carried by riders.

2. (See quot.) *Obs.*

1767 *Doc. Col. Hist. N.Y.* VII. 937 Reservations were made of particular Lots under the names of some members of the Council and public officers. . . . These shares have been distinguished among the Inhabitants of that part of the Country by the name of Riders.

3. In a Virginia rail fence, the top rail, placed in a crotch of crossed stakes or rails at each fence corner.

1789 ANBUREY *Travels* II. 323 Above these stakes is placed a rail of double the size of the others, which is termed the rider, which, in a manner, locks up the whole, and keeps the fence firm and steady. **1903** FOX *Little Shepherd* xxx, The worm fences had lost their riders and were broken down here and there. **1944** *Harper's Mag.* March 375/1 Or he'd say, 'George, I want you to put new riders on the fence,' and George would say, 'I'll ride you, old man, that's what I'll do.'

4. **=circuit rider.** *Colloq.*

1884 CRADDOCK *Tenn. Mts.* 15 The rider says there's some holp in prayer. *Ib.* 143 All them Peels . . . war gone down ter the Settlemint ter hear the rider preach.

5. One experienced in the work done on horseback on a cattle ranch.

1888 *Cent. Mag.* Feb. 502/2, I had with my wagon a Pueblo Indian, an excellent rider and roper, but a drunken, worthless, lazy devil. **1894** *McClure's Mag.* July 101/1 The cowboys or 'riders' of each ranch cut out the cows of its brand. **1930** *Denver Post* 22 Jan. II. 9/3 When I sent the riders out, I told them we would bunch the cattle at the crossing on Troublesome [Creek].

As the last term in **black, bog, circle, circuit, ditch, fence, line, mail, night, out, pony, pony express, post, range, rough, Royal, saddle, sign, sleigh, swing, tail, trail rider.**

rider ˈraɪdɚ, *v. tr.* To strengthen (a rail fence) with riders. Also **ridered,** *a.*

1760 WASHINGTON *Diaries* I. 155 Good part of my New Fencing that was not Ridered was leveld. **1858** WARDER *Hedges & Evergreens* 151 In Delaware . . . worm-fences, not ridered, were to be five feet high. **1946** [see **staked and ridered (b)**].

***ridge,** *n.* In combs.: (1) **ridgeback,** a razorback hog, *colloq., obs.;* (2) ***board,** the highest part of a divide or watershed, *rare;* (3) **buster,** a plow for opening ridges, *colloq.;* (4) **path,** (see quot.); (5) ***pole,** the crest of a mountain range, *rare;* (6) **pole pine, =lodgepole pine;** (7) **prairie,** (see quot.), *obs.;* (8) **road,** a road along the crest of a ridge; (9) **runner,** a hillbilly, hayseed, rustic, *colloq.*

(1) **1872** *Harper's Mag.* April 663/2 She told me it was a 'ridgeback'—a 'jumping alligator,' a 'sub-soiler.' — (2) **1869** W. MURRAY *Adventures* 10 [The] ridge-board of the vast water-shed . . . slopes northward to the St. Lawrence. — (3) **1931** *Walters* (Okla.) *Herald* 19 Feb. 6/4 (*advt.*), Farm Implements 1 1-row ridge buster. — (4) **1849** PARKMAN *Ore. Trail* (1944) 271 And a smaller trail, known as 'the Ridge-path,' leads directly across the prairie from point to point.

(5) **1788** MAY *Jrnl. & Lett.* 29 [We] began to ascend Alleghana. . . . At ten o'clock we were on the ridge-pole. — (6) **1885** ROOSEVELT in *Cent. Mag.* June 225/2 The forest was composed mainly of what are called ridge-pole pines, which grow close together, and do not branch off until the stems are thirty or forty feet from the ground. — (7) **1882** *Econ. Geol. Illinois* II. 73 The prairies are therefore of two classes—those that are a little elevated and rather level near the lower course of the streams, and more elevated and rolling prairies on the higher ridges. The latter are the so-called 'ridge prairies.' — (8) **1817** *N. Amer. Rev.* IV. 185, I have returned by the ridge road. **1886** LOGAN *Great Conspiracy* 305 And what can that purpose be, but to throw his augmented right . . . along the ridge-road, upon Centreville? [**1945** *Democrat* 3 May 1/6 The hailstorm seems to have done its greatest damage along the old Indian Ridge road, from Cedar Fork Church on the south to the region of Gosport on the north and east.] — (9) **1931** *K.C. Times* 10 Sep. (*heading*), Just Ridge Runners. **1943** *Nat. Geog. Mag.* May 596/1 They want to stalk us 'ridge runners' to see us scald a hog, or weave a rag carpet, or get baptized.

As the last term in **beech, cane, chestnut, dividing, flint, Indian, mountain, oak, pine, post oak, prairie ridge.**

***riding,** *n.* and *a.*

1. Designating agricultural implements upon which the operators ride. Cf. **buggy cultivator.**

1868 *Iowa State Agric. Soc. Rep. 1867* 151 Not many riding cornplanters are in use. *Ib.* 156 The corn . . . is cultivated according to the fancy of the farmers; some with shovel & some with barshear plows & others use the riding cultivator. **1901** *World's Work* May 720/1 Corn is planted and fertilized with the aid of special machinery, worked with a 'riding' cultivator, and cut by horse-power. **1924** CROY *R.F.D. No. 3* 24 The farmers tried to make up for it with increased machinery—riding plows, tractors, headers, trucks. **1948** *Democrat* 7 Oct. 8/2 For Sale . . . one International riding cultivator, in good shape.

2. In special combs.: (1) **riding carriage,** a vehicle in which persons ride, *obs.;* (2) **mule,** a mule suitable for riding; (3) **page,** a page who rides in the discharge of his duties; (4) ∗**place,** a fording place on a stream; (5) **postmaster,** a postmaster who carries mail on a horse, *obs.;* (6) **rock,** (see quot.), *obs.;* (7) **twice,** (see quot.), *obs.*

(1) 1792 BELKNAP *Hist. New-Hampshire* III. 117 White ash . . . serves for the frames of . . . riding carriages. **1796** *Ann. 4th Congress* 2 Sess. 2685 On every four-wheel riding carriage except phaetons and stage wagons, [is a tax of] six shillings per wheel. — **(2) 1846** in *Calif. Hist. Soc. Quart.* XXI. 217 My riding mule was the most refractory of all. **1849** in *Wagons West* (c1930) 102 Many from this place [St. Joseph] & Independence are going with Pack mules . . . most of them will start soon & pack feed on their riding mules. — **(3) 1880** LAMPHERE *U.S. Govt.* 24/1 [There are employed] for the Senate Chamber; 3 riding pages, and 1 page for the office of the Secretary. — **(4) 1679** *Conn. Rec.* 27 We went to the river . . . to the old rideing place. **1730** HEMPSTEAD *Diary* 219 Wee made a fence of Brush & poles & Thorn Trees to Stop the Riding place next Packer farm.

(5) 1737 *Pa. Gazette* 27 Oct., Henry Pratt is appointed Riding Postmaster for all the stages between Philadelphia and Newport in Virginia. — **(6) 1859** BARTLETT 365 *Riding rock,* a conspicuous rock at a ford, used to show the depth of the water and the safety of crossings. — **(7) 1843** CARLTON *New Purchase* I. 137 Many horses indeed have two riders, a mode of horsemanship called in the Purchase 'riding twice.'

As the last term in **black, bog, circle, circuit, fence, line, log, night, out, rail, sign, sleigh riding.**

∗**riffle,** *n.* [This word in sense **1.** may be a variant of earlier ∗**ripple.** Lambert records Pa. G. *riffel,* meaning riffle, ripple. See note *s.v.* **whiffet,** *n.*[1]]

1. A shoal, reef, or rocky obstruction in a river or a piece of shallow, rapid, or broken water caused by this.

1792 in *Amer. Sp.* XV. 383 Thence . . . to a hickory by a Riffle in the river. **1804** CLARK in *Lewis & C. Exped.* I. (1904) 205 [We] passed a very bad riffle of rocks in the evening. **1904** *Recreation* (N.Y.) April 288/1 The fish was darting here and there, now in deep water, then in shallow, now splashing on the riffles, then doubling on his trail like a hunted whitetail. **1948** *Sat. Ev. Post* 23 Oct. 36/2 In the lingo of our Rogue River guides, a riffle is anything between a foaming cataract and white-water rapids heavily sprinkled with boulders.

b. *To make the* (or *a*) *riffle,* to cross a riffle or rapid, to succeed in an undertaking. *Colloq.*

1857 *Phoenix* (Sacramento) 13 Sep. 3/3 He could not make the 'riffle.' **1875** *Atlantic Mo.* May 557 If I can make a riffle I want to git to Washington Territory yet. **1911** SAUNDERS *Col. Todhunter* 19, I'll try if I can make the riffle. **1950** *Dly. Ardmoreite* (Ardmore, Okla.) 14 Feb. 8/1 [The] Rexroat girls [were] doing their best trying to win first in the basketball tournament but they couldn't quite make the riffle.

2. *Mining.* A bar, slat, or other obstruction placed across the bottom of a sluice box or other gold-washing apparatus to arrest particles of gold.

1850 KINGSLEY *Diary* 120 Finished the riffles to the machine today. **1910** J. HART *Vigilante Girl* 51 Sometimes the riffles would be clogged with coarse gold. **1948** JOHNSTON *Gold Rush* 57/1 The yellow metal sank to the bottom and lodged in the riffles.

attrib. **1857** *Hutchings Mag.* July 5/1 As often as is necessary, the apron, riffle-bars, and bottom are cleaned of the sand and gold that has concentrated upon them. **1876** RAYMOND *8th Rep. Mines* 349 About one-half of the ore going though the mill is saved by means of riffle-sluices. **1882** *47th Congress* 1 Sess. H.R. Ex. Doc. No. 216, 570 The dry earth, sand, or gravel . . . falls on the adjustable riffle board . . . the finer particles of dirt and dust being thrown away by the current behind before falling on the riffle-bed. **1883** KNIGHT *Supp.* 824/2 *Sluices,* . . . boxes joined together, set with riffle blocks, through which is washed auriferous earth.

b. riffle box, a cradle or boxlike contrivance having riffles or obstructions along the bottom for catching particles of gold.

1850 A. T. JACKSON *Forty-Niner* (1920) 38 We caught an Indian cleaning up our riffle box Saturday night. **1889** MUNROE *Golden Days* 110 [A Long Tom] is simply a long trough ending in a 'riffle box.' **1948** *This Week Mag.* 10 July 20/1 Water was brought . . . and poured over riffle-boxes which were rocked back and forth by hand.

3. (See quot.)

1890 *Cent.* 5174/2 *Riffle,* . . . a piece of plank placed transversely in, and fastened to the bottom of, a fish-ladder.

∗**riffle,** *v. tr.* To ruffle in a slight or rippling manner. — *a***1904** S. E. WHITE *Blazed Trail Stories* vii. 118 The breeze and sun played with the prairie grasses, the breeze riffling them over. **1926** *Ladies' Home Jrnl.* Nov. 228 Even the wail of music from the Palace of Dance barely riffled his preoccupation.

∗**riffler,** *n.* =**riffle box.** Also **riffler box.** *Obs.* — **1839** *Amer. R.R. Jrnl.* 15 Feb. 98 Across the bottom of this lowest trough, bars are placed dividing the 'riffler,' as it is called, into different apartments. **1850** KINGSLEY *Diary* 122 Made a panning trough to pour quicksilver from the riffler into and fix the pump. *Ib.* 137 It requires great care in making both these and the riffler boxes in order to have them hold quicksilver.

riffling ˈrɪflɪŋ, *a.* Forming a riffle or rapid. — **1754** *N. Eng. Hist. & Gen. Reg.* XXII. 408 The navigation to Norridgewalk is considerably difficult by reason of the rapidity of the stream, and riffling falls. **1911** J. F. WILSON *Land Claimers* ix. 123 She . . . heaved her catch up out of the grip of the riffling water.

∗**rifle,** *n.*

1. A firearm the barrel of which is grooved to insure greater accuracy and penetration for the bullet.

From present evidence this term app. arose among those German gunsmiths in Pa. who first made rifles. Some such German word as *riffel,* groove (in a rifle) may be the source of the word in sense **1.**

1772 D. TAIT in *Travels Amer. Col.* 537 Others took the Cock off his rifle and Sixteen carrots of Tobacco. **1775** J. ADAMS in *Familiar Lett.* (1876) 65 They [i.e., Congress] have voted ten companies of riflemen to be sent from Pennsylvania, Maryland, and Virginia, to join the army before Boston. These are an excellent species of light infantry. They use a peculiar kind of musket, called a rifle. **1809** WEEMS *Marion* (1833) 75 O! that we had been there to aid with our rifles, then should many of those monsters have bit the ground. **1947** *Newsweek* 24 Feb. 57/3 [He] killed a wildcat with a high-speed .22-caliber rifle.

b. A rifled pistol. *Rare.*

*c***1852** in STOWE *Key* 175/1 A man told me . . . he would shoot me, and pulled a 'rifle' out of his pocket and showed it to me.

2. A cannon the barrel of which is rifled.

1885 *Cent. Mag.* March 740 Her battery . . . consisted of two seven-inch rifles. **1898** *Scientific Amer. Supp.* XLV. 16/1 A battery of six 6-inch rifles, two being carried in sponsons on the gun deck on each broadside.

3. In obs. combs.: (1) ∗**rifle club,** in the South after the Civil War, an organization ostensibly for rifle practice but really for the overthrow of the carpetbag regime; (2) **coat,** =**rifle frock;** (3) **cracker,** a rifleman; (4) **doctor,** one who pretends to bewitch a rifle, *rare;* (5) **dress,** =**rifle frock;** (6) **frock,** a long, loose-fitting shirt or blouse worn by a rifleman, cf. **hunting shirt;** (7) **frolic,** (see quot. 1775), also (*cap.*) as the title of a painting by Gayle P. Hoskins (1887——); (8) **gun,** =**rifle 1;** (9) **man,** a soldier armed with a rifle rather than with a musket; (10) **match,** a match or contest in rifle-shooting; (11) **pan,** *transf.* a rifle; (12) **picker,** =∗**prick;** (13) **pistol,** a pistol having a rifled barrel; (14) **ranger,** a ranger armed with a rifle; (15) **rule,** rule by force, cf. **Beecher's Bible;** (16) **shirt,** =**hunting shirt,** also **rifle shirted,** *a.;* (17) **shoot,** =**rifle match;** (18) **whisky,** cheap or inferior whisky, cf. ∗**Minié rifle.**

(1) 1876 *Cong. Rec.* 9 Aug. 5347/1 They call themselves 'rifle clubs' and 'saber clubs.' We have them in every county in South Carolina and in some counties we have several. **1879** TOURGEE *Fool's Errand* 295 The Klan, and its more subtle and complete successors, under various and sundry names, 'Rifle-Clubs,' 'Sabre-Clubs,' 'Bulldozers,' and so forth, had fully established themselves throughout the country. — **(2) 1877** *Rep. Indian Affairs* 5 The coat [ought] to be in shape like the old fringed rifle-coat or blouse. — **(3) 1835** HOFFMAN *Winter* II. 165 Ah! There's my stout rifle-cracker. — **(4) 1843** R. CARLTON *New Purchase* xvii. 131 Let the rifle-doctor conceal in his hand a bullet small enough for the purpose.

(5) 1853 B. F. TAYLOR *Jan. & June* 207 You never wore a 'rifle dress.' — **(6) 1776** *Battle of Brooklyn* II. iii, Rifle guns and rifle frocks, will be as cheap in their camp tomorrow, as cod heads in New Foundland. **1823** COOPER *Pioneers* xxxiii, Having thrown a rifle frock over his shirt, . . . [a man] had issued from his retreat in the woods. — **(7) 1775** in A. TOMLINSON *Military Jrnls.* 77 We had a rifle frolick. [Note: 'Shooting at a mark, for liquor.'] **1949** *Chi. Tribune* 20 March (Grafic Mag.) 13/3 A companion picture to 'The Rifle Frolick,' also painted for Samworth, is entitled 'Trade from the Monongahela.' — **(8) 1747** in CHALKLEY *Scotch-Irish Settlement Va.* I. 529 They were robbed of . . . a rifle gun (double tricked). **1775** *Warren-Adams Lett.* I. 58 They do Execution with their Rifle Gun at an Amazing Distance. **1935** T. WILLIAMSON *Woods Colt* 50 Clint can remember the rifle-gun's been hangin' up there on its two pegs, along with the bullet pouch an' the powder horn that goes with it. — **(9) 1775** *Remembrancer* I. 132/1 The Congress have ordered one thousand more markesmen, or, as we call them, riflemen, to be raised. **1830** *Mechanics' Press* (Utica, N.Y.) 10 April 172/1 Our unlucky rifleman, gained the trunk of a large tree, around which he continued to retreat. **1946** *Sierra Club*

Bul. Dec. 36 Under this cover, riflemen spurted forward, tossed grenades through the doorway in the wall of the next tunnel.

(**10**) *c***1845** *Big Bear Ark.* 33 He was a general referee . . . whether it was a horse swap, a race, a rifle match, or a cock fight. **1880** MARK TWAIN *Tramp Abroad* 626 [German newspapers] contain . . . no information about . . . yachting-contests, rifle-matches, or other sporting matters of any sort. **1949** *Chi. Tribune* 2 March (Grafic Mag.) 13/1 It shows how a company of roistering backwoodsmen and others would have conducted a rifle match in the spring of 1775. — (**11**) **1827** COOPER *Prairie* xxiii, It is not every savage that carries . . . as good a rifle-pan as this old friend of mine. — (**12**) **1846** MCKENNEY *Memoirs* I. 74 He then pushed his rifle-picker through the hole. — (**13**) **1848** *Campaign Flag* (Maysville, Ky.) 18 Aug. 1/5 The blacks all had rifle pistols or six barrelled revolvers. **1883** MARK TWAIN *Life on Miss.* xxix, I rose and drew an elegant rifle pistol on him. — (**14**) [**1828** BERNHARD *Reise* I. 89 Die meisten Compagnien haben Infanteriegewehre mit Bajonetten nach englischen Modell, und nur die *riflemen rangers* haben *rifles* oder gezogene Buchsen.] **1835** *Harvardiana* II. 36 Washington is . . . petitioning first to scour the woods with his rifle rangers. **1853** *Harper's Mag.* Dec. 121/2 There was a battle on the 12th of September between the Appeyate Indians and a company of rifle rangers.

(**15**) **1857** T. H. GLADSTONE *Englishman in Kans.* 252 And that day, the 29th of November, 1854, the slaveholding interest, from which there is no appeal, achieved the first of its great bowie-knife victories, and witnessed the establishment of rifle-rule in Kansas. — (**16**) **1778** *Essex Inst. Coll.* XLIII. 9 Brown or some other kind of your own fabrick in Stead [is ordered] to make Rifle Shirts or Frocks principally. **1793** *Gazette of U.S.* 24 Aug. (Th.), '1520 Rifle Shirts' were advertised for, *inter alia*, by the Treasury Department. **1839** C. F. HOFFMAN *Wild Scenes* 30, I had heard of some of his feats before coming into this region, and expected of course to see one of those roystering, 'cavorting,' rifle-shirted blades that I have seen upon our western frontier. — (**17**) **1888** *Boston Jrnl.* 22 Dec. 1/8 On Christmas morning there will be a rifle-shoot at Cider Mill Pond Range. **1892** *Boston Chron.* 26 Nov. 1/5 Rifle Shoot. Thanksgiving Practice by Company B, First Regiment. — (**18**) **1856** *Louisville Courier* 8 Nov. 2/6 They supplied them with rifle whisky gratis. **1863** E. KIRKE *Southern Friends* iii. 49 Thirsty natives, imbibing certain fluids known at the South as blue ruin, bust-head, red-eye, tangle-foot, rifle-whiskey, and devil's dye.

As the last term in **air, cat-and-rat, Deckhard, eight square, hunting, Kentuck, Kentucky, Maynard, Mississippi, Missouri, muzzle-loading, pea, revolving, sixteen-shooter, squirrel, Whitney's, Winchester (repeating) rifle.**

rifler ˈraɪflɚ, *n.* A rifleman. *Obs.* — **1775** *Amer. Hist. Rev.* VI. 318 Dr. Appleton abroad p.m. saw 120 Riflers f'm Maryland on their March to the Camp. **1807** BARLOW *Columbiad* 195 Morgan in front of his bold riflers towers.

riflist ˈraɪflɪst, *n.* A rifleman. *Obs.* — **1883** SWEET & KNOX *Through Texas* 580, I am going to have the figure on the monument represent an Alamo riflist in full uniform.

rift rɪft, *n.* [App. f. **riff*, an obs. var. of **reef*.] **1.** A barrier or obstruction in a stream, or a fall or rapid caused by this. Also **riftling. 2.** The wash of the surf on a beach or shore. **3. rift timber,** (see quot.).

(**1**) **1727** *Doc. Hist. N.Y. State* I. 459 The French . . . have no way but to come up from Montreal to the Lake against a Violent stream, all full of Rifts & Falls & Shallows. **1773** in *Amer. Sp.* XV. 383/2 West fifty six poles to a riftling in the Creek. **1879** *Scribner's Mo.* Nov. 21/1 In one hanging rift close by the bank. . . . I took at five casts fifteen fish. — (**2**) **1866** STEDMAN *Poetical Works* (1873) 238 Light falls her foot where the rift follows after. — (**3**) **1875** TEMPLE & SHELDON *Hist. Northfield, Mass.* 14 Oak, or rift timber, as it was called, i.e., timber that could be easily split into clap-boards and shingles, was the only kind thought to be fit for use for buildings and fences.

***rig,** *n.*

1. A vehicle, esp. one complete with its furnishings and the animals that draw it. *Colloq.*

1831 in *Mich. Hist. Mag.* XI. 472 Breakfast swallowed we stepped into our next rig. **1859** in *S.W. Hist. Ser.* XI. (1942) 99 Three Frenchmen . . . had a good wagon and two yoke of oxen. . . . They were very anxious to dispose of the whole 'rig.' **1917** FREEMAN & KINGSLEY *Alabaster Box* 53 The wagon-shed behind the Brookville House sheltered an unusual number of 'rigs.' **1946** WILSON *Fidelity* 68 A driver of a hired rig from the county seat could not hope to get back for a day or two.

transf. **1893** CUSHING *Story of P.O.* 358 The only vehicle he could procure was an ox team with a certain indescribable paraphernalia, called a 'rig,' attached to a so-called wagon.

2. A plant, outfit, equipment, etc., for a particular purpose, as the engine, derrick, etc., for sinking wells.

1845 *Niles' Reg.* 25 Oct. 128/3 The new rig works to a charm. **1885** *Santa Fe Wkly. New Mexican* 24 Sep. 2/4 He purchased for $1,800 the Dorifee ten-horse power artesian rig. **1949** *Dly. Ardmoreite* (Ardmore, Okla.) 4 Dec. 1/6 The rig was moved onto the lease to clean out the well, a producer in which the flow of oil had been clogged by formations of paraffin.

3. *W.* A saddle; riding equipment in general. Cf. **double rig(ged) saddle.**

1849 KINGSLEY *Diary* 41, I also saw a Spanish rig for horse riding which in part I think superior to ours. **1914** BOWER *Flying U Ranch* 14, I've noticed that a hoss never has any respect or admiration for a swell rig. **1944** ADAMS *W. Words* 128 rig Short name for saddle.

As the last term in **cat, dandy, double, hay, party, schooner, sea, well rig.**

Rigdonite ˈrɪgdənˌaɪt, *n.* (See quots.) *Obs.*

1845 *Warsaw* (Ill.) *Signal* 10 Feb. 3/5 Thefts from the Rigdonites are numerous as ever, notwithstanding the 400 police. **1847** HOWE *Hist. Coll. Ohio* 284 The Mormons . . . [are] now divided into three factions, viz.: the Rigdonites, the Twelveites, and the Strangites. The Rigdonites are the followers of Sidney Rigdon, and are but a few in number. **1890** *N. & Q.* V. 184/2 Sidney Rigdon's followers were or are called *Rigdonites.*

***rigging,** *n.*

1. The exterior leather trappings of a saddle.

1847 HENRY *Campaign Sk.* 25 For the first time had the pleasure of riding a mustang with complete though rude Mexican rigging. **1923** J. H. COOK *On Old Frontier* 112 The California rider used a center-fire or broad single cinch, hung center from the rigging of his saddle.

2. The equipment, apparatus, or outfit needed for a particular kind of work (see quot. 1905).

1849 THOREAU *Week on Concord* 68 They had teams with rigging such as is used to carry barrels. **1895** JEWETT *Life of Nancy* 244, I don't want to move my riggin' nowhere for the sake o' two trees. **1905** *Forestry Bureau Bul.* No. 61, 44 *Rigging*, the cables, blocks, and hooks used in skidding logs by steam power.

3. rigging loft, the place above the stage of a theater or the framework of beams from which the scenery is raised or lowered.

1870 O. LOGAN *Before Footlights* 95 Then there are men up in the rigging loft who attend to the flies and the curtain wheel. **1888** *Scribner's Mag.* Oct. 438 Looking upward from the floor of the stage, he would call them [the beams] the gridiron; standing on them, he would speak of them as the rigging-loft.

riggite ˈrɪgaɪt, *n.* (See quot.) *Rare.* — **1771** FRANKLIN *Autobiog.* 282 This, and my being esteem'd a pretty good riggite, that is, a jocular verbal satirist, supported my consequence in the society.

Riggs's disease. [f. J. M. *Riggs* (1810–85), Amer. dentist.] An inflammation of the sockets of the teeth, usu. resulting in loosening them. — **1900** MARK TWAIN *My Boyhood Dreams* (1928) 261 (R.), If you don't know what Rigg's Disease of the Teeth is, the dentist will tell you. **1936** G. V. BLACK *Operative Dentistry* IV. 55 For one thing, many dentists rebelled against this use of the term 'Riggs' disease' to indicate this condition.

***right,** *a., adv.,* and *n.*

1. *n.* In colonial times, an individual settler's portion of the land at the disposal of a town. *Obs.*

In quot. 1694 app. used also for a child or other dependent in whose behalf a claim to land was made.

1635 *Watertown Rec.* I. I. 2 No Foreainer . . . shall have any benefit either of Commonage, or Land undivided . . . except that they buy a man's right wholly in the Towne. **1686** *Plymouth Rec.* 185 To stand by them . . . to defend theire wrights of lands. **1694** *N.C. Col. Rec.* I. 415 Anne Stuart Senr proveth 6 rights. *Ib.* 393 Mr Tho Lepper has proved Ten rights whose names are as followeth. . . . Caleb Calloway enters ffoure Rights. **1756** *Essex Hist. Coll.* XLIII. 278 To be sold . . . also a Right of Land in Falmouth in Casco-Bay. **1794** S. WILLIAMS *Nat. Hist. Vt.* 337 In the grants of land that were made by him, there were three rights in each township reserved for religious purposes.

2. Short for **right field, right fielder.**

1867 *Ball Players' Chron.* 8 Aug. 6/3 The nine will be as follows: . . . Devyr, short; Waterman, left; Dick Hunt, center; Peters, right. **1949** *Telephone Reg.* (McMinnville, Ore.) 4 Aug. 2/1 Jimmy 'Whiskers' Beard then drove both in with a single to right.

3. In hunting, a bird which when flushed flies up on the fowler's right.

1874 LONG *Wild-Fowl* 179 The experienced sportsman will usually kill his 'right' and 'left' easily.

4. *a.* In the names of positions on an American football team.

1896 CAMP & DELAND *Football* 344 Instructions to Right End. . . . You should help the right tackle block his man. *Ib.* 345 Instructions to Right Half-Back. . . . You are responsible for the hole in this play. **1904** in P. H. DAVIS *Football* (1911) 446 Army vs. Yale. . . . Yale. . Right Guard, R. C. Tripp, '06.

5. *adv.* Straightway, at once. Cf. ***right up.**

1783 in *Amer. Hist. Rev.* (1872) I. 338/1, I should be glad I cood come Rite home with my slaves, for my vessel will not last to proceed farr. **1849** LONGFELLOW *Kavanagh* xxix, If you don't go right about your business, I will come down. **1901** *Munsey's Mag.* XXIV. 800/1 (*OED*), Yes, I'll be right down.

6. In special combs.: (1) **right along,** see ∗**along 2.** (4); (2) **bower,** see **bower;** (3) **field,** in baseball, that part of the outfield to the right of an observer at the home plate; (4) **fielder,** (*a*) a baseball player stationed in the right field, (*b*) a ball hit to the right field in baseball, *rare;* (5) **short,** formerly in baseball, a position behind the base line running from first to second base, occupied by a tenth player, but now played by the second baseman, also the player occupying this position, also **right shortfielder, right shortstop,** *obs.;* (6) **smart,** (*a*) a considerable amount, a good deal, (*b*) also attrib., a development from constructions (see quot. 1836) in which "smart" is sensibly an adj., *colloq.* [for **right smart chance,** see ∗**chance 1.**]; (7) ∗**up,** at once, right away, *colloq.*

(3) 1857 *Spirit of Times* 29 Aug. 404/3 Enterprise Club. Maxfield, catcher; . . . Davis, right field; Knight, second base. **1949** *News-Herald* (Marshfield, Wis.) 19 July 9/4 Corbett hit a change of pace pitch on a line into right field for the second Tomahawk hit. — **(4)** (*a*) **1867** *Ball Players' Chron.* 25 July 1/4 The right fielder was active at times, once making a very handsome stop. **1949** *Telephone Reg.* (McMinnville, Ore.) 4 Aug. 2/1 Sexton, Willamette right fielder, was a ball of fire at the bat, with four hits in five trips to the plate. (*b*) **1867** *Chi. Times* 26 July 5/2 Stearns then sent up a good right fielder, on which he got half way around.

(5) 1866 *Wilkes' Spirit of Times* 2 June 214/1 It being the first of a series to test the advantages of a right short-fielder in base-ball games. **1867** *Ball Players' Chron.* 11 July 2/3 Smith struck a grounder to right short. **1867** CHADWICK *Base Ball Reference* 84 [Let] the second baseman play at right short. **1886** CHADWICK *Art of Pitching* 86 [The second baseman] is required to cover second base and to play 'right short stop.' — **(6)** (*a*) **1842** BUCKINGHAM *Slave States* II. 327, I asked here, whether the people made much maple-sugar in this neighbourhood; when the gentlemen . . . answered, 'Yes, they do, I reckon, right smart.' **1949** NORDYKE *Cattle Empire* 81 Heard a right smart about you, Pincham. (*b*) **1836** DUNLAP *Mem. Water Drinker* (1837) I. 80 His father is building a right smart house for him. **1865** KELLOGG *Rebel Prisons* 395 There is a right smart heap of Sherman's men coming down through here. — **(7) 1833** A. FERGUSSON *Notes* 229 A steward or a cabin-boy . . . assures you that he is going *right up* or *right off* to do your errand. **1844** *Knickerb.* XXIII. 100 His first thought doubtless would be for an omnibus 'right up.'

b. In phrases: (1) *right in the woods,* (see quot. 1784); (2) ∗*right of way,* (*a*) the right to construct a railroad, *rare,* (*b*) a strip of land along which a road, esp. a railroad, is built, (*c*) designating a man who surveys or opens up a right of way; (3) *right off the reel,* at once, directly, *colloq.;* (4) *right of pre-emption,* see ∗**pre-emption.**

(1) 1784 SMYTH *Tour* I. 144 In some parts [of N.C.], each person, in possession of a plantation, has what is called a right in the woods; by which he is entitled to the property of a certain proportion of the live stock that runs wild. **1884** *Cent. Mag.* Jan. 444/2 In some parts of the Chesapeake region, and perhaps elsewhere, a customary 'right in the woods' pertained to every planter, and was matter of sale and purchase. — **(2)** (*a*) **1838** *Indiana H. Rep. Jrnl.* 23 Sess. 101 Mr. Blair introduced bill No. 32, to grant the right of way to Illinois. (*b*) **1883** *Rep. Indian Affairs* p. xxii, I had the honor to submit to the Department . . . the draft of a bill . . . to grant a right of way to the Carson and Colorado Railroad Company. **1918** *Essex Inst. Coll.* LIV. 205 This figure included all bridging, masonry, grading, rights of way, fences. **1949** *Boston Sun. Globe* 1 May (Fiction Mag.) 13/5 My suggestion is that you put some guards out there patrolling the right-of-way. (*c*) **1891** *Harper's Mag.* Nov. 886/2 The first men to follow the engineers . . . are 'the right-of-way men.' **1906** LYNDE *Quickening* 77 He can't any more'n fire me, like he did the Southwestern right-o'-way man. **1924** MCARTHUR *Ore. Geog. Names* 143 Solomon Abraham acted as right-of-way agent, and platted several communities. — **(3) 1835** *Vade Mecum* (Phila.) 14 Feb. 3/1 Where's my old man—tell me that—where's Tom Bloomberg—tell us right off the reel. **1899** ADE *Fables in Slang* 27 He could tell you quick—right off the Reel.

As the last term in **civil, constitutional, corn, county, equal, feeding, head, homestead, hunting, improvement, Indian, land, mill, parchment, planting, pre-emption, settlement, Southern, squatter, squatter's, State, tomahawk, trackage, water, wood right(s).**

rigolet ˌrɪgəˈlɛt, *n.* [See note.]

"*Rigolet* . . . is a diminutive formation from French *rigole,* 'canal' " (Read, 180). "In the central part of the Valley the word was used for 'creek' " (McDermott, *Glossary,* 134).

A small stream, rivulet, or strait.

[**1719** in PIERRE MARGRY *Découvertes* VI. (1888) 251 Nous reconnusmes que c'estoit le Rigolet du Diable; il est fort étroit. . . . A 3 lieues dans le dit rigolet (etc.).] **1775** ROMANS *Nat. Hist. Florida* 227 On this river they are not in such plenty at the freshes as below, at the *rigolets,* on pearl river, and at the *Riviere aux Boeufs.* **1817** DARBY *Louisiana* 356 *Rigolet*—A water that flows both ways. **1883** *Harper's Wkly.* 3 March, Our boat is spreading her pinions for flight through the Rigolets, that sinuous waterway leading to Lake Borgne. **1949** *N.O. Times-Picayune Mag.* 3 April 14 They set out for the Rigolets aboard the steam yacht Marie.

b. (See quot.) *Rare.*

1770 MEASE *Narrative* 65 Pass'd through the Rigolets [below New Orleans] which are low marshy Islands and at Noon came to the Place which is the Rendezvous of the Geese, Outards &ca.

∗**rim,** *n.* In combs.: (1) **rim fire,** (*a*) designating or pertaining to cartridges having the igniting substance disposed in the outer edge, rather than in the center, of the base, (*b*) (see quot. 1927); (2) **rimrock,** see as a main entry.

(1) (*a*) **1868** NORTON & VALENTINE *Rep. Munitions War* 27 It is impossible to explode the rim-fire cartridges, except by a concussion made by the hammer. **1936** *Sears Cat.* (ed. 173) 814 Rim-Fire Smokeless Kopper Koted Bullets. (*b*) **1894** *Harper's Mag.* Feb. 350/2 Tom Bailey called it [the saddle] 'a d—— rim-fire.' **1927** RUSSELL *Trails* 3 He wasn't so much for pretty; his saddle was low horn, rimfire, or double-cinch; sometimes 'macheer.'

rimrock ˈrɪmˌrɑk, *n.*

1. Remaining portions of country rock which once formed the sides or banks of rivers.

1860 GREELEY *Overland Journey* 350 It is one of the arts of the miner to know just where to tunnel through the 'rim rock' so as to strike what was the bottom of the lake. **1873** LAWRENCE *Silverland* 161 The alluvium aforesaid, in many cases, is found to rest in a perfectly well-defined channel. . . . These troughs, varying in width from four hundred to a thousand feet or so, are lined and floored by 'rim-rock' and 'bed-rock' of greenstone, granite, or serpentine. **1876** RAYMOND *8th Rep. Mines* 122 The external character of this deposit is that of a broad channel . . . , with a well-defined rim-rock on the northern side.

2. Rock or rocks on the rim of a channel, basin, cliff, etc. Also attrib.

1898 *Scribner's Mag.* XXIV. 571/1 It was a long, hard day's pull up the northern side of the mountain to the 'rim-rock' in deep snow. **1939** *Southwestern Lore* Sep. 39 The finished Folsom point (from a rimrock work floor) has the most highly divergent base type, the convex or 'wavy' with 'ears.' **1948** *Time* 11 Oct. 21/1 Below the snow-dusted rimrock of the high Rockies, aspen gleamed like brass.

b. Also as a verb (see quot.).

1949 *World-Herald Mag.* (Omaha) 18 Sep. 18/5 Cattle raisers destroyed the flocks [of sheep] by clubbing, shooting, dynamiting, . . . poisoning, and stampeding them over cliffs—a practice sometimes called rim-rocking.

3. rimrock bighorn, an extinct race of bighorns.

1942 Nat. Pk. Service *Fading Trails* 50 West of the Rockies, the rimrock bighorn found the rugged lava-bed country of the Great Basin to its liking.

rincon rɪŋˈkon, *n. S.W.* [Sp. *rincón,* corner, nook of land.] A piece of land, esp. a small round valley or nook suitable for a house or village site. Also as a place-name.

1847 *Calif. Star* (S.F.) 20 March 4/2 All the ungranted tract . . . lying and situated between Fort Montgomery and the Rincon, and known as the water Lots, . . . will be surveyed and divided into convenient building Lots. **1888** *Outing* Nov. 129/2 Halting for lunch at the *rincon* (Spanish for inner corner) of the range, [we] eyed some of the finest scenery outside a modern theatre. **1932** *D.N.* VI. 232 Rincon. Originally meaning a piece of ground or part of one's property, the term is now used for a little round valley, pocket, or hole, generally one in which a man has his house and corrals. **1950** *L.A. Times Midwinter* 3 Jan. 23/1 We acquired a little cabin on the Rincon.

attrib. and *transf.* **1881** in *Amer. Sp.* XXIV. (1949) 266/1 On our right, in the 'rincon,' we find a large table groaning under liquors and confectionery free for all. **1884** in LINDLEY *Calif. of South* 205 The message from the Rincon Indians made my heart ache.

∗**ring,** *n.*

1. A clique or faction, orig. of politicians, who act in concert for their own ends which are not in the public interest.

1862 *Independent* 13 Feb. 4/4 [Parties] are more responsible in regard to the characters of those they nominate than are those . . . profligate rings that are so apt to take the control of a merely local election. **1905** Steffens in *McClure's Mag.* Feb. 337/1 In the Senate there is a small ring (called the Steering Committee) which is coming more and more to be the head of the United States Senate. **1946** Adams *Album Amer. Hist.* III. 269 The cartoons of Thomas Nast in *Harper's Weekly* did much to bring about the downfall of the Ring in 1871.

attrib. **1875** *Chi. Tribune* 2 July 4/7 The Philadelphia *Inquirer* would object to enlarging Gov. Tilden's sphere of usefulness if any of Peter B. Sweeney's Ring-spoils should be traced to his hands. **1903** *McClure's Mag.* Nov. 92/1 Philadelphia had a bad ring mayor. **1950** *N.O. Times-Picayune* 22 Jan. 1/4 Ring promises are seldom kept, as New Orleanians know to their sorrow and cost.

2. In special combs.: (1) **ring bit,** a severe bit having a ring for slipping over the lower jaw of a horse; (2) **fire,** (see quot. 1852), also as verb in fig. use, *colloq.;* (3) **heart,** a defect in lumber caused by a ring shake in the tree from which it comes; (4) **hunt,** a hunt in which a number of persons form a large ring and drive all the animals before them toward the center where they are ruthlessly slaughtered, also **ring hunting,** cf. **ring fire;** (5) **maul,** (see quot.); (6) **oak,** (see quot.); (7) **relievo,** a children's

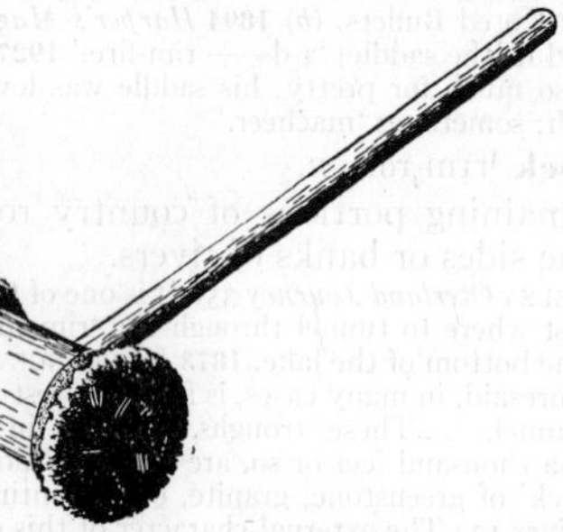

Ring maul

game resembling prisoner's base; (8) **road,** a circular course for a group of horsemen drawn up one behind the other; (9) **rot,** (see quot.); (10) **service,** a marriage service in which a ring is used; (11) **shake,** (see quot. 1905); (12) **-streaked-and-striped,** marked with rings, streaks and stripes, possibly from the Bible phrase "ringstraked and spotted" in Gen. 30:35, *colloq.*, cf. ***ringed,** *a.;* (13) **tail, -tailed,** see as main entries; (14) **toss (game),** a game in which rings are tossed, usu. at an upright stick or peg.

(1) 1894 *Harper's Mag.* March 520/2 The Mexican 'punchers' all use the 'ring bit' and it is a fearful contrivance. **1897** Hough *Story of Cowboy* 64 And still more cruel was the 'ring bit,' with its circle slipped over the lower jaw of the horse. — **(2) 1852** Reynolds *Hist. Illinois* 194 Sometimes the hunters made what they called 'ring fires.' They set fire to the grass and leaves around a considerable tract of country, so as to enclose a number of deer, and other animals. **1859** Taliaferro *Fisher's R.* 46 'Squire, I'll talk all round you. I'll ringfire you with Scripter. — **(3) 1874** Knight 564/1 *Clear-stuff*, boards free from knots, wane, wind-shakes, ring-hearts [etc.]. — **(4) 1799** J. Smith *Remark. Occurr.* (1870) 85 We met with some Ottawa hunters, and agreed with them to take, what they call a ring hunt, in partnership. . . . This put an end to our ring hunting this season. **1924** Dillin *Ky. Rifle* 10 In 1849 the last animal drive or 'Ring Hunt' was held by the pioneers at Beech Creek, Clinton County [Pa.].

(5) 1935 *Ada* (Ohio) *Herald* 1 Nov., A third type was called a ring-maul, the two striking ends protected with iron rings. — **(6) 1709** Lawson *Carolina* 92 White Iron, or Ring-Oak, is so call'd from the Durability and lasting Quality of this Wood. — **(7) 1891** *Amer. Folk-Lore* IV. 224 Ring Relievo. . . . The game continues until all players of the side that had the start are made captives. — **(8) 1843** Haliburton *Attaché* 1 Ser. II. iv. 59 First and foremost, a ring-road is formed, like a small race-course. — **(9) 1905** *Forestry Bureau Bul.* No. 61, 44 *Ring rot*, decay in a log, which follows the annual rings more or less closely.

(10) 1905 *Springfield W. Republican* 23 June 14 The officiating clergyman was Rev. C. C. P. Hiller, and the ring service was used. — **(11) 1905** *Scientific Amer. Supp.* 25 March 24433/1 The defect known as cupshake, ringshake, . . . consists in a partial or entire separation of two consecutive annual rings, and appears on a cross section as one or more splits running concentrically around the log. **1949** Collingwood & Brush *Knowing Your Trees* 117 The same feature, however, reduces the value of this wood for many purposes and is characterized in many trees as 'ring shake' or 'wind shake.' — **(12) 1884** Mark Twain *H. Finn* xxiii. 227 (R.), He was painted all over, ring-streaked-and-striped. **1908** —— *Capt. Stormfield* 267 (R.), Our young saints wear wings all the time—gold, and variegated, and rain-bowed, and ring-streaked-and-striped ones. — **(14) 1879** Howells *Lady of Aroostook* 88 A young person . . . played shuffle-board and ring-toss on the deck of the Aroostook. **1947** *Harper's Mag.* Nov. 476/2 We rode on the Ferris wheel, took our chances in a few ring-toss games, and then . . . went to the main attraction: the race track.

b. In the names of animals: (1) **ringbill,** = **ring-necked duck;** (2) **-billed,** used in the name of, or with reference to, the **ring-necked duck;** (3) **-billed gull,** the common or lake gull, *Larus delawarensis;* (4) **neck,** (*a*) = **ring snake** (*a*), also **ring-necked snake,** (*b*) a ring plover, (*c*) = **ring-necked duck;** (5) **-necked duck,** the marsh bluebill, *Nyroca collaris*, widely distributed throughout North America; (6) **perch,** (see quots.); (7) **snake,** (*a*) any of various American snakes of the genus *Diadophis*, as *D. punctatus*, (*b*) a snake fabled to roll along like a hoop (see quot. and cf. **hoop snake**).

(1) 1856 Audubon *Birds of Amer.* VI. 320 In shape, the Tufted Duck, or Ring-bill, as it is called in Kentucky, resembles the Scaup or Flocking Fowl. **1888** Trumbull *Names of Birds* 60 Ring-Necked Duck: Ring-Necked Scaup. . . . At Chicago [it is known as the] Ring-Bill. **1949** Kitchin *Birds Olympic Peninsula* 46 Far better if they had been officially christened 'ring-bill,' the common name used by the hunters. — **(2) 1883** *Nat. Museum Bul.* No. 27, 160 *Fulix collaris*. . . . Ring-billed Blackhead. **1917** *Birds of Amer.* I. 137 Ring-necked Duck. *Marila collaris*. . . . [Also called] Ring-billed Duck.— **(3) 1831** J. Richardson *Fauna Bor.-Amer.* II. 421 *Larus zonorhynchus*, . . . Ring-billed Mew-Gull. **1844** *Nat. Hist. N.Y., Zoology* II. 309 The Common gull . . . , although called the Ring-billed Gull in the books, has received no other popular name than Brown Winter Gull. **1937** Stone *Bird Studies at Old Cape May* 540 Ring-billed Gulls will often remain on the beaches throughout the winter. — **(4)** (*a*) **1791** W. Bartram *Travels* 274 There are many other species of snakes in the regions of Florida and Carolina; as the . . . copper belly, ring neck, and two or three varieties of vipers. **1949** *Nature Mag.* April 171/2 If a female slimy salamander is attacked by a ring-necked snake as she guards her eggs, she will exude a sticky slime from her skin. (*b*) **1844** *Nat. Hist. N.Y., Zoology* II. 209 The Ring Plover, or Ring-neck as it is commonly called in this State, arrives here about the beginning of May. **1917** *Birds of Amer.* I. 264 Piping Plover. *Aegialitis meloda*. . . . [Also called] Ringneck. (*c*) **1917** *Ib.* 137 Ring-necked Duck. *Marila collaris*. . . . [Also called] Ring-neck.

(5) 1831 J. Richardson *Fauna Bor.-Amer.* II. 454 *Fuligula rufitorques*, . . . Ring-necked Duck. **1948** *Dly. Oklahoman* (Okla. City) 31 Oct. D. 4/1 Other wild fowl found in reasonable numbers in Oklahoma are the ring-necked duck (blackjack), the Baldpate (widgeon) . . . and the Scaup (bluebill). — **(6) 1891** *Cent.* 5188/1 ring-perch. . . . The common yellow perch of North America, *Perca flavescens*. **1947** Brown *Outdoors Unlimited* 233 'Ring' perch, or yellow perch as they are more widely called, offer the earliest fishing in this part of the country. — **(7)** (*a*) **1778** Carver *Travels* 487 The Ring Snake is about twelve inches long. **1836** Edward *Hist. Texas* 76 One will meet . . . at times with that beautiful, small, harmless creature, the ring-snake. (*b*) **1899** *Animal & Plant Lore* 87 The 'ring snake' will, by taking its tail in its mouth, roll like a hoop.

As the last term in **cattle, council, dinner, ear, gold, grant, gum, helper, Indian, larigo, machine, political, prayer, railroad, senatorial, Tammany, toe, treasury, Tweed, Wall Street, whisky ring.**

***ringed,** *a. ringed, striped and speckled*, made up of various elements, used in allusion to the complex make-up of the Free-Soil party. *Obs.* Cf. **ring-streaked-and-striped.** — **1848** *Argus* (Albany) 23 Sep. 363/2, I have just returned from a ringed, striped and speckled 'sore-head' demonstration at Sharon Springs.

* **ringer,** *n.*[1]

1. One who enters a contest under false pretenses by keeping secret his identity and past performances.

1890 *Stock Grower & Farmer* 9 Aug. 8/2 At the same time 'Andy Croker' is the most notorious 'ringer' on the turf. **1928** Foy & Harlow *Clowning Through Life* 188 We had scarcely made the match when we were given a secret tip that Bennett was a 'ringer.' **1947** *Newsweek* 24 Nov. 60/3 As a ringer in the Sadie Hawkins race, she was last heard of pursuing a panic-stricken Dogpatcher.

b. Anyone who attaches himself to a group to which

he does not belong, as a voter who votes in a district outside his own.

1896 G. ADE *Artie* xi. 100 About a dozen ringers followed us in and stood around rubberin'. **1904** *N.Y. Tribune* 8 Nov. 3 The Democratic leaders today started to send a lot of alleged 'ringers' across the line into West Virginia to vote tomorrow. **1928** *Manch. Guard. Wkly.* 26 Oct. 335/2 Perhaps seventy-five were really newspaper men and women, the others being what the American language calls 'ringers,' 'gate-crashers,' or 'dead-heads.'

2. =**dead ringer.** *Slang.*

1894 O. HENRY *Cabbages and Kings* x. 180 The man was a ringer for the pictures of the fat Weary Willie in the funny papers.

***ringer,** *n.*[2] A ringing cheer. — **1901–2** *Rep. Kans. State Bd. Agric.* 360 (*Cent.*), The air was rent with cheers. Auctioneer Judy called for a . . . ringer for the man who has sold the highest-priced beef steer in the world.

ringster 'rɪŋstɚ, *n.* **1.** A member of a political ring. **2.** A member of a price-fixing ring.

(1) **1875** *Chi. Tribune* 15 Dec. 4/1 The support secured for Mayor Cobb was sufficient . . . to defeat the unholy alliance of ringsters and politicians by which Boardman's nomination was first obtained. **1908** *Nation* 16 April 344/3 Hereafter the word [grafter] cannot be lightly used as a synonym for any malefactor at the head of a corporation, or any political ringster. — (2) **1878** *Cong. Rec.* 20 March 1915/1 As the honest contractor will not go into a business where he has to evade the law, the ringster has it all his own way. **1904** TARBELL *Hist. Standard Oil Co.* I. 107 'Deserters,' 'ringsters,' 'monopolists' were the terms applied to [the refiners who had joined Rockefeller in creating a monopoly].

***ringtail,** *n.*

1. A raccoon; also as a nickname for a member of a political faction. *Obs.* Cf. **coon 2. b, roarer,** *n.* **1.**

1840 *Boston Transcript* 15 April 2/1 When the Registry Law was first spoken of, the tail of the Democratic party, the roarers, buttenders, ringtails, . . . talked strong about nullification and all that. **1844** *N.O. Picayune* 30 Sep. 257/5 It aided the fun not a little to see the mischievous monkey . . . bite into his arm, and hang on like a 'ring-tail' to a bough. **1949** *New Yorker* 1 Oct. 63/2.

2. ringtail cat, =**cacomistle.**

1940 *Mt. Hood Guide* xxv, No open season on . . . such small furbearing animals as fisher, marten, civet cat, ringtail cat, and beaver.

3. =**ring-tailed,** *a.* **2.** *Slang.*

1832 PAULDING *Westward Ho!* I. 124, I got tired of making fun of the ring-tail-roarer. **1859** *La Crosse D. Union* 25 Oct. 2/4 Here lies James D. Potter, Who lived . . . as a Methodist Exhorter, With a regular ring-tail snorter. **1909** RYE *Quirt & Spur* 81 Ain't he a 'ring-tail tooter' boys? **1913** *Sat. Ev. Post* 1 Nov. 66/4 Scotty always said that when he got the dough from his old man's estate he was going to have a ring-tail-peeler of a time.

***ring-tailed,** *a.*

1. ring-tailed bassaris, cat, =**cacomistle.**

1853 SITGREAVES *Exped. Zuni & Colo. Rivers* 45 The Ring-tailed Bassaris . . . is common in some parts of California, where it is tamed by the inhabitants, and kept by them for the purpose of catching rats and mice. **1917** *Mammals of Amer.* 108 Ring-railed Cat. . . . [Also called] Mountain Cat, Raccoon Fox. **1949** *L.A. Times* 17 May 1/3 The curiosity of a ring-tailed cat at the Hoover Dam powerhouse yesterday caused a blackout of a wide area of California, Arizona and Nevada.

2. Designating a person or thing that is out of the ordinary, a "rare specimen," a "caution." *Slang.*

1828 *Western Mo. Rev.* June 15 The *snapping turtle, the ring tailed painter, the best horse, dog and gun,* &c. have been successive additions. **1837** BIRD *Nick of Woods* I. 56 My name's Ralph Stackpole, and I'm a ring-tailed squealer! **1916** *Amer. Mag.* Sep. 21/1 The man that pulls *his* cork will sure be some ring-tailed peeler!

b. ring-tailed roarer, (see first quots.). *Slang.*

1830 *Painesville* (O.) *Telegraph* 15 June 1/5 *Ringtailed Roarers*—A most violent fellow, a Crockett. **1871** DE VERE 224 A specially fine fellow of great size and strength is called a *ring-tailed roarer.* **1947** *Chi. Tribune* 2 Nov. IV. 9/2 The 'ring-tailed Roarers' of the pioneer days shout their raucous delight, unsubtle, earthy, outlandish, direct.

3. ring-tailed marlin, (see quots.).

1844 *Nat. Hist. N.Y., Zoology* II. 254 The Ring-Tailed Marlin, *Limosa Hudsonica,* . . . is not as common along our coast as the Marlin. In Boston it is called the *Goose-bird.* **1942** Nat. Pk. Service *Fading Trails* 157 Market hunters of Boston called all godwits 'goose birds,' but perhaps the most widely used name for the Hudsonian godwit was 'ring-tailed marlin' because of the white band on its upper tail coverts.

ringtum ditty. (Variously spelled.) A dish of cheese cooked together with bacon, onions, tomatoes, corn, and other ingredients.

1911 Williams Pub. Lib. Assoc. *Ariz. Cook Book* 99 Rinktum Ditty. **1913** *Ladies' Home Jrnl.* Oct. 47/2 Rictum-Dity. **1948** *Ada* (Okla.) *Ev. News* 2 July 6/1 We enjoyed Rum-Tum-Diddy, a dish made of corn, bacon, cheese, tomatoes, onions and other mysterious ingredients.

rio 'rio, *n. S.W.* [Sp. *río,* river.]

1. A river, chiefly in proper names. (See also quot. 1897.)

1686 *Rel. Florida* 109 There being no great store of *Maes* in the Town, the Governour made us march to another about half the league from *Riogrande,* or the great River. **1810** *Amer. Republic* (Frankfort, Ky.) 19 Oct. 4/3 The United States, then, offered to cede a territory, between the Colorado and the Rio Bravo, as large as the Northern States, including New-York. **1847** *Santa Fe Republican* 30 Oct. 2/4 A war party of the Apaches charged into the Rio. **1897** HOUGH *Story of Cowboy* 20 Each stream [is] called a rio, or river, no matter how small it may be. **1939** *New Mexico* Dec. 5/1 Giant *rios* form the veins for the rich flowing lifeblood of these fertile lands. **1949** *Pacific Discovery* Jan.–Feb. 4/2 From there we crossed the continental divide by pack train and dropped down to the Río Gavilán on the west slope.

2. a. Rio Grande quail, prob. the scaled quail *q.v.* **b. Rio Grande trout,** a trout, *Salmo virginalis,* found in the Rio Grande and other western streams.

(a) 1854 in *Spirit of Times* (1857) 28 March 57/2 O. Virginiana . . . is generally superseded on that stream, by what is known here [Austin, Tex.] as the Rio Grande quail. — **(b) 1883** *Nat. Museum Bul.* No. 27, 426 *Salmo spilurus.* Rio Grande Trout. Upper Rio Grande and Basin of Utah. **1896** JORDAN & EVERMANN *Check-List Fishes* 291.

***riot,** *n.* As the last term in **abolition, draft, Orange, race, squatter riot.**

riot call. A call for additional means to deal with a riot. — **1902** LORIMER *Lett. Merchant* 237 They had to turn in a riot call and bring out the reserves before they could break up Hank's little Boston tea-party. **1905** *N.Y. Ev. Post* 7 Nov. 2 Charges of illegal voting resulted in disturbance which the police were unable to subdue, and a riot call was sent in.

rip rɪp, *n.* [See note.]

The etymology of this word and the place of its first occurrence are doubtful. Webster suggest **ripple* as a source, the *OED* suggests a relationship with **rip, v.;* in both senses, however, the Amer. evidence is about a century earlier than the British usage shown in the *OED.* Cf. ***ripple,** ***rippling,** below.

1. A place in the sea where the water is violently disturbed by the meeting of opposing tides.

1775 ROMANS *Nat. Hist. Fla.* App. p. lxxxviii, You will see a rip appear like breakers. **1807** *Mass. H.S. Coll.* 2 Ser. III. 73 Ships in storms get within the dangerous rips which lie off the island. **1882** GODFREY *Nantucket* 311 Standing here, one can see the 'rips' in the distance.

2. A stretch of broken water in a river, a rapid.

1791 in ADMIRAL JAMES *Journal* 195 We passed several very dangerous places, which they there [on the Kennebec R.] termed 'rips,' which was a confused number of rocks and large stones in the direct way we were obliged to pass, and which generally had a fall of some few feet. **1839** HOLMES *Explor. Aroostook River* 7 The existing obstacles which present themselves to the present navigation of this river, are, the 'rips,' which are occasioned principally by loose boulders of rock. **1882** HUBBARD *Moosehead Lake* 61 A canoe would have to be carried around the 'rip.' **1947** *Sat. Ev. Post* 8 March 20/3 'It's your log and you're riding it,' Rory said, 'but watch the rips ahead.'

3. Short for **ripple.*

1867 T. LACKLAND *Homespun* II. 271 Sometimes he could not help giving a rip of laughter that drew the eyes of the whole school round to him in an instant.

4. *like rips,* energetically, violently. *Colloq.*

1901 HARBEN *Westerfelt* iv. 42 An' she said Jasper Webb swore like rips when the administrator tol' him the trade wus closed with Luke as yore agent. **1904** —— *Georgians* 133 I've got girls of my own, . . . and I feel like rips for one when she has to stand up and sing or say anything in public.

***rip,** *v.* In colloq. and slang combs., usu. obs.: (1) **rip-roaring,** *a.* first-rate, superior, hilarious, full of vim; (2) **-roarious,** *a.* uproarious, violent, tumultuous; (3) **-roariously,** *adv.* in a rip-roaring manner; (4) **sneezing,** *a.* lively; (5) **sniptious,** *a.* (see quot.); (6) **snorter,** *n.* a person or thing regarded as markedly superior or striking; (7) **snorting,** *a.* =**rip-roaring,** *a.;* (8) **staver,** =**rip-snorter.**

(1) **1834** CARUTHERS *Kentuckian* I. 62 There was a rip-roaring sight of slight o' hand and tumbling work there. **1905** PHILLIPS *Social Secretary* 104 It takes a pretty clever man, Miss Talltowers, to make a grand, supreme, rip-roaring ass of himself. **1928** *Sat. Ev. Post* 12

May 69/1 He had had a riproaring time. **1948** *Nat. Hist.* April 177/3 Impulsively he boarded a train for Chicago—the new, booming town of the Midwest, rip-roaring, wild, full of adventure. — (2) **1830** *N.Y. Constellation* 11 Sep. 2/5 The English traveller had put up at a little log tavern on the banks of the Savannah, where the *riproarious* conduct took place. **1890** *Harper's Mag.* April 796/2 Robert J. Burdette . . . divides his waning buzz of rip-roarious approbation between two mettlesome, cavorting, prankish steeds in the great American journalistic circus. — (3) **1834** CROCKETT *Narr. Life* 78 The next day it rained rip-roariously. — (4) **1834** CARUTHERS *Kentuckian* I. 101 They always wind up at the little end with a ripsneezing dance.

(5) **1830** *Va. Lit. Museum* 6 Jan. 479 *Sniptious and Ripsniptious,* 'Smart, spruce.' *South and West.* — (6) **1840** *Crockett Almanac* 20/1 Of all the ripsnorters I ever tutched upon, thar never war one that could pull her boat alongside of Grace Peabody. **1885** *Santa Fé Wkly. New Mexican* 20 Aug. 2/6 Any galoot who wants the Ripsnorter for a year can have it left at his bar-room on payment of three red chips in advance. **1945** *Democrat* 30 Aug. 2/3 But our bobcats are ripsnorters like wildcats are supposed to be. — (7) **1846** *Yale Lit. Mag.* XI. 336 (Th.), What a rip-snorting red head you have got! **1932** *Blue Valley Farmer* (Okla. City) 28 Jan. 2/3 A rip-snortin', sincere and fearless man, friend of the people because he is of the people, who ought to, but probably won't, be elected president. **1949** *Time* 5 Sep. 12/3 These were hell-roaring, rip-snorting affairs with the loudest & longest speeches you ever heard. — (8) **1833** *Sketches D. Crockett* 144 In ten minutes he yelled enough, and swore I was a ripstavur.

b. *To let her rip,* to let a thing go at full speed. Also, rarely, **let-her-rip-itiveness,** *n. Colloq.* or *slang.*

1846 *N.O. Picayune* 31 Aug. 648/2 Why in the name of h—ll's eternal flints don't the engineer pitch in more pine knots and crack on more steam? *Let* her rip. **1857** *S.F. Call* 11 Jan. 1/1, I . . . decided that there was a good deal of honesty of purpose hid under an assumed appearance of let-her-rip-itiveness. **1910** *Out West* Jan. 61 Git up more steam—this ain't a funeral! Let her rip!

c. *To rip and tear,* to be in a state of activity or agitation, to storm and rave. *Colloq.*

1873 MARK TWAIN & WARNER *Gilded Age* xxvii. 249 (R.), A man wants rest, a man wants peace—a man don't want to rip and tear around all the time. **1884** MARK TWAIN *H. Finn* xxi. 207 (R.), It was perfectly lovely the way he would rip and tear.

* **ripper,** *n.* **1. ripper bill.** (See quot. 1914.) Also **ripperism,** *n. Slang.* **2.** (See quot.)

(1) **1893** *Columbus* (O.) *Dispatch* 8 Nov. Let us hope that ripperism, the tool of persons and partisans, is at an end. **1895** *Ib.* 1 April 4/2 The Merryman ripper bill looks very much as if the Republicans of this city were going to the legislature for offices. **1914** *Cyclo. Amer. Govt.* III. 229/1 Ripper Bills. A term applied to acts of state legislatures for the reorganization of city governments, intended to turn incumbents out of office, and to put in a new set of officials. — (2) **1930** HENRY *Conquer. Plains* 65 Both drovers and cowboys called an unfortunate transaction 'bad medicine' and a bad failure 'a ripper.'

As the last term in **double ripper.**

* **ripple,** *n.* =**riffle,** *n.* **1.** Cf. **snag ripple.**

1755 *N.H. Prov. Papers* VI. 431 The chief of ye way [there were] swift water falls and Ripples. **1812** MELISH *Travels* II. 87 We engaged a young man to take us over a bar, here called a *ripple,* a little way below. **1941** BALDWIN *Keelboat Age* 71 The breaking of the water over the bars and chains was known to the boatmen as ripples, or riffles.

b. *To make the ripple,* =**riffle,** *n.* **1. b.**

1874 in FLEMING *Hist. Reconstruction* II. 42 He said he . . . would let me have it on my giving him the money. Told him I was not able to make the ripple.

c. ripple box, =**riffle box.** Also **ripple bar,** =**riffle** *n.* **2.** *Obs.*

1853 PAYSON *Golden Dreams* 93 These partitions corresponded simply to the ripple-bars of the common rocker. **1853** *Alta California* (S.F.) 31 May 2/1 Repeated instances have come to our knowledge when the amount of gold saved has been doubled by a little alteration or improvement made in the ripple-box.

* **rippling,** *n.* =**riffle,** *n.* **1.** *Obs.* Cf. * **ripple,** *n.*

1745 POTE *Jrnl. Captivity* 55 [It was] Likewise verey bad Paddling, on account of Ripplings and falls. **1755** L. EVANS *Anal. Map Colonies* 20 In Half a Mile [you] come to a little gentle Rippling, where the River may be forded on Horseback. **1832** WILLIAMSON *Maine* I. 57 Here are ripplings, to avoid which, a canal was cut twenty rods in length.

* **riprap,** *n.* A foundation or protecting wall made of loose stones.

1833 *Md. Hist. Mag.* XIII. 314 The ripraps directly opposite . . . will effectually secure the Bay. **1882** *Cong. Rec.* 7 Aug. 7006/1 The bridge . . . shall be built with the piers parallel to the current, leaving the water-way unobstructed by riprap or piling, or other obstructions. **1949** *Sat. Ev. Post* 9 July 49/1 These earthen walls are as much as twenty-five feet high, seeded to grass to prevent outside erosion and faced with rock riprap where there is any danger of flood waters reaching the basins.

transf. **1857** *Knickerb.* XLIX. 277, I once knew a druggist . . . who got along so well in dealing in all sorts of rip-raps . . . that he at last undertook to go heavily into the fancy segar-case business.

attrib. **1822** *Niles' Reg.* 15 June 241/1 So much has been said about the 'Rip Rap contract,' we have commenced the publication of the report and the papers that accompanied it. **1838** J. CHILDS *Western Railroad* (1839) 25 (Ernst), To guard the embankments by rip-rap walls. **1871** *N.Y. Herald* 15 Sep. 8/6 The stone, it appears, was for use on the rip-rap wall at the southerly end of the Hudson River.

b. (See quot. 1876.)

1835 *Franklin Repository* (Chambersburgh, Pa.) 1 Sep. 2/4 The Gineral [is a little] recruited by going down to the Rip Raps. **1863** KETTELL *Hist. Rebellion* II. 481 President Lincoln . . . went across from Fortress Monroe to a spot . . . about one mile below the Rip Raps. **1876** KNIGHT 1946/2 *Rip-rap* . . . a foundation of loose stones. The artificial island in Chesapeake Bay, which is thus formed, is named the Rip-raps.

riprap ˈrɪpræp, *v.* [f. the noun.] *tr.* and *absol.* To make a riprap for (a river) or across (a swamp), to protect (a river bank) by a riprap.

1848 *Soc. of N.Y. Aldermen* No. 9 (B.), If, in constructing a bulkhead, it should be determined to rip-rap to low-water mark. **1903** *N.Y. Times* 15 Sep., Congress will be asked to riprap the entire river where there is danger of the current cutting through to the old course. **1943** DEVOTO *Yr. of Decision* 332 They had to dig tracks and fell trees and level off centers high up on mountainsides, pry boulders out of their course, riprap swamp patches, sometimes bridge brooks that could not be crossed otherwise.

b. Hence **riprapped,** *a.,* **riprapping,** *n.*

1883 *American* VI. 297 The stream will be confined within permanent barriers by rip-rapped banks and levees. **1884** *Harper's Mag.* Sep. 504/1 Cliff ledges . . . [are] connected one terrace above the other, by . . . a natural riprapping of fallen fragments.

Rip Van Winkle. [The name of the principal character in Irving's well-known story.] *transf.* One who is unresponsive to change or behind the times; an animal that hibernates. Also attrib.

1849 *N.O. Picayune* 21 July 1/6 A person absent for three weeks, on returning, almost fancies that he has been taking a Rip Van Winkle slumber. **1856** HOFFMAN *Night Watch* 255 Why, Col. Murray, you are the veriest old 'Rip Van Winkle.' Have you also been asleep twenty years? **1861** QUINT *Potomac & Rapidan* (1864) 57 The village of one street was of the Rip Van Winkle order. **1875** BURROUGHS *Winter Sunshine* 141 By mid-October, most of the Rip Van Winkles among our brute creatures have lain down for their winter nap.

b. (See quots.) *Obs.*

1833 *Advocate* (Shelbyville, Ky.) 28 Sep. 2/4 Wm. C. Preston, of South Carolina, in one of his furious tirades, applied to the State of North Carolina, the somewhat degrading epithet of 'the Rip Van Winkle of the South.' **1846** *Warrock's Alm. 1847* 22 North Carolina, Rip Van Winkle [State]. **1870** MACRAE *Americans* I. 246 The 'Rip Van Winkle State' [N.C.] has got an awakening now, and slavery will no longer retard her progress by diverting her proper share of white immigration into the Free States.

c. In derivatives alluding to backwardness or old fogyism such as that of Rip Van Winkle after his twenty-year sleep. *Colloq.*

1829 *Mechanics' Press* (Utica. N.Y.) 5 Dec. 28/1 His Rip VanWinkleish habits asked no more than to pursue 'the even tenor of their way.' **1831** ROYALL *Southern Tour* II. 96 A low raised ignorant woman, into whom one of those Godly *Rip Van Winkle-thumps* from New York, had instilled holy, pious feelings. **1842** KIRKLAND *Forest Life* II. 228 [Reading an old-fashioned book] was counted among my Rip-Van-Winkle-isms. **1852** *Harper's Mag.* Aug. 420/2 A Pilgrim from the back woods . . . had just been awakened from a Rip-Van-Winkleish existence of a quarter of a century by the steam-whistle of the Erie Railroad.

Also **Rip Van Winkledom,** the Catskill Mountain region, alleged scene of Rip's long sleep.

1892 *Outing* April 48 (*title*), A Cyclist's Visit to Rip Van Winkledom. *Ib.* 50/2 Surely we are already in the confines of Rip Van Winkledom!

d. Also as a verb.

1901 *Interstate Manufacturer* (St. Louis) 25 Jan. 1/2 There is but one logical inference, gentlemen, and that is, we are asleep. We have Rip Van Winkled it to a finish.

* **rise,** *n.*

1. a. (See quot.) **b. rise ball,** in baseball, a pitched ball that travels upward. *Rare* or *obs.* Cf. * **upshoot.**

(a) **1905** *Forestry Bureau Bul.* No. 61, 44 *Rise,* the difference in diameter, or taper, between two points in a log. — (b) **1886** *Outing*

July 480/2 He is weak in catching a rise ball and in getting the ball started for second.

2. a. *The rise of*, a little more than. **b.** *to make a rise*, to be successful, to win or make money. **c.** *and the rise*, and more. All *colloq.*

(a) 1834 in J. S. BASSETT *Plantation Overseer* 66, I muste plante the rise of a hundred aceres in coten. **1905** O. HENRY *Roads of Destiny* 141, I've seen the rise of $50,000 at a time in that tin grub box. — **(b) 1836** *Quarter Race Ky.* (1846) 24, I thought I'd make a rise on chuck-a-luck. **1851** HOOPER *Widow Rugby* 20 No matter how I make an honest rise, I'm sure to 'buck it off' at farrer. — **(c) 1853** *S. Lit. Messenger* XIX. 220/2 He pretended to be thirty and the rise, but was, at the least, fifty. **1859** BARTLETT 367 The phrase 'and the rise,' is used in some parts of the South to mean 'and more'; as, 'I should think there were a thousand and the rise.'

As the last term in **June, red rise.**

***rise,** *v.* **1.** *tr.* To exceed (a number or amount). **2.** *how d'ye rise*, (see quot. 1848). Both *colloq.*

(1) 1838 in MATHEWS *Writings* (1843) 82/1 Brother George counted the strokes of his arm upon the cushion, and thinks he rose a hundred in the course of the sermon. **1877** JEWETT *Deephaven* 133, I like well enough to see a hog that'll weigh six hundred, . . . but for my eatin' give me one that'll just rise three. — **(2) 1839** *Spirit of Times* 10 Aug. 267/1 (We.), How do you rise? **1846** CORCORAN *Pickings* 47 He commenced—'How are you, Squire—how d'ye rise?' **1848** *R.I. Words* (Bartlett MS), *How d'ye rise*, a western salutation meaning how do you get along.

***risibilities,** *n. pl.* The risible faculties. *Humorous.* — **1856** CARTWRIGHT *Autobiog.* 142, I had very hard work to keep down my risibilities. **1860** HAWTHORNE *Transformation* III. 161 An Italian comedy . . . [was] effective over everybody's risibilities except his own. **1911** *Everybody's Mag.* April 471/1 Scrambled eggs are only moderately funny, . . . but a hard-boiled egg is unfailing in its appeal to the risibilities, and a fried egg is a scream from start to finish.

***rising,** *a.* and *n.*

1. Fully as much as, rather more than. *Colloq.*

1777 *N.J. Archives* 2 Ser. I. 371 The Horse Royal Oak . . . is a beautiful jet black, . . . and rising nine years old. **1812** *N.Y. Ev. Post* 10 Nov. 2/2 *New-Hampshire* has chosen federal members to Congress, and federal electors for President by a majority rising *Three Thousand!* **1896** WILKINS *Madelon* 123 Old man in there, lived 'round these parts risin' eighty years.

b. *rising of*, upwards of, in excess of. *Colloq.*

1817 PAULDING *Lett. from South* II. 121 'How much wheat did you raise this year?' 'A little rising of five thousand bushels.' **1896** HARRIS *Sister Jane* 41 'How old is your baby?' inquired Mrs. Beshears. 'A risin' of five months,' replied the mother.

2. In combs.: (1) **rising examination,** ?an examination given for finding if students should be promoted, *obs.;* (2) **seat,** (see quot. 1891); (3) ***sun,** *(a)* the East, in Indian speech, *(b)* a quilt pattern depicting the sun when rising, also attrib.

(1) 1859 M. LABORDE *Hist. S.C. College* 35 The first rising examination was held on the 25th November and the several classes were advanced to the next higher grade. — **(2) 1809** M. LEE *Quaker Girl of Nantucket* 28 (Th. Supp.), In the sing-song drawl once peculiar to the tuneful exhortations of the rising seat, he thus held forth. **1891** *Cent.* 5194/1 *Rising-seat*, . . . In a Friends' meeting-house, one of a series of three or four seats, each raised a little above the one before it, and all facing the body of the congregation. These seats are usually occupied by ministers and elders. — **(3)** *(a)* **1841** COOPER *Deerslayer* xxvii, You are a man whose fathers came from beyond the rising sun; we are children of the setting sun. *(b)* **1895** CRADDOCK *Mystery Witch-Face Mt.* 185 Some [quilts] were of the 'log cabin' and 'rising sun' variety. **1935** LINCOLN *Cape Cod Yesterdays* 109, I ducked my tousled head under the . . . 'rising-sun comforter' and fell asleep in spite of the racket.

As the last term in **bran, hop, salt rising.**

ritzy 'rɪtsɪ, *a.* Orig. **Ritzy.** [f. César *Ritz*, a Swiss (d. 1918), and the palatial hotels bearing his name which he built or assisted in building in Paris, London, N.Y., etc.] Smart, vulgarly ostentatious. *Slang.*

1924 *Collier's* 4 Oct. 41/1 Gentleman George dropped his Ritzy manner like it was a hot poker. **1948** *Chi. Tribune* 11 Jan. I. 21/1 In other countries women prefer the long, ritzy Parisian product because it's so pretty. **1949** *Ib.* 30 Sep. III. 6 That's the ritziest club in school!

Also **ritzily,** *adv.*

1928 *Amer. Sp.* III. 349 With one indifferent glance 'round, they whirl ritzily out to Beverly Hills.

***river,** *n.*

1. A stage of water in a river sufficient to insure navigation. *Colloq.*

1853 *Hunt's Merch. Mag.* XXIX. 59 The downward freight . . . was usually sent to Augusta, with instruction to ship it to Savannah if there was a river.

2. In combs.: (1) **river ague,** ague prevalent in river swamp areas, cf. **river fever;** (2) **claim,** a mining claim along a river; (3) **county,** a county adjacent to or traversed by a river; (4) **drive,** in logging, the action of floating or guiding logs down a river, also attrib.; (5) **driving,** conducting saw logs down a river; (6) **farm,** a farm along a river; (7) **fever,** a fever of a type found in regions adjacent to a river or rivers, cf. **river ague;** (8) **flat,** *(a)* a level extent of land along a river, *(b)* a flatboat for use on a river; (9) **roller,** a riverman or boatman, *slang, rare;* (10) ***side,** *(a) local,* that side of New Orleans near the river, *(b)* designating a style of hat, *obs.;* (11) **sluicing,** hydraulic mining along a river, *obs.;* (12) **trace,** a trace or way along a river; (13) **trader,** one who trades along a river from a boat, *obs.;* (14) **work,** work done on a river.

(1) 1845 HOOPER *Suggs* (1928) 112 The 'river ager' made Sol shake worse than that, that fall. — **(2) 1856** *Butte Rec.* (Bidwell, Calif.) 15 March 3/1 Gambling has about ceased, a slug ante, with the limited privilege of going a horse blind, or a whole river claim better, being the extent of bets that we have heard lately. **1897** *Consular Rep.* Oct. 146 Creek and river claims shall be 500 feet long. — **(3) 1864** *Ohio Agric. Rep.* XVIII. cxxiii, There are ten other counties which might with equal propriety be termed 'river counties.' **1870** W. W. FOWLER *Ten Yrs. in Wall St.* 310 Another was a clergyman, from one of the river counties, who had taken the early train down to the city that morning. — **(4) 1929** KELLOGG *Trails & Tales* 82 A woodsman with his river-drive boots came up and looked on at what we were doing. **1937** WILSON *Aroostook* 105 The 'river-drives' were the consummation of turning out the timber.

(5) 1854 BULLARD *Now-a-Days* 65 River drivin' is the pootiest part of loggin', I think. **1908** S. E. WHITE *Riverman* v. 50 How does river-driving strike you? **1937** WILSON *Aroostook* 108 Chronologically, 'river-driving' ended the lumberjack's working year. — **(6) 1891** SLOAN *Fogy Days* 167 Mr. Obediah . . . owned a fine river farm. **1934** VINES *Green Thicket World* 36 Cindy joined in this reminiscence and laughed at the spectacle of the little Glaze boys in the sand beds and plum thickets wanting to tend one of Lat's river farms. — **(7) 1853** STOWE *Key* 27/1 His young master was taken violently down with the river fever. — **(8)** *(a)* **1800** HAWKINS *Sk. Creek Country* 47 On the right side, off from the river flats, the land is waving. **1835** HOFFMAN *Winter in West* II. 60 The prairies . . . resemble what at the North are called 'river-*flats*,' or natural meadows. *(b)* **1829** *Free Press* (Tarboro, N.C.) 27 Nov., The Subscribers will proceed to sell at the Grove, . . . Two excellent River Flats. — **(9) 1837** BIRD *Nick of Woods* I. 58 I'm for any man that insults me! log-leg or leather-breeches, green-shirt or blanket-coat, land-trotter or river-roller.

(10) *(a)* **1936** ARTHUR *Old New Orleans* 5 Visitors [to New Orleans] asking directions are frequently mystified by the expressions 'woods side' and 'river side.' These naive terms are local parlance for east and west. *(b)* **1878** GUILD *Old Times* 46 Now we have the daisy, the sundown, the riverside, and the gipsey hat, costing from twenty-five to fifty dollars each, and which do not cover two inches of the crown, and two must be had for every season, making eight per year. — **(11) 1871** RAYMOND *3d Rep. Mines* 128 *River sluicing.*—The future of the region under consideration will depend to a great degree on finding an outlet for its vast quantity of hydraulic dirt. — **(12) 1835** SIMMS *Yemassee* II. 115 After a while came the tread of a horse rapidly driving up the river-trace. — **(13) 1852** FLEISHMANN *Wegweiser* 102 Auch gibt es an allen Städten des Flussgebietes sogenannte River Traders, welche die Flat-boats zur Aufstapelung der Produkte (gewissermassen als Waarenlager) gebrauchen. — **(14) 1865** *Atlantic Mo.* April 423/1 The John Adams . . . was an old East-Boston ferry-boat, . . . admirable for river-work. **1903** WHITE *Forest* 95, I instanced, too, some of the feats of river-work these men could perform.

b. In similar combs. of obvious meaning or sufficiently explained in the quots.: (1) **River Bands,** (2) **boss,** (3) **Brethren,** (4) ***channel,** (5) **diggings,** (6) **divide,** (7) **driver,** (8) **farmer,** (9) **gambler,** (10) **gambling,** (11) **gap,** (12) **gold,** (13) **hog,** (14) **horn,** (15) **Indians,** (16) **jack,** (17) **man,** (18) **pig,** (19) **pilot,** (20) **pirate,** see as a main entry, (21) **placer,** (22) **rat,** (23) **runner,** (24) **thief,** (25) **town.**

(1) 1778 CARVER *Travels* 59 Near the River St. Croix reside three bands of the Nawdowessie Indians, called the River Bands. — **(2) 1903** S. E. WHITE *Forest* viii. 94 There was Jimmy, the river boss who could not swim a stroke. **1924** SHEPHARD *P. Bunyan* 83 Joe generally took care of takin' the logs out for Paul, and done the scalin', and he was the best river-boss Paul ever had. — **(3) 1865** BELCHER *Relig. Denominations U.S.* 913 Others were organized into a body called, *The River Brethren*, partly from the locality in which they were first found, near the Susquehanna and Conestoga, and chiefly from their baptisms being celebrated only in rivers. **1949** *Newsweek* 18 July 62/3 The Old Catholic Churches, branches of Judaism, the Mennonites, Two-Seed-in-the-Spirit Predestinarian Baptists, Dunkers, and River Brethren are objectivistic. — **(4) 1871** RAYMOND *3d Rep. Mines* 185 So far we have no more than cracked the shell of our mines, the core and heart still lying in the hills and old river-channels. **1880** INGHAM *Digging Gold* 46 The class of deposits known as the ancient river channels or the 'blue lead' of California . . . are gold-bearing gravels found deep beneath the surface.

(5) 1851 WOODS *Gold Diggings* 13 The 'river diggings' include the bars and auriferous portions of the channels of the tributaries of the Sacramento and San Joaquin, during their passage through the foot-hills. — **(6) 1876** RAYMOND *8th Rep. Mines* 68 The lateral ridges or present river-divides terminate to the east of them abruptly. — **(7) 1848** BARTLETT 276 *River Driver*, a term used by lumbermen in Maine, for a man whose business it is to conduct logs down running streams, to prevent them from lodging upon shoals or remaining in eddies. **1910** *Springfield W. Republican* 7 July 14 Maine lumbermen enjoy telling the casual summer visitor how great is the skill of their cant men and river drivers. — **(8) 1894** *Outing* XXIV. 57/1 One of the 'river-farmers,' as we style the owners of fat bottom-lands, had asked me to join him for a day's 'slopping round.' — **(9) 1898** HARRIS *Tales* 84 Dish yer preacher-lookin' man wuz one er dem ar river-gamblers, what you heard folks talk 'bout. **1938** ASBURY *Sucker's Prog.* 279 Another of the river gamblers . . . had found a haven in Cincinnati.

(10) 1866 MOORE *Women of War* 308 Before the war he had lived at Memphis and on the river, following the cognate and equally infamous branches of business, negro-trading and river gambling. — **(11) 1834** *S. Lit. Messenger* I. 98 It appears to have cut its way through three lofty mountains in succession, affording a more sublime exhibition of river gap landscapes than I have witnessed in any other part of the state. — **(12) 1890** HARTE *Heritage of Dedlow Marsh* 209 If we happen to strike river gold, thar's the stream for washing it. — **(13) 1902** S. E. WHITE *Blazed Trail* lvi. 384 And now we've gone and bust, just because that infernal river-hog had to fall off a boom. **1944** NUTE *Lake Superior* 211 Along the main stream a well-worn path was beaten by the feet of the river pigs, or river hogs, as the drivers were termed. — **(14) 1829** *Western Mo. Rev.* III. 16 A wooden trumpet, called a river horn [was] formerly used by keel and flat boat navigators on the western waters.

(15) *(a)* **1680** HUBBARD in *Mass. H.S. Coll.* 2 Ser. V. 33. **a1704** *Mass. H.S. Coll.* 2 Ser. V. 33 Betwixt Kenebecke and Connecticut were . . . the River Indians, such who had seated themselves in several commodious plantations up higher upon Connecticut river. **1910** HODGE *Amer. Indians* II. 392/2 *River Indians.* Used by Hubbard . . . as a collective term for the Indians formerly living on Connecticut r. above the coast tribes. *(b)* **1774** *Doc. Hist. N.Y. State* I. 765 These Tribes have generally been denominated River Indians and consist of about Three hundred Fighting Men. **1907** HODGE *Amer. Indians* I. 786/2 Mahican. . . . An Algonquian tribe that occupied both banks of the upper Hudson r., in New York. . . . To the Dutch they were known as River Indians. — **(16) 1908** WHITE *Riverman* 43 Only at the very last . . . did the river-jacks . . . zigzag calmly to shore. — **(17) 1876** *Cin. Commercial* 17 March, River men, to-day, are recognizing the superior value of negro labor in steamboat traffic. **1902** WHITE *Blazed Trail* 331 The riverman always mysteriously appeared at one side or the other. **1926** RICKABY *Ballads* 236 *Riverman.* A shanty-boy employed on the drive. A driver. — **(18) 1944** [see **river hog**]. **1947** *Sat. Ev. Post* 8 March 20/1 River pigs bristled all around him, men who hadn't seen a town or a saloon for nine months. — **(19) 1838** FLAGG *Far West* I. 42 This story probably owes its origin to an event of actual occurrence . . . at a cliff called by the river-pilots 'Hanging Rock.' **1890** LANGFORD *Vigilante Days* (1912) 338 Captain Ankeny, an old river pilot, . . . knew every crook and rock in the channel.

(21) 1948 JOHNSTON *Gold Rush* 56/1 Many a river placer had yielded more dollars per cubic yard than cents per yard held by those mountainsides. — **(22) 1884** *Harper's Mag.* March 513/1 Observe the river-rats clustering about the groggeries. **1905** *Forestry Bureau Bul.* No. 61, 44 *River rat*, a log driver whose work is chiefly on the river; contrasted with Laker. (N[orthern] F[orest].) **1946** *So. Sierran* Aug. 3/2 The Thunder God of the Colorado protected the river rats today! — **(23) 1913** O. A. ROTHERT *Hist. Muhlenberg Co.* (Ky.) 393 The coal barges were taken up and down the river by men known as 'river runners.' — **(24) 1859** BARTLETT 368 *River-Thief*, one of a class of thieves in New York city who in boats prowl about vessels at night and plunder them. **1882** MCCABE *New York* 518 Another dangerous class of criminals are the river thieves, or 'River Pirates.'

(25) 1853 *Harper's Mag.* March 566/1 Scenes not in all respects unlike it have heretofore occurred . . . in certain of the chivalric river towns of the Southwest. **1938** ASBURY *Sucker's Prog.* 212 When they came ashore they demanded women and whisky, and the river towns provided both in great abundance.

c. Designating land or particular kinds of land or formations immediately adjacent to a river, as (1) **river bluff,** (2) **bottom,** (and variants), (3) **canyon,** (4) **hill(s),** (5) **hummock land,** (6) **land,** (7) **meadow,** (8) **prairie,** (9) **swamp.**

(1) 1817 S. BROWN *Western Gazetteer* 203 The garrison is situated on the river bluffs. **1902** WEBSTER *Virginian* xxv, Against the empty ridge of the river-bluff lay the moon. — **(2) 1752** GIST *Journals* 75 The River Bottoms . . . were a Mile wide and very rich. **1809** CUMING *Western Tour* 323 The river bottom lands generally yield from eighteen hundred to two thousand pounds to the acre. **1819** E. DANA *Geog. Sk.* 188 The river cane bottom land, we suppose to be equal in fertility to any on the continent. **1946** *Negro Digest* Aug. 14/2 Negroes from the cotton fields and sweltering river bottoms came there to lay down their burdens of work and woe. — **(3) 1888** MUIR *Picturesque Calif.* 2 Into these main river-cañons innumerable side-cañons and gorges open. — **(4) 1818** FLINT *Lett. from Amer.* 103 The high grounds every where seen from the river, are called the river hills. **1842** *Amer. Pioneer* I. 431, I was coming to the river hill. **1948** *Democrat* 29 April 4/2 The river hill, while not yet quite subdued, is nothing like the formidable barrier that it once was.

(5) 1883 SMITH *Geol. Survey Ala.* 456 Nearly all of township 16 in this county is second-bottom or river-hummock land. — **(6) 1781** PETERS *Hist. Conn.* 242 One acre commonly yields . . . from 40 to 60 bushels [of Indian corn] on river land. **1872** EGGLESTON *End of World* 283, I have only kept the river land. **1938** *L.A.* Map 28. — **(7) 1854** THOREAU *Walden* 256 In October I went a-graping to the river meadows. **1892** *Vt. Agric. Rep.* XII. 142 Fifty to seventy-five bushels of corn are raised on the river meadows. — **(8) 1817** S. BROWN *Western Gazetteer* 45 There are two kinds of these meadows—the *river* and *upland* prairies. — **(9) 1737** WESLEY *Journal* I. 402 Most river-swamps are overflown every tide by the river which runs through or near them. **1855** SIMMS *Forayers* 209 The river swamp is our hope just now.

d. In the names of plants: (1) **river birch,** (see quots. 1884, 1897); (2) **cottonwood,** (see quot.); (3) **elm,** (see quot. 1817–8); (4) **grape,** a species of wild grape, *Vitis vulpina*, found along rivers in the eastern and southern states, cf. **chicken grape;** (5) **grass,** grass growing in or near a river (see also quot. 1889); (6) **maple,** (see quot.); (7) ***weed,** any one of various American aquatic plants of genus *Podostemon*, also attrib.

(1) 1884 SARGENT *Rep. Forests* 161 Red Birch. River Birch. . . . Used in the manufacture of furniture, woodenware, wooden shoes, ox-yokes, etc. **1897** SUDWORTH *Arborescent Flora* 142 *Betula lenta.* Sweet Birch. . . . River Birch (Minn.). **1947** *Chi. Tribune* 2 Nov. VIII. 12/3 Here one sees river birch, mixed hardwoods, white pines, and oaks. — **(2) 1884** SARGENT *Rep. Forests* 172 *Populus heterophylla*. . . River Cottonwood. Swamp Cottonwood. — **(3) 1817–8** EATON *Botany* (1822) 496 *Ulmus nemoralis*, river-elm, grove-elm. **1852** MARCY *Explor. Red River* (1854) 76 It is fringed upon each side with . . . river-elm. — **(4) 1817** DARBY *Louisiana* 356 *Vitis riparia* . . . River grave [*sic*] vine. **1901** MOHR *Plant Life Ala.* 108 The river grape . . . [is] also found on the bare ledges of these bluffs.

(5) 1856 *Porter's Spirit of Times* 18 Oct. 113/2 The Carp must be angled for . . . in the vicinity of banks of weeds, water-lilies, or river-grass. **1889** VASEY *Agric. Grasses* 25 *Panicum Texanum* (Texas Millet). . . . In some localities it is known as river grass. — **(6) 1851** SPRINGER *Forest Life* 25 It is said that the wood of this tree [Rock Maple] may be easily distinguished from the Red, or the River Maple. — **(7) 1832** WILLIAMSON *Maine* I. 128 We have, also, . . . *Oar-weed, River-weed*, and *Succory*, as common herbs. **1901** MOHR *Plant Life Ala.* 532 Podostemon abrotanoides. . . . Riverweed. . . . Carolinian area. Eastern Pennsylvania, Tennessee, and Georgia.

e. In the names of fishes: (1) **river bass,** any one of certain species of fresh-water fish, esp. black bass, found in the eastern U.S.; (2) **chub,** (see quot.); (3) **herring,** *(a)* the mooneye, *Hiodon tergisus*, *(b)* =**alewife.**

(1) 1857 *Spirit of Times* 11 April 86/2 The Oswego (sometimes known as the 'river bass') is the heavier fish, often attaining to eight pounds weight. **1890** HOWELLS *Boy's Town* 30 There were men who were reputed to catch at will, as it were, silvercats and river-bass. — **(2) 1884** GOODE *Fisheries* I. 617 The 'Horny-head,' 'River Chub,' or 'Jerker' is one of the most widely-diffused of fresh-water fishes. — **(3)** *(a)* **1842** *Nat. Hist. N.Y., Zoology* IV. 266 [The river mooneye] is known under the popular names of *Herring, River Herring*, and *Toothed Herring*. *(b)* **1884** *Cent. Mag.* April 909 The different townships on Cape Cod protect the alewife, or 'river herring.' **1945** *Nat. Geog. Mag.* Sep. 262 Springtime drives salt-water alewives upstream to spawn. . . . A few, canned, enter the domestic market as 'river herring.'

3. In colloq. phrases: (1) *River(s) and Harbor(s) Bill*, a congressional bill appropriating funds for the improvement of rivers and harbors, the most outstanding example of pork-barrel legislation, cf. **pork-barrel bill;** (2) *to sell down the river*, formerly to punish a slave by selling him to a sugar-cane plantation owner on the lower Mississippi where slave conditions were at their worst, also transf.; (3) *to get on the river*, to find employment on a river, esp. on a steamboat; (4) *to follow the river*, to work on a river steamboat; (5) *to go down the river*, of a slave, to go to a new owner as a result of having been sold down the river; (6) *to send up the river*, to send a prisoner condemned in New York City up the Hudson River to Sing Sing prison, also transf.

(1) **1846** *Whig Almanac 1847* 38 The River and Harbor bill . . . was vetoed by the President. **1944** *Chi. D. News* 21 March 10/1 So the omnibus Rivers and Harbors 'pork barrel' bill is before the House of Representatives as privileged business. [**1949** *Ib.* 14 April 18/7 Rivers and harbors appropriations are being hinted with an idea of influencing wavering votes or causing some votes to change.] — (2) **1852** STOWE *Uncle Tom* xi, I've had one or two of these fellers, and I jest sold 'em down river. **1894** MARK TWAIN *P. Wilson* ix, Ole Marse Driscoll 'll sell you down de river. **1949** *Dly. Ardmoreite* (Ardmore, Okla.) 4 Dec. 1/1, I think we are, as a people, a little inclined to sell our own state down the river in our thinking. — (3) **1875** MARK TWAIN *Old Times* i. 14 Boy after boy managed to get on the river. — (4) **1885** GRANT *Personal Mem.* I. 288 There were also many men . . . whose occupation had been following the river in various capacities from captain down to deck hand.

(5) **1893** MARK TWAIN *P. Wilson* iii, Percy Driscoll slept well the night he saved his house-minions from going down the river. — (6) **1901** FLYNT *World of Graft* 98 He was doin' fence work in York, an' I helped send 'im up the river for eight years. **1946** *Chi. D. News* 5 March 8/3, I done it. Send me up the river. Give me the hot seat.

As the last term in **big, East, fresh, fresh-water, Great, Green, high, logging, lost, Mud, Muddy, old, pine, Red, rogue's, salt, sunfish, upper, wade, wading, York River(s).**

river pirate. 1. One who engages in thievery and other piratical activities on or along a river. *Obs.* **2.** (See quot.)

(1) [?**1849** JUDSON *B'hoys of N.Y.* 30 (We.), Alvorado began to see how well his friend and rival River Pirate was situated.] **1860** HOLMES *E. Venner* xi, Richard Venner did not turn out to be the wife-poisoner, the defaulting cashier, the river-pirate, or the great counterfeiter. **1887** *Courier-Journal* 31 Jan. 8/1 The drift from above caused by the rise has about all passed, and the river-pirates were busy in their skiffs collecting it. — (2) **1932** HARRY WILLIAMS *Legends Great Southwest* 260 What is a river pirate? . . . One engaged in . . . smuggling . . . across the border.

***Rivoli,** *n.* The refulgent hummingbird, so called after André Masséna (1758–1817), created duc de Rivoli in 1808. In full **Rivoli hummingbird.** — **1892** TORREY *Foot-Path Way* 139 Mr. Henshaw recalls an experience with a nest of the Rivoli Humming bird [Eugenes fulgens), in Arizona. **1917** *Birds of Amer.* II. 181 The tail of the male Rivoli is slightly forked while that of the female is double rounded.

roach rotʃ, *n.*[1] [A euphemism for **cockroach.* See quot. 1837.] Any one of the various annoying or destructive insects usu. called cockroaches, as *Blattella germanica* and *Periplaneta americana.* Also attrib.

1837 B. D. WALSH tr. *Comedies Aristophanes* (1848) 89 (*footnote*), 'Cock-roaches' in the United States . . . are always called 'roaches' by the fair sex, for the sake of euphony. **1853** P. PAXTON *Yankee in Texas* 163 Texas, in fact, may be entomologically divided into . . . the ant country and the roach and flea country. **1950** *N.O. Times-Picayune Mag.* 15 Jan. 5/2 It's a lucky thing that the species of scorpion found in the South is not as deadly to humans as it is, say, to a roach.

***roach,** *n.*[2]

1. A roll of hair brushed upward. Also attrib.

1884 HARRIS *Mingo* 43 Nor was his ideal of feminine beauty reached by the village belles, with their roach-combs. **1898** DELAND *Old Chester Tales* 93 His yellow hair . . . every afternoon was curled up into a long, sleek roll called a 'roach,' and tied with a blue ribbon. **1944** CLARK *Pills* 217 Men reddened by the hot spring sun were freshly shaved and their hair was combed back in long dampened or oiled roaches.

b. An upward curve in the back of an animal.

1889 *Cent. Mag.* Jan. 335/1 [The Texas pony has] a very long body, with a pronounced roach just forward of the coupling.

2. roachback, an animal with an upward-curved back.

1874 *Vt. Bd. Agric. Rep.* II. 402 Old Brown Dick was a roach-back . . . while the buckskin . . . was a regular hollow or sway back. **1893** ROOSEVELT *Wilderness Hunter* 266 Any bear with unusually long hair on the spine and shoulders . . . is forthwith dubbed a 'roach-back.'

3. roach mane, a horse's mane trimmed short so as to present an upward curve.

1781 *Royal Georgia Gaz.* 8 March (Th.), A Black Horse, about 13 and an half hands high, half roach main. **1835** J. T. IRVING *Indian Sk.* II. 4 She was mounted upon a little wall-eyed, cream-coloured pony, with a roach mane and a bobtail.

***roach,** *v.*

1. *tr.* To trim or clip the mane of (an animal). Also **roaching,** *n.*

1818 *Missouri Gazette* 25 Dec. 4/5 His mane has been divided, and laid on both sides of his neck, and that part that laid on the left side, cut off as if to roach him. **1903** *N.Y. Ev. Post* 24 Oct., When brought to market he [the mule] undergoes the process of 'roaching,' which consists of removing all the hair of poor quality and scanty growth. **1919** WILSON *Ma Pettengill* 29, I had the boys . . . put each one of the cunning little mites [mules] into the chute and roach it so as to put a bow in its neck.

2. To brush (one's hair) upward and to the back.

1853 BALDWIN *Flush Times Ala.* 108 His hair was roached up, and stood as erect and upright as his body. **1929** A. ELLIS *Life* 86 Henry's hair was roached back.

roach dace. (See quot.) — **1842** *Nat. Hist. N.Y., Zoology* IV. 208 The Roach Dace. *Leuciscus pulchellus.* . . . According to Dr. Storer this species is found in the Eastern States.

roached rotʃt, *a.*

1. a. Of a horse's mane: Trimmed into a roach mane *q.v.* **b.** Of hair: Trimmed and brushed upward.

(a) **1790** *Augusta* (Ga.) *Chronicle* 13 March 3/1 (Th. Supp.), A Bay Horse, roached mane and a small switched tail. **1891** *Appeal-Avalanche* (Memphis) 26 April 7/2 Strayed . . . one dark bay colt, roached mane and end of tail cut off. **1948** *Capital-Democrat* (Tishomingo, Okla.) 17 June 10/4 Black saddle horse. One white foot. White spot in forehead. Mane roached. — (b) **1856** CARTWRIGHT *Autobiog.* 141 This young man had a mighty bushy roached head of hair. **1944** DUNCAN *M. Graham* 91 There were twenty-seven big, little, and middlin'-sized boys and girls, giggling and whispering about the master's roached, curly red hair.

2. roached back(ed), an upward-curving back, having such a back.

1776 *N. Eng. Chron.* 25 Jan. (Th.), Strayed or stolen, a sorrel horse—roach'd back, 3 white feet. **1844** W. L. BROWN *Scribblings & Sk.* 176 (Th.), The two [horses] with roatched backs, and ears glued to their necks, were scrambling. **1894** MARK TWAIN *Tom Sawyer Abroad* ix. 355 (R.), Roached-backed animals that he said was hyenas.

***road,** *n.*

1. =buffalo trace. *Obs.*

1765 CROGHAN *Journal* 13 We came into a large road which the buffaloes have beaten, spacious enough for two wagons to go abreast, and leading straight into the Lick. **1886** Z. F. SMITH *Kentucky* 22 The hardy explorers took one of these roads, or buffalo traces, as they are called and known even yet.

2. The track over which railroad trains travel.

1832 HONE *Diary* I. 59 The Mohawk and Hudson road is travelled by the power of a steam locomotive engine; the Saratoga, by a horse-power. **1889** *Gallup* (N.M.) *Gleaner* 18 March 1/3 Roadmaster J. Fogarty spends but little time at home, his attention being required on the road a greater portion of the time. **1918** *Essex Inst. Coll.* LIV. 218 They should be run as one road, thus doing away with the expensive separate staffs, repair shops, freight houses, etc.

3. In combs.: (1) **road beat,** (see quot.); (2) **bed,** the graded surface of a road, esp. of a railroad; (3) **belt,** a belt signifying an agreement with Indians for the maintenance of a road, *obs.;* (4) **boat,** a boat serving as a railroad or ferry, *obs.;* (5) **brand,** *W.* (see quot. 1874); (6) **cart,** a light, two-wheeled, one-horse vehicle, for one or two passengers, cf. **road sulky;** (7) **circus,** a traveling circus; (8) **district,** a district in which the maintenance and construction of roads are locally controlled; (9) **engine,** a railroad engine for use on a line of road as distinguished from a yard or switch engine; (10) **glass,** a road lamp, *obs.;* (11) **grader,** a wheeled vehicular device having an adjustable steel blade or scraper designed to throw dirt from the side to the center of a road; (12) **lottery,** a lottery to raise money for roads; (13) **ma-**

chine, a machine used in building roads, a road scraper; (14) **ometer,** a device for measuring distance along a road, *obs.;* (15) **precinct,** =**road district;** (16) **ranch,** a business establishment beside a road, *rare;* (17) **runner,** =**chaparral cock,** also transf.; (18) **scraper,** an apparatus drawn by a draft animal or animals, used for excavating, esp. in road construction; (19) **show,** a theatrical show on tour; (20) **sulky,** =**road cart;** (21) **trotter,** (*a*) a horse that travels a road by trotting, (*b*) (see quot.), (*c*) a road agent, *q.v.* as a main entry.

(1) **1895** *D.N.* I. 399 Road-beat, part of the highway under the control of a single path-master. N.Y. e., s.e., Canada. — (2) **1840** TANNER *Canals & Railroads* 258 *Road bed,* that part of a rail-road upon which the superstructure reposes. **1949** *Chi. D. News* 6 July 14/3 Its ammunition can be plucked from any roadbed. — (3) **1765**

Road cart or road sulky

CROGHAN *Journal* 156 [We] delivered them [*sc.* Indians] a Road Belt . . . to open a Road from the rising to the setting of the Sun. — (4) **1851** *De Bow's Review* XI. 667 It should be accomplished . . . by a draw-bridge or road boat.

(5) **1874** McCOY *Cattle* 7 The slight brand put on the stock at the time [i.e., when the herd is started to market over the trail] is called a road brand, in contradistinction to the ranch brand, which is usually put on the animal when young. **1939** ROLLINS *Gone Haywire* 144 In addition, there was on all the beasts, for purposes of identification, a slightly seared road brand. — (6) **1883** *Harper's Mag.* Aug. 390/2 The common road cart—with wooden springs—costs $15. **1944** *Democrat* 14 Sep. 2/1 Reminds us of the time that the horse hitched to the roadcart ran away with Walter Coate. — (7) **1899** G. ADE *Fables in Slang* 83 These two Troupers began their Professional Career with a Road Circus. — (8) **1838** *Indiana H. Rep. Jrnl.* 23 Sess. 87 The committee on roads [shall] be instructed to inquire into the expediency of increasing the size of road districts in this state. **1949** *Ill. Agric. Assoc. Rec.* Oct. 4/2 A majority of the road districts are at present unable to furnish road service consistent with the demands of the road users. — (9) **1886** *Walla Walla Union* 24 Nov. 3/4 The 'hog' will haul nine loaded cars up the heavy Alto grade, while the ordinary road engine had a hard tussel to haul four or five.

(10) **1883** *Cent. Mag.* Oct. 927/2 His road-glasses illuminate the wayside: our modern travellers use stronger lenses, and see things through and through. — (11) **1934** WEBSTER. **1948** *Time* 12 Jan. 29/2 Up past the cathedral on the road to Cali stands a broken-down road grader. — (12) **1806** *Balance* V. 31/2 No. 17628, drawn a prize of One Thousand Dollars, in the Road Lottery, was sold at Norman's Lottery-Office. — (13) **1884** *N.Y. Wkly. Tribune* 2 April 17/3 (*advt.*), Lamborn Road Machine easily operated. **1949** *Democrat* 24 Feb. 1/1 The site . . . will be used for parking the large number of cars . . . and other road machines which the department operates. — (14) **1848** CLAYTON *Latter-Day Saints' Emig. Guide* i, The distances from point to point are shown as near as a *Roadometer* can measure.

(15) **1858** *Texas Almanac 1859* 22 They shall also lay off these counties into road precincts, appointing an overseer for each, and designating all the hands liable to work on roads in each precinct. — (16) **1927** SIRINGO *Riata* 76 We came to the still smoking ruins of the Jim Greathouse road-ranch, a saloon and store. — (17) **1856** *Hutchings Mag.* Nov. 201/2 The Road-Runner is seldom seen in trees, unless pursued very closely. **1903** O. HENRY *Roads of Destiny* 374 Hush up, you old locoed road runner. **1949** *Nat. Hist.* Dec. 471/1 Coyotes, roadrunners, and rattlers are to be expected in the desert that lies between the southern California coastal range and the muddy Colorado. — (18) **1902** *Sears Cat.* (ed. 112) 514/3 Our Steel Road Scrapers are made from heavy plates of steel specially hardened and are superior to any drag scraper on the market. **1945** *Chi. D. News* 6 Jan. 5/6 The Gary plant . . . assembles bulldozers and road scrapers for overseas use. — (19) **1944** *Ithaca Jrnl.* 15 Nov. 2/2 'Blossom Time,' a road show, will appear on the stage of the Strand Theater Thursday evening. **1949** *Reader's Digest* Dec. 149/1 He had just received an advance from the manager of a reputable road show.

(20) **1853** *Knickerb.* XLII. 53 A well-built iron-gray was brushing up behind me in a road-sulky. **1868** WOODRUFF *Trotting Horse* 255 The little bay mare . . . in the battered road-sulky, kept making her long, low, sweeping stride directly in his wake. — (21) (*a*) **1868** WOODRUFF *Trotting Horse* 82 [Natural pacers] are often fine lasting road-horses, able . . . to make such fast brushes by pacing that no road-trotter can get by them. (*b*) **1917** *Birds of Amer.* II. 212 Horned Lark. *Otocoris alpestris alpestris*. . . . [Also called] Prairie Bird; Road Trotter; Wheat Bird. (*c*) **1921** *Okla. Chronicles* I. 83 The only way this 'road trotter,' as he was locally known, could be disposed of was to pay him a sum of money . . . and remain in possession of the claim or leave.

b. Used chiefly with reference to persons and groups: (1) **road agent,** see as a main entry; (2) **commissioner,** a county or local official who looks after, or plans the construction of, roads in his district; (3) **company,** a traveling theatrical company; (4) **cutter,** one employed to cut away brush and trees for the construction of a road; (5) **driver,** one who drives a horse on the roads; (6) **gang,** a group of prisoners sentenced to work on roads, also **county, state road gang;** (7) **hog,** a person who usurps more of a road than he should, also **road hogging;** (8) **hunter,** one who sought out a route for an emigrant train, *obs.;* (9) **Indians,** (see quot. 1910); (10) **inspector,** =**road supervisor,** *obs.;* (11) **master,** (*a*) an employee of a railroad who has charge of road maintenance in a division, (*b*) an official in charge of constructing and maintaining roads in a particular district; (12) **monkey,** (see quot. 1905); (13) **overseer,** a person charged with the upkeep of a stretch of road; (14) **star,** an actor or actress of exceptional success in road shows; (15) **supervisor,** a local official charged with looking after the roads; (16) **walker,** =**track walker.**

(2) **1829** in COMMONS *Doc. Hist.* I. 235 Spent the day in the board of Road Commissioners. **1948** *Sat. Ev. Post* 31 July 35/1 Me bein' the road commissioner, I reckon I'll haf to be there to sit on the stand with the committee. — (3) **1900** *Everybody's Mag.* II. 583/2 In the years of association which I have had . . . with 'road companies' I have become familiar with the types. — (4) **1755** *Lett. to Washington* I. 99 The Man is well known by Several in the Garrison, having hunted for them when they Covered the Road-Cutters. **1880** *Lumberman's Gaz.* 7 Jan. 28 After the log-makers come the 'road-cutters,' who clear away the brush and small logs.

(5) **1897** *Boston Jrnl.* 4 Jan. 2/2 The half-mile track is convenient of access to road-drivers from the city. — (6) **1904** *Charlotte Observer* 17 Aug. 5 The small negro boy who attempted to set fire to the residence was sentenced to 18 months on the county road gang. **1931** *Randolph Enterprise* (Elkins, W.Va.) 1 Jan. 1/1 We got the roads broke good and we didn't have a state road gang with the big snow plow to open up the roads early in the morning either. **1948** *Chi. D. News* 1 May 1/3 A 'deaf mute' from Arizona has been sentenced to 12 months on a Virginia road gang—because he talked too much. — (7) **1893** *Outing* June 210/1 There were few 'road hogs' to drive them into ditches. **1934** MORRIS *Digging in Southwest* 80 Road-hogging is one of the most anti-social characteristics in the world. **1949** *Sun. World-Herald Mag.* (Omaha) 22 May 7/1 California can be rough on the road hog. — (8) **1846** *Ore. Spectator* 25 June 2/2 We learn with regret, that the company of road hunters which started from Polk county, has returned unsuccessful and discouraged. — (9) **1858** T. S. WOODWARD *Reminiscences* (1939) 37 After this the Tuckabatchys, Ninny-pask-ulgees, or Road Indians . . . and Conaligas all forted in. [**1910** HODGE *Amer. Indians* II. 73/1 Ninnipaskulgee ('highroad people,' from Creek *nini-paski* 'swept road,' *algi* 'people'). A former band or tribe of Upper Creeks, probably near Tuckabatchi, Elmore co., Ala.]

(10) **1854** THORPE *Master's House* 212 He abused the road inspectors,—abused the jail,—and the world generally, and Jack in particular and especially. — (11) (*a*) **1856** *N.Y. Herald* 12 Jan. 1/4 James Flood is road master of his section; any obstruction being on the track it is the duty of the flagman to exhibit his red flag. **1947** BEEBE *Mixed Train Dly.* 98 A handsome green- and gold-painted Packard limousine with flanged wheels for the exclusive use of the roadmaster adds a panache of de luxe urbanity that might well be

envied by more comprehensive railroad systems. (*b*) **1857** *Spirit of Times* 31 Oct. 130/1 He has held various offices of distinction, such as Roadmaster, Town Clerk, and Overseer of the Poor. **1887** JACKSON *Between Whiles* 200 She saw . . . Sandy Bruce, . . . road-master, ship-owner, exciseman. — **(12) 1895** *Stand.* 1542/2. **1905** *Forestry Bureau Bul.* No. 61, 45 *Road monkey*, one whose duty is to keep a logging road in proper condition. (N[orth] W[oods] L[ake] S[tates Forest].) — **(13) 1834** in *Atlantic Mo.* XXVI. 334 For mending roads, two instruments are used here, which many road-overseers in Virginia have long been vainly urged to employ. [**1944** DUNCAN *M. Graham* 57 Jeremiah, on road-overseeing, court duty, or taking criminals to Bardstown, left his eldest son to take his place, and he was gone oftener and oftener and for more days at a time.] — **(14) 1895** *N.Y. Dramatic News* 7 Dec. 11/4 Mr. Shea, already well established as a 'road' star, has quite captured New York also.

(15) 1869 *Rep. Comm. Agric. 1868* 348 The immediate supervision of construction and repairs is generally under the direction of local 'road supervisors.' **1949** *News-Reporter* (McMinnville, Ore.) 4 Aug. 6/2 Again we call attention of our road supervisors to the bridge across Cozine creek. — **(16) 1897** *Voice* 4 March 8/1 The train was flagged by a road walker only a few feet away from the obstruction of stone and dirt on the track.

c. In colloq. and slang phrases: (1) *fair road for stumps*, *fig.* a difficult way; (2) *to road brand*, *W.* to brand (cattle) with a road brand, also transf. and **road branding;** (3) * *on the road(s)*, (*a*) traveling, or while traveling, as a salesman or lecturer, (*b*) tramping, living as a tramp, (*c*) in allusion to a sentence to work as a convict on roads; (4) *to go over the road*, to begin serving a prison sentence; (5) *to hit the road*, to set out, depart.

(1) 1834 SIMMS *G. Rivers* I. 65, I reckon he's in a fair road for stumps. — **(2) 1874** McCOY *Cattle* 83 As fast as the drover receives the various detachments of his drove, they are by his own men driven to some previously secured corral, and when all are in and the herd is complete the job of road-branding begins. **1883** SWEET & KNOX *Through Texas* 175 He was rounded-up himself, and road-branded for the long trail. **1943** DALE *Cow Country* 48 Often the owner of a trail herd 'made it up' by adding to his own cattle many animals purchased from other ranchmen. . . . This made it necessary that the animals be 'road branded' before starting. — **(3)** (*a*) **1880** *Bradstreet's* 17 April 1/3 A large proportion of the business this season has been done on the road. **1948** Calif. Acad. Sciences *News Letter* Nov. 3 Mr. Ferguson lives in Omaha during the winter months—when he is not on the road with Audubon Screen Tours. (*b*) **1897** *Forum* Feb. 735 It is the man who wilfully and knowingly makes a business of crime . . . that I have found in largest numbers 'on the road.' **1917** MATHEWSON *Sec. Base Sloan* 30 It'll be mighty hard to get into freight cars. . . . Thirty cents won't last long on the road. (*c*) **1904** *Charlotte Observer* 17 Aug. 5 Dora Minor was given four months on the roads for larceny. — **(4) 1924** W. M. RAINE *Troubled Waters* xix. 200 It's right good of you, Miss Ruth, to come and see the old man before he goes over the road.

(5) 1927 SIRINGO *Riata* 60, I had to get these out of 'soak' for him, before he could hit the road again.

As the last term in **back, bayou, blaze, branch, broad, brush, buffalo, cable, California, caribou, chair, charcoal, coal, corduroy, country, county, cross, dirt, dug, elevated, emigrant, emigration, farm, float, fore-and-aft, glade, good, government, grapevine, hack, hill, horse, huckleberry, ice, Indian, iron, line, local, log, main, mud, mule, National, natural, neighborhood, Oregon, Pacific, panhandle, plank, plantation, pole, portage, rail, ribbed, ridge, ring, rock, rolling, Santa Fe, sea, section, settlement, shell, short, side, skid, snake, stage, state, steam, strap, telegraph, three-notch, tote, trading, turnpike, wagon, war, western, white man's, Wilderness, wood road(s).**

***road**, *v. intr.* To travel on a road. Also ***roading**, *n.* — **1884** *Boston Herald* March, The horse . . . can trot better than 3 minutes and can road easily 10 miles per hour. **1890** *Atlantic Mo.* April 524/1 She accomplished forty-three miles in three hours and twenty-five minutes. This was great roading.

road agent.

1. *W.* A highwayman.

1863 J. L. FISK *Exped. Rocky Mts.* 23 He had thrown away [his purse] in the grass, taking us for 'road agents.' **1880** HAYES *New Colo. & Santa Fe Trail* 155 And this was a fair specimen of the doings of the 'road agents.' **1945** *Reader's Digest* June 92/1 No stagecoach robbery of consequence occurred until 1852, when road agents garnered an express box yielding $7500.

Hence **road agentry.**

1947 DOWNEY *Lusty Forefathers* 323 When Vigilantes took over law enforcement, highway robbery was apt to increase, for they simply drove the crooks out of town and some took to road agentry.

b. road agent('s) spin, a way of spinning a revolver backward, instead of forward, on the trigger finger, cocking and releasing the hammer as it comes under the thumb.

1908 BEACH *Barriers* 25 It was the old 'road-agent spin,' which Gale as a boy had practised hours at a time. **1944** ADAMS *W. Words* 128/2 road agent's spin A gun spin made just the reverse of the single roll; sometimes called the *Curly Bill spin*.

2. *N. Eng.* A roadmaster or surveyor.

1945 PEARSON *Country Flavor* 56 It is the political discussions, all the way from who will be the next road agent to who will be the next president.

* **roadster,** *n.*

1. A highwayman, a tramp, a wanderer.

1890 LANGFORD *Vigilante Days* (1912) 315 Henry Plummer was chief of the band; . . . Cyrus Skinner, fence, spy, and roadster. **1901** *Scribner's Mag.* April 427/1 [He] was already a confirmed roadster, with an inordinate love for tobacco, and a well-developed taste for drink. **1936** *Reader's Digest* Nov. 31, I myself went on the road at 17, and remained there till I was 20; I thus met hundreds of 'tourists,' [i.e., tramp printers] or 'roadsters,' as they called themselves.

2. A buggy or light carriage suited to travel on the road. Also an automobile, esp. an open, single-seated car with a place for baggage or a rumble seat in the back.

1892 *York Co. Hist. Rev.* 68 The former [repository and office] carries a fine line of . . . everything in light and heavy work from the most substantial farm truck to the lightest finished roadster. **1908** *Scientific Amer.* 8 Feb. 104 Cadillac. . . . Model G—Roadster, $2000. **1925** *Sat. Ev. Post* 4 July 51 Chevrolet for Economical Transportation. . . . Roadster, $525.

roanoke ˌroəˈnok, *n.* [f. Algonquian name of a kind of shell bead, f. the root *rár*, rub, polish, abrade. In **2.** below, in allusion to Roanoke, Va., and Roanoke Island, poss. a different word. See Hodge.]

1. A kind of wampum used in the Virginia country. Now *hist.*

1624 SMITH *Gen. Hist. Va.* III. 58 *Rawranoke* or white beads . . . occasion as much dissention among the Salvages, as gold and siluer amongst Christians. **1705** BEVERLEY *Virginia* III. 4 Upon his Neck, and Wrists, hang Strings of Beads, Peak and Roenoke. **1900** *Harper's Mag.* March 511 Silver bangles, and ear-bobs, and strings of roanoke. **1944** FOOTNER *Rivers of East. Shore* 137 For currency, the Nanticokes used 'roanoke' and 'peake,' sometimes called 'wampum-peake,' two kinds of shell. Roanoke was made out of conch shell and was dark purple in color.

2. a. Roanoke chub, (see quot.). **b. Roanoke grape,** an excellent red grape thought to have originated on Roanoke Island.

(a) 1883 *Cent. Mag.* July 376/2 In portions of Virginia they are called chub, southern chub, or Roanoke chub. — **(b) 1855** in SCHMIDT *Briefe* 123 De Bow's Commercial Review, ein ausgezeichnetes und sehr belehrendes Blatt, theilte im September 1848 mit, dass in Carolina und Mississippi eine ausgezeichnete einheimische rothe Traubensorte Roanoke grape genannt, gebaut wird, die von der Insel Roanoke stammt.

***roarer,** *n.* **1.** A nickname for a member of a certain faction in the N.Y. Democratic party in the elections of 1840. (Cf. **ringtail 1.**) **2.** An oil gusher. Both *obs.* — **(1) 1840** *Boston Transcript* 15 April 2/1 The tail of the Democratic party, the roarers, buttenders, ringtails, . . . and indomitables, talked strong about nullification. — **(2) 1887** CREW *Treat. on Petroleum* 227 We have no right, perhaps, to expect a continuance of the 'roarers,' or 'gushers' as they are termed.

As the last term in **Mississippi, ring-tail(ed), Tuscaloosa roarer.**

* **roaring,** *a.* and *n.*

1. (See quot. 1917.)

*c***1834** CATLIN *Indians* II. 13 It was in the midst of the 'running season,' and we had heard the 'roaring' . . . of the herd when we were several miles from them. **1917** *Mammals of Amer.* 41/2 The combined bellowing, or 'roaring' as it is called, of the [buffalo] bulls in the breeding time can be heard for miles.

2. roaring camp, *W.* A mining camp where drinking, gambling, prostitution, etc., went unchecked. Also (*cap.*) as the name of a particular camp.

1871 HARTE (*title*) The Luck of Roaring Camp, and Other Sketches. **1936** DRURY *Editor on Comstock* 19 Whether the Washoe zephyrs were blustering or still, the Comstock was always a roaring camp, especially after lamps were alight. **1948** JOHNSTON *Gold Rush* 46/2 The romance of historic days clings to the small towns and settlements which were once the 'roaring camps' of yesteryear.

3. Roaring Forties, a. A colloq. designation for the region along Broadway and adjacent streets in New York City between Fortieth and Fiftieth streets. **b.** The 1840's, in allusion to the political and social changes of that time. *Colloq.*

(a) **1934** WEBSTER. **1938** ASBURY *Sucker's Prog.* 428 From about 1880 to the middle 1890's, when they began to creep into the Roaring Forties, the most important of the first-class houses, . . . were concentrated in the old Tenderloin district. — (b) **1943** DEVOTO *Yr. of Decision* 8 This reawakening, which was to give historians a pleasant phrase, 'the Roaring Forties,' contained some exceedingly material ingredients. **1949** *Ind. Mag. Hist.* March 3 During the 'Roaring Forties,' with its campaign slogans . . . 'The Reannexation of Texas and the Reoccupation of Oregon' and 'Fifty-four Forty or Fight,' George Bancroft, the most honored historian of the age, often phrased his concluding paragraphs in hyperboles.

***roast,** *n.* As the last term in **corn, digger, oyster, steak, wiener roast.**

***roast,** *v.* **1. roast corn,** corn roasted on the cob. Also attrib. **2. roast out,** a New England clambake. Both *obs.*

(1) **1848** *Knickerb.* XVIII. 217 The roast-corn frolics . . furnish sources of enjoyment. **1874** COLLINS *Kentucky* I. 112 [We went] through clouds of dust and over hot sands, with . . . only roast-corn for food. — (2) **1832** *Boston Transcript* 14 July 2/3 The roast-out is a very different affair, it is a merry-making in which both ladies and gentlemen unite.

roasted corn. =**roast corn.** Also **roasted green corn.**

*c*1774 CRÈVECOEUR *Sk. 18th-Cent. Amer.* (1925) 123 We commonly make it [beer] with pine chips, pine buds, hemlock, fir leaves, roasted corn, dried apple-skins, sassafras roots, and bran. **1776** in *R.I. Hist. Soc. Tracts* XIII. 87 Our dinner was some sliced gammon, fried . . . with corn and beans, and some roasted corn. *c*1880 T. R. HAZARD *Jonny-Cake P.* (1915) 51 If possible, the heavenly old cook's rye griddle-cakes, as well as her wholly rye jonny-cakes, were sweeter than newly gathered boiled or roasted green-corn.

***roaster,** *n.* As the last term in **apple, peanut roaster.**

roasting ear. An ear of corn roasted or suitable for roasting.

1650 in ALVORD & BIDGOOD *Trans-Allegheny Region* (1912) 123 Some of the Inhabitants came, and brought us roasting eares. **1705** BEVERLEY *Virginia* III. 15 They delight much to feed on Roasting-ears; that is, the Indian Corn, gathered green and milky, . . . and roasted before the Fire, in the Ear. **1949** *World-Herald Mag.* (Omaha) 18 Sep. 2/1 A motorist came out of a cornfield with an armful of roasting ears.

attrib. **1812** MARSHALL *Kentucky* 128 [They] had exhausted all that kind of supply [i.e., corn] long before the succeeding crop was fit for use, even in the roasting-ear state. **1854** DAVIS *Farm Bk.* 43 Spread manure in the roasting ear patch. **1946** FOREMAN *Last Trek* 67 Later in June they promised to be ready at 'roasting-ear time'—after the middle of August.

***robber,** *n.* **1. robber's roost,** a rendezvous or hide-out for robbers, also with reference to the New York Stock Exchange (see quot. 1885). **2. robber tariff,** a high protective tariff. Also attrib.

(1) **1879** WILLIAMS *Pacific Tourist* 290/1 The Soledad is a wild and rugged cañon, a 'Robber's Roost,' but was never the home of that notorious outlaw, Tiburcio Vasquez. **1885** *Harper's Mag.* Nov. 839/1 The guerrillas . . . have formerly fixed the unsavory appellations of 'Hell's Kitchen' and 'Robber's Roost' upon certain localities of the floor. **1927** SIRINGO *Riata & Spurs* 235 Later it was taken to the Robbers' Roost, fifty miles east of Hanksville, where the Wild Bunch used twenty-dollar gold pieces for poker chips. — (2) **1890** *Cong. Rec.* 12 Aug. 8452/2 [The burning of Indian corn as fuel] is heralded as an evidence of . . . the operation of this 'robber tariff.' **1894** *Ib.* 31 Jan. 1755/2 Under our robber-tariff system there was a license granted . . . to rob the farmers and laborers of the country.

As the last term in **bank, camp, dog, emigrant, mail, sluice, train robber.**

***robe,** *n.*

1. A blanket-like garment or rug made, or resembling one made, of a dressed skin or skins. Also attrib.

1805 LEWIS in *L. & Clark Exped.* II. (1904) 376, I have also observed some robes among them of beaver, moonox, and small wolves. **1850** GARRARD *Wah-To-Yah* iii. 55, I returned . . . with full complements of goods for robe trading. **1939** HARRIS *Purslane* 100 'Are you plenty warm?' 'Chilly a little. Pull the robe up.'

2. robe hide, (see quots.).

1904 in *Kans. Hist. Soc.* IX. 44 The robe hides, those killed late in the fall and early winter, being best, brought better prices—sometimes as high as five dollars each. **1943** LAURA V. HAMNER *Short Grass* 24 This was winter . . . the fur was heavier and the [buffalo] hides were classed as 'robe hides' and brought better prices.

3. *To cast one's robe,* of an Indian: To go on the war-path. *Obs.*

1814 BRACKENRIDGE *Views La.* 254 Frequently when unsuccessful, they 'cast their robes,' as they express it, and vow to kill the first person they meet, provided he be not of their own nation.

As the last term in **bath, beaver, bishop's, black, buffalo, buggy, Crow, endowment, lap, Little, resurrection, sleigh, Small, wolf robe(s).**

Robert (of) Lincoln. A bobolink.

1839 *Boston Transcript* 8 June 2/4 Our old friend, Robert Lincoln, the celebrated minstrel, better known by the abbreviation of Bob Lincoln, or Boblink, is on his usual visit. **1855** BRYANT *Poetical Works* (1903) 230 Robert of Lincoln bestirs him well. **1887** *Our Dumb Animals* Aug. 35/2 Robert-of-Lincoln came. Bobolink is a very dandy-looking fellow.

***robin,** *n.*

1. A large, red-breasted thrush, *Turdus migratorius.*

1703 SEWALL *Diary* II. 74 The Robbins cheerfully utter their Notes this morn. **1884** MERRIAM *Mammals of Adirondacks* 17 In the autumn . . . immense flocks of Robins . . . come to feed upon the handsome berries of the mountain ash trees. **1949** *Chi. Tribune* 19 Oct. 24/3 The over-ripe hawthorn fruits upon which robins are gorging themselves apparently pack quite an alcoholic kick.

attrib. and *fig.* **1823** COOPER *Pioneer* 9 Did ye think to stop a full grown buck with . . . that robin pop-gun in your hand? **1867** *Common Sense Cook Book* 54 Robin pie. . . . Lay ten or twelve robins, previously rolled in flour, [in a pie dish]. **1948** *Reader's Digest* March 73/2 May is . . . a robin strutting across Boston Common.

b. In the names of various other birds. Also attrib. and with specifying terms. Cf. **robin redbreast, robin snipe.**

1884 COUES *N. Amer. Birds* 632 *Tringa.* . . . Robin Sandpiper. Bill about as long as, or rather longer than, the head. **1917** *Birds of Amer.* I. 231 Knot. *Tringa canutus.* . . . [Also called] Robin-breast; Beach Robin; Red-breast. *Ib.* 140 Buffle-Head. *Charitonetta albeola.* . . . [Also called] Dopper; Robin Dipper; Little Black and White Duck (male).

2. (See quot.) *Obs.*

1877 BARTLETT 534 *Robin,* a flannel undershirt.

3. The name, or part of the name, of various fishes.

1884 GOODE *Fisheries* I. 393 The 'Sailor's Choice' . . . bears several other names, being known about Cape Hatteras as the 'Robin' and 'Pinfish.' **1894** *Outing* XXIV. 263/2 The robin grunted vigorously as I relieved him of the hook. **1896** JORDAN & EVERMANN *Check-List Fishes* 489 *Cephalacanthus volitans.* . . . Flying-robin; Mucielago.

4. In special combs.: (1) **robin redbreast,** =**robin 1;** (2) **-run away,** the ground ivy, *Nepeta hederacea;* (3) ***-'s-egg,** a bluish-green color, usu. attrib.; (4) **shot,** shot of a size suitable for shooting robins, *obs.;* (5) **snipe,** (*a*) =**red-breasted sandpiper,** (*b*) (see quot.); (6) **snow,** a snow in the spring after the return of the robins; (7) **wheat,** a haircup moss; (8) **wood,** a tree or shrub, prob. of the family Rosaceae, having berries of which birds are fond, *obs.*

(1) **1689** SEWALL *Diary* I. (1878) 242 Some say they saw a Robin-Redbrest to-day [4 Jan]. **1774** FITHIAN *Journal* I. 232 Not a bird, except now & then Robbin-Redbreast is heard to sing in this Feverish Month. **1949** *Hobbies* Oct. 155/1 Robin Redbreast—most familiar of North American birds—has thrived as man's close neighbor. — (2) **1784** in *Mem. Acad.* I. 461 *Glecoma.* . . . Ground Ivy. Gill-go-over-the-Ground. Robin-run-away. A decoction of the leaves is esteemed by the common people a remedy for the jaundice. **1945** *Mass. Audubon Soc.* Jan. 285, I must have been given half a dozen different names for the one plant—robin-runaway, gill-over-the-ground, ground ivy, etc. — (3) **1873** PHELPS *Trotty's Wedding* xiv, In her upper drawer . . . she saw her robin's-egg sash and gloves. **1918** LINCOLN *Shavings* 256 The said mill arms were painted a robin's-egg blue. — (4) **1792** PRENTICE *Fugitive Ess.* 145 We stand, nor dread the windy storm, Nor all the robin-shot, that rattle From those on t'other side the battle. **1844** *Knickerb.* XXIII. 440 [Get] half a dozen pounds of No. 4 shot. None of the fine mustard-seed or robin.

(5) (*a*) **1832** *N.Y. Mirror* 7 April 317/2 In the woods the throstle and on the beach the robin-snipe whistle to the breeze. **1949** KITCHIN *Birds Olympic Peninsula* 100 Amid these excitables are flocks of red-breasted knots or 'robin snipe.' (*b*) **1917** *Birds of Amer.* I. 229 Dowitcher. . . . Other names [include] Robin Snipe; Sea Pigeon; Driver; [etc.]. — (6) **1857** THOREAU *Journal* IX. 286 The slight robin snow of yesterday . . . is already mostly dissipated. — (7) **1886** BERGEN in *Pop. Sci. Mo.* XXIX. 368 The birds are not the only harvesters of the pretty moss known as robin-wheat. — (8) **1831** AUDUBON *Ornith. Biog.* I. 304 The common name of it is Robin Wood.

As the last term in **Alaska, blind, blue, Canada, Columbian, English, gold, golden, ground, marsh, Oregon, pop, round, sea, swamp, wake, western, wood robin.**

roble ˈroble, *n. S.W.* [Sp., in Amer. Sp. applied to various oaks.] (See quots.)

1879 WILLIAMS *Pacific Tourist* 273/1 The Paso Roble Springs (the name means Pass of Oaks) most used, have been analyzed with the following results. **1888** LINDLEY *Calif. of South* 334 The Mexican 'Roble,' *Quercus lobata*, is one of the grandest trees and forms natural parks of great extent. **1914** SAUNDERS *With Flowers & Trees* 11 In the language of Spanish-Californians the valley oak, which is deciduous, is called *roble*.

Rochester knockings. Knockings or rappings on walls, furniture, etc., alleged to be spiritual manifestations, so called from Rochester, N.Y., where such knockings early attained notoriety. *Obs.* Cf. **spiritualism.** — **1868** GREELEY *Autobiog.* 234, I believe I heard vaguely of what were called 'The Rochester Knockings' soon after they were first proclaimed, or testified to, in the Spring of 1848. **1896** HASWELL *New York* 444 This year [*c*1847–48] witnessed the rise of modern 'spiritualism,' through the delusion or deception then known as 'the Rochester Knockings.'

* **rock,** *n.*

1. A rockfish, esp. the striped bass.

1698 THOMAS *Pensilvania* 14 There are prodigious quantities of . . . the large sort of Fish, as Whales . . . Rock, Oysters. **1796** HAWKINS *Letters* 38 This is the most valuable creek known here for fish in the spring and summer. Sturgeon, trout, perch, rock, red horse. **1894** *Scribner's Mag.* May 603/2 The epicure . . . would go wild with the display and the ridiculous cheapness of . . . June fish, rock [etc., at the mouth of the Rio Grande R.]. **1948** *Trailways Mag.* Fall 11/1 The striped bass—better known as rockfish or just plain rock in the haunts of its native Chesapeake Bay—is an introduced species on the Pacific coast.

2. (See quot. 1881.)

1766 STORK *Acct. E. Florida* 52 The oysters are so plentiful here, that nothing is more common, than at low water, to see whole rocks of them. **1881** INGERSOLL *Oyster Industry* 247 *Rock.*—A growth of native oysters massed into a rock-like bottom or ridge. (Chesapeake and southward.) **1883** *Nat. Museum Bul.* No. 27, 214 Whenever the solid beds or 'Rocks' were encountered, they were found to be long and narrow ridges.

3. Short for **Plymouth Rock 1.** and **2.**

1801 J. ALLYN *Sermon* (22 Dec.) 34 May the rock of the pilgrims . . . be associated with those christian virtues. **1823** THACHER *Military Jrnl.* 27 A visit of a few days to my friends at Plymouth, gave me an opportunity to pay my respects to the *rock.* **1942** WEYGANDT *Plenty of Pa.* 278 No flock of mixed blood to this day but shows Barred Rock blood, and you pass, on any day's round, flock on flock of pure-blooded Rocks.

4. *W.* Mineral ore.

1830 *Workingman's Gaz.* (Woodstock, Vt.) 28 Oct. 38/1 The surface is almost covered with rock, all which contains gold in greater or less quantities, and which is obtained by breaking or pounding the rock. **1896** SHINN *Story of Mine* 78 The quartz prospector . . . only pans out a few ounces of powdered rock. **1948** *L.A. Times* 12 Jan. II. 8/3 (*heading*), Ruby Mine Runs Into Rich Rock.

b. A piece of money, usu. pl. and often in the phrase *pocket full of rocks. Slang.*

1840 *N.O. Picayune* 31 July 2/2 He was just on the eve of leaving town with his 'pockets full of rocks.' **1857** in *Amer. Sp.* XXI. (1946) 118/2 There he lost his every mopus. . . . All the rocks and all the mint drops. . . . All his money, in a word. **1927** SANDBURG *Songbag* 433 Save up your pennies and put away your rocks.

5. (See quot.)

1905 *Forestry Bureau Bul.* No. 61, 18 In forest description rock refers to those characteristics of the underlying formation which affect the forest; as for example, its outcrop, composition, and the rapidity of its disintegration.

6. In combs.: (1) **rock bluff,** a bluff consisting chiefly of rock; (2) **bottom,** the very bottom, the fundamental basis, also transf., usu. attrib. in the sense of the lowest possible, cf. **bedrock, bottom rock;** (3) **breaker,** a machine for crushing stones; (4) **coal,** (see quot.), *obs.;* (5) **codder,** (see quot.); (6) **crusher,** =**rock breaker;** (7) **cut,** a way, esp. for a railroad, cut through a rock or rocky formation, also **rock cutting;** (8) **drill,** a drill or boring machine for penetrating rock; (9) **dusting,** (see quot.); (10) **fence,** (see quot.); (11) **fight,** the collecting of rock bass in great numbers at a place where their upstream journey for spawning is barred by a waterfall, *obs.;* (12) **fishery,** a place where rockfish are caught; (13) **Fort,** (see quot.), *obs.;* (14) **garden,** (see quot. 1909); (15) **honey,** (see quot.); (16) **hound,** =**rock sharp,** also **rock hounding;** (17) **house,** (see quots.); (18) * **pile,** jail, in allusion to prisoners' being sometimes forced to break rocks; (19) **punch,** (see quot.); (20) * **ribbed,** *a.* firm, uncompromising; (21) **road,** a road paved with rocks; (22) **rooted,** *a. fig.* firmly or unalterably fixed in opinion or policy; (23) **sharp,** a mineral expert, cf. sense **4.** above; (24) **slide,** a mass of rock and earth precipitated as a landslide; (25) **vein,** *W.* a quartz vein containing gold deposits, cf. **quartz 1.**

(1) 1886 WINCHELL *Walks & Talks* 53 We have seen . . . the rock-bluffs bounding . . . the basins of the great lakes. — **(2) 1866** *Ore. State Jrnl.* 24 Nov. 2/2 A sound democrat, or 'rock bottom,' never shrinks from the requirements of his master. **1884** *Lisbon* (Dak.) *Star* 10 Oct., Boots, shoes and rubbers in great variety and at rock-bottom prices. **1904** HARBEN *Georgians* 200 Now cool off, an' let's git down to rock bottom. **1939** WHITE *One Man's Meat* 67 It represented the ultimate simplicity, the absolute economic rock bottom. — **(3) 1874** RAYMOND *6th Rep. Mines* 409 It may be necessary to separate from the massive pieces the fine ore and clay . . . without sending them through the rock-breakers. **1896** SHINN *Story of Mine* 218 All larger fragments roll into the jaws of a rock breaker. — **(4) 1913** O. A. ROTHERT *Hist. Muhlenberg Co.* (Ky.) 389 The early blacksmiths called this fuel 'rock coal,' thus distinguishing it from charcoal.

(5) 1896 *Boston Transcript* 21 Nov. 20/1 Rock codders . . . [are] small boats that go out for a day's fishing. — **(6) 1897** *McClure's Mag.* Nov. 79/1 The surrounding hills echo with . . . the continual churning sound of rock-crushers. **1945** *Boulder* (Colo.) *D. Camera* 29 Nov. 2/4 Left Hand Cañon road . . . is in the best condition that the editor has seen it, due to the installation of an efficient rock crusher. — **(7) 1873** BEADLE *Undevel. West* 139 From Wasatch we pass through a long rock-cut and tunnel. **1873** MARK TWAIN & WARNER *Gilded Age* 419 By and by there is Newark, . . . the marshes, then long rock-cuttings, devoted to the advertisement of patent medicines. — **(8) 1876** RAYMOND *8th Rep. Mines* 37 Had it not been for the Burleigh rock-drill the work would have been abandoned long since. — **(9) 1932** *Durant* (Okla.) *D. Democrat* 10 March 4/5 By rock dusting, a practice made mandatory by the 1929 legislature, this coal dust is mixed with an equal amount of rock dust, the latter lowering the ignition point of the mixture.

(10) 1896 *D.N.* I. 423 *Rock fence*, a stone wall. N.Y.c. — **(11) 1784** SMYTH *Tour* I. 89 There is a very extraordinary circumstance, however, attends these falls [near Halifax, N.C.] every spring, about the eighth of May; it is called the rock fight. — **(12) 1945** *Md. Conservationist* 22/1 There was experienced during August, 1945, unprecedented mortality in the rock fishery and, to a far lesser extent, among menhaden. — **(13) 1842** BUCKINGHAM *E. & W. States* III. 225 Not long after leaving Peru [Ill.], we passed on our right, a singular promontory, called by some Rock Fort, and by others Starved Rock. — **(14) 1909** WEBSTER, rock garden. *Hort.* A garden laid out in a rocky situation, adapted for alpine and dwarf plants. **1943** DAMON *Sense of H.* 93 Sometime during the second summer noticed that down one slope of what I had intended as a rock garden a broad band of taller, greener plants was running.

(15) 1815 KIRBY & SPENCE *Intro. Entomology* I. 323 What is called rock-honey in some parts of America . . . is the produce of wild bees, which suspend their clusters . . . to a rock. — **(16) 1922** *Dly. Ardmoreite* (Ardmore, Okla.) 10 Jan. 6/2 Interesting Tale of Work in Africa Told by Texas Rock Hound. **1949** *Nat. Hist.* May 220/1 There are numerous semiprecious stones to interest the 'rock hound.' **1949** *Desert Mag.* June 31/1 In all my rockhounding I have never seen sand fly so fast. — **(17) 1883** SMITH *Geol. Survey Ala.* 438 Underneath the overhanging cliffs, or 'rock houses,' as they are termed, grow abundantly some of our rarest and most beautiful ferns. **1948** DICK *Dixie Frontier* 26 Along the rivers in certain places the rocks projected out over the banks. Hunters and early settlers sometimes lived in the shelter of these for months. They were known as rock houses. — **(18) 1927** EUBANK *Horse & Buggy Days* 127 We were . . . given 30 days on the rock pile or the privilege of leaving town on the first rattler out, which took us into Memphis. **1948** *Sat. Ev. Post* 23 Oct. 132/3 Everybody was dead-pan and silent. But disciplined—like convicts on a rock pile. — **(19) 1887** *N.Y. Tribune* 7 April 2/2 Granites . . . are a rough kind of sorbets. They are sometimes called rock punch and rock ice-cream, and are made of fruit juice, sugar and water.

(20) 1887 *Courier-Journal* 3 May 414 Mr. Straus is a rock-ribbed Democrat. **1911** HARRISON *Queed* 292 Various feelings had gradually stiffened an early general approval into a rock-ribbed resolve. — **(21) 1850** *Western Journal* IV. 75 If rock and lumber were equally convenient, I would make rock roads. **1903** FOX *Little Shepherd* iii, There were towns . . . with rock roads running through them in every direction and narrow rock paths along these roads. — **(22) 1890** *Cong. Rec.* 7 June 5802/1 Every rock-rooted advocate of the gold standard is in favor of [this provision]. **1902** CLAPIN 339 *Rock-rooted*, a qualification applied to the Democratic party, fondly by its members, and in derision by its foes. — **(23) 1873** in *Amer. Sp.* XXIV. (1949) 266/2 They bored everything, from a lime-rock to a sandbank, in search of oil, and never struck it, despite the predictions of professional geologists, oil wizards and rock-sharps generally. **1877** *Amer. Union* (S.F.) 30 Aug. 1/3 Both were employed on the *Enterprise*—Dan as the 'rock sharp' and Mark as the 'funny man.' — **(24) 1877** *Field & Forest* II. 186 Pointing to a rock-slide composed of masses of stone ranging in size from a pebble to the enormous boulder, he said, 'These are the graves.' **1949** *Sky Line Trail* Oct. 8/2 The aggressive action of these mighty rock walls was evident everywhere—great rock slides, waterfalls, melting glacier and snow grinding down into smaller portions on their downward course.

(25) 1843 *Quincy* (Ill.) *Herald* 17 Feb. 4/1 The gold is found we are informed in what miners term 'rock veins.'

b. In the names of animals: (1) **rock bass,** any one of various fishes of the family Centrarchidae esp. common in the streams of eastern and upper central North America, also used of a sea bass, as the black sea bass, *Centropristes striatus*, of the Atlantic Coast, or the cabrilla, *Paralabrax clathratus*, of the Pacific Coast; (2) ***bird,** the purple sandpiper; (3) **chuck,** the yellow-bellied marmot *q.v.;* (4) **cod(fish),** a variety of true cod found on rocky bottoms and ledges; (5) **crab,** any one of various crabs, as *Cancer irroratus*, found on rocky shores; (6) **dog,** the pika or little chief hare; (7) ***fish,** see as a main entry; (8) **oyster,** an oyster found growing upon a rock and not in a bed, also an oyster-like bivalve, esp. *Hinnites giganteus* of the Pacific Coast; (9) **plover,** =**rock bird;** (10) **rabbit,** =**rock dog;** (11) **snipe,** =**rock bird;** (12) **squirrel,** the bushy-tailed ground squirrel, *Citellus variegatus grammurus*, of the western U.S., also the eastern chipmunk; (13) **sturgeon,** (see quot.); (14) **swift,** the white-throated swift, *Aëronautes saxatalis saxatalis*, of western North America; (15) **woodchuck,** =**hoary marmot;** (16) **wren,** any one of several wrens of the genus *Salpinctes*, found in the rim-rock region of the West.

(1) [?**1740** *Importance of Jamaica* 39 There are also . . . Rock-bass Herrings, . . . Old-wife, Sherks so voracious, that one of them snapped off a Negroe's Leg in Kingston Harbour.] **1815** *Lit. & Phil. Soc. N.Y. Trans.* I. 496 White, black, and rock basse, are also seen in great numbers. **1911** *Rep. Fisheries 1908* 308/2 *Cabrilla*, a name applied indiscriminately to several serranoid fishes of the southern coast of California. They are also called 'rock bass,' 'kelp salmon,' 'Johnny Verde' [etc.]. **1947** DALRYMPLE *Panfish* 119 Rock Bass will take minnows, too, and gladly. — **(2) 1708** OLDMIXON *British Empire in Amer.* I. 312 The Rock-Birds [of Virginia] . . . love Society so well, that whenever they see Mankind, they will perch upon a Twig near the Person, and sing the sweetest Airs in the World. **1796** MORSE *Univ. Geog.* I. 212 Spotted Tring. Rock bird. *Tringa maculata.* **1917** *Birds of Amer.* I. 232 Purple Sandpiper. *Arquatella maritima maritima.* . . . Also called Rock Plover; Rock-bird; Rockweed Bird. — **(3) 1913** *Outing* Jan. 451 (*caption*), Not a woodchuck, but a 'rockchuck.' **1947** DEVOTO *Across Wide Missouri* 162 Robes, either with or without the hair, were made from . . . beaver, . . . wolf, or even rockchuck. — **(4) 1838** S. PARKER *Tour Rocky Mts.* 198 The rock codfish were not known to inhabit the waters about the mouth of the Columbia, until the present year. **1911** *Rep. Fisheries 1908* 310/2 The name 'grouper' is also applied to the rock cod of southern California. **1949** *Lincoln Co. News* (Oceanlake, Ore.) 4 Aug. 1/1 Rock and ling cod, ten pound flounders and even salmon were the specimens landed.

(5) 1837 WILLIAMS *Florida* 105 The Rock Crab is common on the Atlantic coast. **1884** GOODE *Fisheries* I. 772 The Pacific Rock Crab does not often occur on the shore between tides. — **(6) 1880** *Rep. Supt. Yellowstone Nat. Pk.* (1881) 42 Rock dog . . . is similar in appearance and habit to the Eastern woodchuck or ground-hog, but much smaller. — **(8) 1881** NASH *Two Yrs. Ore.* 85 The Tide has run nearly out this evening; a good chance for some rock-oysters. **1913** LONDON *Valley of Moon* 278 Some oysters first—I want to compare them with the rock oysters. — **(9) 1888** TRUMBULL *Names Birds* 182 It is the Rock-bird, Rock-Plover, and the Rock Snipe at Rowley and Salem, Mass.

(10) 1881 FARROW *Mt. Scouting* 207 The rock rabbit is very small being only five or six inches long and has pointed ears. **1913** *Outing* Jan. 450 (*caption*), One of the oddest citizens of the Park is this little chap—also known as Coney or Rockrabbit. — **(11) 1835** AUDUBON *Ornith. Biog.* III. 558 Their marked predilection for rocky shores has caused them to be named 'Rock Snipes' by the gunners of our eastern coast. **1917** *Birds of Amer.* I. 232 Purple Sandpiper. *Arquatella maritima maritima.* . . . Other Names.—Rock Sandpiper; Rock Snipe; Rock Plover. — **(12) 1868** *U.S. Geol. Survey Rep.* (1873) 73 Now and then the small sage-rabbit, *Lepus artemisia*, the little rock-squirrel, *Tamias quadrivittatis*, and the sage-hen, or the cock of the plains, are seen. **1917** *Mammals of Amer.* 184/2 The food of Rock Squirrels consists of pinyon nuts, acorns, and juniper berries. **1936** *Univ. Ariz. Gen. Bul.* 3, 78 This species (*Otospermophilus grammurus*) is commonly called the rock squirrel.—**(13) 1883** *Nat. Museum Bul.* No. 27, 493 *Acipenser rubicundus.* . . . Stone Sturgeon; Rock Sturgeon; Red Sturgeon. Mississippi Valley; Great Lakes, and northward. —**(14) 1869** *Amer. Naturalist* III. 186 [Of] the Rock Swift (*Panyptila melanoleuca*), a few . . . breed in some cliffs near [San Diego]. **1874** COUES *Birds N.W.* 265 White-throated or Rock Swift.

(15) 1893 ROOSEVELT *Wilderness Hunter* 124 We heard the shrill whistling of hoary rock-woodchucks. — **(16) 1858** BAIRD *Birds Pacific R.R.* 357 *Salpinctes Obsoletus.* Rock Wren. . . . High central plains through the Rocky mountains to the Coast and Cascade ranges. **1939** LINCOLN *Migration* 84 Examples are the Pine Warbler, Rock Wren, Field Sparrow, Loggerhead Shrike and Black-headed Grosbeak.

c. In the names of plants: (1) **rock chestnut oak,** the chestnut oak, *Quercus prinus*, of the eastern states; (2) **club moss,** =**festoon pine;** (3) **dogwood,** (see quot.); (4) **elm,** the cork elm, or the wood of this, also the slippery elm, *Ulmus fulva*, or the American elm; (5) **fern,** the evergreen wood fern, *Dryopteris marginalis;* (6) **grape,** (see quot.); (7) **maple,** a sugar maple, or lumber obtained from this; (8) **oak,** see as a main entry; (9) **pine,** (*a*) the jack pine, *Pinus banksiana*, (*b*) (see quot. 1905); (10) ***rose,** (see quots.); (11) **saxifrage,** the early saxifrage, *Micranthes virginiensis*, of eastern North America; (12) **tripe,** (see quot. 1866); (13) **wheat,** (see quot.).

(1) 1810 MICHAUX *Arbres* I. 23 *Rock chestnut oak* . . . seul nom donné à cette espèce dans les Etats de New-York et de Vermont. *Rock* et *rocky oak*, . . . dans cette même partie. **1897** SUDWORTH *Arborescent Flora* 156 *Quercus prinus.* Chestnut Oak. . . . [Also called] Rock Chestnut Oak (Mass., R.I., Pa., Del., Ala., Ill.). — **(2)** [**1771** J. R. FORSTER *Flora Amer. Septentr.* 48 *Lycopodium rupestre*, rock Club-moss.] **1843** TORREY *Flora N.Y.* II. 511 *Selaginella rupestris.* . . . Small Rock Clubmoss. . . . Dry rocky places: not rare. — **(3) 1819** *Western Rev.* I. 230 The *Cornus polygama* of the flora of Louisiana. . . . Its vulgar names are Rock-dogwood or White-berry. — **(4) 1833** TRAILL *Backwoods* 106 The son of a naval officer of some rank in the service busily employed in making an axe-handle out of a piece of rock-elm. **1897** SUDWORTH *Arborescent Flora* 180 *Ulmus pubescens.* . . . Slippery Elm. . . . [Also called] Rock Elm (Tenn.). *Ib.* 181 *Ulmus americana.* White Elm. . . . [Also called] Rock Elm. **1902** *Sears Cat.* (ed. 112) 608/2 Made of best selected and well seasoned rock elm; finished antique oak.

(5) 1898 A. M. DAVIDSON *Calif. Plants* 72 The rock fern or Polypodium came above the ground so quickly that it was hard to catch the leaves unrolling. — **(6) 1862** *Rep. Comm. Patents 1861: Agric.* 485 'Rock grape,' *Vitis rupestris.* . . . Grapes small, black. — **(7) 1775** *R.I. Hist. Soc. Coll.* VI. 4 The timber [is] large and of various kinds, such as Pine, Oak, Hemlock and Rock Maple. **1832** BROWN *Sylva* 104 In the extensive country of Genesee, both species the sugar maple and the black sugar maple, *A. nigrum* are indiscriminately called *Rock Maple* and *Sugar Maple.* **1842** *Lowell Offering* II. 274 A huge rock-maple fire was burning brightly on the old kitchen hearth. **1949** *Sat. Ev. Post* 12 March 68/4 They were cumbrous structures built of rock maple, with the frame bored full of holes about a foot apart. — **(9)** (*a*) **1894** *Amer. Folk-Lore* VII. 100 *Pinus Banksiana*, shore-pine, rock-pine, Grand Lake section of Penobscot River. (*b*) **1897** SUDWORTH *Arborescent Flora* 20. **1905** *Forestry Bureau Bul.* No. 66, 33 The rock pine (*Pinus ponderosa scopulorum*), commonly called bull pine or yellow pine, is a variety of the western yellow pine of the Rocky Mountains, which it closely resembles.

(10) 1860 CURTIS *Woody Plants N.C.* 109 *Hypericum.* Of this we have five woody species, all with yellow flowers, one of which (*H. Prolificum*) is occasionally cultivated under the name of *Rock Rose.* **1885** HAVARD *Flora W. & S. Texas* 527 *Selaginella lepidophylla*, Spring. (Siempre Vive; Rock Rose.) Very remarkable moss-like plant. — **(11) 1817–8** EATON *Botany* (1822) 448 *Saxifraga virginiensis*, rock saxifrage. . . . On and near ledges of rocks. **1840** DEWEY *Mass. Flowering Plants* 45 *S*[*axifraga*] *Pennsylvanica*, Water Saxifrage, and *S. Virginiensis*, Rock Saxifrage, are named from their usual habitations. — **(12) 1866** LINDLEY & MOORE *Treas. Botany* 1172/2 *Tripe de Roche.* This name, or that of Rock Tripe, is given in North America, in consequence of the blistered thallus, to several species of lichens belonging to *Gyrophora* and *Umbilicaria*, but especially to the latter. **1907** *St. Nicholas* July 847/1 'Rock-tripe,' another lichen, has been eaten in the arctic regions in times of famine. **1950** *Chi. Tribune* 19 Jan. 12/3 Among these [unfamiliar foods] may be mentioned rock tripe (a lichen), skunk, porcupine, prairie dog. — **(13) 1842** BUCKINGHAM *Slave States* II. 286 A new kind of wheat has been lately introduced into this part of Virginia, called the Rock Wheat, from the circumstance that a few years ago a single head of wheat, of peculiarly large size and product, was seen growing out of the crevice of a rock in a wheat field.

d. In phrases: (1) **Rock of Gibraltar*, designating a kind of coat, *obs.;* (2) *rock and brandy*, rock candy and brandy; (3) *rock and rye*, rock candy and rye whisky, also fig.

(1) **1787** *Md. Hist. Mag.* XXI. 141 Mrs. Galloway . . . attended by her admiring Spouse in his Rock of Gibraltar Coat. — (2) **1872** POWERS *Afoot & Alone* 109 You, Mr. Ox-driver, with your Baptist and Methodist, and Rock and Brandy, why don't you throw that sapling from the road? — (3) **1880** *Cong. Rec.* 23 April 2692/1 These heroes were . . . the cream, or . . . the very 'rock and rye' of the democracy. **1884** *Ib.* 21 April 145/2 The breechless sons of the Lothians were not averse to a wee drop of 'rock and rye.' **1946** *Chi. D. News* 4 June 10/3 The only way to conquer a cold is by virtually drowning yourself in liquids—orange juice, hot lemon tea, rock-and-rye, etc.

As the last term in **anvil, barred, bass, bed, blossom, bottom, building, bull, calico, cap, cement, chawed, chimney, cotton, custom, cut, door, gold, grave, hanging, hard, jack, lost, medicine, oyster, Pawnee, pay, pictured, Pilgrim, pine, Plymouth, pulpit, red, riding, rim, sacrifice, saddle, sheep, shell, wall rock(s).**

***rock,** *v.*

1. *tr.* To throw stones at, to chase, throwing stones. *Colloq.*

1836 *Public Ledger* (Phila.) 30 Aug. (Th.), Jacket over coat,—rock him! rock him! cried the boys of Marblehead, 'rock him round the corner.' **1872** HOLMES *Poet* 379 The boys would follow after him, crying, 'Rock him! Rock him! He's got a long-tailed coat on!' **1947** *Harper's Mag.* Jan. 67/2 We use to rock him home from school ever' noon.

2. *To rock out, W.* To separate (gold) from auriferous gravel by means of a rocker. *Obs.*

1862 in *Pacific N.W. Quart.* XXXIV. 44 They rocked out some $15 or $20.00. **1897** LEONARD *Gold Fields Klondike* 26 In some instances enough gold was rocked out to make a first payment on the claims before sluicing was possible.

rockahominy ˌrɑkəˈhamənɪ, *n.* [f. Algonquian, cf. Virginian *rokahamĕn*, meal from parched corn. **Hominy** is from the same source.] Indian corn parched and pounded into a fine powder; hominy. Now *hist.*

1674 in JILLSON *Dark & Bl. Ground* 18 [They] gave him Rokahamony for his journey. **1738** BYRD *Dividing Line* (1901) 144 Rockahominy . . . is parcht Indian Corn reduc'd to powder. **1913** *Outing* Jan. 448/1, I am too sybaritic to relish John Muir's diet of dried and pulverized bread crumbs or Horace Kephart's famous rockahominy. **1942** in *Amer. Sp.* XIX. 71 'An he'd look for other powerful, simple food,' Mr. Travis goes on, 'such as *rockahominy*, or *pinole* or *coal-flour*. Under whatever name, it's corn, parched in clean ashes until it bursts, then sifted and blown clean and pounded to a coarse flour.'

rockaway ˈrɑkəˌwe, *n.* [*Rockaway*, N.J. (f. Lenape *regawihäki*, sandy land), where such carriages were made.]

1. A four-wheeled pleasure carriage, orig. one having a standing canopy top and removable side curtains. Also attrib. Now *hist.* Cf. **Germantown 1.**

Rockaway or Germantown (sense 1)

1845 NOAH *Gleanings* 174, I keep a little Rockaway wagon. **1846** LOWELL *Letters* I. 121 Dr. Liddon Pennock has driven by me in his rockaway. **1895** *Outing* XXVII. 5/2 The rockaway shaft had been broken only the day before. **1944** CLARK *Pills* 292 Everywhere carriage makers turned out fancy . . . 'cutunders,' 'rockaways,' . . . and 'heavy duties.' **1948** RITTENHOUSE *Vehicles* 19 Rockaway or depot wagon. The name of this wagon indicates its customary use. Body was 36 inches wide on floor; wider across top.

2. a. rockaway carriage, =**rockaway 1. b. Rockaway clam,** a clam from Rockaway Beach, New Jersey.

(a) 1846 *Spirit of Times* 9 May 121/1 The price of a 'Rockaway' carriage which will carry eight persons depends very much on its finish. **1904** T. E. WATSON *Bethany* 210 In the old-fashioned rockaway carriage, the young preacher was driven . . . to the Roberts home. — **(b) 1878** *Billings' Farmer's Allminax* 10 If i could hav mi coice, to be thoroly kontented with things az i find them in this world, or be a Rockaway klam, i would be the klam. **1944** *N. & Q.* Sep. 84/1 He walked from the theater to his hotel 'full ov munny all over, and az well ballasted az tho i had a bushell and a half ov Rochaway klams on mi boddy.'

***rocker,** *n.*

1. =**cradle 1.** Now *hist.*

1830 *Boston Transcript* 15 Dec. 2/3 The surface mines, which are of very inferior importance, require no other labour than that necessary in washing the earth in *rockers*, or large inclined troughs with mercury. **1851** MRS. CLAPPE *Lett. from Calif.* 90 A man busily engaged in working a rocker, a much smaller and simpler machine [than the long tom]. **1948** JOHNSTON *Gold Rush* 40/2 Miles Goodyear died, and was buried in a rocker.

attrib. **1850** A. T. JACKSON *Forty-Niner* (1920) 18 Worked out the claim and before I moved the Tom, tried some of the rocker tailings.

2. =**rocking chair.**

1852 in STOWE *Key* 135/2 Will be sold, . . . Hair-seat Chairs, Sofas, and Rockers. **1948** *Time* 21 June 3 He plants himself in his rocker and begins to rock and think.

3. *W.* (See quot. 1876.)

1853 B. F. TAYLOR *Jan. & June* 155 Then who says, the boys sha'n't skate? Who grudges them the 'rockers'? **1876** KNIGHT 1958/2 *Rocker*, . . . a low-down skate with a rounding sole.

4. rocker sieve, *W.* A miner's cradle or rocker, a cradle-like device for washing out mud from the contents of a dredge.

1869 *Overland Mo.* III. 301/2 The united crash of pebbles on hundreds of quickly agitated rocker sieves, sounded in his ear like the roar of a cotton factory. **1883** *Nat. Museum Bul.* No. 27, 575 Cradle or Rocker Sieve, for washing the contents of the dredges.

As the last term in **Boston, cane, cradle, gold, gum, hand, joe, kitchen, mission, Salem, self, Shaker, shoofly, Virginia, willow rocker.**

***rocket,** *n.* A form of school or college cheer. Cf. **skyrocket.** — **1868** in *Westminster Gaz.* 26 Sep. (1901) 3/1 Three cheers . . . were given with a will, followed by the usual tiger and 'rocket.' **1879** *Princeton Book* 387 The twofold tradition in regard to the origin of the college cheer, or Nassau rocket.

***rockfish,** *n.*

1. Any one of various groupers found in the waters off Bermuda, Florida, etc.

1731 CATESBY *Carolina* I. p. xxxii, Common Names of the Fish of Carolina [include]. . . . Sun-fish, Black-fish, Rock-fish. **1896** JORDAN & EVERMANN *Check-List Fishes* 375 *Mycteroperca bonaci.* Marbled Rockfish. West Indies, Pensacola to Brazil. **1911** *Rep. Fisheries 1908* 310/2 Grouper (*Epinephelus*). . . . The different species are known as 'red grouper,' . . . 'rock-fish,' etc.

2. The striped bass, *Roccus saxatilis.*

1815 *Lit. & Phil. Soc. N.Y. Trans.* I. 503 The largest rock-fish . . . are called green heads. **1884** GOODE *Fisheries* I. 425 In the North it is called the 'Striped Bass,' in the South the 'Rock-fish' or the 'Rock.'

3. The log perch, *Percina caprodes.*

1882 *Nat. Museum Bul.* No. 16, 499 *P. caprodes.* . . . Log Perch; Rockfish. **1889** *Cent.* 2851/3 A darter, *Percina caprodes*, of the family *Percidæ* and subfamily *Etheostominæ*, inhabiting American fresh waters, [is] also called *hog-molly, log-perch*, and *rockfish.*

4. The killifish *q.v.*

1883 *Nat. Museum Bul.* No. 27, 451 Bass-fry; Rock-fish. . . . This species is very abundant in shallow and brackish waters. It is the largest of the cyprinodents.

5. (See quot.)

1891 *Cent.* 5207/2 *Rockfish*, . . . one of several species of serranids. (Local, U.S.)

As the last term in **grass, yellow-backed rockfish.**

Rockies ˈrɑkɪz, *n. pl.* The Rocky Mountains.

1827 JEDEDIAH SMITH *Letter* 12 July in Off. Indian Affairs, Wash., D.C., I allude to the country of the Great Salt Lake, West of the Rockies. **1890** *Stock Grower & Farmer* 26 April 5/3 The falling weather has been general on the eastern slope of the Rockies. **1949** *Nat. Hist.* Dec. 438/3 He led the first expedition across the Great Plains and into the Rockies to find the headwaters of the Arkansas River.

***rocking,** *n.*

1. *W. Mining.* The action of using a rocker (sense **1.**). *Obs.*

1850 AUDUBON *Western Jrnl.* (1906) 202 The men began 'rocking' yesterday, one cradle, and get about a dollar an hour. **1896** SHINN *Story of Mine* 42 We started to rocking with my water.

2. rocking chair, a chair mounted upon rockers. Cf. **Shaker rocking chair.**

1766 in *Hobbies* (1949, Sep.) 50/2, 1st Mo. 1766, to a rocking Chair for andrew hunter 3/. **1768** *Ib.* 50/3 By one Childs Rocking Chear 3/9. **1830** *Collegian* 93 Next sat Airy luxuriating in a cushioned rocking-chair. **1896** HARRIS *Sister Jane* 30, I rose from my rocking-chair and walked nervously about the room. **1948** *L.A. Times* 30 July II. 4/6, I would like to organize a movement to rescue that vanishing American institution, the rocking chair.

One form of rocking chair *c*1840

rock oak. a. =**rock chestnut oak.** Also attrib. **b.** The California blue oak, *Quercus douglasi.*

(a) 1699 *Conn. Rec.* IV. 304 Running eastward three hundred rod to a rock-oak tree markt. **1773** *Ib.* XIV. 172 Resolved that the rock-oak aforesaid with stones about it is the southwest corner of Midletown. **1897** SUDWORTH *Arborescent Flora* 156. **1949** COLLINGWOOD & BRUSH *Knowing Your Trees* 224 Sometimes this tree is called rock oak or mountain oak because it grows on high, rocky slopes, but its more common name, chestnut oak, refers to its leaves which are similar to those of the chestnut. — **(b) 1860** GREELEY *Overland Journey* 349 Black and rock-oak are found in some of the mountain valleys. **1897** SUDWORTH *Arborescent Flora* 160 *Quercus douglasii.* ... (California) Rock Oak.

***rocky,** *a.* and *n.*

1. *n.* A rock bass of eastern North America. *Rare.*

1890 *Outing* July 289/2 The best fly-fishing for 'rockies' on Cayuga Lake exists along the west shore.

2. *a.* **a.** Disreputable, coarse. **b.** Hard, difficult. Also tired out, unwell. *Colloq.* or *slang.*

(a) 1851 A. T. JACKSON *Forty-Niner* (1920) 82 [The men] told stories, some of them pretty rocky. **1891** *Univ. of Mich. Daily* 18 March, Last year it [the filling of programs for the Junior Hop on the night before] was pronounced 'rocky' by all. — **(b) 1873** MILLER *Amongst Modocs* 71 We may have a rocky time down there, my boy. **1898** POST *10 Years Cowboy* 56, I don't believe I'm a coward, but there are things about this business that are a little bit too rocky for comfort. **1945** MATHEWS *Talking* 69, I ... shore felt rocky this mornin'.

3. Rocky Ford, a muskmelon of a netted variety, orig. one grown around Rocky Ford, Colorado. Also attrib.

1899 ADE *Fables in Slang* 2 There came into the room a tall, rangy Person with a Head in the shape of a Rocky Ford Cantaloupe. **1916** *Farmers' Bul.* No. 707, 22 The Rocky Ford melon is not a new variety of melon. **1939** HARRIS *Purslane* 302 He made room for the gift near the mail bag. 'Rocky Fords—the sweetest that grow. We like them for breakfast with red ham gravy.'

4. rocky oak, =**rock chestnut oak.**

1801 MICHAUX *Histoire des Chênes* 6 Chêne chataignier (des montagnes). *Mountain Chesnut Oak, Rocky Oak.* **1810** —— *Arbres* I. 23 *Rock chesnut oak,* ... seul nom donné à cette espèce dans les Etats de New-York et de Vermont. *Rock* et *rocky oak,* ... dans cette même partie.

Rocky Mountain.

1. *pl.* A great mountain range in the western part of North America. Also attrib.

1802 in *Med. Repository 1803* 238 In the fall of 1800 I was on an excursion, on horseback, through the plains that are situated between the Sascatchievan and Mississourie Rivers, along the rocky mountains. **1900** *Cong. Rec.* 31 Jan. 1354/1 The Rio Grande River ... rises in the Rocky Mountains in Colorado. **1949** *Lubbock* (Tex.) *Morn. Avalanche* 23 Feb. I. 1/6 Warmer weather also prevailed over the northern Rocky mountain states.

transf. **1855** BESTE *Wabash* I. 250, I should have gladly ... taken boat in the underground river [in Mammoth cave] and have floated to the 'rocky mountains,' as they term a vast ridge of stalactites in one of these immense halls.

b. Rocky Mountaineer, an inhabitant of the Rocky Mountain region.

1870 *Rocky Mt. News* (Denver) 16 July 2/3 But to come back to Chicago, Rocky Mountaineers are made much of in the Garden City—so long as their 'rocks' will hold out.

2. In the names of animals: (1) **Rocky Mountain elk,** the California wapiti, *Cervus nannodes;* (2) **goat,** (*a*) =**mountain goat,** (*b*) =**Rocky Mountain sheep;** (3) **hare,** (see quot.); (4) **locust,** a migratory grasshopper, *Melanoplus spretus,* formerly traveling in large hordes west of the Mississippi River, cf. **traveling grasshopper;** (5) **rat,** the bushy-tailed wood rat, *Neotoma cinerea,* also **Rocky Mountain wood rat;** (6) **sheep,** the bighorn, *Ovis canadensis,* or a related species; (7) **whitefish,** (see quot.); (8) **wood tick,** (see quot.).

(1) 1877 *Rep. Supt. Yellowstone Nat. Pk.* 11 Over 2,000 hides of the huge Rocky Mountain elk ... were taken out of the park in spring of 1875. — **(2)** (*a*) **1842** *Nat. Hist. N.Y., Zoology* I. 112 Rocky Mountain Goat ..., larger than the common goat. **1949** *Canadian Alpine Jrnl.* May 55 Even on this first day we had seen elk, moose, Rocky Mountain goats, and bighorn. (*b*) **1880** *Rep. Supt. Yellowstone Nat. Pk.* (1881) 40 The web-footed ... white sheep, or Rocky Mountain goats are numerous in many of the adjacent snowy regions. — **(3) 1851** in SCHOOLCRAFT *Indian Tribes* (1853) III. 104 The Rocky Mountain hare, or, as it is libelously called, 'jackass rabbit,' was abundant. — **(4) 1878** *Rep. Comm. Agric. 1877* 264 The Rocky Mountain Locust, or Grasshopper of the West. **1892** KELLOGG *Kansas Insects* 24 The State was invaded by the Rocky Mountain Locust in 1866. **1930** HENRY *Conquer. Plains* 319, I recall that when coming home late one afternoon for supper I stepped back surprised to see what became known as Rocky Mountain locusts covering the side of the house.

(5) 1859 BAIRD *Mammals N. Amer.* 499 Rocky Mountain Rat. **1868** *Amer. Naturalist* II. 534 Rocky Mountain Wood-Rat (*Neotoma cinerea*). On the banks of the Missouri above Fort Union, were frequently seen large nests. — **(6)** [**1804** CLARK in *Lewis & C. Exped.* I. (1904) 239 We precured two horns of the animale the french Call the rock Mountain Sheep.] **1817** S. BROWN *Western Gazetteer* 202 Rocky Mountain Sheep are the most common animal. **1949** *Life* 16 May 119 They saw a wealth of big game, including 100 rare Rocky Mountain sheep. — **(7) 1884** GOODE *Fisheries* I. 542 Rocky Mountain Whitefish—*Coregonus Williamsoni.* ... It is found throughout the Rocky Mountain region, in cold, clear lakes. — **(8) 1947** *Chi. D. News* 27 Aug. 32/1 They ... exposed themselves to two types of tick—the Lone Star tick, known technically as amblyomma americanum, and the Rocky Mountain wood tick, known as dermacentor andersoni.

b. Also (1) **Rocky Mountain bear,** (2) **chipmunk,** (3) **dormouse,** (4) **flying squirrel,** (5) **grasshopper,** (6) **ground squirrel,** (7) **trout.**

(1) 1838 in *Frontier* XI. (1931) 289/1 We then rode to the spot, and took a fair survey of a Rocky Mt. bear. He was dark brown, about the color of a buffalo. — **(2) 1878** HINTON *Arizona* 336 The Rocky Mountain chipmunk is uncommon. — **(3) 1828** RICHARDSON in *Zoological Jrnl.* III. 517 Rocky Mountain Dormouse. — **(4)** *Ib.* 520 Rocky Mountain Flying Squirrel.

(5) 1909 WEBSTER 944/1 The allied migratory Rocky Mountain grasshopper (*M*[*elanoplus*] *spretus*) ... sometimes travels in vast hordes in the region west of the Mississippi. — **(6) 1826** GODMAN *Nat. Hist.* II. 144 The Rocky Mountain Ground-Squirrel, *Sciurus Lateralis.* ... First seen by Lewis and Clark. — **(7) 1892** LUMMIS *Tramp Across Continent* 36 The Rocky Mountain trout is not nearly so beautiful as the princes of the Maine and New Hampshire brooks. [**1938** THOMPSON *High Trails* 36 The black-spotted, sometimes called cutthroat or native or Rocky Mountain, will weigh from one and a half pounds to two and a quarter.]

3. In the names of birds found in the Rocky Mountain region, as (1) **Rocky Mountain antcatcher,** (2) **bluebird,** (3) **blue jay,** (4) **chickadee,** (5) **flycatcher,** (6) **goldeneye,** (7) **screech owl,** (8) **song sparrow,** (9) **swallow,** (see quots.).

(1) 1825 BONAPARTE *Ornithology* I. 6 [The] Rocky Mountain Antcatcher, *Myiothera obsoleta,* ... is one of those beings which seem created to puzzle the naturalist. — **(2) 1858** BAIRD *Birds Pacific R.R.* 224 *Sialia Arctica.* ... Rocky Mountain Blue Bird. ... Rocky

Mountain range and south to Mexico. — (3) **1872** *Harper's Mag.* Dec. 20/2 The eyes of the ornithologist are dazzled with the dark blue-green iridescent plumage of the bold and fearless Rocky Mountain blue jay. — (4) **1853** SITGREAVES *Exped. Zuni & Colo. Rivers* 68 The Rocky Mountain Chicadee. . . . I found quite abundant in the San Francisco mountain, New Mexico.

(5) **1839** AUDUBON *Ornith. Biog.* V. 302 Rocky-Mountain Flycatcher. *Muscicapa Nigricans.* — (6) **1869** *Amer. Naturalist* III. 83 Rocky Mountain Golden-eye (*Bucephala Islandica?*). I saw some dark headed ducks, perhaps this species, . . . high up the Little Blackfoot River. — (7) **1887** RIDGWAY *Man. N. Amer. Birds* 262 Higher Rocky Mountains, from Colorado to eastern Montana (Fort Custer). . . . *M[egascops] asio maxwelliæ.* Rocky Mountain Screech Owl. — (8) **1878** *Nat. Museum Proc.* I. 417 *Melospiza fasciata,* [var.] *δ. fallax.*—Rocky Mountain Song Sparrow. — (9) **1917** *Birds of Amer.* III. 84 Cliff Swallow. *Petrochelidon lunifrons lunifrons.* . . . [Also called] Crescent Swallow; Rocky Mountain Swallow; Moon-fronted Swallow.

4. In the names, often occasional, of trees and plants found in the Rocky Mountain region, as (1) **Rocky Mountain barberry,** (2) **bean,** (3) **bee plant,** (4) **corn,** (5) **flower,** (6) **gentian,** (7) **juniper,** (8) **pine,** (see quots.).

(1) **1871** *Amer. Naturalist* V. 66 We find the rocky slopes all yellow in some places with the flowers of the Rocky Mountain Barberry. . . . This is *Berberis aquifolium* of the author. — (2) **1850** JOHNSTON *Notes* I. 268 Among the horticultural productions were two which were new to me. One was the Rocky Mountain bean, which had pods from 12 to 18 inches in length, growing in pairs, and about the thickness of a common French bean. — (3) **1909** *Cent. Supp.* 125/1 The *Rocky Mountain bee-plant* (also called bee-weed) is one of the spider-flowers, *Cleome serrulata.* **1938** HEWETT *Pajarita Plateau & Its Ancient People* 106 Vegetable pigments, such as the black made from the Rocky Mountain bee plant (cleome), were abundant for pottery decoration. — (4) [**1845** *Farmers' Cabinet* 15 Jan. 189/1 Some variety of corn that grows very large, like the 'Ohio' or 'Rocky Mountain,' might be best.] **1849** EMMONS *Agric. N.Y.* II. 263 Rocky-mountain corn . . . is cultivated at present only as a curiosity.

(5) **1892** *Amer. Folk-Lore* V. 98 *Coreopsis tinctoria,* Rocky Mt. flower. Mansfield, O. — (6) **1937** *Range Plant Handbook* w81 Western fringed gentian, sometimes called Rocky Mountain fringed gentian, . . . is one of the commonest of the range gentians and one of the most beautiful of western wild flowers. — (7) **1898** SUDWORTH *Forest Trees U.S.* 35 Juniperus scopulorum Sargent. Rocky Mountain Juniper. **1949** COLLINGWOOD & BRUSH *Knowing Your Trees* 135 The twigs of the Rocky Mountain juniper, *Juniperus scopulorum,* are four-sided, with leaves arranged alternately in pairs. — (8) **1882** *Cent. Mag.* Sep. 779/1 The narrow valley and the steep declivities . . . [were] heavily timbered with the red fir and the Rocky Mountain pine (*Pinus ponderosa*).

5. In miscellaneous combs. of obvious meaning, as (1) **Rocky Mountain boy,** (2) **finery,** (3) **hunting ground,** (4) **Indian,** (5) **region,** (6) **trapper.**

(1) **1832** *Cong. Deb.* 9 June 3397 If the Government wanted the services of those Rocky Mountain boys, they must pay for it. — (2) **1847** PARKMAN in *Knickerb.* XXX. 236 Several gaudy articles of Rocky Mountain finery . . . garnished the walls. — (3) **1850** GARRARD *Wah-To-Yah* x. 130 The hardy frequenters of the Rocky Mountain hunting grounds and beaver streams. — (4) **1819** P. WAKEFIELD *Excursions in N. Amer.* 331 We saw some straggling parties of Rocky Mountain Indians. **1865** *Wkly. New Mexican* 22 Sep. 1/3 After an experience of several years with the Rocky Mountain Indians, I am compelled to the conclusion that it is impossible to civilize the adult Indians.

(5) **1884** GOODE *Fisheries* I. 542 Rocky Mountain White-fish—*Coregonus Williamsoni.* . . . It is found throughout the Rocky Mountain region, in cold, clear lakes. **1900** *Cong. Rec.* 24 Jan. 1122/1 In our own . . . Rocky Mountain region you would find an optimistic enumerator who would go through a mining district. — (6) **1849** PARKMAN *Oregon Trail* (1944) 101, I defy the annals of chivalry to furnish the record of a life more wild and perilous than that of a Rocky Mountain trapper. **1913** LONDON *Valley of Moon* 104 Del Hancock was . . . going I don't know where to raise a company of Rocky Mountain trappers to go after beaver.

6. **Rocky Mountain spotted fever,** a febrile non-contagious disease occurring in the Rocky Mountain region, and transmitted to people through the bite of a wood tick which is found chiefly on small rodents, esp. ground squirrels.

1934 WEBSTER. **1949** J. B. HERRICK *Memories* 79 His investigation of Rocky Mountain spotted fever . . . is well known.

***rod,** *n.*

1. =**lightning rod.**

[**1750** FRANKLIN *Writings* I. 102 Would not these pointed rods probably draw the electrical fire silently out of a cloud?] **1755** *S.C. Gazette* 24 July, The House of Mr. John Raven . . . was struck with Lightening, altho' it had an electrical Rod fixed to one of the Chimnies. **1851** CIST *Cincinnati* 216 The whole country, of which Cincinnati is the business centre, purchases these rods. **1908** *Sat. Ev. Post* 5 Dec. 30/2 If the thunder-bolt is above a certain size . . . the rod cannot hold and it will jump off and do a lot of damage, maybe.

2. *pl.* The drawrods beneath a freight car, used esp. with reference to rides secured on these by tramps.

1907 LONDON *Road* 24 The tramp, snugly ensconced inside the truck, . . . has the 'cinch' on the crew—or so he thinks, until some day he rides the rods on a bad road. **1924** J. TULLY *Beggars of Life* 56, I beat it through De Kalb last night on the rods of a mannerfest meat train. **1949** *Omnibook* Oct. 9/1 He had not traveled alone since he was a kid riding the freight trains, fly style as they called it, hanging on the rods.

transf. **1949** *L.A. Times* 31 May 15/4 He was riding the rods—of a Greyhound bus.

3. *W.* = ***ramrod.** *Slang.*

1902 *Out West* June 624 The Rod he raised me to 30 dollars a month while the fall work was going on. **1924** FRANKS *Seventy Yrs. Texas* 73 The boss of the outfit was called the 'ramrod' or 'rod.'

4. A revolver or pistol. *Slang.*

1926 *Collier's* 19 June 32/4 A masked gun mob suddenly busted into the huge ballroom with rods in their hands. **1927** *Amer. Mercury* Dec. 407/2 Here's a rod. Blow your brains out if you want to.

5. ***rodman,** a surveyor's assistant who carries the rod in surveying.

1856 WHIPPLE *Explor. Ry. Route* I. 5 The chainmen and rodmen being ignorant of their duties, little more than teaching them could this day be accomplished. **1903** *N.Y. Ev. Post* 31 Oct., He began in 1880 as a rodman, driving stakes for the surveyors. **1949** *Chi. D. News* 23 April 1/1 At least 53 members of the University of Illinois football squad, listed as part-time 'rodmen' collected $32,350.

As the last term in **electric, fishing, forty, Franklin, lightning, mineral, mining, red, sampling, silver, trunk, wagon, wantage, withe rod.**

***rod,** *v. tr.* To provide (a building) with lightning rods. *Obs.* — **1879** PECK *Peck's Fun* (1882) 19 (We.), A lightning rod peddler was struck by lightning [while] trying to induce the farmer to let him rod the barn. **1897** F. C. MOORE *How to Build a Home* 64 A dwelling of his . . . was rodded in the best manner.

rodder ˈrɑdɚ, *n.* One who erects lightning rods. *Rare.* — **1879** STOCKTON *Rudder Grange* xiii, I don't see how the rodder would 'a' got his ladder at all if the dog hadn't made an awful jump at him, and jerked the ladder down.

rode rod, *n.* [See note.] A rope for securing an anchor.

The origin of this expression is unknown. Its early appearance in this country, and Kipling's use of "roding" (see quot. 1897 below) cast doubt on its having originated here. Cf. OE. *rād-pytt,* ?draw-well.

1634 WOOD *N. Eng. Prospect* (1865) 45 They are constrayned to . . . hale their Boats by the sealing, or roades. **1726** PENHALLOW *Indian Wars* 58 [They] quit one of their boats by cutting their roads and lashings. **1884** J. P. BAXTER in *Doc. Hist. State of Maine* III. 85 (*footnote*), Boats roads. The word roads, . . . is not found in the dictionaries, but is doubtless from the Anglo-Saxon, *rad, raed,* ready, preparatory. It is a small rope used in mooring a boat. [**1897** KIPLING *Captains Courageous* iii. 57 Dan . . . twitched once or twice on the roding, and . . . the anchor drew up at once. *Ib.* viii. 153 Three boats found their rodings fouled.]

rodeo ˈrodɪˌo, roˈdeo, *n.* [Sp. in sense 1. An Amer. borrowing.]

1. A roundup of cattle, usu. held once a year on western ranches, for the purpose of branding, counting, inspecting, etc.

1844 FARNHAM *Travels in Calif.* 347 In the spring, yearling calves are collected by an appointed *rodea* of cattle. **1881** ROMSPERT *Western Echo* 172 Each spring the commissioners of each county appoint a captain for the *round-up* or *rodere.* **1950** *Boston Globe Mag.* 8 Jan. 1/5, I told him we were mighty anxious to make a rodeo on his range soon as it was handy for him.

b. Cattle that are being rounded up. *Rare.*

1897 HOUGH *Story of Cowboy* 21 This is an old cattle country. Countless *rodeos* have crossed these hills.

2. A public exhibition of features of the round-up, such as lassoing, riding, etc. Also attrib.

1914 BOWER *Flying U Ranch* 16 They have them rodeos on a Sunday, mostly, and they invite everybody to it, like it was a picnic. **1945** *Pueblo* (Colo.) *Star-Journal* 3 June 7/3 Nine girls at the Pueblo ordnance depot will don cowboy hats, bright shirts, and jeans to vie for the honor of rodeo queen. **1947** *Reader's Digest* Oct. 112/1 More than 700 independent rodeos are staged in the United States each year.

b. *transf.* Any one of various contests of an indicated kind. *Colloq.*

1927 *My Okla.* July 23/1 Oklahoma is going to have a state-wide baby rodeo next year. **1936** *La. Conservation Rev.* July 1/3 The Louisiana Tarpon Rodeo at Grande Isle will next September celebrate its ninth year. **1949** *Democrat* 13 Jan. 8/6 He is one of the original organizers of the Alabama Deep Sea Fishing Rodeo.

3. rodeo ground, the place where a rodeo is held.

1892 ATHERTON *Doomswoman* xxiv, The platform on one side of the circular rodeo-ground. **1945** *Steamboat* (Colo.) *Pilot* 19 July 1/7 His first choice for a site would be across the river on the rodeo grounds.

Rodman gun. [Gen. T. J. *Rodman* (1815–71), Amer. soldier.] A smoothbore, muzzle-loading gun or cannon cast with a hollow core and cooled from the interior. *Obs.* — **1862** MOORE *Rebellion Rec.* V. II. 420, I could clearly distinguish the sharp, crashing thunder of our Rodman guns from that produced by the enemy's pieces. **1863** KETTELL *Hist. Rebellion* II. 429 The gun known as the Union or Rodman gun is a 15-inch columbiad.

roeblingite ˈroblɪŋˌaɪt, *n.* [Named for W. A. *Roebling* (1887–1926), an Amer. civil engineer.] (See quot. 1909.)

1909 *Cent. Supp.* 1148/2 roeblingite. . . . A mineral regarded as consisting of calcium silicate with calcium-lead sulphite, which occurs in white, massive form at Franklin Furnace, New Jersey. **1935** PALACHE *Minerals Franklin & Ster ing Hill* 21/2 Here were first found nasonite, . . . roeblingite [etc]. **1949** *Rocks & Minerals* March–April. 112 Roeblingite, Franklin, N.J., chalky masses W. Willemite, etc.

rogan ˈrogən, *n.* [f. Algonquian. Cf. Ojibway *onâgan*, bowl.] A bowl or other receptacle made of wood or bark. Cf. **birchbark rogan.**

1791 in *Pub. Champlain Soc.* XXI. 523 We are obliged to roast all & make water by immersing red hot stones into a roggan of Snow. **1894** *Outing* Nov. 127/1 The 'rogans,' or water-tight vessels of birch bark, [were] beautifully stitched with roots, and trimmed around the opening with colored porcupine-quills. **1941** MCCOWAN *Naturalist* 191 On a shelf above my desk is a rogan, an Indian canister made from birch bark.

Rogerene ˈrɑdʒəˌrin, *n.* [John *Rogers*, (1648–1721), a nonconformist of colonial Conn.] A member of a small religious sect of Baptist origin in Connecticut, whose doctrines and practice are opposed to some of the formal usages of churches, participation in military service, etc. Also **Rogerene Quaker.**

1754 HEMPSTEAD *Diary* 625 A Co[m]pany of the Rogerens . . . held their meeting after our meeting was over. **1820** *Niles' Reg.* XVIII. 366/1 A contagious disorder is now raging among the sect known by the name of Rogereen Quakers in Grotan. **1865** *Mass. H.S. Coll.* 4 Ser. VII. 584 [John Rogers was] the founder of the sect of Rogerenes, of whom a small number still remain. **1943** *N. Eng. Quart.* March 3 On a wooded hill above Mystic, Connecticut, live the remnants of a little-known religious sect called the Rogerenes, or sometimes Rogerene Quakers.

Rogers Group. A group of statuettes, many of them relating to the Civil War, modeled by John Rogers (1829–1904), an American sculptor. — **1880** *Mfgr. & Builder* Nov. 3 Rogers' Groups of Statues. **1933** *Old Time N. Eng.* Jan. 99/1 The well-known 'Rogers Groups,' so popular fifty years ago, were conceived in the belief that the average American would appreciate and enjoy in his home the reproductions of familiar subjects rather than the classic forms.

***rogue,** *n.*

1. A pirate ship. *Obs.*

1689 SEWALL *Diary* I. 278 Two Rogues to windward of us, which the Man of War keeps off but can't come up with them. **1707** *Boston News-Letter* 7 April 2/2 The Shallops give account of such a Ship seen this week . . . ; 'Tis feared to be a Rogue by his working.

2. Rogue River Indians, the Shasta Indians, who formerly lived on the Rogue River in Oregon. *Obs.*

1851 in SCHOOLCRAFT *Indian Tribes* (1853) III. 155 Joe, the head chief of the Rogue's river Indians, . . . claims the Shasté tribes as properly his subjects. **1861** IVES *Colo. River* 116 It was first used during the campaign in Southern Oregon against the Rogue River Indians, in 1856.

3. rogues' gallery, a collection of photographs of criminals. Also attrib.

1864 NORTON *Army Lett.* 223 The process of transportation affords excellent opportunities for taking photographs of 'black-legs,' etc., for the Rogues' Gallery. **1901** RIIS *Making of Amer.* 272 The 'gallery' at Headquarters is the rogues' gallery, not generally much desired. **1949** *Sat. Ev. Post* 16 April 175/2 It seemed his vanity had been wounded by a rogues'-gallery shot which all the papers were using.

4. Rogue's Island, river, (see quots.). *Obs.*

1824 BUCHANAN *Sketches* I. 77, I well recollect the time when thieves and murderers of Indians fled from impending punishment across the Susquehannah where they considered themselves safe; on which account this river had the name given to it of *'the rogues' river.'* I have heard other rivers called by similar names. **1865** *Atlantic Mo.* Feb. 190/2 Rhode Island—then sometimes called Rogue's Island, from her paper-money operations—refused to give up the refugee rebels.

roiler ˈrɔɪlɚ, *n.* [f. **roil v.*, to salt fish.] (See quot.) — **1891** *Cent.* 5212/2 *Roiler*, a machine for salting small fish, as a revolving box turned by means of a crank. (North Carolina.)

rokeage ˈrokɪdʒ, *n.* [See quot. 1910.] (See quot. 1848 and cf. **nocake, pinole.**) — **1848** BARTLETT 278 *Rokeage*, or *Yokeage*, Indian corn parched, pulverized, and mixed with sugar. **1910** HODGE *Amer. Indians* II. 394/1 *Rokeag*, . . . spelled also *roucheag* and *rokee*. The word is from Quiripi (Quinnipiac) *rok'hig*, abbreviated from *rokehigan*, and . . . means '(what is) softened.'

roleo ˈrolɪˌo, *n.* [f. **roll*, *v.*+rod*eo*.] A contest in birling logs.

1934 WEBSTER. **1948** *Chi. Tribune* 6 July 1. 1/4 The others learned that the roleo is like a rodeo—except that instead of riding ornery bronchos, the contestants ride on floating logs that spin so fast the water churns up like a lawn sprinkler. **1949** *Boston Globe Mag.* 9 Oct. 8/1, I only wish your dad could see you roll at the Roleo.

***roll,** *n.*

1. A package of paper money, money in general.

[1836 DUNLAP *Mem. Water Drinker* (1837) I. 65 His father took him apart and bestowed on him a roll of hard dollars.] **1846** *Dollar Newspaper* (Phila.) 22 April 4/6 He also had a roll which he said contained $600. **1907** WHITE *Arizona Nights* 31, I ain't got four bits. I got my roll lifted off'n me. **1929** F. E. MCCLINCHEY *Joe Pete* 44 Mabel visited the Big Johns and showed them her roll of bills.

2. The rolled-up bedding and other personal belongings of a cowboy. Cf. **bedroll.**

1881 FARROW *Mt. Scouting* 148 Each of the 'rolls' contains sufficient to make a complete shelter tent, a warm bed, and to afford each man a change of clothes. **1907** WHITE *Arizona Nights* 157 'Rolls' were scattered everywhere. A roll includes a cowboy's bed, and all of his personal belongings. When the outfit includes a bed-wagon, the roll assumes bulky proportions. **1947** *Trail & Timberline* June 95/1 Be certain to pack your roll in a tough dufflebag and to carry breakable items on your back.

3. A cut of beef so designated.

1884 *Harper's Mag.* July 299/1 The division is made into . . . loins, ribs, mess, plates, chucks, rolls, rumps.

As the last term in **bank, bed, blanket, Boston, butter, feed, frankfurt, log, muck, Parker House, penny, slicker roll.**

***roll,** *v.*

1. *tr.* To transport (leaf tobacco) by rolling a large hogshead tightly packed with it along a road or way. *Obs.* Cf. ***rolling 1.**

1724 JONES *Present State* 55 The Tobacco is rolled, drawn by Horses, or carted to convenient Rolling Houses, whence it is conveyed on

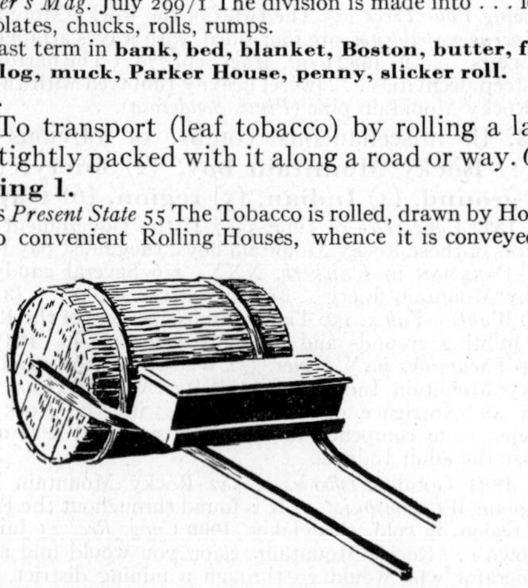

Tobacco hogshead used to roll (sense 1) tobacco

Board the Ships in Flats or Sloops, &c. **1884** *Cent. Mag.* Jan. 446/2 The cask was strongly hooped, and then rolled by human strength along the hot and sandy roads often fifteen or twenty miles to the inspector's warehouse.

2. *S.* To crush (sugar cane) by passing it between rollers. Cf. **rolling season.**

1862 *N.Y. Wkly. Tribune* 22 March 6/2 All the cane grown is never rolled (the term for grinding for sugar), as about 25 per cent has to be saved for seed.

3. *S.* To prepare (cottonseed) for planting by wetting and rolling it about on a flat surface overspread, usu., with ashes.

1865 TURNER *Cotton* 44 The seed should be rolled, previous to planting, in a preparation of ashes, stable manure, and water, which is easily done, and embodies two distinct advantages.

4. To rob (a person who is drunk or otherwise helpless) by, or as if by, turning him over in searching through his pockets. *Slang.*

1873 in *Amer. Sp.* XXIV. (1949) 266/2 When one of these fellows makes a raise by 'rolling a drunk' (i.e., taking the valuables from the pockets of a drunken man on the sidewalk). **1880** *Pacific Metropolis* (S.F.) 12 June 6/3 [At] Mission, between Third and First, ... where the hoodlum 'rolls' fallen drunks. **1948** *St. Paul Dispatch* 17 Sep. 16/5 He wasn't 'rolled' in Minneapolis of $700 and he is sorry about having three men and two women arrested.

5. To make (a cigarette) by placing tobacco as a filler in a small piece of paper and fashioning it into a roll. Also *to roll one's own, to roll a smoke. Colloq.* or *slang.*

1913 *Sat. Ev. Post* 1 Nov. 5/1 Buck rolled a brown-paper cigarette, employing none but the fingers of his left hand. **1923** MULFORD *Black Buttes* 226 Roll me a smoke an' tell me about it. **1925** OWEN P. WHITE *Them Was Days* 47 Those five old-timers ... who 'rolled their own.' **1949** *Exciting Western* May 16/2 They sat down and rolled smokes.

6. In combs.: (1) **roll stone,** a stone which has been rounded by attrition or friction; (2) **way,** a place, as a slope or chute on the bank of a river, to which logs are brought preparatory to further transportation, also the logs piled up at such a place.

(**1**) **1845** FRÉMONT *Exped.* 124 We halted ... on the most western fork of Laramie river—a handsome stream ... with clear water and a swift current, over a bed composed entirely of boulders or roll stones. **1872** *Vt. Bd. Agric. Rep.* I. 688 A young man ... brought me a fine specimen of gold from a rollstone he found, while digging a well. — (**2**) **1855** *Mich. Gen. Statutes* (1882) I. 995 It shall be lawful for such company to cause such rollways or jams to be broken. **1902** WHITE *Blazed Trail* 92 The roll-ways are then broken, and the saw logs floated down the river to the mill. **1947** *Sat. Ev. Post* 8 March 54/3 This was not fear of a fist, of a log bouncing off a rollway or squeezed out of a jam.

b. With adverbs and prepositions in colloq. expressions: (1) *To roll in,* (*a*) to retire to bed, (*b*) to arrive, as in a vehicle, (*c*) to bring in large quantities; (2) *to roll off,* to cover (a certain distance) on a bicycle; (3) *to roll out,* (*a*) to begin a journey, depart (see also quot. 1931), (*b*) to get up, as by unrolling from blankets; (4) *to roll up,* (*a*) to secure (a large number of votes) in an election, (*b*) to build (a log cabin) by rolling the logs for the walls into place, cf. **rolling,** *n.* **2.**

(**1**) (*a*) **1890** *Stock Grower & Farmer* 17 May 5/3 The older hands soon rolled in, leaving him and the kids around the fire. (*b*) **1904** O. HENRY *Heart of West* 270 The invited guests ... rolled in from the Gila country, from Salt River, from the Pecos. **1916** DU PUY *Uncle Sam* 38 Meantime the genial examiner had rolled in upon the bank. (*c*) **1914** ATHERTON *Perch of Devil* 173 A moving picture show rolls in dimes. — (**2**) **1895** *Outing* XXVI. 361/1, I had rolled off seventy-seven miles. — (**3**) (*a*) [**1846** BRYANT *California* (1848) 19 Business detaining me a short time, I did not overtake the wagon, until it had 'rolled,' as the teamster's expression is, about a mile from its starting point.] **1850** L. V. LOOMIS *Jrnl. Birmingham Emigrating Co.* 13 They hitched up and 13 men, 5 wagons and 23 Horses rolled out. **1923** J. H. COOK *On Old Frontier* 34 We will roll out tomorrow. **1931** *Amer. Sp.* VII. Oct. 12 'To roll out' also meant to prepare and depart from membership with the company [of emigrants]. (*b*) **1884** W. SHEPHERD *Prairie Exper.* 237 The cook's voice shouts 'Roll out.' **1931** *Amer. Sp.* VII. Oct. 12 When a pioneer awoke and arose in the morning, he 'rolled out.' — (**4**) (*a*) **1859** *La Crosse Union* 24 Oct. 2 He ought ... to pitch in and help roll up a big majority for Randall. **1877** *Cong. Rec.* App. 24 Feb. 123/2. **1900** *Ib.* 23 Jan. 1103/2 They answered them by rolling up a plurality of 5,665 votes for the member from Utah out of a total vote of 67,805. (*b*) **1919** in *Maine My State* 310 New clearings opened out and new log houses were rolled up on every hand.

c. In other phrases: (1) *To roll logs,* (*a*) in preparing land for cultivation, to dispose of logs by rolling or otherwise bringing them together for burning, also transf., cf. **logrolling,** (*b*) in logging, to guide or float logs down a stream; (2) *Roll the Cover,* a now unidentifiable game; (3) *to roll bones,* to shoot dice, *slang;* (4) *as easy as rolling off a log,* see *****log,** *n.* **5.** (1).

(**1**) (*a*) **1823** in SWEET *Religion* 166, I had at that time three strong black men, and a boy and as many black women, who could help us burn brush, and roll logs. **1834** *Sun* (N.Y.) 24 May 1/2, I take this opportunity, to wright to you by my Job, who is taken the first drove he ever driv, and I want you to roll logs a leetle for him, if so he suits you. **1854** DAVIS *Farm Bk.* 28 Rolled logs for mr Jones. (*b*) **1902** WHITE *Blazed Trail* 195, I'll get you a gang of bully boys that will roll logs till there's skating in hell! — (**2**) **1902** PIDGIN *Q. A. Sawyer* 239 After this game others followed in quick succession. There were 'Pillow,' 'Roll the Cover,' 'Button, Button, Who's Got the Button?' 'Copenhagen,' and finally 'Post Office.' — (**3**) **1931** *K.C. Times* 24 June, Those college men who are digging for mastodon skeletons in Texas are not the first students to roll bones.

*** rolled,** *a.* **1. rolled oats,** husked oats crushed between heated rollers. Also attrib. and **rolled oatmeal. 2. rolled steak,** steak rolled around some stuffing and baked.

(**1**) **1888** *Puget Sound Gazetteer* July 12/1 The peculiar aroma of the old system is not imparted to the rolled oatmeal or the flour. **1888** HARGIS *Graded Cook Book* 514 Breakfast. Rolled Oat. **1901** GRINNEL *Gold Hunting in Alaska* 5 For breakfast, rolled oats mush, baking powder biscuit [etc.]. — (**2**) **1883** RITTENHOUSE *Maud* 204, I got dinner—green peas, mashed potatoes, rolled steak with dressing and bread pudding and didn't spoil a thing.

*** roller,** *n.*

1. a. An undulation in the surface of the land, a ridge. *Obs.* **b.** In baseball, a batted ball that rolls along the ground. **c.** (See quot.) **d.** (*cap.*) =**Holy Roller.**

(**a**) **1849** KINGSLEY *Diary* 88 The land on the left rises in rollers from 10 to 50 feet. **1850** COLTON *3 Years Calif.* 321 Our course ... lay among mountain spurs, till we reached the rollers, which ridge the plain of the San Joaquin. — (**b**) **1880** *Chi. Inter-Ocean* 15 May 7/1 Flint sent a roller to Crane, and he touched the first batter on the way to second. **1949** *Fargo* (N.D.) *Forum* 23 July 8/8 Corcoran's roller, on which there was an error, enabled Erickson to count, making it 3 to 2. — (**c**) **1891** *Cent.* 5214 *Roller,* ... the rockfish or striped-bass, *Roccus lineatus.* [Maryland.] — (**d**) **1928** *Amer. Mercury* Oct. 182/1 To the true Roller every word in his theological vocabulary ... and every moral experience, no matter how trivial, is a symbol of forces whose presence inspires him to delirium.

2. In combs.: (1) **roller bearings,** (see quot.); (2) **boy,** a boy who inks the rollers in a printing office; (3) **cloth,** a roller towel, *obs.;* (4) **coaster,** an amusement device consisting of a kind of serpentine railway with many dips and curves, having carlike vehicles for passengers, also attrib.; (5) **mill,** (see quots. 1876, 1883); (6) **rink,** a rink for roller skating; (7) **skate,** a skate mounted on small wheels; (8) **skater,** one who skates on roller skates; (9) =**skating rink,** =**roller rink;** (10) **worm,** (see quot.).

(**1**) **1895** WAIT *Car-Builder's Dict.* 107 Roller-bearings. Journal bearings in which the load is carried upon small cylindrical rollers inserted between the shaft or axle journal and the bushing or box which surrounds it. These cylinders roll between the journal and the box bearing, thus substituting rolling friction for rubbing friction. — (**2**) **1849** *Knickerb.* XXXIV. 12 Our very roller-boy has got principles, or else he would be discarded indignantly down the stairs of this office. **1896** HOWELLS *Impressions & Exper.* 27 He became a roller-boy, and served long behind the press. — (**3**) **1862** G. HAMILTON *Country Living* 11, I become acquainted ... with the *modus operandi* of 'roller-cloths.' **1877** PHELPS *Story of Avis* 224 A roller-cloth would do, dear. — (**4**) **1903** *Boston Transcript* 7 Oct. 16 The cable cars run over routes that would shame a Coney Island roller coaster. **1946** *Trail & Timberline* May 67/1 The incomparable scenic vistas, the roller coaster grades, the hairpin curves, the altitudes of the summits and the labored speed cannot be approached anywhere else on this continent. **1949** *Travel* Dec. 19/1 Scarcely less spectacular were the roller coaster, the Ferris Wheel and Luna Park.

(**5**) **1876** KNIGHT 1964/1 *Roller-mill,* a machine for bruising flaxseed, before grinding under edge-stones and pressing. **1883** *Ib. Supp.* 763/1 *Roller Mill,* ... a mill in which wheat is made into flour by a cracking process, by passing between rollers consecutively arranged in pairs. **1939** *These Are Our Lives* 36 We raised forty-three bushels, and I hear the price is going to be fair at the roller mill. — (**6**) [**1884** *Milnor* (Dak.) *Teller* 27 June, Only a few months ago and we read with dismay the approach of the roller rinktum.] **1885** *Wkly. New Mexican Rev.* 26 Feb. 3/5 In Santa Fe a roller rink can be kept open all summer, the nights being so delightfully cool. **1949** *Chesterton* (Ind.) *Tribune* 7 April 6/1 Healthful and pleasant recreation at the Atlas Roller Rink. — (**7**) **1863** *Rep. Comm. Patents 1861* I. 280 A roller skate provided with two rows of tubular adjustable rollers, and the whole constructed and operating as shown and described. **1946** PARTRIDGE & BETTMANN *As We Were* 151 Winter skating was not enough, and in the midst of the Civil War one James L. Plimpton introduced the roller skates. — (**8**) **1869** *Nat. Chronicle* (Boston) 9 Jan. 7/2 A good roller-skater may be a very poor ice-skater, and *vice* *versa.* — **(9) 1884** *N.Y. Wkly. Tribune* 13 Aug. 4/3 Down at the roller skating rink having an awfully good time. **1949** *Time* 18 April 25/1 The village board . . . should wake up, give the kids a roller-skating rink.

(10) 1899 *Dept. Agric. Yrbk. 1898* 259 A caterpillar known as the bean leaf-roller or 'roller-worm' is injurious in the Gulf States to leguminous plants.

As the last term in **ball, black, crap, double, gin, high, Holy, log, river, shade, snow, stone, strawberry leaf, tobacco roller.**

rolliche 'ralɪtʃɪ, *n.* [Du. *rolletje*, little roll. See quot. 1924.] (See quot. 1899.)

1830 *Boston Transcript* 21 Dec. 2/2 If reading the above has given you the lock-jaw, why then certes, you will lose your share of the *cooks, ruletjis, smoked geese and sour krout.* **1864** *Rio Abajo Press* 24 May 1/2 He would call for olykrocks, krollers, rollitjes, etc., with a cup of tea. **1899** VANDERBILT *Flatbush* 105 'Rolliches' were made of fat and lean beef cut in pieces somewhat larger than dice, highly seasoned, sewed in tripe, and boiled for several hours. They were then placed under a press and were eaten cold. **1924** LAMBERT *Dict. Pa.-German* 126 rolitsch . . . f, rollichie (small pieces of beef stuffed in bags of tripe, pickled in diluted vinegar, sliced, fried and served with gravy). Dutch rolletje. **1949** KURATH *Word Geog. Eastern States* 24/2 *Rollichies* for meat roulades . . . , and *thick-milk* for curdled milk, have probably always been Dutch family words and are disappearing fast.

b. (See quot.)

1844 SEDGWICK *Tales & Sk.* 79 He received a rooletjeer (doughnut) from the kind hand that had supplied this diurnal want of nature . . . for the last forty years.

* **rolling,** *n.* and *a.*

1. *n.* Conveying tobacco or other goods by means of a hogshead that rolls as it is drawn along a road. *Obs.* Cf. **rolling house, place, road,** in 4. below.

1696 *Md. Laws* (1765) xxiv. § 8 For the rolling or transporting Tobacco or Goods by land. **1856** OLMSTED *Slave States* 360 Until within a recent period, much tobacco has been brought to market, from the more remote districts of North Carolina and Virginia, by a very rude method, called 'rolling.'

2. A logrolling *q.v.*, or a house raising, the logs for the walls being rolled into place. *Obs.* Cf. *to roll up* (*b*).

1847 in HOWE *Hist. Coll. Ohio* 358 Many times were we called from six to eight miles to assist at a rolling or raising.

3. *a.* Of land: Undulating, resembling the swell of the ocean. Also fig.

1804 CLARK in *Lewis & C. Exped.* I. (1904) 45 Found the prarie composed of good Land and plenty of water roleing & interspursed with points of timber land. **1842** in THOMPSON *M. Jones* (1872) 34 Ther minds is too shaller and rollin; they haint got no foundation, and all the skoolin you could put into 'em wouldn't stay no longer nor so much manure on the side of a red sandhill. **1949** *Green Caldron* (U. of Ill.) Nov. 38 His rolling fields are cultivated on the contour.

4. In combs.: (1) **rolling bank,** (see quot.); (2) **chair,** a wheel chair; (3) **dam,** a dam constructed with

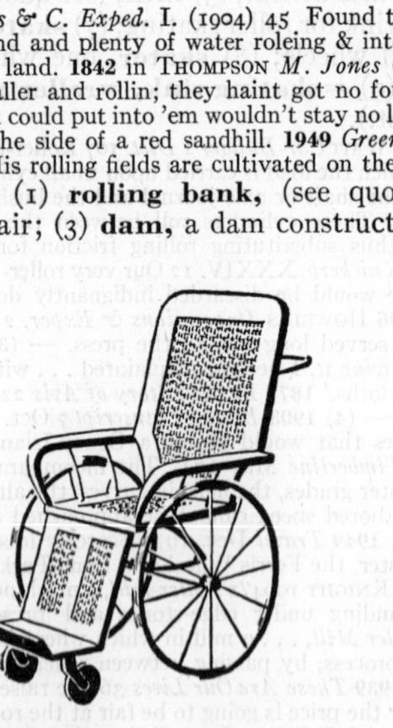

Rolling chair or invalid chair

sluiceways so that the surplus water passes over its top, *obs.;* (4) **exercise,** (see quot. 1807), *obs.*, cf. * **exercise,** *n.;* (5) **frolic,** = **logrolling 1;** (6) **house,** *local*, formerly a warehouse where tobacco was inspected and from which it was shipped abroad, *obs.;* (7) **John,** (see quot.); (8) **mustang,** some form of gambling game; (9) **place,** = **rolling house,** *obs.;* (10) **plant,** (see quot.), *obs.;* (11) **prairie,** prairie land having an undulating surface; (12) **press,** (see quot.), *obs.;* (13) **road,** (*a*) *local*, a road over which hogsheads of tobacco and sometimes other commodities were rolled, now *hist.*, (*b*) a road over rolling country; (14) **screen,** a screen used in the sifting of grain; (15) **season,** the time of the year when sugar cane is ground, *obs.;* (16) **towel,** a roller towel; (17) **weed,** (see first quot. and cf. **tumbleweed).**

(1) 1902 *Forestry Bureau Bul.* No. 34, 25 Logs which were cut and skidded in the fall were hauled during the winter to the shore of some stream, where they were piled in huge tiers on the 'banking grounds,' as they were called on the Susquehanna, or 'landings' or 'rolling-banks,' in northern New York. — **(2) 1876** in *Harper's Mag.* Nov. (1913) 820/1 We went out to the [Philadelphia exhibition] grounds the next day and rolled about in what they call rolling chairs. **1946** *Democrat* 30 May 4/4 For Sale—One rolling chair and one corn sheller. — **(3) 1815** *N.Y. Lit. & Phil. Soc. Trans.* I. 151 A rolling dam was made over the river, and a canal of one hundred rods was cut. — **(4) 1807** MCNEMAR *Ky. Revival* 61 The rolling exercise . . . consisted in being cast down in a violent manner, doubled with the head and feet together, and rolled over and over like a wheel, or stretched in a prostrate manner, turned swiftly over and over like a log. **1847** HOWE *Hist. Coll. Ohio* 46 '*Bodily exercises,*' . . . have been classified by a clerical writer as 1st, the *Falling* exercise; 2d, the *Jerking* exercise; 3d, the *Rolling* exercise [etc.].

(5) 1822 WOODS *English Prairie* 213 Rolling frolics, are clearing wood-land, when many trees are cut down, and into lengths, to roll them up together, so as to burn them, and to pile up the brushwood and roots on the trees. **1835–7** HALIBURTON *Clockmaker* 1 Ser. xxvii. 262 Is it a vandew, or a weddin, or a rollin frolic, or a religious stir, or what is it? — **(6) 1705** *Va. State P.* I. 97 The same storage shall be paid, as is directed by an Act appointing Rowling houses, &c. **1728** *Md. Hist. Mag.* XVIII. 12 John Ensor [is appointed] overseer of the roads . . . from Brittains Ridge Rolling house to the extent of that hundred. **1884** *Cent. Mag.* Jan. 436/1 By the beginning of the eighteenth century private 'rolling houses' . . . had become common. — **(7) 1881** INGERSOLL *Oyster Industry* 247 *Rolling John*, a detached sponge drifting about the bottom. (Florida.) — **(8) 1931** WILLISON *Here They Dug Gold* 236 Along the other wall are ranged a half-dozen tables devoted to poker, faro, chuck-a-luck, rolling mustang, twenty-one, keeno and paddle-wheel. — **(9) 1708** *Md. Hist. Mag.* XVII. 218 But the Slovenly Planter will be ashamed to have his Tobacco brought to These Townes and Rolling places.

(10) 1864 WEBSTER 1146/3 *Rolling-plant*, the locomotives and vehicles of a railway. — **(11) 1820** in *Mo. Hist. Soc. Coll.* III. (1908) 16 Left camp shortly after 6 A.M., & traveled over rolling prairies. **1949** *Boston Sun. Globe* 1 May (Fiction Mag.) 3/2 This was rolling prairie with mottes of timber and brush thickets. — **(12) 1787** CUTLER in *Life & Corr.* I. 269 Another great curiosity was a rolling press, for taking the copies of letters or any other writing. A sheet of paper is completely copied in less than two minutes, the copy as fair as the original, and without effacing it in the smallest degree. — **(13)** (*a*) **1696** *Md. Laws* (1765) xxiv. § 8 The Governor of this Province, hath caused four Rolling Roads to be marked and cleared. **1714** *Md. Hist. Mag.* XVIII. 8 Petition of William Summers . . . [concerning] having cleared a Rolling Road. **1859** BARTLETT 370 *Rolling-Roads*, so called in Maryland and Virginia, from the old custom of rolling tobacco to market in hogsheads. . . . This mode of transportation was still in use twenty years ago. (*b*) **1893** *Outing* XXII. 133/1 To Rosalia and Oakesdale was a fair rolling road. — **(14) 1780** *N.J. Archives* 2 Ser. IV. 175 The merchant and country boults, hoisting works and rolling screen are all in good order.

(15) 1833 SILLIMAN *Man. Sugar Cane* 14 Rains . . . occur during the rolling or grinding season. — **(16) 1869** STOWE *Oldtown Folks* 263 We performed our morning ablutions, refreshing our faces and hands by a brisk rub upon a coarse rolling-towel of brown homespun linen. — **(17) 1888** *Cent. Mag.* Jan. 453/2, I secured a 'tumble-weed' or 'rolling-weed,'—one of those globular perennials of the plains that when dead is pulled up by the wind and goes rolling around over the prairies at the mercy of the blast. **1891** *Cent.* 6527/2.

As the last term in **ball, log, sugar, tobacco rolling.**

roll-top desk. A writing desk having a slatted flexible cover that may be drawn down or rolled back out of the way.

1887 *Trial H. K. Goodwin* 15 That shows the position of the roll-top desk which was in the front office. **1923** HERRICK *Lilla* 173 A young woman looked up from the roll-top desk where she was running over a typed list of names. **1947** *Duluth* (Minn.) *News-Tribune* 19 Jan. 7/4 The ex-officeholder slams down his rolltop desk.

romal rə'mæl, *n. W.* [Sp. *ramal*, strand of a rope.] (See quots.) — **1927** RUSSELL *Trails* 2 These cow people were generally strong on pretty, usin' plenty of hoss jewelry, silver-mounted spurs, bits, an' conchas; instead of a quirt, used a romal, or quirt braided to the end of the reins. **1944** ADAMS *W. Words* 130/2 romal A flexible whip made on the bridle reins when they are fastened together.

***Romanite,** *n.* =**Rambo.** — **1817** [see **Rambo**]. **1840** *Louisville Pub. Adv.* 3 July 1/6, 27 Bbls. Pippin and Romanite Apples in store and for sale by Heth & Halbert.

roncador ˌraŋkəˈdor, *n.* [Sp., name of a fish that makes a hoarse, snoring noise when taken from the water.] Any one of various sciaenoid fishes of the Pacific Coast, also with specifying adjective. Cf. **red roncador.** — **1882** *Nat. Museum Bul.* No. 16, 572 *Sciæna stearnsi*, . . . Roncador. **1890** *Cent.* 3290/2 *Kingfish*, . . . a sciaenoid fish, the little roncador, . . . common on the coast of California: so called in the San Francisco markets.

ronco ˈraŋko, *n.* [Sp., "hoarse" in Amer. Sp. sense shown here. Cf. **roncador.**] (See quots.) — **1883** *Nat. Museum Bul.* No. 27, 442 *Micropogon undulatus*. . . . Croaker; Ronco; Verrugato (Cuba). . . . This is a food-fish of small size but good quality. . . . In the Southern States it is abundant. **1896** JORDAN & EVERMANN *Check-List Fishes* 384 *Hæmulon*. . . . Roncos or Grunts. . . . *Hæmulon plumieri*. . . . Ronco Ronco; Ronco Arará. *Ib.*, 397 *Bairdiella ronchus*. . . . Ronco; Corvina. Atlantic coasts of tropical America, generally common in the West Indies.

rondo ˈrando, *n.* [App. an Amer. borrowing of F. *rondeau*, rondo. Not in French dictionaries in the sense of a gambling game.] (See quot. 1938.) Also **rondo coolo.**

1849 *N.O. Picayune* 22 July 2/5 There are two billiard tables here, and on one they play 'rondo' at night. **1873** BEADLE *Undevel. West* 90 The 'Big Tent' . . . is filled with tables devoted to monte, faro, rondo coolo, fortune-wheels, and every other species of gambling known. **1938** ASBURY *Sucker's Prog.* 276 Rondo, also spelled Rondeau, is played with a stick and nine small ivory balls on a pool table, or any table with pockets. The balls are rolled across the table with the stick to the pocket diagonally opposite the roller. . . . At least one ball must go into the pocket, and at least one must remain outside. **1949** *L.A. Times* 9 April 4/1 A measure, AB 356, . . . would include draw poker with 'faro, . . . rondo, tan, fan-tan, . . . or any banking or percentage game played with cards, dice or any device.'

attrib. **1851** *Cin. D. Commercial* 21 Oct. 2/3 A rondo table in Fifteenth, near Sycamore, . . . was broken up and the tables and fixtures thrown into the street.

b. One of two possibilities in playing rondo, the other being "coolo."

1849 *N.O. Picayune* 22 July 2/5 The roll is made, and 'rondo' is the result.

ronquil ˈraŋkɪl, *n.* [Sp. *ronquillo*, dim. of *ronco*. Cf. **ronco.**] Any of various fishes of the northwest coast of North America, esp. *Bathymaster signatus.* — **1882** *Nat. Museum Bul.* No. 16, 619 *Icosteidæ* (The Ronquils). . . . This group, as at present constituted, is composed of three very diverse genera, each of a single species, inhabiting the deeper waters of the North Pacific. *Ib.* 623 *B[athymaster] signatus*, . . . Ronquil. **1884** GOODE *Fisheries* I. 361 An allied form is *Bathymaster signatus* Cope, the 'Ronchil,' found in deep water from Puget Sound northward.

***roof,** *n.*

1. roof garden, a garden on the flat roof of a building, esp. one where refreshments and entertainment for patrons are provided. Also attrib.

1893 HOLLEY *Samantha at World's Fair* 286 Why, the very elevator you rode up to the ruff garden on wuz made by a woman. **1917** COMSTOCK *Man* 343 They were at a roof garden restaurant. **1948** MENJOU & MUSSELMAN *It Took 9 Tailors* 16 He rented a projector and some films from New York to show his roof-garden customers this interesting novelty that, up to that time, most of them had only read about in the newspapers.

2. *To raise the roof*, to create a noisy disturbance, to make loud and angry protest. *Slang.*

1907 *St. Nicholas* XXXIV. 589/1, I guess I'd better let her in, or she'll raise the roof. **1949** *Sat. Ev. Post* 9 April 56/4 If it's over two dollars a night she raises the roof.

As the last term in **cabin, clapboard, dirt, gambrel, hurricane, monitor, saw tooth, shake, snow, split, tin roof.**

***rookie,** *n.* A beginner in baseball. Also attrib. *Slang.*

1913 *Chi. Record-Herald* 1 March 12/2 Cal tried out Lefty Delano, a New Brunswick southpaw rookie. **1944** *Chi. D. News* 21 Oct. 11/1 They expressed themselves . . . as willing to trade . . . for the rookie outfielder. **1950** *Chi. Tribune* 1 Feb. III. 1/3 The $100,000 . . . is believed to be the highest price ever paid a rookie untried in professional baseball.

***room,** *n.* **1. room clerk,** = ***clerk,** *n.* **3. 2. roommate,** one who shares the same room or rooms with another or with others. **3. room trader,** (see quot. 1900).

(1) **1916** DU PUY *Uncle Sam* 49 The room clerk had suggested that it was the custom of the hotel that guests without baggage should pay in advance. **1924** WITWER *Roughly Speaking* 14 The hotel manager, haughty room clerks, . . . and the rest of the help entered the tourney with a vim. — (2) **1789** DUNLAP *Father* IV. i, We were room-mates at Halifax. **1949** *Chi. D. News* 13 Aug. 5/4 No girl is allowed to step in another prisoner's room unless she is a roommate. — (3) **1887** *Courier-Journal* 7 May 7/3 New England again became weak in company with Reading, both being especially heavy sufferers from the operation of the bearish room-traders. **1900** NELSON *A B C Wall St.* 158 *Room trader*, a man who is a member of an exchange and speculates for his own profit and loss.

b. *To room-keep*, (see quot. 1871).

1871 DE VERE 491 The new word, *to roomkeep*, arising from the exigency which forces impoverished Southern families to content themselves with renting a few rooms and keeping house in them, has not yet obtained currency. **1911** HARRISON *Queed* 213, I don't find anything in the tenets of my religion that requires you to go off and room-keep with Professor Nicolovius.

As the last term in **ash, assembly, baggage, baile, bar, bargain, board, bride's, bunk, call, chapter, check, checking, cloak, clock, clothes, comfort, desk, dormitory, drawing, duffle, dwelling, family, feed, fire, flake, freight, gold, grade, grave, hall, inquiry, issue, ladies, lint, living, local, long, lunch, mover's, news, oyster, packing, pick, poker, pool, rest, sales, sample, setting, shed, side, sink, sitting, snag, sporting, square, stage, state, study, ticket, ward, wash, waste, weave, wine, wood room.**

***room,** *v. intr.* To occupy a room or rooms, to lodge.

1817 *Essex Inst. Coll.* VIII. 241 We are boarding with two of the college students, and room with them. **1859** GRATTAN *Civilized Amer.* I. 193 A good deal of notoriety was about the same time given to the fact of the same gentleman having, not merely 'roomed' with but actually slept with a member of the Federal Senate. **1911** O. HENRY *Rolling Stones* 178 Stickney roomed at 45 West 'Teenth St.

roomage ˈrumɪdʒ, *n.* Space or capacity. *Obs.* — **1843** WHITTIER *Poetical Works* (1894) 20/2 Pack [my ship] with coins of Spanish gold, From keel-piece up to deck-plank, The roomage of her hold. **1865** BURRITT *Walk to Land's End* 209 Mat and seat the rotunda of St. Paul's, and the nave of Westminster, to every foot of their magnificent roomage.

roomer ˈrumɚ, *n.* One who rents a room in a private home or lodging house, usu. one who gets his meals elsewhere.

1871 BAGG *At Yale* 46 *Roomer*, a word used by landladies to designate a lodger or occupant of a room who takes his meals elsewhere. **1923** WATTS *L. Nichols* 68 Some rented out to roomers from cellar to attic. **1949** *Chi. Tribune* 30 Dec. 3/4 In one south side area . . . 3,580 families plus 646 roomers were found to be living in dwelling units built for 1,127 families.

rooming house. A house other than a hotel in which rooms or apartments, usu. furnished, are rented. Also attrib.

1893 *Spectator* 16 Sep. 366/1 We go to no hotel, but look for what Americans call a 'rooming house,' i.e., a house which lets furnished apartments. **1927** *Scribner's Mag.* March 231/1 Three houses up the street was Hirsch's rooming-house. **1949** *Sat. Ev. Post* 25 June 55/1 A rooming-house keeper had a chance to appraise such workings when an out-of-town couple rented one of her rooms.

Roorback ˈrurbæk, *n.* [The name of an imaginary traveler in the U.S. in whose alleged book of travels a statement damaging to the character of James K. Polk (1795–1840) was said to occur. See Mencken, *Supp.* I. 293.] A falsehood circulated for political effect. Also attrib.

1844 *Republican Sentinel* (Richmond, Va.) 4 Oct. 3/3 The rapid succession of events in the 'Roorback' line, has satisfied us, that the whole matter is a *quiz* or a *forgery*. **1913** BLYTHE *Fakers* 176 He saw the headlines in the other papers calling it a roorbach and him a fool. **1947** *Chi. D. News* 27 March 6/1 The roorback stage of the closing days of the campaign broke wide open today with appeals to racial and religious prejudice coming to the surface in many sections of the city.

b. Also as a verb. *Obs.*

1848 *Campaign Flag* (Maysville, Ky.) 15 Sep. 1/5 Whiggery was galvanized into renewed life by discovering that there was two lives of Gen. Cass about, differing a bit from each other, and could not help *Roorbacking* over the discovery. **1858** *Phoenix* (Sacramento) 14 Feb. 1/3 One of the distinguished members for this ill-fated county has 'Roorbacked' it, and 'gone a cool 100 better.'

Roosevelt elk. An elk or wapiti, *Cervus canadensis roosevelti*, found on Vancouver Island and in the Olympic Mountains region.

1902 STONE & CRAM *Amer. Mammals* (1922) 34 Roosevelt's Elk. *Cervus occidentalis* Smith. Larger and darker coloured, with heavier horns. **1923** *Outing* April 3/1 The Olympic peninsula . . . contains vast, unmapped forests. . . . teeming with the lordly Roosevelt elk. **1947** *Mazama* Dec. 43/1 Herds of Roosevelt elk, estimated at between 4,000 to 5,000 head, roam there.

Rooseveltian ˌrozəˈvɛltɪən, *a.* Of or pertaining to Theodore Roosevelt (1858–1919), President of the U.S. (1901–9). *Colloq.*

1908 *Sci. Amer.* 25 Jan. 59/3 In this advanced twentieth century we had fondly hoped that the 'nature faker' at least was a product of the Roosevelt age of literature. **1924** *Amer. Mercury* Feb. 180/1 Every act of Gifford's since Roosevelt died shows his half-way perception of the Roosevelt tactics. **1949** *Sat. Ev. Post* 2 July 19/1 It tickled the fancy of editors, especially the anti-Rooseveltian majority.

b. Used also with reference to Franklin D. Roosevelt (1882–1945), President of the U.S. (1933–45). Hence **Rooseveltiana,** *n.*

1948 *Chi. Tribune* 1 Feb. 1. 37/3 It is a typical example of Rooseveltian democracy where charity is invited where it is not needed. **1950** *Chi. Sun-Times* 24 Jan. 23/2, I have collected the critical Rooseveltiana as well as the adulatory.

Rooseveltism ˈrozəˌvɛltɪzəm, *n.* The political philosophy or practice of Theodore Roosevelt (1858–1919), President of the U.S. (1901–9).

1909 *Wkly. Ardmoreite* (Ardmore, Okla.) 24 Feb. 8/1 Quarantine Lifts March 4. . . . Get Rid of Rooseveltism. **1913** *Industrial Worker* (Spokane) 10 April 2/2 The false economics of the Metropolitan editor is the result of mixing progressive Rooseveltism with conservative Bergerism. **1929** *Collier's* 9 March, Samuel G. Blythe . . . described the inauguration as 'an enormous cocktail, a dash of vaudeville, a fillip of imperialism, a jigger of militarism, a sufficient quantity of expansion, filled, to the top with Rooseveltism, shaken well and served.'

* **roost,** *n.*

1. A place in a forest or woods to which wild birds come regularly to roost and nest.

1845 COOPER *Chainbearer* xiv, Multitudes of pigeons . . . were frequently found in their 'roosts,' as the encampments that they made in the woods were often termed in the parlance of the country. **1923** J. H. COOK *On Old Frontier* 4 Countless flocks . . . [would] congregate at what were called 'roosts.' **1948** *Dly. Ardmoreite* (Ardmore, Okla.) 18 April 18/6 A single roost near Baltimore, Md., is estimated to contain 230,000 crows.

b. *transf.* A resting place.

1858 HOLMES *Autocrat* 164 The world has a million roosts for a man, but only one nest. **1891** C. ROBERTS *Adrift Amer.* 23, I selected what appeared to me to be about the best spot for a roost, and . . . made a fairly comfortable bed.

2. *To rule the roost,* to exercise authority, to be master. *Colloq.*

This expression is prob. not of American origin. The *OED* shows that *roast* was formerly often spelled *roost.* The now well differentiated terms *roast* and *roost* may have been confused in pronunciation as well as in spelling. Hence the original idea of the expression which the *OED* records as *to rule the roast, s.v. roast,* may well have been that of the expression as it is here given. *To rule the roost,* spelled in just this manner, occurs certainly as early as John Heywood's *The Playe of the Four PP* (c1545). Although *roost* is here rhymed with *boast,* to explain the passage as meaning "to rule the roast" appears uncalled for by the context.

If on the other hand the original idea of the expression was "to rule the roast," the form here shown is prob. an attempt at rationalization.

c1769 in *W. & M. Coll. Quart.* 1 Ser. XVI. 175 They say she rules the Roost, it is a pity, I like her Husband vastly. **1893** *Boston Jrnl.* 20 April 5/3 England Rules the Roost. Her Ships at Hampton Roads Admittedly the finest. **1934** CARMER *Stars Fell* 69 After all the Confederates that killed her man was dead Aunt Jennie ruled the roost round here. **1950** *Time* 16 Jan. 82/2 Fond of old-fashioned virtues, he rules his roost with a hand of iron.

***roost,** *v.* [Cf. *EDD roost in,* in similar sense.] *tr.* To watch (wild turkeys) to see where they roost and so be able to kill them early the following morning. *Colloq.* — **c1845** W. T. PORTER *Big Bear Ark.* 149 Sum peeple murder the turkis this time o' year by *roosten em* (finding their roosts). **1945** *Democrat* 4 Jan. 2/2 One night recently Irby roosted some turkeys in Satilpa swamp.

* **rooster,** *n.*

1. A weathercock.

1832 *Boston Transcript* 2 June 2/1 The proprietors of the 'Old North,' proposing to make some repairs and alterations, . . . voted to remove the gallant Rooster, who has been perched at the top of the steeple ever since the dedication of the Meeting House in 1721. **1881** *Harper's Mag.* March 530/2 Every house [in Albany] was . . . surmounted by a rooster.

2. A cock or representation of a cock used as a symbol of the Democratic party.

1843 *Quincy* (Ill.) *Herald* 24 Nov. 2/4 The Democratic papers announce almost every victory with the heading of a crowing rooster. **1876** *S.F. Wkly. Examiner* 24 Aug. 3/1 It takes fourteen good-sized roosters to do the Montgomery (Ala.) *Advertiser's* crowing over the recent Democratic victory in that State. **1948** *Chi. D. News* 5 Oct. 14/1 The committee had grabbed the party name and the rooster symbol. . . . The legislature did not give Truman back the party name and the rooster.

attrib. **1856** *Spirit of Age* (Sacramento) 6 March 2/3 Nothing that we have ever witnessed or heard tell of, by way of a general jollification, exceeded that of the 'Rooster boys' last night.

3. The cock or hammer of a firearm. *Colloq.*

This sense and **1.** above reflect a tendency to be jocular about the widely discussed verbal squeamishness of Americans concerning certain words, esp. "cock." Cf. **b.** below.

1856 *Porter's Spirit of Times* 1 Nov. 140/2 Well now, daddy, says he, I lost the *rooster* off the lock of my gun. **1932** RANDOLPH *Ozark Mt.* 37 Buck he was feelin' kinder mean an' narvish-like anyhow, so he drawed his ol' horse-pistol an' pulls back th' rooster. **1950** *Amer. Mercury* Jan. 89/1 He reports that the local experts with the shotgun do not 'cock' it. Instead, they 'pull back both roosters.'

Rooster (c1750) used as a weather vane

b. rooster-roach, a cockroach. *Jocular.*

1869 *Alaska Times* (Sitka) 11 Sep. 1/4 This includes of course all the invited and uninvited guests, such as rooster-roaches, aldermanic rats, big bugs and dorgs.

4. (See quot.) *Obs.*

1871 DE VERE 262 Rooster . . . indicates a bill, or proposed law, which will benefit the legislators—and no one else—for as the rasorial fowl scratches for his sustenance, so his figurative namesake is supposed to scratch the dunghill of modern legislation.

5. A colloquial name for the violet, in allusion to the pastime mentioned in the quots. Also **rooster-fight, rooster-fighting,** *n.* Cf. **7. a.** below, and see * **hen,** *n.* **1, chicken fight, fighter,** *s.v.* * **chicken,** *n.* **5. b.**

1884 ROE in *Harper's Mag.* June 94/1 [The] purple violets . . . were slaughtered by hundreds, for the projecting spur under the curved stem at the base of the flower enabled the boys to hook them together and 'fight roosters,' as they termed it. **1916** *D.N.* IV. 345 *Rooster-fight,* a violet: so called [in Tenn.] from the practice of 'fighting' them together to see which would pull the other's head off. **1946** RICHTER *Fields* 231 In April they played Hens and Roosters, yoking their wild white and blue violets to see which would get its head pulled off.

6. (See quot.)

1905 *Forestry Bureau Bul.* No. 61, 38 *Gooseneck,* . . . a wooden bar used to couple two logging trucks. (Gen[eral].) Syn.: rooster. ([Pacific] C[oast] F[orest].)

7. a. rooster-heads, (see quot. 1894). **b. rooster redbird,** a male redbird. **c. rooster's egg,** (see quots.).

(a) 1894 *Amer. Folk-Lore* VII. 94 *Dodecatheon Meadia,* var., shooting stars, roosters' heads, Santa Barbara Co., Cal. **1934** VINES *Green Thicket World* 171 One not thicketed might have felt sorry for the blue daisies, white daisies, roosterheads. [**1947** *Atlantic Mo.* July 41/2 Spring not only brought tadpoles but blue hyacinths upon which I could feed my soul, and dogwood and peach blossoms and big bunches of rooster-head violets that the children picked in the woods and brought to me.] — **(b) 1940** STUART *Trees of Heaven* 190 It is a pretty redbird. It is the rooster redbird. — **(c) 1899** GREEN *Va. Word-Book* 308 *Rooster's egg,* a small hen's egg. **1899** *Animal & Plant Lore* 12 A 'luck egg' is the egg of a rooster; also called a 'rooster's egg.' De

Kalb Co., Ill. **1914** *D.N.* IV. 152 *Rooster's egg,* a fertilized egg. [Me.]. . . . In Mass. rooster's egg is used facetiously for a large egg.

As the last term in **dominique, weather rooster.**

* **roosting,** *n.*

1. =**pigeon roost.** *Obs.*

1869 *Mich. Laws* I. 213 No person . . . shall use any gun . . . to maim, kill, or destroy any wild-pigeon or pigeons within their roostings.

2. In combs.: (1) **roosting ground,** an area upon which wild fowls roost; (2) **party,** a marauding party, *obs.;* (3) **place,** = * **roost,** *n.* **1;** (4) **pond,** a pond upon which wild ducks stay at night.

(1) 1860 *Md. Laws.* cix. § 1 No person shall . . . shoot at or shoot any water fowl bedded in flocks, either upon the feeding or roosting-grounds of said water fowl. — **(2) 1809** WEEMS *Marion* (1833) 183 Learning next morning, that a roosting party were out, Marion detached my brother Colonel Horry . . . to attack them. — **(3) 1812** WILSON *Ornithology* V. 103 [Wild pigeons] return . . . in the evening, to their place of general rendezvous, or as it is usually called, the roosting place. **1946** BENT *Life Hist. N. Amer. Jays, Crows, Titmice* 244 The crows return to their roosting place early in the afternoon. — **(4) 1874** LONG *Wild Fowl* 161 The ducks will be seen coming from the roosting-ponds.

* **root,** *n.* In combs.: (1) **root beer,** a beverage prepared with extracts obtained from various roots, also attrib.; (2) **bread,** prob. a breadlike preparation from the cowish, *obs.;* (3) **cake,** prob. a preparation from the roots of the coontie, *obs.;* (4) **collar,** (see quot.); (5) **digger,** an Indian who subsists chiefly on roots, cf. **digger,** *n.;* (6) **doctor,** *local,* ?=**vegetable doctor;** (7) **eater,** an Indian belonging to any one of various tribes or groups noted for dependence upon roots for food; (8) **fence,** (see quot. 1792); (9) **washer,** (see quots.).

(1) 1843 *Knickerb.* XXII. 85 [Let] the temperance halls and the root-beer *perambulatories* make answer. **1941** *Harper's Mag.* Oct. 556/1 Inside, all was just as it had always been, except there was more Coca Cola and not so much Moxie and root beer and sarsaparilla. **1948** *Atlantic Mo.* Feb. 31/2 Kathie had a root beer float that only cost a dime. — **(2) 1806** ORDWAY in *Jrnls. Lewis & O.* 352 We bought a little dark couloured root bread which is not good but will Support nature. — **(3) 1670** *S.C. Hist. Soc. Coll.* V. 166 Here we had nutts and root cakes such as their women useily make as before. — **(4) 1905** *Forestry Bureau Bul.* No. 61, 19 *Root collar,* that place at the base of a large tree where the swelling which is the direct result of the ramifications of the roots begins.

(5) 1831 in A. H. ABEL *F. Chardon's Jrnl.* (1932) 346 Many of these [Snake Indians] go by the name which signifies Root digger, because they live by digging roots. **1873** BEADLE *Undevel. West* 420 Here [in the Indian Territory] are sixty thousand red men who are neither hunters nor root diggers; they are agriculturists, herdsmen and mechanics. **1947** DEVOTO *Across Wide Missouri* 432 'Root-digger' . . . describes all the tribes, most of them superior tribes, that lived in localities where there were staple crops of edible roots and bulbs. — **(6) 1890** *N.Y. Age* 19 April (Th. Supp.), Carmier was what people call down here a root doctor. — **(7) 1836** IRVING *Astoria* I. 276 Another class [of the Snake Indians], the most abject and forlorn, . . . are called Shuckers, or more commonly Diggers and Root eaters. **1907** HODGE *Amer. Indians* I. 390/2 The root-eaters were supposed to represent a low type of Indian. — **(8)** [**1792** BELKNAP *Hist. New-Hampshire* III. 108 When the roots [of the mast pine] have been loosened by the frost, they are . . . cut and dug out of the ground, and being turned up edge way, are set for fences to fields.] **1853** LOWELL in *Putnam's Mo.* II. Nov. 459/2 Sometimes a root-fence stretched up its bleaching antlers. — **(9) 1819** *Plough Boy* I. 123 Root washer, an improved one for washing potatoes, turnips, &c. **1876** KNIGHT III. 1976/2 *Root-washer,* a machine which usually consists of a slatted cylinder revolving in a tank of water.

b. In slang phrases: (1) *To come (the) roots over,* to trick, take advantage of; (2) *to grab a root,* to pitch in, do one's part; (3) *to play roots on,* to deal with severely.

(1) 1856 *Times* (Sacramento) 23 Jan. 2/1 A well known merchant on J street was yesterday charged by a teamster with coming 'roots' [of all evil!] over him to amount of $30. **1916** H. L. WILSON *Somewhere in Red Gap* viii. 327 Some silly game he tried to come the roots over folks with. — **(2) 1880** *Harper's Mag.* May 913/2 One more wicked than them all sang out that old army slang, 'Grab a root!' — **(3) 1890** HARTE *Waif of Plains* 88 He'd hev played roots on them Injins afore they teched ye.

As the last term in **ague, alum, arrow, balsam, bear, beaver, bellyache, big, biscuit, bitter, black, blood, bowman's, bread, buck, butterfly, cancer, chocolate, Choctaw, clay, consumption, convulsion, coon, cotton, cough, cucumber, dragon, eel, fern rattlesnake, fever, fever and ague, fishing, flag, flat, gag, gopher, grass, gravel, grease, grub, harvest, hunting, Huntington, Indian, kidney, knot, large-flowered button snake, leather, licorice, man, mesquite, mouth, musquash, nerve, orange, papoose, pepper, pink, pleurisy, poke, polecat, puccoon, putty, rattlesnake, red, rheumatism, rich, rotten, sassafras, Seneca rattlesnake, Seneca snake, soap, spice, squaw, star, throat, tobacco, tule, unicorn, whisky, yellow root.**

* **root,** *v.*

1. *intr.* (See quot.) *Slang. Obs.*

1856 HALL *College Words* (ed. 2) 395 *Root,* . . . to study hard.

2. To shout, cheer, or work enthusiastically *for* the success of an athletic team or of an individual. *Slang.* Cf. * **rooter,** *n.*

1889 *N.Y. Semi-Wkly. Tribune* 5 Nov. 5/4 Murphy has done little but 'root' for the Giants this year. **1897** FLANDRAU *Harvard Episodes* 164 The fellows who had promised to vote for Wolcott . . . were beginning now to 'root' for him vigorously. **1949** *Lisle* (Ill.) *Advt.* 11 March 1/1 Now we'll have our own home-town team to root for.

3. *root hog or die,* and variants, an expression, often of imperative force, indicating the necessity of either working hard or suffering undesirable consequences. *Colloq.*

1834 CROCKETT *Narr. Life* 118 We therefore determined to go on the old saying, root hog or die. **1845** *St. Louis Reveille* 5 Jan. 1/6, I found I was wasting away lying there, and determined to reach the springs 'come what may'—'root pig or die.' **1949** *L.A. Times* 8 May (Home Mag.) 10/3 They raised you in the stern tradition of 'root, hog, or die!'

b. With attrib. force.

1853 PAIGE *Patent Sermons* III. 193 (Th.), Obliged to go upon the root-hog-or-die principle. **1875** *Chi. Tribune* 8 Dec. 8/3 A tax-eating official . . . could add to the wealth of the State with his little hoe on a good farm if the Root-hog-or-die law was carefully read to him and enforced. **1881** PIERSON *In the Brush* 16 The swine were of the original 'root-hog-or-die' variety.

* **rooter,** *n.* One who gives enthusiastic support, esp. to an athletic team. *Slang.* Cf. * **root,** *v.* **2.**

1894 *U. of Chi. Wkly.* 6 Dec. 107/2 The supporters of the maroon . . . yelled defiance to the Michigan rooters. **1898** *Dly. Ardmoreite* (Ardmore, Okla.) 12 July 3/3 Our ball boys . . . go to Gainesville in the morning to play a series of three games with the rooters of that burg. **1949** *Ward Co. Independent* (Minot, N.D.) 21 July 4/3 The rooters are happy when the home team wins.

As the last term in **piny woods, prairie rooter.**

* **rope,** *n.*

1. *W.* =**lasso.**

1850 GARRARD *Wah-To-Yah* xix. 217 [Beavers are as] shy as a coyote as runs round camp to gnaw a rope. **1927** JAMES *Cow Country* 103 He didn't want to tell the new hand not to whirl his rope in a corral full of horses, on account he figgered the stranger ought to know that without being told. **1949** GANN *Tread of Longhorns* 37 The standard length of a rope is thirty-three feet.

2. In combs.: (1) **rope-apples,** (see quot.), *obs.;* (2) **broken,** (see quot.); (3) **corral,** *W.* a corral made with ropes (see quot. 1944); (4) **elevator,** (see quot.); (5) **ferry,** a ferry operated by, or consisting of, a rope (see quot. 1788); (6) **funeral,** a hanging, *rare;* (7) **lasso,** =**lasso;** (8) **railway,** (see quot.), *obs.;* (9) **-spinning,** an exhibition of skill in twirling a rope.

(1) 1709 LAWSON *Carolina* 109 Rope-Apples . . . are small apples, hanging like Ropes of Onions. — **(2) 1882** BAILLIE-GROHMAN *Camps in Rockies* 99 She was not even 'rope-broken,' i.e. accustomed to the rope-halter. — **(3) 1902** WISTER *Virginian* xviii, After the rope corral we had to make this morning . . . the ropes was all strewed round camp. **1944** ADAMS *W. Words* 131/1 rope corral A temporary corral at the cow camp, made by three or four cowhands holding ropes between them to form an obtuse U, and used to pen saddle horses until they can be caught for saddling. **1948** *Sierra Club Bul.* March 25 Not too near the exact center of women's camp, could packers set up their rope corral in which to feed grain and saddle up? — **(4) 1876** KNIGHT 1979/2 *Rope Elevator,* an elevator in which the platform or cage is raised and lowered by means or a rope and winding mechanism.

(5) 1771 in *N. Eng. Mag.* ns. XII. 350/1, I arrived at a place called the Rope Ferry. **1788** CUTLER in *Life & Corr.* I. 399 [The] boat . . . is a rope-ferry, and by a large block through which the large rope passes, and a tackle at each end of the boat, the stream carries the boat from side to side without oars, setting poles, or rudder. **1897** *Outing* XXIX. 564/1 To cross the river by the old rope ferry. **1931** WILLISON *Here They Dug Gold* 75 Here stands the town's original building, the double cabin of Jack Jones and John Smith, both grown rich during the Gregory rush by the rope ferry across the Platte. —

(6) **1895** *Cong. Rec.* 15 Jan. 1003/2 The judge feels that he has sent enough men to the penitentiary and attended enough rope funerals of the outlaws of that [Indian] country to make it a very paradise of peace. — (7) **1884** W. Shepherd *Prairie Exper.* 37 A man, armed with a rope-lasso, catches a calf by throwing it over his head. — (8) **1876** Knight 1983/1 *Rope-railway,* a railway on which the cars are drawn by ropes wound upon drums rotated by stationary engines. — (9) **1927** James *Cow Country* 124 The man packing that name had won first prize in the bucking horse contest and first in rope-spinning also.

For *to draw the rope,* see ***draw,** *v.* **6.** (1).

As the last term in **bale, baling, calf, catch, drag, grass, lariat, lash, picket, railroad, rawhide, stake, swing, tie rope.**

Rope ferry or wire ferry

***rope,** *v.*

1. *tr.* To catch (a horse, calf, etc.) with a rope, to lasso. Also absol.

1853 P. Paxton *Yankee in Texas* 38 If he [the horse] has been once properly 'roped,' all that is necessary is to get one upon his neck. **1923** Bower *Parowan Bonanza* 65 She . . . can sling a pack or rope a critter better than lots of men that draw wages for doing it. **1949** *This Week Mag.* 9 April 19/2 He roped and branded an' rode fence lines.

b. To capture or tie (a person) with, or as with, a rope. Also fig. *Colloq.* or *slang.*

1848 Ruxton *Life Far West* i, Maybe you'll get 'roped' (lasso'd) by a Rapaho. **1890** *Stock Grower & Farmer* 18 Jan. 3/2 It is hoped they [stockmen] will succeed in roping a few of the thieves. **1916** Du Puy *Uncle Sam* 120 Peterson should be 'roped.' **1950** *Chi. Tribune* 23 Jan. IV. 6 And where I can keep an eye on you until I've got you roped and branded *Rover* boy!

2. To entice (a victim) in the interests of gamblers or of a gambling establishment. Also intr. or absol. *Slang.*

1877 in Asbury *Underworld of Chi.* (1941) 90 Charles P. has not been down to see his beloved since he roped that fellow to stand the drinks. **1938** Asbury *Sucker's Prog.* 271 Another who sometimes roped for the Elite was George W. Post, a notorious confidence man.

b. *To rope in* (or *into*), to ensnare, deceive, take in.

1840 *N.O. Picayune* 18 Sep. 2/2 The persons rightly concluded it was an effort to rope 'in,' and told Trainer so. **1885** *Wkly. New Mexican Rev.* 2 July 4/3 Smokey Jones claims that he was roped into this snap by Chicago sharpers. **1950** *Time* 6 Feb. 21/2 He will probably rope the victim into his favorite charity, the Margaret MacMillan Memorial Fund.

3. (See quot.)

1883 S. Bonner *Dialect Tales* 23 This person was engaged in the curious operation of 'roping' her hair—that is, dividing it into small strands, each one of which was wrapped tightly to its end with a white cotton string.

***roper,** *n.*

1. *W.* One who uses a lasso.

1808 Pike *Sources Miss.* 160 Taking the wild horses, in that manner, is scarcely ever attempted, even with the . . . most expert ropers. **1927** James *Cow Country* 103 To begin with, we seen he was no roper, not while he was on the ground, anyway. **1948** *Denison* (Tex.) *Herald* 1 July 9/2 The calves stole the show from the ropers last night as they refused to stay down after being roped and tied.

b. A horse trained to assist his rider in roping.

1947 *Reader's Digest* Oct. 113/2 It took Rambo three years to train his two horses—a roper and a dogger.

2. A person who acts as a decoy, esp. one who secures clients for a gambling establishment. Also **roper in.**

1840 *N.O. Picayune* 31 Oct. 2/3 He had not well landed on the Levee, so famous for cotton bags, sugar, . . . 'ropers in,' and other 'dry goods.' **1874** Pinkerton *Expressman & Detective* 26 Porter had been promoted by me to be a sort of 'roper.' **1892** Quinn *Fools of Fortune* 207 There is, however, a class of 'ropers' who do rather more than 'dirty' work. **1948** Dick *Dixie Frontier* 165 In one instance a 'roper' led an Old Kentuckian into the den where a special game was in progress.

***roping,** *n.*

1. Ensnaring, taking in, entrapping. Also **roping in.** Also attrib.

1840 *N.O. Picayune* 15 Sep. 2/4 Henry H. Taylor . . . went the 'big figure' in the 'roping in' business. **1848** Bartlett 278 *Roping in,* cheating. A very common expression in the South-western States. **1916** Du Puy *Uncle Sam* 121 A detective less experienced in roping might have considered an opportunity to go to this man's hotel with him as a piece of good fortune.

2. The action of lassoing stock with a rope, often as an event in a rodeo contest. Also attrib.

1889 *Arizonan* (Phoenix) 7 April 3/2 Charley McGary won the roping and tieing contest, three steers, in the very poor time of four minutes and thirty-four seconds. **1907** White *Arizona Nights* 274 The roping and throwing and branding . . . filled our days with . . . the unusual. **1949** *L.A. Times* 12 July II. 2/5 A grave beside the barn on the former Will Rogers ranch . . . became the final resting place of Soap Suds, once the greatest humorist's favorite roping horse.

roque rok, *n.* [An arbitrary coinage f. **croquet.*] A form of croquet played on a court having a border or surrounding embankment.

1899 *Boston Transcript* 15 Sep. 6/5 The players of the new croquet, having developed a new and scientific game, have adopted a new name, and call it roque. **1906** *Springfield W. Republican* 30 Aug. 16 A 16-years-old lad who never before had played in a big tournament won the national championship at roque. **1921** *Cleveland Enterprise* 23 April 6/3 Roque is a health builder.

attrib. **1909** *Chi. D. News* 12 Aug. 8/1 They are holding a roque tournament at Norwich, Conn.

roram 'roram, *n.* Also **rorum.** [Origin unknown.] A woolen material faced with fur, used for making hats; a hat made of this. Also **roram hat.** *Obs.*

1796 *Aurora* (Phila.) 2 Jan. (Th.), Richard Robinson has on hand an assortment of Beaver, Castor, and Roram Hats. **1811** *Niles' Reg.* 21 Dec. 292/1 Philip J. Hahn . . . makes and sells . . . rorum, castor, or common fur hats. **1845** Drake *Pioneer Life Ky.* 231 Other arrangements were being made for the life before me, such as . . . purchasing a white roram hat.

Roscoe's yellowthroat. [Wm. *Roscoe* (1753–1831), a British historian and philanthropist.] =**Maryland yellowthroat.** *Obs.* — **1831** Audubon *Ornith. Biog.* I. 124 Roscoe's Yellow-Throat. *Sylvia Roscoe.* . . . In general appearance, this species so much resembles the preceding, that had not its habits differed so greatly from those of the Maryland Yellow-throat, I might have been induced to consider it as merely an accidental variety. **1839** Peabody *Mass. Birds* 313.

***rose,** *n.* In combs.: (1) **rose acacia,** (see quot. 1898); (2) **blanket,** "a blanket of fine quality, having a rose, or a conventional device resembling a rose, worked in one corner" (*Cent.*); (3) ***bud,** (*a*) a debutante, used attrib., cf. ***bud,** *n.*[2] **1,** (*b*) **Rosebud Senator,** Senator Henry B. Anthony (1815–84), of Rhode Island, *obs.;* (4) **catarrh,** (see quot. and cf. **rose cold, fever**); (5) **City,** Portland, Ore., a nickname; (6) **cold,** a form of hay fever attributed to a rose pollen; (7) **fever,** =**rose cold;** (8) **-flowering locust,** the honey locust, *Robinia viscosa;* (9) **-flowering raspberry,** the purple-flowering raspberry, *Rubus odoratus;* (10) **gas burner,** (see quot.), *obs.;* (11) **pogonia,** (see quot.); (12) **rust,** (see quot.).

(1) **1833** Eaton *Botany* (ed. 6) 306. **1852** Motley *Correspondence* I. 129 The acacias (rose acacias) under my window . . . are not leafless. **1898** Creevey *Flowers of Field* 482 Rose Acacia. . . . *Robinia hispida.* . . . A shrub indigenous south of Virginia. . . . It grows from 3 to 8 feet high, and bears large, rose-colored blossoms. — (2) **1759** *Newport Mercury* 26 June 3/2 Just Imported by Simon Pease, jun. . . . best Rose Blankets. **1820** *Columbian Centinel* 8 Jan. 3/4 A great variety of Dry Goods. . . . Rose Blankets. **1895** *Pittsburgh Gaz.* 15 Aug. 2/3 (*advt.*), 300 pairs rose blankets. — (3) (*a*) **1885** *Harper's Mag.* March 544/2 The girls have gone to a 'rose-bud' dinner at the Mays', though I can't say I approved of it. **1890** *Cent. Mag.* Aug. 582 They flutter their brief hour in society. . . . Some of them hold on like grim death to rosebud privileges. (*b*) **1885** *Cong. Rec.* 21 Jan. 908/1

[H. B. Anthony] was called 'the rosebud Senator,' . . . as a tribute to the healthful glow which mantled his cheek, or from the fact that . . . he constantly wore a bud or other flower. — **(4) 1888** HUNTER *Encycl. Dict.* VI. 184/2 *Rose-catarrh, rose-fever,* . . . a catarrh or slight fever like hay-asthma, prevailing in parts of the United States.

(5) 1905 *N. Eng. Mag.* Sep. 11/2 It might appropriately be called the 'rose fair' as Portland is termed the Rose City. **1948** *Time* 31 May 18/1 Riley . . . had been charged by Portland's influential City Club with negligence in stamping out vice in the Rose City. — **(6) 1872** M. WYMAN *Autumnal Catarrh* 4 The popular name, 'Hay Fever,' . . . has been applied to the 'June Cold' or 'Rose Cold.' **1946** URBACH & GOTTLIEB *Allergy* 509/2 Terms such as rose cold and peach cold are today of little more than historical interest, although a rare case may, in fact, be due to the aroma from roses or other blossoms. — **(7) 1851** WORTLEY *Travels in U.S.* III. 22 [Hay asthma] is known in the U.S., and is called there, rose-fever. **1949** TUFT *Clinical Allergy* 220 This has given rise to such terms as 'rose fever' or 'goldenrod fever' because symptoms appear coincident with the blossoming of these flowers. — **(8) 1810** MICHAUX *Arbres* I. 38 *R[obinia] viscosa.* Rose flowering locust. **1832** BROWNE *Sylva* 299 The rose-flowering locust is not so large as the preceding species. **1897** SUDWORTH *Arborescent Flora* 263 *Robinia viscosa.* Clammy Locust. . . . Rose-Flowering Locust (Tenn.). — **(9) 1847** WOOD *Botany* 249 Rose-flowering Raspberry. Mulberry. . . . Fruit broad and thin, bright red, sweet. **1847** DARLINGTON *Weeds & Plants* 125 Odorous Rubus, Rose-flowering raspberry. . . The fruit of this is pleasantly flavored, but is rarely perfected under cultivation.

(10) 1876 KNIGHT 1984/1 *Rose Gas-burner*, a burner giving a circle of small flames. — **(11) 1907** *St. Nicholas* Aug. 939/1 The *Pogonia* group is represented by the rose-pogonia or snakemouth. — **(12) 1817–8** EATON *Botany* (1822) 498 *Uredo rosae-centifoliae*, rose rust. . . . On the leaves of the centfoil rose.

b. In the names of animals: (1) **rose-breasted finch,** the house finch; (2) **-breasted grosbeak,** a grosbeak, *Hedymeles ludovicianus*, usu. black and white, with a rose-colored breast, also attrib.; (3) **bug,** the rose beetle, *Macrodactylus subspinosus;* (4) **fish,** a rose-colored fish, esp. a marine food fish, *Sebastes marinus*, also attrib.; (5) **fly-catching warbler,** the red-faced warbler; (6) **tanager,** (see quot.); (7) **warbler,** (see quot.); (8) **worm,** (see quot.).

(1) 1884 COUES *Key to Birds* (ed. 2) 348 *C[arpodacus] f[rontalis] rhodocolpus,* . . . Rose-Breasted Finch. — **(2) 1810** WILSON *Ornithology* II. 135 [The] Rose-Breasted Grosbeak . . . [is found] in the state of New York, and those of New England. **1949** Calif. Acad. Sciences *News Letter* Feb. 2 A group of ornithology students in Central Park excitedly recorded the first rose-breasted grosbeak song of the year. — **(3) 1800** *Mass. Spy* 1 Oct. (Th.), He suggests that the Rosebug is the pre-existing state of those worms. **1916** EATON *Idyl of Twin Fires* 207, I frequently pick rose bugs . . . before breakfast, very early, when they are still sleepy. — **(4) 1721** *Essex Inst. Coll.* XLII. 223 We spy'd the Fin of a Whale . . . , & Supposing it to be a Rose fish, ran forward to see it. **1884** GOODE *Fisheries* I. 262 The Rose-fish is much esteemed as an article of food. **1949** *Fishing Gaz.* Oct. 33 Gloucester's rosefish fleet now fishes long distances from port in present craft.

(5) 1884 COUES *Key to Birds* (ed. 2) 314 *Cardellina*, . . . Rose Fly-Catching Warblers. — **(6) 1884** COUES *Key to Birds* (ed. 2) 318 *P[yrangea] æstiva*, . . . Rose Tanager. Summer Red-Bird. — **(7) 1889** *Cent.* 819/2 *C. rubra* is the rose warbler, entirely red with silvery auriculars; . . . found in Texas and southward. — **(8) 1891** *Cent.* 5233/1 *Rose-worm* . . . , the larva of the common tortricid moth, *Cacœcia rosaceana*, which folds the leaves of the rose and skeletonizes them.

b. ∗**rose of Sharon,** (see quot. 1931).

1860 DARLINGTON *Weeds & Plants* 67 Syrian Hibiscus. Rose of Sharon. Shrubby Althæa. **1931** CLUTE *Plants* 63 The rose of Sharon (*Althaea Syriaca*) and the wind-rose (*Papaver argemone*) are not true roses.

As the last term in **bridal, Carolina, Cherokee, Chickasaw, cotton, jack, Kentucky, Macartney, moss, prairie, rock, Safrano, sensitive, summer, swamp rose.**

roseate spoonbill. A wading bird, *Ajaia ajaja*, with bare head and throat, and pink plumage.

[**1785** LATHAM *Gen. Synopsis Birds* III. 16 Roseate Spoonbill, *Platalea Ajaja*. . . . The plumage is a fine rose-colour.] **1813** WILSON *Ornithology* VII. 123 Roseate Spoonbill: . . . inhabits the sea shores of America from Brasil to Georgia. **1948** *Highway Traveler* Dec. 8/1 The roseate spoonbill, one of the oddest of birds, has a long spatulate bill which gives it a grotesque appearance in spite of its soft, delicate pink plumage.

∗**rosebay,** *n.* As the last term in **American, California, Catawba, Lapland, mountain rosebay.**

rosemary pine. The Georgia, loblolly, or short-leaf pine of the southeastern states. Also attrib.

1859 G. W. PERRY *Turpentine Farming* 26 Rosemary pine.—There is less of this kind of pine than any other that is used for turpentine. **1931** MATTOON *Forest Trees Okla.* 22 The shortleaf pine, also known as yellow or rosemary pine, is widely distributed throughout the eastern part of the State. **1932** W. KELLEY *Inchin' Along* 187 The bee . . . rose until it was near the top of a rosemary pine tree.

∗**rosette,** *n.* Any one of various diseases which attack specific plants, usu. causing rosetting of the leaves and stunted growth. Also attrib. — **1892** *Dept. Agric. Rep. 1891* 370 Dr. Smith has this year given considerable attention to peach rosette in Georgia. **1924** *Farmers' Bul.* No. 1414, 2 Symptoms of wheat rosette . . . first become evident in the spring after growth of the healthy plants is well started. *Ib.* (Pref.), The rosette disease is recognized in the field in the spring by stunted and rosetted plants.

∗**rosin,** *n.* In combs.: (1) **rosin back,** (see quot.); (2) **heel,** (see quot. 1826), *obs.;* (3) **plant,** =next; (4) **weed,** (see quot. 1917); (5) **wood,** =prec.

(1) 1920 C. R. COOPER *Under Big Top* 170 She is trained to the 'rosinback,' as the ring horse is called. — **(2) 1826** FLINT *Recoll.* 319 [The people of Western Florida] are a wild race, with but little order or morals among them; they are generally denominated 'Bogues,' and call themselves 'rosin heels.' **1866** W. REID *After the War* 416 'The rossum heels live in thar,' a newsboy on the train informed me. — **(3) 1839** in *Mich. Agric. Soc. Trans.* VII. 419 *Silphium gummiferum.* . . . Rosin-plant. — **(4) 1831** *Jamestown Jrnl.* 13 July 1 Sunflowers and rosin-weed . . . abound [in Wis.]. **1917** KEPHART *Camping* II. 57 The compass-plant or rosin-weed (*Silphium laciniatum*) that once abounded on the prairies of the Mississippi valley, from Minnesota to Texas . . . is a tall plant with long, stiff leaves, that do not grow horizontally but with their edges perpendicular. **1941** R. S. WALKER *Lookout* 55 There are a few species of rosin-weeds, but none, perhaps, attracts more general notice than the kind that grows six feet tall. It is sometimes called prairie dock and bears yellow flowers.

(5) 1854 BARTLETT *Personal Narr.* I. 94 Rosin wood, or creosote plant, a most disgusting, strong-smelling shrub.

ross rɔs, *v.* [f. ∗*ross, n.*, the scaly outer portion of the bark of trees.] *tr.* To divest (a log) of its rough outer surface preparatory to hewing or sawing. Also **rossing,** *n. attrib.*

1853 STRICKLAND *Twenty-seven Yrs.* II. 230 As soon as the tree is felled, a person, called a liner, rosses and lines the tree on each side. **1876** KNIGHT 1984/1 Rossing-machine. *Ib.* 1985/1 Rossing Attachment for Saw-Mill. **1878** *Vt. Bd. Agric. Rep.* V. 109 It injures a tree to ross it.

rosser 'rɔsɚ, *n.* A rossing machine (see also quot. 1905). — **1876** KNIGHT 1984/2 A common use of the rosser is in saw-mills, . . . to remove the bark from the log in advance of the path of the saw. **1905** *Forestry Bureau. Bul.* 61 *s.v.* Rosser. One who barks and smooths the ride of a log in order that it may slide more easily.

Ross's goose. A small white goose, *Chen rossi*, occurring in the western U.S., esp. California, as a migrant, named by John Cassin in 1861 for Bernard R. Ross (1827–74), factor of the Hudson's Bay Co., and correspondent of the Smithsonian Institution.

1874 COUES *Birds of Northwest* 553 Anser Rossii, Bd. Horned Wavy; Ross' Goose. [**1928** *Condor* Sep.–Oct. 293 *Chen rossi.* In winter this goose occurs fairly commonly in the Sacramento and San Joaquin valleys.] **1949** *L.A. Dly. News* 9 Nov. 8/6 The following limits of migratory game birds may be imported: . . . geese and brant, except Ross' goose, 6 in any combination not exceeding 2 Canada geese or whitefronted geese and brant.

∗**roster,** *n.* (See quot.) — **1891** *Calif. Statutes* 31 March 454 The Secretary of State is hereby authorized to compile, publish, and distribute one thousand copies of a State Blue Book or Roster.

∗**rot,** *n.* **1.** =**boll rot. 2.** =**rotgut whisky.** Both *obs.*

(1) 1819 *Niles' Reg.* XVI. 416/1 The *rot* is said to be making sad work among the cotton, in different parts of the southern states. **1856** *Rep. Comm. Patents 1855: Agric.* 233 The 'rot' has been attributed to a variety of causes, such as changes in the atmosphere, . . . and to the growth of fungi. — **(2) 1860** GREELEY *Overland Journey* 201 A grocery devoid of some kind of 'rot,' as the fiery beverage was currently designated, was to them a novel and most distasteful experience.

As the last term in **bitter, black, boll, grape, hoof, ring, water rot.**

Rotarian ro'tɛrɪən, *n.* and *a.* [f. ∗*Rotary*, used in the name of the organization.] A member of a Rotary Club. Of or pertaining to such a club.

1915 *Chi. Herald* 9 Nov. 10/5 The Rotarians will observe 'Moving Picture day' at a luncheon in the crystal room of the Hotel Sherman. **1923** R. HERRICK *Lilla* 181 Lilla, on opening the newspapers, often found his name and a brief report of his remarks at a Rotarian lunch. **1949** *Telephone Reg.* (McMinnville, Ore.) 4 Aug. 5/2 Over 100 Rotarians and their wives took part in the annual Rotary picnic held by the McMinnville club Friday night.

Hence **Rotarianism.**

1922 *Nation* 19 April v, Do you know your state? How it stands in intelligence, rotarianism, bootlegging, evangelism, crime?

* **rotary,** *n.*

1. (*cap.*) = **Rotary Club.**

1944 JOHNSON *As I Dare* 275 When the members of the Denver Rotary attend Eastern conventions they wear ten-gallon hats. **1947** *So. Sierran* April 1/1 You should know how much more deliberate and painstaking was the similar committee of Rotary in making a check-up of my past record.

2. In combs.: (1) **Rotary Club,** one of a group of local organizations of a type begun in Chicago in 1905, and affiliated in an organization known as Rotary International; (2) **lock,** a lock the body of which is round; (3) **plow,** a huge mechanically propelled vehicle or vehicular apparatus provided with a suitable plowlike blade or rotary brush and used for removing snow from roads and railroads, also **rotary snowplow,** cf. next; (4) **steam snow shovel,** app. a snow shovel for clearing railroad tracks of snow, operated by being pushed by an engine.

(1) 1921 *Rural Organization* 86 Is a *Rotary Club* a community council? **1948** *Dly. Ardmoreite* (Ardmore, Okla.) 20 April 1/2 Ardmore Rotary club will entertain the boys who graduate this spring from the Ardmore high school at their meeting Wednesday noon. — **(2) 1856** *Spirit of Times* (N.Y.) 13 Dec. 247/3 Place the Rotary Lock on your street door, and it is absolutely Burglar proof. **1893** CUSHING *Story of P.O.* 408 The postal clerks are not permitted to have keys to open the rotary locks. — **(3) 1890** *Boston Transcript* 29 Jan. 1/4 The big rotary plough has been dug from the snow in Cascade cañon. **1941** SKINNER *Soap Behind Ears* 178 I'll see again the beauty of the huge rotary snow-plough whirling the drifts from the Minnesota tracks. **1949** *Time* 14 March 87/1 The stiff bodies of frozen cattle broke the blades of rotary snowplows in blizzard-bound Montana. — **(4) 1890** *Railways of Amer.* 156 A Rotary Steam Snow-shovel in Operation (From an instantaneous photograph.)

* **rotgut,** *n.*

1. = **rotgut whisky.** *Slang.*

1819 QUITMAN in Claiborne *Life Quitman* I. 42 Whiting and I had to treat to 'red-eye' or 'rot-gut,' as whiskey is here called. **1923** MULFORD *Black Buttes* 220 Yes, even a drink of rot-gut would 'a' bought you! **1946** *Time* 7 Oct. 10/2 For 50 years we have been hearing how the drought-smitten Jayhawkers were poisoning themselves on bootleg rotgut because we couldn't get decent liquor.

2. (See quots.) Also **rotgut minnow.**

1884 GOODE *Fisheries* I. 618 [The shiner] has no tangible importance as a food-fish. Its flesh spoils very quickly after the fish is taken from the water, hence the name 'Rot-gut Minnow,' applied to it in Alabama. **1933** *Amer. Sp.* Feb. 52 Stone rollers, n. Small sucker-like fish, about four or five inches long, which feed in large schools. They are also called *rot-guts,* because their intestines are said to turn black and decay within a few moments after death.

3. a. rotgut tobacco, (see quot.). **b. rotgut whisky,** whisky of a very cheap, inferior quality. *Colloq.* or *slang.*

(a) 1877 RUEDE *Sod-House Days* 57 They have a brand called 'Old Style,' some of Catlin's (St. Louis) cheap rotgut tobacco, and from that price up. — **(b) 1850** A. T. JACKSON *Forty-Niner* (1920) 12 Half the men in sight were full of rot-gut whiskey. **1927** BROMFIELD *Good Woman* 140 A glass filled many times with the rot-gut whiskey that Hennessey sold.

rotogravure ˌrotəgrəˈvjur, *n.* [L. *rota,* wheel, + *gravure,* as in *photogravure.*] Photogravure printed on a rotary press. Also attrib.

1917 *Sunday Herald* (Boston) 24 May, Rotogravure Section. **1924** *Lit. Digest* 31 May 35/1 Beauty contests and bathing-girl parades, which make fine pictures for the rotogravure supplements of the Sunday papers, . . . are 'harmful in every way' to the girls themselves and the devil's own method of advertising. **1950** *L.A. Times* Midwinter 3 Jan. 93 The Finest in Printing is Rotogravure.

* **rotten,** *a.* In combs.: (1) **rotten limestone,** (see quot. 1846), also attrib.; (2) **quartz,** *W.* gold-bearing quartz that is partially decomposed; (3) **root,** prob. black root rot.

(1) 1846 LYELL *Second Visit* II. 42 The common name for the marlite, of which this treeless soil [in Ala.] is composed, is 'rotten limestone.' **1868** *Rep. U.S. Comm. Agric.* (1869) 69 The sand marls of the rotten limestone group of this State. — **(2) 1850** *Calif. Courier* (S.F.) 18 Oct. 2/3 Two gentlemen, by the name of Fisher . . . have recently engaged in extracting gold from what is termed rotten quartz. — **(3) 1867–8** *Ill. Agric. Soc. Trans.* VII. 548 What is called 'rotten root'—a disease that has been fatal to the apple tree in the southern part of the state.

* **rough,** *a., adv.,* and *n.*

1. *n.* A rough draft. *Obs.*

1699 SEWALL *Diary* I. 502 Agree for 15£ and draw a rough of it and take his hand to it. **1710** *Harvard Rec.* I. 395 A rough of sundry Articles was drawn up. **1796** *Steele P.* I. 144 A rough of a letter which may at some future period compose part of a circular.

2. In combs.: (1) **rough-edge,** sawed lumber the edges of which are not trimmed or sized, also **rough-edge plank,** *colloq.;* (2) **gambler, gambling,** (see quot.), *slang, obs.;* (3) * **Heads,** meaning obscure, app. a nickname for certain soldiers, *obs.;* (4) **house,** an uproar, row, noisy sport, also attrib., cf. **roughhouse,** *v.;* (5) **houser,** one who creates a roughhouse, transf. in quot.; (6) **lock,** any rough-and-ready means of braking a load or vehicle, as by the use of chains securing a wheel or wheels to the vehicle's frame or load, cf. **rough-lock,** *v.;* (7) **neck,** (*a*) a rough, uncouth, uncultivated fellow, a rowdy, *slang,* (*b*) *W.* a member of a drilling crew in the oilfields; (8) **oak,** = **iron oak;** (9) * **rider,** see as a main entry; (10) **sc(r)uff,** a person of very low class, *collect.* the rag, tag, and bobtail; (11) **skin,** a ruffian (see also quot. 1859), *obs.;* (12) * **stuff,** boisterous or violent behavior, *slang.*

(1) 1851 *Fla. Plant. Rec.* 441 Received 4 Rufedge Plank 20 feet long from Dr. Turnbulls mill. **1855** DAVIS *Farm Bk.* 220 Sent to Mr Crocker's mill for rough edge. **1856** *Fla. Plant Rec.* 468 Wagon brought 9 scantlin 10 Rufedg planks. — **(2) 1865** *Ore. State Jrnl.* 28 Oct. 2/2 Two 'rough gamblers,' a new name for thieves, were found hanging from a hay frame, at Virginia City, Montana Territory. *Ib.* 30 June 312 'Rough Gambling.'—That's what they call robbing the stage over in Idaho. — **(3) 1760** *N.J. Archives* XX. 472 *Camp at Oswego.* . . . We have now here . . . one Battalion of the Royal Americans, three of the New-York and Jersey Blues, with Gage's Light Infantry, 100 of the Ruff Heads, and two Provincial Regiments. — **(4) 1887** M. ROBERTS *Western Avernus* 54 He called the bridgeman a very opprobrious name, and for a moment there was great danger of a 'rough house' out of hand. **1946** *Casper* (Wyo.) *Tribune-Herald* 29 March 9/3 Rocky, with his striking black hair and roughhouse tactics in the ring, has become a gallery idol.

(5) 1904 *N.Y. Ev. Post* 2 Jan., In fiction, whether it is historic, society, or the work of literary rough-housers. — **(6) 1886** *San Jose* (Calif.) *Mercury* June 3/1 If he thinks the logs will slide and overtake his team, he puts a chain around some of them, making what he calls a rough lock. **1923** EZRA G. WADE *Early Days at Paonia* (MS) 2 We put chain rough-locks on each rear wheel. **1929** A. J. DICKSON *Across Plains* 108 Here it was necessary to put on the rough locks, since emigrant wagons [*c*1864] were seldom fitted with brakes. — **(7)** (*a*) **1836** CROCKETT *Exploits* 58 You may be called a drunken dog by some of the clean shirt and silk stocking gentry, but the real rough necks will style you a jovial fellow. **1946** *Reader's Digest* July 30/2 That stinking roughneck has simply no feeling for antiquity. (*b*) **1948** *Chi. Tribune* 5 Dec. I. 14/3 Among today's roughnecks you'll find college men—petroleum engineers and geologists. **1949** *Sat. Ev. Post* 16 April 39/3 Immediately after the blow-in, roughnecks pumped heavy mud down the bore hole for thirty-eight consecutive hours and succeeded in clamping a blow-out preventer on the casing. — **(8) 1847** DARLINGTON *Weeds & Plants* 308 *Q[uercus] obtusiloba. . . .* Obtuse-lobed Quercus. Barrens White Oak. Post Oak. Rough Oak. . . . The wood is very durable. **1892** APGAR *Trees Northern U.S.* 153 *Quercus stellata,* . . . Post-oak, Rough or Box White oak. . . . A medium-sized tree, 40 to 50 ft. high, with very hard, durable wood.

(10) 1831 *Boston Transcript* 1 Oct. 1/2 The roughscruf of St Louis called my deliverer a Watchenago. **1904** *Atlantic Mo.* March 301 The only nationalities more hated by the trade-unionist are the political rough-scuff of Europe, . . . such as the Armenians, Greeks, and Syrians. — **(11) 1840** *Jamestown* (N.Y.) *Jrnl.* 28 Oct. 2/6 Some hardy roughskins from the pine knots up the Alleghany were sauntering up town. **1859** BARTLETT 371 *Roughskins,* a gang of Baltimore bullies. — **(12) 1913** LONDON *Valley of Moon* I. iv, There's goin' to be rough stuff down there in a minute. **1948** GARDNER *Lonely Heiress* 168 She isn't built right to withstand a lot of rough stuff.

b. In the names of birds: (1) **rough-billed pelican,** (see quot. 1891); (2) **-legged falcon,** = next; (3) **-legg(ed) hawk,** a large hawk, *Buteo lagopus sanctijohannis,* or a related species, having feathers extending to the toes, cf. **black hawk;** (4) **-winged swallow,** a swallow of the American genus *Stelgidopteryx,* as the bridge swallow, *S. serripennis.*

(1) 1785 LATHAM *Gen. Synopsis Birds* VI. 586 Rough-billed Pelican. . . . This species . . . is found in some parts of America. **1891** *Cent.* 5241/1 *Rough-billed,* . . . having a rough horny excrescence on the beak: specific in the phrase *rough-billed pelican, Pelecanus trachy-*

rhynchus (or *erythrorhynchus*). This remarkable formation is deciduous, and is found only on adult birds during the breeding season. — (2) **1811** Wilson *Ornithology* IV. 59 Rough-legged Falcon. *Falco Lagopus.* **1864** *Amer. Naturalist* III. 518 The Rough-legged Falcon and Black Hawk are the same. **1874** Coues *Birds N.W.* 755/3 Falcon, rough-legged. — (3) **1811** Wilson *Ornithology* IV. 60 The Rough-legged Hawk measures twenty-two inches in length. **1948** *Trail Riders Bul.* June 23/1 The most wide-awake member of the community, spotting a skulking coyote or a dangerous rough-leg hawk in the offing, broadcasts a warning to all concerned. — (4) **1838** Audubon *Ornith. Biog.* IV. 595 In its general appearance . . . the Rough-winged Swallow is extremely similar to the Bank Swallow. **1945** *Nat. Geog. Mag.* June 738 Something of a Hermit Is the Rough-winged Swallow.

3. In phrases: (1) *rough-and-ready*, *rough-and-tumble*, see as main entries; (2) *to rough board*, to cover with rough boards, *colloq.;* (3) *to rough-lock*, (see quot. 1884), also **roughlocking,** see **rough lock;** (4) *to rough through*, (see quot.); (5) *Rough on Rats*, a proprietary rat poison; (6) *to get rough with*, to treat or deal with in a severe manner, *colloq.*

(2) **1849** Browne *Poultry Yd.* 87 Rough-board it [a poultry house] from the apex downward by the sills to the ground. — (3) **1859** Marcy *Prairie Traveler* iii, Rough-locking is a very safe method of passing heavy artillery down abrupt declivities. **1884** W. Shepherd *Prairie Exper.* 197 The hind-wheels were rough-locked, that is, a large linked chain was tied round the rim of the wheel in such a way that the wheel rides upon the chain, which drags along and cuts into the ground. **1940** Stuart *Trees of Heaven* 194, I can stand with my weight on the brake beam and rough-lock both hind wheels. — (4) **1874** McCoy *Cattle* 369 It is a proposition upon which cattle feeders differ, whether it is most profitable to full feed Texan cattle on grain or 'rough them through,' or 'range' them upon the plains during winter and fat on the grass the succeeding summer.

(5) **1884** *N.Y. Wkly. Tribune* 23 Jan. 7/4 Seven members of the family . . . have been poisoned by a decoction known as 'Rough on Rats.' **1941** Alley *Random Thoughts* 141 While he was under the water he got strangled, and that caused him to 'throw up' the 'Rough-on-Rats.' — (6) **1931** *K.C. Times* 23 July, We are going to get rough with him.

As the last term in **bear, hazel rough.**

***rough-and-ready,** *a.* and *n.*

1. (*cap.*) = **Old Rough-and-Ready.** Also transf.

1846 *Dollar Newspaper* (Phila.) 15 July 2/2 'Rough and Ready' gave him his parole immediately. **1847** *Rough & Ready* (Louisville) 13 Dec. 2/3 The 'Rough and Ready,' as published by us, . . . was the first paper to advocate the claims to the Presidency of the *honest* 'old man' . . . whose homely cognomen it bears. **1948** Johnston *Gold Rush* iv/1 Rough and Ready [was] settled in 1849 by Wisconsin emigrants led by A. A. Townsend, an army captain who had served with Gen. Zachary Taylor, 'Old Rough and Ready,' in the Mexican War.

b. Rough-and-Ready boys, ?the political adherents of Gen. Zachary Taylor (1784–1850). *Obs.*

1848 *Santa Fe Republican* 22 Jan. 2/1 Some of the 'Rough and Ready' boys, 'hell bent on getting some hair,' fired several times at them, and pursued them so closely that one of them abandoned . . . a large gourd of *aguadiente.*

2. (See quots.) *Obs.*

1855 Beste *Wabash* II. 48 A rough-and-ready is a flat scaffolding raised upon springs and four very slight wheels: above the scaffolding, are suspended two benches, one before the other: poles, at the four corners, support a leather awning and leather curtains hang on rings all round. **1890** *N. & Q.* V. 21 There is nothing very refined and respectable about the belongings of a Down-East logger. Compare *rough-and-ready*, a kind of hat; wrap-rascal, a coarse cloak.

***rough-and-tumble,** *a.*, *adv.*, and *n.*

1. The haphazard give-and-take of rough, adventurous living, struggling, etc. *Colloq.*

1840 Dana *Two Years* xxviii. 306, I had spent nearly a year [on the brig] and got the first rough and tumble of sea-life. **1897** *Cent. Mag.* May 104/2 You have gone through all the rough and tumble of army service and frontier life.

2. *a.* and *adv.* Characterized by a disregard of all rules and formalities, irregular, disorderly. Also in a rough or irregular manner.

1818 Palmer *Travels U.S.* 131, I understand the question is generally asked, *Will you fight fair, or take it rough and tumble?* **1856** G. D. Brewerton *War in Kans.* 280 We are inclined to believe that the Hickory Pointers must be a very 'rough and tumble'—not to mention pugnacious — set of gentlemen. **1905** *Forestry Bureau Bul.* No 61, A *rough and tumble landing* is one in which no attempt is made to pile the logs regularly. **1950** *Esquire* Feb. 116/4 Ben . . . had spent most of his life in the bitter, rough-and-tumble scramble of getting to the top in the oil business.

roughhouse ˈrʌfˌhaus, *v. tr.* and *intr.* To handle roughly, to deal boisterously *with.* Also *to roughhouse it.*

1902 Wilson *Spenders* 436 You rough-housed the boy considerable yesterday. **1908** Sinclair *Metropolis* 57 She's always wanting to rough-house it. **1948** *Parents' Mag.* March 122/2 She apparently loves it whenever I roughhouse with her a bit.

***roughness,** *n.* Hay, fodder, corn shucks, etc., as distinguished from grain. *Colloq.*

1813 in *East Tenn. Hist. Soc. Pub.* XI. 99 Did not draw aney rufness for our teeme. **1869** *Overland Mo.* III. 127 All over the South they feed a horse 'roughness,' (any kind of fodder, as distinguished from grain). **1897** *Scribner's Mag.* XXII. 635/2 If Dave put up corn, or 'roughness,' or meat that year it would be a surprisingly small quantity.

transf. **1846** *Knickerb.* Oct. 313 There can't nobody stay here to save souls without some kind of *roughness* to keep up natur'.

***roughrider,** *n.*

1. A western cowboy, sometimes used of Theodore Roosevelt (1859–1919).

1888 Roosevelt in *Cent. Mag.* Feb. 505/2 The rough-rider of the plains, the hero of rope and revolver, is first cousin to the backwoodsman of the Southern Alleghanies. **1900** Mark Twain *Speeches* (1910) 355 (R.), We have tried for governor an illustrious Rough Rider. **1929** E. W. Howe *Plain People* 16, I wish to apologize at this late day for once treating the rough rider, Charley Irwin, of Wyoming, very inconsiderately.

2. (See quot. 1914.)

1898 *Dly. Ardmoreite* (Ardmore, Okla.) 5 May 1/3 If Muskogee and Guthrie fill the ranks of Roosevelt's regiment of rough riders it will not be because the distinction of a place in the regiment goes begging here. **1914** *Cyclo. Amer. Govt.* III. 236/1 *Rough Riders*, a popular designation given the First United States Volunteer Cavalry organized by Leonard Wood and Theodore Roosevelt for service in the Spanish-American War, and recruited largely from the cowboys of the western plains. **1949** *Chi. D. News* 24 June 16/1 Teddy's Rough Riders Near End of Trail.

attrib. **1930** Ferber *Cimarron* 254 At sight of Yancey Cravat in his Rough Rider uniform of khaki, U.S.V. on the collar, the hat brim dashingly caught up on the left side with the insignia of crossed sabers, they were snared again in the mesh of his enchantment. **1944** Clark *Pills* 191 The naval victory costumes were topped with roughrider hats adorned with crossed sabers.

rounce rauns, *n.* [In **1**, f. G. *rams*, *ramsch*, in a similar sense. In **2.** app. a different word of obscure origin.]

1. (See quots.)

1855 in *Cal. Hist. Soc. Quart.* VIII. 352 Had a great rounce game, a little noise but no fun. **1864** Dick *Amer. Hoyle* (1866) 478 The game of Rounce, as played in the United States, is derived from the German game of *Ramsh*, and in its principal features resembles Division Loo. **1891** *Cent.* 5242/2 *Rounce*, . . . a game of cards, played with a full pack by not more than nine persons. Each player starts with fifteen points, and for every trick he takes subtracts one from the score; the player who first reaches zero wins.

2. In marbles (see quot. 1922).

1888 Eggleston in *Cent. Mag.* May 78/1 Their cries of 'rounses,' 'taw,' . . . and 'vent' might often be heard. **1922** *D.N.* V. 187 *Rounce*, a call given when one's taw is so placed that he cannot shoot at the ring or at an opponent. If he calls 'Rounce' he may select a convenient place to shoot from, unless his opponent first calls, 'Vence ye rounce.'

***round,** *a.*, *n.*, *prep.*, and *adv.*

1. *n. Baseball.* An inning. *Obs.*

1907 *St. Nicholas* July 819/1 That round began with the score a tie. Each side had made two runs.

2. *a.* In combs.: (1) ***round ball,** (see quot. 1867), *obs.;* (2) **black Virginian walnut,** (see quot.), *obs.;* (3) **corn,** (see quot.), *obs.;* (4) ***head,** (see quots.); (5) ***house,** see as a main entry; (6) **-leaved maple,** the vine maple, *Acer circinatum*, found in northwestern North America; (7) **-leaved violet,** (see quot. 1891), also **round-leafed violet;** (8) **log,** designating structures made of logs not split or hewn; (9) **-posted,** *a.* of a chair, having round upright posts for support; (10) **potato,** (see quots.), *colloq.;* (11) **rimmer,** (see quots.), *obs.;* (12) **sauce,** (see quot. 1859 and cf. **long sauce**), *obs.;* (13) ***-sman,** (see quot. 1891); (14) **stone,** (see quot. 1891); (15) **timber,** (see quot.); (16) **trip,** a complete trip to a destination and back again, also attrib.; (17) **up,** see as a main entry; (18) **wood,** = **mountain ash.**

(1) **1841** *N.O. Picayune* 25 May 2/2 We would go to Cleveland ourselves just for one game of round ball, provided we could not enjoy it at less cost. **1867** *Ball Players' Chron.* 18 July 4/2 This game of rounders . . . was brought to our country by the early emigrants, and was called here 'base ball' or 'round ball.' **1871** CUTTING *Student Life Amherst* 112 'Wicket' and 'Round Ball,' were quite common once, though of late years, 'Base Ball' has entirely superceded them. — (2) **1785** MARSHALL *Amer. Grove* 66 *Juglans nigra.* Round black Virginian Walnut. . . . Upon being bruised [the leaves] emit a strong aromatic flavour, as doth also the external covering of the fruit. — (3) **1889** *Cent.* 1268/3 *Round corn*, a trade-name for the grain of a class of yellow maize with small, round, very hard kernels. — (4) **1829** ROYALL *Pennsylvania* I. 152 [Professed Christians] have a number of names here, as in other States, 'Grey-backs, Round-heads, &c.' **1863** MOORE *Rebellion Rec.* V. I. 24 Two companies of the Pennsylvania 'Roundhead' regiment . . . were cut off by the rebels. **1902** CLAPIN 341 Roundhead. In the North-West, frequently said of a Swede.

(6) [**1846** BROWNE *Trees Amer.* 93 *Acer circinatum*, The Circinal-leaved Maple. . . . Round-leaved Maple, Britain.] **1869** W. MURRAY *Adventures* 128 A silver beech or round-leaved maple relieved the sombre color with lighter hues. **1892** APGAR *Trees Northern U.S.* 88 Round-leaved or Vine Maple. . . . A small tree or tall shrub . . . ; cultivated; from the Pacific coast. — (7) **1818** *Mass. H.S. Coll.* 2 Ser. VIII. 168 Among our herbaceous wild plants, the first that appear are the delicate claytonia, the graceful three-lobed hepatica, [and] the round-leaved violet, with its fine nodding blossoms. **1891** *Cent.* 6761/3 *Round-leafed violet*, *Viola rotundifolia* of cold woods in eastern North America. — (8) **1873** HAYCRAFT *Elizabethtown, Ky.* 7 Samuel Haycraft was born August 14, 1795, . . . in a double, round-log cabin. **1884** MARK TWAIN *H. Finn* xxxii, Phelps's was one of these little one-horse cotton plantations . . . [having a] round-log kitchen, with a big broad, open but roofed passage joining it to the house. — (9) **1845** *Knickerb.* XXV. 444 The chairs around the room were the same strait-backed, withe-bottomed, round-posted, unpainted seats that they had been from my earliest recollection. **1857** HAMMOND *No. Scenes* 170 The horns on his [a buck's] head were like an old-fashioned round-posted chair.

(10) **1801** *Hist. Review & Directory* I. 150 Round potatoes. *Solanum Tuberosum.* **1899** GREEN *Va. Word-Book* 309 Round-potatoes, *n. pl.* Irish potatoes, distinguishing from *long-potatoes*, or sweet-potatoes. — (11) **1842** C. MATHEWS in *Bro. Jonathan* Extra 26 Nov. 35/2 All over the region of East Bowery . . . the powerful class of Round-Rimmers; a fraternity of gentlemen, who, in round, crape-bound hats . . . carry dismay and terror wherever they move. **1848** BARTLETT 279 *Round-rimmers*, hats with a round rim; hence, those who wear them. In the city of New York, a name applied to a large class of dissipated young men by others called Bowery Boys and Soaplocks. — (12) **1857** *Knickerb.* XLIX. 273 They'd blamed all the long and round sauce in a kitchen-garden for not growing up into a hickory pole. **1859** ELWYN *Glossary* 95 Long *sarse*, and short *sarse*, and round *sarse*, are not unfrequently applied to different vegetables: carrots, beets, and potatoes are so called, according to their respective dimensions. — (13) **1868** *N.Y. Herald* 31 July 6/5 Patrolman Jas. Mee . . . is hereby appointed roundsman on the force. **1891** *Cent.* 5246/1 *Roundsman*, . . . a police officer, of a rank above patrolmen and below sergeants, who goes the rounds within a prescribed district to see that the patrolmen or ordinary policemen attend to their duties properly, and to aid them in case of necessity. **1903** *N.Y. Ev. Post* 27 Nov. 2 Several hundred patrolmen reported to-day for examination for promotion to the rank of roundsman. — (14) **1883** *Cent. Mag.* XXVI. 221/2 Gangs of street paviors were seen and heard here, there, and yonder, swinging the pick and ramming the roundstone. **1891** *Cent.* 5246/1 *Roundstone*, . . . small round or roundish stones collectively, used for paving; cobblestone. (Local, U.S.)

(15) **1905** *Forestry Bureau Bul. 61*, Round timber. Pine trees which have not been turpentined. (S[outhern] F[orests].) — (16) **1860** *Dinsmore's Amer. R.R. Guide* Sep. 142 Round trip tickets. **1890** *Brighton* (Colo.) *Reg.* 25 Jan. 1/4 The railway company has rehashed its round-trip rate, from suburban towns to Denver. **1948** *Sierra Club* (So. Calif. Chap.) *Sched.* 128, 21 The amount for a round trip from central Los Angeles to Harwood Lodge is $1.50. — (18) **1848** THOREAU *Maine Woods* 59 The wood was chiefly yellow birch, spruce, fir, mountain-ash, or roundwood, as the Maine people call it, and moose-wood. **1850** *N. Eng. Farmer* II. 159 In the spring of 1847, one of my neighbors took from the forest some small mountain ash, or round-wood, as it is sometimes called.

b. In the names of animals: (1) **round clam,** (*a*) =**quahog,** cf. **hard clam,** (*b*) (see quot.); (2) **-crested duck,** =**hooded merganser;** (3) **-horned elk,** the American elk or wapiti, cf. **American elk, elk;** (4) ***robin,** =**cigar fish;** (5) **-tailed muskrat,** a vole, *Neofiber alleni*, found in swamps in Florida, cf. **Florida water rat;** (6) **whitefish,** =**Menominee whitefish.**

(1) (*a*) **1843** *Nat. Hist. N.Y., Zoology* VI. 217 This species is the common Round Clam, much prized as an article of food. **1883** *Nat. Museum Bul.* No. 27, 233 *Venus mercenaria* . . . is the 'quahaug,' or 'round clam.' (*b*) *Ib.* 241 *Saxidomus aratus* . . . is the 'Round Clam' of the Pacific coast. — (2) **1731** CATESBY *Carolina* I. 94 The round-crested Duck. . . . The Head is crowned with a very large circular Crest. **1917** *Birds of Amer.* I. 112. — (3) **1781–2** JEFFERSON *Notes Va.* (1788) 57. **1842** *Nat. Hist. N.Y.*, *Zoology* I. 119 The American Stag . . . is called in various parts of the country, . . . *Wapiti*, *Grey Elk*, and *Round-horned Elk*. — (4) **1709** LAWSON *Carolina* 159 We have another sort of Pearch, which . . . are distinguish'd from the other sorts, by the name of Round-Robins; being flat, and very round-shap'd. **1911** *Rep. Fisheries 1908* 314/2 Round robin (*Decapterus punctatus*), a food fish found along the coast from the Gulf to Woods Hole. It is also called . . . 'scad.'

(5) **1917** *Animals of Amer.* 256 Round-Tailed Musk-Rat. . . . A large, rat-like rodent much resembling the Musk-rat, but having a round tail. **1938** MATSCHAT *Suwannee River* 31 Recently the round-tailed muskrat, or Florida water rat, has been found in Okefenokee. — (6) **1883** *Nat. Musemum Bul.* No. 27, 417 *Coregonus quadrilateralis.* . . . Round Whitefish. . . . Lakes of New England; Upper Great Lakes [etc.].

3. *prep.* Of time: About, approximately. *Colloq.*

1928 F. N. HART *Bellamy Trail* iii. 92 It must have been round quarter to nine.

As the last term in **all, board, boarding, hand, hog, run, sun, tear, walk round.**

***roundabout,** *n.* **1.** An armchair the arms and back of which are made on two adjacent sides. In full **roundabout chair. 2.** A wrapper or dressing gown worn by women.

Roundabout chair

(1) **1840** *Knickerb.* XVI. 115, I sat in my roundabout chair the other evening. **1844** *Lowell Offering* IV. 175 [He sat] in a large flag-bottomed 'roundabout' on the opposite side of the fireplace. **1936** F. C. MORSE *Furniture* 170 'Roundabout' chairs are met with in inventories from 1738 under various names,—'three-cornered chair,' 'half round chair,' 'round about chair.' — (2) **1841** *S. Lit. Messenger* VII. 525/1 The garment is a long, loose roundabout, connecting in front with strings, and is much worn, even at the present time. **1895** WIGGIN *Village Watch-Tower* 103 Mother had let her slip on her new green roundabout over her nightgown.

***rounder,** *n.*

1. One accustomed to make the rounds of low resorts, a petty criminal; a man about town. Also transf. *Slang.*

1854 *Cong. Globe* App. 17 Jan. 1220/3, I have always found him [President Franklin Pierce] a very kind and agreeable man,—what the 'rounders' in New York would term a 'glover.' **1879** DALY in J. F. Daly *A. Daly* 330 [We] are old 'rounders' and familiar with the voice, gait and peculiarities of most of the actors and actresses on the American stage. **1947** PAUL *Linden* 89 You could find better uses for your money than paying for those other rounders' rum and loose women.

b. (See quot. 1903.)

1881 *Bradstreet's* 29 Jan. 51/4 The 'rounder' in alms-taking is headed off. **1903** *Charities* 3 Oct. 283 The class of persons known as 'rounders,' people who go from one hospital to another seeking advice and treatment, a species of medical mendicants.

2. *W.* A cowboy engaged in rounding up cattle.

1890 *Gate City Herald* (Deep Creek Falls, Wash.) 23 Oct. 1/4 At eleven o'clock the . . . majority of the rounders galloped away toward the 'chuck' wagon for dinner.

*__roundhouse,__ *n.*

1. A building of a circular form, concentric with the pivot of a turntable, in which railroad engines are cleaned and subjected to minor repairs.

1856 FERGUSSON *America* 249 The engine-house has stalls for forty-six engines. It is open in the centre; and this arrangement is said to be equally convenient, while it is much less expensive, than the 'round-house,' where all is covered in. **1898** HAMBLEN *Gen. Manager's Story* 62, I walked out, and strolled over to the round-house, to have a look at the engines. **1949** *L.A. Times* 26 April 20/3 Like all roundhouses, its hub is a great circular turntable that can spin big locomotives around like the second hand on a stop watch.

attrib. **1895** *Chi. Strike of 1894* 214 A number of switch tenders, yard clerks, flagmen, tower men, and roundhouse men left their work. **1948** *Chi. Tribune* 11 April I. 1/2 A strike of 10,000 firemen and roundhouse workers of the Pennsylvania railroad was called today for April 14.

2. In special combs.: (1) **roundhouse curve,** (see quot. 1912); (2) **left, punch, right,** an unscientific looping or swinging blow with the fist.

(1) **1910** *Amer. Mag.* June. 224/2 The first curves discovered were of the variety now known as the 'barrel hoop' or 'round house.' **1912** C. MATHEWSON *Pitching* 19 When I first joined the Giants, I had what is known as the 'old round-house curve,' which is no more than a big, slow outdrop. — (2) **1920** *Collier's* 3 July 34/4 He swung a roundhouse left, square to the Kid's unprotected face! **1945** *Chi. D. News* 31 Aug. 25/3 Doty nailed him with a roundhouse right last night. **1949** *Boston Globe* 12 June (Fiction Mag.) 2/2 He waded into the freight's fireman, throwing roundhouse punches right and left.

*__roundup,__ *n. W.* The driving together of cattle scattered over a wide area for counting, establishing ownership, etc.

1873 in *Ann. Wyoming* V. (1927) 74 The herders of this Co. start a Round-up tomorrow. Each ranch sends a man. . . . Then each man picks out his stock and drives them in. **1907** MULFORD *Bar-20* 6 Bar-20's northern line was C 80's southern one, and Skinny Thompson took his turn at outriding one morning after the season's round-up. **1950** *Boston Globe Mag.* 8 Jan. 2/2 They had cooperated agreeably in the matter of round-ups, or rodeos as they were called down there.

transf. **1880** *Harper's Mag.* Feb. 380/2 Why, we old fellows have a round up 'most every year in Denver, and talk and laugh over those times. **1949** *Lincoln Co. News* (Oceanlake, Ore.) 4 Aug. 3/4 Another periodic survey of censorship conditions . . . shows no major barriers have come down since the last roundup of the situation.

attrib. **1885** *Wkly. New Mexican Rev.* 26 March 1/6 Round-up parties have already been started for that section. **1893** ROOSEVELT *Wilderness Hunter* 23 Close beyond the trees on the further bank stood the two round-up wagons. **1920** HUNTER *Trail Drivers Texas* I. 313 The round-up boss would let no one ride through the herd and . . . unnecessarily disturb them. **1944** *Chi. D. News* 27 April 16 Roundup Time [title of a cartoon].

b. The group or company of cowboys, horses, etc., engaged in a cattle roundup.

1878 in *Colo. Mag.* XVI. (1939) 152 Most of the round-up gone; a few still lingered at the bar; two of whom inspired by bad whiskey . . . spurred their horses up onto the hotel piazza. **a1918** G. STUART *On Frontier* II. 178 It was a novel sight to witness the big spring roundup pull out.

c. A canvass or check up, a settlement.

1886 *Phila. Times* 3 May (*Cent.*), That exception . . . will probably be included in the general round-up tomorrow. **1904** CRISSEY *Tattlings* 42 A hatchet-faced lawyer . . . made a quick round-up of the representatives of the corporate interests and vested rights of the state.

d. A bringing together by the police of criminals and suspicious characters.

1890 *Chi. Record* 17 Jan. 12/1 A 'round-up' of all suspicious characters was begun. **1903** *N.Y. Times* 23 Sep., Thirty-three alleged members of East Side gangs were arrested by detectives in a round-up Monday night. **1949** *L.A. Times* 21 April 8/3 Continued roundup by the Immigration Service of aliens illegally in Southern California had netted approximately 1000.

e. =**rodeo 2.**

1914 *World's Work* Feb. 444/2 During the three days of The Round-Up, a constant stream of humanity pours into Pendleton. **1948** *Great Falls* (Mont.) *Tribune* 18 Sep. 5/4 Malta is preparing to welcome at least 5,000 people this weekend when the two-day fall roundup will be staged.

As the last term in **horse, rabbit, spring roundup.**

*__round up,__ *v.*

1. *W. tr.* To drive (livestock) together into a compact herd, to collect or bring in.

This use occurs in Australia as early as 1847 (see the *OED*). The use in this country is app. an independent development. No evidence is at hand to substantiate the claim made in quot. 1891 below.

1876 *Cong. Rec.* 30 June 4309/2 [The Mexican raiders] 'round up' a herd of cattle, and start with them at a full run for the Rio Grande. [**1891** *Harper's Mag.* July 211/1 The word 'round-up' originated in the southern Alleghanies.] **1925** TILGHMAN *Dugout* 24 The men had little difficulty in rounding up some twenty head. **1949** *Sky Line Trail* Oct. 18/1, I met some cowboys rounding up strayed horses.

absol. **1907** MULFORD *Bar-20* 15 They shore outer be here now. They rounded up last week.

Hence **rounding-up,** *n.*

1876 WHILLDIN *Descr. W. Tex.* 16 It soon became evident that a place near us had been selected for 'rounding up.' **1880** *Cimarron News & Press* 15 July 2/4 Rounding up and branding in small parties is in progress throughout the country.

b. *transf.* To capture or bring in (persons).

1885 *Wkly. New Mexican Rev.* 15 Jan. 2/5 Mr. Twitchell went down to 'round-up' the gang and was so far successful as to spot the leader. **1910** *N.Y. Ev. Post* 24 Dec. Supp. 1 At least four successful attempts to round up these fortune-tellers have been made.

2. *intr.* To come to a stop, as for camping or spending the night. *Colloq.*

1885 (*newspaper*), We have reached the point where we intend to round-up for the night. **1911** HARRISON *Queed* 6 Trucks were rounding up for stable and for bed.

rousement ˈrauzmənt, *n.* A rousing demonstration, general and noisy enthusiasm. Usu. *pl. Colloq.*

1883 *Congregationalist* 27 Sep. (*Cent.*), Deep strong feeling, but no excitement. They are not apt to indulge in any more rousements. **1904** *Springfield W. Republican* 23 Sep. 2 Gen. Scott made his famous trip westward really to present his military figure to the people and arouse their enthusiasm. But the rousement failed to come. **1920** *Harvey's Wkly.* 10 July 9/1 At the San Francisco convention it was expedient to put the 'rousements' first.

rousseau ruˈso, *n.* [App. f. F., "a red-haired fellow."] (See quot. and cf. **rubbaboo.**) — **1886** *Outing* Dec. 249/1 The other more favorite dish is rousseau, when it [pemmican] is thrown into the frying pan, fried in its own fat, with the addition, perhaps, of a little salt pork, and mixed with a small amount of flour or broken biscuit.

*__roustabout,__ *n.* A deck hand or water-front laborer, a general laborer.

1868 *Putnam's Mag.* Sep. 342/2 As the steamer was leaving the levée, about forty black deck-hands or 'roustabouts' gathered at the bows. **1909** RICE *Mr. Opp* 172 The roustabouts crowded along the rail, ready to make her fast. **1949** *L.A. Times* 9 April 2/3 Roustabouts from the Clyde Beatty circus appeared to offer any manual labor needed.

transf. and *attrib.* **1928** J. P. MCEVOY *Show Girl* 31, I couldn't afford to get involved in the papers with any roustabout play boys either.

rouster ˈraustə, *n.* =prec. — **1883** *American* VI. 40 Men . . . who used to be rousters, and are now broken down and played out. **1945** FUGINA *Upper Mississippi* 53 Deckhands on raftboats were usually called 'roosters' or 'rousters.'

*__rout,__ *v. tr.* To awaken (someone), to cause (someone) to get *out* of bed.

1787 CUTLER in *Life & Corr.* I. 287 The people at the White House were gone to bed, but I soon routed them. **1852** WHITMORE *Diary* 1 July, Got routed out early this morning. **1892** *N.Y. Sun* 8 May 2/7 He ran to a neighbouring farmhouse, routed out the people.

*__route,__ *n.*

1. A way or road over which mail is regularly carried.

1792 *Ann. 2d Congress* 58 The route by which the mails are at present conveyed shall in no case be altered. **1874** *Rep. Postmaster-General* 209 Each railway post-office clerk . . . is required to attach to each package . . . a facing or label slip bearing the address of the package, the office or route upon which it was made up.

2. The way along which a newsboy regularly delivers papers.

1841 *Jamestown* (N.Y.) *Jrnl.* 5 May 2/4 He succeeded in obtaining possession of a route for a morning penny paper. **1890** H. O. WILLS *Twice Born* 26, I carried a 'route' for the Troy *Daily Press.*

3. The way or course of a line of railroad.

1846 *De Bow's Review* 1 Jan. 23 From the point Atlanta, as a centre, routes projected and in course of construction radiate in every direction.

4. In combs.: (1) **route agency,** an agency for providing or letting mail routes to individuals or contractors; (2) **agent,** (*a*) a postal employee assigned to duty on a railroad train who receives, assorts, and delivers mail along the route, and accompanies it in transit between post office and railroad station or steamboat, *obs.*, (*b*) a road agent *q.v.*, *obs.;* (3) **step,** an order of march in which the men break step, and need not maintain silence.

(1) **1867** Locke *Swingin' Round* 141 We shel hev Post Offisis, and Collectorships, and Assessorships, and Furrin Mishns, and Route Agencies, and sich. — (2) (*a*) **1849** *Hunt's Merch. Mag.* XXII. (1850) 51 The proper duty of the route agents is the care and delivery of the mails. **1880** Tourgee *Invisible Empire* 416 They did not intend to allow any negro route agents, . . . or negro brakesmen, on the road. (*b*) **1897** Lewis *Wolfville* 197 It's shorely the need of money drives this Slim Jim to turnin' route-agent an' go holdin' up the stage. — (3) **1867** *Atlantic Mo.* March 272/2 The 'route step' is an abandonment of all military strictness. **1911** *Infantry Drill Reg.* (*War Dept.*) 99 *Route step* and *at ease* are applicable to any marching formation.

b. *To go the route*, in baseball, to pitch an entire game. *Slang.*

1913 *Chi. Record-Herald* 16 March VIII. 1/5 This was the first complete battle Cicotte has pitched, and he was watched closely to see if he could go the route. **1948** *Chi. Tribune* 8 May II. 3/3 Bill Voiselle went the route for the Braves.

As the last term in **flume, milk, mule, overland, paper, pony express, school, stage, star, through, Utah, wagon route.**

* **route,** *v. tr.* To send or direct (someone or something) over a particular route. Also **routing,** *n.*

1894 *Forum* Oct. 253 Outside agencies and travelling agents . . . secure the routing of passengers and freight by their respective [railroad] lines. **1899** *N.Y. Ev. Post* 28 Jan., [Telegraphic] messages from the United States are generally routed as follows. **1932** Beck *Wonderland* 105 If a request for information comes to the Secretary or Assistant Secretaries of the departments, the letter is routed down the line to the subordinate clerk or officer who had the matter in charge.

b. To arrange (mail) in the order of delivery.

1893 Cushing *Story of P.O.* 235 Here are the carriers themselves, engaged in 'routing' the mail.

c. routing clerk, (see quot. 1889).

1888 *N.Y. Tribune* (F.), As the messages drop they are taken out, slid through steam rollers that copy them, and drop them on a revolving, endless belt, that takes them off to the routing clerks and the messengers. **1889** Farmer 465/1 *Routing Clerks*, clerks in the U.S. Telegraph Service who despatch messages.

***rover,** *n.* **1.** ?A plover. *Rare.* **2.** A nickname for a native or inhabitant of Colorado. — (**1**) **1780** *Narragansett Hist. Reg.* I. 100 Went to the harbor's mouth a gunning and killed one rover. Carried him over to Boston Neck and left him. — (**2**) **1872** *Harper's Mag.* Jan. 317/2 Below will be found a careful compilation of the various nicknames given to the States and people of this republic. . . . Colorado, Rovers. **1902** Clapin 341.

roving commission. A commission appointed by Congress for a special investigation, usu. with vaguely defined authority; authorization or instruction given by Congress to an official, allowing him considerable freedom of operation. — **1867** *Cong. Globe* 22 March 273/2, I think it would be safer to leave this matter [of certain state claims] to the direct inspection of the War Department, than to send out a roving commission. We have had enough of these roving commissions. **1894** *Cong. Rec.* 25 April 4098/1 Is it a legitimate expenditure of the public money to send up consuls with roving commissions to hunt up commerce for a certain class of our people?

* **row,** *n.* In colloq. phrases: (1) *To have a hard row to hoe*, and variants, to have a difficult thing to do, or a dreary prospect; (2) *to have a new* (or *another*) *row to hoe*, to have a new venture or undertaking before one; (3) *to hoe one's own row*, to work independently or without assistance, to hold one's own in an encounter; (4) *to hoe a big row*, to fulfill the duties of a position admirably; (5) *not to amount to a row of beans*, not to amount to anything; (6) *to be at the end of one's row*, to have exhausted one's resources, to be played out.

(**1**) **1835** Crockett *Tour* 69, I never opposed Andrew Jackson for the sake of popularity. I knew it was a hard row to hoe; but I stood up to the rack. **1848** Lowell *Biglow P.*, Poems (1890) II. 48 Ef you're arter folks o'gumption, You've a darned long row to hoe. **1898** Hamblen *Tom Benton's Luck* 104, I've had a pretty tough row to hoe down there in New York. **1948** *Sat. Ev. Post* 14 Aug. 106/3 I'd like to be a surgeon, but it's a long row to hoe. — (**2**) **1836** Crockett *Exploits* 28, I have a new row to hoe, a long and a rough one, but come what will I'll go ahead. *Ib.* 95 Our worthy was discharged from the company, and compelled to commence hoeing another row. — (**3**) **1841** *Knickerb.* XVII. 362 Our American pretender must, to adopt an agricultural phrase, 'hoe his own row,' . . . without the aid of protectors or dependents. **1895** *Cent. Mag.* July 378/2, I wouldn't marry a man that couldn't work in open daylight for a livin'. I'd ruther hoe my own row. — (**4**) **1900** *Cong. Rec.* 7 April 3899/1 Any man who can serve in Congress twenty-five years, hoe as big a row as Bland did, and grow all the time, is big enough for any position whatsoever.

(**5**) **1903** *N.Y. Times* 17 Sep., The letter of Buchanan suspending us doesn't amount to a row of beans. — (**6**) **1904** Harben *Georgians* 2 The old chap certainly is gettin' desperate. . . . It's my opinion he's at the end o' his row.

As the last term in **bald head, bald-headed, check, cotton, down, fence, heap, newspaper, rum, skid, turn, windrow.**

rowdy ˈraudɪ, *n.* [Poss. f. **rowdy,** *a.*] A rough, lawless, quarrelsome, pugnacious person.

1820 J. Flint *Lett. from Amer.* 264 These I must call Americanisms, and will subjoin some examples: Rowdy—Blackguard. **1833** in *Amer. Sp.* VIII. (1933) 76 In Virginia they call an itinerant, a rowdy, in New York a loafer, and in Georgia a cracker. **1919** *Maine My State* 331 A tough looking rowdy . . . aimed a blow at him. **1948** Dick *Dixie Frontier* 201 These 'rowdies,' as they were termed, would fortify themselves with whisky.

b. rowdy hat, a hat of a style much affected by certain rowdies. *Obs.*

1850 Ryan *Adventures* I. 41, I confess I felt some surprise on beholding his Oceanic Majesty suddenly appear on deck—quite fresh from the coral caves of his dominions, as we were informed, wearing a bran-new New York 'rowdy' hat, and with a face as black as the ace of spades.

As the last term in **fire, Illinois rowdy.**

rowdy ˈraudɪ, *a.* [Prob. f. **row, n.*] Of a rough, disorderly, or uncouth nature.

1823 Faux *Memorable Days* 324 A line of houses on the lonely road to Missouri is . . . kept up by these Rowdey robbers and murderers for the reception of travellers, and villians to rob them. **1839** *N.O. Picayune* 20 April 2/3 They talk of removing the seat of government from rowdy Harrisburg to some decent place, say Philadelphia. **1947** *Time* 20 Oct. 5/1 It was the week's rowdiest game.

b. Difficult or hard. *Rare.*

1838 *S. Lit. Messenger* IV. 119/1 He's had rowdy work. poor soul, dodging through the swamps to keep out the way of the enemy.

c. Also **rowdiness, rowdyish, rowdyism.**

1841 J. Q. Adams *Diary* 529 All this was as false and hollow as it was blustering and rowdyish. **1842** *Chi. American* 30 Aug., Let the police be more energetic . . . or we shall soon gain a reputation for rowdyism. **1894** *U. of Chi. Wkly.* 25 Oct. 8/2 A few of the 'Varsity students in a fit of pique allowed rowdyism to overcome their collegiate training. **1945** *Newsweek* 17 Sep. 63/2 He complained against GI drunkenness and rowdiness. **1949** J. B. Herrick *Memories* 26 Like the country boys' rowdyish horning or 'shivareeing' the newly wedded couple.

rowdy ˈraudɪ, *v.* [See the noun.] *tr.* and *intr.* To bully (someone), to behave in the manner of a rowdy. Also **rowdying,** *n.*

1825 Paulding *J. Bull in Amer.* 209 Notwithstanding . . . their being regulated and rowdied, . . . not one [emigrant] in a thousand ever goes home again. **1839** *N.O. Picayune* 26 Feb. 2/4 There *is* more quiet and less rowdying here than in Boston, with all its anti-drinking, anti-bellringing and other anti-noise making laws. **1887** *Courier-Journal* 18 Feb. 1/3 There was a good deal of noise and 'rowdying.'

***rowed,** *a.* As the last term in **check, eight-, twelve-rowed.**

row flat. A flatboat propelled by rowing. *Obs.* — **1777** *N.J. Archives* 2 Ser. I. 335 If it suits the purchaser, [he] may have the use of a row flat and landing. **1790** *Pa. Packet* 27 Sep. 3/4 Taken up a-drift in the river Delaware, on the 12th inst. a Row Flat.

* **rowing,** *n.* **1. rowing machine,** a gymnasium apparatus for exercise as in rowing. **2. rowing weight,** =prec. *Obs.*

(**1**) **1872** *Rep. Comm. Patents 1871* 495 William B. Curtis . . . [claims this] combination, in a rowing machine, . . . all constructed, arranged, and operating substantially as described. **1911** Harrison *Queed* 89 He went around like a museum guide, introducing . . . to the visitor under its true names and uses . . . a rowing-machine, the horizontal and parallel bars [etc.]. — (**2**) **1867** *Harper's Mag.* Oct. 656/1 Some ingenious man has constructed a piece of apparatus called a 'rowing weight.' . . . Eight hundred strokes on the rowing weights are equivalent to a three mile pull. **1887** *Cent. Mag.* June 179/2 Rowing-weights were not invented until two years later.

* **Roxbury,** *n.* [*Roxbury*, Mass.] **1. Roxbury Russet,** a variety of long-keeping apple originally grown in New England. Also **Roxbury Russeting. 2. Roxbury waxwork,** (see quots.).

(**1**) **1821** Thacher *Amer. Orchardist* 136 *Roxbury russeting* . . . is one of the best known, and most valuable fruits in Massachusetts. **1834** *Sun* (N.Y.) 23 Sep. 4/1 The sweet side of the apple is of a bright yellow colour, and the sour side of the same colour as the Roxbury Russet. **1949** *Amer. Forests* Sep. 20/1 Some of the apples sound familiar: Smoke House, Roxbury Russet, Jonathan, Baldwin. — (**2**) **1870**

Amer. Naturalist June 215 Bittersweet (*Celastrus scandens*), also called Roxbury Waxwork, . . . is a hardy climber. **1892** *Amer. Folk-Lore* V. 94 *Celastrus scandens*, Roxbury wax-work. E. Mass.

***royal,** *a.* In combs. (usu. *cap.*): (1) ***Royal Arch Mason,** one who has received the seventh degree in the York rite in American masonry; (2) **Chinook salmon,** =**Chinook salmon,** cf. **tyee 2,** and see **king salmon, quinnat salmon;** (3) **flush,** a straight flush *q.v.* in which the ace is the highest card, also **royal straight flush;** (4) **fox,** (see quots.), also **royal red fox;** (5) **palm,** an ornamental palm, *Roystonea regia*, of southern Florida and Cuba; (6) **refugee,** during the Revolutionary War, a loyalist seeking protection under the British crown, *obs.;* (7) **Rider,** a member of an order auxiliary to the second Ku-Klux Klan; (8) **tern,** a large tern, *Thalasseus maximus*, found in the southern states, cf. **Cayenne tern;** (9) **walnut moth,** =**regal moth.**

(1) **1830** *Williams's N.Y. Ann. Reg.* 208 There are 130 Chapters of Royal Arch Masons in the State of New York, and over 400 Lodges. **1898** A. G. Mackey *Hist. Free-Masonry* 1282 Several Royal Arch Masons in the upper part of South Carolina . . . had received their degrees in Master's lodges. **1945** *Boulder* (Colo.) *D. Camera* 31 Oct. 2/4 He is an active member of the . . . Royal Arch Masons. — (2) **1908** *Pacific Mo.* April 412/1 In the past few years Fancy Sockeye has taken its place in the markets with the Royal Chinook salmon packed on the Columbia River. — (3) **1889** *Olympia* (Wash.) *Rev.* 12 July 8/5 You kept muttering something about jack pots, royal flushes . . . putting up dukes, pasting somebody on the nob, and a lot of other things I couldn't understand. **1907** Harris *Bishop & Boogerman* 163 The hand I've dealt you is known as a royal straight flush, an' it sweeps ever'thing before it. **1949** *Lubbock* (Tex.) *Morn. Avalanche* 23 Feb. II. 4/3 Does five of a kind beat a royal flush with the deuces wild? — (4) **1905** Elliot *Check List Mammals* 382 *Vulpes regalis.* . . . Royal Fox. **1917** *Mammals of Amer.* 73/1 Royal Red Fox.—*Vulpes regalis.* . . . Northern Plains from Dakota to Alberta, east to Manitoba and Minnesota.

(5) **1861** *Smithsonian Rep. 1860* 440 The Palm, . . . [found] in large groves, between Capes Sable and Romano, . . . was called 'Royal Palm,' and said to grow 120 feet high. **1940** *Nat. Geog. Mag.* Jan. 139/2 In one section we found royal palms towering 110 feet in the air. — (6) **1778** *Mass. Spy* 15 Oct. 2/3 All the Royal Refugees in this city are desired to meet at a certain time and place, to deliberate on matters of the greatest importance. — (7) **1923** *N.Y. Times* 4 June 3/5 The congregation had had no warning that the Klansmen and Royal Riders were to attend the service. — (8) **1858** Baird *Birds Pacific R.R.* 859 *Sterna Regia.* . . . The Royal Tern. . . . Atlantic coast of the southern and middle States and California. **1917** *Birds of Amer.* I. 59/2 The Royal Terns were largely exterminated in many sections of their range by the gunners of the millinery trade some years ago. — (9) **1893** Ballard *Among Moths & Butterflies* 236 The oval earth-casket which this caterpillar made was much more complete than the one which held the chrysalis of my Royal Walnut Moth. **1909** *Country Life* Oct. 654/3 The brown and yellow coloring of the Royal Walnut moth seems commonplace compared with the gorgeousness of its earlier existence.

As the last term in **Palmetto, pennyroyal.**

***Royalist,** *n.* In the American Revolution, a supporter of the king and the British government. Now *hist.*

1780 in *Hist. MSS Comm.* 9th Rep. II. App. III. 193 He perfectly knows every inch of the country, is greatly beloved by the American troops, and if entrusted with a body of what is called Royalists will induce great part of [the] rebels to desert. **1809** Freneau *Poems* II. 186 To a Concealed Royalist. **1871** *Scribner's Mo.* II. 44 As the Army of the Revolution passed. . . . Royalists and Republicans were out of doors to see the goodly show.

rubbaboo ˈrʌbəˌbu, *n.* [Prob. f. an Indian word.] (See quots. and cf. **rousseau.**)

1857 *Jrnl. Peter Jacobs* 72 The food that is generally prepared and eaten in these regions by voyageurs is what is called 'ahrubuhboo.' I do not know what the word itself means. I spell it as I hear it pronounced. **1869** *Trans. Chi. Acad. of Sci.* I. II. 177 *Rubbaboo* is a favorite dish with the northern voyageurs. . . . It consists simply of pemmican made into a kind of soup by boiling in water. Flour is added when it can be obtained, and it is generally considered more palatable with a little sugar. **1886** *Outing* Dec. 249/1 We have two ways of preparing this [pemmican]—one called rub-a-boo; when it is boiled in a great deal of water, making a soup [etc.].

***rubber,** *n.*

1. (See quot.) *Obs.*

1825 Pickering *Inquiries Emigrant* (1831) 71 One [practice is] in common use in the Eastern part of Maryland, of girls taking a '*rubber*' of snuff—that is, taking as much snuff as will lie on the end of the forefinger out of a box, and rubbing it round the inside of the mouth!

2. An overshoe made of rubber. Usu. *pl.* Cf. **rubber overshoe** in **5. b.** below.

1842 *S. Lit. Messenger* VIII. 516/2 The *younkers* who would go 'a Maying,' very prudently provided themselves with rubbers and tippets before encountering the rough southeaster. **1945** *Chi. Tribune* 24 June VII. 1 When the chickens start to dust vigorously, hunt your rubbers.

3. A brake on a vehicle. *Obs.*

1850 in Glisan *Jrnl. Army Life* 32 The third vehicle, having no rubbers, or brakes, to the wheels, went so fast . . . that the driver was thrown from his seat. **1894** Searight *Old Pike* 145 The 'rubber,' called brake at this day, was not in use when the National Road was first thrown open for trade and travel. Instead, . . . saplings, cut at the summit of the hills, were shaped and fashioned to answer the ends of the 'rubber,' and at the foot of the hills taken off and left on the roadside.

4. Short for **rubberneck.** *Slang.*

1922 *Sunset* Dec. 10/2, I became what is known as a 'rubber'—one who has no money for stakes but who is fascinated by 'rubbering' at the play of those who have.

5. In combs.: (1) **rubber check,** (see quot. 1928), *slang;* (2) **currency,** (see quot.); (3) **neck,** see as a main entry; (4) **pine,** (see quot.); (5) **prince,** a man who has become wealthy in the rubber business; (6) **soled,** of shoes, having soles of rubber or of rubberized material; (7) **stamp,** *fig.* one who merely echoes the views of another, a person or thing making no independent contribution to a matter or situation, also attrib., *slang.*

(1) **1928** *Sunday Express* 2 Dec. 2/6 After a while the club came to an unfortunate end, due to what Americans call 'rubber checks,' i.e., the type that comes bouncing back from the bank. **1949** *This Week Mag.* 17 Sep. 21/4 She had bought the car and paid for it with a rubber check. — (2) **1904** *N.Y. Ev. Post* 22 Nov. 8 Speaker Cannon talked disparagingly of 'rubber currency,' this being his interpretation of the word 'elastic.' — (4) **1948** *Pacific Discovery* Nov.–Dec. 20/2 Short needles, short cones, and a rubbery stem are the equipment with which the white-bark pine resists a constant wind; and its stems are so tough that the mountaineers call it the 'rubber pine.' (5) **1904** O. Henry *Cabbages & Kings* 4 Frank Goodwin, an American resident of the town . . . [was] a banana king, a rubber prince. — (6) **1884** *Harper's Mag.* Jan. 304/1 If you can buy . . . a pair of rubber soled shoes, and a [tennis] racket, . . . you may readily gratify your whim. **1897** *Outing* July 377/1 A pair of rubber-soled lacrosse or tennis shoes, are first-rate for wear about camp. — (7) **1934** Webster. **1948** *Chi. Sun-Times* 12 April 35/4 He has been more of a rubber stamp voter than most so-called 'machine' officeholders.

b. Designating various articles, chiefly of wearing apparel, made of rubber or rubberized material, as **rubber blanket, boot, coat, overshoe, poncho, shoe.**

1850 in *Soc. Calif. Pioneer Quart.* VII. 21 We . . . spread over it our rubber blankets. **1902** McFaul *Ike Glidden* 158 On the end of the rope was fastened a bundle tied and wound up in a rubber blanket. — **1863** G. Hamilton *Gala-Days* 271 The man who gave rubber-boots to women did more to elevate woman than all theorizers . . . that were ever born. **1949** *This Week Mag.* 17 Sep. 17/2 Barnes found a pair of rubber boots in the trunk compartment. — **1850** Kingsley *Diary* 157, I put on my Rubber Coat and built a chimney outside the tent. *a*1918 G. Stuart *On Frontier* I. 69 Rubber coats and shoes were unknown at that time. — **1823** *Salem Observer* 29 Jan., 200 pair Rubber Over Shoes. **1945** *Suburban List* 8 Feb. 19/5 Boys' 3-buckle Rubber overshoes, sizes 11 to 6, $2.79 to $2.98. — **1865** in *Kans. Hist. Quart.* VII. 42 Go down to Laramie with wagon and get beef, bacon, and rubber blankets or ponchos. — **1844** *Knickerb.* XXIV. 284 Old rubber-shoes! old rubber-shoes! Humble theme for heavenly Muse. **1870** Emerson *Soc. & Solitude* 257 Newton was a great man, without telegraph, or gas, or steam coach, or rubber shoes.

As the last term in **log and husk, street rubber.**

***rubber,** *v.* **1.** *intr.* =**rubberneck,** *v.* **2.** To listen *in* or eavesdrop.

(1) **1896** G. Ade *Artie* xi. 100 About a dozen ringers followed us in and stood around rubberin. **1950** *Chi. Tribune* 24 Jan. III. 1, I just saw Moon Mullins out in the alley rubbering up here. — (2) **1920** Lewis *Main Street* 189 Say, did you hear me putting one over on these goats that are always rubbering in on party-wires? I hope they heard me! **1948** *Southern Folklore* Sep. 191 She's always rubberin' on a party line.

rubberneck ˈrʌbəˌnɛk, *n.* One much given to craning his neck in gaping and staring at persons and things, a sight-seer. Also **rubberneck tour.** Cf. **rubberneck,** *v.*

1900 *Everybody's Mag.* II. 585/2 Could anything be more eloquently expressive than the phrase 'rubberneck,' to characterize the offensively inquisitive and peering person? **1915** *Chi. Herald* 8 Nov. 4/2 The black and tans from the southern states . . . have been taken on a rubberneck tour. **1949** *Nat. Geog. Mag.* Dec. 783/2 Twice daily a horse-drawn stage leaves the Plaza on a 'rubberneck' tour.

b. rubberneck bus, wagon, a vehicle used in taking people on sight-seeing tours.

1908 LORIMER *J. Spurlock* 321 The Major inquired loudly of Horton, the Governor's secretary, whether he was 'runnin' a blank rubberneck waggon.' **1943** M. FLAVIN *Journey in Dark* 174 On the rubberneck wagons the fellow with the megaphone would point it out and say: 'Residence of Stanley Adams, financier and banker.' **1949** *Chi. D. News* 13 Aug. 5/6 That's the relatively harmless impression of Skid Row seen from the rubber-neck busses.

Rubberneck wagon *c*1890

rubberneck ˈrʌbɚˌnɛk, *v. intr.* To crane the neck and peer about inquisitively in the manner of a rubberneck. — **1896** G. ADE *Artie* iii. 23, I stood around there on one foot kind o' rubber-neckin to find an openin. **1949** *N.O. Times-Picayune Mag.* 10 April 5/1 Motorists ask for mangled grills, fenders, delay ambulances as they jam into traffic to rubberneck.

Hence **rubbernecking,** *n.* Also attrib. — **1943** M. FLAVIN *Journey in Dark* 175 The Elliott Wyatt house was off the route of the rubbernecking wagons. **1950** *Sat. Ev. Post* 4 Feb. 57/2 The Rim Road provides rewarding rubbernecking all through the year.

***Rube,** *n.* Orig. ***Reuben,** ***Rueben.** (Also not *cap.*) A hayseed or country jake. *Slang.*

1804 Reuben's "Nutbrown Maid" in *The Nightingale* 284 But she, tho' conscious of his worth, Had chose a youth more rare; A rustic Reuben was his name. **1855** *Herald of Freedom* 8 Sep. 2/5 [Letter signed 'Reuben Rustic.'] **1890** BIFF HALL *Turnover Club* 49 And I overheard one of a knot of Ruebens standing on a corner say [etc.]. **1896** G. ADE *Artie* i. 8 If I had time I'd go over to that church and make a lot o' them Reubs look like thirty-cent pieces. **1949** *Sat. Ev. Post* 12 Feb. 20/1 Generations of comedians have vulgarized Peoria as the symbol of the rube and the boob.

attrib. **1901** *World's Work* Aug. 1101/1 The spieling artist knows his crowd. If it is what is technically known as the 'Reub element' from the country, it is impossible to put the color on too thick. **1915** *Chi. Herald* 24 Nov. 18/4 He come back to the rube town an' he come near gettin' lynched. **1923** C. J. DUTTON *Shadow on Glass* 81 One of your rube detectives should come over to my cottage.

***ruby,** *n.* In combs.: (1) **ruby-crowned kinglet,** an American kinglet, *Regulus calendula;* (2) **-crowned warbler,** =prec.; (3) **-crowned wren, =ruby-crowned kinglet;** (4) **lily,** (see quot.); (5) **-throated hummingbird,** the common hummingbird, *Archilochus colubris*, of eastern North America.

(1) **1844** *Nat. Hist. N.Y., Zoology* II. 64 The Ruby-Crowned Kinglet . . . feeds on small seeds, on insects which infest trees, and their lurking larvae. **1946** STANWELL-FLETCHER *Driftwood Valley* 182 Ruby-crowned, as well as golden-crowned, kinglets hang every dark green spruce with chains of bubbling, rippling melody. — (2) **1785** PENNANT *Arctic Zool.* II. 413 Pine, Yellow, and Ruby-Crowned Warbler. **1917** *Birds of Amer.* III. 221 Ruby-crowned Kinglet. *Regulus calendula calendula*. . . . Other Names.—Ruby-crowned Wren; Ruby-crown; Ruby-crowned Warbler. — (3) **1758** G. EDWARDS *Gleanings Nat. Hist.* I. 95 The Ruby-crowned Wren . . . hath [on top of the head] a spot of an exceeding fine red or ruby colour. **1834** AUDUBON *Ornith. Biog.* II. 547 The Ruby-crowned Wren is found in Louisiana and other Southern States, from November until March. **1917** *Birds of Amer.* III. 221. — (4) **1915** ARMSTRONG & THORNBER *Western Wild Flowers* 36 Ruby Lily. Chaparral Lily. *Lilium rubescens*. White, pink. Summer. Cal., Oreg. . . . A glorious plant, from two to five feet tall, with leaves mostly in whorls, with rippled edges. (5) **1823** JAMES *Exped.* I. 265 *Trochilus colubris*—Ruby-throated hummingbird. **1945** MATHEWS *Talking* 27 Even the nest of the ruby-throated hummingbird, like a lichen-covered eyecup on a lichen-covered limb, seems proper and harmonious.

As the last term in **Arizona, bead ruby.**

***ruck,** *n.* Rubbish, nonsense. *Colloq.* — **1885** MARK TWAIN *Letters* (1917) II. xxv. 460 (R.), Flowers and general ruck sent to him by Tom, Dick, and Harry from everywhere. **1890** *Scribner's Mag.* Aug. 159 [He] wears gloves, and takes his meals private in his room and all that sort of ruck.

Ruckerize ˈrʌkəˌraɪz, *v. intr.* To proceed in the manner followed at the Baltimore Convention in 1836 where, in the absence of any representative from Tennessee, E. Rucker, a citizen of that state, was allowed to cast his state's votes. *Obs.* — **1856** NANCY N. SCOTT *Mem. H. L. White* 336 This latitudinarian proceeding gave rise to the phrase 'Ruckerize,' which was then and afterwards used to describe that and other similar contrivances.

ruckus ˈrʌkəs, *n.* [?f. *ruc*tion and rump*us*.] A noisy disturbance or uproar. *Slang.*

1907 *D.N.* III. iii. 226 *Rukus*, a violent altercation or personal encounter. (Northwest Arkansas.) *a***1909** O. HENRY *Roads of Destiny* xiii. 210 There shall be rucuses in Salvador. **1949** WEYGAND *Hoosier* 9 The Pittsburgers . . . contrived to stir up a ruckus with the village boatmen.

ructious ˈrʌkʃəs, *a.* [f. **ruction.*] Extremely annoyed, difficult. *Slang.* **1830** *Phila. Chronicle* 12 Aug. 1/6 'Swapp'd, ructious, and something clever—O I understand you now,' said I. **1897** *Kissimmee* (Fla.) *Valley* 3 March 1/6 T. P. Howard is having a ruxious old time splitting rails for T. H. Anier as the timber is so tough.

Rudbeckia rʌdˈbɛkɪə, *n.* [f. *Rudbeck*, surname of two Swedish botanists at Uppsala before Linnaeus.] Any plant of the North American genus *Rudbeckia* of the family Carduaceae; a coneflower. — **1819** WARDEN *Statistical Acct. U.S.* II. 325 The natural meadows [in Ky.] are covered with . . . the purple-flowered rudbeechia [*sic*]. **1901** MOHR *Plant Life Ala.* 48 Fleabanes, Rudbeckias, and other tall, coarse composites are characteristic of the prairie flora.

***ruddy,** *a.* **1. ruddy duck,** a small American duck, *Erismatura jamaicensis rubida*, the flesh of which resembles that of the canvasback. **2. ruddy turnstone, =horsefoot snipe** (*a*).

(1) **1813** WILSON *Ornithology* VIII. 128 The Ruddy Duck is fifteen inches and a half in length. [**1893** *Outing* Oct. 68/2 She described the duck closely and I guessed they were 'ruddies.'] **1948** *Dly. Oklahoman* (Okla. City) 31 Oct. D. 4/1 The chunky little ruddy duck . . . is one of the most unsuspicious of birds. — (2) **1917** *Birds of Amer.* I. 270/1 The Black, or Black-headed, Turnstone (*Arenaria melanocephala*) averages a trifle smaller than the Ruddy Turnstone. **1945** *Mass. Audubon Soc. Bul.* Feb. 19 The Ruddy Turnstone, Dowitchers, Knot and Godwits have been reported among the shore birds from these clam flats.

rue anemone. A small American wild flower, *Anemonella thalictroides*, resembling both the meadow rue and the anemone.

1817–8 EATON *Botany* (1822) 174 *Anemone thalictroides*, rue anemone. **1884** ROE *Nature's Story* 182 Burt now appeared with a handful of rue-anemones. **1939** *Nat. Geog. Mag.* Aug. 225/2 The rue anemone . . . presents a happy combination of beautiful foliage.

ruffed grouse. The mountain pheasant, *Bonasa umbellus*, of the eastern half of the U.S. See **Oregon ruffed grouse,** and cf. **ruffled grouse.**

[**1752** G. EDWARDS *Gleanings Nat. Hist.* I. 79 The Ruffed Heath-cock, or Grous.] **1858** BAIRD *Birds Pacific R.R.* 641 Where this bird [the bobwhite] is called quail, the Ruffed Grouse is generally called partridge. **1949** *Amer. Forests* Dec. 12/1 It is difficult to see a ruffed grouse in its nest—a rough affair of twigs built on the ground and sheltered by a tree stump or log.

***ruffian,** *n.* Short for **border ruffian.** Also **ruffianism.** *Obs.*

1855 *Herald of Freedom* 26 May 3/5 The same gang of ruffians, are the effects of the same cause. *Ib.* 30 June 4/6 Such is the ruffianism that seeks to extend its sway over Kansas.

attrib. **1856** *Herald of Freedom* 12 Jan. 2/3 Neither the Yankees in Kansas, nor the Free State soldiers who assembled at Lawrence, ever offered to deliver up their arms, or promised obedience to the infamous enactments of the Ruffian Barons. **1858** *N.Y. Tribune* 23 Jan. 6/1 The Ruffian State Ticket has triumphed in Leavenworth County [Kansas] by nearly 300 majority. **1877** JOHNSON *Anderson Co., Kans.* 220 In 1856 he and his son David Baldwin, then a mere boy, were taken prisoners by Major Buford and his Ruffian party.

As the last term in **Free-Soil border, Missouri ruffian.** Also **border, Missouri ruffianism.**

***ruffle,** *n.*

1. a. The calyx of a cotton bloom. **b.** Something resembling a ruffle (see quots.).

(a) 1856 *Rep. Comm. Patents 1855: Agric.* 109 Upon opening such a ruffle, this small spider was almost invariably found snugly ensconced in its web. **1874** *Rep. Comm. Agric. 1873* 162 The egg of the boll-worm is usually placed in the so-called ruffle or envelope of the flower. — **(b) 1862** AGASSIZ *Contrib. Nat. Hist. U.S.* IV. 88 Four [of the bunches of organs on the jellyfish] are elegant sacks, adorned, as it were, with waving ruffles projecting in large clusters. **1872** COUES *Key to Birds* 18 The condor has a single ruffle all around the neck, of close, downy feathers.

2. a. ***ruffle shirt,** a person of some means, an aristocrat. Also attrib. **b. ruffle-shirter,** (see quot.). Both *contemptuous* and *obs.*

(a) 1830 *Amer. Sentinel* (Phila.) 27 Aug. 2/2 Where a dinner is to be got up, a few mechanics are procured to take the first rank, and the ruffle shirts fall into the rear. **1831** *American* (Harrodsburg, Ky.) 22 July 3/1 General Jackson and his friends are lessening the burthens of the people, by . . . placing the Tax, on Wines, Rum, . . . and fine cloth such as the *Rufle* [*sic*] *shirt* gentry wear. **1855** in TURNER *Cotton* (1865) 120 It is all sheer ruffle-shirt cant, to ridicule selling anything a man has to spare. — **(b) 1842** *Knickerb.* XIX. 305 Many a taunt . . . was thrown at the ruffle-shirters [i.e., upper-class, private-school boys], as the town boys called them.

***ruffled,** *a.* **1. ruffled grouse, =ruffed grouse. 2. ruffled oat, ?=side oat.** *Obs.* **3.** ***ruffled shirt,** designating one clad in a ruffled shirt, also **ruffled-shirted,** *a. Contemptuous* and *obs.*

(1) 1850 S. F. COOPER *Rural Hours* 13 Our Partridge or Pheasant, or Ruffled Grouse, as we should rather call it, is a more hardy bird. **1944** NUTE *Lake Superior* 295 That same day I saw many ruffled grouse. — **(2) 1849** *Rep. Comm. Patents: Agric.* (1850) 289 The ruffled oat is very much cultivated, and highly esteemed. — **(3) 1830** *Amer. Democrat* (Lebanon, Ohio) 14 Aug. 4/1 These *new* mechanics are composed of *Lawyers, dismissed office holders,* and *ruffled shirt loungers.* **1835** LONGSTREET *Ga. Scenes* 85 The *ruffled-shirted* little darlings of the present day [would be] under the discipline of paregoric. **1876** *Harper's Wkly.* 26 Aug. 691/1 They belonged to the class which the ward politicians of to-day sneer at as ruffle-shirted and silk-stockinged.

***rug,** *n.* **1.** (See quot.) *Obs.* **2. rug-rag,** a rag suitable for use in making a rag rug. — **(1) 1792** BELKNAP *Hist. New-Hampshire* III. 129 There is a natural tough sward commonly called a *rug,* which must either rot or be burned before any cultivation can be made. — **(2) 1885** JEWETT *Marsh Island* 55 I've got nothin' to wear over me except old things that's only fit, and ought by good rights to be took for rug-rags.

As the last term in **braided, buffalo, drawn-in, hooked, lap, Navaho, rag, scatter, steamer rug.**

***rugged,** *a.* Strong, hardy, robust.

1731 J. HEMPSTEAD *Diary* 241 A Rugged Hardy young man . . . went to the House of Samll Parke. **1816** PICKERING 167 Englishmen notice our use of *rugged,* in this sense, as a peculiarity; in expressions of this kind—a rugged, i.e., robust child; rugged health. **1890** *Harper's Mag.* April 747/2 She is not what you would call a rugged-looking baby.

ruinatious ˌruɪnˈeʃəs, *a.* (See quot. 1871.) *Colloq.* — **1845** JUDD *Margaret* 210 The War was very ruinatious to our profession. **1871** DE VERE 629 *Ruinatious,* an enlarged and intensified form of *ruinous,* frequently used in the West and South.

***rulable,** *a.* Permissible acording to the rules. — **1889** *N.Y. Produce Exch. Rep.* 305 It shall be rulable to reject any . . . packages varying widely in color or quality from the bulk of the lot. **1890** L. C. D'OYLE *Notches* 170 He would take a cigar—not considered exactly fair, perhaps, but 'rulable' (occasionally) according to the standard of the country.

***rule,** *n.* **1.** *pl.* The sessions of a court. Also **rule-day,** a day appointed for hearing a particular case. *Obs.* **2. rule book,** a book containing the rules according to which, usu., a game, such as baseball, is played. Fig. in examples given.

(1) 1815 in *Niles' Reg.* IX. 370/2 Appear at the clerk's office of our said superior court of law for Henrico county at the rules to be holden for the said court. **1816** *Ib.* 370/1 [He] did not appear at the rule-day, on the 16th of the last month. — **(2) 1910** W. M. RAINE *B. O'Connor* 13 The situation was one not covered in the company's rule book. **1948** GARDNER *Lonely Heiress* 99 There are times when a lawyer throws the rule book away, when he has to go by hunches.

As the last term in **five-minute, gag, ground, machine, Negro, rifle, shotgun, unit, white rule.**

***rum,** *n.*

1. "Used generically as a hostile name for intoxicating liquors" (*OED*). Also, used predicatively, "wet," anti-prohibition.

1855 *N.Y. Wkly. Tribune* 15 Sep. 4/3 The Legislature is heavily Democratic and Rum. **1858** HOLMES *Autocrat* 219 Rum I take to be the name which unwashed moralists apply alike to the product distilled from molasses and the noblest juices of the vineyard. **1868** in GEORGE EASTON *Travels in Amer.* (1871) 26 A dollar sunk in the sea is a dollar lost, but a dollar spent for rum may cause the loss of many more.

2. In combs.: (1) **rum baron,** one who became wealthy through the illegal liquor traffic during the prohibition period (1920–33); (2) **bud,** (see quot.), *obs.;* (3) **cherry,** the wild black cherry, *Padus serotina* (see quot. 1949); (4) **fleet,** during the prohibition period (1920–33), vessels engaged in rum-running, *obs.;* (5) **interest,** those interested in the rum or liquor traffic as manufacturers or dealers; (6) **party,** a party favorable to the liquor interests; (7) **row,** (*cap.*) during the prohibition period (1920–33), a place outside the prohibited area where liquor ships gathered; (8) **runner,** one engaged, esp. during the prohibition period (1920–33), in bringing into the U.S. prohibited alcoholic liquor, also **rum running;** (9) **sucker,** (*a*) a confirmed rum-drinker, a toper, *slang,* (*b*) a local name for a variety of moss.

(1) 1923 *Westm. Gaz.* 4 April 8/5 Reminiscences are inevitable in any gathering of rum barons. — **(2) 1848** BARTLETT 280 *Rum-Bud,* . . . a redness occasioned by the detestable practice of excessive drinking. Rum-buds usually appear first on the nose. — **(3) 1836** LINCOLN *Botany* App. 129 *Prunus . . . virginiana,* (wild-cherry, rum-cherry, cabinet-cherry.) . . . In dense forests, it grows to a very great height. **1949** COLLINGWOOD & BRUSH *Knowing Your Trees* 256 They have a pleasant, slightly bitter taste and are sometimes used in a beverage called 'cherry bounce' hence the name 'Rum Cherry.' — **(4) 1923** *Westm. Gaz.* 4 April 8/5 Off shore is the rum fleet. **1948** *Democrat* 4 Nov. 6/1 Rum fleets were active around the Grand Banks.

(5) 1883 *Cent. Mag.* Sep. 782/2 Such a righteous restoration of the law to its own place will be claimed . . . by the rum interest as a victory for them. — **(6) 1855** *N.Y. Wkly. Tribune* 29 Sep. 2/3 There are in Maine, as elsewhere, four parties: The Republican, Democratic, Whig, and Rum parties. **1894** MARK TWAIN *Pudd'nhead Wilson* xi. 556 (R.), There was a strong rum party and a strong anti-rum party. — **(7) 1923** *Lit. Digest* 26 May 52/2 Small consignments are carried from there down to the 'Rum Row' of ships anchored beyond the three-mile limit of the Long Island and New Jersey shores. **1947** PAUL *Linden* 399 The same group of smugglers that used to run Chinamen and dope over the Vermont border, did yeoman service between Rum Row and the Linden marsh. — **(8) 1920** *N.Y. Times* 19 Sep. 6/1 The Detroit rum runners have had a good deal of notoriety. **1924** *Lit. Digest* 31 May 38/1 Rum-running in New York has received at least a temporary setback. **1924** *Collier's* 24 June 6/1 There is an apparent openness about the traffic, at least as regards the rum-running fleet under British registry. **1949** *Chi. Tribune* 20 Dec. 20/3 F. F. Van de Water . . . attributed the term [the real McCoy] to a notorius rumrunner, Bill McCoy. — **(9)** (*a*) **1844** *Akron Buzzard* 25 June 2/1 The effect of this nefarious traffic upon the inebriate, from the moderate drinker to the confirmed rum-sucker, was most lucidly portrayed. **1888** *Voice* 10 May, If rum-suckers kill fool Prohibitionists we consent. (*b*) **1892** *Amer. Folk-Lore* V. 105 *Polytrichum commune,* rum-suckers. Stratham, N.H.

b. In the names, chiefly obs., of drinks prepared from rum, as **rum-and-gum, cocktail, grog, punch, salad, sling.**

1861 NEWELL *Orpheus C. Kerr* I. 212 [The South Carolina gentleman] clears a mighty track of everything that bears the shape of . . . peach-and-honey, irrepressible cocktail, rum-and-gum. — **1861** *Harper's Mag.* Jan. 150/2 Measures of the most vital importance are first introduced in rum-cocktails, then steeped in whisky, after which they are engrossed in gin for a third reading. **1942** KENNEDY *Palmetto Country* 6 Coconut milk is also used in the concoction of rum cocktails. — **1806** *Balance* V. 142/3 A certain candidate has placed in his account of Loss and Gain. . . . : Loss. 720 rum grogs. — **1921** *Pub. Col. Soc.* XXIV. 195 It was always found necessary to substitute for 'Whiteface' a mixture called 'rum-punch.' — **1859** MACKAY *Tour* I. 45 Streak of lightning, cock-tail, and rum-salad, are but a few of the names of the drinks which are consumed at the bar. — **1827** *Mass. Spy* 25 July (Th.), It vas not a rum sling; no, nor a gin sling; no, nor a mint vater sling. **1845** *Big Bear Ark.* 43 Curse that rum sling—there was too much sugar in it.

c. In designations, usu. contemptuous, for places where rum is sold, as **rum hole, joint, mill, palace, shanty.**

1834 *Sun* (N.Y.) 14 May 2/3 There is, at the present time, in this city, a rum-hole, a house of prostitution, an apothecary shop, and a coffin-ware-house, *all under one roof.* **1887** ALDEN *Little Fishers* v, I'll hunt out towns where the fellows have just been left to stay in the streets, or else go to the rum-holes. — **1928** *Sunday Express* 24 June 8/4 One of our men started a row with one of these birds. . . . They fought in a rum-joint and everyone joined in. — **c1849** PAIGE *Dow's Sermons* I. 144 Every rum-mill, groggery and tippling-shop . . . is a trap set by the devil to catch those who are guilty of not having over three cents. **1889** BARRERE & LELAND I. 238/1 *Charter the bar, charter the grocery, to* (American), to buy all the liquor in a groggery or 'rum-mill' and give it away freely to all comers. — **1890** BIFF HALL *Turn-over Club* 193 He would go to the leading rum palace in the place and make arrangements [etc.]. — **1843** *Yale Lit. Mag.* VIII. 117 The landlord of this same Wild Goose Hotel had become notoriously infamous as keeping one of the most unconscionable rum shanties in the land.

d. In phrases: (1) *Rum and Tar*, used with reference to a local Whig faction, one of the leaders of which dealt extensively in rum and tar, *obs.;* (2) *Rum, Romanism and Rebellion*, (see quot. 1914).

(1) **1851** GREEN *Twelve Days* 98 The Whig party of that city [New Haven, Conn.] divided, and the *Palladium* clique (better known as the *Rum* and *Tar* party) succeeded in securing the nomination of one of the editors of the *Palladium* as the Whig candidate for Congress. . . . The Rum and Tar candidate was defeated by a very large majority. — (2) **1884** S. D. BURCHARD in *N.Y. Herald* 30 Oct. 5/5 You represent all the virtues. Mr. Cleveland represents Rum, Romanism and Rebellion. **1914** *Cyclo. Amer. Govt.* III. 241/1 *Rum, Romanism and Rebellion*, a phrase characterizing the Democratic party, used by Rev. Samuel D. Burchard, spokesman of a delegation of Protestant clergymen, October 30, 1884, in an address in New York City. **1948** *Newsweek* 8 Nov. 21/1 They had paraded for 'Tippecanoe and Tyler, too,' and denounced 'Rum, Romanism, and Rebellion.'

As the last term in **bay, forty rod, Indian, monkey, Negro, New England, northeast, pokeberry, Yankee rum.**

rumba ˈrʌmbə, *n.* [Amer. Sp., prob. of African orig.] A dance imitative of a Negro Cuban dance characterized by violent and sensuous movements. Also **rumba band,** a band playing music for this type of dance.

1934 WEBSTER. **1944** *Harper's Mag.* June 53/1 The Colony employed a rumba band and, almost alone among Chicago clubs, such single-featured stars as Carmen Miranda, Connie Boswell, and Maxine Sullivan. **1949** *This Week Mag.* 12 March 33/4 Now, however, the rumba is taught.

Also **rumba,** *v. intr.*

1943 *Sat. Ev. Post* 1 May 30/1 He asked you if you'd rumba, yes, But not for the duration.

***rumble seat.** In some types of automobiles, a folding seat behind, and unprotected by, the top of the car. Also attrib. and transf.

1931 *K.C. Times* 26 Oct., A goodly number of the younger set . . . had contracted a rumble seat cold the previous night. **1944** *Chi. D. News* 22 July 3/1 The mayor and his delegates just managed to grab the outer rim of the rumble seat of the Truman bandwagon. **1948** RITTENHOUSE *Vehicles* 7 The term 'rumble seat' began with carriages.

***Rumford,** *n.* [Sir Benjamin Thompson, Count *Rumford* (1753–1814), an American-born physicist.] *attrib.* Designating various devices used in cooking or heating. Now *hist.*

[**1803** *Med. Repository* 185 This is an addition of what the inventors term a sliding mantle-piece, and valve or damper, to the fire-place, with slanting jambs, recommended by Count Rumford.] **1811** *Agric. Museum* I. 42 The dinner was principally prepared hot on the ground, by means of a portable Rumford kitchen. . . . The utility of the portable Rumford had not probably been experienced in the field on any previous occasion in New England. **1845** THOREAU *Journal* I. 388 An annual rent . . . entitles him to the benefit of all the improvements of centuries,—Rumford fireplace, back plastering, Venetian blinds. **1937** MARION LANSING *Mary Lyon Through Her Letters* 230 All marveled at the Rumford oven, given by Deacon Safford. . . . This Rumford oven was a sheet iron box with a compartment beneath in which the fire was built.

rummery ˈrʌmərɪ, *n.* A low dive where rum is sold. *Slang. Obs.* — **1846** *Quincy* (Ill.) *Whig* 29 Jan. 2/3 The friend . . . saw a person who had just drank, put three cents down as pay. He, turning to the young man, asked him if it could be a three cent rummery. **1898** *Advance* 12 Nov., His re-election does not prove that the people of the state are going to sell out to the rummeries.

rummy rʌmɪ, *n.* and *a.* [In **1.** f. **rum* +*y*.]

1. *n.* **a.** (See quot. 1907.) *Slang.* **b.** (*cap.*) *pl.* (See quot.) *Slang. Obs.*

(**a**) **1851** GREEN *Twelve Days* 55 The learned counsel of the rummies opened his defence . . . the court adjourned, and the rummies repaired to *another bar* to congratulate each other upon the success of the morning. **1907** *D.N.* III. 198 *Rummy, n.* A drunkard; one who favors the liquor traffic. **1922** *Lit. Digest* 30 Dec. 32/1 The lying labels, proclaiming to the trusting rummies that the whiskey is 'pure and unadulterated, soothing as mountain dew, guaranteed 110 proof,' etc., are pasted on the hooch. — (**b**) **1890** C. L. NORTON *Polit. Americanisms* 96 *Rummies*, a local name for the political opponents of the temperance party in Maine.

2. A social card game in which points are scored by melding sets of three or four cards of the same rank, or sequences of three or more cards of the same suit. Also **rummy game,** Cf. **cooncan, gin rummy.**

The source of the word in this sense is not known. It may not have originated in this country, the present earliest evidence leaving that point in doubt. The earliest form of the word appears to have been "rhum" (see first quot. below).

Rumford oven beside a fireplace

[**1913** *Chi. Record-Herald* 2 March v. 6/1, I never found on one of them The kale I lose at rhum.] **1915** *Chi. Herald* 30 Nov. 15/4 This gave him the idea the game was rummy and he spread the nines on the table. **1918** in F. A. POTTLE *Stretchers* 285 Opposite the stove Capt. Summers . . . and Lt. Chambers of Evanston, Ill. are playing Rummy on Summers' cot. **1949** *Lubbock* (Tex.) *Morn. Avalanche* 23 Feb. II. 4/7 Take the night when you have been unavoidably delayed at the lodge or the rummy game. **1949** *N.Y. Times Mag.* 3 April 25 (*legend*), Between shows, the prime entertainers of the Big Show go for a game of rummy.

3. *a.* Affected by, or pertaining to, rum.

1834 *Jamestown* (N.Y.) *Jrnl.* 29 Jan. 1 The Massachusetts Masons . . . like the rummy deacon, who fell from his horse—have merely 'got off to get on better.' **1843** *Amer. Pioneer* II. 372 He departed, muttering curses loud and deep, and in a voice peculiarly *rummy.* **1864** WEBSTER 1156/3 *Rummy* . . . of, or pertaining to, rum; as, a rummy flavor.

***rump,** *n.*

1. (*cap.*) *pl.* (See quot.) *Obs.*

1842 BYRDSALL *Hist. Loco-foco Party* 178 Hence the Equal Rights Party became divided within itself; the majority for union called the opposing minority Rumps, and the latter called the majority Buffaloes.

2. In combs.: (1) **rump congress,** (*a*) the Congress of the Civil War and Reconstruction period, in which there were no representatives from the southern states, also ***rump government,** *obs.,* (*b*) the last Congress that met under the Articles of Confederation, *rare;* (2) **convention,** a nominating convention composed of a minority or remnant of a party; (3) **President,** (see quot.).

(1) (*a*) **1861** *Richmond* (Va.) *Examiner* 4 Dec. 3/3 It may very reasonably be doubted how far General Sherman or his officers would suffer schemes so vitally important to the Rump Government to leak out through the indiscretions of loquacious volunteers. **1867** LOCKE *Swingin' Round* 136 Clear out the rump congress. **1877** BEARD *K. K. K. Sketches* 17 There was no logical plan supporting that system of political manœuvres set in motion by the 'Rump Congress.' (*b*) **1889** *Cent. Mag.* April 803/2 It was indeed a Rump Congress. — (**2**) **1872** *Newton Kansan* 31 Oct. 3/2 Delegates to the rump convention of W.B. Chamberlin openly charged him with packing the convention. **1903** *N.Y. Times* 28 Aug., The Bryan following

will walk out after having made their protest. Then will come a rump convention. **1948** *Milwaukee Jrnl.* 18 July 1/7 Both were named by acclamation at a rump convention of southern Democrats. — (3) **1866** *Ore. State Jrnl.* 15 Sep. 3/2 A 'Rump President.'—It would seem, according to his theory, that [Johnson] . . . is not the President of the United States, but only the States that voted for him.

∗**run,** *n.*

1. (See quot.) *Obs.*

The first British evidence, with reference to Australia, in *OED* is dated 1826.

1658 *Brookhaven Rec.* 3 This land and the grass thereof for a range, or run, for to feed horses or cattle on . . . I have sold.

2. An upper and a lower millstone operating as a unit.

1798 *Smithtown Rec.* 351 The grist mill house . . . [will] carry three run of stones with three Bolting mills. **1847** HOWE *Hist. Coll. Ohio* 157 The stream at present furnishes power for twenty two runs of stone. **1885** GRANT *Pers. Memoirs* I. 493 Every plantation . . . had a run of stones propelled by mule power, to grind corn for the owners and their slaves.

3. The amount of sap that flows when sugar maples are tapped; the amount of maple sugar made at a particular time.

1822 *Farmer's Diary* (Canandaigua, N.Y.) C3r Sugar makers may venture to set seven or eight hundred pails to one of these pans, . . . in case of extra ordinary runs, which, however, do not often happen. **1890–3** TABER *Stowe Notes* 40 The early runs are not so sweet as the later. **1896** *Vt. Agric. Rep.* XV. 33 Car loads of the last run of the Vermont maple orchards are sent to these cities each year. **1898** N. E. JONES *Squirrel Hunters of Ohio* 21 A 'run' of sugar-water was not dependent upon a special act of Congress. **1949** *Highway Traveler* Feb. 17/2 In the average season of a month—from the middle of March to the middle of April—sap can be expected to run on about half of the days, while on two to five days there will be 'good runs.'

4. In mining, a mill run *q.v.*

1852 WHITMORE *Diary* 16 Oct., Tended stamps. Made a very good runn this week. **1882** *47th Congress* 1 Sess. H.R. Ex. Doc. No. 216, 450 A small run was made by the McLaughlin & Cassell mill, at Central.

5. *Baseball.* The completion by a player of a circuit of the bases under prescribed rules, a score.

1856 *Spirit of Times* 6 Sep. 13/3 At the time of the adjournment the score stood fifteen runs in favor of the Union, and twelve runs for the Baltic. **1910** *Spalding's Base Ball Guide* 131 Off Summers, 3 hits, 4 runs in 5 at bats in 1–3 inning. **1945** *Chi. D. News* 4 Oct. 12/1 They started in and accumulated enough runs in the first inning to put the game on ice.

6. A platform or a similar place for the loading and unloading of wagons.

1870 *Huntington Rec.* III. 585 The said land . . . [is] sufficient . . . to build two runs, so called, or three runs . . . to load brick at. **1920** COOPER *Under Big Top* 226 Many a man [is saved] from injury at the unloading runs.

7. *Football.* The action of running on the part of a player advancing the ball.

1893 STAGG & WILLIAMS *Amer. Football* 43 In defending his territory against these runs the end stands at the most remote part of the field for assistance to help him.

8. *W.* The act of running on the part of settlers rushing to take up desirable land in areas newly made available for settlement.

1894 *Dly. Ardmoreite* (Ardmore, Okla.) 30 April 2/1 Buckskin Joe and his followers are camped at Marlow preparatory to making a run on the Fort Sill country tomorrow. **1901** *World's Work* June 894/1 Hitherto the settlers made a 'run' for the homesteads. **1948** *Dly. Oklahoman* (Okla. City) 16 May E. 3/2 The nine great land openings began in 1889 with the 'run' into the area now occupied by Oklahoma City, Guthrie, Norman, Stillwater and other cities.

9. *W.* A stampede by a herd of cattle.

1903 A. ADAMS *Log of Cowboy* 38 We may never have a run the entire trip.

10. (See quot.)

1912 G. M. HYDE *Newspaper Reporting* 29 [The reporter] is ordinarily put on a *beat*, or *run;* this is simply a daily route or round of news sources which he follows as regularly as a policeman walks his beat.

11. In colloq. phrases: **a.** *To get the run upon,* (see quot.). **b.** *To keep* (or *lose*) *the run of,* to keep (or fail to keep) in touch with or informed about.

(a) **1848** BARTLETT 280 'To get the run upon one,' is to make a butt of him; turn him into ridicule. — (b) **1862** MAURY in Corbin *Life M. F. Maury* 212, I shall . . . very much wish to keep the run of public sentiment. **1893** MARK TWAIN *£1,000,000 Bank-Note* 29 You couldn't afford to lose the run of business and be no end of time getting the hang of things again when you got back home. **1918** LINCOLN *Shavings* 320, I kind of lost run of the time.

As the last term in **blockade, buffalo, century, dead, dog, dry, earned, fall, forced, glade, home, partridge, sap, slate, strawberry, test, unearned run.**

∗**run,** *v.*

1. *tr.* To survey, mark out, or establish (a line, bound, or course).

1641 *R.I. Col. Rec.* I. 114 Mr. Porter . . . and Mr. Jeoffreys shall run the line between the Touns. **1660** *Essex Inst. Coll.* XXXVII. 229 Mr. John Gardener . . . [is] desired . . . to Run the bounds betwixt Bostone, Charlstown and Lynn . . . by a merridian Compass. **1775** *Jrnl. of Nicholas Cresswell* (1925) 57 Very busy with Captn. Knox all this week running the courses of his plantation and jaunting about the neighborhood. **1802** ELLICOTT *Journal* 203 The chiefs gave a strong talk against running the line. **1950** *Va. Mag. Hist. & Biog.* Jan. 103 He began to run the line of the first side of the ten-mile square territory being set apart.

2. To agree upon, bring forward, endorse, or support in an election for office. Cf. **17.** below.

1789 *Maryland Jrnl.* 2 Jan. (Th.), It was agreed to run the following ticket in their respective Districts. **1792** HAMILTON *Works* VIII. 286 To be run in this quarter as Vice-President. **1892** *Courier-Journal* 3 Oct. 4/4 The Democrats are running candidates in every district in the state.

3. To navigate (a stream or part of a stream) in a canoe or other boat.

1805 LEWIS in *L. & Clark Exped.* III. (1905) 23 There were five shoals neither of which could be passed with loaded canoes nor even run with empty ones. **1875** MARK TWAIN *Old Times* ii. 37 Each of our pilots ran such portions of the river as he had run when coming upstream. **1901** THOMPSON *Me. Woods* 73 Stair Falls may be run, if there is a fair pitch of water. **1949** *Sat. Ev. Post* 9 April 32/2 The same thing had happened three days before when the Indian had flatly refused to run some white water.

b. To go up or down (a stream) in fishing.

1879 *Scribner's Mo.* Nov. 20/2 In running a grayling stream, the feeling is one of peace and quietude.

4. To manage, carry on, boss (a business, enterprise, etc.).

1827 *Mass. Spy* 3 Oct. (Th.), Running a Bank. **1864** *Dly. Telegraph* (London) 23 Dec. 5/5 'To run' is a . . . modern American locution. You may 'run' anything—a railroad, a bank, a school, a newspaper. **1920** LEWIS *Main Street* 386 Sister Bogart about half runs his church. **1950** *Dly. Ardmoreite* (Ardmore, Okla.) 14 Feb. 6/7 Take good care of the players, work hard, and above all don't try to run the ball club.

b. *Agric.* To operate or have in operation (a plow), to cultivate (a crop).

1839 in BASSETT *Plantation Overseer* 117, I have got my cotton land the half of it cleaned up and is running four plows. **1879** TOURGEE *Fool's Errand* 84 No nigger shant be allowed to . . . run no crop on his own account hereafter.

c. Used with reference to political domination or management.

1872 *Newton Kansan* 31 Oct. 3/2 This man aspires to run Harvey county by such trickery. **1886** ROOSEVELT in *Cent. Mag.* Nov. 74/1 The men who take part in and control, or, as they would themselves say, 'run' [political machines] . . . are familiarly known as machine politicians. **1905** STEFFENS in *McClure's Mag.* Feb. 339/2 The good people took the bribes and let the best people run the government.

d. *Stock exchange.* To carry on (a deal) or secure (a corner) involving some commodity.

1875 *Chi. Tribune* 2 July 7/3 Sturges was running a corner. **1888** *Economist* 27 Oct. 7/3 He has worked upon the fear of the short interest that a corner might be run.

e. To operate (a game of chance).

1885 *Santa Fé Wkly. New Mexican* 10 Sep. 4/4 They ran games at Houston until the town became unpleasant, and then came to Las Vegas. **1903** A. ADAMS *Log of Cowboy* 260 Every gambling house ran from two to three monte layouts.

f. To control, direct, or guide (a person).

1888 BRYCE *American Commonw.* I. I. ix. 115 It is often said of the President that he is ruled, or as the Americans express it, 'run,' by his secretary. **1890** S. HALE *Letters* 242 Cornelia is running me, and she is really just the right sort. **1949** *Sat. Ev. Post* 23 April 130/4 You're my father and all that, but I'll be damned if you run me any more.

5. To chase or shoot (buffalo) on horseback.

1833 CATLIN *Indians* I. 219 On this journey we saw immense herds of buffaloes; and although we had no horses to *run* them, we successfully *approached* them on foot. **1889** *Nat. Museum Rep. 1886–7* 470 Next to the still-hunt the method called 'running buffalo' was the most fatal to the race, and the one most universally practiced. **1900** DRANNAN *Plains & Mts.* 300, I met about thirty Kiowa Indians going out to run the buffalo near there. **1949** NORDYKE *Cattle Empire* 264 Horses are furnished for the care of the cattle and for other useful purposes, and they must not be used to run wild horses, or buffalo, or antelope.

6. To tease or josh. *Colloq.*

1835 HONE *Diary* I. 134 This is a club . . . where they sup, drink champagne and whiskey punch, talk as well as they know how, and run each other good-humouredly. **1860** HOLLAND *Miss Gilbert* 349 Now what's the use of running a feller? **1872** MARIETTA HOLLEY *My Opinions* (1891) 411 'But,' says I, not wantin' to run anybody to their backs, 'she thought it was her spear to marry.'

7. To float, drive, or conduct (lumber or logs) down a stream.

1840 *Jamestown* (N.Y.) *Jrnl.* 26 Feb. 2/3 The streams are lined with lumber, ready at the proper season, to be run to market. **1896** *Monthly Weather Rev.* Nov. 407 The driving of piles in the Mississippi River . . . to hold a 'sheer boom' for the purpose of running the logs.

8. To entice (a Negro slave) off or away from his master. *Obs.* Cf. ***kink,** *n.* **2. c.**

1844 *St. Louis Reveille* 26 Nov. 2/1 The plan was to bargain with the slave to run him to Canada for a stipulated sum. **1863** BROWNE *Four Years in Secessia* (1865) 288 The rogues grew very communicative, and told us how much money they used to make . . . by . . . 'running a kink,' and other entertainments.

9. To lay off or plow out (rows or furrows).

1851 *Fla. Plantation Rec.* 348, 3 [slaves] Running Roes for Cain. **1885** CRADDOCK *Prophet* 3 It might be marveled that so many furrows were already run.

10. To slip by without paying (something), to evade. Cf. *to run* (one's) *board* in **20.** (5) below.

1867 LACKLAND *Homespun* 68 My conscience will never fully acquit me . . . of the guilt of having *run* that toll of a penny on many an occasion.

11. To meet the needs of, or be sufficient for, to support (a person or group).

1871 MARK TWAIN *Sk. New & Old* 95, I had . . . unsalable turnips enough to run the family for two years! **1909** WASON *Happy Hawkins* 280 She was in the habit of estimatin' just how little nourishment it would take to run her to the next feed.

12. To examine (a net) for fish.

1880 *Harper's Mag.* May 855/2 The boatman . . . turns directly back and 'runs the net'—passing the cork line through the hands. *Ib.* 856/1 The net is 'run' twice or three times and is then taken up.

13. To publish (an advertisement, story, etc.) in a newspaper.

1884 NYE *Baled Hay* 202 He wouldn't run any of his ads. **1912** G. M. HYDE *Newspaper Reporting* 30 [If] the editor decides not to print the story, he *kills* it; otherwise he *runs* it. **1950** *Time* 16 Jan. 65/3 With his vigorous news pages, Dana ran blistering editorials against Boss Tweed, the Credit Mobilier and the Whisky Ring.

14. *W.* (See quot. 1894.) Also transf. Cf. **running brand.**

1894 *McClure's Mag.* July 101/2 [The brand] is simply drawn, or 'run' upon the hide, using a long, sharp-pointed, hot iron rod for a pencil; and those so made are called 'running brands.' **1897** LEWIS *Wolfville* 179 'That's straight,' says Dave Tutt, 'you-alls can't run no brand on melodies.'

15. *intr.* Of maple trees: To produce or furnish sap.

*c***1774** CRÈVECOEUR *Sk. 18th Cent. Amer.* (1925) 99 Our trees will afford sugar for a long time. . . . They will run every year, according to the seasons, from six to fifteen days.

16. To float down a stream, used esp. of ice.

1805 CLARK in *Lewis & C. Exped.* II. (1904) 8 The drift wood beginning to run. **1807** GASS *Jrnl.* 61 The weather became very cold, and the ice began to run in the river. **1884** ROE *Nature's Story* (1902) 192 Don't go out again when the ice is running.

17. To be a candidate for a political office. Cf. **2.** above.

1826 *Va. Herald* (Fredericksburg) 22 Nov. 3/1 Mr. Pitcher is elected Lt. Governor, by a large majority over Mr. Huntington, who ran on the same ticket with Mr. Clinton. **1912** NICHOLSON *Hoosier Chron.* 54, I'd go into their counties and spend every cent I've got fighting 'em if they ever ran for office again. **1949** *Downers Grove* (Ill.) *Rep.* 31 March 1/2 Anyone in America has the right to run for office.

18. To serve as a runner or tout *for* a boardinghouse. Cf. **runner,** *n.* **4.**

1891 C. ROBERTS *Adrift Amer.* 228, I went with him to the house he was running for.

19. In substantival combs.: (1) ***runabout,** a light open-topped buggy, a light automobile of a roadster type; (2) **around,** see as a main entry; (3) ***away,** (*a*) the action of a horse or team that bolts or dashes away out of control, also **runaway horse,** (*b*) =**runway 1;** (4) **in,** a quarrel or row, *slang;* (5) ***off,** see as a main entry; (6) ***out,** (*a*) a body of water that runs off or makes out from another, (*b*) in baseball, retiring a player by running him out, see **21.** (3) (*d*) below; (7) **round,** (*a*) a side channel in a river which comes back into the stream, (*b*) =**run-around 1,** *colloq.;* (8) **way,** see as a main entry.

(1) **1891** *Cent.* 5272/3. **1899** ADE *Fables in Slang* 155 He took her riding in his new Runabout every Evening. **1949** *Chi. Tribune* 18 Sep. 34/2 Among some 70 old-time cars will be a one cylinder 1904 Cadillac runabout, several Stanley steamers, and 'tin lizzies' of pre-World War I vintage.—(3) (*a*) **1850** GARRARD *Wah-To-Yah* xxi. 258 Three of the muleteams made handsome runaways. **1946** THOMPSON

Runabout or elliptic of a cut-under type

Amer. Daughter 34 There were few people, thereafter, who didn't see them, for Thompson runaways became legendary. **1949** *Chi. D. News* 11 Aug. 3/4 A runaway horse and wagon collided with a parking meter. (*b*) **1891** *Fur, Fin, & Feather* March 182/1 To one who has sat all day on a Herkimer county (New York) runaway without seeing anything, the deer would seem to be 'pretty tolable plenty.'—(4) **1908** BEACH *Barrier* 123 We might have lived here all our days and never had a 'run-in.' **1927** *Sat. Ev. Post* 24 Dec. 24/1 My radical style of publicity resulted in frequent run-ins with the fundamentalists.

(6) (*a*) **1818** T. HULME *Jrnl.* 1 July, This Bayou is a run out of the main river, round a flat portion of land, which is sometimes overflowed. (*b*) **1868** CHADWICK *Base Ball* 66 We give the first letters of fly, tip, run out, and home run. **1877** *Nat. League Constitution & Rules* 41 An assist should be given to each player who handles the ball in a run-out or other play of this kind. **1916** BANCROFT *Handbook* 82 Runout. When a base runner [etc.]. — (7) (*a*) **1848** THOREAU *Maine Woods* 51 The frequent 'run-rounds' which come into the river again, would embarrass an inexperienced voyager. (*b*) **1857** *Knickerb.* XLIX. 97 There comes us [*sic*] a 'run-round' on the end of our pen-finger. **1879** WEBSTER *Supp.* 1577/3 *Run-round,* . . . a felon or whitlow. (*Vulg. U.S.*)

20. In colloq. phrases with nouns: (1) *To run into the ground,* to overdo, carry to excess; (2) *to run a saw on,* to make (someone or something) the object of jesting or ridicule, also *to run it on;* (3) *to run* (*for*) (*one's*) *luck,* to trust to luck; (4) *to run the bases,* to make the circuit of the bases in baseball; (5) *to run one's board,* to leave without paying for one's board; (6) *to run the river,* to be employed on a river steamer; (7) *to run cattle, W.* to graze, range, or care for cattle; (8) *to run the mail,* to carry the mail over a particular route; (9) *to run liquor,* to get illicit liquor to market.

(1) **1836** *Quarter Race Ky.* (1846) 16 It's no use to run the thing into the ground. **1884** GRONLUND *Coöp. Commonwealth* 74 After having run this Social 'Order' into the ground, it will be supplanted by a new principle. — (2) **1841** *N.O. Picayune* 9 May 2/2 Here we detected an embryo wag of the first water, actually trying to 'run a saw' upon us with our own sheet [newspaper] in his hand. *a***1846** *Quarter Race Ky.* 68 'Running a Saw' on a French Gentleman. By 'Ginsangandson,' of Philadelphia. **1899** C. KING *Trooper Galahad* 110 The members of the troop . . . thought to 'run it' on the 'doughboy' captain. — (3) **1841** LONGFELLOW in S. Longfellow *H. W. Longfellow* I. 391, I have to run for luck as to horses, which is not so agreeable. **1877** CAMPION *On Frontier* 7 We determined to 'run our luck' and 'play our own hand.' — (4) **1845** in *Appletons' Ann. Cyclo.* XXV. 77/2 A player, running the bases, shall be out if the ball is in the hands of an adversary or on the base, or the runner is touched by it before he makes his base. **1907** *St. Nicholas* June 693/2 'Yes,' laughed Chub, 'we run bases.'

(5) **1897** HOWELLS *Open-eyed Conspiracy* vii, It will be quite enough for the hotel-keeper if they run their board. I shall have to pay for it.

— (6) **1901** CHURCHILL *Crisis* 7, I thought I'd made a mistake to let him run the river. *Ib.* 296 He owns two slaves now who are running the river. — (7) **1907** WHITE *Arizona Nights* 87, I didn't see them any more after that until I'd hit the Lazy Y, and had started in runnin' cattle in the Soda Springs Valley. **1929** DOBIE *Vaquero* 13 When we gathered cattle, we said that we were on a 'cow hunt,' a 'cow work,' a 'work,' or a 'cow drive,' or maybe we said we were out 'running cattle.'— (8) **1929** F. E. MCCLINCHEY *Joe Pete* 26 Every year one of the Island Indians had a contract with the Government to 'run the mail.' — (9) **1934** CARMER *Stars Fell* 155 He started runnin' liquor just to get money to carry his girl to parties.

For *to run the blockade, to run one's face*, see the nouns.

b. Also (1) *To run a match*, (2) *to run post*, (3) *to run the guard*, (4) *to run meat*, (5) *to run the trail*, (6) *to run in the range*, (7) *to run a Mick*, (8) *to run the cards*, (9) *to run haunts*, (see quots.).

(1) **1804** *Fredericktown* (Md.) *Herald* 10 March 3/3 Col. Burr is going to run a match for the Governor's cup in the State of New-York. — (2) **1848** BRYANT *California* xxii. 281 Besides keeping the Indians in subjection, they [*sc.* pickets] run post with a monthly correspondence. — (3) **1848** *Santa Fe Republican* 2 April 1/2 Patrick Duffy . . . was shot recently while attempting to 'run the guard' with two other soldiers. — (4) **1850** GARRARD *Wah-To-Yah* i. 15 The next time you run meat, don't let the horse go in a trot and yourself in a gallop.

(5) **1851** WM. KELLY *Across Rocky Mts.* (1852) 234 Some of the men ran the trail a long distance, without being able to bring them to view. — (6) **1858** WOODWARD *Reminiscences* (1939) 136, I was left to 'run in the range.' — (7) **1863** BROWNE *Four Years in Secessia* (1865) 288 'Running a Mick' was to get an Irishman drunk; induce him to enlist for two or three hundred dollars; obtain five times that sum from citizens desirous of procuring a substitute [etc.]. — (8) **1884** HARRIS in *Cent. Mag.* Nov. 122 I'll run the cards and see what they say. — (9) **1900** *Cong. Rec.* 11 Jan. 784/2 When the dogs would rush in there was not a thing up there [in the tree], and the darkies would immediately say 'Let's go home; that dog was running haunts.'

21. In phrases with adverbs: (1) **To run off*, (*a*) to survey or mark out boundaries, (*b*) (see quot.), *rare*, (*c*) *W.* to stampede or drive off (cattle and horses), usu. preliminary to stealing them, (*d*) to terrorize and drive away, (*e*) to steal, (*f*) to turn out on a typewriter; (2) **to run on to*, to run across; (3) **to run out*, (*a*) to survey or ascertain the bounds of tracts, areas, etc., (*b*) of plants, to degenerate, lose vigor, (*c*) of a breed of persons or animals, to degenerate or decline in character or virtue, (*d*) in baseball (see quots.), cf. ***run out** in **19.** (6) (*b*) above, (*e*) to drive out (grass), take the place of, (*f*) to yield or produce, (*g*) to vanquish (a competitor), to force (someone) to leave or run away; (4) **to run over*, (see quots.); (5) **to run up*, (see quot.).

(1) (*a*) **1748** WASHINGTON *Diaries* I. 8 We began at ye Boundary Line . . . and run of two Lots. (*b*) **1846** *De Bow's Review* 11 Sep. 134 Embracing the notion of the *depreciation*, or 'running off' of cotton, is a question of great importance. (*c*) **1857** W. CHANDLESS *Visit Salt Lake* II. iv. 195 Mormons, in their turn, say that Californian emigrants continually 'ran off' their horses and lived on their cattle. **1890** M. E. RYAN *Told in Hills* 307 When was it the stock was run off from camp? (*d*) **1862** WINTHROP *John Brent* xvi. 183 But then he knows ther ain't no Utes round here to stampede his animals or run off any of his gals. **1901** HARBEN *Westerfelt* 220 He was here the night they run him off. **1949** GANN *Tread of Longhorns* 57 The city rulers felt that the marshal should have stopped the jail delivery, and for his failure to do so, he was run off the job. (*e*) **1846** *Dollar Newspaper* (Phila.) 4 Nov. 3/3 Bryant Hines, who 'run off' a large number of slaves . . ., has been taken in Florida, and is now in the Eutaw jail. **1882** HARTE *Flip* 20 He's down on tramps ever since they run off his chickens. (*f*) **1901** MERWIN & WEBSTER *Calumet 'K'* 106 Now, we'll write to Mr. Brown—no . . . ; I'll do that one myself. You might run off the other and I'll sign it. — (2) **1902** WISTER *Virginian* ii, Meet a man once and you're sure to run on to him again. — (3) (*a*) **1671** *S.C. Hist. Soc. Coll.* V. 298 Another Surveyor . . . doth proffer to run out all parcells of land above 500 Akers at a Penny per Acre. **1842** *Amer. Pioneer* I. 379 A young man . . . made known his desire to have a district to run out. **1905** COLE *Early Oregon* 28 When school closed I assisted them in running out their land claims. (*b*) **1838** *Mass. Agric. Survey 1st Rep.* 128 The herds-grass and red top, entirely run out by the second and third years after sowing. **1878** KILLEBREW *Tenn. Grasses* 98 English Rye Grass . . . is said to impoverish land rapidly and will run out in a few years. (*c*) **1863** *Rep. Comm. Agric. 1862* 48 We often hear the complaint that the breed [of swine] has 'run out.' **1867** LOWELL *My Study Windows* 97 The New England breed is running out, we are told! (*d*) **1867** CHADWICK *Base Ball Reference* 139 A player is 'run out,' when he is caught between two bases and is put out by one or other of the fielders. **1916** BANCROFT *Handbook* 82 When a base runner is trapped between bases by two opponents with the ball who walk toward each other until one of them can put him out, he is said to be 'run out.' (*e*) **1872** *Vt. Bd. Agric. Rep.* I. 281 Some farmers have thought that it [*sc.* oxeye daisy] runs out [timothy]. **1878** *Ill. Dept. Agric. Trans.* XIV. 295 Kentucky blue grass was best adapted for a good dairy farm; it would run out all other grasses. (*f*) **1876** RAYMOND *8th Rep. Mines* 19 The Sunderland, with a furnace of 15 tons of daily capacity, ran out 1,500 flasks last year. (*g*) **1877** WANAMAKER in Appel *Biog. Wanamaker* (1930) 87 Dry Goods people . . . would spend fabulous sums 'to run John Wanamaker out.' **1946** FOREMAN *Last Trek* 195 The agent announced his intention of running out of the country any such preacher who might appear. — (4) **1857** *Hoyle's Games* (Amer. ed.) 288 *Run Over.*—Should you wish to bet more or 'bluff' off your adversary. **1864** DICK *Amer. Hoyle* (1866) 173 If bets are not limited, he [the player] can bet or 'run over' as much as he pleases.

(5) **1891** *Cent.* 5271/3 *To run up*, . . . to execute by hanging: as, they dragged the wretch to a tree and ran him up. (Western U.S.)

22. In phrases with prepositions: (1) *To run across*, to come upon, to meet; (2) **to run against*, to compete with in an election; (3) **to run around*, to plow by passing on both sides of the drill; (4) **to run on*, (see quot.); (5) **to run over*, to treat unfairly or slightingly; (6) *to run round*, (*a*) in surveying, to traverse the bounds of (a piece of land), (*b*) = **to run around;* (7) **to run through*, to cultivate lightly and rapidly; (8) *to run upon*, to make a butt of.

(1) **1884** MARK TWAIN *H. Finn* viii. 64 (R.), I had run across that camp-fire. **1887** J. HAWTHORNE *Tragic Myst.* viii, The young man who happens to run across one of them and to make a good impression on her, may be accounted lucky. — (2) **1831** *Boston Transcript* 12 May 1/1 He . . . was afraid I want a true republican; and wanted to know if I did n't run against Gov. Smith last year down there in Maine. — (3) **1843** in TURNER *Cotton* (1865) 68 Hence, I say, 'as early as possibly convenient,' after the plant is up, 'plough out the middles well, the wide way, having first run around the plant with a scooter-plough.' **1855** DAVIS *Farm Bk.* 156 With the plows we have run around . . . in all 70 acres. — (4) **1841** WEBSTER 514/2 *To run on* . . . to press with jokes or ridicule; to abuse with sarcasms; to bear hard on.

(5) **1836** *Quarter Race Ky.* 23, I would not advise any man to try to run over me. — (6) (*a*) **1748** WASHINGTON *Diaries* I. 5 We set out early with Intent to Run round ye sd Land. (*b*) **1856** DAVIS *Farm Bk.* 24 Eliza Wright run round the corn in the apple orchard. — (7) **1853** T. D. PRICE *Diary* (MS) 6 July, Finished running through the corn. — (8) **1852** *Knickerb.* XXXIX. 403 It takes a long while for some men to learn to take it coolly when they are run upon.

run-around ˈrʌnəˌraund, *n.*

1. A felon or whitlow. *Colloq.*

1872 TALMAGE *Sermons* 224 Some hypochondriac with a 'run-around' or a 'hang-nail.' **1913** LONDON *Valley of Moon* 352 His finger was hurting too much, he said. . . . 'It might be a run-around,' Saxon hazarded.

2. =**bull pen 1. b.** *Slang.*

1900 *Dly. Ardmoreite* (Ardmore, Okla.) 1 May 4/3 This morning the three bellicose prisoners were taken from the run-around and placed in the dungeon of the jail. **1932** *Durant* (Okla.) *D. Democrat* 8 Jan. 1/3 Now a three-inch topping of concrete is being laid on the run-around of the jail, which is also a part of the roof of the lower part of the county building.

3. A channel around a dam in a stream.

1904 *Elect. World & Engin.* 13 Feb. 305 (*Cent. Supp.*), A few hundred feet below the main dam the bed of the runaround again joins the river.

4. Avoidance, evasion. Also *to give one a run-around. Slang.*

1915 *Chi. Herald* 2 Dec. 13/4 Pitts is satisfied that he is the victim of the grandest run-around ever put over on a boxing promoter. **1944** STOUT *Not Quite Dead Enough* 34 You're giving me a run-around. **1948** GARDNER *Lonely Heiress* 152 We want to know the truth with no more run-around.

***runner,** *n.*

1. (See quot.) *Rare.*

1709 LAWSON *Carolina* 162 Runners . . . have Holes in the Sand-Beaches and are a whitish sort of a Crab.

2. One of the two long pieces of wood or metal upon which a sled or sleigh slides.

1762 *Boston News-Letter* 7 Jan. 3/3 Wanted, a pair of good runners. **1815** RICHARDSON *Diary* 3 Started in the stage with 4 Pass. at 11 A.M. Dined at Meriden and arrived at New Haven at 5 P.M. Travelled on runners today but it was bad sleighing. **1949** *Nat. Geog.*

Mag. Oct. 474/1 When they travel, the Kutchin use a sled made of two runners with both ends turned up.

transf. **1829** *Va. Herald* (Fredericksburg) 28 Feb. 3/2 The Stage upset three times; they came to Kingston on wheels and thence to Newark on runners.

b. A heavy timber or structure serving as a temporary supporting track or way for a heavy object that is being moved.

1815 *Niles' Reg.* IX. 201/1 [We] moved the one-half of the arch off sideways, forty-six feet, on to the runner one hundred and eighty-five feet long. **1881** *Harper's Mag.* Jan. 195/2 We ran our engine on runners—simple runners made of planking.

c. A skate or a blade of a skate.

1860 WORCESTER 1348/1 *Skate*, . . . a sort of shoe . . . furnished with an iron runner, used to slide or travel on the ice. **1902** *Sears Cat.* 753/3 The runner of this skate is made of cold rolled steel. **1948** *Time* 2 Feb. 52/3 She practiced her first figures—learning to do eights, brackets and counters; to skate on the inside or outside edge of the runners (never on the flat of the blade).

3. A blacksnake.

1795 in S. WILLIAMS *Nat. Hist. Vt.* (ed. 2) I. App. 485 In a field in Connecticut, . . . I approached with caution within twenty feet of a black snake, about seven feet long, having a white throat, and of the kind which the people there call runners or choking snakes. **1855** SIMMS *Forayers* 549 We got glimpse of a few runners (black-snakes), but they were quite too swift of foot for the hunters.

4. One who solicits patronage, as for a boardinghouse, hotel, store, etc. Cf. **emigrant runner.**

1824 *Microscope* (Albany) 21 Feb. (Th.), Our wholesale property-speculators and their gentry in livery, called runners. **1883** *Harper's Mag.* Nov. 814/1 The runners for several livery-stables offered to provide special transportation. **1948** *Chelsea* (Mass.) *Rec.* 30 Nov. 8/7 Unethical lawyers, plus their hired 'runners,' probation officers, jail attaches and police officers were 'selling' justice in the courthouse corridors to ignorant criminal defendants.

b. One who endeavors to secure votes for a person or cause. *Obs.*

1800 *Mass. Mercury* 27 June (Th.), A couple of runners attended a numerous meeting, and made their usual display of eloquence upon the occasion. **1830** *Wiscassett* (Me.) *Citizen* 20 Aug. 3/4 These Runners are employed to tell the uninformed people great stories about 'the *Tariff*'—Gen. Jackson's economy—the good times he will bring about, and such like silly and false stories.

c. *W.* One who went in advance of a caravan to procure provisions, and provide for other needs of those coming later. *Obs.*

1844 GREGG *Commerce of Prairies* I. 88 A party of *avant-couriers*, known in the technical parlance of the Prairies as 'runners,' soon began to make preparations for pushing forward in advance of the caravan.

5. In the names of fishes: **a.** The blackfish or tautog, *Tautoga onitis.* **b.** An amber fish, *Elagatis bipinnulatus.* **c.** (See quot.)

(**a**) **1814** MITCHELL *Fishes N.Y.* 399 Tide black-fish or runners. The name of this fish is derived from the colour of its back and sides. — (**b**) **1884** GOODE *Fisheries* I. 332 This West Indian fish, known at Key West as 'Skipjack' or 'Runner,' . . . usually moves in small schools of a dozen or two individuals. **1897** *N.Y. Forest, Fish, & Game Comm. 2d Rep.* 238 *Elagatis bipinnulatus.* . . . Runner. . . . This tropical species has once before been recorded from Long Island. — (**c**) **1896** JORDAN & EVERMANN *Check-List Fishes* 346 *Caranx crysos.* . . . Hard-tail; Runner; Jurel; Yellow Mackerel. . . . Cape Cod to Brazil.

6. A prisoner allowed to act as a messenger and to perform other offices about a prison.

1833 T. HAMILTON *Men & Manners* I. 176 [At the Boston prison] there is, however, a class of men, consisting of ten or twelve, called *runners* and *lumpers*, whose duty consists in moving about the yard. **1912** DREISER *Financier* 679 Some of the prisoners, after long service were used as 'trusties' or 'runners,' as they were locally called; but not many.

7. One who pursues buffalo on horseback. *Obs.*

1837 IRVING *Bonneville* II. 180 The 'runners,' mounted on the fleetest horses, were full tilt after the buffalo.

8. =**base-runner.**

1845 in *Appletons' Ann. Cyclo.* XXV. 77/2 A player, running the bases, shall be out . . . if the runner is touched by it [the ball] before he makes his base. **1857** *Spirit of Times* 7 Feb. 372/3 Mr. Thos. Leavy, (otherwise called Blue Top), mans the first base, and rare it is, that a runner reaches the first base, if the ball is passed up quickly. **1948** *Lawton* (Okla.) *Constitution* 4 July 12/2 If the pitcher doesn't keep the runners close to base, the best catcher in baseball can't throw them out.

9. The engineer of a locomotive.

1874 FORNEY *Catechism of Locomotive* 547 Every locomotive runner should . . . have an exact knowledge of the engine intrusted to him. **1901** *Munsey's Mag.* XXV. 749/1 A new express locomotive . . . glided up to the platform under the hand of . . . one of the most experienced runners on the road.

10. One who accompanies a fire engine to a fire as a hanger-on. *Obs.*

1881 *Harper's Mag.* Feb. 372/1 The boys . . . [were] not members of the companies but only 'runners' with the engines. **1899** BREEN *Thirty Years* 74 If they happened to reach the same street at the same time, . . . the 'runners' or outside attaches of each machine would manage to collide.

11. (See quot. 1881.)

1881 INGERSOLL *Oyster Industry* 247 *Runner.*—Vessels engaged in transporting oysters from the grounds to the market; they also buy the stock they carry. (Chesapeake.) **1891** *Cent.* 5274/1.

12. *Football.* A player who runs with the ball.

1890 *Outing* Feb. 386/2 It was left to Princeton and Yale to . . . generalize it into the principle that has made runners and rushers alike in the rushing game of the last four years. **1893** STAGG & WILLIAMS *Amer. Football* 43 The end-rusher has to meet the runner under most trying circumstances. **1922** *Outing* May 65/2 As Gilroy drove his way down the field Hunt counted the yards by fives—'Five—ten—fifteen—' and so on till the runner hurled himself across the line.

13. One who directs or carries on a business.

1893 M. HOLLEY *Samantha at World's Fair* 4 His parents . . . [were] good respectable . . . people . . . and runners of a cheese factory.

14. a. runner bird, =**road runner. b. runner-plank,** (see quot.).

(**a**) **1885** *Santa Fé Wkly. New Mexican* 17 Sep. 4/2 One of the greatest enemies of snakes in Arizona is the runner bird. — (**b**) **1886** *Leslie's Pop. Mo.* XXI. 387/2 The transverse-piece; known in all ice-boats as the runner-plank. *Ib.*, The mast is stepped directly over the center of the runner-plank.

As the last term in **bank, base, black, blockade, boarding-house, buffalo, double, elk, emigrant, engine, fore, hotel, Indian, locomotive, mud, ox, prairie, ridge, river, road, rum, sleigh, slip, tideland, turkey, wood runner.**

***running,** *n.* and *a.*

1. The surveying or marking out of a boundary line. Cf. ***run,** *v.* **1.**

1662 *Dedham Rec.* IV. Ensigne Daniell Fisher and Edward Richards were mutually chosin . . . to setle and determine the runinge of the Devision line. **1706** *Providence Rec.* XI. 105 The reunning of the devideing line betweene the lands of Providence & ye lands of Pautuxett. **1797** *Ann. 5th Congress* I. 305 The running and marking of the boundary line, between the colonies of East and West Florida, and the territory of the United States, have been delayed by the officers of His Catholic Majesty.

2. The act of standing as a candidate for office. Cf. ***run,** *v.* **2.** and **17.**

1830 *Wiscassett* (Me.) *Citizen* 20 Aug. 3/2 Such politicians . . . bet on a candidate's *running* for the Chief Magistracy of the Union or of a single State, precisely as they would bet on the *running* of a *race horse.* **1870** *Nation* XI. 1 He has never failed in getting such offices as he wanted, the record of his 'running' being about as good as that of any man in the country.

3. Teasing or scolding, an occasion of this. *Colloq.* Cf. ***run,** *v.* **6.**

1832 S. SMITH *Life J. Downing* 158, I feel a little put out with Dr Burnham for an unhansome running he gave me 'tother day. **1902** J. CORBIN *Amer. at Oxford* 16 The freshman breakfast is nothing in the world but a variation of the 'running' that is given newcomers in those American colleges where fraternity life is strong.

4. (See quot. 1849.) Cf. ***run,** *v.* **5.**

1839 TOWNSEND *Narrative* 158 They have listened to the garrulous hunter's details of 'approaching,' and 'running,' and 'quartering.' **1849** PARKMAN *Oregon Trail* 91 The method of hunting called 'running,' consists in attacking the buffalo on horseback and shooting him with bullets or arrows when at full speed.

5. *Baseball.* An inning. *Obs.*

1856 *Spirit of Times* 13 Dec. 245/1 The game was exceedingly well contested, and took each side eleven runnings, and from 9 A.M. till 1 P.M., before it was concluded, when the game stood 22 to 24.

6. Of animals: Rutting. *Colloq.* Cf. **running season** (*b*), **running time** (*b*).

1879 VIVIAN *Wanderings in Western Land* 36 The American moose . . . sheds the velvet off his horns about the beginning of September; and commences 'running' about the middle of that month, remaining with the cows about five or six weeks.

7. Conducting or guiding logs down a stream. Cf. ***run,** *v.* **7.** and ***driving 2.**

1880 *Michigan Rep.* XXXVIII. 603 Kelsey was to manage the logging in the woods and running of the logs to the mill.

8. In combs.: (1) **running ball,** ?a buckshot, *obs.;* (2) **board,** (*a*) (see quot. 1843), *obs.*, (*b*) a board or narrow platform along the side of a locomotive, streetcar, or automobile; (3) **brand,** *W.* (see quots.); (4) **business,** (see quot. 1849), *obs.;* (5) **catch,** (see quot. 1868); (6) **exercise,** an emotional state fallen into by a person's attempting to run away from the emotional manifestations aroused at revivalistic religious services, *obs.;* (7) **gear,** see as a main entry; (8) **horse,** *W.* a horse used for riding on hunts, scouting expeditions, etc., as distinguished from a pack animal; (9) **iron,** *W.* a straight or only slightly curved iron rod used by brand-blotters in an effort to avoid suspicion if apprehended, also transf.; (10) **mate,** (*a*) a horse that serves as a pacemaker for another or that works with another, (*b*) a candidate running on the same ticket with another, but for a subordinate office, often used of a candidate for Vice-President; (11) **plate,** a light steel horseshoe used on race horses; (12) **season,** (*a*) the season at which buffalo travel from one grazing region to another, (*b*) the rutting season for deer; (13) **set,** (see quot.); (14) **slough,** (see quot.); (15) **time,** (*a*) =**running season** (*a*), (*b*) =**running season** (*b*), (*c*) the time usually devoted to a certain activity, schedule time.

(1) 1757 WEBB *Orders* 42 The Men for Guard in Camp ye Covering & Working Party's to Lode their First Cartrages with Runing Ball for which Porpos a Proper Proportion of Powder & Ball will Be Deliv.d to Each Corp from ye Artilery. **1809** E. CUMMING *Western Tour* 19, I proceeded for Middleton, . . . first loading one of the barrels of my gun with a running ball. — **(2)** (*a*) **1817** *Essex Inst. Coll.* VIII. 240 [We] were obliged to give it up after being at the expense of putting on running boards, and hiring two men to pole her up. **1843** *Amer. Pioneer* II. 271 Keel-boats . . . were provided with running boards, extending from bow to stern, on each side of the boat. . . . The crew, divided equally on each side, set their poles near the head of the boat, and bringing the end of the pole to their shoulders, with their bodies bent, walked slowly down the running board to the stern. (*b*) **1864** WEBSTER 1158/1 *Running board,* a narrow platform extending along the side of a locomotive. **1923** WATTS *L. Nichols* 235 She sat down on the running-board of the car. **1948** *Dly. Ardmoreite* (Ardmore, Okla.) 20 July 1/7, I went through water up to the running board for some distance. — **(3) 1883** SWEET & KNOX *Through Texas* 160 The other, called a running brand, is a long piece of iron curved at the end. **1934** *Denver Post* 4 Aug. 10/3 A running brand . . . [is] a brand made with a straight poker called a 'running iron,' and used like a pencil. — **(4) 1809** KENDALL *Travels* III. 296 On the Province Point . . . I was taught to expect to find a store inhabited, and in the bustle of the *running* business. **1849** AUDUBON *Western Jrnl.* 53 Matamoras contains many Mexicans who do both a wholesale and retail 'running business,' that is, smuggling.

(5) 1858 *Chadwick Scrapbook* (E. J. Nichols). **1868** CHADWICK *Base Ball* 45 A running catch is made when the ball is caught on the fly while the fielder is on the run. **1885** ——— *Art of Pitching* 140 Running Catch.—These catches are among the prettiest a fielder can make. — **(6) 1834** *Biblical Repertory* VI. 350 The running exercise was also one of the varieties, in which the person was impelled to run with amazing swiftness. **1847** HOWE *Hist. Coll. Ohio* 46 '*Bodily exercises*' . . . have been classified by a clerical writer as 1st, the *Falling* exercise; 2d, the *Jerking* exercise; 3d, the *Rolling* exercise; 4th, the *Running* exercise. **1903** *Ohio Archaeol. Pub.* XII. 249 The running exercise was nothing more than, that persons feeling something of these bodily agitations, through fear, attempted to run away, and thus escape from them. — **(8) 1837** IRVING *Bonneville* II. 183 Some of the men, throwing themselves upon the 'running horses' kept for hunting, galloped off to reconnoitre. **1846** WEBB *Altowan* I. 191 They had hoped to find the baggage-animals and the running-horses.—**(9) 1894** *McClure's Mag.* July 101/2 The running-irons, or *guachos,* . . . are now considered bad form by progressive cattlemen. **1945** *Everybody's Digest* Aug. 89 Of a dying man, the puncher might say: 'Death's got the runnin' iron on him brandin' him for the Eternal Range.' **1949** NORDYKE *Cattle Empire* 84 A clever rustler could take a hot running iron and alter some brands into new designs, completely obscuring the old ones.

(10) (*a*) **1868** WOODRUFF *Trotting Horse* 284 He has been . . . especially great for his knack at going with a running-mate. **1890** *Stock Grower & Farmer* 29 March 7/1 Dandy had a running mate that was just as different from him as could be. (*b*) **1902** WHITLOCK *13th District* 61 There were . . . pictures of the candidate himself, . . . and pictures, too, of his 'running mate,' the candidate for vice-president. **1947** *Dly. Oklahoman* (Okla. City) 21 Sep. 6–D/5 No man would run for president with a woman running mate. — **(11) 1877** CAMPION *On Frontier* 18 The shoes [were] taken off our horses and replaced by 'running plates.' — **(12)** (*a*) **1833** CATLIN *Indians* I. 249 The '*running season,*' which is in August and September, is the time when they congregate into such masses in some places, as literally to blacken the prairies for miles together. **1851** M. REID *Scalp Hunters* iv, 21 It was now the 'running season,' but none of the great droves had crossed us. (*b*) **1868** *Amer. Naturalist* II. 471 Then begins the running season, when bucks grow careless, or fearless, or both. — **(13) 1932** *Atlantic Mo.* CL. 473 The running-set is the sole survival [in the Ky. mountains] of an ancient dance brought to this country in the eighteenth century. It is a dance of great beauty and wildness, executed with swiftness, and yet so smoothly that there is never any cessation of rhythm, sustained by a clap of the hand and a glide, sometimes a shuffle of the feet, and on occasions accompanied by a fiddle. — **(14) 1875** *Amer. Naturalist* IX. 387 Sometimes these ponds [in the river bottoms in Ill.] unite, retain a permanent connection with the stream and, at low water, flow towards it with a slow current, forming what are called 'running sloughs.'

(15) (*a*) **1806** CLARK in *Lewis & C. Exped.* V. (1905) 294 It is now running time with those animals. (*b*) **1890** L. C. D'OYLE *Notches* 60 The loud, shrill, snorting whistle peculiar to the buck in 'running' time. (*c*) **1911** HARRISON *Queed* 143 Queed . . . pulled into supper only three minutes behind running-time.

b. In the names of plants: (1) **running blackberry,** the swamp blackberry, *Rubus hispidus,* or a related species; (2) **myrtle,** see ***myrtle,** *n.* **1;** (3) **oak,** a species of small shrubby oak found on the coast from North Carolina to Florida; (4) **peanuts,** a variety of peanuts having many branching tendrils that grow along the ground; (5) **swamp blackberry,** (see quots.).

(1) 1814 BIGELOW *Florula Bostoniensis* 122 *Rubus trivialis.* Low or running blackberry. Dewberry. . . . Fruit large, black, sweet. **1919** STURTEVANT *Notes on Edible Plants* 507 *R[ubus] hispidus.* Running Blackberry. Swamp Blackberry. — **(3) 1676** SEWALL *Diary* I. 26 They call [them] running Oak, etc. **1832** BROWNE *Sylva* 287 Like the upland willow oak, it is confined to the maritime parts of the Carolinas, Georgia and the Floridas, where it is called Running Oak. **1945** MATHEWS *Talking* 19 When a blackjack is chopped down, or blown down by a tornado or cyclonic winds, a hundred 'running oaks' will spring up to take its place. — **(4) 1946** *Democrat* 16 May 1/1 If you do not have sufficient running peanuts to fatten all of your hogs you should plant grain sorghum.

(5) 1843 TORREY *Flora N.Y.* I. 217 *Rubus hispidus.* Running Swamp Blackberry. . . . Swamps and wet woods; sometimes in rather dry, but shady situations. **1857** GRAY *Botany* 121 *R[ubus] hispidus.* (Running Swamp-Blackberry.) . . . Fruit of a few large grains, red or purple, sour.

As the last term in **base, blockade, buffalo, log running.**

running gear.

1. The moving or working parts, as wheels, pulleys, etc., of a mill, cotton gin, or the like.

1662 *East-Hampton Rec.* I. 201 Mr Backer shall have seven pounds for this yeare for tendinge the mill and maintayninge the running geares that is coggs and rounds. **1725** *N.-Eng. Courant* 18–25 Jan. 2/2 The Wind . . . carry'd off the Top of the Mill, with the shaft, Vanes, and running Geer, and brake them to Pieces. **1834** in BASSETT *So. Plant.* 73 The runinge geares that is hear I cant under take to pick a crop with them. **1901** MERWIN & WEBSTER *Calumet 'K'* 262 'Where is he now, Max?' 'Down in the cellar putting in the running gear for the "cross-the-house conveyors."'

2. The ropes or chains used to work or set sails, yards, etc.

1838 COOPER *Homeward B.* xx, The standing rigging are the bones and gristle; the running gear the veins in which her life circulates. **1856** KANE *Arctic Explor.* II. 48 We can burn hemp and cast-off running-gear.

3. That portion of a vehicle below the bed or body.

1857 STROTHER *Virginia* 230 A shadowy group was dimly visible, a carriage mounted on the running-gear of a wagon, and drawn by four horses. **1924** BECHDOLT *Tales* 363 The boy was driving a span of horses hitched to the running-gear of a lumber-wagon. **1948** DICK *Dixie Frontier* 208 The driver . . . fastened a big deep box on the axle or the front wheels of a wagon running-gear.

***runoff,** *n.*

1. An instance of running off or leaving the rails by a locomotive or car.

1855 *Chi. W. Times* 9 Aug. 1/8 The frequency of these run-offs demands the special attention of all railroad directors. **1872** HUNTING-

TON *Road-Master's Ass't* 87 It is best always to keep spare [switch] rods on hand, to be used in case of a run-off.

2. The amount of water that runs off a particular area during a rain or from a stream or spring. Also attrib.

1893 *Rep. Geol. Survey 1892–3* 149 The run-off, that is, the quantity of water flowing from the land. *Ib.* 150 For comparison with this run-off map a similar map showing the mean annual precipitation is introduced. **1947** *Reader's Digest* April 80/1 The humus holds the irrigation water like a mammoth blotter. There is never any runoff. **1950** *World-Herald Mag.* (Omaha) 8 Jan. 4/3 The New York State runoff average is 45 per cent.

3. In some of the southern states, a second primary election (see quot. 1924). Also **runoff election, runoff primary.**

1924 *Lit. Digest* 6 Sep. 8/2 Texas . . . has a double primary. If no one has a majority in the first primary election, a later 'run-off' primary is held, in which the voters choose between the two candidates receiving the highest number of votes at the first balloting. **1947** *Chi. D. News* 22 Oct. 25/3 Jenkins placed second in yesterday's primary and will contest with Mayor Earl J. Glade in the runoff Nov. 4. **1949** *L.A. Times* 4 May 1/2 He is convinced that the mayoralty candidates in the coming runoff election knew nothing about it.

runtee ˈrʌnti, *n.* [Origin obscure. Hodge suggests F. *arrondi*, rounded. Cf. Du. *rondte*, a round object.] "A circular piece of flat shell drilled edgeways and probably strung and originally used as an ornament" (Hodge). *Obs.*

1705 BEVERLEY *Virginia* III. 59 They also make Runtees of the same Shell, and grind them as smooth as Peak. **1883** *Bureau Amer. Ethnol. 2d Rep.* 229 There is quite a close resemblance between these objects [beads] and the 'runtees' of the early writers. [**1893** *Harper's Mag.* Dec. 215 In America these Dutchmen discovered Indian money, and at once turned the shell heaps of Long Island into mints. The Dutch Midas was slow but sure in making four blue and eight white beads equal to a penny.]

runway ˈrʌnˌwe, *n.*

1. A path, track, or way customarily followed by animals.

1835 [in deer runway *q.v.*]. **1837** *N.Y. Mirror* 28 Oct. 141/1 [The deer] kept swimming along the shore, close under the steep bank, looking up at it every now and then, as if in search of a 'runway' which would carry him back again into the depths of the forest. **1913** *Collier's* 6 Dec. 15/2 The deer broke its own neck in a runway. **1949** R. J. SIM *Pages from Past* 58 The snood . . . was a slipnoose of fine brass wire set in a runway and attached to an upright spring-pole.

b. The underground passageway used by a mole; the way or course run by a fish.

1870 WARNER *Summer in Garden* vii, 60 The mole . . . had rooted up the ground like a pig. I found his run-ways. **1894** *Outing* XXIV. 453/1 After a minute's rest, to let him settle in his runway, I made a cast.

c. A place in which fowls may run.

1871 LEWIS *Poultry Book* 8 The hennery should be placed in a warm, dry location . . . with runways ample to allow of plenty of exercise. **1913** LONDON *Valley of Moon* 459 A goodly portion was devoted to white-washed henhouses and wired runways wherein hundreds of chickens were to be seen. **1949** *Sat. Ev. Post* 9 April 59/2 He even had a plan for one in his desk; the runways were to be painted green outside and whitewashed inside.

2. The bed or channel of a stream.

1874 B. F. TAYLOR *World on Wheels* 250 Like the dusty 'run-ways' of thy brooks, soft pulses have grown dry and dumb. **1879** WEBSTER 1577/3.

3. An artificial track or open way serving as a gangway or road.

1883 HOWE *Country Town* (1926) 36 Pushing this into my wagon with the assistance of his wife, after we had first made a runway of boards, I hauled him to Fairview. **1904** *N.Y. Sun* 9 Aug. 1 The women became hysterical and stampeded for the wagon runway in the middle of the [ferry]boat.

b. (See quot.)

1905 *Forestry Bureau Bul.* No. 61, 39 *Gutter road*, The path followed in skidding logs. . . . [Also called] runway.

rural free delivery. The free delivery of mail on routes passing through rural districts. Also attrib.

1892 *Cong. Rec.* 28 May 481/1 [Mr. Watson of Ga.] is perfectly consistent in advocating a rural free delivery system which would mount carriers on horseback and send them to every habitation in the land to deliver and collect the mails. **1908** *Sat. Ev. Post* 5 Dec. 18/1 They couldn't cold deck anybody on the rural free delivery routes. **1944** CLARK *Pills* 255 These included arbor days, famous southern battles, the birthdays of southern statesmen and military figures, and days on which there was to be no rural free delivery.

* **rush,** *n.*[1] In combs.: (1) **rush bottom,** (*a*) a chair having a bottom made of plaited rushes, in full **rush-bottom chair,** (*b*) a bottom where rushes grow; (2) **collar,** (see quot.); (3) **lily,** (see quots.).

(1) (*a*) **1778** *Pa. Archives* 6 Ser. XII. 31 Publick sale . . . 1 Rush bottom chair—11s. **1874** B. F. TAYLOR *World on Wheels* II. iii. 209 There is a chair—a low rush-bottom chair. **1923** DEEPING *Secret Sanctuary* xiii, He moved to sit down, and she saw him take one of the straight-backed rushbottoms. (*b*) **1831** PECK *Guide for Emigrants* II. 105 In all the rush bottoms they [cattle] fatten during the severe weather on rushes. — (2) **1936** *D.N.* VI. 521, I have learned that the article (called also *rush collar*) was a cheap kind of horse collar, manufactured frequently in prisons. It was usually constructed of a sort of a matting (perhaps woven from dried flag plants) and was used for temporary purposes, particularly on fat-necked horses, during the time that special oversized collars were being made for them. — (3) **1884** W. MILLER *Dict. Names of Plants* 119/2 *Rush-Lily*, the genus *Sisyrinchium.* Purple, *Sisyrinchium grandiflorum.* White. *Sisyrinchium grandiflorum var. album.* **1891** *Cent.* 5278/1 *Rush-lily*, . . . a plant of the more showy species of blue-eyed grass, *Sisyrinchium*, especially *S. grandiflorum*, a species with bright-yellow flowers, native, in northwestern America, occasionally cultivated.

As the last term in **arrow, bald, bayonet, black, chairmaker's, dark-green club, sand, scouring rush.**

* **rush,** *n.*[2]

1. A good recitation. *College slang. Obs.* Cf. * **rush,** *v.* **1.**

1847 *Yale Banger* 22 Oct., In dreams his many *rushes* heard. **1871** BAGG *At Yale* 47.

2. = **stampede 2.**

1849 *Hunt's Merch. Mag.* XX. 60 In May, the gold itself began to come into the town. And then began the rising and the rush. **1868** WHYMPER *Alaska* 227 Minute specks of gold have been found by some of the Hudson's Bay Company's men in the Yukon, but not in quantities to warrant a 'rush' to the locality. **1947** PEATTIE *Sierra Nevada* 60 The discovery in 1859 of a glittering silver bonanza in Washoe County, Nevada, started a frantic rush over the mountains to Virginia City.

3. A general scrimmage or mass encounter between the students of two or more different classes. Cf. * **rushing 1. b.**

1860 *Yale Lit. Mag.* XXVI. 22 As a basis, a Rush tacitly assumes that it is promoting a rivalry that is proper and praiseworthy. **1916** EASTMAN *From Deep Woods* 68 The two classes met in a first 'rush.'

4. rush line, in football, the line of players who carry or sustain the brunt of attack. Also transf.

1887 *Cent. Mag.* Oct. 891/2 Across the field stretch the foot-ball infantry, the 'rush-line,' or 'rushers.' **1906** *Life* 4 Oct. 366 We hear of a surprising prevalence among the young men of brains who come nowadays from the universities of the disposition to get into the political rush-line and have something to say about government. **1921** PAINE *Comr. Rolling Ocean* 3 He tore through a rush-line.

5. Designating a time or function relating to the efforts made in colleges to have students seen and evaluated before being invited to join certain fraternities or sororities, as **rush party, smoker, week.** Cf. * **rush,** *v.* **2,** * **rushing 1.**

1899 QUINN *Pa. Stories* 60 It was not long before Theta Chi gave him a bid to a rush smoker. **1931** *K.C. Times* 24 Sep., Aunt Phoebe Tilden read where so many colleges are having rush parties. **1944** GREELEY (Colo.) *D. Tribune* 24 Sep. 3/5 Formal rush week for all sororities on the campus will be Oct. 1 to Oct. 6.

6. Designating a time (or piece of work, etc.) when there is an unusual effort made for quickness of completion or delivery, as (1) **rush edition,** (2) **hour,** (3) **job,** (4) **order,** (5) **season,** (6) **telegram,** (7) **work.**

(1) **1901** C. MOFFETT *Careers of Danger* 38 Already the mail clerks are swarming at the pouches, like printers on a rush edition. — (2) **1898** *Westm. Gaz.* 28 Oct. 8/3 Trailer cars can be put on during the 'rush hours,' mornings and evenings. **1928** *Hearst's International* Aug. 101/1 I'm makin' the rush-hour express uptown as usual. — (3) **1901** MERWIN & WEBSTER *Calumet 'K'* 126 But if you ever try to put me on a rush job, I'll quit and buy a small farm. **1904** *N.Y. Ev. Post* 16 Aug. 3 The contractors kept the men at work, as it was a 'rush' job. — (4) **1913** *Chi. Record-Herald* 9 March 4/7 The rush order had caught him short a few hundred bands. **1950** *N.O. Times-Picayune Mag.* 5 Feb. 1/8 The customer . . . placed a rush order for a cake to give her estranged friend.

(5) **1906** SINCLAIR *Jungle* 124 Liable again to be kept overtime in rush seasons. — (6) **1903** *N.Y. Times* 24 Aug., Out in the Yellowstone National Park, probably beyond the reach of a rush telegram. —

(7) **1904** *N.Y. Herald* 17 Sep. 1 He stated that in six weeks rush work would be required to repair the boilers to make them serviceable.

b. *With a (perfect) rush, in a rush, on the rush,* in a hurry.

1841 *N.O. Picayune* 10 Dec. 2/2 They all traveled round to the old brushing ground where they 'go it with a rush.' **1845** SOL. SMITH *Theatr. Apprent.* 152 When you find yourself in possession of *four aces,* go it with a perfect rush. **1876** MARK TWAIN *Tom Sawyer* xviii. 149 He is always in such a rush that he never thinks of anything. **1898** *McClure's Mag.* X. 352 The gray-backs came through with a rush. **1901** JAMES *Sacred Fount* 75 Last night she was on the rush.

As the last term in **cane, center, dead, end, flag, gold, land, mining rush.**

***rush,** *v.*

1. *intr.* To make a good or perfect classroom recitation, to pass an examination with success. *Colloq.*

1848 *Yale Banger* 23 Oct., Then for the students mark flunks, even though the young men may be rushing. **1887** *Lippincott's Mag.* Aug. 291 The students gather in the recitation-rooms, where they 'rush' or 'flunk,' according as they have studied the night before or been 'out on a lark.'

b. *To rush it,* to do a thing energetically. *Colloq.*

*a***1856** in HALL *College Words* (ed. 2) 365 Leg it, put it, rush it, streak it. **1859** BARTLETT 375 The old negro is rushing it with his fiddle.

For *to rush the growler,* see ***growler, *n.* 2. b.**

2. a. To make (a fellow student) the object of a rush (cf. ***rush,** *n.*[2] 3). **b.** To keep company with a girl assiduously. **c.** To bestow attention on (a student) in connection with his or her joining a fraternity or sorority. Cf. ***rushing 1.** All *colloq.* or *slang.*

(a) **1876** *S.F. Dly. Ev. Post* 2 Oct. 3/6 The entire Sophomore Class at Williams College has been suspended for 'rushing' Freshmen. — (b) **1899** F. NORRIS *McTeague* 226 Marcus had 'taken up with' Salna a little after Trina had married, and had been 'rushing' her ever since. — (c) **1924** MARKS *Plastic Age* 62 He ought to be a good man for the fraternity. . . . We've got to rush him sure. **1946** THOMPSON *Amer. Daughter* 173 There were a lot of students who weren't rushed or pledged who found solace in the Y, in literary or musical clubs, but not Dora.

3. *tr.* **a.** To make (a region) the scene of a gold rush. *Obs.* **b.** (See quot.)

(a) **1878** I. L. BIRD *Rocky Mts.* 215 Even their [*sc.* Indians'] 'reservations' do not escape seizure practically; for if gold 'breaks out' on them they are 'rushed.' — (b) **1889** *Electrical Rev.* 30 Nov. 10/4 Nearly all [telegraph operators] are ambitious to send faster than the operator at the receiving station can write it down, or in other words to 'rush' him.

***rusher,** *n.*

1. An energetic, aggressive, "go-ahead" person. *Slang.*

1839 *N.O. Picayune* 27 March 2/2 'Aint he a rusher?' bawls out still a third, and exclamations of this kind rent the air. **1889** *Cent. Mag.* Oct. 874/1 The pretty girl from the East is hardly enough of a 'rusher' to please the young Western masculine taste. **1902** MCFAUL *Ike Glidden* 121 She's such a rusher 'twon't take her no time if I kin only git her.

transf. **1841** *N.O. Picayune* 7 Feb. 2/1 They had better make for the box-office in double-quick time, for if there is not a perfect 'rusher' of a house to hear that song of '*Sixty-two-hoo-hoo-hoo*' to-night, our reckoning is wrong.

2. *W.* One who participates in a rush to a newly found mining area, or to a region just opened to settlers. Cf. ***rush,** *n.*[2] **2, *rush,** *v.* **3. a.**

1871 DE VERE 629 *Rushers,* in California and all the gold-bearing districts of the West, is the comprehensive name of persons going to the mines. **1892** *Current Hist.* Nov. 433 As many of the 'rushers' are very poor, there is sure to be great suffering in the territory.

3. *Football.* A player in the rush line.

1883 *Atlantic Mo.* May 682/1 A handsome check of an attempt to break through the line of rushers, in a scrimmage . . . is recognized. **1893** POST *Harvard Stories* 25 The brown oval would go curving and spinning over the heads of the rushers.

As the last term in **center, gold rusher.**

***rushing,** *n.* and *a.*

1. Special attention paid by members of a fraternity or sorority to a new student to decide whether the student should be invited to membership. Also **rushing season, week.**

1878 *N. Amer. Rev.* March 236 'Hazing,' 'rushing,' secret societies . . . are unknown at Oxford and Cambridge. **1929** *Dly. Maroon* (Chi.) 8 Oct. 2/1 No pledges are made until the fourth day of rushing week. **1946** *Life* 18 Nov. 114/2 Howard has a normally lively interest in extracurricular activities like football, swimming, college dances . . . fraternity and sorority rushing. **1949** *Reader's Digest* Aug. 69/1 The rushing season, during which freshmen are pledged to the various houses, was in full swing.

b. (See quot.) *Rare.*

1888 BRYCE *Amer. Commonw.* III. VI. cii. 454 (*footnote*), Sophomores and freshmen have a whimsical habit of meeting one another in dense masses and trying which can push the other aside on the stairs or path. This is called 'rushing.'

2. rushing business, thriving, prosperous business.

1881 MARSHALL *Through Amer.* (1882) 93 Each and all of these have done a 'rushing' business during the past year. **1915** *Lit. Digest* 21 Aug. 338/2 All this time the soda-water stands were doing a rushing business.

***Russ,** *n. local.* [See quot. 1851.] A kind of stone and concrete pavement. In full **Russ pavement.** *Obs.*

1849 G. G. FOSTER *N.Y. in Slices* 9 The sight of the here-and-there patches of good, solid, smooth Russ pavement, puts us in a good humor. **1851** ROSS *In New York* 15, I must speak of a new form which is called the 'Russ Pavement,' named after Horace P. Russ, Esq., who first introduced it. **1896** HASWELL *New York* 542 The grooved and square-block pavement, known as the 'Russ,' was laid in Broadway but in a few years the surface of the blocks, from the hardness of the material, became so smooth as to impede traffic over them.

Russell Barlow knife, see **barlow.**

russet-backed thrush. A thrush, *Hylocichla ustulata.* Also **russet-back, russet thrush.**

1876 WHITMAN *Spec. Days* 86 Down in the apple-trees . . . were three or four russet-backed thrushes. **1881** WHITMAN *Diary* (1904) 58 The song of the catbird, wren, or russet thrush within hearing. **1917** *Birds of Amer.* III. 231 Russet-backed Thrush. *Hylocichla ustulata ustulata.* . . . Other Name.—Russet-back. *Ib.* 232/2 The Russet-backed Thrush must be considered as one of the positively beneficial birds. **1949** KITCHIN *Birds Olympic Peninsula* 198 The russet-backed thrush is decidedly a summer bird in western Washington.

***Russeting,** *n.* As the last term in **Roxbury, Shippen's Russeting.**

***Russian,** *a.* In combs.: (1) **Russian America,** a name for Alaska prior to its purchase by the U.S., *obs.;* (2) **breakbone fever,** (see quot.); (3) **stove,** a stove of a now undefinable type, *obs.;* (4) **thistle,** (see quot. 1931).

(1) **1811** tr. HUMBOLDT *Political Essay* II. 269 The new denominations of *Russian America,* or *Russian possessions in the new continent,* ought not to induce us to believe that the coast of the *Basin of Beering,* the peninsula *Alaska,* . . . have become Russian *provinces.* **1818** *Ann. 17th Congress* 1 Sess. 2139 Until 1816 the settlements of this Power did not reach to the southward of 55°, and were of no consideration, although dignified by them with the title of Russian America. *a***1918** G. STUART *On Frontier* I. 91 We called to them in Chinook jargon, which is understood by all Indians from here up to Russian America (now Alaska). — (2) **1904** *D.N.* II. 379 dengue, n. La grippe when first introduced into the oil country was called *dengue* and Russian *breakbone fever.* Not confined to oil regions. — (3) **1812** in *Essex Antiq.* I. (1897) 185 Great saving of fuel, and promotion of warmth and comfort. The Subscriber, having obtained a complete model of the most improved Russian Stove. — (4) **1931** CLUTE *Plants* 56 A prickly relative of the World's Fair plant, the saltwort (*Salsoli kali*), invaded America a generation or so ago and spread to the waste places where it became known as the Russian thistle and Russian cactus, though not closely related to either cactus or thistles. **1948** *Popular Western* June 27/2 He cached it in the roadside growth of Russian thistle.

Russia turnip. (See quot.) *Obs.* — **1819** COBBETT *Year's Residence* 101 The *Ruta Baga* is a sort of turnip well known in the State of New York, where, under the name of *Russia* turnip, it is used for the Table from February to July.

***rust,** *n.* (See quot.) See also **ash, black, French, rose rust.** — **1877** BARTLETT 543 *Rust,* discoloration in mackerel, sometimes caused by leakage of the brine in which they are packed.

rusticoat potato. A variety of potato with reddish-brown skin. *Colloq. Obs.* — **1775** in *Boston Transcript* 26 April III. 12/7, I have a fine prospect of a Crop of Rusty Coats Portators and winter Squashes this fall. **1782** J. ADAMS *Familiar Lett.* 404 But how much more luxurious it would be to me to dine . . . upon rusticoat potatoes with Portia!

***rustle,** *n. To get a rustle on,* to get a move on. *Colloq.* — **1892** CRANE *Maggie* (1896) 101 Hi, you, git a russle on yehs! **1899** C. W. GORDON *Sky Pilot* xxi, It's about time for me to get a rustle on.

***rustle,** *v.*

1. *tr.* To acquire (something) by putting forth effort; to collect, get together, forage around for. Freq. with *up. Colloq.*

*a*1846 *Quarter Race Ky.* 94 He nailed my thumb in his jaws, and rostled up a handful of dirt and throwed it in my eyes. **1891** *Advance* 29 Jan., Some of the members have arranged . . . to go out on the hills and 'rustle up' wood. **1924** MULFORD *Rustlers' Valley* vi, I can rustle you a snake in a minute. **1947** *Chi. Herald-Amer.* 2 Nov. (Comics) 5 Jist loan me . . . this shotgun an' some shells, an' we'll rustle all the food you kin eat.

b. To round up or herd together (livestock), esp. as a professional cowboy or ranchman. Also with *in, up. Colloq.*

1896 DICE *Counterfeiting Exposed* 30 [He] 'rustled' up a good big herd of cattle. **1903** A. ADAMS *Log of Cowboy* 53 Our foreman . . . sent Honeyman to rustle in the horses. **1910** RAINE *B. O'Connor* 88 Thought you was rustling cows for a living somewheres in burnt Arizona.

c. To acquire (livestock) by theft, to steal. *Colloq.*

1893 *Aberdeen* (S. Dak.) *Sun* 5 Jan. 7/4 Rustling cattle is an exciting trade and very profitable, but extremely hazardous. **1908** *Pacific Mo.* July 37/1 It was a good deal more profitable to 'rustle' calves than to raise them. **1948** *Range Riders Western* May 30/1, I ain't ever rustled a cow in my life.

2. *intr.* To move energetically or hurriedly, to look out *for oneself.* Also with *around. Colloq.*

1872 R. B. JOHNSON *Very Far West* 195, I've rustled upwards from a picayune printin' office down to New Orleans. **1884** MARK TWAIN *H. Finn* xii, We'll rustle around and gather up whatever pickin's we've overlooked. **1916** BOWER *Phantom Herd* 243 He turns you out thinking he'll let you rustle for yourself awhile.

***rustler,** *n.*

1. A lively, industrious, ambitious person. Cf. ***hustler.**

1872 MARK TWAIN *Roughing It* 333 But pard, he was a rustler! You ought to seen him get started once. **1901** GRINNELL *Gold Hunting in Alaska* 47 His companion was a 'rustler.'

b. An animal particularly given to foraging about for its provender, usu. **good rustler.** Cf. ***rustling,** *a.* **2.**

1881 ROMSPERT *Western Echo* 190 He is a good rustler and will find enough to live on. **1890** *Harper's Mag.* April 689/2 The California sheep . . . are of unusual size, known as 'rustlers,' because they must rustle about for their food. **1948** *Chi. Tribune* 9 Oct. 9/4 The flockmaster prefers his Karakuls for they are hardy, good rustlers, and require a minimum of care.

c. A cook on a ranch.

1887 *Scribner's Mag.* II. 508/1 The cook on a ranch used to be called a 'rustler.' **1902** CLAPIN 343 *Rustler,* . . . formerly, a ranchman's term for a cook, on a ranch, from the fact that the work incumbent to it requires considerable activity and energy.

2. A cattle thief.

1882 *N. Mex. Terr. Rep.* 98 The trail of the rustlers . . . was found. **1924** MULFORD *Rustlers' Valley* 219 Reckon they're watchin' for th' rustlers. **1947** *Denver Post* 25 Feb. 26/7 Well organized gangs . . . are 'mechanized rustlers' operating giant tandem trucks over little-traveled routes across the adjacent state lines into South Dakota and Nebraska.

b. rustlerdom, a region infested with cattle thieves. *Rare.*

1897 HOUGH *Story of Cowboy* 291 It was legally impossible to do so in any of the courts sitting in rustlerdom!

As the last term in **box, camp, cattle, horse rustler.**

***rustling,** *n.* **1.** Active, ambitious effort. Cf. ***hustling,** *a.* **2.** *W.* The stealing of cattle. Cf. **cattle rustling.**

(1) **1872** R. B. JOHNSON *Very Far West* 191 'Rustling' is an Americanism, denoting the process of fighting against odds for a living. **1909** O. HENRY *Roads of Destiny* 198 Both of us had seen rough times and plenty of rustling and danger. — (2) **1903** A. ADAMS *Log of Cowboy* 93, I know a few of the simple principles of rustling myself. **1947** *True* Nov. 92/3 All over the West there came a sudden and violent upswing in rustling.

***rustling,** *a.* **1.** Brisk, active, up-and-coming. *Colloq.* Cf. ***hustling,** *a.* **2.** Of range animals: Accustomed to foraging for themselves. Cf. ***rustler 1. b.**

(1) **1882** *Cent. Mag.* Aug. 508/2 To do a rustling business is to carry on an active trade. **1902** *Greenwood* (Ark.) *Democrat* 22 May 1/6 The rustling editor of the Greenwood Democrat was in town Saturday. — (2) **1890** *Stock Grower & Farmer* 29 March 4/2 The condition of rustling animals is . . . deplorable.

***rusty,** *a.* and *n.*

1. An encounter, fight, skirmish. *Slang. Obs.*

1835 BIRD *Hawks* II. 245 Neversomever, I'll try for a spell ag'in, and the next'll be a right-down rusty! **1837** ——— *Nick of Woods* I. 93 It war my idea to send a messenger after your party, in hopes your men would join us in the rusty.

2. In combs.: (1) **rusty blackbird,** a blackbird, *Euphagus carolinus,* found in the U.S. principally in migration and in winter, also **rusty-winged blackbird;** (2) **crow blackbird,** =prec.; (3) **-crowned falcon,** the sparrow hawk, *Falco sparverius;* (4) **dab,** a sand dab, *Limanda ferruginea,* common on the N. Eng. coast; (5) **flounder,** (see quot.); (6) **gold,** (see quot. 1881); (7) **grackle, =rusty blackbird;** (8) **stagbush,** (see quot.).

(1) **1851** GLISAN *Jrnl. Army Life* 89 Of the birds and animals not usually eatable, there are the . . . rusty-winged blackbird, blue-bird, buzzard, crow. **1946** *Nat. Geog. Mag.* Sep. 314/2 One finds nesting such birds as . . . Bonaparte's gull, rusty blackbird, and black-poll warbler, all of which range to the southward. — (2) **1844** *Nat. Hist. N.Y., Zoology* II. 137 The Rusty Crow Blackbird. *Quiscalus Ferrugineus.* . . . Their geographical range extends from 24° to 68° north. — (3) **1872** COUES *Key to Birds* 214 Rusty-crowned Falcon. . . . Crown ashy-blue, with a chestnut patch. **1917** *Birds of Amer.* II. 90. — (4) **1839** STORER *Mass. Fishes* 141 *P[latessa] ferruginea.* . . . The Rusty Dab. This species is occasionally brought to our market, in the winter season only.

(5) **1884** GOODE *Fisheries* I. 197 The Sand Dab, or Rough Dab, *Hippoglossoides platessoides,* also sometimes known as the Rusty Flounder, is taken in winter by the line fishermen of New England. — (6) **1872** TICE *Over Plains* 227 In the refining crucible this 'rusty gold' gives a regulus of 99 per cent. **1881** RAYMOND *Mining Gloss., Rusty gold,* Pac., free gold, which does not easily amalgamate, the particles being coated, as is supposed, with oxide of iron. — (7) **1811** WILSON *Ornithology* III. 41 [The] Rusty Grakle . . . frequents corn fields. **1917** *Birds of Amer.* II. 263 Rusty blackbird. . . . [Also called] Rusty Grackle. — (8) **1897** SUDWORTH *Arborescent Flora* 339 *Viburnum ferrugineum.* . . . Rusty Stagbush.

b. *To cut a rusty,* to cut a shine or dido (see also quot. 1920). *Colloq.*

1837 NEAL *Charcoal Sk.* (1838) 111 It won't do for us to be cutting rusties here at this time o' night. **1852** in *Mich. Hist. Mag.* IX. 397 Our Indians have been cutting up all sort of rustys. . . . most important . . . is the killing of Col. March and his company (80 in number), by the Camanches. **1920** HUNTER *Trail Drivers Texas* I. 300 [In cowboy lingo] '*cutting a rusty*' . . . means doing your best.

Rutherfordite ˈrʌðərfərdˌaɪt, *n.* [f. *Rutherford* Co., N.C.] (See quot. 1891.) — **1857** DANA *Mineralogy* 209. **1891** *Cent.* 5282/3 *Rutherfordite,* a rare and imperfectly known mineral found in the gold-mines of Rutherford county, North Carolina: it is supposed to contain titanic acid, cerium, etc.

***Rutland,** *n.* **1. Rutland beauty,** a species of bindweed, *Convolvulus sepium,* cultivated as a hedge. **2. Rutland wriggle,** (see quot.). *Obs.*

(1) **1847** WOOD *Botany* 444 Rutland Beauty . . . is cultivated as a shade for windows, arbors, &c. **1892** *Amer. Folk-Lore* V. 101. — (2) **1817** PAULDING *Lett. from South* I. 235 [American bucks] walked with the genuine *Rutland wriggle;* that is to say, on tiptoe, and with a most portentous extension of the hinder parts.

***rye,** *n.*

1. =**rye whisky.** Also a drink of this.

1890 *Buckskin Mose* 248 But for the quantity of rye we had all of us been swallowing, the others must have seen through this impudent operation. **1913** LONDON *Valley of Moon* 392 Some drink rain and some champagne . . . ; But I will try a little rye. **1949** *Sat. Ev. Post* 23 April 26/1 He ordered a double rye, downed it before I was halfway through my drink.

2. In combs.: (1) **rye-and-cornmeal,** =next, *obs.;* (2) **rye and Indian,** (*a*) bread made of a mixture of rye and cornmeal, in full **rye and Indian bread,** also **rye and Indian pudding,** (*b*) designating a region where such bread is commonly used, *obs.,* (*c*) **rye and Indian cloth,** cloth made of cotton and linen, *obs.;* (3) **coffee,** a drink prepared from roasted grains of rye or from toasted rye bread, now *hist.,* cf. **coffee essence;** (4) **drop-cake,** a drop-cake made of rye meal; (5) **gin,** gin made from rye, *obs.;* (6) **jack and bitters,** a drink made of rye, *obs.;* (7) **mush,** (see quot.); (8) **whisky,** whisky made from rye or from rye and malt, cf. **Monongahela rye whisky.**

(1) **1892** *Nation* 3 March 168/2 The receipts which I selected were mush, Johnny cake, and Boston rye-and-cornmeal bread. — (2) (*a*) **1805** *Pocumtuc Housewife* 6 Johnny cake or hoe cakes are a good change from Rye and Indian bread. *c*1880 HAZARD *Jonny-Cake P.* (1915) 27 This bread ['Rhineinjun'], vulgarly called nowa-days rye and Indian bread, in the olden time was always made of one quart of

unbolted Rhode Island rye meal to two quarts of the coarser grained parts of ambrosia [i.e., corn meal]. **1947** BEROLZHEIMER *Regional Cookbook* 52 Corn alone made too dry a bread, so it was combined with rye to make a bread called 'rye 'n' Injun.' **1949** *Sat. Ev. Post* 12 March 26/2 We had brown bread, johnnycake, rye and Indian pudding, and many other things that I would like to taste just once more. (*b*) **1839** *N.O. Picayune* 9 April 2/2 Hardly a mail arrives but we receive some 'rie-and-injun' country paper from the 'Far West' or 'Down East' with [Please Exchange] . . . written on the margin. (*c*) **1867** *Beadle's Mo.* May 431/1 The best rye an' indian cloth we could make, they wouldn't allow more'n a shillin' a yard for, pay out o' the shop. — **(3) 1769** *Boston Gazette* 16 Oct. 1/3 And as true Daughters of Liberty, they made their Breakfast upon Rye Coffee, and their Dinner was partly made of that sort of Venison called Bear. **1877** RUEDE *Sod-House Days* 99 Most people out here don't drink real coffee, because it is too expensive. . . . So rye coffee is used a great deal—partched brown or black according to whether the users like a strong or mild drink. [**1898** HARPER *S. B. Anthony* I. 14 A drink of 'coffee' [was] made by browning crusts of rye and Indian bread, pouring hot water over them and sweetening with maple syrup.] — **(4) 1891** JEWETT in *Atlantic Mo.* May 617 Rye drop-cakes, then, if they wouldn't give you too much trouble.

(5) 1858 *Harper's Mag.* May 854/2 Prior to the period of the general Temperance Reformation in New England, . . . every shopkeeper sold codfish and rye gin. — **(6) 1830** SANDS *Writings* II. 240 All her aches and symptoms had disappeared, in consequence of having taken . . . a glass of rye-jack and bitters. — **(7) 1871** DE VERE 41 In some parts of the West, another mush is frequently used, but as it is made of rye after the manner of a Hasty Pudding, it is called *Rye Mush.* — **(8) 1785** in RAMSEY *Tennessee* (1853) 297 Good distilled rye whiskey, at two shillings and six pence per gallon. **1853** *S. Lit. Messenger* XIX. 88/2 Ned Ellet . . . had taken in charge one Nash, a horse-thief, and also a tickler of rye whisky. **1948** *New Yorker* 6 Nov. 62/2 A glass, to them, is simply a *glass*, . . . rye whiskey is *rye*.

S

Saba bean. [*Saba*, an island in the West Indies.] A now unidentifiable kind or variety of bean. *Obs.* — **1793** *Holyoke Diaries* 128 Planted Corn & Beans & Sabea Bean. **1815** *Ib.* 162 Planted beans, Giraud, Saba & Cranberry.

sabatin ˌsabəˈtin, *n.* [Origin unknown.] (See quot.) — **1895** KING *New Orleans* 67 There were . . . potatoes, sabatins (a kind of egg-plant), figs, bananas, pecans, pumpkins.

Sabbaday ˈsæbəˌde, *n. N. Eng.*

1. A colloquial contraction of "Sabbath day."

*c*1772 *Essex Inst. Coll.* LVI. 292 Thare was in the yeare 1738 a great athcak one sabbady. **1841** *N.O. Picayune* 7 April 2/2, I go to meetin twice every Sabba-day. **1935** LINCOLN *Cape Cod Yesterdays* 5, I knew that, when I next dressed, it would be in the prim and stiff and spotless garments befitting what Grandmother often said her mother used to call 'Sabba' Day.'

2. Sabbaday house, (see quot. *a*1870). *Obs.*

*a*1870 CHIPMAN *Notes on Bartlett* 375 *Sabba'day-Houses.* Cottages near a church had for warmth, &c., at recess of public worship.—Old New England use. **1891** EARLE *Sabbath* 102 The 'noon-house,' or 'Sabba-day house' or 'horse-hows' . . . was a place of refuge in the winter time, at the noon interval between the two services.

* **Sabbath,** *n.* In combs.: (1) **Sabbath-day house,** = **Sabbaday-house;** (2) **-keeper,** one who observes Saturday, the seventh day of the week, as a day of rest and worship; (3) **warden,** formerly in N. Eng., an officer to enforce laws governing Sabbath observance, *obs.*

(1) **1887** EGGLESTON in *Cent. Mag.* April 906/2 This extreme scrupulosity about Sabbath-keeping was doubtless the moving cause of the building of the 'Sabbath-day houses.' **1936** *D.N.* VI. 556 Sabbath-day houses, Sunday houses. These were small two-roomed houses, built not far from a meeting house. . . . (They are found outside Connecticut, also; for example, in Fredericksburg, Texas.—Ed.) — (2) **1844** RUPP *Relig. Denominations* 73 There were many other severities practised upon the Sabbath-keepers in New England. **1901** STILLMAN *Autobiog. Journalist* I. 5 All who did not hold to the finest scruple of conscience . . . were excluded from the communion as a precaution against the Sunday keepers becoming a majority in the church and taking it away from the Sabbath keepers. — (3) **1766** *Duxbury Rec.* 340 Jacob Peterson and Robert Samson were chosen Sabbath Wardens.

b. *To travel beyond the Sabbath,* (see quot.). *Obs.*

1826 FLINT *Recoll.* 178 It is a common proverb of the people, that when we cross the Mississippi, 'we travel beyond the Sabbath.'

Sabbath ˈsæbəθ, *v. intr.* To spend the Sabbath. *Rare.* — **1730** B. LYNDE *Diary* (1880) 17 Sabbathed at Mr. Claps, and at Lord's Supper with him. **1732** *Ib.* 27 Sabbath'd at York.

Sabbatia səˈbetɪə, *n.* [Liberatus *Sabbati*, eighteenth-century It. Botanist.] A genus of erect, unbranched annual or biennial herbs of the family Gentianaceae. Also (not *cap.*) a plant of this genus. Cf. **American centaury.**

1847 DARLINGTON *Agric. Botany* 260 S. angularis, *Pursh.* . . . Angular Sabbatia. Centaury. **1891** *Cent.* 5286/3 The various species are called most often by the generic name *Sabbatia*, and sometimes by the book-name *American centaury.* **1949** *Nat. Hist.* June 278/3 On grassy, pine-sprinkled savannas, in the company of gaudy sabbatias, insignificant burmannias, and orange habenarias, this curious plant spreads its leafy rosettes.

* **Sabbatical,** *a. Educ.* Denoting a time of absence from duty for purposes of study and travel given to school teachers at certain intervals. Also absol. and transf.

1903 *N.Y. Ev. Post* 19 Sep., Professors Willcox and Kendall will be absent during the year on sabbatical leave. **1946** HOWE *We Happy Few* 18 Then when Papa had his sabbatical, we went to Paris. **1949** *Time* 18 Dec. 12/2 Kennan announced that he was leaving the State Department 'on sabbatical leave.'

sabe ˈsæbɪ, *n.* [See next.] Understanding, knack, practical knowledge. *Colloq.* Cf. **savvy,** *n.*

1875 HARTE in *Scribner's Mo.* Dec. 244 A little keer and a little *sabe* on my part, and there's that family in the gulch made comfortable. **1913** LONDON *Valley of Moon* 311 We ain't got the *sabe*, or the knack, or something or other. **1931** *Lariat* April 53 (Bentley), You ain't got much sabe.

sabe ˈsæbɪ, *v. W.* [Sp. *saber*, to know. See note.] To understand or comprehend. *Colloq.* Cf. **savvy,** *v.* and see *no sabe* (or *savvy*) *s.v.* * **no,** *adv.* and *a.* **3.**

Our evidence for this verb and for **sabe,** *n.*, and for **savvy,** *n.* and *v.*, indicate that they are all new borrowings from the Spanish in the Southwest and not continuations of the *savey, savvy,* given in the *OED q.v.*

1850 *Calif. Courier* (S.F.) 6 Sep. 2/3 Ha! *Sabe* that? **1879** *Scribner's Mo.* Oct. 814/2, 'I sabe.' The Judge dropped into slang as Silas Wegg descended to poetry. **1913** *Sat. Ev. Post* 1 Nov. 66/4 You saved the Titan Company a makeover and another day's pay for seventy extra people! *Sabe?*

Saber Club. (See quots.) *Obs.* — **1876** *Cong. Rec.* 9 Aug. 5347/1 They call themselves 'rifle clubs' and 'saber clubs.' We have them in every county in South Carolina and in some counties we have several. **1879** TOURGEE *Fool's Errand* xl. 295 The Klan, and its more subtle and complete successors, under various and sundry names, 'Rifle-Clubs,' 'Sabre-Clubs,' 'Bull-dozers,' and so forth, had fully established themselves throughout the country.

Sabines ˈsebinz, *n. pl.* [f. *Sabine* River.] (See quots.) — **1945** *Reader's Digest* March 77/1 With 20,000 other Creoles, Cajuns, . . . Sabines—the mixed folk of south Louisiana—Alcée is going to trap muskrats. **1947** *Chi. Tribune* 21 Dec. (Grafic Mag.) 9/2 With the approval of the Southern Baptist Convention, he began missionary work among the Sabines, a term used colloquially for the forgotten people of Bayou Grand Caillou and Bayou du Large, the swamp rivers running to the Gulf of Mexico.

Sac sæk, *n.* ["Osākiwŭg, 'people of the outlet,' or, possibly, 'people of the yellow earth,' in contradistinction from the Muskwakiwuk, 'Red Earth People,' a name of the Foxes" (Hodge 471/1).]

1. An Indian of an Algonquian tribe formerly living in Michigan, later in Wisconsin and Illinois, and now in Oklahoma, Iowa, and Kansas. Also *pl.*, the tribe of such an Indian. Cf. **Sauk.**

[**1670** *Relations des Jésuites* (1858) 98/1 Leur langue . . . est la même que celle des Saki. **1722** COXE *Descr. Carolana* 48 The Nations who dwell on this River, are Outogamis, . . . Sacky, and the Poutouatamis.] **1804** *Fredericktown* (Md.) *Herald* 30 June 2/4 On their passage down the Missouri, five of their party were killed by the Sacquias. **1810** *Ann. 12th Congress* 1 Sess. 1858 A considerable number of Sacs went . . . to see the British superintendent. **1900** *Cong. Rec.* 26 Jan. 1221/1 What was the number of Indians . . . known as the Sac and Fox of the Mississippi, residing in the State of Iowa?

2. Attrib. with **chief, Indian, nation, tribe.**

1789 *Ann. 1st Congress* 41 [The treaties] with the sachems and warriors of the Wyandot, Delaware, . . . and Sac nations, . . . appear to have been negotiated [etc.]. **1840** *Niles' Reg.* 8 Aug. 356/2 The Sac and Fox Indians and Winnebagoes have had a talk. **1862** *Harper's Mag.* Sep. 463/2 The household traps and plunder of a Sac chief. **1877** JOHNSON *Anderson Co., Kans.* 137 The Sac and Fox tribes of Indians were located on a reservation in Franklin and Osage counties.

sacahuista ˌsɑkəˈwistə, *n. S.W.* [Amer. Sp. *zacahuiscle* (<Nahuatl).] (See quot. 1931.) Also attrib. — **1896** *Houston* (Tex.) *D. Post* 19 April, For some four or five hours my pony stumbled around in the sacuista grass. **1931** DAYTON *Western Browse Plants* 15 Plants of the related genera, sotol (Dasylirion) and sacahuista or beargrass (Nolina), are also sometimes machine-cut or shredded, like soapweed, as emergency feed or silage, especially for cattle.

sacalait ˈsækəˌle, *n.* [See quot. 1937, and W. A. Read in *Internat. Jrnl. Amer. Linguistics*, Oct. 1945, p. 237–8.] A name applied locally to various fish, as the crappie and killie.

1884 GOODE *Fisheries* I. 407 The Crappie—*Pomoxys annularis.* . . . Other names are . . . 'Sac-a-lait' and 'Chinquapin Perch' in the Lower Mississippi. *Ib.* 466 *Fundulus grandis*, is known at Pensacola by the name of 'Sac-à-lait.' **1931** READ *La.-French* 67 In Louisiana the final *t* of *sacalait* is silent and the word is pronounced by the French in French fashion; by the English approximately like *sackalay*, with the chief stress either on the first or on the last syllable. **1937**——in *Zeitschrift* LXI. 82 *Sacalait*, The Louisiana name for the Crappie (*Poxomis annularis* Raf.), commonly thought to have been suggested by the beautiful white flesh or the silvery appearance of this fish. The actual source of the name is Choctaw *sakli*, 'trout,' French *sac à lait* being merely a typical example of folk etymology. On Bernard Romans' *Map of Florida*, 1774, the name of a lagoon appears as *Sakale*. **1949** *N.O. Times-Picayune Mag.* 16 Oct. 20/3 If you run out of bait while the bream, sacalait, and other fish are practically jumping into your boat, then the lily is your friend.

sacaton ˌsækəˈton, *n.* [Amer. Sp. *zacatón* (<Nahuatl), in same sense.] A coarse perennial grass of the Southwest, *Sporobolus wrighti*. In full **sacaton grass.**

1846 ABERT *Exam. N. Mex.* 29 As there were no pasture grounds near the village, I was forced to buy 'zacate' for my mules. **1886** *Outing* Dec. 223/2 We came upon a caved-in well, a wide hollow with a black bottom, covered with high rank grass, the Mexican *zacaton.* **1936** MCKENNA *Black Range* 177 The Indians . . . crept from rock to rock; they crawled like snakes from one bunch of sacatone to another. **1937** NICHOL *Natural Vegetation Ariz.* 197 Today much of this drifting sand with sparsely scattered clumps of sacaton grass. **1942** CASTETTER & BELL *Pima & Papago Agric.* 22 Along the edges and in the openings of the forests of these two drainages, sacaton grass (*Sporobolus Wrightii*) thrives.

sacatra ˈsækətrə, *n.* [F., of obscure origin.] (See quot.) — **1859** BARTLETT 375 *Sacatra*, the name given in Louisiana to the offspring of a griffe and a negress.

sachamaker ˈsetʃəˌmekɚ, *n.* [See next.] =next. *Obs.* Cf. **sagamore.**

1675 *Doc. Hist. N.Y.* XII. 519 The 20th inst. three of the Nevisans Sachemakas, were here with me. **1682** *Indian Laws & Tr.* III. 696 The said Sachemakers doe hereby acknowledge themselves fully satisfyed. **1687** BLOME *Isles & Terr. in Amer.* 103 Another made a Speech to the Indians, in the Name of all the Sachamakers or Kings. **1701** WOOLEY *Journal N.Y.* (1902) 44 When we were at dinner . . . , a Sackmaker or King came in with several of his Attendants.

sachem ˈsetʃəm, *n.* [f. some Algonquian word as *sachimau*, *sakimau*, chief.]

1. An Indian chief or sagamore. Now *hist.*

1622 MOURT *Relation* 113 They brought vs to their Sachim . . . very personable, gentle, courteous, and fayre conditioned. **1771** TAYLOR *Voyage* 197 Their *Sachems* and chief warriors call an assembly. **1839** *Mass. H.S. Coll.* 3 Ser. IX. 93 Before this country was visited by the Europeans, it is believed that the sagamore and sachem . . . came to their offices by hereditary right. **1945** WEBSTER *Town Meeting Country* 12 Eight traders were killed by Indians subject to Sassacus, sachem of the Pequots.

b. The common kingbird, *Tyrannus tyrannus*, of the eastern states, noted for its pugnacious defense of its nest.

1643 WILLIAMS *Key* 94 *Sachim:* a little Bird about the bignesse of a swallow, or lesse, to which the *Indians* give that name because of its *Sachim* or Princelike courage and Command over greater Birds, that a man shall often see this small Bird pursue and vanquish and put to flight the Crow, and other Birds farre bigger than it selfe. **1871** DE VERE 379 The Scissor-tail (*Tyrannus carolinensis*) . . . does not shrink from attacking even hawks and eagles in defence of his young. The Narragansett Indians and other tribes called him, in appreciation of his bravery, the Sachem.

2. The head of any government, a political leader.

1684 *Doc. Hist. N.Y. State* I. 402 Wee have put ourselves under the Great Sachim Charles that lives over the Great Lake. **1776** J. ADAMS *Works* IX. 387 The patricians, the sachems, the nabobs, call them by what name you please, sigh, and groan, and fret. **1817** *Mass. Spy* 2 April (Th.), There is a respect due to our sachems, which this vulgar state of things diminishes. **1856** *Ill. State Reg.* (Springfield) 1 May 1/5 He is high priest, the great sachem of abolitionism. **1861** *Charleston* (S.C.) *Mercury* 29 March 1/2 The Sachems of the Black Republican party did not appreciate the peculiarity of the times when they enacted the Morrill Tariff. **1949** *Sat. Ev. Post* 11 June 109/1 The home-office sachems have more time for reflection, but they are in some danger of becoming elder statesmen, nodding over dispatches from the battlefield.

3. A governing officer of the Tammany Society in N.Y. City or one of its early associated societies, esp. **Grand Sachem,** the chief officer of a Tammany Society.

[**1786** in KILROE *St. Tammany* 95 The example of these holy Sachems, has had a great effect.] **1787** *Ib.* 120 The members of St. Tammany's Society in the City of New York are requested to meet at their wigwam. . . . By the order of the Sachem. **1861** *N.Y. Herald* 7 Jan. 5/1 'The braves, warriors and sachems of the Columbian order' will 'rally round the council board.' **1905** *Springfield W. Republican* 15 Dec. 1 Congressman W. Bourke Cockran was elected grand sachem of Tammany Hall in New York last week.

4. A water pipe or hose. *Rare.*

1889 S. HALE *Letters* 226 Peter Larkin came and coupled the sachem and turned on the ram.

5. sachem snake, (see quots.).

1842 *Nat. Hist. N.Y., Zoology* III. 39 In Suffolk county, a large snake resembling this [milk snake] has been described to me under the name of Sachem Snake. **1910** HODGE *Amer. Indians* II. 402/1 A Long Island serpent, probably the milk-snake, has been called sachem-snake.

As the last term in **Indian, Mohegan, squaw, sub, Tammany sachem.**

sachemdom ˈsetʃəmdəm, *n.* The district governed by a sachem. *Obs.*

1764 HUTCHINSON *Hist. Mass.* I. 459 There seems to have been two cantons or sachemdoms of the Cape Indians. **1794** STILES *Hist. Judges of Charles I.* 109 King Philip's war . . . was attended with exciting an universal rising . . . of the Indians through New-England, except the Sachemdom of Uncas, at Mohegan. **1859** [see **sachemship**].

sachemess ˈsetʃəmɪs, *n.* The wife of a sachem. *Obs.* — **1761** NILES *Indian Wars* II. 327 When the sachemess, or squaw sachem, . . . saw the fate of her husband, she was more flexible.

sachemic ˈsetʃəmɪk, *a.* Of or pertaining to a sachem. *Obs.* — **1781** S. PETERS *Hist. of Conn.* 56 Such as did not acknowledge his sachemic power, were compelled to suffer death. **1885** J. S. KINGSLEY *Stand. Nat. Hist.* VI. 163 The sachemic office was hereditary [among the Five Nations], descending, not from father to son, but to the sister's children.

sachemship ˈsetʃəmˌʃɪp, *n.* The office or jurisdiction of a sachem. Now *hist.*

1651 *Conn. Rec.* I. 228 Hee is not satisfied in Saquassens being exalted vnder our power to great Sachemship. **1859** BARTLETT 375 *Sachemdom*, or *Sachemship*, the government or jurisdiction of a sachem. **1880** *Lib. Universal Knowl.* X. 870 [The Oneidas were] divided into three clans . . . and nine sachemships. **1881** L. H. MORGAN *Houses Amer. Aborigines* 28 Fifty Sachemships were created and named in perpetuity.

***sack,** *n.* In combs.: (1) **sack pants,** loose-fitting trousers, *obs.;* (2) **suit,** a man's suit having a sack coat.

(1) **1856** KANE *Arctic Explor.* II. 98 [My outfit] consists of— . . . an extra jumper and sack-pants for sleeping. — (2) **1895** *N.Y. Dramatic News* 6 July 14/4 Four button sack suit, $25. **1908** O. HENRY *Options* 194 One of them . . . 'roller-coasters' flew the track and killed a man in a brown sack-suit. **1943** in MENCKEN *Supp.* I. (1945) 462/1 Our *lounge suits* are their *sack suits.*

b. *To hold* (or *to be left to hold*) *the sack,* to be left in the lurch. *Colloq.*

1904 W. H. SMITH *Promoters* 343 They are the ones that are always left to hold the sack. **1949** *Chi. D. News* 8 Aug. 10/4 It seems to me that Uncle Sam is holding the sack right now.

As the last term in **bed, carpet, coffee, cotton, crocus, dressing, grip, meal, medicine, pack, paper, possible, tobacco, son-of-a-gun** (or **bitch**)**-in-a-sack.**

***sack,** *v. Logging. tr.* and *intr.* To follow a log drive and roll into deep water those logs that have grounded or lodged (see also 2nd quot. 1905). Also **sacking,** *n.* and *attrib.*

1860 *Harper's Mag.* XX. (*OED*), Another frequent and laborious part of the drive is sacking. **1902** WHITE *Blazed Trail* 334 Intense rivalry existed as to which crew 'sacked' the farthest down stream in the course of the day. **1905** *Forestry Bureau Bul.* No. 61, 45 *Sack the rear, to,* to follow a drive and roll in logs which have lodged or grounded. *Ib., Sack the slide, to,* to return to a slide logs which have jumped out. **1908** WHITE *Riverman* 12 The moving of them [*sc.* stranded logs] was deferred for the 'sacking crew.'

***sacker,** *n.* One who "sacks" logs in a drive. — **1902** S. E. WHITE *Blazed Trail* lii. 360 It was noon. The sackers looked up in surprise.

Sacramento ˌsækrəˈmento, *n.* [Name of a river and of the capital city of California.] In combs.: (1) **Sacramento fever,** app. a form of typhoid pneumonia, *obs.;* (2) **perch,** a fresh-water fish, *Archoplites interruptus*, something like the perch, found in the Sacramento and other rivers of the Pacific Coast; (3) **pike,** the squawfish or yellowbelly, *Ptychocheilus oregonensis*, or a related species.

(1) **1849** JOHNSON *Sights Gold Region* 189 This produces the disease known as the Sacramento fever, resembling the congestive fever of the north, but more fatal. — (2) **1883** *Nat. Museum Bul.* No. 27, 461. **1911** *Rep. Fisheries 1908* 315/1 *Sacramento perch* . . . , sunfish of the Sacramento and an excellent food fish. **1947** DALRYMPLE *Panfish* 186 The Sacramento Perch, *Archoplites interruptus*, . . . is high on the Westerner's list of game-and-eating fishes. — (3) **1883** *Nat. Museum Bul.* No. 27, 487 Sacramento 'Pike'; 'Whitefish.' . . . In cold streams

its flesh is excellent. **1947** DALRYMPLE *Panfish* 320 There is very little difference between this fish and the Squawfish, or Sacramento Pike.

* **sacred,** *a.* In combs.: (1) **sacred bean,** the American lotus or water chinquapin, *Nelumbo lutea;* (2) **concert,** a term allegedly used in N.Y. City for Sunday musical concerts, to avoid the appearance of desecrating the Sabbath, *obs.;* (3) **dance,** (see quot.), *obs.;* (4) **desk,** the pulpit; (5) * **fire,** a ceremonial fire burned as a rite by Indians, esp. by those of the Pueblo tribes of New Mexico; (6) **Harp,** (also not *cap.*) the title of any one of several songbooks esp. popular in the South, a songbook having this title, also **Sacred Harp singing,** a community singing in which such a book is used.

(1) **1817–8** EATON *Botany* (1822) 361 Sacred bean. . . . A most superb plant. **1919** HOUSE *Wild Flowers N.Y.* I. 97 The Indian Lotus or Sacred Bean (*Nelumbo nelumbo* (Linnaeus) Karsten), with large pink flowers, is frequent in cultivation. — (2) **1855** BUCHELE *Land* 303 Schon vor Jahren wurde durch sogenannte 'Sacred'-Concerte der Anfang gemacht. — (3) **1858** in *Minn. Hist. Bul.* II. (1918) 505 Among the Dakotas a most remarkable society exists which is called Wakan wachepe, or Sacred Dance, of which the medicine sack is the badge. — (4) **1772** *Boston Gazette* 28 Sep. (Th.), [That they] should select a Runagate to be their Monitor from the sacred desk. **1866** *Cong. Globe* 24 Jan. 401/3, I have seen in the sacred desk what were called eloquent clergymen, full Africans.

(5) **1849** *31st Congress* 1 Sess. Sen. Ex. Doc. No. 64, 68 The old man and his daughter . . . were tending the sacred fire at Pecos. **1899** CUSHMAN *Hist. Indians* 364 The women . . . [were] seated on skins close to the place of burial or sacred fire. — (6) **1854** *(title)*, Sacred Harp A Collection of Psalm and Hymn Tunes, Odes, and Anthems. **1933** JACKSON *White Spirituals* 94 B. F. White and E. J. King produced the first edition of the *Sacred Harp* in Hamilton, Harris County Georgia, in 1844. **1944** *Democrat* 13 July 3/3 The Five-County Sacred Harp Singing Convention will be held at Huxford, Alabama, on July 27th. Come and br[i]ng your sacred harp.

* **sacrifice,** *n.*

1. In baseball, a bunt to allow a base runner to advance but resulting in the putting out of the batter, in full **sacrifice hit.** Also **sacrifice hitter.**

1880 *Chi. Inter-Ocean* 29 June 8/2 Anson's sacrifice hit and out advanced Williamson to third. **1889** *Sporting Life* (Phila.) 14 Aug. 5/3 Smith . . . is one of the best sacrifice hitters in the profession. **1893** *Chi. Record* 8 July 2/1 Reilly's sacrifice, followed by Allen's single and a wild pitch, brought him around with a score. **1948** *McAlester* (Okla.) *News-Capital* 3 July 6/1 Duncan combined two walks, a sacrifice hit, and an infield putout to score one run and take a first inning lead.

2. sacrifice rock, among American Indians, a rock, esp. one of peculiar appearance or shape, regarded as sacred. *Obs.*

1802 *Mass. H.S. Coll.* 2 Ser. III. 7 [The Indians] still however preserve a regard for sacrifice rocks, on which they cast a stick or stone, when they pass by them.

* **sacrifice,** *v.* **1.** *intr.* In baseball, to make a sacrifice hit. **2.** *tr.* To enable (a base runner) to advance as the result of a sacrifice.

(1) **1912** *Amer. Mag.* May 114/1 The batter twice attempted to sacrifice, failed and was forced to hit. **1948** *Chi. Tribune* 27 March II. 3/1 You're going to be called on more than any one player on the team to sacrifice. — (2) **1915** *Chi. Tribune* 13 Oct. 13/2 In the second Luderus led with a single and was sacrificed ahead. **1948** *Green Bay* (Wis.) *Press-Gazette* 12 July 15/1 Kubiak got life on the miscue to open the inning and was sacrificed to second by Johanson.

* **saddle,** *n.* [The origin of the word in sense **1.** is not clear. It may be related to *EDD sattle, v.*, to induct a minister into a charge.]

1. ?The charge or fee paid by an officer upon the assumption of his duties. *Rare.*

1773 *Md. Hist. Mag.* XV. 57 The strongest reason ag[ains]t High fees to officers is the Saddles they Pay, & if by a Law they were obliged to swear they payed no saddles &c I would willingly give them Liberall Allowances, as it would secure the Residence of the Principall Officers among us.

2. A pair of numbers in a policy game (see quot. 1938).

1882 MCCABE *New York* 551 If a single number is chosen and drawn, he wins $5; two numbers constitute a 'saddle.' **1938** ASBURY *Sucker's Prog.* 92 *Saddle*—Two numbers to appear anywhere on the list. Odds, 32 to 1. *Station Saddle*—Two numbers to appear at specified positions on the list. Odds, 800 to 1. *Capital Saddle*—Two of the first three numbers drawn. Odds, 500 to 1.

3. (See quot.)

1905 *Forestry Bureau Bul.* No. 61, 45 *Saddle*, the depression cut in a transverse skid in a skid road to guide the logs which pass over it. (P[acific] C[oast] F[orest].)

4. In combs.: (1) * **saddleback,** (see quots.), in full **saddleback caterpillar;** (2) **-backed,** *a.* placed astride like a saddle, *obs.;* (3) **-bag John,** a nickname for Gen. John Pope (1822–92), *obs.;* (4) **blanket,** a blanket for use under a saddle; (5) **colored,** *a.* of a tan color, *colloq.;* (6) **gun,** a short, light gun for carrying on horseback; (7) **horn,** the pommel of a saddle, cf. * **horn,** *n.* **1;** (8) **leaf,** (see quot. 1931); (9) **man,** a traveler on horseback, *obs.;* (10) **mat,** *W.* a kind of saddle blanket; (11) **mule,** a mule suitable for riding; (12) **pockets,** saddlebags; (13) **riders,** =prec., *rare;* (14) **Rock,** *local* (see quot. 1891), said to have been so called from a rock of this name in Little Neck Bay, Long Island, in full **Saddle Rock oyster;** (15) **scabbard,** (see quot. 1944); (16) **string,** a string attached to a saddle for tying things on it; (17) **train,** *W.* a train or procession of animals carrying packs or passengers, *obs.;* (18) * **tree,** (see quot. 1891 and cf. **saddleleaf**); (19) **wise,** *adv.* athwart, across, *obs.*

(1) **1891** *Cent.* 5297/2 *Saddleback*, . . . the larva of the bombycid moth *Empretia stimulea:* so called on account of the saddle-like markings on the back. **1908** KELLOGG *Amer. Insects* (ed. 2) 384 The saddle-back caterpillar, *Sibine* (Empretia) *stimulea*, has a striking squarish green blotch on the back. **1928** LEONARD *Insects N.Y.* 535 S[ibine] stimulea Clem. Saddle-back. — (2) **1878** J. H. BEADLE *Western Wilds* xxx. 487 Colorado is divided nearly down the center by the main chain of the Rocky Mountains—or, in miner's phrase, 'saddle-backed across the range.' — (3) **1884** *Cent. Mag.* Oct. 815 Pope was saddled with the title of 'Saddle-bag John,' in memory of his famous order about head-quarters being on horseback. — (4) **1737** in *So. Hist. Jrnl.* V. 89 Yet saddle blanket and pistol holsters could not be made so neatly with you. **1817** FORDHAM *Narr. Travels* 98 My cloak and saddle-blanket, spread on the floor, form my couch. **1949** *Southwestern Jrnl. Anthrop.* Winter 383 On one trip he carried with him one 'chief blanket' and three saddle blankets.

(5) **1854** THORPE *Master's House* 260 That 'saddle-colored' nigger grinning at me . . . would be all the better for about 'forty-five,' well laid on. — (6) **1886** *Outing* April 7/1, [I] had with me the little forty-sixty Winchester saddle gun. **1949** *10 Story Western* May 21/1 They jerked the saddle guns from their scabbards. — (7) **1856** A. CARY *Married* 184 The bridle rein was twisted around the saddle horn. **1949** *Boston Sun. Globe* 1 May (Fiction Mag.) 12/5 He eyed the canteen that some thoughtful person had slung over the saddle horn. — (8) **1820** in MATHEWS *Mem. Charles Mathews* (1839) III. 149 If you have not got any in the grounds, a saddle-leaf is beautiful. **1931** CLUTE *Plants* 39 The tulip tree (*Liriodendron tulipifera*) was called saddle-leaf because the young leafblades in the bud were bent back across the petiole in such a way as to retard the growth of the tip and make it appear as if cut square across. — (9) **1819** AMPHLETT *Emigrant's Directory* 71 *Saddle-men*, as they are termed here, command the best attentions of the host.

(10) **1883** *Cent. Mag.* Aug. 523/1 Mats, called 'cocas,' . . . are much sought after by California ranchmen as saddle-mats. — (11) **1826** in *Overland to Pacific* II. 163, I bought a Saddle mule . . . for $100. cash—The Price is high, but the mule is very good. **1915** YOUNG *Hard Knocks* 165 Get up on that saddle mule. — (12) **1903** STILES *Four Years* 243, I carried nothing on my horse save a pair of very contracted saddle pockets and the cape of my overcoat. **1931** DOBIE *Coronado's C.* 208 He gathered enough of the nuggets to fill his saddle pockets. — (13) **1856** *Porter's Spirit of Times* 1 Nov. 140/1 Drawing a bottle out of his *saddle riders*, says he, boys, here is to the old Spirit. — (14) **1852** *Lantern* (N.Y.) II. 158/1 Oyster House sages . . . acknowledge that for a consideration they will puff anything from Saddle Rock Oysters to Fancy Soap. **1865** BROWNE *Four Years in Secessia* 279 The stewing of 'Saddle-Rocks' in a chafing dish, or the preparation of a lobster salad, was as far as I had ever advanced in the mysteries of the cuisine. **1891** *Cent.* 5298/1 *Saddle-rock*, . . . a variety of the oyster, *Ostrea virginica*, of large size and thick, rounded form.

(15) **1898** CANFIELD *Maid of Frontier* 185 His horse came up to his ranch . . . with the gun still in the saddle scabbard. **1944** ADAMS *W. Words* 137/1 saddle scabbard A heavy saddle-leather case in which to carry a rifle or Winchester when riding. The gun fits in as far as the hammer, leaving the stock exposed. — (16) **1907** WHITE *Arizona Nights* 102 My eyes filled with tears from the wind of our going. Saddle strings streamed behind. — (17) **1861** *Harper's Mag.* Feb. 299/2 Fortunately, a saddle-train which had passed to Genoa . . . returned a little after daylight. **1896** SHINN *Story of Mine* 51 Saddle trains were started for passengers before any vehicle could get over the passes. — (18) **1843** *Penny Cyclo.* XXV. 34/2 *Tulip-tree.* . . . In America where it is native, it is also known by the names White

wood, Canoe wood, Saddle-tree. **1891** *Cent.* 6525/3 *Tulip-tree*. . . . An old name, *saddletree* or *saddle-leaf*, refers to the form of the leaf. — **(19) 1830** *Ky. Reporter* 17 Feb., A loin of mutton was on the table, and a gentleman opposite took the carving knife in hand. 'Shall I cut it saddlewise?' said he. **1867** De Voe *Market Ass't* 71 'Shall I cut this loin of mutton saddle-wise?' 'No,' said his friend. 'Cut it bridle-wise, for then we may have a chance to get a *bit* in our mouths.'

b. *S.* (See quots.) *Colloq.*

1937 *D.N.* VI. 621 His cheery greeting to a horseman to *light and look at his saddle* is about the most hospitable invitation to dinner to be encountered. **1944** Clark *Pills* 54 'Ride up and get down and look at your saddle!' was a southern countryman's favorite greeting.

As the last term in **California, cow, cowboy, cross, double rig, gig and, hogskin, Indian, macheer, Mexican, Mexican peak, McClellan, mountain, sawbuck, side, Spanish, squaw, stock, wagon saddle.**

* **saddle,** *v.*

1. *tr.* To fasten (a bird's nest) on a limb somewhat in the manner of a saddle.

1831 Audubon *Ornith. Biog.* I. 303 The nests were fixed to a horizontal bough, but were not *saddled* upon it so deeply as those of the Wood Thrush are. **1881** *Amer. Naturalist* XV. 217 [The nest of the short-legged pewee] was saddled to a horizontal limb after the fashion of our wood pewee. **1940** *U.S. Nat. Museum Bul.* No. 176, 321 It was about 30 feet from the ground, saddled on a horizontal branch of a maple over the trail.

2. a. (See quot.) **b.** *To saddle the market,* (see quot.).

(a) 1857 H. E. Bishop *Floral Home* 139 The logs are notched at each end, upon the under side, 'Saddled' or ridged upon the upper, and piled up cob-house fashion. — **(b) 1870** Medbery *Men Wall St.* 137 Saddling the market, is to foist a certain stock on the street.

saddle-bag ˈsædl̩bæg, *v. intr.* To catch on an obstruction and double about it in a manner suggestive of saddlebags. *Colloq.* — **1884** Mark Twain *H. Finn* xiii, They went a-floating down, stern first, about two mile, and saddle-baggsed [*sic*] on the wreck. **1905** *Forestry Bureau Bul.* No. 61, 45 *Saddlebag*, as applied to a boom, to catch on an obstruction and double around it.

* **saddler,** *n.* **1.** A saddle horse. *Colloq.* **2.** * **saddler sergeant,** (see quot.).

(1) 1888 *Boston Jrnl.* 16 June 1/1 Another auction sale of choice family horses (including matched pairs and saddlers). **1904** *N.Y. Tribune* 17 July, Mrs. Roosevelt rode her favorite saddler Yganka. **1949** *Boston Sun. Globe* 1 May (Fiction Mag.) 11/2 Gil had more saddlers than he needed. — **(2) 1891** *Cent.* 5298/1 *Saddler-sergeant*, . . . in the United States a non-commissioned staff-officer of a cavalry regiment.

* **saddlery,** *n.* Saddles and other articles made by a saddler. Also attrib.

1711 *Boston News-Letter* 22 Oct. 2/2 To be Sold . . . Pipes, Sadlery, Bunting, Millenary Goods [etc.]. **1787** *Md. Gazette* 1 June 3/3 Saddlery tools, in sets. **1815** *Niles' Reg.* IX. 35/2 Plated saddlery and carriage mounting of all kinds . . . are manufactured. **1894** *Scribner's Mag.* May 603/2 The sewing-machine . . . has been followed [on ranches] by . . . revolvers, saddlery, and cotton goods.

saddy ˈsædɪ, *n. Pa.* [f. next.] A curtsy. *Colloq.* — **1870** *Nation* 28 July 56/2 The child was directed to 'make a saddy.'

saddy ˈsædɪ, *v.* [See quot. 1924.] *intr.* To curtsy, to say "thank you." Also **saddying,** *n.*

1835 Crockett *Tour* 34 It would do you good to see our boys and girls dancing. None of your stradling, mincing, sadying. **1859** Bartlett 375 *To Saddy*, to bob up and down; to curtsy like a child. Probably a child's corruption of *Thank ye*, applied to the curtsy which accompanies the phrase. **1924** Lambert *Pa.-German* 129 saddi . . . thank you (usually used by elders in reminding a small child to say 'thank you'). Probably a corruption of 'sag Dank.' **1948** Mencken *Supp.* II. 206 Heydrick added *butter-bread* (Ger. *butter-brot*), *saddy* thank you (probably from Ger. *sag dank*) [etc.].

saengerfest, see **fest,** *n.*

* **safe,** *n.* As the last term in **fire, fruit, match, patent, salamander, saloon safe.**

* **safe,** *a.*

1. In baseball, not "out," secure in not being retired or put out.

1856 *Spirit of Times* 27 Dec. 276/3 He instantly makes for the first base, and if he can reach it without being hit by the ball from the hand of an adversary, he is safe, and not 'out.' **1949** *Democrat* 22 Sep. 2/5 Magoon bobbled the ball and all hands were safe.

b. Of a hit (or batted) ball: Enabling the batter to reach a base.

1867 *Ball Players' Chron.* 6 June 2/3 Flagg afterward made his base by a safe hit, and Parker also. *Ib.* 2/1 Sumner secured his 1st base on a safe ball to left field. **1881** *Detroit Free Press* 22 Sep. 6/2 Whitney was batted for seven safe hits.

2. *Polit.* Designating a man, esp. a candidate for office, who is not likely to disturb vested interests, dependable. *Colloq.*

1862 Lowell *Biglow P.* 2 Ser. iii. 109 Long 'z ye sift out 'safe' canderdates thet no one ain't afeared on. **1905** Steffens in *McClure's Mag.* XXIV. 352/2 The gubernatorial chair [in R.I.] never had amounted to much more than an empty honor for 'safe men.'

3. safe deposit, a place for storing valuables, usu. attrib.

1783 in Sparks *Corr. Revol.* IV. 27 West Point . . . may be made a safe deposit where every military article may be kept in good order and repair. **1880** W. Newton *Serm. Boys & Girls* (1881) 338, I went down in the vaults of one of our great safe-deposit buildings. **1886** *Encycl. Brit.* XXI. 145/1 The public safes or safe-deposits erected in most of the great cities of America and in London. **1896** *Typographical Jrnl.* 1 July p. iii (*advt.*), Safe Deposit Vault. . . . Finest and only vault of the kind in the State. **1917** *Ladies' Home Jrnl.* Oct. 1/1 A registered bond is more desirable unless you have safe-deposit facilities—then the coupon bond is generally preferred. **1950** *Banking* Jan. 80/3 New York now has uniform provision for banks, savings banks and safe deposit companies.

* **safety,** *n.*

1. *Football.* The action of a player, in preventing his opponents from making a touchdown, of downing the ball and so rendering it "dead" on, above, or behind his own goal line when his side has given the ball the impetus which brought it to or across the goal line. Also the score, now 2 points, given the opposing team as a result of such action. Cf. **safety touchdown.**

1881 in P. H. Davis *Football* (1911) 469 If the game still remains a tie the side which makes four or more safeties less than their opponents shall win the game. **1893** *Outing* Dec. 73/1 With Newell, he blocked Brooke's punt, and forced Pennsylvania to a safety. **1950** *Chi. Tribune* 26 Feb. 20/2 A blocked kick and safety can be credited against him.

2. A safe hit in baseball.

1917 Mathewson *Second Base Sloan* 105 Billy White led off with a safety to left. **1949** *Fargo* (N.D.) *Forum* 23 July 8/8 The Red Sox got seven safeties off Steve Wylie, colored Minot hurler.

3. In combs.: (1) **safety barge,** (see quot. 1859), now *hist.* [such barges were app. used only on the Hudson

Safety barge or barge (sense 1)

River]; (2) **chain,** (see quots.); (3) **fund,** see as a main entry; (4) **razor,** (see quot. 1876); (5) **touchdown,** = * **safety 1.**

(1) 1825 in *Amer. Sp.* XXI. (1946) 236 At the same place was also stationed the Commerce, Capt. Seymour, with the elegant safety-barge, Lady Clinton. **1859** Bartlett 376 *Safety Barge*, a passenger boat towed by a steamboat at such a distance from it as to avoid all apprehension of danger to the passengers. **1945** Adams *Album Amer. Hist.* II. 217 The Lady Clinton was one of two 'safety barges' put into operation by the Fulton Company to meet competition on the Hudson River. — **(2) 1853** Felt *Customs N. Eng.* 130 Females have appeared with gold chains as part of their attire. Particularly those denominated *safety chains*, for the neck, have been increasingly used by both sexes, for the past twenty years, attached to the watch. **1909** Webster, safety chain. . . . An auxiliary watch chain, secured to the clothes, usually out of sight, to prevent stealing of the watch. — **(4) 1876** Knight III. 2018 Safety-razor. A razor having guards at each side of the edge to prevent nervous and infirm persons from accidentally cutting themselves in shaving. **1931** *K.C. Times* 4 Nov., The Raytown News believes Tarzan should write a testimonial for some safety razor company.

(5) **1887** *Cent. Mag.* Oct. 889/2 A 'safety' touch-down counts two points against the side which makes it.

safety fund.

1. A fund provided by the New York banking law of 1829, requiring all chartered banks of the state to deposit initially with the state treasurer three percent of their capital stock, to be used, if needed, for the redemption of their notes. Also attrib. Now *hist.*

1830 *Williams's N.-Y. Ann. Reg.* 167 Banks subject to the operation of the Safety-Fund Act, passed 1829. **1834** THORBURN *Forty Years'* 149 What unanswerable argument he used, I know not, but strongly suspect it was in the shape of a safety-fund note. **1855** *Knickerb.* XLV. 471 Wouldn't he have skinned me if he could, with his discount, one and a quarter per cent for safety-fund money? **1936** G. W. DOWRIE *Money & Banking* 187 The safety fund established by the State of New York in 1829 was the forerunner of the Canadian safety fund for the redemption of bank notes and of the present Federal Deposit Insurance Corporation in the United States.

2. safety fund bank, a bank that contributed to the safety fund. *Obs.*

1832 *Cong. Deb.* 8 March 2074 Suppose one of these safety fund banks to be established in a country village. **1857** *Harper's Mag.* Dec. 115/1 All the banks . . . should receive at par . . . the notes of certain specified Safety-Fund Banks.

Safrano səˈfrɑno, *n.* [?f. * *saffron.*] A variety of tea rose. In full **Safrano rose.** *Obs.*

1869 S. B. PARSONS *On the Rose* 48 *Safrano.* . . . Its half-opened bud is very beautiful, and of a rich, deep fawn color. **1876** WARNER *Gold of Chickaree* 234 'Have you?' said Hazel, intent upon placing a Safrano rose. **1942** *Stand. Plant Names* 565/1 Safrano. T[ea Rose]. [Introducer:] (Beauregard 1839.)

* **sag,** *n.*

1. A depression, shallow ravine, low place. *Colloq.*

1727 in *Amer. Sp.* XV. 387/1 Thence along the North Side of the Mountains . . . to a Corner Several Saplins by a Sagg. **1891** *Outing* Oct. 73/2 A sleek, dark back is just visible over the rim of a slight 'sag.' **1950** *Boston Globe Mag.* 5 Feb. 3/3 Soon's they drop into the next sag out of sight, it might be a good idea for you boys to take your rifles and go into the house.

attrib. **1887** *Virginia* (Nev.) *Rep.* 18 Nov. 3/2 A teamster was driving his team along the borders of the little lake, which is merely a sag-pond.

2. A lull or decline in prices or business activity. *Colloq.*

1891 *Daily News* (London) 4 March 2/2 In the American market there is a slight but general 'sag.' **1897** HOUGH *Story of Cowboy* 334 Then in time came . . . the 'sag' in the cattle business. **1949** *Time* 23 May 83/2 Some new car dealers were feeling a sag in their own sales.

sagaban ˈsægəbən, *n.* Also **sagabon.** (See quots.)

1859 BARTLETT 376 Sagaban. The root of the *Apios tuberoso,* used as food by the Indians of the North-west. **1931** CLUTE *Plants* 30 A more famous potato is the mic-mac potato (*Apios tuberosa*) whose tubers were undoubtedly the first potatoes to be sent to Europe from our country. The Indians called this plant *Sagabon* and from this Sag Harbor, on Long Island, is said to have derived its name. **1941** MCDERMOTT *Glossary* 135 sagaban, n. The groundnut, potato bean, or wild bean.

sagaciate səˈgæʃɪˌet, *v. S.* [?f. *sagacity.*] *tr.* and *intr.* To get along, endure (see also quot. 1933). *Slang.*

1832 *Boston Transcript* 2 Aug. 2/3 Well, Clem, how do you sagatiate dis lubly wedder? **1890** *Amer. Folk-Lore* III. Dec. 311 *Sagatiate,* . . . came into use here [in Phila.] between 1853 and 1859, being used only in the phrase, 'How does your corporosity sagatiate the inclemency of the weather?' **1933** *Amer. Sp.* Feb. 52 Segashiate, *v.* To move about, to progress. Used in a jocular fashion. Talley (*Negro Folk Rhymes,* 1922, p. 200) says that among the Southern Negroes segashuate means to associate with. **1949** *Sky Line Trail* Oct. 22/1 Howdy do, Mr. Gooberpatch. How does yo' sagaciate dis lubbly wedder?

sagakomi sɑˈgækəmɪ, *n.* [Can. F., f. Algonquian. Cf. Chippewa *sagâkcmin,* smoking-leaf berry.] (See quot. 1941.) *Obs.*

1703 LAHONTAN *New Voyages* II. 53 They are forc'd to buy up Brasil Tobaco, which they mix with a certain Leaf of an agreeable Smell, call'd *Sagâkomi.* **1778** CARVER *Travels* 31 A weed that grows near the great lakes, in rocky places, . . . is called by the Indians Segockimac. **1805** CLARK in *Lewis & C. Exped.* I. (1904) 266 Two men of the N W Compy arrive with letters and Sackacomah. *Ib.* III. (1905) 273 A young Chief . . . produced for us to eate . . . cranberries & Sackacomey berries, in bowls made of horn. **1941** MCDERMOTT *Glossary* 135 sacacomi, saccacomi, Ind. . . . The bearberry. Also, the smoking mixture made from the leaves of this shrub. Sometimes mistakenly written *sac-à-commis.*

sagamité səˌgɑməˈte, *n.* [Can. F., f. Algonquian. Cf. Ojibway *kisagamitew.* See Read, *La.-French,* 105 f.] A gruel or hominy made of corn.

[**1632** SAGARD *Le Grand Voyage du Pays des Hurons* 137 Le pain de Mais, et la sagamite qui en est faicte, est de fort bonne substance, et m'estonnois de ce qu'elle nourrit si bien qu'elle faict.] **1744** *Present State of Country & Inhabitants of Louisiana* 22 They were employed in . . . making Sagamité and baking it. **1821** NUTTALL *Jrnl.* 116 A mother weeping over the grave of her son, poured upon it a great quantity of Sagamitty (or hominy). **1895** *Proc. Amer. Antiq. Soc.* April 179 If, as often occurred, they had no meat, and did have an oil or fat of any kind, they used it to give body and flavor to their *sagamité.* **1931** READ *La.-French* 106 The eighteenth century saw the evolution of such English forms as *shaggamitie, sagamitty,* and *sagamite;* the nineteenth century, *sagamity* as well as *sagamité.* The preferable spelling in English is now *sagamité.*

sagamore ˈsægəˌmor, *n.* [f. the Abnaki name for the chief or ruler of a tribe.] An Indian chief or leader. Now *hist.* Cf. **Indian sagamore** *s.v.* * **Indian,** *a.* **6,** and see **sachamaker.**

1613 PURCHAS *Pilgrimage* 628 The said Sagamos lost the pipe. *c***1618** STRACHEY *Virginia* 160 Many provinces . . . [are] governed in chief by a principall commaunder or prince . . . who hath under him divers petty kings, which they call Sagamoes. **1751** GIST *Journals* 72 This Beaver is the Sachemore or Chief of the Delawares. **1843** HAYWARD *Gazetteer of Maine* 88 Each tribe, however, had its own sagamore, subject or tributary to the Bashaba. **1919** *Maine My State* 104 At Mattawamkeag, the Sagamores of the Indian village welcomed them with hospitality.

b. Used as a title with the given name of a particular Indian.

1632 *Mass. Bay Rec.* I. 102 [He] shall give Saggamore John a hogshead of corne for the hurt his cattell did him in his corne. **1677** HUBBARD *Narrative* I. 76 Sagamore Sam, old Jethro, and the Sagamore of Quohaog, were taken by the English. **1758** J. WILLIAMS *Redeemed Captive* 25 An Indian came to the City (Sagamore George of Pennacook) from Cowass. **1834** WHITTIER *Poetical Works* (1894) 496/1 He who harms the Sagamore John Shall feel the knife of Mogg Megone.

c. Sagamore's head, app. some American tree not now identifiable. *Rare.*

1741 P. COLLINSON in *Mem. Bartram* (1849) 148 The butter-nut . . . with the Medlar and Sagamore's head.

sagamoreship ˈsægəmorˌʃɪp, *n.* The territory ruled over by an Indian sagamore. Also the office of a sagamore. *Obs.*

1654 JOHNSON *Wonder-w. Prov.* 66 This Towne lies in the Saggamooreship, or Earldome of Aggawam. **1687** BLOME *Isles & Terr. in Amer.* 232 The three Kingdoms, or Sagamorships of the Mattachusets, . . . were now . . . reduced. **1760** NILES *Indian Wars* I. 178 Philip being now become the next heir to the crown, or sagamoreship doubtless studied some method of revenge on the English for his brother's death.

sagaunash səˈgɔnəʃ, *n.* [App. Amer. Indian.] In Indian parlance, an Englishman, a white man (see also quot. 1910).

1825 W. BIGGS *Narr. Captivity* 13 He asked me if I was a Sagenash, (an Englishman). **1904** WHITE *Silent Places* 68, I know the language of the saganash. **1910** HODGE *Amer. Indians* II. 408/1 Sagaunash ('Englishman'). A mixed-blood Potawatomi chief, better known as Billy Caldwell, born in Canada about 1780. . . . Sagaunash died at Council Bluffs, Iowa, Sept. 28, 1841, aged about 60 years.

* **sage,** *n.*[1]

1. = **sagebrush.**

1805 LEWIS in *L. & Clark Exped.* II. (1920) 29 The wild hysop sage . . . and some other herbs also grow in the plains and hills. **1913** BARNES *Western Grazing Grounds* 43 [There are] many varieties of sage. **1949** *Amer. Forests* Oct. 43/1 The best sage is usually found in canyons or natural pockets in the land, near water.

2. In combs.: (1) **sagebrush,** see as a main entry; (2) **bush,** a bush of sage; (3) **chicken,** a prairie chicken; (4) **chipmunk,** (see quots.); (5) **cock,** a large grouse, *Centrocercus urophasianus,* found on sagebrush plains in the western U.S.; (6) **fowl,** = prec.; (7) **grouse,** = **sage cock;** (8) **hare,** = **sage rabbit;** (9) **hen,** (*a*) the sage grouse, esp. the female, (*b*) (*cap.*) (see quot. 1863), hence **Sage Hen State,** (*c*) a girl, *slang,* cf. * **quail 3;** (10) **rabbit,** any one of various western rabbits, as *Sylvilagus nuttalli,* usu. regarded as a species related to the cottontail of the East; (11) **sparrow,** any one of various sparrows found in the sagebrush regions of the West; (12) **squirrel,** (see quot.); (13) **thrasher, thrush,** (see quot. 1917); (14) **willow,** a gray willow, *Salix tristis.*

(2) **1807** GASS *Journal* 204 Sage bushes . . . grow in great abundance on some parts of these plains. **1944** *Reader's Digest* March 66, I was travelling with four other women through the sagebush country of eastern Oregon and we stopped at Burns early one morning. — (3) **1850** *Alta California* (S.F.) 6 Oct. 2/3 For the last week we have been feasting on sage-chicken and wild ducks. **1945** *Craig* (Colo.) *Empire-Courier* 25 July 1/1 Deer, Elk, Geese, Ducks, Sage Chickens, Bear, Trout Fishing. — (4) **1891** *N. Amer. Fauna* V. 7 The most common diurnal mammals are the Great Basin or Sage Chipmunk (*Tamias minimus pictus*) and a small Spermophile (*Spermophilus townsendi*). **1939** HAMILTON *Amer. Mammals* 144 The little sage chipmunk (*Eutamias minimus pictus*) has been known to feed extensively upon the larvae and pupae of a webworm that was stripping the sagebrush.

(5) **1839** WISLIZENUS *Journey to Rocky Mts.* (1912) 73 A bird that feeds on this plant, the so-called sagecock or cock of the plains (*Tetrao Uriphasianus*), has precisely the same taste. **1917** *Birds of Amer.* II. 30/1 The Sage Cock has a sharp cackle. — (6) **1869** *Amer. Naturalist* III. 82 [The] Sage Fowl (*Centrocercus urophasianus*) . . . is very rare [near Fort Benton]. — (7) **1876** DODGE *Black Hills* 124 Packs of the sage grouse are occasionally encountered. **1948** *Pacific Discovery* Jan.–Feb. 14/2 Sage grouse in the valley sage; . . . showy primroses on the cliffs—these are the Teton country. — (8) **1868** *Amer. Naturalist* II. 536 The Sage Hare (*Lepus artemisia*) . . . is more rare near Fort Benton. — (9) (*a*) **1841** WILLIAMS *Tour to Ore.* (1843) 14 The sage hen is found here also. They are somewhat less than the turkey hen, and are supposed to live on the sage leaves. **1944** *Reader's Digest* August 47 A tourist entered the best restaurant in a small Montana town. 'Watcha got?' he growled. 'Sage hen,' answered the waiter. (*b*) **1863** *Walla Walla* (Wash.) *Statesman* 6 June 1/7 The inhabitants of Nevada are called Sage Hens. **1894** *N.Y. Wkly. Tribune* 7 March 4/3 Nevada [is] . . . called the Sage Hen State. **1946** MCWILLIAMS *So. Calif. Country* 172 Nevadans are 'sage hens.' (*c*) **1939** *New Mexico* Dec. 19/1 Cow pokes, waddies and range bosses . . . are welcome here tonight to this great social event. This also applies to the beautiful little sage hens.

(10) **1846** SAGE *Scenes Rocky Mts.* iv, [The] sage rabbit . . . is nearly three times the size of the common rabbit, and of a white color, slightly tinged with grey. **1879** GOODE *Cat. Animal Resources U.S.* 20 *Lepus sylvaticus.* . . . Sage Rabbit. — (11) **1884** COUES *Key to Birds* 375 *Amphispiza.* . . . Sage Sparrows. **1940** GABRIELSON & JEWETT *Birds Ore.* 566 The Sage Sparrow has been known from Oregon since Bendire (Brewer 1875) found it breeding near Camp Harney. — (12) **1936** BAILEY *Mammals Ore.* 154 Citellus mollis mollis (Kennicott) Sage Squirrel; Piute Squirrel. — (13) **1913** GOODWIN *As I Remember Them* 296 When the night came the sage thrashers and mocking birds took up the refrain and kept it up till morning. **1917** *Birds of Amer.* III. 175 Sage Thrasher, *Oreoscoptes montanus.* . . . Also called Sage Thrush. **1942** LILLARD *Desert Challenge* 111 Cactus wrens, sage thrashers, flycatchers, and other birds obtain their water from insects, morning dew, and rain pools under boulders. — (14) **1846** EMERSON *Rep. Trees & Shrubs Mass.* 256 The sage willow is a slender, hoary plant, or a spreading tufted bush. **1940** FASSETT *Aquatic Plants* 189 S. cándida Flügge. Sage Willow.

b. Designating areas covered by sagebrush, as (1) **sage country,** (2) **desert,** (3) **hill,** (4) **hillock,** (5) **plain,** (6) **prairie.**

(1) **1850** SAWYER *Way Sketches* 73 We now drove nine miles down the river over a sage country. — (2) **1845** FRÉMONT *Exped.* 161 The dark and ugly appearance of this plain obtained for it the name of the Sage Desert. **1869** J. R. BROWNE *Adv. Apache Country* 513 In the alkali plains and sage-deserts and rugged mountain ranges of Nevada, you find him with his pick and shovel. **1870** PINE *Beyond the West* 215 There are [in Oregon] many . . . sage deserts. — (3) **1845** FRÉMONT *Exped.* 227 [Some of the Indians] appeared to have been out on the sage hills to hunt rabbits. — (4) **1848** BRYANT *California* ix. 13 The plain . . . is covered with wild sage, with a few occasional blades of dead bunch-grass between the sage-hillocks.

(5) **1844** in *Calif. Hist. Soc. Quart.* IV. 347 Made 25 miles over Sage plains deep ravines clay Bluffs &c. **1948** *Pacific Discovery* Jan.–Feb. 11/1 The sage plains to the south had been pre-empted and were denied it. — (6) **1856** REID *Desert Home* 11 This shrub is the *artemisia,*—a species of wild sage or wormwood,—and the plains upon which it grows are called by the hunters who cross them the *sage prairies.*

As the last term in **black, blue, hummingbird, Indian, mountain, prairie, salt, sweet, thistle, white, wild sage.**

* **Sage,** *n.*[2] In nicknames of famous men: (1) *Sage of Ashland,* Henry Clay, in allusion to his home in Kentucky; (2) *of Chappaqua,* Horace Greeley, so called in allusion to the name of his experimental farm in Westchester County not far from New York City; (3) *of Concord,* Ralph Waldo Emerson, of Concord, Mass.; (4) *of Monticello,* Thomas Jefferson, so called from the name of his estate in Virginia; (5) *of Wheatland,* James Buchanan, in allusion to his home in Pennsylvania.

(1) **1848** *Literary Amer.* 25 Nov. 356/3 The Sage of Ashland was the author of this great public work. — (2) **1872** *Harper's Wkly.* 1 June 426/3 The Cincinnati candidate is already 'Old Horace,' 'Old Honesty,' . . . 'Old White Hat,' . . . 'the Sage of Chappaqua.' **1942** BERREY & VAN DEN BARK *Amer. Thesaurus Slang* 184 The Ghost, Old White Hat, Prince of Journalists, Sage of Chappaqua, *Horace Greeley, journalist.* — (3) **1846** *Dollar Newspaper* (Phila.) 4 Nov. 32 A Poem by Ralph Waldo Emerson is worthy of the 'Sage of Concord,' and more than worth the price of the beautiful Souvenir. **1942** BERREY & VAN DEN BARK *Amer. Thesaurus Slang* 184 Columbus of Modern Thought, Sage of Concord, *Ralph Waldo Emerson, poet and philosopher.* — (4) **1800** *A Solemn Address to Christians & Patriots* 15 As a learned and experienced statesman, Mr. Jefferson rises superior to the level of his rivals; he is the author of the declaration of independence [etc.]. . . . Such is the sage of Monticelli [*sic*]. **1839** M. PENCIL *White Sulphur P.* 19 It was here in the shade of these elms, that the sage of Monticello was wont to spend so much of his time. **1912** G. D. NICHOLSON *Hoosier Chron.* 196 If you're going back to the Sage of Monticello, how do you think he would answer that?

(5) **1860** PRENTICE *Prenticeana* 264 They don't call the President the 'sage of Wheatland' any more, and the title was nothing but chaff during the canvass.

***sage,** *n.*[3] See ***sedge.**

sagebrush ˈsedʒˌbrʌʃ, *n.*

1. Any of several species of *Artemisia,* esp. *A. tridentata,* growing wild on the western plains and plateaus; a plant of such a species.

1852 JAMES AKIN *Jrnl.* (1919) 16 Not much grass plenty sage brush for use. **1890** CUSTER *Following Guidon* 71 The dull sage-brush, or greaseroot, or the sparse buffalo-grass, were all that the sun spared from its scorching rays. **1949** *Prairie Schooner* Spring 27 A few hundred yards further on through the sagebrush and cactus and we were at our destination.

b. An area covered by sagebrush.

1907 WHITE *Arizona Nights* 27 Onpeacable citizens Texas Pete used to plant out in the sage-brush. **1940** *Pop. Sci. Mo.* May 112 He traditionally sprang on his pony and galloped off into the sagebrush to track down his man.

Hence **sagebrusher,** (see quots.).

1908 *Sat. Ev. Post* 29 Aug. 4/3 [In Yellowstone Park] a Sagebrusher is a person who takes in his own camping outfit. **1949** *Nat. Geog. Mag.* June 750/1 We made assorted and innumerable new friends of the road. 'Sagebrushers' such traveling campers are called in western lingo.

2. *W. attrib.* Denoting a process or method of treating gold and silver ores with a strong tea or extract brewed from sagebrush on the assumption that it would facilitate the amalgamation of the gold and silver. *Obs.*

1877 W. WRIGHT *Big Bonanza* 139 The wonders performed by the 'sage-brush process,' as it was called, were being heralded through the land. **1896** SHINN *Story of Mine* 84 A mill on the Comstock . . . advertised reduction of ores by the 'sage-brush method.'

3. sagebrush state, a state in which sagebrush grows in abundance, esp. (*cap.*) Nevada, a nickname.

In quot. 1908 "Nebraska" is app. an error.

1904 *N.Y. Ev. Post* 6 May 7 A senator from one of the 'sagebrush' States—Mr. Newlands of Nevada. **1908** JOHNSON *Pacific Coast* 208 Nebraska is known as the Sagebrush State, and in general I suppose it merits the name, but when one reaches the vicinity of the famous divorce town of Reno . . . the landscape is distinctly pastoral and agricultural. **1942** LILLARD *Desert Challenge* 79 Patriots of the Sagebrush State have frequently expressed sorrow and indignation at the way individuals have made millions of dollars in Nevada only to spend them elsewhere.

4. Denoting areas in the West largely overgrown by sagebrush, as (1) **sagebrush country,** (2) **desert,** (3) **flat,** (4) **land,** (5) **plain,** (6) **range.**

(1) **1864** *Old Piute* (Virginia, Nev.) 17 May 2/1 What do you think, pharisees and publicans of other lands, of our '*poor, miserable, sagebrush country,*' now. — (2) **1888** *Amer. Humorist* (London) 2 June 3/3, I expect to see the sagebrush deserts of Nebraska and Nevada under cultivation. **1942** STEGNER *Mormon C.* 345 Nevada conjures pictures of dusty ghost towns and endless sagebrush deserts. — (3) **1907** WHITE *Arizona Nights* 191 We began to toil in the ankle-deep sand of a little sage-brush flat. **1949** *Amer. Forests* Nov. 11/1 Application of water to the sagebrush flats of western valleys and plains by irrigation produces crops unmatched in eastern states. — (4) **1900** *Cong. Rec.* 3 Feb. 1474/2 The land is arid sagebrush land. **1942** STEGNER *Mormon C.* 40 The Saints made it plain that sagebrush land was fertile if it got water.

(5) **1863** in *Mont. Hist. Soc. Contrib.* I. (1876) 214 Plenty of . . . greasewood, and sage-brush plains. **1948** *Chi. Tribune* 10 Oct. VII. 22/6 The pronghorn antelope, noted for their curiosity, watch the visitors with interest on the sage brush plains. — **(6)** **1902** MARK TWAIN in *Harper's Mag.* Feb. 431 No poking around all over the sagebrush range an hour and a half in a mass-meeting crowd for *him.* **1945** *Newsweek* 26 March 94/2 Aerial coyote hunting is most successful over the sagebrush range at about 500 feet.

5. a. sagebrush chipmunk, =**sage chipmunk. b. sagebrush whisky,** illicit liquor made out in the sagebrush. *Obs.* Cf. **brush whisky.**

(a) **1908** BAILEY *Harmful & Beneficial Mammals* 9 Sagebrush Chipmunk [is] the smallest and sprightliest of all our chipmunks. — **(b)** **1876** *Silver City* (Ida.) *Avalanche* 28 Feb. 3/1 Nick has been punishing an immense amount of sage brush whisky lately, and has consequently become almost utterly worthless. **1947** CHALFANT *Gold, Guns, & Ghost Towns* 62 There are only 65 graves—largely called into use because of sage-brush whiskey, poor doctors, some killed.

Sag Nichts. A name given the Locofocos or Democrats by the Know-Nothings. Also attrib. Now *hist.*

Bartlett's def. of this term (see quot. 1859) is in error. Cf. quots 1860, 1945.

1856 *Western Citizen* (Paris, Ky.) 16 May 3/1 At the recent elections in Chicago, the Sag Nichts were sad. **1856** *Dollar Times* (Cin.) 18 Sep. 2/8 We have not been beaten by the *Sag-Nicht* Democracy by no means. **1859** BARTLETT 376 Sag-Nichts. The German rendering of the political term *Know-nothing,* it being made on the principle that those who *know* nothing had better *say* nothing. **1860** G. D. PRENTICE *Prenticeana* 211 The Sag Nichts pretend that they attempted no resistance to the Know Nothings at the late election. **1945** MENCKEN *Supp.* I. 316/2 Nor [has the *DAE* mention] of the *Sag Nichts* who opposed the Know Nothings before the Civil War.

Hence **Sag Nichtism.** *Obs.* Cf. **locofocoism.**

1856 *Western Citizen* (Paris, Ky.) 18 Jan. 3/1 It is *Sag Nichtism* and nothing more.

saguaro sə'gwɑro, *n.* Also **sahuaro.** [Amer. Sp. in sense **1.**]

1. A tall treelike cactus, *Carnegiea gigantea,* found in desert regions in the Southwest. Cf. **Carnegiea, giant cactus.**

1856 *Wide West* (S.F.) Oct. 4/6 There are in this region a few Indian rancharies, to which the *Papagos* resort to gather the fruit of the *sugarro.* **1864** MOWRY *Ariz. & Sonora* 161 Gradually appear the palo verde, the mesquit, and a greater variety of cacti, and on the hillside scattered saguaras. **1948** *Nat. Hist.* April 182 The arms of the Saguaro reach heavenward as though in supplication.

attrib. **1881** *Amer. Naturalist* XV. 982 By far the most conspicuous and remarkable form is the *Cereus giganteus,* locally known as the 'saguara' cactus. **1912** LUMHOLTZ *New Trails* 48 An essential part of the festival is the drinking of wine, produced by mixing the sahuaro sirup in a certain proportion of water and allowing this to ferment. **1924** *Cent. Mag.* July 386 There is a singular charm of the sahuaro forest, a charm of elegance. **1942** CASTETTER & BELL *Pima & Papago Agric.* 148 Then, after the sahuaro harvest in July, the second planting, consisting chiefly of maize and teparies, was made on the same land. **1948** *Ariz. Republic* (Phoenix) 27 Feb. 10/6 All previous records for Saguaro National Monument were broken last month.

2. saguaro woodpecker, a woodpecker, *Centurus uropygialis,* that often nests in the stem of the saguaro cactus. Cf. **Gila woodpecker.**

1884 COUES *Key N.A. Birds* (ed. 2) 488 Saguaro Woodpecker. **1917** *Birds of Amer.* II. 163.

Sahaptin, see **Shahaptan.**

saibling 'saɪblɪŋ, *n.* [G. (<*Sais,* ancient capital of Lower Egypt.)] **1.** A char, *Salvelinus alpinus,* introduced into the U.S. from Europe. Also attrib. **2.** The Sunapee trout, *S. aureolus.*

(1) **1884** GOODE *Fisheries* I. 501 The Saibling is, in its habits, perhaps more similar to the well-known Blue-backed Trout, or Oquassa Trout of Rangely Lake, Maine, than to our Brook Trout. *Ib.* 504 In selecting a place in which to deposit the saibling eggs . . . , the Commissioner of Fisheries has endeavored to find a lake as similar as possible in depth and temperature to the larger Swiss lakes. — **(2)** **1911** *Rep. Fisheries 1908* 315/1 Saibling (*Salvelinus aureolus*), the Sunapee trout of Maine and New Hampshire.

∗**sail,** *n.* In combs.: (1) **sail carriage,** a piece of fire-fighting equipment of a now unidentifiable kind, *obs.;* (2) ∗**fish,** any one of various large sea fish of the genus *Istiophorus;* (3) ∗**maker,** in the U.S. Navy, a warrant officer in charge of all articles made of canvas; (4) **maker's mate,** (see quot. 1881).

(1) **1829** *Mass. Laws* 237 The said Firewards . . . are hereby authorized . . . [to appoint] twenty men to each Sail Carriage. *Ib.* The said Firewards shall have the care . . . of the public Engines, Hose and Sail Carriages, Fire Hooks and Ladders. — **(2)** **1879** GOODE *Cat. Animal Resources U.S.* 39 *Histiophorus americanus.* . . . Sail-fish.— Atlantic Coast of America. **1903** T. H. BEAN *Fishes N.Y.* 405 The sailfish lives in the warmer parts of the Atlantic, ranging northward to France and, occasionally, to Cape Cod. — **(3)** **1794** *Ann. 3d Congress* 1426 There shall be employed, in each of the said ships, . . . one sail-maker, one carpenter. **1839** *Knickerb.* XIII. 43 The sailmaker . . . proceeded to sew him up in his hammock. **1881** *Naval Encycl.* 713/2 [A] sailmaker . . . [receives] from $700 to $1800 a year as pay. — **(4)** **1794** *Ann. 3d Congress* 1426 The following petty officers . . . shall be appointed by the captains of the ships: . . . one cockswain, one sail-maker's mate, two gunner's mates. **1881** *Naval Encycl.* 713/2 [A] sailmaker's mate [is] a petty officer of a man-of-war, working at sail-making under the directions of the sailmaker.

As the last term in **fire, Mohegan sail.**

∗**sail,** *v. To sail in* (or *into*), to attack (someone) boldly, to go into something without hesitation or restraint. *Colloq.*

1856 M. THOMPSON *Plu-ri-bus-tah* 69 'Sailing in,' without regard to Any of the Laws of 'Fancy.' **1868** *Cong. Globe* 2 May 2353/2 How he would sail into them! **1911** LINCOLN *Cap'n Warren's Wards* 202 So sail in and show us what you're made of.

∗**sailing,** *n.* and *a.* In combs.: (1) **sailing car,** (see quot.), *obs.;* (2) ∗**date,** the time when a passenger train leaves on a long run; (3) ∗**master,** formerly in the U.S.

One type of sailing car

Navy, a warrant officer next below a lieutenant who navigated the vessel and assisted the executive officer ["The grade was merged in that of *master* in 1862" (W. '09)]; (4) ∗**orders,** orders or directions pertaining to land travel, esp. of a wagon train, *obs.;* (5) **sucker,** =**quillback.**

(1) **1884** KNIGHT *Supp., Sailing Car,* a car . . . rigged with sail . . . used on the railroads on the plains, by telegraph repair parties. — **(2)** **1944** *U. Pacific Time Table* 9 July 7 [The Streamliner City of San Francisco] makes 10 round trips each month; see page 2 for sailing dates. — **(3)** **1779** *N.H. Comm. Safety Rec.* 194 Appointed—Curtice Sailing Master of the Armed Ship Hampden. **1907** O. HENRY *Roads of Destiny* 113, I gave orders to the sailing-master that the arms, ammunition, and provisions were to be landed at once. — **(4)** **1857** STACEY *Journal* 44 We received our sailing orders this morning. **1878** I. L. BIRD *Rocky Mts.* 158 My sailing orders were 'steer south, and keep to the best beaten track.'

(5) **1820** RAFINESQUE in *Western Rev.* II. 301 Sailing Sucker. *Catostomus velifer.* . . . It has received the vulgar names of Sailor fish, Flying fish, and Skinback, because, when it swims, its large dorsal fin appears like a sail, and it often jumps or flies over the water for a short distance.

∗**sailor,** *n.*

1. *local.* (See quot.) *Obs.*

1785 PENNANT *Arctic Zool.* II. 401 Black-Poll [Warbler]. . . . Inhabits during summer, Newfoundland and New York; Called in the last, *Sailor.*

2. In combs.: (1) **sailor fish,** (see quot.); (2) **plant,** (see quot.); (3) **-s' choice,** a name applied locally to any one of various fishes (see quot. 1911).

(1) **1820** RAFINESQUE in *Western Rev.* II. 301 *Catostomus velifer*. . . . It has received the vulgar names of Sailor fish, Flying fish, and Skinback, because, when it swims, its large dorsal fin appears like a sail, and it often jumps or flies over the water for a short distance. — (2) **1891** *Cent.* 5306/3 *Sailor-plant*, . . . the beefsteak-plant or strawberry-geranium, *Saxifraga sarmentosa*. — (3) **1850** in EASTERBY *S.C. Rice Plant.* (1945) 102 Alick has given us fish nearly every day, but not very choice ones, today he has brought a whiting and a sailors choice for the first. *c***1860** in GOODE *Fisheries* I. 399 The 'Sailor's Choice' makes its appearance in our waters about the month of April and continues with us until November. **1911** *Rep. Fisheries 1908* 315/1 Sailor's choice (*Lagodon rhomboides*). . . . The name is also applied to the pigfish (*Orthopristis chrysopterus*) in South Carolina.

* **Saint,** *n.* Also * **saint.**

1. *pl.* The members of the Tammany Society. *Obs.*

1812 PAULDING *Beauties of Brother Bull-us* 38 Brother Hector *Bull-us* is of all men living the best fitted to . . . play tricks for the entertainment of the *Saints* of Tammany.

2. A Latter-Day Saint or Mormon.

1833 *Ev. Star* (Independence, Mo.) July 111 The saints must shun every appearance of evil. **1885** *Wkly. New Mexican Rev.* 5 Feb. 1/6 He said the saints were being persecuted in Arizona. **1949** *Miss. Valley Hist. Rev.* March 630 The Saints began their exodus from Nauvoo in February, 1846.

3. St. Jonathan, the patron saint of the U.S. Also **St. Jonathan's Day,** the Fourth of July, or Forefathers' Day. *Obs.*

1855 *U.S. Rev.* XXXV. 106 But we sons of Columbia . . . will invoke no saint but St. Jonathan, . . . resolving that henceforth and for ever St. Jonathan shall be the patron-saint of the universal Yankee nation —and the Fourth of July, St. Jonathan's Day. **1856** *Spirit of Times* 27 Dec. 272/2 Our New England cousins celebrated their great anniversary of St. Jonathan's Day by a dinner and banquet, on Monday evening, at the Astor House.

4. In special combs.: (1) * **Saint Andrew's cross,** a wood plant, *Ascyrum hypericoides*, having petals in the form of an X; (2) **Domingo grebe,** (see quot.); (3) **Jacob's dipper,** the pitcher plant; (4) **Joseph('s) rod,** =**ocotillo,** *rare;* (5) **Louis,** designating a kind of limestone found near St. Louis, Missouri; (6) **Louisan,** a native or inhabitant of St. Louis; (7) **Lucas thrush,** (see quot.); (8) **Michael('s) pear,** a variety of pear, also attrib.; (9) * **Nicholas,** Santa Claus; (10) **Patrick's Day,** a holiday, March 17, celebrated esp. by Irish-Americans; (11) * **Peter's wort,** any plant of the genus *Ascyrum*, also the snowberry; (12) **Tammany,** see **Tammany.**

(1) **1738** BYRD *Dividing Line* (1901) 111 Abundance of St. Andrew's cross in all the woods. **1869** FULLER *Flower Gatherers* 245 The *Crux Andreae* or St. Andrew's Cross, is interesting from the regularity of its parts. **1931** CLUTE *Plants* 78 Our St. Peter's wort . . . and the St. Andrew's cross . . . are scarcely better situated since they are not the original plants so named but are obliged to bear names transferred from European species. — (2) **1883** *Nat. Museum Bul.* No. 27, 177 *Tachybaptes dominicus*. Saint Domingo Grebe. . . . North to Rio Grande Valley, in Texas, and Lower California. — (3) **1931** CLUTE *Plants* 78 As in other cases, saint's names have been attached to various indigenous species through sheer fancy. This is probably true of St. Jacob's dipper (*Sarracenia purpurea*). — (4) **1853** SITGREAVES *Exped. Zuni & Colo. Rivers* 40 On the hills about the creek were growing numerous cacti; also the St. Joseph rod, (*Foquera spinosa*,) which being in full bloom, looked beautiful.

(5) **1862** DANA *Manual Geol.* 307 The St. Louis limestone (250 feet thick), overlaid by ferruginous sandstone (200 feet). **1879** *Encycl. Brit.* (ed. 9) X. 350/2 St. Louis group.—Limestones with shale, in places 250 feet. — (6) **1905** *St. Louis Globe-Democrat* 2 July (Mag. Sect.) 7/3 The average St. Louisan seldom takes his meal in Quaker silence. **1948** *Time* 1 March 43/1 The arch itself, said proud St. Louisans, would mark their city like the Eiffel Tower or the Washington Monument. — (7) **1873** *Amer. Naturalist* VII. 327 The St. Lucas thrush (*H*[*arporhynchus*] *cinereus*) . . . agrees with the thrasher . . . in being thickly speckled with brownish-black. — (8) **1837** HAWTHORNE *Twice-told Tales* (1879) I. 118 They strung him up to the branch of a St. Michael's pear tree. **1849** *N. Eng. Farmer* I. 368 From Colonel F. R. Bigelow, Medford, very good St. Michael pears. **1871** *Harper's Mag.* Dec. 57/1 [She] helped herself as she liked to . . . the delicious greengages, and 'St. Michael' pears. — (9) **1773** *N.Y. Gazette* 26 Dec. 3/1 Last Monday the Anniversary of St. Nicholas, otherwise called St. A Claus, was celebrated at Protestant-Hall, at Mr. Waldron's, where a great Number of the Sons of that ancient Saint celebrated the Day with great Joy and Festivity. **1828** *Spirit of Seventy-Six* (Frankfort, Ky.) 28 Feb. 4/1 The stockings were hung by the chimney with care, In hope that St. Nicholas soon would be there. **1949** *Chi. D. News* 8 Dec. 20/2 Americans have transformed Santa Claus from a sad-eyed generous St. Nicholas of 1,600 years ago into a smaller, jollier, plumper red-suited Christmas hero.

(10) [**1791** *N.Y. Magazine* March 178/1 Thursday being the 17th of March, the festival of St. Patrick was celebrated in this city.] **1844** *Quincy* (Ill.) *Herald* 22 March 2/1 St. Patrick's Day . . . was observed by our Irish citizens in a suitable and becoming manner. **1948** *Dly. Ardmoreite* (Ardmore, Okla.) 21 March 11/4 He was the only man in Ardmore dressed for the occasion on St. Patrick's day. — (11) **1785** MARSHALL *Amer. Grove* 14 *Ascyrum Hypericoides*. St. Peter's Wort. . . . The flowers are sparingly produced at the tops of the stalks. *Ib.* 82 *Lonicera Symphoricarpos*, Indian Currants, or St. Peter's Wort, . . . often sends off a few weak trailing branches lying upon the ground. **1894** TORREY *Fla. Sketch-Book* 28 St. Peter's-wort, a low shrub, thrives everywhere in the pine barrens. **1931** [see **Saint Andrew's cross**].

As the last term in **Latter-Day, winter saint.**

* **Saintess,** *n.* A Mormon woman. *Obs.* — **1876** *Ogden* (Utah) *Freeman* 9 Dec. 3/1 She was a Mormon Saintess whose parents never believed in free schools. **1888** *Ogden* (Utah) *Union* 23 June 4/1 The young Saintesses had a good conference yesterday.

sala ˈsælə, *n. S.W.* [Sp., an Amer. borrowing.] A large hall.

1834 A. PIKE *Sketches* 96 The sala, or long hall, . . . was garnished with vast quantities of buffalo meat. **1898** ATHERTON *Californians* 19 Mrs. Polk would sing these old love-songs of Spain to the accompaniment of the guitar which had entranced her caballeros in the *sala* of her girlhood. **1926** CATHER *Death Comes* 55 (Bentley), Lujon and his two daughters began constructing an altar at one end of the sala.

* **salad,** *n.* **1. salad bird,** (see quot. 1808). **2. salad tree,** the redbud, *Cercis canadensis.*

(1) **1808** WILSON *Ornithology* I. 21 [Goldfinches] pass by various names expressive of their food, color, &c. such as Thistle-bird, Lettuce-bird, Sallad-bird [etc.]. **1917** *Birds of Amer.* III. 13. — (2) [**1756** KALM *Resa* II. 204 Sallad-trä . . . i god jord.] **1813** MUHLENBERG *Cat. Plants* 42. **1897** SUDWORTH *Arborescent Flora* 252 *Cercis canadensis*. Redbud. . . . Salad Tree (Del.).

As the last term in **chicken, head, poke, raw, rum, Shawnee, Waldorf salad.**

salal ˈsælæl, *n.* [See quot. 1896.] The fruit or berries of *Gaultheria shallon*, a small shrub found on the Pacific Coast; also the shrub or its wood.

[**1805** CLARK in *Lewis & C. Exped.* III. (1905) 274 An old woman presented . . . a kind of Surup made of Dried berries which is common to this Countrey which the natives Call Shele wele (*She-well*).] **1866** LINDLEY & MOORE *Treas. Botany* 522/2 The Shallon or Salal of the north-west coast of America. **1896** *Garden & Forest* IX. 292 Salal, or Sallal.—A Chinook Jargon word, from the last two syllables of *klkwu-shala*, the Chinook name of the fruit of the plant. **1940** *Mt. Hood Guide* 14 Perhaps the most abundant shrub is the salal, in some places almost the sole forest cover.

attrib. **1885** *Pacific Journal* (Oysterville, Wash.) April 6/1 It was originally covered by a growth of hemlock, some fir and spruce, interspersed with . . . alder and sallal thickets.

b. salal berry, the berry of this plant (see quot. 1838).

1838 S. PARKER *Tour Rocky Mts.* 202 The salalberry is a sweet and pleasant fruit, of a dark purple color, and about the bigness of a grape. **1868** WHYMPER *Alaska* 50 We went ashore two or three times, and had several luscious though unsatisfying meals of 'salmon' and 'salall' berries. **1945** MACDONALD *Egg & I* 80 The blue grouse were also very plentiful, but the salal berries which they gorged on gave them an odd bitter taste.

* **salamander,** *n.*

1. In the southeastern states, a pocket gopher, *Geomys tuza.* Cf. **painted, red-backed, tiger salamander.**

1805 LEWIS in *L. & Clark Exped.* I. (1904) 289 Their work resembles that of the salamander common to the sand hills of the States of South Carolina and Georgia. **1885** *South Fla. Sentinel* (Orlando) 8 April 1/6 The gophers (Florida salamanders) proved its [the garden's] destruction. **1943** POWELL *Home Again* 225 The small burrowing rodent about the size of a rat and looking like a chipmunk with his ears clipped off, which others call the gopher, we called the salamander.

2. A fireproof iron safe, in full **salamander safe.** *Obs.*

1840 *Hunt's Merch. Mag.* II. 280 The Salamander Safe. **1852** *Ib.* XXVI. (Feb.) 256 In April, 1833 I [C. J. Gayler] patented my 'Double

Fire Proof Safe.' The same year the name 'Salamander' was applied to it, for the reason that one had been subjected to a very intense heat for a long time, and fully protected its valuable contents. **1870** W. W. FOWLER *Ten Yrs. in Wall St.* 360 In one corner stood a large salamander safe.

3. A small portable stove, usu. burning coke.

1852 HAWTHORNE *Blithedale Rom.* v. (1885) 42 She has been stifled with the heat of a salamander stove. **1873** *Chi. Tribune* 3 Feb. 1/7 It caught fire from the 'salamander' used in drying the plaster.

*salary, *n.* In combs.: (1) **salary day,** the day on which salaries are paid; (2) **grab,** see as a main entry; (3) **judge,** a judge who receives a salary rather than fees; (4) **list,** a list of those who regularly receive salaries; (5) **loan shark,** one who loans money at an excessive rate, taking as security an assignment on the borrower's wages; (6) **man,** a man who receives a salary; (7) **officer,** an officer who receives a salary; (8) **steal,** the action of legislators of increasing their salaries, *obs.*, cf. **salary grab;** (9) **system,** a system in which services are paid for by salaries; (10) **wing,** the arm used by a baseball pitcher in pitching, *slang.*

(1) 1870 O. LOGAN *Before Footlights* 92 These envelopes are all prepared before 'salary-day' arrives. — **(3) 1789** *Ann. 1st Congress* 784 We must have a double suit of salary judges, attorneys general, marshals, clerks, and constables. — **(4) 1845** SOL. SMITH *Theatr. Apprent.* 21, I supposed (of course) that I should immediately be placed upon the salary list.

(5) 1914 KEATE *Destruction Mephisto's Web* 123 In the exposé of grafts, the Salary Loan Shark should be placed at the head of the list. **1915** *Chi. Herald* 10 Nov. 8/1 We first began to put real curbs on the extortionate pawnbroker and the 'salary loan shark' when public-spirited citizens obtained legal protection for the business under public supervision. — **(6) 1719** *Mass. Bay Currency Tracts* 193 Salary Men, Ministers, School-Masters [etc.] . . . are pincht and hurt more than any. **1824** *Baptist Mag.* IV. 358 The situation of clergymen is quite different from other men, even other *salary* men. — **(7) 1816** *Ann. 14th Congress* 2 Sess. 240 The only difference between a salary officer and a per diem, is simply in the mode of payment, and not in the amount. — **(8) 1873** *Cin. Commercial* 1 March 1/2 (*heading*), The Salary Steal Defeated in the House. — **(9) 1880** MARK TWAIN *Tramp Abroad* 585 When we borrowed the feeing fashion from Europe a dozen years ago, the salary system ought to have been discontinued, of course.

(10) 1912 C. MATHEWSON *Pitching* 273, I got the idea from 'Patsy' Flaherty, a Boston pitcher who has his salary wing fastened to his left side.

salary grab. (Also *cap.*) An act of Congress, March 3, 1873, by which the members made substantial retroactive increases in their own salaries. Also **salary grabber, salary grab session.** Now *hist.* Cf. **back salary grab, grabber.**

1873 *Tribune Almanac 1874* 25 The Salary Grab. . . . The back pay dates from March 4, 1871. **1875** *Chi. Tribune* 5 Oct. 2/3 Tipton, the Nebraska salary-grabber, and a young man named Weir, . . . have been advertised for weeks by monster posters, personal drumming, etc. **1886** ALTON *Among Law-Makers* 138 The people of the country were furious when they heard of this 'salary-grab.' **1887** *Nation* 8 Dec. 452/3 A notorious illustration of what may happen . . . was the once renowned 'salary-grab session,' when the retiring members voted to increase their salaries retroactively just before Congress expired. **1895** MYERS *Bosses & Boodle* 126 The 'Salary grab,' was passed by this Congress.

*sale, *n.*

1. In combs.: (1) **sale bill,** a notice of a sale; (2) **block,** a block, stump, etc., upon which slaves were exposed for sale, *obs.;* (3) **brand,** (see quot.), cf. **vent,** *n.;* (4) **crop,** a crop grown to be sold; (5) **day,** *S.* a day, esp. the first Monday of each month, upon which public auctions are held, *obs.;* (6) **garden,** a garden in which vegetables are raised for sale, *obs.;* (7) **money,** money obtained from a sale, *obs.;* (8) **note,** (see quot.), *obs.;* (9) **stable,** a large barn or other building where horses and mules are kept for sale.

(1) 1929 E. W. HOWE *Plain People* 142 In course of time we disposed of the job office, and lost the profit from printing sale bills. **1929** *Randolph Enterprise* (Elkins, W.Va.) 21 March 5/2 From sale bills printed at this office we note [etc.]. — **(2) 1887** HARRIS in *Cent. Mag.* April 847/2 The prisoner was made to stand on the sale-block so that all might have a fair view of him. — **(3) 1844** GREGG *Commerce of Prairies* I. 186 No matter how many proprietors a horse or mule may have had, every one marks him with a huge hieroglyphic brand which is called the *fierro*, and again, upon selling him, with his *venta*, or sale-brand. — **(4) 1850** *Rep. Comm. Patents 1849: Agric.* 131 Our forefathers . . . [were] at too great a distance from market to cultivate any other as a *sale* crop than tobacco.

(5) 1844 in BOUCHER & BROOKS *Correspondence addressed to Calhoun* (1930) 228, I will try and get a meeting 1st Monday in June. You know we can get no meetings of importance except on Sale days. **1887** in *Cent. Mag.* April 841/2 Only last sale-day you mighty nigh jolted the life out of Bill-Tom Saunders. — **(6) 1851** CIST *Cincinnati* 191 J. S. Cook, has recently commenced a sale garden and nursery. — **(7) 1656** *Suffolk Deeds* II. 246 [He] hath hereby full power and Authority . . . out of the Sale money to satisfye himselfe the aforesaid sume of forty sixe pounds. — **(8) 1862** BOUVIER *Law Dict.* II. 495/2 *Sale note*, a memorandum given by a broker to a seller or buyer of goods, stating the fact that certain goods have been sold by him on account of a person called the seller to another person called the buyer. — **(9) 1839** *Spirit of Times* 16 March 23/1 (We.), Sale stables. **1939** ROLLINS *Gone Haywire* 17 The final goal was the 'livery, feed & sale stable' of Comford & Raymond.

2. *pl.* In combs.: (1) **salesgirl,** a girl or woman employed to sell merchandise; (2) **lady,** a saleswoman; (3) **manager,** a company official in charge of sales; (4) **molasses,** molasses bought at a store, as distinguished from that made at home, also **sale molasses,** *obs.;* (5) **people,** those employed to sell goods or merchandise; (6) **resistance,** (see quot. 1927); (7) **room,** a room in which sales are made; (8) **talk,** a talk by a salesman designed to sell goods, also transf.

(1) 1887 *Courier-Journal* 2 Feb. 4/7 In order to cripple his old partner, he offered superior inducements to the sales girls to go with him. **1945** *Chi. D. News* 5 Dec. 15A/5 Salesgirls in department stores snicker with slangy disrespect. — **(2) 1856** *Dem. State Journal* (Sacramento) 1 Nov., Wanted—By a young lady, a situation as Saleslady in a dry goods . . . or millinery store. **1931** *K.C. Star* 29 Aug., We understand an Atchison motor car dealer is going to use salesladies in his business. — **(3) 1928** *Sat. Ev. Post* 12 May 6/3 Sales manager said he wanted to broaden my influence. — **(4) 1854** H. H. RILEY *Puddleford* 92 Longbow . . . used sales-molasses for common, . . . most every day. **1863** RANDALL *Pract. Shepherd* 147 Cow's milk . . . is generally mixed with a little 'sale' molasses [for young lambs].

(5) 1876 *Scribner's Mo.* Feb. 599/2, I walked through the crowds of purchasers and salespeople. **1928** *Publishers' Wkly.* 9 June 2370 Special lectures for groups of sales people from the local stores. — **(6) 1927** *Haldeman-Julius Quart.* July–Sep. 6/2 The presumptuous impulse of the public to do its own wanting is known to the ad men as 'sales resistance.' **1948** *Family Circle* June 70/1 At the end of the carpet I did what you do—wriggled my toes, teetered back and forth on my fallen arch, scowled, nibbled at my upper lip, and tried to suck up my sales resistance. — **(7) 1840** *Knickerb.* XVI. 226 A crowded audience [was ejected] from his sales-room, because an unlucky wight had the temerity to bid six-pence for a tattered copy of Paradise Lost. **1892** *York Co. Hist. Rev.* 85 The salesroom . . . carries a fine line of . . . dress goods. — **(8) 1931** *K.C. Times* 26 Aug., The patient was reluctant until a strong 'sales talk' by the M.D. overcame objections. **1945** *N. Eng. Homestead* 22 Sep. 20/2 You just can't do it with your eyes shut and by listening to a sales talk.

As the last term in **auction, bargain, bargain and, door-to-door, dump, fire, forced, mark down, old horse, package, sheriff, sheriff's, short, succession, tax, wash, washed sale.**

salea sɑˈleə, *n. W.* [Sp. *zalea*, an undressed sheepskin.] (See quots.) — **1897** INMAN *Old Santa Fe Trail* 56 A *salea*, or raw sheepskin, made soft by rubbing, was put on the animal's back, to prevent chafing. **1944** ADAMS *W. Words* 137/2 salea A raw and softened sheepskin placed on a pack animal's back for padding beneath a pack-saddle.

*Salem, *n.* In combs.: (1) **Salem cloth,** app. cloth made in Salem, Oregon, noted for its linen and woolen mills; (2) **grass,** velvet grass, *Holcus lanatus;* (3) **rocker,** a type of rocking chair evolved in New England having a high comb-back and thick scroll seat and characteristically painted and decorated.

(1) 1864 *Ore. State Jrnl.* 12 Nov. 4/3 Parson Bros have on hand a large supply of Salem Cloth especially adapted to the wants of Military Companies in making uniforms. — **(2) 1749** FRANKLIN *Writing* II. 386, I threw in . . . a bushell of Salem Grass or Feather-Grass. **1909** *Cent. Supp.* 544/3 Salem grass. The velvet grass. — **(3) 1928** J. C. LINCOLN *Silas Bradford's Boy* 5 In the Salem rocker by the window sat his mother.

Salemite ˈseləmˌaɪt, *n.* A native or inhabitant of Salem, Mass. *Obs.* — **1702** C. MATHER *Magnalia* (1853) I. 72 Some of the passengers . . . came over with those of our first Salemites. **1708** *Essex*

Inst. Coll. X. 77, [I] found at our house when we came back the Salemites.

saleratus ˌsæləˈretəs, *n.* [f. L. *sal*+*aeratus*, aerated salt.]

1. A name originally used for potassium bicarbonate, but later applied to sodium bicarbonate or baking soda. Also transf.

1837 S. GRAHAM *Treatise on Bread* 46 (Ernst), Pearlash or saleratus is also used by them [*sc.* public bakers] in considerable quantities. **1882** BAILLIE-GROHMAN *Camps in Rockies* 56 The baking powder, or 'saleratus' (the grandest word in the trapper's very abridged dictionary), cannot be found. **1908** O. HENRY *Options* 66 And here was a man whose saleratus you had et.

2. In obs. and rare combs.: (1) **saleratus factory,** a place where saleratus is manufactured; (2) **lake,** *W.* a lake the waters of which are alkaline; (3) **pond,** =prec.; (4) **wagon,** a wagon allegedly for hauling saleratus, *jocular;* (5) **water,** alkaline water.

(1) 1849 CHAMBERLAIN *Ind. Gazetteer* 186 In the county . . . [is] an extensive saleratus factory. — **(2) 1851** WM. KELLY *Across Rocky Mts.* (1852) 219 Which, at the distance, I took for a large saleratus lake dried up by evaporation. — **(3) 1860** in A. D. H. SMITH *Narrative Sam. Hancock* (1926) 64 Our route was through a beautiful plain interspersed with many of the salaratus ponds peculiar to this country. — **(4) 1924** SHEPHARD *P. Bunyan* 9 He 'worked for him on the Big Onion,' or 'was with him the spring of the Round Drive,' or 'had a brother who drove the saleratus wagon for Paul.'

(5) 1877 JEWETT *Deephaven* 61 We tried clear alcohol, and saleratus-water.

b. Denoting various breads made with saleratus, as (1) **saleratus biscuit,** (2) **bread,** (3) **cake.**

(1) 1853 WEBSTER *Improved Housewife* 130 Salaeratus Biscuit. **1948** *Chi. Tribune* 5 Dec. (Comics) 9 Fried eggs! Sizzlin' in squares o' pork! Hashed spuds, browned in what 'uz left o' the sizzle. Salaratus biscuits. Hmmm Mah-hhhh. — **(2) 1872** *Harper's Mag.* Jan. 221/2 The meal was a substantial one of fried bacon, saleratus bread, corn-dodgers, and coffee. **1890** *Harper's Mag.* Oct. 651/2 A wife, who gave us saleratus bread and a bowl of pork fat for supper and breakfast. — **(3) 1846** *Knickerb.* XXVII. 510 The white sal-æratus cake and the 'water bewitched' are quickly devoured.

salina səˈlinə, *n. W.* [Sp., an Amer. borrowing.] A salt spring, lick, pond, etc.; a salt mine or saltworks.

1844 GREGG *Commerce of Prairies* I. 176 The danger from the Indians and the privations experienced in an expedition to the *Salinas* are such, that it is seldom sold in the capital for less than a dollar per bushel. **1890** PEARY in *Sci. Amer. Supp.* LXII. 11710/3 Less than three miles of level swampy *salinas* reach to the surf of the Pacific. **1940** JAEGER *Calif. Deserts* 110 The Owens Lake gopher is restricted to the immediate vicinity of the vanishing salina.

saline fund. A fund, used for educational purposes, which accrues to a state from the sale of salt lands within its borders. Cf. **salt reservation.** — **1844** *Indiana Senate Jrnl.* 29 Sess. 171 That class of children designated in the resolution . . . will participate in the benefits arising from the saline fund.

salinera ˌsælɪˈnɛrə, *n. S.W.* [Amer. Sp. in same sense.] A salt-pit. — **1856** WHIPPLE *Explor. Ry. Route* II. 53 The salineras or salt-pits upon the plains between Rio Pecos and the Del Norte will become another important source of mineral wealth to the settlers of New Mexico.

Salisbury steak. (See quot. 1945.) — **1934** WEBSTER. **1945** MENCKEN *Supp.* 429 During World War I an effort was made by super-patriots to drive all German loans from the American vocabulary. *Sauerkraut* became *liberty cabbage, hamburger steak* became *Salisbury steak.*

Salish ˈselɪʃ, *n.* [f. a native word meaning "people."] (See quot. 1910 and cf. ***flathead.**)

1910 HODGE *Amer. Indians* II. 415/2 Salish. . . . Formerly a large and powerful division of the Salishan family, to which they gave their name, inhabiting much of w. Montana and centering around Flathead lake. **1938** THOMPSON *High Trails* 160 Tribes on the Columbia River practiced such a custom, considered themselves in consequence as having pointed heads, and therefore distinguished the Salish whose heads were not thus deformed as 'flatheads.' **1947** DEVOTO *Across Wide Missouri* 10 The Flatheads . . . were the principal group or tribe of a people who called themselves the Salish, meaning 'the people.'

attrib. **1849** in *Ann. 31st Cong.* 1 Sess. Sen. Ex. Doc. 52 (1850) 170 The *Salisk* or *Flat Head* Indians occupy from Bitter Root river, a fork of the Columbia, all the country drained by that stream down to what is called the Hell Gate. **1940** *Mt. Hood Guide* 25 The lands of these mid-Columbia people . . . felt the full force of conflict of three tribal families: the Salish tribes of the east, the lower Chinook tribes of the west, and the Sahaptin tribes to the south. **1950** *Nat. Hist.* Feb. 52/2 The rigid stylization and stark simplicity of Salish sculpture echo recent trends in modern art.

b. The language of these Indians.

1940 SMITH *Puyallup-Nisqually* 20 Although the language of the Puyallup-Nisqually is classified as Salish, the people themselves used no special language names.

Salishan ˈselɪʃən, *a.* Of or pertaining to the Salish Indians. — **1903** JAMES *Indian Basketry* 51 They are of the Salishan stock. **1910** [see **Salish**].

saliva curl. =**spit curl.** *Obs.* — **1855** BESTE *Wabash* II. 235 All her hair was rolled off her face, except two little 'saliva curls,' as they are called in America.

***Sall,** *n.* Also **Sally.** A generic name for a colored woman. *Obs.* Cf. **Sambo.**

1813 in *Pub. Col. Soc.* X. 140 Let's tell horrible tales of black Sall, And of babies curl'd headed and yellow. . . . [Note:] Though not recognized in the dictionaries, 'Sall' appears to be a generic name for a negress, as Sambo is for a negro. **1855** in *Pub. Col. Soc.* X. 140 Miss Smith makes cotton pincushions for the antislavery fair; and Master Smith thinks he should like to marry 'Sally dear.' [**1944** FOOTNER *Rivers of East. Shore* 265 'Sally-go-naked' was the name of the rough cloth for the field hands made of flax fibers. It had to be beaten on a wooden block before it could be cut and sewn.]

***salmon,** *n.*

1. (See quots.)

1849 LANMAN *Lett. Alleghany Mts.* 65 *Their* salmon is none other than the genuine pickerel of the North and South. **1884** *Cent. Mag.* April 908/1 The pike-perch becomes a 'salmon' in the Susquehanna, Ohio, and Mississippi rivers.

2. In combs.: (1) **salmon bake,** a social gathering at which salmon is baked and eaten; (2) **belly,** the belly of a salmon prepared for food by pickling; (3) **berry,** any one of various plants or their fruits of the genus *Rubus,* as the cloudberry, white-flowered raspberry, *R. parviflorus* and *R. spectabilis* of the Pacific Coast region; (4) **cache,** (see quot.), *obs.;* (5) **cannery,** a place where salmon are canned commercially; (6) **canning,** the canning or preserving of salmon, also attrib.; (7) **chuck,** a stream [Chinook *chuck*] in which salmon abound; (8) **house,** a temporary dwelling erected by Indians engaged in taking salmon, *obs.;* (9) **killer,** (see quot. 1891); (10) **pile game,** a variety of domestic chicken, *obs.;* (11) **pool,** (see quot. 1890); (12) **season,** the time when salmon are taken for curing or canning; (13) **trout,** any one of various American fishes, as the namaycush and the Dolly Varden *qq.v.*

(1) 1919 *D.N.* V. 58 A merry crowd . . . participated in a most enjoyable salmon-bake. — **(2) 1883** GOODE *Fish. Industr. U.S.* (Fish. Exhib. Lit. 1884 v.) 32 (*OED*), Pickled salmon belly is a favourite delicacy of the region. — **(3) 1844** in *Ore. Hist. Quart.* XXXIV. 359 A salmon berry . . . , by being put into the mouth of a fish [salmon], destroys the charm, and they [Indians] are at liberty to sell to anyone who wishes to buy. **1940** *Mt. Hood Guide* 14 The reddish brown thimbles of the salmon berry also ripen in July. — **(4) 1844** LEE & FROST *Oregon* 177 Salmon caches . . . are cellars which they [*sc.* the Dalles Indians] dig in the sand, where they deposit . . . the fruits of their summer's toil, and their winter's hope.

(5) 1891 WELCKER *Tales 'Wild & Woolly West'* 10 Attached to the salmon cannery was a store. **1911** JENKS & LAUCK *Immigration Problem* 219 During the year 1909 some 3,000 of the Chinese were employed in the salmon canneries in Oregon, Washington and Alaska. — **(6) 1882** *Harper's Mag.* Dec. 13/1 The salmon-canning establishments are large unsightly structures. **1919** J. COBB *Canning Fishery Products* p. ix, Salmon canning is the most important fish canning industry of the Pacific coast. — **(7)** *a***1915** MUIR *Travels Alaska* (1917) 196 On October 30 we visited a camp of Hoonas at the mouth of a salmon-chuck. — **(8) 1844** LEE & FROST *Oregon* 242 The Indians were now all engaged in the salmon harvest, and we met with them in their salmon houses at the Dalls. — **(9) 1884** GOODE *Fisheries* I. 458 The name 'Salmon-killer' is applied to them about Seattle. **1891** *Cent.* 5315/2 *Salmon-killer,* a sort of stickleback, *Gasterosteus aculeatus,* var. *Cataphractus,* found from San Francisco to Alaska and Kamchatka, and destructive to salmon-fry and -spawn. **1896** JORDAN & EVERMANN *Check-List Fishes* 324.

(10) 1871 LEWIS *Poultry Book* 55 Salmon Pile Game.—Coloring of hens is a buff or straw color, underlined with white, and has a rich creamy or salmon-colored look. — **(11) 1866** *Mass. Rep.* 32 (*Cent.* s.v. *Pool*[1]). **1886** H. P. WELLS *Salmon-Fisherman* 128 Nothing about salmon-fishing will probably astonish the experienced trout-fisherman . . . more than . . . a 'salmon-pool.' **1890** *Cent.* 4618/3 *Salmon-pools,* eddies where the salmon collect. Formerly, in some parts of New England, these pools or eddies were numbered, and the fishermen living near the streams had certain rights in them. — **(12) 1841** in *Ore. Hist. Quart.* XXXV. 161 The Salmon season has already commenced. — (13) **1705** *Boston News-Letter* 22 Oct. 2/1 Our men were refresh'd with variety of Fish, especially Salmon Trouts, some whereof 2 foot long. **1911** *Rep. Fisheries 1908* 311/2 In different localities the individuals . . . are known by the local names 'salmon trout,' 'namaycush,' 'togue' [etc.].

As the last term in **Alaska, black, calico, Chinook, dog, dogtooth, fall, herring, hoopid, humpback, jack, king, lake, landlocked, lost, Mackinaw, Ohio, Pacific, red, sea, Sebago, shad, silver, siscowet, spring, Susquehannah, tyee, white salmon.**

salometer səˈlɑmətɚ, *n.* An instrument for measuring the salinity of water, a salinometer. *Obs.* — **1849** LANMAN *Lett. Alleghany Mts.* 158 When tested by a salometer, . . . it [the water] ranges from twenty to twenty-two degrees. **1860** MAURY *Phys. Geog. Sea* (Low) ii. § 102 (*OED*), The salometer confirms it.

***saloon,** *n.*

1. A place where intoxicating liquors are sold and drunk.

The efforts made by owners of saloons to avoid this term and to invent "new and mellifluous" names in its place are commented upon by Mencken in his *Supp.* I. 268.

1841 *S. Lit. Messenger* VII. 764/1 After going into the saloon (grogshop) to 'freshen the nip'— . . . they led me into the upper tier of boxes. **1902** WHITE *Blazed Trail* 155 He arrived out of breath in a typical little mill town consisting of the usual unpainted houses, the saloons, mill, office, and general store. **1949** *Columbus* (O.) *Sun. Dispatch* 16 Oct. C. 1/3 He returned to Westerville in 1887 and opened a saloon at a new location on State St.

2. The main room or compartment of a railroad parlor car. *Obs.*

1859 *First Impressions New World* 214 It is neatly fitted up with little 'state' rooms, with sofas all round. There were four of these besides a general saloon in the middle; but the whole was greatly inferior to the elegance of Mr. Tyson's car on the Baltimore and Ohio Railway. **1891** *Harper's Mag.* March 581/1 Then came the more spacious saloon reserved for the smokers, and furnished with a *buffet*.

3. In combs. (sense **1.**), as (1) **saloon boat,** (2) **keeper,** (3) **loafer,** (4) **man.**

(1) **1873** *Kalama* (Wash.) *Beacon* 7 June 1/1 Mr. Angell has taken his stock upon a 'saloon boat,' and is trading with the fisheries below on this side of the river. — (2) **1860** in *Vogue* 1 Oct. (1944) 157, 'I never said all Democrats were saloon-keepers. What I said was all saloon-keepers are Democrats.' **1949** *Nat. Hist.* Dec. 440/1 Billy McPhee, rotund Fairbanks saloonkeeper, brought his fist down on the mahogany bar, causing the glassware to jingle. — (3) **1874** PINKERTON *Expressman & Detective* 160 He formed the acquaintance of several old saloon-loafers. — (4) **1875** LEWIS *Quad's Odds* 274 (We.), 'Did he lif in Chicago?' asked the saloon-man. **1903** *N.Y. Ev. Post* The saloon men of Tennessee have not, perhaps, the literary finish . . . of their brethren in the Empire State.

Also *saloon band, building, business, experience, furniture, lounger, safe.*

As the last term in **anti-, beer, berth, bowling, candy, coffee, concert, dancing, Dutch beer, gambling, ice cream, lager beer, liquor, original package, oyster, shaving, whisky, wine saloon.**

saloonatic səˈlunətɪk, *n.* [f. *saloon* and lun*atic.*] A saloonkeeper or one who favors the saloon system. *Slang. Obs.* — **1878** BEADLE *Western Wilds* 386 The principal saloonatic had secured a rare attraction: a band of fifteen Chippeways were performing the 'war dance' before the door. **1909** RICE *Mr. Opp* 95 We will hurl grape and cannister into the camps of the saloonatics until they flee the wrath to come.

Hence **saloonatically,** *adv. Rare.* — **1895** *Columbus* (O.) *Dispatch* 3 July 4/3 Sunday was such a dry day, saloonatically speaking, in New York, that persons in this vicinity report that they were 'spitting cotton' on Monday.

saloonist səˈlunɪst, *n.* A saloonkeeper.

1870 *Terr. Enterprise* (Virginia, Nev.) 3 March 3/2 (*heading*), New Saloonists. **1888** *Seattle Post-Intelligencer* 13 Nov. 3/1 A number of vagrants . . . had taken possession of the place, and the saloonist was afraid to eject them. **1946** *Chi. D. News* 8 Nov. 18/2 Saloonists voted out of business in the Woodlawn local option election talk of going to court to upset the vote.

***salt,** *n.*

1. In combs.: (1) **salt batterer,** prob. a stick or pestle for breaking up lumps of salt, *rare;* (2) ***box,** a frame building the outlines of which suggest a saltbox, usu. attrib.; (3) **bread,** salt-rising bread, see **salt rising** as a main entry; (4) **creek,** a creek the water of which is salty; (5) **dome,** *Geol.* in sedimentary rocks, a dome-shaped anticlinal fold the center of which is a mass of rock salt, also attrib.; (6) **haying,** the harvesting of salt-grass hay; (7) **lick,** see as a main entry; (8) **log,** a log in which notches have been cut to hold salt for livestock; (9) **reservation,** an area of salt lands reserved to itself by a state government for use in the public interest; (10) ***rheum,** any one of various skin eruptions, as eczema, cf. **3.** (4) below; (11) **river,** see as a main entry.

(1) **1848** *N.O. Picayune* 21 Aug. 2/2 Hannah had thumped her with a salt batterer in the back of the neck. — (2) **1876** INGRAM *Centennial Exp.* 717 [The cabin] was built of logs in the 'salt-box' style and entirely open in front. **1944** *Sat. Review* 2 Sep. 30/1 (*advt.*), New England saltbox in scenic New York setting. **1948** *Chi. Tribune* 9 Oct. 5/1 The building, one of the 'salt box' type, was the Mulford farmhouse that goes back to about 1680. — (3) **1843** OLIVER *Eight Months* 76 There were Johnny cake and hoe cake, pone bread and dodger, salt bread and milk bread, pumpkin and other pies. — (4) **1639** *Portsmouth Rec.* 8 It is Mutually agreed . . . that these quanteties [be grown]. . . . William Hutchinson ffour Hundreth [on the] North side of ye salt Crick. **1748** ELIOT *Field-Husb.* i. 3 Last Fall I began upon it and drew a Ditch of four foot wide from a large Salt Creek. **1938** MATSCHAT *Suwannee River* 96 They are cut by winding salt creeks and are broken here and there by little hammocks of cedar and scrub pine.

(5) **1928** *Bunker's Mag.* Jan. 21 The first salt dome oil field discovered in Texas was at Spindletop. **1929** *Texas Mo.* Feb. 213 As in all salt dome fields, the producing area was limited. — (6) **1860** *Harper's Mag.* Aug. 336/1 He could get well helping the Deacon all one summer on the smack and the salt-haying. — (8) **1800** HAWKINS *Sk. Creek Country* 45 They select a place of good food, cut down a tree or two, and make salt logs. — (9) **1837** W. JENKINS *Ohio Gaz.* p. x, Laws were passed for leasing the school lands, and salt reservations.

(10) **1809** KENDALL *Travels* I. 325 [The disease] of which I heard the name in every one's mouth, is the *salt rheum.* **1877** BURDETTE *Rise & Fall of Mustache* 291 'Centennial Cordial and American Indian Aboriginal Invigorator' . . . has positively no equal for the cure of . . . salt rheum.

b. In similar combs., usu. obs., sufficiently defined in the quots.: (1) **salt block,** (2) **boilery,** (3) **catchers,** (4) **chuck,** (cf. **salmon chuck**), (5) **factory,** (6) **furnace,** (7) **gauge,** (8) **gourd,** (9) **lake,** (10) **manufactory,** (11) **question,** (12) **sick.**

(1) **1876** KNIGHT 2023/1 *Salt-block,* an apparatus for evaporating the water from a saline solution. The technical name for a salt-factory. — (2) **1858** GOVE *Letters* 341 Numerous salt boileries are erected on the shores; from four gallons of water they obtain nearly one gallon of pure dry salt. — (3) **1735** *Ga. Hist. Soc. Coll.* II. 51 About six at night I crossed the salt-catchers, being the head of the Cambake river, in a small canoe. — (4) **1868** WHYMPER *Alaska* 45 An Indian, paddling in his 'frail kanim' on the great 'salt chuck' or sea, was swallowed—canoe and all—by a great fish.

(5) **1835** HOFFMAN *Winter in West* I. 76 At the mouth of the glen we paused to look at a salt factory. **1837** W. JENKINS *Ohio Gaz.* 85 It has . . . ten or twelve salt factories. — (6) **1822** FOWLER *Journal* 124 The Smoke appeered like that of a Salt furnis. **1847** HOWE *Hist. Coll. Ohio* 263 His pack-saddle [was] stolen by the boilers, . . . thrown into the salt furnace, and destroyed. — (7) **1864** WEBSTER 1166/3 *Salt-gauge,* an instrument used to test the strength of brine or salt-water. — (8) **1918** E. WALLER *Illinois* 79 Salt gourd, a gourd in which salt was kept. It usually had an opening in the upper part of one side and was hung up by the stem. — (9) (*a*) **1799** *Amer. Acad. Mem.* II. II. 77 The *mossy plant,* growing in abundance in the bottom of the salt lake, . . . in shallow places may be seen almost covering the whole of it. **1859** BARTLETT 326 These playas . . . are also called 'salt lakes' from the nitrous efflorescence with which they are often covered when dry. **1901** *Amer. Rev. of Reviews* XXIV. 309/1 Throughout the Staked Plains, numerous small and picturesque salt lakes lie nestled among cliffs of sandstone. (*b*) **1826** COOPER *Mohicans* xvii, The enemies of the great king across the salt lake are his enemies.

(10) **1777** *Ky. Petitions* 44 If the Claimants do not immediately erect Salt manufactories at the different springs [etc.]. **1869** *Mich. Gen. Statutes* I. (1882) 436 The inspector shall not . . . have any interest whatever, directly or indirectly, in any salt manufactury. — (11) **1864** *Index* (London) 2 June 343/1 Soon after the blockade many thought that we [confederates] should 'go up' on the salt question—couldn't salt our meat, and should be starved into subjection. — (12) **1868** *Rep. Comm. Agric. 1867* 97 In Duval county, Florida, a disease vulgarly named 'salt-sick,' supposed to result from eating plants growing near salt water, has been fatal [to cattle].

2. Designating areas of a salt or alkaline nature, as (1) **salt bottom,** (2) **cove,** (3) **desert,** (4) **flat,** (5) **meadow,** (6) **plain,** (7) **prairie,** (8) **region.**

(1) **1859** BARTLETT 377 *Salt-Bottom,* a plain or flat piece of ground covered with saline efflorescences. — (2) **1704** *Providence Rec.* XIV. 279 The one halfe of that Salt Cove. . . . Called the Round Cove. — (3) **1846** BRYANT *California* (1848) 170 We commenced our preparations for the long and much-dreaded march over the great Salt Desert. — (4) **1816** *Niles' Reg.* X. 354/1 The Saline is a valuable salt flat.

(5) **1656** *New Haven Rec.* I. 288 It was don . . . by the cattell hurrying downe in to ye salt meddows. **1742** *Duxbury Rec.* 272 The town also voted that David Allen should improve the town's salt meadow marsh this present year. **1833** CATLIN *Indians* I. 219 We came in contact with an immense saline, or 'salt meadow,' as they are termed in this country, . . . some hundreds of acres of the prairie which were covered with an incrustation of salt. **1939** *L.A.* Map 29. — (6) **1791** W. BARTRAM *Travels* 68 Low salt plains . . . produce Barilla, Sedge, Rushes, &c. **1884** ALDRIDGE *Life on Ranch* 135 The Salt Plains form a desert, some seven or eight miles across in either direction, of perfectly level sand. — (7) **1836** *S. Lit. Messenger* II. 354 In the peninsula of Michigan . . . I saw for the first time a salt or wet prairie which is only a swampy meadow, grown up in a rank, coarse, sedgy grass. **1859** BARTLETT 377 *Salt Prairie*, in Texas and New Mexico, the tracts of salt efflorescence which often cover a wide space. — (8) **1832** BAIRD *Valley Miss.* 123 The 'salt region' extends 15 miles along the [Kanawha] river. **1843** N. BOONE *Journal* 221 Mounds of the same material show from afar projected against the horizon in the Salt region.

b. Designating places or formations where salt in some form occurs, as (1) **salt bluff,** (2) **-grassy isthmus,** (3) **hole,** (4) **lick,** see as a main entry, (5) **mountain,** (6) **pit,** (7) **swamp.**

(1) **1865** PIKE *Scout & Ranger* (1932) 119 On its banks was a salt bluff, which rendered it brackish. — (2) **1898** N. BROOKS *Boys of Fairport* 195 That flat, marshy, salt-grassy isthmus . . . connected the hilly peninsula of Fairport with the mainland. — (3) **1691** *Jamaica* (L.I.) *Rec.* I. 391 What salt holles shall fall in ye sd. meadow ye sd. Mr. Whitte to make up with mowable meadow. **1894** *D.N.* I. 333 *Salt holes*, pool holes of small size filled with salt water. Frequent in marshes. [N.J.]

(5) **1803** *Ann. 8th Congress* 2 Sess. 1504 There exists about one thousand miles up the Missouri . . . a salt mountain. — (6) **1856** WHIPPLE *Explor. Ry. Route* II. 53 The salineras or salt-pits upon the plains between Rio Pecos and the Del Norte will become another important source of mineral wealth to the settlers of New Mexico. — (7) **1765** J. BARTRAM *Diary* 14 July, We walked in his Salt swamps where I observed ye small palmeto which never grows to A tree but shoots A number of leaves from ye root abot 4 foot high.

3. In the names of plants: (1) **salt cedar,** an ornamental shrub or small tree, *Tamarix gallica*, which grows in the warmer parts of the U.S.; (2) ***grass,** any of various grasses, as *Distichlis spicata*, or some species of *Spartina*, found in salt flats, meadows or marshes, or on arid alkaline plains in the west, also attrib.; (3) ***marsh,** see as a main entry; (4) **rheum weed,** (see quot. and cf. **1.** (10) above); (5) **sage,** a variety of greasewood found in the West; (6) ***weed,** an annual plant of the genus *Atriplex* found in the dry alkaline regions of the West; (7) **wood,** a shrub, *Purshia tridentata*, valued as winter forage in some regions in the West.

(1) **1881** *Harper's Mag.* April 731/1 Salt cedars and stunted live-oaks . . . were the only trees growing from the thin soil. **1929** DOBIE *Vaquero* 290 The salt-cedars are low, and for hundreds of miles not a tree marks the course of the river. — (2) **1704** *Providence Rec.* XIV. 279 A piece of Ground . . . beareth a sort of salt Grass which is Called Thatch. **1834** AUDUBON *Ornith. Biog.* II. 377 Their flight was precisely similar . . . when perched on the branches of trees, stakes, or stalks of salt grass hay. **1843** FRÉMONT *Explor. Rocky Mts.* 21 There was a bluish grass . . . called by the voyageurs '*herbe salée*' (salt grass). **1936** *Ann. 74th Cong.* 2 Sess. Sen. Doc. 199, 77 At the highest elevations within the type were such true forage plants as Rothrock and black gramas, . . . and in certain situations saltgrass and galleta. — (4) **1847** WOOD *Botany* 400 C[*helone*] *glabra*. Snake-head. Salt-rheum Weed. . . . A plant of brooks and wet places.

(5) **1913** BARNES *Western Grazing Grounds* 57 Salt sage (*Atriplex*) is the one most generally called by the generic name sage by stockmen all over the West. **1931** [see **cenizo**]. — (6) **1806** LANGSDORFF *Voyages* (1817) 469 We arrived there, but found a low boggy plain, overgrown with nothing but the salt weed, *salsola*. **1881** *Macmillan's Mag.* July 237/1 Vegetation wholly fails [in the Bad Lands of Wyoming], save here and there a bunch of salt-weed. — (7) **1812** STUART *Narratives* 82 The Bottoms during this days march were extensive, covered principally with Saltwood.

As the last term in **alum, black, Indian, Onondaga salt(s).**

***salt,** *v.*

1. *intr.* Of passenger pigeons: ?To secure salt. *Obs.*

1770 in T. PENNANT *Arctic Zoology* II. (1785) 325 When they [wild pigeons] come a salting (as they term it) which they do every morning . . . repairing to the marshes near the sea-side.

2. *tr.* To provide (livestock) with salt.

1819 SCHOOLCRAFT *Mo. Lead Mines* 35 [Horses] subsist themselves in the woods, . . . nothing more being required than to look after them, to see that no bells are lost, that they are duly salted, and that they do not go astray. **1903** FOX *Little Shepherd* xxi, Sheep ran bleating toward him, as though he were come to salt them.

b. *To salt the cow to catch the calf*, to achieve one's end by indirect means. *Colloq.*

1834 CROCKETT *Autobiog.* (1923) 44, I went on the old saying, of salting the cow to catch the calf.

3. To make away with or kill (a person). *Slang.*

1840 SIMMS *Border Beagles* (1855) 258 This agent of his excellency . . . once fairly salted, . . . we shall have no trouble for some time to come.

4. *W.* To make (a mine, claim, etc.) appear valuable by secretly supplying it with a small amount of gold dust, high-grade ore, or precious stones. *Slang.*

[**1851** in *Pioneer* (S.F.) (1854) Nov. 274 The miners are in the habit of flattering the vanity of their fair visitors, by scattering a handful of 'salt' (which, strange to say, is *exactly* the color of gold dust,—through the dirt before their dainty fingers touch it; and the dear creatures go home firmly believing that mining is the prettiest pastime in the world.] **1866** *Columbia* (Calif.) *Citizen* 11 Aug. 3/2 We must devise some means of making the claim appear rich to some prosperous greenhorn. . . . I've got it! We'll salt it! **1902** *Everybody's Mag.* Feb. 188/1 We'll salt Barney's claim for him . . . and set him a-finding it. **1949** *Nat. Geog. Mag.* May 569/2 One group salted a Rocky Mountain mine with uncut stones bought in Rotterdam and sold stock in this 'diamond mine.'

Hence **salted,** *a.*, **salting,** *n.*

1852 in *Pioneer* (S.F.) (1855) March 145 The quicksilver which was procured at the Ranch, for the testing of the quartz, the victims declared was 'salted;' and they accused the *rancheros* of conniving at the fraud. **1856** *Santa Barbara* (Calif.) *Gazette* 21 Feb. 2/5 The best yield I have seen is eighteen cents to the pan, and this was without any 'salting.' **1862** *Calif. Mag.* Jan. 355/1, I lost my $2,000 by buying a 'salted' claim. **1949** *This Week Mag.* 15 Oct. 27/4 They are occasionally called upon by unscrupulous characters whose main object is to sell them a 'salted' mine.

5. To cover or prepare (the carcass of a deer) with poison so that it may serve as a bait in poisoning wolves. *Rare.*

1891 *Fur, Fin, & Feather* 187/2 [The buffalo-hunter] brings down a deer, whose carcass is generously 'salted' with a white powder, which is odorless, but deadly.

6. **To salt down*, (*a*) to store (money) away or put it in safekeeping, also *to salt away*, (*b*) to reprimand or "dress" down. Both *colloq.*

(*a*) **1849** N. P. WILLIS *Rural Lett.* viii. 355 'Calm as the shadow of a rock across the foam of a cataract,' would be a neat thing to 'salt down' for Calhoun or Van Buren. **1870** OLIVE LOGAN *Before Footlights* 479 The money for admission having been counted over, and salted down by the lecturer, the latter locked the door. **1885** *Daily News* 3 Nov. 5/2 He was 'salting down' money for the joint benefit of Ward and himself. **1902** R. W. CHAMBERS *Maids of Paradise* vii. 126 No one to hinder you from salting away as many millions as you can carry off! **1931** *K.C. Star* 19 Sep. It is a well known fact that all gamblers salt away their ill-gotten gains and die inordinately rich. — (*b*) **1904** *Springfield* (Mass.) *W. Republican* 9 Sep. 6 Senator Depew salts down William Allen White who has stated that the senator tried to bully the president into [etc.]. **1913** LONDON *Valley of Moon* 61 You're too fresh to keep. . . . You need saltin' down.

***salter,** *n.* **1.** (See quot.) **2.** One who salts cattle. See also **black, mine, sea salter.** — (1) **1891** *Cent.* 5319/1 *Salter*, . . . a trout about leaving salt water to ascend a stream. (New Eng.) — (2) **1903** *N.Y. Ev. Post* 30 Sep. 7 The 'salters' . . . have reported a good grazing season.

salt lick. A place to which animals resort to lick the ground for impregnated saline particles (see quot. 1796).

1751 GIST *Journal* 42 Upon the N Side of Licking Creek . . . are several Salt Licks, or Ponds, formed by little Streams or Dreins of Water. **1796** MORSE *Amer. Geog.* I. 663 The terms Salt Lick and Salt Spring are used synonymously, but improperly, as the former differs from the latter in that it is dry. **1802** ELLICOTT *Journal* 15 The salt lick, or spring, is situated in the bed of a small creek. **1949** *Tenn. Hist. Quart.* March 3 The country abounded in sulphur springs and likewise the salt 'licks' around which congregated buffalo, deer, and elk.

attrib. **1755** L. EVANS *Anal. Map Colonies* 29 Great Salt Lick Creek is remarkable for fine Land.

***salt marsh.**

1. (See quot. 1882.) *Obs.*

1836 SIMMS *Mellichampe* iv, [The pony] smells . . . as if it had fed on cane-tops and salt-marsh all its life. **1882** G. C. EGGLESTON *Wreck of Red Bird* 28 The little marsh islands . . . are simply bars of mud on which a kind of rank grass, called salt marsh, grows.

2. In combs.: (1) **salt marsh caterpillar,** (see quot. 1891); (2) **fly,** (see quot.); (3) **hay,** hay made from salt grass; (4) **terrapin, turtle,** the diamondback terrapin.

(1) **1854** EMMONS *Agric. N.Y.* V. 225 *Spilosoma acræa.* Salt marsh Caterpillar. **1891** *Cent.* 5320/1 Salt-marsh caterpillar, the hairy larva of an arctiid moth, *Spilosoma acraea,* one of the woolly-bears, which feeds commonly on the salt-grass of the sea-coast of New England. — (2) **1862** *Harper's Mag.* Nov. 737/2 The *Simulia æstuarium* — 'Salt-marsh fly'—is a nuisance found every where ... near salt marshes. — (3) **1655** *N.H. Probate Rec.* I. 31, I give unto my Sonne-inlaw ... the farthermost stack of Salt Marsh hay. *c***1680** HULL *Diaries* 243 Being salt-marsh hay, it smothered, and did not hastily burn. — (4) **1872** *Proc. Amer. Philos. Soc.* XII. 475 The salt-marsh terrapin. **1911** *Rep. Fisheries 1908* 317/2 [Salt-water terrapins] are also called 'salt-marsh turtle' and 'diamond-back.'

salt rising. A batter or dough of salt, flour, or corn meal and water or milk, used for leavening.

1833 TRAILL *Backwoods of Canada* (1846) 137 [The wife of a Canadian settler] must know how to manufacture *hop-rising* or *salt-rising* for leavening her bread. **1846** FARNHAM *Prairie Land* 333 They make a large loaf in their iron ovens which is fermented by what they call *salt-rising.* **1898** HARPER *S. B. Anthony* I. 161 The process of yeast-making was ... not well understood by the average housekeeper, so a substitute was found in 'salt-risings.'

b. Attrib. with **biscuit, bread, loaf.**

1907 *N.Y. Ev. Post* (s.-w. ed.) 20 June 4 The general suffrage seems to go to ... Virginia ham, salt-rising biscuits, apple dumpling. — **1865** *Atlantic Mo.* April 400/1 Maggie ... described the process of making 'salt-rising' bread. **1947** *Atlantic Mo.* Dec. 112/2 Gone, too, with these luscious homemade loaves are other substantial and tasty favorites: 'salt rising' bread [etc.]. — **1846** FARNHAM *Prairie Land* 138 When tea-time approached, ... the 'salt risin' loaf ... [was] put to baking. **1890** *Harper's Mag.* Jan. 282/2 The rich brown salt-rising loaf.

salt river.

1. A river up which the tide comes to, or almost to, its source. *Obs.*

1659 *Providence Rec.* I. 97 A percell of land ... lieth upon the salt River at the furthermost side of the towne boundes. **1704** *Ib.* V. 224 Sd Cove ... lieth adjoyneing to the North side of the salt River called Pautuckett. **1791** W. BARTRAM *Travels* 31 Numerous small rivers and their branches ... they call salt rivers, because the tides flow near to their sources.

2. (*cap.*) Used attrib. in the sense: Rude, uncultivated, backwoodsy, esp. with reference to speech. *Obs.* or *hist.*

In this and the following uses, the term seems to allude to a particular stream, poss. Salt River in Kentucky, regarded as the place par excellence for the "roarers," "screamers," and rowdies of the backwoods.

1835 FLINT in *Athenæum* 511/2 There is, in fact, a well-known rivalry between the collectors of the Downing dialect of New England, and the Crocket or Salt River dialect of the South and West. **1835** *Knickerb.* VI. 177 She grew up the oddest compound of ... prose-poetry, mock-sublime, Jersey-Yankeeism, and Salt-river slang and roaring, that it has ever been my fortune to meet.

b. Also **Salt River roarer, screamer,** a half horse half alligator (*q.v.*) rowdy or backwoodsman. *Slang.*

1830 *Columbia Co. Reg.* (Bloomsburg, Pa.) 7 Sep. 1/4 'Stop, friend!' exclaimed one of the Salt River Roarers, stepping deliberately up to him, 'are you a voter?' **1835** *Knickerb.* VI. 178 This tender mourner of the album and the beech could out-face a Salt-river roarer in West country slang. **1947** CONWAY *Midland Humor* x, The ring-tailed roarers and Salt River screamers of the half-horse and half-alligator breed, both male and female, were ordinarily combinations of physical might and mother wit which enabled them to outsmart invaders from other regions.

3. *To row* (someone) *up Salt River,* and variants, to overcome, vanquish, often with reference to political defeats. *Slang.*

1830 *Cin. Chronicle* 2 Jan. 1/2 He replied he did'nt 'smoak me,' and unless I cut cable in short order, he'd roar me up salt river. **1832** *Spirit of Times* (N.Y.) 28 April 3/1 He 'rowed' Stanberry 'up a salt creek,' and is now *being* tried by the House of Representatives for his unlucky propensity. **1861** *N.Y. Herald* 5 Jan. 7/1 There must be compromise, or the whole confederacy must go to Salt river, and Hon. Massa Greeley with it. **1910** *N.Y. Ev. Post* 1 Oct., That imaginary stream called 'Salt River,' up which defeated candidates are supposed to be rowed, is one of the most felicitous of all our political Americanisms, although its authorship is unknown.

b. (See quots.)

1838 *Bentley's Misc.* IV. 588, 'I can drink till the world gets too old to move. While another man rows up Salt River, I'm only putting the fire out in the forest.' [Note:] Rowing up Salt River is a slang term for getting intoxicated; and putting the fire out in the forest signifies quenching the thirst, or internal fire, caused by previous sling drinking. **1842** UNCLE SAM *Peculiarities* I. 89 When the Yorker was quite 'up Salt River'—decidedly intoxicated—he went to sleep. **1852** *Chi. Democrat* 11 Nov., One Thomas Holt, lately a clerk in the Chicago Post Office, when last seen, ... was on his way up 'Salt River' with Gen. Scott. **1941** BALDWIN *Keelboat Age* 97 It'd shore be harder'n rowin' up Salt River to find a cleverer parcel o' fellers 'n them keelers.

* **salt water.**

1. *attrib.* Designating newcomers, esp. slaves, recently arrived from overseas. *Obs.*

*c***1797** LATROBE *Journal* 63 The ferryman ... is one of several who are children of a man and woman, negroes, brought from Africa—called here salt-water negroes. **1818** FEARON *Sketches* 93 If I had my will there should never be a salt-water man employed in the States. **1855** F. DOUGLASS *My Bondage* 323 The salt water slave who hung in the guards of a steamer ... has, by the publicity given to the circumstance, set a spy on the guards of every steamer departing from southern ports.

2. In combs.: (1) **salt-water chub,** (see quot.); (2) **marsh,** a salt marsh; (3) **marsh hen, meadow hen,** (see quot. 1890); (4) **minnow,** (see quot.); (5) **perch,** (see quot.); (6) **tailor,** (see quot. 1859); (7) **teal,** (see quot.); (8) **terrapin,** the diamondback terrapin; (9) **trout,** a local name for a weakfish; (10) **vegetables,** (see quot.), *obs.*

(1) **1884** GOODE *Fisheries* I. 269 At the mouth of the Chesapeake [the tautog is called] 'Salt-water Chub.' — (2) **1754** *Ga. Col. Rec.* VI. 427 [The land was] bounded on the back by a Salt Water Marsh. **1834** AUDUBON *Ornith. Biog.* II. 269 [The fish crows] alight on large mud flats bordering the salt-water marshes. **1883** *Nat. Museum Bul.* No. 27, 155 Louisiana Clapper Rail. Salt-water marshes of Gulf coast. — (3) **1835** AUDUBON *Ornith. Biog.* III. 35 The Salt-Water Marsh Hen swims with considerable ease. **1844** *Nat. Hist. N.Y., Zoology* II. 259 The Saltwater Meadow-Hen, *Rallus crepitans,* ... appears along the shores of this State about the latter end of April. **1890** *Cent.* 3640/1 The clapper-rail, *Rallus crepitans* or *longirostris:* more fully called *salt-water marsh-hen* or *salt-marsh hen.* — (4) **1883** *Nat. Museum Bul.* No. 27, 452 *Fundulus grandis.* ... Killifish; Mummichog; Salt-water minnow. Atlantic coast of Southern United States.

(5) **1889** FARMER 141/2 In New York it [the chogset] is known ... as the Salt Water Perch. — (6) **1859** BARTLETT 469 In the towns on the Potomac, the Blue fish is called a *Salt-water tailor.* **1883** *Nat. Museum Bul.* No. 27, 448 Skipjack; Salt-water Tailor; Horse-mackerel. ... This is a food-fish of great importance. **1911** *Rep. Fisheries 1908* 317/2 The 'salt-water tailor' is the bluefish ... of North Carolina, Virginia, and Maryland. — (7) **1844** *Nat. Hist. N.Y., Zoology* II. 327 The Ruddy Duck, *Fuligula Rubida,* ... is frequently called the Saltwater Teal. — (8) **1842** *Nat. Hist. N.Y., Zoology* III. 10 The Salt-water Terrapin ... is the well known and justly prized Terrapin of epicures. **1911** *Rep. Fisheries 1908* 317/2 The salt-water terrapin (*Malaclemmys palustris*) is very highly prized for food. — (9) **1737** BRICKELL *N. Carolina* 234 The Salt-Water Trouts ... have blackish and not Red Spots. **1884** GOODE *Fisheries* I. 362 About Cape Cod they are called 'Drummers' ... [and in] the Southern Atlantic States ... 'Sea Trout' and 'Salt-water Trout.' **1911** *Rep. Fisheries 1908* 316/2 Squeteague (*Cynoscion regalis*). ... It is known as ... 'shad trout,' 'sea trout,' and 'salt-water trout' in the Middle and South Atlantic states.

(10) **1859** BARTLETT 378 Salt-water vegetables, in New York a cant term for oysters and clams.

Saltzburgher ˈsɔltsˌbɜgə, *n.* A member of a group of colonists from Salzburg, Austria, who settled in Georgia. *Obs.*

1737 *Ga. Col. Rec.* III. 135 The use of the Missionaries and Schoolmaster for the Saltzburghers, [£]50. **1739** in MCCALL *Hist. Georgia* I. 92 We the Saltzburghers, and inhabitants of Ebenezer, ... [intreat] your excellency ... [to send] another transport of Salzburghers, to be settled at Ebenezer. **1741** *Ga. Col. Rec.* III. 385 [The] Saltzburghers, ... with the Saltzburghers that went before, were settled in a Town called by them Ebenezer.

salutatorian səˌlutəˈtorɪən, *n.* [f. next+*-an.*] The member of a graduating class in high school or college, usu. the second highest student in scholastic rank, who delivers the salutatory address on commencement day. Cf. **valedictorian.**

1847 WEBSTER 978/2. **1871** BAGG *At Yale* 592 The 'Salutatorian' is in like manner the 'second best.' **1904** *N.Y. Ev. Post* 4 March 7 By vote of the Yale faculty there will be no appointment of valedictorian and salutatorian after the present year. **1948** *Capital-Democrat*

(Tishomingo, Okla.) 3 June 2/3 The 'Citizenship Award' went to Lewis Nance, class salutatorian.

∗**salutatory,** *a.* and *n.*

1. *n.* An address given by a student at commencement, esp. the salutatory oration given by the salutatorian.

1779 *N.J. Archives* 2 Ser. III. 670 John Woodford [gave] the Salutatory in Latin. **1881** RITTENHOUSE *Maud* 13 Mabel, ten times as smart as all the rest put together, . . . [was] not even given the salutatory. **1941** *Harvard Univ. Reg.* 31 Even the stock joke of *pulcherrimis puellis* in the Latin salutatory, which the Corporation tried to prohibit in the eighteenth century, survives.

2. A printed address of greeting to the readers of the first issue of a newspaper or magazine. *Obs.*

1869 MARK TWAIN *Salutatory* (1923) 15 (R.), Your new editor feels called upon to write a 'salutatory' at once. **1887** *Lit. World* (Boston) 25 June 206/2 In his salutatory the editor declares his paper to be 'a very modest effort to assist in a practical way the "Literary Movement in Chicago." '

3. *a.* Pertaining to an address of greeting, used esp. of the oration delivered by the salutatorian at the opening of commencement exercises.

1670 *Mass. H.S. Coll.* 4 Ser. I. 13 Our class declaimed their last declamations . . . with an oration salutatory and valedictory. **1779** *N.J. Archives* 2 Ser. III. 670 The exercises . . . [included a] salutatory latin oration by George Merchant. **1856** *S. Lit. Messenger* XXII. 68/2 This gentleman . . . was graduated [at Princeton] in 1791, having the Salutatory Oration in Latin assigned him. **1949** J. B. HERRICK *Memories* 24 It was my especial honor to deliver the Latin Salutatory Address.

Hence **salutatorily,** *adv.* By way of greeting. *Obs.* — **1847** WEBSTER 978/2. **1863** A. D. WHITNEY *F. Gartney* vi, 'Well, Melindy,' said Mrs. Griggs, salutatorily.

∗**Sam,** *n.*[1] [In **1.** short for **Uncle Sam.** In **2.** and **3.** the well-known proper name.]

1. A member of the Know-Nothing party. Also Uncle Sam or the U.S. Government (see quot. *a*1870). *Obs.*

1855 *Prairie News* (Okalona, Miss.) 7 June 3/1 The [Know-Nothing] Council is divided on the Jonathan and Sam question. . . . The Sams are anti-foreign and anti-Catholic. **1855** M. THOMPSON *Doesticks* 244 [The Know-Nothings made me] solemnly swear . . . death and destruction to all foreigners, and eternal fidelity to 'Sam.' **1856** J. L. CHAPMAN (*title*), Americanism versus Romanism, or, the Cis-Atlantic Battle between Sam and the Pope. *a*1870 CHIPMAN *Notes on Bartlett* 378 *Sam*, a nickname given, as referring to their cant about Uncle Sam, to the Know-Nothing or Native American party. **1875** *Cin. Enquirer* 1 July 1/1 It took to its bosom 'Sambo,' and then 'Sam;' then more 'Sambos,' and when it had got all the 'Sambos' in the land it kicked 'Sam' out, or shut his mouth, I don't know which.

Hence in derivatives: **Samite, Sammyism.** *Obs.*

1856 *Louisville Democrat* 10 July 3/2 A fellow with a fiddle now followed the Mayor, scraping away, at the instigation of these brave 'Samites.' **1862** in THORNTON *Glossary* II. (1912) 522 A secret organization . . . named *Know-Nothing-ism* or *Sammyism*, from the boasted exclusive devotion of the fraternity to the U.S.

Also **Sammy Know Nothing.**

1856 *Jackson Picket Guard* (Elkton, Md.) 24 Sep. 3/1 See to it Sammy Know Nothing.

b. *To see Sam*, to become impressed with the merits or popularity of the Know-Nothing party. *Obs.*

1855 *N.Y. Wkly. Tribune* 27 Oct. 1/4 Of course, Crippen and Jones have both 'seen Sam,' whether they will or will not confess it. **1866** *Cong. Globe* 18 Jan. 308/1 Just at the close of the polls I looked back over my shoulder, and saw 'Sam' a short distance behind.

2. Sam Hill, a euphemism for "hell." *Colloq.*

1839 *Havanna* (N.Y.) *Republican* 21 Aug. (Th.), What in sam hill is that feller ballin' about? **1927** JAMES *Cow Country* 77 What the Sam Hill do you think we are out here, servants? **1948** *Salt Lake Tribune* 18 Dec. 10/7 He wondered who the Sam Hill the 'senator' was.

3. Sam Peabody, (see quot. and cf. **Peabody bird**).

1909 *D.N.* III. 415 Sam Peabody, n. The white-throated sparrow, which seems to say poor old Sam Peabody, Peabody, Peabody.

Sam sæm, *n.*[2] Short for next. *Obs.* — **1867** DIXON *New Amer.* II. 13 Sam—all negroes there are Sams—may be a Methodist. *Ib.* II. 15 Since the South has been made free for Sam to live in, he has turned his back to the cold and friendly North, in search of a brighter home.

Sambo ˈsæmbo, *n.* [See note.] A nickname for a Negro. Also in a generic sense.

This word is prob. of African origin. In the Congo *nzambu* means a monkey, but Turner (p. 155) finds Sambo used as a name among the Gullahs, a use which he relates to Hausa (northern Nigeria) *sambo*, the name given the second son in a family. The Amer. use may well be a borrowing from slaves and not a continuation of *OED Sambo* 1. See also *zambo* in Santamaría and Friederici.

1704 *Boston News-Letter* 2 Oct. 2/2 There is a Negro man taken up supposed to be Runaway from his Master, . . . calls himself Sambo. **1745** *Va. Gazette* 16 May 4/2 Ran away from the Subscriber's Quarter . . . the following Negro's, viz. Sambo, . . . Aaron, . . . Berwick. **1841** *N.O. Picayune* 12 Jan. 2/2 Literally speaking, the Sambos and their 'lubly' Dinahs were going the whole figure. **1947** LUMPKIN *Southerner* 63 No set of laborers on earth, save the sambo's, can make a cotton and corn crop, on three pounds of bacon and a peck of meal a week.

sammy ˈsæmɪ, *v.* [App. an extension of ∗*sam, v.*, which is older in this sense.] *tr.* and *intr.* (See quots.)

1891 J. W. STEVENS *Leather Manuf.* iii. 24 Sammieing. This term . . . I have failed to learn the origin of. . . . It appears to have originated in the Western and Southern states, for in the East, 'hardening' is generally used when the leather is hung on poles or in the lofts to dry out a certain percentage of moisture, in order to prepare it for splitting and stuffing. **1897** C. T. DAVIS *Manuf. Leather* (ed. 2) 416 If the light color is desired, the leather is hung up and allowed to harden, as it is termed in the East, or to sammy, as it is termed in the West, for setting.

samp sæmp, *n.* [See quot. 1895.]

1. Corn broken into a coarse, ricelike form, boiled and eaten, usu., with milk and sugar.

1643 WILLIAMS *Key* (1866) 41 From this the English call their Samp . . . eaten hot or cold with milke or butter. **1783** PATTEN *Diary* 474, I took 3 bushels of corn to Deacon Smiths Mill and two of it ground and one made into Samp. **1895** GERARD in *N.Y. Sun* 30 July, Samp, from 'nasaump,' 'softened by water,' A Narragansett name for a pottage made of unparched meal. **1948** *Chi. Tribune* 11 Jan. VII. 16/1 She reached up to her cookbook shelf and took down her collection of hearty cold weather recipes: . . . samp pinked with paprika and cooked slowly and carefully, sukiyaki with paper thin steak, . . . chowders and stews.

2. In combs. now obs. or hist.: (1) **samp mill,** a mill in which corn intended for samp was ground; (2) **mortar,** a mortar in which corn was reduced to a coarse meal (see also quot. 1856); (3) **pan,** a pan in which samp was cooked; (4) **porridge,** (see quot.).

(1) **1761** *Huntington Rec.* II. 448 Jacob Brush should have Lyberty to Build a samp Mill in the Meeting house Brook. — (2) **1713** HEMPSTEAD *Diary* 30 I was at home al day fixing Sampmorter & killing Sheep. **1825** WOODWORTH *Forest Rose* I. ii, Didn't you get up softly and put the big samp-mortar in your place? **1856** FERGUSSON *America* 492 Our kind friends carried us to a place [near Fairfield, Conn.] called 'The Samp Mortar.' There is . . . a deep, roundish, but irregular cavity in the rock nigh a foot broad, and as deep, in which it is said the Indians were wont to pound their maize. *c*1887 in *Amer. Sp.* (1948) April 115/2 The sound of the samp-mortar might be heard resounding through the woods in the evening or early morning. — (3) **1850** *Harper's Mag.* Nov. 729/2 Among the relics preserved . . . [is] a samp-pan that belonged to Metacomet, or King Philip. — (4) **1935** *Col. of Conn.* 12 Samp porridge: . . . The corn meal was boiled in water. . . . Salt was added. . . . Sometimes dried huckleberries were added. . . . It was eaten hot or cold with milk.

∗**sample,** *n.* In combs.: (1) **sample ballot,** (see quot. 1897); (2) **case,** a case in which a traveling salesman carries samples; (3) ∗**room,** a barroom or saloon, *colloq.*; (4) **trunk,** a very strong, specially fitted trunk in which a commercial salesman carries samples.

(1) **1897** *Cong. Rec.* 18 Feb. 1970/1 [The law of Illinois] provided, also, that accompanying these ballots should be eight 'instructive ballots'—ballots prepared for the instruction of the voters, sample ballots. **1898** *Mo. So. Dakotan* I. 73 If a voter had to vote on the merits of every law passed by the legislature, he would probably throw away his sample ballot in disgust and go afishing. — (2) **1890** BIFF HALL *Turnover Club* 38 But he opened his sample-case and started to expatiate upon the merits of his goods. — (3) **1865** SALA *Diary* II. 46 Sometimes the bar is at the side, screened off, and genteelly disguised under the name of 'sample room.' You enter ostensibly to purchase cherries, and immediately 'put yourself outside' a 'tot' of Bourbon. **1896** *Chi. Record* 13 Jan. 11/6 For Sale—Corner Sample-room . . . license paid. **1938** HART *New Yorkers* 180 The 'quiet trade' sipped their gin at 'sample rooms' such as Haan's on the site of the present Hotel McAlpin. — (4) **1887** C. B. GEORGE *40 Yrs. on Rail* 178 Commercial travelers with their heavy sample trunks did not exist as in these later times. **1915** *Current Affairs* 25 Jan. 8/2 (Ernst), Salesmen's sample trunks.

sampling rod. (See quot.) — **1886** *Harper's Mag.* July 208/1 On arrival at the city they [*sc.* cereals] are sampled by means of a hollow iron sampling-rod, whose valve opens to admit the grain as the rod is thrust into the hatches of a vessel, or the interior of a car, and closes so as to retain the sample when it is drawn out.

Sancho ˈsæntʃo, *n.* Also **sancho.** [Sp. proper name.] **1.** In the game of sancho pedro, the nine of trumps. **2. sancho pedro,** a gambling card game derived from auction pitch—so called from the trump cards sancho and pedro, cf. **pedro sancho.**

(1) **1880** DICK *Amer. Hoyle* (ed. 13) 210 *Sancho* . . . may be taken with any trump higher than the Nine. **1899** CHAMPLIN & BOSTWICK *Cyclo. Games & Sports* (ed. 2) 7/2 The nine of trumps (called Sancho) [counts] nine points. — (2) **1890** *Cent.* 4356/2 *Pedro*, . . . in the game of sancho-pedro, the five of trumps. **1899** CHAMPLIN & BOSTWICK *Cyclo. Games & Sports* (ed. 2) 7/2 *Pedro Sancho, or Sancho Pedro*. . . . Any number of persons may play.

* **sand,** *n.*

1. Courage, grit, determination. *Slang.* See **f.** (3) below, and cf. **bottom sand, sandiness.**

1875 HARTE *Tales of Argonauts* 71 Blank me if I didn't think he was losing his sand. **1903** *Out West* Jan. 57 Lieut. Richard Roberts [was] rough and loud, ever ready with a blow for brawlers and laggards, but a man of 'sand.'

2. In combs.: (1) **sand artist,** one who makes crude sculptures in sand; (2) * **bag,** a strong cloth or canvas bag partially filled with sand and used as a weapon by thugs; (3) **bagger,** see as a main entry; (4) **bar,** a deposit of sand in the form of a bar, ridge, shoal, etc., found in or along rivers or coasts, cf. **sandbar willow** under **d.** (1) below; (5) **barge,** a barge used in transporting sand; (6) **blow,** (see quots. and cf. **sand burst**); (7) **boat,** ?= **sand barge;** (8) * **box,** (*a*) (see quot.), (*b*) a construction around the end of the axle of a wagon to prevent sand from getting into the hub, cf. **talking box;** (9) **burst,** a cone-shaped sink resulting from the breaking out of fountains of water mixed with sand, mud, and bituminous shale in the New Orleans area during an earthquake in 1811, *obs.*, cf. **sand blow;** (10) **collar,** "the mass of eggs, embedded in firm jellylike matter, of any gastropod of the genus *Natica* or allied genus. It has the shape of a bottomless saucer broken at one side, and is coated with fine sand" (W. '09); (11) **creek,** *W.* a creek the flow of which is greatly impeded by sand, cf. **dry creek;** (12) **dollar,** (see quots.), *obs.*, cf. **c.** (6) below; (13) **line,** designating a city located in a sandy region, *rare;* (14) **painting,** *W.* a representation suggestive of a picture made, usu. by an Indian medicine man in a healing ceremony, by pouring various colored sands, crushed flowers, powdered rock, charcoal, corn meal, etc., on a flat sandy surface; (15) **pie,** moist sand patted or molded into the shape of a pie, *colloq.;* (16) * **stone,** see as a main entry; (17) **storm,** a windstorm that drives along a cloud of sand [one example, 1774, of this term relating to Africa, is recorded in the *OED*—the term was apparently coined anew here]; (18) **whirl,** *W.* a sand spout, cf. **b.** (10) below; (19) **work,** ?a fortification of sand, *rare.*

(1) **1931** *Amusements* (Atlantic City) 11 July 38 Sand Artists are popular always—at Convention periods their subjects become topical. — (2) **1887** *Courier-Journal* 17 Jan. 2/6 He was struck with a sand-bag. **1903** ELY *Evolution Indust. Soc.* 127 If I knock you down with a sand-bag and rob you, is that to be called competition? — (4) **1781–2** JEFFERSON *Notes Va.* (1788) 5 The Missisipi, below the mouth of the Missouri, is always muddy, and abounding with sand bars. **1806** *Ann. 9th Congress* 2 Sess. 1111 The sand bars . . . extended so far into the bend as to leave little more than the breadth of the boat. *a***1918** G. STUART *On Frontier* II. 17 The river was low and full of sand bars.

(5) **1840** DANA *Two Years* 203, I had got everything in order—patch upon patch, like a sand-barge's mainsail. — (6) **1846** [see **sand burst**]. **1903** *D.N.* II. 328 sand-blow, *n.* A small mound raised by gas blowing up through sandy soil during earthquakes. They are very common in the vicinity of New Madrid, Missouri. — (7) **1754** *N.J. Archives* XIX. 336 The least of the two Whales, mentioned in this Paper two Weeks since to be run ashore a little to the Southward of the Hook, was last Thursday brought into this Harbor by a Sand Boat from Rockaway. — (8) (*a*) **1859** BARTLETT 379 *Sand-Box*, a primitive sort of spittoon, consisting of a wooden box filled with sand. (*b*) **1930** BANNING *Six Horses* 365 Even his coach was comparatively silent. All couplings were so well leathered fore and aft that one was conscious only of the dull clucking sound from the sand boxes (around the axles). — (9) **1846** LYELL *Second Visit* II. 176 Within a distance of a few hundred yards, were five more of these 'sand-bursts,' or 'sandblows,' as they are sometimes termed here.

(10) **1918** LINCOLN *Shavings* 159 They walked along the beach, picked up shells, inspected 'horse-foot' crabs, jelly fish and 'sand collars.' — (11) **1846** SAGE *Scenes Rocky Mts.* xiii. We soon came to a large sand creek. **1907** COOK *Border & Buffalo* 96 In the sand creek at the south end of the grove were several holes of fresh water. — (12) **1830** *Day's N.Y. Bank Note List* 16 Aug. 4/3 List of Counterfeit Coins. . . . *Sand Dollars*, such as have been cast in sand, are generally worth 100 cents, but bear no premium. **1836** M. A. HOLLEY *Texas* x. 183 The greatest part of the silver coin was of the description called provincial or hammered and sand dollars,—a coin of the Revolution made by the Mexican patriots before they obtained possession of any of the mints. — (13) **1894** *Harper's Mag.* LXXXVIII. 943/1 The harbor is bad, like those of all the sand-line cities. — (14) **1900** W. HOUGH in *Smithsonian Rep.* (Nat. Mus.) 467 The ceremonial sand painting of the Hopi and Navajo, where the most beautiful effects are secured by allowing sand in slender streams of different colors to fall from the hand guiding it over the surface to form designs. **1948** *Chi. D. News* 9 Aug. 7/1 Sandpainting is done to heal the sick.

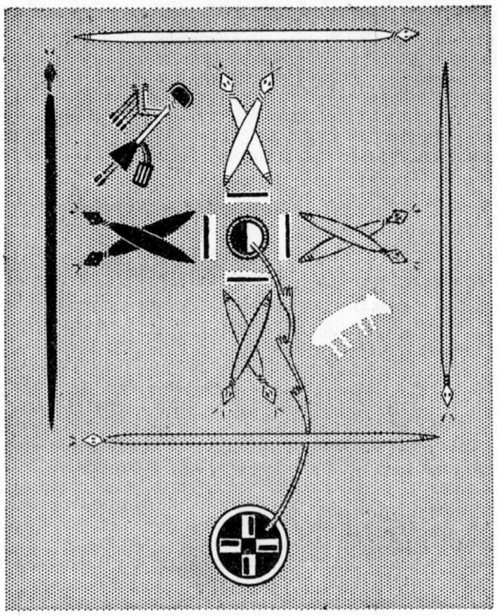

Sand painting

(15) **1835** C. F. HOFFMAN *Winter in West* I. 148 A bevy of rosy little girls . . . were making 'sand pies' on the bank of the river. — (17) **1870** KEIM *Sheridan's Troopers* (1885) 19 Sand storms in the summer are certainly not climatical considerations the most inviting. **1949** *Nat. Geog. Mag.* Sep. 385 Refugees from a Sandstorm Shake the Dust from Their Gear. — (18) **1890** *Stock Grower & Farmer* 4 Jan. 7/2 You see objects like enormous giants moving across the waste swiftly. They are sand-whirls. — (19) **1846** in R. DOUBLEDAY *Jrnl. Maj. Philip Barbour* (1936) 26 Another sand work has been commenced by the Mexicans and considerably forwarded.

b. In combs. of obvious meaning or sufficiently explained in the quots.: (1) **sand auger,** (2) **board,** (3) **club,** (4) **draw,** cf. * **draw,** *n.* **5,** (5) **hog,** (6) **iron,** (7) **lapper,** see as a main entry, (8) **ore,** (9) **sink,** (10) **spout.**

(1) **1900** *Nation* LXXI. 15 Nov. 390/1 One of those little, waltzing whirlwinds, so characteristic of the Southwest and known to frontiersmen of our speech as 'sand-augers.' — (2) **1846** *30th Congress* 1 Sess. H.R. Ex. Doc. No. 41, 441 We saw many axletrees, wagon tongues, sand-boards, and ox yokes, that had been broken and cast aside. **1876** KNIGHT 2025/1 *Sand-board*, . . . a bar over the hind axle and parallel therewith. It rests upon the hind hounds where they cross the axle. — (3) (*a*) **1873** *Winfield* (Kans.) *Courier* 11 Sep. 1/7 A weapon of a peculiarly dangerous and for a time mysterious nature . . . is a sand club, formed by filling an eel skin with sand. (*b*) **1912** *Punch* 15 May 380/2 Incidentally I am pleased to know that Americans call a niblick a sand club. — (4) *a***1909** P. A. RYDBERG *Contrib. U.S. Nat. Herb.* III. 470 (*Cent. Supp. s.v. draw*), A sand draw is a

subterranean stream. On the surface is seen only a broader or narrower band of pure sand, marking the channel.

(5) **1904** *N.Y. Ev. Post.* 11 Jan. 3 The men who are employed as 'sandhogs' or excavators in the caisson for the new Manhattan Bridge. **1949** *Nat. Hist.* Oct. 363/2 Nature's little 'sand hog' [mole] depends on broad flat forefeet and strong claws. — **(6) 1796** MORSE *Univ. Geog.* I. 464 The Rev. Dr. Jared Eliot, of Killingworth, invented sand-iron, or the making of iron from black sand, in 1761. — **(8) 1805** D. MCCLURE *Diary* (1899) 131 The country abounds with Sand or bog oar. — **(9) 1839** F. A. KEMBLE *Jrnl.* 142 He followed it up by assuring me that there were what he called sand-sinks under the mud, and that whatever was placed on the surface would not only sink through the mud, but also into a mysterious quicksand of unknown depth and extent below it.

(10) 1872 *Chi. Tribune* 24 Dec. 2/7 Half a dozen 'sand-spouts'—columns of sand drawn up by whirlwinds—were to be seen on the Twenty-two Mile Desert yesterday afternoon.

c. In the names of birds and other creatures: (1) **sand bird,** one of various birds, esp. a snipe or a sandpiper, found on the seashore, a shore bird; (2) **bug,** a small burrowing crustacean, *Emerita talpoida*, found in sand (see also quot. 1855); (3) **codling,** a local name for the toadfish; (4) **cricket,** (see quot. 1891), cf. **Jerusalem cricket, niño de la tierra;** (5) ***dab,** (see quot. 1891); (6) **dollar,** any one of various flat, round sea urchins, as *Echinarachnius parma*, cf. **2.** (12) above; (7) **fiddler,** the fiddler crab, cf. ***fiddler,** *n.* **1;** (8) **flounder,** any one of various flounders, esp. the windowpane; (9) **hornet,** "a sand-wasp, especially of the family *Crabronidae*, some of which resemble hornets" (*Cent.*); (10) ***lizard,** (see quot. 1933); (11) **peep,** a familiar name for various small sandpipers, so called from their note, also attrib.; (12) ***rat,** a pocket gopher or pouched rat, also transf., cf. **red sand rat;** (13) **shark,** a small voracious shark of the genus *Odontaspis*, also called **shovel-nose** *q.v.;* (14) **shoal duck,** =**pied duck;** (15) ***sucker,** (*a*) (see quot.), (*b*) (see quot. 1896); (16) **whiting,** (see quots.).

(1) 1709 LAWSON *Carolina* 151 The Sand-Birds are about the Bigness of a Lark, and frequent our Sand-Beaches. **1832** WILLIAMSON *Maine* I. 149 Beach, or Sand-bird is about the size of a swallow. **1917** *Birds of Amer.* I. 234 White-rumped Sandpiper. . . . [Also called] Sand-bird; Bull Peep. — **(2) 1855** OGILVIE *Supp.* 346/2 *Sand-bug*, a hymenopterous insect, the *Ammophila arenaria*. (American.) **1884** GOODE *Fisheries* I. 779 The Sand Bug . . . is rather an odd species of Crab, related to the Hermit Crabs. — **(3) 1817** in *Amer. Mo. Mag.* II. 204 The fishermen . . . call it [*Opsanus cerapalus*] by the name of *Yellow-Kusk, Sand Codling, Slimer*, etc. — **(4) 1884** J. S. KINGSLEY *Stand. Nat. Hist.* II. 185 Throughout the Rocky Mountain region . . . are found several species of large, fierce-looking insects . . . popularly known as sand-crickets. **1891** *Cent.* 5329/3 sand-cricket. . . . One of certain large crickets of odd form common in the western United States and belonging to the genus *Stenopelmatus*. . . . It is erroneously considered poisonous by the Mexicans.

(5) 1891 *Cent.* 5239/3 sand-dab. . . . A kind of plaice, the rusty dab, *Limanda ferruginea*, found along the Atlantic coast of the United States, especially northward. **1903** T. H. BEAN *Fishes N.Y.* 726 *Limanda ferruginea*. . . . Sand Dab. . . . This is also known as the rusty dab. — **(6) 1883** *Nat. Museum Bul.* No. 27, 123 The so-called 'Sand Dollar,' (*Echinarachnius parma*), inhabits the east coast. **1893** HALE *N. Eng. Boyhood* 148 Here we had our first real knowledge of what sea-urchins are, and what people call 'sand dollars.' — **(7) 1852** WILEY *Life in South* 30/1 *Sand-fiddler*, . . . the local name for a small animal of the shell-fish kind, which abounds on the [N.C.] beach. **1863** *Harper's Mag.* Aug. 356/2 The grotesque amphibious 'Sand-fiddlers' and the little darkeys are the only exponents of energy. — **(8) 1842** *Nat. Hist. N.Y., Zoology* IV. 296 The pigmy flatfish, *Platessa pusila*, . . . is known in the markets under the name of Sand Flounder. **1893** *Stand.* 470/3 *Daylight*, (Local, U.S.) The sand-flounder or windowpane . . . ; named from its translucency. — **(9) 1881** *Harper's Mag.* Dec. 75/1 The fluttering butterfly . . . is pounced upon in mid-air by the great sand-hornet.

(10) 1928 *Bunker's Mag.* Jan. 73 The little sand lizards so common in West Texas possess the same ability to snap off their tails when they get into a tight corner. **1933** DITMARS *Reptiles of World* 99 The Sand Lizard or Striped Race-Runner, *C[nemidophorus] sexlineatus*, is the only species of its genus ranging into the southeastern portion of the United States. — **(11) 1872** COUES *Key to Birds* 254 This species [the least sandpiper] and the last [the semipalmated sandpiper] are usually confounded under the common name of 'sandpeeps.' **1935** LINCOLN *Cape Cod Yesterdays* 130 Another delicacy, so he said, which was always served in that camp once a season, was a sandpeep pie. — **(12) 1846** in EMORY *Military Reconn.* 388 Piles of loose earth, like small ant hills . . . are formed by the sand rats or gophers. **1911** WRIGHT *Winning Barbara Worth* 109 For the love av Gawd is ut ye, ye owld sand-rat? **1917** J. A. MOSS *Officers' Man.* 485 Sand-rat, an officer or soldier on duty in the rifle pit at target practice. — **(13) 1884** GOODE *Fisheries* I. 671 The Sand Shark—*Odontaspis littoralis*. This species . . . is found on our coast from New England southward to Charleston. **1949** *Fishes Western N. Atlantic* I. 104 Although plentiful, the Sand Shark is of little commercial importance at present. — **(14) 1813** WILSON *Ornithology* VIII. 91 [The pied duck] is called by some gunners the Sand Shoal Duck, from its habit of frequenting sand bars. **1844** *Nat. Hist. N.Y., Zoology* II. 326 This Duck, well known on this coast under the name of Skunk-head, and Sand-shoal Duck on the coast of New-Jersey, is not, however, very abundant.

(15) (*a*) **1881** INGERSOLL *Oyster Industry* 247 *Sand-Sucker*, Holothurians, Nereids, and other soft animals buried in the low-tide sands, and showing tentacles. (Florida, Gulf coast.) (*b*) **1896** JORDAN & EVERMANN *Check-List Fishes* 401 *Menticirrhus undulatus*. . . . California Whiting; Sand Sucker. Southern California, north to Santa Barbara. **1911** *Rep. Fisheries 1908* 318/2. — **(16) 1909** *Cent. Supp.* 1445/2 Sand whiting, *Menticirrhus americanus*, of the south Atlantic and Gulf coasts of the United States. **1911** *Rep. Fisheries 1908* 318/2 The sand-whiting (*M[enticirrhus] saxatilis*) . . . is abundant from Chesapeake Bay to Texas.

d. In the names of plants and trees: (1) **sand bar willow,** (see quot. 1891); (2) **blackberry,** a variety of blackberry found in the eastern states; (3) **brier,** =**horse nettle;** (4) ***bur,** any one of various plants, esp. the annual *Franseria acanthicarpa*, of the western states, and the bur grass, also the prickly calyx of such a plant, see **f.** (2) below; (5) **cherry,** the fruit of the dwarf cherry, *Prunus pumila*, of the Great Lakes region, or a related species, *P. besseyi*, of the western states, also the plant bearing such a fruit; (6) **dock,** (see quot.); (7) **flower,** the pasqueflower, *Pulsatilla ludoviciana;* (8) **grape,** an American wild grape, *Vitis rupestris* or *V. lincecumi;* (9) **grass,** any one of various American grasses, as *Triplasis purpurea*, found in sandy areas, cf. **purple sand grass;** (10) **jack,** (see quot.); (11) **lily,** (see quot. 1909); (12) **myrtle,** a smooth dwarf shrub, *Leiophyllum buxifolium*, found along the coast from New Jersey southward; (13) **orache,** (see quot.), *obs.;* (14) **pine,** (*a*) a smooth-barked pine, *Pinus clausa*, found in sandy regions, esp. in Florida, (*b*) (see quot.); (15) **plum,** (see quots. 1843, 1909); (16) **puff,** (see quot.); (17) **ragweed,** (see quot.), *obs.;* (18) **reed,** =**beach grass;** (19) **rush,** (see quot.), *obs.;* (20) **spur,** (see quot. 1909); (21) **strawberry,** (see quot.); (22) **verbena,** "any West American verbenaceous plant of the genus *Abronia*, having flowers somewhat resembling those of the verbena" (W. '09); (23) **violet,** the bird's-foot violet.

(1) 1884 SARGENT *Rep. Forests* 168 *Salix longifolia*. . . . Sand-Bar Willow. . . . Very common throughout the Mississippi River basin, and reaching its greatest development in the valleys of Oregon and northern California. **1891** *Cent.* 6929/1 Sandbar willow, *Salix longifolia*, a small tree often forming dense clumps of great beauty on river sandbars and banks. It is very common throughout the Mississippi basin, and reaches its greatest development in northern California and Oregon. — **(2) 1843** TORREY *Flora N.Y.* I. 217 *Rubus cuneifolius*. . . . Sand Blackberry. . . . Abundant in New-Jersey. **1901** MOHR *Plant Life Ala.* 541 Sand blackberry. . . . The 'Topsy' variety of blackberry originated from this species. — **(3) 1819** *Western Rev.* I. 93 [Among] the trees and plants peculiar to this [Ky.] region . . . [is] *Solanum Carolinianum*, Sand briar. **1894** *Amer. Folk-Lore* VII. 95 *Solanum Carolinense*, . . . sand-brier, radical, West Va.; bull-nettle, Perrysville, Ind. — **(4) 1834** A. PIKE *Sketches* 48 To add to our comforts, the ground here was covered with sand-burs. **1904** *Topeka Capital* 11 June 4 A sandbur will grapple on to a man's tail and stay there all day. **1943** L. V. HAMNER *Short Grass* 249 They made bedfellows of the sandburs in the breaks.

(5) 1778 CARVER *Travels* 30 Near the borders of the Lake [Michigan] grow a great number of sand cherries. **1843** TORREY *Flora N.Y.* I. 195 Sand Cherry. . . . Sandy and rocky shore; Highlands of New York; rare. **1923** J. H. COOK *On Old Frontier* 95 We passed through the sandhill country at the season when the sand cherries were ripe. **1949** *World-Herald Mag.* (Omaha) 3 July 2/1 Patches of sun-sweetened sand cherries . . . covered the tallest sand hills and the blowouts to the north. — **(6) 1915** ARMSTRONG & THORNBER *Western Wild Flowers* 88 Sand Dock. *Rumex venosus*. . . . The small inconspicuous flowers develop into clusters of showy valves or wings. — **(7) 1934**

WEBSTER. **1941** SETON *Trail of Artist-Naturalist* 186 The sandflowers fade and shrivel to the ground. — **(8) 1856** FERGUSSON *America* 273 In 1799 . . . a Frenchman . . . was making several barrels of wine every year, out of grapes that were found growing wild and abundantly, on the heads of the islands on the Ohio river, called sand-grapes. **1891** COULTER *Bot. W. Texas* I. 62 Abounding in the sandy post-oak woods of eastern Texas it is called 'post-oak grape' or 'sand-grape.' **1915** HUSMANN *Testing Grape Varieties* 15 *V[itis] rupestris* (sand, sugar, or rock grape). . . . Open places in poor soils and along gravelly banks and ravines. — **(9) 1857** GRAY *Botany* 556 *T[ricuspis] purpurea.* (Sand-Grass.) . . . In sand, Massachusetts to Virginia along the coast, and southward. **1894** *Amer. Folk-Lore* VII. 104 *Calamagrostis longifolia*, sand-grass, Central Neb.

(10) 1884 SARGENT *Forests N. Amer.* 153 *Quercus cinerea* Michaux. . . . Upland Willow Oak. Blue Jack. Sand Jack. — **(11) 1909** WEBSTER, sand lily. A white-flowered scapose liliaceous plant (*Leucocrinum montanum*) of the western United States. **1929** *Encycl. Brit.* XIX. 939/1 Sand Lily . . . native to plains and mountain valleys from South Dakota and Nebraska west to California. — **(12) 1814** PURSH *Flora Amer.* I. 301 *Ammyrsine buxifolia.* . . . Being known by the name of Sand-myrtle among the inhabitants of New Jersey. **1943** PEATTIE *Great Smokies* 266 They are . . . tangled growths of rhododendrons, . . . with some amounts of mountain laurel, blueberry, smilax, and occasionally sand myrtle. — **(13) 1833** EATON *Botany* (ed. 6) 46 *[Atriplex] arenaria*, sand orache. . . . Stem reddish, angular, very branching; about a foot high. — **(14)** *(a)* **1884** SARGENT *Rep. Forests* 199 *Pinus clausa.* . . . Sand Pine. Scrub Pine. Spruce Pine. **1901** MOHR *Plant Life Ala.* 131 The dead tops and branches of the sand pine (*Pinus clausa*) . . . increase the impression of aridity on these desolate shores. *(b)* **1897** SUDWORTH *Arborescent Flora* 23 *Pinus contorta.* Twisted Pine. . . . Sand Pine (Oreg.).

(15) 1843 TORREY *Flora N.Y.* I. 194 Beach Plum. Sand Plum. Low, with straggling branches, seldom thorny. **c1870** CHIPMAN *Notes on Bartlett* 379. **1909** *Cent.* 1022/3 *Sand-plum, Prunus Watsoni*, a shrub of sandy lands from Nebraska to Arkansas. — **(16) 1915** ARMSTRONG & THORNBER *Western Wild Flowers* 104 Sand Puffs. *Abronia sclsa.* . . . This plant is . . . delicately tinted and . . . decorative in form. — **(17) 1819** *Western Rev.* I. 93 Peculiar to this [Ky.] region . . . [is] a *Capraria multifida*, Sand Ragweed. — **(18) 1879** *Scribner's Mo.* Sep. 651/1 After laboriously cleaning their fish, they laid them among the sand-reeds. — **(19) 1803** LEWIS in *Jrnls. L. & Ordway* 55 The banks appear every where to abound with the sand or scrubing Rush.

(20) 1909 WEBSTER, sand spur. . . . Common bur grass. **1942** RAWLINGS *C. Creek* 11, I . . . found myself in the middle of a patch of sandspurs waist-high. — **(21) 1915** ARMSTONG & THORNBER *Western Wild Flowers* 240 Sand Strawberry. *Fragaria Chiloensis.* . . . A charming plant. — **(22) 1898** A. M. DAVIDSON *Calif. Plants* 174 The wild four-o'clock and the sand verbena are classed in this group [of beautiful weeds]. **1950** *Amer. Forests* Jan. 20/3 Here along the sandy open trails sparse of pines are sand verbena, buttercups, lupine and larkspur. — **(23) 1880** COOKE in *Harper's Mag.* Dec. 87/1 When I was married to Ethan, . . . if he didn't fetch me a big bunch of sand-violets . . . for to match my eyes and my skirt. **1893** *Amer. Folk-Lore* VI. 138 *Viola pedata*, sand violet. Conn.

e. Denoting areas and land formations where or in which sand predominates, as (1) **sand barren,** (2) **beach,** (3) **bluff,** (4) **bottom,** (5) **butte,** (6) **desert,** (7) **field,** (8) **hammock,** (9) **hill, lot,** see as main entries, (10) **mountains,** (11) **prairie,** (12) **wash.**

(1) 1766 in DARLINGTON *Mem. Bartram & Marshall* 438, I thrice visited the River St. John, often landed upon each shore, exploring the swamps and hummocks, pine barrens, and sand barrens. **1870** EMERSON *Soc. & Solitude* 144 In Massachusetts, we fight . . . the blowing sand-barrens with pine plantations. — **(2) 1709** LAWSON *Carolina* 151 The Sand-Birds . . . frequent our Sand-Beaches. **1907** *St. Nicholas* July 791/1 They finally ran the boat on the little sand beach. — **(3) 1834** PECK *Gaz. Illinois* 352 [The] sand bluffs of the Mississippi, in Warren and Mercer counties . . . furnish convenient landings for steam boats. **1862** MOORE *Rebellion Rec.* V. II. 165 The yellow sand bluff rises to the height of a hundred and fifty feet. — **(4) 1864** *Harper's Mag.* Nov. 694/1 Desert mesas and sand-bottoms formed the characteristic features of our journey.

(5) 1868 *Life Among Mormons* 14 The sand buttes of the Platte were as the Rocky Mountains in miniature. — **(6) 1869** BROWNE *Adv. Apache Country* 50 After coursing along the belt of the great sand-desert on the left, we struck into the Colorado bottom. — **(7) 1836** *S. Lit. Messenger* II. 664 You half-starved old sand-field Jersey Kill-Deer! **1873** COZZENS *Marvellous Country* 236 The great plateau of the West, with its sand-fields sparkling in the sunshine, stretched out as far as the eye could reach. — **(8) 1839** in W. KENNEDY *Texas* I. 40 At that time the main channel was situated one-third of the distance from Decrow's house to the sand hammocks.

(10) 1805 DUNBAR *Life* 319 The great prairies commence near the Cadeaux nation & extend 300 miles west to the Sand mountains as they are termed, i.e. the great Chain separating the waters of the Mississippi from those which fall to the westward. — **(11) 1834** *Visit to Texas* 115 [The town] is situated on a sand Prairie, where are hardly any signs of vegetation. **1846** SAGE *Scenes Rocky Mts.* xviii, There was not a drop of water to allay our thirst short of the river, fifteen miles distant,—over an open sand-prairie. **1857** WILLIS *Convalescent* 243 Our journey of the next day, over the sand-prairies to Siasconset . . . must be the theme of still another letter. — **(12) 1906** *Out West* Feb. 94 Only ten years ago a silver nugget weighing thirty-one pounds was found in a sand-wash near Globe. **1948** *Sierra Club* (So. Calif. Chapter) Sched. 129, 69 The campsite will be in a sand wash at the mouth of the Fan Hill Canyon.

f. In colloq. phrases: (1) *To knock the sand from under one*, to upset one's calculations or intentions; (2) *to stick like a sandbur*, to stick most pertinaciously; (3) *to have sand in one's craw*, and variants, to be full of "grit" or courage, cf. **1.** above; (4) *to throw sand in the wheels*, (see quot.); (5) *to raise sand*, to create a disturbance.

(1) 1847 ROBB *Squatter Life* 73 [He was] conning a most powerful speech, one that would knock the sand from under Hoss. **1851** GREEN *Twelve Days* 121, I never had the sand so knocked from under me before in my life. — **(2) 1870** EGGLESTON *Queer Stories* 53 It sticks to you like a sandburr. **1914** BOWER *Flying U Ranch* 76, I'm sticking to the truth like a sand burr to a dog's tail. — **(3) 1872** *Newton Kansan* 5 Dec. 3/3 We hope to see Mr. Pettibone with sufficient 'sand in his craw' for this new position [of police judge]. **1881** *N.Y. Times* 18 Dec. 4/3 To have 'sand in one's craw.' To be determined and plucky. Equivalent to 'grit.' **1884** MARK TWAIN *H. Finn* viii, When I got to camp . . . there warn't much sand in my craw. — **(4) 1877** BARTLETT 793 To *throw sand in the wheels*, to cast obstructions in the way of an undertaking.

(5) 1944 CLARK *Pills* 305 They were galloping up and down the road catching fly balls, running all over the hill encircling the bases, scaring horses and raising sand in general.

As the last term in **black, blowing, buttermilk, Jersey blue, orange, silver, sugar, wheat sand.**

* **sandbag,** *v. tr.* To fell (a person) with a sandbag. Also **sandbagging,** *n.*, and transf.

1887 *Courier-Journal* 2 Feb. 6/2 The next day Claytor turned up at Central Station with a fairy story that he had been sand-bagged on his way home. **1901** *Cong. Rec.* 23 Jan. 1345/1 [This district] is lying in wait, as it were, from one year's end to the other, awaiting an opportunity to sandbag the public. **1929** *Sat. Ev. Post* 7 Dec. 5/1 Occasionally a more than ordinarily obdurate author will be sandbagged in a dark alley and shipped across the Mohave Desert. **1948** *Chi. Tribune* 15 Feb. I. 32/3 The sandbagging of congress last year touched a tender spot.

sandbagger ˈsændˌbægə, *n.*

1. A robber or ruffian who uses a sandbag to stun his victim. Also transf.

1882 PECK *Sunshine* 203 Suppose all the men that have been robbed in the past year by cowardly sandbaggers, could have 'put up their hands.' **1893** *Chi. Tribune* 26 April 6/4 One of the Chicago papers recently complained that Illinois had no first-class highwaymen. It must have overlooked the legislative 'sand-baggers.' **1929** C. E. MERRIAM *Chicago* 343 A matter to be carefully watched here [in subcommittees of the city council] is room for blackmail, even in the case of worthy measures unless the sandbaggers are offset by those of an opposite persuasion.

2. A sailboat upon which bags of sand are used as ballast.

1894 *Outing* XXIV. 477/2 [He] enjoys the sea in every form, whether racing in a sandbagger, cruising in a schooner, or taking his ease beneath the shady awning of a big steam yacht. **1948** *Sat. Ev. Post* 9 Oct. 140/3 Several smaller craft have been acquired, including . . . the racing sloop Annie—one of the fastest Long Island 'sandbaggers.'

* **sand hill.**

1. *pl.* A locality or region where there are hills or dunes composed of, or covered with, sand. Also as a proper name.

1806 *Ann. 9th Congress* 2 Sess. 1134 The great chain or dividing ridge, [is] commonly known by the name of the sand hills. **1884** *Cent. Mag.* June 280/1 The young man would attend to all that was to be done at Sand Hills. **1949** *Prairie Schooner* Spring 27 The sheep camp at the mouth of Reno Creek is one of several which dot this valley and the adjoining sandhills of the Cheyenne country.

Hence **sand-hillers,** (see quot. 1886).

1850 E. P. BURKE *Reminisc. Ga.* 205 These people are known at the South by such names as crackers, clay-eaters, and sand-hillers. **1886** *Amer. Philol. Assoc.* XVII. 46 Common Southern expressions [include] . . . *sandhillers*, poor whites of sandy districts. **1947** LUMPKIN *Southerner* 151 With their pasty faces, scrawny necks, angular ill-nourished frames, straw-like hair, they seemed to me no different from the real 'sand-hillers.'

2. Short for **sand-hill crane.** *Colloq.*

1938 MATSCHAT *Suwannee River* 186 He seen the sandhills a-dancin' their matin' dance.

3. In combs.: (1) **sand-hill crane,** the brown crane, *Grus canadensis tabida*, also the little brown crane, *Grus canadensis;* (2) **whooper,** the whooping crane, *Grus americana.*

(1) **1805** CLARK in *Lewis & C. Exped.* III. (1905) 176 Jo [Fields] killed a Sand hill Crane. **1891** *Cent.* 5330/3 *Grus canadensis* . . . properly applies only to the northern brown or sand-hill crane somewhat smaller . . . [than] the southern brown or sand-hill crane, *Grus mexicanus* or *G. pratensis.* **1949** *Nat. Hist.* Oct. 378/1 Once heard, the far-reaching call of the sand-hill crane is a sound that never can be forgotten. — (2) **1938** MATSCHAT *Suwannee River* 188 The large sandhill whoopers flew over the water.

b. Also (1) **sand-hill boy,** (2) **country,** (3) **lake,** (4) **pony,** (5) **region,** (6) **tackey.**

(1) **1858** *S. Lit. Messenger* XXVI. 230/1 We had . . . a class of sand hill boys and gopher trapping girls. — (2) **1923** J. H. COOK *On Old Frontier* 95 We passed through the sandhill country at the season when the sand cherries were ripe. — (3) **1923** J. H. COOK *On Old Frontier* 95 Our guide escorted us to one of the sandhill lakes, then unnamed. — (4) **1813** *Raleigh* (N.C.) *Minerva* 19 Nov., Arrived, . . . the northern, eastern, southern, and western transport fleets of gigs, single and double chairs, and sand-hill ponies.

(5) **1913** BARNES *Western Grazing Grounds* 65 These latter species are . . . most common . . . in the sandhill region of western Nebraska. — (6) **1861** in CHESNUT *Diary* 58 They were sandhill tackeys—those fastidious ones, not very anxious to fight with anything, or in any way.

sandia sɑn'diə, *n. S.W.* [Sp. *sandia*, watermelon.] A watermelon. Also attrib. in place-names. — **1846** ABERT *Exam. N. Mex.* 29 In the evening a lad brought me some 'melones' and 'sandias.' **1888** WALLACE *Land of Pueblos* 51 Not very far away to the southeast we trace, in aerial tints of supreme beauty, the serrated ridges of the Sandia mountains.

San Diegan. A native or inhabitant of San Diego, Calif. — **1901** *World's Work* Oct. 1270/2 The railroad situation the San Diegans and their new fellow-citizens at the eastern end of the county have bravely undertaken to solve. **1949** *L.A. Times* 3 May II. 9/3 Two San Diegans will accompany the world's smallest plane to England and Ireland for aviation pageants in July.

***sandiness,** *n.* The quality of having "sand" or pluck. *Slang.* See ***sand 1.** — **1897** FLANDRAU *Harvard Episodes* 31 Their persistent 'sandiness' compelled his admiration.

sandlapper 'sændˌlæpɚ, *n.* (Also *cap.*) (See quots.) *Slang.*

1836 SIMS *Mellichampe* viii, He is some miserable overseer—a sandlapper from Goose Creek. **1903** *Outlook* 7 Nov. 576 A South Carolinian mentioned that the people of his State were often nicknamed 'sandlappers.' **1942** KENNEDY *Palmetto Country* 65 Before the Civil War, crackers were often called 'sandlappers,' because their children 'contracted the habit of eating dirt.' **1948** MENCKEN *Supp.* II. 608 Their State has also been called the *Rice State*, the *Iodine State*, the *Swamp State* and the *Sand-lapper State.*

sand lot. An unoccupied piece of sandy ground or vacant lot in or adjacent to a city, freq. serving as the scene of unorganized games and sports. Also attrib.

The term first came into use in San Francisco from the fact that the followers of Dennis Kearney held meetings on a lot of this kind on the west side of the city. Cf. **Kearneyism, Kearneyite.**

1882 G. A. SALA *Amer. Revisited* II. 201 Colossal fortunes, illimitable speculations, and sand-lot agitators. **1885** *Mag. Amer. Hist.* Feb. 201/2 One Dennis Kearny . . . made his headquarters in what were known as the 'Sand Lots,' near San Francisco. **1898** ATHERTON *Californians* 37 She drew Helena into a sand lot opposite. **1949** *Highway Traveler* Feb. 20 These 'nobs' were the target of Dennis Kearney, famous sandlot orator of the 70's.

b. sandlotter, a Kearneyite, or a member of any radical political element. *Slang.*

1887 *Advance* 17 Feb. 107 [The California Chinese Mission] raised the last year in California $3,756, hoodlums, sandlotters and politicians to the contrary notwithstanding. **1894** *Nation* 12 July 20/2 The decent people . . . outnumber the Sand-lotters and other anarchists by five to one.

***sandpiper,** *n.* As the last term in **Baird's, Bartram's, Bonaparte's, least, long-legged, pectoral, red-backed, red-breasted, semipalmated, solitary, spotted, stilt, telltale, Wilson's sandpiper.**

***sandstone,** *n.* **1. sandstone bluff, butte,** a bluff or butte composed of, or covered with, sandstone. **2. sandstone water,** water occurring in sandstone formations. Cf. **freestone water.**

(1) **1846** W. G. STEWART *Altowan* I. 114 On its right bank runs a low range of sandstone bluffs cut down perpendicularly to the green sward. **1872** BOURKE *Journal* Nov. 25 Passed between two sandstone buttes. — (2) **1818** *Amer. Jrnl. Science* I. 219 The inhabitants no longer speak of their 'sandstone water,' but every where [one] hears of 'limestone water.'

As the last term in **bastard, Ohio sandstone.**

Sandwich (glass). A kind of pressed glass made at Sandwich, Mass., in the first half of the past century, and widely copied in recent years.

1935 LINCOLN *Cape Cod Yesterdays* 164 The buttery shelves of every house in our town were filled with Sandwich glass at that period. **1947** COFFIN *Yankee Coast* 276 [There are] long shelves across the north windows, every inch of them covered with Sandwich glass drinking the pure north light. **1949** *L.A. Times* 28 Aug. (Home Mag.) 11/3 Probably the three other pieces are Sandwich, too, and of the same or only slightly later date.

***sandy,** *a.* In combs.: (1) **sandy cotton,** ginned cotton which, because of unfavorable weather conditions during harvest, has sand mixed with it, cf. **sandy crop;** (2) **creek voyage,** (see quot.), *obs.;* (3) **crop,** a crop (as of cotton) that has sand in it; (4) **-hill crane,** =**sand-hill crane,** *obs.;* (5) **mocking bird,** (see quot.); (6) **toad,** (see quot.).

(1) **1881** *Bradstreet's* 15 Oct. 241/4 But rather [it is] on account of 'sandy cotton.' — (2) **1831** A. S. WITHERS *Chron. Border Warfare* 62 The destruction of the Roanoke settlement in the spring of 1757, by a party of Showanees [*sic*], gave rise to the campaign, which was called by the old settlers, the 'Sandy creek voyage.' — (3) **1881** *Bradstreet's* 15 Oct. 241/4 Last year's crop, however, was not a sandy crop. — (4) **1819** THOMAS *Travels* 210 A bird inhabits this country, called the *sandy hill Crane.* Its size is remarkable. **1825** W. BIGGS *Narr. Captivity* 21, I had . . . sandy-hill cranes, boiled in leyed corn, which made a very good soup.

(5) **1891** *Cent.* 5333/2 Sandy mocking-bird, the brown thrush, or thrasher. — (6) **1870** BEADLE *Utah* 471 The 'horned toad or 'sandy toad,' scientifically ranked *Phrynosoma*, is found on all the high, dry plains . . . [and] is calloused on the belly like an alligator.

b. Also **sandy barren, bottom land.**

1845 *Cultivator* ns. II. 253 Upon some of the Wabash sandy bottom lands, the corn is fine. **1849** CHAMBERLAIN *Ind. Gazetteer* 278 Intermixed with them [*sc.* the timbered lands] are sandy barrens, and swamps.

Sanforize 'sænfəˌraɪz, *v.* Also **sanforize.** [*Sanford* L. Cluett, the Amer. inventor of the process.] *tr.* To treat cotton or linen woven fabrics by a patented process which virtually eliminates later shrinkage. Also **sanforized,** *a.*, **sanforizing,** *n.*

1939 WEBSTER (*New Words*). **1944** CLARK *Pills* 221 A frugal backwoods customer adequately sized up the complications of the 'sanforized' era in men's clothing when he sauntered into the Harbour Pitts store. **1948** *Time* 11 Oct. 91/3 The company was also lucky in its Vice President Sanford Cluett, the original families' only remaining executive. Cluett was an experiment-minded man. His tinkering had turned up Sanforizing. **1950** *Esquire* Feb. 13/3 They are well cut, Sanforized and non-run.

San Franciscan ˌsænfrən'sɪskən, *n.* and *a.* **1.** *n.* A resident or native of San Francisco, California. **2.** *a.* Of or pertaining to San Francisco, California.

(1) **1875** *Scribner's Mo.* July 277/2 San Franciscans are remorseless critics. **1949** *L.A. Times* 6 June 2/5 San Franciscans wear overcoats and furs even in the summer. — (2) **1885** BAYLOR *On Both Sides* 227 The glasses rattled as if in a San Franciscan earthquake.

sang sæŋ, *n.* Short for "ginseng." *Colloq.*

1843 CARLTON *New Purchase* I. 256 The storekeeper was obliged to book the nine and a quarter cents, to be paid in 'sang.' **1897** W. E. BARTON *Sim Galloway's D.* The sang was short this year. **1948** DICK *Dixie Frontier* 32 He spent some time digging ginseng, or 'sang' as they called it.

attrib. **1859** BARTLETT 379 In Alleghany Co., Maryland, is Sang Run near which is a well-known 'sanging ground.' *Ib.*, *Sang-Hoe*, the implement used in gathering ginseng. **1932** W. KELLEY *Inchin' Along* 51, I go up on de hill to dig san' yarbs.

b. sang digger, one who digs sang (see also quot. 1927).

1878 in SUMMERS *Ann. S.W. Va.* 1657 These hill-sides are a godsend to 'sang-diggers.' **1927** EUBANK *Horse & Buggy Days* 53 The trail of death which lasted for twenty years started over the ownership of a 'sang-digger' hog, and before the reign of blood ended 120 lives had been wiped out by the rifle and the six-shooter. **1943** PEATTIE *Great Smokies* 193 A mountain man once described to me a party of 'sang diggers.

sang sæŋ, *v. intr.* To gather sang.

1848 BARTLETT 282 *Sang* . . . is or was also used in Virginia as a verb; *to go a sanging,* is to be engaged in gathering ginseng. **1877** *Field & Forest* III. 40 Why, I have sanged all over [the mountain]. **1892** ALLEN *Blue-Grass Region* 249 In the wildest parts of the country . . . entire families may still be seen 'out sangin'.'

sanguillah saŋ'gwɪlə, *n. local.* [Poss. f. Amer. Indian, but Turner, 200, records *sangalo* (f. Mende, Sierra Leone) as the Gullah word for a wild duck.] Any one of various song birds found in the Southeast.

1809 RAMSAY *Hist. S.C.* II. 333 Of the birds of Carolina the following are the principal: Bald eagle, fishing hawk, . . . nut-hatch great and small, sanguillah, wild pigeon. **1910** WAYNE *Birds of S.C.* 110 This oriole is a summer resident known on the coast as the 'Sanguillah.' **1949** SPRUNT *So. Carolina Bird Life* 495 One name [for the orchard oriole] which is sometimes heard in the Low-country, though not often, is the Indian name 'Sanguillah.'

sanguin 'sæŋgwin, *n.* [Prob. fanciful f. **sanguine.*] (See quot.) *Obs.* — **1881** VAWTER *Prison Life* 112 The bottle contained a fiery liquor, called by the Johnnies in those days, 'sanguin.'

***Sanguinaria,** *n.* [See note.]

This L. name was applied to the genus in 1732 by Dillenius (1687–1747), a German botanist, in allusion to the blood-like juice of the plants. In L. the word was applied to a plant reputed to stanch blood.

A genus of perennial American herbs having only one species (see quot. 1891). Also (not *cap.*) a plant of this genus. Cf. **puccoon.**

1834 TRAILL *Backwoods* 180 The blood-root, sanguinaria, or puccoon, as it is termed by some of the native tribes, is worthy of attention from the root to the flower. **1839** BRYANT *Poetical Works* (1903) 185 The quick-footed wolf . . . crushed the flower of sanguinaria, from whose brittle stem The red drops fell like blood. **1841** PARK *Pantology* 414 Lobelia . . . and sanguinaria, or blood root, have also emetic properties. **1891** *Cent.* 5334/1 Sanguinaria. . . . In *bot.*, a genus of polypetalous plants of the order *Papaveraceæ*, the poppy family, and tribe *Eupapavereæ*. . . . The only species, *S. Canadensis,* the bloodroot, is common throughout eastern North America.

***sanitary,** *a.*

1. Tending to promote health.

1853 KANE *Grinnell Exped.* 298 All hands went out for a sanitary game of romps in the cold light. **1865** LOWELL in *N. Amer. Rev.* Oct. 606 Solitary communion with Nature does not seem to have been sanitary or sweetening in its influence on Thoreau's character. **1872** FISKE *Myths & Myth-Makers* 61 In Sweden sanitary amulets are made of mistletoe-twigs, . . . [as] a specific against epilepsy and an antidote for poisons.

2. (*cap.*) *absol.* The U.S. Sanitary Commission, or a Sanitary Fair. *Obs.*

1864 *Our Daily Fare* (Phila.) 13 June 40/2 (*heading*), How the Sanitary is Working in the Field. **1865** *Atlantic Mo.* Feb. 233/2, [I shall attempt] to answer for others the very questions which my fortnight with the Sanitary has answered for me. **1867** *Ib.* April 422/1 To this hour, therefore, the 'Sanitary' looms up in the eye of the people at home.

3. Belonging to, or provided by, the Sanitary Commission. *Obs.*

The adj. here partakes of the nature of an absolute used attributively.

1865 *Atlantic Mo.* Feb. 242/1 Two to three Sanitary wagons, loaded with hospital stores of all sorts, . . . move with each army corps. **1866** MOORE *Women of War* 359 A lady was on the Sanitary boat with comforts for the sick. **1867** *Atlantic Mo.* April 422/1 The connection which the people had with the army was in a very large walk of experience, carried on through 'Sanitary' agencies.

4. Sanitary Commission, an organization created by the U.S. Government in 1861 to look after the care of sick and wounded soldiers and their dependents. Also any one of various commissions set up by different agencies to have supervision over matters relating to health and sanitation.

1861 *Rep. Sanitary Comm.* 5 By direction of the Sanitary Commission, I respectfully submit the following report. **1898** *K.C. Star* 19 Dec. 2/5 The sanitary commission's work can all be done by a state veterinarian. **1923** WYATT *Invis. Gods* 176 The president of the so-called 'Sanitary commission' . . . railroaded the infamous anti-civil service act through the State legislature. **1949** J. B. HERRICK *Memories* 1 A clearer war memory is that of the fair of the Sanitary Commission, held in Chicago in the summer of 1865.

attrib. **1865** KELLOGG *Rebel Prisons* 327 Another supply of Sanitary Commission stores reached us while in this condition. **1866** LOWELL *Biglow P.* 2 Ser. p. lxix, Being asked to write it out as an autograph for the Baltimore Sanitary Commission Fair, I added other verses. **1947** *Mich. Hist.* Sep. 296 We had on United States Army regulation caps and pants, but a brown Sanitary Commission overcoat and blouse hid our dress and perhaps saved us from detection.

5. Sanitary Fair, during the Civil War, one of various fairs conducted to raise funds for the work of the U.S. Sanitary Commission. Now *hist.*

1864 *Harper's Mag.* April 707/1 The great movement of the early spring is the Sanitary Fair for the United States Commission. **1876** INGRAHAM *Centennial Exp.* 688 At the Chicago Sanitary Fair in the winter of 1864, no less a sum than $16,000 was raised entirely by this means. **1946** ADAMS *Album Amer. Hist.* III. 161 Its work was supported by private contributions and more particularly by Sanitary Fairs.

San Jose scale. [f. *San Jose,* Calif., where this scale (of Asiatic origin) was first introduced into the U.S.] A scale insect, *Aspidiotus perniciosus,* injurious to fruit trees.

1887 *Calif. State Bd. Agric. Biennial Rep. 1885–86* 12 Reports come in rapidly from various sections of the State of the appearance of the San José scale, even so far north as Geyserville, in Sonoma County. **1915** HAWORTH *G. Washington* 150 Being untroubled by San José scale and many other pests that now make life miserable to the fruit grower. **1938** C. S. BRIMLEY *Insects of N.C.* 110 A. perniciosus Comst. San Jose Scale. State-wide on apple, peach, plum, etc.

sanko 'sæŋko, *n.* [Origin unknown.] (See quot.) *Rare.* — **1856** *Porter's Spirit of Times* 18 Oct. 109/1, I can show the handsomest pair of matched family *puppies* that there is in this State [Mass.]—perfect little sankoes, seven weeks old.

San Luiseños. Indians of a Shoshonean stock in southern California, so called from San Luis Rey, the principal Spanish mission in their territory. — **1861** *Los Angeles Star* 21 Sep. One feature is perhaps unfortunate in that the alleged culprit is a Dieguiño, whilst his triers are of the rival tribe of San Luiseños.

sannup 'sænʌp, *n.* [f. an Abnaki term meaning a man.] An ordinary warrior as distinguished from a chief (see also quot. 1902). Now *hist.*

1628 *Mass. H.S. Coll.* 3 Ser. VIII. 177 Sanops must speak to sanops, and sagamores to sagamores. **1792** BELKNAP *Hist. New-Hampshire* III. 378 Our family [included] . . . my late mother's daughter, whom I therefore called my sister, her sanhop, and a pappoose. **1855** *Knickerb.* XLV. 430 The good minister . . . beheld the 'senap' laid out, drunk as a piper, by the road-side. **1902** *Amer. Folk-Lore* 257 *Sánnup.* An old New England word for a married male Indian, the term corresponding to squaw for a woman.

b. (See quot.)

1947 COFFIN *Yankee Coast* 63 A boy . . . is also a *sannup,* the old Algonkian for warrior, if he misbehaves.

Sanpet 'sænpɛt, *n.* [App. a native name.] (See quot. 1910.) Also attrib. — **1842** WILLIAMS *Tour to Ore.* (1921) 76, I was told that the Sanpach Indians would sell their wives for horses; and sometimes kill their horses and eat them, in case of hunger. **1910** HODGE *Amer. Indians* II. 451/1 Sanpet. A body of Ute formerly occupying San Pete valley and Sevier r., central Utah. . . . They are now included under the collective name of Uinta Ute.

Santa 'sæntə, *n.* A colloq. shortening of **Santa Claus.**

1913 *Sat. Ev. Post* 6 Dec. 50/1 If you want to act the part of Santa this Christmas. **1943** LYON *And So to Bedlam* 38 You could feel Santa's hot breath on the back of your neck. **1949** *Oak Leaves* (Oak Park, Ill.) 24 Nov. 5/5 Santa sent two telegrams to the editor yesterday from the North Pole.

***Santa Anna.** *S.W.* Also **Santa Ana.** [Antonio Lopez de *Santa Anna* (or *Ana*) (?1795–1876), a famous Mexican general.] (See quots.) Also attrib.

1903 *Cin. Enquirer* 3 May II. 2/5 An occasional norther, or 'Santa Ana,' as they are called, brings with it a stifling, overwhelming sandstorm that blinds, kills, buries and sweeps on . . . very like an Oriental typhoon. **1915** *Nat. & Science on Pac. Coast* 22 Known locally as Santa Anas, these wind storms constitute the most disagreeable feature of the weather in the great valley of the south. **1946** *Pasadena* (Calif.) *Star-News* 3 Nov. 13 'Santa Ana' winds were sweeping across the higher mountains

Santa Claus. [f. Du. *sinterklaas* (<*Sant Nikolaas*).]

1. Saint Nicholas, according to the modern conception, a jolly old man clad in a characteristic fur-trimmed red costume, represented as the bringer of gifts, esp. to children, on Christmas Eve. Cf. **Belshnickle.**

1773 [see ***Saint Nicholas**]. **1823** COOPER *Pioneers* iv, Remember there will be a visit from Santa-claus to-night. **1949** *Chi. D. News* 8 Dec. 20/2 Americans have transformed Santa Claus from a sad-eyed, generous St. Nicholas of 1,600 years ago into a smaller, jollier, plumper red-suited Christmas hero.

attrib. and *transf.* **1886** STAPLETON *Major's Christmas* 201 Papas and mammas . . . planned the Santa Claus performance which was to come when the inquisitive eyes were closed in slumber. **1934** *Amer. Mercury* May 5/2 The Santa Claus theory of relief may be appropriate to a genuine emergency like an earthquake or a big fire.

b. The U.S. thought of as a Lady Bountiful to other nations.

1909 *Chi. D. News* 10 Aug. 8/3 Uncle Sam is by no means an impartial Santa Claus. **1948** *Time* 19 Jan. 19/3 The Federal Government comes forward again as Santa Claus himself. **1949** *L.A. Times* 16 May II. 4/5 Citizens still allow our government to be a Santa Claus to the whole world.

2. a. Christmas time. *Rare.* **b.** Gifts, presents, etc., such as are exchanged at Christmas. *Colloq.*

(a) 1830 WATSON *Philadelphia* 242 The 'Belsh Nichel' and St. Nicholas . . . is the same also observed in New York under the Dutch name of St. Claes. — **(b) 1939** *These Are Our Lives* 22 One Christmas we ask him for fifty dollars for some clothes and a little Santy Claus for the chil'en.

Santa Cruz. A rum obtained in Santa Cruz, an island in the West Indies. Also attrib. *Obs.*

1846 *Dollar Newspaper* (Phila.) 19 Aug. 2/2 Is it a respectable spree over champagne, in a respectable hotel, . . . as distinguished from a debauch over whiskey and Santa Cruz, in a low 'groggery,' among 'loafers'? **1856** *Western Citizen* (Paris, Ky.) 13 June 1/5 'Has thee any good Jamaica rum?' 'No, sir.' 'Any Santa Cruz?' **1869** MARK TWAIN *Innocents* 149 The uneducated foreigner could not even furnish a Santa Cruz Punch.

Santa Fe. [Name of the capital of New Mexico.] In combs. now obs. or hist.: (1) **Santa Fe expedition,** an expedition to Santa Fe, esp. a quasi-military and commercial expedition sent out by the Republic of Texas to lay claim to eastern New Mexico in 1841; (2) **road,** =**Santa Fe trail;** (3) **tea,** (see quot.); (4) **town,** any one of various towns in New Mexico east of the Rio Grande, an area once designated by Texas as a county in Texas; (5) **trader,** one who transported goods, esp. over the Santa Fe trail, for trade in Santa Fe, New Mexico; (6) **trail,** a road or trail over which trade was conducted from about 1822 to about 1880 between Independence, Missouri, and Santa Fe, New Mexico; (7) **wagon,** a wagon used on the old Santa Fe road or trail.

(1) 1834 in *N. Mex. Hist. Rev.* II. (1927) 304 Your Company is . . . the smallest escort that has heretofore accompanied a 'Santa Fe' expedition. **1841** *N.O. Picayune* 9 Nov. 2/1 The Courier seems to doubt the accuracy of the information respecting the safe arrival of the Santa Fé Expedition, at its place of destination. **1842** *Ib.* 18 Jan. 2/3 The prisoners taken in the Santa Fé expedition had arrived at Mexico. — **(2) 1844** GREGG *Commerce of Prairies* II. 63 Our courts of justice have since dealt with those who killed Chavez, in 1843, on the Santa Fé road. **1867** *Wkly. New Mexican* 4 May 1/3 General Hancock's Indian expedition . . . [was] bound for Fort Larned, on the Santa Fe road. — **(3) 1859** BARTLETT 379 *Santa Fé Tea*, an infusion of leaves of the *Alstonia theæformis*, used in New Mexico. — **(4) 1841** *N.O. Picayune* 3 Sep. 1/6 The principal part of both the population and trade connected with the Santa Fe towns are supposed to lie on the east side of the river, and within the Texan boundary.

(5) 1839 *Boston Transcript* 3 March 2/1 Some of the heaviest Santa Fee traders lay in their entire supplies in this city [Pittsburgh]. **1851** HOWE *Hist. Coll. Great West* 316 At an early day, when the Santa Fe traders traveled in small parties, they were frequently attacked by the wild prairie Indians. **1943** DALE *Cow Country* 4 The emigrants to Oregon, the Santa Fe traders, and the Mormons, had before 1856 established several well-defined trails across the plains. — **(6) 1850** GARRARD *Wah-To-Yah* x. 125 [We] followed the Santa Fe Trail, which kept the river bank. **1949** *Dly. Oklahoman* (Okla. City) 9 Oct. (Mag. Sect.) 2/3 Trails for freight, marchers and explorers across the state began with the Santa Fe trail in 1822. — **(7) 1843** in *Miss. Val. Hist. Rev.* VI. 107 Past Some 40 or 50 Santa-fee waggons sitting out on there Spring Expedition. **1848** PARKMAN in *Knickerb.* XXXII. 95 Here we saw his large Santa Fe wagons standing together.

Santa Fean ˌsæntəˈfeən, *n.* A resident or citizen of Santa Fe, New Mexico.

1840 *Boston Transcript* 8 Feb. 2/1 This fair Santa Féan must be more bewitchingly beautiful than even the 'blushing beauties' of . . . the City of Brotherly Love. **1885** *Wkly. New Mexican Rev.* 1 Jan. 4/2 A lady well known and beloved by many Santa Feans, died suddenly of heart disease. **1941** FERGUSSON *Southwest* 279 By 1932, summer visitors, like Indians, threatened to become a disaster as well as an asset; and the ever alert Santa Feans had to save the towns from a second Texas Invasion.

Santa Lucia fir. The bristlecone fir, *Abies venusta*, found in the Santa Lucia mountains in southwestern California. — **1905** *Calif. Acad. Sci.* Occasional Papers IX. 7 Santa Lucia Fir is found in only a few cañons of the Santa Lucia Mountains in Monterey County. **1948** *Sierra Club Bul.* March 137 Among these were the Santa Lucia fir, *Pinus sabiniana*, (Digger pine), *Pinus monticola*, and hosts of others.

Santee sænˈti, *n.*[1] [Of obscure origin. App. a native word.]

1. *pl.* or *collect.* (See quot. 1910.)

1714 LAWSON *Hist. Carolina* (1903) 33/1 There happened also to be a burial of one of them, which ceremony is much the same as that of the Santees. **1854** SCHOOLCRAFT *Indian Tribes* IV. 155 After passing the settlement of the French Huguenots, . . . he visited the 'Seretees or Santees,' (Zantees), some of whose customs he described in passing. **1910** HODGE *Amer. Indians* II. 461/1 Santee. A tribe, probably Siouan, formerly residing on middle Santee r., S.C., where Lawson in 1700 found their plantations extending for many miles.

2. A kind of cotton. *Obs.*

1820 *Western Carolinian* 25 July, *Cotton*—Sea-Island, 35 *a* 37½ cts. lb.—Santee, 30 *a* 32. **1824** *Catawba Journal* 7 Dec., Santees [have been sold] at 19 a 21.

santee sænˈti, *n.*[2] [Origin unknown.] (See quot.) *Obs.* — **1819** SCHOOLCRAFT *Mo. Lead Mines* 98 The *santee*, consisting of two stones, 3 feet long, and 3 feet 6 inches wide, . . . [which] reach from the bottom of the ash-pit, to a foot above the basin-stone, . . . keeps the lead, slag, &c. from running into the fire arch, and is an important part of the [ash] furnace.

Santee sænˈti, *n.*[3] [f. Dakota *Isañyati*, "to pitch tents at knife lake" (i.e., Mille Lacs, Minn.).] *pl.* or *collect.* Indians comprising the eastern division of the Dakotas (see quot. 1910). Also attrib.

1858 EDWARD D. NEILL *Hist. Minn.* 51 The first [division of Sioux] are called the Isanyati, the Isasti of Hennepin, after one of the many lakes at the head waters of the river, called on modern maps, by the unpoetic name of Rum. **1867** *Harper's Wkly.* 5 Oct. 629 (*caption*), A Village of the Santee Indians near Fort Thompson, Minnesota. **1910** HODGE *Amer. Indians* II. 460/2 Santee. . . . An eastern division of the Dakota, comprising the Mdewakanton and Wahpekute, sometimes also the Sisseton and Wahpeton. **1949** *Chi. Tribune* 1 Sep. 20/1 The Winnebago Omaha, Santee, Sioux, and Ponca tribes of the Winnebago reservation number 5,000 Indians living on 70,000 acres.

santo ˈsanto, *n. S.W.* [Sp. in same sense.] A small statue or image of a saint. — **1834** A. PIKE *Sketches* 146 The santos and other images had been brought from Mexico. **1941** FERGUSSON *Southwest* 27 They took over adobe huts and filled them with battered furniture, noseless wooden santos, torn Navajo blankets, . . . and Indian ceremonial garments.

∗**sap,** *n.* In combs., chiefly with reference to the sap of the sugar maple tree: (1) **sap bush,** =**sugar bush;** (2) **cider,** cider made from maple sap; (3) **freshet,** a freshet in the spring at the time of making maple sugar; (4) **house,** a house in which maple sugar is processed or kept; (5) **neckyoke,** =**sap yoke;** (6) **orchard,** =**sugar grove;** (7) **pine,** the pitch pine, *Pinus rigida*, or the loblolly pine, *P. taeda;* (8) **run,** an unusually free flow of sugar maple sap, also **sap-running time;** (9) **spout,** a spout through which sugar maple sap is drawn from the tree; (10) **suck,** =**sapsucker** *q.v.* as a main entry; (11) **sucking woodpecker,** a sapsucker, esp. the yellow-bellied woodpecker, *Sphyrapicus varius;* (12) **sugar,** =**maple sugar;** (13) **works,** a place where maple sugar is made; (14) **yoke,** a piece of wood fitted for use on one's neck and shoulders for carrying sap buckets suspended on each side, cf. **sap neckyoke.**

(1) *a***1882** WEED *Autobiog.* 12, I now look with great pleasure upon the days and nights passed in the sap-bush. — **(2) 1845** COOPER *Chainbearer* xx, I don't think anything of bringing you . . . a little water, . . . nor should I had we any beer or sap-cider. — **(3) 1852** *Knickerb.* XXXIX. 477 Somebody . . . has been describing '*The Pleasures of Maple-Sugar-Making in the Country*,' . . . [including] the sudden 'sap-freshet.' — **(4) 1939** WOLCOTT *Yankee Cook Book* 338 Any one who . . . returns to the sap house with a lilting heart [etc.].

(5) 1920 in ADAMS *Pioneer Hist.* (1923) 315, I recall things of long ago . . . the dash churn, spinning wheel, pod auger, sap neck-yoke [etc.]. — **(6) 1861** *Boston Herald* 12 April 2/6 Owners of sap orchards can afford to work day and night. **1941** *L.A.* 247 A sap orchard is kind of a grove like. — **(7) 1808** PIKE *Sources Miss.* II. App. 54 The whole of this course lays through ridges of pines or swamps of pinenet, sap pine, hemlock, &c. **1832** BROWNE *Sylva* 238 In swamps, . . . [the wood] is light, soft, and composed almost wholly of sap; it is then called Sap Pine. **1897** SUDWORTH *Arborescent Flora* 26 *Pinus tæda.* Loblolly Pine. . . . Sap Pine (Va., N.C.). *Ib.* 27 *Pinus rigida.* Pitch Pine. . . . Sap Pine (lit.). — **(8) 1875** BURROUGHS *Winter Sunshine* 119 A 'sap-run' seldom lasts more than two or three days. **1919** CUNNINGHAM *Chronicle* 77 Beyond it [is] the big maple bush, where three thousand pails are set out at sap-running time. — **(9) 1878** *Vt. Bd. Agric. Rep.* V. 105 We now have the Eureka sap spout, the tin bucket [etc.]. **1949** *Highway Traveler* Feb. 16/2 A sap spout, or 'spile' as your boss may call it, is driven into the opening with a few taps of a hammer, then it's your turn to perform.

(10) 1889 RILEY *Pipes o' Pan* 41 The catbird in the bottom, and the sap-suck on the snag. — **(11) 1862** *Ill. Agric. Soc. Trans.* V. 732 The wounds made by the Sap-Sucking . . . Woodpecker are carried down to the wood. — **(12) 1800** D'ERES *Memoirs* 63 The squaws in particular, would make me many and valuable [presents] . . . , consisting of sap-sugar. *a*1871 in DE VERE 418 The boys enlivened by . . . whiskey sweetened with sap-sugar, and small beer. **1895** JEWETT *Nancy* 105 [She] handed us sap sugar on one of her best plates. — **(13) 1849** *Knickerb.* XXXIII. 279 '*The Sugar Bush*' has vividly recalled to memory . . . the pale-blue smoke curling up from the 'sap-works.' — **(14) 1878** *Vt. Agric.* V. 105 The sap was lugged with sap yoke and pails on their shoulders. **1923** ADAMS *Pioneer Hist.* 312 One neighbor whittled out brooms for several families. Another gauged the sap yokes, and another made ox yokes.

Sap neckyoke

b. Designating containers for sugar maple sap, as (1) **sap bucket,** (2) **gatherer,** (3) **kettle,** (4) **pan,** (5) **trough,** (6) **tub.**

(1) 1845 JUDD *Margaret* I. 12 [Here were] frows, sap-buckets, a leach-tub. **1949** *Chi. Tribune* 13 March 1. 6/4 Spiles on tapped maple trees are slowly filling sap buckets in 500 sugar groves in Indiana. — **(2) 1874** *Vt. Bd. Agric. Rep.* II. 719 The 'sap-gatherer' or 'draw-tub,' as it is called, is a hogshead containing from one hundred to one hundred and fifty gallons. — **(3) 1904** WALLER *Wood-Carver* 51, [I] drew trees and sheep and loggers' camps on the flat stones beneath the crotch set for the sap-kettles. — **(4) 1874** *Vt. Bd. Agric. Rep.* II. 729 Russia iron is the best material for home made sap pans as the niter can be removed from it more easily.

(5) 1804 FESSENDEN *Orig. Poems* (1806) 41 Your love I well repaid By . . . a sap-trough neatly made. **1897** ROBINSON *Uncle Lisha's Outing* 84 These 'ere boots . . . [are] stiffer'n sap troughs. — **(6) 1872** *Vt. Bd. Agric. Rep.* I. 215 When I was a boy I purchased one hundred sap tubs, and commenced sugaring on my own hook.

c. In combs. of obvious meaning or sufficiently explained in the quots., as (1) **sap boiler,** (2) **boiling,** (3) **porridge,** (4) **sour,** (5) **tree.**

(1) 1876 KNIGHT 2028/1 *Sap-boiler,* a furnace with pans for evaporating the sap of the maple. — **(2) 1877** BARTLETT 793 *Sap-Boiling,* the boiling of sap from maple-trees, for the purpose of making sugar. — **(3) 1842** *Amer. Pioneer* I. 346 'Sap porridge,' . . . when made of sweet corn meal, and the fresh sacarine juice of the maple, afforded both a nourishing and a savory dish. **1948** DICK *Dixie Frontier* 290 Corn-meal mush was a regular supper dish. In the spring it was made with maple sap and was known as sap porridge. — **(4) 1888** *Boston Jrnl.* 15 Sep. 2/4 A new disease . . . among the grape vines of the Santa Ana and San Gabriel valleys of California . . . is termed the sap-sour.

(5) 1843 *Knickerb.* XXII. 161 One felled the proper trees, taking care to leave the sap-trees, the sugar-maple, untouched.

As the last term in **bull, pine, winesap.**

***sap,** *v. tr.* To split off or remove the sap from bolts used in making boards or shingles. Also **sapping machine** (see quot. 1875). — **1776** DUNBAR *Life* 30 Old Jammie begun to rive; Isaac & a new Negro bolting. Young Jammie Saping. *Ib.*, 4 Men at stave making with the assistance of a Boy to sap. **1875** KNIGHT, *Sapping-machine,* a circular saw for slabbing balks and sawing bolts for shingle stuff.

sapajou ˈsæpəˌdʒu, *n.* [F., a South American monkey.] = **opossum.** *Rare.* — **1824** SINGLETON *Letters* 124, I also saw here [in New Orleans], a curious animal from the south of Georgia, called sapajou, which suspends itself by its tail.

***sapling,** *n.*

1. = **sapling pine.** *Obs.*

1809 KENDALL *Travels* III. 53 The yellow or red pine, (*pinus pinea,*) [is] called by the French colonists *sapin,* and by the English corruptly sapling. **1868** *Harper's Mag.* March 419/1 Intermixed with the most valuable pines in the American forests are many trees of the character I have just described. The lumbermen call them 'saplings,' and generally regard them as different in species from the true white pine.

2. sapling flax, (see quot.). *Obs.*

*c*1833 in *N. Eng. Quart.* X. (1937) 281 At one time, among the farmers of Kentucky, there was a great rage for what was called 'the sapling flax,' a kind that grew much larger than that usually raised, the seed of which sold for I do not know exactly how much.

3. sapling pine, the apple pine or white pine, *Pinus strobus.*

1810 MICHAUX *Arbres* I. 17 Pinus strobus, *White pine . . . pumkin pine . . . , Sapling pine . . .* ; denominations secondaires dans les Etats de Vermont, New-Hampshire et le District de Maine. **1832** BROWNE *Sylva* 242 The secondary denominations of Pumpkin Pine, Apple Pine and Sapling Pine . . . are derived from certain accidental peculiarities. **1851** J. S. SPRINGER *Forest Life* 41 The sap or outside of the sapling Pine is much thicker than that of the pumpkin Pine.

As the last term in **bull, persimmon sapling.**

sapo ˈsɑpo, *n.* Also **sarpo.** [Sp. in Amer. Sp. sense shown here.] A toadfish, esp. *Opsanus pardus,* found on the Gulf Coast. — **1879** *Nat. Museum Proc.* II. 336 These fish were called in Pensacola by the names 'Sea Robin' and 'Sarpo;' the latter being doubtless a corruption of the Spanish 'Sapo,' meaning 'toad.' **1896** JORDAN & EVERMANN *Check-List Fishes* 466 *Porichthys notatus.* . . . Cabezon; Sapo. Pacific Coast from Puget Sound to Panama.

sapper ˈsæpɚ, *n.* [f. **sap,* *n.* + *-er.*] (See quots.) *Obs.* — **1822** *Amer. Jrnl. Sci.* V. 147 On this shaft [of a rotary saw machine] are the saws and sappers. . . . The sappers which are crooked pieces of iron, steel edged, . . . cut the sap off a log. **1891** *Cent.* 5339/3 sapper. . . . A chisel used in some sawing-machines to cut away waste or sap-wood and reduce a log to a cylindrical shape.

sappy clubs. (See quot.) *Obs.* — **1868** ROSE *Great Country* 381 The Grant clubs of the country are now called 'sappy clubs.' Undoubtedly because they are short and sweet affairs.

sapsago sæpˈsego, *n.* [f. G. *Schabzieger,* in same sense.] (See quot. 1846.) — **1846** WORCESTER 630/2 *Sapsago,* . . . a kind of Swiss cheese, of a dark olive-green color. . . . *Farm. Ency.* **1877** BARTLETT 551.

sapsucker ˈsæpˌsʌkɚ, *n.* A bird belonging to any one of several varieties of small woodpeckers, esp. those of the genus *Sphyrapicus.* Also transf. Cf. **red-naped, Williamson's sapsucker.**

1805 *Lewis & Clark Exped.* VI. (1905) 187, [I saw] the small woodpecker or sapsucker as they are sometimes called. **1866** *Wkly. New Mexican* 29 Dec. 2/3 This style of argument is peculiar to the Gazette and the coterie of government 'sap suckers' who control its columns. **1946** STANWELL-FLETCHER *Driftwood Valley* 182 A pair of red-breasted sapsuckers, heads, breasts, and hind necks a vivid rose, are, as they tap for grubs in branches of the willow tree, nearly the most beautiful of all.

saque ˈsekɪ, *n. S.W.* Corruption of **acequia.** *Rare.* — **1847** J. T. HUGHES *Doniphan's Exped.* (1907) 91 A large saque interrupted our progress.

sarape, see **serape.**

Saratoga ˌsærəˈtogə, *n.* [f. *Saratoga* Springs, N.Y.]

1. A fashionable type of summer resort.

[**1852** MITCHELL *Dream Life* 156 All the lax gaiety of Saratoga palls on the appetite.] **1856** F. DE WARD *Summer Vacation Abroad* 78 Bath [England] is well known as the Saratoga of the British realm. **1915** A. KILMER in *Leaves of My Life* 101 Buxton is an English Saratoga.

2. = **Saratoga trunk.**

1874 B. F. TAYLOR *World on Wheels* 72 It is not a carpet-bag, nor a valise, nor a Saratoga, but a leather portmanteau. **1897** GUNTER *Don Balasco* xi, [A dandy's] three trunks . . . [gave] the captain of the *Flying Fish* more disgust than all the Saratogas of the ladies.

3. In combs. denoting luggage used by tourists to Saratoga Springs, food served there, etc., as (1) **Saratoga bandbox,** (2) **basket,** (3) **bend,** (4) **chicken,** (5) **chips,** see as a main entry, (6) **corn cake,** (7) **potatoes,**

cf. **Saratoga chips, (8) powders, (9) trunk, (10) walk, (11) water, (12) wave.**

(1) 1877 W. WRIGHT *Big Bonanza* 417 Monk . . . hates the sight of one of those ponderous specimens of architecture in the trunk-line known as the 'Saratoga bandbox.' — **(2) 1884** RITTENHOUSE *Maud* 276 Then we bought five bolts of satin ribbon for the 'Saratoga baskets.' — **(3) 1879** PECK *Peck's Fun* 155 (We.), These young Ripon people . . . have learned all the Boston dips, and Saratoga bends. — **(4) 1943** *Harper's Mag.* Dec. 42/1 For a five-dollar bill a lawyer will swear that his mother is a Saratoga chicken. **(6) 1889** *Hood's Cook Book* 2 For Saratoga corn-cake the white kind [of corn meal is used]. — **(7)** [**1876** HENDERSON *Cooking* 194 Nothing deteriorates more by getting cold or keeping than fried potatoes (with the exception of Saratoga fried potatoes, which are served cold).] **1880** MARK TWAIN *Tramp Abroad* 574, I have made out a little bill of fare: . . . Porter-house steak. Saratoga potatoes. **1890** McALLISTER *Society* 100, I had . . . Spanish mackerel, Saratoga potatoes, soft shell crabs [etc.]. — **(8) 1830** *Huntingdon* (Pa.) *Courier* 15 Sep. 4/4 Carpenter's Saratoga Powders for making *Congress Spring or Saratoga Waters.* — **(9) 1858** *N.Y. Tribune* 26 July 3/1 The Saratoga Trunk is an article that has been a theme of story for some time. **1943** DAMON *Sense of H.* 70 In Hannah's attic is a round-topped Saratoga trunk, bigger than a doghouse, containing two hoop skirts and several hats which seem to us ridiculous.

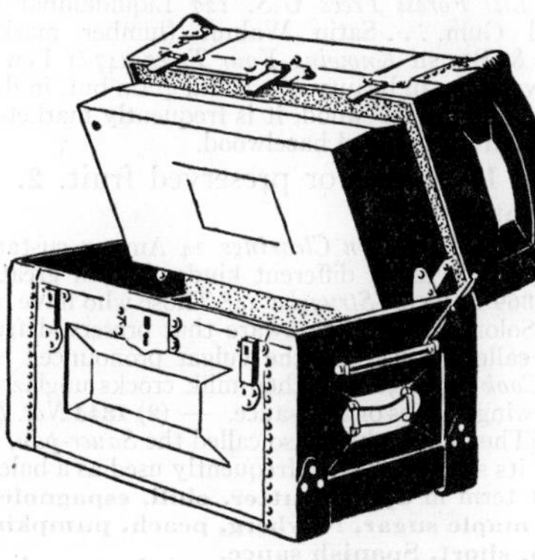

Saratoga trunk

(10) 1890 BARRERE-LELAND II. 195 The Saratoga walk is said to be the latest fashionable gait for women. One who describes it says that 'the first requisite is to throw your shoulders back, the chest forward, chin up, and stomach in, and then walk, wriggling head, limbs, body, and especially bustle.' — **(11) 1829** *Amer. Advertiser* (Phila.) 29 July 3/6 (*advt.*), Fresh Saratoga or Congress Spring Water. **1893** *Harper's Mag.* Jan. 323/1 In front of me was the sign: 'Saratoga water. All you wish for five cents.' — **(12) 1884** NYE *Baled Hay* 223 A raven-black Saratoga wave, hanging on the back of a chair, has been known to turn white in a single night.

Saratoga chips. Potatoes sliced as thin as possible, soaked in cold water, and then dried and fried, so called because such potatoes were first served at Saratoga Springs, N.Y. Cf. **potato chip, Saratoga potatoes.**

[**1865** SALA *Diary* II. 346 These potatoes are the *specialité* of the place—the 'maids of honour,' the whitebait of Saratoga. . . . They are eaten with game, they are eaten with sherry-cobblers, and they are eaten with ice-creams.] **1880** ROE *Army Lett.* 262 The Saratoga chips were delicate and crisp and looked nice. **1947** *Reader's Digest* Feb. 95/2 She compromised on a dozen Lynnhaven oysters, mulligatawney soup, a broiled lobster drenched with butter, Saratoga chips, and a fancy ice cream.

attrib. **1919** MORLEY *Haunted Bookshop* (1921) 88 We discussed some plans for a prune and Saratoga chip campaign.

***sarcophagus,** *n.* (See quot.) *Obs.* — **1871** DE VERE 538 *Sarcophagus* almost universally serves in America to designate the metallic burying-cases, which are largely used to transport bodies from distant places to their last home, and presents a striking instance of the preference given here to the high-sounding terms, however unmeaning and inappropriate they may be.

***sardine,** *n.*

1. (See quots.)

1877 BARTLETT 551 *Sardines*, . . . menhaden prepared in resemblance to the sardines prepared in Europe. **1911** *Rep. Fisheries 1908* 370/1 The silver anchovy (*Anchovia browni*) . . . is also known as 'sardine' and 'spearing.' *Ib.* 316/1 Different species [of silversides] are known as . . . 'merit-fish,' 'sardine,' 'California smelt' [etc.]. **1949** PALMER *Fieldbook Nat. Hist.* 440 Atlantic Herring. *Clupea harengus.* . . . Fry 3–4 in.; fried crisp, 'whitebait'; larger, canned as 'sardines'; full-grown, fresh or dry, 'red herring.'

b. sardine cannery, a place where sardines are canned.

1884 *Nat. Museum Bul.* No. 27, 1064 Sardine cannery. . . . Miniature models of the cans, soldering implements, &c., are shown in position. Camden, Me.

2. (See quots.) *Colloq.*

1856 Sacramento item (Th.), The many lads . . . seemed to think the actor very green; But who, I ask, is most of a sardine? **1861** *New Haven Palladium* 27 Dec. (Chipman), We 'Old Whales' or, as we [*sc.* sailors] are sometimes termed, 'Sardines,' are not supposed by some 'land-crabs' to have much of a taste for [roast fowl]. **1870** LUDLOW *Heart of Continent* 118 The name for a spindling little fellow, whom the plainsman does not wish to compliment, is '*You Sardine.*'

sardine sɑrˈdin, *v. tr.* To crowd or pack (people) closely together. *Colloq.* — **1896** *Advance* 24 Dec. 916/2 [We have room for] 200, yet there are 350 people outside . . . , and in some way we are going to sardine them in.

Sarge sɑrdʒ, *n.* In the Army, a colloquial shortening of "Sergeant." — **1867** GOSS *Soldier's Story* 98 You look hungry too, Sarg. *Ib.* 258 Sarge, the Colonel has got his mad up, and you'll be sent into the stockade. **1946** *Chi. D. News* 23 Feb. (Comics), Is that the way you choked the Japs, Sarge?

Sarracenia ˌsærəˈsiniə, *n.* [After D. *Sarrazin*, of Quebec.] A genus of American bog herbs; also (not *cap.*) a pitcher plant typical of this genus. Also attrib.

1765 J. BARTRAM *Diary* 3 Sep., Lost ye long leaved Saracena ever since we left Charls town but ye hooded kind is very common. **1809** RAMSAY *Hist. S.C.* 345 Sarracenia, dionea muscipula, and many others . . . reward the curiosity and industry of the student of nature. **1855** SIMMS *Forayers* 485 The yellow and purple saracenia, and the blue flag, you will gather along the swamp. **1949** *Nat. Hist.* June 281/1 Anesthesia from Sarracenia extracts does not produce numbness, does not destroy nerve tissue, and is longer acting.

***sarsaparilla,** *n.* A beverage flavored with sarsaparilla. Also **sarsaparilla soda.**

1844 UNCLE SAM *Peculiarities* I. 43 On the outside . . . is printed the following thirsty announcement: . . . Congress Water, Sarsaparilla Soda, Ginger Champaign [etc.]. **1865** *Atlantic Mo.* Jan. 59/1 I have not heard his opinions concerning . . . sarsaparilla, or ginger-pop. **1940** MENCKEN *Happy Days* 233, I . . . even gagged at drinking more than two or three bottles of sarsaparilla.

***sash,** *n.* **1.** (See quots.) **2.** ***sash saw,** a thin narrow saw used in a frame. Also attrib. Cf. **gate saw.**

(1) 1838 *Civil Engineer* I. 148/1 [Potomac Aqueduct.] Wales, or stringers, twelve by six inches, to guide sheet piling, called in America the lower and upper *sash.* **1875** KNIGHT 959/1 *Gate-saw*, a mill-saw

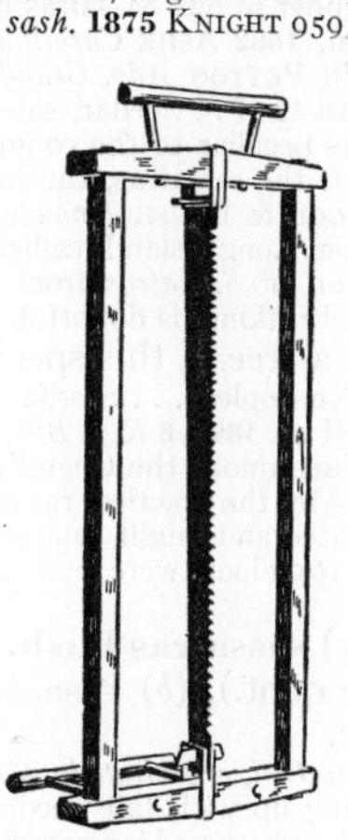

Sash saw

which is strained in a *gate* or *sash* to prevent *buckling.* — **(2) 1866** *Ore. State Jrnl.* 23 June 4/5 We have on hand a full set of Mill Irons for a sash saw mill. **1913** O. A. ROTHERT *Hist. Muhlenberg Co.* (Ky.) 224 After running a horse-power 'upright saw' or 'sash saw' for a number of years he put in a circular saw run by steam.

sashay sæˈʃe, *n.* [See next.] **1.** A trip or journey. *Slang.* **2.** (See quot.)

(1) 1900 G. ADE *More Fables in Slang* 184 Lutie never got out of her Dream until she made a bold Sashay with a Concert Company. **1935** H. L. DAVIS *Honey in Horn* 15 If you yank him out for any all-night sashay on these roads, you ought to be ashamed of yourself. — **(2)**

1940 *Square Dance* 40 The Sashay is a series of short quick steps directly to the side, either to the right or to the left. . . . The gent holds the lady's left hand in his right, and her right hand in his left.

sashay sæˈʃe, *v.* [f. F. *chassé.*] *intr.* To glide or move, orig. as in dancing; to go, go about. *Colloq.*

1836 *Franklin Repository* (Chambersburg, Pa.) 4 Oct. 1/3 If you don't sashay across, button your lip, and go home quietly, you and I will have to promenade all round, and swing corners into the watch house. **1878** Hart *Sazerac Lying Club* 83 S'pose, gentlemen, that we sashay up to the bar. **1947** *Mazama* Oct. 4/1 Saturday evening we'll sasshay over to the Highland Grange and join a neighborhood dance.

Also *tr.*

1928 Nason *Sgt. Eadie* 130 What the hell good a rifle does to me sashayin' these jugheads up an' down the road, I don't know. **1944** Pennell *Rome Hanks* 189 Take them guns thar—tuck 'em from the Yanks at the fust battle of Manassas, an' been a-farin' 'em eveh since an' sashayin' 'em all oveh hell an Vuhginny.

sashrary ˈsæʃrerɪ, *v.* [Corruption of **certiorari.*] *tr.* To have the records of (a case) reviewed by a superior court by virtue of a writ of certiorari. *Slang. Obs.* — **1840** Kennedy *Quodlibet* 229 So what does he do but sashrary the case! **1867** *Harper's Mag.* June 134/1 The Judge, thinking such action might possibly be 'sasherrarrerd,' relucted at acting upon the suggestion.

saskatoon ˌsæskəˈtun, *n.* ["Probably a corruption of *misâskwatomin,* which is the name applied to the fruit in the Cree dialect of Algonquian, signifying 'fruit of *misâskwat,* the tree of much wood.' " (Hodge).] A shadbush of the northern U.S. and Canada. Also *pl.,* the berries of this.

1902 *Amer. Folk-Lore* 257 Saskatoon. . . . The name, in the Canadian Northwest, for a species of berry and the bush upon which it grows. The word is of Blackfoot origin. **1940** *Mt. Hood Guide* 13 This plant is the shadbush of New England, the Juneberry of the Midwest, the Saskatoon of western Canada. **1949** *Sat. Ev. Post* 9 July 60/1 She said she had never tasted saskatoons before.

attrib. **1949** *Sat. Ev. Post* 12 Feb. 52/4 The saskatoon pie was as good as it looked.

sassafras ˈsæsəˌfræs, *n.* [f. Sp. *sasafrás.* The ultimate origin is obscure. It may be from American Indian. See quot. 1949 below and cf. *OED.*]

1. A North American aromatic tree, or species of tree, *Sassafras variifolium* (or *S. albidum*) of the laurel family.

[**1577** Frampton tr. Monardes *Joyfull Newes* II. 46 Of the Tree that is brought from the Florida, whiche is called Sassafras.] **1602** Brereton *Virginia* 12 The finder of our Sassafras in these parts, was one Master Robert Meriton. **1682** Ashe *Carolina* 6 The Sassafras is a Medicinal Tree. **1774** in Peyton *Adv. Grandfather* (1867) 127 The forest of Kentucky consists of . . . cedar, sassafras, wild cherry and many other descriptions peculiar to the country. **1826** Cooper *Mohicans* ix, They brushed the sassafras, causing the faded leaves to rustle. **1949** Collingwood & Brush *Knowing Your Trees* 244 The Narraganset Indians on Long Island called the wood 'asauakapamuch.' The derivation of *Sassafras* from Latin words meaning 'rock-breaking,' or 'salt-breaking' is doubtful.

b. The wood of a tree of this species.

1728 *Boston Rec.* 222 No Popler, . . . Sassifax, Black ash, Basswood, or Ceder Shall be Corded up. **1897–8** *Rep. Bur. of Amer. Ethnol.* I. 422 Sassafras is tabued as fuel among the Cherokee, as also among their white neighbors, perhaps for the practical reason that it is apt to pop out of the fire when heated and might thus set the house afire. **1921** Deam *Trees of Indiana* 165 Floors were made of sassafras to keep out the rats and mice.

2. In combs.: (1) **sassafras bush,** a young sassafras; (2) **laurel,** (*a*) (see quot.), (*b*) = **sassafras 1;** (3) **soap,** see as a main entry.

(1) **1848** G. C. Furber *Jrnl. of Private in Mex.* 54 The field, or the larger part of it, growing up with tall weeds and sassafras bushes. **1944** Clark *Pills* 261 The graveyard is scraped bare of crab grass, . . . Johnson grass and sassafras bushes to give them a 'cared-for' appearance. — (2) (*a*) **1866** Lindley & Moore *Treas. Botany* 821/2 *O*[*reodaphne*] *californica* is a common tree in the mountainous parts of California, where it goes by a variety of names, such as Mountain Laurel, Spice-bush, Balm of Heaven, Sassafras Laurel. (*b*) **1878** Hoblyn *Dict. Medicine s.v., S. officinale,* or Sassafras Laurel, grows in North America.

sassafras soap. ?Soap scented with sassafras, or perhaps homemade "lye soap," so called because it was stirred in making with a sassafras stick.

In making soap at home the use of a sassafras stick was practically universal (see quot. 1921). Two of the quots. below hint that the soap was too strong for use on the face.

1860 Holland *Miss Gilbert* 108 Arthur took his accustomed seat at the head of the table, with Leonora at his right hand, . . . [in an] atmosphere of sassafras-soap. **1863** Taylor *H. Thurston* 137, I never washed my face with sassafras soap. **1898** Westcott *D. Harum* xii, He performed his ablutions (not with the sassafras soap). [**1921** Deam *Trees of Indiana* 165 To successfully make soap, it was necessary to stir the contents of the kettle with a sassafras stick.]

sass tea. Short for **sassafras tea.* — **1847** Robb *Squatter Life* 72 The matron of the house boiled him some hot 'sass-tea,' which, the old man said, relieved him mightily. **1950** *Chi. Tribune* 28 March 14/3 Here at Strawberry Patch we not only doctor with 'sass tea,' but often have it for supper.

***satin,** *n.*

1. satin bell, (see quots.).

1898 A. M. Davidson *Calif. Plants* 123 Mariposas are . . . sometimes called globe tulips, . . . the satin-bell or fairy's lantern. **1915** Armstrong & Thornber *Western Wild Flowers* 58 Satin-bell. White Globe Tulip. *Calochortus albus.* **1925** Jepson *Flowering Plants Calif.* 237 C[alochortus] albus Dougl. White Globe Lily. . . . Also called Snow-drops, Indian Bells, and Satin Bells.

2. satin walnut, (see quots.).

1901 *Daily Chron.* 22 Aug. 7/5 'Sweet gum' is the name most generally used in the United States, and the wood was a drug until its name was changed by a smart trader to 'satin walnut.' **1927** Sudworth *Check List Forest Trees U.S.* 127 Liquidambar styraciflua Linnæus. Red Gum. . . . Satin Walnut (lumber markets). **1949** Collingwood & Brush *Knowing Your Trees* 247/1 Few American woods equal sweetgum in beauty of natural grain but, in deference to the prejudice against 'gum' wood, it is frequently marketed as satin walnut, Circassian walnut and hazelwood.

***sauce,** *n.* **1.** Stewed or preserved fruit. **2.** ***sauce pan,** (see quot.).

(1) **1845** Kirkland *Western Clearings* 24 Among custards, cakes, and 'saase' or preserves, of different kinds, figured great dishes of lettuce [etc.]. **1869** Barnum *Struggles* 248 Those who have heard John E. Owens in 'Solon Shingle,' are aware that preserved fruits are in New England called 'sauce,' by the vulgar pronounced 'sass.' **1884** F. E. Owens *Cook Book* 322 Earthen milk crocks unglazed are best adapted for stewing berries or any sauce. — (2) **1844** *Nat. Hist. N.Y., Zoology* VI. 57 [The king crab] is also called the *Sauce-pan,* in allusion to the shape of its shield, which is frequently used as a bale for boats.

As the last term in **apple, butter, chili, espagnole, garden, long, maple, maple sugar, Newberg, peach, pumpkin, round, Shaker peach, short, Spanish sauce.**

sauerkraut ˈsaʊrˌkraʊt, *n.* Also **sourcrout.** [The quots. indicate that this is an Amer. borrowing f. Germans in this country.] Finecut cabbage slightly fermented in a brine of its own juice.

1776 Leacock *Fall Brit. Tyranny* III. v, Don't leave me, and you shall have plenty of porter and sour-crout. *a***1813** Wilson *Foresters* 9 Torrents of Dutch from every quarter came, Pigs, calves, and *saurcraut* the important theme. **1863** P. S. Davis *Young Parson* 48 [You] eat the best of roast beef, while I have to put up with sauerkraut and spec. **1946** Hibben *Cookery* 135 Wash the sauerkraut in several waters.

Hence **sauerkrauter,** a German. *Slang.*

1869 *Terr. Enterprise* (Virginia, Nev.) 24 April 3/1 The man handed it over, but could not speak English (he was a regular 'sour-krauter').

b. *To look sauerkraut at,* to look at in an exceedingly displeased manner. *Rare.*

1846 Corcoran *Pickings* 11 Here the Dutchman looked sourcrout at the tall, thin gentleman in the seedy black suit.

sauger ˈsɔgɚ, *n.* [Origin obscure. Poss. f. Amer. Indian.] A pike perch, *Cynoperca* (syn. *Stizostedion*) *canadense,* smaller than a wall-eyed pike.

1882 *Nat. Museum Bul.* No. 16, 526 *Stizostedium canadense.* . . . Sauger; Sand-pike; Gray-pike; Horn-fish. **1911** *Rep. Fisheries 1908* 311/1 The name [horsefish] is also applied to the sauger. **1947** Dalrymple *Panfish* 220 One or two pounds is about the average for adult Saugers.

Sauk sɔk, *n.* Variant of **Sac.**

1806 Pike *Sources Miss.* I. App. 20 The Sauks and Reynards are planting corn. **1852** Reynolds *Hist. Illinois* 8 They claimed relationship with the Pottawatamies, and perhaps the Sauks and Foxes also. **1946** Foreman *Last Trek* 187 Treaties were thus made with the following tribes: Delawares, Kansa, Sauk and Foxes and Foxes of the Mississippi, Sauk and Foxes of the Missouri.

attrib. **1949** *Ill. State Hist. Soc. Jrnl.* June 204 They missed the enemy completely and had to be content with burning a Sauk Indian village and destroying its crops.

sault su, *n.* [A new borrowing f. a 17th-century F. spelling *sault* of *saut,* leap, jump.] A waterfall or rapid.

1600 HAKLUYT *Voyages* III. 234 The Captaine prepared two boats to goe vp the great River to discouer the passage of the three Saults or falles. 1809 A. HENRY *Travels* 16 The Sault de Saint-Louis . . . is the highest of the *saults*, falls, or *leaps*, in this part of the Saint-Lawrence. 1850 LANMAN *Haw-hoo-noo* 227 Their principal village stands . . . at the head of the *Sault* or Falls. 1944 NUTE *Lake Superior* 216 The greatest body of fresh water in the world . . . descends some twenty feet over a ledge . . . , creating the famous rapids, the 'sault' in French parlance.

* **sausage,** *n.* Used to designate various implements for cutting or grinding meat and forcing it into suitably prepared intestines or casings, as (1) **sausage cutter,** (2) **filler,** (3) **grinder,** (4) **gun,** (5) **machine,** (6) **stuffer.**

(1) 1854 *Pa. Agric. Rep.* 127 A model of a Sausage cutter was exhibited. — (2) 1848 D. P. THOMPSON *L. Amsden* 104 Jim Walker . . . was to our house . . . to borrow a sassage-filler for his wife. — (3) 1876 KNIGHT 2031/2 *Sausage-grinder,* . . . a machine for mincing

Early (*c*1875) type of sausage stuffer

meat for sausages. 1949 *Chi. Tribune* 20 Feb. VII. 6/7 See this sausage grinder. Just like new. — (4) 1869 *Overland Mo.* III. 130 Swine's flesh, bread, sage, and other matters of nourishment and seasoning, chopped fine, . . . [are] squirted out into links from the end of a sausage-gun. 1933 *Old-Time N. Eng.* July 14/1 The meat division contains many kinds of grinding mills, mincing knives, sausage 'guns' for forcing the chopped meat into the casings.

(5) 1859 BARTLETT 380 *Sausage-machine.* A machine for chopping or mincing meat for the purpose of making sausages. — (6) 1845 *Knickerb.* XXV. 406 It is ten to one that there lurks beneath it [the Yankee countenance] the knowledge of . . . some 'self-acting back-action sausage-stuffer.' 1876 KNIGHT 2032/1 *Sausage-stuffer.* . . . A device for stuffing cleaned intestines with sausage-meat. 1946 *Agric. Hist.* April 97/1 In that process two implements were used, the sausage grinder, which was fastened to a table and turned by hand, and the sausage stuffer, likewise operated by hand.

savagerous sə'vædʒərəs, *a.* and *adv.* Also **sevagerous, salvagerous.** [Fanciful as if f. *savage* and danger*ous*.] Fierce, savage, savagely. *Slang.* Cf. **servigrous,** *a.*

1832 TROLLOPE *Domestic Manners Amer.* xiii. I. 182 The visitor took it [*sc.* a dagger] up, and examining it with much emotion, exclaimed, 'What! do you really jab this into yourself sevagerous?' 1843 *Spirit of Times* (Phila.) 25 Aug. (Th.), The Editor calls his savagerous enemy a remarkably pious and moral young man. 1857 T. H. GLADSTONE *Englishman in Kans.* 206 My white brother was not very communicative, but . . . said he was '. . . nary lick afeard, not by a long sight, but he kinder druther keep tracks a little ways off such a salvagerous, onairthly set.' 1925 KRAPP *Eng. Lang.* I. 115 Fantastically coined or combined words, as . . . *savagerous, savigrous.*

transf. 1943 *Quincy* (Ill.) *Herald* 3 March 2/4 The 'Captain's' effort at *nigger poetry* in the last Whig is truly extatically savagerous.

b. savagerous wildcat, a rowdy, "half horse and half alligator." *Obs.*

1836 *S. Lit. Messenger* II. 287 In regard, . . . to that class of south western mammalia who come under the generic appellation of 'savagerous wild cats.'

savanero ˌsɑvə'nero, *n. S.W.* [Sp. *sabanero,* in the Amer. Sp. sense shown here.] A herdsman. *Obs.* — 1844 GREGG *Commerce of Prairies* I. 183 One person, called the *savanero,* has the charge of the mules at night, which are all turned loose without tether or hopple with the *mulera* or bellmare, to prevent them from straying abroad.

savanilla ˌsævə'nɪlə, *n.* [Origin obscure.] A local name for the tarpon. — 1884 GOODE *Fisheries* I. 611 [The tarpon is] the 'Savanilla' of Texas. 1911 *Rep. Fisheries 1908* 317/2.

* **savanna,** *n.* Also **savannah, Savannah.** [The *Savannah* spelling is the result of confusion between * *savanna* and *Savannah,* Ga.]

1. =**pine savanna.** *Obs.*

1865 *Reader* 23 Sep. 236/3 The army has been moving through magnificent pine-woods—the savannahs of the South, as they are termed.

2. =**savanna sparrow.**

1909 *Auk* XXVI. Oct. 361 A curious misapprehension as to the significance of the current English name of *Ammodramus sandwichensis savanna* seems to exist in ornithological literature as revealed by its orthography. Wilson distinctly refers to the city of Savannah as the locality where he states he first discovered the species (A.O., III, 55) and he so spells its name in the English title. Its specific name, however, he gives as 'savanna.' In our current literature this last appears as the method of spelling the bird's name in English, which is clearly misleading. 1937 STONE *Bird Studies at Old Cape May* 900 The breeding Savannahs appear very pure white below and the black streaks stand out boldly while the yellow eyebrow is conspicuous

3. In combs.: (1) **savanna bunting,** =**savanna sparrow;** (2) **crane,** =**sand-hill crane;** (3) **cricket,** (see quots. 1791, 1842); (4) **finch,** =**savanna sparrow;** (5) **frog,** =**savanna cricket,** *obs.;* (6) **grass,** conjugated paspalum, *Paspalum conjugatum;* (7) **partridge,** a prairie chicken, *obs.;* (8) **sparrow,** a small white and brown sparrow, *Passerculus sandwichensis savanna,* or a related variety.

(1) 1844 *Nat. Hist. N.Y., Zoology* II. 161 The Savannah Bunting is quite common in this State. 1917 *Birds of Amer.* III. 25. — (2) 1791 W. BARTRAM *Travels* 220 Amongst other game, they brought with them a savanna crane which they shot in the adjoining meadows. — (3) 1791 W. BARTRAM *Travels* 276 There is yet an extreme diminutive species of frogs, which inhabits the grassy verges of ponds in savannas; these are called savanna crickets. 1842 *Nat. Hist. N.Y., Zoology* III. 70 *Hylodes gryllus.* . . . At the South, it is called Savannah Cricket. 1853 *Harper's Mag.* Nov. 771/1 The chirp of the savanna-cricket . . . fell upon my ear. — (4) 1783 LATHAM *Synopsis Birds* III. 270 Savannah Finch. 1811 WILSON *Ornithology* IV. 72 Savannah Finch . . . is probably the most timid of all our Sparrows. 1839 AUDUBON *Ornith. Biog.* V. 516 The Savannah Finch was found . . . on the Rocky Mountains and about the Columbia River.

(5) 1827 WILLIAMS *W. Florida* 29 Except the little savanna-frog, these embrace all the species with which we are acquainted. — (6) 1859 G. W. PERRY *Turpentine Farming* 9 The land needs no cultivation, but every kind of turf should be turned over, such as . . . wire grass, savanna grass and broom-sage grass. — (7) 1808 PIKE *Sources Miss.* 73 My Indians killed fifteen partridges, some nearly black, with a red mark over their eyes, called the Savanna partridge. — (8) 1811 WILSON *Ornithology* III. 55 The female of the Savannah sparrow is five inches and a half long. 1942 PEATTIE *Friendly Mts.* 194, I come upon savanna sparrows, singing from fence posts.

* **save,** *v. W. tr.* To secure by killing, to kill. *Slang. Obs.*

1833 J. HALL *Harper's Head* 38, I knew I had *saved* him [the buck]. 1849 KINGSLEY *Diary* 34 One of our sailors struck a porpess this morning but did not save him. 1877 CAMPION *On Frontier* 344 The boys [were] anxious to lose no chance of 'saving' an Indian.

For *to save one's life,* see * **life b.** (1).

* **savings bank.** A container in which coins may be saved, esp. one with a coin slot and openable only after the insertion of a certain number of coins. Cf. **penny savings bank.**

1869 ALCOTT *Little Women* II. 12 [He brought] every kind of tinware, from a toy savings-bank . . . to a wonderful boiler. 1936 *Sears Cat.* (ed. 173) (*index*), Savings Banks. 1949 *L.A. Times* 25 Sep. (Home Mag.) 8/3 As the demand for home savings banks increased inventors used a multitude of commonplace subjects of the contemporary scene as models for the animated portions of the banks.

savvy 'sævɪ, *n.* Also **savey.** [See **sabe,** *v.*] =**sabe.** *Slang.*

1870 HARTE *Chiquita* 9 Hedn't no savey—hed Briggs. 1947 *Time* 3 March 26/3 The aviation industry had bid heavily for the war-taught savvy of top-ranking officers. 1949 *Amer. Forests* Dec. 20 When a farmer of the Louisiana bayou country wants bacon he heads for the woods. Whether he gets it is likely to depend upon the savvy and shiftiness of his hog dogs.

savvy 'sævɪ, *v.* [See **sabe,** *v.*] *intr.* =**sabe,** *v. Slang.* Cf. *no sabe* (or *savvy*) *s.v.* * **no,** *adv.* and *a.* **3.**

1878 Hart *Sazerac Lying Club* 220 'Yosh,' he replied, 'me heap savvy; most Injun he only savvy moon.' **1923** Mulford *Black Buttes* 148 None of 'em is goin' to get her. Savvy me? **1949** *True* Jan. 61/3 When there are ladies present, we say it in Mexican. The hounds savvy either.

* **saw,** *n.* In combs.: (1) **saw brier,** any one of various species of brier, as the bull brier or the common cat brier; (2) **crew,** (see quot.); (3) **dust,** see as a main entry; (4) **gang,** a group of workmen engaged in getting out saw logs; (5) **gin,** a cotton gin in which the fibers of cotton are torn from the seed by toothed disks or circular saws, also **saw-ginned,** *a.;* (6) **grass slough,** a slough in which sawgrass abounds; (7) **gummer,** a device for deepening and enlarging the spaces between the

Early type of saw gin

teeth of a worn saw, cf. **gummer 1;** (8) **log,** a log of a suitable size and length for sawing into lumber; (9) **mill log,** =prec.; (10) **mill town,** a town that has sprung up at a sawmill; (11) **mill work,** a sawmill, *obs.;* (12) **palmetto,** a common dwarf palmetto, *Serenoa serrulata,* of the South, also a similar palm, *Paurotis wrighti,* of southern Florida; (13) **set,** *local,* a slit made perpendicularly in the lower part of the ear of a domestic animal as a mark of ownership; (14) * **tooth,** an ownership mark or notch made in the ears of cattle; (15) **tooth roof,** (see

Saw logs on a log wagon

quot. 1909); (16) * **whetter,** one whose business is sharpening saws, cf. (6) below.

(1) 1806 *Ann. 9th Congress* 2 Sess. 1142 The saw briar, single rose briar, and china root briar [grow near the Washita R.]. **1821** Nuttall *Travels Arkansa* 180 This route was . . . often entangled with brambles, and particularly with the tenacious 'saw-brier' (*Schrankia horridula*). **1944** Clark *Pills* 261 The graveyard is scraped bare of crab grass, blackberry and 'saw' briers, Johnson grass and sassafras bushes to give them a 'cared-for' appearance. — **(2) 1905** *Forestry Bureau Bul.* No. 61, 29 *Bank,* . . . the logs cut or skidded in one day above the required amount and held over by the saw crew or skidders. — **(4) 1902** White *Blazed Trail* 9 The 'saw gangs,' three in number, prepared to fell the first trees.

(5) 1801 Miller & Whitney in *Amer. Jrnl. Science* XXI. 222 The machine for separating cotton from its seeds, [is] commonly called the Saw Gin. **1851** *De Bow's Review* X. 335 This will be another great advantage . . . in bringing the saw-ginned cotton . . . to the point. **1882** *Cent. Mag.* Jan. 477/2 Several minor modifications of the saw-gin . . . seem to have merits. — **(6) 1942** Kennedy *Palmetto Country* 15 After much suffering from the sun, water, sawgrass, snakes, and mosquitoes, the soldiers found the Seminoles had taken a stand in a cypress hammock fronted by a deep sawgrass slough. — **(7) 1859** *Rep. Comm. Patents 1858* 565 Improved Saw Gummer. **1865–6** *Ill. Agric. Soc. Trans.* VI. 52 Saw Gummer: N. F. Stone & Co. — **(8)** [**1756** in Fries *N.C. Morav. Rec.* I. (1922) 160 Brick was made; corn gathered; and saw-logs hauled.] **1825** *Vt. Aurora* (Vergennes) 1 Sep. 4/4 The subscriber will pay *cash* for 2000 sound pine Saw Logs, or any less quantity, delivered at his Mill in Vergennes. **1948** *Hungry Horse News* (Columbia Falls, Mont.) 17 Sep. 1/6 Bids will be opened at the Hungry Horse project next Wednesday for the sale of 5,475,000 board feet of standing 'saw log' timber in the Hungry Horse reservoir. — **(9) 1843** *Yale Lit. Mag.* VIII. 406 There are multitudes of people in the land, . . . whose first idea when coming to the premises would be, what lots of saw-mill logs there are here.

(10) 1941 *Yankee* Dec. 32/2 Nioi, up the Saru River valley, was a sawmill town of a type familiar in the West. — **(11) 1654** *Suffolk Deeds* II. 26, I Edward Colcott . . . doe hereby giue . . . vnto Thomas Rucke . . . one third parte of a saw mill worke. **1739** W. Stephens *Proc. Georgia* I. 402 One Tyrrel, appointed Director of the Saw-Mill Work at Old Ebenezer. — **(12) 1797** Hawkins *Letters* 85 The whole country was a pine barron, with wire grass and saw palmetto. **1942** Kennedy *Palmetto Country* 4 Shrub-like saw palmetto underlies the pine flatwoods from Florida northward into South Carolina. — **(13) 1943** *Democrat* 14 Jan. 4/6 Reddish brindle muley-headed yearling . . . swallowfork and under sawset in right. **1944** *Ib.* 13 April 4/4 One yellow heifer . . . marked crop the right, swallow fork and saw set in the left. — **(14) 1779** *N.J. Archives* 2 Ser. III. 231 A red heifer . . . with a half crop in the left ear . . . and a saw-tooth on the same.

(15) 1909 Webster, saw-tooth roof. . . . A roof composed of two or more parallel simple roofs and in section like the teeth of a saw, esp., one having a slope of each member very steep to receive windows. **1942** Asher & Heal *Send No Money* 58 It had plenty of windows, a sawtooth roof to provide light, and it was airy and spacious. — **(16) 1789** *Boston Directory* 196 Pike Timothy, saw whetter.

b. In the names of animals: (1) **sawbelly,** (*a*) the summer herring, *Pomolobus aestivalis,* (*b*) the branch herring, *P. pseudoharengus;* (2) * **bill,** (see quot. 1872); (3) **cut,** the pine sawyer, *Monochamus confusor,* or its larva, also **saw-cut grub;** (4) **-toothed grain beetle,** a beetle, *Silvanus surinamensis,* the larvae of which destroy stored grain; (5) **whet,** the Acadian owl, *Cryptoglaux acadica,* the smallest of the North American owls, in full **saw-whet owl;** (6) * **whetter,** used erroneously for the Canada jay, *rare,* cf. (16) above; (7) **worm,** (see quot. and cf. **saw cut**).

(1) (*a*) **1884** Goode *Fisheries* I. 582 Around the Gulf of Maine this species is also known by the names 'Kyack' or 'Kyauk,' 'Saw-belly,' and 'Cat-thrasher.' (*b*) **1903** T. H. Bean *Fishes N.Y.* 200 The branch herring, river herring or alewife . . . [is] the sawbelly of Maine. **1949** Palmer *Fieldbook Nat. Hist.* 438 Alewife, Sawbelly. *Pomolobus pseudoharengus.* — **(2) 1763** tr. DuPratz *History Louisiana* (1858) I. 235 We are disturbed in the night, by the hideous noise of the numberless water-fowls, that are to be seen on the Mississipi, such as cranes, flamingo's, wild geese, herons, saw-bills, ducks, &c. **1872** Coues *Key to Birds* 178 In the . . . *Momotidæ* (motmots or sawbills), the middle and outer toes are perfectly coherent for a great distance. — **(3) 1859** *Harper's Mag.* July 164/2 Our disciple of nature . . . hears the busy chirp of the 'saw-cut' under the bark. *Ib.* 165/1 The flies are carefully put away, another footlink is attached to the line—the saw-cut grubs are substituted. Down glide the larvæ . . . and in a few minutes up comes the fish. — **(4) 1895** *Dept. Agric. Yrbk. 1894* 287 The saw-toothed grain beetle . . . is of common occurrence in granaries, in groceries, . . . and in barns.

(5) 1834 Audubon *Ornith. Biog.* II. 567 The Little Owl is known in Massachusetts by the name of the 'Saw-whet,' the sound of its love-notes bearing a great resemblance to the noise produced by filing the teeth of a large saw. **1949** *Amer. Forests* Oct. 23/1 The saw-whet owl has a peculiar voice suggesting the sound of a saw being filed; hence its name. — **(6) 1784** J. Belknap *Jrnl. Tour* (1876) 10 The Dr. saw a blue bird, with a white head, which is said to be a *saw-whetter,* alias *carrion-bird.* — **(7) 1885** *Library Mag.* April 292/2 [The ivory-bill's] principal food is a large flat-headed timber-worm, known in the South as *borer* or *saw-worm.*

As the last term in **band, belt, buck, buzz, crosscut, cylinder, drag, foxtail, gang, gin, ice, mill, muley, sash, shingling, slab, tooth, web, whip, wood saw.**

* **saw,** *v.* In slang phrases: (1) *To saw gourds,* to snore; (2) *to saw the air,* in baseball, to swing at and miss a pitched ball; (3) *to saw wood,* to continue at what one is about, unmindful of what others are doing.

(1) 1870 Ludlow *Heart of Continent* 91 In five minutes . . . we were all 'sawing gourds' together in the land of Nod. **1934** in Wentworth. — **(2) 1880** *Chi. Inter-Ocean* 19 May 2/5 Shaffer sawed the air three times without hitting anything, and retired. — **(3) 1894** *Cong. Rec.* 24 Jan. 1347/2 Is it possible that the framers of the bill hold a grudge against the voters who 'sawed wood' last November? **1908** O. Henry *Options* 75 During all these wintry apostrophes, Barbara, cold at heart, sawed wood—the only appropriate thing she could think of to do.

sawbuck ˈsɔbʌk, *n.* [Du. *zaagbok* in sense **1.**]

1. A sawhorse in which two supports at each end cross each other and so form a rack for holding that which is sawed. Also fig.

[**1842** UNCLE SAM *Peculiarities* I. 41 Add to these . . . several piles of wood in the street, which some niggers are industriously sawing into 'sizes for firing' at their cross-legged mills.] **1862** *Rep. Comm. Patents 1861: Agric.* 141 The sheep is then laid upon his back in a kind of sawbuck. **1878** B. F. TAYLOR *Between Gates* 237 [The horse] made a sawbuck of her legs. **1948** *Sat. Ev. Post* 10 July 83/2 I'd roped everything around the ranch—calves, hounds, horses, fence posts, sawbucks.

b. Attrib. in the sense of "sawbuck-like."

1855 M. THOMPSON *Doesticks* 322 Macduff . . . stands over the conquered Macbeth in a grand saw-buck attitude. **1900** *Scribner's Mag.* Sep. 270/2, I never tired of seeing the two Indians throw the hitches by which they fastened tents, boxes, heads, or anything at all, to the sawbuck attachments on the pack-saddles.

Sawbuck or buck

c. A horse. *Rare.*

1882 BAILLIE-GROHMAN *Camps in Rockies* 366 Dismounting from my tired 'sawbuck,' I proceeded to examine the arrangement.

2. A ten dollar bill, in allusion to the X-shaped ends of a sawyer's sawbuck. Cf. **double sawbuck,** *s.v.* ***double 4. f.**

[**1850** *Knickerb.* XXXVI. 297 Send me the two double 'saw-bucks.'] **1852** *Ore. Statesman* 13 Nov. 1/1 Dod rabbit it, there goes another 'saw-buck,' on the plag'uey jack. **1892** *Outing* June 216/2 I'se got two sawbucks lef', an' up dey goes on de ole hoss. **1950** *Nature Mag.* March 167/2 Originally *vignettes* were pictures of buildings, . . . such as the illustration of the U.S. Treasury building on the back of the Federal Reserve sawbuck.

3. Short for next.

[**1869** MARK TWAIN *Innocents* 58 The saddles . . . consisted of a sort of saw-buck with a small mattress on it.] **1880** NYE *B. Nye & Boomerang* 67 This summer, however, I will get me a little blue jackass and put a sawbuck on his back, . . . and I will hie me to the mines. **1933** CHELEY *Camping Out* 461 While the Government has adopted the aparejo as its pack saddle, the cross-tree or sawbuck is the best one for ordinary use.

4. sawbuck (pack) saddle, a type of pack saddle the end pieces of which suggest those of a sawbuck.

1907 WHITE *Arizona Nights* 17 We skirmished around and found . . . a sawbuck saddle with kyacks. **1913** *Outing* Jan. 425/1 The most practical equipment for pack animals is the ordinary crosstree or sawbuck pack saddle for all-around use. **1938** THOMPSON *High Trails* 138 If you are going on a camping trip you utter an instinctive protest as your packer cinches up the 'sawbuck' packsaddle and loads his animal.

***sawdust,** *n.*

1. *attrib.* Designating persons and things connected with a circus, or with a tent revival meeting.

[**1844** JOE COWELL *Thirty Yrs. Among Players* 65 Would apply to me that coarse but common combination of words 'horse—and sawdust' manager.] **1883** *Cent. Mag.* March 746/1, I was not flattered at being taken for a sawdust artist. **1887** CUSTER *Tenting on Plains* 380, I hardly knew whether I was myself or the venturesome young woman who spends her life in taking airy flights through the paper-covered circles in a saw-dust ring. **1895** *N.Y. Dramatic News* 5 Oct. 16/3 Eddie Arlington . . . has left the ranks of the sawdust field and embarked in the paths of financial journalism. **1949** *Amer. Sp.* April 101 He had given up baseball in his prime to become one of the greatest preachers of the sawdust circuit.

b. sawdust path, trail, used in phrases, usu. fig., in allusion to going down a sawdust covered aisle to the altar in a tent meeting as a sign of repentance or conversion.

1913 *Collier's* 26 July 7/3 And down the aisle, 'hitting the sawdust trail,' they come in ones and twos and dozens, until 476 have stood before that multitude to shake the evangelist's hand and signify their intention of starting another life. **1942** STEGNER *Mormon C.* 155 Mormonism has never since its first years used the sawdust trail technique best exemplified in modern times by the Holy Rollers. **1946** HOLBROOK *Lost Men* 312 Many of these suddenly patriotic pleaders . . . like repentant sinners at a revival, hurried down the sawdust path. **1948** *Dly. Ardmoreite* (Ardmore, Okla.) 23 July 6/3 The white-haired old corporation attorney, mad at both the republicans and the democrats, had come to hit the sawdust trail for Henry Wallace.

2. In combs.: (1) **sawdust country,** a region in which most of the timber has been cut off and sawed into lumber, also attrib., *rare;* (2) **pudding,** (see quots.), *obs.*

(1) **1894** *Home Missionary* Oct. 327 It might seem wise to let the little churches organized in this 'sawdust country' drop into oblivion. *Ib.* 328 These small, rural, sawdust-country churches are to our city churches what mountain rills are to rivers. — (2) **1840** SPARKS ed. Franklin *Works* I. 85 The guests . . . were surprised to see nothing before them but two puddings made of coarse meal, commonly called *sawdust puddings.* **1844** UNCLE SAM *Peculiarities* I. 166 A sawdust pudding . . . [is] a capital fritter, made of the scrapings produced when meat is so frozen as to be separated into pieces by a saw.

***sawed,** *a.*

1. Intoxicated, fooled, "hacked." *Slang.*

1833 A. GREENE *Life D. Duckworth* II. 176 He was seldom downright drunk; but was often . . . most infernally sawed. **1847** FIELD *Drama in Pokerville* 199 The thoroughly 'sawed' victim made way for him as if he had been the cholera incarnate! *a*1856 in HALL *Coll. Words* (ed. 2) 461.

2. ***sawed-off,** short, under average height, also absol. *Slang.*

1887 GEORGE *40 Yrs. on Rail* 22, I remember . . . the little sawed-off cars jolting along the uneven track. **1901** WHITE *Westerners* 220 Most marvellous was a clean-limbed, deep-chested, slender running horse, accompanied by a sawed-off English groom. **1902** LORIMER *Lett. Merchant* 160, I didn't understand football, but understood that little sawed-off. **1947** *Time* 1 Sep. 46/1 The Cowboy and his sawed-off sidekick, Long Tom, were blowing some varmints to kingdom come.

b. sawed-off shotgun, a shotgun having its barrel or barrels cut off short, app. first used by express messengers but now chiefly by criminals.

[**1897** *Scribner's Mag.* Nov. 575/1 In his hand Pete held a shot-gun of the kind used by express messengers, with sawed-off barrels and heavy charges of buckshot in them.] **1898** *Ib.* Jan. 86/2 There was another roar from the messenger's sawed-off shotgun. **1916** DU PUY *Uncle Sam* 11 Who is there around here who has a sawed-off shotgun? **1948** *So. Bend* (Ind.) *Tribune* 15 Aug. II. 13/3 The Johnston office made a ruling that a criminal can't use a sawed-off shotgun or a tommy-gun in pictures.

***sawing,** *n.* (See quot.) *Obs.* — **1857** *Mich. Agric. Soc. Trans.* VIII. 166 'Sawing' . . . means working against each other, or *one* trying to dip the sheep on one side whilst the *other* is trying to do the reverse.

***sawyer,** *n.*

1. The larva of any one of various large beetles, as the pine sawyer, *Monochamus confusor,* that infest dead trees, also the katydid.

1789 ANBUREY *Travels* II. 452 [In Va.] the log huts in which the soldiers reside . . . [have been] nearly destroyed by an insect that . . . preys upon the solid part of the timber; and these insects . . . have

Sawyers (sense 2) in a stream

the appellation of sawyers. **1804** LEWIS in *L. & Clark Exped.* VI. (1905) 127 The green insect known in the U' States by the name of the sawyer or chittediddle was first heard to cry on the 27th. of July. **1908** KELLOGG *Amer. Insects* 285 The sawyers, various species of the genus *Monohammus,* are beautiful brown and grayish beetles.

2. A log or tree caught in a river so that the upper portion of it sways up and down on or just beneath the surface in such a way as to menace navigation. Now *hist.* Cf. **chicot, sleeping sawyer.**

The *EDD* records *sawyer* in the sense of "a fallen tree, floating down stream" with an example of *a*1848.

1790 FORMAN *Journey* (1888) 44 Another dangerous obstruction is a tree becoming undermined and falling into the river . . . the limbs wear off, and the body keeps sawing up and down with great force, rising frequently several feet above the water, and then sinking as much below. These are called 'sawyers,' and often cause accidents to unsuspecting navigators. **1883** MARK TWAIN *Life on Miss.* xl, At this point begins the pilot's paradise; a wide river . . . [with] no bars, snags, sawyers, or wrecks. **1944** DUNCAN *M. Graham* 130 Gangs of chainmen yanked out the midstream 'sawyers'—clearing a path for the steamboat that was coming.

3. a. A smart, witty fellow. **b.** ?A horse of an inferior kind. Both *slang* and *obs.*

(a) 1853 *Oregonian* (Portland) 23 April 1/1 By casually meeting each other . . . quite an intimacy sprung up between the two 'sawyers.' — **(b) 1853** *Alta California* (S.F.) 2 May 2/4 A Purse of $300, mile heats, best 2 in 3, to a sulky, between second-rate 'sawyers,' came off yesterday afternoon over the Pioneer Course.

4. A lumberman who converts trees into sawlogs.

1880 *Lumberman's Gaz.* 28 Jan. 1/3 A Wisconsin lumber-camp is divided into 'choppers,' 'sawyers' and 'swampers.' **1913** *Outing* April 120/2 Sawyers and axemen spring away as the great tree hurtles down. **1942** RICH *We Took to Woods* (1948) 75 They haven't shown, however, what it means . . . to have as the boon companions of one's four-year-old son a bunch of the hardest and toughest teamsters, sawyers, border-jumpers and general roustabouts that ever came down a tote road.

5. (See quot. 1884.)

1884 GOODE *Fisheries* I. 659 The Bowfin or Johnny Grindle—*Amia calva*. . . . It occurs in the Great Lakes, where it is called 'Dogfish' and 'Sawyer.' **1911** *Rep. Fisheries 1908* 308/1.

As the last term in **bob, sleeping, whip, wood sawyer.**

* **saxifrage,** *n.* As the last term in **Pennsylvania, rock saxifrage.**

* **Saxon,** *n.* **1.** Short for next. **2. Saxon merino,** a breed of fine-wooled sheep, also attrib.

(1) 1852 *Mich. Agric. Soc. Trans.* III. 142 A few full blood Saxons; the rest are a grade sheep. **1883** ALLEN *New Farm Book* 419 The Saxon . . . is one of the varieties of the pure-bred Merino. — **(2) 1854** *Pa. Agric. Rep.* 65 There is not a Merino or Saxon Merino Sheep on the ground. **1893** G. W. CURTIS *Horses, Cattle* 250 It is believed that Mr. Berry was the first to apply the name 'Black-Tops,' and that he did so to distinguish them from the light colored, delicate Saxon Merinos.

* **Saxony,** *n. attrib.* Designating a breed of sheep developed in Saxony, Germany. *Obs.*

1831 PECK *Guide* 173 Little is said or done to . . . introduce the marino, or saxony breed. **1842** *Nat. Hist. N.Y., Zoology* I. 112 The quality of the fleece was still farther improved in 1824, by the introduction of what are termed *Saxony sheep*. **1863** *Rep. Comm. Agric. 1862* 47 About the year 1824, and subsequently, occurred the 'Saxony speculation' which resulted in the importation of individuals of the Saxony breed by Judge Hayes.

* **Say,** *n.*[1] [Thomas *Say* (1787–1834), Amer. naturalist.] In the names of birds (see quots.).

1825 BONAPARTE *Ornithology* I. 20 [The] Say's Flycatcher, *Muscicapa Saya*, . . . now before us is a male. **1917** *Birds of Amer.* II. 200 Say's Phœbe. *Sayornis sayus*. . . . Other Name.—Say's Pewee. **1944** *Nat. Geog. Mag.* June 694/2 The floor of the Canyon, on the other hand, a mile below, is in the Lower Austral zone, with such birds as Say's phoebes, ash-throated flycatchers [etc.].

* **say,** *n.*[2] In poker, a player's turn to bet or pass.

1857 *Spirit of Times* 17 Oct. 104/1 He cannot take any action therein until after all the players to the left have had their 'say.' **1887** KELLER *Draw Poker* 23 The next say belongs to the next player to the left. **1903** *Out West* June 725 It was North's ante and Foley had the first say.

* **say,** *v.*

1. *quasi-interj.* Used to call attention to a statement or question. *Colloq.*

1852 *Lantern* (N.Y.) I. 122/1 Say—d'you run with our machine? **1853** *Ib.* III. 363/1 The colloquialism 'say!' justifies our claiming this appalling interrogative as a genuine *Americanism*, and as such we shall request all our beloved pupils to prepare their reply. **1912** NICHOLSON *Hoosier Chron.* 169 Say, the janitor service in this old ark is something I couldn't describe.

2. *Poker. intr.* To bet or pass at one's turn.

1887 KELLER *Draw Poker* 23 If no straddle has been made, the first player to the left of the age must 'say.'

Saybrook platform. A platform of church discipline and polity adopted by a synod of the Connecticut Congregational Church at Saybrook in 1708. Now *hist.*

1825 NEAL *Bro. Jonathan* I. 5 [He had been] defeated at his own game—Divinity—with his own weapons—the Saybrook platform, and Bible. **1879** *Cong. Rec.* 21 Feb. 1715/2 The 'Saybrook platform' was the formula into which the really liberal . . . principles of their religion had been cramped and crowded. **1945** WEBSTER *Town Meeting Country* 44 In 1708, the General Court called delegates to a synod at Saybrook. These twelve clergymen and four laymen drew up the famous Saybrook Platform.

* **scab,** *n.* A workman who accepts lower wages than those prescribed by a trade union, or who refuses to join a union; one who works after a strike has been called, or in the place of a union man on strike. *Slang.*

1806 in COMMONS *Doc. Hist.* III. 74, I concluded at that time I would turn a scab. **1889** SALMONS *Burlington Strike* 259 The man who takes the place of another when that other engages in a struggle with a corporation, is a 'scab.' **1948** CHAPLIN *Wobbly* 6 There was surely no doubt about what the scabs and Pinkertons were doing.

attrib. **1881** *Chi. Times* 11 June 2/2 Three hundred saloon-keepers of New York have joined hands with the striking brewers by refusing to purchase scab beer. **1892** *Chronicle* (Cin.) June 2/1 Mr. Murth still runs a scab bakery, all he says to the contrary notwithstanding. **1947** *Railroad Telegrapher* May 261/1 The small amount of scab operations was not paying expenses.

* **scab,** *v.*

1. *tr.* and *intr.* To work as a scab. Also *to scab it, to scab on. Slang.*

1806 in COMMONS *Doc. Hist.* III. 75 Their business was to watch the Jews that they did not scab it. **1898** *Scribner's Mag.* Oct. 445/2, I won't scab any man's job. **1917** SINCLAIR *King Coal* 298 Is there anybody here who'll scab on his fellows? **1942** LILLARD *Desert Challenge* 90 Nearly everything in Reno, for example, is organized, except tencent-store girls, who scab readily.

b. *transf.* To treat an employee better than fellow employers would.

1920 *Nation* 3 July 11/2 If I should pay you more than other department stores do, my crowd would say I was scabbing on them.

2. *tr.* To ostracize (a worker) as a scab, or to declare (a shop) a nonunion organization and to boycott it. *Slang.*

1806 in COMMONS *Doc. Hist.* III. 73, I was liable to be scabb'd. . . . If I did not join the body, no man would set upon the seat where I worked; . . . they would neither board or work where I was unless I joined. *Ib.* 77 In a little time after this his shop was scabbed.

scabbard, *n.* As the last term in **saddle, shoulder scabbard.**

* **scabbard fish.** The cutlass fish, *Trichiurus lepturus*, or any of several related species, found along the coasts of the southern U.S.

1883 *Nat. Museum Bul.* No. 27, 437 *Trichiurus lepturus.* Silvery Hair-tail; Scabbard-fish; Sabre-fish; Silver Eel. Warm seas. On the east coast of the United States north to Cape Cod. **1897** *N.Y. Forest, Fish & Game Comm. 2d Rep.* 236 [The] scabbard fish . . . is very rarely seen in [Gravesend Bay]. **1903** T. H. BEAN *Fishes N.Y.* 403 The scabbard fish frequents warm seas and ranges north to Cape Cod and Lower California.

scabbarding 'skæbədɪŋ, *n.* [f. **scabbard*, a scaleboard used by printers.] The spacing of lines of type by inserting scaleboards between them. *Obs.* — **1786** CUTLER in *Life & Corr.* II. 270 Size of the paper, scabbording of the lines, . . . scabbording of the prefaces . . . were all particularly specified in the contract. **1818** *N. Amer. Rev.* May 118 If a printer, he is adroit at *scabbarding*.

* **scabious,** *n.* Any of various plants of the genus *Erigeron*, as the sweet scabious *q.v.* — **1830** LINDLEY *Intro. Nat. Syst. of Botany* 200 *Erigeron philadelphicum* and *heterophyllum* . . . are commonly sold under the name of Scabious.

scabish 'skæbɪʃ, *n.* [f. **scabious*.] The evening primrose, *Oenothera biennis*, or a related plant. Also the scabious *q.v.*

1817–8 EATON *Botany* (1822) 364 *Œnothera biennis*, scabish, tree-primrose. . . . Phosphorescent. **1874** *Vt. Bd. Agric. Rep.* II. 779 *Heteraspis pubescens.* Very common on the scabish. **1891** *Amer. Folk-Lore* IV. 149 A very rough, coarse, rank-growing weed in the swamps, which I think now was some kind of Aster, grandmother called *Scabish.* **1892** *Ib.* V. 96 *Œnothera fruticosa*, scabbish. N.H.

scad skæd, *n.*[1] [See note.]

Origin obscure. It is not clear that all the senses shown are of the same word. In **3. scads** may be a rationalized pl. of *skad*, listed in the *EDD* as a variant of *scald* in the sense of a great number, a good deal. See *EDD s.v. scald, v.* and *sb.*[2] 14, and note its variant forms.

1. A dollar. *Slang.*

1809 *Amer. Mag.* Nov. 1 (Ernst), This land of our dads . . . is a dinger at nailing the scads. **1876** *Ventura Free Press* (San Buenaventura, Calif.) 8 Jan. 4/1 He'd deal for you both night and day, Or as long as he had a scad. **1942** LILLARD *Desert Challenge* 192 That's me! Come out with the scads.

2. *W.* A fleck of gold remaining in a goldpan after a washing; all the gold in a pan that has been washed. *Obs.* Cf. **scale gold.**

1863 in *Mont. Hist. Soc. Contrib.* III. (1900) 137 Bill sang out 'I have found a scad.' I returned for answer, 'If you have one I have a hundred.' He then came down to where I was with his scad. It was a nice piece of gold. *Ib.*, I panned the pan of dirt and it was a good prospect; weighed it and had two dollars and forty cents; weighed Bill's scad and it weighed the same. Four dollars and eighty cents!

3. *pl.* A great many, a large quantity, "scadoodles." *Colloq.*

1869 [see **scadoodles**]. **1904** W. H. SMITH *Promoters* 52 England . . . found she could raise scads of opium in India, but had no market for it. **1948** *Redbook Mag.* April 88/2 While you can buy scads of pigeons at $2 apiece, you'll pay $25 to $30 and up for reasonably good birds.

***scad,** *n.*[2] The cigarfish. Cf. **big-eyed, mackerel scad.** — **1882** *Nat. Museum Bul.* No. 16, 432 *Decapterus punctatus.* . . . Scad; Round Robin.

scadoodles skəˈdudl̩z, *n.* [App. fanciful f. **scad**+*oodles.*] (See quot.) *Slang. Obs.* — **1869** *Overland Mo.* III. 131 A Texan never has a great quantity of any thing, but he has 'scads' of it, or 'oodles,' or 'dead oodles,' or 'scadoodles,' or 'swads.'

***scaffold,** *n.* As the last term in **cotton, tobacco scaffold.**

* **scaffold,** *v.*

1. *tr.* Of American Indians: To expose (a corpse) on a scaffold. *Obs.*

1775 ADAIR *Indians* 323 [They] scaffolded their dead kinsman. **1805** CLARK in *Lewis & C. Exped.* I. (1904) 325 An Indian woman was scaffeled in the Indian form of Deposing their Dead. **1814** BRACKENRIDGE *Views La.* 225 An Indian chief . . . was scaffolded here some years ago.

2. To place (furs, skins, etc.) on a scaffold for drying or for safe keeping, frequently with *up. Obs.*

1799 J. SMITH *Acct. Captivity* 39 Sometime in February, we scaffolded up our fur and skins. **1804** CLARK in *Lewis & C. Exped.* I. (1904) 197, I scaffeled up the Deer & returned. **1808** PIKE *Sources Miss.* 2 [The Sacs] were employed in spearing and scaffolding a fish. **1846** *De Bow's Review* I. 455 State any improvement you are familiar with in the scaffolding of cotton?

***scaffolder,** *n.* (See quot.) *Obs.* — **1860** G. VANDENHOFF *Dramatic Reminiscences* 107 The company was, in fact, a Show-company —scaffolders—that played in booths in summer, and in winter, betook themselves to small theatres.

scalage ˈskelɪdʒ, *n.* [f. **scale, v.*] The amount by which anything is scaled down, the amount which timber measures. — **1853** *Cong. Globe* 1 March 961/1 Gentlemen . . . will come in, who have got their scalage at eighty-seven and a half cents on the dollar. **1878** *Michigan Rep.* XXXVI. 168 Allen agreed to deliver . . . merchantable lumber . . . [equivalent] to the total scalage of the logs delivered.

scalawag ˈskæləˌwæg, *n.* Also **scallywag.** [See note.]

The origin of this term is not clear. The *EDD* lists *scallag* (f. Gaelic *sgalag*, a servant, husbandman, rustic) used in the Hebrides for "a poor being who for mere subsistence becomes a predial slave to another. . . . Five days in the week he works for his master: the sixth is allowed to himself for the cultivation of some scrap of land on the edge of some moss or moor." *Scallag* and *scalawag* may be related.

1. A scamp, loafer, rascal.

1848 BARTLETT 284 *Scalawag*, a favorite epithet in western New York for a mean fellow; a scape-grace. **1869** J. R. BROWNE *Adv. Apache Country* 183 [She] had been eight days at this infernal place among a set of scallywags who didn't understand her lingo. **1903** *McClure's Mag.* Sep. 462 The honest, conservative citizen remains at home, while the able scalawag runs his organization.

b. Also attrib., possibly in some instances in allusion to sense **3.** below.

1888 BRYCE *Amer. Commonw.* II. II. xliv. 164 A group of such 'scallawag' members . . . increase their legislative income by levying this form of taxation [blackmail] upon the companies of the State. **1891** WELCH *Recoll. 1830–40* 123 It would be a very 'scalawag' Indian to whom he would answer tan-ta-gig-egac (no trust). **1906** *Nation* 12 July 27 Those scalawag appointees of McKinley's . . . have recently had to be removed from the consular service in China. **1907** *Cin. Enquirer* 10 July 6/1 In anticipation of statehood the territories seem to have been overrun by a lot of scalawag politicians.

2. A poor or worthless animal. Also **scalawag steer.**

1854 *N.Y. Tribune* 24 Oct. (*Cent.*), The number of miserable 'scallawags' is so great that . . . they tend to drag down all above themselves to their own level. **1873** *Chi. Tribune* 2 Feb. 12/6 Inferior—Light and thin cows, heifers, stags, bulls, and scallawag steers . . . 1.75@ 2.20. **1902** LORIMER *Lett. Merchant* 15 Like feeding his weight in corn to a scalawag steer that won't fat up.

3. A Southerner who supported the Congressional plan of reconstruction after the Civil War; a white Republican in the South. Also attrib. Now *hist.*

1862 *Charleston* (S.C.) *Mercury* 9 Aug. 1/3 This invaluable class is composed . . . of ten parts of unadulterated Andy Johnson Union men, ten of good lord and good devil-ites, five of spuss and seventy-five of scallowags. **1867** *Nation* V. 12 Dec. 470/1 And it is not surprising that the Macon (Ga.) *News* has to print in full the names of thirteen persons such as above described (as having 'voted the Scalawag ticket.') **1911** SIMONS *Social Forces in Amer. Hist.* 298 The army of men that were thus marshaling the negroes for the Republican party was made up in part of Northern adventurers ('carpet-baggers') and so-called Southern 'Union men' ('scalawags'). **1946** *Democrat* 24 Oct. 4/1 It wasn't this cringing spirit which enabled our forefathers . . . to retain control of the voting machinery and run the scalawags and carpetbaggers out of the state.

scalawaggery ˈskæləˌwægərɪ, *n.* The rule or motivating principles of scalawags. *Rare.* — **1911** HARRISON *Queed* iv. 45 The Morning *Post* was an old paper. . . . It had crucified carpet-baggism and scalawaggery upon a cross of burning adjective.

* **scald,** *n.* A disease of plants resembling wilt.

1791 W. BARTRAM *Travels* 208 The traders and Indians call this disease the water-rot or scald. **1895** *Stand.* 1590/3 *Scald*, a destructive disease of cranberries, due to a sphaeriaceous fungus: applied also loosely by farmers and fruit-growers to any sudden wilting or decay, of unknown origin, of leaves and fruit. **1899** *Farmers' Bul.* No. 91, 10 Tip Burn, Leaf Burn, or Scald. This disease of the [potato] leaves . . . is often confused with early blight. **1916** *Ib.* No. 727, 28 Sun scald sometimes occurs during the winter on the south or southwest side of the trunks, especially in the case of high-headed trees.

As the last term in **cold, fire, hog scald.**

***scale,** *n.*[1] A spree or drinking frolic. *Obs.* — **1825** PICKERING *Inquiries Emigrant* (1831) 27 Though they are seldom seen drunk, when on a 'scale,' or drinking frolic, [the Americans] are often seen near half-and-half. **1835** TODD *Notes* 37 Bacchanalian orgies [in New York City] are called *scales.*

* **scale,** *n.*[2]

1. A piece of money. *Slang. Obs.*

1871 DE VERE 296 Among the less generally known terms [for money] are . . . *wherewith, shadscales*, or *scales*, 'for short.' **1874** B. F. TAYLOR *World on Wheels* 28 But promise him a 'scale'—scale, skilling, shilling.

2. In combs.: (1) **scale-bark,** *fig.* rough-and-ready in appearance and manners, *rare;* (2) **bug,** any of numerous insects of the family Coccidae, which are destructive to plants; (3) **carp,** a variety of the common carp that is normally scaled, as distinguished from the leather carp and the mirror carp; (4) **gold,** *W.* gold that occurs in small scales or flecks, *obs.*, cf. **scad,** *n.*[1] **2.**

(1) **1837** BIRD *Nick* I. 101 Thar may be something of the scale-bark and parsimmon about me. — (2) **1883** *Cent. Mag.* Oct. 811/2 The orange's worst enemy is a curious insect, the scale-bug. **1895** M. GRAHAM *Stories of Foot-Hills* 90 I'd stick at home closer'n a scale-bug to an orange-tree. — (3) **1878** *Rep. Comm. Fisheries* VI. p. xlii, About half of the scale carp . . . remained in Baltimore. **1903** T. H. BEAN *Fishes N.Y.* 167–8 Three varieties are recognized, the scale, the mirror and the leather carp, based chiefly on the scaling of the body. — (4) **1850** *Calif. Courier* (S.F.) 18 July 2/3 The gold was found in lumps of a large size, and no scale gold whatever was found in this location.

***scale,** *n.*[3] An estimate of the amount of lumber in a given log, logs, or standing timber. Also attrib. — **1877** *Mich. Rep.* XXXIV. 376 To conclude the parties in that respect by his scale. *Ib.* XXXV. 521 The scale bill showed four hundred and ninety three thousand five hundred and seventeen feet of white pine. **1903** WHITE *Blazed Trail Stories* 43 The firm agreed to pay six dollars a thousand, merchantable scale, for all saw-logs banked at a rollway.

In various senses, as the last term in **bill, cattle, counter, cushion, fluted, hay, log, oyster-shell, peach, platform, Rocket, red, San Jose, shad, spring, twelve-back scale(s).**

* **scale,** *v.*

1. *tr.* To reduce (something) in amount, to reduce (an amount) according to a fixed scale. Freq. with *down.* Also * **scaling,** *n.*

1790 *Ann. 1st Congress* 1161 If the Government . . . finds that it will work an evil . . . to discharge those notes . . . at their nominal value, they are not to be blamed for scaling them. **1882** *Nation* 21 Sep. 232/2 All the others must be equally conscious of their deserts in order to get a proper proportion when the 'scaling down' comes. **1911** HARRISON *Queed* 292 Public institutions . . . could consider themselves lucky if they did not find their appropriations scaled down by a fourth or so.

2. *Lumbering.* Of timber: To produce, measure, or work out at (a given amount of lumber).

1853 LOWELL in *Putnam's Mag.* Nov. 466/1 Their eye, accustomed to reckoning the number of feet a tree will *scale*, is rapid. **1911** J. F. WILSON *Land Claimers* 78, I can figure out how much your trees will scale.

b. To measure (logs) or estimate the yield of (timber).

1867 LOWELL in *Atlantic Mo.* Jan. 27, I expect I can Scale a fair load of wood with e'er a man. **1903** WHITE *Blazed Trail Stories* 48 Not a log do I scale for ye, Jimmy Bourke. **1945** SERVICE *Ploughman* 282 She pulled up her skirt and I measured her calf just above the knee. 'Go easy, Son,' said the old mossback. 'Remember you ain't a-scalin' a log.'

3. To proportion (votes) according to a scale. *Rare.*

1856 HAMBLETON *H. A. Wise* 29 The vote was then taken, and was scaled on the principle of allowing each county represented a number equal to its Democratic vote in the presidential election of 1852.

4. To grade or rank.

1890 *Stock Grower & Farmer* 29 March 5/1 Rams must weigh 110 pounds in carcass, clip 25 pounds of wool, and scale 75 points to be standard. Ewes . . . can be scaled or not.

5. * *To scale off,* of the weather: To clear off, become fair. *Colloq.* [Cf. *EDD scale wind,* a scattering wind.]

1898 F. H. SMITH *C. West* 60, I guess she'll scale off. . . . The glass is a-risin', too.

* **scaled,** *a.* In the names of birds: (1) **scaled dove,** (see quot. 1891), also **scale dove;** (2) **partridge,** a partridge, *Callipepla squamata,* found in the Southwest; (3) **quail,** =prec.

(1) **1884** COUES *Key to Birds* (ed. 2) 570 *Scardafella inca.* . . . Inca Dove. Scaled Dove. **1891** *Cent.* 5370/1 *Scale-dove,* . . . an American dove of the genus *Scardafella,* as *S. inca,* or *S. squamata,* having the plumage marked as if with scales. **1917** *Birds of Amer.* II. 52. — (2) **1858** BAIRD *Birds Pacific R.R.* 646 Scaled or Blue Partridge. . . . Valley of Rio Grande of Texas. . . . Most abundant on the high broken table lands and mezquite plains. **1880** *Cimarron News & Press* 30 Dec. 1/5 The scaled partridge or blue quail has a short, full, soft crest. — (3) **1874** COUES *Birds N.W.* 441 Blue Quail . . . is also called the Scaled Quail, from the peculiar appearance of the plumage of the under parts. **1917** *Birds of Amer.* II. 8/1 The Scaled Quail is a desert species.

scale house. A place where large scales, as those for weighing animals, are kept. Also attrib. *Obs.*

1754 *S.C. Gazette* 5 Feb. 3/1 A Scale-House Beam, Scales and Weights, compleat. **1868** *Ill. Agric. Soc. Trans.* VII. 442 In this division of the stock yards there are three scale houses. **1885** *Rep. Indian Affairs* 80 To the southeast . . . is one large cattle corral, . . . with scales and scale-house.

scaler ˈskelɚ, *n.*[1] (See quot. 1926 and cf. **log, lumber scaler.**)

1877 *Mich. Rep.* XXXIV. 376 The contract . . . is held not to impower the scaler to go into the percentage. **1926** RICKABY *Ballads* 237 *Scaler.* The man who computed the amount of lumber in the logs cut. He computed this by a mathematical process based on the diameter of the log at the smaller end. As he scaled each log, he marked it. He usually worked at the landings. **1948** *Sat. Ev. Post* 24 Jan. 30/3 The scaler computes the board-foot content.

* **scaler,** *n.*[2] (See quot.) — **1891** *Cent.* 5370/3 *Scaler,* . . . an instrument resembling a currycomb and usually made of tin, used for removing scales from fish.

scaling law. A Texas law providing for proportionate payment of claims against the government. *Obs.* — **1851** *Hunt's Merch. Mag.* XXV. 739 The last issues are made under the act of 20th March, 1848, usually known as 'the scaling law.'

* **scalloper,** *n.* One who gathers scallops. — **1881** INGERSOLL *Oyster Industry* 247 *Scalloper,* a scallop-fisher. **1887** GOODE *Fisheries* v. II. 570 The scallopers will tell you everywhere that the more they [scallops] are raked the more abundant they become.

scallyhoot ˈskælɪˌhut, *v. W.* [Origin obscure.] *intr.* (See quot. 1889.) Cf. **callyhooting.**

1869 *Overland Mo.* III. 128 A mustang . . . [will] 'get up and scally-hoot' a short distance. **1889** FARMER 473/1 *Scallyhoot, To,* to be off; to skedaddle. A Texas form. **1903** O. HENRY *Roads of Destiny* 96 Same old Whipperwill Creek skallyhootin' in and out of them motts of timber.

* **scalp,** *n.*

1. In fig. use, esp. of political victories or defeats (see quots.). *Colloq.*

[**1850** *Cong. Globe* App. 21 Feb. 190/3 The hon. member said . . . he would either have our votes or our *scalps.*] **1872** *Ib.* 16 Feb. 1076/3 [This hall is not] as the honorable Senator from Mass. of today would have it, an arena for the exhibition of political scalps. **1921** *Unpartizan Review* Jan.–March 7 The American Federation of Labor regards it as the equivalent of compulsory arbitration, and is out for the political scalps of those who voted for it. **1947** *Steamboat* (Colo.) *Pilot* 13 Feb. 2/4 Certain livestock groups of the state have been out after the official scalps because of cutbacks in the grazing allotments in the West.

2. In combs.: (1) **scalpblade,** =**scalp knife,** *rare;* (2) **bounty,** a bounty paid by a colony or government for the scalp of an enemy, *obs.;* (3) **chant,** among Indians, a chant indicating that an enemy scalp has been secured, *obs.;* (4) **dance,** (see quot. 1920), also **scalp dancing,** now *hist.;* (5) **feast,** among Indians, a feast of rejoicing over securing scalps, *obs.;* (6) **halloo,** a shout given by Indians to announce the taking of an enemy's scalp, *obs.;* (7) **hunter,** one who hunts to secure enemy scalps, often to obtain the bounty on them, *obs.;* (8) **lifting,** the taking of scalps, *obs.;* (9) **lock,** a long lock of hair left on the crown of the head by some American Indians as a challenge to their enemies; (10) **mark,** the mark or scar made on the head by the removal of the scalp, *obs.;* (11) **money,** =**scalp bounty,** *obs.;* (12) **music,** the chant or song of Indians upon securing scalps, *obs.;* (13) **pole,** a pole upon which Indians displayed the scalps of their enemies, *obs.;* (14) **song,** a song by Indians announcing success in securing scalps, *obs.;* (15) **vote,** a vote in a colonial assembly providing for the payment of a bounty for Indian scalps, *obs.;* (16) **whoop, yell,** =**scalp halloo.**

(1) **1850** GARRARD *Wah-To-Yah* xvii. 201 'When an Injun's a "gone beaver," we take a knife like this,' pulling out his long scalpblade. — (2) **1747** *New Hampshire Prov. P.* V. 532 Mr. Saml Walton . . . has inlisted twenty men to go out after ye Indians upon the scalp Bounty. **1829** COOPER *Wish-ton-Wish* xxviii, The Sergeant hath a right to claim the scalp-bounty, for the man that is slain. — (3) **1884** *Cent. Mag.* May 138/1 But mingling with these unpleasant sounds came the rapid movement of the scalp-chant, *hum, hum, hum.* — (4) **1791** J. LONG *Voyages* 35 The dances among the Indians are many and various, . . . [including] the scalp dance. **1855** ROSS *Fur Hunters* 28 Here was gambling, there scalp-dancing; laughter in one party, mourning in another. **1920** DRUMM *Jrnl. Fur-Trading Exped.* 104 The scalp dance is the most hideous of all Indian customs. . . . They placed their trophies on the end of lances and for hours would sing and dance, not infrequently reacting in pantomine all the events leading up to the scalping. Both the men and women participated.

(5) **1846** SAGE *Scenes Rocky Mts.* xx, The murderers had the impudence to ask a scalp-feast. — (6) **1782** KNIGHT in *Metcalf Narratives* (1821) 49 The Indian told me, that was my big Captain, and gave the scalp halloo. **1886** Z. F. SMITH *Kentucky* 400 The dependent inmates of the houses were [never] entirely exempt from the echo of . . . the scalp halloo that sent tidings of another victim to savage atrocity. — (7) **1835** BIRD *Hawks* I. 79 He acquired a singular reputation as a bold and successful scalp-hunter. — (8) **1881** *Harper's Mag.* April 659/2 William and Mary's classical course for his young braves . . . would not improve them in deer-stalking or scalp-lifting. — (9) **1826** COOPER *Prairie* xviii, A large and gallant scalp-lock seemed to challenge the grasp of his enemies. [**1945** MATHEWS *Talking* 80 She tied on his scalplock made of buffalo-tail tuft and wild-turkey bristle.]

(10) **1866** WHITTIER *Snow-Bound* 261 How the Indian hordes came down. . . . And how her own great-uncle bore His cruel scalp-mark to four-score. — (11) **1704** in G. SHELDON *Hist. Deerfield, Mass.* (1895) I. 299 That the sum of Sixty Pounds be allowed and Paid to the Petitioners. . . . as Scalp money, to be equally Divided amongst them. **1724** *Ib.* 425 My account of scalp money from Col Partridge much exceeds your act in many particulars. — (12) **1898** *McClure's Mag.* Feb. 382/2 He moved in the direction of his desire, chanting the Apache scalp-music. — (13) **1800** HAWKINS *Sk. Creek Country* 82 The two last towns raised the scalp pole. **1873** COZZENS *Marvellous Country* 124 The scalp-pole was handed round by the oldest of the squaws. — (14) **1823** JAMES *Exped.* III. 60 Two or three other little detached squads were now seen to approach, also singing the scalp song. **1835** SIMMS *Yemassee* II. 78 The warriors . . . [howled] out the sanguinary promise of the scalp-song.

(15) **1746** *New Hampshire Prov. P.* (1871) V. 424 We . . . pray that your Excellency will be pleased to give proper encouragement to all suitable Persons that may appear as Volunteers to go out on ye first scalp Vote as well as the Vote for fifty Volunteers on Wages. — (16) **1792** BRACKENRIDGE *Mod. Chivalry* (1937) 58 A warrior . . . separates it [*sc.* a scalp] from the head, giving, in the mean time, what is called the scalp yell. **1829** COOPER *Wish-ton-Wish* xxv, 'Tis the scalp-whoop, and the warriors are very glad. **1947** *Nat. Geog. Mag.* July 108/1 The hundreds of scientists being marshaled there are pioneers more potent than any who fought when war drums rolled along the Mohawk, scalp yells quivered on the Valley air, and the frontier was aflame.

Also *scalp taker, taking, trophy, visit,* etc.
As the last term in **green, Indian, wolf scalp.**

scalp skælp, *v.* Also †**sculp.** [f. the noun.]

1. *tr.* To mutilate (a vanquished enemy) by taking his scalp in the manner of an American Indian. Now *hist.*

1693 *Mass. Province Laws* VII. 395 [He] found his Brother killed & scalped. **1709** J. LAWSON *Hist. Carolina* 4 Generally, when they take any Prisoners, (if the English be not near to prevent it) sculp them, that is, to take their Hair and Skin of their Heads, which they often flea away, whilst the Wretch is alive. **1881** *Rep. Indian Affairs* 103, I succeeded in capturing the Indian . . . that murdered and scalped a poor, innocent, old white man. **1946** FOREMAN *Last Trek* 141 Here he met two Osage men, shot and scalped one.

fig. **1849** HAWTHORNE in J. Hawthorne *N. Hawthorne & Wife* II. 384, I shall do my best to kill and scalp him in the public prints. **1871** BAGG *At Yale* 252 The Fresh of '72 were for a time in the habit of wearing caps made of paper, . . . so that if they chanced to be 'scalped' their loss would be trifling. **1891** *Cent.* 5372/1 *Scalp*, . . . in *Amer. polit. slang*, to destroy the political influence of, or punish for insubordination to party rule.

2. To level off. *Colloq.*

1825 LORAIN *Pract. Husbandry* 335 The Yankee farmer first chops the fallen timber, then scalps off the grubs level with the ground. **1895** *Stand.* 1591/3.

3. To buy and sell frequently on a stock exchange for the sake of small, quick gains, also *to scalp the market.*

1886 *Harper's Mag.* July 213/2 [The scalper buys] any quantity of grain that may be offered, sells it at an advance of 1/8 cent per bushel, thus scalps the market **1897** *Boston Globe* 29 Aug. (Ernst), The broker himself would be selling the stock at 104 in New York, thereby 'scalping' one-fourth and making a handsome profit at no risk. **1902** LORIMER *Lett. Merchant* 201 Then I saw what looked like a safe chance to scalp the market for a couple of cents a bushel.

4. *intr.* (See quot. and cf. ***scalping, *n.* 2.)

1889 FARMER 473/1 *Scalp, To.* . . . To drive a hard bargain. . . . To speculate in unused railway tickets.

***scalper,** *n.*

1. One who takes the scalp of an enemy, in the manner of an American Indian. *Obs.* or *hist.*

1760 NILES *Indian Wars* I. 174 This reminds me of an account we had of a notable old scalper among [the Indians]. **1841** COOPER *Deerslayer*, v, My gifts are not scalpers' gifts, but such as belong to my religion and colour. **1900** DRANNAN *Plains & Mts.* 60 When the story of my killing the two Indians got out, I came to be generally called 'the boy scalper.'

2. A scalping knife.

1837 BIRD *Nick of Woods* II. xviii. 245 Captain Ralph Stackpole did . . . meet another Injun-savage in the woods . . . with gun, axe, and scalper. **1947** DEVOTO *Across Wide Missouri* 32 The Company is sending . . . 100 dozen 'common scalpers' and 55 dozen more expensive knives for murder with style.

3. One who secures tickets and sells them at unofficial or unauthorized prices. Cf. **ticket scalper.**

1869 *Harper's Mag.* Sep. 623/2 Where theatres are all the run, And bloody scalpers come to trade. **1879** *Chi. Tribune* 8 March 5/4 All the above-named scalpers were arrested . . . and taken to the Armory and placed in the bull-pen. **1949** *L.A. Dly. News* 9 Nov. 48/1 How would you like to buy a pair of tickets without having to pay anything extra to a scalper?

4. (See quot.) *Obs.*

1847 J. C. MCCOY *Hist. Sk. Cattle Trade* 292 So soon as an incoming train is announced nearing the stock yards, the hurrying tramps of solicitors, called 'Scalpers,' may be heard hustling toward the unloading platform. If there is a shipper on the train whose stock is not consigned, they . . . [present] the business cards of the commission firms which have the Scalpers employed.

5. On a stock exchange, a trader who seeks small profits on quick transactions.

1886 *Harper's Mag.* July 213/2 The 'Pit' is the scalper's delight. **1903** *N.Y. Ev. Post* 26 Sep., The buying was only moderately brisk and mainly confined to small scalpers.

***scalping,** *n.*

1. The action of taking an enemy's scalp. Also attrib. or as adj. *Obs.*

1750 in TEMPLE & SHELDON *Hist. Northfield, Mass.* 381 Our Men will not venture out after the Enemy on any Scalping Act whatsoever. **1757** *Lett. to Washington* II. 62 Order them out in Parties with some of Your Men a Scalping. **1835** WHITTIER *Mogg Megone* (1894) 500/2 Norridgewock . . . plucks his father's knife away, To mimic, in his frightful play, The scalping of an English foe. **1883** SWEET & KNOX *Through Texas* 39 A silver-handled hunting-knife . . . would be handy in case any scalping would have to be done.

fig. **1850** GALLAHER *Western Sk.-Book* 389 He regarded the cutting to pieces, or, as he sometimes expressed it, the 'scalping and tomahawking' of a beautiful hymn, which the judgment and good taste of the church has sanctioned . . . as a grievous outrage.

2. The selling, usu. at exorbitant rates, of tickets obtained for speculative purposes. Cf. ***scalper, *n.* 3, and **ticket scalping.**

[**1833** KEMBLE *Record* 296 Some of the lower class of purchasers, inspired by the thrifty desire for gain said to be a New England characteristic, sell these tickets, which they buy at the box-office price, at an enormous advance, and smear their clothes with treacle and sugar and other abominations, to secure from the fear of their contact of all decently-clad competitors, freer access to the box-keeper.] **1882** *Nation* 5 Oct. 276/2 A corporation like the Pennsylvania Railroad must protect itself against loss through 'scalping.' **1945** *Chi. D. News* 8 Oct. 3/1 Those fined . . . denied scalping.

3. (See quot. 1900.) Also attrib. or as adj. Cf. **grain scalping.**

1888 *Economist* 20 Oct. 6/3 There is a fair amount of scalping trade, but the public show little interest in the list. **1897** *Boston Globe* 29 Aug. (Ernst), The whole history of the rise and fall of the arbitrage or scalping business is a story of the perfection of telegraphic communication. **1900** NELSON *A B C Wall St.* 158 *Scalping*, following the varying changes of the market, and taking small profits or losses with the rapidity with which the market fluctuates.

4. In special combs.: (1) **scalping dance,** =**scalp dance,** *obs.;* (2) **knife,** a knife especially suitable for scalping a vanquished enemy; (3) **party,** a party or group out to secure enemy scalps, *obs.*

(1) **1755** *N.J. Archives* XIX. 488 The antient King of the Mohawks . . . came down with some of his Warriors . . . and made their Appearance also among the Ladies on the Assembly Night, where they danced the Scalping Dance with all its Horrors, and almost terrified the Company out of their Wits. — (2) **1756** WASHINGTON *Writings* I. 353 Ensign Smith & 12 men of the Regiment . . . took a number of . . . scalping knives. **1830** *Mechanics' Press* (Utica, N.Y.) 13 Feb. 111/3 He was equipped with his leather hunting shirt, bullet pouch, and scalping knife. **1949** *Sat. Ev. Post* 15 Oct. 98/3 For a time he carried a dry box-elder stick; he imagined it to be a tomahawk or a scalping knife. — (3) **1711** *Conn. Col. Rec.* (1870) V. 280 [Ordered] that the souldiers . . be impowred . . . to act offensively against the said enemy, if they shall continue to send out their scalping parties upon any of the said frontiers. **1867** PARKMAN *Jesuits in N. Amer.* 337 Small scalping-parties infested the Huron forests. **1949** *N.Y. Times Bk. Rev.* 5 June 26/2 The Winooski was a highway for Algonquin scalping parties to and from Deerfield.

***scaly-bark,** *n.*

1. The scaly-bark hickory or its nut.

1856 REID *Desert Home* 187 At length, we saw him descend a tree, whose bark was exceedingly rough—in fact, crisped outward in great, broad pieces, or scales of a foot long, and several inches broad, that looked as though they were about to fall from the tree. For this reason, the tree is known among backwoodsmen as the 'scaly bark.' **1883** HARRIS *Nights* (1911) 250 Man come 'long en ax me how does de wum git in de scaly-bark. **1909** CALHOUN *Miss Minerva* 66 You can get all the . . . scalybarks and fig leaves . . . you want to.

2. scaly-bark hickory, the shagbark hickory, *Carya ovata*, so called from the appearance of its bark. Cf. **flying-barked hickory.**

1781–2 JEFFERSON *Notes Va.* (1788) 37 Scaly bark hiccory. *Juglans alba cortice squamoso.* **1814** PURSH *Flora Amer.* II. 637 This useful tree is known by the name of Shell-bark Hickory, Shag-bark and Scaly-bark Hickory, on account of its bark, which is torn in loose fragments. **1897** SUDWORTH *Arborescent Flora* 113 *Hicoria ovata.* . . . Shagbark (Hickory). . . . Scalybark Hickory (W.Va., S.C.).

b. Attrib. with **nut.**

1775 ADAIR *Indians* 360 Filberts . . . are as sweet and thin-shelled, as the scaly bark hiccory-nuts. **1906** O. HENRY *Rolling Stones* 8, I saw . . . a little flaxen-haired man with a face like a scaly-bark hickory-nut.

***scamp,** *n.* The bacalao, *Mycteroperca falcata*, a southern fish so called because of its ability to steal bait without being caught; also the closely related species *M. phenax.* Cf. ***nibbler, *n.*

1882 *Nat. Museum Bul.* No. 16, 538. **1884** GOODE *Fisheries* I. 413 Another fish of this genus *Mycteroperca falcata*, is called at Pensacola by the name 'Scamp.' **1896** JORDAN & EVERMAN *Check-List Fishes* 375 *Mycteroperca falcata phenax*, . . . Scamp; Bacalao.

***scamp,** *v. tr.* To skimp, to save. *Colloq.* — **1894** C. MERRIWETHER in *Nation* 16 Aug. 116/2 If three or four dollars more are added for rent, the tenant either scamps the life out of himself and family, or crops the land to death.

scamper-down. A rollicking dance. *Obs.* — [**1820** MEAD *Travels* 67 North Carolina camper downs, or what would be more descriptive, scamper dances, were the favourite figures of the party.] **1847** HOWE *Hist. Coll. Ohio* 121 It is doubtful if the anniversary of American independence was ever celebrated in Cleveland by a more joyful and harmonious company, than those who danced the scamper-down, . . . forty-six years ago in the log cabin of Major Carter.

* **scantling,** *n.* Used collect. for lumber or timber, esp. yellow pine, of small dimensions.

1743 *Ga. Col. Rec.* VI. 68 The Reverend Mr. Bolzius [petitioned] this Board to allow him a Quantity of Boards, Planks, and Scantling. **1831** PECK *Guide* 188 Scantling is usually estimated the same as plank or boards, one inch thick. **1903** *Amer. Architect* 8 Aug. 43 Joist and scantling of various kinds . . . have been put together in what has sometimes been called basket-framing.

* **scape,** *n.*

1. The sound made by exhaust steam issuing from a "scape pipe." *Rare.*

1878 BEADLE *Western Wilds* xxiii. 373 Steamboat Spring, from which the water bursts forth at brief intervals with a loud 'cough' like the 'scape' of a slowly moving distant steam-boat.

2. In combs.: (1) ***scapegrace,** the red-throated diver or loon, *Gavia stellata;* (2) **pipe,** the escape pipe of a steamboat, *colloq.*

(1) 1835 AUDUBON *Ornith. Biog.* III. 24 In the neighbourhood of Boston, and along the Bay of Fundy, they are best known by the names of 'Scape-grace' and 'Cape-racer.' **1917** *Birds of Amer.* I. 15 Red-throated Loon. . . . [Also called] Cape Racer; Scape-grace. — **(2) 1838** FLAGG *Far West* I. 51 The stern roar of the scape-pipe, gave evidence of the fearful power summoned up to overcome the flood. **1842** *S. Lit. Messenger* VIII. 65/2 The old cotter's wood trees on its [the Ohio River's] sandy margin, had never then heard the noise of the 'scape-pipe. **1882** *Harper's Mag.* Jan. 169/2 Aft of the pilot-house the twin "scape-pipes' rise from the engine room. **1949** HUNGERFORD *Wells Fargo* 22 This craft, in her neat coat of immaculate white, and her yellow stacks, 'scape pipes and upper works, and her gayly striped paddle-houses, was a pretty sight.

scap net. [?f. **scoop net.**] A net used for catching bait or fish. — *a***1841** HAWES *Sporting Scenes* I. 212 [Jerry's] learning did not extend much beyond a 'scapnet,' and an 'eelspear.' **1892** *Harper's Mag.* Dec. 115/2 Sou'westers, fishing-tackle, scap-nets [etc.] . . . filled up the rest of the window.

* **scare,** *v. To scare out* (or *up*), to frighten (game) out of concealment. Hence, *fig.*, to bring to light, discover. *Colloq.*

1841 *Letter* 12 July (MS), We had 'the best music that has been scared up' for a long time. **1846** *Spirit of Times* 25 April 97/1 He is also to send us the rattles of the biggest snake ever scared up in 'Old Norf Caline.' *a***1861** WINTHROP *J. Brent* 137, I allowed 't would pay to scare up a dance. **1874** LONG *Wild-Fowl* 142 We probably won't scare out any very large batches of ducks. **1907** FREEMAN *Lavinia* 298 I'll see if Almira can't scare you up a cup of coffee.

scarehead ˈskɛrˌhɛd, *v. tr.* To give (a story) a prominent headline, to place (an item) in such a headline. Also **scareheaded,** *a.*

1889 HOWELLS *Hazard of Fortunes* II. 281 He read . . . the deeply scareheaded story of Conrad's death. **1902** NORRIS *Responsibilities of Novelist* 300 The name of the leading lady or leading man is 'scareheaded' [on theater bills] so that the swiftest runner cannot fail to see. **1911** HARRISON *Queed* 219 The *Chronicle* . . . scareheaded a jaundiced account of the affair.

scaresome ˈskɛrsəm, *a.* (See quot. 1859.) *Colloq. Obs.* — **1845** JUDD *Margaret* 275 It's cruel skeersome about there. **1859** BARTLETT 383 *Scaresome* or *Skeersome,* frightful.

scarf skɑrf, *n.* [Origin obscure. ?f. *kerf.* Cf. **scarf,** *v.*] **1.** A line or groove cut in the body of a whale. **2.** A V-shaped or diagonal cut through a limb or tree.

(1) 1851 MELVILLE *Moby-Dick* 331 The blubber in one strip uniformly peels off along the line called the 'scarf.' **1874** C. M. SCAMMON *Marine Mammals* 63 A scarf is cut along the body and through the blubber. — **(2) 1863** *Maine Agric. Rep.* VIII. 36 The bark of the stock opposite the scarf with a thin sliver of wood is cut down. **1887** BILLINGS *Hardtack* 180 When an army first went into camp trees were cut with the scarf two or three feet above the ground.

scarf skɑrf, *v.* [Origin obscure. Cf. **scarf,** *n.*] *intr.* To cut off the blubber of a whale. — **1851** MELVILLE *Moby-Dick* 332 And thus the work proceeds; . . . the mates scarfing, . . . and all hands swearing occasionally. **1887** GOODE *Fisheries* v. II. 278/1 The second mate 'scarfs,' or cuts the body blubber.

scarily ˈskɛrılı, *adv.* In a frightened manner. *Colloq.* — **1845** SIMMS *Wigwam & Cabin* 1 Ser. 107 My heart . . . [was] jumping up and down as scarily as a rabbit's. **1880** HOWELLS *Undiscovered Country* 133 The light . . . was held scarily aloft above the head of an elderly woman who surveyed them with an excited face.

* **scarlet,** *a.* In combs.: (1) **scarlet azalea,** (see quot.); (2) **basil,** (see quot.); (3) **bugler,** a showy plant, *Penstemon centranthifolius,* common from California to Utah in desert regions; (4) **gilia,** a gilia *q.v.* of a scarlet color; (5) **haw,** (see quot.); (6) **ibis,** an ibis, *Guara rubra,* found in tropical America; (7) **letter,** a scarlet A, formerly used as a mark or symbol which one convicted of adultery was forced to wear, also transf., cf. * **A, 1;** (8) **maple,** (see quot. 1916); (9) **oak,** (see quot. 1916); (10) **paintbrush,** a handsome painted cup, *Castilleja miniata,* found on the Pacific Coast, also **scarlet painter's brush;** (11) **salamander,** (see quot.); (12) **snake,** (see first quots.); (13) **sparrow,** =next; (14) **tanager,** a handsome black-winged tanager, *Piranga erythromelas;* (15) **trumpet vine,** ?the trumpet creeper.

(1) 1868 *Rep. Comm. Agric. 1867* 306 The common scarlet Azalea (*Azalea calendulacea,*) hybridized by the pollen of the yellow Azalea (*Azalea Pontica,*) produced flowers finely variegated with the colors of the parent plants. — **(2) 1901** MOHR *Plant Life Ala.* 115 *Clinopodium coccineum,* the scarlet basil, is a low undershrub with dazzling flame-colored flowers. — **(3) 1902** *Out West* May 512, I love . . . June's 'scarlet-bugler,' February's shower of 'shooting-stars' minute. **1947** *So. Sierran* May 4/2 As we passed through the foothill area we noted . . . scarlet bugler, blue-lip penstemon, golden yarrow and a few early yuccas. — **(4) 1846** ABERT *Exam. N. Mex.* 23 They did not get any [game], but brought some beautiful specimens of the scarlet gilia.

(5) 1860 CURTIS *Woody Plants N.C.* 82 Scarlet haw (*Cratægus coccinea*). . . . The fruit is bright red. — **(6)** [**1785** PENNANT *Arctic Zool.* II. 458.] **1813** WILSON *Ornithology* VIII. 41 Scarlet *Ibis* . . . is found in the most southern parts of Carolina. **1839** AUDUBON *Ornith. Biog.* V. 62, I have found the Scarlet Ibis less numerous than even the Glossy Ibis. **1883** *Nat. Museum Bul.* No. 27, 144 Scarlet Ibis. . . . Accidental (?) in Louisiana and Southern Texas. — **(7)** [**1837** HAWTHORNE *Twice-Told Tales* (1879) 219 Sporting with her infamy, the lost and desperate creature had embroidered the fatal token in scarlet cloth, with golden thread and the nicest art of needlework; so that the capital A might have been thought to mean Admirable, or anything rather than Adulteress.] **1850** HAWTHORNE (*title*), The Scarlet Letter. **1872** *Cin. Times & Chron.* 28 May 2/1 A grand mass meeting in Gotham the other night consecrated Apollo Hall by unfurling therein the scarlet letter—we mean banner—of Woodhull and Free Love. **1882** *Int. Review* March 301 Polygamy is the scarlet letter upon the brow of this young commonwealth which proclaims her deep shame and forbids her entrance into the sisterhood of States. **1944** CARRINGTON *Safe Convoy* 112 However, a few minutes later when the unwanted visitor arrived, she directed her venomous tongue against the daughter whom she branded from head to foot with verbal scarlet letters. — **(8) 1813** MUHLENBERG *Cat. Plants* 95 Scarlet, white, red, or soft maple. **1916** SETON *Woodcraft Man.* 292 Red, Scarlet, Water, or Swamp Maple (*Acer rubrum*) A fine tree the same size as . . . [silver maple]. Noted for its flaming crimson foliage in fall, as well as its red leaf-stalks, flowers, and fruit earlier. — **(9) 1775** *Amer. Husbandry* I. 376 Scarlet oak . . . [is used] in ship building. **1832** BROWNE *Sylva* 266 The Scarlet Oak is first seen in the vicinity of Boston. **1916** SETON *Woodcraft Man.* 282 Scarlet Oak (*Quercus coccinea*) Seventy to 80 or even 160 feet high. Scarlet from its spring and autumn foliage color. **1949** *Amer. Forests* Sep. 45/1 Girl Scouts . . . come each Saturday to help clear out dead wood and trash and to plant seedlings of willow and scarlet oak.

(10) 1898 A. M. DAVIDSON *Calif. Plants* 142 The other flower . . . has several common names, painted cup, scarlet painter's brush, Indian plume, etc. **1941** FERGUSSON *Southwest* 234 Michaelmas daisies and scarlet paintbrush form soft tapestries against the warm gray of chamiso tipped with sunny yellow. — **(11) 1842** *Nat. Hist. N.Y., Zoology* III. 81 The Scarlet Salamander, *Salamandra coccinea,* . . . appears to dwell almost constantly on land. — **(12) 1842** HOLBROOK *N. Amer. Herpetology* III. 127 *Rhenostoma coccinea.* . . . The Scarlet Snake. *Ib.*, The 'Couleuvre écarlate' (Scarlet Snake) of Bosc is quite another animal, doubtless the *Calamaria elapsoidea.* **1891** *Cent.* 5381/2 Scarlet snake, *Osceola elapsoidea,* of the southern United States, which is bright-red with about twenty black rings, each inclosing a white one. It thus resembles a poisonous snake of the genus *Elaps,* but is quite harmless. **1941** SCHMIDT & DAVIS *Field Book Snakes* 194 The scarlet snake is a rather uncommon burrowing snake. — **(13)** [**1764** G. EDWARDS *Gleanings Nat. Hist.* III. 278/1 The Scarlet Sparrow . . . [came] from Mr. Brook, Surgeon, of Maryland in North America.] **1917** *Birds of Amer.* III. 79 Scarlet Tanager. *Piranga erythromelas.* . . . [Also called] Pocket-bird; Scarlet Sparrow. — **(14) 1810** WILSON *Ornithology* II. 42 [The] Scarlet Tanager . . . is one of the gaudy foreigners . . . that regularly visit us from the torrid regions of the south. **1949** *Boston Globe* 14 Aug. (Fiction Mag.) 11/1

My great-uncle . . . [was] watching a flock of scarlet tanagers take off from the woods.
(15) 1709 LAWSON *Carolina* 95 The Scarlet Trumpet-Vine bears a glorious red Flower.

* **scat,** *n. Like* (or *quicker than*) *scat*, in a great hurry. *Colloq.*

1833 J. S. JONES *Green Mt. Boy* I. iii, I'll have the square discharge him quicker than s'cat. **1889** MARK TWAIN *Conn. Yankee* 480 But the scheme fell through like scat. **1897** ROBINSON *Uncle Lisha's Outing* 86 One o' the boys . . . hed his fork into 't . . . quicker 'n scat. **1909** STRATTON-PORTER *Girl of Limberlost* 325 Quicker 'an scat there was her ma a-whirling.

scats skæts, *n. pl.* Short for "scattered votes." *Rare.* Cf. ***scattered,** *a.* — **1808** *Mass. Spy* 9 Nov. (Th.), Democratic 'Scats,' 26.

* **scatter,** *v.* **1. scattergun,** a shotgun. *Colloq.* Cf. **shot scattergun, two scattergun. 2. scatter rug,** a small rug of a type used on vacant portions of a floor, a throw rug.

(1) 1836 H. R. HOWARD *Hist. V. A. Stewart* 140, I have a choice scatter-gun. **1923** J. H. COOK *On Old Frontier* 4 Pidgeon shooting was good . . . for anyone who owned or could borrow a 'scatter-gun.' **1947** BUMP *Ruffed Grouse* 39 From the stag and wild boar of the mediaeval sons of Diana to the grouse and pheasant of contemporary scattergun enthusiasts, there has been a tendency to prize male specimens. — **(2) 1934** WEBSTER. **1946** *Negro Digest* Aug. 51/1 Its large living room has a vaulted ceiling and arched beams, and the floor is covered with deer skins and scatter rugs.

***scattered,** *a.* Of votes: Tallied from scratched tickets or from tickets the count of which has been delayed until after most of the other votes have been counted. *Obs.* — **1808** *Mass. Spy* 4 May (Th.), The Federal Senators are certainly chosen, unless scattered votes are uncommonly numerous. **1841** G. COMBE *Notes U.S.* I. 97 If an individual voter is not satisfied with the 'ticket' of his party, he may erase any names from it he pleases, and add others. . . . These votes are regarded as thrown away, and technically are said to be 'scattered.'

***scatterer,** *n.* One who is unsettled, a stray person. *Rare.* — **1840** SIMMS *Border Beagles* 31, I wouldn't advise a lad to go up into the Yazoo now while it's unsettled . . . and none but scatterers about.

* **scattering,** *a.* Of votes: Cast for candidates receiving only a small number of votes, as a write-in candidate on a scratched ticket. *Obs.*

1766 J. ADAMS *Diary Works* II. 185 There were six different hats with votes for as many different persons, besides a considerable number of scattering votes. **1813** *National Intelligencer* (Wash., D.C.) 6 Nov. 3/2 A majority of the whole number being necessary to a choice, and there being 605 scattering votes, no decision by the people was made, and the Legislature elected the lowest of the two. **1888** *Amer. Almanac* 225 The 2,143 'Scattering' votes for President in 1884 were cast for St. John, Prohibition.

* **scenic,** *a.* In combs.: (1) **scenic artist,** a person in charge of the stage scenery in a theater; (2) **line,** a line of railroad that passes through especially beautiful country; (3) **railroad, railway,** a miniature railway running through beautiful artificial scenery, forming an attraction at fairs, etc.

(1) 1840 *Spirit of Times* 21 Nov. 456/3 (We.), C. L. Smith . . . is the scenic artist of the Theatre. **1908** *J. Cohn's Off. Theatrical Guide* XIII. 58 Academy of Music. . . . Frank Platzer, scenic artist. — **(2) 1906** *Scribner's Mag.* July 87/1 The Grand Trunk Pacific . . . will be a scenic line. — **(3) 1901** *Pan-Amer. Exposition, Buffalo* (folder), The Midway will have the choicest of the world's amusement novelties. There will be a Trip to the Moon, . . . Scenic Railway and Rivers. **1949** *Travel* Dec. 19/1 Its first scenic railroad was one of the wonders of that time.

* **schedule,** *n.*

1. *pl.* "In the State of Rhode Island, the printed 'Acts and Resolves' of the General Assembly" (B. '59).

1836 (*title on binding*), Schedules of the General Assembly [of R.I.]

2. A plan in accordance with which something is to be done, a timetable.

1864 NORTON *Army Lett.* 282 That is all that ever caused the name to be printed on anything but time-tables and schedules of a one-horse railroad. **1866** C. H. SMITH *Bill Arp* 21 We tried our durndest to comply with your schedule. **1911** PERSONS *Mass. Labor Laws* 109 Most important of these enforced concessions was the temporary reduction to a ten-hour [factory] schedule at Fall River.

b. A program. *Rare.*

1904 *N.Y. Ev. Post* 12 May 1 Never has there been such a large schedule of speakers at a meeting of the Rapid Transit Commission as this afternoon.

3. In combs. in the sense of scheduled, provided for by a schedule, as **schedule return, speed, time.**

1837 PECK *Gaz. Illinois* 68 In each county a school commissioner is appointed, to . . . receive schedule returns of the number of scholars that attend each school. — **1903** WISTER *Philos. 4* 10 A delayed train makes the last few miles high above schedule speed. — **1881** HAYES *New Colorado* 94 [The engineer] rounded the curves in about half of schedule time. **1908** O. HENRY *Options* 204 The San Augustine Rifles got back home on schedule time.

b. In phrases: *Ahead of, according to, on schedule.*

1885 *Cent. Mag.* Jan. 397/2 The conductor of the Bleecker street car . . . must have got ahead of his schedule. **1906** O. HENRY *Rolling Stones* 23 Tuesday, the day set for the revolution, came around according to schedule. **1909** *Springfield W. Republican* 19 Aug. 10 The train was running exactly on schedule when the party left it.

* **schedule,** *v.* **1.** *intr.* To file a list or schedule (see quot.). *Obs.* **2.** *tr.* To plan, arrange, or announce for a definite time, also *ppl. a.* **3.** *To schedule out*, to depart, make off, as if in accordance with a schedule. *Slang. Obs.*

(1) 1855 *Chi. W. Times* 20 Sep. 1/3 Sherman, late editor of the defunct Beardstown *Gazette*, last week scheduled—i.e., took the benefit of the insolvent law of this state, and turned out his property, under oath, to his creditors. The schedule of his assets was as follows. — **(2) 1898** PAGE *Red Rock* 478 The trial would come off as already scheduled. **1904** *N.Y. Ev. Post* 30 Sep. 1 The archbishop is scheduled to speak this afternoon at the Academy of Music. **1907** M. C. HARRIS *Tents of Wickedness* 188 Dinner . . . was not eaten till two hours after its scheduled time. — **(3) 1890** BIFF HALL *Turnover Club* 89 But I expect that when the surgeon files his bill for alimony I will be forced to schedule out.

***scheme,** *n.* (See quot. 1856.) *Obs.* — **1853** ROOT & LOMBARD *Songs Yale* 22 His bleared eyes gleam o'er that horrid scheme! **1856** HALL *College Words* (ed. 2) 400 The printed papers which are given to the students at Yale College at the Biennial Examination, and which contain the questions that are to be answered, are denominated *schemes.*

As the last term in **colony, Mississippi, Silver scheme.**

schemy 'skimɪ, *a.* Artful, scheming. *Colloq. Rare.* — **1891** THANET *Otto the Knight* 250 He was schemy, too.

Schenectady skəˈnɛktədɪ, *n.* [f. Du. *Scheaenhechstede*, f. native Indian name.] Used attrib. with reference to various river craft built in Schenectady, N.Y., as **Schenectady barge, bateau, boat.** *Obs.*

1768 JOHN LEES *Journal* (1911) 43 The Schenectady Batteaus are navigated with but three men, they hold at most 14 Rum Barls. generally only 12, Cost usually from 8 to 9 pounds N.Y. Currency a Batteau. **1805** PIKE *Sources Miss.* I. App. 3, I have therefore hired two Schenectady barges. **1807** C. SCHULTZ *Travels* I. 4 Those called Schenectady boats are generally preferred. . . . These boats are built very much after the model of our Long Island round-bottom skiffs, but proportionable larger, being from forty to fifty feet in length. **1836** IRVING *Astoria* I. 144 Another [boat] was of a larger size, . . . and known by the generic name of the Schenectady barge.

schepel, see **skipple.**

schepen 'ʃepən, *n.* [Du., sheriff, justice.] In the Dutch settlements of New York, a municipal officer with duties similar to those of an alderman. Now *hist.*

1660 in *New Haven Col. Rec.* (1856) II. 339 [They] verified their declaration . . . before the court of the burgermasters & schepens of this towne of New Amsterdam. **1664** in *N.Y. State Lib. Hist. Bul.* No. 2, 147 Jacob Kip, and Jaques Cousseau, are also Chosen to the Office of Schepens, in this City of New Yorke. **1809** J. ADAMS in *Scribner's Mo.* XI. 576/2 There is not a Burgomaster, Pensionary, Counsellor, or Schepen—and there are near five thousand of them all—who does not understand this subject better than Hamilton did. **1896** EARLE *Colonial Days N.Y.* 240 A judgment was recorded from each burgomaster and *schepen* as to what punishment would be proper.

* **Schismatic,** *n.* A member of one of the seceding religious groups of about 1800, distinguished from the New Lights by a difference of opinion about the part to be played by faith and blind impulse. *Obs.* — **1807** MCNEMAR *Ky. Revival* 42 On this occasion, as far as the way was opened for a separation the subjects of the revival, who were sincere in their profession, generally came forth, and united with the seceding body, which were distinguished by the name of *Schismatics.* **1834** *Biblical Repertory* VI. 339 There sprang up that fruitful crop of heresy and schism, that afterwards assumed the shape, as well as the name, of *New Lights, Schismatics, Marshallites, Unitarians,* and *Shakers.*

schlemiel ʃləˈmil, *n.* [App. f. Chamisso's well-known story, *Peter Schlemihl*, of the unfortunate wretch who sold his shadow to the devil.] (See quots.) *Slang.*

1919 *S.F. Hebrew* 23 May 1/3 'Schlemiel' is the familiar Yiddish name for an unlucky person. **1932** *N.Y. Times* 10 Nov. 23/7 If they expect to beat me by having their names writ in, they're schlemiels—saps, if you get me. **1945** *Sat. Review* 6 Oct. 21/1 The fourth was an amiable schlemiel who had just about enough sense to sit down when he was tired.

schnitz ʃnɪts, *n.* Also **snits.** *local.* [G., chip, piece cut off, in the Pa.-G. (and south G.) sense shown here.] Apples cut up and dried. Also **schnitz pie.**

1848 *Knickerb.* XXXI. 222 A Dutchman smiles when he sees snits and scralls. **1869** *Atlantic Mo.* Oct. 483/1 The rest of the family gathered in the kitchen, and labored diligently in preparing the cut apples, so that in the morning the 'schnitz' might be ready to go in. **1940** *Sat. Ev. Post* 30 March 42/3 No account of the Amish is complete without a mention of shoo-fly pie and schnitz pie. **1945** *Amer. Sp.* Dec. 254 A good housewife of York, Pennsylvania, in an interview with a radio commentator, replied to his question, 'But just what are snits?' with a laugh and the answer, 'Why everybody knows what snits is.'

b. *schnitz and knep,* [*schnitz un knepp,* quartered apples and dumplings], dried apples and dumplings boiled with pork or, more often, ham.

1869 *Atlantic Mo.* Oct. 484/1 'Schnitz and knep' is said to be made of dried apples, fat pork, and dough dumplings, cooked together. **1929** *Sat. Ev. Post* 23 March 166/3 'What are you having for supper, mom?' 'Schnitz and kneps,' said Mrs. Holzoppel heavily. **1947** Berolzheimer *Regional Cookbook* 282, I would like to eat again a dish my boyhood knew . . . we called it Schnitz and Knepp.

schnitzel 'ʃnɪtsl̩, *n.* [G. in same sense.] A small piece of meat, a cutlet. *Obs.* — **1854** *Pioneer* (S.F.) Nov. 318 Eggs, coffee, toast, and now and then, a chop or a 'snitzel,' is the order given from thousands of people.

schnorrer 'ʃnɔrɚ, *n.* [Yiddish.] (See quot. 1942.) Also attrib. and **schnorring,** *n. Slang.*

1906 *Charities* 17 Feb. 695/2 His wife doesn't have to work, the 'schnorrer' game is going so well now. *Ib.*, This has been an open winter for . . . 'schnorring' and the other games. **1942** Berrey & Van den Bark *Amer. Thesaurus Slang* 422 Schnorrer, a Jewish mendicant who begs at the doors of synagogues or other Jewish places.

* **scholar,** *n. Scholar of the house,* (see quot. 1925). *Obs.*

1667 *Harvard Rec.* I. 49 The schollars of the house shall take a strict account of all the Buildings, Chambers, studyes, & fences. **1774** *Yale Laws* 22 The Scholar of the House . . . shall be obliged to view any damage done in any Chamber. **1843** Belden *Sk. Yale College* 86 Scholars on this foundation are to be called 'scholars of the house.' **1876** *Scribner's Mo.* April 769/1 We cannot pause to describe those shadowy functionaries [at Yale], the Beadle and the Scholar of the House. **1925** *Pub. Col. Soc.* XVI. 870 Scholar of the House, term applied to one whose duty it was to take account of the College Buildings, chambers, studies, fences, etc.

Schoodic salmon, trout. The landlocked salmon or trout of the Schoodic Lakes of Maine. — **1872** *N.Y. Agric. Soc. Trans. 1871* 352 An eleven pound Schoodic salmon is the largest on record. **1884** Goode *Fisheries* I. 470 The 'Land-locked' or 'Fresh-water' Salmon, known also . . . in different parts of Maine as 'Schoodic Trout,' 'Sebago Trout,' or 'Dwarf Salmon,' probably never visit salt water.

* **school,** *n.*[1]

1. A college or university.

1767 Fithian *Journal* I. 1 A letter to my Father, begging him to put me to School. **1904** *Delineator* Oct. 657 College pillows are of blue denim, with 'Yale' embroidered in white; of crimson, with 'Harvard' in white letters; . . . and similarly with the names and colors of other schools.

2. In combs.: (1) **school article,** an article of agreement drawn up by a schoolteacher and those who employ him, *obs.;* (2) **bus,** a bus, usu. provided at public expense, for taking pupils to and from a public school; (3) **butter,** an insulting expression of unknown origin and meaning used to schoolboys, *obs.;* (4) **district,** see as a main entry; (5) **entertainment,** entertainment consisting of plays, dialogues, speeches, etc., such as are often given in schools; (6) **farm,** a farm, or farm land, the income from which goes toward the support of a school or schools, also a farm, connected with a school, on which students work to defray their expenses; (7) * **house,** see as a main entry; (8) **land,** land set aside for the support of public schools, also attrib.; (9) **pin,** a pin worn by a student to show what school or class he or she is a member of; (10) **report,** a report on the condition of a school or schools; (11) **reservation,** land set aside by the federal government for school purposes; (12) **reserve,** = prec.; (13) **rick,** a school district, *local* and *obs.;* (14) **route,** the route traversed by a school bus; (15) **section,** a section of government land given to a state government by the federal government for the support of public schools, cf. **sixteenth section;** (16) **ship,** a ship on board which a nautical training school is conducted; (17) **town,** a town sufficiently large to maintain its own schools; (18) **wagon,** (see quot.), *obs.*

(1) 1878 Guild *Old Times* 330 John Smith has signed the school article, and Jim will be here to-morrow. — **(2) 1908** *Suburban Life* July 48/1 (*caption*), The School Bus. **1939** Reeder (*title*), A Manual for the School Bus Driver. **1949** *L.A. Times* 31 May 15/3 Uncollected Federal taxes on school bus fares over a period of four years have been demanded of some 200 residents of Santa Monica Canyon. — **(3) 1835** Longstreet *Ga. Scenes* 84, I fell down . . . , running after that fellow that cried 'school-butter.' **1912** *D.N.* III. 588 When he yelled *schoolbutter* at us, we yanked him off the wagon and blackened his eyes.

(5) 1920 Lewis *Main Street* 218 It was the sort of farce which is advertised in 'school entertainment' catalogues. — **(6) 1734** *Mass. H. Rep. Jrnl* XII. 110 A Petition of the Town of Reading, praying for a Grant of Land for a School Farm of the quantity of two thousand acres. **1871** *Rep. Indian Affairs* (1872) 589 A school-farm of 50 acres of excellent land affords employment for the boys and a large part of the supply for the table. **1898** *K.C. Star* 20 Dec. 2/5 Ex-President Grover Cleveland has decided to abandon the 'school farm' which he . . . undertook earlier in the Summer. — **(8) 1649** *Suffolk Deeds* I. 91 Humphrey Johnson of Roxbury granted unto William Chenie of Roxbury twenty Acres of land in Roxbury bounded wth . . . the schoole lands & Richard Peacocks northwest. **1911** *Okla. Session Laws* 3 Legisl. 242 The Commissioners of the School Land Office shall cause the land to be appraised. **1946** *Dly. Ardmoreite* (Ardmore, Okla.) 15 Dec. 2/3 The state school land commission Monday will receive bids on Oil and Gas leases on 30 tracts of state-owned land. — **(9) 1903** White *Blazed Trail Stories* 99 You wear your school-pin still, so you are not yet 'out.'

(10) 1830 *Williams's N.Y. Ann. Reg.* 192 An additional column was annexed to the forms for school reports, which accompanied the revised statutes. — **(11) 1842** *Niles' Reg.* 11 June 233/3 A bill relating to the school reservations in the states of Alabama and Mississippi, was . . . passed. — **(12) 1908** *Indian Laws & Tr.* III. 360 The Secretary of the Interior . . . [is] authorized to cause that part of the Cheyenne school reserve . . . to be appraised. — **(13) 1789** in Parmenter *Hist. Pelham, Mass.* 227 Each School Rick Shall Build and Maintain their own School Houses. **1797** *Ib.* 228 The Assessors Shall Commit District Lists of the Assessment of every School Rick to their Trustees. — **(14) 1946** Thompson *Amer. Daughter* 118 Ole Gunderson took over the school route, his hired man Arlee Davis, driving.

(15) 1835 *Indiana Mag. Hist.* XXII. 438 This was an action brought by the Trustees of a school Section for money due on two years rent. **1918** *Statutes at Large* XL. II. 2237/1 School section allowed Montana in lieu of lands in Huntley irrigation project. **1949** *World-Herald* (Omaha) 15 May F. 8/4 A railroad subsidiary, the Lincoln Land Company, had bought from the state a school section in the southwest corner of the county. — **(16) 1841** *S. Lit. Messenger* VII. 7/2 The means of creating officers [for the navy] . . . are to be derived from the school-ship. **1903** *N.Y. Times* 7 Oct. 6 The annual graduation exercises of the schoolship St. Mary's were held last night on board the ship. — **(17) 1898** Dunbar *Folks from Dixie* 235 Miltonville had just risen to the dignity of being a school town. — **(18) 1899** Wyeth *Forrest* 112 The vehicle was a school-wagon or light carriage, much used in that section of the country [north Ala.] before the war. It had steps and a door of entrance from behind, and the seats were parallel along each side.

b. In combs. of obvious meaning or sufficiently explained in the quots., as (1) **school Bible,** (2) **block,** (3) **bond,** (4) **election,** (5) **exhibition,** cf. * **exhibition,** (6) **fund,** (7) **keeping,** (8) **law,** [*OED* has one app. sporadic example, 1650, and marks the expression *obs.*], (9) **lot,** (10) **meeting,** (11) **money,** (12) **rate,** (13) **system,** (14) **tax,** (15) **teaching.**

(1) 1796 Weems *Letters* II. 35 Subjoind. is his list of such books as he thinks will sell well, . . . viz. Small school Bibles. — **(2) 1946** *Chi. D. News* 28 March 10/6 The grownups park their cars bumper to bumper in a school block. — **(3) 1873** *Winfield* (Kans.) *Courier* 18 Sep. 2/3 School Bonds are selling at 90 cents. **1950** *Time* 20 Feb. 68/2 For the first time, the chamber indorsed a proposed school bond issue. — **(4) 1903** *Evanston* (Ill.) *Press* 11 April, The readers of The Press will note the call for the annual school election in another column of the paper.

(5) 1883 Howells *Woman's Reason* xv, She used to act in the school exhibitions. **1946** Wilson *Fidelity* 6 Any kind of program could be given there: a school exhibition, a political speaking [etc.]. —

(6) **1812** MELISH *Travels* II. 428 The *school fund* [in N.Y.] amounts to 483,326 Dollars. **1900** *Cong. Rec.* 31 Jan. 1353/2 We have a magnificent permanent school fund from this lease money and from the sale of our land. **1914** *Cyclo. Amer. Govt.* III. 256/1. — (7) **1651** *Dedham Rec.* III. 191 The time of Couent, in ye schoole keepeing, being expired wt. may be the resolution of ye Town. **1775** in JOHNSTON *N. Hale* 139 School keeping is a business of which I was always fond. **1882** THAYER *From Log-Cabin* 238 How would you like to try your hand at school-keeping, James? — (8) **1873** *Harper's Mag.* March 631/1 The new school law of Maryland authorizes the establishment of . . . schools for colored children. **1946** *Chi. D. News* 2 March 4/4 The Conference Committee announced a plan to study the school laws and make recommendations for changes. — (9) **1720** *Lunenburg* (Mass.) *Rec.* 18 Ye. School Lott [shall] be Laid out as Near ye Center of ye house lotts as May be. **1772** PATTEN *Diary* 280, I went to Col Goffes and james Vose to Draw a lease of the privilege of building a Saw mill on the School lotts with jacob McQued and john Orr. **1859** BARTLETT 176 *Gospel Lot*, a lot set apart in new townships for a church, on the same principle as a school lot. New York.

(10) **1834** *Jamestown* (N.Y.) *Jrnl.* 26 Nov. 1/6 This is about the fortieth time I have been to School Meeting on this spot. **1883** HOWE *Country Town* (1926) 34 At the school-meetings he was the second to speak. — (11) **1757** *Duxbury Rec.* 323 [The town] voted that . . . a Committee . . . make up accounts with the Town's trustees, about the Town's stock of School money. **1832** WILLIAMSON *Maine* II. 677 Each town being required to raise a sum in school-money, equal to 40 cents a person. **1871** EGGLESTON *Hoosier Schoolm.* 221 Ralph found himself . . . glad to hear from Mr. Means that the school-money had 'gin aout.' — (12) **1660** *Dedham Rec.* IV. 18 Jonathan Fayerbanke Senior . . . made it apeere that his youth is aboue age to pay to the Schoole Rate and is therefore abated 4*s*, 9*d*. — (13) **1830** *Williams's N.-Y. Ann. Reg. 1830* 191 The first returns under the present school system were made in 1816. **1911** PERSONS *Mass. Labor Laws* 218 We should know how many children . . . the school system could no longer control, as well as those it still retains. — (14) **1789** *Mass. Acts. & Resolves* 12 Whenever the Rents and Incomes of the School Lands . . . shall be insufficient . . . , the said District may . . . grant such School Taxes as may be necessary. **1920** LEWIS *Main Street* 43, I don't like some of these retired farmers who come here to spend their last days—especially the Germans. They hate to pay school-taxes.

(15) **1846** *Indiana Mag. Hist.* XXIII. 459 After he came to the west his occupation was that of school-teaching. **1912** NICHOLSON *Hoosier Chron.* 421 This school-teaching ain't good for you.

c. Designating persons and groups having to do with a school or schools: (1) **school agent,** an agent for a particular school; (2) **commissioner,** a public official elected or appointed to superintend the schools of a county or state, a member of a school board; (3) **committee,** a school board, so called esp. in New England, Delaware, and North Carolina, also attrib.; (4) **director,** a local officer in charge of the district schools, a member of a school board; (5) **ma'am,** see as a main entry; (6) **physician,** a physician employed at public expense to look after the health of children in public schools; (7) **society,** a private organization for the support of schools, *obs.;* (8) **superintendent,** a person in charge of the public schools in a city or county; (9) **trustee,** one who acts as trustee for school properties, a member of a school board.

(1) **1879** *Harper's Mag.* July 215/2 The rival school agents . . . were very fortunate in their contracts with the professors. — (2) **1838** *Indiana H. Rep. Jrnl.* 23 Sess. 126 It [shall be] the duty of school-commissioners to appoint township trustees. **1917** SINCLAIR *King Coal* 117 Observing a bulge on the right hip of the School-Commissioner, Hal put out his hand toward it. — (3) **1787** *Hist. Pelham Mass.* (1898) 226 Voted Not to Devid the School Quarter where Dea. John Crawford is School Committee Man. **1883** *Cent. Mag.* Sep. 654/2 A few years ago, the school committee in one of the towns decided on a change of geographies. **1945** *Suburban List* 8 Feb. 10/3 The school committee could not keep the buses running. — (4) **1890** *Stock Grower & Farmer* 4 Jan. 7/3 All justices of the peace, constables, school directors and mayordomos of acequias [in N. Mex.] shall be elected. **1914** *Cyclo. Amer. Govt.* III. 254/2 School directors in general manage and control the schools, buildings and the school property.

(6) **1911** PERSONS *Mass. Labor Laws* 181 The child must also present a certificate from a school physician. — (7) **1754** HEMPSTEAD *Diary* 623, I Rid out in the Neck to hear the Clerk of the School Society. **1812** *Ann. 12th Congress* 1 Sess. 2255 The Trustees of the Georgetown Lancaster School Society. — (8) **1923** HERRICK *Lilla* 117 The larger cities had begun to pay high salaries for their school superintendents. **1944** PENNELL *Rome Hanks* 5 My mother . . . would have had me a preacher or a banker or a smalltown school superintendent. — (9) **1844** *Indiana Senate Jrnl.* 29 Sess. 292 A bill to authorize the school trustees of congressional townships to act as examiners of common school teachers. **1898** DUNBAR *Folks from Dixie* 240 The younger men thought that he was rather overplaying his rôle of school trustee.

d. *The school of hard knocks,* life and its varied experiences. *Colloq.*

1931 *K.C. Star* 23 Oct., Looks as if Carnera and Tunney are fraternity brothers in the school of hard knocks.

For *not to care whether school keeps or not,* see ***keep,** *v.*

As the last term in **blab, boarding, burro, business, calomel, city, colored, common, congressional, consolidated, county, district, English, field, first day, fitting, free, Freedman's, grade, graded, graduate, grammar, high, Indian, intermediate, Jim Crow, law, library, ma'am, man, manual labor, military, mission, mission sewing, mixed, Negro, neighborhood, new, old, old cornfield, parental, pay, plantation, prep, professional, public, reform, scientific, secondary, select, select boarding, spelling, state normal, state reform, State Superintendent of, summer, Superintendent of, theological, town, ungraded, union, Virginia, ward school(s).**

***school,** *n.*[1] In combs.: (1) **school bass,** (see quot.); (2) **cod,** (see quot.); (3) **fish,** any fish, as the menhaden, that usu. appears in schools or shoals; (4) **lobster,** (see quot.).

(1) **1884** GOODE *Fisheries* I. 372 The smaller fish of the species [the red drum] are called simply 'Bass,' or 'School Bass.' — (2) **1814** MITCHILL *Fishes N.Y.* 368 The Shoal-cod, or School cod, (*Gadus arenosus,*) . . . is taken on the level and sandy bottoms. — (3) **1876** GOODE *Fishes of Bermudas* 11 The smaller school-fishes. — (4) **1884** GOODE *Fisheries* I. 783 In and about Vineyard Sound, Massachusetts, two varieties of Lobsters . . . are distinguished as 'School Lobsters,' 'Rock Lobsters.'

school district.

1. An area established as the unit for the local administration of schools.

1809 KENDALL *Travels* I. 128 There are thirteen school districts [in Berlin, Conn.]. **1851** *Fox River Courier* (Elgin, Ill.) 12 Nov. 2/2 The Directors of School District No. 6 in West Elgin would say to the inhabitants thereof, that the Schoolhouse is now undergoing thorough repairs. **1948** *Hungry Horse News* (Columbia Falls, Mont.) 17 Sep. 2/1 This is one of Montana's largest school districts for area, stretching to the continental divide, and exceeding 100 miles in a north-west-southeast direction.

2. In combs. of obvious meaning, as (1) **school district board,** (2) **election,** (3) **library,** (4) **meeting.**

(1) **1898** *K.C. Star* 21 Dec. 2/2 A case . . . involved the question whether, as to railroad legislation, the legislatures of theoretically sovereign states should be reduced to the level of city councils or school district boards. — (2) **1893** *Harper's Mag.* April 708/1 The right of suffrage [for women] . . . is confined to municipal and school-district elections. — (3) **1910** BOSTWICK *Amer. Pub. Library* 6 Similar to these [town libraries], . . . were school-district libraries. — (4) **1830** S. SMITH *Life J. Downing* 92 Resolved, That it be recommended . . . [to call] school district meetings.

***schoolhouse,** *n.* In combs.: (1) **schoolhouse campaign,** (see quot.), *obs.;* (2) **lot,** =**school lot;** (3) **preacher,** (see quot.).

(1) **1914** *Cyclo. Amer. Govt.* 1209/2 The so-called 'schoolhouse campaign' of 1876, conducted throughout the rural districts of several western states, was strictly educative in purpose and did much to develop sound views upon problems pertaining to the currency. — (2) **1814** *Boston Selectmen* 113 Proposals were received from Mr. David Greenough respecting the terms of purchase of part of the school house lot. — (3) **1872** *Harper's Mag.* March 638/2 The State of Maine has an order of clergy called 'schoolhouse preachers,' who farm it, or work at some trade during the week, and on Sunday 'exercise their gift.'

For **(little) red schoolhouse,** see **red schoolhouse.**

As the last term in **district, log, red schoolhouse.**

schoolma'am ˈskulˌmam, *n.* Also **school-madam.** A schoolmistress. Cf. **Yankee schoolma'am.**

1831 *Ladies' Mag.* (Boston) IV. 557 [It] obliged me to stay the longest in the houses where there were most children and of course where there was the most work to do, and the least time to make the school Ma'am comfortable. **1833** BOARDMAN *Amer. & Americans* 69 The Americans, in their aversion to the use of the terms master and mistress, have attacked those antient and honourable compound words school-master and school-mistress; the former being superseded by preceptor, the latter by preceptress, or more commonly by the awkward appellation of school-madam. **1948** MENCKEN *Supp.* II. vi, In the field of speech of homicidal endeavor I have received contributions from generals and admirals, privates and seamen; in that of pedagogy from the presidents of universities and country school-ma'ams.

Also **schoolmarm.** Cf. **Yankee schoolmarm.**

1841 *N.O. Picayune* 23 Feb. 2/1 What will the 'school marm' say when she reads the following extract of a letter? **1949** *Sky Line Trail* Oct. 22/2 Yestiddy he pulled de cat's tail an' sassed de schoolmarm.

Hence **schoolma'amish, schoolmarmish.**

1887 Frederic *Seth's Brother's Wife* 24 She was held to be too serious and 'school-ma'am-ish' for pleasant company. **1948** *Time* 19 Jan. 73/2 *Pacific Spectator* tries hard not to be parochial or schoolmarmish.

***schoolmaster,** *n.* As the last term in **old field, Yankee schoolmaster.**

schooner ˈskunɚ, *n.*[1] [App. f. **scoon, v.*, see note.]

The story that the word originated about 1713 in Gloucester, Mass., when the first schooner was supposedly launched, is commonly repeated. A bystander is reported to have exclaimed, "Oh, how she scoons!" And the captain is said to have replied, "A scooner let her be!" This story, as quoted in Babson's *Hist. Gloucester* (1860), p. 252, was first recorded in 1790. It is unsupported, however, by any New England evidence for the use of *scoon* or *scun*, a Sc. and northern Eng. dialect word, meaning 'to skim along the surface of the water.'

Schooner (sense 1)

1. A fore-and-aft-rigged vessel, orig. having but two masts, with the smaller sail on the foremast.

1716 *Boston Rec.* XXIX. 231 James Manson ye Skooner Mayflower from North Carolina. **1834** Peck *Gaz. Illinois* 18 [Lake Michigan] affords fine navigation for schooners and steam boats. **1949** *Chi. D. News* 22 April 9/1 She was swept into a stormy sea from a schooner on a cruise.

b. schooner-of-war, a schooner-rigged warship. *Obs.*

1836 Audubon *Ornith. Biog.* III. 391 During several weeks which I spent . . . on board the United States schooner-of-war the Spark.

2. Short for **prairie schooner.**

1842 *Juliet* (Ill.) *Courier* 2 Feb. 4/4 Who can forget . . . 1840? Its imposing processions—its innumerable collection of log cabins, flags, schooners, coon skins, catch penny devices [etc.]. **1902** *Out West* Aug. 203 Well, I hustled off and got three fifteen-foot schooners and piled up seventy-five valises. **1949** *Sat. Ev. Post* 18 June 31/2 The wind-tortured canvas of the schooner swelled, and the words painted on its sides moved like living things: In God We Trusted—In Kansas We Busted.

transf. **1892** *Outing* Feb. 359/2 The herd is 'strung out' by the time the last watchmen are through breakfast and have gotten the cook and his 'schooner' under sail.

b. schooner-wagon, =prairie wagon. *Obs.*

1882 *Cent. Mag.* July 345/1 Deacon Joel, passing her, alone in his schooner-wagon, should insist upon her riding.

3. In combs. in sense **1**, as (1) **schooner barge,** (2) **load,** (3) **man,** (4) **navigation,** (5) **rig,** (6) **-rigged,** (7) **smack,** (8) **yacht.**

(1) 1819 *Western Rev.* I. 361 The River is navigated by steam boats, barges, keel boats, schooner barges [etc.]. — **(2) 1884** Cable *Dr. Sevier* 130 Richard saw him . . . superintending the unloading of a small schooner-load of bananas. — **(3) 1914** Steele *Storm* 270 Then he scrutinized the rank of schooner-men flanking me. **1941** *Christian Sci. Mon.* 9 Aug. (Wkly. Mag. Sect.) 15 (*title*), Cruises with the schooner men of Maine. — **(4) 1819** E. Dana *Geog. Sk.* 199 Fort St. Stevens stands on the west bank of the Tombigbee, at the head of schooner navigation.

(5) 1866 *Outing* VIII. 23/2 In addition to her propelling power she has a schooner rig. — **(6) 1804** *State P.* (1819) V. 35 Several vessels of the above description, which are mentioned to be schooner-rigged. **1894** *Bul. U.S. Fish Comm.* 209 A fleet of larger smacks, mostly schooner-rigged, engage in trolling along the keys and reefs for the larger surface-feeding fishes. — **(7) 1884** *Nat. Museum Bul.* No. 27, 674 Schooner-smack 'Storm King.' — **(8) 1897** *Outing* XXX. 335/2 The happy owner of a small yacht . . . is no worse off in this particular than he who owns a steamer or a schooner-yacht.

As the last term in **bull, clipper, crab, fruit, lumber, mountain, news, prairie, scow, steam, trading, turnpike, whaling schooner.**

schooner ˈskunɚ, *n.*[2] [Origin obscure. It may be, as *OED* suggests, a fanciful use of prec.] A tall beer glass.

1877 Bartlett 557 A Bowery merchant affirms that the resemblance of the Brooklyn bridge to a German's nose lies in the fact that schooners move under it. **1904** Mackaye *Panchronicon* 247 Bring me a schooner of light lager. **1948** *Chi. Sun-Times* 7 Sep. 28/3 After a three-day vacation a good loving wife often is not talking to her husband except to scold him about spilling schooners over dainty dresses of her friends.

schute, *n.*, see **chute,** *n.*

***Schuttler,** *n.* Also ***Schutter.** A make or type of wagon, so called from its maker. In full **Schuttler wagon.**

1898 *Dly. Ardmoreite* (Ardmore, Okla.) 24 June 6/2 Peter Schuttler Wagon Sold and Warranted by T. K. Kearney, Ardmore, Ind. Ter. **1912** Dawson *Pioneer Tales* 70 Thousands of Esponshays, Schutters, and Jacksons, groaned and creaked across the plains in the sixties. **1934** Barrows *Ubet* 173 His mess wagon was a three-inch Schuttler, with a double box and excellent canvas covers well stretched over the bows.

Schuylkill ˈskulkɪl, *n.* [A river and county in Pennsylvania.] Used in now obsolete specific names (see quots.). — **1854** Elliott *Fruit Book* 247 Schuylkill . . . [also called] Cape Grape. . . . Its value is only as a wine grape. **1883** *Nat. Museum Bul.* No. 27, 491 Schuylkill Cat . . . is one of the best known and most esteemed of our cat-fish.

Schwenkfelder ˈʃvɛnkˌfɛldɚ, *n.* A member of a religious sect founded by Kaspar Schwenkfeld (1490–1561), of Silesia (see quot. 1883).

1789 Morse *Amer. Geog.* 213 The Germans [in Pa.] . . . consist of Lutherans, . . . and Swingfelters, who are a species of Quakers. **1844** Rupp *Relig. Denominations* 663 Schwenkfelders are a denomination of Christians. **1883** *American* VI. 372 The Schwenkfelders, who are now extinct in Europe, linger on in Pennsylvania. **1942** Weygandt *Plenty of Penna.* 171 The Schwenkfelders have given up their distinctive hoods and shoulder capes of white.

Schwenkfeldian ʃvɛnkˈfɛldɪən, *a.* Belonging to the sect of Schwenkfelders. — [**1876** R. Barclay *Inner Life* 243 In 1734, forty Schwenkfeldian families travelled to England, and finally emigrated to Pennsylvania.] **1888** Schaff *Hist. Christian Ch.* VI. 574 He founded a new sect . . . which is perpetuated among the Schwenkfeldian congregations in Eastern Pennsylvania.

***Science,** *n.* =**Christian Science.** Also attrib. — **1915** *Chi. Herald* 22 Nov. 1/2 (*heading*), Science Reader Killed By Auto. **1946** *Christian Sci. Jrnl.* Dec. 616 We called on a practitioner to learn what this Science was.

As the last term in **Christian, domestic science.**

scientific school. A school in which technological subjects are taught.

1847 *Cat. Harvard Univ.* 60 The courses of instruction in the Scientific School are intended to commence with the next academic year. **1868** *Ore. State Jrnl.* 11 July 1/2 It was proposed to establish scientific schools in connection with Harvard and Yale. **1870** *Rep. Comm. Educ.* 52 The argument . . . is a plea for artisan, art, industrial, and scientific schools as a part of the common school system.

***Scientist,** *n.* Short for **Christian Scientist.**

1895 *Amer. Art Jrnl.* 26 Jan., The solo singer, however, was a Scientist, Miss Elsie Lincoln. **1914** E. Stewart *Lett. Woman Homesteader* 12, I certainly got as warm as the most 'sot' Scientist that ever read Mrs. Eddy could possibly wish. **1946** *Christian Sci. Sentinel* 26 Jan. 162 We had just concluded our Sunday services and another young Scientist and I had gone up on deck together.

***scissorbill,** *n.* A term of contempt (see quots.). Also attrib. *Slang.*

1871 *Atlantic Mo.* Nov. 566/2 Pootiest band of hogs in Tulare County! There's littler of the real sissor-bill nor Mexican racer stock than any band I have ever seen in the State. **1913** *Industrial Worker* (Spokane, Wash.) 1 May 5/3 Scissorbill is a localized slang term. Here it refers to the 'home-guard' worker, who is filled with bourgeoise [*sic*] ideas and ethics. It ordinarily describes a worker who has some source of income other than his wages. **1949** *Boston Globe* 14 Aug. (Fiction Mag.) 9/5 What you young scissors-bills lookin' for now?

* **scissors,** *n. pl.* **1.** A parlor game in which a pair of scissors is passed in turn to each of the players seated in a circle. **2.** *To give* (someone) *scissors,* to get the better of, overcome, to give a severe scolding. *Colloq.*

(1) **1865** CATE *Two Soldiers* 191 We were introduced to an amusing game or play called 'scissors.' — (2) **1847** ROBB *Squatter Life* 31 Thar is a fellar of the inimy who's dead bitter agin us and our town, so you must gin him scissors! **1893** in WENTWORTH.

scissortail(ed) flycatcher. A flycatcher found in the southern states and Mexico.

1858 BAIRD *Birds Pacific R.R.* 169 *Milvulus forficatus,* Scissor-tail, Swallow-tailed Flycatcher, . . . [is the] 'Bird of Paradise' of the Texans. **1945** *Mass. Audubon Soc. Bul.* Feb. 19 The Scissor-tailed Flycatcher (seen in Gloucester in August, 1942, by Miss Louise Seymour), over a thousand miles from its normal range, is a notable occurrence among accidentals. **1945** MATHEWS *Talking* 10 The quail whistled from all over the ridge, and scissor-tailed flycatchers chattered over the trees in intricate nuptial flights.

scoke, see **skoke,** *n.*[1]

scoldenore ˈskoldəˌnor, *n.* [Of obscure origin. See quot. 1945.] =**old squaw.** — **1873** THAXTER *Isles of Shoals* 109 Boats go out after sea-fowl, . . . [among which are] old wives, called by the natives *scoldenores.* **1945** MCATEE *Nomina Abitera* 32 At a venture, I would suggest that the name 'Scoldenore' . . . is a contraction of 'Scolding Whore.'

* **scoop,** *n.*

1. A newspaper "beat." Cf. * **beat,** *n.* **5,** and see * **scoop,** *v.* **2. b.**

1874 *Macomb* (Ill.) *Eagle* 23 Nov. 1/2 Owing to a slight misunderstanding, the *Sentinel* found itself without a copy of the decision, and for a time a terrible scoop seemed imminent. **1902** LORIMER *Lett. Merchant* 107 This is a bully scoop for you, boys. **1948** *Chi. Sun-Times* 18 March 53/4, I thought for sure I would pick up a scoop or two, just listening to Hollywood's two foremost gossipers gossip.

2. (See quots.)

1881 INGERSOLL *Oyster Industry* 247 *Scoop,* a light kind of dredge. (Chesapeake.) **1911** *Essex Inst. Coll.* XLVII. 14 Today, a long plank or pole called a 'scoop' drawn by horses and having a plank for a man to stand on, drags all the hay at once to the stack.

3. In combs.: (1) **scoop net,** a dip net, cf. **scap net;** (2) **shovel,** an implement consisting of a broad, flat scoop fitted to a handle, used for scooping up loose earth, coal, etc.; (3) **shovel bonnet,** a scoop bonnet, *obs.;* (4) **shovel canoe,** a canoe the shape of which is suggestive of a scoop shovel, *rare;* (5) **wagon,** a Conestoga wagon, in allusion to the resemblance of its body to a huge scoop, *obs.*

(1) **1758** *Pa. Gazette* 12 Jan. 3/3 John Beals . . . makes and mends all Sorts of Nets; Such as Seine Nets, Casting Nets, . . . Scoop Nets. **1896** *Boston Transcript* 21 Nov. 20/1 The fish are then dipped out with great scoop nets, and are sold to the cod fishermen. — (2) **1855** THOMPSON *Doesticks* 218 [The picture] is either a female rag-picker with a scoop-shovel, or a Virginia wench with a hoe-cake in her hand. **1898** *McClure's Mag.* Jan. 216/1 The fireman [had not] interrupted for an instant the steady pendulum-like swing of the fire-door and the scoop-shovel. — (3) **1884** MARK TWAIN *H. Finn* xvii, One was a woman in a slim black dress . . . and a large scoop-shovel bonnet. — (4) **1850** HINES *Voyage* 160 With the help of . . . a couple of scoop-shovel canoes, we succeeded in crossing without accident.

(5) **1935** J. W. COLEMAN *Stage-Coach Days* 173 The coming of the railroads in the Bluegrass a decade or two before the opening of the war between the states sounded the death knell for these turnpike freighters, or 'scoop wagons.'

As the last term in **mud, Navarino, stone scoop.**

* **scoop,** *v.*

1. *tr.* To obtain, take, or get, often surreptitiously, in a wholesale or thorough manner. *Colloq.*

1850 COLTON *3 Years Calif.* 440 [The Roman Catholic church] could scoop up whole tribes of savages, dazzling them with the symbols of religion. **1900** BONNER *Hard Pan* 3 White Pine scooped the last dollar he had.

2. To get the advantage of, vanquish, take *in* (a person). *Slang.*

1866 *Harper's Mag.* Oct. 680/1 Tell him he'll have to send this other fellow some more beans, for I've got him scooped [at draw-poker]. **1889** *Boston Jrnl.* 30 March 2/3 The Mexican Consul . . . [charged] from $3 to $4 for passports to cross the Mexican line, and scooped in many tenderfeet. **1916** THOBURN *Stand. Hist. Okla.* II. 750 They had just been 'scooped,' with no chance to present their side of the case, and they were dumbfounded.

b. *Newspaper.* To get ahead of (a rival) in securing or publishing news. Cf. * **scoop,** *n.* **1.**

1898 *Boston Jrnl.* 17 Oct. 3/6 You don't suppose I am going to let her get scooped on the news of this engagement, do you? **1911** FERBER *Dawn O'Hara* 9 He left them in the ditch on the big story of the McManus indictment, and the whole town scooped him. **1948** Calif. Acad. Sci. *News Letter* April 3 We were scooped by the Bay Area papers on his short story of the Ulong frog.

3. To propel oneself by rowing as with a scoop. *Rare.*

1886 STOCKTON *Mrs. Lecks* 50, I'll never leave this place if I have to scoop myself out to sea with an oar.

4. *intr.* Of a whale: To feed, to take in large mouthfuls of brit.

1887 GOODE *Fisheries* v. II. 264 Again the whale may be 'scooping' or feeding.

* **scooper,** *n.* (See quot.) *Obs.* — **1857** *Ill. Agric. Soc. Trans.* II. 313 The scooper, which was a large, clumsy machine, and very heavy, was used for breaking up prairies.

scooping net. =**scoop net.** — **1806** LEWIS in *L. & Clark Exped.* III. (1905) 350 The Clatsops Chinnooks &c. in fishing employ . . . the scooping or dipping net with a long handle. **1835** AUDUBON *Ornith. Biog.* III. 565 Negroes were there amusing themselves by raising shrimps . . . with scooping nets.

* **scoot,** *n.* **1.** (See quot.) **2. scoot berry,** a local name for the twisted-stalk found in the eastern states. **3. scoot train,** (see quot.), *obs.*

(1) **1905** *Forestry Bureau Bul.* No. 61, 36 Dray, a single sled used in dragging logs. One end of the log rests upon the sled. (N[orthern] F[orest].) . . . [Also called] go-devil, lizard, scoot [etc.]. — (2) **1891** *Amer. Folk-Lore* IV. 149 Streptopus roseus I learned to call Scoot-berry, long before I understood why it was so called. The sweetish berries were quite eagerly eaten by boys, always acting as physic, and as the diarrhoea was locally [in New Hampshire] called 'the scoots,' the plant at once received the name. — (3) **1902** CLAPIN 350 Scoot train. An express train; one that omits stopping at a particular station.

* **scooter,** *n.*

1. *S.* A long, narrow plow used for opening or breaking rather than for stirring the soil.

1820 in *Henderson's N.C. Almanack* (1823) 25 The ridges are opened with a small plough called a scooter, something like a shovel plough. **1867** *Harper's Wkly.* 2 Feb. 69/2 A small plow called a 'scouter' is then used to cut the furrows for the seed. **1944** CLARK *Pills* 281 By colloquial designations the various strange shapes were known to the trade as sweeps, shovels, scooters, twisters, half shovels, muley twisters, half sweeps, bull tongues, buzzard wings, scrapers and subsoilers.

attrib. **1842** in TURNER *Cotton* (1865) 55 The next operation to be performed, as early as possibly convenient, is to plough out the middles well, the wide way, with a good shovel-plough, having first run around the young plant with a scooter-plough. **1920** *3d Nat. Country Life Conf. Proc.* 46 The same old hoe and the same old scooter plow are brought forth at the same time of the year. **1944** CLARK *Pills* 160 A farmer in Alabama wanted '. . . 6½ bu of meal 3 Avury scooter stocks, 10 weeding hoes no 3, 3 sixteen inch sweeps.' **1950** *Democrat* 9 March 8/5 For Sale . . . fertilizer distributors, turning plows, scooter stocks.

2. A sailboat for use on water or on ice. Cf. **ice scooter.**

1903 *N.Y. Times* 13 Dec., The 'scooter' . . . is built with a bottom and a deck which are duplicates of each other. **1913** *Nation* 9 Jan. 37/1 The 'scooters' of the Great South Bay, little flat-bottomed boats with runners attached underneath.

scootist ˈskutɪst, *n.* One who operates a scooter (sense **2.**). *Rare.* — **1903** *N.Y. Times* 13 Dec., The 'scootist' who uses the most judgment in selecting his course on ice or water is the victor.

* **score,** *n.*

1. *Baseball.* A batting list. *Rare.*

1893 CAMP *College Sports* 292 The batsmen must take their positions . . . in the order in which they are named on *the score.*

2. In combs.: (1) * **scorebook,** a book in which the grades or marks of students are recorded, *obs.;* (2) * **card,** (*a*) (see quot. 1895), also attrib., (*b*) in baseball, a printed card used for keeping a record of the runs, hits, errors, etc., also transf.; (3) **hacker,** =**scorer 1;** (4) **keeper,** in baseball, one who keeps a record of the scores, hits, errors, etc.

(1) **1871** BAGG *At Yale* 584 If by chance a student should get hold of the score-book of his division he would not be able to make out very closely the significance of the hieroglyphics contained therein. — (2) (*a*) **1894** *Vt. Agric. Rep.* XIV. 109 By awarding all prizes . . . under the decenial or score-card system, every exhibitor may have the

evidence of merit, or cause of failure, to consider at leisure. **1895** *Stand.*, score-card. . . . In exhibitions of poultry, a rating card. (*b*) **1946** *Chi. D. News* 29 June 6/6 Your newspaper is to be commended for publishing a 'Score Card' of the manner in which our representatives vote on issues which affect us so intimately. **1948** *Chi. Tribune* 5 March III. 3/4 It will take more than a scorecard to tell who is who among the Cubs when they square off here Saturday for the launching of the spring exhibition grind. — (**3**) **1926** RICKABY *Ballads* 124 Scorehackers, hewers, choppers, sawyers, Road-cutters join in. — (**4**) **1880** N. BROOKS *Fairport Nine* 40 The score-keepers had to allow them a home run for Jake Coombs. **1930** *Randolph Enterprise* (Elkins, W.Va.) 27 Nov. 4/2 The score keepers ran out of scoring blanks.

As the last term in **batting, box, Chicago score.**

***score,** *v.*

1. *tr.* To prepare (a log) for hewing by slabbing off the outer part of it with an ax. Also absol.

1752 in *Travels Amer. Col.* 320 Four hands schooring. *Ib.* 320, I finished hewing in the forenoon three at schooring. **1852** REGAN *Emigrant's Guide* 85 John Adams and I scored the timber . . . that is, cut it diagonally with our axes to the depth of the hewer's chalk lines, each stroke of the axe about four inches distant. **1923** ADAMS *Pioneer Hist.* 310 Logs were cut and hauled by some, scored and hewed by others.

2. To castigate (a person or thing), to berate or denounce severely. *Colloq.*

1812 PAULDING *J. Bull & Bro. Jon.* 107 [She] fell upon Beau Napperty, and scored him at such a rate, that [etc.]. **1892** LOUNSBERRY *Studies in Chaucer* III. 223 Even poor Lipscomb . . . was soundly scored for his grossness and vulgarity. **1903** *N.Y. Times* 5 Dec. 5 Bishop Burgess in a sermon which he delivered yesterday plainly scored 'Parsifal,' although he did not once mention the name of the opera.

***scorer,** *n.* **1.** An axman who scores or slabs off the outer portions of a tree trunk in preparation for the work of the hewer. **2.** A sharp cut or slash, as with a switch or whip. *Colloq.*

(**1**) **1752** in *Travels Amer. Col.* 320 Hewed timber with 8 schooars. **1853** STRICKLAND *Twenty-seven Yrs.* II. 281 The hewer then follows with his broad axe, and cleans off all the inequalities left by the scorers. **1880** *Lumberman's Gaz.* 7 Jan. 28 The scorers and liner fell the trees and roughly trim the two opposite sides. — (**2**) **1845** HOOPER *Simon Suggs' Adv.* 24 He came down with a *scorer* across Simon's shoulders.

scoriac ˈskorɪˌæk, *a.* [f. **scoria.* App. first used by Poe.] Having the nature of scoria, lava-like. Also transf.

1847 POE *Ulalume* 15 These were days when my heart was volcanic As the scoriac rivers that roll. **1848** SARAH A. LEWIS *Child of Sea* II. v. 9–10 Scoriac streams from every artery dart And one red boiling consumes her heart. **1878** LANGLEY in Newcomb *Pop. Astron.* 280 Views which regard . . . the spots as analogous . . . to scoriac matter.

***scoring,** *n.* A severe scolding, castigation. *Colloq.* — **1863** *Harper's Mag.* March 569/1 We had not paid our circuit preacher . . . and we expected a scoring from the elder.

scorpene ˈskɔrpin, *n.* [Poss. an Amer. borrowing f. Sp. *escorpina*, as suggested in *OED*, but the evidence is weak.] A fish, *Scorpaena guttata*, found off the coast of southern California. — **1884** GOODE *Fisheries* I. 263 This species [*Scorpæna guttata*] is known by the names 'Scorpene,' 'Scorpion,' and 'Scolpin.' **1896** JORDAN & EVERMANN *Check-List Fishes* 433.

***scorpion,** *n.* [In sense **2.** prob. a modification of **scorpene.**]

1. *S.* Any one of various harmless lizards, esp. those of the genus *Sceloporus.* Cf. **pine barren scorpion, stinging lizard.**

1709 LAWSON *Carolina* 131 The Scorpion Lizard, is no more like a Scorpion, than a Hedge-Hog; but they very commonly call him a Scorpion. **1838** GOSSE *Letters* 188 A day or two since I had the pleasure of discovering, in a little hollow, beneath a decaying log, a nest of our commonest lizard (*Agama undulata*), vulgarly called here [*sc.* in Alabama] the Scorpion. **1944** *Democrat* 10 Aug. 2/3 A scorpion was found in a Grove Hill bathtub Tuesday morning.

2. (See quot. and cf. **scorpene.**)

1884 GOODE *Fisheries* I. 259 The names 'Cabezon,' 'Sculpin,' 'Scorpion,' [etc.] . . . are applied to this species [*Scorpænichthys marmoratus*].

3. In combs.: (1) **scorpion bile,** inferior whisky, *slang, obs.;* (2) **bug,** (see quot.); (3) **lizard,** see **1.** above, quot. 1709; (4) **mouse,** =**grasshopper mouse;** (5) **weed,** the seaside heliotrope, found chiefly in saline regions.

(**1**) **1865** MARK TWAIN *Sketches* (1926) 163 Our reserve [voters were] . . . full of chain-lightning, sudden death and scorpion-bile. — (**2**) **1891** *Cent.* 5411/1 *Scorpion-bug,* a large predaceous water-beetle whose raptorial fore legs suggest a scorpion; a water-scorpion. — (**4**) **1890** *Stock Grower & Farmer* 4 Jan. 7/2 The most curious of all was a little beast that I shall name the 'scorpion mouse' because it appears to feed upon scorpions exclusively.

(**5**) **1947** *Desert Mag.* April 12/3 April possibilties . . . scorpion weed, . . . fiddleneck and crownbeard.

***Scotch,** *a.* In combs.: (1) **Scotch broom,** (see quot. 1891); (2) ***cap,** (see quot. 1900), also attrib.; (3) **-Irish,** *collect.* persons of Scottish and Irish ancestry, also those from northern Ireland, also attrib.; (4) **-Irisher,** a person of Scotch-Irish ancestry; (5) **rickey,** a rickey made with Scotch whisky.

(**1**) **1817–8** EATON *Botany* (1822) 471. **1868** GRAY *Field Botany* 100 *C[ytisus]* (or *Sarothamnus*) *scoparius,* Scotch Broom. Shrub, from Europe. . . . Hardy in gardens N.; running wild in Virginia. **1891** *Cent.* 5412/1 *Scotch broom,* an American designation of the common broom, *Cytisus scoparius.* — (**2**) **1827** in H. C. DALE *Ashley-Smith Explor.* (1918) 245 The under brush, hasle, oak, briars, currents, goose berry, and Scotch cap bushes [etc.]. **1900** WEBSTER *Supp.* 186/2 *Scotch cap,* the wild black raspberry . . . ; also, the salmon berry. — (**3**) **1744** *Mass. H.S. Coll.* 1 Ser. VII. 177 The inhabitants [of Lancaster, Pa.] are chiefly High-Dutch, Scotch-Irish, some few English families, and unbelieving Israelites. **1828** J. HALL *Lett. from West* 295 Scotch-Irish Pennsylvania claims the honour of his [Hugh Glass's] nativity. **1949** KURATH *Word Geog. Eastern States* 2/2 The Scotch-Irish and the Palatine Germans from Pennsylvania and from overseas constituted the main elements in the population of these southern highlands. — (**4**) **1823** COOPER *Pioneers* xxxiii, I was out among the Scotch-Irishers.

(**5**) **1913** *Outing* Feb. 575/2 Later in the Major's dining-room . . . Tompkyns had mixed his second Scotch rickey.

***scotcher,** *n.* One who assists or helps out another. *Colloq.* — **1860** *Harper's Mag.* Jan. 279/2 The Rev. Judson Noth, a local Methodist preacher, . . . was one of the best 'scotchers' that occupied the 'Amen Corner.'

***Scott,** *n.* **1. Scott Law,** app. a local option law, in allusion to the Scott Act, so called, of the Canadian Parliament (1878) granting local option to counties and cities. *Rare.* **2. Scott's oriole,** an oriole, *Icterus parisorum,* found in the Southwest, named for Gen. Winfield Scott (1786–1866).

(**1**) **1891** S. M. WELCH *Recoll. 1830–40* 84 There were no 'Prohibition Parties' at that time, nor 'Maine' nor 'Scott' laws; only individual temperance mania. — (**2**) **1917** *Birds of Amer.* II. 255 Though it ranges as far north as southern Utah and Nevada, Scott's Oriole is most a bird of the Mexican border as far as its presence in this country is concerned. **1934** *Nat. Geog. Mag.* LXVI. 122 The female Scott's oriole, too, in her plain grayish brown and yellow, is known to sing nearly as well as the male, though not so loud nor so prolonged a song.

scoundrelizing ˈskaʊndrəˌlaɪzɪŋ, *n.* Playing the scoundrel. *Obs.* — **1835** *Knickerb.* VI. 446 But there is a pestilent pack of fellows in New York, . . . that spend their days and nights in *scoundrelizing,* to use a term of their own.

***scour,** *v. intr.* Of a plow or plowshare: To become brightly polished by friction with the soil and so slice through the ground smoothly. Also fig., to succeed, do well. *Colloq.*

1863 in SANDBURG *Lincoln* II. (1939) 472 Lincoln told him just after delivering the [Gettysburg] speech that he had regret over not having prepared it with greater care. 'Lamon, that speech won't *scour.* It is a flat failure and the people are disappointed.' On the farms where Lincoln grew up as a boy when wet soil stuck to the mold board of a plow they said it didn't 'scour.' **1871** in *Amer. Sp.* V. (1930) 44 He will find that such thievish pranks will not scour in this soil. *a*1909 *Amer. Encycl. Agric.* 742 (*Cent. Supp.*), In the average soil there [*sc.* Eastern U.S.] the cast-iron plow would scour perfectly. **1948** *Sat. Ev. Post* 7 Feb. 109/1 Then his old moldboard plow wouldn't scour, and after we'd sharpened it he broke the beam.

***scouring,** *a.* **1. scouring plow,** prob. a plow that scours and so turns the furrow slice neatly (see quot. 1943). **2. scouring rush,** any one of various species of plants of the genus *Equisetum,* esp. *E. hyemale,* suitable for use in scouring wood or metal (see also quot. 1847).

(**1**) **1856** *Rep. Comm. Patents 1855: Agric.* 170 It was ploughed as near it as possible with a double-shovel scouring plough. **1861** *Ill. Agric. Soc. Trans.* IV. 204 [The corn is] plowed four times in its cultivation . . . , the two last times with scouring plows. **1943** CROW *Amer. Customer* 71 He bought old sawmill blades with which he made self scouring plows which cut through the soil as clean as a razor. — (**2**) **1817–8** EATON *Botany* (1822) 273 *Equisetum hyemale,* scouring rush. **1847** EMORY *Military Reconn.* 13 We find in the bottoms . . . scouring rush (*Equisetum hyemale,*) a powerful diuretic upon horses. **1899** GOING *Flowers* 251 The horsetails, or scouring-rushes, . . . shed spores.

∗**scout,** *n.*[1]

1. In baseball: **a.** A fielder. *Obs.* **b.** (See quot. 1912.)

(a) **1856** *Spirit of Times* 27 Dec. 276/3 One of these swiftly-delivered balls, when stopped by a skillful batsman, is sure to give the outmost scout employment. **1870** EMERSON *Misc. Papers, Plutarch* Wks. (Bohn) III. 347 They are like the baseball players, to whom the pitcher, the bat, the catcher, and the scout are equally important. — (b) **1912** *Amer. Mag.* June 204/2 Scout—A supposed judge of ball players employed by the larger clubs to watch the playing of men in small leagues, colleges and in independent leagues to recruit good players. **1949** *Athletic Jrnl.* Oct. 20/1 The scout should familiarize himself long before the season starts with the types of defense that have been used by opponents in the past.

2. good scout, a person of an understanding, cheerful, helpful sort. *Colloq.*

1912 NICHOLSON *Hoosier Chron.* 129 Dad's a good old scout and he's pretty sure to do it. **1929** H. L. GATES *Lipstick* 212 Be like Jerry Dillon now—good scout, Jerry—never sober no more.

3. In obs. combs.: (1) **scout horn,** (see quot. 1884); (2) **man,** a scout or spy; (3) **path,** a trail along which scouts or scouting parties usu. pass.

(1) [**1855** P. PAXTON *Capt. Priest* 183 He contented himself . . . keeping his hands busy with the scoot-horn wetting the sails.] **1884** *Nat. Museum Bul.* No. 27, 779 *Scout-horn,* a wooden pole having a piece of a leather boot-leg fastened to one end so as to form a scoop. . . . Used in former years to wet the sails of small vessels in order to make them set flat and hold the wind when sailing close-hauled. — (2) **1739** W. STEPHENS *Proc. Georgia* I. 457 Three of the Scout-men, straggling unwarily into the Woods, were attacked. **1795** PUTNAM in *Memoirs* 407 A few Spyes or Scout men under proper direction will afford every reasonable Protection against the Small Sculking parties of Savages. — (3) **1750** in TEMPLE & SHELDON *Hist. Northfield, Mass.* 378 About twelve or fifteen Indians Way-laid the Scout-Path from Fort Dummer to Colerain.

b. *on the scout,* on the dodge in an effort to escape officers of the law. *Colloq.*

1891 O'BEIRNE *Leaders Ind. Territory* 74/1 Paul was arrested and Ben Dillard fled from the locality, and spent some four years on the scout, after which he gave himself up.

As the last term in **day, eagle, girl, government, Indian, land, Union scout.**

scout skaʊt, *n.*[2] Also **schout.** [Du. *schout,* bailiff, sheriff.] In the Dutch settlements of New York, a local officer vested with judicial functions. *Obs.*

1660 in *New Haven Col. Rec.* (1856) II. 339 [They] verified their declaration on ye other side specefied, being in the hands of the schout Nicasius De Sille. **1664** in *N.Y. State Lib. Hist. Bul.* No. 2, 159 Scout, Burgomastrs. & Schepens ordered to summon a court. **1695** *Doc. Hist. N.Y. State* I. 631 Wee doe give & graunt unto the said Pattentees . . . full power & authoritie to Elect & nominate a certaine officer amongst themselves to execute the place of a Scoute. **1896** EARLE *Colonial Days N.Y.* 237 The *schout* judged this epithet to be a slander and an affront to the Secretary.

b. (See quot.)

1885 *Harper's Mag.* May 840/1 With him is Cornelis vander Huyghens, the *Schout Fiscal,* whose office corresponds with our attorney-general and sheriff.

scouter ˈskaʊtɚ, *n.* [App. a new formation inspired by "scout" meaning a boy scout.] An adult who is actively engaged in boy scout work.

1934 WEBSTER. **1938** *Dly. Ardmoreite* (Ardmore, Okla.) 1 March 3/6 About 75 scouters attended the conference from eight north Texas councils. **1948** *Lawton* (Okla.) *Constitution* 4 July 3/5 A large number of cubbers and scouters were present with their families.

Scovilite ˈskovɪlaɪt, *n.* [See quot. 1851.] One of a criminally disposed band of thieves and ruffians who fomented trouble on the Carolina frontier before the Revolution and were opposed by the Regulators *q.v. Obs.* Cf. ∗**cracker,** *n.* **1.**

1851 JOHNSON *Traditions* 45 The culprits . . . appealed to the royal governor for protection, and he sent a commissioner among them to adjust their differences. This was Colonel Schovel, who, instead of redressing the grievances on both sides, armed the depredators and paraded them for battle; they were, consequently, called Schofilites. **1855** SIMMS *Forayers* 217 All these rascals, Scophilites, Yahoos, foragers, tories, . . . are all in the king's commission. *Ib.* 218 The Scophilites and Yahoos, sir, were notorious long before the beginning of the war. **1899** E. MCCRADY *Hist. S.C. Royal Govt.* 595 He conferred a high commission to suppress these disorders on a man whose name was variously written, Scovil or Schovel or Schofield. . . . The Governor . . . sided with the Scovilites, his creatures.

scow skaʊ, *n.* [f. Du. *schouw,* in same sense.] A large, flat-bottomed river boat, usually serving as a ferryboat or lighter.

1669 in MUNSELL *Ann. Albany* IV. 10 The Governor hath given me Orders . . . to provyde a scow to help ye souldiers in their provision of fire wood. **1714** HEMPSTEAD *Diary* 34, I workt at huttons al day about ye horse Boat or Scow. **1843** CARLTON *New Purchase* 230 But whether the embarkation has been in skows, or 'perogues,' and other troughlike vessels, was uncertain. **1947** *Reader's Digest* Oct. 162/2 They made the trip to Fort Yukon in two open motorboats, with a small scow.

b. Attrib. with **boat, gang, load, schooner.**

1828 FLINT *Geog. Miss. Valley* I. 230 The ferry flat is a scow-boat. — **1891** *Scribner's Mag.* Oct. 483/1 The oyster next falls into the hands of the 'scow-gang,' men whose specialty it is to remove them from the floats. — **1714** HEMPSTEAD *Diary* 38, I fetched ye Scow load of Railes & Posts. **1947** *Mich. Hist.* Dec. 438 It was in this same never-say-die spirit that he got a scowload of horses ashore. — **1913** LONDON *Valley of Moon* 269 At the foot of Castro street . . . the scow schooners, laden with sand and gravel, lay hauled to the shore in a long row.

Also *scow-built, scow-like, scow-shaped.*

As the last term in **cattle, dumping, ferry, mud, oyster, snag, steam, stone, trading scow.**

scow skaʊ, *v.* [f. the noun.] *tr.* and *intr.* To cross by means of a scow, to transport (something) in a scow. *Colloq.*

1749 W. DOUGLASS *Summary* I. 460 The ferry is about 80 rod, and . . . runs 2 or three knots, scowed over in about 9 minutes. **1751** MACSPARRAN *Diary* 58 He and a Boy . . . were Scowing wood. **1929** W. HEYLIGER *Builder of Dam* 39 From this point I will scow the supplies over to the job.

∗**scrabble,** *n.* A scanty growth. *Colloq.* See **hard scrabble.** — **1896** ADE *Artie* 113 There was a scrabble of soft beard on his chin.

∗**scrag,** *n.*

1. Any one of various small whales having the skin near the tail covered with protuberances. In full **scrag whale.** Also **scrag right whale, scrag-tail whale.**

1701 WOLLEY *Journal N.Y.* (1902) 47 A Scrag-tail Whale is like another, only . . . his bone is not good. **1725** DUDLEY in *Phil. Trans.* XXXIII. 258 The Scrag Whale is near a-kin to the Fin-back. **1835** MACY *Hist. Nantucket* 28 A whale, of the kind called 'scragg,' came into the harbor. **1874** C. M. SCAMMON *Marine Mammals* 67 Our observations, however, make it certain that there is a 'scrag' Right Whale in the North Pacific. **1884** GOODE *Fisheries* I. 31 The Scrag is of special interest on account of its influence in first developing the whaling industries of Nantucket.

2. scrag-tailed mustang, a mustang having a scraggy tail. *Rare.*

1865 *Harper's Mag.* Nov. 700/1 Scrag-tailed mustangs, galled mules and burros, were in requisition at prices that inspired in their owners sentiments of profound affection for their property.

scram skræm, *v.* [f. ∗*scramble.*] *intr.* To depart at once, "beat it." Usu. imperative. *Slang.* — **1930** *Ev. Jrnl.* (N.Y.) 14 Jan., Bill comes from Philadelphia, which has made him a little behind on the latest slang. For example, they still say 'Beat It!' over there when they mean 'Scram!' **1945** SERVICE *Ploughman* 196 You scram, or I'll beat you to a pulp—see?

∗**scramble,** *v. tr.* (See quot. 1864.) Also transf.

1864 WEBSTER 1183/3 *Scramble,* to mix and cook in a confused mass; as, to scramble eggs. **1865** *Atlantic Mo.* June 656/1, I might have scrambled you, or boiled you, or made a pasch-egg of you. **1903** *Munsey's Mag.* May 247/1 She scrambled eggs and bacon, and ate them. **1948** *Dly. Ardmoreite* (Ardmore, Okla.) 10 June 6/4 As a naturalist he has camped out in a tent in sub-zero weather, so cold eggs would freeze before they could be scrambled.

b. scrambled egg, an egg that has been scrambled. Usu. *pl.*

1864 SALA in *Dly. Telegraph* 9 Feb., Bring me . . . some scrambled eggs. **1884** F. E. OWENS *Cook Book* 65 Scrambled eggs . . . must not be hard. **1950** *Chi. Tribune* 7 March II. 3/3 Really hungry breakfasters can take care of two scrambled eggs apiece.

∗**scrap,** *n.* **1. scrap basket,** a basket for scraps or remnants, esp. of cloth; a waste basket. **2. scrap house,** a house in which scrap material is kept. *Rare.*

(1) **1895** WILLIAMS *Princeton Stories* 270 Tucker tossed his cap and Symington's gracefully into the scrap-basket. **1914** S. H. ADAMS *Clarion* 21, [I] hung the scrap-basket on the stenographer's ear when she tried to hold me up to sign some letters, jumped out of the fifth-story window, and here I am. — (2) **1872** HUNTINGTON *Road-Master's Ass't* 32 Notice the kegs and barrels full of bent and broken

spikes, and the loose piles of the same article around every car-house, shop or depot, or in the scrap-house.

***scrape,** *n.* Crude turpentine scraped from the scarred surfaces of turpentine pines. In full **scrape turpentine.**

1856 OLMSTED *Slave States* 343 It is occasionally . . . scraped off, and barreled by itself. It is, therefore, known in market as 'scrape.' **1863** E. KIRKE *Southern Friends* ix. 109 Shining flakes of 'scrape turpentine.' **1884** SARGENT *Rep. Forests* 517 The following grades of turpentine are recognized in the trade: . . . 'Scrape' or 'Hard Turpentine'—the product of the scrapings of the boxes. **1896** *Pop. Sci. Mo.* Feb. 470 The product thus obtained is 'scrape,' or 'hard turpentine.'

b. *The whole scrape*, the whole caboodle. *Rare.*

1834 C. A. DAVIS *Lett. J. Downing* 359 All the old Continental States got together and agreed upon a government for the hull scrape on 'em.

As the last term in **buck, shooting, water scrape.**

***scrape,** *v.* **1.** *tr.* To level (ground) or clear its surface of weeds, grass, etc., preparatory to planting a crop. *Obs.* **2.** To cultivate (cotton) to a shallow depth and thin with hoes or special plows.

(1) **1647** WILLIAMS *Letters* (1874) 146 The Indian hills . . . [are] only scraped or levelled. **1772** *Md. Hist. Mag.* XIV. 150 We want a good Season much, most of our tob[acc]o ground being Scraped. — (2) **1827** *Western Mo. Rev.* I. 82 The cotton . . . is thinned carefully, and plows, in the form of scrapers, are used, as the technical phrase is, to scrape it out. **1867** *Harper's Wkly.* 2 Feb. 69/2 This makes it easy to follow with the hoes and 'scrape' the cotton, which means to cut out the surplus growth to the width of the hoe, technically called a half stand.

***scraper,** *n.*

1. A heavy, two-handled scoop drawn by oxen or horses and used chiefly for excavating, as in road-making; or a mechanized contrivance for digging or removing dirt.

1815 THOMAS B. HAZARD *Nailer Tom's Diary* (1930) 442/2 Delivered C. R. Potter p[ai]r Scrapers and a Chain to hich horseis with. **1931** DOBIE *Coronado's C.* 156 And somewhere in the gravel down under the bluff a rich mine that a few mules and scrapers might uncover in a day. **1949** *Columbus* (O.) *Sun. Dispatch* 16 Oct. c. 1/1 Heavy road equipment, such as bulldozers and scrapers, will be available to park officials in building roads.

Scraper (sense 1) or team shovel

2. A plow for use on a plowstock for comparatively shallow cultivation of row crops, esp. cotton.

1827 [see **scrape,** *v.* **2.**]. **1850** in TURNER *Cotton* (1865) 117, I have used the scraper for ten years, and believe I had the first one ever tried in Mississippi. **1944** CLARK *Pills* 282 By colloquial designations the various strange shapes were known to the trade as . . . buzzard wings, scrapers and subsoilers.

3. A dredge for taking oysters, scallops, etc.

1881 INGERSOLL *Oyster Industry* 247 *Scraper*, a small dredge. Chiefly spoken of with reference to scallops. (New England.) **1887** GOODE *Fisheries* v. II. 571 For a rocky bottom a dredge is used which has the blade immovably fastened to the arms; otherwise it does not differ from the 'kettle-bail' and it is known as a 'scraper.'

As the last term in **buck, chimney, cotton, dirt, foot, hog, horse, Mississippi, road, snow, tree, wheel scraper.**

***scraping,** *n.* **1.** = **scrape,** *n. Obs.* **2.** The first process in the cultivation of cotton in which the plants are thinned and freed from grass and weeds. **3. scraping boat,** = ***scraper 3.**

(1) **1832** BROWNE *Sylva* 232 The scraping is a coating of sap which becomes solid before it reaches the boxes. — (2) **1842** in TURNER *Cotton* (1865) 55 Under this treatment, the time-consuming and worse than useless operations of bar-shearing, scraping, and chopping out are saved. **1868** *Putnam's Mag.* II. 48 It is now the first of May. The seed has come up, and the process of 'scraping' has begun. The earth is taken from both sides of the row with a proper implement drawn by a mule. — (3) **1880** *Bradstreet's* 15 Sep. 8/1 It is noted that in Chesapeake waters there are . . . 550 scraping boats.

scrapple ˈskræpl̩, *n.* [A dim. of **scrap.*] Scraps of meat, usu. pork, boiled with cornmeal or flour, and allowed to set. Usu. sliced and fried (see also quot. *c*1870). Cf. **poor-do.**

1855 *Rural New Yorker* 10 Feb. 47/3, I observe a call for a recipe for making 'Scrapple,' and some other homely dishes. *c***1870** CHIPMAN *Notes on Bartlett* 387 *Scrapple*, equal parts of buckwheat flour and wheat flour boiled in the liquor produced in making 'Head-Cheese,' and used as 'Hasty Pudding' is after cooling.—Pennsylvania. **1920** BOK *Americanization* 213 Bok was telling Kipling one day about the scrapple so dear to the heart of the Philadelphian as a breakfast dish. **1949** *Amer. Sp.* April 113/1 Scribblin Mush, *n.* Scrapple. [Richland Co., S.C.]

***scratch,** *n.*

1. Short for **scratch hit.**

1917 C. MATHEWSON *Sec. Base Sloan* 153 He secured but one clean hit, a two-bagger, and a very doubtful 'scratch.'

2. In combs.: (1) **scratch awl,** a form of awl used by carpenters for marking timber, planks, etc.; (2) **coat,** (see

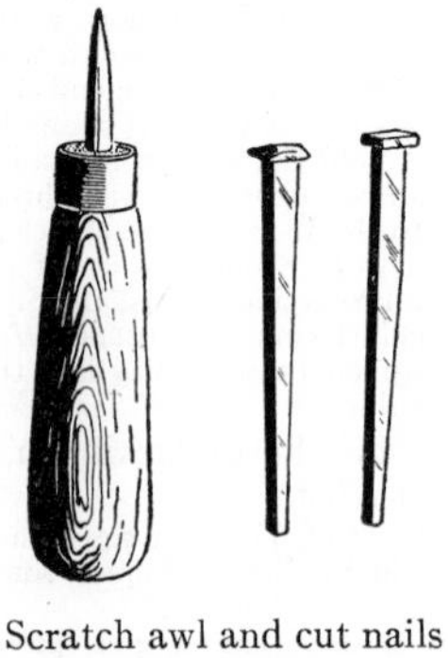

Scratch awl and cut nails

quot. 1891), also **scratch-coated;** (3) **grass,** a common species of tearthumb, *Tracaulon sagittatum;* (4) **gravel,** designating something that is tough or pertinaceous, *rare;* (5) **hit,** in baseball, a hit that barely enables the batter to reach first base, also **scratch hitter;** (6) **lot,** ?a poor, scrappy lot, *rare;* (7) **match,** a match which ignites upon being scratched on a rough surface; (8) **paper,** (see quot. 1905); (9) **rake,** (see quot.), *obs.;* (10) **team,** an inferior athletic team; (11) **ticket,** (see quot.); (12) **vote,** a vote or ballot that has been scratched.

(1) **1894** ROBINSON *Danvis Folks* 238 The carpenter . . . was bustling about with a square and scratch-awl. — (2) **1823** COOPER *Pioneers* xi, Festoons and hieroglyphics met the eye in vast profusion along the brown sides of the scratch-coated walls. **1853** FOWLER *Home for All* 44 My own [finish] consists simply of a coat of common mortar, . . . [put on] just as you would put on the scratch-coat of an inside wall. **1891** *Cent.* 5418/2 *Scratch coat*, in *plastering*, the rough coat of plaster first laid on. . . . It is named *scratch-coat* from the fact that it is usually roughened by scratching the surface with a pointed instrument before it is set hard, in order that the next coat may more strongly adhere to it. — (3) **1790** DEANE *N.-Eng. Farmer* 114/2 There are several other grasses produced in this country, as quitch grass, dogs grass; and scratch grass, resembling arsmart, on the uplands. **1833** EATON *Botany* (ed. 6) 275 *Polygonum sagittatum*, prickly knotweed, scratch grass. **1891** *Amer. Folk-Lore* IV. 148 *P. Hydropiper* was *Smartweed* [in N.H.], and *P. sagittata, Scratch-grass.* — (4) **1862** MOORE *Rebellion Rec.* V. II. 306 It was a fair stand-up, knock-down and scratch-gravel fight between the two iron-clad nondescripts—the Union Essex and the rebel Arkansas.

(5) **1886** *Outing* July 477/2 Many is the man who does much towards producing runs, and yet . . . at the end of the season stands below the 'scratch' hitter. **1917** MATHEWSON *Sec. Base Sloan* 166 Four men faced Chase in the third, the first getting a scratch hit, the second sacrificing him to the next bag. **1947** *Dly. Oklahoman* (Okla. City) 11 Aug. 13/1 Two scratch hits were allowed Henryetta by Clifford White of Perry as the hard-hitting Merchants won. — (6) **1927** BENÉT *J. B.'s Body* 9 'Well, they're a scratch lot,' said the skipper. — (7) **1891** WELCH *Recoll. 1830–40* 359 (*footnote*), Locofoco or scratch matches first came into use about [1840]. — (8) **1905** *D.N.* III. 93

Scratch-paper, paper used for memoranda. 'The commandant doesn't like for you to use the delinquency blanks as scratch-paper.' **1942** BRONSON *Pricking Thumb* 158 He . . . brought a pad of yellow scratch paper out of his pocket, and spent fifteen or twenty minutes making notes. — **(9) 1876** *Vt. Bd. Agric. Rep.* III. 614 Any man who ever held the old Kimball Rake, usually called the 'man killer,' or 'scratch rake.'

(10) 1909 *Harper's Wkly.* 13 Nov. 21/2, I just hate to play against these 'scratch' teams. — **(11) 1859** BARTLETT 386 *Scratch Ticket*, properly *scratched ticket*, an election ticket with one or more names of candidates erased. — **(12) 1888** BRYCE *Amer. Commonw.* I. I. xiv. 203 Surprises and scratch votes are not uncommon.

* **scratch,** *v.*

1. *Polit. tr.* To cancel or scratch from a ticket or ballot the name of (a candidate) who is the party's choice, in order, usu., to vote for a candidate from another party; to mark (a ballot) in this manner. Also absol. Cf. **scratched ticket,** * **scratcher 2.**

1841 *Whig Almanac* 3 Messrs. Ritner and Shulze, the Harrison Senatorial Electors, were *scratched* by a number of voters. **1888** BRYCE *Amer. Commonw.* II. III. lxvi. 494 The number of candidates is often so great . . . that many who would be glad to 'scratch' or 'paste' have really no data for doing so. **1949** *Western Polit. Quart.* March 107 Thousands of voters scratched their ballots.

2. *intr.* To make *for* with all speed, to turn or swing, to move or depart in haste. *Colloq.*

1847 ROBB *Squatter Life* 109, I'm cussed if I hadn't to turn round, too, and scratch for the snag agin! **1875** MARK TWAIN *Old Times* iii. 49 I've got to scratch to starboard in a hurry. **1903** WHITE *Blazed Trail Stories* 5 This little town will scratch fer th' tall timber . . . when the boys goes in to take her apart.

3. In colloq. phrases: (1) *To scratch for oneself*, to look out for one's own interests; (2) *to scratch gravel*, to go or depart in the utmost haste, to work hard for a living; (3) *to scratch a hit*, to secure a scratch hit in baseball.

(1) 1850 WATSON *Camp-Fires Revol.* 30 Then each one had to scratch for himself. **1856** A. CARY *Married* 304 Shaking off the other child, [she] told him to scratch for hisself a time, while she began to prepare the supper. — **(2) 1834** *Richmond* (Ind.) *Palladium* 18 Jan. 1/1, I thought I'd go home—and so I *scratched gravel* for Tennessee. **1898** WESTCOTT *D. Harum* xxv, Till I was consid'able older 'n you be I had to scratch grav'l like all possessed. — **(3) 1912** C. MATHEWSON *Pitching* 109 Then, after two had been put out, another scratched a hit.

scratched ticket. *Polit.* A ticket which has been scratched by the voter. — **1859** [see **scratch ticket**]. **1870** MAVERICK *Raymond & N.Y. Press* 340 A citizen wishing to vote a 'scratched' ticket, putting the name of Hans Breitmann, Republican German, in place of that of Timothy Finnegan, Democratic Irishman, finds [etc.]. **1887** *Courier-Journal* 18 Feb. 1/3 At the suggestion of one of the Democratic judges the scratched tickets were separated.

* **scratcher,** *n.*

1. (See quots.) *Slang.*

1859 MATSELL *Vocabulum* 77 *Scratcher*, a forger; a copyist. **1894** *N.Y. Amer. Rev.* April 454 The actual forger [in a professional forgery gang] . . . is known among his associates as the 'scratcher.'

2. (See quot. 1888.)

1880 *Scribner's Mo.* Feb. 621/2 Mr. Evarts will be obliged to look among the 'scratchers,' . . . for the indorsement of . . . Civil Service reform. **1888** M. LANE in *America* 1 Nov. 16 *Scratchers*, voters who erase from the ticket the name of any candidate for whom they do not wish to vote.

3. (See quots. 1891, 1905.)

1887 *Phila. Ledger* 30 Dec. (*Cent.*), He [a bank-teller] would not enter deposits in his scratcher after a certain hour. **1891** *Cent.* 5418/2 *Scratcher*, . . . a day-book. (U.S.) **1905** *Forestry Bureau Bul.* No. 61, 19 *Scratcher*, an instrument used for marking trees. It usually consists of a hooklike gouge fastened to a flat, elliptical iron hoop.

* **scratching,** *n.*

1. *pl.* A place to which wild turkeys resort for scratching and feeding.

1845 *Big Bear Ark.* 148 Bout the fust ov Octobur we ginerally takes to huntin rigler in the scratchins. **1846** THORPE *Myst. Backwoods* 63, I hunted the gobbler always in the same 'range,' and about the same 'scratchins.'

b. scratching place, a place to which pinnated grouse resort for scratching and feeding.

1810 in WILSON *Ornithology* III. 110 To some select and central spot where there is very little underwood, they [*sc.* grouse] repair from the adjoining district. From the [mating] exercises performed there, this is called a *scratching place*.

2. (See quot.) *Obs.*

1857 BORTHWICK *3 Years in Calif.* 144 The Americans called it 'scratching,' which was a very expressive term for their [Chinese miners'] style of digging.

3. The failure to support a candidate, usu. by marking out or erasing his name from a ticket (see also quot. 1902).

[**1860** MORDECAI *Virginia* 92 Each third year, one of the members should be *elected out*. . . . This ostracising process was termed *scratching*.] **1882** *Nation* 16 Nov. 422/1 The 'scratching' movement, one among the several small beginnings of the overwhelming Independent sentiment of to-day, was started in New York in 1879. **1902** CLAPIN 351 *Scratching*, an electioneering dodge, which consists in distributing narrow slips of paper gummed on the back, and bearing printed names of candidates, so that voters may readily rearrange the ballots to suit their own preferences.

* **scrawl,** *n.* (See quot. 1828.) — **1828** WEBSTER, *Scrawl*, . . . in *New England*, a ragged, broken branch of a tree, or other brush wood. **1845** JUDD *Margaret* I. 169 She crossed the Porta Salutaris and all the scrawls of the stump fence.

scrawny ˈskrɔnɪ, *a.* [App. variant of *EDD scrawmy* in same sense, and perhaps not an Americanism.] Irregular, straggling, lanky, unshapely. Also **scrawniness.** *Colloq.*

1833 STOWE in C. E. Stowe *Life* (1889) 70 This envelope was written in a scrawny, scrawly, gentleman's hand. **1863** HAWTHORNE *Our Old Home* 385, I often found, . . . [in] my dear countrywomen . . . , a certain meagerness, (Heaven forbid that I should call it scrawniness!). **1897** H. MONROE in *Columbus* (O.) *Dispatch* 4 Feb. 7/7, I saw . . . the scrawny, ragged men and women shuffling lackadaisically from door to door.

b. (See quot.) *Colloq.*

1859 ELWYN *Glossary* 97 Scrawny. Whence this word comes, I have no idea. It is heard, in this country, in two senses: a very thin person is called scrawny. . . . 'I always drink this water of a morning, when I come along, and feel a kind o' scrawny like,' evidently meaning that it refreshed him; feeling as one very naturally does in a hot summer's morning, languid and debilitated.

* **screamer,** *n.* A person or thing of unusual size, strength, capabilities, etc. *Slang.* Cf. **Alabama, Kentuck screamer.**

1818 WEEMS *Drunkard's Looking Glass* 18 Here I come! a screamer! yes, d——n me, if I an't a proper screamer; just from Bengal! **1859** TALIAFERRO *Fisher's R.* 46, I want to talk all night with you on Scripter. I've hearn you was a reg'lar built screamer in that way, and I want to try my hand with you. **1909** WASON *Happy Hawkins* 42 I'd allus heard 'at he was a rip-snortin' screamer, an' here he was talkin' low an' level like. **1944** SHAPIRO *Yankee Thunder* 30 He's a real screamer and I'm proud to have him in the family.

* **screech owl.** Any one of various small American owls of the genus *Otus*, esp. *O. asio* of the eastern states. Cf. **Florida, Mexican, red screech owl.**

1671 OGILBY *America* 147 The Bird both common and peculiar [to N.E.] are thus recited: . . . The long-liv'd Raven, th' ominous Screech-Owl, Who tells, as old Wives say, disasters foul. **1812** WILSON *Ornithology* V. 83 Red Owl. . . . This is . . . well known by its common name, the Little Screech Owl. **1884** HARRIS in *Cent. Mag.* Nov. 121 The screech-owl would shake and shiver in the depths of the woods. **1949** *Amer. Forests* Oct. 23/2 The weird call of the more or less familiar screech owl is probably the best known of all the owls.

* **screen,** *n.* As the last term in **fire, rolling, wind, window screen.**

* **screenings,** *n. pl.* Wheat or polished rice of second-grade quality.

1824 SINGLETON *Letters* 111 Their usual fare, is, a peck of corn in the ear a week, which they must break in their hand-mills; and the *grit*, or refuse, a Rice, like the western *screenings* of wheat. **1867** SIMMONDS *Dict. Trade Products* Supp., *Screenings*, a name in the United States for the inferior wheat that is removed by the screens and fans. **1900** *Yearbk. U.S. Dept. Agric.* 135 (*Cent. Supp.*), 9,400 pounds of screenings, and 3,500 pounds of brewer's rice.

* **screw,** *n.*

1. (See quot. 1851.) *College slang. Obs.*

1810 *Harvard Lyceum* 8 Sep. 102 Haunted by day with fearful screw. **1851** HALL *College Words* 265 An excessive, unnecessarily minute, and annoying examination of a student by an instructor is called a screw. . . . The instructor is often designated by the same name. . . . At Bowdoin College an imperfect recitation is sometimes thus denominated. **1855** S. WILLARD *Memories of Youth* I. 256 Apprehension of the severity of the examination, or what in after times, by an academic figure of speech, was called screwing, or a screw, was what excited the chief dread.

2. A form of press for baling ginned cotton. *Obs.* Cf. **cotton press 1, cotton screw, packing screw.**

1824 *Catawba Jrnl.* 23 Nov., I will sell . . . a prime fifty saw Gin, a Screw, &c. **1852** *Fla. Plantation Rec.* 72, I will Commence getting timbers for the Screw.

3. In combs.: (1) **screw auger,** an auger having spiral channels, also transf.; (2) **auger grist mill,** a type of grist mill in which water power was utilized by means of a device suggestive of a screw auger, *rare;* (3) **bean,** the screw-pod mesquite, *Prosopis pubescens,* of the Southwest, or its curiously twisted spiral pod; (4) **dock,** a dock in which a vessel could be raised from the water by the aid of large screws, *obs.;* (5) **fly,** a fly, *Chrysomyia macellaria,* the eggs of which produce screw worms; (6) **mesquite,** =next; (7) **-pod mesquite,** the screw bean *q.v.;* (8) **stem,** any plant of the genus *Bartonia,* the stems of which are sometimes spiral or twisted; (9) **timber,** timber for erecting or repairing a screw (sense **2.**), *obs.;* (10)

Screw (sense 2), packing screw, cotton screw, or cotton press

wood, =**screw-pod mesquite,** *obs.;* (11) **worm,** (see quot. 1891)—so called from its resemblance to a small screw; (12) **worm fly,** =**screw fly;** (13) **wrench,** ?an early type of monkey wrench, *obs.*

(1) 1792 IMLAY *Western Territory* 114 The juice [of the maple] was found to ooze as effectually from an incision made with a screw auger of ¾ of an inch diameter. **1812** *Ann. 12th Congress* 1 Sess. 1446 The inventor of that useful instrument the screw-auger, . . . was an inhabitant of New England. **1840** WEBSTER *Letters* (1902) 671, I have heard of Thompson's Medicine, some called 'screw auger,' some called 'wild-cat.' **1891** *N. & Q.* VI. 204 The real screw auger is an American invention, dating back to the year 1774. — **(2) 1835** A. PARKER *Trip to Texas* 78, I was much amused to see the 'screw auger grist mills' on the bank of the river. — **(3) 1866** LINDLEY & MOORE *Treas. Botany* 930/1 *Prosopis pubescens,* . . . is the Screw-bean or Screw Mezquit of the Americans. **1877** HODGE *Arizona* 246 The bean . . . which is called the screw bean, resembles a bunch of the alder tags and is screw shaped. **1946** *So. Sierran* Nov. 2/3 Another species of mesquite is the screw-bean. — **(4) 1838** STEVENSON *Sketch* 30 The second method, which savours more of originality, is called the Screw-dock, the operation of which I witnessed on one occasion in the harbour of New York. **1896** HASWELL *New York* 311 The Screw Docks, incorrectly so termed, . . . were necessarily removed in this year in order to open South Street.

(5) 1884 R. ALDRIDGE *Life on Ranch* 191 We were a good deal troubled in the summer of 1882 by what is called 'screw fly,' an insect which lays eggs on any raw place that an animal may happen to have from which are hatched out a number of screw worms. **1945** MATHEWS *Talking* 20 Sometimes their hides were torn, thus inviting screw flies.— **(6) 1866** [see **screw bean**]. **1867** *Amer. Naturalist* I. 400 The food of these [bush] rats . . . [includes] the curious spirally-twisted fruit of the 'screw-mezquite' (*Strombocarpa pubescens*). **1881** *Ib.* XV. 30 Another [species is] called the screw mezquit . . . , on account of its short pods being closely twisted into the shape of a screw. — **(7) 1884** SARGENT *Rep. Forests* 62 *Prosopis pubescens.* . . . Screw Bean. Screw-Pod Mesquit. Tornilla. . . . [Reaches] its greatest development within the United States in the valleys of the lower Colorado and Gila rivers. **1897** SUDWORTH *Arborescent Flora* 251. — **(8) 1817–8** EATON *Botany* (c1822) 202 *Bartonia paniculata,* screwstem. **1847** WOOD *Botany* 454 *C[entaurella] autumnalis.* . . . Screw-stem. . . . *C. Moseri.* . . . Moser's Centaurella or Screw-stem. — **(9) 1855** DAVIS *Farm Bk.* 225 A day of jobwork 4 hands getting screw timbers.

(10) 1844 GREGG *Commerce of Prairies* II. 78 In the immediate vicinity of El Paso there is another small growth called *tornillo* (or screw-wood), so denominated from a spiral pericarp. — **(11) 1879** *Diseases of Swine* 208 Ticks, screw-worm, and the large horse or cow fly have destroyed many animals. **1891** *Cent.* 5422/2 *Screw-worm,* the larva of a blow-fly, . . . which deposits its eggs or larvæ on sores on living animals. **1949** *Southwestern Hist. Quart.* April 436 When a calf is infected with screwworm, often the mother will lick the wound until clean, thus destroying the larvae that eat the flesh of the animals. — **(12) 1908** KELLOGG *Amer. Insects* 344 A flesh-fly of serious importance is the terrible screw-worm fly, . . . which lays its eggs on flesh . . . and often in the nasal passages of domestic animals and human beings. **1917** KEPHART *Camping* I. 250 Worst of all flies . . . is the screw-worm fly (*Compsomyia macellaria*), a bright metallic-green insect with golden reflections and four black stripes on the upper part of the body. — **(13) 1850** *N. Eng. Farmer* II. 235 The above cut represents the Patent Adjustable Screw Wrench, invented by L. Coe, of Worcester.

As the last term in **ball, cotton, gin, packing, tobacco screw.**

∗**screw,** *v. tr.* To press (hay or cotton) in bales or bundles with force exerted through a screw. *Obs.*

1713 HEMPSTEAD *Diary* 26, I spent most of ye day about fitting Mr Coits press & Screwing 1 bundle hay. **1823** THATCHER *Military Jrnl.* 46 Next in the martial procession are a train of carts, loaded with fascines and hay, screwed into large bundles of seven or eight hundred weight. **1849** *Knickerb.* XXXIII. 359 At the base of a high cliff I looked up and saw . . . a mass of solid, shining gold, as large as a bunch of screwed hay!

∗**scrimmaging,** *n.* The carrying out of a scrimmage or skirmish by small bodies of enemies. *Obs.* — **1776** R. LINCOLN *Papers* (1904) 3 They have Scrimageing from there every Day. **1853** SIMMS *Sword & Distaff* (1854) 135 We've had a mighty sharp scrimmaging here for more than three hours.

scrimshaw ˈskrɪmʃɔ, *n.* Also **scrimshandy,** etc. [See note.]

This term, numerous forms of which are shown in the quots., is of obscure origin. The *OED* suggests that a surname, Scrimshaw, "if not actually the source, may have influenced the form of the word." With reference to the source suggested in quot. 1853 below, Du. *schrimpen,* to wrinkle, and *schrong,* carved out (see *WNT*) may be pertinent, since scrimshaw work is often characterized by dainty filigree designs. Because of its interest, the term is illustrated with unusual fulness here.

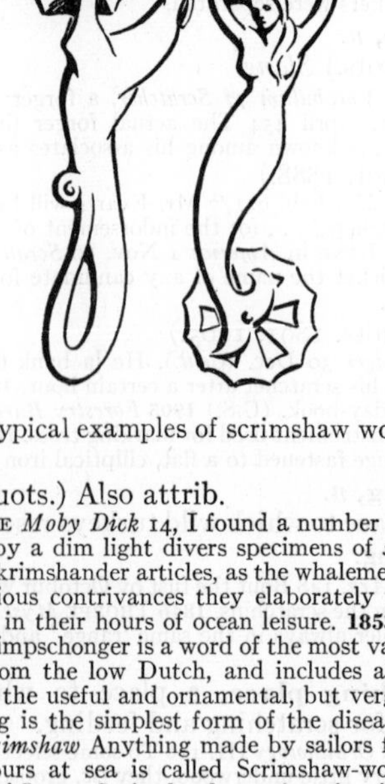

Typical examples of scrimshaw work

1. (See quots.) Also attrib.

1851 MELVILLE *Moby Dick* 14, I found a number of young seamen . . . examining by a dim light divers specimens of *skrimshander.* *Ib.* 302 Other like skrimshander articles, as the whalemen call the numerous little ingenious contrivances they elaborately carve out of the rough material, in their hours of ocean leisure. **1853** PAYSON *Golden Dreams* 61 Schrimpschonger is a word of the most varied significance. It is derived from the low Dutch, and includes all those kinds of labour between the useful and ornamental, but verging more on the latter. Whittling is the simplest form of the disease. **1864** *Hotten's Slang Dict., Scrimshaw* Anything made by sailors for themselves in their leisure hours at sea is called Scrimshaw-work. **1883** CLARK RUSSELL *Sailors' Lang., Scrimshandy,* an Americanism signifying the objects in ivory or bone carved by whalemen during their long voyages. **1883** *Internat. Fisheries Exhib. Cat.* (London) 198 Collection illustrating the games, amusements, literature, art-work of the fishermen; musical instruments, carvings ('scrimshandy'), &c. **1948** *Atlantic Mo.* Jan. 106/2 There is no bookish evidence to show how the bits of carved bone and whale's teeth came to be so delightfully called—skimshander, skrimshander, scrimshont, scrimshant, and finally, scrimshaw. **1949** *Highway Traveler* April 35/2 Not to be overlooked is the scrimshaw display, the only native American art except that of the Indians.

2. Used as a verb (see quots.). Also **scrimshawing,** *n.*

1850 N. Kingsley *Diary* 161 There is plenty of time to tinker or read or do any kind of 'Scrimshonging' anyone feels disposed to do. **1882** E. K. Godfrey *Nantucket* 65 The word 'skrimshonting' is often heard, and is applied to the doing of any small job requiring ingenuity, like the carving of a whale's tooth or the making of a small box. **1883** *Internat. Fisheries Exhib. Cat.* (London) 207 Walrus tusks scrimshawed, and frame made of walrus ivory. **1887** Goode *Fisheries* v. II. 231 Scrimshawing is . . . the art . . . of manufacturing useful and ornamental articles at sea. **1948** *Atlantic Mo.* Jan. 108/1 The Whaling Museum on Johnny Cake Hill . . . displays a shelf of skrimshandering tools made by hand on the whaleship *Awashonks.*

Hence †**schrimpschonger,** one who does scrimshaw work.

1853 Payson *Golden Dreams* 62 With us, it manifested itself chiefly in making ornamental dippers of coconut shells, and a certain necromantic puzzle, for which one of the crew, himself a confirmed schrimpschonger, had furnished the model.

* **scrip,** *n.*

1. A certificate of indebtedness issued as currency, or in lieu of money.

1790 Freneau *Poems* (1795) 429 Vast loads [he] amass'd of scrip, and God knows what. **1831** *Cong. Deb.* 4 Jan. 405 The bill, in fact, proposed an exchange of scrip for land. **1898** *Kissimmee* (Fla.) *Valley Gaz.* 18 Feb. 3/5 It is suggested that scrip be issued for the amount. **1943** Menefee *Assignment* 211 The workers are no longer paid in 'scrip' usable only in the company stores.

b. = **fractional scrip.** *Obs.*

1873 G. Hamilton *Twelve Miles* 216 The widow who bestowed her ten-cent scrip may have been really more benevolent. **1880** Howells *Undiscovered Country* 142 'There,' she said, handing Egeria some bits of scrip, 'it's ten cents apiece to the Junction.' **1887** Billings *Hardtack* 63 This was before scrip was issued by the government to take the place of silver.

2. A certificate or warrant redeemable in land to an amount described on the warrant; land scrip.

Usu. issued by the U.S. Government, either to private claimants or to states under the Morrill (*q.v.*) Act of 1862, but also by state governments and land companies controlling large land grants.

1828 *Texas Laws* (B. '59, p. 192), So much of the vacant lands . . . shall be surveyed and sectionized . . . as will be sufficient to satisfy all claims for scrip sold, soldier's claims, and head-rights. **1884** *Cong. Rec.* 10 June 4994/2 [The lumbermen] have long been in the habit of getting it [pineland] under different forms of scrip, under the soldiers' additional scrip, under the Sioux half-breed scrip, under the Cherokee scrip, and every other damnable kind of scrip that could be had. **1892** *Harper's Wkly.* 9 April 342/2 This land either belongs to R. H. Sayre who has located it with Valentine Scrip or to the State of Colorado.

As the last term in **agricultural, city, college, Confederate, county, fractional, half-breed, Kansas, land, Price Raid, state, treasury, trust scrip.**

scrip skrɪp, *v. tr.* To secure (land) in redemption of land scrip. *Rare.* — **1882** *Cent. Mag.* Sep. 769/1 They 'scrip' the adjoining sections of Government land, or take it up with desert land claims.

scrod skrɑd, *n.* [Origin unknown.] (See quots. and cf. **escrod.**)

1841 *Spirit of Times* 16 Oct. 396/2 (We.), Supplied with a few ship biscuit, a dried scrod, a bottle of good swizzle [etc.]. *c***1870** Chipman *Notes on Bartlett* 388 *Scrod.* . . . In Mass. pronounced *scrōde* and used to designate a small fish split and slightly salted. Comp. Ger. *schroeder.* **1884** Goode *Fisheries* I. 201 In the vicinity of Cape Ann the young Cod, too small to swallow a bait, are sometimes known to the fishermen as 'Pickers,' and throughout all Eastern Massachusetts the name 'Scrod,' or 'Scrode,' is in common use. **1949** *Chi. Tribune* 25 Feb. II. 4/6 As served in famous Boston restaurants, scrod is simply a tail piece of filleted haddock or cod dipped in oil, then bread crumbs and broiled in a moderate oven.

scrod skrɑd, *v.* [?f. prec.] (See first quot.) — **1891** *Cent.* 5425/3 *Scrod,* . . . to shred; prepare for cooking by tearing in small pieces: as, *scrodded* fish. **1895** *Standard* 1607/1.

scrofulaweed ˈskrɔfjələˌwid, *n.* The downy rattlesnake plantain, *Goodyera pubescens.* — **1833** Eaton *Botany* (ed. 6) 160 *Goodyera pubescens,* rattle-snake leaf, scrophula-weed, adders' violet. **1836** Lincoln *Botany* App. 101 *Goodyera . . . pubescens,* (rattlesnake leaf, scrophulaweed).

***scrouge,** *n.* (See quot.) *Obs.* — **1851** Hall *College Words, Scrouge,* an exaction. A very long lesson, or any hard and unpleasant task, is usually among students denominated a *scrouge.*

scrouger ˈskraʊdʒɚ, *n.* [?f. **scrouge, v.*] A person or thing extraordinary or startling in size, capacities, etc. *Colloq.*

1822 [see **Alabama screamer**]. **1840** *N.O. Picayune* 31 Oct. 2/1 Get ready for a scrouger, boys. **1861** Newell *Orpheus C. Kerr* I. 230 We had one of the she-critters aboard—and she was a scrouger, I tell ye!

***scrouging,** *a.* Huge, thumping. *Obs.* — **1846** Sol. Smith *Theatr. Apprent.* 209 Away he goes to Cincinnati—plays a very successful engagement there—has a scrouging benefit.

* **scrub,** *n.*

1. A domestic animal, esp. a horse or cow, of an inferior or mongrel breed. Also in generic sense. Cf. **old field, palmetto scrub.**

The *OED* records this term in the sense of "a breed of cattle distinguished by their small size" with quots. from 1555 to 1581. The application shown here may not have originated in this country.

1812 *Columbia Centinel* 31 Oct. 2/3 May the usefulness of our Institution be acknowledged;—its *speed* drive *scrubs* from the *course.* **1868** *Iowa State Agric. Soc. Rep. 1867* 130 A few of our farmers have half and one-fourth blooded young bulls and heifers, a cross with the scrub and short-horns. **1888** *Harper's Mag.* Jan. 325/1 The colonel's horse—an old 'scrub' he had borrowed—'bucked.' **1905** *Springfield W. Republican* 28 July 5 The term 'scrub' is applied, by agricultural writers, to cattle that have no particular breeding, no matter how good or bad they may be.

b. = **scrub race** *q.v.* as a main entry. *Obs.*

1831 *Amer. Turf Reg.* Nov. 144 There was also a purse, for three year old colts, bred in the counties of Dutchess or Columbia, and a $50 scrub. I did not stay to see, nor have I heard, who won the scrub.

2. Tobacco of an inferior quality. *Rare.*

1840 *N.O. Picayune* 20 Sep. 2/5 The stock on hand for sale is now reduced to less than 500 hhds., a great part of which consists of scrubs.

3. (See quots.) *Obs.*

1866 Carpenter *At White House* 96 'Well,' continued Mr. Lincoln, . . . 'I belonged . . . to what they call down South, the "scrubs"; people who do not own slaves are nobody there.' **1907** H. Binns *A. Lincoln* 27 He was now increasingly conscious . . . of a destiny before him, incompatible with the circumstances either of a 'Southern Scrub' or of a poor farmer in the backwoods of Indiana.

4. A ball player not belonging to the first or best team; usu. pl., a team made up of such players.

1893 Camp *College Sports* 140 He'd rather play against any team in the association than against the 'scrubs.' **1910** *N.Y. Ev. Post* 15 Oct. (Supp.) 1 These men, wrapped in gray blankets, who line the low fence surrounding the field on the day of the big game, are the 'scrubs,' or second team men. **1949** *Sat. Ev. Post* 18 June 100/2 He did lead and train a team of castoffs, though, which seemingly by sheer zeal managed to beat the scrubs, the second team and, finally, the first string.

b. (See quot. 1910.)

1896 White *Real Issue* 66 Just before school was called Piggy Pennington was playing 'scrub.' **1910** *D.N.* III. 447 Scrub, n. A game of baseball played by a half dozen or more persons (when there are not enough to 'choose up' for two nines). **1917** Mathewson *Second Base Sloan* 126 At the end of a week or so they were playing 'scrub' every noon-hour.

5. Attrib. or as adj.

a. Designating a domestic animal that is common or poor, of an inferior or mongrel breed or stock.

1823 Cooper *Pioneers* xvii, Billy Kirby would then be seen, sauntering around the taverns, the rider of scrub-horses, the bully of cockfights. **1872** *Ill. Dept. Agric. Trans.* IX. 204 A common scrub hog can scarcely be found in the country. **1948** *Minneapolis Morn. Tribune* 28 Sep. 11/5 She couldn't resist givin' him a Home, even though she had to admit that he was a very *ugly* lookin' scrub cat.

Esp. **scrub race horse,** a horse run in scrub races. Cf. **scrub race.**

*a***1918** G. Stuart *On Frontier* II. 201 Among them [were] two fairly good 'scrub' race horses. **1947** Price *Trails I Rode* 190 He had put in most of his life travelling around the country with some kind of an old scrub race horse.

b. With reference to breeds or types of such animals or to such stock in general.

1839 *Indiana H. Rep. Jrnl.* 23 Sess. 232 Those [calves] of our scrub breed will only bring 3. **1858** C. Flint *Milch Cows* 50 The term 'native,' or 'scrub,' is applied to a vast majority of our American cattle, which, though born on the soil, and thus in one sense natives, do not constitute a breed, race, or family. **1897** *Kissimmee* (Fla.) *Valley Gazette* 22 Dec. 2/3 Unfortunately, these cattle are of the scrub type and run very light in weight. **1949** *N.O. Times-Picayune Mag.* 22 May

8/1 With the tick, Louisiana had a dying livestock industry—fewer than 600,000 scrub, rawboned cattle.

c. Designating trees that are small or dwarfed, or a *hill* or *land* overgrown by such trees.

1779 *Mass. H.S. Proc.* 2 Ser. II. 472 [We] came over skrub land this day. **1788** M. DEWEES *Jrnl.* (MS) 5v Left the foot of the mountain and cross scrub hill. **1816** U. BROWN *Jrnl.* I. 275 [I] journeyed some times a long on the margin of the River Potomac, and some times a little in those scrub Hills. **1836** in *Ore. Hist. Quart.* XXXVIII. 359 There are a fiew scattering trees along streams and scrubb ceader on the Black hills in the neighbourhood of Ft. William on Larimies fork. **1883** SMITH *Geol. Survey Ala.* 226 *Barrens soil* from near Cluttsville, Madison county. . . . Vegetation [includes] . . . scrub hickory, wild gooseberry, blackberry. **1900** C. C. MUNN *Uncle Terry* 165, I had an ugly hour's scramble over the rocks and through a tangle of scrub spruce and briers. **1947** *Democrat* 11 Sep. 6/3 Scrub palmetto covers about 3,500,000 acres of the Florida flat lands.

Esp. (1) **scrub birch,** a species of low dwarfed birch; (2) **oak,** see as a main entry; (3) **pine,** any one of various American dwarf pines, esp. the Jersey pine and the coastal form of the lodgepole pine, or the wood of such a pine, cf. **northern scrub pine.**

(1) 1817–8 EATON *Botany* (1822) 204 *Betula glandulosa*, scrub birch, . . . very abundant in the marshes about Stockbridge, Mass. **1891** *Cent.* 560/3 Several Shrubby species are widely distributed in mountainous and arctic regions, as . . . the scrub birch (*B. glandulosa*). — **(3) 1791** in *Pub. Champlain Soc.* XXI. 517 A high point of Rocks & scrub pine. **1849** *31st Congress* 1 Sess. Sen. Ex. Doc. No. 64, 131 A large portion of the inhabitants are . . . gathering *piñones*, an edible fruit of the piñon, the common scrub pine of the country. **1949** *Sat. Ev. Post* 9 April 162/3 In front of the fireplace was a coarse-haired bearskin, scarred with burns from the snapping embers of scrub pine and cottonwood.

d. Designating a person or place that is thought of as inferior or contemptible, as **scrub aristocrat, politician, tavern.**

1840 KENNEDY *Quodlibet* 158 If he . . . makes a little fortune, we call him a . . . Scrub Aristocrat. **1848** IRVING *Knickerb.* (rev. ed.) VII. i, He enabled every scrub-politician to measure wits with him. **1853** *Harper's Mag.* April 583/1 These houses were 'groceries,' a sort of scrub-tavern quite common in the western world, where very cheap and very bad liquor is sold to the miners.

e. Of or pertaining to athletic teams made up of players that are not among the best (cf. **4.** above), as (1) **scrub captain,** (2) **center,** (3) **crew,** (4) **eleven,** (5) **game,** (6) **half,** (7) **match,** (8) **nine,** (9) **quarterback,** (10) **team.**

(1) 1895 WILLIAMS *Princeton Stories* 180 He paid very little attention to anything except the scrub captain's orders and the admonitions of the coachers. — **(2) 1920** CAMP *Football without Coach* 63 You will have your regular center playing against a scrub center. — **(3) 1891** *Cent.* 5427/2 *Scrub crew, nine*, etc., in contests or games, a crew, nine, or the like, the members of which have not trained beforehand. **1901** FORD *House Party* 202, I rowed better than he, having been on the 'varsity scrub crew. — **(4) 1892** J. L. FORD *Dr. Dodd's School* 5 The school eleven . . . were playing a practice game of football with a scrub eleven enrolled for the occasion.

(5) 1880 N. BROOKS *Fairport Nine* 173 During the summer, several 'scrub' games had been played by the Fairports. — **(6) 1893** WILLIAMS *Princeton Stories* 180 The scrub halves had fallen on him from the other direction to keep him from being shoved back. — **(7) 1867** *Ball Players' Chron.* 7 Nov. 1/1 A scrub match was arranged with seven of the Star nine and two others against ten in the field. — **(8) 1884** NYE *Baled Hay* 69 When I get in sight the 'scrub nine' close up. — **(9) 1895** WILLIAMS *Princeton Stories* 179 The Scrub Quarterback.

(10) 1887 *Cent. Mag.* Oct. 895/1 The 'University team' . . . is pitted daily against a second, or 'scrub,' team of somewhat larger numbers. **1947** *Chi. Tribune* 29 Jan. 29/2 Perhaps football could be cleaned up if it had more scrub teams.

* **scrub,** *v.*

1. *To scrub along*, to scrape along. *Colloq.*

1901 S. MERWIN *Calumet K.* xi. 202 The rest of the road had to scrub along as best it could.

2. In combs. of obvious meaning, as (1) **scrub-day,** (2) **man,** (3) **mop,** (4) **woman.**

(1) 1873 PHELPS *Trotty's Wedding* vi, They have their 'scrub-days' and their dress-days. **1912** IRWIN *Red Button* 227, I won't be fit for a thing to-morrow an' it's scrub-day, too! — **(2) 1905** *Cleveland Plain Dealer* 24 Jan. 3 Once a soldier in the army of the great white czar, now a scrubman in one of the large department stores. — **(3) 1865** *Harper's Mag.* April 665/1 You can make brooms and scrub-mops . . . to sell. — **(4) 1885** *Cent. Mag.* Jan. 463/1 The men who control the theaters . . . are omnipotent to decide the casting of a tragedy or the pay of a scrub-woman. **1931** *K.C. Star* 31 Dec. 12 The scrub woman . . . is making a trip down the Mississippi River in an old flatboat.

* **scrubby,** *a.* **1. scrubby oak,** = **scrub oak. 2. scrubby pine,** = **scrub pine.** Both *obs.*

(1) 1775 SCHAW *Jrnl. of a Lady of Quality* (1923) 190 They were reviewed on a field mostly covered with what are called here [in North Carolina] scrubby oaks, which are only a little better than brushwood. **1850** E. S. SEYMOUR *Sk. Minnesota* 156 The first and last two miles of our morning's ride was through groves of scrubby oak. — **(2) 1779** R. PARKER in *Pa. Mag. Hist.* XXVII. 405 The Country from Albany to Scanactady is a very light sandy soil that produceth little else but scrubby Pines.

scrub oak. Any one of various American dwarf oaks. Cf. **barren, black, seaside scrub oak.**

These include *Quercus ilicifolia* and *Q. prinoides* of New England and the Middle States, *Q. catesbaei* and *Q. myrtifolia* in the South, and various western species.

1766 J. BARTRAM *Diary* 13 Jan., About one o'clock we came to Round-Lake, . . . almost surrounded with palmetto, pine, and scrub-oak. **1923** J. H. COOK *On Old Frontier* 6 This timber was a sort of scrub oak or blackjack. **1949** *Amer. Forests* Sep. 7/1 A great white pine forest once spread over the acres now covered with blueberries and scrub oak.

attrib. **1779** *Mass. H.S. Proc.* 2 Ser. II. 474 The land the Army came by this day is very poor, chiefly skrub oak plains. **1884** CRADDOCK *Tenn. Mts.* 118 The few necessities . . . were in readiness to be transported . . . to Melinda's old home on Scrub-Oak Ridge. **1947** CAHALANE *Mammals* 365 One pair of these pockets can carry as many as twenty-seven scrub-oak acorns.

b. A single oak of this kind.

1814 PURSH *Flora* II. 631 Quercus Banisteri. . . . This shrub, about four or six feet high, covers large tracts of ground wherever it occurs, called Oak-barrens; it is known by the name of Bear Oak, Black Scrub Oak, and Dwarf Red Oak. **1927** BENÉT *J. B.'s Body* 83 The grey skirmish-line, . . . waits for a flicker of blue in the scrub-oaks ahead. **1945** MATHEWS *Talking* 22, I believe that no one has ever written a poem about a blackjack. . . . As a matter of fact, they go by any number of names, such as scrub-oak, jack-oak [etc.].

scrub race. A race between "scrub" horses. Hence **scrub racer, scrub racing.** Also transf. and fig. Cf. **scrub race horse** *s.v.* **scrub,** *n.* **5. a.**

1804 *Fredericktown* (Md.) *Herald* 10 Mar. 3/3 His antagonists seem sanguine enough for any bet, that he is either to be distanced, or will make but a scrub race for the amusement of the Gentlemen of the turf. **1807** IRVING *Salmagundi* xv. 405 He set out with a determination . . . to start in the scrub-race for honor and renown. **1836** *Knickerb.* VIII. 693 A new owner was on his back, and tearing through the pine barrens like a scrub-racer. **1841** *Ib.* XVII. 276 The gentler sex . . . [have] the aid of such beaux as they can inveigle from amusements better suited to the dignity of the sex, such as drinking, scrub-racing. **1894** *Outing* XXIV. 145/1 In a scrub race the helmsman cracks on until the lee gunwale is almost on a level with the water.

b. (See quot. 1914.)

1868 *N.Y. Herald* 10 July 6/5 The lines of division between the old republican and federal parties having entirely disappeared with the dissolution of the federal party, there was in 1824 a beautiful scrub race for the Presidency. **1914** *Cyclo. Amer. Govt.* III. 274/1 *Scrub Race for the Presidency*, a derisive phrase applied to the personal contest for the presidency in 1824–5, between John Quincy Adams, Henry Clay, Andrew Jackson, and William H. Crawford, in which regularly organized parties were lacking. The electors failing to make a choice, the House of Representatives chose Adams.

scrumptious ˈskrʌmpʃəs, *a.* and *n.* [Poss. f. dial. *scrumptious*, mean, stingy, but cf. * *sumptuous.*]

1. *n.* The gallant or fitting thing. *Colloq.*

1857 UNDERHILL & THOMPSON *Elephant Club* 159 He said his brother would see tu me, and do the scrumptious while he was gone.

2. *a.* **a.** Nice, stylish, first-class. **b.** Fastidious, hard to please. Both *colloq.*

(a) 1830 S. SMITH *Life J. Downing* 50 The General Court . . . all had their hats off, and [were] looking pretty scrumptious. **1920** LEWIS *Main Street* 17 Probably the lumber yard isn't as scrumptious as all these Greek temples. **1949** *L.A. Times* 16 June 11/2 From the first wonderful bite to the last delicious crumb 'They're *simply scrumptious!*' — **(b) 1835** KENNEDY *Horse Shoe Robinson* I. 87 I'm not over-scrumptious which. **1845** JUDD *Margaret* II. 314, I don't mean to be scrumptious about it, Judge.

scud grass. (See quot.) *Rare.* — **1775** ROMANS *Nat. Hist. Florida* 129 *Scud grass* vulgarly called Scots grass is a noble grass on poor land.

∗**scull,** *n.* A large piece of bark removed from a tree for use in making a bark canoe. *Rare.* — **1846** THORPE *Myst. Backwoods* 77 The 'scull' (scroll of bark) is then opened, and braces inserted to give the proper width to the gunnels of the canoe.

sculduggery, see **skulduggery.**

sculling float. A flat-bottomed sculling boat. *Obs.* — **1874** LONG *Wild-Fowl* 89 The sculling-float . . . is rarely used in the pursuit of ducks where they are to be found in any considerable numbers. *Ib.* 230 They may also be approached, by using ordinary caution, in a sculling-float.

∗**sculpin,** *n.* As the last term in **daddy, sea sculpin.**

scup skʌp, *n.*[1] and *v. local.* [Du. *schop*, a swing.] **1.** *n.* A swing. **2.** *v.* (See quot.) Both *obs.*

(**1**) **1848** BARTLETT 288 *Scup*, . . . a swing. A New York word. **1850** S. WARNER *Wide, Wide World* xi, What'll you give me if I'll make you a scup one of these days? — (**2**) **1848** BARTLETT 288 *To scup*, . . . to swing. Common in New York.

scup skʌp, *n.*[2] Short for next.

1848 BARTLETT 288 *Scup*, . . . a small fish abounding in the waters of New York and New England. In Rhode Island they are called *scup;* in New York, paugies, or porgies. **1873** *Rep. Comm. Fisheries* I. 74 The scup are known to be schooling, wandering fish of the high seas, and come from the Gulf Stream and from the Florida Cape. **1911** *Rep. Fisheries 1908* 313/2 ['Pogy' is applied to] the scup (*Stenotomus chrysops*) along the southern coast. **1939** *L.A.* Map. 233.

scuppaug skəˈpɔg, ˈskʌpɔg, *n.* Also **skippaug.** [f. native Narraganset name, *mishcùppaûog*, given in allusion to its scales being close together.] A marine fish, *Stenotomus versicolor*, of the Atlantic Coast, or a related fish, *S. chrysops*.

1807 *Mass. H.S. Coll.* 2 Ser. III. 57 The skapaug in shape somewhat resembles the roach. **1842** *Nat. Hist. N.Y., Zoology* IV. 260 The Mossbonker. *Alosa menhaden*. . . . At the east end of the island, they are called *Skippaugs* or *Bunkers*. **1860** *Harper's Mag.* Nov. 755/1 We . . . spent two hours or more in pulling out scupping. This is a species of perch, plump and white, weighing from one to three pounds. **1911** *Rep. Fisheries 1908* 315/2 Scup, (*Stenotomus chrysops*). . . . Common local names are 'scuppaug,' 'paugy,' . . . etc. **1949** KURATH *Word Geog. Eastern U.S.* 21/2 *Pogy* rimes with *stogy* . . . and denotes an entirely different fish—the *scup* or *scupaug* of southeastern New England.

Also **scupping,** *n.*

1882 E. K. GODFREY *Nantucket* 146 If you like fishing, . . . go out for a day's sport,—either bluefishing, sharking, or scupping, or all combined.

scuppernong ˈskʌpərˌnɔŋ, *n.* [Name, f. Algonquian, of a small river and lake in Tyrrell Co., N.C., where this grape was discovered in the 18th century. See Hodge *s.v.*]

1. A cultivated variety of the southern muscadine, *Muscadinia rotundifolia*, or its large, sweet, plumlike fruit.

1829 *Free Press* (Tarboro, N.C.) 27 Feb., Among them the Scuppernong, a native of North Carolina, growing in a swamp. **1867** MUIR *Thousand-Mile Walk* (1916) 49 Another name for this grape is the Scuppernong, though called 'muscadine' here [Georgia]. **1944** *Democrat* 14 Sep. 2/1 This year it was a box full of assorted varieties of scuppernongs.

2. =**scuppernong wine.**

1846 *Spirit of Times* 25 April 97/1 A keg of 'Scuppernong' is on its way to us, having been shipped from Wilmington, N.C. **1877** in FLEMING *Hist. Reconstruction* II. 61, 62 Supplies for South Carolina: . . . scuppernong, sparkling Moselle [etc.].

3. In combs. of obvious meaning, as (1) **scuppernong family,** (2) **grape,** (in 1887 quot. =**scuppernong wine**), (3) **grapevine,** (4) **hock,** (5) **ice cream,** (6) **pie,** (7) **preserves,** (8) **sherbet,** (9) **vine,** (10) **vineyard,** (11) **wine.**

(**1**) **1868** *Rep. Comm. Agric. 1867* 425 The Scupernong family of grapes never fails [in La.]. — (**2**) **1811** *Raleigh* (N.C.) *Star* 7 March 40/2 Doctor James Mease . . . having seen Mr. Blount's account of the Scuppernong Grape, . . . has requested of us to procure for him some specimens of the vine. **1887** *Courier-Journal* 8 May 18/5 Here's some of that scuppernong grape. **1944** *Democrat* 14 Sep. 2/1 He has . . . many arbors of scuppernong grapes. — (**3**) **1857** *Harper's Mag.* May 746/1 The dwellings in the Piny Woods . . . almost always have . . . a trellis supporting an extensive scuppernong grape-vine. **1904** PRINGLE *Rice Planter* 98 In addition to these they have a most prolific pear tree and a very large scuppernong grapevine. — (**4**) **1848** *Rep. Comm. Patents 1847* 471 For Scuppernong Hock, I put in the juice three pounds of double refined sugar per gallon.

(**5**) **1944** *Democrat* 7 Sep. 2/1 There seem to be a lot of folks who have never tasted . . . scuppernong ice cream. — (**6**) **1903** *Outlook* 7 Nov. 584 A scuppernong pie . . . was the first grape pie I had ever eaten. — (**7**) **1939** HARRIS *Purslane* 3 Dale . . . sent Kate hurriedly to the pantry for some scuppernong preserves. — (**8**) **1944** *Democrat* 7 Sep. 2/1 No later than last Sunday we did eat some scuppernong sherbet. — (**9**) **1939** *These Are Our Lives* 76 We has two scuppernong vines. **1944** *Democrat* 14 Dec. 1/5 In a corner of the yard the deer became entangled in a growth of scuppernong vines.

(**10**) **1848** *Rep. Comm. Patents 1847* 470 Profits of a Scuppernong Vineyard. — (**11**) **1825** *Catawba Jrnl.* 2 Aug., The editor . . . having had a taste of the Scuppernong wine from North-Carolina, extols it in the highest terms. **1887** *Cent. Mag.* July 335/2 [She] begged Mrs. Colonel Ledbetter to give her her recipe for making the scuppernong wine she had heard so much praised. **1948** *Sat. Ev. Post* 3 April 91/1 The selection represented . . . at least one real sacrifice—a bottle of North Carolina scuppernong wine, his last.

scurvy-leaves. (See quot.) *Rare.* — **1674** JOSSELYN *Two Voyages* 80 Water-plantane, called in *New-England* water Suck-leaves, and Scurvie-leaves, you must lay them whole to the leggs to draw out water between the skin and the flesh.

∗**scuttle,** *n.* **1. scuttle door,** an opening in the roof of a house or the trap-door of such an opening. **2. scuttle stairs,** a stairs leading to a scuttle door. — (**1**) **1860** *Harper's Mag.* Aug. 428/1 There was a scuttle-door in the roof of the house, with a convenient stairway leading to it. — (**2**) **1943** PEATTIE *Journ. into Amer.* 43 'That's the scuttle stairs,' said the soft voice from the shadows below.

∗**scuttler,** *n.* A striped lizard, *Cnemidophorus sexlineatus.* — **1886** *Amer. Philol. Assoc. Trans.* XVII. 46 *Scuttler* or *streakfield* (striped lizard).

scythe-whet. A local name for the veery or Wilson's thrush. — **1871** LOWELL *My Study Windows* 22 My walk under the pines would lose half its summer charm, were I to miss that shy anchorite, the Wilson's thrush, nor hear in haying-time the metallic ring of his song, that justifies his rustic name of 'scythe-whet.'

∗ **sea,** *n.* In combs.: (1) ∗**seaboard,** see as a main entry; (2) **corn,** the mass of yellow egg capsules of such marine snails as the whelks; (3) **drift,** any flotsam, esp. vegetable and animal matter cast up on the seashore; (4) **food,** food taken from the sea, as fish, shellfish, etc., also attrib.; (5) **island,** see as a main entry; (6) ∗**lawyer,** (see quot.); (7) **oats,** a sand-binding tall grass, *Uniola paniculata*, found along the southern coast of the U.S., so named from its oatlike panicles; (8) **pea jacket,** =**pea jacket;** (9) **potato,** (see quot.); (10) **rig,** clothes worn at sea; (11) **road,** "a line of communication over the sea; the route taken by ships between two places" (*OED Supp.*); (12) **shore cotton,** (see quot.), *obs.;* (13) **side,** see as a main entry.

(**2**) **1885** J. S. KINGSLEY *Stand. Nat. Hist.* I. 333 [The eggs of the whelk] are laid in hemispherical capsules, yellow in color, piled up in a heap, and presenting an appearance well-described by the name 'sea-corn' applied to them by the New England fishermen. — (**3**) **1816** *East-Hampton Rec.* IV. 396 If any person or persons shall cart . . . more than two loads of seaweed or sea-drift from the beach . . . they so offending shall forfeit the sum of five dollars. **1891** *Harper's Mag.* Sep. 592/1 Many among them have gathered to themselves a respectable covering of soil from the various sorts of sea-drift. — (**4**) **1836** *Knickerb.* VIII. 423 She said that she had come to Screamy Point to get 'sea-food.' **1906** *N.Y. Ev. Post* 10 March 5 Up State residents are among the best customers of the sea food, fruit and produce dealers in the downtown open markets. **1944** BARBOUR *Eden* 166, I was dining with some friends at a popular seafood restaurant in Miami.

(**6**) **1940** RIESENBERG *Golden Gate* 134 Among the seamen who managed to get a longer stay ashore were those waylaid by 'sea lawyers,' shysters who snared crews into saloons and tapped big brief-cases, assuring Jack that 'They can't haze us.' — (**7**) **1894** COULTER *Bot. W. Texas* III. 545 *U*[*niola*] *paniculata.* (Sea Oats.) . . . Drifting sand along the coast, southern Texas to New Jersey. **1947** *Nat. Geog. Mag.* Sep. 337/2 Those who love the wildness of the Land of the Sea would prefer to see the dune covered with a flowing golden robe of sea oats.— (**8**) **1734** *N.J. Archives* 1 Ser. XI. 392 A Servant Man named Lawrence Stakepole . . . had on a Felt Hat, an old Sea-Pea-Jacket lined with red [etc.]. — (**9**) **1891** *Cent.* 5445/3 *Sea-potato*, . . . an ascidian of some kind, as *Boltenia reniformis* or *Ascidia mollis.* (Local, U.S.)

(**10**) **1840** DANA *Two Years* 6, I made my appearance on board at twelve o'clock, in full sea-rig, and with my chest, containing an outfit for a two or three years' voyage. **1865** A. D. WHITNEY *Gayworthys* 127 Gershom was to . . . sign his shipping articles and go with his uncle to get his 'protection,' and his sea rig. — (**11**) **1893** *Columbus* (O.) *Dispatch* 9 Nov., If fish disappeared from the sea-road and fiords. **1907**

T. C. MIDDLETON *Geog. Knowl. Discov. Amer.* 25 The Vivaldi brothers of Genoa, who in 1291, essayed a sea-road to India. — **(12) 1802** DRAYTON *S. Carolina* 134 That raised on lands adjacent to the sea and salt water, called *island* or *sea shore cotton*, being black seed, is preferred to the *green seed* cotton.

b. In the names of birds, fishes, and other creatures: (1) **sea bass,** see as a main entry; (2) **clam,** the surf clam, *Spisula solidissima*, or a related species, found on beaches on the Atlantic Coast; (3) ***duck,** *N. Eng.* an eider duck; (4) **goose,** (*a*) a phalarope, (*b*) (see quot.); (5) ***perch,** the black sea bass (see also quot. 1911) [the identity of the fish or fishes referred to in the first two quots. is uncertain]; (6) **quail,** (*a*) a turnstone, (*b*) Cassin's auklet, *Ptychoramphus aleuticus;* (7) ***raven,** a sculpin, *Hemitripterus americanus*, of the Atlantic Coast; (8) **robin,** see as a main entry; (9) **salmon,** (*a*) a salmon that lives in the sea, (*b*) (see quot.); (10) **terrapin,** a sea turtle, *obs.;* (11) **tiger,** ?a sea lion, *rare;* (12) **toad,** (*a*) a sculpin, (*b*) a toadfish; (13) ***trout,** (*a*) any one of several weakfishes, esp. the squeteague *q.v.* [it is not clear what fish is referred to in the first quot.], (*b*) (see quots.).

(2) 1765 J. BARTRAM *Diary* 29 July, There is many clam shels of different sises cast on y[e] shore by y[e] waves y[e] very same with our sea clams: very white: & perfect as if y[e] fish was just taken out. **1935** LINCOLN *Cape Cod Yesterdays* 49 Away out, along the outer bar, almost two miles from shore and only get-at-able when the tide was at full ebb, were the large 'sea clams.' — **(3) 1835** AUDUBON *Ornith. Biog.* III. 343 We saw a great number of 'sea Ducks,' as the gunners and fishermen on that coast, as well as on our own, call the Eiders and some other species. **1917** *Birds of Amer.* I. 147/1 The Massachusetts gunners call them [*sc.* eiders] Sea Ducks for they seem to prefer the outer ledges jutting into the sea. — **(4)** (*a*) **1835** AUDUBON *Ornith. Biog.* III. 118 The gunners of Eastport, who knew them under the name of Sea Geese, spoke of them as very curious birds. **1880** *Harper's Mag.* Sep. 504/2 A quaint apparent exception, and the only one, to the universal rule of rapine . . . was a little bird somewhat larger than a sand piper—the sea-goose, so called. (*b*) **1891** *Cent.* 5440/3 *Sea-goose*, . . . a dolphin: so called from the shape of the snout.

(5) 1765 ROWE *Diary* 86 We caught above sixteen dozn. of pond and sea perch. **1807** *Mass. H.S. Coll.* 2 Ser. III. 57 The sea perch is very large and excellent: it is caught in the spring. **1911** *Rep. Fisheries 1908* 308/2 Chogset (*Tautogolabrus adspersus*) . . . is also called 'cunner,' 'sea perch,' 'perch,' [etc.]. — **(6)** (*a*) **1888** TRUMBULL *Names of Birds* 186 In Connecticut at Saybrook and Lyme, [*Arenaria interpres* is called] Sea Quail. **1891** *Cent.* 5445/3 *Sea-quail*, . . . the turnstone, *Strepsilas interpres*. (Connecticut.) (*b*) **1917** *Birds of Amer.* I. 20 Because of its plump shape and size, it [Cassin's auklet] has been called a 'Sea Quail.' — **(7)** [**1672** JOSSELYN *N. Eng. Rarities* 29 Sea-Raven.] **1836** J. RICHARDSON *Fauna Bor.-Amer.* III. 50 The Sea-raven . . . inhabits the cod-banks on the coast of New York, Nova Scotia and the Gulf of St. Lawrence. **1897** *N.Y. Forest, Fish, & Game Comm. 2d Rep.* 244 Sea Raven. . . . Spawns in November. — **(9)** (*a*) **1842** *Nat. Hist. N.Y., Zoology* IV. 241 The Common Sea Salmon. *Salmo salar.* **1871** *Harper's Mag.* Aug. 466/1 Whether this fish be really a 'landlocked salmon'—that is to say, a true sea salmon that has changed its habits to such an extent as to dwell permanently in the fresh-waters—is the subject of inquiry. (*b*) **1909** WEBSTER 1907/3 *Sea salmon* . . . either of two weakfishes, *Cynoscion nebulosus* and *C. nobilis*.

(10) 1847 *Knickerb.* XXIX. 494 The staid and lofty lawyer . . . was bargaining with an old African woman for a lot of sea-terrapins. — **(11) 1874** B. F. TAYLOR *World on Wheels* 228 The thing was a sea-tiger, and resembled an exaggerated seal. — **(12)** (*a*) **1842** *Nat. Hist. N.Y., Zoology* IV. 52 The Common Bull-Head, *Cottus virginianus*, . . . is known [as] Sea Robin, Bull Head, Sea Toad, and Pig Fish. **1884** GOODE *Fisheries* I. 258 On our Atlantic coast are found several species of this family [Cottidae], generally known by the name 'Sculpin,' and also by such titles as . . . 'Sea-toad,' and 'Pig-fish.' (*b*) **1891** *Cent.* 5449/3 *Sea-toad* . . . the toadfish, *Batrachus tau*. — **(13)** (*a*) **1766** STORK *Acct. E. Florida* 52 Those mostly made use of . . . [include the] cat-fish, sea-trout, and black-fish. **1884** GOODE *Fisheries* I. 362 With the other members of the genus [the squeteague] is spoken of under the name 'Sea Trout.' **1911** *Rep. Fisheries 1908* 316/2 Squeteague (*Cynoscion regalis*) . . . is known as 'gray trout,' 'sun trout,' 'shad trout,' 'sea trout,' and 'salt-water trout' in the Middle and South Atlantic states. (*b*) **1884** GOODE *Fisheries* I. 267 From San Francisco southward, the names 'Rock Trout' and 'Sea Trout' are common. **1911** *Rep. Fisheries 1908* 315/2 *Sea trout*, a name given to . . . the spotted rock trout or greenling . . . south of San Francisco.

Also in other combs. sufficiently defined in the quots., as (1) **sea brant,** (2) **craw,** (3) ***drake,** (4) ***horse,** (5) ***lion,** cf. ***coaster,** *n.* **3,** (6) **mink,** (7) ***pigeon,** (8) **shad,** (9) **shark,** (10) **spider,** (11) **spin,** cf. **horse-foot crab.**

(1) 1888 TRUMBULL *Names of Birds* 99 To some at Portsmouth, N.H., [*Oidemia deglandi* is known as] Sea Brant. **1891** *Cent.* 548/3 *Sea-brant*, . . . the brant- or brent-goose. — **(2) 1884** GOODE *Fisheries* I. 783 On the coast of Rhode Island, Lobsters are sometimes called 'Sea-craws,' from their resemblance to the fresh-water Cray-fish. — **(3) 1861** COUES in *Phila. Acad. Nat. Sciences Proc.* 240 [Eiderducks] are universally known as 'Sea-ducks,' the males being always distinguished as 'Sea-drakes.' — **(4) 1917** *Birds of Amer.* I. 80 Fulmar. *Fulmarus glacialis glacialis.* . . . [Also called] Molly Hawk; John Down; Sea Horse.

(5) 1890 *Stock Grower & Farmer* 16 Feb. 3/3 The purchase, in 1886, of ten thousand head of scrubby south Texas cattle, 'dogies' or 'sea lions,' at very high prices, was the cause of the great losses by the Delano-Dwyer company. **1929** DOBIE *Vaquero* 20 The 'coasters,' or 'sea lions,' as people sometimes called the longhorned cattle of the coast country, could swim like ducks and were as wild. — **(6) 1888** GOODE *Amer. Fishes* 123 The King-Fish . . . [is] known as . . . the 'Sea Mink' in North Carolina. **1911** *Rep. Fisheries 1908* 311/2 King-fish (*Menticirrhus saxatilis*), a food fish found on the coasts of the Middle and South Atlantic states, and occasionally on the Gulf coast. It is called . . . 'sea mink' in North Carolina. — **(7)** (*a*) **1871** *Harper's Mag.* July 190 Another mollusk, one of the shell-less kind, is a great soft body, of the shape and size of a half-grown pigeon; the resemblance to the latter being so great, it has obtained the name sea-pigeon. **1885** HOLDER *Marvels of Animal Life* 169 One of the sea-slugs, a great green creature, commonly known on the [Florida] reef as the sea-pigeon. (*b*) **1909** WEBSTER 1907 *Sea pigeon* . . . the dowitcher. *New Jersey.* — **(8) 1883** *Nat. Museum Bul.* No. 27, 476 *Clupea mediocris.* . . . Mattowacca; Sea Shad; Shad. Atlantic coast of North America. — **(9) 1814** MITCHILL *Fishes N.Y.* 483 Long-toothed Sea shark. *Squalus Americanus.* . . . This fish is occasionally taken at the very city of New York.

(10) 1843 *Nat. Hist. N.Y., Zoology* VI. 2 The Sea spider, or Spider-Crab, is very common on the coast of this State. — **(11) 1782** CRÈVECOEUR *Letters* 146 Each master of a family [in Nantucket] is obliged to allow him two hundred horse feet, (*sea spin,*) with which this primitive priest fertilizes the land of his glebe.

As the last term in **green, inland sea.**

sea bass. [Cf. Du. *zeebaars.*] Any of the fishes of the family Serranidae, esp. the black sea bass *q.v.* or the white sea bass, a jewfish, *Stereolepis gigas*, of the California coast (see also quot. 1883).

1765 ROGERS *Acct. N. Amer.* 68 In the sea adjacent to this island [Long Island] are sea-bass and black-fish in great plenty, which are very good when fresh. **1821** WELBY *Visit* 211 Fish is well supplied here [in Philadelphia] in quantity but not in variety; it has hitherto chiefly consisted of a coarse kind called *Sea Bass*, but now the Shad fishery is just commencing. **1883** *Nat. Museum Bul.* No. 27, 442 *Sciaena ocellata.* . . . Poisson Rouge; . . . Sea Bass; Spotted Bass. . . . This is a rival of the drum in size and is vastly more important as a food-fish. **1900** NORRIS *Blix* 129 There were . . . sheaves of fishing-rods, from the four-ounce wisp of the brook-trout up to the rigid eighteen-ounce lance of the king-salmon and sea-bass. **1949** *L.A. Times* 5 May IV. 3/8 Sea-bass schools are showing up, too, with catches being made in Catalina waters.

***seaboard,** *n.*

1. The area or land adjacent to the Atlantic Coast. Cf. **Atlantic, Pacific seaboard.**

1788 ASBURY *Journal* II. 37 The Gnats are almost as troublesome here, as the mosquitoes in the lowlands of the seaboard. **1838** STEVENSON *Sketches* 122 This class includes all . . . those which run to and from Boston, New York, Philadelphia, Baltimore, Charleston, Norfolk and the other ports on the eastern coast of the country, or what the Americans call the Sea-board. **1949** *Amer. Sp.* XXIV. 252 On the seaboard there is a multiplicity of words [for this custom].

2. a. seaboard cotton, (see quot.). **b. seaboard slave states,** those slave states on the Atlantic seaboard. Both *obs.*

(a) 1812 MELISH *Travels* I. 27 The principal islands where it is raised are St. Symons and Cumberland; but it is planted, and comes to maturity, in all the other islands along the coast . . . and is thence called *seaboard cotton*. — **(b) 1859** J. REDPATH *Roving Editor* 155 But, in the Seaboard Slave States, I have yet to meet the first Southerner who believes that the condition of the Northern negroes is superior to the condition of the Southern slaves.

sea island.

1. *pl.* The chain of islands off the South Carolina, Georgia, and Florida coasts. Also attrib.

1763 *Hist. Coll. S. Carolina* II. 468 Marshes . . . abound much on the sea Islands. **1810** *Western Chron.* (Columbia, Tenn.) 17 Nov. 2/5 The Georgia Sea Island cotton planters have lost half of their crops by the late storms. **1880** HARRIS *Uncle Remus* p. xiii, The dialect of the cotton plantations . . . [differs from] the lingo in vogue on the rice plantations and Sea Islands of the South Atlantic States. **1895** *Dept. Agric. Yrbk. 1894* 123 The storm of August 26, 27, 28, 1893, [was] familiarly known as the 'sea islands storm.'

2. Ellipt. for next. Also attrib.

1803 J. DAVIS *Travels* 78 Of cotton there are two kinds; the sea-island and inland. The first is the most valuable. **1856** *Rep. Comm. Patents 1855: Agric.* 319 [It is believed] that the 'Georgian,' or 'Short-staple,' is the Sea Island, carried into the interior. **1916** *Farmers' Bul.* No. 787, 7 [Egyptian cotton] will continue to be used by many mills . . . until the Sea Island growers improve their product.

3. sea island cotton, a long silky-fibered cotton, *Gossypium barbadense*, which, before the coming of the boll weevil, was extensively grown in the coastal region of the southeastern states. Also attrib.

1805 MICHAUX *Travels* 345 *Sea Island Cotton* . . . has a deep black seed, and very long fine wool. **1844** in TURNER *Cotton* (1865) 282 The first bale of Sea Island cotton that was ever produced in Georgia, was grown by Alexander Bisset, Esq., of St. Simon's Island, and I think in the year 1778. **1897** *Kissimmee* (Fla.) *Valley* 2 June 1/4 The exhibit of sea-island cotton from Ocala and Gainesville attracts much attention. **1949** MURRAY *This Our Land* 189 The sea island cotton planter early discovered that marsh mud was both the cheapest and most profitable manure.

∗**seal,** *n.*

1. In the early N. Eng. Church, a sacrament. *Obs.*

1637 *Essex Inst. Coll.* I. 39/1 He refuseth to come to Assembly and to p[ar]take in ye seales. **1648** *Platform Church-Discipline* (1772) 10 Their elders in their own church shall receive none to the seals but visible saints.

2. A strip of easily torn metal put on a railroad boxcar to seal it.

1885 *Santa Fé Wkly. New Mexican* 10 Sep. 3/7 John Hubbard, breaking seal of railroad car; two years. **1949** *Sat. Ev. Post* 4 June 121/2 Consequently, when the seals were put on the boxcar doors, those cars often contained a mixture of presses, lathes, desks, filing cabinets, tools and parts.

3. seal fat, *a.* very fat and sleek. *Colloq.* [The first element in this expression is prob. ∗*seal*, the animal.]

1848 RUXTON *Life Far West* ii, 'Any buffalo come in?' 'Heap, and seal-fat at that.' **1898** CANFIELD *Maid of Frontier* 112 The weather'll be warmer an' my horse seal fat.

As the last term in **beech, car, consular, express, golden, harbor, near, state seal.**

∗**seal,** *v.* [Cf. Rev. 7: 3 ff.] *tr.* In the Mormon Church, to reserve (a woman) as a spiritual wife *q.v.* to a particular man. Also transf. Cf. ∗**sealing,** *n.* **2.**

1845 *Quincy* (Ill.) *Whig* 1 Nov. 2/3 Still while all these iniquitous proceedings were going on, it was the common practice for these wicked plotters to boldly and blasphemously proclaim before the people in the presence of hundreds that had been 'seal-up' to them, that such a doctrine was false, and he that practiced it was a scoundrel, and the woman that admitted it no other than a harlot. **1922** *Nation* 28 June 768/1 A celestial marriage is a secret Temple rite where men have dead women 'sealed' to them as their wives for eternity, and unattached women are sealed to dead husbands. **1944** *Chi. D. News* 29 Sep. 1/5 She explained how she was forced into plural marriage and 'sealed' to defendant Wesley Lebaron 'up in a canyon just about my 14th birthday.' **1948** *Amer. Folk-Lore* Jan.–Mar. 28 An illegitimate child appeared thrice in a dream, each time insisting that it be sealed legitimately to the family in appropriate temple ceremonies.

b. Used of men reserved to particular women.

1845 *Quincy* (Ill.) *Whig* 1 Nov. 2/3 Men's wives and daughters were secretly married at night-time to this Young, H. C. Kimball, William Richards and others, and, in the dark night, were attending the secret lodges until most of the 'Seventies' were thus sealed. **1908** DELLENBAUGH *Canyon Voyage* 174, I met two [wives], and he was besides that 'sealed' to one or two Pah Ute women.

Hence **sealed,** *a.*

1856 FERRIS *Mormons at Home* 114 The extra wives of the Mormons are called by some of them 'spirituals,' by others sealed ones, while our landlady calls them 'fixins.' **1857** *Harper's Mag.* Feb. 404/1 In Utah, Judge Drummond . . . instructed them to indict all 'sealed' persons who had not been legally married.

∗**sealing,** *n.*

1. Acquiring public land with the intention of settling upon it. *Obs.*

1732 in *Amer. Sp.* XX. (1945) 275 Whether it is fit altogether to prohibit a trade which encourages the sealing of lands that without it would remain as a desart.

2. Among Mormons, the ceremony or action of taking a spiritual wife. Cf. ∗**seal,** *v.*

1856 FERRIS *Mormons at Home* 114 These left-hand marriages are called sealings. **1882** WAITE *Adv. Far West* 137 These marriages are always performed in their sacred and secret Temple, in a singular manner, and are called 'Sealings.' **1942** STEGNER *Mormon C.* 178 Those are the first processes—baptism and the sealing of one's wife and family.

3. sealing water, water in the trap of a water drain which serves to cut off noxious fumes from the sewer. *Obs.*

1884 *Cent. Mag.* Dec. 260/2 The current thus produced is to carry the sealing-water with it. **1885** *Ib.* Jan. 259/1 The whole volume of sealing-water is rarely removed with a single motion.

∗**seam,** *n.* **1. seam dampener,** a device for dampening the seam of an article before ironing. **2. seam diggings,** gold diggings in an earth seam or narrow stratum. Both *obs.* — **(1) 1887** *Sci. Amer.* 26 March 202/2 A seam dampener has been patented . . . for use in laundries. — **(2) 1873** RAYMOND *Silver & Gold* 25 Among what may justly be ranked as new discoveries is a description of gold-bearing deposits denominated 'Seam Diggings.'

seapoose ˈsipus, *n.* [See note.]

This term is derived f. Munsee (a Delaware subtribe) term, *sepoûs, sepuus, sipus*, a brook, small river. See Ruttenber, *Indian Names* 95, and Hodge, I. 437 *s.v. Esopus.* The first element has been erroneously identified with the English word *sea*, and such forms as those in sense **2.** have resulted in *sea puss, sea purse*, found, without explanation, in some dictionaries. The *Ling. Atlas* (see quot. 1939 below) shows the persistence in the Southampton, L.I., area of the word in what was no doubt its original meaning and pronunciation.

1. *Southampton, L.I.* (See quots. 1874, 1939.)

1650 *Southampton Rec.* I. 69 [They] are to have for their paines 3s per day at the seapoose. **1653** *Ib.* 94 Mr Rayner & Iohn White are appointed & left to agree (if they can) with the miller concerneing the alteration of his mill to ease the towne of the burthen of opening the sepoose. **1658** *Ib.* 132 Ian, 10 1658 at a towne meeting it was granted by the towne that Mr Raynor and Iohn Iessup shall have 6 acres granted them yf it bee to be had in the ten acre lotts, instead of the meadow which was digged vp for the west sepoose. **1665** in B. F. THOMPSON *Hist. Long Island* I. (1843) 333 It is concluded that John Jessup shall call forth thirty men to goe to the west sepoose, and if any refuse to goe, being warned, they shall pay to ye town five shillings. **1874** *Southampton Rec.* I. 69 'Seapoose' is an Indian word and signifies 'little river' as found in these records it almost always refers to the inlet connecting Meacox bay with the ocean. *Ib.* 85 Seapoose was the inlet connecting Meacox bay with the ocean, opened by digging, but soon closed up again. **1939** *Ling. Atlas* Map 40 The map shows the terms creek . . . inlet . . . and [sijpuws] (sea puss?), denoting a tidal stream or a shallow arm of the sea. . . . Attention is called . . . to [sijpuws] on Long Island.

2. (See quot. 1891.)

*a*1841 HAWES *Sporting Scenes* I. 102, I kept watch of him—when I came to a sea poose—I went in and to the east of it. **1891** *Cent.* 5445/3 *Sea-purse*, . . . a swirl of the undertow making a small whirlpool on the surface of the water; a local outward current, dangerous to bathers. Also called *sea-pouce* and *sea-puss.* (New Eng. and New Jersey coasts.) **1904** *N.Y. Tribune* 29 May, McDonald was a good swimmer, but, getting caught in a sea puss, was shot out to the deep sea with great velocity.

∗**search,** *v. Search me*, I have no idea, I don't know at all. *Colloq.* — **1904** O. HENRY *Cabbages & Kings* (1916) 47 'What's her tonnage?' 'Search me!' said Smith, 'I don't know what she weighs in at.' **1917** MCCUTCHEON *Green Fancy* 56 'Wasn't it an automobile accident?' 'Search me.' **1950** *Boston Globe* 9 April (Comics) 1 What's she up to, Sam? Search me, Linda!

∗**searcher,** *n.* **1.** In colonial times, an official inspector of leather, or of meat. **2.** (See quot.) Both *obs.*

(1) 1642 *Mass. Bay Rec.* II. 19 The said searchers . . . shall seale & marke such leather as they shall find sufficient. **1654** *Boston Rec.* 118 Chosen for Searchers and packers of Flesh and Fish: William Dinsdayle and John Barrell. **1689** *Southampton Rec.* II. 305 Manassah Kempton [was] chosen sealer and searcher of leather. — **(2) 1859** BARTLETT, Searcher. An instrument resembling an auger, used in the inspection of butter, to ascertain the quality of that contained in firkins. New England.

sea robin.

1. Any one of several gurnards of the genus *Prionotus.*

1814 MITCHILL *Fishes N.Y.* 430 Gurnard, or Sea Robin, *Trigla lineata.* **1894** *Outing* XXIV. 263/2 Here's a sea-robin! A curious grunting fellow, 10 in. long, with a great fin, like a butterfly's wing, projecting from each side of his throat. **1949** *Fishes Western N. Atlantic* I. 104 The recorded diet . . . includes alewives (*Pomolobus*), . . . sea bass (*Centropristis*), sea robin (*Prionotus*).

b. A toadfish.

1879 *Nat. Museum Proc.* II. 336 These fish were called in Pensacola by the names 'Sea Robin' and 'Sarpo.' **1911** *Rep. Fisheries 1908* 315/2 Sea robin . . . is also applied to the toadfish (*Apsanus tau*) in the Gulf.

2. (See quot.)
1891 *Cent.* 5447/1 Sea-robin, . . . the red-breasted merganser, *Mergus serrator.* (Rowley, Mass.)

* **seaside,** *n.*

1. In the names of various plants and trees sufficiently defined in the quots.: (1) **seaside alder,** (2) **arrow-grass,** (3) **grape,** (4) **oat(s),** (cf. **sea oats**), (5) **scrub oak.**

(1) 1785 MARSHALL *Amer. Grove* 20 The Species are, 1. *Betula-Alnus glauca.* Silver-Leaved Alder. . . . *Betula-Alnus maritima.* Seaside Alder. **1909** *Cent. Supp.* 29/2 Seaside alder, *Alnus maritima,* found in wet ground in Delaware and Maryland, near the coast, and also in Indian Territory. — **(2) 1843** TORREY *Flora N.Y.* II. 261 *Triglochin maritimum.* Seaside Arrow-grass. . . . Salt marshes on the Island of New-York, and on Long Island. — **(3) 1837** WILLIAMS *Florida* 37 The seaside grape, different kinds of plumbs, and custard apples are frequently found in the hammocks. **1889** *Cent.* 2600/2 Seaside grape, a name given to several species of *Coccoloba* growing up the sea-shore, especially to *C. uvifera.* — **(4) c1729** CATESBY *Carolina* I. 32 The Sea-side Oat. . . . I observed growing no where but on Sand-Hills; so near the Sea, that at high Tides the water flows to it. **1891** *Cent.* 5831/1 spike-grass. . . . The genus *Uniola,* especially *U. paniculata* (also called *sea* or *seaside oats*), a tall coarse grass with a dense heavy panicle, growing on sand-hills along the Atlantic coast southward.
(5) 1901 MOHR *Plant Life Ala.* 473 *Quercus myrtifolia.* . . . Seaside Scrub Oak. . . . Coast from South Carolina to Florida, west to Alabama.

2. seaside finch, an Atlantic Coast salt-marsh sparrow, *Ammospiza maritima.*
1811 WILSON *Ornithology* IV. 68 Sea-side Finch. . . . This species derives its whole subsistence from the sea. **1839** PEABODY *Mass. Birds* 326 The Seaside Finch . . . visits the interior only when driven by easterly storms. **1917** *Birds of Amer.* III. 30.

3. seaside resort, a resort at the seaside.
1879 *Harper's Mag.* July 163 Nowhere else in all sea-side resorts will he be likely to get so much . . . elbow-room. **1901** FLYNT *World of Graft* 137 They went on a jaunt to a sea-side resort on their profits in the transaction. **1904** *Country Life* July 290/2 What is perhaps the most curious village in the world . . . is being built at Terminal Island, a seaside resort in southern California.

* **season,** *n.*

1. "In the southern U.S., 'a shower of rain or period of damp weather suitable for setting out tobacco and other plants' " (*OED*).
1724 JONES *Virginia* 39 They transplant and replant [tobacco] upon Occasion after a Shower or Rain, which they [in Va.] call a Season. **1856** *Fla. Plant. Rec.* 161 They have had fine Seasons on Chamoonie Since I ritten to you before and the cotton crope looks mutch better in concequence of the Seasons. **1918** *D.N.* V. 19 This cotton needs a good season.

2. In combs.: (1) **season check,** (see quot. 1905); (2) **passenger,** a railway passenger who travels on a season ticket, *rare.*
(1) 1887 KIRKLAND *Zury* 32 Ye see that thar season-check in the butt-end? **1905** *Forestry Bureau Bul.* No. 61, 33 *Check,* a longitudinal crack in timber caused by too rapid seasoning. . . . Syn.: season check. — **(2) 1856** W. H. SWIFT *Mass. Railroads* 14 There is a return of the Commutation or Season Passengers, for the years 1852, 1853, and 1854.
As the last term in **bloody, branding, camp meeting, closed, fall, grasshopper, hay, lapping, long, lumbering, maple sugar, open, pigeon, pork, rolling, running, rush, salmon, shucking, sleighing, sugar, track season.**

* **seasoner,** *n.* "A seaman or fisherman who hires for the season; by extension, a loafer; a beach-comber" (*Cent.*).

* **seasoning,** *n.* A fever or other illness often suffered during the first year of settling in a new country. *Obs.*
[**1670** DENTON *Brief Descr. N.Y.* 17 The Climate [of N.Y.] hath such an affinity with that of England, that . . . the name of seasoning, which is common to some other Countreys hath never there been known.] **1705** BEVERLEY *Virginia* IV. 69 The first Sickness that any New-Comer happens to have there, he unfairly calls a Seasoning. **1724** JONES *Virginia* 50 Abundance of Damps and Mists . . . makes the People subject to Feavers and Agues, which is the Country Distemper, a severe Fit of which (called a *Seasoning*) most expect, some time after their Arrival in that Climate. **1843** in MARY CONE *Life Rufus Putnam* (1886) 130 In the midst of all this the mumps and perhaps one or two other diseases prevailed and gave us a seasoning.

* **seat,** *n.*

1. A place of employment. *Rare.*
1806 in COMMONS *Doc. Hist.* III. 77, I was afraid if he dismissed me that I could not get another seat in the city, for the next employer would be under the necessity of discharging me likewise.

2. A membership on a stock exchange.
1882 MCCABE *New York* 337 A seat in the Board costs about $6000, and is the absolute personal property of its owner. **1900** NELSON *A B C Wall St.* 15 Memberships . . . are called seats. **1948** *Time* 14 June 90/2 All who buy and sell on the floor must own Stock Exchange seats, which are currently worth about $65,000 apiece (1929 price: $625,000).

3. In combs.: (1) * **seat board,** a board or plank placed athwart a wagon box for the driver or passengers to sit on; (2) **-mate,** one who shares a seat with another, esp. in school; (3) * **of justice,** a county seat, *obs.;* (4) **of the courts,** =prec., *obs.*
(1) 1873 J. H. BEADLE *Undevel. West* iii. 70 The wagon made fearful lurches, and our seatboard rattled over it in every direction. — **(2) 1859** *Ladies' Repository* Nov. 645/1 She will tickle the neck of her seat-mate with a bit of grass. **1903** WIGGIN *Rebecca* 61 Her seat-mate, Emma Jane, had made up a little mound of paper balls. — **(3) 1806** *Ann. 9th Congress* 2 Sess. 1005 Uniontown being the seat of justice for Fayette county, Pennsylvania. **1849** CHAMBERLAIN *Ind. Gazetteer* 288 Lawrenceburgh, the Seat of Justice of Dearborn county, is situated on the Ohio river. — **(4) 1789** *Pa. Mag.* VI. 117 The name of the principal Town or Seat of the Courts is Louisbourg.
As the last term in **amen, anxious, back, barrel, buggy, cane, car, county, deacon, flanker, front, guard, hinge, lock, mill, mourner's, rising, rumble, singer's, spring, wagon, whirligig seat.**

* **seat,** *v.*

1. *tr.* To establish (a plantation or estate); to furnish (land) with settlers; to occupy as settlers. *Obs.* or *hist.*
1620 in BRADFORD *Hist.* 117, I would that the first plantation might hear be seated. **1719** *Md. Hist. Mag.* XVIII. 9 They have seated plantations on the extreme parts of the Garrison Ridge. **1784** WASHINGTON *Writings* X. 366 It would give me pleasure to see these lands seated by particular societies. **1896** P. A. BRUCE *Econ. Hist. Va.* I. 553 The first [condition], to use the technical term in vogue, was to 'seat' the new plantations. A very broad interpretation of what constituted a seating in the eyes of the law prevailed in the Colony.

2. In colonial N. Eng., to assign seats to people in a meetinghouse in accordance with their social position in the community (see also quot. 1828). *Obs.* or *hist.*
1646 *N. Eng. Hist. & Gen. Reg.* (1850) IV. 229 The names of people as they were seated in the meeting-house were read in Court; and it was ordered that they should be recorded. **1718** SEWALL *Diary* III. 208 Visited Mrs. Bethiah Kitchen. . . . She treated Capt Osgood very roughly about Seating the Meetinghouse. **1787** in *Hist. Pelham Mass.* (1898) 264 Voted that . . . those that have no Pews and pay the highest taxes, shall have their choice of Pews by paying the sum which was offered for them when they were formerly seated. **1828** WEBSTER, In New England, where the pews in churches are not private property, it is customary to *seat* families for a year or longer time; that is, assign and appropriate *seats* to their use. **1895** G. SHELDON *Hist. Deerfield, Mass.* I. 484 A committee was chosen to new seat the meeting house, according to age, estate and qualifications.

* **seated,** *a.* **1. seated land,** (see quot. 1877). *Obs.* **2. seated tribe,** a tribe of Indians settled on a reservation in the West.
(1) 1680 *Doc. Col. Hist. N.Y.* XII. 632, [I] haue made severall Surveys both of seated & Unseated Lands. **1877** W. H. BURROUGHS *On Taxation* 208 In Pennsylvania, prior to 1844, seated lands, that is, lands occupied by residence, or cultivation, could not be sold for taxes. — **(2) 1870** D. R. KEIM *Sheridan's Troopers* 292 Half of the remainder of acres are cultivated by the bands living within the limits of Kansas, and the seated tribes of the Indian Territory.

seater ˈsitɚ, *n.* **1.** *Va.* A settler established on land. **2.** *N. Eng.* One who assigns or assists in assigning the seats in a meetinghouse. Both *obs.*
(1) 1653 *Va. House of Burgesses* 90 Provided that such seaters settle advantageously for security. **1822** *Amer. Beacon* (Norfolk) 19 Feb. 2/2 Mr. Clay quoted several laws of the colony of Virginia, passed near two centuries ago, providing that the true owner should compensate the seater of land. — **(2) 1693** *Braintree Rec.* 29 Seaters of the Meeting hous. **1739** in G. SHELDON *Hist. Deerfield, Mass.* (1895) I. 483 Voted that . . . shall be a Com'tee to Determine how many Persons their shall be Seated in Each Pue & to make return thereof to ye Seaters. **1895** G. SHELDON *Hist. Deerfield, Mass.* I. 485 The seaters carried their point at this meeting.

* **seating,** *n.*

1. The establishment of a town or colony. *Obs.*
[**1652** *Cal. Va. State P.* I. 2 Payment is to be made seaven yeares after the first grant, or seating thereof, and not before.] **c1669** *Doc.*

Hist. N.Y. State I. 87 The seating of towns together is necessary in these parts of America, especially upon the Maine Land. **1699** *Phil. Trans.* XXI. 441 At the first Seating of Maryland there were several Nations of Indians in the Country. **1779** *Ky. Petitions* 53 From the first-seating of This Town both the inhabitants and travilers has found it very inconvenient to get across the Kentucky River.

2. The action of assigning seats in a meetinghouse. Also attrib. Now *obs.* or *hist.*

1685 SEWALL *Diary* I. 119 Mrs. Harris and Baker present their mutual offences against each other as to their seating before Mr. Willard and the Overseers. **1753** *Amherst Rec.* (1884) 17/2 Voted 4 that these Ruels in seating be by mens age Estats & Qualifications. **1891** EARLE *Sabbath* 49 Many men were unwilling to serve on these seating committees, . . . protesting against it on account of the odium that was incurred.

Seattleite si'æt|,aɪt, *n.* A native or inhabitant of Seattle, Washington. — **1939** *Alaska D. Press* (Juneau) 19 July 3/5 Seattleites are guests of Boyles. **1947** PERRY *Cities of Amer.* 162 Seattleites whose thirst can't be quenched by beer and wine are dependent either on the state-owned liquor stores or on their private clubs for a taste of the ardent.

Seaver's Sweet. A variety of apple. *Obs.* — **1847** IVES *N. Eng. Fruit* 46 *Cann Apple.* . . . This apple is cultivated by some, under the name of Seaver's Sweet.

Sebago sɪ'bego, *n.* **1. Sebago salmon,** a landlocked salmon, *Salmo sebago*, found in Lake Sebago, Me. **2. Sebago trout,** =prec.

(1) 1883 *Nat. Museum Bul.* No. 27, 425 Sebago Salmon. . . . Saint Croix River and lakes of Maine. Extensively introduced into other lakes and into streams southward. **1911** *Rep. Fisheries 1908* 315/1 The land-locked salmon, or fresh-water salmon, or Sebago salmon . . . , is found in fresh waters, generally landlocked. — **(2) 1884** GOODE *Fisheries* I. 470 The 'Land-locked' or 'Fresh-water' Salmon, known also . . . in different parts of Maine as 'Schoodic Trout,' 'Sebago Trout,' or 'Dwarf Salmon,' probably never visit salt water.

***secede,** *v.*

1. *To secede from the Union*, of a state: To withdraw from the federal Union.

1825 JEFFERSON *Writings* I. 20 Possibly their colonies might secede from the Union. **1861** *N.Y. Herald* 3 Jan. 5/4 Several of the Southern States . . . directed conventions to be held by the said several States in order to secede from the Union. **1941** ALLEY *Random Thoughts* 3 My uncle, honestly believing that a State did not have the right to secede from the Union, at once enlisted.

2. seceded state, one of the southern states that seceded from the Union. *Obs.*

1861 in KETTELL *Hist. Rebellion* I. 293 Kentucky has determined that the proper course for her to pursue is to take no part in the controversy between the government and the seceded states but that of *mediator* and *intercessor*. **1866** F. KIRKLAND *Bk. Anecdotes* 35/1 The condition of the seceded States and the course to be pursued with the garrison at Fort Sumter, were discussed.

b. Also **seceded territory,** (see quot.). *Obs.*

1861 *N.Y. Herald* 20 May 1/7 The embryo Territory of Arizona . . . is therefore viewed in the light of a seceded Territory.

3. seceding state, a state that secedes, or has seceded, from the Union. *Obs.*

1833 MADISON in Benton *30 Years' View* I. 357/2 A seceding State mutilates the domain, and disturbs the whole system from which it separates itself. **1888** LOWELL *Lit. & Polit. Addresses* 211 The Democratic party was quite as efficient in bringing that war upon us as the seceding States themselves.

***seceder,** *n.* One who advocated the secession of a state from the federal Union, a southerner belonging to a seceding state. *Obs.* Cf. ***Baptist.**

1833 MARSHALL in Logan *Great Conspiracy* 28 Numerous important historical facts . . . remove the foundation on which the Nullifiers and Seceders have erected that super-structure which overshadows our Union. **1860** *Boston Transcript* 19 Dec. 2/1 Some of the leading seceders, especially those members of Congress, . . . are a little confused. **1887** BILLINGS *Hardtack* 22 These events [at Fort Sumter] . . . opened the eyes of the 'Northern Doughfaces' . . . to the real intent of the Seceders.

secesh sɪ'sɛʃ, *n.* and *a.* [f. **secession.*]

1. *n.* A term used by Northerners in a jocular or disparaging manner for a Confederate soldier, a seceder. Also collect.

1861 NORTON *Army Lett.* 32 The guards soon found the *secesh* to be a great hog that was wandering round in the woods. **1862** *Esmeralda Star* (Aurora, Nev.) 23 Aug., Fortunately however for the secesh they made no attempt to carry out their threats. **1901** STILLMAN *Autobiog. Journalist* I. 332 My backwoodsmen . . . meant to go to 'shoot secesh,' not to be regular infantry. **1944** PENNELL *Rome Hanks* 41 He thought you were a Secesh.

2. *a.* Of or pertaining to the Southern Confederacy or to a secessionist.

1861 NORTON *Army Lett.* 35 We dug *secesh* potatoes to roast. **1868** *Ore. State Jrnl.* 8 Aug. 1/3 Seymour is a good enough Secesh Democrat for that branch of the party. **1945** BOTKIN *My Burden* 113 Young Master Frank ride over to Vicksburg and jine the Secesh army, but Old Master just go on like nothing happen.

Also *secesh chicken, Colonel, conscription, cousin, fellow, flag, goose, gun, member, opinion, regiment, resolution, state*, etc.

b. In the predicate: Having the opinions of the southerners during the Civil War; sympathetic toward the South.

1863 BOUDRYE *Fifth N.Y. Cavalry* (1868) 339 An oyster man. . . . Was Union on the York, but Secesh on James river. **1865** *N.Y. Ev. Post* 28 Sep. 1/1 He's right smart secesh before they all come. **1887** BILLINGS *Hardtack* 234 So many who really were 'secesh' claimed to be good Union men, it came latterly to be assumed that the victim was playing a false role.

secesh sɪ'sɛʃ, *v.* **1.** *intr.* To secede, withdraw. **2.** *To get seceshed*, to get separated. *Colloq. Obs.*

(1) 1861 MOORE *Rebellion Rec.* I. III. 126 He has plenty of money, which I find is a good thing to secesh with. **1867** LOCKE *Swingin' Round* 23, I seceshed with 100 niggers to git 200. — **(2) 1862** LOWELL *Biglow P.* 2 Ser. iv. 119 We've succeeded in gittin' seceshed an' dissolved.

Seceshdom sɪ'sɛʃdəm, *n.* =**Secessia.** *Obs.* — **1861** *N.Y. Tribune* 23 Nov. 8/1 Private advices from Seceshdom speak of the elation which succeeded the first excitement produced by the arrest of Mason and Slidell.

secesher sɪ'sɛʃɚ, *n.* A southern secessionist. *Slang. Obs.* — **1861** *N.Y. Herald* 2 July 8/2 'Mammy' complains bitterly that the dirty 'seceshers' have spoiled her business. **1866** F. KIRKLAND *Bk. Anecdotes* 105/1 'Long come two or free hundred ob dem seceshers.

seceshly sɪ'sɛʃlɪ, *adv.* In the manner of the secessionists. *Rare.* — **1862** *Congregationalist* 7 Feb. (Chipman), Some sour, seceshly inclined tavern-keeper.

Secessia sɪ'sɛʃɪə, *n.* The land of the secessionists or the Southern Confederacy. Also transf. *Obs.*

1861 *Carrolton* (Ill.) *Press* 1 March 2/3 The information contained in the following item is highly suggestive of the actual condition of affairs in 'Secessia.' **1866** F. KIRKLAND *Bk. Anecdotes* 461/1 'Yes, indeed,' broke in fair Secessia. **1882** SALA *Amer. Revisited* I. 22 He informed me confidentially that he was an habitual blockade-runner, and that he was 'all over quinine and spurs'; both being just then articles of prime necessity in Secessia.

***secession,** *n.*

1. The withdrawal from the Union of one of the states composing it, esp. with reference to the Confederate States. Now *hist.* Cf. **anti-secession.**

1830 *Cong. Deb.* 10 May 948/2 Make good the charge, prove the injury, and they [the people of N.Y.] will consent to the secession [of S.C.] to-morrow. **1846** *Dollar Newspaper* (Phila.) 25 March 2/2 Several petitions have been presented to the Legislature of Massachusetts, praying for the recall of its members in Congress, and its secession from the Union. **1860** LONGFELLOW in S. Longfellow *H. W. Longfellow* II. 409 Secession of the North from freedom would be tenfold worse than secession of the South from the North. **1884** BLAINE *20 Years of Congress* I. 573 The purpose of the secession . . . [was] the establishment of an independent slave-empire. **1941** FERGUSSON *Southwest* 32 After dinner speakers find secession a popular theme; newspapers editorialize about the 'high plains empire' and its right to independence.

2. Widely used attrib., esp. during or just after the Civil War, as **secession army, badge, bonnet, Congress, dinner, ordinance, party, senator, sympathizer.**

1862 in MCCLELLAN *Own Story* 347 There is in front of us to impede our advance the secession Army of the Rappahannock, so called. — **1886** POORE *Reminisc.* II. 80 It was not uncommon to meet on Pennsylvania Avenue a defiant Southerner openly wearing a large Virginia or South Carolina secession badge. — **1863** HOPLEY *Life in South* I. 137 At an annual State exhibition in Georgia, a lady presented a 'Secession bonnet,' of home manufacture. — **1861** *Richmond* (Va.) *Examiner* 6 Sep. 1/4 Anti-President Jeff. Davis, in his message to the Secession Congress, asserts that the Confederate States took up arms in defence of their liberties. — **1865** *Wkly. New Mexican* 4 Aug. 2/2 It was fashionable for some folks, to rend their linen over the fancied wrongs of the South, and to preside 'with dignity,' at secession dinners. — **1860** *Boston Transcript* 21 Dec. 2/5 The official despatch to the President, announcing the passage of the Secession Ordinance, was received last evening. — **1861** *Charleston* (S.C.)

Mercury 14 Feb. 3/2 The secession party in Virginia are worse than defeated. — **1861** in E. McPherson *Polit. Hist. Great Rebellion* (1864) 391/2 A caucus was held in this city [Washington] by the Southern Secession Senators. — **1861** in Linton *Life Whittier* 136, I do not like to find fault with the Administration, as in so doing I seem to take sides with the secession sympathisers of the North.

Also *secession family, feeling, minister, movement, orator, proclivity, sentiment, slippers, sympathy, ticket,* etc.

b. secession convention, any of the state conventions convened in the South to consider or declare secession from the Union. *Obs.*

1860 *Boston Transcript* 19 Dec. 4/2 The South Carolina Secession Convention. **1893** Page in *Harper's Mag.* Dec. 10/2 Here [in Richmond] sat and deliberated the Secession Convention during the period when Virginia stood as the peace-maker between the two sections.

c. secession flag, any one of various flags adopted by the seceding states or by the Confederate Government. *Obs.*

1861 *Alexandria* (Va.) *Gaz.* 27 April 2/2 Secession flags wave from almost every other house. **1863** Hopley *Life in South* I. 283 Before the confirmed Secession of Virginia from the Northern States' Government, the 'Secession flag,' as an indication of the prevailing sentiment, was set floating from many public buildings and private dwellings. **1866** F. Kirkland *Bk. Anecdotes* 582/1 Miss Lee wore upon her bonnet a miniature silken secession flag.

secessiondom sɪˈsɛʃəndəm, *n.* (Also *cap.*) = **Secessia.** *Obs.* — **1862** E. Kirke *Among Pines* 63 This, the reader will please remember, was the state of things . . . in the *very heart* of Secessiondom. **1868** *N.Y. Herald* 1 July 6/4 But New York has had enough experience of the dogmatic philosophers of secessiondom.

secessioner sɪˈsɛʃənɚ, *n.* = **secesher.** *Slang. Obs.* — **1863** *Harper's Mag.* July 282/1 The pesky officers using up on them seceshioners roads all the stuff that was sent to make breeches. **1865** *Nation* I. 457 We ha'n't no use for secessioners, not for nothin'.

secessionism sɪˈsɛʃənˌɪzəm, *n.* The principles or doctrines of those who advocated secession from the Union at the time of the Civil War. Also fig. *Obs.*

1861 *N.Y. Herald* 10 July 2/2 The sudden conversion of the Baltimore *Sun* from secessionism to Unionism, pure and unadulterated, was quite as astonishing as the unexpected appearance of the new comet. **1865** *Nation* I. 38/1 So outspoken is its secessionism that it has lately been warned by the military that its course must change or its publication stop. **1898** *Voice* 5 May 6/5 Lincoln . . . found himself in possession of a bankrupt government, confronted by an arrogant secessionism.

secessionist sɪˈsɛʃənɪst, *n.* One who during the Civil War period advocated the secession of a state from the Union, a supporter of the Southern Confederacy.

1851 *Harper's Mag.* Dec. 120/1 The same division prevailed in the Congressional contest, the nominees being Unionists and Secessionists. **1861** *Alexandria* (Va.) *Gaz.* 2 May 2/7 The secessionists sunk several vessels in New Inlet, blocking up the channel. **1943** DeVoto *Yr. of Decision* 480 Then in that dawn Edmund Ruffin, the most honored Virginia secessionist, pulled the lanyard of a cannon on Morris Island that was trained on a fort in Charleston Harbor, and the military phase began.

b. Also attrib. or as adj.

1869 Brace *New West* 277 The region about Los Angeles . . . was somewhat secessionist, or at least opposed to the Government, during the war. **1944** Pennell *Rome Hanks* 328 [The name] was that of a Pro-Slavery Vice-President of the United States and as black-hearted a Secessionist Brigadier as ever mounted an overbred hunter.

transf. **1948** *Time* 5 July 20/3 The secessionist Dixiecrats might stay hitched if the Democratic platform went no further on civil rights than the generalizations of the 1944 plank.

Seckel ˈsɪkl, *n.* Also **Seckle.** [See quot. 1817, under 2.]

1. Short for next.

1852 *Horticulturist* VII. 48 Those [pears] of merit which were in season with the Seckel and Virgalieu . . . are as follows. **1890** *Cent.* 4343/3 The Seckel is an American variety—the fruit small, but unsurpassed in quality.

2. Seckel pear, a variety of sweet, juicy pear, usu. reddish brown in color. Also a pear of this variety.

1817 W. Coxe *Fruit Trees* 159 Seckle Pear.—So called from Mr. Seckle of Philadelphia, the proprietor of the original tree. **1943** *Christian Sci. Mon.* 27 Feb. (Mag. Sect.) 12/5 Among other words I miss . . . the variant 'sickel' for seckel. I never heard anyone say anything but 'sickel pear.' **1949** *N.O. Times-Picayune Mag.* 21 Aug. 23/1 Among those best known are Bartlett, Bosc, Kieffer, and Seckel pears.

seco ˈseko, *n.* Corruption of **acequia.** *Obs.* — **1862** *Harper's Mag.* May 742/1 The vineyards were but partially cultivated, and the secos, or ditches for the irrigation of the land, were entirely dry.

* **second,** *a.* and *n.*

1. *n. pl.* Tobacco leaves of an inferior quality or the plants that produce them (see also quot. 1896). *Obs.* Cf. **tobacco seconds.**

1656 *Va. Statutes* (1823) I. 399 Wee . . . Doe . . . enact that what person or persons soever shall . . . suffer or cause to be tended any tobacco commonly called seconds and slips shall for so doing pay 2000 lb. of tobacco. **1724** Jones *Virginia* 117 They have a Law against Seconds, . . . [intended] to prohibit all Persons from manufacturing a second Crop from the Leaves that sprout out from the Stalk after the first Leaves are cut off. **1775** *Amer. Husbandry* II. 80 These *seconds* . . . do not usually grow so high as the first plant, but notwithstanding they make very good tobacco. **1896** P. A. Bruce *Econ. Hist. Va.* I. 383 There were stringent regulations to prevent the tending of seconds, which, putting forth after the original leaves had been pulled from the stalk, were . . . mean in texture.

2. *Parliamentary.* An act or utterance in which a motion is seconded; one who seconds a motion.

1812 *Ann. 12th Congress* 1 Sess. 1462 The Speaker said he conceived that every motion must receive a second before it could be announced from the Chair. *Ib.* 1472 A reversal of the rule that the plurality of the members is to govern . . . [would] make the mover and his second superior to the whole body. **1894** T. B. Reed *Manual Gen. Parl. Law* 77 No second is required in the House of Representatives to an ordinary motion. **1915** H. M. Robert *Rules of Order Rev.* 36 The chair should repeat the motion before calling for a second.

3. Short for "second base" or "second baseman."

1867 *Ball Players' Chron.* 13 June 2/1 Marsh, second, and Spencer, third, played well. **1949** *Fargo* (N.D.) *Forum* 23 July 8/7 Jessen walked to open and advanced to second on a passed ball.

4. *a.* Of a theater balcony, circle, or tier: Next above the first balcony, circle, or tier.

1825 in James Agate *These Were Actors* (1943) 94 The stairway leading to the second tier of boxes was so thronged, that it was impossible for those who were in to get out by that way. **1871** *Chi. Ev. Jrnl.* 26 Aug., Above the first balcony is the second balcony. **1896** Birkmire *Planning Amer. Theatres* 46 Seats are arranged as follows: . . . first box-tier, 32 boxes, 160 people, second box-tier, 32 boxes.

5. In combs.: (1) **second bank,** a bluff or embankment that rises from river bottom land, *obs.*, cf. **second bottom;** (2) **board,** (see quot. 1909); (3) **church,** the church in a particular community established next after the first one of the same denomination, cf. * **first,** *a.* **1. b;** (4) **class,** a class of mail comprising newspapers and other periodicals, also attrib.; (5) **-class car,** a railroad car for second-class passengers, *obs.;* (6) **-classman,** at Annapolis, a third-year man; (7) **degree,** (*a*) in the early history of Harvard, the M.A. degree, *obs.*, (*b*) (see quot. 1796 and cf. * **degree**); (8) **faller,** (see quot.); (9) **field,** formerly in baseball, the centerfield; (10) **floor,** the floor of a building next above the ground floor; (11) **girl,** a maid of lesser rank who assists a first maid, esp. in the more menial tasks of a household [cf. G. *das zweitemädchen* in the same sense]; (12) **-hand land,** (see quot.), *obs.;* (13) **low ground,** = **second bottom,** *obs.;* (14) **maid,** = **second girl;** (15) **man,** (*a*) an Indian sub-chief, *obs.*, (*b*) a man who assists a manservant or hired man, cf. **second girl, second maid;** (16) **papers,** the final papers granting citizenship to one who has applied for it; (17) **principal meridian,** (see quot. and cf. **principal meridian**), *obs.;* (18) **quality,** (see quot.), *obs.;* (19) **reader,** the member of a Christian Science church elected to read from the Bible in the Sunday service; (20) **section,** ?capital punishment, *rare;* (21) **soil,** (see quot.), *obs.;* (22) **summer,** (see quot.), *obs.;* (23) **table,** the table set and served after the first, often for children, servants, etc., also fig.; (24) **termer,** one serving a second term in a prison; (25) **work,** such household work as is done by a second girl or a second maid, *qq.v.*

(1) **1777** in *Amer. Sp.* XV. 390/1 He was sitting alone on a seckond bank of the Iland near the edge of the water. **1817** S. Brown *Western Gazetteer* 52 *Rising-Sun*—Is delightfully situated on the second bank of the Ohio. **1823** James *Exped.* I. 62 The second banks . . . are here raised about seventy feet. — (2) **1855** *Chi. W. Times* 29 March 1/4 The market at the Second Board, which was a strong one at the opening, closed 1–2 per cent off. **1909** Webster 1909/1 *Second board, . . .* the second call on exchanges . . . ; on the New York Stock Exchange,

the second printed list of sales, for the period from 12 M. to 2 P.M. — (3) **1827** R. Knight *Six Principle Baptists* 290 The Gloucester Second Church . . . was organized about 1780. — (4) **1863** *Statutes at Large* XII. 705 The second class embraces all mailable matter exclusively in print, and regularly issued at stated periods. **1917** *Patterson's Mag.* June 124/3 The government contemplates piling another burden on the publishers by forcing a parcel post rate on all second class matter beyond the third zone. **1946** *Chi. Sun-Times* 11 July 24/4 Second class, which is periodicals, newspapers and magazines, carried at subsidized rates, brings in 2.5 per cent of total revenue but costs 12.6 per cent of total expenses.

(5) **1843** *Hunt's Merch. Mag.* IX. 482 In the disbursements for 1843, are included two new long coaches, one mail-carriage, one second class car. **1883** *Harper's Mag.* Nov. 968/2 In this country first, second, and third class cars are not common on our railways. — (6) **1888** Dorsey *Midshipman Bob* 128 His class-mates backed him to a man, so did the second-classmen. — (7) (*a*) **1671** Sewall *Letter-Book* I. 18 Sir Bayly intends to see the College in the spring; in order to the taking of his 2d Degree. **1704** *Boston News-Letter* 24 July 4/1 Mr. Thomas Weld . . . took his Second Degree at Cambridge on the 5th Instant. **1734** in B. Pierce *Hist. Harvard* App. 137 Whosoever . . . shall . . . act contrary to any of these prohibitions . . . shall be liable to be denied his second degree. (*b*) **1796** in *Statutes of Va.* (1835) II. 5/6 All murder which shall be perpetrated by means of poison, or by lying in wait, or by any other kind of wilful, deliberate and premeditated killing . . . shall be deemed murder of the first degree; and all other kinds of murder shall be deemed murder of the second degree. **1821** Jefferson *Writings* I. 70 [In 1796] the Virginia legislature introduced the new terms of murder in the first and second degree. **1950** *Chi. Tribune* 19 Feb. 4/5 There are four other possible verdicts: second degree murder with life imprisonment the maximum penalty [etc.]. — (8) **1905** *Forestry Bureau Bul.* No. 61, 46 *Second faller*, the subordinate in a crew of fallers. (P[acific] C[oast] F[orest].) — (9) **1857** *Spirit of Times* 5 Sep. 4/2 G. H. Brooks, second base, J. A. Bogert, third base, S. Saunders, second field.

(10) **1846** E. Waylen *Reminiscences* 230 Meals were taken in a capacious dining room on the first floor. [Note:] Called the 'second-floor' in America. **1912** T. R. Sullivan *Heart of Us* 49 They climbed into a light, airy room occupying the entire second floor. — (11) **1871** Howells *Wedding Journey* 25 The human wave is beginning to sprinkle the pavement with cooks and second-girls. *c***1895** Norris *Vandover* 61 A respectable-looking second girl hurried past him carrying her prayer-book. — (12) **1893** *Scribner's Mag.* June 699/1 The days of 'looking' Government timber are wellnigh over. The land-looker is now engaged in estimating what is called 'second-hand land,' the land of private owners. — (13) **1771** *Va. Gazette* 7 Feb. 3/2 It is all first and second low Grounds, very level and will produce any Thing usually cultivated in this Colony. — (14) **1943** *Chi. D. News* 2 Aug. 1/5 A typewritten sheet giving . . . the duties of the second maid.

(15) (*a*) **1772** in *Travels Amer. Col.* 505 A young man who I had sent two Days ago with a Message to Emistisiguo and 2d Man of the Little Tallassies was Returned. (*b*) **1905** *Washington Star* 24 Nov. 20 Wanted—a thoroughly competent white second man. — (16) **1913** *Industrial Worker* (Spokane) 1 May 8/2 Zbrowsky was denied his second papers in Montesano recently. — (17) **1834** Peck *Gaz. Illinois* 93 The '*Second Principal Meridian*' is a line due north from the mouth of Little Blue river in Indiana. — (18) **1829** B. Hall *Travels N. Amer.* III. 220 The different kinds of cotton are, 'first quality white,' 'second quality white,' and 'yellow.' — (19) **1896** *N.Y. Tribune* 27 Sep. 11. 2/4 Those who had heretofore been known as pastors were hereafter to be known as readers, their titles to be First Reader and Second Reader, and were to be officially appointed by the church. **1947** *Christian Sci. Jrnl.* LXV. 330/1 [She] has just completed a term of three years' service as Second Reader in The Mother Church.

(20) **1838** Drake *Tales from Queen City* 32 It is rumored, perhaps without any foundation, that in cases of great emergency, more than one of these commanders, have seriously threatened a resort to the salutary influence of the 'second section.' — (21) **1857** *Ill. Agric. Soc. Trans.* II. 347 In some sections of the state, in digging wells, a 'second soil,' so called is found about eighteen or twenty feet below the surface, wherein wood, tree tops and bark of trees are imbedded in a black soil similar to the upper. — (22) **1808** Ashe *Travels* 194 The summer is not violently hot, being tempered by a perpetual breeze; and the autumn [in Ky.] is distinguished by the name of the Second Summer. — (23) **1850** *Cong. Globe* 11 March 500/2 Upon steamboats they [*sc.* Negroes] are seated at the 'second table.' **1856** *Ib.* 9 Aug. 2015/1 If we vote for Mr. Buchanan we shall come in at the second table, and can never expect to sit at the first table. — (24) **1889** *Columbus* (O.) *Dispatch* 25 Sep., The established belief [is] that second-termers are numerous.

(25) **1878** Cooke *Happy Dodd* 125 She would make a good child's nurse, or she could do second work.

For **Second Advent, second base, bottom, day,** see as main entries.

Second Advent.

1. *attrib.* Designating persons believing in the imminence of the second coming of Christ, or the doctrines, organizations, etc., of such persons.

1844 Rupp *Relig. Denominations* 668 Second Advent Believers. [Account] by N. Southard, Editor of the Midnight Cry. **1847** Lowell *Biglow P.* 1 Ser. iv. 61 An excellent deacon of my congregation (being infected with the Second Advent delusion) assured me [etc.]. **1860** Holmes *E. Venner* xxiv, Some of the Second-Advent preachers had been about, and circulated their predictions among the kitchen-population of Rockland. **1891** McClintock & Strong *Cyclo. Biblical Lit.* XI. 53/1 On the 18th of May, 1842, the 'Second Advent Association of New York City and Vicinity' was formed.

2. Second Adventism, the belief of the Second Adventists.

1880 *Harper's Mag.* Jan. 184/1 The year 1840 marked a new era in the progress of Second Adventism.

3. Second Adventist, =**Adventist.** Cf. **Millerite.**

1849 in Wellcome *Hist. Second Advent Message* 580 Wm. Miller, distinguished as the founder of the sect known as '*Second Adventists*, or *Millerites*,' recently died at his residence in the State of New York. **1891** Holmes *Over Teacups* 313 No melodramatic display of warring elements, such as the white-robed Second Adventist imagines, can meet the need of the human heart.

secondary school. A school intermediate between an elementary school and college, a high school.

1835 *S. Lit. Messenger* I. 275 Secondary schools . . . [teach] the rudiments of Arithmetic, Geography, English Grammar [etc.]. **1894** *Harper's Mag.* May 964/1 This principle . . . will make a great simplification in secondary-school programmes. **1945** *English Journal* March 137/1 At least four features of the situation demand attention in the secondary schools.

second base. *Baseball.*

1. The base furthest from the home plate.

1845 in *Appletons' Ann. Cyclo.* XXV. 77/2 The bases shall be from 'home' to second base, forty paces [etc.]. **1912** Mathewson *Pitching* 202 Sheckard flied out to Seymour, Kling being held on second base. **1949** *Telephone Reg.* (McMinnville, Ore.) 4 Aug. 2/5 He favored his left knee, which he injured in a slide into second base in a recent game.

attrib. **1867** *Ball Players' Chron.* 31 Oct. 1/1 In Gibney they have a well-known second base player—not an out-fielder.

2. The player stationed at second base. In full **second baseman.**

1856 *Spirit of Times* 20 Dec. 260/3 Wells, as second base, is excellent, and any balls that come in his range are almost sure to be caught. **1867** *Ball Players' Chron.* 4 July 1/4 Without making any movement to deliver, [Martin] would suddenly turn and face the second baseman. **1880** N. Brooks *Fairport Nine* 24 George Bridge, their second base, was the decentest boy of the gang. **1949** *Milwaukie* (Ore.) *Rev.* 28 July 4/2 The club is bolstered by the return to the lineup of Eddie Basinski, second baseman.

b. The position played by this player.

1867 *Ball Players' Chron.* 27 June 3/2 Mr. Olmsted at second base, and Messrs. Anderson and Hope in the field, were deserving of praise. **1886** *Outing* April 104/1 Terry, '85 of Yale, was offered the position of second base of the metropolitan nine. **1948** *Time* 3 May 20/1 He played second base and shortstop on the high-school team.

second bottom. The second or higher level of bottom land by a stream. Also **second bottom land.** Cf. **second bank.**

1691 in *Amer. Sp.* XV. 390/1 On ye second bottom of ye upper back Creek. **1788** Lett. in Imlay *Western Territory* (1797) 595 Next to these are what is called second bottoms, which are elevated plains, and gentle rising of the richest uplands, and as free from stone as the low or first bottom. **1808** F. Cuming *Western Tour* 377 When wide they [benches] constitute what are called bottoms, as first, second and third bottom counting from the river upwards. **1926** *Hutchinson* (Kans.) *News* 19 June, Fritz Tarnstrom of Roxbury, . . . has a good test crop of a new variety of wheat on second bottom land. . . . John Hahn of Inman has another very good test on second bottom land.

second day. 1. second-day dress, a dress worn by a bride on the day after her wedding. **2. second-day wedding,** (see quots.). Both *obs.*

(1) **1898** Hall *Aunt Jane* 163, I had on my 'second-day' dress, the prettiest sort of a changeable silk. — (2) *a***1860** Judd *Hist. Hadley* (1905) 238 There were occasionally, second-day weddings, or wedding festivities kept up the second day. **1877** Bartlett 566 *Second-Day Wedding*, a reception or evening party given by the parents of the bridegroom, or by the new-married couple in their own house, soon after their marriage.

secret 'sikrɪt, *n.* [f. Du. *sekreet*, a privy. "Thans [*c*1935] in N.-Ndl. alleen in zeer platte taal" (*WNT*).] A privy. *Obs.* — **1787** *Md. Gazette* 1 June 1/2 To be rented, a three story Brick House, . . . [with] a large Smoke House and Secret, a large yard [etc.].

*** secretary,** *n.*

1. *Secretary of Congress,* under the Articles of Confederation, the officer who acted as secretary to the Continental Congress. *Obs.*

1778 *Jrnls. Cont. Congress* XI. 611 Resolved, . . . that the Committee of Commerce, the Marine Committee, the Committee of Treasury, Board of War and Ordnance, and secretary of Congress, be authorized to increase the salary of their clerks. **1789** *Ann. 1st Congress* 34 The committee appointed the 13th of April to confer with a committee of the House of Representatives, upon the future disposition of the papers in the office of the late Secretary of Congress, made a report.

b. *Secretary of* (or *for*) *Foreign Affairs,* a title formerly applied to a federal officer now known as the Secretary of State.

1781 *Jrnls. Cont. Congress* XIX. 43 Resolved, That an office be forthwith established for the Department of Foreign Affairs . . . ; That there shall be a secretary . . . to be stiled 'Secretary for foreign affairs.' **1789** *Ann. 1st Congress* 51 Resolved, That the Secretary of Foreign Affairs under the former Congress be requested to peruse the said convention.

c. (*cap.*) Ellipt. for **Secretary of the Treasury, Secretary of State.** Often as a title.

1795 HAMILTON *Works* VII. 108 In this respect the Comptroller is a check upon the Secretary. **1861** *Charleston* (S.C.) *Mercury* 14 Feb. 2/5 The Secretary further says that nine or ten millions will be required before the 4th of March. **1865** *Nation* I. 706 Secretary Seward has advised the North Carolinians . . . to ratify the Constitutional Amendment. **1894** *Harper's Mag.* April 804/1 Secretary Carlisle issued a circular offering $50,000,000 ten-year five-per-cent. bonds for public subscription. **1950** *Time* 13 March 17/2 Secretary Acheson was in the drab, denlike hearing room on the Capitol's first floor to talk about next year's budget.

d. A secretary for a territory of the U.S.

1807 *Ann. 10th Congress* 1 Sess. 2813 Each of the Secretaries of the Mississippi, Indiana, Louisiana, and Michigan Territories, appointed under the authority of the United States [shall] be entitled to the annual sum of one thousand dollars. **1880** *Cimarron News & Press* 17 June 2/2 W. G. Ritch has been confirmed by the senate as secretary of the territory.

e. (*cap.*) In the names of cabinet members, as (1) **Secretary of Agriculture,** (2) **of commerce,** (3) **of Labor,** (4) **of State,** see as a main entry; (5) **of the Interior,** (6) **of the Navy,** (7) **of the Treasury,** (8) **of War,** (formerly sometimes **Secretary at War,** after British usage).

(1) **1889** *Stat. at Large* XXV. 659 The Department of Agriculture, shall be an Executive Department, under the supervision and control of a Secretary of Agriculture. **1938** WHITE *One Man's Meat* 14 Of course my turkey and I constitute a branch of farming which the Secretary of Agriculture does not necessarily take into consideration. — (2) **1903** *Outlook* LXXIII. 471/2 The special interest which has attached to the anti-trust legislation, and the powers conferred by it upon the new Secretary of Commerce. **1950** *Time* 27 Feb. 86/3 Secretary of Commerce Charles Sawyer welcomed bids for the Government-owned, World War I-spawned Inland Waterways Corp. — (3) **1913** *Chi. Record-Herald* 1 March 6/1 The Secretary of Labor will have many duties, including that of endeavoring to adjust industrial controversies. **1948** *Chi. D. News* 24 Aug. 18/3 The new Secretary of Labor, . . . announces that the 'closed shop' agreements . . . should be revived.

(5) **1849** *Whig Almanac 1850* 22/1 The head . . . the Secretary of the Interior, is appointed in the same manner as other heads of departments. [**1861** *N.Y. Herald* 1 Jan. 1/5 The position ostensibly assigned to him is claimed to be the Secretaryship of the Interior.] **1948** *Time* 11 Oct. 22/3 He promised to appoint, 'with great pleasure,' a Secretary of the Interior from the West. — (6) **1798** *Ann. 5th Congress* 584 Resolved, That this bill . . . [be entitled] 'An act to extend the privilege of franking letters and packets to the Secretary of the Navy.' **1868** HAWTHORNE *Notebooks* I. 84 When I asked him whether it would be well to make a naval officer Secretary of the Navy, he said, 'God forbid.' **1950** *Chi. Tribune* 1 March 1/8 This action . . . violated promises made to the witnesses by the committee, the secretary of the navy, and the secretary of defense. — (7) (*a*) **1789** *Ann. 1st Congress* 71 Whenever the Secretary of the Treasury shall be removed from office by the President of the United States, . . . the assistant shall . . . have the charge and custody of the records. **1946** *N. & Q.* Feb. 165/1 The Secretary of the Treasury ordered the needed paper. (*b*) **1861** *Charleston* (S.C.) *Mercury* 29 March 1/2 The Secretary of the Treasury of the Confederated States publishes the following important notices. **1865** *Ib.* 14 Jan. 1/1 The special report of the Secretary of the Treasury, . . . shows that there have been imported into the Confederacy . . . 8,632,000 pounds of meat. — (8) (*a*) **1778** J. ADAMS *Familiar Lett.* 355 The new secretary at war makes a vast parade of the number of men in their service by land and sea. **1789** *Ann. 1st Congress* I. 39 A report from the Secretary of War, on the negotiations of the Governor of the Western Territory with certain northern and northwestern Indians. **1843** CATLIN *Notes* II. (1848) 1 With a permission gained from the Secretary at War. **1950** *Time* 6 March 98/3 Afterward, when little 'Jemmy' Monroe became President, he offered Calhoun the job of Secretary of War. (*b*) **1862** *Charleston* (S.C.) *Mercury* 20 Nov. 1/2 We have great hope that, in the Hon. James A. Leddon a competent Secretary of War for the great emergencies upon the Confederate States, will be found.

2. secretary bookcase, a writing desk or escritoire the top of which serves for books.

1834 *Amer. R.R. Jrnl.* III. 726/1 Premium for Secretary Book Case. **1855** *Chi. W. Times* 18 Oct. 1/7 A secretary book case, of very handsome black walnut, . . . has six large drawers, . . . writing desk, etc.

As the last term in **cabinet, class, desk, field, Governor Winthrop, home secretary.**

Secretary of State.

1. A cabinet officer of the U.S. Government in charge of all foreign affairs.

1789 *Ann. 1st Congress* 90, I likewise nominate Thomas Jefferson, for Secretary of State. **1846** POLK *Diary* (1929) 62 Forty or fifty persons . . . called; among them the Russian Minister, Secretary of State and the Secretary of the Navy. **1925** BRYAN *Memoirs* 176, I next met him after I became Secretary of State. **1950** *World-Herald* (Omaha) 19 Feb. VI. 1/2 Wright County Republicans went on record as demanding the removal of Secretary of State Acheson.

b. An officer with corresponding duties in the cabinet of the Confederate States. *Obs.*

1863 *Harper's Wkly.* 7 Feb. 83/1 It takes the dispatches of rebel agents some seven months to come to hand, and the rebel Secretary of State naïvely mentions to one of his emissaries that his No. 2 has arrived, but that Nos. 1, 3, 4, 5, and 6 are still missing.

2. An officer of a state government whose chief duty is the making and keeping of records.

1803 *Mass. Reg.* 35 *John Avery,* Secretary of State.—Office, Floor of the New State-House. **1844** *Niles' Reg.* 10 Feb. 384/1 From the annual statement prepared at the secretary of state's office, we learn that 33 of the 35 officers in the state last year [etc.]. **1946** *Dly. Ardmoreite* (Ardmore, Okla.) 6 Dec. 7/7 Gov. Robert S. Kerr appointed Miss Manton secretary of state when Carter resigned in November.

*** Secret Service.** A branch of the U.S. Treasury Department concerned with discovering and preventing counterfeiting, with protecting the President, and, in wartime, with espionage.

1867 BAKER *Hist. U.S. Secret Service* 34 There is nothing in the Secret Service that demands a violation of honor, or a sacrifice of principle, beyond the ordinary rules of warfare. **1945** *Athol* (Mass.) *D. News* 14 May 6/2 Not since the lethargic days . . . has the Secret Service had to deal with any one like Truman. **1949** *Dly. Ardmoreite* (Ardmore, Okla.) 4 Dec. 5/2 To combat this the secret service was established on July 5, 1865.

attrib. **1880** LAMPHERE *U.S. Govt.* 66/2 The Secret Service Division sprung from an annual appropriation made for the prevention and punishment of counterfeiting. **1900** *Westm. Gaz.* 25 May 7/3 Secret service agent Brown took the accused man in charge [at San Francisco]. **1950** *Nature Mag.* March 168/1 The nation is divided into fifteen Secret Service Districts for the suppression of counterfeiting and related tasks.

*** section,** *n.*

1. In the public-land survey, a portion of land one mile square (640 acres), forming 1/36 of a township.

1785 *Jrnls. Cont. Congress* XXVIII. 209 The plats of the townships . . . shall be marked by subdivisions into sections of 1 mile square. **1849** CHAMBERLAIN *Ind. Gazetteer* 420 North of Eel river are about 40 sections of barrens intermixed with small prairies. **1950** *Chi. Tribune* 23 Feb. II. 2/4 On a typical small ranch, one section (one square mile) is owned in fee simple but its value is based on its grazing rights on 10 abutting sections.

Attrib. with **boundary, corner, map, road.**

1902 WHITE *Blazed Trail* 114 Officials had run careless lines through the country along the section-boundaries. — **1817** *Niles' Reg.* XII. 97/2 At the distance of every mile, between the township corners, *section* corners are established. **1947** *Mich. Hist.* Sep. 319 He traced it up to the section corner and discovered that the cruiser had signed his name on the tree. — **1882** *Nation* 14 Sep. 220/2 The section map . . . indicates that a portion of this tract had in 1880 from 6 to 11 inhabitants to the square mile. — **1877** RUEDE *Sod-House Days* 141 The supervisor was at the P.O. and informed me he wanted me to work on the road on Monday and Tuesday. That is to pay my poll tax. We are to work on the section road that is my southern boundary line.

b. Often followed by a number to indicate its position in a township.

1837 W. Jenkins *Ohio Gaz.* 119 Its territory consists of sections 5, 6, 7 [etc.]. in township 11, and range 21. **1903** *Indian Laws & Tr.* III. 8 Section sixteen shall become a part of the reservation heretofore set apart for the use and occupancy of the Torros band. **1949** *Sierra Club Bul.* June 111 Matthes Lake lies in sections 30 and 31, at the southern end of a U-shaped valley parallel with Matthes Crest and to the east.

c. section line, the boundary line of a section, often designating or alluding to a road that follows such a line.

1872 *Newton Kansan* 12 Sep. 2/4 The farmers . . . are leaving space for a road along the section lines. **1919** McCarter *Cornerstone* 22 He is trying to get Mrs. Helm and her son to shut up our road and force us to sell this little place to him and Mrs. Helm so they can run section-line roads. **1948** Jacobs *We Chose Country* 24 We bowled along, climbing past snatches of woods and the straight section-line roads to a high plateau.

2. A region or part of the country thought of as an area set apart by geographical or cultural lines, a quarter or district.

"Since the French Revolution this word has been much used here instead of *part, quarter,* &c." (Pickering).

1814 M. Carey *Olive Branch* 186 To sow discord, jealousy and hostility between the different sections of the union, was the first and grand step in their career. **1861** *N.Y. Herald* 7 Jan. 4/4 The slave states not only pay their debts, but pay them better than any other section of the country. **1950** *Dly. Ardmoreite* (Ardmore, Okla.) 1 March 8/1 Old-timers can't figure out the record lack of snow in some sections of the country.

3. *Railroad.* A division of a sleeping car constituting an upper and lower berth, or, when these are not made up, two double seats facing each other.

1866 *Pathfinder* (Boston) Dec. 30 Double or single berths or sections in sleeping cars. **1910** Raine *B. O'Connor* 11 Down the aisle to the vacant section opposite her [went] a procession whose tail was composed of protesting trainmen.

b. (See quot. 1890.)

1872 *Newton Kansan* 3 Oct. 3/2 The caboose and the next three cars to it of the 1st section was badly smashed up. **1890** *Railways of Amer.* 162 But the more usual way of handling extra trains, when circumstances will permit, is to let them precede or follow a regular train upon the same schedule. The train is then said to be run in 'sections,' and a ten minutes' interval is allowed between them. **1948** *Chi. Tribune* 11 April (Comics) 1 Ho! the second section! And no flagman out from the train we stopped.

c. (See quot. 1890.)

[**1851** Watkin *Trip* 76 Ultimately the railway was laid out with substantial and permanent works, as a single line of the six feet gauge, and opened in sections; the first section having been 'operated' in 1841, and the last only a few weeks back.] **1883** Sweet & Knox *Through Texas* 121 He superintended the hands working in that section. **1890** *Railways of Amer.* 156 Each of the supervisors of road has his assigned territory divided into 'sections,' from five to eight miles in length. **1949** *Chi. D. News* 18 Feb. 4/2, I also have worked on the section.

Attrib. with **boss, gang, hand, house.**

1870 *Terr. Enterprise* (Virginia, Nev.) 22 Oct. 3/1 The clothes of the section boss caught upon the brake . . . as he was in the act of jumping off. **1947** Lumpkin *Southerner* 163 The deacon was section boss on the railroad. — **1890** *Railways of Amer.* 156 At least twice a day track-walkers from the section-gangs pass over the entire line of road. **1949** *Chi. D. News* 2 Aug. 7/1 Murphy worked on section gangs during the summer. — **1873** *Newton Kansan* 27 Feb. 3/2 A drunken section hand . . . laid down upon the railroad track to take a nap. **1949** *Chi. D. News* 2 Aug. 7/1 An old Burlington Railroad section-hand thinks a young worker today has a better chance of rising to the presidency of the railroad than he did 40 years ago. — **1869** Wm. H. Jackson in *Time Exposure* (c1940) 183 Decided to board at the section house rather than cook ourselves. **1946** Thompson *Amer. Daughter* 16 Occasionally we passed through tiny country towns with their inevitable grain elevators, one-roomed dull-red depots, and companion section houses.

As the last term in **comic, fractional, half, reserve, reserved, school, second, sixteenth, sleeping, sports section.**

sectionalism ˌsɛkʃənl̩ˌɪzəm, *n.* Confinement of interest to a particular section, sectional feeling or interests.

1855 *N.Y. Wkly. Tribune* 14 July 4/3 As well attempt to reason with a north-east storm as with this narrow sectionalism. **1903** *Out West* March 370 This magazine . . . keeps its oar in for no sectionalism. **1949** *Américas* Sep. 13/1 Sectionalism has its . . . ideological, political, and social aspects.

sectionalist ˈsɛkʃənl̩ɪst, *n.* One who has excessive sectional feeling.

1858 W. P. Smith *Bk. Railway Celebrations* 258 Whatever disunionists or sectionalists may do or say—the more they try to tear us apart, the more the iron road and lightning wire must bind us together. **1862** in Dicey *6 Mos. Federal States* II. 86 There were abolition fanatics there [in the North], it was true—sectionalists, traitors, brothers of Southern secessionists. **1948** *Miss. Valley Hist. Rev.* Dec. 419 Shakespeare and Goethe, Milton and Moliere were likewise 'sectionalists.'

sectional party. A political party devoted primarily to the interests of one section.

1849 A. MacKay *Western World* I. 225 Perhaps the most purely sectional party in this country is that of the Nullifiers. **1858** Douglas in Logan *Great Conspiracy* 67, I am opposed to organizing a sectional party, which appeals to . . . Northern passion and prejudice against Southern institutions. **1902** G. C. Eggleston *D. South* 314 A strong political party at the North . . . was a strictly sectional party in its composition, having no existence anywhere at the South.

sectionize ˈsɛkʃənaɪz, *v.*

1. *tr.* To survey (land) into sections (sense **1.**) to facilitate disposing of it to individual settlers.

1828 *Laws of Texas* Nov. (B.), So much of the vacant lands of the republic [of Mexico] shall be surveyed and sectionized, as will be sufficient to satisfy all claims. **1949** *Surveying & Mapping* Jan.–Mar. 31/2 Long before Florida was sectionized by ranges and townships, rulers of the Old World bestowed favors on a selected few supporters by granting them titles to vast parcels of land in America.

2. To give (a political party) a sectional character. *Obs.*

1856 *Ill. State Reg.* (Springfield) 31 July 1/3 Our efforts to prevent the great American party from being sectionized or abolitionized have been successful.

3. *absol.* Of Indians: To permit reservation lands to be divided off into sections for purposes of white settlement. Also **sectionizing,** *n. Obs.*

1871 *Rep. Indian Affairs* (1872) 185 [Various tribes] were induced either to sectionize, or in some way to admit white settlers. **1873** Beadle *Undevel. West* 399 He is the only Choctaw in the district who is in favor of sectionizing and admitting white immigration.

securityship sɪˈkjurətɪˌʃɪp, *n.* The condition of standing security for another person. *Obs.* — **1797** *Steele P.* I. 149 He has engaged in it purely to exculpate him from his Security Ship for his brothers. **1854** Benton *30 Years' View* I. 117/2 [Nathaniel Macon] was opposed to securityships, and held that no man ought to be entangled in the affairs of another.

***sedan,** *n.* An automobile having both the front and the back seats inclosed in the same compartment. Also attrib. — **1922** *Short Stories* Feb. 98/1 The sedan had been equipped with an exhaust foot warmer or heater. **1948** *Herald-Press* (St. Joseph, Mich.) 14 Aug. 5/1 Besides making some substantial changes in its present sedan models it plans to put a hard top convertible into production.

* **sedge,** *n.* Also * **sage.**

1. *S.* =**sedge grass.**

1799 Weld *Travels* 79 This sedge, as it is called, is a sort of coarse grass, so hard that cattle will not eat it, which springs up spontaneously, in this part of the country [in Va.] on the ground that has been left waste. **1805** Parkinson *Tour* 53 The whole of the different fields were covered with . . . what is called sedge—something like speargrass upon the poor limestone in England. **1950** *Time* 13 March 69/1 Ames Plantation [is] a 27,000-acre expanse of quail-rustled sedge and woodland with a great ante-bellum mansion.

2. In combs.: (1) * **sedge boat,** a boat for transporting sedge, *obs.;* (2) **broom,** *S.* a broom for sweeping the floor made of broom sedge; (3) **field,** *S. attrib.* in the sense of an old or worn-out field covered with broom sedge; (4) **grass,** see as a main entry; (5) **ground,** ground overgrown with sedge or broom sedge; (6) **hen,** a local name for the clapper rail.

(1) **1839** *Knickerb.* XIII. 503 Sedge-boats could pass with their sails set. **1843** *Ib.* XXII. 33 Here two negro boatmen . . . had consented to . . . row us out in their new sedge-boat. — (2) [**1849** *Rep. Comm. Patents: Agric.* (1859) 462 Corn brooms are driving broom-sedge, as an article for sweeping floors, out of every humble dwelling in the Union.] **1945** Botkin *My Burden* 62 Nice dirt floors was the style then, and we used sage brooms. Took a string and tied the sage together and had a nice broom outen that. — (3) **1867** Harris *Sut Lovingood* 30 I'se allers intu sum trap whut wudn't ketch a saidge-field sheep. **1905** N. Davis *Northerner* 42 That sort of talk is what Hugh calls 'sedge-field Democracy.'

(5) **1667** *Plymouth Rec.* I. 95 Graunted unto James Clarke a certaine . . . p[ar]te of the pond or sedge ground. **1740** *Mayflower Descendant* XI. 5 Richard Mayo & Rebecca Mayo . . . [sold] that lot

of Medow or sedge ground lying in Eastham. **1910** C. HARRIS *Eve's Husband* 30 That look of relief and timid animation, like signs of early spring upon the poor brown sedge-ground of an old field. — **(6) 1888** TRUMBULL *Names of Birds* 127 At Pocomoke City, Md., and at Eastville, Va., Sedge-Hen. **1890** *St. Nicholas* June 638/1 We got forty-two sedge-hens, on a high tide. **1917** *Birds of Amer.* I. 204.

As the last term in **Carey's, dry spiked, fox, New England, swamp sedge.**

***sedge grass.** Also ***sage grass.** *S.* (See quot. 1903 and cf. **broom sedge.**)

1886 *Consular Rep.* Jan. 40 Those hundreds of thousands of acres of once valuable Southern lands . . . [are] now lying to waste in worthless 'sage grass.' **1902** MOORE *Songs & Stories* 21 With a bundle of 'sage-grass' in his arms, as evidence that he had been on the errand on which he had been sent. **1903** *D.N.* II. 328 *Sage-grass*, sedge-grass. Also called 'broom-sage.' [s. e. Mo.] **1949** *Chi. Tribune* 27 Feb. VII. 1/1 It must be a very special kind of dog that will run swiftly thru sage grass, briars, cornstalks and other hampering vegetation, smelling out the pretty little striped birds.

Sedition Act, Law. A law of July 14, 1798, passed by the Federalist-controlled Congress to suppress opposition to the government. *Obs.*

1798 *Newport Mercury* 24 July 2/2 (*heading*), Sedition Act. **1800** *Aurora* (Phila.) 19 May (Th.), He replied that he was not at liberty to say—we had a sedition law—which will soon be done away. **1814** J. ADAMS *Works* VI. 518 If these things are so in Virginia, . . . where the sedition act, the gag law, was so unpopular; where can we look . . . [for] a candid freedom of the press? **1942** PADOVER *Jefferson* 260 Perhaps the most scandalous case under the Sedition Act took place in Jefferson's own Virginia.

***see,** *v.*

1. *Not to be able to see it*, to be unable to see the propriety, rightness, etc., in (a situation, policy, etc.). *Colloq.* or *slang.*

1850 *Calif. Courier* (S.F.) 14 Nov. 2/2 This may be all right—but if it is, we cannot see it. **1877** RUEDE *Sod-House Days* 8 The hack driver wanted us to go with him to Osborne, but the fare was $3.50 (trunks extra) and we 'could not see it.' **1945** MARSHALL *Santa Fe* 98 Fred then tried to interest the Burlington in his idea [but] the Burlington couldn't see it. [**1950** *Chi. Tribune* 17 Feb. 4/5 Some of his own party can't see Truman either.]

2. *tr.* To bribe (persons), to interview for the purpose of influencing, esp. by some form of bribery. *Slang.*

1867 *Ball Players' Chron.* 12 Dec. 4/2 This, that or the other 'professional' is 'seen'—that is the professional term for the act of bribery—and lo and behold! the second game between the rival clubs is marked by a signal defeat. **1906** *N.Y. Ev. Post* 8 Jan. 7 When a corporation desires legislation, that is, legislation that requires that legislators should be 'seen,' it sends its bill to Albany, not infrequently in charge of an ex-member. **1927** *Scribner's Mag.* March 269/2 It was found that most of the State's witnesses who could identify them . . . had been 'seen,' which means being bought off.

3. To understand (a person). *Colloq.*

1872 E. EGGLESTON *End of World* xxiii. 158 '[I] See yer,' said Bill, trying in vain to draw his coat. **1873** BEADLE *Undevel. West* 369 'Marshal's got a good thing, though.' 'I *see* you; best place to make money in the United States.'

4. To forecast or prophesy. *Colloq.*

1927 *Boston Herald* 19 Sep., 58 seats seen for Cosgrave.

5. *To go to see a man*, and variants (see quots.). *Slang.*

1867 *Ball Players' Chron.* 12 Sep. 3/1 Although they were all out, at the bases, and the rest of our nine having gone to see a man there was nobody to take the bat. **1942** BERREY & VAN DEN BARK *Amer. Thesaurus Slang* 102 *Go for a drink.* . . . Go see a dog,—a dog about a man or a man about a dog. **1948** *Chi. Tribune* 21 Mar. (Comics) 15 I'm in a rush—gotta see a dog about a man!

seecatch ˈsikætʃ, *n.* [Russ. *sekach.*] An adult male fur seal. — **1881** H. W. ELLIOTT *Rep. Seal Isl. Alaska* 42 The 'see-catchie' which have held the harems from the beginning to the end of the season, leave for the water. **1884** GOODE *Fisheries* I. 77 One old 'See-catch' was pointed out to me . . . as an animal that was long known to the natives as a regular visitor.

seecawk ˈsikɔk, *n.* (See quot. 1891.) *Obs.* — **1879** *Amer. Punch* Nov. 121/2 Indian Meal.—The repast of the buffalo-steak, fried dog, or baked seecawk. With us it is ground corn. **1891** *Cent.* 5464/1 seecawk . . . [Cree Indian.] The common American skunk, *Mephitis mephitica.*

***seed,** *n.*

1. (See quot.) *Rare.*

1825 JOHN NEAL *Bro. Jonathan* II. 73 'Hello, you! major! — where's the seed?' Here 'tis, answered the driver, taking out the keg of powder.

2. (See quot. 1851.) *Slang. Obs.* [App. f. ***hayseed.** Cf. *EDD* 6, "a term of contempt applied to a person."]

1849 *Yale Tomahawk* 27 Nov., But we are 'seeds' whose rowdy deeds Make up the drunken tale. **1851** HALL *College Words* 266 *Seed.* In Yale College this word is used to designate what is understood by the common cant terms, 'a youth'; 'case'; 'bird.' **1852** *Yale Tomahawk* May (Hall), Each one a bold seed, well fit for the deed.

3. In combs.: (1) ***seed bag,** (see quots.), *obs.;* (2) **Baptist,** (see quot.), *obs.;* (3) ***bed,** *S.* a small, specially prepared plot or area in which sweet potatoes are placed to produce draws, cf. ***draw,** *n.*[2] **2;** (4) **cache,** a cache for seed; (5) ***cake,** =**cottonseed cake;** (6) **catalogue,** a mail order catalogue in which seeds are advertised for sale; (7) **cigar,** a cigar made from seed leaf tobacco; (8) **cookie,** a cookie that has caraway seed sprinkled on it; (9) **oil mill,** a mill in which cottonseed is processed; (10) **planter,** a device for planting seeds,

Early (*c*1875) form of seed planter or sower

obs.; (11) **sower,** a mechanical implement for sowing seed; (12) **spot,** (see quot.); (13) **store,** a store which specializes in selling seed; (14) **tick,** any one of various ticks, esp. the cattle tick, in its first or young stage; (15) **tick coffee,** any one of various coffee substitutes in use in the South during the Civil War, *obs.;* (16) **warehouse,** a seed store, a warehouse in which seed is stored; (17) **year,** (see quot.).

(1) 1864 GESNER *Coal, Petrol.* (1865) 32 To prevent communication between any particular portion of the well and the pumping tube, a bag of linseed, called a 'seed bag,' is sent down to the required place. This bag, encircling the tube, soon swells . . . , and forms a water-tight joint. **1890** *Harper's Mag.* Oct. 727/2 He went to Tarentum, witnessed the methods of boring for salt, and the exclusion by 'seed bags' of fresh water and petroleum. — **(2) 1839** CASWALL *America* 314 A miserable sect of Seed Baptists, or Snake Baptists, is said to exist in the west, who carry the Calvinistic system to a tremendous length. They hold that all mankind are divided into two classes, the seed of the woman and the seed of the serpent. The seed of the woman are necessarily saved, and the seed of the serpent necessarily lost. — **(3) 1837** WILLIAMS *Florida* 111 The potato is planted in seed beds. — **(4) 1917** WILL & HYDE *Corn Among Indians* 290 The Mandan seed ears were carefully braided and dried by themselves, and were then stored with extra care in a special seed-cache.

(5) 1881 *Harper's Mag.* Oct. 726/2 The mass of kernels left is made into seed-cake, a most desirable food for stock. — **(6) 1907** *Suburban Life* Jan. 30/2 Send for a long list of seed catalogues. **1949** *Nat. Geog. Mag.* Aug. 164 Our Summer Crookneck of today, named as a variety in seed catalogues as early as 1828, appears to be the same as a squash described by Champlain in 1605. — **(7) 1892** *York Co. Hist. Rev.* 47 J. S. Overbaugh & Co., manufacturers of Fine Seed and Havana Cigars. — **(8) 1861** STOWE *Pearl Orr's Isl.* I. 26 She gave it nuthin but these 'ere little seed cookies. — **(9) 1881** *Harper's Mag.* Oct. 726/2 There are now fifty-nine seed oil mills in the South.

(10) 1850 *Rep. Comm. Patents 1849* 151 Having thus fully described my improved grain and seed planter. **1863** *Rep. Comm. Patents 1861* I. 313 The attachment to hand corn or seed planters of a tube [etc.]. — **(11) 1848** *De Bow's Review* VI. 133 Seed-Sowers, &c. **1874** *Vt. Bd. Agric. Rep.* II. 236 Sow seed with a seed sower at the rate of four pounds per acre. — **(12) 1901** *Forestry Bureau Bul.* No. 61, 20 *Seed-spot*, a small area, usually in a burn or in an opening in the forest, which is sown with tree seed. — **(13) 1833** A. FERGUSSON *Notes Tour*

U.S. 21, I frequently visited the *seed-store* of Mr Thorburn. **1947** *Democrat* 16 Oct. 4/4 It is today in a state of near ruin, with feed and seed stores occupying the first floor. — **(14) 1705** BEVERLEY *Virginia* IV. 66 Seed-Ticks are no where to be met with, but in the track of Cattle. **1889** CUSTER *Tenting on Plains* 139 What was most aggravating were two pests of that region, the seed-tick and the chigger. **1917** KEPHART *Camping* I. 255 The meanest ticks to get rid of are the young, which are known as 'seed-ticks.'

(15) [**1865** in RIDLEY *Battles* (1906) 478 The old woman asked us if we would have sweet potato coffee. Rye, okra seed, parched wheat and meal coffees are our national substitutes for the pure bean.] **1888** *Cent. Mag.* Sep. 266/1 With 'seed-tick' coffee and ordinary brown sugar costing fabulous sums and almost impossible to be obtained, it is small matter of wonder that the unsatisfied appetite of the rebel sharpshooter . . . often impelled him . . . to call a parley with the Yankee across the line. — **(16) 1863** *Horticulturist* Jan. 6 (*advt.*), Alfred Bridgeman, Seed Warehouse, Etc., 876 Broadway New York. **1874** *Rep. Comm. Agric. 1873* 213 The department is not a seed-warehouse. — **(17) 1905** *Forestry Bureau Bul.* No. 63, 7 The year of abundant seeding is called a seed year.

b. In the names of, or with reference to, plants: (1) ∗**seed box,** a North American plant, *Ludwigia alternifolia*, having a boxlike seed vessel; (2) **cane,** (see quot. 1892); (3) ∗**corn,** (*a*) grains of Indian corn for planting, also attrib., (*b*) *to make seed corn off one*, to get the better of one, *colloq.;* (4) **cucumber,** the single-seed cucumber, *Sicyos angulatus;* (5) **forest,** (see quot.); (6) **hemp,** (see quot. 1862); (7) ∗**leaf,** broad-leaved tobacco used for cigar wrappers, a variety of tobacco having exceptionally broad leaves, in full **seed-leaf tobacco,** also attrib.; (8) **squash,** a squash kept for its seed; (9) **tree,** (see quot. 1905).

(1) 1817–8 EATON *Botany* (1822) 341 *Ludwigia alternifolia*, seed box. . . . Damp. **1843** TORREY *Flora N.Y.* I. 237. **1893** *Amer. Folk-Lore* VI. 142 Seed-box. West Va. — **(2) 1829** SHERWOOD *Gaz. Georgia* (ed. 2) 255 The stacks or banks in which seed cane is preserved during winter, are called mattresses. **1892** *Mod. Lang. Notes* Nov. 393 *Seed cane*—the seed or plant cane . . . of the first year's growth.—Also the cane reserved for planting. — **(3)** (*a*) **1619** *Va. House of Burgesses* 17 Yet are wee at this tyme very much unprovided of any good seed-corn. **1831** HOLLEY *Texas* (1833) 103 They were compelled . . . to obtain their seed-corn over land. **1948** *Durant* (Okla.) *D. Democrat* 1 July 5/1 Farmers will be able to see just about everything imaginable in the way of seed corn experiments. (*b*) **1845** HOOPER *Simon Suggs' Adv.*, There aint nobody round here kin make seed corn off o' me at cards. — **(4) 1792** IMLAY *Western Territory* 211 Papaw. This fruit grows upon a tree from twelve to twenty-six feet high. It is in shape more like a seed cucumber than any thing else. It is ripe about midsummer. **1890** WIGGIN *Timothy's Quest* 199 We're goin' to pickle seed cowcumbers to-morrer.

(5) 1905 *Forestry Bureau Bul.* No. 61, 20 *Seed forest*, a forest composed wholly or mainly of trees grown from seed. — **(6) 1765** WASHINGTON *Diaries* I. 213 Began to pull the Seed Hemp—but was not sufficiently ripe. **1862** *Rep. Comm. Patents 1861: Agric.* 114 The male [hemp] is called the blossom-hemp, and the female the seed-hemp. — **(7) 1852** *Hunt's Merch. Mag.* XXVII. 555 The 'seed leaf' is raised on the Miami River. **1895** *Dept. Agric. Yrbk. 1894* 145 The seed-leaf, or Havana, tobacco is produced in such quantities and such excellence as to give a distinct character to localities in Massachusetts, Connecticut [etc.]. **1910** MARK TWAIN *Speeches* 267 (R.), I bought what was called a seedleaf cigar with a Connecticut wrapper. — **(8) 1825** NEAL *Bro. Jonathan* I. 188 A hanging shelf . . . loaded with cheeses; ropes of onions . . . seed-squashes. — **(9) 1896** *Vt. Agric. Rep.* XV. 87 They always leave a sufficient number of seed trees. **1905** *Forestry Bureau Bul.* No. 61, 20 *Seed tree*, any tree which bears seed; specifically a tree which provides the seed for natural reproduction.

c. *in the seed*, said of cotton that has not been ginned.

1829 A. SHERWOOD *Gaz. Georgia* (ed. 2) 259 Suppose, again, that government should erect at every man's door a Tariff Cotton Gin, which should give every man as much ginned cotton as he delivered in the seed. **1833** in BASSETT *Plantation Overseer* 54 You wanted to now how much coten you had in the seede.

As the last term in **ague, Anguilla, basswood, bird, black, bur, cotton, fever and ague, flax, gourd, green, gulf, hay, heart, Hogan, jump, jumping, lop, manzanita, meeting, moon, mustard, Osage orange, persimmon, pumpkin, Shaker, stick, two, wooden cucumber seed.**

∗**seed,** *v. Sports. tr.* In a tournament, to arrange contestants and teams in such a way that there is little possibility that the best teams or players may meet in the early contests.

1909 WEBSTER. **1924** in *Word Study* XXI. (1946) May 5/1 This year for the first time the draw has been seeded. **1950** *Chi. Tribune* 16 March IV. 1/8 The team that was seeded second has won four of the last five tournaments.

∗**seeding,** *a.* **1. seeding machine,** (see quot. 1876). **2. seeding plow,** (see quot. 1876). Both *obs.*

(1) 1831 *21st Congress* 2 Sess. H.R. Doc. No. 50, 3 Planting, seeding, mowing, and thrashing machines. **1876** KNIGHT 2088/1 *Seeding-machine* . . . an implement for sowing seed. The term, in its general sense, may include machines for planting in hills, drills, or broadcast, but it is confined more usually to machines for distributing seed in drills or broadcast. — **(2) 1862** *Rep. Comm. Patents 1861: Agric.* 643 Ploughs, Subsoil, . . . Plough, Seeding. **1876** KNIGHT 2088/2 *Seeding-plow*, a plow with a box, which drops or scatters seed in the furrow or on the fresh-turned earth.

∗**seedling,** *n.* As the last term in **Dearborn's, Virginia seedling.**

∗**seedy,** *a.* **1.** (See quot. 1851.) *Slang. Obs.* **2. seedy buckberry,** (see quot.).

(1) 1848 *Yale Gallinipper* Nov., And snowballs falling thick and fast As oaths from seedy senior crowd. **1850** *Yale Battery* Feb., A *seedy* Soph beneath a tree, practicing *Trigonometry.* **1851** HALL *College Words* 267 *Seedy*, rowdy, riotous, turbulent. — **(2) 1894** *Amer. Folk-Lore* VII. 93 *Andromeda ligustrina* . . . seedy buckberry, West. Va.

∗**seek,** *v. tr.* To endeavor to experience (religion). Also absol. *Colloq.*

[**1824** SINGLETON *Letters* 75 With the field-slaves [in Va.], Sunday is usually a holiday; wherein they deck themselves for frolic, or for their unintelligible methodist meetings; where those, who are tender in spirit, are said to be 'seeking.'] **1881** MCLEAN *Cape Cod Folks* 155 As for Rebecca, they said she had given up 'seekin' religion,' and had returned to the world. **1898** DUNBAR *Folks from Dixie* 19 You don't mean to tell me dat you's gwin 'bout heah seekin' wid yo' har tied up in ribbon? . . . ef yo' wants yo' soul saved, tek it off.

∗**seeker,** *n.* One seeking for religion. *Colloq.*

1801–3 J. LYLE *Diary* (MS) 39 When I spoke to seekers I cautioned them aginst depending on a Jesus yet unknown. **1836** GILMAN *Recoll.* (1838) 270 (*footnote*), Persons of colour . . . become *seekers* in any church, and under any leader they prefer. **1890** *Harper's Mag.* Jan. 285/2 Every negro in the county was there— . . . hardened sinners who had never even been seekers at the mourners' bench—they were all there.

As the last term in **gold, health, home, land seeker.**

seepweed ˈsipˌwid, *n.* [∗*seep* + ∗*weed.*] A low, smooth-leaved shrub, *Suaeda intermedia*, of the alkali regions of the West, thought to be an indication of ground water. — **1931** DAYTON *Western Browse Plants* 36 Several undershrubby species of seepweed, often called sea blite (*Dondia* spp.) and of molly (*Kochia* spp.), notably green molly (*K. americana*), furnish a fairly copious supply of small leaves and slender twigs of moderate palatability in dry, saline areas of the West. **1938** GOODDING *Native & Exotic Plants* 60 Dondia spp.—Seepweed.

seepy ˈsipɪ, *a.* (See quot.) *Colloq.* — **1859** BARTLETT 393 Seepy land is land under cultivation that is not well drained. Maryland and Virginia.

see-saw pan. (See quot.) *Obs.* Cf. **bascule pan, tilt pan.** — **1833** SILLIMAN *Man. Sugar Cane* 100 The syrup flows, readily, into the evaporating vessels—which are the . . . bascule pans, called also, tilt or see-saw pan.

sego ˈsigo, *n.* [Shoshonean Indian.] A showy-flowered perennial plant, *Calochortus nuttalli*, or its edible bulb (see also quot. 1875). Also **sego lily.**

1851 HOWE *Hist. Coll. Great West* 432 Hogs fatten on a succulent bulb or tuber, called the Seacoe, or Seegose Root, which is highly esteemed as a table vegetable by the Mormons. **1852** STANSBURY *Gt. Salt Lake* 160 *Sego* . . . is much used by the Indian tribes as an article of food. **1875** *Amer. Naturalist* IX. 18 The general Indian name of 'Sego' is applied indiscriminately to all the edible bulbs of [s. Utah]. **1947** *L.A. Times* 2 Jan. I. 2/1 Utah's beautiful float depicted a beehive and the flower of the State of Utah, the sego lily.

∗**segregate,** *v. tr.* (See quot.) *Obs.* — **1881** RAYMOND *Mining Gloss., Segregate*, Pac. To separate the undivided joint ownership of a mining claim into smaller individual 'segregated' claims.

∗**segregation,** *n.* (See quot.) *Obs.* — **1866** *Ore. State Jrnl.* 6 Jan. 3/1 Divorces are now called 'Segregations.'

segt sekt, *n.* [App. f. Du. *zicht*, reaping hook.] (See quot.) *Obs.* — **1775** ROMANS *Nat. Hist. Florida* 178, I would advise the introduction of the short scythe and hook, called in New York government segt and mat hook.

segundo seˈgundo, *n.* (See quot. 1944.)

1903 ADAMS *Log Cowboy* 299 Flood inquired if there was any sub-foreman, or segundo as they were generally called. **1944** ADAMS *W. Words* 140 segundo. . . . Spanish, meaning *second, immediately following the first.* The assistant trail boss, or second in command. **1949** *Boston Sun. Globe Mag.* 3 April 1/2 What have you got a segundo for?

*__seine,__ *n.* As the last term in **drag, gill, purse seine.**

*__seiner,__ *n.* A seine boat. Cf. **purse seiner.** — **1880** *Harper's Mag.* Aug. 340/1 There were . . . trawlers, draggers, riggers, [and] seiners. **1906** J. B. Connolly *Out of Gloucester* 8 She's a seiner out of Gloucester.

*__select,__ *a.* In combs.: (1) **select council,** the upper of two legislative bodies which together form a city council; (2) **councilman,** a member of a select council; (3) **court,** in N. Eng., a court of selectmen, *obs.;* (4) **man,** see as a main entry; (5) **school,** a school that secures its pupils chiefly from select or well-to-do families (see also quot. 1898), also **select boarding school;** (6) **townsman,** in N. Eng., a selectman, *obs.;* (7) **watch,** *N. Eng.* a body of night watchmen selected to patrol the streets of a town and serve as policemen, *obs.*

(1) **1796** *Phila. Ordinances* (1812) 90 The said freemen shall . . . also elect, by ballot, twelve persons . . . to be members of the select council. **1822** *Mass. Laws* VIII. 735 The administration [in Boston] . . . shall be vested in . . . one select Council, . . . to be denominated the Board of Aldermen; and one more numerous Council, . . . to be denominated the Common Council; which Boards in their joint capacity, shall be denominated the City Council. — (2) **1892** *York Co. Hist. Rev.* 14 Mr. Stauffer is a native of this city and is select councilman for eight years. — (3) **1677** *Plymouth Laws* 184 Complaint is made that the order of Court made June 1675 concerning Celect Courts that there should be but two in a towne annually [etc.]. **1681** *Ib.* 192 It is enacted by this Court That each Towne of this Gov[e]r[n]ment doe provide a booke wherein shall be entered all those orders of Court as are or shalbe made for direction of said Celect Courts by the Secretary.

(5) **1831** Peck *Guide* 246 Belleville Academy . . . is a select boarding school for boys. **1898** C. O. Parmenter *Hist. Pelham Mass.* 229 From 1825 to 1850 it was not uncommon to have a term of school during the autumn for the more advanced pupils, which was termed a 'select school.' **1903** *Cong. Directory* (57th Congress Sess.) 21 Attended common and select schools there. — (6) **1648** *Suffolk Deeds* III. 454 Benjamine Ward doth hereby binde himself . . . to pay vnto . . . ye present Select Townesmen of Boston . . . three pounds per Annm. **1649** *Springfield Rec.* I. 215 The Select Townsmen shal have full power and authority to Lay out all common Highways. **1664** *Ib.* II. 55 No Inhabitant shall sell or in any manner pass away his house lott . . . before he hath made the Select Townsmen acquaynted who his Chapman is. — (7) **1699** *Boston Rec.* 238 And it was then unanimusly agreed by all the above sd. Justices & Selectmen that a Select watch was most sutable for this town. **1707** *Ib.* 43 Voted the continuance and Support of the Select watch for the year ensueing.

selectman sə'lɛktmən, *n.*

1. In N. Eng., one of a board of town officers elected to execute the orders of the town meeting.

1635 in Frothingham *Hist. Charlestown, Mass.* 51 An order [was] made by the inhabitants of Charlestowne at a full meeting for the government of the Town by Selectmen. **1776** M'Robert *Tour* 24 Boston . . . is governed by seven men chosen yearly, called *select men.* **1885** *Boston Jrnl.* 8 Jan. 1/6 The Selectmen [of Watertown] have voted to protest against the action of Cambridge in using the streets of the town to lay out their Stony Brook water main. **1948** *Reader's Digest* May 23/2 The selectmen are handling town business in a freight car down where the station was.

2. (See quot. 1789.) *Obs.*

1789 Anburey *Travels* II. 236 *Select Men* . . . are a kind of overseers to their meeting-houses, who regulate the affairs of the parish, and report persons for non-attendance at worship, compelling those walking in the streets, or travellers, on a Sunday, to go to some place of worship. **1804** *Ga. Republican* 15 May 4/2 The select men of the Church and society of Midway will receive proposals.

*__self-,__ *prefix.* In combs.: (1) **self-addressed,** *a.* addressed to oneself; (2) **binder,** a harvesting machine which binds into bundles the grain which it cuts; (3) **binding,** *a.* denoting a harvesting machine that binds as well as cuts grain; (4) **boarder,** one who provides and prepares his own food, also **self-boarding;** (5) **cocker,** a self-cocking firearm, esp. a revolver; (6) **cocking,** *a.* denoting a pistol or revolver the hammer of which can be raised and released by pulling the trigger; (7) **feeder,** in mining, a device which automatically supplies ore to the stamp mortars of a stamp mill; (8) **heater,** a type of stove, *obs.;* (9) **hunt,** *v.* of a dog, to hunt without the direction of a trainer or owner; (10) **made lawyer,** a lawyer having no scholastic legal training; (11) **made man,** a man who has attained success by his own efforts; (12) **poise,** poise attained through self-command, also transf.; (13) **propeller,** an engine or machine that propels itself; (14) **raker,** an attachment for a harvesting machine for raking and depositing the cut grain in convenient piles, a harvester having such an attachment; (15) **rising flour,** flour from wheat, buckwheat or corn to which baking powder and salt have been added in the proper proportion for biscuits, griddlecakes, etc.; (16) **rocker,** a chair provided with springs that assist in keeping it in motion when set to rocking.

(1) **1904** *Delineator* Dec. 1084 If you will send a stamped self-addressed envelope, we will tell you where you can take a course. **1949** *Ev. Northwestern* (Chi.) 11 April 1/3 A stamped, self-addressed envelope should be enclosed for the return of the manuscript. — (2) **1877** Ruede *Sod-House Days* 113 Henry and John went to see a selfbinder at work. **1943** Crow *Amer. Customer* 186 The machine bore little resemblance to a modern self binder which had not yet been dreamed of. — (3) **1883** *Scientific Amer.* 3 March 138/3 An improved bundle separating attachment for self-binding harvesters has been patented. — (4) **1849** Chamberlain *Ind. Gazetteer* 60 The

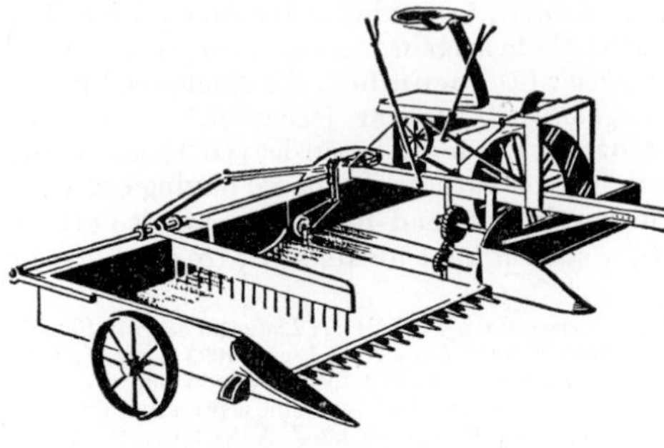

Early (*c*1868) type of self-binder

expense for board is materially lessened by associations for the purpose, also by individual self-boarding. **1885** (letterhead of N.Y. State Normal & Training School), Board, fuel, washing, lights, $3 to $4 per wk. Self-boarders can live much cheaper.

(5) [**1863** *Battle-Fields of the South* I. 125 An Adam's self-cocker (unloaded).] **1902** White *Blazed Trail Stories* 150 It was wonderful work, rattling fire, quicker than a self-cocker even. — (6) **1880** *Cimarron News & Press* 23 Dec. 3/1 Mr. T. O. Boggs of Tramperos, while in the act of drawing a self-cocking pistol from his pocket, accidentally discharged it. **1902** Hulbert *Forest Neighbors* 161 Four shots, as fast as the self-cocking revolver could pour the lead into his body. — (7) **1876** Raymond *8th Rep. Mines* 48 The adoption of self-feeders reduces the expenses of treatment of ores to about $1 per ton. **1882** *47th Congress* 1 Sess. H.R. Ex. Doc. No. 216, 587 The mechanism . . . is driven by the cam shaft similarly to the self-feeders, over which so much ingenuity has been expended to regulate the delivery of ore to the mortars. — (8) **1903** *N.Y. Sun* 22 Nov., A social reunion around the 'self-heater' where they played as children. — (9) **1768** Washington *Diaries* I. 284 The hounds havg. started a Fox in self huntg., we followed. **1770** *Ib.* 369 Found some dogs that were self hunting.

(10) **1852** Fleischman *Wegweiser* 146 Hütet Euch dabei vor sogenannten *Selfmade Lawyers* (Winkeladvokaten), sondern wendet Euch an einen Rechtsgelehrten. — (11) **1832** *Cong. Deb.* 2 Feb. 277 In Kentucky, almost every manufactory known to me is in the hands of enterprising self-made men. **1948** *Sat. Ev. Post* 16 Oct. 166/3 He was a self-made man, with the usual hard outer shell and the usual tenderness beneath. — (12) **1854** Lippincott *Haps & Mishaps* 2 There is a maturity of thought . . . a self-poise about him, which impress you. **1860** Emerson *Conduct of Life* 177 A self-poise belongs to every particle. **1884** *Cent. Mag.* Jan. 453/2 He displayed excellent qualifications for either soldier or civilian—self-poise, a quick intelligence, close application. — (13) **1881** *Harper's Mag.* Jan. 205/2 The steam engines were self-propellers. **1936** *Reader's Digest* Nov. 70 What to call the new vehicle [the automobile] was a serious question. . . . Fearful and wonderful were some of the . . . verbal inventions which contended for favor. 'Polycycle,' 'petrocar,' 'autofiacre' and 'self-propeller' all were in actual use. — (14) **1857** *Ill. Agric. Soc. Trans.* II. 120 A self raker . . . may be just as simple in its structure as some *hand raker.* **1868** *Mich. Agric. Rep.* VII. 285 Thirty reaping machines were entered for trial, eight of which were self-rakers. **1879** *Scribner's Mo.* Nov. 134/2 The self-raker . . . drops it [*sc.* wheat] in convenient little bunches.

(15) **1854** *Placer Times* (S.F.) 7 March 1/4 Among the advantages of the Self-Raising Flour, are: The saving of time in preparing it for

the oven, and the certainty of results in any climate. **1930** *Randolph Enterprise* (Elkins, W.Va.) 20 Nov. 4/3 Girls love to make 'skillet biscuits' with a self-rising flour when out camping. — **(16) 1893** *Harper's Mag.* April 800/1 The chair he sat in was a self-rocker—a little invention of his own. **1909** RICE *Mr. Opp* 97 She's going to select a plush self-rocker for the congregation to give the new preacher.

Selkirk's violet. A violet, *Viola selkirki*, found in the northern states. — **1843** TORREY *Flora N.Y.* I. 70 Selkirk's Violet. . . . Woody hill-sides in the western part of the state. . . . A well-marked, but rare species. **1869** FULLER *Flower Gatherers* 110 One is called *Selkirk's* violet.

∗**sell,** *v.*

1. ∗*To sell out*, to betray (someone) for a price, to change one's position or allegiance as a result of corrupt influence. *Slang.*

1857 *Lawrence* (Kans.) *Republican* 2 July 1 If the *Times* has not been 'sold out' to the Border Ruffian party, it looks very much as if it had been 'chartered.' **1870** *Nation* 6 Jan. 1/1 The opposition candidate for the Speakership, . . . in the opinion of the bystanders, 'sold out' to his competitor. **1901** NORRIS *Octopus* 446 You've sold us out, you. **1945** *Somerset News* 8 March 1/3 At least one young, honest lawyer with high principles who will agree to keep out of petty local politics and thus be in a position to assure his clients they will not be sold out.

b. (See quot. 1870.)

1870 MEDBERY *Men Wall St.* 137 To 'sell out' a man, is to sell down a stock, which another is carrying, so low that he is compelled to quit his hold, and perhaps to fail. **1902** NORRIS *Pit* 323 He's going to try to sell us out, is he? All right. We'll sell, too.

For *to sell short*, see ∗**short**, *to sell down the river*, see ∗**river.**

2. *tr.* To advocate or speak highly of (something or somebody) in order to secure a desired attitude toward. *Slang.*

1925 *Publishers' Wkly.* 5 Dec. 1863 An Advertising Campaign to Sell New York as the Printing Center of the World. **1949** *Dly. Ardmoreite* (Ardmore, Okla.) 4 Dec. 1/1 One of the first tasks that Oklahoma has to accomplish . . . is to sell itself to its own people.

b. *To sell* (*on*), to bring (a person) to a desired evaluation of something. *Slang.*

1916 *Amer. Mag.* March 50/1 I'd make my readers want to enlist. I'd 'sell' them the army. **1926** *Publishers' Wkly.* 30 Jan. 328/1 This book-dealer took a longer route by which to coax the dollars from the young man, first selling him on the significance of St. Valentine's Day to the lover. **1947** *Dly. Ardmoreite* (Ardmore, Okla.) 14 Nov. 6/2 A few million middle-class Americans, touring the world can do more to sell the world on what America really is . . . than by all other devices that can possibly be conceived.

c. *To be sold on*, to be enthusiastic about. *Slang.*

1929 B. HALL & J. J. NILES *One Man's War* 114 After that Captain Bouche was surely sold on me as a pilot. **1930** *Canning Trade* 9 Feb. 117/1 There wasn't anybody any more sold on fresh cherries than we were.

∗**seller,** *n.* **seller three, ten,** etc. Used on a stock exchange to characterize a transaction in which the seller has the right to deliver to the buyer on one day's notice to him property bought within three, ten, etc., days. Cf. ∗**buyer,** *n.*

1849 *Hunt's Merch. Mag.* XX. 670 Fifty-six, buyer 20; 3rd broker—55¾, seller 10. **1869** MARK TWAIN *Innocents* 368 One forty-niner—damaged—at £23, seller ten, no deposit. **1888** *Economist* 20 Oct. 18/3 Sales were made on the Chicago Stock Exchange yesterday of . . . $5,000 Gas 5s at 83 3/8; $10,000 at 83 3/8, seller 3.

As the last term in **best, dirt, notion, pool seller.**

∗**selling,** *n.* As the last term in **best, pool, short selling.**

selling out. A betrayal, esp. a political one, for a price. *Slang.* — **1857** *Lawrence* (Kans.) *Republican* 4 June 3 No humiliating compromise is proposed, and no selling out. **1888** BRYCE *Amer. Commonw.* III. IV. lxxxiii. 110 When this transfer of the solid vote of a body of agitators is the result of a bargain with the old party which gets the vote, it is called 'selling out.'

sell-out ˈsɛlˌaut, *n.* An agreement arrived at by collusion to the detriment of legitimate private or public interests. *Slang.*

1883 HAY *Bread-Winners* 151 How much did the Captain give you for that sell-out? **1890** *Advance* 1 Feb. 3 The proposed sell-out of the State of North Dakota to the infamous Louisiana Lottery Company. **1906** *Watson's Mag.* Jan. 262 (*Cent. Supp.*), The Tariff Act . . . was an ungodly and unblushing sell-out to the Sugar Trust.

b. *Commerce.* The disposal of all of a commodity as the result of an unusual demand. Also attrib. *Slang.*

1934 WEBSTER. **1948** *So. Bend* (Ind.) *Tribune* 15 Aug. III. 2/1 The Indiana and Michigan games at home will be complete sellouts before game time. **1950** *Time* 27 Feb. 62/2 By week's end Lotte Lehmann had sung four sell-out recitals.

semester səˈmɛstɚ, *n.* [G., in related sense.] One of the two periods of instruction into which the school year of approximately thirty-six weeks is usually divided.

In modern usage this term is used with varying significations in different schools. See Kemp Malone in *Amer. Sp.*, Dec. 1946, p. 267.

1881 *Missouri Univ. Cat.* 40 The Juniors and Seniors . . . spent the balance of the semester in studying simple methods of teaching physics. **1895** *Univ. Nebraska Calendar 1895–6* 33 The year is divided upon the semester plan. Each semester has eighteen weeks. **1949** Univ. Okla. *News of Mo.* April 1/1 The new scholarships will provide $75 a semester for those who are chosen.

b. semester hour, (see quots.).

1946 *Amer. Sp.* Dec. 267 Alongside *semester* there has arisen, in the jargon of registrars, the expression *semester hour* as a name for a unit of measure used in recording and certifying academic 'credits' for courses taken. **1949** Univ. Okla. *News of Mo.* April 7/3 A semester hour . . . represents one hour per week of class work and at least 2 hours of additional study, for half the school year.

∗**semi-,** *prefix.* In combs.: (1) **semi-abolitionized,** *a.* halfway in favor of abolition, *obs.;* (2) **arid,** *a.* of an area, having very little rain; (3) **bolson,** (see quot. 1910 and cf. **bolson**); (4) **horse,** half horse, cf. **half horse (and) half alligator,** *jocular, rare;* (5) **monthly,** *a.* of a publication or service, coming out or occurring twice a month, also absol. and as adv.; (6) **occasional,** *a.* occurring or operating every now and then, *colloq.;* (7) **occasionally,** *adv.* every now and then, *colloq.;* (8) ∗**palmated,** *a.* see as a main entry; (9) **sleigh,** a vehicle somewhat resembling a sleigh, *rare;* (10) **weekly,** *a.* appearing, arriving, etc., twice a week, also absol.

(1) 1861 *Richmond* (Va.) *Enquirer* 17 Dec. 2/2 It was at a time when our people were all semi-abolitionized. — **(2) 1898** *Pop. Sci. Mo.* LII. 466 In the semiarid region the struggle for existence is so great. **1900** *Cong. Rec.* 31 Jan. 1353/1 We urge the adoption of a harmonious system of irrigation laws in all of the arid and semiarid States and Territories. **1929** *Texas Mo.* March 341 Practically all the cotton producing lands of West Texas lie within what is usually termed the 'semi-arid' section. — **(3) 1910** *Jrnl. Geology* Feb.–Mar. 141 Those bolsons whose surface water in times of flood reaches some river thoroughfare, some lower bolson, or the ocean, . . . may be called semi-bolsons. **1911** FORBES *Irrigation & Agric. Practice* 92 In the semi-bolson this central feature is poorly developed or even entirely lacking. — **(4) 1861** *N.Y. Herald* 10 July 3/1 In the Southwest are not far from 8,000 Union Guards, . . . provided with all the means requisite for carrying the war into Arkansas and sweeping out secession from the semi-horse and demi-alligator State.

(5) 1851 CIST *Cincinnati* 75 These are semi-monthlies. **1860–6** *Rep. Postmaster-General* 19 The present contract provides for an additional monthly trip between New York and San Francisco, making the service tri-monthly instead of semi-monthly as heretofore. **1895** *Univ. Nebraska Calendar 1895–6* 250 The Hesperian is the pioneer paper of the University, published semi-monthly. — **(6) 1850** in *Yankee Humour* (1853) 113 Semi-occasional intoxication. **1878** *Cong. Rec.* 14 June 4612/1 A semi-occasional ship carries the mails. — **(7) 1854** *Knickerb.* XLIII. 323 He preached semi-occasionally, at a private house. **1928** *Atlantic Mo.* April 504 To still a third group it seems to be a loose society of those who are interested in listening, semi-occasionally, to discussions of the good. — **(9) 1841** G. POWERS *Hist. Sk. Coos* 41 Sleeper contracted with Wheeler to take him and his family on to this semi-sleigh and semi-sled, and carry them to Newbury.

(10) 1791 JEFFERSON in S. K. Padover *Jefferson* (1942) 197 Besides this, Fenno's being the only weekly or semi-weekly newspaper. **1833** in BARNES *Memoir of T. Weed* (1884) 49 Put Millard Fillmore on your list for the Semi-Weekly. **1950** *World-Herald Mag.* (Omaha) 12 March 2/1 Semi-weeklies are published in . . . Red Cloud and Sidney.

semicolon butterfly. An American butterfly, *Polygonia interrogationis*, having markings suggestive of semicolons. — **1841** T. W. HARRIS *Rep. Insects Mass.* 219 Semicolon Butterfly. . . . Under-side of the wings in some rust-red, . . . with a pale gold-colored semicolon on the middle of the hinder pair. **1854** EMMONS *Agric. N.Y.* V. 207 Semicolon Butterfly. . . . There seems to be some variety in the markings of this butterfly, though the general pattern is much the same.

seminar ˈsɛməˌnɑr, *n.* [G., prob. an Amer. borrowing direct from Germany and independent of the British borrowing of about the same date.] An informal meeting of students with a leader, esp. a university course or a meeting of advanced students doing research under the guidance of a professor. — **1889** *Harper's Mag.* Jan. 273/2 In New York and Washington, if I am not misinformed, 'seminors' are held at regular intervals, at which a clever woman coaches other clever women in the political, literary, and ethical topics of the day. **1948** *Time* 16 Feb. 12/3, I meet a seminar on that campus one afternoon a week one term a year, but my main job is at the Huntington Library.

* **seminary,** *n.* **1.** =**seminar. 2. seminary dude,** a contemptuous designation for a foppish seminary student or graduate. *Rare.*

(1) 1879 *Ann. Rep. Johns Hopkins Univ.* 56 Seminary of American History. **1889** *Academy* 17 Aug. 103/2 The 'seminary' system seems to be making way [at Johns Hopkins], especially in the department of philology. The seminary is an association of the teachers, fellows, and scholars . . . for the prosecution of original studies by means of discussion and criticism. **1891** *Cent.* 5485/1–2 *Seminary,* . . . a seminary course: imitated from German use. Also *seminar.* — **(2) 1891** GARLAND *Main-travelled Roads* (1922) 22 W'y, you damned seminary dude, I can break you in two!

Seminole ˈsɛməˌnol, *n.* [Creek *Simanóle*, runaway, separatist.]

1. An Indian of a Muskhogean tribe, orig. composed of Creeks from the towns on the Chattahoochee River, who moved down into Florida after the destruction of the native tribes there by the British and their allies in the eighteenth century; also *pl.*, the tribe of such an Indian.

1789 *Amer. State P.: Ind. Affairs* I. 15 Some of the most southern towns of the Lower Creeks, or Seminoles, are within the territory of Spain. **1866** F. KIRKLAND *Bk. Anecdotes* 318/2 He fainted at the spectacle, and was soon after butchered by a Seminole. **1885** *Cent. Mag.* Aug. 602/2 The Creeks and Seminoles have not improved as much as the three other tribes, and are not considered so bright and energetic. **1946** *Nat. Geog. Mag.* Jan. 53/2 The later Seminole, who were primarily an offshoot of the Creeks and Hitchiti, were also a Muskhogean people.

Attrib. with **Indian, inhabitant, nation, tribe.**

1797 MORSE *Amer. Gazetteer s.v. Calos.* Not far from this is a considerable town of Seminole Indians. **1881** *Rep. Indian Affairs* p. lv, [They] were willing to incorporate the whole Seminole tribe into their nation. **1900** *Cong. Rec.* 2 Feb. 1455/2 In the Seminole Nation the survey and appraisement is already finished. **1945** TRYON *Poor Man* 3 There are bougainvillea in various hues, the flame-colored Florida honeysuckle (so-called) and the bell-like stone-crop, symbol of fertility to the original Seminole inhabitants of this paradise.

Also *Seminole father, influence, squaw.*

b. A local name for the canebrake rattlesnake, *Crotalus horridus.*

1938 MATSCHAT *Suwannee River* 27 Three kinds of rattlesnakes—the diamondback, the timber or Seminole (which the swamp folk insist is the 'wife of the diamondback') [etc.]. **1944** *Sat. Ev. Post* 9 Sep. 13/2 The bright-colored canebrake rattlers or 'Seminoles,' [are] as beautiful as they are deadly.

2. The language of the Seminole Indians.

1848 *S. Lit. Messenger* XIV. 482/2, I concluded at the time [that the opera] was written in Seminole, as the only word which I distinctly heard was en ca. **1857** *Knickerb.* XLIX. 634 The title given the place is *Atseena Otee,* which the largest landed proprietor says is Seminole for Cedar Key.

3. Seminole war, the war of 1817–18 or that of 1835–42, carried on by the U.S. against the Seminole Indians.

1818 *Repub. Constellation* (Winchester, Va.) 11 July 2/1 Gen. Jackson . . . obtained full proof that the Spanish authorities at Pensacola had been active in fomenting the Seminole war. **1831** in BENTON *30 Years' View* I. 167/2 The deliberations of the cabinet of Mr. Monroe on the occurrences of the Seminole war. **1869** *Ore. State Jrnl.* 2 Jan. 2/2 The Seminole war in Florida lasted about 7 years and cost $100,000 and 15,000 lives. **1948** *Fla. Hist. Quart.* July 35 Had not the Seminole war intervened, there is little question that the settlement of the present Taylor county would have begun ten years earlier than it did.

Seminolian ˌsɛməˈnolɪən, *n.* and *a.* A Seminole Indian; of or pertaining to such an Indian. *Obs.* — **1817** *Niles' Reg.* XIII. 191/1 Those negroes . . . together with the barbarous Seminolians, have been robbing and murdering the frontier inhabitants. **1818** *Ib.* XV. 200/2 Little doubt is entertained but there will soon be a final termination of the Seminolian war.

* **semipalmated,** *a.* Denoting various birds that have toes that are semipalmate or joined only partially with a web.

a. semipalmated plover, a plover, *Charadrius semipalmatus,* that breeds in the arctic region and appears as a visitor in various parts of the U.S.

1828 BONAPARTE *Synopsis* 296 The Semi-palmated Plover . . . [is] common all along the sea coast of the union. **1883** *Nat. Museum Bul.* No. 27, 147 *Ægialites semipalmatus.* Semipalmated Plover. . . . Nearly the whole of America, but breeding only far northward. **1950** *Newsweek* 16 Jan. 48/2 He had captured several semipalmated plovers, which somewhat resemble sandpipers.

b. semipalmated sandpiper, an American peep, *Ereunetes pusillus.*

1808–13 WILSON & BONAPARTE *Ornithology* (1831) III. 63 *Tringa semipalmata.* . . . Semipalmated Sandpiper. **1939** LINCOLN *Migration* 30 Shore birds of this size as a Semipalmated Sandpiper, banded on Cape Cod.

c. semipalmated snipe, the willet or stone curlew, *Catoptrophorus semipalmatus.*

1813 WILSON *Ornithology* VII. 27 Semi-palmated Snipe . . . is one of the most noisy and noted birds that inhabit our salt marshes in summer. **1839** PEABODY *Mass. Birds* 369 The Semipalmated Snipe . . . [is] known by the name of Willet. **1917** *Birds of Amer.* I. 246.

d. semipalmated tattler, =prec.

1831 J. RICHARDSON *Fauna Bor.-Amer.* II. 388 *Totanus semipalmatus,* Semipalmated Tatler.

señal senˈjɑl, *n. S.W.* [Sp. sign, mark, in Amer. Sp. sense shown here.] (See quot.) *Obs.* — **1844** FARNHAM *Travels in Calif.* 347 At this meeting, all the cattle of the settlement are gathered into immense *carals* or pens, and the ears of each cow having been marked by a peculiar cut, called señal, ownership of the calf following her, is easily made apparent.

* **senate,** *n.*

1. The upper and smaller branch of a state assembly or legislature. Also attrib. Cf. **state senate.**

1777 HAMILTON *Works* VII. 498 In your time your [N.Y.] Senate . . . will be liable to degenerate into a body purely aristocratical. **1786** J. ADAMS *Works* IX. 548, I cannot conceive why the [Mass.] Senate did not concur with the House. **1840** *Niles' Reg.* 7 March 4 The bill to abolish imprisonment for debt in Louisiana . . . was sent to the senate. **1946** *Democrat* 21 Feb. 1/7 Mr. Glover, who aspires to fill the Senate seat once held by his father, is a resident of Leroy.

2. (*cap.*) The upper house of the U.S. Congress, composed of two senators from each state.

1776 A. ADAMS *Familiar Lett.* 227 Whether you are in the American Senate or on board the British fleet, is a matter of uncertainty. *c***1808** J. ADAMS *Works* VI. 531 We have in fact, an aristocratical branch to our government, and that is, the senate. **1949** *Chi. D. News* 6 July 14/6 It has squeezed through the Senate by two votes.

b. A similar body in the government of the Confederate States. *Obs.*

1865 *Charleston* (S.C.) *Mercury* 12 Jan. 1/3 On motion of Mr. Barnwell, of S.C., the Senate adjourned.

3. In special combs.: (1) **Senate amendment,** an amendment made by the Senate to a bill; (2) **calendar,** the list of bills before the Senate, showing the order in which they are to be considered; (3) * **chamber,** the chamber or hall in which a senate regularly meets; (4) **Committee,** a committee chosen by the Senate to perform some specific function; (5) **district,** =**senatorial district;** (6) **report,** (see quot.).

(1) 1868 *N.Y. Herald* 4 July 3/2 The Senate Amendments to the Special Tax Bill. — **(2) 1880** *Harper's Mag.* Aug. 484, 800 [bills] remained unfinished on the Senate calendar. **1947** *Democrat* 9 Oct. 1/3 A fruitless attempt was made to get the measure on the Senate calendar for a vote. — **(3) 1785** WASHINGTON *Diaries* II. 372 We proceeded to business in the Senate Chamber. **1884** *Cent. Mag.* May 63/2 The Senate Chamber and court rooms [of the capitol in Albany, N.Y.] are almost finished. **1912** NICHOLSON *Hoosier Chron.* 603 It was almost too much for my composure to behold her there, beyond question the best-dressed woman in the senate chamber. — **(4) 1881** *Ore. State Jrnl.* 15 Jan. 4/2 One of the annual illustrations of the Democratic sense of humor . . . is the appointment of Mr. Vest to the chairmanship of the Senate Committee on Civil Service Reform. **1925** BRYAN *Memoirs* 386 It was submitted to the Senate Committee on Foreign Relations. **1949** *Amer. Forests* Nov. 41/1 Senator Anderson's bill for forest regulation was not considered by the Senate Committee on Agriculture.

(5) 1821 *Const. State of N.Y.* Art. 1. Sect. v, The State shall be divided into eight districts, to be called Senate districts. **1850** *Mich. Gen. Statutes* I. (1882) 76 The legislature shall . . . divide the state into senate districts. **1881** *Ib.* 107 This state shall be and is hereby divided into thirty-two senate districts. — **(6) 1896** *Statutes at Large* XXVIII. 621 The executive and miscellaneous documents and the reports of each House of Congress shall be designated as 'House Documents,' 'Senate Documents,' 'House Reports,' 'Senate Reports,' thus making two classes for each house.

Also *senate clerk, document, investigating committee, lobby, printer,* etc.

* **senator,** *n.*

1. =**state senator.**

1780 *Const. of Mass.* Part II, Chap. I § 2. I Forty persons to be Councillors and Senators for the year ensuing their election. **1792** IMLAY *Western Territory* 171 It has been the crude practice [in Ky.] hitherto, that each county should have two delegates and one senator to represent them. **1873** *Harper's Mag.* March 573/1 The terms of Senators range from one to six years. **1950** *Dly. Ardmoreite* (Ardmore, Okla.) 14 Feb. 1/6 He was a staunch leader in that party and served as senator from Carter county.

2. One of the two representatives sent by each state to the U.S. Senate.

1787 *Constitution* Art. I. Sect. III, The Senate of the United States, shall be composed of two Senators from each State. **1846** POLK *Diary* (1929) 127 If a proposition such as they suggested was made, it must come from the Pennsylvania Senators. **1949** D. O. MCGOVNEY *Amer. Suffrage* 8 The Farmers decided that senators should be chosen by state legislatures. On this point the Constitution was amended in 1913 to turn over the election of senators to 'the people.'

3. * **senatorship,** the office or position of a state or federal senator.

1851 LONGFELLOW *H. W. Longfellow* II. 208 Sumner came to dinner in very good spirits, feeling better about his senatorship. **1910** J. HART *Vigilante Girl* 204 He has an itch for office, although he has no chance for the senatorship. **1948** *Minneapolis Morn. Tribune* 28 Sep. 6/4 The senatorship is of greater importance to the citizens of Minnesota than is the governorship.

4. (*cap.*) Prefixed as a title to the surname of a senator.

1852 STOWE *Uncle Tom* ix, Senator Bird was drawing off his boots. **1904** *Springfield W. Republican* 9 Sep. 6 Senator Depew salts down William Allen White, who has stated that the senator tried to bully the president. **1949** *Amer. Forests* Sep. 5/1 A bill designed to assure that funds for timber access roads be used only for that purpose has been introduced by Senator Cain of Washington.

5. **senator-elect,** a senator who has been elected but who has not yet assumed the duties of his office.

1867 *Harper's Wkly.* 26 Jan. 49 (*heading*), Hon. Roscoe Conkling, New York Senator Elect. **1949** *Sooner Mag.* June 10/2 In early December the senator-elect and his wife flew to Washington.

As the last term in **carpetbag, cotton, ex-, junior, railroad, rosebud, secession, senior, silver, state senator.**

* **senatorial,** *a.*

1. Of or pertaining to a state senate, to the federal Senate, or to a senator.

1778 *Essex Co. Convention Result* 52 The senatorial convention may be composed of delegates from the several towns. **1790** MACLAY *Deb. Senate* 199 But as the matter, strictly speaking, was not *senatorial*, or such as belonged to us in our capacity as a public body, . . . it was withdrawn. **1889** *N.Y. Times* 8 Sep., The investigation by the Senatorial commission into the dressed beef combine was resumed. **1903** *Christendom* 13 June 350/1 An insurance policy against senatorial boodling ought to carry a very big premium rate. **1949** *So. Wkly.* 16 Nov. 1/1 A move to the left . . . is definitely indicated by the results of the New York Senatorial election.

2. In special combs.: (1) **senatorial courtesy,** the deference due a senator, esp. in the matter of appointments to offices in his state; (2) **district,** (*a*) a division of a state or territory entitled to elect a senator to the state or territorial assembly or legislature, (*b*) also attrib.; (3) **ring,** a ring or clique of senators.

(1) **1884** THAYER *From Log-Cabin* 279 A custom of the United States Senate called 'Senatorial courtesy' . . . [is] the custom of allowing senators to designate who should be appointed to fill certain offices in their respective states. **1949** *Chi. D. News* 16 March 22/1 Senator Harry Byrd took a long-needed swing at the custom of 'senatorial courtesy.' — (2) (*a*) **1829** *Va. Herald* (Fredericksburg) 14 Feb. 2/1 Yesterday, the substitute of Mr. Allen, graduating the Senatorial Districts, was lost by an equal division. **1948** *Dly. Ardmoreite* (Ardmore, Okla.) 23 July 14/6 This Senatorial district of Carter county is the birthplace and home of Joe. (*b*) **1834** *Cong. Deb.* 17 Feb. 567 The friends of the State and national administrations have recently had meetings in nearly every town, to elect delegates for their council and senatorial district conventions for the present year. **1851** *Mich. Gen. Statutes* I. (1882) 141 A duplicate statement of the votes given for senator . . . [is] to be delivered by him to the senatorial district canvassers. — (3) **1873** *Newton Kansan* 13 Feb. 4/2 [He] has been bitter in hostility to what he called the senatorial ring.

* **send,** *v.*

1. *absol.* To transmit a telegraphic message by operating the "key" of the sending instrument. Also **sending,** *n.*

1873 *Independent Defender* (S.F.) 15 Nov. 3/1 The operator . . . excitedly telegraphed back, don't send so d——d fast. **1891** *Salt Lake Times* 18 April 1/1 The fearless, manly telegrapher is the man who sends even, well spaced Morse—fast, of course, but steady withal, and sends 'all the time.' . . . Telegraphers identify friends by their 'sending' or writing. [**1949** *World-Herald Mag.* (Omaha) 19 June 16/5 It is well known among telegraphers . . . that an experienced man can identify the sender of a message by certain traits peculiar to each individual.]

2. In phrases: (1) *To send in,* of a baseball pitcher, to throw or deliver (balls) to the batter, *rare;* (2) * *to send out, S.* to agree to leave the details of a trade to the judgment of disinterested bystanders, *obs.;* (3) * *to send up,* (see quot. 1905).

(1) **1871** *N.Y. Herald* 22 Sep. 4/6 Wolters . . . never sent the balls in better than on this occasion. — (2) **1800** W. TATHAM *Agric. & Commerce* 81 Sometimes settling this price by mutual agreement of the parties, and at other times having recourse to what is called *sending out: I will truck for your horse, with such and such articles, and send out.* — (3) **1902** WHITE *Blazed Trail* 82 He was engaged in 'sending up'; that is he was one of the two men who stand at either side of the skids to help the ascending log keep straight and true to its bed on the pile. **1905** *Forestry Bureau Bul.* No. 61, 46 *Send up, to,* in loading, to raise logs up skids with cant hooks, or by steam or horse power.

* **send-off,** *n.* **1.** A sending off or starting of contestants in a race. **2.** A good-will demonstration given a person or persons setting off on a journey, a start, also transf. *Colloq.*

(1) **1856** *Porter's Spirit of Times* 25 Oct. 131/2 Shockoe got the send-off with the word. **1875** *Chi. Tribune* 15 July 1/3 There was considerable jockeying, and . . . an even send-off [in the boat race] was not obtained. — (2) **1872** MARK TWAIN *Roughing It* 332 One of the boys has passed in his checks, and we want to give him a good send-off. **1903** ADE *People You Know* 44 Proposing to every Girl the first time he met her . . . seemed to him such a cordial Send-Off for a budding Friendship. **1950** *Time* 6 March 92/3 The little town of Punxsutawney gave him a sendoff worthy of its first citizen to enlist in World War II.

Sene sin, *n.* Abbreviation of "Senior." *Slang. Obs.* — **1846** *Yale Banger* 10 Nov., The Freshman Class . . . from time immemorial the target for all the venomed darts of rowdy Sophs., magnificent Juns., and lazy Senes. **1850** *Ib.* 2 Dec., A rare young blade is the gallant Sene.

Seneca ˈsɛnɪkə, *n.* ["Seneca ('place of the stone,' the Anglicized form of the Dutch enunciation of the Mohegan rendering of the Iroquoian ethnic appellative *Oneida*)" (Hodge).]

1. A Seneca Indian, usu. *pl.* as a tribal designation.

[*c*1614 in *Doc. Col. Hist. N.Y.* I. opp. p. 11 (*map*), Senecas.] **1664** *Mass. H.S. Coll.* 4 Ser. VI. 531, 3000 of the Seneckes, a people in league with the Mohawkes beyond them, are gathered together. **1699** *Va. State P.* I. 67 At last one of the great men & one Sinker (Seneca) came over to us. **1823** J. M. DUNCAN *Travels U.S.* II. 77 The Five Nations were the Mohawks, Oneydas, Onondagoes, Cayugas, and Senecas. **1874** B. F. TAYLOR *World on Wheels* 31 The painted Senecas and the smoky Onondagas went gliding about like vanishing shadows. **1946** FOREMAN *Last Trek* 66 The Seneca are New York Indians, most of whom still reside in that state.

Also the language of these Indians.

1949 *Int. Jrnl. Amer. Linguistics* Jan. 24/2 We asked him to tell us in English the meaning of the part which he had just read in Seneca.

b. (See quots.)

1848 *N.Y. Hist. Soc. Col.* II. 346 They [Indians] are very fond of a game they call 'senneca' played with some round rushes, similar to the Spanish leather-grass, which they understand how to shuffle and deal as though they were playing with cards. **1944** ADAMS *Album Amer. Hist.* I. 93 From the Indians the Puritans learned the medicinal value of snakeroot, or seneca as it was sometimes called.

2. In combs.: (1) **Seneca grass,** the odoriferous holy grass, *Hierochloë borealis,* of the northern states; (2) **Indian,** an Indian of the Seneca tribe, also *pl.*, the tribe of such an Indian; (3) **Indian oil,** =**Seneca oil;** (4) **nation,** the nation composed of the Seneca Indians; (5) **oil,** crude petroleum found in the region formerly occupied by the Seneca Indians, now *hist.;* (6) **rattlesnake-root,** =next, *obs.;* (7) **snakeroot,** (see quot. 1891).

(1) **1814** BIGELOW *Florula Bostoniensis* 245 *Holcus odoratus.* Seneca grass. . . . An erect, early grass, with a small panicle of short flowers. **1857** GRAY *Botany* 574 *H[ierochloa] borealis.* . . . Vanilla or Seneca Grass. . . . Moist meadows, Mass. to Wisconsin, and northward. — (2) **1684** *N.H. Hist. Soc. Coll.* II. 199 The sd Mohauck, Senacar, or other Indians, [shall] be paid out of such monies as shall be raised in

the sd Province. **1790** HILTZHEIMER *Diary* (1893) 24 Oct. 164 There were present six Seneca Indians, Cornplanter, Half Town, Great Tree, John, William, and James Huxhing. **1900** *Cong. Rec.* 26 Jan. 1232/2 Among the Seneca Indians a singularly beautiful belief prevailed. — **(3) 1805** T. M. HARRIS *Jrnl.* 46 The Seneca Indian Oil in so much repute here [near Pittsburgh] is Petroleum. — **(4) 1779** *N.H. Hist. Soc. Coll.* VI. 326 Near the end of this lake is the famous town of Kanadagago, the metropolis of the Seneca Nations. **1846** POLK in *Pres. Mess. & P.* IV. 428, I herewith transmit . . . a memorial addressed to the President and the Senate in relation to the treaty . . . of May 20, 1842, with the 'Seneca Nation of Indians.'

(5) 1795 J. SCOTT *U.S. Gazetteer s.v. Allegany,* In this county is Oil creek: It flows from a spring much celebrated for a bitumen resembling Barbadoes tar, and is known by the name of Seneca Oil. **1860** *N.Y. Tribune* 14 April 3/1 The mineral oil of this region was known to the Indians by the name of Seneca Oil. **1932** *Old-Time N. Eng.* Oct. 64/2 It continued to be used as a medicine and later was sold under the name of Senaca Oil. — **(6) 1738** *Va. Gazette* 30 June 4/2 *The Seneca Rattle-Snake Root* must be of more extensive use than any Medicine in the *Materia Medica.* **1830** WATSON *Philadelphia* 616 About the year 1739, I saw much said in the Gazettes of the newly discovered virtues of the Seneka rattlesnake root. — **(7)** [**1764** REUTER *Wachau* 571.] **1798** MORSE *Amer. Geog.* 415 Among others are the ginseng, Virginia snake root, Seneca snake root, an herb of the emetic kind. **1891** *Cent.* 5725/3 Seneca snakeroot, *Polygala Senega* of eastern North America. It sends up several stems from hard knotty rootstocks, bearing single close racemes of white flowers.

* **senior,** *a.* and *n.*

1. A student in the last year of the regular four-year course in a college or high school. Cf. * **senior sophister.**

1741 in HALL *College Words* 318 No Freshman shall be saucy to his Senior. **1893** POST *Harvard Stories* 70 Randolph presented him with . . . the advice to learn as soon as possible to tell a Senior from a Freshman. **1949** *Desplaines Valley News* (Summit, Ill.) 28 Oct. 1/2 At Argo high school those are every-day words in every senior's vocabulary.

Attrib. with **dormitory, oration, rhetorical, society.**

1851 in HALL *College Words* 270 The custom of delivering Senior Orations . . . is, I think, confined to Washington and Jefferson Colleges in Pennsylvania. **1871** BAGG *At Yale* 169 Senior-society men never mention their own society in the presence of others. **1881** *Ore. State Jrnl.* 8 Jan. 5/3 Prof.'s Johnson and Spiller will take charge of the senior and junior rhetoricals. **1907** *St. Nicholas* May 604/2 [His] belongings were already stowed away in his locker in the Senior Dormitory on the floor above.

b. (See quot. 1847.)

1847 WEBSTER 1006/3 *Senior,* . . . one in the third year of his course at a theological seminary. **1912** *Chi. Theol. Sem. Reg.* May 48 Seniors began to worry over their theses.

2. In special combs.: (1) **senior bachelor,** (see quot.), *obs.;* (2) **class,** see as a main entry; (3) **college,** a college offering the last two years' work required for the bachelor's degree; (4) **high school,** a secondary school comprising grades 9 to 12, or 8 to 12; (5) **preacher,** in the Methodist Church, a preacher superior in rank to another with whom he is associated in a common service; (6) **prom,** a students' formal dance attended by seniors and their friends; (7) **senator,** a senator who has served longer in the Senate than the other senator from his state; (8) * **sophister,** a student in the fourth and last year of a college course, also transf., *obs.;* (9) **year,** the fourth and last year of a high-school or college course.

(1) 1851 HALL *College Words* 270 *Senior bachelor,* one who is in his third year after taking the degree of Bachelor of Arts. — **(3) 1899** *Univ. of Chi. Reg.* 37/1 The Faculties of the Schools of Arts, Literature, and Science have been organized as follows: (1) The Faculty of the Junior Colleges; (2) The Faculty of the Senior Colleges [etc.]. **1920** S. P. DUGGAN in Klapper *College Teaching* 28 Some other degree . . . [may be granted] at the end of the Senior College. **1942** *Bul. Vanderbilt Univ.* 69 The College is divided, for certain purposes, into the Junior College and the Senior College. — **(4) 1934** WEBSTER. **1949** *L.A. Times* 23 June II. 5/1 Then they enter senior high school, and become 'juniors' and then seniors.

(5) 1845 *Indiana Mag. Hist.* XXIII. 212 The senior preacher in his second sermon commenced the controversy on the subject of Arianism. — **(6) 1893** *Outing* Feb. 389/2 They were always a sort of alumni gathering, similar to the president's reception at the Art building—these hot senior 'proms' in Alumni Hall. **1949** *World-Herald Mag.* (Omaha) 14 Aug. 23/2 He invited me to the Senior Prom. — **(7) 1885** CRAWFORD *Amer. Politician* 137 The next vacancy . . . would have occurred in about a year's time, at the expiration of the senior senator's term of office. **1949** *Sat. Ev. Post* 18 June 18/3 Clyde Hoey, the senior senator, . . . still adorns himself as befits his office, in a sugar scoop coat and a gates-ajar collar. — **(8) 1690** SEWALL *Diary* I. 314, I would not have you send any to me whoes Book-Debts are old enough to be senior Sophisters, being of more than three years standing. **1766** in PEIRCE *Hist. Harvard* 246 The Senior Sophisters shall attend the Tudor *A* on Mondays. — **(9) 1796** MORSE *Univ. Geog.* I. 420 The undergraduates are not permitted to attend them [*sc.* medical lectures] till their senior year. **1924** S. S. COLVIN *Intro. to H.S. Teaching* 12 A number of high schools offer in their senior year a vocational course. **1945** *Beloit College Bul.* June 16 And now our Senior year has literally flown by.

senior class. 1. A class in college or high school made up of those in the fourth year of the regular academic course. **2.** (See quot.)

(1) 1766 T. CLAP *Hist. Yale College* 14 The Senior Class were removed to Milford. **1871** CUTTING *Student Life Amherst* 40 For the Exhibition, four orators are now chosen in each society from the Senior class. **1900** WINCHESTER *W. Castle* 25 Wesley and Chester went to the city of Dorchester on some business for the Senior class. **1946** *Democrat* 13 June 3/3 They recently cabled the senior class. — **(2) 1816** *Ann. 14th Congress* 2 Sess. 270 Those [in the militia] over thirty-one, and under forty-five years of age, shall be called the senior class of militia.

senioric sinˈjɔrɪk, *a.* Of or pertaining to a college senior. *Rare.* — **1871** BAGG *At Yale* 167 Fifteen senioric shirt-bosoms were adorned by as many new badges.

señita senˈjitə, *n.* Also **senita.** *S.W.* [Origin obscure. App. dim. of Sp. *seña,* sign, mark, token. Not in Santamaría.] =**old-man cactus.**

1907 MEARNS *Mammals Mex. Boundary* 66 Cereus schottii *Engelmann.* Schott Cactus; Sinita. **1932** *Ariz. Agric. Exp. Sta. Bul.* 141, 24 The cactus family is represented in our flora by . . . pitahaya, or organ pipe cactus, and señita, or old man [etc.]. **1948** *So. Sierran* May 5/2 The Organ Pipe and Senita (Old Man) Cacti are similar except the Senita has whiskers.

señor senˈjɔr, *n.* [Sp., an Amer. borrowing.]

1. A Spanish gentleman or one of Spanish descent.

1847 *Santa Fe Republican* 4 Dec. 2/3 The Santa Fe House also expects to figure some day *seminaria proximo,* all of which the Senors and Senoras shall have timely notice of. **1880** CABLE *Grandissimes* 223 He ventured to reveal the foregoing incidents to the señor.

2. (*a*) A title of respect used before a man's name, equivalent to *Mr.* (*b*) Used as a form of address.

(*a*) [**1884** *Santa Fe Republican* 1/4 [Indians] drove off all the stock belonging to Senor el Padre.] **1866** *Weekly New Mexican* 22 Dec. 1/3 Married. . . . Mr. James Edgar Griggs formerly of New Jersey, to Miss Eugenia E., daughter of Señor Don Cristoval Ascarate. **1925** BURNS *Saga of Billy the Kid* 24 Señor McSween was a young lawyer looking for a good town in which to settle. (*b*) **1890** *Cent. Mag.* Dec. 178 Señor, I have made an important discovery. **1907** WHITE *Arizona Nights* 285 'Señor,' said he, 'you're off your feed.' **1946** *Chi. D. News* 26 Feb. 8/4 (*caption*), We're All Anxious with You, Senor.

señora senˈjorə, *n.* [Sp., an Amer. borrowing.] A Spanish lady. Also a title of respect, equivalent to *Mrs.*

1841 *N.O. Picayune* 10 April 2/4 The Señoras of Santa Fé and Taos invariably wear veils over their heads. **1863** *Rio Abajo Press* 28 April 1/2 Senora Tules . . . screamed and ran back to the kitchen. **1893** *Harper's Mag.* April 786/1 The dark eyes of the gallant dons and lovely senoras still smile on us from the faces of their descendants.

señorita ˌsenjəˈritə, *n.* [Sp. in sense **1.**]

1. *S.W.* A young Spanish lady or one of Spanish descent.

[**1823** QUITMAN in Claiborne *Life Quitman* I. 85 The belles . . . 'tote' their fans with the air of Spanish señoritas.] **1912** HOUGH *Story of Cowboy* 127 Some wandering teamster . . . met and wooed and married the senorita. **1948** *P.C.C. Chronicle* (Pasadena, Calif.) 7 May 2/1 Gay caballeros and beautiful senoritas danced under the warm California sun.

2. Any one of several small, beautifully marked kelpfish of the California coast. Also **señorita fish.**

1882 *Nat. Museum Bul.* No. 16, 604 *Pseudojulis.* . . . Señoritas. *Ib., P. modestus.* . . . Senorita; Pesce Rey. **1884** GOODE *Fisheries* I. 275 The Señorita-fish, of California. At Monterey, California, this species, *Pseudojulis modestus,* is known as, 'Pescerey'; southward it is called 'Señorita.' **1896** JORDAN & EVERMANN *Check-List Fishes* 413 *Iridio semicinctus.* . . . Kelpfish; Señorita. . . . Santa Barbara Islands to Cerros Island. *Ib., Oxyjulis modestus.* . . . Señorita. . . . Monterey to Guadalupe Island. *Ib.* 467 *Gibbonsia evides.* . . . Kelpfish; Senorita. . . . South to Point Conception.

* **sense,** *n.* As the last term in **cattle, cow, horse, realizing sense.**

* **sensitive,** *a.* In combs.: (1) **sensitive brier,** any one of various plants, esp. prostrate herbs of the genus

Schrankia, as *S. uncinata*, that are sensitive to the touch; (2) **fern,** a North American fern, *Onoclea sensibilis*, the leaves of which tend to fold together when plucked or when wilting; (3) **pea,** any one of various North American plants of the genus *Chamaecrista*, as *C. fasciculata* and *C. nictitans*, having leaflets that droop or wilt upon being touched; (4) **rose,** =**sensitive brier.**

(1) **1802** ELLICOTT *Journal* 287 The sensitive briar, (*mimosa instia.*) this beautiful and singular plant, is common to the poor, sandy land. **1869** *Amer. Naturalist* III. 163 Along the steep banks of the creeks and ravines, the sensitive Brier (*Schrankia*) is to be found. **1941** R. S. WALKER *Lookout* 58 Sensitive brier's runners cling to the ground and are tough and spiny. — (2) **1814** BIGELOW *Florula Bostoniensis* 257 Sensitive fern. . . . Low grounds. Perennial. **1943** SMITH *Explor. Biology* 90/2 In some species, such as the sensitive fern, these spore-making organs are borne on a special branch. — (3) **1843** TORREY *Flora N.Y.* I. 190 *Cassia Chamæcrista.* Partridge Pea. Sensitive Pea. . . . Sandy fields: Staten Island; Long Island. rare in the interior of the State. **1907** BAILEY *Cyclo. Amer. Agric.* II. 309/2 Partridge pea, Sensitive pea, Magothy Bay bean (*Cassia Chamæcrista*). — (4) **1892** *Amer. Folk-Lore* V. 95 *Schrankia uncinata*, sensitive rose. West and South.

* **separate,** *n.*

1. (*cap.*) *pl.* (See quot. 1931.) Also attrib.

1810 in SWEET *Religion* (1931) 5 The New-Light-stir being extensive, a great number were converted to the Lord. . . . Having thus separated themselves from the established churches, they were denominated Separates. *a***1817** DWIGHT *Travels* III. 64 Of the number, who finally filled up its extent, were Calvinistic, Arminian, Sabbatarian, and Separate Baptists. **1842** TRACY *Gt. Awakening* 317 About a year afterwards, (October 9, 1745), a Separate church was organized at Mansfield. **1919** *Census: Religious Bodies 1916* II. 126/2 The strict Calvinistic doctrines of election, reprobation, and fatality have never been accepted by the Separate Baptist churches. **1931** SWEET *Religion* 44 The origin of the terms Separate and Regular came from the Great Awakening in New England. The Separates were those who were particularly revivalistic and separated from the churches which did not support the revival, thus they became known as *Separates*. Those who did not thus separate were known as *Regulars*.

2. An article or document issued separately, an off-print.

1884 MERRIAM *Mammals of Adirondacks* 3 Pages 9–107 (comprising the first instalment) appeared in Vol. I, separates issued in October, 1882. **1894** *Harvard Teachers' Assoc. Leaflet* No. 11, 4 The geographical report . . . might be reprinted in the annual report of the superintendent of public instruction, from which 'separates' could be struck off. **1946** *So. Sierran* Oct. 3/1 The finished detailed contour map and report will appear in the American Alpine Journal with enough separates published for those who are interested.

***separate,** *v. tr.* (See quot.) — **1888** *Civil Service Comm. 4th Rep.* 51 A statement of the number of persons who have been 'separated' from the classified service by removal, resignation, and death cannot be made.

separating machine. A machine that separates or sorts. *Obs.* — **1862** *Rep. Comm. Patents 1861: Agric.* 648 Threshing and separating machines, Grain. **1885** *Harper's Mag.* Jan. 286/1 The date given . . . is as near as possible to the time when the machines . . . became accepted successes: . . . 1840.—Sole-leather 'separating' machine.

* **separation,** *n.*

1. The formal dismissal of an employee, student, etc., by his superiors. *Obs.*

1779 JEFFERSON *Writings* II. 179 The separation of these troops would be a breach of public faith. **1888** *Civil Service Comm. 4th Rep.* 51 The number of such 'separations' from the classified departmental service [follows]. **1897** FLANDRAU *Harvard Episodes* 229 He would feel [sorrow] at what the official college gracefully terms the 'separation' of Billy from the University.

2. The withdrawing or seceding of a portion of a state from the whole unit, or of a state from the Union. Also attrib. *Obs.*

1785 J. SEIVER in Ramsey *Annals of Tenn.* (1853) 317 At the time of our declaration, we . . . thought your Legislature had fully tolerated the separation. **1832** WILLIAMSON *Maine* II. 532 The General Court employed measures calculated to cool and abate the high Separation-fever. **1862** KETTELL *Hist. Rebellion* I. 133 Troops were stationed at the polls to over-awe Union voters, and thus the vote for 'separation' was raised to 104,913 against 47,238 for 'no separation.'

As the last term in **grade separation.**

***separationist,** *n.* **1.** An advocate of the right of a state to withdraw from the Union. **2.** A believer in the rigid separation of white people and Negroes. Both *obs.* — (1) **1833** CAREY *Olive Branch Once More* 11 Dec. 17 There is not in this part of the country one separationist in one hundred of our citizens. — (2) **1888** CABLE in *Contemporary Rev.* March 452 No excellence . . . can buy for a 'man of colour,' from these separationists, any distinction between the restrictions of his civil liberty and those of the stupidest and squalidest of his race.

* **Separatists,** *n. pl.* **1.** Seceders from various American denominations, esp. the Separates *q.v.* **2.** Members of a communistic society of German origin established at Zoar, Ohio, in 1817. *Obs.*

(1) **1781** PETERS *Hist. Conn.* 199 The Bowlists, Separatists, and Davisonians, are peculiar to the Colony. . . . The second permit only the elect to pray. **1809** KENDALL *Travels* I. 291 It is divided into three societies, exclusive of a society of anabaptists, and another of *separatists*, or of the *new light*, which it either now does, or lately did, contain. **1875** NORDHOFF *Communistic Societies U.S.* 69 Rapp [founder of 'Harmony Society'] and his adherents . . . were denounced as Separatists [*c*1787]. — (2) **1875** NORDHOFF *Communistic Societies U.S.* 99 Zoar [Ohio] is the home of a communistic society who call themselves 'Separatists,' and who founded the village in 1817.

***separator,** *n.* As the last term in **cockle, corn, gold, wheat separator.**

sepawn, see **supawn.**

September butter. Butter made during September. *Rare.* — **1839** *Mass. Agric. Survey 2d Rep.* 71 June butter . . . and September butter . . . are generally of a superior quality to that made at other seasons.

sequia ˈsekɪə, *n.* Also **zequia.** Shortening of **acequia.**

1846 in BRYANT *California* xxxiv. 396 The Pimos Indians . . . irrigate the land by water from the Gila, as did the Aztecs, . . . the remains of whose sequias, or little canals, were seen by us. **1857** M. REID *War Trial* (B.), As the mustang sprang over the zequia, the flowing skirt of the manga was puffed forward. **1870** LUDLOW *Heart of Continent* 183, I found a number of 'sequis,' or distributing ditches, already run.

Sequoia sɪˈkwɔɪə, səˈkwɔjə, *n.* Also **Sequoyah.** [See note.]

No doubt after Sequoya (Cherokee *Sikwayi*), the famous Cherokee Indian who devised a syllabary of the Cherokee language. Stephan Ladislaus Endlicher (1804–49), who first used the word as a genus name, was a Hungarian ethnologist as well as a botanist, and might well have known of Sequoya's unique services to his people.

1. A genus of trees which includes the big tree *q.v.* and the giant redwood of California. Also (not *cap.*) a tree of this genus.

[**1847** ENDLICHER *Synopsis Coniferarum* 198 Sequoia sempervirens. . . . Habitat in America borealis occidentalis ad sinum Nutka. Sequoia gigantea. . . . Habitat in California. **1866** *Treas. Bot., Sequoia* (including *Wellingtonia*). A genus of the *Abietinæ* tribe of *Coniferæ* from North-western America, closely allied to *Sciadopitys*.] **1869** MUIR *First Summer in Sierra* (1911) 349 Ran over the Tuolumne divide and down a few miles to a grove of sequoias that I had heard of, directed by the Don. **1900** BRUNCKEN *N. Amer. Forests* 12 Of all the forests of the world these have the most gigantic trees, barring only the Sequoias of California. **1949** *Nat. Geog. Mag.* June 763 (*legend*), Oldest in the Mariposa Grove of giant sequoias in Yosemite National Park, this tree has seen its 3,800th birthday.

b. Attrib. with **bark, National Park, redwood, tree.**

1875 *Cin. Enquirer* 2 July 5/1 We ate our first lunch under a great Sequoia tree named 'Illinois.' **1878** *Harper's Mag.* Jan. 244/1 How shall we explain the rise of the sap in the great sequoia-trees of California? **1944** *Nat. Geog. Mag.* June 695/2 From Pasadena a half day's drive took us to the Sequoia National Park in the mid-Sierras, where we were soon driving among trees that were giants when Columbus was a little boy. **1944** STAFFORD *Boston Adv.* 107 Embedded pictures of a Sequoia redwood through which a man could walk. **1948** *Pacific Discovery* Mar.–Apr. 10/1 The thickness and relative fire resistance of Sequoia bark after about forty years give them an added advantage over other trees.

2. A proposed state name (see quots.), in allusion to Sequoya, a Cherokee Indian (*c*1760–1843) who distinguished himself by devising a syllabary of his native language.

[**1885** FOSTER *Se-quo-yah* 26 Then and there, she named her child Se-quo-yah, which in the musical language of his people means 'he guessed it.'] **1905** *Lit. Digest* 23 Dec. 947/2 If two new States are created in Oklahoma and Sequoyah (Indian Territory), this part of the Southwest will have twelve Senators, the same as New England. **1917** GITTINGER *Formation of Okla.* 210 The name adopted for the proposed state was Sequoyah, selected in honor of the 'Cherokee Cadmus.' **1930** FERBER *Cimarron* 217 These were for separate statehood for the Indian Territory, the state to be known as Sequoyah, after the great Cherokee leader of that name. **1948** *Dly. Oklahoman* (Okla. City) 16 May E. 14/3, 1905—Sequoyah convention at Muskogee prepared constitution for Indian Territory to be admitted as the 'State of Sequoyah.'

3. *attrib.* Of or pertaining to Sequoya's syllabary. Cf. **Sequoyan,** *a.*

1902 *Out West* Feb. 176 In 1797, John Arch . . . translated the third chapter of St. John into Sequoyah-syllabic characters.

Sequoiene sɪˈkwɔɪˌin, *n.* (See quot. and cf. **Sequoia.**) — **1923** *Arrow Points* March 51 Too, an alkaloid Sequoiene is distilled from the needles of this tree.

Sequoyan sɪˈkwɔɪ·ən, səˈkwɔjən, *a.* Of or pertaining to the syllabary devised by Sequoya (*c*1760–1843), a Cherokee Indian. Cf. **Sequoia.**

1885 Foster *Se-quo-yah* 148 In 1869 . . . a committee was appointed to select arithmetics, a geography and history to be translated into the Se-quo-yan alphabet for the use of schools. *Ib.* 214 The matrix for the Se-quo-yan type is kept in custody of the Nation, and the full Cherokee is in no danger of being corrupted by vicious literature. **1923** *Arrow Points* March 51 His name is signed in the Sequoyan alphabet.

serape səˈrɑpɪ, *n. S.W.* [Amer. Sp. *sarape* (poss. f. Amer. Indian) in same sense.] A shawl or blanket worn as an outer garment, esp. by Spanish-Americans.

1834 A. Pike *Sketches* 138 Everything is new, strange, and quaint; . . . the zarape or blanket of striped red and white. **1853** Brewerton *With Kit Carson* (1930) 150 The sides of their rooms are provided with huge rolls of serapes (a kind of coarse blanket, which forms one of their articles of trade with the adjoining provinces, being largely manufactured by the women of the country). **1916** Bower *Phantom Herd* 68 He had finished [his work] with an old Mexican serape draped around his person for warmth. **1950** *Chi. Tribune* 1 March 20/3 The feminine counterpart of the serape is the rebozo.

sereno səˈreno, *n.* [Sp. in same sense.] A night watchman.

1884 *Cent. Mag.* Sep. 667/2 Presently the old *sereno*, wrapped in his long cloak, stood beside her. **1895** G. King *New Orleans* 147 A regular force of night watchmen was formed, serenos they were called, from their calling out the state of the weather and the hour of the night. **1904** Churchill *Crossing* 493 A sereno . . . was crying the hour. **1950** *N.O. Times-Picayune Mag.* 12 Feb. 9/1 The [New Orleans] police were called 'serenos.'

* **sergeant,** *n.* In combs.: (1) **sergeant attendant,** in colonial times, a town officer charged with attendance upon courts and the execution of local ordinances, *obs.;* (2) **clerk,** (see quot.); (3) **fish,** a fish of the family Rachycentridae, as *Rachycentron canadus,* marked with stripes resembling those on the sleeve of a sergeant's uniform (see also quot. 1896); (4) * **major,** the cockeye pilot, *Abudefduf marginatus.*

(1) **1640** *R.I. Col. Rec.* I. 101 Henry Bull is chosen Sargeant attendant for this yeare. **1641** *Ib.* 112 Thomas Gorton and Henry Bull are chosen Sergeant Attendants. — (2) **1895** *Outing* XXVII. 252/1 [The new military code] changes the title of the brigade sergeant-major to that of sergeant-clerk. — (3) **1883** *Nat. Museum Bul.* No. 27, 448 *Elacate canadus.* . . . Sergeant-fish; Snooks; Ling. **1896** Jordan & Evermann *Check-List Fishes* 369 *Centropomus undecimalis.* . . . Robalo; Sergeant-fish; Snook; Brochet de Mer. Coasts of Florida and Texas southward among the West Indies to Surinam or beyond. **1944** Barbour *Eden* 36 There was always the good chance of catching an errant sergeant fish or snook. — (4) **1876** Goode *Cat. Fishes of Bermudas* 38 The fish is sometimes called the 'Sergeant-major,' in allusion to the chevron-like bands of yellow on the sides. . . . Its accidental occurrence at Newport, R.I., has been recorded. **1898** Jordan & Evermann *Fishes N. & Middle Amer.* 1561 Abudefduf saxatilis (Linnaeus). (Pintana; Cow-Pilot; Cockeye Pilot; Jaqueta; Majarra Raiada; Demoiselle; Sergeant Major.)

As the last term in **desk, general, hunt, saddler, top sergeant.**

***sermon,** *n.* As the last term in **Artillery, century, convention, election, lesson, trial sermon.**

serpentin ˈsɜpənˌtin, *n.* [F. in same sense.] A paper streamer or ribbon, thrown into the air and allowed to unroll at times of rejoicing. — **1894** *Nation* 22 March 215/2 They shouted unmusical songs, threw confetti, serpentins, and paper darts among the ladies. **1948** *So. Sierran* Feb. 3/1 At midnight balloons were released, and serpentine filled the air.

***Serpents,** *n. pl.* The Shoshoni, a tribe of Shoshonean Indians. *Obs.* — **1843** De Smet *Lett. & Sk.* 62, I visited . . . many other tribes, such as the . . . Cheyennes, Serpents, Crows, [etc.].

Serranos sɛˈrɑnos, *n. pl. S.W.* [Sp. in Amer. Sp. sense shown here.] (See quot. 1910.)

1858 *S.F. Bulletin* 5 Nov., The true native Americans of the wild forests—such as the Yumas, . . . Mohaves and Serranos—predominate. **1888** Lindley *Calif. of South* 382 Palm Valley . . . belongs to a reservation of the Cerranos, whose captain, Old Francisco, is believed to be a hundred and twenty years old. **1910** Hodge *Amer. Indians* II. 512/2 Serranos. . . . A Shoshonean division with a common dialect, centering in the San Bernardino mts., s. Cal., n. of Los Angeles, but extending down Mohave r. at least to Daggett and n. across the Mohave desert into the valley of Tejon cr. **1946** McWilliams *So. Calif. Country* 26 The Serranos and the Gabrieleno were associated with the Mission San Gabriel.

* **servant,** *n.* An immigrant intending or destined to become a servant or indentured servant in America. Now *hist.*

1721 *N.-Eng. Courant* 6 Nov. 4/1 A Ship lately bound from Dublin to Virginia with Servants, were oblig'd by the Servants (who rose upon the Ship's Crew and kill'd two of them) to put back into another Port. **1769** *Boston Chron.* 25 Sep., Arrived from Ireland, The Ship King of Prussia, Arthur Darley, master, has on board 30 Servants. **1856** Olmsted *Slave States* 228 The term *servant* was, I believe, always applied, in the provincial days of Virginia, to white men and women, who were bound to service for a limited time, and the term slaves, to those held for life. **1896** P. A. Bruce *Econ. Hist. Va.* I. 573 The term 'servant' has been misinterpreted in modern times in the light of menial signification which the expression has gradually acquired. **1949–50** *Ga. Rev.* Winter 368 These 'Servants' were white men and women, too poor to pay passages from England or to bring money with them.

* **service,** *n.*[1] In combs.: (1) **service car,** a railroad car used for construction, repair, maintenance of way, etc.; (2) **pension,** a stipend paid at regular intervals by the government to one who has served a prescribed time in the U.S. Army or Navy; (3) **station,** an establishment where motorists may secure gasoline, oil, tire service, etc., also attrib., cf. **filling station;** (4) **train,** a train operated by a railroad company for purposes of construction, maintenance of way, etc.

(1) **1868** *Comm. & Fin. Chron.* VI. 457/1 Of the remainder 212 are freight cars, 15 service cars. **1881** *Rep. Ala. R.R. Comm.* I. 64 Number of service cars . . . 7. — (2) **1887** *Nation* 24 Feb. 160/1 A little band of greedy schemers . . . have been diligently pushing the 'service pension' project, which would place on the roll every man who ever served three months in the Union Army. **1914** *Cyclo. Amer. Govt.* II. 668/2 A service-pension is granted to one who has been in military service for a prescribed length of time, usually without regard to the existence of any injury or disability of service origin. — (3) **1922** S. Lewis *Babbitt* x, He ought to have taken it [*sc.* a car] to the service-station and had the battery looked at. **1949** *Clearing-Stickney* (Ill.) *Bul.* 28 Oct. 5/1 With the Choremaster Snow Plow, walks, drives and service station aprons come clean in a hurry. — (4) **1881** *Rep. Ala. R.R. Comm.* I. 106 Service train [was] thrown from track.

As the last term in **classified (civil), curb, field, forest, immigration, Indian, jitney, news, package, pony express, Reclamation, revenue-cutter, ring, signal, star, wagon service.**

* **service,** *n.*[2]

1. serviceberry, the fruit of the serviceberry bush.

[**1784** Asbury *Journal* I. 477 The child he fed with . . . sawice berries.] **1843** Talbot *Journals* 49 Had an abundance of haws and sarvice berries. **1919** Wilson *White Indian* 221 Service berries. Small berries similar in size and color to blueberries and huckleberries. Found plentifully in the mountains of the West. They grow on bushes. Used by Indians for food.

2. =next.

1805 Lewis in *L. & Clark Exped.* II. (1904) 239 The survice berry differs somewhat from that of the U. States. **1915** Armstrong & Thornber *Western Wild Flowers* 216 Service-berry. June-berry. *Amelanchier alnifolia.* . . . When thickets of this shrub are in bloom on mountainsides the effect is very pretty. **1949** *Desert Mag.* April 9/3 Serviceberry and Fremont barberry or desert barberry will blossom profusely.

3. serviceberry bush, any one of various American trees or shrubs of the genus *Amelanchier.*

1807 Gass *Journal* 136, I saw service-berry bushes hanging full of fruit. **1894** *Outing* July 306/1 The undergrowth was poplar, serviceberry bushes and other shrubs.

Also **service bush.**

1839 Audubon *Ornith. Biog.* V. 464 The nest was in the branch of a small service bush. **1914** E. Stewart *Lett. Woman Homesteader* 19 There were . . . service-bushes and birches that shut off the ugly hills on the other side.

4. * **service tree,** the American mountain ash, *Sorbus americana,* or the serviceberry bush.

1737 Brickell *N. Carolina* 71 The Service Tree groweth to be very large, and beareth long Leaves like those of the Ash Tree. **1824** Doddridge *Notes* 84 The service trees were the first in bloom in the spring.

1943 PEATTIE *Great Smokies* 275 Ordinarily the 'sarvice' tree becomes arrayed with heavy creamy-white bloom by the first part of April.

servigrous sɚˈvɪgrəs, sɚˈvaɪgrəs, *a.* Also **sevigrous.** = **savagerous.** Also **servigerously,** *adv. Colloq.*

1835 LONGSTREET *Ga. Scenes* 207 'Pretty sevigrous, but nothing killing yet,' said Billy Curlew, as he learned the place of Spivey's ball. **1898** HARRIS *Tales* 312 Kaze Marse 'Lisha is de mos' servigrous white man in deze parts. **1938** MATSCHAT *Suwannee River* 81 Ary fowkses knows as how onion juice, rubbed in servigerously, sprouts hair like weeds after a rain, iffen so bee ye stand in the sun.

sesame grass. = **gama grass.** — **1791** MUHLENBERG *Index Florae* 179 *Tripsacum dactyloides*, Sesame-grass. **1829** EATON *Botany* (ed. 5) 426. **1857** GRAY *Botany* 582 *Tripsacum.* Gama-Grass. Sesame-Grass. . . . *T. dactyloides.* . . . It is sometimes used for fodder at the South, where better is not to be had.

sesquicentennial ˌsɛskwɪsɛnˈtɛnɪəl, *n.* The celebration of a one hundred and fiftieth anniversary. Also as adj.

1880 *London & Prov. Mus. Trades Rev.* 15 Nov. 3/1 The Sesquicentennial of Baltimore was celebrated during the second week of October. **1888** *Advance* 9 Aug., The sesquicentennial celebration of the church. **1925** *N.Y. Times* 15 Oct. 16/4 The 150th anniversary of the adoption of the Declaration of Independence will be officially observed . . . at the grounds of the Sesquicentennial Exposition.

***session,** *n.* As the last term in **bull, court of (general), executive, extra, extraordinary, fall, joint, lame duck, long, panic, regular, salary grab, short, special session(s).**

***set,** *n.*

1. Of a river flatboat crew: A position from which to begin concerted action. *Obs.*

1826 FLINT *Recoll.* 25 They raise their pole, walk forward in Indian file, and renew their 'set,' as the phrase is, again. **1843** *Amer. Pioneer* II. 271 The crew . . . walked slowly down the running board to the stern—returning at a quick pace to the bow for a new sett.

2. A suitable place to set a trap for an animal. *Rare.*

1834 A. PIKE *Sketches* 33 He took it on foot, with his six traps on his back, obtained a set for all of them, and went back to camp.

3. (See quot.) *Obs.*

1865 TURNER *Cotton* 30 Upon level land, I require a set of hands to plant ten acres per day, length of rows averaging four hundred and forty yards; a set of hands is one harrower, one opener one to sow seed, and one to cover.

4. A young oyster or the crop of young oysters in a given locality.

1887 GOODE *Fisheries* v. II. 540 (*footnote*), There is no word in the Northern States for infant oysters, except the terms 'set,' 'spat' [etc.]. **1906** *N.Y. Ev. Post* 23 Aug. 7 The oyster 'set' in Connecticut waters this year is a success.

As the last term in **back, bone, check, dead, off, parlor, reverend, running, saw, square, thick, water set.**

***set,** *a.*

1. Ready, prepared. In phrases, as *get set, all set. Colloq.*

1844 GREGG *Commerce of Prairies* I. 51 Each teamster vies with his fellow . . . and it is a matter of boastful pride to be the first to cry out —'All's set!' **1893** *Outing* XXII. 154/1 At the words 'Get set!' the arms are raised, the knees slightly bent, and . . . the starter braces his legs apart. **1947** *Trail & Timberline* June 92/1 His 'All set!' is the signal for the lead man to move smoothly out along the ledge.

2. In combs.: (1) **set bowl,** a fixed lavatory bowl with running water and drainpipe; (2) **gun,** a loaded and cocked gun set up in such a way as to be discharged by a person or animal that touches a string attached to the trigger; (3) **hoop,** ?a very heavy temporary hoop used in barrel-making; (4) **pole,** a fishing pole left anchored for a time; (5) **tub,** a fixed tublike receptacle in which clothes are washed.

(1) **1899** HOWELLS *Ragged Lady* 185 He sympathized with her in her wish that there was a set-bowl in her room. — (2) **1882** *Cent. Mag.* March 723/2 Various kinds of traps, set-guns, and dead-falls are also employed against [the black bear]. — (3) **1850** *Rep. Comm. Patents 1849* 382 Revolving cylinders [are] to be used for the bending of . . . coopers' sett hoops. — (4) **1859** *S. Lit. Messenger* XXVIII. 143/2 Bill . . . 'lowed he'd watch the set pole.

(5) **1884** HOWELLS *Silas Lapham* (1891) I. 66 I'll do the wash . . . , said Mrs. Lapham. I presume you'll let me have set tubs.

***set,** *v.*

1. **To set oneself down,* to settle, take up one's abode. *Obs.*

[**1637** *Conn. Col. Rec.* I. 10 Mr. Haine & Mr. Ludlowe shall goe . . . to parle with the bay aboute our settinge downe in the Pequoitt Countrey.] **1818** FEARON *Sketches* 224 The squatter . . . 'sets himself down,' upon land which is not his own.

2. *To set up,* (*a*) (see quot.), (*b*) to treat, often *to set 'em up, colloq.,* (*c*) with *to,* to court (a girl), *colloq.*

(*a*) **1848** BARTLETT 372 At public auctions an article is sometimes 'set up,' or 'started,' by the auctioneer at the lowest price at which it can be sold. (*b*) **1851** A. T. JACKSON *Forty-Niner* (1920) 92 You can't do anything in this country without setting 'em up first. **1931** *K.C. Times* 6 Aug., While the Judge was new at the business the courthouse folks informed him that it was customary to 'set 'em up' to the gang there, too. **1948** *Copper Camp* 174 Skib always insisted that combatants part as friends—after the usual formality of 'setting them up' for the house. (*c*) **1874** ALDRICH *P. Palfrey* vi, I'd wager a cookey, now, young Dent has ben settin' up to that Palfrey gal, an' there's ben trouble. **1886** *Harper's Mag.* Dec. 42/1 Why don't he set up to Sally Brent?

3. *tr.* To start or kindle (a fire) with malicious intentions. Also *to set out fire,* to start a backfire *q.v.*

1843 OLIVER *Eight Months* 63 Where the country is becoming settled, the inhabitants generally are opposed to 'setting out fire,' the risk to houses, crops, and fences being often very great. *Ib.* 64 This setting out 'fire to meet fire,' as it is termed, may appear, at first sight, a somewhat hazardous experiment. **1895** CRADDOCK *Mystery Witch-Face Mt.* 2 The fire . . . was 'set out' in the woods with the mission to burn only the leaves and undergrowth. **1906** *N.Y. Ev. Post* 15 Nov. 3 Two fires in tenement house letter boxes were set to-day at an early hour. **1950** *Dixie Roto Mag.* 8 May 16/2 Why do people set fire to the woods?

4. **To set back,* to cost. *Slang.*

1933 *OED Supp. s.v.,* That the automobile will set some guy back a lot of dough. **1946** *Reader's Digest* Sep. 10/1 Some bugs are, unfortunately, not much affected even when liberally dosed with DDT. One is the cotton boll weevil, an insect which sets us back perhaps $100,000,000 every year.

5. In substantival combs.: (1) ***setback,** (see quot. 1877); (2) **-back euchre,** (see quot. 1899); (3) ***-down,** (see quot. 1907), *slang;* (4) **-fired,** stupid, "all fired," *slang;* (5) **out dance,** ?among Indians, a dance upon setting out on a journey, *rare;* (6) ***-up,** (*a*) the call or order to sit down to a meal, (*b*) personal bearing or carriage, (*c*) in billiards, pool, etc., a position of the balls which makes it easy for a player to score, also an arrangement or situation, (*d*) a prize fight, game, etc., that has been "fixed," all *colloq.* or *slang.*

(1) **1877** BARTLETT 572 *Set-back,* the reflux of water made by a counter-current, by the tide from the sea meeting the flow of a river, by a dam, &c. **1895** REMINGTON *Pony Tracks* 139 The crane takes off from his grassy 'set back' in a deliberate manner. — (2) **1845** *Big Bear Ark.* 176 It may be crack-loo, poker, brag, or set-back-euchre. **1899** CHAMPLIN & BOSTWICK *Cyclo. Games & Sports* (ed. 2) 299/2 *Set-back Euchre.* . . . At the opening of the game each player's score is credited with five points. When he makes a point it is subtracted from the score, and when he is euchred he is set back two points, which are added to his score. He whose score is first reduced to nothing, wins. — (3) **1900** FLYNT *Tramps* 105 (F.), He will almost always give a beggar a set-down. **1907** LONDON *Road* 28 At the very next house I was given a 'set-down.' Now a 'set-down' is the height of bliss. One is taken inside, very often is given a chance to wash, and is then 'set-down' at a table. — (4) **1882** *Harper's Mag.* Dec. 129/1 I'm afeared I hev ben a set-fired bigoted old man.

(5) **1791** J. LONG *Voyages* 35 The dances among the Indians . . . [include] the set out dance. — (6) (*a*) **1843** CARLTON *New Purchase* I. 180 When the 'set up' is ordered, the gentlemen instantly seat themselves alongside, and partly under the table. (*b*) **1890** T. C. CRAWFORD *Eng. Life* 147 [English soldiers] have a set-up not to be found in any of the soldiers of the Continental armies. (*c*) **1895** *Outing* XXVI. 66/1, I found an easy set-up and pocketed fifteen straight. **1932** GRAYSON *Leaders* 455 It was one thing, however, to reorganize the Union Pacific on paper and give it a new and more hopeful financial set-up. (*d*) **1929** *Variety* 10 April 23/3 Because of the continuous set-ups and the assured frame the pug was as below par as the hero was physically handicapped.

settable ˈsɛtəbl̩, *a.* Of land: Capable of being planted with corn. *Rare.* — *a***1656** BRADFORD *Hist.* 260 They should only lay out settable or tillable land.

***settee,** *n.* (See quot.) — **1891** *Cent.* 5527/3 *Settee,* . . . a small part taken off from a long and large sofa by a kind of arm: thus, a long sofa may have a settee at each end partly cut off from the body of the piece.

***setter,** *n.* A device in a typesetting machine. — **1876** *Centennial Exp.* 208 All the preceding letters . . . were shoved along to the left upon the stick by a small piece of metal, called the 'setter.'

*setting, *n.*

1. a. A Quaker family meeting. *Rare.* **b.** *Keep your setting,* keep your seat. *Colloq.*

(a) 1825 NEAL *Bro. Jonathan* II. 163 It was a 'setting'—a sort of religious exercise, after a 'visitation.' — **(b) 1864** TROWBRIDGE *Cudjo's Cave* 93 Keep yer settin', keep yer settin', Mr. Villars. **1901** WILKINS *Portion of Labor* 97 Keep your settin', keep your settin'.

2. In combs.: (1) ***setting out,** the gifts made to a bride or a newly married couple, or equipment provided to start them off in married life; (2) **pole,** a pole used to propel a boat, a punting pole; (3) **room,** a living room, a sitting room; (4) ***up,** (*a*) a person's size and build, (*b*) a useful gift to a bride or to a newly married couple, both *rare.*

(1) 1833 GREENE *Dod. Duckworth* II. 35 She would be likely to receive a pretty penny by way of marriage dowry; or, as the people expressed it, a good setting out. **1893** HOLLEY *Samantha at World's Fair* 632 A silver bedstead the Sultan is a-goin' to give to his daughter as a part of her settin' out when she marries. — **(2) 1645** *Conn. Rec.* I. 473, 2 owers, 2 setting poles, an halespeare. **1753** WASHINGTON *Diaries* I. 65, I put-out my setting Pole to try to stop the Raft. **1882** THAYER *From Log-Cabin* 193 James was standing on deck, with the setting-pole against his shoulders. **1941** DORSEY *Master of Miss.* 9 The boats went downstream gaily, slightly aided by oar or setting-pole. — **(3) 1741** *N.H. Probate Rec.* III. 30, I give to my beloved Wife . . . ye furniture of ye Chamber over our Setting room. **1854** TROWBRIDGE *M. Merrivale* 312 Don't get excited. We're here now in Robert's comfortable sett'n'-room. **1904** GLASGOW *Deliverance* 312 'Where is he now?' 'Complaining over some bills in his setting-room.' — **(4)** (*a*) *a***1861** WINTHROP *J. Brent* 236, I've got a daughter myself, . . . jest about your settin' up. (*b*) **1877** COOKE *Huckleberries* (1896) 33, I guess I'll let her hev that 'ere brown 'nd white heifer for a settin' up.

*settle, *v.*

1. *intr.* Of a place: To be settled or occupied. *Colloq.*

1806 CLARK in *Lewis & C. Exped.* VII. (1905) 398 The Lands on the lower portion of that river is settling fast. **1907** LILLIBRIDGE *Trail* 271 We were on the other side of the river, before the country settled up.

2. *To settle down,* to take up one's abode as a settler. Cf. ***set,** *v.* **1.**

1818 FEARON *Sketches* 222 A man purchased a quarter, or half section, for the purpose of *settling down.*

3. *tr.* (*a*) To cause the grounds of (coffee) to sink, (*b*) to cause (a boat) to sink, *rare,* (*c*) to melt (snow), *rare.*

(*a*) **1846** FARNHAM *Prairie Land* 332 The coffee is drawn back and settled with an egg. **1883** *Harper's Mag.* March 578/1 Should the coffee be settled with an egg or with fish-skin? (*b*) **1847** LANMAN *Summer in Wilderness* 34 We ran into a downward-bound steamer, and settled her to the bottom. (*c*) **1888** *Forest & Stream* 15 March 147/2 The frequent chinooks have settled the snow faster than it fell.

***settled,** *a.* **1.** Of a country: Peopled with settlers. **2.** Of soap: Refined by fusing in weak lye or water.

(1) 1792 IMLAY *Western Territory* 149, I take notice only of the settled country. **1840** IRVING *Wolfert's Roost* 259, I had relatives in Lexington, and other settled parts. — **(2) 1898** G. H. HURST *Soaps* 228 Three chief varieties of hard soap . . . known as 'curd,' 'fitted,' or, in America, 'settled,' and 'run' soaps. **1906** LAMBORN *Modern Soaps* 329 White settled soap made from tallow does not fulfil these requirements.

*settlement, *n.*

1. The action of settling in a new country.

1675 *Conn. Rec.* II. 249 More to the number of eleven [are] prepareing for setlement. **1872** TICE *Over Plains* 43 The concentration of the cattle trade here retards the growth, settlement, and improvement of the rich agricultural country. **1911** *Indian Laws & Tr.* III. 671 Executive order of June 14, 1879, . . . is hereby amended so as to permanently withdraw from settlement . . . all those tracts.

b. *pl.* Inhabited or settled areas, communities, etc., as contrasted with the wild country beyond the frontier.

1737 BRICKELL *N. Carolina* 116 The Mountain-cat . . . seldom appeareth or approacheth near the Settlements. **1848** BRYANT *California* iv. 54 We met four trappers from the Rocky Mountains, returning to the 'settlements.' **1913** J. B. ELLIS *Lahoma* 81 Them moccasins will do famous until I can get you shoes from the settlements.

With words indicating the nationality of those making the settlement.

1707 *Mass. Province Acts* VIII. 211 Committees of both Houses [shall] be appointed to Consider . . . Whither it be practicable to Insult the French Settlements in Nova-Scotia? **1775** ADAIR *Indians* 261 They were in the horse-pen, preparing that day to have set off with their returns to the English settlements. **1872** MCCLELLAN *Golden State* 75 On his way, at the Mohave settlements on the Colorado, all the party except Smith and two others were killed by the Indians. **1919** *Maine My State* 315 Our Swedish settlement today has three saw mills.

c. A part of a southern plantation reserved for the use of Negroes, either as living quarters or for farming. *Obs.*

1839 KEMBLE *Residence in Ga.* 18 There are four settlements or villages (or, as the negroes call them, camps) on the island. **1865** in FLEMING *Hist. Reconstruction* I. 351 The inspector of settlements and plantations will . . . give them [*sc.* Negroes] a license to settle such island or district. **1884** *Cent. Mag.* April 859/2 The owner of broad acres finds it profitable to divide them into 'settlements' and rent them to the 'hands.'

2. A sum of money or other property given a pastor in addition to his salary. *Obs.*

1755 *Essex Inst. Coll.* XXI. 156 Voted . . . forty Pounds in the year 1756 for his Settelment. **1781** PETERS *Hist. Conn.* (1829) 232 Finding the Doctor's design was to become a churchman, the people demanded the settlement given him twelve years before. *a***1840** N. EMMONS *Works* I. p. xxvii, Before the war began, my people punctually paid my salary, and advanced one hundred pounds of my settlement a year before it was due by contract.

b. "A pastor's homestead as furnished by a parish, by a gift either of land, with or without buildings, or of money to be applied for its purchase" (*Cent.*).

*a***1840** N. EMMONS *Works* I. p. xxvii, I had just purchased a settlement, and involved myself in debt.

3. In combs.: (1) **settlement company,** a company formed to place settlers in particular regions, *obs.;* (2) **duty,** a duty incumbent upon one who settles upon a grant of land, also attrib., *obs.;* (3) **Indian,** a peaceful Indian living in a village or settlement designated by white settlers, *obs.;* (4) **master,** a master or teacher living in a settlement, *colloq.;* (5) **right,** the right to acquire a certain amount of land for a settlement, *obs.;* (6) **road,** a road which serves a settlement, *colloq.;* (7) **store,** a store that serves the needs of a settlement.

(1) 1857 in *Dana Great West* 226 We, the undersigned, do hereby agree to form an Octagon Settlement Company. — **(2) 1853** STRICKLAND *Twenty-seven Yrs.* I. 89 On condition that they would become actual settlers on the land, and perform certain settlement duties, which consisted in chopping out and clearing the concession lines. *Ib.* 174 The place I had selected to watch for them was an old settlement duty-road, which had been cut out some years before. — **(3) 1740** *S.C. Hist. Soc. Coll.* IV. 94 A free Negro . . . used to Scout with some Negroes and Settlement Indians as their Captain. **1775** ADAIR *Indians* 344 Our Settlement-Indians were at this time closely hunted, many were killed, and others carried off. — **(4) 1867** *Atlantic Mo.* Nov. 611/2 Backwoods melodies . . . had been invented for native ballads by 'settlement' masters.

(5) 1784 FILSON *Kentucke* 37 The Settlement and pre-emption rights arise from occupation. **1838** *S. Lit. Messenger* IV. 294/2 All settlement rights were saved, . . . and we set about making new settlements. — **(6) 1843** CARLTON *New Purchase* I. 89, I have travelled all day long upon a neighbourhood or settlement road. — **(7) 1843** R. CARLTON *New Purchase* I. 142 After long and arduous toils they contrive to barter some produce at the settlement store for sugar, tea, coffee and paper.

As the last term in **by, college, dead, European, final, frontier, German, homestead, Indian, Kentuck, lower, marine, out, pine, Shaker, squatter, White settlement.**

*settler, *n.*

1. One who settles in a new country.

1654 [in **first settler**]. **1739** W. STEPHENS *Proc. Georgia* I. 469 One Bunyon, a Builder of Boats and a Settler there, had . . . built a large Ferry-Boat. **1839** A. WILSON *Foresters* 83 Settlers.—A term usually applied in America to those persons who first commence the operations of agriculture in a new country, by cutting, clearing, and actual settlement. **1947** *Commonweal* 23 May 139/2 Each settler was allowed a minimum of 40 acres and settlers drew lots for the land.

collect. **1890** *Rep. Secy. Agric. 1889* 265 The settler . . . is growing a better crop of maize in all the eastern counties of the Centennial State than is the farmer of Michigan. **1925** BRYAN *Memories* 219 The settler . . . had invited in a relentless and apparently unmanageable power.

b. actual settler, one who actually lives in a newly settled region, as distinguished from a land speculator. *Obs.*

1779 *Ky. Petitions* 51 [We] pray that every Actual settler . . . may be entituled to Draw a free lott. **1838** C. NEWELL *Revol. Texas* 187 None but *actual settlers* could hold land in Texas, except perhaps by purchase from a *native* Mexican. **1899** in *Cong. Rec.* (1900) 17 Jan.

891/1 A large number of citizens . . . are actual settlers and home builders upon certain odd-numbered sections of public land.

c. One of the founders of a town. *Obs.*

1701 *Phila. Ordinances* (1812) 1 At the humble request of the inhabitants and settlers of this town of Philadelphia. *c***1870** CHIPMAN *Notes on Bartlett* 395 *Settler*, 1. . . . the founder of a town, one who makes or gains a settlement.—New England.

2. In the possessive in combs.: (1) **settler's ax,** any ax used by a settler, symbolizing the complete destruction of the forest; (2) **elm,** prob. a big elm dating back to the time of the first settlers, thriftily cut down and sawed up before its value as lumber had deteriorated, *rare.*

(1) **1863** TAYLOR *H. Thurston* 277 No settler's axe had cut away a single feather from the ragged plumage of the hills. **1881** *Harper's Mag.* April 659/2 With the . . . disappearance of the game before the settler's axe . . . the conditions of the Indian himself have radically altered. — (2) **1858** HOLMES *Autocrat* xi. 296 The hubs of logs from the 'Settler's ellum,' Last of its timber,—they couldn't sell 'em.

As the last term in **back, Dakota, first, Free Soil, homestead, new, old, out, pre-emption, tomahawk, western settler.**

settling clerk. In N.Y. City a clerk who represents a bank in the bank clearing house. — **1896** WHITE *Money & Banking* 240 Each bank sends to the clearing house—a delivery clerk and a settling clerk. **1902** LORIMER *Lett. Merchant* 52 Bill Harris had found out that he was no good as a settling clerk.

* **setwork,** *n.* A method of making strong barrels and other containers by bending and setting the staves; a vessel or container made by this method. Also attrib. *Obs.*

1720 SEWALL *Diary* III. 276 [I] bid him leave off working at his Trade of Set-Work Coopering. **1824** DODDRIDGE *Notes* 146, I have seen him make a small neat kind of wooden ware called set work. **1843** *Amer. Pioneer* II. 110 In a few months . . . a sufficient amount of nice setwork pails were made.

b. setwork cooper, a cooper who makes barrels by setwork. *Obs.*

1691 SEWALL *Letter-Book* I. 119, I received of Edward Spalding and Joseph Tompson, Executors of Will. Needham of Boston, N. E., Setwork Cooper, Fifty pounds. **1701** *Boston Rec.* 10 [No one] Shall Kindle or make any fire . . . within two rodds of any wooden house, warehouse, wood pile or any other combustable matter . . . except in Ship Carpenters building yards, Sett work coopers, and Ropemakers works.

* **seven,** *a.* and *n.* In combs.: (1) **seven bark,** see as a main entry; (2) **building,** prob. a building in a row of seven such houses erected as boarding places on or near Capitol Hill, Washington, D.C., *c*1850, *obs.;* (3) **-by-nine,** small, inferior, insignificant, trivial, *colloq.;* (4) **Cities,** several ancient towns of New Mexico, now thought to have been pueblos of Zuñi, whose reputed wealth first induced the Spaniards to come to the Southwest, now *hist.*, cf. **Cibola 1;** (5) **Council Fires,** (see quot.); (6) **figure,** denoting a large sum, suggestive of at least a million (dollars), *rare;* (7) **men,** a group of seven men, elected annually in some N. Eng. towns to have charge of various public matters of local concern, *obs.;* (8) **Mule Barnum,** (see quot.), *obs.;* (9) **Nations,** (see quot. 1910); (10) **pence,** a dime, also attrib., *obs.;* (11) **plate stove,** a stove made of seven plates bolted together, *obs.;* (12) **shooter,** a Spencer seven-shot rifle or carbine, or a revolver holding seven cartridges; (13) **sleepers,** [prob. f. G. *siebenschläfer*, a dormouse], (see quot.); (14) **thirty,** a U.S. Government bond (see quot. 1890), *obs.;* (15) **up,** all-fours, a card game, also attrib.; (16) **-year apple,** a tropical shrub, *Casasia clusiaefolia*, or its apple-like fruit; (17) **-year itch,** a type of itch allegedly requiring seven years for healing, also transf., *colloq.;* (18) **-year locust,** ?=**seventeen-year locust.**

(2) **1884** *Cent. Mag.* March 645/2 Gaunt rows of 'six buildings' and 'seven buildings' were erected here and there, principally as boarding-houses to accommodate the members of Congress and those who had business with them during the winter. — (3) **1840** *Spirit of Times* 11 April 63/3 (We.), A little 7-by-9 sheet. **1855** M. THOMPSON *Doesticks* 102 Wanted to see the world; so started for the seven-by-nine State of Rhode Island. **1894** *Cong. Rec.* 11 Jan. 743/2 Those little two penny, seven-by-nine protection furnaces were replaced by the magnificent Democratic furnaces. — (4) **1857** DAVIS *El Gringo* 58 The first knowledge the Spaniards of Southern Mexico had of this country was about the year 1530, when it was known as the country of the seven cities. **1895** *Amer. Hist. Ass. Rep. 1894* 92 In the spring of 1540 Francisco Vasquez Coronado . . . found the Seven Cities of Cibola. **1949** *Exciting Western* May 90/1 The great Captain Coronado prepared to march against the Seven Cities.

(5) **1910** HODGE *Amer. Indians* II. 514 Seven Council Fires. The league of the Dakota . . . existing previous to the migration of the Teton from Minnesota to Missouri r., and commemorated later in ceremony and tradition. — (6) **1908** LORIMER *J. Spurlock* 77 If I had gone to the Governor, recanted, and told him that I was engaged to Miss Grey, he would have given me a seven-figure blessing. — (7) **1636** *Ipswich Rec.* 20 Feb., The seven men shall have no power to grant any Land in . . . the Cow pasture. **1656** *East-Hampton Rec.* I. 103 It is ordered by the 7 men that for the payment of the towne rate wheate shalbe paid [etc.]. — (8) **1885** *Mag. Amer. Hist.* April 394/2 Seven Mule Barnum.—A nickname applied by Republicans to Mr. Barnum of Connecticut, who is said to have used the words 'seven mules,' in a cipher dispatch meaning 'seven thousand dollars.' — (9) **1793** *Mass. H.S. Coll.* 3 Ser. V. 137 While at Navy Hall, a deputation from the Seven Nations of Canada arrived. **1910** HODGE *Amer. Indians* II. 515/1 Seven Nations of Canada. The 7 tribes signified are the Skighquan (Nipissing), Estjage (Saulteurs), Assisagh (Missisauga), Karhadage, Adgenauwe, Karrihaet, and Adirondax (Algonkins).

(10) **1880** *Harper's Mag.* Oct. 804/2 Poor Len had to borrow a quarter here, and a seven-pence there. **1896** J. C. HARRIS *Sister Jane* 144, I gave her a sevenpence piece, and left her. — (11) **1854** *Maysville Eagle* 2 Nov. 1/5 Coal Heating Stoves, . . . 6 plate Hall " ", 7 " " " " " ". — (12) **1860** *Charleston* (S.C.) *Mercury* 6 Nov. 3/5 (*advt.*), Allen & Wheelock's seven shooters. **1866** F. KIRKLAND *Bk. Anecdotes* 659/2 The infantry consisted entirely of West Virginia Union troops, armed with the Spencer seven-shooter. **1884** F. Y. HEDLEY *Marching through Ga.* (1890) 131 Trenches were occupied by dismounted cavalry, armed with seven-shooters. — (13) **1795** *Amer. Philos. Soc.* IV. 122 In the vicinity of Philadelphia, the *Dipus Americanus* is called, by some persons, the *Seven-Sleepers.* — (14) **1867** *Harper's Wkly.* 26 Oct. 674/4 No difference is made in the price of the 2d series of Seven-Thirties and any other series. **1890** *Harper's Mag.* Oct. 700/2 They were known by the name of 'seven-thirties' from their rate of interest.

(15) **1830** *N.Y. Constellation* 11 Sep. 2/5 Some tugged at the bottle, . . . and some played seven-up. **1846** *Spirit of Times* (N.Y.) 11 July 229/1 Said to be one of the best 'seven up' players in all Texas. **1939** ROLLINS *Gone Haywire* 36 One of the visitors spread a blanket and on it began a game of seven-up. — (16) [**1730** *Phil. Trans.* XXXVI. 434 The Seven Years Apple . . . ripens in seven or eight Months Time.] **1884** SARGENT *Rep. Forests* 95 *Genipa clusiæfolia*. . . . Seven-Year Apple. . . . The large insipid fruit . . . [is] popularly but incorrectly supposed to require seven years in which to ripen. **1933** SMALL *Southeastern Flora* 1257 (*Genipa clusiifolia* Jacq.—Seven-year Apple.) Coastal sand-dunes and hammocks, near the coast, S pen. Fla. and Florida Keys. — (17) **1899** CHESNUTT *Conjure Woman* 154 Lawsuits wuz slow ez de seben-yeah eetch. **1909** CALHOUN *Miss Minerva* 10 She got the seven-year itch. **1949** *Chi. D. News* 23 June 47/1 He stuck around like the 7-year itch. — (18) **1930** FERBER *Cimarron* 45 Her tone was that of one who speaks of prairie dogs, seven-year locusts, or any other Western nuisance. **1950** *Chi. Tribune* 18 Jan. 12 Like the seven year locust—the interior decorating bug moves from room to room.

sevenbark ˈsɛvən͵bɑrk, *n.* Ninebark *q.v.* Also any one of certain species of hydrangea, or the bark of such a plant.

1762 CLAYTON *Flora Virginica* 77 *Spiræa floribus albis, foliis opuli.* Sevenbark. **1806** LEWIS in *L. & Clark Exped.* IV. (1905) 49 The seven bark or nine bark as it is called in the U' States is also common [near Ft. Clatsop]. **1901** MOHR *Plant Life Ala.* 535 *Hydrangea arborescens.* . . . Wild Hydrangea. Sevenbark. . . . Western Ohio Valley to Missouri, south to Florida, Mississippi, and Arkansas. *Ib.* 536 *Hydrangea quercifolia*. . . . Oak-leaf Hydrangea. Sevenbark. . . . The bark, 'sevenbark,' is used in domestic medicine. **1931** CLUTE *Plants* 128 *Hydrangea arborescens* appears to be two barks short, at least it was known as seven barks!

* **seventeen,** *a.* and *n.*

1. (See quot.) *Obs.*

*a***1827** in *Pub. Col. Soc.* XXV. 47–8 In the beginning of the year 1768, . . . the house of Representatives of Massachusetts voted to send a circular letter to the legislatures of the several provinces, upon the alarming state of affairs with the mother country. . . . Seventeen members only voting for it, & ninety two against. These numbers therefore were used in a political manner—Seventeen being called the Tory number.

2. seventeen-year locust, the periodical cicada, *Cicada septendecim*, which remains underground seventeen years (in the South, thirteen) before maturity.

1817 *Columbian Centinel* 14 May 1/4 The southern papers have announced that the present is the year for the appearance of what is called, in rural language, the Seventeen Years Locust. . . . The insect lives above ground about two months, and 17 years in it. **1843** *Farmers' Cabinet* 15 July 368/1 Some discussion in regard to the exact year in which the seventeen year locusts make their appearance is now going on in the various newspapers. **1907** *St. Nicholas* June 746/2 Seventeen-year locusts in emerging from their long life in the ground build similar chimneys or turrets. **1950** Calif. Acad. Sci. *News Letter* March 1 The new film, 'Animals Unaware,' contains, among other things, the interesting life history of the seventeen-year 'locust' or cicada.

Also **seventeen-year cicada.**

1870 *Amer. Naturalist* III. 106 The eggs and young of the seventeen-year Cicada. **1950** *Chi. D. News* 13 Jan. 42 The periodic or 17-year cicada lives the longest of any known insect, spending most of its life underground in the nymph stage before emerging.

* **seventh,** *a.* In combs.: (1) **Seventh-Day Adventist,** a member of a millenarian sect of Adventists who observe the seventh day as the true Sabbath, hence **Seventh-Day Adventism,** also attrib.; (2) **-Day Baptist,** one of a group of Sabbatarian Baptists organized in Rhode Island in 1671, also a Seventh-Day German Baptist, also attrib.; (3) **-Day German Baptist,** a member of a small Sabbatarian sect with monastic tendencies, composed of seceders from the Dunkers in Pennsylvania.

(1) 1875 *Amer. Cyclo.* XIV. 745/2 Seventh Day Adventists . . . originated as early as 1844. **1947** PERRY *Cities of Amer.* 142 At Milam Park . . . you can see little groups gathered around speakers who may be holding forth on anything from *El Communismo* to Seventh Day Adventism. **1949** *Telephone Reg.* (McMinnville, Ore.) 4 Aug. 1/8 Construction on a new school for the Seventh Day Adventist denomination of McMinnville started Monday. — **(2) 1703** *Pa. Hist. Soc. Mem.* IX. 185 One William Davis, a Seventh-Day Baptist, had a dispute with him [George Keith] in the Keithian meeting-house. **1846** *Dollar Newspaper* (Phila.) 21 Jan. 3/3 The Committee on Vice and Immorality are at present engaged upon petitions from Seventh-day Baptists, in which they protest against being fined for carrying on their usual worldly pursuits on the Christian Sabbath. **1901** STILLMAN *Autobiog. Journalist* I. 5 The relations of the historic First Seventh Day Baptist Church at Newport with the churches observing the 'Lord's-Day Sabbath' were always most kindly. **1948** *Nat. Geog. Mag.* Aug. 170/1 Still a stronghold of Seventh-Day Baptists, for whom Saturday is the Sabbath, Westerly [Rhode Island] prints the only Sunday evening newspaper in the United States. — **(3) 1867** DIXON *New Amer.* II. 308 In a very short time this [Baptist] body was divided into Old School Baptists, . . . Seventh-day German Baptists, Tunkers [etc.]. **1903** *Encycl. Amer.* VIII. *s.v.*, A small body of seventh-day German Baptists, with five churches and some 200 members, is usually included among the Brethren.

* **seventy,** *a.* and *n.*

1. (*cap.*) **a.** In the Mormon Church, an elder especially commissioned for missionary service, usu. *pl.* as the name of an organization of such elders. **b.** *Committee of Seventy*, a citizens' committee formed in 1871 in New York City for the purpose of breaking the political power of the Tweed Ring. Now *hist.*

(a) 1841 *Times & Seasons* (Nauvoo, Ill.) 16 Aug. 514/1 The Saints are informed that the quorum of the Seventies have withdrawn their fellowship from Elder Jesse Turpin, until he made satisfaction, to said quorum for his conduct. **1846** *Voree* (Wis.) *Herald* April 4/2 By the Law of God there can be but seven seventies, and *no one has a right to that priesthood except he travel and preach to the nations.* **1943** DEVOTO *Yr. of Decision* 317 Lee was a Seventy (just below the high priesthood in the organization) and he was also one of the Sons of Dan, one of the prophet's Gestapo. — **(b) 1871** *Nation* 7 Sep. 153/1 The committee of seventy . . . have already begun operations. **1872** *N.Y. Herald* 2 Nov. 2/3 The Committee of Seventy Boxes. The Committee of Seventy will provide at its boxes for voters, on the day of election, the following tickets, in bunches. **1914** *Cyclo. Amer. Govt.* III. 468/3 A Committee of Seventy was formed in September, 1871, which brought about the destruction of the Ring.

2. In combs.: (1) **Seventy-niner,** (see quot.), *obs.*; (2) **-six,** used allusively with reference to 1776, the year of the Declaration of Independence, also attrib., cf. *Sons of Seventy-six;* (3) **-sixer,** (see quots.), *obs.*

(1) 1928 FOY & HARLOW *Clowning Thro' Life* 135 As California had its Forty-Niners, so the Leadville Argonauts are spoken of in local history as Seventy-Niners. — **(2) 1801** *Ky. Herald* (Lexington) 10 Feb. 2/4 The patriots of seventy six—hallowed be the earth that pillows their heads. **1806** *Balance* V. 2/2 False philosophy and seventy-six fever still predominate. **1880** B. S. HEATH *Labor & Finance Revol.* (1891) 32 Our patriotic fathers of '76 fought seven long years. — **(3) 1806** FESSENDEN *Democracy Unveiled* II. 162 Seventy-sixer, a cant word adopted by some of our mushroom patriots, to designate the men who first asserted American Independence in the year 1776. **1812** PAULDING *J. Bull & Bro. Jon.* (1814) 109 He bought one of those cocked hats usually called seventy-sixers, from having been in fashion about that time. **1837** *S. Lit. Messenger* III. 8 Here is a Gotham . . . weekly. . . . I say its a perfect seventy-sixer.

severalty Indians. App. Indians holding property individually in contrast with those who hold land in common. *Obs.* — **1866** *Rep. Indian Affairs* 256 The severalty Indians, who are mostly of the Pottawatomie band, take most interest in the school.

* **severe,** *a.* Vicious, powerful, headstrong. *Colloq.*

1829 *Western Mo. Rev.* III. 120 They were in the habit of managing a wild, or, as the phrase was, a 'severe' colt. **1889** *Harper's Mag.* Jan. 270/1 He never killed a man who did not deserve killing. . . . He is called in the language of the country [Ky.], a 'severe' man. **1907** WHITE *Arizona Nights* 5 'Trailer,' said he sadly, 'is a little severe.'

sewan 'siwɑn, *n.* Also **seawant.** [Du. (<Algonquian) *sewan, zeawant.* Cf. Narraganset *siwân* "unstrung shell beads."] Wampum. Now *hist.*

1627 *N.Y. Hist. Soc. Coll.* 2 Ser. II. 346 As an employment in winter they make sewan, which is an oblong bead that they make from cockle shells. **1701** G. WOLLEY *Jrnl. N.Y.* (1902) 38 Their Money is called *Wampam* and *Sea-want*, made of a kind of Cockle or Periwinkle-shell, of which there is scarce any, but at Oyster-Bay. **1843** *Nat. Hist. N.Y., Zoology* VI. 217 From the internal purple part of the shell, the colored beads of the aborigines were formerly manufactured, constituting the *sewan* or *wampum.* **1881** *Harper's Mag.* March 537/2 The medium of commerce was *seawant* better known as wampum, which was simply a number of strung shell beads. **1905** *Olde Ulster* Dec. 372 The Currency at the Esopus was *sewan* or wampum (clam shell beads).

* **Seward,** *n.* [Wm. H. *Seward* (1801–72), Amer. statesman and Secretary of State (1861–69).]

1. Seward Whigs, (see quot. 1914). *Obs.*

1855 HAMBLETON *H. A. Wise* 233 The very few Democrats in the Legislature voted generally against the resolutions, and the Seward Whigs . . . seem to have gone in a body for them. **1914** *Cyclo. Amer. Govt.* III. 300/2 *Seward Whigs*, a name given in New York politics, to distinguish those approving Seward's course in the U.S. Senate in 1850 regarding the compromise measures.

Hence **Sewardism, Sewardite.** *Obs.*

1855 *Herald of Freedom* 18 Aug. 1/5 The majority of the free State party adopt the doctrine which Bennett of the Herald has branded as Sewardism—they cry, 'leave Slavery alone where it already exists,' but 'no more slave states.' **1855** *N.Y. Herald* 19 Nov. 8/3 Sewardism does not merely lose power, but position. **1855** *N.Y. Wkly. Tribune* 22 Dec. 3/2 He is denounced as an apostate, a 'Sewardite,' a 'Black Republican.' **1856** *Western Citizen* (Paris, Ky.) 28 March 3/2 The party in Ohio has purged itself of Abolitionism, as it did . . . in New York, where it rid itself of the Sewardites.

Also **Seward party, ticket.** *Obs.*

1855 HAMBLETON *H. A. Wise* 234 Two other resolutions were adopted . . . to indicate that the Seward party are not favorable to the Know Nothings. **1855** *N.Y. Herald* 6 Nov. 4/4 Thurlow Weed says that the New York Herald concedes the election of the Seward ticket.

2. Seward's Folly, Icebox, Alaska, acquired by the U.S. from Russia in 1867, Seward being the Secretary of State at the time.

1883 WRIGHT *Among Alaskans* 13 It was the outcropping of this idea that caused the land, at the time of its purchase, to be loudly called 'Seward's Folly.' **1947** *Newsweek* 20 Jan. 27/1 'Seward's Icebox' was empty last week, almost as bare of food and the necessities of life as its own tundra. **1948** KERWIN *Civil-Military Relationships* 39 We have often had the best of international horse-trading—from the Revolutionary debts owed to France, . . . down to . . . the shrewd purchase of Alaska, 'Seward's folly.'

Sewee 'siwi, *n.* [App. a native name.] (See quot. 1910.) Also attrib.

1677 *S.C. Hist. & Gen. Mag.* XI. 85 [At] Sewee . . . the Sewee Indians are seated. **1709** LAWSON *Carolina* 10 Some Sewee Indians [were] firing the Canes Swamps, which drives out the Game. **1856** W. J. RIVERS *Sk. Hist. South Carolina* 38 The Santees, Seewas, and Etiwans . . . lived between Charleston and Savannah. **1910** HODGE *Amer. Indians* II. 515/2 Sewee. A small tribe, supposedly Siouan, formerly living in E. South Carolina.

b. Sewee bean, (see quot. 1909).

1737 WESLEY *Journal* I. (1909) 402 Sewee-beans, [are] about the size of our scarlet, but to be shelled and eaten like Windsor beans. **1909** *Cent. Supp.* 121/2 Seewee bean, the small lima, or butterbean, preferred in the southern United States to the large lima.

sewellel səˈwɛləl, *n.* [f. *shewallal,* Chinook name for a robe or blanket made of the skins of these animals, erroneously understood by Lewis and Clark as the name of the animal, which was really called *ogwoollal.*] The mountain beaver, *Aplodontia rufa,* found in a limited area in the Pacific Northwest.

1806 LEWIS in *L. & Clark Exped.* IV. (1905) 109 *Sewelel* is the Chinook and Clatsop name for a small animal found in the timbered country on this coast. **1833** *Polit. Examiner* (Shelbyville, Ky.) 9 Feb. 2/1 The sewellel is an animal resembling the squirrel, the fur of which is highly valued by the natives. **1940** *Mt. Hood Guide* 21 Not a true beaver, the sewellel or mountain beaver, . . . finds his natural abode in burrows in the earth.

***sewing,** *a.* and *n.* In combs.: (1) **sewing bee,** a social gathering of women who meet to sew, usu. for benevolent purposes; (2) **bird,** a clamp, part of which is

Sewing bird

shaped like a bird or bird's beak, used for holding material that is being sewn by hand; (3) **circle,** a group of women who meet regularly to sew for charitable purposes, a meeting of such a group, also attrib.; (4) **frolic,** =**sewing bee,** *obs.;* (5) **hall,** a room or hall in which plaited straw hats were sewn, *obs.;* (6) **machine,** a machine for sewing or stitching cloth; (7) **-machine agent,** one who sells sewing machines by house to house canvassing; (8) **-machine girl,** a girl who operates a sewing machine, *obs.;* (9) **society,** a society or group of women, usu. in a particular church, organized to sew for charitable purposes, a meeting of such a society.

(1) **1880** *Harper's Mag.* Aug. 354/2 There is church twice a month, sewing bees, and apple-butter stirrings. **1914** E. STEWART *Lett. Woman Homesteader* 90 It was to be a sewing-bee, a few good neighbors invited, and all to sew for Grandma. **1949** *N.O. Times-Picayune Mag.* 13 Feb. 2/2 Time was when a taffy pull was a gala group activity on a par with a sewing bee or a barn raising. — (2) **1857** *Spirit of Times* 21 Nov. 192/3 (*advt.*), Gold Bracelets, Gold Pencils, Sewing-Birds. **1876** WARNER *Gold of Chickaree* 318 If you want . . . a thimble or a sewing-bird, or any little trifle like notepaper or a clotheshamper, help yourself. **1949** R. J. SIM *Pages from Past* 10 Who can say when the ancestor of the sewing bird made its appearance on the edge of the table? — (3) **1846** *Knickerb.* XXVII. 373 As if I too belonged to a sewing-circle, and read charity sermons. **1900** MUNN *Uncle Terry* 74 They were the subject of much after-church and sewing-circle talk. **1943** CROW *Amer. Customer* 205 These were loaned free to sewing circles which worked on the making of uniforms. — (4) **1822** WOODS *English Prairie* 213 Picking cotton, sewing, and quilting frolics, are meetings to pick cotton from the seeds, make clothes, or quilt quilts. (5) **1864** *Harper's Mag.* Oct. 578/2 Later still [in Providence, R.I.] 'sewing halls' were established. — (6) **1847** *Rep. Comm. Patents 1846* 101 A very beautiful and perfect sewing machine has been patented this year. **1949** *This Week Mag.* 9 Oct. 24/2 Why won't the sewing machine work? — (7) **1873** BAILEY *Life in Danbury* 58 [He] knocked down two sewing-machine agents with the other end. **1912** N. WOODROW *Sally Salt* 123 The sewing-machine agent awaited them. **1946** *Reader's Digest* Dec. 36/1 In California, a former sewing-machine agent became famous as 'Rainmaker' Hatfield. — (8) **1871** in W. D. ADAMS *Dict. of Drama* (1904) I. 150 'Bertha, the Sewing-Machine Girl,' A Play by Charles Foster, was first performed at the Bowery Theatre, New York in Aug. 1871. — (9) [**1842** DICKENS *Amer. Notes* I. 109 They have among themselves [at the State Hospital in Boston] a sewing society to make clothes for the poor.] **1845** KIRKLAND *Western Clearings* 120 Emma and her Mother did not join the sewing society. **1920** *3d Nat. Country Life Conf. Proc.* 96 The 'steered' committee . . . gathers up the neighborhood discussion from the . . . sewing society.

sex appeal. Personal charm, esp. that based upon physical make-up, tending to draw together persons of opposite sex. Also attrib.

1926 *New Republic* 21 April 275/2 At the end of several years of familiarity with the movies and their ways I am inclined to think that their greatest contribution to contemporary thought has been the invention and popularization of the phrase 'sex appeal.' The person of average intelligence finds the words funny. Yet when I was invited to be one of the (presumably hundreds of) judges in the Shubert Sex Appeal Contest, in a letter which alarmingly began, 'Dear Mr. Seldes, Have you got sex appeal?' I regretted that the cautious Shuberts had not offered to pay all expenses. **1931** *K.C. Times* 24 Aug., Jeff Roark . . . has issued a warning against the 'sex appeal' magazine solicitors, as he terms them. **1949** *Your Physique* June 7/2 The lure that is so predominate these days of artificiality is the so called 'glamour'—or sex appeal.

sexology ˌsɛksˈɑlədʒɪ, *n.* [**sex* + **-ology.*] The scientific study of matters pertaining to sex. — **1902** WM. H. WALLING (*title*), Sexology. **1915** S. C. TAPP (*title*), Sexology of the Bible; the Fall and Redemption of Man a Matter of Sex.

S.G.Q. Abbreviation of "Sound of the Goose Question." *Obs.* Cf. ***goose,** *n.* **4. a.** — **1855** *Herald of Freedom* 14 April 2/5 The triumph of the pro-slavery party is overwhelming and complete. . . . Kansas is saved! . . . Kansas has proved herself to be S.G.Q.

shack ʃæk, *n.*[1] [See note.]

App. f. Amer. Sp. *jacal,* earlier written *xacal* and pronounced as though written *shacal* (<Aztec *xacalli,* wooden hut). Prob. a more primitive form of the borrowing is seen in shackle *q.v.,* of which *shack* may well be a shortening. See J. Platt, Jr., in *N. & Q.* Ser. x. XII. 306/2. Cf. **jacal.**

A poor hut or shanty.

1878 *Rep. Indian Affairs* 42 Too much praise cannot be given to these homesteaders for . . . the erection of this building, while they, themselves, were living in shacks. **1901** WHITE *Westerners* 222 Then yere's the cookee's shack. **1949** *Chi. D. News* 10 Nov. 18/5 Losick says he plans to live in his little shack from now on.

attrib. **1885** *Home Missionary* March 426 The rude shacklike store, has changed to an imposing structure of stone or brick. **1891** RYAN *Told in Hills* 191 From their tones one would gather the impression that all the splendors of a metropolis were as nothing when compared with the luxuries of 'shack' life in the 'bush.' **1908** *Pacific Mo.* Jan. 2/2 In a little 'shack' saloon at the Owyhee mines he made some remark about the merits of his six-shooter. **1942** STEGNER *Mormon C.* 28 There are in Mormondom very few of the typical western shack-towns with derailed dining cars and false-fronted stores. **1947** PRICE *Trails I Rode* 41 Red Lodge . . . was then a little shack town.

b. A room or roomlike structure serving various purposes. *Colloq.*

1939 *Denver Post* 2 Jan. 16–B/6 Other work will include the building of a ski shack. **1947** *Christian Sci. Mon.* 15 Jan. 9/1 Al's [ham radio] station, like most of the other 75,000 American amateurs, is a bedroom converted into what they call a 'shack.' **1948** *Sat. Ev. Post* 25 Dec. 22/2 The caboose has other loving titles: the ambulance, anchor, . . . rest room, rough rider, shack, shanty.

As the last term in **claim, cook, feed, frame, log, mess, picket, pole shack.**

***shack,** *n.*[2] (See quots.) — **1891** *Cent.* 5539/1 *Shack,* . . . in the fisheries, bait picked up at sea by any means, as the flesh of porpoises or of sea-birds, refuse fish, etc., as distinguished from the regular stock of bait carried by the vessel or otherwise depended upon. Also *shack-bait.* (New Eng.) **1904** *Mass. Comm. Fisheries Rep.* 78 At first a shack trip referred particularly to a voyage on which cheap species of fishes constituted the bulk of the catch. *Ib.,* Such fish, tumbled in together, without effort at classification, are known as shack.

***shack,** *n.*[3] A railroad brakeman. *Slang.* — **1907** LONDON *Road* 213 As the freight got out of Philadelphia she began to hit up speed. Then I understood what the shack had meant by suicide. **1947** BEEBE *Mixed Train Dly.* 313 The stock was valuable and a roundup was imperative, but, as the shacks and hoggers of the S.V. were unaccustomed to the saddle, a score of professional cowpokes were engaged for the task.

***shack,** *v.*[1] Also **shag.** [App. the same word as *EDD* **shack* (*q.v. s.v.* **shake, v.* 5), of a horse: to go at a jog-trot.]

1. (See quots.) *Colloq.*

[**1860** *Bella Union Melodeon Songster* 15 She was butty as a shack-horse.] **1890** *N. & Q.* IV. 214 *Shack.* . . . This word was formerly common in the New England States among ball players. . . . To *shack* for another player meant to chase wild or fly balls for him. **1891** *Cent.* 5539/1 *Shack,* . . . to go after, as a ball batted to a distance. (Local, U.S.) **1900** *D.N.* II. 58 Shack. 1. To gather tennis balls. . . . 2. To go in search of, hunt up a person or thing. **1949** J. B. HERRICK *Memories* 6, I was of little worth except to chase or 'shag' balls in the field.

2. To go or ride along at a slow, ambling gait. *Colloq.*

1916 H. Titus *I Conquered* ii. 31 Yonder [was] a man shacking along on a rough little horse, head down, listless. **1947** *Sat. Ev. Post* 8 March 53/1 Each winter Steve shacked in to Barry's camp a couple of times, sat in the log office a day and shacked out.

shack ʃæk, *v.*[2] [f. **shack,** *n.*[1]] *tr.* To build up into a shack. *Rare.* — **1919** Cady *Rhymes of Vt.* (1923) 59 Our sugarhouse was jest a shack, Shacked up 'regardless,' bit by bit.

shacker ˈʃækɚ, *n.* [In 1890 quot. f. **shack,** *v.*[1], in 1902 quot. f. **shack,** *n.*[2]] (See quots.) *Colloq.* — **1890** *N. & Q.* IV. 214 The *shacker* stood behind the catcher to intercept, or to chase any ball that might pass the latter. **1902** *Boston Transcript* 20 Aug. 13/6 A 'shacker,' as the vessels which bring fresh cod and haddock to T wharf are called.

shackle ˈʃækḷ, *n.* =**shack,** *n.*[1] *Obs.* — **1890** *Advance* (Chi.) 18 Sep., I found lots of families living in the most miserable shackles.

***shad,** *n.*

1. =**shad-belly coat.** *Obs.*

1856 Cozzens *Sparrowgrass P.* 137 If it were not for the broad-brimmed hat, and the straight coat, which the world's people call 'shad,' I would be a Quaker.

2. =**shadbush.**

1886 *Harper's Mag.* June 149/1 Kites, tops, hoops . . . all appear in due season as regularly as . . . the blossoms of the 'shad.' **1938** Damon *Grandma* 73 There was not so much to enjoy on coming in the front gate of the picket fence: merely maple, shad, ferns, periwinkle.

3. Used locally with qualifying terms, as **Alabama, stink, tailor, white-eyed, winter, yellow-tailed shad.**

1788 Schöpf *Reise* II. 67 Winter-Shad nannte man einen Fisch, welcher sich den ganzen Winter durch in diesem und den übrigen virginischen Flüssen findet, und in grosser Menge in Nezen gefangen wird. **1884** Goode *Fisheries* I. 569 In North Carolina . . . the names 'Yellow-tail' and 'Yellow-tailed Shad' are occasionally heard [for the menhaden]. *Ib.* 608 In the Potomac . . . [the hickory Shad] is called the 'Tailor Shad.' *Ib.* 610 In the Chesapeake region . . . [the mud shad is known as the] 'Winter Shad,' or 'Stink Shad'; . . . in the Saint John's River as the 'Stink Shad,' or 'White-eyed Shad.' **1896** Jordan & Evermann *Check-List Fishes* 282 *Alosa alabamæ.* . . . Alabama Shad, Gulf Coast of United States.

4. A local name for the crappie.

1903 T. H. Bean *Fishes N.Y.* 460 Among the many names which have been applied to the crappie are: . . . John demon, shad, white croppie.

5. In special combs.: (1) **shad-bellied,** (*a*) of a coat, cut so that it slopes away in front, (*b*) of persons, thin- or flat-bellied, lank; (2) **belly,** (*a*) a term of contempt for a Quaker or preacher, *obs.*, (*b*) =next; (3) **-belly coat,** (see quot. 1859); (4) **-belly fence,** (see quot.); (5) **box,** a floating box used by fish culturists for hatching shad, also **shad-hatching box;** (6) **eater,** (see quot.), *obs.;* (7) **fyke,** (see quot. and cf. **fyke,** *n.* **1**), *obs.;* (8) **pole,** a pole used in setting a shad net; (9) **scales,** (see quot.), *obs.;* (10) **slide,** an artificial passage permitting shad to pass an obstruction in a stream; (11) **wallow,** (see quot.).

(1) (*a*) **1832** Kennedy *Swallow Barn* II. 5 A shad-bellied blue bob-tail coat . . . was well adapted to show the breadth of his brawny chest. **1891** *Cent. Mag.* Feb. 540 Put him into a shad-bellied drab and he would still have retained traces of dudishness. (*b*) *a***1846** *Quarter Race Ky.* 163 Do I know it, you no-souled, shad-bellied, squash-headed, old night-owl you! **1857** *S. Lit. Messenger* XXV. 305/1 He is a keen-made man, of the shad-bellied, weazel pattern. **1871** Stowe *Sam Lawson* 8 He was kind o' mournful and thin and shad-bellied. — (2) (*a*) **1851** *Polly Peablossom* 80 Stop, there, you eternal shad-belly. **1859** Bartlett 396 Drab coats of this shape are worn by Quakers, who are hence sometimes called *shad-bellies.* **1902** Mark Twain in *Harper's Mag.* Feb. 441 Just about eligible to travel with this bilk here—Shadbelly Higgins—this loud-mouthed sneak. (*b*) **1852** *S. Lit. Messenger* XVIII. 680/1 He had . . . doffed the cassock, or, rather, the shad-belly, for the gown. — (3) **1842** *Spirit of Times* (Phila.) 18 March (Th.), 'What do you ask for this?' said a gentleman in a shad-belly coat. **1859** Bartlett 396 *Shad-Belly Coat,* one which slopes gradually from the front to the tails, and has no angle. **1891** Welch *Recoll. 1830–40* 181 For an office, or careless coat, the frock was sometimes exchanged for a bottle green 'shad-belly' coat. — (4) **1917** *D.N.* IV. 399 Shad-belly fence, n. A fence made thus: two stakes are driven so as to cross each other. A rail is laid on them with one end in the notch and the other on the ground. Half way, more or less, to the lower end, two more stakes are driven astride the rail, and another rail laid in the same way, and so on.

(5) **1884** Goode *Fisheries* I. 409 These eggs were placed in shad boxes. **1884** *Cent. Mag.* April 901/1 Green's Shad-Box. These, and the invention of Mr. Seth Green's floating shad-hatching box, were really all the important improvements or experiments made. — (6) **1871** De Vere 631 *Shad-eaters,* is the slang term very generally applied to members of the Legislature of the State of Connecticut—from an imaginary fondness for the excellent shad caught in those rivers. — (7) **1848** Bartlett 152 The large bow-nets in New York harbor, used for catching shad, are called *shad-fykes.* — (8) **1852** *Knickerb.* XXXIX. 572 We remarked that the shad-poles had almost entirely disappeared from the Hudson. **1884** Roe *Nature's Story* 197 A moment later a shad-pole gyrated past me. — (9) **1872** De Vere 296 *Money* itself has in the United States . . . probably more designations than any other object . . . [as] *wherewith, shadscales,* or *scales.*

(10) **1876** Goode *Classif. Animal Resources U.S.* 37 Shad-slides, used in the rivers of North Carolina. — (11) **1884** Goode *Fisheries* I. 606 The favorite spawning grounds of the Shad, or 'Shad Wallows,' as they are termed by the fishermen, are on the sandy flats.

b. In the names of animals: (1) **shad bass,** a rockfish, *obs.;* (2) ***bird,** =**shad spirit;** (3) **fly,** (*a*) any one of various insects, esp. May flies, that appear about the time shad enter the rivers, (*b*) an artificial fishing fly for catching shad: (4) **frog,** =**leopard frog;** (5) **herring,** (*a*) =**fall herring,** (*b*) the thread herring, *Opisthonema oglinum;* (6) ***salmon,** a fish of the family Coregonidae, such as the Otsego bass; (7) **shiner,** a young shad; (8) **spirit,** Wilson's snipe, *Capella delicata;* (9) **trout,** (see quot.); (10) **waiter,** (see quot. 1911).

(1) **1790** *Pa. Packet* 1 March 3/3 William Robinson, Junr. . . . Hath for Sale. . . . Shad bass (or rock) and Halibut in barrels. — (2) **1883** in Trumbull *Names of Birds* 157 [In Del.] snipe are called shad-birds by many of the fishermen. — (3) (*a*) **1836** T. Power *Impressions* II. 295 Myriads of a winged insect called the shad-fly; these covered and crowded every building, filled the water and the air. *a***1862** Thoreau *Maine Woods* 237 We met with ephemeræ (shad-fly) midway, about a mile from the shore. (*b*) **1884** *Nat. Museum Bul.* No. 27, 944 Fly-Books. Containing salmon, black bass, shad, grayling, and trout flies. — (4) **1791** W. Bartram *Travels* 276 The shad frog, so called in Pennsylvania from their appearing and croaking . . . at the time people fish for shad, is a beautiful spotted frog. **1897** *Chambers's Encycl.* V. 13/1 Widely distributed in the United States are two forms —the Shad- or Leopard-frog . . . and the Wood-frog.

(5) (*a*) **1814** Mitchill *Fishes N.Y.* 452 Long-Island Herring. *Clupea mattowacca.* . . . Some call this fish the *shad herring* and some the *fall shad.* **1903** T. H. Bean *Fishes N.Y.* 197. (*b*) **1842** *Nat. Hist. N.Y., Zoology* IV. 265 The Spotted Thread Herring . . . appears in our waters about the beginning of September, where it is often called the Shad Herring. — (6) **1842** *Nat. Hist. N.Y., Zoology* IV. 248 The Common Shad Salmon . . . occurs in Lakes Erie and Ontario, and in the smaller lakes in the interior of the State. **1850** S. F. Cooper *Rural Hours* 376 It is a shad-salmon, but is commonly called the 'Otsego Bass,' and is considered one of the finest fresh-water fish in the world. — (7) **1832** Williamson *Maine* I. 158 There are two or three varieties [of shiner], one is like the minnow, another 'the shad-shiner.' — (8) **1844** *Nat. Hist. N.Y., Zoology* II. 35, [I] was told that it was the Shad Spirit, announcing to the scholes of shad, about to ascend the river, their impending fate. **1883** *Cent. Mag.* Oct. 923/1 The fishermen . . . have dubbed its author the 'shad spirit.' **1917** *Birds of Amer.* I 227 Wilson's Snipe. *Gallinago delicata.* . . . [Also called] Shadbird; Alewife-bird; Shad Spirit. — (9) **1911** *Rep. Fisheries 1908* 318/2 Squeteague (*Cynoscion regalis*). . . . It is known as . . . 'shad trout,' 'sea trout,' and 'salt-water trout' in the Middle and South Atlantic states.

(10) **1879** Goode *Cat. Animal Resources U.S.* 57 *Prosopium quadrilaterale.* . . . Shad-waiter. **1911** *Rep. Fisheries 1908* 318/1 The Menominee whitefish . . . is also locally known as . . . 'shad-waiter.'

c. In the names of plants: (1) **shadbush,** see as a main entry; (2) **flower,** (*a*) =**shadbush,** (*b*) whitlow grass; (3) **scale,** (see quot. 1913).

(2) (*a*) **1836** Lincoln *Botany* App. 185/1 Shad-flower. *Aronia.* **1843** Torrey *Flora N.Y.* I. 225. **1861** Wood *Botany* 329 *Amelanchier.* Shad-Flower. Small trees or shrubs. (*b*) **1893** *Amer. Folk-Lore* VI. 137 *Draba verna,* shad flower. West Va. — (3) **1905** *N.Y. Ev. Post* 3 June, I remember one plant, peculiar, I believe, to the Utah desert, called 'shad scale,' whose leaves are so salty that when you touch your finger to them and then put it to your tongue, you can easily taste the salt. **1913** W. C. Barnes *Western Grazing Grounds* 57 There is another favorite forage bush known as shad scale (Atriplex canescens). **1942** Lillard *Desert Challenge* 168 A scrawled sign points to two wavering ruts through the sagebrush or shad scale: 'Golden Pheasant Mine, 5 Mi.'

Also in various names for the shadbush, as (1) **shad-berry,** (2) **blossom,** (3) **blow,** (4) **tree.**

(1) **1847** Wood *Botany* 245 *A*[*melanchier*] *Canadensis.* . . . Shad Berry. June Berry. Wild Service Berry. . . . Fruit pleasant to the taste, ripening in June. **1897** Sudworth *Arborescent Flora* 212 *Amelanchier canadensis.* . . . Service-tree. . . . Shad Berry (Fla.). — (2) *a***1817** Dwight *Travels* I. 42 *Shad-blossom.* This tree grows about fifteen feet in height. **1893** *Outing* July 285/1 Against this darker back-

ground stood out the silver of young poplar and the delicate white flower of the 'shad blossom.' — (3) **1846** BROWNE *Trees Amer.* 282 *Amelanchier canadensis.* The Canadian Amelanchier. . . . [Also called] Wild Pear-tree, Sugar Plum, June Berry, Shad-blow, Shad-flower. **1892** *Amer. Folk-Lore* V. 95 *Amelanchier Canadensis.* . . . sugar plum; shad-blow. N.H. — (4) **1818** *Mass. H.S. Coll.* 2 Ser. VIII. 169 The latter part of May appear . . . among the trees, the elm, ash, beech, aronia or shad tree, yellow and white birch, and red and sugar maples. **1832** WILLIAMSON *Maine* I. 114 Among the shrubs of the largest size is the *Boxwood*, or 'shad-blossom.' . . . It grows 15 or 18 feet in height, has a gray bark, flowers in May, about the time the shad and their fellow travellers ascend the rivers in the spring, and is therefore called 'shad tree.' **1880** *Harper's Mag.* June 70 Yonder on the wooded slope the feathery shad-tree blooms like a suspended cloud of drifting snow.

As the last term in **back, bug, chicken, Connecticut, fall, gizzard, gold, hardhead, hickory, mackinaw, mountain, mud, Ohio, Ohio gold, stink, white-eyed, winter, yellow-tailed shad.**

shadbush ˈʃædˌbuʃ, *n.* [See note.]

"It was called shad-bush by the settlers along the Atlantic coast because its blooming was supposed to mark the season when the shad ascended the rivers to spawn" (Clute, 23).

Any one of various American shrubs, or small trees of the genus *Amelanchier.* Cf. **Maybush, May cherry, June berry.**

1817–8 EATON *Botany* (1822) 181 *Aronia botryapium*, shad-bush, june-berry. *a***1862** THOREAU *Cape Cod* 152 The Shadbush (*Amelanchier*), Beach Plums, and Blueberries, . . . were very dwarfish. **1905** *N.Y. Ev. Post* 29 July 5 The only tree which has buds at all like that of the beech, is the shadbush or June berry, *Amelanchier Canadensis.* **1942** WEYGANDT *Plenty of Penna.* 121 That shadbush had been left for love of its bloom by some backwoodsman clearing here a hundred years ago.

b. (See quot.)

1891 *Cent.* 5539/3 *Shad-bush.* . . . The name is sometimes given (erroneously) to the flowering dogwood, Cornus florida.

* **shade,** *n.*

1. A form of parasol. *Obs.*

1846 *St. Louis Reveille* 1 Jan., A full assortment of Umbrellas, Parasols, Parasolettes and Shades . . . at the lowest market prices. **1888** DALY *Lottery of Love* 21 Put up your shade, it's raining.

2. A device, consisting usu. of a length of stiff cloth mounted on a roller, for use at a window to regulate light, etc. Cf. **shade-cord, -roller.**

1867 A. J. EVANS *Vashti* xviii, Though a rose-coloured shade was lowered, the sash had been raised. **1900** BONNER *Hard-Pan* 87 She saw the split and ragged shades in the windows. **1910** TOMPKINS *Mothers & Fathers* 335 The room is absurdly dark; suppose you pull up that shade. **1949** *Sat. Ev. Post* 19 March 103/2 We'll be needing new shades in the kitchen soon.

3. In combs.: (1) **shade card,** a color chart; (2) **-cord,** a pull-cord on a window shade; (3) **grown,** *a.* (see quot.); (4) **hat,** a woman's or girl's hat having an unusually broad brim to protect the wearer's complexion from the sun; (5) **-roller,** (see quot. 1909); (6) **tree,** a tree, usu. planted or set out, valued for its shade.

(1) **1886** *Delineator* Nov. 403 These Shade Cards show 290 shades of Briggs' Imported Silk and Floss. — (2) **1904** RIIS *Roosevelt* 298 When he passed each window [he] would seize the shade-cord and give a little abstracted pull. — (3) **1906** *Springfield W. Republican* 10 May 15 The growing of wrapper tobacco in tents, or, in other words, shade-grown wrappers. — (4) **1871** *Harper's Mag.* Dec. 57/2 Shade hats, nubias, and fancy rigmaroles were not then invented. **1907** HARRIS *Tents of Wickedness* 112 'Worse than ever!' cried the girl, throwing herself down in one of the big wicker chairs and taking off her shade hat.

(5) **1851** CIST *Cincinnati* 245 Shade and map-rollers, turning in ivory, done in a superior style. **1909** *Cent. Supp.* 1205/3 Shade-roller, . . . a roller resting upon supports in a window or other place, upon which a window-shade, curtain, awning, screen, or map may be rolled. — (6) **1806** *Balance* 22 July 228 (Th.), It is to be regretted that a shade tree, useful and ornamental as the poplar, should be in danger. **1944** CLARK *Pills* 264 Life with its many treacherous hazards and ineffective diet spared a large number of persons to enjoy a peaceful and leisurely old age of chewing tobacco and dipping snuff on porches and under shade trees.

As the last term in **brush, corn, window shade.**

* **shade,** *v. tr.* To reduce or lower (prices or rates) slightly. *Colloq.*

1875 *Chi. Tribune* 27 Oct. 6/4 Prices are not strong, the quotations being shaded on fair orders. **1898** WESTCOTT *D. Harum* 17 Mebbee we c'd shade the price a little. **1913** STRATTON-PORTER *Laddie* ix, He said Mr. Pryor had shaded his price.

***shader,** *n.* (See quot. 1839.) — **1839** *S. Lit. Messenger* V. 314/1 The people . . . have a mortal aversion to fine spreading trees; which under the *horrible* name of '*shaders*' they extirpate in the most cruel manner. **1895** *Dept. Agric. Yrbk. 1894* 466 Thus the box elder, an excellent shader in certain portions of the West, is a failure as soil cover in others.

shadine ʃæˈdin, *n.* [f. * *shad*+*-ine*, on the analogy of * *sardine.*] **1.** The round herring, *Etrumeus sadina.* **2.** (See quot.)

(1) **1782** CRÈVECOEUR *Letters* 132 Near Pochick Rip . . . they catch their best fish, such as, . . . cod, smelt, perch, shadine, pike, &c. **1842** *Nat. Hist. N.Y., Zoology* IV. 263 The Spotted Shadine. . . . Our species does not appear to be common. — (2) **1884** *Nat. Museum Bul.* No. 27, 1041 An effort was made a few years ago to introduce menhaden canned in oil, under the name of 'American sardines,' 'American boneless sardines,' and 'shadines.'

shadow potatoes. (See quots.) — **1909** FARMER *Boston Cook-Book* 314 Shadow Potatoes (Saratoga Chips). **1941** *Ib.* 413 Shadow Potatoes or Saratoga Chips. Slice as thin as possible (using vegetable slicer). Soak 2 hours in cold water, changing water twice. Dry and fry.

shadrach ˈʃædræk, ˈʃedræk, *n.* [Name of one of the three Hebrews preserved unharmed in the fiery furnace (Dan. 3).] (See quot. 1841.) — **1841** WEBSTER II. 581/2 *Shadrach*, in the smelting of iron, a mass of iron in which the operation of smelting has failed of its intended effect. (*Local.*) **1891** *Cent. Mag.* Dec. 178 This mineral is a piece of what the iron-workers call shadrach.

* **shady,** *a.* **1.** (See quot. 1859.) **2.** *To keep shady*, to keep quiet so as to escape notice or detection, also *to keep* (someone) *shady. Colloq.*

(1) **1859** MATSELL *Vocabulum* 78 *Shady*, quiet; out of sight; not easily found. **1872** EGGLESTON *End of World* 174 He disappeared, and he's been shady ever since. — (2) **1847** FIELD *Drama in Pokerville* 81, I kep' shady, Miss Fanny, bress de Lord, I did. **1887** STOCKTON *Hundredth Man* xii, I've promised to keep him shady. **1897** CLOVER *Paul Travers' Adv.* 51, I guess I can fix you out if you hang around here, but keep shady.

* **shaft,** *n.*

1. A memorial obelisk or column.

1837 EMERSON *Poems* (1904) 159 Bid Time and Nature gently spare The shaft we raise to them and thee. **1873** HARTE *Stories & Poems* (1914) 217 The gray shaft that commemorated the Morristown dead of the last civil war obliterated the past. **1910** *N.Y. Ev. Post* 29 Sep., The gravestone is 'the marble shaft' or 'the simple stone which marks the spot where his mouldering dust is deposited.'

2. In combs.: (1) **shaft furnace,** (see quot. 1876); (2) **house,** a structure at the entrance to a mine shaft for housing the hoisting machinery, also attrib.

(1) **1871** RAYMOND *Mines* 378 Smelting in Shaft Furnaces. **1876** KNIGHT 2128/2 *Shaft-furnace*, . . . one in which the ore, in a state of division, is dropped down a chimney through the flame. — (2) **1871** RAYMOND *3d Rep. Mines* 344 The quartz is brought from the mine, unless the mill is in or near the shaft-house, in wagons. **1914** ATHERTON *Perch of Devil* 355 Not daring to summon the shaft house man, he was sneaking down the ladder. **1917** SINCLAIR *King Coal* 176 They came to the shaft-house of Number Two.

As the last term in **elevator, prospect, prospecting, sun shaft.**

* **shafting,** *n.* **1.** The sinking of a shaft, also collect., the shafts of a mine. **2.** "A darkening of the shaft, or quill of a feather, as in some breeds of poultry" (*Cent. Supp.*).

(1) **1871** RAYMOND *3d Rep. Mines* 297 Aggregate of shafting over 5,000 feet. **1874** ALDRICH *P. Palfrey* vii, After four weeks of drifting, and shafting, and all manner of prospecting, they failed to find it again, and gave up. **1876** RAYMOND *8th Rep. Mines* 273 About 1,000 feet of shafting and drifting will represent the amount of work done. — (2) **1897** *Dept. Agric. Yrbk. 1896* 462 Shafting on the back will also help the black stripe in the saddles.

shaganappi ˌʃægəˈnæpɪ, *n.* [f. Cree *pisaganâbiy, pishaganâpi*, in sense shown here.] (See quot. 1910.) Cf. **babiche.**

1873 G. M. GRANT *Ocean to Ocean* 122 Shaganappi . . . does all that leather, cloth, rope, nails [etc.] . . . are used for elsewhere. **1880** *Scribner's Mo.* July 442/2 Should any part break in the course of a thousand-mile journey, shaganappi, or buffalo raw-hide thong, is in requisition. **1892** in C. W. GORDON *Life J. Robertson* 329 In the old days . . . every one had his pocket full of shaganappi. **1910** HODGE *Amer. Indians* II. 518/1 Shaganappi. Thongs of rawhide used for rope or cord. *Shaganappi*, or 'Northwestern iron,' was an important factor in the economic development of the N.W., where it was a god-send to the mixed-bloods and white settlers.

shagbark ˈʃægˌbɑrk, *n.*

1. Any one of several closely related species of hickory, esp. *Carya ovata*, having bark of a shaggy or scaly character; a tree of such a species or its nut. In full **shagbark hickory, shagbark hickory nut.**

1751 J. BARTRAM *Observations* 67 A great hill, cloathed with large Magnolia, . . . shagbark-hickery, chestnut and chestnut-oak. **1777** *Mass. Hist. Soc. Proc.* 2 Ser. II. 236 [Buy me] a bushel or two of shagbarks. **1831** *Boston Transcript* 22 Aug. 2/4 These insects are extravagantly fond of shagbarks, or American Walnuts. **1938** DAMON *Grandma* 98 A row of lofty shagbark hickory nuts were the only signs of former human interest. **1949** *Sat. Ev. Post* 16 April 147/2 They moved under the chestnut oaks and the shagbarks.

b. The wood or bark of the shagbark hickory.

1869 STOWE *Old-town Folks* 483 Ef the deacon hain't come down with his shagbark! **1894** *Advance* 20 Sep. 606/2 The teacher could be seen . . . carrying his blazing torch of shagbark. **1920** HOWELLS *Vacation of Kelwyns* 16 [He looked] as if he were hewn out of hickory, with the shag-bark left on in places.

2. shagbark walnut, shagbark hickory. Also attrib. with *tree*. Cf. **large-fruited shagbark walnut.**

1802 *Mass. Spy* 10 March (Th.), The growth of shagbark walnuts has been remarkably slow. **1827** J. Q. ADAMS *Memoirs* VII. 323 In my summer-house nursery two more of my shagbark walnut-trees have come up. **1947** BEROLZHEIMER *Regional Cookbook* 52 The shagbark walnuts, the hickory and the butternut trees dropped bushels of food for them.

b. The nut of a shagbark walnut tree.

1843 STEPHENS *High Life N.Y.* II. 27 The head of the pin was as big as a shag-bark walnut. **1878** STOWE *Poganuc People* 220 The frost ripened the shag-bark walnuts.

shagreened cutworm. A species of cutworm, *Feltia malefida*, native to the southern states and South America. — **1884** *Rep. Comm. Agric.* 292 The Shagreened Cut-Worm . . . , which has also been noticed to feed upon the cabbage-plant, appears to be confined to the Southern Atlantic States. **1928** *Insects of New York* 662 F. malefida Gn. Shagreened Cutworm. Essex Co; Brooklyn. Probably strays from the South.

Shahaptan ʃəˈhɑptən, *n.* Also **Sahaptin.** [f. *Sâptini*, *pl. Sahâptini*, the Salish name for these Indians. See also quot. 1918.] *pl.* or *collect.* The Nez Percé Indians. Also the language they spoke.

1845 *Quincy* (Ill.) *Whig* 6 Dec. 2/3 The Keyuse and Nezperces, or Seheptans, . . . are represented as having made most commendable advancement in agriculture. **1918** REES *Idaho* 109 Their earliest home was upon the Columbia River and when they were pushed southward the Salish called them 'Shahaptans,' meaning 'strangers from up the river.' **1940** SMITH *Puyallup-Nisqually* 22 If he spoke Sahaptin, it is also certain that he spoke Salish. **1947** DEVOTO *Across Wide Missouri* 11 Ethnologists use the name which the Flatheads bestowed on them, the Shahaptan, of uncertain meaning but perhaps a designation of the country they lived in.

Hence **Shahaptian,** *a.*, of or pertaining to these Indians.

1903 JAMES *Indian Basketry* 261 These rare and beautiful baskets were made by the different tribes belonging to the Shahaptian linguistic stock. **1940** *Mt. Hood Guide* 25 The lands of these mid-Columbia people . . . felt the full force of conflict [with] . . . the Sahaptin tribes to the south.

* **shake,** *n.* [See **shook.**]

1. A long, split, unplaned shingle or clapboard.

1772 *R.I. Commerce* I. 420 We herewith send you all the Shakes we can yet get in. **1845** *Cincinnati Misc.* I. 164/2 It was a small one-story house, shingled with what they call 'shakes,' all over the West and Southwest. **1923** SAUNDERS *So. Sierras Calif.* 30 Now and then a decaying cabin of shakes split from the forest . . . spoke of some forgotten miner's aspirations of yester year. **1948** DICK *Dixie Frontier* 26 Boards of this kind, commonly called shakes in the North, were three or four feet long and six or eight inches wide.

b. *pl.* (See quots., and cf. **shook 1.**) *Obs.*

1820 SCORESBY *Arctic Regions* I. 207 (*footnote*), The staves [of casks taken apart are] closely packed up in a cylindrical form, constituting what are called *shakes* or *packs*. **1841** DANA *Seaman's Man.* 122 *Shakes*, the staves of hogsheads taken apart.

2. Fever and ague. Usu. *pl. Colloq.*

1825 PAULDING *J. Bull in Amer.* 9 Even if the poor man should happen . . . to be free from the ague; or 'shake,' as they call it. **1886** EBBUTT *Emigrant Life Kans.* 118 Ague was rather prevalent in the summers on the creeks, but I never had a fit of the 'shakes' myself. **1948** *Chi. Tribune* 2 May IV. 3/1 The pioneer was not the rosy-cheeked powerful man of legend, but more usually a sallow and fever-ravaged figure living between spells of the shakes.

attrib. **1897** R. G. THWAITES *Afloat on Ohio* 186 We are now in the heart of the 'shake' country.

b. An attack of this.

1839 *N.O. Picayune* 10 Feb. 2/2 This is the day that i have the ague i had a shake this fore Noon. **1888** J. J. WEBB *Adventures* 62 He had a good 'shake,' and being without a doctor or medicine, the prospect of a rapid journey was rather discouraging.

3. a. *pl.* A section of country marked by large fissures or cracks in the earth caused by earthquakes. *Obs.* **b.** An earthquake. *Colloq.*

(a) 1833 *Sketches D. Crockett* 108 [They] asked me if I didn't want to go down to the Shakes, and take a bear hunt. **1847** CUMINGS *Western Pilot* 142 The neighborhood of that once little lake is now called 'The Shakes.' The earthquake put a mark on that place which time only will eradicate. — **(b) 1887** *Courier-Journal* 7 May 2/1 The Arizona Shake. **1907** *Westminster Gaz.* 12 April 3/2 That earthquake at San Francisco—the 'shake,' as the local papers lightheartedly called it within a fortnight. **1949** *L.A. Times* 14 May 1/4 Newspaper and police switchboards were flooded immediately with requests for information on the shake.

4. (See quot.)

1909 WEBSTER 1934/2 *Shake*, . . . short for *milk shake* or *egg shake*, etc., beverages of milk, or milk and eggs, flavored and shaken thoroughly.

5. In combs. (sense **1.**) of obvious meaning, as (1) **shake bucket,** (2) **cabin,** (3) **house,** (4) **maker,** (5) **roof,** (6) **shanty,** (7) **shop.**

(1) 1884 *Nat. Museum Bul.* No. 27, 270 Shake-bucket for transferring oysters to and from tubs. — **(2) 1885** SPRING *Kansas* 64 Big Springs in the autumn of 1855 was a place of four or five shake-cabins and log-huts. — **(3) 1857** *Lawrence* (Kans.) *Republican* 9 July 3 You are always welcome to his [a squatter's] log or shake house. **1888** *Kans. Hist. Coll.* (1890) IV. 249 To save the town-site from jumpers, several shake houses were built. — **(4) 1901** J. MUIR *Our National Parks* 298, I found many shake-makers at work in it, access to these magnificent woods having been made easy by the old mill wagon road. **(5) 1850** *Knickerb.* XXXVI. 73 They live in their cabin with its 'shakes roof' and mud-chimney. **1947** *Mich. Hist.* June 178 It was a small log cabin with a shake roof. [**1950** *Amer. Forests* Feb. 17/1 It was noted that practically every shack nestled among the pines had radio aerials on their shake rooftops.] — **(6) 1901** J. MUIR *Our National Parks* 356 Every one of the frail shake shanties is a centre of destruction, and the extent of the ravages wrought in this quiet way is in the aggregate enormous. — **(7) 1856** ROPES *6 Months in Kans.* 56 At a little 'shake' shop, we see tubs and pails.

6. In slang phrases: **a.** *To be no great shakes*, not to be of unusual importance or excellence. Also *to be some shakes*, to be unusual or important.

1837 *N.Y. Mirror* 23 Dec. 207/3 Come, Bill, taint no use sitting all day on this log—let's take to our axes again — the earthquake's no great shakes after all. **1894** *Life* 6 Sep. 156/2 It ain't no great shakes to find out sumthin' you don't know. **1929** *Texas Mo.* Jan. 26 Jesse James might be a great guy up in Missouri, but Rube Burrow was 'some shakes' down in Texas, yes, sir! **1950** *Esquire* Feb. 41/2 No great shakes is the sand but the scenery's sensational.

b. *To give* (something or someone) *the* (*cold*) *shake*, to get rid of, give the slip. Cf. **cold shake.**

1875 in J. F. DALY *Life A. Daly* 215, I desire to give the 'Two Orphans' a shake. **1883** MARK TWAIN *Life on Miss.* iii. 27 But none of them herded with Dick Allbright. They all give him the cold shake. **1909** WARE *Passing English* 84/2 Do you give me the cold shake?

As the last term in **dumb, fair, milk, oak, ring, swamp shake(s).**

* **shake,** *v.*

1. To forsake (someone), to leave (a place). *Slang.*

1872 MARK TWAIN *Roughing It* 337 He never shook his mother. . . . He give her a house to live in, and town lots, and plenty of money. **1876** ——— *Tom Sawyer* xxxv. 271 Now these clothes suits me, and this bar'l suits me, and I ain't never going to shake 'em any more. **1910** J. HART *Vigilante Girl* 52 Let's shake this deadfall. Come along, we'll go over to the Arcade.

2. * **shakedown,** in colloq. and slang uses: **a.** =**break-down,** *n.* **1.**

1845 *Xenia Torch-Light* 31 July 1/7 The organ struck up, from which he concluded that some sort of 'shake down,' was about to commence. **1908** SINCLAIR *Metropolis* 226 When he felt like dancing a shakedown, he could take a run out to God's country.

b. (See quot.) *Obs.*

1859 MATSELL *Vocabulum* 78 Shakedown. A panel-thief or badger's crib.

c. An act of extortion. Cf. **4.** (1) below.

1902 S. Low to N.Y. Aldermen, To the historic phrase 'blackmail' . . . have been added, as words of similar evil omen, the new and expressive terms shake-down and rake-off. **1947** *Chi. Tribune* 4 July 3/3 Four Chicago gangsters, having served one third of their 10 year terms in connection with a million dollar shakedown of the movie industry, have filed petitions for parole.

d. shakedown cruise, in the U.S. Navy, a cruise made for testing out a newly commissioned man-of-war and for accustoming the crew to the ship.

1934 WEBSTER. **1949** Calif. Acad. Sciences *News Letter* Sep. 3 On a 'shakedown' cruise August 22–26 aboard the *U.S.S. Mulberry*, samples of rock were obtained from the bottom in depths down to 600 feet.

3. ∗**shakeup,** (*a*) a hastily constructed building, also attrib. in the sense of makeshift, *slang, obs.*, (*b*) a change of personnel or a reorganization in an office or other organization, *colloq.*, cf. **4.** (2) below.

(*a*) **1873** BEADLE *Undevel. West* 728 Moorehead is a rather rough looking frontier town, consisting of . . . 'shake-ups' of pine lumber. *Ib.* 823 A man with ten thousand cattle upon the range, is content to . . . sit on a hickory 'shakeup' chair, sleep on shucks, live in a board or log 'shantie.' (*b*) **1887** *Courier-Journal* 6 Feb. 2/2 No Shake-up Probable. **1900** B. MATTHEWS *Confident To-Morrow* 145, I hear there's been another shake-up in the office. **1926** *Chi. Tribune* 20 March 19/3 A big shakeup, with a number of players forced off of teams because of the pro taint, was predicted.

4. In colloq. and slang phrases: (1) ∗*To shake down*, to extort money from, cf. ∗**shakedown c;** (2) ∗*to shake up*, to reorganize; (3) *to shake a leg*, to hurry, get busy.

(1) **1899** *Chi. Record* 26 June 4/6 While working and shaking down a candidate for the purpose of compelling him to cough up, do you favor a plain massage, or the Swedish movement? **1949** *L.A. Times* 5 May 1/3 Ferguson . . . accused them of trying to 'shakedown' Mickey Cohen of $5000. — (2) **1930** A. NEVINS *Henry White* 59 It had also been settled that the subordinate force of the legation was to be shaken up. — (3) **1920** C. R. COOPER *Under Big Top* 219 Six good men! Shake a leg, now! **1925** H. L. FOREST *Trop. Tramp Tourists* 44 Isn't that guy ever going to wait on us? . . . Call him over here. Tell him to shake a leg.

∗**shaker,** *n.*

1. (*cap.*) A member of a dwindling celibate and communistic religious sect, introduced in America in 1774, whose devotions include a characteristic shaking or dance.

This sect, the principle location of which is at New Lebanon, N.Y., is of British origin (1747) and came to this country under the guidance of Mother Ann Lee, whom they regarded as the female incarnation of one of the dual, male and female, principles of God. Their official name is "The United Society of Believers in Christ's Second Appearance."

1784 BELKNAP *Jrnl. Tour to White Mts.* (1876) 20 [His] wife had run away with the Shakers and carried off 25 of his dollars. **1818** PALMER *Journal* 89 We rode out between the two Miamis, of which land, report spoke so high, intending to call at Union, a celebrated settlement of *Shakers*, about thirty miles from Cincinnati. **1896** *Peterson Mag.* March 253/1 The years of watch-care which she had given to the child left in her charge, had created in her heart a love which the Manifesto taught to be earthly and unworthy a devout Shaker. **1949** *Newsweek* 18 July 62/3 These groups, like the Shakers, have experimented with communal living.

2. (See quot.) *Obs.*

1845 LYELL *Second Visit* I. 60 Large grasshoppers, with red wings [are] called here [in N. Eng.] shakers.

3. Short for **Shaker bonnet.**

1881 *Harper's Mag.* May 854/2, The bonnet . . . is far too fine. I will buy you a shaker at the store. **1905** WIGGIN *Rose* 9 Rose had tried on . . . children's gingham 'Shakers,' mourning bonnets for aged dames [etc.].

4. A container in which drinks are mixed by shaking. Cf. **cocktail shaker.**

1889 J. G. WOOLLEY *Seed No. 1 Hard* (1893) 96 The bartender . . . makes the bits of ice, the spoon, the shaker, the strainer, the glasses, fairly play a tune.

5. A container for salt, pepper, etc., having a perforated top.

1910 TOMPKINS *Mothers & Fathers* 29 Miss Elsie would be terribly shocked at this shaker. **1950** *Chi Tribune* 4 May (editorial page).

6. In obs. combs. (sense **1.**): (1) **Shaker bonnet,** a woman's or girl's plain bonnet fitting the head snugly at the sides but flaring at the front and having a puff or hood at the back; (2) **community, = Shaker village;** (3) **dance,** a devotional dance engaged in by Shakers (see quot. 1842); (4) **family,** (see quot. 1837), also attrib.; (5) **herbs,** a vegetable medicinal preparation put up by the Shakers; (6) **potato,** a variety of potato developed by the Shakers; (7) **rocker,** =next; (8) **rocking chair,** a rocking chair made, or of a type made, by the Shakers; (9) **scents,** perfume made by the Shakers; (10) **seed,** seed grown and sold by the Shakers; (11) **village,** a community or settlement composed of, and managed by, Shakers.

(1) **1856** RICHARDS *V. Life* (1912) 77 We went down town this morning and bought us some shaker bonnets to wear to school. *c***1898** CHRISTIAN *Days* 72 Hearing a noise in the yard the night before, [he] jumped up and put on one of the children's shaker bonnets and went out to investigate. — (2) **1817** *Niles' Reg.* XII. 371/1 At Enfield, Vermont, he visited the '*Habitation of the Shaken [sic] community*,' to use their own phraseology, or in more familiar language the Shaking Quakers. **1920** HOWELLS *Vacation of Kelwyns* 171, I thought of having the scene partly in a Shaker community. — (3) **1842** DICKENS *Amer. Notes* xv, These people are called Shakers from their peculiar form of adoration, which consists of a dance, performed by the men and women of all ages, who arrange themselves for that purpose in opposite parties; the men first divesting themselves of their hats and coats, which they gravely hang against the wall before they begin; and tying a ribbon round their shirtsleeves, as though they were going to be bled. **1871** *Scribner's Mo.* II. 657 They could not have produced a divertisement more exquisitely absurd than the Shaker dance. — (4) **1837** MARTINEAU *Society* II. 55 There are fifteen Shaker establishments or 'families' in the United States. **1920** HOWELLS *Vacation of Kelwyns* 24 The caravan of the Kelwyns drew up under the elms at the gable of the old Shaker Family house. **1947** *New Yorker* 23 Aug. 44/3 That's our name for the house a Shaker family lives in.

(5) **1830** *Boston Transcript* 15 Dec. 3/4 Shakers' Herbs . . . just received from the Shakers at Canterbury, prepared in their best manner. **1842** KIRKLAND *Forest Life* II. 113 Here's . . . patent pills—cure anything you like—ague bitters—Shaker yarbs. — (6) **1861** *Ill. Agric. Soc. Trans.* IV. 104 The product of the said half acre . . . [is] ninety-five and a half bushels of fine sized tubers, . . . the variety being the 'Shaker Potato,' flesh white. — (7) **1882** *Cent. Mag.* March 761/2 [I] sat down in the Shaker rocker. **1898** E. C. HALL *Aunt Jane* 4 The chairs were ancient Shaker rockers, some with homely 'shuck' bottoms. — (8) **1866** A. D. WHITNEY *L. Goldthwaite* xii, Miss Craydocke . . . came and placed her Shaker rocking-chair beside her. **1881** *Harper's Mag.* Sep. 579/1 Adams . . . perched on the arm of a scarlet Shaker rocking-chair. **1893** *Ib.* Feb. 476/2 He wrote, not at his desk, but sitting in a Shaker rocking-chair, with a pad upon his knee. — (9) **1867** DIXON *New Amer.* II. 81 Needing a little rose-water, I asked a friend where the best might be got. 'You must apply,' he said, 'at any of the stores where they sell Shaker scents.'

(10) [**1829** *Va. Herald* (Fredericksburg) 7 Feb. 1/2 Just received, from the Shakers at Enfield, Connecticut, a general assortment of Garden Seeds.] **1835** TODD *Notes* 12 Tradesmen exhibit . . . such sort of placards as . . . 'Shakers' seed sold here,' meaning the society of Shakers forming a religious community near Troy, whose garden seeds are much approved. **1854** GREATREX *Whittlings* 368 Shaker fruits and seeds are held in high estimation, and always find a market. [**1947** *New Yorker* 23 Aug. 48/2 The Shakers here at New Lebanon were the first people in the United States to sell seeds in little packages.] — (11) **1824** in H. M. BROOKS *Gleanings* IV. 125 An assortment of Steel & Silver Pens, from the Shaker Village. **1867** DIXON *New Amer.* II. 80 This village is Mount Lebanon, . . . known to scoffers as a comic institution unattached, under the name of the Shaker Village. **1887** *Courier-Journal* 12 Feb. 5/1 He gave Dines $675 on coming to the Shaker village last fall.

b. In combs. of obvious meaning, as (1) **Shaker barn,** (2) **bucket,** (3) **cap,** (4) **chair,** (5) **cloak,** (6) **pail,** (7) **sweater, yarn.**

(1) **1848** *Knickerb.* XXXII. 76 We should like some of our country friends . . . to go into a Shaker barn. **1947** *New Yorker* 23 Aug. 46/2 A good many Shaker barns are built like ours. — (2) **1849** AUDUBON *Western Jrnl.* 152 Some of the mules drank five buckets of water . . . (the common shaker buckets). — (3) **1883** *Cent. Mag.* Feb. 525/1 A bonnet, hey? . . . It looks like a Shaker cap. — (4) **1866** A. D. WHITNEY *L. Goldthwaite* x, She rocked herself back and forth in the Shaker chair. **1876** MRS. WHITNEY *Sights & Insights* I. ii. 8 The ladies were gathered in the end piazza. . . . There were . . . two comfortable low Shaker chairs.

(5) **1905** WIGGIN *Rose* 154 She slipped on her gray Shaker cloak. — (6) **1861** *Harper's Mag.* Feb. 422/1 Old 'Dexter' . . . never had anything to drink but raw whisky, which he bought at a neighbouring grocery every morning, and brought home in a Shaker pail. — (7) **1902** *Sears Cat.* (ed. 112) 870/2 Men's Heaviest Shaker Fine All Wool Sweater. . . . Made from fine clean Shaker yarn with extra heavy neck, tail and cuffs.

Also *Shaker brush, cart, distilled water, fare, flannels, fruit, lady, meeting, missionary, priest, rose water, settlement, sister, vegetable*, etc.

Shakerdom ˈʃekərdəm, *n.* The region occupied by Shakers, or Shakers collectively. *Obs.*

1861 HOLLAND *Lessons in Life* 87, I object to their Style of life and piety, and to everything outside of Shakerdom. **1876** GLADDEN *Work-*

ing People & Employers 203 Shakerdom has but one prophet, and his name is Frederick Evans. **1891** HOLMES *Over Teacups* 66 Your imaginary wholesale Shakerdom is all very fine, said I.

Shakeress ˈʃekərɪs, *n.* A Shaker woman. — **1829** *Ladies' Mag.* (Boston) II. 411 The dress of the Shakeresses was extremely simple and plain . . . a white gown . . . a white handkerchief . . . a white muslin cap. **1880** HOWELLS *Undiscovered Country* 203 A score of young Shakeresses . . . sorted and cleaned these simples.

Shakerism ˈʃekəˌrɪzəm, *n.* (See quot. 1859.)

1807 R. McNEMAR *Ky. Revival* 95 If *Shakerism* were properly understood, there is no man in his senses could persecute it. **1859** GRATTAN *Civilized Amer.* II. 351 Shakerism, although the word is not legitimately adopted into the language by any good authority, is the generally received designation applied to the belief and practices of the singular sect of Christians, called Shakers, from the strange agitations and movements of their religious dances, but who call themselves the Millennial Church, or United Society of Believers. **1948** *Chi. Tribune* 23 May 13/1 Shakerism always has emphasized equality of sexes, labor, and property.

* **shaking,** *n.* and *a.*

1. *pl.* Attacks of fever and ague. *Rare.*

1833 in *Mich. Hist. Mag.* XVIII. 56 The ague is very prevalent at this place [Somerfield, Mich.]. We work at the smith's shop ourselves because the smith has the 'shakings.'

2. In combs.: (1) **shaking ague,** fever and ague or an attack of this, *obs.;* (2) **Quaker,** a Shaker or, *pl.*, the sect of Shakers; (3) **shoe,** a vibrating shoelike trough that drops grain from the hopper of a mill into the eye of the millstone; (4) **table,** (see quot. 1876).

(1) 1791 S. SEWALL *Diary* III. (1882) 238 My wife had a very bad night . . . had such a shaking Ague-Fit. **1835** LONGSTREET *Ga. Scenes* 210 Nancy was cured sound and well by it, of a hard shakin' ager. **1855** SIMMS *Forayers* 164 Dick could easily simulate the sufferings of one seized with 'the shaking agy.' — **(2) 1782** *N.H. Hist. Soc. Coll.* I. 239 The people called Shaking Quakers, came to Mr. (Joseph) Flint's. **1864** NICHOLS *Amer. Life* II. 30, I have never seen a more remarkable people than the American Shakers, or, as they are sometimes called, Shaking Quakers. **1948** *Christian Cent.* 7 Jan. 27/1 The last six surviving members of the once flourishing community of Shakers or 'Shaking Quakers' at Mount Lebanon, N.Y., have moved across the state line and joined the neighboring colony in Hancock, Mass. — **(3) 1850** *Rep. Comm. Patents: 1849* I. 351, I claim . . . as new . . . the arrangement of the horizontally sliding screen and shaking shoe. — **(4) 1854** *Calif. Chronicle* (S.F.) 16 May 3/5 These mills all use stamps and shaking tables with quicksilver. **1876** KNIGHT 2131/1 Shaking-table. (*Metallurgy.*) A form of separator in which the slimes or comminuted ores are agitated in the presence of water.

b. In obs. expressions referring to quaking areas of insecure foundation, as (1) **shaking marsh,** (2) **meadow,** (3) **prairie.**

(1) 1850 DRAKE *Treatise* 339 In a few places, however, this stratum of mud and water is from eight to ten feet deep. These are known by the name of 'shaking marshes,' and are dangerous to cross with horses. — **(2) 1748** ELIOT *Field-Husb.* i. 8, I think there is reason to believe that the shaking Meadows have been formerly Bever Ponds. **1763** MILLS *Pract. Husb.* I. 137 Mr. Eliot's contrivance to drain a piece of shaking meadow, as he calls it. — **(3) 1888** CABLE *Bonaventure* 143 Far out over the vast marshy breadths of the 'shaking prairie,' two still clouds . . . sparkled.

Shalam colonist. [?f. Heb. *shalom,* well-being, peace.] A member of a Faithist colony near Las Cruces, New Mexico. *Obs.* — **1885** *Wkly. New Mexican Rev.* 23 April 3/4 The new bible used by the Shalam colonists . . . is purported to have been written by Dr. Newbrough, under inspiration.

shallon ˈʃælən, *n.* =**salal.**

1806 LEWIS in *L. & Clark Exped.* IV. (1905) 52 The *Shallon* is the production of a shrub which I have heretofore taken to be a species of loral. **1814** PURSH *Flora Amer.* I. 284 This elegant evergreen shrub is in high esteem among the natives on account of its berries, which they call Shallon. **1866** LINDLEY & MOORE *Treas. Botany* 522/2 The Shallon or Salal of the north-west coast of America.

* **sham,** *n.*

1. (*cap.*) *pl.* A secret organization in South Carolina that sought to continue the work of the Ku-Klux Klan after the disbanding of that organization. *Obs.*

[**1877** BEARD *K.K.K. Sketches* 155 The 'sham,' or counterfeit edition of the K.K.K., had no organized existence in either of the remaining Southern States.] *Ib.* 158 A resolution of *sine die* adjournment was actually passed, and the members having exchanged sad farewells and wept on each other's necks in view of the gloomy prospect before them, the 'Shams,' as they were derisively called, became masters of the situation.

2. (See quot. 1891.) Also **sheet sham.**

1891 *Cent.* 5547/1 sham. . . . A false pillow-cover; a pillow-sham. . . . A strip of fine linen, often embroidered, put under the upper edge of the bed-coverings and turned over, as if forming the upper end of the sheets. *c***1900** KING *When I Lived* (1937) 186 No pillow or sheet shams, or indeed any kind of sham, ever desecrated the solid reality of those monumental structures. **1946** THOMPSON *Amer. Daughter* 19, I took Sue's tiny room with its magazine pictures pasted on the walls and embroidered shams over the pillows.

attrib. **1902** *Sears Cat.* (ed. 112) 938/3 By far the best sham holder and once tried you will use no other.

shambler ˈʃæmblɚ, *n.* A horse that shambles. *Rare.* — **1861** WINTHROP *Canoe & Saddle* 219 Shabbiest led off on his shambler in quite another direction from mine.

* **shambles,** *n. pl.* A slave market. *Obs.* — **1852** STOWE *Uncle Tom* xlv, An older sister went to the shambles to plead with the wretch . . . to spare his victims. **1860** ABBOTT *South & North* 177 There is no longer occasion to buy and sell your fellow-men in the shambles.

Shamocrat ˈʃæməˌkræt, *n. Hist.* A Democrat who opposed Stephen A. Douglas and popular sovereignty with reference to slavery and indorsed James Buchanan (1791–1868), fifteenth President of the U.S. (1857–61). Also **Shamocratic,** *a. Obs.*

[**1855** *N.Y. Wkly. Tribune* 17 March 4/1 The last stronghold of the Sham Democracy has been overthrown.] **1856** *Iroquois Republican* (Middleport, Ill.) 31 July 2/4 Mr. Crandall was very severe, not only with Mr. Fillmore, but also upon the present Administration, and the platform of the Buchanan Shamocrats. **1858** *N.Y. Tribune* 11 Feb. 6/5 The very mention of Kansas by a Shamocratic [i.e., Democratic] speaker was the signal for a lateral elongation of the mouth. . . . The distinguished orators on the occasion were all old-line Pierce-Buchanan Shamocratic men.

* **Shanghai,** *n.* Also **shanghai.**

1. A long frock coat. In full **Shanghai (over)coat.** *Obs.*

1855 M. THOMPSON *Doesticks* 297, I could forgive thy Shanghae coats. **1856** *Porter's Spirit of Times* 22 Nov. 190/3, I have doffed the shanghai and donned the shooting-jacket. **1873** BAILEY *Life in Danbury* 11 He wore a Shanghai overcoat. **1901** HARRIGAN *Mulligans* 137 He wore a long black coat, termed 'shanghai.'

2. In various senses (see quots.).

1857 UNDERHILL & THOMPSON *Elephant Club* 86 His hat was an antiquated shanghae—black on the crown and light underneath the brim. **1880** *Scribner's Mo.* Jan. 365/1 The 'shanghai' is the glaring daub required by some frame-makers for cheap auctions. **1880** *Cimarron News & Press* 30 Sep. 2/4 Of late years . . . there are but few rough, bony shanghais, in the shape of oxen and steers, brought from Texas and from the West. **1881** INGERSOLL *Oyster Industry* 248 *Shanghai,* a long, slender oyster. **1898** KING *Warrior Gap* 168 He had a simply fabulous opportunity—a chance to buy out a mine that experts secretly told him was what years later he would have called a 'bonanza,' but that in the late sixties was locally known as a 'Shanghai.' **1910** *Pub. Miss. Hist. Soc.* XI. 88 We built on the east side of Matubba Creek [in Miss.] a nice six-room, chinked and plastered, loghouse, with a row of frame 'Shanghai,' servants' houses, cribs, stables, etc. *Ib.* 95 The male school was built 'Shanghai fashion,' that is of rough, upright lumber.

3. *Mil.* Designating a rapid manner of marching or drilling formerly in use at West Point. *Obs.*

1858 *S. Lit. Messenger* XXVI. 17/2 It is called in the familiar language of the camp, by the name of the 'Shanghai Drill.' *Ib.*, 18/1 They think the 'double quick' or 'Shanghai trot' too undignified for their years and ponderosity. **1867** HARRIS *Sut Lovingood* 196 A long necked passenger . . . cum rushin out in a shanghi trot.

4. *pl.* Long, slender legs. *Rare.*

1863 NORTON *Army Lett.* 187 He asked me if I could march twenty-five miles and not be sick. That was a thrust at my 'shanghais.'

5. Shanghai fence, (see quot.). *Obs.*

1862 *Ill. Agric. Soc. Trans.* V. 692 Many men . . . are compelled to make . . . 'Shanghai' or 'Bloomer' fences (two-boarded fences).

shanghai ˈʃæŋhaɪ, *v.* [Thought to have originated *c*1850 in San Francisco with reference to the practice of securing sailors by foul means for long voyages, often to Shanghai, China.] *tr.* To overpower (someone) by drugs or other means and ship him as a sailor, usu. in order to secure premium money. Now *hist.*

1871 *N.Y. Tribune* 1 March (De Vere) Before that time they would have been drugged, shanghaied, and taken away from all means of making complaint. **1949** *Boston Globe* 12 June (Fiction Mag.) 1/1 The bucko mate had sized him up in a Brooklyn waterfront saloon, slipped knockout drops in his beer and shanghaied him.

b. To entice, inveigle, or otherwise take (anyone) out of his usual environment.

1892 *S.F. Chron.* 17 Sep. 3/7 He says that Norris had refused to prosecute him for shanghaiing him out of the country. **1949** *N.O. Times-Picayune* 6 March 1/2 He said that he had been shanghaied into the French Foreign Legion.

shanghaier ˈʃæŋˌhaɪɚ, *n.* One who shanghais others. *Rare.* — **1926** J. Black *You Can't Win* xii. 152 Here I learned to beware the crafty shanghaier with his knockout drops.

Shanghaism ˈʃæŋhaɪˌɪzəm, *n. Polit.* The action on the part of a candidate of running for office on more than one ticket. *Obs.* **1859** *La Crosse D. Union* 22 Oct. 2/2 There will not be a remnant of Shanghaism left in Wisconsin.

*****shanks,** *n. pl.* As the last term in **caribou, long, moose, yellow shanks.**

Shanpips ˈʃænpɪps, *n. pl.* [Origin unknown.] A secret society reputed to have existed formerly among the Mormons. *Obs.* — **1857** *Cong. Globe* App. 24 Feb. 289/3 They suppose that there is a secret society existing there, called *Danites, Shanpips*, or *Destroying Angels.*

shanty ˈʃæntɪ, *n.* [See note.]

Earlier thought to be f. Irish *sean-tig* (*-toig*), an old, miserable hut, but more recently derived f. Canadian French *chantier*, a log hut, *q.v.* in *OED* with 1st example 1880. Max Förster in Herrig's *Archiv* 107 (1901), 112–14, favored the Irish origin and explained *chantier* as a borrowing of shanty, not its source. Evidence so far found favors Förster's view. Cf. **chienté.**

1. A cheap, flimsy, hastily erected cabin, hut or shack.

1822 Z. Hawley *Tour* 31 [These people] lived in what is here [Ohio] called a *Shanty.* **1886** Poore *Reminiscences* II. 342 He gave him seed to sow, a shanty to live in, and some land to till. **1948** *Dly. Ardmoreite* (Ardmore, Okla.) 19 April 3/3 The wind whipped into town and toppled the little shanty.

Shanty (sense 1) of logs

b. With defining terms indicating the materials used.

1836 *Quarter Race Ky.* (1846) 14, I noticed many a . . . fellow force his skeary nag up to the opening in the little clapboard shanty. **1857** Willis *Convalescent* 256, I am thinking now of building a pine shanty in the glen. **1860** Greeley *Overland Journey* 180 We stopped beside a stone and mud shanty of very rude construction. **1881** Romspert *Western Echo* 70 Many little pole and adobe-shanties deck this pretty level bank. **1942** Kennedy *Palmetto Country* 41 The veterans had no shelter but the small board shanties in which they were housed.

c. Applied esp. to a house used by lumbermen. Cf. **shanty boss, boy, gang, man, team,** in **2.** below.

1846 Farnham *Prairie Land* 208 The solitary wood-chopper, whose 'shantee' [is] hidden among the trees. **1926** Rickaby *Ballads* 237 *Shanty.* Any of the several buildings comprising a logging camp. In the plural, means a camp. Thus: 'To the shanties he will not go.' **1943** *Reader's Digest* Dec. 71/1 More than one lumberjack has been awakened in the night by strange sounds coming from the shanty where the explosives are kept.

d. Used, in depreciation or contempt, of more pretentious structures.

1848 Cooper *Oak Openings* I. 26 This term 'shanty,' . . . by a license of speech, . . . is often applied to more permanent residences. **1862** Cumming *Hospital Life* 32/2 [The] house called a hotel . . . is a perfect shanty. **1884** Hedley *Marching through Ga.* 251 A veteran regiment occupied the old railroad eating-house known as 'Big Shanty.'

e. Short for **shanty boat.**

1938 *Sat. Ev. Post* 15 Oct. 58/2 We moved on to a shanty moored to the one where we had been chatting.

f. The caboose of a train.

1947 Beebe *Mixed Train Dly.* 331 The first section . . . from Prosser east to Chireno is a motor coach and [the] . . . second is a mixed freight and passenger with the cash fares in its homely red-painted shanty. **1948** *Sat. Ev. Post* 25 Dec. 69/2 To understand what the shanty means to its crew, picture the 512 on its run on a blustery, sleeting night.

2. (See quot. 1942.) *Slang.*

1913 *Industrial Worker* (Spokane) 17 July 3/2 Fellow worker Scott then began . . . by putting a couple of shanties over his optics. **1942** Berrey & Van den Bark *Amer. Thesaurus Slang* 121 Blackened Eye. Blinker, . . . painted peeper, shanty, shiner, smoked lamp.

3. In combs.: (1) **shanty boat,** a river boat provided with living quarters similar to those of a shanty, also **shanty boatman;** (2) **boater,** one who lives in a shanty boat; (3) **boss,** (see quot.); (4) **boy,** (see quot. 1926), also as the title of a song; (5) **cake,** a kind of cake formerly eaten by those living in shanties, *obs.;* (6) **family,** a family of people living in a shanty; (7) **gang,** a gang of lumberjacks; (8) **Irish,** very poor Irish people living in shanties; (9) **man,** (*a*) =**shanty boy,** (*b*) =**shanty boater;** (10) **team,** a timber team; (11) **town,** a poor section of a city or town full of ramshackle or makeshift cabins or shacks; (12) **village,** a village composed of shanties.

(1) 1879 Bishop *4 Months in Sneak-Box* 59 The shanty-boatman looks to the river . . . for his life. *Ib.*, The sweeps, or oars, . . . govern the motions of the shanty-boat. **1887** *Courier-Journal* 25 Jan. 2/3 A murder occurred . . . on a shanty-boat near Vidalia. **1945** Fugina *Upper Mississippi* 27 Every fall the river was filled with shanty boats, also called 'John boats,' bound for Saint Louis and New Orleans. — **(2) 1935** *Lit. Digest* 17 Aug. 20/3 The latter is usually a solid citizen who resents being called a 'shanty-boater.' **1945** *Chi. D. News* 5 Dec. 11A/3 They are shanty-boaters . . . living on a little craft moored in a cove not too far from New Orleans. — **(3) 1905** *Forestry Bureau Bul.* No. 61, 33 *Chore boy,* one who cleans up the sleeping quarters and stable in a logging camp, cuts firewood, builds fires, and carries water. . . . [Also called] shanty boss. — **(4)** *c***1847** in Roland P. Gray *Songs of Maine Lumberjacks* (1924) xvii, 'T was in Jim Lockwell's shanty this song was sung with glee, And that's the end of 'The Shanty Boy,' and it was composed by three. **1926** Rickaby *Ballads* 237 *Shanty-boy.* A member of a logging crew. A lumber-jack. In the golden days of logging the woodsman evidently preferred the name 'shanty-boy.' At least it is the word he uses most generally in referring to himself. Probably owes its prevalence to the Irish. **1950** *Amer. Mercury* March 344/2 He knew the life of the shanty-boys and their lore.

(5) 1846 *Knickerb.* XXVIII. 340, [I] became a proficient in making that unleavened bread known, *inter sylvas*, as 'shanty cake.' **1853** Strickland *Twenty-seven Yrs.* II. 76 They . . . fried some venison with slices of bacon, which they set before us with a hot shanty-cake and a good cup of tea. — **(6) 1872** Brace *Dangerous Classes N.Y.* 152 The shanty-family are never quite so poor as the tenement-house family. **1944** *Reader's Digest* July 108 The income of the shanty family that has no definite occupation is incredibly low, perhaps eight dollars a year in cash. — **(7) 1894** *Outing* XXIV. 94/2 A shanty gang had turned a drive of square timber out of the branch. — **(8) 1925** Dos Passos *Manhattan Transfer* 102 And add to that the ignorance of these dirty kikes and shanty Irish that we make voters of before they can even talk English. **1949** *Newsweek* 1 Aug. 44/3 [She] is said to have called herself 'a vindictive old shanty Irish so-and-so.' — **(9)** (*a*) **1829** J. Mactaggart *Three Years* I. 241 The *Shantymen* live in hordes of from thirty to forty together; throughout the day they cut down the pine trees. **1893** *Scribner's Mag.* June 702/2 The typical shantyman works only fitfully in summer. **1926** Rickaby *Ballads* 38 Give a shanty-man old rye and nothing goes wrong. (*b*) **1944** *Reader's Digest* July 107 There has been no census of shanty-men, for census is the Government and shantyboaters don't like the Government.

(10) 1878 *Lumberman's Gaz.* 6 April, The last of the shanty-teams of the season have about gone through here. — **(11) 1888** *Seattle Post-Intelligencer* 30 Nov. 8/5 Comparatively few of the cabins in what is known as 'Shantytown' are located on railroad property. **1948** *Nat. Geog. Mag.* Aug. 235/2 Irish workmen . . . lived with their families in temporary shanty towns. — **(12) 1858** Hale *If, Yes, & Perhaps* 126 But his extempore train chose to stop at a forsaken shanty-village on the Potomac. [**1876** *Harper's Wkly.* 30 Sep. 802/1 The fire by which the greater part of 'Shantyville' . . . was swept away occurred on the afternoon of Saturday, the 9th inst.]

As the last term in **bark, board, boarding, brush, bush, claim, cook, fishing, frame, log, lumber, mud, oyster, palmetto, plank, pole, rag, redwood, rum, shake, slab, switch, timber shanty.**

shanty ˈʃæntɪ, *v. intr.* To live (*out*) in a shanty. Also **shantying,** *n.*

1840 Hoffman *Greyslaer* I. 60, I never shanty out without a large fire. **1857** Hammond *Wild Northern Scenes* 197 They shantied on the outlet, just at the foot of the lake. *Ib.* 212 When we got back to our shantyin' ground, we were tuckered out you may believe. **1926** RICKABY *Ballads* 47 Shantying I'll give o'er when I'm landed safe on shore, And I'll lead a different life.

* **shape,** *n.* Condition, mode or state of being. *Colloq.*

1865 NORTON *Army Lett.* 249, I got through it all in good shape. **1902** MACGOWEN *Last Word* 349 He's in bad shape now. **1930** *Randolph Enterprise* (Elkins, W.Va.) 16 Oct. 3/3 The road from here to Elkins is splendid, but east of the ridge is in bad shape.

* **shape,** *v.*

1. *intr.* To tend in a certain direction, to assume a particular aspect. *Colloq.*

1865 NORTON *Army Lett.* 278 As things are shaping I do not much think I shall try. **1903** *N.Y. Times* 10 Sep., Matters are shaping for an effort on the part of the organized teamsters.

2. *To shape over*, to refashion. *Rare.*

1875 WHITNEY *Life Lang.* iv. 53 The same influences helped . . . to shape over certain pronominal elements into the personal endings *anti*, *masi*, and *ti*.

3. *To shape up*, to put (something) into proper shape; to fatten cattle. *Colloq.*

1885 *Harper's Mag.* Jan. 277/1 An experienced workman finishes the work of setting out by 'shaping up' the hides. **1890** *Stock Grower & Farmer* 8 March 3/1 All the replies received have been 'shaped up,' compiled and condensed. **1939** C. L. DOUGLAS *Cattle Kings of Texas* 219 The plan had been to hold and shape up near Phoenix . . . and then to push on to market with fattened stock.

b. =**1.** above.

1907 *Springfield W. Republican* 2 May 3 It is not at all certain that matters will shape up so as to permit them to do this. **1919** HOUGH *Sagebrusher* 90 We're waiting . . . until things kind of shapes up. **1921** PAINE *Comr. Rolling Ocean* 293 Here is how it shapes up to me.

shaped notes. Also **shape notes.** *Music.* Notes whose heads are shaped (triangle for *fa*, oval for *sol*, square for *la*, diamond for *mi*, etc.) to assist those learning to sing by the old sol-fa system. Cf. **buckwheat notes.**

1932 RANDOLPH *Ozark Mt.* 248 Right hyar is whar I get in some good licks for shape-notes, too. **1943** PEATTIE *Great Smokies* 220 Presently prizes were offered in ballad and folk-song singing, fiddle contests were encouraged, the shape-note singers were received with open arms. **1945** *Chi. Tribune* 18 Nov. VII. 1/5 We sang from song books printed with old time shaped notes. **1949** *Nat. Geog. Mag.* July 23/2 So you want to know something about shape notes, do you?

shapeleel ˈʃæpəˌlil, *n.* (See quots. 1807, 1909.)

1805 CLARK in *Lewis & C. Exped.* III. (1905) 186 Those beeds the[y] trafick with Indians still higher up this river for roabs, Skins, cha-pel-el bread, beargrass &c. **1807** GASS *Journal* xix. 199 Here we got some Shap-e-leel, a kind of bread the natives make of roots, and bake in the sun; and which is strong and palatable. **1909** SHAW *Chinook Jargon* 21/2 (Chinook,—Tsapelil). (Yakima,—saplil;—bread.) Wheat; flour, or meal; a loaf; grain. Example: Hiyu sapolil milite,—there is much flour.

* **share,** *n.*

1. *On* (or *upon*) (*the*) *shares*, in accordance with an agreement by which the collaborators in an undertaking are to receive specified portions of the gain.

*a*1656 BRADFORD *Hist.* 185 [The vessel] was rudly manned, and all her men were upon shars, and none was to have any wages but ye m[aste]r. **1792** BELKNAP *Hist. New-Hampshire* III. 216 Men can always be had to go on shares, which is by far the most profitable method, both to the employers and the fishermen. **1820** FLINT *Letters* 267 He has on his property a great number of people who rent land *on shares*, (a term formerly explained to you.) **1945** BOTKIN *My Burden* 30 Most of all the niggers was farming on the shares.

2. In combs.: (1) **share capital,** the entire capital represented by shares; (2) **crop,** see as a main entry; (3) **hand,** a hand or tenant who crops on shares; (4) **man,** one who shares in the gains of a fishing voyage, *obs.*; (5) **mart,** a stock exchange, *rare;* (6) **system,** a system of farming in which a landlord and a tenant share in the risks and proceeds of a crop; (7) **tenant,** =**share cropper.**

(1) **1885** WELLS *Practical Economics* 251 (*footnote*), The share capital and funded and floating debts of the railroads of the United States, for the year 1883, have been estimated at $6,765,000,000. — (3) **1911** JENKS & LAUCK *Immigration Problem* 83 Italian cotton tenants are showing the cotton growers of how much value careful cultivation, kitchen gardens and small store accounts may be to the cotton 'share hand' and tenant. — (4) **1687** *Conn. Rec.* III. 425 Fishermen . . . shall not presume to break off their voyage, . . . without the consent of the owner, master and share-men.

(5) **1870** MEDBERY *Men Wall Street* 19 In all the great European share-marts there is a general executive organization. — (6) **1831** FOWLER *Tour New York* 76 The *share*, or *halving system*, as it is called, is not very extensively practiced. **1881** *Bradstreet's* III. 354 It is claimed also that the share system now so much in vogue enforces reliance on the single crop. — (7) **1937** *Amer. Mag.* July 164/1 The share-tenant, which Prender has been at times during his life, is a little better off than the share-cropper. **1944** FAST *F. Road* 120 All of them living on the old acreage, all of them going to get off or be share tenants when the land is sold.

As the last term in **home, house, oil, thatch share.**

share crop.

1. share-crop system, a system of farming in the South in which a tenant is supplied by the landlord with certain necessities and receives for his labor a share or portion of the crop he makes. Also **sharecropping (system).** Cf. **share system.**

The custom of sharecropping was adopted in the South at the close of the Civil War, when it was necessary to come to some agreement with the newly freed slaves to induce them to remain on the plantations and work as formerly. Many systems were tried out, but the share-crop one proved popular.

[**1867** in EASTERBY *S.C. Rice Plant.* (1945) 231 This will be cheaper in the end than the contract or share of the crop system.] **1907** *Springfield W. Republican* 25 April 1 It is claimed that the difficulties of the South with the immigration laws can be met by reviving the old-time 'share-crop' system. **1945** BOTKIN *My Burden* 225 That was the beginning of the sharecropping system. **1949** *Reader's Digest* Aug. 128/2 Three fourths of the state's cotton is grown by landowners. . . . Sharecropping is unknown.

2. Also as a verb *tr.* and *intr.* To farm or raise (a crop) on shares. Also transf.

1937 *Atlantic Mo.* Nov. 625/1, I wanted to own my own land and not have to rent or share-crop for a living. **1944** *Chi. D. News* 2 Dec. 4/6 The Capone gang owned several locals of the hotel and restaurant workers in Chicago, and had Lou Romano share-cropping them. **1945** *Reader's Digest* Nov. 26/1 He found hundreds of blacks who share-cropped cotton.

b. sharecropper, one who farms the land of another for a portion or share of the harvest. Also attrib. Cf. **share tenant.**

1929 L. R. GOTTSCHALK *Era French Rev.* 33 Most of them had become . . . like our sharecroppers, farmed a piece of land for a stipulated portion (generally half) of the harvest. **1948** *Chr. Sci. Mon.* 8 April 6 Perhaps, if you're a sharecropper, it doesn't make much difference. **1948** *Harper's Mag.* Nov. 97/1 He failed to argue Snow out of the belief that there was some good in the sharecropper system.

* **shark,** *n.* **1.** =**land shark.** *Obs.* **2.** (See quots. 1856 and 1914), *obs.* in earlier sense, *slang.* **3.** (See quot.) *Obs.*

(1) **1841** *Cultivator* VIII. 53 When you arrive in a new settlement, *beware of sharks.* **1873** EGGLESTON *Myst. Metrop.*52 He knows how to deal with these sharks. — (2) **1853** ROOT & LOMBARD *Songs of Yale* 45 No more look out for sharks. **1856** HALL *College Words* (ed. 2) 421 In student language, an absence from a recitation, a lecture, or from prayers, prompted by recklessness rather than by necessity, is called a *shark.* He who is absent under these circumstances is also known as a shark. **1914** *N.Y. Ev. Post* 5 Jan. 6 [The] 'shark' known to the American college world . . . [is] primarily, the student who devours and digests learning with ease . . . and, secondarily, one who excels in any line of activity. **1920** LEWIS *Main Street* 47 Ella is our shark at elocuting. She's had professional training. — (3) **1859** BARTLETT 397 *Shark*, a lean, hungry hog. Western.

As the last term in **bone, bonnet-headed, college, dog, gospel, gurry, land, mackerel, mining, money, oil, pension, prairie, salary, sand, shoal sand, soul, Wall Street, war shark.**

sharking ˈʃɑrkɪŋ, *n.* (See quot. 1859.) Also attrib. *Obs.*

1859 BARTLETT 397 *Sharking*, fishing for sharks. **1881** in GODFREY *Nantucket* 146 No summer expedition is complete without one 'sharking expedition.' **1882** GODFREY *Ib.* 329 A visit can be made to the 'sharking grounds.'

* **sharp,** *a.* In combs.: (1) * **Sharp Knife,** (see quot.), *rare;* (2) **shin,** (*a*) one of the sharp-edged, wedge-shaped fragments of a coin cut to secure small change, *obs.*, (*b*) =next; (3) **-shinned hawk,** a widely distributed North American hawk (see quot. 1812); (4) * **shooter,** (*a*) (see quot.), *obs.*, (*b*) (see quots.), (*c*) any one of several hemipterous insects that injure cotton bolls; (5) * **tail,** a sharp-tailed grouse or duck, also collect.; (6) **-tailed duck,** (see quot.); (7) **-tailed finch,** =**sharp-tailed sparrow;** (8) **-tailed grouse,** a western grouse, *Pedioecetes phasianellus;* (9) **-tailed sparrow,** a North

American sparrow, *Ammospiza caudacuta*, often found about salt marshes.

(1) 1888 M. LANE in *America* 25 Oct. 15 Sharp Knife, Andrew Jackson. — **(2)** (*a*) **1787** GRIEVE in Chastellux *Travels N. Amer.* I. 328 (*footnote*), In the country, almost all the specie of every denomination was cut by individuals, and appeared under the forms of half, quarter, and eighth parts, the latter of which received the name of *sharp shins.* **1832** KENNEDY *Swallow Barn* I. 103 It is not of the value of a sharpshin. **1860** MORDECAI *Va.* 278 Purses and pockets were not proof against sharp-shins. Money is said to burn the pockets of some folks—sharp-shins cut the pockets of all. (*b*) **1912** BARROWS *Mich. Bird Life* 264 There were Sharp-shins everywhere—sweeping about through the woods, beating about just over the tree tops. **1949** HADLEY *Indiana Birds* 20/1 The sharp-shin dashes with great speed from out of some shady nook, or place of concealment, and strikes down and carries off its quarry in the twinkling of an eye. — **(3) 1812** WILSON *Amer. Ornithology* V. 116 Sharp-Shinned Hawk—*Falco velox*. . . . Edges of the inside of the shins, below the knee, projecting like the edge of a knife, hard and sharp, as if intended to enable the bird to hold its prey with more security between them. **1949** SPRUNT & CHAMBERLAIN *S. Carolina Bird Life* 158 Everything that has been said about the Sharp-shinned Hawk can be said about Cooper's Hawk in enlarged terms. — **(4)** (*a*) *c***1856** in *Amer. Sp.* XXIV. (1949) 266/1 The Sharp-shooters, or pikes, from the mighty Missouri and its tributaries, are often made the butts of their better provided fellow-citizens. (*b*) **1894** SEARIGHT *Old Pike* 110 There were two classes of wagoners, the 'regular' and the 'sharpshooter.' . . . The sharpshooters were for the most part farmers, who put their farm teams on the road in seasons when freights were high, and took them off when prices of hauling declined. **1930** OMWAKE *Conestoga Teams* 100 At the time of year when farmers were not busy on their farms, they often carried freight in their wagons, and they were called by the regular wagoners, militia or sharpshooters. (*c*) **1901** *U.S. Dept. Agric. Yrbk.* 377 (*Cent. Supp.*), Early cotton . . . avoids to a great extent damage to the plant by the boll-worm, cotton worm, and sharp-shooters, as well as by a large number of fungous diseases.

(5) 1891 *Cent.* 5554/2 *Sharptail*, . . . the sharp-tailed grouse. **1917** *Birds of Amer.* I. 128 Pintail. *Dafila acuta*. . . . [Also called] Peak-tail; Sharp-tail; Spirit-tail. **1948** *Shelby* (Mont.) *Promoter* 16 Sep. 1/6 Shooting hours for pheasant and sharptail will be from 8 in the morning to 5 at night. — **(6) 1909** WEBSTER 1937/1 *Sharp-tailed duck*, . . . the pintail duck. *Local, U.S.* — **(7) 1811** WILSON *Ornithology* IV. 70 The Sharp-tailed Finch is five inches and a quarter long. — **(8)** [**1785** PENNANT *Arctic Zool.* II. 306 Sharp-tailed Grouse.] **1804–6** CLARK in *Lewis & C. Exped.* VI. (1904) 12 The Prairie Fowl common to the Illinois are found as high up as the River Jacque above which the Sharpe tailed Grows (grouse) commence. **1945** *Nat. Geog. Mag.* June 735 'Hoot, Mon!' Says the Sharp-tailed Grouse, Like a Doughty Scot. — **(9) 1831** WILSON *Ornithology* II. 260 *Fringilla Caudacuta*, Wilson. Sharp-tailed sparrow.

b. sharp stick, *fig.* in phrases as the name for some dire instrument of compulsion or punishment. *Colloq.*

*a***1846** *Quarter Race Ky.* 120 The boys were all after him with 'sharp sticks' and 'hot bricks.' **1848** BARTLETT 295 'He's after him with a sharp stick;' i.e. he's determined to have satisfaction, or revenge. Western. **1871** *Trenton State Sentinel* 26 May (De Vere 631), The New York *Tribune* is still after Senators Carpenter, Conkling, and others, with a very sharp stick.

As the last term in **bug, bunko, card, gospel, monte, poker, weather sharp.**

sharper 'ʃɑrpɚ, *n.* [f. **sharp, a.*] (See quots.)

1859 *N.Y. Wkly. Tribune* 8 Oct. 3/1 Raritan canal-boats, New-Haven sharpers, yachts, and even the East River pilot-boat O.K., are on the grounds. **1881** INGERSOLL *Oyster Industry* 248 *Sharpers*, elongated, protruding, sharp-ended oysters, dangerous to the feet in moving about the reefs. (Gulf coast.) **1887** GOODE *Fisheries* V. II. 548 Some [oysters] however, growing separately, . . . [are] distinguished as 'sharpers,' from the fact that the ends of their shells are unusually sharp.

sharpie 'ʃɑrpɪ, *n.* [f. the adj. **sharp.*]

1. "A long, sharp, flat-bottomed sailboat. (*Local U.S.*)" (W. '64). Also attrib.

1860 in *Outing* (1913) March 688/2, I took some of the skiffs and sharpies behind the Emma S. . . . and we went down to Whig Inlet. **1895** *Outing* XXX. 488/1 A balance-lug sail . . . was subsequently replaced by a sharpie sail and jib. **1948** *Sat. Ev. Post* 9 Oct. 140/3 Several smaller craft have been acquired, including . . . a seventy-five-year-old New Haven sharpie.

2. A sharper or cheat. *Slang.*

1942 BERREY & VAN DEN BARK *Amer. Thesaurus Slang* 422 Clever Crook . . . sharper, sharpie, sharpshooter, slicker, etc. **1944** *Chi. D. News* 4 Nov. 6/1 Central characters of both plays are engaging high-binders and sharpies who are not exactly thieves, but more than slightly overoptimistic in their use of the mails and other people's money.

* **Sharps,** *n.*

1. Used, usu. in the possessive, with reference to firearms of a type devised by Christian Sharps (1811–74), an American inventor. Now *hist.*

Through a misapprehension of the inventor's name, this term often appears as *Sharp's*.

1853 *S.F. Commercial Advt.* 9 Dec. 2/2 We were shown yesterday one of Sharp's patent rifles, capable of shooting thirty-six shots in three minutes. **1860** *Charleston* (S.C.) *Mercury* 6 Nov. 3/5 (*advt.*), Sharps' Four shooters. **1912** CRUMPTON *Two Boys* 99 When we reached New York, he gave me a little four barrel Sharp's pistol with one hundred cartridges. **1949** *Boston Globe* 17 July (Fiction Mag.) 5/2 There were . . . boxes of ammunition of all sizes, from the smallest to the big, blunt-nosed .50 caliber Sharps ammunition still used by some of the old-timers.

2. Sharps rifle, a breech-loading hunting rifle characterized by a lever breechblock action, patented by Sharps in 1848. Cf. **Beecher's Bible.**

1854 BARTLETT *Personal Narr.* I. 78 My Sharp's rifle . . . loaded at the breech and primed itself. **1929** B. DAVIS *Geronimo* 161 His gun, an antiquated Sharps rifle, had gone off accidentally. **1947** *True* Nov. 90/2 Many still clung to the heavy-caliber Sharp's rifle.

b. Also (ellipt.) **Sharps.**

1908 MULFORD *Orphan* 169 My breach-loading sharps, .50 calibre. **1947** *Sat. Ev. Post* 14 June 20/3 Hopalong would have plugged the scoundrel instanter with his trusty Sharps.

Also **Sharp-rifleism,** the policy in Kansas during the troubles over slavery of ruling by means of Sharps rifles. *Rare.* Cf. **Beecher's Bible.**

1856 *Ill. State Reg.* (Springfield) 19 June 4/2 This is all characteristic of Beecher Sharpe-rifleism.

Shasta 'ʃæstə, *n.* [See note.]

1. An Indian or (*pl.* or *collect.*) a small tribe or division of Indians belonging to the Shastan linguistic family of northern California and Oregon. Also attrib.

The first quots. given below show that Hodge's explanation of this word as "apparently the name of a well-known Indian of the tribe living about 1840 near the site of Yreka" is in error. *Shasta* is clearly from the name (of unknown significance) of the tribe.

1814 in *MSS Jrnl. A. Henry & D. Thompson* (1897) II. 817 They said they were of the Walla Walla, Shatasla and Halthypum (Cayuse) nations. **1827** PETER SKENE OGDEN in *Ore. Hist. Quart.* XI. 213, I have named this river Sastise River. There is a mountain equal in height to Mt. Hood or Vancouver, I have named Mt. Sastise. I have given these names from the tribe of Indians. **1838** PARKER *Exploring Tour* 258 The Umbaquâ nation . . . are divided into six tribes; the Sconta, Chalula, Palakahu, Quattamya, and Chastà. **1851** in SCHOOLCRAFT *Indian Tribes* (1853) III. 161 This man was afterwards dispatched . . . to make another attempt to assemble the Shasté tribes. **1855** *Crescent City* (Calif.) *Herald* 27 Oct., Amongst them were recognized some of the Shastas, who are represented as having been the last to retreat. **1903** JAMES *Indian Basketry* 79 The fine white grass, used by the Shastas in the manufacture of their baskets is gained from great elevations in the mountains.

b. The language of these Indians.

1851 in SCHOOLCRAFT *Indian Tribes* (1853) III. 151 Higher on the main river, the prevailing language is the Shasté.

2. In the names of plants: **Shasta daisy, fir, lily,** (see quots.).

1893 *Stand.* 2248/1 *Shasta daisy*, a large, showy, cultivated variety of the ox-eye daisy. **1946** *Mazama* Dec. 29/1 The floor of this little hanging alpine meadow was partially covered with blue lupine, with here and there a Shasta daisy. — **1897** SUDWORTH *Arborescent Flora* 58 *Abies magnifica*. Shasta Fir. . . . [Also called] Shasta Red Fir (var. *Shastensis*). *Ib.* 76 *Cupressus macnabiana*. Macnab Cypress. . . . [Also called] Shasta Cypress (Cal.). **1949** COLLINGWOOD & BRUSH *Knowing Your Trees* 106 Red Fir, also known as red-barked fir, Shasta fir and golden fir, is found on high mountain slopes and meadows from southern Oregon and northern California southward. — **1915** ARMSTRONG & THORNBER *Western Wild Flowers* 34 Shasta Lily is a variety with a small bulb. **1937** MCFARLAND *Garden Bulbs in Color* 155 There are several varieties of this Washington or Shasta Lily.

shats ʃæts, *n. pl. local.* [Origin obscure. See quot. 1941 below and cf. **longschat pine,** and **longshucks** and **shortshucks.**] (See quots.)

1895 *D.N.* VIII. 393 shats: dry pine leaves or needles. Worcester, Co., Md. **1941** *Nature Mag.* Feb. 139 The Eastern Shore of Maryland yields a precinctive name for pine needles (as it does for so many things) in shats, meaning, presumably, things that are shattered down. **1942** [see **diddledees**].

*shave, *n.* An exorbitant discount on a note, or a premium charged for allowing a contract to be changed. Cf. **close shave, half shave.**

1839 *Spirit of Times* 12 Oct. 373/1 (We.), The greater the shave, the more we want the money. **1855** *Chi. Times* 27 Jan. 2/2 When it [currency issued by certain banks] was offered at the very bank that had loaned it, . . . the sucker offering it was compelled to stand a shave of from *ten to twenty per cent.* **1898** WESTCOTT *D. Harum* 157 You've bled her fer shaves to the tune of sixty odd dollars in three years, an' then got your int'rist in full.

*shave, *v.* **1.** *tr.* To discount (a note) at an exorbitant rate of interest. **2.** To charge (a person) an exorbitant discount rate on a promissory note, to cheat. Both *slang* and *obs.*

(1) **1807** IRVING *Salmagundi* 309 Those who *shave notes of hand* . . . are the most respectable, because, in the course of a year, they make more money. **1848** W. ARMSTRONG *Stocks* 37 Ketchum, Rogers, and Bement . . . do an immense business in shaving notes. **1896** FREDERIC *Damnation of T. Ware* 40 People tacitly inferred that he 'shaved notes.' — (2) **1817** PAULDING *Lett. from South* II. 167 A man is obliged to go to a broker to get shaved, as the phrase is, as often as to a barber. **1837** *Jamestown* (N.Y.) *Jrnl.* 10 May 2/2 Men are so accustomed to be shaved, that . . . [they] look on one who is content with less than 2 per cent a month as an incorrigible flat.

***shaved,** *a.* **1. shaved head,** an Indian. **2. shaved meat,** ?jerked meat. Both *rare.* — (1) **1846** SAGE *Scenes Rocky Mts.* iv, A thousand 'shaved heads' are upon us, half frozen for hair! — (2) **1808** PIKE *Sources Miss.* App. III. 44 The travelling food of the dragoons . . . consists of . . . wheat biscuit and shaved meat, well dried, with a vast quantity of red pepper.

shavee ʃeˈvi, *n.* A person whose note is discounted exorbitantly. *Rare.* — **1819** *Niles' Reg.* 20 Nov. 185/2 Every man who has 100 dollars is *shaving,* and everyone that wants $100 is trying to get *shaved.* . . . *Shavers* and *shavees* are the bulk of the male population.

*shaver, *n.* One who discounts notes at exorbitant rates. *Obs.* Cf. **note shaver.**

1807 IRVING *Salmagundi* 309 Your higher order of *shavers,* your true bloodsuckers of the community . . . grow rich on the ruin of thousands. **1812** PAULDING *J. Bull & Bro. Jon.* 111 He had put it [the cash] in the hands of a shaver, as they called him, . . . who had placed it out at two per cent a month. **1859** *Harper's Mag.* June 137/1 Feels Arnul was a great shaver of small notes.

shave rush. (See quots.) — **1821** NUTTALL *Travels Arkansa* 53 A friable bed of dark-coloured argillaceous and sandy earth . . . [contains] blackened impressions of leaves of an oak, . . . with *Equisetum hiemale* or Shave-rush, and other vegetable remains. *Ib.* 78 It is from the prevalence of the cane, and the shave-rush (*Equisetum hiemale*), that the cattle are kept in tolerable condition.

shavetail ˈʃevˌtel, *n.*

1. *Mil.* An army mule. Also attrib. *Slang.*

1846 *N.O. Delta* 31 Aug. 366/2 [This mule] was followed by Shavetail Kicky, Esq., who, in a few pertinent remarks, expressed his ass-ent to the proceedings. **1897** LEWIS *Wolfville* 168 My off-wheel mule—a reg'lar shave-tail—is bad med'cine. **1927** DIXON *Life of 'Bill' Dixon* 31 We put in twenty days breaking the 'shave-tails.' *Ib.* 34 By this time our 'shave-tail' mules were under fairly good control.

2. (See quot. 1918.) Also attrib. *Slang.*

1899 T. HALL *Tales* 8–9 Not once . . . has the boy asked his advice even about a camping place, which is quite customary and proper with 'shave-tail' officers. **1918** *Everybody's Mag.* Jan. 113/3 A new second lieutenant is a 'shavetail.' **1950** *Time* 20 March 95/1 By confiding Japanese secrets to a bewildered Burma campaign shavetail . . . , Francis throws the enemy for a loss and the U.S. brass into a tizzy.

*shaving, *a.* and *n.*

1. The discounting of notes at exorbitant rates, the business of buying and selling notes at excessively profitable rates. *Obs.* Cf. **note shaving.**

1816 *Niles' Reg.* X. 334/2 It ought to come, to relieve the people from the harpies that prey upon their labor in the '*shaving*' of notes. **1818** FEARON *Sketches* 13 The only business which was good for anything . . . was shaving, i.e. buying and selling bank-notes. **1838** *N.Y. Advertiser & Exp.* 21 March 3/1 The Star says *shaving* is at present quite a monopoly.

2. In combs., chiefly obs.: (1) **shaving bank,** (see quot.); (2) **horse,** =**drawhorse;** (3) **mill,** (see quot. 1859); (4) **saloon,** a grandiloquent term for a barber shop; (5) ***shop,** a bank or a broker's office where notes or certificates are discounted at exorbitant rates; (6) **ticket,** a ticket entitling the holder to a shave or to shaves in a barber shop.

(1) **1848** BARTLETT 295 Banks, when they resort to any means to obtain a large discount, are also called shavers, or shaving banks. — (2) **1800** in *Bul. Dept. Hist. Queen's Univ.* No. 12, 11 On January 22nd, 1800, we find the entry, 'made a rack and a shaving horse.' **1946** *Agric. Hist.* Oct. 229/2 The workman sat astride the shaving horse. — (3) **1781** *Indep. Chronicle* (Boston) 19 July 3/3 A small boat, one of the noted Shaving-Mills, which continually infest our bay, was captured. **1859** J. L. LOCKE *Sketches* 32 Soon after the Revolutionary struggle commenced, this vicinity was occasionally frequented by 'Shaving Mills,' as the barges of British Marauders were called, in which they used to come to plunder the settlers of their cattle, sheep and poultry and frequently commit personal outrages. **1876** *Wide Awake* 243/2 A new 'shaving mill' . . . did double work of destruction. — (4) **1846** CORCORAN *Pickings* 171 This shaving saloon is like himself—queer, very queer. **1855** MARRYAT *Mts. & Molehills* 306 In the 'shaving-saloons' the accommodation these establishments afford is indispensable to the California public. **1867** *Ore. State Jrnl.* 17 Jan. 3/3 New Shaving Saloon, Willamette Street.

Shaving horse, shingle horse, or draw horse

(5) **1836** CROCKETT *Exploits* 29 Placing one million of the public funds in some little country shaving shop with no more than one thousand dollars capital. **1862** *N.Y. Tribune* 24 June 2/1 The only question was whether it [currency inflation] should be done by the banks and shaving-shops, or by the Government. — (6) **1864** *Hist. North-Western Soldiers' Fair* 82 W. A. Hetteck, Sherman House, [gave] 6 shaving tickets with 10 shaves each.

*shawl, *n.* **1. shawl society,** (see quot.). *Obs.* **2. shawl straps,** a pair of straps joined by a handle for carrying shawls, etc.

(1) **1871** BAGG *At Yale* 141 Psi U used to be called the 'shawl society,' in the old days when the wearing of that garment was deemed to smack somewhat of aristocracy and exclusiveness. — (2) **1873** PHELPS *Trotty's Wedding* xviii, The baby's swallowed the shawl-straps! **1902** *Sears Cat.* 906/3 Good, Solid Shawl Straps, with heavy stitched handles and ring, with two straps. Price, each, 3 feet . . . 20c.

As the last term in **Bay State, blanket, Stella shawl.**

Shawmut ˈʃɔmət, *n.* [f. the place-name, of Indian origin, "neck of land."] A variety of apple. *Obs.* — **1849** *N. Eng. Farmer* I. 226 Shawmut.—This is a good apple till the latter part of May.

Shawnee ʃɔˈni, *n.* Also **Shawano, Shawonese,** etc. [Shawnee *Shawunogi,* southerners.]

1. A member of an important Algonquian tribe of Indians, orig. resident on the Savannah River; in *pl.* the tribe. Also attrib. and collect.

1728 in HILDEBURN *Cent. of Printing* 94 Two Indian Treaties . . . between the Honourable . . . Lieut. Governour of the Province of Pennsylvania, . . . And The Chiefs of the Conestogoe, Delaware, Shawanese and Canawese Indians. **1755** *Lett. to Washington* I. 149 The Cherokees have taken up the Hatchet against the French & Shawnesse. **1786** *Mag. Amer. Hist.* I. 177/2 Some few Shawness . . . come in frequently. **1837** BIRD *Nick of Woods* I. 15 The Shawnee and the Wyandot still hunted the bear and buffalo in the cane-brake. **1949** *Democrat* 30 June 7/4 Several Shawnee towns were set up in various places over the state [of Alabama].

b. The language of these Indians. *Obs.*

1792 BRACKENRIDGE *Mod. Chivalry* (1937) 61 It will be necessary for him only to talk Irish, which he might pass for the Shawanese.

2. In special combs.: (1) **Shawnee haw,** (see quots.); (2) **salad,** (see quot. 1822); (3) **tree,** (see quot.); (4) **wood,** (see quots.).

(1) **1909** *Cent. Supp.* 1208/3 *Shawnee-haw,* . . . the larger withe-rod, *Viburnum nudum. Shawnee-wood,* . . . the western catalpa or catawba-tree, *Catalpa speciosa.* **1948** YOUNGKEN *Pharmacognosy* 843 Substitutes and Adulterants [are] the barks of other species of *Viburnum* notably *V. nudum* L. commonly known as Shonny Haw or

Shawnee Haw, *V. cassinoides* L. or With-rod, *Viburnum Lentago* L. or Sheepberry. — (2) *c*1780 in COATES *Outlaw Yrs.* 8 Gathered some herbs on the bottoms which some of the company called Shawnee Sallad. **1822** *London Hort. Soc. Trans.* 1 Ser. IV. 445 *The Hydrophyllum Virginicum* is called by the Americans of the Western States, *Indian Sallad*, or *Shawanee Sallad*, because these Indians eat it as such, when tender. Some of the first settlers do the same. **1931** CLUTE *Plants* 31 At least three plants commemorate them: the Shawnee haw (*Viburnum nudum*), the Shawnee salad (*Hydrophyllum Virginicum*), and the Shawnee tree, also called Shawnee wood (*Catalpa speciosa*). — (3) **1931** [see prec.]. — (4) **1852** *De Bow's Review* XII. 272 Shawnee wood or big-leaved cucumber (magnolia glauca) is found. **1907** HODGE *Amer. Indians* I. 213 The western catalpa, larger Indian bean, or Shawnee wood (*C. speciosa*). **1931** [see **Shawnee salad**].

Shawnese ʃɔˈniz, *a.* [Prob. f. the *-ese* pl. of **Shawnee**, on the analogy of such words as Chin*ese*, Japan*ese*, etc.] Of or pertaining to a Shawnee or the Shawnees. *Obs.*

1748 WEISER *Journal* 32, I made a Present to the old Shawonese Chief. **1826** FLINT *Recoll.* 231 A rich commandant . . . married a Shawnese wife. **1846** *Xenia Torch-Light* 11 June 3/2 A letter [has been] lately received by him from an Indian named John Wolf, of the Shawanese tribe.

***shay,** *n.* (See quot.) — **1905** *Churchman* 18 Nov. 804 A 'shay' . . . is a kind of fishing boat.

* **Shays,** *n.* Used attrib. and in the possessive with reference to an insurrection in 1786–87 against the government of Massachusetts, raised by Capt. Daniel Shays (1747–1825). Now *hist.*

1790 in *Journal Wm. Maclay* (2nd. ed. 1927) 209 In their former attempts to sink them [i.e., the state debts] they raised Shay's insurrection. **1798** MANNING *Key of Liberty* 54 This Shais afair neaver would have hapned if the peopel had bin posesed of a true knowledge of their Rights. **1833** *Jamestown* (N.Y.) *Jrnl.* 13 Feb. 1/3 The Shay's insurrection in Massachusetts has been frequently alluded to of late as affording a parallel to the course expected from South Carolina. **1949** *Social Studies* May 234/2 From 1780 to his death in 1793, he was continuously elected governor of Massachusetts except during Shays' Rebellion.

Shaysite ˈʃezaɪt, *n.* Also **Shayite.** A follower of Daniel Shays in the insurrection of 1786–87. *Obs.*

1787 *Maryland Jrnl.* 21 Dec. (Th.), Hail Congress, Conventions, Mobs, Shayites, and Kings. **1792** *Mass. Spy* 13 Dec. (Th.), [He] acts like one of those who were called warm Shaysites, in whom there was much guile. **1798** MANNING *Key of Liberty* 46 They would call them Jacobines, Shasites, Disorganisers & Enemyes to all government. **1836** R. C. TORREY *Hist. Fitchburg, Mass.* 87 Capt. Shattuck was a distinguished Shaysite of Peperell.

* **she,** *pron.* In combs.: (1) **she-balsam,** (see quot. 1884); (2) * **cat,** *fig.* something regarded as particularly fierce or severe, *slang;* (3) **cattle,** *W.* cows, *colloq.;* (4) **corn,** (see quot.), *obs.;* (5) **stock, stuff,** =**she cattle;** (6) * **wolf,** (see quot.).

(1) **1884** SARGENT *Rep. Forests* 210 *Abies Fraseri.* . . . Balsam. She Balsam. High mountains of North Carolina and Tennessee. **1943** PEATTIE *Great Smokies* 113 They listen with interest, . . . remembering the times they have hurried to the nearest she-balsam, cut off a hunk of bark and brewed it into a kidney tea. — (2) **1932** *K.C. Star* 18 March 34 This last winter has been a regular she-cat. — (3) **1885** *Santa Fé Wkly. New Mexican* 20 Aug. 4/1 There are now on the ranges of New Mexico sufficient she-cattle to fully stock the territory in five years. **1903** A. ADAMS *Log of Cowboy* 12 The contract called for a thousand she cattle. — (4) **1705** BEVERLEY *Virginia* II. 29 The other has a larger Grain, and looks shrivell'd with a Dent on the Back of the Grain, as if it had never come to Perfection; and this they call *She-Corn.*

(5) **1923** EVARTS *Tumbleweeds* 87 The herd would have been worked on the spot, . . . the she stuff . . . being allowed to scatter. *Ib.* 88 But there were . . . no she-stock on the range. — (6) **1945** MENCKEN *Supp.* I. 308 Even Mrs. Lincoln had a nickname, to wit, the *She-wolf.*

***shearer,** *n.* An animal that yields a fleece through shearing. — **1864** *Ohio Agric. Rep.* XVIII. 236, I now have the best shearers I have ever kept. **1898** *Mo. So. Dakotan* I. 46 This class of lambs are found to be a little better shearers.

* **shearing,** *n.*

1. (See quot.) *Obs.*

1822 WOODS *Residence* 257 Discounting of notes is called shearing, and is sometimes much practised.

2. In combs. with reference to the shearing of sheep, as **shearing band, camp, contest, corral.**

1866 *Iowa State Agric. Soc. Rep. 1865* 218 The shearing contest was lively. **1872** POWERS *Afoot & Alone* 300 A party . . . squatted around a fire by the shearing-camp. **1883** *Cent. Mag.* Oct. 817/1 In all . . . large [Indian] villages are organized shearing bands, with captains, that go from ranch to ranch in the shearing season. **1884** W. SHEPHERD *Prairie Exper.* 151 A few tumble-down open sheds guided you to the shearing corral.

* **shearwater,** *n.* =**black skimmer.** Cf. **Audubon's, dark-bodied shearwater.**

1709 LAWSON *Carolina* 150 Shear-Waters are a longer Fowl than a Duck; some of them lie on the Coast, while others range the Seas all over. **1813** WILSON *Ornithology* VII. 85 Black Skimmer, or Sheerwater. *Rhincops nigra. Ib.* 87 The Sheerwater is most frequently seen skimming close along shore about the first of the flood. **1883** *Cent. Mag.* Sep. 652/2 [Among the] birds on Cape Cod is . . . the black skimmer, or shearwater. **1949** SPRUNT & CHAMBERLAIN *S. Carolina Bird Life* 282 This remarkable looking bird is common on the South Carolina coast, where it is almost invariably called 'Shearwater.' . . . It is true that the Black Skimmer shears the water, but it is not a shearwater.

sheathing paper. Building paper.

*c*1790 COXE *View U.S.* 62 The produce, manufacturers, and exports of Pennsylvania . . . [include] sheathing and hanging paper. **1801** *Ann. 7th Congress* 2 Sess. 1225 Articles paying fifteen per cent. ad valorem . . . [include] cartridge and sheathing paper. **1876** *Vt. Bd. Agric. Rep.* III. 239 The other three sides are boarded tightly, and lined with sheathing paper.

shebang ʃəˈbæŋ, *n.* [Origin obscure. Poss. a variant of * *shebeen*, a low public house, or from the same source (Irish) as this.] A poor, usu. temporary, habitation. Also attrib. *Slang.*

1862 WHITMAN *Spec. Days* 27 [I am] among the groups around the fires, in their shebang enclosures of bushes. **1867** B. TAYLOR *Colorado* 60 A dwelling-house is invariably styled 'shebang.' **1887** HINMAN *Corp. Si Klegg* 355 And two hours later they would swarm around the sutler's 'shebang' like flies around a molasses barrel. **1947** BEEBE *Mixed Train Dly.* 141 Denny's Hogan is a small but scrupulously clean hunter's shebang.

transf. *c*1870 CHIPMAN *Notes on Bartlett* 398 *Shebang,* . . . an engine-house. **1871** BAGG *At Yale* 47 Shebang, rooms, place of abode. Also a theatrical or other entertainment in a public hall. **1872** MARK TWAIN *Roughing It* 327 You're welcome to ride here as long as you please, but this shebang's chartered. **1917** FREEMAN & KINGSLEY *Alabaster Box* 29 If we didn't want to sell this old shebang we'd be dumb idiots.

b. Often in the colloq. phrase *the whole shebang.*

1895 *Stand.* 1648/1 More widely, almost any matter of present concern, thing, business; as tired of the whole *shebang.* **1948** *Dly. Ardmoreite* (Ardmore, Okla.) 9 May 21 Wade and me claims the whole shebang!

shecoonery ʃəˈkunərɪ, *n.* An alteration of **chicanery. Rare.* — **1845** THOMPSON *Chron. Pineville* 47 This town's got a monstrous bad name for meanery and shecoonery of all sorts. *Ib.* 48 He dwelt upon the verdancy of his neighbors, and the shecoonery which had been practised upon them.

* **shed,** *n.*

1. An open porch of a house.

1778 CARVER *Travels* 46 Before the doors are placed comfortable sheds, in which the inhabitants sit, when the weather will permit. **1856** OLMSTED *Slave States* 630, I observed remarkably comfortable, though cheap and rude, quarters for the negroes—each cabin being of good size, with brick chimney, and a broad shed or gallery before the door.

2. In combs.: (1) **shed chamber,** *N. Eng.* a room under a shed roof; (2) **kitchen,** a shed room used as a kitchen; (3) **porch,** =**shed;** (4) **room,** *S.* a ground-floor room jutting out from a house or cabin, and usu. having a separate roof, a lean-to room.

(1) **1889** COOKE *Steadfast* 74 Hiram Perkins, the hired man, . . . slept in the 'shed chamber.' **1922** A. BROWN *Old Crow* 483 The bed . . . was the old four-poster he had packed away in the shed chamber. — (2) **1872** EGGLESTON *End of World* 62 Got a mustache onto the top story of his mouth, somethin' like a tuft of grass on the roof of a ole shed kitchen. **1886** STAPLETON *Major's Christmas* 267 They followed her . . . to a shed kitchen, where there was a cook stove and a sink. — (3) *c*1850 BAGBY *Old Va. Gentleman* 250 Under a hastily-made shed-porch in front of the house will be found a number of rocking-chairs. — (4) **1835** LONGSTREET *Ga. Scenes* 205 She pointed to an open shed-room adjoining the room in which we were sitting. **1888** *Cent. Mag.* Oct. 897/1 She went quietly to her little shed-room at the end of the porch. **1936** KROLL *Share-cropper* 93 There were two shed rooms behind, and they cooked in a rehabilitated smokehouse.

As the last term in **brush, buggy, car, cotton, freight, snow, storm, tobacco, train, water, wheel, woodshed.**

***shed,** *v. intr.* To slope like the roof of a shed. *Rare.* — **1857–8** *Ill. Agric. Soc. Trans.* III. 538 The roof may pitch both ways, or shed at the ends, presenting a gable end in front.

*** shedder,** *n.* A crab during one of its stages (see quots.). In full **shedder crab.**

1843 *Nat. Hist. N.Y., Zoology* VI. 11 During this interval, they are known under the name of Soft-shell crabs, or Shedders and are sought after with great avidity. **1848** *S. Lit. Messenger* XIV. 684/1 We will purchase a few shedder-crabs in the market. **1873** *Forest & Stream* 11 Sep. 75/1 Use shedder crabs or clams for bait. **1947** BROWN *Outdoors Unlimited* 245, I had caught weakfish with shrimp, alive and dead, with shedder crab, with blood and sand and tapeworms, with squid, alive and tinned.

As the last term in **horse, ink shedder.**

*** sheep,** *n.* In combs.: (1) **sheep barn,** a barn for housing sheep; (2) **camp,** *W.* a camp serving as headquarters for sheep herders; (3) **corral,** a corral for sheep; (4) **feeder,** (see quot. 1906); (5) **fever,** an intense desire to go into the sheep business; (6) **grower,** one who breeds and raises sheep on a large scale; (7) **herd,** *W.* a herd of sheep; (8) **herding,** *W.* the action or occupation of herding sheep; (9) **-killing dog,** a dog that makes a practice of killing sheep; (10) **meat,** mutton, cf. **sheep's meat;** (11) **mountains,** mountains where mountain sheep range; (12) **nanny tea,** a tea made from sheep droppings, valued as a folk remedy, cf. **nanny-plum tea;** (13) **range,** a range suitable for sheep; (14) **rock,** (see quot.); (15) **-'s gray,** a gray woolen fabric, orig. homemade, also attrib., *obs.;* (16) **shearer machine,** a machine for shearing sheep; (17) **-'s meat,** mutton; (18) **spread,** *W.* = **sheep ranch;** (19) * **-'s wool,** (see quot. 1911), also attrib.; (20) **wagon,** the wagon of a sheep herder; (21) **yard,** ?a yard where in colonial times sheep were penned on occasion, *rare.*

(1) 1868 *Mich. Agric. Rep.* VII. 47 Twelve half-blood Cotswold sheep . . . were put in the pens, at the south end of the sheep barn. **1919** CADY *Rhymes of Vt.* (1923) 164, I knew a farmer's wife that said 'You'll find me at the sheep barn dead.' — **(2) 1869** MUIR *First Summer in Sierra* (1911) 85 Though only a sheep camp, this grand mountain hollow is home, sweet home, every day growing sweeter, and I shall be sorry to leave it. **1939** ROLLINS *Gone Haywire* 114 He had stopped at a sheep camp and played casino with three herders. — **(3) 1847** SUTTER & CLERKS *New Helvetia Diary* (1939) 85 Passengers. . . . Truebody (his family moved back again to the Sheep Corral). **1865** *Harper's Mag.* June 12/1 He undertook to find accommodations in a vacant sheep-corral. — **(4) 1862** *Rep. Comm. Patents 1861: Agric.* 128 Cheyney was at that time a noted sheep-feeder. **1906** *N.Y. Ev. Post* 27 Oct. Sat. Supp. 1 A 'sheep feeder' is a man who receives the animals from the ranges into the feed lots, where they are fattened for market, and he is distinguished from a 'breeder,' who grows his sheep on the range.

(5) 1868 *Iowa State Agric. Soc. Rep. 1867* 408 The 'sheep fever' has proved the 'nub,' and wool-growers are rather disgusted. **1868** BRACKETT *Farm Talk* 27 A sheep-fever, or mania, rages throughout a portion of the country. — **(6) 1868** *Rep. Comm. Agric. 1867* 233 It is a matter well worthy the attention of sheep-growers. **1948** *New Yorker* 11 Sep. 25/1 In 1944, the sheepgrowers made their first large-scale attempt to solve the labor problem, by legally bringing in a hundred and fifty sheepherders from Mexico. — **(7) 1867** *Wkly. New Mexican* 2 Feb. 1/4 A band of Mescalero Apaches . . . made a descent upon a sheep herd a few miles below Las Cruces. **1880** *Cimarron News & Press* 19 Aug. 1/7 The Apaches made a raid upon the sheep herds of Valencia county. — **(8) 1891** C. ROBERTS *Adrift Amer.* 245 Sheep-herding will almost disappear when the wild beasts of Texas are extinct. **1948** *New Yorker* 11 Sep. 24/3 Present-day Americans seem to be temperamentally unfitted to sheepherding. — **(9) 1864** *Ohio Agric. Rep.* XVIII. 388 And the millions of money that are thus annually lost by the farmars [*sic*] of Ohio, are just as causlessly [*sic*] lost as in the case of loss by sheep killing dogs. **1872** *Newton Kansan* 29 Aug. 4/2 Sheep-killing dogs are generally great cowards. **1898** E. C. HALL *Aunt Jane* 18 Job set there, lookin' like a sheep-killin' dog. **1938** J. R. SIMMONS *Feathers & Fur on Turnpike* 75 We might as well include the sheep-killing dog.

(10) 1859 BARTLETT 398 *Sheep-Meat.* Mutton is often so called in the West. **1884** *Gringo & Greaser* 1 Jan. 2/3 [We] munch our tortiers and sheepmeat on the wing. — **(11) 1900** *Scribner's Mag.* Sep. 271/1 It seemed like a fairy-tale to be there, with the sheep mountains all around. — **(12) 1873** HAYCRAFT *Elizabethtown, Ky.* 151 Then sheep-nannie tea was prescribed; about a quart of that condiment swallowed down at night was certain to effect a cure. — **(13) 1901** *World's Work* July 991/1 The finest reproduction of the western yellow pine I have ever seen was on a sheep range in Arizona which had been judiciously grazed for over twenty years without a break. — **(14) 1859** COOPER & SUCKLEY *Nat. Hist. Washington Terr.* III. 137 Several rocky prominences in northern California . . . have the name of 'Sheep rocks,' where the bighorn exists.

(15) 1713 *Boston News-Letter* 2 Feb. 2/2 A Servant Man Named James Holms . . . [has] dark Sheeps gray coloured Stockings. **1852** *Mich. Agric. Soc. Trans.* III. 489 One piece of sheeps-gray cloth. **1889** *Cent. Mag.* Jan. 462/1 Then we had resort to coarse sheep's-gray jacket and trousers. — **(16) 1868** *Mich. Agric. Rep.* VII. 361 G. S. Wormer & Son, Detroit, [exhibited] 1 American sheep shearer machine. — **(17) 1833** J. STUART *Three Years N. Amer.* II. 126 The people, and especially the less rich classes, dislike mutton, which they call sheep's-meat. **1837** MARTINEAU *Society* II. 46 The inhabitants may be put in the way of obtaining tender 'sheep's meat.' — **(18) 1945** *Greeley* (Colo.) *D. Tribune* 13 March 1/6 Loss of trained men for several types of semi-skilled jobs on a sheep spread is a major cause for the drop. — **(19) 1883** *Nat. Museum Bul.* No. 27, 126 Fully 75 per cent. in value of all the Florida Sponges marketed are of the Sheepswool variety. **1911** *Rep. Fisheries 1908* 316/1 *Sheepswool,* the highest grade of Florida commercial sponges.

(20) 1914 E. STEWART *Lett. Woman Homesteader* 8 About noon the first day out we came near a sheep-wagon. — **(21) 1792** *Mass. H.S. Coll.* 1 Ser. III. 146 Clerks of the sheep yard are appointed.

See also as main entries **sheep common, -Eaters, *head, herder, man, ranch, *-shead, *skin.**

b. In the names of, or with reference to, plants: (1) **sheep apple,** a sheepnose apple; (2) **berry,** (*a*) the black haw, *Viburnum prunifolium,* (*b*) the nannyberry, *Viburnum lentago,* or its black edible drupe; (3) **laurel,** a dwarf shrub, *Kalmia angustifolia,* resembling mountain laurel and poisonous to stock (see quot. 1810); (4) * **-nose,** any of several varieties of apple, also attrib. [This term may not be of American origin. In *N. & Q.* 170 (Jan.–Jun., 1936) p. 183, it is said to be a Somerset dial. name for a kind of apple]; (5) **poison,** (see quots.); (6) **saffron,** *S.* sheep sorrel or a medicinal preparation made from it; (7) **-'s teats berry,** the fruit of a blackberry, *Rubus canadensis.*

(1) 1899 VANDERBILT *Flatbush* 280 There were 'sheep apples,' in shape like flattened cheeses, that grew in the pasture-lots on low trees just high enough to entice the boys to climb after them. — **(2)** (*a*) **1814** PURSH *Flora Amer.* II. 709 Sheep-berry. *Viburnum prunifolium.* **1897** SUDWORTH *Arborescent Flora* 338 Stagbush. . . . [Also called] Sheepberry (N.J.). (*b*) **1817–8** EATON *Botany* (1822) 510 *Viburnum lentago,* sheepberry. . . . Berries black, oval, and pleasant-tasted: somewhat mucilaginous. **1884** SARGENT *Rep. Forests* 94 Sheep-berry. Nannyberry. . . . Wood heavy, hard, close-grained, compact. **1948** [see **Shawnee haw**]. — **(3) 1810** MICHAUX *Arbres* I. 35 *Mountain laurel,* . . . dénomination la plus générale. *Sheep laurel,* . . . nom secondaire. **1869** FULLER *Flower-Gatherers* 138 And here is a third species, the *Angustifolia,* commonly termed, 'Sheep-Laurel.' **1897** SUDWORTH *Arborescent Flora* 315 *Kalmia latifolia.* Mountain Laurel. . . . [Also called] Sheep Laurel (Pa., Ohio). — **(4) 1817** W. COXE *Fruit Trees* 125 Bullocks Pippin . . . is more generally distinguished by the vulgar name of Sheep-nose, from a supposed resemblance between the form of the apple and that part of a sheep. **1888** CRADDOCK *Despot* 82 He be right yander in that thar sheep-nose apple-tree. **1943** DAMON *Sense of H.* 234 The Sheepnose, for example, had an interesting shape and a name just right.

(5) 1814 BIGELOW *Florula Bostoniensis* 103 *Kalmia angustifolia,* . . . a low shrub with rose coloured flowers, very common in low grounds, and known by the names *sheep poison, lambkill, low laurel,* &c. **1884** W. MILLER *Dict. Names of Plants* 124/2 'Sheep-poison,' Californian. *Lupinus densiflorus.* — **(6) 1835** LONGSTREET *Ga. Scenes* 210, I reckon sheep-saffron the onliest thing in nater for the ager. **1850** LEWIS *La. Swamp Doctor* 151 How we . . . were perfectly unanimous in the conclusion that 'sheep safern' were wonderful 'truck!' **1856** CARTWRIGHT *Autobiog.* 135 The next time those monkey-catchers come they bring sheep-saffron. — **(7) 1942** WEYGANDT *Plenty of Penna.* 296 These sheep's teats berries were a delicious fruit, coreless, melting, with a piquant individual flavor.

As the last term in **ancon, bush, Dall, grade, mountain, otter, Rocky Mountain, water, wild, woolly sheep.**

*** sheep,** *v.*

1. *tr.* (See quot. 1889.) Also transf.

1889 *Cent. Mag.* Jan. 448/1 The sheep-man represents to the cattle-man that his only possible course is to take his band across the cattle-man's range—to 'sheep' him, in the local phrase. **1912** R. A. WASON *Friar Tuck* xxxiv. 232 'What is it?' sez he, examinin' my face to see if I was 'sheepin' him.

2. In colloq. phrases: (1) *To sheep in,* ?to sow (wheat) by having it trodden in by a herd of sheep, *obs.;* (2) *to sheep off,* to graze (a region) out with sheep.

(1) 1873 *Harper's Mag.* Nov. 910/2 Wheat thus 'sheeped in,' as they call it, has borne sixty bushels per acre. — **(2) 1901** *Cong. Rec.* 1

March 3284/1 The country was all sheeped off, not a young tree growing. **1922** ZANE GREY *To Last Man* i, I see no sense in a sheepman goin' out of his way to surround a cattleman an' sheep off his range. *Ib.* iv, But what if you throwed your sheep round my range an' sheeped off the grass so my cattle would hev to move or starve?

* **sheep common.** A colonist's share or right in common land used for pasturing sheep. *Obs.*

1677 in SHELDON *Hist. Deerfield, Mass.* I. 180 Let out to Philip Matt on my 18 cow commons and 4 sheep commons at Pocumtuck, all the intervale land. **1792** *Mass. H.S. Coll.* 1 Ser. III. 156 The property is very unequally divided, varying from one sheep commons right to fourteen hundred sheep commons right. **1882** GODFREY *Nantucket* 89 The owner of 1/20 part of an original share of land . . . would own . . . thirty-six sheep commons (meaning thirty-six undivided 1/20th parts) of a certain share in each of the old divisions.

Sheep-Eaters 'ʃipˌitɚz, *n. pl.* [Referring to mountain sheep.] "A division of Shoshoni said to have lived in w. central Idaho on the Lemhi fork of Salmon r., and on the Malade. . . . They numbered 90 in 1904, but are no longer separately enumerated" (Hodge). Also attrib.

1865 *Rep. Indian Affairs 1864* 175 These [Tukuarika] bands are generally known as 'the Sheep-Eaters,' and their number is estimated at one thousand. **1890** LANGFORD *Vigilante Days* (1912) 135 That notorious scoundrel . . . bought a squaw from the Sheep Eater tribe of Bannack. **1940** *Places to See in Wyo.* xiii/1 Only the Sheepeaters . . . were known to inhabit the region permanently.

* **sheephead,** *n.* = **sheepshead.**

1743 CATESBY *Carolina* II. p. xxxii, Common Names of . . . Sea Fish [include]: . . . Sea-Tench, Sheephead, Eel. **1864** NORTON *Army Lett.* 212 Sheephead, shaped like a pumpkin seed with teeth exactly like a sheep's, . . . [are abundant]. **1894** TORREY *Fla. Sketch-Book* 51, I never saw so much as a sheep-head or a drum lying at his feet.

sheepherder 'ʃipˌhɝdɚ, *n.*

1. *W.* One who herds sheep, esp. in unfenced country.

1871 *Republican Rev.* 13 May 1/2, 150 Krowas, killed two sheep herders. **1913** *Outing* Jan. 428/2 In other sections of the West, where sheep herders commonly use it, it [crosstree hitch] is locally called the 'sheepherder's hitch.' **1948** *New Yorker* 11 Sep. 24/3 There is a chronic shortage of sheepherders in this country.

2. sheepherder's delight, whisky. *Slang. Obs.*

1873 *Harper's Mag.* Feb. 479/1 A peddler, . . . after taking several drinks of my sheepherders' delight, . . . went off and stole his own pack. **1878** B. F. TAYLOR *Between Gates* 281 The man . . . has just tipped a tumbler of what he calls in his random recklessness, . . . 'the sheep-herder's delight.'

* **sheepman,** *n.* Chiefly *W.* A sheep-breeder, one who owns large herds of sheep.

1868 MUIR *Thousand-Mile Walk* (1916) 202 Inasmuch as he [coyote] is fond of mutton, he is cordially detested by 'sheep-men' and nearly all cultured people. **1892** *Vt. Agric. Rep.* XII. 154 The successful sheep men of the State are . . . breeding for mutton or for roughbred Merinos. **1948** *Great Falls* (Mont.) *Tribune* 27 Sep. 9/5 Coyote control plans will be discussed by Cascade county sheepmen this afternoon.

sheep ranch. *W.* A ranch devoted to the breeding and raising of sheep. Also attrib.

1875 *Cong. Rec.* 20 Feb. 1537/1 This is not the sheep-ranch proposition. **1901** *Outlook* 17 Aug. 908/1, I am going to start a sheep ranch on my claim. **1947** *Amer. Wkly.* 2 Nov. 10/1 He told her . . . his uncle . . . had bequeathed him a huge sheep ranch.

Also as a verb. Hence **sheep rancher.**

1879 HOWELLS *Lady of Aroostook* 65 They cattle-range in West Virginia, too. They may sheep-ranch, too, for all I know. **1904** *Country Life* July 287/1 The Montana sheep-rancher figures that the wool will pay all expenses, leaving the increase for his profit. **1948** *Gainesville* (Tex.) *D. Reg.* 2 July 4/4 Marshall was seeking a new answer to an old problem of the sheep rancher.

* **sheepshead,** *n.* Any one of several fishes having some resemblance to the head of a sheep (see note).

These fishes include: **a.** A large food fish (*Archosargus probatocephalus*), abundant on the Atlantic and Gulf coasts. **b.** An allied fish of Florida, *Salema rhomboidalis* (syn. *Archosargus unimaculatus*). **c.** The fresh-water drumfish (*Aplodinatus grunniens*) of the Great Lakes and the Mississippi Valley. **d.** The dollarfish, *Poronotus triacanthus.* Cf. **lake sheepshead.**

1643 WILLIAMS *Key* (1866) 138 *Taut-añog,* Sheeps-heads. **1687** BLOME *Isles & Terr. in Amer.* 119 The Sheepshead, so called, from the resemblance of its Mouth and Nose to a Sheep, is a Fish much preferred by some. **1789** MORSE *Amer. Geog.* 205 In the rivers and bays are plenty of sheeps-head, black-fish, herring. **1897** *Outing* XXX. 435/2 Most abundant . . . was the 'sheepshead' (freshwater drum), a good-looking, silvery fish. **1909** WEBSTER 1939/1 *Sheepshead,* . . . the salema.

b. Used attrib. with **killifish, lebias, minnow,** to designate a killifish, *Cyprinodon variegatus,* of the Atlantic and Gulf coasts.

1814 MITCHILL *Fishes N.Y.* 441 Sheep's-Head Killifish. . . . Lives in the salt water. **1842** *Nat. Hist. N.Y., Zoology* IV. 215 The Sheepshead Lebias . . . [is] used as bait. **1896** JORDAN & EVERMANN *Check-List Fishes* 314 *Cyprinodon variegatus.* . . . Sheepshead Minnow. Cape Cod to the Rio Grande.

c. sheepsheading party, a social group that fishes for sheepshead. *Rare.*

1814 MITCHILL *Fishes N.Y.* 394 The outfit of a sheep's heading party is always an occasion of considerable parade and high expectation.

2. a. sheepshead gull, (see quots.). **b. sheepshead porgy,** (see quot.).

(a) 1813 WILSON *Ornithology* VII. 76 By many it [the common tern, *Sterna hirundo*] is called the Sheep's-head Gull, from arriving about the same time with the fish of that name. **1844** *Nat. Hist. N.Y., Zoology* II. 305 The Silvery Tern, *Sterna argentea,* . . . is sometimes called the *Little Sheepshead* Gull. — **(b) 1884** GOODE *Fisheries* I. 394 A fish known as the 'Sheepshead Porgy' is said by Stearns to be common about the Florida Reefs.

* **sheepskin,** *n.*

1. A diploma. *Colloq.*

1804 D. WEBSTER *Private Corr.* I. 173 Feeling some anxiety about your 'sheep-skin,' I wrote to Merrill. **1888** TANNER *Lobby* 370 When asked by the late Chief Justice Church where his 'sheep-skin' was, he replied that he never had but one sheepskin in his life, and that his father gave him when one of his sheep died. **1949** *St. Paul Pioneer Press* 19 June 1/4 Under the GI Bill of Rights, the dogged, over-age collegian . . . bought his sheepskin at the price of uncounted mental, physical and spiritual outlay.

2. (See quots.) *Colloq.*

1939 WOLCOTT *Yankee Cook Book* 346 Some people call the [maple] syrup [boiled down and poured on snow] 'sheepskins.' **1943** DAMON *Sense of H.* 107 The snow-hardened sirup, called 'maple wax' or, if in thin large sheets, 'sheepskins,' is such delicious eating that no one minds . . . large and frequent tastings.

sheer boom. A boom in a stream for shunting logs in a desired direction.

1876 KNIGHT 2141/1 *Sheer-boom,* . . . a boom in a stream to catch logs and direct them toward a log-pond. One end is moored to the shore, and it has rudders . . . to catch the force of the current obliquely, and thus maintain its position at a certain angle across the direction of the stream. **1896** *Mo. Weather Rev.* Nov. 405/1 The formation of the gorge is supposed to have been caused by the driving of piles in the Mississippi River . . . to hold a 'sheer boom' for the purpose of running the logs . . . into the Zumbra River for safe harbor. **1948** *Miss. Valley Hist. Rev.* Dec. 437 The sheer booms of the logging company were diverting so much water that the navigability of the main channel was seriously diminished.

* **sheet,** *n.* [In sense **1.** poss. derived from, or influenced by, Du. *schoot* in a similar sense. Cf. quot. 1846 below and see *WNT s.v. schoot* (III) 5.]

1. A large piece *of* gingerbread baked on a flat tin or in a shallow pan. *Obs.*

1825 NEAL *Bro. Jonathan* I. 108 Walk into you, any time, for half a sheet o' gingerbread. **1846** FARNHAM *Prairie Land* 31 It was . . . a pair of luscious brown sheets of gingerbread, which he had purchased at a Dutch farm-house. **1865** *Atlantic Mo.* June 665/2 Not a young farmer came into Hanerford . . . , who did not . . . buy a sheet of gingerbread . . . [for] the drive homeward.

2. sheet writer, (see quot. 1895).

1895 *Funk* 2736/1 sheet-writer, *n. Horse-racing.* A book-maker's assistant who records bets made. **1901** H. ROBERTSON *Inlander* 31 She had intercepted her young daughter . . . in time to prevent an elopement with a pool-room sheet-writer.

For **sheet sham** see **sham 2.**

As the last term in **blanket, box, cooky, dope, style, tally, three, wagon sheet(s).**

* **sheet iron.** In obs. combs.: (1) **sheet-iron band,** used facetiously for a callithumpian band; (2) **hat,** (see quot.); (3) **oil-tank,** an oil-tank made of sheet iron.

(1) 1851 HALL *Manhattaner* 146 The happy couple . . . would have seen . . . a modest card of anonymous authority, calling on the Sheet-Iron-Band to appear that night for duty. — **(2) 1846** *Spirit of Times* (N.Y.) 18 April 88/1 His hat was what is commonly termed a 'sheet-iron' hat, being destitute of nap, and resembling a battered chimney pot. — **(3) 1880** *Harper's Mag.* Dec. 65 Tremendous sheet-iron oil-tanks . . . are to store away 2,000,000 barrels of 'dollar-crude.'

* **sheldrake,** *n.* As the last term in **hooded, summer, swamp Weaser sheldrake.**

* **shelf,** *n.*

1. A shelf fungus.

1907 *St. Nicholas* July 846/1 'Shelves,' often called 'devil's bread,' . . . grow on woodland stumps and trees and logs.

2. In combs.: (1) **shelf back,** (see quot. 1925); (2) **goods,** (see quot. 1944); (3) **hardware,** =prec.; (4) **worn,** of goods, slightly worn from having been long on a shelf.

(1) **1925** J. A. HOLDEN *Bookman's Gloss.* 97 *Shelf-back*, the back of a book, on which the title is lettered. **1931** *Publishers' Wkly.* 9 May 2322 It . . . is strongly bound and has the name of the periodical stamped in gold on cover and shelfback. — (2) **1899** *Caddo Herald* 3 March 1 They have opened up a first-class stock of Hardware, consisting of a general line of Shelf Goods. **1944** CLARK *Pills* 309 There was an endless demand for miscellaneous hardware items listed in the catalogues as 'shelf goods.' — (3) **1865** *Ore. State Jrnl.* 18 Nov. 3/2 Goldsmith and Friendly . . . [are] displaying to the Public an Immense Stock of . . . Shelf Hardware. **1892** *York Co. Hist. Rev.* 57 The stock embraces . . . a large line of heavy and shelf hardware. — (4) **1887** TOURGEE *Button's Inn* 188 [The invention's] out of season, . . . creased and shelf-worn. **1944** CLARK *Pills* 214 At best the ready-made clothes were poor in quality. They were notoriously shelf-worn and moth-eaten. Many of them had seen one or two seasons in a large city store before they reached the crossroad shelves.

As the last term in **chimney, hanging, open shelf.**

* **shell,** *n.*

1. A person's head, mouth, or body. *Colloq.*

1678 B. TOMPSON *Poetical Works* 125 Too big for my poor shell to Comprehend. **1845** *Knickerb.* XXV. 212 'Shut your shells!' answered Tom, in high dudgeon. **1906** F. LITTLE *Lady of Decoration* 95 My old shell is too exhausted to move.

2. A bare, rough, or unpretentious building with little or no furniture. *Colloq.*

1852 STOWE *Uncle Tom* xxxii, They were mere rude shells, destitute of any species of furniture. **1880** *Harper's Mag.* Dec. 43 Which one of the old shells have you taken? **1920** HOWELLS *Vacation of Kelwyns* 5 Even the summer shell was little known in the early eighteen-seventies.

3. Used allusively with reference to Hard Shells and Soft Shells in politics and religion. *Obs.*

1856 W. A. PHILLIPS *Conquest of Kans.* 131 There was an English clergyman; a Baptist preacher from Missouri, of what particular 'shell' I cannot say, for he kept his religion within it while at Topeka. **1858** *N.Y. Tribune* 30 Jan. 5/4 Indeed, the old Hards are perfectly appalled by the hardihood and recklessness of the barnburners upon this Lecompton matter. It is a subject of remark here [Washington] that the New-York Shells seem to be changing their relations, the Softs having turned to Hards, while the Hards are becoming relatively Softs.

4. A light boat or canoe, esp. an extremely light, long, narrow racing boat.

[**1858** HOLMES *Autocrat* 196, I run along ripping it up with my knife-edged shell of a boat.] **1867** *Harper's Mag.* Oct. 654/2 Look at these beautiful 'shells,' resting one above the other on the brackets on either wall. **1875** *Fur, Fin & Feather* (ed. 3) 114/2 For weeks I have paddled my cedar shell in all directions. **1949** *Time* 4 July 34/1 Harvard oarsmen noted with some surprise that the Eli shell was still even with them.

attrib. **1857** *Spirit of Times* 18 July 309/2 The oarsmen of the Unknown, pulling for the first time in a shell boat, pulled a very crooked course. **1871** *Harper's Mag.* July 186 The shell-boats . . . made such good time that in 1869 a general challenge was given. **1891** *Harper's Wkly.* 19 Sep. 715/2 The aquatic event of the day was the eight-oared shell race for the S.I.A.C. challenge cup.

5. A cartridge for a pistol or other firearm. Also attrib.

1874 *Field & Stream* 13 Aug. 11/3 A discussion has been going on of late as to the respective merits of paper and metallic shells in breech loading shot guns. **1879** VIVIAN *Wanderings Western Land* 360 An empty cartridge case (called here [Calif.] a 'shell') found close by, was also of the Remington pattern. **1908** CHAMBERS *Firing Line* 165 The agile herd bounded past far out of shell-range. **1949** *Chi. Sun-Times* 10 May 16/4 Outside was an ejected shell case, marked 'E.C.-42.'

6. In special combs.: (1) **shellbark,** see as a main entry; (2) **beans,** beans shelled before cooking, as distinguished from string beans, also a variety of such beans; (3) **bluff,** a bluff composed largely of a shell deposit; (4) **comb,** a comb of tortoise shell; (5) **cracker,** (see quot. 1891); (6) **dance,** (see quot.), *rare;* (7) * **fish,** a trunk-fish, also with specifying term; (8) **game,** a sleight-of-hand gambling game in which a pea or small pellet and three walnut shells are used, thimblerig, also attrib.; (9) **man,** a thimblerigger; (10) **marble,** (see quot. 1891); (11) **money,** a form of wampum or peag, cf. **allocochick;** (12) **pot,** (see quot.), *obs.;* (13) **quail,** (see quot.); (14) **rock,** a hard rocklike formation consisting largely of sea shells; (15) **worker,** =**shellman,** also transf., *slang.*

(2) **1868** HAWTHORNE *Notebooks* II. 88 We had shell-beans, green corn, and cucumbers from our garden. **1947** PAUL *Linden* 59 On the other side of the house was a tomato patch, . . . shell beans climbing on poles that were never exactly straight or plumb, some squash and pumpkin vines. — (3) **1765** J. BARTRAM *Diary* 25 Dec., This shell-bluff is 300 yards more or less along the river's bank. — (4) **1858** SIMMONDS *Dict. Trade, Shell-comb*, a lady's comb for the hair, or a toilet comb, made of tortoiseshell. **1898** I. H. HARPER *S. B. Anthony* I. 50 Her abundant hair was braided in four long braids, which cousin Margaret sewed together and wound around a big shell comb.

(5) **1891** *Cent.* 5565/3 shell-cracker. . . . A kind of sunfish, *Eupomotis speciosus*. Florida. **1947** DALRYMPLE *Panfish* 180 The name 'Shellcracker' comes from his habit of feeding on small crustaceans, as does the Pumpkinseed. — (6) **1837** *S. Lit. Messenger* III. 391/1, I was informed that this was called by the Indians the Pole Cat Dance though our friends were disposed to distinguish it by the more agreeable . . . name of the *Shell Dance*. — (7) **1896** JORDAN & EVERMANN *Check-List Fishes* 424 *Lactophrys triqueter*. . . . Trunk-fish; Rock Shellfish. . . . West Indies, north to the Bermudas; Key West and Pensacola. *Ib.*, *Lactophrys trigonus*. . . . Common trunk-fish; Chapin; Shell-fish. West Indies, north to Bermuda and Key West. — (8) **1890** BIFF HALL *Turnover Club* 169 Would endeavour to make a collection of Japanese coins, with their cards and a shell game. **1903** *N.Y. Times* 26 Sep. 9 The shell-game man had ceased from troubling. **1948** MENJOU & MUSSELMAN *It Took 9 Tailors* 137 That racket makes the shell game look as innocent as hopscotch. — (9) **1891** QUINN *Fools of Fortune* 348 The simplicity of the apparatus enables the 'shell' man to carry his outfit with him in his vest pocket wherever he may go. **1947** *Amer. Sp.* XXII. 162 There are today two fairly well defined types of professional *shell-men* operating.

(10) **1848** DANA *Mineralogy* 350 Fire marble, or lamuchelle, is a dark brown shell marble. **1891** *Cent.* 5566/2 *Shell-marble*, . . . an ornamental marble containing fossil shells. — (11) **1851** J. F. W. JOHNSTON *Notes N. Amer.* II. 465 From the purple interior of this shell the *wampum* or shell-money of the Indians was prepared. **1907** HODGE *Amer. Indians* I. 546 Shell money and ornaments, composed of strings of dentalia, used by Indians. — (12) **1790** *Mass. Spy* 24 June (Th.), A negro man, saw, and caught, a small turtle, or what is more generally known [in Va.] by the name of shellpot. — (13) **1884** COUES *Key to Birds* (ed. 2) 593 *Callipepla*. . . . Shell Quail. . . . One U.S. species. . . . *C. squamata*. . . . Scaled Partridge. Blue Quail. — (14) **1837** WILLIAMS *Florida* 56 The bank is formed of concrete shell rock. **1891** *Scribner's Mag.* Oct. 475/1 The 'natural beds' . . . are known as . . . 'Shell Rock,' 'Cohansey beds' [etc.]. **1895** *Dept. Agric. Yrbk. 1894* 520 The shell rock was laid down in thickness only 3 to 4 inches.

(15) **1896** G. ADE *Artie* xii. 109 He's better 'n any o' them shell-workers that used to graft out at the government pier. **1903** ——— *People You Know* 150 Joel and the Shell-Worker [a shyster lawyer] moved the Old Gentleman up to a Table in the Front Room.

b. Designating land or areas where marine shells are abundant in the soil, as (1) **shell hammock (land),** (2) **land,** (3) **prairie.**

(1) **1886** I. D. HARDY *Oranges & Alligators* 145 What is by many people of experience held to be the very best of all the Florida lands—high 'shell-hammock' land. **1887** *South Fla. Sentinel* (Orlando) 16 Feb. 1/9 This [land] is what they call a shell hammock. — (2) **1837** WILLIAMS *Florida* 56 The soil is rich shell land. — (3) **1883** SMITH *Geol. Survey Ala.* 500 The belt of what is called in this county 'shell prairie' is about five miles wide.

c. Designating ways, walks, etc., surfaced with marine shells, as (1) **shell drive,** (2) **highway,** (3) **road,** (4) **walk.**

(1) **1887** CUSTER *Tenting on Plains* 273 The best part of all our detention was the shell drive along the ocean. — (2) **1908** CHAMBERS *Firing Line* 146 The little cavalcade made a startling clatter on the shell highway. — (3) **1836** T. POWER *Impressions of Amer.* II. 99 We soon gained the shell road however, and found it as good as the streets of Mobile. **1944** *Sat. Ev. Post* 9 Sep. 67/1, 'I saw Myrtle's friend walking on Shell Road,' I said. — (4) **1884** CABLE *Dr. Sevier* 454 [Mary was] breaking the silence . . . by the soft grinding of her footsteps on the shell walk.

As the last term in **bean, carpet, clam, coffee, corncob, cradle, egg, gold, Hard, Indian, paper, patty, peanut, pecan, Pilgrim, rice, shotgun, soft, tusk shell.**

* **shell,** *v.*

1. *tr.* To remove (the grains of Indian corn) from the cob, to free (ears of corn) of the grains.

1639 *Md. Archives* I. 79 All contracts made for paym[en]t in Corne shall be understood of Corne shelled & a barrell of new Corne tendred in payment. **1813** *Steele P.* II. 708, I Sold Sixty Bushels Corn . . . to be delivered at your plantation at the river on Monday next, please to have it Shelled and delivered that day. **1852** REGAN *Emigrant's Guide* 321 As general rule the corn is never shelled or taken off the cob till wanted for use. **1949** *N.O. Times-Picayune Mag.* 8 May 2/2 He's back again, . . . tending 200 baby chicks, 125 hens, five pigs (climbing into a corn crib, shucking and shelling the feed).

b. With *off, out* (see quot. 1825).

1803 CUTLER in *Life & Corr.* II. 125 In bad weather, shell out your corn. **1825** NEAL *Bro. Jonathan* I. 53 The former . . . gives them [*sc.* his neighbors] notice, that he is ready to 'shell out'; or in other words, to undergo a husking. **1830** S. SMITH *Life J. Downing* 38 Uncle Joshua will have to shell out his bushel of corn. **1845** HOOPER *Taking Census* 163 Taking an ear of corn . . . and shelling off a handful, she commenced scattering the grain.

2. *To shell over*, to hand over, pay up. *Slang. Obs.*

1848 *Jamestown* (N.Y.) *Jrnl.* 26 Feb. 3/2 The County has two treasurers, . . . each calling on the Collectors of taxes to shell over. **1857** *Knickerb.* XLIX. 34, I reckoned I could make him shell over.

b. Also *to shell out the corn*, in same sense. *Slang. Obs.*

1841 *N.O. Picayune* 30 April 1/6 He is induced to be thus particular, (being like ten thousand of his neighbors,) not exactly prepared to 'shell out the corn,' and wipe out old scores.

shellbark ˈʃɛlˌbɑrk, *n.*

1. The scaly-bark hickory, or a tree of this species. Also the thick shellbark hickory or king nut. In full **shellbark(ed) hickory.** Cf. **shagbark.**

1759 in HALSEY *Four Great Rivers* (1906) 21 The Timber in these Parts . . . consists of . . . red Oak Hazel Bushes, Ash and Gum together with Butternut and Shellbark, Hiccory in plenty. **1785** MARSHALL *Amer. Grove* 69 *Juglans alba ovata.* Shell-barked Hickery. . . . There are several varieties of this in America. **1814** PURSH *Flora Amer.* II. 637 Juglans alba. . . . This useful tree is known by the name of Shell-bark Hickory, Shag-bark and Scaly-bark Hickory, on account of its bark, which is torn in loose fragments like the preceding. **1948** DICK *Dixie Frontier* 46 Some of these torches and blazing arrows were made of flax captured from a settler's cabin and wrapped in the inner fiber of shellbark hickory, which was oily and burned readily.

attrib. **1881** PIERSON *In the Brush* 23 He gave orders . . . to get the shell-bark-hickory torches that they had provided to light us home. **1950** *Pa. Dutchman* Jan. 3/4 Those favorite trees, especially of the shellbark family have disappeared.

b. Bark that is scaly or flaky. *Rare.*

1845 DRAKE *Pioneer* 230, [I] found the old hickory . . . quietly as ever casting off now and then his 'shell bark.'

2. The nut of such a tree. In full **shellbark nut.**

1799 *Columbian Mirror* (Alexandria, D.C.) 15 Feb. 3/4 Thomas Simms Has just received, and has for sale at his Grocery Store . . . , a quantity of Excellent. . . . Shellbark Nuts, by the barrel or smaller quantities. **1832** WATSON *Hist. Tales N.Y.* 54 Among the latter [items of Indian diet] were chesnuts, shellbarks, walnuts. **1948–9** *N.W. Ohio Quart.* Winter 13 Two or three did not get in until dark bearing the big loads of fine shellbarks.

shelled corn. Corn removed from the cob.

1676 *Md. Archives* II. 560 No ordinary keeper shall demand above . . . 4 lib. Tob[acco], ffor a Peck of Indian shell'd Corn. **1809** CUMING *Western Tour* 175 The usual produce of an acre of this . . . soil, is from forty to fifty bushels of shelled corn. **1950** *Chi. Tribune* 20 March IV. 1/3 The class of Illinois shippers primarily affected would be those who consign shelled corn to far western states.

* **sheller,** *n.*

1. A device for shelling corn, peas, etc.

1859 *Rep. Comm. Patents 1858* I. 361 The nature of this invention relates . . . to the form and arrangements of the shellers. **1880** *Lib. Universal Knowl.* I. 164 For harvesting, we have mowing, reaping and binding machines, shellers, fruit-pickers, etc. **1948** *Democrat* 6 May 1/7 This sheller does not shell crowder peas satisfactorily.

2. (See quot. 1881.)

1881 INGERSOLL *Oyster Industry* 248 *Shellers*, persons who open clams for market. (New Jersey.) **1887** GOODE *Fisheries* V. II. 593 As many as two dozen shellers are at work at one time. **1894** *D.N.* I. 333.

3. ?A hard-shelled crab.

1886 MITCHELL *R. Blake* 261 Don't know shellers. Why ther's them, an ther's paper shells, and ther's soft shells, . . . and them's all crabs.

As the last term in **corn, pecan, soft sheller.**

* **shelter,** *n.* In combs.: (1) **shelter belt,** a row or group of trees affording protection from snow and wind, also attrib.; (2) **half,** one half of a shelter tent; (3) **hedge,** a hedge that affords shelter for a garden or other ground; (4) **tent,** a small tent, usu. for two persons, having two poles and a ridge rope.

(1) **1869** *Rep. Comm. Agric. 1868* 197 For a shelter belt, . . . this [maple] will be found suitable. **1910** MRS. H. WARD *Canadian Born* 335 The thin background of a few taller trees,—the 'shelter-belt' of the farm. **1945** *Boulder* (Colo.) *D. Camera* 30 Nov. 2/1 The Great Plains shelterbelt project has been pronounced an outstanding success. — (2) **1924** *Scribner's Mag.* Dec. 648/1 Have you a haversack, shelter-half, pack carrier? **1949** *Sat. Ev. Post* 25 June 36/2 The first soldiers I encountered were two youths sleeping beneath a shelter half that bagged with a puddle of water. — (3) **1858** WARDER *Hedges & Evergreens* 43 [The hemlock spruce] soon forms a . . . close shelter-hedge. *Ib.* 240 The common cedar is very efficacious and much used for producing a shelter-hedge. — (4) **1865** SALA *Diary* I. 279 The warriors carried the component parts of the 'shelter-tent' on the tops of their knapsacks.

Sheller (sense 1) (*c*1900), corn sheller, or hand sheller

shenanigan ʃəˈnænəgən, *n.* [See note.]

Origin obscure. It is not likely a development from Sp. *chanada*, a trick or deceit (see *Amer. Sp.* II. 488). Webster regards Irish *sionnachuighim*, "I play tricks," as a prob. source. A poss. source is dial. or argot G. *schinagel, schinäglen*, suggested by Leo Spitzer in *Amer. Sp.* XXIII. (1948) 210–13. The term appears to have come into use first in California.

Treacherous conduct, trickery, nonsense, foolery. *Colloq.*

1855 *Town Talk* (S.F.) 25 April 1/2 'The d——l!' exclaimed Kentuck, 'are you quite sure? No shenanigan?' **1856** in *Calif. Hist. Soc. Quart.* IX. (1930) 62 Bought. . . . Livery Stable, in Co with H. C. Carpenter; paid $250 down & $250 to be paid in six months tryed to play chinanigan but couldn't make it rip. **1897** *Outing* XXIX. 483/1 He is with a man who is firmly kind, but who will stand no shinanigan. **1948** *Pauls Valley* (Okla.) *D. Democrat* 1 July 2/4 The shenanigans and social customs of that time caused sincere wonder what the result of letting down the bars of gentility would produce.

One form of shelter tent

Shenkbeer ˈʃɛnkbɪr, *n.* (See quot.) *Obs.* — **1871** DE VERE 142 The other extreme, an exceedingly weak and insipid beverage, *Shenkbeer*, the *Schenkbier* of Germany, is so called because it has to be put on draught (*schenken*) as soon as it is made, for fear of turning sour if not immediately consumed.

shepherd('s) holland. A kind of holland cloth. *Obs.* — **1644** *Wyllys P.* 73 A good shephard holland strong & white. **1693** Sewall *Letter-Book* I. 137 One p[iec]e Shepard's Holland or course Bag-Holland.

***sheriff,** *n.* Used in the possessive in combs.: (1) **Sheriff's Deadline,** (see quot.); (2) **hammer,** usu. *fig.* a hammer or gavel used by a sheriff at a sheriff's sale; (3) **jury,** a special jury, *obs.;* (4) **prison,** (see quot.); (5) **sale,** a public sale of property conducted by a sheriff in compliance with a writ of execution.

(1) **1944** Adams *W. Words* 48 In early days the Nueces River in Texas was called the *Sheriff's Deadline* because the numerous outlaws would not let a sheriff cross west of it. — (2) **1865** *Atlantic Mo.* April 510/1 In process of time, 'debts of honor' and the sheriff's hammer had dissipated his entire clientage of blacks. — (3) **1820** *Boston Selectmen* 9 Sep., A special jury . . . commonly called a sheriff's jury, to try a claim . . . for compensation for land. **1830** *Williams's N.Y. Ann. Reg.* 254 Sheriff's Jury (City of New-York) for the year 1830. — (4) **1882** McCabe *New York* 418 Ludlow Street Jail . . . is sometimes called 'The Sheriff's Prison.' All persons arrested under process issued by the Sheriff of the county of New York are imprisoned here.

(5) **1798** *Pittsburgh Gaz.* 6 Oct. 1/2 (*advt.*), Sheriff's Sales. **1825** *Ohio Patriot* (New Lisbon) 29 Oct. 1/1 Sheriff's Sales . . . 2 stills, 12 still-tubs, 2 cooling-tubs, 2 singling-kegs and 1 doubling-keg. **1947** *Steamboat* (Colo.) *Pilot* 30 Jan. 2/8 The electric light plant . . . was sold at sheriff's sale.

sheriffcy ˈʃɛrɪfsɪ, *n.* The office of sheriff. *Rare.* — **1841** in Jilson *Dark & Bloody Ground* 91 He remained in service for six months, . . . returning to the duties of his Sheriffcy [etc.].

***Sherman,** *n.* [In (1), (2), and (3) in allusion to John *Sherman* (1823–1900), U.S. Senator from Ohio; in the others the allusion is to Gen. W. T. *Sherman* (1820–91), of Civil War fame.] In combs.: (1) **Sherman Act,** a congressional act in force from 1890 to 1893 for artificially maintaining the price of silver through compulsory government purchase of silver bullion; (2) **Antitrust Act, Bill, Law,** a piece of legislation passed by Congress in 1890 prohibiting combinations in restraint of interstate or foreign trade; (3) **note,** one of the legal-tender treasury notes, redeemable in coin, issued in 1890 under the provisions of the Sherman Act; (4) **-'s bummers,** (see quots.), *obs.;* (5) **-'s hairpin,** a twisted railroad rail (see quot.) in the wake of Sherman's march to the sea; (6) **-'s monument,** (see quot.), *obs.*

(1) **1892** *Dem. Platform* in K. Porter *Nat. Party Platforms* 162 We denounce the Republican legislation known as the Sherman Act of 1890. **1947** *Atlantic Mo.* June 73/1 In 1890 the Sherman Act was passed to 'appease the restive masses,' but it would be fifty years before Thurman Arnold would demonstrate, briefly, that the Act could be made to work. — (2) **1890** *Nation* 27 March 250/1 The debate on Senator Sherman's Anti-Trust Bill is an advantage to the country. **1899** Gunton *Trusts & Public* 42 The Sherman anti-trust law . . . foreshadow[s] what is likely to come. **1908** *Independent* 16 July 137/1 In 1890 Congress enacted the Sherman Anti-Trust act. **1948** *Duncan* (Okla.) *D. Banner* 1 July 1/3 The U.S. Supreme Court . . . held that officers of the company and the firm itself had violated the Sherman anti-trust law. — (3) **1894** Muhleman in Nelson *A B C Wall St.* 104 The Secretary of the Treasury is to redeem the 'greenbacks' and 'Sherman notes' in gold. **1897** *Daily News* (London) 10 Dec. 5/1 The second feature of the Secretary's plan . . . is the retirement of all the outstanding greenbacks and Sherman notes. **1900** *Cong. Rec.* 11 Jan. 776/1 Sherman notes . . . are all to be disposed of under this bill. — (4) **1870** MacRae *Americans* I. 289 These foraging parties, which came to be known in the South as 'Sherman's bummers,' swarmed over the whole country in troops. **1917** Morgan *Recoll.* 239 The inhabitants were in mortal terror of the lawless crew known as 'Sherman's bummers,' who rode on the flanks of his army, accounts of whose fiendish outrages were on every tongue.

(5) **1947** Lumpkin *Southerner* 72 He had traced his weary way along the route of mutilated railroads: . . . looked on rails turned and twisted in grotesque shapes around trees—'Sherman's hairpins' they were called—which had been melted on the fires of burning ties to make them pliable and useless. — (6) **1917** Morgan *Recoll.* 244 The solemn-looking chimneys standing guard over the former sites of once happy homes were called by the natives 'Sherman's monuments.'

***sherry,** *n.* **1. sherry cobbler,** a cobbler in which sherry wine is used. **2. sherry cordwainer,** =prec. *Humorous. Rare.*

(1) **1839** Barnes *Memoir T. Weed* (1884) 73 (We.), Thirst not for sherry cobblers. **1855** Beste *Wabash* I. 85, I chose the far-famed sherry cobler. **1910** Douglas ed. Parkman *Oregon Trail* 361 *Sherry cobblers, brandy toddy,* beverages composed of spirits and water, sweetened. — (2) **1840** *N.O. Picayune* 11 Aug. 2/4 You are now revelling in anticipation of the dozen dozens that you are yet to drink —rum juleps, . . . and toddies, and slings, and cock-tails and sherry cordwainers.

sherryvallies ˈʃɛrɪˌvælɪz, *n. pl.* [f. Polish *szarawary,* introduced by Gen. Charles Lee (1731–82), who for a time was aide-de-camp to the king of Poland. See quots. 1778, *a*1857.] (See quots.) *Obs.*

1778 C. Lee *Memoirs* (1792) 430 If you find them to be green breeches patched with leather, and not actually legitimate sherry vallies, such as his Majesty of Poland wears, . . . I will submit. **1835** Hoffman *Winter in West* I. 91 That short man yonder . . . is just raising his blue cotton frock to thrust his hand into the fob of his sherrivalleys. **1848** Bartlett 296 *Sherryvallies,* . . . pantaloons made of thick velvet or leather buttoned on the outside of each leg, and generally worn over other pantaloons. They are now chiefly worn by teamsters . . . . When journeys were made on horseback, sherryvallies were indispensable to the traveller. *a***1857** *Lower Norfolk Co. Va. Antiquary* I. 99, I remember some writer . . . made particular mention of his [Gen. Charles Lee's] trousers or overhauls, as she called them. But he came out with an answer and begged to set her right, assuring her they were neither trousers nor overalls, but Sherryvallies, such as were worn in his Majesty the King of Prussia's service.

***shield,** *n.* **1.** A policeman's badge. **2. shield of liberty,** a patriotic emblem of the U.S. Both *rare.*

(1) **1903** *N.Y. Ev. Post* 29 Oct. 3 The ex-policeman . . . turned in his shield in September. **1904** O. Henry *Trimmed Lamp* 84 They'll take away my shield and break me. — (2) **1864** *Wkly. New Mexican* 27 May 1/4 On the other side [of the two-cent piece] there is the shield of liberty, bearing the words, 'God our Trust.'

As the last term in **arrow, Indian, water, windshield.**

shift boss. A boss in charge of a shift of miners.

1876 Raymond *8th Rep. Mines* 166 Rates of wages: . . . Foremen, per day, $8.00. Shift-bosses, per day, $6.00. **1896** Shinn *Story of Mine* 226 Each level of the mine has therefore three shift bosses. **1943** *Copper Camp* 65 With guns they forced a shift boss to lead them to the powder magazine.

***shifting,** *n.* and *a.* **1. shifting engine,** a switch engine. **2. shifting-top buggy,** a buggy with a top that folds back. Both *obs.*

(1) **1878** Pinkerton *Strikers* 219 D. M. Watt . . . ordered an employee to descend from a shifting engine and change the switch. **1887**

Shifting-top buggy

Courier-Journal 4 May 4/5 Two men . . . were struck by a shifting engine last night and instantly killed. — (2) **1856** *Mich. Agric. Soc. Trans.* VII. 61 John Patton . . . [exhibited] shifting top buggy. **1865** *Wkly. New Mexican* 17 Feb. 2/3 For Sale. A Shifting Top Buggy.

***shilling,** *n.* **1. shilling pavement,** the sidewalk or pavement on the shilling side of Broadway in New York City. **2. shilling side,** the west side of Broadway in New York City, esp. about Vesey Street, where a cheaper trade was conducted than on the other side of the street. Both *obs.*

(1) **1849** G. G. Foster *N.Y. in Slices* 4 Nothing could more effectually stamp you as vulgar than to be seen stumbling over the crockery-crates and second-hand furniture of the shilling pavement. — (2) **1850** *Knickerb.* XXXV. 91 An animal of the 'porcine genus' . . . was reposing on the shilling-side of the great thoroughfare. **1870** M. H. Smith *20 Years Wall St.* 197 On the dollar side or on the shilling side of the street he intended to create a business. **1922** Wanamaker in Appel *Biog. Wanamaker* (1930) 132 He found himself on the wrong side of Broadway, the shilling side, next to the old Astor House.

As the last term in **Baltimore, bay, Boston, Mexican, New England, New York, Yankee, York shilling.**

*__shimming,__ *n.* The action of filling up a space with a shim. — **1872** HUNTINGTON *Road-Master's Ass't* 78 When ballast is frozen so that track can not be surfaced by tamping, it is done by *shimming.* **1880** FORNEY *Car-Builder's Dict.* (*Cent.*), Shimming has been used in fitting on car-wheels when the wheel-seat of the axle was a little too small.

* **shimmy,** *n.* A formerly popular jazz dance somewhat like the fox-trot accompanied by simulated shivering. Also *to shake a shimmy. Slang.*

1919 *N.Y. Sun* 16 Jan., I was dancing the shimi shiver. **1924** P. MARKS *Plastic Age* 275 That music was enough to make a saint shed his halo and shake a shimmy. **1947** PAUL *Linden* 347 Big Julie was singing 'The Old-Time Religion' with a voluptuous shimmy as part of the accompaniment.

attrib. **1948** *Time* 23 Feb. 21/2 Gilda Gray, famous oldtime shimmy dancer and *Ziegfeld Follies* star, was seriously ill at Sedalia, Colo. **1949** *Chi. Tribune* 15 Sep. 7/4 The former shimmy queen said she was married at 11, a mother at 12.

shimmy 'ʃɪmɪ, *v. intr.* To dance the shimmy. Also **shimmying,** *n.* and *a.*, and transf.

1919 *Lit. Digest* 26 April 47/1 'Jazz' . . . has aggravated the feet and fingers of America into a shimmying, tickle-toeing, snapping delirium. **1920** *Chi. Herald & Examiner* 2 Jan. 14/3 When you shimmy you must pay the fiddler. **1928** GALSWORTHY *Swan Song* II. xiii. 217 He . . . watched the dancing on deck—funny business nowadays, shimmying, bunnyhugging, didn't they call it? **1947** *Sat. Ev. Post* 15 March 162/4 My Adam's apple began to shimmy up and down.

*__shin,__ *n.* As the last term in **sharp, sore shin.**

* **shin,** *v.*

1. *intr.* To walk, move around, bestir oneself. *Slang.*

1837 NEAL *Charcoal Sk.* (1838) 106 Shin it, good man . . . ; shin it as well as you know how! **1879** *Harper's Mag.* Aug. 386 'Tain't much of a kerridge . . . , but I cal'late it's a little better'n shinnin' it. **1904** *N.Y. Sun* 31 Aug. 2 He might find it difficult to shin around the corners of political dilemmas.

2. To borrow or try to borrow money, usu. with *around. Slang.* Cf. **shinning,** *n.*, and **shinny,** *v.* **1.**

1834 A. GREENE *Perils Pearl St.* 125 Shinners may be divided into two classes: those who shin from necessity, and those who shin from profit. **1845** *N.Y. Comm. Adv.* 13 Dec. (B), The Senator was shinning around, to get gold for the rascally bank-rags, which he was obliged to take. **1890** *Cong. Rec.* 18 Sep. 10188/2 They find a difficulty in shinning around to borrow money.

shindig 'ʃɪnˌdɪg, *n.* [Origin obscure. Poss. f. *shin*+ *dig*, a blow on the shin, as suggested in 1st. quot.] **1.** (See quot.) *Obs.* **2.** A more or less noisy party or carouse, a dance, a shindy. Both *slang.*

(1) **1859** BARTLETT 400 *Shin-Dig*, a blow on the shins. Southern. — (2) **1873** HARTE *Mrs. Skagg's Husbands* 139 'Is this a dashed Puritan meeting?' . . . 'It's no Pike County shindig.' **1911** HARRISON *Queed* 229 He found a group of men . . eagerly discussing the shindig. **1949** *L.A. Dly. News* 9 Nov. 19/2 Four of the Southland's top square dance callers will be on hand for the shindig.

* **shine,** *n.*

1. A caper, trick, or prank. *Colloq.*

1835–7 HALIBURTON *Clockmaker* 1 Ser. xvii. 143, I met . . . a real conceited lookin critter as you een amost ever seed, all shines and didos. *a*1861 WINTHROP *J. Brent* 31, I don't feel so sharp set on lettin' you hev that black after that shine. **1869** *Oldtown Folks* 235 She needn't think she's goin' to come round me with any o' her shines.

2. (See quot.) *Obs.*

1851 HALL *College Words* 278 *Shine.* At Harvard College this word was formerly used to designate a good recitation.

3. A polish given a pair of shoes, a job at shining shoes. Also attrib.

1869 *Terr. Enterprise* (Virginia, Nev.) 5 Oct. 3/1 A boy in the 'shine' line, who came through on the railroad from the States a couple of months since, . . . is now in an impecunious state in the way of raiment. **1871** *Galveston News* 4 May (De Vere), As I left the cars, an imp with smutty face, Said: Shine? **1894** *Advance* 27 Dec. 458/1 A little boot-black . . . shivered in the March wind and waited for shines. **1948** *Pauls Valley* (Okla.) *D. Democrat* 4 July 14/4 If customers have to spend a dollar for a haircut, they'll probably just skip the shoe treatment, shine boys fear.

4. A Negro. *Slang.*

1934 WEBSTER. **1946** THOMPSON *Amer. Daughter* 69 Honest to Gawd, that shine done christened the mule after some of them sweepstake nags.

5. In colloq. and slang phrases: (1) *To cut a shine,* to cut a caper or dido; (2) *to take the shine off,* to surpass (somebody), to lower (a person or thing) in the eyes of others; (3) *to take a shine to,* to take a fancy or liking to; (4) *to come a shine over,* to impose upon; (5) *to make a shine with,* to make a good impression upon.

(1) **1819** A. PIERCE *Rebelliad* 72 Peele Dabney gaz'd, Sikes cut a shine. **1856** SIMMS *Eutaw* 387 (Th.), Look you, old woman, don't be cutting any shines now. — (2) **1834** C. A. DAVIS *Lett. J. Downing* 23 The review of Captain Finny's company did take the shine off them are Boston and Salem sogers. **1948** *Chi. Tribune* 31 Oct. 18/3 There are indications of a demand thruout the country for books that reveal the shoddy side of the Roosevelt administration and take the shine off the New Deal. — (3) **1840** *Crockett Almanac* 14, I wonst had an old flame I took sumthin of a shine to. **1946** HODGINS *Mr. Blandings Builds Dream House* 11, I think you could get it for less, . . . if he really took a shine to his prospective buyers. — (4) **1847** ROBB *Squatter Life* 151 They couldn't come any of them thar shines over him.

(5) **1847** ROBB *Squatter Life* 137 To make a shine with Sally, I sent over word that I would . . . bring with me my fust *pledge of affection,* meanin' the parasol.

As the last term in **monkey, moon, sunshine.**

* **shine,** *v.*

1. *tr.* In night hunting, to cause (the eyes of the quarry) to shine by the use of a light. Cf. **fire-hunting 2.**

1833 FLINT *D. Boone* 25 He had *shined the eyes* of a deer. **1885** *South Fla. Sentinel* (Orlando) 10 June 2/2 They took the small boat and pulled to the nearest key to shine deer. **1945** MATHEWS *Talking* 119, I attempt to 'shine' a pair of eyes on the ground or in the trees.

fig. **1843** HAWKS *D. Boone* 23 Rebecca Bryan completely *shined his eyes*; and after a time, . . . [they] were married.

2. *intr.* To succeed. *Slang.*

1839 *N.O. Picayune* 9 April 2/4 At a Methodist Camp Meeting he would certainly shine, for he could fill any ten-acre lot in existence as easily as little Brown does the Camp street theatre. **1859** BARTLETT 401 *To Shine,* . . . to get along, succeed. Western.

3. *tr.* To polish (shoes).

1866 F. KIRKLAND *Bk. Anecdotes* 375 Black yer boots, Sir? Shine them up! **1879** *Caddo* (Indian Terr.) *Free Press* 4 April 3/4 'Sartin, boss, shine 'em up in less'n no time,' said he.

transf. **1885** BAYLOR *On Both Sides* 417 A ragged gamin . . . offered to 'shine' me for a 'dime.' **1888** *Cent. Mag.* July 462/2, I shined a young feller this mornin'.

b. *absol.* To engage in shining shoes.

1872 *Harper's Mag.* March 637/1 Charles Lewis . . . still lives and 'shines' on the shores of the majestic Susquehanna. **1887** *Ib.* June 161/1 While he was 'shining' I asked his price, which he said was ten cents.

4. In colloq. or slang phrases: (1) *To shine around* (one), to make an effort to win the friendship or affection of (someone); (2) *to shine up to,* to play the lover toward.

(1) **1841** *Jamestown* (N.Y.) *Jrnl.* 10 June 4/1, I had a great mind tu go off and shine round some other gal, jest for spite. **1901** WILKINS *Portion of Labor* 454 You needn't come shinin' round Ellen and me. — (2) **1882** *Cent. Mag.* Oct. 827 It was then that David first set out to shine up to her. **1948** GARDNER *Lonely Heiress* 190 It might be a good plan to shine up to Marilyn Marlow.

* **shiner,** *n.* Any one of various small, silvery cyprinoid fishes found in American fresh waters, as the redfin, *Luxilus cornutus,* the chub, *Notemigonus crysoleucas,* the dollarfish, menhaden, etc.; also with a specifying term.

1792 *Mass. H.S. Coll.* 1 Ser. I. 113 [The lake] is supplied with pickerel, large perch, eels, shiners. **1814** MITCHILL *Fishes N.Y.* 364 Cryptous broad shiner. *Stromateus cryptosus.* . . . A curious and beautiful fish. **1864** *Maine Agric. Soc. Returns 1863* 101 Where he takes shiners in quantity he may fail to secure a solitary trout. **1884** GOODE *Fisheries* I. 322 'Blunt-nosed Shiner,' . . . sometimes varied to 'Pug-nosed Shiner,' is in common use in the New York market and in Narragansett Bay. *Ib.* 616 The Golden Shiner—*Notemigonus chrysoleucus* . . . is a sluggish fish, frequenting ponds, bayous, and cut-offs. **1942** CANNON *Mountain* 205 He must be after shiners; there ain't any frogs there.

As the last term in **moon, New York, red-sided, shad shiner.**

* **shingle,** *n.*

1. A small board, brass plate, etc., bearing a name and used as a sign, as of a doctor's or lawyer's office; often *to hoist, hang out,* etc., *one's shingle,* to give public notice of one's profession or occupation.

1842 *Spirit of Times* (Phila.) 18 May (Th.), One William Dermott hoisted his shingle yesterday. **1852** WEED *Lett. from Europe* 508 We only find plain Hiram Powers, whose 'shingle,' as we express it, hangs out to indicate his Studio. **1880** INGHAM *Digging Gold* 321 We saw a shingle out, 'Rooms to Let.' **1949** *Newsweek* 22 Aug. 58/3 Jobless, Metcalf put out his shingle as a food consultant.

2. In combs.: (1) **shingle bee,** a "bee" at which shingles are made, *obs.;* (2) **bundle,** a bundle of shingles, cf. ∗**bundle,** *n.* **2;** (3) **cake,** (see quot. 1915), *obs.;* (4) **-caped overcoat,** an overcoat with two or more overlapping capes, *obs.;* (5) **horse,** =**frowhorse;** (6) **mill,** a mill where shingles are made; (7) **oak,** an American oak, *Quercus imbricaria,* suitable for shingles; (8) **rack,** (see quot.); (9) **sunbonnet,** a sunbonnet so made that pieces of a stiff material, usu. cardboard, can be inserted in the sides to stiffen them, cf. **slat sunbonnet;** (10) **titles,** land titles that overlap each other, *obs.,* cf. **shingle,** *v.* **1;** (11) **weaver,** (see quots.), *obs.;* (12) **whittling,** whittling on a shingle as a meditative pastime, *colloq.;* (13) **willow oak,** =**shingle oak;** (14) **yard,** (see quot.).

(1) **1868** MRS. M. J. CARRINGTON *Absaraka* 141 Shingles were rived from Bolts sawed by the men, and many a 'shingle bee' was held, at night, to expedite work and convince the skeptical that shingles, or anything else, could be made or *done,* when it *had* to be. — (2) **1880** MARK TWAIN *Tramp Abroad* 156 (R.), The roaring of the wind through the shingle-bundles. — (3) **1872** *Harper's Mag.* June 97/1 She had eaten nothing since morning save a reminiscence of her youth in shape of a molasses 'shingle-cake,' purchased of an old '*mauma*' on the wharf at Georgetown. [**1915** *D.N.* IV. 240 *shingles, n. pl.* [In a list of colonial cookery terms.] Cookies like Tories, cut in oblong pieces of the shape of shingles.] — (4) **1889** *Harper's Mag.* Aug. 386/1 [In] a shingle-caped overcoat . . . he sat gravely and sturdily down amid his peers.

(5) **1925** *Old-Time N. Eng.* April 175 And we here show the homemade Shingle Horse . . . seated by which, with the oaken block leaned into its fork, Enos Lewis split shingles, near Haggersville, Bucks County, in 1890. — (6) **1858** SIMMONDS *Dict. Trade, Shingle-mill* a saw-mill for cutting planks or logs into shingles. **1879** *Mich. Gen. Statutes* I. (1882) 552 Any person being in the possession or having the control of any saw-mill, shingle-mill [etc.]. — (7) **1841** PURSH *Flora* II. 627 The Shingle Oak rises to about forty or fifty feet. **1860** CURTIS *Woody Plants N.C.* 36 Shingle Oak. . . . In Illinois, it has been used for shingles, probably for want of a better material. **1945** DARLINGTON *Higher Plants Mich.* 25 Some of these are not at all common, such as blue ash . . . , shingle oak . . . and black-jack oak. — (8) **1895** *Stand.* 1653/2 *Shingle-rack,* a wagon or sleigh made for hauling shingles. — (9) **1856** S. ROBINSON *Kansas* 306 A woman dressed in bright-red calico, . . . and shingle sun-bonnet, sat there sewing on a muslin of gay colors.

(10) **1833** FLINT *D. Boone* 244 Almost every tract was covered with different and conflicting titles—forming what have been aptly called 'shingle titles.' **1853** HAWKS *D. Boone* 129 Almost all the titles conferred in this way became known as 'the lapping, or shingle titles.' — (11) **1859** BARTLETT 401 Shingle-Weaver. A workman who dresses shingles. **1888** J. Q. BITTINGER *Hist. Haverhill* (N.H.) 412 On one occasion the story-teller, whilst making a visit to the camp of the 'shingle-weavers,' as they were familiarly called, . . . entertained them. — (12) **1851** HALL *Manhattaner* 50 He would . . . betake himself to shingle-whittling, or any other Yankee recreation which is as soothing to troubled nerves. — (13) **1817** S. BROWN *Western Gazetteer* 24 [There are] three [species] of willow oak, upland, swamp, and *shingle,* so called from its being an excellent material for shingles. — (14) **1895** *Stand.* 1653/2 *Shingle-yard,* a place where shingles of all kinds are stored for sale.

b. Designating buildings or parts of buildings covered with shingles, as **shingle church steeple, cottage, roof, sugarhouse.**

1810 IRVING in P. M. Irving *Life W. Irving* I. 245 [Helping young artists] would, I am satisfied, be more pleasing in the sight of Heaven . . . than building a dozen shingle church steeples. — **1839** BRIGGS *H. Franco* II. 206 The house was a little shingle cottage with a projecting roof. — [**1749** HEMPSTEAD *Diary* 528 Mostly Wooden houses covered with Long Ceder Shingle Roof & Sides.] **1831** *N.H. Hist. Soc. Coll.* V. 52 The shingle roof had been chiefly removed for a covering of zinc. **1904** *N.Y. Ev. Post* 2 April 5 The shingle roof of his house leaked. — **1869** *Rep. Comm. Agric. 1868* 56 Board and shingle sugar-houses.

Also **shingle-roofed,** *a.*

1792 POPE *Tour S. & W.* 28 At 10 o'Clock espied a Shingle roofed House, occupied by a Family of New-Yorkers. **1847** HOWE *Hist. Coll. Ohio* 273 A hewed log and shingle-roofed building . . . was the first tavern. **1874** COLLINS *Kentucky* I. 23 They burn several towns, one with 120 houses (of which 80 were shingle-roofed).

c. Designating machines employed in making or finishing shingles. Cf. **shingle mill.**

1802 *Mass. Spy* 17 Nov. (Th.), Dr. French of Conn. has invented a Shingle Dressing Machine. **1847** *Rep. Comm. Patents 1846* 90 One patent has been granted this year for an improved shingle-cutting machine. **1850** *Ib. 1849* 431 Some half dozen shingle machines have been patented within the year. **1858** SIMMONDS *Dict. Trade, Shingle-machine,* an American machine for riving, shaving, and joining shingles, which is capable of making 30,000 per day. **1876** KNIGHT 2151/2 *Shingle-planing Machine,* a machine in which roughly rived or sawn shingles are faced by planing in the direction of the grain of the wood.

As the last term in **bundle, cedar, cypress, joint, pine, tin shingle(s).**

∗**shingle,** *v.*

1. *tr.* To file overlapping claims on (a piece of land), to put several liens on (a property). Cf. **shingle titles, shingling system.**

1832 CLAY *Speeches* (1842) 221 The same tract was not unfrequently entered various times by different purchasers, so as to be literally shingled over with conflicting claims. **1869** *Cong. Globe* 7 Jan. 239/1 Where else are great cities built upon a soil shingled with mortgages drawing enormous rates of interest? **1886** Z. F. SMITH *Kentucky* 187 Thus were the means and the inducements furnished to *shingle* over one claim with another. **1892** *Ky. Centenary Celebr. by Filson Club* 137 There were few 'locations' that were not 'shingled' by opposing claims.

2. To cut (hair) as a barber, usu. to cut (the hair) very short. Also absol. and **shingled,** *a.*

1857 HOLLAND *Bay-Path* 232, I don't s'pose . . . there's anybody in the settlement can shingle like me. **1883** HOWE *Country Town* (1926) 25 He shingled hair in a superb manner. **1907** *St. Nicholas* June 712/1 [With] Rob's merry tousel of the shingled head, . . . Fritzi felt her keenest grief and shame appeased.

3. To cover like a shingled roof. *Rare.*

1858 HOLMES *Autocrat* 33 [A] middle-aged female, with a parchment forehead and a dry little 'frisette' shingling it.

4. (See quot.) *Obs.*

1859 BARTLETT 401 *To Shingle,* to chastise. A shingle applied *a posteriori* is a favorite New England mode of correcting a child.

∗**shingling,** *a.* and *n.* **1. shingling saw,** a saw used in a shingle mill. **2. shingling system,** (see quot. and cf. **shingle titles, shingle,** *v.* **1.**). *Obs.* — (1) **1860** *Harper's Mag.* Aug. 422/2 A Good Miller Wanted. . . . He must . . . be a man who can file a Shingling Saw and keep it in good order . . . and run the machine. — (2) **1816** D. THOMAS *Travels Western Country* (1819) 269 This controversy with that of Wyoming, and the *shingling system* in other parts of the State [Penna.], has made titles to land so very uncertain, that no inconsiderable part of this State is still wilderness, while New York and Ohio are well peopled in less favorable situations.

shingly ˈʃɪŋglɪ, *a.* Shaped like a shingle, covered with shingles.

1856 GOODRICH *G. Go-ahead* 195 Mr. Fuz was a man of middle height, but of great breadth, his body being rather flat and shingly. **1857** WHITTIER *Poetical Works* (1894) 152/1 The painted shingly town-house, where The freeman's vote for Freedom falls. **1863** G. HAMILTON *Gala-Days* 107 The rustic stone city . . . looks so attractive, so different from our hasty, brittle, shingly American, half-minute houses.

∗**Shining Mountains.** (See quots.)

1847 COYNER *Lost Trappers* 158 They [Rocky Mountains] were called by some of the first discoverers, the Shining Mountains, from the fact that the higher parts are covered with perpetual snows, which give them a luminous and brilliant appearance. **1918** REES *Idaho* 105 Because the many ridges gleamed brightly when the sun shone upon them he called the range the 'Shining Mountains.' **1947** DEVOTO *Across Wide Missouri* 2 Sometimes they were called the Shining Mountains.

shinleaf ˈʃɪnˌlif, *n.* "A plant of the genus *Pyrola,* properly *P. elliptica,* said to be so named from the use of its leaves for shinplasters" (*Cent.*).

1817–8 EATON *Botany* (1822) 416. **1821** *Mass. H.S. Coll.* 2 Ser. IX. 154 Plants, which are indigenous in the township of Middlebury, [Vt., include] . . . *Pyrola rotundifolia,* Shin leaf. *Pyrola secunda,* One-sided shin leaf. **1903** AUSTIN *Land of Little Rain* 193 Pines raise statelier shafts and give themselves room to grow gentians, shinleaf, and little grass of Parnassus in their golden checkered shadows. **1948** *Green Bay* (Wis.) *Press-Gazette* 13 July 11/4 Huge clumps of ostrich ferns and the shin leaf could be found.

∗**shinner,** *n.* **1.** (See quot. 1844.) **2.** One who begs for money. **3.** One who moves about quickly. All *colloq.* or *slang* and *obs.*

(1) **1831** *Boston Transcript* 21 July 2/1 They complain that the City Councils permit *hucksters* and *shinners* to evade the laws made for their protection. **1844** *Spirit of Times* (Phila.) 11 Feb. (Th.), Certain

cunning men, . . . not farmers . . . , have purchased shabby looking carts, backed them up among the wagons, and every market day made them regular stands for the sale of beef, mutton, veal, &c. These men are called 'shinners.' — (2) **1834** A. GREENE *Perils Pearl St.* 125 Shinners may be divided into two classes: those who shin from necessity, and those who shin from profit. *a***1859** *N.Y. Ev. Post* (B.), No 'short shinner' feared rebuff, Who sued for pelf. — (3) **1837** NEAL *Charcoal Sk.* (1838) 107 Berry . . . [was not] well calculated for a 'shinner' of the first class.

shinnery 'ʃɪnərɪ, *n. W.* [Variant of cheniere *q.v.*] (See quots.) Also attrib. Cf. **oak shinnery.**

1901 *Rev. of Reviews* XXIV. 310/1 It ['creeps'] is due mainly to an insufficiency of nourishment in the grass, particularly in pastures where 'shinnery' or dwarf oak trees abound. **1913** W. C. BARNES *Western Grazing Grounds* 268 Scrub Oak (Quercus gambelii Q. undulata). Known also as 'shin oak.' This is the scrub oak of the western ranges, especially in the Southwest, where it forms as on the Texas staked plain great areas called 'shinneries.' **1946** *Okla. Game & Fish News* March 4/1 They located crow roosts in the shinnery motts west of Elk City.

* **shinning,** *n.* Borrowing or trying to borrow money. *Colloq. Obs.*

1839 *Jamestown* (N.Y.) *Jrnl.* 20 Nov. 1/5 A shinning . . . is borrowing money to take up his own notes with. **1843** STEPHENS *High Life N.Y.* I. 5 Mr. Beebe's out a shinning now. **1853** *LaCrosse Democrat* 6 Dec. 2/6 Shinning [is] on the decline. . . . Stocks are rising. **1871** DE VERE 306 This process of *shinning* is resorted to whenever the merchant or banker is *short.*

shinny 'ʃɪnɪ, *v.*[1] **1.** *intr.* = * **shin,** *v.* **2.** *Obs.* **2.** To climb, esp. by using the arms and shins, usu. with *up.* Also **shinnying,** *n.*

(1) **1851** *De Bow's Review* X. 585 He has never been known to be hard pressed, or obliged to 'shinny,' (as it is sometimes inelegantly called). — (2) **1888** DALY *Lottery of Love* 18 The way you shinnied up the side of the ship . . . converted me on the spot to the Blooming costume. **1906** *Washington Post* 22 May 2 As its girth precluded 'shinnying.' Gladden procured a ladder. **1948** *Chi D. News* 1 March 8/3 He plans to go right on shinnyin' up telephone poles indefinitely. **1950** *Ib.* 11 March 6/1 If the reporters didn't like it, they could go shinny up a tree.

shinny 'ʃɪnɪ, *v.*[2] [f. * *shinny,* the boys' game. Cf. *EDD shin your side,* a call to one who has trespassed too far into the lines of his opponents.] *To shinny on one's own side,* to keep in one's place, attend to one's own affairs. Also *shinny-up-your-own-alley,* app. a form of shinny.

1866 C. H. SMITH *Bill Arp* 144 Let 'em shinny on their own side, and git over among the folks who don't want us reconstructed. **1880** *Mining News* (Ruby Hill, Nev.) 24 April 1/2 He was all-fired sharp—used to wax me at 'shinny-up-your-own-alley' every time. **1890** BIFF HALL *Turnover Club* 145 Make your complaint over there—we have all we can do to shinny on our own side.

shin oak. [Origin obscure. App. f. * *shin* + * *oak* (cf. **shin wood**), but see also **chinquapin oak, cheniere, shinnery,** and note quot. 1913 below.] (See quots. 1844 and 1913.)

1844 GREGG *Commerce of Prairies* II. 200 Black-jacks . . . [are] intermixed with a very diminutive dwarf oak, called by the hunters 'shin-oak.' **1889** *Harper's Mag.* Dec. 121/2 The dwarf shinn-oaks . . . were overlaid here and there with a fine filmy network of love-vine. **1913** WOOTON *Trees & Shrubs N. Mex.* 57 The Shin-Oak or Shinry (*Quercus havardii*) is a low deciduous-leaved shrub, rarely over 3 feet high.

shinplaster 'ʃɪn,plæstə, *n.* A contemptuous term for privately issued paper certificates or script poorly secured and hence of little value; a government note of small denomination. Also attrib. Cf. **fractional currency.**

This term has been applied especially to (*a*) Revolutionary script, (*b*) forms of currency issued after the depression of 1837, and (*c*) the paper money in small denominations issued by the federal government at the beginning of the Civil War.

(*a*) **1824** *Microscope* (Albany, N.Y.) 15 May (Th.), We advise our friends to exchange their 'shin plasters' for 'solid charms' as soon as may be. [**1830** NEILSON *Recollections* 140 In some States, notes for such small sums as 6¼ and 12½ cents . . . are issued, and during the war with Britain bank notes for one cent . . . were quite current. Half, and quarter dollar notes are common every where.] — (*b*) **1838** *N.Y. Advertiser & Exp.* 3 Feb. 1/2 The manner in which the bank and shin-plaster whigs bamboozle poor General Harrison . . . is very affecting. **1839** MARRYAT *Diary* I. 54 Dealers, in general, give out their own bank-notes, or as they are called here, shin plasters, which are good for one dollar, and from that down to two and a-half cents. **1853** BALDWIN *Flush Times Ala.* 1 That halcyon period, ranging from the year of Grace, 1835, to 1837; that golden era, when shin-plasters were the sole currency. **1948** DICK *Dixie Frontier* 124 After the panic of 1837 various citizens, and particularly business houses, issued small bills to be used in change. These, commonly called 'shin plasters,' served for a time, but at best were only as good as the issuing agent. — (*c*) **1866** GOSS *Soldier's Story* 36 Though not acknowledging any superiority, at that time, of the value of greenbacks over their shinplaster currency, they much preferred the former, in payment, to their own. **1869** J. BILLINGS in *Ore. State Jrnl.* 2 Jan. 1/3, I gave one ov them a 50 cent shinplaster. **1874** *Chi. Times* 11 June 4/2 Willful Wallowing in the Slough of Shinplaster Inflation.

b. (See quots.)

1840 *Louisville Pub. Adv.* 4 July 2/2 The State Bonds, *alias* Shinplasters, paid out to contractors on the public works, were passing at par, in Louisville. **1949** *Southwestern Hist. Quart.* Jan. 295 There were in use as money not only the notes of state banks but also 'shinplasters,' a name popularly given to notes issued in Texas by private firms and municipal corporations in denominations usually of less than one dollar.

As the last term in **California, Confederate, Tennessee, treasury, wildcat shinplaster.**

shin wood. The American yew or ground hemlock, *Taxus canadensis.*

1778 CARVER *Travels* 505 Shin Wood . . . proves very troublesome to the hasty traveller, by striking against his shins. **1813** MUHLENBERG *Cat. Plants* 93. **1836** EDWARDS *Hist. Texas* 66 The names of the trees . . . [and] shrubs . . . [include] the Prickly Ash, the Shin-wood [etc.].

* **ship,** *n.* In combs.: (1) **ship canal,** a canal through which ships may be taken; (2) **channel,** a channel used by ships; (3) **house,** a large shedlike structure over a slip or dock where ships were built, *obs.;* (4) **railroad,** = next; (5) **railway,** a projected railway for conveying ships across land (see quots.), *obs.;* (6) **-'s cousin,** a term of contempt, poss. inspired by * *ship's husband,* for an agent who attends to the business of a ship in port, *obs.;* (7) **-'s lawyer,** a poor lawyer, a sea lawyer, *obs.;* (8) **stuff,** (*a*) a coarse or low-grade wheat flour, (*b*) material for use in making or repairing a ship.

(1) **1798** I. ALLEN *Hist. Vermont* 268 A ship canal would be the means of importing salt. **1837** *Knickerb.* IX. 294 Who, ten years since, would have thought of a *ship canal* from the lakes to the ocean! **1914** STEELE *Storm* 57 We approached the mouth of the ship-canal. **1928** *Chi. Tribune* 5 Aug. 25/2 He formulated plans to cut three ship canals forty feet deep and two hundred feet wide. — (2) **1775** in SPARKS *Corr. Revol.* I. 73 The ship-channel . . . runs between the east head of Long Island and the south point of Deer Island. **1875** MARK TWAIN *Old Times* iv. 61 Ship channels are buoyed and lighted. — (3) **1825** N. ADAMS *Ann. Portsmouth* 388 Two ship houses are sufficiently extensive to cover the largest ships employed in the Navy. **1880** MARK TWAIN *Tramp Abroad* 274 Sometimes one of these monster precipices had the slight inclination of the huge ship-houses in dockyards. — (4) **1880** *Bradstreet's* 15 May 8/2 James B. Eads, of Mississippi jetties fame, has laid before the House Committee . . . the Eads scheme of a ship railroad.

(5) **1881** *Chi. Times* 12 March 14/2 Captain Eads . . . will spend a month in making an inspection of his ship-railway route [across the Isthmus of Tehuantepec]. **1888** *Harper's Mag.* Feb. 379/2 A ship-railway has also been surveyed across the Florida peninsula to save the 600 miles of distance around and through the straits. — (6) **1823** COOPER *Pioneers* (1832) xxxiv. 378 'You're a ship's cousin, I tell ye, Master Doo-but-little,' roared the steward; 'some such matter as a ship's cousin, sir.' **1840** DANA *Before Mast* viii, However useful and active you may be, you are but a mongrel,—a sort of afterguard and 'ship's cousin.' — (7) **1894** *Cong. Rec.* 31 May 5547/2 [Judge Turner] decided that I might pass as 'ship's lawyer' to practice in this court. — (8) (*a*) **1771** WASHINGTON *Diaries* II. 23 Sold all the Flour I have left: . . . ship stuff at 8/4 pr. Cwt. **1833** BOARDMAN *America* 16 The following inscriptions, which I copied from the sign-board of a feed store. . . . Coarse and fine homony, Buckwheat, Cracked corn, Oats, ship stuff. (*b*) **1884** SARGENT *Rep. Forests* 511 A few small mills saw oak from the immediate neighborhood into ship-stuff and car lumber.

b. *Not to give up the ship,* not to despair or desist from an undertaking—in allusion to the famous dying words of Captain James Lawrence, "Don't give up the ship," at the taking of the *Chesapeake,* June 1, 1813.

1816 JEFFERSON *Writings* (1899) X. 4 My exhortation would rather be 'not to give up the ship.' **1892** MARK TWAIN *Amer. Claimant* 161 (R.), We'll not give up the ship yet.

As the last term in **battle, cabin, clipper, Kentucky, missionary, packet, practice, prairie, school, steam, tobacco, trader, wind ship.** Also **alcaldeship, bullyship, chargéship, township.**

***ship,** *v.*

1. *tr.* To transport or dispatch (goods, etc.) by rail or other land transportation. Also absol.

1857 *Harper's Mag.* Sep. 459/2 A few of the more enterprising operators . . . thought nothing of shipping two or three thousand tons per annum. **1859** *Ib.* 425/2 Sug . . . knows that it is to his interest to ship by our line. **1916** WILSON *Somewhere* 133 You can't expect us to be shipping steers every month. **1930** BAILEY *Cyclo. Horticulture* 2498/1 To ship at least a carload of fruit constantly, one needs to have about 1,000 to 1,200 trees of each variety in full bearing.

2. *intr.* Of perishable goods: To stand shipment.

1867 *Ill. Agric. Soc. Trans.* VII. 510 It ships well, and is a very good peach.

***shipment,** *n.* The act of shipping goods by land; a consignment of goods so shipped.

1798 I. ALLEN *Hist. Vermont* 268 Spring and fall shipments are seasonably made to New York. **1840** *Niles' Reg.* 4 July 278/1 The shipments [of coal] for the week . . . were 11,898 tons. **1925** FOSTER *Trop. Tramp Tourists* 144 The big mining camps at the top of the hill were calling for a large shipment of lumber. **1950** *Chi. Tribune* 21 March 4/6 The tip on which horsemeat mislabeled tenderloins of beef was seized came from Texas, where shipments of 3,600 pounds, 1,911 pounds and 8,000 pounds had been seized since March 9.

Shippen's Russet(ing). (See quot. 1817.) *Obs.* — **1817** W. COXE *Fruit Trees* 124 Shippens Russeting . . . is a large flat apple, of an irregular form. **1833** *Genesee Farmer* 15 June 190/1 Roxbury Russet. Shippen's Russet.

***shipper,** *n.*

1. One who ships goods by land.

1840 *Niles' Reg.* 4 April 80/2 Principal transportation lines have resolved to give the shipper or owner the full advantage of the reduction of twenty cents per barrel [of flour]. **1923** BLAISDELL *F. T. Comm.* 268 In the case at issue the steel companies were held to be only shippers —customers of the railroads. **1950** *Chi. Tribune* 21 March 4/6 Dr. O. W. Seher, head of federal meat inspection in Chicago, said his department . . . would ask indictment of two of the shippers.

2. A commodity that is shipped or suitable for shipping.

1881 *Tenth Census* III. III. 19 English s' ippers consist of leaf and strips. **1887** *Courier-Journal* 19 Jan. 8/1 For the best quality Clarksville or Harkinsville district shipper, $50 [was] awarded to Mr. Hana.

***shipping,** *n.*

1. *attrib.* Designating commodities suitable or intended for shipping. Cf. **steam shipping.**

1812 STODDARD *Sk. Louisiana* 126 Various articles, usually denominated naval stores, are produced here; such as hemp, pitch, tar, turpentine, and shipping timber. **1863** *Ill. Agric. Soc. Trans.* V. 669 These remarks are particularly applicable to those heavy descriptions of tobacco known in Virginia as heavy shipping leaf. **1869** *Ib.* VII. 420 Choice to extra, and second class shipping steers, remained throughout the month moderately steady. **1881** *Tenth Census* III. III. 194 Dark Shipping tobacco is generally raised on rich lots. [**1930** BAILEY *Cyclo. Horticulture* 2504/2 For shipping, Alexander, Briggs (Red May), Early Hale, Dewey, Imperial, Sneed, Elberta, and Salway are recognized as standards.]

2. In special combs.: (1) **shipping center,** a place from which shipment can most conveniently be made; (2) **ore,** (see quots.); (3) **point,** a town or city from which goods are shipped.

(1) **1887** *Courier-Journal* 9 May 4/1 The business of shippers and shipping centers [has] been becoming better adjusted gradually to the new order of things. — (2) **1876** RAYMOND *8th Rep. Mines* 242 The ore-vein . . . yields a large portion of 'shipping' or first-class ore. **1882** *47th Congress* 1 Sess. H.R. Ex. Doc. No. 216, 201 A shaft is down 75 feet, exposing a 3-foot vein, 15 inches of which is high-grade or shipping ore. — (3) **1872** *Ill. Dept. Agric. Trans.* IX. 173 This is quite a shipping point, over the Chicago and Alton Railroad. **1904** TARBELL *Hist. Standard Oil Co.* I. 94 The same rate was put on refined oil from Cleveland, Pittsburg and the creek, to Eastern shipping points.

***shirk,** *v.*

1. *N. Eng. tr.* To shift (responsibility) *off upon* (or *onto*) someone.

1838 HAWTHORNE *Notebooks* (1932) 69 The horse he pronounced 'a dreadful nice horse to go; but if he could shirk off the work upon the others, he would.' **1845** LOWELL *Letters* I. III, I would almost give half the rest of my life if I might shirk off upon somebody else all that is generally considered the pleasant result of a literary reputation. **1861** PHILLIPS *Speeches* (1863) 368 Burden it [cotton] by taxes with the full cost of a slaveholding government, . . . a tax it has never yet felt, having shirked it on to the North.

2. *intr.* To shift *for* oneself. *Obs.*

1843 MATHEWS *Writings* 71/1 As for Harvest, let him shirk for himself. **1853** *Harper's Mag.* Oct. 708/2 He determined, as he expressed it, to 'leave the old homestead, and shirk for himself.' **1874** *Vt. Bd. Agric. Rep.* II. 422 They are then turned into the pasture to shirk for themselves.

shirr ʃɜ, *n.* [Origin unknown.] **1.** (See quots.) **2.** (See quot. 1891), also a band of fabric gathered on both sides. Also attrib.

(1) **1858** SIMMONDS *Dict. Trade Products* 341/2 *Shirr,* an insertion of elastic cord between two pieces of cloth. **1876** KNIGHT 2157/1 *Shirr,* . . . an elastic cord inserted in cloth or between two pieces. — (2) **1891** *Cent.* 5578/2 *Shirr, shir,* . . . a puckering or fulling produced in a fabric by means of parallel gathering-threads. **1902** *Delineator* Dec. 623 A shirr-string, run through an underfacing, provides the means of closing.

shirr ʃɜ, *v.* [Origin unknown.] **1.** *tr.* To make shirrs or gathers in (a garment or fabric). **2.** (See quot. 1909.)

(1) **1891** *Cent.* 5578/2. **1896** *Godey's Lady's Bk.* Feb. 223/2 Pretty shades may be made by simply taking a piece of crepe paper . . . and shirring it several times, leaving sufficient at the top to form a full ruffle. — (2) **1891** *Cent.* 5578/2. **1909** WEBSTER 1944/1 *Shirr,* . . . to break (eggs) into a dish with cream or crumbs and bake in the oven or cook in hot water on the fire.

shirred ʃɜd, *a.*

1. (See quots.)

1847 WEBSTER 1023 *Shirred,* . . . a term applied to articles having lines or cords inserted between two pieces of cloth, as the lines of India rubber in shirred suspenders. **1876** KNIGHT 2157/1 *Shirred Goods,* . . . goods with elastic cords (*shirrs*) interwoven in suspenders, garters, etc.

2. Gathered, ornamented with gathered trimmings.

1860 S. WARNER *Say & Seal* lxxii, A simple plain shirred spring bonnet of blue and white silk. **1891** EARLE *Sabbath* 91 The good wives' heads bore . . . 'shirred lustring hoods.' **1900** *19th Cent.* XLVIII. 791 A perfectly-fitting gown . . . [with] ruffles and finely-shirred lace. **1907** WIGGIN *Old Peabody Pew* 114 Dark-haired Nancy under the shadow of her shirred hat.

3. shirred eggs, eggs poached or baked in cream, crumbs, etc.

1883 SALA *Amer. Revisited* I. 302 That woman's shirred eggs and sugar-cured ham should immortalise her. **1941** F. M. FARMER *Boston Cook Book* 126.

Also **shirrer,** a receptacle in which eggs are shirred.

1902 F. M. FARMER *Boston Cook Book* 97 The shirrers should be placed on a tin plate, that they may be easily removed from the oven. **1941** *Ib.* 126 Break an egg into a cup and carefully slip into shirrer.

***shirt,** *n.*

1. =**hunting shirt.** *Obs.* Cf. **shirt battalion, shirtman.**

1805 LEWIS in *L. & Clark Exped.* II. (1904) 378 The shirt of the men is really a commodious and decent garment.

2. In combs.: (1) **shirt battalion,** a battalion of soldiers wearing hunting shirts, *obs.;* (2) **bosom,** the front of a shirt, a shirt front; (3) **man,** a rifleman in the Revolutionary armies (see quot. 1788); (4) ***sleeve,** (*a*) used attrib. to denote a person, as a worker, in his shirtsleeves, or actions, events, etc., that are straightforward and honest, (*b*) esp. **shirtsleeve diplomacy;** (5) **sleeved,** *a.* appearing in shirt sleeves; (6) **tail,** the lower part of a shirt, esp. the rear portion, see **b.** (1) below; (7) **-tail boy,** a small boy accustomed to wear only a long shirt, *colloq.;* (8) **-tail chase,** a chase by shirt-tail boys, *rare;* (9) **-tail parade,** (see quot.); (10) **waist,** see as a main entry.

(1) **1776** MARSHALL *Diary* 5 June 75 Past three, I went to Paul Fooks's. He went with me on the commons, where the Third and the Shirt Battalions were exercising. — (2) **1840** *Spirit of Times* 25 April 87/1 (We.), One clean shirt bosom and collar. **1911** *N.Y. Ev. Post* 2 Feb. 6 Annoying, is it not, to sit in your chair and have your shirt bosom rise up out of your waistcoat? **1943** POWELL *Home Again* 70 It looked as if it were made by taking two of those false shirt bosoms occasionally seen in the past . . . and fastening them back to back. — (3) **1775** *Pa. Gazette* 16 Aug. 2/3 The damn'd shirtmen, as they are emphatically called by some of his [the loyal governor's] minions. **1788** W. GORDON *Hist. Independence U.S.A.* II. 112 Colonel Woodford had not more than 300 shirtmen (as they call the riflemen, on account of their being dressed in their hunting shirts.) **1949** *Sat. Ev. Post* 9 July 74/4 Apparently because they feared the port city and naval base would eventually fall into the hands of the British, the

shirtmen and other citizens helped spread the conflagration. — (4) (*a*) **1855** M. THOMPSON *Doesticks* 320 The prompter would . . . suddenly disappear, until some fresh delinquency called for another shirt-sleeve advent. **1864** SALA in *Daily Telegraph* 27 Sep., The people are going to elect shirt-sleeve aldermen that work all day. **1908** *Pall Mall Gaz.* 20 April 2/2 The Congressmen have a preference for what they picturesquely describe as 'Shirt-sleeve Ambassadors'—men who they think will labour for their country's interests and scorn social fascinations. (*b*) **1933** CHINARD *Honest J. Adams* 141 [It] has led the United States to depart from the traditional rules of old-fashioned diplomacy, . . . to present their propositions as ultimata and to adopt the so-called shirt-sleeve diplomacy, of which John Adams may well be considered the first exponent. **1946** *Chi. D. News* 9 March 6/1 It was one of the most outspoken ever delivered by a Secretary of State, long and hardy though the American tradition of shirtsleeve diplomacy is.

(5) **1869** LOWELL *Poetical Works* (1896) 415/1 In this brown-fisted rough, this shirt-sleeved Cid, . . . My lungs draw braver air. **1883** MARK TWAIN *Life on Miss.* xxxviii, The shirt-sleeved passengers c'eansed themselves at a long row of stationary bowls in the barber shop. — (6) **1856** DERBY *Phoenixiana* 128 The San Diego Light Infantry in full uniform, consisting of Brown's little Boy in his shirt-tail, fired a National salute with a large bunch of fire crackers. **1949** *Chi. Tribune* 30 Sep. 20/3 The shirt tails of uninhibited youth ceased to flutter outside the beltline. — (7) **1845** HOOPER *Simon Suggs' Adv.* 13 From the time he was a 'shirt-tail boy,' [his wits] were always too sharp for his father's. **1876** in GUILD *Old Times* (1878) 411, I traversed these granite hills and beautiful vales as a shirt-tail boy. — (8) **1855** WILLIS *Convalescent* 35 The event of the past month, to my children, has been a shirt-tail chase and capture of a 'possum. — (9) **1905** *D.N.* III. 94 *Shirt-tail parade,* a nocturnal parade of students wearing night-shirts over their clothes to celebrate an athletic victory.

b. In phrases: (1) *To make a (straight) shirt-tail,* to run so fast that one's shirt-tail flutters out behind, *slang, obs.;* (2) *to keep one's shirt on,* to retain one's calm or composure, be patient, *slang;* (3) *to wave the shirt,* =*to wave the bloody shirt q.v., s.v.* ***bloody shirt;** (4) *to tear one's shirt,* to make a serious blunder, make oneself ridiculous, *slang.*

(1) **1841** *Spirit of Times* 7 Aug. 270/3 (We.), It was your intention to make a 'straight shirt-tail' from old Kentuck for your village. **1846** W. G. STEWART *Altowan* I. 174 [He] leaped into the river, . . . and made a shirt-tail across the prairie on the other side. — (2) **1854** HARRIS in *Spirit of Times* (N.Y.) 447/3, I say, you durned ash cats, just keep yer shirts on, will ye? **1904** W. H. SMITH *Promoters* 15, I'll tell you how, if you'll keep your shirt on. **1920** SANDBURG *Smoke & Steel* 62, I can keep my shirt on. — (3) **1888** *S.F. News Letter* 4 Feb., The machine had nominated Blaine and connubiated with Tammany and waved the shirt. — (4) **1891** SLOAN *Fogy Days* 246 In my article on 'Prohibition in Atlanta,' it reads about the ministers, that ''twas tho't that some of 'em tore their shirts.'

As the last term in **bald-faced, barrel, bloody, boiled, crocus, ghost, hickory, hunting, log, logging, mackinaw, red, rifle, ruffle, ruffled, soft, split, sport, stag, stuffed, sweat, war shirt(s).**

***shirted,** *a.* As the last term in **hickory, hunting, ruffled-shirted.**

shirtee ʃɜ'ti, *n.* A false shirt front. *Obs.* — **1806** *Mass. Spy* 30 July (Th.). **1818** *Lancaster* (Pa.) *Jrnl.* 5 Aug. (Th.), A shirt, if you can afford it. But if you can't, then a shirtee, with pretty broad ruffles.

***shirting,** *n.* As the last term in **hickory, Negro shirting.**

shirtwaist 'ʃɜtˌwest, *n.* A loosely fitting waist, with or without collar and cuffs, the bottom of which is tucked under a skirt or trousers.

1879 *Harper's Bazaar* 14 June 377 Kilt suits made here have the pleats stitched to a belt at the waist, and are then buttoned to a white shirt waist. **1902** *Sears Cat.* (ed. 112) 819/3 Three Hundred Dozen Men's Regular $1.50 Shirtwaists to go at 50 Cents. **1948** *Chi. D. News* 7 May 1/3 Grandma's Shirtwaist Returns—Maybe you call it the New Look.

attrib. **1887** PERRY *Flock of Girls* 30 The child was a small slender creature for a long time, . . . [with] simple unfurbelowed shirt-waist frocks. **1911** BURGESS *Find the Woman* 108 Bessie was dancing with President Roosevelt at a shirtwaist ball! **1928** *Chi. Tribune* 26 June 10/5 The 'shirt waist girl' wore a wide belt with a large showy buckle.

Hence **shirtwaisted,** *a.*

1900 *Nation* 19 July 55/1 There is always in evidence a swarming, excited, and exciting crowd of young women, low-shoed and shirt-waisted.

shitepoke 'ʃaɪtˌpok, *n.* [f. the common vulgar word for excrement+*poke,* a bag,—from the bird's action when flushed.] A name applied to a heron and sometimes to other birds. *Colloq.*

1775 *First Book Amer. Chronicles* 13 They drummed with their drums, and piped with their pipes, and running to and fro like shitepokes on the muddy shore. **1799** B. S. BARTON *Fragments Nat. Hist. Pa.* I. 18 Ardea virescens. Commonly called S——e-Poke. **1854** *S.F. Sun* 14 Dec. 2/3 [Californians eat] any thing that wears feathers—from cranes, shitepokes, buzzards and crows, to sparrows and tom-tits. **1948** MENCKEN *Supp.* II. 176 The green heron [is] commonly known elsewhere as the *shitepoke.*

b. Used as a term of opprobium. Also *as crazy as a shitepoke,* quite crazy.

1936 LUTES *Country Kitchen* 19 Of course I'll return it—when they've returned all the molasses and sugar and eggs and everything else they've borrowed in the last year—the old shitepoke! **1943** WOOD *W. Reed* 133 He'd be all right with a little rest, but sometimes, after a more severe ordeal by snow and silence, a man would come out crazy as—they had a word for it here—as a shitepoke, the big awkward heron that seemed to have no sense at all.

***shittimwood,** *n.* **1.** A southern sapotaceous tree, *Bumelia lanuginosa.* **2.** (See quot.) **3.** The silver-bell tree, *Halesia carolina.* Cf. **chittamwood.**

(1) **1884** SARGENT *Rep. Forests* 102 *Bumelia lanuginosa.* . . . Gum Elastic. Shittim Wood. . . . Wood heavy, soft, weak. **1905** *Forestry Bureau Bul.* No. 66, 33 The mesquite, wild china, and shittimwood . . . reach up into the State [Kans.] from the south. — (2) **1884** SARGENT *Rep. Forests* 41 *Rhamnus Purshiana.* . . . Bearberry. Bear Wood. Shittim Wood. . . . The bark . . . possesses powerful cathartic properties. — (3) **1894** *Amer. Folk-Lore* VII. 94 *Halesia tetraptera,* shittimwood, West Va.

shivaree ˌʃɪvə'ri, *n.* [Variant of **charivari, n.*] A noisy demonstration, esp. as a serenade for a newly wedded couple, a racket, a confused medley of noises.

"The present distribution of *shivaree* and other terms for the custom is shown on the accompanying map. It is common to all of Canada and much of the United States. Only in the Eastern seaboard states and parts of the South is the word seldom encountered" (*Amer. Sp.* Dec. 1949, 251).

1843 CARLTON *New Purchase* II. 231 The musicians . . . [let] off at each repetition of the demand peals of shiver-ree. **1850** A. T. JACKSON *Forty-Niner* (1920) 23 The boys . . . gathered and gave the couple a shivaree. **1949** *Time* 25 July 34/2 The custom of noisily serenading a couple on their wedding night is called a *shivaree* (from the French *charivari*) in the Mississippi Valley, *belling* in Western Pennsylvania, *skimmelton* in the Hudson Valley, *horning* in Rhode Island.

shivaree ˌʃɪvə'ri, *v.* [f. prec.] *tr.* To annoy, serenade, or drive off (a person) with a shivaree.

1843 in *Amer. Sp.* XXIV. (1949) 251 At a later period, Edward Livingston, esq., was *sherri-varried* here [in New Orleans]. **1872** EGGLESTON *End of World* 294 And among the manly recreations which they have proposed to themselves is that of shivareeing 'that Dutchman, Gus Wehle.' **1910** *Guide* July 139/1 A crowd . . . started out to 'shivaree' (mob and din to madness) the dreaded old man. **1949** J. B. HERRICK *Memories* 26 Boys . . . imagined it was smart and funny, like the country boys' rowdyish horning or 'shivareeing' the newly wedded couple.

***shoal,** *n.* In combs.: (1) **shoal cod,** =**shoal water cod;** (2) **duck,** (see quot. 1891 and cf. **sand shoal duck**); (3) **mark,** a marker for river pilots that indicates shoal water; (4) **water cod,** (see quot.); (5) **water duck,** =**shoal duck;** (6) **water trout,** (see quot.).

(1) **1839** STORER *Mass. Fishes* 120 Several varieties . . . are known by the names of 'Rock Cod,' 'Shoal Cod,' &c. — (2) **1807** *Mass. H.S. Coll.* 2 Ser. III. 54 The birds, which frequent this and the adjacent islands, are . . . the wild goose; the brant; the shoal duck [etc.]. **1891** *Cent.* 5580/1 *Shoal-duck,* . . . the American eider-duck, more fully called *Isles of Shoals duck,* from a locality off Portsmouth in New Hampshire. — (3) **1875** MARK TWAIN *Old Times* iv. 77 [He] then began to work her warily into the next system of shoal marks. — (4) **1884** GOODE *Fisheries* I. 201 [Cod] which live near the shores, but which are less closely limited to the reefs, . . . are called 'Shoal-water Cod,' 'Shore Cod,' 'Inshore Cod' [etc.].

(5) **1874** LONG *Wild-Fowl* 136 The seeds . . . are the favorite food of mallard and other shoal-water ducks. — (6) **1884** GOODE *Fisheries* I. 488 At Grand Haven there are two forms of Mackinaw Trout, known as the 'Shoal-water Trout' and the 'Deep-water Trout.'

As the last term in **mussel shoals.**

***shock,** *n.*

1. A number of matured stalks *of corn* cut and brought together in an upright position. Cf. **corn shock.**

[**1835** GRIFFITHS *Two Yrs.* 63 Indian corn is cut in October, when from sixty to seventy hills of corn are set together in what is called a hock, or stack, four hills being bent down to one another, and twisted for the purpose of supporting the hock, which is tied round the top with a pumpkin-vine to keep it together.] **1863** NORTON *Army Lett.* 174 He came out . . . like a mouse from a shock of corn. **1920** *3d Nat. Country Life Conf. Proc.* 156 You will notice the cornfield and shocks of corn standing sentry.

2. shock corn, corn put up in shocks.

1865 *Ill. Agric. Soc. Trans.* V. 27 So long as the present system of . . . placing shock-corn on the ground . . . shall prevail. **1925** R. R. SNAPP *Beef Cattle* 179 Before the silo became common, corn fodder or shock corn was used extensively for wintering cattle.

∗**shock,** *v. tr.* To place (corn, or corn tops) in compact shocks.

1755 HEMPSTEAD *Diary* 657, I rid down to the Cornfield & helpt to shock up some Corn Topps that was cut yesterday. **1868** *Iowa State Agric. Soc. Rep. 1867* 210, I protect my vines in Winter by shocking corn-fodder around them. **1944** *Chi. D. News* 5 July 10/2 Cutting, shocking, and husking corn—familiar enough—but detasseling? Who ever bothered about a corn tassel, and why detassel?

Hence **shocked corn.**

1944 CLARK *Pills* 162 At least many of the scribes of the southern Israel cried out loudly in their rebuke of the Northwest for shipping a poor grade of immature shocked corn to the South.

shoddy ˈʃɑdɪ, *a.* Of a person: Pretentious by virtue of ill-gotten wealth, etc., but inferior in moral worth, character, and breeding—first used of those who made fortunes in army contracts during the Civil War by supplying inferior goods known as "shoddy." Esp. **shoddy aristocracy.**

1862 *Cong. Globe* 7 July 3164/1 The anxiety of the 'shoddy' politicians to assail that address. **1865** *Daily Telegraph* (London) 4 Dec. 5/6 A few of the codfish, shoddy, and petroleum aristocracy. **1882** McCABE *New York* 226 The acquaintance of some wealthy shoddy family is formed. **1946** PARTRIDGE & BETTMANN *As We Were* 62 A 'shoddy aristocracy' sprang up, best known for its reckless buying of costly luxuries and its pretentious vulgarity.

b. Also **shoddydom, shoddyite, shoddy(o)cracy.** *Obs.*

1863 NORTON *Army Lett.* 169 Shoddycracy is pretty large in New York, . . . the hideous offspring of the monster war. **1864** *Crisis* (Columbus, O.) 17 Feb. 31/2 Let Shoddyites, contractors all, Fall down and worship Uncle Ned. **1870** M. H. SMITH *20 Years Wall St.* 199 A marble palace was to be erected on that site that would make all Shoddydom red with envy. **1902** CLAPIN 359 *Shoddyocracy*, people who have become rich by making contracts for shoddy goods, or in any other disreputable way.

shoddyize ˈʃɑdɪˌaɪz, *v.* (See quot.) *Obs.* — **1871** DE VERE 299 A verb, even—to *shoddyize*—has been made to supply an apparent demand.

∗**shoe,** *n.* In combs.: (1) **shoe bench,** a shoemaker's bench; (2) **boot,** ?a boot of superior elegance, *obs.;* (3) **buttoner,** a small metal contrivance having a semicircular bend or hook at one end used for fastening button shoes; (4) **department,** the place in a department store where shoes are kept for sale; (5) **findings,** *pl.* supplies, materials (except leather), and tools for shoemakers, cf. ∗**findings;** (6) **maker's tree,** sumach, *rare;* (7) **peg,** see as a main entry; (8) **stand,** a place suitable for engaging in selling shoes; (9) ∗**string,** see as a main entry; (10) **town,** a town in which shoemaking is the principal industry.

(1) **1841** *Knickerb.* XVII. 262 A few weeks' rumination on the shoe-bench, or cogitation on the tailor's board, is sufficient to perfect either. **1891** *Harper's Mag.* June 57/1 An express wagon was . . . loaded with the old shoe bench. — (2) **1789** *State Gazette of N.C.* (New Bern) 19 March, He carried off with him . . . a pair of shoe-boots. **1818** ROYALL *Lett. from Ala.* 106 [He] swore vengeance against every shoe-boot gentleman in the Bluff. **1845** HOOPER *Simon Suggs' Adv.* 23 If he was only to see one o' them fine gentlemen in Augusty, with his . . . shoe-boots a-shinin' like Silver. — (3) **1881** RITTENHOUSE *Maud* 34, I'll bet my prettiest shoe-buttoner that Alice and Fred are engaged. **1905** O. HENRY *Roads of Destiny* 138 Old Urique keeps anywhere from $50,000 to $100,000 . . . in a little safe that you could open with a shoe buttoner. — (4) **1887** *Courier-Journal* 2 Feb. 6/7 He will be assigned to the shoe department.

(5) **1836** in COMMONS *Doc. Hist.* VI. 37, 20 dollars . . . it must cost him [the journeyman cordwainer] for shoe-findings, tools and implements. **1892** *York Co. Hist. Rev.* 26 H. B. Beard, Wholesale and Retail Dealer in Harness and Saddlery, Shoe Findings, &c. — (6) *c*1845 *True Picture* 22 The tree from which these tubes [i.e., spiles used in tapping sugar-maple trees] are made, is admirably adapted for the purpose growing somewhat like the elder, only its branches are straighter and contain more pith. It is usually called in Illinois the shoemaker's tree, its botanical name I do not know. — (8) **1887** *Courier-Journal* 6 Feb. 3/6 For Sale—A Good Shoe Stand—Stock and fixtures. . . . Schlesinger's Shoe Store.

(10) **1883** in WELLS *Practical Economics* 106 The best educated factory population in New England is that found in your 'shoe-towns.' **1896** *Internat. Typog. Union Proc.* 25/1 Brockton, Mass., is another well organized shoetown.

b. In other combs. of obvious meaning or sufficiently explained in the quots., as (1) **shoe clerk,** (2) **drummer,** (3) **fitter,** (4) **hospital,** (5) **-maker loo,** (6) **parlor,** (7) **pegging machine,** (8) **pocket,** (9) **-shine box,** (10) **-shine boy,** (11) **-shine emporium,** (12) **-shine** (or **shining) parlor,** (13) **store,** (14) **track.**

(1) **1931** *K.C. Times* 18 Sep., The up to date shoe clerk has learned it's no use showing a woman customer the first ten pair. — (2) **1944** CLARK *Pills* 118 Shoe drummers, like representatives from dry-goods houses, brought trunks filled with actual goods as samples. — (3) **1868** *Harper's Mag.* Sep. 549/1 Women are now . . . shoe-fitters—that is, they do the lighter hand-work on ladies' shoes, put in the elastic in Congress and other gaiters. — (4) **1919** *Polk St. Journal* (S.F.) 27 June 3/3 Calif. St. Shoe Hospital.

(5) **1813** in KITTREDGE *Old Farmer* (1904) 95 Tom Teazer, well known at the grog shops for a dabster at shoemaker loo, . . . and all the village moon-cursers came in for their portion of the wreck. **1833** NEAL *Down-Easters* I. 71 Do you play checkers? . . . or shoe-make-loo [*sic*]? **1904** KITTREDGE *Old Farmer* 96 'Shoemaker loo' was a round game at cards. — (6) **1906** *Washington Post* 29 April 9 Dainty society women performed the menial task of shining men's shoes. The improvised shoe parlor was in All Souls' Unitarian Church. — (7) **1883** KNIGHT 806/1 *Shoe Pegging Machine*, a machine which takes the pegs in the strip, feeds and cuts them, and pegs on the sole. **1894** HOWELLS in *Harper's Mag.* June 44/1 Somehow that shoe-pegging machine must come in. — (8) **1876** KNIGHT 2162/2 *Shoe-pocket*, . . . a small leather pocket attached to a saddle for the purpose of carrying one or more extra horseshoes. — (9) **1945** *This Week Mag.* 1 Sep. 2/3 The first lucky child went into business with a shoe-shine box made for him by a GI.

(10) **1931** *K.C. Times* 29 Oct., Cecil, the Negro shoe shine boy at the City barber shop, has organized a band. — (11) **1930** *Randolph Enterprise* (Elkins, W.Va.) 20 Nov. 1/3 Charley Anderson now has the finest shoe shine emporium. — (12) **1898** *K.C. Star* 21 Dec. 1/4 Mrs. Edna Maxwell . . . ran a shoe shining parlor on West Ninth street. **1911** FAIRCHILD *Greek Immigration to U.S.* 127 In 1904 there were but three shoe-shine parlors in the hands of Greeks in the city. **1949** *Time* 31 Jan. 39/1 The 550 people who had crowded into the old New Orleans dance hall above the shoeshine parlor and magazine stand stamped and crowed. — (13) **1789** *Boston Directory* 175 Bond and Bryant, shoe-store. **1860** MORDECAI *Virginia* 221 His house . . . was bought and demolished by Mr. Hubbard, to make room for his extensive shoe-store. **1949** *World-Herald Mag.* (Omaha) 14 Aug. 23/1, I worked as cashier in a shoe store. — (14) **1725** *Lancaster Rec.* 239 This day Capt Blancher saw some shoe tracks. **1808** PIKE *Sources Miss.* 47 Finding some to be shoe-tracks, he conceived it to be the establishment of some traders. **1848** BRYANT *California* xvii. 223, I saw a plain and fresh shoe-track.

c. In colloq. phrases: (1) *Blast my old shoes*, an expression used for emphasis; (2) *the shoe is on the other foot*, the situation is reversed.

(1) **1835** LONGSTREET *Ga. Scenes* 6, I'll see you a fair fight, blast my old shoes if I don't! — (2) **1939** HARRIS *Purslane* 179, I tell him if he had the waitin' on him to do the shoes would be on the other foot. **1945** *Nation* 17 March 290/2 Recently, much to British chagrin, the shoe was on the other foot.

As the last term in **bed, brake, Canadian, club, Congress, cowhide, French fall, gum, horse, India rubber, low-quarter, Monroe, Negro, over, ox, plantation, rubber, shaking, short-quartered, sleigh, snow, whipporwill's shoe(s).**

shoepack ˈʃuˌpæk, *n.* Also **shoepac.** [Rationalized f. Lenape *shipak* (<*machtschipak*, bad shoe, as compared with a moccasin).] A shoe somewhat like a moccasin (see quots. 1824, 1917). Cf. **pack,** *n.*

1755 *Lett. to Washington* I. 99 It would be a good thing to have Shoe-packs or Moccosons for the Scouts. **1824** J. DODDRIDGE *Notes* 144 Those who could not make shoes, could make shoepacks. These like mocassons were made of a single piece of leather with the exception of a tongue piece on the top of the foot. This was about two inches broad and circular at the lower end. To this the main piece of leather was sewed, with a gathering stich. The seam behind was like that of a mocasson. To the shoepack a soal was sometimes added. **1917** KEPHART *Camping* I. 157 A 'shoe-pac' or 'larrigan' is a beef-hide moccasin with eight to ten-inch top, and with or without a light-flexible sole. **1949** *Boston Globe Mag.* 18 Dec. 8/1 Pulling on high, laced shoe-packs, he studied the pre-dawn sky with thoughtful brown eyes.

shoe-peg ˈʃuˌpɛg, *n.*

1. A small wooden peg used to fasten shoe soles to the uppers or to each other.

1854 LIPPINCOTT *Haps & Mishaps* 13 The Yankee having whittled a lot of unsaleable shoe-pegs into melon seeds. **1860** HOLMES *E. Venner* iii, Manufactures [of Pigwacket Centre], shoe-pegs, clothes-pins, and tin-ware. **1876** KNIGHT III. 2162/1 Shoe-pegs are said to have been invented by Joseph Walker, of Massachusetts, about 1818.

2. A variety of Indian corn, or the grains of such corn, somewhat resembling the pegs used in shoemaking. Also attrib.

1856 DAVIS *Farm Bk.* 27, I planted the shoe peg corn on the lower part of the T ditch. **1876** HARTE *Drift from Two Shores* 141 The honest Connecticut farmer was quietly gathering from his threshing-floor the shoe-pegs. **1942** WEYGANDT *Plenty of Penna.* 96 There were no varieties of sweet yellow corn in those days . . . that have never [*sic*] rivaled, in my estimation, the shoepeg or evergreen for juiciness and sweetness.

***shoestring,** *n.*

1. A variety of tobacco. *Obs.*

1784 SMYTH *Tour* II. 129 There are seven different kinds of tobacco, . . . named Hudson, Frederick, Thick-joint, Shoe-string [etc.].

2. A small amount of money, usu. in phrases, esp. *on a shoestring. Colloq.*

1904 *Cosmopolitan* May 89 He speculated 'on a shoe-string.' **1949** *Time* 14 March 91/3 He had parlayed a $3,000 shoestring into a textile empire that last year grossed $288 million. **1949** *Ward Co. Independent* (Minot, N.D.) 21 July 1/3 They accomplished their elegance on a shoestring, too.

b. Used attrib. in the sense of small, petty, contemptible, esp. **shoestring gambler.** *Colloq.*

1891 QUINN *Fools of Fortune* 494 The gamblers, aside from a lot of 'hangers on,' known as 'shoestring' or 'tin horn' gamblers, do not figure in the criminal records. **1923** B. M. BOWER *Parowan Bonanza* xi. 137 The little shoestring propositions that go broke and leave empty houses behind them. **1926** J. BLACK *You Can't Win* xiii. 185 Consequently the cheap cheaters and tinhorn, shoestring gamblers never got a footing there.

3. =**lead plant.** Cf. **devil's-shoestrings.**

1899 *Mo. So. Dakotan* I. 175 The active air is loaded with the spicy breath of burned mint and shoe-string. **1913** CATHER *O Pioneers!* 36 The wild flowers disappeared, and only in the bottom of the draws and gullies grew a few of the very toughest and hardiest: shoestring, and ironweed, and snow-on-the-mountain. **1929** BELL *Kansas Vocabulary* 190 In Iowa, years ago, old settlers counted that it would be good farming land where the *shoestring* grew.

4. Potatoes cut in long stringlike pieces, usu. *pl.* Also **shoestring potato.** Cf. **shoofly potato.**

1931 B. STARKE *Touch & Go* x. 156, I . . . found that the word 'shoestrings' on the menu really meant Julienne potatoes. I ate every last shoe-string. **1935** MITCHELL *America* 221 It was 'Antlers T Bone Shoe Strings.' Just that. . . . It would be a pity to explain it, but what you get if you order it is a steak and potatoes. **1940** *Amer. Mercury* Sep. 72 When old Fred Harvey started turning a shoestring potato into a 2500-mile string of railroad eating-places, he launched a 'matrimonial bureau' the likes of which these United States had never seen.

5. In special combs.: (1) **shoestring catch,** in baseball, a catch close to the ground made while running; (2) **district,** a political district laid out in a long narrow strip so as to be of advantage to those who designed it, as the Sixth Congressional District in Mississippi laid out in 1874 to exclude a large Negro population, cf. **Gerrymander,** *v.;* (3) **path,** a narrow path; (4) **tie,** a narrow necktie.

(1) **1926** *N.Y. Times* 11 Oct. 25/2 Hafey ran up on it and tried to make a shoestring catch of it, missed it, and the ball got past him for a double. **1946** *Chi. Sun* 2 July 25/8 Harry Lowrey failed in an attempted shoestring catch of Bill Cox' hit in the second inning. — (2) **1878** *Cong. Rec.* App. 13 June 478/2, I will promise to meet him on the northern border of 'the shoe-string district.' **1882** *Ib.* 13 Feb. 1105/1 The Shoe-string district in Mississippi . . . is child's play to the skillful carving of our Pennsylvania artists in fraud. [**1923** MCGROARTY *Hist. Los Angeles Co.* I. 218 In 1908 the 'Shoestring Strip' connecting Los Angeles with San Pedro and Wilmington was annexed to the city, completing the consolidation of the city and its harbor.] **1950** *Chi. Tribune* 5 March III. 1/8 A 'shoestring' district, the 7th circles Chicago and takes in all of suburban Cook county except Evanston, Oak Park [etc.]. — (3) **1897** *Pop. Sci. Mo.* L. 309 Bad roads and shoestring paths . . . fringe them. — (4) **1902** NORRIS *Pit* 337 His shoestring tie straggled over his frayed shirt front. **1924** *McNaught's Mag.* April 250 The banker from Des Moines . . . may wear . . . a shoestring tie.

b. In colloq. or slang phrases: (1) *To tie one's own shoestrings,* to take care of one's own affairs, to exercise one's independence; (2) *to walk on one's shoestrings,* to be quite destitute.

(1) **1854** THOREAU *Walden* 85 Rescue the drowning and tie your shoestrings. **1902** G. C. EGGLESTON *D. South* 166 For many of the services of a valet, Arthur had no use whatever. It was his habit, as he had long ago said, to 'tie his own shoe strings.' — (2) **1888** *St. Louis Globe-Democrat* 16 Feb. (F.), I was literally walking on my shoe strings.

For *to draw to a shoestring and obtain a tanyard,* see ***draw,** *v.* **6.**

shongsasha ʃɔŋˈsæʃə, *n.* (See quot.) *Rare.* — **1848** PARKMAN in *Knickerb.* XXXI. 113 The Big Crow produced his pipe and filled it with the mixture of tobacco, and *shongsasha,* or red willow bark.

***shoo,** *v. tr.* To urge or cause (persons) to go in a desired direction by gentle means. *Colloq.*

1903 *N.Y. Sun* 17 Nov. 12 The police shoo everybody to the south side of the loop. **1923** B. M. BOWER *Parowan Bonanza* xiii. 151 You're supposed to shoo a lady gently before you down the aisle.

shoofly ˈʃuˌflaɪ, *n.* [f. "*shoo, fly.*"]

1. Originally in the name of a nonsense song (see quot. 1927), and of a shuffling dance. Hence **shoofly shoe,** a shoe especially suited for this dance.

*c***1865** in S. SPAETH *Read 'Em & Weep* (1927) 64 Shoo, fly, don't bother me! **1874** WARNER *Clown Songster* 30 I'll show him my shoofly shoe. **1927** S. SPAETH *Read 'Em & Weep* 63 'Shoo, Fly, Don't Bother me!' This was the most popular nonsense song of the Civil War. It was revived many years later in 'Captain Jinks of the Horse Marines,' Ethel Barrymore's first play. The words were by Billy Reeves and the music by Frank Campbell. **1942** LILLARD *Desert Challenge* 218 Several music halls offered a miscellany of entertainment such as bar acts, the shoofly and cancan, jokes, pantomime ballet, Negro dances, monologues in dialect.

2. Used as an expression of disappointment or disgust, or for a thing the proper name of which does not come readily to mind. Also designating a thing regarded as somewhat superior or nice. *Colloq.*

1867 *Chi. Republican* 24 July 8/1 [Baseball] players invariably say 'Shoo-fly,' when they make a miss. **1870** *Alaska Times* (Sitka) 30 April 2/3 They were amazed at beholding weavels, maggots and shooflies march out in columns innumerable. *Ib.* 21 July 3/2 'Shoo Fly' cocktails, 'Can Can' toddies, or any other drinks . . . are always to be had . . . at the Charter Oak Saloon. **1879** *Glendale* (Mont.) *Atlantis* 28 Dec. 4/4 A Dutchman drove rapidly along Main Street, with a new shoo-fly attached to his wagon, making forty flips a second and striking back and forth with the vigor of a hewgag. **1946** RICHTER *Fields* 278 Huldah had gone with Amy MacMahon, a red shoofly ribbon low on both their necks.

3. shoofly potato, =**shoestring potato.** Cf. ***shoestring 4.**

1876 HENDERSON *Cooking* 195 There is a machine which comes for the purpose of cutting shoo-fly potatoes; it costs two dollars and a half. The potatoes are cut into long strips like macaroni, excepting that the sides are square instead of round.

4. A kind of rocker for small children, consisting of a seat mounted between supports representing horses, swans, etc. Also **shoofly hobby horse, rocker.**

One form of shoofly rocker

1887 *Chi. Tribune* 27 Nov. 16/7 Shoo Fly Hobby Horse, 75c. **1902** *Sears Cat.* 1125/1 Shoo Fly. Upholstered in cretonne. Painted in dapple gray. Bent rocker and hair tail. . . . Swinging Shoo Fly Rockers . . . easy to operate, no danger of child falling out. **1947** *Chi. Tribune* 30 Dec. 15/1 The Teaneck, N.J., library has installed something called a shoo-fly, an enclosed rocker in which little Elmer—or young Sally—can rock his head off.

5. (See quot. 1909.) Also attrib. *Slang.*

1904 *N.Y. Ev. Post* 4 June 2 Lack of discipline is still apparent in the Police Department, notwithstanding the restoration of the 'shoofly' system. **1909** L. F. FULD *Police Administration* 456 (Th.), [Let us now consider] the employment of spies, who are usually called 'shoo-flies.' These spies may be patrolmen in citizen's clothes, uniformed roundsmen sent out from headquarters, superior officers in citizens clothes or private citizens.

6. *Railroad.* A temporary track to enable trains to pass an obstruction in the regular line. [In quot. 1929 app. applied to a train.]

1905 *N.Y. Ev. Post* 29 July 1 The Southern Pacific Company's 'shoo-fly' around the tracks now submerged will be completed in a few days. **1929** *Macon* (Ga.) *Telegraph* 2 July (News of Twenty Years Ago), There comes into Macon every morning on the Eatonton Shoo Fly a very old white woman named Mary Loring. **1947** BEEBE *Mixed Train Dly.* 159 The last week in August, 1941, the line was blocked, paradoxically enough, by a tremendous snowslide and it was found cheaper to build a shoo-fly about a thousand yards long rather than dig it out at the time.

attrib. **1945** MARSHALL *Santa Fe* 141 They put Kingman and Morley to work running a shoofly switchback up over the mountain, nearly 8,000 feet in the air.

7. (See quot. 1949.) In full **shoofly pie.**

1938 HARK *Hex Marks Spot* 254 Eggs and sausage and fried potatoes and flannel cakes and coffee, with perhaps a slab of 'shoofly' on the side—there's a breakfast, now, that gives a person something to go on. **1940** *Sat. Ev. Post* 30 March 42/3 No account of the Amish is complete without a mention of shoo-fly pie and schnitz pie. **1949** *Life* 14 Nov. 12/2 What are the ingredients of a shoo-fly pie, a regional dish of Pennsylvania? . . . Molasses, baking soda, brown sugar, flour, shortening, salt and boiling water. According to some folklore experts, the term 'shoo-fly' comes from the sweet, syrupy substance of the pie, which attracts flies that have to be shooed away.

Also in the title of a song.

1945 (*song title*), Shoo-fly Pie and Apple Pan Dowdy.

shook ʃʊk, *n.* [See note.]

Origin obscure. *OED* records *shaken*, of a cask taken to pieces and bound up compactly for transport 1557——. *Shaken hogshead* occurs in an example of 1792 from the Kentucky area, but *shook* was app. quite as much used here as *shaken*, and in its adj. use may have given rise to **shook,** *n.*, just as *shaken* may be related to **shake,** *n.* **1.**

1. A set of staves, boards, headings, etc., sufficient for a hogshead, barrel, box, packed in a compact bundle for transport.

1810 *Columbian Centinel* 13 Jan. 3/1 Eight thousand Hhd Hoops, and 250 Molasses Hhd Shooks, for sale. **1819** *Mass. Stat.* 19 June, For shooks and empty barrels, four cents. **1842** *Amer. Pioneer* I. 138 [He] threw overboard all the puncheon shooks and about fifty barrels of flour. **1897** *Cong. Rec.* App. 31 March 12/2 Any ordinary person of fair ability can look into a car loaded with box shooks and easily determine about how many thousand feet of lumber it contains.

b. (See quot. and cf. ∗**shake,** *n.* **1.**) *Obs.*

1860 GREELEY *Overland Journey* 162 'Shooks,' or split saplings of cotton-wood, . . . incline gently to the transverse or longer sides.

2. *attrib.* or as *adj.* Of or pertaining to a hogshead or other container in a "knocked down" or "shaken" condition. Also in the sense of shake *q.v.* sense **1.**

1763 in *Pub. Col. Soc.* XIX. 388, 10,000 Shook Hogsheads sent to the foreign Islands for Molasses. **1860** GREELEY *Overland Journey* 162 The unchinked, barely shook-covered houses . . . are decidedly the cooler and airier. **1888** *Amer. Almanac* 275 Occupations of the People of the United States. . . . Stave, shook and heading makers. **1940** CUMMINGS *Amer. & His Food* 150 The Fruit Growers' Supply Company, turned out at low cost the 'shook' wood boxes in which the fruits were marketed.

shook ʃʊk, *v. tr.* To reduce (a cask) to shooks (see also quot. 1841). *Obs.*

*c***1800** Gravestone epitaph in *Harper's Mag.* XXII. 283/2 Now food for worms, Like an old rum-puncheon, marked, numbered, and shooked. **1841** WEBSTER II. 593/2 *Shook*, to pack staves in casks. **1849** COOPER *Sea Lions* xxiii, [By] shooking the casks, room might be made aboard . . . for all my [seal]skins.

∗**shoot,** *n.*

1. (See quots.) *Obs.*

*c***1826** STANLEY *Jrnl.* 242 These constant changes of the [Miss.] river, would seem an insurmountable obstacle to any extensive cultivation on the banks. We saw one or two instances where a *shoot*, for this is the term properly applied to the stream, and a *cut off* to the land between the old & new channel, of a mile or two in length, shortened the course of the river twelve or fifteen miles. **1839** *N.O. Picayune* 23 April 2/4 Several times on the trip he had, in order to shorten it as much as possible, taken short cuts, *shutes* as they are called. **1870** MACRAE *Americans* II. 160 Sometimes the [Mississippi] river makes a vast detour, returning after a sweep of twenty or thirty miles to near the spot from which the detour began. At these points it sooner or later makes a new channel for itself across the neck of land. This is called a shoot, and as soon as it becomes deep enough, steamers and rafts avail themselves of it to shorten the distance.

2. A smooth, precipitous way down which logs or cotton bales are allowed to slide. Cf. **chute 3.**

1848 BARTLETT 300 *Shoot*, or *Shute*, a passage-way on the side of a steep hill or mountain down which wood and timber are thrown or slid. **1863** HOPLEY *Life in South* II. 333 On many of the Southern rivers there are wooden landings, with . . . 'shoots,' or long wooden slides for the cotton to be passed down the banks to the boat. **1876** CROFUTT *Trans-continental Tourist* 122 The logs are slid down the mountain sides in 'shoots.'

3. A narrow passageway through which cattle or sheep are driven. Cf. **chute 4.**

1868 *Ill. Agric. Soc. Trans.* VI. 319 Each railroad has one thousand feet of platform . . . provided with 'shoots,' leading directly into the yards and pens. **1881** A. A. HAYES *New Colo.* v. 66 There were a small cabin, a stable, sheds, a pump at the spring, three corrals connected by 'shoots,' or narrow passages.

4. *Baseball.* A pitched ball that curves or shoots away from a direct line.

1885 CHADWICK *Art of Pitching* 14 Pitchers frequently have full command of one kind of a 'curve' or 'shoot' of a ball. **1886** ——— *Art of Batting* 34 What batsmen require . . . is to practice against . . . the various 'shoots.'

5. (See quot.)

1905 *Forestry Bureau Bul.* No. 61, 22 A shoot is a sprout which has not reached a height of 3 feet.

6. In colloq. phrases now obs.: (1) *To take the shoot*, to set forth boldly, to enter upon an indicated course of action; (2) *to take a shoot after*, to take a liking to; (3) *to be on the shoot*, to be ready to shoot, to be on the warpath, also *to be on the cut and shoot;* (4) *to come on a straight shoot*, to proceed in a direct, forthright manner.

(1) **1837** BIRD *Nick of Woods* II. 15 Then for rifle-butt, knife, and hatchet! . . . Take the shoot with full pieces, and let the skirmudgeons have it handsome! **1843** CARLTON *New Purchase* II. 105 Pushed by the two on land [the horse] took the 'shoote;'—in this case a plunge . . . into water a little over nine feet deep! **1883** HAY *Bread-Winners* 252, I had to take the other shoot—he hadn't the sand to help. — (2) **1847** ROBB *Squatter Life* 143 That gal . . . wur about the pootyest creatur . . . I ever took a *shute* arter. — (3) **1873** MILLER *Amongst Modocs* 308 No one cared, so long as he fought with men who 'came from the shoulder,' or were on the 'cut and shoot.' **1890** *Cent. Mag.* Feb. 524/1 Some folks called him the 'Taos Terror' . . . , for he was on the shoot every time. — (4) [**1853** *Oregonian* (Portland) 12 Feb. 2/5, I saw him last making a straight shute for the code commissioners, with a humble petition for the situation of clerk.] **1904** W. H. SMITH *Promoters* 72 You can't come at things on a straight shoot any more.

As the last term in **blizzard, down, fire, log, out, pay, rifle, timber, turkey, two, up shoot.**

∗**shoot,** *v.*

1. *intr.* Of corn: To put out young ears and silk.

1775 in RAUCK *Boonesborough* 179 Corn planted 26 or 27 of April was tasseled or shot. **1851** *Polly Peablossom* 20 It was as vivifying as a shower of rain on corn that is about to shoot and tassel.

2. *tr.* To blast (an oil or gas well) with dynamite or nitroglycerin in an effort to start or increase its flow. Cf. ∗**shooting,** *n.* **1. a.**

1888 *Scribner's Mag.* May 576/1 [Explosives] are used in the petroleum industry to 'shoot' the wells, so as to remove the paraffine which prevents the flow of oil. **1897** *Kissimmee* (Fla.) *Valley Gazette* 1 Dec. 1/8 Sixty quarts of nitroglycerine had been hauled here for the purpose of shooting a gas well. **1946** *Nat. Geog. Mag.* Sep. 273/1 Shooting oil wells pays better than shooting ducks, and there's more money in milk than in moonshine.

3. To give up or quit. *Slang.*

1883 HAY *Bread-Winners* 249 If I had all the cash he takes in to-night, I'd buy an island and shoot the machine business.

4. *Baseball.* To throw (a ball) swiftly.

1912 E. V. COOKE *Baseballogy* 17 Shoot the ball to second. **1912** MATHEWSON *Pitching* 273 Flaherty would shoot the ball over to first as before.

5. In motion pictures, to photograph or film.

1916 B. M. BOWER *Phantom Herd* ii. 22 He . . . debated whether it should be 'shot' with two cameras or three. **1948** *Trail Riders Bul.* Jan. 19/1 In the meantime the scene was shot, the cameras swung around and the story was being unfolded in the heart of the Rockies.

6. To remove (stumps, etc.) by blasting with an explosive.

1931 *Randolph Enterprise* (Elkins, W.Va.) 19 March 8/3 John Vanpelt was shooting stumps with dynamite.

7. In phrases: (1) *To shoot center*, of a rifle, to shoot very accurately; (2) *to shoot one's grandmother*, (see quot. 1859), *slang;* (3) *to shoot that hat*, and variants (see quots. 1877, 1903), *slang*; (4) *to shoot off one's mouth*, to talk with obnoxious freedom, with little regard for propriety, *slang;* (5) *to shoot up*, (*a*) to shoot at (a person) in a lawless, reckless manner, (*b*) to rush or ride through (a place) shooting wildly or recklessly in all directions, (*c*) to consume, all *slang;* (6) *to shoot the chutes*, to slide or go down a precipitous incline in a specially made type of toboggan, boat, etc., cf. **chute,** *n.* **6;** (7) *to shoot a jam*, (see quot.); (8) *to shoot it out*, to fight with firearms to a decision, *colloq.*

(1) **1848** Ruxton in *Blackw. Mag.* LXIV. 575 'This old tool' (tapping his rifle) 'shoots "center," she does.' **1853** Brewerton *With Kit Carson* (1930) 184 There were rough frontiersmen who boasted no 'possibles' beyond the good rifle made by Jake Hawkins which always 'shot centre.' **1948** *Westerners' Brand Book* 49 She's a genooine Hawken and she shoots plumb centre. — (2) **1855** Haliburton *Nature & Hum. Nature* II. 297 You showed her she had shot her grandmother. **1859** Bartlett 402 *To Shoot one's Grandmother*, is a common though vulgar phrase in New England, and means, to be mistaken, or to be disappointed; to imagine oneself the discoverer of something in which he is deceived. The common phrase is, 'You've shot your granny.' — (3) **1876** *Ed. Burton's Songs* (B.), The slang the gang is using now, You'll hear from every lip; It's shoot the hat! and get it boiled; And don't you lose your grip. **1877** Bartlett 585 To say, 'Shoot that dress,' is meant to convey the idea that the dress is inferior. **1903** Farmer & Henley VI. 188/1 *Shoot that (hat, man—anything)!* . . . a mild imprecation, 'Bother!' — (4) **1864** *Rocky Mt. News* (Denver) 3 Aug. 4/2 The last case of any interest was that of a Dutch married woman . . . who was taxed $17.80 for 'shooting off her mouth' against the virtue and morality of a neighboring maiden. **1948** *Chi. D. News* 1 Oct. 16/3 You would think that a psychiatrist would know better than to shoot off his mouth on a subject which he is evidently unqualified to discuss.

(5) (*a*) **1890** *Stock Grower & Farmer* 21 June 3/1 Three cowboys shot each other up. **1912** Wason *Friar Tuck* 198 A cattle man is never satisfied unless he has grabbed what he wanted away from someone else, an' then shot him up a little for kickin' about it. (*b*) **1890** *Stock Grower & Farmer* 18 Jan. 5/2 This so enraged the boys that they began shooting up the town. **1906** *Out West* Feb. 125 It was a safe and popular pastime to 'shoot up the town.' **1949** *Boston Sun. Globe* 1 May (Fiction Mag.) 3/5 Red wanted to shoot up the ranch Western style. (*c*) **1926** J. Black *You Can't Win* xii. 161 They grew so despondent over their plight . . . they decided to 'shoot up' the small portion of white stuff they had left. — (6) **1895** *N.Y. Dramatic News* 30 Nov. 17/4 Shooting the Chutes, the latest craze that has struck the town, is . . . drawing large crowds. **1896** *Ib.* 11 July 10/2 Last week the delightful occupation known as shooting the chutes was shown in full swing. — (7) **1905** *Forestry Bureau Bul.* No. 61, 46 *Shoot a jam, to*, to loosen a log jam with dynamite. — (8) **1912** Raine *Brand Blotters* 327 Had he shown any sign of indecision, they would have taken a chance and shot it out.

***shooter,** *n.* As the last term in **bean, biscuit, cap, crap, double, five, market, navy (six), Negro, seven, sharp, six, sixteen, square, trouble, two shooter.**

* **shooting,** *n.*

1. a. Starting the flow in an oil or gas well by blasting. Cf. ***shoot,** *v.* **2. b.** Short for **shooting affair, affray.**

(**a**) **1879** Vivian *Wanderings in Western Land* 385 The 'shooting' is done with what is here called 'No. 3, giant powder,' a sort of slow dynamite which is quicker and less violent in its action than black powder. — (**b**) **1944** Clark *Pills* 73 Deaths and births were likewise publicized around the stoves. Shootings, scrapes and cuttings were reported, and all of their details discussed.

2. In combs.: (1) **shooting affair, affray,** an encounter in which enemies, usu. two, fight with firearms, esp. pistols; (2) **bee,** a shooting match, *rare;* (3) **cracker,** a firecracker, *obs.;* (4) ***match,** (see quot. 1896), also *the whole shooting match*, "the whole caboodle," see **caboodle,** *colloq.;* (5) **scrape,** an outbreak in which shooting occurs, *colloq.;* (6) ***star,** any of various plants of the genus *Dodecatheon*, esp. the American cowslip, *D. meadia;* (7) ***stick,** a gun, *obs.;* (8) **tree,** in frontier times, a tree supporting a mark for shooting at in testing a new rifle or supply of gunpowder, *obs.*

(1) **1871** *Republican Rev.* 13 May 1/2 Two shooting affairs took place at Elizabethtown on Wednesday last. **1879** *Cimarron News & Press* 27 Nov. 3/2 A shooting affray occurred in Otero in which Harry Bassett, the livery stable keeper, was killed. — (2) **1890** *Harper's Mag.* Dec. 160/1 Progressive shooting bees . . . had been held. — (3) **1867** *Amer. Philos. Soc. Proc.* X. 344 There was also a loud report, described as resembling the noise of a large shooting-cracker. **1890** Howells *Boy's Town* 110 The boys began to celebrate [Christmas] . . . with shooting-crackers and torpedoes. — (4) **1896** *D.N.* I. 424 shooting-match: any kind of meeting, from a church service to a dance. **1946** *New Yorker* 25 May 16/3 Sometimes I think I'll live to see the end of the whole shooting match.

(5) **1831** *Boston Transcript* 30 June 2/2 They came pretty near having a shooting scrape here yesterday. **1949** Gann *Tread of Longhorns* 76 Their first meeting came near ending in a shooting scrape. — (6) **1857** Gray *Botany* 272 *D[odecatheon] Meadia. . . .* Very handsome in cultivation. In the West called Shooting-Star. **1882** *Cent. Mag.* Sep. 772/1 In early June there blooms a unique flower called the shooting star, shaped like a shuttle-cock. **1949** Howell *Marin Flora* 217 The shooting stars are early bloomers and, like rosy-fingered Aurora who precedes dazzling Phoebus, their bright and cheery flowers of late winter are harbingers of the floral flood that comes with spring. — (7) **1846** *Quincy* (Ill.) *Whig* 12 Feb. 2/5 If she persists in denying our *title* to Oregon, may she find our Yankee *shooting-sticks* in full play about her *form.* **1866** F. Kirkland *Bk. Anecdotes* 237/2 Sambo . . . fell back in confusion when the 'shooting stick' was brandished toward his own breast. — (8) **1843** Oliver *Eight Months* 164 If a stranger goes up to the door of almost any house in the backwoods, and looks about him, he rarely fails to see, at the distance of twenty rods, a tree hacked and hewed, sometimes nearly through; it is the shooting tree, and the hacking is done with an axe to get out the bullets.

b. *As sure as shooting*, quite sure or certain. *Colloq.*

1851 Howe *Hist. Coll. Great West* 311 'Hurra, Bill,' roared out Glass, as he saw the animal rushing toward them, 'we'll be made "meat" of, sure as shootin'!' **1947** *Field & Stream* June 19/2 Sure as shootin' . . . one of these days one of my customers will be coming in and telling me he caught a fish with one of your jackets.

As the last term in **bay, boat, chicken, crap, fire, jack, line, pass, point, six, slough, trouble, turkey shooting.**

shootist 'ʃutɪst, *n.* One who shoots, a marksman. *Slang. Obs.*

1864 *Gold Hill* (Nev.) *News* 15 Jan. 3/1 (*heading*), A Shootist. **1876** *Guardian* (San Bernardino, Calif.) 8 Jan. 3/1 Mr. Craig is the champion shootist of the State. **1898** Canfield *Maid of Frontier* 177 He was knowed to be a shootist and there weren't nobody hankerin' for the job of bringin' him in.

* **shop,** *n.* In combs.: (1) **shop butcher,** *local*, a butcher who sells meat on occasion, usu. from a wagon, *obs.;* (2) **call,** (see quot.), *obs.;* (3) **clerk,** one who sells goods in a shop; (4) **note,** a note or bill of credit exchangeable for goods in a shop, *obs.;* (5) **sugar,** ?sugar procured in shops, as distinguished from that made at home, *obs.*

(1) **1896** Haswell *New York* 378 Until the claim of the market butchers of having the exclusive privilege of selling meats, and that only in the public markets for which they paid a tax, was disputed by the 'shop butchers' as they were termed, and supported by the general public, meats and vegetables could only be obtained in the public markets. — (2) **1865** *Three Yrs. Among Working Classes U.S.* 186, I have seen as many as four shop-calls (meetings) in the course of a day upon as many different kinds of work. — (3) **1911** Harrison *Queed* 151 There is your public, . . . shop-clerks, stenographers [etc.]. — (4) **1739** W. Douglass *Discourse Currencies* 23 Many factors . . . send Home a high Account of Sales, by the Shopkeepers giving a great Advance in Consideration of a very long Credit, and to be drawn out in Shop Notes. **1770** *Md. Hist. Mag.* III. 245 We have . . . stated an Account to shew at one View, what Part of each Shop-Note is for the Articles prohibited. *Ib.* XII. 368 The following will Answer the Shop note you wrote for—July 4: 1770 Bought for Cha: Carroll Esqr. By Mr. Harding of Dennis Dougherty.

(5) **1687** Sewall *Letter-Book* I. 74 If the mony hold outt send a barrel or two of shopp sugar and 3 or 4 sugar loves. **1714** *Boston News-Letter* 18 Jan. 2/2 To be Sold by Mr. Thomas Cushing at his Shop; . . . Shop Sugar by the Barrel or quarter of a Hundred.

b. *To give the best one has in the shop*, and variants, to put forth one's best effort. *Colloq.*

1870 Duval *Big Foot Wallace* (1873) 66 (We.), I resolved that I would give them the best ready-made fight I had 'in the shop.' **1939** *These Are Our Lives* 143 If Thelma comes botherin' you, give her all you've got in your shop.

As the last term in **bake, barber, beauty, best, blacksmith, bucket, cabinet, candy, car, carpenter, carriage, cent, closed,**

cooky, coon barber, custom, delicatessen, drug, druggist, dry-goods, frame, gift, gospel, grocery, gun, hock, junk, lager beer, machine, Old Curiosity, open, policy, print, rat, shake, shaving, smith, soda, sweat, variety, wagon, weave, wildcat shop.

* **shop,** *v.*

1. *tr.* To dismiss or "fire" (a person). *Slang.*

1915 H. L. WILSON *Ruggles of Red Gap* iv. (1917) 76 It seemed probable that I should be shopped by Mrs. Effie for what she had been led to believe was my rowdyish behaviour. *Ib.* xvii. 308, I would have shopped the fellow in an instant, . . . had it been at any other time. He was most impertinent. **1928** E. WALLACE *Gunner* xiv, If you'd done any jobs with him, as sure as death he would have shopped you.

2. *To shop around,* to look around in quest of something.

1922 J. D. HACKETT in *Management Engineering* Feb., During the war, although orders greatly exceeded production, absentism increased. Men took days off to 'shop around,' knowing that if unsuccessful they would be welcomed back. **1931** *K.C. Times* 8 Aug., Aw, well then, we'll shop around a bit.

* **shore,** *n.* In combs.: (1) **shore bell,** (see quot.), *obs.;* (2) **bug,** any insect of the family Saldidae; (3) **cod,** (see quot. 1909); (4) **dinner,** a dinner featuring various sea foods; (5) **fishery,** (see quot.), *obs.;* (6) **lark,** the horned lark—so called because it frequents beaches; (7) * **line,** designating a road or railroad along a shore; (8) **-sman,** see as a main entry; (9) **state,** one of the states bordering on the shore of the Atlantic.

(1) **1851** WM. KELLY *Across Rocky Mts.* (1852) 32 For we did not pass a solitary shanty that a shore bell (the signal of goods for shipment) was not rung, much to the annoyance of the passengers. — (2) **1894** COMSTOCK *Man. Study Insects* 134 Some of the Shore-bugs dig burrows, and live for a part of the time beneath the ground. **1904** KELLOGG *Amer. Insects* 202 By the edge of pond or stream may be found . . . the smaller, soft, long-oval, long-legged, running shore-bugs. — (3) **1888** GOODE *Amer. Fishes* 339 'Bank Cod' and 'Shore Cod' are commercial names. **1909** WEBSTER 429/3 Fishermen on the New England coast distinguish: . . . shore, or native, cod, those from near their own shores. — (4) **1895** *Outing* XXVI. 408/2 Happy-Go-Lucky Beach is proud of their achievements . . . in the ordering of and presiding at a good shore-dinner. **1947** PAUL *Linden* 267 It was arranged for the party to eat at the Massasoit a shore dinner cooked by Jeff.

(5) **1767** T. HUTCHINSON *Hist. Mass.* (1768) II. 445 In what they call a sedentaire and we a shore fishery we shall always outdo them. — (6) **1771** J. R. FORSTER *Cat. Anim. N. Amer.* 12 Shore Lark. *Alauda alpestris.* **1893** *Scribner's Mag.* June 760/2 The artificial destruction of forest, and extension of the open country toward the Atlantic, have resulted in the eastward spread of many prairie birds, such as the shorelark and the bobolink. — (7) **1862** *Rep. Comm. Patents 1861: Agric.* 344 The shore-line road from Boston to New York crosses a large number of these marshes in the State of Connecticut. **1872** *Travelers' Official Ry. Guide* Jan. Table 69, New Haven, New London and Stonington Railroad. Operated by New York and New Haven Railroad, as Shore Line Division. — (9) **1871** *Harper's Mag.* July 188 It is a shameful omission on the part of the people of the shore States, as well as those of the interior, that [etc.].

b. (See quot. and cf. * **Eastern Shore.**)

1945 *Somerset News* 22 March 1/3 If, as Shore opponents of the repealer say, no Shore senator or delegate could hope to be re-elected next year if he voted for repeal, why then weren't Shore delegates men enough to stand up and be counted.

shoresman ˈʃorzmən, *n.* [Var. of * *shoreman* in the same sense.] One who remains on shore but is engaged in, or connected with, the fishery business.

1872 TALMAGE *Sermons* 56 Some plain shoresman in rough fishing smack . . . brings them ashore in safety. **1883** GOODE *Fisheries U.S.* 22 To the class of 'shoresmen' belong (1) the capitalists who furnish supplies and apparatus for the use of the active fishermen; (2) the shopkeepers from whom they purchase provisions and clothing; and (3) the skilled labourers who manufacture for them articles of apparel [etc.]. **1884** *Nat. Museum Bul.* No. 27, 839 *Halibut flitching knife.* . . . Used by shores-men to cut off flitches or strips of halibut for smoking and fins for pickling.

* **short,** *a., n.,* and *adv.*

1. *n.* A broker who sells for future delivery securities or commodities which he does not have at the time of the sale.

1849 G. G. FOSTER *N.Y. in Slices* 19 Some wild-looking 'short' . . . rushes down and hysterically inquires of his obliging neighbor, Mr. Smith, whether he hasn't a few hundred over. **1898** *Chi. Times-Herald* 5 April 8/1 Shorts showed their uneasiness by covering. **1949** *L.A. Times* 22 May II. 35/4 It was not in wheat . . . but in soybeans that the shorts took the worst beating.

b. *pl.* Short sales, the supply needed to meet short-sale contracts.

1868 *Terr. Enterprise* (Virginia, Nev.) 11 Feb. 3/2 We believe . . . this rise is attributable to 'cornering' of the 'shorts' below. **1881** *Harper's Mag.* April 734/2 'Spots,' 'futures,' 'longs,' and 'shorts' were unknown terms. **1902** NORRIS *Pit* 345, I'm going to buy in my July shorts.

2. In baseball, the shortstop or the position covered by this player.

1856 *Spirit of Times* 4 Oct. 86/1 The Eagle Club now made a very judicious change by placing . . . Mr. Place as short, which effectually prevented their opponents from making any more such scores as was done in the first innings. **1880** *Chi. Tribune* 29 June 8/3 Irwin covered third, and Corey short. **1949** *Democrat* 22 Sep. 2/5 The next batter hit sharply to short.

3. *a.* Having an insufficient amount of securities or commodities to meet obligations, pertaining to a transaction in "shorts."

1849 *Hunt's Merch. Mag.* XXI. 118 If he does not own the stock [which he has sold for future delivery] he is 'short,' or what is the same thing, a 'bear.' **1875** A. DALY *Big Bonanza* (1884) 20 The market opened lively with a demand for speculative shares by those who have been 'short' of the leading stocks. **1885** *Harper's Mag.* Nov. 842/1 He 'buys in' by purchasing stock to meet a 'short' contract.

4. In combs.: (1) **short bit,** see * **bit,** *n.* **2. c.** (3); (2) **bite,** grass that does not attain much height, *rare;* (3) **Boys,** (see quot. 1851), *slang;* (4) **cut,** a more direct way, also fig.; (5) **ear,** (see quot.), *obs.;* (6) **five,** a short, cheap, five-shot revolver, *rare;* (7) **game,** app. a short card game, cf. **short cards;** (8) **growth,** ?a tendency to be small or undersized, *obs.;* (9) **Hills,** a region in or near Washtenaw County, Mich., also attrib., *obs.;* (10) * **horn,** *W.* (see quot. 1944), *slang;* (11) * **horse,** a racehorse that cannot race the maximum distance, a "short runner," *rare;* (12) **order,** a restaurant order à la carte, also attrib., cf. **f.** (2) below; (13) **-quartered shoe,** a low-quarter shoe, *obs.;* (14) **road,** (see quot.); (15) **session,** before the twentieth amendment went into effect Oct. 15, 1933, the session of Congress beginning in December of even-numbered years and ending on March 3 following; (16) **shoulder,** "an undisputed proposition. *Rare*" (Th.); (17) **six,** (*a*) a kind of cigar, *obs.,* (*b*) a small candle, six of which weigh a pound [cf. *EDD* * *short sixteens*], cf. **f.** (1) below; (18) **sweetening,** sugar, *colloq.;* (19) **term,** a term of office shorter than a full term, usu. the remainder of a full term vacated by death or resignation.

(2) **1865** TURNER *Cotton* 83 It is objected to this country by planters and others taking their cue from them on account of its 'short bite' and sterile pasturage, as they are pleased to call it. — (3) **1851** *Harper's Mag.* July 276/1 A large number of Germans . . . were attacked by a gang of desperadoes from New York, known as 'Short Boys.' **1880** *Cong. Rec.* 12 April 2327/1 We should protect the ballot-box from violence, . . . from the 'short boys' and '*dead rabbits*' of this country. — (4) **1835** AUDUBON *Ornith. Biog.* I. 158 Large streams are now found to exist, where none were formerly to be seen, having forced their way in direct lines from the upper parts of the bends. These are by the navigator called *short-cuts.* **1931** *K.C. Times* 12 Aug., However, if you want to make a short cut to fame, don't go out to beat Mr. Miller's record. **1949** *L.A. Times* 5 July III. 5/5 Originally intended as a wagon road to Sturtevant Camp the trail was built . . . as a short cut to Sturtevant's land on the west fork of the San Gabriel Canyon and Newcomb's holdings at Chilao.

(5) **1851** HALL *College Words* 188 At Jefferson College, Pennsylvania, a student of a sober or religious character is denominated a *long ear.* The opposite is *short ear.* — (6) **1913** MULFORD *Coming of Cassidy* 317 Now here's your short-five. — (7) **1851** *Alta California* (S.F.) 11 Sep. 2/4 A number of witnesses . . . stated that they had heard . . . that eucre and other short games had been played, . . . but that none of them had ever been so unfortunate as to 'get stuck' at the games. — (8) **1919** DUNN *Indiana* II. 792 In my early childhood days I saw some men cut a hole through a tree and pass a delicate child through the opening, in order to cure it of a so-called 'short growth.' — (9) **1835** HOFFMAN *Far West* I. 166 My way, after going a mile or two from the village, led through oak openings of rolling land, called 'the Short Hills,' which I can best assimilate to a collection of enormous graves—the tombs of households, if you choose—thrown confusedly together

upon a perfectly level surface. **1840** in *Mich. Agric. Soc. Trans.* (1853) 285 Beyond the ranges of elevated cones which bound the shorthill district, the country continues broken for about a mile, and then subsides to a gently rolling or undulating surface.

(10) 1888 *Outing* Nov. 129/2 Besides a few snipe killed at a swamp called by Shorthorns 'cineky,' from the Spanish *sienica*, we still depended upon Uncle Sam's subsistence stores for our daily bread. **1944** ADAMS *W. Words* 143/1 shorthorn One not native to the cattle country, a tenderfoot. — **(11) 1890** BIFF HALL *Turnover Club* 119 Twelve m., purchase one pool on a short horse at Saratoga. — **(12) 1906** O. HENRY *Four Million* 103 The clatter of steel, the screaming of 'short orders,' the cries of the hungering and all the horrid tumult of feeding men. **1950** *N.O. Times-Picayune Mag.* 12 Feb. 9/1 Lash got a job as a fry cook in a short order restaurant. — **(13) 1807** IRVING *Salmagundi* xi. 285 She wore a pair of short-quartered high-heeled shoes. **1832** DUNLAP *Hist. Amer. Theatre* 27 We see the beaux of 1761, with . . . their silk stockings, short-quartered shoes, and silver or paste buckles. — **(14) 1905** *Forestry Bureau Bul.* No. 61, 38 *Go-back road*, a road upon which unloaded logging sleds can return to the skidways for reloading, without meeting the loaded sleds en route to the landing. (N[orthern] F[orest].) Syn.: short road.

(15) 1828 COOPER *Notions* II. 262 But the usual practice is to let the bodies separate, at the end of what is called the 'short session.' **1906** *K.C. Star* 3 Dec. 2/2 Both houses of Congress were to meet today for the short session. — **(16) 1849** *Knickerb.* XXXIII. 543, I believe it's reduced to a positive 'short shoulder' that the Jersey Quakers eat more pickled sturgeon than any other class of people. — **(17)** *(a)* **1838** BURTON *Comic Songster* 188 Give me some short six's. **1882** *Harper's Mag.* March 639/2 'Have you a spare cigar?' 'Yes, Sir,' (extending a short six.) *(b)* **1890** J. JEFFERSON *Autobiog.* 146 The very cornerstone of Juliet's balcony contained twenty pounds of the best 'short sixes.' — **(18) 1850** *Quincy* (Ill.) *Whig* 19 Nov. 2/2 He put . . . all the money she had in short sweetening, and left her without a cent. **1948** DICK *Dixie Frontier* 291 'Short sweetening,' or maple sugar, was also obtained in its raw state from the trees. — **(19) 1868** *N.Y. Herald* 15 July 5/2 The General Assembly to-day elected . . . General J. C. Abbott [U.S. senator] . . . for the short term. **1883** *Harper's Mag.* Sep. 642/1 Supreme Judge (short term) Martin D. Follet.

See also **short cards, change, Hairs, *meter,** as main entries.

b. In combs. with reference to baseball: (1) **short field,** the shortstop position or the fielder who plays this position; (2) **fielder,** the fielder who plays short field; (3) **fielding,** playing the position of short field; (4) **stop,** see as a main entry.

(1) 1856 *Spirit of Times* 6 Dec. 229/1 *Adams*, as short field has for many years, been deservedly distinguished. **1898** *K.C. Star* 18 Dec. 3/2 He will be found at short field on the senatorial team next season. **1948** *N.Y. Times* 25 April S1/6 Jack Conway was shifted to the short field. — **(2) 1857** *Spirit of Times* 18 July 309/3 He is a splendid short fielder. **1885** CHADWICK *Art of Pitching* 92 It is necessary that the short fielder should be a man of quick perception. **1949** *L.A. Times* 1 June IV. 2/6 In softball an extra man is used as a shortfielder who may be played in any defensive position. — **(3) 1867** *Ball Players' Chron.* 8 Aug. 1/4 The play was the perfection of short-fielding.

c. In terms pertaining to a stock exchange: (1) **short interest,** (see quot. 1900); (2) **market,** (see quot.); (3) **sale,** a contract made for the sale of securities or goods which the seller does not yet possess but which he expects to buy at a future time for less than his sale price; (4) **selling,** (see quot. 1900); (5) **trading,** =prec.

(1) 1866 *Comm. & Fin. Chron.* III. 75/2 During the week a moderate short interest has been drawn out by the dullness of the market. **1900** NELSON *A B C Wall St.* 159 *Short interest*, that interest in the market which is represented by the aggregate sales of men who have sold at a price with the expectation of buying in at a cheaper price. **1949** *Time* 30 May 73/1 By mid-May, the short interest had risen 130,058 in a month to 1,628,551 shares. — **(2) 1900** NELSON *A B C Wall St.* 159 *Short market*, an oversold market, with the aggregate contracts for the delivery of stocks exceeding the supply at a certain range of prices. — **(3) 1870** W. W. FOWLER *Ten Years in Wall Street* 31 Many devices are resorted to by the ring to induce short sales by the bears. **1911** *Amer. Year Book 1910* 385/2 All of these bills were directed against the use of 'options,' 'short sales,' and transactions in 'futures.' — **(4) 1888** *Economist* 10 Nov. 7/2 The situation, instead of being an encouragement to short selling, suddenly turned distinctly bullish. **1900** NELSON *A B C Wall St.* 159 *Short selling*, selling stocks and borrowing them for immediate delivery. When finally bought in the borrowed stock is returned. **1932** *Blue Valley Farmer* (Okla. City) 3 March 6/6 Short selling was conducive to a stable market.

(5) 1900 NELSON *A B C Wall St.* 19 In this case (short trading) the rule of trading says that the interest belongs to your broker.

d. In the names of, or with reference to, plants: (1) **short bean,** a now unidentifiable bean or variety of bean (see quot. 1790), *obs.;* (2) **corn,** ?corn of a short-eared variety, *rare;* (3) **cotton,** =**short-staple cotton,** *obs.;* (4) **grass,** used attrib. to designate a region where low prairie grass grows naturally; (5) **-hair grass,** (see quot.); (6) **-leaf pine,** a species of pine having relatively short leaves or needles, esp. *Pinus echinata;* (7) **-leaved pine,** =prec.; (8) **sauce,** (see quot. 1859); (9) **shucks,** (see quot.); (10) **-staple cotton,** any of several varieties of cotton, esp. the green-seeded cotton *q.v.*, having a relatively short staple; (11) **straw (pine),** =**shortleaf pine.**

(1) 1767 SAMUEL DEANE *Diary* (1849) 321, I planted short beans, sowed cauliflowers and apple seeds, being increase of the moon. **1790** DEANE *N.-Eng. Farmer* 20/2 The short bean is so called from its shape. — **(2) 1786** WASHINGTON *Diaries* III. 143 Measured . . . 19 Barrls. of long Corn and 6 of Short. — **(3) 1854** SIMMS *Southward Ho!* 249 Their cry is 'war,' even in the midst of prosperity, and when short-cotton is thirteen cents a pound! — **(4) 1844** GREGG *Commerce of Prairies* II. 139 We succeeded in reaching a spot of shortgrass prairie. **1945** PEARSON *Country Flavor* 33 It may have been on the short-grass, lonely prairies or in the sandy-soiled, piney regions of the South. **1948** *Gainesville* (Tex.) *D. Reg.* 2 July 4/4 On the short-grass ranges of the west, a ewe survives an average of six years.

(5) 1913 BARNES *Western Grazing Grounds* 70 A short wiry but nutritious grass known locally as short-hair grass (*Calamagrostis brewerii*), . . . will stand an immense amount of grazing without being completely killed out. — **(6) 1796** HAWKINS *Letters* 24, [I] came to oak, and short leaf pine. **1883** HALE *Woods & Timbers N.C.* 210 All the oaks grow here [in Mecklenburg Co.]; also . . . short-leaf pine and some walnut. **1947** *Democrat* 31 July 4/1 A new disease . . . is already doing great damage to the short-leaf pines in other sections. — **(7) 1743** CATESBY *Carolina* App. p. xxii, The Short-leav'd Pine is usually a small tree. **1802** DRAYTON *S. Carolina* 10 The high lands are covered with different kinds of oak . . . and short leaved pine. **1897** SUDWORTH *Arborescent Flora* 27 *Pinus virginiana*. Scrub Pine. . . . [Also called] Shortleaved Pine (N.C.). — **(8) 1809** RITSON *Poetical Picture* 76 Their long sauce, and their short sauce too, About their boats are laid in view. **1859** BARTLETT 255 Beets, carrots, and parsnips are *long sauce*. Potatoes, turnips, onions, pumpkins, etc. are *short sauce*. — **(9) 1897** SUDWORTH *Arborescent Flora* 27 *Pinus virginiana*. Scrub Pine. . . . [Also called] Short Shucks (Md., Va.).

(10) 1802 *Steele P.* I. 341 Short Staple, or Green seed Cotton if the best Quality, 16 Cents. **1891** CHASE & CLOW *Industry* II. 7 If they [*sc.* fibers] are long, the cotton is called long-staple cotton; if short, short-staple cotton. **1949** *Reader's Digest* Aug. 128/1 It is a short-staple cotton that came to the state via Texas and Oklahoma. — **(11) 1859** G. W. PERRY *Turpentine Farming* 22 We proceed now to the notice of the common short-straw pine. **1946** *Democrat* 26 Dec. 1/1 The following native pines are listed in the order of . . . susceptibility . . . slash (short straw for gum production).

e. In the names of animals: (1) **short-billed curlew,** the Hudsonian curlew; (2) **-billed (marsh) wren,** a small wren, *Cistothorus stellaris*, that frequents marshes; (3) **-legged pewee (flycatcher),** a species of wood pewee, *Myiochanes richardsoni*, found in western North America; (4) **neck,** (see quot. 1844); (5) **-nosed gar,** a ganoid fish, *Cylindrosteus platystomus*, of the eastern and central U.S.

(1) 1813 WILSON *Ornithology* VII. 22 The Esquimaux Curlew, or as it is called by our gunners on the sea-coast, the Short-billed Curlew, is peculiar to the new continent. **1917** *Birds of Amer.* I. 252. — **(2) 1844** *Nat. Hist. N.Y., Zoology* II. 58 The Short-Billed Wren . . . does not appear to be a numerous species in this State. **1874** COUES *Birds N.W.* 37 The Short-billed Marsh Wren . . . occurs along the whole Atlantic coast. **1917** *Birds of Amer.* III. 195. — **(3) 1839** AUDUBON *Ornith. Biog.* V. 299 Short-Legged Pewee Flycatcher. *Muscicapa Richardsonii*. **1858** BAIRD *Birds Pacific R.R.* 189 Short-legged Pewee. . . . High central dry plains to the Pacific; Rio Grande valley, southward to Mexico; Labrador. **1881** *Amer. Naturalist* XV. 217 The short-legged pewee . . . does not seem to be rare throughout this southern country. — **(4) 1844** *Nat. Hist. N.Y., Zoology* II. 242 The Pectoral Sandpiper, *Fringa Pectoralis*, . . . passes under the various names of Meadow Snipe, Jack Snipe, and Short-neck. **1917** *Birds of Amer.* I. 233.

(5) 1883 *Nat. Museum Bul.* No. 27, 492 *Lepidosteus platystomus*. . . . Short-nosed Gar. Great lakes; rivers of the Ohio and Mississippi Valleys, southward to the Rio Grande; Florida. **1911** *Rep. Fisheries 1908* 310/2 The short-nosed gar . . . is smaller than the preceding and has the same geographic distribution.

f. In phrases: (1) *To come to short sixes*, to fight it out, *rare;* (2) *in short order*, without delay, summarily; (3) *to sell short*, *(a)* to sell stock or goods on a stock exchange which the seller does not have at the time of the sale, *(b) fig.* to treat unfairly, *slang;* (4) *to go short*, =prec. *(a)*.

(1) **1834** SIMMS *Guy Rivers* I. 187 If you be not satisfied, why the sooner we come to short sixes the better. — (2) **1834** SIMMS *Guy Rivers* I. 204 Be off now in a hurry, or I shall fire upon you in short order. **1902** E. BANKS *Autobiog. Newspaper Girl* 27, I dressed myself in short order. — (3) (*a*) **1852** *Hunt's Merch. Mag.* XXVI. 738 The writer of the *Aurora* phillipic complains of the practice of 'selling short.' **1949** *Time* 20 June 77/1 Professional speculators, who had been selling wheat short while the price was edging down, took heavy losses. (*b*) **1946** *Democrat* 27 June 2/2 Experience has shown that it doesn't pay to sell that outfit short. **1949** *Milwaukie* (Ore.) *Review* 28 July 5/4 You're a sucker if you sell this town short. — (4) **1870** MEDBERY *Men Wall St.* 192 [He] not seldom gives his broker the order to go short 500 shares on every stock called. **1902** NORRIS *Pit* 325 Crookes and his clique had sold five million bushels, 'going short,' promising to deliver wheat that they did not own.

As the last term in **long, New England, right, stub short.**

shortage ˈʃɔrtɪdʒ, *n.* A deficit or deficiency. Also attrib.

1868 (Newspaper, April), The 'shortage war' between the shippers of grain and the skippers who carry it, is practically over. **1880** *Harper's Mag.* Oct. 726/1 In an aggregate of six carloads there was only a shortage of thirty pounds. **1946** *Chi. D. News* 6 March 1/8 You can't have four to five years of war creating a big hole of shortages then, have the war end suddenly and expect to fill that hole right away.

short cards. A card game in which complete packs are not used. Also attrib.

1845 HOOPER *Simon Suggs' Adv.* 134 Thar never were a *peaceabler* or more *gentlemanlier* game o' short cards played. **1873** in *Amer. Sp.* XXIV. (1949) 266/2 The Barbary Coast is now alive with 'jay-hawkers,' 'short-card sharps.' **1938** ASBURY *Sucker's Prog.* 286 Short card games predominated, the favorites being Brag, Poker, Seven-Up and Whist, although Checkers, Chess, Cribbage and Backgammon were also frequently played for large stakes.

short change. Money in the form of "change" which falls short of the correct amount. Also attrib.

1908 SINCLAIR *Metropolis* 351 Three times in a single day in another of these great caravansaries, Montague was offered short change. **1922** C. SANDBURG *Slabs of Sunburnt West* 6 Beat up the short change artists. **1928** FOY & HARLOW *Clowning Thro' Life* 81 Our Peanut and juice vendors were all short change artists.

short change, *v. tr.* In returning "change" in a transaction, to return less than the proper amount. Also to bamboozle, or cheat in any way. *Slang.*

1903 G. ADE *People You Know* 30 Brad was out in the back Townships short-changing the Farmers. **1931** *K.C. Times* 31 Dec. 16 One day we almost succeeded in short changing a blind woman. **1944** STOUT *Not Quite Dead Enough* 30 As for the young man, he wasn't in Leon Furey's class as a physical specimen, and they had short-changed him a little on his chin, but he would pass. **1946** *Chi. D. News* 17 May 1/6 He has never been short-changed in an arbitration case.

Hence **short changer, short changing.**

1920 C. R. COOPER *Under Big Top* 205 The gambling and the graft of the side shows, the short-changers in the 'connection,' the constant form of Temptation ever beckoning! **1948** *Dly. Ardmoreite* (Ardmore, Okla.) 18 April 2/6 School boards and school administrations are short-changing the children of America by failing to sponsor school orchestras.

Short Hairs. (See quot. 1914.) Also attrib. *Obs.*

1867 *Ball Players' Chron.* 4 July 2/1 Being assisted by their brutish followers of the short-hair grade, they generally manage to make large hauls of plunder. **1875** *Nation* 1 April 218 A very real division of the Democratic party in this city into two sets of politicians known familiarly as 'Short Hairs' and 'Swallow Tails'—the former comprising the rank and file of voters, and the latter 'the property owners and substantial men.' **1914** *Cyclo. Amer. Govt.* III. 308/1 *Short Hairs,* a term . . . denoting the common man and 'toughs' in politics in contradistinction to the fashionable 'swallow tails.'

Shortia ˈʃɔrtɪə, *n.* [Named after Chas. W. *Short* (1794–1863), Amer. botanist.] A genus of perennial plants of the family Diapensiaceae, also (not *cap.*) a smooth, stemless plant, *S. galacifolia,* found in western North Carolina.

1839 GRAY *Letters* 178 So I say, as this is a good North American genus and comes from near Kentucky, it shall be christened *Shortia.* **1877** *Field & Forest* Sep. 40 More than once I was greeted with the query 'Found "Shortey" yet?' By which I suppose was meant the mythical Shortia of Michaux, for which any enthusiastic young or old botanist is at liberty to hunt. **1891** *Cent.* 5589/2 Shortia. . . . . There are but 2 species . . . long thought the rarest of North American plants, and famed as the plant particularly associated with Asa Gray, who first described it from a fragment seen in Paris in 1839, with a prediction of its structure and relationship, verified on its first discovery in flower in 1877. **1948** *Hyde Park Shopper* (Chi.) 29 April 8/5 The rare flower, shortia, is found only in the mountains of North Carolina and Japan.

* **short meter.**

1. (See quot. *c*1870.) Also attrib. *Obs.*

1836 L. BEECHER *Plea for Colleges* 71 Half-made, selfmade men . . . are united only in their contempt of a regular education, and their eulogies of modern mental supremacy, and a short metre course. ***c*1870** CHIPMAN *Notes on Bartlett* 403 *Short Metre,* . . . a short course, as of study, &c.

2. (See quot. 1877.) Also as adv. *Obs.*

1833 S. SMITH *Life & Writings Downing* (We.), I guess I can work it out in short metre. **1847** LOWELL *Biglow P.* 1 Ser. ii. 26 Ef it worn't fer wakin' snakes, I'd home agin short meter. **1853** HALIBURTON *Sam Slick's Wise Saws* (1859) 41, I might just as well make short meter of it, and sell him at once. **1858** *Harper's Mag.* Sep. 567/1, I will hurry through the crowd and into the pulpit in short metre. **1877** BARTLETT 587 *Short Metre,* . . . in a short period; soon. To make short metre of a thing or piece of work is to do it quickly.

shortstop ˈʃɔrtˌstɑp, *n. Baseball.*

1. An infielder who covers the territory between second and third base. Cf. **right shortstop.**

1857 *Spirit of Times* 25 July 324/3 Second Nine Fahys, pitcher; . . . Smith, short stop. **1867** *Ball Players' Chron.* 13 June 2/1 This rule puts upon the short-stop or first baseman the duty, in case of 'called' passed balls, of running up to take care of the home base, leaving the catcher to throw to the pitcher at his position. **1950** *Dly. Ardmoreite* (Ardmore, Okla.) 1 March 10/5 The brilliant shortstop underwent a hernia operation in the off season and has orders to take it easy for a while.

2. The work of a fielder in the shortstop position. Also transf.

1860 in *Amer. Sp.* XXII. 205/1, I thought our fusion would be a 'short stop' to his career. **1865** *Wilkes' Spirit of Times* 19 Aug. 387/3 His catching, together with the short-stop of O'Conner, were the marked features of the Pastimes' play. **1950** *Nature Mag.* March 131/2 A sudden lunge with the net will often cut off its escape. If the net misses, a lucky shortstop may nab the lizard in passing.

3. The position in which the shortstop plays.

1867 *Ball Players' Chron.* 20 June 6/1 The playing of O. Foster at short stop was fine. **1945** *Chi. D. News* 31 Aug. 25/4 A question-mark ballplayer is slated to play short-stop for them.

Also, rarely, **short-stopper.**

1867 *Harper's Wkly.* 14 Sep. 590/1 They had, on the eighth ballot unanimously elected him a member of their Club in the position of 'short-stopper.'

Shoshonean ʃəˈʃonɪən, *a.* and *n.* [f. next.] **1.** *pl.* The Shoshoni Indians. **2. Shoshonean stock,** the linguistic stock to which these Indians belong.

(1) **1921** HALL *Yosemite Nat. Park* 51 The Mono . . . are an offshoot from the Paiutes and other Shoshoneans of Nevada and the Great Basin country. **1940** JAEGER *Calif. Deserts* 117 In historic times the Mohave Desert had fallen almost entirely into the hands of the Shoshoneans. — (2) **1903** JAMES *Indian Basketry* 158 The Panamint woman, of Death Valley, California, of Shoshonean stock, in harvesting the sand-grass seed, . . . carries in one hand a small funnel-shaped basket and in the other a paddle made of wicker work. **1949** *L.A. Times* 25 April II. 2/4 Original inhabitants . . . are believed to have been of the Shoshonean stock.

Shoshoni ʃəˈʃonɪ, *n.* [See note.]

"The origin of the term Shoshoni appears to be unknown. It apparently is not a Shoshoni word, and although the name is recognized by the Shoshoni as applying to themselves, it probably originated among some other tribe" (Hodge, II. 556/2). Cf. quot. 1918 below.

An Indian of a northern tribe of the Shoshonean branch of the Uto-Aztecan family; also, *pl.*, the tribe.

1805 LEWIS in *L. & Clark Exped.* II. (1904) The Shoshoenes may be estimated at about 100 warriors. **1848** BRYANT *California* xi. 152 One of the men called himself a Utah, the other a Shoshonee or Snake. **1918** REES *Idaho* 111 The name comes from two Indian words, 'Shawnt,' meaning 'abundance,' and 'shaw-nip,' 'grass,' which was etymologically changed to the euphonious name Shoshoni and in English conveys the thot of 'abundance of grass.' **1947** *Desert Mag.* Dec. 32/3 The Washoes . . . have long been of interest to anthropologists because their language differs so radically from that of the Paiutes and Shoshones.

attrib. **1806** LEWIS in *L. & Clark Exped.* V. (1905) 4 The Shoshone man was displeased because we did not give him as much venison as he could eat. **1881** ROMSPERT *Western Echo* 358 Small parties of Indian squaws, girls, papooses, and some old men, of the Shoshone and Winnemucca tribes, . . . would run along each side of the train and ask for biscuits. **1944** ROSS *Westward* 93 Sacajawea helped to guide the Lewis and Clark Expedition across America and back in 1804–6.

It is now accepted as historical fact that without this young Shoshone slave President Jefferson's two adventurous envoys, with their twenty-nine picked men, would never have come through to the Western Ocean. **1950** *L.A. Times* 19 Feb. v. 8/1 The savage Shoshone Indians finally came over from Lake Hughes, drove out the Paiutes and slaughtered their herd of sheep.

b. The language of these Indians. *Obs.*

1843 MARRYAT *M. Violet* xiv, I addressed him in Shoshone, which beautiful dialect is common to the Comanches, Apaches, and Arrapahoes.

* **shot,** *n.* and *a.*

1. (See quot.)

1880 *Scribner's Mo.* Aug. 492/2 The ordinary gill or drift net used for shad fishing in the Hudson is . . . divided into 'shots'. If a passing sloop or schooner catches it with her center-board or her anchor, it gives way where two of these shots meet, and thus the whole net is not torn.

2. *a.* Intoxicated. *Slang.* Cf. **3. b.** (1) (*a*) below.

1864 *Harper's Mag.* May 856/2 He again sat down by the fire, . . . by which time he was pretty well 'shot.'

3. In combs.: (1) **shot bag,** (*a*) a bag in which a hunter carries his shot, powder, etc., (*b*) a bag of a strong, closely woven fabric in which shot is put up for transport and sale; (2) **borer,** a bark beetle, *Scolytus rugulosus,* also **shot-hole borer;** (3) **bush,** (*a*) the Hercules'-club, *Aralia spinosa,* (*b*) (see quot.); (4) **gold,** placer gold found in pellets somewhat like small shot, *obs.;* (5) **gun,** see as a main entry; (6) **-hole borer,** see **shot borer;** (7) **ore,** a kind of iron ore (see quots. 1843, 1860); (8) * **pouch,** (see quot. 1888); (9) **scatter gun,** a shotgun, *colloq.*

(1) (*a*) **1638** *Md. Archives* IV. 32 Goods [include] . . . one fowling piece & shott bagge. **1784** SMYTH *Tour* I. 180 Shot bag and powder-horn . . . hang from their necks over one shoulder. **1845** HOOPER *Suggs* (1928) 79 A stake was set up close to the goal which was nearest the river, and from its top hung a huge shot-bag of crimson cloth, covered with beautiful bead-work, and filled with the silver money which was bet on the result of the game. (*b*) **1872** MARK TWAIN *Roughing It* 24 We also took with us a little shot-bag of silver coin. **1948** *Reader's Digest* May 51/1 He'd bring home the cash and put it in a shot bag. — **(2) 1890** E. A. ORMEROD *Injur. Insects* (ed. 2) 331 I found that the cause of the injury was the 'Shot-borer' Beetle (as it is called in America). **1916** *Farmers' Bul.* No. 763, 2 The shot-hole borers or barkbeetles burrow into the bark. — **(3)** (*a*) **1784** *Amer. Acad. Mem.* I. 431 *Aralia.* . . . Berry-Bearing Angelica. Shot Bush. . . . Common in new plantations. **1902** CLAPIN 360 *Shot-bush,* . . . a prickly tree shrub, also humorously called *tear-coat.* A Southern term. (*b*) **1891** *Cent.* 5590/3 *Shot-bush,* . . . the wild sarsaparilla, *Aralia nudicaulis:* from its shot-like fruit. **1949** PALMER *Fieldbook Nat. Hist.* 276/2 The plant is known as shotbush, rabbit's-root, wild licorice, and false sarsaparilla. — **(4) 1873** ARNY *Items regarding N. Mex.* 76 The gold found in the gulches is shot-gold mostly. **1874** RAYMOND *6th Rep. Mines* 303 The gold is 'shot' gold, found on a sandstone bed-rock. **(7) 1804** *Mass. H. S. Coll.* 1 Ser. IX. 255 Ledge or shot ore, yields nearly 25 per cent. of good iron. **1843** *Nat. Hist. N.Y., Geology* IV. 438 Bog iron is found in grains both loose and forming small masses in the soil. . . . It has the local name of *shot ore.* **1860** *Harper's Mag.* April 597/1 The ore . . . is composed of a very pulverulent although closely compacted mixture of small angular grains of magnetic iron ore, or magnetite, with small round granules of phosphate of lime or *apatite.* Such ore is called 'shot ore' by the miners, from its crumbling easily into small fragments. — **(8) 1888** TRUMBULL *Names of Birds* 111 Others at Detroit, and the 'punters' of St. Clair Flats, refer to the species [the ruddy duck] still as Fool-Duck, Deaf-Duck, and Shot-Pouch. **1917** *Birds of Amer.* I. 152. — **(9) 1891** SLOAN *Fogy Days* 27 They [dwellers in Piedmont hills] entertain supreme contempt for the lower country and city folks, . . . who know nothing of signs and shot-scatter guns.

b. In phrases: (1) *shot in the neck,* (*a*) drunk or partially drunk, *slang,* (*b*) a drink of liquor, *slang, obs.;* (2) (*by*) *a long shot,* (by) a great deal, *colloq.*

(1) (*a*) **1830** *Cherokee Phenix* (New Echota, Ga.) 21 April 4/3 *Counsel.* What do you mean by *corned? Witness.* I mean, pretty well *shot in the neck.* **1870** *N.O. Picayune* 17 March (De Vere), When I tried to help him up he offered to fight me, saying that he was not drunk, but only shot in the neck. (*b*) **1851** *Polly Peablossom* 180 The two then exchanged a 'shot in the neck.' — **(2) 1848** BARTLETT 215 Mr. Divver offered a resolution summarily removing the superintendent, and was quickly told . . . that he was going too fast by a long shot. . . . *Proceedings in the Case of Dr. Reese.* **1917** MCCUTCHEON *Green Fancy* 258 He fooled men a long shot keener than you are. **1946** *Chi. D. News* 6 March 2/5 That does not mean by a long shot that all 20-odd million Germans in the zone are whooping it up for Marshal Stalin.

As the last term in **BB, beaver, big, brace, buck, center, clean, crack, cross, first, grape, half, hip, kidney, line, low, mould, mustard seed, pistol, polecat, robin, single, sitting, sling, slung, squirrel shot.**

* **shote,** *n.* Also * **shoat.** An idle or contemptible fellow. *Slang. Obs.*

1800 WEEMS *Washington* (1877) 40 The poorest shoat, if wearing the proud epaulette of a Briton, might command a Wolfe, if so unlucky as to be an American. **1836** *S. Lit. Messenger* II. 664 You poor wretched shote! **1869** STOWE *Oldtown Folks* 134 Where a plague is that lazy shote of a boy?

shotgun ˈʃɑtˌgʌn, *n.*

1. A smoothbore gun for shooting shot.

1776 in RAUCK *Boonesborough* 250 They were prevented from carrying anything away except one shot gun without any ammunition. **1853** GLISAN *Jrnl. Army Life* 118 My first success in deer hunting was with a shot-gun. **1949** *Chi. D. News* 22 Nov. 12/7 The sin of attempting to shoot down a Piper Cub airplane with a shotgun.

b. With a defining term.

1848 COOPER *Oak Openings* I. 47 He and Gershom . . . [took] four pieces of fire-arms; one of which was, to use the language of the west, a double-barrelled 'shot-gun.' **1881** *Ore. State Jrnl.* 1 Jan. 7 We keep a full line of Breech and Muzzle-Loading Shotguns. **1886** *Milnor* (Dak.) *Teller* June, Guess I'll go for the galoot with a two-scatter shotgun. **1938** MATSCHAT *Suwannee River* 55 'Trembling earth, the Seminoles called it,' he told the twelve-gauge shotgun in his hand.

c. A long, boxlike wooden building. Also attrib.

1944 CLARK *Pills* 56 There was no wiser spot on earth than the porches which jutted out from the long shotgun buildings, or the whittling circles about their stoves. **1945** BOTKIN *My Burden* 98 They had to go out and live in sod houses and little old boxed shotguns and turn their Negroes loose. **1948** *Christian Sci. Mon.* 8 April 6 But there's a new type of house on the Delta, relatively speaking, the shotgun house. Rectangular, with no porches, erected row on row after the manner of company houses in the northern coal fields, it is so called 'because you can stand at the front door and shoot a shotgun shell out the back.'

d. Used allusively with reference to a **shotgun marriage** or **wedding.**

1944 *Reader's Digest* Sep. 82/1 The original wedding, following the war with Spain, was of the shotgun variety, with Uncle Sam holding the gun. **1944** CLARK *Pills* 73 If, by chance, there happened to be a little element of the shotgun mixed up in an unexpected and sudden taking of the marriage vows, the news was far more exciting and got around faster.

2. In special combs.: (1) **shotgun driveller,** a frontiersman's contemptuous term for one who uses a shotgun rather than a rifle, *rare;* (2) **marriage,** = **shotgun wedding,** *colloq.;* (3) **messenger,** an express messenger armed with a shotgun, cf. **sawed-off shotgun;** (4) **prescription,** (see quot. 1917), *colloq.;* (5) **shell,** a shell or

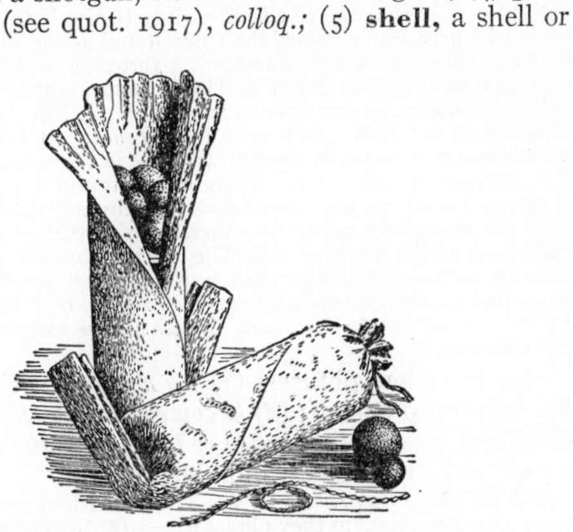

Early (*c*1865) type of shotgun shell loaded with buck and ball

cartridge for a shotgun; (6) **wedding,** a wedding resulting from indiscretions on the part of the couple, and one in which the groom participates under duress, also transf., *colloq.*

(1) 1843 CARLTON *New Purchase* I. 123 Who but a wretched dandy and shot-gun driveller . . . will fire at a flock, killing two and wounding twenty? — **(2) 1929** E. W. HOWE *Plain People* 267 Two people cordially disliked me for years because I thought it best to mention very briefly and respectfully their shot gun marriage. **1947** *Harper's Mag.* Dec. 507/1 It has no business to function—this shotgun marriage of a loyally Catholic people and a Communist government. — **(3) 1893** *Chi. Tribune* 24 April 3/1 He also has pictures of 'Mike' Tovey, a 'shot gun' messenger. **1949** HUNGERFORD *Wells Fargo* 43 The driver and the shotgun messenger alighted, and scraping away the snow, built a great fire to keep horses and passengers warm. — **(4) 1917** KEPHART *Camping* I. 246 The more popular dopes are 'shot-gun prescriptions,' compounded on the principle that if one ingredient misses another may hit. **1926** DE KRUIF *Microbe Hunters* 155 And now Pasteur, with his characteristic impetuousness . . . became more arrogant than ever with the old-fashioned doctors who talked Latin words and wrote shot-gun prescriptions.

(5) 1944 *Reader's Digest* March 44 But these, instead of bein' loaded with one solid slug, were packed with buckshot, so that the round looked like a huge shotgun shell. **1949** *This Week Mag.* 15 Oct. 27/4 They remove the shot from a shotgun shell. — **(6) 1927** BENÉT *J. B.'s Body* 131 'A shotgun wedding,' he said, . . . 'wasn't like that.' **1950** *Calif. Citrograph* Jan. 89/2 Werdel . . . characterized the Brannan plan as a 'shotgun wedding between agriculture and labor.'

b. With **policy, quarantine, rule, system,** in the sense of enforced with a shotgun or by violence. *Colloq.*

1880 *Cong. Rec.* 10 March 1450/1 The shot-gun policy, which worked so well in 1876, . . . has been continued to the present time. — **1883** *Cent. Mag.* July 431/1 To the merchant, 'shot-gun quarantines' throughout the southern Mississippi valley explained themselves. — **1881** HAVILAND *Woman's Work* 502 Shot-gun rule still continued. — **1893** *Cong. Rec.* 5 Oct. 2171/2 You were not able to produce a single instance of intimidation or violence . . . in the period in which you say the elections were conducted under the 'old shotgun system.'

As the last term in **plantation, sawed-off, Tennessee shotgun.**

shotgun ˈʃɑtˌgʌn, *v. tr.* To make (one's way) by means of a shotgun. *Rare.* — **1882** G. A. SALA *Amer. Revisited* I. 87 And our people sabred and shot-gunned their way to liberty.

* **shoulder,** *n.* In combs.: (1) **shoulder draw,** (see quot.); (2) **-hitter,** see as a main entry; (3) **holster,** =next; (4) **scabbard,** (see quot.); (5) **stone,** a stone used as a shot in the shot-put, *obs.;* (6) * **strap,** a soldier, esp. an officer; (7) **striker,** =**shoulder-hitter,** also **shoulder striking,** *colloq., obs.*

(1) 1944 ADAMS *W. Words* 143/2 shoulder draw A draw made from a shoulder holster under the arm pit. — **(3) 1944** [see **shoulder draw**]. **1948** *Westerners' Brand Book* 51 It was also a prophetic suggestion of the shoulder holster. — **(4) 1927** SIRINGO *Riata* 136 Under his left arm young Harden had a powder-and-ball pistol, in what afterwards became famous as the 'Wess Harden [a noted desperado] shoulder scabbard.' The writer still has one of those shoulder scabbards to be worn under the clothing, out of sight, which he has had for over forty years.

(5) 1791 *Wheeleys Baptist Ch. Min.* July (Univ. N.C. MS), Brother Richard Burch Came before the Church and acknowledged himself guilty of joining with the wicked in . . . throwing the Shoulder Stone. — **(6)** [**1863** WHITMAN *Diary* 50 There is a rather notable absence of military uniforms on the floor of the house; . . . I do not see a single shoulder-strap.] **1895** REMINGTON *Pony Tracks* 241 One by one the 'shoulder-straps' crawl in through the hole in the tepee. — **(7) 1852** *S.F. Picayune* 24 March 2/5 There is in this city a party of from a dozen to twenty young men, known usually as 'shoulder strikers,' who are constantly going about creating disturbances. **1856** *Alta California* (S.F.) 19 May 2/1 The election bullies, the notorious 'shoulder-striking' gang, . . . are terror stricken by the exhibition of yesterday. **1866** LOWELL *Biglow P.* 2 Ser. p. lvii, *Shoulder-hitters:* I find that *shoulder-striker* is old, though I have lost the reference to my authority.

b. In colloq. phrases: (1) *To overleap one's shoulders,* to overextend oneself; (2) *to come from the shoulder,* to be open and straightforward; (3) *to do from the shoulder,* to accomplish by one's own unaided efforts.

(1) 1834 SIMMS *Guy Rivers* II. 102 The pedler had somewhat 'overleaped his shoulders,' as they phrase it. — **(2) 1873** MILLER *Amongst Modocs* 308 No one cared, so long as he fought with men who 'came from the shoulder,' or were on the 'cut and shoot.' — **(3) 1943** HOLT *Carver* 233 All of this work Professor Carver had to do from the shoulder.

As the last term in **Boston, short shoulder.**

* **shoulder,** *v. tr.* To cross the shoulder of (a mountain). *Rare.* — **1891** *Harper's Mag.* Sep. 578/1 Jo struck across country to shoulder Ouse Mountain.

shoulder-hitter ˈʃoldɚˌhɪtɚ, *n.* A ruffian, bully, or rowdy. *Slang.* Cf. **shoulder striker.**

1855 M. THOMPSON *Doesticks* 228 [At] the Bowery Theatre . . . adolescent 'shoulder hitters' and politicians in future take their first lessons in rowdyism. **1903** LEWIS *Boss* 60 There were a round twenty of my Tin Whistles, each a shoulder-hitter and warm to shine in the graces of Big Kennedy. **1938** ASBURY *Sucker's Prog.* 124 In many cities the rowdy element—the plug-uglies of Baltimore and the bullies and shoulder-hitters of New York and Philadelphia—had already begun to acquire the power and influence which were destined to prove so useful to the politicians in perpetuating the rule of their corrupt machines.

Also **shoulder-hitting,** *a.*

1861 *N.Y. Herald* 1 Jan. 4/4 The feudal sovereignty of a shoulder-hitting *régime* has the acknowledged background, the impregnable defence, of municipal robbery.

* **shout,** *n.* An occasion of shouting as an expression of religious emotions. *Colloq.*

1862 E. W. PEARSON *Lett. Port Royal* 27 We asked Cuffy if they considered the 'shout' as part of their religious worship. *Ib.* 34 They had a 'Shout,' which I had heard distinctly at three o'clock in the morning. **1867** *Nation* 30 May 432/2 The true 'shout' takes place on Sundays or on 'praise' nights through the week. **1947** *Time* 8 Sep. 25/3 Last fortnight he got up another shout in Summerville, a county seat in the northwest corner of the state.

As the last term in **dead, live, war shout.**

* **shout,** *v.* **1.** *intr.* To say something significant or to the purpose. *Slang.* **2.** Of a thing: To be obvious or conspicuous. *Colloq.* **3.** To be vociferous about something. *Slang.*

(1) 1875 *Scribner's Mo.* Nov. 142/1 Said he, perversely, 'Now yer shoutin'!' **1911** SAUNDERS *Col. Todhunter* 99 'You're shoutin' now, Colonel,' agreed Sim. — **(2) 1892** *Pall Mall Gaz.* 25 July 3/1 Figures which, to use an Americanism, fairly 'shout.' — **(3) 1901** FLYNT *World of Graft* 175 I'm shoutin' 'bout the days when the coin came easy.

* **shouter,** *n.* One who loudly supports a political candidate. *Slang.* — **1875** *Wkly. New Mexican* 13 Oct. 2/1 The Carleton and Perea 'shouters,' got up a procession with banners, transparencies and noise. **1904** *Rochester Post Express* 26 May 4 The canvass of the state was very thorough, Hearst shouters being busily engaged in every city and village.

* **shouting,** *a.* and *n.* **1. shouting bee,** an occasion when there is much shouting as a result of religious emotion. *Obs.* **2. shouting Methodist,** a Methodist who shouts during religious excitement. Also attrib.

(1) 1902 HARBEN *A. Daniel* 116 He's come nigher . . . to turn me into the right way than all the shoutin'-bees I ever attended. — **(2) 1851** *Polly Peablossom* 87 Forgeron was from that time 'a shouting Methodist.' **1875** BURROUGHS *Winter Sunshine* 23 About the only genuine shouting Methodists that remain are to be found in the coloured churches. **1923** J. H. COOK *On Old Frontier* 231 A great revivalist of the shouting Methodist school, who could soon have great numbers of blind followers under the influence of 'the power.'

* **shove,** *v.* * *To shove out,* to depart, to set out *for.* Also * *to shove off. Colloq.*

1856 MARK TWAIN *Adv. of T. J. Snodgrass* (1928) 31 (R.), I shoved out for the Massasawit House. **1895** ——— *How to Tell a Story* (1900) 232 (R.), So he . . . tuck his lantern and shoved out thoo de storm. **1949** *Sierra Club Bul.* June 24 When we reached Charlotte Lake, he and his side-kick, *Snake,* simply shoved off and went home.

* **shovel,** *n.*

1. *S.* =**shovel plow.** See * **twister.**

1854 DAVIS *Farm Bk.* 32 Working in the shops making sweeps & shovels.

2. In combs.: (1) **shovel bill,** a shovel fish; (2) **-billed cat,** (see quot.); (3) **bonnet,** a slat bonnet *q.v., colloq.;* (4) **cake,** ?a flat cake shaped somewhat like a shovel, *obs.;* (5) **cultivator,** a farm cultivator having a number of small shovels on it; (6) * **fish,** the paddlefish, *Polydon spathula,* cf. **flat nose** and **shovel nose;** (7) * **head,** the shovel-nosed sturgeon, *Scaphirhynchus platyrhynchus;* (8) **nose,** a shovel-nosed fish (see quots. and cf. **sand shark**); (9) * **plow,** see as a main entry; (10) **stiff,** a laborer on a railroad section gang, *slang;* (11) **sweep,** *S.* a solid sweep somewhat resembling a large shovel; (12) **weed,** the shepherd's purse.

(1) 1944 *Chi. D. News* 17 July 21/1 If you are a born hillbilly, . . . you jab at . . . red-horse, shovel-bills, and other strangely named creatures of the river. — **(2) 1890** *Geol. Survey Tex. Rep.* 487 Of the catfish there are four kinds, channel cats, yellow cats, mud cats, and shovel-billed cats. — **(3) 1901** CHURCHILL *Crisis* 324 It was a shovel bonnet, with long red ribbons that tied under her chin. — **(4) 1858** *Acc. Newport* (De Vere), Shovel-cakes are still to be had by a hungry generation, and the griddles of Mrs. Durfee in the Tea-house at the Glen, shall not want an historian as they have not wanted troops of lovers.

(5) 1869 *Rep. Comm. Agric. 1868* 236 They are sometimes very expeditiously covered . . . with the mold-board or the shovel cultivator. **1930** *Lerna* (Ill.) *Wkly. Eagle* 7 Feb. 2/1 Public Sale. . . . One sulky plow; one Blackhawk corn plow; . . . two shovel cultivators. — **(6) 1816** D. THOMAS *Travels Western Country* (1819) 211 The *shovel fish* or *flat nose* is another species of sturgeon. **1911** *Rep. Fisheries 1908* 313/1 Local names are 'spoonbill,' 'duckbill cat,' and 'shovelfish.' — **(7)** [**1881** *Cassell's Nat. Hist.* V. 45 The second genus, called the Shovel-head (*Scaphirhynchus*), is represented by a single species, . . . found in the Mississippi.] — **(8) 1709** LAWSON *Carolina* 155 Of these [sharks] there are two sorts; one call'd Paracooda-Noses; the other Shovel-Noses. **1894** *Outing* XXIV. 60/2 The big 'pike' was slow in its movements, and Jack had plenty of warning before the shovel-nose showed in the rapid right at his feet. **1911** *Rep. Fisheries 1908* 317/1 The various species [of sturgeon] are known as 'lake sturgeon,' 'white sturgeon,' 'shovelnose,' etc.

(10) 1913 *Voice of People* (N.O.) 20 Nov. 1/3 Two thousand shovel stiffs . . . just came out on strike on the Pacific Great Eastern Railway. **1936** LAUT *Romance of Rails* 116 The Irish-American . . . became on the rails the grader, the shovel and pickaxe brigade, the contractor and, in not a few cases, the president of the rail on which he had begun as a 'shovel stiff.' — **(11) 1944** CLARK *Pills* 264 Like an ancient and stubby shovel sweep which had been dragged through too many long furrows, the force of life in these individuals was gradually blunted and worn away. — **(12) 1893** *Amer. Folk-Lore* VI. 137 *Capsella bursa-pastoris*, shovel weed. Penobscot Co., Me.

b. In colloq. phrases: (1) *shovel and tongs*, with energy, relentlessly; (2) *to put in one's shovel*, to interest oneself in a matter, to "put in one's oar."

(1) 1843 STEPHENS *High Life N.Y.* I. 40 Arter rolling up his shirt sleeves and spitting on his hands . . . , he went at it shovel and tongs. **1857** *Lawrence Republican* 13 Aug. 3 Of course it pitches into the Free-State men pellmell, shovel and tongs, head over heels. — **(2) 1884** MARK TWAIN *H. Finn* v. 31 (R.), Who told the widow she could put in her shovel about a thing that ain't none of her business?

As the last term in **canal, cotton, ditching, horse, ox, scoop, steam, team shovel.**

shovel plow. *S.*

1. A plowshare shaped somewhat like the blade of a ditching shovel. See * **twister.**

The 1801 example of *shovel plough* in the *OED* app. refers to a different implement.

1805 PARKINSON *Tour* 492 There is what they [i.e., the Americans] call a shovel-plough, something like a paring-spade, that I do not think worth describing. **1842** in TURNER *Cotton* (1865) 55 The next operation to be performed, as early as possibly convenient, is to plough out the middles well, the wide way, with a good shovel-plough, having first run around the young plant with a scooter-plough. **1932** W. KELLEY *Inchin' Along* 53 All his plowshares he shined until they glinted by scraping them in the earth . . . his various sized shovel-plows, his scooters and scrapers.

2. shovel plow stock, a light wooden plow stock to the "foot" of which a shovel plow is or may be attached.

1850 in TURNER *Cotton* (1865) 35 This stick of wood is rounded below, and fastened to a shovel-plough stock. **1852** *Ib.* 15 These I would cover with a board, . . . with a hole bored in the centre one inch from the upper edge, and screwed on the foot of a common shovel or scooter plough stock.

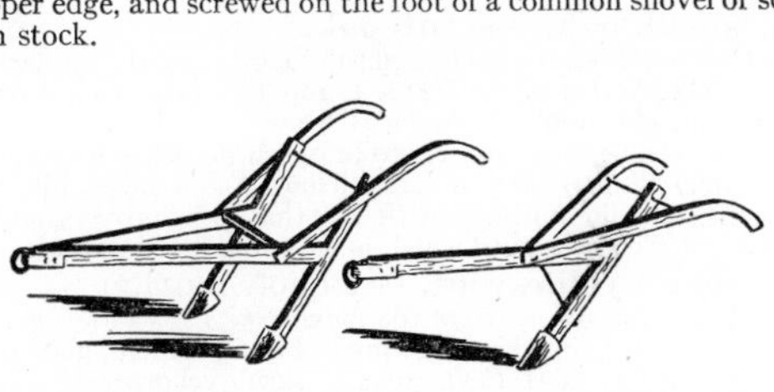

Homemade shovel plow stocks of single and double type

***shover,** *n.* One who passes counterfeit money. *Slang.* — **1859** *U.S. Police Gaz.* (N.Y.) 14 May 4/3 A 'shover' named Flynn, . . . obtained a quantity of 'queer' and went with it to Mrs. Beemer's house and left it on her table. **1896** *Cin. Enquirer* 21 Aug. 6/7 This is about the fourth time . . . that McCullough has been made the victim of shovers of the queer.

* **show,** *n.*

1. An opportunity for doing something, a chance.

The *OED* records one ex., of 1579, of *show* in this sense, but it was app. a nonce use.

1856 *Spirit of Times* 6 Sep. 11/2 If not always the winner, he has been able . . . to [give] his friends and backers a 'fair show' for their money, even if they were betting odds! **1903** *Out West* June 726 I've got a show for this money, and you two gentlemen can bet on the side. **1926** ROBERTS *Time of Man* 207 You got no show, Sallie Brown.

2. = **show-down.**

1887 KELLER *Draw Poker* 29 The previous bettor may . . . call for a show for that amount.

3. In combs.: (1) **showboat, -down,** see as main entries; (2) **dress,** a dress worn by a slave while being shown for sale, *obs.;* (3) **town,** a good town in which to give theatrical performances; (4) **window,** a display window in a store.

(2) 1853 STOWE *Key* 164/1 Gay calico was bought for them to make up into 'show dresses,' in which they were to be exhibited on sale. — **(3) 1888** E. O. SEILHAMER *Hist. Amer. Theatre* I. 81 Williamsburg, Annapolis, New York and Philadelphia—were mere villages in comparison to what is called 'a good show town' in the theatrical slang of this age. **1946** *This Week Mag.* 10 Aug. 4/2 St. Louis, never a world-beater as a show town, wasn't in the market. — **(4) 1840** *N.Y. Mirror* 9 May 367/3 The show-windows of the picture-stores in Broadway exhibit very attractive things. **1914** BOWER *Flying U Ranch* 33 Where do you keep him when he ain't in the show window? **1947** MOTLEY *Knock on Any Door* 22 A man walked by the shop and looked down into the show window.

b. In various colloq. phrases in the sense of affair, chance, matter, concern, as (1) *The show is over,* (2) *to go on with the show,* (3) *to have no show,* and variants, (4) *the whole show, to boss the whole show.*

(1) 1797 H. W. FOSTER *Coquette* 138 The show is over, as we yankees say; and the girl is my own. — **(2) 1867** LOCKE *Swingin' Round* 243 The delegashens bein all in, it wuz decided to go on with the show. — **(3) 1868** WHYMPER *Alaska* 282 'Show,' or 'colour,' from the indications of gold in gravel or sand, are words used in various shapes. 'I have not a show' means I have no chance. **1884** MARK TWAIN *H. Finn* iii. 18 (R.), A poor chap would stand considerable show with the widow's Providence. **1907** WHITE *Arizona Nights* 73 The bad man takes you unawares. . . . He don't give you no show, and sooner or later he's going to get you in the safest and easiest way for himself. — **(4) 1889** *Daily News* (London) 9 Feb. 6/1 The U.B. endeavoured . . . to control the funds and operations of the League—to 'boss the whole show,' . . . making use of a familiar American expression. **1901** MCCUTCHEON *Graustark* 123 We seem to be the whole show here. **1922** A. BROWN *Old Crow* 31, I hate the whole blamed show.

As the last term in **baby, beauty, bench, big, bunko, Creole, dime, floor, horse, medicine, minstrel, monkey, Negro, nickel, picture, road, side, snow, store, Tom, wagon, wild west show.**

* **show,** *v.*

1. show-me, used attrib. in the sense of demanding demonstration, believing only upon direct evidence. *Colloq.*

1909 *N.Y. Ev. Post* 19 April 88 Everything indicative of the 'show me' club. **1947** *Chi. Tribune* 14 Oct. 1/1 Many Republicans and Democrats are taking a 'go slow' and 'show me' approach to the problem of foreign relief.

b. Show Me State, Missouri, a nickname.

1909 *N.Y. Ev. Post* 19 April 88 Everything indicative of the 'show me' State of Missouri. **1948** *Democrat* 2 Dec. 7/2 There is a doubt about Mr. Truman's claim to fame as the first chief executive to hail from the 'Show Me' state.

2. In phrases: (1) *To show down,* in poker, to display one's cards, also fig.; (2) *to show foot,* to put the foot forward preparatory to action, *rare;* (3) *to show leg,* to run away, *rare;* (4) *to show out,* to make a display of oneself, to show off, *colloq.*

(1) 1879 *Caddo* (Indian Terr.) *Free Press* 20 June 4/2 The officials at Washington have tried another game of bluff and been obliged to show down a losing hand. **1902** LORIMER *Lett. Merchant* 234 They just had to . . . pass you the pot when you showed down. **1904** W. H. SMITH *Promoters* 129 Don't show down till you're called. — **(2) 1825** NEAL *Bro. Jonathan* I. 269 Carter . . . began to 'show foot' for another, and more active demonstration. *Ib.* 271 [The wrestlers] drew up—made play—showed foot—half locked—sprang at each other. — **(3) 1837** BIRD *Nick of Woods* I. 120 I'll fight for you, or run for you, . . . shake fist or show leg. — **(4) 1889** MARY E. WILKINS *Far-away Melody* (1890) 258 See that old lady trailing her best black silk by. . . . Ain't it ridiculous how she keeps on showing out?

showboat ˈʃoˌbot, *n.* A river boat provided with a theater and carrying a troupe of actors who give plays at various stops along the stream.

1869 *Atlantic Mo.* July 82/2 Jealousy may be as rife on a Mississippi show-boat as in the antechamber of any court in Europe. **1909** RICE *Mr. Opp* 98 A new and handsome Show Boat will tie up at the Cove. **1946** *This Week Mag.* 10 Aug. 4/2 Captain Bill is a relic from a past century—the never-say-die proprietor of America's last river show-boat.

attrib. and *transf.* **1949** *In Kentucky* Summer 43/1 Visitors from miles around came to the city for showboat entertainment. **1949** KITCHIN *Birds Olympic Peninsula* 15 When hatched, the little black 'grebelings' have a way of riding on the parent's back, a pretty sight, and one hums 'Here comes the Show Boat' as she glides through the reeds with her deck load!

showdown ˈʃoˌdaʊn, *n.* [Cf. * **show,** *v.* **2.** (1).]

1. In poker, a play in which a bet is called and the hands of the players are shown.

1884 *Gringo & Greaser* 15 Feb. 2/2 In the show down Estevan held only a bobtail flush. **1898** W. C. MORROW *Ape, Idiot* 159 Never disclose your hand except on a showdown. **1946** MOREHEAD & MOTT-SMITH *Penguin Hoyle* 132 When the hands are shown in the showdown, the player showing the highest-ranking poker hand takes in the pot.

2. In a business or other deal, an action bringing matters to an issue, an open disclosure of plans, means, etc.

1895 *Chi. Strike of 1894* 32 Where I had to deal with the devil and wanted a show-down, ... I had enough sense to know that my only hope was to go into partnership with him. **1904** *N.Y. Globe* 28 March 2 A 'show-down' disclosed the fact that all the district leaders were with him. **1949** *News-Herald* (Marshfield, Wis.) 19 July 4/4 The House un-American Activities Committee held a showdown, closed-door session on their demands to investigate ... the Alger Hiss trial.

* **shower,** *n.*

1. A shower bath, or a place for taking such a bath.

1851 *Knickerb.* XXXVIII. 178, I must go and take a 'shower' in the adjoining bath-room. **1892** *Outing* Jan. 303/2 The old boat house had no modern arrangements for 'showers.' **1947** *Mazama* Oct. 2/1 The installation of showers will have to be put aside until such times as the Committee sees its way clear of present obligations.

attrib. **1932** *K.C. Times* 3 Feb. 16 One should be in the shower room after a Business Men's Gym Club meeting and see the swell line of hotel towels.

2. A party at which presents are given to a person, esp. to a prospective bride, or to an institution.

[**1891** *Standard* 1660/2 Shower.... An abundant supply; as, a *shower* of gifts.] **1905** *D.N.* III. 94 *Shower*, a party given a prospective bride, at which she receives presents of some one kind. **1925** *Chattanooga* (Tenn.) *Times* 11 Oct. 29/1 Miss Gladys Hanes ... will give a shower in her honor on Thursday. **1945** *Boulder* (Colo.) *D. Camera* 1 Nov. 8/5 There will be a shower of dishes and silverware; each member has been asked to bring any odds and ends of dishes or silver, to be used by the Shrine until complete new sets can be purchased—the Shrine's dishes and silver were lost in the fire last spring. **1949** *Democrat* 22 Sep. 5/2 (*caption*), Mrs. Jack Fleming is Honored at Shower.

b. Also with defining terms. Cf. **kitchen shower, linen shower.**

1945 *E. Jefferson Sentinel* (Edgewater, Colo.) 26 July 5/4 Mrs. Don Noyce will be hostess at a stork shower Friday evening honoring Mrs John Murray. **1947** *Woodlawn Booster* (Chi.) 20 Aug. 1/4 On July 21st thirty people attended a miscellaneous shower given in honor of the bride. **1949** *L.A. Times Home Mag.* 8 May 14/3 Wedding showers, though not strictly comme il faut, are a particularly warmhearted American custom.

As the last term in **dry, moon, snow shower.**

* **showing,** *n.* A display or performance of an indicated kind. — **1869** *Rep. Comm. Agric. 1868* 51 This is a very meager showing, but an export of ten times the amount would be worse. **1902** LORIMER *Lett. Merchant* 141, I would feel a good deal happier over your showing if you would make a downright failure or a clean-cut success once in a while.

showt'l ˈʃotl, *n.* (See quot. 1910, and cf. **sewellel.**) Also with defining terms.

1859 BAIRD *Mammals N. Amer.* 354 This animal ... is now called Showt'l. **1910** HODGE *Amer. Indians* II. 558/1 Showtl. A name of a species of rodent (*Haplodon rufus*) of parts of the Oregon-British Columbia region, known as the *sewellel* (q.v.) or *shavt'l*, the name of this animal in the Nisqualli and closely related Salishan dialects. **1947** CAHALANE *Mammals N. Amer.* 550 Others taken from various Indian languages of the Northwest, are *showt'l* or *showtl, squallah,* and *sh'auch.*

* **showy,** *a.* **1. showy ladyslipper** (or **lady's slipper**), a pink-and-white-flowered American orchid, *Cypripedium reginae.* **2. showy orchid, orchis,** a North American orchid, *Galeorchis spectabilis.*

(1) **1857** GRAY *Botany* 454 Showy Lady's Slipper.... The most beautiful of the genus. **1939** *Nat. Geog. Mag.* Aug. 271/2 They are distinctive but not entirely unique in the possession of a sac or slipper-like lip, which may be less than half an inch long ... in some of the small-flowered species, or an inch and a half in the moccasin flower ... or the showy ladyslipper. — (2) **1857** GRAY *Botany* 443 Showy Orchis.... On hills in rich woods, New England to Kentucky. **1890** *Cent.* 4141/3 The common American species of *Orchis* is *O. spectabilis,* the showy orchis. **1939** *Nat. Geog. Mag.* Aug. 268/2 From April to June showy orchids must be sought in rich woods of the East and Middle West.

* **shredder,** *n.* A machine for shredding (1) stalks of sugar cane in the grinding process, (2) the stalks of corn, with the ears, leaves, and husks, for ensilage, (3) wheat.

(1) **1887** *Cent. Mag.* Nov. 113/2 The canes ... [go] first to a 'shredder.' — (2) **1907** BAILEY *Cyclo. Amer. Agric.* II. 412/1 Shredders are now growing in favor, which strip the husks from the ears and at the same time tear or chop the fodder into very fine particles. — (3) **1909** *Cent. Supp.* 1214/1 Shredder.... Prepared whole wheat is fed between each pair of rolls and is torn into long threads.

shrew mole. Any mole of the genera *Scalopus* and *Scapanus.* Also with defining term.

1826 GODMAN *Amer. Nat. Hist.* I. 84 The shrew-mole is found abundantly in North America, from Canada to Virginia. **1842** *Nat. Hist. N.Y., Zoology* I. 17 The Shrew-mole has a wide geographical range. **1905** ELLIOT *Check List Mammals* 466 *Neurotrichus gibbsi....* Gibbs' Shrew Mole. *Ib.* 467 *Neurotrichus gibbsi major....* Large Shrew Mole. *Ib., Neurotrichus gibbsi hyacinthinus....* Hyacinthine Shrew Mole.

* **Shrewsbury,** *n.* **1.** An oyster taken from the Shrewsbury River in New Jersey. **2. Shrewsbury fever,** (see quot.). *Obs.*

(1) **1841** *Spirit of Times* 16 Oct. 394/1 (We.), The larder will be found to contain ... several kinds of the finest oysters, including the most splendid 'Shrewsbury!' **1868** ROSE *Great Country* 25 They [oysters] are called by many names; 'saddle rocks,' 'blue points,' and 'Shrewsburys,' being the most popular. — (2) **1849** *Knickerb.* XXXIV. 423 Although in these mountain districts we feel comparatively free from apprehension of the cholera, we have had an impressive reminder of the pestilence in the ravages which a disease, called the Shrewsbury fever, has made in a family living a few hundred feet behind us.

* **shrike,** *n.* As the last term in **Great American, loggerhead, migrant, northern shrike.**

shrimp gumbo. Gumbo in which shrimps are the principal ingredient. — [**1805** in *Amer. Pioneer* II. 233 This last [gumbo] is made of every eatable substance, and especially of those shrimps which can be caught at any time.] **1938** MATSCHAT *Suwannee River* 255 The supper was fresh shrimp gumbo, hot and highly spiced.

Shriner ˈʃraɪnɚ, *n.* A member of the Order of Nobles of the Mystic Shrine, established in the U.S. in 1872.

1889 in *Hist. Imperial Council* (2nd. ed. 1921) 92 His name was used as 'one of the original Thirteen Shriners' that were mentioned as the formative Body who instituted the Mystic Shrine in 1871. **1904** *Pittsburgh Gaz.* 14 July 10 Many bands were composed entirely of Shriners, robed in gaudy yet beautiful costumes of the lands of Mohammed. **1949** *Chi. D. News* 13 Aug. 5/7 We saw many out-of-town visitors—Shriners and Legionnaires.

* **shrub,** *n.*

1. shrub oak, = **scrub oak.**

1778 CARVER *Travels* 508 The Shrub Oak is exactly similar to the oak tree. **1832** WILLIAMSON *Maine* I. 109 The *Shrub* Oak grows 8 or 10 feet in height. **1907** *St. Nicholas* May 620/2 He wore ... stout shoes, [and] strong gray trousers to brave shrub-oaks and smilax.

attrib. **1829** *Western Mo. Rev.* April 604 A few miserable, stinted shrubberies of a diminutive growth, like that, which covers our shrub-oak plains, called musquito wood, is only found at intervals.

2. shrub yellowroot, (see quot. 1891).

1785 MARSHALL *Amer. Grove* 168 *Xanthorhiza simplicissima.* Shrub Yellow Root.... This shrub ... might be employed to good purpose in dying cloaths. **1891** *Cent.* 5602/3 shrub-yellowroot.... A low shrubby ranunculaceous plant, *Xanthorrhiza apiifolia,* of the Alleghany region. Its bark and its rootstock are deep-yellow and bitter, and were once used by the Indians for dyeing. **1933** SMALL *Southeastern Flora* 511 X. simplicissima.... Yellow-root. Shrub yellow-root.

As the last term in **chaparral, high water, indigo, papaw, raspberry, strawberry, sweet, sweet-scented, tallow, tobacco shrub.**

* **shuck,** *n.*

1. The husk of an ear of corn. Usu. *pl.*

[**1782** WASHINGTON in Haworth *George Washington* 52 My countrymen are too much used to corn blades and corn shucks and have too little knowledge of the profit of grass land.] *a***1805** *Steele P.* II. 864 Anderson ... cribbed 40 wagon Loads of corn in shucks. **1824** SINGLE-

TON *Letters* 82 What in New England is called the husk of corn, in Virginia is called the *shuck.* **1850** GARRARD *Wah-To-Yah* xiv. 175 The shucks are dried and cut in slips, one and a half inches broad by three in length. . . . When the shuck lights, the burning roll is drawn in the tube. **1948** *Democrat* 15 July 1/4 During the next few weeks cribs should be well cleaned of all old shucks and corn.

b. (See quot. 1859.)

1859 BARTLETT 404 *Shucks.* . . . At the South, where the word is most in use, it is also applied to the shells of oysters. **1881** INGERSOLL *Oyster Industry* 248.

2. (See quot.) *Obs.*

1871 DE VERE 47 During the Civil War . . . the original Blue Backs of the Confederacy (so-called in opposition to the Green Backs of the Union) soon became known as Shucks, a name sufficiently significant of their evil repute as a circulating medium.

3. In combs.: (1) **shuck basket,** *S.* a basket, usu. a dilapidated or worn-out one, for shucks; (2) **beans,** (see quot. 1913); (3) **bed,** a bed having a shuck mattress; (4) **bottom,** a chair bottom made of plaited corn shucks, also attrib.; (5) **-bottomed chair,** a chair having a shuck bottom; (6) **cigar,** *S.W.* a roll of tobacco inclosed in a corn shuck for smoking; (7) **cigarette,** a cigarette the wrapper of which is a piece of corn shuck; (8) **cigarillo,** a small shuck cigar, *rare;* (9) **collar,** see as a main entry; (10) **doll,** a doll made of a corn shuck, cf. **corncob doll;**

Shuck dolls of a type used by Iroquois Indian children

(11) **footmat,** a mat, usu. circular, made of plaited shucks; (12) **hat,** a hat for girls and women made of shucks; (13) **house,** *S.* on a farm, an outhouse in which shucks are stored; (14) **mattress,** a mattress filled with shucks; (15) **pen,** *S.* a pen, usu. of rails, where shucks are kept, esp. for use as fodder; (16) **rack,** *S.* a rack in which shucks for cattle are placed; (17) **tea,** a tea made of shucks, valued as a folk remedy; (18) **tick,** a bedtick filled with shucks.

(1) **1866** C. H. SMITH *Bill Arp* 123 My worldly possessions . . . [included] a shuck basket full of some second-class vittels. — (2) **1913** KEPHART *So. Highlanders* 292 Green beans in the pod are called snaps, when shelled they are shuck-beans. **1949** *Sat. Ev. Post* 16 April 146/4 Bubbly aroma of shuck beans, fat back, gritted bread and gravy mingled with the hickory-smoke incense. — (3) **1844** KENDALL *Narr. Santa Fé Exped.* II. 97 He gave us . . . a shuck bed to sleep upon. — (4) **1872** EGGLESTON *End of World* 282 Jonas . . . was sitting on a 'shuckbottom' chair. **1898** E. C. HALL *Aunt Jane* 4 The chairs were ancient Shaker rockers, some with homely 'shuck' bottoms.

(5) **1841** *S. Lit. Messenger* VII. 775/1 The more provident part of the slaves . . . [manufacture] shuck-bottomed chairs, mats, shuck collars, brooms, and the like. **1888** EGGLESTON *Graysons* xxxi, He drew up another shuck-bottomed chair. — (6) **1841** KENDALL in *N.O. Picayune* 26 June 2/2 Of the Mexican population [at San Antonio, Tex., the men are] . . . extremely fond of smoking *shuck cigars.* **1850** GARRARD *Wah-To-Yah* xviii. 211 In my dreams, *rebozas,* black eyes, and shuck cigars were mixed in admirable confusion. — (7) **1905** O. HENRY *Roads of Destiny* 141 He rolled a shuck cigarette. — (8) **1850** GARRARD *Wah-To-Yah* xii. 165 After rolling up and smoking a shuck *cigarillo,* [he] coiled himself before the fire in his one blanket to sleep.

(10) **1941** *Yankee* Dec. 39/2 They list shuck dolls at 25 cents and 50 cents, colored splint fly swatters are 30 cents. — (11) **1945** BOTKIN *My Burden* 83 Most everybody kept a shuck footmat 'fore their front doors. — (12) **1943** HOLT *Carver* 162 They were taught how to sew, cook, and make shuck hats. — (13) **1856** *Fla. Plantation Rec.* 487 I, Renty, gitten sills to go under shucke house. — (14) **1851** *Knickerb.* XXXVII. 393 There was but an apology for a bed-stead, with a 'shuck' mattress on it. **1944** WILSON *Passing Inst.* 135 There was plenty of slumber in the days of shuck mattresses and straw mattresses and feather beds.

(15) **1844** *S. Lit. Messenger* X. 486/1 The neighbor aforesaid had the comforts of a shuck-pen, in which to console himself for the night. **1895** HARRIS in *Scribner's Mag.* Dec. 726/2 Jeff, the little beagle, could have whipped a shuck-pen full of them without ever showing his teeth. — (16) **1854** DAVIS *Farm Bk.* 118 Split a few rails & hauled to shuck rack. . . . Made shuck rack in the garden. — (17) **1888** *Whitewater* (Wis.) *Reg.* 23 Feb., Oftentimes the simplest remedies, such as pine-water or shuck-tea, were made to serve a timely and efficient turn. — (18) **1884** MARK TWAIN *H. Finn* xx. 168 (R.), My bed was a straw tick—better than Jim's, which was a cornshuck tick; there's always cobs around about in a shuck tick.

b. In phrases, usu. to denote something that is poor or worthless. Cf. **shucks,** *interj.*

1843 W. T. THOMPSON *Major Jones's Courtship* 48 Tom Stallins had . . . one grate big yaller cur, what wasn't worth shucks to trail. **1892** DUVAL *Young Explorers* 196 I'll make him foller you to Jeriko, and he'll fill your hide so full of holes it won't hold shucks. **1911** SAUNDERS *Col. Todhunter* 33 Fetchin' and carryin' for the girls, . . . don't count for shucks. **1949** *Sat. Ev. Post.* 5 March 122/3 Birdie Elkins can't orate for shucks.

c. Esp. *to light a shuck,* (see quot. 1905). *Colloq.*

1905 *D.N.* III. 86 light a shuck, v. phr. To go in a hurry, to move on, to keep away from danger. n.w. Ark. **1947** *True* Nov. 108/2 But the Espinosas lit a shuck for the mountains.

As the last term in **honey, long, short shucks.**

*__shuck,__ *v.*

1. *tr.* To remove the husk from an ear of (corn).

[**1754** *N.C. Morav. Rec.* I. (1922) 107 Finished gathering and shucking corn from the 1st field.] **1772** in *W. & M. Coll. Quart.* XIV. 39 Just so these Ears; when shucked the husk and grain seem really more than the shuck could contain. **1834** NOTT *Novellettes* II. 144 The farmers occasionally employed the mountaineers to . . . shuck corn. **1949** J. MONAGHAN *This is Ill.* 173 The huskers snatched ears from the stalks, shucked and threw them against the wagons' bang boards.

b. *transf.*, esp. with reference to undressing. *Colloq.*

*c***1845** *Big Bear Ark.* 55 Young men in *my* time'd just get in a spree, sorter open thar shirt collars, and shuck themselves with a growl, and come out reddy-made men. **1857** *Spirit of Times* 10 Oct. 81/3 The Hoosier, who evidently thought the mate was coming to answer his challenge, began to strip or 'shuck himself,' as he called it, for a fight. **1908** O. HENRY *Options* 76 Please shuck the hide off that letter and read it. **1950** *Chi. Tribune* 28 March 14/3 We then realize 'tis time to shuck our itchy woolies and to drink tonics 'to thin the blood.'

c. *To get shucked out,* to be bested or overcome. *Colloq.*

1865 MARK TWAIN *Jumping Frog* (1875) 32 (R.), He didn't try no more to win the fight, and he got shucked out bad.

d. To open (oysters or quahogs).

1879 *Harper's Mag.* June 64/1 The oysters are generally shucked early in the morning. **1891** W. K. BROOKS *Oyster* 17 He said that . . . he could 'shuck' thirty-six oysters a minute. **1947** BEROLZHEIMER *Regional Cookbook* 62 Buy quahogs shucked or have the fishman shuck them. **1949** R. J. SIM *Pages from Past* 75 After being brought ashore the oysters are opened or 'shucked' by means of tools peculiar to that purpose.

2. *intr.* Of corn: To yield a specified amount of grain upon being shucked.

1871 *Ill. Agric. Soc. Trans.* VIII. 240 The hills of corn in a field planted five feet apart each way, and with four stalks to a hill, will not shuck any more corn per hill than those [etc.]. **1874** EGGLESTON *Circuit Rider* 12 The first comers . . . spent the time looking at the heap [of corn], and speculating as to how many bushels it would 'shuck out.'

shuck collar. *S.* A cheap homemade horse collar of selected shucks plaited into heavy strips which are then suitably placed beside each other and securely sewed. Also **shuck horse collar.** Cf. **flag collar.**

1781 *Va. State P.* I. 589 Many of these horses are sent with 'shuck-collars.' **1841** [see **shuck-bottomed chair**]. **1896** READ *Jucklins* 128, [I saw] . . . a red-looking negro, with a string of shuck horse collars. **1944** CLARK *Pills* 278 A fifty-cent shuck collar was good enough for an ordinary plow mule, but a sturdier collar was desirable for heavier work.

shucker 'ʃʌkɚ, *n.*

1. (*cap.*) *pl.* (See quot.) *Rare.*

1836 IRVING *Astoria* I. 276 Another class [of the Snake Indians], the most abject and forlorn, . . . are called Shuckers, or more commonly Diggers and Root eaters.

2. One who husks corn. Also a machine for this purpose.

1874 EGGLESTON *Circuit Rider* 17 He started the whiskey bottle on its encouraging travels along the line of shuckers. **1882** *Cent. Mag.* Oct. 874/1 Two 'gin'r'ls' . . . proceed to divide the shuckers into two parties. **1948** *Sat. Review* 27 March 26/3 As these giant shuckers made of rubber and steel march down the rows, the frozen, bleeding hands, the husking bees are quietly retreating into history.

3. One who shucks oysters.

1879 *Harper's Mag.* June 64/1 In the shining pans in front of the shuckers are quarts of clean . . . oysters. **1900** *Everybody's Mag.* Sep. 204 In the shucking room the cars are surrounded by the shuckers, each provided with a knife and a can that hooks upon the side of the vehicle, which is soon emptied of its contents. **1913** *Survey* 3 May 171/1 The fastest adult shuckers seldom ever make more than a dollar a day after years of experience.

As the last term in **corn, oyster shucker.**

shucking 'ʃʌkɪŋ, *n.*

1. A husking bee. *Colloq.*

1817 ROYALL *Lett. from Ala.* 31, I only got a little lively at brother I's shucking. **1903** *D.N.* II. 329 shucking, n. A husking bee. 'There will be a shucking and a dance at the Widow Smith's to-night.' s.e. Mo. **1948** DICK *Dixie Frontier* 129 Before the shucking began, it was customary . . . for two men to form a saddle with their hands and carry the host around the corn pile.

b. Removing the shells of nuts or oysters.

1845 KIRKLAND *Western Clearings* 101 We were soon well pelted with nuts, and busily engaged in freeing them from their aromatic wrappers—an operation which we of the West call 'shucking.' **1879** *Harper's Mag.* June 64/1 Here the chief interest centres—the 'shucking' or opening of oysters. **1948** *Amer. Sp.* XXIII. 298/1 The commercial *shucking* is done in a *shucking house.*

c. *local.* (See quot.)

1946 *Dly. Ardmoreite* (Ardmore, Okla.) 6 Dec. 7/6 Proposals for streamlining [legislative processes] . . . would include a prohibition against 'shucking,' the practice of substituting a wholly new bill for one already on the calendar.

2. In combs. with reference to husking corn, as (1) **shucking bee,** (cf. **husking bee**), (2) **peg,** (cf. **husking peg**), (3) **season,** (4) **song.**

(1) **1852** *Knickerb.* XL. 45 At a 'shucking-bee,' as they have to work, the feasting is gratis, for those who would feast. — (2) **1886** EBBUTT *Emigrant Life* 180 The hand is armed with a 'shucking-peg,' either of wood or iron fastened on with a thong,—which tears open the shucks on the ears of corn. **1946** ADAMS *Album Amer. Hist.* III. 376 *Above* is a shucking (or husking) peg that was used every fall during the 1880's. — (3) **1824** SINGLETON *Letters* 100 In 'shucking' seasons, the slaves split the welkin with their boisterous glee. — (4) **1855** *Putnam's Mo.* Jan. 77/2 The following shucking song has nothing to recommend it to public attention, save the questionable rhyme to 'supper.'

b. With reference to oysters (see quots.).

1879 *Harper's Mag.* June 64/1 At the first glance into a shucking-house it looks terribly dirty. **1881** INGERSOLL *Oyster Industry* 248 *Shucking stand,* a rude table, with boxed sides, etc., at which oysters are opened. (South.) **1884** *Nat. Museum Bul.* No. 27, 220 On each side of each alley are numerous stalls, each fitted with a 'shucking trough,' or box-like receptacle for the oysters. **1949** *Fishing Gaz.* Oct. 92/2 A few minutes after the oysters arrived, they were being transferred to the shucking house.

shucks ʃʌks, *interj.* [f. ***shuck,** *n.* **1.**] An exclamation of disgust, regret, impatience, etc. *Colloq.*

1847 FIELD *Drama in Pokerville* 68 And Mr. Bagley was there . . . [to shoot] any gentleman who might say 'shucks!' **1916** PORTER *David* 107 Shucks! It'll take more'n you ter make me think a crow can sing. **1949** *Boston Globe Mag.* 4 Dec. 11/3 Why, shucks! Amy must be grown-up . . . maybe married.

***shuffle,** *n.* As the last term in **cornfield, cross, sunflower shuffle.**

***shuffler,** *n.* **1.** A scaup duck, also attrib. **2.** The coot, *Fulica americana.*

(1) **1845** HOOPER *Taking Census* (1928) 111 Sol . . . went under the water in the 'Buck Hole,' 'like a shuffler duck with his wing broke.' **1852** BAIRD in Stansbury *Gt. Salt Lake* 324 Little Blackhead Shuffler. Found across the continent. **1874** COUES *Birds N.W.* 573. — (2) **1889** *Cent.* 1252/1 The common or bald coot of Europe is *F. atra;* that of America is *F. americana,* sometimes called *shuffler.* **1917** *Birds of Amer.* I. 214.

shun-pike 'ʃʌnˌpaɪk, *n.* A way, esp. a side road, for avoiding a tollgate on a turnpike. Now *hist.*

1853 W. McMURRAY *Speech* 28 March 17/1 (Th. Supp.), The Oswego Canal . . . has been called a 'shun pike.' **1881** PIERSON *In the Brush* 27, I saw tracks leading off into the woods, and was told that they were known as 'shunpikes.' **1903** STOCKTON *Captain's Toll-Gate* 6 A road . . . branched off from the turnpike . . . [and] entered the pike again beyond the toll-gate, and . . . it had seen a good deal of travel, which, in time, gave it the name of the shunpike. **1947** *Harper's Mag.* Oct. 332/1 Resentment against the turnpikes had risen. In some areas farmers built 'shunpikes' around the toll-collection houses.

***shut,** *n.* As the last term in **cold, deer, flower shut.**

***shut,** *v.* In noun combs.: (1) **shutdown,** (*a*) the action of closing off or stopping something decisively, *rare,* (*b*) the discontinuance of work at a factory, oil well, etc., also attrib.; (2) **-eye flavor,** (see quot.), *rare;* (3) **-in,** a person confined to the house by sickness or infirmity, also attrib. or as adj.; (4) **out,** a failure to score on the part of the loser in a contest, also attrib., cf. **b.** (2) below; (5) **pan,** the act of being secretive, also as adj., close-mouthed, *colloq.*

(1) (*a*) **1857** *Knickerb.* XLIX. 35, 'I'll be just exactly shot if you *don't!*' he added with a patent diabolical shut-down. (*b*) **1884** *New Mex. Review* (Santa Fe) 9 Dec. 1/5 The last shut-down there threw 1,400 men out of employment. **1931** *K.C. Star* 6 Aug., Oil Men in Air as Murray Shutdown Order Hangs Fire. **1950** *Chi. Tribune* 23 March VI. 1/1 Soon after the shut-down was disclosed, the house voted to give 750 millions more to the Reconstruction Finance corporation which administers the program. — (2) **1848** LOWELL *Biglow P.* I. Ser. p. x, I was not backward to recognize in them [*sc.* verses] a certain wild, puckery, acidulous (sometimes even verging toward that point which, in our rustic phrase, is termed *shut-eye*) flavor, not wholly unpleasing, nor unwholesome, to palates cloyed with the sugariness of tamed and cultivated fruit. — (3) **1904** *Prosp. Mass. Blind Assoc.* 2 The lonely and the unbusy, the shut-ins in body and in mind. **1948** *Chesterton* (Ind.) *Tribune* 28 Oct. 11/5 They will travel to the homes of shut-in members and sing several songs used on Sunday mornings. — (4) **1889** *Pueblo* (Colo.) *Opinion* 21 July 4/5 The Springs were 'fated' from the start, and narrowly escaped a shut out. **1949** *Minot* (N.D.) *D. News* 22 July 8/8 He led his Grand Forks team to a one-hit shutout victory over Duluth.

(5) *a***1865** in McCLELLAN *Own Story* (1881–5) 161 The President [Lincoln] . . . said: 'Well, Mr. Blair, I was obliged to play shut-pan with you last night.' **1889** *Cent. Mag.* Sep. 704/1, I shall be very 'shut pan' about this matter. **1949** *Sat. Ev. Post* 18 June 31/1 Barlow . . . sat his horse a few feet distant, his carbine in the crook of his arm, his face as shut-pan as an Injun's above the red calico of his shirt.

b. In phrases: (1) *To shut down on,* to clamp down on, as by suppression or dismissal; (2) *to shut out,* in baseball, to prevent (an opposing team) from scoring or from winning a single game.

(1) **1886** JAMES *Bostonians* 149 She thought it prudent not to attempt to cut short the phase . . . prematurely—an imputation she should incur if, without more delay, she were to 'shut down,' as Verena said, on the young connoisseur. **1891** WILKINS *N. Eng. Nun* 106 She's been sewin' boots for Allen over at Wayne, but I heard the other day he was goin' to shut down on her. — (2) **1881** *N.Y. Herald* 17 July 10/3 The Domestics were shut out in every inning up to the eighth, when by bunching their hits they scored two earned runs on a single by Mahny. **1894** *Spalding's Base Ball Guide* 40 Nichols . . . shut out the St. Louis team without a game to their credit out of four games played. **1922** *Lit. Digest* 27 May 57/1 Another Robertson, of Yale, shut out Princeton without a hit.

***shut,** *adv.* Used colloq. with certain verbs to denote consummation or completeness of an action, equivalent to "to."

1744 FRANKLIN *Acct. Fire-Places* 19 The Door may be . . . commonly kept close shut. **1884** *Cent. Mag.* Nov. 13 [He] pushed the ground-glass door shut. **1902** WISTER *Virginian* xiv, Car wheels clicked over the main-line switch. A train-hand threw it shut after. **1924** MULFORD *Rustlers' Valley* xii, No one cared to light another lamp until . . . the shutters [had been] slammed shut.

shute, see **chute.**

***shuttle,** *n.* **1. shuttle line,** a line of railroad over which shuttle trains operate. **2. shuttle train,** (see quot. 1891).

(1) **1943** MENFFEE *Assignment* 113 Establishment of a railroad shuttle line to Detroit. — (2) **1891** *Cent.* 5607/1 *Shuttle train,* . . . a train running back and forth for a short distance like a shuttle, as over a track connecting a main line with a station at a short distance

from it. **1923** *World Almanac* 503/2 A shuttle train runs between 50th Street and 59th Street on Sixth Avenue.

* **shy,** *a.* Short, lacking, without, originally a poker term. Also with *of, on. Colloq.*

1887 KELLER *Draw Poker* 28 The worst of all poker habits, owing the pool, or 'going shy,' as it is called, results from the non-observance of this very important rule. **1895** *Denver Times* 5 March 1/3 (*headline*), J. W. Shannon, Burglar, . . . Was Shy Several Fingers. **1916** BOWER *Phantom Herd* 80 If they're shy on the number [of costumes], they better set down and make enough. **1948** *Democrat* 1 April 1/1 Gould's gobbler . . . had a beard which was just a bit shy of 12 inches.

shyster ˈʃaɪstɚ, *n.* [Prob. f. some G. slang term based on *scheisse*, excrement. Cf. *scheisserei, scheisser, scheisskerl.*]

1. A term of contempt for an unscrupulous, tricky, mean person, often applied to lawyers. *Slang.*

1846 *Subterranean* (N.Y.) 11 July 2/4 *Shyster.* 'That we can't do, you know, as it is opposed to all precedent.' **1857** *Spirit of Times* 1 Aug. 344/1 A party guilty of suing for his stakes back, when given up by the stake-holder of his opponent, is a 'shyster,' and should be put in Coventry, and warned off the course. **1876** *Wkly. Comanche* (Tex.) *Chief* 22 June 2/1 It costs an editor $15 to call a Buffalo lawyer a 'shyster.' **1923** CATHER *Lost Lady* 104, I suppose it takes longer to make an architect than it does to make a shyster. **1949** J. MONAGHAN *This is Ill.* 90 He had known . . . shysters, pickpockets, loafers.

attrib. **1870** MEDBERY *Men Wall St.* 123 Not a few individuals of the 'shyster' class . . . are ready to break their word. **1872** MARK TWAIN *Roughing It* 487 Next we come to his Excellency the Prime Minister, . . . a lawyer of 'shyster' caliber. **1875** *Chi. Tribune* 2 Nov. 4/6 There are also some miscellaneous provisions directed against shyster corporations.

2. shyster lawyer, a lawyer of a low, pettifogging type, devoid of professional honor. *Colloq.*

1849 G. G. FOSTER *N.Y. in Slices* 20 He must . . . wait next day for the visits of the 'shyster' lawyers—a set of turkey-buzzards whose touch is pollution and whose breath is pestilence. **1923** VANCE *Baroque* 176 His shyster lawyer . . . called on me one day to protest against what he was pleased to term my persecution of his client. **1950** *Dly. Oklahoman* (Okla. City) 23 March 18/3 Behind this commercialized vice racket were grafting politicians . . . , shyster lawyers . . . , and unscrupulous property owners.

shystering ˈʃaɪstərɪŋ, *a.* and *n.* The activities of a shyster, living as a shyster; tricky, unscrupulous. *Colloq.*

1860 *Knickerb.* LVI. 458 Outside of a kind of twopenny shystering smartness and snap-judgment genius, Dovey was . . . rather a cross between a Dutch dumpling and a one-horse blower. **1872** in R. G. WHITE *Amer. View Copyright* 40 At Monday's session an-unprepossessing person . . . made a 'shystering,' pettifogging speech. **1882** HOWELLS *Modern Instance* xvii, I shouldn't like shystering. **1895** *Wkly. Examiner* (S.F.) 19 Sep. 2/6 Those sharp practices generally passing under the name of shystering.

* **Sibley,** *n.* A bell-shaped tent, often quite large, devised by Gen. Henry Hastings Sibley (1811–94) allegedly on the pattern of Sioux tepees and often used in the U.S. Army in the West. Usu. attrib., esp. with *tent.*

1861 QUINT *Potomac & Rapidan* (1864) 53 The Sibley tents, which our men use, are well ventilated at the top, by a hole coverable at pleasure. **1861** *Alexandria* (Va.) *Gazette* 11 May 1/6 One hundred men of the New York Firemen Zouaves have been directed to erect these (the Sibley army tents) near Benning's Crossroads. **1895** REMINGTON *Pony Tracks* 50, I will recount some small-talk current in the Sibley tepees. **1944** PENNELL *Rome Hanks* 31, I went over to the flys of the Sibley which were still supported by the bushes we had hung them on.

b. Sibley (heating) stove, a small portable stove of a type devised by Gen. Sibley.

1867 in CUSTER *Tenting on Plains* 516 We are in our tent, and enjoying a pleasant fire from our Sibley stove. **1947** PRICE *Trails I Rode* 53 We had a little Sibley heating stove about the size of a water bucket for the bed tent.

* **sick,** *a.* and *n.* In combs.: (1) **sick barracks,** *S.* on plantations, a building where sick slaves were cared for, *obs.;* (2) **spinner,** (see quot.); (3) **stomach,** (see quot. 1823), *obs.*

(1) 1847 *Fla. Plantation Rec.* 302 Dye and Tempy in sick Barracks. — **(2) 1880** *Bradstreet's* 4 Dec. 2/1 'Sick spinners' [are] men who hire out as substitutes for operatives [in textile mills] who are obliged to be absent from work by sickness or otherwise. — **(3) 1815** DRAKE *Cincinnati* 182 A disease called by the people the *Sick-stomach*, has prevailed . . . for several years. **1823** W. H. KEATING *Narr.* 48 A very fatal disease had prevailed during the last summer; it is well known to the west under the name of the sick stomach, or milk sickness, and is supposed to be produced by drinking milk, which has become unwholesome from some cause or other; many persons died of it last year. **1837** PECK *New Guide* 81 There is a disease that afflicts many frontier people called by some 'sick stomach.'

As the last term in **milk, plaster, salt sick.**

* **sicken,** *v. tr.* To stupefy (fish), so that they may readily be taken. *Rare.* — **1872** *Fur, Fin & Feather* (ed. 2) 71 [No] person shall . . . sicken fish . . . in any stream, . . . [by any preparation] of a sickening, intoxicating, or destructive quality.

sickishly ˈsɪkɪʃlɪ, *adv.* (See quot. 1841.) — **1841** WEBSTER II. 600/2 *Sickishly,* in a sickish manner. **1880** *Lit. World* (Boston) 24 April 139/1 Most writers upon him are either unpleasantly bitter or sickishly sweet.

* **sickle,** *n.* In combs.: (1) **sickle bar,** the cutter bar on a mowing machine; (2) **bill,** the long-billed curlew, in full **sicklebill curlew;** (3) **-billed thrush,** = **sicklebill;** (4) **grass,** a species of sedge, *Carex crinita,* or the tearthumb, *Tracaulon arifolium;* (5) **pod,** an American species of rock cress, *Arabis canadensis;* (6) **weed,** (see quot.).

(1) 1862 *Ill. Agric. Soc. Trans.* V. 224 No 'tricks of the trade' such as . . . elevating the sickle bar above the proper cutting point were permitted to prevent a fair test. — **(2) 1872** COUES *Key to Birds* 262 *Numenius,* Long-billed Curlew. Sickle-bill. **1893** ROOSEVELT *Wilderness Hunter* 93 The sicklebill curlews . . . had for the most part gone southward. **1909** *Sunset* Jan. 70/2 The long-billed curlew, or sickle-bill, as it is often called (*numenius longirostris*), is a plentiful resident in all suitable localities. — **(3) 1872** COUES *Key to Birds* 75 Sickle-billed Thrush. California Mockingbird. . . . Coast Region of California. — **(4) 1854** *Mich. Agric. Soc. Trans.* VI. 149 In the low grounds are . . . marsh grass, sickel grass, three kinds of red top [etc.].

(5) 1833 EATON *Botany* (ed. 6) 24. **1843** TORREY *Flora N.Y.* I. 55 Sickle-pod. Turkey-pod. . . . Rocky woods and hill sides. **1898** CREEVEY *Flowers of Field* 279 Sickle-pod . . . has sessile stem-leaves, acute at apex and base. — **(6) 1784** *Amer. Acad. Mem.* I. 440 *Polygonum foliis sagittatis, caule aculeato.* . . . Sickleweed. . . . Blossoms white, tinged with red.

* **sickness,** *n.* As the last term in **milk, mine, rail, winter sickness.**

* **side,** *n.* and *a.*

1. ?A quantity or weight of tobacco. *Rare.* [Cf. *EDD* * *side,* sb.⁴, as a measure of cherries or currants, 63 lbs.]

1650 *Essex Probate Rec.* I. 119 Two sides of pork, four sides and five roles of tob[acco].

2. One half of a cowhide or oxhide.

1732 *S.C. Gazette* 128/1 To be sold, . . . about 600 sides of Leather in the Fatts, the greatest part of them tann'd. **1779** *Narragansett Hist. Reg.* I. 37 Returned home with a side of sole leather of Godfrey Hazard's. **1885** *Harper's Mag.* Jan. 274/2 The hides are . . . cut through the middle of the back to separate them into 'sides.'

3. In noun and adj. combs.: (1) **side bacon,** bacon from the side of a hog; (2) **-bar whiskers,** = **sideburns;** (3) * **bone,** a disease of horses causing the cartilages in the side of the hoof to turn to bone, also the bony structure resulting from this disease; (4) **card,** in a poker hand having a pair, any card not paired, in other games, a nontrump card; (5) **door pullman,** a boxcar or freight car, *jocular;* (6) **grade,** a slight grade or slope such as is found in rolling prairie land, *rare;* (7) **harrow,** a harrow for use on the sides of row crops; (8) **hobbled,** of a horse, hobbled by having a forefoot and the hind foot on the same side fastened together, cf. * **line,** *v.* **3,** and **sideline,** *v.* in **4.** below; (9) * **line,** (*a*) an auxiliary line of goods, a subordinate or secondary occupation or business, (*b*) **side line hobble,** *W.* a hobble used in side-lining a horse, cf. **4.** (2) below; (10) * **mark,** (*a*) a mark or object on the side of a river enabling a steamboat pilot to get his bearings, (*b*) (see quot.); (11) **meat,** bacon or pork from the side of a hog; (12) **money,** money earned or secured on the side, cf. **d.** (2) below; (13) **order,** an order for something in addition to that provided on a bill of fare, cf. **d.** (1) below; (14) **stepper,** one who avoids issues, *colloq.,* cf. **side-step,** *v.* in **4.** below; (15) **tackle,** the right or left tackle on a football team; (16) **trip,** an excursion that is incidental to a trip; (17) **walker,** (*a*) one who idles about or loafs on sidewalks, (*b*) (see quot.); (18) **yard,** a yard at the side of a dwelling.

(1) 1850 Sawyer *Way Sketches* 108 [For] each man . . . [should be provided] fifty pounds of smoked side bacon. **1905** O. Henry *Roads of Destiny* 140 Frijoles and side-bacon would do me about as well. — **(2) 1882** Peck *Sunshine* 55 He was a red-faced man, with these side-bar whiskers. — **(3) 1886** *Amer. Agriculturist* (*Cent.*), Heaves, curb, spavin, sidebone, and ringbone are the most ordinary ailments in horses. **1891** *Cent.* 5614/3 Side-bones occur chiefly in the fore feet of draft-horses, and are an occasional cause of lameness. — **(4) 1857** *Hoyle's Games* (Amer. ed.) 288 Should two or more hands come together of equal value in pairs, the better hand is decided by the highest side cards. **1864** Dick *Amer. Hoyle* (1866) 63 *Side-Cards*, lay cards.

(5) 1895 *Columbus* (O.) *Dispatch* 23 Oct. 7/7 'Hobo' . . . was first applied to the knight of the 'side-door Pullmans' by brakemen. **1913** *Industrial Worker* (Spokane) 21 Aug. 4/4, I will have to take the side door pullmans with the rest of the boys. — **(6) 1860** *Ill. Agric. Soc. Trans.* IV. 37 [The Lancaster steam plow] could not maintain its position, on even an easy side grade. — **(7) 1844** in Turner *Cotton* (1865) 174, I have been using, for some time, the plough in the cultivation of the Sea Island cotton, with advantage, and I intend, this year, further to facilitate my work by the side-harrow and the cultivator. **1944** Clark *Pills* 283 In the warerooms or crowded along the aisles . . . were the assembled implements such as middle busters . . . side harrows, spring tooth cultivators [etc.]. — **(8) 1806** Lewis in *L. & Clark Exped.* IV. (1905) 317 We had all our horses side hubbled and turned out to graize. **1884** *Gringo & Greaser* 15 Feb. 2/2 Estevan Lopez thought he was a kicking mule and not being side hobbled let fly the business end against the doors. — **(9)** (*a*) **1890** *N.Y. Tribune* 9 March (*Cent.*), Wanted—Salesman to carry as a side-line a new line of advertisement specialty. **1931** *K.C. Star* 15 Dec. 23 Cooking is only a side-line. **1950** *Time* 3 April 84/3 Adolphus also took some side-lines: he built the Adolphus Hotel in Dallas, and brought the first diesel engine patents from Switzerland to the U.S. (*b*) **1923** Mulford *Black Buttes* 264 He . . . put side line hobbles on the two extra horses.

(10) (*a*) **1875** Mark Twain *Old Times Miss.* v. 90 That pilot can . . . give you such a lot of head-marks, stern-marks, and side-marks to guide you. (*b*) **1905** *Forestry Bureau. Bul.* No. 61, 30 *Bark mark*, a symbol chopped into the side of a log to indicate its ownership. . . . Syn.: side mark. (N[orthern] F[orest].) — **(11) 1873** Beadle *Undevel. West* 482 Two bright-eyed, graceful, copper-colored *senoritas* bring me a supper of coffee, side meat, eggs, and *tortillas de mais*. **1949** Kurath *Word Geog. Eastern U.S.* 14/1 In northern Pennsylvania and seemingly also in the Buffalo sector *side pork*, a blend of Northern *salt pork* and the Pennsylvania term *side meat*, has become established. — **(12) 1928** *Sat. Ev. Post* 10 March 185/3, I thought I could make a little 'side money' during my vacation. **1947** *Sports Afield* Feb. 19/1 With the subtlety of a bull moose, this rental agent was working up some 'side money.' — **(13) 1900** Ade *More Fables* 205 His Brain felt as if some one had played a Mean Trick on him and substituted a Side-Order of Cauliflower. — **(14) 1909** *N.Y. Ev. Post* (s.-w.) 1 March 1 Had not Mr. Fairbanks been a really wonderful side-stepper, their essential differences might have long ago become public property.

(15) 1891 *N.Y. Tribune* 20 Oct. 5/4 He was of fine presence, standing six feet high, and was side-tackle on his college football team. — **(16) 1929** L. F. Carr *Amer. Challenged* 3 He was forced to borrow money for a little side trip to New York. **1946** *Mazama* Dec. 36/2 A short side trip this day was to Dollar Lake. — **(17)** (*a*) **1849** G. G. Foster *N.Y. in Slices* 96 A filthy, ragged, idiotic vagabond, herding with negroes and low sidewalkers in the holes and corners of the City. (*b*) **1891** *Cent.* 5617/2 *Side-walker*, . . . a laterigrade spider; a spider which walks or moves sidewise or otherwise with apparently equal ease, as *Salticus scenicus*. — **(18) 1846** H. N. Moore *Fitzgerald & Hopkins* 10 Antoinette and I were of the same age—playmates—and the side-yard was our playground. **1922** Tarkington *Gentle Julia* 8 A boy of her own age emerged from the 'side-yard.'

For **sidebar, burns, hill, judge, -kick, saddle, show, track, walk, wheel, winder,** see as main entries.

b. In combs. of obvious meaning or sufficiently explained in the quots.: (1) **side boom,** (2) **canyon,** (3) **check,** (4) **comb,** (also transf.), (5) **corset,** (6) **draw,** (7) **jam,** (8) **judge,** see as a main entry, (9) **paddle steamer, wheel,** (10) **partner,** (11) **porch,** (12) **road,** (13) **room,** (cf. **hall bedroom**), (14) **stay,** (15) **tie,** (on a railroad).

(1) 1879 *Lumberman's Gaz.* 1 Oct., Side-booms have been stretched along wherever there is any danger of logs escaping. — **(2) 1858** Ives *Colo. River* (1861) 104 The intervening country is cut up by side cañons and cross ravines. **1949** *Sierra Club Bul.* June 6 Over to the right, a side canyon appears, drops slowly to our level, opens up to show a passageway to Woods Lake. — **(3) 1895** *Stand.* 2269/2 *Side-check*, a check-rein that passes at the side of a horse's head instead of between the ears. **1904** *Cin. Enquirer* 30 Nov. 6 An Englishman, lately arrived in this country, protests against the side-check. — **(4) 1824** *Mo. Intelligencer* 8 May 3/3 Tortoise Shell, Tuck and Side Combs. **1853** B. F. Taylor *Jan. & June* 85 [There are] hens with very delicate side-combs, like our sweethearts. **1944** *Sears Cat.* (ed. 189) 559 Use the large comb for center back in an upsweep . . . and the side combs will keep straggly side ends in place.

(5) 1944 Clark *Pills* 193 Corset makers supplied hose supporters, or side corsets, called 'Langtry lengtheners' with long coupled straps which could be fastened to the corset at one end and to stockings at the other. — **(6) 1907** Cook *Border & Buffalo* 229 At this edge of that side-draw, and up the main draw a little. — **(7) 1905** Wiggin *Rose* 60 There remained now only the great side-jam at Gray Rock. This had been allowed to grow, gathering logs as they drifted past, thus making higher water and a stronger current on the other side of the rock. — **(9) 1846** *Hunt's Merch. Mag.* XV. 69 On the Delaware, his contrivance . . . did away with Doctor Franklin's objections to the side paddle wheel. **1941** Seton *Trail of Artist-Naturalist* 117, I set out eagerly at the end of June, taking the Crandell Line side-paddle steamer *Vanderbilt* at Lindsay.

(10) 1890 *N.Y. Ev. Post.* 23 May (Th. Supp.), The arrest was made by the witness's side partner, it being his night off. **1931** Dobie *Coronado's C.* 127 He and me had been side pardners—reg'lar yoke mates, you might say—for years. I guess we broke enough horses together to furnish a dozen outfits going up the trail. — **(11) 1879** Stockton *Rudder Grange* xiii, We sat on the side porch, where it was shady. **1922** Tarkington *Gentle Julia* 104 Florence sneezed frequently as she sat upon the 'side porch.' — **(12) 1861** in Logan *Great Conspiracy* 295, I sent down Col. Morell . . . to open a road down to Opequan Creek, within five miles of the camp at Winchester, on the side-roads I was upon. **1943** *Nat. Geog. Mag.* April 403/1 South of Pittsburg [N. Hampshire], on a side road, is the first wooden covered bridge that crosses the Connecticut. **1950** *Chi. Tribune* 2 April 38/1 This good pavement lasts for only two or three miles . . . no towns, no houses, no side roads. — **(13) 1884** Howells *S. Lapham* iii, The chambers were to be on the three floors above, front and rear, with side-rooms over the front door. **1893** ——— *Coast of Bohemia* 61 It's over the door, four flights up; it's what they call a side room. **1898** Randell *Amer. Politician in Eng.* 278 The girl . . . shared my little 'side-room'; they call hall-rooms that way in Boston. — **(14) 1852** Ellet *Pioneer Women* 201 All men . . . were required to pull at the side stays, or short ropes attached to the upper side of the wagons, to prevent their upsetting.

(15) 1872 Huntington *Road-Master's Ass't* 14 Side-ties (ties next the joint) should be of equal width and laid the same distances from the joint.

c. In the names of plants and animals: (1) **side-liner,** (see quot.); (2) **oat,** (*a*) a species of oat in which the drooping panicle has branches on one side, esp. the Tartarian oat, *Avena orientalis*, (*b*) *pl.* (see quot. 1909), also attrib.; (3) * **saddle,** see as a main entry; (4) **winder,** see as a main entry; (5) **wiper,** = **sidewinder 1.**

(1) 1891 *Cent.* 5615/2 *Sideliner*, . . . a sidewinder, sidewiper, or massasauga. — **(2)** (*a*) **1856** *Ill. Agric. Soc. Trans.* II. 105 My Tartarian oat . . . is a side oat, but has a thick, stiff straw. **1862** *Ib.* V. 196 He sows four bushels of seed to the acre, of black Tartarian or, as sometimes called, horse mane or side oats. (*b*) **1909** *Cent. Supp.* 1216/1 *Side-oats*, . . . a grama grass . . . ranging from New Jersey to the Rocky Mountains and southward into Mexico. **1910** Thornber *Grazing Ranges Ariz.* 277 This is the case with such species as blue grama, crowfoot or mesa grama, . . . side-oats grass, . . . and spike grass.

(5) 1877 Hodge *Arizona* 226 Another kind [of rattlesnake], called the side wiper, from its peculiar habit of locomotion sideways, instead of ahead, is found through most of the valleys and plains.

d. *On the side*, (1) in addition, as a side order *q.v.*, (2) in addition to one's ordinary duties, as a subordinate occupation, an extra. *Colloq.*

(1) 1884 *Bad Lands Cow Boy* (Little Missouri, Dak. Terr.) 7 Feb. 1/5 'Gimme that snake rare—milk gravy on the side,' was hallooed to the cook. **1890** *Road* (Denver, Colo.) 19 April 7/2 Gim me some Manitou [Spring Water] on the side. **1916** *Lit. Digest* 18 March 766/3 'Beef stew and a cup of tea for me,' the new arrival said. 'Bossy in a bowl—boiled leaves on the side,' sang the waiter. — **(2) 1893** *Cong. Rec.* 18 Dec. 360/1 He will have no pension attorney, for a silent partner, no relative doing business 'on the side' with that bureau. **1912** Nicholson *Hoosier Chron.* 406 Hope you don't mind my doing a small job on the side.

e. *To be on the good side of*, to be in favor with (someone). *Colloq.*

1896 Mark Twain *Tom Sawyer* i. 345 (R.), I reckon he's somebody they think they better be on the good side of.

4. In combinative verbal expressions: (1) **side-corral,** *fig.* to shunt away from a particular subject, *rare;* (2) **-line,** (see quot. 1869 and cf. * **line,** *v.* **3,** and **side-hobbled**); (3) **-step,** to step to one side, often fig., to evade (an issue), also **side-stepping,** *n.*, cf. **side-stepper** in **3.** (14) above; (4) **swipe,** of vehicles, to collide or strike glancingly, also transf.; (5) **track,** see as a main entry; (6) **walk,** to provide (a street) with a sidewalk, also **sidewalked,** *a.;* (7) **-wind,** of a horse, to jump aside with a bucking motion.

(1) 1903 O. HENRY in *McClure's Mag.* Dec. 145/2, [I wished] to show her that I was on about the family receipt, and couldn't be side-corraled off of the subject. — **(2) 1869** in MATHEWS *Beginnings* 156 In addition to the usual methods of hoppling a horse, the Texans often 'side-line' him, by tying a fore to a hind leg. **1936** BARNARD *Rider* 156 We had to side-line it to get a bridle on it. — **(3) 1901** *Scribner's Mag.* April 422/1 Skipper pricked up his ears, raised his head, and side-stepped stiffly. **1906** *Springfield W. Republican* 27 Sep. 8 The Idaho republicans are deftly side-stepping the anti-Mormon issue. **1932** *Blue Valley Farmer* (Okla. City) 17 March 6/5 When America is grappling with things fundamental, tired and disgusted with side-stepping, buck-passing and plain lying . . . the country must content itself with a stone when it asked for bread. — **(4) 1904** *Phila. Ev. Telegraph* 12 Nov. 16 The west-bound St. Louis Express, while pull-

Side-lined horse

ing on to a siding, was sideswiped by the east-bound Pittsburg Limited. **1945** *Las Animas* (Colo.) *Leader* 25 July 2/4 He passed a truck and had his arm sticking out of the car window and it was sideswiped by a passing truck.

(6) 1871 HOWELLS *Wedding Journey* 229 Up the odd side-walked street stretched an aisle of carriages. **1884** *Harper's Mag.* March 516/2 There is no store, no post-office, no sidewalked street—no nothing. **1893** *Home Missionary* March 543 Miles of streets have been opened, graded, planked, and sidewalked. — **(7) 1927** JAMES *Cow Country* 105 The stranger had seemed at home from the time the horse side-winded out of his tracks.

As the last term in **batting, bay, broad, burn, calico, clear, East, hill, Indian, New, off, out, red, river, sea, shilling, slab, southern, West, white side(s).**

* **side,** *v.*

1. *tr.* To provide (a structure) with a side or sides. Also with *up*, and fig.

1681 *East Hampton Rec.* II. 109 To ye Carpentr for ye Gallery for sideing up the Gable End of ye Meetinghouse 1-7-0. **1827** COOPER *Red Rover* I. 35 [It's] cloth that would do to side a house with. **1874** TAYLOR *World on Wheels* 119 [In the afternoon] the morning's frame was . . . raised, roofed and sided, and a doctrine or so put into it to keep house. **1877** *Rep. Indian Affairs* 40 Two dwelling-houses and one school-house have been sided up with weather-boards.

2. *S.* To plow (a row crop) close to the drill.

In the first quot. the reference is app. to the pulling of dirt up to and around hills of cotton with hoes.

1829 in COMMONS *Doc. Hist.* I. 237 Hoes sidleing cotton in No. 2. **1847** *Fla. Plantation Rec.* 244, 9 plows sideing cotton in brickyard cut. **1886** PAGE in *Cent. Mag.* June 200/2, I tell Hannah I ain' done sidin' meh corn.

* **sidebar,** *n.* A buggy having longitudinal sidepieces furnishing support to the body. In full **sidebar buggy.**

1884 *N.Y. Herald* 27 Oct. 1/2 J. B. Brewster sidebar top Buggy Sleigh, sets of Double and Single Harness. **1899** TARKINGTON *Gentleman from Ind.* vii, Here and there the trim side-bar buggy of some prosperous farmer's son . . . flashed along the road. **1944** HOLTON *Yankees* 106 Buggies as I knew them at home were one of two kinds, side-bar or Goddard.

sideburns ˈsaɪdˌbɜnz, *n. pl.* Burnsides. Also in allusion to the period when these were in fashion. Cf. * **Burnside 1,** and **sidebar whiskers.**

1887 *Chi. Jrnl.* 1 Aug., McGarigle has his mustache and small side burns still on. **1949** *Nat. Geog. Mag.* Sep. 317/1 Every man in town seemed to have grown sideburns. **1949** *Courier-Journal* (Louisville, Ky.) 3 Sep. 7/2 Mr. Kane's last was one of those bosomy historicals, full of crinoline and sideburns.

* **sidehill,** *n.*

1. sidehill plow, (see quot. 1876).

1830 *N.C. Spectator* (Rutherfordton) 13 Aug. 1/3 The *patent revolving side hill plough* has, according to them, the following advantages. **1876** KNIGHT 2173/1 *Sidehill Plow,* a plow whose cutting apparatus is reversible, so as to throw its furrow-slice to the right or left. . . . This enables the lead horse . . . to return in the furrow just made, the plow throwing the soil down hill while traveling in either direction.

2. In the names of, or with reference to, fabulous creatures especially adapted for travel on hillsides, as (1) **sidehill critter,** (2) **dodger,** (3) **gouger.** Cf. **prock.**

(1) 1849 WILLIS *Rural Letters* 93 It's a side-hill critter! Two off legs so lame, she can't stand even. — **(2) 1935** in B. A. BOTKIN *Treas. Amer. Folklore* (1944) 645 Sidehill Dodger. It lived on the sides of hills only. It had two short legs on the up-hill side. It burrowed in hillsides, having a number of such burrows and was always dodging in and out of these. — **(3) 1947** *Mich. Hist.* March 50 Fierce animals invented to frighten greenhorns like the 'sidehill gouger' and the 'hui-ja,' combine prankster and tall humor. **1949** *Sat. Ev. Post* 19 March 149/2 He obliged with some scintillating stories about sidehill gougers and a dozen other nonexistent but fascinating animals.

b. sidehill winder, (see quot.).

1922 *D.N.* 188 *Sidehill winder.* A badger with the right foreleg abnormally short. New Eng.

Sidebar buggy with top down

side judge. (See quot. 1889.)

1846 *Knickerb.* Oct. 360 The attorneys . . . in company of the supreme court judge and the 'side-judge,' take the opportunity of having a bit of fun. **1889** *Cent.* 3247/1 *Side judge,* a designation sometimes given to a magistrate, or each of two magistrates, of inferior rank, associated with a magistrate of higher grade for the purpose of constituting a court. **1914** *Cyclo. Amer. Govt.* III. 308/2 In Pennsylvania there has been from early times a system of judges not learned in the law, who sit beside the regular judge. . . . The side judges have little influence on the decision of cases, for they cannot lay down any principles of law before the jury.

side-kick ˈsaɪdˌkɪk, *n.* Also **side-kicker.** A partner or very close friend. *Slang.*

1904 O. HENRY *Cabbages and Kings* 103 Billy was my side-kicker in New York. **1922** R. PARRISH *Case & Girl* 335 He's Hogan's side-kick. **1948** *Democrat* 4 Nov. 6/1 We call a close friend a 'side kick.'

transf. **1949** *Hobbies* Oct. 137/1 Money . . . has been a 'side-kick' for thousands of years, yet we are still unacquainted with it.

sideling ˈsaɪdlɪŋ, *n.* Also **sidling.** (See quot. 1859.) Also attrib. *Obs.* — **1825** W. STRICKLAND in *Reports on Canals* 25 The passing or sideling places are formed by solid cast iron branches. **1859** BARTLETT 406 *Sidling,* a place at which to turn off on a railroad to wait for a passing engine.

* **sider,** *n. W.* (See quot.) *Obs.* — **1869** *Overland Mo.* III. 126 The mighty herd . . . [has] 'siders,' who keep the stragglers out of the chaparral.

As the last term in **East, out, sea, West sider.**

* **sidesaddle,** *n.*

1. =next. Also attrib.

1817–8 EATON *Botany* (1822) 447 *Sarracenia purpurea,* side-saddle. . . . In marshes. **1839** in *Mich. Agric. Soc. Trans.* VII. 418. **1947** *U.S. Dispensatory* 1579/1 Sarracenia. Side-saddle Plant. Pitcher Plant. Huntsman's Cup. Water Cup.

2. sidesaddle flower, the common pitcher plant, *Sarracenia purpurea*, or its flower.

1738 CATESBY *Carolina* II. 69 *Sarracena*. . . . The under Part of the Flower . . . [resembles] somewhat the Seat of a Side-Saddle, from which in Virginia it has received its Name of Side-Saddle Flower. **1850** *N. Eng. Farmer* II. 12/2 By taking up, in the autumn, the *Sarracenia*, or Side-Saddle Flower, with the wet moss attached to its roots, . . . it will flourish. **1886** S. HALE *Letters* 169 Margy's glass pail [was] full of . . . side-saddle flower. **1949** *Nat. Hist.* June 280/3 The numerous colloquial names applied to the species of Sarracenia—pitcher plant, sidesaddle flower, trumpet, huntsman's horn—aptly describe the hollow tubular leaves that serve this genus as insect traps.

b. Californian sidesaddle flower, (see quot.).

1891 *Cent.* 5616/3 *Darlingtonia Californica* has been called *Californian sidesaddle-flower*.

side show. At a circus, fair, etc., an attraction or exhibition of minor extent or importance. Also attrib. and transf.

1846 DURIVAGE *Stray Subjects* 115 He seceded from the Caravan and set up a 'side show,' travelling with the Menagerie as an independent satellite. **1886** HOWE *Moonlight Boy* 73 One of his songs related to a side-showman at a circus. **1910** FRANCK *Vagabond Journey* 276 The secretary was a man . . . with the voice of a side-show barker. **1949** *Time* 7 Feb. 58/2 In the sideshow world of the Sunday supplements . . . pterrifying pterodactyls often rub wings with faded Broadway butterflies.

sidetrack ˈsaɪdˌtræk, *n.* A railroad siding. Also attrib.

1835 *Maine Farmer* 18 July, One of the principal dealers here has offered to lay a side track from the road to his own storehouse. **1876** CROFUTT *Trans-continental Tourist* 41 Waterloo is a small side-track station. **1945** *Track* June 12 Old rail is used in sidetracks.

Also **sidetracking,** sidetracks collectively.

1892 A. E. LEE *Hist. Columbus, Ohio* II. 209 Sidetracking amply sufficient for the great mass of sojourning special trains was provided.

sidetrack ˈsaɪdˌtræk, *v.*

1. *tr.* To run (a train, car, etc.) onto a sidetrack. Also transf. or fig.

1880 *Cimarron News & Press* 19 Feb. 4/3 Short skirts are now worn for dancing dresses, and the gentlemen are no longer obliged to wait for the ladies to side-track their trains before they can pass. **1881** *Chi. Times* 14 May, [The corn] has been side-tracked and kept in the sun and rain somewhere along the road. **1886** *Leslie's Mo.* June 722/1 The next freight-train was to be side-tracked. **1900** *Cong. Rec.* 7 Feb. 1616/1 The power given to the Secretary of the Treasury to issue bonds at his pleasure effectually sidetracks the Congress. **1945** *Chi. D. News* 14 July 6/3 The Jap war would be sidetracked and ultimately settled on a compromise-peace basis.

Hence **sidetracked,** *a.*, stationed on a sidetrack. Also fig.

1889 *Las Cruces* (N.M.) *News* 15 Nov. 1/3 Among the new regulations inaugurated on the first of the month is that all headlights of side tracked locomotives . . . shall be concealed by curtains at night. **1911** WRIGHT *Winning Barbara Worth* 184 Don't get yourself sidetracked by the notion that this whole project is for the benefit of the dear people.

2. *intr.* Of a train, to move onto a sidetrack; also, of a person, to shunt a train onto a sidetrack. Also transf.

1888 *Harper's Mag.* March 650/1 One train had side-tracked to await the train from the opposite direction. **1898** HAMBLEN *Gen. Manager's Story* 185 The conductor came up and asked if I was going to sidetrack there. **1950** *Chi. Tribune* 29 March 18/5, I sit down to write Something lovely and lyrical But always sidetrack To the lightly satirical.

b. *To sidetrack on, fig.*, to leave the main subject for (something else).

1893 *Advance* 8 June, The business of the minister is to preach the gospel, not . . . to sidetrack on great moral issues.

sidewalk ˈsaɪdˌwɔk, *n.* [See note.]

The British evidence in the *OED* for this word is sporadic and hardly in the American sense. The term has been regarded by British observers and commentators as an Americanism; see quots. 1851, 1859, 1896.

A paved walk or way for pedestrians beside a street or road. Cf. **board, plank sidewalk.**

[**1790** *Mass. Centinel* XII. 13 Feb. 180/3 A certain big Grocer in Ann-Street . . . with his empty chests, barrels and kegs, . . . not only renders the side passage impassable [etc.].] **1793** *Boston Rec.* XXVII. 212 Voted, that sixty pounds be allowed by the Selectmen . . . for compleating the highway leading from the Bridge into the Town—provided the side Walks be paved with Brick or flat Stones similar to Union Street. **1851** WORTLEY *Travels* 20 The street . . . is particularly handsome; it is exceedingly wide with excellent and very broad *trottoirs* (which they call here [Albany, N.Y.] side-walks). **1859** GRATTAN *Civilized Amer.* I. 99 The middle of the streets is filled with snow several feet high, the channels overflowing, and the flag-ways, or 'side-walks,' covered with ice in patches. **1896** PHIPSON in *D.N.* I. 431 Many of your most concise and handy expressions, however, the English obstinately refuse to adopt, such as . . . *track, sidewalk*, the meanings of which can only be expressed in England by a circumlocution. **1945** *This Week Mag.* 1 Sep. 4/2 The 'papooses' skip rope or play marbles on the sidewalk with the rest of the small fry.

attrib. **1856** STOWE *Dred* I. 24 She has . . . a taste for side-walk flirtation. **1875** *Chi. Tribune* 15 Aug. 16/4 The bridge-tenders, side-walk-inspectors, and street employees . . . were paid off. **1925** *Sears Cat.* (ed. 150) 751 Improved extension sidewalk skates. **1949** *Nat. Geog. Mag.* Oct. 509 Announcer Ed Stevens interviews an Eskimo lass, . . . in a KFAR sidewalk forum.

b. sidewalk dealer, a trafficker in small wares on, or immediately adjacent to, a sidewalk.

1870 *Scribner's Mo.* I. 114 The sidewalk dealers . . . find extortion a losing game. **1872** *Atlantic Mo.* May 552/1 [The dog dealer] delivers himself of no 'patter,' like that of the sidewalk dealer in sundry small wares. **1882** MCCABE *New York* 268 The sidewalk dealers appear to drive a thriving trade.

Also *sidewalk farmer, huckster, song, space, tree*, etc.

sidewheel ˈsaɪdˌhwil, *n.*

1. One of the large paddle wheels used on a side-wheel steamer.

1845 TYLER in *Pres. Mess. & P.* IV. 367 Side wheels have been ordered, as being best tested and least liable to failure. **1945** FUGINA *Upper Mississippi* 89 Much of the steering was done by means of the side-wheels.

Hence **side-wheeler,** a side-wheel steamboat (see also quot. 1926).

1866 W. REID *After War* 204 At last a light side-wheeler came steaming down the river for us. **1926** *Amer. Sp.* I. April 369/2 They [*sc.* baseball players] are 'south-paws' or 'port-siders' or 'side-wheelers' when they are left handed. **1949** J. MONAGHAN *This is Ill.* 102 A few side-wheelers . . . remained on the rivers for a generation after the turn of the nineteenth century.

2. *attrib.* Designating various boats that use side-wheels.

Side-wheeler used in river traffic

1857 MAURY in Corbin *Life M.F. Maury* 135 She was a side-wheel steamer. **1862** MOORE *Rebellion Rec.* V. II. 136 The small iron-clad and the side-wheel gunboats were badly crippled. **1887** *Courier-Journal* (Louisville) 17 Jan. 3/6 The Louisville and Evansville Mail Line will wheel their large side-wheel packets into line to-day. **1891** WELCH *Recoll. 1830–40* 140 They seemed to have reached the ultimatum of perfection for side wheel 'steamboats.' **1948** *Westerners' Brand Book* 17 By 1847, a number of iron hull, side-wheel ocean steamers were being constructed by the government for service on the Atlantic and Pacific routes.

* **sidewinder,** *n.*

1. Any one of several small rattlesnakes, as the horned rattlesnake and the massasauga, *qq.v.*, so called in allusion to its peculiar sidewise method of looping itself along. Also **sidewinder rattlesnake.** Cf. **side-liner, side-wiper.**

1875 YARROW in *100th Meridian Rep.* V. 535 They were also seen in Arizona, and are called 'side-winders' by the settlers, owing to their peculiar lateral progressive motion. **1906** *Out West* Feb. 136 It is . . . a land of the side-winder, the Gila monster, the scorpion and the centipede. **1949** *Nat. Hist.* May 212/2 Among other interesting tracks are the slanting 'ladder-rung' trails of the sidewinder rattlesnakes.

transf. **1906** *McClure's Mag.* XXVI. 414 You never could tell where Texas Pete was goin' to jump next. He was a sidewinder and a diamond-back and a little black rattlesnake all rolled into one. **1949** *World-Herald* (Omaha) 15 May F. 8/3 The trouble never actually reached the 'Draw, you sidewinder!' phase but it had some unique angles.

2. (See quot.)

1905 *Forestry Bureau Bul.* No. 61, 46 *Side winder*, a tree knocked down unexpectedly by the fall of another.

***siding,** *n.*

1. The boarding forming the side or sides of a frame building, a piece of lumber suitable for such boarding. Often collect.

1829 COOPER *Wish-ton-Wish* xvii, [The dwellings were] constructed of a firm frame-work, neatly covered with sidings of boards. **1874** LONG *Wild-Fowl* 89 Strips of weather-boarding, or 'siding,' as it is called out West, may be made to take their place. **1950** *Chi. Tribune* 29 March 16/5 Now, all the advantages of conventional siding without any of the disadvantages.

attrib. **1858** WILKIE *Davenport* 266 Machinery, one Muley, one Rotary, one Lathing, ... one Siding Saw. **1876** KNIGHT 2568/2 Siding-tiles are used as a substitute for weather boarding. *Ib.* 2749/2 *Weather-board*, lapping siding-boards for houses. *Ib.* 2175/1 *Siding-machine*, a machine for sawing timbers, or re-sawing boards into thin stuff for weather-boarding. **1918** *Amer. Builder* April 83 Our Southern Pine products include ... siding and flooring material.

2. a. *S.* The action of plowing a row crop close to the drill (cf. ***side,** *v.* **2.**). **b.** The reduction of timber to desired dimensions.

(a) 1852 in TURNER *Cotton* (1865) 16 At this first working, unless in lands already very soft, I should advise the siding to be close and to be done with some plough which would break and loosen the earth deep about the roots of the young plant. — **(b) 1875** KNIGHT 908/2 *Forming.* (*Shipbuilding.*) ... This consists in:—*Siding;* ... *Molding;* ... *Beveling.* **1879** *Lumberman's Gaz.* 15 Oct., But mulays were used in siding down for the gang.

***siege,** *n.* A long period devoted to a single purpose or spent in a single occupation, esp. a period of prolonged illness, strain, or difficulty.

1833 CATLIN *Indians* I. 71 [Bogard was] just retiring from a ten years' siege of hunting and trapping in the Rocky Mountains. **1840** DANA *Two Years* 287 From this we escaped, having had a pretty good siege with the wooding. **1862** *Atlantic Mo.* May 558/1 We have had a siege of it. **1898** E. C. HALL *Aunt Jane* 9 She was as pale and peaked as if she had been through a siege of typhoid. **1902** HARBEN *A. Daniel* 58 For a while they have a siege of discontent.

sierra sɪˈɛrə, *n.* [Sp. in sense **1.** An Amer. borrowing.]

1. A ridge or range of hills or mountains rising in peaks suggestive of the teeth of a saw. Cf. **High Sierra.**

[1759 tr. VENEGAS *Nat. Hist. Calif.* II. 260 S. E. of this sierra, or ridge of mountains, were some white cliffs; and on them great numbers of Indians.] **1844** GREGG *Commerce of Prairies* II. 77 The sierra which separates the waters of this river and those of the Rio Pecos was always visible on our left. **1888** *Outing* Dec. 219/2 When Castle Mountain and the steel-pointed sierra behind have swerved to the right, we see northward the great glacier—nourishing the childhood of the Bow with its milky meltings. **1949** *L.A. Times* 8 May III. 6/6 As you ride over the sierra of Santa Ynez ... you will enjoy the beauty of the country that is the handiwork of God.

attrib. **1873** BEADLE *Undevel. West* 255 From noon till 5 p.m. we endure the thumping of a Concord coach over the Sierra spurs. **1903** NORTH *Mother of Calif.* 104 The large sections of the Peninsula which are not sierra regions are usually either wide deserts or hot barren llanos, or plains. **1925** BRYAN *Papago Country* 194 Each of the parts is a lozenge-shaped mountain mass of the sierra type of topography. **1947** PEATTIE *Sierra Nevada* 77 Although the John Muir Trail takes top honors in sheer mileage of superlative scenery, many other Sierra trails rival it in variety and charm.

2. (Usu. *cap.*) Often used in combs., esp. in the names of, or with reference to, animals and plants found in the Sierra Mountain region, as (1) **Sierra bighorn,** (2) **big tree,** (3) **creeper,** (4) **grouse,** (5) **hare,** (6) **heather,** (7) **hermit thrush,** (8) **(Nevada) jay,** (9) **juniper,** (10) **pine,** (11) **red fox,** (12) **State.**

(1) 1942 Nat. Pk. Service *Fading Trails* 50 A small and lighter-colored form called the Sierra bighorn lived in the Sierra Nevada of California. **1949** *Sierra Club Bul.* June 119 The Sierra Bighorn ..., occurs only in the wildest and least accessible regions of the Sierra mainly between the Palisades and Mount Whitney. — **(2) 1906** *Out West* March 176 The cones of one of our redwoods—the Sierra Big Tree— ... are ... the size of a hen's egg. — **(3) 1941** LOFBERG *Sierra Outpost* 222 Yes, it was a Sierra creeper, working its way up the rough crevices of the bole. — **(4) 1904** *Auk* 412 *Dendragapus obscurus sierrae*—Chapman Sierra Grouse. ... California (forested portions of Transition and Boreal zones), north to Fort Klamath, Oregon. **1947** PEATTIE *Sierra Nevada* 33 There are ... warm slopes of manzanita and chinquapin where the Sierra grouse drums its resonant 'thunk, thunk.'

(5) 1941 LOFBERG *Sierra Outpost* 59 A Sierra hare feeding on stiff weed-stem tips must have attracted the coyote's attention. — **(6) 1911** CHASE *Yosemite Trails* 232 Here I met my first Sierra heather (Bryanthus) with one sprig of rosy blossoms still waiting for me. — **(7) 1917** *Birds of Amer.* III. 236/1 The Sierra Hermit Thrush (*Hylocichla guttata sequoiensis*) is slightly darker and decidedly larger than the Monterey. — **(8) 1884** COUES *Key to Birds* 422 *Cyanocitta stelleri frontalis*, ... Sierra Jay. **1917** *Birds of Amer.* II. 220/2 In the Rocky Mountain section of the United States ... [is found] the Blue-fronted Jay or Sierra Nevada Jay. — **(9) 1869** MUIR *First Summer in Sierra* (1911) 220 A still hardier mountaineer is the Sierra juniper (*Juniperus occidentalis*), growing mostly on domes and ridges and glacier pavements. **1949** TRESIDDER *Trees of Yosemite* 27 It touches shoulders with Mountain Hemlock and, occasionally, with White-Bark Pine, while the Sierra Juniper is a neighbor of the rocks.

(10) 1879 WILLIAMS *Pacific Tourist* 226/2 An avalanche has come down and our way lies through the tangled trunks of these huge Sierra pines. — **(11) 1917** *Mammals of Amer.* 73/1 Sierra Red Fox.—*Vulpes necator*. ... High Sierra above 6000 feet altitude in California. — **(12) 1851** *S.F. Picayune* 23 Sep. 2/1 We shall not be surprised to see, at a day not far distant, Senators and Representatives from the Sierra State [California], take their seats in Congress.

Sierran sɪˈɛrən, *a.* and *n.*

1. *n.* A native or inhabitant of the Sierra Nevada Mt. region; also a member of the Sierra Club.

1906 *Out West* May 393 About one hundred Mazamas, Appalachians and Sierrans were gathered around a camp-fire. **1923** *Outing* April 28/2 Equipped with these data, a compass and a set of maps, the dauntless, city-bred Sierran plunged daily into the fastnesses of the mountains. **1948** *So. Sierran* Feb. 1/3 Many Sierrans who hiked the trails twenty and more years ago, will be interested to know what has happened to one of their favorite gathering places, Colby's Ranch.

2. *a.* Of or pertaining to the Sierra Nevada Mts.

1873 HARTE *Stories & Poems* (1914) 216 It was in a Sierran solitude, where I had encamped. **1886** ——— *Snow-bound* 3 Darkness had accompanied a Sierran stage-coach towards the summit. **1902** *Out West* Oct. 440 The tender herbage of the high Sierran meadows is not sustaining. **1947** *Sierra Club Bul.* March 7/2 The earlier expedition followed one of the heaviest of recent winters, and was more arctic than Sierran.

***sieve,** *n.* As the last term in **market, rocker sieve.**

siffleur siˈflɜ, *n.* [F. in Can. F. sense shown here.] **=hoary marmot.** Cf. ***whistler 2.**

1843 T. J. FARNHAM *Travels* 110/2 Abundance of game exists, such as elk, deer, antelope, ... a few grizzly bears and siffleurs, which are eaten by the Canadians. **1936** MCCOWAN *Animals Canadian Rockies* 19 French Canadian voyageurs of fur trading days, shouldering boats and bales across Athabasca Pass, saw these animals basking on the rocks and hearing their clear shrill call, named them *Siffleur* or Whistler. **1949** *Canadian Alpine Jrnl.* May 32 They dined on 'delicious siffleur' which tasted on the tongue like 'very delicate mutton or the fat of sucking pig.'

attrib. **1858** in WHEELER *Selkirk Range* (1905) 141 The Sposshewan Indians make robes of siffleur skins.

***sifter,** *n.* As the last term in **deerskin, hominy sifter.**

***sight,** *n.*

1. In poker, a show of hands. Also *to call a sight.*

1823 LONG *Hoyle's Games* 162 If he calls *a sight*, the cards must be shown in rotation, the player who calls showing last, and the best hand wins the pot. **1850** BOHN *Handbook Games* 381 Should one of the party over-reach the amount that is in possession of an adversary, a '*sight*' may be demanded. **1887** *Courier-Journal* 23 Jan. 15/7 Then a rule sprang up that a man should be allowed a sight for his money.

2. (See quots.)

1848 BARTLETT 303 In North Carolina the distance that can be seen on a road is called a sight. **1891** *Cent.* 5620/2 *Sight*, ... a straight stretch of road, as one along which a sight may be taken in surveying; a line uninterrupted by a bend or an elevation: as, go on three sights, and stop at the first house. Also called *look.* (Western U.S.)

3. (See quot. 1891.)

1849 KINGSLEY *Diary* 74, I began on some wheels for wheelbarrows but had a hard sight to get the lumber suitable for them. **1891** *Cent.* 5620 *Sight*, ... an opportunity for doing something; an opening; a chance; a 'show': as, he has no sight against his opponent. (Colloq.)

4. One of the nails in the ends of a billiard table.

1864 DICK *Amer. Hoyle* (1866) 419 A line is drawn down the centre of the table, from the centre nails or sights in the head and lower cushions. **1899** CHAMPLIN & BOSTWICK *Cyclo. Games & Sports* (ed. 2)

81 The first [spot], opposite the second 'sight,' is sometimes called the light red spot, the second, opposite the sixth 'sight,' the dark red spot.

5. In combs.: (1) **sight bill,** =**sight draft;** (2) **check,** a check payable at sight; (3) **draft,** a draft payable on presentation; (4) **pea,** the front sight on a rifle, *rare;* (5) **piece,** a gun sight, or the piece of metal upon which this is mounted; (6) ***reading,** reading or translating a foreign language at sight; (7) **tree,** (see quot.); (8) **writer,** one who in typing watches the keyboard.

(1) **1853** *S. Lit. Messenger* XIX. 89/2 Mr. Thompson agreed to accommodate him with a sight bill on his correspondent in Raleigh. **1887** *Courier-Journal* 5 May 7/3 Eastern exchange was firm, and there were more buyers than sellers of New York sight bills at 80¢ per $1,000 premium. — (2) **1863** E. KIRKE *Southern Friends* 232, I enclose you sight check of Branch Bank of Cape Fear on Bank of Republic, for $10,820. — (3) **1850** *Fla. Plantation Rec.* 60 Your favor of the 22d. ult. enclosing sight draft on Messrs. Habersham for $200 has been duly received. **1903** O. HENRY *Cabbages & Kings* 209 It's a sight-draft on your president man for twenty thousand dollars. — (4) **1838** GOSSE *Letters* 269 The muzzle of his rifle just projecting in front of the board, so that the light may fall on the sight-pea.

(5) **1835** HOFFMAN *Winter in West* II. 171 (*footnote*), The long western rifle has three sight-pieces on the barrel. **1874** LONG *Wild-Fowl* 24 [The] sight-piece [should be] small and close to the muzzle. — (6) **1891** W. R. HARPER in *Univ. Chi. Official Bul.* 111, 9 Schedule of Courses offered in Higher Academy. . . . Department of Greek. . . . Sight-reading. **1899** QUINN *Pa. Stories* 170 He never called us up on the regular lesson, . . . but kept us for the sight-reading. — (7) **1917** KEPHART *Camping* II. 66 All trees that stand directly on the line of survey have two chops or notches cut on each side of them, without any other marks whatever. These are called 'sight trees' or 'line trees' (sometimes 'fore and aft trees'). — (8) **1918** OWEN *Typewriting Speed* 143 Many sight writers use all the fingers.

b. In phrases: (1) *To draw a sight upon,* to take aim at, also fig.; (2) *by a darned* (*considerable, long*) *sight,* by a good deal, usu. in negative expressions, *slang* or *colloq.;* (3) **in sight,* (see quot. 1900).

(1) **1834** *Cong. Deb.* 25 Feb. 691, I supposed for once in my life I saw gentlemen in the open field, and might be able to draw a fine sight upon them. **1848** DRAKE *Pioneer Life Ky.* 218 You must . . . watch till the dawn of day when the animal comes to drink, and then 'draw a sight' upon his head. — (2) **1834** C. A. DAVIS *Lett. J. Downing* 41 'Gineral, do you want another report?' 'Not by a darn'd sight.' **1844** *Republican Sentinel* (Richmond, Va.) 22 June 1/2 These animals begin to venture out a little of nights, since the Baltimore Convention, but are slyer by a long sight than foxes. **1884** MARK TWAIN *H. Finn* i, I asked her if she reckoned Tom Sawyer would go there, and she said not by a considerable sight. **1896** HARRIS *Sister Jane* 63 That ain't all by a long sight. — (3) **1900** NELSON *A B C Wall St.* 148 *In sight.* Merchandise available for immediate use, and a term applied to grain, cotton and coffee. **1905** *N.Y. Ev. Post* 28 Oct. 6 With . . . all the material in sight, . . . the small builders are beginning to fear that some will be unable to complete contracts.

As the last term in **back, California, globe, heap, hind, pinhead sight.**

***sight,** *v.* **1.** *tr.* To take aim at (see also quot. 1881). **2.** *intr.* To look *around. Colloq.* **3.** *To sight in,* to align (railroad ties) by means of a sighting device.

(1) **1871** *Harper's Mag.* Dec. 48/2 No sooner, however, did he 'sight,' or try to sight, the horseman in question, . . . than the thumping against the ribs again began. **1881** INGERSOLL *Oyster Industry* 248 *Sight,* to be able to see oysters at the bottom and direct tongs to them (Virginia). — (2) **1891** RYAN *Pagan* 40 Naw, I ain't hunting, . . . but as I was sightin' around the mountain, big Bill Riker, he come up to me. — (3) **1872** HUNTINGTON *Road-Master's Ass't* 16 A more ready method of laying the 'leading ties' is to 'sight them in' by the use of 'target boards.'

***sighted,** *a.* As the last term in **double, globe sighted.**

***sightly,** *a.* (See quot. 1828.)

1828 WEBSTER, *Sightly,* . . . open to the view; that may be seen from a distance. We say, a house stands in a sightly place. **1873** MARK TWAIN & WARNER *Gilded Age* 165 The University up there, on rising ground, sightly place, see the river for miles. **1912** *Buffalo Commercial* 2 June 12 The hotel occupies a sightly location.

***sign,** *n.*

1. Evidence in the form of tracks, broken twigs, etc., indicating the recent presence of men, usu. Indians.

1692 *Va. State P.* I. 44 We Ranged about to see if we could find ye tract of any Indians, but we could not see any fresh signe. **1822** FOWLER *Journal* 97 The men are all feerfull of meeting With the Indeans as We . . . Have maid So much Sign in the Snow that the[y] will track us up. **1883** RITCH *Illust. N. Mex.* 103 Probably the Apache has been seen in the neighborhood for the last time, but the pioneers have not lost the habit of watching for his 'sign.'

b. Of animals, usu. with defining terms.

1804 CLARK in *Lewis & C. Exped.* I. (1904) 68 Great Deel of Elk Sign. **1853** P. PAXTON *Yankee in Texas* 117 Nothing leaves a *mark* to him [*sc.* a Texan], he only sees *sign,* whether of bird or beast, friend or enemy. You hear of *turkey sign, bear sign, hog sign, cow sign, Indian sign,* etc. **1946** R. PEATTIE *Pac. Coast Ranges* 213 There is one cougar sign, however, that you may discover along the trail, and that is little heaps of earth pawed up at intervals of about a hundred yards, perhaps from pure playfulness and high spirits.

c. *To cut a sign,* to come across evidence of Indians, game, etc. *Colloq.*

1893 REMINGTON in *Harper's Mag.* LXXXVIII. 72/2 He chased the Indians off his ranch whenever he 'cut their sign.' [**1914** D. W. ROBERTS *Rangers* 137, I took a scout immediately and 'cut sign' for the trail.]

2. In a sign language, the movement, gesture, etc., which identifies or represents a particular person or tribe. *Obs.*

1857 *Lawrence* (Kans.) *Republican* 11 June 4 It is not easy to forget your *sign,* you are Col. Buchanan, and I am right glad to see you. **1870** KEIM *Sheridan's Troopers* 221 Each tribe, to begin with, has its name in sign.

3. In combs.: (1) ***signboard,** a board, usu. on a post beside a road, bearing directions or information for

Once common type of roadside signboard

travelers, cf. **mile board;** (2) **camp,** see as a main entry; (3) **jack,** a laborer whose work has to do with large billboards; (4) **manual,** a sign made by the hand or hands, the system of signs made in this way; (5) **rider,** *W.* =**line rider,** (see also quot. 1907); (6) **riding,** the work of a cowboy sign rider; (7) **talker,** one who uses a sign language.

(1) **1829** ROYALL *Pennsylvania* II. 38 You scarcely go a mile in Pennsylvania but you see a *Preacher*—as signboards are called. They point out the road, but never travel it. **1883** *Wheelman* I. 298 They found a sign-board pointing to Swampscott and Lynn. — (3) **1906** *N.Y. Ev. Post* 17 Aug. 2 The 'sign-jacks' find regular employment from the bill-poster and street advertising companies. — (4) **1833** CATLIN *Indians* I. 116 [The chief's] orders and commands . . . were uniformly given by signs manual. **1871** *Rep. Indians Affairs* (1872) 472 We labored under many great disadvantages in . . . having to depend on the 'sign-manual' altogether.

(5) **1885** SIRINGO *Texas Cow Boy* 176 To turn back any cattle that might slip by the 'signriders.' **1907** COOK *Border & Buffalo* (1938) 308 It all sounds well, but how about that dead Indian down in the tules? He was a sign-rider. He was making a big circle around their camp to see if he could find any signs of approaching enemies. — (6) **1902** A. MCGOWAN *Last Word* 176 'No, this wasn't herding,' Jim added, 'it was something almost as lonesome, though—sign riding.' — (7) **1907** COOK *Border & Buffalo* (1938) 430 Amos was a good sign-talker, and tried to talk to him, but he was stoical and silent.

As the last term in **bear, beaver, cattle, deer, dollar, electric, hog, Indian, possum, snake, tin, water sign.**

***sign,** *v.*

1. *intr.* (See quot.)

1888 *Amer. Folk-Lore* I. 161 *Sign,* constantly used in Washington as a term for marking off the land for corn or potatoes.

2. In phrases: (1) *To sign off,* (*a*) to withdraw from membership in a religious body, to change one's church membership *to* another denomination, also **signing off,** (*b*) (see quot.), both *obs.;* (2) *to sign up,* to secure the signature of (a person), as to a contract, to sign.

(1) (*a*) **1838** EMERSON *Works* I. (1903) 143 In the country neighborhoods, half parishes are *signing off*, to use the local term. **1878** STOWE *Poganuc People* 12, 'I'm glad father signed off to the 'Piscopalians. . . .' 'My papa won't ever sign off.' *Ib.* 27 After the close of the [Revolutionary] war . . . the revolution came which broke up the State Church and gave to every man the liberty of 'signing off,' . . . to any denomination that pleased him. (*b*) **1859** BARTLETT 407 *To Sign off*, to release a debtor by agreeing to accept whatever he offers to pay; to give a receipt in full of all demands. An expression common among merchants. — (2) **1903** A. H. LEWIS *The Boss* 186 You can tell by th' way they go to bat, whether th' Blackberry has signed up to them to kill our franchise. **1945** *This Week Mag.* 21 April 11/2 Dick Jess, the Babe's manager, signed her up and changed her name to Peggy O'Neill.

* **signal,** *n.* In combs.: (1) **signal bearer,** one who carries the flags, etc., used by surveyors; (2) **camp,** a camp or place from which signals are sent; (3) **Corps,** the branch of the U.S. Army in charge of signal communications and information, also attrib.; (4) **kit,** a kit of articles used by signalmen; (5) **office,** a government bureau in charge of signaling (see **signal service** (*b*) quot. 1891); (6) **service,** (*a*) a system of communication by signals, or an organization operating such a system (see (*b*) quot. 1891), also fig., (*b*) also attrib.; (7) **smoke,** smoke serving as a signal or sign to those at a distance, cf. **smoke signal;** (8) **staff,** =**signal tower,** *rare;* (9) * **station,** =**flag station;** (10) * **tower,** in railroading, a small tower or structure where signals, often semaphores, are set or controlled.

(1) **1854** WHIPPLE *Explor. Ry. Route* I. 5 The parties at present are divided as follows: Mr. Albert Campbell, surveyor; . . . Messrs. Jones and Gaines, signal bearers [etc.]. — (2) **1884** *Cent. Mag.* April 827/1 Charles Caywood . . . kept the signal camp in the swampy woods back of Grimes's house. — (3) **1865** *Atlantic Mo.* June 753/1 Lieutenant Clemens of the Signal Corps, put off from the tug in a launch. **1949** *Democrat* 30 June 2/2 Signal corps officials said the walls, floor, and ceilings of the new chamber are covered with wedge-shaped hunks of fiberglass. — (4) **1887** BILLINGS *Hardtack* 396 Details of men were made from the various regiments . . . to learn the use of the 'Signal Kit,' so called. The chief article in this kit was a series of seven flags.

(5) **1872** *Harper's Mag.* Dec. 151 The appropriation by Congress to the Signal-office, with a view to the interests of agriculture as well as of commerce, was one of the results. — (6) (*a*) **1871** *Harper's Mag.* Aug. 406/1 The *military system* is one of the most . . . valuable features . . . of this Signal Service for the benefit of commerce. **1898** CANFIELD *Maid of Frontier* 105 The signal service inside of my shirt has never failed to telegraph me when to look out for the blue wind. (*b*) **1887** *Nation* 12 May 404/3 The information [in a guidebook] includes . . . the signal-service flags, postal rates [etc.]. **1891** *Cent.* 5624/2 *Signal-service Bureau*, from 1871 to the end of 1890, a bureau of the United States War Department, . . . having charge of military signaling and military telegraph-lines, and of the collection and comparison of meteorological observations, and the publication of predictions of the weather based upon them. **1893** *Harper's Mag.* March 489/1 On our way to the cars we read a Signal Service bulletin announcing the temperature in New York to be 24°. — (7) **1834** A. PIKE *Sketches* 58 This day we had seen a large signal-smoke rise to the right behind a mountain. **1943** BENÉT *Western Star* 9 Old riders in the saddle of the past, Old sergeants, carrying Apache lead, Old signal-smokes, grown meaningless at last. — (8) **1833** *Amer. R.R. Jrnl.* II. 548/3 Signal staffs are erected, by means of which information can be transmitted from one end of the road to the other. — (9) **1876** CROFUTT *Trans-continental Tourist* 50 *Barton*, a signal station of very little importance. **1887** *Courier-Journal* 2 Feb. 3/2 The train stopped about a mile from Jeffersonville, at a signal station.

(10) **1900** *Everybody's Mag.* II. 445/1 There has been erected a special signal tower at the great Horseshoe Curve on the Pennsylvania. **1917** MATHEWSON *Second Base Sloan* 15 Eight burnished rails . . . crossed their path, under a big signal tower.

As the last term in **bootjack, smoke, train air, war signal.**

sign camp. *W.* (See quots. 1926, 1944.)

1885 SIRINGO *Texas Cow Boy* 159 We . . . established 'Sign' camps around the entire range. **1926** BRANCH *Cowboy* 95 'Sign camps' were occasionally established about an entire range. There were two men to each camp; their work was to herd back all cattle that might have drifted across the 'line.' The ride of each man was from his 'sign camp' half-way toward the next camp. **1944** ADAMS *W. Words* 144/1 sign camp A building or dugout where the cowboy sleeps and cooks his meals while line riding.

transf. **1897** LEWIS *Wolfville* 2 We'll show Red Dog an' sim'lar villages they ain't sign-camps compared with Wolfville.

* **signer,** *n.* One of those who signed the American Declaration of Independence in 1776.

1820 *Niles' Reg.* XVII. 441/1 There now remain but four signers of the declaration of independence. **1881** *Harper's Mag.* March 530/2 Tradition whispers that in 1736 Philip Livingstone, one of the signers of the Declaration, saved the life of this historical elm. **1949** *Sun. World-Herald Mag.* (Omaha) 10 April 13/2 If you want to start right off at the top, get a manuscript dealer to assemble for you a set of the 'signers' of the Declaration of Independence.

b. Great Signer, Thomas Jefferson (1743–1826), author and thirty-second signer of the Declaration of Independence. *Rare.*

1883 *Harper's Mag.* July 319/2 When the great Signer stopped talking the countryman rushed for his hat.

signist, see **pure signist.**

siki ˈsikɪ, *n.* [Origin obscure.] (See quot.) *Obs.* — **1807** *Mass. H. S. Coll.* 2 Ser. III. 58 The siki, or common clam, is found on the borders of the lagunes and in several other parts of the island.

* **silent,** *a.* In combs.: (1) **silent partner,** a partner who is not active in the management of a firm; (2) **system,** (see quot. 1891), cf. **Auburn system;** (3) **vote,** the vote of those whose choice cannot be predicted, also **silent voter.**

(1) **1828** WEBSTER, *Silent*, . . . not acting; not transacting business in person; as a silent partner in a commercial house. **1898** *McClure's Mag.* X. 499/1 In this firm J. D. Fish, president of the Marine Bank, was to be a silent partner. **1946** FOREMAN *Last Trek* 127 The collections in the Indiana State Library are replete with references to 'silent partners.' — (2) **1836** T. POWER *Impressions of Amer.* I. 226 Auburn, celebrated for its prison, regulated upon what is called the 'silent system.' **1891** *Cent.* 5628/1 *Silent system*, a system of prison discipline which imposes entire silence among the prisoners, even when assembled together. — (3) **1884** *Judge* 12 Nov. 149/2 To the Silent Voter, who was to make himself Felt for Cleveland: Tell me where you are and all will be forgiven. **1934** WEBSTER. **1936** *Durant* (Okla.) *D. Democrat* 2 Nov. 2/4 The regents and police pensions amendments have the best chances of carrying, but even they are endangered by the 'silent vote.'

* **silk,** *n.*

1. *collect.* The fine soft styles of an ear of Indian corn.

[*c***1662** JOHN WINTHROP in *N. Eng. Quart.* X. (1937) 126 There groweth within the Huske upon the Corne a matter like small threads which appeare out of the top of the Eare like a tuft of haire or Silke.] **1757** in WOODWARD *Ploughs* (1841) 279 Don't Top till ye Silk dies & ye Corn grows hard. **1834** *Beardstown* (Ill.) *Chron.* 20 Dec. 4/2 If a silk receives no farina from any source, it will be barren and no grain be connected with it. **1948** *Savings News* Jan. 6/2 One drop of pollen falling from the tassel, perhaps on the same stalk or perhaps two miles away, would fertilize one ovary in the silk.

b. *in silk(s)*, of Indian corn, at the stage of development when the silk is most conspicuous.

1774 FITHIAN *Journal* I. 212 The Corn is beginning pretty generally to tassel, & I saw one hill in Silk. **1784** SMYTH *Tour* I. 295 This state of it is denominated *the Corn being in Silks.* **1847** DRAKE *Pioneer Life Ky.* 52 By the month of August the corn is in silk.

2. The lash of a whip.

1841 *N.O. Picayune* 11 March 2/3 Maria was fed on the heaviest doses of silk from the first jump out. **1873** MILLER *Amongst Modocs* 368 The driver . . . snapped the silk under the heels of his leaders. **1947** PRICE *Trails I Rode* 240, I don't hear his brake blocks squeak as he pulls his six to a stop, or hear the snap of his silk as he swings them into a lope when leaving.

b. silk-popper, a stagecoach driver. Also *knight of the silk. Obs.* or *hist.*

1896 SHINN *Story of Mine* 167 Even that aristocrat of the fraternity, the lordly 'silk-popper,' flicking his playful whip . . . skillfully steered his loaded stages along the precipices. **1949** HINKLE *Sierra-Nevada Lakes* 278 Such were the famous knights of the silk—'Curly Bob' Gearhart, Johnny Wilson, . . . and Prince Lewis.

3. A variety of cotton. Also attrib. *Obs.*

1850 in TURNER *Cotton* (1865) 111 The Silk Cotton seed sent to J. V. J. was grown here, the second crop from seed sent me by my friend Col. H. W. Vick, of Vicksburg. **1851** *De Bow's Review* X. 568 '*Silk*' I planted this year.

4. In special combs.: (1) **silk ball,** (see quot. 1884), *obs.;* (2) **bunting,** (see quot. 1891); (3) **crab,** a mature female crab; (4) * **grass,** (see quot. 1891); (5) **plant,** a species of plantain, *Plantago rugeli;* (6) * **stocking,** see as a main entry; (7) **tassel bush, tree,** (see quot. 1909);

(8) **top palmetto,** (see quot. 1890); (9) **train,** (see quot. 1947); (10) * **weed,** any one of various American plants of the genus *Asclepias*, also attrib.

(**1**) **1741** W. STEPHENS *Proc. Georgia* II. 135 Silk Balls . . . were to be taken at a good and certain Price. **1884** *Science* 9 May 562 The term 'silk-balls' was doubtless employed at times to designate cocoons but that is quite different from 'raw-silk' and 'raw-silk balls,' which . . . might more appropriately apply to the twisted hanks of raw silk. — (**2**) **1884** COUES *Key to Birds* 387 *Spiza*, Silk Bunting. **1891** *Cent.* 5630/1 *Silk-bunting*, . . . an American bunting of the genus *Spiza* (formerly *Euspiza*), as the black-throated *S. americana*, whose plumage is peculiarly close and smooth. — (**3**) **1942** GRAHAM & BEAVEN *Chesapeake Biol. Lab. Pub.* 52, 9 It is at this final molt that the female . . . becomes a silk . . . crab. — (**4**) **1743** CLAYTON *Flora Virginica* 152 Yucca flore albo, foliorum marginibus filamentosis. Silkgrass. **1775** ROMANS *Nat. Hist. Florida* 156 *Silk Grass* grows on the most barren sand hills of Florida (called black Jack ridges) . . . the root having been found by experience to wash woollen the cleanest and whitest of any thing yet known. **1891** *Cent.* 5630/2 silk-grass. . . . The Adam's-needle or bear-grass, *Yucca filamentosa:* in allusion to its fiber, which has been the subject of some experiment, but has not been brought into use.

(**5**) **1806** *Ann. 9th Congress* 2 Sess. 1142 The silk plant, wild endive, wild olive [etc., grow] . . . along the river side. **1852** STANSBURY *Gt. Salt Lake* 175 Among the springs was found . . . a plant I had not before seen—called by some of the men silk-plant. **1894** *Amer. Folk-Lore* VII. 96 *Plantago Rugelii*, . . . silk-plant, Fla. — (**7**) **1907** LYONS *Plant Names* 571 G[arrya] elliptica Dougl. Pacific border U.S. Silk-tassel tree, Quinine bush. **1909** WEBSTER, silk-tassel tree. A California cornaceous tree (*Garrya elliptica*), having silky aments. **1949** HOWELL *Marin Flora* 211 The graceful catkins of the staminate plants make the silk tassel bush one of the most beautiful shrubs in the chaparral. — (**8**) **1884** SARGENT *Rep. Forests* 217 Silk-top Palmetto. Semi-tropical Florida. **1890** *Cent.* 4249/1 *Silk-top palmetto*, the name in Florida of *Thrinax parviflora*, found there and in the West Indies: a tree some 30 feet high, turned to minor uses. **1897** SUDWORTH *Arborescent Flora* 103. — (**9**) **1909** *Harper's Wkly.* 4 Dec. 11/1 If a limited loses time and gets in the way, the limited has to fret on a siding while the silk train roars by in a whirlwind of dust. **1947** *N. & Q.* July 51/1 The silk train—carrying a cargo of raw silk valued at several millions of dollars and roaring west-to-east across the Continent on a faster-than-passenger schedule—is only a little less than ten years dead. . . . It is certain that by 1909 a silk train, serving a single purpose, had acquired a personality in the railroad family. **1949** *Boston Globe* 12 June (Fiction Mag.) 2/5 You heard of the silk train?

(**10**) **1784** *Amer. Acad. Mem.* I. 424 The seeds are contained in large pods, and are crowned with white down, . . . resembling silk, which has occasioned the name of Silkweed. **1854** EMMONS *Agric. N.Y.* V. 263 Silkweed insect, 124. *Ib.* 124 This insect is common on the silkweed . . . in June and July. **1940** STUART *Trees of Heaven* 48 There is the musty smell of ironweeds, milkweeds, silkweeds, clusters of smartweeds, jimson weeds, and bull grass on the lazy wind.

b. *fine as silk*, very fine indeed. *Colloq.*

1836 CROCKETT *Exploits* 64 'That's fine,' say I. 'Fine as silk, colonel, and leetle finer,' says the other. **1905** BELASCO *Girl of Golden West* (1925) I. 61, 'I trust the Girl who runs the Polka is well?' . . . 'Fine as silk, Mr. Ashby.'

As the last term in **bark, corn, Indian, milkweed, Virginia, wild, wrapping silk.**

silk sɪlk, *v.*

1. *intr.* Of corn: To produce or put forth the silk.

1783 S. DEANE *Diary* (1849) 354 Some of my corn silked. **1876** *Wkly. Comanche* (Tex.) *Chief* 22 June 3/3 Corn that is now silking and tasseling will make without any more rains. **1902** *Mo. Weather Rev.* July 346/1 The month closed with the . . . oat harvest far advanced . . . , corn mostly silking or earing. **1948** *Democrat* 3 June 1/3 This worm usually waits until corn bunches for tasseling or begins to silk before they attack.

2. *tr.* To free (a roasting ear) of its silks in preparing it for use as food.

1847 DRAKE *Pioneer Life Ky.* 52 My first business in the morning was to pull, and husk and silk enough [corn] for breakfast. **1892** *York Co. Hist. Rev.* 59 [They] make a specialty of . . . 'silkers' for silking corn.**1939** HARRIS *Purslane* 77 She shucked and silked twelve roas'n' ears.

silkaline ˈsɪlkəˌlin, *n.* Also **silkolene.** A soft cotton fabric resembling silk. Also attrib.

1896 *Internat. Typog. Union Proc.* 64/1, 12 yds. silkaline, $1.80. **1911** O. HENRY *Rolling Stones* 197 The last wrinkle and darn of their blue silkolene cotton tights had vanished from the stage. **1918** *Sears Cat.* (ed. 137) 1164/1 A beautiful rose design in a border Silkoline.

silker ˈsɪlkɚ, *n.* A device for removing the silks from green corn. *Rare.* — **1892** [see **silk,** *v.* **2.**].

* **silk-stocking,** *n.*

1. (See quots. 1891, 1914.)

1891 *Cent.* 5630/1 *A silk-stocking*, a person of this [luxurious or wealthy] class. **1914** *Cyclo. Amer. Govt.* III. 309/1 *Silk Stockings*, a derisive appellation bestowed by the 'practical politicians' upon those citizens of wealth and high social position who occasionally interfere in politics in support of some reform measure or candidate. **1929** W. A. WHITE *Masks in Pageant* 233 Roosevelt was an unknown young silk-stocking in the Civil Service Commission.

2. *attrib.* Designating or pertaining to the wealthy.

1798 *Ann. 5th Cong.* 1948 If they wished to place them in a ridiculous point of view, or to procure for them the name of the *Silk Stocking Company*, or any other term of derision, they could not take a more effectual course to obtain it. *c***1840** in BUCKINGHAM *E. & W. States* II. 117 'Prime Havannas' . . . are only dealt out to his [Van Buren's] 'silk-stocking and ruffle-shirt friends.' **1903** *N.Y. Ev. Post* 30 Oct. 2 Political conditions change even in the 'silk stocking' quarter—the middle reaches of Manhattan, between 14th Street and 96th Street. **1948** *Time* 5 July 20/2 In as chairman . . . went 47-year-old Hugh Scott Jr., a three-term Congressman from a suburban Philadelphia 'silk-stocking' district.

b. Esp. **silk-stocking gentry,** (see quot. 1891).

1812 JEFFERSON *Writings* XIII. 163, I trust . . . the Gores and Pickerings will find their levees crowded with silk stocking gentry, but no yeomanry. **1891** *Cent.* 5630/1 Silk-stockings . . . were formerly regarded as extravagant and reprehensible, and as worn by men were regarded as an indication of luxurious habits; hence, the *silk-stocking gentry* or *element*, the luxurious or wealthy class.

* **silky,** *a.* **silky cornel, silky panic grass,** (see quots.). —**1891** COULTER *Bot. W. Texas* I. 150 *C[ornus] sericea.* Silky cornel. . . . Common in the Atlantic States and extending into eastern and northern Texas. **1894** *Ib.* III. 502 *P[anicum] lachnanthum.* (Silky Panic-grass.) . . . Dry plains, western Texas.

* **silver,** *n.*

1. In miscellaneous combs.: (1) **silver bonanza,** a rich silver mine; (2) **brick,** a bricklike mass of silver, also transf. in allusion to the silverites, cf. **gold brick 2;** (3) **claim,** *W.* a claim to an area selected for silver-mining purposes; (4) **exchange,** (see quot. 1879); (5) **gray,** see as a main entry; (6) **Land,** a nickname for Nevada; (7) **palace (sleeping) car,** an especially luxurious passenger car having scroll work, velvet upholstery, potted ferns, organ with hymn books, etc.; (8) **sand,** white sand of a kind sometimes used on floors; (9) **spike,** a railroad spike made of silver and used in the ceremonies held upon the completion of the Pacific railroad, cf. **golden spike;** (10) **state,** (*a*) (*cap.*) Nevada, a nickname, also, rarely, Colorado, (*b*) a state producing silver or advocating the free coinage of silver; (11) **strike,** *W.* the discovery of a rich silver-mining area; (12) **top,** (*a*) ?a mug of beer, *rare*, (*b*) a condition of grass in which the upper part whitens.

(**1**) **1906** *Out West* Feb. 94 Through it flowed much of the wealth from the silver bonanzas and the silver leads of the section are still rich. — (**2**) **1869** BROWNE *Adv. Apache Country* 295 'Struck it rich!' 'Silver bricks!' and 'Pay rock!' hummed and drummed through the air. **1876** RAYMOND *8th Rep. Mines* 354 Individuals are constantly carrying out bags of gold and gold bricks and some silver bricks. **1896** *Harper's Wkly.* 8 Aug. 779/3 Among the 'silver bricks' put out by these 'confidence men' of modern politics the following may be further cited. — (**3**) **1902** MARK TWAIN *Double-Barrelled Detective Story* (1928) 308 (R.), His silver-claim was at the other end of the village. — (**4**) **1879** *Scribner's Mo.* Oct. 823/1 Along Chestnut street are the 'silver exchanges,' otherwise gambling rooms,—dozens of them, with wide-open doors, and music playing. **1948** *Popular Western* June 25/2 'Well—if it ain't the ex-marshal!' grunted the outlaw who had held up a Silver Exchange down in the Nevada diggings.

(**6**) **1863** *Gold Hill* (Nev.) *News* 31 Oct. 2/1 Since our advance into this section of Silver Land, we have made this discovery as to the whereabouts of our old acquaintances. **1942** LILLARD *Desert Challenge* 187 Each virgin province in Silver Land was a glittering El Dorado. — (**7**) **1867** *Chi. Republican* 24 July 5/3 We have swept through from New York to Chicago in the Silver Palace Sleeping-Cars, without changing a single car. **1881** MARSHALL *Through Amer.* (1882) 145 Passengers bound West now change into the 'silver palace' cars of the Central Pacific. **1947** BEEBE *Mixed Train Dly.* 174 It was on the Silver Palace cars of the Colorado narrow gages that John Morrisey dreamed of spending the profits from the *Highland Mary* [Mine]. — (**8**) **1889** MELLICK *Story Old Farm* 54 No carpets were to be seen, the floors being covered with silver sand drawn into fanciful figures by a skillful use of the sweeping brush, in which the housekeepers took much pride. — (**9**) **1869** *N.Y. Times* 12 May 1/2 In presenting the silver spike to Dr. Durant yesterday, in performance of his part in the exercises attending the laying of the last rail of the great Pacific Road. **1906** *Out West* Feb. 100 The last rail was spiked with a silver spike made from the last bullion taken out of the famous 'Tough-nut' lead at Tombstone.

(10) *(a)* **1866** *Eastern Slope* (Washoe, Nev.) 15 Sep. 4/1 The Silver State struck it rich when they elected H. G. Blasdel to the Gubernatorial chair. **1946** *Trail & Timberline* May 74/1 Colorado miners had been looking for gold but silver became of such importance that when the Territory became a state in 1876, it was known as the Silver State and Georgetown was called the Silver Queen. *(b)* **1885** *Wkly. New Mexican Rev.* 8 Jan. 4/2 All the silver states and territories [should] organize to resist the effort which the single standard advocates are making in congress to suspend the coinage of silver. **1944** *Chi. D. News* 1 June 10/2 Twelve senators from the silver states—Idaho, Utah, Montana, Nevada, Colorado and Arizona—constructed that pipeline. — **(11) 1942** LILLARD *Desert Challenge* 237 Rumors of a great gold and silver strike in Washoe reached the California mining camps. **1947** PERRY *Cities of Amer.* 190 Great silver strikes began to be made at Leadville, Aspen, Creede, and others. — **(12)** *(a)* **1840** *N.O. Picayune* 14 Aug. 2/2 It is hot . . . hot enough for an ice-cream or a Silver Top. *(b)* **1890** *Amer. Naturalist* XXIV. 970 It is probable that these leaf-hoppers are responsible for much of the 'silver-top.'

2. Designating individuals or groups having to do with silver: (1) **silver bloc,** a group in Congress composed of the senators from the silver-producing states of Idaho, Utah, Montana, Nevada, Colorado and Arizona, cf. **silver congressman;** (2) **camp,** the temporary quarters of silver miners; (3) **congressman,** (see quot. and cf. **silver bloc**); (4) **hunter,** one who prospects for silver; (5) **freighter,** *W.* a wagoner who hauls silver ore, *obs.;* (6) **king,** a man of importance in the silver industry, cf. **5.** (8) below.

(1) 1944 *Chi. D. News* 1 June 10/2 The congressional silver bloc is at work again. **1950** *Time* 20 March 18/1 The silver-haired spokesman of the silver bloc swings a big club: chairmanship of the Judiciary Committee which passes on all claims against the Government and judiciary patronage. — **(2) 1895** *Home Missionary* Aug. 222 My husband, though a gold miner, was among the first locators in the little silver camp of Castle. **1949** *Rocks & Minerals* May–June 234/2 Creede was one of Colorado's famous silver camps in the 1890's. — **(3) 1944** *Chi. D. News* 1 June 10/2 In 1934 the silver congressmen managed to run a pipeline into the United States Treasury. — **(4) 1877** W. WRIGHT *Big Bonanza* 486 Two mining superintendents were one day discussing the bonanza, when one of them said to his brother silver-hunter [etc.].

(5) 1896 SHINN *Story of Mine* 1 An old Nevadan silver freighter . . . walked all day long for many . . . years beside his high ore wagon. — **(6) 1882** G. A. SALA *Amer. Revisited* I. Pref. x, 'Railway Kings,' 'Silver Kings,' 'Corn Kings,' 'Pork-Packing Kings,' 'Hotel Kings,' were all kind to me.

b. Designating persons and groups of persons seeking to restore silver to coinage after the demonetization act of Feb. 12, 1873, sometimes in nicknames of persons prominent in the political agitation attendant upon this situation, as, (1) **silver baron,** (2) **beetle,** (3) **bug,** (cf. **goldbug 2.**), (4) **cabal,** (5) **Democrat,** (cf. **gold Democrat**), (6) **Dick,** (7) **Knight of the West,** (8) **man,** (9) **party,** (10) **Republican,** (cf. **gold Republican**), (11) **senator,** (12) **-tongued orator.**

(1) 1885 *Cent. Mag.* Sep. 804 Is it the 'silver-barons' or the 'gold bugs' [who are responsible for the depression]? — **(2) 1896** *Harper's Wkly.* 12 Sep. 902/3 It was the silver-worshippers who . . . because they were 'silver-beetles,' supposed their opponents must of necessity be 'Gold-bugs.' — **(3) 1893** *Nation* 29 June 467/1 The very little game which our silver-bugs . . . are trying to play on us. **1896** *Harper's Wkly.* 1 Aug. 763/1 What's to save the people from the Western Silver-Bugs Cornerin' the market an' a -puttin' on their lugs. — **(4) 1901** *N. Amer. Rev.* Feb. 271 The silver cabal won at every point.

(5) 1896 BRYAN in *Rev. of Reviews* Aug. 174 Our silver Democrats went forth from victory unto victory. **1900** *Harper's Wkly.* 22 Sep. 900/3 Bryan's election would mean a Silver Democrat house, and would practically assure a Silver majority in the Senate in 1901. — **(6) 1900** *Cong. Rec.* 7 April 3898/2 The benignant philanthropy of 'Silver Dick' [i.e., Richard B. Bland (1835–99)] will be discussed and applauded by the historian. — **(7) 1897** R. L. METCALF *Great Fight for Silver* 316 'The Silver Knight of the West,' William Jennings Bryan, of Nebraska, set the convention on fire. — **(8) 1879** *Bradstreet's* 22 Oct. 5/1 The silver men are as violent and rampant as ever. **1903** *Nation* 12 Feb. 124/1 Patterson might easily fail at the next election if there were a fresh schism among the silver men. — **(9) 1893** *Fortnightly Rev.* LIII. 765 The Silver party in the United States insists . . . that the legislation of 1873 was smuggled through Congress by corrupt practices. **1896** *Harper's Wkly.* 18 July 700/2 This speech attracted attention, and was endorsed by the entire silver party.

(10) 1898 *N. Amer. Rev.* Jan. 19 If the People's party be merged, it will be in a new body that shall include advanced Democrats, . . . Silver Republicans, and men of reform views in any other body. **1914** *Cyclo. Amer. Hist.* III. 312/2 Silver Republicans. Those Republicans who in 1896 followed Senator Teller and other western leaders in opposition to the gold policy of the main body of the party. — **(11) 1893** *Dly. Ardmoreite* (Ardmore, Okla.) 2 Nov. 1/5 The silver senators have beaten the gold bugs to a standstill. — **(12) 1943** *Harper's Mag.* Dec. 41/1 The Bryan forces often sent emissaries over to the Brooklyn socialists in 1896 to enlist their votes for the silver-tongued orator.

3. Of or pertaining to the use of silver as money: (1) **silver certificate,** a certificate or piece of paper currency issued by the U.S. Treasury against a deposit of silver; (2) * **dollar,** see as a main entry; (3) **fip,** = **fip,** *obs.;* (4) **pay,** pay in silver, *obs.;* (5) **quarter,** a quarter of a dollar; (6) **Scheme,** (see quots.), *obs.;* (7) **standard,** *(a)* the legal weight and fineness of silver in silver coins, *(b)* a monetary standard in terms of silver, also attrib.; (8) **trade dollar,** = **trade dollar.**

(1) 1882 *Statutes at Large* XX. 165 Silver certificates, when held by any national-banking association, shall be counted as part of its lawful reserve. **1932** GRAYSON *Leaders* 380 The Act of 1886 . . . had authorized the issue of silver certificates in smaller denominations than $10. — **(3) 1843** CARLTON *New Purchase* I. 257 He emptied all the contents on the counter, viz: two silver fips, three 'chaw'd bullits.' — **(4) 1654** *Portsmouth Rec.* 63 Tenn pounds . . . to bee payde at the Rate of silver pay. **1672** *East-Hampton Rec.* I. 347 A case tried . . . in a matter of Debt to the vally of foure shillings in Sillver pay. **1688** *N.J. Archives* 1 Ser. II. 29 There will be perhaps 20 percent loss between [country pay] & silver pay.

(5) 1874 EGGLESTON *Circuit Rider* 253 Postage cost a silver quarter on every letter. — **(6) 1744** in *Pub. Col. Soc.* III. 2 An Account of the Rise, Progress, and Consequences of the . . . Silver Scheme, in the Province of the Massachusetts Bay. **1895** in *Ib.* 14 A number of Boston merchants formed an association, afterwards known as the Silver Scheme, the purpose of which was to issue bills, which, like the Merchants' Notes of 1733, should be on a silver basis. — **(7)** *(a)* **1831** *Cong. Deb.* 22 Feb. p. cxl/2 An error . . . committed in establishing the money unit 'of the value of a Spanish dollar' . . . may be corrected by adhering to the established and existing silver standard. *(b)* **1896** *Harper's Wkly.* 8 Aug. 779/3 The difference of exchange is equal to a bounty equal to the difference between the value of silver and gold on favor of silver-standard countries. **1900** *Cong. Rec.* 17 Jan. 905/1 The great majority of mankind was standing on the silver standard. **1903** *Nation* 12 Feb. 124/2 The gold standard countries are to use gold and the silver standard countries are to use silver. — **(8) 1873** *Statutes at Large* XVII. 427 On the reverse of the silver trade-dollar, the weight and fineness of the coin shall be inscribed.

b. Of or pertaining to the efforts to remonetize silver after its demonetization in 1873, as (1) **silver bill,** (2) **convention,** (3) **heresy,** (4) **plank,** (5) **question.**

(1) 1889 *Cent.* 553/2 [The] Bland Silver Bill . . . reëstablished the silver dollar containing 412½ grains troy of standard silver as a legal tender; but its special feature was a clause requiring the Treasury to purchase every month not less than two million nor more than four million dollars' worth of silver bullion and to coin it into dollars. — **(2) 1885** *Wkly. New Mexican Rev.* 12 Feb. 2/4 The silver convention recently held in Denver passed some very sensible resolutions. — **(3) 1896** *Harper's Wkly.* 12 Sep. 891/1 When Mr. Bryan and the silver heresy have been finally beaten we may expect a return of the prosperity which gladdened the land before this assault was made upon the nation's honor. **1900** *Cong. Rec.* 14 Feb. 1807/1 Such counties as Jasper and Greene, counties which were heretofore Republican, went hellbent for the silver heresy. — **(4) 1892** *Chi. Tribune* 2 July 1/3 Carey did this by means of an amendment containing the language of the silver plank adopted by the Chicago convention.

(5) 1877 *Harper's Mag.* March 627/2 The joint resolution providing for the appointment of commissioners to attend an international conference on the silver question was defeated in the House. **1900** *Harper's Wkly.* 15 Sep. 876/3 He says that Bryan is right on the silver question.

4. In the names of plants: (1) **silver beard grass,** (see quot.); (2) **bell (tree),** a tree, *Halesia carolina,* of the southeastern states, cf. **Carolina silver-bell tree, shittim-wood;** (3) **birch,** the American gray birch or paper birch, *Betula papyrifera;* (4) * **maple,** an American maple, *Acer saccharinum,* with leaves silvery white underneath; (5) * **pine,** a white pine, *Pinus monticola,* found in the West; (6) **poplar,** the white poplar, *Populus alba;* (7) ***rod,** a white-rayed goldenrod; (8) **spruce,** any one of various spruces having pale leaves, found in the western U.S.; (9) **top palmetto,** the silver thatch, *Coccothrinax argentea*, with leaves white on the under side.

(1) **1884** VASEY *Agric. Grasses* 121 *Andropogon argenteus,* Silver Beard Grass. From W. S. Robertson, Muscogee Ind. — (2) **1785** MARSHALL *Amer. Grove* 57 Silver-Bell Tree. . . . The Corolla is of one petal, bell'd and bellied. **1847** DARLINGTON *Weeds & Plants* 218 The *Halesia*, or Silver Bell, two species of which . . . are common in cultivation. **1943** PEATTIE *Great Smokies* 156 In the Great Smokies the silverbell is sometimes a forest giant 100 feet high. — (3) **1848** THOREAU *Maine Woods* 81 It is a country full of evergreen trees, of mossy silver birches and watery maples. **1949** *Prairie Club Bul.* June 5 We will . . . visit the woodland area, consisting . . . of . . . stately blue spruce and Norway pine, and silver birch. — (4) **1765** J. BARTRAM *Diary* 9 Sep., Low ground full of very large timber . . . silver maple horn beam elm walnut. **1846** D. J. BROWNE *Trees Amer.* 95 Silver Maple, Silver-leaved Maple, [in] New York. **1949** *L.A. Times* May 1 (Home Mag.) 33/2 The silver maple, A. dasycarpum, is also native to the Eastern and Central United States.

(5) **1869** MUIR *First Summer in Sierra* (1911) 69 Well may this shining species be called the silver pine. **1948** *Pacific Discovery* Nov.–Dec. 20/1 A closely related tree, the silver pine (*Pinus monticola*), occurs here and there at elevations of about 8,000 feet. — (6) **1847** DARLINGTON *Weeds & Plants* 332 Silver Poplar. . . . Some of the grass-plats in the public squares of New York have been quite overrun by the wide-spreading suckers of this tree. **1947** *Mazama* Dec. 1/1 The brilliant autumn colors of the oak, silver poplar, alder and maple trees against the background of mountain pines, made this a memorable trip. — (7) **1907** LYONS *Plant Names* 434 Note-worthy indigenous species are S. bicolor L., White or Pale Golden-rod, Silver-rod, Silver-weed, Belly-ache-weed; S. Canadensis L. . . . High or Double Golden-rod [etc.]. **1941** R. S. WALKER *Lookout* 53 In late summer a person going on foot meets the silver-rod, the only known white species of golden-rod. — (8) **1868** BOWLES *Colorado* (1869) 63 The silver spruce is the one gem of the trees; a sort of first cousin of the evergreen we call the balsam fir in our New England yards. **1949** HINKLE *Sierra-Nevada Lakes* 231 Before he died, Webber . . . had made himself a pioneer in the conservation of fish, and had helped to replenish Prussian and other European forests with the seeds of the great silver spruce, *picea amabilis.* — (9) **1884** SARGENT *Rep. Forests* 218 Silver-top Palmetto. Brickley Thatch. Brittle Thatch. Semi-tropical Florida.

5. In the names of animals: (1) **silver bass,** (see quot.); (2) **cat,** ?a catfish, *Ameiurus albidus*, of a whitish appearance; (3) ***eel,** ?a cutlass fish found on the coasts of the southern U.S.; (4) **fin,** any one of various fresh-water minnows, as a satinfin, that have the lower fins largely white; (5) **fox,** a color variety of the red fox, a neckpiece made of the fur of this animal, also attrib.; (6) **gray,** see as a main entry; (7) **hake,** a hake, *Merluccius bilinearis*, found on the northern N. Eng. coast and esteemed as a food fish; (8) **king,** the tarpon, cf. **2.** (6) above; (9) **perch,** any one of various fishes, as the crappie, *Pomoxis annularis*, having silver coloring; (10) ***pike,** (see quots.); (11) **salmon,** a salmon, *Oncorhynchus milktschitsch*, found on the north Pacific Coast; (12) **tip,** see as a main entry; (13) **tongue,** =**song sparrow;** (14) **whiting,** (see quot.).

(1) **1884** GOODE *Fisheries* I. 612 'Silver Bass,' *Hyodon selenops*, . . . is confined to the rivers of the Southern States. — (2) **1890** HOWELLS *Boy's Town* 30 There were men who were reputed to catch at will, as it were, silvercats and river-bass. — (3) **1857** *Spirit of Times* 4 April 70/2 There is the perch, . . . and the snake-like silver-eel (hardly a fish). **1882** JORDAN & GILBERT *Syn. Fishes N. Amer.* 910 (*footnote*), This species [*Trichiurus lepturus*] is known as 'Sabre-fish' and 'Silver Eel,' on the coast of Texas. — (4) **1883** *Nat. Mus. Bul.* No. 16, 179 Silver-fin. . . . Pennsylvania and Central New York to Mississippi Valley. **1903** T. H. BEAN *Fishes N.Y.* 145 The silverfin ranges from western New York to Virginia and west to Minnesota and Arkansas.

(5) **1792** CARTWRIGHT *Labrador Jrnl.* 378 Silver-fox. A black-fox, with white king-hairs dispersed on the back of it. **1806** CLARK in *Lewis & C. Exped.* IV. (1904) 88 The Silver Fox . . . is very rare even in the countrey where it exists. **1918** LINCOLN *Shavings* 225 If you knew what a silver fox costs . . . you would be more careful in your language. **1946** *Progress* March 66/2 Albert Leonard . . . was largely responsible for perfecting the foods now used on silver fox and mink ranches. — (7) **1884** GOODE *Fisheries* I. 240 The Silver Hake commonly inhabits the middle depths of ocean. **1903** T. H. BEAN *Fishes N.Y.* 692 The whiting is known by the additional names of hake and silver hake. — (8) **1889** *Scribner's Mag.* Aug. 164/1 No one could boast of having even hooked a 'Silver King.' **1948** *Chi. Tribune* 20 June 17/5 This 'silver king' responds enthusiastically to summer time angling. — (9) **1820** *Western Rev.* II. 53 *Pomoxis annularis.* . . . Vulgar names Gold-ring and Silver-perch. Found in August at the falls [of the Ohio R.], probably permanent. **1855** BAIRD in *Smithsonian Rep. 1854* 331 The Silver Perch, *Corvina argyroleuca*, . . . is not unfrequently brought to market in New York. **1947** DALRYMPLE *Panfish* 254 The White Perch . . . goes by the names 'Silver Perch' and 'Sea Perch.'

(10) **1870** *Amer. Naturalist* IV. 109 The frost-fish are occasionally seen with a few herring in the small ditches, and are known then by juvenile anglers as the 'silver pike.' **1947** DALRYMPLE *Panfish* 271 [The] 'Silver Pike' . . . has no spots, as does the true *Esox lucius*, Great Northern, but is silvery-colored, with the back pale green. — (11) **1878** in JACKSON *Alaska* (1880) 209 A silver salmon, weighing thirty-eight to forty pounds, is sold for fifteen or twenty cents. **1948** *Trailways Mag.* Fall 11/3 At least two varieties of salmon—silver and chinook—are also found in diminishing numbers. — (13) **1884** COUES *N. Amer. Birds* 371 *Melospiza fasciata*, . . . Song Sparrow. Silver tongue. — (14) **1911** *Rep. Fisheries 1908* 318/2 The surf-whiting (*M[enticirrhus] littoralis*), also called the 'silver-whiting,' is common from the Carolinas to Texas.

As the last term in **cut, fire, flat, free, Navaho, wire silver.**

***silver dollar.** A silver coin of the U.S. worth 100 cents.

The U.S. silver dollar was authorized by Congress in 1792 and first issued in 1794. Its weight was changed in 1837 from 416 grains to 412.5 grains of standard silver. In the first quots. below the term is used with reference to the Spanish peso or piece of eight (i.e., eight reales), current in the Amer. colonies at the time of the Revolution.

[**1781** *R.I. Col. Rec.* IX. 478 We estimate the dame the said Robert Lawson hath sustained in his said vessel at five hundred silver dollars. **1782** THOMAS B. HAZARD *Nailer Tom's Diary* (1930) 39/2 Mumford Hazard Bought Thomas R. Robinsons White horse for 70 Silver Dollars.] **1804** FESSENDEN *Orig. Poems* (1806) 159 Pewter platter, Which cook-maid Dolly scours so white, It shines like silver dollar bright. **1872** POWERS *Afoot & Alone* 273 When I arrived in Los Angeles I had just one silver dollar left. **1950** *Travel* Feb. 12 The thousands of John Does will take even a little silver dollar-sized abalone if they can get away with it.

***silver gray.**

1. An elderly man, a member of the home guard *q.v. Obs.*

1813 W. WIRT in *Memoir* (1849) I. 356 Every man [in Richmond, Va.] had to rush with his musket, to the square:—even the 'silver greys' (and parson Blair among them) flew to arms.

2. (*cap.*) A conservative member of the Whig party supporting the Compromise of 1850 (see quot. 1859). Also attrib. Now *hist.*

1851 QUENTIN *Reisebilder* II. 116 Aber 40 Deputirte der alten Farbe, Silvergreys genannt, . . . den Saal verlassen und einen neuen Konvent nach Utica ausgeschrieben haben. **1853** *Knickerb.* XLII. 653 'Woolly-Heads' were 'about,' and 'far-off the coming shone' of dignified 'Silver-Grays.' **1859** BARTLETT 408 *Silver Grays.* This term originated in the State of New York, and was applied to the conservative portion of the Whig party. . . . It was observed that many were men whose locks were silvered by age, which drew forth the remark from some one present, 'There go the silver grays.' **1884** BLAINE *20 Years of Congress* I. 524 Among the representatives of New York . . . [was] Ex-Governor Washington Hunt, whose Silver-Gray conservatism had carried him into the Democratic party. **1949** *Pa. Dutchman* 7 July 1/1 He . . . incidentally drifted into active politics, with the 'Wooley Head' element of the Whig Party and against the 'Silver Greys.'

Hence **Silver-Grayism.** *Obs.*

1855 *N.Y. Wkly. Tribune* 12 May 4/2 It is the doctrine of the most ancient fogyism, . . . the essential oil of decayed Silver-Grayism.

3. silver-gray fox, =**silver fox.** Also attrib.

1778 *Essex Inst. Coll.* XLIX. 109 Sold . . . 3 silver gray fox skins. **1847** EMORY *Military Reconn.* 405 Amongst the animals, we have . . . the silver-grey fox, (*canis cinerea argentus*). **1917** *Mammals of Amer.* 75/1 The Cross Fox and the Black, or Silver Gray, Fox are merely color phases of the Red Fox.

4. silver-gray squirrel, (see quot.).

1857 *Rep. Comm. Patents 1856: Agric.* 66 [The southern grey or Carolina squirrel, *Sciurus carolinensis*] is known among hunters as the 'Silver-grey Squirrel.'

silverism sɪlvəˌrɪzəm, *n.* The political doctrines of the silverites (see **silverite 2.**). *Obs.* — **1895** *Forum* Feb. 674 The panic of '93 was . . . due to two socialistic crazes: silverism and protectionism. **1906** *Springfield W. Republican* 20 Sep. 2 They are helping him [Mr. Bryan] to bury the silverism of his earlier period.

silverite ˈsɪlvəˌraɪt, *n.*

1. (*cap.*) A citizen of Silver City, Nevada. *Rare.*

1877 W. WRIGHT *Big Bonanza* 122 Here the Silverites determined to make the Indians smell 'villainous saltpeter.'

2. One of those who during the period (*c*1885–96) of agitation over the coinage of silver favored the use of silver as a monetary standard, a bimetallist. Now *hist.* Cf. * **crime,** *n.* **1.**

1886 *Science* VII. 267 The attempt is made to cast a slur upon the 'silverites' by calling them inflationists. **1900** *Cong. Rec.* 14 Feb. 1775/1 The battle of the standards was fought and lost by the Silverites in 1896. **1948** *Sat. Ev. Post* 10 July 71/2 The Silverites thought they could raise wages and farm prices by modifying the gold standard to permit the free coinage of silver at 16 to 1.

b. A member of the silver bloc *q.v.* Also attrib.

1942 Lillard *Desert Challenge* 51 Continued silverite agitation and the presence in Congress of twelve new senators from Western states admitted in 1889 led to the Sherman Silver Purchase Act of 1890. **1944** *Chi. D. News* 1 June 10/2 Not being satisfied with the benefits already won for silver producers at the expense of the nation, these silverites now demand that any international monetary stabilization scheme be based not only on gold, but on silver also.

silverling 'sɪlvəlɪŋ, *n.* =**silverite 2.** *Obs.* — **1902** *Nation* 6 March LXXIV. 189/2 Mr. McKinley . . . was a silverling as long as silver was popular; when doubts arose, he became a straddle-bug.

silvertip 'sɪlvɚˌtɪp, *n.* A grizzly bear with hairs silvery-colored at the tips. Also **silver-tipped bear, silvertip grizzly.**

1880 *Rep. Supt. Yellowstone Nat. Pk.* 40 Silver-tipped bear.—This animal is nearly destitute of a mane, and is somewhat smaller, less powerful and ferocious than the true grizzly. **1890** *Outing* Aug. 381/1 The 'silver tip' was surprised at a banquet of 'service berries' and killed by a single well directed bullet. **1923** J. H. Cook *On Old Frontier* 138, I caught sight of a very large silver-tip grizzly lying down. **1947** DeVoto *Across Wide Missouri* 113 Their companions succeeded in killing the silver-tip with four more shots.

simball 'sɪmbl, *n.* Also **cymbal.** *N. Eng.* [Variant of **cymbal.*] A kind of doughnut.

1828 Webster, *Cimbal*, a kind of cake. **1865** A. D. Whitney *Gayworthys* 36 After they had popped corn, and roasted apples, and eaten simballs, . . . they had all gone to bed. **1867** O. W. Holmes *Guardian Angel* xix, The genteel form of doughnut called in the native dialect *cymbal* . . . which graced the board with its plastic forms. **1899** Wilkins *In Colonial Times* 19 Here's a piece of sweet cake and a couple of simballs.

simlin 'sɪmlɪn, *n.* Also **cymbling, simblin, simmin.** [Variant of **simnel.*] =**simnel.** Also attrib. and transf.

1775 *Jrnl. Nicholas Cresswell* (1925) 95 The rest plundered about the plantation and got some young cabbages, squashes and Cimbelines. **1804** Clark in *Lewis & C. Exped.* I. (1904) 188 [The Arikara] raise great quantities of Corn Beens Simmins &c. **1884** Craddock *Tenn. Mts.* 171, I'll break that empty cymlin' of a head of yourn. **1911** Saunders *Col. Todhunter* 96 You impudent little simlin'-headed runt, you! **1949** *Nat. Geog. Mag.* Aug. 164 Fruits like our present White Bush Scallop or Cymling were accurately illustrated by the French botanist Matthias Lobel in 1591.

'simmon 'sɪmən, *n.*

1. A colloq. shortening of **persimmon.** Also attrib.

1834 *Knickerb.* III. 36 They seemed to me to fall just as fast as if I was shakin down 'simmons. **1881** *Harper's Mag.* April 729/2 An' pleased they wuz ter see it—pleased as boys in 'simmon-time. **1904** O. Henry *Roads of Destiny* 350 That's why you see me cake-walking with the ex-rebs to the illegitimate tune about 'simmon-seeds and cotton.

b. In colloq. phrases (see quots.).

1839 *S. Lit. Messenger* V. 378/2 The longest pole, you know, takes the simmon. **1850** Lewis *La. Swamp Doctor* 50 We all cum down like 'simmons arter frost.

2. 'simmon beer, =**persimmon beer.**

1775 Boucher *Glossary* p. l, Brown linen shirts, and cotton jackets wear, Or only *wring-jaw* drink, and *'simmon beer.* **1894** *Outing* Jan. 274/1 Apple cider, 'simmon beer, Christmas comes but once a year. **1945** Botkin *My Burden* 66 'Simmon beer was good in the cold freezing weather too.

* **simnel,** *n. S.* A kind of squash or gourd.

1648 Plantagenet *Descr. New Albion* 28 Strawberries, Mulberries, Symnels, Maycocks and Horns like Cucumbers. **1705** Beverley *Virginia* iv. 56 [The people of Va.] find them very delicious Sauce to their Meats; . . . such are the Red-buds, Sassafras-Flowers, Cymnels, Melons, and Potatoes. **1709** Lawson *Carolina* 77 [There are] Squashes, Simnals, Horns, and Gourds.

simoleon sɪ'molɪən, *n.* [Origin obscure. Poss. f. Simon *q.v.* meaning a dollar, on the analogy of **napoleon*, a former French coin.] A dollar. *Slang.*

1896 G. Ade *Artie* 63 He said I could have it for four hundred samoleons. **1903** *K.C. Dly. Times* 23 Dec. (*Cent. Supp.*), She wears a dress—it cost no less Than ninety-five simoleons. **1948** *Range Riders Western* May 24/2 My share was five thousand simoleons.

* **Simon,** *n.* Also **simon.**

1. a. A kind of game. **b.** A dollar. *Slang.* Cf. **simoleon. c.** Short for **Simon-pure,** the real thing. All *obs.*

(a) 1853 P. Paxton *Yankee in Texas* 205 After playing 'Simon,' 'What is my Thought Like?' and a dozen similar games, one of the company arose. — **(b) 1859** *Harper's Mag.* Sep. 572/2, I was first in say, and bet a *Simon.* — **(c) 1875** Burroughs *Winter Sunshine* 21 The fish-crow, whose helpless feminine call contrasts strongly with the hearty masculine caw of the original Simon.

2. Simon Legree, a hard taskmaster, in allusion to the cruel slave dealer in Mrs. Stowe's *Uncle Tom's Cabin* (1852).

1912 *Lit. Digest* 30 March 657/1 At last, after the long junket through the South, on which all managers are Simon Legrees, is ended, comes a welcome day when the new uniforms are donned [at the start of a new baseball season]. **1949** *Retail Coalman* Nov. 18/1 At least $20 is going into a kitty to help Lewis pay for some dead horses which he has managed to scrape up during his tenure as the miners' Simon Legree.

3. Simon-pure, *a.* genuine, real, authentic. *Colloq.*

The earliest evidence for this use is American, but as a noun *Simon Pure* (f. the name of a Quaker in Mrs. Centlivre's *A Bold Stroke for a Wife* (1717)) is at least as early as 1815 in British use.

1840 *Maysville* (Ky.) *Eagle* 22 April 3/1 The Globe . . . or indeed any other paper of the *Simon Pure democracy.* **1856** *Ill. State Reg.* 15 May 3/2 The real simon pure democracy have been looking to him, more than any other man as their candidate. **1945** *Boulder* (Colo.) *D. Camera* 24 Nov. 4/2 All is not 'Simon pure' in the Big Six conference.

b. Simon Pures, a dyed-in-the-wool conservative faction in the Democratic party. *Obs.*

1830 *Me. Democrat* (Saco) 1 Sep. 2/1 Some of our Simon Pures, who during the last War were fighting against these very federalists, [are] now in full communion with them. **1848** *Field Piece* (Chi.) 16 Aug. 2/4 The 'Simon Pures' of the Democracy, are after the bolters with strong sticks.

simp sɪmp, *n.* Colloq. abbreviation of **simpleton.* — **1916** B. M. Bower *Phantom Herd* vii. 112 You can set some simp at it that don't know any better. **1931** *K.C. Times* 19 Dec. 22 He is just one more simp that is going, and he doesn't know where.

***simpleton,** *n.* (See quot. 1891.) — **1891** *Cent.* 5639/3 *Simpleton*, . . . the American dunlin, purre, or ox-bird. **1917** *Birds of Amer.* I. 237.

simplified spelling. Any one of several methods of spelling English words with greater phonetic consistency than is shown in conventional spelling.

1899 Mark Twain *Simplified Alphabet* (1917) 256 (R.), I have had a kindly feeling toward Simplified Spelling from the beginning of the movement three years ago. **1948** *New Republic* 2 Feb. 27/2 He also—without announcing the fact—got rid of the simplified spelling that has spoiled the big *Standard* as a whole for many readers. **1949** *Time* 21 March 34/1 The House of Commons debated the pros & cons of his bill to make simplified spelling compulsory in all British schools.

sinch, see **cinch,** *n.*

***singer,** *n.* As the last term in **blues, coon, Ethiopian singer.**

singers' seat. A seat or bench in a meetinghouse for the choir. [Cf. *EDD singing seat* in the same sense.]

1777 *Plymouth Church Rec.* I. 353 Deacon Crombie, our former Chorister, had left ye usual Singer's Seat. **1861** Stowe *Pearl Orr's Isl.* I. 72 Aunt Ruey . . . had in her youth been one of the foremost leaders in the 'singers' seat.' **1878** ——— *Poganuc People* 102 The singers' seat . . . was *our* singers' seat.

* **singing,** *n.*

1. Short for "singing school." *Obs. Colloq.*

1872 Eggleston *End of World* 118 She had walked to and from meeting and 'singing' with Humphreys. **1877** Bartlett 595 *Singing*, in Pennsylvania, a singing-school.

2. In combs.: (1) **singing exercise,** a manifestation of strong religious emotion (see quot.), *obs.;* (2) **fish,** the midshipman, *Porichthys notatus*, or an allied fish; (3) **gallery,** a choir loft; (4) **lecture,** a church service consisting of both preaching and specially rehearsed singing, *obs.;* (5) **meeting,** a church or community meeting for singing, *obs.*; (6) **Quaker,** a Quaker given to singing under religious excitement, *obs.*

(1) *a***1844** *Ohio Arch. and Hist. Pub.* XII. (1903) 249, I shall close this chapter with the singing exercises. . . . The subject in a very happy state of mind would sing most melodiously, not from the mouth or nose, but entirely in the breast, the sounds issuing thence. . . . It was most heavenly. — **(2) 1884** GOODE *Fisheries* I. 253 The *Batrachidæ* are represented on the Pacific coast by the 'Singing-fish,' or 'Toad-fish,' *Porichthys porosissimus.* **1896** JORDAN & EVERMANN *Check-List Fishes* 466. — **(3) 1818** BENTLEY *Diary* IV. 513 The amphitheatrical form of Singing galleries placed . . . in front of pulpits has had great favour. **1883** C. C. PERKINS *Hist. Handbook of Ital. Sculpt.* 139 [Della Robbia began] a series of ten alto-reliefs . . . in 1433 for the balustrade of a singing-gallery (cantoria) in the Cathedral. — **(4) 1723** *N.-Eng. Courant* 3 June 2/1 On Thursday last a Singing Lecture was held at the Brick Church in Cornhill, and the Rev. Dr. Cotton Mather preach'd. **1779** E. PARKMAN *Diary* 96 A Singing Lecture at ye Request of ye Singing School.

(5) 1766 CUTLER in *Life & Corr.* I. 14 In the evening a singing meeting in the school-house; sang well. **1802** COWLES *Diary* 66 Cousin T. called after singing meeting. **1860** ABBOTT *South & North* 120 There is no church here, no village school, no singing-meeting, no social winter-evening gatherings. — **(6) 1684** I. MATHER *Providences* (1856) xi. 241 Observe the blasting rebukes of Providence upon the late singing and dancing Quakers. **1704** S. KNIGHT *Journal* 78 Says the woman are you singing quakers?

As the last term in **community, Negro, Sacred Harp singing.**

* **single,** *a.* and *n.*

1. *Baseball.* A one-base hit.

1858 *Chadwick Scrapbook* (E. J. Nichols). **1880** *Chi. Inter-Ocean* 29 June 8/3 Force's winning run came off a wild throw by Ward, a sacrifice, and single. **1948** *Herald-Press* (St. Joseph, Mich.) 14 Aug. 7/2 Green also bashed out a triple and single during the game.

Also **single-baser.**

1879 *Chi. Tribune* 3 May 5/1 Dalrymple led off with a single-baser.

b. Of a hit: Enabling the batter to get only to first base.

1880 N. BROOKS *Fairport Nine* 183 Dan Morey followed with a single base hit which put Eph to third base. *Ib.* 186 Eph Mullett . . . made a two-base hit, Dan Morey following him with a single hit, which sent Mullett to third base.

2. In special combs.: (1) **single action,** (see quot. 1909); (2) **bob,** a mark made in the ears of domestic livestock to indicate ownership; (3) **buggy,** a light buggy to be pulled by one horse; (4) **-decked car,** a railroad stock car having only one tier for animals; (5) **decker,** a house having but one suite of rooms on a floor, *obs.*, also a boat with only one deck; (6) **foot,** a racking gait of a horse in which each foot strikes the ground singly and there are alternately one and two feet on the ground, also **single-foot rack;** (7) **footed,** *a.* (see quot.); (8) **footer,** a horse that singlefoots, also transf.; (9) **-handed poker,** poker in which there is no drawing of additional cards after the deal, cf. **draw poker;** (10) **hander,** a boat operated by one person; (11) **jack,** in mining, a heavy, short-handled hammer used in hand drilling; (12) **-leaf piñon,** the single-leaf pine, *Pinus monophylla;* (13) **letter,** formerly a letter not exceeding a certain weight, *obs.;* (14) **rail,** denoting a railway on which cars travel on one rail, either straddlewise or suspended from it; (15) **-seed(ed) cucumber,** the star cucumber, *Sicyos angulatus;* (16) **shot,** of firearms, capable of firing only one shot without reloading; (17) **spruce,** the white spruce, *Picea glauca*, or the balsam fir, *Abies balsamea;* (18) **standard,** a monetary standard based on one metal only, esp. the gold standard, also attrib.; (19) **star,** used in allusion to Texas, cf. **Lone Star;** (20) **sticker,** a sailboat with only one mast; (21) **stick vessel,** =prec.; (22) **tax,** a proposed tax by which the unearned increment, or the economic rent, of land would be taken as the sole source of public revenue; (23) **taxer,** one who advocates the single tax; (24) **track,** a railroad having only one set of rails, also attrib., also as verb, to construct (a railway line) with a single track; (25) **tree,** see as a main entry; (26) **way,** =**single track.**

(1) 1909 WEBSTER 1961/3 single-acting. . . . Having simplicity of action;—said esp. of a firearm in which the trigger has to be cocked by hand. single action, *n.* **1947** *True* Nov. 30/1 The most famous of all revolvers . . . is the single-action Colt introduced in 1873. — **(2) 1887** *Scribner's Mag.* II. 508/2 Words used in connection with . . . life on the plains: . . . *singlebob*, a slit ear dropping down. — **(3) 1944** CLARK *Pills* 290 There was a growing demand for family surreys and single buggies. — **(4) 1868** *Ill. Agric. Soc. Trans.* VII. 460 Sheep arrive here from the west in single decked cars.

(5) 1896 HASWELL *New York* 332 James P. Allaire had constructed in Water Street . . . a four-story house designed for many tenants. It was the first house constructed proper or exclusively for tenants in this city. It is what is now termed a 'single-decker,' that is, but one suite of rooms on a floor. **1945** FUGINA *Upper Mississippi* 1 The boat was a single decker. — **(6) 1867** HARRIS *Sut Lovingood* 191 [He] started fur the back door, still on his all fours, in a single foot rack. **1882** STILLMAN *Horse in Motion* 117 Single-foot is an irregular pace, . . . distinguished by the posterior extremities, moving in the order of a fast walk and the anterior ones in that of a slow trot. **1934** VINES *Green Thicket World* 28 The fast singlefoot, if anything, was easier on the touchous rider. — **(7)** *a***1864** W. S. CLARKE (W.), Many very fleet horses, when overdriven, adopt a disagreeable gait, . . . in which the two legs of one side are raised almost . . . simultaneously. Such horses are said to *single*, or to be *single-footed.* — **(8) 1887** *Harper's Mag.* Sep. 490 He rode single-footers. **1891** *Ib.* Aug. 365/2 A single curb [is] lightly reining his quickly moving single-footer. **1897** LEWIS *Wolfville* 41 If they's single-footers like me an' ain't wedded none; . . . they wishes they has a wife a whole lot. — **(9) 1844** *N.O. Picayune* 19 Feb. 1/2 The judge of the court, after losing a year's salary at single-handed poker and whipping a person who said he didn't understand the game, went out and helped Lynch a man for hog-stealing!

(10) 1890 *Harper's Mag.* Sep. 594/1 If their pleasure be taken in a single-hander they are unhappy. **1893** *Outing* XXII. 145/2 The cost of a single-hander depends on the size of the boat. — **(11) 1923** BOWER *Parowan Bonanza* 12 Knock it [gold ore] off in chunks with a single-jack and gadget. — **(12) 1897** SUDWORTH *Arborescent Flora* 18 *Pinus monophylla*, . . . Single-leaf Pinon. . . . Fremont's Nut Pine. **1949** COLLINGWOOD & BRUSH *Knowing Your Trees* 20/2 Singleleaf pinyon is characteristically a low spreading tree. — **(13) 1792** *Ann. 2d Congress* 60 And every double letter shall pay double the said rates; every triple letter, triple; every packet weighing one ounce avoirdupois, to pay at the rate of four single letters for each ounce; and in that proportion for any greater weight. — **(14) 1833** *Amer. R. R. Jrnl.* II. 820/1 (*heading*), Suspension or Single Rail Railway.

(15) 1840 DEWEY *Mass. Flowering Plants* 114 *S[icyos] angulatus.* Single-seeded Cucumber. Grows also on the banks of streams. **1847** WOOD *Botany* 270 Single-seed Cucumber. . . . Fruit ½′ long, ovate, spinous, 8–10 together in a crowded cluster, each with one large seed. — **(16) 1886** *Harper's Mag.* Oct. 793/2 The types adopted by the United States navy are the Hotchkiss revolving cannon and rapid-firing single-shot guns. **1897** *Outing* XXIX. 566/1, I gave my rifle—a single-shot express by Henry, with the falling-block system—to one of my men to hold. — **(17) 1810** MICHAUX *Arbres* I. 18 *White* or *Single spruce* . . . dénomination également en usage dans les Etats du Nord, le District de Maine et la Nouvelle-Écosse. *a***1817** DWIGHT *Travels* I. 38 The single spruce . . . is the link between the Hemlock and the white spruce, and is also used for Beer. **1832** BROWNE *Sylva* 93 *Abies alba* . . . in New Brunswick and the state of Maine [is called] *Single Spruce.* **1909** *Webster* 1961/3 *Single spruce* . . . the balsam fir. — **(18) 1885** *Wkly. New Mexican Rev.* 8 Jan. 4/2 All the silver states and territories [should] organize to resist the effort which the single standard advocates are making in congress to suspend the coinage of silver. **1898** *Rep. Monetary Comm.* (Indianapolis Conv.) 97 Any attempt to [use both silver and gold] . . . will result in a single standard of the cheaper of the two metals. — **(19) 1839** *Columbian Reg.* (New Haven, Conn.) 12 March 4/2 The committee of the Texan Congress in their report on this subject state, that in consequence of the single star being refused admission into our sisterhood, the flag should be altered accordingly.

(20) 1893 *Boston Jrnl.* 13 April, The boat . . . will be in all the special races arranged for the big single stickers by the New York and other clubs. **1894** *Outing* XXIV. 193/1 The English way of rigging a single-sticker is being adopted in all our new racing craft. — **(21) 1886** *Outing* IX. 123/1 He asserted he could build a sloop which could beat any of the American single stick vessels. — **(22) 1879** GEORGE *Progress & Poverty* 383 A single tax on the value of land would hardly lessen the number of conscious taxpayers. **1896** *Harper's Wkly.* 15 Aug. 823/2 Delaware is the stamping-ground of the Single-Tax advocates. **1950** *World-Herald Mag.* (Omaha) 26 March 9/2 The once prominent single tax movement, no longer a red hot political issue, is one which has continued on unobtrusively. — **(23) 1889** *20th Cent.* 6 April, He says that is a fair question which no Single-taxer ever answers, but that if it is evaded the whole single-tax theory vanishes. **1947** *Time* 29 Dec. 64/3 A lecture by Single-Taxer Henry George convinced George Bernard Shaw that modern society was ill-made and needed to be completely rebuilt. — **(24) 1832** *Amer. R.R. Jrnl.* I. 245/1 The entire length of single track [is] yet to be laid. **1874** *Boston & Chi. Ry. Trust Co. Bill* (Bay State Transp. League) 8 It will cost to single track the Massachusetts Central to Shelburne Falls $3,000,000. **1898** *McClure's Mag.* March 390/1 When running a first-class train on a single-track branch, I had orders to meet [etc.]. **1918** *Essex Inst. Coll.* LIV. 196 To lessen the expense, only a single track was at first laid.

(26) **1832** *Amer. R.R. Jrnl.* I. 17/1 This kind of Rail road . . . was called the 'single way.'

* **single,** *v.*

1. (See quot.) Cf. **singlefoot,** *v.*

1864 WEBSTER 1233/3 Many very fleet horses, when overdriven, adopt a disagreeable gait, which seems to be a cross between a pace and a trot, in which the two legs of one side are raised almost, but not quite, simultaneously. Such horses are said to *single,* or to be *single-footed.*

2. * *To single out,* (see quot.).

1905 *Forestry Bureau Bul.* No. 61, 46 *Single out, to,* to float logs, usually cypress, one at a time, from the woods to the float road. (S[outhern] F[orest].)

3. *Baseball.* Of a batter: To secure a one-base hit.

1916 *Chi. Tribune* 7 Oct. 13/1 In the ninth the first man up singled. **1949** *Democrat* 22 Sep. 2/5 The first St. Michael batter singled.

singlefoot ˈsɪŋgl̩ˌfʊt, *v.* [f. the noun.] *intr.* Of a horse: To go in the gait known as singlefoot. Also of a horseman: To ride at this gait.

1890 *Harper's Mag.* Jan. 246 The horse often singlefoots faster than he trots. **1903** O. HENRY *Heart of West* 64, I singlefoots up beside him on my bronc. **1934** VINES *Green Thicket World* 28 He could singlefoot as fast as any other horse could run. **1950** *Chi. Tribune* 4 April II. 7/4 It was something to see . . . singlefooting it around the house from the back, Carter on his buckskin horse—lifted a little in the saddle—lariat swinging low and easy.

singletree ˈsɪŋgl̩ˌtri, *n.* [Altered form of * *swingletree,* poss. because of association with doubletree *q.v.*]

1. The swinging bar to which the traces of a horse are attached, a swingletree.

1841 WEBSTER II. 609/1 A single-tree is fixed upon each end of the double-tree when two horses draw abreast. **1913** LONDON *Valley of Moon* 351 The leaders . . . darn near sat down on their singletrees when I . . . slammed on the brake. **1936** *Sears Cat.* (ed. 173) 943/3 Heavy Full-Strapped Single-tree Varnished hickory. Wrought steel drop hooks.

2. "A heavy horizontal bar sometimes used to spread the loop of a hoisting chain to prevent crushing the load" (Webster '09).

Sing Sing ˈsɪŋsɪŋ, *n.* [f. Delaware *assinesink,* at the small stone.] A state prison at Ossining, New York. Also transf.

[**1830** *Mechanics' Press* (Utica, N.Y.) 9 Jan. 69/3 The state prison at Sing Sing is not yet finished.] **1870** EMERSON *Soc. & Solitude* 13 'Tis an extempore Sing-Sing built in a parlor. **1949** *Time* 7 March 29/1 They sat in the death house at Sing Sing while their lawyers battled up to New York's highest court.

* **sink,** *n.*

1. Short for **sinkhole.**

1791 W. BARTRAM *Travels* 246 The ground . . . presented to view those funnels, sinks and wells in groups of rocks, amidst the groves. **1816** *Mass. Spy* 17 July (Th.), The only entrance into the [Mammoth] Cave is from the bottom of what the inhabitants call a 'sink' which is a deep cavity in the earth, at the bottom of which there is generally a current of water. **1947** *Nat. Geog. Mag.* Feb. 139/2 Limestone here has collapsed into a sizable sink.

2. =**sinkbox.**

1793 T. B. HAZARD *Nailer Tom's Diary* (1930) 148/2 John Congdon workt on Skif. I went to the old mill after aboard for Sink. **1856** LEWIS *Amer. Sportsman* 284 It is better . . . to have two or more double-barrelled guns in the sink. **1874** LONG *Wild-Fowl* 252 The brush may be thrown off, and the labor of towing about the 'sink' avoided.

3. In combs.: (1) **sink boat,** =next, cf. **sneak boat;** (2) **box,** (see quot. 1903); (3) * **hole,** a hole in the surface of the earth, freq. shaped somewhat like an inverted cone, formed by the action of water on the soil or underlying rock, also transf.; (4) **room,** *N. Eng.* a room having a sink, esp. a room near a kitchen in which utensils are kept and the coarser operations involved in cooking are performed, also attrib.

(1) **1853** *Md. Laws* 220 If any person or persons shall use any sink boats . . . while engaged in shooting at . . . wild fowl, he or they shall be subject to a fine. **1877** BARTLETT 33 A friend in Maryland informs me that the usual term there is *Sink-boat,*—so called, because the whole body of the boat is below the surface. — (2) **1872** *Md. Laws* 76 Every applicant . . . shall pay to the Clerk of the Circuit Court . . . for a sink box, twenty dollars, . . . for each and every gunning season. **1903** *N.Y. Sun* 8 Nov., A sinkbox . . . is a coffin-shaped boat with extending platforms, that sinks into the water until the platforms rest on the surface. **1945** *Md. Conservationist* 4/1 The receipts . . . from hunters' licenses, duck blind licenses, pushers' licenses, sneak boat and sink-box licenses were $142,005.90. — (3) **1749** in *Amer. Sp.* XV. 392/1 Thence . . . to a small Hiccory Bush and a Hiccory Stake near a Sink Hole. **1895** *Stand.* 1674/2 *Sink-hole,* . . . a place in a marsh where it is too soft to make a road, and which the winter's cold does not freeze over. **1949** *Reader's Digest* June 45/1 The French industrialist behaves as if he believed his country were headed toward the sinkhole. — (4) **1833** *Trial E. K. Avery* 55, [I] found him in the sink room. **1869** STOWE *Oldtown Folks* 66 The conversation was interrupted by a commotion in the back sink-room. **1887** WILKINS *Humble Romance* 331, I hadn't any more'n shut the sink-room door.

As the last term in **alkali, lime, limestone, sand, wash sink.**

* **sinker,** *n.*

1. A muffin, biscuit, or dumpling, now esp. a doughnut. *Slang.*

1870 BEADLE *Utah* 223 Our favorite dinner, when we could get the meat, was of fried ham and 'sinkers.' **1906** *N.Y. Ev. Post* 10 Dec. 14 'Sinkers,' corn cakes, cream puffs, 'cookies,' and other standard foodstuffs. **1917** J. A. MOSS *Officers' Manual* 485 *Sinkers,* dumplings. **1950** *L.A. Times* 3 Jan. 2/8 Sinkers and coffee, folks, get your doughnuts here.

2. A small, pear-shaped object of stone or metal, used by Indians app. as a weight. Cf. **buckshot sinker.**

1872 *Amer. Naturalist* VI. 649 (*footnote*), These 'plummets,' or 'sinkers,' as they are more commonly called in New England, are of quite common occurrence in the vicinity of Salem. **1881** *Smithsonian Rep.* 657 Sinkers and hammer-stones occur on most sites.

3. (See quot.)

1905 *Forestry Bureau Bul.* No. 61, 34 *Deadhead,* a sunken or partly sunken log. . . . [Also called] sinker.

* **sinking,** *a.*

1. Of streams or springs: Disappearing from sight, running into a sinkhole.

1780 in SUMMERS *Ann. S.W. Va.* 733 Parker Atkinson [is to be overseer of the road] from the hollow of Doe Creek to the Steep Bank of Sinking Creek. **1781** in *Amer. Sp.* XV. 392/2 Thence . . . to a Walnut and two hoopwoods in Chaplains line near a small Sinking Spring. **1784** *Ib.* 392/1 Thence . . . to three white oaks by the head of a Sinking run. **1870** BEADLE *Utah* 443 West of the Iron Mountain range are a score of 'sinking creeks.' **1946** *Nat. Speleological Soc. Bul.* July 1/2 The number of sinks, sink-holes and sinking streams indicate that underground drainage channels extend . . . along soluble beds of limestone.

2. sinking chill, (see quot.). *Obs.*

1850 DRAKE *Treatise* 313 According to Doctor Deming, a large proportion of its diseases are intermittent and remittent fevers; many cases of the former, called by the people, 'sinking chills,' are decidedly malignant.

Siouan ˈsuən, *a.* Pertaining to the Sioux Indians.

1889 *Amer. Naturalist* XXIII. 75 The Siouan group had its habitat on the prairies between the Mississippi and Missouri. **1917** MOOREHEAD *Stone Ornaments Amer. Indian* 408 The area has been inhabited in historic times by Algonkin, Siouan, Iroquoian, Muskhogean and one or two other stocks. **1949** *Sky Line Trail* Oct. 12/1 The Siouan and other tribes native to the Great Lakes were tireless travellers.

Sioux su, *n.* [F., shortening of *Nadowessioux,* from Chippewa *Nadowessi,* "little snake, enemy."] *pl.* The largest and best-known of the Indian tribal groups of the Siouan stock. Cf. * **cutthroat 2, Yankton Sioux.**

1805 LEWIS in *L. & Clark Exped.* I. (1904) 258 The Indians in our neighbourhood are frequently pilfered of their horses by the Ascares, Souixs and Assinniboins. **1865** *Cin. D. Gazette* 3 Oct. 3/6 It is thought, however, that the Sioux and Cheyennes are not half whipped. **1946** *Sat. Review* 8 June 37/3 The historical section also shows how the Sioux could weather the disappearance of the buffalo.

attrib. **1808** PIKE *Sources Miss.* 14 His design was to winter with some of the Sioux bands. **1853** *La Crosse Democrat* 17 May 2/6 Persons wishing to locate in the valley of the Root River [in eastern Minnesota] or on any part of the 'Sioux Purchase' will find the route . . . far more convenient. **1872** *Chi. Tribune* 25 June, The characters are a mixed set having among them guerrillas, trappers, Sioux braves [etc.]. **1949** *10 Story Western* May 39/1 The little party of Sioux hunters stopped by the Yellowstone, just below its confluence with the Rosebud.

Also, *sing.,* an Indian belonging to a tribe of this group. In full **Sioux Indian.**

1827 COOPER *Prairie* xxx, The keen weapon . . . meeting the naked breast of the impetuous Sioux, the blade was buried to the buck-horn haft. **1945** *Reader's Digest* April 69 In Deadwood, S.D. Mike Turning Bear, a Sioux Indian, was charged with stealing 20 head of horses.

b. The language of these Indians. In full **Sioux language.**

1915 YOUNG *Hard Knocks* 78 My Indian friend . . . began to talk Sioux to them in an excited manner. **1932** VESTAL *Sitting Bull* 22 The meadowlark, in particular, speaks such good Sioux that it is known as the Sioux bird. **1949** *Amer. Photography* Jan. 40/1 Following a speech in Sioux language, in which God was asked for rain, the real Sun Dance now started.

Also *Sioux cattle, chief, man, nation, pipe, pony, reservation, squaw, war,* etc.

***sir,** *n.*

1. (See quot. *c*1870.) *Obs.*

1789 *Essex Inst. Coll.* XXV. 311 One of them fired and killed my honoured Sir. *c***1870** CHIPMAN *Notes on Bartlett* 408 *Sir,* not infrequent for father; said of parents by children; and of a father by his wife. Salem, Mass., until near 1840. . . . E.g. 'Your sir,' the mother would say to her child respecting his father, her husband.

2. Added to *yes* or *no* as an intensive. *Colloq.* Cf. **no sir-ee.**

1799 *Aurora* (Phila.) 8 Aug. (Th.), Yes Sir! and [France] has been successful beyond any former experience. **1861** BERKELY *Sportsman* 146 In American parlance, to say 'No, sir,' laying a long emphasis on the last syllable, is to give a contradiction of a very flat sort. **1888** CRADDOCK *Despot* 40 Yes, sir. . . . None like 'em now. **1906** FREEMAN *By Light of Soul* 398 'You don't mean to say they did all that?' said the other woman. 'Yes, sir, they did.'

***siren,** *n.* **1.** An eel-shaped American amphibian of the family Sirenidae. **2.** (See quot.)

(1) [**1765** J. ELLIS tr. Linnaeus in *Phil. Trans.* LVI. 192, Dr. Garden's very rare two-footed animal . . . must be a new and very distinct genus, and should most properly have the name of *Siren.*] **1796** MORSE *Univ. Geog.* I. 224 The Siren or Mud-iguana, a fish of the order, *Branchiostegi,* . . . was first observed by Dr. Garden of Charleston (S.C.). **1947** SHERMAN C. BISHOP *Handbook of Salamanders* 467 Nothing is known of the breeding habits of Siren in nature, and the very young have not been described. — **(2) 1891** *Cent.* 5655/3 *Siren,* . . . one of the *Sirenia,* as the manatee, dugong, halicore, or sea-cow; any sirenian.

***sirup,** *n.* As the last term in **maple, mush, New Orleans sirup.**

***sirup,** *v. To sirup off,* in making maple sugar, to remove from the pan or evaporator the sirup resulting from the preliminary boiling of the sap. — **1872** *Vt. Agric. Rep.* I. 216 One should make it a point to syrup off quite often as the continued boiling of the same sweet for a long time will color it.

sis sɪs, *n.* Short for **sister. Colloq.*

1835 *Knickerb.* VI. 293 All the friends called her sister,—which, as the half was easier to be bandied about than the whole,—soon dwindled into 'sis.' **1891** RYAN *Pagan* 133 Folks call boys 'bud' sometimes, jist like they call girls 'sis.' **1948** SAMUEL W. TAYLOR *Man With My Face* 43 'Oh, pipe down, sis,' Curly said. 'I'm trying to talk business.'

siscowet ˈsɪskəwət, *n.* [See note.] (See quots.) Cf. **cisco.**

"A name, with many variants, such as *siskowet, siskiwit, siskowit, siskwoet, ciscovet,* etc. . . . The name is a Canadian French contraction and corruption of the cumbersome Chippewa name *pemitewiskawet,* 'that which has oily flesh' " (Hodge).

1847 LANMAN *Summer in Wilderness* 159 A fish called ciscovet, is unquestionably of the trout genus, but much more delicious. **1900** *Outing* May 160/1 The lake trout . . . is the 'siscowet' or 'siskawetz' of Lake Superior. **1945** GRAY *Pine, Stream & Prairie* 104 The fish begin to slide into the trough . . . the fat siscowet, full of meat and oil.

b. siscowet salmon, =prec.

1882 *Nat. Museum Bul.* No. 16, 318 Siscowet Salmon . . . is probably a local variety rather than a distinct species.

sissified ˈsɪsɪfaɪd, *a.* Effeminate. *Colloq.* — **1905** J. C. LINCOLN *Partners of Tide* iv, To be seen with girls was not so 'sissified' in his mind as it used to be. **1921** R. D. PAINE *Comr. Rolling Ocean* i. 10 The campus . . . thought him a bit sissified. **1950** *Time* 24 April 44/1 James J. ('Big Jim') Jeffries . . . observed that the fight game has become so sissified that 'I'd rather see a wrestling match.'

sissiness ˈsɪsɪnɪs, *n.* Effeminateness. *Colloq.* — **1926** *Harper's Mag.* Feb. 350/2 In spite of his funny sissiness there was not a dog in town that did not love him.

sissy ˈsɪsɪ, *n.* and *a.*

1. *n.* **a.** =**sis. b.** An effeminate man or boy.

(a) 1846 *Dollar Newspaper* (Phila.) 22 April 1/7 'Sissy Jane' smoothed back my hair, and smiled at me. **1934** VINES *Green Thicket World* 15 He's the very buck that run my sissy crazy. — **(b) 1899** T. HALL *Tales* 131 Well, you are a sissy. **1911** FERBER *Dawn O'Hara* 42 The hero is a milk-and-water sissy, without a vital spark in him. **1948** *Sat. Review* 31 Jan. 5/2 These hockey players are big sissies.

2. *a.* Effeminate, girlish.

1891 *Harper's Mag.* Aug. 485/2 [He] sat near me, deep in conversation with a young gentleman with sissy whiskers. **1909** *The Fra* Feb. 69/1 The sissy-boy and the mollycoddle were not in evidence. **1947** *Chi. Sun* 14 Oct. 23/2 Specialists in football are making the game sissy.

sissyish ˈsɪsɪ·ɪʃ, *a.* =**sissy,** *a. Colloq.* — **1889** HOWELLS *Hazard of Fortunes* II. 64 The New York fellows . . . were both sissyish and fast.

***sister,** *n.*

1. *pl.* Mormon wives. *Rare.*

1858 GOVE *Letters* 361 Some of the 'sisters' tell me that the rooms inside of this mansion are only lathed up some six feet, so every word that is spoken in one room can be heard in the adjoining one.

2. In combs.: (1) **sister city,** a city thought of as having a status similar to that of another; (2) **Feebe,** a form of game, *obs.;* (3) **state,** a state associated with others in the federal Union; (4) **union,** a labor union thought of as having aims and a status similar to those of another.

(1) 1831 *Boston Transcript* 13 July 2/1 In your remarks upon the late prevalence of crime, some reflection is obliquely made upon a sister city. **1948** *Chi. Tribune* 4 April VI. 2/5 Gulfport, a modern port, is in sharp contrast to her sister city. — **(2)** *c***1845** W. T. PORTER *Big Bear Ark.* 103 Who always threaded my needle and has kissed me in particler, in playin of . . . Sister Feebe. *Ib.* 157 All took to kissing, and then to playing 'Sister Phebe.' — **(3) 1777** *Boston Rec.* 285 We are sure, that very large, & much wanted Supplies, the Property of this State & expected here, are now ordered into some of the Sister States. **1798** I. ALLEN *Hist. Vermont* 225 The right of the people of Vermont to be admitted a sister State into the union was acknowledged. **1948** *Sat. Ev. Post* 24 April 90/3 After being captured by the Federals, she participated in the travail of her Southern sister states. — **(4) 1874** *Internat. Typog. Union Proc.* 14 A member of a union going to work in the jurisdiction of a sister Union upon permit is amenable to the law of the latter Union. **1896** *Ib.* 49/2 We also suggested to the International officers the idea of printing and mailing blank resolutions to sister unions to be filled out.

b. *sisterhood, the states making up the Federal Union.

1839 [see **single star**]. **1878** BEADLE *Western Wilds* 126 This [State], the most loudly blowed and persistently advertised of the whole sisterhood, has been knocking for admission into the Union since 1849.

In full **sisterhood of states.**

1832 *Cong. Deb.* 16 June 3627 Can you forget . . . the constitution you have sworn to support, the sisterhood of States which has cherished you? **1900** *Cong. Rec.* 25 Jan. 1207/2 A condition precedent to her admission into the sisterhood of States, was . . . an express prohibition against polygamy.

As the last term in **Shaker, sob, vixen, weak sister.**

***sit,** *v.* In phrases: (1) *To sit by,* to be near or present, to sit up to a table for a meal, *colloq.;* (2) **to sit in,* to join a group in playing cards, etc., *colloq.* [*OED* has one ex., of 1599, in the sense "to have a place as a player *at* a game"]; (3) **to sit up,* (see quot. 1856), *colloq.;* (4) *to sit pretty,* to be in a most advantageous position, *slang;* (5) *to sit up nights, fig.* to work hard, to be anxious, spare no pains, *colloq.*

For *to sit like a bump on a log,* see ***log,** *n.* **5.** (4).

(1) 1845 KIRKLAND *Western Clearings* 109 Mr. and Mrs. Lightbody sat by, but Mr. Poppleton was again the spokesman. **1888** KIRKLAND *McVeys* 273 He 'set by,' and resting his forehead on his arm was sound asleep when she came back in five minutes with bread, and milk, and cold meat. — **(2) 1868** S. HALE *Letters* 44 Before we got to lunch two Englishmen *sot in.* **1922** MCNEAL *When Kansas Was Young* 187 A Texan . . . suggested to Major Drumm that he would like to 'sit in' but that he was somewhat hampered in the way of cash. — **(3) 1846** MCKENNEY *Memoirs* I. 138 'Sit up, sit up, stranger, and join us,' said the hardy settler. **1856** S. WARNER *Hills of Shatemuc* xvi, 'Will you sit up, cousin?' . . . : the meaning of the request being that he should move his chair up to the table. **1894** WILLIAMS *Pembroke* 38 If you don't set right up an' eat it, it will be gettin' cold. — **(4) 1931** *K.C. Star* 31 Oct. 12 He is sitting prettier today than thousands of people in other lines of endeavor. **1943** *Harper's Mag.* June 85 They were sitting pretty.

(5) 1855 B. YOUNG in *Jrnl. of Discourses* II. 320/2 If you persecute us, we will sit up nights to preach the Gospel. **1910** *N.Y. Ev. Post* 4 Aug. (Th.), The President is reported as . . . sitting up nights waiting for Mr. Ballinger to come round and hand in his resignation.

sitcup ˈsɪtkʌp, *n.* [Origin unknown.] (See quot.) *Rare.* — **1857** W. CHANDLESS *Visit Salt Lake* II. IX. 291 A large ball of sitcup, dry stuff, looking like buffalo chips, in reality made of juniper berries.

sit-down ˈsɪtˌdaʊn, *n.* An act of sitting down, as on the occasion of a friendly visit or a rest. *Colloq.*

1777 in H. S. ALLAN *John Hancock* (1948) 244, I have some of your wine left for you. I wish to have one sitdown with you in my poor habitation. **1878** MRS. STOWE *Poganuc P.* xiii. 111 After tea there came the genial hour of the social sit-down in front of the andirons. **1898** *Jrnl. Sch. Geog.* Oct. 315 At intervals of two miles [in Burma] . . . are 'sit-downs,' generally a favorite tree selected because of its dense and wide spreading shade, beneath which all native travellers have their sit-down and smoke.

b. A meal taken while sitting down. *Slang.*

1926 J. BLACK *You Can't Win* vi. 67 She'll give you a sit-down for yourself, chances are, but bring back a 'lump' for us.

c. sit-down strike, an occasion when workmen, in an effort to secure more wages or improvements in working conditions, remain at their places of employment but refuse to work.

1936 *Dly. Oklahoman* (Okla. City.) 3 Nov. 12/3 The International Mercantile Marine late in the day cancelled the sailing of the S.S. Manhattan, scheduled for Wednesday, because of a 'sit down' strike by seamen in New York harbor. [**1948** *Chi. D. News* 30 July 1/4 An auburn-haired ex-model continued a 'sitdown' in the mansion of a millionaire Friday.]

* **site,** *n.* As the last term in **county, mill, town site.**

sitio ˈsɪtɪˌo, *n. S.W.* [Sp., site, place, situation. Cf. Amer. Sp. sense of a large farm or cattle ranch.] (See quot. 1859.) Now *hist.*

1825 *Austin P.* II. (1924) 1202 The twelfth article of the law says the Empresarios shall receive (5) five Sitios (Leagues) of pasture land. **1834** *Jamestown* (N.Y.) *Jrnl.* 19 Nov. 2/2 The law allows a married man [in Texas] to have not exceeding a Sitio. **1859** BARTLETT 409 The sitio is a league of land of 5,000 varas, and is equal to 4,428 English acres. **1948** *True* May 123/2 The land was to be apportioned to the settlers at the rate of one *sitio* (4,428 acres) to each family that went in for cattle farming.

Sitka ˈsɪtkə, *n.* ["Prob. meaning 'on Shi,' the native name of Baranof id." (Hodge).]

1. *pl.* or *collect.* (See quot. 1910.)

1873 *Alaska Herald* (S.F.) 9 July 4/2 The Hydahs, Chilcats, Tarkous, Ouchanons, and Sitkas participated. **1879** MORRIS *Pub. Service Alaska* 14 In the fall of 1877, a potlatch was given at Sitka by Jack, chief of the Sitkas, and it is estimated correctly he gave away on that occasion 500 blankets. **1910** HODGE *Amer. Indians* II. 582/2 Sitka. . . . A Tlingit tribe, named from their principal town, on the w. coast of Baranof id., Alaska.

2. *attrib.* In the names of trees and animals found in the Northwest, usu. in the region of Sitka, Alaska.

1884 SARGENT *Rep. Forests* 580 The most valuable tree of this region [Alaska] is the Sitka cedar (*Chamæcyparis Nutkaensis*). *Ib.* 178 *Chamæcyparis Nutkaensis*. . . . Yellow Cypress. Sitka Cypress. **1890** BALLOU *New Eldorado* 146 The white spruce, called the Sitka pine, rises to a height of from a hundred and fifty to a hundred and eighty feet. **1917** *Birds of Amer.* III. 222/2 The Sitka, or Grinnell's Ruby-crowned, Kinglet (*Regulus calendula grinnelli*) is similar to the more widely distributed Ruby-crown. **1948–49** *Antioch Review* Winter 408 This would be the first step toward cutting off the magnificent Douglas fir and Sitka pine from 300,000 acres.

b. Esp. **Sitka spruce,** a tall spruce, *Picea sitchensis*, found on the northwestern coast of the U.S. Also the wood or lumber of this.

1895 FUNSTON *Botany Yakutat Bay* 328 The great bulk of this forest is composed of Sitka spruce. **1949** *Prairie Lumberman* Oct. 38/1 Sitka spruce is tough, even-grained and soft-textured.

* **sitter,** *n.* (See quots.) Cf. **flag-pole sitter.**

1868 *Ore. State Jrnl.* 19 Dec. 2/5 'Sitters,' as they are called, . . . sit about on chairs [in saloons] to sleep off the effects of drink. **1905** J.M. RICHARDS *With John Bull & Jonathan* 139 The greater privacy of the hotels in England greatly impressed me, as no 'loungers,' or 'sitters' as they are called in America, are allowed to frequent them. **1938** HART *New Yorkers* 183 Bowery barkeeps employed homeless men and women as 'sitters' to shiver near the fire on wintry nights and thus evoke the sympathy of cash customers who would treat them to drinks to the great profit of the house.

* **sitting,** *n.* and *a.* In combs.: (1) * **sitting room,** that part of a poultry house where hens sit, *rare;* (2) **shot,** a shot made from a sitting position; (3) **-up party,** a group of friends who sit up with a corpse on the night before interment; (4) **-up visit,** a visit to a mother soon after the birth of her child when she is again able to sit up, *obs.*

(1) **1850** BROWNE *Poultry Yard* 89 In the sitting room . . . [the hen] may remain in perfect quietude till she hatches her brood. — (2) **1874** LONG *Wild-fowl* 151 If it was later in the day, it might be to our advantage to try a sitting-shot. **1894** ROBINSON *Danvis Folks* 24, I never missed a settin' shot in my life. — (3) **1944** CLARK *Pills* 268 There was a commingling of sorrow and joviality in the 'sitting up' parties of the South. — (4) **1761** *Holyoke Diaries* 49 Made Mrs. Ropes a Sitting up visit. **1772** A. G. WINSLOW *Diary* 15, I made a setting up visit to Aunt Suky.

b. *Sitting of the Solstices,* (see quot.). *Obs.*

1851 HALL *College Words* 279 It was customary, in the early days of Harvard College, for the graduates of the year to attend in the recitation-room on Mondays and Tuesdays, for three weeks, during the month of June, subject to the examination of all who chose to visit them. This was called the *Sitting of the Solstices*. . . . The time was also known as the *Weeks of Visitation.*

As the last term in **family, fence sitting.**

Siuslaw saɪˈuˌslɔ, *n.* [App. a native name.] (See quot. 1910.) — **1856** in *34th Cong.* 3 Sess. H. R. Ex. Doc. 37, 9 Your estimate for a remittance on account of fulfilling treaties with certain bands of Gillamooks, Scinslaw, Kala-Walset, Coosa Bay, and other tribes, cannot be counted on. **1910** HODGE *Amer. Indians* II. 584/2 Siuslaw. A small Yakonan tribe formerly living on and near Siuslaw r., w. Oreg. It is now nearly extinct, a few survivors only being on the Siletz res.

Siwash ˈsaɪwɑʃ, *n. N.W.* [Chinook Jargon, f. F. *sauvage.*] An Indian of the northern Pacific Coast. Also attrib. and transf.

1847 PALMER *Journal* 150 Si-wash Indians. **1890** *Puyallup* (Wash.) *Commercial* 17 Oct. 7/4 A stolid Siwash and his wife were seated on a box in front of a Puyallup store from noon till 8 p.m. **1902** WHITE *Blazed Trail Stories* 138 Billy! . . . come down here, you siwash. **1912** *Country Life* Dec. 69/1 The Siwash dogs are in the majority; they are a cross between a wolf and a dog, and usually gray or white in color, but occasionally black. **1949** *Boston Globe* 15 May (Fiction Mag.) 3/2 The Siwash showed him a poke of coarse gold.

b. Siwash coat, a kind of Mother Hubbard; **Siwash dollars,** (see quot. and cf. **hiaqua**); **Siwash onion,** (see quot.).

1852 SWAN *Three Years' Residence* (1857) 155 This garment is still used by old women, and by all the females when they are at work in the water, and is called by them their *siwash coat*, or Indian gown. — *Ib.* 158 A species of small shell, of a cylindrical shape, pointed at one end, slightly curved, and resembling a nearly straight horn, . . . passes as money among them, and is called *Siwash* dollars. — **1945** *Senior Scholastic* 23 April 19/3 *Kamas*—a staple food in the early days. A bulbous root, sometimes called the siwash onion.

c. The trade language or jargon used by the Siwashes and those having dealings with them.

1902 *Skagway Dly. Alaskan* 23 Aug. 3/1 The governor was forced back upon his ability to talk siwash, hoping thereby to control the Indian vote. **1908** BEACH *Barrier* 56 Address me in Siwash or in English unless we are alone.

d. A small college regarded as typical of its class. *Slang.*

1947 *Time* 13 Jan. 59/2 His comparatively small (31 million) audience . . . includes collegians (from Harvard to Siwash) and their professors. **1948** *Chi. Maroon* 6 Feb. 10/4 Old Siwash forged into a twelve point lead and the game began to assume the proportions of a rout.

siwash ˈsaɪwɑʃ, *v. intr.* To camp out in the open without shelter, using only such natural materials as may be at hand.

1904 *Churchman* 21 May 626, I have a lame shoulder, the result of continuous 'siwashing' and sleeping in the snow. **1922** *Outing* Feb. 219/1, I made a practice of lying out or 'siwashing it' in the open woods o' nights. **1946** STANWELL-FLETCHER *Driftwood Valley* 94 Since we can't carry the additional weight of a tent, we will have to siwash under trees.

* **six,** *a.* In combs.: (1) **six-and-a-quarter cents coin,** (see quot.), *obs.;* (2) **bits,** see * **bit,** *n.* **2. b;** (3) **building,** prob. a building in a row of six such houses erected as boarding places on or near Capitol Hill, Washington, D.C., *c*1850, *obs.;* (4) **Companies,** six mutual aid societies originating in California *c*1850 for helping Chinese emigrants, and representing six districts in the province of Kwantung; (5) **figures,** largely, extravagantly, in hundreds of thousands, cf. **seven figure;** (6) **gun,** = **six shooter;** (7) **-handed Virginia reel,** ?a Virginia reel arranged for three couples; (8) **mule,** used attrib. to designate conveyances drawn by six mules, or a team of six mules; (9) **Nations,** the confederation of Iroquois Indians as enlarged in the early eighteenth century by the addition of the Tuscarora to the Five Nations, also at-

trib., cf. **Six United Nations;** (10) * **pence,** (see quot. 1848), *obs.;* (11) **plate stove,** a stove consisting chiefly of six plates so cast as to be bolted together, now *hist.*, cf. **five-plate stove, ten-plate stove;** (12) **Principle Baptists,** see as a main entry; (13) **-rail fence,** see **rail fence 2;** (14) **reel,** ?=**six-handed Virginia reel,** *obs.;* (15) **shooter,** a revolver capable of firing six shots without reloading, also attrib. and transf., also as verb; (16) **shootering,** the firing of a six shooter, *rare;* (17) **shooting,** *a.* of firearms, capable of firing six shots without reloading; (18) **spotted mite,** (see quot. 1909); (19) **States,** the six New England states, *rare;* (20) **United Nations,** =**Six Nations,** *obs.;* (21) **week(s),** see as a main entry.

(1) **1880** N. BROOKS *Fairport Nine* 125 The fourpence ha'penny, or six-and-a-quarter-cents coin, . . . circulated then. — (3) **1884** [see **seven building**]. — (4) **1876** W. M. FISHER *Californians* 58 All these are commonly spoken of as 'The Six Companies.'

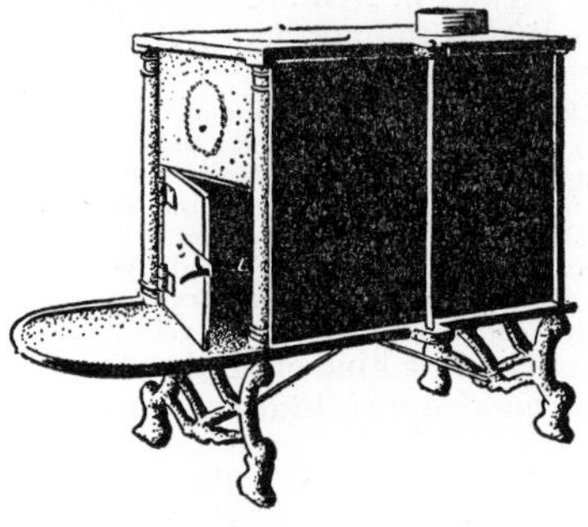

Six plate stove *c*1770

(5) **1873** MARK TWAIN & WARNER *Gilded Age* xiii. 123 (R.), Harry . . . always talked in six figures. — (6) **1912** RAINE *Brand Blotters* 336 My carbine was gone. It was too far for a six-gun. **1949** *Exciting Western* May 62/2 Bleakly he touched the six-gun that dragged his coat pocket. — (7) **1836** *S. Lit. Messenger* II. 355 In the background is seen . . . a true old-fashioned six-handed Virginia reel. — (8) **1843** in *Miss. Valley Hist. Rev.* VI. 109 Move On with 18 carts, one 6 mule waggon, & 2 2 mule waggons. **1873** HARTE *Tales of Argonauts* 202 Mr. Titherick . . . was then driving a six-mule freight wagon. **1895** REMINGTON *Pony Tracks* 5 Now the general steps out of the car and hands the commission into a six-mule ambulance. — (9) **1710** in J. W. LYDEKKER *Faithful Mohawks* (1938) 28 And as a sure Token of the sincerity of the Six Nations, we do in Our own and in the Names of all, present Our Great Queen with these Belts of Wampum. **1813** *Niles' Reg.* IV. 400/1 The *Six Nations* are the Mohawks, Oneidas, Onondagoes, Senecas, Cayugas, and Tuscaroras. **1949** *Pa. Hist.* April 101 Washington's decision to suspend the Presque Isle operation was a result of a determination to keep the Six Nations Indians at peace.

(10) **1818** FEARON *Sketches* 13 A beggar . . . was relieved with a Spanish silver piece called a sixpence: it was the sixteenth of a dollar. **1848** BARTLETT 135 The half real of $\frac{1}{16}$ of a dollar is called in New York a *sixpence.* **1891** WELCH *Recoll. 1830–40* 169 It was common, particularly in New England, to call a sixpence or a half dime, a *fip.* — (11) **1820** *Columbian Centinel* 1 Jan. 3/3 Elijah Vose, Jr. . . . Offers for Sale . . . Six Plate Stoves. **1949** *Hist. Rev. Berks Co.* (Pa.) Oct. 142/1 [It was] a further development of the rectangular six-plate stove by the addition of an inner food-baking compartment opening on the side. — (14) **1835** LONGSTREET *Ga. Scenes* 12 Off went the party to a good old republican six reel.

(15) **1844** *Nauvoo* (Ill.) *Neighbor* 24 July 3/1 Joseph . . . opening the door two or three inches with his left hand, discharged one barrel of a six shooter (Pistol) in the entry, from whence a bullet grazed Hyrum's breast. **1890** *Stock Grower & Farmer* 21 June 3/1 A terrible six-shooter sermon came to us from Socorro county last week. Three cowboys shot each other up. **1904** P. FOUNTAIN *Great North-West* xx. 242 (*footnote*), I never was so near six-shootering myself as I was that night. **1950** *Chi. Tribune* 23 March 10, I never carry guns! My fists are my six-shooters! — (16) **1909** O. HENRY *Roads of Destiny* 371 We heard a yelling and a six-shootering, and a lot of galloping. — (17) **1851** in *Iowa Jrnl. Hist.* (1949) Jan., A Man's best friend here [Calif.] is a good six shooting *Revolver.* **1858** VIELE *Following Drum* 224 A belt full of pistols, a sword buckled to the side, and a six-shooting rifle, composed his supply of fire-arms. — (18) **1890** *Rep. Secy. Agric. 1889* 341 Since the appearance of the Six-spotted Mite of the Orange in 1886, the Florida press has made frequent reference to it. **1909** *Cent. Supp.* 816/1 Six-spotted mite . . . one of the leaf-mites or 'red spiders' of the family *Tetranychidæ* . . . found commonly on the orange in Florida and California. — (19) **1945** WEBSTER *Town Meeting Country* 183 That same difference between the people of 1910 and those of 1940 can be seen all over the Six States.

(20) **1752** W. TRENT *Journal* 96 We join with the Six United Nations of Indians. **1776** *Va. State P.* I. 273 The said Six United Nations . . . did grant to the said Traders . . . all that Tract of Land.

As the last term in **Connecticut, Cuba, currency, government, number, Seventy, short six(es).**

Six Principle Baptists. (See quots. 1919, 1931.) Also attrib.

1830 *Williams's N.Y. Ann. Reg.* 345 Six Principle Baptists—Churches 15; Ministers 30; Communicants 1500. **1919** *Census: Religious Bodies 1916* II. 102/1 A number of members withdrew and in 1653 organized the General Six Principle Baptist Church, the six principles being . . . : Repentance, faith, baptism, laying on of hands, resurrection of the dead, and eternal judgment. **1931** SWEET *Religion* 43 Those Baptists who held to the rite of the 'Imposition of Hands' as a symbol of the receiving of the Holy Spirit as an essential, were known as 'Six Principle Baptists,' and in the early colonial period there was a division among the Baptists in Rhode Island over this question.

* **sixteen,** *a.*

1. sixteen shooter, a magazine rifle capable of firing sixteen shots without reloading. In full **sixteen-shooter rifle.** *Obs.*

1865 RICHARDSON *Secret Service* 480 He and his companions were now armed with sixteen-shooter rifles, revolvers, and bowie-knives. **1875** *Chi. Tribune* 2 Dec. 3/2 He was armed with a sixteen-shooter. **1894** EGGLESTON in *Harper's Mag.* Feb. 475/1 George had a sixteen-shooter.

Hence **sixteen-shooting liquor,** liquor that is especially cheap or "mean." *Rare.*

1893 JAMES *Cow-Boy Life* 26 Let some fiend incarnate tank up with 'sixteen shooting liquor,' take a pistol and shoot into a passenger train, and it is the 'cow-boys.'

2. *sixteen to one,* the legal coinage ratio of gold and silver established by laws passed in 1834 and 1837, esp. used as a campaign cry by those Democrats in 1896 who advocated the free and unlimited coinage of silver at this ratio. Also attrib.

See *Amer. Sp.* April 1944, p. 119.

1854 BENTON *30 Years' View* I. 443/2 The value of gold is 16 to 1 over silver. **1894** *Nation* 7 March 352/2 If all the 16-to-1 men and the international-agreement men and the straddlers . . . could be forced to go off with the Populists, . . . the country would first rise up and call them blessed. **1903** *Forum* July 4 Mr. Bryan seems determined to drag into the next campaign the obnoxious ghost of sixteen to one. **1948** *Annals Iowa* Oct. 415 A craze for the 'free and unlimited coinage of silver at the ratio of 16 to 1' was sweeping over the country.

As the last term in **sweet sixteen.**

sixteenth section. In a surveyed township, the section numbered sixteen, granted to the state by the federal government for school purposes. Also attrib. Cf. **reserved section, school section.**

1785 *Jrnls. Cont. Cong.* XXVIII. 378 There shall be reserved the lot N 16, of every township, for the maintenance of public schools, within the said township. **1837** WETMORE *Gaz. Missouri* 72 This mine is on a tract of school-lands, commonly called sixteenth section. **1880** *Cimarron News & Press* 9 Sep. 2/1 Under our organic law each 16th and 32d section of public land is reserved for school purposes. **1914** *Cyclo. Amer. Govt.* III. 256/1 The states admitted between 1802 and 1848, except Texas, received the 16th section in each surveyed township of public domain. **1949** *Democrat* 8 Sep. 8/3 All state-owned lands, including the sixteenth section school lands, are public and are sanctuaries for wild life.

* **sixty,** *n.* **1.** *like sixty,* with extreme quickness, efficiency, etc. *Colloq.* **2. sixty-niner,** one who took part in a Montana gold rush in 1869.

(1) **1839** *N.O. Picayune* 8 March 2/4 If they du come to hard blows the Maine boys 'll flax out them are Brunswickers like sixty. **1907** WHITE *Boniface to Bank Burglar* 362, I hed tew do five miles, en like sixty, tew. **1949** *Chi. Tribune* 5 Nov. 10/3 He . . . loaded it with the hull can, tamped her in, lit the fuse, an' run like sixty. — (2) **1921** *Frontier* Feb. 6 Not far from where these hardy miners work their sluice-boxes is the site of the once busy mining camp of Moose City, founded by the sixty-niners.

six week(s). *attrib.* Designating various quick-growing plants.

1763 *Holyoke Diaries* 58 Sowed 6 w(ee)ks beans. **1775** ADAIR *Indians* 406 The smaller sort of Indian corn . . . ripens in two months from the time it is planted; though it is called by the English, the six weeks corn. **1859** *Ill. Agric. Soc. Trans.* III. 503 Early yellow six-weeks [beans] and early Valentine (long red mottled,) are excellent for snaps. **1894** COULTER *Bot. W. Texas* III. 533 *B[outeloua] aristidoides.* . . . Six-weeks mesquit. . . . Western Texas to California.

b. Esp. **six-weeks grass,** any one of various quick-growing grasses, esp. *Poa annua*, found in the Southwest.

1925 BRYAN *Papago Country* 375 The cattlemen call this the six-weeks grass. **1932** *Ariz. Agric. Exp. Sta. Bul.* 141, 26 The summer annuals are represented by numerous six-weeks grasses.

***size,** *v.*

1. *tr.* To sum up or take the measure of (something); to estimate, to form an opinion about (a person, thing, etc.). Usu. with *up*.

1877 MARK TWAIN *Punch, Brothers, Punch!* 73 Somehow, it [a lawsuit about a cat] seemed to 'size' the country [Bermuda]. **1885** *Santa Fé Wkly. New Mexican* 24 Dec. 2/5 They know everybody can 'size up' a man at a glance. **1917** B. MATTHEWS *These Many Years* 205, I was always greeted . . . with the transfixing glance which seemed to 'size me up,' to use our expressive Americanism. **1945** GARDNER *Golddigger's Purse* 35, I always like to plan my campaign after I've sized up my man.

b. *intr.* To turn out, amount to, or compare with, to prove to be upon investigation.

1884 NYE *Baled Hay* 126 Time, at last, makes all things size up in proper shape. **1914** JAMES *Ivory Tower* 91 The question of what Gray's 'interest' . . . might size up to.

2. *To size* (someone's) *pile*, to match or equal an opponent, to bet with, estimate correctly someone's resources. *Colloq.*

1840 HALIBURTON *Clockmaker* 3 Ser. xi, Come, I'll size your pile. . . . Plank down a pile of dollars . . . of any size you like, and I'll put down another of the same size. **1891** SLOAN *Fogy Days* 48 Doctors didn't try to size your pile.

b. Also allusively.

1889 MARK TWAIN *Conn. Yankee* 300, I was resolved he should have at least one [bath] . . . , if it sized up my whole influence and bankrupted the pile.

sizzler ˈsɪzlɚ, *n.* Also **sizzer.** A person or thing that sizzles or is sizzling hot. Also fig. *Colloq.*

1848 *Free Soil Minstrel*, They've called us sizzlers long enough, We now begin to boil. **1897** *Chi. Tribune* 5 July 6/4 The last cracker will have cracked, the last torpedo will have popped, the last 'sizzer' will have hissed. **1901** *Emporia Kans. Gaz.* 19 July, The drought, which is a sizzler and frier and boiler, is a good thing for Kansas. **1904** G. H. LORIMER *Old Gorgon Graham* ii. 37 Satan may be down in Arizona cooking up a sizzler for the corn belt.

Skagit ˈskægɪt, *n.* [App. a native name.] *pl.* or *collect.* (See quot. 1910.)

1854 *Pacific Railroad Rep.* I. (1855) 433 The Skagits raise a considerable quantity of potatoes, and have, besides, a natural resource in their kamas. **1903** JAMES *Indian Basketry* 53 The Skagits and Lummis are to the extreme north. **1910** HODGE *Amer. Indians* II. 585/2 Skagit. A body of Salish on a river of the same name in Washington, particularly about its mouth.

***skate,** *n.* As the last term in **cheap, club, roller skate(s).**

skeesicks ˈskizɪks, *n.* Also **skeezicks.** [Origin unknown.] A good-for-nothing, a rascal, often used playfully. *Colloq.*

1850 *Frontier Guardian* 2 Oct. (Th.), Though Kister, that skeezecks, with Hall at his back Should come again thieving. **1892** *Amer. Folk-Lore* V. Sep. 236 *Skeezicks.* . . . In my boyhood, in western New York, the word was applied to persons, usually children, who had been in mischief, and where the prank had caused sorrow to person or damage to property. **1939** ROLLINS *Gone Haywire* 117 Eb Hawkins, that ol' skeesicks you met on th' railway train an' liked, is th' feller that's acted as th' owners' agent in sellin' rights to your uncle.

skeeter ˈskitɚ, *n.* Colloq. shortening of **mosquito.* Also transf.

1839 *Spirit of Times* 14 Dec. 495/2 (We.), I was fast asleep, and dreaming dat a big skeeter was a bitin me. **1904** O. HENRY *Heart of West* 112 Got up, the little skeeter, and licked Ross. **1949** *Boston Globe* 15 May (Fiction Mag.) 2/3 It don't take no brains to send four guys out in the bresh to git eat up by skeeters, does it?

***skein,** *n.* A metal thimble protecting the spindle of a wooden axle. Cf. **thimble skein.**

1847 *30th Congress* 1 Sess. H. R. Ex. Doc. No. 41, 517 The lower 'skeen' of the spindle was broken. **1881** *Rep. Indian Affairs* 402 Skeins, wagon, $2\frac{1}{4} \times 6\frac{1}{2}$ inch. **1948** *Democrat* 25 Nov. 5/2 We have . . . cast iron Skeins . . . for two-horse wagons formerly popular in this territory: Studebaker, Chattanooga, and Weber.

***skeleton,** *n. attrib.* Designating land or water conveyances of an especially light structure.

1846 *Spirit of Times* 18 April 90/2 This match was made to go in 'skeleton wagons.' **1858** HOLMES *Autocrat* 189 My own particular water-sulky, a 'skeleton' or 'shell' raceboat. **1867** LACKLAND *Homespun* 181 A fly, a sulky, or a skeleton gig could be seen somewhere about the yard.

***skew,** *a.* **1. skewball,** (see quots.). [Cf. *EDD skewbald*, a horse colored brown and white.] **2. skew-gee,** *a.* of a person, confused, mixed up, uncertain. *Colloq.*

(1) **1920** THOMAS *Ky. Superstitions* 221 In corn-husking, a blue-spotted red ear brings the best luck. It is called in the Kentucky mountains a 'skew ball.' . . . Mountains. **1946** RICHTER *Fields* 149 Some ears were red and some were blue, but most were skewballs with red and blue pied together. — (2) **1897** BRODHEAD *Bound in Shallows* 165 When folks gets all skew-gee brooding on things, why, it seems only right to straighten 'em out.

Skein or thimble skein in place on an axle

***skid,** *n.*

1. (See quot. 1905.) Also attrib.

1800 TATHAM *Tobacco* 11 *Skids* are two or more strong saplings or other pieces of long timber, upon which timber hogsheads, &c. are rolled. **1851** *Harper's Mag.* Sep. 518/1 New 'skids' are nicely peeled, by hewing off the bark smoothly, and plentifully as well as calculatingly laid along the road. **1890** *Oregonian* (Portland) 3 Jan. 3/2 During the period of the 'skid' method it was necessary for one man to follow the team, . . . [to] lubricate the 'skid' with oil so that the logs would slide easily. **1905** *Forestry Bureau Bul.* No. 61, 46 *Skid*, a log or pole, commonly used in pairs, upon which logs are handled or piled (Gen.); or the log or pole laid transversely in a skid road (P[acific] C[oast] F[orest]). **1948** *Time* 30 Aug. 2/3 In the old days of logging, skids were placed athwart the road five or six feet apart.

2. In special combs.: (1) **skid greaser,** (see quot. and cf. **1.** above); (2) **road,** (*a*) in lumbering, a road or way along which logs are dragged or skidded, usu. across transverse supporting logs, to a desired place, (*b*) = next; (3) **row,** a place in a city where derelicts and petty criminals congregate and where cheap saloons, rooming houses, etc., abound [see quot. 1944, prob. the orig. meaning, from **skid road** (*b*)], also attrib. and transf.; (4) **way,** (see quot. 1893).

(1) **1893** *Atlantic Mo.* Feb. 194/2 The 'skid-greaser,' . . . halting at every two steps to grease the worn skid over which the logs were about to pass. — (2) (*a*) **1880** *N.Y. Adirondack Survey 7th Rep.* 176 Advised that lumbermen had cut 'skid-roads' on which logs were drawn . . . , I changed the route. **1944** W. BLAIR *Tall Tale Amer.* 172 The cream made enough butter to feed the camp and grease the skid roads, to boot. (*b*) **1928** *Survey* 1 Aug. 457/2 He then drifted into that part of the city called the skid-road, and heard a man speaking from a box. **1940** *Amer. Mercury* Dec. 412 Most of the skid-road bars provide either a floor show with a few hard-bitten bosom-heavers or a hill-billy band. — (3) **1944** *N. & Q.* Nov. 120/2 A skidrow . . . is not a red light district. It is the district (mostly in western cities) where unskilled workers, in ordinary times gather to look for jobs—a district of employment agencies, cheap flop-houses, etc. **1949** *Chi. D. News* 13 Aug. 1/1 A lone policeman walks along a sidewalk on Skid Row. **1950** *Chi. Tribune* 28 March 14/3 He saw one on Feb. 8 at Sheridan rd. and Thorndale av. This was, of course, a skid row robin—an old bachelor or widower too tired of it all to travel south with the gang. — (4) **1878** *Lumberman's Gaz.* 6 April, These pole roads can be laid in the 'branch roads' direct to the skidways. **1893** *Scribner's Mag.* June 707/1 The skidway consists of two logs or timbers about ten feet apart, laid perpendicular to the log-road and well blocked up, upon

which a tier of logs is placed ready to be loaded. **1944** NUTE *Lake Superior* 210 It was dragged by horses to the skidways, and there placed . . . on a pile of logs awaiting the teams.

* **skid,** *v.*

1. *tr.* To drag (logs), usu. on skids, in lumbering operations.

1878 *Lumberman's Gaz.* 6 April, Not one-fifth of the logs cut and skidded . . . have been banked. **1924** SHEPHARD *P. Bunyan* 47 And when the crooks finally was all out of that there piece of road, there was enough of it to lay around a round lake we skidded logs into that winter. **1949** *Sat. Ev. Post* 18 June 112/3 Did you ever see a tractor skidding logs out of the woods?

Hence **skidding,** *n.* Cf. **steam skidding.**

*c***1873** in RICKABY *Ballads* (1926) 66 Bull Gordon, the Yankee, on skidding was full, As he cried 'Whoa-*hush*' to the little brown bulls. **1926** RICKABY *Ballads* 237 *Skidding.* The process of drawing the saw-log from where the tree was felled to the skidway. The log was dragged by oxen or horses. The skidding of larger logs was facilitated by the use of a go-devil. **1949** *Amer. Forests* Oct. 37/1 Skidding is made easier and cheaper by moving the mill to the logs.

2. (See quot.)

1905 *Forestry Bureau. Bul.* No. 61, 46 *Skid*, . . . as applied to a road, to reenforce by placing logs or poles across it.

3. *intr.* Of a timbered area: To produce a given number of board feet of lumber when logged.

1902 WHITE *Blazed Trail* 49 That 'seventeen' white pine . . . won't skid over three hundred thousand.

skidder ˈskɪdɚ, *n.* (See quot. 1905.) —*c***1870** in EARL C. BECK *Songs Mich. Lumberjacks* (1941) 37 The choppers and the sawyers They lay the timber low. The skidders and the swampers, They haul it to and fro. **1905** *Forestry Bureau Bul.* No. 61, 47 *Skidder.* 1. One who skids logs. (Gen[eral].) 2. A steam engine, usually operating from a railroad track, which skids logs by means of a cable. (Gen.) Syn.: steam skidder. 3. The foreman of a crew which constructs skid roads. (P[acific] C[oast] F[orest].)

skiddoo skɪˈdu, *v.* [?f. *skedaddle.* Said to have been first used by Thomas A. Dorgan (d. 1929), a cartoonist.] (See quot. 1929.) Also **23 skiddoo.** *Slang.*

1904 *N.O. Sun. Sun* 31 Jan., Say, Skidoo, look out. **1929** *Cent. Mag.* (Autumn) 66 A quarter of a century ago the expression '23 Skiddoo' was on every one's tongue. It was the equivalent of the more modern invitation to 'take the air,' and was generally used in speeding the unwelcome guest. **1949** *New Yorker* 2 April 26/3, I skiddoo and take a trip.

skiddy ˈskɪdɪ, *n.* [Origin unknown.] A type of carriage. *Obs.* — **1868** *N.Y. Herald* 22 July 1/2 Carriages, Second Hand Skiddy, Coupe and light Rockaways, eight leather top Buggies, all in good order.

Skidi ˈskidi, *n.* [Prob. from a native word meaning wolf.] (See quot. 1910.) Also **Skidi Pawnee.**

1910 HODGE *Amer. Indians* II. 589/2 Skidi. . . . One of the tribes of the Pawnee confederacy . . . , sometimes called Wolf Pawnee, and by the French Pawnee Loup. **1937** *Southwestern Lore* June 11 There was one band, the Skee-dee (Wolf) that did sacrifice to the Morning Star. **1947** DE VOTO *Across Wide Missouri* 292 The Skidi Pawnees, one of the principal divisions of the nation, while out on the fall hunt met a band of Oglala Sioux.

***skiff,** *n.* As the last term in **log, mackinaw skiff.**

skijoring skɪˈdʒorɪŋ, *n.* [Norwegian *skigjöring,* "ski-doing."] A winter sport in which a skier is pulled along over ice or snow by a horse or an automobile. Also attrib. or as adj.

1910 *Country Life* Dec. 205/1 In January . . . there are skee-jumping, . . . skee-joring and horse racing. **1935** *Denver Post* 25 Feb. 16/4 Thor Groswold, well known in the skiing world, captured the *skijoring* race, an added event. **1939** Union Pac. R.R. *Snow Sports* 17 Charges for sports in the valley are, . . . ski-joring (horses for skijoring, with experienced driver) $2.00 per hour or $1.00 for half hour.

Also **skijor,** *v. intr.*

1942 PEATTIE *Friendly Mts.* 293 At Saranac Lake they skijor by automobile. **1947** *Steamboat* (Colo.) *Pilot* 13 Feb. 2/8 Some of the boys skijored into town from there.

skilly-pot ˈskɪlɪˌpɑt, *n.* [Du. *schildpad,* a turtle.] (See quot. 1909.) Also attrib.

1807 IRVING *Salmagundi* iv, Harsimus— . . . famous place for *skilly-pots;* Philadelphians call 'em tarapins. **1851** *De Bow's Review* XI. 53 Skillpot Turtle. . . . The most common kind here. **1909** WEBSTER 1968/5 *Skilpot* . . . the red-bellied terrapin.

skilts skɪlts, *n.* [?Variant of **kilts.*] (See quot. 1845.) *Colloq.* — **1845** JUDD *Margaret* I. 9 Her father and elder brother wore . . . a sort of brown tow trousers known . . . as skilts . . . reaching just below the knee, and very large, being a full half yard broad at the bottom. **1885** EGGLESTON in *Cent. Mag.* April 892/2 'Skilts' . . . came in time to take the form of the modern trousers.

* **skim,** *n.* and *a.*

1. a. A thin sheet of ice. *Colloq.* **b.** The expression or look in one's eye. *Rare.*

(a) 1869 MARK TWAIN *Innocents* 206 [Lake Tahoe] never has even a skim of ice upon its surface. **1945** PEARSON *Country Flavor* 15 In the late fall, boys and girls, walking to school, stopped and looked at the skim of ice on the brook. — **(b) 1894** REMINGTON in *Harper's Mag.* Feb. 355 [They] can tell when and where he is going to strike as quickly as a boxer who knows by the 'skim on the eye' of his opponent.

2. skimback, a. The creek chub, *Semotilus atromaculatus.* **b.** =**quillback.**

(a) 1820 RAFINESQUE in *Western Rev.* II. 239 [The] Bigback Chubby, *Semotilus dorsalis*, . . . is found in the Kentucky, and several other rivers. Vulgar names, Big back Minny or Chub, Skimback, &c. — **(b)** *Ib.* 301 Sailing Sucker. *Catostomus velifer.* . . . It has received the vulgar names of Sailor fish, Flying fish, and Skimback, because, when it swims, its large dorsal fin appears like a sail, and it often jumps or flies over the water for a short distance. **1888** GOODE *Amer. Fishes* 437 The 'Spear-fish,' 'Sail-fish,' 'Quill-back' or 'Skim-back' of the Ohio River is a fish often seen in the markets.

3. skim diggings, *W.* very thin deposits of placer gold. *Obs.*

1897 LEONARD *Gold Fields Klondike* 23 There was a general fear that these might be only 'skim diggings.'

4. * **skim-milk,** *a.* weak, washed-out, second-rate. *Colloq.*

1835–7 HALIBURTON *Clockmaker* 1 Ser. xxviii. 274 It was none o' your skim-milk parties, but superfine uppercrust real jam. **1891** RYAN *Pagan* 82 He ain't one o' yer skim-milk, dauncy ones. He's as stout as a young bull. **1932** *K.C. Times* 27 April 16 Don't pray cream on Sunday and live skim-milk the remainder of the week.

* **skimmer,** *n.*

1. A plow designed to be run quite flat and shallow. *Obs.*

1814 J. TAYLOR *Arator* 139 Thenceforth the tillage consists of a streak or furrow of a mere weeding plough called a skimmer, cutting with two wings twenty-four inches—drawn by one horse. **1854** in COMMONS *Doc. Hist.* I. 210 Three skimers ploughing Tobacco.

2. (See quots.)

1881 INGERSOLL *Oyster Industry* 248 *Skimmer*, flat, shallow pans of tin or zinc, with perforated bottom, in which the openers empty their measures of oysters, and where the liquor is allowed to drain away. **1884** *Nat. Museum Bul.* No. 27, 221 The oysters are thus run into a sheet-iron or zinc receptacle called the 'skimmer' . . . and are there cleaned of shell fragments.

3. (See quots.)

1881 INGERSOLL *Oyster Industry* 248 *Skimmer*, the *Cyprina islandica*, or big beach clam. (South shore of Long Island.) **1891** *Cent.* 5671/3 *Skimmer*, . . . one of several bivalves whose shells may be used to skim milk, etc. **1949** R. J. SIM *Pages from Past* 65 The big surf clam, or skimmer (*Mactra solidissima*, Chemn.), lies bedded down in great colonies off shore.

4. skimmer hat, (see quot. 1830). *Obs.*

1830 WATSON *Philadelphia* 176 Other articles of female wear . . . [include] a 'skimmer hat,' . . . of a very small flat crown and big brim, not unlike the present Leghorn flats. **1840** A. M. MAXWELL *Run through U.S.* II. 18 Fellows called Tunkers . . . wear little white *skimmer* hats, *Anglice lilly shallows.*

As the last term in **black skimmer.**

skimming dish. A boat or yacht of light draft. *Colloq.* — **1884** in *Outing* VIII. 58/1 These [light-draught boats] are the 'skimming-dish,' the 'pumpkin-seed' and the 'flat-iron' models. **1897** *Ib.* XXX. 337/1 The boats entering this year's races will probably be all of one general type as to hull-saucers and skimming-dishes.

* **skin,** *n.*

1. In miscellaneous obs. senses: **a.** A whip. **b.** Cribbing. *College slang.* (Cf. * **skin,** *v.* **1.**) **c.** = * **sheepskin. d.** Short for **skin game.**

(a) 1845 SIMMS *Wigwam & Cabin* 2 Ser. 91 Only you be quiet; or we'll have to give you the skin. — **(b) 1855** in E. C. PORTER *Songs of Yale* (1860) 40 'Twas plenty of skin with a good deal of Bohn. — **(c) 1860** *Ib.* 69 Oh, worthless sheep, thy fleece all golden Might catch a foolish Jason's eyes, But never one who had beholden, Though from afar, the 'skin' we prize. — **(d) 1899** TARKINGTON *Gentleman from Ind.* vii. We been running no skin. . . . You gotter prove it was a skin.

2. In combs.: (1) **skin balloon,** (see quot.); (2) **canoe,** a canoe made of skins stretched over a frame, cf. **bull boat;** (3) **faro,** a skin game at faro, *slang, obs.;* (4) **game,** a gambling game in which the players have little or no chance of winning against the bank or table, also **skin card game,** and transf.; (5) **government,** (see quot.), *obs.;* (6) **granny,** a skinflint, *rare;* (7) **hunter,** one who hunts wild animals for their skins; (8) **lodge,** an Indian lodge made by stretching skins over a framework, cf. **tepee;** (9) **trade,** fur trade, *obs.;* (10) **trader,** one who trades for skins or furs, *obs.;* (11) **trapper,** one who traps animals for their skins.

(1) **1895** *Outing* XXVI. 399/1 The balloon is a 'skin balloon' made of silk. — (2) **1806** in *Overland to Pacific* I. (1932) 106 Lieutenant Wilkinson . . . [had a] skin canoe, made of four buffalo skins and two elk skins; this held three men besides himself and one Osage. **1870** *Amer. Naturalist* IV. 597 Let us take a small skin canoe and spend a day on the river. — (3) **1882** MCCABE *New York* 545 'Skin faro,' the only game played here, offers no chance whatever to the player. — (4) **1868** M. H. SMITH *Sunshine & Shadow* 405 The square game . . . is played only by gentlemen, and in first-class houses; . . . the skin game . . . is played in all the dens and chambers, and in the thousand low hells of New York. **1890** *Portland* (Ore.) *Examiner* 30 Oct. 4/1 The sharpers played him with a skin card game. **1947** *Trail & Timberline* April 65/2 The Denver Post brands their plan a 'skin game.'

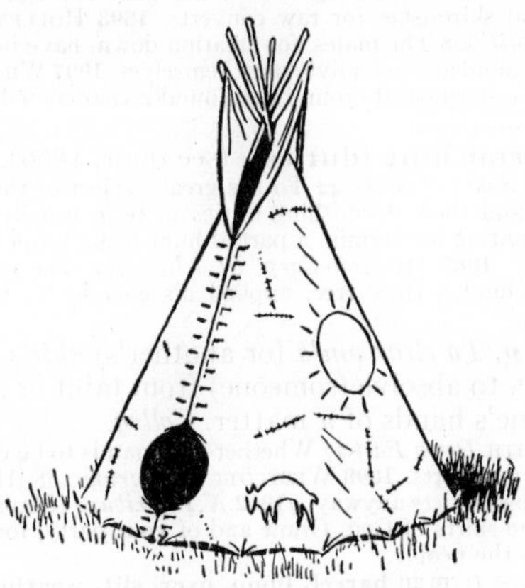

Skin lodge or tepee

(5) **1900** *Cong. Rec.* 25 Jan. 1165/2 It is not what some people have called 'skin' government—government according to the color of the skin. — (6) **1821** R. B. THOMAS *Farmer's Almanack for 1822* 23–31 July/2 Farmer Simkins . . . is no *skin-granny,* and never thinks to grow rich by starving his cattle with meadow hay all winter, that he may sell his English in the Spring. — (7) **1886** ROOSEVELT in *Outing* March 611 The brutal skin-hunters and meat-butchers of the woods and prairies have done their work. **1897** HOUGH *Story of Cowboy* 331 Hunter and trapper, skin hunter, gambler . . .—all mingled in an eddy and boil of tumultuous, vigorous life. — (8) **1823** JAMES *Exped.* I. 187 The travelling huts, or as they are usually denominated, skin lodges, are neatly folded up, and suspended to the pack-saddle of the horse. **1885** *Rep. Indian Affairs* 35 In 1879 not a family lived . . . in anything, but a canvas or skin lodge. **1943** DEVOTO *Yr. of Decision* 298 A skin lodge with an open flare at the top and raised dampers along the edge is, after all, an air conditioner. — (9) **1710** BYRD *Secret Diary* (1941) 186 About 5 o'clock Robin Hix and Robin Mumford came to discourse about the skin trade. **1772** ROMANS in P. L. Phillips *Notes on B. Romans* 120 Mobile will . . . become the only Mart, for the Skin Trade from the Chactaw, Chickesaw, and Upper Creek Nations.

(10) **1841** COOPER *Deerslayer* i. 7 Am I a man like to let any sneaking, crawling, skin-trader get the better of me in a matter that touches me as near as the kindness of Judith Hutter? — (11) **1837** IRVING *Bonneville* I. 92 These, though generally included in the generic name of free trappers, have the more specific title of skin trappers.

b. Designating buildings of a flimsy, non-fireproof construction. *Obs.*

1844 J. COWELL *Thirty Yrs. Among Players* 64 Price put in force some fire-proof law prohibiting all canvass or skin-deep establishments. **1881** MARSHALL *Through Amer.* (1882) 88 There are no 'skin' buildings in modern Chicago.

c. In slang phrases: (1) *To get under* (one's) *skin,* to annoy or irritate (one) severely; (2) *to be no skin off* (one's) *back, knuckles,* to work no hardship upon one, to be no concern of (one).

(1) **1934** WEBSTER. **1945** MENCKEN *Supp.* 84 Todd's sneer at imaginary American inventors of the term got under Pickering's skin.— (2) **1906** *Out West* March 246 The 'Statehood fight' concerns the territories only, and is 'no skin off the knuckles' of California. **1944** FAST *F. Road* 229, I know that. It's no skin off your back.

As the last term in **bear, beaver, blue, buck, bunko, coon, copper, cow, coyote, doe bear, dog, dry, eel, fox, frog, hen, hog, Lincoln, lion, lodge, moose, muskrat, musquash, onion, ox, persimmon, pig, plebe, raccoon, red, rough, sheep, skunk, sore, summer, tiger, turn, weasel, whisky, yellow skin.**

* **skin,** *v.*

1. *intr.* To plagiarize or cheat on a recitation or examination. Also **skinning,** *n. Slang. Obs.*

1835 TODD *Student's Manual* 115 Should you allow yourself to think of going into the recitation-room, and there trust to 'skinning,' as it is called in some colleges. **1854** in E. C. PORTER *Songs of Yale* (1860) 63 But now that last Biennial's past, I 'skinned' and 'fizzled' through. **1871** BAGG *At Yale* 632 Whether the Williams men were too honest or too stupid, or too closely watched, to skin successfully, does not appear.

b. Also *tr.* (See quots.)

1837 *Yale Lit. Mag.* II. 138 A student is said to *skin* a problem, when he places the most implicit faith in the correctness of his neighbor's solution of it. **1871** BAGG *At Yale* 641 A high-stand man who was well up on mathematics, . . . in consideration of $10, was to attempt to 'skin him through' his 'Puckle' Annual.

2. *tr.* To exhaust the fertility of (land) or the ore from (a mine). Also * **skinning,** *n.* and *a.*

1843 in TURNER *Cotton* (1865) 62 To the planter who is satisfied merely to plod along, the inanimate imitator of some skinning neighbor, this sketch will appear a tedious and uninteresting detail. **1850** *Cultivator* ns. VII. 369 Many of the original settlers . . . moved west . . . to run another round of 'skinning' and starving. **1907** WHITE *Arizona Nights* 164 For a while they tried gold washing, but I had the only pocket—and that was about skinned.

3. To plow merely the surface of (the ground). Also * **skinned,** *a.*, deprived of woods or forest (see also quot. 1912).

1861 *Ill. Agric. Soc. Trans.* IV. 373 If he has not a good team he will find himself skinning the ground or resting his animals. **1907** *N.Y. Ev. Post* (s.-w-. ed.) 18 July 6 Lands in the watershed of the Mohawk range cost a dollar an acre for 'skinned' wood-lots. **1912** MATHEWSON *Pitching* 218 The diamond at Marlin is skinned—that is, made of dirt, although it is billed as a grass infield.

4. *intr.* To shin or climb *up* something. *Colloq.*

1871 MARK TWAIN in *Galaxy* Jan. 156/1 The beaver skun up a tree. **1916** WILSON *Somewhere* 312, I guess you can see plain enough now he ain't no rabbit, the way he skinned up that tree.

5. *tr.* (See quot. 1871.) *Slang.*

1871 OLIVER E. WOOD *West Point Scrap Book* 338 To get skinned.—To get reported for some offense. **1929** J. PARKER *Old Army* 201 He rarely has to 'skin' or 'report' a cadet for delinquency.

6. a. To spread out or display (a hand at cards). *Slang.* **b.** To look at one's own (cards) by opening them slightly.

(a) **1873** MILLER *Amongst Modocs* 44 Four aces! and what else? Skin 'em out, skin 'em out! **1884** CARLETON *Thompson St. Poker Club* (1889) 42 Mr. Williams proudly skinned out three jacks and a pair of kings. — (b) **1884** CARLETON in Wilder *Wit & Humor* VI. 1141 Mr. Williams . . . skinned his cards, . . . and said he would 'Jess—jess call.' **1895** *Cornhill Mag.* Aug. 174 Each man skinned his cards and tried his hardest to look disappointed. **1896** ADE *Artie* 11 He had to . . . skin his cards three or four times.

7. To beat (a person or thing) all hollow, to eclipse, outdo, esp. with *a mile. Slang.*

1862 *Charleston* (S.C.) *Mercury* 9 Aug. 1/5 They were 'skinning' the soldiers of other regiments the 'tallest kind.' **1901** O. HENRY *Cabbages & Kings* 47, I guess you've got us skinned on the animal and vegetation question. **1913** LONDON *Valley of Moon* 309 The Porchugeeze has got us skinned a mile. **1931** *K.C. Star* 16 Nov. 20 Her falling tears have Niagara skinned a mile.

8. *intr.* To slip *through,* to get by without much to spare.

1902 LORIMER *Lett. Merchant* 142, I would feel a good deal happier . . . if you would make a downright failure or a clean-cut success once in a while, instead of always just skinning through this way. **1920** CAMP *Football without a Coach* 57 The best a runner can hope for is a chance to skin through that opening before it ceases to exist.

9. *tr.* To peel (a note) from a roll of money.

1903 O. HENRY *Cabbages & Kings* 84 Henry skinned a twenty off his roll. **1908** LORIMER *J. Spurlock* 294 The Major skinned a hundred-dollar bill from his roll.

10. In phrases: (1) *To skin the cat,* (see quot. 1893); (2) *to skin mules,* to drive a team of mules, *slang,* cf. **mule**

skinner; (3) *to keep one's eye(s)* (or *eyeteeth*) *skinned*, see ***eye**, *n.* **b.** (2).

(1) **1845** JUDD *Margaret* II. 199 The boys . . . [were] snapping-the-whip, skinning-the-cat, racing round the Meeting-house, or what not. **1893** *Amer. Folk-Lore* VI. 143 A boy hangs by the hands from a trapeze, and passes his legs through the circle formed by the wooden rod and the upper part of his body. Boys commonly 'skin the cat' both forwards and backwards. **1946** WILSON *Fidelity* 145 There we learned to skin cats, hang by our toes, walk the pole with perfect balance [etc.]. — (2) **1923** *D.N.* V. 221 John's a-skinnin' mules now. **1948** *Capital-Democrat* (Tishomingo, Okla.) 10 June 11/1 Mr. Armstrong came to Oklahoma before the turn of the century and started 'skinnin'' mules.

***skinner,** *n.*

1. During the Revolutionary War, a member of a marauding gang usu. roaming in territory between the British and American lines in Westchester County, N.Y., and professing allegiance to the American cause. Usu. *pl.* and *cap. Obs.*

1775–83 THACHER *Military Journal* (1823) 285 Banditti consisting of lawless villains within the British lines have received the names of *Cow-boys* and *Skinners*. **1821** COOPER *Spy* xviii, The skinner . . . had been left alone by . . . his gang. **1850** S. F. COOPER *Rural Hours* 372 They must have known that this part of the country was not peopled until after the Revolution, and consequently no fear of Cow-Boys or Skinners could have penetrated into this wilderness.

2. In miscellaneous slang senses, chiefly obs.: **a.** One who skins a lesson. (Cf. **skin,** *v.* **1.**) **b.** A knife suitable for skinning an animal. **c.** ?A plow that breaks only the surface of land. **d.** Short for **mule skinner.**

(a) 1871 BAGG *At Yale* 632 A desperate skinner, going up to recite an examination of which he knew nothing, has laid upon a lower edge of his instructor's desk a page or more of mathematical formulæ. — **(b) 1872** *Amer. Naturalist* VI. 223 The specimen could have been used as a knife, or 'skinner,' although now its edge is too irregular and dull for skinning. — **(c) 1873** *Newton Kansan* 24 April 3/3 [As] the breaking season is near at hand . . . farmers . . . should . . . buy a Skinner. — **(d) 1924** *Scribner's Mag.* Dec. 645/1 The skinner with the longest words travels the fastest. **1947** *Time* 1 Sep. 17/3 But at least there will be no language difficulty, for these mules will have U.S. skinners.

As the last term in **bull skinner.**

***skinning,** *n.* As the last term in **mule, shadow skinning.**

***skip,** *n.*

1. A poor or inferior animal.

1892 *Courier-Journal* 2 Oct. 21/6 Pigs and skips $4.25 @ 5.05. **1911** QUICK *Yellowstone N.* 303 A collection of skips an' culls an' canners that was sure a fraud on the Injuns.

2. In combs.: (1) **skipjack,** a kind of boat; (2) **mackerel,** (see quots.); (3) **straight,** (see quot.).

(1) **1882** *Cent. Mag.* July 359/2 The skip-jack is another curious and by no means ungainly craft, evolved out of the sharpie by adding to the latter a rising floor. **1946** *Sat. Ev. Post* 11 May 56/3 There are special types of Chesapeake boats such as the skipjack and the log canoe. — (2) **1884** GOODE *Fisheries* I. 433 The Bluefish.—*Pomatomus saltatrix*. . . . About New York they are called 'Skip Mackerel.' **1911** *Rep. Fisheries 1908* 316/1 *Skipmackerel*, a name applied to the bluefish about New York. — (3) **1887** KELLER *Draw Poker* 17 Efforts have been made to introduce into the game of Draw Poker what is known as the 'skip' straight—a sequence of alternate cards.

***skip,** *v.*

1. *intr.* To leave, make off, often with *out. Colloq.*

1865 GRIGSBY *Smoked Yank* (1891) 188 Thirteen [paroled men] . . . skipped out to-day. **1879** VIVIAN *Wanderings Western Land* 28 Unless in the case of a she-bear defending her young, they will always 'skip' (run off) as fast as they can. **1922** PARRISH *Case & Girl* 123 He skipped out mighty sudden.

b. *To skip one's bail*, to run away while free on bail.

1900 *Cong. Rec.* 5 Feb. 1521/2, I should like the gentleman to know that one lot of those ballot-box stuffers are in jail and every one of the others has skipped his bail.

2. *Skip to My Lou*, the one-line refrain of a play party song. Also the game or dance which is accompanied by this song.

1887 *Courier-Journal* 6 Feb. 14/5 The young people were to be engaged in playing 'Skiptummerlou,' which being interpreted means 'Skip-to-My-Lou,' a game strangely like a quadrille. **1942** FLORENCE WARNICK *Play Party Songs* 7 Pretty as a redbird, prettier too, Skip to my Lou, my darling.

skippaug, see **scuppaug.**

***skipper,** *n.* A snapping beetle, also with a defining term. *Obs.* Cf. **hobomok skipper.** — **1792** BELKNAP *Hist. New-Hampshire* III. 181 Skipper, *Elater oculatus*. **1813** BINGLEY *Animal Biog.* (ed. 4) III. 143 The Night-Shining Skipper. In the savannas of most of the warmer parts of America, these insects are to be seen in great abundance.

skipple ˈskɪpl, *n.* Also **schepel.** [Du. *schepel.*] A measure of about three-fourths of a bushel.

1654 *New Haven Col. Rec.* (1858) II. 72 A skepple (wch is aboute three peckes) for a beavor skin. **1703** in MUNSELL *Ann. Albany* IV. 169 The Plentive . . . demands . . . 96 Gilders in Beavers and 2 schepels of wheat. **1769** SMITH *Tour* 27 The Measures introduced originally by the Dutch are still in vogue [in n.w. New York]. A Morgan of Land contains somewhat more than Two Acres and a Skipple is about 3 Pecks. **1901** *N. & Q.* 9 Ser. VIII. 283/2 The Skipple-measure or Short Bushel of New England. **1937** E. E. GARDNER *Folklore from Schoharie Hills* 20 The first skipple of wheat planted kernel by kernel and hoed like corn yielded eighty-three skipples.

b. skipple stone, (see quot.). *Rare.*

1796 *Aurora* (Phila.) 13 Sep., Not far from Albany, among the Dutch A skipple-stone is used to balance weight On horse-back borne.

***skirmish,** *v. intr.* To scurry or scout *around. Colloq.*

1864 MARK TWAIN *Sk.* (1926) 129 He goes through the camp-meetings and skirmishes for raw converts. **1893** HOLLEY *Samantha at World's Fair* 608 The males, for creation down, have been left free to skirmish round and get a livin' for themselves. **1907** WHITE *Arizona Nights* 17 We skirmished around and found a condemned army pack saddle with aparejos.

b. skirmishing (duties), (see quot. 1866). *Obs.*

1866 GOSS *Soldier's Story* 42 To the great neglect of their personal cleanliness, and their skirmishing duties (a term usually applied to the act of hunting for vermin, a partial hunt being termed driving in the pickets). **1887** HINMAN *Corp. Si Klegg* 254 The general . . . , squatting behind a large tree, applied his energies to the work of 'skirmishing.'

***skirt,** *n. To clear one's* (or another's) *skirts*, to avoid any blame, to absolve (someone) from taint or suspicion, to wash one's hands of a matter. *Colloq.*

1854 S. SMITH *Down East* 27 Whether this man is to be convicted or not, I clear my skirts. **1898** WESTCOTT *D. Harum* 168 [He] cal'lated to clear his own skirts anyway. *a***1902** *N.Y. Tribune* (Clapin), You [do not] clear the skirts of Gen. Grant and of your party, for the basest treachery to the people.

As the last term in **barrel, hoop, over, slit, weather skirt.**

***skitter,** *v.* **1.** *tr.* To cause (an object) to skim or skip along a surface. Also **skittered,** *a.*, **skittering,** *n.* **2.** To make (an object) skim or sail through the air. Both *colloq.*

(1) **1883** *Cent. Mag.* July 383/2 The angler, standing in the bow, 'skitters' or skips the spoon or bait over the surface. *a***1888** in GOODE *Amer. Fishes* 37 When taken with a skittered minnow or bright fly on a light rod, we do not hesitate to class as a game fish the White Perch. **1903** WHITE *Forest* 246 Does yon trout to-day fancy the skittering of his food, or the withdrawal in three jerks? — (2) **1907** *Harper's Mag.* Feb. 460 The younger boy skittered rocks at a chicken-hawk.

skoke skok, *n.*[1] [Massachuset *m'skok*, that which is red.] =**pokeweed.** Also attrib.

1778 CARVER *Travels* 517 Gargit or Skoke is a large kind of weed, the leaves of which are about six inches long. **1846** WHITCHER *Bedott P.* v. 50 She said he must take skoke berries and rum right off. **1949** *Nature Mag.* April 194/1 Folklore has it that the young shoots of skoke, or inkberry, or pokeweed are delicious.

skoke skok, *n.*[2] [App. f. Delaware *s'kakawunsh.*] =**skunkweed.** — **1896** *Garden & Forest* IX. 292/2 *Skoke*, . . . *Symplocarpus fœtidus*. . . . Skoka is a variant of the name. **1910** HODGE *Amer. Indians* II. 595/1 *Skoka*, a name among herbalists for the skunk-cabbage.

Skokomish skoˈkomɪʃ, *n.* [f. *kaw*, fresh water, +*mish*, people, i.e. river people.] (See quot. 1910.) Also attrib. Cf. **Skykomish.**

1845 WILKES *U.S. Expl. Exped.* IV. 411 After passing further down the canal, they found the Scocomish tribe, who inhabit its southern end. **1856** in *34th Cong.* 3 Sess. H.R. Ex. Doc. 37, 71 The foregoing table does not include . . . the Skokomish and the Chemakums. **1883** *Amer. Antiquarian* V. 136 The Twana or Skokomish Indians have given three potlatches within fifteen years. **1910** HODGE *Amer. Indians* II. 595/1 Skokomish ('river people'). A body of Salish who, according to Eells, form one of three subdivisions of the Twana. . . . They live at the Mouth of Skokomish r., which flows into the upper ends of Hoods canal, Wash., where a reservation of the same name has been set aside for them. **1939** *Corporate Charter Skokomish Ind. Tribe* 1 The Skokomish Indian Tribe shall, as a Federal corporation, have perpetual succession.

skookum ˈskukəm, *n.* and *a.* *N.W.* [Chinook Jargon, powerful, evil spirit, f. Chehalis *skukum.*]

1. *n.* An evil spirit, ghost, demon, disease.

1838 PARKER *Exploring Tour* 336 Evil spirit, skookoom. Hell, skookoom. **1844** LEE & FROST *Ten Years Ore.* 180 The way now being prepared, he [medicine man] approaches his patient, and, after a painful and persevering effort, with his mouth applied as a cupping-glass, he transfers the 'sko-kum,' or 'tam-an-a-was,' or disease, wholly or in part from the patient to himself! **1846** O. JOHNSON *Route Across Rocky Mts.* 54 Holding their clenched hands above the head, several loud shouts are uttered in as frightful a manner as they are able. They then open their fingers gradually, to allow the terrified Scocum, (evil spirit,) to make his escape. **1900** *Ore. Hist. Soc. Quart.* I. 185 The benefits of his fishery had gone, not to the people, but to the wicked skookum.

b. (See quot.)

1895 *Outing* July 303/1 Hardly had we eaten dinner when in came a stalwart buck. 'Skookum?' No, we had no skookum (bread). 'Shot?' No, no shot.

2. *a.* Strong, powerful.

1847 PALMER *Journal* 150 *Sko-kum* Strong, stout. **1852** SWAN *Three Years Residence* (1857) 321 He always thought that my skookum medicine was what cured him. *a***1915** MUIR *Travels Alaska* (1917) 266 We were startled by Captain Tyee shouting, 'Skookum chuck! Skookum chuck!' (strong water, strong water), and found our canoe was being swept sideways by a powerful current. **1949** *Sierra Club Bul.* June 105 Billy and Pete were skookum, and I was pretty good myself in those days.

3. skookum-house, jail.

1885 *Cent. Mag.* April 842 [An Indian] had recently been arrested by the agent, put in the 'skookum-house' (jail), and fined sixty dollars for having two wives. **1894** WISTER in *Harper's Mag.* Sep. 514/1 Maybe he catch E-gante, maybe put him in skookum-house (prison)? **1904** O. HENRY *Whirligigs* 232 The skookum house for yours!

skouk skaʊk, *n.* [f. a note the bird often makes when flushed.] The green heron, *Butorides virescens. Colloq.* Cf. ***poke,** *n.* **2.** and **shitepoke.** — **1794** MORSE *Amer. Geog.* 165 Green Bittern. Poke. Skouk. *Ardea virescens.* **1832** WILLIAMSON *Maine* I. 145 The Skouk is as large bodied as a partridge . . . and is vulgarly called a 'shite-poke.'

skulduggery skʌlˈdʌgərɪ, *n.* Also **sculduggery.** [App. Amer. variant of **sculduddery*, obscenity, regarded by Leo Spitzer in *Amer. Sp.* XIX. (1944) 25 ff., as an Amer. bowdlerizing of the earlier term.] Tricky, rascally conduct. *Colloq.*

[**1856** *N.Y. Herald* 7 Jan. 8/3, I doubt amid all the leading and minor schemes of 'schulduggy' whether but little else will be done in the Legislative Assembly.] **1867** RICHARDSON *Beyond Miss.* 134 From Minnesota had been imported the mysterious term 'scull-duggery,' used to signify political or other trickery. One often heard, even from educated men, remarks like this: 'Do you see Smith and Brown whispering there in the corner? They are up to some scull-duggery.' **1872** *Cin. Commercial* 22 May (Supp.) 2/4 They . . . were ready to take any road out of their misgovernment, carpet-baggery, and skullduggery, from which it is useless to deny they have . . . suffered. **1949** *Sat. Ev. Post* 4 June 107/1 There always had been skulduggery and nothing much could be done about it.

skullcap speedwell. The marsh speedwell. — **1817–8** EATON *Botany* (1822) 508 *Veronica scutellata*, scull-cap speedwell. **1821** *Mass. H.S. Coll.* 2 Ser. IX. 157 Indigenous in the township of Middlebury [Vt. is] . . . *Veronica scutellata*, Scull-cap, speedwell.

skulljoe ˈskʌlˌdʒo, *n.* [Origin unknown.] (See quot.) — **1884** GOODE *Fisheries* I. 228 At Provincetown a Haddock salted and dried after being split is called by the name of 'Skulljoe,' or 'Scoodled Skulljoe.'

skunk skʌŋk, *n.* [f. the Algonquian name of the animal.]

1. Any one of several weasel-like mammals of the genus *Mephitis*, or of closely related genera, well known for their power of ejecting an offensive-smelling secretion.

1588 HARIOT *Briefe & True Report* D2r *Saquenúckot* & *Maquo'woc;* two kindes of small beastes greater than conies which are very good meat. **1634** WOOD *N. Eng. Prospect* 22 The beasts of offence be Squunckes, Ferrets, Foxes. **1781** PETERS *Hist. Conn.* (1829) 191 The Skunk is also peculiar to America. . . . He is black striped with white. **1882** *Vt. Agric. Rep.* VII. 69 He believes the raccoon and the skunk are beneficial to the farmers in the destruction of vermin. **1950** *Nat. Geog. Mag.* March 401/1 Sometimes, when skunks come out from under the barn and are trapped, they must be killed.

Also the flesh of this used as food.

1950 *Chi. Tribune* 19 Jan. 12/3 With white flesh, skunk tastes somewhat like chicken.

b. With specifying terms (see quots.). Cf. **black, spotted skunk.**

1917 *Mammals of Amer.* 132/2 Western Striped Skunk, or California Skunk.—*Mephitis occidentalis occidentalis. Ib.*, Mearns Hooded Skunk, or Northern Hooded Skunk.—*Mephitis macroura milleri.* . . . It reaches the United States only in Southern Arizona.

c. In miscellaneous applications (see quots.).

1850 *Amer. Whig Review* XI. May 474/2 A severe defeat at a game of draughts was formerly, and, probably now is, termed 'a skunk.' **1860** *Ill. Agric. Soc. Trans.* IV. 346 These skunks of the insect world [chinch bugs] are . . . many-sided, like the common house fly. **1877** *Vt. Dairymen's Assoc. Rep.* VIII. 67 [Cheese that has deteriorated] in the vernacular is called skunks.

d. The fur of the skunk.

1862 TAYLOR in *Life & Lett.* 404 Sables are so expensive as to be vulgar and skunk . . . is infinitely handsomer. **1949** *Fur Trade Rev.* 17 March 7/3 Europeans are now showing much more interest in all kinds of cheaper priced skunk than they are in the higher priced eastern and central blacks and shorts.

2. A contemptible person.

1840 SIMMS *Border Beagles* I. 89 You can tell the people what a darned skunk of a fellow that Watson is. **1925** TILGHMAN *Dugout* 54 Are you crying for that skunk that took you from home? **1947** *Mazama* Oct. 5/2 Now the skunks will steal anything they can get their hands on, even summit boxes that they can have no possible use for.

Also **skunkishness.**

1924 *Collier's* 12 Jan. 9/1 He put the raise down to the inherent skunkishness of landlords.

3. In combs.: (1) **skunk bear,** the wolverine; (2) **bird,** (see quot.); (3) **blackbird,** the bobolink; (4) **duck,** (see quot.); (5) **farmer,** one who raises skunks for their pelts, also **skunk farming;** (6) **head,** (*a*) the extinct pied duck, (*b*) the surf scoter, *Melanitta perspicillata*, also attrib.; (7) **horse,** (see quot.), *rare;* (8) **porpoise,** (see quots.); (9) **skin,** the skin of a skunk; (10) **trap,** a trap for taking skunks.

(1) 1876 LUDLOW *Rep. on Yellowstone* 65 *Gulo Luscus.* . . . In this region, they were spoken of as the 'Skunk-bear;' farther south they were called 'Carcajou.' **1949** *Sat. Ev. Post* 22 Jan. 97/1 It is sometimes called 'skunk bear' for this reason, although it cannot spray its scent as a skunk can. — **(2) 1836** *Penny Cyclo.* V. 30/1 [The male bobolink's] variegated dress, . . . from a resemblance in its colours to that of the quadruped, obtained for it the name of 'skunk-bird' among the Cree Indians. — **(3) 1841** *N.O. Picayune* 19 March 2/4 The intarpriter he sot tu and talked to him agin, as fast as a skunk blackbird. **1941** *Nature Mag.* March 139 If a Floridian were asked what the skunk blackbird is, he would be nonplussed. — **(4) 1917** *Birds of Amer.* I. 143 Labrador Duck. *Camptorhynchus labradorius.* . . . [Also called] Pied Duck; Skunk Duck. *Ib.* 151 Surf Scoter. *Oidemia perspicillata.* . . . [Also called] Skunk-head; Skunk-head Coot; Skunk-top.

(5) 1912 *Country Life* 1 Nov. 39/1 As there is little difficulty in skunk farming on polygamous lines I had more males than I needed. *Ib.* 40/1 These are the problems to be solved by the skunk farmer. — **(6)** (*a*) **1842** *Nat. Hist. N.Y., Zoology* II. 326 This Duck [the Pied Duck, *Fuligula labradora*], well known on this coast under the name of *Skunk-head*, and *Sand-shoal Duck* on the coast of New-Jersey, is not, however, very abundant. **1875** *Fur. Fin & Feather* (ed. 3) 119 Of the various fowl called vulgarly coot, are the pied-duck (the skunk head), the velvet-duck [etc.]. (*b*) **1917** *Birds of Amer.* I. 151 Surf Scoter. . . . [Also called] Baldpate; Skunk-head; Skunk-head Coot [etc.]. — **(7) 1805** *Balance* 22 Oct. 339 (Th), A couple of impostors are exhibiting a piedbald or skunk horse, which they call a zebra, at the price of two shillings for grown persons. — **(8) 1884** GOODE *Fisheries* I. 16 The best known species on the Atlantic coast are the 'Skunk Porpoise,' or 'Bay Porpoise,' *Lagenorhynchus perspicillatus.* **1884** *Nat. Museum Bul.* No. 27, 632 The Skunk Porpoise . . . is very common off New England. — **(9) 1769** in RICHARD SMITH *Tour Four Great Rivers* (1906) 11 Hans [Mohican Indian] . . . lives near the kaatskill & had a Scunk Skin for his Tobacco Pouch. **1862** TAYLOR in *Life & Lett.* 404 With my pelisse of raccoon and my cap of skunk-skin, I take my daily walk.

(10) 1894 WISTER in *Harper's Mag.* 908/1 Did you ever see a skunk-trap? **1938** WHITE *One Man's Meat* 15 My time, puttering, reading bulletins, . . . setting skunk trap, at estimated hour basis of what I might have earned by putting my time to better advantage.

b. In the names of, or with reference to, plants: (1) **skunk apple,** (see quot.), *obs.;* (2) **bush,** (see quots. 1909, 1913); (3) **cabbage,** see as a main entry; (4) **currant,** the fetid currant, *Ribes glandulosum,* of the eastern states; (5) **grape,** (see quot.); (6) **spruce,** (see quot. 1894); (7) **-tail grass,** the American squirrel-tail grass, *Hordeum jubatum;* (8) **weed,** (*a*) the skunk cabbage, *Symplocarpus foetidus*, also the American hellebore, (*b*) (see quot.).

(1) 1817 W. COXE *Fruit Trees* 169 The Skunk Apple. . . . The name is derived from a nest of that animal found at the root of the original tree, in Middlesex county New-Jersey. — (2) **1909** SCHNEIDER *Woody Plants Pike's Peak* 139 Dense but limited thickets of the plum (*Prunus americana*), the skunk bush (*Rhus trilobata*), or the wolf berry (*Symphoricarpos occidentalis*) are frequent in open places. **1913** WOOTON *Trees & Shrubs N. Mex.* 107 The Rue Family (*Rutaceae*) is represented in New Mexico by 2 species of the Hop Tree or what is sometimes called Skunk Bush (*Ptelea*). **1949** *Amer. Cattle Producer* April 19/2 Texas and Oklahoma ranchers are using airplanes to spray areas infested with sandplum, skunkbush . . . and sumac. — (4) *a*1817 DWIGHT *Travels* II. 312 Three sorts of currants are found in the forest; the red, the black, and a peculiar kind, called Skunk currants. **1942** PEATTIE *Friendly Mts.* 162 Undergrowth and ground cover are sparse, with swamp black currant, skunk currant, mountain ash, and mountain maple the principal shrubby species.

(5) **1909** WEBSTER 1970 *Skunk grape*, the fox grape. — (6) **1894** *Amer. Folk-Lore* VII. 99 *Picea alba*, . . . skunk-spruce, Mt. Desert, Me., Washington Co., Me., Islands of Penobscot Bay, Me. **1948** *Atlantic Mo.* Sep. 25/1 The muskeg reeks and the stench of the skunk spruce fills the breathless air. — (7) **1920** *Mont. Extension Service Bul.* 45, 97 Skunk-tail grass . . . has sometimes been planted as an ornamental grass but the seeds are mostly carried by clinging to passing animals and in hay. — (8) (*a*) **1738** CATESBY *Carolina* II. 71 II. 71 *Arnum Americanum, Betæfolio.* The Scunk Weed. **1762** CLAYTON *Flora Virginica* 141 Polyandria. . . . Dracontium foliis subrotundis vulgo Skunck-weed. **1784** *Amer. Acad. Mem.* I. 407 Scunk Cabbage. Scunkweed. *Ib.* 409 In collecting the roots particular care ought to be taken that the *white hellebore*, or *poke root*, which some people call scunk weed, be not mistaken for this plant. (*b*) **1909** WEBSTER 1970 *Skunkweed*, . . . the polemoniaceous plant *Navarretia squarrosa* of California.

c. Denoting products obtained from skunks and used in folk remedies, as (1) **skunk fat,** (2) **grease,** (3) **oil.**

(1) **1877** RUEDE *Sod-House Days* 170 We intend to get some skunk fat; that is good for all kinds of sores, rheumatism, etc., and for greasing boots. **1948** *Chi. Tribune* 28 March VII. 1/4 For inflammation of the joints, one rubbed on snake oil, fish worm oil, or skunk fat. — (2) **1920** THOMAS *Ky. Superstitions* 112 Rheumatism is treated with skunk grease or red-worm oil. . . . Western Kentucky. — (3) **1920** THOMAS *Ky. Superstitions* 101 Croup is treated with skunk oil, taken internally and applied externally.

d. In obs. colloq. phrases: (1) *To skin one's own skunks*, to do one's own dirty work; (2) *to kill another skunk*, to create another stench or scandal.

(1) **1813** *Portsmouth Oracle* 20 Nov. 2/3 We here choose to let Mr. Madison '*skin his own skunks.*' **1922** KEPHART *So. Highlanders* 143 Moonshining in itself may be only a peccadillo, a venial sin—let the Government skin its own skunks. — (2) **1863** KETTELL *Hist. Rebellion* II. 582 The President hesitated in making another change in the war department, or, as he himself expressed [it] . . . , 'to kill another skunk.'

skunk skʌŋk, *v.*

1. *tr.* To defeat utterly, to keep an opponent from making a single point or score in a game. Also fig. *Slang.*

1846 BURNHAM *Stray Subjects* 135 In the second hand of the third game, I made high, low, game, and 'skunked' him, outright, again. **1904** CRISSEY *Tattlings* 365 A certain trio of choice scamps from the city hall gang would make a strong committee that could skunk the enemy. **1944** DUNCAN *M. Graham* 170 Lincoln, with a short, logical speech in which no words were wasted, 'skunked' his adversary.

b. *passive.* To be utterly defeated or beaten *out* of something, to fail of success. *Slang.*

1843 *Quincy* (Ill.) *Herald* 24 Nov. 2/1 The Legislature will be Democratic by an overwhelming majority; and it is more than probable that the Whigs have been 'skunked.' **1848** BARTLETT 209 A presidential candidate who fails to secure one electoral vote is also *skunked.* **1877** W. WRIGHT *Big Bonanza* 541 'Skunked, by the holy spoons,' cried he. **1890** HASKINS *Argonauts Calif.* 250, I got skunked once out of a good claim. **1898** WESTCOTT *D. Harum* 6 Wa'al, to tell ye the truth, I was so completely skunked that I hadn't a word to say. **1948** *Field & Stream,* June 86/2, I have fished on opening day in the snow . . . , only to get skunked.

c. (See quots.) *Obs.*

1851 HALL *College Words* 284 *Skunk*, at Princeton College, to fail to pay a debt; used actively; e.g. to skunk a tailor, i.e. not to pay him. **1859** BARTLETT 410 A student who leaves college without settling up, is said to skunk his bills.

2. (See quot.)

1891 *Cent.* 5679/2 *Skunk*, . . . to cause disease in or of; sicken; scale, or deprive of scales; said of fish in the live-well of a fishing-smack. (New Eng.)

3. *intr.* To slink *away. Rare.*

1894 HARTE *Bell Ringer of Angel's* 147 You heard how the new Sheriff . . . skunked away with his whole *posse* before one-eighth of my men.

skunk cabbage. Any one of various plants emitting, esp. when bruised, a strong odor.

In the East and Northeast this name is applied commonly to the perennial herb, *Symplocarpus foetidus*, less commonly to the pitcher plant, *Sarracenia purpurea*, and, in early times, to the American hellebore. On the Pacific Coast it is applied to the plant *Lysichiton camstschatcense.*

1751 ELIOT *Field-Husb.* iii. 66 Take the Roots of Swamp Hellebore, sometimes called Skunk Cabbage, Tickle Weed. **1792** J. BELKNAP *Hist. of New-Hampshire* III. 127 The *arum*, or skunk cabbage, has been found very efficacious in asthmatic complaints. **1836** AUDUBON *Ornith. Biog.* III. 478 There he lies, snugly squatted beneath the broad leaves of the 'sconk cabbage' or dock. **1950** *Chi. Tribune* 28 March 14/3 Some watch for skunk cabbages poking mottled brown snouts thru the swamp muck.

Also **skunk's cabbage.**

1849 KINGSLEY *Diary* 15 The fruit grows on the extreme top with a blow or flower resembling our Skunks Cabbage. **1868** BEECHER *Norwood* 91 The great, succulent leaves of the skunk's cabbage were fully expanded.

b. skunk cabbage brandy, cheap or poor liquor. *Contemptuous. Rare.*

1832 *Boston Transcript* 28 May 2/3 Such blades ought to . . . have nothing to drink but skunk-cabbage brandy.

skunkery ˈskʌŋkərɪ, *n.* A place where skunks are bred for their furs.

1890 *Stock Grower & Farmer* 21 June 6/2 The skunkery is paying 200 per cent on the capital invested. **1897** *Boston Transcript* 11 Sep. 24/3 Minks have been bred for their skins in so-called minkeries, just as is being done with the skunks in what might be termed skunkeries. **1902** *Amer. Folk-Lore* 258 Interesting also are *skunkery* and *skunk*-farm, applied to places where skunks are kept or raised for profit.

* **sky,** *n.*

1. In baseball, a batted ball that rises high in the air. *Obs.* Cf. ***fly,** *n.* **1, sky ball,** ***skyrocket 1,** ***skyscraper 3.**

1857 *Spirit of Times* 21 Nov. 180/1 There is a cricketer in the [baseball] club who bats fine balls; but they are often caught, as they are what are called skys. [**1867** *Harper's Wkly.* 14 Sep. 590/2 He was at the bat, so to speak, and intended doing his level best in giving Sheridan, Sickles, Hancock, and others a few 'skyers,' as he had done Stanton.]

2. In combs.: (1) **sky ball,** = ***sky 1,** *obs.*; (2) **blue,** *a.* true blue, dyed-in-the-wool, *rare;* (3) **-cutter,** designating an inferior breed of hogs, *rare;* (4) ***lark,** the horned lark or a related species, also the Missouri skylark *q.v.;* (5) **pipit,** =**Missouri skylark;** (6) ***rocket,** see as a main entry; (7) **scraper,** see as a main entry; (8) ***-scraping,** *a.* very high, or rising high, as of buildings or prices; (9) **tavern,** a tavern in the upper story of a building, *rare.*

(1) **1867** *Chi. Times* 27 July 5/1 The sky ball of their opponents was also neatly held. — (2) **1874** *Calif. Reporter* (S.F.) 15 Aug. 1/4 Joe dearly loves fun, and will have it as often as possible, while his mother-in-law is a rigid, old-fashioned sky-blue Baptist. — (3) **1858** *Spirit of Times* 20 Feb. 390/2 Smith . . . raised . . . a large number of hogs of the most exaggerated 'sky-cutter' breed, and which used to run wild in the woods. — (4) **1781–2** JEFFERSON *Notes Va.* (1788) 74. **1858** BAIRD *Birds Pacific R.R.* 403 *Eremophila Cornuta.* . . . Sky Lark; Shore Lark. **1874** COUES *Birds N.W.* 44, I saw no Skylarks after about the middle of September. **1907** *St. Nicholas* Oct. 1147/1 Down in the meadow a skylark is singing.

(5) **1884** COUES *Key to Birds* (ed. 2) 286 *Neocorys*, Sky Pipits. — (8) **1891** *Boston Jrnl.* Nov., When entire streets are built with sky-scraping buildings, what disadvantages there will be. **1895** *Congreg. Ch. 9th Council Min.* 160 The poor man's cottage . . . is taxed two or three times as much, in proportion, . . . as the sky-scraping block of the millionaire. **1904** *N.Y. Ev. Post* 12 March 10 Skyscraping Prices at Last Brandus Picture Sale. — (9) **1827** MELLEN *Chronicle of '26* 25 What with . . . Sky-taverns, Wall-street springs and watering halls, New York will loom. . . . The grandest, gayest, sharpest, sickliest of our clime.

As the last term in ***blue-sky.**

* **sky-,** *prefix.* In fanciful slang formations, usu. obs.: (1) **skyfalute,** *v.* to cut didoes, to "highfalute," *rare;* (2) **-godlin,** *adv.* obliquely; (3) **-hooting,** =**callyhooting.**

(1) **1856** *Knickerb.* XLVII. 616 Well—we got ter skyfaluting about, and there was licker around, and pooty good rum. — (2) **1869** *Overland Mo.* Aug. 128 A mustang . . . will run 'skygodlin.' — (3) **1922** WILSON *Merton of Movies* 5 Skyhootin' around in here, leavin' the

front of the store unpertected for an hour or two, like your time was your own.

Esp. **skyugle,** *v.* (see quots. 1864, B '77).

1864 *Army & Navy Jrnl.* 11 July (B.), He had scyugled along the front, when the Rebels scyugled a bullet through his clothes; . . . he should scyugle his servant, who . . . had scyugled three fat chickens for a supply of ice; . . . after he had scyugled his dinner, he proposed to scyugle a nap. **1877** BARTLETT 600 *Skyugle, Scyugle,* a queer word that originated with the Union soldiers during the late war. . . . 'It has not only a variety, but a contrariety of meanings.' **1877** W. WRIGHT *Big Bonanza* 375 It would do your hearts good to see that dog show off what a sense of appreciation he's got of me. Fellers, his gorgeous tail then stands aloft, he skyugles about. **1883** HARTE *Poetical Works* 145 And all of Smith's pigs were skyugled to boot.

Also as a noun.

1864 *Army & Navy Jrnl.* 11 July (B.), A corps staff officer . . . informed me that he had been out on a general scyugle.

Skykomish skaɪˈkomɪʃ, *n.* [f. *skaikh,* inland, +*mish,* people.] Indians who once lived along or in the vicinity of the Skykomish River in the state of Washington. Cf. **Skokomish, Snohomish, Snoqualmie.**

1856 in *34th Cong.* 3 Sess. H.R. Ex. Doc. 37, 77, I received a letter from you appointing me the local agent for the Snohomish, the Snoqualmi, and the Skiquamish tribes of Indians. **1930** HAEBERLIN & GUNTHER *Puget Sound Indians* 30 The Snohomish, Skykomish and Snuqualmi shared with the Klallam and Cowichans the use of woven blankets of mountain goat wool, dog hair, or a combination of feathers and fireweed. **1940** SMITH *Puyallup-Nisqually* 303 The Skykomish and Snoqualmie used mountain-goat wool but not dog wool.

***skyrocket,** *n.*

1. = ***sky 1.** In full **skyrocket ball.** *Obs.*

1857 *Spirit of Times* 7 Feb. 373/1 Mr. Smith is famous amongst Base Ball Players, for his '*Sky-Rocket Balls.*' **1867** *Detroit Post* 21 Oct., Clark, by a sky rocket to left field, let Kelly, Brown, and Phelps home. **1868** *N. Eng. Base Ballist* 20 Aug. 10/4 He acquitted himself well, sending up a sky rocket ball to the left field.

2. (See quots.)

1867 *Ball Players' Chron.* 25 July 2/2 After cheers had been interchanged, and the Nationals had let off a 'sky rocket'—namely, a sort of finish to three cheers, with a 'hiss—boom—ah!'—an adjournment was had to the clubhouse, where a very nice collation had been prepared. **1947** PERRY *Cities of Amer.* 222 He is such a stimulating lecturer that many of his classes are preceded by a 'skyrocket': a Wisconsin yell reserved for its heroes.

skyrocket ˈskaɪˌrɑkɪt, *v. tr.* and *intr.* To rise (or be sent) up rapidly, often of sales, prices, etc. *Colloq.*

1909 WEBSTER. **1923** *Nation* 22 Aug. 181 The supply runs short and prices go skyrocketing. **1950** *D. Oklahoman* (Okla. City) 26 Feb. 1/1 The price might skyrocket immediately.

***skyscraper,** *n.*

1. A bird that flies high. *Obs.*

1840 MATHEWS *Politicians* v. vi, I wish I had a brace of the sky-scrapers broiled for a luncheon. **1855** SIMMS *Forayers* 52 Open to the sky-scrapers, and the bouncing wild cats.

2. A high hat or bonnet. Also attrib. *Obs.*

1847 J. A. EAMES *Budget of Letters* 397 She gave me a black silk bonnet . . . which stuck right up in the air after the fashion of the old 'sky scrapers.' *a*1885 in *Cent. Mag.* XXXV. 950/1 Milliner's wire . . . was used to give outline to the skyscraper bonnets of the day.

3. *Baseball.* A ball hit or thrown high into the air. Also attrib.

1866 *N.Y. Herald* 27 June 5/5 Goodspeed made three handsome fly catches; Mehl, Sweet and Dupignac each paying their share of attention to the 'skyscrapers.' **1907** *St. Nicholas* Sep. 996 A 'skyscraper' throw to first.

4. A tall building.

1883 *Cent. Mag.* Sep. 724/1 The Georgia man . . . writes to the 'American Architect' to say that the American mind requires 'sky-scrapers.' **1913** LONDON *Valley of Moon* 82 The way led uptown, past . . . the Fourteenth Street skyscrapers. **1949** *Nat. Geog. Mag.* April 421/2 When he enters a skyscraper, he can reflect that its erection was made possible, in part, by the discoveries of Henry Bessemer.

b. Skyscraper man, modern civilized man.

1943 GOETHE *Sierran Cabin* 2 'Tis a far cry from Peking Man to Skyscraper Man.

***slab,** *n.*

1. A member of a slab company *q.v. Obs.*

1837 GREENE *Glance at N.Y.* 218 There also the 'slabs,' . . . with their arms and accoutrements of all kinds, are dragged on muster days, to share the glory of the volunteers.

2. In baseball, the pitcher's box. *Slang.*

1898 *Outing* July 424/2 In the fifth McCullum went on the slab, and held Northwestern down to one hit for the balance of the game.

3. *W.* A cement or concrete road.

1930 *Durant* (Okla.) *D. Democrat* 4 Nov. 1/6 Efforts are being made to have the road opened for traffic Wednesday, but considerable dirt is to be removed from the concrete yet, and it is likely that the slab will not be opened before Thursday. **1947** *Amer. Mercury* Jan. 69/1 No doubt *slab,* which is short and picturesque, arose partly because 'concrete highway' is a cumbersome and unimaginative expression.

4. In combs.: (1) **slab bonnet,** =**slat bonnet,** *rare;* (2) **bridged,** *a.* (see quot.), *obs.;* (3) **car,** a car or truck used in or about a sawmill for conveying slabs; (4) **company,** a military company made up of irregular, disorderly, "slab-sided" recruits, *obs.;* (5) **pit,** a place where the slabs from a sawmill are burned; (6) **saw,** a saw in a sawmill for cutting up slabs; (7) **shanty,** a shanty made of slabs; (8) **sides,** chap, fellow, *humorous;* (9) **wood,** firewood made of slabs from a sawmill.

(1) 1891 RYAN *Pagan* 46 The face could scarcely be seen in the great shadows of a slab bonnet. — **(2) 1866** LOWELL *Biglow P.* 2 Ser. p. lxii, Whoever has driven over a stream by a bridge made of *slabs* will feel the picturesque force of the epithet *slab-bridged* applied to a fellow of shaky character. — **(3) 1879** *Lumberman's Gaz.* 19 Dec., [The refuse] will fall into the slab car. — **(4) 1841** *Boston Transcript* 10 May 1/1 He had like many other officers who command 'slab' companies, a troublesome set of fellows to deal with.

(5) 1879 *Lumberman's Gaz.* 19 Dec., An elevator . . . is intended to be used in getting the slabs and clippings into the slab-pit. — **(6) 1879** *Lumberman's Gaz.* 19 Dec., The refuse will be run to the slab-saw and cut-up. — **(7) 1845** *Knickerb.* XXVI. 411 There are houses of all grades provided, from the slab shanty to the comfortable frame-dwelling. **1944** KAHN *Cable Car Days* 103 We finally arrived at the next depot, which was nothing but a slab shanty. — **(8) 1851** *Polly Peablossom* 83 How are you, old slab-sides? — **(9) 1871** STOWE *Sam Lawson* 13 Cack allers had slab-wood a plenty from his mill. **1941** WHITE *One Man's Meat* 261 He hasn't delivered the cord of slabwood he said he was going to bring me.

***slab,** *v.* **1.** *tr.* To convert into thick, flat pieces. **2.** *To slab off,* (see quot. 1859).

(1) 1866 LOSSING *Hudson* 70 There are also several mills for slabbing the fine black marble of that locality. **1893** *Advance* 11 May, A section of one thirty feet in diameter is to be slabbed. — **(2) 1835** CROCKETT *Tour* 212 You must take notice that I am slabb'd off from the election. **1859** BARTLETT 411 *To Slab off,* to throw aside as useless, like the outside piece of a log.

slabber gang. A group of saws that remove the outer slabs from logs. — **1871** *Winnebago Co. Press* (Neenah, Wis.) 1 July 2/2 The slabber and stack gangs are arranged on one side of the mill and the double rotary and pony gang on the opposite side.

slack-water ˈslækˌwɔtɚ, *v. tr.* To dam or impede (a stream) so as to produce stretches of deeper water for navigation.

1862 *Cong. Globe* 30 June 3033/1 If you slackwater the Susquehanna a few hundred miles up into New York, and then build a canal to Lake Erie, you will have navigation for your gunboats. **1874** COLLINS *Kentucky* I. 54 Flat boats and water craft descending the slack-watered rivers, from a point above slack water, [are] not to pay tolls.

Hence **slack-watering,** *n.* and *a.*

1850 DRAKE *Treatise* 250 The slack-watering of the Kentucky River, has very materially improved the health of the people living along its banks. **1903** *N.Y. Ev. Post* 5 Sep., The rapids near Keokuk, where the famous slack-watering works are now in operation.

slack-water navigation. River navigation made possible or improved by the erection of dams and locks to secure increased depth in the stream.

1824 in *Amer. R.R. Jrnl.* I. (1832) 452/1 Canals, or slack water navigation, can be effected. **1830** *Williams's N.-Y. Ann. Reg.* 116 One half canal and one half slack water navigation. **1877** W. H. BURROUGHS *On Taxation* 28 It is difficult to see how the advantages of slackwater navigation . . . can be brought within the range of local objects.

***slam,** *n.*

1. (See quot. 1909.)

1884 RITTENHOUSE *Maud* 296 Oh! did I tell you that Mr. Hough to atone for his 'slams,' said, 'I did want to make one gallant speech, but I hardly dared, about how remarkably well you looked Tuesday night.' **1909** WEBSTER, slam. . . . An uncomplimentary personal remark. *Slang.*

2. In combs.: (1) **Slam Bangs,** one of the political factions that opposed the Whigs, also attrib., *obs.;* (2) **Bangers,** =prec.

(1) **1837** *Jamestown* (N.Y.) *Jrnl.* 29 Nov. 2/2 Tory Executive power in its most tyrannical form combined in this country with the Fanny Wrights, the Loco Focos, and the Slam Bangs in order to break down the Whig party and Whig principles. **1838** MAYO *Polit. Sk. Washington* 19 See the infatuated proceeding . . . of the Slam-Bang-loco focos. — (2) **1840** *Maysville* (Ky.) *Eagle* 25 April 3/2 It is a subject of congratulations with all the Whigs, that the 'Slam-bangers,' 'Buttenders,' *id est omne genus*, did not get a much heavier majority.

***slam,** *v. tr.* and *intr.* To make caustic remarks about (a person), to be severely critical of. *Slang.* Cf. ***slam,** *n.* **1.**—**1884** RITTENHOUSE *Maud* 291 When I and Mr Hough arrived late Dr Benson and Mr Parsons slammed right and left at the tardiness. **1916** H. L. WILSON *Somewhere in Red Gap* ii, 57 Couldn't even agree on the same kind of cocktail. Both slamming the waiter.

***slam-bang,** *v. tr.* To attack or denounce. *Colloq.* — **1846** H. N. MOORE *Fitzgerald & Hopkins* 145 And go it the critters did, for they slambanged and pommelled each other not so slow. **1888** *Voice* (N.Y.) 12 July, You might as well denounce the legal profession because of the shysters . . . as to slam-bang newspapers because there are recreant editors.

* **slang,** *n.*[1] In slang combs.: (1) **slang-whang,** abusive or ranting utterance, balderdash, nonsense; (2) **-whanger,** a low, noisy talker or writer, also **slang-whangery;** (3) **-whanging,** the making, writing, or publishing of noisy, ranting, abusive harangues, also attrib. or as adj.

(1) **1834** BRACKENRIDGE *Recollections* 183 The dullest practised speaker is at home, compared to the young lawyer of genius, . . . who has acquired nothing of the ordinary *slang-whang.* **1859** *Harper's Mag.* July 164/1 Don't allow their vulgar slang-wang to have the slightest effect upon you. — (2) **1807** IRVING *Salmagundi* vii, These knights, denominated editors, or *slang-whangers*, . . . may be said to keep up a constant firing 'in words.' **1839** *N.O. Picayune* 9 March 2/1 Two of the Nashville papers . . . are getting to be uncommonly interesting, at least to those of their patrons who like to see papers filled with nothing but political slang-whangery. **1892** T. & A. FITCH *Better Days* 304 The Tucson Star . . . used to be the chief of slangwhangers. **1950** *Chi. Tribune* 24 April 20/3 The titles 'Ice Capades' and 'Borscht Capades' are examples of the numerous blends and portmanteau words spawned by slang-whangers and by Advertisea, the tenth Muse. — (3) **1809** *Essex Reg.* 20 May (Th.), Federal Slangwhanging. **1836** *Crockett Exploits* 84 By his slang-whanging [he] drew a considerable crowd around us. **1870** *Nation* 27 Jan. 58/1 The world would be in a dreadful state if a slang-whanging magazine or newspaper writer had only to call persons whom we all honor and admire Borgias. **1904** *Buffalo Commercial* 13 July 4 A clean campaign—one free from gross personal abuse and slang-whanging.

As the last term in **stump, tea, Texas slang.**

slang slaŋ, *n.*[2] [Du. *slang*, a water pipe or hose.] (See quot.) *Obs.* — **1890** *N. & Q.* V. 6 *Slang.*—I remember in the Adirondacks, a boatable channel or stream connecting a small lake with the Raquette river. Our boatman called it 'the Slang.' He could not tell me whether *slang* was a proper name, or a common noun.

* **slant,** *n.* **1.** A way of regarding a thing, point of view. **2.** A glance or look. Both *slang.*

(1) **1905** *N.Y Ev. Post* 28 Jan. 5 The titles of articles on this subject bear an extremely pessimistic slant. **1930** *Randolph Enterprise* (Elkins, W.Va.) 16 Oct. 4/6 The whole slant of the issues for the coming campaigns is in behalf of the average citizen. — (2) **1911** E. FERBER *Dawn O'Hara* viii. 109 You're supposed t' take a slant at th' things an' make up your mind. **1928** *Collier's* 18 Aug. 25/3, I took a slant and saw two fellows just nailing up an advertising banner.

slapjack ˈslæpˌdʒæk, *n.* A flapjack. *Colloq.* Cf. **corn slapjack.**

1809 IRVING *Knickerb.* IV. vi., To these [the Van Nests of Kinderhook] . . . we are indebted for the invention of slap jacks. **1882** THOMAS HUGHES *G.T.T.* 164 Willy initiated me into the mysteries of making 'slapjacks.' **1941** *L.A.* Map. 289.

***slapper,** *n.* **1.** A window shutter. *Rare.* **2.** (See quot.) *Obs.* See also **back slapper.** — (1) **1843** CARLTON *New Purchase* I. 45 [The] window was a cubit square and had a flapper or slapper hung with leathern hinges. — (2) **1891** *N. & Q.* VI. 129 Sometimes a further degradation occurs, and the toothsome fritter becomes a slapper. I never heard this word, but I have often seen it in this city [Philadelphia]. You will frequently observe a placard bearing the word 'Maryland slappers' in the window of some fourth-rate eating-house.

slapstick ˈslæpˌstɪk, *n.* A large paddling implement consisting of two boards hinged at one end but loose at the other, used by clowns and actors in low comedy to deal other performers light but resounding whacks. Also low comedy or farce such as that in which such contrivances are used.

1896 *N.Y. Dramatic News* 4 July 9/3 What a relief, truly, from the slap-sticks, rough-and-tumble comedy couples abounding in the variety ranks. **1907** *Weekly Budget* 19 Oct. 1/2 The special officer in the gallery, armed with a 'slap-stick,' the customary weapon in American theatre galleries, made himself very officious amongst the small boys. **1949** *Sky Line Trail* Oct. 27/1 A laugh-laden pageant of everything from mock tragedy to slap stick comedy, the show brought out talents hitherto unsuspected.

slash slæʃ, *n.*[1] [Origin obscure. Perhaps suggested by * *slashy, a.*, wet, miry.]

1. A low, wet, swampy or marshy area, often overgrown with bushes, canes, etc. Usu. *pl.* Also attrib.

1652 in *Amer. Sp.* XV. 392/2 Beginning neer a wett slash. **1690** *Ib.* 393/2 One thousand one hundred twenty nine acres . . . beginning at a great pine by a piny Branch or Slash side. **1789** HAWKINS *Letters* 89 This slash looks beautiful covered with reed to a considerable extent. **1816** D. THOMAS *Travels Western Country* (1819) 230 *Slashes*, means flat clayey land which retains water on the surface after showers. From this comes the adjective, *slashy.* **1885** *N.H. Forestry Comm. Rep.* June 98 Forbid . . . the setting of fires between the first of May and the first of October, in any slashes, old pasture, field, or other place.

b. A particular area of this nature. Cf. *Mill boy of the slashes.*

1843 *Junius Tracts* Sep. 50 He and I were born close to the slashes of Hanover. **1893** E. COUES *Hist. Lewis & Clark Exped.* II. 729 (*footnote*), What is now the most fashionable part of Washington . . . was just such a place when I was a boy. It was always called 'The Slashes.' **1904** T. E. WATSON *Bethany* 6 The grocery . . . stood on the flat, called the 'slashes.'

c. (See quots.)

1877 BARTLETT 602 *Slash-Ground*, land on which the brush has been cut and left lying. New York. **1899** GREEN *Va. Word-Book* 340 *Slashes*, . . . small places of standing water after a heavy rain, usually in roads.

2. slash pine, any one of various pines that grow in slashes, or low coastal regions, as *Pinus caribaea*, and the loblolly and shortleaf pines. Also attrib. Cf. **black slash pine.**

1882 HOUGH *Elem. Forestry* 328 Varieties [of *Pinus taeda*] are known in North Carolina as 'Swamp Pine,' 'Slash Pine,' **1884** SARGENT *Rep. Forests* 516 The naval stores . . . in the United States are principally produced from . . . the loblolly pine (*Pinus Tæda*), and the slash pine (*Pinus Cubensis*). **1949** *Democrat* 28 July 1/3 Both have plots on which they have set out slash pine seedlings. **1950** *Amer. Forests* Jan. 34/1 It falls victim to the competition of loblolly and slash pines, oaks, and red gum, which begin their height growth in the first year.

As the last term in **black, cypress, huckleberry, meadow, mill, spring, timber, water, wind slash.**

slash slæʃ, *n.*[2] [?Short for * **slashing,** *n.*]

1. (See quot. 1905.) Also attrib.

1881 *Harper's Mag.* Oct. 688/2 Crawling through the densest slash of burned and fallen timber. **1905** *Forestry Bureau Bul.* No. 61, 47 *Slash.* 1. The débris left after logging, wind, or fire. 2. Forest land which has been logged off and upon which the limbs and tops remain, or which is deep in débris as the result of fire or wind. **1949** *Pacific Discovery* Jan.–Feb. 4/1 The river knew well the flashing draft of lightning fires in the grass but not the consuming roar of a slash fire.

2. The tops, branches, etc., of trees so felled as to impede, or give protection from, an enemy (see also quot. 1887). *Obs.*

1886 MITCHELL *R. Blake* 16 Both sides were 'falling' trees to construct breastworks, abatis, and slashes. **1887** BILLINGS *Hardtack* 380 The territory covered by these fallen trees was called *the Slashes*, hence *Slashing.*

* **slash,** *v.*

1. *tr.* To beat or tread down. *Rare.*

*c***1834** CATLIN *Indians* II. 18 We will take that buffalo trail, where the travelling herds have slashed down the high grass.

2. To clear (land) or cut down (timber) in an unplanned, destructive manner. Also **slashed,** *a.*

1843 *Yale Lit. Mag.* VIII. 332 His eye wandered far away over acres of slashed timber. **1857** *Quinland* I. 33 During the summer we 'slashed' about forty acres. **1885** *Cent. Mag.* April 836 He would have plenty to do 'slashing,' i.e., cutting down the trees preparatory to burning them.

3. To reduce or cut down (salaries, etc.) severely. Also * **slashing,** *a.*

1885 *Walla Walla* (Wash.) *Union* 1 Oct. 3/2 Look out for a slashing 'ad,' from Sam Lesser's clothing emporium. **1906** *Washington Post* 29 April 6 A Disposition was manifested in the Senate Committee to slash the salaries of members of the commission. **1910** *Springfield W. Republican* 8 Dec. 8 It is not a pleasant thing to slash a presidential message to this extent.

*****slasher,** *n.* One who cuts down timber in a destructive or wasteful manner. *Rare.* — **1886** *Leslie's Mo.* June 450/2 [We] can say to the Eastern slashers, 'Go ahead and chop down your forests.'

slashett slæʃˈɛt, *n.* A small slash. *Rare.* — **1876** in *Amer. Sp.* XV. 393/2 Thence . . . to a marked white oak in a slashett.

*** slashing,** *n.*

1. Felling timber, esp. doing this so that the trees fall in heaps suitable for burning. Also the mass of felled trees resulting from this.

1822 *Port Folio* XIII. 68 The act of hewing down the timber is called *slashing.* **1857** *Quinland* I. 34 When it came dry in the spring, we burned the 'slashing' we had made the previous summer. **1887** BILLINGS *Hardtack* 380 When a line of works was laid out through woods, much *slashing,* or felling of trees, was necessary in its front.

2. An area where timber has been cut or blown down.

1840 *Jamestown* (N.Y.) *Jrnl.* 1 July 2/5 On Monday, the body of Mr. Brown was found in a slashing. **1894** *Outing* XXIV. 186/2 We got into a spruce thicket or an old 'slashing'—the track of a hurricane. **1940** *Telephone Reg.* (McMinnville, Ore.) 4 Aug. 1/4 The Dayton fire department was kept moving Friday with four fires during the afternoon—three of them in brush and slashings and one . . . a field fire.

b. *pl.* =**slash,** *n.*[1] **1.**

1864 T. WEED in *Nichols Amer. Life* II. 215 Cattle . . . were turned out to 'browse' in the 'slashings.'

*** slat,** *n.*

1. Short for **slat bonnet;** one of the strips used in such a bonnet. *Colloq.*

1880 *Harper's Mag.* March 578/2 [She] goes to prayer-meetin' in her calico slat. **1891** *Cent. Mag.* Feb. 489 From the end of the tunnel formed by the uncompromising pasteboard slats a shrewd, hard, yellow, cadaverous face peers out. **1944** *Chi. Tribune* 6 Aug. VII. 1/8 Nettie's gay sunbonnet flopped dismally when its pasteboard slats became wet.

2. A rib, usu. in the pl. *Slang.*

1898 HAMBLEN *Gen. Manager's Story* 33 There's nothing much the matter with him; few of his slats stove in, that's all. *a***1906** O. HENRY *Trimmed Lamp* 162 What they need is a man to come home and kick their slats in once a week.

3. In combs.: (1) **slat bonnet,** (see quot. 1944); (2) **cattle-car,** a cattle-car the sides of which are of slats; (3) **sunbonnet,** =**slat bonnet.**

(1) 1880 *Harper's Mag.* March 577/1, I can go to prayer-meetin' in my slat bunnit well enough. **1944** *D.N.* Nov. 60 *slat-bonnet: n.* A sun-bonnet whose 'brim,' instead of being stiffened by starch, is made

Slat bonnet

of a rectangular cloth folded and stitched in parallel rows about one inch apart to form long pockets into which strips of lightweight cardboard may be thrust. Douglas Co. Common. (W.W.) — **(2) 1884** KNIGHT *Supp.* 179/1 *Cattle Car,* . . . a car for live stock. . . . Among the various kinds may be mentioned: . . . combined cattle and box car, . . . Box cattle-car, . . . Slat cattle-car. — **(3) 1878** *St. Nicholas* Oct. 797/1 As soon as they had thrown off their slat sunbonnets. . . . Nimpo was seized with a bright idea. **1945** *Chi. Tribune* 2 Sep. VII. 1/1 Miss Nannie Hamilton added a yellow slat sunbonnet to her display of chocolate cakes, eggs and butter.

*** slate,** *n.*

1. A list of candidates prepared beforehand for appointment, nomination or election.

1854 in *Calif. Hist. Soc. Quart.* VIII. 206, 90 votes on Stony Bar slate. **1868** M. H. SMITH *Sunshine & Shadow* 317 In that little room . . . the 'slates' of ambitious and scheming politicians [have been] destroyed. **1949** *Chi. D. News* 19 Dec. 1/4 The rest of the slate will consist of present officeholders.

2. In combs.: (1) **slate-colored hawk,** =**sharp-shinned hawk;** (2) **-colored junco,** (see quots.); (3) **-colored snowbird,** =prec.; (4) *** maker,** one who makes or assists in making a political slate; (5) *** making,** preparing a political slate; (6) **River pea,** a variety of pea, now unidentifiable, *obs.;* (7) **run,** ?a run or stream that flows over a slaty formation, *obs.;* (8) **smasher,** one who refuses allegiance to a political slate.

(1) 1812 WILSON *Ornithology* VI. 13 [The] Slate-colored Hawk . . . is a native of Pennsylvania, and of the Atlantic states generally. **1844** *Nat. Hist. N.Y., Zoology* II. 17 The Slate-Colored Hawk . . . is noted for its attacks on the poultry yard. — **(2) 1895** *Trans. Md. Acad. Sci.* 336 Junco hyemalis. Slate-colored Junco. **1949** [see **slate-colored snowbird**]. — **(3) 1884** MERRIAM *Mammals Adirondack Region* 19 Amongst the fallen timber were large numbers of Slate-colored Snowbirds. **1949** *Dly. Oklahoman Mag.* (Okla. City) 4 Dec. 16/4 One of Oklahoma's most abundant winter birds, the little slate-colored junco or snowbird is very distinctive. — **(4) 1868** *N.Y. Herald* 9 July 7/3 The slate makers were nigh frantic about the presentation of Mr. Greeley's name. **1946** *Chi. D. News* 19 Dec. 1/4 The party slate-makers were picking a mayoral candidate.

(5) 1904 CRISSEY *Tattlings* 391 The agreement among the members of the slate-making department to keep mum . . . must be observed to the letter. **1949** *Chi. Tribune* 22 Dec. 1/1 It was learned that the slate making was pervaded by heat and bitterness. — **(6) 1800** TATHAM *Agric. & Commerce* 61 Plant black-eyed peas, Slate river peas, or cuckold's increase, in the interstices. — **(7) 1807** GASS *Journal* 51 We passed a run on the south side called a slate run. — **(8) 1869** *Cin. Enquirer* March (Clapin), Gen. Grant . . . is a great slate-smasher.

b. In phrases: (1) *To break the slate,* (see quot. 1888); (2) *to make up a slate,* (see quot.).

(1) 1865 *Harper's Mag.* July 228/2 Sometimes he [Lincoln] would 'break the slate,' as he called it, of those who were making a list of appointments. **1888** BRYCE *Amer. Commonw.* II. 458 The list so settled is now a Slate, unless some discontented magnate objects and threatens to withdraw. To do so is called 'breaking the slate.' — **(2) 1892** WALSH *Lit. Curiosities* 1014 *Slate, to make up the.* In American political slang this signifies the secret understanding by which the leaders of a political party determine among themselves before the meeting of a nominating convention the names of the candidates for office which they desire and which they will endeavor by all their influence, open or covert, to have put in nomination by the convention.

As the last term in **blue, draw, wooden slate.**

*** slate,** *v.* **1.** *tr.* To place the name of (a person) on a political slate. **2.** To free (coal) from pieces of slate.

(1) 1804 *Steele P.* I. 441 The Federalists have not nor do they intend slating a candidate. **1913** *Chi. Record-Herald* 6 March 3/6 Franklin D. Roosevelt, New York state senator, is slated for a position in an important department of the Wilson administration. **1946** *Chi. D. News* 4 Jan. 12/2 Polish leaders thought one of their race should be slated for sheriff or treasurer. **1949** *Chi. Tribune* 22 Dec. 1/1 The ward committeemen at their conclave rejoiced over the slating of Capt. Gilbert, who they feel sure harbors no 'silly ideas.' — **(2) 1859** *Rep. Comm. Patents 1858* I. 705 Improvement in Machines for Slating Coal.

slather ˈslæðɚ, *n.* [Origin obscure.] A large quantity, a good deal, much. Usu. *pl. Colloq.*

1876 MARK TWAIN *Tom Sawyer* vii. 75 They got slathers of money—most a dollar a day. **1911** FERBER *Dawn O'Hara* 142 It's going to be slathers of fun. **1950** *Chi. Tribune* 23 Feb. 12/3 Now, since seeing 'slathers' in such good company, I am wondering if a colloquialism is a slang expression which is becoming respectable.

*****slaughter,** *n.* **1. slaughter chute,** a chute leading to a slaughterhouse. **2.** *****slaughterhouse,** (see quot.). *Obs.* — **(1) 1932** *Blue Valley Farmer* (Okla. City) 17 March 2/6 We appreciate there must be some service charges on stock occupying expensive terminal yards on the way to the slaughter chutes. — **(2) 1789** in CIST *Cincinnati* (1841) 197 Guards . . . are allowed me at present, for the protection and defense of this *slaughter-house,* as some in this country, (Kentucky,) are pleased to term the Miami purchase.

*** slaughter,** *v.* **1.** *tr.* To destroy (forests and timber) by wasteful and excessive cutting. **2.** *Polit.* To defeat or overwhelm. *Colloq.*

(1) 1896 *Vt. Agric. Rep.* XV. 85 Our lumber forests are being slaughtered. **1903** WHITE *Blazed Trail Stories* 47 Fitzpatrick would not have the pine 'slaughtered.' — **(2) 1903** *N.Y. Ev. Post* 5 Oct. 3 McLaughlin's lieutenants are openly declaring that they will 'slaughter' the McClellan-Grout-Fornes ticket. **1929** C. E. MERRIAM *Chicago* 280 He was . . . again slaughtered by Sweitzer in the primaries of 1915.

*** slave,** *n.*

1. (See quot.) *Rare.*

*c***1838** CATLIN *Indians* II. 213 This tribe [Sacs and Foxes] has a society which they call the 'slaves,' composed of a number of the young men of the best families in the tribe, who volunteer to be slaves for the term of two years.

2. In obs. or hist. combs. with reference to slavery in the South: (1) **slave breeder,** a slave-owner primarily interested in selling slaves and their offspring; (2) **breeding,** the breeding or rearing of slaves for the market; (3) **case,** a legal case involving or relating to a slave or to slaves; (4) **code,** laws in the different states for the management of slaves and the protection of slavery, also attrib.; (5) **coder,** an advocate of slavery and slave codes; (6) **driver,** see as a main entry; (7) **driving,** of or pertaining to the driving or superintending of Negro slaves; (8) **land,** the South; (9) **pen,** a sheltered inclosure for slaves awaiting sale; (10) **power,** the political power in the federal government wielded by southern slave owners before the Civil War; (11) **property,** property consisting of slaves; (12) **quarter,** the place on a plantation occupied by the slaves, usu. *pl.;* (13) **-raising state,** a northern state in which slaves were raised and sold to southerners; (14) **rearing plantation,** a wornout plantation upon which the raising and selling of slaves was of primary concern; (15) **state,** see as a main entry; (16) **warehouse,** a structure in which slaves were kept while awaiting sale; (17) **yard,** a yard or inclosure where slaves were kept while awaiting sale.

(1) 1846 MACKENZIE *Van Buren* 276 [Canada] would now have been ruled by . . . the South Carolina and Virginia slave breeders and slave owners. **1867** DIXON *New Amer.* I. 16 Missouri . . . was then a slave state, with a sparse but fiery population of slave-breeders and slave-dealers. — **(2) 1840** CHANNING *Works* (1886) 783/2 The northern slave States . . . have acquired a new interest . . . by humbling themselves to the condition of slave-breeding and slave-trading communities. **1861** *N.Y. Tribune* 27 Dec. 7/2 Perhaps your next publication will altogether defend . . . slavery, slave-breeding and slave-trading. — **(3) 1836** *Niles' Reg.* 26 Nov. 208/3 Another slave case. **1843** *Ib.* 19 Aug. 385 The Slave Case in Cincinnati. — **(4) 1835** CHANNING *Works* (1886) 703/1 'The slave can acquire nothing,' says one of the slave codes, 'but what must belong to his master.' **1860** G. W. BUNGAY *Bobolink Minstrel* 24 [We'll] wipe out the slave-code teachers. **1893** *Harper's Mag.* April 701/1 The Legislature which assembled at Pawnee in July adopted the slave code of Missouri *en bloc,* . . . compelling every official, candidate, and voter to take an oath to support the fugitive-slave law.

(5) 1859 *Kans. Hist. Coll.* (1902) VII. 546 If it denied the power to exclude, and asserted the power to protect, the slave-coders would vote for it and the republicans and Douglasites against it. — **(7) 1830** *Cong. Deb.* 10 May 939/1 Here they may live and flourish, until some slave-driving politician and planter of South Carolina . . . again chains them to a miserable dependence on South Carolina cotton and British looms. **1872** *Newton Kansan* 5 Sep. 4/3 The clothes he is in . . . belong to the . . . slave-driving Democracy. — **(8) 1838–9** F. KEMBLE *Jrnl. Res. Georgia* (1863) 24 One of them . . . anywhere out of slave land would be able to earn fourteen or fifteen dollars a month for himself. — **(9) 1835** REED & MATHESON *View* I. 32 It was at Washington we first saw the slave-pen. It is usually a sort of wooden shed, whitewashed, and attached to the residence of a slave-dealer. **1901** CHURCHILL *Crisis* 35 Mr. Lynch's slave pen had been disgorged that morning.

(10) 1842 CHANNING *Works* (1886) 898/2 To unite with Texas . . . would be to ensure the predominance of the slave power. — **(11) 1810** *Steele P.* II. 632 Being daily more & more disgusted with Tide Swamp and Slave property I should be glad to receive Terms or proposals for from 50 to 80 Negroes. **1862** *N.Y. Tribune* 9 May 6/4 Is slave-property safer now than it was two years ago? — **(12) 1837** MARTINEAU *Society* II. 49 The slave-quarter is large. **1891** *Scribner's Mag.* X. 100 In the rear . . . were the slave quarters. **1948** *Sat. Ev. Post* 23 Oct. 100/4 It was up this very river bed, back in slavery times, that the Negroes used to slither at night to make contact from the slave quarters of one plantation to the other. — **(13) 1819** *N.Y. Advt.* 6 April 2/1 It is idle to hope that the number of slaves will be diminished in the slave-raising states by the liberty of exporting them to the west. **1853** STOWE *Key* 143/2 The immense acquisition of slave territory . . . now opens so boundless a market to tempt the avarice and cupidity of the Northern slave-raising States. — **(14) 1863** J. H. SIMPSON (*title*), Horrors of the Virginia Slave Trade and of the Slave-rearing Plantations.

(16) 1852 STOWE *Uncle Tom* xxx, A slave-warehouse in New Orleans is a house externally not much unlike many others. — **(17) 1866** MOORE *Women of War* 308 War had charms for him far beyond the milder horrors of the slave-yard and the smaller risks of the gaming-table. **1880** CABLE *Grandissimes* 121 Faintly audible to the apothecary . . . came from a neighboring slave-yard the monotonous chant and machine-like tune-beat of an African dance.

b. In other terms of obvious meaning or sufficiently explained in the quots.: (1) **slave auction,** (2) **baron,** (3) **car,** (4) **catcher,** (5) **catching,** (6) **cloth,** (7) **depot,** (8) **government,** (9) **-holders' rebellion,** (10) **holding state,** (11) **lumberman,** (12) **melody,** (13) **oligarch,** (14) **-owning state,** (15) **-owning Unionist,** (16) **question,** (17) **soil,** (18) **song,** (19) **system,** (20) **territory.**

(1) 1839 CHANNING *Works* (1886) 787/1 Men whose reports of us determine our rank in the civilized world, associate with us the enormities of the slave-trade and of slave auctions. **1901** CHURCHILL *Crisis* 40 Was it possible that these people were coming to a slave auction? — **(2) 1934** BURGESS *Reminiscences* 3 My first memories are of . . . courteous slave barons, and of ignorant, slovenly, poor white trash. — **(3) 1859** J. REDPATH *Roving Editor* 266, I have seen slave-pens and slave-cars filled with the unhappy victims of the internal and infernal trade, who were travelling for the city of New Orleans. — **(4) [1765** TIMBERLAKE *Memoirs* 28 The old [Indian] warrior, commonly called the Slave Catcher of Tennessee, invited us to his camp.] **1882** WHITMAN *Spec. Days* 259 The members [of the Democratic nominating conventions were] . . . slave-catchers, pushers of slavery.

(5) 1864 WEBSTER 1241/2 *Slave-catching,* the business of searching out and arresting fugitive slaves, to return them to their masters. — **(6) 1944** CLARK *Pills* 205 Especially was this true in the South where large quantities of work or slave cloth was purchased prior to the war. — **(7) 1834** FEATHERSTONHAUGH *Slave States* (1844) 37 She stated that he had been decoyed to a public slave-depôt in the skirts of the city, had been seized and detained there, and was going to be sold into the Southern States. **1865** RICHARDSON *Secret Service* 64 Along the streets, you saw the sign, 'Slave Depot—Negroes bought and sold.' — **(8) 1853** STOWE *Key* 123/1 Is there not the same dread through all the despotic slave governments of America? — **(9) 1861** *Chi. Tribune* 19 July 1/2 Senator Pomeroy's bill for the suppression of the slave-holders' rebellion, enacts that slavery be immediately abolished by proclamation. **1865** RICHARDSON *Secret Service* 328 From the outbreak of the Slaveholders' Rebellion his name was one of the brightest in that noble but unfortunate army.

(10) 1815 *Niles' Reg.* VIII. 66/1 Among the slave-holding states themselves, the progress of the black and white population has been steady and equal. **1873** HOWELLS *Chance Acquaintance* i, Dr. Ellison . . . was too much an abolitionist to live in a slaveholding State with safety. **1946** ADAMS *Album Amer. Hist.* III. 44 Across the Missouri River in the slaveholding state of Missouri lay such well established towns as Weston and Kansas City. — **(11) 1856** OLMSTED *Slave States* 153 Slave-Lumbermen . . . are mostly hired by their employers at a rent . . . paid to their owners. — **(12) 1891** *Atlantic Mo.* June 813/2 The younger and progressive Negroes . . . are giving up, too, the old slave melodies. — **(13) 1864** *Ore. State Jrnl.* 5 Nov. 1/5 We, the 'slave oligarchs,' [have] governed the Yankees till within a twelve month. — **(14) 1828** COOPER *Notions* II. 296 The confederation is nearly equally divided into slave-owning, and what are called free states.

(15) 1862 *N.Y. Tribune* 20 Jan., The slave-owning Unionists of Kentucky are extremely tenderfooted upon the Slavery Question. — **(16) 1830** *Cong. Deb.* 25 Jan. 46/2 The weakness of the South, as connected with the slave question, exposes us to . . . constant attacks. **1866** F. KIRKLAND *Bk. Anecdotes* 123/1 Mr. Calhoun . . . did not think the slave question . . . would produce a dissolution of the Union. — **(17) 1854** BENTON *30 Years' View* I. 18/1 These treaties (Indian and Spanish) . . . extinguished slave soil in all the United States territory west of the Mississippi. — **(18) 1881** *Harper's Mag.* May 818/2 The plaintive slave songs . . . have won popularity wherever the English language is spoken. **1949** *Reader's Digest* May 96/1 When they began to sing the stirring melancholy songs of bondage which we know as 'spirituals' (then called 'slave songs'), they made a deep impression. — **(19) 1838** HALIBURTON *Clockmaker* 26 (We.), I don't pay to upholders of the slave system. **1862** *N.Y. Tribune* 9 May 6/4 Is the slave system stronger politically [because of the efforts of Southern congressmen]? **1950** *Time* 6 March 98/3 His Southern colleagues were dreaming of the new states to be won for the slave system in the great Southwest.

(20) 1842 JOSEPH STURGE *Visit to U.S.* 13 The grand slave-holding conspiracy for revolutionizing Texas, and annexing it to the American Union, as a slave territory. **1854** BENTON *30 Years' View* I. 18/1 There was not a ripple of discontent . . . at this mighty transformation of slave into free territory. **1949** HUNGERFORD *Wells Fargo* 54 The tension between the Northern abolition states and the Southern slave territory was boiling up to its climax.

3. Used as a prefix, usu. with loss of the final *-e*, in obs. expressions: (1) **Slaveownia,** the slave-owning states; (2) **slavite,** one who favors or upholds slavery; (3) **slavocracy,** a dominant or powerful class made up of slaveowners and those favoring slavery; (4) **slavocrat,** a member of the slavocracy; (5) **slavocratic,** *a.* of or pertaining to the slavocracy.

(1) **1862** *N.Y. Tribune* 21 March 6/4 [The Confederate] officers besought them . . . to recall . . . the reputation of Slaveownia for valor and chivalry. **1885** *Mag. Amer. Hist.* April 395/1 Slaveownia.—The word . . . did not come into general use. — (2) **1831** *Liberator* 8 Jan. 1/2 (Th. Supp.), To say that a clerical slavite is bound to follow his own precepts, is preposterous. *Ib.* I. 115 (*Cent.*), The most abominable . . . spectacle which the wickedness of war presents in the sight of Heaven is a reverend slavite. **1854** *N.Y. Tribune* 2 Aug. 7/3 Now, these meetings are the easiest things in the world—they are nothing but *snap* meetings, and they show nothing more clearly than the weakness of the slaveites. — (3) **1840** *Ill. State Reg.* (Springfield) 22 Jan. 2/2 The reign of the slaveocracy is hastening to a close. **1941** BUCKMASTER *Let My People Go* 163 Committees of the Georgia and South Carolina legislatures made quite sure that certain Northern 'doughfaces' understood the position of the slavocracy on the question of secession. — (4) **1855** *Herald of Freedom* 25 Aug. 2/6 When the time arrives for the *slaveocrats* to call on you and by the force of arms attempt to make you bow down and worship the gods they have set up, or leave the Territory then 'resist unto blood.' **1868** *Putnam's Mag.* May 596/1 There meet . . . the freedman and the once slavocrat.

(5) **1857** *Lawrence* (Kans.) *Republican* 18 June 2 He excoriated this miserable slaveocratic sham, which rejoices to call itself 'National democracy.'

As the last term in **Congo, contraband, cotton, field, plantation, pro-slave.**

slave driver. One having charge of slaves or supervising them while at work.

1807 IRVING *Salmagundi* iii, Beautiful, O most puissant slave-driver, as are my wives, they are exceeded by the women of this country. **1856** *Jackson Picket Guard* (Elkton, Md.) 24 Sep. 1/5 Our Heavenly Father, . . . help us to shiver the Union into atoms rather than to concede to Southern demons, in the form of slave-drivers, one inch of the disputed territory. **1885** BAYLOR *On Both Sides* 212 There was a dreadful slave-driver . . . carrying a wand with an iron tip heated red-hot.

b. *transf.* One in charge of others at work, a difficult or cruel taskmaster.

1840 DANA *Two Years* 128 You've got a driver over you! Yes, a *slave-driver*—a *negro-driver!* **1901** MERWIN & WEBSTER *Calumet 'K'* 189 Do you think it would be worth something to the men who hire you for a dirty slave-driver to be protected from a strike?

* **slavery,** *n.* In obs. combs.: (1) **slavery amendment,** an amendment to the federal constitution dealing with slavery; (2) **extension,** the extension or spreading of slavery to new regions; (3) **extensionist,** one in favor of the spread of slavery into new areas.

(1) **1865** COX *8 Yrs. in Congress* 406 Mr. Buchanan . . . proposed to save us from war by slavery amendments. — (2) **1848** MCKEE *National Conventions* (1901) 67 The political conventions recently assembled at Baltimore and Philadelphia . . . [have nominated] candidates neither of whom can be supported by the opponents of slavery extension. **1886** LOGAN *Great Conspiracy* 35 Threats and counter-threats of Disunion were made on either hand by the opponents and advocates of Slavery-extension through annexation. — (3) **1848** *Field Piece* (Chi.) 14 June 1/3 They have now consummated the crowning outrage by combining with slavery extensionists to disgrace New York, and exclude her from the councils of the nation.

As the last term in **anti-, domestic, pro-slavery.**

slave state. A state in the U.S. in which, before the Civil War, slavery was legal. Also attrib. Cf. **border, seaboard slave state.**

1809 *Ann. 10th Congress* 2 Sess. 428 In the slave States the allowance for the subsistence of a negro, is one peck of corn per week. **1857** BENTON *Exam. Dred Scott Case* 20 The owner cannot carry his slave State law with him into the Territory. **1902** *Out West* Feb. 164 All his life—though born in a 'slave State'—a consistent hater of human slavery, Mr. Valentine was among the most outspoken opponents of recent American policy in the Philippines. **1949** *Chi. Tribune* 25 Sep. 28/5 Had it not been for the work and influence of James Lemen and his sons Illinois would have been a slave state.

slaw slɔ, *n.* [Du. *sla* (< *salade*), salad.] = **coleslaw.** Also attrib. Cf. **hot, warm slaw.**

1861 WINTHROP *C. Dreeme* 157 Pad of butter. Plate of slaw, ready vinegared. **1883** KNIGHT *Supp.* 359/1 *Fruit Slicer*, an open-bottomed box with a follower, to contain fruit, and slipped back and forth in grooves over a knife fixed like that of a slaw-cutter beneath.—*Wharry.* **1945** *Chi. D. News* 13 Oct. 4/3 The general, with great gusto, polished off . . . a bowl of slaw.

slawbank ˈslɔbæŋk, *n.* [Du. *slaapbank*, sleeping bench.] (See quot. 1894.) *Obs.* — **1679** *New Castle Court Rec.* 298 Chests tables Chaires & slaapbank. **1894** EARLE *Customs Old N. Eng.* iv. 113 A form of bedstead called a slawbank was common enough in New York, New Jersey, Delaware, and Pennsylvania until this century. . . . We will give them the Dutch name slawbank, from *slaapbancke*, a sleeping-bench.

***sled,** *n.* As the last term in **bob, clipper, corn, covered, dog, dumping, ground, half, hand, log, logging, ox, traverse, wagon, wood sled.**

sledding ˈslɛdɪŋ, *n.*

1. Conveying things on sleds; riding or coasting on a sled; also weather conditions affecting this.

1682 *Jamaica Rec.* I. 232 A way through the saide Lucasses Medow for sleding of hay. **1726** *N.-Eng. Courant* 26 Feb. 2/2 The Sledding being now over, Country Loads of Oak Wood are sold. **1833** WATSON *Hist. Tales of Phila.* 157 There was also much sledding down the streets and hills descending to Pegg's run. **1890** JEWETT *Strangers* 36, I heard say yesterday that there was good sleddin'. **1945** PEARSON *Country Flavor* 109 Then, after the January thaw and before one of the big snows of the ground-hog time, there is usually a period of good sledding.

b. *six weeks sledding in March,* ?a late spring. *Obs.*

1818 BENTLEY *Diary* IV. 505 We have an old saying, 6 weeks sledding in March.

2. *fig.* Getting on with a job, earning a living, etc., usu. modified by an adj., as **bad, hard, smooth, tough sledding.**

1839 GREELEY in *Corr. R. W. Griswold* (1898) 26 Payments are slack still, and we have rather hard sledding. **1888** *Cong. Rec.* 1 May 3589/1 For the farmer, in those days, there was mighty bad sledding on the road to Hard Scrabble. **1898** *N.Y. Ev. Post* 21 Oct. 1 Professional labor agitators do not always have smooth sledding in the field of politics. **1924** CROY *R.F.D. No. 3* 47 It was the duty of the 'contest manager' on the newspaper to originate some new feature each day, and often it was hard sledding. **1946** *Sierra Club Bul.* Dec. 34 Heavy weapons men would have tougher sledding still.

***sledge,** *n.* As the last term in **box, dog, hand, logging, mail, old sledge.**

sled-tender. (See quot. 1905.) — **1850** E. S. SEYMOUR *Sk. Minn.* 202 One-sled tender, who helps to load, and also aid in cutting off the limbs. **1905** *Forestry Bureau Bul.* No. 61, 47 *Sled tender*, a member of the hauling crew who accompanies the turn of logs to the landing, unhooks the grabs, and sees that they are returned to the yarding engine. (P[acific] C[oast] F[orest].)

* **sleep,** *n.* Among Indians or in imitation of them: A day, the measure of time between one sleeping period and the next.

1670 *S.C. Hist. Soc. Coll.* V. 166 The Caseeka . . . was within one sleep of us. **1761** NILES *Indian Wars* II. 582 He proposed . . . to return in 10 nights, or sleeps. **1844** GREGG *Commerce of Prairies* II. 298 Distances are represented by days' journey, which are oftener designated by camps or 'sleeps.' **1919** CODY & COOPER *Buffalo Bill* 312 It was many sleeps away. **1947** *Steamboat* (Colo.) *Pilot* 2 Jan. 6/4 He held up two fingers and said in a voice that did not seem to waver: 'Maybe so. Two sleeps more, you git out.'

***sleep,** *v. To sleep up,* to catch up on one's sleep. *Colloq.* — **1884** MARK TWAIN *H. Finn* vii, We laid off after breakfast to sleep up, both of us being about wore out.

* **sleeper,** *n.*

1. (See quot. 1864.) Also fig.

1856 *S.F. Bulletin* 4 Dec. 2/2 Some were waiting for 'sleepers,' others were telling some other betters a certain card was going to win, dead 'sure.' **1864** DICK *Amer. Hoyle* (1866) 208 A bet [in faro] is said to be a sleeper, when the owner has forgotten it, when it becomes public property, any one having a right to take it. **1896** G. W. DICE *Counterfeiting Exposed* 25 [He] was on a 'dead card' and liable to be 'swiped for a sleeper.' **1939** ROLLINS *Gone Haywire* 16 A Dakota miner had been detected attempting to steal 'sleepers' from the faro table.

2. A railroad car arranged with compartments and berths for sleeping.

1881 MARSHALL *Through Amer.* (1882) 108 You can have your dinner brought to you in your 'sleeper' and served privately in your section. **1917** SINCLAIR *King Coal* 348, I came down on that sleeper last night. **1948** *Chi. D. News* 17 Aug. 1/3 A mail car, a baggage car and a sleeper for train crew members also left the tracks.

b. sleeper train, a train made up of sleepers.

1881 MARK TWAIN *Speeches* 258 (R.), I must change cars there and take the sleeper train.

3. W. (See quot. 1907.)

1907 WHITE *Arizona Nights* 78 A sleeper is a calf that has been ear-marked, but not branded. **1934** LOMAX *Amer. Ballads* 411 Along with the strays and the sleepers, The tailings must turn from the gate. **1949** *Boston Sun. Globe* 1 May (Fiction Mag.) 2/1 He described the condition of the range and its waterings, . . . gave a tally of the sleepers and mavericks he had branded.

Also **sleeper branding, sleeper marked.**

1894 *McClure's Mag.* III. 113/1 It is these ear-marks, . . . which makes the practice of 'sleeper branding' possible. **1943** L. V. HAMNER *Short Grass* 97 Again cattle were 'sleeper marked,' that is marked but left unbranded.

4. In miscellaneous senses: **a.** ?A dormitory. *Rare.* **b.** In a foot race, a competitor whose capabilities are not known; in a horse race, a horse with a poor record in previous races that unexpectedly wins. *Slang.* [See Parke Cummings, *Dict. of Sports*, 408/1 for a fuller explanation of this term.] **c.** (See quot.)

(a) 1754 *S.C. Gazette* 1 Jan. 4/1 The sleeper 15 feet square, and was built this year. — **(b) 1892** *Outing* March 454/2 [Harmar was] beaten by Wells, a 'sleeper' from Amherst. **1941** BERREY & VAN DEN BARK *Amer. Thesaurus Slang* 731 Sleeper, a horse which is not doing its best, proven when it unexpectedly wins. **1948** *Redbook Mag.* April 66/2 Down the homestretch they battled neck and neck—the unknown N.Y.U. 'sleeper' and the supposedly invincible McKenley. — **(c) 1909** *N.Y. Ev. Post* (s.-w. ed.) 26 April 1 Attempts to smuggle gowns and women's wearing apparel by means of so-called 'sleepers,' or trunks which are brought over on the steamships without being accompanied by the owner.

5. (See quot.) Also **sleeper fire.**

1944 *New Yorker* 7 Oct. 38/2 The smoke was coming from a 'sleeper fire.' Sleepers are a very common sort of forest fire. They are caused most frequently by lightning, and they smolder for several hours in the wet woods before they start to burn in earnest, as the weather clears and the sun dries out the forest.

As the last term in **colonist, Pullman, seven, Soul, through, tourist sleeper(s).**

***sleeping,** *n.* or *a.* In combs.: (1) **sleeping attorney,** an attorney secretly retained to sleep in the same lodging that jurors sleep in, so as to be near to influence their decisions in a case, *rare;* (2) **bag,** a canvas or waterproof bag, usu. warmly lined and padded, for the use of one sleeping out of doors; (3) **car,** =**sleeper 2,** also attrib., cf. **emigrant, Pullman sleeping car;** (4) **chair,** (see quot.); (5) **coach,** =**sleeper 2;** (6) **over,** sleeping late (see also quot. 1851); (7) **sawyer,** a sawyer (sense **2.**) wholly submerged; (8) **section,** a berth or compartment on a sleeper or Pullman; (9) **train,** a train made up of sleepers.

(1) 1809 KENDALL *Travels* I. 184 It has been found that a *sleeping attorney* may be rendered very profitable. — **(2) 1856** KANE *Arctic Explor.* I. 196 We crawled into our reindeer sleeping bags. **1946** *Trail Riders* Oct. 10/2 I'm tired, I'm off to my sleeping bag and nightshirt. — **(3) 1839** *Mechanics' Mag.* 5 Jan. 240 The introduction of the newly-invented sleeping cars on our railroads. **1901** CHURCHILL *Crisis* 324 In Shreve's time the cabins were curtained off, just like these new-fangled sleeping-car berths. **1950** *Time* 27 March 24/2 In one year he spent more than one-third of his nights in sleeping cars. — **(4) 1874** KNIGHT 481/2 Car-seats . . . made reclining, for night travel, . . . are termed 'sleeping-chairs.'

(5) 1870 *Pathfinder Railway Guide* Oct. 1 Palatial *Drawing Room* and Sleeping Coaches. — **(6) 1827** *Harvard Reg.* Sep. 202 They have indulged in the luxury of 'sleeping over.' **1851** HALL *College Words* 284 *Sleeping over,* a phrase equivalent to being absent from prayers. **1871** BAGG *At Yale* 570 On Sunday mornings, too, there is an unusual amount of 'sleeping over,'—breakfast being often cut as well as chapel by the votaries of Morpheus. — **(7) 1807** SCHULTZ *Travels* II. 30 *Sleeping Sawyers* are the same as those just mentioned, except that their motion is entirely under water. **1819** SCHOOLCRAFT *Mo. Lead Mines* 224 When the tree does not reach within two or three feet of the surface of the water, they [the sawyers] are called *sleeping sawyers.* **1941** BALDWIN *Keelboat Age* 78 The most dangerous, the so-called sleeping sawyers, never broke surface but might come up unexpectedly and stave in the bottom of the boat as it passed over. — **(8) 1881** MARK TWAIN *Speeches* 258 (R.), I asked the young man in the ticket-office if I could have a sleeping-section. — **(9) 1860** W. H. COOK *Letters* (1946) 18 Nov. 67 Immediately after we left for Manchester in a Sleeping train their being no change of the Sleeping train from here to Manchester.

***sleepy,** *a.* In the names of plants and animals (see quots.).

1817–8 EATON *Botany* (1822) 459 *Silene antirrhina,* sleepy catchfly . . . Flowers small. **1891** *Cent.* 5691/2 *Sleepy duck,* the ruddy duck, *Erismatura rubida:* also called *sleepyhead, sleepy coot, sleepy brother.* (Atlantic coast, U.S.) *Ib.* 5951/1 *S[tipa] viridula,* var. *robusta,* of Mexico, New Mexico, etc., is reported to have a narcotic effect upon horses, and is called *sleepy-grass.* **1923** ADAMS *Pioneer Hist.* 615 Great tree black snakes, known as 'sleepy johns,' very harmless but frightful to meet, were often seen hanging by their tails from the limbs of trees.

***sleeve,** *n.* As the last term in **angel, balloon, bishop, shirt sleeve.**

***sleeve button.** (See quot.) *Slang.* — **1888** WHITMAN *Nov. Boughs* 71 In the slang of the New York common restaurant waiters . . . codfish balls [are known] as 'sleeve-buttons.'

sleigh sle, *n.* [Du. *slee* (<*slede*), in same sense.]

1. A vehicle on runners used on snow or ice.

[**1696** in MUNSELL *Ann. Albany* III. 18 It is resolved . . . to Present . . . Two good and sufficient horses, & a Slee.] **1703** SEWALL *Diary* II. 91 Corps is brought to Town in the Governours Slay. **1799** *Ann. 7th Congress* 2 Sess. 1429, I got into the sleigh, and went off. **1892** *S. Dak. Hist. Coll.* I. 60 Over this mail route, in February, 1871, came H. R. Vaughn, 'in an open one horse sleigh.' **1947** *N.Y. Times Mag.* 2 Feb. 18/4 We always had to hitch her to the ring on the wall while we got out the sleigh.

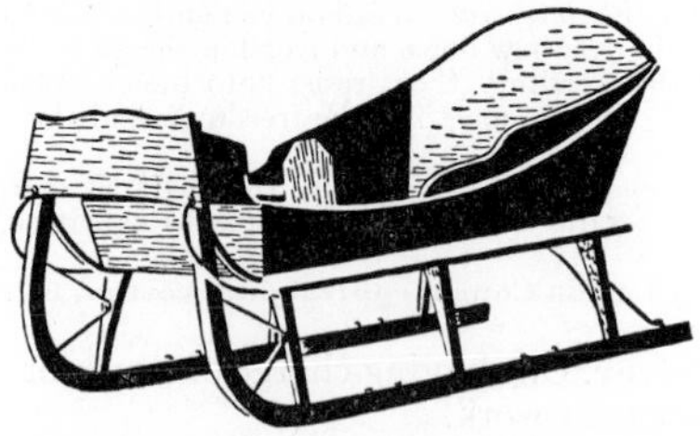

One type of sleigh (sense 1)

b. A small vehicle of this kind for a child, having a tongue by which it may be pulled.

1869 *Boyd's Business Directory* 58 Wheelbarrows and Childrens' Sleighs. Newell & Sperry, Jordan.

c. The bone of the upper jaw of a sperm whale.

1874 SCAMMON *Marine Mammals* 75 Next to and above the bone of the upper jaw (which is termed the 'coach' or 'sleigh').

2. In combs.: (1) **sleigh bed,** a name now applied to a type of bed made *c*1820–60 having solid headboards and footboards rolled outward at the top; (2) **bell,** one of the small bells, usu. of globular shape, attached to sleigh harness or to the sleigh itself; (3) **bottom,** the lower portion of a sleigh (see quot.); (4) **box,** the box or body of a sleigh; (5) **chaise,** ?a chaise on runners, *obs.;* (6) **dog,** a dog that pulls or helps to pull a sleigh; (7) **haul,** a way over which logs are hauled on sleighs; (8) **runner,** = * **runner 2;** (9) **shoe,** a protective covering of iron for the runner of a sleigh.

(1) 1934 WEBSTER. **1942** WEYGANDT *Plenty of Penna.* 222 In the sale of the old homestead in Middleburg there were . . . a field bed of curly maple, a sleigh bed in cherry. — **(2) 1772** *Boston Gaz.* 3 Feb. 3/2 About midnight I heard a noise at a distance, which I soon found to be sley-bells. **1885** CRAWFORD *Amer. Politician* 10 The sleigh bells tinkled unceasingly as the sleighs slipped by the window. **1945** PEARSON *Country Flavor* 108 Sleigh bells jingled; white clouds came back from the mare's nostrils. — **(3) 1842** *Lowell Offering* II. 61 But when the company is large, sleigh bottoms might be used [in the place of sleds]. These hold more and are equally as convenient to handle. — **(4) 1855** HOLBROOK *Among Mail Bags* 142 He drew from the sleigh-box . . . a revolver. *c***1873** DE VERE *MS Notes* 186 *Bobs,* short, stout sleds, 2 of which are gen[erally] placed under 1 sleighbox or wagon box.

(5) 1782 *Rec. N.H. Comm. Safety* 305 Ordered . . . To pay . . . for use of Sley Chaise. — **(6) 1806–8** PIKE *Sources Miss.* 72 My sleigh dogs brought me ahead of all by one o'clock. **1947** *Mich. Hist.* Sep. 319 Bango was not a good sleigh dog, at least in the woods. — **(7) 1902** WHITE *Blazed Trail* 258 The old-fashioned, picturesque ice-road sleigh haul will last as long as north-woods lumbering. — **(8) 1747** *Boston Gaz.* 22 Dec., A pair of handsome slay runners. **1949** *Sat. Ev. Post* 9 July 52/2 All at once, Uncle Pete pulled up the horses, and the squeal of sleigh runners stopped. — **(9) 1799** *Essex Inst. Coll.* LIV. 108, 3 [Tons] . . . Sleigh Shoes . . . 24 [dollars]. **1825** *Columbian Centinel* 5 Jan. 3/1 For sale by James Fullerton . . . Steel Sleigh

Shoes. **1845** J. W. NORRIS *Chi. Directory* 112 Stove Plates, Paint Mills, Sleigh Shoes of every description.

b. Also (1) **sleigh-drive, -driving,** (2) **frolic,** (3) **frolicker,** (4) **load,** (5) **man,** (6) **mark,** (7) **path,** (8) **ride,** (9) **rider,** (10) **riding,** (11) **robe,** (12) **stage,** (13) **track.**

(1) 1868 WHITTIER *Poetical Works* (1894) I. 273 Sleigh-drives on the mountain ways Defy the winter weather. **1886** EBBUTT *Emigrant Life* 221 The Mississippi River . . . was now frozen over, and was alive with people skating, sliding, and sleigh-driving on its broad surface. — **(2) 1772** *Boston Gaz.* 3 Feb. 3/2 Snow falling . . . brings to my mind a scene I was witness to about three weeks ago past; which I would recommend to the serious consideration of all lovers of sley-frolicks. — **(3) 1772** *Boston Gaz.* 3 Feb. 3/2 The ingenuity of some of those nocturnal Sley-frolickers, had added the Drum and Conk-shell, or Pope-horn, to their own natural, noisy, abilities. — **(4) 1767** HILTZHEIMER *Diary* (1893) 1 Jan. 12 Three sleigh-loads of us went to Darby to Joseph Rudolph's. **1802** *Mass. Spy* 24 March (Th.), A lad, seated on the fore part of a sleigh load of goods, was suddenly pitched off before one of the runners.

(5) 1758 R. EASTBURN *Narr. Captivity* 5 [He] reported, That our Slaymen were all taken by the Enemy. — **(6) 1855** *Knickerb.* XLV. 354 Already the sleigh-marks on the old snow were hidden. — **(7) 1758** *Mayflower Descendant* X. 187 We Have Constantly Kept a Good Slay Path out in One Plais. **1798** I. ALLEN *Hist. Vermont* 269 The changeable wether on the sea cost at Boston, &c. spoils the sleigh path. — **(8) 1770** HILTZHEIMER *Diary* (1893) 2 April 20 Took a sleigh ride, the 'five mile round,' with wife, sister, and son Tommy. **1947** *Steamboat* (Colo.) *Pilot* 2 Jan. 1/6 The Newcomers club will hold a sleigh ride Friday night. — **(9) 1833** *Knickerb.* I. 207 Arrived at the Plains, the sleigh riders stopped at a tavern. **1883** *Wheelman* I. 434, I was making my first trial of it [i.e., a bicycle] in the snow, among the sleigh-riders.

(10) 1931 *Randolph Enterprise* (Elkins, W.Va.) 1 Jan. 1/1 It [the snow] made good sleigh-riding all winter. — **(11) 1853** STRICKLAND *Twenty-seven Yrs.* I. 192 Sleigh-robes are commonly made of bear or buffalo skins dressed with the hair on. The most fashionable are racoon or wolf. Several of these skins are sewn together, with the tails of the animals stitched to the bottom of the robe. **1947** V. H. CAHALANE *Mammals* 73 Head-hunters slowly decimated these to sell their scalps to taxidermists, and the hides to tanners to make sleigh robes. — **(12) 1873** *Cin. Commercial* 6 March 2/2 Think of an all night's ride in a sleigh stage on the open prairie, with the thermometer 18° below zero. — **(13) 1854** TROWBRIDGE *M. Merrivale* 369 A good sleigh-track was already broken on the village road. **1876** J. BURROUGHS *Winter Sunshine* IV. 96 The fox . . . stepped with great care and precision into a sleigh-track.

c. sleigh-ride, *v. intr.*, to ride in a sleigh. Also transf.

1807 IRVING *Salmagundi* i. 8 He recollects perfectly the time when young ladies used to go sleigh-riding at night. **1845** JUDD *Margaret* III. 407 In winter, we sleigh-ride, coast, skate, snow-ball. **1869** MARK TWAIN *Innocents* 156 She would like well to sleigh-ride. **1949** *Summit Valley Times* (Argo, Ill.) 1 Dec. 4/3 Santa, who now reigns the Christmas card realm, in 1919 managed to sleighride onto only a handful of cards for children.

As the last term in **beer, bob, box, buggy, close, covered, double, Dutch, family, hack, hand, Indian, log, lumber, mail, omnibus, ox, pleasure, pod, semi-, stage, wood sleigh.**

sleigh sle, *v. intr.* and *tr.* [f. the noun.] (See quot. 1806.)

1728 SEWALL *Letter-Book* II. 264 They waited there for convenient snow to slay it to Salem. **1806** WEBSTER 281/1 *Sley*, to ride or convey in a sley. **1900** STOCKTON *Afield & Afloat* 249 She sometimes went sleighing. **1941** WILDER *Little Town on Prairie* 278 She was sure now that he would not ask her to go sleighing.

sleigher ˈsleɚ, *n.* One who rides in a sleigh. — **1861** *Harper's Mag.* Jan. 236/1 Away the merry sleighers bound, With jingling sound of bells.

sleighing ˈsle·ɪŋ, *n.*

1. Riding in a sleigh for pleasure; the condition of the snow or ice that permits this.

1764 J. ROWE *Diary* (1903) 71 Went with Mrs Rowe a Slaying. **1772** *Boston Gaz.* 3 Feb. 3/2 Another considerable Quantity of Snow falling, enough to give us the prospect of Sledding, and also Sleying (as it is called) again, brings to my mind a scene I was witness to about three weeks ago past. **1832** WILLIAMSON *Maine* I. 100 During the whole of it [January], in many years, the sleighing is poor. **1947** *N.Y. Times Mag.* 2 Feb. 18/3 Grandfather, with whom I did my sleighing, had a Morgan horse.

2. In combs.: (1) **sleighing party,** a number of people taking a sleigh ride together, the occasion of such an amusement; (2) **time,** a time suitable for sleighing.

(1) 1775 BURNABY *Travels* 88 In the winter, when there is snow upon the ground, it is usual to make what they call sleighing parties. **1807** IRVING *Salmagundi* ix, He remembers once to have been on a sleighing party with her. **1950** *Time* 27 March 116/3 The social committee of the Horse Cooperative Marketing Association, which cans horse meat, had to cancel a sleighing party because it could find no horses to pull the sleighs. — **(2) 1837** NEAL *Charcoal Sk.* (1838) 177 We whole-souled people always plant sich articles in sleighing-time. **1889** R. T. COOKE *Steadfast* xxv. 272 'Tain't none too often we get sight of anybody here in sleighin' time.

b. Also **sleighing frolic, match, ride, season, weather.**

1816 *Mass. Spy* 10 April (Th.), Either at a ball, party, sleighing match, or in a hack, the Spanish minister had signified something about the Floridas. **1818** FESSENDEN *Ladies Monitor* 73 She makes her beau, for ball or sleighing-ride, Her chief fan-flirter, and her shopping guide. **1832** *Boston Transcript* 23 Jan. 2/2 Twenty-nine captains of vessels and steam boats had a sleighing frolic at Albany one day last week. **1860** E. COWELL *Diary* 20 This being the first 'sleighing weather' this winter, . . . the Concert was constantly being interrupted by the sleigh bells. **1882** MCCABE *New York* 401 During the sleighing season runaways are of daily occurrence.

* **sleuth,** *n.* A detective.

1872 H. P. HALSEY in *Fireside Companion* (*title*), Old Sleuth the Detective (Pearson *Dime Novels* 192). **1901** O. HENRY *Cabbages & Kings* (1916) 59 Goodwin followed at increased speed, but without any of the artful tactics that are so dear to the heart of the sleuth. **1949** *Chi. D. News* 4 Aug. 1/7 These alone convinced him that a smart, big-time crew had been outsmarted by his sleuths.

sleuth sluθ, *v. tr.* To track a person.

1905 *Rev. of Reviews* Sep. 254/2 In the midst of the disputation enter Benton who has been sleuthed by the detectives. **1909** GUNTER *Prince Karl* 269 You sleuth her to Buffalo and I will get you a raise in salary.

Hence **sleuthing,** *n.* and *a.*

1900 G. ADE *More Fables* 193 He called himself a Reformer, and he did all his Sleuthing in the line of Duty. **1946** *Reader's Digest* Sep. 76/1 Izzy knew nothing of sleuthing procedure; he simply knocked on the door. **1948** *News-Palladium* (Benton Harbor, Mich.) 14 Aug. 5/1 A new course in scientific sleuthing will be offered at Michigan State College this fall.

***slew,** *n.*[1] and *v.*, see ***slough,** *n.* and *v.*

slew slu, *n.*[2] [Origin obscure. Irish *sluagh* in the same sense has been suggested. See *Amer. Sp.* Feb. 1947, 20.] A great many, a lot. Often *pl. Colloq.*

1840 THOMPSON *Green Mt. Boys* II. 268 He has cut out a road, and drawn up a whole slew of cannon clean to the top of Mount Defiance. **1897** ROBINSON *Uncle Lisha's Outing* 2, I've seen slews on 'em [ducks] on the ma'shes. **1945** *Chi. D. News* 13 Jan. 4/6 Only it seems they weren't, by and large. Seems slews of them were isolationists.

* **slew,** *v.* **1. slew-eyed,** squint-eyed. **2. slew-foot,** a foot that is turned out more than usual, often in names. Both *colloq.*

(1) 1807 IRVING *Salmagundi* iv, Vernon *slew-eyed*—people of Brunswick, of course, all squint. — **(2) 1896** (*title*), Slew Foot Pete. **1943** *Christian Sci. Mon.* (Mag. Sect.) 27 Feb. 12/5 'Slew-eyed' is here, but not 'slew-foot.' **1947** *Trail Riders Bul.* Feb. 20/2 Jest like Sluefoot sez, there's them there rattlers holed up for the wintuh, an' all friz stiff's a bride's first biscuits.

slewer ˈsluɚ, *n.* [Origin unknown.] A low, common person (see also quot. 1889). — **1848** W. T. THOMPSON *Major Jones's Sk. Travel* 107 They say here [in Phila.] that they [the servant girls] aint nothing but slewers—but I seed sum that I would tuck for respectable white galls if I had seed 'em in Georgia. **1889** BARRERE & LELAND 220/1 About fifty years ago in Philadelphia it was usual to speak of balls frequented by factory girls as 'slewers.'

* **slick,** *a.*, *n.*, and *adv.*

1. A member of a band of regulators in Jackson County, Alabama. Also attrib. or as adj. *Obs.*

1833 *Niles' Reg.* XLIV. 202/2 Several of the defendants . . . had admitted that they and others, as members of the association commonly called the 'slick company,' had made the arrest and given the lashes; but that they did so as a punishment, under the slick law, for the crime. . . . It was insisted further, that the slicks had done much good.

2. (See quot.) *Obs.*

1836 WESTON *Visit* 59 (*footnote*), ['Slick'] sometimes means 'insolence,' for they often say 'Give me no slick.'

3. An oily surface on the sea. Also **slick water.**

1849 D. WEBSTER *Private Corr.* III. 333 You have seen on the surface of the sea, those smooth places, which fishermen and sailors call 'slicks.' **1875** MARK TWAIN *Old Times Miss.* 289 (R.), The lines and circles in the slick water over yonder are a warning. **1906** *Scribner's Mag.* Sep. 314 So out they went, chasing slicks and occasionally striking a school of big fish.

transf. **1948** *Nat. Geog. Mag.* Aug. 213/1, I stood up . . . to see if the riffle had a 'slick,' an opening in the rocks where most of the water pours through in a smooth V pointed downstream. **1949** *Sat. Ev. Post* 14 May 102/4 Each of 'em's got a rubber bag full o' bright yeller, stain—marker dye, I think they call it. An' when a flier's forced down he releases it an' it makes a bright yeller slick, so's he can be spotted easy from the air an' mebbe picked up. See?

4. *W.* (See quots.) Also **slick ear.**

1890 *Stock Grower & Farmer* 12 July 6/3 Seven of them were branded, the remainder were 'slicks,' or horses which had run wild from birth. **1926** BRANCH *Cowboy* 52 They found in their herds 'slick ears,' as they called those yearlings that had been missed in the round-ups of the season before. **1934** LOMAX *Amer. Ballads* 411 No Maverick or slick will be tallied In that great book of life in His home. **1947** PRICE *Trails I Rode* 72 Any man not belonging to the big outfits that got a slick ear (a maverick) was branded in a lot of people's minds as a cattle rustler.

5. **=laurel slick.**

1934 WEBSTER. **1949** *Nature Mag.* Nov. 422/2 In North Carolina the rhododendron jungles go by the name of 'slicks.'

6. *a.* and *adv.* In colloq. or slang comparisons, as (1) *slick as (bear's) grease,* (2) *slick as molasses,* (3) *slick as a whistle.*

(1) **1811** *Mass. Spy* 20 March 4/1, I hop'd I should pass Slick as greese down the current of time. **1832** PAULDING *Westward Ho!* I. 119, I wish I may be utterly ornswoggled if he didn't tip it off as slick as bear's grease, anyhow. **1904** STRATTON-PORTER *Freckles* 256 She took us to be from McLean's gang, slick as grease. — (2) **1847** LOWELL *Biglow P.* 1 Ser. iv. 52 To the people they're ollers ez slick ez molasses. **1906** *Springfield W. Republican* 16 Aug. 1 Two years ago everything was made as slick as molasses for Lieut.-Gov. Roberts. — (3) **1830** S. SMITH *Life J. Downing* 36 He's lost it, slick as a whistle. **1855** *Pioneer* (S.F.) Oct. 2/7 My sweetheart has turned out untrue, and *socked* me as *slick as a whistle.*

b. Also in less frequent phrases (see quots.).

1830 *Indiana Palladium* (Lawrenceburgh) 31 July 4/1, I got here last week in the ben franklin, shes as slick as beeswax I tell you. **1832** *Polit. Examiner* (Shelbyville, Ky.) 8 Dec. 4/1 Deby is a monstrous nice gal, she's about as slick as an elephant's tush, mind I tell you. **1837** BIRD *Nick of Woods* I. 222 If I didn't fetch old dug-out through slicker than snakes. **1948** *Popular Western* June 99/1 It's all planned and carried out as slick as a buffalo calf's nose.

c. *slick and clean,* completely. *Colloq.*

1857 *Quinland* II. 119 You'll be slick and clean out of the muss. **1900** DRANNAN *Plains & Mts.* 583 That fire wiped me out slick and clean.

As the last term in **laurel slick.**

***slick,** *v.*

1. *tr.* To subject (a person) to vigilante justice, to lynch. *Obs.* Cf. **slick,** *n.* **1.**

1836 H. R. HOWARD *Hist. V. A. Stewart* 20 On the day they published that they would be there to slick him, he had eighteen friends who came to his assistance.

2. Used in colloq. phrases: (1) *To slick back* (or *down*), to make (the hair) lie smooth, also transf.; (2) *to slick off,* to polish off, make elegant; (3) *to slick up,* (*a*) to tidy up (a place), to make oneself clean and neat, (*b*) *passive,* of a person, to be cleaned up and made attractive or presentable, sometimes *to get slicked up,* cf. **slicking up.**

(1) **1839** C. A. DAVIS *Lett. J. Downing* 25 Every hair on it [was] slicked down with a dipped candle. **1878** STOWE *Poganuc People* 153 The minit that Dr. Cushing . . . got folks kind o' slicked down and peaceable, Zeph would git up and stroke 'em all back'ards. **1922** WILSON *Merton of Movies* 23 There was Merton in the natty belted coat, with his hair slicked back in the approved mode. — (2) **1846** LOWELL *Biglow P.* 1 Ser. i. 2 The parson kind o' slicked off sum o' the last varses. — (3) (*a*) **1828** *Richmond Enquirer* 22 Aug. 4/1 (Th.), She calls it 'slicking up the room.' **1867** *Atlantic Mo.* May 571/2 'Where's Kate?' 'Up stairs, a-slickin' up.' **1918** LINCOLN *Shavings* 79 Mother was always a great one for keeping things slicked up. **1948** *Family Circle* June 96/2 It's always serious when they slick up for a girl! . . . Especially when they use *slickum* on their hair. (*b*) **1831** S. SMITH *Life J. Downing* 134 My clothes had got so shabby, I thought I better hire out a few days and get slicked up a little. **1876** MARK TWAIN *Tom Sawyer* xxxiii. 263 Come down when you are slicked up enough.

slickens ˈslɪkɪnz, *n.* *W.* [App. f. **slick, n.,* finely powdered ore.] (See quots.)

1882 *Cent. Mag.* XXV. 337 It is the lighter soils of the hydraulic mines and the pulverized matter from the quartz-mills of the mining region which constitute 'slickens.' **1894** *N.Y. Tribune* 1 Feb. 1/3 Above 500 acres . . . will be covered with 'slickens,' washings from the mines in the mountains, and thus be rendered valueless. **1902** *Out West* July 19 A peculiar necessity arose here, and was met (after fierce fighting) by 'anti-slickens' legislation—merely law to keep the gold-hunter up-stream from water-shoveling his hills down upon the top of your farm. **1949** *Nat. Hist.* March 129/1 Their 'slickens' clogged the Sacramento, and the salmon run fell off along its upper tributaries.

transf. *a***1915** MUIR *Travels Alaska* (1917) 109 The meals . . . [included] a cup of muddy, semi-liquid coffee like that which the California miners call 'slickens.'

***slicker,** *n.*

1. A long, loose, oilskin waterproof coat.

1881 ROMSPERT *Western Echo* 181 Good or bad, they must take it, with no shelter but a gum-coat, called a *slicker.* **1923** MULFORD *Black Buttes* 250 Heavy drops of rain warned them to get into their slickers. **1949** *Sky Line Trail* March 19/2 Every hiker should be supplied with a slicker or raincoat—just in case.

b. **slicker roll,** a cowboy's roll wrapped in, or consisting of, his slicker.

1924 MULFORD *Rustlers' Valley* vi, Matt slipped the glass jar into his slicker roll.

2. A smooth, clever trickster or cheat. Also attrib. *Colloq.* Cf. **city slicker.**

1900 FLYNT *Notes Itinerant Policeman* 62 Pickpockets! . . . You just bring the slickers in. **1936** *Sat. Morn. Advt.* (Durant, Okla.) 14 March 1/3 (*heading*), 'Slicker' Insurance Agents Better Be A Bit Wary Now. **1950** *Dixie Roto Mag.* 21 May 15/1 Some slicker sold the boss on the idea of selling this wasted advertising space.

3. A silverfish or fish moth.

1902 L. O. HOWARD *Insect Bk.* 380 Order *Thysanura.* The insects of this order are usually of very small size. . . . They comprise the little insects known as springtails, bristletails, fishmoths or slickers.

4. (See quot.)

1948 DICK *Dixie Frontier* 234 In Missouri in the thirties occurred the 'Slicker War,' in which a large number of citizens known as 'Slickers' cleared out a nest of counterfeiters.

slickings ˈslɪkɪŋz, *n.* ?Slick-greens, i.e. the young leaves of a cabbage before it matures. *Obs.* — **1847** FIELD *Drama in Pokerville* 53 'A little of the roast, if you please.' . . . 'None of the stuffin'!' 'Some of the slickin's!'

slicking up. The action of cleaning up and making presentable. *Colloq.*

1843 CARLTON *New Purchase* I. 72 The caps . . . were worn expressly as the wives themselves said—'to save slicking up every day, and to hide dirt!' **1855** *Mich. Agric. Soc. Trans.* VI. 495 The farm needs a good deal of slicking up to make the general appearance equal to what nature has done for the land. **1907** *Springfield W. Republican* 9 May 1 Denver has been having her period of spring slicking up.

***slide,** *n.*

1. The mass of rock and earth dislodged by a landslide.

1841 WHITTIER *Poetical Works* (1894) 173/2 Loose rock and frozen slide, Hung on the mountain-side. **1874** RAYMOND *6th Rep. Mines* 296 The shaft passes 45 feet through 'slide,' and then 155 feet on the vein. **1910** *Country Life* Nov. 42 The tail end of a ten-mile slide, showing a mountain railroad choked with heaps of trees, telegraph poles, and debris.

2. An otter or beaver slide.

[**1770** CARTWRIGHT *Labrador Jrnl.* 50 Arriving at the head of Long Pool, I met with the sliding of an otter.] **1842** *Nat. Hist. N.Y., Zoology* I. 40 The steel trap is placed . . . at the bottom of one of their slides. **1884** MERRIAM *Mammals Adirondack Region* 89 The borders of the lakes and streams of the Adirondacks offer numerous examples of these slides. **1947** CAHALANE *Mammals N. Amer.* 198 In a few minutes the minor bumps are worn away and the wet bodies have made the slide as slick and smooth as any metal slide on a school playground.

3. (See quot. 1858.)

1858 SIMMONDS *Dict. Trade Products* 349/1 *Slide,* a place in a river for timber-logs or rafts to go down. **1880** *Lumberman's Gaz.* 7 Jan. 28 The government constructs 'slides' for the passage of timber around shoals or rapids where there are no canals.

4. (See quot.)

1879 *Harper's Mag.* Nov. 889/1 Some [corrals] have what are called 'slides,' or passages gradually narrowing until but one animal can pass, and he, as he cannot turn around, can be easily branded.

As the last term in **beaver, fish, hook, land, log, rock, shad, snow slide.**

***slider,** *n.* (See quots. 1884, 1910.) Also **slider terrapin.**

1883 *Science* I. 149/2 The heart of the 'slider' terrapin. **1884** GOODE *Fisheries* I. 155 The 'Red-bellied Terrapin' . . . is also known under the names 'Potter,' 'Red-fender,' and 'Slider.' **1910** HART *Vigilante Girl* 88 They have some mud-turtles there called 'sliders.' **1944** MORRIS *They Hop & Crawl* 157 The slider is at home in the quieter portions of streams and rivers.

***slim,** *n.* [Poss. f. or influenced by G. *schlimm.*] Of a person or his health: Not well. *Colloq.*

1815 HUMPHREYS *Yankey* 40, I guess I be [homesick]; . . . I feel pritty slim. **1858** *Salem* (Ill.) *Advocate* 1 Jan. 3/2 Will looks rather 'slim,' as if he had been putting in the holiday's fast. **1902** L. RICHARDS *Mrs. Tree* 167 Mother's slim, I tell ye.

slimer ˈslaɪmɚ, *n.* [f. **slime.*] A toadfish, *Opsanus tau.* — **1817** in *Amer. Mo. Mag.* II. 204 The fishermen . . . call it by the name of *Yellow-Kusk, Sand Codling, Slimer,* etc.

slime table. An apparatus as a platform or inclined table for the treatment of slime in mining. — **1883** RITCH *Illust. N. Mex.* 91 A slime table or 'buddle' . . . is for treating the dust or powdered ore. **1919** FAY *Glossary of Mining* 624/1.

***sling,** *n.* As the last term in **brandy, gin, hot, mint, Mother Hubbard, rum sling.** See also **ax, gun sling.**

sling slɪŋ, *v.*[1] *intr.* To take a sling, to drink alcoholic liquor. Also **slinging,** *n. Obs.*

1833 J. E. ALEXANDER *Transatlantic Sk.* II. 7 He used to sling considerable heavy. **1840** HALIBURTON *Clockmaker* 3 Ser. xi, I ordered a pint o' the best [toddy], and so we slinged. **1867** SMYTH *Sailor's Word-Book* 632 On the American coast . . . the custom of *slinging* prevails . . . extensively, even where intoxication is despised.

***sling,** *v.*[2]

1. *tr.* In various colloq. or slang uses, chiefly obs.: (1) To fling or toss (the foot) in dancing; (2) to handle (dishes or drinks), to mix; (3) in a card game, to play (one's cards); (4) to put on style, often with *on;* (5) to shoot (lead) from a firearm; (6) to tell a story.

(1) 1834 *Knickerb.* III. 34 When she dances she slings a nasty foot. **1879** *Cimarron News & Press* 20 Nov. 3/2 A tenderfoot can sling his heels higher at a baile than the average old timer. — **(2) 1872** *Newton Kansan* 28 Nov. 3/3 The way he'll sling the flowing bowl. **1889** H. O'REILLY *50 Yrs. on Trail* 7 As junior waiter . . . I could sling dishes around with the best of them. **1902** LORIMER *Lett. Merchant* 236 Hired a fancy mixer to sling together mild snorts . . . for the ladies. — **(3) 1873** *Winfield* (Kans.) *Courier* 15 Feb. 1/5 [Jo] slings his cards with an enviable dexterity. — **(4) 1875** *Scribner's Mo.* Nov. 142/1 You sling on too much style! **1878** BEADLE *Western Wilds* 184 [She] slung more style than a speckled show-horse.

(5) 1879 TOURGEE *Fool's Errand* 259 It's enough for you to have her sling a lump of cold lead through your carcass. — **(6) 1896** HARTE *Poetical Works* 183, I kin not sling a fairy tale of Jinnys fierce and wild. **1899** ——— *Mr. J. Hamlin's Med.* 173 He jest slung yarns about his doins' thar.

b. Also in slang phrases: (1) *To sling ink,* to write; (2) *to sling hash,* to serve as a waiter or waitress in a restaurant.

(1) *a***1867** BROWNE *Works* (1876) 322 You axe me, sir, to sling sum ink for your paper. **1873** BEADLE *Undevel. West* 142 All who could sling ink became correspondents. — **(2) 1889** *Gallup* (N.M.) *Gleaner* 27 March 3/2 A portion of the Mobile Minstrels of Albuquerque are slinging hash in Gallup and practicing for a long walk in the near future. **1906** O. HENRY *Four Million* 108 I'm going back there and ask her to marry me. I guess she won't want to sling hash any more when she sees the pile of dust I've got. **1947** MOTLEY *Knock on Any Door* 201 She slings hash on North Clark Street.

2. The verb stem used in combs.: (1) **sling-fist, foot,** boxing, fighting, foot racing, *rare;* (2) **shot,** (*a*) =

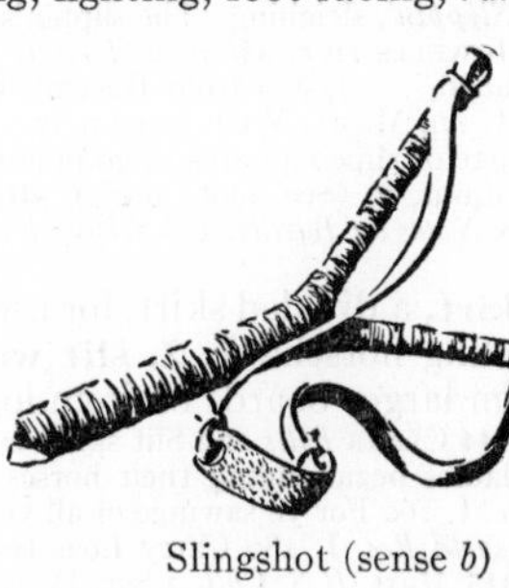

Slingshot (sense *b*)

***blackjack,** *n.* 3, (*b*) a contrivance for shooting pebbles, etc., consisting essentially of a forked stick to which rubber bands are fastened, also attrib.

(1) 1824 SINGLETON *Letters* 65 Accustomed from boyhood to athletic sports, in an infinite series, the Virginians are muscular and elastic in limb; and leaving draughts, whist, backgammon, and chess, for the evening; they are out at sling-fist, and sling-foot; or outjumping, or outrunning each other. — **(2)** (*a*) **1849** KINGSLEY *Diary* 77 Many are getting up sling-shots, . . . but I hope we shall never have occasion to use them. **1891** H. HERMAN *His Angel* 149 He made a ghastly horrible sling-shot by filling a heavy tumbler with the iron tops screwed off from the fire-irons, and tying the lot in a handkerchief. **1904** *N.Y. Ev. Post* 24 June 2 The guards are authorized to carry slingshots . . . heavily loaded with lead. (*b*) *Ib.* 3 Nov. 1 A keeper in Central Park charged the boy with shooting birds and squirrels in the park with a powerful slingshot. **1923** CATHER *Lost Lady* 16 They had behaved like wild creatures all morning;—cutting sling-shot crotches [etc.]. **1949** *Reader's Digest* Sep. 96 He was caught in the eighth row of a burlesque theater armed with a slingshot.

***sling-drinking,** *a.* Designating a person or persons habituated to drinking sling. *Slang. Obs.* — **1835** PAULDING *J. Bull & Bro. Jon.* (new ed.) 146 She denounced them for a tobacco-chewing, . . . sling-drinking set. **1838** UNCLE SAM in *Bentley's Misc.* IV. 586 A 'sling' drinking, bullying braggadocia from the 'old dominion'—(Virginia or Kentucky).

slinger ˈslɪŋɚ, *n.* One who drinks sling habitually. *Obs.* See also **gin, hash, ink slinger.** — **1807** JANSON *Stranger in Amer.* 299 There is a numerous set of people in the Southern States, called *slingers,* and another, styled *eleveners.*

***slink,** *n.* **1.** (See quot.) *Obs.* **2. slink weed,** (see quots.).

(1) 1883 ZEIGLER & GROSSCUP *Alleghanies* 157 What's a slink? A year-old deer. When past a year old, the male deer is called a spike-buck. — **(2) 1889** *Chambers's Encycl.* IV. 401/1 This species [*Epilobium angustifolium*] with several others is common in North America, where it is sometimes called . . . slink-weed, from a belief that it causes cows to 'slink' or miscarry. **1909** *Cent. Supp.* 1230/1 slinkweed. . . . The swamp loosestrife, *Decodon verticillatus.*—Red or Cardinal slinkweed, the cardinal-flower, *Rapuntium cardinale.*

***slip,** *n.*[1]

1. "An opening between wharves or in a dock" (W. '28); a ship's berth.

1796 *Gazette of U.S.* 6 Aug. (Th.), The abominable custom of filling up slips and docks with similar materials. **1868** *N.Y. Herald* 1 July 5/6 The Williamsburg ferry was attempting to enter the slip. **1909** *Sunset* Jan. 88/1 'Move forward, please—boat's in the slip,' came the raucous voice of a deckhand. **1946** *Christian Sci. Mon.* 20 July (Mag. Sect.) 9 Curve of the 'El' in Its Heyday Makes a Frame for Photograph of Manhattan's Financial District From Coenties Slip.

2. A mountain pass.

1788 CUTLER in *Life & Corr.* I. 427 Came through Dunning's Slip, where the river divides Dunning Mountains, and in a short distance passed through another Slip. **1858** in *Amer. Sp.* XV. 393/2 Beginning on 2 beeches, dogwood and maple in a slip in the mountain above the forks of sd branch.

3. *Bookbinding.* (See quots.)

1876 KNIGHT 2211/2 *Slip,* . . . the end of the twine to which the sheets are sewed, serving to attach the book to the boards. **1894** *Amer. Dict. Printing* 511 *Slip,* a cord used in fastening the back of a book.

4. *pl.* Bedroom slippers. *Colloq.*

1893 HOLLEY *Samantha at World's Fair* 155, I took my old slips, that had been my faithful companions for over two years. **1898** WESTCOTT *D. Harum* xviii, There's a pair of bedroom slips lined with lambs' wool.

5. In combs.: (1) **slip bars,** =**slip gap;** (2) **cleat,** a movable cleat, *rare;* (3) **gap,** (see quot. 1859); (4) **rail,** =prec., *obs.*

(1) 1681 *Southampton Rec.* II. 88 The said Iohn Woodruff is to keep a pair of slip bars for a highway. **1719** *Southold Rec.* II. 485 Gates or convenient slip bares may be set up upon the before mentioned open ways. — **(2) 1873** BEADLE *Undevel. West* 41 Many plant trees for posts, using 'slip cleats,' that the wires may be moved every year or two on the growing tree. — **(3) 1859** BARTLETT 167 A *Slip gap* is a place provided in a fence, where the bars may be slipped aside and let down. **1945** BOTKIN *My Burden* 54 He'd beat her out there, put her head between the slip gap where they let the hogs into the pasture. — **(4) 1725** *Huntington Rec.* II. 356 Benjamine Scudder shall have Liberty to Run his fence into the water or harbour . . . on condition the sd. Benjamin scuddar his heirs and assigns shall and do keep a good pair of slip Rails Convenient for the passing and Repassing of teams and carts.

As the last term in **Albany, call, canary, clay, cow, deposit, facing, ferry, policy, trip, yellow slip.**

***slip,** *n.*[2]

1. A shoot or sprout from a sweet potato or a piece of a potato vine used in planting. Cf. **potato slip,** and see **eye slip.**

1798 HAWKINS *Letters* 323 Planted potato slips. Planted red pepper. **1862** E. W. PEARSON *Lett. Port Royal* 105 Sweet potatoes, planted with slips in July. **1927** EUBANK *Horse & Buggy Days* 10 Father planted cabbage plants and sweet potato slips.

b. A sweet potato developed from such a slip (see quot. 1850).

1848 in COMMONS *Doc. Hist.* I. 199 November: . . . 15, 16, 17, 20, 21, digging slips. **1850** BURKE *Reminisc. Georgia* 126 The sweet potato . . . is of two kinds, called yams and slips. The yams are raised by planting the root in the spring as our farmers do the Irish potato, then when the tops of these are about six inches high, slips are cut from them and planted on another piece of ground. . . . The potato obtained in this way is called the slip, and is long and slender in form while the yam is short and thick. **1864** in EASTERBY *S.C. Rice Plant.* (1945) 312, I have comence Diging my slips at ganderlos on monday.

2. Chiefly *N. Eng.* "A long seat or narrow pew in churches" (W. '28).

"When there is a door, they are called pews; when without doors and free to all, slips. This, I believe, is the difference between them" (B. '48).

1823 *East-Hampton Rec.* IV. 426 That four slips be hired out . . . and the money for which they are hired, be applied towards painting the meeting house. **1853** STOWE *Key* 22/1 A beautiful quadroon girl . . . sat in one of the slips of the church. **1906** CHURCHILL *Coniston* 15 Jethro Bass . . . sat in the rear slip.

3. In combs.: (1) **slip crop,** a crop of sweet potatoes grown from slips; (2) **field,** a field for potato slips; (3) **potato,** a sweet potato grown from a slip; (4) **runner,** in policy gambling, a person who carries slips of paper with the winning numbers to the stations where the bets were made; (5) **ticket,** (see quot.).

(1) **1865** TURNER *Cotton* 133 As soon as the vines are sufficiently grown, say on the first of June, they commence planting the 'slip crop.' This is done by taking the vines from the seed beds, and laying along the top of other beds, and covering a part of the vines with dirt, when they immediately take root, and grow a better crop than from the seed. — (2) **1848** in COMMONS *Doc. Hist.* I. 197 Feb. . . . 12, making slip field fence. — (3) **1862** E. W. PEARSON *Lett. Port Royal* 72 They will probably be set to planting slip-potatoes. *Ib.* 111 The slip-potato crop is the only crop by which to judge of the negroes' capacity to take care of themselves. **1865** *Nation* I. 747/1 It was just time then to dig the slip potatoes. — (4) **1901** HARRIGAN *Mulligans* 65 The waiting policy players added to the hub-bub by their mutterings of discontent at the tardiness of the slip-runner.

(5) **1888** BRYCE *Amer. Commonw.* II. III. lxvi. 493 A slip ticket is a list, printed on a long strip of paper, of the persons . . . recommended by the same party or political group for the posts to be filled up at any election.

* **slip,** *v.*

1. *tr.* To provide (a church) with slips. *Rare.*

1837 in CHIPMAN *Hist. Harwinton* 82 Voted to Slip the meeting house.

2. In a post office, to provide (a bundle of letters, etc.) with a direction slip.

1887 *Postal Laws* 361 Letter and circular mail must always be properly 'faced up,' slipped, and tied in packages.

3. To deliver, hand, or give. *Colloq.*

1926 J. BLACK *You Can't Win* vi. 69 A woman had just slipped me a dime an' was standin' in the front door.

4. *intr.* To lose grip of things, to decline in proficiency.

1930 *Publishers' Wkly.* 22 Feb. 933/2, I must be slipping for I turned in a measly 78 on No. 4 in the Lenz-Rendel book.

5. slip-shuck, in harvesting, to jerk or snap (an ear of corn) from the stalk so as to leave most of the husk on the stalk. Usu. **slip-shucked,** *a.*, denoting ear corn from which most of the shuck has been removed.

1850 *Rep. Comm. Patents 1849: Agric.* 155 A barrel of corn must be closely slip-shucked to average . . . a bushel of shelled corn. **1905** PRINGLE *Rice Planter* 228 The corn . . . has done very well—814 bushels of slip-shuck corn on seven acres. **1924** RAINE *Land of Saddle-Bags* 29 At 'gathering time,' he hangs sacks of slip-shucked corn [from pulleys] and lets them slide down by gravitation. **1944** *Democrat* 13 April 4/4, 1,000 bushels good slip-shucked ear corn.

Also **slip-shucking,** *n.*

1938 *Amer. Sp.* Oct. 237 *Slip-shucking* should be added to the list of corn-husking terms. . . . It is an expression frequently used by older farmers in Iowa, and it means to partly break and partly snap the ears of corn.

6. In phrases: (1) *To slip up,* (*a*) to make a mistake or to fail, (*b*) to abscond; (2) *to slip a cog,* (see quot. 1909).

(1) (*a*) **1854** *Jrnl. of Discourses* II. 67/2 Some men think the way they are going to be saviors is to get as many wives as they can, and save them; now, they may slip up on that. **1866** *Wkly. New Mexican* 14 July 2/1 The knowledge that he has 'slipped up' and been exposed is more than sufficient punishment for the offense. **1923** DUTTON *Shadow on Glass* 247 All of us slipped up. (*b*) *a***1855** J. F. KELLY *Humors* 263 Dr. P. St. C. Smith 'slipped up' one day, leaving the well done community of Boston and the environs, for fields more congenial to his peculiar talents. — (2) **1909** *Cent. Supp.* 270/1 To slip a cog, to make a single unsuspected mistake in one's work or calculations. **1931** *K.C. Star* 17 Nov. 24 Someone slipped a cog in Concordia on Armistice day when no one remembered to put out the flags.

***slipe,** *n.* "A distance" (B. '48). *Obs.* — **1835** CROCKETT *Tour* 145 Well, I've got a long slipe off from my steamboat. **1843** *Missouri Reporter* 19 May (Th.), They do not begin to be the party, 'by a long slipe.'

* **slipper,** *n.* **1. slipper-down,** (see quot.). *Obs.* **2. slipper-noose,** a noose with a slipknot. Cf. **slippy-noose.**

(1) **1848** BARTLETT 310 Slipper-Down. A vulgar name in some parts of Connecticut for hasty pudding. The etymology is obvious. — (2) **1857** *Quinland* II. 43 The students had fastened up a number of small cords, by means of a 'slipper-neuse,' in which they suspended their books. **1875** BURROUGHS *Winter Sunshine* 162 [The rabbit] will put his head through the boy's slipper-noose.

As the last term in **Cinderella, Congress, Indian, lady's, secession slipper.**

slippery elm.

1. One of the red elms, *Ulmus fulva*, having a slippery inner bark.

1748 DRAKE *Pioneer Life Ky.* 73 Of the whole forest the red or slippery elm was the best. **1836** *Knickerb.* VIII. 73 Beware of a person . . . [vending] barks of prickly ash and slippery-elm. **1905** *Forestry Bureau Bul.* No. 66, 37 The slippery elm . . . is a smaller tree than the white elm.

attrib. **1882** PECK *Sunshine* 293 Canned peaches, that swim around in a pint of slippery elm juice in a tin can. **1889** COOKE *Steadfast* 118 [You] keep a wettin' his lips with that slipp'ry ellum tea in the mug. **1948** *Atlantic Mo.* Nov 69/1 These Sassafras leaves, when chewed, at once set up a mucilaginous slime in the mouth, like that of Slippery Elm twigs, which country children love to taste.

b. Short for next.

1882 C. B. LEWIS *Lime-Kiln Club* 112 He was . . . handed a piece of slippery elm to keep his throat moist during his oration. **1899** A. BROWN *Tiverton Tales* 69 'Slippery elm left by my dear father from his last illness,' she read. **1949** *Time* 21 March 56/3 For another duel he had an open wound in his left arm; doctors wanted to amputate, but he refused and trusted in a poultice of slippery elm.

c. slippery-elm bark, the mucilaginous inner bark of the slippery elm.

1780 in *Travels Amer. Col.* 640 Bear fat is preserved sweet and pure by putting in a bunch of the Slippery Elem bark into it when rendering. **1846** THORPE *Myst. Backwoods* 76 A little pounded slippery-elm bark is used to caulk the seams [of the canoe]. **1946** RICHTER *Fields* 4 She put her basket on the counter, lifting out bunches of dried sang and slippery elm bark.

2. The flannelbush, *Fremontia californica*, of the Pacific Coast.

1884 SARGENT *Rep. Forests* 26 Slippery Elm. . . . The mucilaginous inner bark used locally in poultices. **1897** SUDWORTH *Arborescent Flora* 272.

* **slipping,** *a.* and *n.* **1.** (See quot. 1895.) **2. slipping bars,** = **slip gap.** *Obs.*

(1) **1895** *D.N.* I. 394 *Slippin'*, sleighing. 'The slippin's pretty good.' Gardner, Mass. **1896** HOWELLS *Impressions & Exp.* 9 The 'slippin',' as the sleighing was called, . . . lasted from December to April. — (2) **1667** *Southold Rec.* I. 229 Master Wells [was] to leav a convenient cart way . . . with a gatte or slipeing bares to go in and out at.

slippy-noose ˈslɪpɪˌnus, *n.* (See quot. and cf. **slipper-noose.**) *Obs.* — *c*1870 CHIPMAN *Notes on Bartlett* 416 *Slippy-noose*, a running knot.—New England.

* **slit,** *a.* **1. slit skirt,** a divided skirt, for use by women when cycling or riding horseback. **2. slit work,** *collect.* thin boards cut from larger boards or from logs. *Obs.*

(1) **1934** WEBSTER. **1944** CLARK *Pills* 202 Slit skirts came into style with the bicycle and ladies began riding their horses like men. — (2) **1636** *Springfield Rec.* I. 160 For ye sawinge of all ye boards & slit worke [etc.]. **1713** *Topsfield Rec.* I. 180 Carry Logs to Saw-Mills to make . . . Slit work. **1815** *Mass. H.S. Coll.* 2 Ser. IV. 55, 70,000 feet of boards, plank and slitwork were cut at the saw mill in the same year.

* **sliver,** *n.* **1.** A slice taken from the side of a small fish for use as bait. **2.** (See quot.) Also attrib.

(1) **1869** *Maine Acts & Resolves* 24 Any person who shall cast or deposit . . . any pumice, scraps or other offal arising from the making of oil or slivers for bait . . . shall pay a fine. **1880** GOODE *Amer. Fisheries: Menhaden* 142 Fresh 'slivers' are preferred to those which have been salted. *Ib.* 147 The slivers (pronounced *slyvers*) are salted

and packed in barrels. — (2) **1883** *Nat. Museum Bul.* No. 27, 336 *Sliver spade*, . . . a kind of spade used when cutting off the head of a whale for severing the connecting pieces of flesh, which are technically termed 'slivers.'

∗**sliver,** *v. To let sliver,* to let slip or fly. *Rare.* — **1847** Robb *Squatter Life* 111 As soon as I clapped peeper on him I let sliver.

slivering ˈslɪvərɪŋ, *n.* The action of cutting a sliver from a fish. Also attrib. — **1877** Jewett *Deephaven* 104 We soon found what 'slivering' meant. **1880** Goode *Amer. Fisheries: Menhaden* 147 The knife used is of a peculiar shape and is called a 'slivering knife.'

slobberhannes ˈslɑbɚˌhanɪs, *n.* [Origin unknown.] "A game of cards for four persons, played with a euchre-pack" (*Cent.*); also a point scored in this game. — **1880** Dick *Amer. Hoyle* (ed. 13) 258 Slobberhannes . . . is an amusing game. *Ib.* 259 If a player scores *all* of the three foregoing points, he receives one point extra, which is called 'Slobberhannes.'

slobgollion, *n.* See **slumgullion 2.**

slooper ˈslupɚ, *n.* ?Error for **whooper.** *Rare.* — **1835** J. Martin *Descr. Virginia* 484 There are two kinds [of swans], so called from their respective notes—the one the trumpeter, and the other the slooper.

slooping ˈslupɪŋ, *n.* The transporting or forwarding of goods in sloops. *Rare.* — **1854** *Budget* (Troy, N.Y.) 2 Aug. (Ernst), He prosecuted the mercantile business in connection with slooping.

∗ **slop,** *n.* In combs.: (1) **slop bowl,** a bowl or basin for slops, esp. a receptacle for the dregs from teacups or coffee cups at the table; (2) **jar,** a covered basin for toilet slops (see also quot. 1949).

(1) **1810** *Columbian Centinel* 25 Aug. 4/2 For sale at Davis & Brown's Silver Ware and Jewellry Store . . . Sugar Basons, . . . Slop-Bowls. **1884** *Harper's Mag.* Jan. 233/2 They presented him with a service of silver-ware richly chased and engraved . . . tea-pot, sugar-bowl, cream-cup, and slop-bowl. **1929** Shelton *Salt-box House* xxvi. 221 Slop-bowls, tea-caddy and cake plates, all decorated with a border of gold stars. — (2) **1857** T. B. Gunn *N.Y. Boarding-Houses* 42 There are also dainty little bits of crochet-work under the soap dish, and tumblers, and a big china slop-jar. **1903** Wiggin *Rebecca* iii. 37 I've tacked up two thick towels back of her washstand, and put a mat under her slop-jar. **1949** *Amer. Sp.* April 113/1 Slop Jar, *n.* Garbage pail. [Edgefield Co., S.C]

∗ **slop,** *v.*

1. *tr.* To feed (a cow or pig) with slop or swill.

1848 Drake *Pioneer Life Ky.* 92 To slop the cows . . . was another [labor]. **1923** Watts *L. Nichols* 23 You got time t' slop them pigs I guess. **1947** *Time* 27 Jan. 21/2 Did you ever slop a hawg?

2. *To slop over, fig.* to do or say more than is wise, through an excess of sentiment, zeal, etc. *Slang.*

1861 Browne *Works* (1876) 117 The prevailin weakness of most public men is to slop over! **1872** *Cong. Globe* 23 Jan. 524/2 Amnesty . . . is magnanimity slopping over. **1902** Phillips *Woman Ventures* 103 She felt that she had told the facts, and that she had avoided 'slopping over.'

Hence **slopover,** an instance of going to excess in or about something. *Slang.*

1908 Gale *Friendship Village* 275, I see 'em all sprinkled along comin' from the funeral—neighbours an' friends an' just folks—an' most of 'em livin' in Friendship peaceful an'—barrin' slopovers—doin' the level best they could.

∗ **slope,** *n.*

1. A sloping or slanting cut made in the ear of a domestic animal to denote ownership.

1662 *East-Hampton Rec.* I. 193 Joseph ffoster marked a horse coult of his owne haveinge . . . a crop on the nere eare and a slope on the hinderpart of the same. **1751** *Portsmouth Rec.* 328 The Ear mark is two Slopes one on each Ear taken out behind the hinder part. **1859** in *Harper's Mag.* XX. 569/1 One stear a stag . . . [with] a slop on the under side of each yeare and the end of the rite yeare.

2. An artificial descent in a stream to facilitate navigation. *Obs.*

1790 *Ky. Petitions* 145 Mills was suffered to be built . . . with ither good locks or slopes sufficient for boats to pass by the dams with safety. **1815–6** *Niles' Reg.* IX. Supp. 165/2 Throw away all your notions of ford-ways, slopes and notches.

3. A continental area that slopes in one general direction, the Pacific or Rocky Mountain slope. Also attrib.

1870 D. R. Keim *Sheridan's Troopers* 140 The fact of old Joe having known the General 'on the slope.' **1932** *D.N.* VI. 233 Slope. The word is used in the West as elsewhere, and possibly somewhat more. The broken country in Eastern Wyoming and Montana was called The Slope Country. **1945** *Dly. Sentinel* (Grand Junction, Colo.) 25 Nov. 14/6 Four Slope Soldiers Due to Arrive in U.S.

Hence **sloper,** one who lives on a slope. Cf. **Pacific sloper.**

1894 *Nation* 12 July LIX. 20/2 We can see no way to improve the education of the Slopers but to leave them in the hands of their pets and favorites.

As the last term in **Atlantic, back, Eastern, over, Pacific slope.**

∗ **slope,** *v.*[1] *tr.* To mark (a domestic animal) with a sloping cut in the ear. *Obs.*

1666 *East-Hampton Rec.* I. 250 One sorrell horse coult . . . slopte on both sides of the right eare. **1705** *Portsmouth Rec.* 273 [A piece] Slopt of from the hinder part of the Said Crop. **1809** *Ib.* 371 The Ear mark of the Creatures of Elizabeth Brightman . . . is a Crop on the right ear, and a piece Slopt of from the hinder part of the said Crop.

slope slop, *v.*[2] [See note.]

This term is regarded in *OED* and *DAE* as of American origin, but it prob. is not. Cf. *EDD loup* (also *lope*) *v.* 7, "To run . . . to run off, escape," and *louper*, "One who flees the country, a vagabond."

intr. To depart, decamp, make off, go. *Slang.*

1830 *Palladium of Brit. N. Amer.* (Toronto) 29 Aug. 224/1 Bad climate indeed, wonder people dont all *slope.* **1839** *Columbian Reg.* (New Haven, Conn.) 26 Feb. 4/2 The collector of Taxes in the town of Livingstone . . . has *sloped* with $2060 of the people's money. **1845** *St. Louis Reveille* 2 Feb. 1/6 He couldn't 'come' the gingerbread, so decided it best to *slope.* **1949** *10 Story Western* May 48/2 He sloped into town that afternoon, a medium-built man with over-sized shoulders.

Hence **sloping,** *n.*

1839 *N.O. Picayune* 12 April 2/3 More Sloping.—One Abraham Charles, of Tazewell county, Missouri, advertises that 'David St. Clair, late a Universal preacher, has run away with my wife Jemima.' **1839** Marryat *Diary* II. 232 Here are two real American words:—'Sloping'—for slinking away; 'Splunging,' like a porpoise.

b. (See quot. 1859.) *Obs.*

1851 *Harper's Mag.* Jan. 188/2 And a shout wafted into the room—'Sloped for Texas!' **1853** *Ib.* VII. 310/1 If he had not 'sloped to Texas,' he had at all events migrated to parts unknown. **1859** Elwyn *Glossary* 104 Slope. This word has become quite common within a short time, but seems confined in its application to the movements of persons of doubtful character. A man formerly ran away; he now 'slopes for Texas.' . . . The word was heard, I believe, first when Texas became the American Alsatia; as, he sloped for Texas, was always understood of one who had cheated his creditors, plundered a bank, or robbed his employers.

∗ **slosh,** *v.*

1. *intr.* To travel about, walk *around*, loaf *about* (see also quot. 1854). *Colloq.*

1854 *Harper's Mag.* IX. 701/2 Saltonstall made it his business to walk backward and forward through the crowd, with a big stick in his hand, and knock down every loose man in the crowd as fast as he come to 'em! That's what I call 'sloshing about'! **1876** Mark Twain *Tom Sawyer* vi. 67 Devils don't slosh around much of a Sunday. **1908** McGaffey *Show-Girl* 58, I sloshed around town for a couple of days.

b. To flounder *around* in talking.

1880 *Harper's Mag.* Sep. 648/1 The Court . . . let him slosh around for a minute.

2. *fig.* To throw or toss (something) *in* or *on* in a hit-or-miss fashion. *Colloq.*

1875 *Chi. Tribune* 3 Sep. 2/5 The Ring-paid scribblers and papers will slosh on the usual amount of whitewash. **1902** *Emporia Gaz.* 29 July, It pours over it the same oleaginous language that it once sloshed on Governor Roosevelt of New York. **1929** W. Heyliger *Builder of Dam* 107 Flowers and Golding . . . poured sand and gravel on top of the cement. Harry Olds sloshed in water. **1945** *Everybody's Digest* Aug. 86 He sloshed on his sombrero and went outta there, heatin' his axles.

∗ **slough,** *n.* Also †**slow,** †**slew,** †**sloo,** †**slue.**

1. A comparatively narrow stretch of backwater; a sluggish channel or inlet, a pond.

1665 *Springfield Rec.* II. 216 There is grannted to Inhabitants of Skeepmuck a highway from ye Slow beyond the Swan pond. **1714** *Charlestown Land Rec.* 217 The said Hunewell hath incroached & inclosed of the high way against his Orchard: between his old house & the Slough or Small Bridge. **1845** N. F. Moore *Diary* (1946) 22 We entered the slough (pronounced here sloo) which brought us out into the Mississippi. **1950** *Chi. Tribune* 10 Jan. 18/3 At 11:57 a.m. on New Year's day, I saw my first robin, near Katydid slough at Willow Springs.

2. In combs.: (1) **slough bass,** (see quot. 1888); (2) **grass,** any one of various tall, stout grasses suited to low, wet lands (see quots.); (3) **hay,** hay made of slough grass; (4) **shooting,** shooting (birds, etc.) in a low, wet region.

(1) **1881** J. A. Henshall *Bk. Black Bass* 142 Slough bass. **1888** *Wildwood's Mag.* (Chi.) June 64 In the north and west both species

are known as 'bass,' with the addition of various adjectives expressive of gameness, coloration, or habitat, as 'tiger-bass,' . . . Yellow-bass; . . . moss, slough, or marsh-bass. — (2) **1860** *Ill. Agric. Soc. Trans.* IV. 488 Then [I] make a band of whatever material I have at hand, (slough grass is preferable). **1880** BESSEY *Botany* 355 *Muhlenbergia glomerata* and *M. Mexicana* constitute the 'Fine Slough Grass' of the Mississippi valley prairies. **1948** *Annals Iowa* July 380 On top of the banked-roof was a layer of loose 'slough grass,' to keep out the rain. — (3) **1871** *Ill. Agric. Soc. Trans.* VIII. 172 The entire bed should be covered with coarse prairie or slough hay. — (4) **1894** *Harper's Mag.* Aug. 457/1 If slough-shooting has a drawback, it is its lack of action.

b. Also **slough bridge, pig, soil, water.**

1874 LONG *Wild-Fowl* 150 Lager-beer . . . is much better to drink than slough-water. **1883** SMITH *Geol. Survey Ala.* 269 *Black prairie slough soil*, eight miles south of Montgomery. *Ib.* 272 The bottom soils . . . [vary] from the stiff black prairie slough lands . . . to light and rather sandy loams. **1905** *Forestry Bureau. Bul.* No. 61, 48 *Slough pig*, usually a second-rate river driver who is assigned to picking logs out of sloughs in advance of the rear. (N[orthern] F[orest].) **1945** BOTKIN *My Burden* 20 They pass the Ku Kluxes right on the slough bridge.

As the last term in **hay, mud, running, saw-grass slough.**

slough slu, *v.* [f. *∗***slough,** *n.* **1.**]

1. *tr.* To mire in a slough, swamp, etc. Usu. passive.

1846 FARNHAM *Prairie Land* 49 It was right good luck . . . that we didn't get *slued* afore we got to town. **1862** STANLEY in Baillie & Bolitho *Victorian Dean* 105 '*Slewed*,' in the extreme west [of the U.S.] is 'sloughed,' 'lost in a swamp.' **1867** *Atlantic Mo.* March 329/1 Many a farmer in those times has seen his load hopelessly 'slewed' within what is now Chicago. **1950** *Chi. D. News* 16 Feb. 8/7 An old man who allows his subordinates to slough a battlewagon on the mud in Hampton Roads has not earned his retroactive pay.

2. *To slough in* (or *up*), to arrest, imprison. *Slang.*

1901 FLYNT *World of Graft* 93 The crooked municipal co- per . . . kep' me from gettin' sloughed up. **1907** LONDON *Road* 162 The constables are . . . sloughin' in everybody in sight.

*∗***slow,** *a.* In colloq. and obs. combs.: (1) **slow bear,** (2) **brand,** (3) **elk,** (4) **garter,** (5) **lizard,** (6) **push powder,** (see quots.).

(1) **1869** *Overland Mo.* III. 129 A hog clandestinely killed outside of camp and smuggled in under cover of darkness, was called a 'slow bear.' . . . 'Mud-lark' signified the same thing. — (2) **1929** DOBIE *Vaquero* 121 The law further required that every brand should be recorded in the county of its origin. A man who had blotted out a brand and put another in its place was naturally chary of putting this new brand on record. He simply ran it, trusting to get the cattle out of the country at the first opportunity. Such an unrecorded brand was called a 'slow brand.' — (3) **1910** W. M. RAINE *B. O'Connor* 209. **1944** ADAMS *W. Words* 147/1 slow elk To kill for food an animal belonging to someone else (as verb); beef butchered without the owner's knowledge (as noun). — (4) **1842** *Nat. Hist. N.Y., Zoology* III. 45 The Striped Snake, *Tropidonotus tænia*, . . . is known under various popular names, such as Green Garter-snake, Slow Garter [etc.]. (5) **1778** CARVER *Travels* 489 The *Slow Lizard* is of the same shape as the Swift, but its colour is brown. — (6) **1909** GEO. B. ELY *Pioneer Days* 267 Then the powder we used was all home-made. . . . [It] was not reliable, and our boys called it 'slow-push' powder.

slows sloz, *n. pl.* (See quot.) — **1851** DUNGLISON *Med. Lexicon* (ed. 11) 564/1 *Milk Sickness, Sick stomach*, swamp sickness, Tires, Slows. . . . A disease occasionally observed in . . . Alabama, Indiana, and Kentucky, which affects both man and cattle, but chiefly the latter.

*∗***slug,** *n.*

1. A heavy piece or lump of crude metal, a gold nugget.

1849 *N.O. Picayune* 6 June 1/6 The gold from that stream is generally in large pieces, more generally termed slugs or coarse, but very fine gold, if you please. **1855** *Golden Era* (S.F.) 21 Jan. 2/7 We took out one slug weighing 60 ounces of pure gold, in the shape of an ox's tongue. **1890** *Electrical Rev.* 19 April 2/4 'That is platinum, and it is worth about $150.' It was an insignificant looking slug.

b. Any one of various large gold coins of irregular shape privately issued in California *c*1850. Now *hist.* Cf. **dobie,** *n.* **2. b.**

1851 *Ore. Statesman* 23 Sep. 2/6 He accordingly 'pungled down' two of Moffat's $50 slugs, and of course, cut the black, there being no red spots in the pack. **1872** POWERS *Afoot & Alone* 303 A shining 'slug,' fresh from the San Francisco mint, [was] laid scrupulously in the place. **1907** *N.Y. Ev. Post* (s.-w. ed.) 5 Sep. 6 A rare relic in the form of an oblong 'slug,' such as passed current in the very early days of California for $50. **1948** *Ore. Hist. Mag.* March 35 A fifty dollar slug, either round or with corners, should have been an imposing pocket piece.

2. A thick lump of bacon. *Colloq.*

1868 *Ill. Agric. Soc. Trans.* VII. 222 Our remedy is to drench them with lard or slugs of fat bacon.

3. *Printing.* (See quots.) Cf. *∗***slug,** *v.* **3.**

1871 RINGWALT *Amer. Encycl. Printing* 416/2 In daily-newspaper offices another species of slug, cast, with the various letters of the alphabet on the top, are used to distinguish the matter set up by the different compositors, and the latter are frequently designated . . . as slug A, slug B, etc. **1893** PHILIPS *Making of Newspaper* 103 'Slug 14' received his 'take' of copy at 2:35 A.M. **1924** *Publishers' Wkly.* CVI. 190/2 *Slugs*, pieces of lead, about 3/4 inch high, and usually 6 or 12 points thick, used as spacing material between lines of type. The bar of metal with the type cast on it by the Linotype or Intertype is also called a slug. **1949** *Manual of Style* 255 The line of matrices is then brought in contact with molten type metal, in which the entire line is cast as one 'slug.'

attrib. **1894** SHUMAN *Steps into Journalism* 27 Most papers use 'big heads' or 'slug heads' over news articles exceeding one-half or two-thirds of a column in length.

4. slug-caterpillar, (see quot. 1891).

1841 GOULD *Invertebrata Mass.* 303 The most common of these slug-caterpillars, in Massachusetts, live on walnut-trees. **1891** *Cent.* 5706/3 *Slug-caterpillar*, one of the footless slug-like larvae of the bombycid moths of the family *Limacodidae.*

*∗***slug,** *v.* **1.** *tr.* and *intr.* Of a bullet: (see quot.). **2.** *To slug up*, to take a slug or drink of liquor. *Slang. Rare.* **3.** (See quot. and cf. *∗***slug,** *n.* **3.**)

(1) **1876** KNIGHT 2217/2 The bullet, when forced to assume the sectional shape of the bore [of a breech-loading firearm] in the act of firing, is said to slug or to be slugged. — (2) **1856** *Porter's Spirit of Times* 6 Sep. 7/1 Let's slug-up and prepare for business. — (3) **1912** G. M. HYDE *Newspaper Reporting* 30 The bit of lead on which the name is printed is called a *slug* and the story is said to be *slugged.*

slugger ˈslʌgɚ, *n.* [f. *∗slug, v.*] **1.** A boxer, prize-fighter, shoulder hitter. *Slang.* **2.** A baseball player who is given to making long, hard hits. Also transf.

(1) **1877** [in **coon slugger**]. **1938** ASBURY *Sucker's Prog.* 362 Half a dozen of Rynders' sluggers immediately rushed upon the brash youth. — (2) **1883** *Chi. Tribune* 3 July 6/5 Poor Burns fell an easy victim to the Cleveland sluggers. **1946** *Ib*, 23 Dec. 14/2 The 'Louisville Slugger' became the standard bat of big league and sandlot alike. **1948** *Denison* (Tex.) *Herald* 2 July 13/1 He quit being just a slugger to be a ballplayer.

As the last term in **coon, home slugger.**

*∗***sluice,** *n.*

1. In gold mining, a trough, flume, or series of riffle boxes through which water bearing auriferous gravel and sand is made to flow and deposit particles of gold.

1851 *S.F. Picayune* 14 Oct. 2/4 In the neighborhood of Rough and Ready, a sluice of fourteen miles in length has been constructed. **1883** *Cent. Mag.* Jan. 327/1 To use [the canyon] as a 'dump' or depository for the 'tailings' or debris of his sluices. *a***1919** G. STUART *On Frontier* I. 89 We purchased water from a ditch company for our sluices. **1948** JOHNSTON *Gold Rush* 18/1 Two or three times their sluices had been robbed, and they were mighty sore and on the lookout for the man who had done it.

2. (See quot. 1905.)

1905 *Forestry Bureau Bul.* No. 61, 37 *Flume*, an inclined trough in which water runs, used in transporting logs or timbers. . . . [Also called] sluice, water slide, wet slide. **1908** WHITE *Riverman* 9 The sluice. . . . had been built a good six feet above the level.

3. In combs. (sense **1.**) now obs. or hist.: (1) **sluice blanket,** = *∗***blanket,** *n.* **2;** (2) **box,** =**riffle box;** (3) **fork,** a forklike implement used in a sluice, also fig.; (4) **head,** a "head" or amount of water sufficient for flushing out a sluice; (5) **way,** see as a main entry.

(1) **1876** RAYMOND *8th Rep. Mines* 74 Paid for sluice-blankets, [$]265.50. — (2) **1857** *Hutchings Mag.* July 7/1 A continuous line of these troughs or 'sluice boxes' the smaller and lower end of each, inserted for three or four inches into the larger end of the next one below, form the 'sluice.' **1948** *Life* 2 Feb. 46/3 With tremendous labor the forty-niners diverted rivers into new channels to get water for their sluice boxes and pans. — (3) **1856** *S.F. Call* 16 Dec. 4/2 As he went—took it *puss*'nal—it commenced raining 'sluice-forks.' **1867** *Terr. Enterprise* (Virginia, Nev.) 29 Jan. 3/1 Some forty or fifty persons [were] busily engaged on Main street . . . with hoes, sluice forks, rakes, etc., in the laudable occupation of sluicing off the mud and accumulated filth. — (4) **1855** *Golden Era* (S.F.) 4 March 1/6 At Eureka there are only twelve sluiceheads of water running. **1856** *S.F. Bulletin* 11 Oct. 1/2 The last gold mining district is the Colorado mines, . . . in which some seventeen hundred sluice-heads of water could be used.

b. Also (1) **sluice mine,** (2) **mining,** (3) **process,** (4) **robber,** (5) **robbing,** (6) **tailing,** (7) **trough,** (see quots.).

(1) **1881** ROMSPERT *Western Echo* 323 In the *sluice* or *gulch* mine the men dig the dirt into the water and mash up the clods, throw out the stones, etc., and the dirt all washes down while the metal sinks to the bottom. — (2) **1867** *Terr. Enterprise* (Virginia, Nev.) 13 Feb. 3/1 Some parties [have commenced] sluice mining at a point on the ravine formerly the site of the old Spanish mill. — (3) **1891** *Cent. Mag.* Feb. 533/2 This auriferous region . . . comprises the places . . . where the sluice and hydraulic processes were invented. — (4) **1869** HARTE *Luck of Roaring Camp* 21 The expatriated party [included] . . . 'Uncle Billy,' a suspected sluice-robber and confirmed drunkard. **1948** JOHNSTON *Gold Rush* 11/1 It has been said that the strong prejudice of which the Chinese were victims was due to their adeptness as sluice robbers.

(5) **1873** BRET HARTE *Mrs. Skagg's Husbands* 121 A young man . . . was hung at Red Dog for sluice-robbing. — (6) **1871** RAYMOND *3d Rep. Mines* 259 The sluice-tailings assay $5 per ton. — (7) **1905** O. HENRY *Strictly Business* 81 Some of 'em [*sc.* women] are natural sluice troughs and can carry out $1,000 to the ton.

As the last term in **gold, mining, tail sluice.**

***sluice,** *v.*

1. *W. tr.* To wash (auriferous sand or gravel) in a sluice. Also absol. Cf. ***sluicing,** and see **ground, river sluicing.**

1850 A. T. JACKSON *Forty-Niner* (1920) 21 [We] washed up two days and sluiced top dirt the rest of the week. **1869** BRACE *New West* 161 In many of these streams, whole hills have been 'sluiced' away. **1921** *Frontier* Nov. 5, I went from Deer Lodge City to Silver Bow, where they were sluicing and where the beginnings of Butte were just showing. **1948** JOHNSTON *Gold Rush* 30/1 It is said that one man returned to his claim and told his partners that they might as well quit sluicing for a few ounces a day, because the source of all gold had been found over on Gold Hill.

2. (See quot. 1905.) Also *intr.*

1877 *Lumberman's Gaz.* 17 Nov. 309 The Chippewa will sluice down on the river mills at least 400,000,000 feet of logs. **1905** *Forestry Bureau Bul.* No. 61, 48 *Sluice,* . . . to float logs through the sluiceway of a splash dam. (N[orthern] F[orest].) **1908** WHITE *Riverman* 53 Three dams had to be sluiced through.

b. *passive.* To be caught in a rush of logs broken away from confinement.

1908 H. DAY *King Spruce* xxv, He knew—that most terrible knowledge of all woods terrors—that he was 'sluiced.'

***sluicer,** *n.* A lumberer who guides logs through a sluice. Cf. **ground sluicer.** — **1893** *Scribner's Mag.* June 715 Sluicer's boot, with calks. **1908** S. E. WHITE *Riverman* iv. 44 The sluicers with their long pike-poles thrust the logs into the chute.

sluiceway ˈslus͵we, *n.*

1. An artificial channel or waterway; a sluice.

1779 *Mass. H.S. Proc.* 2 Ser. II. 461 The sluceway was broke up. **1873** LAWRENCE *Silverland* 165 The long tunnel becomes a 'sluice-way;' through the whole length of which 'sluice-boxes' are laid. **1947** PEATTIE *Sierra Nevada* 27 The landscape is strewn with relics of heroic labors, abandoned mine shafts, . . . moldering sluiceways, crater-like excavations.

fig. **1858** *Beecher's Life Thoughts* 185 Some people . . . always make a drain or sluiceway by which the heavenly stream of God's favors escapes from them.

2. (See first quots.)

1851 *Harper's Mag.* Sep. 517/2 For taking logs down mountain sides, . . . we construct what are termed dry sluice-ways, which reach from the upper edge of a precipice down to the base of the hill. **1905** *Forestry Bureau Bul.* No. 61, 48 *Sluiceway,* the opening in a splash dam through which logs pass. **1947** *Sat. Ev. Post* 8 March 54/3 He loped up and down river spreading his crew, guarding at danger points, sending messages to dam watchers to close or open sluiceways.

***sluicing,** *n.*

1. The mining of gold by means of a sluice. Also attrib. or as adj.

1851 in *Pioneer* (S.F.) (1854) July 24, I confess that I intend some day, when I feel statistically inclined, to favor you with some profound remarks upon the claiming, drifting, sluicing, ditching, fluming and coyoting politics of the 'diggins.' **1857** *Hutchings Mag.* July 6/1 Sluicing . . . is a mode of mining particularly adapted to those localities where it becomes desirable to wash large quantities of dirt, and where the descent is sufficient to operate advantageously. **1882** *47th Congress* 1 Sess. H.R. Ex. Doc. No. 216, 107 But little sluicing is now done except by Chinamen.

b. sluicing claim, a mining claim upon which sluicing is carried on.

1852 *Mt. Echo* (Downieville, Calif.) 19 June 2/2 The Bank Diggins and sluicing claims at Cox', Goodyear's & other bars in our vicinity are paying good wages. **1882** *47th Congress* 1 Sess. H.R. Ex. Doc. No. 216, 105 The Fox Creek and Boulder Creek sluicing claims have uniformly done well.

2. A sluice or sluiceway used in gold-mining.

1869 HARTE *Luck of Roaring Camp* 67 It contained a rough, oblong box,—apparently made from a section of sluicing. **1885** *Wkly. New Mexican Rev.* 29 Jan. 4/2 Here large reservoirs and about two miles of substantial sluicing are to be constructed, and improved hydraulic machinery put in.

slum slʌm, *n.* [App. f. **slumgullion.**]

1. (See quot. 1917, and cf. **slumgullion 1. c.**)

1847 J. MITCHELL *Reminisc. College* 117 Though the son of Vulcan found the pork and cabbage harmless, I am sure that slum would have been a match for him. **1871** BAGG *At Yale* 246 An olla podrida, hashed up from the remnants of yesterday's dinner, and fried into a consistency which baffled digestion, . . . was known as 'slum,' and was served both dry and wet. **1917** J. A. MOSS *Officers' Man.* 485 *Slum*—a stew of meat, potatoes and onions, mostly potatoes and onions. **1928** *Sat. Ev. Post* 12 May 117/2 His steaming mess kit full of slum.

2. =**slumgullion 1.** Also attrib.

1868 *Terr. Enterprise* (Virginia, Nev.) 1 May 3/1 The fine metal contained in the slum is saved on a slum table attached to the machine. **1872** *Chi. Tribune* 25 Nov. 5/5 She [Mrs. Minnie Myrtle Miller] sketched the life of the poet [Joaquin Miller] in the mines, where he wheeled dirt and shoveled slum for one month. **1890** *Scientific Amer.* 31 May 341/1 The alternate rise and fall of the hopper [in an ore concentrator is] caused by the vertically sliding beam, the slums, light gravel, etc., passing off through the waste flume at every upward motion.

slumgullion ͵slʌmˈgʌljən, *n.* [See note.]

App. a fanciful formation. With ref. to sense **1**, cf. *EDD gul'ion,* sb.3, mud. In sense **1. c.** cf. *EDD scabby-gullion,* a stew of hashed meat and potatoes. In sense **3.** cf. **gullion,* a worthless wretch.

1. *Mining.* The thick viscid refuse or mud of the sluice boxes, generally of highly-colored red ferruginous clay and water.

1850 A. T. JACKSON *Forty-Niner* (1920) 30 The mud we were sending down the stream buried them under slumgullion. **1887** HARTE *Millionaire & Devil's Ford* 146 We preach at them for playing in the slumgullion, and getting themselves splashed. *a***1915** MUIR *Travels Alaska* (1917) 109 The meals are all alike—a potato, a slice of something like bacon, some gray stuff called bread, and a cup of muddy, semi-liquid coffee like . . . 'slumgullion.' **1948** WESTON *Mother Lode* 82 The miners . . . insisted on calling it 'Slumgullion,' because when it rained the knee-deep adobe mud was no small problem.

b. (See quots.) *Slang.*

1879 WILLIAMS *Pacific Tourist* 44/1 The weary passengers . . . were glad to regale themselves on pork and beans, corn bread, and 'slumgullion'— he Far Western name for tea. **1942** DALE *Cow Country* 121 In most cases 'slumgullion,' a kind of bread pudding made from cold biscuits, sugar and raisins marked the limit of his culinary imagination.

c. A stew of meat and vegetables, esp. potatoes and onions.

1902 LONDON *Daughter of Snows* 45 'What do you happen to call it?' 'Slumgullion,' she responded curtly, and thereafter the meal went on in silence. **1904** E. ROBINS *Magnetic North* iv. 59 'Mix 'em with cold potatoes in a salad.' 'No, make slumgullion,' commanded O'Flynn. **1936** McKENNA *Black Range* 250 A large caldron was sitting over the fire. It must have had two gallons of the slumgullion in it.

2. (See quots.) Also **slobgollion.**

1851 MELVILLE *Moby-Dick* 465 It is called slobgollion; an appellation original with the whalemen. . . . It is an ineffably oozy, stringy affair, most frequently found in the tubs of sperm, after a prolonged squeezing, and subsequent decanting. **1891** *Cent.* 5708/2 *Slumgullion,* . . . offal or refuse of fish of any kind; also, the watery refuse, mixed with blood and oil, which drains from blubber.

3. A low, worthless fellow. *Slang.*

1869 LELAND *Hans Breitmann Ballads* 61 Should I in the Legislature as your slumgullion stand. **1926** J. B. AMES *Valley of Missing Men* viii, She is . . . a whole lot too good for that lump o' slumgullion she lives with.

slump,** *v. intr.* (See quot. 1851.) Also as noun. *Slang. Obs.* — **1851** HALL *College Words* 284 Slump. . . . At Harvard College, a poor recitation. *Ib.* 285 To make a poor recitation. *a1856** *MS Poem* in HALL *College Words* (1856) 433 At recitations, unprepared, he slumps, Then cuts a week, and feigns he has the mumps.

slung shot. A weapon, used chiefly by criminals, consisting of a shot or other weight attached to a flexible handle or strap.

1842 *Spirit of Times* (Phila.) 29 Aug., Davis's companion struck him three violent blows with a slung-shot over the head. 1850 *Quincy* (Ill.) *Whig* 26 Nov. 2/6 In the 'Killer' gang to make up for disparity of age and strength, the slung shot was adopted as the most effective weapon they could use. 1938 ASBURY *Sucker's Prog.* 362 Half a dozen of Rynders' sluggers immediately rushed upon the brash youth and smote him hip and thigh with fists, bottles, chairs, slung shots, and other weapons.

Hence **slung-shotter.**

1868 *Alta California* (S.F.) 6 May 5/4 San Francisco has had a surplus of low-flung thieves, garroters, burglars, slung shotters, and such like fellows of the baser sort.

slunker ˈslʌŋkɚ, *n.* [App. f. or related to **slunk*, *a.*, cast prematurely (of calves). Cf. **lunker.**] (See quot.) — 1903 GOODE & GILL *Amer. Fishes* 527 These spent females [*sc.* sturgeons] are called 'slunkers,' and are of little value.

***slur,** *v. tr.* To coat or cover (a wall) with plaster. *Obs.* — 1885 *Harper's Mag.* March 531/1 The rear wall is slurred, and from it three windows open into a garden.

***slush,** *n.*

1. Rubbishy literature. Also attrib.

1896 *Daily News* 23 Jan. 6/1 Two stout volumes of what the American editor would have called 'delirious slush.' 1916 B. M. BOWER *Phantom Herd* vii. 112 You want those stories worked up in a lot of darned, sickly slush melodramas.

2. In special combs.: (1) **slush fund,** in the Army and Navy, a fund derived from selling refuse fat, grease, etc., and used to get small luxuries for the men, also a contingent fund appropriated by Congress, and administered at the discretion, usu., of the Secretary of the Treasury, in later use, a fund for bribery, corruption etc.; (2) **investigation,** an investigation with reference to funds for bribery and corruption; (3) **money,** money for surreptitious purposes.

(1) 1864 *Rio Abajo Press* 5 July 2/2 The polite Commissary informed us that they received twelve dollars a barrel for the [coffee] grounds, and thus added materially to the 'slush fund.' 1874 *Cong. Rec.* 17 April 3166/1 We have had this 'slush-fund' since 1866. 1938 ASBURY *Sucker's Prog.* 299 They gave liberally to a slush fund which he collected periodically and distributed where it would do the most good. — (2) 1929 *Chi. Tribune* 30 Jan. 1/8 The state capital shared with Chicago in the developments of the Sanitary district pay roll slush investigation yesterday. — (3) 1842 J. F. COOPER *Wing-and-Wing* II. 20 They were only put there yesterday . . . a little slush-money did it all.

***smack,** *n.* A fishing vessel having a well in which fish may be kept alive, a well boat (see quot. *a*1891). Cf. **schooner smack.**

1850 *S.F. Herald* 26 Oct. 1/4 It was almost as unsuccessful as the baling out of the hole of a fishing smack would be. 1888 *Outing* March 513/1 She proved to be one of those peculiar crafts called a 'smack,' which ply between Havana and the coast of Florida. *a*1891 *Fisherman's Memorial Bk.* 70 (*Cent.*), Many of them were made into smacks, so-called, . . . by building a water-tight compartment amidships, and boring holes in the bottom to admit saltwater.

Also **smackee.**

1894 *U.S. Fish Comm. Bul.* 209 The fish, consisting of grunts, snappers, groupers, porgies, etc., are brought to market alive in the wells of the smackees.

smack smæk, *v. tr.* To convey in a smack. — 1880 *Harper's Mag.* Aug. 350/2 The jigger . . . taking a haul of fish, 'smacking' a load of lobsters, wood, or ice. *Ib.* Sep. 499/1 The schooner Marthy . . . 'smacked' fish regularly to Portland.

***smack,** *adv.* **1. smack dab,** *adv.* entirely, directly. *Colloq.* **2. smack smooth,** *a.* entirely (see also quot. 1848). *Obs.*

(1) 1902 HARBEN *Abner Daniel* 14 It'll be started inside of the next yeer an' 'll run smack dab through my property. 1949 *Oak Leaves* (Oak Park, Ill.) 24 Nov. 5/5 He said he wanted one printed 'smack dab on the front page' inviting all the kids in the villages to come out for the parade. — (2) 1833 S. SMITH *Life Downing* (1834) 28 (We.), [He] rolled them up in piles and sot fire to 'em again and burnt 'em up smack smooth. 1848 BARTLETT 409 *Smack smooth*, at the West, a term applied to land which is thoroughly cleared: i.e. smoothly cleared; level.

***smacked,** *a.* (See quot.) *Obs.* — 1886 *Amer. Philol. Assoc. Trans.* XVII. 46 List of common Southern expressions: . . . *smacked* (ground—as smacked corn).

***smacker,** *n.* A dollar. *Slang.* — 1920 *Chi. Herald & Examiner* 2 Jan. 14/2 Along comes Earl Gray and knocks off the U.S. treasury for 13,000,000 smackers. 1947 FAIR *Fools Die on Friday* 32 Two hundred and fifty smackers is quite a chunk of dough for a working girl to dig up.

***small,** *a.* In combs.: (1) ***small-bore,** *fig.* petty, mean, contemptible, *colloq.;* (2) **boy,** a young boy, usu. applied to boys of about five to ten years of age regardless of their size; (3) **farmer,** one who farms on a small scale, almost or entirely without hired help, also attrib.; (4) **farming,** farming performed on a small scale; (5) **generals,** see quot. 1889 *s.v.* ***general 1;** (6) **hominy,** see **hominy 1. b;** (7) **Nation,** (see quot.), *rare;* (8) **note currency,** currency consisting of notes of small value, *obs.;* (9) **planter,** one who engages in planting on a relatively small scale, *obs.*, cf. **small farmer;** (10) ***potato,** see as a main entry; (11) **Robes,** a subtribe of the Siksika Indians—a translation of their native name, *Inuksiks, obs.;* (12) **time,** *a.* petty, insignificant, also absol., chiefly *theatrical slang;* (13) ***town,** such theatrical performances as are often given in small towns, also attrib. in the sense of mean, paltry, insignificant, hence **small townish,** *a., colloq.*

(1) 1900 *Cong. Rec.* 14 Feb. 1804/2 No small-bore, two-by-four, radical politicians can hurt that great court. — (2) 1786 WASHINGTON *Diaries* III. 86 That Cowper Jack and Day, with some small boys and girls, . . . were assisting the farmer. 1889 *Atlantic Mo.* April 465/1 A small boy who first sees a military parade wishes to be a soldier. 1950 *Chi. Tribune* 10 Jan. 18/3 As weather sharps well know, those favorite harbingers of the vernal season, migrant robins, are not due for some time, their advent depending upon the unwitting offices of our small boys. — (3) 1835 HOFFMAN *Winter in West* I. 79 They were chiefly plain people, small farmers and graziers. 1913 LONDON *Valley of Moon* 327 The district . . . was 'small-farmer' country in which labor was rarely hired. — (4) 1880 *Scribner's Mo.* Oct. 843/1 Small farming means, in short, meat and bread for which there are no notes in the bank. 1898 WESTCOTT *D. Harum* 171 Small farmin' ain't cal'lated to fetch out the best traits of human nature.

(7) 1851 in CUSHMAN *Hist. Indians* 89 In 1771, the eastern district of the Choctaw Nation was known as Oy-pat-oo-coo-la, signifying the 'Small Nation.' — (8) 1838 *Speeches D. Barnard* vi, And allow our banks to furnish a better small-note currency. — (9) 1863 *Rep. Comm. Agric. 1862* 60 Cuba tobacco is, next to sugar, most in favor with small planters.

(11) 1832 CATLIN *Indians* I. 52 The Blackfeet proper are divided into four bands or families, as follows: . . . the 'Blood' band, of 450 lodges; and the 'Small Robes.' — (12) 1924 *Collier's* 2 Feb. 8/1 Pat was playing the string of comparatively small time through up-State New York. 1948 *Chi. Tribune* 11 Jan. (Comics) 1 You don't know that smalltime political boss, he's shifty and treacherous. 1949 *Boston Globe* 15 May (Fiction Mag.) 2/3 He don't fool around with no small-time stuff. — (13) 1881 *Harper's Mag.* Jan. 223/2 Cosmopolitans, they do not sink into the ruts of small-town life. 1890 BIFF HALL *Turnover Club* 136 He and Will McConnell were playing the entire mob in small town. 1931 CONCANNON *St. Patrick* xiv. 189 The smooth paths of a smug small-townish officialdom. 1946 *Chi. D. News* 6 April 6/1 He was a dapper small-town politician and business man.

b. In the names of, or with reference to, plants: (1) **small-bolled cotton,** a variety of cotton having small bolls, *obs.;* (2) **buckeye, =red buckeye;** (3) **cherry, =red cherry;** (4) **-flowered buckeye, papaw,** (see quots.); (5) ***fruits,** *pl.* (see quots.); (6) **-fruited hickory,** a variety of hickory bearing fruit of comparatively small size; (7) **grain,** any one of various cereals, as wheat, oats, barley, etc., having grains smaller than those of Indian corn, also attrib.; (8) **magnolia,** the sweet bay, *Magnolia virginiana;* (9) **-nut hickory,** (see quot.); (10) **red cherry, =red cherry;** (11) **-toothed aspen,** the quaking aspen, *Populus tremuloides*, cf. **large-toothed aspen.**

(1) 1835 in COMMONS *Doc. Hist.* I. 184 Small bold cotton was backward in this country owing to the dry spring. — (2) 1832 BROWNE *Sylva* 226 The Yellow *Pavia* . . . is here called *Big Buckeye*, to distinguish it from the *Pavia rubra*, . . . which is called *Small Buckeye.* 1846 ——— *Trees* 115 The Small Buckeye is a slender-growing tree or shrub. — (3) 1832 BROWNE *Sylva* 135 Red Cherry Tree. *Cerasus borealis*. . . . [In] Maine and Vermont, it is called *Small Cherry* and *Red Cherry.* — (4) 1901 MOHR *Plant Life Ala.* 92 The delicate white-flowered spikes of the small-flowered buckeye (*Æsculus parviflora*). *Ib.* 507 *Asimina parviflora*. . . . Small-flowered Papaw. . . . Carolinian and Louisianian areas.

(5) 1879 WEBSTER *Supp.* 1579/1 *Small fruits*, fruits raised in market-gardens. 1892 CROZIER *Dict. Bot. Terms* 164/2 *Small fruits*, a horticultural term for certain low-growing perennial, fruit-bearing

plants and their product, including the strawberry, raspberry, blackberry, gooseberry, currant, huckleberry, and cranberry. The term includes grapes, but excludes cherries. **1950** *Scientific Mo.* April 212 The story of the evolution of the groups from which our small fruits have been derived is shrouded in the mists of the geological past. — **(6) 1847** DARLINGTON *Weeds & Plants* 306 The small fruited Hickory, *C[arya] microcarpa*, . . . is distinguished by its very small fruit. **1919** STURTEVANT *Notes on Edible Plants* 149 Small-fruited Hickory. Eastern North America. The nuts are edible but not prized. **1938** BROWN *Trees Northeastern U.S.* 169 Small-fruited Hickory [is] . . . an upland species preferring hillsides and rich woods, often in admixture with other hardwoods. — **(7) 1786** in *Va. Hist. Mag.* XL. 366 The Country [near Lexington, Ky.] . . . Produces . . . every thing but Wheat & small grain which cannot produce untill the Land is worked about 10 years. **1839** BUEL *Farmer's Companion* 197 The small-grain crops are the greatest exhausters of the fertility of the soil. **1892** *Courier-Journal* 1 Oct. 12/6 Churchill Hand-made Sour-mash Whisky. 40 per cent small grain. — **(8) 1785** MARSHALL *Amer. Grove* 83 Small Magnolia, or Swamp Sassafras, . . . grows naturally in low, moist, or swampy ground. **1868** GRAY *Field Botany* 43 Small M[agnolia] or Sweet Bay, [grows] wild in swamps N. to New Jersey and Mass. — **(9) 1860** CURTIS *Woody Plants N.C.* 44 Small-nut hickory (*C[arya] microcarpa*). The nut is roundish.

(10) 1849 EMMONS *Agric. N.Y.* II. 317 Small Red cherry. Seasoned. — **(11) 1911** *Storrs* (Conn.) *Agric. Exp. Sta. Bul. 69*, 390 The Large-toothed Aspen resembles the Small-toothed Aspen with which it is frequently confused.

c. In the names of birds and fishes: (1) **small-headed flycatcher, warbler,** (see quots.); (2) **-mouth (black bass),** =next; (3) **-mouthed (black) bass,** a valuable fresh-water game fish, *Micropterus dolomieu*, cf. ∗**large,** *a.* (3); (4) **mud hen,** (see quot.); (5) **pewee, =green-crested flycatcher;** (6) **silverside,** (see quot.).

(1) 1812 WILSON *Ornithology* VI. 62 [The] Small-headed Flycatcher . . . [is a] very rare species. **1839** PEABODY *Mass. Birds* 297 The Small-headed Flycatcher . . . has been found in Ipswich. **1870** *Amer. Naturalist* III. 577 Small-headed Flycatcher . . . This rather apocryphal species is given by Peabody as having been met with at Ipswich by Dr. Brewer. **1902** RIDGWAY *Birds of N. & Middle Amer.* II. 709 *Wilsonia microcephala* Ridgway. Small-headed Warbler. . . . I am unable to satisfactorily dispose of this hypothetical species to any other. — **(2) 1884** GOODE *Fisheries* I. 401 The Small-mouth shares with the Large-mouth in the Southern States the names 'Jumper,' 'Perch,' and 'Trout.' **1897** *Outing* Aug. 438/1 A small-mouth black bass was the prize first tried for. **1949** *Sat. Ev. Post* 14 May 5/3 You can distinguish between Large-Mouth Black Bass and Small-Mouth Black Bass if you look for their special characteristics. — **(3) 1882** *Nat. Museum Bul.* No. 16, 485. **1883** *Cent. Mag.* July 376/2 There are but two well-defined species, the large-mouthed bass and the small-mouthed bass. **1947** *Collier's* 29 Mar. 32/1 The smallmouthed black bass, for which I wouldn't trade any fish when it comes to making for interesting angling, belongs to the sunfish family. — **(4) 1917** *Birds of Amer.* I. 205 Virginia Rail. *Rallus virginianus*. . . . [Also called] Small Mud Hen; Fresh-water Marsh Hen.

(5) 1839 PEABODY *Mass. Birds* 295 The Small Pewee . . . is a very common summer bird. **1844** *Nat. Hist. N.Y., Zoology* II. 112 The Small Green-crested Flycatcher, or Small Pewee . . . , winters in Mexico. **1917** *Birds of Amer.* II. 207 Acadian Flycatcher. . . . [Also called] Green Flycatcher; Small Pewee. — **(6) 1814** MITCHILL *Fishes N.Y.* 446 Small Silverside. *Atherina notata*. . . . Upper jaw somewhat jutting.

smaller ˈsmɔlɚ, *n.* "An ordinary-sized drink of liquor" (Th.). *Slang. Obs.* — **1829** *N.Y. Mirror* 7 Nov. 138/2 'Sixteen smallers,' cried R——ds, 'it is deerskin.' **1839** *S. Lit. Messenger* V. 66/1 Bill . . . had just commenced, after taking a 'smaller' himself, to serve out the liquor to them.

∗**small potato.**

1. *pl. fig.* A person or thing regarded as trivial, insignificant, paltry, etc. Also *small potatoes and few of* (or *in*) *a hill. Colloq.*

1831 *Boston Transcript* 1 April 2/1 When a person is guilty of a mean action, or takes much pains to make himself rediculous, it is often said in relation to the circumstance, 'small potatoes,—rather small potatoes, and few in a hill.' **1836** CROCKETT *Exploits* 25 This is what I call small potatoes and few of a hill. *c***1849** PAIGE *Dow's Sermons* I. 199 Political foes are such very small potatoes, that they will hardly pay for skinning. **1948** *Proc. Acad. Pol. Sci.* May 12 The $7 billion was of course pretty 'small potatoes' compared to the vast inflationary borrowings of the federal government.

2. Attrib. in sing. with **affair, enemy, highness, man, politician, reader.**

1840 *N.O. Picayune* 19 Aug. 2/1 Creole readers, Yankee readers, small potato readers, . . . hope you are well this morning. **1849** G. G. FOSTER *N.Y. in Slices* 102 Like monkeys and small-potato politicians, they have their appointed end. **1861** *N.Y. Herald* 2 July 4/5 Old Abe need not trouble himself about the injuries which such small potato affairs may endeavor to inflict upon him. **1863** *Rio Abajo Press* 14 April 2/2 Their acts have shown them to be the smallest kind of 'small potatoe' enemies. **1880** *Harper's Mag.* Oct. 708 Yer small-p'tater men Will kin' o' work t' th' bottom uv the ben. **1896** HASWELL *New York* 331 He [Bennett], in the *Herald* also proclaimed Gilbert Davis as the Governor of the Island, and later was in the habit of referring to Governor Seward as his 'small potato highness,' and Horace Greeley as 'a galvanized squash.'

∗**smart,** *a.* In combs.: (1) **smart Aleck, aleck,** (*a*) a bumptious, conceited know-it-all, also attrib., (*b*) also **smart alecky, alexist;** (2) **chance,** see ∗**chance,** *n.* **1;** (3) **grass,** smartweed; (4) **hooping,** (see quot.), *obs.*

(1) (*a*) **1865** *Carson* (Nev.) *Appeal* 17 Oct. 2/3 Halloa, old smart Aleck—how is the complimentary vote for Ashley? **1930** *Sat. Ev. Post* 13 Dec. 15/2 We live dumb and we dress dumb, you said, and thought maybe of that Leslie Schlegel with his Smart-Aleck clothes and ways. **1948** *Confectioner's Jrnl.* June 73/1 The violator feels he is a 'smart-aleck' in being able to get away with flagrant violations for a time without getting caught. (*b*) **1909** F. CALHOUN *Miss Minerva*, You 'bout the smart Alexist jack-rabbit they is. **1948** *Denison* (Tex.) *Herald* 2 July 4/6 Few grown-ups enjoy an encounter with a smart-alecky child. — **(3) 1845** JUDD *Margaret* II. 212 The geese . . . left only may-weed, smart-grass, and Indian tobacco. — **(4) 1800** TATHAM *Tobacco* 54 [One method] of forming the hoop of tobacco hogsheads . . . resembles the method used in the construction of pales and tubs, called flat hooping; and the other is of the kind used for hooping casks for ordinary occasions, called smart hooping.

b. In colloq. phrases: (1) *smart as a steel trap* (or *whip*), extremely alert, brisk, clever; (2) *smart to work, N. Eng.* energetic, not lazy.

(1) 1833 S. SMITH *Life J. Downing* 224 He'd come up again as smart as a steeltrap. **1860** *Mountaineer* (Salt Lake City) 24 March 120/4 Mr. A—— was a prompt and successful business man, 'smart as a whip,' as the Yankees say. **1946** FAIR *Crows Can't Count* 45 She's shrewd—smart as a whip. — **(2) 1890** JEWETT *Strangers* 137, I've be'n a smart woman to work in my day. **1902** FREEMAN *Six Trees* 91 The old woman always was smart to work.

smart smɑrt, *v.* [f. ∗*smart, a.*] **1.** *tr.* To make spruce or neat. Also **smarted up. 2.** *To get smarted up*, to spruce up, to be made smart or acquainted with new things. Both *colloq.*

(1) 1782 DALRYMPLE *Journal* 13, I shall have but little time to smart myself. **1891** COOKE *Huckleberries* 251, I'm a goin' to stop till she's outdoors again and pootty well smarted up. — **(2) 1831** *Boston Transcript* 3 May 1/2 It looks as natral as the hogs, Just as you used to be, When you got smarted up to go And take a walk with me. **1867** HOLMES *Guardian Angel* 359 He had got 'smarted up,' as his mother called it, a good deal.

∗**smartness,** *n.* Extreme cleverness or shrewdness, esp. to one's own advantage. — **1842** DICKENS *Amer. Notes* (1850) 171/1 This smartness has done more in a few years to impair the public credit . . . than dull honesty . . . could have effected in a century. **1890** *Spectator* 26 April, Mr. Blaine . . . instructed his supporters in the Press and on the platform to proclaim the 'smartness' of his scheme.

smarty ˈsmɑrtɪ, *n.* and *a.*

1. *n.* A smart aleck *q.v. Colloq.*

1861 *Calif. Mag.* Aug. 39/2 'Juvenile smartys' are interesting, even to a vagabond. **1903** *Outing* April 51/2 Grace turns her head on those 'smarties.' **1947** *Atlantic Mo.* Oct. 60/2, I called him Smarty because he was an awful sassy customer and used to talk back a lot.

2. *a.* Having the characteristics of a smarty. *Colloq.*

1883 MARK TWAIN *Life on Miss.* xxxiii. 370 In the old times, the barkeeper owned the bar himself, and was gay and smarty and talky. **1913** *Good Housekeeping* Nov. 202/2 Once I was 'smarty' just to see How *very* 'smarty' I could be.

∗**smash,** *n.* **1.** An outside success, a hit. *Slang.* **2.** ∗**smash-up,** a collision or wreck. *Colloq.*

(1) 1931 *Dly. Express* 21 Sep. 9/3 The magnates who had contracted to buy the picture indulged in fits of doubt concerning its prospects as a box-office 'smash.' — **(2) 1856** M. J. HOLMES *L. Rivers* 35 The old lady, sure of a *smash-up* this time, had attempted to rise. **1931** *K.C. Times* 3 Oct., What could run more typically true to form than a smashup when that bee got up a motorist's pants leg a short time ago?

As the last term in **brandy, mint, whisky smash.**

∗**smash,** *v.*

1. *intr.* (See quot.) *Obs.*

1809 in P. H. MUSSER *James Nelson Barker* (1929) 32 Quincy concluded to day reading a speech begun yesterday, in which, to use a cant congressional phrase—he *smashed!* that is—he lost himself in his volume of notes—feigned illness, and sat down.

2. *tr.* To handle (baggage), esp. in a rough, careless manner. Cf. **baggage-smasher.**

1865 *Atlantic Mo.* April 386/1 New trunks [were] more recklessly smashed, than would be possible at a later hour. **1872** BRACE *Dangerous Classes N.Y.* 317 They were mere children, and kept life together by . . . 'smashing baggages' (as they called it), and the like.

3. In the passive: To be greatly infatuated by, often *to be smashed on. Colloq.* Cf. ***crush,** *n.* **1,** ***mash,** *v.* **2.**

1883 WILDER *Sister Ridnour* 153, I had so often heard my brother and his friends laughing about this or that girl that was 'smashed' or 'over ears in love.' **1888** GUNTER *Mr. Potter* ix. 113 My gracious! If the widdah is not smashed on the Australian!

***smasher,** *n.* **1.** A spirituous drink. **2.** =**baggage-smasher.** Both *obs.*

(1) **1849** G. G. FOSTER *N.Y. in Slices* 96 A good-looking female bar-keeper . . . dispenses smiles and smashers. — (2) **1851** *True Standard* (S.F.) 6 March 2/2 Some of their countrymen coming up with wheelbarrows, offered to transport it much cheaper, whereupon the 'Smashers' fell on them and beat them unmercifully. **1873** *Cottonwood Observer* (Alta, Utah) 26 July 3/4 The smasher flung the bag up against the wall savagely, and then threw it on the floor and stamped on it and jumped up and down on it, as usual.

As the last term in **brandy, slate smasher.**

smashfulness ˈsmæʃfəlnɪs, *n.* Propensity for breaking or smashing *Rare.* — **1887** *Courier-Journal* 15 Feb. 4/3 The general smashfulness of the average baggageman . . . [has] long created suspicion in the public mind.

***smear,** *n.* **1.** (See quot.) **2.** Short for next. Both *obs.* — **(1) 1877** BARTLETT 614 *Smear,* food; hash; grub, especially a society spread or supper. — (2) **1891** THANET *Otto the Knight* 330 You an' Bulah Norman wud . . . be projickin roun' my kitchin for light bread an' smear.

smearcase ˈsmɪrˌkes, *n.* [G. *Schmierkäse,* cheese for smearing on (something).] =**cottage cheese.**

1829 ROYALL *Pennsylvania* I. 171 A dish, common amongst the Germans, . . . is curds and cream. It is very palatable, and called by the Germans *smearcase.* **1835** *Vade Mecum* (Phila.) 31 Jan. 2/7 Drink Champagne, and eat smear-cases. **1894** *Harper's Mag.* Jan. 218/2 The 'cookey' (koekje), noodles, hodgepodge, smearcase, rullichies, cold-slaw, and other dishes that survive in New England. **1949** *Sat. Ev. Post* 23 April 80/3, I took large helpings of ham and potatoes, *schmierkase,* and green salad with tomatoes.

smeared dagger. (See quots.) — **1871** C. V. RILEY *3d Mo. Ent. Rep.* 70 The Smeared Dagger . . . is another insect which is occasionally found upon the Grape vine. **1883** W. SAUNDERS *Insects Inj. Fruits* 325 The Smeared Dagger, *Apatella oblinita.*

***smee,** *n.* Also **smees.** (See quot. 1888.) — **1888** TRUMBULL *Names of Birds* 38 In New Jersey, at Manasquan . . . the pintail duck is known as Smee. *Ib.* 39 Most of us . . . call it Sprig-tail, but I suppose its real name is Smees. **1917** *Birds of Amer.* I. 128.

smellage ˈsmɛlɪdʒ, *n. local.* [App. f. ***smell**+lo*vage.*] Fragrant vegetation, esp. lovage, *Levisticum officinale.*

1836 LINCOLN *Botany* App. 110 [*Ligusticum*] *levisticum,* (smellage,) leaves many. . . . Medicinal. **1855** *Mich. Agric. Soc. Trans.* VI. 149 The plants on the uplands are Columbo, . . . smellage, skoke or garget root. **1889** ROSE T. COOKE *Steadfast* iii. 43 A nosegay of lavender, damask roses, smellage, old man, clove pinks [etc.].

smelling committee. (See quots.) *Obs.* — **1877** BARTLETT 614 *Smelling-Committee,* persons appointed to conduct an unpopular investigation. The phrase originated in the examination of a convent in Massachusetts by legislative order. **1888** WALLACE *Carpetbag Rule* 104 The colored members . . . elected a permanent chairman of the caucus, and that chairman appointed a committee of three to ferret out all the schemes which looked anything like money schemes. This committee was styled 'the smelling committee.'

smell lemon. A variety of gourd (see quot. 1838). — **1838** GOSSE *Letters* 196 With these are interspersed occasional plants of the little Smell Lemon (*Cucurbita ovifera?*). The fruit is about the size of a small orange, perfectly round; its appearance is beautiful, the hue being bright glossy red, with stripes of yellow running round, like the meridian lines on a globe. The smell is very fragrant. **1871** DE VERE 415 The little Smell-Lemon (*Cucurbita ovifera*), the fruit of which is about the size of a small orange, bright glossy red, with stripes of yellow.

***smelter,** *n.* A smelting works. Hence **smelterman.** Cf. **custom smelter.**

1876 RAYMOND *8th Rep. Mines* 275 The Winnamuck Company shut down its smelter. **1883** RITCH *Illust. N. Mex.* 35 A few reduction works, smelters and stamp mills have been erected. **1896** *Columbus* (O.) *Dispatch* 4 Sep., The millionaire smelterman. **1914** ATHERTON *Perch of Devil* 9 The horizons . . . had always been obscured by the poisonous haze of smelters.

smelt minnow. The silvery minnow, *Hybognathus nuchalis.* — **1884** *Nat. Museum Bul.* No. 27, 481 *Hybognathus regius.* . . . Smelt Minnow. . . . Sometimes sold in early spring as 'smelt,' to which it bears almost no resemblance except in size and color.

***smethe,** *n.* (See quot.) — **1888** TRUMBULL *Names of Birds* 38 Others at Tuckerton refer to it [the pintail duck] as *Smethe.*

smidgen ˈsmɪdʒɪn, *n.* Also **smitchin, smidgeon.** [See note.]

Cf. *smidge, smitch* in the same sense in *D.N.* III. 65, and *smitch,* a particle, bit, in *OED* and *EDD.* Also cf. *midgan, midjan,* (pronounced [ˈmɪdʒɪn]), a small fragment, scrap, in *EDD.* Prob. all related to ***midge,* anything very small.

A small bit or part. *Colloq.*

1845 KIRKLAND *Western Clearings* 71 They wouldn't have left a smitchin o' honey. **1883** BEADLE *Western Wilds* 615 Not a smidgeon left—just bodaciously chawed up and spit out. **1886** *Amer. Philol. Assoc. Trans.* XVII. 43 *Smidgen,* 'a small bit, a grain,' as 'a *smidgen* of meal,' is common in East Tennessee. **1949** *New Yorker* 9 July 11/2 Yearning, we have no doubt, for a smidgen of Broadway glamour.

***smile,** *n.* A drink of liquor. *Colloq.* Cf. **papaw smile.**

1839 *Spirit of Times* 24 Aug. 294/3 (We.), We all agreed to take another 'smile.' **1866** *Calif. Leader* (S.F.) 25 Aug. 3/2, I am Martin; take a *smile* with me. **1908** FOHLIN *Salt Lake City* 37 Full, h'm, never was insulted to take a smile in my life. **1949** BEEBE & CLEGG *U.S. West* 302 It is no task for the imagining . . . to pass the hospitable doors of Barry and Patten's in Montgomery Street for a 'smile' at the invitation of the Emperor Norton.

***smile,** *v.*

1. *intr.* To drink, to take a smile. *Colloq.*

1845 *St. Louis Reveille* 29 April 2/4 He can't be very unhappy, for he 'smiles' so often. **1894** *S.F. Midwinter Appeal* 24 Feb. 1/4 We will ask him to 'smile' with us.

Hence ***smiler,** a drinker.

1856 *Spirit of Times* 29 Nov. 211/1 Tom Tit, a very ugly customer, . . . made straight for the bar-room and scattered all the smilers, and knocked their glasses into a thousand sparkles

b. *tr.* To take (a drink). *Obs.*

1857 *Knickerb.* XLIX. 42 And having smiled about three fingers all round . . . I inquired [etc.].

2. *I should smile,* used to emphasize a sentiment of willingness, unwillingness, etc. *Colloq.*

1883 HOYT *Bunch of Keys* 48 (We.), Single room? Well, I should smile. **1889** MARK TWAIN *Conn. Yankee* 112 They actually wanted *me* to put in! Well, I should smile. **1891** *Youth's Companion* LXIV. 138 Sing for nothing? Well, I should smile!

***smith,** *n.*

1. The carpenter frog, *Rana virgatipes* (see quot.).

1938 MATSCHAT *Suwannee River* 67 There is one frog [in Okefenokee swamp] that sounds like dozens of hammers striking against an empty barrel, and the natives call him the 'smith.'

2. Smith and Wesson, a pistol of a particular make, so called from the inventors. Also attrib. and in possessive.

1860 *Charleston* (S.C.) *Mercury* 6 Nov. 3/5 (*advt.*), Smith & Wesson's seven shooters. **1881** ROMSPERT *Western Echo* 115 The second ball from my Smith & Wesson stretched him struggling upon the earth with a bullet through his lungs. **1947** *Newsweek* 25 Aug. 19/3 His customer . . . had just bought a Smith & Wesson police special and a box of cartridges.

b. Also, erroneous, **Smith and Weston.**

1867 DIXON *New Amer.* I. 34 The new arm of the west, called a Smith-and-Weston, is a pretty tool. **1919** WINANS *Modern Pistol* 84 The smaller Civilian and Police Colt have not quite as good a stock . . . ; the same applies to . . . the Smith & Weston.

3. smith shop, a workshop in which a smith follows his trade.

1710 *Boston Rec.* 105 Ordered That Compl[ain]t be made. . . . Ag[ains]t Enoch Greenliefe for makeing a Smith Shop in his buildings. **1857** *Ill. Agric. Soc. Trans.* II. 360 As smithshops were almost unknown in the country, horses were seldom shod. **1892** *York Co. Hist. Rev.* 68 The wheelwright and smithshop [is] 26×68 feet in area.

b. Also **smith's shop.**

1651 *Dedham Rec.* III. 79 Whensoeuer the said shopp shall be no longer vsed for a smithes shopp . . . , then it shall be remoued. **1705** *Boston News-Letter* 22 Oct. 2/1 A fire broke out in a Smith's Shop. **1800** HAWKINS *Sk. Creek Country* 30 At the public establishment there is a smith's shop.

As the last term in **black, gold, house, jaw smith.**

Smithfield ham. (See last quots.)

1908 *Sat. Ev. Post* 31 Oct. 25/2 Next to singing a hymn, nothing gives him so much pleasure as Smithfield ham. **1924** *Concrete Highway Mag.* Sep. 215 Almost due south from Suffolk . . . is Smithfield, the home of the famous Virginia Smithfield hams, grown on a peanut diet and cured with smoke of the burning shells. **1947** BEROLZHEIMER *Regional Cookbook* 188 Smithfield Ham. . . . The hogs fatten rapidly by foraging in the peanut fields after the crop is harvested, special care is taken in curing and smoking.

Smithsonian smɪθ'sonɪən, *a.* [f. J. L. M. *Smithson* (1765–1829), Eng. physician and founder of the Smithsonian Institution.]

1. Of or pertaining to Smithson or to the Institution which he founded. Also short for next.

1840 *Niles' Reg.* 7 March 11/3 Mr. Adams rose ... to make a report from the select committee on the Smithsonian bequest. **1851** *Santa Fe Gazette* 26 April, The Smithsonian Library contains near five thousand volumes. **1874** *Rep. Comm. Agric. 1873* 358 Among the important apparatus ... recently procured may be mentioned a Smithsonian barometer. **1883** *Charleston* (W.Va.) *Ev. Call* 25 Sep., We may look for a listing of these discoveries, at no distant day, which the Smithsonian may put out. **1948** *Nat. Hist.* April 178/3 Dall proposed that if the Smithsonian would match that sum, he'd devote the entire summer to scientific exploration of the northland.

2. Smithsonian Institution, an institution at Washington, D.C., endowed by J. L. M. Smithson (see quot. 1835).

1835 JACKSON in *Pres. Mess. & P.* III. 187 A bequest [has been made] to the United States by Mr. James Smithson, of London, for the purpose of founding 'at Washington an establishment under the name of the Smithsonian Institution, for the increase and diffusion of knowledge among men.' **1896** *Cong. Rec.* App. 6 Feb. 489/1 The Egyptian mummies across yonder in the Smithsonian Institution are not more dead than these plans. **1950** *Nat. Hist.* Feb. 96/1 Valuable pieces from the Smithsonian Institution will be exhibited.

b. Also **Smithsonian Institute.**

1892 DUVAL *Young Explorers* 180 Lawrence picked up among the debris, several of the most delicately cut obsidian spear and arrow heads I had ever seen, and I believe he sent them subsequently to the Smithsonian Institute. **1947** *So. Sierran* Nov. 3/3 We wished we had asked the weather experts at the Smithsonian Institute Solar Observatory Station atop Table Mountain for today's forecast.

* **smithsonite,** *n.* Carbonate of zinc.

A French geologist, Beudant, in 1832 first used "smithsonite" for carbonate of zinc. Dana, and after him other American geologists continued this usage, but in British English and in French "calamine" denotes the carbonate. See *OED s.v. Calamine.*

1856 DANA *Rudim. Treat. Min.* 86 Carbonate of Zinc (Calamine, Smithsonite) is abundant in many of the localities of lead ores. **1922** *Mineral Resources 1919* (Bur. Mines) I. 245 The ores [in n. Ill.] are galena, smithsonite, sphalerite. **1942** *Ark. Geol. Survey Bul.* VI. 45 The only zinc minerals of common importance in Arkansas are sphalerite, smithsonite and calamine.

* **smithy,** *n.* A blacksmith. Also **village smithy.**

This sense apparently has arisen through a misunderstanding of the word in Longfellow's "The Village Blacksmith" (see quot. 1839 below, and *Amer. Sp.* XVI. 151–2).

[**1839** LONGFELLOW *Poetical Works* (1893) 14/2 Under the spreading chestnut tree The village smithy stands.] **1847** *Graham's Mag.* April 262/1 Was he some Smithy, grim and old, Whose anvil iron changed to gold? **1900** *Everybody's Mag.* Jan. 36/2 The smithy and his mate opened their 'establishment' within a few hours of their arrival, and did a 'roaring trade.' **1945** *Nat. Geog. Mag.* Jan. (*advt.*), Far more wondrous is his mastery over metals than that of his storied ancestor ... the village smithy.

* **Smock,** *n.* A variety of peach. *Obs.* — **1866** *Rep. Comm. Agric. 1865* 193 *Smock.*—A well known late variety, very productive, and valuable as a market peach. **1868** *Mich. Agric. Rep.* VII. 429 The most extensive for market are: Early Crawford, next, Early Barnard, Hale's Early, Late Crawford, and Smock (free).

* **smoke,** *n.*

1. ?A quantity of tobacco. *Obs.*

1792 *Hebron* (Conn.) *Rec.* (MS), Pepoon, Silas, ... 1 clock, 1 smoke 7/16. **1801** *Ib.*, Pepoon, Joseph, ... 1 silver watch, 3 smokes 3rd rate.

2. A spell at smoking a pipe, cigar, etc.

1835 LONGSTREET *Ga. Scenes* 213 *Mrs. B.* [*to Mrs. S.*]. Well, let's light our pipes, and take a short smoke, and go to bed. **1900** *Outing* June 304/1 The leading men of the Snake and Antelope fraternities meet together, and, after a ritualistic smoke, set the time when the ceremonies shall begin. **1946** *Chi. D. News* 23 Nov. 21/2 Just let Quagmire try to sneak a quick smoke—wow! He's a regular bloodhound.

3. Cheap whisky, or a concoction of wood or denatured alcohol used for this.

1904 O. HENRY *Cabbages & Kings* (1916) 49 On the bottles of ... Scotch 'smoke' ... behind the little counter the dust lay thick. **1928** *Daily Tel.* 9 Oct. 11/3 Twelve additional deaths today are attributed to week-end 'jags,' which have been traced to 'speak-easies' in the New York East-end, where the liquor is known as 'smoke.'

4. In combs.: (1) **smoke dance,** among the Osage Indians, a solemn dance in honor of those who have recently died; (2) **fire,** (see quot.), *obs.;* (3) **house,** see as a main entry; (4) * **jack,** (see quots.); (5) **jumper,** (see quots.), also **smoke jumping;** (6) **signal,** =**signal smoke;** (7) **stack,** (*a*) the funnel of a steamboat, (*b*) the tall chimney of a factory or other building, (*c*) the chimney of a locomotive; (8) **summer,** (see quot.), *obs.*, cf. **Indian summer;** (9) **talk,** a meeting of two or more people at which informality and friendliness are fostered by smoking, an informal talk made while smoking; (10) **wagon,** (*a*) a railway train, (*b*) a revolver, both *rare.*

(1) **1945** MATHEWS *Talking* 82 Then on the afternoon of the fourth day they have the Smoke Dance, or Give-Away Dance, during which the singers honor some of the families with their own song. — (2) **1877** RUEDE *Sod-House Days* 89 The easiest way, and one much used here, to get rid of mosquitoes in the evening is to make a 'smoke fire' before the door and let the smoke blow into the house. — (4) **1891** *Cent.* 5719/1 *Smoke-jack,* ... on railways, a hood or covering for the end of a stove-pipe, on the outside of a car. **1909** WEBSTER 1981/1 *Smokejack,* ... a movable stack over the smokestack of a locomotive engine in a round-house stall.

(5) **1945** *Chronicle-News* (Trinidad, Colo.) 15 Oct. 2/5 A famous army paradoctor and several forest service smoke jumpers prepared today to bail out over western Montana's rugged timberlands to rescue an unidentified hunter, reported wounded accidentally. **1949** *Chi. D. News* 9 Aug. 5/2 The units are made up of parachuting firefighters christened 'smokejumpers.' **1949** *Amer. Forests* Oct. 18/2 Smoke jumping is a hazardous occupation. — (6) **1873** COZZENS *Marvellous Country* 65 After leaving the Organos Mountains we had noticed Indian smoke-signals. **1949** *Nat. Geog. Mag.* Sep. 372 Gone Are the Prairie Schooner, Campfire, and Smoke Signal of Indian Days. — (7) (*a*) **1859** *Harper's Mag.* April 606/1 [It was exciting] to listen to ... the hoarse breath of the smoke stacks as it came from the rosin-fed furnaces. **1941** DORSEY *Master of Miss.* 73 The smokestack rose majestically thirty feet above the deck. [**1949** *Time* 11 April 94/2 This ship is the first of three $12 million, smokestackless streamliners for the American President Lines' round-the-world service.] (*b*) **1859** *Cairo City* (Ill.) *Gaz.* 8 July 3/1 A number of mischievous boys, ... lighting a bunch of fire crackers, ... threw them into the smoke stack. **1949** *Rocks & Minerals* March–April 125/2 The smokestacks and blackened buildings are not easily seen from the highway because of the great mounds of dump material. (*c*) **1871** *Cong. Globe* App. 27 Jan. 67/3 In the region around Lake Superior it was cold enough ... to freeze the smoke-stack off a locomotive. **1880** *Harper's Mag.* March 557/1 A freight train ... [was] thrown into lurid illumination by the sparks from the smoke-stack. — (8) **1855** BESTE *Wabash* II. 285 The Indian summer was now beginning. ... It extends through the three autumn months, and is often called the 'smoke summer,' owing to the haze which then pervades the atmosphere. — (9) **1893** *Boston Jrnl.* 25 March 2/2 The Association of Railroad and Steamboat Agents of Boston held a smoke-talk at the Tremont House last evening. **1907** *Springfield W. Republican* 24 Jan. 16 The Amherst club enjoyed the first of a series of informal banquets and smoke-talks to be held this winter.

(10) (*a*) **1853** *La Crosse Democrat* 13 Dec. 3/2 You get into one of these smoke wagons. (*b*) **1912** WASON *Friar Tuck* xxiii, As we drew closer, we made our smoke-wagons ready.

b. *Watch my smoke,* watch me go or perform. *Slang.*

1910 RAINE *B. O'Connor* 70 Watch my smoke. **1921** PAINE *Comr. Rolling Ocean* 10 Suspend judgment and watch my smoke.

As the last term in **big, fairy, holy, horse, medicine, prairie, signal smoke.**

* **smoke,** *v.*

1. *intr.* Among Indians, to exchange friendly greetings or to hold council by smoking. *Obs.*

1725 in *Travels Amer. Col.* 102 The Indians presented me with their pipes to Smoak out of (it being their Custom). **1754** *Mass. H.S. Coll.* 3 Ser. V. 42 They have never invited us to smoke with them, (by which they meant the Commissioners had never invited them to any conference). **1827** COOPER *Prairie* xxv, He was not privileged then to smoke at the great council-fire of his nation. **1870** KEIM *Sheridan's Troopers* 189 If the band accepts the pipe and smokes, the request is granted, and the warriors of the band extend their cooperation.

2. *tr.* To thicken and harden (a skin shield) by exposing it to smoke. *Obs.*

1833 CATLIN *Indians* I. 241 [By] the process of '*smoking the shield*' ..., the skin is kept tight whilst it contracts to one-half of its size.

3. Among the Sacs and Foxes, to obtain (a horse) by observing a special custom involving the act of smoking. *Obs.*

*c*1838 CATLIN *N. Amer. Indians* II. 213 *Smoking horses* is another of the peculiar and very curious customs of this tribe.

4. To haze (a college freshman) by subjecting him to excessive tobacco smoke. *Obs.* Cf. **smoking out.**

1850 in HALL *College Words* (1856) 435 I would not have you sacrifice all these advantages for the sake of smoking future Freshmen. **1880** *Harper's Mag.* Nov. 950/1 They hazed and smoked Freshmen.

5. To furnish with tobacco. *Colloq.*

1897 MARK TWAIN *Following Equator* 129 He will . . . feed you and slake you and smoke you with the best that money can buy.

smoked Yankee. Also **smoked Yank.** A Negro. *Slang. Obs.* or *hist.*

[**1829** BRAUNS *Belehrungen* 18 Der Volkspott hat dem armen Afrikaner hier den Namen *Smoked-Beef* (geräuchertes Rindfleisch) gegeben.] **1864** *Wkly. New Mexican* 10 June 2/3 In Baltimore they call the negro soldiers, who are abundant there, 'smoked Yankees.' The smoked ones like the title. **1888** GRIGSBY *Smoked Yank* (1891) 92 The line on either side was a line of living, human skeletons, . . . not exactly smoked Yankees, but the smoked skeletons of Yanks. *Ib.* 233 [He] dubbed me 'The Smoked Yank.' **1949** J. MONAGHAN *This is Ill.* 84 Hundreds of freed slaves—'smoked Yankees'—followed the armies.

* **smokehouse,** *n.*

1. A building in which meat or fish is cured by means of dense smoke.

1746 in *Lower Norfolk Co. Va. Antiquary* I. 110 (*footnote*), I . . . bequeath to my wife Mary the free use & occupation of my dwelling house . . . with the Kitching, Store house smoke house, Hen house and new Shade joining to my dwelling house. **1819** *Va. Herald* (Fredericksburg) 19 May 1/5 The improvements are a good frame House containing four rooms, a kitchen, smoke-house and stable, all in good repair. **1949** *Time* 28 March 21/3 Tipton's farmers had the relaxed air of men who have plenty of meat in their smokehouses.

attrib. **1892** MARK TWAIN *Amer. Claimant* 23 (R.), Crushed by a log at a smoke-house raising. **1949** J. B HERRICK *Memories* 4, I was permitted to open the smokehouse door.

b. *fig.* Anything full of smoke or having the appearance of a smokehouse. *Rare.*

1835 M. THOMPSON *Doesticks* 35, [I] rode to the railroad for the last time in the four-wheeled smoke-house.

c. A prison. *Obs.*

[**1857** GRIFFITH *Autobiog. Female Slave* 138 The 'lock-up' . . . had once been used as a smoke-house, but since the erection of a new one, was employed for . . . confining negroes.] **1863** P. S. DAVIS *Young Parson* 79 He could play ball without the fear of being penned in the smokehouse for it. **1889** *N.Y. Herald* 10 Jan. 8/4 [In Wilmington, Del., in 1740] the prison or 'cage,' sometimes called 'smoke house,' was a small one story brick building.

2. a. A building in which persons are exposed or subjected to smoke in order to disinfect them. **b.** A building for disinfecting anything by the use of smoke.

(**a**) **1792** BENTLEY *Diary* I. 394 At the Smoak house below the college, no representations that I had come from Salem would save me from a Smoaking. **1828** SHERBURNE *Memoirs* 29 There were little smoke-houses [for victims of smallpox] erected on a remote part of the island. — (**b**) **1924** CROY *R.F.D. No. 3* The supers for the beehives must be cleaned and taken to the smokehouse.

* **smoker,** *n.*

1. *pl.* A grade of tobacco.

1881 *Tenth Census: Tobacco Culture* 15 Types of tobacco produced in different sections. . . . Domestic Cigar Tobacco and Smokers. **1895** *Dept. Agric. Yrbk. 1894* 145 Mahogany and yellow wrappers and smokers give a distinct character to localities in Virginia, North and South Carolina, and eastern Tennessee.

2. A railway car designed for the use of those desirous of smoking.

1882 *Alta California* (S.F.) 25 July 1/8 At a convention of drummers held in the smoker it was unanimously resolved that her seat was reserved . . . for the balance of the season. **1922** J. A. DUNN *Man Trap* 154 The third coach . . . was the smoker. **1950** *Time* 27 Feb. 23/3 Twoscore others rode in the head car, the smoker.

3. (See quots.)

1888 TRUMBULL *Names of Birds* 198 Sickle-Bill Curlew. . . . Known also at Pleasantville [N.J.] to some of the gunners as *Smoker* or *Old Smoker* (the bill curving downward like the stem of a pipe). **1917** *Birds of Amer.* I. 251 Long-billed Curlew. . . . [Also called] Sabre-bill; Smoker.

4. A social occasion or party at which the guests smoke and chat.

1899 *N.Y. Journal* 7 Sep. 1/3 Smoker at the Waldorf-Astoria for the sailors of the Olympic. **1945** *Roundup* (Mont.) *R.-Tribune* 15 Feb. 1/2 Musselshell post No. 18 is hereby extending an invitation to all ex-servicemen home on furlough, to attend the annual smoker at the Legion hall, Saturday, February 17.

5. A smoking jacket.

1904 WALLER *Wood-Carver* 230 He sat before the library fire in his leather smoker.

As the last term in **Johnny, rush, stag smoker.**

***smokery,** *n.* = ***smokehouse 1.** *Rare.* — **1794** T. COOPER *America* 132 His *smokery* for bacon, hams, &c. is a room about twelve feet square.

* **smoking,** *n.* In combs.: (1) **smoking bag,** (see quot.), *obs.;* (2) **bean,** (see quot. 1909), *colloq.;* (3) **car,** = * **smoker 2;** (4) **out,** the action of hazing a college freshman by subjecting him to excessive tobacco smoke, *obs.;* (5) **tobacco,** tobacco esp. prepared for smoking.

(**1**) **1849** MCLEAN *Notes* I. 59 Here we borrowed a 'smoking-bag,' containing a steel, flint, and tinder. — (**2**) **1897** SUDWORTH *Arborescent Flora* 235. **1909** *Cent. Supp.* 1233/2 smoking-bean. . . . The catalpa or Indian bean, *Catalpa Catalpa:* so called from the custom of boys of smoking the pods. — (**3**) **1856** *Herald of Freedom* (Lawrence, Kans.) 1 April 1/7 Why not have a chewing car as well as a smoking one; a vile, filthy place with the floor full of holes, and any quantity of red-hot stoves? **1949** *Sat. Ev. Post* 25 June 106/3 Bell . . . recalls a smoking-car incident in Minnesota just a few years back in which five men introduced themselves to one another. — (**4**) **1871** BAGG *At Yale* 252 'Smoking out' is generally practised upon Freshmen before they become known as individuals.

(**5**) **1796** MORSE *Univ. Geog.* I. 259 Snuff, chewing and smoaking tobacco [are produced in the U.S.]. **1834** HAWTHORNE *Twice-told Tales* (1879) I. 116 Especially was he beloved by the pretty girls along the Connecticut, whose favor he used to court by presents of the best smoking tobacco in his stock. [**1923** MULFORD *Black Buttes* 17 They've got lots of smokin' up to Sheridan, Too bad you was so busy at McLeod that you couldn't buy none.] **1944** CLARK *Pills* 77 He wanted, at once, a pound of Missing Link chewing tobacco, a half pound of smoking tobacco and a package of cigarette leaves.

* **smoky,** *a.*

1. a. Foggy, misty. **b.** Used esp. of mountains covered with mist. Also as a proper name. **c.** (See quot.)

(**a**) **1768** *Essex Inst. Hist. Coll.* XIV. 262 This week much smoky. **1802** A. ELLICOTT *Jrnl.* 8 The morning was very smoky. **1824** DODDRIDGE *Notes* xxxi. 266 The smokey time commenced, and lasted for a considerable number of days. — (**b**) **1825** NEAL *Bro. Jonathan* I. 105 See'd him jess now, comin' over the smoky mountain there. **1885** CRADDOCK *Prophet* 1 The peaks of the Great Smoky Mountains are like some barren ideal. — (**c**) **1899** *Scribner's Mag.* XXV. 13/2 Cowboys often call vicious horses 'smoky' horses.

2. a. Smoky City, Pittsburgh, Pa., a nickname. **b. Smoky pie,** (see quot.,—a name apparently invented by Coues).

(**a**) **1850** *Elk Co. Advocate* (Ridgway, Pa.) 15 June 2/4 Your valued letters to us come regularly to hand from the 'Smoky City.' **1949** *Highway Traveler* Feb. 41/2 Today the city has the courage to smile at the wiseacre who calls her, 'the smoky city.' — (**b**) **1884** COUES *Key to Birds* 419 *Psilorhinus,* Brown Jays. Smoky Pies.

* **smooth,** *a.* and *adv.*

1. *absol.* "A meadow, or grass field" (B. '48). *Obs.*

1845 JUDD *Margaret* I. 105 On the smooth in front of the house, her . . . chickens were peeping.

2. Fine, first-class. *Slang.*

1893 W. K. POST *Harvard Stories* 210 'Well, you'll have a rattling good time down there.' 'A smooth time, you mean,' corrected Rattleton. **1944** *Chi. Tribune* 10 Dec. (Grafic Mag.) 4 Watch those people whom you consider smooth; see how they dress.

3. In combs.: (1) **smooth-barked pine,** (see quot.); (2) **bore,** (*a*) a gun having an unrifled bore, also transf., (*b*) also as adj.; (3) **-bored gun,** a smoothbore; (4) **mouth,** (see quot. 1944); (5) **sumac,** (*a*) the red sumac, *Rhus glabra,* (*b*) (see quot.).

(**1**) **1788** SCHÖPF *Reise* II. 276 Die *Smooth-barked-Pine,* glatte Kiefer. —Sie hat 2 Nadeln in jeder Scheide, von 3–5 Zoll Länge, übrigens wie die vorhergehenden gebildet. . . . Die Rinde am unter Stamm ist etwas rauh, wird aber weiter hinauf glatt und weiss. — (**2**) (*a*) **1812** *Niles' Reg.* II. 398/1 It was the best smooth bore he ever shot with in his life. **1869** MARK TWAIN *Innocents Abroad* 146 (R.), Canon Fulbert . . . the old smooth-bore. **1907** LILLIBRIDGE *Trail* 27 His finger was on the trigger of the old smoothbore. (*b*) **1799** *Ann. 7th Congress* 2 Sess. 1402 One had a rifle, and the other a smooth-bore piece. **1886** LOGAN *Great Conspiracy* 322 A smooth-bore battery of the Enemy . . . is driven back. **1902** WHITE *Blazed Trail* 129 He was armed with an old-fashioned smooth-bore muzzle-loader. — (**3**) **1775** ADAIR *Indians* 275 He could not discharge it, as it was double-tricker'd, contrary to the model of their smooth-bored guns. — (**4**) **1944** ADAMS *W. Words* 148/1 smooth mouth An aged horse. **1945** *Hardin* (Mont.)

Tribune-Herald 15 Feb. 7/4 Horses—1 bay mare, smooth mouth, weight 1,750.

(5) (*a*) **1814** BIGELOW *Florula Bostoniensis* 71 Smooth Sumach. . . . A common species of Sumach found about fences and borders of fields. **1901** MOHR *Plant Life Ala.* 600 Smooth Sumach. . . . The leaves are used for tanning and dyeing. (*b*) **1897** SUDWORTH *Arborescent Flora* 275 *Rhus copallina.* Dwarf Sumach. . . . Smooth Sumach.

smörgåsbord ˈsmɔrgəsˌbɔrd, *n.* [Sw. an appetizer, lit. "sandwich table."] A relish or appetizer, usu. at a Scandinavian dinner, also the meal itself (see quot. 1926 and cf. etymology).

1926 *Ladies' Home Jrnl.* Nov. 150/2 The 'Smorgesbord,' or bountifully supplied refreshment table, is a Scandinavian institution, though it is said the custom originated in ancient Russia. **1949** *Chi. D. News* 29 Nov. 18/7 There were ample liquid refreshments and smorgasbord. **1950** *Chi. Tribune* 9 Jan. 24/2 He should know that at a smorgasbord you wait on yourself.

transf. **1948** MENJOU & MUSSELMAN *It Took 9 Tailors* 176 Instead the studio offered me the lead in a piece of *smörgåsbord* called *The Sorrows of Satan*, a novel by Marie Corelli. **1949** *Chi. Tribune* 6 March VII. 1/2, I . . . wasted much time watching gay little juncoes, . . . scarlet cardinals and even arrogant jays and crows at my smorgasbord.

***smudge,** *n. attrib.* Designating things used in a smudge for repelling mosquitoes.

1882 G. C. EGGLESTON *Wreck of Red Bird* 55 'What is a "smudge box," Ned?' 'Simply a shallow box of earth set upon a post, to build a smudge upon.' **1846** *Knickerb.* XXVIII. 341 You make a large 'smudge' fire outside that the smoke may drive these [insects] away. **1902** WHITE *Blazed Trail* 148 Thorpe's old tin pail was pressed into service as a smudge-kettle. **1903** ——— *Forest* 112 Your smudge-pan may drive away the mosquitoes.

***smudge,** *v. tr.* To make a smudge in (a place) to repel mosquitoes, etc.; to cause (a fire) to emit dense clouds of smoke. Also **smudging,** *n.*

1846 FARNHAM *Prairie Land* 314 This process is more briefly designated by its technical name of '*smudging.*' **1860** *Harper's Mag.* Aug. 296/2 The blankets were spread in the tents, the tents smudged, or mosquito nets hung. **1866** *Ib.* Jan. 265/2 The others sat by the fire and 'smudged' it. **1891** *Cent.* 5722/1 *Smudge*, . . . to make a smudge in; fumigate with a smudge: as, to smudge a tent so as to drive away insects.

***smut,** *n.* In combs.: (1) **smut face,** (see quot.); (2) **grass,** a West Indian grass, *Sporobolus elongatus*, common in the southern states; (3) **mill,** a smut machine for cleaning wheat of smut.

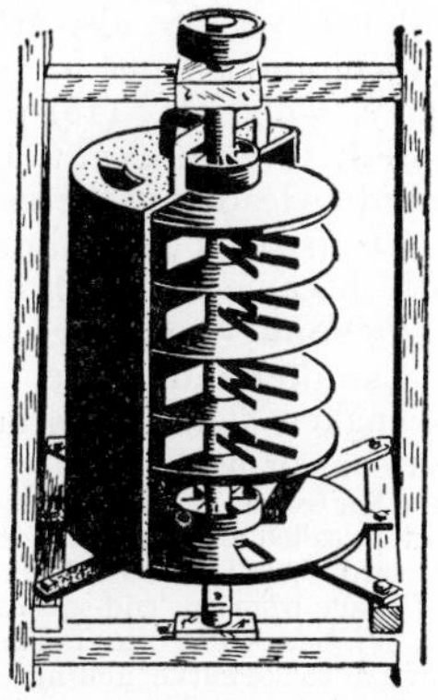

Early (*c*1848) form of smut mill

(1) **1893** ROOSEVELT *Wilderness Hunter* 265 They insist on many species; not merely the black and the grisly, but . . . others with names known only in certain localities, such as the range bear, the roach-back, and the smut-face. — (2) **1884** VASEY *Agric. Grasses* 63 *Sporobolus Indicus.* . . . is called smut grass from the fact that after flowering the heads become affected with a black smut. **1894** COULTER *Bot. W. Texas* III. 518 Smut-Grass. . . . Introduced in rather moist land throughout the southern United States. — (3) **1818** *Niles' Reg.* XV. 80/2 A *smut mill*, for cleaning wheat of smut, is in operation at Plattsburg. **1871** DE VERE 547 *Smut-mill* or *smut-machine*, designates in the farmer's language a part of the flouring-mill which breaks and separates grains of wheat affected with smut.

***smutty,** *a.* In the names of birds (see quots.). — **1884** COUES *Key to Birds* 425 *Perisoreus canadensis fumifrons*, . . . Smutty-nosed Jay. *Ib.* 783 *Priofinus melanurus*, Smutty-nosed Shearwater. **1917** *Birds of Amer.* I. 148 Scoter. *Oidemia americana.* . . . [Also called] Gray Coot; Smutty Coot.

S.N. *attrib. Polit.* Abbreviation of **Sag Nichts** (Say Nothing). *Obs.* — **1855** *N.Y. Wkly. Tribune* 26 May 1/3 The tall, sun-burned voters were collected into groups discussing K.N. and S.N. matters . . . , in rather a quiet, listless way.

snab snæb, *n.* [Prob. fanciful.] A pretty girl, esp. one fashionably dressed. *College slang. Rare.* — **1891** *Outing* Nov. 103/2 There were a number of the New Haven 'snabs,' and Harry fancied he detected there amid a group the beautiful Miss Hastings.

***snag,** *n.*

1. A tree trunk or large branch embedded in the bottom of a river, bayou, etc., in such a way as to be dangerous to boats. Cf. ***planter,** ***sawyer.**

1804 CLARK in *Lewis & C. Exped.* I. (1904) 44 We got fast on a Snag Soon after we Set out. **1841** FALCONER *Letters & Notes* (1930) 66 We passed the wrecks of two steamers, which had been sunk by striking snags. **1897** DANA *Recoll. Civil War* 26 It was reported . . . that Bayou Macon was full of snags. **1949** *Pacific Northwest Quart.* April 102 Thus, with profits in sight that would pay for their steamers twice over, owners wagered their vessels against the snags of the Missouri.

b. Any impediment or difficulty.

1829 KIRKHAM *Eng. Grammar* 207 He has run against a snag. **1949** *Reader's Digest* July 60/1 But once more those currency snags!

c. (See quot.) *Rare.*

1831 ROYALL *Southern Tour* II. 110 This snag, (I mean a Vermonter) was *pretty tolerable clever.*

2. In combs.: (1) **snagboat,** a powerful boat, often double-bottomed, for removing snags and other obstructions from waterways; (2) **chamber,** the front part of the hull of a river steamer, made into a water-tight compartment as a safeguard against the boat's sinking if snagged, *obs.;* (3) **room,** =prec., *obs.;* (4) **scow, vessel,** =**snagboat,** *obs.*

Snagboat

(1) **1832** *Cong. Deb.* 3 May 2722 The snag boat had been employed in improving the navigation of the Mississippi. **1949** *N.O. Times-Picayune Mag.* 15 May 12/3 He designed the snagboat, the Heliopolis, himself. — (2) **1829** B. HALL *Travels in N. Amer.* III. 364 All the boats on the Mississippi are now fitted with what is called a snag-chamber. **1838** STEVENSON *Sk.* 110 Several steamers are built with false bows, called 'snag-chambers,' as a palliative of the danger arising from accidents of this kind. — (3) **1820** *Niles' Reg.* XVIII. 112/2 The *steam boat* Columbus from New Orleans to Shipping port, was . . . saved from sinking by having a snag room. — (4) **1847** LANMAN *Summer in Wilderness* 21 The snag-vessels can extricate them from their dangerous positions. **1907** STEWART *Partners of Providence* 176 The white snag-scow . . . did keep the snags pulled out of the mouth of the Missouri.

b. *To catch on* (or *hit*) *a snag*, to encounter a difficulty, to meet one's match. *Slang.*

1887 STUART CUMBERLAND *Queen's Highway* 277 In rough Western parlance a man who falls in with such a player 'catches on a snag,' and it is said that every one who visits the North-West comes across sooner or later the snag on which he is to catch. **1949** *Dallas Morn. News* 9 May II. 10/1 Czechoslovakia's nationalization of private enterprises hit a small snag when it encountered a snake farmer, Dr. Frantisek Kornalick.

* **snag,** *v.*

1. *tr.* Usu. in passive: To be pierced by a snag, said esp. of river steamers.

1807 GASS *Journal* 229 One of our best horses got snagged today, and was left here. **1836** J. HALL *Statistics of West* 239 Twenty-four [boats were] snagged, and *five* destroyed by being struck by other boats. **1898** POST *10 Years Cowboy* 62 The folks used to talk of that flatboat getting snagged. **1926** *Chi. Drovers' Jrnl.* 1 May 4/2 Since the William M. Johnson snagged herself to death, no steamboat has ever tried to climb as far up the Gasconade as this.

fig. **1833** *Polit. Examiner* (Shelbyville, Ky.) 22 June 4/1, I will agree to be shot with a paper wadding if there ar' room enough in the whole clearing for a man of ordinary parts to stand on five minutes at a time, without getting snagged by some tape and cotton yarn dealer in the street. **1852** PHILLIPS *Speeches* (1863) 38 A great mind, anchored in error, might snag the slow-moving current of society.

b. *intr.* and *passive.* To be caught on a snag. Also transf.

1866 *Harper's Mag.* Nov. 810/1 A Mississippi steamer, that snagged and went down on 'Yazoo Bend.' **1891** C. ROBERTS *Adrift Amer.* 211, I started to haul my line in, but found I was snagged. **1893** *Outing* XXII. 123/1 When the hook is snagged or fast in a tree it is often handy to be able to reel in.

2. To break down, defeat, or trip. Also fig. *Slang.*

1842 *Ainsworth's Mag.* II. 556 Feller citizens, jine me in snagging 'em. **1848** E BENNETT *Mike Fink* 11/2 Open, Deb, . . . or by all the fishes of the Dead Sea, I'll snag this old door. **1898** *N.Y. Journal* 17 Aug. 6/6 The travellers thought to snag him.

* **snagged,** *a.* Pierced or caught by a snag.

1851 WORTLEY *Travels in U.S.* 112 In the papers will you often see whole columns, headed, 'Snagged,' containing a melancholy list of boats. **1867** RICHARDSON *Beyond Miss.* 21 A snagged steamer. . . . Our steamer . . . [would] shudder with horror at every snag grating against her hull. **1872** C. KING *Mountaineering in Sierra Nev.* 174, I made a dash for the snagged mule.

snaggers ˈsnægəz, *v.* [?f. * *sniggers*, a minced oath.] *I snaggers!* a mild imprecation. *Slang. Obs.* Cf. **snugger,** *v.* — **1831** *Workingman's Gaz.* (Woodstock, Vt.) 19 Jan. 129/3, 'I snaggers,' said another, 'no more would you n't; for he is n't knee-high to a toad.' **1833** A. GREENE *Life D. Duckworth* I. 92 Say nothing worse than—Darn it, I snaggers!

snagging ˈsnægɪŋ, *n.* An instance of a boat's being pierced by a snag. *Obs.* — **1851** HALL *Manhattaner* 179 There may sometimes occur a snagging, . . . with perhaps a collision. **1880** MARK TWAIN *Tramp Abroad* 95 [He] had gone to bed with his head filled with impending snaggings, and explosions, and conflagrations.

* **snaggy,** *a.* Of a waterway: Abounding in snags.

1806 CLARK in *Lewis & C. Exped.* V. (1905) 380 The Sand bars . . . confined the [river] to a narrow Snagey Chanel. **1864** HOSMER *Color-Guard* xii, We passed into snaggy lakes at last. **1887** *Harper's Mag.* July 270/2 [The] snaggy, rafted, convoluted course was by universal avoidance relegated to an isolation almost insulting.

* **snail,** *n.* **1.** Any oyster drill, as *Urosalpinx cinerea.* Also **snail bore. 2. snail bird, hawk,** the everglade kite, *Rostrhamus sociabilis plumbeus,* which feeds on snails.

(1) **1881** INGERSOLL *Oyster Industry* 248 *Snail-Bore.*—Mollusks of the genus *Urosalpinx,* etc. (New Jersey.) **1884** GOODE *Fisheries* I. 696 These small 'Snails,' 'Drills,' 'Borers,' and 'Snail-bores,' as they are variously called, belong to several species. — (2) **1917** *Birds of Amer.* II. 63 Everglade Kite. . . . Snail Hawk. . . . Tropical Florida. **1942** Nat. Pk. Service *Fading Trails* 167 One victim of the sudden recession of 'glades water was the Everglade kite or snail bird.

* **snake,** *n.*

1. (*cap.*) An Indian belonging to any one of various Shoshonean tribes; also, *pl.*, any of these tribes. Cf. **6. d.** below.

These Indians are said to have been so called because of the adroit manner in which they concealed themselves when discovered. They glided away into the grass, sagebrush and rocks with the subtlety of snakes. See Drumm *Jrnl. of a Fur-Trading Exped.* 106.

1821 J. FOWLER *Journal* 55 Last night on Counting them over find now four Hundred of the following nations—Iltans—Arrapohoes—Kiawa Padduce—Cheans—Snakes. **1842** *Jrnl. Medorem Crawford* (1897) 13 They were a war party of Sues & Shians who had been to fight the Snakes. **1901** *Ore. Hist. Soc. Quart.* II. 257 These tribes held as slaves members from . . . the Rogue River Indians, Shastas, Klamaths, Modocs, and occasionally some from the Snakes. **1940** *Places to See in Wyo.* xxiv/2 Shoshones were also referred to as Snakes or the Snake People.

b. In full **Snake Indians.**

1791 *Mass. H.S. Coll.* 1 Ser. III. 24 The tribes of Indians [were called] . . . the Blackfeet tribe, the Snake Indians [etc.]. **1864** *Washoe* (Nev.) *Star* 19 Nov. 2/1 The Snake Indians have been able to keep themselves supplied with guns and ammunition by confederating themselves with the Mormons. **1920** DRUMM *Jrnl. Fur-Trading Exped.* 106 Snake Indians. This tribe was so generally known by this term as to almost obscure the family name of Shoshoni.

2. *pl.* Used as an interjection. *Slang.*

1839 *Spirit of Times* 17 Aug. 283/3 (We.), Snakes! such a row! **1894** WISTER in *Harper's Mag.* Sep. 509/1 Snakes! but it feels good.

3. = **black snake 3.**

1863 *Ladies' Repository* Aug. 488/1 [The teamster] made his snake ring again as he cracked it around his head.

4. *pl.* Delirium tremens. Also allusively. *Colloq.* Cf. **7.** (13), (15) below.

1865 *Harper's Mag.* Nov. 701/1 He is only taking a parting smile at the snakes. **1892** *Courier-Journal* 3 Oct. 3/4 A crazy man, with 'snakes' jumped overboard. **1942** BERREY & VAN DEN BARK *Amer. Thesaurus Slang* 157 Delirium tremens. Barrel fever, . . . shivery-shakes, snakes, snakes in the boots.

5. (See quot. 1896.)

1870 *N.Y. Herald* 1 July 4/5 The ordinance against . . . the setting off in the streets of fireworks known as 'snakes' . . . will be vigorously enforced. **1896** HASWELL *New York* 545 There was then [*c*1860], and for some years after, an article of fireworks known as a snake from the tortuous manner of its motion when ignited.

6. In special combs.: (1) **Snake Baptist,** see **Seed Baptist;** (2) * **box,** (see quot. 1891); (3) **curve,** in baseball, an alleged extremely baffling curve, *rare;* (4) **dance,** see as a main entry; (5) **den,** a place where a number of snakes are found hibernating together; (6) **estufa,** the room in which the Hopi Indians keep the snakes used in their snake dance; (7) **fence,** a zigzag or worm rail fence, also **snake fencing;** (8) * **head,** the loosened end of a strap rail driven upward through the floor of a passenger car, to the danger or injury of the passengers, now *hist.*, cf. **snake-rail** (*a*), * **snake's head,** and **b.** (4) below; (9) **headed,** *a.* very angry, *slang, rare;* (10) * **hole,** (see quot.), *slang, obs.;* (11) **Hunter,** during the Civil War, one of a body of Federal partisans organized to combat the Moccasin Rangers, *obs.;* (12) **kiva,** = **snake estufa;** (13) **medicine,** whisky, also attrib., *slang;* (14) **-oil (balm),** a contemptuous name for a quack remedy; (15) **poison,** whisky, *slang, obs.;* (16) **pole,** an oxgoad, *obs.*, cf. **snake-poled,** *s.v.* * **snake,** *v.* **1. c.** below; (17) **priest,** one of the Indian leaders in the snake dance (sense **1.**); (18) **rail,** (*a*) a strap or flat iron railroad rail, the ends of which frequently became loose, forming snakeheads, *obs.*, cf. (8) above, (*b*) **snake-rail fence,** = **snake fence;** (19) **-'s head,** = * **snakehead** above, cf. **b.** (9) below; (20) **sign,** sign of snakes, *obs.;* (21) **story,** a tall story in the manner of a bear or fish story.

(2) **1891** *Cent.* 5725/1 *Snake-box,* . . . a faro-box fraudulently made so that a slight projection called a snake warns the dealer of the approach of a particular card. **1903** LEWIS *Boss* 374 They [are] handin' him out every sort of brace from an 'end-squeeze' . . . to a 'snake-box.' — (3) **1907** *St. Nicholas* June 720/1 The umpire . . . could throw an 'up shoot' and a 'snake curve' and never half try.

(5) **1824** J. DODDRIDGE *Notes* 79 The next attempt to destroy a snake den took place between New Lancaster and Columbus in the state of Ohio. **1891** M. E. RYAN *Pagan of Alleghanies* 95 The Good Man was leading me right over the snake-den to hear things that are good for me. — (6) **1893** DONALDSON *Moqui Pueblo Indians* 69 The snake estufa at Walpi is hewn out of the solid sandstone of the mesa. — (7) **1805** PARKINSON *Tour* 48 Snake-fences . . . are rails laid with the ends of one upon the other, from eight to sixteen in number in one length. **1855** OLIPHANT *Minnesota* 70 Occasionally, but very rarely, a bit of snake-fencing indicates a settler. **1948** DICK *Dixie Frontier* 104 The commonest fence was that variously known as the worm, snake, or Virginia fence. It was made in a zigzag pattern. — (8) **1848** BARTLETT 315 *Snake-Head,* an object of dread to travellers on railways. . . . Serious accidents have been caused by them. **1891** WELCH *Recoll. 1830–40* 31 One of the ever present fears of travelers riding on those strap rails were the so-called 'snake heads.' **1943** POWELL *Home Again* 53 The snakeheads—the thin rail, under the weight of the train, would buckle, pull loose from the spikes that held it to the

stringers, and strike against the bottoms of the cars. — **(9) 1920** B. CRONIN *Timber Wolves* viii. 137 Anyhow, they's no need to get snake-headed about it.

(10) 1927 *Scribner's Mag.* March 266/2 Much of the graft formerly vested in the 'district' is now turned over to the heads of municipal chauffeur and taxi license bureaus, the keepers of 'snake-holes' (hidden prohibition saloons), . . . and hotel keepers. — **(11) 1862** *N.Y. Tribune* 3 June 5/1 Fremont has 'Snake-hunters,' gathered from the same class. **1866** F. KIRKLAND *Bk. Anecdotes* 406/1 Captain Baggs got up . . . a company of 'Snake-Hunters.' — **(12) 1900** *Outing* June 305/1 It is in the Snake kiva that the snake charm liquid is made. **1911** *Nat. Geog. Mag* Feb. 125/2, I saw a priest ascending the ladder leading from the Snake kiva. — **(13) 1865** *Harper's Mag.* Aug. 276/2 A fine spring of water, aided by a little snake-medicine, set us all right. **1901** CRANE *Monster* 199 [You] got up agin some snake-medicine licker. — **(14) 1927** BENÉT *J. B.'s Body* 294 Crooked creatures of a thousand dubious trades, . . . sellers of snake-oil balm and lucky rings. **1947** PAUL *Linden* 333, I liked to hear the barker, and to see who fell for his spiel and bought the Snake Oil, at fifty cents a bottle.

(15) 1889 L. C. D'OYLE in *Cornhill Mag.* Jan. 51 It was variously called for as tangle-foot, snake-poison, . . . chain-lightning, or other fancy name, but it was *never* called for as *whisky*. — **(16) 1830** in W. T. COGGESHALL *Poets & Poetry* (1860) 84 With snake-pole and a yoke of oxen. — **(17) 1900** *Outing* June 305/2 Then, like a flash, the Snake priests dart upon them grabbing in their hands all they can pick up. **1911** *Nat. Geog. Mag.* Feb. 107/1 The old faith of the Hopis is guarded and taught with care by the Antelope and Snake priests. — **(18)** *(a)* **1862** *N.Y. Tribune* 26 June 1/4 The loose end of a snake rail threw the first car from the track. *a*1877 *Ib.* (B.), The Winchester Railroad was built many years ago with the snake-rail, the ends of a large number of which, having become unfastened, spring up and down whenever a train passes. *(b)* **1948** *Scientific Amer.* Sep. 41/3 They made ramrods of Hickory for their rifles, and fenced in their cleared land with snake-rail fences. **1949** *Boston Globe* 14 Aug. (Fiction Mag.) 10/3 The waxing moon's light lay green-white upon the new grass with the barred shadows of the snake-rail fence across it. — **(19) 1847** HONE *Diary* II. 328 The detail of loss of life by boiler-bursting, collisions, and snakesheads is as regular a concomitant of the breakfast-table as black tea. **1918** *Essex Inst. Coll.* LIV. 197 An unpleasant feature of primitive railroad travel was the 'snake's head' or end of a loosened rail punching through the floor of the car.

(20) *a*1846 *Quarter Race Ky.* 93, I couldn't see no snake sign. — **(21) 1826** *Va. Herald* (Fredericksburg) 6 Sep. 3/2 The New-York Spectator will probably class this with the Snake stories of the day. **1835** *Sentinel & Star in West* (Philomath, Ind.) 27 June 32/2 We relate the following circumstances without fear of being accused of merely telling a *snake story.* **1945** FUGINA *Upper Mississippi* 196 This is a snake story, I must admit, but it happens to be a true one because I saw it.

b. In the names of plants: (1) **snake bite,** (see quot. 1909); (2) **cactus,** the brain cactus, *Pediocactus simpsoni*, so called from the manner of its growth along the ground; (3) **collards,** app. a contemptuous term for collards, *rare;* (4) *****head,** =**balmony,** cf. **6.** (8) above; (5) **lily,** (see quot.); (6) *****mouth,** *(a)* (see quot. 1931), also **snakemouth arethusa,** *(b) pl.* (see quot.); (7) **plantain,** (see quot.); (8) **root,** see as a main entry; (9) *****-'s head,** *(a)* =**balmony,** cf. (4) above, *(b)* (see quot.), cf. **6.** (19) above; (10) **-'s master,** (see quots.); (11) *****tongue,** (see quot.); (12) **violet,** (see quot.); (13) **weed,** see as a main entry.

(1) 1905 *Outlook* 7 Nov. 580 He pointed out a white flower he called snake-bite which he said he would rub on if one of the creatures bit him, and that would take out the poison. **1909** *Cent. Supp.* 1233/3 snake-bite. . . . 1. The nodding wake-robin, *Trillium cernuum.*—2. The blood-root, *Sanguinaria Canadensis.*—3. The wild lettuce, *Lactuca Canadensis.* — **(2) 1910** HOLDER *Channel Islands* 156 The choya cactus, the snake cactus, and the ordinary tuna abound. **1946** *Trail & Timberline* May 75/2 Five varieties of cacti were found, among which was a large snake cactus. — **(3) 1832** KENNEDY *Swallow Barn* 232 The heirs of Swallow Barn . . . are hereafter to be pestered with this fine garden of wankopins and snake-collards. — **(4) 1784** *Amer. Acad. Mem.* I. 464 Snake-head. . . . Common by fences and amongst bushes in moist land. **1869** FULLER *Flower Gatherers* 271 We had still another flower . . . that Jimmy Carroll called *Snake-head.*

(5) 1833 EATON *Botany* (ed. 6) 189 *Iris versicolor*, snake lily, blue flag. — **(6)** *(a)* **1817–8** EATON *Botany* (1822) 397 Snake-mouth arethusa. . . . About 8 inches high, in damp places. **1931** CLUTE *Plants* 108 Thus the little orchid, *Pogonia ophioglossoides*, though called snake-mouth, has a technical name which means like a snake or adder's tongue. *(b)* **1894** *Amer. Folk-Lore* VII. 96 *Chelone*, sp., snake-mouths, Banner Elk, N.C. — **(7) 1839** in *Mich. Agric. Soc. Trans.* VII. 414 *Plantago lanceolata.* Snake plantain. — **(9)** *(a)* **1834** AUDUBON *Ornith. Biog.* II. 150 The Snake's Head grows on the banks of rivers and swamps, in the Middle and Southern States. **1885** *Outing* VII. 180/1 Another stout herb with a spike of curiously formed white flowers is snakes-head. *(b)* **1915** ARMSTRONG & THORNBER *Western Wild Flowers* 572 Snake's Head. *Malacothrix Coulteri.* White. Spring. California.

(10) 1841 W. KENNEDY *Texas* I. 133 A root called snakes'-master, which grows abundantly in the pinewoods, is said to be an efficient remedy for the reptile's venom. **1844** M. C. HOUSTON *Texas* (1845) 244 In order, I suppose, to make one's mind easy [about rattlesnakes], you are told that 'the Indians' know an herb, which they call the 'snake's master.' — **(11) 1844** *Lexington Observer* 3 July 1/3 The velvet Geraniums were . . . familiarly known as Snaketongue! — **(12) 1893** *Amer. Folk-Lore* VI. 138 *Viola pedata*, . . . snake violet; horse-shoe violet. Swansea, Mass.; Boston, Mass.

c. In the names of birds and other creatures: (1) *****snake bird,** any one of various fish-eating birds of the genus *Anhinga* found in swamps along the southern coasts of the U.S., cf. **anhinga, Grecian Lady, water-turkey;** (2) *****charmer,** (see quot.); (3) **doctor,** *(a)* the dragonfly, cf. **snake feeder,** *(b)* =**hellgrammite;** (4) **feeder,** see as a main entry; (5) **hawk,** (see quot. 1917); (6) **killer,** the chaparral cock or road runner; (7) **maid,** ?a dragonfly, *obs.;* (8) **worm,** (see quot.).

(1) 1791 W. BARTRAM *Travels* 132 Here is . . . in the waters all over Florida, a very curious and handsome species of birds; the people call them Snake Birds. **1944** KANE *Bayous of La.* 134 Every foot of available space is crowded with birds of many kinds: Louisiana herons of many shading hues; . . . the shiny black ibis; the curious anhinga or 'snake bird.' — **(2) 1863** C. C. HOPLEY *Life in South* I. 93 Another sweet songster is the cat-bird, or 'snake-charmer,' thus named from its cry of alarm, as the popular belief is, when a snake is near. — **(3)** *(a)* *c*1862 BAGBY *Old Va. Gentleman* 92 [The water is] full of all manner of nasty and confounded 'mud-kittens,' 'snap'n turtles,' and snake doctors. **1946** RICHTER *Fields* 255, I seed a bee bird last summer. It's no bigger'n a snake doctor. *(b)* **1891** *Cent.* 5725/2 Snake-doctor, . . . the dobson or hellgrammite. **1948** *Field & Stream* July 42/2 Various stages of the dobson are known as . . . chippers, water grampus, . . . flip-flaps, snake doctors.

(5) *c*1728 CATESBY *Carolina* I. 4 They are said to prey upon Lizards and other Serpents; which has given them by some the name of Snake-Hawk. **1873** *Amer. Naturalist* VII. 202 Numbers of exquisitely graceful swallow-tailed kites or 'snake hawks' . . . were seen sailing about. **1917** *Birds of Amer.* II. 60 Swallow-tailed Kite. . . . Other Names.—Swallow-tailed Hawk; . . . Fork-tailed Kite; Snake Hawk. — **(6) 1872** MCCLELLAN *Golden State* 242 Woodpeckers, snake-killer, cuckoo, fish-hawk, . . . king-fisher, humming-bird . . . made up the rare and large variety of birds inhabiting California. **1917** *Birds of Amer.* II. 126 Road-Runner. . . . [Also called] Snake Killer; Lizard Bird. — **(7) 1863** C. C. HOPLEY *Life in South* I. 87 'Yes, that's a fly; one kind of fly.' ''Tain't no fly; that's a snake maid.' — **(8) 1891** *Cent.* 5726/1 *Snakeworm*, one of the masses of larvæ of certain midges of the genus *Sciara* . . . [which] often migrate in armies forming a snake-like body a foot or more long.

d. Of or pertaining to the Snake Indians, as (1) **Snake country,** (2) **horse,** (3) **nation,** (4) **squaw,** (5) **tribe,** (6) **warrior.**

(1) 1825 in DALE *Ashley-Smith Explor.* (1918) 157 The Snake country. . . . Mr. Smith understood as being confined to the district claimed by Shoshone Indians. **1844** LEE & FROST *Oregon* 211 He found a stone that he had picked up . . . in the Snake country. — **(2) 1843** TALBOT *Journals* 45 The trappers prefer Snake Indians and Snake horses before any race of men or horses in the world. — **(3) 1807** GASS *Jrnl.* 154 This . . . is the same river, whose head waters we saw at the Snake nation. **1841** WILLIAMS *Tour to Ore.* (1921) 42 We are now among the Snake nation and Flat Head Indians. — **(4) 1812** LUTTIG *Jrnl.* 106 This Evening the Wife of Charbonneau a Snake Squaw, died of a putrid fever.

(5) 1819 E. DANA *Geog. Sk.* 54 Of these natives, . . . the Snake tribe is the largest. **1837** IRVING *Bonneville* II. 48 These are of that branch of the great Snake tribe called Shoshokoes, or Root Diggers. **1910** HODGE *Amer. Indians* II. 606/1 The principal Snake tribes were the Walpapi and the Yahuskin. — **(6) 1938** THOMPSON *High Trails* 53 The Snake warriors got ready for an attack as soon as the moon should come up.

7. In colloq., often nonsensical and obs., phrases, the significance of which is usu. clear from the quots, as (1) *To whip the snake*, (2) *there are no snakes*, etc., (3) *to fall a snake*, (4) *by the snakes of Babylon*, (5) *to wake snakes, (and walk your chalks)*, (6) *as sure as snakes*, (7) *a sin to snakes*, (8) *to make snake*, (9) *to be some snakes*, (10) *like killing snakes*, (11) *to be above snakes*, (12) *as cold*, etc., *as* *a snake in August*, (13) *to have snakes in one's boots*, (14) *why in snakes*, (15) *to see snakes*, cf. **4.** above.

(1) **1766** J. BARNARD in *Mass. H.S. Coll.* 3 Ser. V. 239 When I first came [in 1714], there were two companies of poor, smoke-dried, rude, ill-clothed men, trained to no military discipline but that of '*whipping the snake*,' as they called it. **1838** *N.Y. Advt. & Exp.* 24 Jan. 2/1 To Hayne, Hamilton, McDuffie, Preston, Thompson and Legare, we see no unkindness in the Northern Press, but it cannot be expected that we can *whip the snake* after John C. Calhoun, in his Cretan labyrinth of political doubling and twisting, though never a word is said that he has not ability. — (2) **1802** DAVIS *Travels* (1803) 325 There are no snakes if *Philadelphia* does not beat Charleston hollow! **1854** S. SMITH *Down East* 331 I'm a-going to have some bread and flour cake . . . or else there's no snakes in Oquago. — (3) **1820** J. HALL *Lett. from West* (1828) 349, 'I killed a hundred of them [*sc.* snakes],' said he, 'in a few minutes, each as large as my leg.' 'I do not dispute it,' replied his friend, 'but would be better satisfied if you would fall a snake or two.' **1855** *Cong. Globe* 31 Jan. 483/1, I say I saw twenty-five [snakes] and I will not fall another snake. **1880** BURNETT *Old Pioneer* 159 Don't you really think you might safely fall a snake or two in the distance? — (4) **1831** *Boston Transcript* 19 July 1/1 By the snakes o' Babylon, Squire, there was Capt'n Joe huggin my Sal around the neck.

(5) **1835** LONGSTREET *Ga. Scenes* 6 Oh, wake snakes, and walk your chalks! **1848** LOWELL *Biglow P.* 1 Ser. 147 *Wake snakes*, to get into trouble. **1872** DE VERE 212 The other meaning . . . makes waking snakes equivalent to 'running away quickly.' **1909** CALHOUN *Miss Minerva* 17 Rabbit up the gum tree, Coon is in the holler Wake-snake; Juney-Bug stole half a dollar. — (6) **1789** *Columbian Mag.* III. 182 As sure as snakes it must be *tarnation* clever fun. **1835** CROCKETT *Life* (1865) 242, I should lose my election as sure as there are snakes in Virginny. — (7) **1841** *N.O. Picayune* 15 Jan. 4/1 Dad sets the dog arter the sheep and me arter the gals—and the way he makes the wool, and I the petticoats fly, is a sin to snakes. **1879** *Caddo* (Ind. Terr.) *Free Press* 4 July 5/2 Two 'coons' of the cyprian type run together the other night across the railroad track, and the way the 'fur and har' flew was a sin to snakes. — (8) **1843** TALBOT *Journals* 42 A party of skirmishers . . . zig-zagging or as it is called 'making snake.' — (9) **1846** *Quincy* (Ill.) *Whig* 17 Feb. 2/2, I borrid one from red-headed Jake, t'other day, and I reckon if you was to have seed it, you'd a said it was some snakes!

(10) **1845** *Big Bear Ark.* 38 At it we went, like killing snakes, so good a man, so good a boy. — (11) **1851** WORTLEY *Travels U.S.* 154 Look at those two tall Kentuckians, with their tufted chins, somewhere about seven feet 'above snakes.' — (12) **1855** SIMMS *Forayers* 246 Inglehardt . . . is about as cold, as cunning, and as venomous as a snake in August. — (13) **1877** HABBERTON *Barton Exper.* ix, He's been plenty high on whisky for two or three days, . . . and they say he's got snakes in his boots now. — (14) **1891** *Scribner's Mag.* Sep. 293/1 Why in snakes should anybody want to be a sculptor?

(15) **1912** *OED s.v. snake, sb.* 2 d. *To see snakes*, to have delirium tremens. *U.S. slang.* **1943** *Democrat* 14 Oct. 2/1 These men, entrusted with enforcing the prohibition laws, are not supposed to see snakes or elephants unless the critters really exist, so their report may be accepted as authentic.

As the last term in **bead, belled, black, blind, blow, blowing, brown, bull, chain, chicken, choking, copper, coral, corn, cow, diamond, diamondback rattle, double-headed, eel, egg, fox, garter, glass, gopher, grass, green, hair, harlequin, hissing, hog-nose(d), hoop, horn, horned, horse, horsehair, house, joint, king, milk, moccasin, northern rattle, pilot, pine, prairie, rattle, rattled, rattletail, red, red bead, ribbon, ring, sachem, scarlet, sheepnose, snow, speckled, striped, swamp, thorn-tailed, thunder, thunder-and-lightning, turkey, two-headed, wampum, whip, worm snake.**

***snake,** *v.*

1. *tr.* To drag or draw (a log or tree) along the ground.

1829 FLINT *G. Mason* 21 (Th.), Logs, sixteen feet in length, could be drawn, or as it is technically phrased, snaked into church. **1880** *Cong. Rec.* 22 Jan. 490/2, I could not fail to recall the wild sublimity of that early day when I snaked saw-logs. **1948** DICK *Dixie Frontier* 28 A horse was used to 'snake' a log right into the house by leading the animal through the cabin.

b. *transf.* and *fig.*

1834 C. A. DAVIS *Lett. J. Downing* 14 We snaked him out of that scrape as slick as a whistle. **1883** *Phila. Times* No. 2810, 4 Some legal loophole . . . through which an evasion or extension can be successfully snaked. **1905** LINCOLN *Partners* 200 If you've got a loose tooth a string and a door'll snake it out as quick as the dentist will. **1946** *Democrat* 24 Jan. 2/3 No boys to snake a 200-pound buck over several miles of rugged country.

c. (See quot. 1859.) Also **snake-poled,** *a.*, soundly beaten with a snake-pole *q.v. Obs.*

1838 DRAKE *Tales Queen City* 92 Many were trampled under foot, some *gouged*, others horribly *snake-poled*. **1852** O. P. BALDWIN *Southern Sk.* 120 (B.), Any gal like me . . . ought to be able to snake any man of her heft. **1859** BARTLETT 421 *To Snake*, . . . to beat; to thrash. Southern.

2. *passive.* To be pierced by a snakehead while traveling on a railroad car. *Rare.*

1855 BESTE *Wabash* I. 172 We were a good deal shaken, though not 'snaked' as sometimes happens . . . when this iron hooping becomes detached, and curling itself up, enters through the floor of a car.

snake dance.

1. A religious dance among Indians, esp. a ceremony in which live snakes are used, observed every two years, chiefly as a prayer for rain, by the Hopi Indians.

1772 in *Travels Amer. Col.* 517 The women danced the Snake dance, the leader haveing her legs Covered with Turpin shells which is filled with small stones on purpose to make a noise. **1877** JOHNSON *Anderson Co., Kans.* 139 [The Sac and Fox Indians] also danced the 'green corn' dance, and the 'snake' dance. **1891** *Bureau Amer. Ethnol. Rep.* VIII. 136 Among the Hopi, particularly at Walpi, the snake-dance is renowned. **1948** *Westerners' Brand Book* 77 The real mystery of the Snake Dance is how they are able to select a date when it will rain.

2. A stage dance in some way suggestive of snakes or of an Indian snake dance. Also a parade of students celebrating some special event, as an athletic victory, by moving in a zigzag manner in Indian file, or such a parade engaged in as a political demonstration.

1895 *N.Y. Dramatic News* 23 Nov. 4 Ida Siddons in her snake dance, two Italian pantomimists and the breathing paintings stood out in the olio like warts on a fat man's face. **1911** BURGESS *Find the Woman* 244 So he . . . went, reminding them of the [football] score and the snake-dance every time he opened a bottle. **1946** THOMPSON *Amer. Daughter* 234 'Okay,' I said, and a few minutes later was a link in a howling, writhing snake dance that weaved itself in and out of the business section. **1948** *Green Bay* (Wis.) *Press-Gazette* 30 June 16/4 The political parties' national conventions and their snake dances are American institutions.

Also as a verb, hence **snakedancing,** *a.*

1922 *Chi. D. Maroon* 3 Oct. 2/1 The public . . . picture . . . howling, snakedancing crowds whenever colleges and universities are mentioned. **1931** F. L. ALLEN *Only Yesterday* 17 Eight hundred Barnard College girls snake-danced on Morningside Heights in New York. **1948** *Time* 26 July 15/3 There they snake-danced under a portrait of Robert E. Lee, flourished Confederate battle flags, and shouted their defiance of Harry Truman.

snake feeder. A dragonfly (see also quot. 1891).

1861 *Ill. Agric. Soc. Trans.* IV. 34 [Suppose] we wished to multiply, artificially, the number of a particular species of *dragon-fly*, or *snake-feeder*. **1883** RILEY *Old Swimmin'-Hole* 11 The snake-feeder's four gauzy wings fluttered by. **1891** *Cent.* 5725/2 *Snake-doctor*, . . . the dobson or hellgrammite. . . . Also [in Ohio] *snake-feeder*. **1904** STRATTON-PORTER *Freckles* 219 The snake-feeders are too full to feed anything—even more sap to themselves. **1949** KURATH *Word Geog. Eastern U.S.* 14/1 The line of demarkation over against the Midland *snake feeder* is remarkably clear and sharp.

snakeroot ˈsnekˌrut, *n.*

1. The root or rhizome of any one of various American plants regarded as useful in cases of snake bite, or the medical preparation made from such a root.

1635 *Relation of Md.* 21 They have a roote which is an excellent preseruative against Poyson, called by the English, the Snake roote. **1713** *Mass. H.S. Coll.* 6 Ser. V. 276 If the measeles coms amongst you, its best to giue sage and baum tea, . . . not too much snake roote. **1784** SMYTH *Tour* I. 290 The inhabitants, and negroes, likewise find and dig great quantities of snake-root. **1901** MOHR *Plant Life Ala.* 672 The roots of this *Gentiana villosa* and *G. ellittii*, under the name of 'Sampson's snake-root,' are used in domestic medicine. **1942** WEYGANDT *Plenty of Penna.* 176, I recalled her cookies, . . . her herbs, her sassafras bark and snakeroot.

attrib. **1859** GRATTAN *Civilized Amer.* I. 62 Snakeroot bitters, timber doodle, egg-nogg, and some others I have only heard of, but have never been tempted with. **1882** *Harper's Mag.* Nov. 855/1 He is no New-Englander, . . . who has never heard of 'snakeroot tea.' **1948** *Hoosier Folklore* March 6 Cold snakeroot tea is the very best of nerve medicines.

2. A plant supplying such a root or preparation.

1709 LAWSON *Carolina* 78 The more Physical [herbs include] . . . Monks Rhubarb, Burdock, Asarum wild in the woods, reckon'd one of the Snake-roots. **1904** BAILEY *Cyclo. Amer. Horticulture* IV. 1673 Snakeroot. Black S. *Cimicifuga racemosa* and *Sanicula Marilandica.* Button S. *Liatris.* Canadian S. is *Asarum.* Seneca S. *Polygala Seneca.* White S. *Eupatorium ageratoroides.* **1948** *Amer. Jrnl. Nursing* Dec. 751/1 The names of the plants have a pleasant old-time ring: gentian, cardamon, . . . snakeroot, condurango.

As the last term in **black, button (rattle), Canada, heart, large-leaved Virginia, Seneca, tall button, Virginia, Virginian, white, wild snakeroot.**

snakeweed ˈsnek͵wid, *n.* Any one of various American plants reputed to be valuable in treating snake bites (see also quot. 1899).

1630 in FORCE *Tracts* I. No. 12, 12 There are some Serpents called Rattle Snakes, that . . . will flye vpon him and sting him so mortally, that he will dye within a quarter of an houre after, except the partie stinged haue about him some of the root of an Hearbe called Snake weed to bite on, and then he shall receiue no harme. **1784** *Amer. Acad. Mem.* I. 475 *Prenanthes.* . . . Snake-weed, Blossoms white. **1899** *Animal & Plant Lore* 118 Ferns are popularly known as 'snake-weeds,' because snakes are supposed to harbor among them. Tennessee. **1943** DAMON *Sense of H.* 155 Take the common dooryard plantain. . . . Samule calls it snakeweed because theoretically he believes it will cure snake bite.

snaking ˈsnekɪŋ, *n.* **1.** The killing of snakes. *Obs.* **2.** Creeping or crawling in a snakelike manner. *Rare.* **3.** The action of dragging (a saw log) *out* of a place.

(1) 1850 JAMES ABBEY *Trip to California* 27 While the boys were eating their cold snack, I started out on the prairie a snaking, and killed ten rattlesnakes. **1862** *Harper's Mag.* June 33/2 The Colonel . . . cried out 'Let the logs alone, and all of you go to snaking.' They piled up fifty-three [rattlesnakes] in the course of the evening. — **(2) 1853** SIMMS *Sword & Distaff* (1854) 94 Keep you quiet now, while I do a little *snaking.* — **(3) 1883** *Harper's Mag.* Jan. 206/1 The snaking out of these logs is another source of casualty to the lumberman.

* **snap,** *n.*

1. *pl.* String beans. Cf. **snap bean.**

*c***1770** JOHN RANDOLPH, JR. *Gardening* (1924) 6 French Beans and snaps are the same. **1841** *N.O. Picayune* 4 May 2/1 What Kentuckian would believe that *porc fumé aux haricôts verts à la Kentucky* in French, was plain *bacon and snaps* in English? **1943** *Sat. Ev. Post* 24 July 90 (Wentworth), He has become rooted in . . . the exacting business of being a Virginian. He has learned to call string beans 'snaps.'

2. (See quot. 1864.) Also attrib.

1845 in BLAIR *Amer. Humor* (1937) 325 I'll never bet on two pair agin! They're peart at the snap game, theyselves; but they're badly lewed this hitch! **1864** DICK *Amer. Hoyle* (1866) 207 *Snap,* a temporary bank, not a regular and established game. [Faro.] **1938** ASBURY *Sucker's Prog.* 280 A few of the river gamesters ran Faro snaps when ashore in St. Louis, but most of them concentrated on Poker.

3. (*cap.*) A game played by young people in which the one who is "snapped" or invited to do so chases another around a ring formed by the players. Cf. * **snap,** *v.* **4. b.** (2).

1865 in RIDLEY *Battles* (1906) 481 Games [in Ga.] soon began—'Thimble,' 'Snap,' and kissing songs. **1944** WILSON *Passing Inst.* 93 Our liveliest game was Snap, a game that used to seem very exciting but now somewhat resembles Drop the Handkerchief.

4. Vim, dash, zip, energy. *Colloq.*

1865 *Harper's Mag.* 145/2 [They] had no snap about them. **1920** LEWIS *Main Street* 415 Snap and speed are his middle name!

5. Something particularly easy or pleasant. *Colloq.*

1877 RUEDE *Sod-House Days* 120 It is no snap, for the straw rolls out fast enough to keep them very busy. **1905** *Denver Republican* 6 Sep. 6/1 The tendency is away from the 'public office is a private snap' idea. **1949** *L.A. Times Home Mag.* 6 Nov. 14/3 Prepared mixes enriched flours, creamy shortenings work for you, making hot breads a 'snap' to prepare.

6. (See quot.)

1881 INGERSOLL *Oyster Industry* 248 *Snaps.*—The most inferior oysters sent to market. (Maryland.)

7. In photography, a snapshot or quick exposure. *Colloq.*

1893 *Amer. Annual Photography* VIII. 251 The exposures were mostly 'snaps.' **1950** *Nat. Geog. Mag.* April 514/1 We . . . eventually secured a few satisfactory snaps of the ordinary garden variety of jump.

8. *pl.* (See quot. 1929.)

1929 R. B. VANCE *Human Factors Cotton Culture* 132 Cotton picked with the cotton burr to save time is known as 'snaps.' **1933** HOLLANDER *Arme Blanken* 288 Deze door 'sledding' verkregen katoen, 'snaps,' brengt wel een lageren prijs op, maar door de groote arbeidsbesparing is het toch vaak voordeelig om dit te doen.

As the last term in **black, Boston, cattle, cold, great, soft, Philadelphia, turtle snap(s).**

* **snap,** *a.*

1. Quick, offhand, held on short notice.

1854 *N.Y. Tribune* 2 Aug. 7/3 Now, these meetings are the easiest things in the world—they are nothing but *snap* meetings, and they show nothing more clearly than the weakness of the slaveites. *c***1870** CHIPMAN *Notes on Bartlett* 422 *Snap,* rapid, quick, off-hand. 'A . . . snap bargain,' &c. **1906** *N.Y. Ev. Post* 27 June 1 Many Tammany men expressed indignation over last night's 'snap' meeting. . . . Notices of the meeting were not sent out until yesterday morning. **1911** LINCOLN *Cap'n Warren's Wards* 136 This judgment was not of the snap variety.

b. snap company, a theatrical company playing short engagements. *Obs.*

1885 *Santa Fé Wkly. New Mexican* 24 Sep. 4/6 It is the custom, during the summer months, for 'snap' companies to travel through the country and gather shekels.

c. snap convention, (see quot. 1914).

1892 *N.Y. Herald* 23 Feb. 3/1 This small army of influential independents was here as a protest against what they term a 'snap' Convention. **1892** *Courier-Journal* 3 Oct. 4/3 His hopes . . . were blasted by the nomination of Dr. J. F. Kimbley by a snap convention or 'conference' of Republican office-holders. **1914** *Cyclo. Amer. Govt.* III. 324/2 Snappers, a nickname applied to the machine Democrats in New York in 1892, who, under the leadership of David B. Hill held a very early state convention on short notice, called a 'snap' convention (Feb. 22, 1892).

d. snap judgment, a hasty, offhand judgment. Also attrib.

1841 *Cong. Globe* App. 14 June 42/3 This extra session of Congress called in time of peace to take snap judgments on the American people. **1860** *Knickerb.* LVI. 458 A kind of twopenny shystering smartness and snap-judgment genius. **1923** BOWER *Parowan Bonanza* 123 I ain't going to give snap judgment on a thing the size of this. **1949** *Chi. Tribune* 24 Aug. 12 You ought to be ashamed of your snap judgment of her!

2. Of gloves: Having a snap fastener.

1893 M. HOWE *Honor* 220 His wife wore . . . short white gloves of the species called 'snap' from the mode of fastening.

* **snap,** *v.*

1. *tr.* (See quots.) Cf. * **snapped,** *a.* **2.**

1874 MCCOY *Cattle* 246 In Central Kansas by far the larger portion of the corn crops are harvested by husking, or snapping the corn from the stalk, leaving the immatured ears and nubbins on the stalks with the fodder. **1877** RUEDE *Sod-House Days* 193 Geo. and I helped Hoot 'snap' corn. 'Snapping' is breaking off the ear from the stalk without husking it. **1948** JACOBS *We Chose Country* 136 The whole family went out, on a cold and sparkling Sunday morning, to 'snap corn,' which means husking it off the stalk.

2. To throw (a ball) with a quick snappy jerk.

1887 *Outing* Oct. 70/1 In a scrimmage he places it on the ground, and at a signal from his quarter, snaps the ball back by a downward and backward pressure with his foot. **1912** MATHEWSON *Pitching* 262 He snapped it to third. **1920** CAMP *Football without Coach* 48 The center would snap him the ball.

3. To take a snapshot of (a person or thing), to take (a picture).

1926 *Phila. Pub. Ledger* 24 March 10/6 He looks much like the man known to many a tourist who stands at the top of the incline on the Island of Capri inviting the photographers to snap him. **1950** *Chi. D. News* 11 Jan. 46/1 He pulled out a small camera from the pocket of his jacket and snapped a picture of the boat.

4. In combs.: (1) **snap and raffle,** a kind of gambling game, *obs.;* (2) **back,** (see quot. 1893 and cf. **snapper-back**); (3) **bean,** a string bean *q.v.* the young pods of which "snap" when broken preparatory to cooking, a dish of such beans, usu. *pl.;* (4) **bug,** =**snapping beetle,** *colloq.;* (5) **-jack bug,** =prec., *obs.;* (6) **law,** (see quot.), *obs.;* (7) **mortgage,** ?a mortgage under the provisions of the snap law, *obs.;* (8) **turtle,** =**snapping turtle.**

(1) 1810 *Monthly Mag.* XXX. II. 416 After that was raffled for, the company began to play with dice, at a game called snap and raffle. — **(2) 1887** *Outing* Oct. 69/2 He it is who, receiving the ball from the 'center- rusher,' or 'snap-back,' as he is more commonly called, passes it to some other player for a kick or run. **1893** CAMP *College Sports* 96 Usually the 'snap-back' [puts the ball in play]. *Ib.* 99 This name [center rusher] has since given place almost entirely to 'snap-back.'— **(3) 1770** in *Va. Hist. Mag.* XLV. 156 A Breast of Veal for Dinner Snap Beans & gooseberry tart. **1855** in BOYD *Alabama* 115 Bacon and greens, . . . snap beans and occasionally other garden vegetables. **1950** *Democrat* 2 March 1/6 The best test of a good snap bean is to break it. If it has lots of snap, it's fresh and tender. And, remember, keep snap beans in a cool place. — **(4) 1834** MCMURTRIE tr. *Cuvier's Anim. Kingdom* 350 North America is extremely rich in this genus. The insect is usually called a Snap-bug. **1879** *Scribner's Mo.* Aug.

497/2 This springing power . . . has given it the improper name of 'Snap Bug.'

(5) c**1845** W. T. PORTER *Big Bear Ark.* 91 You have seed one of them Snapjack bugs. — (6) **1863** *Cong. Globe* 7 Jan. 226/1 We had in operation [in Mass. until 1840] a terrible system, sometimes designated a snap law, by which a creditor could go, even in the night, and strip the debtor of everything he had in the world. — (7) **1902** A. D. MCFAUL *Ike Glidden* xviii. 138 The hours which others allotted to repose were spent by him in pursuing claims under snap mortgages. — (8) **1841** H. PLAYFAIR *Papers* I. 32 'Half-horse, half-alligator,' with a 'streak of the snap-turtle,' is the usual appellation of those amphibious men who spend their lives on the banks, and as boatmen on the waters of the Mississippi.

b. In colloq. phrases: (1) *snap the whip,* (see quot. 1896); (2) *snap and catch ('em),* = ∗**snap,** *n.* **3;** (3) *snap-up around the chimney,* some now indefinable children's game, *obs.;* (4) *snap into* (or *out of*) *it,* to hurry, move with sprightliness.

(1) **1853** RICHARDS *V. Life* (1912) 28 We played snap the whip at recess to-day and I was on the end and was snapped off against the fence. **1896** *D.N.* I. 424 *Snap the whip,* a boys' game in which a line of boys with hands joined run sharply and one end of the line suddenly stops, the other going round it in a circle. — (2) **1857** *Quinland* I. xiii. 192 Then began the fun. Some danced, some played snap and catch. **1914** *D.N.* IV. 112 snap and catch 'em, n. phr. A children's game. [Kansas.] — (3) **1867** T. LACKLAND *Homespun* I. 133 Then the old-fashioned family games begin, . . . snap-up around the chimney [etc.]. — (4) **1918** in F. A. POTTLE *Stretchers* (1930) 239 Oh, snap into it! We want to get this done. **1929** H. L. GATES *Lipstick* 4 You look dead over there. Snap out of it and come for a shuffle.

∗**snapped,** *a.* **1.** *S.* Drunk. *Slang. Obs.* **2.** (See quot. 1925.)

(1) **1840** *S. Lit. Messenger* VI. 514/1 'Quit, Daniel, you'r *snapped,*' she said. **1851** *Polly Peablossom* 46 Bennett and Smith were both at the grocery, the latter about two-thirds snapped. — (2) **1868** *Iowa State Agric. Soc. Rep. 1867* 126 Feed in open lots from seventy-five to one hundred bushels of corn in the ear, snapped or pulled. **1925** R. R. SNAPP *Beef Cattle* 353 The term 'snapped corn' is applied to corn that has been gathered with the inner layers of the husks remaining on the ears.

∗**snapper,** *n.*

1. =**snapping turtle.**

1796 *Aurora* (Phila.) 17 May (Th.), The crocodile throats of the gentle snappers or mud tortles in the Jersey market. **1886** *Scientific Amer.* 11 Dec. 370 The snapper has a voracious appetite. **1938** MATSCHAT *Suwannee River* 24 Large snappers may weigh a hundred pounds, and it is claimed that they live for more than a century.

b. Also as the name of other animals and birds.

1842 BUCKINGHAM *E. & W. States* III. 101 Rattlesnakes, copper-heads, ground-vipers, and snappers—all of the venomous class of serpents—are occasionally found. **1891** *Cent.* 5727/2 *Snapper,* . . . one of various American flycatchers (not *Muscicapidæ*) which snap at flies, often with an audible click of the beak; a flysnapper.

c. As the name of plants (see quots.).

1840 DEWEY *Mass. Flowering Plants* 75 Touch-me-not, or Jewel Weed . . . [is] often called *Snapper.* **1892** *Amer. Folk-Lore* V. 93 *Silene cucubalus,* snappers. Salem, Mass.

2. A cracker at the end of a whip. Usu. transf. in the sense of a word or phrase giving a smart or pointed finish to something.

1835 HOFFMAN *Winter in West* I. 179 *Jim* cracked his snapper. **1857** HOLLAND *Bay Path* xiv, You'd a said twenty lashes . . . and Mr. Moxon would 'a said twenty Amens on the end on 'em for a snapper. **1895** MARK TWAIN *How to Tell a Story* 226 (R.), A humorous story finishes with a nub, point, snapper, or whatever you like to call it. **1903** G. BRADFORD in *N.Y. Ev. Post* 29 Sep. 8 Senator Carmack . . . is simply adding a snapper to the lash of his vigorous denunciation of the whole Philippine policy. **1949** *Newsweek* 19 Dec. 13/3 Then came the snapper: 'No matter by what method we achieve security, we'll not achieve it in a bankrupt economy.'

3. A glassworker who uses a tongs called a snap-dragon.

1903 *K.C. Star* 12 Dec. (Th. Supp.), Eighteen 'snappers' of the Kansas window glass factory returned to work today.

4. (See quot.) *Obs.*

1914 *Cyclo. Amer. Govt.* III. 324/2 *Snappers,* a nickname applied to the machine Democrats in New York in 1892, who, under the leadership of David B. Hill, held a very early state convention on short notice, called a 'snap' convention (Feb. 22, 1892).

5. snapper-back, in American football, the player, usu. the center, who puts the ball in play. Cf. **snap-back.**

1887 in P. H. DAVIS *Football* 475 Rule 12 altered so as to prohibit interference with the snapper-back until the ball is in motion. **1893** *Ib.* 483 The snapper-back [is] to have full and undisturbed possession of the ball. **1921** *Official Football Guide* 17 One of the two men standing on either side of and next to the snapper-back (commonly known as guards).

As the last term in **alligator, anti-, bastard, black, brown, fly, gray, lane, mangrove, red, red-bellied snapper.**

∗**snapping,** *a.* In combs.: (1) **snapping beetle,** any one of numerous beetles of the family Elateridae; (2) **bug,** =prec.; (3) **mackerel,** (see quot. 1842); (4) **tortoise,** =**snapping turtle;** (5) **turtle,** see as a main entry.

(1) **1868** *Rep. U.S. Comm. Agric.* (1869) 93 These insects [*sc.* Elateridae] are known in Europe by the common name of 'skip-jacks,' or 'spring beetles,' and in America as 'snapping beetles.' **1874** *Dept. Agric. Rep.* (1873) 155 Mr. N. B. Moore, Manatee, Florida, . . . forwarded with his letter specimens of an insect, which proves to be the *Pyrophorus physoderus,* . . a species of snapping-beetle. — (2) **1860** *Ladies' Repository* XX. 263/2 There is a singular little insect known in Indiana as the 'snapping bug.' **1874** *Dept. Agric. Rep.* (1873) 162 As the larvae of *Melanactes,* a species of *Elater* or 'snapping-bug,' are said to be luminous, it is possible [etc.]. — (3) **1842** *Nat. Hist. N.Y., Zoology* IV. 131 From the avidity with which they seize even an unbaited hook, they [*sc.* young bluefish] have received . . . the name of *Snapping Mackerel.* **1888** GOODE *Amer. Fishes* 150 Young Bluefish are in some parts of New England called 'Snapping Mackerel.' — (4) **1809** THOMAS ASHE *Travels* 201 The Indians call this by a name which implies the snapping tortoise. **1840** *Knickerb.* XVI. 54 The . . . snapping-tortoises, frogs, squirrels, and such small deer, are their flocks and herds.

snapping turtle. Any one of various large, voracious water turtles of the family Chelydridae, esp. *Chelydra serpentina.* Also a soft-shelled turtle.

1784 SMYTH *Tour* I. 338 One kind of them bites very fiercely when incensed . . . ; these are called *Snapping Turtles.* **1846** LYELL *Second Visit* II. 156 On the shore of the lake we caught a tortoise, called here the snapping-turtle. **1884** GOODE *Fisheries* I. 153 The 'Snapping Turtle,' is very widely distributed. **1950** *Time* 23 Jan. 1/3 A long fleshy tail with alligator-like crests marks this unpleasant creature as a snapping turtle.

attrib. c**1866** BAGBY *Old Va. Gentleman* 48 A true Virginian . . . [must have] snappin'-turtle eggs. **1872** EGGLESTON *End of World* 24 This was spoken in a staccato, snapping-turtle way.

b. A person having the characteristics of a snapping turtle. *Slang.*

1808 SCHULTZ *Travels* (1810) II. 145, I am a Mississippi snapping turtle: have bear's claws, alligator's teeth, and the devil's tail; can whip *any man,* by G—d. **1857** *Spirit of Times* 10 Oct. 82/1 With a quick but easy hit from the shoulder, he caught the 'snappin' turkle' smack between the eyes, and knocked him right into the river.

c. (See quots.)

1920 HUNTER *Trail Drivers Texas* I. 297 An arrangement for holding the cattle while they are being branded is called a 'squeezer' or 'snappin' turtle.' **1944** ADAMS *W. Words* 148/2 snappin' turtle A narrow branding chute.

snapping ˈsnæpɪŋ, *adv.* Intensely, used of cold. *Colloq.*

1857 in A. ALLEN *P. Brooks* (1900) I. 201 It is snapping cold here today. **1876** *Wide Awake* 19/1 The night was snapping cold. **1905** WIGGIN *Rose* 93 The snapping cold weather and the depth to which the water was frozen were aiding it.

snarky ˈsnɑrkɪ, *a.* Irritable, short. *Rare.* — **1915** H. L. WILSON *Ruggles of Red Gap* xii. (1917) 209, I had received a rather snarky letter from him demanding to know how long I meant to remain in North America.

∗**snarl,** *n.* A large number, a swarm. *Colloq.*

1775 *Broadside Verse* (1930) 141/2, I see another snarl of men. **1860** HOLLAND *Miss Gilbert* 386 A snarl of people that didn't care anything about me. **1904** *N.Y. Tribune* 10 April, A veritable snarl of street urchins took possession of several benches in Lincoln Park.

∗**snatch,** *v.* **1.** *tr.* To arrest. *Slang.* **2.** To bring (a steamboat) quickly into a desired course. *Rare.* **3.** *To snatch* (a person) *bald-headed,* see ∗**bald-headed. 4.** *To be snatched,* (see quot.). *Obs.*

(1) **1860** *Harper's Mag.* Jan. 284/1 Colonel M'G—— . . . was 'snatched' for a violation of the same law. — (2) **1875** MARK TWAIN *Life on Miss.* ii. 40 Mr. Bixby . . . shouted through the tube. . . . 'Put her hard down! snatch her! snatch her!' — (4) **1877** BARTLETT 619 'Don't be snatched,' i.e., do not be in too great a hurry. South-western.

b. snatch team, (see quot. 1944).

1905 *Forestry Bureau Bul.* 61, *s.v.* **1944** ADAMS *W. Words* 148/2 snatch team. A strong team used to supplement another on a hard pull.

*__snatcher,__ *n.* __1.__ The conductor of a horsecar. *Slang. Obs.* __2.__ (See quot. 1932.) *Slang.*

(1) **1885** WHITMAN in *N. Amer. Rev.* Nov. 434, What did you do before you was a snatcher? **1886** ——— *November Boughs* 406 The conductor is often call'd a 'snatcher' (i.e. because his characteristic duty is to constantly pull or snatch the bell-strap, to stop or go on). — (2) **1932** *Tulsa D. World* 7 March 10/5 'Snatchers' or kidnapers have not been as busy in Tulsa as they have in other cities. **1949** *L.A. Times* 17 May IV. 4/6 He owned the car used by the snatchers.

As the last term in **bank, buck, cradle snatcher.**

*__sneak,__ *n.*

1. A scout. *Rare.*

1845 SIMMS *Wigwam & Cabin* I Ser. 45, I was a leetle too anxious to be altogether so careful as a good sneak ought to be.

2. In combs.: (1) **sneak boat,** a light boat of shallow draught used by duck shooters, cf. **Barnegat sneak-boat, -box, sink boat;** (2) **box,** =prec., also attrib.; (3) **thief,** (see quot. 1859); (4) **thieving,** stealing without using force or violence, as by sneaking into places left unlocked or unguarded.

(1) **1853** *Md. Laws* 220 Any person or persons [who] shall use any sink boats, sneak boats or floats, . . . shall be subject to a fine. **1898** *Kissimmee* (Fla.) *Valley Gaz.* 28 Jan. 3/5, I found Carr in his new sneak boat duck shooting. **1949** R. J. SIM *Pages from Past* 78 The garvey and the sneak boat are old inventions native to Barnegat Bay. — (2) **1875** *Fur, Fin & Feather* (ed. 3) 120 Each gunner hiding his little sneak-box boat in the point of meadows . . . awaits the coming of the broad-bill flocks. **1883** KNIGHT *Supp.* 826/2 The New Jersey sneak box is from 12′ to 14′ in length. **1906** *Atlantic Mo.* Aug. 240 The very moment one is captain of only a sneak-box one becomes arrogant. — (3) **1859** MATSELL *Vocabulum* 82 *Sneak-thief,* a fellow who sneaks into areas, basement-doors or windows, or through front-doors by means of latch-keys, and entering the various apartments, steals any thing he can carry off. **1928** F. N. HART *Bellamy Trial* i. 17 The front door was slightly ajar, and thinking that sneak thieves might have broken in, he pushed it farther open. — (4) **1884** *Cent. Mag.* March 653/2 The offences are nearly all trivial, most of them being petty larceny and sneak-thieving. **1892** *Advance* 31 March, The designed effect of it [a gerrymander] may be termed a kind of political sneak-thieving.

b. *To lead from a sneak,* in card-playing, to lead from a weak suit.

1891 THANET *Otto the Knight* 269 These primitive players led from 'sneaks.'

As the last term in **bank, dead sneak.**

*__sneaker,__ *n.* A soft-soled, noiseless shoe, usu. of canvas. *Colloq.*

1895 *Standard Dict.* **1900** G. ADE *More Fables* 193 His Job on this Earth was to put on a pair of Pneumatic Sneakers every Morning and go out and investigate Other People's Affairs. **1949** *Desert Mag.* April 18/1 The best attire for hiking . . . may be high boots and breeches, or levis and sneakers, or shorts and sandals—depending on the terrain.

*__sneeze,__ *n.* __1. sneezeweed,__ any one of several American perennial plants of the genus *Helenium,* the odor of which is said to cause sneezing. __2.__ *__sneezewort,__ =prec.

(1) **1837** DARLINGTON *Flora Cestrica* 487 False Sun-flower. Sneezeweed. **1880** CABLE *Grandissimes* 244 A frenzied mob of weeds and thorns wrestled . . . for standing-room—rag-weed, smart-weed, sneeze-weed. **1915** ARMSTRONG & THORNBER *Western Wild Flowers* 538 Sneeze-weed. *Helenium Bigelowii.* . . . The flowers are from an inch and a half to two inches across. — (2) **1840** DEWEY *Mass. Flowering Plants* 132 *H[elenium] autumnale.* Sneezewort. False Sun Flower. . . . bitter; fields; August. **1891** *Cent.* 5730/2 *Sneezeweed.* . . . Less properly called *sneezewort.*

snell snɛl, *n.* [Origin obscure. Cf. Du. *snelgaren,* refuse thread from a cotton spinnery.] A short piece of gut, horsehair, etc., used in fastening a fishhook to a longer line.

1846 *Spirit of Times* 9 May 126/2 [The bass] was taken with a jointed rod, with a single gut snell, after half an hour's play. **1883** *Cent. Mag.* July 381/2 Reeling up his line to the snell of the hook, . . . he turned his left side to the riffle below. **1897** *Outing* XXIV. 331/2 Hooks mounted on strong gut snells.

snell snɛl, *v.* [f. the noun.] *tr.* To tie (a fishhook) to a line. Also **snelled,** *a.* — **1891** *Cent.* 5730/2. **1893** *Outing* XXII. 123/2 Double-snelled Aberdeen, sizes 1 and 2, are very satisfactory hooks.

*__sniff,__ *n.* __1.__ An insignificant person. *Slang.* __2.__ (See quot. *a*1922.)

(1) **1890** GUNTER *Miss Nobody* xii, Going to marry that little sniff? — (2) **1917** HERGESHEIMER *3 Black Pennys* xxiv, After dinner, when they were playing sniff. *a*1922 in APPEL *Biog. Wanamaker* 336 His own favorite game was 'sniff,' played with dominoes.

*__snifter,__ *n.* A dram or small drink of liquor. Also a globular-shaped glass, somewhat smaller at the top, to intensify the aroma of the liquor served in it.

1848 DURIVAGE & BURNHAM *Stray Subjects* 110 'Cobblers for the party,'—'snifters for the crowd,'—or 'slugs for the entire company.' **1910** McCUTCHEON *Rose in Ring* 90 You need a snifter of brandy. **1943** BAKER *Trio* (1946) 103 She was sitting beside me holding a brandy snifter.

*__snifty,__ *a.* __1.__ Disdainful, proud, inclined to sniff. *Slang.* __2.__ (See quot. and cf. __nifty.__)

(1) **1889** K. MUNROE *Golden Days* xvii. 188 If you notice me getting anyways snifty . . . you just bump me down hard. **1902** G. H. LORIMER *Lett. Self-made Merchant* xviii. 268 Clytie said . . . that spirits were mighty snifty and high-toned. — (2) **1891** *Cent.* 5731/1 snifty. . . . Having an inviting odor; smelling agreeably: as, a *snifty* soup. [Slang, U.S.]

*__snipe,__ *n.*

1. In miscellaneous colloq. and slang uses: **a.** (See quot. 1900.) **b.** A cigar or cigarette butt. **c.** (See quot.)

(a) **1870** MEDBERY *Men Wall St.* 131 In street *argot,* they are 'snipes' and 'lame ducks.' **1900** NELSON *A B C Wall St.* 159 *Snipe,* an obsolete term for a curbstone broker. — (b) **1889** *N.Y. Herald* 2 Jan. 4/4 Farewell, old year; adieu, dear pipe; Goodbye, cigar; goodbye, old 'snipe.' **1899** FLYNT *Tramping* 397 *Snipe,* cigar-butts. **1931** *K.C. Star* 9 July, He'll be darned if he is going to shoot cigarette snipes. — (c) **1906** *N.Y. Ev. Post* 21 Feb., 'Snipes,' in the vernacular of the Panhandle and the Santa Fé, are . . . section men.

2. snipe hunt, hunting, a prank played upon one not familiar with the sport in which, under the guise of having him hold a bag for snipes to run into, he is left at night in a lonesome or disagreeable place. Also fig.

1904 FLEMING *Documents re. Reconstruction* No. 2. 3 And one of the night games was much like 'snipe hunting.' **1934** *Chi. D. News* 10 Jan. 7/1 There are times when reporters are holding the bag in an off the record snipe hunt.

As the last term in **black, blind, bullhead, Drummond's, English, fall, German, grass, gray, gutter, horsefoot, marsh, meadow, mud, prairie, red-bellied, red-breasted, robin, rock, semipalmated, squat, squatting, stone, white, Wilson, Wilson's, winter snipe.**

sniptious ˈsnɪpʃəs, *a.* [?f. **snippy.*] (See quots. 1830, 1893.) *Colloq.* Cf. **ripsniptious.**

1827 *Mass. Spy* 24 Oct. (Th.), We mought paddle our canoes together pretty snipshush like. **1830** *Painesville* (O.) *Telegraph* 15 June 1/5 *Sniptious*—Finically nice. **1893** M. A. OWEN *Voodoo Tales* 123 She hatter 'splain w'y she feel so snipshus (pert).

Snohomish snoˈhomɪʃ, *n.* [Indian term of uncertain meaning.] (See quot. 1910.) Cf. **Skykomish.**

1854 *Pacific Railroad Rep.* I. (1855) 432 Below the Sinakomish come the Stoluchquamish, (river people) or as the name is usually corrupted, Steilaquamish, whose country is on the stream bearing their name. **1903** JAMES *Indian Basketry* 53 The Snohomish and Skohomish peoples occupy the opposing sides of the upper portion of the Sound. **1910** HODGE *Amer. Indians* II. 606/2 Snohomish. A Salish tribe formerly on the s. end of Whidbey id., Puget sd., and on the mainland opposite at the mouth of Snohomish r., Wash. Pop. 350 in 1850. The remnant is now on Tulalip res., Wash., mixed with other broken tribes. **1940** SMITH *Puyallup-Nisqually* 17 In the Puyallup-Nisqually dialect the word means butte or rump but informants thought it might mean something else in the dialects of either the Twana or Snohomish.

Also **Snohomish Indian.**

1874 *Field & Stream* 20 Aug. 18/3 This assertion was verified afterwards by a Snohomish Indian. **1892** BOSTON TILICUM *Puyallup Indians* 26 They say he is a Snohomish Indian.

snollygoster ˈsnɑlɪˌgastɚ, *n.* [App. a fanciful formation.] ?A pretentious boaster (see also quot. 1895). *Slang. Obs.* — **1862** EMMETT *Black Brigade* (*Cent. Supp.*), We am de snollygosters An' lubs Jim Ribber oysters. **1895** *Columbus Dispatch* 28 Oct. 4/3 A Georgia editor kindly explains that 'a snollygoster is a fellow who wants office, regardless of party, platform or principles, and who, whenever he wins, gets there by the sheer force of monumental talknophical assumnacy.'

snook snuk, *n.* [See note.] **1.** *S.* A morsel of food, a bite. *Colloq.* **2.** (See quot.) Both *obs.*

In sense **1.** app. a variant of **snack* in the same sense. Cf. **snucks.** Sense **2.** may be f. **snook,* to pry about, search out, sneak. See *EDD snook, v.* 4.

(1) **1869** *Overland Mo.* III. 129 Many a Rebel cavalry-man . . . had sometimes gone forty-eight hours without a 'snook' of any thing. **1872** POWERS *Afoot & Alone* 92 Come, set up, stranger, and take a snook. — (2) **1891** EARLE *Sabbath* 76 The ancient tithingman was pre-eminently a general *snook*, to use an old and expressive word,—an informer, both in and out of meeting.

snoop snup, *n.* (See quots. and cf. next.)

1891 *Cent.* 5733/2 snoop. . . . One who snoops, or pries or sneaks about; a snooper. **1891** *Amer. Folk-Lore* IV. 160 *Snoop.*—This word I have frequently heard in New England, used both as a verb and as a noun. It implies sneaking, spying, prying around. **1948** *Time* 3 May 19/3 Every cop, . . . stool pigeon and neighborhood snoop in Detroit was working overtime.

snoop snup, *v.* [f. Du. *snoepen* in sense **2. a.** below.]

1. *intr.* To pry into, loiter stealthily, sneak about or around.

1832 SANDS *Writings* II. 291 The world has realms wherein to *snoop.* **1891** *Amer. Folk-Lore* IV. 160 In Worcester, [Mass.], where there are no resident families of Dutch descent . . . , it would be said: 'They caught him snooping at the door,' that is, peeping and listening. **1949** *Exciting Western* May 38/2 We know the sheriff's snooping around.

Hence **snooping,** *n.*

1945 *Nation* 31 March 350/2 After all these years of well-financed private and government snooping.

2. a. (See quot.) **b.** *tr.* To pick or take *up.* Both *obs.* or *rare.*

(**a**) **1848** BARTLETT 318 *To Snoop.* . . . Applied to children, servants, and others, who clandestinely eat dainties or other victuals which have been put aside, not for their use. — (**b**) **1880** *Harper's Mag.* Dec. 91/2, I should be snooped up in the fust gale.

snooper ˈsnupɚ, *n.* [f. **snoop,** *v.*] One who snoops.

1891 *Cent.* 5733/2. **1928** *Chi. Tribune* 11 July 10/4 Prohibition Commissioner Doran has warned dry snoopers to stop gunplay against innocent citizens. **1950** *Chi. D. News* 14 April 18/3 Another thing is that snoopers often get snooped on, in retribution.

* **snoozer,** *n.* A city urchin who sleeps about in boxes, stairways, etc. Also as a vague appellative.

*c***1860** in BRACE *Dangerous Classes N.Y.* 112 If you want to be snoozers, . . . you'll hang up your caps and stay. **1909** *Sunset* Feb. 154/2 The old snoozer's been after the Lost Mexican mine for two years. **1921** R. D. PAINE *Comr. Rolling Ocean* iv. 65 Do you mean to say that the wonderful old snoozer had the grit to cruise out to your country at his age?

Snoqualmie snəˈkwalmɪ, *n.* [f. the native name, meaning "people of the moon," their legendary belief being that they came from the moon.] (See quot. 1910.) Cf. **Skykomish.**

1856 in *34th Congress* 3 Sess. H.R. Ex. Doc. 37, 82, I have charge over . . . the Suquamish or Seattle tribe. **1910** HODGE *Amer. Indians* II. 606/2 Snoqualmu. A Salish division which formerly occupied the upper branches of a river of the same name in Washington and which numbered 225 in 1857. **1940** SMITH *Puyallup-Nisqually* 23 Informants spoke of Sahaptin-speaking relatives among the Snoqualmie.

attrib. **1824** in *Wash. Hist. Quart.* III. 213 We stopped at the Soquamis village situated in the bay of the same name. *Ib.* 214 In the afternoon passed a large house belonging to some of the Sannikamis tribe on the E. side of the channel. **1856** in *34th Congress* 3 Sess. H.R. Ex. Doc. 37, 33 Local agent Hill [was] in charge of the Snoqualmi Indians.

snore snor, *n.* [Du. *snoer*, a string.] (See quot.) *Obs.* — **1848** BARTLETT 318 *Snore*, . . . a string with a button on one end to spin a top with. This term is retained by the boys of New York

* **snore,** *v.* Chiefly *N. Eng. I snore*, a mild oath. *Colloq.*

1709 *Mass. Spy* 30 Dec., In one village you will hear the phrase 'I snore,'—in another, 'I swowgar.' *c***1815** PAULDING *Amer. Comedies* (1847) 34, I snore, I think the young fellows must have lost their gumption. **1897** ROBINSON *Uncle Lisha's Outing* 124 Wal, I snore, if it don't look like one.

snout beetle. Any beetle of the group Rhynchophora, so called because the head is more or less prolongated into a beak.—**1862** *Rep. Comm. Patents 1861: Agric.* 603 The family *Curculionidae* of authors includes . . . the 'snout-beetles' or 'weevils.' **1909** *Cent. Supp.* 1235/1 *Scarred snout-beetle*, any member of the family *Otiorhynchidae*, so called on account of a scar at the tip of the rostrum characteristic of this family of beetles.

snouted weevil. A snout beetle. *Obs.* — **1832** WILLIAMSON *Maine* I. 171 *Curculio quircus*, Snouted Weevil.

* **snow,** *n.*

1. In or with reference to Indian speech: A year.

1778 CARVER *Travels* 250 [Indians] in the interior parts . . . count their years by winters; or, as they express themselves, by snows. **1843** MARRYAT *M. Violet* xv, They would come every snow to the lodge of our Manitou. **1873** MILLER *Amongst Modocs* 242 One late and severe spring-time many thousand snows ago. **1919** WILSON *White Indian* 41 She [an Indian woman] said she was sixty-two 'snows' (years) old when I came.

2. In miscellaneous combs.: (1) **snow banner,** a stream of loose snow blown from a mountain peak, often of a pinkish color and extending horizontally for several miles like a huge banner; (2) **belt,** a region or area where winter snowfall is consistently deep every year; (3) * **bird,** see as a main entry; (4) **blockade,** a stoppage of traffic on a road or railroad caused by snow; (5) **course,** a layer or stratum of snow considered with reference to its water content, cf. **snow survey, surveying;** (6) **fence,** a fence or barrier so placed as to protect a road or railroad from snow; (7) **fort,** a protective structure of snow built by children in snowballing; (8) **mobile,** a motor-driven vehicle for use in snow, having runners for front wheels and tractor wheels in the rear; (9) **plow,** see as a main entry; (10) **roof,** = **snow shed,** *obs.;* (11) **service,** the service in behalf of the government rendered by snow surveyors; (12) **shed,** a shed built over a railroad track to protect it from snow; (13) **shoe, slide,** see as main entries; (14) **surveyor,** one who makes snow surveys to determine the amount of water for irrigation purposes to be expected from given depths of snow, cf. **snow survey, surveying.**

(**1**) **1894** MUIR *Mts. of Calif.* (1916) I. 47 The most magnificent storm phenomenon I ever saw . . . was the peaks of the High Sierra, back of Yosemite Valley, decorated with snow-banners. **1948** *So. Sierran* March 2/2 We passed peak after peak covered with dazzling new snow, each with great wind-driven snow banners. — (**2**) **1886** HUTCHINGS *Heart of Sierras* 331, I speak from personal observation, after several delightful sleigh rides over that snow belt with Joe Mulligan. **1933** *Amer. City* Sep. 53/1 Old-fashioned winters have not been as prevalent in the snow belt in the last few years as they were ten or twenty years ago. — (**4**) **1872** MCCLELLAN *Golden State* 367 The protracted snow blockade on the overland road . . . demonstrated that but little interruption need be anticipated. **1891** *N.Y. Tribune* 6 March 5/4 A Durango, Col., dispatch says the snow blockade is still on, but the rotary snowplough expects to have the road opened by Saturday next. **1928** *Amer. City* March 111/1 Who can state the annual cost of snow blockades in the vast northern territory that includes nearly half the area of the United States and practically all of Canada?

(**5**) **1931** *Popular Mechanics* Dec. 903/1 The procedure now consists in determining the water content of the snow cover, along suitably selected 'snow courses' in each river basin, by cutting and weighing samples of snow at intervals along each course, these measurements being made at the same points each year. **1949** *Sat. Ev. Post* 9 Jan. 92/1 Twice a year, during the early spring, I have to go up into the mountains on snowshoes to read the snow courses. — (**6**) **1872** *Laramie* (Wyo.) *Independent* 23 Jan. 3/2 An immense quantity of snow fence and snow shed material has been unloaded at this place. **1945** *Nat. Geog. Mag.* Sep. 292 The entire male population, . . . seemed to be mending the snow fences along the roads. — (**7**) **1853** G. C. HILL *Dovecote* 200 Some of us took to building snow forts near the school house. — (**8**) **1934** *Christian Sci. Mon.* 23 March, During the trip south, the tractors came upon the snowmobile with which the first Byrd expedition had experimented in trying out mechanical surface transport.

(**10**) **1869** BRACE *New West* 183 For miles it is covered with snow-roofs made of heavy timber; indeed, it is said that forty miles of these roofs must be made before the road will be safe from avalanches and snow-drifts. — (**11**) **1935** *Popular Mechanics* May 688/1 It is to the snow service the government looks to keep water in streams. — (**12**) **1868** *Ore. State Jrnl.* 22 Aug. 2/3 The Pacific Railroad advertises for a thousand men to build snow sheds on the summit. **1949** *Reader's Digest* Jan. 120/1 Miles of snowsheds were built at the fearful price of $6 an inch. — (**14**) **1931** *Popular Mechanics* Dec. 903/1 The methods of the snow surveyor are entirely different from the old plan of sizing up the mountain snowfield. **1948** *Sat. Ev. Post* 31 Jan. 31/2 During winter 1000 snow surveyors roam the Northwest.

b. In other combs. of obvious meaning or sufficiently explained in the quots., as (1) * **snowball,** cf. **c.** (1) below, (2) **blizzard,** (3) **disease,** (4) **eater,** (5) **roller,** (6) **scraper,** (7) **shower,** (8) **snake,** (9) **spit,** (10) **squall,** (11) **storm,** (12) **survey,** (13) **surveying.**

(**1**) **1834** *Sun* (N.Y.) 20 March 2/2 A huge looking 'yaller gall' was hammering away at the eyes of a small white man . . . because he called her a *snow* ball. **1857** *Spirit of Times* 10 Jan. 302/2 We entered the furthest box, and in a moment the little darkey thrust in his head with, 'What's the order, gents?' I ordered a 'son of Didymus and the author of Lamentations;' as did my friends. Snowball departed, and in a moment returned. — **(2) 1902** T. A. BROWN *Hist. N.Y. Stage* I. (Index) 671/2 Snow Blizzard, The. **1949** *Rider's Reader* (Chi.) Dec. 2/2 It can and has paralyzed the necessary traffic operations of cities throughout the country where an extremely heavy snow blizzard has occurred. — **(3) 1842** DE SMET *Letters* (1843) 193 The cold moreover was so uninterruptedly severe that during the hunting season, which lasted three months, such a quantity of snow fell that many were attacked with a painful blindness, vulgarly called 'snow disease.' — **(4) 1886** *Science* 12 March 242/2 Warm west winds . . . are here [in e. Colo.] often called Pacific winds, also 'snow-eaters' and 'zephyrs.' **1933** CHELEY *Camping Out* 197 It was the Chinook wind, a warm, dry wind which melts snow quickly and carries the moisture off on the wind without ever wetting the earth. The Indians call it the 'snow eater.'

(5) 1945 PEARSON *Country Flavor* 107 The farmer . . . joined forces with a neighbor and his team on the snow roller. . . . Heavy and solidly built, it resembled two barrels made of staves, with open spaces between the longitudinally nailed bars. — **(6) 1851** in GREELEY *Autobiog.* (1868) 551 We met with a bad accident at 4 P.M., when 45 miles from Baltimore, our snow-scraper catching against some part of the track. **1884** KNIGHT *Supp.* 826/2. — **(7)** [**1779** in *Tenn. Hist. Quart.* (1915) March 57 Windy and showers of Snow

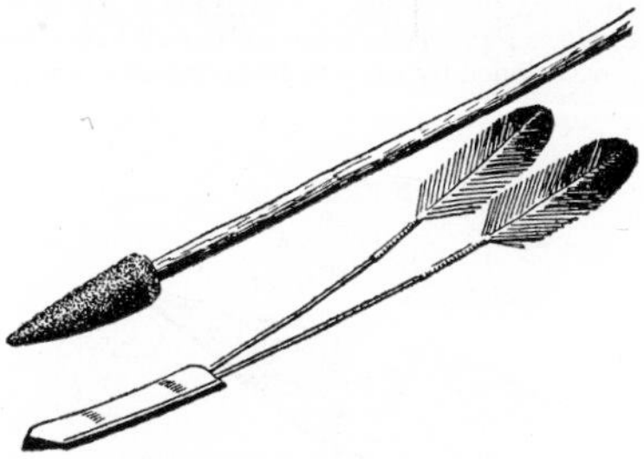

Types of snow snakes

latter part of the day.] **1811** *Cramer's Alman. 1812* (Pittsburgh) 6 Variable with rain and snow showers. **1949** *Chi. Tribune* 17 Nov. 22/3 Recent 'squaw-winter' weather culminated in brisk snow showers the night of Nov. 2. — **(8) 1844** BROWN in *Edin. Jrnl.* I. 327 They [Cherokee Indians in New York] stroll about the woods shooting squirrels and foxes; and in winter amuse themselves with their snow-snakes, which are long smooth sticks of hard wood, sometimes tipped with silver, which they send to an extraordinary distance over the smooth surface of the snow. **1888** *Science* XI. 37/1, I was recently surprised at not finding the snow-snake in the collection of Iroquois implements at the Museum of Natural History. — **(9) 1877** RUEDE *Sod-House Days* 176 Last Thursday we had a little snow spit—just enough to see the snow fall—but we could not see it on the ground.

(10) 1775 *Mass. H.S. Proc.* 2 Ser. II. 287 The weather is attended with Snow Squalls. **1849** KINGSLEY *Diary* 55 We have had one or two quite heavy snow squalls this morning. **1911** *Nat. Geog. Mag.* June 521/1 At Lake O'Hara . . . snow squalls were not infrequent on the higher summits. — **(11) 1771** A. G. WINSLOW *Diary* 8, I was prevented dining at unkle Joshua's by a snowstorm. **1843** *N.Y. Wkly. Tribune* 13 Feb. 1/4 The most severe snow storm known for several years occurred in that section on the 5th. **1943** *Amer. City* Aug. 47/1 There were two violent snowstorms which blocked traffic for a few hours. — **(12) 1931** *Popular Mechanics* Dec. 905/1 In the semi-arid west, where the storage and regulated distribution of water play a part in some of the leading industries, the value of the advance information obtained through snow surveys is obvious. — **(13) 1942** LILLARD *Desert Challenge* 117 Snow surveying, a methodical measurement of depth and water content of the seasonal pack in the mountains, enables the Nevada Agricultural Station . . . to forecast the summer's water supply with an accuracy as high as ninety-five per cent. **1944** *Amer. City* Oct. 67/3 Snow surveying as conducted by the Los Angeles Water Department and illustrated on the following page consists of the following steps.

c. In the names of plants: (1) ∗**snowball,** any one of various white-flowering plants, as the Jersey tea, also attrib., cf. **b.** (1) above and see **swamp snowball;** (2) **ball bush,** (see quot. 1931); (3) **ball hardhack,** (see quot.); (4) ∗**berry,** a name applied to various plants and shrubs, as a North American shrub, *Symphoricarpos racemosus*, the blolly, *Chiococca alba*, and the creeping snowberry *q.v.*, also attrib.; (5) ∗**-drop,** see as a main entry; (6) **-lily,** (see quot.); (7) **-on-the-mountain,** a spurge, *Euphorbia marginata*, having white bracts; (8) ∗**-plant,** (see quot. 1891).

(1) 1867 LACKLAND *Homespun* 239 Snow-balls, too, were growing in immense clusters in that yard. **1949** *Chi. Tribune* 23 Nov. 14/3 Chilly weather is fairly common around Decoration day, and the Chicago name for such spells when we were a boy was 'snowball winter.' It was so called, we think, because it often coincided with the blooming of snowball bushes. — **(2) 1931** CLUTE *Plants* 48 Guelder rose, a common name of the snow-ball bush (*Viburnum opulus sterilis*), is said to be properly elder rose. **1949** [see ∗**snowball** above]. — **(3) 1817–8** EATON *Botany* (1822) 478 *Spiraea opulifolia*, nine-bark, snowball hard-hack. — **(4) 1803** JEFFERSON in *Lewis & Clark Exped.* VII. (1905) 393 We call it the snow-berry bush, no botanical name being yet given to it. **1948** *L.A. Times Home Mag.* 19 Dec. 22/2 The Symphoricarpos racemosus snowberry shrub stages a Christmas prelude by covering itself with great quantities of pure white, wax-like berries.

(6) 1912 *Country Life* 1 April 39/1 The most noticeable and abundant flower on all slopes is the avalanche lily, (*Erythronium Montanum*), called also snow lily, deertongue, and addertongue. — **(7) 1880** T. MEEHAN *Native Flowers* 2 Ser. I. 77 Snow on the Mountain. . . . Particularly attractive to the traveller over . . . western railroads. **1939** *Nat. Geog. Mag.* Aug. 229/1 When massed in gardens or beside the road, snow-on-the-mountain plants . . . give strikingly handsome effects. — **(8) 1874** *Field & Stream* 13 Aug. 5/3 One of the grandest [sights] . . . in our mountains is the exquisite plant, the snow plant of the Sierra. **1891** *Cent.* 5342/2 The only species, *S[arcodes] sanguinea*, is a native of the Sierra Nevada in California, and is known as *snow-plant* from the place of its growth. **1940** *Ore. Guide* 20 Deeper in the forest grow the waxy Indian pipe, the blood-red snow plant, and the rare moccasin flower.

d. In the names of animals, esp. birds: (1) **snow flea,** a small leaping insect, esp. of the genus *Achorutes*, common in the East in early spring; (2) **goose,** see as a main entry; (3) **owl,** the snowy owl, *Nyctea nyctea*, which is found in the northern parts of the U.S. in winter; (4) **quail,** the white-tailed ptarmigan.

(1) 1868 *Amer. Naturalist* II. 53 The little insects called snow-fleas . . . are found in winter at the foot of trees. **1943** DAMON *Sense of H.* 106 Snow fleas . . . have a disagreeable habit of putting an end to their brief existence by drowning themselves in sap buckets. — **(3) 1811** WILSON *Ornithology* IV. 53 Snow Owl: *Strix nyctea*. . . . Inhabits the coldest and most dreary regions of the northern hemisphere. **1947** BEEBE *Mixed Train Dly.* 341 The Laramie's lonely right of way . . . abounds with rabbits, cock pheasant, partridge, deer and, in the high-timber stretches, great snow owls, wildcats and an occasional bear. — **(4) 1895** W. R. OGILVIE-GRANT *Game Birds* I. 45 In the Rocky Mountain region it is generally known by the very appropriate name of 'White' or 'Snow' Quail.

As the last term in **evening, hominy, hunting, mountain, onion, robin, sugar snow.**

∗**snow,** *v.* In phrases: (1) *To be snowed in*, to be forced to remain in a particular place by heavy snow, hence **snowed in,** *a.;* (2) *to snow under*, *fig.* to overwhelm or predominate over, *colloq.;* (3) *to be snowed up*, =*to be snowed in.*

(1) 1859 *No. California* (Union) 18 May 2/4 A hunter who has been 'snowed in' on the head waters of the Tuolumne river, arrived at this place last week . . . with a fine lot of forty skins. **1904** *N.Y. Ev. Post* 5 Feb. 3 The Wabash is devoting all its energies to clearing the line of delayed and snowed-in trains. **1949** *L.A. Times* 20 May 1/2 A total of 11 inches fell at Mt. Wilson, with 5 in the following May when Big Bear was snowed in. — **(2) 1880** E. KIRKE *Garfield* 32 Democrats vied with Republicans . . . in snowing him under with congratulations. **1950** *Chi. Tribune* 24 Feb. 1/8 The Communists also were being snowed under. — **(3) 1867** *Harper's Mag.* 2 Feb. 78/1 Railroad travel was everywhere obstructed, even the lines as far South as Virginia and Maryland being 'snowed up.' **1869** BRACE *New West* 183 To have a train snowed up in this desolate region, 200 miles from any inhabited district, would be no joke.

∗**snowbird,** *n.* (See quots.) *Slang.* — **1905** *N.Y. Ev. Post* 20 Nov. 6, 28 per cent. deserted after three months, and were presumably 'snowbirds,' that is, men who enlist to get food and clothing during the winter months. **1923** *Nation* 31 Oct. 487 In winter, when building is at a standstill in the North, northern workmen, 'snow birds' or 'white doves' in Negro parlance, flock south.

As the last term in **black, eastern, Lapland, Oregon, western snowbird.**

∗**snowdrop,** *n.*

1. Any one of various plants and trees, as the common anemone, the fringe tree, the snowberry, etc., having flowers that are suggestive of snow. Also attrib.

1737 BRICKELL *N. Carolina* 22 Narcissus, Daffodil, Snow-Drops [are found here]. **1863** E. W. PEARSON *Lett. Port Royal* 159 There are a few snow-drops, very pretty. **1892** *Amer. Folk-Lore* V. 97 *Symphoricarpus racemosus*, snow-drop. Mansfield, O. **1943** DAMON *Sense* *of H.* 111 On the south side of the house a snowdrop blossom has gone by and lusty bunches of daffodil spears are up.

2. * **snowdrop tree,** = **fringe tree.**

1785 MARSHALL *Amer. Grove* 33 *Chionanthus virginica.* Virginian Snowdrop Tree. The bark . . . is accounted by the natives a specific. [**1866** LINDLEY & MOORE *Treas. Botany* 270/2 *Chinonanthus,* the Snowdrop tree of North America.]

b. = **silver bell tree.**

1813 MUHLENBERG *Cat. Plants* 46 Silverbell tree, or Four-winged Snow-drop tree. **1846** BROWNE *Trees Amer.* 366 *Halesia tetraptera,* The Common Snowdrop-Tree. **1897** SUDWORTH *Arborescent Flora* 323 *Mohrodendron dipterum.* . . . Snowdrop-tree. *Ib., Mohrodendron parviflorum.* . . . Small-flower Snowdrop-tree.

snow goose. Any one of several North American geese of the genus *Chen.*

[**1771** J. R. FORSTER *Cat. Animals N. Amer.* 16 Snow Goose, *Anas nivalis.*] **1823** JAMES *Exped.* I. 266 *Anas* (*Anser,* Briss.) *hyperborea*—Snow goose. **1917** *Birds of Amer.* I. 156/1 The Snow Goose is a western bird, closely resembling the Greater Snow Goose, which is confined mainly to eastern North America. **1949** *Clearing-Stickney* (Ill.) *Bul.* 28 Oct. 1/5 There are now about 500 blue geese, snow geese and Canadian geese there.

b. Also with specifying terms.

1883 *Nat. Museum Bul.* No. 27, 157 *Chen hyperboreus albatus* (Cass.). Lesser Snow Goose. *Ib., Chen rossi* (Baird). Ross's Snow Goose. **1889** *Cent.* 2576/1 *Blue snow-goose, Anser* or *Chen cærulescens,* a North American goose closely related to the snow-goose. **1909** WEBSTER 1985/2 The greater snow goose (*C. hyperborea nivalis*) occurs chiefly on the Atlantic coast; the lesser snow goose (*C. hyperborea*) on the Pacific coast and in the Mississippi Valley. **1949** SPRUNT & CHAMBERLAIN *S.C. Bird Life* 110 Lesser Snow Goose. . . . This beautiful little goose is about the size of the brant, and, except for the Greater Snow Goose, could hardly be mistaken for anything else.

snowplow ˈsnoˌplaʊ, *n.*

1. Any one of various plowlike contrivances for removing snow from a road or railroad.

1792 BELKNAP *Hist. New-Hampshire* III. 79 When a deep snow has obstructed the roads, they are in some places opened by an instrument called a snow plough. It is made of planks, in a triangular form, with two side boards to turn the snow out on either hand. **1848** *Amer. R.R. Jrnl.* 13 May 305 This apparatus is said, by the inventor, to answer for a *snow-plough* as well as *cow-remover.* **1950** *L.A. Times* 26 March 1/3 Snowplows were used to clear roads in the San Jacinto Mountains.

attrib. **1943** *Amer. City* Aug. 47/3 There are also 46 water sprinklers to which snow-plow blades are attached in winter for this work.

2. In skiing, an act or instance of slowing down or stopping by spreading the rear ends of the skis outward from the line of progress, pressure being exerted on the heels. Also attrib.

1939 WEBSTER (*New Words*). **1947** *Mazama* Jan. 1/2 This could be a giant slalom with wide gates that a good snowplow can negotiate, but stiff enough so there will be real competition. **1948** *Ib.* Feb. 1/1 The class was well attended and all were doing snowplow turns at the end of the session.

snowplow ˈsnoˌplaʊ, *v. intr.* In skiing, to slow down or stop by executing a snowplow (sense **2.**). Also **snowplowing,** *n.*

1912 *Country Life* Dec. 65/2 'Stemming' is really but 'snow-ploughing,' and consists in running one skee straight and letting the other one slip sideways. **1939** WEBSTER (*New Words*). **1947** *Sierra Club Bul.* Nov. 88 Snowplow at least five yards, under control, to a standstill from a direct descent.

snowshoe ˈsnoˌʃu, *n.*

1. A racket-like footgear enabling the wearer to walk on the surface of soft snow. Also attrib.

1666 *Doc. Hist. N.Y. State* I. 72 Ye french . . . made use of Indian snow shoes which hath the very form of a Rackett tyed to each foote. **1772** in MORSE *Univ. Geog.* I. 100 As the Indians were hunting, some of them saw a strange snow-shoe track. **1825** *Vt. Aurora* (Vergennes) 25 Aug. 1/5 Rogers and his men proceeded on snow shoes, . . . the snow being at least four feet deep. **1917** EATON *Green Trails* 27 Down from the attic come the snowshoes, the thongs are tested, moccasins are oiled, and we are off for the deep woods. **1949** *Nat. Geog. Mag.* Oct. 474/1 She . . . repaired snowshoes, and performed virtually all of the camp drudgery.

Also **horse snowshoe,** (see quot.). *Obs.*

1886 HUTCHINGS *Heart of Sierras* 331 The horse snow-shoe is made of one inch ash plank, thirteen inches long by eleven wide.

b. A ski.

1886 *Calif. Maverick* (S.F.) 13 Feb. 6/6 The snow-shoes . . . consist of long, narrow boards turned up at one end, which are laced to the feet, and which, having smooth under sides, are used like sleds in descending the mountains. **1948** *Nev. Highways* April 22/2 He got through on skis (they were called snowshoes at the time . . .), when other means had failed and the mail was delivered.

attrib. **1867** *Terr. Enterprise* (Virginia, Nev.) 14 March 3/1 The snow-shoe race came off at the appointed time. . . . Miss Mary Kinney, a child but eight years of age, with a pair of shoes three times as long as herself, was one of the competitors. **1890** *Silverton* (Colo.) *Miner* 1 March 2/3 The snow-shoe rider moves with a constantly accelerating motion, and we may say that his speed at the finish approximates . . . 500 feet per second.

2. In special combs. explained by the quots., as (1) **snowshoe dance,** (2) **disease,** (3) **evil.**

(1) *c***1836** CATLIN *Indians* II. 139 The *snow-shoe dance* . . . [is] danced with the snow-shoes under the feet, at the falling of the first snow. **1841** BUCKINGHAM *America* I. 76 Another dance, among the tribe of Ojibbeways, is called the 'snow-shoe dance,' from its taking place at the first fall of snow in the winter. — (2) [**1829** HEAD *Forest Scenes* 66 Indeed, so certain is the effect produced by the exercise upon persons not trained to it, that the Canadians have a name for the complaint it brings on. They call it the '*mal à raquette,*' which is a violent inflammation and swelling of the instep and ancles, attended with severe pain and lameness.] **1891** *Cent.* 5736/2 *Snow-shoe disease,* a painful affection of the feet occurring in arctic and subarctic America after long journeys on snow-shoes. — (3) **1809** A. HENRY *Travels* 68 The *snow-shoe evil* . . . proceeds from an unusual strain on the tendons of the leg, occasioned by the weight of the snow-shoe, and brings on inflammation.

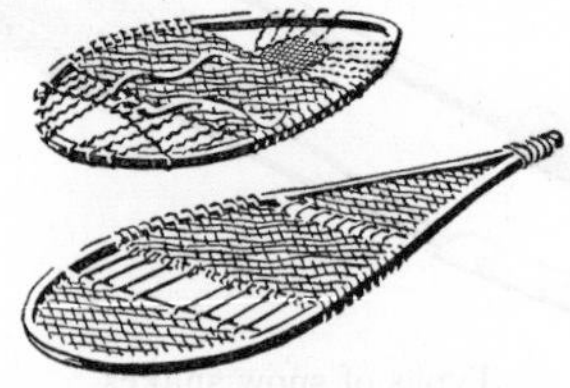

Types of snowshoes

b. snowshoe rabbit, (see quot. 1890). Also **snowshoe hare.**

1890 *Cent.* 4924/2 *Snow-shoe rabbit,* that variety of the American varying hare which is found in the Rocky Mountains. . . . It has been described as a distinct species, *Lepus bairdi.* **1917** *Mammals of Amer.* 274 Our Jack Rabbits and Snow-shoe Rabbits are not Rabbits, but Hares. **1921** *Frontier* May 11 In a zig-zag pattern in the snow were the tracks of the snow-shoe hares. **1948** *Milwaukee Jrnl.* 18 July 6/2 Anybody with any suggestions for keeping snowshoe hares alive in captivity should write, care The Journal.

Also *snowshoe country, cramp, lace, man,* etc.

snowshoe ˈsnoˌʃu, *v. intr.* To go on snowshoes or skis. Also **snowshoeing,** *n.*

1882 *Harper's Mag.* April 697/2 This sort of snow-shoeing [using Norwegian skis] is said to excel coasting, or even tobogganing. **1907** *St. Nicholas* Aug. 885/2 As the winter wore on, snow-shoeing, skating, skeeing kept them together for hours. **1947** *Christian Sci. Mon.* 1 March III. 7/4 Our four-mile-away neighbor has snowshoed by several times since then.

Hence **snowshoer,** one who uses snowshoes, a skier.

1867 *Terr. Enterprise* (Virginia, Nev.) 12 March 3/2 A race for a gold buckle, free to all lady snow-shoers, was also announced. **1890** *Silverton* (Colo.) *Miner* 1 March 3/2 During the storm, the big tree on Anvil, which was generally known as the starting point for snow shoers and the toboggan club, was blown down. **1947** *Sports Afield* Dec. 132/2 Only the skier, the snowshoer, the hunter, the winter hiker see these things.

snowslide ˈsnoˌslaɪd, *n.*

1. A sudden sliding of a mass of snow, or the snow involved in this.

1841 WHITTIER *Poetical Works* (1894) 11/1 Dazzling and white! save where the bleak, Wild winds have bared some splintering peak, Or snow-slide left its dusky streak. **1906** *N.Y. Ev. Post* 19 March 9 A snowslide which came down yesterday at the Liberty Bell mine damaged the tramway and considerable trestle work. **1949** *Sierra Club Bul.* Feb. 9/2 The possibility of snow slides, and, more, of extensive avalanches, is ever a challenge to the knowledge and alertness of ski mountaineers.

2. (See quot.)

1905 *Forestry Bureau Bul.* No. 61, 48 *Snow slide,* a temporary slide on a steep slope, made by dragging a large log through deep snow which is soft or thawing; when frozen solidly, it may be used to slide logs to a point where they can be reached by sleds. (N[orth] W[oods].)

***snowy,** *a.* In combs.: (1) **snowy egret,** a small white egret, *Egretta thula;* (2) **heron,** =prec.; (3) **plover,** a ring plover, *Charadrius nivosus,* of the West.

(1) **1895** *Stand. Dict.* 1698/3 *Snowy egret* or *heron,* an entirely white egret (*Ardea candidissima*) ranging from New York to Chile. **1949** SPRUNT & CHAMBERLAIN *S. C. Bird Life* 11 Among Sass's observational records of value were his rediscovery of breeding colonies of the Snowy Egret in South Carolina in 1908. — (2) [**1785** LATHAM *Gen. Synopsis Birds* III. I. 92.] **1828** BONAPARTE *Synopsis* 155 The Snowy Heron . . . inhabits both Americas. **1949** SPRUNT & CHAMBERLAIN *S.C. Bird Life* 85 Snow Egret. . . . Local Names: Snowy Heron. — (3) **1872** COUES *Key to Birds* 245 Snowy Plover . . . several lateral tail feathers entirely white. **1949** *Nat. Hist.* May 232/1 The snowy plover, most beguiling bird to be found on a Southern California beach, has been called a variety of names, but none of them are derogatory, because the adjective 'cute' is used as a prefix for all.

***snub,** *n.* (See quot.) — **1891** *Cent.* 5737/1 *Snub,* . . . a stake, set in the bank of a river or canal, around which a rope may be cast to check the motion of a boat or raft. (U.S. and Canada.)

***snub,** *v. tr.* To check or stop (an animal or thing) with, or as with, a line turned around a post or reel, to draw *up* close.

1868 *Harper's Mag.* May 822/2 He smashed out the window, and thrusting out his bristling head . . . shouted. . . . 'Snub her, boys: consarn her! Snub her!' **1888** *Cent. Mag.* March 660/1 The newly caught animal . . . is taught this by being violently snubbed up. **1895** *Outing* XXVII. 224/1, I kept him [*sc.* a fish] snubbed up too closely for him to get a start. **1907** WHITE *Arizona Nights* 152 In such case he [*sc.* a calf] was snubbed up short enough at the end of the rope. **1947** *Sat. Ev. Post* 8 March 51/1 McKechnie rushed, and stopping him was like snubbing a white-pine log coming off a rollway.

***snubber,** *n.* (See quot.) — **1853** *Oregonian* (Portland) 12 March 1/5 A *snubber,* may it please the court, . . . snubs the boat when she heaves to on the heel-path shore, and unships the whiffletrees in passing a lock.

snucks snʌks, *n. pl. To go snucks,* "to share equally" (B. '77). *Obs.* Cf. *EDD to go snacks s.v.* *snack. — **1872** EGGLESTON *End of World* 183 You'll get the 'old man' down on you, if you let a bird out of the trap in which he goes snucks.

***snuff,** *n.* In combs., chiefly *S.:* (1) ***snuffbox,** a species of tortoise, *rare;* (2) **brush,** =**snuff stick;** (3) **dipper,** (see quot. 1944); (4) **dipping,** taking snuff by dipping; (5) **stick,** a small stick, usu. a twig of black-gum, with one end chewed until it is reduced to a brush, used in dipping snuff; (6) **-takers,** (see quot.), *obs.*

(1) **1877** BARTLETT 699 The most celebrated [terrapin] is the *diamond-back;* there are also the *yellow-bellies, red-bellies, loger-heads, snuff-boxes,* &c. — (2) **1882** in HOLLANDER *Arme Blanken* 47 We approached the spot, where sat a wretched woman, with a snuff brush in her mouth. — (3) **1845** GREEN *Texian Exped.* 137 We believe the most filthy of all practices is that of your 'snuff-dippers.' **1896** *Amer. Missionary* Oct. 324 One sister who had been a snuff-dipper for more than twenty years was enabled by God's grace to give up the habit. **1944** *D.N.* Nov. 70 *snuff-dipper:* n. One who uses snuff by dipping the brush into the snuffbox and inserting the snuff into the mouth. — (4) **1860** M. W. DISHER *Powells in Amer.* (1934) 65 But the ladies have a habit which is, I think, still more disgusting. That is 'snuff dipping' which is openly practised in the South, and privately indulged in, in the North. **1950** *Reader's Digest* March 39/2 The company figured a northern crew would be unhappy down here in the land of snuff dipping.

(5) **1870** W. BAKER *New Timothy* 103 Love her, and that snuff-stick 'tween her lips? **1913** MORLEY *Carolina Mts.* 170 When a mountain woman refers to her 'toothbrush' the snuff-stick is what she means. **1938** MATSCHAT *Suwannee River* 109 The women drank scuppernong wine, expanded cheerfully in the glow it produced, and sucked their snuff sticks. — (6) **1873** *Harper's Mag.* Sep. 589/2 Mr. Seward and his friends were filled with consternation, while a feeling of exultation equal in strength pervaded the minds of the Silver-Grays, or Snuff-takers, as the conservative Whigs were termed by their radical brethren.

b. In phrases: (1) *in great snuff,* showily, gaily, also *in high snuff,* in high feather, *colloq.* or *slang;* (2) *to rub snuff,* to dip snuff, also *to chew snuff.*

(1) **1829** ROYALL *Pennsylvania* I. 26 One of the females . . . was dressed in great *snuff,* (as we say in the west). **1840** DANA *Two Years* 149 The Sandwich-Islanders rode down, and were in 'high snuff.' — (2) **1849** *Knickerb.* XXXIV. 117 The 'gude woman' sat in the corner 'rubbing snuff,' or 'dipping.' **1891** RYAN *Pagan* 105 [Does] your deity of the lower world . . . chew snuff?

***snuffer,** *n.* A porpoise. *Colloq.* — **1884** GOODE *Fisheries* I. 14 The little Harbor Porpoise, *Phocaena brachycion* Cope, [is] known to the fishermen as 'Puffer,' 'Snuffer,' 'Snuffing Pig.' **1911** *Rep. Fisheries 1908* 314/1.

snug,** *v. tr.* To conceal from the owner, to steal. *Slang. Obs.* — *a1859** in BARTLETT 424 I'd stuff watches, drop pocket-books, . . . but I'd never condescend to snug dogs.

snugfist ˈsnʌgˌfɪst, *n. attrib.* Designating one who spends money grudgingly. *Rare.* — **1837** *Jamestown* (N.Y.) *Jrnl.* 26 July 1/1 'That won't make the pot boil,' said an old snugfist farmer.

snugger ˈsnʌgɚ, *v. I snuggers,* a mild oath. *Slang. Obs.* Cf. **snaggers,** *v.* — **1843** STEPHENS *High Life N.Y.* II. 202, I snuggers, it made me feel streaked all over.

snum snʌm, *n. By snum,* by gosh! *Colloq. Obs.* — **1825** NEAL *Bro. Jonathan* II. 315 By snum; but you're a precious fellow!

snum snʌm, *v. intr. I snum,* I swear. *Colloq.*

1839 *Yale Lit. Mag.* IV. 357 (Th.), I snum, 'taint the thing for me. **1890** M. J. HOLMES *Marguerite* (1896) 200, I snum if I can do it. **1916** WILSON *Somewhere* 333 Now, I snum! Here she's two-thirty!

sny snaɪ, *n.* "A localism in use along the Mississippi and Missouri Rivers, signifying a narrow passage between an island and the shore. The word is Missouri French, derived from *chenal,* channel" (Ramsay, *Mark Twain s.v.*). — **1893** MARK TWAIN *Tom Sawyer Abroad* 24 (R.), Ef we slips acrost de river [at Hannibal] to-night arter de moon's gone down, en kills dat sick fam'ly dat's over on the Sny. **1945** STEWART *Names on Land* 213 So also the boatmen of New France did not say *chenal* for a river-channel, as a Parisian would, but they said *chenail,* and the word in English became *sny.*

***soak,** *n. In soak:* **a.** Under consideration, ready. **b.** In pawn. **c.** Of persons: In jail. All *slang.*

(**a**) **1833** *Polit. Examiner* (Shelbyville, Ky.) 15 June 4/1, I have had a speech in soak these six months. **1872** STILL *Underground Railroad* 151 Contrary to the laws of North Carolina, he had lately married a free girl, which was an indictable offense, and for which the penalty was then in soak for him—said penalty to consist of thirty-nine lashes. — (**b**) **1845** *St. Louis Reveille* 10 April 2/3 Printer's fee, $250, not paid—but the poet begged hard, and left his hat 'in soak' that fits our devil. **1932** *Blue Valley Farmer* (Okla. City) 10 March 5/6 Everything we had is either gone or in soak. — (**c**) **1869** *Terr. Enterprise* (Virginia, Nev.) 14 Sep. 3/1 There are a good many of the 'boys' over there in 'soak.' **1880** NYE *B. Nye & Boomerang* 15 He made a compromise by offering to put Pythias in soak while the only genuine Damon went to see his girl.

***soak,** *v.* **1.** *tr.* To pawn, put "in soak." **2.** To lambast, beat up, hit hard. **3.** To cheat, charge exorbitantly. All *slang.*

(1) **1882** SALA *Amer. Revisited* (1885) 382 'Hock my sparks,' 'soak my gems,' and 'Walker my diamonds.' . . . American euphemisms for the act of pawning your jewellery. **1928** FOY & HARLOW *Clowning Thro' Life* 205 And then I soaked my overcoat at Simpson's. — (2) **1892** *Columbus* (O.) *Dispatch* 29 July, To-day's Washington Post 'soaks' it to the Southern Democrats in the House. **1912** DREISER *Financier* 8 Don't you let any of 'em [the boys] give you any lip. If they do, soak 'em. — (3) **1895** *N.Y. Dramatic News* 23 Nov. 2/2 This little scheme sometimes . . . enables the photographer to 'soak' them. **1913** LONDON *Valley of Moon* I. xii, Dog-cheap is what I call it, when I think of the small rooms I've ben soaked for.

b. soak-about, (see quot. 1890).

1888 *Cent. Mag.* Jan. 369/2 The young master saw the boys playing at the boisterous and promiscuous 'soak-about.' **1890** HOWELLS *Boy's Town* 83 Soak-about . . . simply consisted of hitting any other boy you could with the ball when you could get it.

***soap,** *n.*

1. Money, esp. that used for corrupt purposes, usu. political. *Slang.*

1836 *Quarter Race Ky.* 24 When you offered to bet on the sorrel, I was out of soap. **1885** *Mag. Amer. Hist.* April 394/2 *Soap.*—Originally used by the Republican managers during the campaign of 1880, as the cipher for 'money' in their telegraphic dispatches. In 1884, it was revived as a derisive war cry aimed at the Republicans by their opponents. **1894** *Cong. Rec.* 18 May 4920/1 A distinguished ex-President, now dead, said that soap was needed in a great campaign.

2. In combs.: (1) **soap boom,** a boom in soap; (2) ***box,** a makeshift stand for a street orator, usu. attrib. and transf.; (3) **boxer,** one who harangues crowds in the open air from, or as from, a soapbox; (4) **day,** the day upon which soap for a household is made, in attrib. use; (5) **fat,** fat used in making soap, in attrib. use; (6) ***fish,** (see quot.); (7) **flakes,** finely flaked soap; (8) **flat,** prob. an alkali flat or dry lake *qq.v.;* (9) **game,** a performance in which a street swindler seems to wrap cakes of soap in five, ten, and twenty dollar bills and then sells them at from one to five dollars each; (10) **gourd,** *S.* a gourd used as a container for soft soap; (11) **grease,** =**soap fat,** also attrib.; (12) **lock,** a lock of hair, esp. a long earlock.

soaped to make it lie smooth, one who wears such a lock, a rowdy or rough, now *hist., slang;* (13) **locked,** *a.* wearing a soap lock, *obs.;* (14) **oil,** (see quot.); (15) **opera,** a daytime radio drama calculated to appeal particularly to housewives, also attrib.; (16) **stick,** a gun, so called from its length and slimness, suggestive of a stirring stick used in making soap, *rare;* (17) * **stone,** see as a main entry; (18) **tail,** ?jocose for "fellow," *rare.*

(1) **1879** in Walsh *Lit. Curiosities* 114, I am looking for a soap boom every day. — (2) **1927** T. C. Pease *United States* 546 The choice of party candidates by manipulation of party conventions and soap-box primaries. **1949** *Time* 25 July 20/2 Midday crowds gathered in the sun to hear soapbox speakers supporting labor solidarity. — (3) **1913** *Industrial Worker* (Spokane) 10 April 4/1 They do want all the publicity that can be given them by the locals, by the soapboxers, and by individual conversation. **1948** *So. Weekly* 3 July 13/3 These stupid things have given tragic substance to the charges made by the soapboxers. — (4) **1805** *Pocumtuc Housewife* (1906) 47 On soap day morning get breakfast out of the way early.

(5) **1836** *Franklin Repository* (Chambersburgh, Pa.) 4 Oct. 1/3 Ever since these black stones were brought to town, the wood-sawyers and pilers, and then soap-fat and hickory-ashes men, has been going down. **1864** Mark Twain *Sketches* (1926) 122 Those who may have kitchen refuse to sell, can leave orders and our soap-fat carts will visit the corner designated. **1877** *Harper's Mag.* Feb. 424/4 All the bits and ends . . . find their way to the soap-fat man and the swill tub. — (6) **1896** Jordan & Evermann *Check-List Fishes* 297 *Synodus fœtens.* Lizard-fish; Lagarto; Soap-fish. Cape Cod to Brazil. — (7) **1934** Webster. **1946** *Sat. Ev. Post* 11 May 18/2 No prizes, soap flakes or baking powder are handed out to the people in the studio. — (8) **1839** Audubon *Ornith. Biog.* V. 256 They . . . alighted . . . on a 'soap flat' of vast extent, where neither boat nor man could approach them. — (9) **1938** Asbury *Sucker's Prog.* 330 Soapy Smith, . . . earned his nickname by his skill at a swindle known as 'the soap game,' which was invented in the early 1880's by a sharper in Leadville.

(10) **1835** Crockett *Tour* 192, I'd give my head for a soap-gourd that Andrew Jackson never made the proposition. **1884** Craddock *Tenn. Mts.* 11 Ye ain't wantin' ter gin Vander the soap-gourd to drink outn'. — (11) **1805** *Pocumtuc Housewife* (1906) 47 Put it in the soap-grease barrel down cellar. **1880** Deming *Adirondack Stories* 165 Large sections of the [bear] flesh were furtively used by the housewives for soap-grease. — (12) **1840** *N.O. Picayune* 30 Aug. 2/2 Howard . . . is described as . . . wearing moustaches and soaplocks. **1858** *Spirit of Times* 23 Jan. 333/2 In the case of Ezra White, he was the chief of a gang of 'soap-locks,' *vice* 'Dead Rabbits.' **1891** Welch *Recoll. 1830–40* 30 [Dickens wore] long hair and earlocks which were then denominated as 'soap-locks,' but deemed vulgar, except for the dudes and 'Bowery boys' of those days. **1948** *Sat. Review* 17 July 23 An 1844 watercolor of Broadway idlers, 'The Soap Locks.' — (13) **1843** in Thompson *M. Jones* (1872) 140 Do you think . . . he could recognize his countrymen in the starched up, soap-locked, high-heeled, sickly-looking dandys of the present day? — (14) **1909** *Cent. Supp.* 801/1 *Soap-oil,* the trade-name of the lowest of four grades of summer yellow cotton-seed oil. It is . . . used in soap-making.

(15) **1939** Webster (*New Words*). **1942** Stegner *Mormon C.* 347 They deal with impressionable virgins caught in the net of polygamy and agonizing worse than any soap-opera heroine through endless difficulties. **1949** *This Week Mag.* 2 July 11/1 Fishing is like soap opera. You listen to it enough and you get interested. — (16) **1835** Longstreet *Ga. Scenes* 219 Wait till you see him lift the old Soap-stick, and draw a bead upon the bull's-eye. — (18) **1851** J. J. Hooper *Wid. Rugby's Husb.* 23 You was feedin' us *soap-tails* on *bull beef.*

b. In the names of plants: (1) * **soap apple,** (see quot. 1891); (2) * **ball,** in the Southwest, the flower head of a species of *Yucca;* (3) **bulb,** = * **soap apple;** (4) **gentian,** = * **soapwort gentian;** (5) **plant,** any one of various plants some part of which may be used as soap; (6) * **root,** (see quot. 1909); (7) * **weed,** any one of various soap plants found in the western and southwestern states, also attrib.; (8) * **wood,** = **deer grass,** *obs.;* (9) * **wort,** = **soap weed;** (10) * **wort gentian,** a gentian, *Dasystephana saponaria,* having leaves resembling those of soapwort.

(1) **1864** Webster 1252/2. **1891** *Cent.* 5741/3 *Soap-plant,* . . . one of several plants whose bulbs serve the purpose of soap; particularly, the Californian *Chlorogluam pomeridianum,* of the lily family. . . . Also called *soap-apple* and *soap-bulb,* and . . . *amole.* — (2) **1907** J. R. Cook *Border & Buffalo* (1938) 396 'Soap-balls,' said Squirreleye, who had been raised in Texas. And so they were. There was a soap-root growing profusely in all this region, with which the Mexicans washed their clothes. From the top of its stalk grew a round, fuzzy ball about four inches in diameter, which would ignite at the touch of a burning match. — (3) [**1876** Lindley & Moore *Treas. Botany* (rev. ed) 1279/2 *Chlorogalum pomeridianum.* . . . The bulbous root, when rubbed in water, makes a lather . . . : hence it is known as the Soap-bulb. **1891** [see **soap apple**]. — (4) **1817–8** Eaton *Botany* (1822) 288. **1840** Dewey *Mass. Flowering Plants* 147 Soap Gentian. The leaves resemble some kinds of Saponaria, or Soapwort. **1869** Fuller *Flower Gatherers* 308 By some botanists this species has been confounded with the . . . *Soap-Gentian.*

(5) **1844** Gregg *Commerce of Prairies* I. 160 Among the wild productions of New Mexico is the *palmilla*—a species of palmetto, which might be termed the soap-plant. **1915** Armstrong & Thornber *Western Wild Flowers* 12 Amole Soap Plant. . . . The bulbs form a lather in water. — (6) **1879** Williams *Pacific Tourist* 233/2 At one time soap-root, a bulb, growing like the stub of a coarse, brown mohair switch, just emerging from the ground, was gathered by the Chinamen. **1909** *Cent. Supp.* 1236/2 *Soaproot,* . . . the soapwort, *Saponaria officinalis.* . . . The soap-plant, *Chlorogalum pomeridianum.* — (7) **1848** Robinson *Santa Fe Exped.* 50 Here the soapweed becomes almost a tree. **1923** J. H. Cook *On Old Frontier* 95 The sand cherries were ripe and at their best, as also were the blossoms on the soapweeds. **1944** Johnson *As I Dare* 328 She was a young woman who had already gone through the various purifying ceremonies at the hands of other women—the thorough purging, the washing in suds of soapweed root. — (8) [**1743** Clayton *Flora Virginica* 41 *Rhexia calycibus glabris.* . . . Soopwood. **1771** J. R. Forster *Flora Amer. Septentr.* 17 *Rhexia virginica,* Soapwood.] **1791** Muhlenberg *Index Florae* 168 *Rhexia,* Soap-wood. — (9) **1890** Custer *Following Guidon* 202 The soapwort with its scentless blossom . . . was really used as a substitute for soap. **1909** [see **soap root**].

(10) **1814** Bigelow *Florula Bostoniensis* 64 Soapwort Gentian. . . . A very fine plant, distinguished by its large purple flowers. **1847** Wood *Botany* 453 Soapwort Gentian. . . . Leaves . . . resembling those of the common soapwort.

As the last term in **cream, sassafras, settled, tooth soap.**

* **soapstone,** *n.*

1. A bedwarmer or footwarmer made of a piece of soapstone.

1887 *Courier-Journal* 29 Jan. 6/2 The Flower Mission . . . has already received and distributed more than two dozen of these soapstones. **1905** Lincoln *Partners* 28 Tempy, you do up that soapstone for his feet. **1946** *Reader's Digest* Jan. 60/1 He jumped shivering into bed and felt the warm, flannel-wrapped soapstone which his mother had tucked between the blankets.

2. In combs. denoting various things made of soapstone, as (1) **soapstone backlog,** (2) **griddle,** (3) **pencil,** (4) **stove.**

(1) **1810** *Columbian Centinel* 27 Jan. 4/2 Just received, a few soapstone Back Logs, of large size. — (2) **1849** *N. Eng. Farmer* I. 252 Cakes on a soapstone griddle required no fat to keep them from sticking. **1891** *Cent. Mag.* Jan. 383 The household utensils were few . . . a soapstone griddle for the tortillas. — (3) **1876** Knight 2201/1 The softer, neater, and greatly superior article, known as soapstone pencils, [is] made from a peculiar stone found near Castleton, Vt. — (4) **1883** *Cent. Mag.* Aug. 596/2 He was sitting . . . with his feet on the hearth of the open soap-stone stove. **1938** Damon *Grandma* 21 A slight concession to modernity was embodied, in the parlor, in the shape of a tall oblong soapstone stove.

soary ˈsorɪ, *a.* Of or pertaining to soaring. — **1861** *N.Y. Tribune* 10 Oct. 6/2 The newspaper correspondents from Western Virginia are a very soary or a very hoaxy set of fellows. **1899** Tarkington *Gentleman from Ind.* ii, The orator winged away to soary heights.

* **sob,** *n. attrib.* Designating persons and writings of an excessively sentimental character, as (1) **sob raiser,** (2) **reporter,** (3) **sister,** (4) **specialist,** (5) **squad,** (6) **story,** (7) **stuff.** *Slang.*

(1) **1917** S. Graham *Priest of Ideal* xxix. 278 Our great sob-raiser who persistently pleads in the *Primer* for all causes which obviously evoke pity and rage. — (2) **1929** *McGraw-Hill Book Notes* 11 Feb., The story in that announcement . . . looked too much like the efforts of a newspaper sob-reporter. — (3) **1912** *Sat. Ev. Post* 7 Dec. 9/3 Of the Daily Blatt's seven sob sisters six had husbands; and of the six it was more or less pure coincidence that five were supported by their wives. **1948** *Time* 26 July 56/2 Winifred Black, the original sob sister, sets the pattern for countless future sob-sister leads. — (4) **1931** *K.C. Star* 3 Nov., It is gratifying . . . that the sob specialists can find practically nothing . . . to be sorry about.

(5) **1912** G. M. Hyde *Newspaper Reporting* 236 The search for human interest material is a modification of the 'sob squad' work of the sensational papers, on more delicate lines. — (6) **1916** *Out West* July 15/1 Didja see what Ripley did t' that sob story of mine? **1949** *L.A. Times* 15 June II. 4/4 How anyone could heed such a sob story is beyond me. — (7) **1920** *Chambers's Jrnl.* 439/2 You ain't a child, and I see that I can't put over any sob stuff with you. **1935** Weekley *Something About Words* 58 *Sob-stuff,* perhaps the most expressive

term in cinema jargon, but one which did not originally belong to that milieu, crossed the Atlantic in 1920.

* **sociable,** *n.*

1. An informal social gathering, often under the auspices of a church.

1826 LONGFELLOW in S. Longfellow *H. W. Longfellow* I. 74 [I] went with them to a little 'sociable' in the evening, where we had dancing. **1893** PHILIPS *Making of Newspaper* 173, I was . . . supplying the managers of rural Sunday-school sociables with charcoal drawings of the donkey with the adjustable tail. **1939** GILBERT *Forty Yrs.* 94 We had baptisms, confirmations, and sociables without end.

2. (See quot. 1876.) *Obs.*

1851 CIST *Cincinnati* 202 Dressing bureaus, sociables, and *vis-à-vis* are sure to catch the visitor's eye and to open the visitor's purse. **1876** KNIGHT 2234/1 *Sociable,* . . . a kind of couch with a curved S-shaped back, for two persons who sit partially facing each other.

As the last term in **church, ice cream, milk, necktie sociable.**

* **social,** *a.* and *n.*

1. = * **sociable 1.**

1872 *Newton Kansan* 22 Aug. 5/5 Parties, balls and socials . . . will be supplied with Fresh Oysters at all times at the old oyster depot. **1886** EBBUTT *Emigrant Life* 58 Sometimes, too, a 'social' is turned into a dance after the Methodists have gone home. **1945** *Bristol* (N.H.) *Enterprise* 15 Feb. 5/3 Thursday, Feb. 15—Adult group social in Parish House.

b. App. a game played on such an occasion.

1946 WILSON *Fidelity* 107 Along in the evening, after we had played Social until every boy had met every girl and sometimes got stuck with an uninteresting partner, the postmaster entertained us with numerous records on his graphophone.

2. In combs.: (1) **Social Band,** a secret organization formed in Missouri in 1854 by those interested in carrying Kansas for slavery, now *hist.;* (2) **hall,** see as a main entry; (3) **library,** see as a main entry; (4) **register,** a register or directory of those who are socially prominent, also attrib.; (5) **sparrow,** the chipping sparrow *q.v.*

(1) **1883** ANDREAS *Hist. Kansas* 90 Secret lodges were organized under various names—'Social Band' [etc.]. **1918** CONNELLEY *Kansas* 349 The new names of some of these societies were: 'The Blue Lodge,' 'The Social Band,' 'Friends' Society' and 'The Sons of the South.' — (4) **1886** (*title*), Social Register, New York. **1947** *Sat. Ev. Post* 15 March 37/1 The Forbeses occupy over a page and a half in the Boston Social Register. **1949** *Sat. Ev. Post* 15 Oct. 142/3 The student body . . . has a heavy sprinkling of millionaires' sons and Social Register families.

(5) **1869** BURROUGHS in *Galaxy Mag.* Aug. 139/2 The social-sparrow, . . . *alias* 'red-headed chipping bird,' is the smallest of the sparrows. **1917** *Birds of Amer.* III. 41 Its confidence in the friendliness of man seems to be no less than that of the Robin and Bluebird, whence one of its names, the Social Sparrow.

As the last term in **basket, book, box, church, dime, gum, ice cream, mum, necktie, pie social.**

social hall.

1. A large hall for assembly purposes, also a building having such a hall.

[**1839** *Ill. Temperance Herald* (Alton) Feb. 2/3 Mr. Reno has enlarged his establishment by adding to it the rooms that were formerly occupied by Social Hall.] **1862** *N. Amer. Rev.* July 209 These dwellings, with the adjoining Council-House, History Office, Social Hall, and Hotel, give honor to the centre of the Mormon city. **1889** Union Pac. R.R. *Ore. & Wash.* 251 A large social hall contains a library and piano. **1948** *Chelsea* (Mass.) *Rec.* 30 Nov. 8/1 Troop 13, Boy Scouts, will meet tonight at 7 o'clock in the social hall of the First Baptist church.

2. A drawing room or salon on a river steamer.

1839 in *N.O. Picayune* (1840) 8 April 4/1 There was a passenger with a violin practising in the Social Hall. **1893** LELAND *Memoirs* 223, I recorded the *bon mots* and merry stories which passed among us all in the *sanctum* in articles for our weekly newspaper, under the name of 'Social Hall Sketches' (a social hall in the West is a steamboat smoking-room).

social library. A library maintained, either by ownership of shares or by payment of subscription fees, by the particular group of persons entitled to use it. Cf. **society library** (*a*).

*c***1765–80** *N. Eng. Hist. & Gen. Reg.* XXII. (1868) 446 We the Subscribers being desirous of purchasing a *Social Library* . . . do severally promise and engage to pay Four Dollars a piece for this purpose. **1809** E. A. KENDALL *Travels* II. 244 In Franklin Place, apartments are occupied by the Boston Social Library, and by the Massachusetts-Historical Society. By *social* is here intended *society;* for, by a perversion of language, the *society-libraries,* of which some account has been given in a former chapter, are so called. **1910** BOSTWICK *Amer. Pub. Library* 7 The joint-stock form of library is in its simplest form a book club, as in the so-called 'social libraries' of Massachusetts.

* **society,** *n.*

1. Chiefly *N. Eng.* A parish or part of a town or settlement having its own place of worship. Also a Protestant church group whose members attend the same place of worship.

1739 *Suffield Doc. Hist.* 275 The Inhabitants of the West part of said Town . . . [ask] to be Set off into a Distinct and Seperate Society. **1775** FITHIAN *Jrnl.* II. 122 This settlement is broken with religious divisions—there is a Baptist Society, now under the direction of one Mr. Lane. **1831** PECK *Guide* 260 The *Christ-ians,* as they are termed, have some societies in Illinois. **1889** FREEMAN *Far-away Melody* (1891) 257 More people went into the Baptist Church, whose Society was much the larger of the two.

2. Among the Indians, a secret organization having some special religious or other significance.

1804 CLARK in *Lewis & C. Exped.* I. (1904) 130 Those who become Members of this Society must be brave active young men who take a Vow never to give back let the danger be what it may. **1886** *Rep. Bureau Amer. Ethnol. 1885–86* 151 The persons admitted into the society are firmly believed to possess the power of communing with various supernatural beings. **1906** *N. Dakota H.S. Coll.* I. 464 Among the Dakotas membership in societies generally is not determined by tribal relations.

3. Short for "Society of Friends." *Obs.*

1849 CHAMBERLAIN *Ind. Gazetteer* 73 The Society have about 5,000 children in this State.

4. A secret club or organization among students, esp. a fraternity.

1871 BAGG *At Yale* 51 The sub-Freshman is pledged to his society months before he approaches the college walls. **1889** *Cent. Mag.* March 799/2 He was a member of neither of these societies, but of Delta Upsilon, a non-secret fraternity. **1915** F. W. SHEPARDSON *Phi. Beta Kappa* 14 On Saturday, Jan. 6, 1781 five members [decided that] . . . the society should disband.

attrib. **1871** BAGG *At Yale* 65 No one without society badge or admission ticket could pass the entrance. *Ib.* 205 No undergraduate can shirk paying his 'society tax.' **1876** *Wide Awake* 99/1 His brother Tom . . . wore a 'society pin.'

5. In special combs.: (1) **society column,** a column in a newspaper devoted to news about those prominent in society; (2) **editor,** an editor in charge of the department in a newspaper which deals with society happenings; (3) **hall,** a hall in which members of a college society meet; (4) * **house,** a house in which members of a college society or of a religious group live or meet; (5) **land,** (see quot. 1889), *obs.;* (6) **library,** (*a*) = **social library,** (*b*) a library maintained in a society, sense **1,** *obs.;* (7) **reporter,** one who reports society news for a paper.

(1) **1931** *K.C. Times* 15 Aug., From the number of times a certain . . . woman's name appears in the society column, it would seem she has a pretty good press agent. — (2) **1880** HARRIS *U. Remus* (1884) 203 'The old man's mind is wandering,' said the society editor. **1949** *Sat. Ev. Post* 7 May 134/4 The society editor came over and perched on the edge of my desk. — (3) **1860** *Ladies' Repository* Jan. 60/2 [We] settled the affairs of the whole world in the society halls. **1887** *Lippincott's Mag.* Aug. 291 Others spend their evenings at the theatre, at their society hall, or in calling on their young lady acquaintances. — (4) **1887** *Lippincott's Mag.* Oct. 574 The candidate is invited to visit the society-house. **1891** EARLE *Sabbath* 105 The New Canaan Church built on the green beside their meeting-house a fine 'Society House.'

(5) **1774** *New Hampshire Prov. Papers* (1873) VII. 24 His Excellency ordered to be read at the Board the Petition of sundry of the Inhabitants of the Society Land for an incorporation for reasons mentioned in said Petition. **1889** W. W. HAYWARD *Hist. Hancock, N.H.* 2 In 1746 John Tufton Mason . . . sold out his right [to Capt. John Mason's share] to a company of twelve men for £1,500 currency. . . . The land not granted for townships was called 'Society Land.' — (6) (*a*) **1809** KENDALL *Travels* I. 136 The number of books, in the respective town or society . . . libraries, is very small. (*b*) **1823** J. & R. C. MORSE *Traveller's Guide* (1826) 14/1 The library [of Amherst Coll.] . . . contains 900 volumes, and the Society libraries have about 400 more. **1837** A. GREENE *Glance at N.Y.* 222 The New York Society Library . . . began [1754] with about 700 volumes. The price of a share was $12.50. — (7) **1888** *St. Louis Globe-Democrat* 29 April (F.), The brainy paragraphs thrown off by one society reporter. **1931** WILLISON *Here They Dug Gold* 229 A society reporter notes a 'white satin bonnet with a delicate spray of flowers and two tiny birds in the act of flying, with a trimming of ostrich feathers.'

As the last term in **abolition, Alumni, Audubon, cent, colonization, Columbian Benevolent, Danite, Democratic, Ebenezer, Education, Emigrant Aid, emigration, fire, Greek letter, immigration, improvement, Ladies' Aid, Massachusetts Aid, medicine, mite, National Colonization, northern emigrant aid, peace, Pilgrim, Pioneer(s'), Republican, school, senior, sewing, shawl, state, state historical, St. Tammany, Tammany, temple, tract, turn, Washington Benevolent, White Cross, Woman's Aid society.**

***sock,** *n.* As the last term in **German, long, Siwash sock(s).**

sockdolager sɑkˈdɑləgɚ, *n.* Also **sogdollager, sockdologer,** etc. [Origin obscure. Poss. a fanciful formation based on **sock* and **doxology*.]

1. A tremendous blow, a finisher. Also fig. *Slang.*

1830 *Va. Lit. Museum* 6 Jan. 479 *Sockdologer*, 'a decisive blow'—one, in the slang language 'Capable of setting a man a thinking.' **1855** *Santa Barbara* (Calif.) *Gaz.* 16 Aug. 4/1 We overheard a poor unfortunate get the following sock-dollager, the other day, from his better half. **1928** *Bunker's Mag.* June 931, 'I shall not vote for you again.' This was a sockdologer.

2. An unusually large or exceptional person or thing. *Slang.*

1838 COOPER *Home as Found* II. 72 There is but one 'sogdollager' in the universe, and that is in Lake Oswego. **1910** *D.N.* III. 458 Sockdologer, a very tremendous person or thing. 'Wasn't that a sockdologer of a man?' **1919** HOUGH *Sagebrusher* 20 'Got him!' said he. 'And he's one sockdollager, believe me!' **1949** *Amer. Dial. Soc. Pub.* April 26.

3. (See quot. 1848.) Also attrib.

1848 BARTLETT 319 *Socdolager*, a patent fish-hook, having two hooks which close upon each other by means of a spring as soon as the fish bites. **1857** *Spirit of Times* 17 Jan. 319/3 We prepared ourselves; that is, each man provided himself with a 'sockdologer' fish-hook and line, strong enough to hold a calf.

sockeye ˈsɑkaɪ, *n.* [f. Salish Indian. See quot. 1887.] An important salmon, *Oncorhynchus nerka*, which in the spring ascends the streams in the Northwest. Also attrib.

1887 GOODE *Amer. Fishes* 481 O Frazer River, where this species is the most important Salmon, it is known as the 'Suk-kegh,' 'Saw-quai' or 'Suck-eye.' **1913** *Industrial Worker* (Spokane) 17 July 4/4 The company has been forcing the slaves at extra speed to turn out extra cans and cases . . . as this is the year of the big sockeye run. **1950** *Amer. Forests* Jan. 42/3 After the steam shovels had started work, somebody remembered that there were steelhead and chinook and sockeye salmon that would be blocked, and something ought to be done to save them if possible.

soco ˈsoko, *n.* [La. F. *soco* (<Choctaw *suko*, muscadine).] (See quot. 1931.) — **1894** CHOPIN *Bayou Folk* 207 They could well afford shoes now, for they had saved many a picayune through . . . selling . . . 'socoes' to ladies in the village who 'put up' such things. **1931** READ *La. French* 106 The French of Louisiana are all familiar with *soco*, the name of the Southern Fox-grape or the berry of the muscadine.

***sod,** *n.* In combs.: (1) **sodbuster,** *W.* a farmer, *slang;* (2) **corn,** *W.* (*a*) (see quot. 1833), also attrib., (*b*) whisky made from such corn, also attrib.; (3) **crop,** the first crop on heavily sodded prairie land; (4) **fence,** (see quot. 1852), *obs.;* (5) **grain,** grain for planting sod ground; (6) **ground,** ground, esp. on a prairie, having a thick heavy sod; (7) **-house claim,** a claim of public land upon which a sodhouse has been built; (8) **land,** prairie land having a heavy sod during the first year of cultivation; (9) **planted,** *a.* planted on sod ground, *rare;* (10) **plow,** (see quot. 1876); (11) **soaker,** (see quot. 1944), *colloq.;* (12) **wheat,** (see quot.), *obs.;* (13) **worm,** (see quots.), also **sod-webworm.**

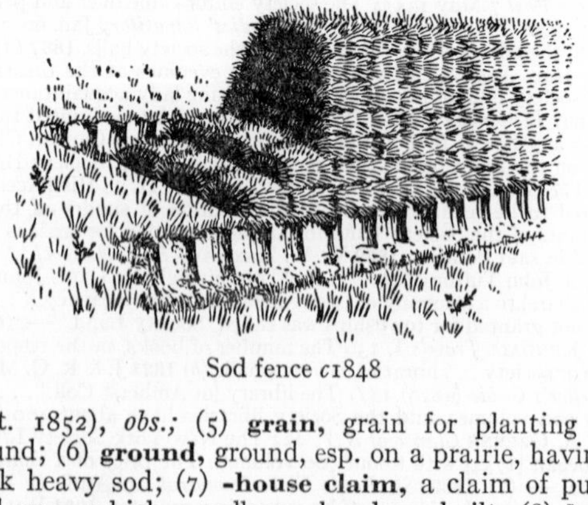

Sod fence *c*1848

(1) **1927** SANDBURG *Songbag* 89 Its tune was familiar to the lonely 'sodbuster.' **1948** *Popular Western* June 12/2 The boardwalks teemed with . . . sodbusters accompanied by work-faded womenfolk in challie sacques and starched sunbonnets. — (2) (*a*) **1833** SHIRREFF *Tour* (1835) 248 Indian corn is dropped into every third furrow . . . and covered with the next cut turf. This crop receives no further cultivation of any kind, is termed sod corn, and said to yield fifty bushels per acre. **1857** *Lawrence* (Kans.) *Republican* 18 June, A man in Illinois, near Bloomington, has invented a sod corn planter. **1913** CATHER *O Pioneers!* 27 John Bergson says to his boys, 'Try to break a little more land every year; sod corn is good for fodder.' (*b*) **1857** ERASTUS BEADLE *To Nebraska in '57* (1923) 73 Followed the Indian trail to the place found the family enjoying themselves over their 'Sod corn whiskey.' **1927** EUBANK *Horse & Buggy Days* 94 They . . . ate their dinners, . . . munching cheese, or oysters or sardines, which was helped along on its onward course by a tumbler or so of sod corn, made in a moonshine still especially for the occasion. — (3) **1848** *Rep. Comm. Patents 1847* 539 This gave a sod crop without tending of thirty to forty bushels per acre. **1930** HENRY *Conquer. Plains* 317 Shallow plowing and broadcasting seed grain—at first for merely sod crops—brought many a defeat and loss. **1950** *Jrnl. Ill. State Hist. Soc.* Spring 37 They learned to plant a 'sod crop' by cutting upturned furrows at intervals with an ax, then dropping in a few kernels of corn. — (4) **1839** J. PLUMBE *Sk. Iowa* 33 A ditch and sod fence, for which the soil is admirably adapted, can be made to answer every purpose. **1852** REGAN *Emigrant's Guide* 348 Sod fences are made by digging a ditch, throwing up the earth on the side next the field to be fenced, and facing the mound with sods, laid flat on each other, having a slope to the field.

(5) **1847** *Hunt's Merch. Mag.* XVI. 294 The land is then ready for 'sod grain.' — (6) **1871** *Ill. Agric. Soc. Trans.* VIII. 238 Next in adaptation is the *sod ground* of our prairie State. **1932** *Randolph Enterprise* (Elkins, W.Va.) 4 Feb. 4/2 Sod ground is about all ploughed and some stubble ground also. — (7) **1945** *Time* 24 Sep. 100/2 Markey's earliest idol was a weather-beaten Indian expert named Mr. Howell, whose unplowed sod-house claim adjoined that of the Jameses. — (8) **1856** *Rep. Comm. Patents 1855: Agric.* 262 They were mostly sown upon sod-land. **1886** EBBUTT *Emigrant Life Kans.* 74 Indian corn does not grow so well as these on sod land. — (9) **1879** *Scribner's Mo.* Nov. 134/1 Where it [*sc.* corn] has been sod-planted it is left untouched.

(10) **1876** KNIGHT 2238/1 *Sod-plow*, a plow long in the share and mold-board, adapted to cut and overturn sod. — (11) **1923** *K.C.* (Mo.) *Star* 23 April, That part of the state known as the short grass country needs a sod-soaker. **1944** *Democrat* 20 July 2/2 A real rain is a gully washer. A little less rainfall may be a sod-soaker. — (12) **1841** *Cultivator* VIII. 147 'Sod wheat' is the term given to the first crop of the prairie. — (13) **1891** *Cent.* 5747/3 *Sodworm*, the larva of certain pyralid moths, as *Crambus exsiccatus*, which destroys the roots of grass and corn. **1925** HERRICK *Man. Injurious Insects* 308 The Sod Webworms. . . . There are at least six species of moths of the sub-family *Crambinæ* . . . whose larvæ feed on various grasses, weeds, and cereals.

b. *sod and pole shanty,* a shanty built of poles upon which pieces of sod are laid.

1897 *Outing* XXIX. 582/2 Midway of its length, the canyon widens enough to admit a sod and pole shanty, and a little patch of alfalfa and pumpkins.

As the last term in **buffalo, prairie sod.**

***soda,** *n.*

1. In faro, the card which shows face up in the deal box before dealing begins. In full **soda card.** Often *from soda* (*card*) *to hock,* (see quot. 1938).

1843 GREEN *Exposure Gambling* 194 The top card, when the deal is first commenced, is called the deal card; this card neither wins nor loses, and on that account is sometimes called the soda card. **1856** *Town Talk* (S.F.) 12 July 1/2 The 'king' was the soda card, and Harry backed the royal piece of pasteboard with one-fourth of his remaining checks. **1902** H. L. WILSON *Spenders* v. 49 Young Bines played the deal from soda card to hock. **1938** ASBURY *Sucker's Prog.* 16 Soda—The first card, exposed face up before bets were made. Said to have been a corruption of zodiac. For many years a common expression was 'from soda to hock,' meaning the whole thing, from soup to nuts.

2. In combs.: (1) **soda biscuit,** a biscuit raised with soda; (2) **butte,** *W.* a butte in an alkaline region; (3) **clerk,** one who prepares and sells drinks, etc., at a soda fountain; (4) **cocktail,** (see quot. 1889); (5) **counter,** a counter or bar at which drinks are served; (6) **cracker,** a thin, crisp flour cracker made from yeast dough to which soda has been added; (7) **fount,** a soda fountain (sense

1.); (8) **fountain,** see as a main entry; (9) **grass,** grass found in an alkaline region; (10) **jerk(er),** =**soda clerk,** *slang;* (11) **mound,** a mound in an alkaline region; (12) **mountain,** (see quot.), *obs.;* (13) **pop,** soda water variously flavored and sold, usu., in tightly capped bottles, also attrib.; (14) **powder,** (see quot. 1890); (15) **prairie,** (see quot.); (16) **shop,** a shop at which soda water is sold; (17) **spring,** a spring the water of which is impregnated with soda, also as a proper name; (18) **squirt,** a social entertainment, *rare;* (19) **squirter,** =**soda clerk,** *rare;* (20) **-water fountain,** =**soda fountain 1.**

(1) **1830** *Albany Journal* 25 Aug. 3/5 Fresh Soda Biscuit, just received from Treadwell's Bakery, and for sale by S. W. Southwick. **1939** WOLCOTT *Yankee Cook Book* 164 Soda biscuits still retain their flavor when they are warmed over in the oven. — (2) **1886** *Cong. Rec.* 14 Dec. 153/2 There are [in Yellowstone Park] hot springs and soda buttes. — (3) **1944** JOHNSON *As I Dare* 220 We went in to ask the soda clerk questions. **1946** *This Week Mag.* 7 Sep. 31/1 Ida forsakes her soda-clerk lover for sleek gent. — (4) **1868** *N.Y. Herald* 2 July 4/1 We have the Fourth of July thrown in with . . . its exhilarating associations so conducive of headaches and soda cocktails. **1889** *Cent.* 1081/1 *Soda cocktail,* a glass of soda-water with a little bitters.

(5) **1846** *Dollar Newspaper* (Phila.) 19 Aug. 4/2 He very importantly asked his friend to enter, went up to the soda counter, and 'reckoned they'd take a little whisky.' **1922** WILSON *Merton of Movies* 64 You would be surprised to see these drug stores where you can go in and sit at the soda counter and order your coffee and sandwiches and custard pie. — (6) **1830** *Stonington* (Conn.) *Phenix* 1 Sep. 3/4 (*advt.*), Fresh Soda Crackers. **1948** MENJOU & MUSSELMAN *It Took 9 Tailors* 35 I would go out and buy a box of soda crackers and make a meal out of *canapés* and champagne. — (7) **1848** *Knickerb.* XXXI. 40 They had not a theatre, nor an oyster-saloon, nor a soda-font, nor a gin-palace. **1908** *Home Herald* (Chi.) 13 May, For example, here is the popular soda-fount drink known as Coca-Cola, absolutely harmless, and probably the most widely used soft drink ever made in our country. — (9) **1846** *30th Congress* 1 Sess. H.R. Ex. Doc. No. 41, 596 We encamp in soda grass.

(10) **1916** *Amer. City* April 373/2 For soda 'jerkers' he paid $2.50 a day. **1948** *Sat. Review* 27 March 28/3 Did a knowledge of Xenophon or Juvenal ever turn a soda-jerker into a tycoon? **1949** *New Yorker* 2 April 72/2 Builders are *constructioneers,* soda jerks are *fountaineers.* — (11) **1878** BEADLE *Western Wilds* 372 The plain is dotted by soda mounds from five to thirty feet in height. — (12) **1871** J. W. BARLOW *Reconn. Yellowstone R.* (1872) 15 Towards the western verge of this prairie a hill of white rock was discovered which, upon investigation, proved to be another of the 'soda mountains,' as they are called by the hunters. Approaching nearer, I found jets of smoke and steam issuing from the face of the hill, while its other side was hollowed out into a sort of amphitheater, whose sides were steaming with sulphur fumes, the ground hot and parched with internal fires. — (13) **1923** *Nation* 25 July 93 Such imps as the beloved demon rum, the comforting demon nicotine, and the flapper demon soda-pop. **1950** *Chi. Tribune* 5 April 22 It was run over by a soda-pop truck when he was playing baseball in the street! — (14) **1820** *Columbian Centinel* 1 July 3/6 Maynard & Noyes continue to prepare Soda Powders, of superior quality. **1890** *Cent.* 4661/2 *Soda powder,* sodium bicarbonate 30 grains, tartaric acid 25 grains.

(15) **1859** BARTLETT 426 *Soda-Prairie,* a plain covered with an efflorescence of soda, elsewhere called natron. — (16) **1820** *Boston Selectmen* 161 All licensed victuallers, retailers, confectioners, and soda shops, must be closed in future on Sundays. **1862** STRONG *Cadet Life W. Point* 128 The records of the soda shop may be found in the archives of the institution. — (17) **1837** IRVING *Bonneville* II. 32 We have heard this also called the Soda spring. **1890** LANGFORD *Vigilante Days* (1912) 79 At last they reached Soda Springs on Bear River. **a1918** G. STUART *On Frontier* I. 147 At Soda springs on Bear river we drank our fill of soda water from a spring on the bank. — (18) **1898** MARK TWAIN *Stirring Times* 319 (R.), The undersigned desires an invitation to the next soda-squirt. — (19) **1898** MARK TWAIN *Stirring Times* 319 (R.), Hurrah for the soda-squirter!

(20) **1858** VIELÉ *Following Drum* 149 A bakery and even a 'pharmacie,' with a most pretentious soda water fountain, are found here. **1892** *Harper's Mag.* Dec. 142 [He] increased the apothecary's business by persuading him to send East for a soda-water fountain. **1902** LORIMER *Lett. Merchant* 217 [He] ran a soda-water fountain in the front of his store.

As the last term in **baking, chocolate, cream, grape, ice cream, sarsaparilla, whisky soda.**

soda fountain.

1. A container from which soda water is drawn off by faucets. Also a counter at which soda water and other soft drinks, as well as light meals, are served.

1824 *Independent Chron.* (Boston) 9 Oct. 3/3 This luxury in a hot and dusty season, together with an ever-flowing Soda Fountain, . . . he flatters himself will ensure a continuance of public patronage. **1855** *Chi. W. Times* 5 July 3/5 The kind-hearted knight of the soda fountain . . . handed her $5. **1920** LEWIS *Main Street* 34 In the Greek candy-store was . . . a greasy marble soda-fountain. **1950** *N.O. Times-Picayune Mag.* 16 April 6/3 About the most striking gadget inside is the soda fountain, nearly 100 years old, originally used in Philadelphia.

attrib. **1876** *Napa* (Calif.) *Reg.* 29 July 4/2 A Woodward avenue drug-store hired a new soda-fountain boy the other day. **1950** *Lincoln Co. Advt.* (Brookhaven, Miss.) 12 Jan., Bill flunked out and has since held jobs briefly as car salesman, oil-station attendant, soda-fountain clerk, hotel night-desk man.

2. *W.* A spring of mineral water containing soda. Also as a proper name.

1842 J. BIDWELL *Trip to Calif.* 10 A distance of 10 miles took us to the Soda Fountain, where we stopped the remainder of the day. This is a noted place in the mountains and is considered a great curiosity. **1878** BEADLE *Western Wilds* 372 The soda-fountains . . . boil furiously with a loud, bubbling noise.

soddy ˈsɑdɪ, *n. W.* A sodhouse.

1877 RUEDE *Sod-House Days* 57 Many of the young bachelors . . . were building their own 'soddies.' **1915** *Lit. Digest* 10 April 831/1 Only in the western counties are there any soddies standing now. **1949** *World-Herald Mag.* (Omaha) 18 Sep. 16/3 During the years from 1870 to 1888 in Nebraska, frame school buildings were rapidly replacing 'soddies.'

Sodom apple. (See quot.) — **1891** *Cent.* 5747/3 *Sodom-apple,* . . . sometimes, in the United States, the horse-nettle, *S. Carolinense,* or some similar species.

sofky ˈsɑfkɪ, *n.* ["The word is derived from the Creek dialect of the Muskhogean language" (Hodge).] Hominy or thin corn gruel used by the Creeks and other southern Indians.

1796 HAWKINS *Letters* 28 [She] gave me a basket of corn for my horses, a fowl, some sofkey (hommony) and ground peas. **1845** HOOPER *Simon Suggs' Adv.* 75 She had scarcely time to cook the sophky for her children. **1916** THOBURN *Stand. Hist. Okla.* I. 262 The fermented hominy which was known as 'tah-fula' . . . was the national dish of the Choctaws. The Creeks had a similar dish known as sof-ky. **1944** BARBOUR *Eden* 49 The basis of the *sofkee* used to be the arrowroot-like starch which is made from the coomtie plant. But the coomtie does not grow abundantly where the Indians are now forced to live, and grits is the ordinary substitute. The mess is flavored up with such wild meat as may be available.

∗ **soft,** *a.* and *n.*

1. (*cap.*) *pl.* (See quot. 1844.) *Obs.*

1844 *Lexington Observer* 14 Aug. 3/2 The locofocos . . . are divided in that State [Mo.], and are known by the distinctive appellations of the '*Hards*' and '*Softs*' in consequence of their views upon the currency question. **1846** *Quincy* (Ill.) *Whig* 31 March 2/1 The 'hards' and 'softs' [of St. Louis] have brought out Mr. Hawken for Mayor. **1946** *St. Louis Globe-Democrat* 18 Aug., The 'Softs' . . . stood for a liberal issue of paper money by the wildcat banks.

2. (*cap.*) *pl.* (See quot. 1914.) Now *hist.* Cf. ∗**Hard-Shell 2, soft-shell 3.**

1853 *N.Y. Tribune* 2 April 3/6 The Softs are composed of the remnants of the Van Buren and Adams party of 1848, and such Hunkers as Secretary Marcy and Gov. Seymour. **1888** BRYCE *Amer. Commonw.* II. II. xlvi. 203 The Hunkers and Barnburners . . . subsequently passed into the 'Hards' and the 'Softs.' **1914** *Cyclo. Amer. Govt.* III. 350/1 The 'Softs,' or 'Soft Shells,' were New York Democrats, in opposition to the regulars, 'Hunkers' . . . or 'Hards.' . . . The 'Softs' made efforts to draw back into the Democratic party the Democratic element of the Free Soil party.

3. *a.* and *attrib.* Of or pertaining to Soft-shell Democrats. Cf. prec.

1853 *Whig Almanac 1854* 41 Average Soft vote, 96,698. **1856** MACLEOD *F. Wood* 299 He could not really be called 'Hard' or 'Soft,' though a member of the latter organization and in full communion with it. **1859** *Harper's Mag.* Nov. 832/2 The 'Soft' chairman was thrown from the platform.

4. In special combs.: (1) **softball,** a form of ball game somewhat like baseball, but played with a larger and softer ball on a smaller diamond, a ball used in this game, also attrib.; (2) **corn,** see as a main entry; (3) **currency,** =**paper currency,** *obs.;* (4) **dollar,** =**paper dollar,** *obs.;* (5) **hat,** a hat which is not hard, a crush or felt hat; (6) **maple,** the red, the silver, or the dwarf maple; (7) **mark,** =**easy mark,** *slang;* (8) **marsh,** (see quots.); (9) **money,** (see quot. 1892), also attrib.; (10)

-shell, -shelled, see as main entries; (11) **shirt,** a shirt to be worn without starching; (12) **snap,** a "good thing," a place or job requiring little or no work, *colloq.;* (13) **spot,** (*a*) *fig.* a lack of sound practical sense, a trace of tenderness or sentimentality, *colloq.,* (*b*) (see quot.); (14) **tack,** (see quot.), *obs.;* (15) **thing,** *fig.* something extremely easy or pleasant, a snap, *colloq.*

(1) **1938** *Chi. Tribune* 2 April 21/3 While playing softball the other day I cracked a line drive toward center field. **1948** *Time* 6 Sep. 34/2 Ripe tomatoes as big as softballs glowed in almost every stall. **1949** *Ward Co. Independent* (Minot, N.D.) 21 July 3/4 A total of 58 softball teams . . . participated in the spring program. — (3) **1851** GREEN *Twelve Days* 33 The politicians were fiercely discussing the 'hard' and 'soft' currency question. — (4) **1776** *Battle of Brooklyn* I. iv, There is not one of those horses but what is worth more than a hundred and fifty soft dollars—consider, Sir!

(5) **1873** MARK TWAIN & WARNER *Gilded Age* xiii. 125 He wore . . , a soft hat, a short cutaway coat. **1893** *Harper's Mag.* May 897/1 A gay, reckless gleam under the wide rim of his soft hat. — (6) [**1778** CARVER *Travels* 496 The Maple. Of this tree there are two sorts, the hard and the soft.] **1807** GASS *Journal* 195 The timber is mostly of the fir kind, with some cherry, . . . soft maple and ash. **1948** JACOBS *We Chose Country* 25 We turned south . . . and saw the farm buildings, clustered behind a great row of soft maples that bordered the road. — (7) **1891** QUINN *Fools of Fortune* 231 He then tells the selected victim that he has found a 'soft mark,' (which in the vernacular of the profession means a particularly gullible dupe), and offers to introduce him. — (8) **1737** WESLEY *Journal* I. 402 Soft marsh . . . is all a quagmire, and absolutely good for nothing. **1775** ROMANS *Nat. Hist. Florida* 30 The soft marshes are those, whose spungy nature allows the water easily to penetrate them. — (9) **1844** *Henry Clay Bugle* (Maysville, Ky.) 11 April 3/3 Mr. Tod . . . endorses the bank doctrines of Gov. Shannon, and declares himself a sort of hermaphrodite, soft money man. **1892** WALSH *Lit. Curiosities* 450 In political parlance, especially during the second half of the decade 1870–1880, . . . 'soft money' . . . was understood [to mean] an irredeemable paper currency such as was advocated by the Greenbackers.

(11) **1900** NORRIS *Blix* 191 With a sensation of positive luxury . . . he put on a 'soft' shirt of blue cheviot. — (12) **1845** HOOPER *Simon Suggs' Adv.* 19 Simon Gets a 'Soft Snap' out of His Daddy. **1904** *N.Y. Times* 2 July 6 The average politician seemed to regard that office as a soft snap, for the performance of whose duties no training was required. — (13) (*a*) **1845** in *Amer. Sp.* XXII. 205/1 He possesses . . . that tact which enables man to detect the *soft spots* in his fellow. **1901** *McClure's Mag.* Dec. 152 [Platt's] delight in music still remains the soft spot which he turns to humanity. (*b*) **1900** NELSON *A B C Wall St.* 159 Soft spot, a weak point in the market. — (14) **1890** GOSS *Recollections* 8 On our arrival in Washington the next morning, we were marched to barracks, dignified by the name of 'Soldiers' Retreat,' where a half loaf of 'soft-tack,' as we had already begun to call wheat bread, was issued.

(15) **1867** CRAWFORD *Mosby* 103 Thinking they had a *soft thing* [they] were inside the house playing cards and drinking. **1898** FORD *Tattle-Tales* 153 Now, if you want a soft thing pay heed to what I write.

b. In the names of, or with reference to, animals: (1) **soft-back,** =**soft-shelled turtle;** (2) **clam,** the long clam, *Mya arenaria,* of the Atlantic Coast, also attrib.; (3) **crab,** =**soft-shell crab;** (4) **gar,** (see quot.); (5) **oyster,** (see quot.); (6) **shell,** see as a main entry; (7) **-shelled,** see as a main entry; (8) **sheller,** a soft-shelled crab, *colloq.*

(1) **1838** GOSSE *Letters* 99 Another Tortoise of even greater size and equal ferocity is the Soft-back (*Trionyx ferox*). It is spoken of as rather rare, but as being occasionally met with in the Cahawba River. — (2) **1855** *Knickerb.* XLVI. 222 Along the strand, . . . these great delicacies, 'soft clams' and sand-crabs may be found. **1867** *Common Sense Cook Book* 10 Hard Clam Fritters . . . are made the same way as soft clam fritters, except the clams must have been previously boiled. **1935** LINCOLN *Cape Cod Yesterdays* 46 The variety with the long, thin shell is a soft clam. — (3) **1772** in *William & Mary Coll. Quart.* 1 Ser. XIV. (1906) 38 Like the shell out of a soft crab, the body of the crab after the shell is off seems by much too large for the shell. **1884** GOODE *Fisheries* I. 776 The terms 'Soft Crab,' 'Paper-shell,' and 'Buckler' denote the different stages of consistency of the shell [of the blue crab]. — (4) **1883** *Nat. Museum Bul.* No. 27, 469 *Tylosurus marinus.* . . . Silver Gar-fish; Soft Gar; Bill-fish; Needle-fish, Atlantic coast.

(5) **1881** INGERSOLL *Oyster Industry* 248 *Soft Oyster.*—The 'Virginia plant,' or southern oyster (Staten Island sound), as distinguished from the 'hard' native oyster. — (8) **1886** MITCHELL *R. Blake* 261 Women is often like soft shellers.

soft corn.

1. A variety of corn the kernels of which are especially rich in soft starch. Also corn which, as a result of unfavorable weather conditions, contains at harvesting an undesirably large amount of moisture, rendering it likely to spoil at germinating time the following spring. Also attrib.

1751 J. BARTRAM *Observations* 60 Last of all was served a great bowl full of Indian dumplings, of new soft corn, cut or scraped off the ear. **1770** *Md. Hist. Mag.* XIII. 72, I Have a great deal of soft Corn at all the Plantations. **1868** *Mich. Agric. Rep.* VII. 160 Early frosts made considerable 'soft corn.' **1947** *Chi. Tribune* 23 July 9/4 Crop experts here and farmers interviewed on the drive warn that the state must prepare for a soft corn crop this fall. They expect frost to strike before much of the corn is matured, leaving it with too high a moisture content to store safely.

2. (See quot. 1859.) Also *to feed on soft corn. Slang.*

1834 CARUTHERS *Kentuckian* I. 98 He's feedin me on soft corn, thought I. **1859** BARTLETT 426 *Soft Corn,* flattery. The more common terms are 'soft sawder' and 'soft soap.' **1948** *Antioch Rev.* Autumn 161 He was all soft corn . . . , but you couldn't be sure, not with a man like Malcolm.

soft-shell ˈsɔftˌʃɛl, *n.*

1. Any one of various aquatic animals, esp. crabs and clams, having a shell that is soft, also one of these prepared as food.

1830 SANDS *Writings* II. 230 The soft-shell of the Red River [is a dish unrivalled in other parts of the world]. **1846** THORPE *Myst. Backwoods* 156 It is Turtle Lake from its abundance of 'green, amphibious soft-shells.' **1886** MITCHELL *R. Blake* 261 Soft shells . . . ain't got no shells really. **1943** PENN *Ecology* XXIV. 11 Here the majority of the 'soft-shells' . . . were found.

2. =**Soft-Shell Baptist.** *Obs.* Cf. **Hard-Shell Baptist.**

1845 *Knickerb.* XXVI. 285 A 'Hard-Shell' recently turned a 'Soft Shell' out of church. **1893** FARMER & HENLEY III. 270/2 The Soft-shells are of more liberal mind [than the Hard-Shells].

3. (See quot. 1914.) Now *hist.*

1853 *N.Y. Tribune* 2 April 3/6 A Soft Shell . . . is a loud stickler for Union and Harmony. **1858** in BARTLETT 426 The terms Hunker, Barnburner, Soft-shell, and Hardshell, have become obsolete, and hereafter we will be known only by the term Democrat. **1914** [see **soft, a.* and *n.* 2.].

4. A variety of walnut having fruit that is relatively soft-shelled.

1888 LINDLEY *Calif. of South* 359 The English walnut comes into bearing in about ten years, and the soft-shell at about six years.

5. In combs.: (1) **Soft-Shell Baptist,** a Baptist holding views more liberal than those of the Primitive or Hard-Shell Baptists, also attrib.; (2) **clam,** =**soft clam;** (3) **convention,** a convention of Soft-Shell Democrats, *obs.;* (4) **cooter,** see **cooter;** (5) **crab,** a crab that has recently shed its shell, the new one not yet being hard; (6) **terrapin,** =next; (7) **turtle,** any one of various aquatic turtles, as *Amyda ferox,* found esp. in southern waters and the Mississippi Valley.

(1) **1845** *Knickerb.* XXVI. 285 They have singular denominational distinctions in the west, among which the 'Hard and Soft Shell Baptists' are most remarkable. **1871** DE VERE 241 The Soft Shell Baptists . . . [allow themselves] to be indulgent to certain worldly usages, and to educate their ministers carefully for the pulpit. **1945** *Chi. Tribune* 19 Aug. I. 9/3 The Rev. Scott Hall, 94, 'Soft-shell' Baptist minister who preached the gospel throughout Kentucky for many years, died last night. — (2) **1818** *Amer. Mo. Mag.* II. 296 Soft shell Clam. These animals . . . are excellent eating. — (3) **1856** *N.Y. Herald* 7 July (B.), The call of the Soft-shell Convention was signed by twelve men of the Free-Soil Buffalo stripe.

(5) **1843** *Nat. Hist. N.Y., Zoology* VI. 11 During this interval, they are known under the name of Soft-shell Crabs, or Shedders. **1883** GOODE *Fishery Industries U.S.* 49 Soft-shell Crabs are . . . seldom taken in marketable quantities excepting on the New Jersey coast. **1891** G. A. SALA in *Times* (London) 22 Feb. 2/3, I heard of the contemplated establishment of a London American club, the scheme of which seemed to comprise unlimited . . . soft-shell crabs [etc.]. — (6) **1846** THORPE *Myst. Backwoods* 17 In the depths of these ponds . . . [is the] soft-shell terrapin. — (7) **1805** in *Wis. Hist. Coll.* XXII. (1916) 218 Passed 2 creeks . . . boath of them had running water in one of them saw Soft Shell Turtle. **1884** GOODE *Nat. Hist. Aquat. Anim.* 152 The food of the soft-shell Turtles consists of small fishes, snails, and other small animals.

***soft-shelled,** *a.* In the names of various aquatic creatures having soft shells, as (1) **soft-shelled clam,** (2) **crab,** (3) **tortoise,** (4) **turtle.**

(1) **1796** *Smithtown Rec.* 129 Any person not an inhabitant . . . taking Soft shelled clams within the limits of said Town shall pay six pence for every bushel. **1855** P. PAXTON *Capt. Priest* 11 The protruding neck of a soft-shelled clam is . . . efficient . . . in quieting the yells. — (2) **1891** *Cent.* 5749/2 *Soft-shelled crab*, the common edible crab of the United States, *Callinectes hastatus*, when it has molted its hard shell and not yet grown another. — (3) **1857** *Rep. Comm. Patents 1856: Agric.* 112 Soft-shelled tortoises . . . can escape by diving. — (4) **1771** *Phil. Trans.* LXI. 267 We call it the *soft shelled Turtle.* **1842** *Nat. Hist. N.Y., Zoology* III. 6 The Soft-shelled Turtle . . . is much esteemed as a wholesome and nutritious article of food. They are said to feed on fish, and the smaller aquatic reptiles. **1950** *Time* 23 Jan. 1/3 The identifying marks of a soft-shelled turtle are a flapjack-shaped body and a long, pointed snout.

b. soft-shelled almond, the common sweet almond, the shell of which is relatively soft.

1856 *Rep. Comm. Patents 1855: Agric.* p. xviii, The 'soft-shelled' almond . . . is the variety recently introduced and distributed by this Office. **1872** *Atlantic Mo.* April 396 What an experimenter he [Jefferson] was with his garden! He tried . . . almonds, bitter almonds, soft-shelled almonds, olives [etc.].

c. Soft-Shelled Baptist, =**Soft-Shell Baptist.**

1871 *N.Y. Herald* 28 July 6/1 He had proved by two soft-shelled Baptist companions that he had never been at a clam bake before.

sog sɑg, *n.* [App. the same word as *EDD sog*, any solid bulk, or f. *EDD sogger*, anything large and heavy.] A large whale. *Colloq.* — **1839** *Knickerb.* XIII. 379 He was a most extraordinary fish; or, in the vernacular of Nantucket, 'a genuine old sog,' of the first water. **1850** CHEEVER *Whale & Captors* 185 She's a beauty! a regular old sog!

∗**soil,** *n.* As the last term in **adobe, buckshot, cane, crawfish, Free, peach, prairie, second, slave, slough, truck, tule soil.**

∗**soilage,** *n.* The fact of soiling or condition of being soiled. — **1926** *Publishers' Wkly.* 22 May 1679/2 One of the practical problems of retail bookselling is the rapid depreciation of stock due to soilage.

soiling corn. [Cf. *OED* ∗*soil, v.*[4] to feed (horses, etc.) on fresh-cut green fodder.] Corn planted to be fed as green fodder. — **1884** *Vt. Agric. Rep.* VIII. 355 [He] would plant soiling corn and not sow. **1888** *Ib.* X. 17 [He] raised no soiling corn.

∗**solar,** *a.* **1.** *absol.* Salt made by solar evaporation. **2. solar match,** (see quot.). Both *obs.*

(1) **1859** *Ill. Agric. Soc. Trans.* IV. 103 Fourteen ounces of salt (solar being the best I ever used) is added. **1869** *Mich. Gen. Statutes* I. (1882) 439 All ground salt manufactured and put up for market, shall be legibly marked . . . 'ground solar,' or 'ground boiled,' or 'ground steam,' or 'ground Chapin,' as the fact may be. — (2) **1862** in CROW *Amer. Customer* (1943) 101 Agents for the Solar Matches wanted in places where not already appointed. The Solar matches are now superseding all other matches now on the market as they contain no sulphur, have no unpleasant smell when burning.

∗**soldier,** *n.*

1. (See quots.) *Obs.*

1832 CATLIN *Indians* I. 42 The chiefs have had to place 'soldiers' at my door . . . to protect me from the throng. **1848** PARKMAN in *Knickerb.* XXXI. 190 There were but few 'soldiers,' a sort of Indian police, who among their other functions usually assume the direction of a buffalo hunt.

2. In miscellaneous senses (see quots.).

1892 *Amer. Folk-Lore* V. 101 *Echinospermum Virginicum*, soldiers. E. Mass. **1902** JORDAN & EVERMANN *Amer. Food Fishes* p. xlviii, The most useful [artificial flies for bass] may be named as follows: Coachman, professor, soldier [etc.]. **1904** P. FOUNTAIN *Great North-West* 224 A bird known locally [in Ohio] as 'the marshal,' and sometimes 'the soldier,' . . . is a very gaudy woodpecker.

3. In combs., usu. in the possessive: (1) **soldier blackbird,** =**red-winged blackbird;** (2) **bug,** any predatory pentastomid bug that sucks the blood of other insects; (3) **-s' bee,** (see quot.), *obs.;* (4) **-s' bounty land,** public land to be given to soldiers in payment for military service, *obs.;* (5) **-'s certificate,** a certificate showing that a soldier is entitled to bounty land, *obs.;* (6) **-'s claim,** (see quot.); (7) **-s' home,** an institution where old or disabled soldiers are taken care of; (8) **-s' land,** land set aside for soldiers as payment for military service, *obs.;* (9) **-s' lodge,** (see quot.), *obs.;* (10) **-'s plume,** (see quots.); (11) **-'s warrant,** =**soldier's certificate;** (12) **vote,** *collect.* the political vote of returned soldiers.

(1) **1917** BAILEY *Sand Dunes Indiana* 134 My coming frightened a whole army of soldier blackbirds into flight. — (2) **1868** *Mich. Agric.* VII. 175, [I] found [them] to be soldier-bugs, with their long harpoon bills thrust into a fine fat slug, and sometimes also into perfect beetles. **1884** *Rep. Comm. Agric.* 391 The Soldier-Bug. An undetermined species of *Podisus* affected wheat in the same manner. — (3) **1863** in ANDREWS *Scraps of Paper* (1929) 207 Every Thursday evening when the army was in town we had gay little parties which we called 'Soldiers' Bees,' . . . and as much more talking was done than sewing, we changed it into 'Soldiers' Buzz.' — (4) **1837** *Jamestown (N.Y.) Jrnl.* 29 March 3/2 Soldiers' bounty lands can . . . be bought at still less.

(5) **1852** GOUGE *Fiscal Hist. Texas* 66 It would be difficult for those who had bought up soldiers' certificates . . . to find purchasers. — (6) **1930** HENRY *Conquer. Plains* 180 Besides, there existed the Military Land Warrants, popularly called Soldiers' Claims, enabling any veteran of the Civil War to receive a Warrant from the Government for a specified part of the public domain without payment. — (7) **1861** *Army Reg.* 343 The paymaster will deduct from the pay of all enlisted men twelve and a half cents per month for the support of the 'Soldiers' Home.' **1900** *Cong. Rec.* 19 Jan. 1001/1 Part of his [the veteran's] meager pension [is] confiscated at Soldiers' Homes. — (8) **1770** WASHINGTON *Diaries* I. 428, I marked two Maples, an Elm, and Hoopwood Tree as a Cornr. of the Soldiers L[an]d. — (9) **1878** *Rep. Indian Affairs* 159 The only party which could bolster him [Chief Spotted Tail] up is made up of the untamed and thoughtless young fellows of his tribe, who have established what is termed a 'soldiers' lodge,' and who have put the whole tribe under martial law.

(10) **1850** S. F. COOPER *Rural Hours* 168 The handsome, large purple-fringed orchis is also found here. . . . The country people call it soldier's plume. **1894** *Amer. Folk-Lore* VII. 100 *Habenaria psycodes*, . . . soldier's plume, N.Y. — (11) **1822** *Ann. 17th Congress* 1 Sess. 162 The holders of those soldier's Warrants Commenced locating them on the tract of land. — (12) **1887** *Nation* 10 March 197/3 The demagogues . . . are always bidding for the 'soldier vote.' **1900** *Cong. Rec.* 15 Feb. 1851/1 The pension attorneys are the organizers and managers of the so-called 'soldier vote.'

As the last term in **bay, buffalo, citizen, convention, dog, old, state, union, wagon, water soldier.**

sold land. (See quot.) *Obs.* — **1824** DODDRIDGE *Notes* 104 We have no districts of 'sold land,' as it is called, that is large tracts of land in the hands of individuals, or companies who neither sell nor improve them.

Soledad pine. [f. *Soledad* (Sp., solitude) River, Calif.] =**Torrey pine.**

1908 SUDWORTH *Forest Trees Pacific Slope* 41 Torrey Pine; Soledad Pine. **1927** ——— *Check List Forest Trees* 16 Torrey Pine. Range.—Southern California (coast near Soledad River in San Diego County); also on Santa Rosa Island. Names in use Soledad Pine (Calif.) [etc.]. **1950** *Amer. Forests* Jan. 19/2 Known also as Soledad pine, Del Mar pine and lone pine, this rare tree is found only in open, scattered stands on the highlands adjacent to the sea.

∗**solicitor,** *n.*

1. One who canvasses and solicits trade, donations, or the like.

1902 CLAPIN 376 *Solicitor*, a canvasser; one who solicits orders. **1926** *Publishers' Wkly.* 15 May 1589 Why can't he leave it to the judgment of the printers? Or to the advertising solicitor?

2. solicitor general, (*a*) the chief law officer of certain states, (*b*) a law officer who assists the attorney-general of the U.S.

(*a*) **1780** *Constitution of Mass.* II. ii. § 1. p. ix, All judicial officers, the attorney-general, solicitor-general, all sheriffs, coroners, and registers of probate shall be nominated and appointed by the Governor. **1879** ABBOTT *Dict. Terms Jurisprudence* II. 485/2 *Solicitor-general*, . . . in some of the states, the title of the chief law-officer, or one corresponding with the attorney-general in other states. (*b*) **1870** *Stat. at Large* XVI. 162 There shall be in said Department [of Justice] an officer learned in the law, . . . to be called the solicitor-general. **1900** *Cong. Rec.* 17 Feb. 1900/1 The oral argument was presented by the gentleman from Ohio, John K. Richards, the Solicitor-General, a most able lawyer and ex-attorney-general of Ohio.

∗**solid,** *a.* and *n.*

1. *n.* A single color.

1883 *Ev. Star* (Washington) 31 Oct. 3/6 Solids are all the go this season. **1908** GALE *Friendship Village* 4 Daisy and wild-rose patterns in 'solid,' and art curtains.

2. *a.* Politically orthodox or regular, unanimous. Cf. **Solid South, solid vote.**

1872 *Chi. Tribune* 14 Oct. 1/3 The Democrats are solid for Greeley in this county. **1905** *McClure's Mag.* 342 And the Republicans do the same in their solid towns when we go in to outbid them. **1949** *So. Wkly.* 16 Nov. 1/2 If the rest of the South stays 'solid,' this will put 157 electoral votes in the Democratic bag.

b. In favor with, esp. in the phrase *to make oneself solid with*, to get in the good graces of. *Colloq.*

1882 PECK *Sunshine* 161, I was pretty solid with him. **1890** *Railways of Amer.* 396 A certain railroad president regales himself in summer on spring water brought in jugs from 100 miles up the road by trainmen who find in this service an opportunity to 'make themselves solid' at headquarters. **1912** NICHOLSON *Hoosier Chron.* 183 I advise you to make yourself solid with her.

3. Of liquor: Straight. *Rare.*

1894 *Outing* XXIV. 49/1 He always took his liquor solid . . . ; he swallowed down two-thirds of a tumbler of raw Appleton rum.

4. In combs.: (1) **solid coin,** =**hard money,** *obs.;* (2) **South,** the states which seceded from the U.S., so called chiefly because of the practically invariable Democratic vote of the area since the Civil War (see also quot. 1885); (3) **sweep,** *S.* a plow or plowshare somewhat resembling a large shovel, not having "wings" as an ordinary sweep does; (4) **train,** a train all the cars of which have the same destination; (5) **vote,** *collect.* votes all of which are "regular" or in strict accord with party lines.

(1) **1789** *Ann. 1st Congress* 169 These articles are paid for principally, if not altogether, in solid coin. — (2) **1876** *Harper's Wkly.* 26 Aug. 691/2 The solid South is the Southern Confederacy seeking domination of the United States through the machinery of the Democratic party and by peaceable means. **1885** *Mag. Amer. Hist.* April 395/1 *Solid South,* . . . latterly the united white vote (Democratic) as opposed to the solid Republican vote of the negroes. **1950** *So. Wkly.* 22 March 3/1 Truman was elected in 1948 in a bold break on civil rights with the solid South. — (3) **1850** in TURNER *Cotton* (1865) 36, I can dirt easily four acres per horse; and can, with the solid sweep, break out four to nine acres per horse, owing to whether rows be four or five feet wide. **1858** *Texas Almanac 1859* 73 This last ploughing may be done with the solid sweep, if the ground is dry, but if wet, then with the turning-plough, while your hands, with trim hoes, make a finish, or lay the crop by. — (4) **1890** *Railways of Amer.* 288 The movement of 'straight' cars and 'solid' trains is comparatively simple.

(5) **1884** *Harper's Mag.* Aug. 472/1 This perception may be due to the withdrawal of a candidate, and the transfer of his solid vote to another. **1943** OTTLEY *New World* 204 In short, a solid vote may conceivably have tremendous influence upon the fretful future of American politics.

b. *solid men of Boston,* the dependable, well-to-do men of Boston. *Obs.*

1812 *Yankee* 30 Oct. 4/4 What will Ebenezer Seaver Esq. say to the butchery of our brave soldiers on the frontiers? And what will the *solid men of Boston,* who gave Seaver his War Dinner, just before his departure for Congress, say to it?

***solidly,** *adv.* Unanimously, as a unit. — **1865** in *Morning Star* (London) 14 March, I was told by a citizen of New York . . . [that] 100,000 Irish votes were given, as he expressed, solidly . . . for General M'Clellan. **1878** *Cong. Rec.* 8 April 2350/1 When I find republicans . . . voting solidly for an Irish Catholic democrat then I know there is a 'cat in the meal-tub.'

* **solitary,** *a.* In the names of birds: (1) **solitary sandpiper,** an American sandpiper, *Tringa solitaria;* (2) **tattler,** (see quot. 1839); (3) * **thrush,** (see quot.); (4) **vireo,** the blue-headed vireo of eastern North America.

(1) **1813** WILSON *Ornithology* II. 54 The Solitary Sandpiper is eight inches and a half long. **1909** *Sunset* Jan. 69/2 The solitary sandpiper (*Totanus solitarius*) is another species that migrates through the upper parts of the Coast and winters in Mexico. — (2) **1839** PEABODY *Mass. Birds* 370 The Solitary Tattler, *Totanus chloropygius,* . . . is very unsuspicious. **1872** COUES *N. Amer. Birds* 259 Solitary Tattler, . . . a shy, quiet inhabitant of wet woods. — (3) **1917** *Birds of Amer.* III. 234 Hermit Thrush. *Hylocichla guttata pallasi.* . . . [Also called] Solitary Thrush. — (4) **1831** AUDUBON *Ornith. Biog.* I. 147 The Solitary . . . Vireo. **1872** COUES *N. Amer. Birds* 121 Blue-headed or Solitary Vireo. [**1892** TORREY *Foot-Path Way* 13 [The Philadelphia vireo's] song is practically certain to be confused with the red-eye's rather than with the solitary's.]

solograph ˈsɑləˌgræf, *n.* [f. *sol,* sun, +*-graph.* Cf. *photograph.*] (See quot. 1858.) Also attrib. *Obs.* — **1851** CIST *Cincinnati* 187 Hawkins, in addition to his daguerrotypes, produces what he terms a *solograph* picture. **1858** SIMMONDS *Dict. Trade Products* 352/1 *Solograph,* a name which has been given to some pictures on paper taken by the talbotype or calotype process.

***solve,** *v. Baseball. tr.* To hit (a pitcher's balls) effectively. *Colloq.* — **1898** *N.Y. Tribune* 22 April II. 1/3 Only in the second inning were the home players able to solve his [the opposing pitcher's] curves.

sombrero sɑmˈbrɛro, *n.* [Sp. in same sense. An Amer. borrowing.] A hat, esp. any of various kinds of broad-brimmed hats worn in the Southwest. Also **sombrero hat.** Cf. **Mexican sombrero.**

1823 G. A. MCCALL *Lett. from Frontiers* (1868) 88 He was met, as he came upon deck, by a man whose medium dimensions and large 'sombrero,' or hat, we at once recognized as those of Diego. **1857** GUNN *N.Y. Boarding-Houses* 177 He wore . . . a broad *sombrero* hat. **1946** *Trail Riders* Oct. 4/1 If you rode up behind a figure garbed in sombrero, plaid shirt, dungarees, and cowboy boots, you couldn't always be sure whether it would be he or she!

Hence fig. (in allusion to "old hat"), and **sombreroed,** *a.*

1906 *Out West* Jan. 49 'Oh, no, you never make it. Too mucho arena!' with an emphatic, disapproving shake of sombreroed head. **1950** *Sat. Ev. Post* 4 Feb. 57/1 Even El Pasoans, to whom Juárez is, after all, pretty ancient sombrero, enjoy taking their out-of-town guests there for the night-clubbing.

* **some,** *a.* and *n.*

1. *n.* **a.** A great deal. **b.** *and then some,* and more than that, something more. *Colloq.* For **some pumpkin(s)** see * **pumpkin 2. b.**

(a) **1850** KINGSLEY *Diary* 159, 30 ounces of amalgam, . . . I think is some for this bar. *Ib.* 163, 80 ounces of amalgam . . . is some & no mistake. — (b) **1908** YESLAH *Tenderfoot S. Calif.* ii. 22 It rains in sheets, in blankets, and in comforters, and then some. **1914** D. O. BARNETT *Letters* (1915) 19, I picked them out with those glasses, and let them have it, and then some!

2. *a.* In predicate position: Remarkable, deserving of special notice. *Colloq.*

1845 *Knickerb.* XXV. 273 The way *he* put in the licks was some. **1849** *N.Y. Tribune* 15 May (B.), That [winter] . . . was admitted by the oldest inhabitant to be 'some' in the way of cold winters. **1863** *Rio Abajo Press* 24 Feb. 2 Our legislature is 'some' in the memorial line. **1888** EGGLESTON *Graysons* xiii, I used to think you wuz some at a hoe-down.

* **some,** *adv.* In colloq. uses.

The uses shown here are given in the *OED* and in the *DAE* as American, but the difference between them and those shown in the *EDD* is slight.

1. Somewhat, to some extent.

1843 WHITTIER in Pickard *Life Whittier* I. 281, I think some of attending the great antislavery convention. **1889** *Internat. Ann., Anthony's Photog. Bul.* II. 206 Having been troubled some of late to get clear results, . . . I have substituted distilled water for ordinary water.

2. In emphatic uses: Very well indeed.

1848 RUXTON *Life Far West* i, That one did shoot some. **1866** LOWELL *Biglow P.* 2 Ser. p. lxxix, Thet night, I tell ye, she looked *some!* **1908** K. MCGAFFEY *Show-Girl* 19, I still retain my pure English, even when I lose my temper, which is going some for a lady.

* **son,** *n.*

1. (*cap.*) *pl.* In the names of organizations, usu. obs. or hist.: (1) *Sons of America,* (*a*) a patriotic society during the Revolutionary period, (*b*) (see quot.), (*c*) a patriotic and benevolent society founded about 1847; (2) *Sons of Dan,* the Danites or Destroying Angels; (3) *Sons of Liberty,* see as a main entry; (4) *Sons of New England,* a local organization made up of those who came originally from New England; (5) *Sons of Seventy-Six,* (see quot. 1891); (6) *Sons of Temperance,* a fraternal and benevolent organization founded to afford mutual assistance among its members against the excessive use of alcoholic liquor, also (*sing.*) a member of this organization; (7) *Sons of the Pilgrims,* a society founded *c*1798, whose members were male descendants of the Pilgrim fathers of Plymouth, Mass.; (8) *Sons of the Sires,* (see quot. 1891 *s.v. Sons of Seventy-Six*); (9) *Sons of the South,* =**Blue Lodge;** (10) *Sons of Veterans,* a society organized in 1879, consisting of sons of members of the Union forces in the Civil War.

(1) (*a*) **1774** FITHIAN *Journal* I. 96 There were parties in Rooms made up, some at Cards; some toasting the Sons of America; some singing 'Liberty Songs.' (*b*) **1865** RICHARDSON *Secret Service* 429 He belonged to a secret organization known as the Sons of America, instituted expressly to assist Union men . . . in escaping to the North. (*c*) **1892** *York Co. Hist. Rev.* 62/1 Born in this country, he is identified with the I.O.O.F. Encampment, and the Sons of America. — (2) **1942** STEGNER *Mormon C.* 153 Joseph's personal bodyguard and one of the most redoubtable of the Sons of Dan had his hair singed. **1943** DEVOTO *Yr. of Decision* 83 One of the Sons of Dan (the 'destroying Angels' of ten-cent fiction), crept up to a window in Boggs's house and shot him. — (4) **1845** *Quincy* (Ill.) *Whig* 11 Dec. 2/1 The Sons of New England in St. Louis are to celebrate the 22nd of this month, the anniversary of the landing of the pilgrims.

(5) **1862** BROWNE *A. Ward: His Book* 254 These brave sons of '76 took no part in the demonstration, but an honored bench was set

apart for their exclusive use. **1891** *Cent.* 5768/1 *Sons of Sires*, or *Sons of Seventy-six*, a name said to have been applied to or assumed by members of the American or Know-nothing party. **1894** C. STICKNEY *Know-Nothingism in R.I.* 4 In certain States we find promulgated orders and announcements of 'The Sons of '76,' and 'The Order of the Star-Spangled Banner.' — **(6) 1840** *Knickerb.* XXVIII. 145 The Sons of Temperance will hold their next celebration to-morrow. **1890** LANGFORD *Vigilante Days* (1912) 272 The circumstances of duress . . . ought not to impair his standing as a Son of Temperance. **1898** WESTCOTT *D. Harum* xxiii, I'm a son o' temp'rance. **1935** BUCKBEE *Saga of Old Tuolumne* 96 The town supported . . . a division of the Sons of Temperance and a choral society — **(7) 1798** *Columbian Centinel* 26 Dec. 2/4 The Feast of the 'Sons of the Pilgrims.' **1799** *Ib.* 28 Dec. 1/4 The following are the Toasts given at the Feast of the 'Sons of the Pilgrims.' — **(8) 1855** (*title*), Sons of the Sires; A History of the Rise, Progress, and Destiny of the American Party. **1891** [see *Sons of Seventy-six*]. — **(9) 1867** DIXON *New Amer.* I. 21 A meeting of Sons of the South was called in Westport. **1883** ANDREAS *Hist. Kansas* 90/2 Secret lodges were organized under various names—'Social Band,' 'Friends' Society,' 'Sons of the South' [etc.].

(10) 1884 *Boston Jrnl.* 6 Sep., Stirring speeches were made by . . . District Commander Atwood . . . and Mr. Chas. Penniman, Chief Mustering Officer of the Sons of Veterans of Minnesota. **1909** WEBSTER 316/1 A lodge or local division of certain patriotic societies connected with past wars; as, a *camp* of the Sons of Veterans.

2. Also (1) *son-of-a-gun* (*stew*), a highly seasoned meat stew or a hash of tripe, kidneys, and haslets, cf. **district attorney 3;** (2) *son-of-a-gun* (or *bitch*)*-in-a-sack*, dried fruit rolled up in dough and steamed in a sack; (3) *son of* (*fair*) *freedom*, a patriotic American, *obs.;* (4) *son of St. Nicholas*, a member of the St. Nicholas Society, founded in 1835 by Washington Irving, its membership being restricted to those who had resided in New York since 1785, or who were descended from a person living in the city at or before that date, *obs.;* (5) *son of the forest*, an Indian, *obs.*

(1) 1933 *Amer. Sp.* Feb. 27/2 When I asked a ranchman who prepares delectable *son-of-a-gun* how to make it, he replied quite seriously, 'I don't know what to call everything, but give me a calf and I can find it for you. You use everything but the hair, horns, and *holler*.' **1937** *D.N.* Dec. 620 A hash or goulash composed of tripe, kidneys, haslets, etc. is happily called *son of a gun* (Slumgullion). **1948** *Chi. Tribune* 28 Nov. (Comics) 12 Umm—do Ah smell 'son-of-a-gun' stew? — **(2) 1927** JAMES *Cow Country* 156 Frank had been inside of the house, showing the new cook how to make . . .'son-of-a-gun-in-a-sack.' **1939** ABBOTT-SMITH *We Pointed* 209 The winter of '86 . . . we cooked a Christmas dinner of deer meat and son-of-a-gun-in-a-sack (Plum duff). **1947** PRICE *Trails I Rode* 44 He could make what we called son-of-a-bitch-in-a-sack that would melt in your mouth. — **(3) 1768** in BUCKINGHAM *Newspaper Lit.* I. 149 The Sons of fair Freedom are hampered once more. **1798** in H. M. BROOKS *Gleanings* IV. 71 Take Notice! Ye Sons of Freedom! **1885** CRAWFORD *Amer. Politician* 18 'And the Irish and German votes,' added Vancouver, with that scorn which only the true son of freedom can exhibit in speaking of his fellow-citizens. — **(4) 1846** *Knickerb.* XXVII. 83 The sable attendants [were] clad in the authentic costumes of a period held in loving remembrance by every true son of Saint Nicholas.

(5) 1826 *Va. Herald* (Fredericksburg) 8 Nov. 3/1 The Choctaw Students, the native sons of the forest, displayed extraordinary aptitude in spel ing. **1878** HART *Sazerac Lying Club* 233 Some white men tackled some Indians in a game of Indian poker to-day; but the sons of the forest rang in a cold deck and cleaned up all the money on the blanket.

sonder ˈzandɚ, *a.* [G. *sonderklasse*, special class.] Designating a class of small racing yachts. Also **sonder class.** — **1913** C. W. ERNST *Letter* (MS), Our yachtsmen, since 1907, talk of 'sonder-boats', sonder class, sonder race,—meaning certain boats recognised by the International Yacht Racing Union.

***song,** *n.*

1. song and dance, a vaudeville act made up, chiefly, of singing and dancing. Also attrib.

1872 *Chi. Tribune* 13 Oct. 5/6 First week of the distinguished song and dance artists. **1880** E. JAMES *Negro Minstrel's Guide* 4 A two-hours' entertainment is quite enough, allowing . . . ten minutes or so each for song-and-dance, stump speech, instrumental solos [etc.]. **1895** *N.Y. Dramatic News* 23 Nov. 13/3 The first double song and dance team was comprised of Wash Norton and Ben Cotton. **1908** McGAFFEY *Show-Girl* 15 That show . . . is a song and dance about this mental telepathy gag.

b. An account or explanation, not necessarily true, and often intended to impress or deceive. *Slang.*

1895 TOWNSEND *Chimmie Fadden* 6 (We.), Den, 'is whiskers gives me a song an' dance. **1949** *Time* 5 Sep. 2/3 Labor Leader Preble . . . was not impressed by 'the song and dance about [Stefan's] mother and sister being persecuted and murdered.'

2. song sparrow, a sparrow, *Melospiza melodia*, of the eastern part of the country, having a song of several notes. Cf. **Arizona, desert song sparrow.**

1810 WILSON *Ornithology* II. 125 [The] Song Sparrow, *Fringilla melodia*, . . . is fond of frequenting the borders of rivers, meadows, swamps. **1880** *Harper's Mag.* June 70 There's the ringing voice of song-sparrow and the bell note of the thrush. **1942** PEATTIE *Friendly Mts.* 194 The first bird song I heard on this morning was the song sparrow at my window at the first gray of dawn.

As the last term in **alumni, bear, cabin, calumet, chronicle, coon, corn, cowboy, death, dropping, gospel, medicine, Negro, peace, plantation, play, scalp, shucking, slave, state, theme song.**

son of liberty.

1. A patriotic American fighting for freedom from British rule, esp. a member of one of several loosely federated societies first organized to oppose the Stamp Act. Also (*cap.*) *pl.*, one of these societies. Now *hist.*

"On February 6, 1765, Isaac Barré had made his famous speech in Parliament which furnished the phrase 'Sons of Liberty' and led to the formation of the well-known pre-Revolutionary organization of that name" (*Pub. Col. Soc.* XXVI. (1924) 29).

1766 in *Pub. Col. Soc.* XXVI. 49 The Sons of Liberty being informed that a Vessel has arrived here with stamped clearances from Jamaica, desire that you would go and demand in their Names those marks of Creole Slavery. **1770** ADAMS *Diary* Wks. II. 243 [The] landlord . . . is a staunch, zealous son of liberty. **1876** *Scribner's Mo.* Jan. 314/1 'The New York Journal' . . . was the sturdy and unpurchasable organ of the Sons of Liberty. **1943** FORBES *J. Tremain* 77 So Rab was one of the semi-secret famous Sons of Liberty, those carefully organized 'mobs' who often took justice into their own hands.

2. (*cap.*) *pl.* (See quot. 1885.) Now *hist.*

1867 *Harper's Wkly.* 30 March 195/1 The organized resistance to the drafts; the plots of the Sons of Liberty at the West; . . . were either denied or extenuated, as seemed most discreet, by the Democratic papers. **1885** *Mag. Amer. Hist.* April 395/2 *Sons of Liberty*, a name assumed by certain secret societies whose purpose was the liberation of Confederate prisoners held at the North during the civil war. An alleged branch of the Knights of the Golden Circle. **1948** *Sat. Ev. Post* 7 Aug. 116/2 Carrington was sent from Washington to help Gov. Oliver Perry Morton, . . . stamp out the Knights of the Golden Circle, a group treasonous to the North, who later became the Sons of Liberty.

Sonora səˈnorə, *n. Calif.* A winter rain from the South, in allusion to the state of Sonora, Mexico.

1911 PLUMMER *Chaparral* 14 The 'Santa Anas,' together with the 'Sonoras,' or southern storms, cause a wide range in the recorded maximum and minimum temperatures. **1919** CHASE *Calif. Desert Trails* 37 The 'Sonoras' or storms, which give this precipitation, are usually confined to the main mountain-ridges.

b. Sonoratown, the Mexican quarter of a town.

1930 BARTLETT *On Old West Coast* 275 He owned a little long, flat adobe on a lot in Sonoratown. **1946** McWILLIAMS *So. Calif. Country* 86 In most cases, the Chinatowns had developed around the adobe huts of Sonoratowns.

Sonoran səˈnorən, *n.* and *a.* Also **Sonoranian, Sonorian.** *S.W.* [f. *Sonora*, a state in northwestern Mexico.]

1. *n.* A native or inhabitant of Sonora.

1862 *Harper's Mag.* June 13/2, I . . . suddenly found myself close by a camp of Sonoranians. **1864** *Ib.* Oct. 560/2 Being thus left at the mercy of . . . roving bands of Apaches and Sonoranians. **1935** BUCKBEE *Saga of Old Tuolumne* 258 The Sonorians placed the court house flag at half mast. **1948** A. K. WILLIAMS *Gold Rush Days* 26 Pack saddles [were] obtained from the Sonorans.

2. *a.* (See quot. 1909.)

1893 COVILLE *Death Valley Exped.* 26 These two belts are correlated respectively with the Lower and Upper Sonoran zones of the desert. **1902** in *Sierra Club Bul.* (1949) Oct. 5/2 There is probably no place in North America where the alpine and the Sonoran floras are in such proximity as they are on San Jacinto Mountain. **1909** *Cent. Supp.* 1241/2 *Sonoran.* . . . Of or pertaining to a long-headed Indian type which is found in the state of Sonora and scattered over the Southwestern parts of the United States.—*Sonoran region, Sonoran zone*, a zoogeographical region instituted by Cope, in 1875, including northern Mexico and adjoining eastern California. As defined by Merriam, in 1890, the Sonoran zone included also the peninsula of Lower California and part of western Texas as well as much of central Mexico. The term was loosely used by Cope, whose map and description do not agree with one another. **1925** JEPSON *Flowering Plants Calif.* 4 The Lower Sonoran Zone comprises three distinctive areas: (a) Colorado Desert or Colorado Sonoran, (b) the Mohave Desert or Mohave Sonoran, (c) the Great Valley or Valley Sonoran.

sontag ˈsɑntæg, *n.* [f. Henriette *Sontag*, G. operatic singer (1806–54).] A knitted or crocheted jacket with long ends that cross over the front and fasten in the back. *Obs.*

1863 A. D. Whitney *F. Gartney* xviii, Faith brought quickly, sontag, jacket and cloak. **1864** *Hist. North-Western Soldiers' Fair* 74 [Donations:] Mrs. Nolden, a sontag, Mrs. Howell, an opera shawl. **1900** Dix *Deacon Bradbury* 45 Did you hear what she said to Mrs. Delane about that worsted sontag she brought?

sooner ˈsunɚ, *n.*

1. *W.* One who enters upon public land to secure choice areas before the official date of its being thrown open for settlement.

1890 *Cong. Rec.* 17 Jan. 657/2 We have recognized the fact that there are 'sooners' there. **1901** *Outlook* 20 July 667/1 It is notoriously the fact that the 'sooners,' who were illegally first on the ground, have not infrequently secured final title to farms which they practically had stolen. **1945** *Chi. Tribune* 2 Sep. (Grafic Mag.) 5/1 On the day of the run the sooner would stake his claim long before the legitimate runners drew near, and he would scrub his pony with soap and water to imitate the lathery sweat of hard running.

b. Any one who acts hastily or prematurely.

1890 *Columbus* (O.) *Dispatch* 7 May, The Governor is quite right in declining to be regarded as a sooner. **1892** *Boston Jrnl.* 2 May 4/7 The word 'Sooners' is a Southwestern descriptive term . . . gradually coming into general use in defining that numerous class of nervously excitable people who insist upon crossing bridges before they come to them. **1903** *Cin. Enquirer* 30 May 12/1 None of the gun sooners ever got the drop on Nick Halpin when he pounded the day Marshal's beat in Tombstone.

2. (*cap.*) One who entered what is now Oklahoma before April 22, 1889, at which time it was officially thrown open to settlement. Also as a nickname for an Oklahoman.

1892 *Pall Mall Gaz.* 28 Sep. 7/1 One of these 'Sooners' got into the territory before the date for opening it up by the Presidential proclamation, by virtue of being an employee on a railroad which entered the territory. **1930** Ferber *Cimarron* 22 They had burned the prairie ahead for miles into the Nation, so as to . . . smoke out the Sooners, too, who had sneaked in and were hiding in the scrub oaks, in the draws, wherever they could. **1948** [see **Okie**].

b. Sooner State, Oklahoma.

1939 *New Yorker* 14 Oct. 73 Oklahoma uses on its road signs a phrase which I first heard in Kansas and never again except in the Sooner State. **1948** *Okla. Cotton Grower* 15 May 2/2 For the Sooner State planter that is perhaps the first major theorem of the business.

Soonerism ˈsunəˌrɪzəm, *n.* The activity of the Oklahoma Sooners. — **1894** *Columbus* (O.) *Dispatch* 19 March, An important case growing out of the 'soonerism' at the Oklahoma opening will be given a hearing. **1945** Marshall *Santa Fe* 232 They watched the line through telescopes and, congratulating themselves on their success in checkmating 'Soonerism,' figured it would take the first settlers on the fastest horses, about ninety minutes to reach Oklahoma.

soopolallie ˌsupəˈlælɪ, *n. W.* and *N.W.* [Cf. Chinook *olallie, olillie*, berry. The prefix is also prob. of Chinook origin.] A buffalo berry (*q.v.*), *Shepherdia argentea* or *S. canadensis*. — **1931** Dayton *Western Browse Plants* 119 Russet buffaloberry, . . . known locally as Canadian, or thornless buffaloberry, . . . soopoo-lalia, or soopolallie (Indians), wild oleaster, and wild olive, ranges from Newfoundland and Labrador to Maine, western New York, the Black Hills, northern New Mexico, eastern Oregon, and Alaska. **1946** Stanwell-Fletcher *Driftwood Valley* 33 Poplars are the chief trees, with an occasional small white birch, and dense thickets of small Shepherdia, or soopolallie, bushes.

soot tea. (See quots. 1877, 1926.)

For an indication of the antiquity and prevalence of the idea that soot is a healing agent see *Handwörterbuch des Deutschen Aberglaubens s.v.* Russ. Cf. *cinder tea* in *OED.*

1842 C. M. Kirkland *Forest Life* I. viii. 71 We stick to thoroughwort,—balmony,—soot tea,—'number six,'—and the like, and avoid, as if for the very life, all 'apothecary medicines.' **1877** Bartlett 627 *Soot-Tea*, a decoction of soot taken from a chimney, believed by some old grannies to be a sovereign remedy for the colic or cholera. **1926** *Bur. Amer. Ethnology Rep.* XLIII. 267 'Soot tea' is given [by Mohegan Indians] to infants to relieve colic. It is prepared by pouring boiling water over a small quantity of soot.

***Sop,** *n.* A derisive term for a Dunker or Tunker *qq.v. Obs.* — **1796** Morse *Amer. Geog.* I. 281 The English word that conveys the proper meaning of Tunkers is Sops or Dippers. **1867** Dixon *New Amer.* II. 184 The Tunkers . . . profess Baptist tenets; and the word 'tunker' meaning to dip a crumb into gravy, a sop into wine, they are described by those who use it, in a very poor joke, as dippers and sops. . . . We English style them Dunkers, by mistake.

soph sɑf, *n.* Short for sophomore. *Colloq.*

1778 Stiles *Diary* II. 277, I appointed Stevens a Soph. Waiter in the Hall. **1842** *Dartmouth* IV. 118 My Chum, a Soph, says he committed himself too soon. **1903** *N.Y. Times* 26 Sep. 5 The freshmen's progress was impeded by the 25 specially organized sophs. **1945** *Jefferson Co. Republican* (Golden, Colo.) 26 Sep. 1/3 The Frosh, being big-hearted, gave the Sophs another chance with the same results occurring.

***sophic,** *a.* **1.** Sophomoric. **2.** Pertaining to knowledge. Both *obs.* — **(1) 1853** in Hall *College Words* (ed. 2) 436 So then the Sophic army Came on in warlike glee. — **(2) 1898** *Rep. Bureau Amer. Ethnol. 1897–8* p. xlv, The sophic activities so highly developed among the tribes of the arid pueblo region.

***sophomore,** *n.* **1.** A second-year pupil in a high school. **2. sophomore class,** a class in college or high school made up of second-year students.

(1) 1906 *Forum* Jan. 363 High school pupils whose average was about the same as that of the high school sophomores of to-day. **1948** *Lisle* (Ill.) *Eagle* 21 Oct. 10/1 Although the freshmen played exceptionally well, they lost to the sophomores with a score of 10–7. — **(2) 1765** Habersham *Letters* 51 He lately entered with honor the Sophomore Class. **1945** *Mt. Holyoke College Bul.* 160 Sophomore honors are conferred by the faculty upon the members of the sophomore class who have taken high rank in the work of the first four semesters.

As the last term in **fresh-, freshman-sophomore.**

sophomoreship ˈsɑfmɔrˌʃɪp, *n.* The condition of being a sophomore. *Obs.*

1698 in *Proc. Mass. Hist. Soc.* VIII. 34 Towards ye End of our Sophymoreship . . . Mr. Leverett saw it convenient to place me ye Lowest in ye class. **1721** *Harvard Rec.* II. 455 The Moiety of £45 Sterling . . . [shall] be paid to him . . . as a Consideration toward reimbursing the charge of his Education in his Sophimorship. **1725** *Ib.* 525 Campbel [shall] be allowed . . . forty pounds for this year of his sophimoreship.

sophomoric ˌsɑfəˈmɔrɪk, *a.* Resembling or suggestive of a sophomore, immature, bombastic, superficial.

1813 *Salem Gaz.* 1 June 3/3 The Address of Mr. Gerry . . . is distinguished by all that sophomoric inflation of style . . . [etc.] which characterise the productions of that miserable old gentleman. **1881** Cable *Madame Delphine* 20 [They were] speculating upon the nature of things in an easy, bold, sophomoric way. **1907** Mark Twain *Christian Sci.* 115 (R.), Their make-up is a complacent and pretentious outpour of false figures and fine writing, in the sophomoric style.

sophomorical ˌsɑfəˈmɔrɪkl, *a.* =prec. — **1839** *Knickerb.* XIV. 204 Its style . . . is labored and sophomorical, to the last degree. **1883** *Science* 27 July 113/2 The paper is decidedly sophomorical.

sora ˈsɔrə, *n.* Also †**saurer.** [Poss. f. Amer. Indian.] The Carolina rail, *Porzana carolina.* In full **sora rail.** Cf. **sorus,** *n.*

1705 Beverley *Virginia* II. 37 The Shores . . . are also stor'd with . . . Snipes, Woodcocks, Saurers [etc.]. **1809** Wilson *Poems & Lit. Prose* I. 172 The Sora was in multitudes at Detroit. **1835** Audubon *Ornith. Biog.* III. 251. **1880** *Dly. Dispatch* (Richmond, Va.) 3 Nov. 2/1 The Mahone party has . . . disappeared as sora disappear when the frost comes. **1945** *Mass. Audubon Soc. Bul.* March 62 A Sora Rail was seen at Milton on January 9.

***sore,** *a.* In combs.: (1) ***sorehead,** a disgruntled, curmudgeonish person, also attrib. or as adj.; (2) ***headed,** *a.* of or like a sorehead, also **sore-headedness,** *colloq.*; (3) **shin,** a disease of young cotton caused by any one of various soil fungi which girdle the stalk near the ground; (4) **skin,** [poss. a variant of prec.], (see prec. and quot. 1909); (5) ***throat,** (see quot.), *obs.*; (6) **tongue,** ?black tongue, *obs.*

(1) 1848 *Albany Wkly. Argus* 12 Aug. 253/3 As no other selection could be supposed so well to represent such a conventicle of 'sore heads,' it is perhaps quite as well it sho'd take that direction as any other. *Ib.* 26 Aug. 270/5 He has been from the first identified with the sore-head faction. **1949** *Boston Globe* 4 Dec. 1/1 Their testimony is still too strong to be brushed aside as gripes of a few soreheads. — **(2) 1855** *Oregonian* (Portland) 17 Feb. 2/2 [This] is another reason for special complaint with the sore-headed gentry of the Salem '*clique.*' **1860** *Marysville* (Calif.) *Appeal* 31 March 2/2 The patriots of the Customs House [are] suffering from the sore-headedness which so often follows an unsuccessful attempt at ascendency in the political scale. — **(3) 1853** in Turner *Cotton* (1865) 165 The *sore shin* has been very destructive to our stands of cotton this season. **1883** Smith *Geol. Survey Ala.* 547 Lice, flea-bugs, and sore-shin generally appear . . . when the cotton is young. — **(4) 1835** Ingraham *South-West* II. 282 Sometimes whole acres together, die with the 'rust,' 'sore skin,' or 'yellow fever.' **1862** *N.Y. Wkly. Tribune* 22 March 6/1 If it be so a crust will form over the top, and the seed will come up with difficulty, and the [cotton] plant will look weak and sick. It is then said to have the 'sore skin,' and is similar to rust. **1909** WEBSTER 1996/2 *S[ore] skin*, a disease of the tobacco plant in which a section of the stem near the ground dries up so as to break the continuity of the sap flow.

(**5**) **1919** DUNN *Indiana* II. 804 In 1842–3 epidemic erysipelas prevailed in a number of counties in southern Indiana, and was known by a number of popular names, as 'black tongue,' 'sore throat,' 'swelled head,' etc. The fatality was great. — (**6**) **1819** R. L. MASON *Narrative* (1915) 28 Passed several dead horses on the road [near Maysville, Ky.]. An infectious disease called the sore tongue had produced their deaths, and was to be found at every stable for hundreds of miles. Men, cows, hogs and sheep were subject to it.

b. *To get* (or *feel, be*) *sore on* (or *over*)*:* (1) To be sore and stiff as a result of exercise or work, *rare;* (2) to be vexed, displeased, or grumpy towards (one), or about (something). *Slang.*

(**1**) **1868** H. WOODRUFF *Trotting Horse Amer.* iii. 54 This is an indication that he has had too much work for his age, and has got sore on it. — (**2**) **1886** POORE *Reminiscences* II. 374 General Gordon felt sore because he had failed to secure the entire Democratic vote of the Senate. **1904** *N.Y. Ev. Post* 13 June 1 Kelley denied the charges and said the patrolman was 'sore' on him. **1931** *K.C. Star* 14 Aug., This is carefully worded and seems to take in everyone, so none of the girls can get sore over being left out.

* **sorghum,** *n.*

1. = **sorghum molasses.**

1874 KNIGHT 683 Defecators for sorghum partake of the character of filters. **1888** *Cent. Mag.* Sep. 766/2 At home and abroad sorghum came to take the place of the vanished sugar. **1949** *Chi. D. News* 24 Oct. 32 (*caption*), It's Molasses Time in Southern Illinois; Sorghum Is Cooked in Special Stove Built Outdoors.

2. In combs.: (1) **sorghum boiler,** one who makes sorghum molasses; (2) **mill,** a mill for crushing sorghum

Sorghum mill

for its juice, also attrib.; (3) **molasses,** molasses made from the juice of sorghum; (4) **patch,** a small area planted in sorghum; (5) **planter,** a device for planting sorghum, *obs.;* (6) **pulling,** a social occasion upon which those present make candy of sorghum molasses by boiling and "pulling" it, *obs.*, cf. **molasses candy pulling;** (7) **skimmings,** the refuse matter skimmed from the juice of sorghum during the process of boiling it into molasses; (8) **stripper,** (see quot.).

(**1**) **1888** *Nation* 5 Jan. 2/2 Now the sorghum-boilers in Kansas are protesting against any meddling with the duty on sugar. — (**2**) [**1863** *Farmer's Oracle* (Spring Lake Valley, Utah) 22 Sep. 69/2 The sorgo mills are now in active operation.] **1934** CARMER *Stars Fell* 195 There's a old sorghum mill close by and you'll see the mash in the road. **1949** *Telephone Reg.* (McMinnville, Ore.) 4/8 A Summerville, Tennessee sorghum mill operator decided it was cheaper to buy gasoline, hooked his new tractor up to replace the mule on the end of the long pole which made the mill go around. — (**3**) **1860** *Mountaineer* (Salt Lake City) 12 May 150/4 We have always paid three dollars per gallon for the sorghum molasses. **1949** *Chi. D. News* 24 Oct. 32/1 (*legend*), The process of turning it into sorghum molasses will continue for the next three months. — (**4**) **1913** CATHER *O Pioneers!* 44 You have a little sorghum patch, maybe? Put a fence around it, and turn the hogs in.

(**5**) **1883** HOWELLS *Woman's Reason* xi, I've got the idea of a sorghum-planter that . . . is going to make somebody's fortune. — (**6**) **1871** DE VERE 287 Among the minor details of the war that produced new terms, may be mentioned the word *sorghum pulling* or tugging. — (**7**) **1880** HARRIS *U. Remus* (1884) 216 It's the meanest bug-juice in town—regular sorghum skimmings. — (**8**) **1876** KNIGHT 2246/2 *Sorghum-stripper*, . . . a knife for stripping the blades from cane-stalks.

* **sorority,** *n.*

1. *N. Eng. Collect.* The female members of a religious body. *Obs.*

1645 PAGITT *Heresiography* (1647) 86 The Synod of New-England maketh not only the fraternity but (as they speak) the sorority to be the subject of the . . . power of the keys.

2. A national or local secret society among women students of a college or, sometimes, of a secondary school. Cf. * **fraternity,** *n.*

[**1888** *Cent. Mag.* XXXVI. 753 The female students, not to be outdone, about a dozen years ago began to organize sisterhoods, from which males were ignominiously debarred from membership, and had meantime succeeded in building up 7 prosperous societies.] **1900** *D.N.* II. 14 Those societies of a social nature . . . are called . . . *fraternities* or *sororities*. **1949** *Oak Leaves* (Oak Park, Ill.) 24 Nov. 21/3 Alpha Kappa sorority celebrated its 25th anniversary at a dinner party last week at the Carleton hotel.

transf. **1946** *Amer. Sp.* April 86 You do not belong to her sorority.

attrib. **1900** *Harper's Mag.* Sep. 490 One saw many of those neat little sorority pins the American girl proudly brings home from boarding-school or college. **1945** MAXWELL *Folded Leaf* 150 The night of the sorority dance it took Spud over an hour to dress. **1948** *Seattle Times* 26 Sep. 4/1 Tonight is the big night for more than 600 University of Washington sorority rushees—tonight is Pledge Night.

* **Sorosis,** *n.* A women's society or club.

"An arbitrary use of the botanical term, adopted as the name of the first club of the kind, founded in 1868" (*OED*).

1873 ALDRICH *Marjorie Daw* 238, I would back our Club against the Sorosis. **1895** *Johnson's Univ. Cyclo.* II. 349/1 In Mar., 1868, the first club exclusively for women, Sorosis, was founded . . . in New York city. **1902** *Out West* May 557 The founding of the first woman's club, Sorosis of New York, was almost simultaneous with the union of the Atlantic and Pacific by the completion of the first transcontinental railway in 1869.

* **sorrel,** *n.* In combs.: (1) **sorrel top,** "a derisive appellation for a red-haired person" (B. '77), also **sorrel-topped,** *a.;* (2) **tree,** see as a main entry; (3) **vine,** the vine sorrel, *Cissus trifoliata.*

(**1**) **1863** E. KIRKE *So. Friends* 58 'Har, you lousy sorrel-top,' said the trader to the red-faced and red-headed bar tender. **1904** O. HENRY *Roads of Destiny* 298 They don't raise 74-inch sorrel-tops with romping ways down in his precinct. **1931** *K.C. Times* 12 Nov. 20 We would like to inform a certain sorrel-topped Central Missouri editor that the name of our sheet is not the Northwest Missourian. — (**3**) **1891** *Cent.* 5777/3 *Sorrel-vine*, . . . a shrub . . . found in tropical America, reaching into Florida.

As the last term in **gentleman's, red, redwood, toad sorrel.**

sorrel tree. An ericaceous tree, *Oxydendrum arboreum*, having sour evergreen leaves.

1687 CLAYTON *Va.* in *Phil. Trans.* XLI. 152 The Sorrel-tree . . . grows plentifully on the South-side of James River in Virginia. *c***1730** CATESBY *Carolina* I. 71 The Sorrel-Tree. The trunk . . . is usually five or six inches thick. **1814** PURSH *Flora Amer.* I. 295 The leaves are of a very pleasant acid taste, from which it has been called Sorrel-tree. **1949** PALMER *Fieldbook Nat. Hist.* 285/3 Sourwood, Sorrel Tree *Oxydendrum arboreum*. . . . Known as elk tree, titi, and by other names.

b. (See quot.)

1909 *Cent. Supp.* 1242/2 sorrel-tree. . . . The stagger-bush, *Pieris Mariana.*

sorus ˈsorəs, *n.* An obs. variant of **sora.** — **1775** BURNABY *Travels* 42 The sorus is not known to be in Virginia, except for about six weeks from the latter end of September.

sosh soʃ, *n.* [f. **social.*] One who has little except social polish. *Slang. Rare.* — **1902** H. L. WILSON *Spenders* xxxi. 367 That's right, son. I knew I could make something more than a polite sosh out of you.

sotana soˈtɑnə, *n. W.* [Sp. in same sense. An Amer. borrowing.] A gown or cassock. *Obs.* — **1877** BRET HARTE *Story of Mine* 392 Running rapidly to Father Pedor's side, he grasped his sotana.

sotol soˈtol, *n. S.W.* [Amer. Sp. *sotol, zotol* (f. the Aztec name of the plant).] Any one of various plants of the genus *Dasylirion.* Also attrib.

1881 *Amer. Naturalist* XV. 874 The home of the sotol is Western Texas, Southeastern New Mexico and Northern Chihuahua. **1905** BRAY *Sotol Country in Texas* 3 In Texas, the main body of the sotol country is embraced in the rough limestone region lying between the breaks of the Devil's River and the front ranges of the Cordilleras near Marathon over 150 miles west. **1942** CASTETTER & BELL *Pima & Papago Agric.* 213 The mature leaves were dried by the Papago in the sun on a sotol mat outside the house.

sots sats, *n. local.* [G. *satz*, sediment, dregs, in Pa.-G. sense shown here.] A leavening agent made from hops.

1799 WELD *Travels* 65 They raise it with what they call sots; hops and water boiled together. **1817** *Niles' Reg.* XII. 165/2 The result was . . . that kind of rising called here 'sotts,' a Dutch term, I presume. **1902** CLAPIN 377 *Sots.* Yeast is so called, in Virginia and Pennsylvania. **1945** *Amer. Sp.* Dec. 254 In their own home district the regionalisms *ponhaus, snits, sots* . . . and a host of others are accepted by the natives of Southern Pennsylvania quite as naively as quaint New England provincialisms.

soufflet su'fle, *n.* [F., prob. in the sense of bellows.] ?A case or brief case. *Rare.* — **1835** *Stimpson's Boston Directory* (Cover), Orders received for . . . Gilchrist's Manifold Letter Copyer, Sermon Cases, and Attorney's Soufflets.

* **soul,** *n.* In combs.: (1) **soul butter,** a contemptuous term for moralizing drivel, *rare;* (2) **driver,** one who took indentured servants, slaves, etc., from place to place to sell them, an overseer of slaves, *obs.;* (3) **shark,** a preacher, *slang;* (4) **Sleepers,** (see quot.), *obs.;* (5) **trap,** a disreputable "joint," *slang;* (6) **weeding,** ?a searching examination, *rare.*

(1) **1884** MARK TWAIN *H. Finn* xxv, Music is a good thing, and after all that soul-butter and hogwash I never see it freshen up things so. — (2) **1774** *Amer. Hist. Rev.* VI. 77 Soul drivers . . . drive them [*sc.* servants and convicts] through the Country . . . untill they can sell them to advantage. **1818** *Mass. Spy* 4 Nov. (Th.), Two men, in the character of soul drivers, lodged in the jail for safe keeping, five negros. **1888** *Cong. Rec.* 2 May 3647/1 Today every old soul-driver of the South is a free-trader. — (3) **1898** HARPER *S. B. Anthony* I. 249 The country is full of these soul-sharks, men who haven't had brains enough to find pulpits or places in the free States. — (4) **1860** *So. Enterprise* (Thomasville, Ga.) 13 June 2/5 Soul Sleepers is the name of a new religious sect which has recently made its appearance at Fairfield, Iowa. . . . They . . . think that the soul is a mortal substance and sleeps within the body until the resurrection.

(5) **1818** WEEMS *Letters* III. 225 This detestable *Soul Trap* was kept by one John Blackfoot. — (6) **1912** N. WOODROW *Sally Salt* 10 Lucy was apparently alarmed at the prospect of a soul-weeding.

Soule sul, *n.* [?f. a personal name.] A variety of wheat. In full **Soule(s) wheat.** *Obs.*

1856 *Rep. Comm. Patents 1855: Agric.* 195 For the most part, we sow the 'Soule' wheat. **1868** *Mich. Agric. Rep.* VII. 424 The midge injured the variety known as the Soules wheat. **1874** *Rep. Comm. Agric. 1873* 220 All the varieties had stood the winter well—quite as well as the Soules and Bluestem.

sou markee. [F. *sou marqué.*] Orig. a French copper coin of low value that circulated to some extent in the U.S.; *fig.*, anything of small value, a trifle.

1826 *Mass. Spy* 5 July (Th.), Who the d——l would give a sumarkee to read the newspapers after breakfast? **1855** *Putnam's Mo.* April 410/1 The deacon'll save every soomarkee on't for the children. **1908** DAVENPORT *Butte Beneath X-Ray* 10 Today Percy is not worth a sou markee. **1936** MCKENNA *Black Range* 268 Marshall drifted from one settlement to another, and he likewise died without a sou marquee.

* **sound,** *a.* and *n.*

1. *n.* (See quot.)

1881 INGERSOLL *Oyster Industry* 248 *Sounds,* oysters grown in Staten Island sound, New York; especially an European brand.

2. *a.* Of currency: Possessing a relatively fixed or stable value.

1841 TYLER in *Pres. Mess & P.* IV. 85 The idea . . . of furnishing a sound paper medium of exchange may be entirely abandoned. **1844** *Lexington Observer* 25 Sep. 2/2 They embrace . . . a sound currency, emanating from the will, and upheld by the authority of the whole nation. **1903** ELY *Evolution Indust. Soc.* 482 The Fabians have been in favor of what is called with us sound currency.

b. Esp. **sound money,** money having a stable value, as gold, or currency based upon gold.

1895 *Nation* 19 Dec. 438/1 He has astonished the friends of sound money. **1913** LA FOLLETTE *Autobiog.* 209 A new heading for the paper [advocated]: . . . Sound money, a dollar's worth of dollar. **1946** *N. & Q.* July 56/2 In the auricular test given to coins, the coin is dropped on a hard surface and its quality gauged by the nature of the resulting ring. The determining factors, as this source points out, have varied over different periods. Yet the principle is old enough and familiar enough to make the term 'sound money' meaningful.

attrib. **1896** *Harper's Wkly.* 25 July 723/1 Sound-money Democrats are not hesitating as to their duty in the present crisis.

3. Holding sound views, esp. in politics, reliable as a politician or party man. *Colloq.*

1865 RICHARDSON *Secret Service* 34 The New Yorker was swift to explain that he was very 'sound,' favoring no compromise which would not give the slave holders all they asked. **1871** DE VERE 266 If he has been in political life before, his record is carefully searched to find out if he is sound, that is, if he has always voted strictly with his party.

For *sound on the goose* see * **goose,** *n.* **4.** *a.*

* **sounding,** *n.* **1.** *pl.* (See quot.) *Rare.* **2.** *attrib.* Designating a barge, boat, or yawl used in river soundings.

(1) **1804** C. B. BROWN tr. *Volney's View Soil U.S.* 174 On each side, it forms eddies or counter-currents, which, aided by the depositions of the rivers, forms the muddy stratum or deposit, termed *soundings.* — (2) **1875** MARK TWAIN *Old Times* v. 79 The pilot . . . goes out in the yawl provided the boat has not that rare and sumptuous luxury, a regularly devised 'sounding-boat.' *Ib.* 85 The paddle-wheel has ground the sounding-boat to lucifer matches! *Ib.* 569 (R.), The next moment the sounding-yawl swept aft to the wheel. **1906** —— *Carl Schurz* 727 (R.), If there were serious doubts he would stop the steamer and man the sounding-barge and go down and sound the several crossings.

* **soup,** *n.* In combs.: (1) * **soup bone,** in baseball, one's throwing or pitching arm, *slang;* (2) **hole,** a hole in a marsh filled with mud and water of a souplike consistency; (3) **-house bill,** (see quot.), *obs.*

(1) **1912** C. MATHEWSON *Pitching* x. 224 'My old soup bone,' says Kilroy, 'was so weak that I couldn't break a pane of glass at fifty feet.' — (2) **1911** *Essex Inst. Coll.* XLVII. 15 Little salt ponds or 'soup holes' . . . cover the marsh. — (3) **1882** *Cong. Rec.* 5 Dec. 31/1 Is not the bill introduced by the gentleman from Pennsylvania commonly called the Soup-house bill? I refer to the bill for the establishment of soldiers' homes throughout the country.

b. In slang phrases: (1) *To leave in the soup,* to leave in the lurch, or in trouble; (2) *from soup to nuts,* from the first to the last course of an elaborate meal, everything.

(1) **1889** *Lisbon* (Dakota) *Star* 26 April 4/2 After collecting a good deal of money, the scoundrels suddenly left town, leaving many persons in the soup. — (2) **1938** [see * **soda,** *n.* **1**]. **1950** *N.O. Times-Picayune Mag.* 16 April 5 Today's drug stores may have everything from soup to nuts, but they can't boast fascinating remedies like Gambler's Luck, Virgin's Milk, . . . or Come-Follow-Me-Boy.

As the last term in **corn, cream, gumbo, Indian corn, squash, sweet potato, terrapin soup.**

* **sour,** *a.* and *n.*

1. *n.* **a.** A facial expression manifesting discontent or bitterness. *Rare.* **b.** (See quot. 1891), also **lemon, strawberry sour. c.** (See quot. 1902.)

(a) **1877** W. WRIGHT *Big Bonanza* 290 His face wears a calm, resigned, chronic 'sour.' — (b) **1889** *Pall Mall Gaz.* 20 June 3/2 Sours are made principally with whisky or brandy, or Santa Cruz rum. **1891** *Cent.* 585/1 *Sour,* . . . an acid punch. [Colloq.] **1932** *K.C. Star* 4 April 18 P. Plug Citizen will have a great mental struggle with himself trying to decide whether to take strawberry or lemon sour. — (c) **1890** *Harper's Mag.* Oct. 708/2 He's so fond of sours. **1902** CLAPIN 377 *Sour,* used for pickles in parts of Pennsylvania. 'Pass the sour.'

2. *a.* In combs.: (1) **sour beer,** (see quot.), *obs.;* (2) **-berry,** (see quot. 1949); (3) **-berry bush,** prob. the lemonade berry or sumac *qq.v.;* (4) **bough,** a variety of apple, *obs.;* (5) **clover,** (see quot.); (6) **-dough,** see as a main entry; (7) **gum,** any one of various trees of the genus *Nyssa,* esp. the tupelo gum, in full **sour gum tree;** (8) **hominy,** (see quot.), *obs.;* (9) **mash,** fermenting grain mash, or whisky made from this, also attrib.; (10) **tupelo,** = **Ogeechee lime;** (11) **wood,** a tree, *Oxydendrum arboreum,* common in the Allegheny region, also attrib.

(1) **1866** GOSS *Soldier's Story* 105 Another genius developed a process for converting Indian meal into beer, by souring it in water. And 'sour beer,' as it was termed, speedily became one of the institutions. — (2) **1909** *Cent. Supp.* 1243/3. **1949** PALMER *Fieldbook Nat. Hist.* 288/3 Cranberry *Vaccinium oxycoccus.* . . . Known as sourberry, moss melons, crowberry, moorberry. — (3) **1847** PALMER *Rocky Mts.* (1904) 76 Occasionally there is a group of quaking aspen, and a few sour-berry bushes. — (4) **1853** FOWLER *Home for All* 146 The sweet and the sour Bough, ripe in July.

(5) **1915** ARMSTRONG & THORNBER *Western Wild Flowers* 262 Sour Clover. *Trifolium fucatum.* Cream-color. Spring, summer. Wash., Oreg., Cal. — (7) **1785** MARSHALL *Amer. Grove* 97 Upland Tupelo-Tree, or Sour Gum. . . . The timber of this tree is . . . much used for hubs of wheels for waggons, carriages, &c. **1857** GRAY *Botany* 162

Nyssa. Tupelo. Pepperidge. Sour Gum-tree. **1916** SETON *Woodcraft Man.* 294 Sour Gum, Black Gum, Pepperidge, or Tupelo (*Nyssa sylvatica*) A forest tree up to 110 feet high; in wet lands. — **(8) 1844** in *Amer. Sp.* XXII. 205/1 In his grave were deposited . . . sour hominy. . . . [This] is the Indian corn, pounded in a mortar by the women, after the manner of our hominy, and boiled, leaving a large quantity of the liquid with it. To this is added a small portion of lye, and it is set away in a vessel till it undergoes a fermentation, after which it is ready to use. — **(9) 1885** CRADDOCK *Prophet* 150 Him an' me run a sour mash still on the top o' the mounting. **1894** ROBLEY *Bourbon Co., Kans.* 97 Ben said they run out of Polk County sour mash, and towards the last he had to chuck in some bay rum. **1902** CLAPIN 185 Another large group [of brands of whisky] is the 'sour-mash' family.

(10) 1810 MICHAUX *Arbres* I. 30 Nyssa capitata, *Sour Tupelo* (Tupelo à fruits aigres), dans l'Etat de Géorgie. **1832** BROWNE *Sylva* 220 The Sour Tupelo first makes its appearance on the river Ogeechee. **1897** SUDWORTH *Arborescent Flora* 311. — **(11) 1709** LAWSON *Carolina* 98 The Sorrel, or Sowr-Wood-Tree, is so call'd, because the Leaves taste like Sorrel. **1887** CRADDOCK *Keedon Bluffs* 189 He clambered out of a clump of sour-wood shoots. **1896** POOL *In Buncombe County* 137 He cut me a whip from a sourwood. **1949** *Nature Mag.* April 165/2 In the southern Appalachians not even a sign would tell me where to look for sourwood honey.

As the last term in **brandy, sap, whisky sour.**

* **sour,** *v.* In phrases: (1) *To sour on*, to take a dislike to (a person or thing) *colloq.;* (2) *to sour onto*, to take, steal, *slang, obs.*

(1) 1862 *Rocky Mt. News* (Denver) 20 Nov. (Th.), Guess the M.P. will 'sour' on William C. **1907** *St. Nicholas* XXXIV. 601/2 Maybe if I get any more soured on Hammond I'll skate over with my trunk and try Ferry Hill. — **(2) 1866** SHANKS *Recollections* 47 Instead of 'souring onto,' i.e. taking without leave each other's rations, they were in the habit [etc.].

source book. [Cf. G. *Quellenbuch.*] A book of fundamental documents, records, etc. — **1899** A. B. HART (*title*), Source-Book of American History. **1913** W. M. WEST (*title*), A Source Book of American History.

sourdough ˈsaʊrˌdo, *n.*

1. One who spends much time in the open, esp. as a prospector, in Alaska, so called from the lump of sour dough saved over from each bread-making to start fermentation in a subsequent baking (see also quot. 1948).

1902 LONDON *Daughter of Snows* 120 Look at the old-timers,—'sourdoughs' as they proudly call themselves. **1948** *Reader's Digest* March 148/2 The term 'sourdough' had so long been applied to the man of the northern wastelands that now all Alaskans call themselves sourdoughs. **1950** *Boston Globe Mag.* 1 Jan. 3/5 Black John stepped into the Tivoli saloon and joined the little group of sourdoughs at the bar.

2. *attrib.* Of or pertaining to dough that is sour.

1900 *Outing* May 153/1 Preparations are made that result in light 'sour-dough' rolls, . . . and steaming coffee. **1927** WALGAMOTT *Remin. Early Days* II. 24 When I returned to camp I found Joe preparing sour-dough biscuits as usual. **1948** A. K. WILLIAMS *Gold Rush Days* 15, I obtained a dutch oven and baked what we called sourdough bread. This was the Mexican way of baking bread.

sousaphone ˈsuzəˌfon, ˈsusəˌfon, *n. Music.* A form of tuba used in brass bands, so called after J. P. Sousa (1854–1932), the American bandmaster who originated it.

1934 WEBSTER. **1936** *Sears Cat.* (ed. 173) 785 Supertone Sousaphones . . . Double B-flat—Full, rich sonorous tone. Bell and mouthpiece are adjustable . . . 52 inches high, 24-inch detachable bell, playing weight 26½ pounds. **1950** *World-Herald Mag.* (Omaha) 16 April 18/2 The sousaphone was likewise named for the famous march king, John Philip Sousa.

***souse,** *n.* A drunkard. *Slang.* — **1915** H. L. WILSON *Ruggles of Red Gap* iv. (1917) 80 You don't look like a periodical souse. **1930** BYRNE *Golden Goat* ix. 71 Mrs. Trelawny-Hocking . . . was an '*alcoolique terrible*,' a most notable souse, in the vulgate.

***soused,** *a.* Intoxicated. *Slang.* — **1902** H. L. WILSON *Spenders* ix. 87 I could see then that he was good and soused. **1930** MAUGHAM *Gent. in Parlour* xliii. 265 He got soused every night.

* **south,** *n.* and *a.*

1. (*cap.*) The southern, esp. the present southeastern, part of the U.S. below Mason and Dixon's line.

1781 FRENEAU *Poems* (1786) 215 Cornwallis has manag'd . . . well in the South. **1850** in A. C. COLE *Whig Party in So.* (1913) 174 We are heartily sick of this everlasting twaddle about the South—the South —that word of talismanic charm with southern demagogues. **1902** BELL *Hope Loring* 4 In the South his business was conducted in a large and generous way. **1949** *Newsweek* 8 Aug. 14/2 He rejects the South's unyielding attitude on states' rights.

b. The Confederate States of America. Now *hist.*

1865 *Chi. Tribune* 15 April 1 The assassin . . . [shouted,] 'the South is avenged,' and then escaped from . . . the theater. **1898** PAGE *Red Rock* 50 Wherever a Southern woman stood during those four years, there in her small person was a garrison of the South. **1950** *N.O. Times-Picayune Mag.* 9 April 18/2 The South woulda won if Stonewall Jackson had lived!

2. *collect.* The inhabitants of the southern states.

1792 in S. K. PADOVER *Jefferson* 203 (*footnote*), North and South will hang together, if they have you to hang on. **1837** *Diplom. Corr. Texas* I. (1908) 180 The North will be opposed and the South in favour of annexation. **1902** MEYER *Nominating Systems* 51 The party enthusiasm of the North greets that of the South.

3. In substantival and adjectival combs. and derivatives: (1) * **South America,** (see quot.); (2) * **Americans,** (see quot. 1859), *obs.;* (3) * **Atlantic,** belonging to the part of the U.S. extending from Delaware and Maryland south to Florida; (4) **-bound,** a train bound for the south, in full **southbound train;** (5) **Carolina,** of or pertaining to the state of South Carolina; (6) **Carolinian,** a native or inhabitant of South Carolina, also as adj.; (7) **Columbia,** South America, *rare;* (8) **Dakotan,** a native of South Dakota; (9) **-eastern states,** those states in the southeastern part of the U.S.; (10) **-end,** the posteriors or buttocks, *colloq.;* (11) **-enders,** a gang of ruffians who formerly operated on the south side of Boston, Mass., *obs.;* (12) **-land,** (*a*) the southern part of the U.S., the southern states, (*b*) southern California; (13) * **-lander,** (*a*) = **Southerner,** *rare,* (*b*) a native or inhabitant of southern California; (14) **-paw,** see as a main entry; (15) **-southerly,** a local name for the long-tailed duck; (16) * **-west,** the southwestern part of the U.S., earlier applied to what is now the South, also attrib.; (17) * **-wester,** a native or inhabitant of the Southwest; (18) * **-western,** designating a territory or state in the Southwest; (19) **-westerner,** a native or inhabitant of the southwestern part of the U.S.

(1) 1943 *Nat. Geog. Mag.* Dec. 764/2 Perhaps the worst of the feud country of this area in earlier times was the isolated mountain pocket 'South America,' about 20 miles from Middlesboro, Kentucky. — **(2) 1859** BARTLETT 430 *South Americans,* that branch of the American or Know-Nothing party which belongs to the South and favors slavery. **1860** *Harper's Mag.* May 860/2 The South Americans they have 23 votes, you know. — **(3) 1884** BLAINE *20 Years of Congress* I. 296 They had taken from the National Government its strongest fortress on the South-Atlantic coast. **1908** *S. Atlantic Quart.* Oct. 332 Gullah: a Negro Patois . . . spoken in the mainland and island regions, bordering the South Atlantic Seaboard. — **(4) 1885** JACKSON *Zeph* vi, I am going on the south-bound train. **1909** O. HENRY *Options* 273, I was on the south-bound, going to Cincinnati.

(5) 1829 *Va. Herald* (Fredericksburg) 21 March 3/4 We all remember the Hartford Convention—and, though last, not least, the South-Carolina and Georgia Resolutions. **1859** *La Crosse D. Union* 3 Nov. 4/3 The conflict . . . originated with the South Carolina Nullification. **1945** MARLOWE *Coaching Roads* 117 Those who had tasted his . . . South Carolina milk punch . . . wondered how anyone who owned him could ever have consented to part with him. — **(6) 1821** ROYALL *Lett. from Ala.* 137 She married a South Carolinian. **1866** GOSS *Soldier's Story* 260 One of the South Carolinian officers came up, and pushed away a big fat fellow. **1950** *This Week Mag.* 11 March 16/2 A drawling South Carolinian, was assigned the task of escorting recruits through the vaccination lines. — **(7) 1819** MEAD *Mississippian Scenes* 36 In South Columbia great republics rise. — **(8) 1889** *N.Y. Semi-Wkly. Tribune* 6 Dec. 13/4 Three ballots were put in the box for the South Dakotans to draw from. **1947** *Denver Post* 23 Feb. A. 10/3 Minnesota lawmakers promised a law banning South Dakotans from their state's fishing holes. — **(9) 1857** *Rep. Comm. Patents: Agric.* 66 This species is a Southern squirrel, and is most abundant in some of the Southeastern States.

(10) 1883 MARK TWAIN *Life on Miss.* iii, He bent stooping forward, with his back sagged and his south end sticking out far. — **(11) 1868** S. SMITH *Autobiog.* 12 We were on the side of Bonaparte, you see—I mean we Boston boys, North-enders and South-enders. — **(12)** (*a*) [**1812** PAULDING *J. Bull & Bro. Jon.* 92 The farms usually called Southlands were principally settled by people who, having a great number of slaves, were great sticklers for liberty.] **1849** WHITTIER *Poetical Works* (1894) 371/2 The South-land boasts its teeming cane, The prairied West its heavy grain. **1950** *Amer. Forests* Feb. 10/1 Dumfries [Va.] is as undistinguished as thousands of other villages on the busy route to the Southland. (*b*) **1898** *Pomona* (Calif.) *Progress* 23 June, Santa Monica, determined to be one of the most progressive cities in the southland, has begun a campaign to rid the city of wooden or metal awnings. **1948** *L.A. Times* 26 Dec. I. 2/2 Early morning hours were cold throughout the Southland, with Palmdale taking chilly honors at 14 degrees. — **(13)** (*a*) **1812** PAULDING *J. Bull & Bro. Jon.* 92 The Southlanders . . . were a set of frank, jolly, hospitable, high-spirited fellows. (*b*) **1949** *L.A. Times* 11 July 1/5 A major earthquake was recorded Saturday night probably in Northern Pacific waters, but it was not the same shock Southlanders felt. **1950** *L.A. Times* 8 Jan. 1/8 Officials told Southlanders there was no need to be alarmed about the [aqueduct] break.

(15) 1813 WILSON *Ornithology* VIII. 93 This Duck is very generally known along the shores of the Chesapeake Bay by the name of South Southerly, from the singularity of its cry, something imitative of the sound of those words. **1917** *Birds of Amer.* I. 141 Old-Squaw. . . . Other Names.—Long-tailed Duck; Long-tail; Swallow-tailed Duck; South-southerly; Old Wife; Old Injin; Old Granny; Old Molly; Old Billy. — **(16) 1853** BALDWIN *Flush Times Ala.* 224 There is no greater error than that which assigns inferiority to the bar of the South-West. **1860** *Harper's Mag.* Sep. 565/1 Captain H—— raved in true Southwest steamboat style for a few minutes. **1880** *Cimarron News & Press* 21 Oct. 2/2 The broad plains of New Mexico at Springer . . . is the great pastoral region of the Southwest. **1949** *Sierra Club Bul.* Oct. 5/1 The San Jacinto Mountains are the southernmost area of true alpine flora in the Southwest States. — **(17) 1867** EDWARDS *Shelby* 231 Colonel Hooper rode to the front, taking with him Captain Lea, and some others of the Southwesters. — **(18) 1806** *N.-Eng. Palladium* (Boston) 30 July 2/1 The President appoints the Legislative Councils in our Southwestern Territories. **1828** COOPER *Notions* II. 328 There is still another establishment [of Shaking Quakers], in one of the southwestern states. **1947** *Newsweek* 6 Oct. 23/2 The Mountain and Southwestern States have 32. — **(19) 1860** WHITMAN *Leaves of Grass* 350 There shall be countless linked hands—namely, the Northeasterner's, and the Northwesterner's, and the Southwesterner's, and those of the interior. **1945** MATHEWS *Talking* 187 It takes courage to call a southwesterner a coyote.

As the last term in **Deep, Far, New, Old, Solid, Sons of the, Sunny, Sweet South.**

* **south,** *adv.* **1.** In or into the South. **2.** *To go south,* (see quots.).

(1) 1834 C. A. DAVIS *Lett. J. Downing* 209 There warn't much in [nullification] . . . , but folks South thought there was. **1852** STOWE *Uncle Tom* xlii, A sister Emily . . . was sold South. **1898** PAGE *Red Rock* 526, I am going South to-night. — **(2)** [**1746** D. BRAINERD *Jrnl.* (1902) II. 204, I asked him [an aged Delaware Indian] whether the Indians of old times supposed there was anything of the man that would survive the body. He replied, Yes. I asked him where they supposed its abode would be. He replied, 'It would go southward.'] **1894** EGGLESTON in *Harper's Mag.* Feb. 470/2 The Dakota tribes believe that the soul, driven out of the body, journeys off to the south, and 'to go south' is, among the Sioux, the favorite euphemism for death.

* **southern,** *a.* and *n.*

1. *n.* **a.** = **Southerner. b.** *pl.* (See quot.) **c.** English such as is used in the South.

(a) 1827 *Spirit of Seventy-Six* (Frankfort, Ky.) 11 Oct. 3/2 The southerns will not long pay tribute. **1848** A. PRENTICE *Tour* 115 The annual migration of the southerns is very suggestive. **1949** MURRAY *This Our Land* 93 Politicians, abolitionists, and fire-eating Southerns kept the country in a state of turmoil. — **(b) 1900** NELSON *A B C Wall St.* 17 Railroad stocks . . . are divided in distinctive groups, including the . . . Granger, Southerns, Pacifics, and Local Transportations. — **(c) 1948** MENCKEN *Supp.* II. 104 This General Southern is spoken in 'the plantation up-country of Georgia and South Carolina.'

2. *a.* Of Indians: Living in what is now the southern or southeastern part of the U.S. *Obs.*

1684 *N.H. Hist. Soc. Coll.* VIII. 252 It [was] very necessary to entertain a number of southern Indians for soldiers. **1724** JONES *Virginia* 19 The Northern and Southern Nations might be managed by Missionaries from the Society. **1792** WASHINGTON *Writings* XII. 172 [They are] endeavoring to disaffect the four southern tribes of Indians towards this country.

b. Of, pertaining to, or characteristic of the southern states.

1798 FESSENDEN *Orig. Poems* (1806) 56 With many a southern negro driver. **1836** *S. Lit. Messenger* II. 111/2 We have known a New Englander laugh at the Southern use of the word clever. **1854** M. J. HOLMES *Tempest & Sunshine* 147 We will . . . pay a visit to Dr. Lacey in his southern home. **1907** *St. Nicholas* May 619/2 He went there . . . in order to receive under his protection slaves who had succeeded in escaping from their Southern masters.

c. Coming from the southwestern part of the U.S.

1890 *Stock Grower & Farmer* 15 Feb. 6/4 Unless the price of southern steers is considerably under that of last season very few will be purchased for Montana.

3. (Often *cap.*) In combs.

Combinations of this kind are so numerous that no effort is made to include all of them here.

(1) **Southern Chivalry,** the chivalrous manners and bearing of refined southern gentlemen (see quot. 1885); (2) **colony,** a colony in the southern part of what is now the eastern U.S.; (3) **Confederacy,** see as a main entry; (4) **congress,** a congress of the Southern Confederacy; (5) **convention,** a convention of southern representatives to express views on the controversial topics of the day, esp. the compromise measures of 1850, *obs.;* (6) **country,** the southern part of the U.S., the southern states; (7) * **Cross,** the battle flag of the Southern Confederacy; (8) **Empire,** the Southern Confederacy, *obs.;* (9) **fever,** = **Texas fever;** (10) **hospitality,** hospitality characteristic of southern people; (11) **league,** one of the military organizations established in the South early in the Civil War, *obs.;* (12) **measure,** a political measure undertaken or inspired by Southerners; (13) **Methodism,** Methodism such as prevails in the South; (14) **question,** a matter which concerns social or economic conditions in the South; (15) **rights,** political rights, particularly with regard to slavery, which those in the South, before the Civil War, felt they had under the federal constitution, also attrib., cf. **northern rights;** (16) **side,** in the federal Congress, that part of the assembly hall occupied by the representatives from the southern states; (17) **states,** the states in the southern part of the U.S., esp. those south of Mason and Dixon's line and east of New Mexico; (18) **tier,** a series, as of counties or states, in southern situations.

(1) 1857 STROTHER *Virginia* 207 But where is Southern chivalry? . . . choked by the maxims of dollar-jingling prudence? **1885** *Mag. Amer. Hist.* XIII. 99 'The Southern Chivalry' was a common phrase before and during the civil war. It was claimed as a proud title by Southerners and their friends, but has always been heard and used at the North with a shade of contempt. **1948** *Chi. Tribune* 20 June 1. 6/4 In 1860 the Democrats were deadlocked for 57 ballots in Charleston, S.C., 'city of secession and southern chivalry.' — **(2) 1724** JONES *Virginia* 18 These . . . are the Indians that make . . . such Disturbance in the Northern and Southern Colonies. **1789** *Ann. 1st Congress* 223 Previous to the late war we had a market in Nova Scotia, Newfoundland, and Canada, all the Southern Colonies, Europe, and Africa. — **(4) 1861** *Charleston* (S.C.) *Mercury* 14 Feb. 2/5 The Convention has also elected seven delegates to the Southern Congress.

(5) 1849 CALHOUN in H. von Holst *J. C. Calhoun* (1899) 325 There is but one thing that holds out the promise of saving both ourselves and the Union, and that is a Southern convention. **1889** J. PHELAN *Hist. Tenn.* 434 The Southern Convention had met at Nashville in May, 1850, as the Whigs said, 'to inaugurate a Southern Confederacy.' — **(6) 1789** *Ann. 1st Congress* 231 However slavery may be condemned in the Eastern States, it is impracticable to cultivate the Southern country without their assistance. **1852** EASTMAN *Aunt Phillis's Cabin* 50 Should the southern country become free . . . it will not be through the efforts of these fanatics. — **(7) 1866** in FLEMING *Hist. Reconstruction* I. 66 The place which has so long been sacred to the 'Southern Cross.' — **(8) 1862** E. KIRKE *Among Pines* 91 This latter organization [Knights of the Golden Order] . . . has for its sole object the dissolution of the Union, and the establishment of a Southern Empire—Empire is the word, not Confederacy or Republic. **1865** KELLOGG *Rebel Prisons* 375 Prisoners found a home there, not unlike . . . many others furnished by the Confederate authorities, in their so-called *Southern empire.* — **(9) 1895** *Dept. Agric. Yrbk. 1894* 78 The losses from the Southern or Texas fever have been almost entirely prevented.

(10) 1819 THOMAS *Travels* 100 The mistress . . . treated us to milk, in the true spirit of southern hospitality. **1945** *Chi. D. News* 7 Feb. 10/3 Perhaps Mr. Harris was denied the Southern hospitality because he was not agreeable company. — **(11) 1861** in LOGAN *Great Conspiracy* 250 Senators entrusted with the representative sovereignty of the States . . . conceive a Conspiracy for the overthrow of the Government through the military organizations, . . . 'Committees of Safety,' Southern leagues, etc. — **(12) 1854** BENTON *30 Years' View* I. 10/1 The non-slaveholding States . . . were successful in producing the compromise, conceived and passed as a Southern measure. — **(13) 1866** in FLEMING *Hist. Reconstruction* II. 243 This general remark applies more fully to Southern Methodism than to any other Southern ecclesiastical system. — **(14) 1878** *N. Amer. Rev.* CXXVII. 102 The Southern question, . . . properly treated, might have delayed this material question for some years. **1900** *Cong. Rec.* 25 Jan. 1171/2 Nobody regrets more than I do that the Southern Senators . . . have reopened this Southern question.

(15) 1851 *Miss. Palladium* (Holly Springs) 23 May 2/2 Thus he compliments the States Rights—Southern rights men, and associations, and especially the democratic party. **1852** *Whig Almanac 1853* 42/2 Candidate of the Southern Rights Party. **1865** PIKE *Scout & Ranger* (1932) 127, I heard nothing now, but clamor about 'Northern aggression,' and 'Southern rights,' wherever I went. **1913** A. C. COLE *Whig Party in South* 180 They called themselves Union men, members of the 'Union and Southern Rights Party.' — **(16) 1860** *Harper's Mag.* May 832/2 Mr. Lovejoy, of Illinois, made a violent speech on the Slavery question. While speaking, he . . . advanced into the area, approaching the 'Southern side' of the House, speaking and gesticulating with great violence. — **(17) 1776** *Jrnls. Cont. Congress* VI. 1039 Resolved, That two other magazines of ammunition . . . be formed, one in the eastern states, and one in the southern states. **1864** *Wkly. New Mexican* 10 June 2/1 Very little money has been realized . . . from the cotton owned by the Southern or Confederate States. **1948** *Chi. D. News* 19 April 10/2 The southern states of course, would be the principal beneficiaries of federal school aid. — **(18) 1860** *Lawrence* (Kans.) *Republican* 22 Nov. 1/5 This road traverses, from Lake Erie to New York, what are known as the 'southern tier' of the counties of the State. **1948** *Green Bay* (Wis.) *Press-Gazette* 13 July 6/6 The wild-eyed crackers from the southern tier were still gnashing their tuskes and hating Truman.

b. In combs. relating to persons: (1) **Southern Baptist,** a Baptist who is a member of a church belonging to the Southern Baptist Convention, also attrib.; (2) **Bourbon,** = ***Bourbon 4;** (3) **brigadier,** =**rebel brigadier;** (4) **brother,** a Southerner, *obs.;* (5) **Democrat,** a member of the Democratic party in the South; (6) **gentleman,** a gentleman in or from the South; (7) **Methodist,** a member of the Methodist Episcopal Church, South, also attrib.; (8) **planter,** a planter or plantation owner in the South, esp. before the Civil War; (9) **Rangers,** (see quot.), *obs.;* (10) **stater,** a native of the southern states, *obs.;* (11) **Union man,** a southern man who favored the side of the Union in the Civil War, *obs.*

(1) [**1866** in FLEMING *Hist. Reconstruction* II. 247 In 1845, when the Southern Baptist Convention was organized, . . . in proportion to the population there were more negroes than white people who were members of our churches.] **1932** *N.Y. Times* 3 Nov. 19/3 The Southern Baptist handbook for 1932 declares Southern Baptists are 'still wasting money in riotous living.' **1949** *Charleston* (S.C.) *News & Courier* 6 Feb. D. 7 Their largest religious denominations in recent years have been Negro Baptist and Southern Baptist. — **(2) 1873** PIKE *Prostrate State* 13 It must be said of the Southern Bourbon of the Legislature that he comports himself with a dignity, a reserve, and a decorum, that command admiration. **1945** *Somerset News* 19 April 1/2 The men who put him over in Chicago represent absolutely the worst elements in this country—cynical city politicians and southern bourbons. — **(3) 1886** POORE *Reminisc.* II. 272 The 'carpet-baggers' from the South were gradually being replaced by ante-bellum politicians and 'Southern brigadiers.' — **(4) 1789** *Ann. 1st Congress* 228 He did not mean to infer that the people of Massachusetts possessed any excellence over their Southern brethren. **1851** *Knickerb.* XXXVIII. 550 Two stout 'Union men' . . . would go out of the way any day to catch a 'fugitive' for a 'Southern brother.'

(5) 1900 *Cong. Rec.* 31 Jan. 1365/1 You can not discuss any question with a Southern Democrat . . . that he does not holler 'Nigger.' **1949** *So. Wkly.* 21 Dec. 3/1 Both the Republicans and the Southern Democrats are reluctant to endorse the plan. — **(6) 1789** *Ann. 1st Cong.* 215 Suppose a member from Massachusetts was to propose an impost on negroes, what would you hear from the Southern gentlemen, if fifty dollars was the sum to be laid? **1852** EASTMAN *Aunt Phillis's Cabin* 27 Mr. Weston will stand for a specimen of the southern gentleman of the old school. **1945** MOLLOY *Pride's Way* 2 Some wit has rather unkindly described a Southern gentleman as a man who won't kick his wife downstairs while he is wearing his hat. — **(7) 1846** *Jrnl. Gen. Conf. M.E. Church S.* I. 105 Southern Methodists were enabled . . . to carry on . . . the ordinary operations of church enterprise. **1872** *Cong. Globe* App. 30 May 478/3 You belonged to the Southern Methodist Church? **1928** *Bunker's Mag.* Feb. 195 There are five conferences of the Southern Methodist Church in Texas. — **(8) 1836** IRVING *Astoria* i. 45 Gorgeous prodigality . . . was often to be noticed in former times in Southern planters. **1947** *Time* 29 Dec. 14/1 A jovial man with a Southern planter's courtliness, he likes good clothes, good living and glittery functions. — **(9) 1741** in FORCE *Tracts* I. No. 4, 74 This the Place where a Body of Horse called the *Southern Rangers,* under the Command of Capt. *James Macpherson,* were station'd for several Years. They were paid by the Government of *Carolina;* but have been discharged for some Time by past.

(10) 1849 *Knickerb.* XXXIV. 219 Speak of your Virginian, your South-Carolinian, and Southern-Staters in general; where are they? **1851** *Harper's Mag.* June 36/2 A Southern-stater, with a spanking wagon-team, and two grinning negroes behind, were new and strange elements in the life of a city. — **(11) 1865** TROWBRIDGE *Three Scouts* ii. 21, I believe Southern Union men are a humbug, gen'ly.

c. In the names of, or with reference to, plants and trees: (1) **southern buckthorn,** a small tree or shrub found in the southeastern states; (2) **corn,** a variety of corn suited to the climate of the southern states; (3) **crabapple,** (see quot.); (4) **linn,** (see quot.); (5) **moss,** the long moss of the southern states; (6) **muscadine,** (see quot.); (7) **pine,** the Georgia pine, or lumber obtained from this, also attrib. and transf.; (8) **red lily,** (see quot.); (9) **spruce pine,** (see quot.).

(1) 1857 GRAY *Botany* 267 *Bumelia lycioides.* (Southern Buckthorn.) Moist grounds, S. Kentucky and southward. — **(2) 1820** *Columbian Centinel* 5 Jan. 4/5 Muson & Barnard. . . . Offer for sale . . . 2000 bushels Southern Corn. **1874** *Rep. Comm. Agric. 1873* 414 It is more trouble to grow Southern corn [than sweet corn]. — **(3) 1901** MOHR *Plant Life Ala.* 61 Southern crabapple (*Pyrus angustifolia*) frequent[s] the openings and borders of the woodlands. — **(4) 1860** CURTIS *Woody Plants N.C.* 79 Southern Linn, (*T[ilia] pubescens,*) . . . is confined to the Lower Districts of the Southern States.

(5) 1886 *Amer. Naturalist* XX. 88 Thus we find disclosures upon so-called Southern moss, Tillandsia, upon ginkgo (*Salisburia adiantoflora*). — **(6) 1868** *Amer. Naturalist* I. 639 The Southern Muscadine . . . is the *Vitis Rotundifolia* of Michaux. — **(7) 1810** MICHAUX *Arbres* I. 17 *Southern pine* . . . et *Red pine* . . . dans les Etats du milieu et du nord. **1852** *Harper's Mag.* Dec. 85 Jackson, the stalwart Hickory; Clay, the graceful Elm; Calhoun, the lofty, erect Southern Pine; all had gone before [Webster]. **1900** E. BRUNCKEN *N. Amer. Forests* 70 Probably the extreme limit, however, for supplying the market with original southern pine on a large scale is fifty years. **1918** *Amer. Builder* April 83 Our Southern Pine products include . . . siding and flooring material. — **(8) 1890** *Cent.* 3454/2 In the four native species of the eastern United States the perianth is colored from yellow to scarlet . . . : the Southern red lily, *L. Catesbæi,* with solitary erect flowers and recurved sepals. — **(9) 1901** MOHR *Plant Life Ala.* 96 The northern limit of the Southern spruce pine (*Pinus glabra*) proceeds very nearly along the same line.

d. In the names of animals, chiefly birds (see quots.).

1857 *Rep. Comm. Patents 1856: Agric.* 86 The Southern shrike (*Lanius ludovicianus.*) . . . breeds largely in the prairie districts. **1874** COUES *Birds N.W.* 407 *Pediœcetes phasianellus* . . . Southern Sharp-tailed Grouse. **1917** *Birds of Amer.* III. 99 Loggerhead Shrike, *Lanius ludovicianus ludovicianus.* . . . [Also called] Southern Loggerhead Shrike; Southern Butcher Bird. *Ib.* 161/2 The Florida, or Southern, Yellow-throat (*Geothlypis trichas ignota*) is found in the southeastern United States. **1917** *Mammals of Amer.* 18/2 Southern Black-tailed Deer.—*Odocoileus columbianus scaphiotus.* . . . Southern California. **1917** *Birds of Amer.* III. 49/1 The Pine-woods Sparrow of Florida and its northern variety Bachman's Sparrow, or Southern Pine Finch (*Peucœa æstivalis bachmani*) are striped Sparrows that are distinctly southern birds.

Southern Confederacy.

1. A discussed or contemplated confederacy embracing the southern portion of the U.S. *Obs.*

1788 MADISON *Writings* V. 80, I have for some time considered him as driving at a Southern Confederacy. **1837** *S. Lit. Messenger* III. 84 He regarded every attempt to unite the South, in support of a Southern President, as a prelude to the formation of a Southern Confederacy. **1860** ABBOTT *South & North* 307 The Southern confederacy shall again have its free North, and its slaveholding South, as now.

2. The Confederate States of America. Now *hist.*

1860 *Charleston* (S.C.) *Mercury* 15 Nov. 2/5 The 'Lone Star' was very suggestive of the additions which may hereafter be made to the Independent Southern Confederacy. **1891** *Harper's Mag.* Dec. 46/2 If England had recognized the Southern Confederacy [etc.]. **1943** DALE *Cow Country* 11 The Five Civilized Tribes . . . had made an alliance with the Southern Confederacy and fought on the side of the South throughout the war.

* **Southerner,** *n.* A native or inhabitant of the southern states.

1828 *Western Mo.* II. 12 A Yankee is a Yankee over the globe. . . . The Southerner, too, is such over the whole globe. **1876** *Dly. Morn. Argus* (San Bernardino, Calif.) 26 Sep. 2/2 Mr. Bushyhead is an old liner in Democracy, a Southerner by birth, sympathizing with secession. **1950** *Harvard Alumni Bul.* 22 April 600/1 Here is the authentic feeling of the progressive Southerner who remains a Southerner in most of what this means of emotion and conditioning.

Southernism ˈsʌðənˌɪzəm, *n.*

1. The qualities characteristic of southern culture or life.

1861 *N.Y. Tribune* 15 July (Chipman), Southernism has raised the standard . . . of social condition. **1911** *Quarterly Reg. Panpresb. Chs.* (London) Nov. 479 New Orleans has its solid *Southernism* before, during, and since the war. **1948** *Ga. Review* Spring 56, I was brought up in the most orthodox late-nineteenth-century Southernism.

2. A word or expression peculiar to Southerners.

1882 *Amer. Missionary* April 108 Aside from African features . . . and some Southernisms in voice and expression. **1886** *Academy* 11 Sep. 174/3 Prof. C. F. Smith of Nashville, read some interesting notes on 'Southernisms.'

southpaw ˈsaʊθˌpɔ, *n.* In baseball, the left hand, a left-handed pitcher. Also **southpaw pitcher.**

1892 *D.N.* I. 227 The president spoke of *south* meaning 'left' in *southpaw*, a left-handed base-ball pitcher; *south-handed* had been mentioned to him by Englishmen. **1913** *Chattanooga* (Tenn.) *News* 20 Sep. 14/5 He also thinks Rose, the southpaw, will be a valuable man. **1948** *Chi. Tribune* 20 April I. 20/5 He waved his big southpaw and ducked under the roof. **1950** *Chi. D. News* 18 March 11/4 Bob Henry, a 19-year-old south paw pitcher from the University of Texas, has been signed by the Chicago Cubs.

Hence **southpaw,** *v. tr.*, and **southpawing,** *n.*

1928 *Dly. Ardmoreite* (Ardmore, Okla.) 12 April 8/1 Herb Pennock southpawed his way the route for the Yankees. **1938** *Chi. Tribune* 4 April 21/1 The White Sox positively refused to be awed today by the southpawing of Larry French. **1949** *Chi. Tribune* 16 May IV. 1/8 The Chicagoans . . . let the title holders have it, 10 to 0, behind Bill Wight's southpawing.

* **Southron,** *n.* = **Southerner.**

1828 *Free Press* (Tarboro, N.C.) 9 Nov., I am a Republican in principle, and a Southron in feeling. **1886** POORE *Reminisc.* I. 530 Many other bitter things were said about him by the Southrons. **1949** *Southwestern Hist. Quart.* April 450 It was a rebellion, and the Southrons gloried in the term 'rebel.'

Southward Indians. Indians dwelling south of a particular region, esp. those south of the Ohio River. *Obs.*

1671 *S.C. Hist. Soc. Coll.* V. 341 Corne from time to time [is] taken out of the plantations by the Kussoe and other Southward Indians. **1725** in *Travels Amer. Col.* 114 If they were in Unity with the Southward Indians they should have no enemy. **1765** G. CROGHAN *Jrnl.* (1904) 61 They brought an Account that the Southward Indians had come to the Lower Towns to War.

* **sovereign,** *n.*

1. The supreme governing power in a country or state. *Obs.*

[**1787** J. ADAMS *Defence of Constitutions* I. 26 The sovereign [in Switzerland] is the whole country.] **1829** JACKSON in Benton *30 Years' View* I. 164/1 These states, claiming to be the only sovereigns within their territories, extend their laws over the Indians. **1861** *Chi. Tribune* 19 July 1/2 None need be afraid that they will be held accountable for past opinions, . . . if they will now . . . acknowledge their allegiance to Virginia and her Confederate States, as their true and lawful sovereigns.

2. An American voter or citizen.

1846 *Ind. Hist. Soc. Pub.* III. 412 This fact illustrates the situation of thousands of the future sovereigns of our beloved State. **1862** *N.Y. Tribune* 7 June (*Chipman*), [Nissen said that he] could not be forced to take an oath of allegiance to the Confederacy. . . . Instantly the 'sovereigns' in attendance pitched upon the audacious recusant. **1869** MARK TWAIN *Innocents* 100, I am a free-born sovereign, sir, an American, sir.

3. In combs.: (1) **Sovereign Squats, Squatters,** terms applied to themselves by the free state settlers of Kansas in derision of the squatter sovereignty doctrine of Stephen A. Douglas, *obs.*, cf. **squatter sovereign;** (2) **state,** one of the states of the U.S.

(1) **1855** *Herald of Freedom* 27 Jan. 2/7 *Resolved*, That we, the Sovereign Squatters of Kansas Territory, . . . are a free and independent people, and regard with contempt and public odium the course pursued here by the Lawrence Association. **1902** *Kans. Hist. Coll.* VII. 420 The free-state settlers in Kansas . . . called themselves and each other Sovereign Squats, in derision of the Douglas proposition. — (2) **1819** MARSHALL *Constitutional Opinions* (1839) 160 The defendant, a sovereign state, denies the obligation of a law enacted by the legislature of the union. **1871** *Harper's Mag.* Dec. 51/1, I'll teach him . . . to go a-cavorting round coercing sovereign States of this Union. **1950** *Boston Globe Mag.* 23 July 7/1, I am Hezekiah Livingstone, originally from the sovereign state of Kaintucky.

b. *To play the sovereign*, (see quot.). *Obs.*

1877 *N. & Q.* 5 Ser. VIII. 186/1 In Western Pennsylvania, when a candidate for office puts on shabby clothes a short time before an election, drinks whiskey with everybody, and shakes hands with everybody, he is said to be 'playing the sovereign.'

* **sovereignty,** *n.* A state or statehood in the Federal Union; the authority possessed by a state in the management of its affairs.

1799 *Ky. Resolutions* in ELLIOT *Debates* IV. (1836) 545 A nullification, by those sovereignties, of all unauthorized acts done under color of that instrument, is the rightful remedy. **1818** *Niles' Reg.* XIII. 298/1 Missouri and Illinois . . . will soon prefer their claims to sovereignty. **1896** *Omaha D. Bee* 18 Feb. 3/5 The chapters of the revised code relating to the sovereignty and jurisdiction of the state . . . escaped defeat.

As the last term in **popular, squatter, state sovereignty.**

* **sow,** *n.* In combs.: (1) **sowbelly,** fat pork from the belly or sides of a hog, *colloq.;* (2) **bosom,** jocose for prec.; (3) * **bug,** (see quot.); (4) **crab,** a mature female crab; (5) * **tit,** the wild strawberry, *Fragaria vesca*, or a species of blackberry, also attrib.

(1) **1867** Goss *Soldier's Story* 205 My captor presented to me a generous slice of 'sow-belly.' **1950** *Reader's Digest* March 41/2, I don't think either of them ever saw more than a peck of black-eyed peas and a side of sowbelly. — (2) **1915** in WENTWORTH. **1936** MENCKEN *Amer. Language* 304, I am informed by a correspondent that in 1933 the pious Los Angeles *Times* printed *sow-bosom* in lieu of *sow-belly.* — (3) **1883** *Harper's Mag.* Jan. 186/1 The common sow-bug (*idotœa*) often illumines the crevices and sea-weeds along our shores. — (4) **1942** GRAHAM & BEAVEN *Chesapeake Biol. Lab. Pub.* 52, 9 It is at this final molt that the female . . . becomes a sow . . . crab.

(5) **1788** CUTLER in *Life & Corr.* I. 410 A white oak . . . has a cavity in the middle covered with sow-tits. **1795** WINTERBOTHAM *Hist. View* III. 395 Sawteat blackberry or bumblekites, *Rubus fruticosus.* **1893** *Amer. Folk-Lore* VI. 141 *Rubus villosus*, 'sow-tit' (teat). N.H. Farrington, Conn., Goshen, Conn.

* **sower,** *n.* As the last term in **guano, seed, timothy, wool sower.**

sozodont ˈsozəˌdɑnt, *n.* [f. the Gk. combining elements *soz-* (<*sozein*, to save, keep)+stem *odont*, tooth.] (See quot. 1877.) Now *hist.*

"And he was so fine to look at with his broad mailed shoulders, and the grand leonine set of his plumed head, and his big shield with its quaint device of a gauntleted hand clutching a prophylactic toothbrush with the motto: 'Try Noyoudont.' This was a tooth-wash that I was introducing" (1889 MARK TWAIN *Conn. Yankee* (1917) xx. 168).

[**1864** in *Reader's Digest* (July, 1948) 139/2 An 1864 ad called Sozodont 'the most convenient, efficacious and beneficial article for the Teeth the world has ever seen.'] **1865** *Evansville* (Ind.) *D. Jrnl.* 26 Sep. 2/4 The teeth themselves, if beautified by the aid of Sozodont, are powerful agents in providing the fascination which leads to marriage. **1877** BARTLETT 631 Sozodont. A certain or uncertain dentifrice, extensively made known by placards on fences and rocks by the roadside. **1891** *Memphis Appeal-Avalanche* 23 April 8/1 No one need be foul-mouthed if they will only use Sozodont and rub it in well. **1948** *Reader's Digest* July 139/1 Then, in 1859, an ingenious New York wholesale druggist, William Henry Hall, started to promote a red liquid called Sozodont—a name coined from Greek words meaning 'save' and 'teeth.' The preparation could have been more accurately named Sozodon't. It was 37 percent alcohol.

transf. **1865** *Republican Banner* (Nashville, Tenn.) 13 Oct. 3/2 Having got through with the first, diluted with about a pint of Robertson County Sozodont, . . . he sought the domicil of his beloved Biddy.

* **space,** *n.*

1. (See quot.) *Obs.*

1877 BARTLETT 631 *Space*, floor. Second space, first floor. Massachusetts.

2. A part of a page or number of lines in a newspaper taken up by a particular contributor's work, and often serving as the basis of his compensation.

1889 *Chi. D. News* 20 April 1/4 The town is full of special correspondents who are writing from imagination and against space. **1893** PHILIPS *Making of Newspaper* 16 The special correspondents who send news by telegraph or post . . . are paid by 'space,' or at so much per column. **1894** SHUMAN *Steps in Journalism* 83 Articles by the beginner are nearly always submitted 'on space.'

3. In combs. with reference to writing or drawing for a newspaper or periodical on the basis of space taken up.

1887 *Westminster Rev.* Oct. 858 The standard of literary excellence in the news columns of the New York press has also been lowered by the general substitution of 'space writing' for the work of salaried reporters. **1892** HOWELLS *Quality of Mercy* 116 He felt that as a spaceman . . . his duty to his family required him to use every means for making copy. **1893** PHILIPS *Making of Newspaper* 44 An ordinary 'space' reporter of today excels in cleverness the 'staff' special writer of twenty years ago. **1902** BANKS *Newspaper Girl* 207 [By] the 'guarantee space' system . . . a member of the staff is guaranteed a stipulated sum of money every week, and as much over that amount as he or she makes by writing at ordinary or special space-rates. *Ib.* 233 Space artists get paid two dollars a single-column cut. **1935** *Amer. Mercury* July 382/2 Let us by law provide that any underpaid newspaperman or impoverished writer may apply to the great journals or news associations, *before his death*, for payment at space rates, for the obituary which is to appear after his demise.

***spade,** *n.* A blade on the rotary wheel of a spader. See also **griddle-spade.** — **1864** *Ohio Agric. Rep.* XVIII. p. xxii, The result [of the operation of the spaders] may be taken as a fair average of what may be expected of the performance of the spades. **1876** KNIGHT 2252/1 The sharp-pointed spades . . . rotate in the direction in which the machine moves.

***spader,** *n.* A machine provided with a rotary device for digging into and pulverizing land. — **1863** *Ill. Agric. Soc. Trans.* V. 255 If the rotary spader does not throw the steel clipper out of place. **1874** KNIGHT 703/1 Other forms of spaders have blades thrust out and retracted as the machine advances.

spading fork. A flat- and broad-pronged fork for spading.

1863 *Horticulturist* March 15 (*advt.*), New York Agricultural Warehouse [has for sale]. . . . Spading Forks, Weeding Forks [etc.]. **1902** *Sears Cat.* (ed. 112) 583/2 D Handle, Capped Ferrule, Spading Fork, four flat steel tines. **1947** *Dly. Oklahoman* (Okla. City) 11 Aug. 12/3, I just stuck a spadin' fork in th' ground for a few fishin' worms and bang, it came gushin' up!

span spæn, *n.* [Du. in same sense.] A pair of draft animals, usu. matched, for harnessing abreast as a team.

1769 *Boston Gaz.* 2 Oct. (Th.), Wanted, a Spann of good Horses for a Curricle. **1860** GREELEY *Overland Journey* 81 We were stalled until an extra span of mules was sent from the other wagon. **1945** MATHEWS *Talking* 8, I got a span of mules from the ranch.

***span,** *v.* [In **1.** prob. f. noun above.] **1.** *intr.* (See quots.) **2. spanworm,** a larva of any geometrid. Also *collect.* Cf. **cotton span worm.**

(**1**) **1828** WEBSTER *Span*, to agree in color, or in color and size; as, the horses span well. [*N. Eng.*] **1891** *Cent.* 5793/2 *Span*, . . . to be matched for running in harness; form a span. . . . [U.S.] — (**2**) **1820** *Amer. Farmer* I. 375/3 What can our obliging correspondents tell us about the . . . best method of destroying that dreadful plague of our orchards, the *span worm.* **1892** KELLOGG *Kans. Insects* 61 The caterpillars . . . loop the body when walking, like a span worm.

***span,** *adv.* [?f. **span*-new, or *spick and *span.*] Entirely, completely. *Colloq.*

1843 STEPHENS *High Life N.Y.* II. 110 The men folks had on span white gloves. **1878** B. F. TAYLOR *Between Gates* 182 [The dresses] have been washed span-clean. **1887** *Lippincott's Mag.* Sep. 360 He got clean span away.

spandy ˈspændɪ, *adv.* and *a.* Chiefly *N. Eng.* [Prob. a variant of *spandal* or *spander.* See *OED* and *EDD* for *spandal new, spander new, span- new.*] **1.** *adv.* Very, perfectly. **2.** *a.* Very good, new. Both *colloq.*

(**1**) **1838** TITTERWELL *Yankee Notions* 116 (We.), I have heard of a ghost that always came in a new coat . . . and a spandy clean dickey. **1848** BARTLETT 322 *Span-clean, Spandy-clean*, very clean; perfectly clean. **1903** WIGGIN *Rebecca* 15 These [shoes] are spandy new. — (**2**) **1868** ALCOTT *Little Women* I. 126 My silk stockings and two pairs of spandy gloves are my comfort.

spang spæŋ, *adv.* [Poss. f. **spang*, *v.* to move rapidly, but cf. *EDD spanghew, adv.*, with a violent jerk.] **1.** Directly, "smack," entirely. *Colloq.* **2. spang up,** very good. *Rare.* Cf. ***bang-up.**

(**1**) **1843** CARLTON *New Purchase* I. 173 She got three times right spang through it. **1898** HARRIS *Tales of Home Folks* 18 [I'll] run right spang over you with my big gray. **1922** TARKINGTON *Gentle Julia* 199 New straw hat right spang the firs' warm day. — (**2**) **1878** HART *Sazerac Lying Club* 96, I seed . . . the minin' superintenders drivin' around with their spang-up teams, and all the population bowin' and scrapin' to 'em.

spango ˈspæŋgo, *n.* [Origin unknown; **spankue** in 1779 quot. may be a different word.] A kind of drink. *Obs.* — **1721** in B. LYNDE JR. *Diary* (1880) 132 Mr. Fiske, Plaisted, etc., at our house, supped here; drink spango. **1779** in *Loyal Verses* (1860) 47 Each in his bowels griping *spankue* feels.

***Spaniard,** *n.* In miscellaneous obs. uses: A Spanish dollar, a cigar, a cloak or shawl. See also **American Spaniard.**

1779 *N.J. Archives* 2 Ser. III. 703 Soft or paper dollars . . . now pass at the rate of near forty for one solid Spaniard at the city of Philadelphia. **1828** *Yankee* I. 328/2 Do they not smoke their spaniard? **1837** *S. Lit. Messenger* III. 227/1, [I] wrapped my spaniard about me.

***Spanish,** *a.* and *n.*

1. *n.* In various obs. uses: **a.** The black Spanish, a breed of domestic fowls. **b.** A fine flavor in a cigar. **c.** A kind of dance.

(**a**) **1850** BROWNE *Poultry Yard* 28 The cross between the pheasant-Malay and the Spanish produces a particularly handsome fowl. — (**b**) **1862** NORTON *Army Lett.* 46, I have been . . . drawing the Spanish out of my cigar. — (**c**) **1891** WELCH *Recoll. 1830–40* 377 The 'Spanish,' a rich, warm, seductive dance, suggestive of black and gold dresses with black lace flowing mantilla and fan.

2. In combs.: (1) **Spanish America,** that part of America once controlled by Spain, or in which Spanish is the principal language; (2) **-American,** see as a main entry; (3) **bit,** a form of bridle bit in which the usual curb chain is replaced by a curb ring, cf. **Mexican bit** and see **d.** (1) below; (4) **brick,** (see quot. and cf. **adobe 1.**), *obs.;* (5) **-Californian,** a Californian of Spanish descent, also attrib. or as adj.; (6) **Creole,** a Creole, esp. one of predominantly Spanish descent, also attrib. or as adj.; (7) **-Cuban War, =Spanish-American War;** (8) **dance,** a dance such as is common in Spain or in Spanish countries; (9) **fever,** (*a*) (see quot.), *obs.*, (*b*) an infectious disease among cattle transmitted by the cattle tick, *Margaropus annulatus*, Texas fever; (10) **grant,** a land grant originally made by the Spanish government, also **Spanish land grant;** (11) **Indian,** (*a*) an Indian belonging to an Indian race of Spanish America, also attrib., (*b*) of a language, made up of Spanish and Indian; (12) **Mexican,** a Mexican of Spanish descent; (13) **monte, =monte 1,** also attrib.; (14) **quarter,** a section in a town or city where Spanish people live, cf. **d.** (7) below; (15) **saddle,** a saddle used by Spaniards, esp. one of heavy and elaborate construction; (16) **sauce,** ?some kind of hot sauce, *obs.;* (17) **spur,** a long-shanked spur much used by Spanish and Mexican riders; (18) **supper,** (see quot.), *colloq.;* (19) **title,** a land title issued by the Spanish government in Mexico; (20) **trail,** *W.* any one of various ways or roads used from early times, esp. a trail or road connecting Santa Fé, New Mexico, and Los Angeles, California, or a road from Salt Lake City by way of Cedar City and Las Vegas to the Mormon settlements in San Bernardino, California; (21) **War, =Spanish-American War.**

(**1**) **1789** MORSE *Amer. Geog.* 480 The whites [in Mexico] are born in Old Spain, or they are creoles, that is, natives of Spanish America. **1856** *34th Congress* 1 Sess. H.R. Ex. Doc. No. 135, I. 42 A river . . . [making] what is called in Spanish America a cañon—that is, a river hemmed in by vertical walls. **1884** *Terr. Rep. N. Mex.* 33 For centuries it [N. Mex.] was a purely military government of a wild and remote province of Spanish-America. — (**3**) **1842** *S. Lit. Messenger* VIII. 466/1 [He stopped] his horse, with the aid of the unmerciful Spanish bit, in full career. **1930** *Colo. Mag.* May 95 We have for example such words as 'riata,' 'chaparejos,' 'sombrero,' and 'corral,' and the Spanish bits and spurs, as reminders of the descent of the industry from the riders of Coronado's day. — (**4**) **1850** *Jrnl. Birmingham Emig. Co.* 1 June, The fort was enclosed by a wall about 11 feet high, made of Adoby's or spanish Brick.

(**5**) **1906** PARSONS *Wild Flowers Calif.* 124 The Spanish-Californian children knew them as 'gallitos.' **1917** SAUNDERS *Western Wild Flower Guide* 158 Canachalgua is one of the most famous of Pacific Coast medicinal herbs, valued alike by Americans, Spanish-Californians and Indians as a febrifuge. — (**6**) **1807** in FOOTE *Texas & Texans* I. 193 These are principally Spanish Creoles, some French, some Americans, and a few civilized Indians. **1880** CABLE *Grandissimes* 224 The Spanish-Creole master had often seen the bull . . . standing in the arena. — (**7**) **1900** *Cong. Rec.* 1 Feb. 1412/1 In a conversation, about the close of the Spanish-Cuban war, . . . he said [etc.]. — (**8**) **1828** MRS. HALL *Letters* 217, I forgot to mention that at all balls and dances at Charleston a favorite dance is the Spanish dance, as they call it, and in *plan* it certainly is a Spanish country dance, but in execution, Oh Heavens! **1837** WILLIAMS *Florida* 117 The Spanish dances are still preferred, by the natives, while the Americans consider cotillions as more genteel. — **(9)** (*a*) **1828** *Richmond Whig* 5 Aug. 2/3 (Th.), The Spanish fever, or 'Dengue,' . . . at once yields to a warm bath and hot tea. (*b*) **1858** *N.Y. Herald* 2 Oct. 5/3 Southern cattle communicate to those of Missouri a disease known as Spanish or Texas fever. **1934** *Rocky Mt. News* (Denver) 22 April E. 15/1 Missouri bushwhackers murdered them under the pretense of defending their own cattle against Spanish fever.

(10) 1826 FLINT *Recoll.* 199 But it is not my intention to dip into the gulph of land-claims, . . . Spanish grants, confirmed claims [etc.]. **1890** *Stock Grower & Farmer* 19 April 6/2 One of the greatest problems congress has had to do with in the past fifty years is the settlement of Spanish and Mexican land grants. **1941** M. L. SMITH *God's Country* 171 They have what they call the old Spanish Grant. — **(11)** (*a*) **1705** ROBERT BEVERLEY *Virginia* 51 By their Accounts, we suppose him to have come from the *Spanish Indians*, some-where near *Mexico*, or the Mines of *St. Barbe.* **1715** *Boston News-Letter* 9 May 2/2 Ran away from his Master, . . . a very likely Spanish Indian Lad. (*b*) **1899** *Atlantic Mo.* June 759/2 Men and women share in the possession of . . . the vitiated but musical Spanish-Indian patois of the Southwest. — **(12) 1848** ROBINSON *Santa Fe Exped.* (1932) 62 The Spanish Mexicans use no chairs, but sit upon the floor on a mat or carpet. — **(13) 1889** *Chi. D. News* 27 April 1/3 There are wheels of fortune, chuck-luck outfits, and Spanish monte tables everywhere. **1891** *Cent. Mag.* April 915 Gambling appeared to be the chief occupation and Spanish Monte the favorite game. — **(14) 1872** POWERS *Afoot & Alone* 270, I entered the city [Los Angeles] near the little, old, mean Spanish quarter, with its red-tiled adobes. **1890** *Internat. Ann., Anthony's Photog. Bul.* III. 339 The baranca . . . [separates] the business part of the town [Santa Barbara, Calif.] from the 'Spanish Quarter.'

(15) 1827 COOPER *Prairie* xviii, A Spanish saddle, too, like a grandee of the Mexicos! **1897** HOUGH *Story of Cowboy* 67 The Spanish saddles of the Southwest were often heavily decorated with silver. **1945** *Elk Mt. Pilot* (Crested Butte, Colo.) 19 July 3/1 For Sale—Practically new modern white coal range; a Spanish Saddle, excellent condition. — **(16) 1928** S. LEWIS *Man Who Knew Coolidge* 70 Hamburg steak and Spanish sauce. — **(17) 1872** MARK TWAIN *Roughing It* 42 The pants were stuffed into the tops of high boots, the heels whereof were armed with great Spanish spurs. **1926** COOPER *Oklahoma* 105 They stopped at a distance and surveyed it, then, touching their horses lightly with their heavily rowelled Spanish spurs, moved closer. — **(18) 1929** DOBIE *Vaquero* 158 The water was good and I took a 'Spanish supper'—tightened my belt up a notch. — **(19) 1880** *Cimarron News & Press* 9 Sep. 1/6 Spanish or Mexican titles to land for grazing or agriculture did not embrace a title to mineral land.

(20) *c***1857** *Kit Carson's Own Story* (1926) 30 We followed the Spanish trail that leads to California. **1942** STEGNER *Mormon C.* 66 More important than any of these was the string of settlements running south and west from Salt Lake City along the Spanish Trail, later known as the Mormon Road. **1950** *Amer. Forests* Feb. 2/2 The old Spanish Trail runs from New Orleans to Houston, thence to San Antonio, and then on to El Paso and Los Angeles. — **(21) 1900** *Cong. Rec.* 8 Jan. 693/2. *Ib.* 30 Jan. 1308/1, I hope the Senator will not confuse in his mind . . . the cost of the Spanish war with the cost of the Philippine war.

b. In the names of plants and trees: (1) **Spanish bayonet,** any of several species of *Yucca*, esp. a rigid, short-trunked plant, *Yucca aloifolia*, of the Southwest (see also quot. 1856); (2) **beard,** =**Spanish moss;** (3) **clover,** (*a*) alfalfa, (*b*) =**Florida clover;** (4) **coffee,** (see quot. and cf. **coffee weed**); (5) **cypress,** (see quot.); (6) **dagger,** one of several species of *Yucca*, esp. *Y. gloriosa;* (7) **larkspur,** see **Spanish cypress;** (8) **moss,** the long moss, *Dendropogon usneoides*, forming tufts hanging upon trunks and branches of trees in the South, cf. **Mississippi moss;** (9) **needles,** see as a main entry; (10) **oak,** any of the red oaks, as *Quercus borealis*, esp. in the South, the wood of any of these trees or any individual tree, cf. **lowland Spanish oak;** (11) **peanut,** (see quot. 1909); (12) **potato,** the sweet potato, *obs.*

(1) 1843 *Knickerb.* XXII. 566 A few white flowers of the Spanish-bayonet . . . [looked] like sentries with white feathers. **1856** FERGUSSON *America* 143 The dwarf palmetto grows abundantly on St. John's Island. It is called the Spanish bayonet, or bayonet palmetto. **1950** *L.A. Times Mag.* 22 Jan. 27/3 These are yuccas, also called 'Spanish Bayonets' and 'Candles of the Lord.' — **(2) 1763** in *Amer. Sp.* XX. (1945) 49 The other excrescence is commonly found upon trees near the banks of rivers and lakes. It is called *Spanish beard.* **1836** EDWARD *Hist. Texas* 89, [I saw] vast quantities of moss, alias Spanish beard, in the lower parts of Texas. **1948** *Travel* Nov. 10/1 The early French labelled it 'Spanish Beard,' the Spanish in retaliation, 'Frenchman's Wig.' — **(3)** (*a*) **1832** *Amer. R.R. Jrnl.* I. 568/2 (*caption*), Alfalfa, or Spanish Clover. **1873** BEADLE *Undevel. West* 448 There at least is a patch of green, a tract grown up in alfalfa or Spanish clover. (*b*) **1889** VASEY *Agric. Grasses* 103 *Richardsonia scabra* (Mexican Clover; Spanish Clover; Florida Clover; Water Parsley [etc.]). — **(4) 1831** AUDUBON *Ornith. Biog.* I. 181 The wild Spanish Coffee. *Cassia occidentalis.* . . . It flowers through the summer, and grows chiefly in old fields, in the Southern States.

(5) 1901 MOHR *Plant Life Ala.* 686 *Gilia coronopifolia.* . . . Spanish Cypress. . . . Frequently cultivated for ornament, under the name 'Spanish larkspur.' — **(6) 1859** A. VAN BUREN *Sojourn in South* 108 A tall 'Spanish dagger' stood leaning its crested head against the veranda. **1939** PICKWELL *Deserts* 25/1 Spanish Daggers bloom in deserts made by mountains like snow-capped Old Baldy. — **(8) 1823** JAMES *Exped. Rocky Mts.* III. 220 The Spanish moss disappears northwardly of the 33d degree of north latitude. **1950** *Reader's Digest* March 119/1 Here is an old pomegranate bush and some old gnarled oaks with gray whiskers of Spanish moss.

(10) 1671 *S.C. Hist. Soc. Coll.* V. 333 This Land bears very good . . . Spanish, & liue oak. **1797** HAWKINS *Letters* 106 The whole of the growth on this path scrub, black and small spanish oak. **1849** *N. Eng. Farmer* I. 50 For durability, Spanish oak is much better than either red or post oak. **1949** *Chi. Tribune* 20 Feb. 30/3 Cedar and mesquite alone are costing Texas ranchers 115 million dollars a year. Add the sage and cactus, and the live oak, Spanish oak . . . and prickly pear and the toll is terrific. — **(11) 1909** WEBSTER, S[panish] peanut, a variety of peanut with small pods, sometimes grown as a forage plant. **1945** *Democrat* 23 Aug. 1/1 Some hogs in the county have already been put on early corn for grazing, some on Spanish peanuts, and the rest on running peanuts within a month. — **(12) 1765** ROGERS *Acct. N. Amer.* 139 This country also has a great variety of vegetables and fruits, as Spanish potatoes, pompions [etc.]. **1830** WATSON *Philadelphia* 718 Colonel A. J. Morris . . . told me that the potatoes used in his early life . . . were called Spanish potatoes.

c. In the names of, or with reference to, animals: (1) **Spanish curlew,** the long-billed curlew or the white ibis; (2) **flag,** a rockfish, *Hispanicus rubrivinctus*, found in California; (3) **horse,** a hardy breed of horse introduced by the Spaniards into the South and Southwest, a horse of this breed; (4) ***lady,** the crimson and gold wrasse, *Bodianus rufus*, found off the Florida coast; (5) **merino,** a breed of sheep introduced from Spain, a sheep of this breed, also attrib.; (6) **oyster,** (see quot.); (7) **plover,** (see quot.); (8) **pony,** =**Spanish horse.**

(1) 1791 W. BARTRAM *Travels* 146 Both species are called Spanish curlews. **1813** WILSON *Ornithology* VIII. 43 White Ibis . . . are usually called Spanish Curlews. **1917** *Birds of Amer.* I. 177/1 The old birds, which are popularly supposed to be of a different species, are usually referred to as 'Spanish Curlews' or 'White Curlews.' **1949** A. SPRUNT *S.C. Bird Life* 222 Long-Billed Curlew. . . . Local names: Sickle-bill; Spanish Curlew. — **(2) 1880** *Nat. Museum Proc.* III. 292 The 'Spanish Flag' . . . is the most brilliantly colored large fish on the Pacific coast. — **(3) 1741** *Col. S.C. Hist. Soc.* IV. 33 The general . . . sent out the Indians to hunt up the Spanish Horses and Cattell. **1890** *Stock Grower & Farmer* 15 Feb. 5/2 The Spanish horse escaped in the wars with Mexico. **1948** *Dly. Ardmoreite* (Ardmore, Okla.) 19 April 8/1 He was a small boy but he remembers the Spanish horse that the preacher rode and how frightened it became over nothing. — **(4) 1888** GOODE *Amer. Fishes* 205 In this limpid pool were . . . rainbow-fish, the Spanish-lady.

(5) 1802 F. L. HUMPHREYS *Life D. Humphreys* II. 346 A Gold Medal . . . is presented to you . . . for your patriotic exertions in introducing into New-England one hundred of the Spanish Merino breed of Sheep. **1890** *Stock Grower & Farmer* 8 March 7/2 Stock Sheep For Sale. . . . Improved with Spanish merino. — **(6) 1709** LAWSON *Carolina* 162 Spanish Oysters have a very thin Shell, and rough on the outside. — **(7) 1917** *Birds of Amer.* I. 246 Willet. *Catoptrophorus semipalmatus semipalmatus.* . . . [Also called] Spanish Plover; Stone Curlew. — **(8) 1876** CROFUTT *Trans-Continental Tourist* 91 Terms heard on the Plains: . . . 'Bronco,' California or Spanish pony. **1929** *Texas Mo.* Feb. 240 A cayuse is a Spanish pony.

d. In the names, now obs. or hist., of various coins of Spanish origin that once circulated in the U.S., as (1) **Spanish bit,** (see also **2.** (3) above), (2) **dollar,** see as a main entry, (3) **half-dollar,** (4) **half-real,** (5) **mill(ed) dollar,** (6) **pistole,** (7) **quarter,** (see also **2.** (14) above).

(1) 1683 *Pa. Col. Rec.* I. 85 The Gov[erno]r telleth Ch[arles] Pickering & Sam[ue]ll Buckley of their abuse to ye Governme[n]t, in Quining of Spanish Bitts and Boston money. **1738** W. STEPHENS *Proc. Georgia* I. 82 One Smith, . . . paying away a few Spanish Bits. *c***1782** JEFFERSON *Writings* I. 243 The tenth [of the dollar] will be precisely the Spanish bit, or half-pistareen. — **(3) 1865** *Atlantic Mo.* May 534/1 Along here, many's the Spanish half-dollar I've picked up myself among the kelp. — **(4) 1848** BARTLETT 139 Fippenny Bit, or contracted Fip. Fivepence. In the State of Pennsylvania, the vulgar name for the Spanish half-real.

(5) **1754** in C. HAZARD *Thos. Hazard* 245 Received of Robert Haszard of South Kingstown . . . two Spanish Milled Dollars. **1781** *Essex Inst. Coll.* XXVI. 115, I received eight Spanish mill dollars. **1806** ORDWAY in *Jrnls. of Lewis & O.* 361 Frazer got 2 Spanish mill dollars from a squaw for an old razer. **1851** MITCHELL *Dream Life* 87 He seems to have great confidence in the value of Spanish milled dollars. — (6) **1693** SEWALL *Letter-Book* I. 137, I have sent you three and twenty Spanish Pistolls. **1745** FRANKLIN *Poor Richard's Almanac 1746* 2. **1831** SLOCOMB *Amer. Calculator* 92 Coins which pass current in the United States [include] . . . an English Guinea, . . . a Spanish Pistole (Silver). — (7) **1831** *Boston Transcript* 18 May 2/3 Spanish quarters of 1794, and French half crowns are also circulating. **1857** *Spirit of Times* 31 Jan. 352/2 The war on the Spanish quarters, shillings, and sixpences, is now raging with unabated fury.

As the last term in **cowpen, Creole Spanish.** See also *to walk Spanish, s.v.* ∗**walk,** *v.* **2.** (5).

Spanish-American, *n.* and *a.*

1. *n.* A native or citizen of a Spanish-speaking country of North America. Also a citizen of the U.S. of Spanish descent.

1811 *Niles' Reg.* I. 14/2 The Creoles—Spanish Americans—i.e. the descendants of Spaniards born in this country. **1890** *Stock Grower & Farmer* 10 May 3/3 The upper and better class of our Spanish-Americans are good intelligent citizens. **1950** *Nat. Geog. Mag.* April 475/1 These two Spanish-Americans . . . had worked as a team for years.

2. *a.* Of or pertaining to Spanish America, or to U.S. citizens of Spanish descent.

1826 *Va. Herald* (Fredericksburg) 19 Aug. 2/1 In that respect the Spanish American people have the advantage of us—they beat us all hollow. **1876** *Reese River Reveille* (Austin, Nev.) 17 Sep. 2/2 Is there any hope for the Spanish-American nations? **1885** *Wkly. New Mexican Rev.* 15 Jan. 4/4 The president in making appointments [must] pay due respect to our Spanish-American populace.

Also **Spanish-American amalgamation process,** =**patio process.** *Obs.*

1864 MOWRY *Ariz. & Sonora* 167 No experiments have been made in working this ore by the patio or Spanish-American amalgamation process.

b. Designating American soldiers who fought in the Spanish-American War (1898).

1900 *Cong. Rec.* 19 Jan. 992/1 The delay in the taking up and considering the pension applications of the Spanish-American soldiers.

3. Spanish-American War, the war between Spain and the U.S. (1898).

1899 *Pres. Mess. & P.* X. 602/1 Spanish-American War. In February, 1895, the natives of Cuba, being dissatisfied [etc.]. **1900** *Cong. Rec.* 15 Jan. 801/1 [From] the cannon on the gunboat Nashville . . . was fired the first shot in the Spanish-American war. **1947** *Steamboat* (Colo.) *Pilot* 30 Jan. 1/8 He served in the Spanish-American war as a second lieutenant.

Spanish dollar. A Spanish or Spanish-American silver coin worth eight reals. Now *hist.* Cf. **silver dollar.**

1684 *N.H. Hist. Soc. Coll.* VIII. 162 Spanish dollars of Seville and Mexico should pass at six shillings the piece. **1756** ROGERS *Journals* 14 Ten Spanish dollars were allowed to each man towards providing cloaths, arms, and blankets. **1818** *Niles' Reg.* XV. 125/1 *Spanish Dollars* appear to be in great demand at this moment. **1894** S. LEAVITT *Our Money Wars* 34 In 1792, . . . people reckoned in pounds, shillings, and pence, and paid in Spanish dollars. **1950** *L.A. Times Home Mag.* 8 Jan. 12/4 This was the quality used in the Spanish dollars, or pieces of eight (worth 8 *reales*), which were everywhere accepted in trade in the early days.

Spanish needles. The dry prickly achenes of beggar-ticks, *Bidens bipinnata*, or of a plant of a related species. Also a plant producing these.

1743 CLAYTON *Flora Virginica* 94 Bidens corona seminum retrorsum aculeata. . . . Spanish-needle. **1821** NUTTALL *Travels Arkansa* 29 The corn-fields . . . are so overrun with . . . seeds of different species of Bidens or Spanish-needles, as to prove extremely troublesome to woollen clothes. **1873** *Winfield* (Kans.) *Courier* 17 July 1/4 Sensations of exquisite joy . . . thrill through it like Spanish needles through a pair of tow linen trowsers. **1946** *Nat. Geog. Mag.* Sep. 340/2 It is a white-flowered member of the same genus of plants as the better-known pestiferous yellow-flowered weed called Spanish needles.

b. Spanish needle grass, a local name for porcupine grass *q.v.*

1941 WILDER *Little House on Prairie* 81 He said it was Spanish needle grass. When it got into the mouths of horses or cattle, it must be cut out of their lips and tongues.

∗**spanker,** *n.* "A light cart suitable for rapid travelling" (*OED*). *Obs.* — **1831** in A. E. LEE *Hist. Columbus* I. 318 Our vehicle, which, in the dialect of the country was called a *spanker,* was intended for four persons.

∗**spar,** *v. tr.* "To aid (a vessel) over a shallow bar by the use of spars and tackles" (*Cent.*). Also absol., and **sparring,** *n.*

1843 TALBOT *Journals* 4 [We became] finally the prey of an insidious sand-bar, where after hours of sparring, . . . we again resume the slow ascent. **1872** *Harper's Mag.* March 542/2 She'll beach herself . . . if Boldman didn't spar her off good. **1872** MARK TWAIN *Roughing It* 21 [I remember] sandbars which we roosted on occasionally, and rested, and then got out our crutches and sparred over. **1883** *American* VI. 40 At low water, the vessel has often to be sparred over sand-bars.

sparada spəˈrɑdə, *n.* [Origin unknown.] A surf fish, *Cymatogaster aggregatus,* of the Pacific Coast. — **1891** *Cent.* 5796/1. **1896** JORDAN & EVERMANN *Check-List Fishes* 403 Sparada. Pacific Coast, from Port Wrangel, Alaska, to Todos Santos Bay.

∗**spare,** *n.* In the American game of bowling, the act of knocking down all the pins in two bowls. Hence **double spare,** a strike.

1843 *Knickerb.* XXII. 327 He was never guilty of a 'spare.' **1879** *Daily News* (London) 2 Sep. 3/1 Younger people . . . sought out the American ten-pin alleys, . . . and, in striving for spares and 'double spares,' esteemed themselves far in advance of their wise elders. **1884** BUNNER in *Harper's Mag.* Jan. 299/2 Strikes and spares were less common.

∗**spark,** *n.* In combs.: (1) **spark arrester,** any contrivance to prevent the escape of sparks from a locomotive; (2) **plug,** a pluglike device designed for screwing into the cylinder head of an internal combustion engine and so connected with the ignition system as to supply an electric spark for combustion, also transf.; (3) **protector,** =**spark arrester,** *obs.*

(1) **1835** *24th Congress* 1 Sess. H.R. Ex. Doc. No. 64, 24 Spark arrester, Alfred C. Jones, Portsmouth Va. **1905** *Forestry Bureau Bul.* No. 60, 29 It should also require the use of efficient spark arresters on all locomotives. — (2) **1908** *Country Life* Dec. 299/1 It won't cause fouling of spark-plugs. **1945** *Time* 30 April 72 Sparkplug of the new program is clear-eyed, billiard-bald President Case. **1945** *Good Housekeeping* Dec. 259/1, I put in four new sparkplugs, a new battery, and fresh bulbs in the headlights. — (3) **1880** *Bradstreet's* 22 May 3/3 There is a law . . . which inflicts a penalty upon companies neglecting to use 'spark protectors.'

∗**spark,** *v.* [Cf. *EDD spark up to,* in the same sense.] *intr.* To court, engage in courtship. Cf. **sparking,** *n.*

1787 TYLER *Contrast* II. ii, She promised not to spark it with Solomon Dyer while I am gone. **1813** PAULDING *Lay Sc. Fiddle* (1814) 192 A young man goes many miles to *spark.* **1890** CUSTER *Following Guidon* 314 Me and Eliza was mighty fond of each other, and off and on we was sparking. **1933** T. WILLIAMSON *Woods Colt* 29 Folks from Hokeville come here to spark.

b. Also *tr.*

1835 KENNEDY *Horse Shoe Robinson* II. 34, I'll be cursed if I wouldn't spark that little fusee myself. **1857** *Atlantic Mo.* I. 26/1 George . . . visited the farm-house for the laudable purpose of 'sparkin' Miss Sally. **1906** GUNTER *Prince in Garret* v, Isn't Ambigue sparking the actress? **1947** *Time* 29 Dec. 39/3 Eddy could then afford to spark the girls to the extent of 50¢.

sparked-back, *n. local.* (See quot. 1917.) — **1888** TRUMBULL *Names of Birds* 186 In Massachusetts . . . at Falmouth, [it is called] Sparked-back, Streaked-back, and Bishop Plover. **1917** *Birds of Amer.* I. 268 Ruddy Turnstone. *Arenaria interpres morinella.* . . . [Also called] Calico-jacket; Sparked-back; Streaked-back.

sparker ˈspɑrkɚ, *n.* One who sparks the girls. *Colloq.* — **1835** LONGSTREET *Ga. Scenes* 177 Come . . . all ye young sparkers, come listen to me. **1882** PECK *Sunshine* 169 These sparkers are looked upon by parents generally as a nuisance.

sparking ˈspɑrkɪŋ, *n.* Courting, making love. Often *to go a-sparking. Colloq.* Cf. ∗**spark,** *v.*

1804 FESSENDEN *Orig. Poems* (1806) 77 She's courted been, by many a lad, And knows how sparking's done. **1807** IRVING *Salmagundi* xv. 396 He went a sparking among the rosy country girls. **1888** EGGLESTON *Graysons* xiii, I've promised the mare to one uv the boys to-night—to—to go a-sparkin' weth.

attrib. **1852** CASEY *Two Yrs.* 49 Verily the Yankees are an ingenious people, and this 'sparking sofa' is their *chef d'oeuvre.* **1935** J. F. KELLY *Architect. Guide for Conn.* 21 Inside the items to be noted are the front stairs, with a finely molded closet string and 'sparking bench.'

sparkleberry ˈspɑrklˌbɛrɪ, *n.* =**farkleberry.** Also attrib.

1860 CURTIS *Woody Plants N.C.* 87 Sparkleberry. . . . The fruit is black and small. **1897** SUDWORTH *Arborescent Flora* 312. **1908** CHAM-

BERS *Firing Line* viii, A superb butterfly . . . came flitting about the sparkleberry bloom.

*sparrow, *n.* As the last term in **Brewer's, bush, chip, chipping, clay-colored, desert, desert song, Eastern Henslow's, English, European house, field, fox-colored, golden-crowned, grasshopper, ground, hair, Henslow's, Ipswich, lark, Lincoln's, Nelson's (sharp-tailed), nightingale, Nuttall's, Oregon vesper, sage, savanna, scarlet, sharp-tailed, social, song, swamp, Texas, Townshend, Townshend fox, tree, vesper, white-crowned, white-throated, wood sparrow.**

***sparse,** *a.* Of population or a settlement: Small and scattered, thin.

1827 SHERWOOD *Gaz. Georgia* 36 The land is poor and population sparse. **1856** EMERSON *Eng. Traits* 63 A sparse population gives this high worth to every man. **1871** HOWELLS *Wedding Journey* 259 The village . . . grows sparser as you draw near the Falls of Montmorenci.

***sparsely,** *adv.* In respect to the condition of a settled area: To a partial or incomplete extent.

1857 OLMSTED *Journey Texas* 365 The country . . . is sparsely settled. **1887** TOURGEE *Button's Inn* 54 Such comfortable lodging was rare in the sparcely-settled region where it stood. **1950** *World-Herald Mag.* (Omaha) 16 April 18/3 In days when Nebraska was sparsely settled, families would leave food on the table and put the latch string out when they left home.

***Spartan Band.** A New York City Locofoco club of 1840. *Obs.* — **1840** *Dly. Nat. Intelligencer* 5 Nov. 3/6 The Spartan Band (Locofoco) gave the Grinnell Club a drubbing.

spar torpedo. (See quot.) *Obs.* — **1917** MORGAN *Recollections* 85 Commander Matthew F. Maury buoyed the places in the river where he afterwards had placed what were probably the first floating mines used in war. We called them 'spar torpedoes' as the mines were attached to an anchored and floating spar.

***spat,** *v. intr.* To speak *up* and argue, to dispute, quarrel. *Colloq.*

1809 KENDALL *Travels* III. 292. The women had not much to say in politics, though now and then they would *spat up.* **1848** BARTLETT 323 *To spat,* to dispute; to quarrel, A low word. New England. **1885** BAYLOR *On Both Sides* 345 'The American ladies *spat* on all occasions, . . . I have read.' . . . 'We don't quarrel any more than any one else,' said Bijou, quite misunderstanding.

***spatter,** *n. thick as spatter(s)* and variants: Very thick or close. *Colloq.*

1823 *Dly. Nat. Intelligencer* 1 May 1/4 *Spatter.* A comparative word, 'as thick as spatter.' **1892** WILKINS *Young Lucretia* 156, I s'pose the berries are as thick as spatters. **1907** WHITE *Arizona Nights* 28 And outfits at that time were thicker'n spatter.

spatterdock ˈspætɚˌdɑk, *n.* Also **splatterdock.** [Origin obscure.] Any one of various plants of the genus *Nuphar* or the related *Nymphaea,* esp. the yellow water lily, *Nuphar advena.*

1813 WILSON *Ornithology* VIII. 30 [He] also eats the seeds of that species of nymphae usually called splatter docks. **1915** ARMSTRONG & THORNBER *Western Wild Flowers* 156 Indian Pond Lily, Spatter-dock *Nymphaea polysepala* (*Nuphar*). . . . In quiet mountain ponds we find these yellow flowers, on stout stems standing up out of the water. **1949** *Amer. Photography* Aug. 516/1 A not unlovely flower is the large yellow pond lily, cow lily, or spatter dock (*Nymphaea advena*).

***spatula,** *n.* **=paddlefish.** In full **spatula fish.** *Obs.*

1763 in *Amer. Sp.* XX. (1945) 50 The *Spatula* has its name from the form of its bill, which is about seven or eight inches long, an inch broad towards the head, and two inches and a half towards the extremity. **1781–2** JEFFERSON *Notes Va.* (1788) 6 [The Miss. R.] yields turtle of a peculiar kind, . . . spatula-fish of 50 lb. weight [etc.]. **1809** T. ASHE *Travels* 255 Trout, gar, pike, mullets, herrings, carp, spatula, a fish of fifty-six pounds weight.

spawn-eater ˈspɔnˌitɚ, *n.* A shiner or smelt, *Hudsonius hudsonius.* — [**1881** *Cassell's Nat. Hist.* V. 131 The Spawn-eater, or Smelt (*Leuciscus hudsonicus*), is a silvery fish . . . about three inches long, and occurs in Lake Superior.] **1896** JORDAN & EVERMAN *Check-List Fishes* 254 *Notropis hudsonius.* . . . Spawn-eater; Spot-tailed Minnow; Shiner. The Dakotas and Lake Superior to New York, and southward to South Carolina.

speakeasy ˈspikˌizɪ, *n.* [Perhaps inspired by *speak-softly-shop.* See Mencken, *Supp* I. 265.] An illicit drinking shop. *Slang.*

1889 *Cheney* (Wash.) *Sentinel* 13 Sep. 1/1 Unlicensed saloons in Pennsylvania are known as 'speak-easies.' **1923** COBB *Kansas* 15, I can tell a speak-easy as far as I can smell it! **1950** *Life* 2 Jan. 54 Moe Smith and Izzy Einstein were the most dreaded prohibition agents who ever closed down a speakeasy.

***speaker,** *n.*

1. Prob. a book of speeches suitable for school children. *Obs.*

1872 in ASHER & HEAL *Send No Money* (1942) xviii, I got a scarf and two speakers [school books] and sum candy razons for chrsmas.

2. *Speaker of the House,* the presiding officer of a house of representatives, as in a state legislature or in Congress.

1792 CUTLER in *Life & Corr.* I. 483 The Speaker of the House sent the Marshal at Arms to summon the Committee. **1832** WILLIAMSON *Maine* II. 10 The Governor . . . could negative as many as thirteen of the Councillors chosen, and also the Speakers of the House. **1949** *N.Y. Times Mag.* 3 July 14/2 A Senate Majority Leader, unlike the Speaker of the House, does not enjoy the help of strong and Spartan rules.

***speaking,** *n.* (See quots. 1863, 1903.) *Colloq.* Cf. **stump speaking.**

1842 BUCKINGHAM *Slave States* II. 245 The farmers of the neighbourhood . . . had come in to attend 'the speaking,' . . . the rival candidates for the governorship being both here . . . 'in the field.' **1863** HOPLEY *Life in South* I. 57 Then came the 'speaking,' as the sermon was called. **1903** *D.N.* II. 331 *Speaking,* a political meeting [s.e. Mo.]. 'There will be a speakin at the cross roads to-morrow and all the candidates will be there.' **1946** WILSON *Fidelity* 6 Any kind of program could be given there: a school exhibition, a political speaking [etc.].

attrib. **1890** *Harper's Mag.* Dec. 138/2 Ev'ry speakin' day—Friday 'twas—I was allers on han' . . . an' sometimes I'd practice the boys 'forehand till they knowed their pieces perfect. **1931** F. L. ALLEN *Only Yesterday* ii. 32 He would win them to his cause, making a speaking trip through the West.

b. speaking leaf, a piece of paper with writing or printing on it—in imitation of, or to suggest, Indian speech. *Obs.*

1804 BURK *Hist. Virginia* I. 109 The whole people were astonished at the prophetic properties of 'the speaking leaf.' **1835** WHITTIER *Poetical Works* (1894) 498/1 Will he make his mark, that it may be known, On the speaking-leaf, that he gives the land?

***spear,** *n.*

1. A filament *of* hair. *Obs.*

1852 STOWE *Uncle Tom* xxv, If they's to pull every spear o' har out o' my head it wouldn't do no good. **1853** G. C. HILL *Dovecote* 96, I'd no notion o' . . . gettin' my hair, every spear on't, pulled out o' my head. [**1868** ALCOTT *Little Women* I. 239 I'd do as much for our Jimmy any day if I had a spire of hair worth selling.]

2. In combs.: (1) **spear dance,** (see quot.), *rare;* (2) ***fish,** a local name for the quillback *q.v.;* (3) ***grass,** any one of various American species of meadow-grass, esp. *Poa pratensis;* (4) **head plug,** a plug of chewing tobacco of this brand, *obs.;* (5) ***man,** (see quot. 1891).

(1) 1791 J. LONG *Voyages* 35 The dances among the Indians are many and various, and to each of them there is a particular hoop. . . . The dead dance. . . . The spear dance [etc.]. — **(2) 1882** *Nat. Museum Bul.* No. 16, 119. **1896** JORDAN & EVERMANN *Check-List Fishes* 238 *Carpiodes velifer.* . . . Spearfish; Sailfish; Skimback. Mississippi Valley and southwestward to Rio Grande and upper Missouri. — **(3) 1747** FRANKLIN in *Amer. Jrnl. Science* IV. 359 The grass which comes in first, after ditching, is spear grass and white clover. **1884** VASEY *Agric. Grasses* 94 *Poa Pratensis.* (June grass, Kentucky blue grass, Spear grass). . . . It forms the principal constituent of pastures. **1939** *Nat. Geog. Mag.* Aug. 222/2 The preeminence of oak, hickory, beech, and chestnut in woodland, and of spear grass, drop-seed, . . . is due mainly to family pride. — **(4) 1902** WHITE *Blazed Trail* 37 He . . . assisted in loading the sleigh with a variety of things, from Spearhead plug to raisins.

(5) 1868 *Rep. Comm. Agric. 1867* 65 The Colorado bug or ten-lined spearman is reported to have produced poisonous effects on several persons who handled them incautiously. **1891** *Cent.* 5804/3 *Spearman,* . . . a book-name for any leaf-beetle of the genus *Doryphora.*

As the last term in **medicine spear.**

***spear,** *v. tr.* In harvesting tobacco, to pierce (the stalk) with a pointed stick. Also ***spearing,** *n.* — **1850** *Rep. Comm. Patents 1849: Agric.* 321 It may be put away in three different modes, by 'pegging,' 'spearing,' and 'splitting.' **1868** *Rep. Comm. Agric. 1867* 181 The plants should . . . be taken up and placed in small heaps of eight or ten plants, . . . to be speared in the field, and then carried on the sticks to the house.

spearing ˈspɪrɪŋ, *n.* [f. Du. *spiering,* a smelt.] (See quots.)

1884 GOODE *Fisheries* I. 612 Our Anchovy has recently been sold in considerable numbers in New York under the name 'Whitebait,' although the fishermen distinguish it from the true 'Whitebait,' the young of the herring, calling it 'Spearing.' **1903** T. H. BEAN *Fishes N.Y.* 359 The common silversides, or spearing, lives in Gravesend bay almost all the year. **1911** *Rep. Fisheries 1908* 307/1 The silver anchovy (*Anchovia browni*) . . . is also known as 'sardine' and 'spearing.'

spec spɛk, *n.* [Short for * *speculation.*] A commercial venture; speculation. *Colloq.*

1794 J. ADAMS *Works* I. 469 Many merchants have already made a noble *spec.* of the embargo by raising their prices. **1885** SIRINGO *Texas Cow Boy* 110, I got them for two and a half cents a piece, therefore made a better 'speck' than before. **1946** *Sat. Ev. Post* 11 May 28/2 The wandering motorist lacks such background and, if he takes the boulevard on spec, presently finds himself going southeast.

* **special,** *a.* and *n.*

1. *n.* A special article or communication to a newspaper.

1867 *Ore. State Jrnl.* 19 Jan. 2/3 A Washington special says that [etc.]. **1894** SHUMAN *Steps into Journalism* 124 The typical 'special' is a long article making some pretentions to exhaustiveness. **1906** *N.Y. Ev. Post* 20 Nov. 8 The Frankfurter Zeitung published a special from Berlin, covering the inaugural lecture of the Roosevelt professor.

2. A free-lance writer for a newspaper.

1877 *Harper's Mag.* Dec. 48/2 The price paid to outsiders, or 'specials,' . . . is about eight dollars per column.

3. In a store, restaurant, etc., a product which is specially featured.

1913 LONDON *Valley of Moon* 337 She had . . . persuaded the proprietor . . . to make a 'special' of her wares.

4. *a.* Of legislation: Having limited application.

1803 *Mass. Priv. & Sp. Statutes* p. iii. (Ernst), Private and special Acts of the Commonwealth. **1917** *Corpus Juris* XII. 773/1 One who is active in procuring the adoption of a special or local statute may not question its constitutionality.

5. In special combs.: (1) **special agent,** an agent whose authority is limited (see also quot. 1880); (2) **car,** a railroad car devoted to a particular use; (3) **correspondent,** a newspaper correspondent employed for a particular purpose; (4) **delivery,** see as a main entry; (5) **deposit,** (see quot.); (6) **election,** an election held at other than the regular time, and for a particular purpose; (7) **enforcement officer,** an enforcement officer with limited authority; (8) **interest,** the private, ulterior interests of a particular group or, *pl.*, the groups having such interests; (9) **partner,** one associated with others in carrying on a business but having only limited authority and liability; (10) **partnership,** (see quot.); (11) **relief,** (see quot.); (12) **request envelope,** an envelope upon which directions for return are printed; (13) **session,** = **extraordinary session;** (14) **student,** a student who does not take a regular course of study, and does not expect to receive a diploma or degree.

(1) 1840 *Hunt's Merch. Mag.* II. 261, I have despatched one of the special agents of this [Post office] department to Europe. **1880** *Harper's Mag.* March 553/2 Connected with the transmission of the United States mails are certain officials called 'special agents.' **1950** *World-Herald Mag.* (Omaha) 9 April 14/5 The special agents searched the house. — **(2) 1889** *Chi. D. News* 23 April 1/2, 'I travel in my own special car,' said he, 'like Jay Gould or Vanderbilt.' **1906** *Springfield W. Republican* 19 July 16 The annual clambake of the Hartford business men's association was held Friday, some 200 arriving in special cars. — **(3) 1865** *Three Yrs. Among Working Classes U.S.* 33 At every point on sea or land where the services of a special correspondent could be of advantage to the public. **1889** *Chi. D. News* 20 April 1/4 The town is full of special correspondents.

(5) 1859 BARTLETT 432 *Special deposit,* a deposit made in a bank subject to the control of the depositor, and which is not made a part of the funds of the bank to be used by it in its business. — **(6) 1866** *Wkly. New Mexican* 22 Dec. 2/2 One of the senators from San Miguel county having resigned, a special election was held. **1949** *Capital Jrnl.* (Salem, Ore.) 27 July 1/1 Final step in perfecting the consolidation will be a special election in Salem within the next few months. — **(7) 1911** *Okla. Session Laws* 3 Legisl. 165 The office of Special Enforcement Officer is hereby established and created. — **(8) 1910** G. PINCHOT *Fight for Conservation* 134 The people of the United States believe that, as a whole, the Senate and the House no longer represent the voters by whom they were elected, but the special interests by whom they are controlled. **1914** *Cyclo. Amer. Govt.* I. 147/2 The successful boss makes use of both of the party machines as a most reliable means of deceiving the public and guarding the special interests which he is hired to guard. — **(9) 1828** KENT *Commentaries* III. 13 The special partners may receive an annual interest on the capital invested, provided there be no reduction of the original capital. **1839** MARRYAT *Diary in Amer.* 1 Ser. II. 251 In America, if a person wishes to become a special partner (a sleeping partner) in any concern, he may do so to any extent he pleases. **1890** *Cent.* 4309/1 If the statute governing partnerships is violated the special partner becomes liable as a *general partner*.

(10) 1859 BARTLETT 432 *Special Partnership.* A partnership limited to a particular branch of business, or to one particular subject.—*Judge Story.* — **(11) 1865** *Atlantic Mo.* Feb. 237/1 The immense collection of back pay, bounties, pensions, and prize-money . . . is Special Relief. — **(12) 1893** *Cong. Rec.* 18 Feb. 1802/2 The issue of special-request envelopes has been going on ever since 1865. **1893** CUSHING *Story of P.O.* 380 There are more special request envelopes issued now than of any other kind. — **(13) 1846** *Whig Almanac 1847* 10/1 Mr. Van Buren called a Special Session of Congress. **1900** *Cong. Rec.* 14 Feb. 1801/1 The governor, by force of public opinion, was forced to call the legislature in special session to pass this election law. **1950** *Time* 3 April 22/3 Dewey proclaimed that the people of New York were going to have rent control even if he had to call a special session. — **(14) 1894** *Harper's Mag.* April 768/2 Yale has discouraged the attendance of 'special' students who are not graduates of any college nor pursuing any of the recognized courses for a degree. **1942** *Gen. Cat. U. of Wis.* 45 [They] may apply to the Executive Committee of the College of Letters and Science for admission as 'special students not candidates for a degree.'

special delivery. Delivery of mail by special messenger ahead of the usual routine delivery schedule; a letter so delivered. Also attrib., and as adv.

1886 RITTENHOUSE *Maud* 368 Eliza brought me a special delivery letter from my good boy. **1904** *Harper's Mag.* Feb. 462/2 And what a lucky chance that brought me a 'special delivery.' **1909** STRATTON-PORTER *Girl of Limberlost* 327 If I'd put them special delivery on the morning train, she'd get them in the late afternoon. **1924** CROY *R.F.D. No. 3* 46 She sent it off with a special delivery stamp. **1947** *Christian Sci. Mon.* 15 Jan. 6/8 A Special Delivery stamp will assure quick delivery of a letter that is sent to a place where extra postmen are employed.

***specialist,** *n.* (See quot. 1900.) Cf. **sob specialist.** — **1900** S. A. NELSON *A B C Wall St.* 130 Specialist.—A broker who confines his attention to one, or a very few stocks. **1912** DREISER *Financier* 81 You could never guess what stock was being 'nursed' or 'washed' or being handled by a specialist.

specialty performer. A vaudeville actor or actress who engages in special types of entertainment. — **1888** G. O. SEILHAMER *Hist. Amer. Theatre* II. 118 But in a letter addressed to Wall, the manager, by Dr. Bayley, a specialty performer, who gave entertainments in this country as early as 1752.

* **specie,** *n.* In combs.: (1) **specie basis,** an amount of specie serving as a basis or reserve for paper money, also fig.; (2) **Circular,** an order issued at the instance of President Jackson in July, 1836, instructing officers of the Treasury to accept only gold and silver in payment for public land; (3) **dollar,** a coined dollar; (4) **-paying bank,** a bank which redeemed its notes in specie, *obs.*

(1) 1832 D. WEBSTER *Works* 397 The general circulation has been extended too far for the specie basis on which it rests. **1863** LOWELL *Biglow P.* 2 Ser. vii. 180 To make a sneakin' truce Without no moral specie-basis. — **(2) 1837** *Cong. Globe* App. 29 Sep. 339 [The money flowed to Mobile] by the aid of the far-famed Specie circular, in 'mint drops' and 'hard currency.' **1894** LEAVITT *Our Money Wars* 69 Mr. Webster [in 1837] ascribed the distress to the interference of the Government with the currency, and to the 'Specie Circular.' — **(3)** *a***1821** BIDDLE *Autobiog.* 238 State Island money [in Pa.] . . . soon depreciated to eight for one specie dollar. **1900** *Cong. Rec.* 1 Feb. 1385/2 The standard specie dollar . . . is the standard and medium by which other things . . . are redeemed. — **(4) 1818** *Niles' Reg.* XIV. 207/2 The incorporated banks of Maryland . . . whose bills are 12 per cent. below the paper of what are called specie-paying banks. **1845** *Big Bear Ark.* 143 It can boast of the only specie-paying bank in the State. **1875** *Chi. Tribune* 6 Oct. 4/4 The Whigs . . . proposed that the Government should receive in payment of public lands the notes of *specie-paying banks.*

As the last term in **corn specie.**

* **speck,** *n.*[1]

1. A plant disease characterized by blasted seed grains, or speckled fruit or leaves.

1771 WASHINGTON *Diaries* II. 24 My Wheat every where being much Injurd, by the Speck or Spot. **1878** *Ill. Dept. Agric. Trans.* XIV. 126 The 'speck' . . . affects some few varieties [of fruit]. **1909** *Cent. Supp.* 1247/2 *White speck of tobacco,* a disease on the leaves of tobacco producing small white spots caused by the fungus *macrosporium tabacinum.*

2. (See quots.)

1877 *Lyceum Nat. Hist. N.Y. Ann. 1876* 311 *Boleosoma Stigmœum.* . . . Known to boys and fishermen as *Speck.* **1891** *Cent.* 5808/2 *Speck,* . . . a percoid fish, *Ulocentra stigmœa* of Jordan, common in ponds of the hill-country from Georgia to Louisiana.

3. A bit, in the least. *Colloq.*

1843 HALIBURTON *Attaché* I Ser. I. ii, I didn't like it a spec. **1889** JEWETT *B. Leicester* 87, I s'pose you ain't kind of flaunted it a little speck. **1934** VINES *Green Thicket World* 153 It would not make a speck of difference in a thousand years.

speck spɛk, *n.*[2] [Du. *spek,* G. *speck,* bacon.]

1. Bacon (see also quot. 1886).

1691 *Ann. Albany* (1850) II. 116 The plaintiff demands 180 lb. *speck.* **1809** *Lancaster* (Pa.) *Jrnl.* 12 Sep. (Th.), He goes out almost every week to eat speck with the country folks. **1886** *Amer. Philol. Assoc. Trans.* App. p. xii, 'Speck' is . . . the generic term applied to all kinds of fat meat. **1936** *Pa. Dutch Cook Book* 11 Speck und Beans (Ham with Green String Beans).

2. speck and applejees, (see quot. 1863).

1842 *Boston Transcript* 14 Dec. 2/3 We noticed and tasted of . . . a dish of *speekland appletjes.* **1863** *Ladies' Repository* Jan. 55/2 'Speck and appeljees' is a slight modification of *speken appeltjes* the name for fried pork and apples among the Hollanders.

* **specklebelly,** *n.* **1.** The white-fronted goose. **2.** =**gadwall. 3.** (See quot.)

(1) 1874 COUES *Birds N.W.* 547 The 'Speckle-bellies,' as they are called in California, associate freely at all times with both the Snow and Hutchins' Geese. — **(2) 1888** TRUMBULL *Names of Birds* 24 Gadwall. . . . Though rather a rare visitant on Long Island, it is known (when it does appear) at Moriches as Speckle-Belly. **1917** *Birds of Amer.* I. 118. — **(3) 1891** *Cent.* 5808/3 *Speckle-belly,* . . . a trout or char, as the common brook-trout of the United States, *Salvelinus fontinalis.*

* **speckled,** *a.* In combs., esp. in local names of birds, fishes, etc.: (1) **speckled alder,** the hoary alder, *Alnus incana;* (2) **belly,** =**speckled brant;** (3) **-bill coot,** the surf scoter; (4) **brant,** (see quots.); (5) **brook trout,** =**speckled trout;** (6) **Canada warbler,** the Canada warbler, *Wilsonia canadensis,* of northern North America; (7) **cheek woodpecker,** =**Texas woodpecker;** (8) **cut-worm,** (see quot. 1909); (9) **garrupa,** see quot. 1884 *s.v.* **garrupa;** (10) **grunt,** (see quot.); (11) **hen,** the small-mouthed black bass; (12) **lady,** (see quot.), *obs.,* cf. **speculator,** *n.;* (13) **mountain trout,** =**speckled trout;** (14) **pea,** *S.* =**whippoorwill pea;** (15) **snake,** app. one form or another of the king snake, *Lampropeltis getulus, obs.;* (16) **thrush,** = ***thrasher;** (17) **trout,** any one of various trout, as the brook trout and the rainbow trout, having a speckled appearance; (18) **woodpecker,** the downy woodpecker.

(1) *a***1862** THOREAU *Maine Woods* 307 The speckled or hoary alder . . . abounds everywhere along the muddy banks of rivers and lakes. **1884** SARGENT *Rep. Forests* 165. — **(2) 1888** [see **speckled brant**]. — **(3) 1888** TRUMBULL *Names of Birds* 103 At Stratford, [Conn., it is known as the] Speckled-Bill Coot. **1917** *Birds of Amer.* I. 151. — **(4) 1888** TRUMBULL *Names of Birds* 11 American White-fronted goose, . . . Laughing goose, . . . known in various parts of the West as Prairie Brant, Speckled Belly, and Speckled Brant. **1917** *Birds of Amer.* I. 158 White-fronted Goose. *Anser albifrons gambeli.* . . . [Also called] Speckled Brant.

(5) 1869 *Rep. U.S. Comm. Agric. 1868* 322 [It is] rank folly to allow so great a delicacy as the speckled brook trout (*Salmo fontinalis*) to become extinct. — **(6) 1865** BURROUGHS in *Atlantic Mo.* May 521/1 The Winter-Wren . . . is one of those birds . . . that, like the Speckled Canada Warbler and the Hermit-Thrush, only the privileged ones hear. — **(7) 1917** *Birds of Amer.* II. 144. **1940** JAEGER *Desert Wild Flowers* 19 The red-shafted flicker and the little speckled-check [*sic*] or cactus woodpecker dig holes in the fibrous trunks and branches. — **(8) 1884** *Rep. Comm. Agric.* 296 The Speckled Cut-Worm. . . . This cut-worm was also one of the species described and figured by us in the first report on the insects of Missouri for 1868. **1909** *Cent. Supp.* 331/1 Speckled cutworm, the larva of *Mamestra subjuncta.*

(10) 1814 MITCHILL *Fishes N.Y.* 406 Speckled Grunts. *Labrus fulvomaculatus.* . . . There are rows of yellow speckled stripes, almost parallel to each other. — **(11) 1888** GOODE *Amer. Fishes* 56 'Marsh Bass,' . . . and 'Speckled Hen' are other names applied to one or both species [of bass]. — **(12) 1910** *Pub. Miss. Hist. Soc.* XI. 92 Negro traders were called 'speculators' by the white people and 'speckled ladies' by the negroes. — **(13) 1877** H. C. HODGE *Arizona* 39 They are well stocked with the real speckled mountain trout. — **(14) 1854** DAVIS *Farm Bk.* 53 Planted early speckled pea (6 weeks) in the gin field.

(15) 1778 CARVER *Travels* 487 The Speckled Snake is an aqueous reptile about two feet and half in length, but without venom. Its skin . . . is used by the Americans as a cover for the handles of whips, and it renders them very pleasing to the sight. **1789** MORSE *Amer. Geog.* 61 Of the Snakes which infest the United States, are the following viz. . . . Speckled. **1836** D. B. EDWARD *Hist. Texas* iv. 76 Occasionally . . . one will meet with a hissing snake, or a green snake—a speckled snake. — **(16) 1912** N. WOODROW *Sally Salt* 11 That speckled thrush is three days earlier than usual. — **(17) 1805** LEWIS in *L. & Clark Exped.* II. (1904) 150 These trout . . . resemble our mountain or speckled trout. **1857** HAMMOND *Northern Scenes* 43 He will not . . . take the speckled trout that we find in [northern N.Y.]. **1902** HULBERT *Forest Neighbors* (1903) 60 Small, bright carmine spots . . . gave him one of his *aliases,* the 'Speckled Trout.' — **(18) 1806** LEWIS in *L. & Clark Exped.* V. (1905) 136 Saw the speckled woodpecker, bee martin and log cock or large woodpecker.

* **spectacle,** *n.* **1.** (See quot. 1856.) *Obs.* **2. spectacle coot, duck,** the surf scoter.

(1) 1779 J. ADAMS *Diary* Wks. (1851) III. 210 Fruit, cakes, ice-cream, *spectacles.* **1856** FERGUSSON *America* 8 Theatrical representations were gradually introduced [into Boston] under the name of 'spectacles,' in connexion with museums, until at last the mask was thrown aside entirely, and theatres are now built and used as such. — **(2) 1844** *Nat. Hist. N.Y., Zoology* II. 335 The Box Coot, Spectacle Duck, . . . is very common on the coast of New-York during the winter. **1917** *Birds of Amer.* I. 151 Surf Scoter. *Oidemia perspicillata.* . . . [Also called] Box Coot; Spectacle Coot; Butterboat-billed Coot.

As the last term in **bridge, double, Franklin spectacles.**

spectacled eider. An Alaskan eider duck, *Arctonetta fischeri,* having eyes set in white plumage rimmed with black. — **1872** COUES *Key to Birds* 292 Spectacled Eider, . . . a whitish space round eye, bounded by black. **1917** *Birds of Amer.* I. 145/1 The Spectacled Eider is essentially an Alaskan Duck.

spectacularity spɛkˌtækjəˈlærɪtɪ, *n.* The quality of being spectacular. *Rare.* — **1883** HOWELLS *Woman's Reason* xii, The bare spectacularity of the keeping . . . must all be eloquent of a boarding-house. **1891** ——— *Imperative Duty* i, Boston . . . was not like Liverpool in a certain civic grandiosity, a sort of lion-and-unicorn spectacularity.

spectatorio ˌspɛktəˈtorɪo, *n.* [f. *spect*acle+or*atorio.*] A form of entertainment, devised by James Steele MacKaye (1842–94), which was to have combined oratorio, spectacle, pantomime, etc. Hence **spectatorium,** the building which was to have housed this production. *Obs.* — **1892** in P. MACKAYE *Epoch* II. 337 A *Spectatorium* . . . is an entirely new species of building, invented and devised for the production of a new order of entertainment entitled a *spectatorio.* **1894** *Pittsburgh Dispatch* 28 Feb., Up to the day when work was abandoned upon the Spectatorium building, $850,000 had been sunk in the enterprise.

Spectorama ˌspɛktəˈræmə, *n.* (See quot.) *Obs.* — **1898** *Chi. Inter-Ocean* 23 Oct. 15/5 The Spectorama on Madison street reminds one of the dream of Steele Mackaye, both in the name and the delightful effects produced. Real water, real boats, are nicely blended with built-up fortifications, and these again blended with painted scene. The sinking of the Merrimac is a very interesting and picturesque exhibition.

spectral owl. The great gray owl, *Scotiaptex nebulosa,* coming rarely as a straggler into the northern and northeastern parts of the U.S.

1884 COUES *Key to Birds* (ed. 2) 509. **1912** W. B. BARROWS *Mich. Bird Life* 310 Great Gray Owl . . . Spectral Owl. **1917** *Birds of Amer.* II. 105.

* **spectrograph,** *n.* An apparatus for photographing the spectrum.

1884 *Amer. Acad. Proc.* XIX. 238 In July, 1876, several photographs of the spectrum of Vega were taken with an apparatus which Dr. Draper called the 'spectrograph.' **1889** *Internat. Ann., Anthony's Photog. Bul.* II. 394 The color sensitiveness of the plate I find out with the aid of my Quartz spectrograph. **1893** *Nation* 16 Feb. 126/2 With the eleven-inch Draper spectrograph nearly a thousand photographs were taken.

Hence **spectrographic,** *a.*

1901 *Sci. Amer. Supp.* 6 April 21122/3 The great importance of the temperature factor in spectrographic investigations is recognized by all observers.

* **speculator,** *n.* A trafficker in Negro slaves. *Obs.*

1852 STOWE *Uncle Tom* xx, I was raised by a speculator, with lots of others. **1899** CHESNUTT *Wife of His Youth* 85 Don't you remember Cicely—Cicely whom you sold, with her child, to the speculator? **1910** *Pub. Miss. Hist. Soc.* XI. 92 Negro traders were called 'speculators' by the white people.

As the last term in **cotton, land, Negro, real estate, ticket speculator.**

*speech, *n.* **1.** Among Indians, a communication relating to matters of concern to an entire tribe or nation. **2. speech belt,** among Indians, a belt of wampum relating to a conference or council. Both *obs.*

(1) **1690** SEWALL *Letter-Book* I. 110 Writt to Mr. Mather . . . enclosing the Print of the Maquas speeches. **1785** DENNY *Journal* 62 Three Shawanee Indians arrived with a speech from their nation. **1808** in *Niles' Reg.* II. 342/2 A Pottawattimie Indian had arrived at the towns, with a speech from the British. — (2) **1753** WASHINGTON *Writings* I. 28 The King . . . offered the French Speech-Belt which had before been demanded.

As the last term in **abolition, buncombe, dinner, free, keynote, palmetto, stump speech.**

*speed, *n.*

1. *Baseball.* The ability of a pitcher to throw balls hard. *Colloq.*

1886 CHADWICK *Art of Batting* 73 Never mind what his speed or twist is. **1910** *Baseball Mag.* Sep. 88/1 He has great speed, when right, knows the batters, and consequently wins many games. **1945** H. W. RAPER *What This World Needs* 219 So many men are like the pitcher. Plenty of speed but poor control.

2. In combs.: (1) **speed cop,** a police officer who enforces speed laws; (2) **wagon,** a motor vehicle, *jocular;* (3) **way,** a road on which the speeding of harness horses is permissible, a road reserved for fast traffic, a race course for automobiles.

(1) **1925** *Dollar Mag.* Dec. 205 Speed-cops are posted on the highways with powerful motor-cycles to catch unwary speeders. **1948** *Sat. Ev. Post* 3 July 77/3 Speed cops still speak politely to me. — (2) **1931** *Randolph Enterprise* (Elkins, W.Va.) 19 Nov. 5/3 We knew there wouldn't be so many speed wagons or death wagons running to and fro. — (3) **1894** *Voice* 28 June, New York has millions of dollars to spend upon its uptown parks and speedways. **1903** *N.Y. Times* 16 Aug., The owners of rapid roadsters are devoting no inconsiderable portion of their summer leisure to spirited brushes on the new speedway. **1947** *Harper's Mag.* Jan. 70/1 He took up the cudgels for a family of nine which was evicted and against a loan shark and a project to widen a street and turn it into a 'speedway.'

As the last term in **schedule speed.**

*speeder, *n.*

1. (See quot. 1876.)

1847 *Knickerb.* XXX. 517 A few [girls] tend the 'warpers,' the 'spoolers,' and the 'speeders.' **1876** KNIGHT 2261/1 *Speeder,* (*Cotton-manufacture,*) a machine invented by Mason as a substitute for the bobbin and fly frame, by which slivers of cotton from the carding-machine are slightly twisted, and thereby converted into rovings. **1900** *Everybody's Mag.* I. 593/1 The 'speeder' . . . rolls two of the slubber's threads into one.

2. One who rides or drives at a rapid rate of speed (see also quot. 1891).

1891 *Cent.* 5814/2 *Speeder,* . . . one who or that which moves with great swiftness, as a horse. **1893** *Columbus* (O.) *Dispatch* 6 Sep., A certain good-fellowship has been established between the speeders and the city, and . . . confidence may be placed in the promises of the local wheelmen. **1948** *Chi. D. News* 20 Sep. 14/5 At long, long last the frantic automobile speeder has met his master, the 'jay walker' on a wheel.

*speedwell, *n.* As the last term in **purslane, skullcap speedwell.**

*spell, *n.*

1. A period of being ill, out of sorts, or irritable; an attack of illness, indisposition, etc.

[**1748** in J. NORTON *Redeemed Captive* (1870) 42 He was taken at sea, June 24, 1746, and died of the bloody flux, after a tedious spele of it.] **1806** W. PETTIGREW *Lett.* 26 Nov. (Univ. N.C. MS), My brother in law has had a Spell of Sickness but is recovered. **1869** STOWE *Oldtown Folks* 171 When Hepsy does get beat out she has *spells,* and she goes on awful. **1896** JEWETT *Pointed Firs* 21 She had also made dark reference to his having 'spells' of some unexplainable nature.

2. *A spell ago* (or *back*), some time ago. *Colloq.*

1834 C. A. DAVIS *Lett. J. Downing* 364 Our folks . . . saw this a long spell ago. **1853** *Knickerb.* XLII. 653 'When?' 'A spell ago—an' more.' **1886** HOWELLS *Minister's Charge* 14, I don't know as you got a letter from me a spell back. **1917** FREEMAN & KINGSLEY *Alabaster Box* 48 There was another party looking at the place a spell back.

3. spellbinder, an orator, esp. a political stump speaker, who holds his hearers spellbound.

1888 *N.Y. Tribune* 15 Nov. 6/1 A big and successful dinner was given at Delmonico's by the Republican Orators—'Spellbinders'—who worked during the recent campaign. **1911** SAUNDERS *Col. Todhunter* 41 Emotional endowment . . . has made Missouri 'spell binders' long famous on the stump. **1948** *Dly. Ardmoreite* (Ardmore, Okla.) 23 July 6/6 Domestic policies that the Wallace party spellbinders have been complaining about thus far in their campaign include civil rights, high prices, housing, the Taft-Hartley act.

Also **spellbinding,** *n.* and *a.*

1896 *N.Y. Wkly. Witness* 30 Dec. 13/1 He prayed to be permitted to try his hand at spellbinding. **1945** *Chi. Tribune* 18 Nov. VII. 1/7 Ray had sat on a railroad track, so engrossed with the talk of a spell-binding orator that he never heard the frate train.

As the last term in **fainting, nooning, play, wood spell.**

*spell, *v.*

1. *tr.* To test (a person) in spelling. *Obs.*

1866 C. H. SMITH *Bill Arp* 171 He then spelt him right straight along on all sorts of big words, and little words. **1867** LACKLAND *Homespun* 138 The hour arrived for us to be spelled round out of the little Walker dictionary.

2. In colloq. phrases: (1) *To spell able,* (see quot.); (2) *to spell baker,* [*baker* was the first word of two syllables in Webster's "Blue-back Speller" and this expression may in some way be an allusion to it] ?to be pretty good, to be up to the mark, *obs.;* (3) *to spell down,* in a spelling match, to spell a word an opponent has missed and so force him to sit down as a token of his withdrawal from the contest; (4) *to spell up,* to go up towards the head of a class by spelling words which others have missed.

(1) **1909** *Cent. Supp.* 2/2 *To spell able,* to be able; to have all the ability and strength needed (for some particular purpose). [Colloq.] — (2) **1868** LONGFELLOW *Poetical Works* (1893) 504/1 If an old man will marry a young wife, Why then . . . he must spell Baker! — (3) **1853** B. F. TAYLOR *Jan. & June* 259 The struggle is, to spell each other down. **1903** FOX *Little Shepherd* iv, [He] spelled them both down before the whole school. **1949** *L.A. Times* 28 April II. 5/8 The whole class had to line up for spelling bees and those who were spelled down generally at least got hardened to it and tried to do a bit better next time. — (4) E. STONE *Life of Howland* i. 17 After many trials, he succeeded in 'spelling up' next to the head [*sc.* of the class].

spelldown 'spel,daʊn, *n.* =**spelling match.** — **1943** *Nat. Geog. Mag.* Dec. 755 Among cherished memories of 'the days of real sport,' the old-fashioned 'spelldown' takes high rank. **1949** *Chi. D. News* 26 Oct. 20/2 The contest for District 8 is the initial spelldown in a series of eliminations.

*speller, *n.* **1.** A seeker *after* something. *Rare.* **2.** A spelling-book.

(1) **1796** PAINE *Writings* III. (1896) 217 John Adams . . . it is known was always a speller after places and offices. — (2) **1864** WEBSTER 1269/2 *Speller,* . . . a book containing exercises in spelling; a spelling-book. **1881** *Harper's Mag.* Dec. 107/2 Mary still keeps the green-covered 'speller' in which she and Sam studied their lessons together. **1947** R. K. LEAVITT *Noah's Ark* 9 Then he [Webster] compiled his Speller.

*spelling, *n.*

1. A spelling bee or spelling school. *Obs.*

1889 RILEY *Pipes o' Pan* 45 How her face used to look in the twilight As I tuck her to spellin'.

2. In combs.: (1) **spelling bee,** a social gathering at which competitive spelling is the chief diversion, also attrib.; (2) **class,** a class in spelling; (3) **club,** a club of those eager to learn to spell, *obs.;* (4) **fight,** =next, *humorous, rare;* (5) **match,** a contest in spelling; (6) ***school,** =**spelling bee;** (7) **tournament,** an elaborate spelling bee.

(1) **1875** *London Times* 16 April 4/4 The 'Spelling Bee,' a New England invention, . . . has made rapid strides over the country [i.e., the U.S.]. **1881** NEVIN *Vignettes of Travel* 154 Witness . . . the sweep of the praying-band or spelling-bee excitement from one ocean to the other. **1949** *Chi. D. News* 16 Dec. 1/7 (*heading*), Here's Last Spelling Bee This Year. — (2) **1871** EGGLESTON *Hoosier Schoolm.* 25 Hence the necessity for those long spelling-classes at the close of each forenoon and afternoon session of the school. **1944** CLARK *Pills* 182 Spelling classes in schools, however, were anything but frolics. — (3) **1882** THAYER *From Log-Cabin* 215 His two cousins . . . were members of his Spelling Club a few years before. — (4) **1876** MARK TWAIN *Tom Sawyer* xxi. 170 There were reading exercises and a spelling-fight.

(5) **1845** in *P.M.L.A.* LVI. (June, 1941) 501, I recollect that it used to be the custom that the head of the first class and the next should choose sides for a 'spelling match' once a week or so. **1946** WILSON *Fidelity* 149 At that time we had a spelling match, with the entire school 'choosed up.' — (6) **1832** *Indiana Mag. Hist.* XV. 241 In the evening I appointed a spelling school at which I invited all the parents to attend. **1883** *Harper's Mag.* Sep. 643/1 We are in a fever about

the Carnival, the paring bee, the spelling school, or whatever it is called. **1948** DICK *Dixie Frontier* 138 Backwoods debating societies, spelling schools, story-telling, and singing helped to while away the time. — (7) **1871** EGGLESTON *Hoosier Schoolm.* 25 Time [elapsed] between the appointing of the spelling tournament and the actual occurrence of that remarkable event.

*** Spencer,** *n.* A breech-loading magazine rifle of a type invented by C. M. Spencer (1833–1922). Usu. attrib.

1869 in *Frontier* IX. (1929) 155 We went out and found one young warrior killed. . . . He was hit by a Spencer ball and must have been shot either by Louis or me. **1873** BEADLE *Undevel. West* 545 My horse, bridle, saddle, lariat, gun (a Spencer) and two Navajo blankets cost me two hundred dollars. **1949** *Exciting Western* May 36/2 The .52 Spencer he kept under the bunk was a souvenir of Malvern Hill.

b. Esp. **Spencer carbine, rifle.**

1866 F. KIRKLAND *Bk. Anecdotes* 660/1 Harris ordered the skirmish line forward, . . . with orders to silence the troublesome battery . . . with the aid of the Spencer rifle. **1872** ROE *Army Lett.* 43, I was given a Spencer carbine to shoot (a short magazine rifle used by the cavalry). **1915** YOUNG *Hard Knocks* 36 Sutherland stood just to one side with his Spencer carbine ready for instant use. **1949** *Nat. Hist.* March 129/2 One of the pursuers did boggle at shooting the children with his .56 caliber Spencer rifle: *It tore them up so.*

***sperling,** *n.* A local name for a young or immature herring. — **1884** GOODE *Fisheries* I. 550 The name 'Sperling,' employed by our own fishermen of Cape Ann to denote the young herrings. **1911** *Rep. Fisheries 1908* 311/1 'Sperling' and 'brit' denote differences in the age of the fish.

sphagnum frog. A frog, *Rana virgatipes*, of medium size, 2 to 2½ inches, discovered at Atlantic City in 1891 in stagnant water where sphagnum moss, water lilies, etc., were growing. — **1934** WEBSTER. **1950** *Nat. Geog. Mag.* April 512/2 Associated with it is another amphibian, the carpenter frog, or sphagnum frog (*Rana virgatipes* . . .). Its hammering call is heard in similar places, but its distribution continues into Georgia.

***sphinx,** *n.* As the last term in **five-spotted, grapevine sphinx.**

*** spice,** *n.*

1. **=spicebush.** *Obs.*

1842 *Cultivator* IX. 82/2 Remove no logs; grub no spice; it costs too much. The bushes afford the finest amusement for fat cattle. **1849** CHAMBERLAIN *Indiana Gazetteer* 389 The prevailing timber is oak, hickory, ash . . . spice and pawpaw.

2. In combs.: (1) **spiceberry,** any one of various aromatic shrubs, esp. the wintergreen; (2) **bitters,** (see quot.), *obs.;* (3) **bush,** see as a main entry; (4) **oak,** (see quot.); (5) **root,** (*a*) the barren strawberry, *Waldsteinia fragarioides,* (*b*) the dewdrop, *Dalibarda repens;* (6) **sweeting,** (see quot.), *obs.;* (7) **tea,** tea made from the roots or leaves of a spicebush; (8) **tree,** (see quot.); (9) **wood, =spicebush,** also attrib.; (10) **wood tea, =spice tea,** also **spicewood tea party.**

(1) **1792** IMLAY *Western Territory* 216 There is a variety of shrubs in every part of the country, the principal of which are the myrtle and spice berry. **1871** DE VERE 404 The queen of them all is said to be the lovely, creeping snowberry . . . ; although others give the prize to the spice-berry. **1897** SUDWORTH *Arborescent Flora* 306 *Eugenia procera. . . .* Red Stopper (Fla.). Spiceberry (Fla.). — (2) **1894** ROBINSON *Danvis Folks* 7 These 'ere spice bitters is compaounded of several nat'ral plants, but the main ingrejencies is fever-bush an' bayberry. — (4) **1807** C. SCHULTZ *Travels* II. 24 Natural fruit and forest trees, which I noticed on the banks of the Ohio: . . . black thorn, Jerusalem oak, or spice oak.

(5) (*a*) **1821** *Mass. H.S. Coll.* 2 Ser. IX. 149 *Dalibarda fragarioides,* . . . Spice-root, dry strawberry, [is indigenous in Vt.]. (*b*) **1833** EATON *Botany* (ed. 6) 120 *Dalibarda repens,* spice root, false violet. . . . Troy, rare. — (6) **1850** *N. Eng. Farmer* II. 359/2 There are several other varieties of apple under the name of Spice Sweeting. — (7) **1856** CARTWRIGHT *Autobiog.* 25 We had sage, bohea, cross-vine, spice and sassafras teas. **1871** DE VERE 395 Spice-tea is . . . made from another laurel common at the South, the spice-bush (*Laurus benzoin*). — (8) **1884** SARGENT *Rep. Forests* 120 *Umbellularia Californica. . . .* California Laurel. Spice Tree. . . . Rogue River valley, Oregon, south through the California coast ranges to San Diego county. — (9) **1756** KALM *Resa* II. 204. **1788** J. MAY *Jrnl.& Lett.* 66, [I] am applying the leaves of spice-wood, soaked in vinegar. **1800** TATHAM *Agric. & Commerce* 61 Particularly cane-brake, sugar-tree, and spice-wood bottom. **1947** *Chi. Tribune* 8 June VII. 9/5 In cars and on foot, the neighbors gathered, Homer bringing in an armload of spicewood branches, moist and fragrant.

(10) **1818** SCHOOLCRAFT *Journal* 46 Mrs. Fisher . . . preferred dittany, sassafras, and spice-wood tea to our hyson. **1852** ELLET *Pioneer Women* 40 She would relate interesting anecdotes . . . of the . . 'spice-wood tea-parties.' **1948** *Hoosier Folklore* March 6 In the spring people drink . . . dittany tea, spicewood tea, and sassafras tea to purify and thin their blood before hot weather.

As the last term in **pond, swamp spice.**

spicebush ˈspaɪsˌbʊʃ, *n.* Any one of various plants of the genus *Lindera,* esp. the feverbush, *L. benzoin.*

1770 WASHINGTON *Diaries* I. 409 The Growth, [is] Walnut, Cherry, Spice Bushes, etca. **1856** BRYANT *Poetical Works* (1903) 185 There the spice-bush lifts Her leafy lances. **1866** LINDLEY & MOORE *Treas. Botany* 821/2 *Oreodaphne californica* is a common tree in the mountainous parts of California, where it goes by a variety of names, such as Mountain Laurel, Spice-bush, Balm of Heaven. **1949** *Mo. Bot. Garden Bul.* April 106 Perhaps the first wild shrub to flower in this state is the interesting spicebush (*Lindera Benzoin*).

attrib. **1903** HOLLAND *Moth Book* 84 Callosamia promethea Drury. . . . (The Spice-bush Silk-moth.) **1905** *Country Life* April 63/1 The Spice-bush Swallowtail (Papilio Troilus) on a daisy.

*** spider,** *n.*

1. An iron frying pan or skillet, orig. and now sometimes provided with long legs for cooking over coals. Cf. *** creeper 3.**

1790 *Pa. Packet* 1 March 3/3 William Robinson, Junr. . . . Hath for Sale . . . bake pans, spiders, skillets. **1858** *Spirit of Times* 13 Feb. 370/1 She set a capacious three-legged skillet or spider on the fire

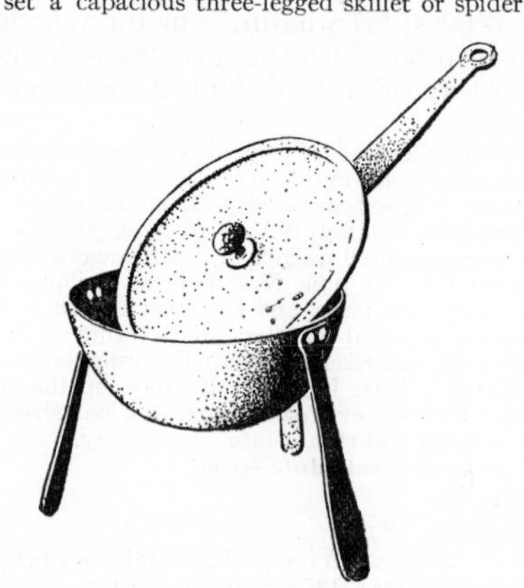

Early form of spider (sense 1) or creeper (sense 3)

to heat. **1949** *Amer. Sp.* April 110/1 Large, hand-shaped loaves, cooked two to a spider or Dutch oven.

attrib. **1870** A. D. WHITNEY *We Girls* v, The flaky spider-cake, turned just as it blushed golden-tawny over the coals. **1920** LINCOLN *Mr. Pratt* 33 She'd been . . . giving 'em spider bread and dried apple pie for breakfast. **1941** *L.A.* Map 285.

2. On a seagoing ship, a rack for a dining table to prevent plates and dishes from slipping off in rough seas. *Obs.*

1855 BESTE *Wabash* I. 45 'But what is this on the table?' I asked. 'A spider.' . . . I knew no more than you what 'a spider' meant on a dinner-table on board ship.

3. (See quot.)

1883 GRESLEY *Gloss. Coal-mining* 230 *Spiders,* . . . see Drum rings. [*Ib.* 91 *Drum-rings,* cast iron wheels, with projections, to which are bolted the staves or laggings forming the surface for the ropes to lap upon.]

4. In special combs.: (1) **spider bent grass,** bent grass or a variety of this; (2) **bird,** the cedar waxwing; (3) **fashion,** (see quot.), *obs.;* (4) **flower,** any plant of the genus *Cleome,* or any of various plants of the genus *Tibouchina,* having long, thin stamens; (5) **lily,** the spiderwort, or any one of various other plants of somewhat similar appearance, as those of the genus *Hymenocallis;* (6) **orchid,** any one of various cultivated plants of the genus *Brassia;* (7) **-wheeled buggy,** a light buggy, *rare;* (8) *** wort,** (see quots.).

(1) **1894** COULTER *Bot. W. Texas* III. 525 Spider bent grass . . . [is found in] low wet land, central Texas to Tennessee. — (2) **1850** *Conn. Public Acts* 5 It shall not be lawful in this State for any person to shoot . . . [any] spider-bird or wax-bird. — (3) **1848** *Knickerb.* XVIII. 499 To this were yoked two tolerably good wheel-horses, and a third in what is technically called 'spider fashion,' that is, in front of the other two. — (4) **1861** WOOD *Botany* 240 Spider Flower. . . . Herbs or shrubs. **1891** *Cent.* 5830/3 *Spider-flower,* . . . a plant of the

former genus *Lasiandra* of the *Melastomaceae*, now included in *Tibouchina*. The species are elegant hothouse shrubs from Brazil, bearing large purple flowers. **1931** CLUTE *Plants* 101 Among the few plants named for the arachnids, are . . . the spiderflower (*Cleome*) named from the long and sprawling stamens like spider's legs.

(5) **1887** *Harper's Mag.* Feb. 351/1 The exquisite white spider-lily, nodding in clusters on long stalks. **1900** BAILEY *Stand. Cyclo. Horticulture* III. 787/2 *Hymenocallis.* . . . Spider Lily, Sea Daffodil. Bulbous plants of about 30 species of the warm parts of the New World. **1949** *Life* 11 April 81 In March purple irises and white spider lilies blossom in a Delta swamp. — (6) **1934** WEBSTER. **1938** MATSCHAT *Suwannee River* 222 Don't they look like tiny green and white spiders? That's why people call them spider orchids. — (7) **1886** ROOSEVELT in *Cent. Mag.* July 338/2 There may be a crowd of onlookers in every kind of trap, from a four-in-hand drag to a spider-wheeled buggy drawn by a pair of long-tailed trotters. — (8) **1847** WOOD *Botany* 172 *C[leome] pungens.* Spiderwort. . . . A common garden plant, with curious purple flowers. **1931** CLUTE *Plants* 44 The spiderwort of the gardens is *Cleome spinosa*, named in reference to its long stamens and stalked petals and pistil which render the flower quite spiderlike in appearance.

As the last term in **calico, hunter spider.**

spiegel iron. [f. G. *Spiegeleisen.*] A kind of pig iron containing a considerable amount of manganese, used in steel-making. — **1880** *Harper's Mag.* Dec. 61/1 From far above the now silent converter there tumbles a fierce rivulet of molten 'spiegel' iron. **1883** KNIGHT *Supp.* 839/2 A spiegel iron in this country . . . made from the New Jersey Franklinite ore . . . has commenced to be universally used in place of the spiegel iron, thus far imported from Germany.

spiel spil, *n.* [Prob. f. the verb *q.v.*] A story, speech, harangue, esp. one of a voluble, cheap, noisy nature. *Slang.*

1896 G. ADE *Artie* xi. 100 There was a long spiel by the high guy in the pulpit. **1901** *U. of Chi. Wkly.* 1 Aug. 1086/2 I'll go to the Pi Gams and give them the same spiel. **1950** *Chi. Tribune* 20 March 22/3 It requires little imagination to consider that such a marvelous critter as the ballyhoo bird, as the subject of a sideshow barker's blatant sales talk, might readily have lent its name to denote the spiel itself.

b. spiel mark, app. an imitation diamond. *Obs.*

1879 *Chi. Tribune* 3 May 8/3 The two prisoners are wanted for swindling a man really named John Smith . . . who . . . was given 200 of those bright, scintillating gems known as spiel-marks for $100 of hard-earned cash which he had with him.

spiel spil, *v.* [G. *spielen*, to play (an instrument). Cf. quot. 1947.] *intr.* To talk, esp. in a high-flown, grandiloquent manner. *Slang.*

[**1870** *Terr. Enterprise* (Virginia, Nev.) 16 July 3/1 The new 'circus' is to be seen at the corner of D street and Sutton avenue—down var der orkan goes a spielin'.] **1894** *S.F. Midwinter Appeal* 10 March 1/3 Tell [the barker] to stop spieling now and then. [**1947** PERRY *Cities of Amer.* 187 At the moment, since Denver's Symphony chooses to spiel only when winter's winds doth blow, the city is hard put to figure a way to utilize this splendid amphitheater.]

Also *tr.*

1904 O. HENRY *Cabbages & Kings* iii. 58 I'll come right back and hear you spiel the rest before bedtime.

spieler 'spilə, *n.* [f. **spiel,** *v.*] An actor or player, a voluble talker, as a "barker" stationed outside an amusement place to attract customers. *Slang.*

1891 QUINN *Fools of Fortune* 334 The game is played with three cards, which are held by the operator, who is known in gamblers' slang as the 'spieler,' in his right hand, between the thumb and first two fingers. . . . The 'spieler' is usually attired after the manner of a well-to-do country farmer or stock-raiser. **1894** *S.F. Midwinter Appeal* 19 May 15/1 Some spielers for the Midway who attempted to lick the Camp gate keeper were sent up for 24 hours. **1947** *Reader's Digest* Sep. 116/2 On the right is the side-show tent, with its glaring posters and strident spieler.

spig sprg, *n.* [Short for next.] (See quot. 1923.) *Slang.*

1922 *Collier's* 2 Sep. 22/2 Pedro! Come out from hiding, you d——d spig! **1923** *19th Cent.* Jan. 122 The Spanish negro natives, now generally called 'Spigs,' are slow to learn English. **1928** S. LEWIS *Man Who Knew Coolidge* II. 116 We need a supply of cheap labor, and where get it better than by encouraging those Wops and Hunks and Spigs and so on to raise as many brats as they can?

spiggoty 'spɪgətɪ, *n.* [Poss. inspired by some such expression, by Spanish-speaking Negroes, as *no speaga de Engleesch.*] A spig *q.v.* Also the language used by spigs. *Slang.* — **1922** H. L. FORSTER *Adv. Trop. Tramp* ix. 132 Just stood around the dock and jabbered a lot of spiggoty talk at me, like I could understand spiggoty! I don't know a word of this damned Spanish, and I'm glad of it! **1934** WEBSTER.

* **spike,** *n.*

1. A spike buck or the spikelike horn of this (see also quot. 1931).

1858 *Harper's Mag.* Oct. 615/2 A young 'spike' . . . made one plunge at the side of his now occupied antagonist. **1870** *Amer. Naturalist* IV. 190 Yet it is the first pair of horns only that are ever 'spikes' in a common *C. Virginianus.* **1931** *Amer. Sp.* VII. Oct. 7 A two-year-old [buffalo] 'bull' having short sharp horns was called a 'spike.'

2. (See quot. 1911.)

*a***1884** in GOODE *Fisheries* I. 298 Fish of this size are sometimes called 'Spikes.' **1911** *Rep. Fisheries 1908* 312/1 Small mackerel are known as 'spikes' (5 to 6 inches long), 'blinkers' (7 to 8 inches long), and 'tinkers' (9 inches long).

3. In combs.: (1) **spike antler,** =**spike horn** (*a*); (2) **bill,** (*a*) (see quot.), (*b*) the marbled godwit, (*c*) the hooded merganser; (3) **buck,** a young male deer in the stage of development in which the antler is a simple spike; (4) **bull,** a young elk having his first or dog antlers, also a buffalo (see quot. 1947); (5) * **grass,** (see quot. 1891); (6) **horn,** (*a*) the spikelike horn of a male deer, also attrib., (*b*) =**spike buck;** (7) * **pole,** a long pole having a spike in the end for punting a boat; (8) **tail,** see as a main entry; (9) **team,** a team of three animals so arranged that one precedes the other two, cf. **spider fashion;** (10) **weed,** an annual California herb of the family Carduaceae (see quot.).

(1) **1902** HULBERT *Forest Neighbors* 239 The hound's fate had shown him what that spike antler could do. — (2) (*a*) **1875** *Fur, Fin & Feather* (ed. 3) 119 The smaller species of loon I have heard variously called the spike-bill, the cape-race [etc.]. (*b*) **1888** TRUMBULL *Names of Birds* 207 In New Jersey at Pleasantville (Atlantic Co.), . . . and Cape May City, [it is called] Spike-Bill, and less frequently, Spike-Bill Curlew. **1917** *Birds of Amer.* I. 241. (*c*) **1888** TRUMBULL *Names of Birds* 74 At Detroit, [the hooded merganser is known as] Spike-Bill. **1917** *Birds of Amer.* I. 112. — (3) **1824** DODDRIDGE *Notes* 127 The spike buck, the two and three pronged buck, the doe and barren doe, figured through their anecdotes. **1949** *Pacific Discovery* July–Aug. 12/2 Wisconsin deer hunters . . . kill and abandon in the woods at least one doe, fawn or spike buck for every two legal bucks taken out. — (4) **1891** *Scribner's Mag.* Oct. 447/2 Usually, in a band of fifty cows, there would be three or four males, including possibly, one or two spike-bulls. **1947** DEVOTO *Across Wide Missouri* 37 Yearlings would be darker and 'spike bulls,' the four-year-olds whose horns had smooth, clean points, would begin to show the colors of maturity.

(5) **1791** MUHLENBERG *Index Florae* 161 *Uniola*, Spike-grass. **1891** *Cent.* 5831/3 spike-grass. . . . One of several American grasses, having conspicuous flower-spikelets. (*a*) *Diplachne fascicularis.* (*b*) *Distichlis maritima* (salt grass). (*c*) The genus *Uniola*, especially *U. paniculata* (also called *sea* or *seaside oats*), a tall coarse grass with a dense heavy panicle, growing on sand-hills along the Atlantic coast southward. — (6) (*a*) **1857** HAMMOND *Northern Scenes* 189 He was a fine two year old buck, with spike horns. **1869** *Amer. Naturalist* III. 553 The first Spike-horn Buck was merely an accidental freak of nature. **1870** *Ib.* IV. 189, I shot on Louis Lake a buck with spike-horns, which was not a yearling, . . . but a *large* buck, of full age and size. (*b*) **1870** *Amer. Naturalist* IV. 190 The spike-horn was shot just as deer were attaining the 'blue coat.' **1902** WISTER *Virginian* 405 [We] caught sight of a vanishing elk. . . . 'A spike-horn, wasn't it?' said I. — (7) **1848** THOREAU *Maine Woods* 39 [The] operation was performed by sticking our two spike-poles into the ground in a slanting direction. — (9) **1848** BARTLETT 324 *Spike Team*, a waggon drawn by three horses, or by two oxen and a horse, the latter leading the oxen or span of horses. **1890** L. C. D'OYLE *Notches* 178, I got there with a loaded waggon, and a 'spike team'—three mules.

(10) **1931** VANSELL *Nectar & Pollen Plants Calif.* 8 Another spike-weed, *C[entromadia] pungens*, is reported as producing good honey in abundance throughout the San Joaquin Valley.

As the last term in **blue, fork, forked, gold, golden, lightwood, silver spike.**

* **spike,** *v. tr.* (See quot. 1900.) Also transf. *Slang.*

1889 in MCILWAINE *Poor White* (1939) 133 Water from biled hops an' poke root, an' sweetened wi' lasses and spiked wi' good strong whiskey. **1900** *D.N.* II. 63 *Spike*, v.t. 1. To get possession of, in any way. 2. To join a fraternity. 3. To fortify a drink by adding wine or spirits. **1949** *This Week Mag.* 7 May 20/2 Drinking water tastes so bad it has to be spiked with lime or orange extract.

* **spiked,** *a.*

1. In the names of various plants, as **spiked alder, buckeye, clover, gama grass, Indian corn, salt grass,** (see quots.).

1789 MORSE *Amer. Geog.* 52 The spiked indian corn is of a similar kind. **1833** EATON *Botany* (ed. 6) 99 *Clethra alnifolia*, spiked alder, sweet pepper bush. **1839** in *Mich. Agric. Soc. Trans.* VII. 420 *Spartina cynosuroides*, Spiked salt-grass. **1888** *Boston Jrnl.* 6 Dec. 2/3 A native forage plant, called 'spiked clover,' is attracting attention in California. **1901** MOHR *Plant Life Ala.* 334 *Tripsacum dactyloides.* . . .

Spiked Gamma Grass. . . . Of some value for forage. *Ib.* 608 *Aesculus parviflora.* . . . Spiked Buckeye. . . . Highly ornamental.

2. spiked buck, =**spike buck.** *Rare.*

1897 *Outing* Feb. 439/1 A strong, young, spiked buck came streaking through the Chêniere with the howling pack close at his heels.

***spikenard,** *n.* An American herb, *Aralia racemosa,* the root of which is used for medicinal purposes.

[**1640** PARKINSON *Theater of Plants* 1744/2 Virginia Spikenard.] **1778** CARVER *Travels* 511 *Spikenard,* vulgarly called in the colonies Petty-Morrell, . . . appears to be exactly the same as the Asiatick spikenard. **1840** DEWEY *Mass. Flowering Plants* 13 Spikenard. . . . [The root] formerly was used in a bruised state upon wounds, and is still employed for some medicinal purposes. **1891** *Amer. Folk-Lore* IV. 148 *A. racemosa* we [in N.H.] generally called by the correct name, *Spikenard,* but we pronounced it with short i, as if Spicknard.

b. With specifying terms: Any one of various other aromatic American plants, as the false spikenard or Solomon's-seal, *Smilacina racemosa.* Cf. **American spikenard.**

1785 MARSHALL *Amer. Grove* 16 *Baccharis.* Plowman's Spikenard. **1843** TORREY *Flora N.Y.* II. 298 *Smilacina racemosa.* . . . Wild Spikenard. . . . Moist grounds, thickets, etc.: frequent. **1857** GRAY *Lessons Botany* 81 A compound raceme . . . [occurs] in the Goat's-beard and the False Spikenard.

c. spikenard tree, (see quot.).

1891 *Cent.* 5832/1 *A[ralia] spinosa,* the angelica-tree, has been called *spikenard-tree.*

***spiker,** *n.* **1.** ?A variety of oyster. *Rare.* **2.** A railroad laborer who drives the spikes holding the rails to the cross-ties.

(**1**) **1842** UNCLE SAM *Peculiarities* II. 5 The oysters you shall have with *my* money shall be spikers, fourteen to the dozen, and real, precious flabbers. — (**2**) **1872** HUNTINGTON *Road-Master's Ass't* 32 Tall spikers usually set the spike leaning from them. **1887** *Scientific Amer.* 18 Jan. 389 There are 32 'spikers' to every five miles of track each man of whom drives 840 spikes a day.

spiketail ˈspaɪkˌtel, *n.*

1. a. A river duck, *Dafila acuta,* of an American species. **b.** =**spike-tailed grouse.**

(**a**) **1888** TRUMBULL *Names of Birds* 38 *Dafila acuta.* . . . At Chicago, Spike-Tail, and less commonly Pike-Tail. **1917** *Birds of Amer.* 128. — (**b**) *Ib.* II. 27 Sharp-tailed Grouse. *Pediœcetes phasianellus phasianellus.* . . . [Also called] Northern Sharp-tailed Grouse; Spike-tail; Pin-tail.

2. *pl.* =**spike-tailed coat.** *Colloq.*

1905 *Brooklyn Eagle* 17 March, After the wedding he . . . sat around all day in his spike-tails. **1950** *Time* 20 March 100/3 He grew tired of being a celebrity, doted on by lecturegoers, lionized at dinner parties where the guests came in 'spiketails, white throat seizings and black ties.'

b. Also **spiketail coat.**

1889 RILEY *Pipes o' Pan* 30 You'll have a little spike-tail coat an' travel with a show! **1928** BRADFORD *Ol' Man Adam* 67 Esau was on hand all dressed up in a spike-tail coat.

spike-tailed ˈspaɪkˌteld, *a.* **1. spike-tailed coat,** a swallow-tailed coat, or dress coat. **2. spike-tailed grouse,** (see quot.).

(**1**) **1870** MARK TWAIN in *Galaxy* May 721/2 Would we not miss a spike-tailed coat and kids? **1896** *Columbus* (O.) *Dispatch* 24 July 1/1 Captain Lloyd wore red, white and blue spiked-tailed coat and the tall hat of Uncle Sam. — (**2**) **1891** *Cent.* 5832/1 *Spike-tailed grouse,* the sharp-tailed, sprig-tailed, or pin-tailed grouse, *Pediœcetes phasianellus* or *columbianus.*

***spile,** *n.* A small wooden or metal spout used for conducting the sap from a maple tree into a pail.

1844 *Knickerb.* XXIII. 444 The clean white-pine buckets, . . . into which the sap drips from the spiles, are made expressly for this use. **1904** ATHERTON *Rulers of Kings* 31 He was inserting the little nickel troughs called spiles into the trees of the maple orchard. **1942** RICH *We Took to Woods* (1948) 127 Ralph and Gerrish tap the trees, going back into the woods across the road on snowshoes, and carrying the pails and spiles by the armload.

***spill,** *v. Stock Exchange.* (See quot.) *Colloq.* — **1870** MEDBERY *Men Wall St.* 137 *Spilling stock.* When great quantities of a stock are thrown upon the market, sometimes from necessity, often in order to 'break' the price.

***spindle,** *n.*

1. A fixture, prob. tall and cylindrical, placed in an advantageous spot as a guide to ships.

1819 *Stat. at Large* III. 535 For the spindle or buoys on the reef running from Cochney's Island . . . , and for that on the rock off the point of Fairweather Island, twelve hundred dollars [shall be appropriated]. **1829** *Ib.* IV. 345 Four hundred dollars for a spindle to be placed on Minot's Ledge [shall be appropriated]. **1904** *Hartford Courant* 19 Aug. 13 What this man was really doing was simply placing a spindle on Magazine Rock. **1925** FORBUSH *Birds of Mass.* I. 159 If in the dead of winter one sees off our coast a large, dark bird flapping slowly along close to the water with outstretched neck and alighting on a spindle or a ledge where it stands nearly upright, probably that bird is the Cormorant.

2. The tassel of Indian corn. *Obs.* Cf. **spindle worm.**

1824 SINGLETON *Letters* 82 They [Virginians] also call, what we [New Englanders] call the spindle, the tassel. **1847** *Knickerb.* XXX. 239 The tall corn, whose spindles were high above your head. **1871** *Amer. Naturalist* V. 245 The corn . . . sent forth a new tassel or spindle.

3. A pine needle.

1865 G. W. NICHOLS *Story of Gt. March* 218 The roots of the trees are buried in the spindles and burrs which have fallen undisturbed for centuries. **1891** *Cent.* 5835/1.

4. In combs.: (1) **Spindle City,** a nickname for Lowell, Mass.; (2) **fever,** app. a fever of a particularly debilitating kind, *obs.;* (3) **-tail,** (see quot. and cf. **spiketail 1. a.**); (4) **worm,** the larva of a noctuid moth, destructive to Indian corn and other plants, also attrib.

(**1**) **1858** *Scientific Amer.* 23 Jan. 153/1 The 'spindle city' is gradually resuming its steady hum of industry. — (**2**) **1836** *Crockett Alman. 1837* 8, I was confined to my bed with spindle fever—my legs were swelled up as big as broomsticks. **1865** *Harper's Mag.* Nov. 705/2 She was took with a spindle-fever till her legs warn't no thicker than your thumb. — (**3**) **1884** S. F. BAIRD *Water Birds N. Amer.* **1890** *Cent.* 4502/3 *Pintail,* . . . the pin-tailed duck, *Dafila acuta.* Also called, from the peculiarity of the tail, . . . *sharptail, spiketail, spindletail.* **1923** W. L. MCATEE *Local Names Game Birds* 15 In local use . . . spindletail (Long Id., N.Y.). — (**4**) **1790** DEANE *N.-Eng. Farmer* 148/1 *Top-worms,* or *spindle-worms,* a white worm . . . which eats off the stem of the [maize] plant. **1854** EMMONS *Agric. N.Y.* V. 243 *Nonagriadae.* . . . They are known by the common name of spindle-worms. **1895** *Stand.* 1200/1 *Nonagrian,* . . . a noctuid moth of *Nonagria* or a related genus, as the spindleworm-moth.

As the last term in **squeeze spindle.**

***spine,** *n.* **1.** ***spinetail,** the spine-tailed swift or the ruddy duck, also attrib. and with specifying term. **2. spine-tailed swift,** (see quots.).

(**1**) **1839** AUDUBON *Synopsis Birds* 33 *Chætura,* Spine-tail. *Ib., Chætura pelasgia,* American Spine-tail. **1884** COUES *Key to Birds* (ed. 2) 457 *Chæturinæ,* Spine-tail Swifts. *Ib.* 580 *Centrocercus.* . . . Spine-tail Grouse. **1917** *Birds of Amer.* I. 152 Ruddy Duck. *Erismatura jamaicensis.* . . . [Also called] Stick-tail; Spine-tail; Dip-tail. — (**2**) **1872** COUES *Key to Birds* 183 *Chæturinæ.* Spine-tailed Swifts. **1889** *Cent.* 908/2 The spine-tailed swifts [are] so called because the shafts of the tail-feathers project beyond the webs.

***spinner,** *n.* As the last term in **hair, sick, tobacco spinner.**

***spinning,** *n.*

1. =**spinning bee.** *Obs.*

1876 *Scribner's Mo.* Jan. 334/1 They had 'bees,' apple-cuts, huskings, quiltings, spinnings, . . . and plenty of weddings and christenings.

2. In obs. combs.: (1) **spinning bee,** a gathering of women for the purpose of spinning, usu. for one of their number or for some worthy cause; (2) **frolic,** =prec.; (3) **match,** =**spinning bee;** (4) **visit,** (see quot. and cf. quot. 1788 *s.v.* **spinning bee**), *obs.,* cf. Du. *spinvisite,* in the sense of a spinning bee.

(**1**) **1788** *Cumberland Gaz.* (Portland, Me.) 8 May, Spinning Bee. On the 1st inst. assembled at the house of the Rev. Samuel Deane of this town, more than one hundred of the fair sex. **1904** *Sun* (N.Y.) 28 Aug. 4 The Martha Washington Benevolent Society . . . met at Sunset the other day for its annual spinning bee. — (**2**) **1845** *Lowell Offering* V. 268 We used to have sewing parties, . . . quilting matches, and spinning frolics. — (**3**) **1769** *Boston Gaz.* 16 Oct. 1/3 Last Thursday about Twenty young Ladies met at the House of Mr. Nehemiah Liscome, here [Taunton, Mass.], on purpose for a Spinning Match: (or what is call'd in the Country a Bee.) **1880** *Harper's Mag.* Aug. 350/1 A spinning match took place at one of the schoolhouses. — (**4**) **1832** TROLLOPE *Domestic Manners* II. 177 Once a year a day is fixed on which some member of every family in a congregation meet at their minister's house in the afternoon. They each bring an offering . . . of articles necessary for house-keeping. . . . These meetings are called spinning visits.

spinose ear tick. A tick, *Octobius megnini,* which infests the ears of horses, sheep, dogs, etc., in some parts of the South. — **1918** *Farmers' Bul.* No. 980, 6 On account of their habits and great vitality, and the wide range of the animals which they infest, complete eradication of spinose ear ticks is a difficult matter.

*__spiral__, *n. Football.* (See quot.) — **1920** W. Camp *Football without Coach* 85 Forward passes are of two kinds, the lob pass and the spiral. . . . The spiral is thrown like a spear and goes more nearly on a line.

* **spirit**, *n.* In combs.: (1) **spirit crab,** prob. the ghost crab, *Ocypode arenaria;* (2) **duck,** any duck, esp. the bufflehead, that dives at the flash of a gun, or is given to sudden appearances and disappearances; (3) **rapper,** one who purports to communicate with spirits by means of rapping, *obs.;* (4) **rapping,** rapping thought to be made by spirits, also attempted communication with spirits by rapping.

(1) **1871** *Harper's Mag.* June 28/1 The spirit-crabs reigned supreme on Loggerhead until the Bos'n took over some of our pet rabbits, the lop-ear kind. — (2) [**1785** Pennant *Arctic Zool.* II. 558 Spirit Duck. . . . Inhabits North America, from Hudson's Bay to Carolina.] **1872** Coues *Birds N.W.* 577 Spirit Duck. . . . I have reason to believe that this Duck . . . nests in Northern Dakota. **1923** W. L. McAtee *Local Names Game Birds* 23 Bufflehead. . . . In local use . . . spirit duck (Que., N.W.T., Calif.) — (3) **1854** O. A. Brownson (*title*), The Spirit-Rapper; an Autobiography. **1859** Bartlett 434 *Spirit-rapper,* a person, who . . . interprets raps produced by an unseen agency on tables, floors, etc., as messages from the other world. **1892** Browne *A. Ward: His Book* 45 Just so soon as a man becums a regular out & out Sperret rapper he leeves orf workin. — (4) **1852** *Lantern* (N.Y.) II. 16/2 Six patients have been admitted into the Indiana Insane Hospital within the past month, whose insanity has been produced by the spirit rappings. **1862** Lowell *Biglow P.* 2 Ser. vi. 164, I worked round at sperrit-rappin' some. **1907** *Cosmopolitan* Feb. 439/1 You've been a-foolin' me, right along, wid all this talk about that Black Death gold-mine, and wid all this spirit-rappin' about the wealth I'd be rollin' in.

b. In miscellaneous expressions with reference to alleged spiritualistic phenomena of the middle of the nineteenth century and later.

1854 (*title*), Spirit Advocate [Rockford, Ill.]. **1863** B. Taylor *H. Thurston* 112 Then there's sperut-raps, as they call 'em. **1867** Dixon *New Amer.* II. 162 He is ready to perform this miracle of Spirit-Act by letter, at any distance, for ten dollars. *a***1882** J. Quincy *Figures of Past* (1883) 279, I am loath to borrow the word impressional from the vocabulary of spirit-mediums. **1896** S. A. Underwood (*title*), Automatic or Spirit Writing, with Other Psychic Experiences.

As the last term in **corn, Great, lynch, shad spirit(s).**

* **spiritual,** *a.* and *n.*

1. *n.* **a.** = **spiritual wife.** *Obs.* **b.** = **Negro spiritual.**

(a) **1852** in *Putnam's Mo.* VI. 147/1 These extra wives are known by sundry designations—some call them '*spirituals.*' **1859** Bartlett 434 *Spiritual,* a Mormon concubine. — (b) **1866** *Harper's Mag.* May 775/1 Maum Rina flavored all her dishes with these 'spirituals,' as they are called among the negroes. **1948** *Parents' Mag.* March 161/2 Folk songs, sea chantys, cowboy songs, spirituals offer a wealth of material.

2. *a.* Spiritualistic, pertaining to spiritualism.

1851 *S.F. Picayune* 29 Oct. 2/4 A National Mass Convention of 'Spiritual Rappers' is to be held at Rochester, New York, in February. **1863** Taylor *H. Thurston* 113 Had the invitation to a spiritual *seance* been given by any one but Mrs. Waldo [etc.]. **1871** in DeVere 245 A Circle is held for Medium Developments and Spiritual Manifestations at Bloomfield-street every Sunday.

3. In obs. combs.: (1) **spiritual widower,** *Calif.* a gold hunter who spends most of his time in prospecting activities away from his wife, cf. **California widow;** (2) **wife,** a wife married for eternity according to the principles of the Mormon Church (see quot. 1877), also transf. and attrib.; (3) **wifery,** the practice of having spiritual wives.

(1) **1872** Powers *Afoot & Alone* 325 That queer Americanism 'grass widow,' is here supplemented by the other one, 'spiritual widower.' — (2) **1843** *Quincy* (Ill.) *Herald* 15 Dec. 3/1 Hyram Smith has had a revelation confirming the spiritual wife system. **1845** *Quincy* (Ill.) *Whig* 1 Nov. 2/3 He was seen sneaking through a garden, to get into a house by the back way, to visit his 'spiritual wives.' **1877** Bartlett 637 *Spiritual Wife,* or simply *Spiritual.* A Mormon extra wife or concubine. So, as among the Millerites in 1843, at Athol, Mass., except that they claimed such a companion as *only* a spiritual partner. **1925** *Ladies' Home Jrnl.* April 38/1 It is considered by the elderly women of Utah a great and sacred privilege to be the spiritual wife of Brigham Young or the Prophet Joseph Smith in the world to come. — (3) **1845** *Quincy* (Ill.) *Whig* 1 Nov. 2/3 To complete this man's reign of power, there was adopted, as I have before alluded to, the system of spiritual wifery. **1870** Beadle *Utah* 83 The apostolic dignitaries did not always agree among themselves, after the establishment of 'spiritual wifery,' in the distribution of female prizes.

* **spiritualism,** *n.* The belief that departed spirits can communicate with the living through a "medium," by means of rappings and other manifestations.

1853 Dix *Transatlantic Tracings* 244 Every two or three years the Americans have a paroxysm of humbug— . . . at the present time it is Spiritual-ism. **1860** Holmes *Professor* 15 Spiritualism is quietly undermining the traditional ideas of the future state. **1902** Mark Twain *Christian Science* 762 (R.), To whom does Spiritualism appeal? **1949** J. Monaghan *This Is Ill.* 62 Along with diverse social experiments such as communism, polygamy, and spiritualism came a popular and intense crusade against slavery.

* **spiritualist,** *n.* A believer in spiritualism.

1853 B. Alcott *Journals* 265 The Spiritualists' Convention . . . is sitting—or sleeping, rather—in the Masonic Temple. **1886** Rittenhouse *Maud* 374 Warren Chase, a spiritualist lecturer conducted the funeral services. **1906** Mark Twain *What Is Man* 44 (R.), Why were the Congregationalists not Baptists . . . and the Atheists Spiritualists.

* **spit,** *n.* In combs.: (1) **spitball,** see as a main entry; (2) **bug,** (see quot.); (3) **curl,** a small lock of hair dampened, orig. with spit, and curled so as to lie flat on the temple, cheek, or forehead, *colloq.;* (4) **devil,** a form of fireworks.

(2) **1891** *Cent.* 5844/2 *Spit-bug,* . . . any spittle-insect. — (3) **1831** *Boston Transcript* 9 Sep. 2/1 What would the reverend Doctor say of the 'spit curls,' and Chinese precision of a modern dandyzette's head gear? **1949** *Home & Life Mag.* 13 Aug. 7/1 Anne Baxter wears bangs and spit curls for her role. — (4) **1887** *Courier-Journal* 21 June 1/1 The deadly explosives . . . turn out to have been innocent roman candles, fire-crackers and spit-devils.

*__spit__, *v. To spit cotton,* see ***cotton 7.** (3).

spitball ˈspɪtˌbɔl, *n.*

1. A pellet made of paper that has been chewed and formed into a small ball.

1846 *Knickerb.* XXVII. 410 [They] crooked pins, made pop guns, ejected spit-balls. **1899** W. James *Talks to Teachers* 92 The spitballs that Tommy is ready to throw. **1940** Mencken *Happy Days* 146 He . . . delighted in writing down the names of boys detected in . . . blowing spitballs at the Salvation Army.

2. (See quot. 1909.) Cf. * **spitter.**

In professional baseball the spit ball is no longer permitted.

1905 *St. Louis Globe-Democrat* 2 July II. 8/5 Strictly speaking, the spit ball was a product of last season, as it was used by one or two American league twirlers then. **1909** Webster 2015/2 *Spitball.* . . . (Usually two words.). . . . A variety of pitched ball produced by moistening one side of the ball with saliva. **1928** G. H. Ruth *Baseball* vi. 75 All spit balls break down, but by turning the wet spot one way or the other the pitcher can make the ball break in or out as he desires.

transf. **1925** E. Fraser & Gibbons *Soldier & Sailor Words & Phrases, Spit Ball:* Hand-grenade. [U.S. Army.]

Hence **spitballer.**

1928 *Chi. Tribune* 7 June 19/4 The Giants . . . made only three hits off his successor, Clarence Mitchell, the southpaw spitballer.

spite fence. A fence erected to spite a neighbor. — **1899** *Everybody's Mag.* I. 70/2 Meanwhile an ordinance was passed making the building of spite fences illegal. **1950** *New Yorker* 8 April 68, I want to get a spite fence.

*__spitter__, *n.* = **spitball 2.** — **1911** *Chi. D. News* 4 April 6/2 He . . . possesses a drop curve ball which is a cross between the knuckle ball and the 'spitter.' **1928** G. H. Ruth *Baseball* vi. 75 The theory of the spitter is simple enough. The ball is wet on one side. Naturally that makes a slippery spot which reduces friction and gives added speed to the opposite side where friction is applied.

* **spittle,** *n.* **1. spittle ball,** = **spitball 1. 2. spittle bug, fly, insect,** a froghopper which, in an immature stage, is enveloped in a white froth.

(1) **1885** Leland *Brand-new Ballads* (ed. 2) 4 As in country schools the urchins cast each one a spittle-ball. — (2) **1882** *Vt. Agric. Rep.* VII. 77 Dr. Cutting spoke of the frog hopper, usually known as the spittle bug on grass. **1891** *Cent.* 5845/1 *Spittle-fly,* . . . a spittle-insect. **1921** *Conn. Agric. Exper. Sta. Bul.* No. 230, 330 The grass-feeding spittle-bug is protected from predaceous and parasitic enemies. **1949** Palmer *Fieldbook Nat. Hist.* 394/2 Spittle Insect, Froghopper *Lepyronia quadrangularis.* . . . Best known from the frothy 'spit' found on plants as a cover, usually for nymphal stages.

spittoon spɪˈtun, *n.* [f. * *spit* + *-oon.*] A cuspidor.

1823 Faux *Memorable Days* 218 No lump sugar, no brandy, no segars, no spitoons are seen at this hotel. **1873** Mark Twain & Warner *Gilded Age* 223 The darky boy who purifies the Department spittoons—represents Political Influence. **1949** *Harvard Alumni Bul.* 24 Sep. 34 Whitman . . . found himself cleaning spittoons.

spitz spɪts, *n.* A Spitzenburg apple. — **1875** BURROUGHS *Winter Sunshine* 151 You are company, you red-cheeked spitz, or you, salmon-fleshed greening! *Ib.* 163 [It] can stand the ordeal of cooking, and still remain a spitz.

Spitzenburg ˈspɪtsn̩ˌbɝg, *n.* [See note.]

The origin is not clear but prob. f. Du. *spitz,* point, pointed, +*berg,* mountain, in allusion to the shape of the apple, the seedling from which it was developed having been found on a hill at Esopus, N.Y.

A red-and-yellow apple of any one of several varieties, as the Esopus. In full **Spitzenburg apple.** Cf. **Newtown Spitzenburg.**

[**1804** CUTLER in *Life & Corr.* II. 153 We had the Spitzbergen apple, from New York.] *a***1817** DWIGHT *Travels* I. 45 The varieties of apple-trees are: . . . Spitzenberg, Holden Sweeting, Fall pippin. **1869** *Rep. Comm. Agric. 1868* 482 [He] names the Baldwin for dessert and cooking, the Spitzenburg for cooking. **1949** J. B. HERRICK *Memories* 5 Father laid in about five barrels of apples, . . . a barrel each of Spitzenburgs and Baldwins.

spizzerinctum ˌspɪzəˈrɪŋktəm, *n.* [App. a fanciful coinage as if f. L. *specie rectum,* the right kind.] Hard money, specie (see also quots. 1926, 1947). *Slang.*

1845 HOOPER *Simon Suggs' Adv.* 40 A hundred and seventy dollars in the clear spizarinctum. **1869** *Overland Mo.* Aug. 128 In March, 1868, they [greenbacks] had gotten no farther west than Marshall [Tex.], and everywhere west of that, when a man named a price, he meant 'spizerinctums' (corrupted from *specie*). [**1926** *Amer. Sp.* I. 268 As for the *raison d'etre* of the Sunbeam Betty organization I cannot say, nor how La Spizzerinktum came to name itself as it did; nor shall I venture to prophesy how long these organizations will remain in existence.] **1947** *Newsweek* 24 Feb. 28/2 Tirelessly he promised 'to put spizzerinctum into the Republican party.' Explaining that 'spizzerinctum' means the 'old get-up-and go,' Sigler was nonplussed when the Democrats found the word also meant: 'Tawdry adornment . . . as on a building; gimcrackery.'

***splash,** *n.* In logging, a body of water suddenly released to carry down logs. Also attrib. and as verb. — **1879** *Lumberman's Gaz.* 23 Aug., Some of these . . . logs may possibly be moved by a splash. **1905** *Forestry Bureau Bul.* No. 61, 49 *Splash,* to drive logs by releasing a head of water confined by a splash dam.

***splasher,** *n.* A piece of oilcloth or a rug to protect a surface from splashings. — **1897** BRODHEAD *Bound in Shallows* 98 Did you notice the splasher? I worked it myself. **1905** BELASCO *Girl of Golden West* (1925) II. 73 A wash-stand, backed by a 'splasher' of white oilcloth, is near the bed.

***spleen,** *v. intr.* To feel angry or sick at the stomach. *Colloq.* — **1885** COOKE in *Congregationalist* (*Cent.*), It is fairly sickenin'; I spleen at it. **1889** ——— *Steadfast* 198 [It] makes me spleen to think on't! **1902** WILSON *Spenders* 31, I spleened against it and let him know it.

***splendiferous,** *a.* Magnificent, very striking. *Jocular.*

The *OED* shows this as an obsolete word in use *c*1460–1546. The modern jocular use may be a new American coinage.

1837 BIRD *Nick* I. 226 At a close hug, a squeeze on the small ribs, or a kick-up of heels, he's all splendiferous. **1882** SALA *Amer. Revisited* (1885) 151 A desire to appear 'splendiferous' and outshine all rival hotels. **1949** *Sat. Ev. Post* 5 March 100/2 Inside are what must have been among the most splendiferous public rooms of that splendiferous period.

splenic fever. =**Texas fever.** — **1869** *Rep. Comm. Agric. 1868* 5 On the breaking out of the splenic fever at the halting places of Texas cattle. **1901** *Amer. Rev. of Reviews* XXIV. 309/2 The altitude . . . prevents the occurrence of splenic fever.

***splint,** *n. attrib.* Designating various things made, or partially made, of wooden splints, as (1) **splint bag,** (2) **basket,** (3) **bonnet,** (4) **bottom(ed) (arm)chair,** cf. **Carver chair,** (5) **broom,** (6) **chair,** (7) **letter case.** Cf. ***split,** *n.* **3.**

(1) **1893** M. A. OWEN *Voodoo Tales,* She ketch up all dem crows an' fling um inter er big splint bag. — (2) **1866** A. D. WHITNEY *L. Goldthwaite* xi, Leslie had hanging upon her finger . . . [the] most graceful of all possible little splint baskets. **1912** I. COBB *Back Home* 66 It was a fad of Aunt Dilsey's to bring one covered splint basket. — (3) **1944** CLARK *Pills* 219 The average wide-brimmed high-crowned country-store hat, like the famous splint bonnets, became a symbol of a kind of simple but raw agrarian dignity and respectability. — (4) **1850** *Knickerb.* XXXVI. 73 She wiped out the seats of some splint-bottomed chairs with her calico apron. **1876** MARK TWAIN *Tom Sawyer* vi, The master, throned on high in his great splint-bottom armchair, was dozing. **1944** DUNCAN *M. Graham* 141 He sat upon the low and narrow splint-bottom chair in complete discomfort. (5) **1843** TORREY *Flora N.Y.* II. 183 Broom Hickory . . . [is] frequently used for making splint brooms. — (6) **1871** TAYLOR in *Life & Lett.* II. 564 An old-fashioned, highbacked splint-chair. **1889** MELLICK *Story Old Farm* 6 Occasionally is to be seen the old-time, white-covered, farm wagon, . . . with splint chairs from the farm-house for seats. — (7) **1887** WILKINS *Humble Romance* 220 There were a few poor attempts at adornment on the walls; a splint letter-case, a motto worked in worsteds.

***splinter,** *n.* **1.** Used in mild oaths. **2. splinter-shinned,** *a.* spindle-shanked. Both *rare.* Cf. **lightwood splinter.**

(1) **1840** SIMMS *Border Beagles* I. 197 By the splinters, you shall see how I shall drive. **1845** ——— *Wigwam & Cabin* 1 Ser. 49 No, darn my splinters, said I . . . if I leave the lad. — (2) **1863** RUSSELL *Diary* II. 79 The question was not worth arguing—the boys were in fact very 'weedy,' 'splinter-shinned chaps,' as another critic insisted.

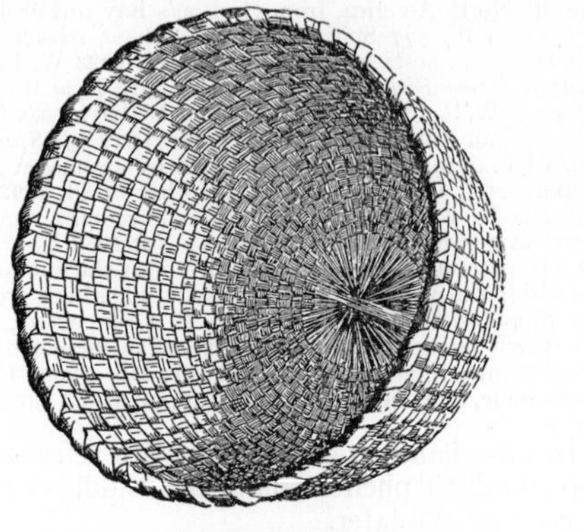

Splint basket

***split,** *n.*

1. (See quot. 1864.)

[**1843** GREENE *Exposure of Gambling* 179 To prevent splitting, the [faro] dealer will 'milk' the cards; that is, draw at the very same time one card from the top and one from the bottom, until the whole pack has been run through in this manner; then one half will win and the other half will lose, and cutting them does not in any wise alter the matter.] **1864** DICK *Amer. Hoyle* (1866) 204 Whenever [in faro] two cards of the same denominations . . . appear in the same turn, the dealer takes half the money found upon such card—this is called a 'split,' and is said to be the bank's greatest per centage. **1908** LORIMER *J. Spurlock* viii, One turn, high card to win, splits barred?

2. A cross *between* one thing and another. *Rare.*

1875 MARK TWAIN *Old Times* 19 You dash-dash-dash-*dashed* split between a tired mud-turtle and a crippled hearse-horse!

3. Designating various objects made in whole or in part of splits or splints, as (1) **split basket,** (2) **bonnet,** (3) **bottom,** see as a main entry, (4) **broom,** (5) **roof,** (6) **-seated chair,** (7) **sunbonnet.** Cf. ***splint.**

(1) **1890** *Harper's Mag.* Jan. 282/1 [He shifted] his white oak split basket from one arm to the other. — (2) **1944** WILSON *Passing Inst.* 137 The split bonnet was the aristocrat of the family. I cannot tell you how to make one, but I know the splits were made of cardboard and had to be removed when the bonnet was washed. — (4) **1848** DRAKE *Pioneer Life* 94 We always used a split broom. . . . A small hickory sapling was the raw material. **1940** WRIGHT *Pioneer Life* 83 Night brought its own household industries: the carding and spinning of wool, the making of split brooms, the coopering of a new tub [etc.]. (5) **1905** *Forestry Bureau. Bul.* No. 61, 49 *Split roof,* a roof of a logging camp or barn made by laying strips split from straight-grained timber. . . . (N[orthern] F[orest].) — (6) **1880** *Scribner's Mo.* March 676/2 It was a split-seated chair, painted green. — (7) **1931** *K.C. Times* 7 Oct., The more she tries on one of these Empress Eugenie hats, the better she likes grandmother's old split sunbonnet.

As the last term in **banana, full, hell to, lickety, oak, over split.**

***split,** *v.*

1. *tr.* To scratch (a political ticket), to vote for candidates of different parties on (a ballot). Cf. ***cut,** *v.* **2,** ***straight 6.**

1842 *Spirit of Times* (Phila.) 14 July (Th.), The cry is raised of 'Vote the whole ticket! Don't split your ticket!' **1905** *N.Y. Ev. Post* 17 Oct. 1 Plenty of talk is heard about intentions to split ballots. **1946** *Chi. D.*

News 20 Nov. 18/5 Democrats . . . decided the country did need a change, and split their ticket.

b. Also absol. and *∗splitting, *n.**

1850 *Quincy* (Ill.) *Whig* 12 Nov. 2/4 Our motto should always be—no splitting—the whole ticket, and nothing but the ticket. **1851** HOOPER *Widow Rugby* 23 Never *split* in my life.

2. (See quots.)

1850 *Rep. Comm. Patents 1849: Agric.* 321 'Splitting' tobacco . . . [is] simply splitting . . . the plant from the top to within a few inches of the bottom, before it is cut down for housing. **1909** *Cent. Supp.* 1256/1 *Splitting*, . . . in harvesting tobacco, the cleaving of the stalk nearly to the base, with the purpose of 'hanging,' i.e. placing it astride a stick for curing.

3. The participle or verb in combs.: (1) **split ballot,** a ballot voted by one who splits the ticket; (2) **cake,** (see quot.), *obs.;* (3) **ear,** a horse whose ear has been split as a mark of ownership, *obs.;* (4) **hickory,** hickory wood that has been split; (5) **mouth (sucker),** the sucker, *Lagochila lacera;* (6) **pine,** (see quot.); (7) **rail,** see as a main entry; (8) **Shirts,** (see quot.), *obs.;* (9) **spoon,** (see quot.); (10) **tail,** (*a*) a cyprinoid fish, *Pogonichthys macrolepidotus,* of California, (*b*) =**spiketail 1. a;** (11) **ticket,** a ticket or ballot bearing names other than those nominated or recommended by a single party or party faction, also a ballot cast by a voter who does not confine his votes to members of a single party, also attrib., cf. **split ballot;** (12) **worm,** the larva of a small moth, *Phthorimaea operculella.*

(1) **1947** *Chi. Tribune* 2 Nov. I. 3/5 To vote a split ballot, the voter should mark the squares before candidates' names, eschewing the party circles. — (2) **1899** VANDERBILT *Flatbush* 113 There was another tea cake which we must consider. . . . These cakes were so thin as sometimes to be called wafers; they were also known as split cakes because, thin as they were, they were split open and buttered before being sent up to the table. — (3) **1869** *Harper's Mag.* Jan. 157/1 To lance a buffalo the hunter must have a horse that . . . is thoroughly trained as a buffalo-horse—a 'split ear,' if possible, for his Indian education is then of service to you. [**1944** ADAMS *W. Words* 151/2 split An earmark made simply by splitting the ear midway from the tip about halfway toward the head.] — (4) **1835** HOFFMAN *Winter in West* I. 245 Presently, however, the landlord entered with an armful of burr-oak and split hickory.

(5) **1882** *Nat. Museum Bul.* No. 16, 144 *Ouassilabia lacera,* . . . Split-mouth Sucker. **1884** GOODE *Fisheries* I. 614 The 'Rabbit-mouth,' 'Hare-lip,' 'Split-mouth,' or 'May Sucker' is found in abundance in many rivers of Tennessee. **1911** *Rep. Fisheries 1908* 317/1. — (6) **1814** BIGELOW *Florula Bostoniensis* 234 The wood [or pitch pine] . . . is chiefly used as a light fuel, under the form of 'split pine.' — (8) **1775** in WILLARD *Letters* 105 It is talked of raising a company of *Split Shirts* immediately. . . . *Ib.* 171 The general uniforms are made of brown Osnaburghs, something like a shirt, double caped over the shoulder, in imitation of the Indians, and on the breast, in capital letters, is this motto, Liberty or Death. — (9) **1930** WILLIAMSON *Amer. Hotel* 197 It was in keeping with the Tremont's silver table-service, which included America's first four-tined forks—called, in derision, 'split spoons'—which did more to abolish the ancient art of 'sword-swallowing.'

(10) (*a*) **1882** *Nat. Museum Bul.* No. 16, 223. **1883** *Ib.* No. 27, 486 The split-tail is 'singularly distinguished from our other *Cyprinidæ* by the great development of the upper lobe of the caudal and its rudimentary rays.' (*b*) **1917** *Birds of Amer.* I. 128 Pintail. *Dafila acuta.* . . . [Also called] Split-tail. — (11) **1836** in MACKENZIE *Van Buren* 262, I was reproached by you for having voted a 'split ticket.' **1875** *Chi. Tribune* 4 Nov. 1/5 Besides the straight tickets thus disposed of, there were about 100 split tickets, which had been also put on a string by themselves. **1949** *So. Wkly.* 9 Nov. 1/2 The registration law was designed to keep split-ticket voters out of Democratic primaries. — (12) **1899** *Dept. Agric. Yrbk. 1898* 122 Another new insect . . . is the so-called tobacco leaf-miner, or 'split worm.'

To split the wind, to split the log, to split rails, see the nouns.

split-bottom ˈsplɪtˌbɑtəm, *n.* A chair the bottom of which is made of long thin splits of wood, usu. white oak. Often attrib.

1838 *S. Lit. Messenger* Jan. 28/1 At this log-house in the prairie . . . [were] split-bottom chairs, tin lamps [etc.]. **1839** *Ib.* V. 209/2 Nor had a windsor chair yet showed his rounded form among the old *split-bottoms* with low seats and tall perpendicular backs. **1866** W. REID *After War* 61 A rather more airy hall still contained the old, split-bottom arm-chairs. **1944** PENNELL *Rome Hanks* 6 We sat in splitbottom rockers for perhaps ten hours.

Also **split-bottomed,** *a.*

1843 *Amer. Pioneer* II. 444 [There were] four split-bottomed chairs. **1944** WILSON *Passing Inst.* 9 Straight-backed, split-bottomed chairs were good enough for the living-room or the dining-room.

split rail. A fence rail split from a tree. Also **split-rail fence.**

1826 FLINT *Recoll.* 206 Scarcely has a family fixed itself, and enclosed a plantation with the universal fence,—split rails [etc.]. **1897** *Essex Antiq.* I. 27 The split-rail fence is also old. Logs, generally of ash, about nine feet in length, and a foot or more in diameter, split the entire length into about sixteen equal parts, formed the rails, which were chamfered at each end. Of such split sections posts were also made, having holes cut in them in the proper places to receive the ends of the rails. **1947** *Mich. Hist.* March 14 They came from log cabins in clearings, from farm houses among stumpy fields with split-rail fences.

transf. and *attrib.* **1949** *Pacific Discovery* July–Aug. 12/1 Such awareness is 'nationalism' in its best sense. For lack of any other short name, I will call this, in our case, the 'split-rail value.'

*∗**splitter,** n.* As the last term in **hazel, rail, straw, wind splitter.**

splitting knife. A knife used for splitting fish, tobacco, etc.

1634 WOOD *N. Eng. Prospect* I. xii. 52 Here likewise must not be forgotten all vtensils for the Sea, as Barbels, splitting-knives, Leads, and Cod-hookes, and Lines [etc.]. **1722** *Broadside Verse* (1930) 115/2 [The] said Daniel still retain'd his splitting knife. **1820** *Amer. Farmer* I. 395 Split down the [tobacco] stalk through the middle near to the bottom . . . with a 'splitting knife.' **1885** *Harper's Mag.* Jan. 276/1 Iron rollers . . . roll or force the hides against a long splitting-knife.

splurge splɜdʒ, *n.* [Poss. imitative, or f. *spl*ash and s*urge.*]

1. An ostentatious display; a conspicuous effort or demonstration.

1830 SANDS *Writings* II. 179 What a splurge she makes! **1857** *Phoenix* (Sacramento) 20 Sep. 1/3 He came back with his stock of goods and made quite a 'splurge.' **1911** *N.Y. Ev. Post* 7 Jan. (Supp.) 3 Not a few manufacturers . . . are persuaded to make a splurge on their own account by sending their own special representative abroad. **1947** *Parade* 23 Feb. 17/3 An electric refrigerator, new radio, and—as a splurge—a dishwasher, are also on the list, but won't be bought for a while.

b. *To cut a splurge,* to make a display, to show off. *Colloq.*

[*c***1847** WITCHER *Bedott P.* 89 She tries to cut a spludge, and make folks think she's a lady.] **1897** *Chi. Tribune* 19 Sep. 37/1 Two shrewd young Hoosiers . . . came to Chicago in 1891 and cut a big splurge in monetary and real estate circles.

2. A sudden lunge. *Rare.*

1840 HOFFMAN *Greyslaer* II. 26 He caught my bullet in the back of his neck, gave a splurge, and was done for.

splurge splɜdʒ, *v.* [See prec.]

1. *intr.* To brag. *Rare.*

1844 *Knickerb.* XXIII. 507 You'll see all their steam-ships and their sail-ships they splurge so much about, lying high and dry.

2. To show off, to make a display.

1843 in THOMPSON *M. Jones* (1872) 100 Cousin Pete was thar splurgin about in the biggest, with his dandy-cut trowsers and big whiskers, and tried to take the shine off everybody else, jest as he always does. **1923** WYATT *Invis. Gods* 15 Enos bought it . . . to splurge around and show off with. **1947** *Chi. Sun* 28 Jan. 17/2 When I got around to furnishing my office, I thought I'd splurge on a good 18th Century English armchair.

b. To hustle, bestir oneself, go ahead.

*c***1845** *Big Bear Ark.* 129 We splurged about till breakfast time, gettin' up and cleanin' guns, countin' balls, and dividin' powder. **1852** *Deseret News* (Salt Lake City) 1 May 1/1 Hurry up the cakes—moderate, but don't *splurge*—slow, but all-fired *sartin.* **1887** T. STEVENS *Around World on Bicycle* I. 189, I don my gossamers . . . , and splurge ahead through the mud.

splurgy ˈsplɜdʒɪ, *a.* Showy, ostentatious. *Colloq.* — **1852** *Yale Tomahawk* May (Hall), They even pronounce his speeches splurgy. **1900** R. GRANT *Unleavened Bread* 221 It may be that I can introduce some of her and her daughter's splurgy and garish misconceptions without making myself hopelessly ridiculous.

*∗**spoil,** n.* In combs., usu. pl.: (1) **spoilsman,** one who shares in political "spoils" or supports the spoils system, also **spoilsmanship;** (2) **system,** the practice of regarding appointive public offices and their emoluments as so much plunder and of awarding them to members of a victorious political party, cf. **merit system.**

(1) **1842** *So. Quart. Rev.* II. 137 What a dazzling vision is here presented for bankrupts . . . and the whole rank and file of spoils-men!

1922 *Nation* 19 April 458/2 The Wilson Administration set a record in spoilsmanship hardly equalled since the days of Andrew Jackson. **1950** *Time* 20 March 18/1 Under the congressional rules which promote men by seniority instead of ability, Spoilsman McKellar wields immense power. — (2) **1838** MAYO *Polit. Sk. Washington* 40 Mr. Jefferson . . . authorized a friend to compromise with the federalists for . . . a guarantee against the spoils system. **1949** *Sat. Ev. Post* 11 June 12/2 We also have, after sixty-six years of the Civil Service, a survival of the spoils system.

b. In miscellaneous combs. having reference to spoilsmen or the spoils system in politics, as **spoils business, cabinet, doctrine, hunter, monger, mongering, party, politics.**

1833 WHITTIER in Pickard *Life Whittier* I. 170, I should as soon think of worshipping the devil with the Manicheans, as to fall down and do homage to Andrew Jackson with the idolatrous 'spoils party' of the day. **1833** CLAY *Speeches* (1842) 303 The Senate . . . [was] where the spoils doctrine . . . was first boldly advanced in Congress. **1837** *Jamestown* (N.Y.) *Jrnl.* 15 Feb. 3/2 The spoil hunters must admit he holds an office under the government. **1855** BAXTER *America* 60 'The spoils cabinet,' 'the disappointed applicants,' 'the eager expectants,' 'the hungry politicians;' such are some of the epithets which met my eye in all American newspapers. **1883** *Cent. Mag.* Oct. 950/1 The spoils business, in fact, is one of the strongest proofs of the prevailing apathy. **1887** *Courier-Journal* 5 May 4/4 Responsible Democratic officials . . . have been accused of spoils-mongering in violation of law. **1891** in *Works of T. Roosevelt* (1926) XIV. 116 But the greater portion still remain outside the classified service, and therefore in the hands of the spoils mongers. **1905** *Forum* April 589 The system which has dragged the schools into spoils politics and fostered corruption.

* **spoil,** *v. To be spoiling for a fight*, or variants, to be extremely eager for a fight. *Colloq.*

1861 MOORE *Rebellion Rec.* I. III. 8 Youthful South Carolina . . . is literally 'spiling' for lack of [a fight]. **1876** *Ventura Free Press* (San Buenaventura, Calif.) 8 Jan. 4/1 He was spoiling for a fight. **1948** WESTON *Mother Lode* 44 Two of the Woods' Crossing party, Colonel James and a man named George, were always 'sp'iling fer a fight.'

b. Also in other expressions (see quots.). *Colloq.*

1874 in *Amer. Sp.* XXII. 205/2 The corn's laid by and I've got nothing to do, and I'm spoiling for a preach. **1893** *Nation* 16 Nov. 368/2 Dr. James Martineau . . . seemed still be to 'spoiling for an argument.'

Spokane spoˈkæn, *n.* [f. a native word of unknown meaning. See the first quot.] *pl.* Any one of several small bodies of Salish Indians on and near the Spokane River in northwest Washington.

[**1838** PARKER *Exploring Tour* 302 They denominate themselves the children of the sun, which in their language is Spokein.] **1894** *Messenger Sacred Heart Jesus* April 273 Colonel George Wright gained a general victory over the . . . Spokanes. **1947** DEVOTO *Across Wide Missouri* 12 The Spokanes . . . were neighbors of the Nez Perces and poor relations of the Flatheads.

attrib. **1838** PARKER *Exploring Tour* 284 We passed to-day several small villages of the Nez Percé and Spokein nations. **1849** in *31st Cong.* 1 Sess. (1850) Sen. Ex. Doc. 52, 170 The Spokan tribe occupy the country between Fort Colville and Saaptin. **1944** ROSS *Westward* 71 She had to learn the Spokane language. . . . This was a difficult task, as the sounds the Spokanes made in speech were like nothing so much as the sounds of husking corn.

spondulics spɑnˈdulɪks, *n.* [Origin unknown.] Money, cash (see also quot. 1865). *Slang.*

1856 M. THOMPSON *Plu-ri-bus-tah* 113 Spondulicks, or ye Tin. **1865** SALA *Diary* II. 280, I paid for my Kissingen in a five-cent 'dingbat,' or 'spondulick'—two of the many names given to the fractional currency. **1884** MARK TWAIN *H. Finn* xiii, I'm derned if *I'd* live two mile out o' town . . . not for all his spondulicks. **1947** MYERS *The 'Guv'* 158 Then I parceled out my stuff and a little spondulix and wished them a Merry Christmas.

Also **spondulic,** *v.*, to provide *with* money. *Rare.*

1871 *Billings' Farmer's Allminax* 4 Thou shalt not spondulick thyself with the dimes ov another.

* **sponge,** *n. S.* (See quots.)

1835 J. MARTIN *Descr. Va.* 246 In this [surface of the Dismal Swamp] (sponge as it is called here) are imbedded innumerable old trees of juniper. **1842** BUCKINGHAM *Slave States* II. 489 The soft and yielding mass of decayed vegetable matter, with which this Dismal Swamp is chiefly covered, is called by the people living near it, Sponge. **1856** OLMSTED *Slave States* 157, I am aware of but a single attempt, as yet, to cultivate the sponge or true swamp soil.

As the last term in **grass, wool sponge.**

spontenacious ˌspɑntəˈneʃəs, *a.* A would-be humorous variant of *spontaneous.* Also **spontenaciously,** *adv. Obs.*

1830 *N.Y. Constellation* 11 Sep. 2/5 Here's a corn-stealer that can drive a wedge spontinaceously through the Table Rock. *c***1845** *Big Bear Ark.* 19 In Arkansaw, feeding as they do upon the *spontenacious* productions of the sile, they [*sc.* 'bar'] have one continued fat season the year round. **1848** *Literary Amer.* 19 Aug. 103/2 A-n-d such stuff for expandin' the ideas, and causin' them to flew spontanaciously.

spook spuk, *n.* [Du., in same sense.] A ghost or specter. Also attrib.

1801 *Mass. Spy* 15 July (Th.), Mine horses I'll to Vaggon yoke, Und chase him quickly;—by mine dunder I fly so swift as any spoke. **1884** *Lisbon* (Dak.) *Star* 31 Oct. 7/4 He was really run out of a fine position by spooks. **1946** *Democrat* 31 Oct. 6/1 Ghosts Abandon Gloomy Mansions . . . New Spook Crop Devotes Their Attention to Ordinary Homes.

b. spook-dancing, dancing by those masquerading as ghosts. *Rare.*

1904 *Charleston News & Courier* 26 Oct. 9 The programme was not confined to corn shucking, but 'spook dancing,' games, etc. played a prominent part.

spook spuk, *v.* [f. the noun.] *tr.* and *intr.* To act like a spook, to haunt, scare. *Colloq.*

1867 LOWELL *Poetical Works* (1896) 477/2 Yet still the New World spooked it in his veins. **1893** LELAND *Memoirs* I. 10 The ghost went with them, and there it still 'spooks' about as of yore. **1944** *Nat. Geog. Mag.* June 669/1 To get photographs of the herds Williams took to the saddle, since a man on foot is liable to 'spook,' or stampede them. **1949** *Sat. Ev. Post* 16 April 152/3 We would have to descend the hillside and work in among the moose, running the risk of spooking them and causing a panicky exodus from the basin.

spooky ˈspukɪ, *a.* Suggestive of spooks, eerie.

1854 *Wide West* (S.F.) 16 July 1/5 After treading many dark passages, the guide, having unlocked all sorts of 'spooky' looking iron doors, . . . ushered us before the tomb. **1907** *St. Nicholas* May 633/1 It was decidedly too spooky for comfort. **1948** *Time* 1 Nov. 90/2 Shakespeare's *Macbeth* is a turbulent melodrama, full of spooky claptrap.

b. *W.* Skittish, easily frightened. *Colloq.*

1926 BRANCH *Cowboy* 12 There were times when the steer would get spooky and mad. **1947** *Westerners' Brand Book* 51 Range cattle . . . were too 'spooky' in those days for man-made bridges.

* **spool,** *n.* In combs.: (1) **spool bed,** a wooden bed popular in the Victorian period the posts, railings, etc., of the head- and foot-pieces of which have spool-like turnings; (2) **cotton,** cotton sewing thread wound on a spool; (3) **thread,** thread wound on a spool, also *spool of thread*, and attrib.

(1) **1932** *Montgomery* (Ala.) *Advt.* 11 Sep., The typical Alabama spool-bed, or as some call it, the button-bed, made of maple is the product of the shop right here at home. **1946** *Democrat* 25 July 4/3 Antique for sale—Antique Spool Bed may be seen at home of Mrs. W. W. Daffin. — (2) **1839** C. F. BRIGGS *H. Franco* I. 28 He is the celebrated Mr. Bulbrief, the importer of spool cottons. **1881** *Rep. Indian Affairs* 384 Spool-cotton, 6 cord, Nos. 20 to 50, white, black and brown . . . dozen . . . 2,833. — (3) **1873** MARK TWAIN & WARNER *Gilded Age* 29 It takes her a week to buy a spool of thread. **1941** *Yankee* Dec. 38/2 Samuel L. Hill, one of the founders, purchased the entire property, renamed it the Nonotuck Silk Company, and began the manufacture of spool thread silk. **1947** *Reader's Digest* Aug. 132 Annoyed when a local department store refused to deliver a spool of thread.

As the last term in **cotton, wire spool.**

***spooler,** *n.* A machine that winds thread on spools. — **1847** *Knickerb.* XXX. 517 A few [girls] tend the 'warpers,' the 'spoolers' and the 'speeders.'

* **spoon,** *n.* In combs.: (1) * **spoonbill,** see as a main entry; (2) **bread,** a form of bread made usu. with corn meal, rice, or hominy, milk, eggs, shortening, and leavening, and baked in a pan or dish from which it is served with a spoon, also **spoon cornbread;** (3) **exercise,** (see quots.), *obs.;* (4) **fish,** =**shovelfish;** (5) **hunt,** a local name for the mountain laurel or calico bush; (6) **strainer,** ?a strainer shaped like a spoon, *rare;* (7) **tree,** (see quot.); (8) **wood,** the wood of the mountain laurel or the tree itself; (9) **wood ivy,** a local name for sheep laurel.

(2) **1906** *D.N.* III. 158 *Spoon corn-bread,* soft corn-bread served with a spoon. **1948** *Chi. D. News* 23 Feb. 12/7 And so I get asked out to dinner, to sample . . . old Aunt Mamie's spoonbread. — (3) **1832** KEMBLE *Record* 111 We . . . took a delightful walk . . . to a place called Hoboken . . . now the favourite resort of a pacific society of

bon vivants, who meet once a week to eat turtle, or, as it is expressed on their cards of invitation, for 'spoon exercise.' **1896** HASWELL *New York* 62 The Turtle Club, afterward known as the Hoboken Turtle Club, was in existence [*c*1816]; notices of its meetings were announced as dividends of twenty or twenty-five per cent., and termed spoon exercise. — **(4) 1838** FLAGG *Far West* I. 107 Another singular variety found is the 'spoonfish,' about four feet in length, with a black skin, and an extension of the superior mandible for two feet, . . . used probably for digging its food.

(5) 1845–7 THOREAU *Journal* 435, I have watered . . . the cornel and spoonhunt and yellow violet, which might have withered else in dry seasons. **1892** *Amer. Folk-Lore* V. 100 *Kalmia latifolia*, spoon-hunt. Mason, N.H. — **(6) 1791** *Ky. Petitions* 184, I give and bequeath . . . one spoon strainer. — **(7) 1770** FORSTER tr. Kalm *Travels* I. 360 The American evergreens are 1. *Ilex Aquifolium*, holly. 2. *Kalmia latifolia*, the spoon tree. — **(8) 1778** CARVER *Travels* 234 They fashion their spoons . . . from a wood that is termed in America Spoon Wood, and which greatly resembles Box Wood. **1949** PALMER *Fieldbook Nat. Hist.* 284/3 Mountain Laurel . . . has been called spoonwood, broad-leaved kalmia, ivy bush, . . . and American laurel. — **(9) 1892** *Amer. Folk-Lore* V. 100 *Kalmia angustifolia*, spoonwood ivy. Conn.

b. In obs. colloq. or slang phrases (see quots.).

1848 J. MITCHELL *Nantucketisms* 42 'That's a great spoon.' Good, promising. **1859** BARTLETT 437 Spoon, 'to do business with a big spoon,' is the same as to cut a big swathe.

As the last term in **berry, horn, Irish, split, watermelon spoon.**

***spoon,** *v. intr.* and *tr.* To lie spoon fashion with another, to fit oneself snugly against (another) while lying down. *Colloq.* Cf. **table spooning.**

1863 *Rio Abajo Press* 18 Aug. 1/3 Giving him a tremendous thump, I again requested him to 'spoon.' **1887** *Harper's Mag.* Dec. 49/2 'Now spoon me.' Sterling stretched himself out on the warm flag-stone, and the boy nestled up against him. **1947** CHALFANT *Gold, Guns, & Ghost Towns* 16 Hey, you fellows! Time to turn over. Spoon! All hands turn over, I say!

***spoonbill,** *n.*

1. =**roseate spoonbill.**

1794 WANSEY *Excursion to U.S.* (1798) 122 There were [in Peale's Museum] Toucans, with their remarkable bills; Spoonbills natives of Georgia [etc.]. **1917** *Birds of Amer.* I. 175/1 Formerly the Spoonbills, or 'Pink Curlews,' as the Florida hunters know them, were extensively shot and their feathers shipped . . . [to be] made into fans. **1942** R. P. ALLEN *Roseate Spoonbill* 3/2 The shooting of egrets in colonies that these birds shared with the 'Pink Curlews' would have had an effect on both species, even though no Spoonbills were actually killed.

2. =**paddlefish.**

1892 J. A. THOMSON *Outline Zool.* 430 The paddle-fish or spoon bill of the Mississippi. **1908** *Cent. Mag.* July 457/1 In Mississippi [the paddlefish is known as] spoon-billed-cat or spooney, and in Arkansas as the spoonbill or spoonbilled sturgeon. **1931** *Sat. Ev. Post* 12 Sep. 135/1 Buffaloes and spoonbills are depressed, like stocks and cotton. Catfish that formerly sold for ten cents now go begging at six.

attrib. **1847** *Knickerb.* XXIX. 332 The shovel or spoon-bill fish is only found in the Alabama and its tributaries. **1882** JORDAN & GILBERT *Syn. Fishes N. Amer.* 83 *Polyodon spatula*, Paddle-fish; Spoonbill Cat. **1933** *Collier's* 16 Sep. 30/4 When the Muscovite Empire got tangled up by the World War, the production of caviar on the Mississippi River was stimulated—pure Russian caviar made from roe of the spoonbill catfish.

spoops spups, *n.* Also **spoopsy.** [Origin unknown.] (See quots.) *Slang. Obs.* — **1851** HALL *College Words* 291 At Harvard College, a weak, silly fellow, or one who is disliked on account of his foolish actions, is called a *spoops*, or *spoopsy*. **1860** *Yale Lit. Mag.* XXV. 192 (Th.), [If he] makes a dull recitation, he is denominated a regular 'spoops.'

***sport,** *n.*

1. Gaming, a gamester or gambler, a gay fellow. Also **sport-a-bout.** *Colloq.* or *slang.*

1856 *Harper's Mag.* Dec. 60/1 The very words 'sport' and 'sportsmen' have been perverted from their old English significations to mean gaming and gamblers. **1876** HARTE *Two Men of Sandy Bar* 91 Ye don't teach old sports like him new tricks. **1920** LEWIS *Main Street* 274 He was nineteen now, tall, broad, busy, the town sport, famous for his ability to drink beer. **1932** *K.C. Times* 29 Feb. 16 Many a young sport-a-bout of today who will eat only the breast of a fowl has a dad who was happy to grab the rumble seat.

2. *pl.* The sports section of a newspaper. Cf. **sports page.**

1923 *Nation* 17 Oct. 25/1 Crime and comic strips, sports and 'columns'—the *Leader* provides them all.

3. Designating articles of clothing suitable for wear by those engaged in sports, as **sport(s) blouse, coat, dress, jacket, shirt, suit.**

1916 H. L. WILSON *Somewhere in Red Gap* v. 188 Beryl Mae Macomber in her sport shirt. *Ib.* 204 A blue-striped sport bloose [*sic*]. **1917** *Ladies' Home Jrnl.* Feb. 96/1 See for yourself just how ravishing the new Sport Dresses are. **1919** MORLEY *Haunted Bookshop* (1921) 142 Posters announcing *The Return of Tarzan* showed a kind of third chapter of Genesis scene with an Eve in a sports suit. **1946** *Chi. D. News* 17 May 35/8 And to think I've been afraid to be seen outside in my new sport coat! **1946** *Reader's Digest* July 85/1 Found in addition were an Army blouse . . . and a sport jacket.

b. sports page, the page in a newspaper devoted to an account of sports, the sporting page.

1930 *Outlook* 8 Jan. 68/1 Naturally it is asking too much of the newspapers to expect them to hire humorists for their sports pages. **1950** *Chi. Tribune* 17 April IV. 1/4 Almost everyone whose name has hit the sports page headlines in the last quarter of a century was there.

***sporting,** *a.* and *n.*

1. Of, pertaining to, or engaged in gambling, drinking, dissipation, etc.

1845 HOOPER *Suggs* (1928) 21 That'll put all his wild sportin' notions out of his head. **1860** MORDECAI *Va.* 252 The field is now chiefly in possession of a class, termed in softened phrase, 'sporting characters.' **1900** GOODLANDER *Fort Scott* 43 This was the first building built for a saloon and sporting purposes in the town. **1928** FOY & HARLOW *Clowning Thro' Life* 148, I am sorry I cannot speak as favorably for his gambling room—which of course was what he meant by 'sporting resort.' **1938** ASBURY *Sucker's Prog.* 156 Even then the so-called sporting element formed a very small proportion of the population.

2. Designating parts or issues of a newspaper having to do with sports, or one who edits or writes such news, as (1) **sporting column,** (2) **editor,** (3) **extra,** (4) **page,** (5) **reporter,** (6) **section,** (7) **writer.**

(1) 1901 *Bookman* Oct. 123/2 Americans . . . have noted the peculiarities of the diction of the writers of the sporting columns. **1930** *Outlook* 8 Jan. 68/3 This is the sort of thing the sporting columns of a big New York daily carried each morning. — **(2) 1857** *Spirit of Times* 1 Aug. 340/2 We see exactly, where 'the sporting editor' of *The Times* has made his fatal mistake about handicaps and handicappers. — **(3) 1890** DAVIS *Gallegher* 90 It was nearly dusk . . . , as he knew by the newsboys calling the sporting extras on the street below. — **(4) 1915** *Lit. Digest* 21 Aug. 360/3 Bozeman Bulger . . . contributes to the sporting page of the New York *Evening World*. **1930** *Sat. Ev. Post* 25 Jan. 12/1 The fillers of space upon the sporting pages of the period were mostly professional sports.

(5) 1890 DAVIS *Gallegher* 212 The honor . . . was given to Andy Spielman, the sporting reporter of the *Track and Ring*. **1930** *Sat. Ev. Post* 25 Jan. 13/1 The moment the baseball season died away, the hordes of sporting reporters were turned loose upon the gridirons. — **(6) 1909** *D.N.* III. 399 Let me have the sporting section of that paper. **1929** *Amer. Mercury* March 338/1 Since the World War the sporting section has grown tremendously. — **(7) 1901** *Bookman* Oct. 123/2 Sporting writers all over the country were in a state of chaos.

3. In special combs.: (1) ***sporting gentleman,** a gambler, *obs.;* (2) **goods,** clothing and equipment for various sports, also attrib.; (3) ***house,** a house frequented by gamblers, a brothel; (4) ***man,** a gambler; (5) **room,** a room in which gambling is carried on.

(1) 1835 INGRAHAM *South-West* II. 10 Two . . . are professed 'black-legs'; or, as they more courteously style themselves, 'sporting gentlemen.' **1862** MOORE *Rebellion Rec.* V. II. 285 They seemed to be of that class to which we apply the term 'sporting gentlemen.' — **(2) 1869** *Boyd's Business Directory* 500 John H. Mann, Importer and Dealer in Guns, Fishing Tackle, Gun Powder, and all Sporting Goods. **1949** *Pacific Discovery* July–Aug. 13/1 Then came the gadgeteer, otherwise known as the sporting-goods dealer. — **(3) 1891** *Cent.* 5857/3 *Sporting-house*, a house frequented by . . . betting men, gamblers, and the like. **1946** THOMPSON *Amer. Daughter* 192 She regaled me with tales . . . of her life when she was young, when she worked in the sporting houses as maid—she said. — **(4) 1833** in M. JAMES *Andrew Jackson* (1937) 7/1 (We.), Sporting men were willing to wager that the deposits would be removed. **1924** MCCONNELL *Frontier Law* 115 All 'sporting men' should leave within a stated time.

(5) 1878 BEADLE *Western Wilds* 46 He strayed into one of our sporting rooms.

***sportsman,** *n.* One who bets on horse races, etc., a professional gambler.

1740 W. STEPHENS *Proc. Georgia* I. 606 The Sportsmen, as Yesterday, took a plentiful Cup in the Evening. **1835** TODD *Notes* 40 The word *Sportsman* here denotes, not a foxhunter, but a gambler by profession. **1878** *Cong. Rec.* 27 March 2093/1 The adroit and sleight-of-hand Stebbins, . . . could handle a ticket as a sportsman would a playing-card.

sposh spaʃ, *n.* [Poss. imitative in origin, but cf. *OED* and *EDD posh* in same sense.] Slush, mud. *Colloq.*

1845 *N.Y. Tribune* 25 Nov. (B.), The streets were one shining level of black sposh. **1877** BURROUGHS *Birds & Poets* 93 Yellow sposh and mud and water everywhere.

Hence **sposhy,** *a.* [cf. *EDD poshy* in same sense], soft, wet, miry. *Colloq.*

1842 *Yale Lit. Mag.* VIII. 96, I can't always decipher quail tracks—specially in *sposhy* weather. **1884** JEWETT *Country Doctor* 22 There's a sight o' difference between good upland fruit and the sposhy apples that grows in wet ground.

***spot,** *n.*

1. A blaze on a tree. *Rare.* Cf. ***spot,** *v.* **1.**

1841 G. POWERS *Hist. Sk. Coos* 115 They made their way by *feeling* of the trees to see if they were *spotted;* but they at length could feel no *spots,* and despaired of finding a settlement.

2. One of the conventional figures or pips on a playing card, also a playing card having a designated number of such pips. *Colloq.*

1843 STEPHENS *High Life N.Y.* II. 215 'Jest so,' sez I, a fli[n]gin down the ten spot o' clubs. **1864** DICK *Amer. Hoyle* (1866) 457 Face cards, having but one spot, may be taken by a deuce or any other card having two or more spots. **1920** MULFORD *J. Nelson* x, I'm layin' down as fine a pair of four-spots as I've ever held.

b. With the value in dollars designated by a number: A bank note, silver certificate, or the like, as a **ten spot, twenty spot.** *Colloq.*

1846 BURNHAM *Stray Subjects* 135, I moved towards the money, but he prevented my raising it, by covering it with a *twenty*-spot. **1857** *Harper's Mag.* Sep. 568/2 I'll take that ten spot, if you please. **1945** SERVICE *Ploughman* 145 At Winnipeg I got rid of my gun for a 'ten spot.'

3. Any one of various fishes, as the red drum, *Sciaenops ocellata,* or the sciaenoid food fish, *Leiostomus xanthurus.* In full **spot fish.**

1875 *Fur, Fin & Feather* 122 You are always welcome to a seat in his boat, if disposed for snipe or duck, or spot-fish. **1879** KILBOURNE & GOODE *Game Fishes U.S.* 37/2 'Spot' is another name erroneously applied to this fish [the red drum], and which is the property of a much smaller species of the same family, otherwise known as 'Lafayette,' or 'Cape May Goody.' **1911** *Rep. Fisheries 1908* 316/2 Spot (*Leiostomus xanthurus*).... [It] is taken with hook and line and in gill nets.

4. In special combs.: (1) **spot cash,** cash paid at once, *colloq.;* (2) **cotton,** cotton on hand for immediate delivery; (3) **rump,** =**Hudsonian godwit.**

(1) **1879** *Bradstreet's* 8 Oct. 4/3 A business Utopia where credit shall be unknown and 'spot cash' an unvarying rule. **1944** DUNCAN *M. Graham* 11 William bought two hundred additional acres, for spot cash. — (2) **1881** *Bradstreet's* 8 Oct. 234/4 The New York cotton market has been very steady . . . for spot cottons. **1950** *Guaranty Survey* 29 March 18 Cotton—Middling, spot, New Orleans. Cents per lb. 12.50. — (3) **1888** TRUMBULL *Names of Birds* 209 At North Scituate, Provincetown, and Chatham [Mass., it is called] Spot-Rump. **1917** *Birds of Amer.* I. 240

b. In colloq. and slang phrases: (1) *In spots,* at intervals, in some respects; (2) *to knock the spots off,* and variants, to surpass, beat decisively; (3) *to go to the spot,* to satisfy completely, "fill the bill"; (4) *to get* (something) *down to a spot,* to get (something) down pat; (5) *to put on the spot,* to place in a perilous position, to murder, also *to be on the spot,* to be in a position of great danger, *to keep off the spot,* to play safe, keep out of danger [said to have originated from the kangaroo court custom described in quot. 1929].

(1) **1852** STOWE *Uncle Tom* xvi, Mammy has a kind of obstinacy about her, in spots. **1900** *Cong. Rec.* 16 Jan. 867/1 It is found in spots, which is something like this wartime prosperity they have talked about. — (2) **1856** *Spirit of Times* 22 Nov. 196/1 Addison County leads the van (or 'knocks the spots off,' as we say here) in Vermont, and is celebrated over the world for its fine horses. **1897** ROBINSON *Uncle Lisha's Outing* 34 If that don't knock the spots out'n all the dancin' ever I ever did see. — (3) **1868** *Putnam's Mag.* I. 670/1 'I hope that last corjul set you up?' 'Yes, Mr. Plunkitt, it went right to the spot.' **1923** NUTTING *Massachusetts* 241 Did ever a dish of apple dowdy go to the spot like that? — (4) **1886** CHADWICK *Art of Pitching* 69 A man who for years has been playing in one position, and who, in that position, has got everything down to a spot.

(5) **1929** *Sat. Ev. Post* 13 April 50/3 He is taken before the penitentiary court, and then Father Time tries him. If the offense is trivial, Father Time may put him on the spot. The spot is a piece of carpet about eight or ten inches square. He takes off his shoes and stands on the spot all day—or perhaps two days—without food. . . . In other places he faces a wall and his nose is placed against a small painted spot. **1930** *Punch* 16 April 442 You get rid of inconvenient subordinates . . . by 'putting them on the spot'—that is deliberately sending them to their death. **1932** *K.C. Times* 28 March 18 We'd be overwhelmed with money in a short time—if we could keep off the spot long enough. **1943** *Sat. Ev. Post* 1 May 19/1, I was on the spot then, and I stood on that spot for two weeks, dripping sweat. **1948** *Chi. Sun-Times* 18 March 38/1 Some of the questions directed at him were obviously designed to put Stassen on the spot.

As the last term in **alkali, black, building, five, four, hard, high, night, polka, seed, soft, tight, two spot.**

***spot,** *v.*

1. *tr.* To blaze (a tree), to mark (a line) by blazing. Cf. ***spot,** *n.* **1.**

1718 *N.H. Probate Rec.* II. 58 One of the said lotts begins at . . . a Beach tree spotted and numbered three. **1792** BELKNAP *Hist. N.H.* III. 75 Where they find the land suitable for a road, the trees are spotted, by cutting out a piece of the bark. **1860** *Harper's Mag.* Feb. 300/1 We had struck the line which our friends had spotted as they past along. **1947** *Ib.* July 82/1 When a tree is spotted with an axe the wood grows over the blaze in a few years.

b. To smooth off a level place on (a timber), as on a railroad tie for a rail.

1857 *Ill. Agric. Soc. Trans.* II. 434 Ties, like common fence posts, . . . were spotted down.

2. To hit with a bullet. *Rare.* Cf. ******pot,* the usual term.

1882 HARTE *Flip* 24 It's an even thing if she wouldn't spot me the first pop.

***spotted,** *a.*

1. Of trees or a trail: Blazed.

1828 SHERBURNE *Memoirs* 192 We could no longer find our way by our spotted trees. **1888** ROOSEVELT in *Cent. Mag.* June 204/1 Some fur-trapper had chopped a deeper blaze than usual in making out a 'spotted line.'

2. In the names of birds, plants, and animals: (1) ***spotted Canada warbler,** =**Canada warbler;** (2) ***cat,** (see quot.); (3) **frog,** (see quot.); (4) **sandpiper,** the teetertail, *Actitis macularia;* (5) **skunk,** (see quot. 1917); (6) **-tail bass,** prob. a spotted bass; (7) **tiger,** a bobcat or ocelot, *obs.;* (8) **weakfish,** a weakfish, *Eriscion nebulosus,* found along the south Atlantic and Gulf coasts; (9) **wintergreen,** an evergreen herb, *Chimaphila maculata,* named from its mottled leaves.

(1) **1844** *Nat. Hist. N.Y., Zoology* II. 91 The Spotted Canada Warbler. *Sylvicola pardalina* . . . is occasionally very rare in New York, or at least in its southern portions. — (2) **1917** *Mammals of Amer.* 152 If one talks with hunters or ranchmen about Ocelots, the probability is that they will refer to them as Leopard Cats or Spotted Cats. — (3) **1867** *Amer. Naturalist* I. 109 Other species of Frogs found in Massachusetts . . . are the Spotted Frog, Marsh Frog, or Pickerel Frog (*Rana palustris* Le Conte); the second species of Spotted Frog [etc.]. — (4) **1813** WILSON *Ornithology* VII. 60 *Tringa macularia,* Spotted Sandpiper. . . . This species is . . . remarkable for perpetually wagging the tail. **1944** *Nat. Geog. Mag.* June 690/1 Some of our North American birds, especially among the water-loving species, are found during the summer from coast to coast and from the Gulf of Mexico to Alaska. . . . Such are the spotted sandpiper and the killdeer.

(5) **1917** *Mammals of Amer.* 135 The Spotted Skunk and its relatives of the genus *Spilogale* are the smallest of the North American Skunks. **1949** *Minot* (N.D.) *D. News* 22 July 2/2 The spotted skunk is often called the hydrophobia skunk. — (6) **1894** *Life* 5 July 14/2, I sat trolling for spotted-tail bass. — (7) **1805** *Ann. 9th Cong.* 2 Sess. 1103 We saw no animals that were not common in all the country of Louisiana, except the spotted tiger, and a few white bears. **1808** SCHULTZ *Travels* II. 144, I thought it as beautiful a spotted tiger or leopard skin as I had ever seen. . . . They are called the spotted tiger in this country [near N.O.]. — (8) **1891** *Cent.* 6858/1. **1947** *Sports Afield* Dec. 20/1 The most popular species is the spotted weakfish, locally called winter trout. — (9) **1846–50** A. WOOD *Class-bk. Bot.* 379 *Chimaphila maculata,* . . . Spotted wintergreen. **1902** *Amer. Folk-Lore* 253 Another plant of the same family is the 'spotted *pipsissewa*' (*C. maculata*), also known as 'spotted wintergreen.'

b. spotted land, (see quot.). *Obs.*

1845 *Cong. Globe* 4 Feb. 242/3 The lands of Missouri were called spotted lands; one strip was good, and another bad.

***spotter,** *n.* **1.** One who assists a surveyor by carrying an object or target used in sighting. *Obs.* **2.** One who seeks out good spots of land. *Rare.* **3.** A spy or detective, esp. one hired by a railroad or streetcar company to watch for dishonesty on the part of the conductor or passengers. Cf. **company spotter.**

(1) **1741** *N.H. Prov. P.* (1871) V. 77, I think the best way of doing it will be by a skillful surveyor or surveyors and chainmen on oath with a proper number of spotters and baggagemen to attend them. — (2) **1847** *Knickerb.* XXIX. 203 The soil is too thin and sandy to raise cotton, except in small and detached patches, on which the 'spotters' have settled. — (3) **1876** *Scribner's Mo.* April 911/2 The stockholders and directors, the 'car-starters' and 'spotters,' . . . were all embalmed in verse and immortalized in song. **1944** KAHN *Cable Car Days* 67 'Spotters' were placed in advantageous positions along the road and in the cars, but every method to detect the fare beaters was unsuccessful.

*__spout,__ *n.* As the last term in **basswood, eave(s), sand, sap spout.**

* **Sprague,** *n.* [Isaac *Sprague* (1811–95), Amer. illustrator.] **Sprague's lark, pipit,** =**Missouri skylark.**

1875 *Amer. Naturalist* IX. 78 There is something I have not quite made out respecting the breeding range of Sprague's lark, *Neocorys Spraguei.* **1917** *Birds of Amer.* III. 171/1 The best known is Sprague's Pipit, called the Missouri Skylark, or sometimes the Prairie Skylark. **1948** *Audubon Mag.* July–Aug. 249/2 The song of Baird's sparrow leads you up to a gently-rolling short grass prairie, where a small colony of Sprague's pipits is discovered.

* **sprangle,** *n.* A straggling cluster or ramification; branching rootlets. Also fig. *Colloq.*

1839 *Jamestown* (N.Y.) *Jrnl.* 20 Nov. 1/4 The most I could git was two or three sprangles of little white things that I stirred up from the bottom of the plate. **1896** *Advance* 21 May 738/1 Skepticism has its roots and spreads its feeding sprangles chiefly in the affections and the will. **1898** *Ib.* 19 May 662/1 This [Philippine] archipelago lies upon the map a great sprangle of intermingled land and water.

sprangly ˈspræŋglɪ, *a.* [Cf. *EDD spranggelin, a.* straggling.] Scraggy, scrawny, spreading. *Colloq.*

1840 HOFFMAN *Greyslaer* II. 25 Following hard on his trail along a hillside overgrown with short sprangly bushes, I saw [etc.]. **1886** *Leslie's Mo.* Oct. 503/1 We can command a view through their sprangly branches. **1945** *Chi. Tribune* 13 May VII. 1/5, I found the breeches [in the Ozarks] to be a sprangly (the word is Donie's) plant with fuzzy stems.

* **spread,** *n.* [See note.]

In sense **1.** regarded in *OED* as being orig. Amer., prob. after Du. *sprei* in same sense. There is a Du. regional form *spreed,* but the *EDD* records *spread* in this sense from Devonshire with evidence dated 1892.

1. A quilt or coverlet, a table cover. Cf. **bedspread, table spread.**

1836 GILMAN *Recoll.* (1838) 251 The bed-curtains and spreads were mostly patterns of gorgeous birds and trees. **1846** THORPE *Myst. Backwoods* 27 An enormously thick-leafed table, with a 'spread' upon it, attracted little attention. **1950** *Chi. Tribune* 13 Jan. 12/6 She'll throw herself across the bed and cry all over that new spread I gave her.

2. In a newspaper, an article given conspicuous treatment, as by display across two or more columns, or facing pages.

[**1858** HOLMES *Autocrat* 131 One gives a 'spread' on linen, and the other on paper—that is all.] **1877** *Harper's Mag.* Dec. 50/1 His remarkable ability is best seen when occasion arises for a 'spread.'

3. In billiards, a rebound of a cue ball from the object ball at a considerable angle from its former course.

1864 DICK *Amer. Hoyle* (1866) 418 Beginners . . . are apt to suppose that, to effect a 'spread,' it is necessary to hit the object ball far from the centre.

4. (See quot. 1900.) Cf. * **spread eagle 3.**

1879 WEBSTER *Supp.* 1579/3 *Spread,* . . . the privilege of demanding shares of stock at a certain price or of delivering shares of stock at another price, within a certain time agreed upon. **1900** NELSON *A B C Wall St.* 160 *Spread.* This is a double stock privilege which entitles the holder to the right to deliver or demand a certain amount of stock on specified terms, or grain price differences between different options, or between the same option in different cities, or between the put and call price.

5. Jam, jelly, peanut butter, etc., suitable for spreading on bread.

1886 STOCKTON *Mrs. Lecks* 40 The one who gets the last biscuit will have somethin' of a little spread on it. **1948** *Amer. Butter & Cheese Rev.* Dec. 6 The public wants a yellow fat spread for its bread.

6. *W.* A cowboy term for a ranch and its appurtenances. Cf. **sheep spread.**

1927 JAMES *Cow Country* 67 He'd paid a big price for the said spread, and he was lord and master there sure enough. **1947** *Trail Riders Bul.* Feb. 20/1, I wuz top bronc buster for the Tumblin' L spread.

* **spread,** *v.*

1. *tr.* To enter or record (an order, sentence, etc.), *on* or *upon* a permanent record.

1845 COOPER *Chainbearer* xix, It will greatly aid the reader . . . if I spread on the record the language that passed. **1894** ROBLEY *Bourbon Co., Kans.* 184 Councilmen Dimon, White and Drake caused the following order to be spread upon the minutes. **1931** *Randolph Enterprise* (Elkins, W.Va.) 26 March 1/5 Resolved that a copy of these resolutions be sent to the family, a copy spread on the minutes of the lodge [etc.].

2. *reflex.* To exert oneself, make a show, display oneself. *Colloq.*

1845 G. A. MCCALL *Lett. fr. Frontiers* (1868) 433 Champion [a horse] brought me safely out of the flat, and *spread himself,* or bounded forward on the broad level plain. **1909** WASON *Happy Hawkins* 248 This afternoon he got to spreadin' himself about how much money the place handled.

3. (*a*) *To spread it on thick,* to exaggerate, *slang,* (*b*) *to spread out,* to expand the scope of one's operations, *colloq.* Cf. **spread-out,** *a.*

(*a*) **1865** MARK TWAIN *Sketches* (1926) 172 Don't you think he is spreading it on rather thick? (*b*) **1901** HARRIGAN *Mulligans* 158 He wanted to 'spread out,' but not in the sense of ostentation or extravagance. *Ib.* 159 Tom 'spread out.' He sold his Chicago possessions and invested the money . . . in Dakota farm lands.

* **spread eagle.**

1. A representation of an eagle with outstretched wings serving as the emblem of the U.S.

1842 *Vt. Militia Act.* Sec. 28, 62 Buttons—gilt, convex, with spread eagle and stars. **1894** ALDRICH *Two Bites* 65 The Stars and Stripes, held in the claws of a spread eagle, decorated the editorial page.

2. Bombast, boastfulness. Usu. attrib., with reference to high-flown patriotic oratory.

1858 *N. Amer. Rev.* Oct. 454 'The spread-eagle style' is chargeable only upon a certain class of writers. **1864** *Wkly. New Mexican* 15 July 2/2 There is no trifling and 'spread eagle' in his [Grant's] bearing and manner. **1890** LANGFORD *Vigilante Days* (1912) 136 There are always those present who, by the command 'Dry up,' 'No spread-eagle talk,' force them to a close. **1948** *Time* 21 June 19/1 The great game of U.S. politics, its deadly seriousness concealed from the unobservant by circus trappings and spread-eagle oratory, was moving swiftly and dramatically toward its quadrennial climax.

3. = * **spread,** *n.* **4.** Also attrib.

1857 *Hunt's Merch. Mag.* July 136 The buyer can call when he pleases, which would compel the 'spread eagle' operator to deliver. **1870** MEDBERY *Men Wall St.* 86 One modification of this is the Spread Eagle, formerly a highly popular style of speculation with capitalists who had plenty of money and a wide-awake broker. **1910** *Encycl. Brit.* (ed. 11) V. 55/1 A combined option of either calling or putting is termed a 'straddle,' and sometimes on the American stock exchange a 'spread-eagle.'

spread-eagleism ˈsprɛdˈiglˌɪzəm, *n.* Exaggerated laudation of the U.S.

1859 G. F. TRAIN (*title*), Spread-Eagleism. *Ib.* p. ix, We cannot fasten an ism on him (except Spread-Eagleism). **1884** *American* VIII. 212 The old-fashioned oration, though greatly abused by spread-eagleism. **1903** W. F. JOHNSON *Cent. of Expansion* 130 At the very moment when he was indulging in such spread-eagleism American ships were being fired upon at the mouths of American harbors.

*__spreader,__ *n.* As the last term in **fertilizer, guano, hay, manure spreader.**

* **spreading,** *a.* In combs.: (1) **spreading adder,** =**hognose snake;** (2) **dogbane,** (see quot.); (3) **frame,** (see quot. 1876); (4) **viper,** =**spreading adder.**

(1) **1842** *Nat. Hist. N.Y., Zoology* III. 52 The Hog-nosed Snake . . . is also called Deaf Adder, Spreading Adder, Hog-nose and Buckwheat-nose. **1948** *Chi. Tribune* 4 April VII. 10/7 The first trick, of course, was to catch and kill your snake—a big bull snake, black snake, cottonmouth, or spreading adder. — (2) *a***1862** THOREAU *Maine Woods* 317 *Apocynum androsæmifolium* (spreading dogbane). — (3) **1850** *Rep. Comm. Patents 1849* 375, I claim . . . the treating of the lap after it comes from the 'spreading frame.' **1876** KNIGHT 2289/1 *Spreading-frame,* . . . a machine in which a number of *stricks* or slivers of flax are spread and conducted to a system of drawing-rollers, whereby they are united and drawn into one. **1891** CHASE & CLOW *Industry* III. 33 The 'spreading frame' to which we were next taken was much like it. — (4) **1887** *Courier-Journal* 15 Feb. 6/6 Early in the fall the girl was playing in a field and was bitten on the arm by a spreading viper.

*__spread-out,__ *a.* Not compact or densely settled, extended in operation or scope. *Colloq.* — **1856** *Porter's Spirit of Times* 18 Oct.

115/1 Arrived at Salem about half past 5 same day—city 'spread out' a good deal, streets very wide—houses far apart. **1887** *Nation* 20 Oct. 302/1 Nearly everybody was [financially speaking] 'spread out.'

***spree,** *n.* As the last term in **cane, horn spree.**

* **sprig,** *n.*

1. =**sprigtail.**

1888 TRUMBULL *Names of Birds* 38 At Baltimore, Washington, [etc., it is known as] . . . Sprig-Tail; this being sometimes shortened to Sprig. **1932** *Book of Birds* I. 102 The pintail, or 'sprig,' as it is known in California, is a far more common duck in western than in eastern North America. **1948** *Chi. Tribune* 25 April IV. 6/1 I've killed, with a .410, doves, quail, teal, shovellers, sprig, canvasback . . . and wild turkey.

2. sprigtail, the pintail duck or the ruddy duck. Also attrib., and (by error) **spring-tail.**

1768 WASHINGTON *Diaries* I. 254 Killd 2 Ducks, viz. a sprig tail and Teal. **1870** *Amer. Naturalist* IV. 49 Pintail Duck. . . . By some it is called Spring-tail. **1874** J. W. LONG *Amer. Wild-Fowl* 199 In sprigtail-shooting it is best to place the decoys to windward of the blind when circumstances will allow. **1949** SPRUNT & CHAMBERLAIN *S.C. Bird Life* 116 American Pintail. . . . Local Names: Sprig; Sprig-tail. . . . The long central tail feathers of the adult male are always noticeable.

b. The sharp-tailed grouse.

1859 in F. HALL *Hist. Colo.* II. 522 Phil killed two sprigtail grouse. **1891** *Cent.* 5862/3 *Sprigtail*, . . . the sharp-tailed or pin-tailed grouse, *Pediœcetes phasianellus columbianus:* more fully *sprig-tailed grouse.*

***sprigtailed,** *a.* In the names of birds (see quots.). — **1872** COUES *Key to Birds* 39 A cuneate tail . . . is also called pointed, in contradistinction to rounded, as in the sprig-tailed duck. **1917** *Birds of Amer.* II. 27 Sharp-tailed Grouse. *Pediœcetes phasianellus phasianellus.* . . . [Also called] Pin-tailed Grouse; Sprig-tailed Grouse; White Grouse.

* **spring,** *n.*

1. In combs. alluding to springtime: (1) **spring beaver,** the skin of a beaver taken in the spring, *obs.;* (2) **chicken,** (*a*) a young chicken, usu. one only a few months old, (*b*) a youthful or inexperienced person, *colloq.;* (3) **drive,** a drive of logs down a stream in the spring; (4) **fever,** (see quot. 1859); (5) **freshet,** a spring flood or overflow in a stream; (6) **poor,** *a. W.* of cattle, poor or lean in spring after a hard winter, *colloq.;* (7) **range,** *W.* a range for cattle in the spring; (8) **rodeo, roundup,** *W.* a rodeo or roundup *qq.v.* that occurs in the spring; (9) **term,** (*a*) the session of a court held in the spring, (*b*) the school term which begins in the spring; (10) **trade,** trade, beginning during the winter, in commodities for sale or use in the spring, cf. **fall trade.**

(1) **1902** HULBERT *Forest Neighbors* 139 It would have made the pelt which the old fur-traders sometimes sold under the name of 'spring beaver.' — (2) (*a*) **1845** *Knickerb.* XXVI. 511 It consisted of a pair of spring chickens. **1917** MCCUTCHEON *Green Fancy* 22 'Ham and eggs, pork tenderloin, country sausage, rump steak and spring chicken,' said Mr. Bacon. (*b*) **1879** TOURGEE *Fool's Errand* 259, I'm no spring-chicken; and . . . I have never listened to more sound and convincing sense. **1947** MYERS *The 'Guv'* 277 Guv, you and the other boys are not spring chickens any more. — (3) **1893** *Scribner's Mag.* June 699/1 A man who had put in a long winter and a spring drive, presented himself at the Company's office. — (4) **1859** BARTLETT 438 *Spring fever*, the listless feeling caused by the first sudden increase of temperature in spring. It is often said of a lazy fellow, 'He has got the spring fever.' **1950** *Chi. Tribune* 28 March 14/3 We old-timers know that the true vernal season is ushered in by that state of lassitude called spring fever.

(5) **1884** W. SHEPHERD *Prairie Exper.* 216 The people, after the spring freshets, must content themselves with very little water. — (6) **1868** *Iowa State Agric. Soc. Rep. 1867* 128, I do not believe in turning them out on watery grass to shift for themselves 'spring poor.' **1905** *McClure's Mag.* XXV. 598 Nowadays we hardly know what is meant by the expression 'Spring poor.' — (7) **1905** *Forestry Bureau Bul.* No. 62, 28 In some of the States there is an area along the lower slopes of the mountains which is called spring and fall range, being used in the early part of the season before stock are driven to the summer ranges. **1913** W. C. BARNES *Western Grazing Grounds* 72 In the Southwest and on the Pacific Coast they have a range known as the spring range. . . . The feed for the most part is foxtail (Hordeum murinum), bronco grass (Bromus rubens), poverty grass. — (8) **1874** HITTELL *Resources Calif.* 282 In the fall there is another season of rodeos, to brand such calves as may have escaped notice at the spring rodeos. **1890** *Stock Grower & Farmer* 22 March 6/4 The stockmen had a meeting March 1st for the purpose of arranging the spring roundup. **1950** *L.A. Times Mag.* 26 Feb. 5/1 Ranchers near Capistrano hold spring roundup in the old tradition of neighbor help neighbor. — (9) (*a*) **1771** *Copley-Pelham Lett.* 139 The tryal . . . must go to the spring term. **1864** *Wkly. New Mexican* 24 June 2/2 The fines . . . during the past spring terms, amounted to Eleven hundred and Fifteen dollars. (*b*) **1854** *Boston Ev. Trav.* 12 July, '*Chip day*,' at the close of the spring term, is still observed in the old-fashioned way. **1904** WALLER *Wood-Carver* 90 She is going to the district school during the spring term.

(10) **1851** [see **fall trade**]. **1890** *Bradstreet's* 18 Feb. 108/4 Spring trade is opening up in Baltimore.

b. In the names of plants and animals: (1) **spring beauty,** (*a*) any one of various plants of the genus *Claytonia*, as *C. virginica*, that flower in the early spring, (*b*) (see quot.); (2) * **bird,** (*a*) the song sparrow, (*b*) (see quot.); (3) **cankerworm,** a cankerworm, *Paleacrita vernata*, that spends the winter in the ground and matures early in the spring; (4) **cress,** a variety of cress, *Cardamine bulbosa*, found in wet places in the eastern states; (5) **herring,** the alewife; (6) **lily,** (see quots.); (7) **mackerel,** (see quot. 1890); (8) **peeper,** a peeper *q.v.*, *Hyla crucifer*, of eastern North America, the smallest of its genus, being about an inch long; (9) **salmon,** =**tyee salmon;** (10) **sunflower,** (see quot.).

(1) (*a*) **1821** *Mass. H.S. Coll.* 2 Ser. IX. 148 Plants, which are indigenous in the township of Middlebury, [Vt., include] . . . *Claytonia virginica*, . . . Spring beauty. **1863** *Rep. Comm. Agric. 1862* 158 These Claytonias . . . go by the name of 'Spring Beauty.' **1946** *Trail & Timberline* May 75/2 Anemones, spring beauties and sedums were in blossom. (*b*) **1915** ARMSTRONG & THORNBER *Western Wild Flowers* 122 Spring Beauty. *Montia parvifolia.* White and pink. Spring Northwest. . . . This charming little flower . . . blooms in late spring, among the ferns and wet grasses near the Yosemite waterfalls and in similar places. — (2) (*a*) **1824** Z. THOMPSON *Gazetteer Vt.* 18 The singing birds are the robin, thrush, . . . springbird, goldfinch, and hangbird. **1832** WILLIAMSON *Maine* I. 143 The Spring Bird is larger than a chipping bird, and is one of the very first to sing the vernal song. (*b*) **1917** *Birds of Amer.* II. 212 Horned Lark. . . . Also called Wheat Bird: Spring Bird; Life Bird. — (3) **1889** *Cent.* 791/3 The spring canker-worm, *Anisopteryx vernata*, is found . . . from Maine to Texas. — (4) **1817–8** EATON *Botany* (1822) 177 *Arabis rhomboides*, spring cress. **1869** *Amer. Naturalist* III. 130 Along streams in open woodlands, we may find the Spring Cress . . . with large, white flowers.

(5) **1839** STORER *Mass. Fishes* 114 The Spring Herring or Alewife. . . . They are still taken in some places in immense numbers. **1950** *Chi. Tribune* 17 Jan. 14/3 The spring herring is known as 'Taunton turkey.' — (6) **1909** *Cent. Supp.* 729/2 Spring lily, the white dogtooth violet or adder's-tongue, *Erythronium albidum*, which flowers in the early spring. **1939** *Nat. Geog. Mag.* Aug. 266/1 Adder's-tongues are also popularly known as 'dogtooth violets' or 'spring lilies,' although they are not true lilies of the genus *Lilium*, and certainly are not in any respect violets. — (7) **1818** *Amer. Mo. Mag.* II. 296 Spring Mackerel. This elegant fish is migratory. **1890** *Cent.* 3561/3 *Spring mackerel*, the ordinary commercial mackerel of good size and quality, sometimes technically named *Scomber vernalis:* distinguished from *fall mackerel.* — (8) **1906** DICKINSON *Frog Book* 139 There are few people in the eastern United States who do not know the voices of the Spring Peepers, although they may not guess who these singers may be. **1950** *Chi. Tribune* 28 March 14/3 Then there are those who listen for choruses of spring peepers. — (9) **1851** in SCHOOLCRAFT *Indian Tribes* (1853) III. 147 The spring salmon, which is by far the best, is apparently identical with that of the eastern States. **1940** SMITH *Puyallup-Nisqually* 235 Since the tyee is generally the earliest to arrive, the term 'spring salmon' is occasionally used as referring only to this species.

(10) **1919** WILSON *White Indian* 219 Balzamoriza. . . . A species of plant with showy yellow blossoms, and velvety leaves, belonging to the sunflower family. Commonly known as 'spring sunflower.' The seeds were used by Indians for food. It grows about one foot high.

2. In combs. relating to or involving a source of water: (1) * **spring box,** a box fixed in a spring so as to form a convenient receptacle for water; (2) **branch,** a branch or brook fed by a spring or by springs; (3) **brook,** =prec.; (4) **creek,** a creek fed by a spring or by springs; (5) **dairy,** (see quot.); (6) **hole,** (*a*) a hole or pool of water at the source or along the channel of a stream, (*b*) an air hole in ice; (7) **house,** a small house built over a spring or brook for the purpose of keeping perishable foods cool; (8) **lot,** an inclosure for horses, cows, etc., having a spring or branch flowing through it; (9) **oil,** (see quot.), *obs.;* (10) **slash,** a slash which heads in a spring; (11) **still,** a whisky still located at or near a spring; (12) **swamp,** a swamp that heads in a spring.

(1) **1917** KEPHART *Camping* I. 221 At a cabin in the Smokies . . . I had a spring box . . . which kept things cool and safe in the warmest weather. — (2) **1650** in *Amer. Sp.* XV. 396/1 Bounded on the North East with a Spring branch or cove. **1826** T. FLINT *Recoll.* 192 [The settlement] is intersected with numerous spring-branches, around which there are always found clumps of trees. **1945** BOTKIN *My Burden* 26 They baptizes me in the spring branch close to where I finds the Lord. — (3) **1852** MARCY *Explor. Red River* (1854) 30 We went on, and in a few miles found a spring-brook. **1888** JEWETT *King of Folly Isl.* 132, I made an arrant out to the spring-brook to see if there was any cresses started. — (4) **1800** HAWKINS *Sk. Creek Country* 57 A fine little spring creek joins on its right bank. **1904** WHITE *Blazed Trail Stories* 76 They came to a glade through which ran a soggy, choked, little spring-creek.

(5) **1823** FAUX *Memorable Days* 129, I saw here a fine Spring dairy; that is to say, a dairy of stone built over a spring of pure cold water continually flowing through, and round it, so that the milk and cream-vessels may stand in water to prevent the butter from turning to stinking oil. — (6) (*a*) **1845** KIRKLAND *Western Clearings* 69 The pony didn't die in the spring-hole. **1902** WHITE *Blazed Trail* 63 Muddy swamp and spring-holes caused endless difficulty. (*b*) **1890–3** TABER *Stowe Notes* 35 The frost-formed spring-holes in the ice. — (7) **1755** in CHALKLEY *Scotch-Irish Settlement Va.* I. 445, 1 spring house, 18 feet long and 12 feet wide. **1805** PARKINSON *Tour* 222 As to butter, the milk can only be kept in springhouses. **1949** *Pa. Dutchman* 28 July 4/1 But there was always a springhouse cooling watermelons. — (8) **1898** HARRIS *Tales of Home Folks* 53 Her voice came from the spring lot. **1938** DAMON *Grandma* 60 The brook was at the foot of the hill in the 'spring-lot.' — (9) **1837** W. JENKINS *Ohio Gaz.* 457 Petroleum or spring oil rises with or near to the gas.

(10) **1681** in *Amer. Sp.* XV. 396/2 From thence with a direct line to the head of the spring slash. **1682** *Ib.*, Up ye sd branch to a white oake att ye mouth of his Spring Slash. — (11) **1869** TOURGEE *Toinette* (1881) 11 That's good whiskey, . . . made by an old Dutchman at a little spring-still up the country. — (12) **1636** in *Amer. Sp.* XV. 396/2 Downe the maine river into the Spring Swamp. **1747** *Ib.*, Thence along the said Mill pond to the Mouth of my Spring Swamp.

b. Also (1) **spring frog,** the green frog or the leopard frog; (2) **keeper,** (see quot. 1859); (3) **lizard,** =prec.

(1) **1842** *Nat. Hist. N.Y., Zoology* III. 62 The Spring Frog . . . is that [species] usually eaten as a delicacy. **1906** M. C. DICKERSON *Frog Book* 171 (*footnote*), The Leopard Frog is called 'Spring Frog' in Florida and 'Grass Frog' in New York. *Ib.* 198 The Green Frog *Rana clamitans*. . . . Called 'Spring Frog' and 'Pond Frog' in various parts of the country. — (2) **1859** BARTLETT 438 Spring-Keeper. A salamander, or small lizard-shaped animal, found in springs and fresh water rivulets, whence the name. **1945** *Amer. Sp.* XX. (Oct.) 230/1 While collecting salamanders near Munson Hill, Virginia, years ago, I was informed by a colored woman that the red salamander (*Pseudotriton ruber*) which I caught in her presence was called a *springkeeper*. — (3) **1892** HARRIS *U. Remus & Friends* 313, I want you ter ketch me sev'n spring lizzuds. **1917** KEPHART *Camping* II. 411 The little red newt (often called 'spring lizard,' although it is not a reptile but a batrachian) is greedily taken by trout and other fish.

3. In combs. relating to resilience: (1) ∗**spring board,** (*a*) (see quot. 1905), (*b*) ?a plank serving as a wagon seat, *obs.*, cf. **buckboard;** (2) **buggy,** a buggy the

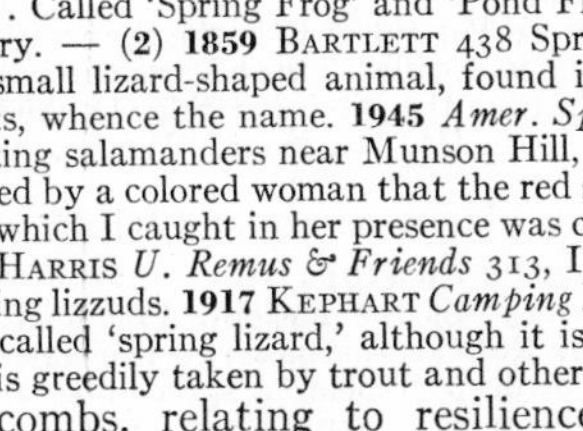

Early type of homemade spring seat for wagon

body of which rests upon springs; (3) **heel,** a shoe in which the outsole is bent over a thickness of leather between the sole and the upper, in full **spring-heel shoe,** also **spring-heeled,** *a.;* (4) **scale**(**s**), a weighing device in which the amount of distortion in a spiral spring or springs is measured in pounds, ounces, etc.; (5) ∗**seat,** a seat resting on springs at its ends and suitable for use on a wagon box or frame, cf. **wagon seat;** (6) **-tooth,** designating a farm cultivator or harrow the teeth of which are on curved steel springs; (7) **vise,** (see quot. 1876).

(1) (*a*) **1883** *Harper's Mag.* Jan. 200/2 These [mortise holes] were intended for the insertion of their iron-shod 'spring-boards.' **1905** *Forestry Bureau Bul.* No. 61, 49 *Spring board,* a short board, shod at one end with an iron calk which is inserted in a notch cut in a tree, on which the faller stands while felling the tree. (P[acific] C[oast] F[orest], S[outhern] F[orest].) (*b*) **1883** STEVENSON *Silverado Squatters* 174 A couple in a waggon, or a dusty farmer on a spring-board toiling over the 'grade' to . . . Calistoga. — (2) **1867** HARRIS *Sut Lovingood* 141 They moves like a cradil on cushioned rockers, ur a spring buggy runnin in damp san'. — (3) **1790** *Pa. Packet* 5 Feb. 3/3 Nathaniel Prentiss [has] . . . Lined & bound spring-heel'd Pumps. **1887** *Courier-Journal* 6 Feb. 9/3 The figure . . . would have regarded with ineffable scorn . . . the ungainly but comfortable 'spring-heels.' *Ib.* 20 Feb. 9/4 Kid and Pebble Spring-heel Shoes by the hundreds. — (4) **1934** WEBSTER. **1945** *Democrat* 30 Aug. 1/5 They might properly be termed the granddaddy of the modern spring scales.

Spring-tooth harrow

(5) **1835** A. PARKER *Trip to Texas* 30 [We] took a wagon, without any spring seats. **1946** WILSON *Fidelity* 75 Buggies, farm wagons with spring seats or split-bottomed chairs for the adults and quilts thrown over hay for the younger ones. — (6) **1930** *Randolph Enterprise* (Elkins, W.Va.) 30 Oct. 8/2 Farm Tools and Machinery . . . 1 spring tooth harrow. **1944** CLARK *Pills* 283 In the stores themselves were the assembled implements such as . . . side harrows, spring tooth cultivators [etc.]. **1948** *Pauls Valley* (Okla.) *D. Democrat* 1 July 11/6 The soil conservation district furnished the spring-tooth harrow. — (7) **1843** *Reg. for Preservation of Arms in Service* 80 Each squad of ten men, a wire and tumbler punch, and a spring vice. **1876** KNIGHT 2292/1 *Spring-vise,* . . . a small vise used for confining the main-spring of a gun-lock when the lock is to be taken apart.

As the last term in **alkali, alum, barrel, boiling, burning, call, canyon, Congress, Creole, door, dug, falling, first breath of, flooding, gas, good-morning-, hair, oil, poplar, Saratoga, soda, suck, sweet, tide, wall, warm, wet-weather springs.**

springerle ˈsprɪŋəlɪ, *n.* [G.] A kind of cooky upon which there is an embossed design (see quot. 1902).

1902 *Sears Cat.* (ed. 112) 794/1 Fancy Cake Roller or Springerle Formen, made of hardwood with twelve assorted deeply hand carved designs. **1942** *Good Housekeeping Cook Book* 757 Springerle. . . . When cool, store in a covered jar for two or three weeks before serving. Makes about 41 springerle. **1949** *Chi. Tribune* 18 Dec. 25/1 Sugar coated Pfeffernusse, crunchy Springerle and Anise Drops.

∗**Springfield,** *n.*

1. *attrib.* Designating firearms made at the government armory at Springfield, Mass.

1813 *Niles' Reg.* IV. 87/2 [The] gun . . . is but one pound and a half heavier than the common Springfield gun. **1888** J. D. BILLINGS *Hard-tack* 270 Plain smooth-bore Springfield muskets soon became Springfield rifles. **1902** *Sears Cat.* 292/1 Cut Down Musket, made from U.S. Springfield Musket Model 1863.

b. *absol.* A Springfield gun.

1863 *Harper's Mag.* May 857/1 The sentinel carefully laid his bright 'Springfield' upon the ground.

2. Springfield hickory, the big shellbark, *Carya laciniosa;* **Springfield nut,** the nut of this tree. Both *obs.*

1810 MICHAUX *Arbres* I. 21 *Springfield hickery* (Hickery de Springfield), autre dénomination donnée à cet arbre [shellbark hickory] dans cet endroit, peu éloigné de Philadelphie. **1814** PURSH *Flora Amer.* II. 637 *Juglans sulcata*. . . . It is called Thick Shellbark Hickory, Springfield or glocester Nut. **1832** BROWNE *Sylva* 176 In the vicinity of Springfield, in Pennsylvania, . . . its fruit is called *Springfield nut.*

∗**sprinkler,** *n.*

1. A machine for spraying or irrigating cotton plants to destroy insects.

1879 *Rep. upon Cotton Insects* (Dept. Agric.) 251 Mr. William T. Robinson, of Huntsville, Tex., has invented a machine that combines a sprinkler and duster, so that dry or fluid poisons may be applied. **1882** *Cent. Mag.* Jan. 477/1 The automatic sprinkler and the rotary dust-blower . . . are the largest and most complete tools.

2. (See quot. 1905.) Also attrib.

1893 *Scribner's Mag.* June 708/1 In freezing weather the sprinkler is run, and . . . [one sees] immense sleigh-loads of logs passing down the road. **1902** WHITE *Blazed Trail* 68 They are supposed to serve . . . a variety of lunches up to midnight for the sprinkler men. **1905** *Forestry Bureau. Bul.* No. 61, 49 *Sprinkler*, a large wooden tank from which water is sprinkled over logging roads during freezing weather in order to ice the surface, (N[orth] W[oods], L[ake] S[tates Forest].) *Ib.*, *Sprinkler sleds*, the sleds upon which the sprinkler is mounted.

As the last term in **street, track sprinkler.**

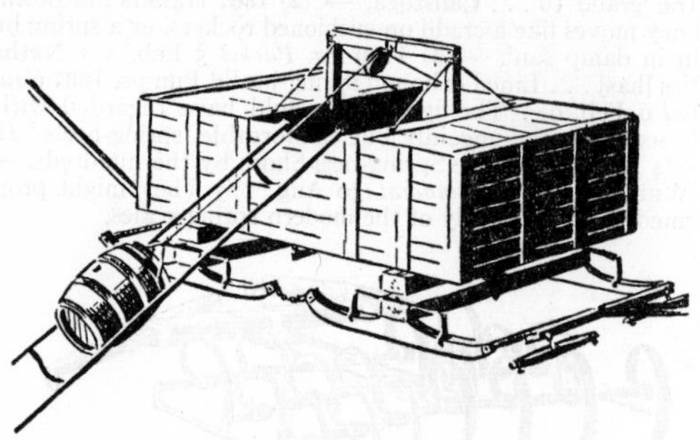

Sprinkler used in logging

***sprout,** *n.* [In sense **1.** (see quot. 1816) f. Du. *spruit*, branch of a river, a small river.]

1. *local.* A branch or mouth of a river. *Obs.*

1758 *Essex. Inst. Coll.* XVIII. 99 We cou'd get no further than . . . about a mile below ye upper Mohaak Sprout. **1816** in *N.Y. Hist. Soc. Col.* II. (1848) 120 The *mouths* of the Mohock they distinguished as the Spruyten, corrupted to, and which may also possibly pass for a translation, the Sprouts. **1841** *N.Y. Hist. Soc. Coll.* I. 143 [tr. of Van der Donck, 1656.] Forty-four miles from the sea this North river is divided. One part by four sprouts ascends the great falls of the Maquas kill.

2. a. (See quot. and cf. *course of sprouts s.v.* ***course.**) *Obs.* **b.** A variety of potato (see also quot. 1949).

(a) 1856 HALL *College Words* (ed. 2) 443 Any *branch* of education is in student phrase a *sprout*. This peculiar use of the word is said to have originated at Yale. — **(b) 1869** *Rep. Comm. Agric. 1868* 240 Michigan White Sprouts. **1949** *Nat. Geog. Mag.* Aug. 172/1 Kale is often called 'borecole,' and in America collards are sometimes called 'sprouts.'

3. In combs.: (1) **sprout flow,** the first flow of water over a rice field after sowing, *obs.;* (2) **land,** (see quot. 1874); (3) **water,** =**sprout flow,** *obs.*

(1) 1856 OLMSTED *Slave States* 471 This is termed the 'sprout flow,' and the water is left on the field until the seed sprouts. **1859** MACKAY *Tour* I. 324 The rice is submitted to three several floodings before it is fit to be harvested. The first, in the early spring, is called 'the sprout flow.' — **(2)** *a***1862** THOREAU *Excursions* 230 In 'sprout-lands' they [*sc.* maples] seem to vie with one another. **1874** *Vt. Bd. Agric. Rep.* II. 493 In Massachusetts the 'sprout lands,' . . . are those which have once been cultivated, but which have since been covered with trees in a natural way from roots remaining in the soil and from seed sown by the winds. **1929** SHELTON *Salt-box House* 40 Daniel grew tall and straight and slim like the young saplings in the sprout-land. — **(3) 1856** in COMMONS *Doc. Hist.* I. 143 He drew off his 'Sprout Water' too rapidly, prostrating his rice to the ground.

As the last term in **bay, mountain sprout(s).**

***sprouting,** *a.* and *n.* **1. sprouting crab grass,** (see quots.). **2. sprouting hoe,** (see quot. 1800).

(1) 1884 VASEY *Agric. Grasses* 37 In the Southern States, . . . there occurs a variety of this grass, called *Panicum proliferum*, var. *geniculatum*, or sprouting crab grass. **1909** *Cent. Supp.* 309/2 *Sprouting crab-grass* . . . is liked by cattle but is hardly worthy of cultivation. — **(2) 1800** TATHAM *Tobacco* 12 The sprouting hoe . . . is a smaller species of mattock that serves to break up any particular hard part of the ground. **1864** *Maine Agric. Soc. Returns 1863* 159 After the beds are thus burnt, . . . they are dug up with a common sprouting hoe.

***spruce,** *n.* In combs.: (1) **spruce chewing gum,** =**spruce gum;** (2) **duff,** (see quots.); (3) **gum,** the resinous exudation from a spruce tree or a balsam fir, used chiefly as chewing gum; (4) **pine,** see as a main entry; (5) **stumpage,** spruce timber as it stands uncut in the forest, also the value of this or the right to cut it; (6) **swamp,** a swamp in which spruce is the prevailing growth; (7) **yellow,** a yellowish brown.

(1) 1940 CUMMINGS *Amer. & His Food* 24 A combination of these two practices appeared in spruce chewing gum. **1946** T. JONES *Skinny Angel* 140 From then on we had only the spruce chewing gum to which Vivian was addicted. — **(2) 1878** *Pop. Sci. Mo.* XIII. 289 'Spruce-duff' . . . is composed of rotten spruce-trees, cones, needles, etc. This 'duff' has the power of holding water . . . , and, when it is thoroughly dry, burns, like punk, without a blaze. **1885** *Outing* VII. 62/1 This forest-mould is composed of partially decayed leaves, logs, bark, cones and needles, and is spoken of generally as 'spruce duff' because found in greater quantities among the spruce trees. — **(3) 1836** *Public Ledger* (Phila.) 21 May (Th.), The down east girls . . . [amuse] themselves . . . by chewing spruce gum. **1947** PAUL *Linden* 251 The Italian women . . . began searching the woods and fields for dandelion greens, slippery elm, spruce gum, and various roots.

(5) 1896 *Vt. Agric. Rep.* XV. 83 Ten years of prolonged life may double the value of spruce stumpage. — **(6) 1652** *Essex Inst. Coll.* V. 266/2 Granted to James Standish the little spruce swamp lying neare his house. **1775** *Mass. H.S. Proc.* 2 Ser. II. 279 We Cross'd the pond and Came to . . . a Spruce Swamp Knee deep in mire. **1947** COFFIN *Yankee Coast* 199 We must have covered three townships easily, and townships mostly alder thickets and spruce swamps. — **(7) 1794** *Mass. H.S. Coll.* 1 Ser. IV. 49 His first attempts in making spruce yellow, were flattering.

b. In the names of birds and other animals: (1) **spruce bird,** (see quot.); (2) **deer,** app. a mule deer, *rare;* (3) **grouse,** a grouse, *Canachites canadensis* or a related species, that frequents forests in the northern part of the U.S.; (4) **hen,** =prec.; (5) **partridge,** (see quot. 1917); (6) **wren,** (see quot.).

(1) 1900 WEBSTER *Supp.* 199/2 *Spruce bird*, . . . the white-winged crossbill (*Loxia leucoptera*). — **(2) 1877** CAMPION *On Frontier* 131 [Of] 'spruce deer,' . . . a few small bands ranged high up the mountains. — **(3) 1844** *Nat. Hist. N.Y., Zoology* II. 206 The Spruce Grouse. . . . The flesh is bitter, and has a peculiar taste as if boiled in turpentine. **1946** STANWELL-FLETCHER *Driftwood Valley* 13 Several times we've scared up coveys of spruce grouse along the trail. — **(4) 1902** HULBERT *Forest Neighbors* 87 Spruce hens and partridges. **(5) 1832** WILLIAMSON *Maine* I. 144 *Quails* are not with us so plenty as in the other States of New-England. . . . Many think the spruce Partridges are the same. **1917** *Birds of Amer.* II. 15/1 There is no such bird as the Spruce Partridge. It is the Spruce Grouse (*Canachites canadensis*); but it is called Spruce Partridge in common parlance to distinguish it from the Birch Partridge (Ruffed Grouse). — **(6) 1917** *Birds of Amer.* III. 194 Winter Wren. . . . [Also called] Spruce Wren.

c. Designating places or regions where spruce prevails. See also **spruce swamp.**

1661 *Rowley Rec.* 115 All the meadow Commonly Called the Spruce meadow. **1759** ROGERS *Journals* 153 The water most of the way [was] near a foot deep, it being a spruce bog. **1817–8** EATON *Botany* (1822) 339 Lily orchis . . . grows from 4 to 6 inches high in the spruce woods on Catskill mountain. **1880** *Harper's Mag.* Aug. 344/2 A rude timber assembly hall [was] . . . erected in a spruce grove.

d. In the names of, or with reference to, insects injurious to spruce trees.

1884 *Rep. Comm. Agric.* 378 The Reddish-Yellow Spruce-Bud Worm . . . was found to be very injurious to the white spruce. **1891** *Cent.* 5868/1 Spruce bud-worm, the larva of a tortricid moth, as *Tortrix fumiferana*, which eats the end-buds of the spruce in northeastern parts of the United States, especially in Maine. . . . Spruce saw-fly, a common saw-fly, *Lophyrus abietis*, whose pale-green larvae defoliate spruce, fir, pine, and cedar in the United States, but especially spruce. **1939** WHITE *One Man's Meat* 90 And I see by the paper that a hundred million parasites have been turned loose in the State this summer, to war on the spruce sawfly. **1945** *Boulder* (Colo.) *D. Camera* 12 Nov. 5/6 W. D. Buchanan is making a reconnaissance, in forest terminology, of the spruce budworm disease.

As the last term in **balsam, beer, big-cone, black, blue, cat, Colorado blue, double, Douglas, essence, hemlock, Menzies, red, silver, single, skunk, tideland, white spruce.**

spruce pine. The bog spruce, *Picea mariana*, of the northeastern states, also any one of various American pines or hemlocks having light, soft wood.

1684 I. MATHER *Providences* (1856) x. 223 Passing through a thick swamp of spruse pine . . . , [the wind] laid all flat to the ground. **1765** J. BARTRAM *Diary* 25 Sep., Ye 2 leaved or spruice pine grows very large in swamps. **1842** *Jrnl. Medorem Crawford* (1897) 19, I noticed the White Pine and the Spruce Pine. **1949** *Boston Globe Mag.* 4 Dec. 11/2 He went up to the white 'Honor Roll' board nailed to a big spruce pine.

∗**sprung,** *a.* Of a horse: Knee-sprung *q.v. Colloq.* — **a1846** *Quarter Race Ky.* 96 'Chest foundered' and hairless, And 'sprung' though she be, She's an eye-sore to others, A good 'un to me. **1902** McFaul *Ike Glidden* 138 He usually drove an old mare, blind of one eye, sprung in both forward legs.

∗**spud,** *n.*

1. (See quots.)

1871 *Amer. Inst. Mining Engineers Trans.* I. 378 A spud, as it is called, that is, a nail resembling a horseshoe nail with a hole in the head, is driven into the timbers. **1876** Knight 2292/2 *Spud,* . . . a spade-shaped implement, used in fishing for broken tools in a well. **1905** *Forestry Bureau Bul.* No. 61, *Spud,* a tool for removing bark.

2. A polished stone implement with a broad blade and a handle, formerly used by the Indians.

1885 *Rep. Indian Affairs* 108 [The Indians are] laying aside the old Indian hoes and spuds. **1896** *Rep. Bureau Amer. Ethnol. 1891–2* 109 The peculiar stones called 'spuds' . . . are usually of a comparatively soft material, carefully worked and polished.

∗**spud,** *v. tr.* and *intr.* (See quots. 1891, 1901.) Also **spudding,** *n.*

1886 *Scientific Amer.* 21 Aug. 116 A 12 inch hole is usually drilled or spudded down to the rock. **1891** *Cent.* 5868/3 spudding. . . . In *oil-well drilling,* a method of handling the rope and tools by which the first fifty or sixty feet of an oil-well are bored by the aid of the bull-wheel, the depth not being sufficient to allow of the use of the working-beam for that purpose. **1901** *Munsey's Mag.* XXV. 746/2 The start is made by 'spudding,' which is done by attaching the drill proper to the rope, and then skillfully tightening and loosening the coils on the drum by hand, thus raising the drill and letting it fall within the tube. **1945** *Craig* (Colo.) *Empire-Courier* 25 July 1/5 Moving in material. Preparing to spud.

Hence **spudder,** *n.* Cf. **bark spudder.**

1929 *Texas Mo.* March 354 Some of the largest wells have been drilled with the lowly spudder. **1946** *Dly. Ardmoreite* (Ardmore, Okla.) 6 Dec. 12/4 He drilled a well 300 feet deep with his own Fort Worth spudder.

spudge spʌdʒ, *n.* [Origin unknown. Cf. next.] App. some kind of gambling game. *Obs.* — **1839** *Columbian Reg.* (New Haven, Conn.) 28 Dec. 4/4 Said a Wolvereen to a Yankee, on board a Mississippi steamer, . . . 'Will you play spudge?'

spudge spʌdʒ, *v.* [Origin unknown. Cf. *EDD* (VI.) *pudge,* to exert oneself, to strain, and Wentworth *pudge up,* to prod, rouse, stimulate.] *To spudge up;* (*a*) To pay or fork over (money), (*b*) to brace up. *Colloq.*

(*a*) **a1855** Kelley *Humors* 386 The clerk explained it, clear as mud; the trio 'spudged up' the amount, looked very sober, and walked out. (*b*) **1881** Jewett *Country By-Ways* 49 I've wondered sometimes, myself, he didn't spudge up and be somebody. **1886** —— *White Heron* 104 I'll spudge up and take right holt.

∗**spun,** *a.*

1. Tobacco twisted into a compact cylindrical roll, prob. for chewing. In full **spun tobacco.** *Obs.*

In Du. *spinnen* was early and freely used of twisting tobacco. Cf. *gesponnen tabak* in *WNT* 2835/1, and see **tobacco spinner, tobacco wheel.**

1706 *Boston News-Letter* 14 Jan. 2/2 [There] will be exposed to Sale . . . twenty nine half Barrels of Leaf, and 40 Rolls of Spun Tobacco. **1748** *N. Eng. Hist. & Gen. Reg.* IV. 176 She continues to sell the best Virginia Tobacco, Cut, Pigtail and spun, of all Sorts. **1803** *Lewis & Clark Exped.* VII. (1905) 235 Indian Presents [include]: . . . 50 lbs. Spun Tobacco.

2. spun truck, spun thread or yarn. *Colloq.*

1851 Hooper *Widow Rugby* 72 Jim Bell . . . had visited town, for the purpose of buying two bunches 'of No. 8, spun truck.' **1898** Harris *Tales* 367 She had gone to town with butter and eggs to exchange for some factory thread—'spun truck' Mrs. Pruett called it.

∗**spunk,** *n.*

1. *To get* (*one's*) *spunk up,* and variants, to become angry or to take courage. *Colloq.*

1834 *Jamestown* (N.Y.) *Jrnl.* 24 Dec. 3/1 My spunk is getting up a leetle about it. **1856** M. Thompson *Plu-ri-bus-tah* 147 How a Woman got her spunk up and left the country. **1873** *Newton Kansan* 27 Feb., Philadelphia has got its spunk up. **1912** N. Woodrow *Sally Salt* 38, I got my spunk up, and I says [etc.].

2. spunk water, rain water that collects in cavities in stumps, used as a folk remedy, esp. for removing warts. Also attrib.

1876 Mark Twain *Tom Sawyer* vi. 65 You got to go . . . to the middle of the woods, where you know there's a spunk-water stump. *Ib.,* Spunk-water, spunk-water, swaller these warts. **1949** *Time* 29 Aug. 7/2 Spunk water, spunk water, wash away my warts!

∗**spunk,** *v. To spunk up,* (*a*) to make love *to* someone, (*b*) to kindle or increase the intensity of a fire, (*c*) to pluck up courage, to encourage (someone) to a show of spirit. All *colloq.*

(*a*) *c***1840** Neal *Beedle's Sleigh Ride* 21, I was spunking up to Sally Jones like all vengeance. (*b*) **1881** Cooke *Somebody's Neighbors* 264 He'd spunked up a fire. **1889** —— *Steadfast* 124 [She was] puttin' on them cedar branches so's to spunk up the fire. (*c*) **1885** Siringo *Texas Cow Boy* 90, I finally spunked up and drawing my pistol proceeded in the direction whence came the groan. **1889** Cooke *Steadfast* 395 You stan' by the parson and spunk him up, dear.

∗**spur,** *n.* Allegedly, a hard, bony process at the end of a horn snake's tail. Also attrib. *Obs.* — **1789** *Amer. Philos. Soc.* III. p. xxiii, The spur of his tail is so venemous [*sic*], as to kill young trees, if by accident it strikes them. **1793** *Mass. H.S. Coll.* 1 Ser. III. 86 The jointed and spur snakes are sometimes met with.

As the last word in **long, Mexican, sand, Spanish, Texas spur.**

∗**spur,** *v. Mining. tr.* To run into (an adjoining claim) with a spur or spurs. *Rare.* — **1861** *Harper's Mag.* Jan. 161/2 The Cedar Mill Company were spurring the Miller Company; the Virginia Ledge was spurring the Continuation; . . . and so on.

∗**spurge,** *n.* As the last term in **cypress, ipecacuanha, mountain spurge.**

spurge nettle. The tread-softly, a stinging weed, *Cnidoscolus stimulosus.* — **1847** Darlington *Weeds & Plants* 289 *Cnidoscolus.* Spurge-nettle. . . . *C. stimulosa.* **1901** Mohr *Plant Life Ala.* 594 *Jatropha stimulosa.* . . . Spurge Nettle. . . . Dry sandy pine barrens.

∗**squad,** *n.* A number of persons working together in some athletic sport.

1902 *Harvard Bul.* 19 March 2/2 The rest of the squad will leave the cage as soon as the ground is dry enough. **1913** *Chattanooga* (Tenn.) *News* 20 Sep. 12/3 As soon as Coach Yost gets back from Europe the squad will be put to work. **1950** *Dly. Ardmoreite* (Ardmore, Okla.) 15 Jan. 14/3 It was the second loss of the season for the Tiger 'A' squad as the unbeaten Cougars took them 47 to 40.

b. squad car, a police patrol car that keeps in communication with headquarters by means of special radio-telephone equipment.

1939 Webster (*New Words*). **1950** *D. Oklahoman* (Okla. City) 26 Feb. 1/2 The ink on the Biltmore hotel register had hardly dried when a detective squad car arrived.

As the last term in **Broadway, shopping, sob squad.**

∗**squadrant,** *n.* =next. *Obs.* — **1665** *Groton Rec.* 14 Sergent James Parker Jam Knop and William Leaken were chosen . . . to determen the seuerall Squadrants and hom shall worke at each squadron successiuly. **1707** *Cambridge Prop. Rec.* 255 The first Lott in ye Sixth Squadrant was layd out.

∗**squadron,** *n.* In colonial times in N. Eng., a division, prob. one of four and orig. square, of town land. *Obs.*

1653 *New Haven Rec.* I. 188 They will in the seuerall squadrons in their turnes worke at the makeing the damm. **1689** *Cambridge Prop. Rec.* 166 Each Squadron [shall] be so proportioned as that lots may not exceed four Score Rods in length. **1724** *Ib.* 294 Voted that Andrew Bordman have his Rights Laid out to him on ye Northerly Side of ye Third Squadron on ye Lower Common.

b. The fourth part of a public road. *Obs.*

1683 *Suffield Doc. Hist.* 100 All the Highwayes belonging to the Towne . . . should be divided into four squaderns.

c. A school district. *Obs.*

1749 *Marlborough Rec.* (*Cent.*), Voted and chose a committee of seven men to apportion the school in six societies or squadrons, . . . taking the northwesterly corner for one squadron.

∗**squall,** *n.* A fit of bad temper. *Rare.* Cf. **snow, sun squall.** — **1807** Irving *Salmagundi* vi. 96 The old gentleman came home in quite a squall; kicked poor Caesar the mastiff out of his way [etc.].

squam skwɔm, *n.* [In **1.** f. Anni*squam,* Mass., a fishing village. In **2.** the source of the application is prob. the same.] **1.** (See quot. 1891.) Also **squam hat. 2. squam duck,** a local name for the eider duck.

(**1**) **1891** *Cent.* 5874/2 *Squam,* . . . an oilskin hat worn originally by fishermen and deep-water sailors; a cheap yellow sou'wester. **1908** *Sat. Ev. Post* 7 Nov. 11/2 The Hard-Rock Man tilted back his 'squam' hat to scratch his head. — (**2**) **1844** Giraud *Birds of L.I.* 332 Eider Duck. . . . This species, so celebrated for the superior quality of its down, . . . is called 'Squam Duck.' **1917** *Birds of Amer.* I. 146.

squanter-squash ˈskwɑntɚˌskwɑʃ, *n.* Also **isquouterquash, -squash, squontersquash.** [Amer. Indian. See quot. 1634 below.] =**squash.** *Obs.* or *hist.*

1634 Wood *N. Eng. Prospect* 15 Muskmillions, Isquouterquashes, . . . and whatsoever growes well in England, growes as well there. *Ib.* 76 In Summer, when their [*sc.* the Indians'] corne is spent, Isquoutersquashes is their best bread, a fruite like a young Pumpion. **1672** JOSSELYN *N. Eng. Rarities* 57 Squashes, but more truly Squontersquashes, a kind of Mellon, or rather Gourd. **1705** BEVERLEY *Virginia* II. 27 Squash, or Squanter-Squash, is their Name among the Northern Indians, and so they are call'd in New-York, and New-England. **1931** CLUTE *Plants* 49 Josselyn . . . wrote the name of a common vegetable cultivated by the Indians as squontersquashes.

Squantum ˈskwɑntəm, *n.* Also **squantum.** [The source of this term appears doubtful. See notes.]

"The place name Squantum is said to be derived from Tisquantum, or Tasquantum, the appellation of a Massachusetts Indian, generally known to the settlers about Plymouth as Squantum or Squanto. . . . In all probability the word goes back to this personal name in the Massachuset dialect of Algonquian, signifying 'door,' 'entrance' " (A. F. Chamberlain in Hodge, II. 629).

"The name explains itself by the verb *musquantam* (he is angry,) and by Roger Williams's remark, 'They (the Narragansett Indians) will say, when an ordinary accident, as a fall, has occurred to somebody: *musquantam mânit* (God was angry and did it)' " (A. S. Gatschet in *Amer. Folk-Lore* XIII. 211).

1. (See quots.) *Obs.*

1630 HIGGINSON *N.-Eng.* 20 Their evil God whom they feare will doe them hurt, they call Squantum. **1654** JOHNSON *Wonder-w. Prov.* 226 Squantam is a bad Divel, and Abbamocho is their good Divell. **1674** JOSSELYN *Two Voyages* 132 They acknowledge a God who they call *Squantam*, but worship him they do not, because (they say) he will do them no harm.

2. An annual celebration held near Boston, which includes ceremonies resembling Indian practices and the eating of sea food, often *the Feast of Squantum.* Also attrib.

1812 *Boston Gaz.* 24 Aug. (Th.), The Squantum Celebration will be this day. . . . The antient celebrators of the Squantum Feast will be honored with the presence of . . . Caleb Strong and William Phillips. **1817** *Mass. Spy* 6 Aug. (Th.), There is an annual festival observed in the neighbourhood of Boston, which is called the Feast of Squantum. **1832** GOODRICH *Syst. Universal Geog.* 106 (*footnote*), The feast of *Squantum* is held annually on the shore to the E. of Neponset Bridge, at a rocky point projecting into Boston Bay. . . . Squantum was the name of the last Indian female who resided there.

b. (See last quots.)

1855 H. A. WISE *Tales for Marines* 21, I wish to all fired smash I was . . . hazin' round with Charity Bunker and the rest o' the gals at a squantum. **1881** *Lippincott's Mag.* Sep. 309/2 The amusements are boating, bathing, shark- and blue-fishing, and going on squantums, or clam-bakes. **1883** in *Amer. Folk-Lore* XV. 259 The Squantum is a peculiar institution of this island (Nantucket), being an informal picnic on the beach-sands, where the dinner is made of fish and other spoils of the sea. **1902** *Ib.*, *Squântum*, a word still in use in Nantucket and some other parts of New England in the sense of 'a good time,' 'merry-making,' 'picnic party,' also 'a high old time.'

* **square,** *n.*

1. A city block; an area, approximately square, bounded by four streets or by streets and avenues.

1770 PITTMAN *Present State* 11 All the streets [in New Orleans] are perfectly straight, and cross each other at right angles, and these divide the town into sixty-six squares, eleven in length by the river's side, and six in depth. **1833** COKE *Subaltern's Furlough* I. 64 The city [Philadelphia] is consequently chequered, as it were, like a chessboard, by these divisions and subdivisions; the squares (as the inhabitants term them) being solid, or blocks of buildings. **1944** *Amer. Sp.* XIX. 37 One lexicographical peculiarity of this [Philadelphia] dialect which is rather widely known is the use of the word *square*, '(city) block.'

b. As a measure of distance.

1827 in COMMONS *Doc. Hist.* IV. 127, I was going to take a walk a square or two. **1923** WATTS *L. Nichols* 354 This machine . . . musta been th' len'th of four-five city squares off. **1950** *Reading* (Pa.) *Eagle* 15 Jan., Willow Manor One Square Beyond Museum.

c. (See quot. 1859.)

1859 BARTLETT 440 *Square.* In the city of New York this term is applied to the open spaces caused by the junction of several streets. 'Chatham square' and 'Franklin square' are triangles! **1950** *Time* 24 April 43/1 He made his way through the after-theater crowd in Times Square.

2. (See quot. 1943.)

[**1787** *Ky. Gaz.* 6 Oct. 2 (*footnote*), Advertisements of no more length than breadth, are inserted for 3s. the first time and 2s. each time after and longer ones in proportion.] **1800** *Impartial Observer* (Natchez, Miss.) 5 May 1/1 Advertisements . . . which exceed a square will be inserted at the same proportionate price. **1877** *Harper's Mag.* Dec. 111/1 These newspaper people set an extraordinary value on their squares, as they call them. **1943** CROW *Amer. Customer* 122 No publisher bothered with anything less than an annual contract for fixed advertising space and the standard space measurement was the 'square,' which meant a space equal in depth to the width of a column—approximately two column inches.

3. The immature flower of the cotton plant together with the three bracts which subtend it. Cf. **cotton square,** and see * **form,** *n.* **1,** and * **square,** *v.* **1.**

1854 DAVIS *Farm Bk.* 83 Cotton shedding squares and young bolls—wants rain. **1927** SANDBURG *Songbag* 253 De farmer say to de weevil: 'What you doin' on de square?'

b. square borer, the boll weevil. *Rare.*

1906 *Westminster Gaz.* 19 Dec. 2/1 The devastation caused by . . . the cotton aphis, the web-worm, and the square-borer.

4. = **square meal.** *Slang.*

1882 in *Frontier* X. (1930) 252/1, I went in sat down and had some dinner . . . ate a square & talked awhile & then made the rest of the way home. **1927** J. BARBICAN *Confess. Rum-Runner* xxiii. 260 We sure was hungry for the dough, for it was weeks since we had roped in our three squares a day.

5. *Mining.* A sample of ore.

1885 *Wkly. New Mexican Rev.* 19 Feb. 4/1 The squares 3×5 inches . . . are sufficient to convince anybody that he has struck a bonanza.

As the last term in **Capitol, cotton, courthouse, eight, form, pitcher's, public square.**

* **square,** *a.*

1. Full, complete. *Colloq.* Cf. **square meal,** and * **square,** *adv.*

1836 *Public Ledger* (Phila.) 25 March 1/1 [A subscription for] 1 square year, $20.00. **1854** *Cong. Globe* 19 May 1231/2 He has . . . a good square quarter of a century yet to devote to the welfare of his country. **1875** *Cong. Rec.* 20 March 107/1 Make it till half past five; that will make square hours.

2. Of a horse's gait: Steady, even. Hence **square-gaited, square-pacer, square-trotter.** Cf. * **square,** *adv.* **b.**

1832 VIGNE *6 Mo. in Amer.* II. 8 The horse . . . is valuable according to his performances as a square or natural trotter, a pacer, or a racker. **1868** WOODRUFF *Trotting Horse* 79 He was a square-gaited horse as a trotter. *Ib.* 81 When a pacer is got to a square trot, he is to be kept at it by the nicest kind of handling. **1886** ROE *Army Lett.* 345 He is what we call a square pacer. **1907** WHITE *Arizona Nights* 294 Dimly could be seen the horses, their flanks swinging steadily in the square trot.

3. In special combs.: (1) **square deal,** in card games, an honest, fair dealing or distribution of the cards, also fig., a fair, honest arrangement or act, *colloq.;* (2) **drink,** (see quot.), *obs.;* (3) **feed,** (see quot.), *obs.;* (4) **fight,** (see quot. 1868); (5) **game,** (see quot.); (6) **meal,** a substantial, satisfying meal; (7) **-necked grain beetle,** a grain beetle, *Cathartus gemellatus;* (8) **nut hickory,** = **mockernut;** (9) **room,** (see quot. 1876), *colloq.;* (10) * **set,** in mining (see quots.); (11) **shooter,** one who is honest and aboveboard, *colloq.;* (12) **steel,** ?steel in the form of square rods, *rare;* (13) **tail,** (see quot.); (14) **thing,** the fair, honest thing, *colloq.;* (15) **timber,** a beam or timber that has been squared, also collect., tree trunks that have been hewed square.

(1) **1883** MARK TWAIN *Life on Miss.* lii, Thought I had better give him a square deal. **1947** MYERS *The 'Guv'* 127, I could never get a square deal . . . in this place. — (2) **1868** WHYMPER *Alaska* 283 A 'square' drink is a 'deep, deep draught.' — (3) **1873** BEADLE *Undevel. West.* 708, [I] never tasted tea, coffee, flour-bread, meat or any one of the things we consider 'square feed' in Indiana. — (4) **1804** CUTLER in *Life & Corr.* II. 162 It was . . . a square fight between the all-important head man of the party and another who ranks as his second. **1868** WHYMPER *Alaska* 283 All over this coast . . . a good 'square fight' is an encounter or 'muss' where the opponents were in earnest. (5) **1938** ASBURY *Sucker's Prog.* 16 Square game—Faro bank which used squared cards exclusively. — (6) **1850** A. T. JACKSON *Forty Niner* (1920) 12 Had two square meals in town yesterday. **1947** *Duluth* (Minn.) *News-Tribune* 19 Jan. 10/1, I want . . . three square meals a day for which I'm willing to pay. — (7) **1895** *Dept. Agric. Yrbk. 1894* 290 An insect of some importance in the South is the square-necked or red grain beetle. — (8) **1875** EMERSON *Trees & Shrubs Mass.* I. 222 The Mockernut Hickory. *Carya tomentosa.* . . . This species is often called the walnut, and is also known by the name of the square-nut hickory. It is also called white heart. — (9) **1829** *Detroit Gaz.* 5 March 4/2 Peggy looked sullen, and put out the fire in the square room. **1876** *Wide Awake* (Boston) 78/2 The children felt as if it was a great thing to have a fire in the 'front room,' or the 'square room,' as Mrs. Drew called it.

(10) **1877** W. Wright *Big Bonanza* 311 In the bottom of this opening or chamber are put down the sills for the first 'squareset' of timbers. **1896** Shinn *Story of Mine* 96 'Square sets' consist of short, square timbers, four to six feet long, mortised and tenoned at the ends so that they can be put together in a series of interlocked cribs and built up in a continuous row or block. *Ib.* 97 Dangers . . . were obviated by the proper use of the square-set timbers. — (11) **1934** Webster. **1949** *Boston Globe* 12 June (Fiction Mag.) 12/4 Captain Mac . . . was known from Seattle to Nome and back again as a square shooter. — (12) **1744** in *Md. Hist. Mag.* XXI. 244, 3 ffaggotts German or Square Steel. — (13) **1942** Nat. Pk. Service *Fading Trails* 153 They called them 'chickens,' 'prairie chickens,' or 'square-tails,' the last name being used to distinguish them from the sharp-tailed grouse. — (14) **1868** in *Cong. Rec.* 19 July (1894) 7692/2 Do the square thing by him [*sc.* the Indian] and he is a honey cooler. **1917** McCutcheon *Green Fancy* 304 If I get the stuff, I'll do the square thing by her.

(15) **1728** *Boston Rec.* 222 Twenty Shillings for Every Range that Shall haue the Quantity of Eight feet of Square Timber. *c*1790 Coxe *View U.S.* 62 The produce, manufactures, and exports of Pennsylvania [include] . . . square timber, scantling, plank [etc.]. **1850** E. S. Seymour *Sks. of Minnesota* 79 One million, three hundred thousand shingles; and fifty thousand feet of square timber.

* **square,** *v.*

1. *intr.* Of cotton: To develop squares. Also * **squaring,** *n.*

1875 *Chi. Tribune* 2 July 7/2 The weather has been hot and moist enough to . . . cause the plant to form and square well. **1948** *Ada* (Okla.) *Ev. News* 4 July 11/4 This is one of the best methods for controlling weevils when cotton is small and before squaring.

2. In phrases: (1) * *To square off,* to assume a posture of defense, to take up the attitude of a boxer, also fig., *colloq.;* (2) *to square it,* to live honestly, to reform, *slang;* (3) *to square back,* to turn back, *rare.*

(1) **1837** Neal *Charcoal Sk.* (1838) 41 If he 'squares off' at a big fellow, he is obliged . . . to hit his antagonist on the knee. **1875** *N.Y. Herald* 17 April (B.), Mr. Fullerton . . . squared off with a vim . . . that sometimes makes victory half assured. **1943** Ottley *New World* 192 When he [Jeffries] squared off with Johnson at Reno, Nevada, July 4, 1910, he took one of the most awful lacings a fighter had ever received in the city. — (2) **1873** in W. Taylor *David* vii, Give a poor fellow a chance to square it for three months. **1903** Hapgood *Autobiog. of Thief* 25 Now that I have 'squared it' I see a good deal of my family. — (3) **1897** Stuart *Simpkinsville* 16 Seen May Day first time on her way to church, an' looked after her—then squared back direct an' followed her.

* **square,** *adv.* Completely, directly. Also with *out. Colloq.* Cf. * **square,** *a.* **1.**

1862 E. W. Pearson *Lett. Port Royal* 103 His heart failed him and he backed square out. **1876** *Cong. Rec.* 5 July 4397/1 If the Senator from Vermont . . . does not like to vote square against [this bill] . . . , this is the right way to defeat it. **1922** Tarkington *Gentle Julia* 213 There's no etiquette in coming right square out and asking how much it was.

b. At a steady, even gait. Cf. * **square,** *a.* **2.**

1868 Woodruff *Trotting Horse* 54 He will trot square again with the rollers on. *Ib.* 68 It is of no use to keep on in *hopes* that he will go square again.

squared circle. The prize ring. *Colloq.* — **1927** Sandburg *Songbag* 398 His big fights were in the 1850's and he defeated Thompson, the Yankee Clipper, the Benicia boy, in the squared circle.

* **squarely,** *adv.* Plainly, unequivocally.

1860 in Victor *Hist. So. Rebellion* I. 89 [This] means simply and squarely, that you intend either to rule or ruin this Government. **1885** *Cent. Mag.* Feb. 511/1 He stands squarely upon observation, experience, induction. **1894** Mark Twain *P. Wilson* xiii, Tom, tell me squarely—didn't he find any fault with you?

squash skwɑʃ, *n.*¹ [f. Algonquian. Cf. the Narraganset word in quot. 1643 below and **squanter-squash.**]

1. The fruit of any one of various species of *Cucurbita*, or the plant producing this.

1643 Williams *Key* (1866) 125 *Askútasquash,* their Vine aples . . . the English . . . call Squashes. **1705** Beverley *Virginia* II. 17 The same Use is made also of . . . Vetches, Squashes, Maycocks [etc.]. **1819** *Plough Boy* I. 183 A squash, taken from the garden of Mr. Wm. Chouty, Londonderry, N.H. on the 2d inst. weighed 311 lbs. **1949** *Nat. Geog. Mag.* Aug. 162 All three species of squashes and pumpkins are native to the Western Hemisphere.

b. With specifying term.

1814 *Bentley Diary* IV. 280 This squash . . . is also called the African Squash. **1847** Darlington *Weeds & Plants* (1860) 142 *Cucurbita Melopepo* . . . Round Squash.

c. The flesh of this fruit cooked as food.

1758 C. Rea *Journal* 70 I've eat this Summer one meal of Squash. one of Turneps, one of Potatoes & one of Onions & no more. **1872** Powers *Afoot & Alone* 254 At dinner he plumped a spoonful of squash on his plate. **1949** *Nat. Geog. Mag.* Aug. 234/2 There were squash, string beans, and mashed potatoes.

d. Also **squash pie, soup.**

1751 J. Bartram *Observations* 62 We dined on Indian corn and squash soop, and boiled bread. **1805** *Pocumtuc Housewife* (1906) 24 Squash Pie with Raisins. **1917** Mathewson *Second Base Sloan* 22, I ain' never eat any of that squash pie.

2. In the names of insect pests: (1) **squash beetle,** a striped beetle, *Diabrotica vittata*, injurious to the leaves of the squash; (2) **borer,** (see quot. 1909), also **squash vine borer;** (3) **bug,** an insect injurious to squash plants, esp. *Anasa tristis*, which feeds upon the leaves of the plant.

(1) **1867** *Amer. Naturalist* I. 163 The Squash Beetle . . . now attacks the squash plants before they are fairly up. **1902** *Amer. Folk-Lore* 259 Squash-beetle (*Diabrotica vittata*) squash-borer (*Trochilium cucurbitae*). — (2) **1891** *Cent.* 5878/1 Squash-borer . . . the larva of an aegerian or sesiid moth . . . which bores the stems of squashes in the United States. **1909** *Cent. Supp.* 1422/2 *Squash vine-borer*, the larva of an American sesiid moth, *Melittia satyriniformis*. It bores into and excavates the stems of squash-vines, especially near the roots. **1945** *Athol* (Mass.) *D. News* 5 July 5/3 The squash vine borer, however, is a creature which does more damage and which is apt to do its damage before you realize what is taking place. — (3) **1846** Worcester 689/1 *Squash-Bug*, . . . a fetid insect destructive to squashes. **1948** *Pacific Discovery* Jan.–Feb. 19/1 The highly magnified photographs show . . . a member of the order of true bugs, the Hemiptera, of which the squash bug is a familiar—and more typical—example.

As the last term in **acorn, bell, blue, bonnet, bush, butter, club, cowhorn, crook-neck(ed), Hubbard, long-neck(ed), marrow, pie, pineapple, seed, squanter, summer, Wabash, warted, wild, winter squash.**

squash skwɑʃ, *n.*² Short for **musquash.** *Obs.*

1678 Phillips *New World of Words* (ed. 4), *Squash*, a little Creature in some parts of America, somewhat resembling an Ichnumon or Indian Rat. **1774** Goldsmith *Hist. Earth* III. 380 But the smell of our weasels, and ermines, and polecats, is fragrance itself when compared to that of the *squash* and the *skunk*, which have been called the Polecats of America. **1796** Morse *Univ. Geog.* I. 201 Another stinkard, called the Squash, is said . . . to be found in some of the southern states.

squashbelly ˈskwɑʃˌbelɪ, *n.* ? = **squash,** *n.*² *Rare.* — **1785** Patten *Diary* 509 We butchered our brindled Cows calf it weighed 44 l. of Veal and we took the skin and the skin of the Calf we killed the 2d Instant to Frenchies to Tan and a small Squashbellys Skin.

squat, *n.*¹ The place where a "squatter" has settled. *Rare.* — **1856** H. V. Huntley *California* I. 196 There will be found nothing sufficiently persuasive to induce an American to 'vamose' his 'squat.'

squat skwɑt, *n.*² [L. *Squat*ina, an angelfish or skate.] An angelfish of the genus *Squatina*. — **1884** Goode *Fisheries* I. 675 *Squatina angelus*. . . . Angel-fish, Angelo or Squat. From San Francisco southward. Not rare. **1891** *Cent.* 5878/2.

* **squat,** *v.*

1. *intr.* To settle on land, esp. public land, without having, or applying formally for, a title to it. Usu. with *in, on, upon,* etc.

1800 *Miss. Terr. Arch.* (1906) 212, I wish also to be instructed for my Conduct towards those people, Squatting or establishing themselves upon the Public Lands. **1829** Marryat *F. Mildmay* xxi, He was a Kentucky man, of the Ohio, where he had 'squatted,' as we say. **1859** Hunter *Western Border Life* 67, I am the rightful claimant to these lands, having squatted here for the last six months. **1901** Duncan & Scott *Allen & Woodson Co., Kans.* 582 John Coleman squatted upon a piece of land in Owl Creek township.

fig. and *transf.* **1813** Paulding *Lay Sc. Fiddle* (1814) 207 They seem to have *squatted* down upon the public reputation, as they did upon the land. **1855** Holbrook *Among Mail Bags* 288 His chair was appropriated by a fatigued neighbor, who 'squatted' on the vacant territory, regardless of 'pre-emption' or pre-session. **1903** Ade *People You Know* 70 If they squatted in a low down Neighborhood, Mrs. Jump was ashamed to give her Address to Friends in the Congregation. **1944** Pennell *Rome Hanks* 3 But what sort of people squatted in Fork City anyway?

b. In passive and reflexive construction.

1809 Irving *Knickerb.* III. viii, The Yankees . . . had the audacity to *squat* themselves down within the jurisdiction of Fort Goed Hoop. **1825** Neal *Bro. Jonathan* I. 219 A person . . . had 'squatted' himself down upon the vacant land. **1857** *Lawrence* (Kans.) *Republican* 30 July 1 Nearly all the timbered claims within four or five miles are already squatted upon. **1894** Robley *Bourbon Co., Kans.* 48 A good part of these lands were squatted on by settlers.

2. To sit and do nothing, cease trying. *Slang. Obs.*

1836 *Crockett's Yaller Flower Almanac* 32 When you come to put in the scientific licks, I squat. *a***1846** *Quarter Race Ky.* 118 As I am utterly unable to do him justice in a description, I'll squat, and let Hooker do it.

3. In combs.: (1) **squat snipe,** (see quots.); (2) **tag,** (see quot.).

(1) **1888** Trumbull *Names of Birds* 176 In Connecticut at Milford, [*Tringa maculata* is called] Squat-Snipe; at Stratford, Squatter. **1917** *Birds of Amer.* I. 233 Pectoral Sandpiper. *Pisobia maculata*. . . . [Also called] Squat Snipe; Squatter; Krieker. — (2) **1891** *Amer. Folk-Lore* IV. 222 Squat Tag. . . . Players . . . may escape being tagged by squatting down. This immunity is only granted to each individual a certain number of times, usually ten, . . . and after his 'squats' are exhausted he may be tagged as in the ordinary game.

squatment ˈskwɑtmənt, *n.* A settlement, land occupied by a squatter. *Obs.* — **1835** *Knickerb.* VI. 176 Hawk-nosed speculators already rode . . . through the muddy Virginia-fence lands of these squatments. **1860** *Chambers's Jrnl.* 21 July 39/2 The ghost of a squatter might prove a less unpleasant neighbour than the squatter himself, dispossessed of his *squatment*.

* **squatter,** *n.*

1. One who settles upon land, esp. public land, to which he has no legal title. Cf. **free squatter.**

1788 Madison *Writings* V. 96 Constituents are only squatters on other people's land. **1829** Hall *Travels* III. 355 It is the fashion to speak slightly of these Pioneers, Squatters, Crackers, or whatever name it pleases them most to be called by, but I must own that I was well satisfied with almost every one of them whom I encountered. **1870** *Cong. Globe* 23 March 2173/3 If there is one term more than another which is opprobious to our people, . . . it is the term 'squatter.' **1948** *Ariz. Republic* (Phoenix) 5 March 1/4 'We're not mad and we don't figure on fightin',' said one bewhiskered old squatter.

transf. **1947** *Reader's Digest* Sep. 173/1 There was the last-minute scramble for tickets, the squatters' rush for the unreserved section.

b. Used in the possessive to designate organizations or establishments formed by, or for the benefit or protection of, squatters. *Obs.*

1854 in W. E. Connelley *Stand. Hist. Kans.* I. 350 No person shall be protected by the Squatter's Association who shall hold in his own right more than one claim. **1877** Johnson *Anderson Co., Kans.* 110 In November, 1858, a Free State squatters' court was organized in the counties of Linn, Anderson and Bourbon, for the trial of contested land claims.

2. = **pectoral sandpiper.**

1888, 1917 [see ***squat,** *v.* **3.** (1)].

3. In combs. (sense **1.**): (1) **squatter law,** a law or system of laws made by squatters for their own governance and enforced by them; (2) **right,** the right or claim of a squatter to the land upon which he has settled, also **squatter's right,** also transf.; (3) **-s' association,** (see quot.), *obs.;* (4) **sovereign, sovereignty,** see as main entries; (5) **State,** (see quot.).

(1) **1856** Phillips *Kansas* 27 A code of 'Squatter Laws' was adopted, which had application to the valley of the Kaw, and in which mutual assistance was pledged to sustain the 'claims' taken, in the absence of other means of legalizing these inchoate titles. **1946** Foreman *Last Trek* 188 White squatters . . . going so far . . . as to parcel out individual selections and inaugurate what they called 'squatter laws' to protect them. — (2) **1857** [see **squatters' association**]. **1873** Beadle *Undevel. West* 417 This is not an 'Indian title,' so called, . . . not a 'squatter's right.' **1947** *Chi. D. News* 1 Nov. 13/3 Every team in the conference has beaten the victoryless Rockets and the Dodgers, who had all but won 'squatters' rights' on the Eastern division cellar, have scored their only two 1947 victories. — (3) **1857** T. H. Gladstone *Englishman in Kans.* 168 During the first stage, mutual protection is given to the squatters by their forming into 'Squatters' Associations;' and the 'squatter-right' to a lot of ground is bought and sold on the strength of the law which emanates from these associations, and which asserts its power by rifle and tomahawk.

(5) **1871** De Vere 659 Kansas . . . appears occasionally as *Squatter State*, from the pertinacity with which squatter-sovereignty was discussed there, and settlers poured in by the two contending parties.

Also *squatter candidate, court, element, home, life, meeting, riot, settlement*, etc.

squatter-butter ˈskwɑtɚˌbʌtɚ, *v. To go squatter-butter*, (see quot.). *Slang. Obs.* — *c***1870** Chipman *Notes on Bartlett* 439 *Squatter-butter*. To go 'squatter-butter,' is to slide down hill 'sitting on one's heels,' as more inoffensively the thing is expressed.—Eastern Massachusetts.

squatteree ˌskwɑtəˈri, *n.* A squatter's cabin. *Rare.* — **1843** Carlton *New Purchase* I. 101 Due east from the capitol about a furlong, was the squateree of uncle Tommy Seymour. *Ib.* 198 The squatteree was . . . built of small round saplings.

squatterism ˈskwɑtəˌrɪzəm, *n.* The principles and practices of squatters. *Obs.* — **1855** *Herald of Freedom* 4 Aug. 4/1 The question of squatterism has passed the period at which discussion is profitable, and reached that at which action is inevitable. **1892** C. Robinson *Kans. Conflict* 54 But some thought it a good opportunity to make an end of squatters and squatterism altogether.

squatterphobia ˈskwɑtɚˌfobɪə, *n.* An inordinate fear of, or dislike for, squatter sovereignty. *Rare.* — **1856** in C. Robinson *Kans. Conflict* (1892) 222 Colonel Lane, . . . came here with the squatterphobia, of which he has been long and dangerously sick—having been bitten in Congress by the Nebraska bill itself.

squatter sovereign. A settler in a U.S. territory, esp. Kansas, who agitated for squatter sovereignty there with reference to slavery. Also attrib. and transf. *Obs.*

[**1848** Calhoun *Works* (1854) IV. 498 The first half-dozen squatters would become the sovereigns, with full dominion and sovereignty over them.] *a***1861** Winthrop *Open Air* 284 When the road grew too hot for us, . . . we jumped over the fence into the Race-Course . . . and there became squatter sovereigns all day. **1900** *Kans. Hist. Coll.* VI. 336 In 1847 Lewis Cass, a democrat from Michigan, gave birth to the squatter sovereign subterfuge—the dogma of the control of slavery or freedom in a territory by the vote of the squatters in that territory.

b. (*cap.*) Stephen A. Douglas. *Obs.*

1855 (*title*), The Squatter Sovereign. **1860** G. W. Bungay *Bobolink Minstrel* 72 Your little Squatter Sovereign Sha'nt be our King!

squatter sovereignty.

1. The right of settlers in a territory to make their own laws, popular sovereignty. Also attrib. Now *hist.*

1854 *Cong. Globe* App. 9 May 586/2 It has been assumed that this bill embraces the principle of squatter sovereignty. **1878** Beadle *Western Wilds* 371 The 'squatter sovereignty' doctrine of Stephen A. Douglas had suited their position. **1898** *Mo. So. Dakotan* I. 58 [A temporary government] would be a practical application for 'squatter sovereignty' in its best sense, and certainly preferable to lynch law.

2. The right of settlers to the lands upon which they have settled. Also fig.

1855 *Knickerb.* XLV. 422 In that part of that beautiful state [Illinois] known as 'Egypt,' many of these wise men have exercised their 'squatter sovereignty' for the last forty years. **1858** *Ill. Agric. Soc. Trans.* III. 645 There are the sixty varieties of plant lice. . . . Their ideas of 'squatter sovereignty' conform to no true democratic or republican platform. **1892** *S. Dak. Hist. Coll.* I. 59 [A] surveyor general . . . was greatly needed when land-seekers preferred not to depend on the rights of 'squatter sovereignty.'

* **squatting,** *a.* and *n.*

1. *n.* The action of the verb squat (sense **1.**). Also attrib. *Obs.*

1809 Irving *Knickerb.* III. vii, This unceremonious mode of taking possession of *new land* was technically termed *squatting.* **1824** Blane *Excursion U.S.* 101 This settling on land which belongs to another person, and clearing and cultivating it without leave, is called Squatting. **1839** Marryat *Diary Amer.* 1 Ser. II. 75 Squatting . . . is taking possession of land belonging to government and cultivating it. **1848** *Ib.* (rev. ed.) V. iii, The city of New Amsterdam was a mere Dutch squatting-place on their territories.

b. (See quot.) *Obs.*

1870 Medbery *Men Wall St.* 168 [He resorted] to what is known in street *argot* as 'squatting.' In other words, he dishonored his own contracts and entered upon a lawsuit to cover his duplicity.

2. *a.* Occupying land in the manner of a squatter. *Obs.*

1839 Irving in *Knickerb.* XIII. 317 The Yankees of Connecticut, those swapping, bargaining, squatting enemies of the Manhattoes. **1848** ——— *Knickerb.* (rev. ed.) V. iii, His first impulse was to . . . kick these squatting Yankees out of the country.

3. squatting snipe, = **squat snipe.**

1781–2 Jefferson *Notes Va.* 77 Besides these, we have The Royston Crow, . . . Squatting snipe [etc.].

squaw skwɔ, *n.* [f. an Algonquian word meaning woman.]

1. An Indian woman or wife.

1634 Wood *N. Eng. Prospect* (1865) 109 If her husband come to seeke for his Squaw and beginne to bluster the English woman betakes her to her armes which are the warlike Ladle, and the scalding liquors. **1704** *Boston News-Letter* 26 June 1/2 After further Examination of the said Squaw they kill'd her also. **1870** Keim *Sheridan's Troopers* 211 Kidnapping another warrior's squaw is an offense which generally results in the death of the offending savage, if caught. **1950** *World-Herald Mag.* (Omaha) 15 Jan. 2/4 Indian women bitterly resent being called 'squaws.'

Hence **squawish,** *a.*

1858 WILKIE *Davenport* 48 The Indian left, doubtless, well assured of the fact, that at *bottom* there is no real enjoyment in the satisfaction of that squaw-ish trait, curiosity.

b. A white woman. *Jocose.*

1642 LECHFORD *Plain Dealing* 49 When they [*sc.* Indians] see any of our English women sewing with their needles, or working coifes, or such things, they will cry out, Lazie *squaes!* 1831 *Boston Transcript* 17 March 2/4 The poor Indian died of his scalding, after enduring for a few days the taunts of his companions, for being defeated by an 'Englishman's squaw.' 1879 *Cimarron News & Press* 20 Nov. 2/2 He spoke of Mrs. Price and Josephine Meeker heap brave squaws. 1949 *Chi. Tribune* 9 Dec. 18/3 Just look at all those squaws on State st.

c. An Indian man lacking in masculine qualities. *Obs.*

1808 PIKE *Sources Miss.* 20, I directed my interpreter to ask how many scalps they had taken, they replied 'none;' he added they were all squaws. 1855 KIP *Indian Council Walla Walla* (1897) 11 To be seen engaged in menial tasks . . . would procure for them [*sc.* Indian braves] the title of squaws.

d. good squaw, a dead squaw. *Rare.* Cf. **good Indian.**

1919 WILSON *White Indian* 36, I was so mad I would have made a few 'good squaws' in quick time.

2. (See quot.) *Obs.*

1830 *Huntingdon* (Pa.) *Courier* 15 Sep. 4/5 American Remedies Wanted. . . . Squaw or Poppoose, (Caulophyllum Tholictroides.)

3. Short for **old squaw.**

1902 *Everybody's Mag.* Feb. 179/1, I think that there is no swifter flier among birds than this garrulous 'Squaw.'

4. =**squaw hitch.**

1913 BARNES *Western Grazing Grounds* 368 There are an endless number of hitches used by western men, as the squaw, the stirrup, the bed and basco.

5. In combs.: (1) **squaw ax,** (see quot. 1832), *obs.;* (2) **camp,** a camp in which squaws and children live while the men are away hunting or fighting, *obs.;* (3) **campaign,** (see quot.), *obs.;* (4) **dance,** among Indians, a dance in which the squaws choose partners, also transf., and attrib.; (5) **fighter,** (see quot.), *obs.;* (6) **fish,** any one of various fish found in the streams of California and the Northwest, esp. the Sacramento pike *q.v.;* (7) **hitch,** a hitch or knot used by packers; (8) **humper,** =**squaw man,** *rare;* (9) **line,** (see quot. 1897 and cf. **tumpline**), *obs.;* (10) **man,** a white man married to an Indian woman, or an Indian who does woman's work; (11) **medicine,** (see quot.), *obs.;* (12) **pony,** (see quot.), *obs.;* (13) **sachem,** an Indian woman who holds the rank of a chief, also transf., *obs.;* (14) **talk,** (see quot.); (15) **wind,** =**Chinook wind;** (16) **winter,** an early cold spell, usu. just before or just after Indian summer; (17) **wood,** *W.* firewood that is easily gathered, or that does not require chopping, also cow or buffalo chips.

(1) 1804 in *Wis. Hist. Coll.* XXII. (1916) 174 They Brought their Squaw axes & kittle to fix and mend for which they Gave us corn & beans Squasshes & C. 1832 *Louisville Directory* 104 [They stunned] the old Indian and squaw . . . by some smart blows with their squaw axes, (as the small axes are called usually handled by the squaws.) 1907 COOK *Border & Buffalo* (1938) 77, I generally went ahead on foot, and with a squaw-ax lopped off such limbs as would strike our packs. — (2) 1840 HOFFMAN *Greyslaer* I. 143 The 'Squaw Camp' of Thayendanagea [was] a lonely fastness where, in time of war, the women and children of his tribe were sequestered for safety. 1885 *Wkly. New Mexican Rev.* 18 June 1/4 Geronimo . . . , in order to mislead the troops and save the squaw camp, kept on with some twenty bucks. — (3) 1895 THWAITES (ed.) Withers *Chron. Border Warfare* 210 From the fact that this first American movement against the savages . . . resulted only in the capture of non-combatants, . . . it was long known as 'the squaw campaign.' — (4) 1893 *Outing* Oct. 11/1 The ceremony over, a squaw dance began. 1946 R. PEATTIE *Pac. Coast Ranges* 296 During the earlier days a squaw dance house, known as the 'Madhouse,' . . . specialized in 'blue ruin' whiskey. 1948 *Atlantic Mo.* Jan. 61/1 Full of energy as a grasshopper, he leads an impromptu Squaw Dance as close to the fire as skin will stand it, and then abruptly heads for bed.

(5) 1832 WILLIAMS *Maine* I. 456 The proud Mohawks, afterwards called the Lenape, *squaw-fighters*, from the proverbial peace-making character of Indian females. — (6) 1881 NASH *Two Yrs. Ore.* 85 The fisherman on this coast calls this the 'squaw-fish,' from this sheltering, maternal interest. 1896 JORDAN & EVERMANN *Fishes N. Amer.* 224 Ptychocheilus oregonensis (Richardson). (Squaw-fish; Chappaul; Sacramento Pike.) 1947 [see **Sacramento pike**]. — (7) 1903 A. ADAMS *Log of Cowboy* 32 He showed me what he called a squaw hitch with which you can lash a pack single-handed. 1946 *Sierra Club Bul.* Dec. 50 Basket, squaw, or diamond hitches were not even part of the military vocabulary of a World War II soldier. — (8) 1936 BARNARD *Rider* 98 Jack Stillwell and that old squaw humper, Johnson, rode in. — (9) 1704 in G. SHELDON *Hist. Deerfield, Mass.* (1895) I. 300 An account of wt plunder was taken from the enemy on the last of Febewary, 1703–4: . . . John Wait A hatchet Zacrye field A squaline Samll warner A squaline Nathll Colman A squaline. 1897 *Boston Transcript* 4 Dec. 16/5 'Squaline' was a leather strap used to fasten on packs or knapsacks to the shoulders of scouts or soldiers on the march.

(10) 1866 *Rep. Indian Affairs* 91 White men . . . have located in the vicinity of the reservation, and are known as squaw men. 1877 COZZENS *Crossing Quicksands* 153 'What's a squaw-man?' inquired Ned. 'One that ain't allowed ter fight, or hunt, or git married, or own hosses; but has tew stay about the camp with the squaws all the time.' 1948 DICK *Dixie Frontier* 23 First came the missionary, hunter-trapper, trader, and Indian countryman, or squaw-man as he was known in the territory north of the Ohio River. — (11) 1857 P. ST. G. COOKE *Scenes & Adventures* 82 It was that which succeeded: for surely the chief, Shu-da-gah-ha, did not believe her, that the Pawnee threw 'squaw medicine' (love powder) on her; that he 'bewitched her.' — (12) 1870 KEIM *Sheridan's Troopers* 217 The herd is always divided into two classes of animals, war and squaw-ponies, the latter being used for carrying burdens. — (13) 1622 MOURT *Relation* 126 The Squa Sachim, or Massachusets Queene was an enemy to him. 1702 in J. W. LYDEKKER *Faithful Mohawks* (1938) 11 (*footnote*), They [the Indians] did admire at first that we should have a Squaw Sachem vizt. a woman King, but they hoped she would be a good Mother. 1832 WILLIAMSON *Maine* I. 459 Their ancient chief . . . was a female and called a Squaw Sachem. — (14) 1905 *Lit. Digest* 12 Aug. 207/1 In the vocabulary of the American Indian, . . . 'squaw-talk' is the term for any kind of foolish, irrelevant, or untrue talk—the kind of talk that 'is good enough for women.'

(15) 1935 H. L. DAVIS *Honey in Horn* 214 A warm squaw-wind eased in from the direction of China. — (16) 1874 B. F. TAYLOR *World on Wheels* 185 Those single-minded, grand old fellows . . . had kicked the light snow of 'squaw winter' from their Spanish-leather boots. 1949 *Chi. Tribune* 4 Nov. 18/3 This week's cold snap may be 'squaw winter,' which is supposed to bring the true Indian summer. — (17) 1914 *Outing* June 191/2 The cooking fire is only the beginning of the possibilities of 'squaw wood.' 1933 CHELEY *Camping Out* 37 'Standing Squaw Wood,' if such is available, is of course always to be preferred over 'Down Squaw Wood.' 1949 *World-Herald Mag.* (Omaha) 19 June 5/2 'Squaw-wood' is ample for a meal.

Also *squaw ancestor, blanket, costume, dance, fashion, garden, mistress, pet, saddle, widow, wife, work,* etc.

b. In the names of plants: (1) **squawberry,** see as a main entry; (2) **bush,** see as a main entry; (3) **cabbage,** *W.* (*a*) =**miner's lettuce,** (*b*) the desert trumpet, *Eriogonum inflatum;* (4) **carpet,** =**mahala mat;** (5) **corn,** a soft-grained variety of Indian corn, often having grains of various colors; (6) **currant,** (see quot. 1909); (7) **grass,** (see first quots.); (8) **huckleberry,** (see quot. 1931); (9) **mash,** variant of **quamash,** *rare;* (10) **root,** any one of various American plants, some of which have roots possessing medicinal or food value, esp. *Canopholis americana*, also the root of one these plants; (11) **vine,** the partridgeberry or the checkerberry *qq.v.;* (12) **weed,** see as a main entry; (13) **whortleberry,** (see quot.).

(3) (*a*) 1915 ARMSTRONG & THORNBER *Western Wild Flowers* 122 Miner's Lettuce. *Montia parviflora*. . . . It is also called Indian Lettuce and Squaw Cabbage. (*b*) 1939 PICKWELL *Deserts* 47/2 When the desert rains have fallen properly, the swollen stems of Squaw Cabbage grow in circles about the Creosote Bushes in the Mohave, like children in ring-around-the-rosy. — (4) 1934 WEBSTER. 1943 GOETHE *Sierran Cabin* 61 One blue-flowered ceanothus, the squaw carpet, adjusts itself to heavy high-Sierran snows, by assuming a matlike form.

(5) 1824 DODDRIDGE *Notes* 90 How widely different is the large squaw corn, in its size, and the period of its growth from the Mandan corn. 1914 E. STEWART *Lett. Woman Homesteader* 151 They had a small patch of land . . . on which was raised the squaw corn that hung in bunches from the rafters. 1948 *Milwaukee Jrnl.* 18 July 2/7 There's pop corn, sweet corn, squaw corn, flint corn, hybrid corn and then there is just plain corn, the kind we get on the radio. — (6) 1909 SCHNEIDER *Woody Plants Pike's Peak* 146 The squaw currant (*Ribes cereum*) occurs in the gullies. 1947 *Desert Mag.* May 28/3 The national park expects a limited showing of Indian paintbrush, redbird, . . . squaw currant . . . and others during May. — (7) 1903 JAMES *Indian Basketry* 89 The squaw grass—Xerophyllum tenax—of the Klickitats' basketry in its natural color is white. 1909 *Cent. Supp.* 544/1 *Xerophyllum tenax* . . . is the bear-grass of Lewis and Clark. Also called *squaw-grass* and *squaw-lily*. 1949 *Pacific Discovery* May-

June 18/2 There were slopes clad with velvety mats of heather interrupted here and there by wavy plumes of squaw grass. — (**8**) **1857** GRAY *Botany* 248 Deerberry. Squaw Huckleberry. . . . Dry woods, Maine to Michigan, and southward. **1931** CLUTE *Plants* 37 The squaw-huckleberry (*Vaccinium stamineum*) is almost the only species in its genus that is inedible. — (**9**) **1806** LEWIS in *L. & Clark Exped.* III. (1905) 333 The natives . . . eat it [i.e., whale blubber] either alone or with the roots of the rush, squawmash [etc.].

(**10**) **1815** DRAKE *Cincinnati* 85 Plants Useful in Medicine and the Arts. . . . *Actea racemosa*—squaw root, the *root* [etc.]. **1891** *Amer. Folk-Lore* IV. 149 *Trillium erectum* we called [in N.H.] *Squaw Root.* **1943** PEATTIE *Great Smokies* 190 The old wives of the mountains today are not averse to taking, sometimes, a dose of squawroot for 'female complaints.' — (**11**) **1850** S. F. COOPER *Rural Hours* 32 It was a perfect bed of the squaw-vine and partridge berry. **1919** STURTEVANT *Notes Edible Plants* 366 *Mitchella repens.* . . . Partridge-Berry. Squaw-Vine. . . . The insipid, red fruits are eaten by children. — (**13**) **1829** EATON *Botany* (ed. 5) 433 *Vaccinium stamineum*, squaw whortleberry.

c. *To trap a squaw*, see ∗**trap**, *v.* **4.**

As the last term in **old, pale face, Seminole, Sioux, Snake, sunck, war squaw.**

squawberry ˈskwɔˌbɛrɪ, *n.* Any one of various plants, as (*a*) the osoberry, *Osmaronia cerasiformis*, (*b*) the deerberry, *Vaccinium stamineum*, cf. **squaw whortleberry,** (*c*) a sumac, as *Rhus aromatica*, or *R. trifoliata*, cf. **lemita, skunkbush,** (*d*) (see quot.), (*e*) a plant or its fruit of the genus *Lycium*, cf. **garambullo, wolfberry.**

(*a*) **1885** ONDERDONK *Idaho* 30 Nuttalia cerasifolia, Squawberry. — (*b*) **1891** *Cent.* 5879/1 *Squaw-berry*, . . . same as *squaw-huckleberry* [*Vaccinium stamineum*]. — (*c*) **1907** LYONS *Plant Names* 396 R[hus] aromatica. . . . Fragrant Sumac, Sweet-scented Sumac, Trefoil Sumac, Squaw-berry. **1931** DAYTON *Western Browse Plants* 96 Their slender twigs are very important in basketry work among the Indians, which is probably the reason that many people call them squawbush or squawberry. — (*d*) **1931** CLUTE *Plants* 37 The squaw-berry (*Mitchella repens*) has brilliant red fruits, but the interior is dry and tasteless. — (*e*) **1937** NICHOL *Natural Vegetation Ariz.* 213 In addition many kinds of chollas and prickly pears are found with squawberries, saltbushes, bur sage. **1944** *Utah Hist. Quart.* July–Oct. 120 Among the native fruits gathered in season were the wild grapes and sour squawberries of the streambanks.

squawbush ˈskwɔˌbʊʃ, *n.* Any one of various shrubs (see quots.).

1832 WILLIAMSON *Maine* I. 125 *Indian Tobacco*, called by the Natives '*Squaw-bush*,' is a perennial herb, or shrub. **1894** *Amer. Folk-Lore* VII. 90 *Cornus stolonifera*, squaw-bush, Penobscot Co., Me. **1909** *Cent. Supp.* 1261/2 *Squaw-bush*, . . . a name of *Cornus stolonifera*, *C. serica.* and *C. Canadensis.* **1909** WEBSTER 2025 *Squaw bush. a.* The cranberry tree. *b.* A sumac of the western United States (*Rhus trilobata*), with unpleasantly scented trifoliate leaves. **1942** STEGNER *Mormon C.* 307 A sheepwagon slept by a squawbush [i.e., a sumac] and a horse grazed on the withered grass.

squawed skwɔd, *a.* Married to a squaw. *Rare.* — **1904** E. ROBINS *Magnetic North* 324 The old miners had nearly all got 'squawed.'

∗**squawk,** *n.* The black-crowned night heron *q.v.*, so named from its cry.

1872 COUES *Key to Birds* 269 *Nyctiardea*, Night Heron. Qua-bird. Squawk. **1897** *Kissimmee* (Fla.) *Valley Gaz.* 2 June 1/4 A squawk, perched on one foot by a century plant, is serenely viewing the exhibit. **1917** *Birds of Amer.* I. 194.

squawweed ˈskwɔˌwid, *n.* Any one of various plants, as (*a*) a horseweed, *Erigeron canadensis*, (*b*) any one of various ragworts, (*c*) =**squawberry** (*c*).

(*a*) **1828** RAFINESQUE *Medical Flora* I. 167 [These plants] were known to the Northern Indians by the name of Cocash or Squaw-weed. **1877** [see **cocash**]. — (*b*) **1848** BARTLETT 328 *Squaw-Weed.* (Lat. *senecio obovatus.*) A medicinal plant used for diseases of the skin. **1857** GRAY *Botany* 231 Golden Ragwort. Squaw-weed. . . . Common everywhere; the primary form in swamps. **1939** *Nat. Geog. Mag.* Aug. 256/2 There are many different kinds of ragworts, or groundsels and squawweeds, as they are also called, distributed throughout the country. — (*c*) **1903** JAMES *Indian Basketry* 73 The Hopi use yucca and fine grass; . . . the Southern California Indians, tule root and squaw weed.

squeak bean. (See quot.) — **1931** CLUTE *Plants* 60 The hard ripe seeds of the honey-locust (*Gleditsia triacanthus*) emit the most delightful squeaks when twisted under foot on a hard surface, as any mischievous schoolboy is aware, and in his vocabulary are known as squeak-beans.

∗**squeaker,** *n.* (See quot. 1900.) In full **squeaker crab.** — **1887** GOODE *Fisheries* V. II. 651 The lady crab, sand crab, or squeaker crab (*Platyonichus ocellatus*), occurs on most sandy shores from Cape Cod to Mexico. **1900** WEBSTER *Supp.* 200/1 *Squeaker*, . . . any crab that stridulates when irritated, as the American lady crab.

∗**squeal,** *v. intr.* (See quot. 1877.) *Slang. Obs.* — *a***1846** *Quarter Race Ky.* 45, I got his hed under my arm an I made him squeal immediantly. **1877** BARTLETT 797 *Squeal*, . . . to 'throw up the sponge.'

∗**squealer,** *n.* **1.** Applied to birds (see quots.). **2.** A complainer. *Slang.*

(**1**) **1877** BARTLETT 797 *Squealer*, (*Charadrius Virginianus*,) the Golden Plover. New England. **1881** *Cent. Mag.* May 100/1 When ready to leave the nest and face the world for itself, it [a young pigeon] is a squealer, or, in market parlance, a squab. **1888** TRUMBULL *Names of Birds* 91 Harlequin Duck, . . . known also as Squealer at Machias Port, Me. — (**2**) **1889** *Columbus* (O.) *Dispatch*, In nine cases out of ten, the editor gives the squealer more privileges in the way of reply than he is entitled to by equity. **1902** MCFAUL *Ike Glidden* 69 If it's anything I hate it's a squealer or a kicker.

squealing hawk. (See quot.) — **1884** *Harper's Mag.* March 622 The red-tailed hawk . . . by some is called the squealing hawk.

squeamy ˈskwimɪ, *a.* Squeamish. *Colloq.* — **1836** GILMAN *Recoll.* (1838) 44, I feel so squeamy-like at my stomach. **1880** *Harper's Mag.* Sep. 582/1 They 'd eet so much sweet it kinder made 'em squeamy.

squeeze play. *Baseball.* A play in which a runner on third base and the batter are in collusion, the runner dashing for the plate the moment the ball is pitched, depending on the batter to bunt the ball into fair territory so that a fielder will not have time to prevent the runner from scoring.

1905 *St. Louis Globe-Democrat* 2 July II. 8/5 Like the spit ball, the squeeze play is not strictly an invention of the present season. **1909** *Collier's* 15 May 29/2 The 'squeeze' play, of which we have heard so much in the past two or three years, is the method of scoring a man from third base on the hit-and-run system. **1949** *Chi. Tribune* 27 Sep. II. 1/8 The mighty Sox . . . had to resort to the squeeze play to score their all-important victory.

transf. **1948** MENJOU & MUSSELMAN *It Took 9 Tailors* 40 This squeeze play left important film companies like Fox, IMP . . . , Keystone, and others out in the cold.

∗**squeezer,** *n.* **1.** (See quot. 1891.) **2.** (See quot.)

(**1**) *a***1871** in HARGRAVE *Hist. Playing Cards* 334. **1891** *Cent.* 5880/2 *Squeezer* . . . *pl.*, a kind of playing-cards in which the face-value of each card is shown in the upper left-hand corner, and can readily be seen by squeezing the cards slightly apart, without displaying the hand. — (**2**) **1920** HUNTER *Trail Drivers Texas* I. 297 Some cattlemen now employ a branding chute where an arrangement for holding the cattle while they are being branded is called a 'squeezer,' or 'snappin' turtle.'

As the last term in **lemon squeezer.**

squeeze spindle. A device which enables the operator of a wheel of fortune or similar gambling device to stop the wheel secretly at a desired place. Also **squeeze wheel.** Cf. ∗**fixed 2. b.** quot. 1901.— **1891** QUINN *Fools of Fortune* 293 It differs from the 'squeeze spindle' already described, only in that it contains three 'arrows' or 'pointers' instead of one, two of which are under control of the operator through the employment of friction at the pivot by means of precisely similar contrivances. **1909** *Sat. Ev. Post* 20 Feb. 38/2 The squeeze wheel? It goes by various names. The gamblers call all such devices 'spindles.'

squeteague skwəˈtig, *n.* [f. a Narraganset term meaning lit. "they make glue," in allusion to the practice of the Indians of making a glue from the swimming bladders of these fish.] The weakfish, *Cynoscion regalis.*

1803 *Mass. H.S. Coll.* 1 Ser. IX. 202 The fishes . . . are called the sheepshead, . . . mackerel, squeterg, grunters [etc.]. **1815** *Ib.* 2 Ser. IV. 289 The fish, common to this bay, are found at Wareham, such as . . . squitteag, scuppeag . . . and alewives. **1895** GERARD in *N.Y. Sun* 30 July, Squeteague, a name of the weakfish, variously corrupted to squettee, squitie, squit, scuteeg, chequet, chickwit, and chickwick. The name probably stands for 'm'skwiteague,' 'stained with red,' referring to the bright salmon-colored tint of the fish's chin. **1903** *N.Y. Ev. Post* 11 Sep., Buzzard's Bay now affords only small squeteage, where large ones once abounded.

b. With specifying terms.

1884 GOODE *Fisheries* I. 365 *Cynoscion maculatum* . . . is of course in every respect very unlike a trout, and the name 'Spotted Squeteague' has been proposed for it. *Ib.* 367 The Silver Squeteague, *Cynoscion nothum*, . . . [is] of an uniform silvery hue.

Squiaelps ˈskwɪˌʌlps, *n.* [App. a name given them by other Salish tribes.] "A division of Salish between Kettle falls and Spokane r., E. Wash.; said by Gibbs to have been one of the largest of the Salish tribes. Lewis and Clark estimated their number at 2,500, in 130 houses, in 1806" (Hodge, *s.v. Colville*). — **1849** in *31st Cong.* 1 Sess. (1850) Sen. Ex. Doc. 52, 170 The *Ponduras* or *Squiaelps* occupy the country east of Colville.

*squid, *n.* An artificial bait used in fishing for squid. Also **squid jig, jigger.**

1861 *Harper's Mag.* March 459/1 These [squid] are caught by means of a 'squid-jig'—a piece of pewter run on a paper of hooked pins. **1866** *Ib.* Nov. 720/2 The men and boys were meanwhile swinging their squids, and sending them . . . fifty yards into the surf. **1876** Knight 2295/2 *Squid-jigger,* a trolling-hook for catching squids for bait. **1911** *Rep. Fisheries 1908* 309/2 Cuttle-fish . . . are caught with a peculiar arrangement of hooks called a 'squid jig.'

squid skwɪd, *v. intr.* (See quot. 1859.) — **1859** Bartlett 442 *To Squid,* to fish by trolling with a squid, either natural or artificial. **1894** *Outing* XXIV. 54/1 The fly-fisher scoffs at squidding.

squinch skwɪntʃ, *v.* [App. a blend of *squ*eeze and p*inch.*]

1. *tr.* To screw up, twist, squeeze.

1835 Longstreet *Ga. Scenes* 202 If I didn't see that fellow wink, and that woman squinch her face, then hell's a dancing room. **1840** Haliburton *Clockmaker* 3 Ser. xi, How it will make her squinch her face, won't it? **1939** *Real Detective Mag.* Aug. 89 She squinched and twisted her too prominent nose in a way that was not at all becoming.

2. To compress or squeeze together.

1843 Stephens *High Life N.Y.* 195 Harnsome gals . . . squinched themselves up to make room for me. **1909** Calhoun *Miss Minerva* 200 [Ladies] got to squinch up their waists and toes.

3. *intr.* To shrink or flinch, to pinch or scrimp. Also **squinching,** *n.*

1843 Stephens *High Life N.Y.* II. 195 Wal, she squinched a trifle and gin a leetle start. *Ib.* 253, [I] poured the glass [of cider] down without squinchin. **1905** Phillips *Social Secretary* 120, I reckon there's a lot of miserable pinching and squinching when the blinds are down.

squinch skwɪntʃ, *a.* and *adv.* [See **squinch,** *v.*] **1. squinch-eyed,** squint-eyed. Also **squinch-eye,** *attrib.* **2. squinch-owl,** a screech owl. Both *colloq.*

(1) **1884** Harris *Mingo* 177 Mrs. Hendrick's brother . . . had been engaged in China in converting (to use a neighborhood phrase) the 'squinch-eyed heathen.' **1907** White *Arizona Nights* 221 A little squinch-eye round face with big bow spectacles came and plumped down beside me. — **(2) 1880** Harris *Uncle Remus* (1884) 89 Word went roun' dat ole man Squinch Owl done kotch nudder watzizname. **1927** Benét *J. B.'s Body* 67 Talk like that and paterollers'll git you, Swinge you all to bits with a blacksnake whip, Squinch-owl carry yo' talk to de paterollers.

*squinny, *v. intr.* (See quot.) *Obs.* — *c***1870** Chipman *Notes on Bartlett* 442 *Squinny,* to make a broad laugh—New England.

*squint, *n.* A narrowing of the eyelids, a screwing up of the eyes or face. *Colloq.* — **1897** Hough *Story of Cowboy* 34 The bright sun causes him to hold . . . [his eyes] well covered with the lids, with a half squint to them. **1900** Bacheller *E. Holden* 118 When we . . . were on our way to the brook with pole and line a squint of elation had hold of Uncle Eb's face.

*squinting, *a. fig.* Tending in an indicated direction. Also as noun. *Colloq.* — **1855** Barnum *Life* 382 The attack had a squinting towards 'black mail.' **1904** *N.Y. Ev. Post* 28 Oct. 7 They inspired some significant paragraphs in the daily papers, squinting at the possibility of a scandal.

*squirarch, *n.* A justice or judge. *Rare.* — **1880** Tourgee *Invisible Empire* xi, The slave-holder was also the squirarch and the legislator.

*squire, *n.* A justice of the peace, a lawyer or judge. Also used as a mere honorific. *Colloq.*

1817 J. Bradbury *Trav. Amer.* 320 He is not in the least danger of receiving a rude or uncivil answer, even if he should address himself to a *squire* (so justices are called.) **1818** Palmer *Journal* 14 The judge, instead of Mr. is sometimes called squire. **1873** Mark Twain & Warner *Gilded Age* 17 'Squire' Hawkins got his title from being postmaster of Obedstown. **1900** Nicholson *Hoosiers* 25 The young attornies, called 'squires,' long clung to the queue as a kind of badge of their profession, and were prone to disport themselves before the rustics in the court yards of strange towns. **1946** Wilson *Fidelity* 53 For several terms he had served as magistrate and thus acquired the title 'Squire.'

b. Squire Birch, (see quot.). *Obs.*

1851 Howe *Hist. Coll. Great West* 193 The tribunal of *Squire Birch,* as the person who personated the judge was called, was established under a tree in the woods; the culprit being usually found guilty, was tied to a tree and lashed without mercy, and then expelled from the country.

*squire, *v. tr.* To marry (someone) in the manner of a squire or justice of the peace. With *together. Rare.* — **1892** *Advance* 16 June, I utterly forgot to utter a word of prayer over them. And so, . . . Mrs. Knowles was 'squired together' again.

*squirm, *v. tr.* To fit or squeeze *into;* to utter with a squirm. *Colloq.* — **1876** Mark Twain *Tom Sawyer* xxi. 171 No matter what the subject might be, a brain-racking effort was made to squirm it into some aspect or other that the moral and religious could contemplate with edification. **1889** Gunter *That Frenchman!* xxi, Here Zamaroff squirms out: 'Do I look like a man who would kill anything?'

*squirrel, *n.*

1. A squirrelfish *q.v.*

1733 Catesby *Carolina* II. 3 The Squirrel . . . is a good eating Fish. **1883** *Nat. Museum Bul.* No. 27, 503 *Diplectrum fasciculare.* . . . Squirrel.

2. (See quots.) *Obs.*

1808 Pike *Sources Miss.* 156 (*footnote*), The Wishtonwish of the Indians, prairie dogs of some travellers; or squirrels as I should be inclined to denominate them; reside on the prairies of Louisiana in towns or villages. **1814** Brackenridge *Views La.* 58 The Prairie dog or Squirrel, is a great curiosity.

3. In combs.: (1) **squirrel bee,** (see quot.), *obs.;* (2) **bot,** (see quot.); (3) **corn,** a handsome wild herb of the genus *Dicentra,* having yellow tubers resembling kernels of Indian corn; (4) **cup,** the hepatica, *Hepatica triloba;* (5) **dog,** a dog useful in hunting squirrels; (6) **fish,** see as a main entry; (7) **frog,** (see quot. and cf. **squirrel tree toad**); (8) **grass,** (see quot.); (9) **gun,** a light gun suitable for shooting squirrels and other small creatures; (10) **hake,** a species of codling, *Phycis chuss,* or a related fish; (11) **hawk,** the ferruginous roughleg, *Buteo regalis,* also **California squirrel hawk;** (12) **hold,** a hold with the hands and feet after the manner of a squirrel, *rare;* (13) **hunt,** a hunt for squirrels, esp. a squirrel bee *q.v.;* (14) ***hunter,** a member of an irregular volunteer Ohio militia that assembled in 1862 for the defense of Cincinnati from attack by a Confederate force under Gen. Kirby Smith; (15) **picker,** one who lives largely on squirrel meat, *contemptuous, rare;* (16) **rifle,** a light small-bore rifle suitable for shooting squirrels and other small game, also attrib.; (17) **shot,** small shot suitable for squirrel shooting; (18) ***track,** a very dim trace or track through the forest, *rare;* (19) **tree toad,** a small green tree-frog, *Hyla squirrella,* found in the southern states, also **squirrel tree frog.**

(1) 1855 Weld *Vacation Tour* 78 These hunts, or, as they are called [in New York], 'Squirrel Bees,' take place at the close of harvest, and are generally attended with a terrible destruction of squirrels and other animals. — **(2) 1891** *Cent.* 3882/3 *Squirrel-bot,* . . . a bot-fly, *Cutiterebra emasculator,* whose larvæ infest the genital and axillary regions of various squirrels and gophers in the United States. — **(3) 1843** Torrey *Flora N.Y.* I. 46 Squirrel Corn. Turkey Corn. . . . Rather common in the western and northern counties. **1915** Armstrong & Thornber *Western Wild Flowers* 170 *Bicuculla uniflora,* a diminutive alpine plant, of Bleeding Heart family. This is called Squirrel Corn and Steer's Head. **1950** *Mo. Bot. Garden Bul.* Jan. 23 For example, Squirrel Corn (*Dicentra canadensis*), was found in southern Missouri at only one locality, in Taney Co., along White River. — **(4) 1850** S. F. Cooper *Rural Hours* 48 Perhaps it is this position [at the foot of trees] which, added to their downy, furred leaves and stems, has given them the name of squirrel-cups. **1919** Cady *Rhymes of Vt.* (1923) 225 Shooting stars, Oxalis, bloodroot, squirrel cup And Injun pipe come sprouting up.

(5) 1855 M. Reid *Hunter's Feast* xix, A good squirrel-dog is a useful animal. **1949** *Democrat* 17 March 7/2 Good squirrel and o'possum dog for sale. — **(7) 1900** Webster *Supp.* 200/1 *Squirrel frog,* a small American tree frog (*Hyla squirilla*). — **(8) 1890** Webster 1398/2 *Squirrel grass,* . . . a pestiferous grass (*Hordeum murinum*) related to barley. In California the stiffly awned spikelets work into the wool of sheep, and into the throat, flesh and eyes of animals. — **(9) 1875** *Fur, Fin & Feather* (ed. 3) 125 Then there are rural gunners . . . provided with quail and squirrel guns. **1949** *Chi. Tribune* 2 Oct. I. 14/4 Some called them [Kentucky rifles] squirrel guns because the owners could bag this most teasing of targets with ease.

(10) 1882 *Nat. Museum Bul.* No. 16, 799 *P[hycis] tenuis,* . . . Codling; White hake; Squirrel-hake. North Atlantic, south to Virginia. **1911** *Rep. Fisheries 1908* 311/1 Different species are known as 'old English hake,' 'squirrel hake,' 'white hake' [etc.]. — **(11) 1858** Baird *Birds Pacific R.R.* 34 *Archibuteo Ferrugineus.* . . . California Squirrel Hawk. . . . This is one of the most handsome of the American Falconidae. **1895** *Dept. Agric. Yrbk. 1894* 219 The rough-legged hawk, and the ferruginous roughleg, or squirrel hawk, . . . are among our largest and at the same time the most beneficial hawks. — **(12) 1858** Harris *Sut Lovingood* 152 He drapped ofen the hoss-rack, but hilt a squirrel-holt ontu the pole wif his paws and his feet, and hung back down. — **(13) 1795** Priest *Travels* (1802) 91 At a squirrel-hunt in Madison county, on the 29th and 30th ult., the hunters rendezvoused at captain Archibald Wood's. **1840** *Niles' Reg.* 11 July 304/2 Squirrel hunt . . . 21,000 squirrels were recently killed at Gratton, by two parties of sportsmen. **1855** M. REID *Hunter's Feast* xix, To make a successful squirrel-hunt two persons at least are necessary. — **(14)** **1863** MOORE *Rebellion Rec.* V. I. 77 Over one thousand squirrel-hunters from the neighboring counties . . . volunteered their services. **1874** COLLINS *Kentucky* I. 111/2 'Squirrel hunters' and volunteer militia from Ohio and Indiana pour in from all directions.

(15) **1857** STROTHER *Virginia* 150, I don't like to be stumped, nor yit to be called a squirrel-picker, by no set-up swell. — **(16)** **1834** NOTT *Novellettes* I. 56 They were differently armed and equipped . . . [with] old-fashioned muskets, squirrel-rifles, horse-pistols, and pocket-pistols. **1948** *Chi. D. News* 10 April 6/2, I have an idea that too much of the squirrel rifle and prairie wagon tradition still runs in the blood-stream of most Americans to permit them [etc.]. — **(17)** **1803** C. PETTIGREW *MS Lett. to E. P.* (Univ. N.C. MSS), I wish you to fetch . . . 4 Lb. of good squirrel shot. **1872** EGGLESTON *End of World* 249 You heerd the buckshot and the squirrel-shot . . . a-rattlin' around. — **(18)** **1844** EMERSON *Experience* Ess. 2 Ser., Western roads, which opened stately enough, . . . but soon became narrower and narrower, and ended in a squirrel track. — **(19)** **1842** *Nat. Hist. N.Y., Zoology* III. 72 The Squirrel Tree-toad . . . inhabits under logs and bark of decaying trees. **1850** JOHNSTON *Notes* I. 137 There are at least two species in the United States—the northern tree-toad and the squirrel tree-toad. **1950** *Nat. Geog. Mag.* April 509/2 My first introduction to the squirrel tree frog (*Hyla squirella*) was at night near Gainesville, Florida.

b. squirrel's jump, as far as a squirrel can jump, a short distance. *Colloq.*

1838 *Knickerb.* XII. 506 Have you ever been as far as a squirrel's jump from it? **1856** *Harper's Mag.* XII. 570/2, I've never been a squirrel's jump *from* it.

As the last term in **antelope, antelope ground, barking, black, burrowing, canyon, cat, chip, chipping, Douglas, earth, federation, flying, four-lined ground, fox, gray, ground, migratory, mountain, mouse, pine, prairie, prairie ground, red, red-belly, rock, Rocky Mountain flying, Rocky Mountain ground, silver-gray, striped, striped ground, whistling squirrel.**

squirrelfish ˈskwɜəlˌfɪʃ, *n.* Any one of various fish which when taken from the water make a noise suggestive of the bark of a squirrel, as (*a*) a grunt, (*b*) the serrano or sandfish, *Diplectrum formosum*, or a related fish, (*c*) the sailor's-choice, *Lagodon rhomboides.*

(*a*) **1803** SHAW *Gen. Zool.* IV. II. 439 Squirrel Sparus *Sparus sciurus*. Size of a common Perch: native of the American seas, where it is known by the name of the Grunt, or Squirrel-fish. **1884** GOODE *Fisheries* I. 398 In some localities they are called also 'Squirrel-fish,' in allusion to the same habit. (*b*) **1867** LATHAM *Black & White* 122 The fisherman . . . [showed] me bastard snappers and squirrel-fish, the like of which I had never seen before. **1884** GOODE *Fisheries* I. 410 The Squirrel-fish is usually to be seen in the markets of Charleston. (*c*) **1889** GOODE *Fisheries* I. 393 The 'Sailor's Choice' . . . [is known] at Brunswick, Georgia, as the 'Squirrel-fish.' **1903** T. H. BEAN *Fishes N.Y.* 562 [The sailor's choice] is also called pinfish, squirrel fish, porgee, yellowtail and shiner.

* **squirreling,** *n.* The hunting of squirrels. Also attrib.

1831 *Maysville* (Ky.) *Eagle* 5 July, Suppose we make a squirriling tour to the country today. **1843** CARLTON *New Purchase* II. 188 Who's goin' squirrillin'? **1943** PEATTIE *Great Smokies* 147 Are you a-fixin' to go squirrelin'?

* **squirt,** *v.* and *n.*

1. a. (See quot. 1851.) *Obs.* **b. squirt clam,** (see quot.).

(a) **1851** HALL *College Words* 292 At Harvard College, a showy recitation is denominated a *squirt.* **1876** TRIPP *Student-Life* 26 He couldn't have read a word, but, as luck would have it, did make a regular 'squirt' on another passage. — **(b)** **1887** GOODE *Fisheries* V. II. 581 In Long Island Sound and at New York it [*Mya arenaria*] is most spoken of as the 'long clam' and 'squirt clam.'

2. squirt gun, a syringe-like device for squirting water, usu. a child's toy. Also transf. and fig.

1803 FESSENDEN *Poetical Petition* 87 With glyster-pipe and squirt-gun There will be dev'lish deal of hurt done. **1865** E. BURRITT *Walk to Land's End* 96 An instrument which American boys would call a squirt-gun is employed [at Reading, England] in making the macaroons. **1894** HOYT *Texas Steer* (1925) III. 39, I won't be made the target for your squirt-gun of wit.

As the last term in **bob, pop squirt.**

squirtish ˈskwɜtɪʃ, *a.* Given to display or ostentation in dress or manner. *Obs.* — **1847** ROBB *Squatter Life* 73 These squirtish kind a fellars ain't perticular hard baked. **1851** HALL *College Words* 292 *Squirtish,* showy; dandified.

squirty ˈskwɜtɪ, *a.* (See quot.) Also **squirtiness.** — **1851** HALL *College Words* 292 *Squirtiness,* the quality of being showy. *Ib.*, *Squirty,* showy; fond of display; gaudy. Applied to an oration which is full of bombast and grandiloquence; to a foppish fellow; to an apartment gayly adorned, &c.

squit skwɪt, *n.* [App. f. **squeteague.**] The squeteague, *Cynoscion regalis.* — **1884** GOODE *Fisheries* I. 362 'Squit,' 'Succoteague,' 'Squitee,' and 'Chickwit' are doubtless variations of ['squeteague']. **1911** *Rep. Fisheries 1908* 317/1.

squizzle,** *v.* **1.** *To let squizzle,* to fire a gun. **2.** To sizzle. Both *rare.* — **(1)** *a1861** WINTHROP *Open Air* 241 The recruit let squizzle and jist missed his ear. — **(2)** **1890** *Detroit Free Press* 2 July, Think of an editor fairly 'squizzling' with the heat.

squmption ˈskwʌmpʃən, *n.* [Origin unknown.] ?A hurry. *Rare.* — **1851** *Polly Peablossom* 60 Hold on, fellers, don't be in such a squmption.

squnch skwʌntʃ, *v.* [Prob. a variant of **scrunch.**] *intr.* (See quot. and cf. **squinch,** *v.*) — **1877** BARTLETT 797 *Squnch,* to stoop or lie down; to squeeze one's self within the smallest compass.

squow skwaʊ, *n.* [?squabble+*row.*] A row or squabble. *Rare.* — **1862** E. W. PEARSON *Lett. Port Royal* 70 It is a peculiar experience to be detective, policeman, judge, jury, and jailer,—all at once—sometimes in cases of assault and battery, and general plantation squows, —then in a divorce case.

sqush skwʌʃ, *v.* [Var. of **squash, v.*] *tr.* To crush, mash, overcome. Also *intr. Colloq.* Cf. Wentworth *s.v.*

1837 NEAL *Charcoal Sk.* (1838) 45 The next time I meet that chap, . . . I'll sqush it with my foot. **1884** MARK TWAIN *H. Finn* xxix, Blamed if the king didn't have to brace up mighty quick, or he'd a' squshed down like a bluff bank that the river has cut under. **1941** *Sat. Ev. Post* 25 Oct. 90 (Wentworth), Sqush that big ox. Sqush him good.

squshy ˈskwʌʃɪ, *a.* Soft and yielding. *Colloq.* — **1891** *Cent. Mag.* Feb. 489 He reposes on three or four feather beds piled one upon another, a patchwork quilt being spread over the squshy mountain.

***stab,** *n. To make a stab at* (or *for*), to make an effort to do something. *Slang.* — **1908** K. MCGAFFEY *Show-Girl* 235, I . . . made a stab for the rail. **1943** *Harper's Mag.* June 87 Surprising numbers of them have seemed almost willing to leave their farms and to make a stab at some other way of life.

stabbist ˈstæbɪst, *n.* A stabber. *Rare.* — **1871** DE VERE 658 The man of violence, who had heretofore been denounced as a murderer, now appeared before the charitable jury as a modest *stabbist,* or, at worst, called a formidable *strikist.*

* **stable,** *n.*

1. a. A booth or stall where certain commodities are dealt in. *Rare.* **b.** (See quot.) *Slang.*

(a) **1886** *Harper's Mag.* July 175/1 The bicycle and tricycle stable was well patronized. — **(b)** **1904** *McClure's Mag.* April 661/1 Kelly and his 'stable' as the retinue of rubbers and 'workout' boxers are known to the devotees of pugilism, had been at Ocean View.

2. In combs.: (1) **stable car,** a form of cattle car, *obs.;* (2) **fly,** a troublesome biting fly, *Stomoxys calcitrans,* sometimes abundant about stables, also a related fly, *Muscina stabulans;* (3) **lot,** an inclosure for horses, cattle, etc., adjoining a stable or stables.

(1) **1890** *Stock Grower & Farmer* 11 Jan. 5/2 The patent stable-car alone delivered 48,000 car loads [to Chicago], which at twenty head to the car would amount to 960,000. — **(2)** **1862** T. W. HARRIS *Treatise Insects Injur. Veget.* 16 The stinging stable-flies (*Stomoxys*). **1892** KELLOGG *Kansas Insects* 116 A cattle pest [from Europe] . . . bids fair to . . . be as troublesome as its nearly related pest, the well-known Stable Fly, or Cattle Fly. **1949** GATES *Field Man. Plant Ecology* 6 Mosquitoes, chiggers, black flies, deer flies, nosee-ums, and stable flies are perhaps the most common. — **(3)** **1896** *Cosmopolitan* XX. 391/2 In the stable lot . . . the grass was grazed so close that the geese could barely nip it. **1946** NIXON *Va. Words* 10.

As the last term in **boarding, brush, exchange, feed, Kansas, log, sale stable.**

staboy stəˈbɔɪ, *v.* Also **stubboy.** [See next.] *tr.* To urge or encourage (dogs or other animals), as by calling 'staboy!' Also fig.

1843 STEPHENS *High Life N.Y.* II. 141, I shook my bridle . . . , and stuboyed the old critter along. **1850** LOWELL *Poetical Works* (1896) 323/2 Like dogs let loose upon a bear, Ten emulous styles [of architecture] *staboyed* with care, The whole among them seemed to tear. **1905** *N.Y. Sun* 15 Nov. (*Cent. Supp.*), Are there not even Brooklynites in remote green outskirts or dusty fringes of ambiguous suburbs who have stubboyed or still stubboy?

staboy stəˈbɔɪ, *interj.* Also **stu boy, steboy, steeboy,** etc. [f. *st* (given in *EDD* as Sc. and Derbyshire exclamation to urge on a dog or horse), +*boy,* an appellative often used to a dog or horse. Cf. **hist-a-boy,** and see *stoo* in *EDD.*] A call used to summon or arouse a dog or other animal. Also in fig. use. *Colloq.*

1774 *Mass. Spy* 29 Dec. (Th.), Stu boy, Stu boy, seize 'em, Jowler, seize 'em. **1843** W. T. THOMPSON *Major Jones's Courtship* 55 The dogs started up sumthing.... 'Steboy; catch him!' ses he. **1848** LOWELL *Biglow P.* 1 Ser. vi. 74 Certain theologic dogmas, . . . when occasion offers, he unkennels with a *staboy.* **1905** *Sun* (N.Y.) 15 Nov. (*Cent. Supp.*), 'Stubboy, stubboy' . . . was the cry used in trying to force those obstinate beasts [*sc.* pigs] into the ways they should go.

* **stack,** *n.*

1. The part of a library in which the main collection of books is shelved, usu. pl. Also attrib.

1884 *Harper's Mag.* Nov. 828/1 The stack-rooms, in which the body of the collection . . . is packed. **1910** BOSTWICK *Amer. Pub. Library* 284 The relation of reading room to stack must be such as to make these [carriers] easily operable. **1946** *Library Quart.* April 128/2 It is a modern brick building, five stories high, and contains, in addition to the stack space, a small reading-room. **1948** *Chi. Maroon* 2 Feb. 12 The Maroons are all assembled with their glasses raised for a toast to the U of C that rings from the towers of Rockefeller to the Harper stacks.

2. stackpole, a pole about which hay or forage is stacked.

1712 HEMPSTEAD *Diary* 12, I got Stack Poles & Stackt hay. **1816** *Ann. 15th Cong.* 1 Sess. 2456, I began by erecting . . . a signal . . . in form of a tripod, made of a ladder and two stack-poles. **1891** READ *Emmett Bonlore* 343 He was almost as high as a stackpole, an' so slim.

3. *dark* (or *black*) *as a stack of black cats,* very dark or black. *Colloq.*

1834 *State Adv.* (Vandalia, Ill.) 26 Nov. 3/1, I should say it was about as dark as a stack of black cats. **1913** LONDON *Valley of Moon* 319 It's pretty still.... An' black as a stack of black cats. **1916** SANDBURG *Chi. Poems* 19 It is dark as a stack of black cats.

As the last term in **double, fodder, smoke stack.**

* **stack,** *v.*

1. *tr.* To shuffle or arrange (cards) in such a way as to facilitate cheating. Also fig. Cf. * *stock* in same sense.

1825 in M. BAYARD SMITH *Forty Yrs. Washington Soc.* (1906) 186 John Randolph observed after counting the ballots, 'It was impossible to win the game, gentlemen, the cards were stacked.' **1896** LILLARD *Poker Stories* 54 The cards were stacked and marked on the back, so that he didn't have any chance at all to win. **1938** NORRIS *Bricks Without Straw* 67 You might make a success of your marriage, but I doubt it. There are too many cards stacked against you. **1948** *Durant* (Okla.) *D. Democrat* 2 July 1/5 His young polltaker detected no signs of 'stacking' the poll for any candidate.

2. *intr.* * *To stack up,* to pile up one's poker chips; *fig.* to measure up or turn out, to pile up. *Colloq.*

1896 ADE *Artie* 10 He'd stack up, you know, an feel in his pockets and then he'd say: I'm forty-seven cents loser. *Ib.* 70 How does the old gentleman stack up? **1921** PAINE *Comr. Rolling Ocean* 71, I wish this trouble hadn't stacked up between us. **1950** *Business Week* 22 April 22/3 For it tells him the productivity of his store, how one department stacks up against another.

* **stacker,** *n.* A machine or part of a machine which stacks straw or hay. Cf. **hay stacker.** — **1864** *Ohio Agric. Rep.* XVIII. 61 The stacker may be easily and quickly raised or lowered, while the machine is in operation, by turning the handcrank. **1914** STEWART *Lett. Woman Homesteader* 15 He couldn't run both the mower and the stacker.

stadthouse ˈstɑtˌhaus, *n.* [Du. *stadhuis,* in same sense.] In regions of former Dutch settlement, a town hall. *Obs.*

See A. Matthews in *D.N.* II. 199 ff. and cf. **state house.**

1666 *Md. Archives* II. 28 The Upper House do think fit . . . that Smith repay the Tobaccos next Year which he hath already received towards the building of the Great Stadt house. **1695** *N.Y. Hist. Soc. Coll.* I. 355 When he arrived he went to ye Stadt House. **1744** in *Pa. Mag.* I. 127 About 4 in the afternoon, the Company broke up, and from thence went to the Stadthouse. **1809** IRVING *Knickerb.* VII. vi, The sturdy Burgomasters called a public meeting in front of the Stadt-house.

* **staff,** *n.*[1] As the last term in **half, Jacob's, signal, verge staff.**

staff stæf, *n.*[2] [f. G. *staffieren,* to fill out, adorn.] "A building material consisting of plaster mixed with fibre, used for temporary ornamental work" (*OED*). — **1892** *Advance* (Chi.) May 19 When mixed the staff is rolled out into slabs to be nailed to the sides of buildings, or made up in blocks . . . for statues, friezes or cornices. **1893** *Offic. Guide World's Columbian Expos.* 21 Staff was invented in France about 1876, and was first used in the buildings of the Paris Exposition in 1878.

* **staff tree.** The false bittersweet, *Celastrus scandens.* Also attrib.

[**1771** J. R. FORSTER *Flora Amer. Septentr.* 11 *Celastrus bullatus.* Staff tree, elegant. Virginia.] **1785** MARSHALL *Amer. Grove* 28 The Staff-Tree.... The Corolla has five petals. **1891** COULTER *Bot. W. Texas* I. 56 *Celastrineæ.* (Staff-tree Family.) Shrubs, with simple and undivided leaves.

* **stag** *n.*

1. Short for **stag party.** *Colloq.*

1904 *Brooklyn Eagle* 28 May 3 The Myrtle Fishing Club will have a stag at Hurman Hub's Park this evening. **1947** *Chi. Tribune* 19 Oct. (Comics) 6 The marchin' and chowder club's throwin' a stag tonight.

2. (See quot. 1905.) Also *to go stag. Colloq.*

1905 N. DAVIS *Northerner* 213 'No man not escorting a lady'—a stag, you know—could go upon the floor. **1923** P. MARKS *Plastic Age* xix, Several of the brothers were going 'stag'; so he felt completely at ease. **1948** *This Week Mag.* 1 May 16/3 The sign read: 'No Stags Allowed.'

Hence **staggish,** *a.*

1852 *Alta California* (S.F.) 16 Jan., It [the ball] was decidedly 'staggish,' with a touch of the 'free and easy.'

3. In combs.: (1) **stag bush,** (see quot.), cf. **rusty stagbush;** (2) **horn,** see as a main entry; (3) **shirt,** ?a lumberman's plaid shirt.

(1) **1884** SARGENT *Rep. Forests* 94 *Viburnum prunifolium.*... Black Haw. Stag Bush. — (3) **1917** KEPHART *Camping* I. 147 A modish and well-fitting shooting suit, or the like . . . is as *outre* as a stag shirt and caulked boots would be on Fifth Avenue.

b. Used to designate activities or gatherings engaged in, or attended by, men only, as (1) **stag dance,** (2) **dinner,** (3) **party.**

(1) **1843** *Amer. Pioneer* II. 61 If perchance a *fiddle* or a *jewsharp* was possessed by any of the inmates [of the fort], it was occasionally brought into requisition, and the monotony disturbed by the hilarity of a *stag dance.* **a1918** G. STUART *On Frontier* I. 82 On Saturday night the miners would get up a stag dance, there being very few women in camp. — (2) **1892** *Harper's Mag.* Jan. 252/1 A stag dinner is a good time that women would like to come to if they could. **1947** *Rocky Mt. News* (Denver) 2 March 22/1 [He] puts on his traditional stag dinner for legislators at his home Wednesday night. — (3) **1854** *Pioneer* (S.F.) May 318 A young lady of this city asked a gentleman, a day or two since, 'Why old bachelors' gatherings were called stag parties?' **1949** *Sat. Ev. Post* 25 June 44/4 Her husband wouldn't take her to a prize fight with a strictly stag party.

c. Also **stag ball, banquet, devilry, picnic, smoker, supper-party.**

1860 *Charleston* (S.C.) *Mercury* 15 Dec. 3/5 In the evening, a brilliant 'Stag' Ball was gotten up. **1869** BOWLES *Our New West* 218 Our Mormon hosts took us . . . to Salt Lake—a 'stag' picnic. **1886** POORE *Reminiscences* I. 311 Colonel Season . . . gave one of his famous 'stag' supper-parties. **1911** HARRISON *Queed* 185 Buck Klinker, returning from some stag devilry at the hour of two A.M. **1912** IRWIN *Red Button* 11 Tommy North . . . came home from a stag smoker drunk. **1947** *Dly. Oklahoman* (Okla. City) 28 Dec. 8/2 Central high-school's Jeffersonian debating society members and alumni met . . . Saturday night for the annual founder's day stag banquet.

* **stag,** *v.*

1. *tr.* (See quot. 1902.) Hence * **stagged,** *a.*

1902 S. E. WHITE *Blazed Trail* xxvii. 190 A gigantic young river man in the conventional stagged (i.e. chopped off) trousers. **1942** RICH *We Took to Woods* (1948) 158 One stags one's pants, one's shirt sleeves, anything that needs to be abbreviated quickly, even one's hair. **1949** *Boston Globe* 14 Aug. (Fiction Mag.) 9/2 Staggin' his pants, by Gosh! . . . He sure is bound to try to be a river-rat.

2. (See quot. 1926.)

c1904 in EARL C. BECK *Songs of Mich. Lumberjacks* (1941) 23 M is for moss we stag our camp with. **1926** RICKABY *Ballads* 198 To 'stag' a camp with moss (stanza 4) was to stuff the cracks of the log shanties with it. It made a very warm camp.

* **stage,** *n.*

1. The depth or level of water in a river, usu. with *of.*

1805 CLARK in *Lewis & C. Exped.* III. (1905) 148 Narrow chanels . . . pass through a hard black rock forming Islands of rocks at this Stage of the water. **1904** *N.Y. Ev. Post* 21 Jan. 2 Pittsburgh may have a forty-foot stage of water. **1948** *Dly. Oklahoman* (Okla. City) 4 June 8/1 He forecast a 29.3 foot stage here Monday—about half a foot below last Tuesday's peak.

2. An omnibus used within a city. *Obs.*

1855 M. THOMPSON *Doesticks* 41 Hereafter you may not mistake a Grand Street stage for a perambulating Circus wagon. **1912** J. MILNE *John Jonathan & Co.* 92 A fleet of motor-buses, which the New Yorkers call 'stages,' short for stage-coaches, meanders up and down it [Fifth Ave.].

3. In combs., usu. obs. or hist.: (1) **stage barn,** a barn on a stage line for the accommodation of stage teams; (2) * **coach,** a game in which each player represents something connected with a stagecoach, as a horse, whip, wheel, one player, the "driver," telling a story and employing the names of these objects, whereupon each player is supposed to act out the part which he or she represents, cf. **old family coach,** *s.v.* ***old,** *a.* **5.** (4); (3) **connection,** the act or means of continuing a journey along a stage route; (4) **darky,** a blackface Negro minstrel; (5) **door Johnny,** a man who frequents the actors' entrance at theaters seeking favorable notice from actresses, *slang;* (6) **dough,** imitation money used on the stage, *slang;* (7) **holdup,** an attack upon a stagecoach for purposes of robbery; (8) ***house,** a tavern on a stage line where horses were kept and changed and passengers served meals; (9) **Indian,** an Indian as depicted on the stage; (10) **line,** a line of stages operated on a schedule, also attrib.; (11) **mule,** a mule used on a stagecoach line; (12) **plank,** a gangplank *q.v.* of a vessel; (13) **post,** =**stage station;** (14) **ranch,** =**stage station;** (15) **road,** a road over which stages travel; (16) ***room,** room for the erection of fishing stages, a room connected with a fishing stage; (17) **route,** a route along which stagecoaches travel; (18) **sleigh,** a sleigh used for conveying passengers; (19) **stand,** =next; (20) **station,** a stopping-place on a stage route.

(1) **1874** B. F. TAYLOR *World on Wheels* 43 Dismantled stage barns . . . were sparsely sprinkled along the route. — (2) **1831** *Boston Transcript* 2 Aug. 2/3 The entertainment happened to be the 'Stage Coach,' which was acted so wretchedly that it was impossible to make head or tail of it. **1892** *Nation* 24 Nov. 397/3 What happened on the demise of the Grand Prince resembled a game of 'stage-coach.' **1935** LINCOLN *Cape Cod Yesterdays* 106 After dinner there were games in the sitting-room and parlors: 'Animal, vegetable or mineral?' 'Consequences,' 'Stagecoach' and, sometimes, charades. — (3) **1869** *Boyd's Business Directory* 62 Stage connections: at Middleburgh for Gilboa, Moresville, Roxbury. — (4) **1888** WARNER *On Horseback* 116 His face was blackened to the proper color of the stage-darky.

(5) **1912** *Out West* Feb. 139/1 No theater can hope to do business without stage door Johnnies. **1950** *Chi. D. News* 15 March 6/4 There is psychology involved in handling the Stage-Door Johnnies. — (6) **1929** *Variety* 29 May 30/4 He had on his stage clothes and a heavy roll of stage dough. — (7) **1912** RAINE *Brand Blotters* 165, I want to know what's being done about that Fort Allison stage hold-up. — (8) **1772** ASBURY *Jrnl.* I. 37 We came to the stage-house through much rain and bad roads. **1907** ANDREWS *Recoll.* 120 The stage-house was a two story building. — (9) **1873** BEADLE *Undevel. West* 517 They are as much unlike the 'stage Indian,' and as much like a tribe of dark Caucasians as it is possible to conceive.

(10) **1830** *Williams's N.-Y. Ann. Reg.* 115 Other principal Stage lines from Albany. **1860** HOLLAND *Miss Gilbert* 285 [He] rode rapidly off to the nearest stage-line station. **1912** DAWSON *Pioneer Tales* 117 The old Trail was passing into decay by this time, the stage lines being abandoned during the summer of 1867. — (11) **1860** GREELEY *Overland Journey* 264 The stage-mules are turned out to feed and rest. — (12) **1865** *Harper's Mag.* Feb. 400/2 She had noticed the sentinel passing to and fro at the shore-end of the stage-plank. **1875** MARK TWAIN *Old Times* i, I would rather be the deck-hand who stood on the end of the stage-plank with a coil of rope in his hand. — (13) **1947** *True* Nov. 106/3 The sheriff . . . followed them closely enough to find two men they had left in gruesome shape at the Ute Pass stage post. — (14) **1882** *Lippincott's Mag.* May 427 (*heading*), A Stage Ranch on the Wyoming Plains. **1912** DAWSON *Pioneer Tales* 90 All stage stations and ranches along the Trail, from the river to Fort Kearney, were very similar of shape and construction.

(15) **1760** *N.J. Archives* XX. 414 To be sold. . . . Two hundred acres of very good land, . . . and lies about a mile from the town, where there is a good landing to take wood for Philadelphia, and joining the stage road from that to Amboy. **1837** JENKINS *Ohio Gaz.* 103 Centerburg . . . [is] on the stage road from Mount Vernon to Columbus. **1943** WOOD *W. Reed* 98 Following the stage road, the party crossed the Colorado River. — (16) **1628** *Mass. H.S. Coll.* 3 Ser. VIII. 164 More [ships] cannot well be there, for want of convenient stage room. **1713** *N.H. Probate Rec.* I. 711, I Give & Bequeath [to my sons] . . . my Stages Stage rooms, boat if any bee [etc.]. — (17) **1819** *Niles' Reg.* XVI. 4/1 The pecuniary receipts of the department . . . [cannot] defray the expenses of any considerable portion of the stage routes alone. **1910** AUGUST SANTLEBEN *Texas Pioneer* 18 A stage route had also been established between San Antonio and Eagle Pass. — (18) **1850** S. F. COOPER *Rural Hours* 518 The stage-sleighs, with four horses and eight or ten passengers, perhaps, occasionally go and come over the ice at that season. — (19) **1856** STOWE *Dred* II. 125 At the first stage-stand, [he] changed him [the horse] for a fresh one. **1926** O. L. SHIPMAN *Taming Big Bend* 188 There were many graves about this old stage stand. **1950** *Dly. Ardmoreite* (Ardmore, Okla.) 30 April c. 18/1 Tishomingo City was recognized as an important stage stand between Fort Washita and Fort Arbuckle.

(20) **1860** G. T. CLARK *Diary* (MS) 10 Drove down to a stage station to see if we could stay. **1945** MATHEWS *Talking* 93, I shall leave my horse at stage station.

As the last term in **accommodation, auto, Concord, dough, fishing, ice, Jersey, mail, minstrel, mountain, mule, opposition, overland, post, water stage.**

***stage,** *v. transf. tr.* To put on, enact, make arrangements for. *Colloq.* — **1924** HASKIN *Amer. Govt.* 437 In combating bootlegging Federal agents staged raids that revealed [etc.]. **1931** *K.C. Times* 17 Aug., Monroe County . . . recently staged a centennial celebration.

stagee steˈdʒi, *n.* A small stagecoach. *Rare.* — **1833** *Hist. Mag.* XIII. 343 We left in a stagee—a little two horse concern.

***stagger,** *n.* **1. staggerbush,** a shrub, *Neopieris mariana,* which is poisonous to stock. **2. stagger-grass,** (see quot.). **3. staggerweed,** a plant of the genus *Delphinium.*

(1) **1847** DARLINGTON *Weeds & Plants* 213 Maryland Andromeda. Stagger-bush. . . . The farmers . . . allege that it is injurious to sheep, when the leaves are eaten by them,—producing a disease called the staggers. **1931** CLUTE *Plants* 27 The strong inner bark of the basswood . . . is also called wicopy . . . as is the calico-bush . . . and the stagger-bush (*Lyonia mariana*). — (2) **1891** *Cent.* 5889/2 Stagger-grass. . . . The atamasco-lily, *Zephyranthes Atamasco:* so called as supposed to cause staggers in horses. — (3) **1855** DUNGLISON *Med. Lex.*, Staggerweed, *Delphinium.* **1932** *Blue Valley Farmer* (Okla. City) 21 Jan. 4/2 Some loss is also caused by sweet clover hay, black locust bark, stagger-weeds and buckeye sprouts.

As the last term in **blind staggers.**

***staghorn,** *n.* In combs.: (1) **staghorn cactus,** =next; (2) **cholla,** (see quot. 1942); (3) **coral,** any of various corals of the genus *Acropara* which branch in such a way as to suggest antlers; (4) **sumac,** a kind of sumac, *Rhus typhina,* whose flower stalks and branches look somewhat like antlers, also **stag's horn sumac,** cf. ***buckhorn 1, velvet sumac, Virginia sumac.**

(1) **1929** DENTON *Naturalist's Diary* (1949) 263 About us were low pines and cedars, oaks, greasewood, stag horn cactus, . . . and desert flowers. — (2) **1942** CASTETTER & BELL *Pima & Papago Agric.* 25 Other characteristic chollas of the paloverde belt are the vari-colored or staghorn cholla (*O. versicolor*), . . . and the long-jointed, dark-spined *O. acanthocarpa.* **1947** *Desert Mag.* April 12/3 April, possibilities: staghorn cholla, hedgehog cactus, prickly pear, brittle bush, apricot mallow, . . . devil's claw, scorpion weed, . . . fiddleneck and crownbeard. — (3) **1884** GOODE *Fisheries* I. 841 Among the true stony corals are the Stag-horn Corals (*Madrepora cervicornis, prolifera,* and *palmata*); the Brain Corals . . . , and many others. — (4) [**1731** MILLER *Gard. Dict. s.v. Rhus,* Virginian Sumach, by some falsely called, The Stag's-horn-tree.] **1785** MARSHALL *Amer. Grove* 129 Stag's-horn Sumach. This grows naturally in Virginia and Pennsylvania. **1898** CREEVEY *Flowers of Field* 481 Stag-horn Sumach. . . . The ends of the irregular branches, covered with a soft, velvety down, give the name stag-horn. **1945** MCATEE *John & Joe* 5 So also do the smooth and staghorn sumacs, persimmon, nannyberry, and black haw, not to mention several shrubs and vines.

***staging,** *n.* Driving a stage or stagecoach. Also attrib.

In British use in this sense 1850——, and called in *OED* "chiefly Anglo-Indian." Prob. of earlier and independent formation in this country.

1840 *S. Lit. Messenger* VI. 381/2 He does not follow the sea nor staging. **1864** *Harper's Mag.* Oct. 563/1 In an ancient adobe building, . . . Mr. Banning carried on his staging and teaming operations. **1894** *Outing* XXIV. 399/2 Stagin' in them days, stranger, was *stagin'*.

***stair,** *n.* As the last term in **box, scuttle stair.**

stairway ˈstɛrˌwe, *n.* Stairs, a flight of stairs.

1708 *Cambridge Prop. Rec.* 262 A Stairway for passage into ye Sd Court house. **1812** *Niles' Reg.* I. 329/1 The stair-ways were immediately blocked up. **1922** PARRISH *Case & Girl* 38 She calmly outgeneraled him again, . . . disappearing herself up the stairway with Miss Willis.

b. A fishway. *Rare.*

1869 HALE *Sybaris* 54 You must take our friend out to see the fish go up his stairways.

stakage ˈstekɪdʒ, *n.* The work of driving stakes in a channel. *Obs.* — **1792** *Ann. 2d Congress* 1356 The stakeage of channels on the sea-coast . . . shall continue to be defrayed by the United States. **1854** PIERCE in *Pres. Mess. & P.* V. 263 All appropriations of this class were confined . . . to the construction of light-houses, beacons, buoys, and public piers and the stakage of channels.

*stake, *n.*

1. Provisions or savings intended to last until better times, a grubstake. Also transf.

1738 Byrd *Dividing Line* (1901) 178 [We] recommended to the men to manage this, their last stake, to best advantage. **1863** *Rio Abajo Press* 21 April 1/1 Not finding any one . . . willing to donate or lend him another 'stake,' he had recourse to Dona Luiza. **1902** White *Blazed Trail* 17, I ain't got no ticket. . . . I blows my stake. **1943** Menefee *Assignment* 87 About mid-November they will return with their 'stake' to attend high school again.

2. (*cap.* in specific uses.) *Mormon Church.* (See quots. and cf. **b.** below.) Also attrib.

[**1833** J. Smith in Linn *Story of Mormons* 120 It is expedient in me that this Stake that I have set for the strength of Zion be made strong. **1839** *Ib.*, I have other places which I will appoint unto them, and they shall be called Stakes for the curtain, or the strength of Zion.] **1883** Schaff *Religious Encycl.* II. 1578 Every city, or 'stake,' including a chief town and surrounding towns, has its president. **1947** Sessions *Cities of Amer.* 39 Each stake president will parcel out the acreages he has agreed to accept among his bishops, and each bishop will divide his commitment among the Saints in his ward.

Hence **Stake House.**

1925 Foster *Larry* (1930) 131 Then we all paraded down to the Stake House (Mormon Districts are called 'Stakes'), where there was a pioneer's meeting.

b. *Stake of* (or *in*) *Zion,* (see quots.). Cf. ***presidency,** *n.* **2.**

1843 H. Caswall *Prophet of 19th Cent.* 90 Other 'churches' established by 'revelations' given to Smith, are called 'Stakes of Zion,' or simply 'Stakes.' **1857** *So. Illinoisian* (Shawneetown) 1 May 1/3 Throughout the States and Territories, at various and convenient locations, the Mormons have what are termed 'stakes in Zion,' and each stake is governed by a Presidency. **1905** *Out West* Sep. 246 The Stakes of Zion, I will explain, are those gathering places of the Saints that are outside of Zion proper—Jackson county, Missouri, where the holy city it is believed will yet be built.

3. In special combs.: (1) **stake car,** a platform railway car, *obs.;* (2) **dock,** a temporary dock built on stakes or piling, *rare;* (3) **driver,** the American bittern, so named because one of its notes resembles the sound made in driving a stake into mud; (4) **horse,** *W.* a horse tethered to a stake; (5) **notice,** a notice of a mining claim made public by being affixed to a stake; (6) **pin,** *W.* a pin used for driving into the ground and staking out an animal; (7) **prairie,** =**staked plain;** (8) **rope,** (see quot. 1944).

(1) **1862** *N.Y. Herald* 18 March 2/1 In the rear was a stake car, upon which was loaded a quantity of furniture. — (2) **1862** *Harper's Mag.* Aug. 311/2 The scows which then [1750] plied between New York and the opposite shore landed their passengers and freight at a stake dock built from this place—a dock which was generally carried away every winter by ice. — (3) **1814** *Mass. H.S. Coll.* 2 Ser. III. 101 Among the birds that are found here [Lancaster, N.H.] are . . . stake-driver or bittern. **1851** in *Amer. Sp.* XX. (1945) Feb. 78 Minott calls the stake-driver '*belcher-squelcher.*' Says he has seen them when making the noise. They go *slug-toot, slug-toot, slug-toot.* **1946** Stanwell-Fletcher *Driftwood Valley* 189 The persistent all-night 'pounding' around the marshes of numerous bitterns (big heronlike birds, sometimes called stake drivers, because their notes resemble stakes being driven into mud) keeps them awake. — (4) **1892** *Outing* Feb. 359/2 Then stake horses are saddled [and] the men in camp eat their meal. (5) **1880** *Cimarron News & Press* 26 Feb. 1/5 Location stake notices were treated with contempt. — (6) **1927** Siringo *Riata* 51 The pony staked out the evening before had pulled up the stake-pin and drifted south. — (7) **1834** A. Pike *Sketches* 42 This Stake Prairie is to the Comanche what the desert of Sahara is to the Bedouin. — (8) **1871** De Vere 130 Texans *twine* or *rope* a horse, . . . and then stake him out with a *stake-rope.* **1944** Adams *W. Words* 153/1 stake rope The Texan's name for the picket rope used to stake horses.

b. In the names of, or pertaining to, fences: (1) **stake and board fence,** a fence made of stakes and boards; (2) **stake and rider(ed) fence,** a rail fence at each corner of which two rails are placed as props and slanted so as to cross each other and support the end of a "rider" or additional rail joining those serving as stakes to the pair similarly placed at the next corner, cf. **staked and ridered;** (3) **stake and wire,** of or pertaining to a fence made of stakes and wire.

(1) **1850** *N. Eng. Farmer* II. 68 On the same farm he also built a line of stake and board fence. — (2) **1829** *Mass. Spy* 11 Feb. (Th.), He met a man in a lane with a stake-and-rider fence on each side. **1846** *Knickerb.* XXVII. 208 Already the 'stake and ridered' fence was beginning to enclose the cleared land. **1950** *Pa. Dutchman* Jan. 3/3 He could do nothing better than to quickly place his gun behind him in a corner of a stake-and-rider fence. — (3) **1868** Brackett *Farm Talk* 116 'Getting out fencing stuff?' 'Yes. I'm going to try some more of the stake and wire sort.'

4. In colloq. phrases: **a.** *To pluck* (or *pull, haul*) *up stakes,* to leave a place, to move, often fig. Cf. **c.** below.

This expression at first app. had reference to a colonial practice regarding boundary stakes of land allotments (see the earliest quots.). See an article by A. Matthews in *The Nation,* Dec. 28, 1899, pp. 483–4.

1640 Lechford in De Vere 185, I am loth to hear of a stay [in N. Eng.], but am plucking up stakes with as much speed as I may. [*a***1658** Bradford *Hist.* 439 They of Hingam presumed to alotte parte of them [i.e., meadow grounds] to their people, and measure & stack them out. The other pulled up their stacks, & threw them.] **1703** Sewall *Diary* II. 76 Went to my Bounds, asserted them, . . . then

Stake and rider fence

ordered Kibbe to pull up the Stakes. **1784** *Mass. H.S. Coll.* 1 Ser. I. 256 And so they plucked up stakes, and came over to this place to fix themselves here. **1843** Stephens *High Life N.Y.* III. 256 'Jonathan,' says he, a risin from the locker, and diggin both hands in his old trousers pocket, 'Jonathan, it's time for us to haul up stakes and go hum.' **1950** *N.O. Times-Picayune Mag.* 16 April 10/2 They just pulled up stakes and left for parts unknown.

b. *To set* (or *drive*) *stakes,* to drive down boundary stakes; also fig., to take up one's abode.

1703 Sewall *Diary* II. 76 Told Mr. Lynde's Tenants what my Bounds were . . . forwarn'd them of coming there to set any Stakes. **1853** *Ore. Statesman* 6 Dec. 1/2 One claim thou may'st own, and then drive your stake, And coyote and crevice till you make or you break. **1906** *Outing* Feb. 605/2 After drifting about several years I finally drove stakes on the Spokane River. **1949** *Boston Globe* 15 May (Fiction Mag.) 6/2 We'll set our stakes, an' I'll slip down to Dawson an' record the claim.

c. *To up stakes,* =**a.** above.

1837 *Jamestown* (N.Y.) *Jrnl.* 6 Sep. 1/6 If we can't go according to that rule, then I say let everyman upstakes and go to Turkey or China. **1843** Stephens *High Life N.Y.* II. 40, I can up stakes, and go hum again in the old sloop.

d. *To move stakes,* to change one's place of settlement.

1862 Harte *Luck of Roaring Camp* 211 He built the shanty for that purpose, lest titles should fall through, and we'd have to get up and move stakes farther down.

e. *To make a stake,* (sense **1.**), to earn some money, make a fortune.

1873 Beadle *Undevel. West* 510 It is a splendid country to travel through; a miserable poor one to stop in to make a 'stake.' **1948** A. K. Williams *Gold Rush Days* 13 Almost any kind of a shelter sufficed for the man who came to make his stake and leave again.

f. *To raise a stake,* =prec.

1883 *Rep. Indian Affairs* 10 They work merely long enough to 'raise a stake.'

As the last term in **claim, corner, grade, grub, home stake.**

***stake,** *v.*

1. *tr.* To provide (a fence) with stakes. Also *to stake and pole, to stake and rider. Obs.* Cf. **staked and ridered.**

1655 *Suffolk Deeds* II. 149 Peleg heath shall make and mayntayne all ye fence where it is now staked Against the orchard. **1662** *Portsmouth Rec.* 116 All out fences . . . being sufishently staked and pould.

1787 WASHINGTON *Diaries* III. 208 Women [were] staking and ridering fence of the said field.

2. To mark (a line or route) with stakes, usu. with *out.*

1668 *Dedham Rec.* IV. 156 Lieft Fisher Joh: Haward and Sergent Fuller are deputed and empowered to laye out this way accordingly and stake or doole the same out as they shall Judge most equall. **1714** SEWALL *Diary* II. 435 Take Mr. Benjamin Mayhew with you . . . and Stake the Line between the Honble. Corporation and him. **1877** JOHNSON *Anderson Co., Kans.* 98 The route was staked out from Ohio City to Fairview.

3. To mark or define (a claim) with stakes. Usu. with *off* or *out.*

1851 *State Jrnl.* (San Jose, Calif.) 15 March 2/1 It was estimated that ten thousand people were on the ground staking off 'claims.' **1852** *N.Y. Wkly. Tribune* 9 Oct. 7/4 A large party went out of Grass Valley on Wednesday last, to stake out claims. **1898** ATHERTON *Californians* 13 In community with his brother-in-law, he staked off a claim. **1949** *Nat. Geog. Mag.* Oct. 507/1 After the meeting I went out to stake my claim.

transf. **1945** *Democrat* 24 May 1/6 The California Oil Company . . . has staked a location for the drilling of a test well. **1949** *Nat. Hist.* April 189/3 Sometimes when the bee hunter finds a nest that has not yet reached its peak of honey production, he will 'stake his claim' by marking the tree so that other hunters will know of his prior discovery.

4. To advance or supply (a person) with a stake or grubstake. Also transf. Cf. **grubstaker.**

1853 P. PAXTON *Yankee in Texas* 219 The jo-fired mean whelp wouldn't stake me. **1917** MCCUTCHEON *Green Fancy* 25 He staked her to a ticket to New York.

5. *absol.* To settle down. *Rare.*

1872 DE VERE 184 Where he settles, there he stakes or sticks his stakes.

* **staked,** *a.*

1. staked and ridered. a. Provided with a stake and rider fence. *Rare.* **b.** Of a fence: made with stakes and riders.

(a) 1852 *Mich. Agric. Soc. Trans.* III. 333 The staked and ridered domicil, lopped over like some old lame hen. — **(b) 1855** *Chi. W. Times* 17 May 3/5 A whirlwind . . . scattered in every direction a strong 'staked and ridered fence.' **1946** FOREMAN *Last Trek* 169 All their farms were inclosed with good rail fences sufficiently high to secure their crops, many of them 'staked and ridered.'

2. staked plain, a treeless plain, esp. (*cap.*) =**Llano Estacado.**

1848 ROBINSON *Santa Fe Exped.* 67 The whole country may well be called, as some maps style it, a staked plain. **1881** ROMSPERT *Western Echo* 137 We were now prepared to cross the *staked plains,* which had been reported to us as a broad, dry, and barren country. **1938** *Bunker's Mag.* Jan. 23 The Staked Plains [were] . . . so-called because the early Spanish explorer-priests marked the trail across the plains with stakes topped by bleached buffalo skulls. **1948** *Sat. Review* 26 June 13/1 Its vast background is that surprisingly varied region of plains and mountains ranging from the Staked Plains of Texas to the Badlands of the Yellowstone.

staky ˈsteki, *a.* (See quot.) *Rare.* — **1877** BARTLETT 652 A staky horse is one that *jibbs,* or stands still when in harness.

* **stalk,** *n.* In combs.: (1) **stalk-borer,** (see quot. 1909); (2) **cutter,** one who or a machine which cuts stalks of cotton or corn from a previous year's crop; (3) **field,** a field in which cornstalks are standing after harvest.

(1) **1884** *Rep. Comm. Agric.* 417 The Stalk-borer (*Gortyna nitela*) was often made the subject of complaint during the past summer. **1909** WEBSTER 2029/3 *Stalk-borer,* the larva of a noctuid moth (*Papaipema nitela*), which bores in the stalks of the raspberry, strawberry, tomato, and other garden plants. — (2) **1825** *Forest Rose* I. lv, Here comes the stalk-cutters, and the apple-pickers, and the cider-grinders. **1850** *Cultivator* ns. VII. 369 We stand much in need of . . . cheap and effective straw and stalk cutters. **1950** *Democrat* 16 Feb. 8/1 For Sale. . . . 1 B.F. Avery Stalk Cutter. — (3) **1845** *Cultivator* ns. II. 125/1 The stalk fields are the main dependance [*sic*] of half the farmers in the country for wintering the stock. **1885** *Rep. Indian Affairs* 93, 750 tons [of hay] . . . with the stalk-fields and other forage will be fair provision for the stock on hand.

As the last term in **corn, long, polk, sassafras, tobacco, twisted stalk(s).**

* **stall,** *n.* The berth of a locomotive in a roundhouse. — **1876** CROFUTT *Trans-continental Tourist* 42 The company have here . . . a round-house with six stalls. **1899** *McClure's Mag.* March 484 The engine . . . is put on the turn-table and sent into her stall.

As the last term in **beef, box, headstall.**

* **stall,** *v. intr.* To engage in delaying activities, to play for time. *Slang.* — **1903** LEWIS *Boss* 23 [If] Big Kennedy shows up to stall ag'inst you, why I should say [etc.]. **1945** *New Republic* 27 Aug. 235/1 American officials did not believe the Japanese were stalling with some ulterior purpose in mind.

* **Stalwart,** *n.* A member of the "machine" faction of the Republican party who supported Grant for a third term, opposed Civil Service reform under President Hayes, and long retained distrust of the South for political purposes. In full **Stalwart Republican.** Now *hist.*

1879 *Cong. Rec.* App. 26 April 89/2, I saw a great company of stalwarts approaching. **1880** *Chi. Tribune* 25 Jan. 4/2 Some of the papers that call themselves 'bloody-shirters' are boasting that Matt Carpenter's election to the Senate is a reinforcement for the 'stalwart Republicans.' **1901** *McClure's Mag.* Dec. 152 [Platt] is merely a stalwart. **1926** *Wks. of T. Roosevelt* XIV. xiv, And with the feud between the 'Stalwarts' and the 'half-breeds' of the Empire State culminating in a positive split.

Hence **Stalwartism,** *n.,* the principles of the Stalwarts. *Obs.*

1879 *Nation* 27 Nov. 355/2 Stalwartism . . . includes indifference or hostility to civil-service reform, and a willingness to let 'the boys' have a good time with the offices. **1882** *Ib.* 16 Nov. 422/2 They have rejected President Arthur and Stalwartism; nor do they take more kindly to Mr. Blaine and Jingoism.

stalwartize ˈstɔlwɚtˌaɪz, *v. tr.* To convert to the principles of the Stalwarts. *Obs.* — **1882** *N.Y. Tribune* 12 April, An attempt is being made . . . to stalwartize the Republican party, . . . convert its majority against its will from Garfield to Stalwart Republicanism. **1882** *Nation* 13 July 22/3 The Administration . . . has been [charged with] trying to 'stalwartize' the party by removals in the civil service.

* **stamp,** *n.*

1. (See quots. and cf. **buffalo stamp, horse stamp.**) *Obs.*

1796 HAWKINS *Letters* 31 They have in the range a place called the stamp, where the horses have salt every spring, and here they gather of themselves at that season. **1828** *Central Watchtower* (Harrodsburg, Ky.) 19 Nov. 1/1 The earth for some distance and the sand hills that constitute their barracks, is trodden firmly by the cattle of the neighbouring country, forming what the herdsmen call a stomp.

2. (See quot.) *Obs.*

1848 BRYANT *California* xxi. 268 A tin coin issued by Captain Sutter circulates among them, upon which is stamped the number of days that the holder has labored. These stamps indicate the value in merchandize to which the laborer or holder is entitled.

3. A piece of fractional currency. *Obs.*

1862 *Washington Republican* 15 Aug. 2/3 The five and twenty-five cents stamps are printed on yellow bank note paper, and the tens and fifties on white paper. **1903** HAPGOOD *Autobiog. of Thief* 21 He went to his father, . . . and got a fifty cent 'stamp.'

b. *pl.* Money, esp. paper money. *Slang. Obs.*

1865 BOUDRYE *Fifth N.Y. Cavalry* 195 The paymaster . . . is relieving himself freely of 'stamps,' as the boys call his greenbacks. **1882** MCCABE *New York* 161 If I had his stamps I wouldn't hang around nights to catch a five-cent fare.

4. Used in combs. with **distributor, man, officer,** with reference to the stamps provided for by the British Stamp Act of 1765. *Obs.*

1765 ROWE *Diary* 88 A Great Number of people assembled . . . to see the Stamp Officer hung in Effigy. **1765** *Gazetteer* [London] 18 Oct. 2/4 Boston, August 26. By a Gentleman who came to town last Friday from Connecticut, we are informed that the *Stamp-man* from that colony had appointed his deputies. **1769** *R.I. Col. Rec.* VI. 591 Mr. Johnston . . . was appointed to the obnoxious office of stamp distributor. **1777** J. ADAMS *Familiar Lett.* 251 Ingersoll, the stamp man and Judge of Admiralty.

As the last term in **Baltimore, buffalo, calico, express, hand, horse, log, post, postage, postage-due, rubber, trading stamp.**

stampedable stæmˈpidəbḷ, *a.* Subject to being stampeded. — **a1861** WINTHROP *J. Brent* 88 Every . . . wagon of the Mormon caravan was in its place. . . . Nothing stampedable there. **1888** *Advance* 19 Jan. 41 This pastor is not a stampedable sort of man.

stampede stæmˈpid, *n.* [Sp. *estampida,* in Amer. Sp. sense similar to **1.** Cf. **stampedo.**]

1. A wild, headlong rush of animals, such as buffaloes, horses, and cattle.

1844 *N.O. Picayune* 26 Feb. 9/4 The loose horses . . . were grazing in a band near the fort, when, in the settled stillness after noontime, the furious onset yell of the Chayennes suddenly arose, and the alarm of a *stampede* at once startled all who were within two miles of the spot. **1872** POWERS *Afoot & Alone* 126 We all leap to our feet, and hear the terrible cry, 'A stampede! a stampede!' **1950** *Pacific Discovery* March–April 6/1 Thunder River issues full-born from a tremendous fissure in the canyon wall to go charging down the canyon like a stampede of wild horses.

transf. **1844** MOORE *Texas* 34 The stampade, or tremendous tramping sound made by these large herds of mustangs, is often heard several miles, and resembles the sound of distant thunder.

b. A sudden fright that causes such a rush. *Obs.*

1844 GREGG *Commerce of Prairies* II. 167 Their horses had taken a *stampede* and escaped. **1846** SAGE *Scenes Rocky Mts.* xxx, One of our pack-horses, also, took the '*stampede*,' and ran off with his entire load.

c. A precipitous rush of people. Also transf.

1846 LONGFELLOW in S. Longfellow *H. W. Longfellow* II. 69 There is a great 'stampede' on Parnassus at the present moment. **1850** *Calif. Courier* (S.F.) 10 Aug. 2/2 The last night of the session is the only real legislative *stampede* which it is the privilege of the House to enjoy. **1948** *Sat. Ev. Post* 14 Aug. 21/1 The West's great periods of expansion have come in stampedes, set off by urges as instinctive as the migration of birds.

2. *W.* Among goldminers, a precipitous unreasoning rush to an area rumored to be fabulously rich in gold or silver.

1851 *S.F. Herald* 28 Nov. 2/2 The news of the discovery of these rich deposites spread like wildfire . . . and produced an intense excitement and a perfect stampede from the old and worn out placers. **1880** INGHAM *Digging Gold* 311 Stampedes were in order all over the State, to points wherever a new district was formed, or quartz mines discovered. **1949** *Amer. Photography* March 147/1 It was a thrill to follow the trail of the stampede of '98.

b. (*cap.*) A form of dance. Also **Stampede dance.**

1856 *Spirit of Times* 13 Dec. 238/2 The following was the programme of dancing [at a party in the Adirondacks, N.Y.]: Part the Fourth—Scotch Reel, Money Musk, Zip Coon, French Four, General Stampede. **1870** DUVAL *Big-Foot Wallace* 263, I see you haven't yet introduced the Texas national dance—the Stampede. **1950** *Chi. D. News* 10 May 10/1 The annual 'Stampede Dance' of the Order of the Builders, State of Illinois, will be held May 20.

3. *W.* =**rodeo 2.** Also attrib.

1948 *Popular Western* June 10/1 Carola was secretary of the Caprock Stampede Committee, in charge of signing up the contestants. **1948** *Ada* (Okla.) *Ev. News* 2 July 1/5 A capacity crowd was on hand for the opening performance of the Hereford Heaven Stampede.

stampede stæmˈpid, *v.* Also †**estampedo.** [f. the noun.]

1. *intr.* Of persons or animals: To rush suddenly and in disorder, to go into a stampede.

1843 MARRYAT *M. Violet* xxix. 29 The animals had estampedoed the whole distance at the utmost of their speed. **1849** *N.Y. Tribune* 12 June (B.), The Virginia Legislature, becoming frightened at the approach of the cholera, have finally stampeded toward the White Sulphur Springs. **1929** J. PARKER *Old Army* 88 And then [they] furiously stampeded on the road back toward Sill.

b. Esp. of a miner: To take part in a stampede (sense **2.**).

1869 *New North West* (Deer Lodge, Mont.) 13 Aug. 3/2 About 15 men stampeded there July 25th. **1876** RAYMOND *8th Rep. Mines* 263 Among the miners who had 'stampeded' to Cedar were many of the best prospectors in the Territory. **1948** JOHNSTON *Gold Rush* 44/2 The miners stampeded to the rich bluff diggin's at Oroville.

2. *tr.* To cause a stampede among (animals).

1844 GREGG *Commerce of Prairies* II. 169 A party of Mexicans . . . stampeded and carried away, not only their own horses, but those of the Texans. **1892** *S. Dak. Hist. Coll.* I. 62 A vast expanse of green prairie, where antelopes had never been startled, nor buffalos stampeded by a locomotive. **1950** *Pacific Discovery* March–April 22/2 The prairie fire . . . invariably stampeded the buffalo and sometimes destroyed entire herds.

transf. **1853** BREWERTON *With Kit Carson* (1930) 66 Some inexperienced mountaineer had given the alarm of Indians during his time of guard at night, or as Western men sometimes express it, 'stampeded the camp.' **1884** *Boston Jrnl.* 11 July, The convention refused to be stampeded. **1950** *Time* 3 April 20/2 A solid, grey, calm man, never rushed to a conclusion, impossible to stampede, he has been in the Senate 27 years.

stampeder stæmˈpidɚ, *n.* One who causes or takes part in a stampede.

1862 *N.Y. Tribune* 5 May 3/2 The leader of the stampeders . . . was killed. **1899** *Harper's Weekly* 8 April 341/1 None of the side gulches—or 'pups' as they were called—were favored by the stampeders. **1950** *Boston Globe Mag.* 15 Jan. 1/1 He realized immediately that most of the hopeful stampeders would never strike it rich.

stampedo stɑmˈpido, *n.* Also **stampido, stampado,** etc. An early form of **stampede,** *n. Obs.*

1826 *Va. Herald* (Fredericksburg) 14 Oct. 2/1 Instantly this prodigious multitude, and there were thousands of them, took what the Spanish call the 'stompado.' **1828** in *Mo. Hist. Rev.* VIII. (1914) 187 A little before daylight, the mules made an abortive attempt to raise a stampido. **1834** *23d Congress* 2 Sess. H.R. Doc. No. 2, 79 A stupid sentinel last night . . . alarmed the camp, and sent off in a *stampedo* the rest of the horses. **1837** IRVING *Bonneville* II. 238 The night attack, the stampado, the scamper . . . will then exist but in frontier story. **1852** BRISTED *Upper Ten Th.* 62 Nearly a hundred slaves . . . had made a stampedo, as the Western men say.

b. A meeting of trappers, Indians, etc. *Rare.*

1847 COYNER *Lost Trappers* 235 Some two months are generally spent by all parties at one of those grand stampadoes.

* **stamping,** *n.*

1. stamping ground, a place frequented by animals. Also, *transf.*, a place where a person is accustomed to be or stay, an early or favorite haunt. *Colloq.*

1786 in *Amer. Sp.* XV. 396/1 Beginning about ½ mile So. of a place well known by the Stamping Ground. **1836** H. R. HOWARD *Hist. V. A. Stewart* 70, I made my way from Milledgeville to Williamson County, the old stamping-ground. **1870** W. BAKER *New Timothy* 176 It's with them fellows as it is with wild animals. You can just keep clear of them if you want, stay far out of their stamping-ground. **1949** *Amer. Cattle Producer* April 14/1 If one of these old-timers could return to his old stomping grounds it would be interesting to hear his comments.

2. stamping place, =prec.

1820 in *Amer. Sp.* XV. 397/2 To a white oak and hickory on top of the Butt Mountain near a stomping place. **1844** *Ib.* To three chesnut Oaks on said ridge in an old Stamping place.

stampler ˈstæmplɚ, *n.* One favoring the Federal Stamp Act of 1799. *Obs.* — **1799** *Ann. 7th Cong.* 2 Sess. 1435 They damned the house tax and the stamp act, and called me a stampler repeatedly. *Ib.* 1454 The unmeaning epithets of *Stamplers* and *Tories* were rudely applied to the friends of the government.

* **stanchion,** *n.* A fixed or stationary device, usu. of metal, fitting loosely around a cow's neck so as to limit the forward and backward motion. Also attrib.

1868 BRACKETT *Farm Talk* 101 What do you think of slip stanchions? **1896** *Vt. Agric. Rep.* XV. 72 The cows in general seem to like swinging stanchions much better than the stationary. **1950** *Hoard's Dairyman* 10 April 272/3 Ceilings and upper walls of his compact, concrete block, 8-stanchion milking parlor and adjoining milk house are lined with 3-8-inch veneer.

* **stand,** *n.*

1. A site or building suitable for business, a place of business, often **old stand.**

1776 *N.J. Archives* 2 Ser. I. 106 Its healthy pleasant and central situation . . . and old accustomed business render it [*sc.* an inn] a most commodious and profitable stand. **1829** *Geneva* (N.Y.) *Gaz.* 19 Aug. 1/2 The subscriber gives notice . . . he will continue the business at the *Old Stand.* **1948** *Dly. Ardmoreite* (Ardmore, Okla.) 28 June 2/4 He has resumed business in the same old stand.

attrib. and *transf.* **1813** *Cramer's Alman. 1814* (Pittsburgh) 52 Beyond these are the stand-merchants, who expose their goods on stands covered with an awning. **1894** *Chi. Rec.* 4 May 2/2 Chicago is still at the same old stand—at the tail end [of league standings].

2. A stallion's performance as a breeder or the place where he is available. Cf. * **stand,** *v.* **1.**

1797 *Steele P.* I. 151 As a covering horse I am of Opinion he would make a very good Stand. **1836** *Russellville* (Ky.) *W. Advt.* 21 Jan. 3/3 (*advt.*), Merlin is now at his stand in Elkton . . . books are opened for those who may wish to enter their mares.

3. A stopping-place or tavern on a regularly traveled route.

1816 U. BROWN *Jrnl.* II. 366 Thence 20 Miles through the Mountains to Widow Merchants (not another Stand for 12 Miles). **1846** *Xenia Torch-Light* 23 July 4/1 Taverns, there were none; and their substitutes, 'stands,' in the phrase of the country, poor and far between. **1919** CADY *Rhymes of Vt.* (1923) 98, I hope our quaint old tavern stands Will keep right on-a-standing. **1948** DICK *Dixie Frontier* 209 The term 'stand' was also used for a tavern along the stage lines.

b. On a theatrical tour, a stop for one or more performances. Cf. **one-night stand.**

1895 *N.Y. Dramatic News* 19 Oct. 11/1 Denver was the second stand of the week. **1900** *Everybody's Mag.* II. 583/2 The next 'stand' was Topeka. **1917** J. F. DALY *Life A. Daly* 195 Each of its 'stands' being supplied in turn with a play and a company strictly limited in the requirements of that piece.

4. A wooden structure, often consisting of a small platform, a bench, and a Bible rest or lectern, from which sermons are delivered during a camp meeting.

1820 DEWEES *Lett. from Texas* 17 [They] came up to the camp ground with the determination of cutting down the stand. **1852** REGAN *Emigrant's Guide* 175 Immediately in front of the pulpit or stand, as it is called, was a square of about four hundred superficial feet, enclosed with a stout railing. **1891** SLOAN *Fogy Days* 159 We were invited down to the stand, as it was about time for the morning services.

b. (See quot.)

1889 *Harper's Mag.* May 902/1 A large wooden shed, called 'The Stand,' without floor or weather-boarding, capable of covering, say, four thousand persons, stood near the centre [of a Ga. camp-meeting ground].

5. A standing growth or crop, usu. of one just germinating and in allusion to its sufficiency for an ordinary yield.

1833 SILLIMAN *Man. Sugar Cane* 12 Every joint sends up cane shoots, and thus contributes to a fuller stand of Cane than when the joints are farther apart. **1869** *Overland Mo.* III. 130/1 Planters everywhere in the South say they have a good 'stand,' when the corn or cotton plants come up thick enough in the rows to insure an ordinary harvest. **1950** *Hoard's Dairyman* 10 April 258/2 Your alfalfa stand may not look too good during these weeks when plans are being made for spring plowing.

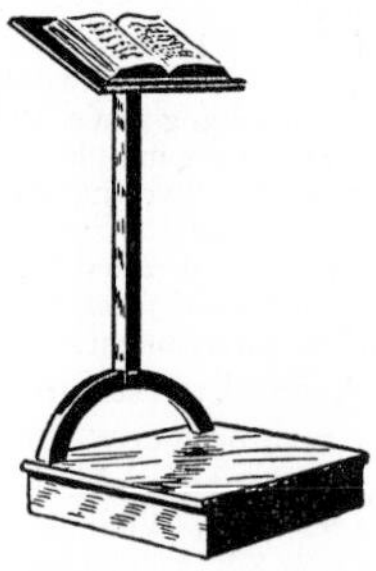

Stand (sense 4) or hand board

b. Used of trees.

1905 *Forestry Bureau Bul.* No. 60, 13 The proportion of sweet birch in the stand is large. **1949** *Democrat* 28 July 4/2 Areas . . . are now showing excellent stands of young timber.

6. The witness box in a court room.

1865 LOWELL *My Study Windows* 209 [Thoreau] had watched Nature like a detective who is to go upon the stand. **1922** PARRISH *Case & Girl* 316 Percival wouldn't go on the stand.

b. *To take the stand on*, to vouch for. *Colloq.*

1907 TARKINGTON *His Own People* viii. 121 [She] is generally believed to be Sneyd's wife, though I could not take the stand on that myself.

7. (See quots.)

1879 VIVIAN *Wanderings Western Land* 207 When in motion they are not so swift as smaller deer, and on this account it is sometimes easy, when they are massed together, to obtain what the hunters call a 'stand,' that is, a chance of firing an unlimited number of shots into the brown before they can get sufficiently far away to be out of shot. **1915** YOUNG *Hard Knocks* 56 In getting a stand of buffalo, the hunter must crawl up unawares without being seen or scented. **1938** J. F. GUYER *Pioneer Life* 25 The killing of these [buffalo] leaders first is the secret of getting a stand (as it is called), when making a killing.

8. A student's rank or standing in a class.

1904 *N.Y. Ev. Post* 17 March 7 The highest stand man of the non-elective scholastic period was Dean Wright of 1868, who attained a stand of 3.71 on a scale of 4.00. **1921** R. D. PAINE *Comr. Rolling Ocean* i. 11, I had a rotten stand in your course.

As the last term in **auction, bee, block, book, candy, caster, check, cigar, dressing, drove, fishing, fruit, gin, grand, hamburger, lunch, music, news, newspaper, one-night, oyster, peanut, pigeon, popcorn, preacher's, preaching, reviewing, shoe, stage, wagon, wash, witness stand.**

***stand,** *v.*

1. *intr.* Of a stallion: To be available for breeding purposes. Cf. ***stand,** *n.* **2.**

1766 *Va. Gazette* 4 April 3/3 Merry Tom Stands at my house, and covers mares at a guinea the leap, or 51. the season. **1801** *Impartial Observer* (Natchez, Miss.) 21 Feb. 3/3 (*advt.*), The noted Horse Pantaloon, will stand the ensuing season . . . at Mr. Jesse Carter's on second creek. **1880** *Cimarron News & Press* 25 March 3/3 The celebrated Stallion Sweeper Will stand the coming season . . . at my ranch.

b. Also *tr.*

1876 *St. Helena* (Calif.) *Star* 26 May 2/4, I propose to stand the above described stallion during the coming season. **1944** *Democrat* 11 May 4/5, I will stand my stallion at Grove Hill every Saturday. Fee $10.00.

2. In noun and adj. combs.: (1) **stand -in,** (*a*) an understanding or "pull," *slang*, (*b*) in motion pictures, one who stands in the place of an actor or actress until the taking of the picture is ready to begin, also transf.; (2) **off,** see as a main entry, cf. **b.** (4) (*b*); (3) **-out,** one who or that which is outstanding; (4) **pat,** of or pertaining to standing pat, see **b.** (5) below; (5) **patter,** one who stands pat, esp. in politics; (6) **pattism,** the quality of standing pat; (7) ***pipe,** a vertical pipe for holding a liquid, often to secure uniform pressure in a supply system; (8) **-up,** ?a cheap eating place at which the patrons eat standing, *obs.*; (9) **-up law,** in Connecticut, an election law (1801–17) which required the electors to indicate their votes in certain elections by standing up, *obs.*

(1) (*a*) **1870** *Food Jrnl.* 1 Nov. 523 The affair is settled amicably by a 'stand in,' which means that the purchaser shall pay the other, or others, a certain sum not to bid against him. **1923** *D.N.* V. 222 He's got a stand-in with the boss. (*b*) **1934** WEBSTER. **1948** *Chi. Tribune* 21 March (Grafic Mag.) 7 Stand-ins . . . are not necessarily doubles, as the pictures here disclose, but do have the approximate heights and body measurements of the stars. **1949** *Sat. Ev. Post* 4 June 17/2 Tobin has . . . acted as Fred Allen's stand-in at a christening. — (3) **1928** *Collier's* 29 Dec. 26/2 When the show opened, this girl had improved in her dancing so amazingly that she was a distinct 'standout.' — (4) **1903** *Nation* 30 July LXXVII. 83/3 Here we have the stock market in total collapse . . . in the piping times of the 'stand-pat' evangel. **1947** *Steamboat* (Colo.) *Pilot* 2 Jan. 2/1 Taft of Ohio is too much on the stand-pat order.

(5) **1904** *Boston Transcript* 16 Feb. 11/2 He was an avowed 'standpatter' on the tariff. **1947** PAUL *Linden* 391 He would shake his head,—sigh deeply, and take a pitying attitude toward the standpatters who, just then, were sold on the 'white man's burden.' — (6) **1909** *Chi. D. News* 10 Aug. 8/1 Altruism and stand-patism do not travel on the same side of the street. **1932** *DAB* VIII. 228 In 1902 he declared himself the champion of that 'Stand-pattism,' which, however much in his colloquial verbiage it may have appealed to his fellow Republicans of that day, soon carried all the connotations of reactionary politics. — (7) **1882** *Wheelman* I. 17 It is the Roxbury stand-pipe. **1896** *Engineering Mag.* X. 1043 These stand pipes have been built in three main classes: a large wrought-iron or even wooden tank raised on a trestle, the same tank supported upon and enclosed by substantial masonry walls, . . . an immense wrought-iron or steel cylinder, filled with water from the ground up. — (8) **1897** MARK TWAIN *Following Equator* 143 (R.), He halted a moment in front of the best restaurant, then glanced at his clothes and passed on, and got his breakfast at a 'stand-up.' — (9) **1817** *Niles' Reg.* XIII. 131/2 Many if not all of the evils which wise and good legislators have sought to obviate by ballot-voting, have resulted from this 'stand-up law.' **1831** *Jamestown* (N.Y.) *Jrnl.* 23 March 2/4 Why did the people of Connecticut complain of the 'stand-up law' which formerly existed in that state?

b. In colloq. phrases: (1) **To stand for*, to put up with or tolerate; (2) *to stand from under*, to avoid or escape something, to get to a place of safety; (3) **to stand in with*, to be in collusion with; (4) **to stand off*, (*a*) of a bet in gaming, to be off or invalid, (*b*) to hold out *for* something, to repel or foil, hold at bay; (5) *to stand pat*, in poker to play a pat hand *q.v.*, *fig.*, to oppose change of any kind; (6) **to stand round*, to be on the alert, mind one's p's and q's (see also quot. 1840); (7) **to stand up*, (*a*) to go through a wedding ceremony, (*b*) to hold up and rob, (*c*) to leave one in the lurch; (8) *to stand up and be counted*, to take a strong or public stand; (9) *to stand up with*, to act as a groomsman or bridesmaid for (someone).

(1) **1896** ADE *Artie* 107 They say they can't stand for that kind o' work. **1938** SMITTER *F.O.B. Detroit* 16 It's against the rules, and besides—I don't stand for it. — (2) **1857** *Chi. Times* 6 Oct., To enable me to stand from under the present crash, I shall offer my entire stock for the next 30 days at a great sacrifice. **1920** HOWELLS *Vacation of Kelwyns* 185 Brother Jasper was standing from under and letting him take the whole responsibility of dispossessing the Kites. — (3) **1882** COOPER *Amer. Pol.* 199 The former quickly allied themselves with the Democrats, and thus carried the State, though Grant's administration 'stood in' with the Radicals. **1905** *McClure's Mag.* 351 But Champlin 'stood in' with Brayton. — (4) (*a*) **1856**

Spirit of Times 6 Dec. 224/1 When a person in throwing dice has thrown *ten*, and another person . . . throws ten also, does the bet stand off, or does the second party lose? **1857** *Ib.* 11 April 88/1 In each case the bet stands off. (*b*) **1878** BEADLE *Western Wilds* 38 He offered him fifty thousand for it, and the feller stood him off for seventy-five thousand. **1925** TILGHMAN *Dugout* 89 Probably that old dug-out is the same one where your mother stood off the Indians.

(5) **1882** C. WELSH *Poker* 12 The gentleman . . . failed to better his hand. The other stood pat. **1884** CRADDOCK *Where Battle Was Fought* 35 Then he drew one card, Estwicke standing pat. **1890** *Stock Grower & Farmer* 29 March 7/1 When it came to them two accomplishments he stood pat. **1948** *Chi. Tribune* 21 March I. 1/7 Britain stands pat in its determination to surrender the Palestine mandate May 15. — (6) **1840** *Knickerb.* XVI. 205, I should have made more by *standing round*, i.e., watching the land-market for bargains. **1845** *Ib.* XXVI. 466, I knew him by the way they 'stood round' when he came along. *a*1861 T. WINTHROP *Life in Open Air* (1863) 148 We was about sick of puttyheads and sneaks that . . . didn't dare to make us stand round and bone in. — (7) (*a*) **1842** *Amer. Pioneer* I. 314 They were married without any previous preparation of nice dresses, bride cakes, or bride maids—he standing up in a hunting dress, and she in a short gown and petticoat of homespun. (*b*) **1897** LEWIS *Wolfville* 319 You don't want to go too close to stand-up your gent. **1897** NORRIS *Stories & Sk.* (1931) 146 That a girl should stand up a stage is extraordinary enough. (*c*) **1906** O. HENRY *Four Million* 122 I'm afraid she'll stand me up when it comes to the scratch. **1946** THOMPSON *Amer. Daughter* 40 It looked as though the blacksmith and the chestnut tree were going to be stood up. — (8) **1904** *Hartford Courant* 12 Aug. 10 Another democratic paper, the 'Sacramento Bee,' follows the example of the 'Chicago Chronicle' and stands up to be counted for Roosevelt. **1945** *Somerset News* 22 March 1/3 Why then weren't Shore delegates men enough to stand up and be counted? — (9) **1859** in *Chi. Tribune* (1929) 10 Nov. VIII. 1/6 We had no one to stand up with us, as we wished to have a simple service. **1917** MCCUTCHEON *Green Fancy* 344 Countess Mara-Dafanda, . . . and Thomas Kingsbury Barnes 'stood up' with the happy couple.

For *to stand up to the rack, to stand a show*, see the nouns.

*****standard**, *n.* As the last term in **gold, limping, silver, single standard.**

* **standard,** *a.* In combs.: (1) **standard dollar,** = **standard silver dollar;** (2) **gold dollar,** a dollar, not necessarily coined, containing gold of an amount and fineness specified by law, which is used as the standard unit of value; (3) **silver dollar,** the regular silver dollar, which was not coined between 1873 and 1878, as distinguished from the trade dollar; (4) * **time,** one of the four clock times for the respective time belts of the United States, adopted by the railroads in 1883 and by Congress in 1918, cf. **central, eastern standard time.**

(1) **1881** *Ore. State Jrnl.* 15 Jan. 2/3 The distribution of standard dollars from the U.S. mints during the month of December amounted to $1,807,481. **1887** *Statutes at Large* XXIV. 635 The trade-dollars recoined under this act shall not be counted as part of the silver bullion required to be purchased and coined into standard dollars. — (2) **1876** in D. K. WATSON *Hist. Amer. Coinage* (1899) 112 After that date [1834], owing to a reduction in the weight of gold required for the standard gold dollar, the silver dollar was made to contain of fine metal almost precisely sixteen times that of the new gold dollar. — (3) **1878** *Statutes at Large* XX. 25 An act to authorize the coinage of the standard silver dollar. **1900** *Cong. Rec.* 11 Jan. 771/1 There were in the United States in 1896 between five hundred and six hundred millions of standard silver dollars. — (4) **1883** *Boston Transcript* 10 Nov. 9/6 The Standard Time for the running of Trains of this road will be changed to conform to the 'Eastern Standard Time.' **1947** *Nat. Geog. Mag.* Sep. 411/1 Some people now living, born before 1883, can remember when the United States, and in fact all the world, had no such thing as standard time.

standee stænˈdi, *n.* **1.** (See quot. 1859.) *Obs.* **2.** One who has to stand in a streetcar or theater.

(1) **1831** *American* (Harrodsburg, Ky.) 25 March 1/5, 'I say Cap'en, what have I got?' 'A standee,' roared a dozen voices. . . . 'Captain, I demand a berth. I am not accustomed to standing up all night amidst such a vulgar set of rascals as you have got here.' **1859** BARTLETT 446 *Standee*, a standing bed-place in a steamer. — (2) **1856** *Knickerb.* March 278 Occasionally the car is brought to a full stop, and the 'standees' are thrown against each other like alley-pins by a 'ten-strike.' **1949** *Time* 30 May 43/1 Inside, with standees five deep, a frankly sentimental audience roared welcome to the ghost.

* **stander,** *n.* In hunting, one who stands at a particular place; esp., in deer hunting, one who occupies a stand.

1836 GILMAN *Recoll.* (1838) 210 They were to scream behind them, and force the deer out to the standers. **1886** *Leslie's Mo.* Sep. 376/2, I could . . . thus perhaps reach our next 'stander' before the deer could find a landing. **1917** KEPHART *Camping* II. 51 The 'standers' in a bear drive are stationed along the main divide, or near it.

* **standing,** *a.* **1.** Of a church: Established. *Obs.* **2. standing cypress,** a handsome perennial herb, *Gilia rubra*, of the southern and southwestern states. **3. standing order,** (*a*) (see quots.), (*b*) (see quots.).

(1) **1748** *N.H. Hist. Soc. Coll.* IX. 9 A Controversy was then subsisting whether they ought to be acknowledged as belonging by Right to the Standing Church. — (2) **1861** WOOD *Botany* 569 Standing Cypress. . . . A splendid herb, . . . bearing at top a long . . . thyrse of scarlet red flowers. **1892** COULTER *Bot. W. Texas* II. 277. — (3) (*a*) **1823** in SWEET *Religion* 119 The word separate came from New England. . . . The Presbyterians there is called the standing order; all who desent from them of whatever denominations are called, and call themselves separates, because they do not adhere to the standing order. **1865** *Harper's Mag.* April 608/1 To pay taxes, for the support of the Presbyterian, or 'Standing Order.' (*b*) **1836** COX *Baptists* 171 The church of 'the standing order' [in Vt.], or congregationalists, is near. . . . The term 'standing order,' refers to the compelled support of this party, by a tax, in the township, . . . but the recent abolition of this exclusive support, has occasioned the more than proportionate increase of other denominations. **1909** WEBSTER 2031/3 *Standing order*, . . . a term formerly used in Connecticut of the Congregational Church, the State church until 1818.

standoff ˈstændˌɔf, *n.* and *a.*

1. *n.* In various colloq. uses: **a.** A situation or contest in which neither party or side wins, or in which gain and loss are equal.

1843 GREENE *Exposure Gambling* 187 Thus, if a man bets on the ace and deuce, and the ace comes to his side, and the deuce to the dealer's side, it is a stand-off, and neither wins. **1876** *Wkly. Mountaineer* (The Dalles, Ore.) 1 July 1/1 What you lose on the ace you win on the ten, —in other words, it is a stand-off. **1950** *Business Week* 22 April 21/1 As of now, it looks like a standoff, with Democrats holding Congress, the Republicans making insignificant gains in the House.

b. A postponement or credit.

1883 HARTE *In Carquinez Woods* (1911) 28 You'd better make it a standoff for twenty-four hours. **1896** *Typographical Jrnl.* IX. 236 Everybody had a 'standoff' at the corner.

c. Aloofness. Cf. **2.**

1885 PORTER *Incid. Civil War* 143 A kind of 'stand-off' between the army and the navy . . . prevented them from working in harmony. **1911** QUICK *Yellowstone Nights* 164, I don't take any high-an'-mighty stand-off from a lunkhead that's stole my melons.

d. A counterbalance.

1888 *Microcosm* Dec. 7 We are willing to allow this judicial estimate . . . to count as a stand-off against all the subsidized commendations. **1890** *Atlantic Mo.* Nov. 672/1 When therefore the lawyer hears the curses . . . of his impatient clients, the preferences of other clients . . . make a complete stand-off.

2. *a.* Aloof, proud. *Colloq.*

1922 ALICE BROWN *Old Crow* xxxiv. 395 She had a direct address country folk liked. She was never 'stand-off,' 'stuck-up.'

staninca stæˈnɪŋkə, *n.* [?Amer. Ind.] (See quots.) Now *hist.* Cf. **persimmon bread.**

[**1772** B. ROMANS in Phillips *Notes on B. Romans* (1924) 124 But the Diospyros Supplys them with a kind of Bread, that is not only in a very great Abundance, but also of a very pleasant and Agreeable Taste, and a Sovereign Remedy against Fluxes.] **1817** J. BRADBURY *Travels* 37 A wooden bowl was now handed round, containing square pieces of cake, in taste resembling gingerbread. On enquiry I found it was made of the pulp of the persimon, mixed with pounded corn. This bread they [Osage Indians] call *staninca*. **1949** *Nat. Hist.* May 222/3 The English naturalist, John Bradbury, while traveling up the Missouri, was received among the Osages and offered a bread called *staninca*, made of the pulp of persimmon pounded with maize.

staple states. The southern, cotton-producing states. *Obs.* — **1785** in *S. Lit. Messenger* XXVIII. 40/2 The giving Congress a power to legislate over the trade of the Union, would be dangerous in the extreme to the five Southern or staple states. **1837** CALHOUN *Works* III. 49 The staple States were wholly opposed to the protective system.

* **star,** *n.*

1. In the U.S. flag, a representation of a star symbolizing one of the states in the Union.

1781 FRENEAU *Poems* (1786) 211 Bid the haughty Britons know They to our Thirteen Stars shall bend. **1856** *Louisville Courier* 8 Nov. 4/3 We are . . . looking forward to that no distant day, when we shall ask and gain admission as a state, and add another star to the banner of our republic. **1944** PENNELL *Rome Hanks* 58 He heard the cannon in salute and something about the new star in the flag for Kansas.

2. A policeman, so called from his wearing a star or badge. Also **star policeman.**

1846 DURIVAGE *Stray Subjects* 150 If his victim knew where to find him or could prove his guilt, he would at once place a 'Star' policeman on his track. **1852** *Lantern* (N.Y.) II. 95/1 Tipple, tipple, lazy Star! All folks wonder where you are, When the victim's shrieking cry Of murder, fills the midnight sky. **1866** *Harper's Mag.* Feb. 356/2 The star assuring Frankie that he would find his mother for him before long.

3. In special combs.: (1) **star boarder,** a boarder, usu. of long standing, having, or regarded as having, special favors or privileges, also transf.; (2) **candle,** a candle of stearine, orig. for measuring luminous intensity; (3) **route,** a mail route other than a railroad, steamboat, or rural service route, so called from being designated with a star or asterisk in postal publications, also attrib.; (4) **router,** one of those who during the Garfield-Arthur administration were charged with having defrauded the government by increasing the compensation on a large number of star routes, now *hist.;* (5) **-s and Bars,** the flag of the Confederate States adopted at Montgomery, Ala., March 4, 1861, often, inaccurately, the Confederate battle flag; (6) **-s and Stripes,** (*a*) the popular name for the flag of the U.S., (*b*) *transf.*, the U.S., (*c*) (see quots.); (7) **service,** the service to the public rendered by the star

Early form of the Stars and Stripes

routes of the Post-Office Department; (8) * **spangled,** of or pertaining to the flag of the U.S.; (9) **Spangled Banner,** (*a*) =**Stars and Stripes** (*a*), (*b*) the title of a patriotic poem written by Francis Scott Key in 1814 and set to music, the national anthem of the U.S., cf. *Order of the Star-Spangled Banner.*

(1) **1877** in ASBURY *Underworld of Chi.* 135 Miss Jessie Curtis, the star boarder at 519 State Street, is looking nice. **1949** *10 Story Western* May 10/2 Rafe was always the star boarder at the Widder Hawley's boardin' house in the Little Rockies. — (2) **1845** *Xenia Torch-Light* 23 Oct. 3/5 Their stock consists, in part, of the following variety, viz.:—Star & Mould candles. **1873** BEADLE *Undevel. West* 573 With them were a number of star candles. — (3) **1880** *Cimarron News & Press* 26 Feb. 2/3 The service on all star routes [shall] be reduced to one trip a week. **1948** *Chi. Tribune* 2 May I. 22/6 Three of these mail dispatches are made by star route service to other roads that do not enter Traverse City. — (4) **1882** *Nation* 30 Nov. 453/1 The Government is the party defrauded by the Star-routers. **1923** GARLAND *Amer. Ind.* 105 It was in the days of the Star Routers, and this was a bogus line, but neither he nor Robe knew it.

(5) **1861** *Richmond* (Va.) *Examiner* 6 Dec. 2/4 The *Stars and Bars* are so like the *Stars and Stripes* that, at an inconsiderable distance, it is difficult to distinguish one from the other. **1927** BENÉT *J. B.'s Body* 214 He . . . thumbed his nose across at the Stars and Bars. **1949** *Time* 21 March 75/1 He proudly displays the Stars & Bars alongside an autographed photograph of Robert E. Lee in his tiny, cluttered office. — (6) (*a*) **1782** E. WATSON *Men & Times Revol.* (1861) 203 He . . . attached to the ship the stars and stripes. **1947** *Nat. Geog. Mag.* July 69/1 The radio was saying that right here in Rome the Stars and Stripes first flew in battle. (*b*) **1809** FRENEAU *Poems* II. 56 O king, my dear king, you shall be very sore, From the *Stars* and the *Stripes* you will mercy implore. **1904** O. HENRY *Roads of Destiny* 357 So the Stars and Stripes ain't landing any marines. (*c*) **1888** WHITMAN *Nov. Boughs* 407 In the slang of the New York common restaurant waiters a plate of ham and beans is known as 'stars and stripes.' **1917** J. A. MOSS *Officers' Man.* 485 *Stars and Stripes*, beans. — (7) **1877** *Cong. Rec.* 3 March 2224/1 Most of us are interested in the star services. It is a service that does not yield much. **1880** *Ib.* 27 Jan. 548/2 The star service is the poor man's mail. — (8) **1806** *Balance* V. 40/2 And pale beam'd the Crescent, its splendor obscur'd By the light of the star-spangled flag of our nation. **1861** NEWELL *Orpheus C. Kerr* I. 40 We raised the Star-spangled particular on the Post-office. — (9) (*a*) **1814** *National Intelligencer* (Wash., D.C.) 27 Sep., And the star spangled banner in triumph shall wave. **1949** *Chi. D. News* 15 Dec. 3 Was the Star-Spangled Banner made in a brewery? (*b*) **1843** *Quincy* (Ill.) *Herald* 3 March 1/1 It is a most beautiful history of that national ballad, 'The Star Spangled Banner.' **1949** *Ward Co. Independent* (Minot, N.D.) 21 July 12/2 The group gave the homemakers creed and sang 'The Star Spangled Banner' and 'Long, Long Ago.'

b. In the names of birds, plants, etc.: (1) **star buzzard,** a hawk, *Asturina plagiata*, having the form and proportions of a buzzard, which ranges from Central America into the southern states; (2) **campion,** the starry campion, *Silene stellata*, found in the eastern states; (3) **cucumber,** (see quot. and cf. **one-seeded star cucumber**); (4) * **fish,** a local name for the dollar fish, *Poronotus triacanthus;* (5) * **flower,** any one of various plants of the genus *Trientalis*, esp. *T. americana;* (6) **-leaved gum,** (see quot.); (7) **nose,** =next; (8) **-nose(d) mole,** the American button-nosed mole, *Condylura cristata*, having fleshy processes resembling a star at the end of the snout; (9) **root,** the plant or root of a species of colicroot, *Aletris farinosa* or *A. aurea*, also a medicinal preparation made of this; (10) **tick,** (see quot.).

(1) **1884** COUES *Key to Birds* (ed. 2) 551 Star Buzzards. . . . A small group of handsome under-sized hawks, peculiar to America. — (2) **1840** DEWEY *Mass. Flowering Plants* 87 C[*ucubalus*] *stellatus*. . . . Star Campion, is a native of this country and State. . . . July; woods. — (3) **1889** *Cent.* 1388/2 One-seeded or star cucumber, the common name in the United States of the *Sicyos angulatus*, a climbing cucurbitaceous annual, bearing clusters of dry, ovate, prickly, one-seeded fruits. — (4) **1884** GOODE *Fisheries* I. 333 The 'Butter-fish' of Massachusetts and New York, sometimes known . . . at Norfolk as the 'Star-fish,' is common between Cape Cod and Cape Henry.

(5) *c***1729** CATESBY *Carolina* I. 33 The Little yellow Star-Flower . . . grows plentifully in most of the open pasture lands in Carolina and Virginia. **1887** *Harper's Mag.* July 303/1 Star-flower, gold-thread, and anemones starred the woods. **1932** HARVEY *Wild Flowers Amer.* 49 Star Flower (*Trientalis Americana*), is a frail little plant that grows in the shade and is sometimes called 'Star Anemone.' — (6) **1916** SETON *Woodcraft Man.* 288 Sweet Gum, Star-Leaved, or Red Gum, Bilsted, Alligator Tree, or Liquidambar (*Liquidambar Styraciflua*). A tall tree up to 150 feet high of low, moist woods. — (7) **1842** *Nat. Hist. N.Y., Zoology* I. 14 The Star-nose burrows in moist places near the surface. — (8) **1826** GODMAN *Nat. Hist.* I. 100 The Star-nose mole frequents the banks of rivulets, and the soft soil of adjacent meadows. **1917** *Mammals of Amer.* 306/2 The tunnels of the Shrew Mole resemble those of the Star-nosed Mole more than those of others. **1948** *Time* 14 June 1/2 This underground dweller is identified by a 22-point star that he wears on his nose. He's a star-nosed mole. — (9) **1743** CLAYTON *Flora Virginica* 38 Stargrass & Starroot. **1789** *Amer. Philos. Soc.* II. p. xx, The root of *Aletris farinosa* is taken in powder, or bruised and steeped in liquor: this root is called star-root. **1843** TALBOT *Journals* 29 External applications: . . . Star root. Rattlesnake plantain [etc.].

(10) **1863** *Ladies' Repository* Oct. 605/1 These ticks reappear much larger in size and with a lustrous circle on their backs, and are then called 'star-ticks,' or 'yearling-ticks.'

As the last term in **blazing, gold, golden, lone, May, road, shooting, Texas, thirteen, war, woodland star(s).**

stare cat. (See quot.) *Obs.* — **1859** BARTLETT 448 Stare-Cat, a woman or girl who amuses herself with gazing at her neighbors. A woman's word.

* **starling,** *n.* Any one of various American birds, esp. the red-winged blackbird, resembling the European starling.

*a***1676** WINTHROP in *Phil. Trans.* XII. 1065 The Ear is cloathed and armed with several strong thick Husks . . . defending it from . . . the Crows, Starlings and other Birds. **1811** WILSON *Ornithology* IV. 31, I was frequently entertained with the aerial evolutions of . . . great bodies of Starlings. **1850** S. F. COOPER *Rural Hours* 49 The red wing black-bird or starling, we have never seen in this country. **1948** *Chi. Tribune* 23 June I. 16/4 The bobolinks . . . have a bubbling, exuberant song that defies imitation by a catbird or even by a starling.

As the last term in **fore-, orchard, red-winged starling.**

* **starry,** *a.* **1. Starry Banner,** =**Stars and Stripes** (*a*). **2. starry flounder,** the California flounder, *Platichthys stellatus.*

(1) **1865** BOUDRYE *Fifth N.Y. Cavalry* p. iii, The Brave Boys . . . have heroically upborne the Starry Banner. **1867** GOSS *Soldier's Story* 50 Once again they were to be under the protecting folds of Liberty's starry banner. — (2) **1884** GOODE *Fisheries* I. 184 The Starry Flounder . . . is known, wherever found, as the 'Flounder,' all others being considered as Bastard or False Flounders. **1911** *Rep. Fisheries 1908* 56/1 The name flounder is variously applied to the flat fishes . . . known as 'American sole,' . . . 'starry flounder,' 'rough limanda' [etc.].

***start,** *v.* **1.** *To start in,* to begin, set to work. **2.** *To start something,* to stir up agitation or commotion. Both *colloq.*

(1) **1866** MARK TWAIN *Sk. New & Old* 298 The showman drummed up his grit and started in fresh. **1932** GRAYSON *Leaders* 444 He . . . immediately started in on his own behalf. — (2) **1917** SINCLAIR *King Coal* 78 Either the man was an agitator, seeking to 'start something,' or else he was a detective sent in by the company.

***starter,** *n.*

1. (*a*) (See quot.), (*b*) one who starts quickly in a race, (*c*) a foundation comb in a beehive, (*d*) a batch of sour cream, etc., used to inoculate milk in making butter or cheese.

(*a*) **1875** BURROUGHS *Winter Sunshine* 116 In the lumber countries, . . . starters are at work with their pikes and hooks starting out the pine logs on the first spring freshet. (*b*) **1893** *Outing* XXII. 154/1 'Starters,' . . . can start like a cannon-ball, literally outclassing, in all distances up to fifty yards, men who hold world's records in the hundred and two-twenty yard dashes. (*c*) **1880** *Harper's Mag.* Oct. 778/1 Into the large frame there may be set eight little one-pound frames, each with its foundation 'starter.' (*d*) **1896** *Vt. Agric. Rep.* XV. 67 This may be done . . . by using a 'starter' made from cream.

2. *As* (or *for*) *a starter,* as (or for) a beginning. *Colloq.*

1873 BEADLE *Undevel. West* 450 He gave me twenty drops of laudanum as a starter. **1884** MARK TWAIN *H. Finn* 321 (R.), For a starter I would go to work and steal Jim out of slavery again. **1947** *Chi. Tribune* 3 Sep. 6/3 As a starter, agents have begun a canvass of small independent food wholesalers.

As the last term in **car, elevator, train starter.**

starting bar. 1. (See 1st quot.) Also transf. **2.** (See quot. 1905.)

(1) **1876** KNIGHT 2310/2 *Starting-bar,* . . . a hand-lever for starting the valve-gear of a steam-engine. **1876** *Scribner's Mo.* Feb. 482/2 The fund subscribed was only the 'starting bar' which sets the train in motion. — (2) **1903** WHITE *Blazed Trail Stories* 36 The other man . . . seized the iron starting-bar and descended. **1905** *Forestry Bureau Bul.* No. 61, 38 *Gee throw,* a heavy, wooden lever, with a curved iron point, used to break out logging sleds. (N[orthern] F[orest].) Syn.: starting bar.

starvation party. (See quots.) *Obs.* — **1865** SALA *Diary* II. 169 In the South they were having their Christmas 'starvation parties,' where you could dance all night if you liked, but get nothing to eat or drink for the very sufficient reason that there was nothing in the larder. **1874** G. C. EGGLESTON *Rebel's Recoll.* 75 The return of the soldiers made some sort of social festivity necessary, and 'starvation parties' were given, at which it was understood that the givers were wholly unable to set out refreshments of any kind.

starved rat. The little chief hare, *Ochotona princeps,* of the Rocky Mountain region.

1884 J. S. KINGSLEY *Stand. Nat. Hist.* V. 81 The miners and hunters in the West know these oddities as 'conies' and 'starved rats.' **1890** *Cent.* 3331/2 [The] starved rat . . . inhabits the mountains of the West as far south as New Mexico and Arizona. **1909** E. T. SETON *Lives Game Animals* IV. 640 The driver calls it 'Coney,' or Rock-rabbit'; and the old miners will tell you it is a 'Starved Rat.'

stash stæʃ, *v.* [Poss. f. *st*ore and *cache.* Cf. **stash,* to stop, end.] *tr.* (See quot. 1949.) *Slang.* — **1934** *Collier's* 26 Jan. 6/1 If it wuzn' stashed (that's a new word that came in with prohibition) jest before the country went dry, it wuz stolen from a Kentucky warehouse, or smuggled from Scotland. **1949** *St. Paul Pioneer Press* 19 June 6/1 The word stashed, from the verb 'to stash' . . . is American slang for 'to put away, as for safe keeping, or in a prepared place.'

statal ˈstetḷ, *a.* Of or pertaining to a state in the U.S. *Obs.* — **1862** E. BATES in *Official Opinions Attorneys Gen.* X. 388, I have no knowledge of any other kind of political citizenship higher or lower, statal or national. **1880** TOURGEE *Invisible Empire* xi, Public education flourished as a part of the statal economy.

***state,** *n.*

1. A British colony in America; one of the commonwealths making up the U.S.

1634 *Mass. Bay Rec.* I. 117 When I shalbe called to giue my voice touching any such matter of this state, wherein ffreemen are to deale, I will giue my vote & suffrage [etc.]. **1776** A. ADAMS *Familiar Lett.* 204 Thus ends royal authority in this State [Mass.]. **1883** *Gringo & Greaser* 1 Sep. 1/1 New Mexico has 1200 miles of railway,—more than the great commonwealth of Nevada which has been a state 19 years. **1946** *Democrat* 3 Jan. 1/2 Alabama's two Senators and nine Representatives to the Congress will discuss in a series of lectures current legislation affecting our State.

b. *pl.* The United States.

1776 CRESSWELL *Journal* 191 Washington, who is Dictator for the present year, has ordered sixteen battalions to be raised (in the States as they call them) under the appellation of Guards or Washington's Life Guards. **1829** *Va. Herald* (Fredericksburg) 8 April 1/4 They resolved with the advice of their few neighbors, to cross into 'the States,' and seek there employment in some of the new manufactories. **1950** *Nat. Geog. Mag.* April 507/1 Recording bird voices was an old story to us, for we had been doing it in the States for years.

c. *pl.* Those states east of the Mississippi River, as distinguished from the unsettled or thinly-settled West.

1805 PIKE *Sources Miss.* (1810) 31 Caught a curious little animal on the prairie which my Frenchman termed a *prairie mole,* but it is very different from the mole of the States. **1876** *Dutch Flat* (Calif.) *Forum* 17 Aug. 5/1 Capt. Gardner and family are now enjoying themselves in the States. **1900** DRANNAN *Plains & Mts.* 61 Col. Fremont had been detailed . . . to command an exploring expedition . . . [to] find a better route from the 'States' to California. **1948** JOHNSTON *Gold Rush* 2/2 First reports of the phenomenal discovery were received in 'the States' with frank incredulity.

attrib. **1890** CUSTER *Following Guidon* 59 General Custer gave them the privilege of first greeting their two States women. **1939** ABBOTT-SMITH *We Pointed* 84 We pulled out of Fort Kearney with the main herd in August, 1883. The states cattle that had been shipped in were very poor. [Note:] Just cattle seems to have been Texas longhorns; states cattle, any others.

d. A representative of a state, a state's attorney. Also *to lose a state,* to lose the support of a majority of the voters in a state.

1787 *Constitution,* Done in Convention, by the unanimous consent of the States present. **1834** HONE *Diary* I. 114 We have lost the State, it is said, from the opposition of the Hicksites. **1894** MARK TWAIN *P. Wilson* xx, Witness after witness was called by the State, and questioned at length.

2. In special combs. (often *cap.*).

These are so numerous that only a relatively small number are here illustrated.

(1) **state capitol,** = ***capitol,** *n.* **1,** also attrib.; (2) **election,** an election held throughout a state for selecting state officers, including federal representatives, also attrib.; (3) **emancipation,** the proposed emancipation of slaves by states, *obs.;* (4) **fair,** a fair at which prizes are awarded for the best farm and home products submitted by the citizens of a state; (5) ***house,** see as a main entry; (6) **land office,** an office in which the management of state lands centers; (7) **line,** the boundary line of a state, cf. **5.** (8) below, cf. **old state line;** (8) **paper,** (see quot. 1891 and cf. **4.** (5) below); (9) **party,** a political party or faction in Kansas which desired Kansas to become a free state, *obs.;* (10) **pauper,** (see quot.), *obs.;* (11) **right,** the right to market a particular product throughout a state; (12) **rights,** see as a main entry; (13) ***room,** see as a main entry; (14) **scholarship,** a scholarship maintained at an educational institution at state expense; (15) **-'s evidence,** see as a main entry; (16) **sovereignty,** political supremacy possessed by a state in the management of its governmental affairs, esp. in pre-Civil War debate, the doctrine that the individual states are essentially sovereign powers associated in voluntary union; (17) **ticket,** the list of candidates for state offices agreed upon by political leaders in a state; (18) **wide,** *a.* comprehending an entire state.

(1) *a***1857** *Mich. Gen. Statutes* I. (1882) 171 The board of state auditors are hereby authorized . . . to procure plans, drawings and estimates for a state capitol. **1949** *Dly. Oklahoman Mag.* (Okla. City) 9 Oct. 2/3 Construction of the state capitol was begun in 1914 and completed early in 1918. — (2) **1798** MANNING *Key of Liberty* 38 In our State Elections for Federal Representatives & Electors, . . . their was not halfe the people brought to act on either side. **1911** *Okla. Session Laws* 3 Legisl. 225 The Governor shall . . . appoint a State Election Board. — (3) **1853** STOWE *Key* 70/1 Such [slaveholders] are most earnest advocates for State emancipation. — (4) **1844** *Farmers' Cabinet* 15 Oct. 73/1 New York State Fair and Cattle Show at Poughkeepsie. **1949** *Ward Co. Independent* (Minot, N.D.) 21 July 1/8 The North Dakota State fair in Minot will open July 25 and close July 30.

(6) **1851** *Mich. Gen. Statutes* (1882) I. 238 Whenever . . . there shall be a vacancy in the office of . . . the state land office, the governor shall have power [etc.]. **1945** *Las Cruces* (N.M.) *Citizen* 15 Feb. 2/2 Two million dollars have been collected by the State Land Office at Santa Fe. — (7) **1783** *Va. Gazette* 20 Dec. 2/3 George R. Clark, Surveyor State Line. **1835** in BASSETT *So. Plant.* 43 The distance from the state line is about 100 miles. **1949** *New Harmony* (Ind.) *Times* 5

Aug. 1/2 His car had no trouble at all in pulling over the many state lines that he crossed on his recent trip to the West. — **(8) 1838** *N.Y. Laws* 246 The comptroller shall immediately thereupon . . . give notice in the state paper that [etc.]. **1850** *Mich. Gen. Statutes* I. (1882) 47 The Legislature shall not establish a state paper. **1891** *Cent.* 5912/1 *State paper,* . . . a newspaper selected, by or pursuant to law, for the publication of official or legal notices. — **(9) 1856** *Kans. Hist. Coll.* (1890) IV. 505 It is announced that the 'State party' intend to order an election shortly.

(10) 1832 WILLIAMSON *Hist. Maine* II. 682 The support of poor persons, who had no legal settlement within the Commonwealth, called State-paupers, has been another heavy charge upon the public funds. — **(11) 1896** *N.Y. Dramatic News* 15 Aug. 3/4 One of the best state rights to Edison's marvelous Vitascope is for sale by John F. Harley. — **(14) 1871** BAGG *At Yale* 38 Forty free State-scholarships were established.

(16) 1787 in *Sp. & Doc. Amer. Hist.* (London, 1844) I. 70 No amendment of the confederation can answer the purpose of a good government, so long as State sovereignties do, in any shape, exist. **1811** *Ann. 12th Congress* 1 Sess. 2159 Our only hope of participating . . . in the rights and blessings of State sovereignty, is built upon the pleasing anticipation of becoming a part of the Mississippi Territory. **1947** LUMPKIN *Southerner* 49 As early as 1862 its first conscription bill had been passed, much as it was deplored by many Southern patriots as contravening all the South was fighting for of 'state sovereignty' and 'individual liberty.' — **(17) 1835** *Jamestown* (N.Y.) *Jrnl.* 4 Feb. 2/3 It was to save . . . the election of the regency state ticket, that these gentlemen stultified themselves. **1912** NICHOLSON *Hoosier Chron.* 342 But the choice of an invulnerable state ticket at this convention is our business and our only business. — **(18) 1911** PERSONS *Mass. Labor Laws* 62 A state-wide organization was sufficient to bring the necessary pressure to bear. **1949** *Gladewater* (Tex.) *Times-Tribune* 31 July II. 2/1 The flower adorned auditorium of the First Methodist church was the scene of a fashionable wedding of statewide interest Wednesday evening.

b. Designating areas set aside by a state for public use or enjoyment, and roads constructed by a state or with state aid, as (1) **state forest,** also attrib., (2) **highway,** also attrib., (3) **park,** (4) **preserve,** (5) **reservation,** (6) **road.**

(1) 1897 *N.Y. Forest, Fish, & Game Comm.* 2d Rep. 130 Two of the parties having built their cottages with timber cut from the adjoining State forests. **1949** *Amer. Forests* Dec. 15/1 The third Tillamook blaze caused such public outcry against the waste of state forest lands that the governor appointed a citizens committee. — **(2) 1883** *Harper's Mag.* Aug. 335/2 Civilization has followed almost exactly the print of the moccasin in the State highway. **1904** *N.Y. Ev. Post* 15 July 7 In fine contrast to the old way of treating the 'big trees' of California is the action of the State Highways Commission in arranging to support the decaying trunk of the 'Grizzly Giant.' **1949** *Lincoln Co. News* (Oceanlake, Ore.) 4 Aug. 4/1 A state highway runs up the valley of the Lemolo River, on the track of a corduroy road of pioneer times. — **(3) 1904** *Mass. Col. Soc. Pub.* VIII. 397 In addition to National Parks, there are in the United States various State Parks. **1950** *Nature Mag.* March 152/2 In 1935 a 1500-acre tract in the heart of the scenic area was set aside for preservation as a State park. — **(4) 1939** WHITE *One Man's Meat* 86 The pond is in fact a State Preserve, and carries a twenty-dollar fine for picking wild flowers.

(5) 1792 *Mass. H.S. Coll.* 1 Ser. I. 287 The whole Six Nations live on grounds, called the State Reservations. **1903** A. B. HART *Actual Govt.* 330 State reservations are simply a setting aside for public use of mountains, valleys, and other places of beauty. — **(6) 1795** *Pittsburgh Gaz.* 6 June 3/3 The great state road leads by the end of the town. **1944** *Sat. Ev. Post* 9 Sep. 65/1 From the house by the state road the little Peters girl had headed into the village on her bicycle.

c. Designating things adopted as symbolic of a state, as (1) **state bird,** (2) **flag,** (3) **flower,** (4) **song,** (5) **tree.**

(1) 1910 J. H. WALLACE, JR. *Ala. Bird Day Book* 8 The Yellow Hammer is the State Bird of Alabama. **1950** *Dly. Ardmoreite* (Ardmore, Okla.) 14 Feb. 5/3 The Oklahoma state bird is the quail. — **(2) 1861** *Charleston* (S.C.) *Mercury* 14 Feb. 2/5 The Convention to-day adopted the State flag. **1950** *Chi. Tribune* 19 Feb. VII. 1/7 She was instrumental in the selection of a state flag. — **(3) 1898** *Land of Sunshine* Feb. 153 At the foot of Mount Lowe . . . are slopes covered in spring with the yellow poppy, the State flower, to which the unromantic name of *eschscholtzia* has been given. **1949** *Exciting Western* May 56/1 The state flower in Kansas is the sunflower. — **(4) 1945** *Chi. Tribune* 19 Aug. VII. 1/8 The youngsters sang the Arkansas state song in soft young voices that mingled with the voice of the river. **1948** MENCKEN *Supp.* II. 546 *Ioway* seems to be preferred by the plain people of the State, and the name so appears in the State song.

(5) 1917 BAILEY *Sand Dunes Indiana* 116 Possibly it was here that the thought of naming the violet, the Indiana State Flower, and the oak, the Indiana State Tree, was born. **1948** *Forest Way* (Chi.) May 5 Illinois is one of 25 states which, by legislative act, have adopted state trees.

3. Designating officials who serve a state in some indicated capacity, as (1) **state auditor,** (2) **clothier,** *obs.,* (3) **forester,** (4) **geologist,** (5) **librarian,** (6) **printer,** (7) **-'s attorney,** (8) **senator,** (9) **superintendent of schools,** (10) **treasurer.**

(1) 1850 *Mich. Gen. Statutes* I. (1882) 57 The secretary of state, state treasurer, and commissioner of the state land office shall constitute a board of state auditors. **1911** *Okla. Session Laws* 3 Legisl. 198 The State Auditor shall, thereupon, issue public building bonds and deliver same to state treasurer. — **(2) 1780** *N.H. Hist. Soc. Coll.* IX. 223 The regimental returns for Shous are to be Made to the State Clothier. **1782** *N.H. Comm. Safety Rec.* 299 He is to be accountable out of his pay as Sub or State Clothier. — **(3) 1909** *Nat. Conservation Cong. Proc.* 60 Forestry is most fortunate in having for its leader there the State Forester. **1911** *Colo. Laws* 420 The State forester shall advise, aid and assist in preventing and extinguishing forest fires on State lands and private lands and in the National Forests in the State. — **(4) 1838** *Indiana H. Rep. Jrnl.* 23 Sess. 30 The act providing for the appointment of a State Geologist not having expired. **1898** *K.C. Star* 18 Dec. 4/2 State Geologist Blatchley . . . said the coal district in western and southwestern Indiana would be the center of Indiana's manufacturing interests within a few years.

(5) 1838 *Indiana H. Rep. Jrnl.* 56 The Speaker also laid before the House the Report of the State Librarian. **1907** *St. Nicholas* July 709/2 If I were a legislature and wanted to appoint a state librarian, I'd never appoint mother. — **(6) 1800** *Steele P.* I. 191 They this day brought on the ballot for State printer. **1911** *Okla. Session Laws* 3 Legisl. 287 It shall be the duty of the State Printer to prepare the plans and specifications for all public printing and binding. — **(7) 1809** KENDALL *Travels* III. 251 There is, in Vermont, as in some of its fellow-republics, no attorney-general for the whole republic, but an attorney-general, or, as it is called, a *state's attorney,* for each particular county. **1949** *Downers Grove* (Ill.) *Rep.* 31 March 13/1 I've heard lots of wild talk about why didn't the state's attorney do this. — **(8) 1798** MANNING *Key of Liberty* 37 The State Senetors are more unknown. **1948** *Time* 13 Dec. 28/3 He had been a state senator, then he went to Washington. — **(9) 1883** *Harper's Mag.* Sep. 642/1 State Superintendent of Schools, John Akers. **1944** JOHNSON *As I Dare* 312 The young woman who saved that situation was now the state superintendent of schools up in Denver.

(10) 1789 *Boston Directory* 205 Public officers include . . . State Treasurer. **1944** JOHNSON *As I Dare* 10 Johnny Page lives in Arizona where he was at one time state treasurer.

Also *state agent, comptroller, executive, game warden, inspector, judge, patrolman, representative, surveyor-general, veterinarian,* etc.

4. Designating things pertaining to the finances of a state: (1) **state aid,** aid given by a state to various projects within its borders carried on in the public interest; (2) **bank,** a bank owned by a state or operating under the laws of a state, also attrib.; (3) **debt,** a debt owed by a state; (4) **money,** money issued by a state before 1789, also state notes circulating as currency, *obs.;* (5) **paper,** *collect.* notes issued by a state and circulating as currency, *obs.,* cf. **2.** (8) above; (6) **stock,** stock or bonds issued by a state; (7) **tax,** a tax levied by a state, as distinguished from a federal tax.

(1) 1856 OLMSTED *Slave States* 136 So, too, with regard to a line from Antwerp to Norfolk, (a proposition to grant State aid for establishing which, was the chief topic of public discussion in Virginia). **1949** *Ill. Agric. Assoc. Rec.* Nov. 9/2 This is a state aid road in Pike county that is impassable many days in the year. — **(2) 1815** MADISON in Leavitt *Our Money Wars* (1894) 47 If the operation of the State banks cannot produce this result [a stable and sufficient currency], the proper operation of a National bank will merit consideration. **1837** *New-Yorker* 25 Nov. 571/3 The State Bank Deposite system failed owing to the incompetency . . . of Mr. Secretary Woodbury. **1950** *Banking* Jan. 78/1 California permits national banks to convert to state banks. — **(3) 1788** *Mass. Spy* 3 April 3/1 A considerable part of the State debt will shortly be extinguished. **1900** *Cong. Rec.* 14 Feb. 1800/1 The enormous State debt . . . had been piled upon the people of Missouri. — **(4) 1781** *Cal. Va. State P.* I. 553 His employees having the choice of receiving Tobacco at the market price in lieu of State or Continental money. **1882** in S. LEAVITT *Our Money Wars* 78 Indiana has generally had the best State money of any of the United States.

(5) 1792 *Steele P.* I. 81, I mention this . . . that those who yet hold State paper may be upon their guard. **1822** *Ann. 17th Congress* 1 Sess. 323 It might have been had in Kentucky for three cents, State paper. — **(6) 1837** PECK *Gaz. Illinois* 59 The Fund Commissioners are authorized to contract loans by issuing state stock at a rate not exceeding six per centum. **1868** *N.Y. Herald* 1 July 9/1 The State stocks were very weak. — **(7) 1796** *Ann. 4th Congress* 2 Sess. 2694 The deficiency of the State tax has been hitherto supplied from the proceeds of vacant lands. **1849** CHAMBERLAIN *Ind. Gazetteer* 115 The whole State tax assessed in 1816, was $6,043.36.

Also *state bonds, credit, dollar,* (*obs.*), *rates, scrip, treasury, warrant,* etc.

5. Designating groups having to do with the government of a state or its military or political affairs: (1) **state assembly,** =**state legislature;** (2) **board,** a group of state officials having charge of various matters, esp. education, of state concern, cf. ***canvasser,** *n.;* (3) **committee,** a committee in charge of the affairs of a political party in a state, also **state central committee;** (4) **convention,** a convention of the leaders of a political party in a state; (5) **court,** a court forming a part of the judicial system of a state, as distinguished from a federal court; (6) **guard,** the National Guard or militia force of a state, also a portion of this force; (7) **legislature,** the legislative body of a state; (8) **line,** the military force of a state enrolled for combat service, *obs.*, cf. **2.** (7) above; (9) **militia,** a term formerly used for the National Guard *q.v.;* (10) **Regency,** =**Albany regency,** *obs.;* (11) **senate,** the upper house of a state legislature, also attrib.

(1) **1782** TRUMBULL *M'Fingal* 94 When in want no more in them [Congress] lies, Than begging of your State-Assemblies. **1818** J. FLINT *Lett. from Amer.* 111 It would be an interesting inquiry to find the number and the names of legislators in the different states assemblies, who are interested in banking concerns. — (2) **1838** COLTON *Indiana Delineated* 45 The State Board . . . express their doubts whether it can be effected except by partial canalling. **1911** PERSONS *Mass. Labor Laws* 185 The state board issues a pamphlet of the laws relating to school matters. — (3) **1848** *Whig Almanac 1849* 6/2 The Hunkers . . . appointed a new State Central Committee, and in due time called another State Convention at Albany. **1884** in *Works T. Roosevelt* XIV. 37 Who has not known numerous instances where the action of a State committee has been reversed by the State convention? **1950** *Chi. D. News* 10 May 18/5 Last Friday's battle . . . of the Republican State Central Committee set a new high for Republican stupidity. — (4) **1779** *Amherst Rec.* (1884) 75/2 Calling a State Convention for the sole purpose of forming a new Constitution. **1861** *N.Y. Herald* 4 Jan. 5/2 It may call a State Convention on the secession question. **1949** *Social Studies* May 234/2 In the State Convention of 1788, his prestige secured the adoption of the Federal Constitution.

(5) **1789** MACLAY *Deb. Senate* 87 If any matter made cognizable in a Federal court should be agitated in a State court, a plea to the jurisdiction would immediately be put in. **1912** NICHOLSON *Hoosier Chron.* 225 The doors of the state courts swing inward to any Hoosier citizen of good moral character who wants to practice law. — (6) **1833** *Niles' Reg.* XLIV. 139/1 We the people, oversetting and nullifying the state guard by the way, who in vain attempted to keep us out. **1898** PAGE *Red Rock* 232 Should they [*sc.* Negroes] plough when they were the State guard! **1947** *Chi. D. News* 15 Jan. 1/1 The state guard is operated by Georgia. — (7) **1787** *Constitution* I. II. § 1 The electors in each State shall have the qualifications requisite for electors of the most numerous branch of the State legislature. **1950** *Lincoln Co. Adv*. (Brookhaven, Miss.) 12 Jan. 10/3 Allen has served . . . in the State Legislature as representative of Lincoln county. — (8) **1855** SIMMS *Forayers* 521, I will reserve Major Sinclair, whom I design to advance to a colonelcy in the state line, for a separate duty. — (9) **1867** EDWARDS *Shelby* 397 General Shelby . . . invested the courthouse, held by four hundred State militia. **1944** CLARK *Pills* 184 It looked at one time like nothing short of the state militia would put down the 'blue-back' speller.

(10) **1830** *Montgomery Republican* (Johnstown, N.Y.) 1 Sep. 3/1 We recollect stating a few evenings since . . . that 'many would support Gen. Root for governor, with no other view than to put down the State Regency.' — (11) **1840** *Niles' Reg.* 25 April 128/1 In 1836, Governor Noble was elected to the state senate. **1950** *Dly. Ardmoreite* (Ardmore, Okla.) 14 Feb. 2/3 All county and district offices will be on the ballot with the exception of the state senate post held by Sen. Joe B. Thompson.

Also *state commission, game department, police, supreme court, textbook commission, troops,* etc.

b. In the names of organizations of a statewide scope: (1) **State Association,** an organization embracing the churches of a particular denomination within a state, also a meeting of representatives of such an organization; (2) **Bar Association,** an association composed of the lawyers admitted to practice in a particular state; (3) **Historical Society,** a society whose members are especially interested in state history; (4) **Teachers' Association,** an association of schoolteachers in a particular state.

(1) **1835** REED & MATHESON *Visit* II. 91 The State Association is the same species of meeting. **1853** BLAKE *Mendon Association* p. iii, The fact was informally communicated to some of the members, at a meeting of the State Association at Wrentham, in June. — (2) **1882** *Nation* 5 Oct. 281/1 The account given by Mr. Rogers, the President of the State Bar Association, . . . is far from encouraging. **1946** *Reader's Digest* May 87/2 A bill came into the executive office requiring all attorneys to join the State Bar Association. — (3) **1848** COOPER *Oak Openings* II. 214 A renowned annalist, whose information is sustained by the collected wisdom of a State Historical Society, does tell us that the enemy possessed both shores of Lake Erie in 1814. **1950** *Jrnl. Ill. State Hist. Soc.* Spring 78 Death claimed another member of the Illinois State Historical Society. — (4) **1868** *Ore. State Jrnl.* 1 Aug. 2/3 The Oregon State Teachers' Association met to hold its eighth annual session. **1900** *Cong. Rec.* 4 Jan. 663/1 He also presented a petition of the State Teachers' Association of Missouri, praying for the establishment in the Indian Territory of free public schools.

c. State Department, a federal department whose head is the Secretary of State and whose chief function is the conduct of the country's foreign affairs. Cf. **Department of State.**

1790 *Ann. 1st Congress* 1505 The resolution laid on the table yesterday, respecting the State Department, was taken up. **1846** POLK *Diary* (1929) 119, I had a full conversation with him [*sc.* Buchanan] on the subject of his transfer from the State Department to the Supreme Court bench. **1950** *Time* 27 March 22/2 They believed that the State Department and the Congress could do better than that.

6. Designating institutions maintained by a state as: (1) **state asylum,** (2) **college,** (3) **experimental farm** (or **station**), (4) **farm,** (5) **hospital,** (6) **library,** (7) **normal (school),** (8) **penitentiary,** (9) **reform school,** (10) **-'s prison,** [*OED* has Br. ev. 1732 for *state prison* but lists *state's prison* as U.S.], (11) **teachers' college,** (or **institute**), (12) **university.**

(1) **1840** *Niles' Reg.* 1 Aug. 342/3 A commission to inquire into . . . the practicability of a state asylum. **1873** *Mich. Gen. Statutes* (1882–3) 528 [He] shall be confined in a state or county asylum. — (2) **1831** PECK *Guide* 256 One sixth part is to be . . . bestowed on a state college or university. **1945** WEBSTER *Town Meeting Country* 239 Going to grammar and high school and then for a year at the state college. — (3) **1876** *Harper's Mag.* Dec. 155/1 The fertilizer control system introduced in Connecticut by the State Experimental Station is working very satisfactorily. **1945** *N. Eng. Homestead* 22 Sep. 16/3 It is being used . . . at the State Experimental Farm. — (4) **1862** *Rep. Comm. Patents 1861: Agric.* 271 In the experiment of the State farm of Massachusetts, the cost of the manure was forty dollars per acre.

(5) **1791** *Phila. Ordinances* (1812) 83 An act to provide for completing the repairs of the Wharf near the State Hospital. **1865** CUMMING *Hospital Life* (1866) 184/2, I never approved of state hospitals, situated as we were. **1949** *L.A. Times* 18 June II. 5/1 Sentence was suspended and he was sent to the State hospital for 'treatment.' — (6) **1833** *Niles' Reg.* XLIV. 114/2 The second story [will] . . . furnish a capacious room for the state library. **1912** NICHOLSON *Hoosier Chron.* 497 He dug diligently in the State Library preparing his case. [**1947** MYERS *The 'Guv'* 86 He went to the state law library in the state house.] — (7) **1891** O'BEIRNE *Leaders Ind. Terr.* 72/2 He went to the state normal, where he graduated at nineteen. **1902** TOMPKINS *Hist. Rec. Rockland Co., N.Y.* 314 Mr. Abram DeBaun, a graduate of the State Normal School, succeeded Mr. Loomis and taught nearly four years. — (8) **1809** CUMING *Western Tour* 170 The publick buildings here [in Frankfort, Ky.], are a state-house, . . . the state penitentiary, and a government house. **1927** J. DOWD *Negro in Amer. Life* 143 There are state penitentiaries, consisting of one large building where men are confined who have committed serious crimes. — (9) **1863** in ADAMS *Pioneer Hist.* (1923) 426 There are at or in the vicinity of Lansing the 'State Reform School,' the 'Michigan Female College' [etc.].

(10) **1827** PICKERING *Inquiries Emigrant* (1831) 92 The inhabitants are chiefly Americans. A 'darned tarnation' pretty sample of them here 'I swear,' some 'I guess,' from the 'State's prison.' **1903** A. T. HADLEY *Freedom & Responsibility* 161 The forger who has managed to escape state's prison by a technicality. — (11) **1868** *Ore. State Jrnl.* 27 June 2/2 It will be gratifying to the friends of education generally, and especially to those who may wish to attend the session of the State Teachers' Institute. **1941** *U. of Ill. Ann. Reg.* 74 Credits may be accepted for advanced standing . . . from a state teachers college. **1950** *Time* 24 April 75/1 Tomorrow's teachers preparing at Cortland State Teachers College, Cortland, New York, will occupy three Georgian style buildings now being constructed. — (12) **1831** [see **state college**]. **1946** THOMPSON *Amer. Daughter* 147 The money Gwyn earned was to help pay her tuition to the state university in September.

As the last term in **abolition, Apache, Atlantic, Baby, back, Badger, banner, Basin, Battle-born, Bay, Bayou, Bear, Beehive, black, Blizzard, Bonanza, border, Border Ruffian, Buckeye, Bullion, carpetbag, Centennial, Central, Chinook, coast, commercial, Confederate, Constitution, Corncracker, Cornhusker, cotton, Cracker, Cranberry, credit, Creole, Diamond, doubtful, down, dry, eastern, Empire, Eureka, Everglade, Evergreen, Flickertail, free, Freestone, Future, Garden, Gem, Golden, Goober, Gopher, grain, Granite, Grasshopper, Green Mountain, gulf, Hawkeye, home, homestead, Hoosier, Hotspur, Iron, Island, Jayhawker, Key, Keystone, Lake, log cabin, Lone Star, maple sugar, middle, Mississippi, Mormon, Mosquito, Mudcat, Negro, New England, North Star, northern, northwestern, Nutmeg, October, old, Old Bay, Old Granite, Old Line, Old Mother, Old North, Old South, original, out, Pacific, Palmetto, Panhandle, Pelican, Peninsula, Pickerel, Pine Tree, pivotal, plantation, planting, prairie, prohibition, provision, public-land, range, Rattlesnake, rawhide, rebel, reconstructed, Republican, repudiated, Rip Van Winkle, Sagebrush, seaboard slave, seceded, seceding, secesh, Secretary of, shore, Sierra, silver, sister, sisterhood of, six, slave, slaveholding, slave-owning, slave-raising, Sooner, southern, southern Atlantic, southwestern, sovereign, squatter, staple, Stubtoe, Sucker, sugar, Sunflower, Swinge-cat, tariff, thirteen, thirteen original, thirteen united, tobacco, turpentine, Twin, United, up, valley, Volunteer, Webfoot, western, wildcat, Wolverine, Wooden Nutmeg, Yankee, York state(s)** or **State(s).**

***state,** *v.*

1. *tr.* To allot (land) *to* an individual or group. *Obs.*

1661 *Topsfield Rec.* 6 The aforsaid fiuehundred acres of land is stated to the inhabitants of the Town . . . to share in the said common. **1699** *Springfield Rec.* II. 78 The said land was first stated to the ministry In Springfield.

2. To establish (a road or way) by authority. *Obs.*

1674 *Conn. Rec.* II. 223 The Court . . . haue now seen cause to state the road thorow Nath: Hayden's quarter. **1692** *Ib.* IV. 68 There may be a roade stated between Conecticut Riuer and the upland. **1705** *Dedham Rec.* V. 340 We have layed out and stated a way from the East street up the Hill towards the house of James Fales four rods wide. **1724** *Cambridge Prop. Rec.* 281 Said Select Men have Nominated & appointed John Stedman and Solomon Prentice . . . to State passages thrû the Same.

***stated,** *a.* In combs.: (1) **stated clerk,** (see quot. 1909); (2) **preaching,** preaching at fixed or set times, *obs.;* (3) **supply,** (see quot. 1861), *obs.*

(1) **1831** PECK *Guide* 259 The Rev. John M. Ellis, of Jacksonville, . . . was stated clerk when the three Presbyteries were in one. **1909** WEBSTER 2035/2 *Stated clerk,* in the Presbyterian churches of the United States, the secretary of a court. — (2) **1861** *Vanity Fair* 30 March 148/1 Twenty or thirty Sioux Indians . . . stated that they had adopted a number of customs in vogue among the whites, such as wearing pantaloons, . . . regular attendance upon, 'stated preaching,' &c. **1863** *Harper's Mag.* May 858/1 A clergyman . . . heard that a portion of the country was without 'the stated preaching of the Gospel.' — (3) **1860** *Harper's Mag.* July 194/1 The New School Meeting . . . 'sot under' Mr. Reuben Kenworthy, Stated Supply. . . . Stated Supplies are at liberty to go away whenever they get tired. **1861** *Contrib. Eccles. Hist. Conn.* 221 Stated supplies . . . [are] men employed to perform the duties of a pastor, but not inducted, in any appropriate way into the pastoral office.

statehood ˈstetˌhʊd, *n.* The condition or status of a state. Also attrib.

1868 *N.Y. Times* 8 June, Why indeed should the Federal Senate . . . be organized on the basis of an extinct statehood? **1893** *Dly. Ardmoreite* (Ardmore, Okla.) 20 Nov. 1/1 A Statehood convention will be held at Kingfisher, O.T., on the 28th of this month. **1950** *L.A. Times Midwinter* No. 3, Jan. 7/1 It was on Oct. 18, 1850, that news of Statehood reached San Francisco.

Statehouse ˈstetˌhaʊs, *n.* [See note.]

In 1902, when the discussion of this term by Albert Matthews appeared in *D.N.* II. 199–224, the *OED* treatment of the word had not appeared. Matthews concluded that Statehouse was "invented" in this country and without any assistance from German or Dutch. The *OED* shows that the combination was in existence as early as 1593, but in its Amer. use the term appears to be a new formation rather than an extension in meaning of the earlier Br. term.

1. The capitol of a colony or state.

1638 *Cal. State P., Colonial Ser. 1574–1660* 268 A levy has been raised . . . for the repair of the Fort at Point Comfort and building a state house at James City [Va.]. **1666** *Md. Archives* II. 28 The Upper House do not think fit to repeal the act for building a State House. **1796** MORSE *Univ. Geog.* I. 620 A large state-house or capitol, has lately been erected on the hill [at Richmond, Va.]. **1893** *Harper's Mag.* May 972/2 Disputes between the rival [parties] . . . threatened to culminate in a riot at the State-house in Topeka. **1949** *Chi. D. News* 6 July 14/6 It was thought around the statehouse that this would bring Kennelly's support.

2. An Indian council house. *Obs.*

1654 JOHNSON *Wonder-w. Prov.* 109 A State-house . . . covered round about, and on the top with Mats. **1666** *S.C. Hist. Soc. Coll.* V. 66 Before the Doore of their Statehouse is a spacious walke. **1751** GIST *Journals* 44 A Kind of State-House of about 90 Feet long, . . . in which they hold their Councils.

stateite ˈstetaɪt, *n.* One favoring statehood for a particular region, in the quots. with ref. to New Mexico. *Obs.* — **1871** *Republican Rev.* 25 Feb. 1/1 The Stateites imagine they have it all their own way about now. **1872** *Borderer* (Las Cruces, N.M.) 8 May 2/4 The stateites under the lead of Diego Archuelta, have held a meeting in Rio Ariba county.

Staten Island. [An island in N.Y. Bay.] *attrib.* **Staten Island herring, lamb,** (see quots.). *Obs.* — **1814** MITCHILL *Fishes N.Y.* 450 Staten-Island Herring. *Clupea mediocris.* Grows very large for a herring, being frequently eighteen inches long, and almost as big as small shad. **1867** DE VOE *Market Ass't* 76 Small old sheep, very poor and thin in flesh, are often dressed up 'lamb fashion' by irresponsible butchers and others, who sell it under the name of lamb, and many years ago such was known as 'Staten Island Lamb.'

***stater,** *n.* As the last term in **Bay, down, Lone Star, southern, up-stater.**

State rights. Also **States' rights.**

1. The body of political rights held to reside in the individual states; the principle of reserving to the states as much power as is possible under the Constitution.

1798 *Ann. 5th Congress* 2022 The powers of our general Government are checked by State rights. **1811** CLAY *Speeches* (1842) 31 Let me inquire what they would have had those to do, who believed the establishment of a bank an encroachment upon state rights? **1949** *Newsweek* 26 Dec. 20/1 The last term, a recent Gallup survey indicated, is more widely thought to mean 'states' rights.'

Hence **State-Righters, States' Righters.**

1948 *Salt Lake Tribune* 29 June 5/3 (*heading*), State-Righters Plan Caucus. **1950** *So. Wkly.* 15 March 5/2 Over in Alabama the Trumanites are making a fight to recapture the State Committee, now controlled by States' Righters.

2. *attrib.* Of or pertaining to factions in political parties.

1839 CALHOUN *Works* III. 391 [Hamilton] is the perfect type and impersonation of the national or Federal school . . . as Jefferson is of the State Rights Republican school. **1843** in HAMBLETON *H. A. Wise* 40 He stated . . . that John Tyler was nominated at Harrisburg, because of his States Rights Republican Whig principles, and that there was . . . a union of National Republicans and States Rights Whigs. **1949** *Fla. Hist. Quart.* Oct. 134 Whigs who were willing to let the defaulted banks go and believed that the 'faith bonds' were unlawful called themselves 'States-right Whigs.'

b. State rights Democrat, a Democrat in the South particularly zealous in his support of the doctrine of State rights.

1858 in BARTLETT 290 There are two parties in the South, called 'National' and 'States-Rights' Democrats. **1884** *Chi. Tribune* 15 March 7/3 Col. Phocion Howard . . . said he was . . . a State-rights Bourbon Democrat from away back. **1948** *Owensboro* (Ky.) *Inquirer* 22 Oct. 3/4 The Texan didn't mention Truman's civil rights program nor the States' Rights Democrats.

c. State rights party, the dominant faction in the Democratic party in the South just before and during the Civil War. *Obs.*

1840 *Louisville Pub. Adv.* 4 July 2/3 Men of the two . . . parties, State Rights and Union, have united for the avowed purpose of carrying out the good old principles of Jefferson and Madison. **1860** *Charleston* (S.C.) *Mercury* 13 Dec. 3/3 The *Picayune* . . . has heretofore been opposed to the State Rights party. **1862** in LOGAN *Great Conspiracy* 409 The leaders [in the South] . . . comprehend what was previously known as the State Rights Party.

Also *State rights banner, feeling, flag, man, member, plank, platform, politics, principle, theory, training,* etc. Chiefly *obs.*

***stateroom,** *n.*

1. A small room on a passenger boat providing sleeping accommodations for one or more passengers.

This use of a term earlier applied to a captain's or superior officer's room on a ship is labeled U.S. in the *OED*, but the first quot. below refers to a Jamaica packet at Burntisland on the Firth of Forth.

1774–5 JANET SCHAW *Jrnl. Lady of Quality* (1923) 22 Our Bed chamber which is dignified with the title of State Room, is about five foot wide and six long. *c***1828** PICKERING *Inquiries* 8 And being the only passenger on board . . . had the privilege of a small apartment to myself, dignified with the name of 'stateroom.' **1836** THORPE *Life* *on Lakes* I. 65 My state room is, in shape, size, and opportunity of ventilation, very like a baker's oven. **1879** HOWELLS *Lady of Aroostook* 20 At either end were four or five narrow doors, which gave into as many tiny state-rooms. **1948** *Chi. D. News* 17 Nov. 2/2 The two big men struggled out of the stateroom, down the passageway, onto the bow.

2. A drawing room or individual apartment on a train. Also attrib.

1853 *So. Standard* (Charleston, S.C.) 31 Aug. 2/5 Messrs. Eaton & Gilbert . . . have built a beautiful car for the Hudson River Railroad which is divided into state rooms of eight feet square. **1904** *N.Y. Times* 14 May 10 The train was made up of a dining car, a stateroom car, and five sleepers. **1949** *Sat. Ev. Post* 21 May 132/3 After he has his passengers tucked away . . . Joseph polishes the several pairs of shoes he finds left in the stateroom shoe boxes.

state's evidence.

1. One who, to lessen his own punishment, turns informer on his associates in crime.

1827 *Spirit of Seventy-Six* (Frankfort, Ky.) 1 Nov. 3/1 Having failed in making a tool of Mr. Buchanan, he thinks it necessary to find a *states evidence* somewhere. **1842** COOPER *Wing-and-Wing* II. 61 Still he gagged a little at the idea of passing for one who peached—or for a 'State's-evidence' as he called it; that character involving more of sin, in vulgar eyes, than the commission of a thousand legal crimes. **1898** CANFIELD *Maid of Frontier* 73 Stealing a hand down now and then to feel the Winchester hugged close under his knee, State's Evidence sped along.

b. The evidence in behalf of the state given by such an informer.

1890 LANGFORD *Vigilante Days* (1912) 300 Long John was admitted to testify under the rule of law regulating the reception of State's evidence. **1905** *Forum* April 532 The public accepted the articles as state's evidence, provided from motives of revenge or penitence.

2. *To turn state's evidence*, to become state's evidence, to give evidence in behalf of the state to obtain leniency.

1796 A. BARTON *Disappointment* 86 Ye turn'd eenformer, and states-evedence, to get the ane half till yere sel. **1806** FESSENDEN *Democracy Unveiled* II. 105 Lyon, . . . by turning States' evidence, has brought out his friend Duane. **1903** *N.Y. Tribune* 20 Sep., He was turning State's evidence and saving himself from punishment. **1949** *Sat. Ev. Post* 5 March 113/3 He helped convict Ford by turning state's evidence.

stateship ˈstetʃɪp, *n.* =**statehood.** *Rare.* — **1884** *Milnor* (Dak.) *Teller* 21 Nov., One of these principles is the right of stateship.

* **static,** *n.* Atmospheric disturbances causing interference with radio reception, also the interference so produced.

1913 *Wireless World* I. 508/1 Communication will also be had with New Orleans, which the static formerly prevented. **1925** *Sat. Ev. Post* 'That's not such a bad jazz piece,' I says, kidding. 'That's static,' explains Trist. **1947** *Chi. Tribune* 21 Aug. 29 Gas low—radio is drowned by static and I'm lost from dodging storm centers.

* **station,** *n.*

1. A pioneer's residence, a plantation. *Obs.*

1677 HUBBARD *Narrative* II. 58 [At] Mount Desart, . . . his Peteroon used to keep his Winter Station. **1780** in *Travels Amer. Col.* 641 Three men were kild and scalped at Leva Todds Station the 27th. **1788** *Mass. Spy* 31 July 3/2 Col. James Robertson's son . . . was killed . . . within a few hundred yards of his father's station.

b. A settlement of one family or several families, fortified against the attack of Indians or other enemies, esp. in Kentucky. *Obs.* or *hist.*

1790 ASBURY *Journal* II. 82 We rode down to Blackmore's station. **1831** AUDUBON *Ornith. Biog.* I. 291 These emigrants [to Ky.] . . . [had] hundreds of miles to be traversed, before they could reach certain places of rendezvous called *stations.* **1833** J. HALL *Harpe's Head* 132 Every here and there a *station*—a rude block-house surrounded with palisades—afforded shelter to the traveller, and refuge, in time of danger, to all within its reach. **1948** DICK *Dixie Frontier* 38 Settlement was made in stockaded communities, which were known as forts in the northern area and east of the mountains, but usually were called stations in the Old Southwest.

2. A single church of the Methodist-Episcopal denomination. Also attrib.

1844 RUPP *Relig. Denominations* 448 A leaders' meeting is composed of class leaders in any one circuit or station, in which the preacher presides. **1910** *Census: Religious Bodies 1906* II. 432/2 The local church . . . may be a single station, or may include two or more congregations.

b. =**mission station.**

1844 LEE & FROST *Oregon* 186 These pages relate to the work at the station, chiefly among the Indians of the Caclasco Village near it. **1883** WILDER *Sister Ridnour* 229 The converts . . . have been for many weeks at the station.

3. A shop or stand. *Rare.*

1855 *Harper's Mag.* X. 418/2 She stopped before a 'station' where hominy grits, buckwheat, flour, etc., were sold.

4. A stopping-place on a stage route. Also with defining term. Now *hist.*

1858 *N.Y. Herald* 2 Oct., As the road to the next station, though only 13 miles, was nearly all up hill, we were one hour and forty-five minutes in realizing it. **1890** LANGFORD *Vigilante Days* (1912) 252 This was the supper station. **1948** *Westerners' Brand Book* 21 The following is the list of stations on the Butterfield Overland mail route from Fort Yuma to San Francisco.

attrib. **1872** MARK TWAIN *Roughing It* 40 The station buildings were long, low huts, made of sun-dried, mud-colored bricks. *Ib.* 45 The station boss stopped dead still.

5. A temporary stopping-place on the underground railway. Now *hist.*

1861 TALLACK *Friendly Sk.* 227 These will either drive him on by night, some six or ten miles, to the next 'station,'—that is, the house of some other person of similar freedom of sentiment. **1907** *St. Nicholas* May 619/2 He went there in order to establish a station on the Underground Railroad;—that is, in order to receive under his protection slaves who had succeeded in escaping from their Southern masters.

6. (See quots.)

1877 W. WRIGHT *Big Bonanza* 307 A 'station' is the place of landing at each level of the mine. *Ib.* 443 The engineers, station-tender, pumpmen, and the watchmen on the lower levels, all occupy positions to which are attached grave responsibilities. **1896** SHINN *Story of Mine* 223 A station is the office for the work done on that mining level, as well as the point where men stop and where freight is shipped or received.

7. =**filling station.**

1945 *Farmington* (N.M.) *T. Hustler* 16 Feb. 2/5 He operated the station the past two years.

8. In special combs.: (1) **station agent,** one who has charge of a railroad station or a station on a stagecoach line; (2) **camp,** a temporary camp erected by hunters or explorers; (3) * **house,** *W.* a stopping-place for stagecoaches; (4) **keeper,** (*a*) one who maintained a place of refuge for slaves fleeing along the underground railway, (*b*) one in charge of a station on the Oregon Trail; (5) **master,** (*a*) a railroad station agent, (*b*) =**station keeper** (*a*); (6) **tree,** (see quots.); (7) **wagon,** an automobile having an inclosed wooden body and seats for nine or ten passengers.

(1) **1855** *Ill. Agric. Soc. Trans.* II. 25 Your letter . . . suggests the active co-operation of this [railroad] company, through its station agents. **1890** *Railways of Amer.* 411 The term 'station-agent' means, practically, the person in charge of a small or medium-sized station. **1948** *Westerners' Brand Book* 21 Louis J. F. Jaeger . . . was the Butterfield station agent at Fort Yuma. — (2) **1820** DEWEES *Lett. from Texas* 17 Gabriel Martin, and five others with myself, left the station camp one morning. **1853** RAMSEY *Tennessee* 106 The party . . . formed a station camp upon a creek. — (3) **1862** E. KIRKE *Among Pines* 227 A large hotel, or station-house, and about a dozen log shanties made up the village. **1912** DAWSON *Pioneer Tales* 111 We were enabled to witness much of this fight from the station-houses. — (4) (*a*) **1898** SIEBERT *Underground Railroad* 115 The coöperation of some zealous station-keeper in the neighboring slave territory seems to account partly for the multitude of stations. **1941** BUCKMASTER *Let My People Go* 75 Many a hungry and desperate fugitive wandered for weeks within the orbits of white station keepers. (*b*) **1949** WEST *Rocky Mt. Cities* 109 The potentialities of the grass plains . . . had been noted for several decades by travelers and station-keepers along the Oregon Trail.

(5) (*a*) **1856** *N.Y. Herald* 12 Jan. 1/4 When any train is irregular, or behind time, . . . the station master must see that the fact is reported to the conductor of the following train. **1949** *N.O. Times-Picayune* Mag. 6 Nov. 21/2 The stationmaster needs to be familiar with—among other things—12 classifications . . . and six postwar tariff adjustments. (*b*) **1872** STILL *Underground Railroad* opp. 691 (*caption*), Station masters on the Underground Railroad. **1941** BUCKMASTER *Let My People Go* 59 The mystification was enhanced logically by the good humor of the operators who forthwith called themselves 'conductor,' 'stationmasters,' 'brakemen,' and 'firemen,' called their houses 'depots' and 'stations,' talked of 'catching the next train.' — (6) **1817** *Niles' Reg.* XII. 99/1 The deputy surveyors are required to note particularly . . . all corner or bearing trees, and all those trees which fall in the lines, called station, or line trees. **1852**

FLEISCHMANN *Wegweiser* 132 Weiterhin notirt der Landmesser die Entfernung jedes Baumes, der unmittelbar auf der Linie steht, und dessen Ort. Man nennt diese Bäume 'Stations-Bäume' (*Station trees*) und bezeichnet sie durch zwei Einschnitte auf jeder Seite. — (7) **1904** *Scientific Amer.* 30 Jan. 99/1 Manufacturers of Electric Broughams, Landaus, . . . Victorias, Station Wagons, Surreys, Tonneaus, Stanhopes. **1950** *Reader's Digest* Jan. 131/2 So in the fall of 1936 four faculty members climbed into a heavily loaded station wagon.

As the last term in **baggage, breakfast, chipping, coach, comfort, dinner, eating, elevated, engine, experiment, feed, feeding, filling, fishing, flag, forest, gas, home, ice, life, life-saving, local, log, mail, meal, migration, mission, Missionary, Mormon, pay, relay, signal, stage, state experimental, swing, tank, telegraph, union, water, watering, way, whaling, wood, wood-and-water, wooding station.**

stave stev, *n. local.* [f. Du. *staaf,* in same sense.] A pig of lead weighing perhaps a hundred pounds or more. *Obs.* — **1683** *Doc. Hist. N.Y. State* III. 512 [R. Livingston agreed] to pay . . . Six Guns, fifty pounds of Powder, Fifty staves of Lead [etc.].

stave bucker. A contrivance provided with fixed slightly curved parallel blades or knives between which stave bolts are forced to reduce them to a uniform size. — **1897** E. W. BRODHEAD *Bound in Shallows* 183 The mill-stacks were misted in vaporous white, stave-buckers were beating away at piles of rugged oak.

* **staving,** *a.* and *adv.* Big, immense, excessively. *Colloq.*

1862 *N.Y. Tribune* 7 Feb. 5/6 A staving dram put him in a better humor. **1898** F. H. SMITH *C. West* 194 They was stavin' good to her. **1902** HARBEN *A. Daniel* 91 He got blind, stavin' drunk.

stavy ˈstevɪ, *a.* Tasting of the staves of a cask. *Rare.* — **1888** *Voice* 23 Feb., Stavy or woody butter from tubs made of green wood.

* **stay,** *v.*

1. *Poker. intr.* To remain in a hand by meeting a bet, ante, or raise.

1861 *Honolulu Comm. Advt.* 10 Aug. 2/6, I said two bits, whereupon he said, 'I will see you if I don't stay but a *minnit.*' **1946** MOREHEAD & MOTT-SMITH *Penguin Hoyle* 130 If the second player does raise three chips, and all the other players drop, the player who opened may stay in by putting three more chips in the pot. **1949** *Fur Trade Rev.* 7 April 7/1, I opened the pot and one other man stayed.

2. In colloq. phrases: (1) * *To stay with,* (*a*) to marry, (*b*) to stick with or keep at (something), (*c*) of food, to give lasting satisfaction; (2) *to stay put,* to stay in place, to remain where one is; (3) *to come to stay,* to become permanent, to secure an established position; (4) * *to stay by,* to stand by or stick with.

(1) (*a*) **1833** A. GREENE *Life D. Duckworth* I. 35 He did not hesitate to pop the question, . . . whether she would 'stay with him.' (*b*) **1887** F. FRANCIS *Saddle & Moccasin* 177 But they couldn't bluff the old man off; he stayed with them. **1907** LONDON *Road* 167 He could not run so fast as I, but he stayed with it. (*c*) **1891** FISKE *Holiday Stories* 128 Stew's good, but they don't stay wid yer. Kin I have somethink solid? — (2) *a***1848** *N.O. Picayune* (B.), The levees and wharves of the First Municipality won't 'stay put.' **1893** *Harper's Mag.* Feb. 349/2 There was some talk, also, of the advantages . . . accruing to those who 'stay put' in this world. **1950** *Chi. Tribune* 20 April III. 10/6 She had to stay put for eight consecutive Saturday nights for the program. — (3) **1863** LINCOLN in E. McPherson *Polit. Hist. U.S Rebell.* 336 I hope it [*sc.* peace] will come soon, and come to stay. **1904** *Hartford Courant* 24 June 10 The national convention came to stay in American politics seventy-two years ago. — (4) **1883** MARK TWAIN *Life on Miss.* xxx, I stayed faithfully by him until his comedy was finished.

* **staying,** *a.* and *n.* **1.** *n.* Lodging for a night. *Rare.* **2.** *a.* Remaining or lasting for some days. *Colloq.*

(1) **1847** *Knickerb.* XXIX. 534 Can we have a staying here tonight? — (2) **1832** TROLLOPE *Domestic Manners* II. 11 Above these rooms was a loft, . . . where I was told the 'staying company' who visited them, were lodged. **1889** *Cent. Mag.* April 840/2 Mrs. Herbert of Alexandria was often asked . . . to fetch a coach-load of her offspring for a 'staying-visit' to the Washingtons.

stay law. A law establishing a moratorium on the payment of judgments or foreclosures.

1822 *Niles' Reg.* 22 June XXII. 266/2 Judge Clark, of Kentucky, sometime since, gave an opinion that a certain act of the legislature of that state, in passing some stop law, stay law or relief law, was unconstitutional. **1868** *N.Y. Herald* 3 July 3/5 Mr. Ingersoll . . . characterized the proviso as a sort of stay law, or a confession that the government was not able to pay its debts. **1894** *Cong. Rec.* 24 Jan. 1349/1 Were it not for the stay law of Dakota, she would be . . . turned over to the manufacturers of Connecticut and Massachusetts under foreclosure of contract of mortgage.

* **steady,** *a.* and *n.*

1. A regular sweetheart. Also **steady beau.** *Slang.*

1900 ADE *More Fables* 179 Lutie then selected for her Steady a young man with Hair who played the 'Cello. **1922** STELLA BENSON *Poor Man* v, She had just mislaid her last steady beau, so she was at the moment a little susceptible. **1949** *Lincoln Co. News* (Oceanlake, Ore.) 4 Aug. 4/5 Girls of 15 in New York talk about their 'steadies,' and refer to other children of similar age as 'going steady.'

transf. **1905** *N.Y. Ev. Post* 22 July, Perk is no mere guide, picked up for the exigencies of a short trip; he is our real 'steady,' engaged for 12 weeks.

2. steady habits, staid and regular habits, esp. as attributed to the people of Connecticut and other parts of N. Eng. Cf. **Land of Steady Habits.**

1800 *Aurora* (Phila.) 23 Dec. (Th.), Steady Habits and Straight Waistcoats. **1806** *Intelligencer* (Lancaster, Pa.) 14 Jan. (Th.), A letter from a Gentleman in the State of Steady Habits to his friend in Newport, Rhode island. **1813** *Mass. Spy* 16 June (Th.), Troops were assembled, ready to repel any invasion of the soil of 'steady habits.' **1827** *Ib.* 4 April (Th.), [I cannot] banish from my mind the old steady habits of Massachusetts. **1864** *Harper's Mag.* March 450/1 It is . . . as vociferous in sounds of . . . industry as any place of its size in the good old State of steady habits.

* **steak,** *n.* **steak fry, roast,** a social occasion upon which people assemble to fry or roast steak and partake of it.

1931 *Durant* (Okla.) *D. Democrat* 3 June 4/5 [They] entertained with a steak fry. **1935** MITCHELL *America* 207 A less evanescent and cloying joy is a steak roast. Get some Americans to take you on one. **1945** *Chi. D. Tribune* 8 Jan. 15/7 We . . . enjoy sleigh rides, and in warmer weather steak fries and picnics.

As the last term in **bear, hamburger, moose, porterhouse, rolled, Salisbury, T-bone steak.**

* **steal,** *n.*

1. A corrupt transaction or deal, often of a political nature, highly remunerative to its perpetrators.

1872 *Dly. Gazette* (Little Rock, Ark.) 1 April, Of all the swindles and steals that have ever been proposed or carried out in our State, this is the largest and boldest. **1947** *So. Sierran* July 3/1 [The] lumbermen's proposed steal of 56,000 acres containing 2,500,000,000 feet of virgin timber has Park Service approval 'for greater ease in administration.'

2. *Baseball.* A safe advance by a base-runner from one base to another without the assistance of a hit, an error, a putout, a base on balls, or a penalty on the defensive team.

1867 *Chi. Times* 26 July 5/2 Norton made first base, but, on essaying Berthrong's steal, he was similarly ousted. **1949** *Oregonian* (Portland) 10 Aug. III. 4/1 Davis overthrew second in an attempt to nail Hale on a steal.

* **steal,** *v.*

1. *Baseball. tr.* Of a base-runner: To achieve a steal *q.v.* sense **2.** Also transf.

1857 *Spirit of Times* 7 Feb. 373/1 He . . . oftentimes steals a run home while the ball is passing from the pitcher to the catcher. **1904** MARK TWAIN *Bequest* 17 (R.), Then he stole a base—as he called it—that is, slipped from the presence, to keep from getting brayed in his wife's discussion-mill. **1949** *Fargo* (N.D.) *Forum* 23 July 8/8 He stole second and scored on Jack Johnson's single.

2. a. Of a ewe: To bring forth (lambs) out of season. **b.** *To steal one's thunder,* to appropriate for one's own use something effective that originated with another. *Colloq.*

(a) 1859 ALLEN *New Amer. Farm Bk.* (1883) 417 If young ewes have stolen lambs, they should be taken away from them immediately after yeaning. — **(b) 1931** *K.C. Times* 1 Aug., It is all right for the other fellow to steal our thunder if he will let our lightning alone. **1950** *Time* 15 May 85/2 Harry Truman is no man to let Congress steal his political thunder.

* **stealer,** *n.* As the last term in **bait, base, corn, Negro stealer.**

* **steam,** *n.* In combs.: (1) **steamboat,** see as a main entry; (2) **boater,** one who works on or about a steamboat, *colloq.;* (3) * **car,** a railway locomotive or a car or train drawn by this; (4) **doctor,** see as a main entry; (5) **doddler,** ?a steam pump, *obs.;* (6) **galley,** a steamboat, *obs.;* (7) **harmonicon,** =**calliope,** *obs.;* (8) * **horse,** a railway locomotive, *obs.,* cf. **iron horse;** (9) **mill,** a mill driven by steam as distinguished from a water mill; (10) **paddy,** an excavating machine operated by steam, so called in allusion to Irish pick and shovel laborers, cf. **steam shovel;** (11) **piano,** =**calliope;** (12) * **road,** a

railroad, also attrib.; (13) **sawyer,** a sawing machine or sawmill, *obs.;* (14) **ship king,** a person dominant in steam shipping, *rare;* (15) **shipping,** shipping carried on by means of steamships; (16) **shovel,** a self-propelled machine for excavating, cf. ***excavator, Orukter Amphibolos, rotatory steam shovel;** (17) **thresher,** a threshing machine operated by steam, also attrib.; (18) **washer,** a steam-driven washing machine, *obs.*

(2) **1907** C. D. STEWART *Partners* 331, I made it up that I would tell him [the Captain] first about me being a steamboater. **1938** *Sat. Ev. Post* 15 Oct. 63/1 The relations of the shanty hunter or fisherman with that other great class of rivermen, the steamboaters, depend, like their other practices, upon the individual.—(3) **1833** *Amer. R.R. Jrnl.* II. 225/2 The [railroad] Steam Car accomplished the distance. **1903** Fox *Little Shepherd* v, 'Steam cars!' they cried.

(5) **1887** *Courier-Journal* (Louisville) 21 Jan. 8/7 The steam-doddler was kept busy all night pumping. — (6) **1825** in *Amer. Sp.* XXI. (1946) 306/2 In the centre of the picture is the James Kent, steam-galley.... At the extremity of the right of the picture, is a steam-galley. — (7) **1897** HOWELLS *Open-eyed Conspiracy* iv, I merely heard you above the steam harmonicon at the switchback. — (8) **1851** *Hunt's Merch. Mag.* XXV. 167 The Atlantic and Pacific shores are connected by bands of Iron and the Steam Horse. **1879** *Las Vegas* (N.M.) *Gaz.* 5 July 1/4 Tuesday at 1 o'clock, the steam horse careered along the flat opposite town. — (9) **1815** D. DRAKE *Cincinnati* iii. 137 The most capacious... building in this place is the Steam Mill. **1880** *Harper's Mag.* Aug. 344/2 The grist from it [*sc.* the tide mill] is said to be of a better quality than from the steam-mills, as being less heated in the process.

(10) **1851** *Ore. Statesman* 29 July 2/7 The 'steam Paddy,' too, is doing wonders among the sand hills down Happy Valley way. **1889** MUNROE *Golden Days* 304 He watched the steam excavators, or 'paddies,' tearing down and levelling the tall hills. — (11) **1895** *N.Y. Dramatic News* 5 Oct. 3/3 Two Johns, Phillips and McVicker,... brought up the rear like a steam piano. **1948** *Ariz. Republic* (Phoenix) 2 March 6/5 It is nothing like the old road Where the 'steam pianners' play. — (12) **1868** *Comm. & Fin. Chron.* VI. 832/3 We are always in a position to furnish all sizes... for both steam and horse roads. **1911** H. S. HARRISON *Queed* xv. 174 The cars are steam-road size. — (13) **1840** *N.O. Picayune* 6 Aug. 2/6 For sale... a first rate steam sawyer. — (14) **1867** *Harper's Wkly.* 23 March 179/1 The chief members of this pool were a well-known steamship king, a heavy curb-stone operator,... and a rich and daring financier.

(15) **1883** *Cent. Mag.* Sep. 693/2 Offices of railroad and mining companies, of steam and other shipping,... next center closest around the financial hub. **1901** *N. Amer. Rev.* Feb. 286 It is our steam shipping that has been aided. — (16) **1879** R. J. BURDETTE *Hawkeyes* 25 The depot policeman looked in to say to him that if he was tired out, he would send in a section hand or the steam shovel to give him a spell. **1949** *This Week Mag.* 7 May 20/1 Steam shovels bite into the square mile of diamond-bearing soil. — (17) **1865** *Atlantic Mo.* XV. 730/2 Thirty steam-threshers only were required. **1906** *N.Y. Ev. Post* 21 July (Supp.) 3 The steam thresher trusts have no hold on the conservative 'black' Amish settlements of Indiana. — (18) **1816** *Niles' Reg.* X. 336/2 It is stated in a New-York paper, that 'a *steam-washer*, an American patent invention, had been some time in use in that city. It was introduced a year or two since, and is said to answer its intended purpose extremely well.' **1830** *Juniata* (Pa.) *Gaz.* 22 July 3/5 The great facility and ease attending the operation of the Angular Revolving Steam Washer, have been for many ages objects devoutly wished for by the fair portion of creation. **1887** *Courier-Journal* 7 May 5/8, I Want Agents To Sell The Missouri Steam Washer.... It works on a new principle, which saves labor and clothing enormously.

b. In combs. of more obvious meaning: (1) **steam calliope,** (2) **cotton-press,** (3) **elevator,** (4) **ferry (boat),** (5) **frigate,** (6) **heated,** (7) **propeller,** (8) **radiator,** (9) **scow,** (10) **siphon,** (11) **towboat,** (12) **whistle.**

(1) **1868** *Terr. Enterprise* (Virginia, Nev.) 29 Aug. 3/1 Even a steam calliope would not cause our firm nerves to tremble as vigorously as this worst of all combinations of unsweet tones. **1950** *World-Herald Mag.* (Omaha) 2 April 20/3 There was a steam calliope and gaudy wagons for small animals. — (2) **1827** in COMMONS *Doc. Hist.* I. 287, I found myself in a steam cotton-press house, where they work... by candle-light, screwing cotton. **1864** NICHOLS *Amer. Life* I. 181 Next are seen... the tall chimneys of the numerous steam cotton-presses. — (3) **1873** *Harper's Mag.* Oct. 714/1 Once at the factory, a steam-elevator raises the hogsheads to the stemming-room, in the upper story. **1943** CROW *Amer. Customer* 197 Steam elevators were also unsatisfactory though a few were installed in buildings not more than four of five stories high. — (4) **1836** *Niles' Reg.* 1 Oct. 80/2 The steam-ferry boat... ran down the boat gen. Jackson in the harbor of New York. **1842** *McDonough P.* 65 The steam ferry which runs from one side of the river to the other lands a short distance below my house. **1946** FOREMAN *Last Trek* 116 A steam ferryboat was in service.

(5) **1814** *Niles' Reg.* 29 Oct. 128/2 The steam frigate Fulton the First was launched at New York October 31. **1886** *Harper's Mag.* June 18/1 The *Chicago* is a steam-frigate. — (6) **1884** *N.Y. Herald* 27 Oct. 2/2 Single Flats, in Excellent order; halls steam heated. **1907** *St. Nicholas* Oct. 1135/1 The European pelicans... in the cold weather of winter have to be placed in a steam-heated building. — (7) **1845** J. W. NORRIS *Chi. Directory* 108 Lake boats from New York to Oswego, and of Steam Propellers from Oswego to Chicago. **1874** *Rep. Comm. Agric. 1873* 147 Double-track railroads, canals vexed with steam-propellers,... and every other fancied boon obtained, she will still remain in comparative poverty. — (8) **1879** *Bradstreet's* 22 Nov. 2/1 In close rooms close stoves are better than steam radiators. **1950** *Amer. Mercury* March 327/2 The man with the hangover ... 'felt as if he had swallowed a steam radiator and some one had gone down to repair it.' — (9) **1854** *Oregonian* (Portland) 15 Feb. 2/2 Mr. Bridges, an engineer on the steam scow *Peyton*, met with a serious injury on Saturday. **1860** in *Amer. Sp.* XXII. 206/1 Accordingly, on the 27th of December he set out, and met it [our freight] on the way on board a petty steam-scow.

(10) **1868** *Rep. U.S. Comm. Agric.* (1869) 171 Wages were paid at the following rates:... For steam syphon: 1 man, at 28 cents. **1907** C. D. STEWART *Partners* 213 A steam siphon is a big steam pipe fixed so that it will blow across the mouth of another pipe that is stuck down in the water; it is like a perfume squirter that is called an atomizer, and when the boilers is turned loose it is like forty thousand Chinamen blowing water on a shirt. — (11) **1815** *Mass. Statute* 7 Feb., His patent steam tow-boats... said patent bearing date the 2 day of April 1814. **1857** DANA *Great West* 347 Vessels... are now for the most part taken up to New Orleans by steam tow-boats. — (12) **1836** *Nat. Intelligencer* 21 Dec. 1/5 It was a steam whistle, played to clear the track which a half mile ahead was occupied with several cows. **1856** EMERSON *Eng. Traits* xiv, The voice of their modern muse has a slight hint of the steam-whistle.

c. In less frequent, often obs., combs., as (1) **steam bakery,** (2) **barge,** (3) **bonnet manufacture,** (4) **flat,** (5) **gin,** (6) **hen,** (7) **loader,** (8) **lumber mill,** (9) **planing mill,** (10) **schooner,** (11) **skidder, skidding.**

(1) **1903** ADE *In Babel* 29 For ten years it had braced itself against the onsweeping rush of big machine-shops and steam-bakeries. — (2) **1901** MERWIN & WEBSTER *Calumet 'K'* 49 Can they have one or more steam barges at Monistogee? — (3) **1846** *Niles' Reg.* 25 April 128/3 Steam Bonnett Manufacture. The straw used in the manufacture of hats is the culms of several kinds of grain or grass. In this country wheat and rye culms are mostly used. — (4) **1837** LUNDY WILLSON *N.J. to Ohio & Return* (1929) 34 We came to Bridgeport. ... The ferry was a steam-flat by which means one goes over much sooner than at the other ferry which is called the rope ferry...; the cost was 25 cents.

(5) **1862** E. W. PEARSON *Lett. Port Royal* 117, I shall have... [the cotton] taken to Beaufort for the steam-gin. — (6) **1845** *Niles' Reg.* LXI. 32/3 The 'steam hen,' a hatching apparatus.... This operation of hatching fowls has been reduced to a science. — (7) **1905** *Forestry Bureau Bul.* No. 61, 49 steam loader. A machine operated by steam used for loading logs upon cars. — (8) **1866** *Rep. Indian Affairs* 92 A large and valuable steam lumber mill was erected on the reservation. — (9) **1877** MCCABE *Hist. Great Riots* 68 The burning premises... proved to be the extensive steam planing mills and lumber yard of J. Turner & Cate.

(10) **1940** RIESENBERG *Golden Gate* 213 When sails were abandoned altogether a small funnel was installed and they [i.e., California coastal trading vessels] were called steam schooners. — (11) **1901** *Munsey's Mag.* XXV. 393/1 The most important improvements in logging methods are the ice roads, steam skidding, and the logging railroad. **1907** BAILEY *Cyclo. Amer. Agric.* II. 337/1 The steam skidder... gathers these logs from a few thousand feet on either side of the track.

steamboat ˈstim,bot, *n.*

1. A boat of considerable size, esp. one for river traffic, propelled by steam.

1785 in T. WESTCOTT *Life John Fitch* 127, I have examined the Principles and construction of Mr. Fitche's Steamboat. **1786** in RUMSEY *Treat. Steam* (1788) Certif. No. 6. He was in the city of Philadelphia ... in the month of September last... when he had an opportunity of seeing what is called the Steam Boat, said to be constructed by Mr. Fitch. **1844** *Edinburgh Jrnl.* I. 230 Curious-looking machines, which the pilots called steamboats, were sailing about in every direction; they looked like factories that had broken loose, and taken to the water, with the beam of the steam-engine working up and down through the roof. *a***1918** G. STUART *On Frontier* II. 31 The gold was ... shipped down the river by steamboat. **1948** *Talladega* (Ala.) *D. Home* 29 May 3/5 Now, like the steamboats they once graced, the whistles and bells are gone.

attrib. **1789** HILTZHEIMER *Diary* (1893) 13 March 151 Mr. Fitch is to be heard on Tuesday on behalf of Rumsey with regard to the steamboat privileges passed in March of 1787.

b. *transf.* (See quot. 1859.) *Obs.*

1819 QUITMAN in Claiborne *Life Quitman* I. 42 Saw for the first time what are termed 'steam-boats,' 'snapping-turtles,' and 'half-horse half-alligators'—a formidable set of fellows, truly! **1835** HOFFMAN *Winter in West* I. 259 Come here, old fellow, and take your treat—you're a steamboat. **1859** BARTLETT 449 *Steamboat*, a term used at the West to denote a dashing, go-a-head character.

c. An exceptionally long, large wagon. In full **steamboat wagon.** *Obs.*

1841 BUCKINGHAM *America* II. 420 The vehicle which conveyed the family to church was called 'the Steam-boat,' from its great length, though drawn on four wheels and by a pair of horses. In it were seats for sixteen persons. **1889** *Harper's Mag.* Aug. 390/2 The mountaineers ... have come down to 'the settlemints' ... bringing in slow-moving ox-drawn 'steamboat' wagons.

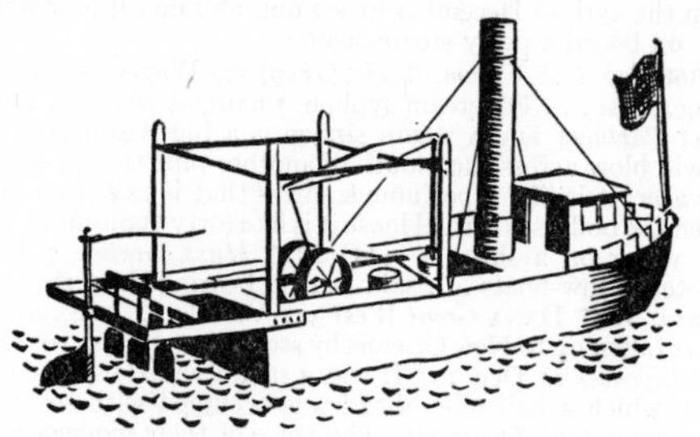

Steamboat of an early (*c*1786) type

2. In special combs.: (1) **steamboat agent,** = **steamboat runner,** *obs.;* (2) **basin,** (see quot. 1837), *obs.;* (3) **gun,** a gun on a steamboat fired to announce its approach to land, *obs.;* (4) **inspector,** one whose duty is to inspect the boilers of a steamboat, *obs.;* (5) **landing,** a place where a steamboat lands to discharge and take on freight, passengers, etc.; (6) **line,** a number of steamboats under one management operating over a particular route; (7) **mail,** mail carried by steamboats; (8) **runner,** a solicitor for a steamboat, *obs.;* (9) **train,** a train that connects with a steamboat, *obs.;* (10) **yard,** a place where steamboats are built or repaired.

(1) **1891** WELCH *Recoll. 1830–40* 155 There was a class of men in Buffalo of a race or type peculiar to themselves.... They were 'steamboat agents;' or, rather, as they finally assumed the title 'General Solicitors!'—(2) **1837** PECK *Gaz. Illinois* 56 A steamboat basin, or harbor, is to be constructed, ... near the termination of the canal. **1866** *Ore. State Jrnl.* 14 April 2/3 At Oregon City the most notable change is the new steamboat basin. — (3) **1845** SIMMS *Wigwam & Cabin* 1 Ser. 83 We had heard the steamboat gun the night before. — (4) **1838** *Niles' Reg.* 13 Oct. 112/2 The steamboat inspectors at Cincinnati ... have condemned the boilers of several boats.
(5) *c***1845** *Big Bear Ark.* 87 We took a lounge down to the steamboat landing. **1949** *No. Dak. Hist.* Jan. 12 There were five steamboat landings. — (6) **1938** ALBION *Square-Riggers* 18 In October 1816, moreover, advertisements announced the beginning of service by 'The Sound Steamboat Line,' with the steamers *Fulton* or *Connecticut* leaving New York five days a week for New Haven, while the *Connecticut* continued three days a week on to New London. — (7) **1827** *Spirit of Seventy-Six* (Frankfort, Ky.) 25 Jan. 1/2 Mr. C. L. Harrison offered a resolution ... to have a *steam boat mail* established between Louisville and New Orleans. — (8) **1847** ROBB *Squatter Life* 101 A steamboat runner came to their aid.... 'Passage up the Missouri, sir?' inquires the runner. **1891** WELCH *Recoll. 1830–40* 155 These men were also called 'steamboat runners.' — (9) **1843** *Hunt's Merch. Mag.* IX. 291 The conductors of the steamboat train, Messrs. Ham & Cook are courteous and attentive. **1897** HOWELLS *Open-eyed Conspiracy* vii, 'When in the world did you come?' 'This morning by the steamboat train.'
(10) **1827** DRAKE & MANSFIELD *Cincinnati* 66 Three Steam-boat Yards, 200 hands.

b. In combs. of obvious meaning or explained in the quots.: (1) **steamboat bug,** (2) **canal,** (3) **captain,** (4) **clerk,** (5) **coal,** (6) **cotillion party,** (7) **engineer,** (8) **law,** (9) **lock,** (10) **man,** (11) **navigation,** (12) **wood.**

(1) **1876** *Field & Forest* II. 4 Among these [fish] I placed a ... steamboat bug, *Belostoma grandis.* **1891** *Cent.* 5920/1 *Steamboat-bug,* ... a water-beetle of large size, or otherwise conspicuous. — (2) **1834** *Amer. R.R. Jrnl.* III. 321/3 She ought, and must, construct a sloop and steamboat canal. **1839** *Indiana H. Rep. Jrnl.* 290, I am directed by the Senate to inform the House of Representatives, that the Senate has passed an engrossed joint resolution No. 199 of the House, relative to a steamboat canal around the falls of Ohio. — (3) **1866** F. KIRKLAND *Bk. Anecdotes* 40/2 She and her husband, a Mississippi steamboat captain, occupied the middle front room. **1883** *Cent. Mag.* June 223/1 Here met the capitalist ... the steam-boat captain, the horse-fancier. — (4) **1849** PARKMAN in *Knickerb.* XXXIII. 4 In his former capacity of steamboat clerk he had learned to prefix the honorary Mister to every body's name.
(5) [**1880** *Bradstreet's* 2 Oct. 5/4 The sizes used are 'lump,' 'steamboat,' 'broken,' and 'pea.'] **1891** *Cent.* 5920/1 Steamboat-coal, coal broken small enough to pass between bars set from 6 to 8 inches apart, but too large to pass between bars less than 5 inches apart. — (6) **1821** HOWISON *Sketches* 325, I have forgot to mention an elegant summer amusement, called the 'Steam-boat cotillion parties.' One of the small steam-boats, that ply upon the East River, is occasionally engaged for an evening, to make an excursion round the islands opposite New York. — (7) **1840** *Knickerb.* XVI. 227 Come, gentlemen, 'fire up, fire up!' as the steam-boat engineer says. **1892** *York Co. Hist. Rev.* 59 He is a machinist by avocation, and an old steamboat engineer. — (8) **1843** *Niles' Reg.* 4 March 14/2 *Steamboat laws.* The bill to amend the act of 1838, for the preservation of the lives of passengers on vessels propelled by steam, was next taken up and after some discussion, passed. — (9) **1838** COLTON *Ind. Delineated* 44 Contracts ... have been made for the construction of a dam and steamboat lock. **1848** *Indiana Gen. Assoc. Doc.* II. 138 The gates of the steamboat lock ... have been rebuilt.
(10) **1846** SOL. SMITH *Theatr. Apprent.* 145 No person had a greater respect for steam-boat men than I had. **1945** FUGINA *Upper Miss.* 48 Steamboatmen sometimes referred to these logs as 'hull inspectors.' — (11) **1821** *Ann. 17th Cong.* 1 Sess. I. 44 The jurisdiction had only embraced steamboat navigation. **1883** *Harper's Mag.* June 80/2 The fact that it [St. Paul] is the head of steamboat navigation on the Mississippi ... is where its strength lies. — (12) **1833** *Sk. D. Crockett* 13 Was [the timber] corded up like steamboat wood? **1883** *Rep. Indian Affairs* 159 They have cut and sold during the past winter a considerable amount of pine timber and steamboat wood.

As the last term in **Mississippi (River), sidewheel steamboat.**

steamboat ˈstim͵bot, *v. tr.* To "take in," swindle. *Slang. Obs.* — **1866** *Ore. State Jrnl.* 8 Dec. 3/2 The poor ignorant people o [*sic*] the North were humbugged, bamboozled, steamboated.

steam doctor. (See quots. 1833, 1919, and cf. **Thomsonian, Thomsonianism.**) Now *hist.*

1830 *Cin. Chronicle* 6 Feb. 2/3 The Mayor was induced ... to issue his warrant for the apprehension of a black man calling himself Caesar Gimsoun, and practising in this city as a *steam doctor.* **1833** COKE *Sub. Furlough* I. 145 Steam doctors, as the Americans call them who ... put in practice the system from which they derive their name—hot-baths and cayenne pepper for every complaint, from a cold and sore throat to the yellow fever. **1919** DUNN *Indiana* II. 790 One of the early medical fads was known as Thomsonianism, 'steam doctors,' etc. This system was inaugurated by an ignorant but energetic charlatan,—'Dr.' Samuel Thomson, who was born in Olmstead, New Hampshire, Feb. 9, 1767. **1949** *N.O. Times-Picayune Mag.* 3 July 13/2 A New Englander ... had settled along the trace and hung out his shingle as a 'steam doctor.'

Hence **steam-doctoring.** *Obs.*

1872 E. EGGLESTON *End of World* xv. 104 Your ma is so took up with steam-doctorin' that she dont believe in nothin' but corn-sweats and such like.

***steam engine,** *n.* As the last term in **Columbian, musical steam engine.**

***steamer,** *n.* In combs.: (1) **steamer basket,** ?a medium-sized basket or hamper having a cover; (2) **corn,** ?corn shipped or brought in by steamboats, *obs.;* (3) **day,** see as a main entry; (4) **dock,** a dock for steam vessels, *obs.;* (5) **edition,** *Calif.* an edition of a newspaper published just after the arrival of a steamer with news and exchanges from the States, *obs.*, cf. **steamer issue;** (6) **fireman,** a stoker on a steamboat; (7) **issue,** *Calif.* an issue or edition of a newspaper esp. designed for sending back to the States and abroad, *obs.*, cf. **steamer edition, steamer paper;** (8) **night,** the night upon which a steamer reaches a particular place; (9) **paper,** an edition of a newspaper immediately before the departure of a mail steamer on which it is sent to distant points, *obs.*, cf. **steamer issue;** (10) **rug,** a warm, blanket-like robe, usu. in various colors and plaid design, used as a covering or lap robe; (11) **trunk,** a small trunk suitable for use in a stateroom on a steamer.

(1) **1909** O. HENRY *Roads of Destiny* 132 They can reach out and pick steamer baskets of the choicest fruit without gettin' out of bed. — (2) **1886** *Harper's Mag.* July 43/1 Successive calls are for . . . No. 2 corn, steamer corn, or No. 2 red winter wheat. — (4) **1870** LOGAN *Before Footlights* 327 On the morning of her arrival from Europe, the Hamburg steamer dock at Hoboken was crowded with an eager throng.

(5) **1850** *Alta California* (S.F.) 29 June 2/3 Our Steamer Edition . . . is now ready for delivery. — (6) **1866** MARK TWAIN *Lett. Sandwich Islands* 15 Steamer firemen do not live, on an average, over 5 years. — (7) **1851** *S.F. Picayune* 14 Oct. 2/4 In our last steamer issue we gave an account of the method of coyote digging. — (8) **1863** E. KIRKE *So. Friends* 234 It was again 'steamer night.' **1889** HARTE *Waif of Plains* vii, It was dark, but, being 'steamer night,' the shops and business places were still open. — (9) **1850** *Calif. Courier* (S.F.) 28 Nov. 2/1 The Steamer Paper.—Our regular issue for circulation through the United States and Europe by the steamship Republic, which sails on Friday the 29th inst., will be ready to-morrow morning, at 10 o'clock. **1851** *S.F. Picayune* 23 Oct. 2/2 We hope our cotemporaries will reserve the article in question for their steamer papers, *as we certainly shall;* it will create, we doubt not, a very favorable impression of California newspapers in the Atlantic States. [**1858** *S.F. Dly. Ev. Bul.* 6 Nov., The Steamer Bulletin double sheet of 8 pages, is published the day before the departure of the mail Steamer, and contains such selections of editorials and other matter from the Daily as may be interesting to parties in the Atlantic States.]

(10) **1890** SUSAN HALE *Letters* 253 It is . . . so cold, . . . that we are sitting close up to the grates . . . and all wound about with the heaviest steamer rug! **1946** HOWE *We Happy Few* 34 Dorothea spread a large woolen steamer rug on the warm pine needles. — (11) **1891** *Scribner's Mag.* X. 513 A number of agile cabin-stewards . . . were bringing aboard an endless variety of steamer-trunks. **1949** *Sat. Ev. Post* 18 June 31/2 She'd take . . . her steamer trunk, if it wouldn't be asking too much of the McAllisters.

As the last term in **banana, day, ferry, fruit, lake, mail, Mississippi, package, packet, palace, side paddle, sternwheel, tank steamer.**

steamer day. *W.* (See quots. 1856, 1910.)

1851 *S.F. Herald* 16 Aug. 2/2 Steamer day in San Francisco is a marked feature of the calendar—it is an era—something to look forward to and date from. **1856** *S.F. Bulletin* 27 Oct. 3/3, I would call your attention to the fact that the approaching day of election occurs on 'steamer day,' or the day before the sailing of the next mail steamer, a day on which our merchants, bankers, business men, and those in their employ will naturally have many duties to perform in preparing for the departure of the mail. **1910** HART *Vigilante Girl* 104 All bills had to be settled on 'Steamer Day' when the bi-monthly steamers sailed for the States.

transf. **1877** WM. WRIGHT *Big Bonanza* 445 Monday in Virginia City is sometimes jocularly termed 'steamer day,' as corresponding to the old 'steamer day' of San Francisco—the day when the steamer sailed for New York, and when all business men were expected to make good all their coin contracts.

***steaming,** *n.* Traveling by steamboat. *Obs.* — **1836** *S. Lit. Messenger* II. 696 Steaming from Washington to Baltimore is an improvement upon that route at least. **1883** CRAWFORD *Dr. Claudius* 140 Miss Skeat also thought sailing much more poetic than steaming.

***steel,** *n.* In combs.: (1) **steel-bowed,** of spectacles, having bows or rims of steel; (2) **climbers,** spurs or strips of steel used by linemen in climbing; (3) **driver,** one who, before the advent of power drills, drove a steel rod in making holes in rock for setting blasting charges; (4) **head,** (*a*) either of two trouts, *Salmo gairdneri* and *S. irideus,* of the Pacific Coast region, (*b*) a local name for the ruddy duck *q.v.*

(1) **1912** I. COBB *Back Home* 8 Her little gray eyes behind her steel-bowed specs were leveled with a baleful, condemning glare. **1915** F. E. LEUPP *Walks about Washington* 33 Lincoln drew from his pocket a pair of steel-bowed spectacles, which he adjusted very deliberately. — (2) **1894** *Outing* XXIII. 355/2 A pair of such steel climbers as linemen fasten to their feet when about to climb telegraph poles. — (3) **1916** in L. W. CHAPPELL *John Henry* (1933) 1 He gave out a popular report of John Hardy, the 'steel-driver . . . famous in the beginning of the building of the C. & O. Railroad.' **1933** L. W. CHAPPELL *John Henry* (1933) 13 If it is to have any bearing on the connection of the steel-driver with Big Bend . . . something more definite [etc.]. — (4) (*a*) **1882** *Nat. Museum Bul.* No. 16, 313 *Salmo gairdneri,* Steel-head; Hard-head. **1949** *Lincoln Co. News* (Oceanlake, Ore.) 4 Aug. 5/2 Wayne . . . came home with two nice chinook and one steelhead. (*b*) **1888** TRUMBULL *Names of Birds* 112 William Wagner, a well known Washington gunner, tells of hearing it called Water-Partridge and Steel-head, on the Patuxent River, Md. **1917** *Birds of Amer.* I. 153/1 They are extremely tough, hardy little birds and gunners know them by such names as Tough-head, Hard-head, Steel-head, etc.

b. *To draw one's steel,* to use one's pistols. *Rare.*

1902 WISTER *Virginian* ii, He has handed Trampas the choice to back down or draw his steel.

steencrout 'stinˌkraʊt, *n. local.* [Du. *steenkruid,* used of various plants.] A stoneweed. — **1833** *Amer. R.R. Jrnl.* II. 504/3 This weed, sometimes called steencrout, stone-weed and wheat-thief, is very troublesome [in New York].

***steep,** *a.* Of a price or amount: High, exorbitant. *Colloq.* — **1856** *Knickerb.* XLVII. 362 He's too steep in his price, anyway. **1901** *Munsey's Mag.* XXIV. 441/1 Forty thousand marks . . . is a pretty steep price even for a royal motorcarriage.

steeplebush 'stipl̩ˌbʊʃ, *n.* The hardhack, *Spiraea tomentosa,* or a related species. — **1817–8** EATON *Botany* (1822) 478 *Spiraea tomentosa,* steeple-bush. **1931** CLUTE *Plants* 45 When the pink inflorescences of *Spiraea tomentosa* appear in the damp meadows, they are so suggestive of church spires as to be known as steeple-bushes.

***steer,** *n.*[1] As the last term in **bay, feeder, pitchfork, Texas steer.**

***steer,** *n.*[2] *fig.* An idea or a suggested course of action. *Slang.* Cf. ***steerer,** *n.* — **1894** C. H. HOYT *Texas Steer* (1925) III. 45 You're going back to Texas to give the voters of my district a steer. What's that steer to be? **1919** T. K. HOLMES *Man from Tall Timber* xxx. 374 That girl from New York gave me the right steer, I do believe.

***steer,** *v. tr.* To guide or entice (a person) into a place where he may be cheated or robbed. *Slang.*

1889 *Cent.* 721/3 bunko-steerer. . . . That one of the swindlers called bunko-men who allures or steers strangers to the bunko-joint or rendezvous. [American slang or cant.] **1908** K. MCGAFFEY *Show-Girl* 29, I would steer no friend of a friend of mine up against a flim flam where there's so many nice girls running loose. **1914** J. H. KEATE *Destruction* 243 Seeing a possibility of a large killing to be made by 'steering' Moore, Heaston was very liberal with expenses.

***steerage,** *n.* Attrib. with **country, mess, officer,** (see quots.).

1881 *Naval Encycl.* 776 *Steerage-officer.* An officer living or messing in the steerage. Steerage-officers in the U.S. navy are clerks, midshipmen, cadet-midshipmen, mates, . . . and all officers ranking with ensign. **1889** *Cent.* 1307/3 *Steerage country* . . . , the open space in the middle of a . . . steerage of a man-of-war not occupied by berths or state-rooms. **1891** H. PATTERSON *Naut. Dict.* 264 *Steerage Mess.* This mess is composed of midshipmen, ensigns, clerks and mates.

***steerer,** *n.* A swindler's accomplice who directs or entices victims to a place where they are fleeced. *Slang.* See **bunco steerer.** — **1875** *Chi. Tribune* 30 Oct. 5/6 The gamblers and their ropers, steerers, and hangers-on maintained a sort of rear guard near the main entrance. **1905** O. HENRY *Strictly Business* 70 On a corner lounged a keen-eyed steerer for a gambling-house.

***steering,** *a.* **1. steering committee, group,** a committee or group, esp. in a legislative assembly, that directs or prescribes the order in which business shall be considered. **2. steering oar,** an oar by which a boat, esp. a broadhorn or river flatboat, is steered. *Obs.*

(1) **1887** *Courier-Journal* 6 Feb. 2/2 A steering committee upon the order of business for the remainder of the session was appointed. **1945** *Reader's Digest* Jan. 54/2 A local Committee of 21 was organized, with a steering group of three members. **1950** *Chi. D. News* 7 Feb. 6/5 He was one of the 'steering' committee of four men. — (2) **1808** KER *Travels* (1816) 30 In endeavouring to run the outside of a sawyer, I ran with my stern athwart it, and unshipped my steering oar, which I lost. **1884** MARK TWAIN *H. Finn* xiii, They lost their steering-oar.

***Stella,** *n.* **1.** A four-dollar gold coin minted in 1879–80, so called from a star on its reverse. **2. Stella shawl,** a now unidentifiable type of shawl. *Obs.*

(1) **1909** *Stevens' Ill. Coin Bk.* 25 Four Dollars—Stella (Patterns) 1879 $25 00 1880 $35 00. **1948** *Numismatic Gallery Mo.* May 2/1 $4.00 Gold Stella, 1879. Flowing Hair. Proof. Very rare $525.00. — (2) **1856** *Porter's Spirit of Times* 4 Oct. 74/1 The 'Stella' Shawls became so common last season that they will hardly be worn by our *elegantes,* at present. **1895** A. BROWN *Meadow-Grass* 176 She snatched her stella shawl from the drawer, threw it over her shoulders, and ran out of the room.

***Steller,** *n.* [G. W. *Steller* (1709–46), G. naturalist.] **1. Steller's jay,** a dark-crested blue jay, *Cyanocitta stelleri,* found in the western states. **2. Steller's duck,** a species of eider duck found in Alaska.

(1) **1828** BONAPARTE *Ornithology* II. 44 The Steller's Jay is one of those obsolete species alluded to in the preface to this volume. **1948** *Pacific Discovery* Jan.–Feb. 14/2 Stellar jays, bald eagles, mountains of wild geraniums, . . . these are the Teton country. — (2) **1883** *Nat. Museum Bul.* No. 27, 162 *Cosmonetta stelleri.* Steller's Duck.

*__stem,__ *n.* In combs.: (1) **stem clam,** (see quot. and cf. **maninose**), *obs.;* (2) **guest,** a regular guest or boarder, *rare* [no doubt after G. *Stammgast* in same sense]; (3) **ware,** *collect.* wine and liqueur glasses; (4) **winder,** a watch which is wound and set by a mechanism connected with the stem, also transf., a person or thing of superior excellence, *colloq.;* (5) **-winding watch,** a watch that is wound by means of the stem, a stem-winder; (6) **wood,** the wood contained in the stem or trunk of a tree.

(1) **1859** BARTLETT 84 The Soft Clam, or Mananosay (*Mya arenaria*) . . . has a long, extensible cartilaginous snout, or proboscis, through which it ejects water; whence it is also called Stem-clam. — (2) **1869** *Atlantic Mo.* July 72/2 His 'stem guests' fell off one by one and sought a quieter neighborhood for their evening potations. — (3) **1929** *Sears Cat.* (Fall) 898/1 One of the newest creations in stemware. **1949** *Ib.* (ed. 198) 716 Gemlike Stemware . . . to bring a glowing sparkle to your table. — (4) **1876** KNIGHT 2373/2 Some of the stem-winders are so constructed that [etc.]. **1892** GUNTER *Miss Dividends* 68 Ain't he a stem-winder? **1948** *Time* 1 Nov. 38/2 Chargé d'Affaires Rafael de la Colina delivered a protest which U.S. diplomats described as a 'stemwinder.'

(5) **1867** *Rep. Comm. Patents 1866* 1115 Either side of the case of the stem-winding watch is opened by pressure upon the head of the winding arbor. **1876** KNIGHT 2373/1. — (6) **1896** *Vt. Agric. Rep.* XV. 83 About 24 cubic feet per acre is added to the stem wood of the merchantable trees annually.

As the last term in **blue, Colorado blue, main, pipe, screw stem.**

*__stem,__ *v.*

1. *tr.* To strip (tobacco leaves) from the stalk, or to remove the stems and midribs from the leaves. Cf. quot. 1887 *s.v.* **stemmery,** *n.*

1724 JONES *Virginia* 40 It lies till they have Leisure or Occasion to stem it (that is pull the Leaves from the Stalk) or *strip* it (that is take out the great Fibres). **1797** IMLAY *West. Terr.* (ed. 3) 248 This done, you stem the tobacco, or pull out the middle rib of the leaf, which you throw away with the stalks as good for nothing. **1898** *Treasury Decisions Customs* II. 967 Persons who have qualified as dealers in leaf tobacco are . . . permitted to strip or stem their tobacco—that is, they may divide the leaf in half and take out the midrib, and may re-sweat the tobacco or leaves thus separated.

2. To remove the stems from (grapes or currants).

1873 *Ill. Dept. Agric. Trans.* X. 61 [Grapes] were stemmed and mashed and put to ferment on the skins for forty-eight hours. **1907** WIGGIN *New Chron. Rebecca* x. 308 Her aunt and her mother were stemming currants on the side porch.

3. *To stem from,* to originate or spring from.

1932 LEWINSON *Race* 166 Its lineage, however, was not Hamiltonian or industrial; rather did it stem from anti-Bourbonism. **1950** *Chi. Tribune* 3 May 22/3 However, the common use of the term may well have stemmed from the fact that 'bits' were often the result of dividing coins of greater value.

*__stemmer,__ *n.* **1. best stemmer,** tobacco most easily stemmed. **2.** A machine for stemming grapes, etc. Both *rare.* — (1) **1887** *Courier-Journal* 19 Jan. 8/1 For best stemmer, usually grown in the Henderson and Owensboro districts, $50 was awarded to Mr. Foster of Hartford, Ohio county. — (2) **1899** *Dept. Agric. Yrbk. 1898* 558 Crushers and stemmers are capable of working up 300 tons of grapes per day.

stemmery ˈstɛmərɪ, *n.* (See quot. 1859.)

1859 BARTLETT 450 *Stemmery,* a large building in which tobacco is stemmed. **1887** *Courier-Journal* 5 May 6/6 At the stemmeries . . . gangs of negroes, big and little, male and female, may be seen dexterously snatching the stem from the leaf. **1897** KILLEBREW & MYRICK *Tobacco Leaf* 283 The work in the stemmeries goes on from November . . . until June.

steno ˈstɛno, *n.* A "stenog" or stenographer *qq.v. Slang.* — **1925** *Sat. Ev. Post* 10 Oct. 22/2 My girl friend who got me in there was steno to the boss. **1947** *Dly. Oklahoman* (Okla. City) 28 Dec. 6/3 Knee-sitting stenos would have had a rough time in those days, girls.

stenog stəˈnɑg, *n.* Short for **stenographer.** Also as verb. *Slang.*

1906 O. HENRY *Four Million* xiv. (1916) 139 Not being able to stenog, she could not enter that bright galaxy of office talent. **1909** *The Fra* March 82/1 The Stenog wanted a new set of curtains. **1922** E. WALLACE *Valley of Ghosts* xxix, It will look better if I put it into police-English than if you dig up the hotel stenog.

stenograph ˈstɛnəˌgræf, *n.* [Gk. *steno-*, narrow, +*-*graph.*] **1.** A report written in some form of shorthand. **2.** (See quot.) — (1) **1856** EMERSON *Eng. Traits, The 'Times'* Wks. (Bohn) II. 118, I saw the reporters' room, in which they redact their hasty stenographs. — (2) **1891** *Cent.* 5930/1 *stenograph.* . . . A stenographic machine; a form of typewriter in which signs and marks of various kinds—dots, dashes, etc.—are used in place of ordinary letters. A number of different machines have been made, essentially type-writers operated by means of a keyboard.

stenographer stəˈnɑgrəfɚ, *n.* [Prob. f. **stenography.*] One skilled in stenography, a shorthand writer. Cf. **court stenographer.**

1796 *Ann. 4th Cong.* 2 Sess. 1607 He also adverted to the attempt at the last session to introduce a stenographer into the House, which failed. **1813** *Ann. 13th Cong.* 1 Sess. 125 Under an order of the House directing stenographers to be admitted by the Speaker . . . the petitioner made application to be received as such. **1906** QUICK *Double Trouble* 147 A stenographer and bookeeper were employed in the counting-room of the Brassfield Oil Company. **1949** *This Week Mag.* 2 April 27/2 Here is this office full of pretty stenographers.

Also **stenographer-typist.**

1918 M. S. OWEN *Typewriting Speed* 59 After a careful study of the poor style of operation of hundreds of stenographer-typists.

*__step,__ *n.* As the last term in **block, route, side, turtle step.**

*__step,__ *v.* With adverbs and prepositions in colloq. and slang expressions: (1) *To step down, transf.* to retire from office, to vacate; (2) *to step lively,* to hurry; (3) **to step out,* (*a*) to die or disappear [Bense *s.v. Step out* regards the Du. past indefinite *stapte uit* (<*uitstappen*), fig. to die, as having prob. inspired this use], (*b*) to take part in social activities, go into company or society; (4) *to step up,* to increase or raise as if by steps or degrees; (5) *to step upon,* to reprove or criticize (one) sharply.

(1) **1890** *Stock Grower & Farmer* 3 May 3/2 If the bureau cannot do this, let the members of it, the lunkheads, step down and resign. — (2) **1891** *Outing* Nov. 147/2 There was . . . the guard's admonition to 'step lively.' **1906** FREEMAN *By Light of Soul* 41 She was told to step lively on the trolley-cars. — (3) (*a*) **1844** *Yale Lit. Mag.* IX. 381 Of the other pieces . . . which have been sent us, some will be found in the present number . . . and the remainder have '*stept out.*' **1902** MCFAUL *Ike Glidden* 277 That is why he stepped out when he did. (*b*) **1907** MARK TWAIN *Capt. Stormfield* 44 (R.), I thought what a figure I should cut stepping out amongst the redeemed in such a rig. — (4) **1920** *Glasgow Herald* 8 July 7 They would suggest that this increase . . . should be 'stepped up' over a period of years. **1949** *Boston Globe Mag.* 25 Sep. 8/2 Dave told about . . . the giant transformers which stepped up the voltage in the transmission station.

(5) **1871** HOWELLS *Wedding Journey* 100 Abjectly I . . . try to give myself the genteel air of one who has not been stepped upon.

stepping mill. A treadmill used as an amusement or as a means of discipline. *Obs.* — **1825** WOODWORTH *Forest Rose* I. i, The Gas-lights, and the Water-works, and the Fire-works, and the Stepping-mill, and all other places of amusement. **1831** ROYALL *Southern Tour* II. 24 When a slave displeases his master, he or she is sent to the Work House or Stepping Mill, as they work and grind alternately.

stereoptician ˌstɛrɪɑpˈtɪʃən, *n.* [f. next.] One who operates a stereopticon. — **1887** *Evans* (Colo.) *Jrnl.* 26 Nov., The great stereoptician . . . showed over one hundred different views.

stereopticon ˌstɛrɪˈɑptɪkən, *n.* [f. Gk. *stere-* (combining form of *stereos,* solid), +*optikon,* relating to sight.] An improved type of projector or magic lantern. Also attrib.

1863 *Hunt's Merch. Mag.* XLVIII. 430 Although the stereopticon was exhibited for a time in the Polytechnic Institute, and in the Hall of Illustration, Regent's Park, London, yet it did not advance beyond the first discovery. J. Fallon, Esq., of Lawrence, Mass., . . . who has devoted thirty years to photology, imported from England one of these instruments for his own family. But under his hands it was developed into something so perfect that his friends desired that others might have the pleasure which he enjoyed. **1894** *Outing* Sep. 49/1, I had seen it projected by a stereopticon lantern fifteen years before, when a boy in America. **1929** E. W. HOWE *Plain People* 47 There was a side show displaying stereopticon views of the war.

stern wheel.

1. A large paddle wheel serving as a propeller at the stern of a steamboat.

1819 *15th Cong.* 2 Sess. No. 78, 12 Double stern wheel for boats, December 10, John L. Sullivan, Boston. **1886** *Outing* VIII. 159/2 There was then 'a flat-boat with a tea-kettle boiler and stern-wheel' plying on Lake Umbagog.

Hence **stern-wheel craft, steamer.**

1849 *N.Y. Herald* 13 Aug. 1/4 The new stern-wheel steamer, sent out by Messrs. Howland and Aspinwall, made a trip up the river. **1856** OLMSTED *Slave States* 368 The boat I was in . . . was a stern-wheel craft. **1949** *Southwestern Hist. Quart.* April 419 Another stern-wheel steamer made the trip to Austin.

b. (See quot. 1859.) *Obs.*

1859 BARTLETT 450 The term is applied to any thing small, petty; as, a 'stern-wheel church.' **1862** LOWELL *Biglow P.* 2 Ser. i. 20 Nary social priv'ledge but a one-hoss, starn-wheel chaplin.

2. Short for next.

1882 RITTENHOUSE *Maud* 73 You can count 6 or 8 queer flats, canoes, rafts, dug-outs, stern-wheels, skiffs [etc.]. **1884** MARK TWAIN *H. Finn* xix, You couldn't tell nothing about her only whether she was a stern-wheel or side-wheel.

3. sternwheel boat, a steamboat having a large paddle wheel at the stern as a propeller.

1836 HALL *Statistics of West* 228 The long struggles of a stern wheel boat to ascend Horse-tail ripple [etc.]. **1887** *Courier-Journal* 15 Feb. 3/3 The New Orleans and Ouachita packet Corona is undoubtedly the fastest sternwheel boat of her size afloat.

stern-wheeler. =**sternwheel boat.** *Colloq.* Cf. **wheelbarrow boat.**

1855 *Harper's Mag.* Dec. 40/2 He got possession of a 'starn-wheeler,' and entered the 'pine-knot business.' **1884** HEDLEY *Marching through Ga.* 422 In its wake . . . lazily floated one of the most diminutive stern-wheelers of the western river class. **1950** *Reader's Digest* March

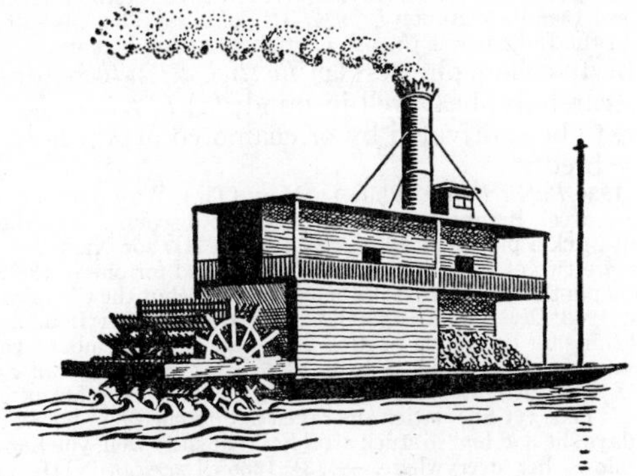

Stern-wheeler or wheelbarrow boat

39/2, I had wanted to work on one of these old-time, coal-burning, cinder-throwing, hard-puffing, back-breaking stern-wheelers.

* **Stetson,** *n.* The trade-mark name of a hat devised by John B. Stetson (1830–1906) about 1865. In full **Stetson hat.** Cf. **Palo Alto hat.**

1902 *Out West* June 623 We'll rig him out complete . . . Chaps, and a Stetson and a gun. *c***1908** F. M. CANTON *Frontier Trails* 16 He got a forty-five-caliber bullet through the brim of his Stetson hat. **1950** *Nat. Hist.* Feb. 92/3 The men . . . dress more picturesquely, wearing the traditional cowboy riding outfit of broad-brimmed Stetson, blue jeans, colorful shirt, and gay neckerchief.

stevedore ˈstivəˌdor, *n.* [See note.]

From Sp. *estibador* in same sense. The spelling "stowadore" in quot. 1788 and the allusion to N.Y. in quot. 1828 suggest Du. *stuwadoor* as an immediate source or influence. *WNT*, however, shows no early use of *stuwadoor*.

A laborer engaged in loading and unloading ships.

1788 *Mass. Spy* 10 July (Th.), 'Stowadores' appeared in the Grand Procession at Portsmouth, N.H., June 26. **1828** WEBSTER *Stevedore*, one whose occupation is to stow goods, packages, &c. in a ship's hold. *New York.* **1882** MCCABE *New York* 366 Gangs of stevedores are busy loading and unloading vessels. **1950** *Chi. D. News* 11 Jan. 1/1 He watched the stevedores in their loading.

***stew,** *n.* As the last term in **box, Brunswick, candy, fortune, molasses, oyster, terrapin stew.**

***stewardess,** *n.* In the Methodist Church, a woman steward. — **1844** LEE & FROST *Oregon* 217 The Rev. J. P. Richmond . . . and O. Lankton, stewardess, were appointed to return with Mr. Lee.

Stewartia st(j)ʊˈartɪə, *n.* Also **Stuartia.** [f. John *Stuart* (1713–92), Marquis of Bute.] A genus of American and Japanese shrubs of the family Theaceae or (not *cap.*) a plant of this genus. Also with specifying term.

1765 J. BARTRAM *Diary* 24 July, The trees common in this rich neck of land is as follows . . . tupelo, water tupelo. shrubs fartle berry stewartia benjamin Cephalanthus halesia. **1831** AUDUBON *Ornith. Biog.* I. 91, I have placed them on a branch of Stuartia. *Ib.* 95 The White-flowered Stuartia. . . . A small tree, with smooth spreading branches. **1891** *Cent.* 6003/1 Two handsome white-flowered species, from the mountains of Virginia, Kentucky, and southward, are sometimes cultivated under the name of *stuartia.* **1930** BAILEY *Cyclo. Horticulture* 3241/1 The stewartias are very desirable ornamental plants.

stib stɪb, *n.* [Origin obscure. "Stile" in the first quot. is app. an error for **stib.**] (See quot. 1891.)

[**1876** F. C. BROWNE in *Forest & Stream* 9 Nov. 212/3 *T. alpina.* Stile.] **1888** TRUMBULL *Names of Birds* 182 F. C. Browne gives Stib in his list of gunners' names at Plymouth Bay. **1891** *Cent.* 5941 *Stib,* . . . the American dunlin, purre, or ox-bird: a gunners' name . . . (Massachusetts.) **1925** E. W. FORBUSH *Birds of Mass.* I. 416.

* **stick,** *n.*

1. A grove of timber. *Rare.*

1860 *Harper's Mag.* March 446/2 We just took lodgings for the night in the big stick, as being more handy to the stream.

2. A baseball bat. *Slang.*

1868 *N.Y. Herald* 4 Aug. 6/5 The Empire seemed out of practice with 'the stick.' **1912** MATHEWSON *Pitching* 3 Now I observed that he had his stick way down by the handle.

3. *pl.* The backwoods, the country, esp. *in the sticks. Colloq.*

1905 N. DAVIS *Northerner* 78 Billy is a cane-brake nigger; he'll take to the sticks like a duck to water when he's scared. **1917** COMSTOCK *Man* 67 He meant, should he come across Burke in 'the sticks,' to take him off for a bear hunt. **1946** *Amer. Sp.* April 116/2 Cow county [is] . . . still used in Calif., referring to rural districts in general, 'the sticks.'

4. In combs.: (1) **stick-and-clay chimney,** a chimney made of sticks covered with, and held in place by, clay mortar, also **stick-and-clay fireplace;** (2) **-and-dirt,** see as a main entry; (3) **-and-mud,** *attrib.* of or pertaining to structures composed of sticks and mud mortar; (4) **back,** the back of a chair having upright rods in it, also **stick chair,** a chair with such a back, a Windsor chair; (5) **ball,** (*a*) app. a form of ball in which a stick or bat is used, *obs.*, (*b*) a form of Indian ball from which lacrosse *q.v.* was developed; (6) **broom,** ?=**brush broom** (*a*); (7) **bug,** (see quot. 1891); (8) **candy,** hard candy in the form of small sticks, usu. with red and white stripes; (9) **chair,** (*a*) a chair made of rods or sticks of wood, (*b*) =**stick gig,** both *obs.;* (10) **chimney** =**stick-and-clay chimney;** (11) **dice game,** a gambling game played by Indians in which sticks with different marks were used, cf. **hand game, Indian poker, stick poker;** (12) **gig,** a light, two-wheeled carriage for one person; (13) **horse,** a stick used by children as a play horse; (14) **poker,** an Indian guessing game in which sticks are concealed and their number or position guessed, cf. **hand game, Indian poker, stick dice game;** (15) **pot,** "a lath-pot for tak-

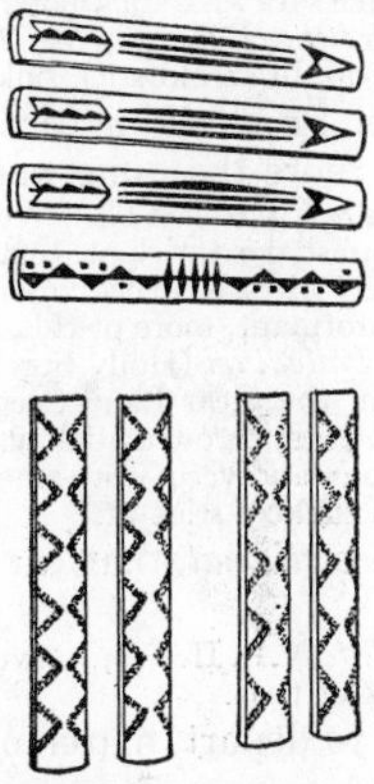

Forms of stick dice

ing lobsters . . . constructed of laths or of any narrow strips of wood" (*Cent.*); (16) **sulky,** =**stick gig.**

(1) **1863** *Ladies' Repository* XXIII. 398/2 A 'stick and clay chimney' on the same ample scale lets out the smoke and lets in the rain. **1932** W. KELLEY *Inchin' Along* 2 At one end of the cabin a stick-and-clay chimney reared its red body above a sloping roof. *Ib.*, The silence remained unbroken until he had built a roaring blaze in the stick-and-

clay fireplace. — (3) **1881** PIERSON *In the Brush* 309 It had a stick-and-mud chimney on the outside, and was without floor of any kind. **1947** HILTON *Sonora* 270 The first thing that I noticed was the fact that the houses were of adobe, instead of the usual stick-and-mud construction. — (4) **1783** *Narragansett Hist. Reg.* II. 314 The Sheriff . . . [shall purchase] Three good large Windsor or Stickback Chairs. **1897** TERHUNE *Old Field* 28 There were a table in the middle of the room, a candle-stand, two rocking-chairs and five upright, all of wood with 'stick backs.'

(5) (*a*) **1824** *Nantucket Inquirer* 12 Jan. (Th.), No person shall play Foot-ball or Poke, Stick-ball or Swinger, within the compact part of the town of Nantucket. (*b*) **1946** *Life* 11 Nov. 91/1 On the Cherokees' Qualla Indian Reservation in North Carolina last month the Wolftown Wolves met the Wolftown Bears in a crucial game of stickball, the roughest sport in the world. . . . The game of stickball, which is a primitive version of modern lacrosse, was centuries old when De Soto led a Spanish expedition through Cherokee territory in 1540. **1950** *Asheville* (N.C.) *Citizen-Times* 26 March IX. 17/2 Before DeSoto came to Western North Carolina in 1540, the clans of the Nation for centuries had been competing in stickball. — (6) **1939** *These Are Our Lives* 45 He brought a chair from the porch to the yard, swept clean in country style with a stick broom. — (7) **1887** A. M. SULLIVAN in H. Keller *Story of My Life* 329, I tried to interest her in a curious insect called a stick-bug. It's the queerest thing I ever saw—a little bundle of faggots fastened together in the middle. I wouldn't believe it was alive until I saw it move. **1891** *Cent.* 5943/1 Stick-bug, . . . any orthopterous insect of the family *Phasmidae* . . . (Local.) **1894** *Harper's Mag.* Feb. 456/1 The form [of walking stick] . . . dubbed 'stick-bugs' and 'prairie alligators,' our *Diapheromera femorata*. — (8) **1886** *Harper's Mag.* June 93/2 The 'stick' candy, which seems to be an indigenous American product, is of ordinary 'A' sugar. **1948** WESTON *Mother Lode* 94 Jars of striped stick candy, rock candy, candies with birds and flowers in the centers [etc.]. — (9) (*a*) **1843** CARLTON *New Purchase* I. 61 The room contained . . . a table, 'stick chairs' and some stools. (*b*) **1860** MORDECAI *Virginia* 275 The modes of conveyance were either by a stage-wagon . . . or on horseback with saddle-bags, or in a stick-chair. **1908** M. JOHNSTON *L. Rand* i, Coach and chaise, curricle and stick-chair, were encountered.

(10) [**1835** in ELLET *Pioneer Women* 410 It had not the ordinary stick and round chimney common to log houses.] **1845** KIRKLAND *Western Clearings* 208 At one side was a stick chimney, . . . finished on the top by the remnant of a stone churn. **1923** ADAMS *Pioneer Hist.* 295 It was a rough log structure with a stick chimney on one end, and within the building a large fireplace. — (11) **1903** S. CULIN in *Amer. Anthrop.* Jan.–Mar. 60 A comparative study of the stick-dice game. — (12) **1825** *Catawba Jrnl.* 17 May, The subscriber . . . is now finishing, about $4,000 worth of work . . . consisting of a Coachee, Chariotee, Phaeton, Panneled and Stick Gigs [etc.]. **1877** BAGBY *Old Va. Gentleman* 1 Once a month the lawyers, in their stick gigs or 'single-chairs,' . . . jogged on to court. — (13) **1896** WHITE *Real Issue* 71 So his lonely way was strewn with broken stick-horses, which he took from the little boys. **1945** BOTKIN *My Burden* 218 One old man been riding one of these stick horses and he been so glad. — (14) **1889** *Puyallup* (Wash.) *Commercial* 6 Sep. 7/2 The stick-poker-odd-or-even-now-you-see-it-and-now-you-don't games started up Sunday . . . with $57 in the pot, and Sam Stomach beating the tom-tom.

(15) **1887** GOODE *Fisheries* V. II. 666 Other names by which they are known to the fisher-men are . . . 'stick-pots,' and 'lath-coops.' — (16) **1868** WOODRUFF *Trotting Horse* 137 Mr. Treadwill used to drive Lady Blanche on the road, in an old stick sulky.

b. *more than one can shake a stick at*, and variants, more than enough; more than one would believe. *Colloq.*

1818 *Lancaster* (Pa.) *Jrnl.* 5 Aug. (Th.), We have in Lancaster as many Taverns as you can shake a stick at. **1830** *Western Mo. Rev.* III. 356 His slang-curses were ultra Kentuckian on a ground of Yankee; and he had, says my informant, more of this, 'than you could shake a stick at.' **1851** *Miss. Palladium* (Holly Springs) 9 May 1/1 Every body knows Uncle Sam, the great Land Speculator out West, who has more acres than you can throw a stick at. **1950** *Chi. Tribune* 17 Feb. 16/3 'Crack,' as noun and verb, is an all-service word with more meanings than you can shake a stick at.

c. *that can shake a stick at*, that can possibly compare with. *Colloq.*

1843 STEPHENS *High Life N.Y.* II. 216, I never sot eyes on anything that could shake a stick at that.

d. *To up sticks*, to depart, march off. *Colloq.* Cf. *to up stakes.*

1839 *Knickerb.* XIV. 141 Why, in the name of common sense, do you not up sticks and off? **1877** *Harper's Mag.* Jan. 213/2 If any man tries hard words with me, I knocks him down, up sticks, and makes tracks.

As the last term in **bait, ball, barley, boom, bow, button, candy, cat, corn, courting, crooked, cross, fire, float, fore, grave, gunning, hickory, hoodoo, hook, jockey, mint, mud, muddling, night, plume, prayer, red, sassafras, shooting, slap, snuff, soap, stove, tobacco, toddy, top, twisting, witch, yard-stick.**

* **stick,** *v.* In combs.: (1) **stick pin,** an ornamental pin, as a tie-pin, that is merely stuck in as distinguished from a safety pin, also (rarely) **stick-pinned,** *a.;* (2) **seed,** any plant having prickly or adhesive fruit, esp. one of the genus *Lappula*, also with a specifying term; (3) **-up,** see as a main entry; (4) **weed,** one of a number of American plants, esp. ragweed, *Ambrosia elatior*, or a species of *Aster*, also with a specifying term, attrib. and fig.

(1) **1903** *N.Y. Sun* 21 Nov. 2 Dr. Amador presented to the President a gold stickpin containing the flag of the new republic. **1909** O. HENRY *Options* (1916) 77 They were . . . pearl stickpinned like other young New Yorkers. **1948** *Reader's Digest* May 26/1 The heavy mustache, wing collar, stickpin and wavy hair parted in the middle are known around the world. — (2) **1843** TORREY *Flora N.Y.* II. 90 Broad-leaved Stickseed. . . . Borders of woods, along fences, and hill-sides. **1939** *Nat. Geog. Mag.* August. 236/2 The tiny, burlike fruits of the stickseeds . . . attach themselves by the score to the clothing of anyone intent on a stroll through fields. — (4) **1743** CLAYTON *Flora Virginica* 102 Verbesina floribus corymbosis, foliis lanceolatis petiolatis . . . White Stickweed. **1808** WEEMS *Washington* (1840) 6 He will . . . stand forth confessed in native stickweed sterility and worthlessness. **1896** P. A. BRUCE *Econ. Hist. Va.* I. 167 The only salt in use among the Indians was the ash of stick weed and hickory.

b. In colloq. phrases: (1) *To stick a pin there* (or *here*), note carefully, bear well in mind; (2) *to get* (or *be*) *stuck after*, to be captivated by or enamored of; (3) *to be stuck on*, =prec.

(1) **1836** *Public Ledger* (Phila.) 1 Nov. (Th.), Why does money become scarce? Because the bankers cannot discount, says the merchant. Stick a pin there. **1861** *Knickerb.* LVIII. 266 Name for name, there are two of the Norman in New-England for one in the South. Stick a pin there—not that it's of any account, but the Chivalry insist on it. **1948** *Dly. Oklahoman* (Okla. City) 7 June 8/1 It might be a good thing for the voters to stick a pin here and remember a thing or two on next election day. — (2) **1865** *Wkly. New Mexican* 15 Sep. 2/3, I got 'stuck' on sight after one of the girls. **1906** MARK TWAIN *Horse's Tale* 335 She untied the raven and fetched him home. . . . In two days she had him so stuck after her that she—well, you know how he follows her everywhere. — (3) **1886** *American* XIII. 14/2 A customer willing to give ten francs for it . . . [was] ridiculed . . . for having been 'stuck' on the canvas. **1949** *N.O. Times-Picayune Mag.* 13 Feb. 8/2 Want to show your girl you're stuck on her? Then take her to a taffy pull.

stick-and-dirt. *attrib.* Designating a chimney or fireplace made of sticks covered with, and held in place by, clay mortar. Cf. **stick-and-clay chimney.**

1885 *Cent. Mag.* March 684 The huge 'stick-and-dirt' fire-place . . . [was] in perfect accord with the figures, the costumes, and the predicament. **1887** *Ib.* May 111/1 The water mirrored the Shinault cabin with its one wee window and 'stick and dirt' chimney. **1948** *Fla. Hist. Quart.* July 40 A double-penned house was one of two log pens united by a hallway and having a 'stick-and-dirt' chimney at the end of each pen.

b. stick-and-dirt road, =**dirt road.** *Rare.*

1943 POWELL *Home Again* 7 There were only the sandy ruts of rude 'stick-and-dirt' roads trailing through the wide expanses of uncut forests of tall long-leaf yellow pines.

* **sticker,** *n.*

1. A narrow slip of paper bearing a printed name that may be pasted on a ballot to facilitate scratching, also a similar slip of paper for other uses. Cf. * **paster,** *n.* **1.**

1871 DE VERE 270. **1888** *Voice* 5 July, [Quotations] printed on *one* side of little slips of paper . . . to be gummed and used as 'stickers' . . . on newspaper wrappers [etc.]. **1911** *N.Y. Ev. Post* 6 Jan. 1 A telegraph company is obliged to accept a 'sticker' on a message intended to fix additional liability on the company in the event of delay in transmission or non-delivery of a message.

2. A thorn or bur.

1889 H. H. MCCONNELL *Five Years a Cavalryman* 34–5 The leaves when submitted to the action of fire in order to burn off the sharp stickers, are used as food for cattle. **1899** GOING *Flowers* 350 When the 'stickers' are at last picked or rubbed off, they fall to the ground.

stick-to-itiveness ˌstɪkˈtuɪtɪvnəs, *n.* Perseverance. *Colloq.* — **1867** in CUSTER *Tenting on Plains* 520 Old Rover, with the stick-to-it-iveness of a fox-hound when once on a trail, was in for [etc.]. **1887** GEORGE *40 Yrs. on Rail* 231 They devote their quick wit and their stick-to-ativeness to 'sponging' for a living.

stick-up ˈstɪkˌʌp, *n.*

1. (See quot.)

1881 INGERSOLL *Oyster Industry* 240 *Stickup*, a long, thin oyster, growing in mud, etc. (Dennis creek, New Jersey.)

2. A criminal who holds up and robs his victims (see also quot. 1905). Usu. **stick-up man.** *Slang.*

1905 *N.Y. Times* 2 Jan. (*Cent. Supp.*), The man . . . is declared to be a typical 'yeggman of the stick-up' class. . . . The 'stick-up' is always a powerful man, whose duties are to intimidate intruders and kill them, if necessary, while the others are at work on a safe. **1949** *Archives Neurology & Psych.* July 86 I'm no stick-up man or nothing like that.

3. A hold-up or robbery. *Slang.*

1945 *Chi. Sun* (Mag. Sect.) 9 Dec. 5/1 For in 25 years of operation in the East they have had no 'stick-ups.' **1950** *Time* 27 March 62/2 Another showed how to 'case' a bank for a 50-G stickup.

* **Stiegel,** *n.* Exceptionally beautiful blown glass made by Henry William Stiegel at Manheim, Lancaster County, Pennsylvania, *c*1765–74. Also any glass somewhat resembling this or made in imitation of it.

[**1906** *Country Life* Dec. 208/3 Among the first successful works and perhaps the most famous, was that at Manheim, Pa. Here Baron Stiegel established a factory about 1769.] **1922** *Ib.* May 49/2 I'd rather have it than any other piece of Stiegel I ever saw. **1949** *Hobbies* June 104/1 Until quite recently the majority of our collectors were in the habit of calling all old blown glass either Stiegel or Wistar.

attrib. **1942** WEYGANDT *Plenty of Penna.* 233, I find fully half as much Stiegel glass in central New Hampshire in the summer as I do cruising hither and yon in Pennsylvania Dutchland the other nine months of the year. **1949** *Hobbies* June 104/2 All can not be the proud possessors of Stiegel sugar bowls in sparking cobalt, creamers in lovely shades of amethyst.

* **stiff,** *n.* and *a.*

1. A rough or clumsy person, a bum or tramp, often **big stiff.** Also transf. *Slang.*

1876 *Silver City* (Ida.) *Avalanche* 19 Feb. 3/3 The gentlemen in attendance were, Colonel P. Nicholson . . . and several 'stiffs.' **1896** ADE *Artie* 17 There I set like a big stiff for five hours. **1949** *Dly. Ardmoreite* (Ardmore, Okla.) 23 Feb. 18/6 A select group of working stiffs in high government circles have run into 20 assorted kinds of complications.

2. stifftail, a local name for the ruddy duck *q.v.*

1888 TRUMBULL *Names of Birds* 112 In the vicinity of Philadelphia . . . and at Savannah, Ga., [it is called] Stiff-Tail. **1917** *Birds of Amer.* I. 152.

For *to keep a stiff upper lip*, see ***keep,** *v.* **2.** (1).

* **still,** *a.*, *n.*, and *adv.*

The noun is from various sources.

1. An individual picture or frame of a motion picture used in advertising.

1934 WEBSTER. **1950** *Time* 24 April 71/1 She made press agents tear up her first publicity stills and shoot another set.

2. In combs.: (1) **still alarm,** a fire alarm given without sounding the public alarm; (2) **baiting,** (see quot.), *obs.;* (3) **fed,** *a.* of an animal, fed with the refuse from a distillery; (4) **feed,** refuse from a still used as feed for hogs or cattle, also as verb; (5) **fish,** to fish quietly, on the analogy of still-hunt *q.v.*; (6) **hunt,** see as a main entry.

(1) **1875** *Chi. Tribune* 6 Nov. 5/4 Engine Company No. 4 answered a still alarm at 6:30 o'clock yesterday. **1911** *N.Y. Ev. Post* 2 March 1 A still alarm brought Engine No. 65 to the scene. — (2) **1859** BARTLETT 451 *Still-baiting,* fishing with a deep line in one spot, as distinguished from trolling. — (3) **1850** *Ann. Sci. Discovery* 98 Much the larger share of this [oil] is of inferior lard, made of mast-fed and still-fed hogs. — (4) **1874** McCOY *Cattle* 221 Cattle are usually still-fed for from six months to two hundred days. *Ib.* 223 In no one year perhaps were there so many cattle put upon still-feed as that of 1873.

(5) **1910** HOLDER *Channels Islands* 126 You can locate him by chumming, and 'still fish' if you can.

b. *still and all,* after all. *Colloq.*

1928 F. N. HART *Bellamy Trial* iv. 104 Still and all, I believe that he was there precisely when he said he was.

As the last term in **blockade, log, moonshine, spring, turpentine, wash, wildcat still.**

stiller 'stɪlɚ, *n.* A steer fed on still-refuse. *Rare.* — **1880** *Cimarron News & Press* 25 Nov. 2/4 The experienced buyer will tell you in a minute whether a 'grasser,' a 'stiller,' a 'straw-tramper,' a 'stabler,' or a field fed bullock is before him.

still hunt. A hunt for game carried on in a quiet or stalking manner. Also transf.

1834 CROCKETT *Narr. Life* 29 Though the school-house might do for a still hunt, it wouldn't do for a drive, and so I concluded to wait until I could get him out. **1855** *Harper's Mag.* Oct. 599/2 Starting on a 'still hunt,' he coursed along the edge of the island. **1879** *Bradstreet's* 22 Oct. 5/1 So far the commissioners have been conducting what we may call a 'still hunt' for facts in various remote quarters of the Dominion. **1918** W. E. CONNELLEY *Stand. Hist. Kans.* I. 289 The terrible 'still-hunt' was usually used. A herd sighted, the hunter secreted himself and fired, killing the leader. **1948** DICK *Dixie Frontier* 241 Sometimes a candidate who was at a disadvantage in speech-making slipped off and went on a 'still hunt'; that is, he visited the people house-to-house and attended small gatherings unheralded.

still-hunt, *v. tr.* and *intr.* To hunt by stalking the game.

1858 *Harper's Mag.* 615/2 An old woodsman . . . had been, without success, still-hunting. **1877** C. HALLOCK *Sportsman's Gaz.* 81 (*Cent.*), The best time to still-hunt deer is just before sunset, when they come down from the hills to drink. **1906** *Munsey's Mag.* Jan. 475/2 Lacy, a seasoned sportsman at twenty-two, still-hunted many a deer.

Hence **still hunter, still hunting.**

1830 *Amer. Turf Reg.* April 406 We went out to a neighboring prairie, where my friend promised if we could find deer to practise his other method of still hunting, which we have just called the *bush-blind.* **1831** AUDUBON *Ornith. Biog.* I. 335 We are now about to follow the *true hunter*, as the Still Hunter is also called. **1905** *N.Y. Ev. Post* 9 Sep., The animals . . . are now the worthy prize of the skilled still hunter. **1923** J. H. COOK *Fifty Yrs. on Old Frontier* 26, I found times that I could slip out of camp for a little still hunting.

Stillson (pipe) wrench. A readily adjustable pipe wrench having a semi-ratchet action by means of which pressure on the handle tightens the grip, invented in 1869 by Daniel C. Stillson.

This term is now considered to be generic, and wrenches of this type or pattern are made by various manufacturers. What is known as the Genuine Stillson, however, having the diamond trade-mark with the name Stillson in it, is made only by the Walworth Co. of N.Y.

1902 *Sears Cat.* (ed. 112) 563/3 The Stillson Pipe Wrench is too well known to require a lengthy description of same. **1903** *Scientific Amer.* 10 Oct. 266/1 Your kit is not complete unless it includes the famous Stillson wrench which is particularly adapted for turning out the best work without crushing the pipe in the least. **1950** *Boston Globe Mag.* 26 Feb. 2/5 He showed how to tighten the connection with his Stillson wrench.

transf. **1949** *Boston Globe* 25 Sep. 1/6 A one-time pipe-fitter on the Illinois Central Railroad, pitcher Ellis Kinder of the Red Sox, gripped his Stillson wrench around the bats of the Yankees and squeezed them into helplessness, 3 to 0.

stilt sandpiper. =**long-legged sandpiper.** — **1872** COUES *Key to Birds* 253. **1946** *Nat. Geog. Mag.* Sep. 313 Think of driving a car within sight of a nesting Hudsonian curlew, stilt sandpiper, or Harris's sparrow!

* **sting,** *n.* **1.** * **sting nettle,** (see quot.). **2. sting ray,** any ray of the family Dasyatidae or allied families.

(1) **1899** GREEN *Va. Word-Book* 364 *Sting-nettle,* . . . the jelly-fish; also called *sea-nettle.* — (2) **1612** SMITH *Virginia* I. 15 Of fish we were best acquainted with Sturgeon, Grampus, Porpus, Seales, Stingraies. **1799** ELLICOTT in Mathews *Life A. Ellicott* 186 Along the Florida Reef . . ., a great abundance and variety of fish may be taken: such as . . . porgys, turbots, stingrays. **1884** GOODE *Fisheries* I. 665 The Sting Ray, *Trygon centrura,* ranges farther to the north than any of the other species.

stinging lizard. *S.* =***scorpion 1.** — **1877** McDANIELD & TAYLOR *Coming Empire* 262 These stinging lizards . . . exactly resembling the picture of the scorpion in the almanacs. **1889** H. H. McCONNELL *Five Years a Cavalryman* 77 The 'scorpion' or 'stinging lizard' abounds.

* **stink,** *n.* In combs.: (1) **stink bug,** (see quots.); (2) **grass,** (see quot.); (3) * **pot,** the musk turtle, also attrib.; (4) **shad,** see * **shad 3;** (5) **weed,** =**jimson weed;** (6) * **wood,** (see quot.).

(1) **1877** BARTLETT 647 *Squash-Bug.* . . . A small yellow bug, injurious to the vines of squashes, melons, and cucumbers. . . . In Connecticut, called a *stink-bug.* **1891** *Cent.* 5950/2 *Stink-bug,* any one of several malodorous bugs, particularly the common squash-bug, *Anasa tristis,* of the *Coreidæ.* — (2) **1894** *Amer. Folk-Lore* VII. 104 *Eragrostis major* . . . stink-grass, Neb. — (3) **1825** *Phila. Acad. Nat. Sciences Jrnl.* IV. 217 The *odorata* is generally known by the name of 'stink-pot,' from its musky odor. **1903** *Nature* 1 Oct. 531/2 Fourteen Stink-pot Terrapins (*Cinosternum odoratum*), . . . from North America [have been added to the London zoo].

(5) **1753** ELIOT *Field-Husb.* iv. 92 Not knowing the botanical Name of this Plant: from its ill and singular Quality we call it Stink-Weed. **1843** TORREY *Flora N.Y.* II. 101 *Datura Stramonium.* . . . Jamestown- or Jimson-weed. Stinkweed. An extract is kept in the shops, which is used in various spasmodic and painful diseases. — (6) **1897** SUDWORTH *Arborescent Flora* 298 *Rhamnus caroliniana.* . . . Indian

Cherry. . . . [Also called] Stinkwood (La.) . . . Stink Berry (Nebr.). Stink Cherry (Nebr.).

*Stinkards, *n. pl.* (See quot. 1763 and cf. **Puants.**) Also **Stinkard language.** *Obs.* — **1763** in *Amer. Sp.* XX. (1945) 50 The nation of the *Natches* is composed of nobility and common people. The common people are named . . . *Stinkards.* **1791** W. BARTRAM *Travels* 466 Those numerous remnant bands or tribes . . . generally speak the Stincard language, (which is radically different from the Muscogulge).

***stinking,** *a.* In the names of trees, as (1) **stinking ash,** (2) **buckeye,** (3) **cedar,** (4) **wood,** (cf. **stinking ash**), (5) **yew,** (see quots.).

(1) **1843** TORREY *Flora N.Y.* I. 133 *Ptelea trifoliata.* . . . Swamp Dogwood. Stinking Ash. . . . On the shore of Lake Erie. — (2) **1897** SUDWORTH *Arborescent Flora* 293 *Æsculus glabra.* Ohio Buckeye. . . . [Also called] Stinking Buckeye (Ala., Ark.). — (3) **1884** SARGENT *Rep. Forests* 186 *Torreya taxifolia.* . . . Stinking Cedar. Savin. **1948** [see **stinking yew**]. — (4) **1817** CUMING *Ohio & Miss. Pilot, Ptelea tomentosa* Raf. . . . The leaves have a strong and disagreeable smell, from which it is vulgarly called *Bois puant* (Stinking wood,) but the flowers have a most fragrant smell.

(5) **1884** *Rep. Comm. Agric.* 126 Stinking yew; Savin. A very rare evergreen tree, resembling the yew, growing in the northwestern part of Florida. **1948** TRESIDDER *Trees of Yosemite* 85 On account of the disagreeable odor which results from bruising the foliage and even the wood, the tree is sometimes known as 'stinking yew' or 'stinking cedar.'

***stir-.** The stem of the verb used in combs. with **cake, net, pudding.** *Obs.*

1838 *Knickerb.* XI. 16 Which will you have for dinner, John, 'taters or stir-pudding? **1845** KIRKLAND *Western Clearings* 168 Her husband . . . mixes stir-cakes for the eldest blue eyes to bake on a griddle. **1872** *Pa. Laws* 481 It shall not be lawful . . . to take, capture or destroy fish by . . . stir-nets.

stirpiculture 'stɜpɪˌkʌltʃɚ, *n.* [f. L. *stirps, stirpis,* stock, stem, + **culture.*] The production of an improved race or stock by careful breeding.

This term appears to have been first used by J. H. Noyes (see below) in connection with the efforts made at Oneida *q.v.* to produce the best possible offspring. In the *OED s.v.,* in a quot. of 1904, the British scientist Sir Francis Galton claims that he coined the word *stirpiculture* and later discarded it for the term *eugenics.* No evidence is at hand to substantiate this claim.

1870 J. H. NOYES *Sci. Propagation* 12 It is one thing to seek in any existing race the best animals we can find to breed from . . . ; and it is another thing to start a distinct family and keep its blood pure by separation from the mass of its race. It is this last method that has produced the Ayrshires, the short-horns, and the Leicesters. It deserved a distinct name, and we will take the liberty to call it stirpiculture. **1900** ESTLAKE *Oneida Community* 101 Until the subject of intuition has become better understood, people will be liable to mistakes in stirpiculture. **1950** *Amer. Mercury* Feb. 205/2 He also published and circulated an immense number of copies of his lectures on Stirpaculture.

Hence **stirpicultural,** *a.,* **stirpiculturist,** *n.*

1891 *Amer. Naturalist* Oct. 932 Of the stirpicultural children only one has since died. **1903** A. J. MCLAUGHLIN in *Pop. Sci. Mo.* Jan. 231 (*Cent. Supp.*), The stirpiculturist, noting the poor physique . . . of some of the immigrants, fears race degeneration. **1948** *Antioch Rev.* Fall 277 It was a major disappointment when the stirpicultural babies turned out to be only a normal, and unusually healthy, batch of kids.

***stirring,** *n.* **1. stirring off,** the action of making sugar from maple sap, sugaring off. **2. stirring plow,** a plow for stirring, as distinguished from breaking, the soil.

(1) **1846** *Knickerb.* XXVII. 211 All . . . were there . . . to witness the grand 'stirring off.' **1881** *Harper's Mag.* April 649/2 The hot syrup . . . was poured into a large . . . kettle for the process of 'stirring off.' — (2) **1857** *Lawrence* (Kans.) *Republican* 28 May 3 Also a great variety of Stirring or Old Ground Plows. **1881** *Rep. Indian Affairs* 95, I have purchased for them . . . 10 stirring plows.

***stirrup,** *n.* As the last term in **doghouse, oxbow stirrup.**

***stitch,** *n.* As the last term in **cat, crazy, draw, Kensington stitch.**

stiver 'staɪvɚ, *n.* [Du. *stuiver,* an Amer. borrowing.] A Dutch coin worth one-twentieth of a guilder, or about two cents. *Obs.*

1676 *New Castle Court Rec.* 47 A horse and man to pay for passage [on the ferryboat] 2 gilders a man with out a horse 10 styvers. **1701** in MUNSELL *Ann. Albany* IV. 141 The assessment . . . [is] approved off, and laid 4½ stuyver upon ye pound. **1788** JEFFERSON *Writings* VI. 458 The new government should by no means be left by the old, to the necessity of borrowing a stiver. **1884** CRADDOCK *Where Battle Was Fought* 171 Lost the last stiver.

***stock,** *n.* and *a.*

1. A hydrant or fireplug. *Rare.* Cf. ***penstock.**

1833 *Niles' Reg.* XLIV. 420/2 A hose was attached to the stock at the corner of William street and Exchange Place.

2. *pl.* (See quot. 1876.)

1854 BARTLETT *Personal Narr.* I. 16 The first step . . . was to construct a frame-work of timber, called the 'stocks,' . . . capable of containing a single mule. **1876** KNIGHT 2391/1 *Stocks,* . . . a frame in which refractory animals are held for shoeing or veterinary purposes. **1892** *York Co. Hist. Rev.* 5 The shop is . . . the only shop in town having kicking stocks.

3. (See quot.)

1891 *Cent.* 5955/1 *Stock* the proceeds of the sale of the catch of a fishing-trip; the net value of a cargo of fish (New Eng.).

4. A socket or receptacle on the dashboard of a vehicle for a whip.

1902 PIDGIN *Q. A. Sawyer* 79 It was never necessary to touch her with the whip. Shake it in the stock and she would not forget it for the next two miles.

5. In combs.: (1) ***stock board,** (*a*) a stock exchange, also attrib., (*b*) a board of even width, as 8, 10, or 12 inches; (2) ***book,** a book in which records are kept of transactions in stock or shares; (3) **chute,** a cattle chute *q.v.;* (4) ***company,** a company of actors employed more or less permanently by the same management and usu. having a central or home-town theater; (5) **fence,** a fence sufficient to restrain large domestic stock, esp. cattle; (6) **fort,** a stockaded fort, *rare;* (7) **gap,** = **cattle guard** (*b*); (8) **gate,** a gate for the passage of stock; (9) **guard,** a heavy guard or railing sufficient to inclose stock; (10) ***jobber,** a stockbroker; (11) **judging,** designating a show or exhibition where livestock is judged; (12) **law,** a law relating to the running at large of cattle; (13) **lot,** = ***lot,** *n.* **1;** (14) ***man,** meaning obscure (see quot.), *obs.;* (15) **note,** a note secured by stocks or bonds; (16) **palace car,** an exceptionally well fitted-out stock car, *rare;* (17) **pea,** ?a variety of pea raised for feeding stock; (18) ***saddle,** *W.* a heavy saddle with a strong tree and steel horn to afford resistance in using a lariat; (19) **ticker,** a telegraphic device which automatically prints stock quotations and other market news on a narrow strip of paper; (20) **watering,** increasing the number of stocks or shares in an enterprise without adding to its assets or resources; (21) ***yard,** an extensive inclosed area having pens and shelters for cattle, hogs, etc., awaiting slaughter, also attrib., usu. *pl.,* cf. **Union Stockyards.**

(1) (*a*) **1865** *Harper's Mag.* Aug. 318/2 Three stock boards . . . were in full operation in San Francisco. **1896** SHINN *Story of Mine* 189 The stockboard valuation put upon the two bonanza mines in that month was $160,000,000. (*b*) **1872** *Ill. Dept. Agric. Trans.* IX. 390 The roof is of stock boards, grooved on both edges. — (2) **1835** COOPER *Monikins* ii, Love was a sentiment much too pure and elevated for one whose imagination dwelt habitually on the beauties of the stock-books. **1887** *Courier-Journal* 6 May 3/1 They had been permitted to examine the stock books of the company. — (3) **1875** *Chi. Tribune* 11 Sep. 2/6 The stock chute and grain-elevator are familiar objects [in Nebraska]. — (4) **1839** *Chi. American* 30 Aug., As a stock company we consider it unsurpassed. **1895** KING *New Orleans* 270 The new enterprise offered all-year-round, legitimate drama, with a fine stock Company of English players.

(5) **1873** *Winfield* (Kans.) *Courier* 7 Aug. 1/5 Many farmers who live in the creek bottoms have open pasture lots fenced with a stock or open post and rail fence. — (6) **1853** RAMSEY *Tennessee* 105 On the mound near the Lick the voyageurs found a stock fort. — (7) **1865** in FLEMING *Hist. Reconstruction* I. 19 Stock-gaps were out of order, and fences built across the track. **1887** *Courier-Journal* 2 Jan. 3/2 Wm. Lacy . . . lost his way and let his horse fall into a stock gap. — (8) **1945** *Chi. Tribune* 12 Aug. VII. 1/3 Then she . . . opens a stock gate, and is on the highway. — (9) **1897** BRODHEAD *Bound in Shallows* 29 On the little main-deck, protected with a heavy stock-guard, numbers of men lounged.

(10) **1833** *Niles' Reg.* XLIV. 370/1 The 'black-leg' in the gambling houses . . . more fairly takes the chances of the play, than the stock-jobber on 'change. **1911** HARRISON *Queed* 107 If a man became the greatest stock-jobber in the world, who would remember him after he was gone? — (11) **1924** CROY *R.F.D. No. 3* 53 They were members of 'pig clubs' [and] went to stock-judging shows. — (12) **1934** VINES

Green Thicket World 56 There was no stock law. **1946** WILSON *Fidelity* 215, I wrote a vigorous protest to the county paper when some one suggested that we needed a stock law to prevent animals from running at large. — **(13) 1865** TURNER *Cotton* 89 It is the construction of the stock lots. — **(14)** *c***1699** *N.J. Archives* (1881) III. 487 Note, All the sd Jurors of inquiry signed as above, except three Stockmen & that one of Stock-parents tho born of this Country.

(15) 1818 *Niles' Reg.* XIV. 3/1 The . . . accommodation of the rest amounts to not less than Six Millions of Dollars . . . including certain things called stock notes. **1840** BANCROFT *Hist. U.S.* III. 232 Philip V. of Spain took one quarter of the common stock, agreeing to pay for it by a stock-note. — **(16) 1871** DE VERE 356 It is to be hoped that the introduction of Stock Palace-Cars on some of the Northern roads will speedily lead to the adoption of more appropriate names [for passenger cars]. — **(17) 1869** *Rep. U.S. Comm. Agric. 1868* 221 The lot intended for peanuts, say next year, has been seeded in stock peas this year. **1901** H. ROBINSON *Inlander* 120 The fields . . . were now luxuriant in stock-peas. — **(18) 1886** *Cent. Mag.* July 340/1 A stock-saddle weighs thirty or forty pounds. — **(19) 1886** *Boston Jrnl.* 17 July 2/3 The Stock Ticker. . . . The exclusive right of the 'ticker' service in the [N.Y.] Stock Exchange . . . has been a constant source of contention. **1946** ADAMS *Album Amer. Hist.* III. 242 Thomas A. Edison, twenty-two years old, in New York looking for a job, invented a stock ticker—and sold his rights for $40,000.

(20) 1870 MEDBERY *Men Wall St.* 158 Such occasional diversions as corners, money lock-ups, wholesale stock-watering, . . . are the indications of forces with large reserves of strength. **1913** LA FOLLETTE *Autobiog.* 459 It was inevitable that the years of stock-watering and promotion . . . should bring . . . financial distress and reaction. — **(21) 1867** *Atlantic Mo.* March 332/2 Out on the flat prairie . . . may be seen the famous 'Stock Yards.' **1924** *McNaught's Mag.* Jan. 15 Nearly 7,000 men and women . . . from stockyard shanties and lake front clubs were asked. **1946** *Chronicle-News* (Trinidad, Colo.) 2 July 3/2 Lifting of OPA ceilings brought a jam of trucks three quarters of a mile long at the Chicago stockyards, deluged with the greatest arrival of cattle and hogs since last January.

b. In combs. of obvious meaning or sufficiently explained in the quots.: (1) **stock car,** (2) **cattle,** (3)

Early (*c*1882) form of stock car

corral, (4) **country,** (5) **grower, growing,** (6) **hay,** (7) **inspector,** (8) **mill,** (9) **minder,** (10) **pen,** (11) **raiser,** (12) **raising,** (13) **ranch,** (14) **rancher,** (15) **ranching,** (16) **range,** (17) **region,** (18) **roundup,** (19) **tender,** (20) **track,** (21) **train,** (22) **water.**

(1) 1858 *Pa. R.R. Ann. Rep.* 14 The rolling stock [included] 188 Eight-wheeled Stock Cars. **1949** *Exciting Western* May 55/1 Another group was bringing the cattle up the Texas trail to ship east in the stock cars. — **(2) 1857** F. L. OLMSTED *Journey Through Texas* 236 This expression 'stock cattle' is constantly used to express the usual herd of cattle bought as herdsmen's stock. It includes here all the cows of a herd, with their calves, and all young cattle under three years of age. **1904** *Indian Laws & Tr.* III. 72 Two hundred and fifty thousand . . . dollars shall be expended in the purchase of stock cattle. — **(3) 1907** S. E. WHITE *Arizona Nights* ix. 156 The stray-herd . . . we pushed rapidly into one big stock corral. — **(4) 1876** in WHILLDIN *Descr. W. Texas* 12 All the small cattle men . . . were poor immigrants, located in the stock country, and possessed of but a few cows.

(5) 1837 PECK *New Guide* 114 Some stock growers have monopolized the smaller farms till they are surrounded with several thousand acres. **1860** GREELEY *Overland Journey* 15 The soil . . . is admirably fitted for stockgrowing. **1936** *Denver Post* 13 Feb. 14/3 A number of sheriffs have written the stockgrowers headquarters pledging complete cooperation. — **(6) 1882** *Maine Agric. Rep.* XXVI. 43 What would be the difference between a ton of English hay and what we call stock hay, or swale hay? — **(7) 1888** ROOSEVELT in *Cent. Mag.* Feb. 507/1 At every shipping point . . . stock inspectors . . . jealously examine all the brands on the live animals or on the hides of the slaughtered ones. — **(8) 1851** CIST *Cincinnati* 169 Stock mills, for grinding corn and cobs together, and other grain for feeding purposes. — **(9) 1829** B. HALL *Travels N. Amer.* III. 218 Gardeners, house servants, and stock-minders—what we should call in Scotland herds; in England, I believe, herdsmen. **1905** PRINGLE *Rice Planter* 239 In the middle of the tract is a little cabin where my father's stock-minder used to live.

(10) 1881 ROMSPERT *Western Echo* 180 The beeves are then driven to the railroad, where there are stock-pens. **1948** *Dly. Ardmoreite* (Ardmore, Okla.) 20 July 1/4 When the sun drops beyond the prairie, cattle will bawl in the barn and stock pens. — **(11) 1836** EDWARD *Hist. Texas* 143 Should they also be *stock raisers,* grazing land shall be added to complete a *sitio.* **1913** BARNES *Western Grazing Grounds* 33 In the phraseology of the western stock-raiser, there are two distinct ranges. — **(12) 1800** HAWKINS *Sk. Creek Country* 30 They have begun to settle out in villages for the conveniency of stock raising. **1847** HOWE *Ohio* 333 [Madison] is principally a stock-raising county. **1945** *Greeley* (Colo.) *D. Tribune* 18 Aug. 1/2 He moved north of Scottsbluff and was intensively engaged in farming and stock raising. — **(13) 1871** *Old & New* June 649/1 The Hacienda of Encarnacion . . . was an 'estancia,' or stock-ranch. **1949** *Prairie Schooner* Spring 48 He applied for a job managing a big stock ranch in Montana. — **(14) 1878** J. H. BEADLE *Western Wilds* vii. 106 The needs of miners and stock-ranchers in the adjacent mountains have built up a few trading towns. **1949** *Chi. Tribune* 17 April 23/1 Stock ranchers, altho their stock lost weight when heavy snow buried pasture grass, say the range lands were never greener.

(15) 1874 JOSEPH G. MCCOY *Cattle Trade* 88 Willis McCutcheon, of Austin, Texas . . . was reared to the business of farming and stock ranching. **1881** CHASE *Editor's Run in N.M.* 38 In extensive stock ranching a man makes no account of distance. — **(16) 1819** E. DANA *Geog. Sk.* 190 These swamps afford the finest stock range imaginable, particularly for hogs. **1913** BARNES *Western Grazing Grounds* 382 Nester, a small farmer generally located within the limits of some stock range. — **(17) 1873** BEADLE *Undevel. West* 794 Western Texas [means] the whole region from the Colorado to the Rio Grande, including the 'stock region,' especially so-called. **1888** *Cent. Mag.* Feb. 507/1 The traveler . . . can hardly believe he is in the great stock region. — **(18) 1885** *Wkly. New Mexican Rev.* 8 June 2/6 About 700 saddle horses are being used in the Watrous stock round-up. — **(19) 1890** LANGFORD *Vigilante Days* (1912) 518 The only habitations of whites . . . were the log cabins of the stock tenders.

(20) 1840 *Knickerb.* XVI. 160 Some of these paths were made by the cattle of the settlers, and were called 'stock-tracks.' — **(21) 1859** BARTLETT 451 *Stock-Train,* a train of railroad cars loaded with cattle. **1898** *McClure's Mag.* X. 403 You're wanted for a stock train. — **(22) 1842** *Cultivator* X. 37 Stock water is obtained in creeks, ponds and springs. **1942** LILLARD *Desert Challenge* 17 The cold winters, which make winter feeding necessary, make control of stock water on the range less important than control of irrigation water, which raises the hay needed for winter feeding.

c. *To take stock in,* to have regard for or confidence in. *Colloq.*

1870 MARK TWAIN *Sk. New & Old* 161 The chance 'theory' concerning seven-up is . . . calculated to inflict . . . pecuniary loss upon any community that takes stock in it. **1945** BOTKIN *My Burden* 50 Old Master's oldest boy, didn't take much stock in church.

As the last term in **black, corn, curb, fancy, full, Georgia, half, Kentucky, live, Louisiana, mining, Morgan, notion, out, paper, Patton, pen, Pilgrim, plow, preferred, she, shovel plow, state, watered, wildcat stock.**

* **stock,** *v.*

1. *tr.* (See quot. 1828.)

1828 WEBSTER, *Stock,* . . . to supply with seed; as, to stock a land with clover or herdsgrass. American farmers. **1863** MITCHELL *My Farm* 70 Shall I stock my land with grass, and sell hay?

2. To provide (a plow or plowshare) with a stock.

1851 *Fla. Plantation Rec.* 354, 1 [slave] Stocking Ploughs and so forth. **1857** *Ill. Agric. Soc. Trans.* III. 489 [The plant-cutter] is made by stocking a plow share similar to a common plow.

3. To issue shares or stocks in (a business enterprise).

1880 *Cimarron News & Press* 18 March 2/2 The Jicarilla placers, close by, have been stocked for just one million. **1908** STEVENS *Liberators* 212 We can easily bond it for six millions and stock it for five millions.

stockade stak'ed, *v. tr.* To protect with a stockade. *Obs.*

1677 *Doc. Hist. N.Y. State* I. 12 The Caiougos . . . intend next spring to build all their houses together and stockade them. **1847** HOWE *Hist. Coll. Ohio* 377 They keep no sentry, and had neglected to stockade or set pickets around the block-house.

Hence **stockaded,** *a. Obs.*

1675 in EASTON *Indian War* 75 A Block House or some stockadoed or palisadoed House or Place. **1756** *Doc. Hist. N.Y. State* I. 478 At the Falls . . . a good stockaded Fort is building, to defend that Pass. **1857** *Atlantic Mo.* Nov. 94/2 The spot was the site of the old blockhouse and stockaded fort.

stockade fort. A fort or fortified place having a stockade as part of its defenses. Now *hist.* Cf. **picket stockade.**

1742 *Essex Inst. Coll.* XLV. 343 He was going to the Lake after his Powder-Horn and his gun, he had left at the Stockade Fort there. **1803** LEWIS in *Jrnls. L. & Ordway* 38 On the point formed by this creek and the river stands an old stockade fort, now gone to decay. **1903** *N.Y. Tribune* 13 Sep., The colonel's daughter was born in a stockade fort.

Stockbridges ˈstɑkˌbrɪdʒəz, *n. pl.* An Algonquian tribe of Indians of the Mahican Confederacy, first known under the name Housatonic, but later named after the village of Stockbridge, Mass. Usu. attrib., esp. **Stockbridge Indian**(s).

1756 in *Hist. MSS Comm. 14th Rep.* App. X. (1895) 7 Deed of Sale of Land from the Stockbridge Indians. **1759** *Newport Mercury* 4 Dec. 2/2, I had 6 Men slightly wounded, and a Stockbridge Indian killed. **1838** VAN BUREN in *Pres. Mess. & P.* III. 429, I transmit for your consideration a communication from the Secretary of War, respecting a treaty before you with the Stockbridge and Munsee Indians. **1894** ROBLEY *Bourbon Co., Kans.* 7 These various tribes of New York Indians, consisting of the remnants of the Senacas, Onondagas, . . . Stockbridges, Munsees and Brothertowns, were called the 'Six Nations.' **1948** *Green Bay* (Wis.) *Press-Gaz.* 30 June 16/5 Stockbridge and Navajo tribesmen will also encamp at Oneida over the coming week end.

* **stocker,** *n.* An animal, esp. a young steer or heifer, intended for butchering but kept until fattened or mature.

1881 *Chi. Times* 1 June, Stockers and feeders were dull and weaker. **1905** *Bur. Plant Industry Bul.* No. 74, 9 Stockers are shipped from the southwest to the Pacific coast, Montana, and Canada to take advantage of feed in those localities when it is unobtainable in the southern breeding grounds. **1947** PERRY *Cities of Amer.* 244 Kansas City stockyards handle more stockers and feeders . . . than any other American market.

attrib. **1942** DALE *Cow Country* 240 The northern plainsmen soon came to look to Texas as a source of supply for stocker cattle. **1946** *Dly. Ardmoreite* (Ardmore, Okla.) 15 Dec. 27/4 Sows weak to 50 lower; stocker pigs steady to 1.50 lower. **1948** *Ib.* 4 May 9/1 One man has consigned . . . 50 stocker cattle for Thursday Sale.

* **stocking,** *n.* **1. stocking basket,** a basket in which a housewife keeps stockings to be mended. **2. stocking weaver,** a now unidentifiable insect. *Obs.*

(1) **1868** A. D. WHITNEY *P. Strong* 150 'That's off my mind!' said mother, . . . turning the stocking-basket bottom up. **1890** *Harper's Mag.* Dec. 146/2, I had some o' the old blue feetin' layin' on my stockin' basket's if they was waitin' to be darned. — (2) **1819** NUTTALL *Travels Ark.* (1821) 181 The crickets, grashoppers [*sic*], catidids, and stocking-weavers, as they are familiarly called, kept up such a loud and shrill crepitation, as to prove entirely irksome.

As the last term in **blue, Christmas, Indian, leather, silk stocking.**

stogy ˈstogɪ, *n.* Also **stogie, stoga.** [Cone*stoga*, Pa.]

1. A heavy, rough shoe or boot. Also attrib.

1847 PALMER *Rocky Mts.* (1904) 217, I paid for a pair of stoga shoes, made in one of the Eastern states . . . four dollars and fifty cents. **1855** *Golden Era* (S.F.) 4 March 2/3 These 'stogy' boots are good enough. **1905** *D.N.* III. 96 Stogies, n. Brogans. 'These stogies won't wear long.'

2. An inexpensive cigar, usu. long and slender. In full **stogy cigar.** Cf. **Pittsburgh stogy.**

1893 *D.N.* I. 237 *Stogies* . . . cheap cigars. **1930** OMWAKE *Conestoga Teams* 118 The Conestoga wagon gave its name to the Stogie cigar, a great thin coarse one, supposed to have been originally a foot long and made for the delectation of the wagoner. **1948** *Herald-Press* (St. Joseph, Mich.) 14 Aug. 5/2 Columbus in 1492 saw his first Indian contentedly puffing away on a stogie.

attrib. **1949** *Painter & Decorator* Oct. 39/1, I remember, as a boy, going into a stogie factory in which stogies were then all hand-rolled. That particular place employed about 500 Stogie rollers, the members of the National Stogie Makers' League.

Stokes's aster. A flower, *Stokesia laevis* (see quot. 1891), named after Jonathan Stokes (1755–1831), an English botanist.

1891 *Cent.* 5958/3 The only species, *S. cyanea*, is a native of the southern United States near the Gulf of Mexico, a rare plant of wet pine-barrens. . . . [They] are grown in large quantities for the London market, under the name of *Stokes's aster.* **1930** BAILEY *Cyclo. Horticulture* 3245/1 Stokes' Aster is one of the choicest and most distinct of American hardy perennial herbs. **1949** *Mo. Bot. Garden Bul.* April 90 Of those groups about a foot high we could use *Anchusa myosotidiflora*, various pinks (*Dianthus*), . . . Stokes aster (*Stokesia*), . . . and *Sedum spectabile.*

stolen base. In baseball, a base reached by a runner who has achieved a steal (sense **2.**).

1889 W. CAMP *College Sports* (1893) 176 Following this column is sometimes one headed S.B., which means 'stolen bases.' **1910** *Spalding's Base Ball Guide* 383 A stolen base shall be credited to the base runner. **1950** *Dly. Ardmoreite* (Ardmore, Okla.) 30 April D. 6/1 Joe Nodar . . . was high on the list in stolen bases.

stomach tooth. (See quot. 1889.)

1875 R. H. DAVIS *Silhouettes* 240 He has one stomach-tooth almost through. **1880** *Harper's Mag.* Sep. 582/1 Cuttin' of his stomach teeth was the end o' him. **1889** BILLINGS *Nat. Medical Dict.* II. 594 Stomach tooth, canine tooth of lower jaw of first dentition, so called because of gastric disturbance frequently accompanying its eruption.

* **stone,** *n.* In combs.: (1) **stone bee,** a gathering of neighbors for removing stones from a piece of land; (2) **boat (sled),** a flat-bottomed sled for transporting stones or other heavy objects for short distances; (3) * **breaker,** a machine for breaking or crushing stone; (4) **car,** a railway car for carrying stone or stones; (5) **clover,** (see quot.); (6) **-coal indigo,** =**pit-coal indigo,** *obs.;* (7) **-coal iron,** ?iron smelted with stone-coal, *rare;* (8) **cotton,** unginned or seed cotton, poss. so called because of verbal modesty about "seed," *obs.;* (9) **crowbar,** some stone object thought to have been used by Indians as a crowbar *q.v.*, *rare;* (10) **dog,** (see quot.), *obs.;* (11) **drag,** =**stone boat;** (12) * **fence,** a mixed alcoholic drink,

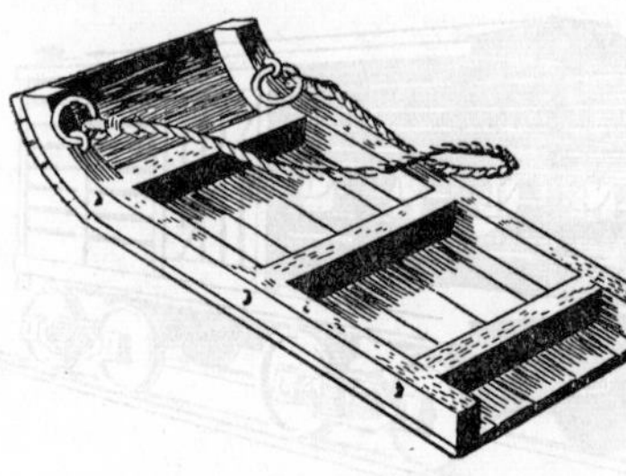

Stone drag or stone boat *c*1848

esp. whisky and cider, *slang, obs.;* (13) **fleet,** (see quot.), *obs.;* (14) **frolic,** =**stone bee;** (15) **Indians,** the Assiniboine, whose tribal name signifies a stone or one who cooks by the use of stones; (16) **jacket,** a prison, *slang, rare,* cf. * *stone jug;* (17) **mill,** a mill built of stones (see also quot. 1876); (18) **pasture,** a stony pasture, *colloq.;* (19) **scow,** a scow for transporting stones, *obs.;* (20) **sloop,** a sloop for transporting stones, *obs.,* (21) * **wall,** see as a main entry.

(1) **1829** COOPER *Wish-ton-Wish* xix, The neighbors will not be backward at the stonebee. **1856** GOODRICH *Recoll.* I. 75 At Ridgefield we used to have 'stone bees,' when all the men of a village or hamlet came together with their draft cattle. **1947** DOWNEY *Lusty Forefathers* 106 It was stone-bees that cleared the fields and built all the stone fences hereabouts. — (2) **1855** WILLIS *Convalescent* 75 A *stoneboat* would run glibly over such shallow snow! **1907** BAILEY *Cyclo. Amer. Agric.* I. 432/1 The sled, commonly known locally as the 'stone-boat sled,' has heavy runners six inches wide, two cross-beams and two raves, and a flexible pole. **1948** JACOBS *We Chose Country* 277 With a full load in the stoneboat, and another on the toboggan, we get a crack-the-whip effect that is as good as the thrills of a roller coaster. — (3) **1869** *Rep. Comm. Agric. 1868* 355 The cost, however, has of late been greatly reduced by the introduction of the 'Blake Stone-Breaker.' **1876** INGRAM *Centennial Exp.* 393 These rollers . . . are adapted for driving stone-breakers or other fixed machinery. — (4) **1881** *Rep. Ala. R.R. Comm.* I. 64 Number of stone cars.

(5) **1850** S. F. COOPER *Rural Hours* 125 The downy 'rabbit-foot,' or 'stone-clover,' the common red variety . . . are all introduced. —

(6) **1827** *Western Mo. Rev.* I. 85 The tin merchants are metamorphosed into traveling book-sellers, and instead of stone-coal-indigo, the people are cheated with catch-penny books and maps. — (7) **1871** W. M. GROSVENOR *Protection* 237 American stone-coal iron sells at about three dollars a ton more than Scotch pig. — (8) **1862** E. W. PEARSON *Lett. Port Royal* 109, I have stored twenty-five thousand pounds of stone cotton on my plantations. — (9) **1871** *Republican Rev.* 18 March 1/3 It was pronounced to be a 'stone crow-bar,' formerly used by the old Aztec inhabitants of this country.

(10) **1892** *N.J. State Geol. Rep.* 138 The low plain [south of Morristown is] . . . equally rich in concretions, which are locally known as 'clay-stones,' 'clay-dogs,' 'stone-dogs,' etc. — (11) **1867** RICHARDSON *Beyond Miss.* 131 One family even rode triumphantly on a stone drag—a broad plank dragged over the ground by two horses. **1902** MCFAUL *Ike Glidden* 26 They attached him to a stone-drag and four of the men stood on it. **1939** *L.A.* Map 168. — (12) **1843** *Ainsworth's Mag.* IV. 239 Anything in the shape of stone-fence will suit my fancy. **1910** J. HART *Vigilante Girl* 207 Did you ever tackle that Jersey beverage called 'Stone Fence'? — (13) **1924** *Pub. Col. Soc.* XXVI. 78 Forty [whaling vessels] were bought by the Federal Government and made up the greater portion of the well-known 'stone fleets' which were sunk at the entrances of the harbors of Savannah and Charleston to the end that the blockade of these ports might be made effective. — (14) **1823** I. HOLMES *Account* 358 If a field has to be cleared of stones, they have what is termed a stone frolic, . . . If Indian corn has to be husked, there will be a frolic for that also.

(15) **1859** *Col. Me. Hist. Soc.* 270 The Assinee Poetuc, or Stone Indians, are said to have been a portion of the Naudawissees on the Mississippi, mentioned in Carver's travels. — (16) **1799** *Aurora* (Phila.) 21 June (Th.), Paragraphs an hundred times more obnoxious than those for which Abijah Adams was dressed in a stone jacket. — (17) **1838** FLAGG *Far West* I. 84 My attention was arrested by that series of substantial stone mills situated upon the shore immediately above. **1876** KNIGHT 2398/2 *Stone-mill,* a machine for breaking or crushing stone. . . . A machine for facing stone. **1898** YOUNG *Jessamine Co., Ky.* 188 There is an old stone-mill at Keene, which was built in 1794. — (18) **1869** STOWE *Oldtown Folks* 125 [I've] heerd that 'ere boy's screeches clear from the stun pastur'. — (19) **1737** J. HEMPSTEAD *Diary* 314, I was at home all day splitting & hewing peices for a Stone Scow.

(20) **1886** *Leslie's Mo.* Feb. 223/1 The harbor is just large enough to store away three or four stone-sloops.

b. In the names of animals: (1) **stone bird,** (see quot.); (2) **carrier, =stone roller, toter;** (3) **cat(fish),** a catfish, *Noturus flavus,* of the Mississippi Valley, having poisonous pectoral spines; (4) * **crab,** a large edible crab, *Menippe mercenaria,* found along the southern coast of the U.S.; (5) * **curlew,** *local* (see quots.); (6) **lugger, =stone roller, toter;** (7) **roller,** the hog molly *q.v.* or a common cyprinoid fish, *Campostoma anomalum;* (8) **snipe,** a long-legged American bird of the genus *Totanus,* also with specifying adj.; (9) **toter, =stone roller.**

(1) **1917** *Birds of Amer.* I. 242 Greater Yellow-Legs. *Totanus melanoleucus.* . . . [Also called] Stone-bird. — (2) **1852** *Mich. Agric. Soc. Trans.* III. 228 Stone Carrier. These are knowing little fish. — (3) **1871** *Amer. Naturalist* IV. 719 The 'stone-cat-fish' were much more active, and shy. **1947** DALRYMPLE *Panfish* 291 So far we have discounted the tiny Stonecats and Madtoms, and briefly appraised most of the lunkers. — (4) **1709** LAWSON *Carolina* 161 The large Crabs, which we call Stone-Crabs . . . are plentifully met withal. **1884** GOODE *Fisheries* I. 773 The Stone Crabs generally live more or less buried beneath the bottom.

(5) **1835** AUDUBON *Ornith. Biog.* III. 510 The Semipalmated Snipe is known . . . from the Carolinas Southward . . . [as the] 'Stone Curlew.' **1917** *Birds of Amer.* I. 246 Willet. . . . Other Names . . . Spanish Plover; Stone Curlew; Duck Snipe. *Ib.* I. 177 The young birds [of the white ibis] before they assume the adult plumage are called 'Stone Curlews' by the fishermen. — (6) **1882** JORDAN & GILBERT *Syn. Fishes N. Amer.* 130. **1935** ROLLINS *Discovery Ore. Trail* 130 (*footnote*), The 'Sucker' was a catostomoid fish, *Catostomus* or *Hypentelium nigricans,* known also, in popular parlance, as stone-roller, stone-lugger. — (7) **1903** T. H. BEAN *Fishes N.Y.* 103 The stone roller has a peculiar physiognomy. **1936** *Amer. Sp.* XI. 317 Stone-roller, n. A small fish common in the Ozark streams. — (8) **1858** BAIRD *Birds Pacific R.R.* 731 Tell Tale; Stone Snipe. . . . A large and handsome species, abundant throughout the United States. **1917** *Birds of Amer.* I. 242 Greater Yellow-Legs. *Totanus melanoleucus.* . . . [Also called] Stone-bird; Stone Snipe; Yelper. *Ib.* 244 Yellow-Legs. *Totanus flavipes.* . . . [Also called] Little Stone-bird; Little Stone Snipe. — (9) **1812** STUART *Narratives* 130 Our almost only resource for food . . . is poor Trout and a species of Sucker which is fat & really excellent, called by Virginians the *Stone-toater.* **1883** *Harper's Mag.* Dec. 103/2 The fishes known as stone-toters, or suckers, are so named from their habit of piling up pebbles into rude mounds, in which their eggs are concealed. **1903** T. H. BEAN *Fishes N.Y.* 104, 113.

As the last term in **arrow, ballast, banner, bark, bird, blue, brown, cat, China, clay, clear, Cleaveland, cliff, Connecticut, cotton, ending, fly, Jersey, Key, lost, mad, mad dog, medicine, metate, oil, peep, photograph, pipe, poisoned, red, roll, round, sand, shoulder, skipper, skipple, soap, traveling, Virginia, Yellowstone.**

Stoneite ˈstonaɪt, *n.* A follower of Barton Warren Stone (1772–1844), an evangelist who shared the enthusiasm of the contemporary revival movement and in 1803 seceded from the Presbyterian Church and subsequently organized churches known simply as "Christian." Cf. **New Light 1,** and **Revival man.**

1824 R. H. BISHOP *Hist. Church Ky.* 130 The people of whom we propose to give a short sketch . . . have usually been called 'New Lights, or Stoneites.' **1856** CARTWRIGHT *Autobiog.* 219 Arianism was rife through all that country [Kentucky], although they called themselves 'Christians,' and were called by the world, New Lights, Marshallites, or Stoneites. (These were two leading Presbyterian ministers, that in the time of a great revival in Kentucky, were disowned by the Synod of Kentucky.) **1948** *Crusader* May 15/1 'The Christian Church,' which name the 'Stonites' had selected.

* **stonewall,** *n.*

1. =stone fence. *Slang.* Now *hist.*

1857 *Santa Barbara* (Calif.) *Gaz.* 29 Jan. 4/3 The drinks ain't no good here—there ain't no variety in them, neither; no white-nose, apple-jack, stone-wall, chain-lightning, railroad, hailstorm. **1947** DOWNEY *Lusty Forefathers* 4 'Switchell. . . . Spiced Cyder. . . . Stone-wall' . . . the effect of the last listed, a potent mixture of hard cider and rum, would resemble a head-on collision with the structure for which it was named.

2. (*cap.*) A title or nickname for Gen. Thomas J. Jackson (1824–63) of the Confederate army, usu. **Stonewall Jackson.**

1862 *Texas Almanac Extra* (Austin) 18 Sep. 1/1 Stonewall Jackson was marching on Baltimore with 40,000 men. **1862** *Houston* (Tex.) *Tri-Wkly. News* 19 Sep. 1/1 Expressions indicative of similar confidence in 'Stonewall' are said to be quite common with Gen. Lee. **1950** *N.O. Times-Picayune Mag.* 9 April 18/3 Me and Stonewall Jackson never surrendered to the Damyankees!

3. Stonewall Brigade, the brigade or troops commanded by Stonewall Jackson. Now *hist.*

1890 HENTY *With Lee in Va.* 107 Bee . . . shouted, 'Look, there is Jackson standing like a stone wall.' . . . Henceforth the brigade was known as the Stonewall Brigade, and their general by the nickname of Stonewall Jackson. **1900** *Everybody's Mag.* Dec. 544/2 The ford at Seaver's . . . was guarded by a part of the famous 'Stonewall Brigade.' **1940** DOUGLAS *I Rode With Stonewall* 217 The Stonewall Brigade changed its camp three times.

4. Stonewall Guard, a secret organization formed in the South after the Civil War to assist in maintaining white supremacy. *Obs.*

1880 *46th Congress* 2 Sess. Sen. Rep. No. 693 p. xvii, The distrust of Democracy . . . was inspired during the days, when the 'Kuklux,' the 'White Brotherhood,' the 'Universal Empire,' and the 'Stonewall Guard' spread terror and desolation over the State. *Ib.* 400 The White Brotherhood, the Invisible Empire, and the Stonewall Guard.

stooge studʒ, *n.* [Origin unknown. See note.] One who serves or cooperates with another in a meanly subservient manner, orig. and often with reference to the stage. *Slang.*

The 1945 quot. refers to an episode of *c*1897. A musician desired Service to help him on the stage by taking the role of an assistant who was to try to play something and make a wretched failure of it. Thereupon the musician was to take over, the excellence of his performance being heightened by the poor playing of his foil.

1913 *Sat. Ev. Post* 1 Nov. 64/4 Ben, I want you to plant one of your stooges in that coop with a couple of smoke-pots, so that we'll get the effect of Jack coming through the thickest of it. **1929** *Variety* 24 July 1/1 Stuges perform on the floor with dead-pan faces and unconscious feet beating out the time-step. **1945** SERVICE *Ploughman* 185, 'I have a good ear, but I can't read music—not fast, that is.' 'That does not matter. Well, I am going to make you an offer. Will you be my *stooge?*' *Ib.* 188 Say, there's an old fellow living in the annex of the Golden North Hotel wants what he calls a stooge. He's a musician too. **1950** *Time* 27 Feb. 25/3 'The party decided his Communist affiliation was too well known.' A stooge was picked instead.

Also as a verb.

1948 MENJOU & MUSSELMAN *It Took 9 Tailors* 91 By prearrangement, Montana used to stooge for Doug whenever visitors came on the lot.

* **stool,** *n.*

1. A bird, either real or artificial, used as a decoy. Also attrib.

1811 WILSON *Ornithology* IV. 84 Two or three live Crows being previously procured as decoys, or as they are called, *Stool-crows.* **1825** *Huntington Rec.* III. 522 No person [shall] be permitted to gun with macheanes or stools in sd Town. *a***1841** HAWES *Sporting Scenes* I. 199 Your man disposes the stool-birds to your leeward, and sails away to stir up flocks miles off. **1893** *Outing* Nov. 137/1 The old-day countless myriads of pigeons have vanished for aye, and with them the 'stool-birds' and netted 'stools,' the 'bough-house' and taut spring-rope. **1949** R. J. SIM *Pages from Past* 62 Here is a hamper of small birds—all solid wood carefully rounded. 'Snipe stools' they are called.

2. (See quot. 1881.)

1869 in *Amer. Sp.* XXIII. (1948) 297/2 He wrote in his diary for July, 1869, that he had just *shelled* some of his oyster land with 900 bushels of *stools*, stools being his name for *cuch* [*sic*]. **1881** INGERSOLL *Oyster Industry* 249 *Stools*, material spread on the bottom for oyster spawn to cling to. **1883** *Nat. Museum Bul.* No. 27, 220 All shells, or other matters suitable for 'stools' or 'cultch,' are put on the shell-heaps on shore for subsequent use.

3. stool pigeon, a pigeon fastened to a stool or perch to serve as a lure for others. *Obs.* Cf. **flutter pigeon.**

1836 IRVING *Astoria* I. 137 One man . . . was used like a 'stool pigeon,' to decoy the others. **1871** DE VERE 211 The *Stool-Pigeon* . . . [literally] means the pigeon, with its eyes stitched up, fastened on a stool, which can be moved up and down by the hidden fowler.

b. *transf.* A person or thing serving as a decoy, a police informer. *Colloq.*

1830 *Working-man's Gaz.* (Woodstock, Vt.) 1 Dec. 79/2 A wag who keeps an oyster cellar in Newark, advertises, among other things, '. . . . stool pigeons trained to catch voters for the next Presidency—warranted to suit either party.' **1850** *Cong. Globe* 18 July 1403/1 Sheltering this aggression, on the part of the United States, behind 'poor New Mexico,' who is only a stool pigeon. **1901** FLYNT *World of Graft* 125 In New York City he [a mouthpiece] is also called a Stool-pigeon. The 'profession' generally speak of him as a Squealer. **1950** *World-Herald Mag.* (Omaha) 12 Feb. 4/3 Lock the stool pigeon up immediately.

4. stool-pigeoning, (see quot.). *Obs.*

*a***1848** *N.Y. Courier & Enquirer* (B.), 'Stool-pigeoning' is for an officer to arrest a party of doubtful or perhaps decidedly bad reputation on suspicion, and making him or her give up money or valuables to obtain liberty, when the officer would set the party free, and nothing would be heard by the public or any one else of the arrest, or anything else connected with it.

As the last term in **Arkansas, dopping, pigeon stool.**

stool,** *v. tr.* and *intr.* To entice (wild fowl) by means of a stool or decoy; of a bird, to come to a decoy. *Obs.* — *a1841** HAWES *Sporting Scenes* I. 55, I'll tell you all about that . . . the next time we're stooling snipe together. **1874** LONG *Wild-Fowl* 209 Widgeon . . . stool well to almost any decoys.

stoop stup, *n.* [Du. *stoep*, in first sense.] Formerly a small porch with seats or benches; now any small porch, veranda, or entrance stairway at a house door. Cf. **Dutch stoop, high stoop.**

The use of *stoop* in the first quot. for a tract of land is puzzling. It may be a different word.

[**1679** in *Md. Hist. Mag.* XIX. 349 The Stoop, 118 acr. Sur[veyed] the 24th March 1679 for George Yates.] **1755** *Essex Inst. Coll.* LII. 78 Houses of one Story & a Stoop to each. **1845** *Knickerb.* XXV. 127 No man can be found who will . . . run up and down one hundred and fifty 'stoops.' **1950** *L.A. Times Home Mag.* 12 Feb. 4/3 A brick stoop and walk were built before a bay window on the driveway side, making a new and smarter entrance.

attrib. **1852** *Harper's Mag.* March 446/1 She gave him the message, standing at the stoop-door. **1904** *N.Y. Ev. Post* 21 Nov. 2 Five Italian bootblacks were charged with 'keeping and maintaining bootblack stands within the stoop line without a licence.'

b. Steps over a fence, a stile. *Rare.*

1897 STUART *Simpkinsville* 135 The cordial relations . . . were still indicated by the well worn 'stoop' set in the dividing-fence between the two gardens.

***stoop,** *v. intr.* In expressions relating to field crops in the production of which much stooping is necessary. *Colloq.* — **1928** *Sat. Ev. Post* 10 March 170/2 He does heavy field work—particularly in the so-called 'stoop crops' and 'knee crops' of vegetable and cantaloupe production. **1949** *Nat. Geog. Mag.* May 573 (*legend*), Most lettuce and asparagus cutting, and similar 'stoop labor,' is done in California by Filipinos, Japanese, and Mexicans.

***stop,** *n.* As the last term in **back, cattle, corporation, dinner, door, fire, short, whistle stop.**

* **stop,** *v.*

1. In noun combs.: (1) **stop ball,** in baseball, a pitched ball which, allegedly, stops just before reaching the batter, *obs.;* (2) **law,** a law placing limitations on proceedings against debtors, *obs.;* (3) **over,** a stop at an intermediate point on a journey, also attrib.; (4) **reel,** on a fishing rod, a reel that can be stopped or locked when a desired length of line has been let out; (5) **sign, signal,** a sign or signal, esp. a red light in a system of traffic lights, directing one to stop.

(1) **1912** MATHEWSON *Pitching* 222 Pitchers . . . are always trying for new curves. . . . Out of the South . . . drift tales each spring of the 'fish' ball and the new 'hook' jump and the 'stop' ball. — (2) **1820** *Ann. 16th Congress* 1 Sess. 1944 Pennsylvania speaks . . . of a stop law to prevent the sale of real and personal property in execution, unless it sells for two-thirds of its appraised value. **1854** BENTON *30 Years' View* I. 5/2 Stop laws—property laws— . . . the intervention of the legislator between the creditor and the debtor: this was the business of legislation. — (3) **1881** *Harper's Mag.* April 767/2 Stop-over tickets . . . give them the privilege of turning their stock out at any place for the winter, and then sending them on in the spring to market. **1885** *Outing* Nov. 150/2 There I took advantage of what, in railroad parlance, is called a 'stop over.' **1948** *Democrat* 19 Aug. 7/4 Fluffy went sight-seeing during a one-night stopover in Buffalo. — (4) **1893** *Outing* XXII. 122/2 Of late years the 'click' or 'stop-reel' has been a favorite—particularly with fly fishermen. . . . One might as well carry a squawking poll-parrot through the brush as a 'stop' reel.

(5) **1949** *Oak Leaves* (Oak Park, Ill.) 24 Nov. 16/1 Also on the council's agenda will be a discussion of proposed stop and go signals at Roosevelt and East avenue. **1950** *Dly. Oklahoman* (Okla. City) 15 Feb. 1/3 A woman in the crowd came forward to say she had seen Walker stop at the stop sign before proceding into the street intersection.

2. In phrases: (1) *To stop by*, see * **by 1;** (2) *to stop off*, to interrupt one's journey for a brief stay at some intermediate point, *colloq.;* (3) *to stop over*, on a journey, to remain at a place after the departure of one's conveyance with the intention of proceeding by one going later, *colloq.*

(2) **1855** *Knickerb.* XLVI. 604 He had 'stopped off,' he said, to see a friend. **1932** GRAYSON *Leaders* 400 Pleased with his success, Armour started home on a visit and stopped off at Milwaukee, then the leading city of the Middle West. — (3) **1857** M. J. HOLMES *Meadow-Brook* xvi, We have stopped over one train. **1922** DEPEW *My Memories* 220 Passing through Albany while he was governor, I stopped over to pay my respects.

* **store,** *n.*

1. A shop or other place of business where goods are kept for sale, a retail shop.

"In the United States and the British Colonies any shop where goods are sold, large or small, is often called a store. This is not mere provincial grandiloquence, as is often supposed, but results from the fact that, when the use grew up, the places in question were really storehouses,—as every 'shop' in a new country must necessarily be" (Greenough & Kittredge *Words and Their Ways* 134).

1721 *Amer. Wkly. Mercury* 16 March 2/2 At a Store under George Mifflins House . . . are several Sorts of English Goods to be sold. **1817** S. BROWN *Western Gazetteer* 54 There are within the precincts of the town . . . five taverns and seven stores. **1948** *Democrat* 1 Jan. 5/3 Our store will be open Wednesday all day.

2. (See quot.) *Obs.*

1775 *Amer. Husbandry* I. 187 Every planter [in Pa.] has his pond at least, but generally a chain of them, on a brook, which always supplies fresh water; in these stores, as they call them, are kept the products of their river-fishing.

3. In combs.: (1) **store bill,** a bill incurred at a store by purchasing on credit; (2) * **boat,** a boat carrying miscellaneous articles for sale; (3) **book,** an account book in which transactions in a store or shop are recorded; (4) **boom,** a boom where sawlogs are held in store; (5) **bought,** *a.* purchased from a store as distinguished from homemade, *colloq.;* (6) **boughten,** *a.* =prec.; (7) **box,** a box in which goods are shipped to a store; (8) **corn,** (see quot.), *rare;* (9) **goods,** goods such as are usu. sold in a store; (10) * **house,** =**store 1;** (11) * **keeper,** one who keeps a store, a merchant; (12) **pay,** payment for produce or other articles by goods from a store instead of by cash; (13) **show,** a moving picture show in a building erected for a store, *obs.;* (14) **street,** a street given over to stores; (15) **ticket,** a ticket accepted in trade at a store; (16) **trough,** a trough in which maple sap is stored temporarily in sugar-making.

(1) **1853** P. PAXTON *Yankee in Texas* 76 A little money was sometimes to be found, if their store bill did not overrun their crops. **1943** *Harper's Mag.* June 85 Well, most of these families had . . . store bills. — (2) **1822** WOODS *Eng. Prairie* 87 The master of the store-boat . . . had freighted his boat with store-goods and fruit. **1864** NICHOLS *Amer. Life* I. 169 Selling supplies to steam-boats, and transferring passengers from the down to the up-river boats, is done on floating store boats, made fast to the shore. **1944** CLARK *Pills* 25 In the Louisiana sugar belt, barge store boats eased along the back ways of sugar plantations receiving stolen goods. — (3) **1740** W. STEPHENS *Proc. Georgia* II. 20 [Upon] looking into the Store-Books, it was found there was a considerable Debt. **1898** PAGE *Red Rock* 446, I want to ax you,—is Mr. Spickit—'lowed to write 'whiskey' down in my sto'-book? **1944** CLARK *Pills* 135 Southerners generally like oysters, both canned and fresh, and many of the store books contain records of numerous purchases of this highly perishable food. — (4) **1871** *Winnebago Co. Press* (Neenah, Wis.) 1 July 2/3 Many of the mills were visited, several going up to the river three miles to the store boom, where as far as the eye could reach the river was filled with one grand mass of logs.

(5) **1932** W. KELLEY *Inchin' Along* 7 Overalls . . . were worn by the men, with only an occasional store-bought suit in evidence. **1941** DANIELS *Tar Heels* 258 Coffee comes in, too, and an increasing amount of the twice-as-much-for-a-nickle colas and store-bought cakes. — (6) **1883** ZEIGLER & GROSSCUP *Alleghanies* 91 Two good-natured-looking young men [were] dressed in . . . 'store-boughten' coats, and homespun pantaloons. **1944** *Christian Sci. Mon.* 25 April (Editorial), Nobody . . . cares for this miserable store-boughten meal. — (7) **1880** N. BROOKS *Fairport Nine* 2 Spare barrels, store-boxes . . . were to be brought in. **1904** STRATTON-PORTER *Freckles* 69, I'll have Duncan get you a ten-bushel store-box the next time he goes to town. — (8) **1843** OLIVER *Eight months* 86 Store, or sod corn, is planted on the breaking up of prairie, the seeds being scattered along every third furrow; and thus the land is ploughed and a crop put in at the same time. — (9) **1822** WOODS *English Prairie* 98 We had about 14,000 lbs. weight of store goods, on board the ark, to be left at this place [Cincinnati]. **1944** JOHNSON *As I Dare* 325 He had ridden a long distance bringing blankets and silver work to exchange for store goods.

(10) **1707** *Boston News-Letter* 27 Jan. 2/2 To be Sold . . . at his Store-House upon the Dock in Boston near the Swing-Bridge, Good Barbadoes Rum & Molasses. *c*1773 in *S. Lit. Messenger* XI. 139/1 Shops . . . are here called Store Houses. **1877** JOHNSON *Anderson Co., Kans.* 63 About this time a store house was built and occupied by a merchant. — (11) [**1741** P. TAILFER *Narr. Georgia* 107 Augusta . . . is principally, if not altogether, inhabited by Indian Traders and Store-keepers.] **1742** *Pa. Gaz.* 13 Jan., [Franklin offers his goods] to country storekeepers. **1886** STAPLETON *Major's Christmas* 83 Store-keepers come, too, with goods as fine as in Bankton. **1949** *Democrat* 8 Dec. 6/2 He's jess waitin' for the storekeeper to bring back the spittoon. — (12) **1845** COOPER *Chainbearer* xix, One pound sixteen, one-third store-pay, is the utmost farthin' I can offer. **1891** WELCH *Recoll. 1830–40* 353 The workmen were to receive . . . only half cash, the remainder in trade—store pay, *i.e.:* in orders on the employers or other stores for such goods as they needed. — (13) **1920** C. R. COOPER *Under Big Top* 59 One block from my destination was a 'store show.' **1927** *Scribner's Mag.* March 285/2 Proprietors of feed-stores and the like who . . . had heard what had happened at Salamanca, N.Y. (where the first permanent moving picture 'store show' was established . . .), closed out their stocks. — (14) **1879** WHITMAN *Spec. Days* 155 Fourth, Fifth and Third streets are store-streets.

(15) **1878** *Rep. Indian Affairs* p. xxxix, Formerly the Indians were imposed upon through a system of brass checks, tokens, and store-tickets. — (16) *a*1797 in IMLAY *Western Territory* (ed. 3) 149 The sap flows into wooden troughs, from which it is carried and poured into store troughs, or large cisterns, in the shape of a canoe, or large manger. **1851** *Knickerb.* XXXVII. 377 He tramped [through the snow] . . . to bring the luscious juice to the 'store-trough.'

Also *store account, boy, clerk, counter, debt, detective, door, front, furniture, gallery, grounds, hours, keeping, proprietor, rent, stuff, window,* etc.

b. Designating products purchased at a store as distinguished, usu., from those made at home: (1) **store boots,** (2) **candy,** (3) **cheese,** (4) **clothes,** (5) **dress,** (6) **flag,** (7) **meal,** (8) **medicine,** (9) **pants,** (10) **sugar,** (11) **suit,** (12) **tea,** (13) **teeth,** (14) **tobacco.**

(1) **1857** STROTHER *Virginia* 238 Nowadays, sence these store boots come in, . . . there hain't no distinctions; . . . everything w'ars boots now. — (2) **1880** MARK TWAIN *Tramp Abroad* 229 By him lay a new jewsharp, . . . five pounds of 'store' candy. **1898** CANFIELD *Maid of Frontier* 207 Dearer than all was a package of American store candy, striped in red, white and blue. — (3) **1863** P. S. DAVIS *Young Parson* 61 On the table: . . . one plate of 'store cheese,' and half a bread-basket of ginger crackers. **1894** *Vt. Agric. Rep.* XIV. 25 A full cream store cheese is run through a grinder. — (4) **1840** *Knickerb.* XVI. 262, I felt an awe of young ladies in 'store clothes.' **1944** JOHNSON *As I Dare* 294 These young men did not want to give up their store clothes.

(5) **1938** MATSCHAT *Suwannee River* 82 I'm right peart when I'm smarted up, in my store dress an' all. — (6) **1878** HART *Sazerac Lying Club* 134 The beholder would never have guessed the materials of which it was composed, or that it was not a regular, Simon-pure, store flag. — (7) **1938** DAMON *Grandma* 12 She said, and she was right, that such meal had a consistency and a flavor that 'store' meal . . . lacked. — (8) **1854** THORPE *Master's House* 77 She wants some store medicine. — (9) **1891** THANET *Otto the Knight* 4 Thar, store pants an' gallowses! Make haste an' putt 'em on! **1942** STENGER *Mormon C.* 126 St. George smart alecs had money to jingle in their store pants.

(10) **1872** DE VERE 206 Store-sugar, or sugar made from the cane. — (11) **1900** ADE *More Fables* 28 People would see him there in his Store Suit. **1944** JOHNSON *As I Dare* 294 The Indian . . . had worn the store suits of the white man and drunk his fire water. — (12) **1843** in *Amer. Sp.* XXII. 206/1 Tisn't none of your spice-wood or yarbstuff, but the rale, gineine store tea. **1882** *Harper's Mag.* Dec. 126/2 The old man drank his store tea in triumph. — (13) **1891** THANET *Otto the Knight* 1 Nobody on the plantation has such beautiful, white store teeth. **1947** *Time* 8 Sep. 22/3 You must have paid plenty for those store teeth, Pop. — (14) **1884** MARK TWAIN *H. Finn* xxi, You borry'd store tobacker and paid back niggerhead.

c. *To keep store,* to have charge of a store as owner or clerk. *Colloq.*

1752 *Pa. Gazette* 25 June 4/3 Where Mr. Samuel Burge kept store. **1873** MARK TWAIN & WARNER *Gilded Age* 19 [The postmaster] 'kept store' in the intervals. **1904** *Cosmopolitan* May 88 He has 'kept store' in a country town.

As the last term in **adobe, auction, beer, bird, boat, book, branch, business, candy, carpet, cash, chain, cheap(ware), china, cigar, clothing, college, commissary, commission, company, corner, country, crockery, delicatessen, department, dime, dog, dollar, drug, druggist, dry-goods, factory, fancy, feed, finding, fish, five-and-ten-cent, floating, flour, flower, flying, food, frame, fruit, furnishing, furniture, general, gift, grain, grocery, gun, hardware, hat, ice cream, Indian, iron, jewelry, junk, leather, linen, liquor, log, meat, mercantile, millinery, Mormon, music, notion, one-piece, one-price, open, outfit, outfitting, package, paint, pastry, picture, plantation, produce, provision, racket, rag, retail, seed, settlement, shoe, state, subsistence, sutler's, thread, tin, tobacco, trade, trader's, trading, traveling, truck, twine, variety, vendue, village, vinegar, wet store.**

* **storm,** *n.* In combs.: (1) **storm cellar,** a cellar fitted up as a place of refuge from a storm; (2) **cotton,** cotton damaged by a storm just before or during the harvest, *obs.;* (3) **dam,** ?a dam capable of holding back waters resulting from a rainstorm, *rare,* cf. **storm water;** (4) **door,** an additional door, sometimes temporary, at an outer entrance for protection in severe or inclement weather [cf. Du. *stormdeur*]; (5) **flag,** a flag used as a signal of an approaching storm (see also quot. 1918); (6) **house,** a structure, sometimes as a temporary addition before an outer door, for protection in stormy weather; (7) **pit, =storm cellar;** (8) **porch,** a porch for the protection of an outer door from storms; (9) **rack,** a rack used on dining tables aboard ships in rough weather to prevent the dishes from slipping off; (10) **shed, =storm porch;** (11) **twister,** a cyclone; (12) **water,** water resulting from a rainstorm, also attrib.

(1) **1929** DOBIE *Vaquero* 151 Storm cellars in north Texas, Oklahoma, and Kansas still preserve its architecture. **1948** *Dly. Ardmoreite* (Ardmore, Okla.) 4 May 1/7 Townsmen saw it swing down upon them and were in their storm cellars when it struck 'with a crash and a roar.' — (2) **1850** *De Bow's Rev.* VIII. 100 The cotton . . . would be the inferior, leafy, or what is called 'storm cotton.' — (3) **1890** *Stock Grower & Farmer* 15 March 7/1 The irrigating dam on upper Cherry Creek [in Colo.] . . . will be the finest if not the largest 'storm dam' in America. — (4) **1878** E. B. TUTTLE *Border Tales* 29 The horses . . . broke loose from the stable, and begun gnawing the storm doors in front of the officers' quarters. **1946** THOMPSON *Amer. Daughter* 59 The one storm door was hung at the south entrance, the other door nailed closed.

(5) **1881** *Naval Encycl.* 789/2. **1896** *Weather Bureau Bul.* No. 80, 7 Two storm flags (red with black centers), displayed one above the other, . . . announce the expected approach of tropical hurricanes.

1918 Farrow *Dict. Mil. Terms* 588 *Storm flag*, in the United States army, the national flag, having 9 feet fly and 5 feet hoist. It is hoisted in stormy or windy weather, and is also to be used as a recruiting flag. — **(6) 1836** Power *Impressions of Amer.* I. 31 She . . . had stump-royal masts, and a storm-house abaft. **1887** *Harper's Mag.* Dec. 119/1 Two men . . . were bending down at the storm-house in front of her parlor-door. — **(7) 1930** Vines *River Goes with Heaven* 259 Well, he can fix him up a storm pit. — **(8) 1879** *Lumberman's Gaz.* 15 Oct. Horses . . . should be protected at every much-used entrance, by storm-porches. — **(9) 1893** Mark Twain *About All Kinds of Ships* 172 (R.), The storm-racks were on the table all the way over.

(10) 1920 Lewis *Main Street* 81 Storm sheds were erected at every door. — **(11) 1904** *Sun* (N.Y.) 23 Aug. 1 The storm twister struck Willow Lakes about 9 o'clock. — **(12) 1899** *Rep. Neb. State Bd. Irrig.* 17 Further development is possible from the storage of storm waters. **1949** *Telephone Reg.* (McMinnville, Ore.) 4 Aug. 1/2 The project will alleviate a serious storm water disposal program.

As the last term in **brain, electric, ice, line, nerve, sand, snowstorm.**

* **story,** *n.* A news article in a newspaper, or material for such an article.

1892 *Harper's Wkly.* 9 Jan. 42/4 An estimate is made of how much space each 'story' will occupy. **1914** S. H. Adams *Clarion* 14 You wouldn't hardly expect me to kill the story. **1948** *Time* 16 Feb. 52/2 The leads are not more readable than the stories—as they naturally should be—but less readable.

As the last term in **bear, continued, detective, feature, first, fish, gold, hard luck, Pilgrim, snake, sob, tall story.**

Stoughton bottle. A bottle containing a tonic, "Stoughton's Elixir," a once popular household remedy (see quots. 1942, 1950).

[**1857** Dunglison *Medical Dict.* (ed. 15) 917/1 Stoughton's Elixir is a compound tincture of gentian.] **1918** *Boston Herald* 15 March 10/4 We turned at once [in the *OED*] to 'Stoughton bottle' and found it not. 'There he sat like a Stoughton bottle.' Is the term strictly American? **1942** Berrey & Van den Bark *Amer. Thesaurus Slang* 574 cold-audience, deadheads, frost, stote an' bottle, *an unresponsive audience.* **1950** *Chi. Tribune* 25 Feb. 1. 8/3 'Like a Stoughton bottle': An American figure of speech for a stupid or inarticulate person. It has fallen into disuse, but it was so common in its heyday a generation or two ago that it gained dictionary recognition. It refers to an old fashioned remedy, much used as a restorative by housewives, called Dr. Stoughton's bitters.

* **stove,** *n.* In combs.: (1) **stove board,** a protective metal mat placed under a parlor stove; (2) **league,** a group of idlers who often sit around a stove, as in a cross-roads store, discussing baseball, also **hot stove league,** *jocular;* (3) **length,** a length corresponding to that of the firebox of a stove, a billet of wood of this length; (4) **lid,** a round metal plate fitting into an opening in the top of a stove or range, cf. **broken stove lid;** (5) **(lid) lifter,** a

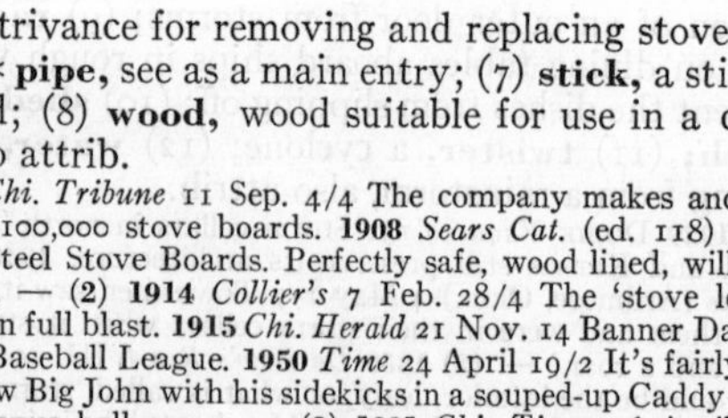

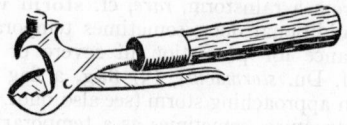

One type of stove lifter

metal contrivance for removing and replacing stove lids, etc.; (6) * **pipe,** see as a main entry; (7) **stick,** a stick of stovewood; (8) **wood,** wood suitable for use in a cook-stove, also attrib.

(1) 1875 *Chi. Tribune* 11 Sep. 4/4 The company makes and sells every year 100,000 stove boards. **1908** *Sears Cat.* (ed. 118) 423/6 Enameled Steel Stove Boards. Perfectly safe, wood lined, will keep their shape. — **(2) 1914** *Collier's* 7 Feb. 28/4 The 'stove league' season was in full blast. **1915** *Chi. Herald* 21 Nov. 14 Banner Day For Hot Stove Baseball League. **1950** *Time* 24 April 19/2 It's fairly easy now to follow Big John with his sidekicks in a souped-up Caddy to the hot-stove-league ball game. — **(3) 1881** *Chi. Times* 16 April, The buyer decides to have it taken to him sawed into stove lengths. **1929** A. J. Dickson *Across Plains* 58 We thereupon chopped down a good-sized tree, which we sawed into stove-lengths and split. — **(4) 1876** Mark Twain *Tom Sawyer* i. 18 She could have seen through a pair of stove-lids just as well. **1922** Tarkington *Gentle Julia* 113 In a room in the cellar, . . . were loosely stored . . . rusted stove lids and flatirons.

(5) 1886 *Harper's Mag.* Nov. 835/1 We'll have a real egg and cinder flip with the hot stove-lifter in it when we get back. **1935** *Montgomery Ward Cat.* (Index), Stove lid lifters. — **(7) 1888** Grigsby *Smoked Yank* (1891) 146 A little bundle of 'fat' pine, as much as a common stove stick would make, when split up fine, brought twenty-five cents in the prison. — **(8) 1867** Locke *Swingin' Round* 159, I held a stick of stove wood suspended over his head. **1919** Cady *Rhymes of Vt.* (1923) 172 Then next we moved the stovewood box. **1946** *Democrat* 24 Jan. 4/6 We have dry oak stove wood, 12-inches. We cut 15-inch stove wood.

As the last term in **barrel, box, brick, buffalo, caboose, camp, cannon, car, close, cook, cooking, dumb, five-plate, Franklin, jamb, Latrobe, monkey, morning-glory, Norwegian, Nott, Russian, salamander, six-plate, soapstone, ten-plate, wood, Yukon stove.**

* **stovepipe,** *n.*

1. A stovepipe hat.

[**1851** *Illust. London News* XIX. 395/2 Every male who wears the present stove-pipe section head-gear.] *a***1861** Winthrop *J. Brent* 209 Men hatted with slouched hat, wash-bowls, and stove-pipes. **1947** *Life* 10 Feb. 64/2 The black felt hat which he had worn . . . was discarded for a 'stovepipe'—the professional attire of lawyers.

2. stovepipe hat, a tall silk hat. Also **stovepipe beaver.**

1852 *Cleveland Plain-Dealer* 20 April, I have been laughing all morning at his queer bob-tailed coat, his stove-pipe hat, and awkward looking boots. **1865** *Washoe* (Nev.) *Times* 4 Feb. 4/1 How changed from him we in the city knew, In stove-pipe beaver, and a long-tailed blue. **1950** *New Yorker* 8 April 91/2 Quite an impressive scene is to watch Hildegarde in a Mr. John's stove-pipe satin hat.

Also **stovepipe Leary,** a type of stovepipe hat, so called from the maker.

1859 *Union No. Calif.* 17 Aug. 1/3 A beautiful stove-pipe 'Leary' and an awful dignity sat on his brow.

* **straddle,** *n.*

1. The action of taking a noncommittal position on a question, esp. a political one, also the position so taken.

1843 *Knickerb.* XXII. 233 These are . . . subjects for the straddle. **1892** *Chi. Tribune* 3 July 12/3 The Democratic plank . . . was adopted as a *substitute* for a protection straddle. **1905** *Springfield W. Republican* 1 Dec. 2 A compromise between free trade and protection that in America would be contemptuously characterized as a straddle. **1948** *Chi. D. News* 2 March 2/6 So, unless some really artistic straddles are invented meanwhile, it is not unreasonable to expect rows in the Democratic platform committee.

2. (See quot. 1864.)

1864 Webster 1304/1 *Straddle*, . . . the position, or the distance between the feet, of one who straddles; as, a wide straddle. **1934** Vines *Green Thicket World* 21 The two springs that were little more than a man's straddle apart boiled up.

3. In poker, a doubling of the blind or ante. Cf. * **straddler 2.**

1864 Dick *Amer. Hoyle* (1866) 177 If the dealer choose, he may, in turn, double the straddle. **1909** Webster 93/2 The ante is usually twice the amount of the blind or the last straddle.

b. capital straddle, (see quot.).

1882 McCabe *New York* 551 A 'capital straddle' is a bet that two numbers will be among the first three drawn, and wins $500.

4. *Stock Exchange.* (See quot. 1877.)

1877 Bartlett 667 *Straddle* . . . means a contract which gives the holder the privilege of calling for the stock at a fixed price, or of delivering it at the same price to the party who signs the contract. **1902** *Longman's Mag.* April 485 The lady's wealth is based on a successful Straddle, operated . . . in—Bristles—Hog's Bristles and Lard.

* **straddle,** *v.*

1. *tr.* To double the amount of (a blind *q.v.* sense **2.** or a bet).

1864 Dick *Amer. Hoyle* (1866) 177 The next player to the left may at his option straddle this bet. **1866** *Wilkes' Spirit of Times* 16 June 249/3 Five chips being the blind, it takes the next man ten to straddle it, and to straddle him will take twenty. **1884** Craddock *Where Battle Was Fought* 34 Only knew vaguely that somebody was 'passing' or 'straddling the blind.'

transf. **1884** *Chi. D. News* 4 July 2/4 The democrats must ante a square tariff-reform declaration. If they attempt to straddle the Ohio blind they will get bluffed.

2. To take an equivocal position on (an issue or question). Also absol.

1884 *Boston Traveller* Aug., Mr. Hendricks has straddled almost every issue of recent years, . . . [but has] remained firm on the negro question. **1906** *N.Y. Ev. Post* 6 Dec. 8 Eleven Senators answered yes, four no, and four straddled. **1948** *Chi. Tribune* 9 May 24/7 He not only straddles both sides of the fence, but tries to sit on top of it to boot, and all at the same time.

Hence *straddling, a. and n.

1892 *Chi. Tribune* 2 July 1/3 The Democratic convention having adopted a straddling plank on silver, he thought that there was no use in embarrassing the party. **1949** *S.F. News* 14 March 14/2 Despite the local board's straddling, the Legislature, fortunately, voted to continue the centers for another year.

3. (See quots.)

1870 W. W. Fowler *Ten Yrs. Wall St.* 128 Going long and short of stocks, at the same time, is what is technically called 'Straddling' the market. **1900** Nelson *A B C Wall St.* 161 A speculator who has bought and is long of one stock, and sold and is short of another, has straddled the market.

straddlebug ˈstrædḷ͵bʌg, *n.* Any one of various long-legged beetles, as the tumblebug. Also attrib. and transf. *Colloq.*

1831 *Working-man's Gaz.* (Woodstock, Vt.) 19 Jan. 130/3 Such a straddle-bug I never seed! **1865** Mark Twain *Sk. New & Old* 31 If he even see a straddle-bug start to go anywheres, he would bet you how long it would take. **1872** *Newton Kansan* 5 Sep. 2/1 We think it well that the people . . . not see quite so much of the straddle-bug business carried on by a few. **1948** *Sat. Ev. Post* 10 July 33/3, I will not support either a conservative or a straddlebug.

b. *W.* (See quots.)

1917 in Wentworth 602/1 We . . . set forth . . . to mark the location of our claims with the 'straddle-bugs.' The straddle-bug . . . was composed of 3 boards set together in tripod form & was used as . . . a sign of occupancy. Its presence defended a claim against the next comer. **1948** *Range Riders Western* May 23/2 Always before, the straddle bug had been a symbol of ownership, a pioneer's first notice to Nature that he had come to tame new land, to grow crops and make a home.

***straddler,** *n.* **1.** A politician who straddles an issue. **2.** One who makes a straddle in poker. Cf. ***straddle,** *n.* **3.**

(1) **1884** *Boston Traveller* Aug., Multitudinous attacks . . . are being made on the record as a straddler of Vice-Presidential Candidate Hendricks. **1896** Moe *Hist. Harvard* 37 Increase Mather . . . was a straddler on the question of bimetalism. — (2) **1946** Morehead & Mott-Smith *Penguin Hoyle* 133 The active player nearest the left of the last straddler must make the first bet in the second betting interval.

***straight,** *a.* and *n.*

1. *n.* In poker, a hand in which cards of different suits form a numerical sequence.

1857 *Spirit of Times* 14 March 24/1 The game of Poker, or Bluff, is sometimes played with a straight. For example: the five cards held in one hand—deuce, tray, four, five and six—is the lowest straight. **1903** O. Henry *Roads of Destiny* 210 He always would play jack, queen, king, ace, deuce for a straight. **1949** *Lubbock* (Tex.) *Morn. Avalanche* 23 Feb. I. 8/7 The last time George took a peek-back squint at that mitt . . . it was a busted straight.

2. *the straight,* the truth. *Colloq.*

1866 C. H. Smith *Bill Arp* 35 You should git the straight of it from one who seen it with his eyes. **1909** R. A. Wason *Happy Hawkins* 198, I ain't heard the straight of it. **1943** in Wentworth 602/1 Tell me the straight of it.

3. *ellipt.* **a.** A regular party member. **b.** =**straight whisky.**

(a) **1887** *Courier-Journal* 20 Jan. 2/5 The 'straights' will caucus this evening. — (b) **1905** O. Henry *Trimmed Lamp* 242, I managed to soak in a little straight or some spilled Martini. **1950** *Business Week* 22 April 24/2 Take a look at the table (above) and you will see that the straights and bonds are making their comeback.

4. In trap shooting: A perfect score.

1903 *Forest & Stream* 21 Feb. 160 (*Cent. Supp.*), In the 10-bird event W. . . . and C. each made a straight.

5. *a.* Genuine, undiluted, esp. of whisky. Cf. **straight whisky.**

1855 M. Thompson *Doesticks* 59 *My* glass of brandy, . . . [which] should have been 'straight,' was also surreptitiously diluted. **1889–90** Barrere-Leland II. 299 In the United States a straight drink means one of unmixed spirits. **1934** Vines *Green Thicket World* 97 He drank a large cup of coffee which was straight.

b. Unmixed with or unaccompanied by anything else.

1859 Bartlett 454 Straight. . . . Even or uniform in quality. A term used in commerce, and particularly among flour-dealers. **1873** Beadle *Undevel. West* 528 We lived on Navajo bread, coffee, and 'commissary butter,' straight. **1895** *N.Y. Dramatic News* 6 July 2/1 Trilby is the only 'straight' theatrical entertainment now left in New York. **1932** Grayson *Leaders* 444 For several years he did a steadily increasing business of a straight brokerage character.

c. whisky (or **Bourbon**) **straight,** undiluted whisky (or Bourbon).

1862 *Harper's Mag.* Aug. 312/1 [The] primer was simply a gill of Bourbon straight. **1864** *Cong. Globe* 21 April 1876/2 From the impassioned tone of the gentleman from Illinois . . . one would suppose that he had been investing in whisky straight. **1889–90** Barrere-Leland II. 299 In the United States . . . whisky straight is the same as neat.

d. Not deviating from a fixed amount or standard.

1889–90 Barrere-Leland II. 299 Thus, if cigars are labelled, 'Ten cents apiece, straight,' it means that no deduction will be made for buying a number of them. **1948** *Chi. D. News* 20 Sep. 18/2 In premedical college Jim S. was a brilliant student—straight A's.

e. Often in phrases (see quots.).

1868 Bowles *Colorado* (1869) 99 We had to take our victual and drink 'straight,'—plain ham and bread and butter and black coffee,—or go without. **1902** McKee *Land of Nome* 234 It was a rude shock, later in the evening, when I saw 'Little Casino' standing by the bar and drinking her whisky straight. **1947** *This Week Mag.* 10 May 13/2 She was a bold . . . camp in days gone by and still drinks her liquor straight.

6. *Polit.* Made up only of persons who support uncompromisingly a party or a principle; of a person, strictly partisan.

1856 *N.Y. Courier & Enquirer* Sep. (B.), The present candidate of the straight Whigs for the Vice-Presidency. **1887** Frederic *Seth's Brother's Wife* 403 You mustn't allow that to lead you into the habit of thinking that all bolters are saints and all straight-party men devils. **1898** *K.C. Star* 18 Dec. 5/7 The straight silver party . . . got only twenty-two out of the forty-five members of the legislature in Nevada. **1944** *Chi. D. News* 25 July 7/6 Few laymen realize that in every presidential election there is a sizeable group of voters who . . . continue to vote the straight party ticket as their fathers did.

b. Of votes: Cast in support of all the candidates of a single party. Cf. ***split,** *v.* **1.**

1892 *Chi. D. News Almanac* 237 Readjuster and straight Republican votes combined. **1904** *Brooklyn Eagle* 9 June 4 One unable to hold his straight party vote in his own city would be a calamity. **1949** *Time* 12 Sep. 21/3 Lausche's name was enough to pull thousands of straight party votes.

7. In combs.: (1) **straight ball,** (see quots.); (2) **car,** a railway freight or express car carrying various goods to a common destination; (3) **flour,** (see quot. 1859 in **5. b.** above); (4) **flush,** in poker, a hand in which all the cards are of the same suit and form a sequence, also transf.; (5) **fours,** four-handed reels; (6) **goods,** the truth, *slang;* (7) **out,** see as a main entry; (8) **poker,** a form of poker in which each player in turn puts up the ante for the rest; (9) **ticket,** a political ticket made up of the regular candidates of a party; (10) ***-up-and-down,** (see quot. 1931), *colloq.;* (11) **whisky,** (*a*) undiluted or pure whisky, (*b*) (see quot.), *obs.*

(1) **1886** Chadwick *Art of Pitching* 27 The 'straight ball' referred to being a ball over the plate and at the height called for. **1916** Bancroft *Handbook* 83 Straight ball. A ball delivered to the bat on a straight line as distinguished from drop balls and curved balls. — (2) **1890** *Railways of Amer.* 288 The movement of 'straight' cars and 'solid' trains is comparatively simple. But there is a very large amount of through freight, particularly of merchandise, that cannot be put into a 'straight' car. — (3) **1883** *Harper's Mag.* June 78/1 Bakers . . . use what is known as 'wheat,' or 'straight' flour. — (4) **1864** Dick *Amer. Hoyle* (1866) 182 The strongest hand you can get is a straight flush. **1903** Marchmont *When I Was Czar* 239 This is no mere bluff I'm putting up: I hold a straight flush. **1946** Morehead & Mott-Smith *Penguin Hoyle* 127 The odds are only 2-to-1 against improving if the straight flush is open at both ends.

(5) **1836** in *Amer. Sp.* XXIV. (1949) 151/1 At it we went and danced straight fours for an hour. — (6) **1892** Wister in *Harper's Mag.* Dec. 138, I'm givin' yu' straight goods, yu' see. **1929** A. Ellis *Life* 293 You know it might be straight goods this time. — (8) **1864** Dick *Amer. Hoyle* (1866) 175 The Age does not use the term 'I pass,' as in Straight Poker. **1894** Robley *Bourbon Co., Kans.* 16 The rest of the time . . . they could play . . . straight poker. — (9) **1856** *Spirit of Times* 6 Dec. 224/1 Mr. Fillmore got a vote in Alleghany Co. of 1488—592 of these were cast on the fusion ticket, and 896 were the Fillmore straight ticket. **1949** *Time* 12 Sep. 21/3 Voters can vote a straight ticket by making one cross at the top of the ballot.

(10) **1869** Mark Twain *Innocents Abroad* 323 (R.), The peak we had to climb looked almost too straight-up-and-down. **1931** *Amer. Sp.* Dec. 94 *straight-up-and-down,* extending uniformly in a vertical direction. 'The hill to Indian Cave "n" Initial Rock is purt nigh straight-up-and-down.' [Cumberland Mts.] — (11) (*a*) **1865** Mark Twain

Sketches (1926) 163 Calaveras possesses . . . 'straight' whisky that will throw a man a double somerset. **1950** *Business Week* 22 April 24/2 When war broke out, distillers . . . started concocting blends of straight whiskey and alcohol. (*b*) **1877** BARTLETT 751 Straight Whiskey means the liquor upon which the excise duty has been paid.

∗**straighten,** *v.* **1.** ∗*To straighten out*, to put back in health. **2.** *To straighten up*, to stand erect; *fig.*, to adopt an honest course in life.

(1) **1873** BEADLE *Undevel. West* 34 A third was positive the Lake Region would straighten me out. — (2) **1897** *Amer. Pediatric Soc. Trans.* IX. 168 After a series of such oscillations . . . he straightens up. **1908** J. WEBSTER *Four-Pools Myst.* xix, He wishes to straighten up and lead a respectable life.

∗**straight-out,** *a.* and *n.*

1. *n.* (*cap.*) *pl.* Apparently the Whigs or one of the factions making up the Whig party. Also **Straight-outers.** *Obs.*

1840 *Nashville Whig* 17 Aug. (Th.), Straight-Outs . . . are the representatives of a hardy race of honest log cabin pioneers, who, however ridiculed for their primitive manners, never fail to make their influence felt at the ballot-box. **1844** *Henry Clay Bugle* (Maysville, Ky.) 11 April 1/5 *The Whigs and Straightouters* of 1840 are girding for the conflict. **1878** GUILD *Old Times* 162 The Straightouts, with their copperas jackets and coonskin caps, were out in full force that night.

2. *a.* Unqualified, open, unconcealed, genuine.

1848 W. ARMSTRONG *Stocks* 9 The Stock is to be delivered and paid for upon a certain day—these are sometimes termed straight out contracts. **1898** *Kissimmee* (Fla.) *Valley Gaz.* 18 Feb. 1/2 The failure of this bill to become a law means a straight-out fight for prohibition. **1912** DREISER *Financier* 57, I don't like it as well as I do the straight-out brokerage business.

3. Of a person or group of persons: Making no exceptions in the support of a party, principle, etc., representing uncompromising members of a party.

1855 WELD *Vacation Tour* 282 The number of political associations in America is as extraordinary as the strange names which they bear. Here are a few of them:—Wild Cats, Woolly Heads, Hunkers, Straight-out Whigs. **1882** *Nation* 3 Aug. 85/1 The Virginia Straight-Out Republican Committee decided . . . not to call a State Convention. **1891** *World Almanac* 75/2 South-Carolina, Democratic 'Straight-out' State Convention . . . put a ticket in the field in opposition to the regular (Tillman) Democratic ticket.

b. Of a political ticket: Straight.

1888 BRYCE *Amer. Commonw.* II. II. l. 269 The electors . . . give little thought to the personal qualifications of the candidates, and vote the 'straight out ticket.'

stram stræm, *n.* [Origin obscure. Cf. *EDD stram, v.*, to walk in a rude, noisy manner.] A hard walk. *Colloq.* — **1869** STOWE *Oldtown Folks* 568, I hed sech a stram this mornin'.

∗**stranger,** *n.*

1. Used vocatively to one who is unknown to the speaker. *Colloq.*

1809 ASHE *Travels in Amer.* 105 'Good morrow, stranger,' (was uttered involuntarily by all) 'how fares it?' **1892** DUVAL *Young Explorers* 22 Hello! strangers, which way are you traveling? **1946** *Chi. D News* 25 May 21 (*comics*), 'Thank yo', stranger' . . . 'Stop calling me "stranger." My name is Walter!'

2. (See quots.) *Obs.*

1833 in *Amer. Sp.* VIII. (1933) 76 Stranger. Anybody not born in Kentucky. *c***1845** *Big Bear Ark.* 121 A barrel of whiskey is called a 'stranger,' from the fact that it is brought from a distance, there being none made in the country.

3. stranger's fever, a fever to which newcomers into an area are thought to be particularly subject, orig. used of yellow fever. *Obs.*

1824 HODGSON *Lett. N. Amer.* I. 52 The *natives* . . . are generally exempt, after the age of from ten to fifteen years, from the yellow, or stranger's fever. **1840** *N.O. Picayune* 24 Sep. 2/1 The Charleston Board of Health reports the death of twenty persons . . .—stranger's fever, four. **1845** GOODMANE *Seven Years* 19 Ague, yellow, bilious, and strangers' fevers, sweep hundreds into untimely graves. **1888** C. L. BACHMAN *John Bachman* 31 Before the close of the summer [of 1815] 'Strangers' Fever,' as it was called, made its appearance in Charleston.

Strangism ˈstræŋɪzəm, *n.* The religious principles of the Strangites. *Obs.* See next. — **1846** *Quincy* (Ill.) *Whig* 31 March 3/1 In the mean time a revelation, by Orson Hyde, has been published, in which he denounces Strangism in the strongest manner.

Strangite ˈstræŋaɪt, *n.* A follower of J. J. Strang (1813–56), who claimed the leadership of the Mormon Church after Joseph Smith's death. *Obs.*

1846 *Quincy* (Ill.) *Whig* 21 Feb. 3/2 The Strangites in Nauvoo are taking advantage of the unsettled state of the Mormons to create dissentions amongst them. **1851** *Ore. Statesman* 23 Dec. 1/5 The Strangites, new lights, settled on Beaver Island, Lake Michigan. **1890** *N. & Q.* V. 184/2 The sect which once lived on Beaver island, in Lake Michigan, were called Strangites.

∗**strangler,** *n.* A member of a vigilance committee (see quot. 1888).

1857 *Phoenix* (Sacramento) 15 Nov. 1/2 Captain Ira Brooks [is] one of the Stranglers' Detectives. **1888** *Cent. Mag.* May 43/1 During the preceding fall the vigilantes—locally known as 'stranglers,' in happy allusion to their summary method of doing justice—had made a clean sweep of the cattle country along the Yellowstone. **1931** WILLISON *Here They Dug Gold* 259 If there's anything in the world these boys are dead sore on, it's stranglers.

strap stræp, *n.*^{1} *N. Eng.* [Origin uncertain. ?Variant of *strip*. Cf. **strappet.**] A strip of land. *Obs.*

1651 in *R.I. Col. Rec.* (1856) I. 234 It is but a strape of land lying in between the colonies of Massachusitts, Plymouth and Conitaquot. **1671** *First Cent. Hist. Springfield* (1899) II. 235 Symon Lobdell desiring a little strap of Meddow. . . . There is grannted unto him five acres of meddow. **1686** *Ib.* 268 John Barber hath granted him a little Strap of Land about two or Three acres to ly from his Land to the fence.

∗**strap,** *n.*^{2} In combs.: (1) **strap game,** a swindling game, perhaps that referred to in the Halliwell quot. below, *obs.*; (2) ∗**iron,** iron in long, narrow strips; (3) **rail,** a railroad rail consisting of a wooden beam to which a thin strap or strip of iron is secured to provide a bearing surface for the wheels of the cars and engine, now *hist.*; (4) **road,** a railroad having strap rails, *obs.*

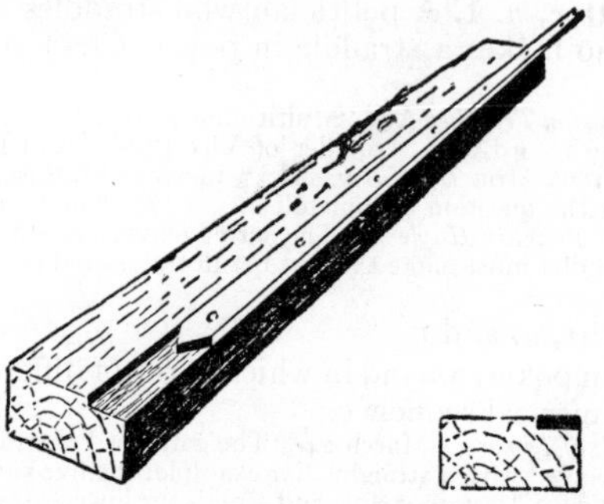

Strap rail *c*1840

(1) [**1847** HALLIWELL, *Fast-and-loose*, a cheating game played with a stick and a belt or string, so arranged that a spectator would think he could make the latter fast by placing a stick through its intricate folds, whereas the operator could detach it at once.] **1847** *Knickerb.* XXIX. 281 He was accused of having 'come the strap-game' over a native. **1873** BEADLE *Undevel. West* 140 A score of 'smart Alecks' relieved of their surplus cash by betting on the 'strap game.' — (2) **1882** *47th Congress* 1 Sess. H.R. Ex. Doc. No. 216, 641 Sometimes only wooden rails are used, but generally they are faced with a light strap iron. **1918** *Essex Inst. Coll.* LIV. 197 On many early American railroads the rails were of strap iron spiked on wooden rails. — (3) **1874** B. F. TAYLOR *World on Wheels* 105 Years ago, he rode on a train of the old Toledo & Adrian Railway—strap-rail at that. **1903** *N.Y. Ev. Post* 19 Sep. 5 The State built a road to Springfield in 1838 . . . with strap rails on wooden stringers. **1948** Mus. Sci. & Ind. (Chi.) *Exhibit Finder* 3 The story of the early days of railroading is further traced by samples showing the progress of rail manufacture from strap rail, flat as a pancake, to the heavy crowned rail of today. — (4) **1861** N. A. WOODS *Prince of Wales in Canada* 357 The first part of the journey was over . . . a 'strap road,' one of the most unsafe varieties of railways ever used. **1891** WELCH *Recoll. 1830–40* 28 It was an ordinary strap road, the moving power was one horse.

As the last term in **back, bell, black, check, hand, head, hitching, latigo, shawl, shoulder, tie strap(s).**

∗**strap,** *v. tr.* To deplete (one) of financial resources. Usu. ∗**strapped,** *a.*, without money, broke. *Slang.*

1851 *Ore. Statesman* 7 Oct. 2/6 We blame the picayune editor most for taking advantage of their 'strapped' condition to cut down their wages. **1880** *Amer. Punch* Feb. 22/1 This last election pretty nearly strapped me for funds. **1949** *Time* 14 March 22/1 There were times in this campaign when we were pretty well strapped.

strappet ˈstræpɪt, *n. N. Eng.* [Dim. of **strap,** *n.*^{1}] A small strip of land. *Obs.* Cf. **strap,** *n.*^{1}

1655 *Springfield Rec.* I. 238 There is granted to John Lamb yt little strappet of land over ye river at ye hay place. **1665** *Ib.* II. 216 Japhett Chapin hath grannted unto him a Strappet of meaddow on ye Mill River. **1686** in *First Cent. Hist. Springfield* (1899) II. 267 John Barber desires a little Strappet of Land about two or three acres from his Land to the fence.

straw strɔ, *n.*[1] [See note.]

This use of *straw* with reference to tumblers or glasses imported from Holland and Germany is app. derived from G. *Stroh* or Du. *stroo*. In both G. and Du. the term has been used in commerce as a measure with reference to smoked fish. In Du. a *stroo* of fish varies from 500 to 1000 depending on the kind. In Bremen and other coastal cities a *Stroh* of herrings was a certain number packed in or tied together with straw, twenty *Stroh* making one load of herring. In Low German a *Stroh* was a container for wax. See *OED s.v. Straw*, sb.[2]

No evidence is at hand for the use of *straw* in advertisements of glassware in England, but obviously it might well have appeared in such places and at a date prior to the occurrences here shown.

1. App. a basket or other container serving as a measure or indication of quantity used in connection with glassware imported from Holland and Germany. *Obs.*

1790 *Columbian Centinel* 15 Sep. 4/2 To be sold, at J. Brazer's Variety-store, A Large assortment of Looking-Glasses. . . . Tumblers, in straws, by the chest or less. **1810** *Ib.* 20 Jan. 3/5 [Sale at Auction] Stock of German and other Goods.—to close the concern, viz.:— 7 cases Dutch half-pint Tumblers, each containing 100 straws. **1810** *Conn. Courant* 1 April 3/3 (*advt.*), A quantity of quart, pint, and half-pint tumblers and wine glasses in straws.

2. straw tumbler, ?a tumbler of a kind usually received in straws (see **1.** above). *Obs.*

1796 *Independent Chronicle* (Boston) 17 Nov. 4/3 [Among Dutch goods from Amsterdam] straw and barrel tumblers. **1800** *Columbian Centinel* 8 Jan. 3/4 [For sale] straw tumblers.

* **straw,** *n.*[2]

1. *collect.* =**pine straw.**

1856 Olmsted *Slave States* 321 There were occasionally young long-leaved pines: . . . the leaves, or *straw*, as its foliage is called here, long, graceful, and lustrous.

2. In combs.: (1) **strawberry, bid,** see as main entries; (2) **bond,** a bond for which the sureties are worthless; (3) **bondsman,** one of the sureties on a straw bond, *obs.;* (4) **boss,** a subordinate boss, *colloq.* [cf. Du. *stroodekkersbaas*]; (5) **broom,** a sedge broom *q.v.;* (6) **dance,** (see quots.), *obs.;* (7) **fiddle,** (see quot. and cf. G. *Strohfiedel*); (8) **poll,** =**straw vote;** (9) ***ride,** a pleasure ride taken by a group in a wagon or hayrack partially filled with straw, also attrib., cf. **hayride;** (10) ***splitter,** an implement for splitting straws preparatory to braiding them, *obs.;* (11) **town,** a town in which straw-plaiting is an important industry, *rare;* (12) **vote,** an unofficial vote or poll taken to indicate the probable outcome of an election or other issue, also **straw voter;** (13) ***worm,** (see quot.).

(2) **1881** *Ore. State Jrnl.* 8 Jan. 7/2 He'd be dashed if any little jack-legged shyster could shove a straw-bond on him. **1899** in *Cong. Rec.* 25 Jan. (1900) 1169/2 [He] was let off on his own recognizance or straw bond, I have forgotten now which. — (3) **1887** *Vindicator* (S.F.) 2 May 1/1 The straw bondsmen have not been quite so active during the past week, but they are still at work, and we are still on their tracks. — (4) **1894** Carwardine *Pullman Strike* 117 These employees . . . [having suffered] the continued oppression of the 'straw bosses,' . . . were in no condition to be trifled with by the Company. **1950** *N.O. Times-Picayune Mag.* 9 April 7/1 Taft is the straw boss of the pair.

(5) **1939** *These Are Our Lives* 27 Somethin' was all time sweepin' de floors; you could hear somethin' like a straw broom go sweep-sweep. — (6) **1841** Buckingham *America* I. 76 The 'straw dance,' among the tribe of the Sioux, consists in making young children dance naked, with burning straws tied to their bodies, to make them tough and brave. *c***1898** Christian *Days* 13 'Uncle Burrell' . . . was very proud of his 'straw dance' . . . he would cross two broomstraws on the floor and begin by dancing around them, then dancing into the straw cross, and never touching or even stirring the straws, repeating this until he had danced into all four spaces. — (7) **1817** in Lincoln *Wilmington Del.* (1937) 321 A concert given by Mr. Sanders on July 18, 1817, opened with . . . Flute, Tambourine and Triangle Basset Horn, and *Straw Fiddle*. 'The Straw Fiddle is a very curious instrument made of Wood and Straw; it has a very soft and agreeable sound, and is quite unknown in this country.' — (8) **1944** *Chi. Tribune* 26 Oct. 12/2 (*heading*), New Deal Area Lifts F.D.R. In N.Y. Straw Poll. **1948** *Chi. Sun-Times* 18 March 35/4 Our famous straw polls, for example, require the expenditure of money. — (9) **1881** Du Chaillu *Land of Midnight Sun* II. 434 A custom which reminded me of the 'straw ride' parties common in the rural districts of the United States. **1943** Tutt *Yankee Lawyer* 6 We had husking and spelling bees, apple-paring bees, singing schools and straw rides.

(10) **1893** Daniel *Scrap-Book* 119 We plaited our hats of straw (I have a straw-splitter now, for which I gave $13; it did good service). — (11) **1864** *Harper's Mag.* Oct. 578/2 Among all the 'straw towns' of Massachusetts is a not very large yet quite enterprising one. — (12) **1887** *S.F. Thunderbolt* 4 Nov. 1 The straw vote taken at the 'Report' office is unreliable. **1948** *Time* 19 Jan. 80/3 Quite obviously, not all of these straw voters were Communists. **1948** *Democrat* 23 Sep. 4/3 The Demopolis Rotary Club held a straw vote on the Presidential Election. — (13) **1859** G. W. Perry *Turpentine Farming* 107 Straw Worm . . . is to be found on the boughs of pines from the latter part of July during the remainder of the season.

As the last term in **broom, long straw.**

* **strawberry,** *n.* In combs.: (1) **strawberry apple,** (see quot.), *obs.;* (2) **bank,** app. a tract containing banks on which wild strawberries grow, also as a proper name; (3) **blond(e),** reddish blond, red-headed, a blond person (see quot. 1880); (4) **bread,** (see quot.), *obs.;* (5) **bush,** a shrub of the genus *Calycanthus*, also an American spindle tree, *Euonymus americanus*, having bright red pods; (6) **cactus,** a low cactus, *Echinocereus enneacanthus*, of the Southwest, having a strawberry-like fruit; (7) **festival,** a sociable or similar gathering at which strawberries are served, also **strawberry-cream festival;** (8) **moon,** the moon or month when strawberries are ripe; (9) **Night,** at Harvard, a student festival; (10) **party,** =**strawberry festival;** (11) **patch,** a small area on which strawberries are cultivated, also as a place-name; (12) **pin cushion,** a pin cushion somewhat resembling a large strawberry; (13) **pink,** a variety of potato, *obs.;* (14) **run,** (see quot.); (15) **shortcake,** a shortcake or biscuit covered with sweetened strawberries, usu. crushed or sliced; (16) **shrub,** any shrub of the genus *Calycanthus* having fragrant dark red flowers; (17) **sour,** see **sour 1. b;** (18) **sundae,** a sundae made with strawberries; (19) **tomato,** any one of various species of ground cherry having edible tomato-like fruit, cf. **cherry tomato;** (20) **tree,** a species of spindle tree (see also quot. 1785).

(1) **1847** Ives *N. Eng. Fruit* 45 *Strawberry Apple.*—This variety originated in New Jersey; it is an early winter fruit. — (2) **1627** in *Amer. Sp.* XV. 398/1 Fifty acres of the same land lying and being a parte of the Strawberry bancke. **1936** *Ib.*, Its present title dates back only 45 years, being known as 'Strawberry Bank' for three centuries before. — (3) **1880** *Scribner's Mo.* Feb. 575/2 In the vernacular of the farm the mulatto-girls are called 'strawberry blondes.' **1884** Nye *Baled Hay* 98 That is what is . . . sprinkling my strawberry blonde hair with gray. **1941** Seton *Trail of Artist-Naturalist* 325 She was a handsome strawberry blonde, but she could cuss and fight and swear and gamble with any man. — (4) **1643** Williams *Key* (1866) 121 The Indians bruise them [*sc.* strawberries] in a morter, and mixe them with meale and make Strawberry bread.

(5) **1847** Darlington *Weeds & Plants* 135 Carolina-allspice. . . . Strawberry-bush. . . . There are several species of this genus cultivated for the fragrance of their rather unsightly flowers. **1860** Curtis *Woody Plants N.C.* 102 Strawberry Bush. . . . The fruit gives the plant a peculiar beauty, for which chiefly it is prized in shrubberies. **1943** Peattie *Great Smokies* 284 Of these, the strawberry bush, called 'hearts a-bustin' with love' by some of our mountain people, dangles its rich glossy crimson fruits from frosty-pink husks and becomes a favorite with many who discover it. — (6) **1911** Wooton *Cacti N. Mex.* 49 One species is locally known as 'strawberry' cactus because of a fancied resemblance in the taste of the fruit. **1948** *Desert Mag.* Aug. 19/3 We caught occasional flashes of the bright red flowers of the strawberry cactus against the rocks. — (7) **1863** *Boston Sun. Herald* 14 June 4/2 (Ernst), Strawberry festivals are the rage here just now. **1880** Farrar *Five Years Minn.* 201 'Strawberry-cream festivals' or 'picnics' in summer, to which only the 'elect' on the church's muster-roll are admissible, afford the younger members of the flock opportunities for pious flirtation. **1940** *Chi. Maroon* 10 May 3/3 Every student is invited to attend the 14th Annual Strawberry festival, sponsored by Phi Sigma Delta. — (8) **1916** Thoburn *Stand. Hist. Okla.* I. 68 The most noted conflict between the Cherokees and the Osages . . . took place at the Claremore Mound in 'the Strawberry Moon' . . . , in 1818. — (9) **1893** Post *Harvard Stories* 134

The night before I left was Strawberry Night at the Pudding. **1897** FLANDRAU *Harvard Episodes* 114 There is Strawberry Night at the Signet, when the First Seven, from the Sophomore Class is taken in, . . . and Strawberry Night at the Pudding.

(10) 1857 *S.F. Bulletin* 6 June 2/2 He . . . thinks well of 'our Sunday School excursions, railroad parties, social sleigh rides, strawberry parties,' as indications of a growing taste for the country. **1900** BACHELLER *E. Holden* 151 He came over one noon in the early summer . . . to tell us of a strawberry party that evening at the White Church. — **(11) 1835** BIRD *Hawks* II. 114 You robbed Elsie Bell's straw-berry patch. **1880** *Scribner's Mo.* Feb. 569/1 We realized the difference between a strawberry farm and a strawberry bed or 'patch,' as country people say. **1950** *Chi. Tribune* 11 March 8/3 No stay-at-homes we, the master and mistress of Strawberry Patch! — **(12) 1864** *Hist. North-Western Soldiers' Fair* 74 [Donations include] 5 strawberry pin cushions . . . 12 bottles perfumery. — **(13) 1854** *Mich. Agric. Soc. Trans.* V. 208 Some of the more approved kinds [of potatoes] are . . . the White, Red, and Strawberry Pinks. — **(14) 1891** *Cent.* 5272/2 *Strawberry run,* a run of fish in the season of the year when strawberries are ripe. . . . (Local.)

(15) 1841 L. B. SWAN *Jrnl.* (1904) 28 We had a new dish, 'Strawberry Short Cake,' very fine indeed. **1949** *Time* 23 May 34/3 Then they adjourned for a buffet lunch of roast beef, beer and strawberry shortcake. — **(16) 1915** ARMSTRONG & THORNBER *Western Wild Flowers* 158 [The] Strawberry Shrub . . . has many other names, such as Sweet Shrub, Carolina Allspice, Wineflower, etc. **1941** R. S. WALKER *Lookout* 59 A wild strawberry shrub with its greenish stems and foliage of the same color when young, becomes very ornamental in late summer. — **(18) 1904** DERVILLE *Other Side of Story* 277 Cool off for the night with 'Chocolate Fridays,' 'strawberry Sundays,' and other popular concoctions. **1930** *Sat. Ev. Post* 9 Aug. 12/1 Alvina Hall sat in a booth . . . and spooned her strawberry sundae daintily out of its aluminum cup. — **(19) 1919** STURTEVANT *Notes on Edible Plants* 432 *P. lanceolata* . . . was among the strawberry tomatoes grown at the New York Agricultural Experiment Station in 1886.

(20) 1785 MARSHALL *Amer. Grove* 11 *Arbutus.* The Strawberry Tree, or Bear-Berry. **1813** MUHLENBERG *Cat. Plants* 25 *Euonymus Americanus,* (burning bush, strawberry tree). **1866** *Ill. Agric. Soc. Trans.* VI. 391 The Strawberry Tree, with its delicate foliage, green wood and beautiful berries.

b. In the names of animals: (1) **strawberry bass,** (see quot. 1867); (2) **bug,** a strawberry borer of some kind, *obs.;* (3) **leaf-roller,** any one of various moth larvae that roll up and eat strawberry leaves; (4) **perch,** the calico bass; (5) **worm,** (see quot.).

(1) 1867 DE VOE *Market Ass't* 294 Calico bass, speckled bass, or partridge-tailed bass.—This fish is also known among our fishermen as the 'strawberry bass.' **1947** DALRYMPLE *Panfish* 81 You'd think there be Strawberry Bass, or maybe even Speckled Bass in there, too. — **(2) 1854** EMMONS *Agric. N.Y.* V. 263 (Index), Strawberry-bugs, 171. **1909** *Cent. Supp.* 1283/1 strawberry-bug. . . . 1. An insect, *Lygus pratensis,* which produces the so-called buttoning of strawberries.—2. The flea-like negro-bug, *Corimelaena pulicaria.* — **(3) 1892** KELLOGG *Kans. Insects* 95 The Strawberry Leaf-roller was first noticed in Kansas as an insect pest in 1880. — **(4) 1883** *Nat. Museum Bul.* No. 27, 461 *Pomoxys sparoides.* . . . Strawberry Perch. . . . This species . . . is esteemed as a food-fish.

(5) 1868 *Rep. Comm. Agric. 1867* 73 A saw fly or strawberry worm, *Emphytus maculatus,* . . . the larvæ of which eat the foliage of the strawberry plants.

As the last term in **barren, Boston, California, dry, emery, English, Illinois, sand strawberry.**

straw bid. (See quot. 1877.) Also **straw bidder, bidding.**

1872 A. KENDALL *Autobiog.* 344 Thenceforward all 'straw-bidding' ceased. **1876** in BARTLETT 669 The House post-office committee has agreed . . . to punish straw-bidders when caught. **1877** BARTLETT 669 Straw Bid, a bid for a contract which the bidder is unable or unwilling to fulfill. **1881** *Bradstreet's* III. 293 The first investigation relative to straw bids occurred, some six years ago.

stray stre, *v. W. tr.* To separate the strays from (a herd). *Colloq.* — **1869** *Overland Mo.* Aug. 126 They are obliged to stop and 'stray' the herd.

* **streak,** *n.*

1. A run *of luck,* good or bad. *Colloq.*

1843 *Knickerb.* XXI. 303, I had 'struck a streak of bad luck.' **1889** MUNROE *Golden Days* 176 You can't never tell when a streak of luck is going to strike you in this business.

b. In baseball (see quots.).

1868 CHADWICK *Base Ball* 20 They got into what is called a 'streak of batting,' that is, one after another made good hits. **1912** MATHEWSON *Pitching* 233 But what's a new hat against a losing streak or a batting slump? **1950** *Dly. Ardmoreite* (Ardmore, Okla.) 30 April D. 6/2 Last year's edition of the Indians set one of the hottest paces in the league before folding with a long losing streak.

2. In phrases: (1) *To start off like a streak,* and variants, to go (or do anything) very fast or instantly, *colloq.;* (2) *to make a streak for,* to hasten towards (a place), *colloq.;* (3) * *a streak of lightning,* a drink of whisky, *rare.*

(1) 1839 *Knickerb.* XIII. 298, I see him yesterday afternoon . . . starting off like a streak, to go to Norridgewock. **1901** *Scribner's Mag.* April 501/1 We worked like streaks. **1920** SANDBURG *Smoke & Steel* 138 Maybe I will light out like a streak of wind. — **(2) 1875** HOLLAND *Sevenoaks* 60 [We'll] make a clean streak for the woods. **1909** WASON *Happy Hawkins* 280 She was in the habit of . . . gettin' it [food] into her in the shortest possible time, an' then makin' a streak for it. — **(3) 1859** C. MACKAY *Life & Liberty* I. 169 'Gin-sling,' 'brandy-smash,' 'a streak of lightning,' 'whisky-skin,' 'mint-julep' [etc.].

* **streaked,** *a.*

1. In the names of plants and animals (see quots.).

1782 CRÈVECOEUR *Letters* 129 Most common are the streaked bass, the blue fish [etc.]. **1820** RAFINESQUE in *Western Rev.* II. 51 Streaked-cheeks River-Bass. *Lepomis trifasciata.* . . . Found in the Ohio and many other streams. **1834** *S. Lit. Messenger* I. 97 The underwood is mostly streaked maple or elkwood. **1884** *Rep. Comm. Agric.* 336 During the past season the Streaked Cottonwood Leaf-beetle has done great damage in portions of Nebraska and Dakota.

2. *To look or feel streaked,* to look or feel alarmed, silly, or uncomfortable. *Colloq.*

1815 HUMPHREYS *Yankey* 57 How streaked I feel all over! **1835** LONGSTREET *Ga. Scenes* 190 A limb . . . fetched me a whipe [*sic*] across the face, . . . giving me for the first time in my life a *sensible* idea of the Georgia expression, 'feeling streaked'; for my face actually felt as though it was covered with streaks of fire and streaks of ice. **1878** BEADLE *Western Wilds* 416, I felt orful streaked, . . . but I knowed 'old blaze' had never failed yet.

***streaky,** *a.* Ashamed, confused. *Colloq.* — **1845** *Big Bear Ark.* 43 That party did look streaky. **1848** *Family Companion* (B.), I never did feel so streaky and mean before.

***stream,** *n.* As the last term in **beaver, Gulf, mining stream.**

* **street,** *n.*

1. (Usu. *cap.*) Wall Street *q.v.*

1863 KIMBALL *Undercurrents of Wall Street* 131 (Flügel), Sufficient of the two millions [could be] launched on the street. **1883** *Nation* (N.Y.) 16 Aug. 132/1 'The Street' begins to play a larger and larger part in the financial world, owing to the enormous amounts of American capital it holds and of foreign capital it distributes. **1888** C. MILLS in *N. Amer. Rev.* Jan. 50 Then it was that the Street began to suspect that money would not always remain at four per cent.

2. In combs.: (1) **street broker,** =**curbstone broker;** (2) **car,** (*a*) a public conveyance that runs through the streets, usu. on rails, cf. **bobtail streetcar,** (*b*) also attrib.; (3) **commissioner,** a city official having supervision of streets; (4) **operator,** =**street broker;** (5) **railroad,** =next, also attrib., *obs.;* (6) **railway,** the physical equipment, esp. the tracks and right of way, of a company operating streetcars, also attrib.; (7) **rubber,** a rubber overshoe; (8) **scraping machine,** a machine for scraping or grading a street, *obs.;* (9) **sprinkler,** a

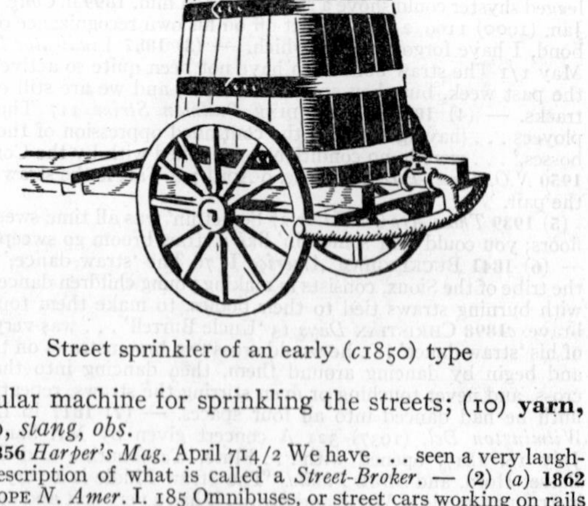

Street sprinkler of an early (*c*1850) type

vehicular machine for sprinkling the streets; (10) **yarn,** gossip, *slang, obs.*

(1) 1856 *Harper's Mag.* April 714/2 We have . . . seen a very laughable description of what is called a *Street-Broker.* — **(2)** (*a*) **1862** TROLLOPE *N. Amer.* I. 185 Omnibuses, or street cars working on rails run hither and thither. **1949** *Trail Riders Bul.* March 19/1 The street cars move quietly and without the city roar. (*b*) **1870** *Rep. Comm.*

Agric. 1869 372 Horse buyers obtain . . . street-car animals, and heavy dray or omnibus horses. **1873** *Newton Kansan* 15 May 1/5 It is proposed to introduce civil service reform among the uncivil street-car conductors. **1950** *Ashville* (N.C.) *Citizen-Times* 26 March IX. 18/5 Occasionally home runs would be hit into the lake or over the fence at the right end of the street car barn. — **(3) 1789** *Phila. Ordinances* (1812) 75 [The] common councilmen shall . . . [do all] things, as the . . . street commissioners were . . . enabled by law to do. **1947** MYERS *The 'Guv'* 175 O'Peal was rumored to be receiving percentages on city contracts while serving as street commissioner. — **(4) 1884** in LEAVITT *Our Money Wars* 277 'The number of brokers in this city has increased immensely,' said an old-time 'Street' operator.

(5) 1859 *Ladies' Repository* Nov. 694/1 The problem of street railroads in Cincinnati has been solved. **1860** in M. W. DISHER *Cowells in Amer.* (1934) 119 Took seats in one of the street railroad-cars in Bowery and set off. **1893** *Boston Jrnl.* 25 March 2/1 The New England Street Railway Company . . . [was organized] to acquire various street railroads in New England. — **(6)** [**1861** *Chambers's Jrnl.* 29 June 416/1 The street railways of the American cities.] **1867** *Mich. Gen. Statutes* I. (1882) 909 Street railway companies may be organized under the provisions of this act. **1906** *Springfield W. Republican* 7 Feb. 10 The cars on the street railway have been installed with electric searchlights. — **(7) 1945** *Roundup* (Mont.) *R. Tribune* 15 Feb. 5/2 Just Arrived! For Women For Men Street Rubbers. — **(8) 1843** *Niles' Reg.* 1 July 279/1 Street Scraping Machine. — **(9) 1867** RICHARDSON *Beyond Miss.* 50 A mechanic had sold a street-sprinkler.

(10) 1816 *Mass. Spy* 6 March (Th.), [When I] see the yard covered with stumps, old hoops, and broken earthen[ware], I guess the man is a horse-jockey, and the women a spinner of streetyarn. **1864** NICHOLS *Amer. Life* I. 23 The young ladies . . . 'spin street yarn.'

As the last term in **business, down, easy, Main, Negro, store, Wall, water street.**

streetage ˈstritɪdʒ, *n.* A tax or charge for the use of a street, or for conveying goods along a street. *Obs.* — **1866** *Md. Rep.* XXV. 87 The defendant . . . charged in addition to the usual freight . . . a further compensation for streetage to the foot of 6th street. **1884** *Reading Morning Herald* 17 April, There has been charged but a nominal sum on the Reading's business for streetage.

streeter ˈstritɚ, *n.* ?A horse suitable for ordinary street driving. *Obs.* — **1896** *N.Y. Herald* 2 April 7/5 The sales included business horses, some heavy workers and chunks, and the nondescript type of animal known as a streeter.

***stretch,** *n.* As the last term in **back, homestretch.**

***stretch,** *v.* **1.** *tr.* In baseball, to play (a hit) for one or more bases further than it would normally permit. **2.** **To stretch out,* (see quot.). *Rare.*

(1) 1897 *N.Y. Tribune* 9 Sep. 4/1 Clark . . . was retired at second trying to stretch the hit. **1949** *Time* 10 Oct. 42/2 They had less reason to thank their own bats than the batty stretch-run performance of the Cardinals. — **(2) 1862** *Harper's Mag.* Sep. 449/1 At the command 'Stretch out!' each waggon falls into its appointed place and . . . we begin our march.

strict construction. An understanding, construing, or interpreting of the U.S. Constitution of 1787 as meaning precisely what is expressly stated in that document. Cf. **elastic clause, liberal construction, limitarian, limited construction.**

1824 in *Sp. & Doc. in Amer. Hist.* II. (1944) 55 Then we cannot perceive the propriety of this strict construction, nor adopt it as the rule by which the constitution is to be expounded. **1853** BALDWIN *Flush T. Ala.* 77 Nor do I recollect of hearing any question debated that did not resolve itself into a question of constitution—strict construction, &c. **1904** *N.Y. Ev. Post* 22 Dec. 6 Tammany has never held to the theory of strict construction as to the purposes for which money may be spent at election time. **1948** *Dly. Ardmoreite* (Ardmore, Okla.) 6 May 9/2 Despite these two deviations from his policy of strict construction, Jefferson is the man responsible for the viewpoint being invoked today in his name as 'True Jeffersonian democracy.'

strict constructionist. One who interprets the U.S. Constitution as meaning what it expressly states. Also transf. Cf. **loose constructionist.**

1836 NANCY N. SCOTT *Memoir H.L. White* (1856) 209, I profess to be what is called a strict constructionist of the Constitution. **1888** *Nation* XLVI. 245/1 He was a strict constructionist, and he was persuaded that the Bible did not forbid such marriages. **1903** W. F. JOHNSON *Cent. of Expansion* 101 He was a 'strict constructionist,' and as the Constitution did not say in so many words that the U.S. might acquire new territory, he denied the ability of the U.S. to do so.

***strike,** *n.*

1. *Baseball.* A hit by a batter or a turn at bat. *Obs.*

1841 *N.O. Picayune* 25 May 2/2 If 'Edith' wishes to see 'a great strike' and 'lots of fun,' let her walk down Water street some pleasant afternoon towards 'set of sun,' and see *the* 'bachelors' make the ball fly. **1845** in *Appletons' Ann. Cyclo.* X. 77/2 Players must take their strike in regular turn. **1867** *Ball Players' Chron.* 4 July 6/2 Their batting was of a superior character, two of their players, Pettingill and Dawson, each making some powerful strikes.

b. A count against the batter, usu. resulting from his unsuccessful attempt to hit the ball or to hit it fair, a fair ball *q.v.*, sense **2.**

1856 *Spirit of Times* 22 Nov. 197/2 The striker should also be compelled to run on such occasions, strike or no strike. **1912** MATHEWSON *Pitching* 12 It put me in the hole with the count two balls and one strike. **1950** *Athletic Jrnl.* Feb. 41/1 Too many batters have a tendency to wait for the perfect strike through the middle (the cripple)—the easiest pitch to hit.

Also allusively in phrases (see quots.).

1944 *Chi. D. News* 22 Nov. 10/3, I sometimes think of the heart patient as a ballplayer with one strike on him. **1949** *Chi. Tribune* 25 Sep. 18/2 Any public building which has reached a certain age, say 20 or 25 years, should be considered to have two strikes on it whenever it is subjected to any safety inspection.

2. Any sudden success, esp. a financial one resulting from finding oil, rich ore, etc. *Colloq.*

1855 H. HELPER *Land of Gold* 296, I may make a 'strike,' but that is mere speculation. **1868** *Putnam's Mag.* Jan. 25 I'll make a strike in Erie. **1904** *Scientific Amer.* 30 Jan. 496/1 Heretofore few signs of oil have been found in the locality, and the 'strike' came in the nature of a surprise. **1949** *Boston Globe* 15 May (Fiction Mag.) 1/1 A couple of cheechakos . . . was in here throwin' their dust around an' braggin' about locatin' a strike on some crick way to hell an' gone up the Stewart.

b. Often preceded by a qualifying term, as **big, lucky, rich strike.**

1853 *Alta California* (S.F.) 15 April 2/3 There are quite a number [of miners] that are making great wages or 'big strikes.' **1853** *Shasta Courier* (Redding, Calif.) 2 July, The bed, as far as it has been prospected, is about two feet in thickness, and in all likelihood will prove a 'lucky strike' to the fortunate discoverers. **1949** *Boston Globe Mag.* 25 Dec. 1/1 Miners, promoters, speculators, followed by the usual riff-raff which follow rich strikes, moved into Wild Horse Valley.

3. In American bowling, the action of knocking down all the pins with one bowl. Also transf. Cf. **ten-strike** (*a*).

1866 LOWELL *Biglow P.* 2 Ser. lix, To make a *strike* is to knock down all the pins with one ball, hence it has come to mean fortunate, successful. **1939** MILLER *Cosmological Eye* 219 *Of Human Bondage* was a great book, he thought. I thought so too and I scored another strike for the constable on my mental blackboard. **1949** *Southtown Economist* (Chi.) 25 Sep. 5/4 You'll score a fashionable 'Strike' . . . striding into a smart 'n pretty pose in this action-ready gabardine Bowlerette.

4. A form of legislative blackmail in which a bill is introduced by a legislator merely for the purpose of getting paid to let the matter drop. Also **strike bill.**

1885 *Cent. Mag.* April 824 The latter, technically called a 'strike,' is much the most common. **1903** HART *Actual Govt.* 135 Another method of influencing legislation is to introduce so-called 'strikes'—bills not intended to be passed, but to be bought or shaken off in some way. **1914** *Cyclo. Amer. Govt.* I. 478 'Strike' bills, or 'regulators' which are introduced by legislators attack some interest for the purpose of being bought off. Behind them is frequently to be found a 'combine' of members, usually bi-partisan, organized for purposes of plunder.

As the last term in **foul, gold, oil, silver, ten, third, wildcat strike.**

***strike,** *v.*

1. *tr.* To take down (tobacco) from the place where it has been curing. *Obs.*

1642 *Md. Archives* I. 153 No attachm[en]t . . . may be layd upon Tobacco afore it be struck in Cask. **1678** *New Castle Court Rec.* 252 A forthy foott house of Tobbacco w[hi]ch was struck & Lay in bulke. **1784** SMYTH *Tour* II. 135 All that is within the house is struck or taken down.

2. Of a line or course: To come out at, to meet.

1798 *Mass. Mercury* 30 Oct. (Th.), Thence south, such a course as will strike William Negro's house. **1802** ELLICOTT *Jrnl.* 179 The articles were then taken . . . up the lake to the point where our road from the hill struck it. **1890** *Cong. Rec.* 8 Aug. 8317/2 The water comes rapidly down [the Potomac R.] until it strikes tide water here at Georgetown.

b. Of a person: To come upon or arrive at, to happen upon.

1808 PIKE *Sources Miss.* 134 In about five miles we struck a beautiful hill. **1881** CHASE *Editor's Run in N. Mex.* 176 [Leadville, Colo.] is the highest point 'we've struck,' as they say here. **1906** *McClure's Mag.* Feb. 342 We seemed to have struck a late season.

c. To meet or find (a person). *Colloq.*

1886 *Cong. Rec.* 4 June 5253/1 He discovers in conversation with him, that he 'knew more about levees than any man he ever struck.' **1901** WHITE *Westerners* 316 Struck Billy down the road a piece.

3. To discover (a lead or pocket of ore); to hit upon (pay dirt). Also fig. and transf.

1835 HOFFMAN *Winter in West* II. 47, I hear that he has lately struck a lead. **1884** MATTHEWS & BUNNER *In Partnership* 63 The young woman had refused to have anything to do with him for a long period; but he seems to have struck pay gravel about two days before my arrival. **1892** *Harper's Mag.* May 906/2 Water is struck at from 600 to 1200 feet. **1942** CHALFANT *Tales of Pioneers* 77 Shorty and his partner struck a rich showing.

b. *To strike it,* to find a rich ore deposit, also fig., often *to strike it rich. Colloq.*

1852 CLAPPE *Lett. from Calif.* 216 When a company wish to reach the bed-rock as quickly as possible, they sink a shaft . . . until they 'strike it.' **1869** J. R. BROWNE *Adv. Apache Country* 295 'Struck it rich!' 'Silver bricks!' and 'Pay rock!' hummed and drummed through the air. **1950** *Newsweek* 16 Jan. 69/1 [He] had received his chance in life in some little mountain mission school in Tennessee and had used his training to strike it rich.

c. *To strike oil,* (1) to tap a source of oil by sinking a well, (2) *fig.* to make a fortune, to strike it rich, *slang.*

(1) **1861** *Appletons' Ann. Cyclo.* 580/1 The oil, when first struck, has . . . been known to burst forth with great violence. **1950** *Business Week* 22 April 46/3 The company drilled 10 dry holes and six gas wells before it struck oil. — (2) **1879** WEBSTER 1580/1 *To strike oil,* . . . to make a lucky hit, especially financially. **1890** *Harper's Mag.* Oct. 727/2 Should he not have 'struck oil' by the time the money reached him, he should use it in paying off his debts.

4. To induce (a person) to pay money on the promise of getting him votes, legislative favors, etc.

1859 MATSELL *Vocabulum* 87 *Strike,* to get money from candidates before an election, under the pretense of getting votes for them; to borrow without intending to pay back. **1894** *Atlantic Mo.* Feb. 248/2 A legislator 'strikes' a corporation, . . . when he introduces some bill calculated to injure it directly or indirectly; his purpose being . . . to compel the corporation to buy him off.

5. (See quot.)

1891 *Cent.* 5991 strike, . . . in the United States army, to perform menial services for an officer; act as an officer's servant: generally said of an enlisted man detailed for that duty.

6. In colloq. phrases with prepositions and adverbs: (1) *To strike for,* to aim at getting or attracting; (2) * *to strike in,* of fish, to arrive in large numbers; (3) * *to strike off,* to mark as being sold or allocated *to* someone; (4) * *to strike out,* see **strike out,** *v.* as a main entry; (5) * *to strike up,* used passively in the sense of (*a*) to be surprised, confounded or unnerved, (*b*) to be attracted by someone, *obs.*

(1) **1867** HOLMES *Guardian Angel* 32 Happening one day to see a small negro girl . . . in a flaming scarlet petticoat, she struck for bright colors in her own apparel. **1897** HOWELLS *Landlord at Lion's Head* 365 He meant to strike for the class of Americans who resorted to those climates; to divine their characters and to please their tastes. — (2) **1756** THOMAS SMITH *Journals* (1821 ed.) 135 The season seems so altered that the fish are struck in, as in May. **1888** *Scientific Amer.* 9 June 352/2 A dispatch from Newfoundland says that the caplin have 'struck in'. This means that the cod . . . has arrived on the banks. — (3) **1777** *Narragansett Hist. Reg.* II. 313 The above mentioned house is struck off the day above mentioned to Mr Silas Niles for 260 Dollars. **1830** *Mass. Spy* 24 Nov. (Th.), A large tract in what is now called the Susquehanna country was struck off to him. (5) (*a*) **1833** S. SMITH *Life J. Downing* 230 At this I was a little struck up. **1843** STEPHENS *High Life N.Y.* I. 15, I never was so struck up in my life, as I was tu see her. *Ib.* 116, I was so struck up in a heap at seeing her in sich a fix. (*b*) **1884** HOWELLS *Silas Lapham* 37 'Seem struck up on Irene?' asked the Colonel.

b. With nouns: (1) *To strike* (one's) *average,* to size up or estimate (one); (2) *to strike bottom,* to reach an ultimate, as in grief, misfortune, etc.; (3) *to strike camp,* to make camp.

(1) **1880** MARK TWAIN *Tramp Abroad* 163 (R.), He did not understand me. I turned and twisted my question around and about, tryin to strike that man's average, but failed. — (2) **1902** MARK TWAIN *Belated Russian Passport* 186 (R.), Within thirty minutes he struck bottom; grief, misery, fright, despair could go no lower. — (3) **1846** SAGE *Scenes Rocky Mts.* xi. It was midnight ere we arrived . . . and struck camp. *Ib.* xvii, [We] struck camp in a small grove of cottonwood.

strike-out ˈstraɪkˌaʊt, *n.* [See note to * **strike out,** *v.*] *Baseball.* A put-out resulting from a batter's being charged with three strikes.

1887 *Courier-Journal* 2 Feb. 8/3 A pitcher is not to receive an assist for a strike-out under the amended rules. **1901** *Denver Republican* 26 Aug. 6/2 The last one he let pass was directly over the plate and scored a strike-out. **1948** *N.Y. Times* 23 May v. 3/1 Koeneke . . . accounted for six of the nine putouts with strikeouts.

attrib. **1928** *Chi. Tribune* 14 June 17/6 Pat Malone, himself of some repute as a strikeout specialist, got little inspiration from the work of the whiff king. **1945** *Greeley* (Colo.) *D. Tribune* 18 July 8/1 Bob Feller, former strikeout king of the junior circuit, still is slipping the third strike past batters.

* **strike out,** *v. Baseball.*

The precise application of this word, and the corresponding noun, is more complicated than is usu. realized. Only general definitions are here attempted. For more detailed information see Parke Cummings, *The Dictionary of Sports.*

1. *intr.* Of a batter: To be retired or put out by a strike-out *q.v.*

1853 *Oregonian* (Portland) 2 July 1/5 No doubt they will find that strikers have struck out. **1907** *St. Nicholas* May 630/1 If I'd had a bat that was any good, I'd have knocked out a home run . . . instead of striking out the way I did. **1948** *Chi. Tribune* 7 March II. 1/4 Schenz struck out.

2. *tr.* Of a pitcher: To retire (a batter) by causing him to be charged with three strikes.

1934 WEBSTER. **1946** *Sat. Ev. Post* 24 Aug. 54/4 Mullins fouled off two pitches and Westbrook struck him out. **1949** *Fargo* (N.D.) *Forum* 23 July 8/7 Nehowig struck out the next two batters.

* **striker,** *n.*

1. One who does odd jobs for another, esp. in the army, a soldier detailed as a servant to an officer.

1836 *Quarter Race Ky.* 20 [He] came and took the mare from his striker. **1867** in CUSTER *Tenting on Plains* 558 Several Indians of a lower grade . . . seems to act as strikers for the rest, attending to the cooking of the meat, and so on. **1948** *Time* 14 June 9/3 He takes the same attitude toward Congress as he would to a striker who fails to put the proper polish on his boots.

b. One of the agents and well-wishers of John A. Murrell (fl. 1826–34), a noted southern outlaw. *Obs.*

1840 MARRYAT *Diary* 90 The other class were the active agents, and were termed Strikers, and amounted to about six hundred and fifty. **1883** MARK TWAIN *Life of Miss.* 315 (R.), Murel's gang of robbers . . . was composed of two classes. . . . The active agents were termed strikers.

c. A runner or ruffian employed by a real-estate company or gambling joint. *Obs.*

1845 HOOPER *Simon Sugg's Adv.* vi, Among her admirers was a young man named Eggleston—a sub-partner, or 'striker,' of the great Columbus Land Company. *a***1871** *Country Merchant* 317 (De Vere), He was one of the most accomplished strikers, or barkers, as they are called, in the employ of the hells. **1893** *Harper's Mag.* April 712/2 Professional 'boomers,' with a retinue of surveyors and cappers and strikers, invaded the State.

d. A low character who preys upon political candidates and public officials.

*c***1855** *Sons of Sires* 90 The 'strikers' are a bold class of marauders, who 'come down' upon a candidate for a place . . . with threats that if he does not give it, they will be down upon him in the Primary Elections. **1873** BEADLE *Undevel. West* 184, I had published a severe criticism of this Judge Smith. His 'strikers' now had me at Court as defendant. **1903** *N.Y. Ev. Post* 18 Nov. 8 The 'striker' for aid has become recognized as a distinct type of Congressional parasite.

2. In baseball, the batter. *Obs.*

1845 in *Appletons' Ann. Cyclo.* X. 77/2 A player running home . . . can not make an ace if the striker is caught out. **1887** *Outing* May 99/1 The new rule . . . gives a left-hand pitcher somewhat of an advantage over a right-hand one when opposed to a right-hand striker.

3. (See quots.) *Obs.*

1872 EGGLESTON *End of World* 171 It was natural enough that the 'mud-clerk' on the old steamboat Iatan should take a fancy to the 'striker,' as the engineer's apprentice was called. **1876** MARK TWAIN *Old Times* i. 12 At last he turned up as apprentice engineer or 'striker' on a steamboat.

4. (See quot.)

1891 *Cent.* 5993/3 striker. . . . In the *menhaden-fishery:* (*a*) The man who manages the striker-boat. A vessel usually has two striker-boats, with one man in each; these row close to the school of fish, observe its course, signal the purse-crew to set the seine, and drive the fish in the desired direction with pebbles which they carry in the boats. (*b*) A green hand who works at low wages while learning the business, but is one of the crew of a vessel.

5. Something unusual or striking. *Rare.*

1898 LAPPENTEUR *Forty Years* 223 'Seven more men gone last night.' This was rather a striker.

As the last term in **machine, shoulder, ten, ward, wildcat striker.**

***string,** *n.*

1. A line *of fence.*

1794 WASHINGTON *Writings* XIII. 20 The string of fence . . . divides the upper from the lower fields. **1854** *Mich. Agric. Soc. Trans.* VI. 177 The strings of fence will average eight and three-quarter rails high. **1903** A. ADAMS *Log of Cowboy* 17 On the Mexican side there was a single string of high brush fence.

2. A whip. *Obs.*

1839 KIRKLAND *New Home* (1840) 14 By some judicious touches of 'the string,' the horses are induced to struggle as for their lives. **1852** BRISTED *Upper Ten Th.* 30 And now the b'hoy . . . lays the string about fearfully.

3. =**string line.**

1857 *Spirit of Times* 30 May 200/1 The player in hand can play at any ball, the largest half of which lies outside the string. **1872** MARK TWAIN *Roughing It* 336 Cheese it, pard; you've banked your ball clean outside the string.

b. (See quot. 1879.)

1848 BAKER *Glance at N.Y.* 11 (We.), I have beat Miss Wilson one string. **1879** WEBSTER *Supp.* 1580/1 *String*, the number of points made, in a game of billiards. **1891** *Cent.* 5994/2 He made a poor string at first, but won.

4. A restriction or condition attached to something. *Colloq.*

1888 *Battle Creek Wkly. Jrnl.* 15 Feb., Bob Ingersoll Says There Is a String to It. **1949** *Sierra Club Bul.* Jan. 4/1 The Corporation . . . made its offer to California—an offer good for six months only, and having several untenable strings attached.

5. In miscellaneous senses: **a.** (See quot.) *Obs.* **b.** A hoax. *Slang.* **c.** (See quot. 1891.) **d.** (See quot.)

(**a**) **1835** SHIRREFF *Tour* 235, I found four travellers, the landlord, and his wife, assembled in a poor habitation, lighted by what they termed a string, or piece of twine, dipt in tallow, and which gave a glimmering light. — (**b**) **1851** BURKE *Polly Peablossom* 92 Of course Mabe was innocent of the 'string.' — (**c**) **1891** *Cent.* 5994/1 *String*, . . . in *printing*, a piece-compositor's aggregate of the proofs of types set by him, pasted on a long strip of paper. The amount of work done is determined by the measurement of this string. **1898** *Milwaukee Sentinel* 11 Jan. 3/1 Printers . . . who found it no unusual thing to 'paste up' 'strings' that averaged more than 1,500 an hour. — (**d**) **1900** DRANNAN *Plains & Mts.* 57 One dozen traps is called a 'string,' and it is considered one man's work, ordinarily, to 'tend a string.'

6. In combs.: (1) **string bean,** (*a*) any one of several varieties of beans grown for the pods which have stringlike fibers along the sutures, also the pod of such a bean, usu. *pl.*, (*b*) attrib. in the sense of countrified, *rare;* (2) **line,** in certain games of billiards or pool, an imaginary line across the table over which a cue ball must pass after being out of play; (3) **piece,** =**stringer 1;** (4) **tie,** a narrow necktie.

(1) (*a*) **1759** *Holyoke Diaries* 20 First Str[ing] Beans ys. year viz. C. W. Beans. **1830** *N.Y. Constellation* 11 Sep. 3/2 We do not call it a string bean, because the pod is *entirely stringless.* **1949** *Nat. Geog. Mag.* Aug. 232/2 There were squash, string beans, and mashed potatoes. (*b*) **1867** *Harper's Mag.* Sep. 537/1 Those old New Hampshire 'musters,' where the 'crack companies' met on a common level with the 'string-bean' organizations. — (**2**) **1867** *Ball Players' Chron.* 24 Oct. 11/2 A ball exactly on the 'string line' is considered within the string. — (**3**) **1834** DAVIS *Letters of Downing* 14 (We.), I have heard it said, that Mr. Van Buren had sawed the string-pieces under the bridge. **1883** *Harper's Mag.* Jan. 199 The track is rudely built and rickety, the rails being heavy strap iron bolted upon string-pieces. **1949** *Sat. Ev. Post* 21 May 23/1 Pat sat on a stringpiece. — (**4**) **1929** *Randolph Enterprise* (Elkins, W.Va.) 28 March 1/2 [He wore a] white vest with a double-decker collar and string tie. **1945** *New Yorker* 27 Jan. 18/3 Only the lack of a black string tie (he was wearing a sharp red bow) marred a considerable resemblance to the Boy Orator of the Platte.

As the last term in **Deb's apron, door, gee, hame, horn, moccasin, red, saddle, shoe string(s).**

***string,** *v.* **1.** *To string along (with)*, to go along with (see quot. 1938). **2.** *To string out*, to draw out or prolong. *Colloq.*

(**1**) [**1790** *Jrnl. of Wm. Maclay* (2d. ed. 1927) 172, I think both Senators and Representatives are tired of making themselves the gazing-stock of the crowd and the subject of remark by the sycophantic circle that surround the President in stringing to his quarters.] **1938** ASBURY *Sucker's Prog.* 17 Stringing along—Betting all odd or even numbered cards to play one way. **1944** *Sat. Review* 23 Sep. 17/2, I wouldn't vote for any other And gladly string along with Struther. — (**2**) **1867** MARK TWAIN *Sk. New & Old* 73 (R.), What is the use of stringing out your lives to a lean and withered old age?

***stringent,** *a.* Of the money market: Tight. — **1870** MEDBERY *Men Wall St.* 69 Money is 'very active,' and the loan market 'stringent.' **1909** WEBSTER 2059/2.

***stringer,** *n.*

1. In the days of strap railroads, the heavy timber to which the strap iron was fastened to form a rail. Now *hist.*

1848 *Rep. Comm. Patents 1847* 72 One patent has been granted for improvements in . . . the manner of fastening it [*sc.* the rail] to the stringers. **1872** HUNTINGTON *Road-Master's Ass't* 37 Common spikes . . . act as so many wedges to split the stringers or rail-plates. **1943** POWELL *Home Again* 53 Our railroad . . . was not much of a railroad in those days. Most of the way . . . it was laid with 20- or 25-pound rail, supported on wooden sills, or stringers.

2. A tale or story concocted to hoax someone. *Obs.*

1850 in *Tall Tales of S.W.* (1930) 99 He never lacked assistance from his acquaintances whenever he had concocted a 'stringer.'

3. A narrow, stringlike vein of ore.

1872 RAYMOND *4th Rep. Mines* 47 It is generally believed they [*sc.* pocket veins] are outlying 'stringers' of the main lode. **1896** SHINN *Story of Mine* 133 Their ledge . . . contained only a very low-grade ore that could not be milled at a profit after a few surface stringers were mined out. **1945** SERVICE *Ploughman* 464, I listened as he talked of stringers and veins and the mother lode.

4. A cord upon which fish are strung as they are caught. *Rare.*

1893 *Outing* XXII. 88/2 Though he had several strikes, his stringer remained dry in his pocket.

stringlet ˈstrɪŋlɪt, *n.* [f. **string*+*let*, after **ringlet.*] A long wisp of hair. *Colloq.* — **1846–52** MRS. WHITCHER *Widow Bedott P.* xv. 154 Them great long stringlets a danglin down her cheeks. **1874** *Vt. Bd. Agric. Rep.* II. 600 Faded-out hair upon either side, with stringlets hanging half-way to the ground from hip and shoulder.

***strip,** *n.*

1. (Usu. *cap.*) =**Cherokee strip 1.**

1873 *Winfield* (Kans.) *Courier* 22 May 2/3 One Henry House, residing on the strip, about five miles south of this place [etc.]. **1926** COOPER *Oklahoma* 23 Most people think it's called the 'Strip' just because it happens to run all the way across the Territory. **1945** M. JAMES *Cherokee Strip* 36, I regretted there were no canals in the Strip so I could start as a towpath boy and become President of the United States.

attrib. **1894** *Dly. Ardmoreite* (Ardmore, Okla.) 28 April 3/5 Nothing of a definite character has been done by the Cherokee council regarding the payment of the Strip money. **1949** *Exciting Western* May 61/1, I was the first white man in this town on Strip-opening day.

2. a. strip carpet, (see quot. 1845). **b. strip loin,** a particular cut of a loin of beef.

(**a**) **1843** *Lowell Offering* III. 90 She had not only the requisite pillow-case full of stockings before she was engaged, but also divers rag-mats and strip carpets. **1845** *Ib.* V. 255 A strip carpet . . . is made of the best remnants of old coats, and overcoats, and waistcoats, and the dark groundwork is relieved by strips of red and green and yellow flannel. — (**b**) **1884** *Harper's Mag.* July 299/1 Tenderloins, striploins, sirloins.

3. Short for comic strip *q.v.*

1923 *Nation* 3 Oct. 340/1 Political cartoons were dropped, but the omnipresent 'strips' and 'comics' appeared in all their sorry glory. **1948** *Chi. Tribune* 28 March (Grafic Mag.) 5/1 Within a year the Alley became a daily strip, built around the bachelor Walt and his neighbors and cronies.

As the last term in **Cherokee, comic, weather strip.**

strip,** *v.* **1.** *S. tr.* =pull,** *v.* **2.** *Colloq. Obs.* **2. strip tease,** (see quot. 1947). Also attrib.

(**1**) **1856** *Fla. Plantation Rec.* 502 Chesley striping foder in school house field today. **1862** in EASTERBY *S.C. Rice Plant.* (1945) 271 Rain Men striping fodder. — (**2**) **1939** WEBSTER (*New Words*). **1947** *Reader's Digest* Sep. 135/2 The blackface minstrel show and the strip tease, act of burlesque in which a girl disrobes piece by piece, are the only forms of theatrical entertainment that originated in the United States. **1950** *Chi. Tribune* 27 April 22/2 Eight women and nine men [were] arrested by state's attorney police in a raid on a Cicero strip tease establishment.

***stripe,** *n.*

1. *pl.* The Stars and Stripes, the flag of the U.S. *Rare.*

1783 in VAN SCHAACK *Life Peter Van Schaack* (1842) 334 The American stripes have already appeared in the Thames, and have been hailed with acclamations of joy.

2. A particular kind of political or religious opinion, a kind, sort, or race.

1850 GARRARD *Wah-To-Yah* viii. 109 The ox-driver . . . was of the same stripe as those to whom the scalps dangling from the Arapaho lance points, originally belonged. **1904** *N.Y. Times* 27 May 8 No Democrat of the Bryan-Hearst stripe could make headway in such an enterprise.

3. *pl.* A striped uniform worn by prisoners. Also fig.

1887 *Courier-Journal* 29 Jan. 3/2 He changed his stripes for a suit of citizens' clothes. **1904** *Brooklyn D. Eagle* 10 June 4 Tammany was . . . whipped into line, and made work for him under ball and chain and in stripes, to the end. **1943** GASSNER & NICHOLS *Best Film Plays 1943–1944* 279/1 Yes, but he's going to be in jail, Trudy, for a long time. He can't do you any good in stripes, honey.

As the last term in **blue, lobo, thirteen stripe(s).** Also **Stars and Stripes.**

***striped,** *a.* In combs.: (1) **striped-back woodpecker,** the common three-toed woodpecker; (2) **bass,** (see quot. 1911), also attrib., cf. ***striper;** (3) **-blue ribbon,** a variety of ribbon cane; (4) **bonito,** (see quot.); (5) **bug,** ?=next, *obs.;* (6) **cucumber beetle,** a greenish-yellow leaf beetle, *Diabrotica vittata,* injurious to cucumbers and other plants; (7) **drum,** the young or common drumfish; (8) **gopher,** a striped spermophile, *Citellus tridecemlineatus;* (9) **ground squirrel,** (*a*) =prec., (*b*) =**chipmunk;** (10) **lizard,** the race runner, *Cnemidophorus sexlineatus;* (11) **maple,** the moosewood, *Acer pennsylvanicum;* (12) **pig,** a fictitious animal used as a symbol of some surreptitious activity, also attrib.; (13) **snake,** a garter snake, esp. *Thamnophis sirtalis;* (14) **squirrel,** any squirrel with stripes on its back, as the chipmunk.

(1) **1869** *Amer. Naturalist* II. 598 Striped-back woodpecker (*Picoides dorsalis*). — (2) **1818** *Amer. Mo. Mag.* II. 295 The striped bass, of New-York, or Rock-fish, . . . is another excellent salt-water fish. **1911** *Rep. Fisheries 1908* 317/1 In the North it [*Roccus lineatus*] is generally called the 'striped bass.' . . . The name is sometimes applied to the white bass (*Roccus chrysops*) of the Great Lakes region. **1949** *News-Reporter* (McMinnville, Ore.) 4 Aug. 6/6 Reports come every day that striped bass fishing is tops in the Coos Bay area. — (3) **1856** *Rep. Comm. Patents 1855: Agric.* 273 The varieties of cane which have hitherto been most cultivated in Louisiana . . . are the 'Striped-blue Ribbon;' . . . the 'Yellow' [etc.]. — (4) **1884** GOODE *Fisheries* I. 316 The common Bonito of England, *Orcynus pelamys,* is what is here-called the 'Striped Bonito.'

(5) **1790** DEANE *N.-Eng. Farmer* 148/2 The *striped bug,* or yellow fly . . . eat[s] and destroy[s] the young plants of cucumbers, melons, squashes and pumpions. — (6) **1934** WEBSTER. **1945** *Athol* (Mass.) *D. News* 9 June 2/7 The striped cucumber beetle is another pest which causes considerable damage to many young plants. — (7) **1884** GOODE *Aquat. Animals* 367 The adult is known as the 'Black Drum,' the young as the 'Striped Drum.' — (8) **1941** SETON *Trail of Artist-Naturalist* 299 Gone . . . also [was] the striped gopher, whose labyrinths are only four inches down, for the plough destroys their safety places, lays open their secret strongholds. — (9) (*a*) **1941** SETON *Trail of Artist-Naturalist* 189 The striped ground squirrels (*Spermophiles*) abounded at Carberry. (*b*) **1947** CAHALANE *Mammals* 379 Other names applied rarely are 'hackie,' chipping squirrel, striped ground squirrel, and just ground squirrel.

(10) **1791** W. BARTRAM *Travels* 278 The striped lizard, called scorpion . . . I have already mentioned. — (11) **1785** MARSHALL *Amer. Grove* 3 American Striped Maple. . . . The bark, especially of the young shoots, is beautifully variegated or striped. **1931** CLUTE *Plants* 42 The striped maple (*Acer Pennsylvanicum*) is the real whistle-wood because its bark is so easily loosened in spring. — (12) **1839** *N.O. Picayune* 31 Jan. 2/3 John Jones was up before the Police Court in Boston the other day for making too free with the 'Striped Pig.' **1839** *Boston Transcript* 11 June 2/3 The soubriquet given to those honorable gentlemen [i.e., informers under Mass. prohibition laws] is 'striped pig' reeves. **1869** *Harper's Mag.* Aug. 450/2 The 'striped pig' very easily outwitted the Statute. But even the striped pig could not carry the whole victory. **1950** *Chi. Tribune* 29 April, These picturesque phrases ['blind pig' and 'blind tiger'] are of rather obscure origin, the original term probably having been 'striped pig.' — (13) **1778** CARVER *Travels* 478 The Wall or House Adder, the Striped or Garter Snake. **1839** in AUDUBON *Ornith. Biog.* V. 601 The snake was the common and apparently innoxious Striped Snake. — (14) **1796** MORSE *Univ. Geog.* I. 203 The Striped Squirrel is still less than the [red squirrel]. **1842** *Nat. Hist. N.Y., Zoology* I. 62 The Striped Squirrel . . . is well known under the various popular names of Hacky, Ground Squirrel, Chipping Squirrel, Chipmuck. **1888** *Ipswich* (Mass.) *Chron.* 15 Sep. 2/4 In some parts of the country a grey ground squirrel is called a gopher. In other parts a striped squirrel or prairie chipmunk is called by that name.

***striper,** *n.* The striped bass *q.v.* (see also quot. 1946).

1946 *News-Age-Herald* (Birmingham) 7 April 1-B/8 The 'stripers' haven't made themselves felt strongly yet in Martin. . . . Technically known as white lake bass this fish had become highly popular in the TVA chain of lakes. **1947** BROWN *Outdoors Unlimited* 288 Stripers will always be here unless netted out. **1948** *N.Y. Times* 23 May V. 5/6 The surfcasting along this beach is excellent when the bass are in-shore, and an occasional striper is taken in this section.

***stripper,** *n.* One seeking a land claim in the Cherokee strip. *Rare.* — **1893** *Columbus* (O.) *Dispatch* 15 Sep., Eager strippers swarmed to-day at the new booth established here last night.

***strong,** *a.* In combs.: (1) ***strong arm,** see as a main entry; (2) **Government Whig,** (see quot.); (3) **grass,** (see quot. and cf. **bear grass**), *rare;* (4) ***handed,** (see quot.), *obs.;* (5) ***hold,** =**strong suit,** *colloq.;* (6) **house,** (see quot.), *obs.;* (7) **suit,** that which one does best, *colloq.*

(2) **1890** C. L. NORTON *Polit. Americanisms* 110 Strong Government Whigs, one of the early divisions of the original Whig party which favored what has since been called 'Centralization,' as opposed to State rights, or the 'Particularists.' This wing of the party adopted the more easily handled name of Federalists . . . after the formal adoption of a Constitution in 1789. — (3) **1808** in DUNBAR *Life* 202 Strong or Bears grass was the vulgar name Mr. Ellicot told me for the Yucca. — (4) **1818** H. B. FEARON *Sk. of Amer.* 222 If he be *strong-handed,* (has property,) he has the trees felled, about one foot from the earth, dragged into heaps, and made into an immense bonfire.

(5) **1927** RUSSELL *Trails* 7 Walking ain't my strong holt an' these boulder bumps don't help me none. — (6) **1797** B. S. BARTON *New Views Orig. Tribes Amer.* p. xxxviii, The Senecas, Mohawks, Onondagos, Cayugas, and Oneidas, constitute the confederacy which has long been known by the name of the Five Nations. This confederacy, or compact, is called by the Indians themselves the Strong-House. — (7) **1865** MARK TWAIN *Jumping Frog* 33 (R.), Jumping on a dead level was his strong suit.

b. *To be strong with,* to be in the favor of. *Colloq.*

1894 MARK TWAIN *Pudd'nhead Wilson* 780 (R.), She's pow'ful strong wid de Jedge.

strong arm. Physical violence, force. Usu. attrib. or as adj. *Slang.*

1828 J. HALL *Lett. from West* 291 When a horse thief, a counterfeiter, or any other desperate vagabond, infested a neighbourhood, evading justice by cunning, or by a strong arm, . . . the citizens formed themselves into a 'regulating company.' **1836** HOLLEY *Texas* 322 This military council . . . distributed lots to the inhabitants, contrary to all law, but that of the *strong arm.* **1901** FLYNT *World of Graft* 17 One of the best illustrations of the indifference of the Chicago police force to the criminal situation in the city, is the freedom with which the 'hold-up' and 'strong-arm' men conduct their operations. **1949** *Lubbock* (Tex.) *Morn. Avalanche* 23 Feb. I. 2/5 Police described [him] as a member of a strong-arm robbery gang.

Also **strong-arm,** *v. tr.,* to exercise force upon. Also fig.

1903 *Mo. Maroon* (Chi.) June 444 If he refused, Phil, who would be near by, was to strong-arm him while Tommy took away the badge. **1950** *N.O. Times-Picayune Mag.* 5 Feb. 6/1 Educators and legislators have long tried to strongarm sororities out of existence.

stroud straud, *n.* [See note.]

"Stroud, Gloucestershire, was noted for its woollen manufactures. The stream which flowed through it was peculiarly adapted for use in dyeing bright colours. The fur companies bought largely of its coloured blankets and its name became a trade-mark for those of the best quality" (Jas. Bain, ed. Alex. Henry *Travels* (1910) 116).

Strouding *q.v.*, or a blanket or garment made of this. Now *hist.*

1683 in C. H. HUNT *Life E. Livingston* 6 Four garments of Strouds. **1748** WEISER *Journal* 31, I made a Present to the old Shawonese Chief Cackawatcheky, of a Stroud, a Blanket [etc.]. **1816** MCKENNEY *Memoirs* I. 309 Strouds are a blue cloth, six quarters wide, with a narrow cord about one inch from the selvage. **1871** *Rep. Indian Affairs* (1872) 459 Not a vestige of Indian costume—as blankets, leggings, strouds, &c.—comes into our schoolroom.

attrib. **1683** in C. H. HUNT *Life E. Livingston* 7 Four Stroud-Coats and Two duffel-Coats. **1765** CROGHAN *Journal* (1904) 60, I gave him a Strowd Shirt, Match Coat [etc.]. **1772** in *Travels Amer. Col.* 553, I also gave him a Stroud Blanket flap. **1939** PINKERTON *Wilderness Wife* 286 The bead ornamentation of the blue stroud covering must have kept three wives busy.

strouding ˈstraʊdɪŋ, *n.* A kind of coarse woolen cloth formerly much used in the Indian trade. *Obs.* or *hist.*

1814 BRACKENRIDGE *Views La.* 201 The merchandise . . . consisted of strouding, blankets, lead, tobacco [etc.]. **1886** *Cent. Mag.* Nov. 33/2 He and his sons gathered hazel-nuts enough to barter at the nearest store for a few yards of blue strouding such as the Indians used for breech-clouts. **1947** DEVOTO *Across Wide Missouri* 32 The Company is sending . . . a variety of cloths too diversified to list here, common cloths, stroudings, plaids, fancy calicos, flannels.

strychnine whisky. Very inferior whisky. *Obs.* — **1859** *U.S. Police Gaz.* (N.Y.) 12 March 2/7 The Perils of Drinking Strychnine Whiskey. **1860** *Harper's Mag.* Aug. 427/2 It was apparent that the man had died from the immoderate use of strychnine whisky.

Stuartia, see **Stewartia.**

* **stub,** *n.*

1. A derogatory term for a person, esp. one who is old or short and stocky. *Colloq.*

1823 COOPER *Pioneers* (1832) 242 What's that, old corn-stalk! you sapless stub! **1865** *Harper's Mag.* Dec. 133/2 In these . . . regions there dwells a stub of the law who is possessed of august presence. **1890** CURTIN tr. Sienkiewicz *With Fire & Sword* 514, I have something to say to this little stub of an officer.

2. The butt or stump of a cigar or cigarette. Also attrib.

1855 M. THOMPSON *Doesticks* 133 Perhaps they expect us to smoke 'stubs,' like the newsboys. **1896** MARK TWAIN *Innocents* 162 It wounds my sensibilities to see one of these stub-hunters watching me . . . and calculating how long my cigar will be likely to last. **1914** BOWER *Flying U Ranch* 187 He spat upon the burnt end of his cigarette stub from force of the habit that fear of range fires had built.

3. A counterfoil (cf. **check stub**). Also the portion of a ticket detached and returned to the purchaser by a ticket collector.

1876 *N. Amer. Rev.* CXXIII. 301 The shipment of large packages, for which check stubs representing only small amounts were retained. **1911** REEVE *Poisoned Pen* 303 'Number 156' Herndon noted as the collector detached the stub and handed it to her. **1950** *Business Week* 22 April 87 Left-handed checkbooks. These please southpaw writers. Stubs are on the opposite side from the conventional checkbook.

4. In combs.: (1) **stub-and-twist,** (*a*) a firearm the barrel or barrels of which are made of a spirally welded ribbon of steel and iron made of stub or horseshoe nails, also attrib., *obs.*, (*b*) (see quot.); (2) **ballot book,** the book or pad remaining when ballots of a certain type are torn out; (3) **book,** a book or pad of stubs of checks, receipts, etc.; (4) **sho(r)t,** (see quot. 1876); (5) **switch,** (see quot.); (6) * **tail,** (see quot.); (7) **tracks,** (see quot.).

(1) (*a*) **1844** *Knickerb.* XXIII. 440 There, Peter, is a true 'stubb-and-twist.' **1861** *Chi. Tribune* 26 May 1/5 When finished the gun presents the appearance of a stub-and-twist rifle. (*b*) **1917** *Birds of Amer.* I. 152 Other names [of the ruddy duck are] . . . Paddy-whack; Stub-and-twist; . . . Dinky; Dickey; Paddy. — **(2) 1911** *Okla. Session Laws* 3 Legisl. 229 The bundle of voted ballots and the stub ballot book, . . . shall be placed in the envelope labeled 'Voted Ballots.' — **(3) 1886** *Rep. Secy. Treasury* 700 Stub-books of stamps . . . [occupy] a very large and rapidly increasing space in the files-rooms. **1902** O. HENRY *Roads of Destiny* 191 Then the stub book of the certificates of deposit. — **(4) 1843** *Knickerb.* XXII. 446, I was flat on my back . . . by the camp-fire, . . . with the 'stub-shot' for a pillow. **1876** KNIGHT 2431/2 *Stub-short; stub-shot.* 1. The unsawed portion of a plank where it is split from the bolt or log. . . . 2. (*Turning*). The portion by which an object to be turned is grasped.

(5) 1909 WEBSTER 2062 *Stub switch,* . . . a switch in which the track rails are cut off squarely at the toe and the switch rails are thrown to butt end to end with the lead rails. — **(6) 1867** SIMMONDS *Dict. Trade* (Supp.), *Stubtail, Stumptail,* names in North America for flour made out of damaged wheat and good wheat ground together. — **(7) 1909** *Cent. Supp.* 1287/2 The parallel tracks of the train-shed of a terminal station are *stub-tracks.*

As the last term in **check, ham stub.**

* **stub,** *v.* **1.** *intr.* To stump *about*, to go *along* heedlessly. *Colloq.* **2. Stubtoe State,** (see quots.).

(1) 1875 LEWIS *Quad's Odds* 480 (We.), The writer will stub along through life with a heart full of joyfulness. **1878** B. F. TAYLOR *Between Gates* 241 An old whaler stubbing about estimated him [a whale] at sixty barrels. **1895** *Stand.* 1783/1 The boy stubs along to school. — **(2) 1890** *Brighton* (Colo.) *Reg.* 11 Jan. 4/1 Montana is the 'stubbed-toe State.' **1934** SHANKLE *State Names* 129 The names *Bonanza* and *Treasure* are typical of the mining area of the State, and *Stubtoe* of the mountainous nature of the western section of the State.

* **stubble,** *n.*

1. The stump or lower part of sugar cane remaining when the crop is cut; sugar cane growing from these stumps, in full **stubble cane.**

1827 in COMMONS *Doc. Hist.* I. 214 Stubbles of Creole cane in new land mark the row. **1856** *Fla. Plantation Rec.* 455 Plantin and Replanting stuble cane. **1897** *Kissimmee* (Fla.) *Valley Gaz.* 19 May 1/4 Well cared for stubble will rattoon for three years in most parts of this state.

attrib. **1881** *Chi. Times* 11 June 7/2 The sugar districts in this state [La.] report . . . Stubble crop good.

2. In special combs.: (1) **stubble plow,** (see quot.); (2) **rye,** rye sown on stubble, *rare;* (3) **shearing, shorn,** (see quot.).

(1) 1876 KNIGHT 2431/1 *Stubble-plow,* . . . one for plowing *old* ground, so called; land which was lately in small grain, not in grass. In contradistinction to *sod*-plow. — **(2) 1802** *Mass. H.S. Coll.* 1 Ser. VIII. 189 The first year, Indian corn; the second, hill rye; the third, stubble rye. — **(3) 1866** *Maine Agric. Soc. Returns 1865* 157 This sheep was stubble shorn, which accounts for one staple being so much longer than the other. Stubble shearing is performed for the purpose of improving the form and cheating the committee at fairs.

***stubble,** *v.* **stubbling in,** (see quot.). *Obs.* — **1825** LORAIN *Pract. Husbandry* 129 The worst system of cultivation in common practice seems to be stubbling in; or annually putting in crops of small grain on stubble grounds.

stubboy, see **staboy.**

* **stud,** *n.*[1]

1. A studhorse or stallion.

1803 CUTLER in *Life & Corr.* II. 142 The famous white stud, an Arabian horse. **1845** *Knickerb.* XXVI. 368 A very large stud broke from the line. **1891** C. ROBERTS *Adrift Amer.* 183 He was a stud, and as fine a horse of his class as I ever saw. **1947** SANTEE *Apache Land* 72 The old stud was a bay and battle-scarred.

b. *To take the stud(s)*, (see quot. 1830). *Colloq.* [Cf. *EDD to take* (*the*) *stunt* (*s.v. stunt* 15) in same sense.]

1797 *Pa. Mag.* VI. 111 Don't you think Mr. Ashleys leading Strings may give way, if the Commy. should take the studd. **1830** *Va. Lit. Museum* 6 Jan. 479 'To take the stud'—to be obstinate: originally applied to a horse that refuses to go on. **1900** HARRIS *On the Wing* 226 I'm a pretty good walker, but if I was to take the studs and lie down in the road, you'd have some trouble.

2. = **stud poker.** Also **studhorse.**

1891 QUINN *Fools of Fortune* 188 Next to the banking games in the estimation of the betters comes poker, both 'draw' and 'stud.' **1920** MULFORD *J. Nelson* ii, He's a travellin' eddicator in th' innercent game of draw—or was it studhoss, Nelson? **1949** *Boston Globe* 26 June (Fiction Mag.) 8/1 It would be real comfortin' for you an' me an' Dixie to play stud in the back of the chuck wagon.

attrib. **1948** *Dly. Ardmoreite* (Ardmore, Okla.) 7 May 6/1 In a real old-fashioned stud game at the club, the boys always take Presto to the cleaners. **1949** *Boston Globe* 15 May (Fiction Mag.) 3/2 The officer . . . stepped over and paused beside the stud table.

3. In combs.: (1) **studfish,** a killifish, *Xenisma stellifer* or *X. catenatum*, also with a specifying term, cf. **horse fish;** (2) **-horse type,** (see quot.), *obs.*, cf. **horse bill;** (3) **poker,** a form of poker differing slightly in the dealing and betting from other forms of the game, also **studhorse poker.**

(1) 1882 *Nat. Museum Bul.* No. 16, 337 *Fundulus stellifer,* Spotted Stud-fish. **1896** JORDAN & EVERMANN *Check-List Fishes* 310 *Fundulus catenatus.* Studfish. Tennessee and Cumberland rivers and clear streams of the Ozark Mountains. — **(2) 1868** *Putnam's Mag.* II. 215 The facts must be stated tersely, handsomely, takingly; the whole must be set off with 'display lines,' 'stud-horse type' (to use the strong technic of the composing-room). — **(3) 1864** DICK *Amer. Hoyle* (1866) 182 Stud Poker . . . in all essential particulars, is like the other Poker games. **1891** C. ROBERTS *Adrift Amer.* 152 Every saloon had a gambling room, where poker, stud-horse poker, faro, . . . and a wheel of fortune were usually hard at it. **1950** *Asheville* (N.C.) *Citizen-Times* 26 March III. 12/1 Three men sat in a small room . . . engaged in a friendly game of stud poker.

***stud,** *n.*[2] The height of a room from floor to ceiling. — **1850** in J. HAWTHORNE *N. Hawthorne & Wife* I. 369 You cannot think how pretty the room looks, though with such a low stud that I have to get acclimated to it. **1886** E. S. MORSE *Jap. Homes* 63 These rooms were unusually high in stud.

***studded,** *a.* As the last term in **high, low studded.**

***studding,** *n.* The height of a room or story in a house. — **1884** Howells *Silas Lapham* iii, Lapham promptly developed his ideas of black walnut finish, high studding, and cornices.

Studebaker (wagon). A well-built and widely known wagon of a type first built by Studebaker Brothers at South Bend, Indiana, in 1852.

[**1874** Goodrich & Tuttle *Hist. State Indiana* 615 (*caption*), Studebaker Bros. Wagon Works, South Bend.] **1881** *Ore. State Jrnl.* 1 Jan. 5/1 [He] has just received a car load of the famous Studebaker wagons. **1889** *Chi. D. News* 20 April 1/4 The most popular outfit is a strong, canvas-covered Studebaker, drawn by two large, stout horses. **1948** *Reader's Digest* April 123/2 From the high seat of a Studebaker wagon, the reins around his neck, he drove a span of horses 50 miles to town.

***student,** *n.* **1.** (See quot.) *Obs.* **2. student lamp,** an adjustable lamp esp. suitable for use by students.

(1) **1848** *Western Boatman* May 103 We should be pleased to have communications on. . . . The Student, or freight hoister, a small vibrating cylinder to hoist freight, supplied by a separate boiler. —

Early type of student lamp

(2) **1873** G. Hamilton *Twelve Miles* 101 The fame of the German Student Lamp was noised abroad. **1877** *Nation* 15 March 158/3 Pratt's Astral Oil. Perfectly Safe. Especially adapted for use in the St. Germain Student Lamp. **1910** Tompkins *Mothers & Fathers* 147 Cora . . . drew their chairs up to the student lamp.

As the last term in **first course, house of, special student(s).**

***studio,** *n.* **1. studio apartment,** orig. an apartment having high ceilings and a maximum of natural light, like an artist's studio; now freq. a one-room attic apartment. **2. studio couch,** a flat couch upholstered like a davenport, usu. with three matching pillows, capable of being opened into a full-sized bed.

(1) **1934** Webster. **1944** *Chi. Tribune* 1 March 25/2 Beau. 2–3 rm. studio apts. — (2) **1936** *Sears Cat.* 506 A studio couch that looks like a beautiful davenport . . . broad comfortable arms and magazine rack in the end. **1946** *Sat. Ev. Post* 3 Aug. 30/1 But you remember my two-room flat And the studio couch on which you sat.

***study,** *n.* As the last term in **field, fire study.**

***study,** *v.*

1. *To study up,* (see quot. 1891). *Colloq.*

1880 Mark Twain *Tramp Abroad* 412, I resolved to devote my first evening in Zermatt to studying up the subject of Alpine climbing. **1891** *Cent.* 6005/3 *study up.* (*a*) To learn by special study or investigation; get up a knowledge of, as for a particular purpose or occasion. . . . (*b*) To seek or get a knowledge of by observation or consideration; observe or reflect upon critically; make up one's mind about. **1946** *Chi. D. News* 25 June 31/3 Ah'll git a li'l closer, an' study up on him!

2. In combs.: (1) **study hour,** an hour or period during which pupils study; (2) **lamp, =student lamp;** (3) **room,** a room in which one studies, a study.

(1) **1873** Tyler *Hist. Amherst Coll.* 178 A legislative body, called the House of Students, enacted laws . . . for the better observance of study hours, etc., etc. **1907** *St. Nicholas* May 663/2 Duty calls with the voice of the bell, for study-hour. — (2) **1830** *Collegian* 231 A rusty old study-lamp hung from the dingy ceiling. **1931** *K.C. Times* 24 Aug., A study lamp . . . will last all through his course. — (3) **1837** *Knickerb.* X. 383 Our study-rooms were contiguous. **1907** *St. Nicholas* Aug. 872/1 You look in the study room and I'll go upstairs.

***stuff,** *n.* (See quot.) *Obs.* Cf. ***stuffy,** *a.* — **1787** J. Q. Adams *Life N. Eng. Town* 66 [She] has rather too much temper, or as it is called in New-England, too much *stuff.*

As the last term in **basket, bill, blue, bread, chin, chip, creek, dry, feed, fencing, hard, hot, rail, rough, she, ship's, sob, store, truck stuff.**

***stuff,** *v. tr.* To put fraudulent votes in (a ballot-box) (see quot. 1950). *Slang.*

1854 *Pioneer* (S.F.) Nov. 293 They saw the Judge and Inspectors of the First Ward polls stuffing the ballot-boxes. **1876** *Gold Hill* (Nev.) *News* 5 Oct. 2/1 Sam Tilden is endeavoring to carry Indiana by stuffing the ballot-boxes. **1950** *Chi. D. News* 18 Feb. 2/6 They're going to 'stuff the ballot box' by illegally voting twice or more.

transf. **1898** *Chi. Times-Herald* 1 April 6/2 It should not relax its efforts to punish those who are responsible for stuffing the registry lists until the guilty ones are lodged in the penitentiary. **1949** *Newsweek* 23 May 18/2 He swamped his opponents by . . . stuffing the election rolls.

b. Also with prepositions and adverbs.

1856 *S.F. Bulletin* 14 May 2/2 The fact of his having stuffed himself through the ballot-box as elected to the Board of Supervisors from a district where it is said he was not even a candidate [is not] any justification for Mr. Bagley to shoot Casey. **1857** *Phoenix* (Sacramento) 20 Sep. 2/3 Head who is a stripling of the petty larceny school, sold his party—whig—in 1850 and stuffed in Ben Burns for Controller for the paltry sum of $40. **1876** *The Dalles* (Ore.) *Tribune* 8 Jan. 1/7, I believe the ballot-boxes were stuffed against me!

***stuffed,** *a.* In combs.: (1) **stuffed ballot,** a fraudulent ballot; (2) **monkey,** (see quot.), *obs.;* (3) **Prophet,** Grover Cleveland (1837–1908), a nickname; (4) **shirt,** a man of insignificant or contemptible abilities but of pompous or imposing manners and appearance, also **stuffed-shirtism,** *slang.*

(1) **1883** *Cent. Mag.* Aug. 631/2 The abuses of the primary in the form of false enrollments, fraudulent expulsions, stuffed ballots, and the like, have developed with equal pace. — (2) **1893** Leland *Memoirs* 38 'Stuffed monkey' was a common by-word, by the way, for a conceited fellow. — (3) **1892** *N.Y. Sun* 25 March, The stuffed Prophet's thirst for the Presidency, now and forever, is inconditioned. **1892** W. S. Walsh *Literary Curiosities* 1037 Stuffed Prophet, an epithet which the New York *Sun* sought to fasten on Grover Cleveland just prior to his nomination as a candidate for the Presidency of 1892. **1945** Mencken *Supp.* 308. — (4) **1913** Cather *O Pioneers!* 144 He characterized Frank Shabata by a Bohemian expression which is the equivalent of stuffed shirt. **1945** Service *Ploughman* 345, I have always resented stuffed-shirtism. **1950** *Reader's Digest* April 62/2 He was always fighting with stuffed shirts.

***stuffer,** *n.* **1. =watch stuffer. 2.** One who stuffs ballot-boxes. *Slang.*

(1) **1840** in *Amer. Sp.* XVI. 231/1 'A stuffer' . . . persuaded Robert that he could not live here in York, without a watch. — (2) **1875** *Chi. Tribune* 9 Nov. 2/4 The first thing to do was to use every means to bring the scoundrelly 'repeaters' and 'stuffers' to justice. **1910** J. Hart *Vigilante Girl* 255 Tower always stands by his stuffers and plug-uglies, to give the Devil his due.

As the last term in **ballot, ballot-box, sausage, watch stuffer.**

***stuffing,** *n.* Advertising pamphlets or literature. *Slang.* Cf. **watch stuffing.** — **1926** *Publishers' Wkly.* 22 May 1712/2 We recommend also less use of stuffing in monthly statements, unless no catalog is mailed out regularly.

***stuffy,** *a. N. Eng.* Sulky, obstinate, bad-tempered. *Colloq.*

1825 Neal *Bro. Jonathan* III. 289 Well then, if you're so stuffy about it. **1862** Lowell *Biglow P.* 2 Ser. iii. 91 It's justifyin' Ham to spare a nigger when he's stuffy. **1890** *D.N.* I. 20 *Stuffy,* sullen, obstinate, ill-humored. [New Eng.]

***stump,** *n.*

1. A platform, orig. a stump, from which an audience may be addressed.

[**1716** in Ann Maury *Memoirs Huguenot Family* (1872) 276, I went down to the Saponey Indian town. . . . There is in the centre of the circle a great stump of a tree; I asked the reason they left that standing, and they informed me it was for one of their head men to stand upon when he had anything of consequence to relate to them, so that being raised, he might the better be heard.] **1775** in Moore *Songs & Ballads Amer. Rev.* 101 Upon a stump, he placed (himself,) Great Washington did he. **1816** *Ann. 14th Cong.* 1 Sess. 1169 His arguments are better calculated for what is called on this side of the river *stump* than for this Committee. **1901** Montgomery *Reminiscences* 9, I thought Mr. Foote the superior of Mr. Davis on the stump. **1949** *Sat. Ev. Post* 2 July 68/3, I would finish a stump speech—yes, sometimes I actually spoke from a stump—and find that Dick had wandered off a mile or so down the road.

2. (See quot. 1835.) Also **stump man.** *Obs.*

1835 TODD *Notes* 34 Candidates of doubtful principles are called *Stumps.* **1840** KENNEDY *Quodlibet* 98 Agamemnon Flag . . . was the only stump man on the ticket. **1844** EMERSON *Poet* Ess. 2 Ser., Our stumps and their politics . . . are yet unsung.

3. A dare or challenge, a test or trial. *Colloq.* Cf. * **stump,** *v.* **1.**

1842 *Warsaw* (Ill.) *Signal* 3 Sep. 3/3 Joe is not good for much, but he said I dare not have him, and I won't take a stump from any body. **1894** *Advance* 18 Oct. 102/3 The bravest thing ye did was to refuse to run the risk fer a mere stump!

4. (See quot.) *Obs.* Cf. * **stump,** *v.* **4.**

1851 HALL *College Words* 294 A *stump,* a bad recitation; used in the phrase, *to make a stump.*

5. In special combs.: (1) **stump city,** a new city in which stumps still abound, *rare;* (2) **corn,** corn planted among the stumps of newly cleared land, *rare;* (3) **country,** a region from which the logs have been cut; (4) **cultivation,** cultivation among the stumps of a newly cleared field, *obs.;* (5) **extractor,** = **stump puller,** cf. **grub puller;** (6) **fence,** a fence made of stumps, also **stump fencing;** (7) **lot,** a lot or field in which stumps

Stump fence

abound, *obs.;* (8) **machine,** = **stump puller,** *obs.;* (9) **puller,** a machine for pulling up stumps; (10) **-stinger,** prob. a long-tailed ichneumon fly, often suspected of being a wood borer; (11) **sucker,** a crib-biter or wind-sucker, also transf.; (12) **swallow,** (see quot.); (13) * **tail,** see as a main entry; (14) **tree,** the Kentucky coffee tree, so called from its lack of small branches; (15) **water,** rain water that has collected in a stump cavity, much valued in folk remedies and magic; (16) **yard,** a yard in which there are stumps of trees.

(1) **1862** *Harper's Mag.* June 133/2 In one of the many stump cities for which Michigan is somewhat noted live two individuals. — (2) **1942** CANNON *Mountain* 310 They set off on the path . . . that cut through the middle of his acre of stump corn. — (3) **1896** *Home Missionary* July 129 Vast tracts of stump country [in Mich.] are as truly virgin soil as if the region had just been discovered. — (4) **1835** LATROBE *Rambler* II. 145 The low country around it, with its 'corduroy roads' and 'stump-cultivation.'

(5) **1847** *Rep. Comm. Patents 1846* 94 Letters patent have been granted for improvements in . . . stump extractors. **1889** HOWELLS *Hazard of Fortunes* I. 105 Then somebody invented a stump extracter, and we pulled them out with a yoke of oxen. — (6) [**1815–16** *Niles' Reg.* IX. (Supp.) 178/1, I observed . . . [a] strong substantial and durable fence, made of white pine stumps.] **1932** *Old-Time N. Eng.* July 12/2 Here are . . . samples of stump fencing and of the more familiar sort known as post and rails. **1942** WEYGANDT *Plenty of Penna.* 30 Other fences surviving from yesterday are stump fences of white pine. — (7) **1865** TROWBRIDGE *Three Scouts* 7 Around them were all the evidences of desolating war,—neglected fields, demolished fences, and orchards converted into stump-lots. **1873** BAILEY *Life in Danbury* 97 If every flying pang had been a drunken plow chased by a demon across a stump lot, I think the observer would understand my condition. — (8) **1858** *So. Cultivator* XVI. 246/1 Mr. J. Q. Estill of Kentucky, furnishes . . . the following description of a cheap stump machine. **1868** LOSSING *Hudson* 54 One of the stump-machines stood in a field near the road. — (9) **1854** *Mich. Agric. Soc. Trans.* V. 505 The afternoon was spent in a trial of plows, a stump puller, and in general conversation. **1947** *Calif. Citrograph* Nov. 40/4 Need a stump puller? Get some well casing, a welding outfit, and make it yourself.

(10) **1849** LANMAN *Lett. Alleghany Mts.* 82 The stump-stinger is remarkable for having attached to the middle of his body a hard and pointed weapon, with which he can dig a hole one inch in depth in the body of even a hickory tree. — (11) **1811** *Chillicothe* (O.) *Supporter* 5 Oct. 3/3 Taken up by Isaac Washburn, one bay mare, supposed to be 14½ hands high, 12 or 13 years old, blind of the right eye, supposed to be a stump sucker, appraised to eighteen dollars. **1900** HARRIS *On the Wing* 73 You had to be broke in, you know. I didn't know whether you was a stump-sucker or a thorough-bred. **1942** MCATEE *Rural Dial. Grant Co., Ind.* 62 *stump-sucker,* . . . a horse that sets its upper teeth on the edge of the manger or other object and gulps air that later may cause it great discomfort. — (12) **1917** *Birds of Amer.* III. 88 Tree Swallow. *Iridoprocne bicolor.* . . . [Also called] White-bellied Swallow; Stump Swallow: Eave Swallow. — (14) **1890** NEWHALL *Trees Northeastern Amer.* 190 Kentucky Coffee Tree, Stump Tree. *G[ymnocladus] disicus.* **1900** H. L. KEELER *Native Trees* (1902) 109 Kentucky coffee tree, stump tree.

(15) **1892** HARRIS *U. Remus & Friends* 290 De way ter git rid er ha'nts wuz ter git some prickly-pear root en bile it in stump-water en sprinkle it 'roun' de yard. **1928** BRADFORD *Ol' Man Adam* 216, I drinks nothin' but stump water and a rattlesnake bit me and died. — (16) **1723** *N.-Eng. Courant* 2 Dec. 1/2 For suppose . . . they should forget where they were, and order their Men . . . to *face about to the Stump-Yard,* or *turn about to the Barn.*

b. Used (sense **1.**) in combs. of obvious meaning, as (1) **stump campaign,** (2) **candidate,** (3) **orator,** (4) **speaker,** (5) **speaking,** (6) **speech.**

(1) **1888** BRYCE *Amer. Commonw.* I. I. x. 132 (*footnote*), The famous struggle of Mr. Douglas and Mr. Lincoln for the Illinois senatorship in 1858 was conducted in a stump campaign. — (2) **1833** in *Amer. Sp.* VIII. (1933) 76 Stump Candidates. A numerous class of high-minded and patriotic worthies, who, having no particular business of their own, are ever ready to attend to that of the public—provided they can get well paid for it. — (3) **1813** JEFFERSON *Writings* XIII. 281 Of this acrimony, the public papers of the day exhibit ample testimony, in the debates of Congress, of State legislatures, of stump-orators. **1888** FERGUSON *Experiences of Forty-Niner* 151 Over the hill . . . [lived] the Dutch blacksmith, politician, and stump orator. — (4) **1844** *Lexington Observer* 24 Aug. 3/1 The mendacity of the Locofoco press, and Locofoco stump speakers, has reached to such a degree, that [etc.]. **1944** DUNCAN *M. Graham* 163 And he did grow less morose, entertaining the Grahams with sidesplitting imitations of stump speakers at political rallies.

(5) **1834** *Boston Atlas* 5 Sep. 2/4 Two candidates . . . having agreed to meet, to have a regular stump speaking match. **1889** *Harper's Mag.* Sep. 554/2 Other occasions . . . were set apart for . . . militia musters, stump-speakings, county court day assemblages. — (6) **1820** FLINT *Lett. from Amer.* 251 The harangues are called stump-speeches. **1894** *Chi. Record* 16 March 1/5 Coxey and Browne are conducting a red-hot stump-speech campaign. **1948** *Newsweek* 18 Oct. 35/3 The big play for the Mexican-Americans in the Southwest drew enthusiastic pro-Wallace crowds to hear his stump speeches.

Also *stump material, oration, oratory, oratress, phrase, slang, tour,* etc.

c. In colloq. phrases: (1) *To whip the devil (a)round a stump,* see * **devil,** *n.* **5;** (2) *from the stump,* from the beginning, *obs.;* (3) *to be up a stump,* to be in a perplexing situation or difficulty; (4) *to take the stump,* to go on a political speaking tour; (5) *to run against a stump,* to encounter a difficulty; (6) *to fool around the stump,* to delay, beat about the bush; (7) *to go on the stump,* = *to take the stump;* (8) *to talk around a five-cornered stump,* see * **five 2. c.** (3); (9) *to put to* (one's) *stumps,* to force (one) to put forth great effort; (10) *in* (or *at*) *the stump,* of timber, unfelled, standing uncut.

(2) **1813** *Niles' Reg.* 4 Sep. 12/2 The *Sylph,* pierced for 24 guns, and carrying 20, of the burthen of 340 tons, schooner rigged, was built and ready for service in '*thirty-three days from the stump.*' **1844** LEE & FROST *Oregon* 289 A house must be built from the stump in a few weeks. — (3) **1829** KIRKHAM *Eng. Grammar* 206 [He will] soon be up a stump. **1944** DUNCAN *M. Graham* 147 For once in his life, work had him so up a stump that he could not snatch a moment for study or reading. — (4) **1852** *N.Y. Wkly. Tribune* 9 Oct. 8/2 Mr. S. will take the stump shortly. **1950** *Time* 3 April 23/2 Pepper hit the road even before Smathers took the stump.

(5) **1871** EGGLESTON *Hoosier Schoolm.* 50 Ralph Hartsook ran against a stump where he was least expecting it. — (6) **1880** *Scribner's Mo.* XIX. 428/2 Thar ain't no use in foolin' round the stump! — (7) **1884** *Cambridge Tribune* 18 July, Blaine is not foolish enough to go on the stump. **1904** *Sun* (N.Y.) 7 Aug. 1 [If someone] informed him that Chauncey M. Depew had turned Democrat and was going on the stump for Parker and Davis . . . , 'he wouldn't bat an eye.' — (9) **1890** MCALLISTER *Society* 317, [I urged] them to show these Britishers what the Yankee could do when put to his stumps. — (10)

1902 WHITE *Blazed Trail* 243 Worth in the stump anywhere from sixteen to twenty thousand dollars. **1905** PRINGLE *Rice Planter* 153 It has been the habit of many to sell the wood to negroes at the stump.

As the last term in **birch, liberty, lightwood, locust, mesquite, pine stump.**

***stump,** *v.*

1. *tr.* To challenge or dare. *Colloq.* Cf. ***stump,** *n.* **3.**

1766 J. ADAMS *Diary* Wks. II. 204 Keen . . . stumped Soule, the moderator, to lay down the money to prevent a tax upon the poor. **1882** THAYER *From Log-Cabin* 73, I stump you to do it. **1948** *Sat. Ev. Post* 11 Sep. 150/4 I'll stump you to jump down.

2. To perplex, confuse, baffle. *Colloq.*

1812 PAULDING *J. Bull & Bro. Jon.* 129 John Bull was a little stumped when he saw Jonathan's challenge. **1910** *Pacific Mo.* Jan. 86/1 When the layman desires to 'stump' the philosopher 'good and hard' he asks him, 'Which was first, the owl or the egg?' **1950** *Time* 3 April 40/2 For once in his triumphant career, crafty old John L. Lewis was momentarily stumped.

3. (See quot. 1828.) *Colloq.*

1828 WEBSTER, *Stump*, to strike any thing fixed and hard with the toe. (*Vulgar.*) **1891** *Harper's Mag.* Feb. 364/2 Mus' be powerful sorrowful ter set at home an' shed tears lest he mought hev stumped his toe on the road.

4. *intr.* To fail, as in a recitation. *Obs.* Cf. ***stump,** *n.* **4.**

The meaning in quot. 1836 is not clear.

[**1836** *S. Lit. Messenger* II. 697 None is more deserving of particular mention, inside and outside, than the Unitarian Church, (although Baltimoreans generally 'stump' on the Cathedral).] **1843** R. CARLTON *New Purchase* iv. 20 It may be supposed our songster chose not to halt or stump from any defect of memory. **1851** HALL *College Words* 294 Stump. At Princeton College, to fail in reciting; to say 'not prepared,' when called on to recite.

5. To make stump speeches, to electioneer in a political campaign.

1838 BIRD *Peter Pilgrim* I. 114, I stumped through my district, and my fellow citizens sent me to Congress! **1905** *Springfield W. Republican* 6 Oct. 8 That year he stumped in Maryland, Virginia, Michigan and throughout a long western trip. **1950** *Business Week* 22 April 21/1 President Truman will make politicking official next month when he stumps to the West.

b. *tr.* To travel or canvass (a state or other area) in a speech-making political tour.

The *EDD* records this use from Lancashire but gives no early evidence.

1855 *Herald of Freedom* 9 June 4/2 With these absurd falsehoods reiterated in every speech did [he] stump the State during the winter. **1897** *Kissimmee* (Fla.) *Valley Gaz.* 31 Dec. 2/1 Ex-State Treasurer Collins is said to have threatened to stump the state in the cause of his innocence.

stumpage ˈstʌmpɪdʒ, *n.* Standing timber, the value of this, or the right to cut it. Cf. **spruce stumpage.**

1835 *Knickerb.* V. 423 The folds of verse are too tender for such rough words as tariff, jobbing, cuts, stumpage, snags, sawyers, etc. **1882** NASH *Two Years Ore.* 224 When the logger is honest, he buys the right to cut from the owner of the land, paying 'stumpage' of about fifty cents per tree. **1900** E. BRUNCKEN *N. Amer. Forests* 81 This has given rise to a peculiar class of people variously known as woodsmen, cruisers, landlookers, whose business it is . . . to buy 'stumpage'—that is, standing timber. **1949** *Sierra Club Bul.* Jan. 8 There is plenty of good sugar pine stumpage elsewhere in the state.

attrib. **1884** *Rep. Comm. Agric.* 142 All stumpage laws should be repealed. **1906** BELL *C. Lee* 318 He leased them the stumpage rights of Sunnymede. **1948** *Democrat* 23 Sep. 1/2 The total stumpage value of timber sold in Alabama last year . . . was $34,076,000.

***stumper,** *n.* In colloq. uses.

1. A question, problem, etc., which stumps or baffles one.

1807 IRVING *Salmagundi* vi, Now this [a new dramatic reading] was 'a stumper.' **1887** *Courier-Journal* 20 Jan. 4/5 The question was sort of a stumper. **1950** *World-Herald Mag.* (Omaha) 16 April 25/4 Fact Chaser His Job Is Thinking Up Radio Quiz 'Stumpers.'

2. A stump speaker.

1849 *Knickerb.* XXXIV. 513 The best 'stumpers' are not always the best qualified for the business of the state. **1896** *Columbus* (O.) *Dispatch* 23 Sep., The secretary of the American Marine association . . . [wrote] to the Republican stumpers asking them to call special attention to the shipping plank.

3. One who challenges or dares another to do something. Cf. ***stump,** *v.* **1.**

1948 *Sat. Ev. Post* 11 Sep. 150/4 Without waiting for them to yell, 'Stumpers go first,' he jumped.

***stumping,** *n.* The delivering of stump speeches. Also attrib.

1844 *Lexington Observer* 18 Sep. 2/3 Gen. Cass has started on a *stumping* excursion for Polk and Dallas. **1860** *Lawrence* (Kans.) *Republican* 22 Nov. 1/5 He was returning from a stumping tour in the Wisconsin district now *mis*represented by the doughface Larabee. **1875** *Chi. Tribune* 5 Oct. 2/3 There is very little stumping in Wisconsin this fall. **1949** *Oregonian* (Portland) 10 Aug. 19/4 His visit will be made during his planned 'stumping' tour of the state after congress adjourns.

***stumptail,** *n.*

1. a. (See quot.) *Obs.* **b.** *attrib.* Designating a person or thing that is damaged or inferior. *Contemptuous.*

(a) 1867 SIMMONDS *Dict. Trade* (Supp.), *Stubtail, Stumptail*, names in North America for flour made out of damaged wheat and good wheat ground together. — **(b) 1861** *Ill. Agric. Soc. Trans.* IV. 323 Not a lot of 'seedlings,' which are often worse than 'stumptail' wheat, in any well supplied market. **1889** MARK TWAIN *Conn. Yankee* 353 (R.), Merlin's sort—stump-tail prophets, as we call them in the profession. **1894** P. L. FORD *P. Stirling* 72 Most residents of New York can remember the 'swill-milk' or 'stump-tail milk' exposures and prosecutions of that summer.

2. stumptail currency, (see quot. 1861). *Obs.*

1861 *Chi. Tribune* 22 May 4 'Stumptail' currency:—At the outbreak of the Civil War, those bank notes secured by Southern state bonds and depreciated Northern issues were called 'stumptail' and were, as the name denotes, circulated at a discount, the discount varying with the market quotations of these southern bonds. **1888** KIRKLAND *McVeys* 236 Here the stranger lugged out . . . bills of all denominations and all kind of banks, those being the days of 'stump-tail' currency.

***stumpy,** *a.* Abounding in stumps.

1673 *Southampton Rec.* II. 253 All the meadow and mowing land . . . standing on the west side of the stumpy marsh. **1875** MARK TWAIN *Old Times* iv. 71 We were shaving stumpy shores. **1897** *Outing* XXX. 328/2 We were passing a cabin surrounded by a few acres of stumpy pasture.

stunt stʌnt, *n.* [Origin unknown.] A feat or performance, esp. of an athletic nature, usu. done for effect. Also attrib. *Colloq.*

1895 *D.N.* I. 400 *Stunt*, . . . one of those convenient words which may be used in almost any connection . . . ; in general it is synonymous with 'thing' and may be used as variously. **1922** WILSON *Merton of Movies* 174 Ain't I a good stunt actress? **1949** *Sky Line Trail* Oct. 23 The Hambone Minstrels drew plenty of guffaws at Stunt Nite in camp.

b. stunt master, (see quot.).

1891 *Amer. Folk-Lore* IV. 228 Stunt Master, or Follow the Leader is a game in which the leader endeavors to stunt the others; that is, perform some feat in which they are unable to follow him.

***sturgeon,** *n.* **1. sturgeon extract,** (see quot.). **2. sturgeon pie,** a compost heap in which sturgeons are the chief ingredient. Both *obs.* — **(1) 1884** *Nat. Museum Bul.* No. 27, 1117 Sturgeon extract. . . . 'This is a novelty, and is what its name indicates, the extract of sturgeon meat, intended to be used for meat or fish sauces, soups, &c.' — **(2) 1841** *Farmers' Cabinet* (Phila.) V. 368 *Sturgeon Pie.* . . . Plough up a bank of earth, and place upon it half-a-dozen sturgeon [etc.].

stuss stʌs, *n.* [Colloq. G. and Yiddish (<Hebrew), joke, nonsense.] A gambling game resembling faro. Also attrib.

1909 WEBSTER. **1911** LEWIS *Apaches N.Y.* 51 What bridge whist is to Fifth Avenue, so is stuss to the East Side. **1929** *Texas Mo.* Feb. 220 Berg learned something new in the stuss games on Second Avenue. **1949** *L.A. Times* 22 May 2/1 The trombonist was a very popular boy named Abel Greenberg, a talented stuss player.

***style,** *n.* In combs.: (1) **stylebook,** a book explaining in detail the plan followed in a particular publishing house of dealing with various matters of publication, as punctuation, capitalization, division of words, etc.; (2) **manual,** =prec.; (3) **sheet,** a sheet of instructions for the guidance of compositors in a printing or publishing house.

(1) 1901 (*title*), Style Book: Adopted and in Use for University Publications. **1942** P. G. PERRIN *Writer's Guide* 741 Most newspapers, magazines, and publishing houses have stylebooks. — **(2) 1945** MENCKEN *Supp.* 536 Nevertheless, the Style Manual of the Department of State . . . grants it to a long list of functionaries. — **(3) 1931** *K.C. Star* 28 Sep., Gilbert wins a tilt with the style sheet.

b. (1) *To put on style*, to assume a proud or arrogant attitude, *colloq.*; (2) *to cramp one's style*, to interfere with one's efforts or pleasure, *slang*.

(1) **1864** *Rio Abajo Press* 5 July 1/3 [J. C. Frémont] was in command of the Department of Missouri, wherein he fizzled in generalship, and put on 'style' that was a scandal to American sentiment. **1877** in H. ASBURY *Underworld of Chi.* opp. 80 May Willard, why don't you take a tumble to yourself and not be trying to put on so much style. — (2) **1931** *New Republic* 8 April 202/2 Too sick to groan I received a few lashes, the squat ceiling and poor light considerably cramping the style of the boss.

As the last term in **Boston, buncombe, dog, fall, family, mission, open, plantation, sucker, Texas, Virginia, wheelbarrow style.**

***styling,** *n.* (See quot.) — **1928** *Publishers' Wkly.* 9 June 2370 Recourse to art for investing conventional merchandise with fresh or added appeal has been the chief reliance of post-war sales strategy. It has been termed 'Styling' in some quarters.

suability ˌsuəˈbɪlətɪ, *n.* Liability to be sued, esp. with reference to states.

1793 JAY *Correspondence* III. 454 The second object of inquiry now presents itself, viz., whether suability is compatible with State sovereignty. **1798** *Ann. 5th Congress* 483 An Act of the Legislature of the State of Kentucky, consenting to the ratification of the amendment of the Constitution of the United States . . . relative to the suability of States. **1838** *U.S. Mag.* I. 159 The first cycle of American nationality was rounded off before the Supreme Court pronounced any formidable judgment on constitutional law, save that which . . . asserted the suability of States.

***sub,** *n.* A substitute printer. *Colloq.* — **1876** *Scribner's Mo.* April 838/1 He consented finally to allow another printer to take his place in the 'Clarion' office—temporarily, and as his 'sub' only. **1896** *Internat. Typog. Union Proc.* 44/2 In the meantime the Call office is overrun with subs.

* **sub,** *v. intr.* To work as a substitute. Hence **subbing,** *n.*

1853 MARK TWAIN *Letters* I. 26 (R.), I am subbing at the 'Inquirer' office. *Ib.*, If I want it, I can get subbing every night of the week. **1879** *University Mag.* Nov. 589 At Cincinnati where he [Edison] . . . 'subbed' for the night men whenever he could obtain the privilege.

* **sub-,** *prefix.* In combs.: (1) **subagency,** a government Indian agency of subordinate rank; (2) **band,** a division of a band of Indians; (3) * **base,** (*a*) (see quot.), (*b*) a secondary base of supplies; (4) **caucus,** a subordinate caucus, *obs.;* (5) **deb,** a girl who is about to become a debutante, *colloq.;* (6) **genation,** the subjection of one race to another, *rare,* cf. **miscegenation;** (7) **irrigation,** a method of irrigating below the surface, cf. **subirrigate,** *v.;* (8) * **soiler,** a razorback hog, *obs.;* (9) * **treasurer,** (*a*) an assistant treasurer of the U.S. in charge of a subtreasury, (*b*) (see quot.), *obs.;* (10) **treasury,** see as a main entry; (11) **trousers,** drawers, *rare;* (12) **way,** (*a*) a tunnel for a metropolitan railway, a metropolitan railway operating underground, (*b*) also attrib.

(1) **1834** *Stat. at Large* IV. 736 The limits of each agency and subagency shall be established by the Secretary of War. **1900** *Rep. Geol. Survey 1898–9* IV. Pl. 44 Subagency of Southern Utes at Navajo Springs. **1950** *Nat. Hist.* Feb. 76/2 This agent, whose official title is Principal-teacher in charge of Havasupai Sub-agency, is teacher, counselor, and friend. — (2) **1810** PIKE *Sources Miss.* I. App. 60 A young man . . . has recently taken the lead in all the councils and affairs of state of this sub-band. **1866** *Rep. Indian Affairs* 210 This sub-band of the Brulés still maintain a distinct organization. — (3) (*a*) **1877** BARTLETT 676 *Sub-Base,* a mop or wash-board. Philadelphia. (*b*) **1903** *Science* 9 Oct. 478 After establishing a sub-base there [at Cape Sabine, Mr. Peary will] force his way northward. — (4) **1800** *Aurora* (Phila.) 8 Jan. (Th.), They would recommend that the [Congressional] library be divided into several small apartments, for the purposes of holding Sub-Caucusses. **1810** *Amer. Republic* (Frankfort, Ky.) 19 Oct. 4/3 It was calculated, both in the cabinet and subcaucuses, that the sum eventually to be paid, for 'the country East of the Mississippi,' would be *eight millions.*

(5) **1921** *Ladies' Home Jrnl.* Jan. 63 Any sub-deb or college girl. **1947** *Time* 6 Jan. 20/3 The season's debutantes danced their way into society while eager sub-debs looked on. — (6) **1864** J. H. VAN EVRIE (*title*), Subgenation: the Theory of the Normal Relation of the Races; an Answer to 'Miscegenation.' — (7) **1880** *Cimarron News & Press* 19 Aug. 1/6 But sub irrigation for wheat would be too expensive. — (8) **1858** C. FLINT *Milch Cows* 362 The class of hogs usually denominated 'subsoilers,' with their long and pointed snouts, and their thin flabby sides. **1899** CUSHMAN *Hist. Indians* 239 [The wild boar's] progeny were styled the 'racers, razor backs, subsoilers, jumpers, and rail splitters,' by the early white settlers. — (9) (*a*) **1837** *Cong. Deb.* 30 Sep. 1164/2, I should not feel authorized to appoint any number of 'new officers,' whether called sub-treasurers, or otherwise. **1870** W. W. FOWLER *Ten Yrs. in Wall St.* 154 At the sub-treasury, they were paid out by Mr. John T. Cisco, the Sub-treasurer. (*b*) **1838** *N.Y. Advt. & Exp.* 20 Jan. 1/3 The Sub-Treasurers in St. Louis,—*this* is now the fashionable name for our Office-holders, — met in St. Louis, . . . to hold a Loco Foco meeting.

(11) **1890** *Columbus* (O.) *Dispatch* 11 July, Four inches of white canvass subtrousers was exposed. — (12) (*a*) **1893** *Mass. Acts & Resolves* 1421 The said board is hereby authorized to lay out and construct a subway for street railway purposes. **1949** *Sat. Ev. Post* 9 April 101/1 There was a west-side subway that crossed town on Fifty-third. (*b*) **1893** *Mass. Acts & Resolves* 1420 The mayor of the city of Boston shall appoint . . . three commissioners . . . to be known as the board of subway commissioners. **1948** *Woman's Day* March 102/3 We're playing subway rush, . . . and I'm the subway guard.

b. Denoting persons of subordinate rank or office, as (1) **sub-agent,** (2) **boss,** (3) **chief,** (4) **clothier,** (5) **Indian agent,** (6) **sachem,** (7) * **treasurer,** see (9) above.

(1) **1818** *Stat. at Large* III. 428 All sub-agents [shall] receive five hundred dollars per annum. **1869** *Overland Mo.* III. 171 Hostilities had commenced with the murder of sub-agent Bolon. **1950** *Nat. Hist.* Feb. 92/2 Besides the white man's law as embodied in the subagent, the Havasupai have their own representation in the form of a local council. — (2) **1881** ROMSPERT *Western Echo* 189 Cow-boys are ranked in the business something like officers in the army. There are foremen, bosses, and sub-bosses, . . . and they are paid according to their experience and ability. — (3) **1844** *Cincinnati Misc.* 137 There were also some sub or half Chiefs. *a***1918** G. STUART *On Frontier* I. 182 It will probably be the cause of civil war among the Blackfeet for those killed were all sub-chiefs. — (4) **1780** *N.H. Hist. Soc. Coll.* IX. 238 The Sub Clother of the Troops in gerrison . . . will Make Returns to Head Quarters. **1781** *Va. State P.* I. 481 The sub-clothier, as he is styled by Congress, . . . is the proper officer thro' whose hands all issues of clothing should pass.

(5) **1846** *Californian* (Monterey) 19 Sep. 4/1, I received a letter of the U.S. Sub-Indian Agent, Dr. E. White, . . . concerning the wallawalla affair. **1937** SCANLAN *Prairie du Chien* 135 They complained of [a] . . . sub-Indian agent who defended men violating liquor laws at Prairie du Chien. — (6) **1838** *Mass. H.S. Coll.* 3 Ser. IX. 91 John Neptune is the lieutenant-governor or sub-sachem.

c. *Educ.* In nouns and adjectives designating a lower or inferior educational status or one occupying such a status, as (1) **subfresh,** (2) **freshman,** (3) **graduate,** (4) **preparatory,** (5) **primary.**

(1) **1850** THAXTER *Poem before Iadma* 14 To assist a poor Sub Fresh at the dread Examination. **1893** *Congregationalist* 21 Sep., Enrollment as freshmen or 'sub-fresh' in the City College. — (2) **1871** BAGG *At Yale* 51 The sub-Freshman is pledged to his society months before he approaches the college walls. **1909** BREWSTER *Life J. D. Whitney* 72 When Josiah went away, he was not even a sub-freshman. — (3) **1864** in *Proc. Inauguration of F. A. P. Barnard* (1865) 7 The hour has come when I am to take my final leave, as President of the College, . . . of you, my young friends, graduates and sub-graduates of the College. — (4) **1898** *Advance* (Chi.) 17 Feb. 206/2 The institution has never had a sub-preparatory department, as several of the young colleges have.

(5) **1895** *Proc. 14th Conv. Instr. Deaf* 293 In subprimary work there is surely an interesting field for the constructive talent.

subirrigate sʌbˈɪrəˌget, *v. tr.* To irrigate (land) by underground irrigation. Cf. **subirrigation** *s.v.* ***sub-,** *prefix.* — **1903** *Scientific Amer. Supp.* 17 Jan. 22616 (*Cent. Supp.*), Where the subsoil transmits water freely, irrigation ditches may subirrigate large tracts of country without rendering them marshy.

* **Submissionist,** *n.* Before the Civil War, one in the South who favored submission to the demands of northerners in the controversies over nullification and secession, or one in the North who favored submission to the demands of the South. *Obs.*

1834 *Savannah Georgian* 8 July 2/6 (Th. Supp.), The Nullifiers call us Submissionists. **1861** *Charleston* (S.C.) *Mercury* 14 Feb. 3/2 Even the worse submissionists agree with them on this point. **1913** A. C. COLE *Whig Party in So.* 189 The disunion men [*c*1851] . . . tried to discredit the Union movement in the eyes of Democrats by applying to it such epithets as 'Federalists,' 'Feds,' 'Submissionists,' . . . 'Dirteaters.' **1949** WILTSE *John C. Calhoun* 87 These were the State Rights and Union party, called by their opponents 'Submissionists'; and the State Rights and Free Trade party, or 'Nullifiers.'

***submit,** *v. Law. tr.* ?To appeal (a case). *Rare.* — **1818** *Niles' Reg.* XIV. 48/2 [He was] fined only $20, and discharged. He submitted the case.

* **subscriber,** *n.*

1. The undersigned. Also as a substitute for the personal pronoun, *I* or *me.*

1744 *S.C. Gazette* 9 Jan. 4/1 Run away some Time since from the Subscriber . . . an Indian Wench. **1767** in COMMONS *Doc. Hist.* I. 245

The one on which the subscriber lives has . . . a large apple orchard. **1870** MARK TWAIN *Screamers* 42 'Let us have Abraham for one of his names.' . . . 'Abraham suits the subscriber.'

2. In the New York Stock Exchange, a non-member broker allowed certain privileges on payment of a subscription fee. *Obs.*

1885 *Harper's Mag.* Nov. 842/2 A 'gutter snipe,' or 'curb-stone broker,' . . . does business mainly upon the sidewalk, and is supremely happy in the light and warmth of the Subscribers' Room or corridor when he can raise shekels sufficient to pay for them.

***subscription,** *n.*

1. Direct sale, by house-to-house methods, of books.

1866 *Ore. State Jrnl.* 23 June 3/4 The Photograph Family Record . . . Sold Only by Subscription. **1897** G. H. P. & J. B. PUTNAM *Auth. & Pub.* (ed. 7) 51 Books sold by subscription (that is, through canvassers).

2. ***subscription book,** a book sold by this method.

1868 *Ore. State Jrnl.* 13 June 3/2 Agents Wanted at once to canvass for the most popular Subscription Books of the season. **1886** *Harper's Mag.* Dec. 162/1 The sale of a successful subscription book is something unrivalled by that of any book in the trade. **1910** BOSTWICK *Amer. Pub. Library* 143 Librarians are regarded by the agents for subscription books as fair game.

3. *To take up* (or *make*) *a subscription,* to collect a fund from a number of persons.

1866 H. PHILLIPS *Hist. Sk. Paper Currency* II. 168 To relieve the army a subscription was taken up by the ladies of Philadelphia. **1897** *Daily News* (London) 22 April 6/3 [Amer. sailor:] Let's make a subscription.

subscriptioneer səbˌskrɪpʃən'ɪr, *v. intr.* To sell a book or books by subscription methods or direct personal canvass. Also **subscriptioneering,** *n.* and *a. Obs.* — **1796** WEEMS *Letters* II. 29 It is a choice work for a subscriptioneering parson. *Ib.* 46 Subscriptioneer there and in its neighborhood. **1805** *Ib.* 210 In 18 hours subscriptioneering I obtained from the Legislature 100 subs. to Sydney.

subscriptionist səb'skrɪpʃənɪst, *n.* A solicitor of subscriptions. *Rare.* — **1853** HAWTHORNE *Eng. Note-Books* I. 51, I wish . . . I had given the poor family ten shillings, and denied it to a begging subscriptionist, who has just fleeced me to that amount.

***subsistence,** *n.* **1. Subsistence Department,** in the U.S. Army, a staff department having charge of the procurement and issue of provisions. *Obs.* **2. subsistence stores,** (see quot. 1891).

(1) 1846 MCKENNEY *Memoirs* I. 222 The duty of providing the rations for the emigrating Indians was referred to the Subsistence Department. **1861** *Army Reg.* 248 Ovens may be built or paid for by the Subsistence Department. — **(2) 1861** in KETTELL *Hist. Rebellion* I. 171 The subsistence stores . . . must last to include the 23rd inst. **1891** *Cent.* 6030/1 *Subsistence stores* . . . , the food-supplies procured and issued for the support of an army. The phrase also covers the grain, hay, straw, or other forage supplied for the sustenance and bedding of animals intended for slaughter. **1918** FARROW *Dict. Mil. Terms* 594.

substanche səb'stæntʃ, *v. tr.* To substantiate. *Slang. Rare.* — **1838** *Lexington Observer* 7 July, He said he was only fending off the blows of her darned old rollin pin, that she could substanche.

substaquilate səb'stækwəˌlet, *v. tr.* To discomfit, overwhelm. *Humorous. Obs.*

1840 *Bentley's Misc.* VII. 624 Then I lay down on the ground right away, and taking a perspective horizontal view of the whole regiment sideways, I wish I may be tee-totally substaquilated if I didn't carry off the entire whole of the seven-and-forty heads. **1842** *Ainsworth's Mag.* II. 151 You estimate I'm flummuxed; but I swear I'll substaquilate you *some* when the day is hot enough for it. *Ib.* 556 If you will all foller my steps to the polling windows, we'll substaquilate the loafing locofocoes in two twos.

substitute broker. One who makes a business of procuring substitutes for military service. Also **substitute brokerage.** *Obs.*

1863 *Cong. Globe* 4 Feb. 714/3 As soon as it seemed to be understood that the government was determined to force men into the army . . . , these substitute brokers made their appearance. **1865** LOWELL in *N. Amer. Rev.* C. 541 We have had shoddy, . . . we have had substitute-brokerage, we have had speculators in patriotism. **1865** *Cong. Globe* 6 Feb. 612/2 A substitute broker, . . . the vilest of mankind, . . . is entitled to a fair trial. *Ib.* 614/3 These substitute brokers in the city of New York have a broker's board and have regular meetings.

substruct sʌb'strʌkt, *v. tr.* To build underneath, as a foundation. *Obs.* — **1850** EMERSON *Representative Men* 57 Metaphysics and natural philosophy expressed the genius of Europe; he [Plato] substructs the religion of Asia, as the base. *Ib.* 131 This seer of the souls [Swedenborg] substructs a new hell and pit, each more abominable than the last, round every new crew of offenders.

subterranean railroad, railway. =**underground railroad.** *Obs.* — **1846** *Cong. Globe* 18 March 523/1 Amend the amendment by adding $50,000 for the perfection of the Bebb and Schenck subterranean railroad, on which to carry their odoriferous friends from Kentucky to Canada. *Ib.* 523/3, I am told that it [the amendment] proposes a subterranean railway for carrying the blacks from Kentucky to Canada.

subtreasury sʌb'trɛʒərɪ, *n.* (Often *cap.*) A subordinate treasury, esp. a branch of the U.S. Treasury or the building housing this. Now *hist.*

Established by acts of 1840 (repealed 1841) and 1846; abolished by an act of 1920.

1837 *Cong. Deb.* 30 Sep. 1164/2 The Secretary . . . [is] required to furnish this House with a statement of the number of sub-treasuries which will be required if the bill . . . should become a law. **1882** MCCABE *New York* 332 The Sub-Treasury [is] a noble edifice of white marble. **1920** *Stat. at Large* XLI. I. 654 The Secretary of the Treasury is authorized and directed to discontinue . . . such subtreasuries.

attrib. **1838** *Diplom. Corr. Texas* I. (1908) 312 The Sub-Treasury Bill is still under consideration in the Senate. **1838** *Lexington Observer* 23 May, The Whigs have elected 71 members, the Sub Treasury Vanites 42. **1856** MACLEOD *F. Wood* 63 President Van Buren's Sub-Treasury system had succeeded to the United States Bank. **1889** *Cent. Mag.* April 810/2 [The] buildings . . . gave way to the old Custom-house and to the United States Sub-Treasury building of to-day.

succahanah ˌsʌkə'hænə, *n.* [App. a native word.] (See quot. 1687.) *Obs.* — **1687** CLAYTON *Va.* in *Phil. Trans.* XLI. 160 [The Indians] drink, I think, little besides Succahanah, that is, fair Water, unless when they can get Spirits . . . from the English. **1708** E. COOK *Sot-Weed Factor* 21, [I] soon got up, To cool my Liver with a Cup Of *Succahana* fresh and clear.

succession sale. "A sale of property to enable the heirs to divide the same" (B. '59). *Obs.* — **1858** *La. Democrat* 20 July (B.), At the succession sale of the slaves belonging to the minor heirs of S. A. and A. X. Baillie . . . long sums were bid.

succotash 'sʌkəˌtæʃ, *n.* [Narraganset *misickquatash* "an ear of corn." Cf. Williams *Key* (1866) 40: "*Manusqussedash,* beanes."] A dish consisting principally of corn and beans boiled together with or without meat. Cf. **winter succotash.**

1751 MACSPARRAN *Diary* 47 Mo[the]r dined with us upon Suckatash and Ham. **1823** THACHER *Military Jrnl.* 213 The landlady brought on the table a dish of succatash, boiled corn and beans. **1892** DUVAL *Young Explorers* 163 The choice pieces of the buffalo had been roasted, and a large camp kettle, filled with 'succotash' (a medley of stewed meat, beans, hominy and peppers). **1949** *Nat. Geog. Mag.* Aug. 159/2 The Indians invented succotash.

b. (See quot. 1859.)

1859 *Ill. Agric. Soc. Trans.* III. 503 The white succotash (a large, round bean,) is most excellent, green or dry. **1938** DAMON *Grandma* 159, I made a good big mess of the first succotash this morning.

c. *Plymouth, Mass.* (See quots.)

*c***1870** *Old Plymouth Receipts,* The soup and the vegetables are then mixed with the water the fowl and beef were boiled in and salt and pepper added. Four quarts of hulled corn having been boiled soft and tender are added to the succotash. **1915** *Pub. Col. Soc. Mass.* XVII. 299 Succotash as made at Plymouth is a soup.

succoteague ˌsʌkə'tig, *n.* (See quot.) — **1884** GOODE *Fisheries* I. 362 The name 'Squeteague' is of Indian origin, and 'Squit,' 'Succoteague,' 'Squitee,' and 'Chickwit' are doubtless variations of this name in different ancient and modern dialects.

***suck,** *n.* and *v.*

1. A salt lick so wet that the animals frequenting it secure salt by sucking rather than licking. Also **suck lick, suck spring.** *Obs.*

1792 in *Amer. Sp.* XV. 398/2 Crossing a drain by the Suck Lick. **1816** *Ib.,* To a Beach and gum by the road side near the suckspring. **1832** C. S. RAFINESQUE *Atlantic Jrnl.* 74 They were called licks by the first settlers, because they noticed that buffaloes, elks and deer went to lick the saline ground, and sucks when they went to suck or drink the saline springs or pools. *Ib.* 76 Licks become Sucks sometimes in the Winter and Spring, in rainy weather: and many Sucks become Licks in the dry season.

2. ***suckfish,** a sucker or suckerfish (see quot. 1896).

1840 SIMMS *Border Beagles* II. 184 There's not a suckfish in Big Black that wouldn't laugh at this for gill-tackle. **1896** JORDAN & EVERMANN *Check-List Fishes* 491 *Caularchus mœandricus.* . . . Suckfish. Pacific Coast . . . , from Vancouver Island to Monterey.

3. a. (See quot.) **b.** A whirling movement of air. Both *obs.*

(a) 1867 *Atlantic Mo.* April 804/2 Three great 'sucks,' as we call them here,—the Ohio, the Missouri, and the Mississippi,—drained out of the land. — (b) 1877 W. WRIGHT *Big Bonanza* 253 Fierce whirls and 'sucks' are formed in the lee of the mountain.

As the last term in **bee, sapsuck.**

***sucker,** *n.*

1. Any one of various fresh-water fishes, as the buffalo fish, black horse, red horse, etc., having lips which suggest that they feed by suction.

1769 in HALSEY *Four Great Rivers* (1906) 45 The other Fish common in the Lake & other Waters . . . are Pickerel . . . Pike . . . Eels, Suckers [etc.]. **1806** CLARK in *Lewis & C. Exped.* V. (1905) 22 With those nets they take the Suckers. **1904** *Springfield W. Republican* 9 Sep. 10 As a boy he used to lie on the rocks, snare suckers, and swim in the pot holes. **1948** *Nat. Hist.* Dec. 454/1 Later in the spring, when the suckers were running up Mink Brook to spawn, old mother owl turned her attention to fishing.

attrib. **1856** COZZENS *Sparrowgrass P.* 63, I could hear . . . the reverberations of the big oathes . . . that had been the running accompaniment to the sucker-fishing on the Nepperhan!

b. In full **sucker fish.**

1841 STEELE *Summer Journey* 222 The people of Illinois obtained their nickname of suckers from the practice of going up the Mississippi when the spring opened for lead, which was the period of the annual voyage up the river of the Succar fish. **1893** *Chi. Tribune* 26 April 6/4 Their principal catch in those days were the buffalo, a species of sucker fish similar to that caught on a sandbar the other day. **1946** *This Week Mag.* 17 Aug. 16/2 Then he leads a worthless, bony, dumb suckerfish up to my hook, seemin' to think me an' the sucker ought to meet each other.

For **sucker-mouth buffalo,** see ***buffalo,** *n.* **2.**

c. With specifying terms.

1814 MITCHILL *Fishes N.Y.* 458 Fresh-water Sucker, *Cyprinus teres*, . . . is extensively employed in the interior districts for food. **1820** RAFINESQUE in *Western Rev.* II. 302 Black-back Sucker. *Catostomus melanotus*. . . . Vulgar names Black sucker and Blue sucker. **1842** *Nat. Hist. N.Y., Zoology* IV. 202 The Large-scaled Sucker, *Catostomus macrolepidotus*, . . . appears to be a common species. **1884** GOODE *Fisheries* I. 614 Numerous other species . . . , belonging to the genera of *Moxostoma, Minytrema*, and *Placopharynx*, are found in the waters of the West and South, all going by the general names of Red Horse, White Sucker, and Mullet.

2. A simpleton, fool, one easily hoodwinked.

1831 *Boston Transcript* 17 Dec. 2/2 It looks very much like a swindling concern, got up to catch suckers. **1898** *Cong. Rec.* 20 Jan. 804/1 The gentlemen who form the platform[s] are always adroit enough to frame them so as to catch the 'suckers' on Election day. **1950** *Time* 27 March 19/3 We are always ready to discuss, to negotiate, to agree, but we are understandably loath to play the role of international sucker.

Hence **sucker list.**

1946 *Collier's* 30 March 32/4 The pickings from phony promotions are so slim, however, that post-office sleuths are getting fewer sucker-list cases all the time. **1948** *Dly. Ardmoreite* (Ardmore, Okla.) 21 April 6/1 The Wallace-for-president movement has given communists a new sucker list to work on.

Also **sucker,** *v. tr.*, to treat (one) as a fool or simpleton. Also to *play (one) for a sucker. Slang.*

1945 SERVICE *Ploughman* 235 Anyway, he's played you for a sucker. **1948** *Chi. Tribune* 27 March I. 1/4 Apparently we are again going to be suckered into approval of a glorified world WPA. **1950** *Ib.* 17 April III. 14 When he gets back to his *pee-pul*, without having suckered me out of any more money—they'll wind *him* up.

3. (Usu. *cap.*) A nickname for an Illinoisan. Cf. **6.** below.

No generally accepted explanation of the reason for this nickname has so far been found. Cf. quot. 1841 under **1. b.** above and see quot. 1886 under **b.** below. Perhaps the best, and certainly the simplest, explanation is that many of the first settlers of Illinois were the dupes of land speculators, i.e., were *suckers* in sense **2.** above.

1834 *Sun* (N.Y.) 23 Aug. 3/2 The Illinois Pioneer gives the following list of nick names adopted to distinguish the citizens of the Western states: In Kentucky they are called Corn Crackers . . . Illinois Suckers. **1835** HOFFMAN *Winter in West* I. 176 There was a long-haired 'hooshier' from Indiana, a couple of smart-looking 'suckers' from the southern part of Illinois. **1901** CHURCHILL *Crisis* 152 The Tall Sucker was on the steps to receive them. **1949** *Chi. D. News* 12 May 14/2 We suckers didn't get back one thin dime.

b. Also **Sucker State,** Illinois. Cf. **6.** below.

1844 *St. Louis Reveille* 7 Dec. 2/3 In stalked a hero from the Sucker State. **1886** *Chi. W. News* 29 April 4/3 Illinois is the Sucker state (sometimes Prairie state), and its people are Suckers; it is supposed the name was derived from the habit of emigrants drawing water from the holes made by crawfish. **1950** *Chi. Tribune* 21 April 22/3 Illinois bears a nickname that irks the pride of its citizens: the Sucker state.

c. A corrupt political worker. *Slang. Obs.*

c1855 in *Sons of Sires* 90 Under this system of Primary Elections, there have grown up a large class of men known in the slang of the city as 'suckers' and 'strikers.' *Ib.* 91 The man who does not wish to be known as taking money in person, puts into these nominating committees these 'strikers' and 'suckers,' and they notoriously sell their votes.

4. An animal or, formerly, a slave woman, that gives suck. *Obs.*

1854 DAVIS *Farm Bk.* 119 Countied 60 head of Sheep 75 of Stock hogs of which 24 are Suckers 59 kiling hogs. We have 28 head of cattle 9 milkers & 10 Suckers. **1863** RUSSELL *Diary* I. 380 'Suckers,' as they are called, are permitted to go home, at appointed periods in the day, to give the infants the breast.

5. (See quot.)

1931 *Daily Express* (London) 2 Sep. 1/5 Before the first pair teed up the United States Golf Association committee passed a special rule permitting 'suckers'—that is, balls embedded in the mud—to be lifted and cleaned without penalty.

6. In combs., usu. occasional and obs., alluding to Illinois as the Sucker State, as **Sucker boot, captain, farmer, mechanic, style, woman.**

1838 FLAGG *Far West* II. 70 If the sucker-farmers don't look to it, the prairie-wolves will get the better of all the geese, turkeys, and *hins* in the barnyard. **1842** *Knickerb.* XX. 298 You should have seen the 'Sucker' women marching to the drum, in martial order. **1848** *Scientific Amer.* 7 Oct. 21/2 Eastern mechanics . . . look down with contempt upon us Hoosier and Sucker mechanics. **1851** GREEN *Twelve Days* 163 The sucker captain soon made his way to the clerk's office. **1857** *Ill. Agric. Soc. Trans.* III. 438 Those farms immediately on the river, with a soil of sandy loam that has been cropped in the usual Sucker style, viz.: Corn and wheat . . . for twenty years, without fallowing, show that they need rest and manure. **1872** *Chi. Tribune* 9 Oct. 4/6 Another invoice of those Celebrated Hand-Made Sucker Boots.

b. Esp. (1) **Suckerland,** Illinois; (2) **Sucker team** app. a team (see quot. 1877) driven by a Sucker from Illinois. *Obs.*

(1) **1839** *Dly. Chi. American* 4 May 2/2 The 'yankee gal' . . . shows a good taste in coming to this *sucker* land. **1860** *Harper's Mag.* March 567/1 The County of Jasper lies on the line between 'Hoosierdom' and the 'Suckerland.' — (2) **1866** *Harper's Mag.* May 682/2 When the streets of Galena, the mining metropolis, were crowded with sucker-teams. **1877** in *Amer. Sp.* XXII. 300 The commerce of the country at this early day [*c*1842] was mostly carried on by Sucker team, a large Pennsylvania wagon with from four to six yoke of oxen to haul it.

As the last term in **black, bog, chub, cow, fine-scaled, gone, gourd seed, hammerhead, hare-lip, hog, honey, horse, May, Missouri, mud, mullet, pale, razor-backed, rum, sailing, sand, stump, swamp, sweet sucker.**

Suckerdom ˈsʌkərdəm, *n.* Illinois. *Obs.*

1846 *Dollar Newspaper* (Phila.) 11 Feb. 4/5 A youth from Sucker*dom* arrived in town and engaged himself at a printing establishment to learn the art and mysteries of printing. **1862** *N.Y. Tribune* 22 March 5/2 One distiller . . . would pay into the Treasury $1,200 a day, or $375,600 a year, if Suckerdom continued thirsty. **1863** *Harper's Mag.* Oct. 713/2 Of some of the localities in Suckerdom . . . the schoolmaster has been shamefully negligent.

***suckerel,** *n.* (See quots.) — **1883** *Nat. Museum Bul.* No. 27, 477 *Cycleptus elongatus*. . . . Missouri Sucker; Suckerel. . . . One of the most interesting of all the suckers. **1884** GOODE *Fisheries* I. 615 The 'Black Horse,' 'Gourd-seed Sucker,' 'Missouri Sucker,' or 'Suckerel' is found chiefly in the river channels of the Ohio and Mississippi.

Suckerism ˈsʌkəˌrɪzəm, *n. collect.* Illinoisans. *Rare.* — **1846** FARNHAM *Prairie Land* 97 We entered on the flood tide of Suckerism that was setting into the narrow, winding door.

***Suckley,** *n.* [Dr. George *Suckley* (1830–69), Amer. surgeon and naturalist.] Used in possessive in names (see quots.). — **1858** BAIRD *Birds Pacific R.R.* 848 *Laurus Suckleyi*. . . . Suckley's Gull. . . . Pacific coast; Puget's Sound. **1869** *Amer. Naturalist* III. 126 Suckley's Salmontrout (*S[almo] Suckleyi*). . . . The first of this splendid salmontrout we met with were at the mouth of St. Regis Borgia creek, which flows down the east slope of the Cœur d'Aleñe Range.

suckwick ˈsʌkwɪk, *n.* [Origin unknown.] = **wicopy 1.** *Obs.* — **1778** CARVER *Travels* 499 The Wickopick or Suckwick appears to be a species of the white wood.

suction engine. A fire engine with a suction pump. *Obs.*

1830 *Mass. Laws* XI. 400 The number of enginemen shall . . . exceed fifty to every hydraulion or suction engine [etc.]. **1851** CIST *Cincinnati* 168 Each of these companies is provided with Fire and Suction Engines and Hose Reel. **1893** HALE *N. Eng. Boyhood* 135 Every engine, therefore, which was good for anything was a 'suction engine,' as it was called; that is, it was able to pump from a well, as well as able to throw water to an indefinite height.

sudadero sudəˈdero, *n. S.W.* [Sp. "sweatcloth."] (See quots.)

"Suadera" (quot. 1876) is from the Amer. Sp. variant *suadero.*

1876 Bourke *Journal* 27 Feb., Then the 'suadera,' or sweat cloth is placed upon the withers. **1944** Adams *W. Words* 158 sudadero. . . . The cowman uses it to mean the leather lining of the skirt of the saddle. This term is sometimes incorrectly applied to the *rosadero.*

Sudan grass. A grass, *Sorghum vulgare sudanense,* sown for hay, esp. in semiarid regions.

1929 Deam *Grasses of Indiana* 325 Sudan grass has only recently been introduced into Indiana and its use as a hay crop is on the increase. **1931** Vansell *Nectar & Pollen Plants Calif.* 23 An observer at Woodland reported sudan grass as an important source of pollen. **1949** *Hoard's Dairyman* 25 Oct. 756/3 Frost-nipped cane, sudan, pig weeds, Johnson grass, and flax are poisonous to cattle and can cause death.

***sudden death.** Cheap whisky. *Slang. Obs.* — **1865** Mark Twain *Sketches* (1926) 163 Our reserve . . . we had . . . kept out of sight and full of chain-lightning, sudden death and scorpion-bile all day. **1877** Burdette *Rise & Fall of Mustache* 160 'The Same,' 'Fast Freight,' 'Bran'an Wa'r,' 'Sherri'neg,' 'Sudden Death,' 'Crusade Drops,' . . . and several other spirits.

sudsing ˈsʌdzɪŋ, *n.* Washing in suds, soaping. Also attrib.

1843 Stephens *High Life N.Y.* II. 20, I'd gin myself a good sudsing in the wash hand basin. **1879** *Scribner's Mo.* Oct. 940/2 As soon as they begin to boil, remove them to the 'sudsing'-water. **1881** McLean *Cape Cod Folks* 167 A good poundin', and boilin', and sudzin', you need.

sudsy ˈsʌdzɪ, *a.* Full of suds, produced by suds. Also transf.

1866 *Harper's Mag.* Sep. 544/2 He's gone! across the sudzy sea. **1884** *Ib.* Sep. 528/2 We then bade adieu to . . . our string of washers still laving their linen in the sudsy stream. **1901** *Munsey's Mag.* XXV. 394/2 There was a pleasant, sudsy cleanliness about the two little rooms. **1948** *Chi. D. News* 2 March 9 (*advt.*), That's the new extra-sudsy 1948 Super Suds! Colgate-Palmolive-Peet has made this new 1948 Super Suds the sudsiest and best of all time.

Suffolk Resolves. *Hist.* Resolves adopted by representatives from towns in Suffolk County, Mass., in September, 1774, denouncing the action of Great Britain and urging actions which led to Independence. Also **Suffolk Resolutions.** — **1784** in *Life & Lett. Charles Inglis* (1936) 146 The American Congress, by adopting certain Resolves sent from Boston . . . and known by the Name of the 'Suffolk Resolves' convinced him that the Congress really aimed at Revolution & Independence. **1933** J. H. Preston *Revolution 1776* 28 In his saddlebags that morning Revere carried letters from Boston, and some high political explosive known as the Suffolk Resolutions.

***suffrage,** *n.*

1. The right of voting as a citizen of a nation or state.

1787 *Constitution* v, No State, without its Consent, shall be deprived of its equal Suffrage in the Senate. **1837** Martineau *Society* III. 164 Foreigners of all ages may scoff at the self-confidence and complacency of young men who have just exercised the suffrage for the first time. **1884** Lowell *On Democracy* 4, I recollect hearing . . . that the doing away with the property qualification for suffrage twenty years before had been the ruin of the State of Massachusetts. **1940** J. T. Adams *Dict. Amer. Hist.* V. 199/1 The educational test for voting has been the most obvious means of exclusion in an age of generally extended suffrage.

2. Attrib. in the sense: Of or pertaining to female suffrage.

1842 *So. Quart. Rev.* II. 244 The whole proceedings of the Suffrage Party . . . were improper. **1886** *Harper's Mag.* Dec. 68/1 They had walked all the way to get me to sign the suffrage petition. **1911** *N.Y. Ev. Post* 14 Sep. (Th.), Whether or not the new woman Mayor would 'make good' was . . . of considerable importance to the future of the suffrage movement. **1931** F. L. Allen *Only Yesterday* 4 There is other news, too: . . . the prospects for the passage of the Suffrage Amendment, which it is predicted will enable women to take 'a finer place in the national life.' **1947** Myers *The 'Guv'* 231 'In just a few days,' said he, 'another state will ratify the Suffrage Amendment.'

As the last term in **anti-, colored, female, Negro suffrage.**

sugan ˈsugən, *n.* Also **soogan, suggan.** *W.* [See note.]

From the available evidence this term (of Irish origin) appears to have been borrowed afresh in this country. Cf. *OED s.v. suggan.*

A coarse blanket or comfort, often one made of patchwork and weighing about four pounds.

1907 White *Arizona Nights* 72 Sitting cross-legged on his 'so-gun' in the middle of the floor, he told us the following yarn. **1939** Rollins *Gone Haywire* 62 The blankets might be of ordinary commercial manufacture, or they might be soogans, otherwise known as suggans—homemade coverlets created from numerous fragments of discarded garments. **1949** *Sat. Ev. Post* 9 April 136/3 After we'd crawled into our soogans that night I told Blackie what had passed between me and the granger over on the Cimarrón.

***sugar,** *n.*

1. Short for **sugar maple,** esp. attrib. See also **2. c.** and **d.** below.

1816 U. Brown *Journal* II. 233 A sugar stump in the Corn which we Imagine nearly south. **1837** W. Jenkins *Ohio Gaz.* 285 The land lies rolling, and is covered with beech and sugar timber. **1839** Plumbe *Sk. Iowa* 62 The prairies are generally . . . surrounded with groves of . . . sugar, lynn, walnut, &c. **1843** Carlton *New Purchase* II. 303 Scamper away, you little grey gaffer, and peep from the dense foliage of that lofty sugar-top!

2. In special combs.: (1) **sugar barberry,** ?jelly made from barberries; (2) **belt,** a sugar-producing region; (3) ***bird,** (see quots.); (4) **boat,** a boat used in the Louisiana sugar industry; (5) **bowl,** see as a main entry; (6) **central,** see ***central 2;** (7) **coast,** the region along the Mississippi in Louisiana where sugar from sugar cane is made on a large scale, cf. **sugar bowl 3;** (8) **cured,** *a.* of ham or pork, prepared for use by a process in which sugar is used; (9) **farm,** a farm or estate upon which sugar is produced from sugar cane; (10) **ham,** a sugar-cured ham; (11) ***house,** (see quot. 1803), cf. **c.** (6) below; (12) **interest,** the sugar-planters, regarded as an economic and political group, also **sugar-growing interest;** (13) **king,** one holding a dominant position in the sugar industry; (14) **kiss,** (*a*) ?a piece of sugar candy, (*b*) **sugar-kiss ticket,** (see quot.), *obs.;* (15) **land,** land noted for the number of sugar maples on it, or used for growing sugar cane; (16) **mule,** (see quot.); (17) **nabob,** =**sugar king;** (18) **rag,** a cloth having sugar wrapped in it used as a pacifier for a baby, a sugar-tit, *colloq.;* (19) **rolling,** the grinding of sugar cane in making sirup or sugar; (20) **sand,** a sandstone of a sugary or grainy texture, cf. **c.** (10) below; (21) **state,** a state in which a large amount of sugar is made; (22) **trust,** a combination of financiers or companies exercising quasi-monopolistic control over the manufacture and selling of sugar.

(1) **1895** A. Brown *Meadow-Grass* 100 Mrs. Pettis . . . had been holding a long conversation with young Mrs. Lamson on the possibility of doing over sugar-barberry. — (2) **1944** Clark *Pills* 25 In the Louisiana sugar belt, barge store boats eased along the back ways of sugar plantations receiving stolen goods. — (3) **1891** *Cent.* 6046/2 *Sugar-bird,* . . . a translation of the Indian name of the American evening grosbeak . . . , which is specially fond of maple sugar. (Local, U.S.) **1949** Hadley *Indiana Birds* 43/1 The tufted titmouse . . . is sometimes called Tom tit also sugar bird and Peter bird. — (4) **1887** *Cent. Mag.* No. 108/1 Sugar-boats . . . carry supplies to the plantations on rivers and bayous. **1945** Botkin *My Burden* 60 They's a old sugar boat in the bayou.

(7) **1839** in Stowe *Key* 41/1 The sugar planters upon the sugar coast in Louisiana had ascertained that [etc.]. — (8) **1844** *N.O. Picayune* 35/3 We have recently tasted something a shade superior in the way of hams. . . . They were of that class got up by E. Davis & Brother of Cincinnati, known as the sugar cured. **1948** Menjou & Musselman *It Took 9 Tailors* 64 The sugar-cured ham melted in our mouths and the beer was only a nickel. — (9) **1818** Darby *Emigrant's Guide* 10 On all those places, except the Vermilion, sugar farms and houses are at this time established to advantage. **1888** Cable *Bonaventure* 201 [She] mentioned the small sugar-farm and orangery of the kinsman Robichaux.

(10) **1838** *N.Y. Advt. & Exp.* 7 Feb. 3/3 The 'Sugar Hams' prepared by E. S. Miller . . . have been considered equal to any. — (11) **1784** *S.C. Gazette* 6 Jan. 1/2 Delivers her [a slave] to the Warden of the Sugar-House, in Charleston. **1803** J. Davis *Travels* 90 The ladies of Carolina, and particularly those of Charleston . . . send both their men-slaves and women-slaves, for the most venial trespass, to a hellish-mansion, called the Sugar-house: here a man employs inferior agents to scourge the poor negroes. **1947** *Sat. Review* 11 Oct. 21/3 Before long he is captured and made to feel the rigors of prison life in the Sugar House under the infamous jailer Cunningham. — (12) **1836** *Diplom. Corr. Texas* I. (1908) 170 This government . . . will not consent to see an independent slave holding community . . . presenting a formidable rivalry to the cotton and sugar growing interests of Louisiana and Mississippi and the whole south. **1881** *Ore. State Jrnl.* 8

Jan. 4/2 He has always favored a tariff policy that protects the Louisiana sugar interest. — **(13) 1898** *K.C. Star* 18 Dec. 15/2 Hop, Skip and Jump are . . . the pet sheep of . . . the children of Mr. Henry O. Havemeyer, the sugar king. — **(14)** *(a)* **1839** BRIGGS *H. Franco* II. 143 There would be [at the party] . . . scandal by the wholesale, besides sugar kisses, and philippinas. *(b)* **1876** *Cong. Rec.* 25 July 4873/2 The conservatives of Portsmouth [Va.], . . . had printed tickets of the smallest possible size, on the thinnest paper, and by folding several in a large ticket and presenting it as their vote they succeeded in filling the ballot-boxes with over a thousand of these small tickets—sugar-kiss tickets as they are called.

(15) 1692 *Va. State P.* I. 44 We marcht to the Suggar Land. **1814** *Niles' Reg.* VI. 393/1 In Louisiana are great quantities of the most valuable 'sugar lands' in the world. **1852** GOUGE *Fiscal Hist. Texas* 84 Texas . . . would have been under no necessity of cultivating . . . her sugar lands. **1883** SWEET & KNOX *Through Texas* 82 In the counties of Fort Bend, Wharton, Colorado, and Brazoria, there is a great deal of the finest sugar-lands in the world. — **(16) 1908** *U.S. Dept. Agric. Farmers' Bul.* 334, 24 Sugar mules are those shipped south to use on the sugar farms of Georgia, Louisiana, and other Southern States. They are taller, larger, and more breedy looking than cotton mules and have heavier bone. — **(17) 1891** S. M. WELCH *Recoll. 1830–40* 157 This southern travel mostly consisted of the sugar 'Nabobs' of Louisiana and rich planters. — **(18) 1855** COOKE *Ellie* 203 Are you going . . . to make a sugar-rag for that baby up there? **1897** M. HARLAND *Old-Field School-Girl* 31 Give me one o' them sugar-rags to stop his mouth. — **(19) 1853** *Harper's Mag.* Nov. 763/1 To the children, 'sugar rolling' is composed of halcyon days.

(20) 1890 J. CARLL *7th Rep. Oil & Gas Fields W. Pa.* 139 Drillers have certain terms—not classical, but expressive and well understood by the craft and by oil men generally—*sugar-sand, clover-seed* [etc.]. — **(21) 1855** *Prairie News* (Okalona, Miss.) 7 June 4/1 The K. N.'s in the sugar State are in a bad way. **1888** THOMPSON *Story La.* 203 Louisiana . . . was a cotton and sugar State and she was at the mercy of the Mississippi River. — **(22) 1888** *Cong. Rec.* App. 9 June 211/2 The next largest trust in the world is the 'sugar trust.' **1910** PINCHOT *Fight for Conservation* 110 The Sugar Trust and the beef-packers . . . injure the average man without good reason.

b. In the names of, or with reference to, plants: (1) ∗**sugar beet,** *attrib.* (see quots.); (2) **berry,** see as a main entry; (3) **birch,** sweet birch, *Betula lenta,* of the eastern U.S.; (4) **bush,** the sugar sumac, *Rhus ovata,* cf. **c.** (1) below; (5) ∗**cane,** see as a main entry; (6) **grape,** the sand grape; (7) **huckleberry,** (see quot.), *rare;* (8) **loaf,** a local term for a variety of cotton, *obs.;* (9) **maple,** see as a main entry; (10) ∗**pear,** (see quot.); (11) **pine,** *(a)* =**coontie,** *(b)* a pine or species of pine, *Pinus lambertiana,* found on the Pacific Coast, also attrib.; (12) ∗**plum,** the shadbush, *Amelanchier canadensis;* (13) **pumpkin,** a sweet-fleshed variety of the common pumpkin; (14) **tree,** see as a main entry; (15) **wood,** a sugar maple or a grove of sugar maples.

(1) 1909 *Cent. Supp.* 713/3 *Larger sugar-beet leaf-beetle, Monoxia puncticolis. Ib.* 1295/3 *Sugar-beet belt,* . . . from southern New York and northern Pennsylvania to northern Nebraska and South Dakota, over large sections of Colorado, Utah, Wyoming, Montana, Idaho, Washington, and Oregon, and in California on the coast side. — **(3) 1751** J. BARTRAM *Observations* 27 The timber was sugar birch, sugar maples, oak and poplar. — **(4) 1931** VANSELL *Nectar & Pollen Plants Calif.* 49 Sugar bush, *R. ovata,* of coastal southern California blossoms in winter. **1949** *Nature Mag.* Nov. 424/1 There is the gray of some manzanitas, the silver of white sage, the dark green of sugar bush.

(6) 1891 COULTER *Bot. W. Texas* I. 63 *V[itis] rupestris.* . . . Sugar grape. . . . In the Valley of Devil's River and westward into the mountains of the Pecos. — **(7) 1860** DARLINGTON *Weeds & Plants* 210 *V[accinium] Pennsylvanicum.* . . . Pennsylvanian Vaccinium. Dwarf Blueberry. Sugar Huckleberry. — **(8) 1848** in TURNER *Cotton* (1865) 101, I beg to call the attention of the planting interest to the early maturity and the productiveness of the cotton called in Mississippi, Sugar Loaf and Prolific. **1865** TURNER *Cotton* 29 The Sugar Loaf, another variety from Mississippi, . . . in some localities in the Gulf States has proved very productive.

(10) 1893 [see **sugarberry 2.**]. — **(11)** *(a)* **1848** DUNGLISON *Med. Lexicon* 80/1 Florida arrow root is derived from *Zamia integrifolia* or *Z. pumila,* Sugar pine. *(b)* **1846** O. JOHNSON *Across Rocky Mts.* 75 It is called Sugar Pine, from the peculiar quality of its gum, which tastes very much like Sugar saturated with Turpentine. **1857** BORTHWICK *3 Years in Calif.* 188 The pine-trees are of an immense size. . . . The most graceful is what is called the 'sugar pine.' **1949** *Sierra Club Bul.* Jan. 6/1 Once cut and milled, that tree will become indistinguishable in the piles of lumber that might have come from anywhere in the sugar-pine belt. — **(12) 1832** BROWNE *Sylva* 216 In the northern section of the Union, it is called *Wild Pear Tree* and *Sugar Plum.* **1893** *Amer. Folk-Lore* VI. 141 *Amelanchier Canadensis,* sugar-plum. Vt. — **(13) 1905** in *Cent. Supp.* 1295/3 Negro or Nantucket Sugar Pumpkin. The true old-fashioned black-warted, shelled pumpkin.

(15) 1809 A. HENRY *Travels* 68 A ridge, or mountain . . . is rocky, and covered with rock or sugar maple, or sugar-wood. **1890–3** TABER *Stowe Notes* 36, I was in the sugar-wood for some time.

c. In expressions relating to the sugar maple (*q.v.* as a main entry) and the making of sirup and sugar from its sap: (1) **sugar bush,** a grove of maples set aside for the production of sirup; (2) **cabin,** a cabin at a sugar camp, also as a place-name, *obs.;* (3) **camp,** see as a main entry; (4) **day,** a day when sugar maple sap flows freely; (5) **grove,** =**sugar bush;** (6) ∗**house,** a shed where maple sugar and sirup are made, cf. **2.** (11) above; (7) **lot,** =**sugar bush;** (8) **month,** the month during which maple sugar is chiefly made; (9) **orchard,** an orchard or grove of sugar maple trees; (10) **sand,** a granular sediment, principally calcium malate and silica, which forms in the process of making maple sugar, cf. **2.** (20) above; (11) **season,** the season when maple sugar is made; (12) ∗**snow,** (see quot. 1932); (13) **town,** a town in a region where maple sugar is made; (14) **trough,** a wooden trough used for maple sap, cf. **sap trough;** (15) ∗**water,** =**maple sap;** (16) **weather,** weather suitable for making maple sugar.

Sugar trough or sap trough

(1) 1823 COOPER *Pioneers* xx, We will stop and see the 'sugar-bush' of Billy Kirby. **1950** *N.Y. Times Mag.* 23 April 46/2 'Sugar bush' is rarely heard in New Jersey, but in Pennsylvania it is the normal term throughout the Yankee settlements. — **(2) 1765** *Lett. to Washington* I. 191 One at the Sugar Cabbins called Fort Littleton Commanded by Capt. Hanee Hamilton. **1765** CROGHAN *Journal* (1904) 124 We travelled . . . to a place called the Sugar Cabins. — **(4) 1854** RILEY *Puddleford* 242 These March days, were 'sugar days.'

(5) 1792 IMLAY *Western Territory* 136 [Settlement in this country] has expanded into fertile fields, blushing orchards, pleasant gardens, luxuriant sugar groves. **1917** EATON *Green Trails* 14 It is a steep way, past a running brook and through a sugar grove. **1948** DICK *Dixie Frontier* 247 These trees grew in clumps, and a clump numbering from one hundred to three hundred trees was chosen for the operation. Such a clump came to be called a sugar grove. — **(6) 1821** W. DALTON *Travels U.S.* 102 There being few farms in this part of the country without maple trees and sugar houses. **1949** *Highway Traveler* Feb. 16/1 Steam from thousands of rustic sugarhouses tinges the crisp mountain air with the aroma of boiling liquid gold. — **(7) 1822** *Farmer's Diary 1823* (Canandaigua, N.Y.) c2ᵛ My sugar lot is in the town of Norway (Herkimer county) and encloses about 50 acres of ground, on which I have set about two thousand pails. **1943** TUTT *Yankee Lawyer* 5 We broke a road through the snow to the sugar lot. — **(8) 1929** F. E. MCCLINCHEY *Joe Pete* 66 During the 'sugar month' Mabel and her two children also lived on sugar and the fish which Big John brought them occasionally. — **(9) 1833** FLINT *D. Boone* 113 The contiguity of a salt lick and a sugar orchard . . . was a very desirable circumstance. **1896** *Vt. Agric. Rep.* XV. 38, [I] would not pay any attention to the matter of pasturage in a sugar orchard.

(10) 1882 *Vt. Agric. Rep.* VII. 64 In the process of sugar making there was a point where it would combine with the lime, making 'sugar sand' or the malate of lime. **1907** BAILEY *Cyclo. Amer. Agric.* I. 429/2 It undergoes further boiling in a special deep pan until the temperature is about 219° . . . when (after the separation of the 'niter' or 'sugar sand,'—an impure malate of lime—by filtration or sedimentation) it is sealed, usually hot, in tin cans. — **(11) 1836** *Penny Mag.* V. 475 It commonly happens, during the earlier part of the 'sugar-season,' that the frost by night . . . is . . . severe. **1929** F. E. MCCLINCHEY *Joe Pete* 19 The sun grew strong enough to melt the snow, the sap began to rise in the maple trees, and the sugar season was on. — **(12) 1861** G. K. WILDER *Diary* (MS) 6 March, It will be a 'sugar snow with a little more.' **1932** WILDER *Little House in Big Woods* 92 It's called a sugar snow, because a snow this time of year means that men can make more sugar. You see, this little cold spell and the snow will hold back the leafing of the trees, and that makes a longer run of sap. — (13) **1881** *Harper's Mag.* April 644 A Sugar Town in the Green Mountains. — (14) **1779** *Mass. Hist. Soc. Proc.* 2 Ser. II. 453 Made Sugar Troughs and katchd. some Sap. **1898** N. E. JONES *Squirrel Hunters of Ohio* 22 The sugar-trough was a short trough two to four feet long made of some light wood. **1946** RICHTER *Fields* 17 She lifted the long bundle from out of the sugar trough.

(15) **1818** BIRKBECK *Letters* 40 Hard by, a range of iron kettles are steaming away; in these the 'sugar water' is evaporating to a syrup of proper consistency. **1890** HOWELLS *Boy's Town* 161 The boys began to go to the woods to get sugar-water, as they called the maple-sap. **1949** *Chi. Tribune* 13 March I. 6/4 Tho the tree flow of sugar water is restricted by lack of sharp freezes and sudden thaws, the spiles' steady drips are yielding three gallons of sap a tree a day in some sections. — (16) **1836** *Penny Mag.* V. 476 About three weeks is a full average of 'sugar weather.' **1894** R. E. ROBINSON *Danvis Folks* 139 It wa'nt no gre't sugar weather.

d. In expressions designating or alluding to frolics and parties in connection with the making of maple sugar, as (1) **sugar bee,** (2) **eat,** (3) **fire,** (4) **frolic,** (5) **lick,** (6) **party,** (7) **supper.**

(1) **1850** LANMAN *Haw-ho-noo* 11 The last sugar-bee . . . was given by an old Dutchman. — (2) **1859** G. K. WILDER *Diary* (MS) 7 April, I was invited to a party, a sugar eat. **1906** *Springfield W. Republican* 7 Feb. 9 A number attended the moving picture entertainment and sugar-eat. — (3) **1853** *Harper's Mag.* March 562/1 Many a night-gathering is there before the blazing 'sugar-fires,' in comfortable wigwams, and odorous clean straw upon the 'ground'-floors. — (4) **1886** *Harper's Mag.* June 92/2 A good many of us have helped in sugar frolics.

(5) **1871** DE VERE 206 The gatherings of young people in the beautiful groves to eat the warm sugar are practically but very prosaically called *sugar-licks.* — (6) **1871** DE VERE 206 Sugar-parties, during which the sap collected in large vessels is boiled down in the still wintry woods, amid much merriment and innocent mirth, are common from Vermont down to Western Virginia. **1907** HOWELLS *Through Eye of Needle* 65, I once went to a sugar party up in New Hampshire. — (7) **1947** BEROLZHEIMER *Regional Cookbook* 53 In New England towns, if sugaring off and a fresh fall of snow coincide, the Ladies' Aid is likely to sponsor a 'sugar supper.'

e. *To bring sugar in one's spade,* ?to be prepared to practice bribery. *Rare.* Cf. **sugaring,** *a.*

1894 *Cong. Rec.* 25 Jan. 1383/1 When you seek to get your voucher approved, bring sugar in your spade, and nothing else.

As the last term in **cake, cistern, corn, cornstalk, country, cut, horse, Indian, long, maple, mosey, mush, sap, sap maple, shop, store, tree, tub, wagon sugar.**

* **sugar,** *v.*

1. *intr.* To make maple sugar.

1778 PATTEN *Diary* 380, I went up to the boys where they was Shugaring but it was dull weather. **1872** *Vt. Bd. Agric. Rep.* I. 215 My brother . . . sugared in what we called the old sugar place.

2. *To sugar off,* to complete the process of boiling maple sap until it is thick enough to crystallize. *Colloq.*

1836 TRAILL *Backwoods of Canada* (1846) 237 Those that sugar-off outside the house have a wooden crane fixed against a stump. **1844** *Knickerb.* XXIII. 441 We will rendezvous about one o'clock, and in the afternoon help 'sugar off.' **1894** *Vt. Agric. Rep.* XIV. 125 Take all that is wanted for maple syrup or honey and sugar it off.

b. *transf.* To amount to after all allowances have been made.

1871 *Harper's Bazaar* 13 March 163/3 It is estimated that his estate would 'sugar off,' as they say in Vermont, at about $200,000.

sugarberry ˈʃʊgɚˌbɛrɪ, *n.*

1. =**hackberry.** Also attrib.

1837 DARLINGTON *Flora Cestrica* 180 Nettle tree. Sugar-berry. **1896** *Chi. Rec.* 17 Feb. 4/6 He laid the groundwork . . . by cutting a sugarberry sprout. **1917** *Lit. Digest* 15 Dec. 22/2 The berries of the hackberry, or sugarberry, as it is called in the South, are dry but have an agreeable taste. **1948** *Fla. Anthropologist* May 19 This vegetation includes sugarberry, banyan, mulberry, papaya, saw palmetto and small plants.

2. A shadbush (see quot.).

1893 *Amer. Folk-Lore* VI. 141 *Amelanchier Canadensis,* sugar pear. Orono, Me. Sugar berry. N. Woodstock, N.H.

sugar bowl. [See note.]

This term may not have been first used in this country, though evidence for it is lacking in the *OED.* "The ordinary small earthenware vessels, used for porridge, soup, milk, sugar, etc., which are historically *bowls,* and are so called in Scotland and in U.S., are always called in the south-east of England, and hence, usually in literary English, *basins*" (*OED s.v. Bowl*).

1. A small bowl-shaped container, usu. of glass, crockery or china, and having two handles and a cover, for sugar at table.

1772 *Boston News Letter* 31 Dec. (*advt.*), Glass sugar bowl. **1936** *Sears Cat.* (No. 173) 641 Open Stock Prices . . . Sugar Bowl . . . 10c. **1949** *Hobbies* June 104/2 All can not be the proud possessors of Stiegel sugar bowls.

2. (*cap.*) *attrib.* Of or pertaining to the bowl (*q.v.*, sense **2.**) at New Orleans.

1936 ARTHUR *Old New Orleans* 39 Appropriately, this firm has donated an antique sugar bowl which will be the annual trophy for the mid-winter 'Sugar Bowl' football contest to be played in New Orleans each New Year's Day. **1946** *Times-Herald* (Washington, D.C.) 28 Dec. 4 (*heading*), Sugar Bowl Bound Panama Limited Wrecked Near New Orleans.

3. (*cap.*) A region, such as southern Louisiana, famous for the amount of sugar it produces.

1945 *Amer. Mercury* 311/1 The Sugar Bowl spilled over, from the Mississippi along the borders of the fecund Louisiana bayous into Georgia and Florida. **1949** *Amer. Forests* Nov. 11/3 We of Colorado will never cease to be grateful for the idea which drove a tunnel thirteen miles through solid granite under the continental divide to carry water . . . to the Sugar Bowl of northeastern Colorado. **1950** *World-Herald Mag.* (Omaha) 12 Feb. 15/3 Residents of the famous Sugar Bowl section of the state have handed down from generation to generation many stories accounting for his motives.

sugar camp. A grove of sugar maples together with all the facilities for producing sirup, as the boiling house, arches, kettles, etc.

1779 PATTEN *Diary* 400, I went to our shugar Camp and covered some fire steads with brush where we had Cabbage and french Turnip seed sowed to preserve them from the Cattle. **1808** PIKE *Sources Miss.* 49 The sugar camp near the stockade was where he made sugar. **1813** *Niles' Reg.* IV. 316/1 Many of our farmers have their 'sugar camp,' of three or four acres. **1949** *Ill. State Hist. Soc. Jrnl.* Sep. 325 Characteristic features of the Illinois country not mentioned at all were the sugar camps (*sucreries*) to which the French repaired in the spring to make maple sugar.

attrib. **1807** in MARSHALL *Kentucky* (1824) II. 415 A line at right-angles will strike the head of Black's and Newman's sugar camp branch. **1845** *Lowell Offering* V. 268 We used to have sugar-camp parties in the woods. **1874** B. F. TAYLOR *World on Wheels* 71 It is . . . a full-grown maple, that gave down the sap for the sugar-camp kettle in your grandfather's time.

* **sugar cane.** In attrib. uses (see quots.). Cf. **Chinese sugar cane.**

1856 *Porter's Spirit of Times* 15 Nov. 172/3 The refuse sugar-cane *bagasse* was being burnt up. **1891** *Cent.* 6046/3 [The] *Sugar-cane beetle,* a scarabæid beetle, *Ligyrus rugiceps,* . . . damages sugar-cane in Louisiana by boring into the canes in the early spring. *Ib.,* [The] *Sugar-cane borer,* the larva of a crambid moth, *Chilo saccharalis,* . . . bores sugar-cane in the southern United States, the West Indies, and elsewhere. **1909** *Cent. Supp.* 161/1 *Sugar-cane brand,* a disease of the leaves of sugar-cane caused by the smut, *Ustilago Sacchari.*

* **sugaring,** *n.*

1. The making of sugar by boiling down maple sap. Also attrib.

1835 THOMPSON *Adv. T. Peacock* 40 My boy, Jock, . . . was fourteen last sugarin'-time. **1896** *Advance* 23 April 607/1 The farmers are hardly getting to sugaring in dead earnest. **1919** CUNNINGHAM *Chronicle* 280 The sugaring party was fortunate in the selection of a day. **1948** *Chi. Tribune* 14 March VII. 17/2 I'm just contrary enough to be thinking about 'sugaring time.'

b. sugaring off, converting maple sap into sugar, or a gathering of neighbors to assist in this and to enjoy a merrymaking afterwards. Also, rarely, the time of year when sap is gathered and boiled.

1836 TRAILL *Backwoods of Canada* (1846) 237 The best rule I can give as to the sugaring-off, as it is termed, is to let the liquid continue at a fast boil. **1903** *Atlantic Mo.* Sep. 383 The 'huskings' and 'sugarings-off' of the old-fashioned rural New Englander. **1904** WALLER *Wood-Carver* 30 I'll hev ter knit from now t'll sugarin-off. **1949** *Downers Grove* (Ill.) *Rep.* 31 March 11/4 When the sap had been boiled to syrup for sugar, it was taken to the classroom for final 'sugaring off.'

attrib. **1938** DAMON *Grandma* 22 Grandma kept several pails hung up along the pipe, for all the world as on a maple tree in sugaring-off time. **1944** JOHNSON *As I Dare* 56 They . . . were famed for their cooking, their 'sugaring-off parties,' and their barn dances where bearded old fiddlers called the turns. **1949** *Highway Traveler* Feb. 39/1 Further boiling is done to reduce syrup to sugar on a smaller arch and pan, the 'sugaring off' rig, or at home on the kitchen range.

c. sugaring down, crystallizing.
1850 S. F. COOPER *Rural Hours* 26 The syrup boils until on the point of graining, as it is called, or in rustic parlance, 'sugaring down.'

2. Bribery. *Slang.*
[**1885** SIRINGO *Texas Cow Boy* 305 His only hope now was to sugar the prosecuting attorney.] **1891** QUINN *Fools of Fortune* 285 This payment is what the 'fakirs' call 'sugaring,' and I have never known one of these officials for whom the dose could be made too sweet. **1902** WHITE *Blazed Trail* 117 The old-time logger found these two individuals susceptible to the gentle art of 'sugaring.'

sugar maple.

1. Any one of several related maples, esp. *Acer saccharum,* from the sap of which sirup is made. Cf. **black, western sugar maple.**
1731 MILLER *Gard. Dict. s.v. Acer,* There is another sort of Maple, which is very common in Virginia, and is known by the Name of the *Sugar Maple.* **1840** COOPER *Pathfinder* xviii, I had a cabin in a grove of sugar maples. **1892** *Vt. Agric. Rep.* XII. 120 [There is] a large supply of the sugar maple, making many valuable orchards. **1944** NUTE *Lk. Superior* 259 The sugar maple is as American as the rail fence or the Kentucky rifle.
attrib. **1791** *Amer. Philos. Soc.* III. 64 The Sugar Maple-tree grows in great quantities in the western countries of all the middle states of the American Union. **1844** *Knickerb.* XXIII. 506 A western orator recently delivered himself of it from the summit of a sugar-maple stump at a political barbacue. **1945** PEARSON *Country Flavor* 11 The grove of gnarled, old, sugar-maple trees is a veteran of many years of intense activity.

2. sugar-maple borer, (see quot. 1881).
1881 *U.S. Entomological Comm. Bul.* No. 7, 103 The sugar-maple borer, *Glycobius speciosus,* . . . bores for several inches into the trunks of healthy trees. **1907** *Suburban Life* May 300/2 The sugar-maple borer is most destructive to the hard and sugar maples in many portions of the country.

sugar tree.

1. =**sugar maple.**
1705 BEVERLEY *Virginia* II. 21 The Honey and Sugar-Trees are likewise spontaneous, near the Heads of Rivers. **1775** FITHIAN *Journal* II. 57 Peggy . . . showed me their Sugar-tree bottom, out of which Mrs. Piper . . . makes yearly, plenty of sugar for her family's use. **1949** *Chi. Tribune* 13 March I. 6/4 The Crane Naval depot encroached upon some fine old sugar trees in Martin county.
attrib. **1783** in *Travels Amer. Col.* 667 The Inhabitants tan leather with beach tree bark they likewise find sugar tree bark will answer. **1790** HILTZHEIMER *Diary* (1893) 10 Nov. 165 Planted some of the American Sugar Tree seed given by Henry Drinker to the Agricultural Society. **1824** DODDRIDGE *Indian Wars* 142 It was made of a sugar tree sapling. **1843** CARLTON *New Purchase* I. 112 Mrs. Seymour entered the parlour with a cake of sugar-tree sugar in her hands.

2. ?The honey locust (see quot.). *Rare.*
1819 E. EVANS *Pedestrious Tour* 299 The sugar-tree produces a sweet pod, like that of a pea, and furnishes very nutritious food for swine.

* **suggestive,** *a.* Hinting at something improper or indecent. Hence * **suggestiveness,** *n.*
1889 GUNTER *That Frenchman!* xi, Her incomparable drolleries and naughtinesses, in some suggestive opera bouffe, some musical debauch. **1914** S. H. ADAMS *Clarion* 130 'The Nymph in the Nightie' . . . [is] rotten with suggestiveness. **1925** *Scribner's Mag.* Oct. 4/2, I liked the story and found it neither smutty nor suggestive.

suggumug ˈsʌgəˌmʌg, *n.* [Origin unknown.] (See quot.) *Rare.* — **1784** *Amer. Acad. Mem.* I. 456 *Bixa.* . . . Bass Wood. White Wood. Suggumug. . . . Blossoms white. In woods. Not common. July.

* **suit,** *n.* A person's head *of* hair or set *of* whiskers or teeth. *Colloq.*
1803 LEWIS in *Jrnls. L. & Ordway* 61 Lorimier . . . is remarkable for having once had a remarkable suit of hair. **1845** JUDD *Margaret* I. 10 His laughter exposed a suite of fair white teeth. *Ib.* II. 216 The face of this gentleman was strikingly marked by a suit of enormous black whiskers. **1903** WIGGIN *Rebecca* 82 Cousin Cyrus . . . says I've got a splendid suit of hair.
As the last term in **bathing, business, courting, cowboy, fall, ice cream, moose, parlor, sack, store, strong, zebra suit.**

* **sulky,** *a. Agric.* Designating riding implements, as **sulky cultivator, harrow, hay rake, plow, rake.**
1865 *Ill. Agric. Soc. Trans.* VI. 49 There were but two competitors, E. B. Skinner, driving a sulky plow [etc.]. **1868** *Iowa State Agric. Soc. Rep. 1867* 140 After the corn is up so that it can be rowed, . . . sulky-cultivators . . . are used. **1872** *Newton Kansan* 22 Aug. 3/6 Agent for the sale of . . . Taylor Sulky Rake. **1876** KNIGHT 2452/1 *Sulky-harrow,* one having a wheeled carriage and seat for the rider. **1881** *Rep. Indian Affairs* 95, I have purchased for them . . . 1 mower and sulky hay-rake. **1948** *Mt. Morris* (Ill.) *Index* 24 Dec. 2/6 Closing Out Sale . . . gang plow, horse pull; sulky plow; wagon box.
As the last term in **double, road, stick sulky.**

sull sʌl, *v.* [?Back formation from * *sullen, a.*] *intr.* (See quots. 1869, 1902.)
1869 *Overland Mo.* III. 127 A mustang . . . will both 'sull,' (have the sulks) and 'buck.' **1902** *D.N.* II. 246 *Sull.* 1. To hold a position with imperturbable obstinacy and a total disregard to surroundings, as a possum, or a hog in a corner. 2. To be in a semicomatose state through pain. Used only of animals. [s. Ill.] **1949** *10 Story Western* May 11/2 Tell them slow motion sons to keep them cattle comin' before this drive balks and sulls.

One form of sulky plow

* **sulphur,** *n.*

1. Used in names (see quots.).
1833 EATON *Botany* (ed. 6) 256 *Peucedanum ternatum,* sulpher wort. **1884** COUES *Key to Birds* (ed. 2) 431 *M[yiodynastes] luteiventris.* . . . Sulphur-bellied Striped Flycatcher. . . . Central Am. and Mexico to Arizona. **1915** ARMSTRONG & THORNBER *Western Wild Flowers* 94 This plant [*Erigonum bakeri*] is quite pretty and conspicuous. . . . There are several other kinds of Sulphur Flower. **1947** PEATTIE *Sierra Nevada* 123 Whether you go traipsing in the northern or the southern Sierra, you will soon see sulphur-flower, the commonest mountain buckwheat, growing in rocks or in pine-needles. **1949** *Pacific Discovery* Jan.–Feb. 8/1 A parallel retardation in the reproductive cycle was observed among the peccaries, wild turkeys, Mearns quail, and some of the smaller birds such as sulphur-bellied flycatchers.

2. a. sulphur bluff, a bluff impregnated with sulphur. **b. sulphur lick,** a lick in soil containing sulphur. Both *obs.*
(**a**) **1807** GASS *Journal* 38 We came to black sulphur bluffs. — (**b**) **1792** in *Amer. Sp.* XV. 398/1 About one mile above the Sulphur Lick.

c. *sulphur and molasses,* a preparation taken as a medicinal tonic. Cf. * *brimstone and treacle* in *OED.*
1846 DURIVAGE *Stray Subjects* 195 'Poor fellow!' chorussed the entire circle . . . 'try the water cure'—'sulphur and molasses!' 'steam,' 'calomel,'—'glass of brandy!' 'mint julep.' **1896** *Wkly. Witness* 2 Dec. 7/3 Our mother gave us lib'rally Of sulphur and molasses. **1950** *Chi. Tribune* 28 March 14/3 There seem to be two schools of home doctoring: Those who swear by sassafras tea, and those . . . who dose with sulphur and molasses.

* **sumac, sumach.** As the last term in **coral, live, mountain, poison, smooth, staghorn, swamp, upland, velvet, Virginia sumac(h).**

* **summer,** *a.* In combs.: (1) **summer boarder,** one who boards in a country place during the summer; (2) **camp,** a camp for health and pleasure open during the summer; (3) **capital,** (see quot. and cf. **summer White House**); (4) **complaint,** diarrhea, esp. of children, during summer, *colloq.;* (5) **cottage,** a cottage, usu. in the country or at a summer resort, occupied during the summer, also **summer cottager;** (6) **game,** (see quot.), *slang, obs.;* (7) **garden,** (*a*) a plot of ground devoted to the culture of plants during the summer, also attrib., (*b*) an outdoor refectory or amusement place for use in summer; (8) **hogan,** (see quot. and cf. **hogan**); (9) **hotel,** a hotel operated for summer visitors and residents, also **summer hotel-keeper;** (10) **kitchen,** an extra kitchen, built adjacent to a house, used for warm-weather cooking (see also quot. 1948); (11) **normal,** (see quot.); (12) **pemmican,** (see quots. and cf. **pemmican**); (13) **rancheria,** *W.* a collection of Indian huts used in summer; (14) **range,** foraging at large by animals during the summer, a region suitable for such foraging; (15) **resort,** a place affording rest and recreation for visitors in summer;

(16) **resorter,** one who frequents summer resorts; (17) **retreat,** =**summer resort;** (18) **school,** a school conducted in the summer, often for training teachers; (19) **skin,** (see quot.), *obs.;* (20) **tent,** (see quot.); (21) **term,** in a school or college a term held during the summer; (22) **White House,** a residence occupied in summer by the President of the U.S., cf. **summer capital.**

(1) **1846** H. N. MOORE *Fitzgerald & Hopkins* 73 And stated also that there were several summer boarders from the city present. **1949** *Sat. Ev. Post* 25 June 47/2 At the end of one unusually arduous summer he put an ad in a Portland paper for summer boarders. — (2) **1893** *McClure's Mag.* I. 242/2 The camp was founded by Mr. Ernest Berkely Balch as a summer camp for boys. **1948** *Sat. Ev. Post* 23 Oct. 87/2 He wants to send every youngster in Lawrence to summer camp for at least two weeks. — (3) **1909** *World To-day* Oct. 1014 We are accustomed to speak of a summer capital. That means the town in which the President owns or hires a summer residence. — (4) **1847** *Amer. Jrnl. Medical Sci.* XIV. 40 On the Endemic Gastro-follicular Enteritis, or 'Summer Complaint' of Children. **1944** CLARK *Pills* 264 A tenant farmer's child took sick with the 'summer complaint' and within a day or two it was dead.

(5) **1840** *Knickerb.* XVI. 253 Mary's father had a summer-cottage in the neighborhood. **1948** *Chi. Tribune* 20 June VII. 12/5 Many summer cottagers will be happy to know that the same house makes a similar type of cream that repels chiggers. **1949** *Sat. Ev. Post* 2 April 25/3 They tag their boats with names such as we haven't seen since the days when it was thought gay to give cute names to summer cottages. — (6) **1889** FARMER 522/1 *Summer Game* (Cant.) playing merely for amusement, or for the benefit of another person with the latter's money. — (7) (*a*) **1868** GRAY *Field Botany* 79 *Pelargonium*, the Geranium, so-called, of house and summer-garden culture. **1901** CHURCHILL *Crisis* 451 Virginia and he would . . . descend to the bench on the lower tier of the summer garden. (*b*) **1882** MCCABE *New York* 660 Castle Garden . . . was converted into a summer-garden, where refreshments were sold and indifferent concerts given. **1903** ADE *In Babel* 29 The Barclays never went to summer-gardens where malt drink is served. — (8) **1912** *Out West* Feb. 109/2 In the summer months, rude 'summer hogans' are constructed, consisting merely of an enclosure of brush or any other material that may be at hand. — (9) **1852** *Harper's Mag.* Aug. 335/2 You lose your personal identity in a great summer hotel, as you would in a penitentiary. **1894** *Harper's Mag.* LXXXIX. 341/2 They are called 'lakes' by the summer hotel-keepers. **1945** *Colo. Springs Gaz.* 29 June 14/3 The ranch includes two fish rearing ponds and a summer hotel property.

(10) **1874** *Southern Mag.* XIV. 124 There was Charley's wife . . . flitting about from house to summer-kitchen. **1893** HOLLEY *Samantha at World's Fair* 158 Miss Growdey wuz a-comin' to the World's Fair as soon as she made her rag-carpet for her summer kitchen. **1948** JACOBS *We Chose Country* 25 The back hall, or 'summer kitchen,' was about the fullest room in the house. — (11) **1898** CANFIELD *Maid of Frontier* 17 She had . . . been sent to . . . one 'summer normal,' an occasional institution intended for the development of teachers. — (12) **1944** *Mil. Surgeon* Aug. 91/1 The kind made in the late winter and early spring, the summer pemmican, was what writers have had in mind who have called this one of the most remarkable dietetic advances of mankind, comparable, for instance, to the invention of the canning process. **1947** DEVOTO *Across Wide Missouri* 163 'Summer pemmican,' the Grade A stuff, was made in late winter and early spring. — (13) **1912** LUMHOLTZ *New Trails* 26 The aboriginal name for the summer rancherias is ooítak, fields. **1925** BRYAN *Papago Country* 351 On the right a faint road goes west through the fields of the summer ranchería of Jeowic. — (14) **1831** PECK *Guide* 105 [Horses] find . . . herbage for the summer range. **1948** *So. Sierran* May 6/1 [The] stock-carrying capacity of Calif. parks amounts to less than one-half of one per-cent of state's summer range requirements.

(15) **1832** *Louisville Public Advt.* 12 July 3/5 He has prepared his House and Garden at the lower end of Jefferson Street, for the purpose of making it a general *Summer Resort.* **1949** *L.A. Times* 23 May II. 4/6 Could it be that this invasion of a wilderness area is the 'foot in the door' approach to the ultimate building of a Palm Springs 'summer resort.' — (16) **1889** *Advance* 19 Sep., At Astoria the summer resorters distribute themselves to the various beaches. **1907** MARK TWAIN *Chapters from Autobiog.* 327 They respected these elegant summer-resorters. — (17) **1847** *De Bow's Review* IV. 263 We condense . . . a sketch of the beautiful summer retreats which are spread along the coasts of the Mississippi. — (18) **1871** EGGLESTON *Hoosier Schoolm.* 1 You might teach a summer school. **1928** *Chi. Tribune* 29 July 10/5 Northwestern university has a summer school. — (19) **1823** JAMES *Exped.* I. 192 Those [bison] skins which are obtained during this season are known by the name *Summer skins.*

(20) **1839** WISLIZENUS *Journey to Rocky Mts.* (1912) 40 In the summer the Indians find it often too cumbersome to carry their tents of skins with them, and so make at every place where they camp so-called summer tents. For this the squaws cut tree branches and wands, put them into the ground in a semi-circle, and cover this little natural tent with a blanket or a hide. — (21) **1853** ROOT & LOMBARD *Songs of Yale* 4 Presentation Day is the sixth Wednesday of the Summer Term, when the graduating Class . . . are presented to the President as qualified for the first degree, or the A.B. **1898** *Chi. Times-Herald* 3 April 37/4 The special preparations for the summer term surpass those of any former year. — (22) **1928** *Chi. Tribune* 2 June 8/5 What we would like to know is, whether President Coolidge in 'choosing' a summer White House among the cool lake breezes of Wisconsin didn't place himself in a 'draft,' so to speak. **1945** *Greeley* (Colo.) *D. Tribune* 4 Aug. 1/6 President Truman has been invited to establish the summer White house in this Pikes Peak region. **1949** *L.A. Times* 15 May 17/5 An American Federation of Labor Painters' Union protested to President Truman the hiring of a nonunion man to paint the summer White House.

b. In the names of birds and other creatures: (1) **summer duck,** a duck, as the wood duck, *Aix sponsa,* that nests and spends the summer in a particular locality as distinguished from one of more migratory habits; (2) **finch,** a sparrow of the genus *Aimophila;* (3) **flounder,** a large flounder of the Atlantic Coast, *Paralichthys dentatus;* (4) **herring,** (*a*) the hickory shad, *Pomolobus aestivalis,* (*b*) (see quot.), also **summer false herring;** (5) **phalarope,** (see quot.); (6) **redbird,** =**summer tanager;** (7) **sheldrake,** a local name for the hooded merganser; (8) **tanager,** a tanager, *Piranga rubra,* of the middle and southern states; (9) **warbler,** =next; (10) **yellowbird,** the yellow warbler, *Dendroica aestiva.*

(1) **1731** CATESBY *Carolina* I. 97 The Summer Duck. . . . They breed in Virginia and Carolina. **1871** LEWIS *Poultry Book* 86 The Wood or Summer Duck . . . one of the finest varieties we have, is easily reared and domesticated. **1945** *Md. Conservationist* 16/2 The wood duck, or summer duck as it is frequently called in Maryland, surpasses it in brilliant coloring. — (2) **1884** COUES *Key to Birds* (ed. 2) 373 *Peucœa æstivalis illinoensis,* Illinois Summer Finch. — (3) **1814** MITCHILL *Fishes N.Y.* 390 [The] Flounder of New-York . . . is called the summer flounder. **1911** *Rep. Fisheries 1908* 308/2 The name ['chicken halibut'] is also incorrectly applied to the summer flounder. — (4) (*a*) **1814** MITCHILL *Fishes N.Y.* 456 Summer Herring of New-York . . . has a row of spots to the number of seven or eight. **1911** *Rep. Fisheries 1908* 311/1. (*b*) **1820** *Western Rev.* II. 174 Summer False Herring. *Hyodon heterurus.* . . . A common species in the Ohio and tributary streams; it appears later than the following, whence it is called Summer-herring.

(5) **1917** *Birds of Amer.* I. 220 Wilson's Phalarope. *Steganopus tricolor.* . . . Other Name.—Summer Phalarope. — (6) *c***1730** CATESBY *Carolina* I. 56 The Summer Red-Bird. . . . They are Birds of Passage, leaving Virginia and Carolina in Winter. **1871** BURROUGHS *Wake-Robin* (1886) 78 The bluebird is not entirely blue; nor will the indigo-bird bear a close inspection, . . . nor the summer redbird. **1917** *Birds of Amer.* III. 81. — (7) **1888** TRUMBULL *Names of Birds* 73 At Stonington, Conn., [the hooded merganser is called] Wood Sheldrake; at Essex same state, Summer Sheldrake. — (8) **1783** LATHAM *Gen. Synopsis Birds* II. 220 Summer T[anager]. *Muscicapa rubra.* . . . A little bigger than an House Sparrow. . . . Inhabits Carolina and Virginia in the summer. **1917** *Birds of Amer.* III. 82/2 Because of his habit of eating honey-bees, the Summer Tanager has been given the name of Bee Bird. — (9) **1891** *Cent.* 6820/2 Summer warbler, the summer yellow-bird of North America; one of the golden warblers. **1917** *Birds of Amer.* III. 126 Yellow Warbler. . . . [Also called] Summer Warbler.

(10) **1810** WILSON *Ornithology* II. 111 [The] Blue-Eyed Yellow Warbler . . . [is the] Summer Yellow-bird [of] Bartram. **1844** *Nat. Hist. N.Y., Zoology* II. 99 The Summer Yellow-Bird . . . is a very common species in our State. **1917** *Birds of Amer.* III. 126.

c. In the names of, or with reference to, plants: (1) **summer crookneck,** a pale-yellow squash, *Cucurbita pepo condensa,* having a curved neck; (2) **fox grape,** (see quot.); (3) **grape,** a sweet wild American grape, *Vitis aestivalis;* (4) **haw,** the May haw or a related plant; (5) *** rose,** (see quot.), *obs.;* (6) **squash,** one of various squashes which mature and are used in summer, also attrib.

(1) **1890** *Amer. Naturalist* XXIV. 731 Summer Crooknecks appeared in our garden catalogues in 1828. **1949** *Nat. Geog. Mag.* Aug. 164 Our Summer Crookneck of today . . . appears to be the same as a squash described by Champlain in 1605. — (2) **1737** BRICKELL *N. Carolina* 92 The Vines that are Spontaneous and produce Grapes in Carolina are of six Kinds, . . . Two of which are call'd the *Summer-Fox-grape* because they are ripe in July. — (3) **1709** LAWSON *Carolina* 102 Two [kinds of fox grapes] . . . are called Summer Grapes. **1901** MOHR *Plant Life Ala.* 101 The vigorous summer grape . . . and the supple jack . . . ascend the highest trees without visible support below the lofty summits. **1949** *Amer. Photography* April 244/3 The summer grape is

somewhat similar to the blue grape. — **(4) 1857** GRAY *Botany* 124 *C[ratægus] flava,* (Summer Haw.) . . . Sandy soil, Virginia and southward. **1868** ——— *Field Botany* 128 *C[ratægus] æstivalis,* Summer Haw of S. States. . . . Large red juicy fruit, pleasantly acid, used for tarts, &c.: ripe in summer. **1884** SARGENT *Rep. Forests* 83.

(5) 1817 W. E. COXE *Fruit Trees* 103 Summer Rose . . . is an apple of singular beauty and excellence. . . . It . . . is brought to market . . . under the name of Harvest apple. — **(6) 1815** BENTLEY *Diary* IV. 346 A more free use has been made of the summer squash than ever before known. **1902** FREEMAN in *Harper's Bazaar* Sep. 766 There was nothing in her larder except a summer-squash pie. **1949** *Nat. Geog. Mag.* Aug. 162 The small, quick-growing forms that are eaten before the rinds and seeds begin to harden are called summer squash and belong to the species *C. pepo.*

d. summer-board, *v,* to keep as a summer boarder. *Rare.*

1903 KATE D. WIGGIN *Rebecca* x. 107 Mother has summer-boarded a lot o' the school-marms.

As the last term in **farewell, goodbye, Indian, second, smoke summer.**

∗**summer,** *v. To summer over,* to keep over summer. — **1872** *Vt. Bd. Agric. Rep.* I. 138 Do not be afraid of summering over a few tons of hay. **1896** *Vt. Agric. Rep.* XV. 39 In what way would you take care of the sugar that is intended to be summered over?

summerer ˈsʌmərɚ, *n.* One who patronizes a summer resort. *Colloq.* — **1881** H. J. WARNER *New Lett. Idle Man* 7 The first week of September brings with it everywhere else a hopeless collapse of 'Summerers.'

∗**sun,** *n.*

1. = sunfish.

1807 GASS *Journal* 29 The fish here are generally pike, cat, sun, perch. **1896** BRUCE *Econ. Hist. Va.* I. 113 There were in the waters of Virginia when first explored, grampus, . . . perch, tailor, sun [etc.].

2. In combs.: (1) ∗**sunburst,** jewels arranged in a piece after the fashion of a conventional representation of the sun and its rays; (2) **cured,** *a.* cured or preserved by exposure to the sun's rays; (3) **dance,** among the Plains Indians, a ceremonial dance performed in honor of the sun, freq. accompanied by public self-torture, also attrib.; (4) ∗**down, downer,** see ∗**sundown** as a main entry; (5) ∗**fish,** see as a main entry; (6) **fisher,** see **sunfish,** *v.;* (7) **jerked,** *a.* of meat, cured by being cut into strips and dried in the sun; (8) **pain,** (see quots.); (9) **parlor,** a glass-inclosed parlor having a sunny exposure; (10) **porch,** a small porchlike room designed to take full advantage of the sunlight; (11) **room,** = **sun parlor;** (12) **round,** a day, *rare;* (13) **set trail,** *fig.* a road or way to extinction; (14) ∗**setty,** *a.* suggesting a sunset, *obs.;* (15) **shaft,** a sunbeam, or shaft of sunlight; (16) **shine cake,** a form of sponge cake; (17) **shine State,** see as a main entry; (18) **umbrella,** a large sunshade.

(1) 1878 ROE *Army Lett.* 189 An immense gold star with a diamond sunburst in the center was above her forehead. **1905** *N.Y. Times* 7 Jan. 14 The Sunburst . . . consists of a large centre diamond with thirty smaller stones set in a double row around it. — **(2) 1877** (*advt.*), Old Judge Sun cured Virginia Smoking Tobacco. **1897** HOUGH *Story of Cowboy* 5 A cow, . . . if driven north and allowed to range on the sun-cured short grasses, . . . might increase [in weight] fairly by one-third. — **(3) 1849** EASTMAN *Dahcotah* p. xxii, The *sun dance* is performed by young [Sioux] warriors who dance, at intervals of five minutes, for several days. **1901** WHITE *Westerners* 68 This was indeed the young hero of the sun dance. **1947** *Sky Line Trail* Feb. 8/2 The Stoney Indians made a large circular tent which we called the Sun Dance Lodge.

(7) 1888 ROOSEVELT in *Cent. Mag.* Oct. 832/1 [He] shares his last bit of sun-jerked venison with you. — **(8) 1832** BAIRD *Valley Miss.* 73 A form of winter or relapsing intermittent fever; is 'periodical head-ache,' or 'Sun pain,' so called . . . from the well known fact, that the fit generally comes on . . . about sun-rise and seldom continues after sun-set. **1855** DUNGLISON *Med. Lexicon, Hemicrania* . . . , pain, confined to one half the head, . . . at times, continuing only as long as the sun is above the horizon; and hence sometimes called *Sun-pain.* **1944** HARNETT T. KANE *Deep Delta Country* 226 For 'sun-pain,' or sunstroke, great care and no little skill are required. — **(9) 1917** MATHEWSON *Second Base Sloan* 114 The fourth house from the corner . . . , the one with the sun parlor on it. **1931** B. S. ALDRICH *White Bird Flying* xix. 206 Through the sun-parlor they went, with its cathedral-glass skylight and its French doors.

(10) 1918 M. B. COOKE *Threshold* 53 Joan went in search of Mr. Farwell and found him reading in the sun porch. — **(11) 1921** *Ladies Home Jrnl.* May 31/3 Gay and colorful is this sun room, as every sun room should be. **1928** *Daily Express* 14 June 12/5 The glass-walled 'sun-room' of the doctor's home in Detroit. — **(12) 1924** A. J. SMALL *Frozen Gold* i. 39, I can generally get on their trail inside a sun-round. — **(13) 1928** FOY & HARLOW *Clowning Thro' Life* 115 The redskins in Kansas, like the Buffalo, were on the sunset trail. — **(14) 1870** A. D. WHITNEY *We Girls* i, We always thought it was a pretty, sunsetty name. **1886** PAGE in *Harper's Mag.* Jan. 306/1 Her arms so white, an' her face sort o' sunsetty.

(15) 1868 A. D. WHITNEY *P. Strong* 156 The maples were splendid in the sunshafts that shot through their bosoms. **1908** CHURCHILL *Mr. Crewe* xiii, He had but to beckon a shining Pegasus from out a sun-shaft in the sky. — **(16) 1888** HARGIS *Graded Cook Book* 362 [Recipe for] Sunshine Cake. **1891** RITTENHOUSE *Maud* 533 Pineapple ice in thin glass sherbet-cups, angel-food, kisses and sunshine cake. **1945** MACDONALD *Egg & I* 94, I had already made sunshine cake, angel food and pound cake. — **(18) 1831** *Boston Transcript* 31 May 3/2 Light Sun Umbrellas . . . are offered at low prices. **1898** M. LEONARD *Big Front Door* 31 A little girl came slowly up the street carrying a sun-umbrella.

b. In the names of plants and fishes: (1) **suncup,** an evening primrose, *Oenothera ovata,* found on the Pacific Coast; (2) ∗**dial,** the common lupine, *Lupinus perennis;* (3) **drop,** any one of various plants of the genus *Kneiffia* of the evening primrose family having flowers that open in daylight, cf. **pine barren sundrop;** (4) ∗**fish,** see as a main entry; (5) ∗**flower,** see as a main entry; (6) **perch,** = ∗**sunfish 1;** (7) **squall,** (see quots.); (8) **trout,** the squeteague.

(1) 1934 WEBSTER. **1947** *Mazama* Dec. 37/2 At the edge penstemon and suncups bloomed brightly. — **(2) 1840** DEWEY *Mass. Flowering Plants* 63 Sun Dial . . . has long been cultivated for ornament in gardens. **1892** *Amer. Folk-Lore* V. 94 *Lupinus villosus,* monkey faces; sun-dial. N. Ohio. — **(3) 1784** *Amer. Acad. Mem.* I. 438 Sundrop. They open about eleven o'clock. **1840** DEWEY *Mass. Flowering Plants* 47.

(6) 1804 LEWIS & CLARK *Exped.* VI. (1905) 174 In this lake there is also . . . Sunperch. **1852** *S. Lit. Messenger* XVIII. 680/1 He was a pretty good live parody on an enormous goggle-eyed sun perch. **1902** GORDON *Recoll. Lynchburg* 117 How full were the holes of craw-fish, turtles, sun-perch, grindles, and of daring, voracious pike. — **(7) 1859** BARTLETT 463 *Sun-Squall,* a term applied, on the coast of New England, to the Medusae, or Sea-Nettles. **1884** GOODE *Fisheries* I. 169 Jelly-fish, or sun-squalls . . . [are] abundant along the New England coast in summer. **1924** *D.N.* V. 288 Jelly fish are 'sunsqualls' for some unknown reason, and a sculpin is a 'scalawag.' [Cape Cod.] — **(8) 1884** GOODE *Fisheries* I. 362. **1911** *Rep. Fisheries 1908* 316/2 [The squeteague] is known as . . . 'gray trout,' 'sun trout,' 'shad trout,' 'sea trout,' and 'salt-water trout' in the Middle and South Atlantic states.

Sunapee ˈsʌnəpɪ, *n.* [f. an Algonquian (Pennacook) name, lit. "south lake."] *attrib.* Designating a species of brilliantly colored char, *Salvelinus aureolus,* found in Sunapee Lake, New Hampshire, and in other lakes in that state and in Maine.

[**1857** *Spirit of Times* 4 April 70/2 In Sunapee Lake, with the single exception of the trout, the fish are the same as in all the ponds.] **1897** *N.Y. Forest, Fish, & Game Comm. 2d Rep.* 186 As the October pairing time approaches, the Sunapee fish becomes illuminated with the flushes of maturing passion. *Ib.* 188 The Sunapee saibling takes live bait readily. **1900** *Outing* May 159/2 The blue-back resembles the Sunapee trout more than any other of the charr species.

b. Also **Sunapee Indians,** Indians of an Algonquian stock living in the vicinity of Sunapee Lake, New Hampshire.

1857 *Spirit of Times* 4 April 70/2 Whilom it was a splendid trout-lake, and the rendezvous of the Sunapee Indians, from whom it derives its name.

∗**sunbonnet,** *n.* As the last term in **shingle, slat, split sunbonnet.**

sunck sʌŋk, *n.* Also **sunk.** [f. Algonquian and prob. related to **squaw.** Cf. Massachuset *sonksq, saunck squauh.*] A female chief of an eastern Indian tribe. In full **sunck squaw.** *Obs.*

[**1662** *Brookhaven Rec.* 7 This writing, made . . . between Weany Sunk, squaw, Anabackus and Iackanapes, all of them residents of Shinecock.] **1663** *Southampton Rec.* II. 36 An agreement between the great Sunk squa Quashawam, and the Indians of Shinecock as followeth. **1797** B. TRUMBULL *Hist. Conn.* I. 347 A treaty was concluded between the United colonies and the six Narraganset sachems, and the sunk squaw or old queen of Narraganset. **1804** *Mass. Hist. Coll.* I Ser. IX. 83 (*footnote*), Awaking one night. . . . and finding his sunck (queen) lying near another Indian, he . . . took his knife, and cut three strokes on each of her cheeks.

b. As the name of an Indian man. *Rare.*

[**1675** *Conn. Rec.* II. 403 They say the Indyans are scattered; the two sachems Suikquens, Nononanto, & ye Queene beeing neere ye Nipmug Country.] **1781** S. PETERS *Hist. of Conn.* 23 Sunksquaw . . . after murdering his Sachem, Quinnipiog, was also declared Sachem by the English Dominion.

sundae ˈsʌndɪ, *n.* Also **sundi, Sunday.** [Time and place of origin obscure, but accepted as an obscuration of Sunday. See Mencken, *Supp.* I. (1945) 376–7.] An individual portion of ice cream served with a sweet sauce, fruit, nuts, whipped cream, etc.

1904 *N.Y. Ev. Post* 21 May, The Sundi, so popular at the confectioner's, can be prepared at home. **1921** TUCKER *Amer. English* 306 *Sunday*, sometimes misspelled 'sundae.' . . . Name said to have been first used, about 1897, at Red Cross Pharmacy, State Street, Ithaca, N.Y. **1948** *Ice Cream Trade Jrnl.* Oct. 80/2 The loss in the sale of ice cream can be traced to the soda fountains where the quantity of ice cream in sodas, sundaes, and milk shakes has been reduced 10 to 30 per cent.

As the last term in **chocolate, ice cream, strawberry sundae.**

***Sunday,** *n.* In combs.: (1) **Sunday comic,** comic pictures in a Sunday paper; (2) **-go-to-meeting(s),** one's best or Sunday clothes, also attrib., usu. with reference to apparel but sometimes in the sense of first-class, *colloq.*, cf. **go-to-meeting,** and see ***meeting,** *n.* **3;** (3) **scholar,** a pupil in a Sunday school; (4) **supplement,** a section or sections of miscellaneous matter forming part of a Sunday newspaper.

(1) **1908** *Nation* 5 Nov. 426/2 We are familiar with the defence of the Sunday comic. — (2) **1831** *Boston Transcript* 12 Dec. 1/1 They tossed on their 'Sunday-go-to-meetings,' and crossed into Jarsey, the route they intended to take lying through that little but interesting State. **1841** *S. Lit. Messenger* VII. 646/2 [He discarded] his 'Sunday go-to-meetin' broadcloth.' **1902** ALDRICH *Sea Turn* 199 The street wasn't what might be called a Sunday-go-to-meeting street, but the neighbors . . . lodged complaints. **1948** *Southern Folklore* Sep. 187 She's wearing her Sunday-go-to-meeting clothes. — (3) **1830** *Williams's N.Y. Ann. Reg.* 194 Leaving Sunday scholars not in other schools . . . 7,006. **1872** MCCLELLAN *Golden State* 406 The Old and New School Presbyterians have . . . 2,600 members and 3,500 Sunday-scholars. — (4) **1929** SMITH *Stray Lamb* (1938) 154, I have no desire to furnish material for the Sunday supplements and medical journals. **1948** *Pacific Discovery* March–April 2/2 The kind of stuff which is so far 'popularized' or rehashed in the Sunday supplements . . . is no longer to be relied upon as science.

As the last term in **Congress, Negro Sunday.**

Sunday ˈsʌndɪ, *v. intr.* To spend Sunday. *Colloq.*

1884 *Lisbon* (Dak.) *Clipper* 13 March, H. R. Turner Sundayed in Fargo. **1888** *Milnor* (Dak.) *Teller* 13 July 8/3 W. H. Pelton and Frank Hammond, two of Forman's jolly young men, Sundayed in town. **1909** RICE *Mr. Opp* 103 You read that Uncle Enoch Siller had Sundayed over at the Ridge.

***sundown,** *n.* and *a.*

1. *n.* A hat with a wide brim.

1878 GUILD *Old Times* 46 Now we have the daisy, the sundown, the riverside, and the gipsey hat, costing from twenty-five to fifty dollars each, and which do not cover two inches of the crown, and two must be had for every season, making eight per year. **1935** LINCOLN *Cape Cod Yesterdays* 81 The girls were dressed in their oldest old clothes, with broad-brimmed straw hats—'sundowns' we used to call them. **1948** DICK *Dixie Frontier* 297 In the summer linen or straw sundowns (sunbonnets) were the normal headgear.

2. *beyond sundown*, in the Far West. *Obs.* Cf. next.

1846 *Hancock Eagle* (Nauvoo, Ill.) 10 April 1/5 Captain Sutter . . . recommends those who intend seeking a new home *beyond* 'sun-down', to get there as soon as possible, in order that they may be able to secure lands *gratis*.

3. *a.* Of or pertaining to the Far West.

1846 *Ore. Spectator* 30 April 2/2 The 'Platte Argus' is the most western paper in the United States. We shall soon have to give in our *sundown* position to some enterprising typo who will be *toting* a press to Oregon. *Ib.* 28 May 2/1 Quite a number of *sovereigns* of Clackamas county met in Oregon City, . . . such was their curiosity to witness, in this '*sun-down*' land, scenes with which they had once been familiar in the *far east.* **1948** *Sat. Review* 15 May 32/3 Pacific Books, a publishing house along the country's sundown rim, has brought out this entertaining book with some fine pictures and attractive end papers.

4. (See quots.)

1897 *Boston Transcript* 5 Aug. 5/1 There are sundown doctors, sundown lawyers and sundown ministers. **1944** *N. & Q.* IV. Aug. 71/2 *Sundown lawyers:* Government employees who practice law after their regular working hours (N.Y. *Herald Tribune*, July 28, 1944, p. 9).

Hence **sundowner,** (see quots.). *Colloq. Obs.*

1890 *N. & Q.* IV. 22 March 250 *Sundowner*, in the phrase, 'he's (or she's) a sundowner,' in the sense of a 'hustler.' **1904** *N.Y. Sun* 14 Aug. 17 The Washington sundowner is so called because he practises a profession, usually medicine or dentistry, after the close of Government office hours, or after sundown.

***sunfish,** *n.*

1. Any one of various small American fresh-water fishes of the family Centrarchidae, resembling perches and usu. brilliantly colored. Cf. **sun perch.**

1685 PENN *Further Acct. Pa.* 9 There is the Catfish, . . . Smelt, Sunfish, &c. **1709** LAWSON *Carolina* 157 Sun-Fish are flat and rounder than a Bream, and are reckon'd a fine-tasted Fish. **1860** *Harper's Mag.* March 488/1 The sun-fish, or 'pumpkin-seed,' as that ragged urchin called it, has an interest attached to it in my eyes that any cooking cannot heighten. **1949** *St. Paul Pioneer Press* 12 Aug. 17/3 Fly fishermen reported excellent results in the evening with poppers and bucktail flies on both crappies and sunfish.

b. sunfish (river) bass, (see quot.).

1820 *Western Rev.* II. 53 Sunfish River-bass, *Lepomis icthetoides*, . . . is found in the Kentucky and tributary streams. Vulgar names White Bass, or Sunfish Bass.

2. *W.* A manner of bucking. Cf. **sunfish,** *v.*

1903 *Wide World Mag.* 548 A broncho named 'E.A.' . . . used a combination of 'sunfish' and 'twister.' **1939** ROLLINS *Gone Haywire* 260 One prodigious forward jump, then a 'sunfish,' and the beast raced into a 'circle buck'—one of the most distressing of all gyrations —'swapped ends,' and stopped short.

As the last term in **black-banded, fresh-water, long-eared, mud sunfish.**

sunfish ˈsʌnˌfɪʃ, *v. W. intr.* (See quot. 1888.) Also **sunfishing,** *n. Colloq.*

1888 ROOSEVELT in *Cent. Mag.* April 854/2 [The bronco] may buck steadily in one place, or 'sun-fish,'—that is, bring first one shoulder down almost to the ground and then the other. **1924** W. M. RAINE *Troubled Waters* v. 52 Neither side-bucking nor pitching, sunfishing nor weaving could shake the lean-loined, broad-shouldered figure from his seat. **1949** GANN *Tread of Longhorns* vii, By the time he was fifteen he could 'ride 'em slick' when the bucker went sunfishing.

Hence **sunfisher,** *n.*

1924 W. M. RAINE *Troubled Waters* v. 47 Rocking chair [an outlaw horse] . . . was a noted fence rower, weaver, and sunfisher.

***sunflower,** *n.*

1. The prickly pear, *Opuntia compressa*, of the eastern states. *Rare.*

1737 BRICKELL *N. Carolina* 23 The Sun-Flower, the Indian-Figg, or Prickly-Pear, the Fruit of this Vegetable is frequently eaten.

2. In combs.: (1) **sunflower calico,** calico having a representation of a sunflower in its pattern; (2) **Democracy,** the Democrats of Kansas, cf. **Sunflower State;** (3) **domain,** Kansas, cf. **Sunflower State;** (4) **oil,** oil derived from sunflower seeds; (5) **quilt,** a patchwork quilt of a sunflower pattern; (6) **shuffle,** a way of shuffling cards, *obs.;* (7) **State,** Kansas, the state flower of which is the sunflower.

(1) *a***1846** *Quarter Race Ky.* 84 [The girls] came pourin out of the woods . . . fixed out in all sorts of fancy doins, from the broad-striped homespun to the sunflower calico. — (2) **1905** *N.Y. Times* 8 Aug. 7/7 The Sunflower Democracy now bows to the Missourian, and offers him anything he wants. — (3) **1932** *K.C. Times* 18 March 18 He has observed that Crawford and Cherokee counties are rather moist spots in that great expanse of aridity, the Sunflower domain. — (4) *c***1770** *Amer. Philos. Soc.* I. 308 The sun-flower oil may prove equally valuable with the best Florence oil, for diet or medicine. **1819** *Plough Boy* I. 43 The sun-flower oil was a subject of conversation. **1833** *Amer. R.R. Jrnl.* II. 218/3 Sunflower oil . . . is worth at least as much as linseed.

(5) **1846** *S. Lit. Messenger* XII. 597/2 Tell Patsy to put on the sunflower quilt that your Miss Adaline Amelia made. — (6) *a***1846** *Quarter Race Ky.* 92 He gin 'em [the cards] the Sunflower 'shuffle,' and I the Big Greasy 'cut,' and pushed 'em back. **1855** OLIPHANT *Minnesota* 134 There was the game of Seven-up, . . . involving the mysteries of the 'Sunflower-shuffle' and the 'big greasy cut.' — (7) **1888** *Harper's Mag.* June 39/1 Her citizens affectionately speak of Kansas as the 'Sunflower State.' **1946** *Life* 18 Nov. 18/2 Irate citizens of the sunflower state will write indignant letters claiming that they have lived in Kansas for years.

As the last term in **false, Oregon, spring sunflower.**

∗sunk, *a.* **1. sunk country,** a region which has been lowered by natural subterranean activity of some kind. **2. sunk hole,** a sink hole. Both *obs.*

(1) **1849** Lyell *2nd Visit* II. 178 He took me to a part of the forest [in La.], on the borders of what is called the 'sunk country.' — (2) **1751** in *Amer. Sp.* XV. 399/2 Thence . . . to a Hiccory Standing near a Sunk Hole. **1834** *Ib.*, Thence . . . to a white oak on the East side of a sunk hole.

∗sunken, *a.* Denoting various areas that are low-lying or submerged, as (1) **sunken land,** (2) **prairie,** (3) **swamp.** *Obs.*

(1) **1647** in *Amer. Sp.* XV. 399/1 Six hundred Acres of Land . . . bounded North Upon a pcell of Sunken Land. **1785** *Md. Hist. Mag.* XX. 47 He did . . . attend him in making a Survey of a Lot or tract of sunken land. — (2) **1791** W. Sargent *Diary* 12 We were halted by a swamp or sunken 'Prairie' in our Front. — (3) **1702** in *Amer. Sp.* XV. 399/2 A part of ye parcell of Land . . . Beginning on ye Sunken Swamp att ye mouth of a branch. **1779** *N.H. Hist. Soc. Coll.* VI. 315 Rocky mountains, sunken swamps and burning plains the whole of the way.

b. sunken grass, grass on a low area. *Obs.*

1682 *Southold Rec.* I. 168 All the borders of meadows & krick thatch with the sunken grass at the mouth of Goose Kreek.

sunny ˈsʌnɪ, *n.* **1.** A sunfish. *Colloq.* **2. Sunny South,** the southern states.

(1) **1835** Audubon *Ornith. Biog.* III. 51 The sunny . . . swam to one side, then to another. **1884** Goode *Fisheries* I. 405 The common 'Sunfish,' 'Pumpkin-seed,' or 'Sunny' of the brooks of New York and New England . . . is everywhere abundant in the Great Lake region and in the coastwise streams from Maine to Georgia. — (2) **1846** *Hunt's Merch. Mag.* XV. 127 The author . . . is a true son of the warm and sunny South. **1950** *Chi. Tribune* 11 March 8/3 Eric the redbird . . . flew by, fat 'n' sassy from a sojourn in the sunny south.

Sunshine State. a. South Dakota. **b.** New Mexico. **c.** Florida. **d.** California.

(a) **1918** Visher *So. Dakota* 60 South Dakota is known as 'the Sunshine State,' not because it surpasses in this respect other states, especially those in the southwest, but because of the contrast between South Dakota and the Eastern States and northern European countries from whence most of the persons not born in South Dakota came. **1947** *Denver Post* 23 Feb. A. 10/3 Wealthier shooters . . . have leased many of the choice waterfowl grounds in the Sunshine state. — (b) **1926** *N.M. Hist. Rev.* Jan. 15 The Sunshine State fears no storm. — (c) **1947** *Time* 17 March 42/2 Employees, too, are happier in The Sunshine State where living is so pleasant and healthful. **1948** *Chi. Tribune* 1 Feb. I. 37/2 The sun shone 58 per cent of the possible time, far more than the normal of 44 per cent and closely approaching the average of 60 per cent for Florida, the so-called Sunshine state. — (d) **1949** *Trail Riders Bul.* March 6/1 The papers say that the snow is slowly melting in California (apologies to the sunshine state).

Supai ˈsupaɪ, *n.* [f. *Havasupai* "blue or green water people."] "A small isolated tribe of the Yuman stock . . . who occupy Cataract canyon of the Rio Colorado in N.W. Arizona" (Hodge). In full **Supai Indians.**

1882 *Atlantic Mo.* Oct. 544/2 Mooney's survivors . . . returned to Prescott to tell the story of . . . the strange people whom they called 'Supais,' that they had seen. **1948** *Desert Mag.* Feb. 9/2 A small tribe of Indians—the Supai—live seven miles upstream. **1950** *Nat. Hist.* Feb. 73/1 The Supai Indians of Havasu Canyon in northern Arizona have the nearest approach to Paradise to be found on the North American continent.

supawn səˈpɔn, *n.* Variously spelled, see quot. 1910. [Ultimately f. Indian, cf. Massachusett *saupáun,* softened by water, but immediately f. Du. *sappaen.*] Boiled corn meal or mush.

[*c***1612** Strachey *Dict. Indian Lang.* (1849) 183 Asapan, *a hasty pudding.* *c***1627** in *N.Y. Hist. Soc. Coll.* 2 Ser. II. 348 When they wish to make use of the grain (maize) for bread or porridge which they call 'Sappaen,' they first boil it and then beat it flat upon a stone; then they put it into a wooden mortar . . . and . . . pound it small, and sift it through a small basket . . . of the rushes before-mentioned.] **1671** in *Amer. Sp.* XXI. (1946) 118/2 Their general Food is Flesh, Fish, and *Indian Wheat,* which stamp'd, is boyl'd to a Pap, by them call'd Sappaen. **1754** in Fries *Moravians in N.C.* II. 530 Now [we] must eat Sapan (Indian Corn Porridge) alone, it is well that we have cows, which affords a little milk to it. **1809** Irving *Knickerb.* 327 [The Van Brummels] were the first inventors of Suppawn, or Mush and milk. **1910** Hodge *Amer. Indians* II. 652/2 *Supawn,* [is] spelled also sepawn, sepon, supaen, suppaen, suppawn, etc., by earlier writers. **1949** Kurath *Word Geog. Eastern U.S.* 17/1 The Midland and the South have *mush,* and this expression is also used to some extent in the New England settlement area beside the terms containing *pudding,* in the Hudson Valley beside the local *suppawn.*

attrib. **1834** Traill *Backwoods* 202 Also a preparation made of Indian corn-flour, called supporne-cake, which is fried in slices, and eaten with maple-syrup, were among the novelties of our breakfast-fare. **1857** *Harper's Mag.* March 461/2 The 'suppawn bell' . . . was the signal for all to eat their 'suppawn' or hasty-pudding, and prepare for bed.

b. (See quot.)

1899 Vanderbilt *Flatbush* 106 'Suppawn' was also made from pumpkins boiled, to which was added wheat flour, making it of the consistency of Indian suppawn; this, like the other, was eaten with cream or milk, and was often used for a late supper.

∗super-, *prefix.* **1. super-battleship,** an exceptionally powerful battleship of the latest and most modern design. **2. super-highway,** a highway of superior construction, usu. with lanes well marked off, for especially fast traffic. Also attrib. **3. super-market,** a large foodstore in which the customers select their purchases from open shelves and pay for them on a cash-and-carry basis.

(1) **1945** *Greeley* (Colo.) *D. Tribune* 17 Aug. 1/6 For instance, besides the super-battleship New Jersey, older battleships like the California, New Mexico and New York were not operating with the third fleet at the time. — (2) **1927** *Amer. City* July 46/1 Added to these influences are county and state highway commissions, and a new form of organization created under a special act obtained for that purpose, known as a Super-Highway Commission. **1938** *L.A. Times* 5 Aug. 10/3 First of eight spans over Superhighway completed. **1947** *Dly. Ardmoreite* (Ardmore, Okla.) 11 Aug. 4/1 This superhighway that cuts through the west half of town, north and south is a rather barren and desolate looking thing. — (3) **1946** *This Week Mag.* 17 Aug. 18/2 It was only a step from his giant supermarket to the crossroads store where Grandmother traded eggs for tea. **1949** *World-Herald Mag.* (Omaha) 14 Aug. 23/1 Pat had a job in a super-market.

∗superintendency, *n.* A region under the direction of a Superintendent of Indian Affairs.

1856 Pierce in *Pres. Mess. & P.* V. 363, I herewith communicate to the Senate . . . two treaties recently negotiated by . . . the superintendent of Indian affairs for the northern superintendency. **1871** *Rep. Indian Affairs* (1872) 171 They receive the largest annuity (per capita) of any Indians in the superintendency. **1946** Foreman *Last Trek* 164 Four superintendencies under the commissioner were designated.

∗superintendent, *n.*

1. A federal official in charge of Indian affairs for a certain area; since 1832 such an official responsible to the Commissioner of Indian Affairs in Washington. In full *Superintendent of Indian Affairs.*

1757 *Lett. to Washington* II. 80 Edm[un]d Atkin his Majestys Agent & Superintendent of Indian Affairs in the Southern District of America. **1867** *Wkly. New Mexican* 9 April 1/3 The Apache Indians (the Coyoteros) in 1864, desired to see Dr. Steck, the then superintendent. **1912** *Indian Laws & Tr.* III. 547 [For] the Indian school at Flandreau, South Dakota, and for the pay of Superintendent, sixty-one thousand five hundred dollars. **1946** Foreman *Last Trek* 147 Agent Beach stated their situation on September 1, 1846, in his report to the superintendent of Indian affairs at St. Louis.

2. *Superintendent of Indian Trade,* the former title of the chief of the national Indian Bureau.

1816 Madison in McKenney *Memoirs* I. 18, I do appoint him [Thomas McKenney] superintendent of Indian trade.

3. A conductor in charge of a train or an official in charge of some other form of transportation. *Obs.*

1835 Breck *Recoll.* 275 'Make room for the ladies!' bawled out the superintendent. **1869** J. R. Browne *Adv. Apache Country* 307 As most passengers desire to get an outside seat [on a stagecoach], . . . it is highly important that you should proceed at once to secure the favorable consideration of the superintendent.

b. A railroad administrative officer, as one in charge of a division.

1843 *Hunt's Merch. Mag.* IX. 389 We do not know a more careful or efficient superintendent than C. L. Lynds, Esq. **1885** *Wkly. New Mexican Rev.* 19 March 4/4 The superintendent of the roads running through Atchison, Kansas, raised an important point.

4. An administrative officer in charge of schools, often *Superintendent of Education,* or *Superintendent of Schools.*

1842 Buckingham *Slave States* I. 360 The Secretary of State [in La.] was made 'Superintendent of Education.' **1881** McLean *Cape Cod Folks* 15, I wrote to the Superintendent of the Farmouth schools. **1911** Persons *Mass. Labor Laws* 186 Elasticity of method . . . is one of the great advantages in the issue of certificates by the superintendents in person. **1946** *Democrat* 8 Aug. 1/6 Supt. D. C. Mathews announces that . . . schools will open the week of September 2nd.

5. (See quot. 1909.) Also **district superintendent.**

1909 WEBSTER 1362/2 Presiding elders [are] . . . now called district superintendents in the M.E. Church. **1912** in SANFORD *Rep. Comm. Judiciary, Meth. Epis. Ch.* 143 The Bishops in the Annual Conference appointed a Superintendent to preside over a District containing more than fifty pastoral charges.

As the last term in **county, division, general, Indian, school superintendent.**

* **superior court. 1.** = **Supreme Court 1.** *Obs.* **2.** The supreme court of a state or an intermediate court between this and the lower courts.

(1) **1686** SEWALL *Diary* I. 118 [He] must be relieved by some Superiour Court, as Chauncery. **1771** in *N. Eng. Mag.* ns. XII. 352/2 The Superior or Circuit Court sits here twice a year. — (2) **1777** *Jrnls. Cont. Cong.* IX. 918 Every commissioner before he sits in judgment shall take an oath to be administered by one of the judges of the supreme or superior court of the state. **1809** KENDALL *Travels* I. 178 The courts of the state are a *superior-court,* which performs the circuit of the counties [etc.]. **1911** *Okla. Session Laws* 3 Legisl. 264 A superior court is created by operation of this act.

supersedure ˌsupəˈsidʒə, *n.* The act of setting aside or superseding. — **1788** HAMILTON in *Federalist* lxxxi, An implied supersedure of the trial by jury, in favor of the civil law mode of trial. **1894** *Forum* Feb. 683 No opportunity to vote out the Cabinet which had just come into power, by supersedure of the Wilcox ministry the day before, could possibly occur before May, 1894.

* **supervisor,** *n.* In some states an elected officer charged with the administration of a town, township or county.

1845 *Sandusky* (O.) *Clarion* 8 March 2/4 Unlike our supervisors in Ohio, the supervisor in New York is the principal official of the *town,* corresponding to our *township.* **1882** A. SHAW in *Fortn. Rev.* Oct. 491 The supervisor is both a town and a county officer. He is general manager of town business, and is also a member of the County Board, which is composed of the supervisors of the several towns. **1905** *N.Y. Ev. Post* 11 Oct. 6 He had been a supervisor of his country for 16 years, and for 12 years chairman of the Board of Supervisors.

b. supervisor of penmanship, (see quot.).

1907 *Springfield W. Republican* 9 May 12 The school board voted that the office of supervisor of penmanship be discontinued. . . . Penmanship was not in itself distinctly educational, like drawing, manual training, music and the other departments over which there are supervisors.

As the last term in **county, road supervisor.**

* **supper,** *n.* As the last term in **box, church, donation, Dutch, egg, ice cream, lap, oyster, pie, possum, Spanish supper.**

* **supple,** *a.*

1. * **supplejack,** a jumping jack. Also transf.

1776 CUTLER in *Life & Corr.* I. 55 They made us several presents of the small affairs in the cabins, . . . such as sweetmeats, cayenne-pepper, supple-jacks, cassada or bread. **1791** in *Jrnl. Wm. Maclay* (1927) 390 Schuyler is the supple-jack of his son-in-law Hamilton. **1832** KENNEDY *Swallow Barn* II. 19 He would . . . spring from the floor upwards, flinging out his arms and legs like a supple-jack. **1904** *N.Y. Times* 8 July 5 Those political supplejacks . . . go about with sanctimonious moan, saying: 'The President is wrong but we must support the President.'

b. The woody vine, *Berchemia scandens.*

1788 SCHÖPF *Reise* II. 286 Ein windendes Staudengewächs dieser Art ist der sogenannte Supple Jack, wovon ich aber weder Blätter noch Blüthe gesehen. Es macht einen hölzernen biegsamen Stamm, einen bis zwey Finger dick, und 40- 50- 60 Fuss lang. **1812** STODDARD *Sk. Louisiana* 169 Most of the low lands are covered with underwood, vines, supple jacks, and cane. **1941** R. S. WALKER *Lookout* 57 Occasionally, an adventurer on foot meets in damp ground near the base of the mountain, a pert specimen of supple-jack.

2. supple sawney, (see quot.).

1888 *Cent. Mag.* XXXVI. 771/1 Jumping-jacks, or 'supple sawneys,' were made of pasteboard, and worked their arms and legs through the medium of a cotton string.

* **supplement,** *n.* As the last term in **colored, comic, Sunday supplement.**

Supreme Bench. The U.S. Supreme Court. — **1845** POLK *Diary* (1929) 39, I had a right to nominate Judge Woodward to the Supreme Bench of the United States. **1900** *Cong. Rec.* 5 Feb. 1520/2 No man who is fit to sit on the Supreme Bench . . . would tolerate that cheap demagogy for half a minute.

* **Supreme Court.**

1. In certain of the colonies and states, a court of general jurisdiction composed of a distinct body of judges, often exercising appellate jurisdiction. *Obs.* Cf. **superior court.**

1709 *N.J. Archives* 1 Ser. III. 458 On search of the Docquet of Causes depending in the Supream Court of her Majestys Province of New Jersey, I find [etc.]. **1785** *Warren-Adams Lett.* II. 261 Mr. Dana is appointed one of the Judges of the Supreme Court [in Mass.]. **1872** MCCLELLAN *Golden State* 417 The Supreme Court of California consists of five judges. **1949** *Chi. D. News* 19 Nov. 6/4 The Supreme Court in Illinois and elsewhere has upheld repeatedly that the journal cannot lie.

b. In New York, orig. a court of general jurisdiction, which also served with state senators as a court of impeachment and appeals; since 1869, a court subordinate to the court of appeals; a similar court in New Jersey.

*a***1817** DWIGHT *Travels* III. 277 The Governour, Chancellor, and Judges of the Supreme Court [of New York] . . . are constituted a Council. **1886** *Nevada Rep.* XIX. 342 The name 'supreme court' . . . is given to courts possessing similar jurisdiction to that given to the district courts in this state. **1914** *Cyclo. Amer. Govt.* III. 532/1 The court of chancery [in N.J.] still stands as of equal dignity with the supreme court. **1947** *Christian Cent.* 13 Aug. 964/2 And in New York, State supreme court Justice Isidore Bookstein ruled that a Buffalo attorney . . . had no right to sue.

c. The highest court in the Cherokee Nation.

1828 *Cherokee Phenix* (New Echota, Ga.) 19 Nov. 2/4 Fifteen dollars was appropriated for the benefit of Joshua Buffington and Alfred A. Hudson for illegal fees collected from them by direction of the Supreme Court 1827. **1885** FOSTER *Se-quo-yah* 195 The supreme court consists of three Judges, one of whom is selected by a joint vote of the National Council as Chief Justice.

2. The highest court in the federal system of courts, in full **Supreme Court of the United States.** Also attrib.

1787 *Constitution* ii. § 2 The President . . . shall appoint . . . Judges of the supreme Court. **1816** *Ann. 14th Congress* 2 Sess. 357 Chief Justice and Associate Justices of the Supreme Court of the United States shall cease to be Judges of the Circuit Courts of the United States. **1900** *Cong. Rec.* 8 Jan. 688/1, I for one think the Supreme Court library should be located in that room. **1949** *Sun. World-Herald Mag.* (Omaha) 22 May 2/2 The Supreme Court that Presidents Roosevelt and Truman appointed has disappointed many New Dealers.

* **sure,** *a.* In colloq. combs.: (1) **sure cure,** *n.* an unfailing remedy; (2) **enough,** *a.* actual or genuine; (3) **fire,** *a.* unfailing, certain; (4) **thing,** see as a main entry.

(1) **1881** *Ore. State Jrnl.* 1 Jan. 1/3 No other preparation . . . will give such universal satisfaction as Dr. Keck's Sure Cure For Catarrh. **1932** *K.C. Times* 15 April 20 If someone wants to make a hit with this column he may do it by revealing a sure cure for a spring cold. — (2) *a***1846** *Quarter Race Ky.* 112 It was a man with a sure-enough fence-rail. **1872** *Republican Rev.* 20 Jan. 2/2 We naturally supposed that we were going to have a sure enough circus. **1914** D. W. ROBERTS *Rangers & Sovereignty* 106 We went 'sure enough' fishing to the . . . River. — (3) **1918** V. O. FREEBURG *Photoplay Making* 57 That photoplay included many 'sure fire' pictures, from the dashing waves to the coiling smoke over a burning village. **1946** *Chi. D. News* 7 June 36/2 Is there one sure fire way to be happy?

sure thing. A certainty, a bet upon which one cannot lose. *Colloq.*

1836 HILDRETH *Dragoon Campaigns* 24, I say, stranger, didn't I say that old 'Slow and Easy' was a sure thing, in the end? **1867** *Ball Players' Chron.* 20 June 3/4 Under the circumstances, the friends of the Quakers thought they had a 'sure thing,' and indeed things looked blue for the Keystones. **1950** *Boston Globe Mag.* 12 Feb. 2/4, I won't bet on a sure thing. I call.

attrib. **1903** HAPGOOD *Autobiog. of Thief* 246 There are several kinds of sure-thing grafters. **1915** YOUNG *Hard Knocks* 39 Newton was a rendezvous for gamblers and 'sure-thing' men. **1947** *Amer. Sp.* XXII. 165 The outside-man nudges the mark, raises the shell slightly, and shows the mark that the pea is there. It is a sure-thing bet.

Also as an adv., certainly.

1896 ADE *Artie* 147 'Sure thing,' says he. **1921** PAINE *Comr. Rolling Ocean* 44 Sure thing! They won't bother to look it up.

* **surf,** *n.* In combs.: (1) **surfbird,** a Pacific Coast shore bird, *Aphriza virgata;* (2) **clam,** a large clam, *Spisula solidissima;* (3) **duck,** the surf scoter; (4) **fish,** any of numerous fishes of the family Embiotocidae, living chiefly off the California coast in shallow water, also attrib.; (5) **man,** a member of the crew of a surfboat, esp. in the life-saving service, also **surfmanship;** (6) **perch,** = **surf fish;** (7) **smelt,** a smelt, *Hypomesus pretiosus,* about

twelve inches long, abundant on the northern Pacific Coast, spawning in the surf; (8) **whiting,** silver whiting.

(1) **1839** AUDUBON *Ornith. Biog.* V. 249 Townsend's Surf-Bird . . . was procured . . . on the shores of Cape Disappointment. **1917** *Birds of Amer.* I. 268/1 Ornithologists have been divided as to whether the Surf-bird should be considered a Plover or a Turnstone. — (2) **1883** *Nat. Museum Bul.* No. 27, 260 Hen Clam, Surf Clam, or Sea Clam. Florida and Gulf of Mexico to Labrador. — (3) **1813** WILSON *Ornithology* VIII. 49 *Anas perspicillata.* Black, or Surf Duck. . . . This duck is peculiar to America. **1857** J. G. SWAN *Northwest Coast* 357 The Colonel saw a 'butter-duck' in a shallow creek. . . . These ducks are the black surf-duck. — (4) **1882** *Nat. Museum Bul.* No. 16, 585 The Surf-fishes. . . . Fishes of the Pacific coast of North America, inhabiting bays and the surf on sandy beaches. **1884** GOODE *Fisheries* I. 276 The Surf-Fish Family . . . forms the most characteristic feature of the fauna of our Pacific coast. **1912** *Out West* May 336/1 The lazy fisherman can sit on the wharf . . . and get his reward of smelt or surf fish.

(5) *a***1878** *Harper's Mag.* LVI. 337/2 The beach will be patrolled by the surf-men every night. **1880** *Scribner's Mag.* Jan. 334 Until 1871 . . . surfmanship was not a standard of qualification. **1903** *N.Y. Tribune* 4 Oct., The surfmen rowed ashore, and the bathing season was at an end. — (6) **1885** *Nat. Museum Proc.* VIII. 134 The Development of the Viviparous Surf-Perches or Embiotocidae of the Pacific Coast. — (7) **1882** *Nat. Museum Bul.* No. 16, 294 *Hypomesus.* . . . Surf Smelts. . . . *H[ypomesus] pretiosus.* . . . Surf Smelt. . . . Pacific coast, from California northward. — (8) **1882** JORDAN & GILBERT *Fishes N. Amer.* 933 M[enticirrus] littoralis. . . . Surf Whiting. . . . South Atlantic and Gulf coast.

* **surface,** *n. attrib.*

1. Designating things or actions connected with traffic on city streets. See also **surface car** in **2.** below.

1867 *Harper's Mag.* June 134/2 Soon afterward he was seen in company with George Lanman . . . talking over some matter about a surface railroad. **1893** *Ib.* April 652/1 Here come . . . the surface vehicles . . . of Manhattan. **1909** *N.Y. Ev. Post* (s.-w. ed.) 4 March 1 On streets leading to these ferries surface travel was blocked by heavily laden vehicles stalled. **1946** *Chi. D. News* 24 April 14/2 A Surface Lines' conductor, off duty, kidnapped a streetcar standing at the end of the line.

2. In special combs.: (1) **surface boat,** (see quot. 1859 and cf. **sink boat**), *obs.;* (2) **car,** a streetcar as distinguished from an elevated or subway car; (3) **coal,** *W.* buffalo chips.

(1) **1851** LEWIS *Amer. Sportsman* 189 The Surface-boat. . . . This artful contrivance for the destruction of ducks we claim as entirely American. **1859** BARTLETT 24 *Battery,* a sort of boat used for duck-shooting in the Chesapeake, in which the shooter lies below the surface of the water. It is also called . . . a Surface-boat, Coffin-boat, Sink, or Box. — (2) **1889** HOWELLS *Hazard of Fortunes* II. 208 He stopped at the corner to wait for a surface-car. **1943** MENEFEE *Assignment* 14 Quantities of anti-Semitic leaflets have been left systematically on the seats of subway, 'El' and surface cars. — (3) **1948** *Southwestern Rev.* Summer 238/1 There were other names for the commodity—surface coal, prairie coal, and Babcock coal were just a few of them.

b. *W.* In expressions relating to mining on or near the surface of the ground, as (1) **surface diggings,** (2) **dirt,** (3) **lead,** (4) **placer.**

(1) **1856** *Spirit of Times* 6 Sep. 13/1 In this section the surface diggings . . . are paying well. **1860** *S.F. National* 19 March 3/3 He, with eighteen others, commenced to strike good surface diggings, going North, from the mouth of the Okenagen river. — (2) **1851** *S.F. Sun. Dispatch* 3 Aug. 3/1 Gold has lately been found in the surface dirt on a hill near the North Fork of the American. **1897** LEONARD *Gold Fields Klondike* 21 They found their claims washed $10 to the pan of surface dirt. — (3) **1906** *Out West* Feb. 87 There grew a swift and dangerous tradition that Arizona was a land of 'surface leads,' and that it was sheer waste of good hope and good money to follow them into the earth. — (4) **1853** *S.F. Comm. Advt.* 9 Dec. 2/2 These two works will supply water for several thousand acres of dry surface placers. **1948** JOHNSTON *Gold Rush* 12/2 The wild, insouciant time of flush production from the surface placers was of comparatively short duration.

surfer ˈsɜfɚ, *n.* A surf scoter. *Colloq.* — **1876** *Forest & Stream* 9 Nov. 212/3 List of Gunner's Names for Birds and Wild Fowl obtained in Plymouth Bay, Mass.: . . . *Pelionetta perspicillata.* Surfer. **1917** *Birds of Amer.* I. 151.

* **surgeon,** *n.*

1. surgeon dentist, a dental surgeon. *Obs.*

The earliest evidence so far found for this term is American, but the first dentists in this country to use the title were from England. They had prob. been accustomed to the expression before they came here.

1768 in H. M. BROOKS *Gleanings* IV. 21 All Persons who have had false Teeth fixt by Mr. John Baker, Surgeon-Dentist. **1836** *Niles' Reg.* 29 Oct. 144/3 The surgeon dentist, Aldis Brainard, . . . was indicted for having as many wives as a sultan. **1851** *Knickerb.* XXXVII. 97 Dr. N. Dodge . . . [is] one of the most experienced, skilful, and popular surgeon-dentists in New-York.

2. surgeon fish, one of numerous fishes of the genus *Acanthurus* and of the family Acanthuridae.

1871 *Harper's Mag.* July 191/2 The terror of all, the surgeon-fish, . . . boldly swims in every quarter, opening and shutting his lancet, threatening to bleed every thing that comes in his way. **1911** *Rep. Fisheries 1908* 317/1 Surgeon-Fish (*Teuthis hepatus*). — This is the Tang common from Carolina to Florida. . . . Also known as 'lancet-fish.'

As the last term in **dental, police, tree surgeon.**

* **surprise party.** An unannounced party given as a surprise to a person. Also transf.

1859 REDPATH *Roving Editor* 86 Was he never at a husking, . . . a bee, a surprise party, a 'social'? **1901** MERWIN & WEBSTER *Calumet 'K'* 268 There's no telling what sort of a surprise party those railroad fellows may have for us. **1950** *Chi. Tribune* 21 April II. 12/3 Mrs. Drake at once arranged a surprise party.

* **surrender,** *n. S.* The surrender of General Lee at Appomattox Court House, Va., April 9, 1865, ending the Civil War.

1881 *Uniontown Press* 15 Jan. 3/3 The determination of the planters in the Canebrake . . . to make a crop this year exceeds that of any previous year since the surrender. **1941** H. BRICKELL *Prize Stories* 26, I never did go to school—I was too old at the Surrender. **1943** HOLT *Carver* 132 Set one of the old people to talking about the days before surrender . . . he would surely relate how he or one of his fellow slaves . . . ran away.

* **surrey,** *n.* [See note.] A four-wheeled, two-seated pleasure carriage, often with a flat rectangular top with fringe along the edges, and sometimes with a cut-under bottom. Now *hist.*

Surrey *c*1900

"'Originally applied to an adaptation of the Surrey cart (an English pleasure cart with an open spindle seat first built in the county of Surrey) introduced into the U.S.A. by J. B. Brewster & Co. of New York in 1872.' (*The Hub* March 1882)" (*OED*).

1895 HOWELLS *Day of Their Wedding* 32 There was . . . a rank of stately hacks and barrouches, and light, wood-colored surreys and phaetons. **1903** *N.Y. Tribune* 27 Sep., When the President drives he prefers the 80-year old surrey which belonged to his father. **1949** *Sun. World-Herald Mag.* (Omaha) 22 May 5/3 In background is a surrey with the fringe on top.

attrib. and *transf.* **1904** *Scientific Amer.* 30 Jan. 75/2 Steam cars of the surrey and runabout types . . . were shown by other manufacturers.

* **surrogate,** *n.* In New York, New Jersey, and a few other states, a county or municipal judicial officer charged with probating wills, settling estates, and, sometimes, appointing guardians for minors and incompetent persons.

1784 *N.J. Archives* XXIII. p. lxxi, An Act to Ascertain the Power and Authority of the Ordinary and his Surrogates. **1834** *Jamestown* (N.Y.) *Jrnl.* 22 Oct. 1/5 Who holds the office of Surrogate in this County? **1885** *Harper's Mag.* May 847/2 The Surrogate of Albany County refused to entertain the application. Application was recently made to the Surrogate of Albany for letters of administration upon the personalty of Mrs. Anneke Bogardus. **1948** *N.Y. Star* 30 June 18/2 Like nearly everybody, we are interested in only one phase of the row going on about the Surrogate's job.

b. surrogates' court, (see quot.).

*c***1830** *Williams's N.Y. Ann. Reg. 1830* 238 Surrogates' Courts, having jurisdiction of testamentary case held by the surrogates of each county.

surround səˈraʊnd, *n. W.* A method of hunting animals by surrounding a herd and driving them over a precipice, into a deep ravine or other place from which they cannot escape. Cf. **antelope surround, cerne, piskun.**

1833 CATLIN *Indians* I. 199 The plan of attack, which in this country is familiarly called a 'surround,' was explicitly agreed upon. **1889** H. O'REILLY *50 Yrs. on Trail* 37 They go out after the buffalo . . . make what is termed a surround . . . then ride in a circle round them. **1932** VESTAL *Sitting Bull* 198 It was plenty there, they made a big surround, and afterward stayed in camp, feasting.

***survey,** *n.* "A district for the collection of the customs, under the inspection and authority of a particular officer" (*Cent.*). — **1791** *State P.* (1819) I. 24 The powers . . . , which respect the sub-divisions of the districts into surveys . . . have likewise been carried into effect.

As the last term in **coast, field, geological, government survey.**

***surveyor,** *n.* As the last term in **county, government surveyor.**

surveyor general. A federal officer in charge of the survey of public lands in a particular area.

1790 *Ann. 1st Congress* 1719 Resolved, That a Surveyor General for the United States be appointed. **1835** JACKSON in *Pres. Mess. & P.* III. 132 Charges . . . may have been made to me against the official conduct of Gideon Fitz, late surveyor-general south of the State of Tennessee. **1900** *Cong. Rec.* 17 Feb. 1903/1 The surveyor-general of that State [Nevada] writes me that there are more inquiries for public land than there have been for years.

***Susan,** *n.* As the last term in **brown-eyed, lazy, sweet Susan.**

***suspend,** *v. tr.* To discipline or punish (a student) by forcing him to withdraw from school for a time. — **1818** in J. MACLEAN *Hist. College of N.J.* II. 175 This morning we suspended one student. **1871** BAGG *At Yale* 256 The combatants . . . who are caught are heavily 'marked' or even 'suspended.'

suspension railway. (See quot. 1876.) *Obs.*

1832 *Amer. R.R. Jrnl.* I. 51/1 We have recently had an opportunity to examine a model of a Suspension Rail Way. **1833** *Ib.* II. 738/3 We were particularly interested with the novelty of a Suspension Railway . . . this truly American invention. **1876** KNIGHT 2464/1 Suspension-railway. A railway in which the carriage is suspended from an elevated track, one carriage on each side of a single track, so as to balance; or suspended between two tracks.

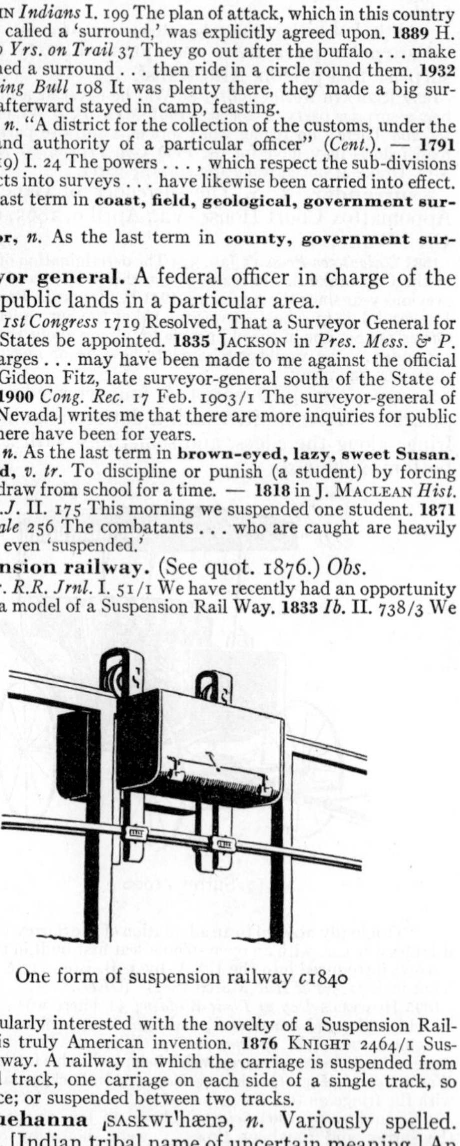

One form of suspension railway *c*1840

Susquehanna ˌsʌskwɪˈhænə, *n.* Variously spelled. See quots. [Indian tribal name of uncertain meaning.] An Indian of an Iroquoian tribe formerly living on the Susquehanna River; also, *pl.*, the tribe. Also **Susquehanna Indians.**

1612 SMITH *Virginia* I. 19 The people differ very much in stature, . . . some being very great as the *Sesquesahamocks*, others very little as the *Wighcocomocoes*. **1676** *New Castle Court Rec.* 39 If the Sasquehannos should aply to you for anything, you are to use them kindly. **1751** *N.J. Archives* 1 Ser. VII. 598 The Susquahannah Indians only want leave from the Mohawks whom they call their Fathers in order to their accepting of a missionary. **1833** KERCHEVAL *History* xxiv, He ran amongst his men, crying out . . . these are our friends the Susquehanoughs. **1940** CLARKE *Bloody Mohawk* 36 The Iroquois, about 1660, turned their attention to the Andastes, or Susquehannocks of Pennsylvania and southern New York

b. Susquehanna purchase, a purchase of land in the region of the Susquehanna River.

1768 in C. HAZARD *Thos. Hazard* 246 To the Company or proprietors of the Susquehanna Purchase . . . I hereby Certify [etc.].

c. Susquehanna salmon, a salmon of a variety found in the Susquehanna River.

1871 *Game Laws* (Penn.) in *Fur, Fin & Feather* (1872) 122 The species commonly known as Susquehanna salmon, pike, perch, jack salmon . . . shall henceforth not be taken . . . during their spawning time.

Susquehannian ˌsʌskwɪˈhænɪən, *n.* A European inhabitant of the Susquehanna region. *Obs.* — **1676** in FORCE *Tracts* I. No. 9, 3 The Susquehanians and Marylanders of friendes being ingaged enimyes (as hath by former letter bin hinted to you).

sussexite ˈsʌsɛksˌaɪt, *n.* (See quot. 1909.) — **1868** G. T. BRUSH in *Amer. Jrnl. Sci.* 2 Ser. XLVI. 242 Sussexite may be regarded as an analogous compound in which 2/3 of the water is replaced by manganese and magnesia. **1909** *Cent. Supp.* 1304/1 sussexite. . . . A hydrous borate of manganese, magnesium, and zinc . . . occurring in white fibrous forms at Franklin Furnace, Sussex county, New Jersey.

sutler('s) store. A store kept by a sutler.

1845 GREEN *Texian Exped.* 276 We had the privilege of buying brandy at the tienda, shop, a kind of sutler store. **1863** *Rio Abajo Press* 27 Jan. 3/1 Sutler Store, Albuquerque, New Mexico. **1923** J. H. COOK *On Old Frontier* 54 Jack went up to the fort, . . . and accidentally left his quirt in the sutler's store.

Suwarrow səˈwɔro, *n.*[1] [A. V. *Suwarrow* (Suvorov) (1729–1800), Russian field marshal.] A type of cavalry boot. In full **Suwarrow boot.** *Obs.* — **1805** *Lancaster* (Pa.) *Jrnl.* 29 March (Th.), [Egbert Taylor advertises] Cossacks, Suwarrows, Buck-straps, Fire-buckets [etc.]. **1860** *Harper's Mag.* Aug. 351/2 He bought himself a pair of Suwarrow boots then [*c*1800] just coming into fashion in the Eastern cities.

suwarrow səˈwɑro, *n.*[2] A variant (f. the Amer. Sp. *sahuaro*) of **saguaro.**

1864 *Harper's Mag.* Nov. 693/1 A difference of opinion exists as to whether the petayah is not a distinct species from the suaro. **1884** SARGENT *Rep. Forests* 90 *Cereus giganteus*. . . . Suwarrow. Saguaro. Giant Cactus. . . . A tall, columnar tree, 8 to 18 meters in height. **1894** *Garden & Forest* 22 Aug. 334/2 The Suwarro . . . dots the . . . mesas of southern Arizona.

swaar swɑr, *n.* [?Du. *zwaar*, large.] A large, medium-late variety of apple of fine quality.

1847 IVES *N. Eng. Fruit* 42 *Swaar*.—This is a large apple, the form round, somewhat flat. **1850** S. WARNER *Wide, Wide World* xxii, 'What a great monster!' 'That's a Swar; they ain't as good as most of the others.' **1875** BURROUGHS *Winter Sunshine* 140 Those late ripeners are the winter varieties—the Rhode Island greenings or swaars of their kind. **1942** *Stand. Plant Names* 241/1.

***swab,** *n. transf.* A naval officer. *Rare.* — **1850** H. MELVILLE *White Jacket* II. xliii. 289 Touch your tile whenever a swob (officer) speaks to you.

swaddle bill. A kind of duck (see quot. 1917). — **1709** LAWSON *Carolina* 151 Swaddle-Bills are a sort of an Ash-Colour'd Duck, which have an extraordinary broad bill, and are good meat. **1917** *Birds of Amer.* I. 126 Shoveller. *Spatula clypeata*. . . . [Also called] Shovel-bill; Swaddle-bill; Butter Duck.

***Swainson,** *n.* [Wm. *Swainson* (1789–1855), Eng. naturalist.] Used in the possessive in the names of species or varieties of birds (see quots.).

1858 BAIRD *Birds Pacific R.R.* 19 *Buteo Swainsoni*, . . . Swainson's Buzzard, . . . [is] more nearly related to a generic form of the Old World (typical *Buteo*) than any bird hitherto discovered inhabiting the continent of America. *Ib.* 252 *Helmitherus Swainsonii*. Swainson's Warbler. . . . South Atlantic States. **1869** *Amer. Naturalist* III. 31 Swainson's Thrush (*Turdus Swainsonii*). . . . Common at Cœur d'Aleñe Mission up to the 22d [of Sep.]. **1917** *Birds of Amer.* III. 85/2 The Mexican, or Swainson's, Cliff Swallow (*Petrochelidon lunifrons melanogastra*) . . . visits Arizona for [breeding]. *Ib.* 105/2 In western North America there is a smaller and darker form of [the warbling vireo] . . . , known as the Western, or Swainson's, Warbling Vireo (*Vireoslyva gilva swainsoni*).

b. Esp. **Swainson's hawk,** a western hawk or species of hawk having a rufous breast-band and white plumage on the under side.

1895 *Dept. Agric. Yrbk. 1894* 222 The food of Swainson's hawk . . . is of much the same character as that of the two preceding species. **1939** LINCOLN *Migration* 79 Observers in the Great Plains saw large flocks of Red-tailed Hawks, Swainson's Hawks and Rough-legged Hawks wheeling majestically in long spirals. [**1945** MATHEWS *Talking* 199 Marsh hawks quarter the ravines. The Swainson's sit on the tops of the blasted trees, waiting for something, but I don't know what, since I have never seen them catch anything.]

* **swale,** *n.* A marshy or moist depression in a level or rolling area. Cf. **ash swale.**

1667 *Dedham Rec.* IV. 135 He may cutt in a place called the Swale, adjoyning to the Ceader Swampe. **1819** THOMAS *Travels* 98 In the country east of the mountains, its use would be very limited, for *swales* are nearly unknown; but in the western parts of New-York, these are so numerous that without it our language would be defective. I define it, a draught in the land which receives and conveys off the superfluous water, without being gullied; moist, but furnishing no stream fed by fountains. **1913** CATHER *O Pioneers!* 83 South of the hill, in a low, sheltered swale, surrounded by a mulberry hedge, was the orchard. **1949** HOWELL *Marin Flora* 15 The wetter swales . . . support rank growths of grasses, sedges, and rushes in the form of large tussocks.

attrib. **1838** *Mass. Agric. Survey 1st Rep.* 19 Considerable quantities of fresh meadow or swale hay is cut. **1873** *Vt. Bd. Agric. Rep.* II. 189 [If] the lightest were swale grass, . . . I would cut it in June.

* **swallow,** *n.* In combs.: (1) **swallow-fork,** (*a*) chiefly *S.* a V-shaped earmark for cattle, suggestive of the fork of a swallow's tail, *colloq.*, cf. * **fork,** *n.* **2,** (*b*) **swallow-fork coat,** a swallow-tailed coat; (2) **-'s tail,** =**swallow-fork** (*a*), *obs.;* (3) * **tail,** see as a main entry; (4) **tree,** (see quot.), *obs.*

(1) (*a*) **1636** *Plymouth Rec.* 1 Every mans marke of his Cattle. . . . Christopher Waddesworth a swallow forke. **1746** *Va. Gazette* 9 Jan., A small Black and White Cow . . . is mark'd with a Crop in the right Ear and a Swallow Fork in the left. **1946** *Democrat* 6 June 2/4 Strayed . . . a red heifer with white star in face, . . . marked swallowfork in left, two splits in right. (*b*) **1912** COBB *Back Home* 308, I still remember his swallowfork coat and his white neckerchief. — **(2) 1667** *Essex Inst. Coll.* XXXVII. 218 Richard Gardner his mark, a swallows taile on ye left ear and a half penny under ye right. **1715** *Topsfield Rec.* I. 189 Taken up by Nathaniel Borman . . . a stray Heifer; . . . a Swallows Tail cut out of both Ears. **1845** *Portsmouth* (R.I.) *Rec.* 387 The Ear Mark of the Creatures . . . is a fork or Swallows tail on the right ear. — **(4) 1812** WILSON *Ornithology* V. 50 This place of repose [for chimney swallows] . . . is usually a large hollow tree open at top, trees of that kind, or *Swallow trees*, as they are usually called, having been noticed in various parts of the country.

As the last term in **chimney, cliff, eave(s), green blue, jug, mud, Republican, rough-winged, sand, stump, tree, white-bellied swallow.**

* **swallowtail,** *n.*

1. =**swallow-fork** (*a*). *Obs.*

1636 *Plymouth Rec.* 1 Mr John Weekes a swallow tayle cut out on the left eare. **1644** *Md. Archives* IV. 288 John Price entred for the mark of his cattell . . . swallow-taile in the left eare & slitt the right eare.

2. (See quot. 1914.) Also **Swallow Tail Democracy** *Obs.*

1875 *Nation* 1 April 218 In this city [New York, there are amon Democrats] two sets of politicians known familiarly as 'Short Hair and 'Swallow-Tails.' **1882** McCABE *New York* 167 The Manhatt Club . . . is the headquarters of what is known in New York as 't Swallow Tail Democracy.' **1914** *Cyclo. Amer. Govt.* III. 464/1 *Swall Tails*, a derisive term applied to men prominent in fashionable circ who have gained some influence in politics.

3. =**swallow-tailed kite.**

1917 *Birds of Amer.* II. 60/2 No other North American bird proaches the Swallow-tail in the grace and beauty of its flight.

4. a. swallow-tailed flycatcher, =**scissor-tail(flycatcher. b. swallow-tailed kite,** a graceful *Elanoides forficatus*, having a deeply forked tail.

(a) 1858 [see **scissortail(ed) flycatcher**]. — **(b) 1872** COUE *to Birds* 211 *Nauclerus* . . . Swallow-tailed Kite.

swaly ˈsweli, *a.* Marshy or swampy. — **1792** *Mass. H.S.* Ser. I. 272 There are pretty large tracts of swaily or swamp **1874** *Vt. Bd. Agric. Rep.* II. 420 The Cotswolds are just the improve springy, swaly pastures.

swammock ˈswɑmək, *n.* (See quot. 1863.) — **1863** *Rep. Agric. 1862* 63 Low hummocks . . . from the fact of their pa ing of the nature of hummocks and swamps, are sometimes swammocks. **1889** *N. & Q.* III. 285 In Florida, the term *hammock* (for a certain description of land), is sometimes abl to *swam-mock.*

* **swamp,** *n.* [See note.]

The earliest available examples of this word occur with to Virginia, but the term had no doubt existed earlier in Great Britain. See the *OED* entries *Swamp* and *Sump.* Th tions into which *swamp* has entered in American use are too to be fully illustrated here. Some, as **swamp angel, a blueberry, cheese, oak, pine, pink, rose, Spanish oak, white oak,** are given as main entries.

1. In the names of trees and shrubs: (1) **swamp buttonwood,** the buttonbush, *Cephalanthus occidentalis;* (2) **cabbage,** =**cabbage palmetto,** cf. **c.** (1) below; (3) **cedar,** a white cedar, *Chamaecyparis thyoides;* (4) **gum,** =**black gum;** (5) **hickory,** the bitternut hickory or the water hickory; (6) **honeysuckle,** the swamp azalea, *Rhododendron viscosum;* (7) **huckleberry,** the highbush blueberry, *Vaccinium corymbosum,* cf. **swamp blueberry** as a main entry; (8) **laurel,** (*a*) the sweet bay, *Magnolia virginiana,* (*b*) the bog kalmia, *Kalmia polifolia;* (9) **magnolia,** =**swamp laurel** (*a*); (10) **maple,** (*a*) the red maple, (*b*) (see quots.); (11) **sassafras,** =**swamp laurel** (*a*); (12) **sumac,** =**poison sumac;** (13) **willow,** the pussy willow.

(1) 1754 ELIOT *Field-Husb.* v. 123 The Brush was . . . Swamp Button Wood, the most difficult to subdue of any Wood I know. — **(2) 1942** KENNEDY *Palmetto Country* 3 Folks outside the region usually think of the palmetto as the tall palm which is locally called the swamp cabbage or cabbage palm. — **(3)** *a***1817** DWIGHT *Travels* I. 39 The swamp cedar . . . is extensively used for shingles. **1868** *Amer. Naturalist* II. 334. — **(4) 1802** ELLICOTT *Journal* 288 In the middle states it is generally found on the common swamp gum, (Nyssa integrifolia). **1834** R. BAIRD *Valley Miss.* xxi. 265 The Cypress and Swamp gum are large in the swampy lands.

(5) 1805 *Ann. 9th Congress* 2 Sess. 1090 The growth, on . . . the highest [places is] handsome oaks, swamp hickory, ash, grape vines, &c. **1938** MATSCHAT *Suwannee River* 161 They alus stuck togither tightern the bark on a swamp hickory. — **(6) 1814** O. O. RICH *Amer. Plants* 23. **1869** FULLER *Flower Gatherers* 59 The *Azaleas*, or *Swamp Honeysuckles*, are beautiful cousins of the Rhodora. **1941** R. S. WALKER *Lookout* 48 Wild honeysuckle, and white swamp honeysuckle are common floral residents. — **(7) 1800** J. MAUDE *Niagara* 8 The swamp huckleberry, a tall shrub like the alder. **1865** BURROUGHS in *Atlantic Mo.* May 520/2 That clump of Swamp-Huckleberry conceals three or four different songsters. — **(8)** (*a*) **1743** CLAYTON *Flora Virginica* 83 *Magnolia Laurifolio*, . . . Swamp-Laurel. **1814** PURSH *Flora Amer.* II. 381 This species is known by the names of Swamp Sassafras, Sweet Bay, Swamp Laurel, and Beaver-wood. **1884** SARGENT *Rep. Forests* 20. (*b*) **1817–8** EATON *Botany* (1822) 325. **1869** FULLER *Flower Gatherers* 138 The farmers around here call it 'Swamp-Laurel.' — **(9) 1813** MUHLENBERG *Cat. Plants* 53 *Magnolia glauca*, Swamp magnolia.

(10) (*a*) **1810** MICHAUX *Arbres* I. 28. **1869** STOWE *Oldtown Folks* 153 Here and there, a swamp-maple seemed all one crimson flame. **1947** *Sat. Ev. Post* 15 March 145/1 The marshy land on both sides of the ridge, land burgeoning with swamp maples, sumac [etc.]. (*b*) **1891** *Cent.* 6099/1 *Swamp-maple*, . . . *Negundo Californicum*, of the Coast . . . in California. **1909** *Ib. Supp.* 1304/2 *Swamp-maple*, . . . the . . . The mountain-maple. — **(11) 1785** MARSHALL . . . or Swamp Sassafras . . . grows . . . PURSH *Flora* II. 381

Chêne chataignier, Swamp's Chesnut Oak.] **1832** Browne *Sylva* 286 Farther south . . . it is called *Chesnut White Oak, Swamp Chesnut Oak*, and . . . *White Oak*. **1940** Deam *Flora Indiana* 383 Quercus Prinus L. (*Quercus Michauxii* Nutt.) Swamp Chestnut Oak. — **(4) 1884** Sargent *Rep. Forests* 172 *Populus heterophylla*. . . . River Cottonwood. Swamp Cottonwood. **1933** Small *Southeastern Flora* 412 P[opulus] heterophylla. . . . (Swamp-cottonwood. Black-cottonwood. Downy-poplar.)

(5) 1907 Lyons *Plant Names* 454 T[axodium] distichum. . . . Southern or Virginia Cypress, Swamp Cypress, Sabino-tree. **1948** *Pacific Discovery* Sep.–Oct. 8/1 These staminate aments show a marked resemblance to those of the swamp cypress, *Taxodium*. — **(6) 1924** Deam *Shrubs of Indiana* 109 Rubus hispidus Linnaeus. Swamp Dewberry. **1942** Tehon *Native Ill. Shrubs* 116 The Swamp Dewberry grows near lakes and marshes, especially at the base of wooded slopes. . . . It ranges from Nova Scotia to Georgia and west to Minnesota and Kansas. — **(7) 1815** Drake *Cincinnati* 76 The botanical resources of this. . . . Forest of the Miami country [include] . . . *Cornus candidissima*, Swamp dogwood. **1931** Clute *Plants* 93 There is also a swamp dog-wood (*Ptelea trifoliata*). — **(8) 1853** Strickland *Twenty-seven Yrs.* II. 49 They construct for temporary purposes, a ruder-built one made out of an entire roll of the bark of the swamp-elm. **1921** Deam *Trees of Indiana* 140 Ulmus americana Linnæus. White Elm. . . . This species is also called water elm, swamp elm, gray elm, bitter elm, sour elm and in southwestern counties it is often called red elm. — **(9) 1833** Eaton *Botany* (ed. 6) 305 *Ribes lacustris*, swamp gooseberry. *a*1862 Thoreau *Maine Woods* 223, I also saw the swamp gooseberry (*Ribes lacustre*), with green fruit.

(10) 1907 Lyons *Plant Names* 242 I[lex] decidua. . . . Swamp or Meadow Holly, Bearberry, Possum Haw. **1938** Matschat *Suwannee River* 118 The older women . . . preferred a pungent drink brewed from the leaves of yaupon, the swamp holly. — **(11) 1814** Bigelow *Florula Bostoniensis* 248 *Nyssa villosa*, Tupelo tree, Swamp Hornbeam. . . . This tree grows in swamps. **1907** Lyons *Plant Names* 322 N[yssa] sylvatica. . . . Pepperidge, Sour Gum, Tupelo, Swamp Hornbeam, Black Gum, Yellow Gum, Beetle-bung, Hornbine, Hornpine, Hornpipe. — **(12) 1814** Pursh *Flora* II. 633 Quercus lyrata. . . . This oak is from eight to fifteen feet high, and known under the names of Over-cup Oak, Swamp-post Oak, and Water White Oak. **1894** Coulter *Bot. W. Texas* III. 414 *Quercus lyrata*. (Over-cup oak. Swamp post oak.) River swamps. **1933** Small *Southeastern Flora* 425 Q[uercus] lyrata. . . . (Overcup-oak. Swamp white-oak. Water white-oak. Swamp post-oak.) — **(13) 1666** *Plymouth Rec.* 87 On the south side and east side of the said land [I] have bounded it with a swamp wood tree. **1668** *Boston Rec.* 41 A white swamp wood [is] by some called a plumb tree.

c. In the names of herbaceous plants: (1) **swamp cabbage, = skunk cabbage,** also attrib., cf. **1.** (2) above; (2) **grass,** any one of various coarse grasses or rushes found in swamps; (3) **hellebore,** the American or false hellebore, *Veratrum viride;* (4) **lily,** any one of various plants growing in low or swamp ground (see quots.); (5) **milkweed,** a common American milkweed, *Asclepias incarnata;* (6) **potato,** (see quot. 1917); (7) **wire grass,** fowl grass, *Poa palustris*.

(1) 1793 in M. Cutler *Life* (1888) II. 292, I am pleased that in the new Edition of Genera Plantarum our Swamp Cabbage (or Dracontium foetodum) is removed to the fourth class, where, according to your observation, it belongs. **1880** *Harper's Mag.* June 66 The swamp-cabbage flower . . . peers above the ground beneath his purple spotted hood. — **(2) 1845** Frémont *Exped.* 206 Only the high swamp grass appeared above. **1950** *Amer. Photography* Feb. 70/2 A pond which I constructed in my studio had all the natural pond growth such as cat-o'-nine-tails, waterlilies, arrowhead, ferns, and swamp grass. — **(3) 1751** Eliot *Field-Husb.* iii. 66 Take the Roots of Swamp Hellebore, sometimes called Skunk Cabbage, Tickle Weed, [illegible]ar Root. **1874** Garrod & Baxter *Materia Med.* (1880) 382 Ameri[illegible]r Green Hellebore; called also Swamp Hellebore and Indian [illegible] — **(4) 1737** Brickell *N. Carolina* 21 Another Weed, vulgarly [illegible] *Swamp-Lillie* . . . grows in the Marshes and low Grounds, [illegible]hing like our *Dock* in its Leaves. **1857** *Knickerb.* XLIX. [illegible]wamp, with green slime, and the swamp-lily moving [illegible]it. **1909** Webster 2090/3 *Swamp lily*, . . . a white [illegible] *Crinum* (*C. angustifolium*) of the southern U.S. [illegible]n *Flora* 321 C[rinum] americanum . . . (Swamp- [illegible]3 *A*[*sclepias*] *incarnata*. (Swamp Milk- [illegible] **1882** *Cent. Mag.* May 153/2 The only [illegible] we would recommend for the wild [illegible] . . . the four-leaved milkweed [illegible]rlington *Higher Plants Mich.* [illegible]owers as the cardinal flower [illegible] (*Asclepias incarnata*) and [illegible] *Comm. Patents 1849:* [illegible] is found in mud and water about 3 feet deep. **1917** Kephart *Camping* II. 374 *Arrowhead, Broad-Leaved.* Swan or Swamp Potato *Sagittaria latifolia* (*S. variabilis*). . . . Tuberous roots as large as hens' eggs, were an important article of food among the Indians. — **(7) 1751** J. Eliot *Field-Husb.* 13 It [i.e., fowl grass] is suppos'd to be brought into the Meadows at Hartford by the Annual Floods, and called there Swamp-wire Grass. **1820** *Plough Boy* I. 310 The other is Fowl Meadow, sometimes called Duck-Grass, and sometimes Swamp-wire-grass.

2. In the names of animals, chiefly birds: (1) **swamp blackbird,** a red-winged blackbird; (2) **garter,** (see quot.), *obs.;* (3) **hare,** (see quot.); (4) **hawk, = marsh hawk;** (5) **owl,** (see quot. 1917); (6) **partridge,** (see quot.); (7) **quail,** (see quot.); (8) **rabbit,** a rabbit, *Sylvilagus aquaticus*, or a related species, found in wet places in the southern Mississippi Valley; (9) **robin,** any one of various thrushes, esp. the wood thrush *q.v.* (see also quot. 1810); (10) **sheldrake,** (see quot.); (11) **sparrow,** a fringilline sparrow, *Melospiza georgiana*, related to the song sparrow and found in swamps in the South and East; (12) **warbler,** any one of various American warblers found in swamps, also with specifying terms, cf. **pine swamp warbler.**

(1) 1794 *Amer. Philos. Soc.* IV. 108 Red-winged-maize-thief. [Note:] Commonly called, in Pennsylvania, the Swamp-black-bird. **1895** *Outing* XXVII. 75/1 A huge flock of swamp blackbirds covered the ground. — **(2) 1842** *Nat. Hist. N.Y., Zoology* III. 45 The Striped Snake, *Tropidonotus taenia*, . . . is known under various popular names, such as . . . Swamp Garter. — **(3) 1891** *Cent.* 6098/3 swamp-hare, . . . a large, long-limbed hare or rabbit, *Lepus aquaticus*, inhabiting the fresh-water swamps and bayous of the southern United States. — **(4) 1892** Harris *U. Remus & Friends* 5 Dey er done broke in ter ketchin' chickens—de goshawk, de swamphawk en de bluedarter.

(5) 1853 *Harper's Mag.* Nov. 771/1 With night came . . . the screech of the swamp-owl. **1917** *Birds of Amer.* II. 101 Short-eared Owl. *Asio flammeus*. . . . [Also called] Swamp Owl. *Ib.* 103 Barred Owl. *Strix varia varia*. . . . [Also called] Swamp Owl. — **(6) 1874** Coues *Birds N.W.* 394 Canada Grouse; Spruce Grouse. . . . [Also called] Spruce Partridge, Wood Partridge, Swamp Partridge. — **(7) 1778** MacKenzie *Diary* I. 256 No birds have been seen yet, except such as remain here [Newport, R. I.] during the Winter, which are the Meadow-lark, or Swamp-Quail, the Snow bird, the Quails, and a few Snipes. — **(8) 1845** Lyell *Second Visit* I. 228, I had heard much of the swamp-rabbit, which they hunt near the coast in South Carolina and Georgia. **1875** *Fur, Fin & Feather* (ed. 3) 136/1 The 'swamp rabbit' inhabits the heavy timbered woodlands and river bottoms. **1949** *N.M. Quart. Rev.* Spring 90 Swamp rabbits . . . with boiled turnips and corn bread, were occasional treats. — **(9) 1769** Smith *Tour* 41 The lively Note of the Swamp Robin, the Red Bird and other Birds from the earliest Dawn is entertaining. **1810** Wilson *Amer. Ornith.* II. 36 In Virginia, he [*sc.* the towhee bunting] is called the Bulfinch . . . in Pennsylvania, the chewink, and by others the Swamp Robin. **1946** Richter *Fields* 189 All Guerdon could hear were the sweet lonesome notes of the swamp robin.

(10) 1844 *Nat. Hist. N.Y., Zoology* II. 318 The Buff-Breasted Sheldrake. *Mergus Merganser*. . . . The female . . . is called Weaser, or Swamp Sheldrake. — **(11) 1811** Wilson *Ornithology* III. 49 [The] Swamp Sparrow, *Fringilla Palustris* [frequents] . . . the immense cypress swamps and extensive grassy flats of the southern states. **1872** Coues *Key to Birds* 138 Swamp Sparrow, . . . a common inhabitant of low thickets, swamps and marshes. **1949** *Boston Globe Mag.* 18 Sep. 10/1 Swamp sparrows twittered and cheeped. — **(12) 1865** Burroughs in *Atlantic Mo.* May 521/2, I have met here many of the rarer species, such as . . . the Blue-Winged Swamp-Warbler. **1917** *Birds of Amer.* III. 156 Connecticut Warbler, *Oporornis agilis*. . . . [Also called] Swamp Warbler.

Also *swamp buck, finch, fly, moccasin, snake*, etc.

3. Designating areas of a low, wet, or marshy nature, or natural formations occurring in a swamp, as (1) **swamp bottom,** (2) **hammock,** (3) **island,** (4) **lot,** (5) **marsh,** (6) **meadow,** (7) **prairie.**

(1) 1845 Simms *Wigwam & Cabin* 1 Ser. 15 A portion of the forest . . . was swallowed up in . . . a swamp-bottom, the growth of which consisted of mingled cypresses and bay-trees. — **(2) 1848** *Rep. Comm. Patents 1847* 388 The rich swamp hammocks have not yet been tested in wheat. — **(3) 1846** Child *Fact & Fiction* 195 They arrived at one of those swamp islands so common at the South. — **(4) 1637** *Dedham Rec.* (1892) III. 33 It is ordered yt . . . their Swampe lotts shall adioyne thervnto. **1715** *Harvard Rec.* II. 427 A Swamp-Lott in the West fields [shall] be Sold. **1880** *Harper's Mag.* June 70 Down in the moist green swamp lot the yellow cowslips bloom along the shallow ditch.

(5) **1750** in *Amer. Sp.* XV. 400/2 A Certain parcell of Swamp Marsh or Sunken ground Lying Contiguous to his unpatented high Land. — (6) **1697** *Cambridge Prop. Rec.* 344 Four Rods of fence, Lyeing att the head of Samuel Hastings Swamp-meadow. **1880** *Harper's Mag.* June 80 Out in the swamp meadow the tall clumps of boneset show their dull white crests. — (7) **1895** G. KING *New Orleans* 44 The rush-covered banks of to-day extended then into vast swamp prairies.

b. Esp. **swamp land,** land, often fertile and cultivable, in a swamp.

1663 *Conn. Hist. Soc. Col.* XIV. 433 One parcel of land . . . being Swamp land. **1701** *Providence Rec.* V. 125 A Certaine ffarme or tract of land Consisting of upland swampe land & Meadow land. **1851** *Chi. D. Jrnl.* 2 Jan. 2/2 The swamp lands in Ohio, granted to the State by a late act of Congress, amount to 303, 329 acres. **1948** *Democrat* 22 April 4/3 Clarke is a great big body of swamp land.

attrib. **1741** TAILFER *Narrative Ga.* (1835) 67 The Land is of Four sorts; Pine Barren, Oak Land, Swamp land Marsh. **1869** *Mich. Agric. Soc. Trans.* VII. 483 All swamp land scrip known as 'general scrip' shall be received in payment of all lands sold under the provisions of this act. **1898** U.S. Geol. Surv. *Water Supp. Paper* 18, 34 The ditch was constructed, probably about 1864, with money from the State swamp-lands funds. **1949** *Chi. Tribune* 17 Nov. 16/3 It was swampland speculators who raised the first outcry.

4. Designating persons who live in or frequent swamps, (1) **swamp angel,** see as a main entry, (2) **Democrat,** (3) **doctor,** (4) **ranger,** (5) **rat,** (6) **sucker.** All *obs.*

(2) **1832** SANDS *Writings* II. 298 Tacitus, speaking of some Swamp Democrat of his day, uses this verb intransitively. — (3) **1850** H. C. LEWIS *La. Swamp Doctor* 22 The swamp doctor must have the unconcernedness of the dissecting-room, and be prepared to swallow his peck of dirt all at once. **1880** *Harper's Mag.* April 798/2 Defendant's counsel called . . . old Dr. B. . . . who delights in calling himself a 'swamp doctor.' — (4) **1880** CABLE *Grandissimes* 29 They were . . . adventurous swamp-rangers, and . . . lively free-livers.

(5) **1867** EDWARDS *Shelby* 410 The 'higher civilization' folks from the North . . . [found] in him a specimen of the green Arkansas 'swamp-rat.' — (6) **1835** SIMMS *Partisan* (1854) 86 Thou art a better swamp-sucker than Ned Travis, and he born . . . in a bush and cradled in a bog. **1853** ——— *Sword & Distaff* 170 He had to deal with old 'swamp suckers,'—hunters as keen and familiar with such places as himself.

b. Swamp Fox, General Francis Marion (1732–95), a celebrated South Carolina patriot and partisan leader during the Revolutionary War. A nickname.

1836 SIMMS *Mellichampe* (*advt.*), The pursuit of the 'swamp fox' by Colonel Tarleton . . . follows closely the several authorities. **1900** *Cong. Rec.* 29 Jan. 1262/2 Marion, the 'Swamp Fox,' . . . and the other men who fought and continued to fight were hiding out. **1949** *Chi. Tribune* 13 Nov. VII. 12/4 There were also frequent hard-riding skirmishes between the British and Tories and the irregular troops led by Francis Marion, the Swamp Fox.

c. In the names of, or with reference to, ailments suffered by those who live in swampy regions: (1) **swamp ague,** (2) **chill,** (3) **fever,** (4) **malaria,** (5) **shakes.**

(1) **1883** HARRIS *Nights* (1911) 47 He aint no sooner make he bow en look 'roun' twel he 'gun ter shake en shiver lak he done bin strucken wid de swamp-ager. — (2) **1932** W. KELLEY *Inchin' Along* 22 She felt the coverings which were thick because of the swamp chills. — (3) **1846** *Knickerb.* XXVIII. 431 And cured the good folks of all their complaints, from swamp-fever to phthisic. **1892** HARRIS *U. Remus & Friends* 301, I been had de measles, en de plooisy, en de swamp fever. **1943** *L.A.* Map 505. — (4) **1901** *Harper's Mag.* Dec. 67 His incautious neglect to fortify himself against the swamp malaria by a glass of straight Bourbon.

(5) **1932** W. KELLEY *Inchin' Along* 223 It de bes' stuff dey is fuh de swamp shakes.

5. In miscellaneous combs.: (1) **swamp angel,** see as a main entry; (2) **branch,** a branch in a swampy region; (3) **broadcloth,** (see quot.), *obs.;* (4) **buggy,** a vehicle (see quots.) used by oil prospectors in swampy regions; (5) **clearing,** a clearing in a swamp; (6) **grant,** a grant by the federal government to a state of the swamp lands within its borders; (7) **hook,** (see quot. 1905); (8) **law,** (see quot.), *obs.;* (9) **manure,** swamp soil used as fertilizer, *obs.;* (10) **muck,** muck obtained from a swamp; (11) **pre-emptioner,** *transf.* an animal living in a swamp, *obs.;* (12) **tacky, = marsh tacky,** *obs.;* (13) **tea,** prob. tea made from *Ledum groenlandicum* or Labrador tea, *obs.;* (14) **wood,** wood, as firewood, cut from trees in a swamp, also a wood or forest in a swamp.

(2) **1726** in *Amer. Sp.* XV. 400/2 Along the said Swamp-Branch to a white Logg. — (3) **1850** LEWIS *La. Swamp Doctor* 110, I donned a suit of 'swamp broadcloth,'—yellow linsey—which clove to my proportions as if it were an integral part of my frame. — (4) **1941** *Nat. Geog. Mag.* June 706 Their 'swamp-buggy' is a seagoing amphibious-looking vehicle. Its 10-foot high wheels are equipped with fat, fin-studded oversized tires which act as propellers; when the odd vehicle leaves the land and takes to water, it begins to swim. **1942** KENNEDY *Palmetto Country* 17 It was here that the 'swamp buggy' was evolved, a contraption that moves with equal facility on water, highway, or bog.

(5) **1932** W. KELLEY *Inchin' Along* 39 The strawberry mare came cropping her way into the swamp clearing. — (6) **1860** *Harper's Mag.* Feb. 401/2, 1,712,040 acres were approved to the several States under swamp grants. — (7) **1877** *Lumberman's Gaz.* 22 Dec., Swamp Hooks, Pevys, Skidding Tongs always on hand. **1905** *Forestry Bureau Bul.* No. 61, 50 *Swamp hook,* a large, single hook on the end of a chain, used in handling logs, most commonly in skidding. — (8) **1832** WILLIAMSON *Maine* II. 173 Nor would they very readily shrink from a 'trial by battle,' or by 'swamp-law,' which seemed to rest much upon the same principle. — (9) **1796** *N.Y. State Soc. Arts* I. 252 Some of the swamp-manures will also produce good harvests of wheat.

(10) **1840** J. BUEL *Farmer's Companion* 73 Peat earth, or swamp muck, is vegetable food, in an insoluble state. **1904** STRATTON-PORTER *Freckles* 118 The wildly leaping heart of Freckles burst from his body and fell in the black swamp-muck at her feet. — (11) **1847** ROBB *Squatter Life* 79 Every new yell of the swamp pre-emptioners, made him [a city man lost in swamp at night] climb a limb higher, and each progression upwards appeared to introduce him to a fresh and hungrier company of mosquitoes. — (12) **1836** SIMMS *Mellichampe* xliii, If you see that little bullet foot of a swamp-tacky freshly put down in the swamp or sand after mine, be sure the skunk's started. — (13) **1839** *Columbian Reg.* (New Haven, Conn.) 26 Feb. 4/3 Cold gander for breakfast, swamp tea and some nut cakes; the latter some consolation. — (14) **1670** *Essex Inst. Coll.* XLII. 47 Marshall Skery hath liberty to Cutt . . . swampe wood w[ha]t he needeth. **1683** *Cambridge Prop. Rec.* 158 We found Cutt seuerall heapes of green Swamp wood. **1814** J. TAYLOR *Arator* 208, [I] cleared and drained some acres of springy swamp, closely covered with swamp wood. **1851** HALL *Manhattaner* 150 A thick swamp wood on our left, and the turbid Mississippi at our right.

As the last term in **alder, ash, back, bay, beech, birch, black, branch, burnt, cane, cat, cattail, cedar, cotton, cranberry, cypress, Dismal, elder, flat, grape, grass, green, gum, hay, hemlock, huckleberry, hunting, inland, laurel, logging, maple, meadow, mosquito, muck, muskeg, Palmetto, peat, pine, poplar, raccoon, reedy, rice, river, salt, spring, spruce, sunken, tamarack, tideland, timber, tule, wet, whiteoak, willow, wood swamp.**

swamp swɑmp, *v.*

1. *tr.,* usu. *pass.* or *reflex.* To mire or bog down in a swamp; to take refuge in a swamp. *Obs.*

1646 *New Haven Col. Rec.* 270 Samuell Marsh . . . [was] seeking cowes, it being in the spring, yn catle being lyable to be swampt. **1654** in HUTCHINSON *Coll. P. Mass. Bay* 263 Ninnigret . . . had swampt himselfe and refused conference with us. **1821** FOWLER *Journal* 25 Some of our Horses . . . Ware Swamped with their loads.

2. Used in mildly profane imprecations. *Obs.*

1764 HUTCHINSON *Hist. Mass.* 436 He has, in like manner, . . . I swamp, and I vum, for I swear, and I vow. **1776** *Battle of Brooklyn* I. iii, Swamp me, if I have not hove up a breast-work. **1815** HUMPHREYS *Yankey* 19, I shood never have swimmed to shore, to all atarnity I swamp it.

3. In logging operations, to do the work of a swamper. Hence **swamping,** *n.*

1851 SPRINGER *Forest Life* 84 An experienced hand . . . 'spots' the trees where he wishes the road to be 'swamped.' **1873** T. H. BALL *Lake Co., Indiana* 353 Getting this timber out in the winter is called 'swamping.' **1946** NEWTON *P. Bunyan* 162 He was working with one of Paul's swamping crews.

b. ?To extricate or remove (a log) from a swamp. *Rare.*

1784 PATTEN *Diary* 480, I swampt out 4 small oak logs the boys saved in cutting wood Ready for hauling out.

swamp angel.

1. One who lives in, or is familiar with, swamps or backwoods regions.

1857 *Jrnl. Discourses* V. 31 Angels who would thus visit us are swamp angels,—they are filthy. **1900–04** *D.N.* II. 332 swamp-angel, n. A young woman from the swamps or backwoods. (Facetious.) [s.e. Mo.] **1949** *Boston Globe* Mag. 18 Sep. 8/1 Some 'swamp angels' will stick right at home till the water reaches into their attic . . . then they'll howl for boats!

b. A member of a southern anti-Negro group. *Obs.*

1876 *Cong. Rec.* 27 Dec. 384/1 If I were to credit what I hear, he was once known as a 'swamp angel.' **1890** *Ib.* 23 Jan. 804/2 'Jim' Tiddell was there with his crowd of 'Swamp Angels' (for this badge was worn by them all—a green silk ribbon with 'Swamp Angel' on it).

2. (*cap.*) A Parrott gun used in the siege of Charleston, S.C., during the Civil War. *Obs.*

1863 in EASTERBY *S.C. Rice Plant.* (1945) 427 We live in daily expectation of the 'Swamp Angel.' **1876** *Cong. Rec.* 19 May 3215/2 The Swamp Angel that hurled its ponderous shells into Charleston would destroy such an establishment from the open sea. **1917** MORGAN *Recollections* 198 My surroundings were not cheerful and my gloomy thoughts were not dispelled by the bursting of a shell from the historic 'Swamp Angel' and the whirring of its fragments which passed unpleasantly close to me.

transf. **1865** *Harper's Mag.* Oct. 673/2 The striking letter . . . is a 'swamp angel' in the attack which is now opening upon the traditions of education. **1882** *Cong. Rec.* 13 Feb. 1106/2 That assertion . . . was a sort of 'swamp angel' shot from his mathematical battery.

3. *local.* The hermit thrush.

1865 BURROUGHS in *Atlantic Mo.* May 522/2 [The hermit thrush is usually found] in damp and swampy localities. On this account the people in the Adirondack region call it the 'Swamp Angel.' **1917** *Birds of Amer.* III. 234.

swamp apple.

1. Any one of various azaleas, as the swamp honeysuckle *q.v.*, or a plant confused with this.

1805 BENTLEY *Diary* III. 166 The young ladies furnished themselves with the Kalmia, swamp apples. **1881** *Harper's Mag.* March 526/1 Both he and his followers were covered with Pinxter *blummies* —the wild azalea, or swamp apple. E. Mass. **1892** *Amer. Folk-Lore* V. 100 *Rhododendron nudiflorum*, swamp apple. E. Mass.

2. (See quot. 1907.) Cf. **honeysuckle apple.**

1846 *Zoologist* IV. 1281 The galls called swamp-apples . . . grow on the small twigs of the swamp-pink, or Azalea viscosa. **1907** LYONS *Plant Names* 63 A[zalea] nudiflora. . . . A parasitic fungus on it is known as Swamp Apple, May Apple, Honeysuckle Apple, Swamp Cheeses. **1944** HOLTON *Yankees* 145 From the wooded end of the swamp we brought in something we called swamp apples.

swamp ash. Any one of various ashes, as black ash and red ash, found in swamps (see quots 1842, 1935).

1815 DRAKE *Cincinnati* 83 The swamp ash . . . and aspen, seem to be confined to the more northern portions of this tract. **1842** Z. THOMPSON *Hist. Vt.* I. 211/2 The Black Ash . . . is commonly found growing on low lands, and in and about swamps; and hence it is sometimes called Swamp Ash. **1889** RILEY *Pipes o' Pan* 37 Clean out o' sight o' home, and skulkin' under kivver Of the sycamores, jack-oaks, and swamp-ash and ellum. **1935** ROLLINS *Discovery Ore. Trail* 22 Stuart's 'white ash' was *Fraxinus oregona* (Nutt). His 'swamp ash' was probably the broad-leaved maple, *Acer macrophyllum*, which Lewis and Clark said 'resembles ash except the leaf.'

swamp blueberry. (See quot. 1870.) Also the fruit of this.

1870 *Amer. Naturalist* IV. 216 The Swamp Blueberry (*Vaccinium corymbosum*) . . . is a very attractive shrub. **1917** BAILEY *Sand Dunes Indiana* 154 There is a chance to study all the sides of a small pond, with the shrub zone of plants in perfect type, such as swamp blueberry, cranberry [etc.]. **1949** *Pacific Spectator* Spring 223 You had to cross the river to an intervale on the other side to find the low swamp blueberries, lighter blue and sweeter than any other kind.

swamp cheese. =**swamp apple 2.** — **1860** DARLINGTON *Weeds & Plants* 214 These succulent excres[c]ences are much sought after by boys who call them 'swamp apples' and 'swamp cheeses.' **1907** [see **swamp apple 2**].

swamper ˈswɑmpɚ, *n.*

1. One who lives in a swamp or swampy region.

[**1735** J. BELCHER in *N.H. Prov. P.* (1870) IV. 878 The B B's Pr——st is a jolly Fellow. I hear he stood Kick and Cuff upon the Road with some Swampeers. **1755** W. DOUGLASS *Summary* II. 245 In February 1689–90, the French, consisting of 500 Coureurs des bois (in New-England they are called Swampiers,) with as many Indians or savages, made incursions upon the province of New-York.] **1775** *N.C. Gaz.* (New Berne) 24 March 3/3 Fellow Dismalites and Swampers, are we not the Men whom God hath appointed to curb the Insolence of Britain. **1857** LONG *Pictures of Slavery* 323, I made an appointment to deliver a temperance address to the 'swampers.' **1891** *Boston Jrnl.* 9 April 2/3 [Alligator oil] has a high reputation among the swampers as a remedy for rheumatism. **1942** KENNEDY *Palmetto Country* 22 Hamp Mizell, a typical swamper, says: 'My father was one of the first to try a boat to get through the swamp.'

transf. **1867** *Ball Players' Chron.* 6 June 3/4 We saw near a regular bull-frog party, for they croaked like regular old swampers.

2. (See quot. 1926.)

1850 E. S. SEYMOUR *Sk. Minn.* 202 One swamper, or road-breaker, who is constantly employed in keeping the roads open. **1926** RICKABY *Ballads* 237 *Swamper.* A man whose work was that of clearing the fallen tree of limbs, knots, etc., and preparing the way generally for the sawyers, who cut the trunks into logs. Also worked at cutting and clearing the roads. The swamper stood on the first and lowest rung of the shanty-boy ladder. **1945** *N. & Q.* June 38/2 Curtis . . . was employed for a time as a swamper in the woods.

transf. **1870** *Terr. Enterprise* (Virginia, Nev.) 21 April 3/1 A 'swamper' is a man who goes with the driver of a 10, 12, or 14-mule team as his assistant—the driver being chief engineer and the swamper first-assistant. **1939** ROLLINS *Gone Haywire* 65 Until the call was given, the average cook permitted nobody to approach the fire except the helper whom he rarely had, and who was known as the flunky, roustabout, swamper, or cook's louse.

b. A man-of-all-work in a saloon.

1907 *Oregonian* 13 Oct. (Th.), He was a swamper in a saloon. **1929** *Collier's* 5 Jan. 33/1 As a result it became pay dirt, and in later years the swamper actually had to pay for his job.

As the last term in **Carolina, master swamper.**

swampine ˌswɑmˈpin, *n.* [f. *∗swamp*+*-ine.*] "A poecilioid fish, *Fundulus heteroclitus*, found on the Atlantic coast of the United States" (*Cent. Supp.*). — **1835** KIRBY *Hab. & Inst. Anim.* I. ii. 122 Another migrating fish was found by thousands in the ponds . . . of Carolina, by Bosc. . . . They belong to a genus of abdominal fishes [Note: *Hydrargyra*] and are called swampines.

swamp oak. Any one of various oaks found in swamps, as the swamp white oak and the pin oak.

1681 *New Castle Court Rec.* 503, 40 perches to a corner marked swamp oake. **1766** J. BARTRAM *Journal* 22 The east banks being . . . full of live and swamp-oaks. **1834** AUDUBON *Ornith. Biog* II. 238 Not a single tree of the species did we find, although there were thousands of large 'swamp oaks.' **1897** SUDWORTH *Arborescent Flora* 152 *Quercus lobata.* . . . California White Oak. . . . Swamp Oak (Cal.). **1921** DEAM *Trees of Indiana* 123 Pin oak . . . is also sometimes called water oak, and swamp oak.

attrib. **1790** DENNY *Journal* 144 March through beech and swamp oak land.

swampoodle swɑmˈpudl, *n. local.* [Fanciful formation.] A low-lying or poor section of a town or city. *Slang. Obs.* — **1871** *Cong. Globe* 15 April 718/1 Passengers . . . will be left out here at this part of the city [of Washington] that . . . is known as Swampoodle. **1894** *Cong. Rec.* App. 1 Aug. 1117/2 A part of that city [Kansas City, Kansas] . . . at one time the suburbs of old Kansas City, Mo. . . . was made up of what you would call here [in Wash.] 'swampoodle.'

swamp pine. Any one of various pines, as the loblolly pine and the slash pine, found in wet or swampy regions.

[**1731** P. MILLER *Gardeners Dict.* (1735) *s.v. Abies*, Species . . ., to be found in the English Gardens, . . . [include] *Pinus; Americana, palustris.* The Swamp Pine.] **1743** CATESBY *Carolina* II. p. xxii, The Swamp Pine grows on barren wet land. **1785** MARSHALL *Amer. Grove* 102 *Pinus Tæda*, Virginian Swamp, or Frankincense Pine, . . . grows to a pretty large size. **1914** E. STEWART *Lett. Woman Homesteader* 7, I have a grove of twelve swamp pines on my place. **1933** SMALL *Southeastern Flora* 5 P[inus] palustris . . . (Slash-pine, Swamp-pine.)

swamp pink.

1. An azalea, esp. *A. viscosa*, found in wet or swampy regions.

1784 *Amer. Acad. Mem.* I. 416 American Honeysuckle. Swamp Pink. . . . Common in low, swampy land. June. **1814** BIGELOW *Florula Bostoniensis* 52 Wild honeysuckle. Swamp pink. . . . A fine flowering shrub, very common among the brushwood in low land. **1892** *Amer. Folk-Lore* V. 100 *Rhododendron nudiflorum*, swamp pink. Parts of N.E. **1894** *Harper's Mag.* Nov. 920/1 The low, marshy meadow Where pale swamp-pinks blow.

2. (See quots.)

1898 CREEVEY *Flowers of Field* 85 Swamp Pink, *Helonias bullata*. . . . A pretty plant, found from New Jersey southward to Virginia. **1909** WEBSTER 2090 *Swamp pink*, . . . grass pink.

swamp rose. A wild rose, *Rosa palustris*. Also *R. carolina* of the eastern states.

1785 MARSHALL *Amer. Grove* 135 *Rosa palustris*, Swamp Pennsylvanian Rose . . . [rises] to the height of four or five feet. **1814** BIGELOW *Florula Bostoniensis* 121 *Rosa Caroliniana.* Swamp rose. . . . This rose grows in swamps and wet grounds, sometimes forming thickets of itself. **1902** *Outing* June 272/2 The Carolina or swamp rose . . . is well known to us all.

swamp Spanish oak. The pin oak, *Quercus palustris*, of the eastern states.

1810 MICHAUX *Arbres* I. 25 *Swamp Spanish oak*, . . . dans les Etats de Pensylvanie et de Maryland. **1832** BROWNE *Sylva* 278 [*Quercus palustris*] is called . . . Swamp Spanish Oak, in Pennsylvania. **1894** COULTER *Bot. W. Texas* III. 417. **1933** SMALL *Southeastern Flora* 429 Q[uercus] palustris. . . . (Swamp Spanish-oak. Pin-oak. Water Spanish-oak.)

swamp white oak. An oak found in the eastern states, *Quercus bicolor;* also the overcup oak, *Q. lyrata,* and the cow oak, *Q. prinus.*

1725 *Cambridge Prop. Rec.* 314 We have Settled ye Line . . . to a Swamp white Oak tree mark'd. **1897** SUDWORTH *Arborescent Flora* 155 Overcup Oak. . . . Swamp White Oak (Tex.). *Ib.* 158 Cow Oak. . . . Swamp White Oak (Del., Ala.). **1945** DARLINGTON *Higher Plants Mich.* 12 Common species are silver maple . . . , swamp white oak . . . , sycamore.

* **swan,** *n.* **1. swan dive,** a fancy front dive in which the arms are spread sideways, the head is tilted backwards, and the body gracefully curved with the back slightly hollowed. Also as verb. **2. swan potato,** (see quot. and cf. **swamp potato**).

(1) **1898** *Swimming Mag.* Oct. 45/2 The diving . . . included forward headers, . . . somersaults and the 'Swan' dive from twenty, thirty, and forty feet. **1912** JACK LONDON *Son of Sun* ii. § 3. 53, I used to swan-dive a hundred and ten feet in the clear. — (2) **1917** KEPHART *Camping* II. 374 *Arrowhead, Broad-Leaved.* Swan or Swamp Potato *Sagittaria latifolia* (*S. variabilis*). In shallow water; ditches. . . . Tuberous roots as large as hens' eggs, were an important article of food among Indians. Roots bitter when raw, but rendered sweet and palatable by boiling.

As the last term in **trumpeter, whistling swan.**

swan swɑn, *v.* [Prob. f. some no. Eng. dial. form of *I warrant.* Cf. *I'se worn ye, I'se warn ye, I'se warran* in *EDD s.v. Warrant.*] *intr.* To swear, declare, used in asseverations and exclamations. Also *swan to man, goodness. Colloq.* or *slang.*

1784 in *Mag. Amer. Hist.* (1878) II. 498/2 Nay, I swan (as the old saying is) we of Boston, after all, are better off than those of New York. **1841** *Jamestown* (N.Y.) *Jrnl.* 24 June 1/3 Well, I swan to man, if old Tyler hain't made a fool of himself. **1917** FREEMAN & KINGSLEY *Alabaster Box* 117 But, I swan! you can't tell that girl nothing. **1931** *K.C. Times* 11 Sep., And now scientists are makin' new experiments so's the old cats can listen again. I swan to goodness.

swanny ˈswɑnɪ, *v. intr.* Variant of **swan,** *v.*

1832 BUCKINGHAM in *N. Eng. Mag.* III. 380 We have '*I swan*' and '*I swanny*' for I swear. **1865** *Harper's Mag.* Feb. 325/1, I swanney, their mother does give 'em such dinners Sundays. **1911** *Boston Herald* 6 Feb. 6/8 He does not say, 'I swanny!'

* **swap,** *v.*

1. *tr.* To cheat in a trade; also, *absol.*, to rob. Also with *off. Colloq.*

1880 HARRIS *Uncle Remus* iv, Den Brer Fox know dat he bin swop off mighty bad. **1888** FERGUSON *Experiences of Forty-Niner* 61 The Crows would rob, or 'swap' as they called it. **1898** HARRIS *Tales of Home Folks* 159 Come, watch me swap him out of his eye teeth.

2. In colloq. phrases: (1) *To swap (a)round,* to move from one place or subject to another; (2) *to swap ends,* (see quot. 1944), hence *swapping ends;* (3) *no time to swap knives,* and variants, no time to change tactics or plans; (4) *to swap lies,* to chat, converse; (5) *to swap stories* (or *yarns, words,* etc.), to converse, tell stories, exchange confidences, etc.

(1) **1873** MARK TWAIN & WARNER *Gilded Age* 307 Husband says Percy'll die if he don't have a change; and so I'm going to swap round a little and see what can be done. **1892** ——— *Amer. Claimant* 205 So the chat would swap around to some other subject. — (2) **1879** *Scribner's Mo.* Oct. 888/1 Tony's mule performed the evolution known as 'swapping ends.' **1944** ADAMS *W. Words* 160/2 swapping ends A movement peculiar to a bronc, where he quickly reverses his position, making a complete half-circle in the air. — (3) **1871** in COLLINS *Kentucky* I. 218 It was 'no time for swapping knives.' **1875** MARK TWAIN *Old Times* vi. 120 It was no time to 'swap knives.' **1884** ——— *H. Finn* xxxii, There warn't no time to swap knives. — (4) **1835** LONGSTREET *Ga. Scenes* 233 He begged me . . . to go home with him and swap lies that night. **1902** LORIMER *Lett. Merchant* 217 Most men dropped into Lem's store of an evening, because there was n't any other place to go and swap lies.

(5) **1887** *Harper's Mag.* Jan. 222/1 Step out here an' less me 'n' you swap a few words. **1888** *Scribner's Mag.* Jan. 24/1 The older men . . . stayed at home and swapped stories. **1897** STUART *Simpkinsville* 152, I s'pose you and Mis' Carroll've been swappin' confidences about garden-truck. **1904** CRISSEY *Tattlings* 412 We didn't swap family secrets for a long time. **1911** BURGESS *Find the Woman* 55 Just a crowd of good fellows that meet every night to swap yarns.

* **Swartwout,** *n.* [See note.] An embezzler. Also attrib. *Obs.*

In allusion to Samuel Swartwout (1783–1856), collector of the port of N.Y. in Jackson's administration, who misappropriated more than a million dollars of public funds and fled to England.

[**1839** *Cong. Globe* App. 17 Jan. 103/3, I am confident . . . every effort will be used . . . to whitewash the black frauds . . . of Swartwout, and black-wash the Administration.] **1845** *Xenia Torch-Light* 23 Oct. 2/4 McNulty, soon after his defeat, joined the Swartwout church. **1853** W. ISHAM *Mud Cabin* 159 And have they no Swartwouts of their own here [in England]?

Swartwout ˈswɔrtwaʊt, *v.* [See note to prec.] *tr.* and *intr.* To embezzle, depart, abscond. *Obs.*

1839 *Ky. Observer* (Lexington) 29 June 3/3 That the Bank, at some time, would fall into the hands of scoundrels, who would *Swartwout* its funds, is altogether probable. **1840** *Knickerb.* XVI. 480, [I] live in daily fear of being compelled to 'absquatulate,' or 'Swartwout.' **1886** POORE *Reminisc.* I. 128 He 'Swartwouted' (to use a word coined at the time) to avoid a criminal prosecution.

Hence **Swartwouting,** *n.*, embezzlement. *Obs.*

1839 *Ky. Observer* (Lexington) 11 May 3/3 (*heading*), More Swartwouting. **1876** *Trial W. W. Belknap* 47 'Swartwouting' is equivalent to embezzlement and official peculation.

Swartwouter ˈswɔrtwaʊtɚ, *n.* [Cf. * **Swartwout,** *n.*] An embezzler who absconds. *Obs.*

1839 *Maysville* (Ky.) *Eagle* 11 Dec. 2/6 (*heading*), A Swartwouter Tripped Up. **1841** *N.O. Picayune* 20 Feb. 2/2 The amount due to the government from defaulting officers—chiefly tax-collectors is estimated at $1,000,000. A good round sum for the *Swartwouters.* **1844** *Spirit of Times* (Phila.) 22 Aug. (Th.), 'An English Swartwouter.'—W.S.W., clerk in a Birmingham bank, absconded.

swather ˈswɑðɚ, *n.* [f. **swath, n.*] (See quot. 1875.) — **1875** KNIGHT, Swather, a device attached to the front of a mowing-machine for the purpose of raising the uncut fallen grain and marking the line of separation between the cut and the uncut grain. **1929** *K.C.* (Mo.) *Times* 26 June, The swather, or windrowing machine, is proving almost as popular as the older combine, which it complements.

* **swear,** *v.*

1. In colloq. noun combs.: **a. swear-off,** an oath or vow of abstinence. **b. swearword,** a profane word, a curseword.

(**a**) **1889** *Valley Bul.* (Solomonville, Ariz.) 27 Dec. 3/1 New Years is almost at hand and all the boys are getting ready to make a big 'swear off.' **1910** HART *Vigilante Girl* ii. 30 'So I stopped drinking. . . .' 'And have you stuck to your swear-off?' — (**b**) **1883** A. M. GOW *Primer of Politeness* 58 A youth who mixed his conversation with many swear-words. **1947** MYERS *The 'Guv'* 174 The doctor sat down on the running board and cussed the fractious machine until he was out of swear words.

2. *To swear out,* to cause (a warrant for arrest) to be issued by making a charge upon oath; to cause a warrant to be issued on (a certain charge).

1895 *Denver Times* 5 March 8/5 During the scuffle, Miss Alderfer . . . saw the 'black jack' up his sleeve, . . . and as a result, swore out the concealed weapons charge. **1912** *Times* (London) 19 Oct. 5/6 The warrant was 'sworn out' by the girl's mother at Minneapolis. **1931** *Randolph Enterprise* (Elkins, W.Va.) 17 Sep. 5/4 Henry Phillips swore out a warrant for Fred W. Elmore for non-support of his children.

* **sweat,** *n.*

1. = * **sweat-cloth.** *Obs.*

1868 *How Gamblers Win* 94 The most systematic game played with dice in this country [U.S.] is known by the euphonious title of 'Sweat.' **1889** *Walla Walla* (Wash.) *Union* 5 Jan. 2/5 Faro, stud poker, and 'Sweat' are the games played.

2. In combs.: (1) **sweatband,** a leather or leather-like band stitched around the inside of the crown of a hat as a protection against sweat; (2) **board,** prob. a board having figures on it used in playing sweat-cloth *q.v.*, or the game itself, *obs.;* (3) * **box,** (*a*) a box into which grapes or figs are packed to undergo a sweat, cf. **sweat house 1. c,** (*b*) (see quot.), (*c*) an exceptionally close or hot place in which a prisoner is put in an effort to make him confess or implicate others (see also quot. 1903); (4) * **cloth,** see as a main entry; (5) **fly,** a small biting fly of a kind esp. troublesome to sweating animals, *colloq.;* (6) **hole,** a hole in which a sweat bath is taken, *obs.;* (7) **house,** see as a main entry; (8) **lodge,** = **sweat house,** *obs.;* (9) **mill,** (see quot.), *obs.;* (10) **shirt,** a loose pull-on shirt of warm material, used chiefly by athletes before and just after exercise; (11) **shop,** a room or shop in which employees work long hours under unsanitary conditions for insufficient wages, also attrib.; (12) **tepee, =sweat lodge.**

(1) *Pall Mall Gaz.* 28 Sep. 2/3 An American chemist . . . threatens us with lead-poisoning from the 'sweat-band.' **1931** *K.C. Star* 28 Aug. He won't even permit a stenciled initial on the sweatband of his hat. — **(2) 1849** *Knickerb.* XXXIV. 253/1 [The lad] must . . . give bonds not to . . . frequent oyster-cellars, . . . billiard-rooms, sweat-boards [etc.]. **1865** *Nation* I. 371 He was recently the owner of a 'sweat-board,' a singular gambling instrument. **1867** Goss *Soldier's Story* v, Fifty to seventy venders of beans, . . . together with small gamblers with sweat-boards, sat on the ground. — **(3)** *(a)* **1888** Lindley *Calif. of South* 361 Small grape-growers find it to their advantage to sell their raisins in the sweat-boxes to those who have made a reputation for their brand. **1900** *U.S. Dept. Agric. Yearbk.* 94 After the figs were dried they were placed in sweat boxes holding about 200 pounds each, where they were allowed to remain for two weeks, to pass through a sweat. *(b)* **1897** *Chi. Tribune* 10 July 1/4 The upper gallery, commonly known as the 'sweat box' in regular theaters. *(c)* **1901** Flynt *World of Graft* 102 They put him in the sweat-box, made him cough, an' you know the rest. **1903** *D.N.* II. 353 Sweat-box, n. A conference in which one or more detectives or police officials question a prisoner in order to elicit information as to his possible connection with a certain crime. **1945** *Dly. Sentinel* (Grand Junction, Colo.) 25 Nov. 13/7 Col. Erich Killinger, chief of the notorious 'sweat box' camp where captured American and British airmen were tortured in hot asbestos-lined cells.

(5) 1843 Oliver *Eight Months* 148 The whole earth and air seems teeming with them, and mosquitoes, gallinippers, bugs, . . . sweat flies, . . . join in one continued attack. — **(6) 1806** Lewis in *L. & Clark Exped.* V. (1905) 61 During the time of his being in the sweat hole, he drank copious draughts of a strong tea of horse mint. — **(8)** Garrard *Wah-To-Yah* ii. 35 A few steps from the outside was a 'sweat lodge' . . . into which the medicine men enter before performing their sacred duties. **1947** *Democrat* 18 Sep. 4/4 One of the unique buildings in every Creek Indian village was the 'sweat lodge,' constructed of logs and dabbed tight with clay. Steam rising from boiling water in these small huts provided for sweat baths. — **(9)** *a***1847** in Howe *Hist. Coll. Ohio* 188 Prior to the year 1800, many families used a small hand-mill, properly called a *sweat-mill.*

(10) 1934 Webster. **1949** *Nat. Geog. Mag.* Dec. 789/1 Their younger brothers, voicing the latest American slang, wore baseball caps and sweat shirts. — **(11) 1892** *Scribner's Mag.* July 22/2 The *sweat-shop* is a place, where, separate from the tailor-shop or clothing-warehouse, a 'sweater' (middleman) assembles journeymen tailors and needlewomen, to work under his supervision. **1949** *Time* 17 Oct. 28/2 Shaw justified *Mrs. Warren's Profession* by blaming it on the sweat-shop wages which capitalism paid the female proletariat. — **(12) 1905** Blankinship *Native Econ. Plants Mont.* 22 This was the species commonly used by the Indians to make the framework of their 'sweat tepees,' which was then covered with skins or blankets and filled with steam produced by pouring water over hot stones.

***sweat-cloth,** *n.*

1. (See quots.)

See quot. 1938. No British evidence is available for the term in this sense, which is given in the *OED* as U.S.

1843 J. H. Green *Exposure of Gambling* 90 Chutter-luck. This game is sometimes called sweat-cloth. . . . This game is played with three dice . . . and a box to throw them from. **1938** Asbury *Sucker's Prog.* 52 Chuck-a-Luck is one of the oldest of dice games, and in England was originally called Sweat-Cloth.

2. (See quot. 1872.)

1848 Judson *Mysteries of N.Y.* 90 (We.), A crowd of darkies were standing before a little table, upon which lay a 'sweat-cloth' or a square piece of oil-cloth. **1857** *Phoenix* (Sacramento) 20 Sep. 1/3 He fell in with a gentleman from his native place, who loaned him fifty dollars, which he invested on a 'sweat cloth.' **1872** De Vere 329 The sweat-cloth, a cloth marked with figures, and used by gamblers with dice.

sweat house. A hut, cavern, lodge, or booth in which sweat baths are taken, esp. by Indians. Cf. **temescal.**

1731 *Bristol* (Va.) *Vestry Bk.* 54 Walthur Childes & Robert Tucker [procession] . . . up Deep Creek to the sweathouse. **1804** Lewis in *L. & Clark Exped.* I. (1904) 365, 3 pieces of scarlet one brace in each, which had been left as a sacrifice near one of their swet houses. *a***1918** G. Stuart *On Frontier* II. 43 At the conclusion of this dance the participants take an emetic and then go to the sweat house. **1940** Smith *Puyallup-Nisqually* 121 Sweat houses were made with floors level with the outer ground.

b. (See quot.) *Rare.*

1849 T. T. Johnson *Sights Gold Region* 155 [The Digger Indians dig] large holes in the ground for sanitory [*sic*] purposes, called *sweat houses.*

c. (See quot.)

1882 *Harper's Mag.* Nov. 872/2 The grapes for raisin-making . . . are removed to an airy building known as a 'sweat-house,' where they remain possibly a month, till the last vestiges of moisture are extracted.

***sweating,** *n.*

1. Torturing to obtain a confession; putting one charged with or suspected of a crime through the third degree *q.v.* (see also quot. 1824). Also attrib.

1824 in J. Hall *Sk. of West* (1835) I. 222 The torture of sweating . . . that is, of suspension by the arms, pinioned behind the back, brought a confession. **1890** *Boston Jrnl.* 10 April 2/3 It is curious that in London and New York at the same time there should be a serious revolt against the 'sweating system.' **1904** *Cin. Enquirer* 21 Oct. 4 He confessed, under sweating, that he broke into several offices.

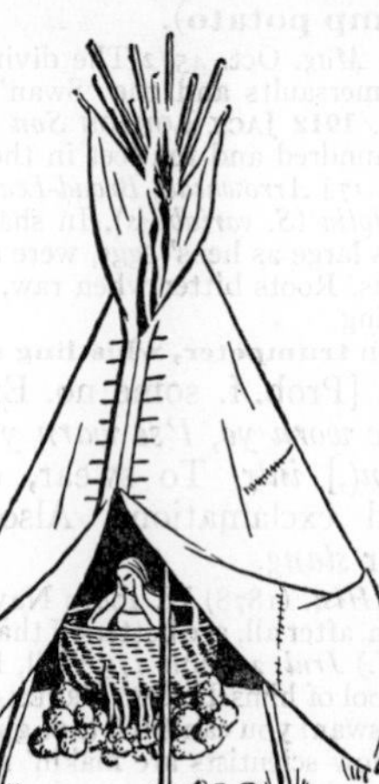

Indian sweat lodge, medicine lodge or temescal

2. (See quot. 1938), in full **sweating out.** *Slang.*

1907 *Hoyle's Games* 411 *Sweating out.* Refusing to bid when nearly out, so as to get out by picking up a few points at a time. **1938** Asbury *Sucker's Prog.* 52 A player was said to be 'sweating' or 'sweating out' if he proceeded cautiously, taking no risks and contenting himself with whatever points might naturally fall to his share; in other words, if he played them close to his vest.

3. In special obs. combs.: (1) **sweating coop, =sweat house;** (2) **kiln,** a crude drying booth used by Indians; (3) **lodge, =sweat house.**

(1) 1751 J. Bartram *Observations* 33 [The conjurers' tents] differ from their sweating coops, in that they are often far from water, and have a stake by the cage. — **(2) 1806** Lewis in *L. & Clark Exped.* IV. (1905) 14 The natives . . . eat these berrys when . . . dryed in the sun or by means of their sw[e]ating kilns. — **(3) 1848** Parkman in *Knickerb.* XXXII. 52 The ashes of some three hundred fires were visible . . . together with the remains of sweating lodges.

***Swedish,** *a.* **1. Swedish bitters,** (see quot.), *obs.* **2. Swedish Nightingale,** Jenny Lind (1820–67), a famous Swedish operatic soprano, a nickname. — **(1) 1890** Billings *Nat. Medical Dict.* II. 629/1 *Swedish bitters,* compound tincture of aloes. — **(2) 1855** Barnum *Life* 296 This speculation . . . must prove immensely profitable, provided I could engage the 'Swedish Nightingale' on any terms within the range of reason.

sweenied ˈswinɪd, ˈswɪnɪd, *a.* [See next.] Affected by sweeny. Also transf. — **1861** *Harper's Mag.* Aug. 421/2 The people have been fed on buncombe, while a lot of spavined, ring-boned, . . . swyneyed, split-headed . . . polleviled politicians have had their noses in the public crib. **1872** *Borderer* (Las Cruces, N.M.) 5 Oct. 2/4 God Almighty only knows the age of 'em! — three footed, one-eyed, sweeneyed, spavined, broken-down ex-livery stable stock, 'political hacks,' and sway-backed horses.

sweeny ˈswinɪ, *n.* [Poss. f. G. dial. *schweine,* atrophy, emaciation, *schweinen,* to become emaciated. Cf. Lambert, *Pa.-G. Dict. s.v. schweining, schwinne,* sweeny.] Atrophy of the muscles of the shoulder of a horse. Also transf.

1832 Kennedy *Swallow Barn* II. 22 He professed to cure the colt's distemper, sweeny, and other maladies. **1883** S. Bonner *Dialect Tales* 48 It gives a poor man's pocket-book the swinney to buy a thrashing machine. **1892** *York Co. Hist. Rev.* 50 Hanes' Liniment is positively the . . . Most Sure and Certain Cure for . . . Sweeney, Scratches, Bruises in animals.

∗**sweep,** *n.*

1. Orig. *S.* A plow (sense **2.**) having flat narrow wings esp. adapted for the shallow cultivation of row crops, as cotton. See also quot. 1842. *Colloq.*

1842 in TURNER *Cotton* (1865) 55, I have now no further use for a plough in its subsequent culture, but use the *sweep*—a kind of horse hoe—I call it a sweep in the absence of a more appropriate name. **1846** *De Bow's Review* II. Sep. 136 After the cotton is hilled the second time, I use almost entirely the *cultivator* or the sweep, or both. **1944** CLARK *Pills* 160 A farmer in Alabama wanted . . . 10 weeding hoes no 3, 3 sixteen inch sweeps. **1948** *Dly. Ardmoreite* (Ardmore, Okla.) 12 April 4/4 This is done by sub-surface tillage, with special kinds of V-shaped sweeps or other equipment.

2. At Yale a man employed to take care of the students' rooms.

1846 *Yale Banger* 10 Nov., A Freshman by the faithful sweep, Was found half buried in soft sleep. **1853** ROOT & LOMBARD *Songs of Yale* 12 A College Sweep went dustily 'round, Plying his yellow broom. **1950** [see ∗**sweeper**].

3. sweep-pole well, a well from which water is drawn by a long sweep. Cf. ∗**reach.**

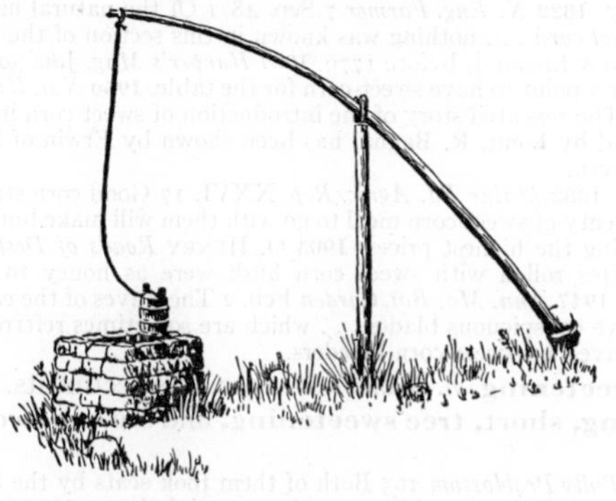

Sweep-pole well with well pole or well sweep

1943 POWELL *Home Again* 57 To make a sweep-pole well, one starts somewhat as one does to make rabbit hash.

As the last term in **buzzard, cotton, shovel, solid, well, wing sweep.**

∗**sweep,** *v. S. tr.* To till or cultivate (a field or crop) with a sweep (sense **1.**). *Colloq.*

1843 in TURNER *Cotton* (1865) 65 It is very desirable, and highly necessary even, that the cotton be swept once after topping it. **1854** DAVIS *Farm Bk.* 48 In the M Jones field, sweeping it. **1856** *Fla. Plant. Rec.* 475 Plows swepen ground peas and siden cotton.

sweepage lot. (See quot.) *Obs.* — **1880** J. MERRILL *Hist. Amesbury, Mass.* 15 These lots were called 'sweepage lots,' probably from the fact that the sea swept one end of them.

∗**sweeper,** *n.* (See quot. 1950 and cf. ∗**goody,** *n.*[1])

1790 *Laws of Harvard Coll.* 58 The Steward shall also engage proper sweepers for the Colleges. **1861** *Macm. Mag.* Feb. 268/2 The rooms [in an American College] were supposed to be taken care of by three or four men called 'sweepers,' whose duty extended only to making the beds daily, and sweeping the rooms occasionally. **1950** *Harvard Alumni Bul.* 22 April 590/3 In early times, *sweeper* was in use instead of *goody,* and even now at Yale College the word *sweep* is retained.

As the last term in **carpet, chimney sweeper.**

∗**sweepings,** *n. pl.* (See quot. 1871.) *Slang. Obs.*

This sense of the term prob. resulted from laws enforcing periodical cleanups of branch mints, when the sweepings (rather valuable in this case) had to be accounted for by those in authority.

1868 *Putnam's Mag.* I. 668/2 The sweepin's of the post-office is about three thousand a-year. **1871** DE VERE 264 *Sweepings* are more exclusively the side-earnings of lucrative offices.

∗**sweep-rake.** (See quot. 1883.) Also **sweep-rake reaper.** *Obs.*

1876 *Vt. Bd. Agric. Rep.* III. 610 The sweep-rake reaper is now so perfect a machine that it will reap grain so badly lodged that it is with difficulty that it can be mown with a scythe. **1883** KNIGHT *Supp.* 876/1 *Sweep Rake,* the rake that clears the table of a self-rake reaper. **1910** *Encycl. Brit.* (ed. 11) XIII. 108/1 An American invention known as the sweep rake was introduced . . . into England in 1894.

∗**sweet,** *a.*

1. In the names of, or with reference to, plants and trees: (1) ∗**sweet bay,** =**sweet magnolia;** (2) **Betsy, Betty,** (see quot. 1907 and cf. **sweet bubby, sweet shrub**), also **sweet Betty bush;** (3) **birch,** any one of several species of birch, esp. *Betula lenta,* found in the eastern states; (4) **bough,** a variety of apple or apple tree; (5) **bubby,** the strawberry shrub, *Calycanthus floridus;* (6) **buckeye,** a plant of the genus *Aesculus,* esp. *A. octandra* of the central states; (7) **goldenrod,** the Blue Mountain tea of the eastern states, also **sweet-scented goldenrod;** (8) **hickory,** prob. the shagbark hickory, the roots of the seedlings being somewhat sweetish, *obs.;* (9) **locust,** =**honey locust;** (10) **magnolia,** a magnolia, *Magnolia virginiana,* abundant in the South and along the Atlantic Coast; (11) **Mary,** a sweet-scented balm, as *Melissa officinalis,* Oswego tea, or a costmary; (12) **pepper (bush),** the white alder, *Clethra alnifolia,* a handsome shrub of the Atlantic states having very fragrant flowers; (13) **shrub,** =**sweet bubby;** (14) **tater,** =**sweet potato,** *colloq.;* (15) **viburnum,** the sheepberry, *Viburnum lentago.*

(1) 1804 DUNBAR *Life* 244 They have a method of boiling it [bear's fat] from time to time upon sweet-bay leaves which restores it or facilitates its conservation. **1897** SUDWORTH *Arborescent Flora* 194. — **(2) 1888** C. E. CRADDOCK *Broomsedge Cove* 464 At the other window a series of straight wands rose up above the sill, and betokened the withered estate of the 'sweet Betty' bushes. **1907** LYONS *Plant Names* 85 [Calycanthus florida] Carolina Allspice, Florida Allspice, . . . Strawberry-bush, Spice-bush, Sweet-Betsies. — **(3) 1785** MARSHALL *Amer. Grove* 18 *Betula nigra.* Black, or Sweet-Birch . . . a large tree, often rising to the height of fifty or sixty feet. **1943** PEATTIE *Great Smokies* 156 From Highland come measurements of . . . a sweet birch fully six feet thick. — **(4) 1850** *Rep. Comm. Patents 1849: Agric.* 281 Of summer apples, the best and most productive are the early-harvest and early sweet-bough. **1906** *Harper's Mag.* April 667 He halted under the sweet-bough and gave one branch a shake.

(5) 1913 M. W. MORLEY *Carolina Mts.* 47 Another shrub that belongs to us and eastern Asia and that tempts one to nibble is what the people here call 'sweet bubbies.' It appears in old-fashioned Northern gardens under the name of sweet-scented or flowering or strawberry shrub. **1945** MCATEE *Nomina Abitera* 12 Strawberry Shrubs. . . . One is fragrant and, therefore, called sweet bubby. — **(6) 1815** DRAKE *Cincinnati* ii. 77 Sweet buckeye [In a list of plants and trees in the Miami country.] **1943** PEATTIE *Great Smokies* 155 Certain it is that the sweet buckeye or horse chestnut is found here up to 125 feet in height. — **(7) 1817–8** EATON *Botany* (1822) 466 *Solidago odora,* sweet-scented golden-rod. . . . This is the true golden-root tea-plant. **1892** COULTER *Bot. W. Texas* II. 189 *Solidago odora . . .* (Sweet Golden-rod). . . . Dry or sandy soil, eastern and southern Texas. — **(8) 1873** BEADLE *Undevel. West* 641 A species of milky weed, with tough, stringy root, in taste resembling the 'sweet hickory' the boys used to pull and chew. — **(9) 1832** BROWNE *Sylva* 161 The Sweet Locust belongs peculiarly to the country west of the Alleghanies. **1884** SARGENT *Rep. Forests* 59.

(10) 1878 WHITMAN *Spec. Days* 123 These perennial blossoms and friendly weeds [include] . . . sweet magnolia, milk-weed, wild daisy. **1897** SUDWORTH *Arborescent Flora* 195. — **(11) 1894** *American Folk-Lore* VII. 96. **1938** DAMON *Grandma* 273 Our old chest of unbleached muslin sheets and ancient homespun blankets was made fragrant, as well as mothless, by the sprays of sweet Mary she laid in it. — **(12) 1836** LINCOLN *Botany* App. 88 *Clethra.* . . . Sweet pepper-bush. **1901** MOHR *Plant Life Ala.* 652 Sweet Pepper Bush. . . . Common in the Coast plain on swampy banks of pine-barren streams. **1944** HOLTON *Yankees* 84 With the perfume of bush honeysuckle and sweet pepper from the swamps on the landward side of the road. — **(13) 1809** RAMSAY *Hist. S.C.* II. 594 Among these are the locust, . . . the wild rose, and the sweet shrub. **1883** HALE *Woods & Timbers N.C.* 173 Sweet shrub (*Calycanthus floridus*)—This plant, now so extensively cultivated, and admired for the rich Strawberry odor of its flowers, is a native of the southern Alleghanies. **1945** *Democrat* 29 March 2/1 Being out turkey hunting some spring afternoon with the air heavy with the scent of wild honey suckle and sweet shrubs, and with the white of the grandaddy graybeards and the dogwoods peeping out from the delicate green of the beeches. — **(14) 1893** *Voodoo Tales* 40 Yo' done fegit bake 'possum an' sweet-taters wid coon gravy. **1895** *Outing* XXVI. 436/2 Is not the African heaven simply a corner on coon, 'possum, chicken, sweet 'taters and corn pone?

(15) 1843 TORREY *Flora N.Y.* I. 305 Sweet Viburnum. . . . The fruit is rather palatable, especially after having been frozen. **1861** WOOD *Botany* 398 Sweet Viburnum. . . . A common tree-like shrub, in rocky woods. **1892** APGAR *Trees Northern U.S.* 114.

b. In similar combs. sufficiently explained in the quots.: (1) **sweet cicely,** (2) **coco,** (3) **elder,** (4) **leaf,** (5) **maple,** (6) **mountain grape,** (7) **sage,** (8) **scabious,** (9) **Susan.**

(1) **1847** WEBSTER 204/3 The sweet cicely of New England is *Osmorrhiza longistylis.* **1884** *Amer. Naturalist* XVIII. 784 Thus in sweet cicely . . . the flowers are in compound umbels. — (2) **1850** *Rep. Comm. Patents 1849: Agric.* 156 In wettish flat lands, several varieties of *Panicum crus-galli* . . . grow vigorously, not unfrequently mixed with *cyperus repens,* sweet coco, or nut grass. — (3) **1832** WILLIAMSON *Maine* I. 107 The former [black elder], called 'Sweet Elder,' has handsome blossoms. — (4) **1814** PURSH *Flora Amer.* II. 451 *Hopea tinctoria* . . . is known by the inhabitants under the name of Sweet-leaf. **1891** *Cent.* 6108/3 sweetleaf. . . . A small tree or shrub, *Symplocos tinctoris,* found in deep woods or on the borders of cypress-swamps in the southern United States. Its leaves are sweet to the taste, greedily eaten by cattle and horses, and they yield, as does also the bark, a yellow dye. Also called *horse-sugar.*

(5) **1787** *Amer. Acad. Mem.* II. II. 156 Sugar Tree or sweet Maple . . . ; very beneficial to the country. — (6) **1915** *Dept. Agric. Bul.* No. 209, 14 *V[itis] monticola* (sweet mountain grape): Texas. . . . [Vine] rather small; good grower. — (7) **1913** BARNES *Western Grazing Grounds* 57 The forage is greatly augmented by the great sage family, especially the sweet sage or 'winter fat' (*Eurotia lanata*). — (8) **1828** RAFINESQUE *Medical Flora* I. 162 *Erigeron Philadelphicum.* . . . Vulgar Names—Skevish, Scabish, Sweet Scabious [etc.]. **1937** *Range Plant Handbook* w67 Annual wild-daisy (*E[rigeron] annuus*) and Philadelphia wild-daisy, misnamed sweet scabious (*E. philadelphicus*), . . . are other wild-daisies with similar properties. — (9) **1891** *Amer. Folk-Lore* IV. 147 Nuphar advena was *Bullhead Lily.* . . . Silene armeria had only the name *Sweet Susan;* never Sweet William, as Gray had it, for this name was reserved exclusively for Dianthus barbatus.

c. Also in more occasional designations as (1) **sweet (-bark) cottonwood,** (2) **onion,** (3) **poplar.**

(1) **1825** in DALE *Ashley-Smith Explor.* (1918) 130 The sweet cottonwood, such as affords feed for horses, is nowhere to be found in the mountains. *Ib.* 146 Here we found a luxurious growth of sweet-bark or round-leaf cottonwood. — (2) **1845** DE SMET *Oregon Missions* 117 The sweet onion . . . bears a lovely flower resembling the tulip. — (3) **1850** L. SAWYER *Way Sketches* 30 We have found no wood since we struck the Platte, except fragments of wagon boxes and a few sweet poplar and cotton wood limbs, brought from the islands by emigrants who have preceded us.

For **sweet corn, fern, gum, potato, -scented,** see as main entries.

2. In miscellaneous combs.: (1) **sweet scents,** perfumery, *obs.;* (2) **sixteen,** the age of sixteen banteringly regarded as the most desirable for a girl; (3) **South,** =**Sunny South,** *obs.;* (4) **springs,** (see quot. 1799); (5) **sucker,** the chub sucker, *Erimyzon oblongus* (see also quot. 1911).

(1) **1794** *Ann. 3rd Congress* 1472 There shall be levied . . . [on all] preparations or compositions, commonly called sweet scents, . . . 5 per cent. ad valorem. — (2) **1833** NEAL *Down-Easters* I. 155 All women wish to be, 'Sweet sixteen.' **1899** H. B. CUSHMAN *Hist. Indians* 215 In the social dance alone were the women allowed to participate, which to the youthful maid of '*sweet sixteen*' was truly bliss. — (3) **1859** WILMER *Press Gang* 69 He left the 'Quaker City,' and removed further toward the 'Sweet South.' — (4) **1786** *Amer. Philos. Soc.* II. 197 A Letter from J. Madison, Esq. to D. Rittenhouse, Esq. containing Experiments and Observations upon what are commonly called the Sweet Springs. **1799** WELD *Travels* 125 In the western part of the county are several medical springs, whereto numbers of people resort towards the latter end of summer. . . . Those most frequented are called the sweet springs, and are situated at the foot of the Alleghany Mountains.

(5) **1884** GOODE *Fisheries* I. 614 The 'Chub Sucker,' 'Sweet Sucker,' or 'Creek-fish' is one of the most abundant and widely diffused of the Suckers. **1911** *Rep. Fisheries 1908* 307 Black Horse (*Cycleptus elongatus*). — A sucker found in the larger streams of the Mississippi Valley. It is also called 'gourd-seed sucker,' 'Missouri sucker,' 'sweet sucker,' and 'suckerel.'

As the last term in **bitter, golden, green, Jersey, pound, Seaver's Sweet.**

sweet corn.

1. Indian corn prepared in various ways (see quots.), esp. by Indians, to preserve it and increase its palatability.

1646 *Mass. H.S. Coll.* 4 Ser. VI. 334 Wequash Cooks brother tooke from him . . . 2 bushell of sweet corne. **1842** *S. Lit. Messenger* VIII. 582/1 They now pull much of their corn while it is in the milk, and dry it carefully in the sun: it is then called 'sweet corn.' **1868** BOLLER *Among Indians* 119 Each family reserves a number of the choicest ears to make a sweet corn for winter use. It is first parboiled, the grains are then carefully picked off the cob, and dried in the sun, . . . then put away in skin bags and carefully hoarded for use on special occasions or in time of scarcity. **1888** in FARMER 480/1 The Shakers . . . originated the drying of sweet corn for food more than fifty years ago, and suggested the modern improved kilns for that purpose. **1917** WILL & HYDE *Corn Among Indians* 118 The Upper Missouri tribes prepared this 'sweet corn' for winter use in two ways: by boiling it in kettles, and by roasting it in fires.

2. Any one of several varieties of corn the kernels of which are rich in sugar and therefore desirable for table use when in the milk stage.

The context of our quot. 1822 states that sweet corn was first brought to the attention of people in New England by a Lt. or Capt. Bagnal of Plymouth, who had taken part in Sullivan's expedition against Indians of the Six Nations. From the region of the Susquehanna in 1779, Bagnal brought back what the Indians he said called papoon corn *q.v.* This corn had a red cob, and the kernels when cut from the cob on which they had been boiled indelibly stained cloth with which they came in contact. Cf. **dyeing corn.** A. T. Erwin in *Jrnl. Amer. Soc. of Agronomy,* vol. 39, (Feb. 1947), 117 ff. regards the Bagnal story as a myth. Cf. quot. 1950 below.

1810 THOMAS JEFFERSON *Garden Book* (1944) 424 Apr. 28. [sowed] Cherokee latter corn in the middle part. Sweet or shriveled corn in the N.W. corner of D°. above Bailey's walk. *a***1817** DWIGHT *Travels N.-Eng.* I. (1821) 48 Maize, of the kind, called sweet corn, is the most delicious vegetable while in the milky stage, of any known in this country. **1822** *N. Eng. Farmer* 7 Sep. 48/1 Of the natural history of the *sweet corn* . . . nothing was known in this section of the country (if in New England) before 1779. **1887** *Harper's Mag.* Jan. 308/1 We make it a point to have sweet-corn for the table. **1950** *Nat. Hist.* May 196/3 The repeated story of the introduction of sweet corn into New England by Lieut. R. Bagnal has been shown by Erwin of Iowa to be a myth.

attrib. **1882** *Maine Bd. Agric. Rep.* XXVI. 17 Good corn stalks . . . with plenty of sweet corn meal to go with them will make butter that will bring the highest prices. **1903** O. HENRY *Roads of Destiny* 364 Cigarettes rolled with sweet corn husk were as honey to Buck's palate. **1947** *Ann. Mo. Bot. Garden* Feb. 2 The leaves of the ear shoot . . . have conspicuous blades . . . which are sometimes referred to as 'flag-leaves' by sweet-corn breeders.

* **sweetening,** *n.* Molasses, sugar, or sweetmeats. *Colloq.* Cf. **long, short, tree sweetening,** and see **bee sweetening.**

1851 *Polly Peablossom* 165 Both of them took seats by the fire; the table between them, and liquor and sweetenin' plenty. **1860** OLMSTED *Back Country* 241 [She] had taken pains to boil in some sweetenin' (molasses) on my account. **1878** HART *Sazerac Lying Club* 116 The Mormons knew not sugar in those days, sorghum syrup . . . answering the purpose for 'sweetening.' **1933** T. WILLIAMSON *Woods Colt* 37 You shore use up a heap o' sweetnin' at your place.

sweet fern.

1. A small American shrub, *Comptonia asplenifolia,* having fernlike leaves of an aromatic scent.

It is not possible to identify positively the plants referred to in some of the quots.

1654 JOHNSON *Wonder-w. Prov.* 81 The sweet Ferne, whose scent is very strong so that some herewith have beene very nere fainting. **1778** CARVER *Travels* 504 Juniper, Shrub Oak, Sweet Fern, the Laurel [are native shrubs]. **1832** WILLIAMSON *Maine* I. 118 *Sweet-fern* is much smaller and of less notoriety, than the Rose-bush, though its leaves are wholesome in diet-drink. **1896** JEWETT *Pointed Firs* 213 The darker green of the sweet-fern was scattered on all the pasture heights. **1950** *Nat. Hist.* Jan. 10/2 Sites on which longleaf pine forests grew had a characteristic ground cover, highly inflammable, of broom sedge, wire grass, sweet fern and gall berry.

2. sweet-fern cigar, prob. an imitation cigar made from the aromatic leaves of the sweet fern.

1869 ALCOTT *Little Women* II. 358 Tommy Bangs will smoke sweet-fern cigars under the bed-clothes. **1905** LINCOLN *Partners* 72 After tying a handkerchief—not too clean and smelling of sweet-fern cigars—over his friend's eyes.

sweet gum. A North American tree, *Liquidambar styraciflua,* the copalm.

1700 *Md. Hist. Mag.* XIX. 367, 127 acre Sur[veyed] . . . for Samuell Baker Lyeing betwixt rumley & delph Creek begun at a bounded sweet gum. **1897** W. E. BARTON *Trouble at Roundstone* 144 The sweet gum was glorious in its autumn dress. **1950** *New Yorker* 11 March 29/1 The uncultivated land growing up in sweet gum and old field pine.

attrib. **1709** LAWSON *Carolina* 95 The sweet Gum-Tree, so call'd, because of the fragrant Gum it yields in the Spring-time, upon Incision of the Bark, or Wood. **1835** *Survey of Property* Nov., (Pettigrew P.), To a littel sweet Gum corner Tree. **1866** C. H. SMITH *Bill Arp* 61, I found Dick ploughing away down in a field close by a sweet-gum swamp. **1949** *Southwest. Rev.* Summer 241/2 All'd go wadin in the water, and look for good sweetgum and hickry sticks.

b. The gum exuded from a cut or bruise on this tree. Also attrib.

1884 J. C. HARRIS *Mingo* 196 Manys en manys de time is I seed yo w'en you gwine atter sweet-gum. **1948** *Democrat* 22 July 8/1 Notice to sweet gum producers—I will buy gum at my home.

∗**sweeting,** *n.* As the last term in **golden, Jersey, pound, red, short, spice sweeting.**

sweet potato.

1. A vine, *Ipomoea batatas*, or its farinaceous root valued as food.

1750 J. BIRKET *Cursory Remarks* 9 They have . . . abundance of . . . the Sweet Potatoe. **1787** WASHINGTON *Diaries* III. 255 Dug the Irish Potatoes in the half Acre of experimental ground (adjoining the ½ Acre of Sweet or Country Potatoes). **1819** THOMAS *Travels* 102 Here we first noticed in this state the sweet potatoe (*Convolvulus batatas*). **1851** *Fox River Courier* (Elgin, Ill.) 12 Nov. 2/6 Very few have the art of keeping sweet potatoes thro' the winter in this latitude. **1949** *Nat. Geog. Mag.* Aug. 168/1 Sweet potatoes were cultivated in Virginia in 1648, possibly earlier, and are said to have been taken into New England in 1764.

b. *Music.* An ocarina. *Colloq.*

1934 WEBSTER. **1945** *New Yorker* 24 March 23/3 Suppose a candidate took it into his head to run on the platform that he could play 'Goodbye, Old Paint,' on the sweet potato better than his opponent. **1949** *Chi. Tribune* 2 Nov. II. 2 My cousin's a hot thistle on the slide whistle—and I'm a neat tweeter on a sweet potater!

2. In combs.: (1) **sweet potato beetle,** any one of various beetles, esp. *Cassida bivittata*, that destroy the leaves of the sweet potato and related plants; (2) **bird,** prob. the Carolina wren, so named from its note, *colloq.;* (3) **patch,** a small area where sweet potatoes are grown; (4) **rot,** a rot which affects sweet potatoes.

(1) **1861** *Ill. Agric. Soc. Trans.* V. 432 The 'Sweet Potato Beetle' . . . depredates upon the leaves and stems of sweet potatoes. — (2) **1912** I. COBB *Back Home* 39 That huckstering little bird of the dead treetops, which the negroes call the sweet-potato bird . . . was calling his mystical wares. — (3) *c***1862** BAGBY *Old Va. Gentleman* 84 There is a wagon-way which runs in a straight line by the sweet-potato patch. — (4) **1890** *Rep. Secy. Agric. 1889* 420 The special subjects under investigation in the laboratory have been . . . sweet-potato rot, pear blight, peach yellows.

b. Designating foods prepared from sweet potatoes: (1) **sweet potato bun,** *obs.*, (2) **coffee,** *rare*, (3) **pie,** (4) **pone,** *obs.*, (5) **pudding,** (6) **soup,** (7) **waffle.**

(1) **1850** MARY RANDOLPH *Va. Housewife* 141 Sweet Potato Buns. Boil and mash a potato, rub into it as much flour as will make it like bread—add spice and sugar to your taste, with a spoonful of yeast; when it has risen well, work in a piece of butter, bake it in small rolls. — (2) **1927** SIRINGO *Riata* 124 We used corn and sweet potato 'coffee' and brown sugar. — (3) **1829** FLINT *G. Mason* 19 There was no . . . deficiency of custards, delicious sweet potatoe pies, and various wild fruits. **1946** THOMPSON *Amer. Daughter* 54 Tom and Gus went hunting, and that night there was roast duck and dressing and sweet-potato pie. — (4) **1847** *Carolina Housewife* 130 Sweet Potato Pone. No. 1. A quart of grated potato, three-fourths of a pound of sugar, ten ounces of butter, half a pint of milk, three table-spoonfuls of powdered ginger, the grated peel of a sweet orange. Rub the ingredients well together, and bake in a shallow plate, in a slow oven. **1877** BARTLETT 686 *Sweet Potato Pone*, sweet potatoes, flavored with spices, and baked in a tin pan.

(5) **1828** LESLIE *Receipts* 21 Sweet Potato Pudding. **1885** *La Cuisine Creole* 198 Sweet Potato Pudding . . . is a Southern dish, and fit to grace the table of an epicure. — (6) **1867** GOSS *Soldier's Story* 227 A friend gave me . . . wheat bread and sweet potato soup. — (7) **1847** *Carolina Housewife* 211 Sweet Potato Waffles. Two table-spoonfuls of mashed potato, one of butter, one of sugar, one pint of milk, four table-spoonfuls of wheat flour; mix these ingredients well together, and bake in a waffle iron. **1941** F. M. FARMER *Boston Cook Book* 104.

∗**sweet-scented,** *a.* **1. sweet-scented shrub,** the strawberry shrub, cf. **sweet bubby, sweet shrub. 2. sweet-scented (tobacco),** a variety of tobacco the leaves of which have an especially agreeable odor. *Obs.*

(1) **1786** WASHINGTON *Diaries* III. 53 Planted . . . 6 of the Sweet scented, or aromatic shrubs in my Shrubberies. **1859** BARTLETT 7 The 'sweet-scented shrub' . . . is also known as Carolina Allspice, the bark and wood having a somewhat spicy flavor. **1893** *Amer. Folk-Lore* VI. 141 *Calycanthus floridus*, sweet-scented shrub. . . . E. Mass. — (2) **1666** *Essex Rev.* XVII. 133 One hogshead of Sweet-sented tobacco, lodgd in Cornewall. **1690** *Va. State P.* I. 25 The sweet scented Tobacco of this Colony may be improv'd. **1800** TATHAM *Tobacco* 4 The different species of the genus have been in former days distinguished in Virginia by the names of Oronoko, sweet scented, and little Frederic. **1816** J. K. PAULDING *Letters from Va.* 165, I see yonder old miserly dog refuse a single chew of his *kitesfoot* for a pretty girl, while that lad of mettle and spirit bids his whole plantation of *sweet-scented* at once, and wouldn't take twice as much for his bargain.

Sweezyites ˈswiziˌaɪts, *n. pl.* [?f. a personal name.] (See quot. and cf. **Holy Roller.**) *Obs.* — **1841** *N.O. Picayune* 2 April 2/5 A new sect of Religionists, so called, has sprung up in Yates county, New York, called the 'Sweezyites, or Holy Rollers,' an appellation applied on account of their exercises being those of rolling upon the floor.

∗**swell,** *n.* As the last term in **Broadway, heavy swell.**

∗**swell-,** the verb stem in combs.: (1) **swell-butted,** (see quot.); (2) **fish,** any one of various fishes capable of inflating their bodies, a puffer or globefish; (3) **front,** a house front that is rounded or curved, a house having such a front, *obs.;* (4) **head,** a person inordinately conceited or vain, also conceit, arrogance, *colloq.;* (5) **shark,** (see quot.); (6) **skull,** designating "busthead" (*q.v.*) whisky, *rare;* (7) **toad,** = **swellfish.**

(1) **1905** *Forestry Bureau Bul.* No. 61, 50 Swell butted, as applied to a tree, greatly enlarged at the base. — (2) **1807** *Mass. H.S. Coll.* 2 Ser. III. 55 The puff fish, or swell fish, or bellows fish, is a cartilaginous fish. **1911** *Rep. Fisheries 1908* 317/1 Swell-fish (*Tetraodontidae*).—The different species are known as 'globe-fishes,' 'puffers,' 'swell-toad,' etc. — (3) **1848** N. DEARBORN *Boston Notions* 350 The building is of brick, with an imposing agreeable swell front projecting twelve feet. **1871** HOWELLS *Wedding Journey* 58 A humble three-story swell-front up at the South End is no longer the place for me. **1886** *Cent. Mag.* May 243/1 In the central house, the 'swell front,' and domed roof of which make it somewhat more pretentious than the wings, are feather and fan palms. — (4) **1845** HOOPER *Simon Suggs' Adv.* iv, As for the present directory, they're all a pack of d——d swell-heads. **1867** G. W. HARRIS *Sut Lovingood* 61 Wif a onintemitant attack of swell-head. **1873** C. GORDON *Boarding-School Days* 35 Where's Bullock and Gracie?—don't see them with you swell-heads lately.

(5) **1891** *Cent.* 5436/1 *S*[*cyllium*] *ventricosum* is the swell-shark, a small voracious species found on the Pacific coast from California to Chili. — (6) **1867** HARRIS *Sut Lovingood* 233 She fotch a glass bottil ove swell-skull whiskey outen the three-cornered cupboard. — (7) **1878** *Nat. Museum Proc.* I. 366 *Chilomycterus geometricus.* Swell-toad. . . . Sold by small boys as curiosities. **1911** [see **swellfish**].

∗**swelled,** *a.* **1. swelled head,** (see quot.). **2. swelled neck,** goiter. Both *obs.*

(1) **1919** DUNN *Indiana* II. 804 In 1842–3 epidemic erysipelas prevailed in a number of counties in southern Indiana, and was known by a number of popular names, as 'black tongue,' 'sore throat,' 'swelled head,' etc. The fatality was great. — (2) **1832** BAIRD *Valley Miss.* 74 Goiter, or 'swelled neck,' once prevailed on the upper waters of the Ohio. **1863** RANDALL *Pract. Shepherd* 152, I never have applied any remedy whatever for 'swelled neck.'

∗**swift,** *a.* and *n.*

1. Short for **swift fox.**

1877 CAMPION *On Frontier* 132 Of foxes there were . . . many 'swifts' —the last-mentioned a species of fox I have rarely met with. **1897** HOUGH *Story of Cowboy* 42 At these red or tawny blotches which lie about over the landscape the coyotes are feeding, then the foxes and swifts.

2. a. swift fox, the kit fox, *Vulpes velox.* **b. swift witness,** ?a witness eager to testify. *Obs.*

(**a**) **1869** *Amer. Naturalist* III. 476 Visiting a steel trap which I had set . . . I was surprised to find in it a Swift Fox. **1917** *Mammals of Amer.* 77/1 The Kit, or Swift Fox, . . . is a much smaller animal than the Red and Gray Foxes. — (**b**) **1857** *Lawrence* (Kans.) *Republican* 11 June 3 [A] lady appeared at the police court yesterday, with a bundle of hair in her hands as 'swift witness' against one Mary Bolle. **1884** BLAINE *20 Years of Congress* I. 383 The stories told by many of these swift witnesses were on the surface absurd.

As the last term in **chimney, northern, rock, spine-tailed, Vaux's swift.**

∗**swifter,** *n.* A drink of liquor. *Slang. Obs.* — **1834** *Sun* (N.Y.) 13 May 2/3 Why, I mean that, after church was out, I went into a porter house and took a *swifter*. *Ib.* 16 May 2/3, I take a *swifter* of a little of the good old gin.

∗**swill,** *n.* **1. Swill-Boys,** (see quot.). **2. swill-milk,** (see quot. 1858). Also attrib. Both *obs.*

(1) **1859** BARTLETT 467 *Swill-Boys*, a gang of New York rowdies. — (2) **1853** *Hunt's Merch. Mag.* XXVIII. 684 The whole business [is] in the hands of the *swill milk* manufacturers. **1858** C. FLINT *Milch Cows* 208 The nefarious traffic in 'swill-milk,' or milk produced from cows fed entirely on 'still-slops.' **1894** FORD *P. Sterling* 72 The press began, too, a crusade against the swill-milk dealers.

*swim, *v. tr.* (See quot. 1864.) *Obs.* — **1790** S. DEANE *N.-Eng. Farmer* 16/2 Swimming the barley before it is sowed, will in great measure prevent [mixture of oats]. **1864** WEBSTER 1339/2 *Swim*, . . . to immerse in water that the lighter parts may swim; as, to *swim* wheat for seed.

*****swimming,** *n.* and *a.* **1. swimming hole,** a deep part of a stream, as a branch or creek, used for swimming. **2. swimming market,** a buoyant market.

(1) **1867** G. W. HARRIS *Sut Lovingood* 25 He wer aimin fur the swimin hole in the krick. **1906** LYNDE *Quickening* 58 His lip curled stiffly at the thought of a girl . . . dividing the sovereignty of . . . the swimming-hole . . . with him. **1947** *Mazama* Oct. 3/2 Mr. Rosenfeld graciously invited the Mazamas to go through his lovely gardens to the swimming hole. — (2) **1870** MEDBERY *Men Wall St.* 138 *Swimming market*, the opposite of a sick market. **1885** *Harper's Mag.* Nov. 841/2 He . . . has a 'swimming market' when all is buoyant. **1900** NELSON *A B C Wall St.* 161.

As the last term in **big swimming.**

*****swindle,** *n.* The price or charge for something. *Slang. Obs.* — **1835** *Knickerb.* V. 146, [I] desired to know what the swindle would be for a new set of buttons. **1871** DE VERE 576 When he [a Western man] wishes to know what he has to pay, he asks, What's the damage? or, not so charitably, What's the swindle?

*****swing,** *n.*

1. *W.* That part of a herd of cattle behind the front and well ahead of the tail. Also attrib. Cf. **swing rider.**

1903 ADAMS *Log Cowboy* 28 The main body of the herd trailed along, . . . guarded by outriders, known as swing men. *Ib.* 91 Quince Forrest . . . rode in the swing on the branded side of the cattle. **1923** MULFORD *Black Buttes* 11 The trail-boss signalled the point and swing men to check the cattle. **1949** *10 Story Western* May 9/2 The cowhands riding the swing and those fetching up the drags rode hunched over in their saddles, cold and miserable.

2. In combs. in some of which the first element has verbal force: (1) **swingdingle,** a kind of logging sled (see quot. 1944), *colloq.;* (2) **ferry,** app. a rope or wire ferry *qq.v.;* (3) **pole,** = **well sweep,** *obs.;* (4) **rider,** *W.* (see quot. 1944); (5) **room,** in post-office jargon (see quot. 1948); (6) **rope,** *W.* the rope used to suspend a load across the back of a pack animal before securing it with a pack rope; (7) **station,** *W.* a station on a stage line where teams are changed.

(1) **1934** WEBSTER. **1944** NUTE *Lk. Superior* 209 At noon a cookee brought a hot lunch to them in the woods by means of the 'swingdingle,' a rude kitchen, or perhaps buffet service, on runners. — (2) **1873** BEADLE *Undevel. West* 758 We traveled northwest . . . , crossing the Klamath River by a 'swing-ferry' soon after daylight. **1919** LEWIS *Free Air* 101 Her car had crossed the Missouri River on the swing-ferry. — (3) **1818** FORDHAM *Narr. Travels* 157 Wells won't dig themselves, and the swing pole and bucket are forever out of order. — (4) **1903** A. ADAMS *Log Cowboy* xx. 312 We swing riders were never out of sight of each other. **1944** ADAMS *W. Words* 161 swing rider One of the riders with a trail herd, riding about one-third of the way back from the point riders.

(5) **1923** *Nation* 12 Dec. 682/2 The First Assistant Postmaster General . . . established an official censorship over the bulletin boards in the workers' 'swing,' i.e., rest rooms. **1948** MENCKEN *Supp.* II. 767 Swing-room. A lunch-room or rest-room. — (6) **1894** WISTER in *Harper's Mag.* April 783/2 The rolls were made, balanced as side packs, and circled with the swing-ropes. **1902** —— *Virginian* 488 He would teach her how to loop and draw the pack-ropes, and the swing-ropes on the pack-saddles. — (7) **1867** *Ore. State Jrnl.* 27 April 4/1 At the swing station at Duck Lake . . . the stage started out at 8 P.M. **1930** BANNING *Six Horses* 280 The distance between stations averaged about twelve and a half miles; but this was to include 'swing stations,' where only stocktenders lived.

b. *swing (a)round the circle,* a political tour. Cf. **swing,** *v.* **3. b.**

1902 PHILLIPS *Woman Ventures* 121 Marlowe found that he must leave town on Wednesday night to go with the President on a short 'swing round the circle.' **1905** *Springfield W. Republican* 6 Oct. 1 Will the appropriated money be available for campaigning swings around the circle?

As the last term in **clear, gloucester, grapevine, western swing.**

*****swing,** *v.*

1. *intr.* (See quot. 1851.) Also with *out. Obs.*

1851 HALL *College Words* 296 At several American colleges, the word *swing* is used for coming out with a secret society badge. . . . Generally, *to swing out* signifies to appear in something new. **1871** BAGG *At Yale* 143 Old graduates seldom 'swing out' except on special occasions.

2. *tr.* To bring around, manage, control.

1873 MARK TWAIN & WARNER *Gilded Age* 405 You will find we can swing a two-thirds vote. **1917** FREEMAN & KINGSLEY *Alabaster Box* 62 But it's going to be a good thing for the creditors, if she can swing it. **1932** LEWINSON *Race* 113 The Negro primary electorate, however was this time swung for Tobin, and Tobin was elected.

3. a. *To swing off,* to desert to another side or party. **b.** *To swing (a)round the circle,* to make an extended political tour of the country, also *swinging round the circle,* and transf. **c.** *To swing a wide loop,* see **wide loop.**

(a) **1861** in M. W. DISHER *Cowells in Amer.* (1934) 327 Virginia has 'swung off' (new phrase) to the side of the traitors. — (b) **1877** WRIGHT *Big Bonanza* 227 This [trip] surpasses any 'swinging round the circle,' political or otherwise, that has ever been done in the United States. **1887** *Chi. Tribune* 2 Oct., President Andrew Johnson originated the phrase 'swinging round the circle' on the occasion of his famous tour to Chicago . . . in September, 1866. **1910** *N.Y. Ev. Post* 29 Oct. 2 To stem the rising tide against him, Col. Roosevelt is to swing around the circle in Brooklyn to-night.

swinge cat. 1. A person of a violent temper. *Colloq.* **2. Swinge-cat State,** (see quot.). *Obs.*

(1) **1835** LONGSTREET *Ga. Scenes* 219 For all you see him in these fine clothes, he's a *swinge*-cat—a darn sight cleverer fellow than he looks to be. **1840** *S. Lit. Messenger* VI. 506/2 She's a *swinge-cat* arn't she? — (2) **1890** *Brighton* (Colo.) *Reg.* 11 Jan. 4/1 South Dakota is the 'swinge-cat State.'

swinging harness. In a fire station, harness designed to be suspended, when not in use, immediately above the horse it is for. *Obs.* — **1889** BRAYLEY *Boston Fire Dept.* 317 The commissioners made arrangements with the patentee of the Speedy swinging-harness to use it in this department.

*****swingle,** *v.* **1.** *****swingletail,** the thresher shark. **2. swingle tow,** = next. *Obs.*

(1) **1832** WILLIAMSON *Maine* I. 161 The Shark, among fishermen, is called the 'maneater,' 'the shovel-nose,' and 'the swingle-tail'; these being varieties of the species. **1911** *Rep. Fisheries 1908* 316 Shark (Notidani).—They are sometimes called . . . 'porbeagle,' 'swingle-tail.' — (2) **1812** *Conn. Courant* 9 June 2/2 He and his wife . . . covered the body up with *swingled tow*, ashes and straw. **1855** *Amer. Inst. N.Y. Trans. 1854* 343 Good crops of potatoes have been grown under swingletow, upon a grass sod.

swingling tow. (See quot. 1828.) Also transf.

1828 WEBSTER, *Swingling-tow,* the coarse part of flax, separated from the finer by swingling and hatcheling. **1843** STEPHENS *High Life N.Y.* II. 173 A son of the President of these United States ought to be noticed for what's inside of his head, and not for such an etarnal swad of swinglin-tow as that are. **1946** *N. & Q.* June 35 (*caption*), Sassafras and Swinglingtow: or, Pinkster Was a Holiday.

*****swipe,** *n.* One who rubs down horses. *Slang.* — **1929** S. ANDERSON in *Mercury Story Bk.* 221, I had taken a job as swipe with one of the two horses Harry was campaigning.

*****swipe,** *v. tr.* To steal. Also *****swiped,** *a. Slang.*

1889 *Seattle Post-Intelligencer* 5 Dec. 8/1 He runs a steel chain through the sleeve, and fastens the chain to the dummy with a padlock. 'By adopting this method,' said the merchant, 'we can stand back and laugh at their vain attempts to "swipe" our goods.' **1931** *K.C. Star* 18 Sep., Don't get nasty because we know as well as you do that these data are swiped from the New Yorker. **1942** PHILIPS *Big Spring* 136 The offending ranchman . . . had been running his cattle in a 'swiped valley.'

*****switch,** *n.*

1. *Railroad.* A sidetrack.

1835 *Mass. Laws* XIII. 461 It shall be the duty of the corporation . . . to enter the said Boston and Lowell rail-road, by . . . proper turn-outs or switches. **1873** *Newton Kansan* 29 May 2/2 It has now 495 miles of track besides switches. **1904** *N.Y. Times* 11 May 3 The rule is to maintain a six-mile speed when entering a switch.

2. In combs. relating chiefly to railroads: (1) **switch-back,** (see quot. 1890), also used of roads and trails for hikers; (2) **ball,** the ball of a ball signal at a switch, *obs.*, cf. *****highball,** *n.* 3; (3) **board,** an apparatus for connecting and combining electric circuits; (4) **engine,** an engine used for switching; (5) **engineer,** the engineer of a switch engine; (6) **hog,** (see quot.); (7) **shanty,** a shanty at a railroad switch; (8) **tower,** a building containing the levers and other appliances for working railway switches; (9) **yard,** an area taken up by railway switches.

(1) **1863** *Harper's Mag.* Sep. 465/1 We descend from our high elevation by gravity, changing our directions at various points by means of what is called a switch-back. **1890** *Railways of Amer.* 8 Another American invention is the switchback. By this plan the length of line

required to ease the gradient is obtained by running backward and forward in a zigzag course, instead of going straight up the mountain. **1947** *So. Sierran* Nov. 1/3 The brilliant yellow aspen, the tree-studded sheer cliffs, and the switchbacks to the ridge were behind us. — **(2) 1878** PINKERTON *Strikers* 152 A militiaman . . . while sitting on the cow-catcher, particularly noticed the position of the switch-ball, which indicated that the train . . . would be thrown off the right track. — **(3) 1873** *Harper's Mag.* Aug. 349/2 The switch-board, to which allusion has been made, is the central ganglion of the whole [telegraphic] system. **1949** *Chesterton* (Ind.) *Tribune* 7 April 4/7 The metal plungers on a horizontal panel at the left of the standard board are arranged to correspond to the lights on the switchboard. — **(4) 1867** *Jamestown* (N.Y.) *Jrnl.* 28 June 3/2 Mary Haycroft was knocked down by a switch-engine. **1948** *Chi. D. News* 2 March 1/3 Four Chicagoans were injured when their auto was struck by a Pere Marquette switch engine.

(5) 1889 SALMONS *Burlington Strike* 355 They went out on a strike, being joined by the switch engineers and firemen. — **(6) 1926** RICKABY *Ballads* 237 *Switch-hog,* A small engine used on log trains. A switch engine. — **(7) 1909** *Harper's Wkly.* 4 Dec. 11/1 The story of the winning of the blue-ribbon of the rails is told in every roundhouse and switch-shanty between the two coasts. **1945** *Tracks* June 48 We were in the switch shanty, getting ready to put in another honest eight. — **(8) 1901** *Munsey's Mag.* XXV. 699/1 The locomotive . . . stopping only once to allow McCann to drop another set of running orders at a switch tower on the next division. **1903** *N.Y. Ev. Post* 30 Dec. 3 A slight blaze occurred in an elevated road switch tower. — **(9) 1888** *Austin* (Tex.) *Statesman* 1 Nov. 6/6 In the switch yards of the Chicago & Alton . . . nearly all the men reported for duty this morning. **1943** *Sat. Ev. Post* 26 June 73/2 By the end of 1942, every old teakettle still on wheels was back in service on branch lines and in switch yards, releasing more powerful engines for main-line duty.

b. In plant and tree names: (1) **switch-bud hickory,** a local name for the pignut hickory; (2) **cane,** small cane, also attrib.; (3) **grass,** (*a*) (see quot. and cf. **quack grass**), *obs.*, (*b*) a western panic grass, *Panicum virgatum;* (4) **-tail pine, =foxtail pine.**

(1) 1884 SARGENT *Rep. Forests* 134 *Carya porcina.* . . . Switch-bud Hickory. . . . Dry hills and uplands; common.—**(2) 1845** *Big Bear Ark.* 132 They circled about among the switch-cane and priscimmon bushes a long time. **1850** DRAKE *Treatise* 197 A considerable growth of small cane;—hence they are called 'switch-cane marshes.' **1861** *Harper's Mag.* Nov. 754/2 Reynard . . . for some half hour amused himself with coursing hither and thither among the switch-cane and briers. — **(3)** (*a*) **1839** BUEL *Farmer's Companion* 232 The quack, switch, or witch grass, a variety of the fiorin. (*b*) **1889** VASEY *Agric. Grasses* 28 Tall Panic Grass; Switch Grass . . . forms a large constituent of the native grasses of the prairies, particularly in moist localities. **1895** *Dept. Agric. Yrbk. 1894* 430 *Switch grass* . . . has powerful creeping rootstocks, and is easily propagated. — **(4) 1865** STUART *Montana as It Is* 78 This is a species of pine very much resembling the 'switch-tail pines' of California.

As the last term in **flying, kick, lickety, stub switch.**

***switch,** *v.*

1. *tr.* To turn (a car, train, etc.) onto another track by means of a switch.

1861 in G. H. PUTNAM *Mem. Publisher* 421 [Each car carried in white letters the caution:] Not to be switched under penalty of death. **1903** *N.Y. Ev. Post* 17 Sep. 1 At Hagerstown the train was switched from the Cumberland Valley Railroad to the Norfolk & Western. **1943** *Chi. Sun* 29 Sep. 8/5 It serves 22 major gateways and has more than 200 places in its territory where cars are switched from one railroad to another.

b. *intr.* Of a railroad line or train: To branch or turn off at a switch. Also fig.

1853 MARK TWAIN *Letter* in *Iowa Journal* 413 (R.), Our train ran back half a mile and switched off another track, and stopped. **1887** DALY *Railroad of Love* 72 The track is ever smooth and straight, 'Tis only when the coupling breaks, Or we switch off, we seal our fate. **1905** *N.Y. Ev. Post* 27 Dec. 3 The freight was switching to this track as the passenger train was leaving it.

2. *fig. tr.* To move or shift (a thing or action) to another place or in another direction.

1860 HOLMES *E. Venner* xvii, Good ministers . . . sometimes contrive to switch off their logical faculties on the narrow side-track of their technical dogmas. **1911** HARRISON *Queed* 53 Suppose it popped into his head some day to switch all that directness and concentrated energy in some other direction.

b. *intr.* To turn *off*, to change sides in a controversy. *Colloq.*

1869 MARK TWAIN *Innocents Abroad* 432 We had all intended to go by diligence to Damascus, and switch off to Baalbec. **1898** WESTCOTT *D. Harum* xli, Did I ever tell you . . . how Lawyer Staples come to switch round in that there railroad jangle last spring?

c. *tr.* To interchange.

1897 *Columbus* (O.) *Dispatch* 18 June 5/2 An opportunity presented itself to 'switch' the bottles.

3. switchback, to ascend a hill in a manner suggestive of a railroad switchback. Also **switchbacking,** *n.*

1913 *Outing* Jan. 498/1 Switch-backing or zigzagging up a hill is simply striking off to the right, for instance, at an angle and then turning off to the left. **1920** *Ib.* July–Aug. 204/1 It is perfectly safe, but the trail switchbacks up a sixty-five degree slope for about a thousand feet. **1947** *Sierra Club* (So. Calif. Chap) *Sched.* 125, 84 We shall have to cross a stream thirty times, switchback to a saddle, climb a firebreak straight up, and crawl over a few rocks to reach the summit.

4. *I'll be switched,* I'll be doggoned. *Colloq.*

1838 *U.S. Mag.* I. 427, I'll be switched if I do. **1920** LEWIS *Main Street* 182 I'll be switched if I'll stand for your thinking I'm nothing but a dollar-chasing —.

switchel ˈswɪtʃəl, *n.* [Origin unknown. Cf. **swizzle*, a name for various intoxicating drinks.] A drink of molasses and water, often seasoned with vinegar and ginger, and sometimes with rum.

1790 FRENEAU *Poems* (1795) 375 For such attempts men drink your high-proof wines, Not spiritless switchel and vile hogo drams. **1834** *Mt. Carmel* (Ill.) *Sentinel* 15 Sep. 1/5 The first go off I took a leetle less New England in my switchell. **1946** *Yankee* Aug. 9 Our grandfathers would be drinking Switchel for refreshment: a mixture of water, ginger, molasses or vinegar, and sometimes rum.

switching yard. *Railroad.* **=switch yard.** — **1894** *Dly. Ardmoreite* (Ardmore, Okla.) 28 March 1/8 There came very near being a disastrous collision . . . in the upper switching yards of the Santa Fe. **1947** *Time* 6 Oct. 3/1 Sixteen men used to tug and sweat to lift one length of rail into place in this Detroit switching yard.

swivel chair. A chair the upper portion of which turns on a swivel. Cf. **whirligig seat.**

1860 HOLMES *Professor* 37 The swivel-chair spins round with me, as if it were giddy with pleasure. **1884** HOWELLS *S. Lapham* i, He continued, wheeling round in his leather-cushioned swivel-chair, and facing Bartley. **1950** *Time* 20 March 26/3 Some of them like to sit in swivel chairs and run things by correspondence.

Swivel chair or revolving chair

attrib. **1948** *Pacific Discovery* March–April 14/1 We might even claim that swivel chair birding is the busy person's method, while armchair birding is the lazy one's. **1949** *Miss. Valley Hist. Rev.* March 579 The *Utah Labor News* said it would be a 'sad mistake' for Roosevelt to appoint a 'swivel chair farmer.'

***sword,** *n.* **1. *sword-bearer,** (see quot. 1841). **2. sword palmetto,** ?the saw palmetto. *Rare.*

(1) 1841 HARRIS *Insects Mass.* 131 One more grasshopper . . . belongs to the genus *Conocephalus,* and . . . bears the specific name of *ensiger,* the sword-bearer, from the long, straight, sword-shaped piercer of the female. **1904** KELLOGG *Amer. Insects* 153. — **(2) 1834** AUDUBON *Ornith. Biog.* II. 236 A growth of rank grass . . . mixed with low bushes and sword palmettoes.

swow swaʊ, *v.* [App. a blend of *swear* and *vow.*] *I swow,* I declare. A mild oath. *Colloq.*

[**1790** *Mass. Spy* 30 Dec. 1/1 In one village you will hear the phrase 'I snore,'—in another 'I swowgar.'] **1843** STEPHENS *High Life N.Y.* I.

104, I swow, Miss Miles, you look as harnsome as a full blown rose. **1886** STAPLETON *Major's Christmas* 38 It's Freckles, I swow.

* **sycamore,** *n.* Any plane tree of the genus *Platanus*, a buttonwood. Cf. **European sycamore.**

1709 LAWSON *Carolina* 100 The Sycamore, in these Parts, grows in a low, swampy Land, by River-sides. **1848** *Santa Fe Republican* 15 Jan. 4/2 A new sort of sycamore tree made its appearance here; it has a bark precisely like our own sycamore tree or button wood, and a leaf resembling our maple. **1949** *News-Herald* (Marshfield, Wis.) 19 July 4/5 In the United States the plane tree is also known as sycamore and buttonwood.

attrib. **1750** T. WALKER *Journal* 56 I Blazed several Trees in the fork and marked T W on a Sycomore Tree. **1815** *Niles' Reg.* VIII. 135/1 We were desirous to see the effect of sinking large Sycamore gums as low down as we could force them. **1888** *Cent. Mag.* Sep. 770/1 A favorite lamp . . . was a saucer of lard with a dry sycamore ball floating in the midst of it. **1890** HOWELLS *Boy's Town* 70 He . . . was attended by two or three other boys from below the Sycamore Grove.

b. The planer tree, *Planera aquatica*. *Rare.*

1897 SUDWORTH *Arborescent Flora* 183 *Planera aquatica*, . . . Sycamore (N.C.).

c. sycamore warbler, a subspecies of yellow-throated warbler.

1886 *Amer. Ornith. Union Check List.* **1945** *Mass. Audubon Soc. Bul.* Feb. 18 This may account for the Yellow-throated Vireo, the Worm-eating Warbler and the Sycamore Warbler which have been seen recently or in years past.

* **Sydney,** *n. Pacific Coast.* [*Sydney*, Australia.] *attrib.* Designating an undesirable or criminal immigrant from Australia who came to California just after the discovery of gold there, as (1) **Sydney bird,** (2) **duck.** Now *obs.* or *hist.*

(1) **1851** in *One Man's Gold* (1930) 197 Chilians, Chinese, British convicts from New South Wales, known as 'Sidney Birds,' Englishmen, Frenchmen. **1935** BUCKBEE *Saga of Old Tuolumne* 22 The discontent quickly spread . . . to the Australian immigrants, who were known as 'Sydney Birds,' and 'clipped ears.' — (2) **1851** *S.F. Dispatch* 13 July 3/3 On board the Senator last Tuesday evening a Sidney duck was taken to the windless [*sic*] and received three dozen lashes for theft on board. **1880** BURNETT *Recollections* 342 The immigrants from Australia consisted in part of very bad characters, called 'Sydney Ducks.'

* **system,** *n.* As the last term in **alcalde, American, Australia, Australian, caucus, common school, convention, convict lease, Dewey Decimal, district, dormitory, elective, Federal Reserve, four shift, gag, honor, lecture, lyceum, manual labor, merit, national banking, object, papering, parole, pass, patrol, peon, Philadelphia, plantation, primary, renewal, salary, school, share, share crop, shingling, shotgun, silent, slave, spoils, Taconic, three shift system.**

T

* **T,** *n.* **1. T dagger,** a type of dagger formerly used by ruffians in New Orleans. *Obs.* **2. T.D. (pipe),** (see quot. 1889). Now *hist.*

(1) **1867** LATHAM *Black and White* 161 The dagger was a remarkable one, with a cross handle like a corkscrew, whence they are called 'T,' or 'cotton-hook' daggers. — (2) **1889** *N. & Q.* II. 114 'T.D. Pipes.' . . . It is said that they took their name from Timothy Dexter, an eccentric capitalist, who in his will left a large sum of money to be expended in the erection of a factory where cheap clay pipes, such as those that now bear the name of 'T.D.'s,' were to be manufactured. **1947** PAUL *Linden* 27 Deacon Parker, known to the boys as T.D., because he smoked the one-cent clay pipes of that name.

T.D. pipe and snuff stick or mop (sense 1)

* **tab,** *n.*[1] As the last term in **eartab.**

tab tæb, *n.*[2] [See note.]

The word * *tab* is given in the *OED* and in Webster as of obscure origin. The other senses of the word are so different from the uses shown here as to suggest that in these American senses **tab** is a different term altogether, being a shortening of * *tabulation.*

1. An account, check, or memorandum of what is owed or expended (see also quot. 1938).

1890 BIFF HALL *Turnover Club* 19 And they knocked off and filed out into the deserted streets, while the Purveyor figured up the 'tabs.' **1938** ASBURY *Sucker's Prog.* 14, 15 *Tabs*—Printed sheets on which the [faro] players noted the cards as they won or lost. *Keeping tabs*—Making this record.

2. a. *To keep tab on,* see * **keep,** *v.* **2.** (3). **b.** *To pick up the tab,* to pay the bill.

(b) **1950** *Chi. Sun-Times* 24 Jan. 27/2 Who's going to pick up the tab when the government is on relief?

tabasco tə'bæsko, *n.* [Name of a river and state in Mexico.] **1.** App. a fiery liquor formerly used in the Southwest. Also (*cap.*) a trade-mark name for next. **2. Tabasco sauce,** (see quot. 1909 in **1.**).

(1) **1876** J. MILLER *First Families* 126 The following popular drinks . . . were all made from the same decoction of bad rum, worse tabasco, and first-class cayenne pepper. **1909** *Cent. Supp.* 1314/1 tabasco. . . The trade-name given to a pungent sauce and to a catsup made from a variety of *Capsicum annuum* . . . and said to be prepared by extracting the pulp of the ripe fruit and so treating it as to retain its flavor, strength, aroma, and color. **1949** *N.O. Times-Picayune Mag.* 18 Sep. 39 Use Tabasco to season seafood, meats, vegetables, soups. — (2) **1894** *Amer. Anthrop.* July 299 The mescal . . . has added to it several kinds of roots and berries, the most important being chilchipin, said to be the basis of the fiery Tabasco sauce. **1942** PHILIPS *Big Spring* 163, I never will forget one old boy who helped himself to Tabasco sauce.

tabby 'tæbɪ, *n.* [See note.] (See quot. 1885.)

This word is app. chiefly confined to the Gullah region along the coast of Georgia and South Carolina. No doubt African slaves brought it to this region. Cf. Gullah *tabi kwus* in Turner 202/1. Arabic *tabix,* cement, mortar, brick, is the source of the African word. The term here shown is app. a different word from *OED Tabby, q.v.,* with esp. attention to the note and sense 6.

1775 *S.C. Hist. Mag.* VI. 91 [The Council of Safety ordered that Fort Lyttelton be repaired with] tappy. **1802** ELLICOTT *Journal* 267 That part of [Frederica] lying immediately on the water . . . was defended by a small battery of tabby work. **1833** SILLIMAN *Man. Sugar Cane* 36 The walls [of the draining rooms] are all constructed of tabby. **1885** EGGLESTON in *Cent. Mag.* April 874/2 A concrete of oyster shells, called 'tabby,' was much used on the southern coast; a wall and columns of this material, built before the Revolution, are still standing. ***c*1943** *Flags of Five Nations* 27 The old 'tabby' house, which it is thought Gwinnett built and where he made his home with his wife.

* **tabernacle,** *n.* A place of worship of the Mormons, esp. (*cap*) the great edifice in Salt Lake City, Utah.

1837 *New-Yorker* 8 July 250/3 The crazy fanatics have their grand tabernacle at a place they call Kirtland. **1852** *Harper's Mag.* Dec. 121/2 The Mormons . . . have finished their Tabernacle. **1892** GUNTER *Miss Dividends* 206 Mormons . . . have come to the Tabernacle from the south and the north, the east and the west.

* **table,** *n.* In combs.: (1) **table board,** board with lodging; (2) **girl,** a girl who waits on tables; (3) **-mountain pine,** "*Pinus pungens,* of the Alleghanies, in Tennessee forming large forests, in Pennsylvania largely made into charcoal" (*Cent.*); (4) **rock,** a flat-topped rock; (5) **spooning,** ?towing, *rare;* (6) **spread,** a cover for a table.

(1) **1883** HOWELLS *Woman's Reason* viii, People must find tableboard at some of the neighboring houses. **1898** PAGE *Red Rock* 113 Captain Stevenson Allen . . . had applied to her for table-board. — (2) **1877** HOWELLS *Out of Question* 14 Our table girls teach school in the winter and are as good as anybody. **1898** *McClure's Mag.* X. 208 A table-girl . . . serves you at a way-side cafe. — (3) **1810** MICHAUX *Arbres* I. 16 *Table mountain pine,* . . . seule dénomination . . . dans la haute Caroline du Nord. **1943** PEATTIE *Great Smokies* 164 The Appalachian forest formation contains, too, a large number of species peculiar to itself, like Carolina hemlock, table-mountain pine, and black locust, which give it character. — (4) **1841** BUCKINGHAM *America* II. 143 Now the rock of Niagara cliffs is not granitic or basaltic, but a slaty shale, lying in horizontal layers, and thus presenting those level surfaces called table-rocks. **1853** MRS. MOODIE *Life in Clearings* 365 The fall of that large portion of the table rock has made the alteration.

(5) **1851** HALL *Manhattaner* 168, I was in the cabin of the tow-boat, which was 'table-spooning' our gallant ship up the Mississippi. — (6) **1856** *Mich. Agric. Soc. Trans* VII. 64 Nall . . . [exhibited] 1 velvet table spread.

As the last term in **banknote, boarding, chair, crap, devil's tea, education, end, extension, extension-leaf dining, high, ice cream, ladies, mission, monte, percussion, rain, second, slime, training, traverse table.**

* **table,** *v. tr.* To postpone action on (a bill, resolution, etc.) by laying it on the table.

1849 *Whig Almanac 1850* 22/1 Senator Westcott tried to table the bill, but failed: it became law. **1916** THOBURN *Stand. Hist. Okla.* II. 715 [The bill] was sent to the council where it was considered, amended, and finally tabled. **1949** *Chi. D. News* 17 May 1/3 It [a bill] had been tabled in the Senate armed services committee for many weeks.

* **tack,** *n.* As the last term in **cold, cut, hard, land, soft, thumb tack(s).**

* **tackle,** *n.* In football, one of the two linesmen playing next to the guards; the position of such a player. Cf. **left tackle, side tackle.**

1893 CAMP *College Sports* 100 The two [players] next the ends . . . were called 'tackles.' **1920** *N.Y. Times* 7 Nov. IX. 1/7 Sherfy started off tackle on the next play, but fumbled. **1947** MOTLEY *Knock on Any Door* 28 He was a big, beefy man who might have played tackle on a college football team ten years earlier.

tackling bag. A stuffed bag suspended and used by football players for indoor practice in tackling. — **1892** *Outing* Jan. 279/2 Their one special piece of apparatus is . . . the tackling bag, and this is . . . necessary to the indoor practice of a football team.

tacky ˈtækɪ, *n.* and *a.* Also **tackey.** *S.* [Origin unknown.]

1. *n.* A small, insignificant horse. *Colloq.*

1800 Tatham *Communications* 81 You are thus asked (in local phrase and expression) to *truck* or *trade* for a horse, a cow, or a little *tackie*, &c. (which last term signifies a poney or little horse of low price). **1884** *Cent. Mag.* Jan. 444/2 The scrubby little 'tackeys' still taken in the marshes along the North Carolina coast are descendants of the wild horses of the colony. **1890** *N. & Q.* IV. 190 In Louisiana the inferior grade of Creole ponies are known as 'tackies.'

2. A hillbilly or cracker. *Colloq.*

[**1835** Simms *Partisan* (1854) 187 As if it wasn't curse enough to be blear-eyed without having every dirty field-tackey whickering about it.] **1896** *Peterson Mag.* Jan. 85/1 One need not look for refinement in a 'tacky.' **1907** Harris *Bishop & Boogerman* 49 He had discovered that the vegetables went to the maintenance of a small colony of 'tackies' that had settled near Shady Dale—'dirt-eaters' they were called.

3. *a.* Dowdy, shabby, common, lacking in good taste. *Colloq.*

1883 Rittenhouse *Maud* 262 Two little cards (with his name printed on them in gilt. Tackey? Ugh). **1931** *K.C. Star* 2 Dec. 28 Englishwomen have the knack of looking tacky even when they are wealthy and titled. **1948** *Miami* (Okla.) *News-Rec.* 30 June 7/6 Dorothy Jean Sigle and Larry Carnes were awarded prizes for the tackiest costumes.

b. tacky party, a party to which the guests come dressed as hayseeds or hillbillies. Cf. **hard times party, social.**

1904 *Charlotte* (N.C.) *Observer* 1 Sep. 2 A tacky party was given at the home of Mrs. G. W. Smithson. **1948** *Duncan* (Okla.) *D. Banner* 1 July 1/1 Mrs. W. E. Chaffin and Bill Proctor won first prizes . . . at the American Legion dance, picnic and tacky party last night.

As the last term in **cane, courting, marsh, piny woods, sand hill, swamp tacky.**

tacky-wax ˈtækɪˌwæks, *n. local.* [**tacky, a.*, sticky, adhesive, **wax.*] Homemade maple sugar candy in small cakes. — **1873** Haycraft *Elizabethtown, Ky.* 172 Then the molasses and tacky-wax made at those camps threw every other delicacy in the shade.

Taconic təˈkɑnɪk, *a.* [See quot. 1891 in **2.** below.]

1. (See quot. 1865 and cf. next.)

[**1833** Hitchcock *Rep. Geol. Mass.* (1835) 84 The summit of the Taconic Range corresponds nearly with the west line of the State.] **1849** Lyell *2nd Visit U.S.* (1850) II. 354, I believe the formations called Taconic, in the United States, . . . to be simply Silurian strata much altered, and often quite metamorphic. **1865** Page *Geol. Terms, Taconic*, a term applied by the late Professor Emmons to the rocks east of the Hudson (from the Taconic range lying along the western slope of the Green Mountains), . . . which consist of slates, quartz-rock, and lime-stones of Lower Silurian or perhaps more properly of Upper Cambrian age. **1892** *21st Ann. Rep. State Geol. Minn.* 116 There is therefore a general alliance between all the outcrops from Little Falls southward that requires them to go together into the same formation whether Archean or Taconic.

2. Taconic system, (see quot. 1891).

1844 Ebenezer Emmons (*title*) The Taconic System; Based on Observations in New-York, Massachusetts, Maine, Vermont and Rhode-Island. **1888** *Amer. Jrnl. Science* Dec. 427 'Taconic system' is only a synonym of the older term 'Lower Silurian,' as this term was used by geologists generally twenty . . . years since. **1891** *Cent.* 6143/1 *Taconic system* (so called from the Taconic Mountains, a branch or continuation of the Green Mountains in southern Vermont, western Massachusetts, and eastern New York); in *geol.*, rocks of Lower Silurian age (or Cambrian, in part, according to the nomenclature of the United States Geological Survey now adopted), more or less metamorphosed, formerly supposed by some geologists to constitute a distinct system.

Also **Taconic age.**

1899 N. H. Winchell *Geol. of Minn.* IV. 65 The Archean granite and gneiss, and the associated rocks of Taconic age, forming the Mesabi iron range, . . . doubtless continue westward beneath the drift to the Boy river.

taconite ˈtækənaɪt, *n.* [f. prec.] (See quots. 1892, 1944.)

1892 *21st Ann. Rep. State Geol. Minn.* 116 The rock struck first is taconyte, a grayish, cherty rock which is abundant on the Mesabi Range [in Minnesota], in connection with the ore. **1944** *Milwaukee Jrnl.* 13 Aug., That word is 'taconite.' Known in the Michigan peninsula as jasper, it is the name given to a low grade iron ore that abounds in the Lake Superior district in billions of tons. **1950** *Newsweek* 20 March 68/3 But if Big Steel should lose its Venezulean ore boats to submarines in a war, taconite would enable it to survive.

Hence **taconitic,** *a.*

1900 N. H. Winchell *Geol. Minn.* V. 738 There is a connective fine layering that forms the periphery of most of the compound or taconitic groups.

tacos ˈtakos, *n. pl. W.* [Sp. *taco*, in Amer. Sp. sense similar to that shown here.] Tortillas spread with a filling, rolled up and fried in fat. — **1934** Franklin School P.-T.A. (Ardmore, Okla.) *Favorite Recipes* 15 To be served with tocos. **1948** *Sat. Ev. Post* 2 Oct. 52/3 Senora Gonzalez does her stuff on such fabulous dishes as . . . *tacos*—crisp folded *tortillas* containing meat, lettuce and tomatoes [etc.].

tad tæd, *n.* [Prob. variant of **toad* in a sense similar to **2.** Cf. ME *taddle*, toad.]

1. In miscellaneous uses (see quots.). *Obs.*

1845 *Cincinnati Misc.* I. 240 Among a certain class in the eastern cities, . . . the word *Tad*, is applied to *one who don't nor won't pay.* **1851** Hall *College Words* 297 At Centre College, Ky., there is a society . . . composed of the very best fellows of the College, calling themselves Tads. **1890** Custer *Following Guidon* 213 These youths [although graduates of West Point] were called 'tads' and 'plebes,' and treated in a half-contemptuous manner by officers [until] . . . they had been in a fight.

2. A person, esp. a child. *Colloq.*

1877 Bartlett 688 *Little tads*, small boys. *Old tads*, graybeards, old men. **1904** Nesbit *Trail to Boyland* 49 That handle has been broken since he was just a tad.

3. ***tadpole, a.** (*cap.*) A Mississippian, a nickname. **b.** (See quot. 1888.)

(**a**) **1845** *St. Louis Reveille* 14 May 2/4 The inhabitants of Mississippi [are called] Tadpoles. **1946** McWilliams *So. Calif. Country* 172 Marylanders are 'crawthumpers'; Kentuckians, 'corncrackers'; Mississippians, 'tadpoles,' and so forth. — (**b**) **1888** Trumbull *Names of Birds* 75 Another name [for the hooded merganser] . . . commonly heard among the 'crackers' of St. Augustine is Tadpole. **1917** *Birds of Amer.* I. 112.

4. tadpole democracy, (see quot.). *Obs.*

1858 *N.Y. Tribune* 25 Jan. 2/4 These men have been christened 'the tadpole Democracy.' They claim to belong to the Free-State party at present, but will join the Democracy when party lines are drawn after Kansas is admitted as a State.

***taffy,** *n.*

1. Flattery, cajolery. Also as verb. *Colloq.*

1879 *Cong. Rec.* 15 April 462/1, [I wish to prevent them from] denouncing me as the coadjutor of the South, distributing 'taffy' to the South. **1889** *Texas Siftings* (N.Y.) 12 Jan. 11/3 I've advertised freely and taffied the editors, and stood beers to the reporters, but I've never had a decent report yet. **1904** *Buffalo Comm.* 2 Sep. 4 Watson the Populist takes no taffy from the democrats.

2. taffy bake, pull, pulling, an occasion upon which young people assemble to make taffy. *Colloq.*

1877 Phelps *Story of Avis* 31 There were twenty-five candy-pulls and taffy-bakes in that town that winter. **1912** *Out West* March 166/2 He wrote with beautiful flourishes, little notes of regret . . . declining all socials, taffy pullings and croquet parties. **1949** *Chi. Tribune* 11 Nov. III. 4/3 There is nothing like an old fashioned taffy pull.

As the last term in **molasses taffy.**

tafia ˈtæfɪə, *n.* [See note.]

The ultimate origin of this word is not known. It was in use in the West Indies as early as 1722 as the name given by natives and Negroes to rum made of sugar cane. The word appears in Malay dictionaries in the same sense. It was admitted to the dictionary of the French Academy in 1762. In U.S. use it is of Negro and Creole origin.

A rumlike spirituous liquor made from sugar-cane juice.

1775 Adair *Indians* 260 The French Alebahma Garrison had been . . . supplied pretty well with corrupting brandy, taffy, and decoying trifles. **1812** Stoddard *Sk. Louisiana* 304 In the neighbourhood of that city [New Orleans] were also twelve distilleries for making taffia. **1882** Buel *Metropolitan Life Unveiled* 526 Before each guest was . . . a vase with capacious and rounded belly, and a small spout, out of which the revelers drank wine or *tafia* (sugar-cane rum). **1946** Tallant *Voodoo in N.O.* 13 Then the others danced, pausing to drink of the contents of the inevitable caldron and quantities of tafia, a strong, raw alcoholic beverage.

Taftian ˈtæftɪən, *a.* Of or resembling Wm. Howard Taft (1857–1930), 27th President of the U.S. (1909–13). — **1913** *Chi. D. News* 3 March 8/1 Thus closes the Taftian era. **1921** *Double Dealer* April 157/1 His chuckle, however, is very Taftian indeed, and he employs it, as does Taft, as a prelude to a story.

***tag**, *n.*

1. A label to be attached to a box, piece of goods, etc.

1835 *Stimpson's Boston Directory* (*cover advt.*), Tags for Dry Goods put up in boxes of 1000. **1866** *Jamestown* (N.Y.) *Jrnl.* 1 June 3/5 [The patent tags] are better than the linen tags and cost only half as much. **1944** *Sears Cat.* (ed. 189) 479A Trappers' Supplies 40 tags $1.00.

b. tag tying, attaching strings to such tags.

1944 HOLTON *Yankees* 87, I wonder if during the last forty years anybody has thought of the once flourishing home industry of tag tying.

2. In special combs.: (1) **tag alder,** (see quot.); (2) **day,** a day upon which funds for some benevolent purpose are solicited, a tag being given each contributor; (3) **tail,** (see quot. 1864), *obs.*

(1) **1891** *Cent.* 6158/2 tag-alder. . . . A name for the alder in the United States, referring to *Alnus incana* or *A. serrulata* in the eastern part, and usually to *A. rubra* on the Pacific coast. [Colloq.] — (2) **1909** *Washington Post* 20 Feb. 3 Monday has been designated as 'tag day' in Alexandria, and the proceeds will be used to improve the children's playgrounds. **1949** *Courier-Journal* 3 Sep. 10/1 The conference agreed [upon] . . . a tag day on which Boy Scouts and Girl Scouts will solicit funds during the Kentucky State Fair. — (3) **1834** C. A. DAVIS *Lett. J. Downing* 311 You are surrounded by such a raft of snuffle-nose, scabby set of tag-tails, that I can't have nothin more to do with you. **1864** WEBSTER 1348/3 *Tag-tail*, . . . a person who attaches himself to another against the will of the latter; a dependent; a sycophant; a parasite.

As the last term in **baggage, bronco, chewing-tobacco, cross, fence, pine, price, squat, tin, tobacco, wood tag.**

tag tæg, *v.* [f. **tag*, a children's game.] *tr.* In certain games, to touch (a player). Also in baseball, to put (a player) out by touching him with the ball. Hence ***tagging**, *n.*

1878 HART *Sazerac Lying Club* 166 One of them, who had been 'tagged' seven times in succession, got tired, and proposed to change to playing house. **1891** *Amer. Folk-Lore* IV. 222 One player, who is 'it,' attempts to tag, or touch, one of the other players. **1924** C. WARDLAW *Fundamentals of Baseball* 44 It is often necessary to slide back to first in order to avoid tagging by the first-baseman. **1947** *Sat. Ev. Post* 8 March 118/4 Earle would throw the potato over the third baseman's head, and then tag the runner out with the real baseball.

transf. **1944** GARDNER *Black-Eyed Blonde* 64 Keep cutting corners, Mason, and I'm going to catch you off first base one of these days, and then I'll tag you out.

Tahoe trout. A large (up to sixty pounds) trout, *Salmo henshawi*, found in Lake Tahoe on the California and Nevada boundary and in nearby regions. — **1902** *Out West* Oct. 431 A magnificent string of Tahoe and Rainbow trout more than repaid us for two days spent in whipping the waters. **1942** LILLARD *Desert Challenge* 104 More common was the cut-throat later famous as the Tahoe trout, . . . the largest trout in America.

tahona tɑˈonə, *n. S.W.* [Sp., a grain mill.] *Mining.* A form of arrastre *q.v.* — **1851** *S.F. Herald* 2 Oct. 2/3 These engines are now effectually working twelve stampers and twelve *tahonas*. **1864** MOWRY *Ariz. & Sonora* 118 The existing hacienda consists of two small patios and . . . three tahonas or arrastras, . . . one melting furnace and one reverberatory, with the requisite sheds.

Tahosa təˈhosə, *n.* [Allegedly f. Amer. Indian.] One of the many names suggested for what is now the state of Idaho. *Obs.* — **c1860** in STEWART *Names on Land* (1945) 302 The House seems to have hit upon the very appropriate name of 'Tahosa' which means Dwellers on the Mountain Tops. **1866** *Beadle's Mo.* June 495/2 Several early attempts were made to organize the new territory, under the successive names of Jefferson, Idaho (Shining Mountains), and Tahosa (Dwellers among the Mountain-tops).

***tail**, *n.*

1. = ***foot**, *n.* **1.** *Colloq.*

1865 *Atlantic Mo.* June 737/2 He is disheartened by always being at the tail of his class.

2. *pl.* A swallow-tailed or full dress coat. *Colloq.*

1909 WEBSTER. **1946** *Chi. D. News* 22 April 8/3 The boiled shirt and the tails are disappearing from our social life, and a good thing, too. **1949** *Democrat* 5 May 3/2 Waiters in tails hover over prosperous-looking men with beautiful, expensively dressed women.

3. In combs.: (1) **tail band,** (see quot.), *rare;* (2) **chain,** (see quot.); (3) **digging,** *W.* = **tail flume,** *obs.;* (4) ***ender,** an athletic team in the last place in league standing, *colloq.;* (5) **flume,** *W.* a flume or digging that serves as an outlet, *obs.;* (6) **fly,** in angling, the fly at the end of a leader; (7) **gate,** (*a*) a gate or barrier in the tail-race of a water mill, in a canal lock, the lower gate, (*b*) the tailboard of a wagon, or a similar part of a railroad car; (8) **hold,** a sitting-down position, *jocular, rare;* (9) **house,** (see quots.); (10) **rider,** (see quot.); (11) **sluice,** (see quot. 1877); (12) **vise,** (see quot.).

(1) **1890** HOWELLS *Boy's Town* 90 The kite . . . had to be hung, with belly-bands, and tail-bands; that is, with strings carried from stick to stick over the face and at the bottom. — (2) **1905** *Forestry Bureau Bul.* No. 61, 50 *Tail chain*, a heavy chain bound around the trailing end of logs as a brake, in slooping on steep slopes. (N[orth] W[oods].) — (3) **1867** *Wkly. New Mexican* 23 Feb. 1/3 [They] had to make tail-diggings of about 160 feet in length to draw off the water. — (4) **1887** *Chi. Inter-Ocean* 7 May (E. J. Nichols). **1889** *S.F. Bulletin* 26 July 1/7 The game was finally won by the tail-enders by a score of 5 to 0. **1948** *Chi. Tribune* 20 June II. 1/8 Eight of the Sox's first dozen victories this season bloomed from double headers, and its things like that that make even tailenders bubble with confidence.

(5) **1867** *Terr. Enterprise* (Virginia, Nev.) 10 Dec. 3/1 It is feared that much damage will be done to the tail-flumes in the canyons. **1882** *47th Congress* 1 Sess. H.R. Ex. Doc. No. 216, 99 The mine . . . is provided with a large dump-house, reservoir, and lengthy tail flumes. — (6) **1869** W. MURRAY *Adventures* 67 For the tail fly I noosed on a brown hackle. **1899** VAN DYKE *Fisherman's Luck* 44 He does not . . . tear the tail-fly out of the fish's mouth. — (7) (*a*) **1853** *S. Lit. Messenger* XIX. 665/1 Bethink you of a fish sailing around the tail-gate of a country-mill. **1875** KNIGHT 1341/1 The head-gate and tail-gate [of a canal lock], . . . with the side-walls, inclose the lock-chamber. (*b*) **1868** *Ore. State Jrnl.* 28 Nov. 2/3 The whole charge—24 buck shot—[passed] through the tailgate of the wagon. **1909** WEBSTER 2106 *Tail gate*, . . . a heavy wooden panel pivoted to the end of a railroad car to form an incline from the car bottom to the rails. — (8) **1878** BEADLE *Western Wilds* 459 The walking was comparatively easy . . . suddenly the walker's breath gave out and he took 'tail hold.' — (9) **1881** RAYMOND *Mining Gloss.*, *Tail-house, tail-mill*, the buildings in which *tailings* are treated. **1888** *Scribner's Mag.* Jan. 22/2 This tail-house, or receiving house [for oil], was a favorite haunt of hers.

(10) **1926** BRANCH *Cowboy* 22 'Tail riders,' cowboys who rode in the rear of moving cattleherds to keep the stragglers in the procession, protected themselves from the dust by pulling their bandannas up to their eyes. — (11) **1871** RAYMOND *3d Rep. Mines* 85 This tail-sluice cost $55,000, and has been exceedingly profitable. **1877** BARTLETT 611 A *tail-sluice* is a sluice below other sluices through which the earth and water passes. — (12) **1864** WEBSTER 1349/2 *Tail-vise*, a small hand-vise, with a tail or handle to hold it by.

b. *W. To roll one's tail*, (see quots.). *Slang.*

1894 REMINGTON in *Harper's Mag.* LXXXVIII. 381/1 They had 'rolled their tails' for Bavicora. . . . [Note:] Cowboy for travelling rapidly. **1944** ADAMS *W. Words* 130 roll his tail Another slang expression for leaving on the run.

As the last term in **beaver, black, blue, boat, bob, broom, buck, cat o' nine, cat o' sixty-nine, club, coon, cotton, cow-hide, dog, fan, forceps, fork, hard, hollow, lobster('s), pigeon, pin, rat, red, ring, sharp, shave, shirt, soap, spike, spindle, spine, split, sprig, spring, stiff, stub, stump, swallow, swallow's, swingle, tag, tattle, top, turkey, white, wiggle, willow, wolf, yellow tail(s).**

***tail**, *v.*

1. a. *tr.* To catch by the tail (a deer that is in the water or otherwise hampered) in order to kill it with a knife. *Rare.* **b.** To upset or throw (a bull or pony) by grasping its tail and tripping or turning it about. Cf. **colear.**

(**a**) **1839** HOFFMAN *Wild Scenes* 61 A man that can't tail a deer, oughtn't to hunt him. — (**b**) **1895** REMINGTON *Pony Tracks* 95 Mr. Bailey . . . in the next instant 'tailed' and threw the bull as it was about to enter the timber. **1897** LEWIS *Wolfville* 203 'What's tailin' a pony?' 'It's ridin' up from the r'ar an' takin' a half-hitch on your saddle-horn with the tail of another gent's pony an' then spurrin' by an' swappin' ends with the whole outfit,—gent, hoss, an' all.' **1929** DOBIE *Vaquero* 15 The safest and most effective thing to do when an old steer ran off was to tail him.

2. In colloq. phrases: (1) *To tail down*, (*a*) to ease (a heavy load or a heavily loaded wagon) down a steep hill, cf. ***tailing 1,** (*b*) (see quot.), (*c*) *W.* to hold (a range animal) by the tail; (2) *to tail up*, (see quot. 1926).

(1) (*a*) **1851** *Harper's Mag.* Sep. 518/1 In this manner the load is 'tailed down' steeps where it would be impossible for the 'tongue oxen' to resist the pressure of the load. (*b*) **1905** *Forestry Bureau Bul.* No. 61, 50 *Taildown, to*, to roll logs on a skidway to a point on the skids where they can be quickly reached by the loading crew. (N[orthern] F[orest].) (*c*) **1929** DOBIE *Vaquero* 288 He was pointed towards Claude, and Claude expected me to 'tail him down' while he mounted his horse. — (2) **1868** *Iowa State Agric. Soc. Rep. 1867* 129 Shelter and good feeding is a sure preventive [for hollow horn], and much cheaper than 'tailing them up' or taking off their hides toward

Spring. **1926** Branch *Cowboy* 101 The cowboys had to 'tail 'em up'—to twist the tail of the benumbed animal until the agony forced it to rise.

*tailed, *a.* As the last term in **bob, red, ring, yellow-tailed.**

*tailer, *n. Stock Exchange.* (See quots.) — **1900** S. A. Nelson *A B C Wall St.* 161 Tailer. Big operators have a following of little traders who tail-on a bull or a bear movement on the theory that to make money it is a good thing to follow in the wake of the successful men. **1902** Norris *Pit* (1922) viii, The 'tailers'—the little Bulls—were radiant.

tailing, *n.

1. a. (See quot. and cf. ***tail,** *v.* **2.** (1).) *Obs.* **b.** *W.* The action of throwing an animal by the tail.

(a) **1792** Belknap *Hist. New-Hampshire* III. 106 Some of the cattle are placed behind it [the load]; a chain . . . attached to their yokes is brought forward and fastened to the hinder end of the load, and the resistance which is made by these cattle checks the descent. This operation is called *tailing*. — (b) **1895** Remington *Pony Tracks* 86 The process of 'tailing' is indulged in, although it is a dangerous practice. . . . A man will pursue a bull at top speed, will . . . grasp (the) tail of the animal, bring it to his saddle, throw his right leg over the tail and swing his horse suddenly . . . to the left, which throws the bull rolling over and over. **1929** Dobie *Vaquero* 15 A thorough tailing usually knocked the breath out of him.

2. *pl.* The refuse or debris resulting from the washing of ground ore.

1853 *Alta California* (S.F.) 31 May 2/1 It is a large sluice or flume, about half a mile long; . . . which receives all the water and tailings which pass from the hundred sluices of the miners along its line. *a*1918 G. Stuart *On Frontier* I. 89 Shallow gulches . . . would not afford any place for sluices to dump tailings. **1950** *Nat. Hist.* April 192/3 It was quartz sand from the tailings of gold mines up country.

attrib. **1860** *Harper's Mag.* April 616/1 Numberless are the 'tailing companies,' whose labors are confined to washing by a more careful method the 'tailings' or refuse discharged from the end of the sluices. **1923** Bower *Parowan Bonanza* 46 He showed me a piece of rock no better than you can pick up on any tailing dump in Goldfield.

fig. **1876** Miller *First Fam'lies* 226 He now found that the entire end of his father's name had been . . . worn or torn away, and hid or covered up forever in the tailings. **1889** Munroe *Golden Days* 268 Come in and take a smile to wash the tailings out of your throats.

As the last term in **bull, dove, pan tailing(s).**

***tailor,** *n.* **1.** =**tailor herring,** or the bluefish, *Pomatomus saltatrix.* **2. tailor bee,** any one of various leaf-cutting bees. **3. tailor herring,** the fall herring or mattowacca, *Pomolobus mediocris.* **4. tailor shad,** see **shad 3.**

(1) **1676** Glover in *Phil. Trans.* XI. 625 In the Creeks are great store of small fish, as Perches, crokers, Taylors, Eels, and divers others. **1709** Lawson *Carolina* 158 The Taylor is a Fish about the bigness of a Trout, but of a bluish green colour, with a forked Tail. **1850** Lanman *Haw-ho-noo* 156 Blue Fish . . . are found on the sea coast as far south as Norfolk (where they are called tailors). **1903** T. H. Bean *Fishes N.Y.* 446 Some of the many names applied to this widely distributed fish are . . . salt-water jack (southern states), tailor (Chesapeake bay), whitefish (Hudson river). — (2) **1867** *Amer. Naturalist* I. 373 The interesting habits of the Leaf-cutting, or Tailor-bee (*Megachile*), have always attracted attention. **1873** *Harper's Mag.* March 595/2 Peggy rolled out her paste reflectively, and lined a deep pan as daintily as the tailor-bee lines her nest with a rose leaf. — (3) **1883** *Nat. Museum Bul.* No. 27, 476 Hickory Shad; Tailor Herring; Fall Herring. . . . This is a comparatively poor fish, yet it is largely sold by unprincipled persons as the true shad. **1911** *Rep. Fisheries 1908* 312/1 Mattowacca . . . is called . . . 'tailor shad,' 'tailor herring,' and 'fresh-water tailor' in the Potomac.

As the last term in **custom, fresh-water, gentleman, man, salt-water, shad tailor.**

take, *v.

1. *tr.* To vanquish, defeat (an opponent). *Slang.* Cf. *to take into camp s.v.* ***camp 7. b.** (3).

1880 *Chi. Inter-Ocean* 11 June 8/1 They Take Troy, The Chicago Club Does Vanquish the Nine of That Classic Village.

2. With adverbs and prepositions in colloq. uses: (1) **To take in,* (*a*) to visit as a part of a journey, to attend or inspect, (*b*) of a school, to begin, also to teach (school); (2) **to take out,* to cease plowing and unharness the draft animal or animals; (3) **to take up,* (*a*) of a school, to begin, (*b*) to destroy (a nest or hive of bees), to collect (honey).

(1) (*a*) **1755** *Essex Inst. Coll.* LII. 80 In our way by the Skuylkill rd. took in ye prop[rieto]rs Gardens. **1886** *Puck's Annual* 16, I might stop over another day and take it in. **1906** *Springfield W. Republican* 4 Oct. 5 American visitors to London would do well to 'take in' some of the lesser-known auction-rooms. (*b*) **1876** Mark Twain *Tom Sawyer* xx, She could hardly wait for school to 'take in,' she was so impatient to see Tom flogged. **1894** *Amer. Missionary* Sep. 324 Here, not quite two years up, we, in the dialect of the country [Miss.], 'took in school.' — (2) **1935** Mudd *Old Boat Rocker* 107 He 'took out,' hung the harness in a tree, left the plow where it was and told the mule to go to the barn. — (3) (*a*) **1876** Mark Twain *Tom Sawyer* xiii, The bell for school to 'take up' tinkled faintly. **1903** Fox *Little Shepherd* iii, When school 'took up' again Chad was told to say them aloud in concert with the others. (*b*) **1880** *Harper's Mag.* Oct. 777/1 This fearless being, however, knew only one way to 'take up the honey,' viz., to brimstone the bees, killing every one. **1885** C. A. Stephens *Adv. Six Young Men* 101 There were numerous bumble-bees' nests in the grass and about the old stumps. We 'took up' not less than ten that forenoon.

b. In colloq. phrases: (1) *To take a tree,* to take refuge behind or up a tree; (2) *to take the hair,* (see quot.), *obs.;* (3) *to take the starch out of,* to deflate, to make less haughty, to tire or weary; (4) *to take a hand in,* to participate in; (5) *to take a brace,* see ***brace,** *n.*[2] **1;** (6) *to take for a ride,* (see first quot.), also transf.; (7) *to take it out on,* to force (another) to bear the brunt of something.

(1) **1835** Simms *Yemassee* II. 168 The foresters took their tree when necessary, as well as their enemies. **1853** P. Paxton *Yankee in Texas* 30 To all appearance the bear had either taken a tree, or else . . . turned upon his tormenting pursuers. — (2) **1858** Peters *Kit Carson* 215 The common expression now in use is that they proceeded to 'take the hair' of their victims. — (3) **1868** T. H. Sheridan in *U.S. Pub. Doc.* No. 1360, 40 The Cheyennes . . . attempted to browbeat General Hazen. . . . I will take some starch out of them before I get through with them. **1868** Mrs. M. J. Carrington *Absaraka* 174/5 Its practical suggestions take all the starch and false pride as to work completely out of the unfortunate human creature. **1939** Pinkerton *Wilderness Wife* 21 The trail led steeply over a granite rise which took the starch out of Robert's knees as he climbed it with two pack-sacks. — (4) **1874** Eggleston *Circuit Rider* 69 The new-comers 'took a hand' in all the sports. **1880** *Harper's Mag.* March 623/1 General Jackson . . . 'took a hand in' as soon as he could, by calling Mr. Eaton to the cabinet.

(6) **1931** F. L. Allen *Only Yesterday* x. 261 Another favorite method was to take the victim 'for a ride': in other words, to lure him into a supposedly friendly car, shoot him at leisure [etc.]. **1947** *Chi. Tribune* 21 July 1/6 They threatened to take him for a ride unless he produced the money. **1947** Cahalane *Mammals* 171 At least one mallard duck took a marten 'for a ride.' — (7) **1943** Menefee *Assignment* 7 They identify themselves with the original Yankees, and overcompensate for their lack of American background by 'taking it out' on other immigrant groups.

***taker,** *n.* As the last term in **census, entry, scalp, snuff, water taker.**

Talapoosa ˌtæləˈpusə, *n.* [Native word of unknown meaning.] (See quot. 1910.) Also an Indian of one of these towns or tribes.

1722 Coxe *Descr. Carolana* 23 Upon or near the Middle of it live the great Nations of the Cusshetaes, Tallibousies, and Adgebaches. **1771** Mease *Narrative* 89 At this Place we met with a Party of Thirteen Creeks or Talapouses, headed by one M'Gillivray. **1910** Hodge *Amer. Indians* II. 677/2 Talapoosa. A comprehensive name for the Creek towns and tribes formerly on Tallapoosa r., Ala.

talk, *n.

1. A powwow or conference among or with Indians; a message or speech sent to or received from them. Now *hist.*

1725 in *Travels Amer. Col.* 102, I answered . . . that I was come with a great talk from all the beloved men of the English. **1807** in *Niles' Reg.* II. 342/2 The enclosed *talk* which has been industriously spread among them needs no comment. **1851** *Miss. Palladium* (Holly Springs) 2 May 3/2 The Indians have had a 'talk' with the commissioners, and agreed to stop stealing. **1949** *Wm. & Mary Coll. Quart.* Jan. 17 In July, 1792, some of the tribes sent a 'talk' to the Spanish Indian agent.

2. talkfest, an informal meeting during which there is much pleasant talk or discussion. *Slang.* Cf. **fest.**

1910 *Chi. D. Maroon* 10 June 1/2 After the roll call a 'talk fest' was indulged in by some of the old timers. **1928** W. A. White *Masks in Pageant* 247 He stepped naturally into supremacy at that talkfest [a political convention] because he had been training for his famous speech. **1949** *Chi. D. News* 26 March 6/1 He objects to the 'talkfests' in Congress which delay legislation favored by the people.

3. a. *To be on talk,* to be under discussion, *rare.* **b.** *that's the talk,* that's right, that's the stuff, *colloq.* **c.** *all talk and no cider,* see ***cider,** *n.* **2.**

(a) **1838** AUDUBON in *Harper's Mag.* LXI. 674/1 Just such an expedition is now *on talk.* — (b) **1857** *Lawrence* (Kans.) *Republican* 11 June 2 Good, good, that's the talk. **1876** MARK TWAIN *Tom Sawyer* ix, 'That's the talk,' said Injun Joe.

As the last term in **baby, big, chalk, long, medicine, Negro, peace, pep, sales, smoke, squaw, war talk.**

* **talk,** *v.*

1. *intr.* To parley, have a conference. *Rare.*

1868 *Harper's Mag.* Feb. 302/2 He told him that it was Pawnee-Killer and some other Sioux chiefs, who were anxious to 'talk.'

2. With adverbs in colloq. use: (1) *To talk back,* to answer back, to indulge in back talk, also *talking back;* (2) *to talk up,* (*a*) to talk freely or boldly *to,* (*b*) to discuss (a matter) in an effort to arouse interest.

(1) **1869** MARK TWAIN *Innocents Abroad* 112 There was no 'talking back,' no dissatisfaction about over-charging, no grumbling about anything. **1887** BILLINGS *Hardtack* 144 Some of the more common ways of showing disrespect were to 'talk back,' in strong unmilitary language. **1946** NEWTON *P. Bunyan* 71 Well, I didn't talk back to Sniffy. — (2) (*a*) **1843** STEPHENS *High Life N.Y.* II. 190, I talked right up to him, as a free-born American ought tu. (*b*) **1872** *Vt. Bd. Agric. Rep.* I. 679 This little conversation led me to talk the matter up with the marble dealers. **1884** *Ib.* VIII. 30 The subject . . . was talked up quite extensively.

3. In colloq. phrases: (1) *To talk against time,* to forestall an undesirable event by talking until a particular time; (2) *to talk baby (talk),* to talk as or as to a baby; (3) *to talk stand,* (see quot.), *obs.;* (4) *to talk to death,* to prevent the passage of (a bill or other legislative measure) by continuing discussion of it until the time of adjournment is reached; (5) *to talk round a five-cornered stump,* see * **five,** *a.* **2. c.** (3); (6) *to talk the bark off a tree,* see * **bark,** *n.*[1] **2. c.** (4); (7) *to talk turkey,* see * **turkey.**

(1) **1838** *Democratic Rev.* I. 44 A minority, however small, who may determine to 'talk against time.' — (2) **1865** *Atlantic Mo.* XV. 495 She never petted him. . . . She never let him talk baby-talk or have any baby-talk talked to him. **1869** LOWELL *My Study Windows* 82 Don't shake that rattle in our faces, nor talk baby to us any longer. — (3) **1871** BAGG *At Yale* 594 To 'talk stand' . . . is, to make the rank and recitation-marks of various men a topic for extended conversation. — (4) **1884** *Boston Herald* 17 Jan., Its danger is it may be talked to death. **1908** STEVENS *Liberators* 304 The opponents of the measure undertook to talk them to death.

* **talkee-talkee,** *n.* A talkative person. *Rare.* — **1877** *Harper's Mag.* Dec. 38/1, I am only giving to these talkee-talkees the right to bully me.

* **talker,** *n.* As the last term in **chalk, sign talker.**

talkie ˈtɔkɪ, *n.* A motion picture accompanied by sound effects, such as spoken words, music, etc.

[**1913** *Munsey's Mag.* March 957/1 The 'movie' had received its full brother in the 'talkie' [i.e., Edison's kinetophone], and a new era had begun in the progress of one of the most amazing of modern amusement enterprises.] **1928** *Ladies' Home Jrnl.* Nov. 25/1 There are already a confusing number of devices for making the talkies. **1949** *Chi. Tribune* 21 Sep. 30/5 He made 218 pictures in all, topped by such epics as the silent 'Vanishing American' and the talkie 'Cimarron.'

* **talking,** *n.* or *a.* In combs.: (1) **talking box,** the wheelbox of a wagon, *obs.,* cf. * **sandbox** (*b*); (2) **iron,** a firearm, *slang;* (3) * **machine,** (*a*) a phonograph, (*b*) the sound-producing mechanism of a talking doll, *rare.*

(1) **1910** J. HART *Vigilante Girl* 139 Same way with them teamsters —you seen how they heerd our talkin'-boxes, and are gittin' ready for us to pass 'em. — (2) **1843** HALIBURTON *Attaché* 1 Ser. ii, I jist hops out of bed . . . and outs with my talkin' irons, that was already loaded. **1944** ADAMS *W. Words* 162 talkin' iron Slang name for a gun. — (3) (*a*) [**1844** *Quincy* (Ill.) *Herald* 9 Feb. 3/2 A German, named Faber, residing in New York, has invented and brought to perfection a talking machine. It is played on by keys like a piano, and can be made to say any thing, in any language, that its inventor desires.] **1844** in *Amer. Sp.* XXI. (1946) 118/2 Why *don't* you go see the Talking Machine, and take little Matilda along with you? **1946** WILSON *Fidelity* 216 The children . . . told us that a man was going to exhibit a talking machine. (*b*) **1897** STUART *Simpkinsville* 110 The little talkin' machine inside it has got out o' fix . . . an' it don't say 'papa' an' 'mama' any more.

* **tall,** *a.* and *adv.*

1. Denoting something regarded as superlative or unusual, remarkable, extravagant, etc. *Colloq.*

1834 in MACKENZIE *Van Buren* 253 Our brethren in Oneida are all 'with one accord united'—look out for a tall majority in O. **1852** *Ore. Statesman* 11 May 1/2 Pretty tall fodder; chickens, hams, pine-apples and o-be-joyful. **1902** WISTER *Virginians* 338 Editors immediately reared a tall war out of [the event].

b. *To walk tall,* to walk handsomely or proudly. *Colloq.*

*c***1845** *Big Bear Ark.* 174 You ort'er bin thar if you aint never seen a man walk *tall;* every time he stept, his legs went out to right angles. **1869** STOWE *Oldtown Folks* 72 You're the fust one . . . that's got into college, and I'm 'mazing proud on't. I tell you I walk tall.

2. Of speech or utterance: Exaggerated, highly colored. Also as adv. *Colloq.*

1842 *Knickerb.* XIX. 221 One of the striking peculiarities of our people is the disposition to talk tall. **1865** SALA *Diary* II. 311 They . . . smack their lips over the 'tall talk.' **1891** *N.Y. Times* 26 Jan. (*Cent.*), A tall yarn about the Jews wanting to buy the Vatican copy of the Hebrew Bible. **1902** ELIZ. L. BANKS *Newspaper Girl* 279 Nor do I think that there is anything 'tall' in this statement. **1938** SMITTER *F.O.B. Detroit* 102 Blame it all—I don't like to tell such tall lies.

Hence **tall talker, tall talking.**

1856 GOODRICH *Recoll.* I. 129 Since everything goes by steam and electricity, tall walking and tall talking are the vogue. **1867** *Ore. State Jrnl.* 25 May 4/1 But the tallest talker and the one that had more cheek than any of us was a certain Jonah Squires.

b. Esp. (1) **tall story,** a story that is highly exaggerated or difficult to believe; (2) **tale,** =prec.

(1) [*c***1845** *Big Bear Ark.* 22 A 'live Sucker' from Illinois . . . had the daring to say that our Arkansaw friend's stories 'smelt rather tall.'] **1846** *Dollar Newspaper* (Phila.) 27 May 4/6 This is a 'tall story,' it is true; but we have no special reasons . . . for calling in question its credibility. **1948** *Durant* (Okla.) *D. Democrat* 4 July 21/1 The writer was accused last week of telling a tall story about the fly fisherman catching catfish with a fly-rod. — (2) **1927** BENÉT *J. B.'s Body* 59 Lincoln, six feet one in his stocking feet, . . . Whose wit was a coon-skin sack of dry, tall tales. **1949** *Nat. Hist.* June 267/1 Looking at the magnificent spectacle, we had to admit that the men who told the tallest tales had been most nearly correct in their descriptions.

3. In special combs.: (1) **tall country,** the mountains, *rare;* (2) **feed,** (see quot. 1848), *obs.;* (3) **girl,** (see quot.), *rare;* (4) **timber,** see * **timber 3.**

(1) **1907** S. E. WHITE *Arizona Nights* 12, I . . . made a climb for the tall country, aiming to wait around until dark. — (2) **1848** G. E. ELLIS *Lett.* (Bartlett MS), [I have heard] *tall feed*—as high grass. **1863** RANDALL *Pract. Shepherd* 371, I might have imagined that it [*sc.* hoofrot] was caused by 'tall feed.' — (3) **1870** MACRAE *Americans* II. 337 In Vermont they speak about *tall* girls, meaning gay.

b. Used of tall species or varieties of trees and plants, as (1) **tall button-snakeroot,** (2) **buckeye,** (3) **gallberry,** (4) **grass.**

(1) **1843** TORREY *Flora N.Y.* I. 325 *Liatris spicata.* . . . Tall Button-Snakeroot. . . . A popular medicine, being employed as a tonic and diuretic. — (2) **1806** SHECUT *Flora Carolinæensis* I. 106 Yellow flowered Horse Chesnut, or Tall Buck Eye, or Deers Eye, . . . a native of the western parts of Pennsylvania and Virginia. — (3) **1860** CURTIS *Woody Plants N.C.* 60 Tall Gallberry, (*I[lex] coriacea,*) . . . grows in similar situations. — (4) **1846** in EMORY *Military Reconn.* 386 The whole country is verdant with the rank growth of the 'tall grass,' as it is called by way of eminence, when compared with that which grows beyond the region of the walnut and the hickory. **1901** MOHR *Plant Life Ala.* 371 *Agrostis altissima.* . . . Tall Bent Grass. . . . New England and New York to North Carolina; California.

tall oil. (See quot. 1948.)

1934 WEBSTER. **1948** *Progress Thru Research* Summer 1/1 The name *tall oil* is an Americanized Swedish-German hybrid. The Swedes, who were active in first developing tall oil, called it tallolja (meaning pine oil) because it is an oily material obtained from pine wood during the manufacture of paper. At the time, however, the term pine oil was already used in Europe and America to describe a different oil obtained from pine trees. To avoid confusion, the Germans, who were among the first to use tall oil extensively, coined the word Tallöl, from the Swedish 'tall' for pine and the German 'öl' for oil. In the United States, this became 'tall oil,' the name by which the product is known today.

* **tallow,** *n.* In combs.: (1) **tallow berry,** (*a*) a partridgeberry or checkerberry, (*b*) the locustberry, *Byrsonima spicata,* of Florida; (2) **bush,** ?= **tallow shrub;** (3) **hunt,** a hunt for buffalo in order to obtain tallow, *rare;* (4) **nut,** the mountain plum, *Vimenia americana,* of Florida; (5) **shrub,** the wax myrtle; (6) **weed,** (see quot.).

(1) (*a*) **1867** DE VOE *Market Ass't* 392 Tallow-berries, or ground-berries. These small red berries are found growing on a small, tender vine resting on the ground, in the cleared woods; and when eaten, they have a sort of sweetish, tallowy taste, but rather pleasant. (*b*) **1884**

SARGENT *Rep. Forests* 28 *Byrsonima lucida*. . . . Tallowberry. Glamberry. Semi-tropical Florida, on the southern keys. — (2) **1835** SIMMS *Partisan* (1854) 387 The prisoners . . . had been made to file into the groves of tallow bushes. — (3) **1821** NUTTALL *Travels Arkansa* 182 The Osages had now returned to their village from a tallow hunt. — (4) **1791** W. BARTRAM *Travels* 94 These shelly ridges have a vegetable surface of loose black mould, very fertile, which naturally produces . . . Tallow-nut, or Wild Lime, and many others. **1884** SARGENT *Rep. Forests* 34 Wild Lime. Tallow Nut. . . . Common and reaching its greatest development in Florida on the west coast.

(5) **1770** FORSTER tr. *Kalm's Trav.* I. 192 Candleberry Tree, Bayberry-bush, [or] Tallow shrub. **1789** ANBUREY *Travels* II. 300 [The candles] were made from the berries of a tree, which is called [in Pa.] the tallow shrub. **1911** *Boston Transcript* 27 May II. 3/7 The early English settlers called this plant [the bayberry] the 'Candleberry tree,' and the Swedes called it the 'Tallow-shrub.' — (6) **1909** *Cent. Supp.* 1317/3 *Tallow-weed*, . . . a native forage plant, *Tetraneuris linearifolia*, of southern and western Texas. . . . Its name is due to its remarkable fattening quality.

As the last term in **bayberry, elk tallow.**

*** tally,** *n.*

1. In baseball, a score, or a total of scores.

1856 *Spirit of Times* 27 Dec. 276/3 One of these swiftly-delivered balls, when stopped by a skillful batsman, is sure to give the . . . striker time to go his rounds in safety, and score one tally as he reaches home. **1868** CHADWICK *Base Ball* 46 *Tally.*—This term applies to the total score of the single innings played, or of the even innings, or of the totals at the close of the match. **1875** *Chi. Tribune* 29 July 5/4 [They] were only two tallies behind at the beginning of the ninth inning. **1949** *News-Herald* (Marshfield, Wis.) 19 July 9/1 Phil Satkowiak homered with none on in the fourth and his teammates added two more tallies.

2. In combs.: (1) * **tally board,** (*a*) a board containing instructions sent along with a tailblock to a shipwrecked vessel, (*b*) (see quot. 1905); (2) **card,** a scorecard, a tally sheet; (3) * **man,** = **scorekeeper,** *obs.;* (4) **pole,** a pole to which a beaver trap is affixed; (5) **sheet,** a sheet on which a tally is kept, esp. one used in keeping a record of votes cast; (6) **wag,** (see quot.).

(1) (*a*) **1882** *Harper's Mag.* Feb. 372/1 The whip or hauling-line . . . is drawn on board with a pulley-block, . . . and a tablet, or tally board. (*b*) **1901** MERWIN-WEBSTER *Calumet 'K'* 11 The red-headed young man . . . came in, tossed a tally board on the desk, and said that another carload of timber had come in. **1905** *Forestry Bureau Bul.* No. 61, 50 *Tally board,* a thin smooth board used by a scaler to record the number or volume of logs. — (2) **1909** *Cent. Supp.* 1317/3. **1928** *Publishers' Wkly.* 14 July 172 Allied with these are tally cards, playing cards, novelties and party favors. — (3) **1857** *Spirit of Times* 23 May 190/3 The tallymen were: Olympic, E. W. Cody; Bay State, W. W. Bragg, jr. — (4) **1889** *Harper's Mag.* Jan. 238/1 Trap and sticks being in place, the tally-pole is moved in parallel with the bank and lightly anchored below the surface of the water.

(5) **1887** *Courier-Journal* 7 May 3/3 The tally sheets of the counties gratuitously distributed at the convention . . . were a great convenience to delegates. **1911** *Okla. Session Laws* 3 Legisl. 77 Such special election commissioner . . . shall receive . . . the ballots, ballot boxes, poll books, tally sheets [etc.]. — (6) **1896** JORDAN & EVERMANN *Fishes N. Amer.* 1199 Centropristes striatus (Linnæus.) (Black Sea Bass; Blackfish; Tally-Wag; Hannahill; Black Will; Black Harry.) **1902** ——— *Amer. Food & Game Fishes* 397 The tally-wag of the Gulf of Mexico is a distinct species of sea bass, *C[entropristes] ocyurus,* occurring in rather deep water, chiefly on the Snapper Banks.

*** tally,** *v. Baseball. tr.* and *intr.* To bring in (a run or a runner), to score. *Colloq.*

1867 *Ball Players' Chron.* 14 Nov. 2/4 Taylor took his first on a muff by Banker and tallied on passed balls. **1931** *Randolph Enterprise* (Elkins, W.Va.) 9 July 5/3 The nine from Randolph had tallied five times in the same frame. **1949** *Fargo* (N.D.) *Forum* 23 July 8/8 Erickson's single tallied West. **1949** *Oregonian* (Portland) 10 Aug. III. 1/5 Byerly's tallied in the first, when Lee Jackson . . . scored on an error by Center Fielder Jerry Leblanc.

*** tallyho,** *n.* (See quot. 1901.) — **1893** *Harper's Mag.* Jan. 287/1 They were . . . easily amused with picture-books, and accustomed not to play auction or tally-ho while their parents read and wrote. **1901** *D.N.* II. 149 *Tally-ho,* a game like hare and hounds.

talma ˈtælmə, *n.* [François Joseph *Talma* (1763–1826), French tragedian.] A large cape or loose, short cloak. *Obs.*

1852 in DONALDSON *Moqui Pueblo Indians* (1893) 26 This talma is pure white; its material I should suppose to be cotton or wool. **1870** M. H. SMITH *20 Years Wall St.* 274 They wear in their office, hats, heavy chignons, grecian bends, and talmas, thrown over their shoulders, which gives them an untidy and bunchy look. **1928** ASBURY *Gangs of N.Y.* 93 Both Turner and Baker threw off their Talmaz and drew pistols.

tamale təˈmɑlɪ, *n.* [f. Amer. Sp. *tamales,* pl. of *tamal* (<Nahuatl) in same sense.] A highly seasoned article of food made of cornmeal and minced meat, and usu. wrapped in a corn husk. Cf. **hot tamale.**

[**1612** SMITH *Descr. Virginia* 17 Their corne they rost in the eare greene, and bruising it in a morter of wood with a Polt, lappe it in rowles in the leaues of their corne, and so boyle it for a daintie. **1691** in *S.W. Hist. Quart.* XXX. (1927) 211 There are five or six kinds of beans—all of them very good, also calabashes, watermelons, and sunflowers. The seed of all of these, mixed with corn make very fine *tamales.* **c1721** *Ib.* XXXI. 132 The Indians returned the favor with young corn, muskmelons, tamales (which are rolls of corn), beans cooked with corn, and nuts.] **1854** BARTLETT *Personal Narr.* I. 107 Tamaules are minced meat, rolled up in corn shucks, and baked on coals. **1913** LONDON *Valley of Moon* 104 They were seated around the table in the kitchen . . . making a cold lunch of sandwiches, tamales, and bottled beer. **1947** *Nat. Geog. Mag.* Feb. 141/2 Nati excelled in making tamales.

attrib. and *transf.* **1888** LINDLEY *Calif. of South* 89 The *tomale* man is another Mexican feature, who is very similar to the hot-corn hawker of Eastern cities. **1928** *Nat. Geog. Mag.* June 664/2 Likewise, Los Angeles in the eighties was a tiny tamale town. **1950** *Chi. Tribune* 4 Jan. II. 2 No torrid tomale is going to toss me for a loss in 1950.

b. tamale pie, a preparation or dish consisting of a lining of cornmeal mush filled with a mixture of meat and a sauce, made of pepper and tomatoes, highly seasoned with chili.

1911 Williams Pub. Lib. Assoc. *Ariz. Cook Book* 220 Tamale Pie. **1947** *Amer. Wkly.* 2 Nov. 36/3 My wife . . . found time a short while ago to discover from some friends, during our stay at a ranch in Colorado, a Mexican dish called Tamale Pie.

c. *the real tamale,* the genuine article, the real stuff. *Slang.*

1897 ADE *Pink Marsh* 92 Some of 'em wuhds you tossed into Misteh Cliffo'd come out o' no small book, no, seh. 'Em 'uz 'e real tomolleys.

tamarack ˈtæməˌræk, *n.* [Algonquian.]

1. Any one of several larches, esp. the red larch of the North, *Larix laricina.* Also a lodgepole pine *q.v.*

1805 CLARK in *Lewis & C. Exped.* III. (1905) 66 The Mountains which we passed to day much worst than yesterday the last excessively bad & thickly Strowed with falling timber & Pine Spruce fur Hackmatak & Tamerack. **1873** MILLER *Amongst Modocs* 2 Column upon column of storm-stained tamarack . . . have rallied here. **1884** SARGENT *Rep. Forests* 195 *Pinus Murrayana*. . . . Tamarack. Black Pine. Lodge-pole Pine. Spruce Pine. . . . Generally confounded with closely-allied *P. contorta* of the coast. **1947** PEATTIE *Sierra Nevada* 160 Lodgepole pine . . . is plain tamarack to many Californians. **1949** *Prairie Lumberman* Oct. 27/1 The larch or tamarack is the only conebearer of the North that hibernates.

attrib. **1842** KIRKLAND *Forest Life* I. 30 Corn-cribs and pig-sties . . . are made of slender tamarack poles, which need no cost of sawing. **1869** *Rep. Comm. Agric. 1868* 176 Frames of canoes . . . are afterwards covered with its bark, sewed with spruce or tamarack (Larix) roots, and the seams calked with spruce gum. **1894** *Outing* XXIV. 94/1 By vigorous working of three paddles we got up a 'tamarack breeze' that carried us rapidly along. **1948** *Green Bay* (Wis.) *Press-Gaz.* 13 July 11/4 The cedar and tamarack bog intrigued me most of all.

2. In special combs.: (1) **tamarack pine,** (see quots.); (2) **swamp,** a swamp in which tamaracks grow.

(1) **1891** *Cent.* 6174/1 *Tamarack-pine,* . . . same as *tamarack,* 2 [*Pinus murrayana* and *P. contorta*]. **1897** SUDWORTH *Arborescent Flora* 23 *Pinus murrayana,* . . . Lodgepole Pine. . . . Tamarack Pine (Cal.). **a1915** MUIR *Travels Alaska* (1917) 61 The 'tamarac pine' or black pine, as the variety of *P. contorta* is called here, is yellowish-green, in marked contrast with the dark, lichen-draped spruce. — (2) **1835** HOFFMAN *Winter in West* I. 169 You generally find a tamarack swamp the favourite covert of [bears]. **1947** *Mich. Hist.* June 185 He had reported these lands as being all cedar and tamarack swamp, with no pine on them.

tambien ˌtɑmbiˈen, *adv. S.W.* [Sp. *también,* in same sense.] Also. Used for emphasis. *Obs.* — **1863** *Rio Abajo Press* 25 Aug. 4/3 And we *tambien,* for similar reasons recommend our farmers to do likewise. **1867** *Wkly. New Mexican* 26 Jan. 2/1 Push their investigations to a thorough examination of his monetary arrangements throughout the territory and his Mormon instincts *tambien.*

tambo ˈtæmbo, *n.* In the lingo of Negro minstrels, a tambourine, or the performer who plays this.

1848 *New Negro Forget-me-not Songster* 32 We plaid dis song, 'on de banjo,' Wid de fiddle and de bones, and ole tambo, Yah, yah, yah! **1863** BEADLE *#1 Ten Cent Song Book* 64 You may talk about your fiddles and de old tambo, But they cannot be compared with the old banjo. **1930** WITTKE *Tambo & Bones* 140 'Tambo' who performed on the tambourine, was expected to go through wild and grotesque maneuvers for the benefit of the audience, while performing on his instrument.

* **tame,** *a.*

1. Designating a pasture of cultivated, as distinguished from wild, grass. Also used of land improved by cultivation.

1857 *Ill. Agric. Soc. Trans.* II. 382 Where tame pasture is resorted to something more needs be done. **1887** BUCK *Handbk. Med. Sci.* V. 9/2 The careful pioneer . . . had his corral . . . where the land had become 'tame.' **1898** *Mo. So. Dakotan* I. 46 As soon as eastern tame pastures are sufficiently formed to receive stock at all.

Also **tame hay (crop).**

1948 *Milwaukee Jrnl.* 18 July 2/2 The tame hay crop has been short compared with recent years. **1949** *News-Herald* (Marshfield, Wis.) 19 July 3/8 Production of barley, tame hay, oats and spring wheat will be below 1948 yields.

2. tame Indian, a friendly Indian.

1863 *N.Y. Tribune* 18 Feb. 1/6 The country above referred to is infested with small bands of roving, and several settlements of what we term tame Indians. [Ariz.] **1894** REMINGTON in *Harper's Mag.* LXXXVIII. 351/1 Some tame Indians, just in from a hunt in the Rio Chico, had seen three fires. [**1948** *Dly. Ardmoreite* (Ardmore, Okla.) 17 May 3/2 He had heard about the Indians up here and wasn't sure whether they were wild or tame.]

Tammanial təˈmenɪəl, *a.* Of or pertaining to the Tammany Society of New York. *Obs.* — **1791** *Amer. D. Reg.* (N.Y.) 16 May, Before them was borne the cap of Liberty; after following seven hunters in Tammanial dress, then the great standard of the society. **1812** *Columbian Centinel* (Boston) 2 Dec. 2/3 The Ticket which prevailed was at first denounced by the Ohio Madisonians as 'Mongrel'—'Clintonian'—and 'Tammanial.'

Tammany ˈtæmənɪ, *n.* [See note.]

This was the name of a Delaware chief, Tamanen, Tammenund, or Tammany, who flourished about 1683. References to him for that year may be found in: *Pa. Archives* I. 62; Wm. Penn *Works* (1782) IV. 305.

1. St. Tammany, a patron saint of America, canonized facetiously about 1770. *Obs.* or *hist.*

1771 W. EDDIS *Lett. from Amer.* 115 The Americans on this part of the continent have . . . a Saint. . . . The first of May is . . . set apart to the memory of Saint Tamina. **1789** *N.Y. Dly. Gaz.* 14 May 470/3 Last Tuesday, being the 12th inst. (or the 1st of May old stile) was the anniversary of St. Tammany, the Tutelar Saint of America. **1816** TUCKER *Lett. from Va.* 114 'By St. Tammany' said he, 'he died like a martyr.' **1945** MARLOWE *Coaching Roads* 119 John Trumbull is said to have suggested the name of St. Tammany, originating from the legends of the famous Indian chief Tamanende, whose 'wisdom, humanity and many virtues' had earned him the title.

b. Sons of St. Tammany, the members of several patriotic societies loosely associated during the Revolutionary period; in later use =sense **3.** *Obs.*

1773 *Pa. Mag.* XXV. 446 The natives of this flourishing Province . . . have adopted a great warrior sachem and chief named Tammany . . . to be the tutelar Saint of this Province. . . . You are requested to meet the children and associates Sons of Saint Tammany at the house of Mr. James Byrnes to dine together and form such useful charitable plans for the relief of all in distress as shall be agreed upon. **1790** *N.Y. Journal* 11 May 3/3 To-morrow . . . the annual feast of St. Tammany will be celebrated by the Sons of St. Tammany & Columbian Order, at their wigwam on the banks of the Hudson. **1846** *Cong. Globe* App. 1 July 1041, I was told that the sons of St. Tammany had degenerated into old hunkers, barnburners, and office-seekers.

c. The name of a parish in Louisiana.

1813 in BRACKENRIDGE *Views La.* 281 Lake Ponchartrain in the parish of St. Tammany, in the state of Louisiana.

2. King Tammany, a variant of **St. Tammany.** *Obs.*

1772 *Pa. Chronicle* 4 May 63/2 A number of American Gentlemen, Sons of King Tammany, met . . . to celebrate the Memory of that truly noble Chieftain. **1782** FRENEAU *Poems* (1786) 308 The Prophecy of King Tammany.

3. A fraternal and benevolent society of New York City, developed out of one of the earlier patriotic societies; the political club identified with this society.

Tammany is a Democratic organization, associated at first with the early Democratic-Republican party, later with the Democratic party.

1790 *N.Y. Dly. Gaz.* 13 April 351/2 To the Independent Electors of the City of New-York. . . . [Signed:] Tammany. **1839** *Jamestown* (N.Y.) *Jrnl.* 23 Jan. 3/2 A change has come over the spirit of Tammany. **1949** *Newsweek* 16 May 21/3 Tammany hadn't expected any further trouble from [him].

b. *pl.* Members of the New York Tammany Society or the Society itself. *Obs.*

1813 *Federal Republican* (Georgetown, D.C.) 13 Aug. 3/2 Armstrong is the idol of Tompkins, Spencer, and all the Tammanies of New York. **1837** *Jamestown* (N.Y.) *Jrnl.* 26 April 2/4 Of the seventeen aldermen, the Whigs have twelve and the Tammanies five. **1842** J. D. HAMMOND *Hist. Pol. Parties N.Y.* (1852) II. 491 The Tammanies entered the hall as soon as the doors were opened, by means of back stairs.

4. In combs.: (1) **Tammany brave,** a member of Tammany (sense **3.**); (2) **Hall,** see as a main entry; (3) **heeler,** a ward heeler working under the auspices of Tammany; (4) **highbinder,** a political speechmaker or grandiloquent leader connected with Tammany; (5) **man,** a member of a Tammany political group; (6) **ring,** a clique of unprincipled politicians connected with Tammany; (7) **sachem,** a political leader associated with Tammany; (8) **Society,** =**Tammany 3,** also **St. Tammany Society;** (9) **Temple,** (see quot.), *obs.* or *hist.;* (10) **tiger,** the symbol of Tammany (sense **3.**); (11) **wigwam,** =**Tammany Hall.**

(1) **1884** *Boston Jrnl.* 11 Oct. 2/3 The Tammany braves are having barbecues. — (3) **1938** ASBURY *Sucker's Prog.* 103 He . . . was associated . . . with the notorious Shang Draper, a Tammany heeler. — (4) **1938** ASBURY *Sucker's Prog.* 35 A favorite rendezvous of William M. Tweed and his gang of Tammany highbinders.

(5) **1817** *N.Y. Herald* 2 April 1/2 Since then they have been Clintonians, Tammany-men, Spencerites, Madisonians. **1868** *Ore. State Jrnl.* 31 Oct. 2/2 The Tammany men attempted to drive them back into line. **1945** *Christian Sci. Mon.* (Ed. page), Since General O'Dyer is a Tammany man, the battered old Tiger displays a fresh grin. — (6) **1872** *Atlantic Mo.* May 642 If Mr. Thomas Nast could have died when the Tammany Ring did, he would have ended his career with a reputation unequalled in the history of political literature. — (7) **1890** *Boston Jrnl.* 1 July 4/1 Richard Croker . . . is to be entertained this week by the Tammany sachems. **1948** *Time* 12 July 62/3 An oldtime Tammany Sachem once remarked that he would rather have the New York *Times* against him than for him. — (8) **1787** *N.Y. Journal* 3 May 3/1 Tuesday last, being St. Tammany's Day (the Tutelar Saint of America) the St. Tammany Society of this City held their Anniversary Meeting, at the Wigwam at Halls. **1872** *Harper's Mag.* April 686/1 The Tammany Society, or Columbian Order, is doubtless the oldest purely self-constituted political association in the world. **1948** *Chi. Tribune* 10 Oct. (Grafic Mag.) 17/2 Aided by his 'Martlings' of the Tammany society, he carried New York City by 100 votes. — (9) **1941** *Sat. Review* 19 July 3/2 On March 11, 1840, the Locofoco newspaper, the New York *New Era,* listed the clubs as follows—the Butt Enders, the Tammany Temple, the Indomitables, the Huge Paws (named for their symbol, a muscular arm grasping a hammer), the Van Buren Association, and the Simon Pures.

(10) **1871** NAST in *Harper's Wkly.* XV. 1056 (*caption*), The Tammany Tiger Loose. **1950** *Time* 28 Aug. 15/3 When election time came around, he would be found, cozy in the corner of the Tammany tiger. — (11) **1868** *N.Y. Herald* 2 July 4/1 This Democratic Convention . . . takes possession of the Tammany wigwam.

Also *Tammany address, aristocracy, candidate, leader, member, robbery, stronghold, ticket,* etc.

Tammany Hall. Any one of the successive buildings which have served as headquarters of Tammany.

1812 *N.Y. Ev. Post* 6 July 3/2 At a meeting of citizens held, in pursuance of public notice, at Tammany Hall [etc.]. **1868** *N.Y. Herald* 7 July 4/1 Outside Tammany Hall . . . a surging mass of humanity congregated. **1924** *Atlantic Mo.* Sep. 315/1 This Tammany Society still lives and owns the structure known as Tammany Hall.

b. =**Tammany 3.**

1880 *Scribner's Mo.* Oct. 863/1 Ex-Governor Lucius Robinson, . . . diverted many votes . . . from the ticket of Tammany Hall, the local organization most powerful in the neighborhood. **1947** *Chi. D. News* 10 June 12/6 In Manhattan, [he] is openly reorganizing Tammany Hall with men and policies of his own making. **1949** *Newsweek* 21 Nov. 27/2 Morris kept charging that Costello was the real ruler of Tammany Hall and that Tammany therefore was inextricably lined with the underworld.

transf. **1854** FRANK SOULÉ *Annals S.F.* 556 They [the Hounds] organized themselves so far that they had a place of regular meeting, or *Head Quarters,* which they called *Tammany Hall,* in a large tent, near the City Hotel. **1940** RIESENBERG *Golden Gate* 91 At a large tent near the City Hotel, dubbed 'Tammany Hall' by a New York member, the Hounds first met.

Tammanyite ˈtæmənɪˌaɪt, *n.* A member or supporter of Tammany (sense **3.**).

1858 *Leslie's Wkly.* 23 Oct. 328/3 He would, no doubt, have been elected, and Judge Waterbury and the pale-faced Tammanyite, Billy Macintyre, might have returned to his crockery and bonded warehouses. **1892** *N.Y. Herald* 21 Feb. 16/1 Many Tammanyites who were accompanied by their wives departed on the Buffalo express at 1:30. **1948** *Time* 12 July 15/1 Celebrating the hall's 162nd anniversary last week, a handful of Tammanyites heard a message from Harry Truman.

Tamoleon təˈmolɪən, *n. local.* [Origin unknown.] A horse of a breed now extinct (see quot.). *Obs.* — **1852** G. W. L. Bickley *Hist. Tazewell Co., Va.* 104 The *Tamoleons* are celebrated for their riding qualities, and when crossed with the cultivator, are, perhaps, equal to any in the United States. They are very docile, and easily kept in good order. They are sorrel, with flax mane and tail, and with the exception of a few small defects about the head, are fine specimens of the species.

∗**tan,** *n.*[1] or *v.* **1. tan bay,** the loblolly bay, *Gordonia lasianthus,* of the southern states. **2. tan toaster,** (see quots.). *Colloq.*

(1) **1884** Sargent *Rep. Forests* 25 Tan Bay. . . . The bark, rich in tannin, was once occasionally used, locally, in tanning leather. **1897** Sudworth *Arborescent Flora* 273. — (2) **1873** C. Thaxter *Isles of Shoals* (1885) 69, I never could understand . . . what they mean by calling a great gale or tempest a 'Tan toaster.' **1895** *D.N.* I. 394 tan-toaster: severe storm. N.H.

As the last term in **black and, valley tan.**

tan tæn, *n.*[2] *W.* Short for *fan-tan,* a Chinese gambling game. *Obs.* — **1873** in *Amer. Sp.* XXIV. (1949) 267/1 The game which is being dealt is 'Than,' or 'Tan,' a kind of odd and even affair; we came to the conclusion that it would be odd indeed if anybody got even by playing it. **1883** Stevenson *Silverado Squatters* 189 Where he might . . . lose his little earnings at the game of tan.

∗**tanager,** *n.* As the last term in **Cooper's, Louisiana, rose, scarlet, summer tanager.**

∗**tanbark,** *n.* **1.** Used in fig. phrases concerning the devil or hell, to indicate great haste or activity. *Colloq.* **2. tanbark oak,** any oak producing tanbark, as the rock chestnut oak or an evergreen species, *Lithocarpus densiflora,* of the Pacific Coast.

(1) **1851** *Polly Peablossom* 153 I'll larrup you worse nor the devil beatin' tan-bark! **1898** Hamblen *Gen. Manager's Story* 129 On this afternoon Dinny saw 'some felly comin' like the divil batin' tan-bark.' **1902** White *Blazed Trail* 192 Old Morrison he's as busy as hell beatin' tan-bark. — (2) **1883** Smith *Geol. Survey Ala.* 296 On the high lands or extensive table-lands [is found] . . . *Q. Prinus,* (the mountain or tan-bark oak). **1949** Howell *Marin Flora* 7 The laurels and tanbark oaks form a more conspicuous part of the forest.

tandem ˈtændəm, *n.* [Origin unknown.] A kind of linen cloth. Also **tandem Hollands.** *Obs.*

1741 *S.C. Gazette* 26 March, Just imported . . . wide garlix, tandem Hollands [etc.]. **1747** *Boston Ev. Post* 18 May 2/2 To be sold cheap . . . Lloyd's Garlets, Tandems, Cambricks, Taffatees. **1758** *Newport* (R.I.) *Mercury* 19 Dec. 4/2 George Hazard . . . has to sell. . . . Yard-wide Tandems. **1761** *Ib.* 28 April 4/3 Just Imported. . . . Russia and ravens duck, Ticklenburgh, dowlas . . . tandems. **1783** *Circular from Hamburg* in *Pa. Gaz.* 26 Nov. 3/1 German cloth of every quality and colour . . . Silesia linens . . . Rough dowlas, Quadruple tandems, Brown Silesias.

∗**tangent,** *n.* (See quot. 1895.) *Obs.* — **1888** Kirkland *McVeys* 147 [They] knew the radius of every curve, and the length of every straight stretch ('tangent'). **1895** *Standard* 1839/1 *Tangent,* . . . a straight stretch of railway-track.

∗**tangle,** *v. tr.* To add spirituous liquor to (water); to spike. *Slang. Obs.* — **1835** Kennedy *Horse Shoe Robinson* I. 256 Some water, Mr. Musgrove, and it will not come badly to my hand if you can tangle it somewhat. **1840** ——— *Quodlibet* 126 Bring us a tumbler of water—tangle it.

tanglefoot ˈtæŋglˌfʊt, *n.*

1. Strong drink of an inferior quality. Also **tanglefoot whisky.** *Colloq.*

1859 Matsell *Vocabulum* 89 Tangle-foot, Bad liquor. **1867** Harris *Sut Lovingood* 113, I got two for one boots, an' old tangle-foot whisky enuf tu fill 'em. *a***1918** G. Stuart *On Frontier* 265 Each dispenser of liquid refreshments had the formula for making 'tanglefoot:'—a quantity of boiled mountain sage, two plugs tobacco steeped in water, box cayenne pepper, one gallon water. **1939** Rollins *Gone Haywire* 176 We heads back ter th' saloon, . . . an' then, goin' inside, we bites off a couple more inches o' th' tanglefoot.

2. *fig.* Something which makes one stumble. Also attrib.

1893 *Advance* 28 Sep., The tangle-foot complications in which it was sure to involve its defenders. **1908** W. R. Hearst in *Westminster Gaz.* 2 Oct. 5/1 The deeper he sinks into the tangle-foot of corruption and contradiction. **1947** Myers *The 'Guv'* 175 Thus things of good and bad report went tanglefoot and the Guv stuck to his last until slow-footed time dragged along his wedding day.

3. A local name for the hobblebush.

1894 *Amer. Folk-Lore* VII. 90 *Viburnum lantanoides* . . . tanglefoot, N.H.

tangle-footed ˈtæŋglˌfʊtəd, *a.* Drunk, awkward, stumbling. *Slang. Obs.*— **1859** Matsell *Vocabulum* 89 *Tangle-footed,* Drunk. **1888** *Voice* 27 Dec., Republican lies . . . are nearly always of this tangle-footed variety, which trip up and throw themselves by their absurdity and self-contradiction.

∗**tangleleg,** *n.* **1.** *pl.* =**hobblebush. 2.** (*a*) =**tanglefoot 1,** also attrib. and fig., (*b*) hence **tanglelegged,** *a.* (see quot.). *Slang. Obs.*

(1) **1817–8** Eaton *Botany* (1822) 510 Hobble-bush, tangle-legs. . . . Stem very flexible and crooked. **1860** Curtis *Woody Plants N.C.* 91 Tangle-Legs. . . . The branches . . . form well secured loops for tripping the feet of inexperienced wayfarers. — (2) (*a*) **1861** *Calif. Police Gaz.* (S.F.) 30 March 2/4, I believe that he . . . did capture one old man known as 'Kentuck,' on Sunday last, . . . laboring under the influence of an over dose of what Sargent denominates 'tangleleg.' **1882** Baillie-Grohman *Camping in Rockies* 6 But my men and I knew too much of Western 'tangle-leg' and its vile poisonous qualities. (*b*) *a***1856** in Hall *College Words* (ed. 2) 461 We give a list of a few of the various words and phrases which have been in use . . . to signify some stage of inebriation: . . . jug-steamed, tangle-legged [etc.].

tanglewood ˈtæŋglˌwʊd, *n.* A region of thick, bushy woods. Also attrib.

1853 N. Hawthorne (*title*), Tanglewood Tales, for Girls and Boys. **1863** Mitchell *My Farm* 158 Within this tangle-wood, I have set a few graftlings upon a wild-crab. **1894** *Advance* 26 April, [The bird] scuttled off in a wild panic through the thick tanglewood.

∗**tank,** *n.*

1. *W.* A natural pond.

In this sense the term is perhaps from Sp. *tanque* similarly used. See quot. 1941. But cf. *OED tank, sb.*[1] **1. b.**

1869 *Overland Mo.* Aug. 130 A 'tank' in Texas is a pond of fresh water. **1890** *Amer. Antiquarian* July 201 The surface is smooth sandstone, with here and there great hollows filled with rain-water. These places are called 'tanks' by the ranchmen. **1941** Fergusson *Southwest* 353 A tank is a dip in the ground which, in good seasons, holds a little water, where stock may drink. Etymologically, it is a descendant of the Spanish tanque, pond.

2. In combs.: (1) **tank car,** a railroad car provided with a large tank for carrying liquids, esp. crude and re-

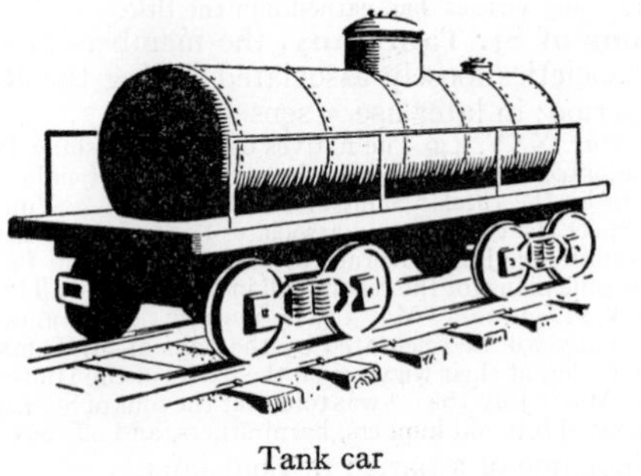

Tank car

fined petroleum, in bulk; (2) **drama,** (see quot. 1891), *obs.;* (3) **station,** (see quots.); (4) **steamer, steamship,** (see quots.); (5) **town,** a small town located on a railroad, hence **tank-towner,** *colloq.;* (6) **train,** a train made up of tank cars.

(1) **1874** Knight 457/2. **1949** *Lubbock* (Tex.) *Morn. Avalanche* 23 Feb. 1. 10/7 The line, however, is still in operation so water can be hauled to Archer City from Olney in tank cars. — (2) **1891** *Cent.* 6180/2 *Tank drama,* a sensational or cheap melodrama in which water is employed in the scenic effects, as in representing a rescue from drowning. (Theatrical slang.) **1898** *Scribner's Mag.* XXIII. 505/2 'Real tubs' [as properties on the stage] lead straight to the 'tank drama.' — (3) **1895** *Stand.* 1839/2 *T[ank]-station,* . . . a railway-station at which there is a tank for supplying water to the locomotives. **1901** *Cosmopolitan* July 254/1 At such intervals in an oil pipe line as the contour of the country requires, there are 'tank stations,'

where are situated two huge tanks, the oil being pumped from one to the other in order to secure the head necessary for it to flow to the next station. — (4) **1891** *Scribner's Mag.* Oct. 608/2 The tank steamship, for carrying oil in bulk, is an American invention. **1901** *Cosmopolitan* July 255/1 The transatlantic trade is chiefly carried on in tank-steamers, huge steel shells in which almost the entire space in the hull is devoted to carrying oil in bulk.

(5) **1913** *Sunset* Dec. 1173/2 There ain't no best hotels in the tank towns we play. **1927** *Cleveland Press* 29 Jan., Some 'tank-towners' from Pennsylvania stood open-mouthed and 'pop-eyed' in the visitors' gallery. **1949** *Sat. Ev. Post* 9 April 82/3 Out they went for sixteen weeks in the theaters, opera houses and musty lodge halls of the tank towns. — (6) **1901** *Munsey's Mag.* XXV. 749/1 Racks for the loading of tank trains.

As the last term in **flush, manure, sheet-iron oil, water tank.**

∗**tank,** *v.* **1.** *tr.* (See quot.) *Obs.* **2.** To drink heavily, hence **tanked up,** drunk. *Slang.*

(1) **1874** J. G. McCoy *Cattle Trade* 251 Many thousands of stock cattle . . . were sold at from one to one and a quarter cents per pound gross weight, to be 'tanked;' that is, the hide, horns, and hoofs taken off, and the balance of the carcass placed in a tank and rendered or steamed; the tallow obtained, the balance was thrown away. — (2) **1897** A. H. Lewis *Wolfville* 254 He don't feel so free to get tanked expansive with Willyum on his mind. **1934** Vines *Green Thicket World* 113 By the time Old Andy was tanked up he looked at the moon.

∗**tankage,** *n.* The residue of slaughterhouses and rendering plants, dried and used as manure and feed. Also attrib. — **1886** *Scientific Amer.* LV. 149/1 A new drier [is] adapted for drying . . . tankage, sewage, clay, fertilizers, etc. **1924** Croy *R.F.D. No. 3* 64 On one wall [was] . . . a large calendar got out by a Chicago tankage company.

∗**tanking,** *n.* (See quots.) — **1891** *Cent.* 6181/1 *Tanking,* . . .the operation or method of treating in tanks, as fish for the extraction of oil, by boiling, settling, etc. **1905** *Forestry Bureau Bul.* No. 61, 51 *Tanking,* the act of hauling water in a tank, to ice a logging road. (N[orthern] F[orest].)

tansy mustard. An herb, *Descurainia pinnata,* having leaves like those of tansy. — **1857** Gray *Botany* 36 Tansy Mustard. . . . Penn. and Ohio to Wisconsin, and southward and westward. **1891** Coulter *Bot. W. Texas* I. 16 Tansy-mustard. . . . One of the most common of western mustards.

∗**tanyard,** *n. bully of the tanyard,* the cock of the walk. — **1845** W. T. Thompson *Chron. Pineville* 18 The doctor could not but feel himself, to use one of his own polished expressions—'bully of the tan-yard.'

For *big dog of the tanyard,* see ∗**big,** *a.* **5.** (3) quot. 1845; *to draw to a shoestring and obtain a tanyard,* see ∗**draw,** *v.* **6.** (4).

Taos taus, *n.* [Sp. *pl.,* adaptation of the native name of their chief pueblo.]

1. Taos Indian, an Indian belonging to a pueblo tribe of the upper Rio Grande region in New Mexico.

1844 Gregg *Commerce of Prairies* I. 86 A Taos Indian who formed one of the Mexican escort, seeing a gun levelled at his commander, sprang forward and received the ball in his own body, from the effects of which he instantly expired! **1887** *Scribner's Mag.* II. 510 Then the saddle-blanket is laid over his withers, with sometimes a *tilpah,* or parti-colored rug, woven and dyed by the Navajo or Taos Indians. **1949** *Travel* March 11/1 Here you meet the tall, dignified Taos Indians.

attrib. **1944** Johnson *As I Dare* 287 Adobe walls around the garden and various nooks and vistas were being built by Taos Indian labor. **1949** *Nat. Geog. Mag.* Dec. 784/1 Coronado's soldiers discovered the Taos Indian community in 1540.

Also **Taos tribe.**

1853 Brewerton *With Kit Carson* (1930) 290 The appellation of '*Taos*' refers more particularly to the '*Valle de Taos,*' so called in honor of the '*Taosa*' tribe of Indians.

2. *attrib.* Designating liquor of a kind made in the vicinity of Taos, New Mexico.

1846 Abert *Exam. N. Mex.* 32 Trains of 'burros' are continually entering the city, laden with kegs of Taos whiskey. **1901** Root *Overland Stage* 229 The vile whisky, some of which was drank by the overland stage-drivers, was by them given the very appropriate name of 'Taos lightning.' **1949** *Nat. Geog. Mag.* Dec. 784/2 Americans . . . trooped in with their long rifles and packs of beavers in quest of riches, romance, and 'Taos lightning.'

Taosans 'tauzənz, *n. pl.* Taos Indians.—**1893** Donaldson *Moqui Pueblo Indians* 101 The Taosans braid 2 side locks of hair with fur or worsted, parting it back and front in the center of the head.

∗**tap,** *v. tr.* (See quot. 1864.) — **1850** A. T. Jackson *Forty-Niner* (1920) 8 'Texas Bill' tapped one of the banks for two thousand dollars and won on the first pull. **1864** Dick *Amer. Hoyle* (1866) 456 In this game [monte], the limit is the bank, the player having the right, at any time, to bet the whole amount, which is called 'tapping the bank.'

tapadera ˌtæpə'derə, *n.* [Sp. in Amer. Sp. sense shown here.] A leather cover for a stirrup serving to protect one's foot in riding through underbrush.

1844 Gregg *Commerce of Prairies* I. 213 The estribos or stirrups are usually made . . . over which are fastened the tapaderas or coverings of leather to protect the toes. **1927** James *Cow Country* 106 The silver was a-shining to the sun at every curve of the horse's body; the long hand-carved tapaderos, along with the wide wings of the rider's chaps, sort of made the movements of the horse and man mighty easy to watch. **1947** *Time* 22 Dec. 64/3 Williams plans to stop calling a rope a rawhide riata and not use words like hackamore, tapaderas and cinch ring.

tapajo tɑ'pɑho, *n. S.W.* [Amer. Sp. *tapaojo* (<*tapar,* to cover, +*ojo,* eye).] (See quots.) *Obs.* — **1847** Ruxton *Adv. In Mexico* 112 (Bentley), I instantly stopped . . . dismounted, and, catching the wildest mule, immediately tied her legs together with a riata, and covered the eyes of all with their tapojos. **1881** Farrow *Mt. Scouting* 121 The blind or 'tapajo,' made of leather with straps and loops, should invariably be used while packing or adjusting a disarranged pack.

tap-borer, *n.* [Prob. an old term that has escaped dictionaries; cf. Du. *tapboor,* in same sense.] (See quot. 1876.)

1633 *N.H. Prov. P.* I. 79 Tapp boarers 4. **1759** *Newport* (R.I.) *Mercury* 26 June 4/3 Imported. . . . Box Pullies and Pins, Gimblets and Tapborers. **1876** Knight 2495/1 *Tap-borer,* a tapering boring-instrument for making spigot or bung holes in casks.

∗**tape,** *n.*

1. a. tape grass, an aquatic plant, *Vallisneria spiralis,* having leaves suggestive of tape. **b.** ∗**tapeworm,** *local,* a ticket of special size used for finding out whether purchased votes were actually voted, in full **tapeworm ticket.** *Obs.*

(a) 1817–8 Eaton *Botany* (1822) 505 Tape grass. . . . In the river Hudson from Waterford to the Highlands. **1840** Dewey *Mass. Flowering Plants* 190 [Our] Tape Grass . . . was considered by Michaux a distinct plant from that of Europe. **1894** Coulter *Bot. W. Texas* III. 421. — **(b) 1875** *Cong. Rec.* 27 Feb. 1890/2 The 'tape-worm' ticket . . . is three inches in length, one-sixteenth of an inch in width. **1878** *Ib.* 6 Feb. 804/2 'Tape-worm tickets' . . . were given to a certain class of voters, and as they were put into the ballot-box the employers of the voters could easily tell whether such tickets were voted or not. **1882** *Ib.* 2 June 4460/1 'The tape-worm' . . . had to be voted as given, and if any poor wretch dared to come to the box with any other [ticket], 'off with his head.'

2. In phrases and expressions used in phrases: **a.** *measure and cut off tape,* a play-party kissing game, cf. ∗**love,** *n.* (6). **b.** *to doctor the tapeline,* to impair the accuracy of a tapeline. Both *obs.*

(a) 1828 *Yankee* July 227/2 When a select party have met together, and they play button—roll the plate—chase the lady, and many other romping-plays, then they kiss wheelbarrow style—measure and cut off tape. — **(b) 1877** W. Wright *Big Bonanza* 428 'Doctoring the tape-line' is a trick that strolling miners have sometimes been known to perform, when the opportunity was found.

Tappahannock ˌtæpə'hænək, *n.* [*Tappahannock,* Va.] A variety of early winter wheat. In full **Tappahannock wheat.** *Obs.* — **1868** *Rep. Comm. Agric. 1867* 349 The 'Tappahannock' is named as the only variety that ripened side by side with the white Mediterranean. **1870** *Ib. 1869* 245 Tappahannock wheat has been widely distributed by the Department since the spring of 1862.

∗**tapper,** *n.* As the last term in **till, wire tapper.**

∗**taps,** *n. pl. Mil.* A signal given orig. with a drum but now usu. with a bugle, for extinguishing lights and going to bed. Also used at the conclusion of a soldier's burial.

1824 *18th Cong.* 1 Sess. H. Doc. 111. 8 March 35 It is his [the orderly's] duty . . . to visit his rooms, at the taps; see that the lights are extinguished; the fires properly secured; the occupants present, and in bed. **1887** Hinman *Corp. Si Klegg* 331 Their ears caught the music of the bugles sounding 'lights out,' or 'taps.' **1919** Hough *Sagebrusher* 300 'Blow "taps," ' he ordered of the bugler near by. **1949** *Oak Leaves* (Oak Park, Ill.) 24 Nov. 22/5 Gathered in their cabins the boys then played the old reliable Ghost game and others until 'Taps.'

∗**tar,** *n.* In combs.: (1) **tar and feathers,** a coating of tar smeared upon a person and then covered with feathers, cf. ∗**tar,** *v.;* (2) **and Turpentine State,** a nickname for North Carolina, cf. **Turpentine State;** (3) **Baby,** in the well-known Uncle Remus story (see quot.

1881), a doll heavily smeared with tar set to catch Br'er Rabbit, also transf.; (4) *barrel, see **b.** (1) and (2) below; (5) **Boiler,** =**Tarheel,** *obs.;* (6) **Burner,** =**Tarheel,** *obs.;* (7) **bush,** any one of various western shrubs characterized by viscidity and a heavy scent; (8) **heel,** see as a main entry; (9) **knot,** *S.* a lightwood knot; (10) **paper,** building paper impregnated with tar or some other bituminous substance, also attrib.; (11) **tree,** (see quot.), *obs.;* (12) **weed,** (*a*) any one of several resinous, glandular plants of California, esp. of the genera *Media* and *Grindelia*, also attrib., (*b*) the waxweed, *Cuphea petiolata.*

(1) **1775** FITHIAN *Journal* II. 25 [He] is now in great fear, & very humble, since he hears many of his townsmen talking of tar and feathers—these mortifying weapons. **1925** BENEFIELD *Chicken-Wagon Family* 310 That's the stuff; give 'em the tar and feathers. **1947** *Sat. Ev. Post* 15 March 151/2 An angry Colonial mob . . . were licking their lips at the thought of tar and feathers. — (2) **1856** *Harper's Mag.* May 854/2 He lost his way among the pine woods that abound in that tar and turpentine State. **1876** INGRAM *Centennial Exp.* 734 He spent his youth in the good old 'Tar and Turpentine State.' — (3) **1881** J. C. HARRIS *Uncle Remus* ii. 20 Brer Fox . . . got 'im some tar, en mix it wid some turkentime, en fix up a contrapshun what he call a Tar-Baby. **1906** MARK TWAIN *Autobiog.* II. 18 (R.), For two years the 'Courant' had been making a 'tar baby' of Mr. Blaine. **1950** *Nat. Geog. Mag.* March 410 Like Floating Tar Babies, 30 Rare Sea Otters Loll on Their Backs along the Pacific Shore.

(5) **1845** *St. Louis Reveille* 14 May 2/4 The inhabitants of . . . North Carolina [are called] Tar-boilers. **1888** WHITMAN *Nov. Boughs* 406 Those from . . . North Carolina . . . [were called] Tar Boilers. — (6) **1775** *N.C. Gaz.* (New Bern) 24 March 3/3 Then arose *Pinuspixterebinthus* the Tar-Burner, who had set more than three Thousand three Hundred four Score and seventeen Kilns. **1808** *Norfolk* (Va.) *Gaz.* 16 March 2/4 (Th. Supp.), According to the arithmetick of the ignorant 'Tarburners,' [this]would amount to eleven hundred and fifty dollars. — (7) **1902** *Out West* Oct. 452 Then there were the innumerable cacti with their brilliant flowers, and the tar bush, the greasewood, *ocatilla,* mountain mahogany. **1949** *Chi. Tribune* 20 Feb. 30/3 Cedar and mesquite alone are costing Texas ranchers 115 million dollars a year. Add the sage and cactus, and the . . . blue oak, creosote, tarbush . . . and prickly pear and the toll is terrific. — (9) **1890** *Cong. Rec.* 23 June 6393/2 Burn some North Carolina tar-knots. . . . That will destroy your malaria.

(10) **1907** *Putnam's Mag.* July 482/1 A whole house covered with tar paper . . . sat complacently upon a hay wagon. **1919** LEWIS *Free Air* 122 Then a lonely, tight-haired woman in the doorway of a tar-paper shack waved to her. **1947** MYERS *The 'Guv'* 41 Nearly two hundred Italians had already been housed there in long rows of shacks roofed with tar paper. — (11) **1707** *N.J. Archives* 1 Ser. XI. 24 No person . . . shall presume to Cut, Fell, or Destroy any Pitch-Pine Trees, or Tar-Trees. — (12) (*a*) **1868** MUIR *Thousand-Mile Walk* (1916) 209 The waxy secretion of its leaves and involucres has suggested its grim name of 'tarweed,' by which it is generally known. **1922** NORRIS *Certain People* 138 The Barbee house was . . . set among a waste of crushed dry grass and odorous tar-weed. **1949** *Sat. Ev. Post* 18 June 108/1 White road dust puffed from beneath her feet and drifted over the tarweed and Queen Anne's lace at the roadside. (*b*) **1893** *Amer. Folk-Lore* VI. 142 *Cuphea petiolata,* tar weed. West Va.

b. In colloq. phrases: (1) *To have one's head in a tar barrel,* to be in a fix or pickle; (2) *as brisk as bees in a tar bucket,* quite brisk, also *as busy as a bee in a tar barrel,* very busy; (3) *to knock the tar out of,* and variants, to beat unmercifully.

(1) **1834** CARUTHERS *Kentuckian* I. 63 Pete had his head in a tar barrel sure enough. — (2) **1840** *Spirit of Times* 8 Aug. 270/3 (We.), Things are . . . as brisk as bees in a tar-bucket. **1859** L. WILMER *Press Gang* 199 He . . . made himself 'as busy as a bee in a tar-barrel.' **1889** COOKE *Steadfast* 197 I've been busier'n a bee in a tar-barrel ever since the folks come home. — (3) **1923** *D.N.* V. 212 *Knock the tar out of,* . . . to beat senseless. [McDonald Co., Mo.] **1942** PHILIPS *Big Spring* 59 You just started out by whaling the tar out of him. **1947** MYERS *The 'Guv'* 248 He beat the living tar out of me two weeks ago.

As the last term in **dead, green tar.**

*tar, *v.* *To tar and feather,* to punish (a person) by smearing him with tar and then shaking feathers on him.

"At Salem, on September 7, 1768, an informer named Robert Wood was stripped, tarred and feathered and placed on a hogshead under the Tree of Liberty on the Common" (*Old Time New England* XX. 30).

[?**1740** *Importance of Jamaica* 19 The old Greek [in Jamaica], mentioned before, took a milder but a more effectual Method to expose one of his [slaves] than Stripes; he had him tarr'd all over, and then roll'd in Feathers. Imagine what a Figure he made.] **1769** *Boston* (Mass.) *Chron.* 30 Oct. 3/2 A person . . . was stripped naked, put into a cart, where he was first tarred, then feathered [etc.]. **1836** E. L. JOHNSTON *Recoll. Loyalist* 44 If a Tory refused to join the people, he was imprisoned, and tarred and feathered. This was a terrible indignity, the poor creature being stripped naked, tarred all over, and then rolled in feathers. **1950** *Chi. Tribune* 18 May II. 4/6 If you don't go to work and support your family we will tar and feather you and ride you on a rail to Brushy creek and throw you in.

b. Hence **tarring and feathering,** with substantival force.

1774 CAPT. EVELYN *Memoir* 28 They are distinguished here by the name of Tories, as the Liberty Boys, the tarring-and-feathering gentlemen, are by the title of Whigs. **1843** *Quincy* (Ill.) *Herald* 12 Jan. 1/4 This is the latest case of tarring and feathering that we have heard of. **1925** BENEFIELD *Chicken-Wagon Family* 304 We don't count tarring and feathering as violence.

Also **tar and feathering.**

1809 IRVING *Knickerb.* IV. iv, The enemy . . . were represented as a gigantic, gunpowder race of men, . . . exceedingly expert at boxing, biting, gouging, tar and feathering. **1890** *Cent. Mag.* Dec. 307 We ain't a tar-and-feathering party.

*tarantula, *n.*

1. A large, hairy American spider of the family Aviculariidae, as the common southwestern species, *Eurypelma hentzi.*

1814 BRACKENRIDGE *Views La.* 59 In the southern parts, both the scorpion and the tarantula exist. **1917** KEPHART *Camping* I. 258 Tobacco juice, by the way, is fatal to scorpions, tarantulas, and centipedes, and will set a snake crazy. **1950** *Nat. Geog. Mag.* April 462/2 Tarantulas were common.

2. In combs.: (1) **tarantula hawk,** =**tarantula killer;** (2) **juice,** inferior whiskey of a particularly vile nature, *slang;* (3) **killer,** any large wasp of the genus *Pepsis* which preys on tarantulas; (4) **wasp,** =prec.

(1) **1878** B. F. TAYLOR *Between Gates* 198 The tarantula hawk . . . pounces upon his victim and makes a needle-cushion of him. **1909** WEBSTER 2114/3. — (2) **1861** *Harper's Mag.* Jan. 147/2 We found a large party assembled, . . . without much to eat and but little to drink, except old-fashioned 'tarentula-juice,' 'warranted to kill at forty paces.' **1931** DOBIE *Coronado's C.* 28 On the second afternoon of our captivity, the Comanches brought in a jug of fire water—regular old tarantula juice—from somewhere and they all got as drunk as a covey of biled owls. — (3) **1867** *Amer. Naturalist* I. 137 The large, red-winged 'Tarantula Killer' . . . is, as far as I know, the largest of the dauber group. **1899** *Cambridge Nat. Hist.* VI. 105 *P[epsis] formosus,* . . . is called in Texas the tarantula-killer. — (4) **1886** VAN DYKE *So. Calif.* 145 The tarantula-wasp is nearly two inches long, with body of deep brilliant blue and wings of deep orange. **1901** ——— *Desert* 190 The tarantula-wasp, with his gorgeous orange-colored body and his blue wings is like a bauble made of precious stones flashing along the ground.

*__tardiness,__ *n.* Lateness at a meeting, class, etc., esp. of pupils in school. — **1828** WEBSTER, Tardiness. . . . Lateness; as the *tardiness* of witnesses or jurors in attendance; the *tardiness* of students in attending prayers or recitation. **1930** *Randolph Enterprise* (Elkins, W.Va.) 2 Oct. 5/4 No business enterprise would tolerate the percentage of absence and tardiness experienced in the schools.

*tardy, *a.* Late for a meeting, appointment, etc.

1638 *Md. Archives* I. 16 Mr. Greene amerced for tardie appearing. **1843** *Yale Lit. Mag.* VIII. 240 We were '*tardy*' at our *matins.* **1905** *Springfield W. Republican* 28 April 9 In all his career he never missed a rehearsal nor was tardy. **1948** *Dly. Ardmoreite* (Ardmore, Okla.) 4 July 21/4 During this time he had been neither absent nor tardy.

*__target,__ *n.* A signal attached to a railroad switch to indicate whether it is open or shut. Also attrib. Cf. **water target.** — **1883** KNIGHT *Supp.* 810/1 These are turned by the target-man by means of a hand-lever. *Ib.,* A common form at ordinary switches is an upright pivoted lever with target on top. **1904** *Chi. Tribune* 18 Aug. 3 The passenger train had the right of way, and the 'target' was against the freight train.

*__target,__ *v. tr.* To have a favorable target at (a switch). *Rare.* — **1893** *Columbus* (O.) *Dispatch* 17 Nov., The crews of both trains claim to have had the crossing targeted.

Tarheel ˈtɑr,hil, *n.*

1. A native of North Carolina, a nickname.

1864 *So. Hist. Soc. P.* II. 232 A poor, starving Tar Heel at Elmira [prison]. **1869** *Overland Mo.* III. 128 A brigade of North Carolinians . . . failed to hold a certain hill, and were laughed at by the Mississippians for having forgotten to tar their heels that morning. Hence originated their cant name, 'Tar-heels.' **1903** *N.Y. Tribune* 20 Sep., The men really like to work, which is all but incomprehensible to the true 'tar heel.' **1945** *Chi. D. News* 31 Aug. 25/3 Shelby's Tarheels return to action tomorrow night.

b. *attrib.* in allusion to next.

1935 *News & Observer* 11 Aug., Members of the Tar Heel delegation succeeded in reaching his elbow. **1949** *Time* 4 April 26/1 But last week Kerr Scott tore up their lists and shook Tarheel professionals to their political roots.

2. Tarheel State, North Carolina, a nickname.

[**1894** *N.Y. Wkly. Tribune* 7 March 4/3 Its sobriquets are the Old North State, the Tar State, and the Turpentine State.] **1942** Kennedy *Palmetto Country* 260 North Carolina became known as the Tar-heel State. **1949** *So. Wkly.* 6 April 7/1 The people of the Tar Heel State definitely do not favor a civil rights program.

* **tariff,** *n.*

1. (See quot. 1940.) Also attrib.

1868 *Rep. Comm. Agric. 1867* p. viii, These monopolies have combined, in their tariff of rates, to discriminate unfairly against farm products. **1898** *Boston Herald* 23 Jan. 14/3 (Ernst), There are indications that tariff sheets are being secretly shaved. **1940** *Quiz* [Quest. 235] What is a tariff in railway service? A tariff is the railroads' published price list from which there can be no deviation.

2. In combs.: (1) **tariff bug,** one who has an unusual idea or enthusiasm about the tariff; (2) **conferee,** see **conferee;** (3) **convention,** a convention or meeting for consideration of problems connected with tariff legislation; (4) **man,** one who favors or advocates a protective tariff; (5) **plank,** a political party's declaration of policy on tariff, as expressed in the party platform; (6) **question,** a controversial question concerning tariff legislation arising from the conflict of interests between different sections of the country; (7) **state,** a state interested in the maintenance of a protective tariff; (8) **wall,** a tariff thought of as a protective wall; (9) **Whig,** a Whig who had formerly been in favor of a protective tariff but *c*1846 became favorably inclined toward a free-trade policy, *obs.*

(1) **1841** [see ***bug,** *n.* **1.**]. — (3) **1831** Hone *Diary* I. 41, I attended the tariff convention this morning. **1842** *Niles' Reg.* 2 April 80 Alabama Tariff Convention. . . . It was agreed . . . that cotton could not be afforded at Mobile at a less price than eight cents a pound. — (4) **1824** *Ann. 18th Cong.* 1 Sess. 2025 'Be of good cheer,' ye tariff-men; in the end you will triumph. **1870** *Nation* 3 March 129 The work of inflation . . . [is] part of an arrangement between the Western inflationists, who want more greenbacks, and the Eastern tariff men, who are opposed to a reduction of duties.

(5) **1884** *Boston Jrnl.* 6 June, The phrase on the tariff plank, that duties shall be placed on imports not for revenue only, elicited a round of applause. **1894** *Cong. Rec.* App. 26 Jan. 79/1 The very author of the tariff plank in the Chicago platform was last fall buried beneath more than 80,000 votes. — (6) **1824** *Ann. 18th Congress* 1 Sess. 2359 When are we to have enough of this Tariff question? **1904** *N.Y. Ev. Post* 27 June 7 On the tariff question . . . there will be a sharp difference of opinion between the White House group and the leaders at the other end of the avenue. — (7) **1830** *Cong. Deb.* 29 April 859/2 Restrictions [were] imposed by the tariff States upon the commerce of the planting states. — (8) **1904** *N.Y. Ev. Post* 28 Jan. 6 If there was a tariff wall separating New England from the Middle States. — (9) **1851** Quentin *Reisebilder* II. 189 Den 'Tariff-Whigs' ward zugerufen, sie möchten sich hüten, den Süden noch mehr zu reizen, welcher, wenn mit den Demokraten des Nordens vereinigt, jeden Schutztarif verhindern könne.

b. In political slogans: (1) *Tariff for revenue* (*only*), a tariff to raise revenue, not to protect industry; (2) *tariff of abominations,* (see quots.).

(1) **1830** *Cong. Deb.* 27 Jan. 84/1 Suppose, Sir, the New England gentlemen were now to join the South in going back to a tariff for revenue. **1880** in McKee *Nat. Conventions* (1901) 183 The Democrats of the United States [declare] . . . a tariff for revenue only. — (2) [**1833** Calhoun *Works* (1856) II. 217 The act of 1828, that 'bill of abominations,' as it has been so often and properly termed.] **1902** D. R. Dewey *Financial Hist. U.S.* 180 The tariff act of 1828 represented the high-water mark of protective legislation before the Civil War; it was generally condemned, and derisively termed the 'Black Tariff' and the 'Tariff of Abominations.'

As the last term in **anti-, black, Dingley, horizontal, nullification, revenue, robber tariff.**

tariffite ˈtærɪf,aɪt, *n.* One who favors a protective tariff. Cf. **high tariffite.** — **1830** *Western Mo. Rev.* III. 376 She is a true tariffite, a hearty and staunch advocate for the genuine American system. **1903** *Nation* LXXVI. 467/1 Mr. Chamberlain . . . follows in the footsteps of William McKinley, as the latter did in those of Lord George Bentinck and the other tariffites of sixty years ago.

tarnished plant bug. A common bug, *Lygus pratensis,* infesting many kinds of plants and often a pest on nursery stock and cultivated plants.

1903 Weed & Dearborn *Birds in Relations to Man* 44 The chinchbug is the type of a large group of the true bugs called the Heteroptera, another typical example of which is the tarnished plant-bug. **1913** Essig *Injurious & Beneficial Insects Calif.* 148 The tarnished plant-bug . . . feeds on almost every kind of plant. **1928** Bailey *Cyclo. Horticulture* 1036/1 (*caption*), Nymphs of the four-lined leaf-bug, and adult of the tarnished plant-bug.

tarp tɑrp, *n.* A tarpaulin. Also attrib. *Colloq.*

1906 *Out West* April 319 The men had unrolled their 'tarps' and spread their beds for the night on the ground in front of the little shack. **1920** *Outing* Dec. 112/3 A common tarp sheet can be set up in half-pyramidal shape, as shown in the accompanying illustration. **1948** *Mazama* Dec. 13/2 Eight of us lay huddled under an outstretched tarp there among the larches by the glacier's edge.

tarrabee ˈtærə,bi, *n. S.W.* [Amer. Sp. *taraba* or Sp. *tarabilla,* in Amer. Sp. sense shown here.] (See quots.) Cf. **hair spinner.**

[**1932** J. K. Ditchy *Les Acadiens Louisianais* 200 Tarabi, instrument ressemblant à une manivelle, employé pour tordre les torons d'une corde; l'ouvrier qui le tient, lui fait faire une rotation continuelle.] **1937** W. A. Read in *Zeitschrift für französische Sprache* LXI. 83 *tarabi,* m. A small grooved tool, used like a crank, for twisting the strands of a rope. Dial.—Opelousas and Southwest Louisiana. **1944** Adams *W. Words* 163/2 tarrabee An all-wood machine, carved by hand from whatever wood the man of the house possesses and used for spinning the threads for making girths.

Tarrateens ˈtærə,tinz, *n. pl.* [See quot. 1907.] Abnaki (*q.v.*) Indians in what is now Maine, esp. those about the mouth of the Penobscot River. *Obs.*

1616 in *Mass. Hist. Soc. Coll.* 3 Ser. VI. 117 On the east of it are the Tarrantines, their mortal enemies. **1634** Wood *N. Eng. Prospect* II. ii. 60 Of the Tarrenteenes or the Indians inhabiting Eastward. The Tarrenteenes saving that they eate mans flesh, are little lesse salvage, and cruell than these Canniballs. **1907** Hodge *Amer. Indians* I. 3/1 By the Puritans they [*sc.* the Abnaki] were generally called Tarrateens, a term apparently obtained from the southern New England tribes; and though that is the general conclusion of modern authorities, there is some doubt as to the aboriginal origin of this term.

***tarrying,** *n.* The practice of unmarried couples, partly undressed, occupying the same bed. *Obs.* — **1775** Burnaby *Travels* 144 A very extraordinary method of courtship, which is sometimes practised amongst the lower people of Mass. . . . is called Tarrying. **1815** *Reviewers Reviewed* 34 Neither your *grave* or *gay* [British] authorities on the subject of 'bundling' and 'tarrying' are worthy of criticism.

tarve tɑrv, *n.* [App. related to **tirve,* **terve, v.,* turn, turn over, bend.] (See quot. 1859.) Cf. Wentworth, *s.v.*

1848 Cooper *Oak Openings* I. 24, I can't say much for your axe, stranger, for this helve has no tarve to 't, to my mind. **1859** Bartlett 473 *Tarve,* a turn, bend, curve. **1917** in Wentworth 624/2 Let me get a tarve on it, & then they can pull it.

Tarzan ˈtɑrzən, *n.* In the adventure stories of Edgar Rice Burroughs (1875–1950), a white man of great strength and agility reared by African apes and hence uncorrupted by civilization. Also **Tarzan-like,** and attrib.

1919 Morley *Haunted Bookshop* (1921) 142 Posters announcing The Return of Tarzan showed a . . . scene with an Eve in a sports suit. **1931** *K.C. Times* 4 Nov., The Raytown News believes Tarzan should write a testimonial for some safety razor company. **1943** *Copper Camp* 214 Butt Block gazed pridefull at his partner, smiled and then with brawny fists pounded, Tarzan-like, upon his hairy chest. **1949** *Chi. Tribune* 5 Dec. IV. 1/1, I know some guys Who possess Tarzan eyes—Eyes that keep swinging from limb to limb.

tasajero ,tɑsəˈhɛro, *n. S.W.* [Amer. Sp. *tasajera,* in the sense shown here.] (See quot.) *Obs.* — **1888** Harlan *Calif., '46 to '88* 219 This tasajero was a long house with no windows but only a low door, and the meat was hung on strips of raw hide stretched across over a fire which smouldered in the middle of the floor.

tasajillo ,tɑsəˈhiljo, *n. S.W.* [Sp. in Amer. Sp. sense shown here.] (See quot. 1934.) — **1894** *Scribner's Mag.* May 596/2 There is an almost unvarying succession of the 'huisatchi,' the 'tasajillo,' the 'coma,' the black ebony, whose wood will sink in water. **1934** *N. Mex. Agric. Exp. Sta. Press Bul.* 716, 2 *Opuntia leptocaulis,* sometimes called tassajillo, is a slender stemmed type of the cactus that grows in all the lower regions of the State.

tasajo tɑˈsɑho, *n. S.W.* [In **1.** f. Sp. *tasajo,* jerked meat; in **2.** f. the Amer. Sp. application of this term to a species of cactus.]

1. Jerked meat. Cf. **tasseau.**

1838 Texian *Mexico vs. Texas* 77 The whole company . . . [had nothing] except some raw *tassajo,* or jerked beef. **1851** M. Reid *Scalp Hunters* xxvi, Our tasajo was all eaten, and we began to hunger. **1929** Dobie *Vaquero* 28 A staple article of diet with many of them

[Texas colonists] was *carne asada*, or *tasajo*—'jerky' (from the Spanish word *charqui*), which is still prepared and used on many Texas ranches.

2. An American cactus of the genus *Opuntia*.

1871 *Overland Mo.* VI. 555/1 On the Apache Mountains one finds that most singular shrub, the *tasajo*. At a distance, a clump of it looks like a number of green Apache spears planted in the ground, twelve or fifteen feet high. **1919** C. G. RAHT *Romance of Davis Mt.* 288 Tasajo. Literally 'dried' or 'jerked' beef. . . . Because of the resemblance in shape of the stem of this plant to the . . . strips of meat used for drying, the name became fastened to the plant. . . . The plant is a 'cereus' probably Cereus greggii. **1942** CASTETTER & BELL *Pima & Papago Agric.* 25 Other characteristic chollas of the paloverde belt are the varicolored or staghorn cholla (*O. versicolor*), tesajo, . . . (*O. leptocaulis*), the arborescent pencil cholla (*O. arbuscula*).

* **task,** *n.* **1.** *S.* A measure of land fixed in terms of the time needed to work it. **2. task hand,** formerly in the South, a slave sufficiently strong and ambitious to be given a task after the completion of which the slave could work for himself or herself. Also **task system.** Now *obs.* or *hist.*

(1) **1850** BURKE *Reminisc. Ga.* 117 If a person is asked the extent of a certain piece of land, he is told it contains so many tasks. **1862** E. W. PEARSON *Lett. Port Royal* 78 Tirah had planted a task of cowpease for the Government. — (2) **1848** *De Bow's Review* VI. 149 The effective force of the plantation numbers 70 task hands. **1859** in EASTERBY *S.C. Rice Plant.* (1945) 151, I lost in one year 28 negroes 22 of whom were *task hands.* **1948** DICK *Dixie Frontier* 82 In Georgia and probably other parts of the cotton kingdom the 'task system' was used. The hands were rated according to their ability and given daily tasks proportionately.

tasseau tɑˈso, *n.* Also **tasso.** (See quot. 1931.) Cf. **tasajo 1.** — **1841** *S. Lit. Messenger* VII. 77/2 The evening banquet of gumbo, tasso, and beef, in every variety of form, was shortly served up. **1931** READ *La.-French* 73 Tasseau, m. *Du tasseau* is the equivalent of 'jerked beef.' Formerly strips of deerskin and fish, too, were dried in the sunshine on a clothes line or wooden support. This word is adapted from St[andard]-Fr. *tasseau*, 'block,' 'bracket,' 'prop.'

* **tassel,** *n.* The inflorescence of a corn plant.

*a***1649** WINTHROP *Hist.* II. 277 [Caterpillars] eat up first the blades of the stalk, then they eat up the tassels, whereupon the ear withered. **1785** WASHINGTON *Diaries* II. 409 The tassel . . . had got too dry for the farina to impregnate the grain. **1824** SINGLETON *Letters* 82 They [Virginians] also call, what we [New Englanders] call the spindle, the tassel. **1948** *Chi. D. News* 9 Aug. 3/3 High School lads begin the final tassel cleanup.

b. *In tassel*, of corn: In the stage of having tassels.

1774 FITHIAN *Journal* I. 207, I was not a little Surprised to see Corn out in Tassel. **1903** *Atlantic Mo.* July 84 The corn was in tassel now, and rustled softly in the fields.

c. (See quot.) *Obs.*

1851 in *One Man's Gold* [Jrnl. of Enos Christman] (1930) 245 In Chester County we did the clean thing and proved ourselves 'Sound corn to the tassel.'

As the last term in **corn, pine tassel.**

* **tassel,** *v. intr.* Of corn: To bloom or form tassels. Also with *out.*

1757 in WOODWARD *Ploughs* (1941) 278 Just before it Tossles it should be plowed & hoed again. **1854** DAVIS *Farm Bk.* 55 The corn near the gin is tasselling. **1887** WILKINS *Humble Romance* 29 His corn tasselled out . . . as soon as anybody's. **1948** *Iowa State Coll. Jrnl. Science* Oct. 86 When moved north to longer days during June at Ames, Iowa, many kinds of corn collected in Guatemala . . . grow to abnorma heights and fail to tassel.

taste test, *n.* [Origin unknown.] A kind of narrow silk ribbon. Now *local.*

1788 *Ky. Gazette* 28 June 2/3 Hugh M'Ilvain, Is now opening at his Store in Lexington. . . . An Assortment of Goods: . . . Taste and garters [etc.]. **1845** JUDD *Margaret* I. 132 The third [beautiful girl] led down from the skies the brilliant Planet Venus, by a bridle of blue taste tied about one of its rays. **1899** GREEN *Va. Word-Bk.* 384 Taste, n. Narrow, thin silk ribbon.

tata ˈtɑtə, *n. S.W.* [Sp. in Amer. Sp. sense shown here.] A title of respect. Also **Tata Grande, =Great Father** *a.*

1838 TEXIAN *Mexico vs. Texas* 16 The Tata padre and the strange gentleman . . . drove away with great speed. **1870** *Republican Rev.* 21 May 3/1 We wish these statements sent to our 'Tata Grande,' and let the Government know our wishes. **1885** *Wkly. New Mexican Rev.* 12 March 3/6 The head chiefs and warriors of the Mescaleros and Jicarillas told your correspondent that he was the first 'tata,' father or agent, who protected them against the encroachment of settlers.

* **tattler,** *n.* A long-billed, limicoline bird of the genus *Totanus* or allied genera. Also with specifying terms. Cf. **Bartram's, solitary tattler.**

1831 [in **semipalmated tattler**]. **1874** COUES *Birds N.W.* 503 In most parts of the West, between the Mississippi and the Rocky mountains, this Tattler, commonly known as the 'Prairie Pigeon,' is exceedingly abundant during the migrations. **1917** *Birds of Amer.* I. 244 Yellow-legs. . . . [Also called] Lesser Long-legged Tattler.

tattletale ˈtætlˌtel, *n.* One who tells tales or secrets. Also attrib. and transf.

1888 CRADDOCK *Despot* 429 I'd strangle that tattle-tale with a mighty good will. **1925** BENEFIELD *Chicken-Wagon Family* 210 A tattletale is a person of no account whatsoever. **1944** ROBSJOHN-GIBBINGS *Goodbye* 49 By the time the white damask had turned a tattle-tale gray and the ruching was flattened to a pancake, along came Dorothy Draper.

Taunton turkey. [*Taunton*, Mass.] The alewife, *Pomolobus pseudoharengus.* — **1850** MRS. A. A. CURTIS *Home Ballads* (Farmer), Taunton turkeys are so thick, We sell them by the rod. **1950** *Chi. Tribune* 17 Jan. 14/3 In Massachusetts . . . the spring herring is known as 'Taunton turkey.'

tautog ˈtɔtɑg, *n.* [Narraganset *tautauog*, pl. of *tautau*, blackfish, but thought by Roger Williams to mean "sheep's-head."] A highly esteemed food fish, *Tautoga onitis*, abundant on the Atlantic Coast. Cf. **blackfish 2.**

1643 WILLIAMS *Key* (1866) 138 Of Fish and Fishing. . . . *Taut-auog*, sheeps-heads. **1775** BURNABY *Travels* 121 Fish are in the greatest plenty and perfection, particularly the tataag or black-fish. *a***1841** HAWES *Sporting Scenes* I. 37, I once crossed over to Faulker's island, to fish for tautaugs, as the north side people call black fish. **1947** COFFIN *Yankee Coast* 296 Near the shore, we have . . . the vast tautogue, which fights like a bull and fills a whole oven with his strong-flavored roasting hulk.

* **tavern,** *n.* As the last term in **coon, log, pumpkin, scrub, sky, wagon tavern.**

Tawakoni təˈwɑkənɪ, *n. pl.* [Regarded by Gatschet as a native word prob. meaning "river bend among red sand hills."] A Caddoan tribe of Indians who in the eighteenth and nineteenth centuries lived on the middle Brazos and Trinity rivers in Texas. Also attrib.

1823 DEWEES *Letters* (1852) 47 They then sent out two spies in a westerly direction to find the Toncoway camps. **1830** *Boston Transcript* 2 Sep. 1/1 War has broken out between the Cherokees, Shawnees, Delawares, . . . and the Tahuacanies, Wacos and Comanches. **1846** *Dollar Newspaper* (Phila.) 8 July 4/2 Represented in this delegation [are] the Camanches, Lipans, . . . To-wah-cah-noes, . . . and Delawares. **1910** HODGE *Amer. Indians* II. 703/1 The Tawakoni and the Waco speak dialects of the Wichita language and sometimes have been considered the same people.

tawkee ˈtɔkɪ, *n.* Also **tawho.** Variants of **tuckahoe 1.**

1725 in NELSON *Indians of N.J.* 78 The families gather the first-fruits of roots, which grow in swamps, not unlike nuts, called *Tachis.* **1772** FORESTER tr. Kalm *Travels* I. 389 This Taw-ho seems to be the same with what the Indians in Carolina call *Tuckahoo.* **1819** *Amer. Farmer* 2 July 107/3 They also eat the dried seeds of the *orantium aquaticum*, called by them tawkee; they were boiled in water, and eat like peas, or made into bread. **1910** HODGE *Amer. Indians* II. 711/2 *Tawkee.* . . . The word . . . is derived from *p'tukwi*, or *p'tukqueu*, in the Delaware dialect of Algonquian, signifying 'it is globular.'

* **tax,** *n.* In combs.: (1) **tax certificate,** a certificate issued or to be issued at a tax sale certifying that the purchaser is entitled to a tax deed on a given piece of land upon the fulfillment of certain conditions; (2) **deed,** a deed to land bought at a tax sale; (3) **dodger,** one who avoids paying taxes; (4) **land,** land taken over by the state for nonpayment of taxes; (5) **sale,** a sale of property, usu. at auction, for delinquent taxes, also attrib.; (6) **title,** a title acquired under a tax sale.

(1) **1878** *Wis. Supreme Ct. Rep.* XLIV. 489 Tax certificates issued to a county cannot be transferred by it without an assignment in writing. **1900** *Okla. Supreme Ct. Rep.* X. 279 A tax certificate represents an interest in real estate. — (2) **1861** *Mich. Acts* 178 An act to authorize the Auditor General to execute second tax deeds, in certain cases. **1945** *Hardin* (Mont.) *Tribune-Herald* 15 Feb. 7/2 The board approved applications for taking tax deed on lands described as follows. — (3) **1876** *Nation* 30 March 202/2 The 'tax-dodger' is one who, finding that the rate of taxation in Boston is too high for his means, flies, with his wife and children to some rural town. **1894** *Cong. Rec.* App. 29 Jan. 277/1 There are tax dodgers under any system which may be inaugurated. — (4) **1882** *Mich. Gen. Statutes* I. 1258

Any person may purchase any parcel of the unsold state tax lands now held by the state.

(5) *c*1830 *Williams's N.Y. Ann. Reg. 1830* 222 And also the anticipated revenue from the tax sales to take place in the spring. **1879** *Mich. Pub. Acts* 16 The auditor general of this state . . . is hereby authorized to execute a second deed upon tax-sale certificates. **1950** *Ill. Munic. Rev.* March 44/1 The assessed real estate can be sold at the annual tax sale to satisfy this special assessment lien. — **(6) 1831** PECK *Guide* 320 Purchasers for taxes, now offer and sell quarters [of land] thus held by tax-titles. **1929** F. E. MCCLINCHEY *Joe Pete* 161 The foreigner had bought up the tax title on his land and intended to hold it.

As the last term in **bachelor's, back, bank, county, grazing, land, mill, occupation, province, school, single, state tax.**

∗ **tax,** *v. tr.* To charge (a person) a certain price, to fix as a charge. *Colloq.*

1848 BARTLETT 351 *To Tax,* to charge; as, 'What will you tax me a yard for this cloth?' i.e. what will you charge for it, or what is the price of it? *c*1849 WHITCHER *Bedott P.* xx. 218 [Jabe Clark] said 'twas worth double the money he taxed; but seein' he was tradin' with the clargy, he wouldnt charge but half-price. **1907** *D.N.* III. 219.

taxable ˈtæksəbl̩, *n.* [f. the adj.] One who or that which is subject or liable to taxation.

1662 *Mag. Amer. Hist.* XI. 39 Every householder and freeman . . . should take up ten shillings per poll . . . for every taxable under their charge. **1770** *N.H. Prov. P.* VII. 257 If any one honest taxable in the Province is comforted in one penny thus saved to him . . . I do Rejoice at the vote. **1855** DAVIS *Farm Bk.* 151 Went to Hamburg & gave in my taxables. **1904** *Newark Ev. News* 24 Aug. 6 A readjustment of local taxables [has been] recently completed by the city Board of Assessors.

taxi ˈtæksɪ, *n.* [See quot. 1947.] A vehicle, usu. an automobile, used in public passenger service the charge for which is usu. computed by a taximeter. In full **taxicab** or †**taximeter motor cab.**

1907 in *N.Y. Times Mag.* (1947) 26 Oct. 28/5 The new taximeter motor cabs, which promise New Yorkers low-price cab service, made their initial trips for the general public yesterday. **1947** *N.Y. Times* 26 Oct. 28/4 Mr. [Harry N.] Allen also coined the word 'taxicab,' which he had copyrighted in Washington. 'The "cab" part was a natural,' he explained. 'The "taxi" came from a French company that made meters for horse cabs, called "taximetres." That means a meter that arranges for the tax. I merely combined the two.' **1950** *Business Week* 22 April 26/1 One lone British-built taxicab is now cruising New York's streets.

attrib., esp. **taxi-driver.**

1932 MORLEY *Swiss Family Manhattan* 205 Fritz intends to be a taxi-driver. **1938** SMITTER *F.O.B. Detroit* 331 He pulled up . . . and opened the door for us like a taxi-cab driver. **1948** *Chi. D. News* 3 Jan. 7/5 Action to ease Chicago's taxi muddle by ridding the streets of 'wildcat cabs' is expected soon.

b. taxi-dance place, a dance hall, cabaret, etc., where girls are available to dance with patrons who pay for the privilege. Also **taxi-dancer,** a girl who works for such a place.

1938 SMITTER *F.O.B. Detroit* 9 On it there was the name of a taxi-dance place over a store on Woodward Avenue. *Ib.* 67 I'm a taxi-dancer but that don't mean I'm your slave.

Taylorism ˈteləˌrɪzəm, *n.* **a.** The political principles or philosophy of Zachary Taylor, twelfth President of the U.S. (1849–50). **b.** A modified Calvinism taught by Nathaniel William Taylor (1786–1858), professor of theology at Yale. Both *obs.* or *hist.*

(a) 1848 *Campaign* (Wash., D.C.) 9 Aug. 176/3 The New York Tribune thus unburdens itself of its repugnance to Taylorism. **1849** *Ib.* 11 April 413/2 The result has a moral for Taylorism. — **(b) 1884** SCHAFF *Religious Encycl.* III. 2306/1 An elaborate system, which . . . powerfully affected theological thought and preaching in America, . . . was called 'Taylorism.'

Taylorite ˈteləˌraɪt, *n.* One who accepts the doctrines of Taylorism. *Obs.* — **1867** DIXON *New Amer.* II. 308 In the Congregational Church . . . there arose endless divisions, including Millennialists, Taylorites, and the strange heresy of the Perfectionists.

T-bone steak. Strictly, a steak containing a T-shaped bone, from the middle portion of the short loin, but often used loosely for a porterhouse steak.

1934 WEBSTER. **1943** *Copper Camp* 92 Where the former two welcomed any stray handout, Dynamite frowned on any contribution less than T-bone steaks and chicken or turkey scraps. **1947** DALRYMPLE *Panfish* 154 Although you don't eat scallops or clams or frogs' legs, or even T-bone steaks every day, you still jump at the chance to tie into such a meal when the opportunity is afforded.

∗ **tea,** *n.* In combs.: (1) **tea-and-coffee splash,** *local.* a social gathering at which tea and coffee are served; (2) **ball,** (see quot. 1909); (3) **bincum,** (see quot.), *obs.;* (4) **clam,** (see quots.); (5) **dance,** a short, usu. informal dance held at tea-time, i.e. in the late afternoon, esp. at schools and colleges, *colloq.;* (6) **hound,** one especially given to frequenting teas, *slang;* (7) **junketing,** a tea or tea party, *obs.;* (8) **spiller,** a participant in the Boston Tea Party, *humorous, obs.;* (9) **water,** see as a main entry.

(1) 1889 *Boston Jrnl.* 28 March 2/3 Rural towns in Pennsylvania indulge in what they call a 'tea and coffee splash.' — **(2) 1905** [see **coffee ball**]. **1909** WEBSTER, tea ball. A perforated metal ball filled with tea leaves, submerged in boiling water to make tea. **1922** NORRIS *Certain People* 135 A silver tea-ball quite enchanted her. **1946** C. R. V. THOMPSON *How to Like Englishman* 163 It must have something to do with the water, which is largely responsible—although tea balls help—for the fact that you can't make really good tea in America. — **(3) 1837** WILLIAMS *Florida* 100 Of this [*sc.* wild thyme] is made the Tea Bincum, which immediately cures the Dangue. — **(4) 1881** INGERSOLL *Oyster Industry* 249 *Tea-clam.*—The quahaug, *Venus mercenaria,* of small size. **1883** *Nat. Museum Bul.* No. 27, 234 Smaller sizes . . . when about one inch in diameter, are called 'tea-clams.'

(5) 1923 WATTS *L. Nichols* 137 Step across the bridges pretty nearly any time you want to—girl—restaurant—luncheon—matinee tea-dance—there you are! **1924** MARKS *Plastic Age* 136 No freshman was allowed to attend the Prom. . . . There was a tea-dance at the fraternity house during Prom week. [**1946** *New Yorker* 2 Feb. 4 A Melba trio plays in the Cafe Pierre, where there is tea dancing daily.] — **(6) 1925** *Scribner's Mag.* Oct. 353/2 He was a regular tea-hound, he was seen at so many teas. — **(7) 1820** IRVING *Sketch Book* No. 7, 116 Mrs. Lamb . . . would give little hum-drum tea junkettings to some of her old cronies. **1852** *Harper's Mag.* July 185/1 There was to be a tea-junketing. — **(8) 1837** PHILLIPS in C. Martyn *W. Phillips* 96 Certainly we sons of the tea-spillers are a marvellously patient generation! **1895** *Advance* 8 Aug. 192/1 Would the old tea spillers and Puritan parents know themselves now?

b. In the names of plants: (1) **teaberry,** the wintergreen, *Gaultheria procumbens,* or its fruit; (2) ∗ **plant,** any one of various wild American plants whose leaves can be used in making a beverage somewhat like tea; (3) ∗ **tree,** the yaupon or a related species, the leaves of which are used in making a kind of substitute for tea, cf. **Indian tea;** (4) **weed,** any one of various meadowsweets; (5) **wheat,** a variety of wheat alleged to have originated from some stray seed found in a shipment of tea, also **China tea wheat,** *obs.*, cf. **China wheat.**

(1) 1837 DARLINGTON *Flora Cestrica* 258 Tea-berry. Spicy Wintergreen. **1895** *Outing* XXVII. 18/1 Tiny white capillaire tea-berries, . . . with a flavor like some rare perfume, and having just a faint suggestion of wintergreen. **1944** *Herb Magic* 8 Wintergreen Leaves (also known as Teaberry)—Very refreshing. . . . An infusion has been considered a valuable remedy for rheumatism. — **(2) 1809** KENDALL *Travels* II. 143 Where the pine only is found, the ground beneath is nearly bare, sustaining but dwarfish plants, such as the partridge-berry, sometimes called the *tea plant* and *Indian tea.* **1894** *Amer. Folk-Lore* VII. 96 *Lantana,* sp., tea-plant, Louisiana. — **(3) 1785** MARSHALL *Amer. Grove* 26 Yapon, or South-Sea Tea-tree . . . grows naturally in Carolina and some parts of Virginia. **1841** W. KENNEDY *Texas* I. 100 Among the latter, may be enumerated . . . red bud, hog wood, the yawpan or tea tree [etc.]. — **(4) 1852** *Mich. Agric. Soc. Trans.* III. 197 My timber is generally oak, with some hickory, indigo weed, tea weed. **1874** *Vt. Bd. Agric. Rep.* II. 775 Common upon flowers of many kinds, especially those of the meadow-sweet or tea-weed. (*Spiraea.*)

(5) 1832 J. MACGREGOR *British Amer.* II. 315 The kind of seed-wheat generally sown . . . [is] known by the distinction of 'tea-wheat.' **1862** *Ill. Agric. Soc. Trans.* V. 197 China Tea Wheat . . . was said to have been taken from a chest of black tea some fifteen years since, by a gentleman in Rensalaer [*sic*] county, New York. **1868** *Iowa State Agric. Soc. Rep. 1867* 141 The first seed wheat I bought in Iowa (in 1853) was called Red River, and when it was grown I recognized at once the Tea wheat of New York.

c. In obs. expressions relating to tea or the tax on tea as a source of friction between Great Britain and the American colonies. Cf. **tea spiller** above.

1773 in *Pub. Col. Soc.* XI. 32 Voted—That a committee be chosen to draw a resolution to be read to the Tea Consignees tomorrow 12 O'Clock, noon, at Liberty Tree: and that Dr. Thos. Young and Church, and Warren be a committee for that purpose, and make a report as soon as may be. **1774** *Ib.* VIII. 86 One of the Tea Commissioners it is said narrowly escaped a Tarring and Feathering one

Day last Week. **1775** *Jrnls Cont. Cong.* III. 370 Tuesday [shall] be assigned for the consideration of the memorials of the Teaholders. **1775** HUTCHINSON *Diary & Lett.* I. 505, I was threatened by the Tea mobs. **1781** PETERS *Hist. Conn.* (1829) 293 [To] exert themselves . . . in favour of the Bostonian tea-merchants.

As the last term in **American, Appalachian, bohea, boneset, breakfast, bush, cambric, Carolina, catnip, chaparral, Chickasaw, clover, desert, elder bark, elder blow, English breakfast, ginger, gum, hemlock, hickory, hot water, iced, Indian, Jersey, Labrador, lap, liberty, low, malt, Mexican, mountain, mullein, New Jersey, Oswego, peach tree, pennyroyal, pepper, pink, prairie, Revolutionary, sass, sheep nanny, sheep nanny plum, shuck, silver, soot, spice, spicewood, store, thoroughwort, Virginia, wafer-ash, wild, worm, yaupon tea.**

* **teacher,** *n.*

1. In the early Congregational churches of New England, a person appointed to give religious instruction. *Obs.*

1642 *Suffolk Deeds* I. 35 The dwelling house of the Reverend Teacher Mr. John Cotton in Boston aforesaid. **1648** *Platform Church-Discipline* (1772) 30 The pastors special work is, to attend to exhortation, and therein to administer a word of wisdom: The teacher is to attend to doctrine, and therein to administer a word of knowledge. **1693** (*title*), Cases of Conscience Concerning Evil Spirits Personating Men. . . . By Increase Mather, . . . Teacher of a Church at Boston in New England. **1788** FRANKLIN *Autobiog.* 347, I rather approv'd his giving us good sermons compos'd by others, than bad ones of his own manufacture, tho' the latter was the practice of our common teachers.

2. In the Christian Science Church, a person prepared and authorized to give class instruction in Christian Science to qualified applicants.

1896 M. B. EDDY *Misc. Writings* 92 The teacher of Christian Science needs continually to study this textbook [i.e., *Science and Health*]. **1945** *Christian Sci. Sentinel* XLVII. 1923 No individual or group of individuals seeking class instruction can possibly receive it if the one claiming to do the teaching has not qualified as a teacher under the Rules in the Manual.

3. In combs., usu. pl.: (1) **teacher bird,** the ovenbird *q.v.*, so called from its note; (2) **-s' association,** an association composed of the schoolteachers in a particular county, state, etc.; (3) **-s' college,** a college for training teachers; (4) **-s' institute,** an assembly of the teachers in a state, county, etc., for discussing their problems and the best methods of teaching, etc., also **teachers' state institute.**

(1) **1934** WEBSTER. **1943** DAMON *Sense of H.* 214 The toads speak as if the water had made them sure, secure, the teacher bird insists, and the unseen veery begins to whirl his silvery circles again. — (2) **1944** *Democrat* 27 Jan. 1/5 (*heading*), Clarke County Teachers Association Program Given. — (3) **1934** WEBSTER. **1949** *Dly. Ardmoreite* (Ardmore, Okla.) 8 Sep. 4/1 They visited Carlsbad Caverns, the Mescalero Apache Indian reservation, . . . and Las Vegas Teachers' college. — (4) **1837** in S. N. SWEET *Teachers' Institutes* 14 Professor Sweet, the founder of Teachers' Institutes, or Temporary Normal Schools, is entitled to the gratitude of all the lovers of science. **1868** *Ore. State Jrnl.* 18 July 2/6 Teachers and others coming from a distance to attend the Teachers' State Institute. **1947** MYERS *The 'Guv'* 25 The Guv's father, having attended teachers' institutes and having served on juries, knew many people in the county seat.

As the last term in **grade, Indian, Negro, nutmeg school, object teacher.**

teacherage ˈtitʃərɪdʒ, *n.* A residence or home for the teachers in a particular community.

1934 WEBSTER. **1936** *Amer. Sp.* Oct. 271 Walking into the corner of his *teacherage* after dark, a lens in his glasses was shattered, a fragment piercing his eye. **1948** *Pageant* Feb.–Mar. 24/2 There she built the Teacherage—the mountaineer's name for the teachers' home.

teacherly ˈtitʃəlɪ, *a.* Relating to the office of a teacher in a church. *Rare.* — *c*1680 HULL *Diaries* 173 Mr. John Norton . . . continued with us three years and upward . . . laboring in God's work, and joined in a teacherly office with us.

teaching elder. An elder, as in the colonial Congregational churches, exercising teaching or pastoral functions (see also quot. 1889).

1642 T. LECHFORD *Plain Dealing* 15 Some Churches have no ruling Elders, some but one, some but one teaching Elder, some have two ruling, and two teaching Elders. **1735** in C. HAZARD *Thos. Hazard* 226 We the Subscribers, Teaching Elders or Pastors of the first gathered. . . . Church in Boston New England. **1889** *Cent.* 1864/3 In churches of the Presbyterian order the pastor of a church is technically called the *teaching elder*, as distinguished from the *ruling elders*, commonly called simply *elders*, who are a body of laymen.

* **teal,** *n.* As the last term in **cinnamon, salt-water teal.**

* **team,** *n.*

1. A grandiose term for an individual of superior endowments. Usu. **whole team,** and often with various embellishments as *the whole team and the dog under the wagon. Colloq.* Cf. * **yellow dog 3.**

1832 *Polit. Examiner* (Shelbyville, Ky.) 17 Nov. 4/2 'Whoop! Aint I a horse?' 'A whole team, I should think,' said Rainsford. **1856** BREWERTON *War in Kans.* 270 Avow yourself ready to declare that Mistress B—— and her fair companion are trumps; and a clear-grit Yankee woman quite equal, upon an emergency, to what, in vulgar parlance, is quaintly styled 'a whole team, and *a dog under the wagon*' to boot. **1861** *Harper's Mag.* April 711/1 The accused sought the advice and counsel of your 'humble servant,' who at that time was considered a full team in the way of managing a criminal case. **1911** LINCOLN *Cap'n Warren's Wards* 170 Mother's the whole team and the dog under the wagon!

2. A pack of dogs that hunt together. *Obs.*

1844 FEATHERSTONHAUGH *Slave States* 111/2 They maintained stout *teams* of dogs until the hunting season commenced by slaying beeves for them. **1851** *Polly Peablossom* 126, I had long promised myself the pleasure of following a good 'team' of *dogs* through these unexplored wilds.

3. (See quot. 1899.)

1849 E. DAVIES *Amer. Scenes* 186 At length I learned that there was a 'team' in the stable. **1899** MUIRHEAD *Baedeker's U.S.* xxx, *Team*, often applied to *one* horse. **1944** WENTWORTH.

4. Short for baseball team *q.v.*

1867 *Ball Players' Chron.* 20 June 3/4 On Thursday, both clubs presented their strongest 'teams,' and the result was a very well contested game. **1910** *Spalding's Base Ball Guide* 361 'No game' shall be declared by the umpire if he terminates play in accordance with Rule 22, Section 3, before five innings are completed by each team. **1949** *News-Herald* (Marshfield, Wis.) 16 July 9/1 The local team began the defense of its Eighth District crown, won last year, at 10 a.m. today against Stevens Point.

5. In combs.: (1) **team boat,** a boat, esp. a ferryboat, propelled by horses on board, also attrib., *obs.;* (2) **play,** play in which members of a team coöperate for a desired end, also **team player;** (3) **shovel,** (see quot. 1876), *obs.*, cf. * **scraper;** (4) * **work,** (*a*) coöperative work by individual members of an athletic team, who subordinate their own interests to the success of the group, also transf., (*b*) (see quot.), *obs.*

(1) **1816** *Niles' Reg.* X. 414/1 The team boat . . . is 62 feet long and 42 feet wide, and propelled by eight horses. **1820** *Columbian Centinel* 12 Jan. 3/1 A Team Boat ferry connects the travel with the eastern shore opposite. **1895** *Forum* May 378 The 'team-boat,' or ferry-boat propelled by horse power, actually ran for some time in competition with steam ferries. — (2) **1886** CHADWICK *Art of Batting* 7 The practical effect of all this is to destroy a batsman's ambition to excel as a 'team player' in batting. **1945** *Somerset News* 19 April 1/1 It is team-play with personalities submerged to the general welfare. **1948** *Chi. Tribune* 22 Feb. II. 4/7 He's a fine team player and a great hitter. — (3) **1876** KNIGHT 2501/2 *Team-shovel*, an earth-scraper. A scoop drawn by horses or oxen, managed by means of handles, and used in removing earth. — (4) (*a*) **1886** *Outing* June 365/1 All three of the college nines were . . . weak in their team-work together to a more or less extent. **1913** *Chi. Record-Herald* 18 March 10/2 Superior team work brought victory. **1950** *Calif. Citrograph* Jan. 91/3 In order to have teamwork we have to keep on good terms and not let little differences grow. (*b*) **1887** H. CAMPBELL *Prisoners of Poverty* 26 Others preferring to send out what is known as 'team work,' [shirt] flaps being done by one, bosoms by another, and so on.

b. *To drive too much team,* to undertake more than one can do. *Colloq.*

1842 *Cultivator* IX. 193/3, I should have accomplished all this, . . . but I undertook to drive *too much team.*

As the last term in **ball, baseball, bell, breaking, breaking-up, bronco, bull, cow, dog, double, five cattle, freight, full, home, Pitt, pod, prairie, scratch, scrub, shanty, snatch, spike, sucker, tote, track, team.**

* **teaming,** *n.* (See quot.) *Obs.* Cf. * **teamwork** (*b*). — **1876** KNIGHT 2501/1 *Teaming*, . . . a certain mode of manufacturing work, which is given out to a boss, who hires a gang or team to do it, and is responsible to the owner of the stock.

teamster ˈtimstɚ, *n.* One who drives a team. Also attrib. Cf. **tote teamster.**

1777 *N.H. Comm. Safety Rec.* 88 The Committee delivered the Several Teamsters. **1817** *N. Amer. Rev.* IV. 183 We there sat down to table with teamsters. **1850** GARRARD *Wah-To-Yah* xxvi. 304 Only a green teamster train. **1927** Benét *J. B.'s Body* 108 Bailey had been a teamster and was a corporal.

***tear,** *n.* A spree, frolic, rampage. Also *to get* (or *go*) *on a tear. Colloq.* Cf. **tear-down.**

1849 G. G. Foster *N.Y. in Slices* 24 It is Thursday night, and a grand 'tear' is to be held in that large and rather aristocratic-looking cellar across the way. **1882** *L.A. Times* 28 March, Ike Clanton came into Tombstone, and 'got on a tear.' **1928** Foy & Harlow *Clowning Thro' Life* 99 The Arkansas River—a shallow, quiet stream which went on a tear once in a while and did some damage. **1949** *Time* 29 Aug. 15/1 Some employers wistfully look back to the days when a red-blooded man could go on a tear.

***tear,** *v.* In combs.: **1. tear blanket, coat,** any one of various prickly plants (see quots.). *Colloq.* **2. tear-down,** = ***tear,** *n. Obs.* **3. tear-round,** a spree or frolic. *Obs.*

(1) **1835** Latrobe *Rambler N. Amer.* I. 213 We found . . . abundance of green-briar or tear-blanket as it is familiarly called. **1897** Sudworth *Arborescent Flora* 265 *Xanthoxylum clava-herculis*. Prickly Ash. . . . Wait-a-bit, Tear-blanket (Ark.). — (2) **1831** *Boston Transcript* 12 Dec. 1/1 They drove up to the door of a village tavern, where they heard the foot-shaking voice of the violin inviting them, while they were up for a 'tear-down,' to go the 'whole figure,' by taking steps in the dance. — (3) **1872** Harte in *Atlantic Mo.* March 350 Maybe ye'd all come over to my house to-night and have a sort of tear-round.

***tearer,** *n.* **1.** *fig.* An elaborate party, a violent storm. **2.** (See quot.) Both *colloq.* and *obs.*

(1) **1835** *S. Lit. Messenger* I. 357/2 A real tearer—a regular turnout—been preparing a fortnight. **1892** S. Hale *Letters* 275 The storm increased as day went on, and by noon was a regular tearer. — (2) **1843** Oliver *Eight Months* 163 Some hunters prefer rifles termed *tearers*—a qualification which, I believe, is given them by increasing the twist of the scroll, and thereby causing the bullet to make a revolution on its axis in shorter space than it would otherwise do. Such guns it is said, are more deadly from making a larger wound.

***tears,** *n. pl.* (See quot.) — **1896** *U.S. Dept., Agric. Div. Veget. Physiol. & Pathol.* Bul. 8, 30 Psorosis, a disease known in Florida as 'tears' or 'gum disease,' is often confounded with foot rot, but is unquestionably quite distinct. . . . Psorosis does not kill the bark entirely.

***tea water.**

1. *N.Y. City.* Water from the tea water pump (see next). Now *hist.*

1870 M. H. Smith *20 Years Wall St.* 34 'Tea water' was expensive. **1938** Hart *New Yorkers* 16 The Tea Water was fed by seepage from the Collect Pond, once a beautiful limpid pool surrounded by hills. **1946** Partridge & Bettmann *As We Were* 132 (*caption*), Tea water delivered at the door.

2. tea water pump, (see quots.). Also attrib.

1782 in De Voe *Market Ass't* (1867) 221 To be shown this day and to-morrow at Mr. Jeroleman's Punch House, at the tea-water pump (New York). **1794** Wansey *Excursion to U.S.* (1798) 219 The water is very bad to drink, except at one pump, in Queen-street, called the tea-water pump. **1832** Dunlap *Hist. Amer. Theatre* 39 Nearly opposite the place where Queen-street ended in Chatham-road, was the celebrated tea-water pump. **1939** Dunshee *Enjine! Enjine!* 57 There is a story of a meeting of the members of Engine Company No. 3, who gathered in the famous old Tea Water Tavern. . . . The Tea Water pump, which stood opposite the tavern, had just received a fresh coat of pea-green paint.

***technic,** *n.* A technical term or expression. *Obs.*

1826 Flint *Recoll.* 86 We began to pull the boat up the stream, by a process, which, in the technics of the boatmen, is called 'bush-whacking.' **1855** *Knickerb.* XLV. 438 [The mare] has a new disease—the staggers, perhaps. . . . I don't know as 'staggers' is the technic. **1875** Emerson *Lett. & Soc. Aims, Greatness* Wks. (Bohn) III. 272, I find it easy to translate all his [Napoleon's] technics into all of mine.

Technicolor ˈteknɪˌkʌlɚ, *n.* [See quots.] The trademark name of a system of making color motion pictures.

1944 *Reader's Digest* Aug. 63 By 1917, however, they thought they had a satisfactory process. Kalmus had named it Technicolor—'Tech' for his alma mater. **1948** *Time* 22 March 85/3 Herbert T., Kalmus, . . the co-inventor, developer, majority stockholder and president of Technicolor, . . . is a graduate of Massachusetts Institute of Technology (after which Technicolor was named).

Hence **technicolored,** *a.*

1949 *House & Garden* July 60 The West is a magnificent overstatement, designed to order for the picture post card trade, technicolored movies and carefree life. **1949** *Time* 12 Dec. 101/1 The Story of Seabiscuit offers impeccable Technicolored performances by several horses.

technological school. A school in which technology is taught. — **1883** *Harper's Mag.* Aug. 327/2 Many graduates from the technological schools of Boston . . . work in these [car] shops. **1914** *Cyclo. Amer. Govt.* III. 635/2 The Division of Higher Education [of the Bureau of Educ.] has charge of the statistics . . . regarding universities, colleges, technological schools, normal schools, and professional schools.

tecolote ˌtekəˈlotɪ, *n. S.W.* [Amer. Sp. (<Nahuatl *tecolotl*) in same sense.] (See quots.) — **1925** Bryan *Papago Country* 392 Tecolote comes from the Nahuatl tecolotl and means owl, specifically the small ground owl. **1928** Mary Austin *Children Sing in Far West* (Bentley), Black beetle and tecolote owl Between two winks their ancient forms will take.

***tedder,** *n.* A machine for stirring and spreading hay to promote its drying. Cf. **hay tedder.**

Tedder, hay tedder, or hay spreader

1868 *Mich. Agric. Rep.* VII. 223 There are important advantages in the use of the tedder for machine-cut grass. **1888** *Vt. Agric. Rep.* X. 18 [He] mows clover in the afternoon and the next forenoon sets the tedder to work. **1941** White *One Man's Meat* 241 There was a tedder stored in one corner.

Teddy bear. A stuffed toy bear of plush or similar material, so called after Theodore ("Teddy") Roosevelt in allusion to his fondness for hunting big game. Also attrib.

1907 *Springfield Wkly. Republican* 11 July 1 Nothing now remains for the president but to denounce the 'Teddy bear'—or else defend it from horrid aspersion. **1948** *Parents' Mag.* March 8/2 His gently gruff appearance is in best Teddy Bear tradition. **1949** *Chi. D. News* 12 Dec. 12/3 Clifford K. Berryman, noted editorial cartoonist for the Washington Star, died Sunday. . . . He was known for creating the famous 'Teddy Bear.' He first drew the cub in 1902 as a joke on President 'Teddy' Roosevelt.

b. (See quots.)

1942 Castetter & Bell *Pima & Papago Agric.* 25 The hottest desert hills are taken over by the teddy bear cactus (*O. Bigelovii*). [**1948** *Nat. Hist.* April 181 The deceptively fussy [? =fuzzy]-looking Cholla Cactus, with her children gathered about her like animated teddy bears, is another native of the southern Arizona desert.]

teest tist, *n.* [Origin unknown.] (See quots.) *Obs.* — **a1870** Chipman *Notes on Bartlett* 473 *Teest*, an anvil used by planishers of tinned plate.—Mass. **1876** Knight 2504/1 *Teest*, a stake or small anvil used by sheet-iron workers.

***teeter,** *n.*

1. The spotted sandpiper, *Actitis macularia*. Also **teeter-peep, tail.**

1842 *Nat. Hist. N.Y., Zoology* I. 247 The Spotted Sand-Lark . . . is known . . . [as] *Teeter* and *Tilt-up*, from its often repeated grotesque jerking motions. **1917** *Birds of Amer.* I. 249 Spotted Sandpiper. . . . [Also called] Teeter-peep; Teeter-tail; Teeterer.

2. teeterboard, a seesaw.

[**1845** Kirkland *Western Clearings* 213, I laid a teterin' board over it, so that if you stepped on it, down you went.] **1855** *Knickerb.* XLVI. 88 We were having a grand time with our 'teeter-boards' up on the highest fence. **1949** Kurath *Word Geog. Eastern U.S.* 16/1 The seesaw is known as a *teeter*, a *teeter board*, or a *teetering board* in all of New England except the southeastern sector.

attrib. and *transf.* **1894** *Cong. Rec.* App. 6 June 915/1 The moneyed men could work the financial 'teeter' board to suit their pleasure. **1909** *Springfield Wkly. Republican* 2 Dec. 3 Lord Rosebery's brilliant teeterboard speech, protesting against the budget and at the same time against its rejection by the House of Lords.

teetery ˈtitərɪ, *a.* Tottery, unsteady. *Colloq.* — **1900** *N.Y. Jrnl.* 25 Nov. 59/2 An attendant was there to help you off if you felt teetery or uncertain. **1905** Rex Beach *Pardners* i. (1912) 34 The orchestra spieled some teetery music.

teething ring. A small ring, usu. of rubber, ivory, etc., for a teething infant to bite on.

1872 MARK TWAIN *Roughing It* xv. 125 (R.), Soothing-syrup! Teething-rings! **1904** CRISSEY *Tattlings* 367, I put away my teething ring and baby 'pacifier' several years ago. **1950** *Chi. D. News* 7 April 1/2 Sandra Haynes, 2, liked her new teething ring—a real, live and remarkably agreeable rattlesnake.

teetotaciously ˌtitoˈteʃəslɪ, *adv.* Totally. *Obs.* — **1833** *Sk. D. Crockett* p. v, The still more delicate repast of a constant repetition of the terms *'bodyaciously,' 'tetotaciously,' 'obflisticated,'* &c. **1889** FARMER 528/1 Teetotaciously.—A Western form, supposed to be an emphatic variant of teetotal.

Tegua ˈtegwɑ, *n.* Also **Tewa.** *S.W.* [See note.]

Hodge *s.v. Tewa* explains the name of these Indians as being the Keresan word for "moccasins." Santamaría thinks the moccasins were so called from the fact that the Tegua Indians wore them.

1. *pl.* or *collect.* (See quot. 1910.) In full **Teguas Indians.**

1844 GREGG *Commerce of Prairies* I. 124 They were only awaiting the arrival of the *Teguas*, Taosas and Apaches, in order to finish their work of extermination. **1846** ABERT *Exam. N. Mex.* 30 They told me they were 'Teguas' Indians. **1893** DONALDSON *Moqui Pueblo Indians* 62 The Tehuas were inured to war and proved a valuable auxiliary to their old kinsmen. **1910** HODGES *Amer. Indians* II. 737/2 Tewa. . . . A group of Pueblo tribes belonging to the Tanoan linguistic family, now occupying the villages of San Ildefonso, San Juan, Santa Clara, Nambe, Tesuque, and Hano, all except the last lying in the valley of the Rio Grande in N. New Mexico. **1948** *Southwestern Jrnl. Anthrop.* Winter 374 No mention of trading with the Tewa was contained in informants' reports.

attrib. **1938** HEWETT *Pajarita Plateau & Its Ancient People* 45 The Tewa origin of the tribal name Navaho is assured.

Hence **Teguan,** *a.*

1858 IVES *Colo. River* (1861) 127 We were joined by the Teguan chief and several of his friends.

2. (Not *cap.*) (See 1st quot. 1932.) Also attrib.

1889 LUMMIS *Land of Poco Tiempo* 49 The men . . . shaped rawhide soles for their *teguas.* **1932** BENTLEY *Sp. Terms* 206 tegua. . . . A handmade moccasin worn by many Mexicans and also by American children in Mexico. *Teguas* are heelless, pointed-toed, ankle-high, and laced in front. They are never made of buckskin although they are often swede [*sic*] together with buckskin string. Teguas are never decorated with beads, etc. as the Indian moccasins frequently are. **1932** DANE COOLIDGE *Fighting Men of West* 158 (Bentley), He found the tegua tracks of an Indian or Mexican who had picked it up.

Tejano teˈhɑno, *n.* *S.W.* [Amer. Sp. in same sense.] A Texan.

1925 OWEN P. WHITE *Them Was Days* 75 The fear of God, as represented by the wrath of the *Tejanos* (Texans). **1927** JAMES *Cow Country* 35 'You don't seem anyways sad about whatever it is that's a-popping,' finally says an old hard-faced Tejano. **1945** M. JAMES *Cherokee Strip* 24 Yessiree, knowed ol' Sam Houston, Bigfoot Wallace, an' all them early Tejanos.

transf. **1925** CHARLES SIMPSON *El Rodeo* 42 (Bentley), The little cowpony Tejano, pricks up his ears.

telautograph tɛlˈɔtəˌgræf, *n.* [f. the Gk. combining form, *tele-+autograph.*] (See quot. 1883.) Also **telautography.**

1883 KNIGHT *Supp.* 880/1 *Telautograph*, an electrical device for transmitting autographs, or copying designs. . . . The possibility of deception and the impossibility of automatic unquestionable record . . . are removed, it is said, by the employment of telautography. **1901** *World's Work* Aug. 1059/1 The perfected 'telautograph' is simple of construction and apparently durable. **1948** *Chi. Tribune* 4 Jan. I. 20/3 The station telegrafer writes it up on the telautograph, which works like a teletype.

telegram ˈtɛləˌgræm, *n.* [f. combining forms (<Gk.) *tele-+-gram*, denoting that which is written at a distance.] A message sent by telegraph.

1852 *Albany* (N.Y.) *Ev. Jrnl.* 6 April (W.), A friend desires us to give notice that he will ask leave . . . to introduce a new word into the vocabulary. It is telegram, instead of telegraphic dispatch, or telegraphic communication. **1852** *Lantern* (N.Y.) I. 184/2 Our Boston correspondent says, that the new name for Telegraphic Despatches, now called Telegrams, should be written *Tell-a-cram.* **1924** H. CROY *R.F.D. No. 3* 233 Josie had expected that they would have to go to the railroad station, the 'depot'—it was the way her father had always sent telegrams. **1945** MENCKEN *Supp.* I. 243 But *telegram*, first recorded in 1852, seems to be an American invention, as is *cablegram*, first recorded in 1868.

As the last term in **rush, weather telegram.**

* **telegraph,** *n.* In combs.: (1) **telegraph blank,** a printed form on which the words of a telegram are to be written; (2) **company,** a company of business associates who operate a telegraph line or lines; (3) **editor,** on a newspaper staff, one who receives and edits news received by telegraph; (4) **line,** a system of communication over which telegrams are sent; (5) **man,** a man in charge of a telegraph office (see also quot. 1939); (6) **operator,** one employed to send or receive telegrams; (7) **post,** a tall pole supporting a telegraph wire or wires, *rare;* (8) **road,** a road along which a telegraph line is built; (9) **station,** a telegraph office.

(1) **1893** PHILIPS *Making of Newspaper* 99 He struck out the formal matter in the heading of the telegraph blank. **1928** F. N. HART *Bellamy Trial* i. 3 [He] had three very sharp pencils and a good-sized stack of telegraph blanks clasped to his heart. — (2) **1859** *N.Y. Tribune* 13 Aug. (Chipman), No party has any such preferential rights over the lines of the American Telegraph Company. **1905** *Indian Laws & Tr.* III. 155 Two hundred dollars for cable anchorages of two telegraph companies . . . is discretionary with the Secretary of the Interior. — (3) **1875** C. F. WINGATE *Views & Interviews* 195 Have been continuously employed on the *Missouri Republican* . . . [as] telegraph editor. **1923** G. C. BASTIAN *Editing Day's News* 9 Inside the News Room . . . [we find the] Managing Editor, . . . Makeup Editor, . . . City Editor. . . . Telegraph Editor [etc.]. — (4) [**1830** *Boston D. Advt.* 17 Oct. 2/5 (Ernst), Telegraph line. The public is respectfully informed that a new line of stages by the above name is established between this city and Hartford.] **1849** *Mich. Gen. Statutes* I. (1882) 944 The owner of any land through which said telegraph line may pass, and railroad corporation on whose right of way the same may be constructed, having first given consent. **1949** MURRAY *This Our Land* 93 The first telegraph line between Washington and Baltimore did not open before 1844.

(5) **1864** DALY *A. Daly* 65 The telegraph man . . . keeps a grocery and the postmaster has a news stand. **1901** MCCUTCHEON *Graustark* 56 Your aunt and I went at once to the telegraph man. **1939** ABBOTT-SMITH *We Pointed* 158 In the spring. . . . I was working . . . for . . . the president of the Montana Stock Association. . . . I was what was called a telegraph man. Our job was to carry messages back and forth about the movements of certain men who were under suspicion. — (6) **1858** W. P. SMITH *Railway Celebrations* 67, 260 firemen, 210 watchmen, 34 telegraph operators. **1937** LYMAN *Ralston's Ring* 296 Hurriedly he left his cubicle and sought out his telegraph operator. — (7) **1902** MOORE *Songs & Stories* 158 An' when Hood's army cum in de Yankees gin us guns an' tole us we had ter fight or be cotch an' hung ter telegraf postes! — (8) **1867** CRAWFORD *Mosby* 192 We took the old telegraph road to within a mile of Stafford Court House. **1894** *Outing* April 43/2, I suddenly found the telegraph road winding through hills and mountains. — (9) **1839** *Knickerb.* XIV. 187 A recent excursion . . . [extended] from New-Brighton to the telegraph station. **1905** O. HENRY *Roads of Destiny* 129 There were telegraph stations ahead.

As the last term in **dial, fire alarm, grapevine, hydraulic, magnetic, moccasin, printing, recording telegraph.**

* **telegraph,** *v. tr.* To reveal (a pitch, blow, etc.) inadvertently, as when a baseball pitcher or a boxer unknowingly reveals his next move. *Slang.* — **1945** E. NICHOLS *Hunky Johnny* 68 Christ, he telegraphs every curve he throws. **1950** *L.A. Times* 7 May (Comics) 13 He doesn't throw that right fast enough. He telegraphs it.

* **telephone,** *n.*

1. An instrument of a type devised by Alexander G. Bell (1847–1922), consisting of a transmitter and receiver so combined and connected as to transmit and receive sounds.

1876 BELL in *Amer. Acad. Proc.* XII. 7 The telephones so constructed were placed in different rooms. **1891** WELCH *Recoll. 1830–40* 423 We now have for daily convenience . . . the telephone. **1949** *Chi. D. News* 29 Nov. 18/2 The telephone now contributes largely to the rescue work.

2. In combs. of obvious meaning, as (1) **telephone booth,** (2) **box,** (3) **call,** (4) **closet,** (5) **directory,** (6) **exchange,** (7) **girl,** (8) **operator,** (9) **pole,** (10) **post.**

(1) **1909** O. HENRY *Options* 261, I hurried to a telephone-booth and rang up the Telfair residence. **1943** LYON *And So to Bedlam* 13 Glass shattered in three nerve-racking smashes just outside the door of the tiny telephone booth. — (2) **1904** *McClure's Mag.* Feb. 405 Golden could snatch only two opportunities to step into the telephone box that morning and ask about copper. — (3) **1910** O. HENRY *Strictly Business* 13 She pointed out to him clearly how it [a play] could be improved by introducing a messenger instead of a telephone call. **1949** *Cleveland Plaindealer* 11 Dec. (Pict. Mag.) 11/1 Telephone calls come in all the time. — (4) **1903** *McClure's Mag.* Nov. 101/2 He strolled to the telephone-closet.

(5) **1913** EATON *Barn Doors & Byways* 81 Personally, we fail to find this sort of thing any more thrilling or 'literary' than the telephone

directory. **1949** *Chi. D. News* 6 May 26/1 The . . . bill . . . would prevent . . . advertisements in periodicals or telephone directories. — (6) **1879** *Bradstreet's* 10 Dec. 1/3 The Edison Telephone Exchange has now connections with Washington and Pekin, Ill. **1947** *Steamboat* (Colo.) *Pilot* 2 Jan. 5/1 The employes of the Oak Creek telephone exchange had a Christmas party on Tuesday afternoon. — (7) **1893** *Chi. Tribune* 2 July 13/3 The telephone girl sits on her high stool and steadily chews gum as she produces alternate order and chaos at her switchboard. **1942** Branson *Pricking Thumb* 22 He waited until the mellifluous voice of the telephone girl came out of its box, like a cuckoo, to inform him, 'The party does not answer.' — (8) **1894** *Life* 19 April 256/1 One of the young lady telephone operators might be listening to our talk and we don't want our telephone taken out. **1949** *Dly. Ardmoreite* (Ardmore, Okla.) 25 Jan. 2/4 Telephone operators were being swamped today with local calls because most housewives were doing their shopping and visiting by phone. — (9) **1920** Cooper *Under Big Top* 122 People were . . . running and climbing trees and telephone poles. **1949** *Dly. Oklahoman* (Okla. City) 11 Sep.

Telephone of an early type

(Sun. Mag.) 15/1 All summer there was but a family group, centering their activities about the telephone pole up the road where they had nested.

(10) **1945** Wallace *Barington* 231 The gunshots fired from behind a telephone post at Anderson's corner awakened Debs at midnight.

As the last term in **lover's, molecular, public telephone.**

telephone 'tɛləˌfon, *v.* [f. the noun.]

1. *intr.* To communicate by telephone.

1880 *Amer. Punch* (Boston) Feb. 19/2 If you want to be polite lend me a dollar and telephone for a coupé. **1894** Howells in *Harper's Mag.* Feb. 371/2, I telephoned at once for Dr. Lawton to come instantly. **1923** Dutton *Shadow on Glass* 29, I telephoned to her, after I called you.

2. *tr.* To transmit (information) or to inform (a person) by telephone.

1883 *N. Mex. Terr. Rep.* 70, I telephoned to Lake Valley the fact of their death. **1894** Howells in *Harper's Mag.* Feb. 378 She telephoned you on the impulse of the moment. **1950** *Lincoln Co. Advt.* (Brookhaven, Miss.) 12 Jan. 4/3 But Bill, who has no job now, actually is at the house nearly every day or telephoning her every hour.

* **telescope,** *n.* A traveling bag consisting of two cases of which the larger slips over the smaller.

Telescope

1896 *Chi. Tribune* 28 June 4/1 A set of the best safe-boring tools were put into a 'telescope' for the Ohio job. **1914** *Outing* June 312/1 The telescope was made of hydraulic canvas (a very heavy, stiff canvas,) with no pasteboard. **1949** *Boston Globe* 5 June (Fiction Mag.) 1/2 Other bundles, valises and telescopes were ranged beyond.

* **telescope,** *v. intr.* Of railroad cars: To crash into each other in the manner of sliding tubes in a telescope. Also *tr.* and **telescoping,** *n.*

1867 *Comm. & Fin. Chron.* V. 6/2 There are two principal dangers which have to be guarded against—the 'telescoping' of cars into each other in case of collision [etc.]. **1881** *Chi. Times* 18 June, A freight of thirty loaded cars . . . collided with the other train, telescoping and completely wrecking several of the cars. **1947** Myers *The 'Guv'* 150 Pullman cars were telescoped and rolled over onto their sides.

telestial tə'lɛstʃəl, *a.* [App. modeled on *celestial* and utilizing the well-known Gk. combining form *tele-*, afar, far off.] (See quots.)

1843 H. Caswall *Prophet of 19th Cent.* 98 The second, or telestial state, is the Paradise reserved for the spirits of the just after death. **1870** Beadle *Utah* 325 They [the Mormons] hold that there are three heavens: the celestial, terrestrial, and telestial, typified by the sun, moon and stars. **1936** *Univ. Ariz. Gen. Bul.* 3, 283 Its three largest ceremonial rooms, designated as the Telestial, the Terrestrial, and the Celestial rooms respectively are symbolically constructed on different levels indicating different degrees of spiritual living.

* **tell,** *v.* **1.** *To tell good-bye,* (see quot. 1859). **2.** *To tell the world,* to state most positively. *Slang.*

(1) **1859** Bartlett 475 To *tell* one good-bye, is the Southern phrase for to bid one good-bye. **1906** *Atlantic Mo.* Aug. 176 A dozen of my students were gathered there to tell me good-by. — (2) **1924** A. J. Small *Frozen Gold* i. 37 I'll tell the world that . . . not all the Mounted Sergeants in the Territories would be able to make him talk.

* **teller,** *n.* As the last term in **first, paying teller.**

* **telltale,** *n.* and *a.* **1.** A yellowlegs or tattler. **2. telltale godwit,** =next. **3. telltale sandpiper,** the greater yellowlegs, *Totanus melanoleucus.*

(1) **1813** Wilson *Ornithology* VII. 57 This species and the preceding . . . are detested [by duck gunners] and stigmatized with the names of the greater and lesser tell-tale, for their faithful vigilance in alarming the ducks with their loud and shrill whistle. **1917** *Birds of Amer.* I. 244/1 'Tattler' and 'Tell-tale' are also popular names for [the greater yellowlegs]. — (2) **1813** Wilson *Ornithology* VII. 57 Telltale Godwit, or Snipe; *Scolopax vociferus.* **1917** *Birds of Amer.* I. 242. — (3) **1823** James *Exped.* I. 4 Among other birds [we] saw the . . . tell-tale sandpiper. **1870** *Amer. Naturalist* IV. 547 Tell-tale Sandpiper (*Gambetta melanoleuca*). . . . Early in May, . . . these birds in company with other *Scolopacidæ* arrive in the neighborhood of Trenton, New Jersey.

temblor tɛm'blɔr, *n. W.* [Sp. in same sense.] An earthquake. Also attrib.

1896 *Land of Sunshine* July 72 One freshet of one Ohio river a dozen years ago took more lives than all the *temblores* in California in a century and a half have taken. **1906** *Out West* May 433 This was the only earthquake in North America comparable with the historic ones which have made the *temblor* a name of terror. **1950** *L.A. Times* 3 Jan. 1/6 The temblor was reported from both Ogden and Logan.

temescal ˌtɛməs'kæl, *n. W.* and *S.W.* [Amer. Sp. *temascal* (<Nahuatl), in sense shown here.] A place for taking a sweat or steam bath. Also attrib. Cf. **sweat lodge.**

[**1780** Clavigero *Storia della Messico* II. 214 Il *Temazcalli,* o Ipocausto messicano, si fabbrica per lo più di mattoni crudi.] **1831** Beechey *Voyage to Pacific* II. 35 A mud house, or rather a large oven, called temeschal by the Spaniards, is built in a circular form, with a small entrance, and an aperture in the top for the smoke to escape through. **1896** *Land of Sunshine* Nov. 235 It was currently believed that he *never* took a bath—but this must be a libel, as he was owner of a *temescal.* **1947** *So. Sierran* May 4/2, I had been especially impressed by . . . the sunflower-like Venegasia on the Temescal Canyon hike.

* **temperance,** *n.* In combs. of obvious meaning, as **temperance mass-meeting, platform, state.**

1873 Beadle *Undevel. West* 402 This radical temperance platform in this latitude excited our astonishment. **1880** *Cong. Rec.* 1 May 2938/1 [He] holds temperance mass-meetings in his district, every month. **1884** W. Shepherd *Prairie Exper.* 166 Two men . . . had been raised in severely temperance States.

As the last term in **Sons of, state temperance.**

temper screw. 1. A link connecting the walking beam and the cable of the drilling apparatus used in boring deep wells. **2.** (See quot.)

(1) *a***1864** Gesner *Coal, Petrol.* (1865) 28 The Temper Screw . . . serves to regulate the descent of the drill, without the inconvenience of lengthening the rope at short intervals. **1883** *Cent. Mag.* July 330/1 The '*temper-screw*' . . . lowers the drilling apparatus inch by inch as it goes down. — (2) **1876** Knight 2529/1 *Temper-screw,* . . . a set screw for adjustment. One which brings its point against a bearing or an object.

∗ temple, *n.*

1. Among American Indians, a ceremonial structure, as a medicine lodge. *Obs.*

1814 BRACKENRIDGE *Views La.* 72, I saw . . . in an open space before the temple or medicine lodge, an enclosure about six feet square. **1895** G. KING *New Orleans* 192 On the island are those inexplicable mammoth heaps of shell, covered by groves of oaks, . . . which were selected by the aboriginal inhabitants as sites for their temples.

2. A place of worship among Mormons. Also attrib.

1843 MARRYAT *M. Violet* xxxix, In 1836, an endowment meeting, or solemn assembly, was called, to be held in the temple at Kirkland. **1844** GREGG *Commerce of Prairies* I. 320 A large lot . . . known as the 'Temple Lot,' upon which the 'Temple of Zion' was to have been raised,—has lately been 'profaned,' by cultivation. **1942** STEGNER *Mormon C.* 178 He arrives at the temple with his garments and temple apron in a little handbag.

3. temple society, (see quot.). *Obs.*

1859 TALIAFERRO *Fisher's R.* 109 The first time I ever heard of temperance societies in that section, the people called them 'temple societies.'

As the last term in **Masonic, Mormon, Tammany Temple.**

temporal ˌtɛmpəˈrɑl, *n. S.W.* [See note.]

From Sp. *temporal, n.*, storm, tempest, poss. as used in some such expression as *terreno de temporal*, with reference to unirrigated land.

A field, portion of land or farm (see also quot. 1890).

1866 MELINE *Two Thousand Miles on Horseback* (1867) 161 Passing through the Carnuel Cañon and San Pedro Pass, I saw some as fine looking fields (*temporales*) of corn and wheat as the most of those in the valley. **1890** *Stock Grower & Farmer* 5 April 3/1 Our mountain farmers, who cultivate the 'temporal,' or land which does not require irrigation, are getting ready to put in a crop. **1894** *Amer. Anthrop.* July 293 This entire region . . . is unadapted for agriculture, yet when the July rains commence the Indians forsake their rancherias and hasten to the *temporales*, where they plant crops of corn, pumpkins, melons [etc.]. **1925** BRYAN *Papago Country* 51 The best hunting season is in the fall in the vicinity of Papago temporales, where the quail congregate to feed on the residue of the crop and seeds of the pigweed.

∗ ten, *a.*

1. *absol.* A ten-dollar bill. *Colloq.*

1829 *Va. Herald* (Fredericksburg) 18 April 3/3 The public are cautioned against receiving spurious 5's 10's and 20 dollar bills, purporting to be on the Bank of Virginia. **1845** SOL. SMITH *Theatr. Apprent.* 23 [He] began counting out tens, twenties, and fifties. **1949** *L.A. Times* 11 April II. 6/1 Right now there is some counterfeit money circulating in Los Angeles. Mostly 10s, 20s and 100s.

2. In combs.: (1) **ten-acre lot,** a lot containing ten acres, any relatively large lot; (2) **cent,** see as a main entry; (3) **-dollar,** *a.* of paper currency and coins, worth ten dollars; (4) **footer,** a room or house only ten feet long, a small place; (5) **-foot pole,** a pole ten feet long, usu. fig. in the phrase *not to touch with a ten-foot pole;* (6) **forties,** a popular name for certain five per cent government bonds issued in 1864, redeemable at any time after ten years, and payable in forty years; (7) **-gallon hat,** *W.* a large broad-brimmed hat, usu. worn by cowboys, cf. **ten-ounce hat;** (8) **∗-hour,** used attrib. with reference to a working day of ten hours, now *hist.;* (9) **-lined,** *a.* of a potato bug, having ten stripes marking its body, hence **ten-liner;** (10) **-ounce hat,** ?a hat weighing ten ounces, *obs.*, cf. **ten-gallon hat;** (11) **∗penny,** a pistareen, in full **ten-penny bit;** (12) **∗pin,** see as a main entry; (13) **-plate stove,** see as a main entry; (14) **-rail fence,** a fence ten rails in height, usu. regarded as a desirable standard; (15) **spot,** see **∗spot,** *n.* **2. b.;** (16) **strike,** see as a main entry; (17) **striker,** (see quot.); (18) **-striped,** *a.* **=ten-lined,** *obs.;* (19) **-twenty-thirty,** designating a cheap show or theater—in allusion to the prices of admission; (20) **up,** (see quot. 1885); (21) **wheeler,** (see quot. 1909).

(1) 1671 *S.C. Hist. Soc. Coll.* V. 284 Tenn acre lotts . . . are laid out to them. **1850** S. WARNER *Wide, Wide World* xxxix, The wheat in that ten-acre lot . . . *ought* to be prostrated too. **1902** ALDRICH *Sea Turn* 232 The old gentleman was swinging across the ten-acre lot on his way to the house. — **(3) 1807** *Ann. 10th Cong.* 1 Sess. 429, I got two of the notes changed, and one, a ten dollar note, was returned on my hands. **1818** *Wkly. Recorder* (Chillicothe, O.) 4 Sep. 32/3 Five and ten dollar bills are in circulation, purporting to be [on] the 'Michigan Bank of Detroit.' **1861** *Chi. Tribune* 19 July 1/8 Lost— . . . a Lady's Portmonnaie, containing a Ten Dollar Gold Piece, and sixty-five cents in change. **1949** *Courier-Journal* 3 Sep. 9/5 The $10 notes are on the Federal Reserve Bank of Richmond, Va. — **(4) 1854** O. OPTIC *In Doors & Out* (1876) 119 Though she had been brought up in a ten footer in an obscure street, she earnestly desired to become what is technically called a 'lady.' **1872** HOLMES *Poet* 26 [Near] the district school-house . . . [was] Ma'am Hancock's cottage, never so called in those days, but rather 'ten-footer.'

(5) 1738 BYRD *Dividing Line* (1901) 52 We found the ground moist . . . insomuch that it was an easy matter to run a ten-foot pole up to the head in it. **1848** MITCHELL *Nantucketisms* 41 *Can't touch him with a ten-foot pole.* He is distant, proud, reserved. **1949** *Chi. D. News* 1 April 2/2 The United States and France, certainly, will not touch the Franco Spain case with a 10-foot pole. — **(6) 1867** *Comm. & Fin. Chron.* V. 459/1 Ten-Forties have been decidedly strong. **1870** W. W. FOWLER *Ten Yrs. in Wall St.* 278 But a new loan at a lower rate of interest (the ten forties) would have to be soon placed upon the market. — **(7) 1928** *Dly. Express* 17 Oct. 3/7 She instinctively recognised that he was a cowboy, even though he did not wear a ten-gallon hat and a jacket embroidered with Mexican dollars. **1949** *Nat. Geog. Mag.* June 739/2 Sheridan's awnings are raised to make room for ten-gallon hats. — **(8) 1840** VAN BUREN in *Pres. Mess. & P.* III. 602 The President of the United States . . . directs that all such persons, whether laborers or mechanics, be required to work only the number of hours prescribed by the ten-hour system. **1911** PERSONS *Mass. Labor Laws* 71 In this two weeks' interval Butler and the ten-hour issue entered together what may thenceforth fairly be called the political arena. — **(9) 1868** *Rep. Comm. Agric. 1867* 65 The Colorado bug or ten-lined spearman is reported to have produced poisonous effects on several persons who handled them incautiously with naked hands. **1876** *Vt. Bd. Agric. Rep.* III. 574 We now come to the chiefest agent among insects in the destruction of the potato, the famous ten-lined potato beetle. *Ib.* 676 Jack Frost . . . must overtake many of the ten liners that supposed themselves safe from cold.

(10) 1893 JAMES *Cow-Boy Life* 28 A little six-bit fellow . . . posing as the cow-boy preacher . . . usually procures a ten-ounce hat with a leather band, a pair of high-heeled boots, and then he is sailing. — **(11) 1835** TODD *Notes* 7 A tenpenny, or pistorine, passing in most Western States for 13 pence, [has] an eagle with the figures 10 beneath it. **1841** *Knickerb.* XVII. 187 The chain . . . was terminated by three seals, three keys, and a ten-penny bit. **1950** *Chi. Tribune* 3 May 22/3 The ten penny bit was a pistareen, a debased Spanish two-real piece rated at from 17 cents to 20 cents. — **(14) 1835** *Knickerb.* VI. 178 She could leap a ten-rail Virginia-fence, like a deer. **1932** W. KELLEY *Inchin' Along* 267 He ran against a ten-rail fence.

(17) 1869 *Overland Mo.* III. 128 Some boasted that one Southerner could 'whale' ten Yankees. Lieutenant J. W. Boothe, of the Seventh Texas Battalion, I am told, first applied to this sort the phrase 'ten-strikers,' which became immensely popular in that State. — **(18) 1869** *Mich. Agric. Rep.* VII. 170 The results of my observations on the Ten-striped Potatoe Beetle, for the year 1868. **1877** *Vt. Bd. Agric. Rep.* IV. 108 Say gave it the scientific name *Doryphora decem-lineata*, or the Ten-striped Spearman. — **(19) 1928** *Chi. Tribune* 9 July 10/4 Dick Ferris' Comedians was one of the leading ten-twenty-thirty cent shows touring the middle west. **1949** *Ib.* 26 Nov. 10/3 If I drop dead from overwork, it will not be inside a 10–20–30 vaudeville theater.

(20) 1841 *Week in Wall St.* 29, I will send you in a check for 'ten up,' and the rest we will arrange tomorrow. **1885** *Harper's Mag.* Nov. 842/2 Brokers demand 'ten up,' or a deposit of ten per cent on the selling value of the stock. — **(21) 1873** Z. COLBURN *Locomotive Engine* 122 One of Hinkley's ten wheelers on the Northern road was altered by taking out the truck frame and putting in another pair of drivers. [**1909** FOWLER *Locomotive Dict.* 91 Ten-Wheel Locomotive. . . . Specifically a locomotive having ten wheels, but commonly applied only to locomotives having a four-wheel front truck and six coupled driving wheels.] **1950** *Time* 15 May 96/2 The Technicolored movie recounts the adventures of a narrow-gauge ten-wheeler on its first run into the Rockies.

As the last term in **seller, upper ten.**

tenas təˈnæs, *a. N.W.* [Chinook (Nootka).] Small. *Obs.* — **1851** *Ore. Statesman* 7 Oct. 2/6 The printers of the *tenas* sheet reply to our communication in the last Statesman by saying they do not think the majority of printers would call them 'rats.' **1879** MORRIS *Pub. Service Alaska* 87 They complained that some years since a party of Sitka Indians had stolen from one of their villages a 'tenas man' (boy).

ten-cent ˈtɛnˌsɛnt, *a.*

1. Worth ten cents.

1846 *Quincy* (Ill.) *Whig* 17 March 3/1 A negro man, who belonged in the country, was seen passing off 'quarter and half eagles' as 'ten cent pieces.' **1874** *Southern Mag.* XIV. 28 These fellows went there swindling and stealing when there was very little to steal, and taking the last ten-cent shinplaster off dead men's eyes. **1920** HOWELLS *Vacation of Kelwyns* 130 From one pocket he brought forth a small wad of greenish paper worth twenty-five cents; from another a ten-cent note.

Hence **ten-center,** something worth ten cents. *Colloq.*

1873 *Caddo* (Indian Terr.) *Free Press* 14 March 4/1 We intend to . . . raise enough to take a ten-center in one of them [kissing] sociables any how.

b. Often somewhat contemptuous. *Colloq.* Cf. next.

1860 M. J. HOLMES *Maude* 26 Dr. Kennedy . . . [bought] for Hannah a ten-cent calico apron. **1893** JAMES *Cow-Boy Life* 23 Reading the lives of such characters as the Younger brothers . . . and ten-cent detective trash, so often sends the small boy on the war-path with blood in his eye. **1908** O. HENRY *Roads of Destiny* 60, I expected to have to typewrite about two thousand words of notes-of-hand, liens, and contracts, with a ten-cent tip in sight.

2. Ten-cent Jimmy, (see quot. 1856). Also transf. *Obs.*

1856 *Cong. Globe* App. 5 Aug. 1169/2 Mr. Buchanan . . . was at one time an advocate of . . . low tariffs and low wages, till he came to be called, as he perhaps deserved to be, 'Ten-Cent Jimmy.' **1864** *Ib.* 12 May 2260/1 Why, Mr. Speaker, I had no idea there were so many ten-cent 'Jimmys' on the intensely loyal side of the House. **1874** *Cong. Rec.* 15 Jan. 667/2 A distinguished statesman [once] said that it would be just as well to have wages ten cents a day, provided the purchasing power of ten cents was equal to what a dollar was then, . . . and I believe that he obtained by that remark the *sobriquet* of 'Ten-cent Jimmy.'

3. ten-cent store, a variety store in which low-priced articles are sold, orig. such a store in which the maximum price of the articles was ten cents. Cf. **dime store, racket store,** and cf. * **five,** *a.*, **2. c.** (2).

1901 H. ROBERTSON *Inlander* 118 The sleepers in the grass-grown churchyard . . . had been removed elsewhere to make room for the thriving innovation known as the 'Ten Cent Store.' **1949** *This Week Mag.* 10 Sep. 5/2 She cruises through a 10-cent store twice weekly.

* **tender,** *n.*[1] Money or other things that may be legally offered in payment. Often **common** or **lawful tender.** Also fig.

1739 W. DOUGLASS *Discourse Currencies* 20 France never made their State Bills a common Tender. **1777** *Jrnls. Cont. Cong.* VII. 36 That it be recommended to the legislatures of the United States, to pass laws to make the bills of credit, issued by the Congress, a lawful tender. **1903** WHITE *Forest* 24 Strange, suggestive words and phrases . . . [are] coined into the tender of daily use.

attrib. **1781** A. ADAMS *Familiar Lett.* 390 A repeal of the obnoxious tender act has passed the [Mass.] House and Senate. **1786** HUMPHREYS *Anarchiad* (1861) 30 Cheat heaven with forms, and earth with tender-laws.

* **tender,** *n.*[2] In football, a backfield man. *Obs.* — **1874** *Boston Transcript* 16 May 2/5 The McGill and Harvard foot-ball eleven, . . . are as follows. . . . Harvard—W. R. Tyler, Lombard and Goodrich (tenders) [etc.].

As the last term in **baby, bar, bridge, camp, chuck, door, hook, lock, sled, stock tender.**

tenderfoot ˈtɛndɚˌfʊt, *n.* Orig. *W.* [?Back formation from * **tenderfooted.**] A new arrival in the West; an inexperienced or young person.

1849 in *Amer. Sp.* XXI. (1946) 227/2 We saw a man in Sacramento when we were on our way here, who was a tenderfoot, or rawheel, or whatever you call 'em, who struck a pocket of gold. **1890** CUSTER *Following Guidon* 172 The frontiersman had then, as now, a great 'despise,' as they put it, for the tenderfoot. **1946** NEWTON *P. Bunyan* 153 A tenderfoot could hardly be blamed for not being posted like we are.

transf. **1887** *Scribner's Mag.* Oct. 508/1 'Pilgrim' and 'tenderfoot' were formerly applied almost exclusively to newly imported cattle.

b. *attrib.* or as *adj.* Inexperienced, belonging to, or consisting of, tenderfeet.

1881 ROMSPERT *Western Echo* 89 Here was the tender-foot outfit, our home a dark cave in the bluff of the Cimaron, seventy-five miles from the smallest settlement. **1891** *Harper's Mag.* July 204/2 His pony . . . [will] slide down a bank which would make our tenderfoot hair stand on end. **1907** PEARY in *Harper's Mag.* Feb. 338 The arrival of this supply of fresh meat created a very agreeable impression, especially upon the 'tenderfoot' members of the expedition and crew.

tenderfoot ˈtɛndɚˌfʊt, *v. To tenderfoot it,* to go about as a tenderfoot. *Rare.* — **1886** HOWELLS *Minister's Charge* 260 His wife wanted to go to Europe a while, and kind of tender foot it round for a year or two in the art centres over there.

* **tenderfooted,** *a. fig.* Designating persons lacking experience, timid, sensitive. *Colloq.*

1842 *People's Adv.* (Carrollton, Ill.) 4 March 2/4 When this was proposed, upon the stump, in the late canvass, how many *tender-footed* democrats united with the Whigs, to ridicule the idea, and prove it *Demagoguism!* **1860** *Marysville* (Calif.) *Appeal* 23 March 2/1 The San Francisco National . . . bluffed the tender-footed adherents of the National Executive into abandonment of the plan. **1883** MARK TWAIN *Life on Miss.* xxvii, Each tourist . . . went home and published a book—a book which was usually calm, truthful, reasonable, kind; but which seemed just the reverse to our tenderfooted progenitors.

tenderloin ˈtɛndɚˌlɔɪn, *n.*

1. A strip of tender meat close to the backbone of a beef, hog, etc., a piece of this. Also attrib. Cf. **pork tenderloin.**

1828 WEBSTER, *Tenderloin,* a tender part of flesh in the hind quarter of beef. [Probably an inexact definition.] **1883** *So. Hist. Soc. P.* XI. 84 Tenderloin steaks are tough behind iron gratings. **1944** *Newsweek* 16 Oct. 107 Thus, a tenderloin chop for the lieutenant becomes an elevenerloin chop.

2. In New York City, a police precinct, orig. one west of Broadway between Twenty-third and Forty-second streets, affording police officers luscious opportunities for graft. Also transf. to similar districts in other cities where gambling, prostitution, etc., flourish. Also attrib.

A policeman named Williams is said to have first used "tenderloin" with reference to the N.Y. vice area. See *Amer. N. & Q.* Oct. 1945, 107–8.

1887 *Harper's Mag.* March 500/2 His precinct is known as the 'Tenderloin,' because of its social characteristics. **1898** *Voice* 6 Jan. 4/3 If laws generally suitable to a city do not suit some slavic, Polish, or other quarter, or some 'tenderloin' district, the local police must pass upon those laws, . . . and give a 'liberal' enforcement. **1903** *S.F. Argonaut* 2 Nov. 273 Portland is not a puritanic city. In fact, its tenderloin is extensive and worse than anything in San Francisco. **1949** *L.A. Times* 15 May II. 5/1 The 1st Ward had most of the city's tenderloin and flop houses.

tenement house. A dwelling house or building divided into separate apartments which are rented out to different families, esp. such a building with certain facilities, such as water closets, shared by several families; an apartment building occupied by persons of the poorer classes of a city.

For the purposes of legal contracts and enforcement of city regulations, "tenement house" has been given technical definitions in certain statutory provisions. The first tenement houses are said to have been erected in New York City about 1835. See the source of quot. 1950.

1859 BARTLETT 476. **1861** WINTHROP *C. Dreeme* 78 A court, . . . serving as a well to light the rear range of a tenement-house. **1913** EATON *Barn Doors & Byways* 131 Across the river and the railway, the land rises up and is crested with tenement-houses, like a long wave, as far as you can see. **1950** *New Yorker* 20 May 74/2 The housing reformers succeeded in persuading the city to enact the 'model' Tenement House Law of 1901.

attrib. **1868** *N.Y. Herald* 1 July 6/5 The case which we reported . . . reveals in a striking manner the evils of the tenement house system. **1923** WATTS *L. Nichols* 225 No more Fresh-Air-Farm picnics for tenement house children.

As the last term in **clapboard, frame, log tenement.**

Tennessee ˌtɛnəˈsi, *n.* [f. Amer. Indian but otherwise obscure. Prob. a mispronunciation of a Cherokee mispronunciation of a Creek name.] A river and a south central state. Used attrib.

1. Designating varieties of fruits, vegetables, etc. *Obs.*

1827 *Western Mo. Rev.* I. 82 The kinds of cotton which are chiefly cultivated, are Louisiana, green seed, or Tennessee, and recently Mexican. **1855** *Amer. Inst. N.Y. Trans. 1854* 594 Indian Millet . . . [is called] 'Tennessee rice.' **1856** *Rep. Comm. Patents 1855: Agric.* 290 The 'Tennessee Milam,' and 'Kentucky Red,' are our best early winter apples. **1890** *Amer. Naturalist* XXIV. 738 In 1884 there appeared in our seedsmen's catalogues, under the name of Tennessee Sweet Potato Pumpkin, a variety very distinct.

2. Designating liquor made in, or coming from, Tennessee. Also absol. *Obs.*

1845 HOOPER *Simon Sugg's Adv.* 53 That light-yaller bottle tho', in the corner thar, that's Tennessee! **1860** *Harper's Mag.* Sep. 571/2 He told Uncle Ned to . . . bring home a gallon of No. 1 gin; and . . . a gallon of Tennessee brand.

3. Designating livestock of a type or breed produced in Tennessee.

1944 *Democrat* 2 Nov. 3/4 For Sale—One Tennessee jack, 12 to 14 years old, weight about 700 pounds, $250. **1947** *Chi. Tribune* 9 Nov. VII. 1/7 We could look at any one of those young Tennessee walking horses and instantly name its father! **1948** *Ib.* 24 March I. 18/3 Arkansas Lady, a 6 year old Tennessee Walking mare, is the mother of twins at the Hereford Manor stock farm, near here.

4. Tennessee itch, a malignant rash breaking out in hot weather. *Obs.*

1804 MICHAUX *Voyage à l'Ouest* 257 On donne dans le pays, à cette maladie, le nom Tennessée Itch (gale de Tennessée).

5. Tennessee warbler, a small olive-green warbler, *Vermivora peregrina*, of the eastern states.

1811 WILSON *Ornithology* III. 83 [The] Tennessee Warbler, *Sylvia Peregrina*, . . . I first found . . . on the banks of Cumberland river in the state of Tennessee. **1903** WEED & DEARBORN *Birds in Relations to Man* 114 The Tennessee Warbler is a very interesting migratory species. **1946** STANWELL-FLETCHER *Driftwood Valley* 195 Just below timber line J. collected a Tennessee warbler and its nest.

6. In miscellaneous combs., usu. obs., of obvious meaning or sufficiently explained in the quots.: (1) **Tennessee marble,** (2) **platform,** (3) **ranger,** (4) **sharpshooter,** (5) **shinplaster,** (6) **shotgun,** (7) **wagon.**

(1) **1947** *Sat. Ev. Post* 8 March 76/3 More than 800 carloads of pink Tennessee marble . . . were used in the walls alone. — (2) **1859** *Harper's Mag.* April 688/1 The 'Tennessee Platform,' . . . opposes the idea of disunion, but advocates retaliation for what the South considers her wrongs. — (3) **1833** [see ***ranger 1. b.**]. — (4) **1895** G. KING *New Orleans* 244 On the summit of the parapet stood the corps of Tennessee sharp-shooters.

(5) **1839** *S. Lit. Messenger* April 272/2 Tennessee *shin-plasters* were rejected. — (6) **1827** COOPER *Prairie* iv, I scorn to slander even a Tennessee shot-gun. — (7) **1857** *Harper's Mag.* Aug. 423/2 In a dream. . . . I had swallowed my big Tennessee wagon, and the great pole stuck out of my mouth. **1910** *Pub. Miss. Hist. Soc.* XI. 87 My father and Mr. Eyre Spann moved from South Carolina together about the year 1838 in 'prairie schooners' or covered wagons, or, as they were then called, 'Tennessee wagons.'

b. Tennessee spinster, ?a spinning wheel. *Rare.*

1830 *Yadkin & Catawba Gaz.* (Salisbury, N.C.) 22 June 1/4 Having commenced manufacturing the Machines commonly known by the name of the *Tennessee Spinster*, the subscriber respectfully informs the public that he is prepared to make, on short notice, . . . any number of those useful articles of household furniture, at only *one hundred dollars* a piece.

As the last term in **Army of the Tennessee.**

Tennesseean ˌtɛnəˈsiən, *n.* and *a.*

1. *n.* A native or resident of Tennessee.

1815 *Niles' Reg.* VII. 373/1 Glory to . . . the hardy and gallant Tennesseeans, Kentuckians and Louisianians. **1851** *Fox River Courier* (Elgin, Ill.) 12 Nov. 2/3 He had one hundred dollars for a Tennesseean who had called at his office that morning. **1945** BOTKIN *My Burden* 184 My mother was Amy Van Zandt Moore and was a Tennesseean.

Also **East, West Tennesseean.**

1818 JACKSON in *Ann. 15th Congress* 2 Sess. App. 20 Jan. 2175, [I] advised you of the appeal I had made to the patriotism of the West Tennesseans. **1845** SOL. SMITH *Theatr. Apprent.* 184 He got rid of any further inquiries from the anxious West Tennesseans. **1846** POLK *Diary* (1929) 128 He had not been in my office or at the President's mansion, . . . except once for a few minutes . . . in company with Hon. John Blair and some other East Tennesseeans.

b. (See quots.)

1865 *Jackson* (Tenn.) *Whig* 4 Nov. 1/2 Jack Harris' leader is speckled Ball [a dog], a native Tennesseean, son of old Boxer, five years old. **1883** JACKSON *Ramona* 453 'Wall, I allow yer've got more right ter 'em 'n—' began Jos, energetically, forgetting himself; then, dropping Tennesseean, he completed in Spanish his cordial assurances that the horses were at Felipe's command.

2. *a.* Of or pertaining to Tennessee.

1853 MCCONNEL *Western Char.* 269 Its dye a favorite 'Tennessean' brownish-yellow. **1869** MARK TWAIN *Sk. New & Old* 50 The paragraphs, . . . into whose cold sentences your masterly hand has infused the fervent spirit of Tennesseean journalism, will wake up another nest of hornets. **1891** *Cent.* 6232/2. **1945** WOODS *Amer. Sayings* 274 A Tennesseean-born pioneer, he was in the tradition of Daniel Boone and other border heroes of his time.

***tennis,** *n.* As the last term in **paddle, platform paddle tennis.**

Tennis Cabinet. (See quot. 1914.) — **1914** *Cyclo. Amer. Govt.* III. 516 Tennis Cabinet. A term applied by the newspaper press to the personal friends of President Roosevelt, some of whom played tennis with him, and with whom he was supposed to have had special confidential relations, even to the extent of conference on important public questions. **1945** *Cleveland Press* 25 Oct. 1 James R. Garfield, in the tennis cabinet of Theodore Roosevelt, was born in this house at Hiram.

***tenor,** *n.* In colonial Massachusetts, the value of a piece of paper money. *Obs.* — **1716** *Mass. H. Rep. Jrnl.* I. 114 That the Bills be of the same tenour with those that are already emitted.

As the last term in **Arizona, middle, new, old tenor.**

***tenpin,** *n.* **tenpin alley,** a bowling alley where tenpins is played.

1835 NICKLIN *Letters Va. Springs* 23 The means of amusement at the Warm Springs, consist of a bagatelle table . . . , a ten-pin alley [etc.]. **1886** POORE *Reminiscences* I. 62 Ten-pin alleys were abundant [in Washington].

b. Also **tenpin ball, rolling.** Cf. next.

1840 *N.O. Picayune* 29 July 2/1 [With] billiard playing, ten pin rolling, eating, smoking [etc.] . . . some of our friends are enjoying rare times at the watering places. **1870** LOGAN *Before Footlights* 120 Finely cut bits of paper, for fatal snowstorms; ten-pin balls, for the distant muttering of the storm. **1895** *Outing* XXVI. 444/1 You rush to the bottom like a ten-pin ball sent spinning down its alley.

c. *To roll tenpins*, to play tenpins.

1841 *Spirit of Times* 2 Oct. 363/3 (We.), I never saw him roll tenpins! **1872** *Newton Kansan* 5 Sep. 4/1 A Texas German . . . lost $12 rolling ten-pins.

ten-plate stove. A stove for both heating and cooking consisting of ten plates bolted together, being essentially a six-plate stove *q.v.* with four plates added so as to provide an oven. Now *hist.*

Ten-plate stove *c*1770

1766 in *Hist. Rev. Berks Co.* (Pa.) (1949) Oct. 144/1 John Waggoner for 1 Large Tenplate Stove with feet—5/10/0 [*c*$14.58]. **1830** WATSON *Philadelphia* 198 Ten plate stoves when first introduced, though very costly, and but rudely cast, were much used for kitchens and common sitting rooms. **1888** in *Pa. Dutchman* 23 June (1949) 7/3 A ten-plate-stove, that weighed a ton, Stood in a wooden-box spittoon. **1931** *Old-Time N. Eng.* Oct. 72/1 The six-plate stove was soon superseded by the ten-plate stove which contained an oven and could be used for cooking as well as heating. It had a large oven door on both sides. **1949** *Hist. Rev. Berks Co.* (Pa.) Oct. 144/2 Just who is responsible for making the pattern, ordering the first casting, and promoting the first ten-plate stove remains obscure at this date.

ten-strike, *n.* In tenpins, a bowl that knocks down all the pins.

1840 *Spirit of Times* 11 July 228/1 (We.), [This] he says is an extra touch—a ten strike and two spare balls. **1886** POORE *Reminiscences* I. 62 Ten-pin alleys were abundant, and some of the muscular Congressmen from the frontier would make a succession of 'ten strikes' with great ease, using the heaviest balls. **1899** CHAMPLIN & BOSTWICK *Cyclo. Games & Sports* (ed. 2) 109/1 If a player makes a ten-strike, the pin may be set up again.

b. (See quot.) *Obs.*

1851 HALL *College Words* 298 *Ten-strike*, at Hamilton, a perfect recitation, ten being the mark given for a perfect recitation.

c. A stroke of unusual luck or success. *Slang.*

1865 SALA *Diary* III. 253 The apothecary . . . was merely actuated by the common greed . . . for doing a 'ten strike'—for making 'their pile.' **1897** LEONARD *Gold Fields Klondike* 54 A very hard country to live in on account of the mosquitoes and poor grub, but healthy and a show to make a ten-strike. **1949** *Chi. D. News* 30 April 6/1 Bowles is credited with a political 'ten strike' in disposing of a possible rival.

***tent,** *n.*

1. tent caterpillar, any one of several gregarious caterpillars which spin large webs on trees, esp. the larva of the moth *Malocosoma americanum.* Also with a specifying term. Cf. **forest tent caterpillar.**

1854 EMMONS *Agric. N.Y.* V. 236 To eradicate completely the tent caterpillar, it will be necessary to give attention to the wild cherry trees. **1884** *Rep. Comm. Agric.* 412 These . . . appeared to be closely allied to, if not identical with, the common Apple-tree Tent-caterpillar (Clisioampa americana) of the Eastern States. **1948** *Nat. Hist.* April 168/2 The egg masses of the tent caterpillars form conspicuous brown rings on the small twigs.

2. *attrib.* Designating a temporary *city, colony* or *town* made up of tenters.

1878 BEADLE *Western Wilds* 103 Along the track west of it had sprung up five tent-towns, whose equals were never seen. **1943** MENEFEE *Assignment* 52 Thousands lived in tent colonies north and south of the city. **1946** FOREMAN *Last Trek* 251 They had hardly been established in their tent city. **1948** *Time* 23 Feb. 39/1 Through the tent city moved a truck with a raised platform, draped in India's tricolor flag.

As the last term in **bark, blanket, brush, bush, cook, grub, guard, house, Indian, log, miners', pup, shelter, summer, wall, war, wedge tent.**

* **tented,** *a.* **1. tented meeting,** a camp meeting held under a tent. **2. tented wagon,** a covered wagon. Both *obs.*

(1) 1898 N. E. JONES *Squirrel Hunters Ohio* 131 Protracted, tented, or camp-meetings increased, following the settlements, and becoming very popular with preachers and people. [**1950** *Reader's Digest* Jan. 85/2 Frakes joined the Methodist Church at an evangelistic tent meeting.] — **(2) 1848** BRYANT *California* i. 14 Long trains of oxen . . . pulling huge tented-wagons, were moving about the streets.

tenter ˈtɛntɚ, *n.* One who lives in a tent. — **1846** *Indiana Hist. Mag.* XXIII. 409 The eating hours were the same as those of the tenters. **1888** *Harper's Mag.* Oct. 801/1 The pretty girl of our civilization, who pushes into the canvas home of the tenters.

tepary ˈtɛpərɪ, *n. S.W.* [Origin obscure, cf. quot. 1912 below.] An annual native bean, *Phaseolus acutifolius,* found in the Southwest, or a cultivated drought-resistant variety developed from this.

[**1716** VELARDE *Relacion* (1926) 309 Los demás frutos de esta Pimería son maíz, frijol pequeño, llamado *tepari* y otras semillas.] **1912** FREEMAN *Southwestern Beans* 582 The name tepary or tepari (Spanish) originated from the Papago word 'stäte päve,' 'stäte' meaning wild and 'päve' having reference to the kind of plant to distinguish it from the 'mon' or bean. **1925** BRYAN *Papago Country* 354 The beans known as tépari . . . are said to be so resistant to drought that the plants may wither three successive times and then, if enough rain comes, mature a crop. **1942** CASTETTER & BELL *Pima & Papago Agric.* 191 The Papago made only one planting of teparies—In July, and harvested in October.

b. In full **tepary bean.**

1912 LUMHOLTZ *New Trails* 318 He had cooked bones of mountain-sheep with tépari beans for us. **1942** CASTETTER & BELL *Pima & Papago Agric.* 92 Archaeological evidence also amply supports the thesis that occurrence of the cultivated tepary bean antedates the coming of the white man in the Southwest.

tepee ˈtipi, *n. W.* [*Tipi* (from the Siouan root *ti* "to dwell," +*pi* "used for").]

1. A conical lodge or wigwam, usu. of skin, used by Plains Indians.

1835 FEATHERSTONHAUGH *Canoe Voyage* I. 338 Here, also, were their spring teebees, which they inhabit at that season. **1903** A. ADAMS *Log of Cowboy* 140 [The camp] had contained nearly a hundred lean-tos, wickyups, and teepees. **1949** *Nat. Geog. Mag.* Oct. 473/2 The northern tepee is covered sometimes with skin and sometimes with bark.

transf. **1948** *Trail Riders Bul.* Jan. 15/2 A trek to Forest Hills found yours truly receiving a typical trail riders' welcome at the lovely 'teepee' of Mr. & Mrs. Dale Carnegie.

2. In combs. of obvious meaning or sufficiently explained in the quots.: (1) **tepee butte,** (2) **cloth,** (3) **cover,** (4) **pole,** (5) **skin,** (6) **trail.**

(1) 1918 VISHER *So. Dakota* 14 The buttes of the plains owe their existence in part to more resistant lenses of rock. Striking illustrations are the 'tepee buttes,' due in certain places (in the Pierre shales) to lenses of fossil shells, and in others (in the Fort Union formation) to lenses of chert. — **(2) 1877** *Rep. Indian Affairs,* Tepee cloth should be discontinued, and . . . log or frame houses should be substituted. — **(3) 1890** CUSTER *Following Guidon* 6 The hides were dressed for robes or tepee covers. — **(4) 1899** *Mo. So. Dakotan* I. 175 Indian . . . had cut and peeled teepe poles. **1939** *Southwestern Lore* Sep. 28 The fact that the poles were left would indicate a habit of cutting fresh poles at each new camp and of moving camp goods by hand or on horseback, rather than on tipi-pole travois. **1949** *Sky Line Trail* Oct. 13/1 Later, when the Indians obtained horses, the foot as well as the buffalo trails became widened by large parties passing with horses dragging tepee poles and travois.

(5) 1917 WILL & HYDE *Corn Among Indians* 133 This was done on the floor itself or upon old tipi skins spread on the ground. — **(6) 1869** *Amer. Naturalist* II. 648 [We] follow upon the dim road or the tepe trail over the broad prairie. **1901** WHITE *Blazed Trail Stories* 118 Alfred said he hadn't seen even a teepee-trail.

tequila təˈkilə, *n.* [Amer. Sp. (<Nahuatl place-name) in sense shown here.] A spirituous drink made from the maguey.

1849 GREGG *Diary & Lett.* (1944) II. 317 So celebrated has this place become, for the manufacture of superior *mezcal,* that that taken from here is known by the name of *Tequila.* **1881** *Amer. Naturalist* XV. 877 This sotol mescal should not be confounded with maguey mescal, or taquile, the product of the maguey plant, *Agave americana.* **1950** *N.O. Times-Picayune Mag.* 1 Jan. 23/3, I should like a keg of tequila.

* **term,** *n.*

1. The period of time for which a public official is elected to office.

1793 WASHINGTON in *Pres. Mess. & P.* I. 138 Since the commencement of the term for which I have been again called into office, no fit occasion has arisen [etc.]. **1886** ALTON *Among Law-Makers* 13 The terms of the Representatives begin at twelve o'clock, noon, on the 4th of March of every odd-numbered year. **1946** *Democrat* 27 June 1/6 This contest is for Senator Bankhead's unexpired term.

2. term paper. *Educ.* A paper written in partial fulfilment of the requirements of a course for a given term.

1934 WEBSTER. **1947** *Staff Lookout* (Denver Pub. Lib.) Winter 12/1 The article was condensed from a term paper prepared while Miss Gross was a graduate student in the University of Denver.

3. term slave, (see quot. and cf. ***redemptioner**). *Obs.*

1889 MELLICK *Story Old Farm* 148 Redemptioners, or term slaves, as they were sometimes called, constituted in the early part of the eighteenth century a peculiar feature of colonial society.

As the last term in **fall, heated, one, presidential, short, spring, summer, third term.**

* **terminal,** *n.* The end of a railroad line, usu. including the switches, sheds, etc. (see also quot. 1909).

1888 *Boston Jrnl.* 7 Aug. 3/2 The Canadian Pacific Road . . . has purchased extensive dock property and terminals at Windsor, opposite Detroit. **1909** WEBSTER 2130/3 *Terminal,* . . . a town lying at the end of a railroad. **1912** IRWIN *Red Button* 93, I have an option on the Hudson Terminal and a mortgage on the Singer Building. **1950** *Chi. Tribune* 15 May 1/4 The cuts in rail service, showed in lessened crowds at the Central, Union, La Salle, and Dearborn stations, which are terminals for the struck roads.

b. *transf.* The end of something, as a telegraph line or bridge, or the place where something ends.

1897 *Boston Globe* 29 Aug. (Ernst), The arbitrage broker required only a private wire . . . with terminals as near as possible to the exchanges in the two cities. **1904** *N.Y. Ev. Post* 29 Sec. 6 The traffic problem presented by the Manhattan terminal of the Brooklyn Bridge.

* **tern,** *n.* As the last term in **bridled, elegant, Forster's, least, Nuttall's, Portland, royal, Wilson's tern.**

terrapin ˈtɛrəpɪn, *n.* ["Terrapin is a diminutive from the *torope* or *turŭpe* of the Virginian and Delaware dialects of Algonquian" (Hodge). Cf. **torup.**]

1. Any one of several edible turtles of the family Testudinidae, living in fresh or brackish water, esp. the diamond-back turtles of the genus *Malaclemys;* loosely, any land or fresh-water turtle. Also one of these used as food.

1672 JOSSELYN *N. Eng. Rarities* 34 The turtle that . . . is called in Virginia a Terrapine. **1705** BEVERLEY *Virginia* III. 14 Their Food is Fish and Flesh of all sorts, and that which participates of both; as . . . a small kind of Turtle, or Tarapins, (as we call them). **1824** SINGLETON *Letters* 71 They do not here [in Virginia] eat the terrapin, which is esteemed a luxury at the north; but they highly relish the sturgeon, which is seldom eaten at the east. **1947** BEROLZHEIMER *Regional Cookbook* 186 Drop live terrapin into boiling water and let stand 5 minutes.

attrib. **1772** in *Travels Amer. Col.* 517 The women danced the Snake dance, the leader haveing her legs Covered with Turpin shells . . . filled with small stones on purpose to make a noise. **1839** *S. Lit. Messenger* V. 376/2 Jane . . . proposed that 'they should all go the next day to hunt terrapin eggs.' **1910** J. HART *Vigilante Girl* 88 The diamond-back costs almost as much in Baltimore as it would if terrapin farms were carved out of the dryest plains of western Texas. **1944** *Harper's Mag.* Aug. 223/2 Others start spinning like tops the minute they hit town and throw off continual sparks in the form of champagne-and-terrapin parties for senators.

b. terrapin soup, stew, soup or stew of terrapin.

1825 PAULDING *J. Bull in Amer.* 16 There was a very suspicious dish on the table, which they called terrapin soup. **1842** *Galveston* (Tex.) *News* 19 April 2/3 Let Maryland boast of her . . . turtles, and oysters, and terrapin stews. **1949** *Time* 12 Dec. 89/1 Union chefs served up the latest gossip as piping hot as the famed terrapin soup.

c. *To walk terrapin*, meaning obscure. *Obs.*

1819 *Ky. Alman. 1820* (Lexington) 30 Drat it if I shouldn't have walked terrapin.

2. (*cap.*) Used with *policy* and *system* with reference to the Embargo Act of 1807 and to the War of 1812. *Obs.*

This use originated with those hostile to the Embargo Act who app. felt that the country was withdrawing from commerce just as a terrapin shuts itself up in its shell. But cf. quot. 1824.

1809 *Ann. 10th Cong.* 2 Sess. 1003 Is the Chinese, or Terrapin system [of commerce] as it is called, to be enforced? **1823** *Niles' Reg.* 15 Nov. XXV. 152/1 The writer ridicules what he calls the 'Terrapin policy.' There was a time when it was *fashionable* to approve it, in its utmost extent. **1824** BLANE *Excursion* 320 But after they had captured a few British men-of-war, the Americans, in allusion to the gun-boats, which were for the most part drawn up ashore, defied the advice of President Jefferson, by calling it 'the Terrapin System.' **1860** MORDECAI *Va.* 320 When we resorted to the terrapin policy of Embargo and Non-intercourse, to prepare for war by depriving ourselves of the means to conduct it, this among other patriotic resolutions was adopted at public meetings, that we should dress in domestic fabrics.

As the last term in **alligator, diamond-back, fresh-water, land, mud, pine barren, salt-marsh, salt-water, sea, slider, soft-shell, water, wood, yellow-bellied terrapin.**

terrell grass. (See quot. 1891.) — **1891** *Cent.* 6246/3 *Terrell grass*, a species of wild rye, or lyme-grass, *Elymus Virginicus*, a coarse grass, but found useful for forage in the southern United States: so named from a promoter of its use. **1901** MOHR *Plant Life Ala.* 388.

* **terrified,** *a.* (Also *cap.*) (See quots.) *Obs.*

1849 *Waukegan* (Ill.) *Chron.* 23 Oct. 2/5 The 'terrified democracy,' *alias* hunker democracy, called by Isaac H. Smith, Esq., held their convention yesterday. **1857** BUNGAY *Off-Hand* 316 We have the Barnburners, known also by the names of 'Softs,' 'Putty-heads,' 'the Unterrified,' and their bitterest opponents, the 'Hards,' 'the Terrified,' &c. **1865** *Washoe* (Nev.) *Times* 14 Oct. 3/1 The terrified Democracy, we mean the class that are heavy on the shoot-their-mouth-off, are likely to have many candidates before their Convention for Congress.

* **territorial,** *a.*

1. Of or pertaining to a territory of the U.S.

1802 *Ann. 7th Cong.* 1 Sess. 1101 It is the interest of the United States to obtain some further security against an injurious sale, under the Territorial or State laws, of lands sold by them to individuals. **1814** BRACKENRIDGE *Views La.* 99 The territorial governor [of Mo.] acts as well in the capacity of a general agent for the United States, as in that of civil magistrate. **1949** *Democrat* 30 June 7/4 Alabama's territorial capital, St. Stephens, was settled by the Spaniards in 1790.

2. In special combs.: (1) **territorial fair,** an exhibition of agricultural and other products sponsored by a U.S. territory; (2) **government,** (*a*) a government set up for a territory of the U.S., (*b*) *first grade of territorial government*, a territorial government having an elected legislature, (*c*) *second grade of territorial government*, a territorial government conducted entirely by federal appointees.

(1) **1872** RAYMOND *3d Rep. Mines* 287 The Territorial fair, . . . was a striking exhibition of the wealth and progress of Colorado. **1890** *Stock Grower & Farmer* 19 July 3/2 For several years the territorial fair has been plodding along without startling success. — (2) (*a*) **1804** *Ann. 8th Congress* 1 Sess. 1062, I believe the Territorial government, as established by the ordinance of the Old Congress, the best adapted to the circumstances of the people of Louisiana. **1907** ANDREWS *Recoll.* 80 All the offices under the territorial government are bought by votes in favor of the bill. **1949** *Time* 4 July 7/1 The productive and gracious economy of Hawaii was paralyzed last week; its territorial government was powerless to act. (*b*) **1831** PECK *Guide* 327 In 1789, the first grade of territorial government was organized and called the 'Western Territory.' (*c*) **1818** *Niles' Reg.* XIV. 48/2 A majority of the votes in Michigan territory is *against* the second grade of territorial government.

Also *territorial appointment, court, debt, library, militia, press, road, status, town.*

* **territorialize,** *v. tr.* To reduce (a state) to the condition of a territory. *Rare.* — **1869** *Cong. Globe* App. 1 April 437/2, I asked, 'What bill? The bill to territorialize the State of Mississippi?'

* **territory,** *n.*

1. Land or country lying outside the states but belonging either to a state or to the federal government.

1787 *Constitution* iv. 3 The Congress shall have Power to dispose of and make all needful Rules and Regulations respecting the Territory or other Property belonging to the United States. **1818** *Niles' Reg.* XV. 116/1 Calculate the immense extent of unappropriated territory . . . which stretches into the north-westernmost angle of the United States. **1949** D. O. MCGOVNEY *Amer. Suffrage* 47 We fall short of a national election in many respects. One is that citizens of the United States residing in the Territories and the District of Columbia have no voice in it.

2. (*cap.*) A particular area of the country not yet admitted to the Union as a state, but organized under an act of Congress with some measure of self-government. Also, sometimes, the government or people of such an area.

1787 in W. M. WEST *Source Book Amer. Hist.* 488 Be it ordained by the United States in Congress Assembled that the said territory for the purposes of temporary government be one district. **1879** HART *Sazerac Lying Club* 112 I'd rather run an ice-cream cart in the State of Nevady than a first-class saloon in the Territory of Montany. **1949** *Nat. Geog. Mag.* Oct. 505/2 And he has poured his profits back into the Territory instead of taking them Outside to spend.

b. territory wool, (see quot. 1920).

[**1920** *Amer. Wool & Cotton Reporter* 24 June 2358/1 Quotations to Manufacturers of Leading Grades of Wool . . . Territory fine staple \$1.70 \$1.80. [Note:] Territory includes wools from the Dakotas, Montana, Nevada, Utah, Colorado, Idaho, Wyoming, New Mexico and Arizona.] **1931** *Ib.* 19 Feb. 4/2 Scoured Territory wools were fairly active. **1950** *Ib.* 2 March 30/2 Some odd lots of fine territory wool such as good even 64s and finer, are being taken off the market from day to day.

3. An area allotted to a commercial traveler or firm throughout which to sell a particular product.

1900 *Cent. Mag.* LIX. 644/2 We've got to begin small. Our territory is Ohio. **1904** CRISSEY *Tattlings* 88 This young reformer . . . had invaded a competitor's territory and put in his own goods. **1950** *Chi. Tribune* 13 July III. 13/6 Good men over 25 will be hired to take over going territories . . . vacated by men who have been promoted.

As the last term in **back, Dakota, free, Illinois, Indian, Kansas, Louisiana, Mississippi, Montana, Northwest, Northwestern, oil, Oregon, Orleans, slave, Washington, western territory.**

* **tertium quid.** (Also *cap.*) (See quots. 1914, 1947.)

1805 *N.-Eng. Palladium* (Boston) 12 July 1/3 If the Tertium Quids offer any stubborn facts, to prevent their having the least effect, it is only necessary to cry, '*O ye are all a set of d——d Tories.*' **1806** *Balance* V. 11/2 He was a deserter, and had either joined the federalists, or the tertium-quids. **1914** *Cyclo. Amer. Govt.* III. 529/2 Tertium Quid was the term applied to the faction led by John Randolph, in Jefferson's administration. **1947** *West. Pa. Hist. Mag.* 23 Each branch of the Republican (or Democratic) party called itself the original party, referring to its adversaries as 'tertium quids' or a 'third something,' as it has been freely translated.

tesquite tes'kite, *n. S.W.* [Amer. Sp. *tesoquite* (<Nahuatl), in same sense.] (See quot.) *Obs.* — **1859** BARTLETT 476 *Tesquite*, an alkaline efflorescence of considerable value which exudes from the earth around many of the lakes, ponds, and marshy grounds, of New Mexico, California, and Arizona.

tessellated darter. A small fish of the eastern states. — **1842** *Nat. Hist. N.Y., Zoology* IV. 20 The Tessellated Darter. *Boleosoma tessellatum.* . . . It is usually seen at the bottom of clear springs or streams, lying for a while perfectly still, . . . suddenly darts off with great velocity at its prey. **1897** *N.Y. Forest, Fish, & Game Comm.* 2 Rep. 241.

* **test,** *n.*

1. = **test well.**

1922 *Dly. Ardmoreite* (Ardmore, Okla.) 8 Jan. 14/3 The test originally was spudded in to drill for the 800 foot gas sand. **1932** *Tulsa* (Okla.) *D. World* 13 March II. 2/3 This test was originally drilled by the Tidal Oil company. **1950** *Dly. Ardmoreite* (Ardmore, Okla.) 1 March 7/3 A contract has been made with the Warren and Bradshaw drilling company for a deep test for oil at Courtney.

2. In combs.: (1) * **test paper,** (see quot. 1891); (2) **pit,** a shallow pit or hole made by a prospector in searching for or testing a mineral deposit, also fig.; (3) **run,** a proof or milling of a given amount of ore for determining its yield; (4) **vote,** a vote, often informal, as an indication of sentiment; (5) **well,** a well made in testing a site for oil.

(1) **1841** *Pa. Rep.* (Wharton) VI. 291 No doubt must remain as to the handwriting of the test paper. **1850** BURRILL *Law Dict.* II. (1860) 522/2 *Test Paper.* In practice. A paper or instrument shown to a jury as evidence. A term used in the Pennsylvania courts. **1891** *Cent.* 6253/1 *Test-paper*, . . . a document allowed to be used in a court of justice as a standard of comparison for determining a question of handwriting. — (2) **1882** *Harper's Mag.* May 897/2 The prospectors sink a well, which they call a 'test pit.' **1896** *Atlantic Mo.* May 606/2 Sinking test-pits through layers of crusted consciousness into depths of fiery nature. — (3) **1876** RAYMOND *8th Rep. Mines* 302 A test-run made upon about three tons showed it to contain 51 ounces of silver and 41 per cent. of lead per ton. **1880** *Cimarron News & Press* 3 June

2/4 Jack Burroughs, the man who made a 'test run' with the Sperry mill, . . . passed the winter in London. — (4) **1856** *Porter's Spirit of Times* 8 Nov. 168/1 The intention . . . [is to] ridicule the mania for taking test votes in railroad cars, steamboats, and everywhere else. **1870** MEDBERY *Men Wall St.* 14 The Stock Exchange . . . on a test vote, . . . could only muster fifty-two members.

(5) **1945** *Democrat* 24 May 1/6 The California Oil Company . . . has staked a location for the drilling of a test well. **1948** *Ib.* 4 Nov. 4/3 Up to the time this well was drilled, Clarke held the distinction of having had the deepest test well in the state.

As the last term in **cattle, fire, love's, nullification, pan test.**

tester bar. A mosquito bar. *Obs.* — **1850** COLTON *Deck & Port* 122 If by good fortune your tester-bar keeps out the musqueto, you fall into the hands of a still worse enemy in the shape of the flea.

***tête-à-tête,** *n.* (See quot. 1864.)

1853 *S.F. Whig* 28 July 3/5 Their stock consists, in part, as follows. . . . Sofas and Tete-a-Tetes—Every style, and a large assortment. **1864** WEBSTER 1368/3 *Tête-à-tête,* . . . a form of sofa for two persons, so curved that they are brought face to face while sitting on different sides of the sofa. **1899** *Boston Traveller* 25 July, It is more than tete-a-tete, larger than a canape.

Teton 'titn, *n.*[1] [A contraction of the native name meaning "dwellers on the prairie."] *pl.* or *collect.* (See quot. 1910.)

1807 DUNBAR *Travels* 18 This trade, as small as it may appear, has been sufficient to render the Tetons independent of the traders of the Missouri. **1840** *N.Y. Mirror* 4 July 12/3 The Rising Elk was the chief of the Tetons. **1873** *Forest & Stream* 9 Oct. 133/1 For several hours we followed on the trail of the Tetons. **1910** HODGE *Amer. Indians* II. 736/1 Teton. . . . The western and principal division of the Dakota or Sioux, including all the bands formerly ranging w. of Missouri r., and now residing on reservations in South Dakota and North Dakota.

attrib. **1840** *N.Y. Mirror* 4 July 12/3 His household was the whole tribe of the Teton Dahcotas. **1941** DICK *Vanguards of Frontier* 131 Father Jean-Baptiste Genin traveled through Minnesota and North Dakota with the Teton Sioux.

Teton 'titn, *n.*[2] *W.* [F. *téton,* a woman's breast.] A mountain of a form suggestive of a woman's breast, often in allusion to the Teton Range in northwestern Wyoming. Cf. **mamelle.**

1855 J. MULLAN *Pac. R.R. Explor.* I. 331 The word 'butte' is 'applied to high elevations of land . . . which occur, as a general thing, in a prairie country.' The Tetons, on the contrary, occur in a mountainous country. **1910** *Out West* Feb. 134 The lonely snow-capped Tetons call to you. **1949** *Mazama* Jan. 1/1 Some of America's finest climbers have explored the Tetons and have established many routes, ranging from the utmost difficulty to simple climbs within the reach of all.

b. Esp. in proper names.

1832 *Ev. & Morning Star* (Independence, Mo.) Oct. 7/1 On the 17th five were again attacked by these Indians at Jackson's hole, near the Three Tetons, and 3 of them were killed. **1872** RICHARDSON *Wonders of Yellowstone* 222 In front of me, at a distance of fifty miles away, in the clear blue of the horizon, rose the arrowy peaks of the Three Tetons. **1949** *Mazama* Jan. 1/1 Teton National Park is a wild-life refuge, with moose, elk, bighorn sheep, deer and many other forms of wild life in abundance.

Tewa. See **Tegua.**

Tewksbury Winter Blush. A variety of apple (see quots.). *Obs.* — **1817** W. COXE *Fruit-Trees* 156 Tewksbury Winter Blush. This apple was brought from the township of Tewksbury in Hunterdon county, New Jersey. **1849** *N. Eng. Farmer* I. 90 Tewksbury Winter Blush.—Very small and beautiful.

Texalite 'tɛksə,laɪt, *n.* [*Texas,* Pa. + *-*lite.*] (See quot.) — **1862** *Amer. Jrnl. Sci. & Arts* 2 Ser. XXXIV. 203 R. Hermann has given the name of Texalite to the hydrate of magnesia from Texas, Pennsylvania.

Texan 'tɛksn, *a.* and *n.*

1. *n.* A native or inhabitant of Texas.

1838 C. NEWELL *Revol. Texas* 27 The Texans were gallantly led to the charge by their commander, John Austin. **1865** RICHARDSON *Secret Service* 99 A Texan on board the boat was very bitter against Governor Houston. **1923** J. H. COOK *On Old Frontier* 53 In our outfit was . . . a large, hungry-looking Texan. **1950** *Newsweek* 20 March 96/2 At this critical juncture, the impetuous Texans threatened to join England unless they were admitted to the Union.

2. *pl.* Texas cattle.

1868 *Ill. Agric. Soc. Trans.* VII. 138 We also put five cows and a buffalo with some Texans about the 20th of June. **1890** *Stock Grower & Farmer* 1 March 3/4 Rules for Shipping Texans.

3. The language or vernacular of Texas people. Also **Texanism,** an expression characteristic of this.

1877 HALE *G.T.T.* 41 The English talk of American dialect, as if I spoke Texan, or could; or as if a Carolinian could speak Yankee. **1948** MENCKEN *Supp.* II. 220 In 1944 John T. Krumpelmann contributed to *American Speech* a small group of Texanisms unearthed from a German travel-book of 1848.

4. *a.* Of or pertaining to what is now the state of Texas.

1832 DEWEES *Letters* (1852) 142 On arriving at that place the Texan troops put to flight seven hundred Mexicans. **1880** *Harper's Mag.* April 667 In that long building over there, Indian caciques, Spanish conquerors, Texan invaders, and American Governors have successively sat in state. **1949** *Chi. Tribune* 20 Feb. (Grafic Mag.) 17/5 On April 21 of that year a Texan army under Gen. Sam Houston defeated the Mexicans at the battle of San Jacinto.

b. In the names of animals and plants.

1859 BARTLETT 218 Jackass Rabbit. (*Lepus callotis.*) . . . It is known also by the names of Mule Rabbit, Texan Hare, and Black-tailed Hare. **1890** *Cent.* 4347/1 Peba, or Texan Armadillo (*Tatusia novemcincta*). **1894** *Harper's Mag.* Feb. 457 The Texan Walking Stick, *Diapheromera denticrus.* **1897** SUDWORTH *Arborescent Flora* 248 *Zygia flexicaulis.* . . . Texan Ebony.

5. a. Texan Ranger, = Texas Ranger. Also transf. **b. Texan Republic,** the republic (1836–45) established by the citizens of Texas after their declaration of independence from Mexico.

(**a**) *a*1846 *Quarter Race Ky.* (1854) 122 (We.), Bill Dean, the Texan Ranger. **1935** BUCKBEE *Saga Old Tuolumne* 450 William H. Worth, formerly a Texan Ranger under Hayes' command, . . . was brought to trial in Sonora on March 6, 1856, in the District Court. — (**b**) **1842** *N.O. Picayune* 4 Jan. 1/6 The Texans . . . represented . . . their object was to invite the New Mexicans to unite themselves to the Texan Republic.

Texas 'tɛksəs, *n.* [Amer. Sp. f. a term used by some east Texas tribe or tribes to mean "friends" or "allies." See Hodge.]

1. An Indian belonging to any one of numerous Texan tribes, the Caddo being the most important, often allied against the Apache. Also attrib.

[**1541** CORONADO in *Colec. Doc. Indias* XIII. (1870) 264 Los teyas estavan contra esto.] **1818** *State P.* (1819) XII. 31 Alonzo de Leon treated the Asimais with the greatest kindness, and called them *Texas,* which in their language signifies 'friends.' **1822** MORSE *Rep. Indian Affairs* II. 373 Indian Tribes between Red River, and Rio del Norte . . . Texas. **1858** *Texas Almanac 1859* 130 The State of Texas . . . set apart twelve leagues of land, upon which the Texas Indians were to be settled by the U.S. Government. **1946** FOREMAN *Last Trek* 162 They participated in an important Indian council presided over by Pierce M. Butler, in which representatives of the Delaware, Caddo, Shawnee, and Texas tribes took part.

2. (Often not *cap.*) A structure on the hurricane deck, immediately behind or beneath the pilot house of a river steamer, serving as officers' or crew's quarters. Cf. **double texas.**

The commonly accepted view is that the custom arose of naming staterooms on Mississippi steamers after states, whereupon the officers' room, being the largest, was named after the largest state. The evidence at hand is not sufficient to substantiate this, or any other, explanation of the origin of this application of the term.

1857 OLMSTED *Journey Texas* 27 To this Texas, inveterate card-players retire on Sundays, when custom forbids cards in the Saloon. **1907** STEWART *Partners* 207, I had the texas all to myself like a little house on top of mine. **1941** DORSEY *Master of Miss.* 226 It had been like pinning a political badge on steamboats when the large cabin, that Shreve had been first to build on the second deck, was dubbed the 'Texas.'

attrib. **1875** MARK TWAIN *Old Times* ii. 31 Here was . . . a tidy, white-aproned, black 'texas-tender,' to bring up tarts and ices and coffee during mid-watch, day and night. **1883** —— *Life on Miss.* xix. 232, I slipped . . . around to the texas-door. **1884** —— *H. Finn* xii, Away down through the texas-hall we see a light! **1950** *Chi. Tribune* 11 Sep. 20/3 The texas tender . . . was, and is, the name of the colored member of the crew who has charge of sweeping out the texas hall and the rooms which border it on either side. It is also the duty of the texas tender to carry coffee up to the pilot at certain hours and to keep the pilot house cleaned up and the floor scrubbed.

b. = Texas deck.

1864 *Quincy* (Ill.) *Herald* 30 Nov. 3/1 She has a wheel built on the pattern of a sidewheel, situated in her stern, ferry boat fashion, and a pilot house and texas where the cabin ought to be. **1942** HEREFORD *Old Man River* 51 On top of the roof was a smaller deck called the texas.

3. In special combs. usu. referring to the state of Texas: (1) **Texas cattle,** cattle raised in Texas, esp. a breed or variety of longhorned cattle found in early times in Texas, also attrib., cf. **Texas longhorn;** (2) **Compromise,** in the joint resolution of Congress providing for the annexation of Texas (1845), the stipulation that slavery should be prohibited in any new states to be formed from Texan territory north of the Missouri Compromise line, and that the slavery question should be decided for itself by every such state to be formed south of that line, also attrib.; (3) **deck, fever,** see as main entries; (4) **itch,** (see quot. 1909); (5) **leaguer,** in baseball, a batted ball that loops over the infielders' heads and yet falls too close in for an outfielder to catch, *slang;* (6) **longhorn,** a longhorned bovine animal of a type once common in Texas, also attrib. in a transf. sense, cf. **Texas cattle;** (7) **Panhandle,** a narrow strip of Texas in the extreme northern part of the state between New Mexico and Oklahoma; (8) **pony,** a cow pony; (9) **question,** the question of whether or not to admit Texas into the Union, *obs.;* (10) **Ranger,** (*a*) a member of a body of armed Texans, orig. Indian-fighters, and later active as soldiers, (*b*) a member of the mounted police of the state of Texas; (11) **saddle,** a heavy stock saddle usu. having a high cantle, a high knobbed pommel, and two cinches; (12) **tree,** the tree of a Texas saddle.

(1) **1857** BRAMAN *Texas* 72 The Texas cattle are descendants, with few crosses, from the old Mexican stocks, and they are well adapted to the country. **1870** *Rep. Comm. Agric. 1869* 16 The investigation [was] instituted to develop the character and cause of the 'Texas cattle disease.' **1893** G. W. CURTIS *Horses, Cattle* 220 Although known as 'Texas Cattle,' the same race extends throughout Mexico, and has been pretty well scattered through the more northern and western territories of the United States. — (2) **1848** POLK in *Pres. Mess. & P.* IV. 608 The Territory of Oregon lies far north of 36° 30′, the Missouri and Texas compromise line. **1857** BENTON *Exam. Dred Scott Case* 102 The Texas Compromise of 1845 omits it [the word 'forever'], and not by accident. — (4) **1873** NEWTON *Kansan* 13 Feb. 3/3 Mayor had a horse with . . . Texas itch. **1909** WEBSTER, Texas itch, *Veter.*, a contagious parasitic skin disease of cattle, usually occurring in winter, caused by the scab mite *Psoroptes communis bovis.* It is accompanied with atrophy of the hair follicles, loss of the hair, and disquamation of the epithelium. Also called *scabies, mad itch,* etc.

(5) **1906** *Cin. Enquirer* 1 April IV. 2/1 Many fans are unaware that the expression 'Texas leaguer' originated in Houston. **1949** *Oregonian* (Portland) 10 Aug. III. 3/5 Johnny Pesky's two bagger, a Texas leaguer which fell at the feet of the hard-trying Johnny Lindell, preceded Williams' homer. — (6) **1908** *Pacific Mo.* July 19/1 Pink got here about the same time but he come of old Texas-longhorn stock. *a***1918** G. STUART *On Frontier* II. 178 None of our cattle were Texas long horns. **1946** *Nat. Geog. Mag.* Jan. 17/1 Cattle then were the rangy Texas longhorns—more head, horns, and tail than thick, juicy steaks. — (7) **1884** ALDRIDGE *Life on Ranch* 92 The ranges in the 'territory' are nearly all fenced, and a good many also in West Kansas and the Texas Panhandle. **1949** *Harvard Alumni Bul.* 24 Sep. 34 [He] took a summer job as a locomotive fireman . . . in the Texas Panhandle. — (8) **1883** RITTENHOUSE *Maud* 206 Last night on the front porch Elmer said, 'The Texas pony is yours.' **1897** HOUGH *Story of Cowboy* 84 A great many persons think that all Texas ponies were 'mustangs,' but the rancher made a sharp distinction between his stock and these wild horses of the plains. — (9) **1844** *Republican Sentinel* (Richmond, Va.) 20 July 3/3 The Texas question has operated with force on the people of Louisiana. **1846** POLK *Diary* (1929) 59 Col. Benton feels that he lost caste with Democracy on the Texas question.

(10) (*a*) **1846** *Whig Almanac 1847* 19/1 Capt. Samuel Walker, at the head of a small company of Texas Rangers, left Point Isabel. **1907** ANDREWS *Recoll.* 163 We were under charge of Colonel Wharton and a detachment of his regiment, the Texas Rangers. (*b*) **1911** *Everybody's Mag.* Sep. 354/1 Two Texas rangers faced Antonio Carrasco and his seventeen thieves sometime in December of 1910. **1948** *Westerners' Brand Book* 51 The newly formed Texas Rangers bought all the Colts they could lay their hands on. — (11) **1877** MINTURN *Travels West* 37 There I saw for the first time a Texas saddle. This saddle was made of a piece of bone covered with strong leather. The bone seemed to be from the back of some animal. The saddle comes high up in front, where the lasso is fastened. **1945** *Democrat* 6 Sep. 4/2 [For Sale]—Good country raised iron gray saddle horse. . . . Also Texas saddle. — (12) **1852** SITGREAVES *Exped. Zuni & Colo. Rivers* 8 Lieutenant Colonel Johnston informed me that he was in the habit of using with good results the common Texas tree, provided with the necessary rings and straps. **1921** *Outing* March 246/3 In roping, the Texas tree gives greater purchase, a very desirable feature when a thousand-pound steer is trying to drag both horse and rider over the landscape.

b. Also in combs., often occasional or obs., of obvious meaning or sufficiently explained in the quots.: (1) **Texas annexation,** (2) **cattleman,** (3) **coaster,** (4) **cotton,** (5) **cow,** (6) **dialect,** (7) **dollar,** (8) **hat,** (9) **herd,** (10) **insurrection,** (11) **lingers,** (12) **lullaby,** (13) **norther,** (14) **northwester,** (15) **steer,** (16) **style,** (17) **trail,** (18) **wagon,** (19) **yell.**

(1) **1845** *Xenia Torch-Light* 31 July 3/1 The National Treasury is open to any and all demands made as the price of Texas Annexation. — (2) **1885** *Wkly. New Mexican Rev.* 8 Jan. 1/2 Texas cattlemen should not be allowed to drive cattle into this territory, not owning any water rights or range privileges, keep them here awhile and escape taxation both here and in Texas. — (3) **1902-1** *Kans. State Bd. Agric. Rep.* 154 Fine specimens have been . . . landed in the hands of the Philistines, with dire results to the offspring—bodies that could not make a shadow, and horns of the old Texas coaster—all from the lack of decent care. — (4) **1838** C. NEWELL *Revol. Texas* 165 The Texas cotton is allowed, in the New Orleans market at least, if not the European, to be superior in quality to that generally produced in the United States.

(5) **1875** *Cimarron News & Press* 7 Aug. 4/4 Texas cows, $12 to $16 per head. **1892** *Outing* Jan. 270/1 The first 'cut out' is a raw-boned Texas cow of gigantic proportions. — (6) **1881** C. M. CHASE *Editor's Run in N. Mex.* 118 They are honest, old-fashioned people, hard-shelled Baptists, speak the Texas dialect with 'thar,' 'whar,' 'befo,' etc., in the broadest style. — (7) **1841** *N.O. Picayune* 21 Jan. 2/3 Several instances of specie being freely exchanged for these notes, at the rate of five Texas dollars for one specie, were known. — (8) **1929** B. DAVIS *Truth About Geronimo* 160 My broad-brim Texas hat jerked back on my head. — (9) **1885** *Wkly. New Mexican Rev.* 25 June 3/6 These are Texas herds which came in via the Pecos trail recently.

(10) **1847** *Whig Almanac 1848* 5/1 The Texas Insurrection, the open and ostentatious drumming up of men, munitions and money throughout the South-west . . . are all matters of public history. — (11) **1895** *Nation* 9 May 358/3 The enervating influence of the climate, giving rise to that which in the southwestern United States is called the 'Texas lingers.' — (12) **1923** J. H. COOK *On Old Frontier* 17 Every man now began to ride very carefully and slowly, riding in circles around and around them, all except myself singing the melody known as the 'Texas Lullaby.' — (13) **1873** ROE *Army Lett.* 87 Then we knew that we were having a 'Texas norther,' a storm that is feared by all old frontiersmen. — (14) **1879** *Cong. Rec.* 1653/2 When one of these Texas northwesters comes this ship has to sail without unloading.

(15) **1865** *Wkly. New Mexican* 8 Sep. 2/3 The facts are . . . the stock, (Texas steers) corralled about seven miles below Las Cruces, for some unknown cause became badly frightened. **1897** HOUGH *Story of Cowboy* 210 He does not like to get his rope muddy for the sake of a Texas steer. **1945** *Texas Almanac & State Indust. Guide* 407 If all the Texas steers were one big steer, he would stand with his front feet in the Gulf of Mexico, one hind foot in Hudson Bay and the other in the Arctic Ocean, and with a sweep of his tail brush the mist from the Aurora Borealis. — (16) **1907** S. E. WHITE *Arizona Nights* 276 The old shiny Colt's forty-five, with its worn leather 'Texas style' holster, became a bedroom ornament. **1940** BABER & WALKER *Longest Rope* 41 He wore his guns Texas style and used them the same way. — (17) **1881** *Cimarron News & Press* 17 March 1/4 The well-known old Texas trail was infested with hostile Indians. — (18) **1853** P. PAXTON *Yankee in Texas* 50 A Texas wagon . . . drawn by those miserably slow oxen—beeves, as a Texan calls them—for which this part of the country is noted. — (19) **1896** *Harper's Mag.* XCIV. 64/1 We raised the Texas yell, and away we went.

c. In the names of plants, trees, and birds found in Texas: (1) **Texas ash,** (see quot.); (2) **bluebonnet,** a lupine, *Lupinus texensis,* common in the Southwest; (3) **bluegrass,** a forage grass, *Poa arachnifera,* that resembles Kentucky bluegrass; (4) **millet,** (see quot. 1909); (5) **moss,** (see quot.); (6) **oak,** the Texas red oak; (7) **persimmon,** (see quot.); (8) **sparrow,** (see quot. 1909); (9) **star,** (see quot.); (10) **thrasher,** a thrasher or species of thrush found in Texas, as the crissal thrasher; (11) **umbrella tree,** =**umbrella tree;** (12) **white oak,** (see quot.); (13) **woodpecker,** a kind of downy woodpecker, *Dryobates scalaris bairdi,* common in western Texas.

(1) **1897** SUDWORTH *Arborescent Flora* 327 Fraxinus texensis (Gray) Sargent. Texas Ash. — (2) **1934** WEBSTER. **1950** *Dly. Ardmoreite* (Ardmore, Okla.) 30 April 11/4 There is a cemetery there in the center of about an acre of Texas Bluebonnets. — (3) **1882** *Rep. Comm.*

Agric. 231 The *Poa arachnifera*, locally called Texas blue grass, has been known for many years as one of the native grasses of Texas. **1885** HAVARD *Flora W. & S. Texas* 530 Other grasses highly prized for pasture or hay . . . [include] Texas Blue Grass . . . native on the prairies of the Brazos. **1889** VASEY *Agric. Grasses* 64 Texas Blue Grass . . . was first described by Dr. John Torrey in the report of Captain Marcey's exploration of the Red River . . . as having been found on the headwaters of the Trinity. — **(4) 1889** VASEY *Agric. Grasses* 25 *Panicum Texanum* (Texas Millet). This grass is a native of Texas, and was first described and named in 1866 by Prof. S. B. Buckley. **1909** *Cent. Supp.* 810/2 Texas millet, *Panicum Texanum*, a leafy branching annual grass of much merit as a hay-grass, native and abundant near the Colorado River of Texas. Also called *Colorado grass, Austin grass, concho-grass* . . . and *bottom-* or *river-grass*.

(5) 1877 BARTLETT 790 New Orleans Moss. (*Tillandsia usneoides.*) . . . Also called Texas Moss, as it is equally abundant in that State. — **(6) 1901** MOHR *Plant Life Ala.* 61 North of the maritime belt, cow oak (*Quercus michauxii*), Texas oak (*Quercus texana*) [etc.]. **1950** *Dly. Ardmoreite* (Ardmore, Okla.) 30 April B. 6/3 Trees native to the park include post oak, . . . Texas oak, . . . and hickory. — **(7) 1885** HAVARD *Flora W. & S. Texas* 458 Other shrubs deserving mention are: The Trefoil Barberry . . . , the well known Texas Persimmon (*Diospyros Texana*). — **(8) 1909** WEBSTER, T[exas] sparrow, a finch (*Arremonops rufivirgata*) of southern Texas and Mexico. It is olive-green above with inconspicuous rufous stripes on the head and yellow on the wing. **1939** *Nat. Geog. Mag.* March 361 Chaparral thickets of the Southwest are home to the inconspicuous Texas Sparrow . . . , once known as the 'green finch.' — **(9) 1907** *Springfield W. Republican* 22 Aug. 6 The fields are dotted with clumps of white golden coreopsis, called the Texas star.

(10) 1878 *Nat. Museum Proc.* I. 119 The nests . . . are . . . readily distinguishable from those of the Texas Thrasher and Mocking-bird. — **(11) 1903** GARCIA *Shade Trees* 16 The Texas Umbrella Tree . . . is a striking tree, and in leaf, bloom, and fruit resembles the China Berry Tree. — **(12) 1901** MOHR *Plant Life Ala.* 100 On these rich uplands [in the prairie region of Ala.] the Texas white oak (*Quercus breviloba*), commonly known in this section as pin oak, is found most frequent. — **(13) 1917** *Birds of Amer.* II. 145/2 The Texas Woodpecker shows the ruling characteristic of its family in its choice of food.

d. In phrases (see quots.). *Obs.*

1830 *Ark. Gaz.* (Little Rock) 4 Aug. 3/1 In the list of accounts sent me, there are many there is no chance on earth to collect—such as the following: . . . —, runaway, gone to Texas; —, gone God only knows where. **1836** *Crockett Alman. 1837* (Nashville) 2, I told my constituents, if they did not re-elect me, they might go to hell, and I'd go to Texas. **1840** *N.Y. Mirror* 21 March 311/3 If a public defaulter absents himself, the rumor is, 'he is gone to Texas.'

Texas deck. (See quot. 1940.)

1875 MARK TWAIN *Old Times Miss.* 70 (R.), She has a fanciful pilothouse perched on top of the 'texas' deck. **1928** BRADFORD *Ol' Man Adam* 27 Tote dat planed lumber up on de texas deck. **1940** in *Amer. Sp.* XVI. 71 The Texas deck of a Mississippi (or Ohio) river steamer is the top deck, surrounding the Texas. **1948** *Sat. Review* 5 June 44/2 Round-trip fares run about $10 a day for staterooms on the cabin decks, slightly higher on the Texas decks.

Texas fever.

1. An extreme desire to go to Texas. *Obs.* Cf. **California fever.**

1825 *Austin P.* II. (1924) 1020 The emigrating, or Texas *fever* prevails to an extent that your *wishes* would no more than anticipate. **1878** *Ill. Dept. Agric. Trans.* XIV. 146 The Texas fever has called away a number.

2. An infectious parasitic fever occurring in cattle and transmitted by the cattle tick. Cf. **Spanish fever.**

1866 *Ill. Agric. Soc. Trans.* VII. 222 Another pest . . . is the 'Texas fever,' 'Spanish fever,' or 'Texas murrain,' as it is variously known. **1929** DOBIE *Vaquero* 22 In 1866, according to unreliable and apparently underestimated figures of the United States Census Bureau, 260,000 head of cattle went north. The drovers of this year generally set forth with no definite market in mind; they encountered frenzied fear of 'Texas fever.' **1949** *Land Economics* Feb. 12/1 It was not until the cattle tick and the deadly Texas fever it carried were eradicated that a livestock economy was feasible in most of the South.

b. Texas fever tick, a cattle tick, *Margaropus annulatus*, which transmits the parasite causing Texas fever.

1913 BARNES *Western Grazing Grounds* 135 An inspector of the Bureau of Animal Industry . . . looks the stock over carefully for evidences of disease, especially Texas fever ticks and mange. **1949** *N.O. Times-Picayune Mag.* 22 May 8/1 The second was a tiny pest, the Texas fever tick.

Texian ˈtɛksɪən, *a.* and *n.*

1. *n.* =**Texan,** *n.* **1.**

1835 *Franklin Repository* (Chambersburg, Pa.) 8 Dec. 1/6 Volunteers are moving from almost every section of the west to the assistance of the Texians. **1892** DUVAL *Young Explorers* 101 Never ask an old Texian ef he'll have coffee, but jess pour it out and hand it to him. **1950** *Sat. Ev. Post* 4 Feb. 4/3 Your writer . . . should at least learn the common appellation assigned to the sons of the Lone Star State is 'Texans' and not 'Texians.'

2. *a.* =**Texan,** *a.*

1836 *Charleston* (S.C.) *Patriot* 16 March, The Texian Banner was the same as that of the United States, with the exception of a single *Star* in the centre, instead of the *thirteen*. **1860** *Charleston* (S.C.) *Mercury* 13 Dec. 4/2 Threatened and impending danger and domestic tranquility admonish Texian freemen that no time is to be lost in looking to their immediate defence under their own flag.

Texican ˈtɛksəkən, *n.* A Texan.

1863 *Lawrence* (Kans.) *Republican* 16 April 2/4 (*headline*), 'Texicans' and 'Injuns' Again. **1915** YOUNG *Hard Knocks* 39 The Texicans had visited the town some five days prior and ran things to suit themselves. **1948** *Sat. Ev. Post* 10 July 80/3 He carries that pistol so that if he meets the Texican again he'll kill him?

transf. **1881** ROMSPERT *Western Echo* 194 It is not *usually* much of a job to catch and throw an animal; but sometimes there is a large, powerful, wild Texican in the bunch, and the boys have some fun.

* **textbook,** *n.* As the last term in **campaign, Democratic Campaign textbook.**

* **thank,** *v.* In colloq. expressions: **1.** *thank fortune!* a phrase of thankfulness. **2.** *thank-you-ma'am*, a slight obstruction or defect, as a hollow, ridge, or drain, in or across a road.

(1) 1845 KIRKLAND *Western Clearings* 44 'Who has Phebe Penniman got tacked to her?' 'Nobody, thank fortune!' said his mother. **1886** *Harper's Mag.* June 98/1 She was in her own coupé, thank fortune! — **(2) 1849** LONGFELLOW *Kavanagh* 56 The driver called them [*sc.* hollows in the snow] 'thank-you-ma'ams,' because they made everybody bow. [**1889** MELLICK *Story Old Farm* 3 The stage rattles on, and reaching a short incline bounces over a 'thankee-marm.'] **1945** PEARSON *Country Flavor* 74 The technical part of road building in those days was simple . . . stones and rocks in the known mudholes; thank-you-ma'ams on the hills.

* **thanksgiving,** *n.*

1. (*cap.*) =**Thanksgiving day.** Cf. **Continental thanksgiving.**

[**1632** *Mass. Bay Rec.* I. 96 The Court . . . hath appoyncted the 13th day of this present moneth [June] to be kept as a day of publique thanksgiuing throughout the seuerall plantacions.] **1778** CUTLER in *Life & Corr.* I. 73 This day [Dec. 30] appointed by Congress as a day of Thanksgiving through the United States of America. **1863** LINCOLN in G. W. Douglas *Amer. Book of Days* 589, [I] invite my fellow citizens . . . to set apart and observe the last Thursday of November next as a day of thanksgiving and praise to our beneficent Father who dwelleth in the heavens. **1949** *Democrat* 24 Nov. 1/7 Thanksgiving in Grove Hill is expected to follow the usual pattern.

attrib. **1788** *Mass. Centinel* 30 July 155/3 Cato . . . [and] one of his brethren of colour . . . were staggering home from a frolic on a thanksgiving eve. **1849** *Knickerb.* XXXIV. 556 This is *Thanksgiving Night*. **1945** WALLACE *Barington* 87 At Thanksgivingtime huge, yellow pumpkins were placed about the store.

2. A blessing or grace said in connection with a meal. *Obs.*

1650 *Harvard Rec.* I. 35 Neither may any Schollar rise from his place or goe out of the Hall at meal-times before thanksgiving bee ended.

3. In special combs.: (1) **Thanksgiving bird,** =**Thanksgiving turkey;** (2) **day,** an American holiday proclaimed annually by the President since 1863 and designed as a day of public thanksgiving for divine blessing [first observed by the Plymouth colony in 1621, proclaimed for the nation by Washington in 1789]; (3) **dinner,** a dinner, usu. especially elaborate, served on Thanksgiving day; (4) **turkey,** a turkey served as a traditionally appropriate part of a Thanksgiving dinner.

(1) 1870 BILL *Florida* 146 Shouldering our Thanksgiving-bird, we reached camp, and were congratulated heartily by our companions. — **(2) 1674** JOSSELYN *Two Voyages* 214, I returned to Boston again, the next day being Thanksgiving day. **1781** PETERS *Hist. Conn.* (1820) 142 Those religionists preach damnation to all people who neglect to attend public worship twice every Sabbath, fasting and thanksgiving day. **1836** *S. Lit. Messenger* II. 746 As ever I hope to eat pumpkin pie thanksgiving day, that's no English trader. **1945** *N. Eng. Homestead* 10 Nov. 8/2 It was not until 1863, and largely through the efforts of Mrs. Sarah J. Hale, that Thanksgiving Day was set each year by presidential proclamation. — **(3) 1830** *Workingman's Gaz.* (Woodstock, Vt.) 1 Dec. 78/2 They have added to the comfort and happiness of those, whose scanty pittance would hardly allow them to enjoy the luxuries of Thanksgiving dinner. **1946** *Chi. D. News* 7 Nov. 6/5 Turkey and the traditional Thanksgiving dinner trimmings are en route to U.S. soldiers all over the world. — **(4) 1829** *Va. Herald* (Fredericksburg) 25 April 4/1 (*heading*), A Thanksgiving Turkey. **1927** BENÉT *J. B.'s Body* 317 Mr. Lincoln's Thanksgivin' turkey, . . . [is] still not carved.

* **that,** *pron.* In colloq. uses.

1. *at that,* even so, into the bargain.

1830 *Mass. Spy* 28 July (Th.), The march was now hurried on, yet slow at that, for I could not walk fast. **1897** *Amer. Pediatric Soc. Trans.* IX. 73 The infant was underfed, and did not receive the correct food at that. **1925** *Red Book Mag.* Oct. 43/2 There was something in her point of view at that.

2. *that's so,* that is true, also *that is so, that so?*

1857 *Knickerb.* XLIX. 86 One of the quaintest, quietest, most musical, and most engaging forms of acquiescence is in the new and popular phrase of 'That's so,' which is working its way into common parlance. **1876** *Cong. Rec.* 3 Aug. 5134/1 That is so. That is what the Chair has ruled. **1891** RYAN *Pagan* 93 'That so?' she said.

* **thatch,** *n.*

1. Any one of various tall, coarse grasses, esp. of the genus *Spartina,* common along the north Atlantic Coast of the U.S. In full **thatch grass.** *Obs.* Cf. **creek thatch.**

1695 *Providence Rec.* VI. 156 That Parcell of Meadow marsh & thatch . . . belongeth to me. **1704** *Ib.* XI. 90 Care might be taken for the orderly Cutting of the thatch Grass. **1797** TRUMBULL *Hist. Conn.* (1898) I. iii, Where lands were thus burned there grew bent grass, or as some called it, thatch, two, three and four feet high.

2. In expressions designating places where such grass grows, as (1) **thatch bank,** (2) **bed,** (3) **cove,** (4) **ground,** (5) **meadow,** (6) **share.**

(1) 1718 *N.H. Probate Rec.* II. 73, I give to Collo. Georg Vaughan all . . . ye marsh and the thatch bank of Crooked lane. **1793** BENTLEY *Diary* II. 67 Our reckoning began in the Thatch bank. — **(2) 1682** *Providence Rec.* XV. 238 Sume kare may bee taken Consarning the thach beeds. **1757** *Smithtown Rec.* 407 On the beach thatch bed we allow six acres and sixteen rods for one lot. **1841** *Huntington Rec.* III. 379 All the several thatch beds & meadow within the said bounds . . . [are conveyed] unto Jacob Scudder. — **(3) 1711** *Providence Rec.* XVI. 66, I give . . . my share of thach Cove. — **(4) 1718** *N.H. Probate Rec.* I. 532 A Peice of Marsh & Thatch Ground Lyeing by the Boare's Head.

(5) 1841 *Huntington Rec.* III. 379 [This Indenture] doth convey a certain piece of thatch meadow. — **(6) 1746** *N.H. Probate Rec.* III. 362, I Give unto my son . . . two thach shares.

* **thaw,** *v. To thaw out,* to free from the effects of cold, to become warm. Also transf. and fig.

1785 CUTLER in *Life & Corr.* II. 228 This cold snowy winter has considerably cooled my zeal, but when I get thawed out, in the spring, perhaps it may return. **1835** INGRAHAM *South-West* I. 33 When vessels in their winter voyages . . . become coated with ice, . . . they seek the genial warmth of this region [the Gulf Stream in the latitude of Baltimore] to 'thaw out,' as this dissolving process is termed by the sailors. **1910** MCCUTCHEON *Rose in Ring* 177 He could save us a lot of trouble if he'd thaw out and hand over some of the money he's hiding.

* **theater,** *n.* **1. theater bee,** =next. *Rare.* **2. theater party,** a social entertainment consisting largely of attendance at a theater; a group of people who go to the theater together.

(1) 1897 FLANDRAU *Harvard Episodes* 268 Returned 'theatre bees' came there to scramble eggs and drink beer. — **(2) 1883** *Cent. Mag.* Sep. 787/1 This City . . . has no more interesting social life than is shown in a report of . . . Mrs. Dash's theater party. **1907** A. THOMAS *Witching Hour* (1925) I. 110 In the same theater party a girl's got to listen or leave the box.

As the last term in **boudoir, marionette, nickel, Orleans theater.**

theme song. A recurring and characterizing melody in a musical performance. Also transf. — **1929** *Variety* 3 April 20/2 Musical accompaniment is agreeable and theme song has possibilities as a ballad plug, being pure musical hoke. **1950** *Chi. Tribune* 17 July 26/3 The theme song is 'Water water everywhere,—but not a drop to drink.'

* **theological,** *a.* **1. theological school,** =next. **2. theological seminary,** a divinity school, a school in which students are trained in theology.

(1) 1807 in *Union Theol. Sem. Va. Centennial Cat.* (1907) 7 The head of the theological school must be the president of Hampden-Sidney College. **1909** *Religion & Life* Pref. Note, This volume comprises addresses made by members of the teaching community of the Meadville Theological School. — **(2) 1810** in *Union Theol. Sem. Va. Centennial Cat.* (1907) 7 It was chiefly from a regard to a theological seminary lately established at this place that I was induced to accept the presidency of Hampden-Sidney College. **1915** *Current Opin.* Feb. 113/1 His reportorial preconception of theological seminaries got a jolt. **1950** *Seminary Rev.* Jan. 2 Evangelical Theological Seminary is one of the graduate professional schools of the Evangelical United Brethren Church.

* **theory,** *n.* As the last term in **rain belt, State rights theory.**

therblig ˈθɜblɪg, *n.* [Coined by F. B. *Gilbreth* (1864–1924), an Amer. engineer, by spelling his name backwards with a slight variation.] One of the units of motion or thought into which the act of doing something may be analyzed. Also attrib.

1931 *Lit. Digest* 17 Jan. 26/2 The motions of the operator are broken down into fundamental motions known as 'therbligs.' **1938** W. G. HOLMES *Applied Time & Motion Study* 219 This therblig covers the duty and activity of the three therbligs, Search, Find, and Select. **1948** E. E. GHISELLI & C. W. BROWN *Personnel & Industrial Psychology* 279 This therblig type of classification of movements is important principally in such problems as classifying the sequence of movements and in the elimination of unnecessary movements.

* **there,** *adv. To have been there,* to have had previous experience, hence to know at first hand. *Colloq.* — **1885** *Wkly. New Mexican Rev.* 29 Jan. 4/5 The Santa Rifles had their first drill at Alhambra hall last night. . . . Nearly all the boys have 'been thar' before, and as a consequence, catch up the command very readily.

thermal belt. A limited area on the sloping side of a mountain in which the vegetation escapes, at least in part, frost damage. Also **thermal zone.** — **1862** *Rep. Comm. Patents 1861: Agric.* 146 The beautiful phenomenon of the 'Verdant Zone' or 'Thermal Belt' exhibits itself upon our mountain sides, commencing about three hundred feet vertical height above the valleys. **1883** ZEIGLER & GROSSCUP *Alleghanies* 192 Horticulturists are just beginning to appreciate the advantages of the thermal or 'no frost' zone.

thermolamp ˈθɜməˌlæmp, *n.* A device for supplying illumination by the use of inflammable gas. *Obs.* — **1802** *Med. Repository* V. 474 The theory of the Thermolamp . . . merely consists of exposing . . . any thing that contains carbon and phlogiston, to a high heat, in a close apparatus. **1805** SILLIMAN *Jrnl. Travels* (1812) I. 237 It is the same thing with the thermo-lamp of which you have heard much in America.

thermos ˈθɜməs, *n.* [Gk., hot.] A bottle so made that liquids may be kept at a desired temperature for a considerable time. Usu. **Thermos bottle,** a trade-mark name for a bottle of this kind.

1908 *Sat. Ev. Post* 15 Aug. 21/1 The Thermos Bottle keeps baby's sterilized milk at feeding temperature day or night. **1948** *Nat. Geog. Mag.* Aug. 233/1 Our host walked down from his house with a gallon thermos of hot coffee. **1950** *Time* 3 April 24/3 Simon began to pack blankets and Thermoses for a fishing trip.

Also **thermos jug.**

1938 NORRIS *Bricks Without Straw* 350 He poured a glass of water from his thermos jug.

theses collector. (See quot. 1814.) *Obs.* — **1759** *Holyoke Diaries* 20 Theses Collectors, (John) Lowell, (John) Warren. **1814** *Harvard Laws* 35 The president, professors, tutors, annually, sometime in the third term, shall select from the junior class a number of theses collectors, to prepare theses for the next year.

Thespian society. A society of amateur actors and actresses. *Obs.*

1845 SOL. SMITH *Theatr. Apprent.* 36, I never knew any good to come from Thespian societies. **1848** *Santa Fe Repub.* 8 Jan. 4/3 Thespian Society—A society of this kind has been formed in our town for the present winter. **1863** MASSETT *Drifting About* 21 A lot of young students started a Thespian Society.

* **thick,** *a.* In combs.: (1) **thick-bark(ed) juniper,** the alligator juniper, *Juniperus pachyphloea,* of the southwestern U.S.; (2) **-billed guillemot,** (see quot. 1917); (3) **-billed parrot,** a green parrot with red markings, *Rhynchopsitta pachyrhyncha,* found in the Southwest; (4) **-joint,** a variety of tobacco, *obs.;* (5) * **set,** (see quots.), *obs.,* cf. **Piper's thickset;** (6) **shellbark hickory,** the king nut, *Carya laciniosa.*

(1) [**1857** *Rep. Explorations Pacific R.R.* (War Dept.) IV. 142 On the Zuñi Mountains, Western New Mexico, . . . is the thick-barked Juniperus.] **1885** HAVARD *Flora W. & S. Texas* 503 Thick-bark Juniper . . . furnishes . . . a yellow, aromatic, transparent balsam. **1897** SUDWORTH *Arborescent Flora* 99. — **(2) 1835** AUDUBON *Ornith. Biog.* III. 142 The Foolish Guillemot . . . lays only a single egg, which is the case with the Thick-billed Guillemot also. **1917** *Birds of Amer.* I. 27 Brünnich's Murre. *Uria lomvia lomvia.* . . . [Also called] Thick-billed Guillemot; Thick-billed Murre. . . . Similar to common Murre . . . ; bill, shorter and stouter. — **(3) 1917** *Birds of Amer.* II. 124 The Thick-billed Parrot appears to be either very stupid or very curious. . . . The birds are most likely to be encountered in the piñon pine forests. . . . In the United States they are found chiefly in the cañons of the Chiricahua Mountains, in Arizona. **1939** LINCOLN *Migration* 103 As an exemplar of vagrant migration from south to north, the Thick-billed Parrot may be cited. — (4) *c***1775** BOUCHER *Glossary* p. l, In *twist-bud, thick-joint, bull-face, leather-coat,* I'd toil all day. **1788** SCHÖPF *Reise* I. 540 Die Maryländischen und Virginischen Tobackpflanzer unterscheiden vielerley Abarten von Toback, nach dessen Wachsthum: also Long-green, Thick-joint, Brazil, Shoestring u.s.w.

(5) (*a*) **1714** *Boston News-Letter* 8 March 2/2 To be Sold . . . very good Thicksetts of all colours. **1762** *Essex Inst. Coll.* LXIX. 277 Had on . . . a Pair of Snuff-colour'd Thickset Breeches. **1809** KENDALL *Travels* II. 26 Jeans, fustians, thicksetts, velvets and other fabrics are manufactured in Providence. (*b*) **1784** SMYTH *Tour U.S.* II. 129 There are seven different kinds of tobacco . . . named Hudson, Frederick, Thick-joint, Shoe-string, Thickset [etc.]. — (6) **1810** MICHAUX *Arbres* I. 20 *Thick shell-bark hickery,* . . . nom donné dans les Etats de l'ouest où elle est le plus souvent confondue avec le vrai *Shell bark Hickery.* **1897** SUDWORTH *Arborescent Flora* 114 *Hicoria laciniosa.* . . Common Names [include] . . . Thick Shellbark Hickory (N.C., Ark.).

* **thicken,** *v.* **1.** *intr.* Of ice: To continue to freeze so as to become increasingly thick. **2.** *tr.* To increase the population of (an area). **3.** *To thicken up,* to become angry. All *colloq.* and *obs.*

(1) **1808** PIKE *Sources Miss.* 42 Ice in the river thickening. — (2) **1814** BRACKENRIDGE *Views La.* 116 It is perhaps good policy in our government . . . to thicken the frontier, and to suffer the intermediate space to fill up gradually. — (3) **1841** COOPER *Deerslayer* iii, You're not thick'ning up about a small remark, I hope. **1844** UNCLE SAM *Peculiarities* I. 161, I don't thicken up without calculation.

* **thicket,** *n.* As the last term in **bay, cedar, curl-leaf, laurel, mesquite, papaw thicket.**

* **thief,** *n.* As the last term in **bunko, canal, cattle, chicken, corn, horse, maize, Negro, panel, river, sneak, timber, water thief.**

* **thimble,** *n.*

1. In the name of, or in allusion to, a play party guessing game involving the hiding and finding of a thimble.

1782 DALRYMPLE *Journal* 36 We have diverted ourselves playing . . . *hide the thimble.* **1833** *Sketches D. Crockett* 49 Plays which had been fashionable when their grandmothers were girls, such as Sell the Thimble . . . were called up and wearied out. **1865** in RIDLEY *Battles* (1906) 481 Games soon began—'Thimble,' 'Snap,' and kissing songs.

2. A short piece of metal tubing attached to the underside of the barrel of a muzzle-loading gun for securing the ramrod.

1835 LONGSTREET *Ga. Scenes* 227 The thimbles were made, one of brass, one of iron, and one of tin. *a***1918** G. STUART *On Frontier* I. 33 From two to four small pieces of iron or brass tubing [were] called thimbles. **1950** *Asheville* (N.C.) *Citizen-Times* 26 March VII. 6/4 This ramrod was carried in thimbles under the barrel.

3. In combs.: (1) **thimble bell,** a small ornamental bell resembling a thimble; (2) **belt,** a belt having loops for cartridges; (3) **bib,** ?a bib nozzle; (4) **party,** a sewing party, *colloq.;* (5) **skein,** a conical sheath for the spindle of an axle, also attrib.; (6) **thrift,** petty thrift.

(1) **1899** CUSHMAN *Hist. Indians* 501 The monotonous tinkling and rattling of the thimble bells and terrapin shells [in the dance] could be heard. — (2) **1901** *N. Amer. Rev.* Feb. 231 The thimble belt, used only by the Americans, is still preferred to the cartridge pouches of the others. — (3) **1897** F. C. MOORE *How to Build a Home* 124 Supply with hot and cold water through 3/4-inch flange and thimble bibbs. — (4) **1906** *Springfield W. Republican* 7 Feb. 5 The women of Christ church will hold a thimble party at the home of Mrs. William Yorrall.

(5) **1865** *Chi. Tribune* 10 April, Manufacturers of Leonard's Patent Seamless Thimble Skeins. **1907** COOK *Border & Buffalo* (1938) 216 He drove into camp with a four-mule team and new thimble-skein wagon. — (6) **1910** C. HARRIS *Eve's Husband* 286 [In] women's characters . . . penuriousness . . . has been reduced . . . to a sort of thimble thrift.

b. In the names of plants and animals: (1) **thimble berry, blackberry,** any one of various American raspberries or blackberries having fruit shaped like a thimble; (2) **eye,** the chub mackerel, in full **thimble-eye(d) mackerel;** (3) **fish,** (see quot.); (4) **flower,** (see quot.); (5) **weed,** the wood anemone, or any one of various plants of the genera *Rudbeckia* or *Petalostemon.*

(1) **1788** HASWELL in Bancroft *N.W. Coast* I. 713 We often met with gooseberries, raspberries, currants, blackberries, strawberries, and thimbleberries. **1883** *Cent. Mag.* Sep. 681/2 The tall thimble blackberries grew in abundance. **1946** STANWELL-FLETCHER *Driftwood Valley* 219 Here the devil's-club gave way, thank God, to a dense growth of alders, azaleas, and thimbleberry. — (2) **1815** *Lit. & Phil. Soc. N.Y. Trans.* I. 422 Thimble eyed, bull eyed, or chub mackerel. (*Scomber grex.*) . . . Comes occasionally in prodigious numbers to the coast of New-York in autumn. **1884** GOODE *Fisheries* I. 303 The Chub Mackerel, . . . or, as it is called the 'Thimble-eye,' . . . closely resembles in general appearance the common Mackerel. **1911** *Rep. Fisheries* 308/1. — (3) **1885** J. S. KINGSLEY *Stand. Nat. Hist.* I. 93 One of the most abundant medusae at times in the neighborhood of the Florida Keys is a Discophore, called by naturalists *Linerges,* and known to fisherman there as the 'thimble fish.' — (4) **1840** DEWEY *Mass. Flowering Plants* 140 *Rudbeckia laciniata.*—Often called Thimble Flower, from the length and size of the cone-part of the flower. **1932** WILDER *Little House in Big Woods* 113 The grass grew green again and the woods were full of wild flowers. Buttercups and violets, thimble flowers and tiny starry glassflower were everywhere.

(5) **1833** EATON *Botany* (ed. 6) 19 *Anemone virginiana,* wind-flower, thimble weed. **1848** BARTLETT 354 *Thimble Weed* . . . is one of the herbs prepared by the Shakers, and is used in medicine for its diuretic and tonic properties. **1931** CLUTE *Plants* 39 Many plants were named for their likeness to other things, as the thimble weed (*Anemone cylindrica*) whose rough heads of fruit were very suggestive of green thimbles. **1949** PALMER *Fieldbook Nat. Hist.* 189/2 Tall Anemone, Thimbleweed. *Anemone virginiana.*

* **thin,** *a.* **1. thin dime,** *fig.* the least amount of money. *Slang.* **2. thin grass,** any one of various plants of the genus *Agrostis* having unusually thin panicles. **3. thin hominy,** see **hominy 1. c.**

(1) **1931** *K.C. Times* 4 Nov., Following the suggestion we frisked every pocket of our old suit and didn't find a thin dime. — (2) **1814** BIGELOW *Florula Bostoniensis* 22 *Trichodium laxiflorum,* Thingrass, . . . is readily known by its very thin, spreading, capillary panicle. **1901** MOHR *Plant Life Ala.* 76 Thin grass (*Agrostis perennans*) with its weak, decumbent stems, occurs [in the 'rock houses' of the Warrior table-land].

* **thing,** *n.* As the last term in **big, good, soft, square, sure thing.**

* **third,** *a.*

1. *absol.* = **third base.**

1857 *Spirit of Times* 10 Oct. 85/2 England, on the third, put out six men. **1917** MATHEWSON *Second Base Sloan* 246 The Billies caused consternation by . . . advancing a man to third on a sacrifice and an error. **1949** *Sat. Ev. Post* 19 March 140/4 The ball was hit sharply into the hole between third and short.

2. In combs.: (1) **third base,** in baseball, the base to the pitcher's right as he faces the home plate, also the playing position centering on this base or short for next; (2) **baseman,** a baseball player stationed at third base; (3) **bottom,** see * **bottom 2;** (4) * **class,** see as a main entry; (5) **clerk,** on a river steamboat, a clerk ranking below the first and second clerks; (6) * **degree,** severe treatment, sometimes brutality, inflicted by police on a prisoner in an effort to secure information from him, also transf.; (7) **house,** see as a main entry; (8) **man,** meaning unknown (see quot.), *obs.;* (9) * **party,** see as a main entry; (10) **rail,** (*a*) (see quots.), *obs.,* (*b*) in some types of electric railways, an additional rail which carries an electric current; (11) **strike,** in baseball, the final strike permitted a batter; (12) **term,** see as a main entry.

(1) **1845** in *Appletons' Ann. Cyclo.* XXV. 77/2 A ball knocked outside the range of the first or third base is foul. **1856** *Spirit of Times* 20 Dec. 260/3 Thomas, as third base—a good batter, but ought to have his eyes on the ball instead of looking over the field. **1866** CHADWICK *Base-Ball Player* 29 The Third Base is quite as important a position as the others, and it requires its occupant to be a good player. **1946** *Chi. Sun* 2 July 25/3 He can start a club that would have a Red Sox star at every position except third base and right field. — (2) **1857** *Spirit of Times* 7 Feb. 373/1 Mr. Scott, their third base man, is always at his post. **1866** CHADWICK *Base-Ball Player* 29 A player who catches with his left hand will not make a good Third Baseman. **1949** *News-Herald* (Marshfield, Wis.) 16 July 9/4 Six of the miscues were charged to third baseman Junior Bauer.

(5) **1883** MARK TWAIN *Life on Miss.* xxxvii, Among the forty-seven wounded were the captain, chief mate, second mate, and second and third clerks. — (6) **1900** *Everybody's Mag.* Nov. 406 From time to time a prisoner . . . claims to have had the Third Degree administered to him. **1949** *Chi. D. News* 5 July 1/1 His first military days are more like the third degree. — (8) **1865** CATE *Two Soldiers* 191 After being entertained with music and conversation we were introduced to an amusing game or play called 'scissors,' also a very laughable one

called 'the third man.' We laughed over these innocent amusements until my sides were sore.

(10) (*a*) **1867** *Comm. & Fin. Chron.* 29 June 808 It is throughout a double track road, and a third rail is laid . . . for the accommodation of the wide cars of that line. **1868** *Ib.* VI. 247/2 The consolidated company . . . intend to . . . lay down a third rail for the wide gauge. (*b*) **1918** MORLEY *Shandygaff* 265 As the door closed I pushed a decrepit clergyman outside, and I hope he fell on the third rail. — **(11) 1867** *Ball Players' Chron.* 11 July 1/2 Birdsall, instead of throwing the ball to Goldie, as is generally done, threw it to Martin at second, thereby cutting off Bailey, for the batsman, not having been put out on the third strike, was forced to run to his base, thereby forcing Bailey to vacate it. **1948** *Time* 10 May 62/3 The catcher couldn't handle Radcliffe's fast drop on one third strike.

b. *To play third fiddle*, to occupy a very inferior position. *Colloq.*

1866 MARK TWAIN *Lett. Sandwich Islands* 9 America . . . is out in the cold now, and does not even play third fiddle to this European element.

* **third class.**

1. The classification of U.S. mail which includes printed matter other than newspapers and periodicals. Also attrib.

1863 *Statutes at Large* XII. 705 The third class embraces . . . all pamphlets, occasional publications, books . . . maps, prints, engravings, . . . cards, . . . seeds, cuttings, bulbs [etc.]. **1894** *N.Y. P.O.* 10 July, Press clippings . . . are mailable at the third class rate of postage. **1949** *Capital Jrnl.* (Salem, Ore.) 27 July 4/2 Postal authorities in Washington are trying to blame the deficit of the post office department on the fact it has to carry third-class mail—which is paid for.

2. Attrib. in the general sense of poor or inferior.

1866 *Rep. Indian Affairs* 288 The soil is extremely light and divided into ridges of sand and marsh, . . . which may be called third-class farming land. **1902** *Harper's Mag.* May 879/1 It is too late to make a third-class student of me.

3. third classman, at the U.S. Naval Academy, a student in his second year. Cf. * **first classman.**

1888 DORSEY *Midshipman Bob* 128 His class-mates backed him to a man, . . . and even the third-classmen were divided.

third house.

1. A burlesque organization made up of newspapermen and hangers-on at a legislative session.

1849 *Alta California* (S.F.) 31 Dec. 1 The solicitude manifested by the members of the legislature to ascertain where they are to get their mileage and per diem, is a subject of much jocularity among the *third house.* **1864** *Gold Hill* (Nev.) *News* 25 Jan. 2/3 Governor Mark Twain: —Understanding from certain members of the Third House of the Territorial Legislature [etc.]. **1912** A. B. PAINE *Mark Twain* I. 244 The two Houses of the last territorial legislature of Nevada assembled January 12, 1864. A few days later a 'Third House' was organized—an institution quite in keeping with the happy atmosphere of that day and locality, for it was a burlesque organization, and Mark Twain was selected as its 'Governor.'

2. A lobby in attendance on a legislative body. Also attrib.

1852 *S.F. Dispatch* 18 Jan. 2/2 The *San Joaquin Republican* contains the Inaugural Message of R. H. Taylor, the Governor of the 3d House or lobby members. **1886** POORE *Reminiscences* II. 44 The people who nightly assembled to see and to take part in the entertainments of the house consisted of . . . master workmen of the third house, the lobby. **1946** THOMPSON *Amer. Daughter* 71 Before the 'Third House' banquet, farmer-politicians sought after him. **1950** *Look* 31 Jan. 24/1 In a state where the Third House, the lobbyists, . . . spend millions every year . . . , a legislator going on a payroll for 75 bucks a week is looked upon as just a precedent-setting price cutter, undermining the foundations of a fine profession.

thirdling law. (See quot.) *Obs.* — **1862** *Harper's Mag.* April 715/1 A law of the State [Georgia] at that time, called a thirdling law, allowed a man to pay one-third of a judgment against him in cash.

third party.

1. *Polit.* A party organized as an independent rival of the two major parties.

1801 F. AMES *Works* (1859) II. 138 He is a very weak or very presumptuously vain man, who can think of organizing a third party. **1884** *Cent. Mag.* Nov. 132 The formulation of these 'third-parties' . . . is on the whole a public misfortune. **1948** *Dly. Ardmoreite* (Ardmore, Okla.) 2 April 6/2 A third party has as much place in American politics as does a third party on a honeymoon.

b. Attrib. with **campaign, man, movement, paper, prohibition.**

1804 *Fredericktown* (Md.) *Herald* 10 Nov. 2/2 We have hitherto used rather more forbearance towards a democratic print published in this city, called the Freeman's Journal, or *third party paper*, than its conduct has entitled it to. **1805** *N.-Eng. Palladium* (Boston) 26 July 2/5 He did not wish (or intend) to support a paper controlled by a third-party man. **1884** *Cent. Mag.* Nov. 150 The only 'third party' movement of note has been captured by a 'politician' who repudiates civil service reform. **1887** *Boston Jrnl.* 23 Aug. 5/4 Some of the well-meaning people who have gone daft upon third party prohibition may not understand it. **1948** *This Week Mag.* 13 June 5/2 Henry Wallace's third-party campaign is unique.

Also **third partyism, partyist.** *Obs.*

1845 *Xenia Torch-Light* 31 July 3/3 The editor of the Voice of Freedom . . . [has] manfully renounced his third partyism. **1889** *Voice* 10 Jan., [They] gloat over the fact that the temperance men in the Republican party outnumber the 'third partyists' seven to one.

third term. An additional term of office for one who has already served two terms, often with reference to the presidency of the U.S.

1833 *Niles' Reg.* XLV. 202/2 A late preposterous suggestion that president Jackson may be induced to stand for a third term of the presidency. **1888** BRYCE *Amer. Commonw.* II. II. xlix. 103 In those [states] which do not [limit the governor's re-eligibility] there seems to exist no tradition forbidding a third term. **1950** *So. Wkly.* 22 March 3/1 The opportunity to solidify a Liberal Democratic Party and stand in history as its creator constitutes one of the greatest appeals the third term has for Harry Truman.

Also **third termer** and (*obs.*) **third termery, termism.**

1876 *Harper's Wkly.* 15 July 584 Cæsarism—Third-Termism Vanquished. **1880** *Chi. Tribune* 1 June 1/7 Everywhere there was unmistakable evidence of an obstinate determination to rescue the Republican party from the rock of third-termism. *Ib.* 2/1 The arbitrary action of Cameron unmasks the purpose of the third-termers. *Ib.* 9 June 1/5 Third-Termism Buried. . . . Boss Government Abolished. **1890** *Cin. Comm.-Gaz.* 30 June, There would be no thirdtermery in it, as he [Cleveland] had not two consecutive terms. **1912** *Harper's Wkly.* 5 Oct. 7/2 Haven't the Third-Termers overreached a bit in California?

* **thirteen,** *a.* In combs.: (1) **Thirteen Colonies,** and variants, the colonies which became the thirteen original states of the Federal Union; (2) **fires,** in Indian speech, the original thirteen states, *obs.*; (3) **stars,** the stars in the original flag of the U.S.; (4) **states,** and variants, the original states making up the Federal Union; (5) **stripes,** the flag of the U.S., the stars and stripes; (6) **-year locust,** an alleged variety of locust, *obs.*

(1) 1776 *Huntington Rec.* III. 6 Yesterday the Freedom and Independence of the Thirteen United Colonies was . . . proclaimed. **1941** S. V. BENÉT *Listen to People* (1942) 471 There are the pretty girls with their hair curled Who represent the Thirteen Colonies. **1949** MURRAY *This Our Land* 73 The migration from the thirteen original colonies to western territories . . . now swelled to a mighty stream. — **(2) 1787** E. DENNY *Journal* 106 As a pledge of remembrance of the thirteen great fires (the thirteen United States), he presented each tribe with thirteen strings of white wampum. **1847** HOWE *Hist. Coll. Ohio* 142 Their people . . . determined to make a permanent peace with the 'Thirteen Fires,' as they called the federal states. — **(3) 1779** *N.J. Archives* 2 Ser. III. 279 The subscriber . . . now keeps a Tavern: . . . he intends to put up the sign of thirteen stars at said house, and is furnished with every necessary for entertainment. — **(4) 1776** *Declaration of Independence*, The unanimous Declaration of the thirteen united States of America. **1806** *Ann. 9th Congress* 1 Sess. 558 The true territory of the United States, . . . the good old United States—part of Georgia, of the old thirteen States. **1886** ALTON *Among Law-Makers* 10 The people of the thirteen original states were represented in the House by sixty-five members. **1950** *Chi. Tribune* 23 Feb. 4/4 Our 13 original states found that survival and progress depend on closer association and common effort.

(5) 1808 *Ann. 10th Cong.* 2 Sess. 77 In the meantime the thirteen stripes were displayed with increasing frequency and numbers along the coasts of Europe. — **(6) 1846** *Dollar Newspaper* (Phila.) 17 June 2/3 The locusts are said to be thirteen years' locusts, having made their appearance before this time in 1833.

***thirteener,** *n.* Something or someone left over, in allusion to thirteen as an unlucky number (see also quot. 1891). — **1849** MELVILLE *Redburn* 56 They were all chosen but me; . . . I was a thirteener. **1891** *Cent.* 6295/2 *Thirteener*, . . . in whist, the last card of a suit left in the hands of a player after the other twelve have been played.

* **thirty,** *a.* and *n.*

1. (See quot. 1895.) Also transf.

1889 *Kansas Times & Star* 7 May, At midnight '30' (the end) flashed out on a large floral 'sounder' and a majority of the guests . . . adjourned. **1895** *Funk's Standard Dict.*, Thirty, . . . among printers and telegraphers, the last sheet, word, or line of copy or of a despatch; the last; the end. **1947** *Sooner Mag.* Nov. 22/2 He had just written the editorial sign '30' to the copy of Volume 20, No. 4, of the publication which he had founded and over which he had presided for 20 years. **1948** *Dly. Ardmoreite* (Ardmore, Okla.) 13 April 1/8 (*heading*), Famed Editor Answers to '30.'

2. In combs.: (1) **thirty-cent,** used attrib. in the sense of cheap, paltry, *colloq.;* (2) **days,** a month; (3) **-six thirty,** the degree of latitude agreed upon in the Missouri Compromise as that north of which no slave state except Missouri would be formed from the Louisiana territory; (4) **years' consumption,** ?consumption that lasts for thirty years, *rare.*

(1) 1944 *Chi. D. News* 31 July 3/6 (*heading*), Sues to Make Uncle Sam Feel Like a 30-Cent Refund. — **(2) 1928** *Publishers' Wkly.* 30 June 2596 The ideal turnover would be about every thirty days or twelve times a year. — **(3) 1857** BENTON *Exam. Dred Scott Case* 150 Northern men who would not agree to spread slavery over the broad expanse of all that half of California, New Mexico and Utah, which lies south of 36°30'. **1865** PIKE *Scout & Ranger* (1932) 105 We pushed on . . . to the famous line of 36°30'. — **(4) 1842** *Lowell Offering* II. 4 Did you ever hear of the 'thirty years' consumption'? a disease at present unknown in New England.

As the last term in **buyer, seven, six thirty.**

* **thistle,** *n.* In combs.: (1) **thistle bird,** a goldfinch; (2) **poppy,** = **prickly poppy;** (3) **sage,** a salvia, *S. carduacea,* found in the western U.S.

(1) 1808 WILSON *Ornithology* I. 21 [Goldfinches] pass by various names expressive of their food, color, &c. such as Thistle-bird, Lettuce-bird [etc.]. **1893** *Scribner's Mag.* June 763/1 'Thistle bird' is another name that he bears. **1939** HARRIS *Purslane* 90 She threw a handful of fruit at a flock of sparrows until she heard the familiar 'Per-chic-o-ree, per-chic-o-ree' and recognized a thistle bird. — **(2) 1908** HORNADAY *Camp Fires on Desert* 32 We also noted three white thistle-poppies. **1911** CHASE *Yosemite Trails* 315 The trail wound among shady flats where grew myriads of the thistle-poppy. — **(3) 1909** WEBSTER. **1947** *So. Sierran* May 4/2 On the desert we noted the exquisite beauty of the thistle sage whose frilled lavender-blue petals and orange stamens also give it the name of Persian Prince.

As the last term in **bull, Canada, Canadian, coyote, English, Russian thistle.**

Thomas('s) elm. [David *Thomas,* of N.Y. State.] The rock elm, *Ulmus racemosa,* of the eastern states. — **1843** TORREY *Flora N.Y.* II. 166 Thomas's Elm. White Elm. . . . Banks of rivers in the western part of the State; rather frequent. **1897** SUDWORTH *Arborescent Flora* 182 Cork Elm. . . . Thomas Elm (Tenn.)

Thompson seedless. A California raisin grape—a popular synonym for the Sultanina, a variety derived from *Vitis vinifera.*

1894 *Land of Sunshine* (Nov.) 121/2 The Thompson's Seedless is a comparatively new raisin grape, yet widely disseminated and well tested. **1906** *Out West* April 341 The varieties of raisin grapes include . . . the seedless varieties of Sultana and Thompson Seedless. **1949** *L.A. Times* 2 July 5/4 Twelve hundred skilled workers are picking, packing and trucking the Thompson seedless grapes.

Thomsonian tɑm'sonɪən, *a.* and *n.* Also **Thompsonian.** [Dr. Samuel *Thomson* (1769–1843), of Mass.]

1. *n.* A believer in or practitioner of a system of medicine advocated by Dr. Thomson, who stressed the use of vegetable preparations and steam baths. *Obs.*

1848 DUNGLISON *Med. Lexicon* 833/1 The Thompsonians are Botanic Physicians. **1850** COLTON *3 Years Calif.* 61 The Indians here are practical Thomsonians or Hydropathists; they sweat for every kind of disease. **1864** NICHOLS *Amer. Life* I. 364 There are . . . chronothermalists, Thompsonians, Mesmerists [etc.].

2. Thomsonian (steam) doctor, a doctor who practices medicine in accordance with the principles approved by Dr. Thomson. Now *hist.* Cf. **steam doctor.**

1830 *Backwoodsman* (Xenia, Ohio) 12 Aug. 1/5 Mr. Litch is one of the Thompsonian steam doctors. **1859** BARTLETT 477 *Thompsonian Doctor,* a physician who follows the Thompsonian practice; also called Steam Doctor. **1948** DICK *Dixie Frontier* 219 Then he went and learned herb remedies from an Indian doctor and the steam system from a Thompsonian doctor.

Also **Thomsonian (medical) system.**

1872 E. EGGLESTON *End of World* xx. 135 One of those little handbooks which the founder of the Thomsonian system sold dirt-cheap at twenty dollars a piece. **1933** ANDREWS *Community Industries Shakers* 100 The sale of the Shaker herbs was promoted by the popularity of the so-called Thomsonian medical system, which 'makes use of herbs only.'

Thomsonianism tɑm'sonɪən,ɪzəm, *n.* Also **Thompsonianism.** The Thomsonian medical system. *Obs.*

1847 *S. Lit. Messenger* XIII. 567/1 There are Medical Schools in Winchester and the City of Richmond; and there are rumors of others founded not only upon the approved principles of Medical Science, but also upon those of Thompsonianism and quackery. **1880** *Harper's Mag.* Jan. 188/2 Nor did either of these important systems fare so hardly at the hands of the 'regular' practitioners as did Thomsonianism, a pure Yankee product. **1919** DUNN *Indiana* II. 790 One of the early medical fads was known as Thomsonianism, 'steam doctors,' etc.

thorite 'θoraɪt, *n.* [*Thor*+*-ite.*] (See quot. 1909.) *Obs.* — **1899** *Boston Transcript* 20 July 12/7 The final trials of thorite will take place within a few weeks. **1909** *Cent. Supp.* 1344/3 *Thorite,* . . . an explosive of the ammonium-nitrate class once experimented with as a bursting charge for shell.

* **thorn,** *n.* In combs.: (1) * **thorn apple,** any one of various haws or their fruit; (2) **fence,** a fence or hedge of some thorny plant or shrub, *rare,* cf. **Osage orange hedge;** (3) **-tail(ed) snake,** = **horn snake,** *obs.*

(1) 1817 S. BROWN *Western Gazetteer* 322 The plants and shrubs [include] . . . pennyroyal, thorn apple, wild hops. **1844** LEE & FROST *Oregon* 89 The natural fruit of this valley is much the same . . . as that upon the Clatsop Plain . . . with the addition of wild cherries, red and black, and the thorn-apple. **1949** *Chi. Tribune* 24 Sep. 10/3 As one bird hopped out to shake itself dry, one or two more would drop down from neighboring thornapples. — **(2) 1843** *Farmers' Cabinet* 15 Jan. 184/1 Our fences are either the worm, post-and-rail, or thorn. — **(3) 1778** CARVER *Travels* 486 The Thorn-Tail Snake . . . receives its name from a thorn-like dart in its tail, with which it is said to inflict a mortal wound. **1836** EDWARDS *Hist. Texas* 76 One will meet with . . . a speckled snake, or a thorn-tailed snake.

As the last term in **all-, American black, black, English, fiery, Osage, Virginia, Washington thorn.**

thorogummite ,θorə'gʌmaɪt, *n.* [f. *thor*ium+*gummite.*] A hydrous silicate of uranium and thorium. *Obs.* — **1889** *Amer. Jrnl. Science* 3 Ser. Dec. 481 We name this mineral *thoro-gummite,* because it is a gummite in which the water has been replaced by the thorite molecule. **1891** *Cent.* 6301/1 *Thorogummite* . . . occurs with gadolinite and other rare minerals in Llano county, Texas.

* **thorough,** *prep.* or *adv.* In combs.: (1) **thorough brace,** (*a*) one of a number of strong leather straps sup-

One end of a thorough brace (sense *a*)

porting the body of a passenger vehicle, as a stagecoach, (*b*) (see quot. 1930), now *hist.;* (2) **braced,** *a.* built with, or supported on, thorough braces, now *hist.;* (3) * **fare,** (*a*) (see quot. 1859), *obs.,* (*b*) (see quot.); (4) **goer,** a person or thing of a superior or thoroughgoing type, *colloq.;* (5) **stitcher,** an out-and-outer, app. used of a member of a political faction, *obs.;* (6) **wort,** any one of various species of *Eupatorium,* esp. the boneset, *E. perfoliatum;* (7) **wort tea,** tea prepared from the leaves of some species of thoroughwort.

(1) (*a*) **1836** T. POWERS *Impressions* I. 299 Here I enjoyed my first lesson in what is familiarly termed riding a rail. . . . The term is derived from a fence-rail being occasionally used to supply the place of a broken thoro'-brace, by which all these stages are hung. **1949** HUNGERFORD *Wells Fargo* 52 Like the Concord, the mudwagon was slung on thoroughbraces. (*b*) **1886** *Leslie's Mo.* Dec. 722/1 The mustangs looked worse than the thorough-brace itself. **1930** BANNING *Six Horses* 399 The term *thorough-brace,* like 'stage,' was also used in the sense of vehicle; it was any conveyance whose body was suspended by rockers upon leather straps or thorough-braces. — (2) **1869** J. R. BROWNE *Adv. Apache Country* 445 Scouts were sent out all over the town of Aurora to secure the best wheeled vehicle . . . preference to be given to a thorough-braced ambulance of Concord manufacture. **1884** JEWETT *Country Doctor* 19 The old-fashioned thorough-braced wagon. — (3) (*a*) **1730** in *Amer. Sp.* XV. 403/1 Opposite to the lower Gap or Thoroughfare of the aforementioned Blew Ridge. . . . At a place called the meeting house by a gap or thoroughfare of the mountains. **1859** BARTLETT 477 *Thoroughfare*, a low gap between mountains; as, 'Thoroughfare gap' in Fauquier county, Virginia. 'Thoroughfare mountain.' Southern. (*b*) **1878** C. HALLOCK *Sportsman's Gaz.* (1883) p. xi/2 *Thoroughfare*, a straight of water, or neck of land connecting two bodies of water, habitually traversed by wild fowl in migrating or passing to and from their feeding-grounds. — (4) **1895** *Outing* XXVI. 388/1 [The polo ponies] are such thoroughgoers in the field that it is difficult to say this or the other is best. **1897** STUART *Simpkinsville* 155 [The widow is] a reg'lar business thorough-goer, she is.

(5) **1840** KENNEDY *Quodlibet* 144 We shall get the custom of the thorough-stitchers. — (6) **1814** BIGELOW *Florula Bostoniensis* 190 Eupatorium perfoliatum, Thoroughwort, Boneset, . . . has acquired great medicinal reputation. **1906** *Harper's Mag.* Oct. 712 The boggy place where she came in all warm seasons of the year for one thing or another: the wild marsh-marigold, good for greens, thoroughwort, and the root of the sweet-flag. — (7) [**1846** LEVINGE *Echoes Backwoods* II. 217 Here an old woman gave me a decoction of a plant which she called *thorough-wort*, and which, I think is a species of eupatorium.] **1863** RANDALL *Pract. Shepherd* 150 The tonic contained in half a dozen teaspoonfulls of . . . thoroughwort (*Eupatorium perfoliatum*) tea, has an excellent effect. **1887** WILKINS *Humble Romance* 84, I'll hev to fix me up some thoroughwort tea.

Thousand Island dressing. Russian dressing with various additions, as cream beaten till stiff, chopped pickle, green pepper, etc. — **1934** WEBSTER. [**1945** MARSHALL *Santa Fe* 106 For years, Bill Gardner, steward on the Kansas City–Chicago run, handed out a special '1001 Dressing,' an improvement on the usual Thousand Island mixture.]

***thrasher,** *n.* Any one of several American birds of the family Mimidae, related to the mockingbird, esp. a bird of the genus *Toxostoma.*

1810 WILSON *Ornithology* II. 84 The Thrasher is a welcome visitant in spring. **1877** *Harper's Mag.* April 662/1 [The catbird] brings forth sounds as mellow and as powerful as those of the thrasher and mocking-bird. **1949** *Democrat* 27 May 4/4 He is soon joined by the thrasher, whose fussy, scolding note indicates that he is peeved at having been awakened so early.

As the last term in **brown, cat, crissal, curve-billed, Le-Conte's, rice, sage, speckled, Texas thrasher.**

***thread,** *n.* **1. thread store,** a store which deals chiefly in thread. *Obs.* **2. thread herring,** (*a*) a species of herring, *Opisthonema oglinum*, of which the last ray of the dorsal fin is long and slender, (*b*) a gizzard shad.

(1) **1839** BRIGGS *H. Franco* I. 128 Her part of the proceeds . . . set her up in an elegant thread and needle store in the Bowery. — (2) (*a*) **1842** *Nat. Hist. N.Y., Zoology* IV. 265 The Spotted Thread Herring . . . has also the names of Thread Herring and Thread-fish, in allusion to its last filamentous dorsal ray. **1890** *Cent.* 3707/3 The name *menhaden* . . . is locally misapplied to the thread-herring, *Opisthonema thrissa.* (*b*) **1884** GOODE *Fisheries* I. 610 In North Carolina [the mud shad is known] as the 'Hairy-back' or the 'Thread Herring.'

As the last term in **Eve's, factory, gold, golden, spool thread.**

***thread,** *v.* **To thread the needle*, (see quot.). *Obs.* — **1838** GOSSE *Letters* 131 Another [feat in rifle-shooting] is 'threading the needle.' An auger-hole is pierced through the centre of an upright board; the orifice is just large enough to allow the ball to pass without touching; and *it is expected* to pass without touching.

***three,** *a.* In combs.: (1) **three-card,** see as a main entry; (2) **cent,** *a.* designating pieces of currency worth three cents; (3) **center,** a low liquor shop at which drinks are sold for three cents, *obs.;* (4) **-cornered cat,** a form of cat ball in which there are three batters; (5) **dollar,** *a.* designating a gold coin authorized in 1853; (6) **-fourths hand,** = **three-quarter hand,** *obs.;* (7) **-lined potato beetle,** (see quot. 1909); (8) ***minute,** *a.* denoting a horse that can cover a mile in three minutes; (9) **month,** *a.* of Civil War soldiers, enlisted for three months, *obs.;* (10) **m's,** (see quots.), *colloq.;* (11) **-notch road,** (see quots.), now *hist.;* (12) **point-two-beer,** beer containing 3.2% alcohol; (13) **-quarter hand,** one able to do three-fourths as much as a full hand *q.v.*, *obs.;* (14) **-rail fence,** a fence three rails high, *obs.;* (15) **sheet,** a poster composed of three sheets; (16) **shift system,** a system of rotating land with three crops, *obs.;* (17) **-twenty-nine,** (see quot.), *obs.;* (18) * **up,** a form of card game, *obs.*

(2) [**1829** *Central Watchtower* (Harrodsburg, Ky.) 13 June 2/4 In how many different ways it is possible to pay $100, without using any other money than pieces of silver, each 3, 5 and 7 cents.] **1851** *Miss. Palladium* (Holly Springs) 2 May 2/3 The three cent pieces authorized by the recent law reducing the postage on letters and newspapers, are now being coined at the Philadelphia Mint. **1880** *Bradstreet's* 25 Aug. 3/2, 3-cent notes may be regarded as practically out of existence. **1890** *Statutes at Large* XXVI. 485 The coinage of the three-dollar gold piece . . . and the three-cent nickel piece [shall] be . . . prohibited. — (3) **1848** BURTON *Waggeries* 65 (We.), I've drinked better stuff than that . . . at a three center in Bosting. — (4) **1867** *Chi. Republican* 24 July 8/1 Many years ago . . . the game was known as three-cornered cat, and as that animal has nine lives, we think this accounts for the number of men required to play the game.

(5) **1858** J. H. HICKCOX *Amer. Coinage* 56 Three Dollar gold coins were coined . . . under an act passed in 1853. **1948** Numismatic Gallery *Cat. U.S. Gold Coins* 56 It is interesting to compare the frequency with which this coin appears as against the $3.00 gold piece of this date. — (6) **1865** *S.C. Statutes at Large 1860–66* 38 After the words 'servant in husbandry' may be inserted, if it be required, the words 'to be rated as (full hand, three-fourths hand, half hand, or one-fourth hand), as the case may be.' — (7) **1876** C. V. RILEY *Potato Pests* 100 The Three-Lined Potato-Beetle, (*Lema trilineata*, Oliv.). **1909** *Cent. Supp.* 1045/3 Three-lined potato-beetle, an American Chrysomelid beetle, *Lema trilineata*, yellow in color and with three black elytral stripes. It feeds on the leaves of the Irish potato. — (8) **1833** *Knickerb.* I. 160 The present Mrs. S. admired his three minute roan. **1874** *Vt. Bd. Agric. Rep.* II. 211 They are able to ride in grand carriages with their three minute blacks hitched thereto. — (9) **1861** *Chi. Tribune* 26 May 1/3 So shameful has been the treatment of many of the three month volunteers, that most of them will certainly return home as soon as their terms expire. **1881–5** MCCLELLAN *Own Story* 53 The time of the three-months regiments was now rapidly expiring.

(10) **1938** DANIELS *Southerner* 136 But it was impressive how directly the town's merchants made their appeal to poverty with the heavy necessities of living—the three M's, meat, meal and molasses. **1941** ——— *Tar Heels* 258 Enough has been written about the 'three m' diet as the hangover of the frontier dietary and the food of slaves. — (11) **1818** in W. T. HARRIS *Remarks* (1821) 139 Occasional injunctions to 'keep the big road,' varied sometimes to 'keep the three-notch road.' . . . [Note:] The tracks or roads from one settlement to another in the woods, are marked by one notch in the bark of the trees for a foot-path, two for a bridle-road, and three for a waggon route. [**1948** DICK *Dixie Frontier* 204 This [the Federal Road, from Ga. to Natchez] was popularly known as the three-chopped way, from the triple blaze the surveyors used in marking the trees.] — (12) **1947** PERRY *Cities of Amer.* 225 Here's a huge Rathskeller where our old friend, three-point-two beer, is on tap. **1948** *Ga. Review* Spring 26 The evening was made merrier by a modest consumption of 3.2 Happiness Beer served gratis in gay paper cups. — (13) **1856** OLMSTED *Slave States* 433 The children beginning as 'quarter-hands,' advancing to 'half-hands,' and then to 'three-quarter hands'; and, finally, . . . to 'full hands.' — (14) **1666** *East-Hampton Rec.* I. 250 A three raile fence shalbe sufficient in all common fences. **1681** *Ib.* II. 102 Thomas Bee doth . . . maintaine a sofficient three raile fence one the beach.

(15) **1890** BIFF HALL *Turnover Club* 157 Why, don't you give a prominent line on your three-sheets to Julie De Mortimer, and isn't she your wife? **1908** MCGAFFEY *Show-Girl* 128 They will leave Flossie, the belle of the village, waiting at the gate any time a burlesque three-sheet shows up on the side of the blacksmith shop. — (16) **1814** TAYLOR *Arator* 126 Those tied by habit to the rotation of corn, wheat, and pasture, or the three shift system, object [etc.]. **1819** AGRICOLA *Ess. Agric.* 22 The system of tillage which has generally been pursued under the name of the three-shift system, has also tended greatly to the destruction of our lands. — (17) **1885** *Mag. Amer. Hist.* April 396/2 Three-Twenty-Nine (329).—During the presidential campaign of 1880 these numbers were chalked by Democrats on every wall and door-step, and fence in the land. Mr. Garfield, the Republican candidate, had been charged with having received as a bribe $329 worth of Credit Mobilier stock. — (18) **1834** NOTT *Novellettes* I. 40 They could indulge in three up, old sledge, whist, or loo. **1840** *S. Lit. Messenger* VI. 294/2 The crowd was . . . playing cards; whist, loo, three-up, and all fours.

b. Used in baseball in such expressions as (1) **three bagger,** (2) **base hit,** (3) **baser,** to designate a hit which enables the batter to reach third base. *Colloq.*

(1) **1881** *Detroit Free Press* 24 Sep. 6/4 Carpenter's three-bagger and Hotaling's single with a passed ball had given the two [runs] in the fifth. **1948** *Herald-Press* (St. Joseph, Mich.) 14 Aug. 7/2 Schultz followed suit with another three bagger, scoring Green. — (2) **1879** *Spirit of Times* 23 Aug. (E. J. Nichols), Three-base hit. **1905** *Denver Republican* 6 Sep. 8/2 Perrine was perforce credited with a three-base hit. — (3) **1871** *N.Y. Herald* 23 Aug. 8/4 Wolters also made a brace

of beautiful 'three basers.' **1950** *Chi. Tribune* 19 April IV. 1/3 The triple with which Adams opened the Sox offensive was the perfect three baser in that it bisected the space between the left and center fielders.

three-card.

1. =next. Also attrib. and fig.

1875 LANDON *Eli Perkins* 122 (We.), We'll hang these three-card fellows to the telegraph pole. **1887** LOWELL *Writings* II. 187 [They] play their three-card trick as subsidies or as protection to labor. **1898** CANFIELD *Maid of Frontier* 109 I've seen low-down greasers playin' three-card, . . . but never any decent white men. **1920** SANDBURG *Smoke & Steel* 175 Pickpockets, yeggs, three card men.

2. three-card monte, a gambling game in which three cards, previously identified, are dexterously thrown face down on the table to deceive the players, who bet upon the position of one of them. Also attrib.

1854 PARKER in Weiss *Life T. Parker* II. 134 Three-card-monte men, and gambling-house keepers. **1938** ASBURY *Sucker's Prog.* 55 Three-Card Monte first appeared in the United States during the early 1830's, when it was introduced into New Orleans from Texas, then a part of Mexico. **1949** *Amer. Milk Rev.* May 42/3 Now he knows you can't beat or cheat Three Card Monte games.

***thriftily,** *adv.* Flourishingly. — **1865** BURRITT *Walk to Land's End* 215 Two of the largest and oldest California pines are growing most thriftily in these gardens. **1894** *Amer. Missionary* Sep. 330 The seed . . . is growing thriftily.

thrip θrɪp, *n. S.* [f. **threepence*. Prob. not of U.S. origin as *OED* has *threpps c*1700.] The English threepenny piece; any coin of little value.

1834 SIMMS *G. Rivers* II. 108 He rewarded [him] with a *thrip* (the smallest silver coin known in the southern currency—the five cent issue excepted). **1880** HARRIS *U. Remus* 221 I'll hunt 'roun' in my cloze an' see ef I can't run out a thrip er two fer you. **1904** CHURCHILL *Crossing* 257 Kentucky can go to the devil, . . . and not a thrip do they care.

***throat,** *n.* In combs.: (1) **throat distemper,** ?diptheria, *obs.;* (2) ***latch,** (see quot.); (3) **rattler,** a drink of liquor, *slang, obs.;* (4) **root,** (see quot. 1884).

(1) *c*1772 HULTON *Letters* 58 There's another terrible disorder, called here [Boston] the throat Distemper, wch attacks Children chiefly, this sometimes Spreads, & sweeps away numbers in a short time. — (2) **1892** *Outing* Feb. 395/1 After the first unfortunate smelt finds its way out of the water the eyes and the solid piece of flesh between the gills, called by the fishermen the 'throat latch,' are used for bait. — (3) **1837** *Harvardiana* III. 238, I was obliged to down with a throat-rattler of West India. — (4) **1784** *Amer. Acad. Mem.* I. 454 Water Avens. Throatroot. Cureall. . . . The root is powerfully astringent. **1884** W. MILLER *Dict. Names of Plants* 200/1 *Geum virginianum,* Throat-root, White Avens.

As the last term in **ash, cut, desert black, sore, white, yellow throat.**

***through,** *adv.* and *a.*

1. Of cattle: Driven or shipped beyond local places. *Colloq.*

1884 *Harper's Mag.* July 297/2 The latter receives most of the 'through Texans,' the old cows, and the 'scrubs' and 'culls' from the better lots. **1890** *Stock Grower & Farmer* 12 April 4/4 The local owners [in Colo.] banded together for a vigorous opposition to the use of their ranges for common trails and bed grounds for these through herds.

2. In combs. relating to trains, railroads, traffic, travel, etc., going on or destined to go beyond intermediate or local points, as (1) **through freight,** (2) **line,** (3) **passenger,** (4) **route,** (5) **ticket,** (6) **train.**

(1) **1843** *Hunt's Merch. Mag.* IX. 388 The through freight from Boston to Albany having been trebled in May and June last. **1900** GARLAND *Eagle's Heart* 316 The train, being a 'through freight,' ran almost as steadily as a passenger train. — (2) **1867** *Comm. & Fin. Chron.* 6 April 447 Pacific Mail Steamship Company's Through Line to California. **1887** *Courier-Journal* 11 Jan. 2/2 Freight going from New York to San Francisco may pass over the various lines of road, making up a through line for perhaps half their regular rates. — (3) **1842** *Phila., Wilmington, & Balt. R.R.* 4th Rep. 8 (Ernst), Through passengers. **1887** GEORGE *40 Yrs. on Rail* 35 Even when tickets began to creep into use, they were at first sold only to through passengers. — (4) **1861** J. DAVIS *Lett., Papers, & Sp.* V. 169 This comparatively short line would give us a through route from north to south in the interior of the Confederate States. **1909** *Boston Herald* 17 Dec. 4/4 A through route from Boston by way of the great lakes to the west and northwest.

(5) **1845** *Boston Transcript* 29 Nov. 3/2 Through tickets may be obtained for Montreal. **1888** *Interstate Commerce Comm. 2d Rep.* 44 Ticket brokers or 'scalpers' . . . deal in unused coupons of through tickets. — (6) **1846** *Boston Traveller* 2 July, Through trains from Boston. **1950** *World-Herald Mag.* (Omaha) 8 May 23/3 When sleepers were hooked on to a through train we enjoyed the luxury of a diner.

Also *through baggage, business, car, express, fare, going, mail, pouch, rates, sleeper, traffic, travel, traveler.*

b. through cut, a water channel cut through land separating two bodies of water.

1846 *Bankers Mag.* I. 368 The summit level of the canal was intended to be supplied with water by means of a throughcut from Lake Michigan. **1898** PAGE *Red Rock* 350 Farther back is a through-cut to the Bend.

***throw,** *n.* As the last term in **free, over, wild throw.**

***throw,** *v.*

1. *tr.* In miscellaneous colloq. or slang uses (see quots.).

1847 RUXTON *Adv. Rocky Mt.* (1848) 256 To 'throw a buffalo in his tracks,' which is the phrase for making a clean shot, he must be struck but a few inches above the brisket. **1870** M. H. SMITH *20 Years Wall St.* 121 Vanderbilt has never been 'thrown' since he commenced his stock speculations. **1921** MULFORD *Bar-20 Three* xv, You got plenty of gall, comin' down here an' throwin' a gun on me, for that!

b. To give the verdict against in a lawsuit. *Colloq. Obs.*

1887 in *Lisbon* (Dak.) *Star* 20 May 2/5, 'I am compelled to throw you in the cost,' said a justice of the peace.

2. To lose (a game or contest) deliberately, for money or other ulterior reasons, orig. with *off* or *up. Colloq.* or *slang.* Cf. ***heave,** *v.* **c.**

[**1857** *Spirit of Times* 10 Oct. 85/2 It has been stated that this was a throw off match; it was not so—each man would do his best.] **1867** *Chi. Republican* 28 July 4/3 The game of Thursday last with the 'Forest City Club,' of Rockford, was 'thrown up' for the purpose of enabling thieving gamblers to make bets against the 'Excelsior Club' of this city. **1868** WOODRUFF *Trotting Horse* 263 It was . . . very unjust to charge Mr. Nodine with throwing the race. **1929** *Sat. Ev. Post* 14 Dec. 13/1 This little rat is asking me to throw the fight. **1949** *Chi. Tribune* 27 Sep. II. 1/6 There's never been an umpire found guilty of anything like the ball-players—throwing games and like that.

3. Used colloq. with adverbs: (1) **To throw down,* (*a*) to discard (a friend or associate), (*b*) to pull (a gun) *on* a person; (2) **to throw in,* to contribute, join *with* (a person) in partnership; (3) **to throw off,* (*a*) =**bar,** *v.*, *obs.*, (*b*) in faro (see quot. 1864), also transf., (*c*) to toss off (a drink); (4) *to throw off on,* (*a*) to belittle, (*b*) to avoid, ignore; (5) **to throw out,* (*a*) to stop cultivating (land), (*b*) to reject (a vote) as invalid, (*c*) in baseball, to put (a runner) out by a throw; (6) **to throw up,* to bring up or mention repeatedly *to* someone as a challenge or taunt.

(1) (*a*) **1896** *Typog. Jrnl.* IX. 281 He was 'thrown down' by his party and he secured the nomination of the Democrats, but was defeated. **1913** BIGGERS *7 Keys to Baldpate* xiii, He'll throw you down some day. (*b*) **1898** CANFIELD *Maid of Frontier* 183 [He] threw his pistol down on Chisolm at three feet distance. — (2) **1904** PRINGLE *Rice Planter* 61 The whole family unite and 'trow een' to make up the sum necessary to bring the wanderer home. **1923** J. H. COOK *On Old Frontier* 125 He said . . . he should be glad to have me 'throw in' with him as a partner. — (3) (*a*) **1829** in COMMONS *Doc. Hist.* I. 235 Hoes still in Groces field, two ploughs throwing off before them. (*b*) **1864** DICK *Amer. Hoyle* (1866) 208 Throwing off a Game.—When a dealer, by a preconcerted plan, allows a player to win, he is said to throw off the game. **1865** MARK TWAIN *Jumping Frog* 34 (R.), Smiley says, 'I do wonder what in the nation that frog throw'd off for?' **1947** MYERS *The 'Guv'* 223 Time after time he slapped the queen of spades down with a thump of the side of his hand on the table as he threw off the 'black Maria' on some particular player. (*c*) **1873** HARTE *Mrs. Skagg's Husbands* 6 He threw off his liquor with a single dexterous movement of head and elbow, and stood refreshed. — (4) (*a*) **1876** MARK TWAIN *Tom Sawyer* xxv. 193 But I bet you I ain't going to throw off on di'monds. **1904** *Charlotte Observer* 27 July 4 Charlotte can no longer throw off on Lincolnton for being behind the times. (*b*) **1896** HIGGINSON *Land of Snow Pearls* 193 It was considered quite proper for a young man and a young woman to 'go together' for months, or even years, and for one to 'throw off' on the other, when attracted by a fresher face, with no explanation or apology.

(5) (*a*) **1856** OLMSTED *Slave States* 241 [They] 'threw out,' to use their own phrase, so much of the land as they had ruined. **1904** PRINGLE *Rice Planter* 63, I have decided to throw out three of my fields. (*b*) **1877** JOHNSON *Anderson Co., Kans.* 78 On the canvass of the vote the probate judge threw out all the returns except the Shannon precinct. (*c*) **1880** *Brooklyn Eagle* 10 Oct. (E. J. Nichols). **1949** *Oregonian* (Portland) 10 Aug. III. 1/4 Barker was thrown out in an attempted steal. — (6) **1870** MARK TWAIN *Sk. New & Old* 276 He would . . . let on to be studying algebra by the light of a smouldering

fire, so that all other boys might have to do that also, or else have Benjamin Franklin thrown up to them. **1884** NYE *Baled Hay* 219 Do not throw it up to us that we are weird and pixycal.

b. throw off, *n.* With reference to a train: A derail.

1874 *Kalama* (Wash.) *Beacon* 20 Jan. 4/2 The passenger train from Tacoma . . . passed the Des Chuttes bridge (near where the 'throw-off' occurred) an hour or two previous to the 'dinkey.'

c. In slang or colloq. phrases: (1) *To throw a fit,* to have a fit; (2) *to throw a bluff,* to work a bluff, run a bluff; (3) *to throw one's hat in the ring,* to become a candidate; (4) *to throw a diamond hitch,* to tie or make a diamond hitch *q.v.*

(1) **1897** FLANDRAU *Harvard Episodes* 132, I don't suppose the creature thought I was throwing a fit like that just for exercise. **1938** SMITTER *F.O.B. Detroit* 32 The lady threw a high-toned conniption fit. — (2) **1911** VANCE *Cynthia* 71 Why didn't you try it, anyhow—throw the bluff, at least? **1923** R. HERRICK *Lilla* 69, I can't throw a bluff with those kids I've known always. — (3) **1932** *K.C. Star* 16 Feb. 22 In the case of J. Ham it is not said that his hat was thrown into the ring. — (4) **1895** REMINGTON *Pony Tracks* 12, I felt like a pack on a government mule, and only wished I had some one to 'throw the diamond hitch over me.' **1902** WILSON *Spenders* 30 He could throw the diamond hitch with his eyes shut. **1947** *Trail & Timberline* May 77/1 There seems to be a number of ways of throwing a diamond hitch, but they all come out about the same.

***thrush,** *n.* As the last term in **brown, ferruginous, fox-colored, golden-crowned, gray-cheeked, hermit, least golden crown, Louisiana water, migratory, mocking, Monterey hermit, New York, New York water, olive-backed, red, red-breasted, red-vented, russet, russet-backed, sage, Saint Lucas, sickle-billed, sierra hermit, solitary, speckled, Townsend fly-catching, varied, water, Wilson's, wood thrush.**

***thumb,** *n.*

1. thumb paper, a paper, card, etc., used by school children to keep their thumbs from soiling the lower inner parts of the pages of their books. [Cf. *EDD thumb-scall,* in the same sense.]

1843 HALL *New Purchase* (1916) 243 To have used . . . any other than the thumb-paper just named, would have been considerably worse than ridiculous. **c1880** HAZARD *Jonny-Cake P.* (1915) 9 Both my hands were required to keep my old dog-eared broken-back'd spelling primer in place, and hold fast to my *thumb* papers, which were always used in those days [about 1810 in Rhode Island]. **1942** WARNICK *Dialect Garrett Co., Md.* 15 *thumb-paper,* n., a book mark; also a small piece of paper used to protect the pages.

2. thumb tack, a tack with a broad, flat head for pressing into soft boards or the like with the thumb. Also as a verb.

1884 RITTENHOUSE *Maud* 278 [He] coolly left me to put the thumb-tacks in my picture by myself. **1931** *Sat. Ev. Post* 11 April 118/2 The engineer who plots the system thumb-tacks to the graph two long strips of paper in the form of an X. **1935** *Montgomery Ward Cat.* 481 Thumb Tacks . . . 7/16 in. Flat heads, one piece.

As the last term in **lady's, trigger thumb.**

***thumb,** *v.* **1.** *tr.* Among gun-fighters, to pull back and release (the hammer of a single-action pistol) with the thumb. *Colloq.* **2.** *To thumb one's nose,* to put one's thumb to one's nose and extend the fingers in a gesture of derision and insult.

(1) **1932** *K.C. Star* 17 May, Then he passed out to the roar of .45s whether he 'thumbed' or 'fanned.' — (2) **1916** B. HALL *One Man's War* (1929) 218 He thumbed his nose with both thumbs at once and told me to climb the Tour d'Eiffel and stay there. **1947** MOTLEY *Knock on Any Door* 119 Behind Ma's back Ang thumbed her nose at him and stuck out her tongue.

thumber ˈθʌmɚ, *n.* (See quot. 1944 and cf. ***fanner.**) — **1932** *K.C. Star* 17 May (*heading*), Two Schools of Old-Time Gunmen The 'Fanners' and The 'Thumbers.' **1944** ADAMS *W. Words* 165 thumber A type of shooter who removes the trigger and guard from his gun and shoots by raising and releasing the hammer with his thumb. He does his shooting at close quarters and relies upon speed for safety.

***thumper,** *n.* ?Short for **crawthumper,* a Roman Catholic. *Obs.* — **1828** COOPER *Notions* II. 327 All that one hears concerning Thumpers and Dunkers, and other enthusiasts, is grossly caricatured.

***thumping,** *n.* The drumming (*q.v.,* sense **2.**) of the ruffed grouse. — **1750** JOHN BARTRAM in George Edwards *Gleanings Nat. Hist.* I. (1758) 80 There is something very remarkable in what we call their thumping, which they do with their wings.

***thumps,** *n. pl.* In animals, esp. horses that have over-exerted, a characteristic throbbing movement of the sides of the chest produced by spasmodic contractions of the diaphragm.

1839 *Spirit of Times* 11 May 114/1 (We.), The Barefoot filly being taken with 'the thumps' was now withdrawn. **a1846** *Quarter Race Ky.* 137 [The dog was] breathing like a horse with the thumps. **1890** *Spec. Rep. Diseases Horse* (Bureau Animal Indust.) 134 Thumps is produced by the same causes which produce congestion of the lungs.

transf. **1881** VAWTER *Prison Life* 158, I know that when I got out I carried in a load [of wood] that gave me the thumps.

b. (See quot. and cf. **buck ague.**) *Colloq.*

1945 *Md. Conservationist* 14/2 Campbell told young Skinner that he had been a victim of the 'thumps' and that older and more experienced hunters had been worse afflicted in their first deer hunt.

***thunder,** *n.*

1. An expressed policy, an argument, vigor or force. *Obs.*

1838 D. WEBSTER *Works* I. 427 Another will exclaim, 'That won't do; that's not my thunder.' **1856** E. G. PARKER *Lesson of '76* 15 No party owns the Revolution. . . . No party can say 'that's my thunder.' No, it is the thunder of America. **1877** *N.Y. Tribune* (B.), Whatever thunder there can be in the present Southern policy [of Pres. Hayes], it is not the thunder of those Republicans who oppose it.

2. In combs.: (1) **thunder-and-lightning snake,** =**thunder snake;** (2) ***bird,** among certain Indians, a mythical bird supposed to cause thunder, also transf.; (3) ***bug,** (see quot.); (4) **cap,** a thunderhead; (5) **gust,** a thunderstorm accompanied by strong wind, also attrib.; (6) **pump,** a local name for the bittern, see next; (7) **pumper,** the fresh-water drumfish, also the American bittern; (8) **snake,** a milk snake or a snake of a related species (see also quot. 1891).

(1) **1842** *Nat. Hist. N.Y., Zoology* III. 39 The Milk Snake . . . is called Chicken Snake, Thunder and Lightning Snake, House Snake, and Chequered Adder. **1907** *St. Nicholas* July 845/1 Another of its many local names is 'thunder-and-lightning snake,' but I cannot imagine why so gentle a serpent should be so named. — (2) **1875** PARKMAN in *N. Amer. Rev.* Jan. 40 The thunder-bird is offended, and all thunder-storms are occasioned by his anger. **1906** MARK TWAIN *Horse's Tale* 330 (R.), In forty-eight hours the Indian encampment was here, illustrious old Thunder-Bird and all. **1947** *Time* 1 Sep. 15/3 In the U.S., Indians still propitiate the Thunderbird with symbolic dances. — (3) **1837** WILLIAMS *Florida* 71 Horse Fly.—*M[usca] equi.* Of these there are five kinds — 1st. the large black, called thunder bug, an inch long. — (4) **1877** *Harper's Mag.* Jan. 297/1 All day long great 'thunder caps' had rolled their still and solemn heights of rounded pearl and shadow upward. **1912** N. WOODROW *Sally Salt* 146 Look at the thunder-caps on the horizon.

(5) **1733** FRANKLIN *Poor Richard's Almanac 1734* 11 Wind southerly thunder-gusts. **1837** *New-Yorker* 8 April 40/2 It is quite comfortable to reflect that thunder-gusts, as well as stage-coaches, must submit to be impeded by those tremendous barriers. **1886** *Harper's Mag.* July 282/2, I have yet to see . . . the bushes that some thundergusts would not prostrate into the mud. — (6) **1941** WILDER *Little Town on Prairie* 36 Up from Big Slough rose the thunder-pumps with their long legs dangling and long necks outstretched, giving their short, booming cry. — (7) **1884** GOODE *Fisheries* I. 370 In the Southern States the name 'Drum' predominates; that of 'Thunder-pumper,' also used for the bittern, . . . is heard along the Mississippi River. **1917** *Birds of Amer.* I. 181 Bittern. *Botaurus lentiginosus.* . . . [Also called] Stake Driver; Thunder Pumper; Butterbump. — (8) **1800** LAMB *Letters* (1935) I. 219 There is an exhibition quite uncommon in Europe . . . a live rattlesnake, . . . whip-snakes, thundersnakes, pig-nose-snakes, American vipers. **1891** *Cent.* 6321/3 *Thunder-snake,* . . . the little worm-snake, *Carphophis* (formerly *Celuta*) *amœna,* common in the United States: apparently so called because forced out of its hole by a heavy shower. **1903** *Current Lit.* April 475/1 Thunder snakes are common in Texas, New Mexico and Arizona.

b. As a softened or euphemistic substitute for "hell" in colloq. expressions as (1) *by thunder,* (2) *go to thunder,* (3) *to give* (or *catch*) *particular thunder.*

(1) **1843** *Yale Lit. Mag.* IX. 79 Wal! You're considerable of a critur now, you are, by thunder! **1870** M. H. SMITH *20 Yrs. Wall St.* 309 'Am I Governor of New York?' 'No, by thunder! Thurlow Weed is.' — (2) **1848** N. AMES *Childe Harvard* 82 A voice . . . replied, 'Please, go to thunder!' **1894** *Outing* XXIV. 125/2 'You go to thunder!' I yelled at him. — (3) **1851** BYRN *Life Ark. Doctor* (Th. 494), I'll give you particular thunder one time, and then perhaps you will stay out of here. **1875** *Chi. Tribune* 21 Sep. 8/4 If the rations happen to be short, the squaw catches particular thunder.

As the last term in **pump thunder.**

thunderation ˌθʌndəˈreʃən, *n.* and *adv.* Used as an intensive or for emphasis, often in oathlike expressions. *Colloq.*

1836 *Crockett's Yaller Flower Almanac* 21, I don't know as I can say he was so all darned thunderation fat. **1856** MARK TWAIN *Adv. Snod-*

grass 23 Thunderation. It [the 'iron horse'] wasn't no more like a hoss than a meetin house. **1911** SAUNDERS *Col. Todhunter* 17 What in thunderation is the matter, suh? **1949** *Sat. Ev. Post* 9 July 86/2 Why in thunderation does he have to play such a hay-in-the-hair?

* **thunderer,** *n.* Anything exceptional of its kind; also (*cap.*) as a nickname for Thomas H. Benton (1782–1858).

1857 *Harper's Mag.* Nov. 727 [The panther] was a thunderer, I tell ye. **1872** *Ib.* Aug. 348/1 Dick talked and vociferated, slashed his rod in the water, hooked a 'thunderer' and let him get away. **1943** DEVOTO *Yr. of Decision* 464 The Thunderer turned demagogue on an almost cosmic scale.

thurl θɜl, *n.* [Origin unknown.] ?The hip joint in cattle. Cf. Webster. *Colloq.* — **1920** *Jrnl. of Heredity* XII. 327, I would call attention to the fact that the heifers were wider through the thurls at five months of age than through the hips, but after they had become mature cows they were wider through (or across) their hips than across their thurls.

* **thus,** *adv.* So, esp. * *thus and so,* a variant of * *so and so. Colloq.*

1873 J. H. BEADLE *Undevel. West* 788 Inquiring of a philosophical native why this was thus, he replied [etc.]. **1904** *N.Y. Ev. Post* 23 April, The statement that matters will result thus and so 'if the crops turn out all right.' **1918** *Nation* 7 Feb. 161/1 They . . . offered us a contract in this, that, or the other company, whose dividend-paying record had been thus and so.

* **thyme,** *n.* As the last term in **Niagara, Virginia, Virginian thyme.**

* **tick,** *n.* **1. tick nation,** (see quot.). *Jocular* and *obs.* **2. tick trefoil,** a plant of the genus Desmodium, so named from its trifoliate leaves and the nature of the joints of the pods which adhere readily to clothing.

(1) **1859** BARTLETT 478 *Tick Nation.* A name given to regions in which ticks abound, and, as the grasses and sandy soil infected by them are peculiar to the poorer parts of the country, it is sometimes used as a term of reproach. — (2) **1857** GRAY *Botany* 99 Tick-Trefoil. . . . Pod . . . roughened with minute hooked hairs by which they adhere to the fleece of animals or to clothing. **1944** *Amer. Scholar* Summer 334 The white and purple prairie clover, black-eyed Susan, tick trefoil, wild licorice, wild bergamot, and rosinweeds adorn the rolling hills.

b. In colloq. expressions: (1) *as full as a tick,* quite full; (2) *as thick as ticks,* very numerous.

(1) **1822** *N.J. Almanac 1823,* Though of love I'm *as full as a tick.* **1852** LODISA FRIZZELL *Journal* (1915) 14 We . . . yoked up our cattle which were as full as *ticks,* started out into the broad road, or roads, for here there are several tracks. — (2) **1917** COMSTOCK *Man* 8 Why folks is as thick as ticks up here.

As the last term in **beggar, cattle, ear, moose, old, seed, spinose ear, star, Texas fever, wood, yearling tick.** See also **bed, feather, shuck tick.**

* **ticker,** *n.*

1. (See quot. 1851.) *Slang. Obs.*

1836 *Harvardiana* III. 123 If any 'Ticker' dare to look, A stealthy moment, on his book. **1851** HALL *College Words* 301 *Ticker,* one who recites without knowing what he is talking about; one entirely independent of any book-knowledge.

2. =**stock ticker.** Also attrib.

1882 MCCABE *New York* 338 Thanks to these 'tickers,' . . . men can watch the market, and buy and sell, miles away from the Stock Exchange. **1885** *Wkly. New Mexican Rev.* 7 May 3/2 The ticker service was partially restored this morning. **1948** *Time* 5 April 83/1 All week long, stock exchange brokers watched the ticker.

b. ticker tape, the paper ribbon upon which stock quotations are printed by a stock ticker. Cf. * **ribbon,** *n.* **2. b.**

1902 WILSON *Spenders* 407 For two days he clung to the ticker tape as to a life line. **1950** *Time* 8 May 11/1 The prices are chalked up on the quote board as they come through on the ticker tape.

* **ticket,** *n.*

1. A sheet of paper bearing the names of several candidates, nominated usu. by a single political party, such a sheet used as a ballot; the list of candidates appearing on such a sheet, or, commonly since 1888, one of the lists in a column on a blanket ballot. Cf. **general ticket 1.**

1755 in FRANKLIN *Hist. Rev. Pa.* 403 Every one votes . . . as privately as he pleases, the Election being by written Tickets folded up and put into a Box. *a***1821** BIDDLE *Autobiog.* 330, I was surprised . . . to find my name on the ticket to be run as Senator. **1903** *Evanston* (Ill.) *Press* 11 April, Several of the friends of Mr. A. W. Kimball have . . . urged him to consent to allow his name to be placed on the ticket.

b. A ballot for or against some proposition.

1876 *Harper's Mag.* Dec. 159/1 A voter came up and asked for a ticket against the school tax.

2. *collect.* The group of party candidates selected for a given set of offices.

1764 W. B. REED in *Life J. Reed* I. 36 [The] Calvinists and the Presbyterians. . . . I believe to a man assisted the new ticket. **1806** *Balance* V. 135/2 In New-York—three distinct tickets are nominated. **1917** SINCLAIR *King Coal* 386 The Supreme Court handed down a decision which unseated him and the entire ticket elected with him. **1950** *Chi. Tribune* 18 May II. 1/1 Duff and his entire statewide ticket bowled over the machine which had controled Pennsylvania since 1860.

3. With specifying terms in either sense **1.** or **2.**

1789 MADISON *Writings* V. 330 The Western ticket . . . is supposed to have prevailed. **1837** *New-Yorker* 14 Oct. 474/2 There was no opposition to the regular Whig tickets. **1910** C. HARRIS *Eve's Husband* 138, I have determined to run on the anti-liquor ticket against Clancy Drew.

4. A playing card.

1870 RAE *Westward by Rail* 187 The card-dealer calls upon him to return the 'ticket.' **1936** ASBURY *French Quarter* 206 The monte operator simply displayed three cards, called 'the tickets,' usually two aces and a queen.

5. A summons given to an offender to appear in court, usu. with reference to traffic violations. *Colloq.*

1930 *Outlook* 12 Feb. 249/1 He wrote the young professor a ticket for speeding. **1948** *Downers Grove* (Ill.) *Rep.* 21 Oct. 1/2 Twenty-one tickets were issued to owners of cars which parked all night without lights.

6. In combs.: (1) **ticket agent,** a railway employee who sells tickets, cf. **general ticket agent;** (2) **book,** (*a*) an official book of ballots, *obs.,* (*b*) railroad tickets so attached as to resemble a small book; (3) **box,** a place where tickets are sold, or a box in which tickets are deposited; (4) **broker,** =**ticket scalper;** (5) **case,** ?a place for selling railroad tickets, *rare;* (6) **chopper,** an employee of a city transportation system in charge of a ticket-chopping machine, also the position held by such an employee; (7) **master,** =**ticket agent;** (8) **office,** an office where tickets are sold, cf. **consolidated ticket office;** (9) **peddler,** one who hands out party tickets at a polling place to be cast as ballots; (10) * **room,** (*a*) a room where a voter gets his ballot, (*b*) a room where railroad tickets are kept; (11) **scalper,** a person who buys tickets, esp. transportation or theater tickets, and disposes of them at other than stated or official prices, hence **ticket scalping;** (12) **speculator,** one who speculates in tickets.

(1) **1861** *Richmond* (Va.) *Examiner* 6 Dec. 3/3 Mr. John M. Parker, for several years the efficient General Freight and Ticket Agent of the Richmond and Petersburg railroad, has resigned his post. **1916** DU PUY *Uncle Sam* 201 The ticket agent thought he remembered selling the man . . . a ticket to Chicago. — (2) (*a*) **1888** *Nation* 19 Jan. 46/2 A full set of ticket-books is to be provided at each polling-place before the polls are opened. (*b*) **1903** E. JOHNSON *Railway Transportation* 152 The original buyer . . . must sign his name on the last page of the ticket-book. — (3) **1851** *Polly Peablossom* 104 Tom Placide was dealing out in the Ticket Box. **1898** *N.Y. Tribune* 13 May 11/2 Mr. Hoy is supposed to stand near the ticket-box and see to it that the pasteboards are dropped into the box. — (4) **1888** *Interstate Commerce Comm. 2d Rep.* 44 Ticket brokers or 'scalpers' . . . deal in unused coupons of through tickets, . . . in the unused portion of excursion tickets [etc.].

(5) **1887** GEORGE *40 Years on Rail* 34 Frequently, a pine box in open air by the side of the track served as the ticket case, and was the only landmark for a station. — (6) **1898** C. B. DAVIS *Borderland of Soc.* 90 She took up with a ticket-chopper on the elevated road. **1939** MILLER *Cosmological Eye* 359 I held innumerable positions, for a day or less often. Among them were the following: dish-washer, . . . ticket chopper, etc. — (7) **1849** *Hunt's Merch. Mag.* XXI. 580 Ticket masters receive from $156 to $720 per annum. **1857** *Harper's Mag.* Feb. 400/1 There was a mail-train . . . which the ticket-master informed me should land me in New York at half-past six. — (8) **1835** INGRAHAM *South-West* I. 221 A noisy crowd was gathering around the ticket-office. **1903** E. JOHNSON *Railway Transportation* 148 Ticket offices are located in the most central sections of the large cities. — (9) **1872** *Chi. Tribune* 6 Nov. 1/6 There were the usual congregations of ticket-pedlers and candidates, serving their country and themselves. **1903** LEWIS *Boss* 59 Go for the blokes with badges—th' ticket-peddlers.

(10) (*a*) **1888** *Cent. Mag.* Dec. 321/2 The voter receives his ballots from a sworn official of the State in a room called the 'ticket-room,' which only one voter is allowed to enter at a time. (*b*) **1907** LILLIBRIDGE *Trail* 172 Within the station itself the shirt-sleeved agent surreptitiously locked the door to the ticket-room. — (11) **1880** *Cong. Rec.* 14 June 4521/1 Thomas P. Mills [was] a ticket-scalper of Indianapolis. **1888** *Boston Jrnl.* 11 Dec. 1/4 Rates Reduced by Ticket Scalping and Commissions. **1948** *Dly. Ardmoreite* (Ardmore, Okla.) 31 May 1/3 Sheriff's deputies arrested a patrol wagon full of ticket scalpers today at the Indianapolis motor speedway. — (12) **1883** JOSEPH HATTON *Henry Irving's Impressions of Amer.* I. 96 (*footnote*), These ticket speculators have regular customers, who willingly pay them the ordinary price they ask rather than bother about going to the box-office.

b. In phrases: (1) *To carry a ticket*, to elect the candidates on a ticket; (2) *to run ahead of* (or *behind*) *one's ticket*, and variants, to get more (or fewer) votes than the other candidates on one's ticket; (3) *the head of a ticket*, the candidate for the most important office indicated on a ticket; (4) *to put a ticket in the field*, to nominate a group of candidates, esp. in response to an independent movement.

(1) **1711** *Pa. Hist. Soc. Mem.* X. 438 Chester carried their ticket entire. **1847** *Yankee Doodle* 10 April 7/2 We carried our ticket, but we had a close job of it. — (2) **1846** *Xenia Torch-Light* 2 April 2/3 He ran ahead of every Whig on the ticket in Preble County. **1904** *N.Y. Ev. Post* 29 Sep. 3 Even the most optimistic admit that it [the state ticket] will run behind the national ticket. **1910** *Ib.* 23 Nov. 8 While the state of the party vote, as such, is indicated by an aggregate new Democratic plurality of 14,068 in the vote on Assembly candidates, Mr. Wilson's plurality for the Governorship was 49,360. It is fair, therefore, to say that he ran 35,000 ahead of his ticket. — (3) **1884** *N.Y. Herald* 7 June 5/2 [The Democrats] can easily win with Tilden's name at the head of their ticket. **1888** *Chi. Inter-Ocean* (F.), The head of the ticket is one of the most vulnerable men who figured in Southern politics in the carpet-bag era. — (4) **1891** *World Almanac* 75 South-Carolina, Democratic 'Straight-out' State Convention . . . put a ticket in the field in opposition to the regular Democratic ticket. **1913** LA FOLLETTE *Autobiog.* 322 The opposition was laying the foundation either for stealing the state convention or else bolting it and placing a third ticket in the field.

As the last term in **abolition, ball, bread, citizens', clean, commutation, Democratic, dollar, electioneering, electoral, emigrant, Free Soil, fusion, general, hard, kiss-joke, limited, liquor, local, locofoco, machine, meal, Mechanics', mileage, mixed, omnibus, package, party, punch, scratch, scratched, secession, shaving, split, state, store, straight, Tammany, tapeworm, through, toleration, transfer, union, walking, war, Webster, yellow dog ticket.**

* **ticket,** *v.*

1. *pass.* To be issued a ticket for accommodations on a train, boat, etc.; to be booked *through to* a place.

1842 LONGFELLOW in S. Longfellow *H. W. Longfellow* I. 415 To borrow the expression of a fellow-traveller, we were 'ticketed through to the depot.' **1859** A. VAN BUREN *Sojourn in South* 17, I was soon 'ticketed' and aboard [the steamer]. **1882** PECK *Sunshine* 165 They thought they were ticketed through to the other place.

2. *tr.* To give a ticket or invitation to (someone).

1860 *Ladies' Repository* May 267/1 There was to be a great ball, and Mrs. Locke's girls were to be ticketed.

b. To supply (a person) with a railroad ticket. Also absol.

1882 *K.C. Jrnl.* 19 Feb., We ticket directly to every place of importance. **1890** *Kingston* (N.M.) *Shaft* 25 Oct. 4/6 We can ticket you at Lake Valley to any point on earth.

* **tickle,** *v.* In combs.: (1) **tickle bender,** ?a fine or superior fellow, *colloq.* and *obs.*, cf. **tickley-benders** *s.v.* **tiddledies;** (2) **grass,** the rough bent or hair grass, *Agrostis hiemalis*, or one of various other American grasses; (3) **match (grass),** the rough bent, *Agrostis hiemalis;* (4) **mouth,** =prec.; (5) **weed,** (see quot.), *obs.*

(1) **1831** *Boston Transcript* 6 Dec. 2/4 Aint he a tickle bender? — (2) **1832** WILLIAMSON *Maine* I. 124. **1840** DEWEY *Mass. Flowering Plants* 234 *T*[*richodium*] *laxiflorum*, Tickle-grass, . . . forms a handsome turf. **1924** CROY *R.F.D. No. 3* 30 The hated barbed ticklegrass was stuffed down trousers. — (3) **1819** *Niles' Reg.* XVII. 143/2 Two elegant imitations of ladies Leghorn hats . . . [were made] from a grass common in the vicinity of Hartford, . . . commonly known as *tickle-match grass.* **1819** *Plough Boy* I. 199 A grass, commonly called *Tickle match*, has lately been used for making hats, by some ladies of Hartford. — (4) **1819** *Amer. Farmer* I. 280 It is known, generally among our farmers, by the name of 'tickle mouth'—although some call it 'wire grass.' **1946** C. H. KNOWLTON (in a letter to the editor 9 July), I asked Dr. Merritt Lyndon Fernald of the Gray Herbarium about the name Tickle-mouth. He said that in his boyhood they always called the [tickle] grass by that name, presumably in Orono, Maine. (5) **1751** ELIOT *Field-Husb.* iii. 66 Take the Roots of Swamp Hellebore, sometimes called Skunk Cabbage, Tickle Weed, Bear Root.

* **tickler,** *n.*

1. A book of memoranda so arranged that on a given day the things to be remembered for that day's work appear on the calendar for that day. (See also quot. 1891.)

1805 *Theatr. Censor* (Phila.) 12 Dec. 16 By inserting this in your *tickler*, you will render a service to the play-going citizens of Philadelphia. **1891** NICHOLS *Business Guide* (ed. 28) 244 *Tickler*, a book containing a memoranda [*sic*] of notes and debts arranged in the order of their maturity. **1906** QUICK *Double Trouble* 166 You'll do for an animated 'office tickler' if you continue to improve. You used to forget all those things.

2. (See quot. 1889.)

1809 WEEMS *Marion* (1833) 162 [The old man held] up a stout tickler of brandy. **1889** *Harper's Mag.* Aug. 388/2 The tickler was a bottle of narrow shape, holding a half-pint—just enough to tickle.

3. (See quot.)

1841–52 T. W. HARRIS *Insects Injur. Veget.* ii. (1862) 105 The largest Capricorn-beetle, . . . found in New England, is . . . the tickler, so named probably on account of the habit which it has . . . of gently touching now and then the surface on which it walks with the tips of its long antennae.

4. (See quot.)

1905 CALKINS & HOLDEN *Art Advertising* 351 A tickler is any small piece of printed matter sent out to keep open a prospective sale on the part of the inquirer.

5. *Electr.* A feed-back coil.

1922 *Wireless World* X. 430/2 The reaction coil (or 'tickler' as it is called over the water). **1925** *Scribner's Mag.* July 44/2 The intricate business of . . . whirling the tickler into place and moving the detector dial to the exact spot.

* **tidal wave.** *fig.* A wave or surge of grief (see also quot. 1892).

1875 MARK TWAIN *Sk. New & Old* 213 A great tidal wave of grief swept over us all when Joan of Arc fell at Waterloo. **1882** *Nation* 9 Nov. 391/1 The so-called tidal wave of 1874 was only a lively ripple compared with this overwhelming flood. **1892** WALSH *Lit. Curiosities* 1053 *Tidal Wave*, an American political figure of speech, applied to an election in which the winning party is returned with an overwhelming and unprecedented majority.

tiddledies ˈtɪdl̩dɪz, *n.* Also **tiddles, tiddly-benders, tickley-benders.** [Origin obscure. Cf. **kittly-benders** and see * *tittle, adv.*, very lightly, in *EDD.*] An expression used with reference to running or skating on ice that has begun to break up, or that is so thin that it bends as one passes over it. Also transf. *Colloq.*

1877 BARTLETT 704 Boys say, 'run tiddlies,' *i.e.* run over ice after it has begun to break up on a sheet of water. **1886** C. C. ABBOTT *Upland & Meadow* 52 (Funk), I have even seen them [*sc.* crows] play at 'tickley benders,' but with the advantage over boys in that they can stay up always, even if the ice goes down. **1888** *Boston Jrnl.* 17 Dec. 3/6 Running tiddledies, or 'tiddledy-benders,' is a great test of character. **1902** LORIMER *Lett. Merchant* 70 You had the old man running tiddledies. **1913** *Outing* Jan. 490 On the delicious tiddly-benders over the brook, though, you could kick a hole through with the toe of your skate, and, lying on your stomach, suck up a drink.

* **tide,** *n.*

1. (See quot.) *Obs.*

1817 *Ann. 14th Cong.* 2 Sess. 1008 In speaking (in the phraseology of the country) of the tides in the Currituck [n.e. coast of N.C.], and the other sounds and inland waters with which it is connected, a regular periodical ebb and flow of the waters is not to be understood, but that change which is produced by the action of a strong and constant wind in driving the water from one sound to another.

2. A rising of the water in a river at a time of heavy rains; a flood or freshet.

1897 BRODHEAD *Bound in Shallows* 104 A hope of early fall 'tides' began to enliven the loggers' conversation. **1903** FOX *Little Shepherd* iii, In the spring, . . . the 'tides' came.

3. In combs.: (1) **tideland spruce,** the Sitka spruce, *Picea sitchensis*, of the northern Pacific Coast; (2) **runner,** (see quot.), *obs.;* (3) **spring,** a spring that ebbs and flows daily; (4) **swamp,** (see quot.); (5) * **water,** see as a main entry.

(1) **1884** SARGENT *Rep. Forests* 206 Tide-Land Spruce. . . . A large tree of great economic value, . . . reaching its greatest development

. . . near the mouth of the Columbia river. **1906** *Out West* March 175 The great Tideland Spruce of the north coast is but little less in dimensions. — **(2) 1877** C. HALLOCK *Sportsman's Gaz.* (1883) 244 These big fellows [weakfish] are designated as 'tide-runners.' — **(3) 1838** FLAGG *Far West* II. 222 From this remarkable *tide-spring* until we reach the Grand Tower, the face of the country has a depressed and sunken aspect, as if once the bed of standing water. — **(4) 1796** *Ann. 4th Congress* 2 Sess. 2694 All tide-swamps, not generally affected by the salts or freshes of the first quality, are rated at six pounds per acre.

∗ **tidewater,** *n.*

1. Water of a given area or in specified streams which is affected by the tides, or a region or area where the waters are so affected.

This term is often used with specific reference to eastern Virginia.

1772 *Va. Statutes at Large* VIII. 564 The extension of the navigation of James river . . . will be greatly promoted by cutting a canal, through the falls, from Westham to the tide water. **1857** *Harper's Mag.* March 434/1 All the swamps bordering the southern tide-water present the same characteristics. **1889** *Cent. Mag.* Feb. 602/1 Long 'tidewaters' . . . ran up to the very foot of the wooded hills. **1904** *N.Y. Sun* 21 Aug. 4 He aspires to be the Republican boss of the Old Dominion, from mountains to tidewater. **1944** FAST *F. Road* 7 It lay in that gently rolling country that makes a broad belt of demarcation between the flat tidewater and the high uplands.

attrib. **1832** KENNEDY *Swallow Barn* I. 179 There are very few villages in the tide-water country of Virginia. **1868** *Rep. Comm. Agric. 1867* p. x, The whole tide-water area . . . is endowed with a climate peculiarly adapted to market gardening. **1884** *Cent. Mag.* April 825/2 Mr. Jones . . . [has] one of those thin, mournful faces common to tide-water Maryland. **1946** *Chi. D. News* 24 April 18/4 Jane, mistress of a prominent white citizen in the Tidewater community, is unjustly accused of murder.

2. a. tidewater red cypress, bald cypress. **b. tidewater spruce, = tideland spruce.**

(a) 1947 BEEBE *Mixed Train Dly.* 11 Above is one of Brooks-Scanlon's wood burners deep in the network of logging lines which the company maintains to exploit its thousands of acres of long-leaf pine and tidewater red cypress. — **(b) 1884** *Rep. Comm. Agric.* 142 Tidewater Spruce.—This variety grows 200 feet high and 8 to 10 in diameter.

tidytips ˈtaɪdɪˌtɪps, *n.* (See quot. 1891.) Also with specifying term.

1888 LINDLEY *Calif. of South* 329 All through the months of March, April, and May, plants of *Layia platyglossa* are scattered over the ground as thickly as star-dust in the sky. The children call it 'tidy-tips,' each golden petal being daintily fringed with white. **1891** *Cent.* 6331/1 *Tidytips*, a Californian composite plant, *Layia* (*Callichroa*) *platyglossa:* a showy plant with bright-yellow rays, frequently cultivated as a half-hardy annual. **1949** *Desert Mag.* May 29/2 An abundance of senecio, white tidytips, . . . and sand blazing star are among the flowers in bloom.

∗ **tie,** *n.* Short for **railroad tie.**

1853 *La Crosse Democrat* 4 Oct. 2/5 The contract [has been let] for furnishing the whole of the ties required for the road. **1894** *Outing* XXIV. 123/2 We were swinging over the ties where the woods bordered the railroad. **1948** *Reader's Digest* Jan. 68/1 We spanned the treeless plains on ties cut from eastern forests.

attrib. **1879** VIVIAN *Wanderings in Western Land* 277 He had been in the summer time prospecting for a tie camp, . . . when he struck some elegant strawberries. **1892** *N.Y. Herald* 21 Feb. 13/1 Coy . . . returned to a tie camp on the Texarkana and Fort Smith Railroad. **1900** *Cong. Rec.* 10 Jan. 754/2 The cutting of tie and bridge timber for the construction of railroads in the Indian Territory. **1946** WILSON *Fidelity* 16 A tie-hack, I might say by way of explanation, was a professional maker of railroad crossties.

Also *tie chopper, contract cutter, maker, plate,* etc.

b. *To count the ties,* to walk along a railroad, usu. said of one, as a tramp, unable to secure a train ticket. *Colloq.*

1912 *Out West* Jan. 79/1 I've counted the ties and slept in the jungles and stole chickens and cooked them in a coal oil can. **1942** DALE *Cow Country* 152 Then he settled down to count the ties And to the next town straightway hies.

As the last term in **ankle, cross, head, hog, oak, rail, railroad, redwood, shoestring, side, string, Windsor tie.**

∗ **tie,** *v.*

1. *tr.* To supply (the roadbed of a railroad) with ties.

1867 *Comm. & Fin. Chron.* 2 Feb. 151 The contract for grading, bridging, and tieing the division of this line between Charito and Aston, Ia. . . . has been awarded. **1883** *Local News* (West Chester, Pa.) II. No. 234, 1 Forty miles of road . . . had to be rebuilt entirely, graded, tied.

2. In combs.: (1) **tie bush,** ?**=hobblebush;** (2) **game,** a game in which the final scores of the opposing sides are equal; (3) **post,** a hitching post; (4) **rail,** a rail or railing to which horses are hitched; (5) **rope,** a short rope used by cowboys for tying together the feet of lassoed cattle, also a mecate *q.v.*, used as a rein; (6) **strap,** (see quot. 1876); (7) ∗**-up,** see as a main entry.

(1) 1836 LATROBE *Rambler* II. 7 The dark and sombre verdure of the sweet-bay, magnolia, tie-bush . . . were now contrasted with the more brilliant colours. — **(2)** [**1856** *Spirit of Times* 6 Sep. 13/3 The Knickerbocker and the Empire Clubs met on Saturday, and the work resulted in a tie, eight innings being played and 21 runs being the aggregate in favor of each side.] **1867** *Ball Players' Chron.* 4 July 2/2 This left the totals at 16 to 16—tie game. **1928** *Collier's* 29 Dec. 17/4 A tie game in football is certainly more thrilling . . . than a one-sided game. — **(3) 1861** *Harper's Mag.* Feb. 424/2 He alighted, . . . carelessly throwing the reins over a tie-post. **1909** CULLUM *Watchers* 32 The only building worth consideration is the hotel. . . . This has a verandah and a tie-post. — **(4) 1920** MULFORD *J. Nelson* 238 He'll never forget my kickin' him off'n th' tie-rail. **1948** *Chi. Tribune* 31 Oct. VII. 20/2 By 10:30 the horses are waiting at the tie rail for the morning ride to the foothills.

(5) 1890 *Stock Grower & Farmer* 4 Jan. 5/2 Tom Davenport . . . had lost his tie rope. **1923** J. H. COOK *On Old Frontier* 19 With one of the 'tie-ropes' which he always carried tucked under his belt, [he] 'hog-tied' the bull. **1944** JOHNSON *As I Dare* 291 She would start across the wide field with a short tie-rope dragging behind her, and the only way we could follow her course was by motion of the alfalfa. — **(6) 1876** KNIGHT 2567/2 *Tie-strap,* (*Saddlery,*) a long strap having a buckle and chape on one end, used as an extra strap to a bridle for tying. **1901** *Munsey's Mag.* XXV. 736/2 The colt . . . was led in, the tie strap was unsnapped from his halter, and he was allowed [etc.].

b. With adverbs and prepositions in colloq. phrases: (1) *To tie into,* to go to work upon, to take to task; (2) *to tie out,* to take out and tie (mail matter) in separate bundles; (3) ∗*to tie to,* to rely upon, to identify one's interests with; (4) ∗*to tie up,* to delay or stop; (5) *to tie up to* (or *with*), = ∗*to tie to.*

(1) 1902 WHITE *Blazed Trail Stories* 71 Just tie tight into her and keep her hustling. **1912** WASON *Friar Tuck* xiv, They girded up their loins, and tied into him a little harder. — **(2) 1883** CUSHING *Story of P.O.* 56 The postmasters at distributing points like Sisson should 'tie out' the little packages of letters intended for offices on the radiating routes. — **(3) 1858** *So. Cultivator* XVI. 17/2, I think it [Chinese sugar cane] will 'do to tie to.' **1909** *N.Y. Ev. Post* 13 Sep. 5 The college must offer in its faculty men whom students can tie to, men who can evoke personal devotion and enthusiasm. **1948** DICK *Dixie Frontier* 21 He isn't a bad man, but he'll never do to tie to. — **(4) 1887** GEORGE *40 Yrs. on Rail* 140, I ran into a snow-storm that tied us up until we were six days making the run. **1907** *Springfield W. Republican* 10 Oct. 16 Traffic west of Springfield was tied up until about midnight.

(5) 1876 *Fur, Fin & Feather* Sep. 144/1 Cutchogue, Long Island, . . . is a good place to 'tie up to' for any one fond of fishing and fowling. **1903** *N.Y. Ev. Post* 5 Dec. 1 When a representative has a navy yard in his district, . . . [he can] make business for that yard . . . by tying up with the other navy yard representatives on the committee. **1928** *Publishers' Wkly.* 30 June 2613 There are . . . well over one hundred booksellers . . . who are tying-up with the national advertising campaign.

tienda tiˈɛndə, *n. S.W.* [Sp. in same sense.] A shop or store.

1844 KENDALL *Narr. Santa Fé Exped.* II. 38, I saw . . . the detestable Salezar, standing in front of a small *tienda*, or store. **1884** HARTE *On Frontier* 139 A part of the shanty was used as a *tienda* or shop. **1912** SAUNDERS *Indian Terraced Houses* 71 Our proximity to the pueblo was indicated by our meeting Indians . . . on their way to the trader's *tienda* beneath the shady cottonwoods at Algodones.

∗ **tier,** *n.*[1] A row, range, or series of contiguous lots, townships, states, or counties. Cf. **second tier, southern tier.**

1693 *Hartford Land Distrib.* 212 One [parcel of land] lyeing in the Same Teere of lotts abutting on a High way. **1824** in COX *Recoll. Wabash* X. 18 The land is sold in tiers of townships. **1856** *Spirit of Times* 18 Oct. 113/1 The great varying hare . . . is no longer to be found in our state, . . . until we reach the northern tier of counties, on the Canada line. **1860** *Cong. Globe* 19 Dec. 139/3 They constitute the first tier of the border slave States. **1949** *Ward Co. Independent* (Minot, N.D.) 21 July 1/3 Each of the big wheat states in the tier from Texas up through North Dakota appears to be coming up with a crop just under that state's all-time record.

∗ **tier,** *n.*[2] *N. Eng.* [So called in allusion to the garment's being tied on, rather than buttoned.] (See quot. 1846.) *Colloq.* Cf. **tire.**

1846 WORCESTER 740/2 *Tier,* . . . a child's apron. **1865** WHITNEY *Gayworthys* 73 She took care of Say; put on her long-sleeved tyers when she sent her out to play. **1892** WILKINS *Young Lucretia* 33 It was Fidelia's white tier. **1902** *D.N.* II. 254 Even among the older people, 'cricket' has mostly given place to 'footstool,' and 'tier' to 'apron.'

tierras tɪ'ɛrəs, *n. pl. W.* [Sp. pl. of *tierra*, earth.] (See quots.) — **1873** *Mining & Sci. Press* 21 March, The screenings and fine stuff [from a quicksilver mine] is called 'tierras.' **1881** RAYMOND *Mining Gloss., Tierras,* . . . fine dirt impregnated with quicksilver ore, which must be made into adobes before roasting.

* **tie-up,** *n.*

1. A place where cattle are tied up for the night. Also attrib.

1851 SPRINGER *Forest Life* 82 At the further end of the 'tie-up' he thinks he hears a little clattering noise. **1882** *Maine Agric. Rep.* XXVI. 50 The farmers throw the dressing out of the tie-up windows. **1949** KURATH *Word Geog. Eastern U.S.* 21/1 *Lean-to* and *tie-up* are common names in eastern Massachusetts, New Hampshire, and Maine for the shed-like addition to the barn in which the cows are housed.

2. A stoppage of work or operations because of a strike, accident, etc.

1889 *Scientific Amer.* LX. 32/3 In the event of a 'tie-up,' or strike, these street boxes would be used. **1948** *Time* 6 Dec. 22/1 The West Coast [shipping] tie-up was being unknotted.

tiff tɪf, *n.* [Origin unknown.] (See quots.) *Obs.*

1814 BRACKENRIDGE *Views La.* 148 The porter's ore, or galena, has always adhering to it, a sparry matter, which the miners call tiff. **1819** SCHOOLCRAFT *Mo. Lead Mines* 70 Tiff, cawk, and sulphate of barytes, are therefore one substance, consisting of the earth barytes united to the sulphuric acid. **1856** FERGUSSON *America* 404 The most remarkable specimens were one of large cubes of galena, weighing 250 to 300 lbs., and various specimens of carbonate of lime, the local name given to which is 'tiff.' **1920** FAY *Glossary* 686/1 Tiff. 1. A common name for calcite in Wisconsin and Missouri zinc fields. 2. Barite in southeast Missouri.

* **tiger,** *n.*

1. Any one of various American animals, esp. a panther, of the cat family.

1709 LAWSON *Carolina* 119 Tygers are never met withal in the settlement; but are more to the westward. . . . It seems to differ from the Tyger of Asia and Africa. **1809** HENRY *Travels* 305, I saw also the skins of foxes, bears, and a small number of panthers, sometimes called tigers, and most properly, *cougars.* [Note to *cougar:*] Felis concolor. **1894** EGGLESTON in *Cent. Mag.* April 849 The panther was long called a 'tyger' in the Carolinas, and a 'lyon' elsewhere. **1946** S. P. YOUNG *Puma* 3 In earlier colonial times the name 'tiger' was applied to the animal [i.e., the puma] in present New York State, then known as New Netherlands.

2. The game of faro (see quot. 1938). Also attrib. *Slang.*

1845 HOOPER *Simon Sugg's Adv.* 55 Of these tables the 'tiger' claimed three—for faro was predominant in these days. **1849** G. G. FOSTER *N.Y. in Slices* 47 The groggeries and tiger dens . . . were in quite a flutter for several hours. **1938** ASBURY *Sucker's Prog.* 15 Tiger—Faro. During the early 1830's a first-rate professional gambler carried his Faro outfit in a fine mahogany box on which was painted a picture of the Royal Bengal Tiger.

transf. **1877** in *Amer. Sp.* XXII. 300 A two storied frame building . . . was opened as a gambling house and named 'the tiger.'

b. (See quots.)

1938 ASBURY *Sucker's Prog.* 30 The Tiger became popular about 1885, and was described in the 1887 edition of *Hoyle's Games* as 'a dreadful innovation.' It is the lowest hand which can be held, the deuce, trey, four, five and seven, and as originally played was better than a straight and not as good as a flush. **1946** MOREHEAD & MOTT-SMITH *Penguin Hoyle* 122 A *big tiger* is a hand in which the king is the highest card, the eight is the lowest card, and there is no pair; a *little tiger* is a hand in which the eight is the highest card, a three the lowest card, and there is no pair.

c. *To fight the tiger*, and variants, to gamble at faro. *Slang.*

For *to buck the tiger* see **buck,** *v.*[1] **1. b.**

1839 *Spirit of Times* 10 Aug. 266/1 (We.), The 'man what fights the tiger' is a gentlemen [*sic*] in comparison. **1845** HOOPER *Simon Sugg's Adv.* iv. 43 Simon believes that he can whip the Tiger. **1853** P. PAXTON *Yankee in Texas* 183 All the rogues is thar fer some reason or nother . . . some to stock a jury, and a pile to 'spread the tiger' an play poker. **1859** *N.Y. Herald* 25 Feb. 1/5 'Fighting the tiger' in the metropolis was an expensive amusement. **1869** MARK TWAIN *Curious Dreams* 83 (R.), Hunting the 'tiger,' or some kindred game. **1907** MULFORD *Bar-20* Reckon I'll hit th' tiger a whirl.

3. As a name for various implements (see quots.).

1848 *De Bow's Review* V. 53, I shall now proceed to consider the subject of . . . refining the sugar by means of pneumatic boxes or *tigers*, as they are called. **1876** KNIGHT 2568/1 *Tiger*, (*Sugar*,) a tank having a perforated bottom, through which the molasses escapes. **1881** RAYMOND *Mining Gloss., Tiger.* . . . A tool for supporting a column of bore-rods while raising or lowering them.

4. A howl or yell concluding a round of cheering.

1856 *Spirit of Times* 8 Nov. 165/1 Mr. Andrews . . . concluded by . . . calling upon the Excelsiors to give three times three and a tiger to the Putnams. **1908** DAVENPORT *Butte Beneath X-Ray* 62 Three Cheers and a Tiger for the Plumbers' Union of Butte. **1945** MARSHALL *Santa Fe* 120 Three Cheers and a Tiger for the A.T. & S.F.R.R.

5. Short for **blind tiger.**

[**1890** *Our Mountain Home* (Talladega, Ala.) 5 Nov. 4/2 He established a 'tige' of his own.] **1905** *D.N.* III. 70 'It looks like there are no *blind-tigers here.*' Universal. The abbreviated form 'tiger' is beginning to be used [in n.w. Ark.].

6. (*cap.*) =**Tammany tiger.**

1903 *N.Y. Times* 1 Oct. 8 For when we let the Tiger into the City Hall we put him in control of pretty much the entire City Government.

7. In combs.: (1) **tiger bass,** =**striped bass;** (2) ***cat,** a western wildcat or lynx, also attrib. and transf.; (3) **frog,** (see quot.); (4) **rattler, rattlesnake,** (see quot. 1909); (5) **salamander,** (see quot. 1909); (6) **skin,** the skin of any one of various American animals formerly known as tigers.

(1) **1888** *Wildwood's Mag.* (Chi.) June 64 In the north and west both species are known as 'bass,' with the addition of various adjectives expressive of gameness, coloration, or habitat, as 'tiger-bass,' . . . black, green, or yellow-bass; . . . marsh-bass, or Oswego-bass. — (2) **1806** CLARK in *Lewis & C. Exped.* IV. (1905) 113 Capt Lewis [has] a Tiger cat skin [coat]. **1886** BURNETT *Lord Fauntleroy* xi, A hefty un she was,—regular tiger-cat. — (3) **1842** *Nat. Hist. N.Y., Zoology* III. 62 The Marsh Frog, *Rana palustris*, . . . is called, in various districts, Pickerel Frog, and also Tiger and Leopard Frog. — (4) **1898** *Smithsonian Rep.* 1183 A study of the present series convinces me that the nearest affinity of the 'tiger rattler' is with the true *Crotalus confluentus* of the plains. **1909** *Cent. Supp.* 1114/2 Tiger rattlesnake, *Crotalus tigris*, a rare species of the Southwest, named from its tawny color and dark cross stripes.

(5) **1909** *Cent. Supp.* 1350/2 tiger-salamander. . . . A book-name for the common large western salamander, *Ambystoma tigrinum.* **1948** HERRICK *Brain of Tiger Salamander* 3 The tiger salamander, to whom this book [of 409 pages] is dedicated, is appropriately named, for within the obscurity of its contracted world it is a predaceous and voracious terror to all humbler inhabitants. — (6) **1734** *Ga. Col. Rec.* III. 93 Left by him, . . . as a Token of Friendship, . . . One Tyger Skin, & Six Buffalo Skins. **1854** WHIPPLE *Explor. Ry. Route* I. 75 Juan Septimo brought for us several excellent robes of wild-cat or tiger skin.

As the last term in **blind, sea, spotted, Tammany tiger.**

* **tight,** *a.* and *n.*

1. *n.* App. a kind of liquor. *Rare.*

1834 CARUTHERS *Kentuckian* I. 23 Won't you join us in a glass of tight?

2. =**tight place.** *Colloq.*

1902 HARBEN *Abner Daniel* xxi. 182 It would tempt five men out of ten if they were inclined to go wrong, and were in a tight. **1942** in WENTWORTH 643 Any time you get in a tight, us is here to do what we can.

3. In combs.: (1) **tighteye,** =**titi,** *colloq.;* (2) **fit,** (see quot.), *slang, obs.;* (3) **line,** (see quot.), *obs.;* (4) **place, spot,** a close place, a difficulty or embarrassment, *colloq.;* (5) **wad,** a miser or skinflint, *slang.*

(1) **1905** W. L. FLEMING *Civil War & Reconstruction* 123 Deep thickets called 'tight-eyes' swarmed with . . . deserters. **1932** BESSIE MARTIN *Desertion Ala. Troops* 50 Besides swamps, the region contained caves and dense thickets or brushes [*sic*], sometimes called 'tight eyes,' where deserters might hide safely. — (2) **1851** HALL *College Words* 302 A good joke is denominated by the students a *tight fit.* — (3) **1882** G. C. EGGLESTON *Wreck of Red Bird* 17 'We fish with tight lines.' 'What are they?' 'Why, long lines with a sinker at the end and no poles.' — (4) **1841** *Jamestown* (N.Y.) *Jrnl.* 31 March 2/4 It speaks of his being in a tight place. **1852** TOWNSHEND (of Ohio) in *H. Rep.* 23 June (Th.), I felt myself in a tight spot. **1932** *K.C. Star* 11 Jan. 16 This is the way old Sol Miller got out of a tight place in his Troy Chief, sixty years ago.

(5) **1900** G. ADE *More Fables* 30 Henry was undoubtedly the Tightest Wad in the Township. **1945** SERVICE *Ploughman* 312 So I became one, and passed the plate in my turn, adjuring the tightwads to come through.

As the last term in **air, hog, pig tight.**

tignon ti'jɔn, *n.* [La. F.] (See quot. 1931.)

1884 *Dly. Inter-Ocean* (Chi.) 2 July 1/5 [The women's heads were] adorned with the traditional head handkerchief of the tignon. **1929**

SAXON *Old. La.* 123 Piquant quadroon girls, wearing their bright-striped *tignons*, moved through the throng. **1931** W. A. READ *La.-French* xx, It may be well to note here some conspicuous features of Louisiana Acadian . . . *Di*, when followed by a vowel, has approximately the value of English *j*, as in *dieu, diable;* 'gn' is sometimes pronounced like English 'y,' as regularly in *tignon*, 'kerchief.'

** **tile,** *n.* **1.** =next. **2. tilefish,** a marine food fish, *Lopholatilus chamaeleonticeps*, of the eastern coast; by extension, a fish of the family Branchiostegidae (see quot. 1911).

(1) 1893 *Worthington's Mag.* I. 150 The Tile should be obtainable in numbers equal to the cod. — **(2) 1881** in *Rep. Comm. Fisheries* IX. 34 One of the tile-fish taken in the morning was boiled for dinner and served with egg sauce. **1911** *Rep. Fisheries 1908* 317/2 Tilefish (*Latilidae*). . . . The California species (*Caulolatilus princeps*) is also known as the 'whitefish' and 'blanquillo.'

tilikum ˈtɪləkəm, *n.* Also **tillicum.** *N.W.* [Chinook, people, friends, relations, folks, etc.] *pl.* The common people as distinguished from those of some rank; friends.

1845 PALMER *Rocky Mts.* (1847) 105 A long time ago the Great Spirit became angry with them, set the mountain on fire, destroyed their towns, turned their *tiye* (chief) and *tilicums* (people) into stone, and cast them in the ocean outside of Cape Lookout. **1878** *Pt. Townsend* (Wash.) *Wkly. Argus* 22 March, The other day, a school-boy having committed an offense, he was tied up, and some of his 'tillicums,' who do not belong to the church party, set up a howl and finally cut him loose. **1920** *Outing* Sep. 275/2 Bart and Bill being old *klos tillicums*, their talk soon drifted to things and folks of other days. **1950** *Amer. Sp.* May 84 From the Jargon, words like *cumtux, ictas, muckamuck*, and *tillicum* frequently appeared.

Tillamook ˈtɪləˌmuk, *n.* Also **Killamook.** [Prob. f. the Chinook name for these Indians.] *pl.* or *collect.* (See quot. 1910.) Also attrib.

1838 PARKER *Exploring Tour* 259 Near the mouth of the Columbia, along the coast, are the Killamooks who are numerous, but their numbers are not known. **1844** LEE & FROST *Oregon* 99 The south side of the Columbia, immediately on the coast, is inhabited by the Clatsops, and to the south of them is the Killemook country. **1910** HODGE *Amer. Indians* II. 750/2 Tillamook. . . . A large and prominent Salish tribe on Tillamook bay and the rivers flowing into it, in N.W. Oregon.

b. The language of these Indians.

1950 *Amer. Sp.* May 82 At heart the Jargon was Indian, a mixture of verbs, modifiers, and a collection of nouns from Indian languages like Nootka, Tillamook, and Chinook.

till-tapper. One who robs tills. Also **till-tapping,** *n.*

1848 JUDSON *Mysteries N.Y.* 111 (We.), The youngsters are in for till-tapping. **1893** *Columbus* (O.) *Dispatch* 14 Nov., The firm has been a loser by persistent till-tapping. *Ib.*, The camera lens closed automatically with the photographs of the till-tappers imprinted on the instantaneous plate. **1903** *N.Y. Times* 7 Oct. 8 Their rank [among criminals] will be about that of tilltappers and pickpockets.

tilma ˈtɪlmə, *n. S.W.* [Amer. Sp. (<Nahuatl) in same sense.] (See quot. 1927.)

[**1780** CLAVIGERO *Storia della Messico* II. 91 Allora un Sacerdote annodava una punta dell' *Huepilla*, o camicia della Sposa con un' altra del *Tilmatli*, o mantello della Sposo, ed in queste ceremonia faceano, essezialmente consistere il contratto matromoniale.] **1844** GREGG *Commerce of Prairies* I. 278 The Pueblos, however, make some of the ordinary classes of blankets and *tilmas*, as well as other woollen stuffs. **1927** CATHER *Death Comes*, The tilma was a mantle worn only by the very poor,—a wretched garment loosely woven of coarse vegetable fibers and sewn down the middle. **1949** MCWILLIAMS *No. from Mexico* 295 Names for items of dress have likewise been appropriated: *sombrero, tilma, rebozo, manta, and sarape.*

** **tilt,** *n.* and *v.*

1. a. = ** **longshanks. b.** =**tilt-up** (*b*).

(a) 1813 WILSON *Ornithology* VII. 50 Long-legged Avoset. . . . The name by which this bird is known on the sea coast is the Stilt, or Tilt, or Long-shanks. **1844** *Nat. Hist. N.Y., Zoology* II. 266 The Lawyer . . . is known under the various popular names of Tilt, Stilt, Long-shanks. — **(b) 1891** *Cent.* 6339/1 A simple tilt is a lath or narrow board with a hole bored through one end. . . . An improved tilt consists of an upright with an arm. . . . Also called *tilter, tilt-up*, and *tip-up*.

2. In combs.: (1) **tilt pan,** (see quot.), *obs.;* (2) **-up,** (*a*) the spotted sandpiper, *Actitis macularia*, (*b*) in fishing, a device placed over a hole in the ice in such a position that it will be tilted, as a signal, by the pull of a fish on the line, cf. **tip-up** (*b*); (3) **wagon,** a covered wagon, *obs.*

(1) 1833 B. SILLIMAN *Man. Sugar Cane* 100 This is so elevated, that the syrup flows, readily, into the evaporating vessels—which are the (now well known,) bascule pans, called also, tilt or see-saw pans. — **(2)** (*a*) **1842** *Nat. Hist. N.Y., Zoology* I. 247 The Spotted Sand-Lark . . . is known . . . [as] *Teeter* and *Tiltup*, from its often repeated grotesque jerking motions. **1917** *Birds of Amer.* I. 249 Spotted Sandpiper. . . . [Also called] Tip-up; Tilt-up . . . from its nervous habit of constantly tilting its body. (*b*) **1891** [see **tilt 1. b.**]. **1899** VAN DYKE *Fisherman's Luck* 128 [A] 'tilt-up' . . . consists of two sticks fastened in the middle, at right angles to each other. — **(3) 1836** T. POWER *Impressions* II. 43 As we thus lay together, I noticed that the upper or promenade deck of the Columbus was completely taken up by a double row of flashy-looking covered carts, or tilt-waggons, as they are called here [Philadelphia]. [**1838** S. WOOD *Lett. from U.S.* 3 In the course of this day's sail, there was pointed out to me, on the bank of the river, the habitation of *a squatter:* it was a log-hut, to all appearance about a month old, and close by it was the tilted wagon which had brought this migratory man and his family to the spot where they had fixed themselves.]

** **tilter,** *n.* **a.** A seesaw. **b.** A swaying motion. **c.** =**tilt-up** (*b*). All *colloq.* and *obs.*

(a) 1727 COMER *Diary* (1893) 17 As I was playing a childish play on a tilter with one Power Merit . . . , I fell. — **(b) 1833** NEAL *Down-Easters* I. 173 A lawyer . . . [with] a tilter in his walk. — **(c) 1891** [see ** **tilt 1. b.**].

tilter ˈtɪltɚ, *v.* [Poss. f. ** *tilt* + ** teet*er*.] *intr.* To seesaw or sway up and down. *Colloq.*

1825 NEAL *Bro. Jonathan* III. 271 The cursed pistol . . . was tiltering too, as if it were just ready to go off, at every jump. **1845** JUDD *Margaret* I. 105 A bobolink clung tiltering to the breezy tip of a white birch. **1895** WIGGIN *Village Watch-Tower* 36 Butterflies . . . perch on the . . . stalks and tilter up and down in the sunshine.

** **timber,** *n.*

1. A forest or wood.

1792 in YOUNG *Jessamine Co., Ky.* 49 [He] shot him in the arm and ran off into the timber. **1855** BOYNTON & MASON *Journey through Kans.* 49 On the opposite side of the grove, called here 'the timber,' we discovered . . . a cornfield. **1909** *The Fra* Feb. 72/2 It was not so long after that there was a Big Meeting in the 'timber.'

2. A person or persons considered with respect to his or their qualifications for specific responsibilities, human material. *Colloq.* Cf. **presidential timber.**

1831 in MACKENZIE *Van Buren* 227 There is but little first rate timber in the democratic ranks. **1891** *Truth* (Louisville) 19 July 7/2 Manager Hanlon will never be able to make a winning team out of the timber he has. **1945** *New Yorker* 10 Feb. 31/2 The treasurer of a department store ought to be as likely a piece of timber as the president of a utility.

3. tall timber, *fig.* the uninhabited forest, used in colloq. phrases as *to break* (*put, pull, strike*) *for* (*the*) *tall timber*, to depart in great haste and without ceremony.

1845 *St. Louis Reveille* 22 Jan. 1/6 Knowing the direction of the trees that stood in the grove, I 'broke for tall timber.' **1846** *Knickerb.* XXVIII. 311, I calculate . . . that he'll put for tall timber one of these days. **1885** SIRINGO *Texas Cow Boy* 212 Jim . . . gave his guards the slip and pulled for tall timber. **1914** D. W. ROBERTS *Rangers & Sovereignty* 128 The 'bad men' . . . began to strike for 'tall timber.' **1949** *Sky Line Trail* Oct. 18/1, I fell off *three times;* finally the disgusted critter took to the tall timber, leaving me to hike onward and to get across the frigid stream as best I could.

Also *to break for high timber.*

1831 *Boston Transcript* 24 June 2/4 Why didn't Van just go and *tell* the old man he wanted to *break for high timber?*

b. Also transf. and attrib.

1854 HAMMOND *Hills, Lakes* 146, I don't deny, that down in the settlements, among fellers that think themselves tall timber, I stretch matters a little. **1948** *Shelby* (Mont.) *Promoter* 16 Sep. 3/6 They especially enjoyed the tall timber country in Northwestern California.

4. In combs.: (1) **timber camp,** a camp of those engaged in getting out timber; (2) **cart,** (see quot.); (3) **cattle,** cattle that range chiefly in timbered regions; (4) **claim,** a timbered area of public land that may be or has been filed upon, also a claim to public land secured upon condition that the claimant plant and cultivate a specified acreage of trees upon the land; (5) **clock,** ?a wooden or New England clock, *rare;* (6) **cruise,** see as a main entry; (7) **doodle,** see as a main entry; (8) **heels,** (see quot.), *slang, obs.;* (9) **hunting,** looking for desirable tracts of timber; (10) **inspector,** an official who inspects timber; (11) **line,** see as a main entry; (12) **looker,** =**timber cruiser;** (13) ** **man,** ?a vessel engaged in the timber trade, *obs.;* (14) **pirate,** =**timber thief;** (15)

raft, a raft of saw logs; (16) **shanty,** a shanty used by those engaged in timbering operations; (17) **shoot,** a chute down which logs are sent; (18) **thief,** one who cuts and sells timber which is the property of another or of the state or national government; (19) **wheels,** (see quot.).

(1) **1879** *Scribner's Mo.* Nov. 21/1 We came across occasional timber camps. — (2) **1883** Knight *Supp.* 894/2 *Timber Cart,* . . . a high wheeled cart for drawing timber. The timber, after the cart is driven over it, is raised to the axle by crank-gearing and tackle. — (3) **1927** Siringo *Riata* 23 Most of them were wild timber cattle which only venture out on the edges of the prairies at night—grazing back to the timber at sunup. — (4) **1857** *Lawrence* (Kans.) *Republican* 4 June, Timber claims . . . may be purchased on better terms than in any place of equal distance from Lawrence. [**1889** Union Pac. R.R. *Ore. & Wash.* 26 Already the homestead, pre-emption and timber culture claims of the new settlers are rapidly absorbing these lands.] **1922**

One form of timber cart

Cather *One of Ours* 51 They had been as far as Mr. Wheeler's timber claim and back.

(5) **1820** J. Hall *Lett. from West* 194 In Goshen . . . he will find land abounding in cheese and timberclocks. — (8) **1877** Bartlett 706 Timberheels. A headlong fellow careless in walking. — (9) **1853** P. Paxton *Yankee in Texas* 21 There could be no more timber-hunting that day.

(10) **1898** N. E. Jones *Squirrel Hunters Ohio* 223 The 'timber inspector' failed to 'hold up' several thousand Canadian robbers, who were engaged in floating American timber across the line. — (12) **1917** Kephart *Camping* II. 64 Timber-lookers may or may not leave evidence of their wanderings . . . they would merely mark the easiest route for a prospective road from the river to some 'bunch' of timber. — (13) **1823** Cooper *Pilot* I. iii. 24 All to burn some old timber-man, or catch a Norway trader asleep! — (14) **1898** N. E. Jones *Squirrel Hunters of Ohio* 227 The timber pirates [were found] responsible for most all the calamities from fire which have befallen the timber lands of [Minn.].

(15) **1819** *Plough Boy* I. 7 The experiment of towing timber-rafts, on our northern waters, . . . is about to be tried. **1889** Munroe *Golden Days* 228 The miner had helped navigate great timber rafts down the Ohio. — (16) **1944** *Nat. Geog. Mag.* June 668/1 At the 'Timber Shanty' in McCall one night, former State Senator Carl E. Brown who operates a big lumber business, told some of his experiences as a pioneer in Idaho. — (17) **1884** *Rep. Comm. Agric.* 172 One of these models represented the timber-shoot, or lade, down which timber can be sent. — (18) **1878** *Rep. Forestry* (Forest Service) I. 9 Too often the forest history of our most valuable woodlands would be a record of the doings of timber-thieves. **1904** Stratton-Porter *Freckles* 208 You've kept the timber-thieves out of this lease. — (19) **1905** *Forestry Bureau Bul.* No. 61, 42 *Logging wheels,* a pair of wheels, usually about 10 feet in diameter, for transporting logs . . . Syn.: big wheels, katydid, timber wheels.

b. Designating or with reference to tracts or areas: (1) **timber belt,** a belt or strip of timbered country or of timber; (2) **bottom,** a timbered area of bottom land; (3) **district,** the country or backwoods, *obs.;* (4) **fall,** an area where timber has been blown down by a storm, cf. **blowdown, fallen timber;** (5) **farm,** a farm in a timbered region; (6) **land,** land that is well wooded, esp. with marketable timber; (7) **lot,** an area of timbered land; (8) **opening,** a place in a forest where there are naturally few trees; (9) **pasture,** a pasture in which there is timber, *obs.;* (10) **patch,** a relatively small timbered area; (11) **prairie,** (see quot.), *obs.;* (12) **slash,** a wet, slashy area overgrown by timber; (13) **swamp,** a swamp in which timber abounds; (14) **township,** a township upon which there is a considerable amount of timber, *obs.*

(1) **1862** *Ill. Agric. Soc. Trans.* V. 212 Along side of a timber belt it would be different. **1889** Munroe *Golden Days* 92 Our adventurers made their slow way after leaving the timber belt of the bottom lands. — (2) **1836** Edward *Hist. Texas* 49 Have I not seen hogs, taken from the timber bottoms, . . . weigh upwards of three hundred and fifty pounds each. — (3) **1836** *Quarter Race Ky.* 22 [He] was, as they brag in the timber districts, twenty foot in the clear, without limb, knot, windshake, or woodpecker hole. — (4) **1907** Cook *Border & Buffalo* (1938) 77 We had to pass through a timber-fall for nearly two miles, where there had been a tornado and the trees had uprooted, and in many cases piled one on top of another.

(5) **1857** *Rep. Comm. Patents 1856: Agric.* 104 This meadow-mouse . . . in timber-farms . . . is doubtless as great a pest . . . as the prairie species. — (6) **1654** *Suffolk Deeds* II. 55 Howses fence or gardens, Tymber Lands broaken & vnbroaken as whatsoeuer elce Appertenances. **1816** U. Brown *Jrnl.* II. 233 This Line Cuts away. . . . Considerable of Their Timber Land. **1946** *Longmont* (Colo.) *Times-Call* 21 June 1/2 A forest service official warned today that three unusual circumstances pose a serious fire threat in timberlands of the Rocky Mountain states. — (7) **1846** Cooper *Redskins* vi, The whole property, mills, taverns, farms, timber-lot and all fall in to young Hugh Littlepage. **1949** *Chi. Tribune* 13 June 17/4 Many woodpeckers, wrens, and other birds choose the timber lots on the farm each year for their homes. — (8) **1845** *Xenia Torch-Light* 31 July 1/1 Many an emigrant . . . [had] 'dotted down' in the midst of the timber-openings. **1860** Greeley *Overland Journey* 15 Interposed between the prairies are miles on miles of gently rolling ridges, thinly covered with white oak, and forming 'oak openings' or 'timber openings.' — (9) **1654** *Suffolk Deeds* II. 44 To haue and to howld. . . . Wth one halfe of all ye said dwelling howses out howses barnes byldings stables orchards gardens fences Woods vnderwoods trees tymber pastures [etc.]. **1668** *Oyster Bay Rec.* I. 21 To hold free land, as a for Said with all previlleges and appertenances, of timber pasters or pastareges.

(10) **1845** Kirkland *Western Clearings* 125 There would be timber-patches that looked at first no bigger than your hand. **1886** Ebbutt *Emigrant Life Kans.* 96 We could not . . . get down to our timber patch. — (11) **1852** M. Reid *Boy Hunters* xxxiv, There are the 'timber prairies' where trees grow in 'mottes' or groves. — (12) **1663** in *Amer. Sp.* XV. 404/1 An irregular Tract of Land Known by the name of Timber slash in Henrico County. — (13) **1627** *Plymouth Col. Rec.* XI. 5 It was agreed in a full Court . . . that they leave all great Tim[ber] swamps for common use. — (14) **1837** *Jamestown* (N.Y.) *Jrnl.* 23 Feb. 2/2 Not more than one third of what is called a timber township [in Maine] is covered with pine timber.

c. In the names of plants and animals: (1) **timber cock, = timberdoodle 2;** (2) **doodle,** see as a main entry; (3) **grouse,** (see quot.); (4) **pine,** any one of various pines the wood of which is valued as timber; (5) **rattler, rattlesnake,** the banded rattlesnake, *Crotalus horridus,* of the eastern and central states; (6) **wolf,** (see quot. 1891), also transf.

(1) **1941** Seton *Trail of Artist-Naturalist* 220 In many places, the forest fires had left a stretch of bare and blackened masts that were the ideal homeland of timber cock, redhead, sparrow hawk, and scores of lesser birds. — (3) **1891** *Cent.* 6340/2 *Timber-grouse,* . . . any grouse of wood-loving habits, as the ruffed grouse, the pine-grouse, or the spruce-partridge. — (4) **1817** S. Brown *Western Gaz.* 10 Between the Mobile and the Perdido, the soil is thin, timber pine, loblolly bay, cypress. **1877** Jewett *Deephaven* 156 No such timber-pines nowadays.

(5) **1936** Barnard *Rider* 51 Some called it the timber rattler or the black diamond rattler. **1950** *Chi. Tribune* 16 May II. 12/2 With him to the zoo went five timber rattlesnakes, which he snagged over the week-end around Galena. — (6) **1876** Dodge *Black Hills* 133 The 'timber' wolf . . . is regarded by frontiersmen as more dangerous than even the great gray wolf of the northern prairies. **1891** *Cent.* 6340/2 *Timber-wolf,* . . . the ordinary large gray or brindled wolf of western parts of North America, *Canis lupus occidentalis.* Though by no means confined to wooded regions, this wolf is so named in antithesis to *prairie-wolf* (the coyote). **1944** Pennell *Rome Hanks* 10 Why should He send a boatload of young rustics from Ioway down the Tennessee to a tanner from Illinois to be killed, mangled and disgraced by a pack of timberwolves from the woods of Georgia and the hills of North Carolina and Virginia? **1949** *Nat. Geog. Mag.* Dec. 830/1, I have heard gossip that a couple of timber wolves survive.

b. *To leave for bigger timber,* to go to a larger place more in keeping with one's talents. *Colloq.*

*a***1855** J. F. Kelly *Humors* 368 I'll go to Boston; I'd be a fool to stay here any longer; I'll leave for bigger timber.

As the last term in **basket, big, board, bottom, bow, cotton, cypress, dead, down, fallen, hardwood, heavy, lodge, maple, mesquite, open, presidential, rail, ranging, rift, round, sassa-**

fras, screw, square, tall timber. See also **bedding timbers, Cross Timbers.**

timber cruise.

1. A trip taken to seek out desirable tracts of timber.

1946 NEWTON *P. Bunyan* 149 Paul and I paddled from Munising over to the Pictured Rocks in his big canoe, for a day's timber cruise. **1949** *Boston Globe* 17 July (Fiction Mag.) 8/1 Hard years in mine and timber cruise had given Flood a certain steadiness and maturity beyond his years.

2. timber cruiser, one who seeks out desirable tracts of timber. Cf. ∗**cruiser,** *n.* **1.**

1894 *Cent. Mag.* March 671/2 The timber-cruiser is a hero. . . . The location of a choice tract of timber is a secret to be guarded with his life. **1949** *Sat. Ev. Post* 16 April 157/1 Some of the timber cruisers, notably the seven Merritts of Duluth, looked as much for iron as for timber and thereby discovered the great Mesabi Range.

timberdoodle ˈtɪmbɚˌdudl̩, *n.*

1. A form of spirituous drink. *Obs.*

1842 DICKENS *Amer. Notes* 26 There, too, the stranger is initiated into the mysteries of . . . Sherry-cobbler, Timber Doodle, and other rare drinks. **1873** *Punch* 17 May 201/2 Any description of beverage possessing the properties of American 'timberdoodle.'

2. (See quot. 1944.) *Colloq.*

1856 *Spirit of Times* 25 Oct. 129/1 While we have been dosing timberdoodles with infinitesimal blue pills, they shall have . . . been doctoring bruins with ounce boluses. **1944** *Mass. Audubon Soc. Bul.* Dec. 263 The Yearly Cycle, Migrations and Flights, Banding Operations, Fight for Survival, and Woodcock Cover, hardly compose a 'full' account of our present knowledge of *Philohela minor*, the Timberdoodle or American Woodcock.

3. A codger, an old fogy. *Colloq.*

1941 SETON *Trail of Artist-Naturalist* 20, I can see him yet go proudly forth to show those 'old timber-doodles' something new.

timberline ˈtɪmbɚˌlaɪn, *n.*

1. In cold or mountainous regions, the line above which timber does not grow. Cf. **cold, dry timberline.**

1867 *Harper's Mag.* June 17/2 A high mountain range divided into innumerable peaks, all of which tower above the timber-line. **1947** *Nat. Geog. Mag.* June 754/2 Above timberline we clambered over loose rock. **1950** *Nat. Hist.* May 212/1 Higher up, near timber line, the picture does become more desolate, however.

transf. **1901** RYAN *Montana* 72 The top of his head had got above timber line and glistened in the sun of early summer.

2. The boundary line of a timbered tract.

1904 STRATTON-PORTER *Freckles* 20 The Boss showed him around the timber-line.

∗**time,** *n.*

1. The unexpired time of an indentured servant, or the time of a slave permitted to seek outside employment on condition that he pay a stipulated amount to his owner. *Obs.*

1705 *Boston News-Letter* 5 Nov. 2/1 This Young man wrote to Mr. Samuel Carpenter, and other Quakers of Philadelphia, . . . who came forthwith to Virginia, and bought his time & brought him to Philadelphia last year. **1843** *Missouri Rep.* 28 Jan. (Th.), I have for sale a very likely yellow woman, . . . [with] between five and six years to serve. The balance of her time will be sold very low. **1865** *Atlantic Mo.* April 509/1 He was the slave of a gentleman who allowed him to buy his time.

2. (See quots. 1878, 1916.)

1856 *Spirit of Times* 18 Oct. 117/1 When time was called the former was one notch ahead. **1878** *De Witt's Base-Ball Guide* 79 When the umpire calls 'time,' play shall be suspended until he calls 'play' again. **1916** BANCROFT *Handbook* 83 Time at bat. The turn at bat of a player. It lasts from the time he takes his position as a batsman until he is put out or becomes a base runner. He is not considered to have completed his time at bat, however, if he be advanced to first base by the umpire on called balls, by being hit by a pitched ball, or on a sacrifice hit. **1948** *Dly. Ardmoreite* (Ardmore, Okla.) 22 Jan. 10/2 During the seventh inning the umpire called 'time.'

3. In combs.: (1) **time alarm,** (see quot.); (2) **belt,** one of the four longitudinal belts or strips, approximately fifteen degrees wide, into which the U.S. is divided for standardizing time; (3) **bill,** a bill or note payable at a given time; (4) **card,** (*a*) a card on which there is a timetable or schedule, (*b*) a card for keeping a record of hours worked or the time of a worker's arrival or departure; (5) **clock,** a clock having a device for recording the time of arrival and departure of employees or the time at which something is done; (6) **deposit,** a deposit in a bank that is to remain for a definite time; (7) **draft,** a draft payable at a specified time; (8) **payment,** an instalment payment; (9) **register,** (see quot.).

(1) **1876** KNIGHT 2572/2 *Time-alarm,* an audible notice at the expiration of a set time. — (2) **1894** *Amer. Ann. Photography* IX. 22 In each of these time-belts, the standard time is one hour faster than in the adjoining time-belt on the West. — (3) **1831** CIST *Cincinnati* 90 This House deals very extensively . . . in time bills on N. Orleans. — (4) (*a*) **1873** *Newton Kansan* 24 April 3/2 The new time card . . . allows the conductors . . . to lay over here. **1904** *Booklovers Mag.* May 663 On every large railway system there is a train not scheduled on the time-card. (*b*) **1891** *Cent.* 6342/2. **1901** MERWIN & WEBSTER *Calumet 'K'* 11 My time cards for the first years figured-up four hundred and thirty-six days. **1938** SMITTER *F.O.B. Detroit* 318 Get me his time-card. I'll fire him.

(5) **1887** GEORGE *40 Yrs. on Rail* 56 [He] pulled a wire leading to a time-clock. **1949** *Sat. Ev. Post* 7 May 120/3 He watched her cross the cannery and put her card in a time clock. — (6) **1851** CIST *Cincinnati* 90 Their policy of taking *time* deposits and allowing eight and ten per cent. interest . . . [has] attracted public attention. — (7) **1863** E. KIRKE *So. Friends* 224 Our banks requiring two home names on time drafts, I have to beg you to honor a small bill at one day's sight. **1875** *Chi. Tribune* 19 Nov. 6/1 An interesting question in relation to the bills of lading accompanying time drafts drawn against consignments has been in litigation several years. — (8) **1927** *Ladies Home Jrnl.* Dec. 45/2 Chrysler dealers are in a position to extend the convenience of time-payments. — (9) **1855** HOLBROOK *Among Mail Bags* 102 The 'time register'—a book in which each clerk is required to enter his name and time of his arrival at and departure from the office.

b. In colloq. phrases: (1) *times that try men's souls,* times of peril and hardship, as, or in allusion to, the short title of the first of the thirteen essays by Thomas Paine which appeared from time to time during the Revolution; (2) ∗*on time,* (*a*) with reference to buying, to be paid for in instalments, (*b*) at the time set, punctually; (3) *by time!* a mild oath; (4) *why* (or *what*) *in time,* and variants, why (or what) on earth; (5) *to be on a time,* to be on a spree, *rare;* (6) *to call* (or *bring*) *to time,* to take up, call to account; (7) *to run like time,* to run fast; (8) *to be up to time,* to be on time; (9) *to have a time with,* to have difficulties with; (10) *to make a time over* (or *about*), to make a demonstration or fuss over or about; (11) *to be in with the times,* to be abreast of the times in one's actions or standards; (12) *to have the time of one's life,* to have an exceptionally fine time; (13) *to call time,* to put a stop to something, cf. **2.** above; (14) *it beats my time,* see ∗**beat,** *v.* **3.** (2); (15) *to make (good) time,* see ∗**make,** *v.* **9.** (3).

(1) **1776** THOMAS PAINE (*title*), Times That Try Men's Souls. [**1847** *Yankee Doodle* I. 246/2 'These are the times that try men's soles,' as the Mexican volunteer said when his shoes were worn out.] **1858** D. K. BENNETT *Chron. N. Car.* 73 The 'Charlotte Whig' believes she was the only remaining relict (in that community) of 'the times that tried men's souls.' — (2) (*a*) **1840** *Spirit of Times* 15 Aug. 277/1 (We.), *On time*, the prices would at once be enhanced. **1920** SANDBURG *Smoke & Steel* 50 They go to an installment house and buy a bed on time. (*b*) **1848** DURIVAGE & BURNHAM *Stray Subjects* 30 S'pose you never heard of burying a man on time! **1905** ATHERTON *Travelling Thirds* 139 The train arrived on time. — (3) **1847** LOWELL *Biglow P.* 1 Ser. ii. 15 By Time, ses he, I du like a feller that aint a Feared. **1865** TROWBRIDGE *Three Scouts* 351 By time, don't that taste good! — (4) **1849** *Corr. R. W. Griswold* (1898) 250 Why in Time don't you come our way and see the boys? **1898** N. BROOKS *Boys of Fairport* 201 What'n time are you fellers up to? **1922** WILSON *Merton of Movies* 5 Merton Gill, what in the sacred name of Time are you meanin' to do with that dummy?

(5) *a*1855 J. F. KELLY *Humors* 185 The captain, being on a time, dashed into a meeting-house, running in at one door, and slap bang out at the other. — (6) **1856** *Repub. Campaign Songster* 59 Absent when the Kansas Bill was called to time. **1894** RITTENHOUSE *Maud* 572 She guys him, and calls him to time sharply. — (7) **1864** E. KIRKE *Down in Tenn.* 118 The current was running 'like time.' — (8) **1869** MARK TWAIN *Innocents* 58 They were always up to time—they could outrun and out last a donkey. **1870** F. FERN *Ginger-Snaps* 67 'The minister' must, like a conductor of a railroad train be 'up to time.' — (9) **1882** RITTENHOUSE *Maud* 149 I've had a 'time' with Mr. Blauvelt.

(10) **1888** *Boston Jrnl.* 31 July 2/5 She doesn't weep at the parting or make any time over it. **1901** *N. Amer. Rev.* Feb. 228 No other troops made such a time about water as the Americans. — (11) **1894** CABLE *J. March* xl, Just that Yankee's being here . . . pulled my wits together . . . because he's in with the times. — (12) **1905** *New Haven Reg.* 16 Feb. 6 President Roosevelt had the time of his life

when he visited the East Side Tuesday evening. — (13) **1940** MENCKEN *Happy Days* 13 When a large china thunder-bug came bouncing down the third-story stairs and a black hair-cloth sofa in the parlor lost a leg they horned in with loud shrieks and lengths of stove-wood, and my grandfather called time.

As the last term in **ball, bell, big, boom, calf, Central Standard, day, dropping, Eastern, Eastern Standard, Eastern War, fast, fishing, flush, fly, God's, good, hard, high, hog-killing, killing, laying-by, lecture, mining, mountain, mountain standard, nooning, one, Pacific, pea, persimmon, picking, pottering, rag, railroad, running, sapping, sap-running, schedule, small, standard time(s).**

timist, n.* (See quot.) *Obs.* — **1884 *Independent Almanac* 18 Only a small company [of Adventists], called '*Timists,*' now venture to fix a definite time for the advent.

timothy ˈtɪməθɪ, *n.* [f. *Timothy* Hanson, an early (*c*1720) grower of this grass.]

1. =**timothy grass.**

1747 FRANKLIN *Writings* II. 313 What [grass seed] you gave me is grown up and proves mere Timothy. **1807** GASS *Journal* 127, [I] saw no clover or timothy, as I had seen on the Missouri and Jefferson river. **1923** WYATT *Invis. Gods* 16 A clump of two of golden-rod, of black-eyed Susan and purple-panicled timothy.

2. =**timothy hay.**

1858 *Harper's Mag.* May 764/1 He lay under the dusty roof, chewing . . . now and then a stem of new-mown Timothy. **1929** DEAM *Grasses of Indiana* 158 Timothy is the principal dry grass crop of the United States.

3. In combs.: (1) **timothy grass,** a meadow grass, *Phleum pratense,* valued for forage; (2) **hay,** hay made from timothy grass; (3) **meadow,** meadow-land sown with timothy grass; (4) **sower,** a device used in sowing timothy grass; (5) **trimmer,** in baseball, a batted ball that skims along near the ground, *rare.*

(1) **1751** ELIOT *Field-Husb.* iii. 57 Herd-Grass (known in Pennsylvania by the name of Timothy-Grass). **1909** BIGELOW *Retrospections* I. 9 [On] a few stalks of timothy grass. . . . I would string as many raspberries as would suffice for my dinner. — (2) **1772** *Pa. Gaz.* 16 April 4/3 (Ernst), Timothy and blue grass hay to be sold. **1885** *Rep. Indian Affairs* 67 They all cut more or less wild grass in addition to what timothy hay is herein enumerated. — (3) **1786** *Pa. Ev. Herald* 12 April 89/1 To be Sold . . . thirty acres of timothy meadow. **1863** *Rep. Comm. Agric. 1862* 80 His own and his neighbor's old and well-established timothy meadows . . . had that year yielded a good crop of cheat. — (4) **1856** *Rep. Comm. Patents 1855: Agric.* 254 Timothy, with us, is generally sown . . . by means of a Timothy sower attached to the drill.

(5) **1869** *N.Y. Herald* 16 Sep. 3/4 [The batter] followed with a good 'timothy trimmer' to left field, on which he made second base.

Also *timothy field, head, seed, sod,* etc.

Timucua tɪˈmukwə, *n.* (See quot. 1910.) Also **Timucuan,** *a.* — **1910** HODGE *Amer. Indians* II. 752/2 Timucuan Family. A group of cognate tribes formerly occupying the greater part of N. Florida, extending along the E. coast from about lat. 28°, below C. Cañaveral, to above the mouth of St. John r. . . . The family designation is derived from the name of one of the principal tribes, the Timucua, Timagoa, Tomoco, or Atimuca, whose territory was about St. Augustine. **1948** *Fla. Anthropologist* Nov. 37 The Timucuan Indians were the most important Florida people.

***tin,** *n.*

1. =**tin sign.** *Obs.* Cf. ***shingle,** *n.*

*c***1845** PAULDING *Amer. Comedies* (1847) 108 I've had my tin up in gilt letters for two months.

2. In combs.: (1) **tin can,** a can made of tinned iron; (2) **coat,** see quot. 1856 *s.v.* ***bobtailed,** *a.* **2,** *obs.;* (3) **dipper,** a dipper (sense **1.**) made of tin; (4) **Lizzie,** an early model Ford automobile, *jocular;* (5) **roof,** a roof of tinned iron; (6) **sign,** a professional man's sign made of tin; (7) **store,** a store where tinware is sold; (8) **tag,** a tag of tin, used in the ears of cattle as a mark, on brands of goods, etc.

(1) **1770** WASHINGTON *Diaries* I. 442, I was to . . . give them a Quart Tinn Can. **1888** *Outing* May 102 The fools, like empty tin cans, are found everywhere. **1950** *Skyline Trail* March 4/2 A large cairn had been built here and a tin can contained all the names of past climbers. — (3) **1783** E. PARKMAN *Diary* 298 Tin Tunnel, /4; two tin dippers, /4. **1856** G. D. BREWERTON *War in Kans.* 257 And then our New England 'Dot' handed us a tin dipper full of clear, cold water. — (4) **1915** *Chi. Herald* 2 Nov. 4/2 Believe me, Mr. Fixit, you're right about the guy who is able to make a tin lizzie out of the cans they tie to him. **1950** *Reader's Digest* April 60/1 It is as simple and homely as an old tin Lizzie.

(5) **1827** SHERWOOD *Gaz. Ga.* 174 The proprietors pledge themselves to furnish it as cheap as a tin roof. **1949** *Nat. Geog. Mag.* Aug. 232/1 A good tin roof was the only modern touch. — (6) **1840** *Knickerb.* XVI. 238 Among the innumerable little tin signs in Wall-street [was] one which bore the name of Brothers Tuck. — (7) **1866** *Ore. State Jrnl.* 23 June 4/1 Eugene City Stove and Tin Store. **1869** *Ib.* 2 Jan. 3/1 By reference to our advertising columns, it will be seen that Mr. B. F. Dorris has opened a new tin store. — (8) **1885** *Wkly. New Mexican Rev.* 15 Jan. 2/6 On left side slit in right ear, tin tag in left. **1902** G. H. LORIMER *Lett. Merchant* x. 127 The head of our sausage department started to put out a tin-tag brand of frankfurts.

b. In combs., now obs. or hist., that refer or allude to N. Eng. peddlers of tinware and other "notions" who were very active during the first half of the nineteenth century, as (1) **tin cart,** (2) **peddler,** (3) **peddling,** (4) **sidesaddle,** (5) **wagon,** (6) **ware.**

(1) **1858** *Harper's Mag.* May 722/2 They were presently provided with a vehicle of the tin cart species for the passengers. **1887** WILKINS *Humble Romance* 12 The tin-cart had been put up in the hotel stable. — (2) **1812** *Beauties of Bull-us* 53 [The] 'feather-merchants, rag-men, tin-pedlars, and horse-jockies' of *Connecticut* are almost to a man *democrats.* **1948** DICK *Dixie Frontier* 120 The Yankee pack peddler was originally a tin peddler. He carried his wares on his back in two large tin trunks, each weighing fifty pounds. — (3) **1837** *S. Lit. Messenger* III. 414 Mr. Hardin . . . is represented . . . to have 'hit at cod-fishery, wooden nutmegs and tin peddling.' **1883** EGGLESTON *Hoosier School-Boy* 99 Ignorant and pretentious men, . . . wanderers from New England, who had grown tired of clock-peddling, or tin-peddling, . . . would get places as teachers. — (4) **1833** ELMWOOD *Yankee among Nullifiers* 17 What right, Gentlemen, have the Yankees to the protection of their looms, their spinning jennies, their wooden nutmegs, their horn gun flints, their tin side saddles.

(5) **1827** *Western Mo. Rev.* I. 85 The tin wagon, pit-coal-indigo, wooden nutmeg, and wooden clock missionaries find the harvest beginning to fall short. — (6) **1832** BUCKINGHAM in *N. Eng. Mag.* III. 377 The cant and slang, as well as the simple local idioms of the *centaur* of Kentucky, are as different from those of the sly, civil jockey, or tin-ware vender of New-England, as [etc.]. **1833** WYETH *Oregon* 32 A yankee tin-ware man in his jingling go-cart. **1947** MYERS *The 'Guv'* 87 A very short time before he was a tinware salesman who had saved up eighteen hundred dollars.

c. In combs. sufficiently explained in the quots., as (1) **tin clad,** (2) **goose,** (3) **kitchen,** (4) **mouth,** (cf. **crappie**), (5) **wedding,** [quot. 1870 is app. in error].

Tin kitchen

(1) **1864** *Amer. Ann. Cyclo. 1863* 680/1 The flotilla on the Mississippi . . . [included] 33 'tinclads,' so called from being less heavily plated than [ironclads]. **1899** *Boston Globe* 4 June 28/8 The term 'tin-clad,' . . . is not remotely connected with the white metal but signifies rather boats heavily planked with oak for the purpose of protecting them somewhat from ravages of bullets. **1949** GOSNELL *Guns on Western Waters* 19 The so-called 'tinclads' were protected by thin iron; they were safe against musketry where covered by their plates of, say, $\frac{1}{4}$-inch thickness. — (2) **1903** *N.Y. Sun* 30 Nov. 5 'The Tin Goose,' an irreverent name for the mace of the House of Representatives, consists of a bundle of 13 ebony rods entwined and bound together with 13 silver bands. — (3) **1828** WEBSTER, Kitchen, . . . a utensil for roasting meat; as, a tin kitchen. **1868** G. G. CHANNING *Recoll. Newport* 161 There were no 'tin kitchens' then to dry up the birds, . . . but roasting was done on a long spit. **1938** MATSCHAT *Suwannee River* 153 The tin kitchen was a boxlike affair, open to the blaze on one side, with iron spits run through it on which the roasts

were skewered. The meats were turned over and over by means of a crank at one end. — (4) **1888** GOODE *Amer. Fishes* 71 *Pomoxys annularis* . . . has other names of local application as 'Tin Mouth,' 'Bridge Perch.' **1903** T. H. BEAN *Fishes N.Y.* 463 Other names of local application are barfish, bitter head, tinmouth, *sac-a-lait* [etc.].

(5) **1863** *Harper's Mag.* Nov. 856/2 Mr. Jones's people made him a tin-wedding visit on the tenth anniversary of his marriage. **1870** MACRAE *Americans* II. 203 Some people have what they call a sugar wedding on the first anniversary, and a tin wedding on the fifteenth; but these are not 'on the card.'

For **tinhorn, pan, type,** see as main entries.

tinaja tiˈnɑhə, *n. S.W.* [See note.]

This is the usual Sp. word for a large earthen jar, often for storing water and other liquids (cf. **2.** below). In Amer. Sp. it must have been used early in our sense **1.** (see quot. 1925) but such a use is not recorded by Santamaría.

1. (See quots.)

1835 COULTER *Upper Calif.* 65 The only water to be had is found in the ravines, frequently at some distance from the road, in excavations called Tinajas, made by the Indians. **1900** *Outing* April 55/1 There are a few water holes and tenejos (tanks) scattered through the mountains. **1925** BRYAN *Papago Country* 256 Rock tanks, called in Spanish 'tinajas,' are natural cavities in the rocks which retain water for longer or shorter periods after rains. **1942** CASTETTER & BELL *Pima & Papago Agric.* 42 During winter, families camped as near as possible to a spring, water hole or *tinaja.*

b. Also in place-names.

1948 *Ariz. Republic* (Phoenix) 29 Feb. II. 3/3 Leave Quitobaquita following the old road to Tinajas Altas.

2. An earthen jar, usu. for water.

1888 WALLACE *Land of Pueblos* 235 The *olla* or *tanaja* was excavated from the ruins of the Montezuma Casas Grandes. **1897** *Land of Sunshine* July 49 Only less scope of decoration characterizes the fewer and larger *tinajones* (storage-jars), made for keeping bread and the like. **1949** *Jrnl. N.Y. Bot. Garden* March 59 The women look like animated tea cozies . . . loaded down . . . with *tinajas* (jars) or rolls of mats made of reeds.

tinhorn ˈtɪnˌhɔrn, *n.* [See quot. 1931.] A gambler of a cheap, flashy, pretentious kind. In full **tinhorn gambler.** *Slang.*

1885 *Wkly. New Mexican Rev.* 26 Feb. 4/2 We have been greatly annoyed of late by a lot of tin horn gamblers and prostitutes. **1931** WILLISON *Here They Dug Gold* 216 Chuck-a-luck operators shake their dice in a 'small churn-like affair of metal'—hence the expression, 'tinhorn gambler,' for the game is rather looked down upon as one for 'chubbers' and chuck-a-luck gamblers are never admitted within the aristocratic circle of faro-dealers. **1950** *Chi. D. News* 6 Feb. 6/1 Run fast, little girl. You're mixed up with a tinhorn.

attrib. **1886** *San Juan Prospector* (Del Norte, Colo.) 4 Sep. 3/7 The Silverton vigilantes have notified the tin-horn element to meander.

* **tinker,** *n.* (See quot. 1891.)

1848 BARTLETT 356 Tinker. Small mackerel. New England. **1886** *Scientific Amer.* LIV. 352/3 Mackerel may be so plenty as to be almost given away, as . . . recently, during the early run of young mackerel or 'tinkers.' **1891** *Cent.* 6347/2 tinker. . . . A small mackerel, or one about two years old; also, the chub-mackerel.

b. Also **tinker mackerel.**

1884 GOODE *Fisheries* I. 304 A considerable school of these fish [the chub mackerel] . . . were taken in company with the Tinker Mackerel. **1911** *Rep. Fisheries 1908* 309/1 Chub mackerel (*Scomber japonicus*) . . . is also called 'tinker mackerel.'

tin pan.

1. (*cap.*) Used allusively (see quot. 1888) during the Hard Cider Campaign of 1840. *Obs.*

1840 in NORTON *Tipp. Songs* (1888) 37 Dying Groans of the Tin-Pan. [Title of a popular song.] **1888** NORTON *Reminisc.* 55 The Van Buren part of the Ohio legislature are in the habit of deliberating upon their measures in secret ere they bring them before the public. This caucus operation has by some means come to be known all over the State as the 'Tin Pan.'

2. A cheap, tinny piano. *Slang.* Cf. next.

1902 BANKS *Newspaper Girl* 139 He tried my voice, sitting down at the 'tin-pan' and asking me to sing something.

3. tin-pan alley, a district frequented by musicians, song writers and publishers, orig. used of the theatrical section of Broadway and suggestive of the tinny quality of the cheap, over-used pianos in music publishers' offices. Hence **tin-pan alleyite.**

1914 GRAU *Theatre of Science* 356 His procedure will be watched by his confreres of 'tin-pan alley' with intense interest. **1929** *Variety* 10 April 25/4 Downey, as a tin pan alleyite, is singing most of the time. **1947** *Newsweek* 1 Dec. 84/3 It claims it could record, press, and ship a new Tin Pan Alley, Broadway, or movie hit to this country in three weeks. **1948** MENJOU & MUSSELMAN *It Took 9 Tailors* 54 The famous *Perils of Pauline,* with Pearl White, inspired a pair of tin-pan-alley tunesmiths to write a popular song about poor Pauline and her hair-raising escapes from death.

4. tin-pan revival, a cheap, noisy revival. *Contemptuous.*

1902 HARBEN *A. Daniel* 178 Sister, that's the trouble with these tin-pan revivals.

tin-pan ˈtɪnˈpæn, *v.* **1.** *tr.* =**shivaree,** *v.* **2. tin-panning,** (*a*) noisy agitation in an effort to arouse enthusiasm for a person, *rare,* (*b*) =**shivaree,** *n.*

(1) **1885** *South Fla. Sentinel* (Orlando) 22 July 1/6 The parties were tin-panned Monday night. — (2) (*a*) **1848** *Albany Wkly. Argus* 5 Aug. 246/5 Notwithstanding the announcement that John Van Buren would be the chief spokesman, and much effort had been made at tin-panning . . . not enough could be collected from the great county of Bristol, to fill the Town Hall. (*b*) **1949** KURATH *Word Geog. Eastern U.S.* 78/2 *Serenade* is the usual term among the folk in Eastern New England . . . , *tin-panning* in Maryland on both sides of the Bay.

tintinnabulation ˌtɪntɪˌnæbjəˈleʃən, *n.* [f. L. *tintinnabulum,* bell.] The ringing, pealing, or jingling of bells; a sound or series of sounds suggestive of this.

Quot. 1831 in *DAE* is improperly dated, Poe's well-known poem, "The Bells," having been written in 1849, though some lines of it were done in 1848.

1845 *MS lett. of W. W. Lord to Mrs. Kinney,* 11 June, Others bore a distinct resemblance to the tintinnabulations of jingled cow bells. **1853** *La Crosse Democrat* 6 Dec. 2/5 The last tintinabulation of the last funeral bell is drowned by the clattering of hurrying feet. **1877** BURROUGHS *Birds & Poets,* The bobolink [has] . . . the qualities of hilarity and musical tintinnabulation. **1950** *Harvard Alumni Bul.* 22 April 596/1 Freedley's contemporaries will remember him as the man who wrote the Pudding song, 'The Tintinnabulation of the Old Cow Bell.'

tintype ˈtɪnˌtaɪp, *n.* A photographic positive taken on a thin iron plate, a ferrotype.

1864 E. W. PEARSON *Lett. Port Royal* 423 You will probably in due course see the tin-types of Rose and Demus. **1926** ROBERTS *Time of Man* 257, I used to take tintypes and cabinets, both. **1947** PAUL *Linden* 272 The old tintypes indicate that she had been handsome, as a young woman, and in middle age.

attrib. **1880** HOWELLS *Undiscovered Country* 3 That round table . . . with its subscription literature and its tin-type album. **1883** *Harper's Mag.* May 818/1 Third Street . . . [abounds] in small restaurants, markets, and 'tin-type' galleries. **1903** O. HENRY *Roads of Destiny* 212 Old man Billfinger, an educated tintype taker. **1941** STUART *Men of Mts.* 70 Somewhere back in a tin-type album . . . I saw a tin-type turning yellow with age. **1949** *Chi. D. News* 21 Sep. 33/4 'A tintype pose, if you please,' said the photographer.

b. *Not on your tintype,* certainly not. *Slang.*

1899 G. ADE *Fables in Slang* 78 Oh, rats! Not on your Tintype. **1948** *Time* 6 Dec. 44/3 Is modern art revolutionary? Not on your tintype, say the moderns.

c. *galloping* (or *jumping*) *tintypes,* motion pictures. *Slang* or *jocular.*

1922 WILSON *Merton of Movies* 96 Me for the jumping tintypes at the hour named. **1949** *Time* 19 Dec. 90/2 Last week moviemen felt pressure from a fading minority which it has used as a villain ever since the movies were galloping tintypes.

tiny herring. A name given by Mitchill to a herring of the Atlantic Coast, perhaps the fall herring, *Pomolobus mediocris. Obs.* — **1814** MITCHILL *Fishes N.Y.* 452 Tiny Herring. *Clupea pusilla.* About six inches long. Three faint lines or stripes, lengthwise along the back.

* **tip,** *n.*[1]

1. (See quots. 1864, 1876.)

1843 *Quincy* (Ill.) *Herald* 12 Jan. 4/4 Hatters' Tips Executed with bronze or colored ink, as may be desired. **1864** WEBSTER 1387/3 *Tip* . . . the lining of the top of a hat;—so called among hatters. **1876** KNIGHT 2578/2 *Tip,* . . . a circular piece of scale or paste board pasted on the inside of a hat crown to stiffen it.

attrib. **1876** KNIGHT 2579/1 *Tip-paper,* a variety of paper of a rigid quality, made for lining the tips or insides of hat-crowns. **1876** INGRAM *Centennial Exp.* 385 The Eickemeyer Hat Blocking Machine Company exhibited . . . a tip-stretcher.

2. *Baseball.* (See quot. 1868.) Cf. **tip bound, tip foul.**

1857 *Spirit of Times* 26 Dec. 261/2 The batsman must run on everything, tips and foul balls. **1868** CHADWICK *Baseball* 18 The last two hands being put out on 'tips'—viz., foul balls, just touching the bat and bounding sharply into the catcher's hands.

3. A light rubber overshoe having only a strap around the heel.

1894 P. L. Ford *P. Stirling* 347 'It's very different,' he was told. 'I put on tips and a mackintosh. You didn't put on anything. And it was pouring torrents.' **1934** Webster.

4. In the names of insects injurious to the terminal buds of plants and trees.

1891 *Cent.* 6351/3 *Tip-worm*, . . . the larva of a gall-fly, *Cecidomyia vaccinii*, which works in the terminal buds of the cranberry-vine. **1905** *Forestry Bureau Bul.* No. 66, 20 The tip-borer . . . in the larval form, destroys the terminal buds of the leading shoots and dwarfs the young pines.

As the last term in **arrow, fly, foul, silver tip.**

Tip tɪp, *n.*² =**Tippecanoe 1.** Also attrib. *Obs.*

1840 *Louisville Pub. Adv.* 11 July 2/2 Young Adams had Tip sent As Minister to Columbia, our States to represent. **1840** in A. C. Cole *Whig Party in South* 61 Last night the Tips had a great celebration here. . . . A select set of singers then sang a Tip song. **1842** *Democratic Press* (Peoria, Ill.) 2 March 1/2 The rest of their acts, . . . are they not embodied in 'coon skin' lyrics, and celebrated in Tip melodies, of the year 1840?

* **tip,** *v.* [The uses shown here belong to different verbs but since none of these are of American origin no attempt is made here to separate them.] In combs.: (1) **tip bound,** in baseball, a ball so hit that it bounds off and is easily caught, *obs.;* (2) **car,** a railroad gravel or coal car the body of which is so pivoted as to facilitate discharging its load; (3) **foul,** in baseball, a foul merely tipped by the batter; (4) **off,** the act of tipping off, esp. a secret warning; (5) **up,** (*a*) =**tilt-up** (*a*), (*b*) =**tilt-up** (*b*), (*c*) (see quot.).

(1) **1867** *Ball Players' Chron.* 6 June 2/2 Jewell, after being missed by Flagg on a tip bound, had his base given him on three balls. **1868** Chadwick *Base Ball* 80 Hatfield . . . was disposed of handsomely on a tip-bound. — (2) **1890** *Railways of Amer.* 146 It would require a separate article to give even a brief description of the different kinds of cars which are now used. . . . Sweeping-car, Tank-car, Tip-car. **1895** Wait *Car-Builders' Dict.* 49 Dump-car. A term used to designate both *drop-bottom, side-dump*, and *tip-cars*, which see. — (3) **1874** *Chi. Inter-Ocean* 7 July 5/1 Schafer was given a life on an easy foul muffed by Malone, and then retired on a tip-foul to the same player. —(4) **1923** Vance *Baroque* xxvii. 176, I traced the tip-off back to him.

(5) (*a*) **1848** Bartlett 356 *Tilt-up*, or *Tip-up*, the popular name of the Sandpiper. **1917** *Birds of Amer.* I. 250/1 The Spotted Sandpiper . . . is popularly nicknamed 'Teeter' or 'Tip-up,' from its nervous habit of constantly tilting its body. (*b*) **1850** S. F. Cooper *Rural Hours* 42 The boys call these contrivances 'tip-ups,' from the bit of stick to which the line is attached, falling over when the fish bite. **1894** *Outing* Jan. 295/1 The 'tip-ups' are the jolliest, and the hand-line the surest, but spearing through the ice is the most comfortable. (*c*) **1917** *Birds of Amer.* III. 150/1 This tilting or waving of the tail up and down . . . has given [the palm warbler, *Dendroica palmarum*] the names Tip-up Warbler and Yellow Tip-up.

b. In phrases: (1) *To tip off*, to make known, esp to give warning, also *tipping off, n., slang;* (2) *to tip one's hat*, to raise or touch the hat in greeting or salutation; (3) *to tip out*, in baseball, said of a batter who is put out by merely tipping the ball so that it is easily caught; (4) *to tip the scales at*, to weigh.

(1) **1896** *Chi. Tribune* 28 June 4/2 The fact that the telegram to her had 'tipped off' the situation made Mrs. Jones particularly downhearted. **1938** Asbury *Sucker's Prog.* 455, I took measures to prevent this 'tipping off,' as it is called. — (2) **1881** Rittenhouse *Maud* 18 Nearly ran over little WmSn at the P. O. and he solemnly tipped his hat. **1898** C. A. Bates *Clothing Bk.* No. 1261 He isn't afraid to tip his hat to any one. — (3) **1857** *Spirit of Times* 10 Jan. 309/1 Our first man took the bat, tipped out, great dependence placed on him. **1868** Chadwick *Base Ball* 95 Williams . . . began by tipping out. — (4) **1884** *Harper's Mag.* June 111/2 Single fish often tipping the scales at from five to seven pounds. **1893** *St. Louis Globe-Democrat* Oct., She tips the scales at 150 pounds.

Tippecanoe ˌtɪpəkəˈnu, *n.* [The native name of an Indian village.]

1. Gen. Wm. Henry Harrison (1773–1841), a nickname alluding to his victory in the battle of Tippecanoe in 1811. Also *pl.*, the political followers of Gen. Harrison. *Obs.* Cf. **Old Tippecanoe.**

[**1835** *Jamestown* (N.Y.) *Jrnl.* 25 March 1/2 Many, very many who have been the zealous supporters of the 'hero of New Orleans,' are ready to unite heart and hand in support of the hero of Tippecanoe.] **1840** *N.Y. Dly. Express* 9 April 2/2 The Tippecanoes have a powwow tonight. **1885** *Mag. Amer. Hist.* April 396/2 Tippecanoe, a nickname of William Henry Harrison, ninth President of the United States, given him because of his victory over the Indians of the Northwest under Tecumseh, in 1811.

b. *attrib.* Designating partisans of General Harrison, songs honoring him, or things named after him.

1840 *Boston Transcript* 20 Feb. 2/2 They are organizing Tippecanoe Clubs in some of the upper counties of Missouri. **1840** *Cong. Globe* App. 2 April 376 [They could] sing a few Tippecanoe songs, and then what a soul-stirring time they had of it! **1840** *Louisville Pub. Adv.* 9 July 2/1 They are 'barking up the wrong tree' in relation to the participation of negroes in the Tippecanoe Celebration. **1840** *Kentucky Rifle* 31 Oct., Old father Adam or uncle Moses . . . [would] be whole-hog *Tippecanoe Boys.* **1841** *N.O. Picayune* 1 April 2/5 A man of genius in Philadelphia has invented a new culinary mixture which he calls Tippecanoe soup. **1886** Poore *Reminiscences* I. 232 Almost every voting precinct had its Tippecanoe Club with its choristers.

2. *Tippecanoe and Tyler too*, a rallying cry used by the Whigs in the campaign of 1840, in which Wm. Henry Harrison and John Tyler were the Whig candidates for President and Vice-President. Also attrib.

1842 *Cong. Globe* App. 11 Jan. 128/3 [These] facts . . . will make those political fanatics—those 'Tippecanoe and Tyler too' politicians, feel [etc.]. **1885** *Mag. Amer. Hist.* April 396/2 'Tippecanoe and Tyler too' was the refrain of a popular song during the Log Cabin and Hard Cider campaign. **1950** *Chi. Tribune* 28 Feb. 12/3 Along with 'O.K.,' 'Tippecanoe, and Tyler, Too!' and 'the latchstring is always out,' it was a catchword of the Log Cabin and Hard Cider Presidential campaign of 1840.

tipple ˈtɪpl̩, *n.* [f. * *tip, v.*] A device for tipping and thus unloading coal cars; a place where such cars are weighed and unloaded. Also attrib. Cf. **coal tipple, ore tipple.**

1880 *Harper's Mag.* Dec. 55/1 Noisy cars . . . rush down the 'incline,' bang against the 'tipple,' and discharge their contents. **1917** Sinclair *King Coal* 134 The tipple-boss reappeared. **1949** *Chi. D. News* 16 Nov. 1/5 The victim was . . . a tipple dust cleaner for the Pennsylvania Coal and Coke Co.

tipsinah ˈtɪpsɪnə, *n.* [See quot. 1910.] (See quot. 1859.)

1859 Bartlett 481 Tipsinah. The wild prairie turnip, used as food by the North-western Indians. **1910** Hodge *Amer. Indians* II. 760 *Tipsinah.* . . . This plant is also known as the Dakota turnip, and tipsinah is derived from típsinna, its name in the Sioux language. **1932** Vestal *Sitting Bull* 6 How savory the steaming soup in the kettle, the big wooden bowls of crisp white tipsin!

attrib. **1860** *Harper's Mag.* Oct. 596/2 An Indian had trudged along before us, digging with his tipsini-stick.

tipsy, *a.* **tipsy parson, pudding,** (see quots.). — **1941** F. M. Farmer *Boston Cook Book* 510 Tipsy Pudding. Flavor with sherry. Pour over slices of stale sponge cake. Chill. Cover with whipped cream, if desired. **1943** Forbes *J. Tremain* 59 The five little squabs, three of each kind of pastry, a wreath of jellied eels (because she said it was a specialty of the house), a tipsy parson—white bread tied into little knots, buttered and baked.

tipteer ˈtɪptɪr, *v.* [?f. Eng. dial. *tipteer, n.*, a Christmas mummer.] (See quot. *a*1870.) *Obs.* — **c1849** Paige *Dow's Sermons* I. 208 You see a gentleman tipteering along Broadway, with a lady wiggle-wagging by his side, and both dressed to kill. ***a*1870** Chipman *Notes on Bartlett* 481 *Tipteer*, to promenade, to show off, to strut, to walk mincingly.

tire taɪr, *n.* [The same word as **tier,** *n.*² but understood as a shortening of * *attire.*] =**tier,** *n.*² *Colloq.*

1846 Worcester 742/2. **1848** Lowell *Biglow P.* 1 Ser. p. xiii, Well-drilled urchins, each behind his tire, Waited in ranks the wished command to fire. **1896** Pool *Buncombe Co.* 262 They were washed and combed and put into red 'tires' and white sun-bonnets.

* **tired,** *a. To make* (a person) *tired*, to annoy, bore, disgust. *Slang.* — **1895** Williams *Princeton Stories* 47 To them Jack turned with some heat, and observed, 'You fellows make me tired. You aren't under-class men now; you're old enough to know better than to size up people by underclass man standards.' **1907** M. C. Harris *Tents of Wickedness* II. vii. 200 'He makes me tired!' exclaimed Leonora, who had imbibed a little slang in these two months.

tire-shrinker. A machine for decreasing the size of wagon and carriage tires. — **1857** *Ill. Agric. Soc. Trans.* II. 171 J. L. Warfield's tire shrinker appeared . . . likely to prove a useful instrument. **1868** *Iowa State Agric. Soc. Rep. 1867* 420 We have invented . . . Sandgreen's combined shears, tire-shrinker and punch. **1881** *Rep. Indian Affairs* 442.

tissue ballot. (See quot. 1885.) Also attrib. Cf. **kiss joke.**

1879 *Cong. Rec.* App. 23 June 120/1 If my friend takes position behind the literal term 'onion skin' or 'tissue ballots,' I do not know whether they were used in Williamsburgh County or not. **1885** *Mag.*

Amer. Hist. April 396/2 *Tissue ballots.*—Ballots printed on thin paper so that a single voter can deposit a number of them at one and the same time without detection. Tissue ballots are believed to have been invented in North Carolina in 1876. **1903** HART *Actual Govt.* 75 The 'tissue ballot' system allows a voter to put in a handful of tickets at once.

tisswood ˈtɪsˌwud, *n. local.* [Origin obscure.] The red bay, also a snowdrop tree.

1897 SUDWORTH *Arborescent Flora* 201 Persea borbonia.... Common Names. Red Bay.... Tisswood. *Ib.* 323 Mohrodendron carolinum.... Common Names.... Tisswood (Tenn.). **1907** LYONS *Plant Names* 306 *M. Carolinum.*... Virginia to Florida, west to Illinois. Silver-bell, Snowdrop tree, Bell tree, Wild Olive tree, Calicowood, Shittim-wood, Tiss-wood. *Ib.* 346 *P. Borbonia.*... Southeastern U.S. Red Bay, White Bay, Isabella-wood, False Mahogany, Tiss-wood. **1933** SMALL *Man. Southeastern Flora* 922 A large tree with bark broken into flat ridges: leaf-blades elliptic or nearly so, 5-15 cm. long, often acuminate at both ends.... Sweet-Bay. Florida-Mahogany. Tisswood. *Ib.* 1036 H. Carolina.... Wild-Olive Tree. Opossum-Wood.... Tisswood.

tiswaw ˈtɪswɔ, *n.* [App. Indian term.] (See quot.) *Obs.* — **1624** SMITH *General Historie* 10 Ground nuts, Tiswaw we call China roots; they grow in clusters, and bring forth a boyer stalke, but the leafe is far unlike, which will climb up to the top of the highest tree.

tiswin tɪsˈwin, *n.* Also **tizwin.** *S.W.* [f. Amer. Sp. *tesgüino*, in same sense. See Santamaría under *tecuín* for numerous variants.] A fermented intoxicating beverage made by the Apache Indians.

1877 *Rep. Indian Affairs* 162 'Tiswin' ... they manufacture from corn, and whiskey [is] obtained from traders. **1881** *Rep. Indian Affairs* 11 There have been several Indians wounded ... at Tis-win parties. **1929** B. DAVIS *Geronimo* 115 Tizwin was a crude beer made of corn, but with a strong alcoholic content.

Also **tiswin drunk.**

1894 *Amer. Anthrop.* July 297 When officers learned that the Apaches were indulging in a 'tizwin drunk' they knew that mischief was afoot. **1948** *Westerners' Brand Book* 46 Kid's father had been killed during a tizwin drunk.

*__tit,__ *n.* As the last term in **bush, gold, least, sow, wren tit.**

*__tithable,__ *n.*

1. Short for **tithable person.** *Obs.*

1653 *Va. House of Burgesses* 88 Northampton County—500 Tithables. **1787** *Ky. Petitions* 111 The settlements of Limestone do not contain ... more than one hundred and fifty Tithables. **1893** *Nation* LVI. 309/2 The population of a Virginian county a hundred and forty years ago was probably considerably more than three times as great as its number of tithables.

2. tithable person, a person of the proper age, as between sixteen and sixty, to be subject to the payment of tithes. *Obs.*

1654 *Va. Statutes at Large* I. 388 Certaine arrears by overchargeing of tithable persons in some counties is now in question. **1713** *N.C. Col. Rec.* II. 11 These are therefore to impower you ... to collect and receive of every Tythable person in the precinct of Chowan twenty pence. **1796** MORSE *Univ. Geog.* I. 627 The poor, unable to support themselves, are maintained by an assessment on the titheable persons in the parish.

*__tithing,__ *n.*

1. tithing house, office, a place where Mormons pay tithes.

1850 *Deseret News* (Salt Lake City) 21 Sep. 115/2 Any information on this account can be obtained ... at the tithing office. **1873** LAWRENCE *Silverland* 48 It did occur to us that if some of the large monies, derived from the weekly contributions in kind to the Tithing House, had been thrown into the streets, so as to make the foul quagmire between the *trottoirs* at least fordable in wet weather, it would have been a sage civic policy. **1879** WILLIAMS *Pacific Tourist* 120/2 It has a 'co-op' store, bishop's residence, and a tithing office. **1950** *L.A. Times* 5 March v. 7/2 Meanwhile the Mormons used the old asistencia as a tithing house until 1857.

2. *__tithingman,__ in colonial New England, an officer chosen to enforce the observance of the Sabbath and to keep order at divine service. *Obs.*

For a full discussion of the office of tithingman in this country see *Johns Hopkins Hist. Studies* No. 1.

1677 *Laws of Mass.* 23 May, To prevent ... Prophanation of the Sabbath ... Tithing man or men shall ... have power in the absence of the Constable to apprehend all Sabbath-breakers. **1721** *Conn. Rec.* VI. 277 Each town ... shall choose two or more Tything Men in each parish or society for divine worship within said town. **1836** *Rev. Stat. Mass.* 180 At the annual meeting, every town shall choose.... Tythingmen, unless the towns shall vote that it is not expedient to choose the same. [Repealed in 1860.] **1895** *Forum* May 377 The interference with Sunday travel by the tithingmen of the Puritan Connecticut towns.

b. (See quot.) *Obs.*

1682 *Plymouth Col. Rec.* XI. 253 In each towne where Indians doe reside euery tenth Indian shalbe chosen by the Court of Assistants or said ouerseer yeerly whoe shall take the Inspection care and oursight of his nine men and present their faults [and] Misdemenors to the ouerseer which said ouerseer shall keep a list of the Names of the said Tithing Men.

titi ˈtaɪtaɪ, *n. S.* [Origin unknown. It may be f. Amer. Indian.] Any one of various large shrubs or small trees of the cyrilla family found in the Gulf States. Also attrib. Cf. **tighteye.**

1827 J. L. WILLIAMS *View W. Fla.* 53 These galls are usually covered with titi and other andromedas, loblolly and other laurels, vacciniums and vines. *Ib.* 54 Titi. A[ndromeda] angustifolia. The titi, in particular, occupies the same situation south of Georgia that the alder does in the northern States. **1883** SMITH *Geol. Survey Ala.* 289 The usual growth in the bottom lands consists of magnolia, bay, ti-ti, sweet-leaf, juniper. **1943** POWELL *Home Again* 8 We failed to appreciate our titi heads thick with bays and magnolias.

b. (See quots.)

1927 SUDWORTH *Forest Trees U.S.* 182 Cyrilla racemiflora Linnaeus. Swamp Ironwood.... Names in use.... Red Titi (Fla.) White Titi. *Ib.*, Cliftonia monophylla (LaMarck) Sargent. Titi.... Names in use Titi (S.C., Ga., Ala., Fla., Miss.) ... Black Titi (Fla.). *Ib.* 217 Oxydendrum arboreum (Linnaeus) de Candolle. Sourwood. ... Titi (S.C.). *Ib.*, Lyonia ferruginea (Walter) Nuttall.... Name in use Titi (Fla.). **1949** PALMER *Fieldbook Nat. Hist.* 285/3 Sourwood, Sorrel Tree *Oxydendrum arboreum.*... Known as elk tree, titi, and by other names.

*__titlark,__ *n.* As the last term in **brown, prairie titlark.**

*__title,__ *n.* In combs.: (1) **title attorney,** a lawyer who specializes in titles; (2) **catalogue,** (see quot.); (3) **insurance company,** an insurance company that insures its clients against loss because of defective titles; (4) **paper,** a deed to property, usu. *pl.*

(1) 1930 *Randolph Enterprise* (Elkins, W.Va.) 23 Oct. 1/5 Mr. Reger ... had a reputation as a title attorney which was surpassed by few. — **(2) 1910** BOSTWICK *Amer. Pub. Library* 175 If they are arranged alphabetically by the chief word in the title, it is a title catalogue. — **(3) 1902** C. J. PIDGIN *Stephen Halton* 260 That was a mighty good idea of yours Mr. Lethbridge—telling me to go to a title insurance company. — **(4) 1805** *Ann. 8th Cong.* 2 Sess. 1122 [They] had the best right imaginable to put faith in the authenticated documents and title papers presented to them. **1861** *Army Reg.* 157 Complete title papers, with full and exact maps, plans, and drawings of the public lands purchased ... will be ... filed in the Bureau of the Corps of Engineers.

As the last term in **clean, improvement, Indian, paper, patroon, shingle, shingling, Spanish, tax title.**

titman ˈtɪtˌmæn, *n.* [f. **tit*, in the sense of small, + **man.*] A man stunted physically or mentally; the smallest pig in a litter. Also attrib. *Colloq.*

1818 FESSENDEN *Ladies Monitor* 113 But vanity oft prematurely calls, Her titman-votaries to your *baby-balls* Where tiny belles, and Lilliputian beaux, ... Strut round the hall. **1854** THOREAU *Walden* 117 We are a race of tit-men, and soar but little higher in our intellectual flights than the columns of the daily paper. **1903** *D.N.* II. 334 *Titman*, the smallest of a litter of pigs. In the North 'runt.' [s.e. Mo.]

*__titmouse,__ *n.* As the last term in **bush, crested, least bush, tufted titmouse.**

tlaco ˈtlɑko, ˈklɑko, *n.* Also **claco.** *S.W.* [Amer. Sp. (<Nahuatl) in same sense.] A coin of small value, worth half a Mexican cuartilla or 1/8 of a real.

1844 KENDALL *Santa Fé Exped.* II. 216 A crowd of poor wretches ... [called] upon every saint in the Mexican calendar to shower down prayers ... if we would but give them a solitary claco. *a***1892** in *D.N.* I. 252 Two thlacks are equivalent to two and a quarter cents of our money. **1912** TWITCHELL *Leading Facts N. Mex. Hist.* II. 132 One quartillo (copper) equals 3 1-8 cents; one tlaco (copper) equals 1 9-16 cents.

Tlinkit ˌtlɪŋkɪt, *n.* [f. a native word meaning "people."] *pl.* Seafaring Indians inhabiting the islands and coasts of southern Alaska. Also **Tlinkit Indians.**

1881 MORGAN *Houses Amer. Aborigines* 17 The phratry also appears among the Thlinkets of the Northwest coast upon the surface of their organization into gentes. **1903** JAMES *Indian Basketry* 50 In Alaska the chief basket-makers are the Tlinkets and Haidas. **1947** *Sierra Club* (S.C. Chap.) *Sched.* 126, 29 The Tlinkit Indians of Alaska call it 'Yahtse-tasha,' meaning 'high mountain that rises back of bay from which water flows.'

* **to,** *prep.*

1. With, to indicate the crop planted on land. *Colloq.*

1833 S. SMITH *Life of Downing* (1834) 28 (We.), [He] planted the ground all over to corn, and potatoes. **1862** *Ill. Agric. Soc. Trans.* V. 154 The land . . . [was] mostly planted to potatoes. **1884** *Vt. Agric. Rep.* XIII. 355 Last year I planted an acre to Sanford corn.

2. *That's all there is to it,* and variants, nothing more is involved in it. *Colloq.*

1888 DORSEY *Midshipman Bob* 230 There's just this to it: if you'll go to any place [etc.]. **1914** CASTLE *Mod. Dancing* 44 Simply *walk* as softly and smoothly as possible. . . . This is the One Step, and this is all there is to it.

* **toad,** *n.* In combs.: (1) **toad bellies,** (see quot.); (2) * **fish,** (see quot. and cf. **sea toadfish**); (3) **grunter,** (see quot.); (4) **head,** (see quots.); (5) **lily,** (see quots. 1784, 1931); (6) **plantain,** prob. the common plantain, *Plantago major;* (7) **sorrel,** (see quots.), also **toad's sorrel;** (8) **stabber,** =next; (9) **sticker,** a sword or knife, *jocular,* cf. **frog sticker;** (10) **strangler,** a heavy rain, *colloq.*

(1) **1931** CLUTE *Plants* 112 The only really characteristic name relating to toads is toad-bellies, applied to the leaves of *Sedum telephium* and allied species. — (2) **1814** MITCHILL *Fishes N.Y.* 473 [The] Puffer. . . . He is called in some places, *toadfish,* because his back is mottled with yellow and dark somewhat like that of a toad. — (3) **1877** *Bartlett* 708 *Toad-Grunter,* the toad-fish, so called from the noise it makes. — (4) **1891** *Cent.* 6361/1 toadhead. . . . The American golden plover, *Charadrius dominicus.* [Cape Cod, Mass.] **1917** *Birds of Amer.* I. 257 Golden Plover. . . . [Also called] Toadhead.

(5) **1784** *Amer. Acad. Mem.* I. 456 *Nymphaea.* . . . Yellow Water Lily. Toad Lily. . . . In ponds and rivers. **1891** *Cent.* 6361/2 toad lily. . . . The white water-lily . . . an old American name. **1931** CLUTE *Plants* 111 The toad-lily, however, is the white water-lily (*Castalia odorata*), apparently named from the belief that toads frequent it. — (6) **1788** J. CARVER *Travels* 517 Toad Plaintain resembles the common plantain, only it grows much ranker, and is thus denominated because toads love to harbour under it. **1836** EDWARD *Hist. Texas* 42 Then there are the herb varieties . . . [such as] the rattle-snake plantain, the toad plantain. — (7) **1892** *Amer. Folk-Lore* V. 102 *Rumex acetosella,* . . . toad's sorrel. Stratham, N.H. **1931** CLUTE *Plants* 111 The toad-sorrel (*Oxalis stricta*) is simply an insignificant weed. — (8) **1939** SMITTER *F.O.B. Detroit* 48 'There you are,' said Russ, snapping the blade open. 'A regular toad-stabber of a thing.' — (9) **1858** *Calif. Spirit of Times* (S.F.) 7 Aug. 1/8 The Judge put his toad sticker atween his teeth, tuk a pistol in won hand, and a slung shot in the other, an sez thru his nose, 'cum on.' **1877** BARTLETT 708 *Toad-Sticker,* a term for a sword, almost universal among our soldiers during the late war. **1944** PENNELL *Rome Hanks* 293 I must have picked up this old toadsticker.

(10) **1938** in WENTWORTH. **1944** *Democrat* 20 July 2/2 A little less rainfall may be a sod-soaker. Some of them may even be called toad-stranglers.

b. *The biggest toad in the puddle,* the one of most importance. *Colloq.*

1877 BARTLETT 42 D. D. F.—is the biggest toad in the puddle.

As the last term in **hop, horn, horned, sandy, sea, squirrel tree, swell, tree toad.**

* **toast,** *n.* As the last term in **cider, cream, French, milk toast.**

* **toaster,** *n.* An electrically operated contrivance by means of which bread is toasted. — **1913** *Sat. Ev. Post* 1 Nov. 37/2 Hotpoint A combination electric toaster and stove. **1948** *Democrat* 2 Dec. 4/4 Frigidaire Ranges, Water Heaters, Sunbeam Mixmasters, Toasters . . . are here.

* **tobacco,** *n.* In combs.

1. In misc. expressions: (1) **tobacco cancer,** a cancer resulting from a chronic sore, as one on the tongue or lips, caused, or thought to be caused, by excessive smoking; (2) **house,** see as a main entry; (3) **Indians,** the Tionontati, an Iroquoian tribe allied with the Hurons—so called because of their large fields of tobacco at the time (1616) when they were first visited by white men, *obs.,* cf. **Tobacco Nation;** (4) **money,** money with which to buy tobacco, cf. **4.** (3) below; (5) **Nation,** =**Tobacco Indians;** (6) **roller,** the driver of a rolling hogshead in which tobacco was conveyed to market, *obs.;* (7) **sack,** a tobacco pouch, in modern use a small cloth sack or bag in which smoking tobacco is sold; (8) **scaffold,** a scaffold upon which freshly cut tobacco is placed for curing; (9) **screw,** a screw used in pressing tobacco, esp. into hogsheads, *obs.;* (10) **seconds,** =**second,** *a.* and *n.* **1,** *obs.;* (11) **shed,** =**tobacco house 1;** (12) **spinner,** one who prepares spun tobacco *q.v., obs.;* (13) **stick,** a stick about an inch in diameter and four or five feet long upon which tobacco is hung to cure in a tobacco barn; (14) **twist,** tobacco in the form of a twisted roll.

(1) **1884** NYE *Baled Hay* 142 Ben Hill died, after suffering intolerable anguish from tobacco cancer, caused by too much smoking. — (3) **1854** SCHOOLCRAFT *Information resp. Indian Tribes* IV. 203 The Eries and Petuns, or Tobacco Indians, who were Wyandots, had been pursued and slaughtered mercilessly in West Canada. — (4) **1862** NORTON *Army Lett.* 124, $42 for postage and tobacco money.

(5) **1867** PARKMAN *Jesuits in N. Amer.* 426 The Wyandots . . . are descendants of the ancient Hurons, and chiefly of that portion of them called the Tobacco Nation. **1940** CLARKE *Bloody Mohawk* 3 Others remained just north of Lake Erie and from their fertile fields of tobacco, were known as the Tobacco Nation. — (6) **1835** LONGSTREET *Ga. Scenes* 125 Just beyond these went three tobacco-rollers. **1860** MORDECAI *Va.* 331 The *tobacco roller,* as the driver (often the owner) was called, sought no roof for shelter, during his journey, sometimes of a week's duration and of severe toil. — (7) **1833** CATLIN *Indians* I. 115 A piece of the 'caster,' which it is customary amongst these folks to carry in their tobacco-sack to give it a flavour. **1926** BRANCH *Cowboy* 153 The one suggestion of woman was a photograph behind the tobacco-sack in the cowboy's shirt pocket. — (8) **1945** BOTKIN *My Burden* 32 Then he drunk the rest of the gallon of buttermilk and went out and laid down on a tobacco scaffold in the yard. — (9) **1832** *Louisville Directory* 174 Jacob A. Horning . . . is prepared to execute . . . every description of work in his line such as . . . tobacco screws. **1853** *La Crosse Democrat* 27 Sep. 1/2 Oil and Tobacco Screws.

(10) **1769** *Va. House of Burgesses* 205 The Acts . . . prohibiting the tending of Tobacco-seconds. — (11) **1880** CABLE *Grandissimes* 192 You may still here and there see one [villa] standing . . . among founderies, cotton and tobacco-sheds, junk-yards, and longshoremen's hovels. **1950** *Pa. Dutchman* (Lancaster, Pa.) March 2/1 He arose to close the tobacco sheds. — (12) **1807** J. R. SHAW *Life* (1930) 74 A certain militia-man by the name of Everman, a tobacco spinner, . . . lived in Lancaster. — (13) **1766** GLOVER *Va.* in *Phil. Trans.* XI. 635 They hang them [tobacco leaves] up by the pegs on Tobacco-sticks, so nigh each other that they just touch. **1776** CRESSWELL *Journal* 166 About 600 men appeared under-armed, with Tobacco sticks in general. **1941** STUART *Men of Mts.* 129 It took two men to hold the cross-bars while one drove spikes in them to hold them fer the heavy terbacker sticks. — (14) **1823** JAMES *Exped.* I. 141 His [Indian] auditors . . . were presently highly wrought up by the sight of two or three little mounds of tobacco twist which were now laid before them. **1925** TILGHMAN *Dugout* 32 Ballard was shredding . . . tobacco twist, into their . . . bean kettle.

2. Designating land, places, or regions where tobacco is grown, as (1) **tobacco bed,** (2) **belt,** (3) **country,** (4) **farm,** (5) **field,** (6) **ground,** (7) **land,** (8) **lot,** (9) **new ground,** (10) **patch,** (11) **plantation,** (12) **state,** (also **tobacco growing state**), (13) **woodland.**

(1) [**1800** TATHAM *Tobacco* 8 The beds, or patches, as they are called, differ in size.] **1819** *Amer. Farmer* I. 62 We have been dreadfully annoyed in our *Tobacco beds,* by a small black insect, called the fly. [**1944** WILSON *Passing Inst.* 32 For days and days the log piles burned, some of them furnishing the basis for a tobacco plantbed.] — (2) **1880** TOURGEE *Bricks* 11 The plantation was just upon that wavy line which separates the cotton region of the east from the tobacco belt that sweeps down the pleasant ranges of the Piedmont region. **1948** *Newsweek* 4 Oct. 14/2 Under pressure from tobacco-belt interests, the Economic Cooperation Administration is no longer discouraging ERP nations from spending scarce dollar balances on American tobacco. — (3) **1885** HOWELLS *Silas Lapham* xiv, Anybody who had ever lived off a tobacco country could tell him better than that. — (4) **1872** *Atlantic Mo.* Jan. 33 His father's tobacco farm on the James was the portion of his brother Randolph.

(5) **1852** J. B. JONES *Col. Vanderbomb* 46 They rode by a large tobacco field. **1904** E. GLASGOW *Deliverance* 120 The wagon rolled between the green tobacco fields. — (6) **1659** *Southold Rec.* I. 87 An other parcell of woodland in Oyster ponnd Lower neck in the Tobackow ground. **1800** W. TATHAM *Tobacco* 6 The condition of soil of which the planters make choice, is that in which nature presents it when it is first disrobed of the woods. . . . This is termed *new* ground, which may be there considered as synonymous with *tobacco* ground. **1859** BARTLETT 181 *Grounds,* 'tobacco grounds,' 'low grounds,' 'corn grounds,' are terms applied to lands in Virginia. — (7) **1659** *Southold Rec.* I. 86 The Tobacco lands . . . hee lately exchanged with Samuell King for his meadowe in the Indian neck. **1792** *Fayetteville* (N.C.) *Gaz.* 25 Sep., Containing upwards of 300 acres, 230 of which is Tobacco Land of the first quality. **1869** TOURGEE *Toinette* xlvi. (1881) 453 The Lovett Lodge plantation amounts to nigh double that. Its all prime terbacker land. **1950** *Amer. Forests* Feb. 11/1 The washing

down of silt from tobacco lands eventually choked up Quantico Creek. — **(8) 1820** *Amer. Farmer* I. 394 The tobacco planter was under the necessity of robbing all the rest of his farm, to keep up the fertility of his *tobacco lots.* — **(9) 1902** G. C. EGGLESTON *D. South* 89 Let's ride to the tobacco new grounds at once.

(10) [**1800** see **tobacco bed. 1904** PRINGLE *Rice Planter* 97 They plant a field of corn, a patch of rice, a patch of cotton, and one of tobacco.] **1939** *These Are Our Lives* 11 Long about that time I break up my tobacco patch with a two-horse plow, harrow it good and run the rows. — **(11) 1676** GLOVER *Va.* in *Phil. Trans.* XI. 627 [They are] so intent on their Tobacco-Plantations that they neglect all other more Noble and advantageous improvements. **1861** *Vanity Fair* 8 June 271/1 Then I've got . . . four tobacco-plantations. — **(12) 1824** *Cong. Deb.* 15 April 2324 The effect of this measure [the tariff bill] on the cotton, rice, and tobacco-growing States will be pernicious in the extreme. **1900** *Cong. Rec.* 31 Jan. 1359/2 Letters are being received by Congressmen from all the wool and tobacco growing States imploring the Representatives to prevent the consummation. **1946** *Newsweek* 28 Jan. 14/2 Cotton and tobacco states . . . will be reminded of the prospective exports. — **(13) 1772** in *Amer. Sp.* XV. 404/2 Two Hundred and thirty Acres of rich Tobacco woodland.

3. Designating or with reference to boats, vessels, etc., used in transporting tobacco, as (1) **tobacco boat,** (2) **canoe,** (3) **drogher,** (4) **fleet,** (5) **ship.** All *obs.* Cf. **tobacco hogshead** in **6.** below.

(1) 1790 FORMAN *Narrative* (1888) 42 He bought me a tobacco boat, loaded her with this product of the country, and got matters and things arranged so that I was ready to accompany the descending fleet. [**1902** *Amer. Folk-Lore* 242 Through corruption, or by jesting alteration of the name, they [i.e., Chebacco boats] were also known as '*tobacco*-boats.'] — **(2) 1781** *Va. State P.* 451 He had proceeded up James River thus far, in search of canoes of the kind needed, viz. 'Sound tobacco canoes.' — **(3) 1745** E. KIMBER *Itinerant Observer* 29 They have also a Kind of Sloops, clumsily built, which may be called Tobacco Druggers, of 70 or 80 Tons Burden. — **(4) 1709** LAWSON *Carolina* 88 We lie near at hand to . . . sell our Provisions to the Tobacco-fleets. **1745** E. KIMBER *Itinerant Observer* 52 There are . . . Inhabitants on the other Side of the Bay, where large Towns abound, and, which are the Rendezvous of the several *Tobacco Fleets* that sail from *Europe.*

(5) 1777 HUTCHINSON *Diary & Lett.* II. 132 The tobacco ship was taken by four sailors only. **1794** *Mass. H.S. Coll.* III. 286 Many of these tobacco ships were owned by Scotchmen, and paid for here in Scotch manufactures delivered the builder. **1889** *Cent. Mag.* April 837/2 To this old manor-house of the Masons, built, in 1739, of Scotch brick brought to the colony as ballast in empty tobacco-ships . . . the Washington family was accustomed to resort.

4. Designating things that relate to the use of tobacco as money, as (1) **tobacco debt,** (2) **fee,** (3) **money,** (cf. **1.** (4) above), (4) **note,** (5) **payment.** All *obs.*

(1) 1662 *Md. Archives* I. 445 All persons that shall tender paymt. in such [English] Graynes . . . shall be allowed for the same as aforesaid which money shall pass in discount of tobacco debts at 2 d. per lb. **1705** *Cal. Va. State P.* I. 97 If any debtor shall neglect to deliver his tobacco debts to the County Agent at the times [etc.]. — **(2) 1733** *Md. Hist. Mag.* XIX. 303, [I must] pay at the Rate of ten shillings per cent. for the Tobacco Fee. . . . I was ready to pay the Tobacco out of my warehouse. **1780** *Va. Statutes at Large* X. 489 An act for regulating tobacco fees, and fixing the allowance to sheriffs, witnesses, and venire-men. — **(3) 1691** *Mass. Bay Currency Tracts* 31 Why may not Paper-mony be as good as Tobacco-mony, Potato-mony, and Sugar-mony? **1834** CARUTHERS *Kentuckian* II. 202 The buckles which their fathers wore in the days of 'tobacco-money.' — **(4) 1760** WASHINGTON *Diaries* I. 136 Gave Captn. Cawsey's Skipper . . . 1 Tobo. Note. **1837** *S. Lit. Messenger* III. 219 Did you not give me a tobacco note to sell for you several weeks ago?

(5) 1705 *Cal. Va. State P.* I. 97 Such notes shall be received in all tobacco payments.

5. In the names of plants and insects: (1) **tobacco beetle,** (see quot.); (2) **fly,** either of two hawk moths, *Protoparce quinquemaculata* and *P. sexta,* cf. **tobacco worm;** (3) **hawk moth,** the adult of the tobacco worm; (4) * **pipe,** the Indian pipe, *Monotropa uniflora;* (5) **root,** (*a*) (see quots.), (*b*) bitter root; (6) **shrub,** (see quot.); (7) **worm,** the larva of the tobacco fly which feeds on the leaves of the tobacco plant.

(1) 1891 *Cent.* 6362/3 tobacco-beetle. . . . A cosmopolitan ptinid beetle, *Lasioderma serricorne,* which . . . is so fond of stored or manufactured tobacco as to become a pest in many manufactories and warehouses in the United States. Also called *cigarette-beetle.* — **(2)** [**1688** JOHN CLAYTON in *Phil. Trans.* XVII. 947 There be various Accidents and Distempers, whereunto Tobacco is liable, as the Worm, the Flie, Firing to Turn, as they call them, French-men, and the like.] **1807** JANSON *Stranger in Amer.* 339 Many planters, . . . knew of no remedy against the devastation produced by the 'tobacco-fly.' **1904** GLASGOW *Deliverance* 126 It was . . . mid-August—the time of the harvest moon and of the dreaded tobacco fly. — **(3) 1838** GOSSE *Letters* 66 This is the Tobacco Hawk-moth (*Sphinx Carolina*), a large but sober-coloured species. The usual food of the larva is the tobacco plant, in which it is found in considerable numbers. — **(4) 1840** DEWEY *Mass. Flowering Plants* 108 Tobacco Pipe . . . is a singular and handsome plant. **1845** JUDD *Margaret* I. 143 She found . . . the curious mushroom-like tobacco pipe.

(5) (*a*) **1845** FRÉMONT *Exped.* 135, I ate here, for the first time, the *kooyah,* or tobacco root, (*valeriana edulis,*) the principal edible root among the Indians. **1919** STURTEVANT *Notes Edible Plants* 589 Tobacco Root. Valerian. Ohio to Wisconsin and westward. (*b*) **1864** *Chambers's Encycl.* VI. 109/2 [*Lewisia*] *rediviva* . . . is called *Tobacco Root* because, when cooked, it has a tobacco-like smell. **1890** *Cent.* 3429/3. — **(6) 1885** HAVARD *Flora W. & S. Texas* 472 First observed as a native plant north of the Rio Grande, is the beautiful Tobacco-Shrub (*Nicotiana glauca*). — **(7)** [**1688** JOHN CLAYTON in *Phil. Trans.* XVII. 947 There be various Accidents and Distempers, whereunto Tobacco is liable, as the Worm, the Flie, Firing to Turn, as they call them, French-men, and the like.] **1737** BRICKELL *N. Carolina* 168 The Tobacco-worm . . . has two sharp horns on its Head, the Body is white and Black, with as many Feet as the former. **1944** *D.N.* Nov. 72 tobacco-worm: n. A large green worm that feeds on green tobacco. Same as *horn-worm.*

6. In expressions of obvious meaning or sufficiently explained in the quots.: (1) **tobacco bag,** (2) **barn,** (3)

Tobacco bags

cask, (4) **crop,** (5) **cutter,** (6) **cutting,** (7) **exchange,** (8) **factory,** (9) **hill,** (10) **hoe,** (11) **hogshead,** (12) **horse,** (13) **knife,** (14) **planter,** (15) **stalk,** (16) **store,** (17) **tag,** (18) **warehouse,** (19) **wheel.**

(1) 1643 WILLIAMS *Key* (1866) 72 Generally all the men throughout the countrey have a Tobacco-bag, with a pipe in it, hanging at their back. **1864** CUMMING *Hospital Life* (1866) 120/2, I hinted to some of the ladies about having tobacco bags made. **1894** *Harper's Mag.* LXXXVIII. 643/1 He would often hand the old man . . . his tobacco-bag, from which Reub would fill his corn-cob pipe. — **(2) 1877** BAGBY *Old Va. Gentleman* 3 Where is your plank to come from, and your logs

One form of tobacco knife or cutter

for new cabins and tobacco barns? **1947** *Sports Afield* Dec. 125/3 Has 12 large tobacco barns, which are now filled with tobacco raised from the base on these farms. — **(3) 1658** *Md. Archives* I. 371 Several Complaints [by masters of ships] have bene made . . . of the vnreasonable Size of Tobacco Caske. — **(4) 1847** ROBB *Squatter Life* 133, [I asked] what'ud be the probable amount of the old man's tobacco crop this season. **1885** BAYLOR *On Both Sides* 208 The result was recorded in . . . tabulated expositions of the imports, exports, cotton-, tobacco-, and corn-crops of the United States for about fifty years.

(5) 1876 KNIGHT, Tobacco-cutter. 1. A machine for shaving tobacco leaves into shreds for chewing or smoking . . . 2. A knife for cutting plug-tobacco into smaller pieces. **1902** *Sears Cat.* 749 Tobacco Cutter with Image. Cast iron, with steel blades. Japanned finish. Price, each . . . 37c. — **(6) 1904** GLASGOW *Deliverance* 161 It'll have to lie over till after tobacco cutting. — **(7) 1867** *Harper's Wkly.* 20 April 253/1 We present on this page a view of the interior of the Tobacco Exchange, corner of Cary and Virginia streets, Richmond. — **(8) 1827** DRAKE & MANSFIELD *Cincinnati* 65 Three Tobacco and Snuff Factories. **1946** WILSON *Fidelity* 205 We drove down to Marse Jeffy's tobacco factory to listen to the Negroes sing as they worked in the stemming room. — **(9) 1763** WASHINGTON *Diaries* I. 183, 170 Tobo. Hills. **1792** POPE *Tour S. & W.* 62 They plant their Corn in Holes at an unequal, tho' never greater Distance than Tobacco Hills, from one another.

(10) 1790 *Pa. Packet* 14 April 3/2 William Perkins, Blacksmith, Makes and sells . . . the best kind of corn or tobacco hoes. — **(11) 1658** *Md. Archives* I. 371 An Act Concearning the Gage of Tobacco Hogsheds. **1759** in COMMONS *Doc. Hist.* I. 112, I shall therefore confine myself to Tobo. Tobo hhds should always be provided the 1st week in September; every morning of the month is fit for striking & stripping. [**1824** SINGLETON *Letters* 58, I also met, what would be a novelty to you, a slave rolling tobacco to market, to Norfolk; the hogsheads are enormously large, from ten to twenty hundred weight, and so screw-pressed and tripple-hooped, that they are revolved along the road by an axle attached to a couple of mules.] — **(12) 1849** *Amer. Farmer* V. 185/2 A 'Tobacco horse' is nothing more than three small sticks nailed together so as to form a triangle, each side being three or four feet long. — **(13) 1876** KNIGHT, Tobacco-knife. A knife for cutting plug-tobacco into pieces convenient for the pocket. It is usually a sort of guillotine knife worked by a lever, and cutting downward onto a wooden bed. — **(14) 1775** *Amer. Husbandry* I. 66 Those who have dealings with London . . . are the tobacco and rice planters. **1867** DIXON *New Amer.* II. 2, I have heard [the phrase] . . . among the tobacco-planters of Richmond.

(15) 1659 *Md. Hist. Mag.* VIII. 31 [He] took tobacco stalks and beat his servants. **1807** IRVING *Salmagundi* xvii. 448 It was not worth a tobacco-stalk. **1899** *Boston Transcript* 14 Jan. 12/2 The 'Caton Chimney' of Kentucky is doubtless an emigrant from the Atlantic coast, with tobacco stalks substituted for catsticks. — **(16) 1809** FRENEAU *Poems* I. 137 This box. . . . Has been unfilled a week or more, And curses the tobacco store. — **(17) 1908** O. HENRY *Roads of Destiny* 54 His dollars had appeared as but tin tobacco-tags. **1944** JOHNSON *As I Dare* 23 Tobacco tags gave me the most enjoyment—the little tin tags which were attached to various brands of chewing tobacco. — **(18) 1732** in *Amer. Sp.* XX. (1945) 275 For the more speedy detecting and punishing the felonious burning of tobacco warehouses. **1867** GOSS *Soldier's Story* 26 The prison was one of the large tobacco warehouses, three stories high. **1948** *Reader's Digest* March 105/2 One merchant loaned the Theatre his tobacco warehouse to use as a workshop. — **(19) 1876** KNIGHT 2585/2 *Tobacco-wheel*, a machine by which leaves of tobacco are twisted into a cord.

As the last term in **blockade, Brazil, broad-leafed, cake, casked, chewing, Clarksville, Connecticut, cowpen, crop, Cuba, dog leg, fig, fine cut, hand, Indian, issue, junk, Kentucky, kitefoot, long green, manufactured, mountain, old field, Oronoco, paper, perique, plug, port, rabbit, rotgut, seedleaf, smoking, spun, store, sweet-scented, top, transfer, trash, Virginia, Virginian, wagon, wild tobacco.**

tobacco house.

1. An open, airy house in which tobacco is cured. Also **tobacco-curing house.**

1652 *Southhold Rec.* I. 17 The Neck over against the east side of the Tobacco house in Oysterpond Meadows. **1705** BEVERLEY *Virginia* IV. 53 Their Tobacco-Houses are all built of Wood, as open and airy as is consistent with keeping out the Rain; which sort of Building is most convenient for the curing of their Tobacco. **1820** *Amer. Farmer* I. 395 The most common size of a tobacco house formerly was 40 feet long by 24 feet wide. **1897** MARK TWAIN *Autobiog.* I. 99 (R.), The woody hill fell sharply away, past the barns, the corn-crib, the stables and the tobacco-curing house.

attrib. **1691** *Va. State P.* I. 27, I have searched in such places as it was suspected ye broad-arrow was unduly putt on ye toba. housedoores. **1760** WASHINGTON *Diaries* I. 134, [I] set a course for the head of the drain that Runs into my Meadow which leaves in the Tobo. House Field. **1775** J. ADAMS in *Warren-Adams Lett.* I. 115 Coll. Harrison of Virginia . . . is very confident that they are making large Quantities [of saltpeter] from Tobacco House Earth in his Colony.

b. A tobacco warehouse.

1887 *Courier-Journal* 13 Jan. 8/5 Mike Billings . . . was apprehended at Levy's tobacco house, in Portland.

2. A business concern dealing in tobacco.

1900 WINCHESTER *W. Castle* 166, I was traveling for a large tobacco house.

Tobin bronze. [John A. *Tobin*, U.S. Navy (*c*1875).] A bronze resistant to corrosion in salt water and hence useful in naval construction. — **1891** *Franklin Inst. Jrnl.* July 54 The Ansonia Brass and Copper Company . . . [are] the sole manufacturers of Tobin Bronze. **1909** *Cent. Supp.* 168/1 *Tobin bronze*, an alloy . . . composed chiefly of copper, zinc, tin, iron, and lead, in varying proportions.

toboggan tə'bɑgən, *n.* [f. Can. F. *tobagan* (<Algonquian word for a drag or hand sled).]

1. A long, narrow sled the front of which is curved upward and to the back.

1829 HEAD *Forest Scenes* 64 A tobogin is a small sleigh, drawn by men, of very simple construction, and capable of conveying from 100 to 140 pounds of clothes or other baggage. **1870** MACRAE *Americans* II. 341 The 'toboggan' (Indian name) is a thin slip of wood about a foot and a half wide, and four to six feet long. The end that goes foremost is curled up, to prevent it from catching the snow, or being checked by any protuberance. **1950** *Chi. D. News* 12 Jan. 20/7, I understand Maggie [a horse] slides down the trail on her haunches, like a toboggan.

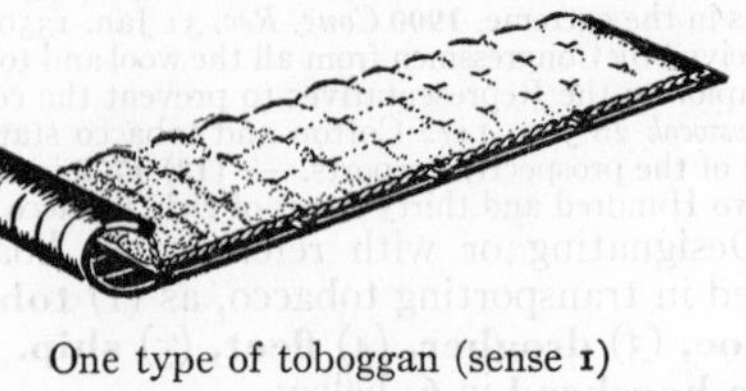

One type of toboggan (sense 1)

b. Attrib. with **carnival, chute, club, course.**

1886 *Outing* March 712/2 A three-day toboggan carnival was concluded on January 27, at the Glen Summit Hotel, Penn. **1890** *Silverton* (Colo.) *Miner* 1 March 3/2 During the storm, the big tree on Anvil, which was generally known as the starting point for snow shoers and the toboggan club, was blown down. **1913** EATON *Barn Doors & Byways* 223 One road runs along the ridge, the other plunges over it and crosses the intervale like the smooth, straight drop of a great toboggan chute. **1934** *Rocky Mt. News* (Denver) 21 Dec. 24/2 The project will include ski jumps, cross-country ski courses, toboggan courses and ice skating.

2. A long-tasselled stocking cap, in full **toboggan cap.**

1902 *Sears Cat.* (ed. 112) 1159/3 Toboggan Caps or Toques. **1928** *Chi. Tribune* 11 June 10/5 Women and children in winter wore toboggan caps which wrapped two or three times around the neck and hung about a yard down the back. **1948** *Pacific Spectator* Winter 83 He had on faded overalls with new blue patches on the knees, and a sweater under the overalls, and a knitted blue toboggan on his head, against the cold.

3. toboggan slide, a long, steep chute for coasting on toboggans. Also a well-known playground fixture, chiefly for children.

1886 *Boston Jrnl.* Nov., The Edmunds and Myrrhline toboggan slides remain unimpaired. **1898** *Land of Sunshine* Jan. 104 Toboggan-slides, flying-trapezes, spring-boards, etc., furnish fun for the bathers. **1948** *Highway Traveler* Dec. 20/2 The four-track toboggan slide is always a busy place.

4. *On the toboggan, fig.* headed for disaster, "on the skids." *Slang.*

[**1889** *Sporting Life* (Phila.) 29 May 1/5 We hope that Worcester is done with its unseasonable tobog, and will work its way toward the top.] **1910** E. A. WALCOTT *Open Door* xii. 153 Do you remember the time I got Conny Mulnix off, when the police had him on the toboggan for the Kinsley affair? **1931** *K.C. Star* 31 Oct. 12 With everything else on the toboggan how can you fancy wheat going up? [**1947** *Christian Cent.* 20 Aug. 999/1 The United States is sliding down the toboggan with 75 per cent of the south a negroid population.]

toboggan tə'bɑgən, *v. intr.* (See quot. 1879.) Also transf. and **tobogganing,** *n.*

1855 OLIPHANT *Minnesota* 27, I must endeavour to explain the accomplishment of trabogginning, which can scarcely be acquired in less than two pic-nics. **1879** WEBSTER *Supp.* 1582/1 *Toboggan*, to slide down hill over the snow, on a toboggan. **1941** LOFBERG *Sierra Outpost* 187 Where granite sloped over a fifty-foot drop, it was ten times quicker to toboggan on snowshoes than to make the long hairpins of the trail. **1950** *Chi. Tribune* 5 Jan. III. 2/2 Two tobogganing Oregon State college athletes were fatally hurt.

Hence **tobogganer, tobogganist.**

1891 *Outing* Oct. 53/1, I challenge any tobogganer to show me greater enjoyment than the cycle's swift flight down the hillside. **1947** *Sierra Club Bul.* March 23/2 The Chamber of Commerce expects . . . a crowd of skiers, tobogganers, snowballers and spectators 'estimated at 8,000 to 10,000 persons per week end.' **1949** *Chi. Tribune* 6 Dec. 22/3 Santa Claus, of course, is always . . . costumed as if he were a primitive French-Canadian tobogganist.

tobosa grass. *S.W.* [The first element may be f. Amer. Sp. *toboso* (<an Indian tribal name), used in

Sonora for *Anagallis arvensis.*] A forage grass, *Hilaria mutica.*

1912 WOOTON & STANDLEY *Grasses N. Mex.* 11 On the mesas Black Grama (*Bouteloua eriopoda*), Tobosa Grass (*Hilaria mutica*), False Needlegrass (*Scleropogon brevifolius*), . . . are characteristic. **1931** DAYTON *Western Browse Plants* 165 It is common and abundant on dry sandy, or adobe plains, . . . frequently in association with creosote bush, mesquite, burrograss, and tobosa-grass. [**1940** CASSADY & GLENDENING *Revegetating Semidesert Range Lands* 2 Barren areas [are] interspersed with well-vegetated areas supporting such plants as tobosa, burro grass, sacaton, tar-brush.]

toby ˈtobɪ, *n.* [Origin obscure. The explanation in quot. 1894 seems hardly plausible.] A stogie. *Colloq.*

1894 SEARIGHT *Old Pike* 144 They [cheap cigars] became very popular with the drivers, and were at first called Conestoga cigars; since, by usage, corrupted into 'stogies' and 'tobies.' **1903** *Westm. Gaz.* 23 May 10/1 The railway ticket office clerk twists and swigs at a 'toby' as he asks you 'Where for, sir?' **1944** WENTWORTH.

tocalote ˌtokəˈlotɪ, *n. W.* [Var. of chicalote *q.v.*] (See quots.)

1909 *Cent. Supp.* 1344/2 Napa thistle, a yellow-flowered star-thistle, *Centaurea Meletensis,* abundantly introduced as a weed in California, apparently diffused from Napa. Also *tocalote.* **1911** RICHTER *Honey Plants Calif.* 977 The bee forage consists of the caterpillar phacelia, phacelia ramosissima and sow-thistle, followed by oak, tocalote, and an abundance of turkey mullein. **1916** *Proc. Iowa Acad. Sci.* XXIII. 490 Broad acres are covered with the Yellow Knapweed or Tocalote.

tod tɑd, *n.* Short for "toddy." — **1797** C. PRENTISS *Fugitive Ess.* 67 Whether thou exercisest thy power in the full bowl of *punch,* . . . or the circling mug of *tod.* **1898** POST *Harvard Stories* 106 With 'tod and tobac.' the party disposed itself about the room.

*toddy, *n.* As the last term in **apple, brandy, possum toddy.**

toddy stick. A small stick for stirring toddy. *Obs.*

1840 *N.O. Picayune* 4 Oct. 2/5 A 'toddy stick' is as spirit-stirring an article as any poet can boast. **1865** *Atlantic Mo.* May 597/1 Old Boody stirs with an appetizing rattle of the toddy-stick. **1867** LACKLAND *Homespun* 179 [The landlord] was twirling the toddy-stick in his customer's punch.

* **toe,** *n.*

1. (*cap.*) *pl.* (See quot.) *Obs.*

1896 HASWELL *New York* 157 The members [of the 'Toe Club' *q.v.*] . . . were designated 'Toes,' and their place of meeting was termed their 'Shoe.'

2. In combs.: (1) **toe calk,** (see quot. 1876); (2) **Club,** (see quot.), *obs.;* (3) **itch,** = **ground itch;** (4) * **nail,** an alcoholic drink, *obs.;* (5) **ring,** a heavy ring or sleeve at the end of a cant hook.

(1) **1859** *Rep. Comm. Patents* (1858) I. 525 Certain indentations are made in the rolls to correspond to the toe-calk. **1876** KNIGHT 2585/2 *Toe-calk,* a prong or barb on the toe of a horse's shoe, to prevent slipping on ice or frozen ground. **1881** *Rep. Indian Affairs* 442. — (2) **1896** HASWELL *New York* 154 It was from a party of young men who were in the habit of meeting at Castle Garden [*c*1823–4] that the 'Toe Club' was formed, one of the first social clubs that was organized in New York. — (3) **1925** BASSETT *Plantation Overseer* 184 Probably refers to the 'toe itch,' due to excessive rain. — (4) *c*1844 R. H. COLLYER *Amer. Life* 7 Various fancy mixtures called, 'Toenails, Bowel Ploughers, Corn Cobs, Eye Snappers,' are retailed.

(5) **1905** *Forestry Bureau Bul.* No. 61, 43 A peavey differs from a cant hook in having a pike instead of a toe ring and lip at the end.

As the last term in **brass, copper, dog, Negro, poor toe(s).**

* **toe,** *v.* In colloq. phrases: (1) *To toe off,* in knitting, to diminish the stitches at the toe of (a stocking or sock) and so complete it, also *toeing off, n.;* (2) *to toe in* (or *out*), to turn the toes in (or out) in walking, also *toeing in, n.;* (3) *to toe up,* to toe the mark.

(1) **1856** M. J. HOLMES *Homestead* II. iii, [She] was toeing off the stocking only that morning commenced. **1904** WALLER *Wood-Carver* 36 There ain't nothin' more ter learn but 'toein' off.' — (2) **1877** BARTLETT 710 *To toe in,* to turn in the toes. **1891** WELCH *Recoll. 1830–40* 116 That peculiar turn of the foot called 'toeing in,' which in the white girl would be called 'pigeon toed.' **1894** *Vt. Agric. Rep.* XIV.120 Avoid a horse which toes in or toes out. — (3) **1901** MERWIN & WEBSTER *Calumet 'K'* 226 If he doesn't toe up, I'll get one and send him the bill.

*toed, *a.* As the last term in **brass, claw, copper-toed.**

*toggle, *v. tr.* To secure or make fast by means of a toggle or toggles. Also fig. — **1836** *Knickerb.* VIII. 207 Has the devil toggled you at last? **1899** *Outing* XXX. 229/1 In the *Mab* and other canoes employing this device, the stick is toggled at one end to the rudder yoke, and at the other to the collar of the deck tiller.

togue tog, *n. local,* chiefly Maine. [f. Can. F.(<Algonquian).] = **namaycush.**

1839 HOLMES *Explor. Aroostook River* 33 The large lake trout, or togues, as they are sometimes called, abound here. **1864** *Maine Agric. Rep.* IX. 132 [The whitefish] will live where the trout will, especially the lake trout, or 'togue.' **1884** GOODE *Fisheries* I. 486 The 'Togue' or 'Tuladi' of the Maine and New Brunswick Indians and lumbermen . . . has been honored with a distinct binomial. **1950** *Boston Globe* 14 May 36/3 Newfound Lake . . . is also an outstanding producer of lake trout or togue.

tola ˈtolə, *n.* Also **tolle.** *S.W.* Short for **atole.** *Obs.* — **1839** FARNHAM *Great Western Prairies* (1841) 77 Our expectations of game and meat subsided into a supper of 'tole'—plain water porridge. **1881** C. M. CHASE *Editor's Run in N. Mex.* 215 For supper, tola, or roasted corn, ground into meal, boiled into a mush, and served with goat's milk and tortillas.

*tolerance, *n.* (See quot. 1905.) — **1898** PINCHOT *Adirondack Spruce* 6 A provisional scale of tolerance is as follows. *Ib.* 30 Black Cherry stands about midway in the scale of tolerance among the trees in the Park. **1905** *Forestry Bureau Bul.* No. 61, 24 *Tolerance,* the capacity of a tree to endure shade.

*tolerant, *a.* (See quot. 1905.) — **1898** PINCHOT *Adirondack Spruce* 5 A selection forest is usually composed of species tolerant of shade. **1905** *Forestry Bureau Bul.* No. 61, 25 *Tolerant,* Capable of enduring more or less heavy shade.

* **toleration,** *n.*

1. *local.* A tax or license for taking clams or oysters. Also attrib.

1796 *Smithtown Rec.* 129 Any person not an inhabitant . . taking Soft shelled clams within the limits of said Town shall pay six pence for every bushel as toleration for taking the same. **1881** INGERSOLL *Oyster Industry* 249 *Toleration,* license to gather oysters or operate beds; paid by every individual annually. (Brookhaven, Long Island.) The money paid is called a *Toleration fee.*

2. Toleration party. *Hist.* A political party in Connecticut *c*1818 made up largely of religious dissenters and other opponents of the Federalist control of the state. Also **Toleration ticket.** *Obs.*

1817 *Niles' Reg.* XII. 128/1 The 'toleration ticket,' so called, has succeeded in this state. **1831** *Jamestown* (N.Y.) *Jrnl.* 23 March 2/4 The 'toleration party' of that state [Conn.] contended for the right of voting by ballot. **1914** *Cyclo. Amer. Govt.* I. 397/2 A coalition between the Democrats (Republicans) and those who dissented from the established church, styled the Toleration party, was then [1817] successful in sweeping the state.

*Tolerationist, *n.* A member of the old Connecticut Toleration party. Now *hist.* — **1819** *Niles' Reg.* XVI. 160/2 All the new members of Congress are 'tolerationists,' or republicans. **1904** MORGAN *Conn. as Colony & State* III. 107 While the success of the Democrats and Tolerationists was due to their unanimity of feeling in favor of a new constitution, the Federalists were by no means united in opposing it.

*toll, *n.* **1. toll bin,** a bin in which the miller's share or toll for grain ground is kept. **2. toll gin,** a cotton gin at which toll is charged for the cotton ginned. Both *rare.* — (1) **1884** HARRIS *Mingo* 230, I was in—about up to my eyes in the toll-bin. — (2) **1896** *54th Cong.* 2 Sess. H.R. Doc. No. 267, 357 With the subdivision of farms an almost new industry was developed in the way of toll gins.

*toll, *v.*[1] *tr.* To bring (an estray) before a public official. *Obs.* — **1829** *Camden* (S.C.) *Journal* 6 June 1/4 Estray. Samuel Kirkland tolls before me, a Bay Horse, eight years old, appraised at thirty eight dollars. **1830** *Augusta* (Ga.) *Constitutionalist* 13 July 1/3 Tolled before me by John H. Stone, . . . one small Bay Horse, four feet ten or eleven inches high, left eye out, and dim sighted in the right.

* **toll,** *v.*[2] *tr.* To lure or decoy (wild creatures) for the purpose of capturing or killing them.

*a*1835 in AUDUBON *Ornith. Biog.* IV. 8 An instance in which I had toled to within a space of from forty to seventy yards off the shore a bed of certainly hundreds of ducks. **1880** *Harper's Mag.* Sep. 510/1 Others fling over bait of ground porgies from boxes along the sides, to 'toll' them [the mackerel] for easier capture. **1893** ROOSEVELT *Wilderness Hunter* 280 A bear carcass will toll a brother bear to the ambushed hunter better than almost any other bait. **1948** *Atlantic Mo.* Sep. 26/1 The geese can be tolled in only when they are moving in big flocks.

fig. and *transf.* **1850** *Deseret News* (Salt Lake City) 17 Aug. 73/2 They were all what you call land pirates once, and didn't think any more of tolling a ship ashore, than a city sharper would think of cheating a country green horn. **1856** *Placer Press* (Auburn, Calif.) 25 Oct. 3/3 Like a wild hog, I am caught in the pen, sir—actually tolled in by you and your dirty *Tribune,* sir. **1927** EUBANK *Horse & Buggy Days* 57 We . . . sought to toll the fair beauty forth to candy pullings.

b. *intr.* To admit of being lured or decoyed.

*a*1835 in AUDUBON *Ornith. Biog.* IV. 7 The Black-heads toll the most readily, then the Red-heads. 1847 LEWIS in Youatt *Dog* 90 The canvass-back toles better than any other duck.

toll bait. Bait for throwing into the water to toll or attract fish. — 1870 *Amer. Naturalist* IV. 516 The 'tole-bait' consists chiefly of menhaden ground very fine. 1887 GOODE *Fisheries* v. II. 594 In the old style of mackerel fishing, . . . clams were chopped up (often with a mixture of menhaden) and sprinkled overboard as 'toll-bait.'

∗**toller,** *n.* In the region of Chesapeake Bay and the sounds of North Carolina, a small dog trained to entice ducks within range of hunters. Also attrib. Cf. ∗**tolling,** *n.*

*a*1835 in AUDUBON *Ornith. Biog.* IV. 7 Most persons on these shores have a race of small white or liver-coloured dog, which they familiarly call the *toler* breed, but which appear to be the ordinary poodle. 1944 *N. & Q.* May 21/1 Dr. William Bruette has an excellent chapter on the toller in his *American Duck, Goose and Brant Shooting.*

b. (See quots.)

1874 LONG *Wild-Fowl* 72 For deep-water ducks, three or four decoys as tolers may be set out. 1947 COFFIN *Yankee Coast* 180 Old Captain Hamilton carved tollers so much more like wild ducks than they were themselves that the ducks gladly sculled up to them and died adoring. 1949 *Reader's Digest* June 140/2 Orville figured to breed and sell his ducks to hunters as tollers.

∗**tolling,** *n.* The luring or decoying of ducks, fish, etc. Also attrib.

[1813 WILSON *Ornithology* VIII. 104 The dog, if properly trained, plays backwards and forwards along the margin of the water. . . . This method is called *tolling them in.*] *a*1835 in AUDUBON *Ornith. Biog.* IV. 6 The usual mode of taking these birds has been . . . by *toling.* 1857 *Spirit of Times* 12 Dec. 227/1 The dog had evidently been well trained in *toling,* for he understood perfectly what he was about. *a*1888 ATWOOD in Goode *Amer. Fishes* 180 The present mode of catching mackerel by drifting and tolling with bait did not come into general use until 1812. 1944 *N. & Q.* May 21/1 George Bird Grinnell . . . remarks that tolling has been out of favor 'for many years,'—and, he adds, 'naturally so, since it is so very destructive.'

tollon, see **toyon.**

Tolman ˈtolmən, *n.* [App. f. a proper name.] A variety of apple, usu. **Tolman sweet(ing),** or a tree producing such an apple.

1822 J. THACHER *Amer. Orchardist* 139 *Tolman sweeting.* . . . It is held in much estimation for family use during the autumn. 1875 BURROUGHS *Winter Sunshine* 155 Now you have got a Tolman sweet. 1903 *Dept. Agric. Yrbk.* 1902 246 In New York and New England the Northern Spy, Roxbury *Russet,* Tolman, and Arctic are among the least susceptible [to sun scald]. 1949 *Boston Globe* 14 Aug. (Fiction Mag.) 11/4 From where we were we could look squarely at the tolman sweet standing all alone with the moonlight making its blossoms burn like candles, so white they were.

toloache toloˈɑtʃɪ, *n. S.W.* [Amer. Sp. (<Nahuatl) in same sense.] =**jimson weed.**

1894 *Scribner's Mag.* May 596/2 [The] 'toloachi,' [and] the 'mariguam,' . . . [are] used by discarded women for the purpose of wreaking a terrible revenge upon recreant lovers. 1912 LUMHOLTZ *New Trails* 280 Close to my tent toloache (*datura*) was in flower. 1948 MATHEWS *Southernisms* 33 In Texas the jimson weed has the Mexican name *toloache.*

Tolowa ˈtɑləˌwɔ, *n.* [App. a native name.] *pl.* or *collect.* (See quot. 1910.)

1853 SCHOOLCRAFT *Indian Tribes* III. 139 The first tribe on the coast were a warlike band called Tol-e-wahs; of whom the Klamaths stand in some awe. 1903 JAMES *Indian Basketry* 53 About Crescent City a few of the Tolowas still live, a bold, warlike people. 1910 HODGE *Amer. Indians* II. 773/1 Tolowa. An Athapascan tribe of extreme N.W. California. When first known they occupied the coast from the mouth of Klamath r. nearly to the Oregon line, including Smith r. valley. They were gathered on a reservation in 1862.

∗**Tom,** *n.* Also ∗**tom.**

1. *W.* =**Long Tom.** Also attrib. Now *hist.*

1839 *Amer. R.R. Jrnl.* VIII. 98 The Rocker is a somewhat different machine, consisting of a 'Riffler,' as in the Tom, except that the bars are concave. 1856 *Harper's Mag.* Oct. 594/2 A stream of water . . . is led through wooden flumes to the 'tom heads.' 1877 WM. WRIGHT *Big Bonanza* 41 He was working with a 'tom' (a contrivance for washing auriferous gravel). 1949 *Boston Globe* 17 July (Fiction Mag.) 9/3 Twenty miles back in the mountains at a round pocket in a circular head he struck a tom-rocker and tried to work his discovery.

b. tom iron, (see quots.). *Obs.*

1853 *Calif. Express* (Marysville) 12 March 3/4 The advantage of the improvement consists in having a sheet of tom-iron, placed over the box containing the rifles, in such a manner as to separate the current of water at the rifle-box and carrying off the coarser stones without at any time clogging the rifles. 1857 *Hutchings Mag.* Jan. 292/1 At the lower end there is a plate of perforated iron called a 'tom iron,' through which the water, dirt and gold pass into a 'riffle box' underneath, where the gold is saved.

2. In special combs. and expressions: (1) **Tom and Jack,** ?=next, (*a*), *obs.;* (2) ∗**Tom and Jerry,** (*a*) a hot drink of sweetened and spiced rum to which beaten eggs have been added, (*b*) a coat or overcoat; (3) ∗**cod,** any one of various small fishes of the genus *Microgadus* that resemble codfish except in size, also applied locally to other fishes, as a kingfish and the bocaccio, cf. **mixed, Pacific tomcod;** (4) **Collins,** (see quots. and cf. **gin rickey**); (5) **-'s Finch,** =**Lincoln's finch,** *obs.;* (6) **show,** ?a touring company featuring *Uncle Tom's Cabin,* also attrib., *slang;* (7) **Tom the Tinker,** (see quot. 1885), *obs.;* (8) **Tom, Tip, and Ty,** (see quot.), *obs.;* (9) **walkers,** stilts, *colloq.*

(1) *c*1844 TOWNES *Hist. Marion* (Ala.) 22 Having seen the show, they . . . regaled themselves with Buck-eye, Apple-jack, Tom and Jack, and other kindred spirits. — (2) (*a*) 1845 GREEN *Texian Exped.* 368 These very men . . . now want, one a '*sherry cobbler,*' one a '*Tom and Jerry.*' 1934 VINES *Green Thicket World* 146 They had made a rift in the talk by making and drinking another Tom and Jerry. (*b*) 1838 *Knickerb.* XII. 313 The intruder . . . [was] wrapped to the throat in a shaggy Tom-and-Jerry. — (3) 1722 *N.-Eng. Courant* 1 Oct. 1/2 Some Fishermen in *Boston* made me pay *Two Pence* for the Sight of a *Tom-Cod* instead of a *Maremaid.* 1852 *S.F. Herald* 29 Nov. 2/1 A silent vow of meditation, portentous of death to tom-cods and other imprudent little fishes that come darting around the city wharves to spend their Sundays. 1949 *Lincoln Co. News* (Oceanlake, Ore.) 4 Aug. 1/1 After a short visit to Siletz Bay about a month ago, those tinsel colored, handsome and tasty tomcod have again put in an appearance. — (4) 1909 *Cent. Supp.,* Tom Collins. . . . A drink made of gin and club-soda and lemon or lime-juice, and sweetened. 1945 MENCKEN *Supp.* I. 254 The addition of sugar converts a *rickey* into a *Tom Collins,* which is supposed to have been named after its inventor, a distinguished bartender of that name, and the substitution of Holland gin for dry gin makes a *Tom Collins* a *John Collins.*

(5) 1834 AUDUBON *Ornith. Biog.* II. 539 Lincoln's Finch. . . . I named it Tom's Finch, in honor of our friend [Thomas] Lincoln, who was a great favourite among us. — (6) 1908 K. MCGAFFEY *Show-Girl* 47 There is something in town besides a 'Tom' show. 1945 *Sat. Review* 6 Oct. 24/2 The version was not the famous George L. Aiken one which was to make 'Tom' show history; it was C. W. Taylor's adaptation. — (7) 1862 *Harper's Mag.* Feb. 373/1 Tar and feathers and the torch were freely used and the violence employed was in a manner personified, and called Tom and Tinker. *Ib.,* Women and children in loyal families turned pale at the name of *Tom the Tinker.* 1885 *Mag. Amer. Hist.* April 396/1 During the Whiskey Rebellion . . . the house of an obnoxious official was pulled to pieces by a mob whose members gave out they were 'mending it.' Mending and 'tinkering' being interchangeable terms, the members dubbed themselves 'tinkers,' and 'Tom the Tinker' was shortly evolved as the popular watchword of the first rebellion against the United States Government. — (8) 1885 *Mag. Amer. Hist.* April 396/2 Tom, Tip and Ty, . . . a party motto common in Ohio during the 'Hard Cider' campaign of 1839. 'Tom' Corwin was running for the governorship of the State, while 'Tippecanoe' (Harrison) and Tyler were the Whig candidates on the Presidential ticket. — (9) 1929 *Augusta* (Ga.) *Herald* 15 Dec., 'Tom-Walkers,' the favorite of youths of a generation ago, have been revived by him.

b. In expressions in which the first element is not etymologically related to that in the preceding groups but is usu. the result of perversion: (1) ∗**tom alley,** (see quot.), cf. **tamale;** (2) **fuller,** see as a main entry; (3) **hawk, ho(c)k, hog,** a tomahawk, *obs.;* (4) **pung,** (see quot. 1895); (5) **tate,** (see quot.).

(1) *c*1900 C. W. GREENE *Lett. to Sir J. A. H. Murray,* When I was a youngster in Massachusetts, we called the gelatinous part of a baked maize pudding, the *tom-alley.* It somewhat resembles in appearance the *tom-alley* of the lobster; but in meaning it comes very near the Mexican, Cuban, and Southern U.S. use of *tamauli* or *tamalli* as the name of a kind of maize pudding. — (3) 1716 CHURCH *Philip's War* 24 A great surly look'd fellow took up his Tomhog, or wooden Cutlash. 1758 POST *Journal* 228 The Indians . . . lay with their guns and tomhocks on all night. 1788 FRENEAU *Poems* (1795) 89 The North American Indians . . . [decorate the corpse of a warrior] with bows, arrows, tomhawks [etc.]. 1821 DODDRIDGE *Backwoodsman & Dandy,* Next I larned to shoot the bow and arrow, throw the tomhok, and handle the rifle. — (4) 1801 *Spirit Farmers' Mus.* 243 That fam'd town, which sends to Boston mart, The gliding Tom Pung, and the

rattling cart. **1825** COOPER *L. Lincoln* xix, Polwarth drove into the little courtyard . . . with all those knowing flourishes . . . which, in the year 1775, were thought to indicate the greatest familiarity with the properties of a tom-pung. **1895** GERARD in *N.Y. Sun* 30 July, Pung, a rude sort of sleigh used for drawing loads of snow by horse; formerly written Tom Pung. The word is a corruption of toboggan.

(5) **1895** JORDAN & EVERMANN *Check-List Fishes* 385 Tom-tate; Red-mouth Grunt.

As the last term in **female, long, mad, Uncle Tom.**

tom tɑm, *v.* [f. the noun] *tr.* To wash (auriferous gravel) with or in a tom. *Obs.* — **1854** *Wide West* (S.F.) 1 Oct. 1/8 The prospects, may be perhaps a cent to the pan, . . . and if a party should attempt to 'tom' it he could not make fifty cents per day.

tomahawk ˈtɑməˌhɔk, *n.* [f. the widespread Algonquian name of this article. See Hodge.]

1. An Indian war club of any one of various types, in later use commonly applied to the hatchet or hatchet-like weapon or tool of the Indians in the eastern U.S.

Types of tomahawks

*c*1612 STRACHEY *Dict. Indian Lang.* (1849) 188 A hatchet, *tacca hacan, tamahaac.* **1701** WOLLEY *Journal N.Y.* 38 They dig their ground with a Flint, called in their Language *tom-a-hea-kan.* *a*1817 DWIGHT *Travels* I. 118 The well known Tomahawk, or war-club, . . . [was] in shape not unlike a Turkish sabre, but much shorter and more clumsy. . . . Since the arrival of the English, they have used fire-arms . . . [and] a small battle-axe, to which they have transferred the name of Tomahawk. **1948** *Nat. Hist.* Dec. 445/1 The warrior immediately smashed open the oyster with his tomahawk.

fig. **1950** *Chi. Tribune* 1 Jan. III. 4/2 A lot of pesky little oxygen atoms are sharpening their tomahawks right now against the day not far hence when you rack up the coal shovel for the season.

With reference to the notching of tomahawk handles by the Indians; cf. ∗**Notchers.**

1817 J. BRADBURY *Travels* 41 (*footnote*), It is customary amongst the Missouri Indians to register every exploit in war, by making a notch for each on the handle of their tomahawks. **1891** *Cent. Mag.* Feb. 523 The handle of the tomahawk he carried had nearly a hundred notches to record the number of his Indian scalps.

2. In combs., usu. obs. or hist.: (1) **tomahawk claim,** (see quot. 1895); (2) **dance,** an Indian dance characterized by flourishing of tomahawks; (3) **entry,** =**tomahawk improvement** or **tomahawk right;** (4) **face,** a hatchet face; (5) **improvement,** a casual improvement, such as the girdling of a few trees or the planting of a little corn, made in order to secure a preemption claim to government land, also the place so improved; (6) **pipe,** (see quot. 1907 and cf. **hatchet pipe**); (7) **right,** (see quot. 1824); (8) **settler,** a settler who has made a tomahawk improvement or who has a tomahawk right to a piece of public land.

(1) **1895** J. WINSOR *Miss. Basin* 229 The valley was spotted with tomahawk claims, as squatters' rights were termed, traceable for years by the lighter color of the wound made by the woodsman's hatchet on the boundary trees. **1948** DICK *Dixie Frontier* 8 Pioneers began to blaze out numerous tomahawk claims. — (2) **1856** EMERSON *Works* V. (1903) 87 They have no Indian taste for a tomahawk-dance. — (3) **1842** *Amer. Pioneer* I. 312 One tract, a few miles above Marietta, is still known as 'Wiseman's bottom,' after the man who made a 'tomahawk entry' at that place. — (4) **1862** E. KIRKE *Among Pines* 248 The Abolitionists have long, lean, tommerhawk faces.

(5) **1803** *Steele P.* I. 374 There were many Tomahawk Improvements. *a*1847 HOWE *Hist. Coll. Ohio* 377 Below the garrison, was an old 'tomahawk improvement' and a small cabin. **1948** DICK *Dixie Frontier* 67 Such species of titles as 'cabin rights,' 'corn rights,' 'sugar-cane rights,' and 'tomahawk improvements' were bought and sold like genuine property. — (6) **1836** HOFFMAN *Winter in West* I. 245 The frontiersman, knocking the ashes from his tomahawk-pipe, passed me a flask of Ohio whiskey. **1907** HODGE *Amer. Indians* I. 536/1 The combination of the iron hatchet with the tobacco pipe as a single implement, often called the tomahawk pipe, became very general in colonial and later times, and as no counterpart of this device is found in aboriginal art, it was probably devised by the whites as a useful and profitable combination of the symbols of peace and war.— (7) **1824** DODDRIDGE *Notes* 100 At an early period of our settlements an inferior kind of land title denominated a 'tomahawk right' . . . was made by deadening a few trees near the head of a spring, and marking the bark of some one, or more of them with the initials of the name of the person who made the improvement. **1948** DICK *Dixie Frontier* 8 Yet these 'tomahawk rights' . . . were recognized by other settlers. — (8) **1788** CUTLER in *Life & Corr.* I. 425 They were tomahawk settlers.

b. In phrases: (1) *To bury the tomahawk,* and variants, to cease hostilities, to conclude peace; (2) *to take up the tomahawk,* and variants, to begin warlike activities; (3) *to play tomahawk,* (see quot.), *rare.*

(1) [**1705** BEVERLEY *Virginia* III. 27 They use . . . very ceremonious ways in concluding of Peace, . . . such as burying a Tomahawk.] **1775** ADAIR *Indians* 315 We in a few days packed up a sufficient quantity [of presents], to bury the tomahawk which the French had thrust into their unwilling hands. **1808** PIKE *Sources Miss.* 86 The two nations had laid aside the tomahawk at my request. **1927** BENÉT *J. B.'s Body* 17 The tomahawk is buried in prairie-sod. — (2) **1765** TIMBERLAKE *Memoirs* 33 The bloody tommahawke, so long lifted against our brethren the English, must now be buried deep, deep in the ground, never to be raised again. **1811** *Niles' Reg.* I. 311/2 Certain deputations from the northern tribes lately visited the southern Indians to induce them to unbury the tomahawk. **1813** *Ib.* IV. 76/2 The society are ready to unbury the tomahawk whenever their country's good requires it. **1896** *Harper's Mag.* 709/2 All the tribes of the upper lakes had taken up the tomahawk. — (3) **1844** POE *Works* (1902) VI. 20 By 'playing tomahawk' he referred to scalping, brow-beating and otherwise using-up the herd of poor-devil authors.

tomahawk ˈtɑməˌhɔk, *v. tr.* To strike or kill with a tomahawk. Also **tomahawked,** *a.* Now *hist.*

1711 *N.C. Col. Rec.* I. 813 The Baron de Graftenried . . . was still alive but supposed only reserved for a more solemn execution, to be tomahawked and tortured. **1795** *Pittsburgh Gaz.* 13 June 3/1 They were scalped and tomahawked in a most shocking manner. **1899** CUSHMAN *Hist. Indians* 440 Sixteen warriors . . . were led out and, in cold blood, tomahawked. **1947** *Nat. Geog. Mag.* July 105/2 Eventually his tomahawked head was spiked on the Indian palisades.

fig. **1852** *Lantern* (N.Y.) I. 223/2 The article in question was fired by a young *savage* in the office, whom they kept for the purpose of tomahawking and scalping the Fogies, one of the most annoying of the literary tribes. **1946** *Dly. Ardmoreite* (Ardmore, Okla.) 15 Dec. 14/3 Four previous times the Bears have battered their way to the top seat, the last time in 1943 when they tomahawked the Redskins from Washington 41–18.

Hence **tomahawking,** *n.*

1835 BIRD *Hawks* I. 120 I'll allow you to be a complete master of the science of tomahawking, skinning, and scalping. **1883** *Harper's Mag.* Feb. 423/1 After a great deal of tomahawking and scalping . . . , the united forces . . . crushed the Tuscaroras.

tomatillo ˌtoməˈtiljo, *n. S.W.* [Amer. Sp. (dim. of *tomate*) in same sense.] (See quot.) — **1933** HARRINGTON *Gypsum Cave, Nev.* 197 *Lycium pallidum* Miers. Tomatillo. Rabbit thorn.

∗**tomato,** *n.* In combs.: (1) **tomato butter,** a smooth paste made by stewing tomatoes; (2) **can,** a cylindrical vessel of tinned iron in which tomatoes are canned; (3) **cushion,** a pincushion suggestive in color, shape and size of a tomato, also **tomato pincushion;** (4) **gall,** (see quot.); (5) **patch,** a small area in which tomatoes are grown; (6) **worm,** a tobacco worm, so called when found on a tomato plant.

(1) **1884** MRS. OWENS *Cook Book* 342 Tomato Butter . . . takes an entire day to cook properly. — (2) **1883** HOWELLS *Woman's Reason* xvii, A few slatternly goats . . . wandered over the dismal expanse, as if to crop the battered tomato-cans. **1950** *Boston Globe Mag.* Feb. 2/3 He had a tomato can half filled with gold dust. — (3) **1864** *Hist. North-Western Soldiers' Fair* 117 [Donations include] 1 pr. infant's shoes, 6 tomato cushions. **1903** WIGGIN *Rebecca* 37 She ran up the back-stairs to . . . a red tomato-pincushion on Rebecca's bureau. — (4) **1891** *Cent.* 6371/3 *Tomato-gall,* . . . a gall made upon the twigs of the grape-vine in the United States by the gall-midge *Lasioptera vitis:* so called on account of its resemblance to the fruit of the tomato.

(5) **1892** RITTENHOUSE *Maud* 555 We were hunting a ball in the tomato-patch back of the stop-net. — (6) **1868** *Mich. Agric. Rep.* VII. 167 In many parts of Michigan, the tomato worm—larvæ of the *Sphinx quinqua-maculata*—have been frightfully abundant. **1892** V.

KELLOGG *Kansas Insects* 3 The larvae of moths and butterflies are the voracious caterpillars, as those of the Codlin Moth, the Tomato-worm [etc.].

As the last term in **bur, cherry, gem, husk, prairie, strawberry, wild tomato.**

* **tomb,** *n.*

1. (*cap.*) *pl.* The New York City prison. Also attrib.

1840 *N.Y. Herald* 20 Feb. 1/5 Our report would be but a dull record of assaults and petty larcenies, but for the following gross case of neglect and inattention to the suffering of the wretched inmates of 'the tombs' which we were called on to investigate. **1852** BRISTED *Upper Ten. Th.* 207 Kelly the carrier, And Lynch the Tombs lawyer a pleader well known. **1881** *Phila. Rec.* No. 3473, 4 One of the worst abuses in the most depraved days of New York City was the prevalence of the Tombs shyster. **1946** *Time* 23 Dec. 58/3 Charnay once posed as a murderer's attorney to get an interview in a cell at the Tombs.

2. *To give one hark from the tomb,* to give one the very devil. *Colloq.*

In allusion to the line "Hark! from the tombs a doleful sound" in a hymn by Isaac Watts.

1884 MARK TWAIN *H. Finn* 263 Then Susan she waltzed in, and if you'll believe me, she did give Hare-lip hark from the tomb.

tombé tɑmˈbe, *n. S.W.* [Origin obscure, poss. f. a native word.] An Indian drum (see quot. 1876).

1848 RUXTON *Far West* viii. 291 Their instruments being generally a species of guitar called *heaca,* a *bandolin,* and an Indian drum called tombe—one of each. **1876** COZZENS *Ariz. & N. Mex.* 394 At the sound of the tombe, the warriors . . . entered the plaza. [Note to *tombé:*] A section of hollow log, about two feet long, and from sixteen to eighteen inches in diameter. Over one end of it is stretched a dried hide, from which the hair has been carefully removed. It is sounded with a stick, similar to that used in beating a bass drum, and produces a most terrific sound, which can be heard for miles on a still night.

tom fuller. [f. Choctaw *tanfula, tahfula,* hominy.] (See quots. 1916, 1948.)

1848 *Ladies' Repository* Sep. 275 Some were beating corn for *tom-fuller,* (a kind of hommony). **1916** THOBURN *Stand. Hist. Okla.* I. 262 The fermented hominy which was known as 'tahfula' (corrupted into English 'tom fuller') was the national dish of the Choctaws. **1948** DICK *Dixie Frontier* 291 A dish known as sof-ky to the Indians, but Americanized into 'Tom Fuller' by the settlers, was made by cracking the shells of certain nuts very fine and putting them, shell and kernel, into a pot containing peas, corn, dry venison, and beans.

attrib. **1891** O'BEIRNE *Leaders Indian Terr.* 24/2 The 'Tonfulla' patch, too, has become a three-hundred-acre field more or less, for some of the farms in the Choctaw and Chickasaw Nations cover 5,000 acres.

Tommy gun. [f. the trade-mark names "Tommy" or "Thompson" (< Gen. John T. Thompson (1860–1940), U.S. Army officer and coinventor).] A light automatic machine gun that may be fired from the shoulder or the hip. Also **tommy-gunner.** *Slang.*

1929 *Sat. Ev. Post* 13 April 54/3 There are three types of machine guns used—Tommy guns, Browny guns and Louie guns. **1947** *Chi. D. News* 14 Oct. 35 I'll have my men cover it with Tommy guns from this bullet proof vault. **1949** *Sat. Ev. Post* 9 July 88/4 A man with a sword across his knees sat on the hood of a jeep, shouting orders to a squad of tommy-gunners.

Tonawandas ˈtɑnəˌwɑndəz, *n. pl.* Indians, esp. Senecas, living on Tonawanda Creek in western N.Y. (See quot. 1910.) Also **Tonawanda Indian.**

1806 Soc. of Friends, Phila. Yrly. Meeting *Acct. Comm.* 42 A visit was also made with the Tonewantas. **1819** EVANS *Pedestrious Tour* 57 The Tondanwandeys are much troubled with the supposed existence of witchcraft. **1844** *Cherokee Adv.* (Tahlequah, Okla.) 16 Nov. 3/3 A Tonawanda Indian, near West Point, New York, recently accomplished, on foot, ten miles in less than an hour. **1910** HODGE *Amer. Indians* II. 777/2 Tonawanda ('confluent stream'). A Seneca settlement on Tonawanda cr., in Niagara co., N.Y. In 1890 there were 517 Seneca and a few other Iroquois on the reservation. **1949** *Ann. Rep. Smithsonian Inst.* 411/2 The Tonawanda Indian Reservation comprises 7,549 acres in Erie and Genesee Counties along Tonawanda Creek, 20 miles northeast of Buffalo, N.Y.

* **tong,** *n.*[1]

1. *pl. N. Eng.* (See quot. 1845.) *Obs.*

1845 JUDD *Margaret* I. 34 The boys dressed in 'tongs,' a name for pantaloons or over-alls. *a*1847 in J. S. HALL *Book of Feet* 138 This continued until long trousers were introduced, which they called *tongs.*

2. *pl.* A long-handled implement having two rakelike or basket-like jaws used to grapple oysters or crabs and bring them to the surface. Cf. **oyster tongs.**

1811 SUTCLIFF *Travels* (1815) 129 These instruments, which are called tongs, are opened wide when the Leads are let down from the boats. **1911** *Rep. Fisheries 1908* 309/2 Crabs . . . are caught with . . . hand lines, spears, and tongs.

3. tongman, =**tonger.**

1881 INGERSOLL *Oyster Industry* 249. **1891** W. K. BROOKS *Oyster* 140 They are exposed to the depredations of both tongmen and dredgers.

tong tɔŋ, *n.*[2] [f. a Chinese word, *t'ang, t'ong,* hall, meeting place.] An association or secret organization among the Chinese in the U.S. Also attrib.

It is said that the first tongs were formed in San Francisco by Chinese who had observed the work there of the Vigilance committees, and who felt that somewhat similar organizations were needed to protect the weaker of their number from the exploitation of their more powerful compatriots. See *Reader's Digest,* Sep. 1941, 133.

1883 *Harper's Mag.* May 831/1 This burial-place . . . is parcelled off by white fences into enclosures for a large number of separate burial guilds, or *tongs,* as the Fook Yam Tong [etc.]. **1928** ASBURY *Gangs of N.Y.* 301 The tongs are as American as chop suey—the latter is said to have been invented by an American dishwasher in a San Francisco restaurant, while the first tong was organized in the Western gold fields about 1860—and finally they became little more than associations for parcelling out gambling and opium smoking privileges. **1948** JOHNSTON *Gold Rush* 15/2 Chinese who were members of two tongs, the Sam-yap and the Yan-wo, were working side by side at Two-mile Bar, on the Stanislaus River.

b. tong war, a war between such organizations.

1928 ASBURY *Gangs of N.Y.* 301 The tong wars appeared to have begun about 1899, and, with the exception of one of two which started over women, were all caused by conflicting gambling interests. **1950** *L.A. Times Home Mag.* 26 March 5/2 The servants of 70 years ago were mostly Chinese whose favorite outdoor sports were tong wars.

Tongas ˈtɑŋgəs, *n. pl.* (See quot. 1910.) — **1860** *North-West* (Portland) 5 July 3/2 A posse of policemen . . . arrested the well-known chief 'Captain John,' and his brother, on a charge of having murdered the Tunghas tyhee. **1910** HODGE *Amer. Indians* II. 778/1 Tongas (. . . named from an island on which they formerly camped). A Tlingit tribe at the mouth of Portland canal, Alaska, numbering 273 in 1880 and 255 in 1890, probably including the Sanya.

tonger ˈtɔŋɚ, *n.* (See quot. 1881.) — **1881** INGERSOLL *Oyster Industry* 249 *Tonger,* one who procures oysters by the use of tongs. **1945** *Reader's Digest* April 114 The tonger operates a pair of rakes that are bolted together, opening and closing scissor-fashion—wide rakes with long limber shafts.

tonging ˈtɔŋɪŋ, *n.* The taking of oysters with tongs. Also attrib.

1869 *Rep. Comm. Agric. 1868* 342 The Baltimore department . . . reports an annual average of eleven million bushels, taken in the legitimate way of dredging and tonging. **1884** *Nat. Museum Bul.* No. 27, 220 The majority of the 'tonging' canoes employ one man and a boy. **1947** *Downtown Shopping News* (Chi.) 20 Jan. 8/3 Oysters are harvested by dredging or by tonging.

* **tongue,** *n.* As the last term in **beard-, black, bull, burnt, crotch, Dakota, deer, forked, lamb's, Mingo, Mohawk, Mohegan, moose, Osage, snake, sore, wooden tongue.**

Tonkawa ˈtɑŋkəwə, *n.* [Said to be f. a Waco word meaning "they all stay together."] *pl.* An Indian tribe making up the Tonkawan linguistic family, living in the eighteenth and nineteenth centuries in central Texas.

1807 DUNBAR *Travels* 45 Tankaways (or Tanks, as the French call them) have no land, nor claim the exclusive right to any, nor have any particular place of abode, but are always moving. **1862** *Texas Almanac Extra* (Austin) 15 Nov. 1/4 Out of all the tribes on the Reserve, the Comanches and Tonkaways alone remained true to our government. **1907** COOK *Border & Buffalo* (1938) 212 We don't want to bulge in on a band of peaceable Tonkawas and play the devil before we know it. **1942** DALE *Cow Country* 191 Under the terms of this treaty the United States during the next few years removed to this region the Osages, Kaws, Poncas, Otoes, and Missouris, and the Tonkawas.

attrib. **1853** in *Southwestern Hist. Quart.* (1949) April 385 They were of the Tonkaway tribe, some thirty in number, and had come to beg. **1862** *Texas Almanac Extra* (Austin) 15 Nov. 1/4 Dr. Sturm took refuge in the Tonkaway camp. **1870** DUVAL *Big-Foot Wallace* 148, I got it from 'Puppy's Foot,' the Tonkawa chief. **1892** ——— *Young Explorers* 34 There was a part of the Tonkewa tribe of Indians encamped not far from Goliad, who at that time professed to be friendly to the Texans.

* **tonnage,** *n. attrib.* Designating a train or car for freight as distinguished from one for passengers. *Obs.* — **1858** W. P. SMITH *Railway Celebrations* I. 92 Equipment of the Marietta and Cincinnati Railway. . . . For Passenger Trains, 24; For Tonnage Trains, 24; making

a Total of 48 Locomotives. **1862** *N.Y. Herald* 11 June 1/2 We took . . . three passenger and fifty tonnage cars.

tonsorial artist. A barber. *Grandiloquent.*

1875 SKINNER *His Centennial Booke* 19 (We.), Now, the men mostly go to a tonsorial artist, (formerly a barber). **1884** *Lisbon* (Dak.) *Star* 15 Aug., Geo. Pickard, the popular tonsorial artist . . . will return to business in a week or two. **1910** *Daily News* (London) 15 Dec. 6 American 'tonsorial artists' are furious at the popularity of the safety razor.

tonsorialist tɑnˈsorɪəlɪst, *n.* =**tonsorial artist.** *Grandiloquent.* — **1869** *New North West* (Deer Lodge, Mont.) 6 Aug. 3/1 Mr. Plummer, the colored tonsorialist . . . has the misfortune to be a 'bloody Hinglishman.' **1919** *Polk St. Journal* (S.F.) 2 May 1/3 (*headline*), Popular Tonsorialist in Race for Convention Meet.

Tonto ˈtɑnto, *n. S.W.* [Sp. *tonto*, fool.] *pl.* A name given to various Indians (see quot. 1910). Also **Tonto Apaches, Tonto Indians.**

1852 SITGREAVES *Exped. Zuni & Colo. Rivers* (1853) 9 He did not return until late in the night, and reported that he had come upon a large encampment of Yampai or Tonto Indians on the edge of a deep ravine. **1910** HODGE *Amer. Indians* II. 783/1 Tontos (Span.: 'fools,' so called on account of their supposed imbecility; the designation, however, is a misnomer). A name so indiscriminately applied as to be almost meaningless. **1949** *Nat. Hist.* May 234/2 Its present name of Tuzigoot—City of the Crooked Water—was given it long decades ago by the Tonto Apaches.

Also **Tonto Apache,** the language of these Indians.

1949 *Travel* Dec. 10/3 Near Clarksdale, Tuzigoot, which in Tonto Apache means 'Crooked Waters,' is the site of three large pueblos.

tony ˈtonɪ, *a.* [f. **tone.*] Stylish, fashionable. *Slang.*

1877 BURDETTE *Rise & Fall of Mustache* 177 He's a toney old cyclopedia on the patter, is old Fitchy. **1879** *Amer. Punch* Dec. 135/1 The most 'tony' thing in the kitchen is the rolling-pin, because it rolls right over even the upper-crust. **1949** *Time* 16 May 77/1 Aside from mellowing him, success has awakened some tony tastes that amuse his acquaintances.

***tool,** *n.* As the last term in **doughboy, fire, fishing tool(s).**

***toot,** *n.* A spree, a drunken fit, often *on a toot. Slang.*

1891 *Cent. Mag.* Nov. 54 Grubbsy's went off on a toot, and they've got nobody to ride. **1941** STUART *Men of Mts.* 132 I've had birds to come down out'n the air and pluck hairs out'n my head to line their nests with when I's gettin' over a big toot. **1949** *N.O. Times-Picayune Mag.* 18 Dec. 5 Only a few old-timers will remember the Yule Eve when New Orleans went on one gigantic raucous toot.

***tooter,** *n.* **1.** One who proclaims loudly. **2.** A hotel runner or a circus barker.

(1) 1863 *Rio Abajo Press* 19 May 2 The nameless party's tooter speaks confidently of the success of its nominee. — **(2) 1886** *Harper's Mag.* Aug. 417/2 The wharf . . . was alive with vehicles and tooters for the hotels. **1897** ROBINSON *Uncle Lisha's Outing* 297 Noisiest of all were the tooters, vociferously proclaiming the wonders of the side shows.

***tooth,** *n.* In combs.: (1) ***toothache,** see as a main entry; (2) ***brush,** *S.* (see quots.), *colloq.;* (3) **carpenter,** a dentist, *colloq.;* (4) **paste,** a paste used in cleaning the teeth, also attrib.; (5) ***pick,** see as a main entry; (6) **saw,** (see quot. 1876), *obs.;* (7) **soap,** a soap for the teeth.

(2) 1913 MORLEY *Carolina Mts.* 170 When a mountain woman refers to her 'toothbrush' the snuff-stick is what she means. **1926** *D.N.* V. 404 *tooth-brush,* n. A chewed twig used in dipping snuff. — **(3) 1846** *Freeman's Journal* (N.Y.) 31 Oct. 137/2 How shocked the gentlemen aforesaid would be, if they heard, as we did the other day, one of their brethren, a dentist, called a 'tooth-carpenter.' **1888** *Chehalis* (Wash.) *Bee* 18 May 3/4 Dr. Boyce, besides being a physician and druggist, is a 'tooth carpenter.' — **(4) 1832** *Amer. R.R. Jrnl.* I. 607/3 (*advt.*), Seidlitz Powders, chloride of Soda, Chlorine Tooth Paste. **1949** *Reader's Digest* July 141/1 The tube virtually turned the dentrifrice business into the tooth-paste business.

(6) 1868 *Ore. State Jrnl.* 31 Oct. 2/2 He is engaged with a company in New York in the manufacture of Brown's patent adjustable tooth saws. **1876** KNIGHT 2596/1 *Tooth-saw.* The dental saw is a fine frame-saw, used for cutting off the natural teeth for the attachment of pivot teeth; for sawing between teeth; or for sawing off the wires of artificial teeth to detach them from the plate. — **(7) 1944** CLARK *Pills* 299 Scattered in with these items were razors, razor straps, tooth soap and brushes.

As the last term in **alligator, black, blind, devil's golden, horse, pivot, saw, spring, stomach tooth.**

***toothache,** *n.* In combs.: (1) **toothache bush,** (see quots.); (2) **grass,** *S.* a tall grass, *Ctenium aromaticum,* having a dense and much awned, one-sided spike; (3) **tree,** the prickly ash.

(1) 1817–8 EATON *Botany* (1822) 519 *Zanthopylum fraxineum,* prickly ash, toothache bush. **1859** BARTLETT 483 *Toothache Bush,* . . . Prickly Ash; so called from its pungent properties, made sensible when applied to an aching tooth. — **(2) 1837** WILLIAMS *Florida* 82 Tooth-ache Grass . . . affects the breath and milk of cows. **1901** MOHR *Plant Life Ala.* 124 Toothache grass . . . [has a] stout aromatic rootstock deeply buried in the compacted sand. — **(3)** *c***1729** CATESBY *Carolina* I. 26 The Pellitory, or Tooth-ach Tree, . . . seldom grows above a foot in thickness. **1775** ROMANS *Nat. Hist. Fla.* 22 Tooth ach tree, with white spines almost an ash leaf. **1941** R. S. WALKER *Lookout* 61 Prickly-ash, or tooth-ache tree grows in certain favored spots, and the hop-tree is occasionally found at both the north end and south end of Lookout.

toothed herring. =**mooneye.** — **1842** *Nat. Hist. N.Y., Zoology* IV. 266 The River Moon-eye . . . is known under the popular names of *Herring, River Herring,* and *Toothed Herring.* **1871** DE VERE 386 The Moon-Eye . . . [is] also known as lake and river herring, and as toothed herring.

***toothpick,** *n.*

1. A bowie knife or dagger.

1848 COOPER *Oak Openings* II. 43 We got our own tooth-picks. **1869** *New No. West* (Deer Lodge, Mont.) 20 Aug. 1/7 The Missourian edged out of 'range,' and putting up his 'tooth-pick,' [etc.]. **1910** J. HART *Vigilante Girl* 135 He loaned him his toothpick.

b. (See quot.) *Obs.*

1863 RUSSELL *Diary* II. 13 In the train which preceded us there was a band of volunteers armed with rifled pistols and enormous bowie knives, who called themselves 'The Toothpick Company.' They carried along with them a coffin, with a plate inscribed, 'Abe Lincoln, died——,' and declared they were 'bound' to bring his body back in it, and that they did not intend to use muskets or rifles, but just go in with knife and six-shooter, and whip the Yankees straight away.

2. (*cap.*) *pl.* (See quots.)

[**1846** *Warrock's Alm. 1847* 22 Arkansas, Tooth Pickers.] **1886** *Chi. W. News* 29 April 4/3 Arkansas is the Bear state and its people Toothpicks from their structure. **1946** MCWILLIAMS *So. Calif. Country* 172 People from Arkansas are 'toothpicks.'

3. Designating various sharp-pointed things as **toothpick collar, shoes, steeple.**

1880 MARK TWAIN *Tramp Abroad* 245 [Lucerne offers] to the eye a heaped-up confusion of red roofs, quaint gables, dormer windows, toothpick steeples. **1891** WELCH *Recoll. 1830–40* 179 A white two-pointed collar coming up and over the chin and lapping, called 'tooth-pick collars.' **1895** *Outing* XXVII. 6/1 A girl . . . gave me the go-by for a patent medicine drummer with tooth-pick shoes. **1947** *True* Nov. 72/1 He wore sharply pointed patent leather shoes, called 'tooth-pick shoes' by most of the reporters who described them.

As the last term in **Arkansas, California, Missouri toothpick.**

***tooting,** *n.* A characteristic sound made in breeding time by pinnated grouse. Also attrib. — **1810** in WILSON *Ornithology* III. 109 This noise . . . is termed *tooting,* from its resemblance to the blowing of a conch or horn from a remote quarter. **1835** AUDUBON *Ornith. Biog.* III. 100 To the Gulls [mud flats or sandy beaches] are what the scratching or tooting grounds are to the Pinnated Grous.

***top,** *n.*

1. *pl.* The upper parts of stalks of Indian corn cut off for use as fodder.

1724 H. JONES *Virginia* 40 Indian Corn is the best Food for Cattle . . . and the Blades and Tops are excellent Fodder, when well cured. **1811** *Agric. Museum* I. 240, [I was] informed of the advantages of using the tops of Indian Corn cut as rye straw. **1945** PEARSON *Country Flavor* 23 She has a crib full of green oats or the tops of sweet corn on which to munch.

2. In combs.: (1) **top crop,** (*a*) (see quot. 1903), (*b*) in mining, an outcrop; (2) **cross,** (see quot. 1909); (3) ***dirt,** *W.* in mining, topsoil, surface soil, cf. **top washing;** (4) **fire,** a forest fire in the tops of the trees; (5) **fodder,** =***top 1.** above; (6) **hand,** *W.* among cowboys, a superior hand; (7) **heavy,** *a.* of the audience in a theater, distributed principally in the upper, lower-priced seats, with a small attendance on the main floor; (8) ***knot,** see as a main entry; (9) **load,** (see quot.); (10) **loader,** in logging, the member of a loading crew who stands on top of a load and directs the placing of logs as they are sent up; (11) **minnow,** (see quot. 1909); (12) **mostly,** *adv.* mainly, principally, *rare;* (13) **-mounter,** in a troupe of acrobats performing together, the one who mounts to the highest position; (14) **notch,** the highest point or degree of excellence, also attrib., *colloq.;* (15) **notcher,** a person or thing of the highest quality, *colloq.;*

(16) **sergeant,** a first sergeant in a military organization; (17) **shelfer,** a person of the highest class, *colloq.;* (18) **stick,** a stick of wood placed on top in a wood fire; (19) **tobacco,** tobacco obtained from the tops of the stalks, *obs.,* cf. **ground leaf;** (20) **tow,** ?the shorter fibers of flax or hemp which are separated by heckling from the fine and long-stapled; (21) **waddy,** *W.* =**top hand;** (22) **washing,** in mining, washing of the top soil, *obs.;* (23) **works,** the head, *slang, obs.;* (24) **worm,** =**spindle worm.**

(1) (*a*) **1854** *Fla. Plantation Rec.* 97, I am wanting rain now but I think that the top crop of cotton will be short. **1903** *D.N.* II. 334 top-crop n. The last picking of cotton. The lower bolls are first to open and are the best. The top bolls are late to open and the cotton in them is not as well matured. (*b*) **1895** *Advance* 19 Dec. 910/3 And it ain't top-crop rock, anyhow. — **(2) 1890** *New Breeder's Gaz.* (Chi.) 28 March (*Cent.*), A filly with three top crosses or a horse with four top crosses can be registered. **1909** WEBSTER 2172/1 *Top cross,* . . . a cross in which superior or pure-bred breeds or individuals (usually males) are mated with inferior stock; a generation of ancestors in which one parent has superior qualities; the product of such a cross. — **(3) 1852** in *Pioneer* (S.F.) (May, 1855) 307 In many places the surface soil, or in mining phrase, the 'top dirt,' 'pays' when worked in a 'Long Tom.' **1876** RAYMOND *8th Rep. Mines* 96 The top dirt has been entirely stripped. — **(4) 1900** BRUNCKEN *N. Amer. Forests* 109 There is something horrible in the slow, steady approach of a top fire.

(5) 1894 *Vt. Agric. Rep.* XIV. 42 The stalks are divided into . . . the tops, or top-fodder (cut off above the upper ear), the husks or shucks, and the butts. — **(6) 1912** BOWER *Flying U* 201 We can both safely consider ourselves top-hands when it comes to lying. **1948** *Sat. Ev. Post* 10 July 87/2, I figger you know enough about ranchin' now to make a top hand. — **(7) 1895** *N.Y. Dramatic News* 2 Nov. 18/1 Lansing Theatre. . . . Human Hearts, 14; top-heavy house. — **(9) 1905** *Forestry Bureau Bul.* No. 61, *s.v.* Top load. A load of logs piled more than one tier high, as distinguished from a bunk load.

(10) 1903 *Outlook* 7 Nov. 586 Jimmy, besides being the best top-loader we had on the job, was one of the jolliest men in camp. **1946** *Sat. Ev. Post* 11 May 41/1 [He would] toss them with the twist that only a real top loader can manage. — **(11) 1883** *Nat. Museum Bul.* No. 27, 471 *Gambusia patruelis.* . . . Top Minnow. . . . Southern United States, from Virginia to Texas. **1909** WEBSTER, top minnow. Any of certain small viviparous cyprinodont minnows, esp. *Gambusia affinis,* abundant in sluggish streams and ditches in the southern United States. — **(12)** *a***1861** T. WINTHROP *Life in Open Air* (1863) 34 A Dish of Pork-and-beans, Topmostly this. There were lesser viands, buttresses to this towering triumph. — **(13) 1895** *N.Y. Dramatic News* 14 Dec. 14/3 The top-mounter of the Athos troupe skipped away during the Chicago engagement. **1896** *Ib.* 11 July 12/3 Willie Milette, the top-mounter of the Milette brother act, made a mis-cue . . . and fell heavily. — **(14) 1833** S. SMITH *Life J. Downing* 203 [To] ride awhile in one [wagon] without any cover to it, finney-fined off to the top notch, . . . [is] enough to tucker a feller out. **1917** MC-CUTCHEON *Green Fancy* 190 He telegraphed last night for four top-notch people to join us.

(15) 1899 ADE *Fables in Slang* 164 They told him he ought to go after the Top-Notchers. **1913** LONDON *Valley of Moon* III. ix. 402 And down here you're a top-notcher at *your* own game. — **(16) 1917** J. A. MOSS *Officers' Man.* 485 *Top Sergeant*—first sergeant. **1949** *Sat. Ev. Post* 26 March 107/1 He became the unofficial top sergeant of the enlisted men. — **(17) 1882** BAILLIE-GROHMAN *Camps in Rockies* 9 The frontiersman calls them, as we have heard, 'top-shelfers'; they are accompanied by their servants from England. — **(18) 1852** *Knickerb.* XXXIX. 203 The 'log' has been placed; the 'back-log' has surmounted it; the 'top-stick' crowns the apex. **1853** B. F. TAYLOR *Jan. & June* 189 Back-stick, fore-stick, top-stick, and superstructure, all were in their places. — **(19) 1658** *Va. Statutes* (1823) I. 488 In case anie person . . . shall false pack anie tobacco, that is, pack anie ground leaves to the quantity of ffive pounds in a hogshead, among his topp tobacco, . . . it shall be lawful for the said com'r to give order for the burning it. *Ib.,* They may have an equal benefit with others in the advance of their topp tobacco.

(20) 1804 in J. ROBERTS *Pa. Farmer* 153, I have never, however, found anything so good for my apple trees, as top tow, laid on the land near the trees. **1871** STOWE *Sam Lawson* 28 So that afternoon beheld Sam arranged at full length on a pile of top-tow in the barn-chamber, hatchelling by proxy by putting Harry and myself to the service. — **(21) 1902** *Out West* Oct. 446 As the right bower is to the joker, so, and more also, the 'top waddy' is to the 'rod.' — **(22) 1850** AUDUBON *Western Jrnl.* 211 These diggings . . . were completely riddled; first by the top washing, and 'dry' washing of the Mexicans. — **(23) 1838** INGRAHAM *Burton* II. 102 You will find a comrade of mine behind the rock a little cracked in the topworks. — **(24) 1790** DEANE *N.-Eng. Farmer* 148/1 *Top-worms,* or *spindle-worms,* a white worm resembling a grub, found in the hose, or socket of a plant of maize, which eats off the stem of the plant, and renders it unfruitful.

b. *top of the heap, fig.* the most advantageous position. *Colloq.*

1855 BARNUM *Life* 342 We will find the honest, hard-working practical farmer at the very 'top of the heap.' **1870** LOGAN *Before Footlights* 127 At the 'top of the heap' is the person who owns the theatre.

3. Designating vehicles: (1) **top buggy,** a buggy provided with a top that may readily be raised or lowered, cf. **covered buggy, shifting-top buggy;** (2) **buggy wagon,** a light wagon having a body the front of which is provided with a seat and top like a buggy.

(1) 1863 *Boston Auditor's Rep. 1862–3* 115 New Top Buggy for use of Superintendent, $275. **1948** *Dly. Ardmoreite* (Ardmore, Okla.) 2 April 10/4 They love the quaint canopy top buggies. — **(2) 1849** *Knickerb.* XXXIV. 266 She started with her husband in an ordinary 'top-buggy' wagon.

b. In obs. designations for other vehicles provided with tops, as (1) **top chaise,** (2) **gig,** (3) **phaeton,** (4) **wagon.**

(1) 1770 *Mass. Gaz.* 23 April 3/2 (Ernst), Top chaises. **1815** *Columbian Centinel* 28 June 3/3 (*advt.*), 4 new bellows top chaises . . . 1 coachee. 1 English built curricle. — **(2) 1868** *N.Y. Herald* 18 July 1/2 Fine Top Gig For Sale. — **(3) 1897** HOWELLS *Open-eyed Conspiracy* v, To issue from the railway station in the midst of those buoyant top-phaetons and surreys, with their light-limbed horses is to be thrilled. — **(4) 1852** BRISTED *Upper Ten Th.* 205, I have a top-wagon. **1884** ROE *Nature's Story* 294 He hastened to harness Thunder to his light top-wagon.

4. In verbal expressions, usu. obs.: (1) **top off,** *W.* (see quot. 1944); (2) **pole,** to finish off (a fence or wall) with a pole placed on top; (3) **-tail,** (see quot. 1891); (4) **-thresh,** to thresh the top or best developed grains of (wheat, etc.); (5) **work,** (see quot. 1898).

(1) [**1908** *Sat. Ev. Post* 4 July 22/2 Twice more in the course of a week he was topped by the buster.] **1927** JAMES *Cow Country* 229 The cowboy was at the ranch that day and topping off a bronk he'd started to break that summer. **1944** ADAMS *W. Words* 167/1 top off To ride first, to take the rough edges off a horse. — **(2) 1737** HEMPSTEAD *Diary* 317, I top poled the fence. **1774**——— PATTEN *Diary* 329, I worked at the highway and jamey and Bob top poled the fence up the back side. **1868** BRACKETT *Farm Talk* 118 If you have a wall, it must be well top-poled. — **(3) 1839** *Knickerb.* XIII. 385 'There she top-tails! there she blows!' added he, . . . after taking a long look at the sporting shoal. **1891** *Cent.* 6389/1 *Toptail,* . . . to turn the tail up and the head down, as a whale in diving. — **(4) 1874** *Vt. Bd. Agric. Rep.* II. 222, I would recommend the plan of top-threshing some of the best grain for seed.

(5) 1882 *Maine Agric. Rep.* XXVI. 342 The Bourassa . . . does well top-worked on a strong stock, and then produces bountifully of apples varying remarkably in size in the same tree. **1898** S. B. GREEN *Forestry Minn.* 301 Top-worked, said of trees that are grafted or budded at some distance above the ground.

As the last term in **bellows, big, brick, cane, canvas, corn, curly, extension, fair, falling, fine, flat, fore, high, no, open, pine, red, silver, sorrel, wagon, yellow top.**

*** topknot,** *n.*

1. A scalp. Now *hist.*

1837 BIRD *Nick of Woods* I. 92 It's time you war tryin your hand at an Injun top-knot. **1850** GARRARD *Wah-To-Yah* xiii. 168 Mind the time we 'took' Pawnee 'topknots' away from the Plattes? **1943** DE-VOTO *Yr. of Decision* 296 These talkers by the campfire have passed a knife under the topknot and ripped scalps from skulls.

2. a. topknot duck, (see quot.). *Obs.* **b. topknot quail,** the California quail *q.v.*

(a) 1850 BROWNE *Poultry Yard* 197 The 'crested,' or 'topknot duck,' a beautiful ornamental tame variety, . . . breeds early. — **(b) 1877** HODGE *Arizona* 223 Two others are similar to the top-knot quail of California. **1935** H. L. DAVIS *Honey in Horn* 1 Blue grouse and top-knot-quail boarded in the brush-piles and thorn heaps by the hundreds all the year round.

As the last term in **Poland topknot.**

toppee tɑ'pi, *n.* A toplock or forelock of the hair of the head. *Obs.* — **1778** F. MARION in *Harper's Mag.* LXVII. (1883) 546 The Lt. Colo recomends to every Soldier to have their hairs Cut short to reach no further down than the top of the collar and thinned upwards to the Crown of the head, the fore top short without toppee & short at the sides.

***topping,** *a. N. Eng.* Domineering, boastful. *Colloq.* — **1815** D. HUMPHREYS *Yankey in Eng.* 30 She's lofty—topping—has her highs—sometimes. **1899** JEWETT *Queen's Twin* 217 Child'n has too hard a time now,—all the responsibility is put on 'em since they . . . get to be so toppin' an' knowin'.

***torch,** *n.* In combs.: (1) **torch basket,** a receptacle in which torches may be placed for illumination, as on a steamboat, *obs.;* (2) * **-light,** *attrib.* designating meetings, processions, demonstrations, etc., in which torches play a conspicuous part; (3) **pan,** = * **fire pan,** *obs.;* (4) **pine** (see quot. 1890), also pine kindling suitable for making a torch.

(1) **1875** MARK TWAIN *Old Times Miss.* 191 (R.), It was inspiring to hear the crews sing, especially if the time were nightfall, and the forecastle lit up with the red glare of the torch-baskets. **1896** ——— *Tom Sawyer, Detective* 354 (R.), Jake slipped down aft with his hand-bag . . . and walked ashore . . . and we see him pass out of the light of the torch-basket. — (2) **1837** *New-Yorker* 30 Sep. 441/3 A Loco-Foco 'Torch-Light Meeting,' auxiliary to the larger concern in Tammany, was held in the Park on Thursday evening. **1844** *Lexington* (Ky.) *Observer* 3 Aug. 3/3 The Whigs of Louisville have a Barbacue . . . and a great Torchlight Procession this evening. **1876** INGRAM *Centennial Exp.* 656 The torchlight parade . . . had served only to increase the excitement for the Fourth. **1948** *Democrat* 11 March 4/1 Thus far we have heard of no Southern torchlight parades in response to his announcement. — (3) **1859** TALIAFERRO *Fisher's R.* 156, I went home, told the fambly, left that night, fambly follered, and all the poor men got for my shootin' thar hosses was O'Pan and my torch-pan. — (4) **1890** *Cent.* 4496/2 *Pitch-pine,* . . . in America, *Pinus rigida,* . . . found from New Brunswick to Georgia. . . . Also called *torch-pine.* **1934** VINES *Green Thicket World* 15 Even Asbury forgot that he wanted to be at home in bed and was ever at hand with torch pine and tow sack.

As the last term in **blow, bog, lightwood torch.**

***torch,** *v. tr.* To catch (fish, etc.) by using torches at night. Also **torching,** *n.* Cf. **herring torching.**

1839 STORER *Mass. Fishes* 111 [The] scarcity [of herring] has been attributed by the fishermen to *torching* them at night. **1887** GOODE *Fisheries* V. II. 502 'Torching' . . . is practiced principally by negroes. Having provided themselves with torches they visit the sandy shores at night and catch the terrapins as they come upon the beach to spawn. **1896** *Boston Transcript* 21 Nov. 20/1 The boats [of the herring fleet] . . . are engaged in 'torching' herring.

***torment,** *n.* Hell. *Colloq.* — **1852** STOWE *Uncle Tom* xviii, I'm gwine to torment. . . . I's gwine straight to torment.

***tormentor,** *n.* (See quots.) — **1839** *Spirit of Times* 10 Aug. 276/1 (We.), The new *tormentors,* or wings nearest to the audience, painted by Bengough . . . have been put up. **1929** *Photoplay* April, Tormentor, a large portable wall draped with special material to prevent echo and resonance on the sound set.

tornadic tɔrˈnedɪk, *a.* [f. next + *-ic.*] Of or pertaining to a tornado.

1884 *Amer. Meteorol. Jrnl.* I. 7 Four series of storms of tornadic character have passed over the states east of the Mississippi River since the beginning of the year. **1890** *Columbus* (O.) *Dispatch* 13 June, These are tornadic conditions. **1950** *Dly. Ardmoreite* (Ardmore, Okla.) 30 April 3/1 Oklahomans can expect more unusual weather Sunday following two days of tornadic conditions.

***tornado,** *n.* "A destructive rotatory storm under a funnel-shaped cloud like a water-spout, which advances in a narrow path over the land for many miles" (*OED*).

1804 *Fredericktown* (Md.) *Herald* 16 June 2/2 Within the vortex before the cloud a column of thick vapour, very black, extending from the earth to the heighth of about 40 feet, and advancing rapidly in the direction of this place was discovered by several inhabitants. . . . The Tornado passed through the centre of the village . . . and was observed to break on a neighboring hill. **1946** *This Week Mag.* 3 Aug. 16/2 Every newspaper reader in America knows of the terrible destructive force of the tornado. **1950** *World-Herald Mag.* (Omaha) 8 May 15/2 Least extensive, but most violent and sharply defined of all storms, the tornado is characterized by the vortex cloud sometimes likened to a funnel, an elephant's trunk or a rope.

attrib. **1815** *N. Amer. Rev.* II. 38 The strength of the wind, and its tornado character, was principally felt . . . between New-London and Newburyport. **1898** C. B. DAVIS *Borderland of Soc.* 92 Wait till you marry and can't get even a tornado insurance company to put a cent on your frizzled self. **1905** *Springfield W. Republican* 19 May 7 Inhabitants of the 'new country' in Oklahoma are digging 5000 tornado cellars.

tornadoish tɔrˈnedo·ɪʃ, *a.* Characteristic of a tornado. *Rare.* — **1889** *Columbus* (O.) *Dispatch* 16 Jan., The storm is going out of the United States across Lake Superior and if so we will escape the greater weight of both its powerful warm, wet, tornadoish right, and cold, snowy, blizzardy left hand.

tornillo tɔrˈnijo, *n.* [Sp. in Amer. Sp. sense shown here.] The screw-pod mesquite *q.v.;* also the bean of this plant.

1844 GREGG *Commerce of Prairies* II. 78 In the immediate vicinity of El Paso there is another small growth called tornillo (or screw-wood), so denominated from a spiral pericarp. **1858** *Harper's Mag.* Sep. 464/1 Mojave rancherias are surrounded by granaries filled with corn, mesquite beans, and tornillas. **1932** D. COOLIDGE *Fighting Men* 154 (Bentley), The Rangers crossed the river and rode through the heavy willows and tornillos.

attrib. **1852** SITGREAVES *Exped. Zuni & Colo. Rivers* 19 They were without provisions, living upon the fruit of the mezquit and tornilla trees. **1902** *Out West* Jan. 51 Tornillo and mesquite limbs dragged across his face and clutched at his wounded arm.

toro ˈtoro, *n. S.W.* [Sp. bull, *toro mejicano,* buffalo.] (See quot.) *Obs.* — **1839** WISLIZENUS *Journey to Rocky Mts.* (1912) 52 The so-called toro is still more suitable for preservation. For its preparation this dried [buffalo] meat is beaten with a stone into a coarse grained powder, and mixed with as much melted buffalo fat and tallow as it will hold. The paste thus formed is pressed as compactly as possible into a bag of buffalo skin, which is then firmly sewed up.

torope, see **torup.**

toroso təˈroso, *n. S.W.* [App. Sp. adj., strong, robust.] A greasewood. — **1912** LUMHOLTZ *New Trails* 215 The small bush toroso, which grows everywhere in the desert region, contains so much resin material that it burns even when green and wet.

torpedal battery. (See quot.) *Obs.* — **1823** *Niles' Reg.* 4 Oct. XXV. 69/1 The *torpedal battery* is calculated either for sea or land defence, and would, perhaps, in certain situations, be more destructive on land than at sea. . . . A single vessel, of sufficient strength and tonnage to carry a full *torpedal battery,* might navigate the ocean alone, and, unconnected with any other force, bid defiance to a navy.

***torpedo,** *n.*

1. Any one of various devices for destroying enemy ships by blowing them up.

1807 IRVING *Salmagundi* xiii, The Society have . . . invented a cunning machine, a *Torpedo,* by which the stoutest line-of-battle ship . . . may be caught napping. **1898** *Boston Ev. Globe* 25 Feb. 2/3 (Ernst), The term [mine] is generally applied to such torpedoes as are fixed in a particular place. **1949** *Sat. Ev. Post* 9 April 128/4 Torpedoes were the only weapon which could really hurt this class of ship.

attrib. **1810** in P. H. MUSSER *James N. Barker* (1929) 39 The Torpedoe Bill passed the Senate yesterday. **1877** KNIGHT 2602/1 *Torpedo-catcher,* a forked spar or boom extending under water, ahead of a vessel, to displace or explode torpedoes. **1891** *Cent.* 6392/2 In the United States a torpedo-school for the navy has been established at Newport, Rhode Island, and for the army at Willett's Point, New York.

2. An explosive concealed where enemy forces will prob. explode it inadvertently.

1863 MOORE *Rebellion Rec.* V. I. 3 The rebels have been guilty of the most murderous and barbarous conduct in placing torpedoes within the abandoned works, . . . in carpet-bags, barrels of flour, etc. **1907** ANDREWS *Recoll.* 196 A fatigue party of my division . . . took up seventy loaded torpedoes.

3. An explosive charge set off to open up an oil well or to start the flow of oil.

1886 *St. Nicholas* Nov. 48/1 A queer-looking, pointed piece of iron, called the 'go-devil,' is dropped down the well, and [strikes] . . . a cap on the top of the torpedo. **1948** *Dly. Ardmoreite* (Ardmore, Okla.) 20 May 13/2 The torpedos are used on old oil wells which have nearly quit producing.

b. torpedo man, a man in charge of using such torpedoes.

1883 *Cent. Mag.* July 330/2 The 'torpedo man' is one of the interesting personages of the oil regions. **1900** *Everybody's Mag.* July 79/2 There are many stories told of the 'torpedo men' of the oil region.

4. A contrivance placed on a railroad track to serve as a signal to an engineer by exploding under the wheels of the locomotive.

1900 *Everybody's Mag.* II. 444/2 Another device that is useful in giving warning to engineers at points unprovided with fixed signals, or in case of fogs which obscure such signals, is the torpedo. **1945** MARSHALL *Santa Fe* 272 The train crew, a bit mystified by the unmanned engine, set out the usual flags and torpedoes.

5. A gangster who is a trigger man or gunman. *Slang.*

1948 *Chi. Tribune* 5 March 1/3 Earlier the committee had heard a story of dynamiting by Chicago 'torpedoes,' skull-cracking and other violence in a Hollywood movie strike. **1949** *Time* 4 July 13/2 Rich, booming, and afloat with dull-eyed suckers, it is an irresistible target for shady operators, con men, burglars, jewel thieves and tired Eastern torpedoes.

6. torpedo boat, a boat from which torpedoes are launched. Also attrib.

1810 FULTON *Torpedo War* 44 It would be difficult for a Torpedo boat to depart from any port of America, and return without being detected. **1886** *Harper's Mag.* June 25/2 [There is] a new type of vessel, called torpedo-boat catchers, whose primary duty is to destroy the torpedo-boats of the enemy. **1942** W. L. WHITE *They Were Expendable* 4 We four are what is left of Motor Torpedo Boat Squadron Three.

As the last term in **air, American, fish, oil, spar torpedo.**

* **torpedo,** *v. tr.* To clear out or start flowing (an oil well) by exploding a torpedo in it. Also **torpedoing,** *n.*

1873 HOWELLS *Chance Acquaintance* vi, He treats me very gingerly, as if I were . . . an inflammable naiad from a torpedoed well. **1879** *Elmira* (N.Y.) *Gaz.* 21 June, Thursday, June 12th, the well was 'torpedoed' with a twenty-quart shot of glycerine. **1893** *Columbus* (O.) *Dispatch* 1 Aug., A success in the oil well at this place is assured as shown by the result of torpedoing last evening.

torreon tore'on, *n. S.W.* [Sp. *torreón,* a large tower.] (See quot. 1932.) — **1931** M. AUSTIN *Starry Adventure* 56 (Bentley), Gard . . . had climbed up and up, quite to the top of the tree, pretending it was a *torreon* from which he was looking for Apaches. **1932** BENTLEY 209 torreon. . . . An outlook hill or mountain usually in a position to command a view of the surrounding plains or valleys. Commonly used in the Southwest.

Early (*c*1885) form of torpedo boat

* **Torrey,** *n.* [John *Torrey* (1796–1873), Amer. botanist.] Used attrib. and in the possessive in the names of plants. Esp. **Torrey pine,** a California pine, *Pinus torreyana,* which in regions of high winds is a low, crooked, or sprawling tree from 25 to 30 feet high, but which away from sea winds has a straight trunk and a height of 50 or 60 feet. Cf. **Del Mar Pine, Soledad pine.**

1843 TORREY *Flora N.Y.* II. 62 *Pycnanthemum Torrei.* Torrey's Pycnanthemum. . . . Dry rocky hill-sides, near Kingsbridge on the Island of New York. **1886** VAN DYKE *So. Calif.* 31 Torrey's Pine is limited to a few square miles upon the table-lands along the coast of San Diego County . . . the only place in the world where it has yet been found. **1948** *Pacific Discovery* Nov.–Dec. 18/1 Changes in temperature and moisture have isolated the Torrey pine to these small 'islands,' many sea-miles apart.

Torreya 'tɑrɪə, *n.* [See prec.] A plant of the genus *Torreya;* the stinking cedar of Florida, *T. taxifolia,* or the California nutmeg, *T. californica.* Also with specifying term. — **1897** SUDWORTH *Arborescent Flora* 102 *Tumion californicum.* . . . California Torreya. **1901** MOHR *Plant Life Ala.* 34 The Torreya . . . and the Florida yew . . . present similar striking instances of a strange localization.

tortilla tɔr'tijɑ, *n. S.W.* [Sp. in Amer. Sp. sense shown here.] A very thin griddlecake, usu. made from cornmeal.

1831 PATTIE *Personal Narr.* 42 She then brought forward some tortillas and milk. **1884** *Gringo & Greaser* 1 Jan. 2/3 [We] munch our tortiers and sheepmeat on the wing. **1949** *Nat. Geog. Mag.* Dec. 820 (*legend*), Tortillas and Coffee Are Spread on the Linoleum-covered Adobe Floor.

***tortoise,** *n.* As the last term in **alligator, box, desert, geographic, gopher, lock, marsh, mud, musk, painted, snapping, wood tortoise.**

torup 'tɑrəp, *n.* [See **terrapin,** of which this is a variant.] = **terrapin.**

1613 WHITAKER *Good Newes from Va.* 42, I have caught with mine angle . . . the Torope or little Turtle. **1894** *Critic* 27 Oct. 268 Farmers and sailors call the big 'snapper' the torup or torop. **1902** *Amer. Folk-Lore* XV. 261 In the early writers the forms *tarapin, terrapene, terebin,* etc., occur, while the negroes of the South have adopted the word as *tarrypin.* Our word *terrapin* is from a diminutive, as Whitaker, who wrote in 1623 unconsciously recorded, when he spoke of 'the *torope,* or little turtle.'

* **Tory,** *n.*

1. During the Revolutionary period, an American partisan of the cause of the British crown, a loyalist. Now *hist.*

1769 *Boston Gaz.* 24 April 3/2 Keep your Rights out of Sight, and you may have any Thing you please. A Tory. **1774** HULTON *Letters* 74 These who are well disposed towards Government (more from interest than principle it's to be feard, as there are few willg to acknowledge the Authority of Parliamt) are termd Tories. **1864** PENNIMAN *Tanner-Boy* 17 [The bitterness of some Canadians toward the United States] is owing to the fact that among their forefathers were to be found many of the Tories of the American Revolution. **1948** *Chi. Tribune* 18 April IV. 5/1 Safe from the British and Tories I lay Till the last of the Redcoats skedaddled away.

attrib. **1775** *Boston Ev. Post* 6 March, Our meek and tender lambs, the Tory Refugees, who have fled to this town for protection, are incessantly inculcating . . . that the people of this province are a set of timid mortals.

2. A person regarded as disloyal, a traitor.

Applied in New England to those who opposed the War of 1812 and in the Confederate States to sympathizers with the Union.

1809 *Ann. 10th Congress* 2 Sess. 1333 The Old Tories and Federalists of the North . . . are not much worse [about violating the embargo acts] . . . than the young Tories and Democrats of the South. **1812** *N.Y. Ev. Post* 28 Oct. 2/4 The war-hawks of that vicinity . . . began abusing him with the usual slang of *Federalist, old Tory,* &c. **1862** *So. Confederacy* (Atlanta, Ga.) 3 May (Th.), The other prisoners were all sharp, intelligent-looking men, no hard-looking cases like Yankee prisoners, and East Tennessee Tories usually are. **1866** W. REID *After the War* 402 Ef you fetch any d— tories heah, that went agin their State, and so kin take the oath, . . . 'twill soon be too hot to hold 'em. **1950** *Chi. Tribune* 27 April 22/6 Present day Tories have taken over the country.

3. a. tory bud, = next. **b. tory weed,** a coarse plant of the genus *Cynoglossum,* the hound's tongue.

(a) **1894** *Amer. Folk-Lore* VII. 95 *Cynoglossum officinale,* tory-bud. N.Y. — (b) **1836** EATON *Botany* (ed. 7). **1876** J. E. TODD *John Todd* 24 After a time [he] returned with some leaves of a plant called 'tory weed,' and told the doctor to apply them to the wound.

As the last term in **British, gentleman, piny woods tory.**

Toryess 'torɪ,ɛs, *n.* A woman loyalist. *Obs.* — **1777** FRANKLIN *Writings* VII. 24 She is a *Toryess* as well as you, and can as flippantly call *Rebel.*

***Toryish,** *a.* Sympathetic to the cause of the American loyalists. *Obs.* — **1860** HOLMES *E. Venner* vii, [Among the guests were] the Vaughans, an old Rockland race, . . . Toryish in tendency in Revolutionary times.

* **Toryism,** *n.* The principles of the loyalists, sympathy with the cause of the British crown. Now *hist.*

1771 J. ADAMS *Diary* Wks. II. 266 John Chandler, Esq. of Petersham, . . . gave us an account of Mr. Otis's conversion to Toryism. **1838** INGRAHAM *Burton* II. 57 Now, major, be careful you are not converted to toryism on the ride. **1888** BRYCE *Amer. Commonw.* III. VI. ciii. 468 The Anglican Clergy were prone to Toryism.

toshence 'tɑʃəns, *n. N. Eng.* Also **torsh, tortience,** etc. [See quots. 1802, 1910.] The youngest child in a family. *Colloq.*

1802 J. FREEMAN in *Mass. H.S. Coll.* 1 Ser. VIII. 97 The Indians of New England had . . . [a] word, which in the dialect of the Nauset Indians was *taushents.* It has been adopted by descendants of the English in many parts of the Old Colony of Plymouth, and is applied as a term of endearment. **1888** L. G. MORSE *Chezzles* 36 Bob . . . is your father's torshent, and the little Barnes girl is her father's; every one in Nipsit calls her little Torsh Barnes. **1910** HODGE *Amer. Indians* II. 787 Toshence. The last of anything; a term local in Massachusetts. . . . The word consists of the two last syllables of *mattasons,* the Massachuset name for the last child of the family. **1912** *Yarmouth Reg.* 29 Nov., I have heard 'toshance' . . . in quite recent years.

* **toss,** *v.* **1.** *toss and catch, fig.* pitch and toss. *Rare.* **2.** *toss 'em boys,* (see quots.). *Obs.*

(1) **1904** *Atlantic Mo.* Oct. 477 The smutty-handed Smoot playing at toss and catch with his conscience and honor. — (2) *c*1775 BOUCHER *Glossary* p. l, At dinner, let me . . . toss 'em boys, and belly bacon see. **1800** *Ib., Toss 'em boys;* chickens: so called, it is supposed, because . . . [they are] run down with . . . [a dog set on] by the phrase *Toss 'em boys.*

totage 'totɪdʒ, *n.* [f. **tote,** *v.*] The carrying of burdens. *Rare.* — **1886** *Boston Herald,* The burro, that patient little beast of general totage.

total abstinent. A total abstainer. *Rare.* — **1882** *Harper's Mag.* Sep. 633/2 They are total abstinents.

tote tot, *n.* [f. the verb.] The position in which a gun is carried. *Rare.* Also a load or burden, or the distance this is carried. *Colloq.*

1867 Goss *Soldier's Story* 260 I've told yer four times to bring that gun ter a tote. **1884** Hill *Colo. Pioneers* 207, I ain't got no wagon, and fo' fowls jist like dat ar, would be a big tote, so I will fotch one at a time, boss, if dat will suit you. **1950** *Pacific Discovery* March–April 9/2 Tuffy loaded our gear into the jeep in order to save the animals the nine-mile tote to the takeoff point.

tote tot, *v.* [See note.]

This term is app. of African origin. Turner, p. 203, finds such forms as *tota, tuta,* to pick up, carry, in Angola and the Belgian Congo. See also *Amer. Sp.* April 1942, 128–9. The earliest available evidence for the term is southern, but, as the quots. below show, it has spread widely in colloq. use.

1. *tr.* To carry (a thing) by one's individual effort, as in one's hands, on the shoulders, etc.

1677 in *Va. Mag.* II. 168, 60 armed men . . . [were] commanded to goe to work, . . . and mawl and toat railes. **1775** in Pusey *Road to Ky.* (1921) 44 We are obliged . . . to toate our packs. **1883** *Harper's Mag.* Jan. 207/1 John Chinaman . . . totes kegs of water . . . up and down the rough declivities. **1949** *Chi. D. News* 13 Aug. 5/3, I picked up my knapsack of clothes and toted it to a new residence.

transf. and *fig.* **1837** *Knickerb.* IX. 263 He 'toted' a wheel-barrow with cake and ale . . . throughout the city. **1883** Mark Twain *Life on Miss.* xxviii, You've got to admire men that deal in ideas of that size and can tote them around without crutches. **1949** *Chi. Tribune* 2 Nov. 1/7 A 'tired business man' . . . stuffs his business troubles in his briefcase and totes them home at night.

b. To lead, conduct, convey (persons).

1769 *Boston Gaz.* 7 Aug. 3/2 The next Morning he was toated on board the Rippon, in a Canoe. **1807** Irving in P. M. Irving *Life W. Irving* I. (1862) 189 At Baltimore. . . . I was *toted* about town and introduced to everybody. **1832** *Boston Transcript* 1 June 2/1 A constable was in special attendance, who toted him off to jail. **1924** Mulford *Rustler's Valley* iii, I don't need no safe conduct, an' you might as well know that ain't why I'm totin' you along with me.

c. To wear or carry about regularly with one.

1823 in Claiborne *Life Quitman* I. 85 The belles . . . 'tote' their fans with the air of Spanish señoritas. **1949** *Amer. Forests* Oct. 11/2 They tote cameras everywhere they go.

Esp. of firearms. Cf. **pistol-toting.**

1883 Sweet & Knox *Through Texas* 13 They said that he 'always went heeled, toted a derringer, and was a bad crowd generally.' **1946** *Cong. Rec.* App. A4019/1 A delegation of thin-lipped citizens, toting impressive-looking hardware, called.

d. To haul or transport (a thing) as in a vehicle.

1836 Gilman *Recoll.* (1838) 50 Fayther . . . wants Master Richard's horse to help tote some tetters. **1946** *Harper's Mag.* Oct. 308/1 The manure in the feed lots is scraped up by a bulldozer and toted away to the field in a spreader.

2. *intr.* or *reflex.* To go.

1845 *Quincy* (Ill.) *Whig* 20 Nov. 2/5 She bade him, 'git off his horse and tote himself into the house.' **1862** Lowell *Biglow P.* 2 Ser. i. 16 Tote roun' An' see ef there's a feather-bed (thet's borryable) in town. **1865** *Atlantic Mo.* April 387/1 Nothing would do but to tote down here to the Crik and make his fortin.

3. In combs. of obvious meaning or sufficiently explained in the quots., as (1) **tote load,** (2) **pole,** (3) **road,** (4) **team,** (5) **teamster,** (6) **trip.**

(1) **1859** Bartlett, Tote-Load. As much as one can carry. Southern. — (2) **1889** *N. & Q.* IV. 107 In the woods of Northern Maine we find *tote-poles,* by means of which logs are carried. — (3) *a*1862 Thoreau *Maine Woods* 222 The Indian was greatly surprised that we should have taken what he called a 'tow' (i.e. tote or toting or supply) road, instead of a carrying path. **1947** *Sat. Ev. Post* 8 March 53/2 Forty miles on the tote road in a day had hit him hard. — (4) **1926** Rickaby *Ballads* 237 *Tote team.* The team used in bringing supplies overland by sled from the trading centres to the camps. **1942** Rich *We Took to Woods* (1948) 232 He flew lumberjacks into camps, when they'd missed the tote team on account of too much conviviality.

(5) **1902** White *Blazed Trail* 84 The tote teamster drove his hay-couched burden to Beeson Lake. **1947** *Sat. Ev. Post* 8 March 20/2 Then toward spring, tote teamsters brought gossip from other camps. — (6) **1924** Shephard *P. Bunyan* 153 So he took him along on this tote-trip he was makin' across the plains.

b. *To tote fair,* to take one's just portion of a burden, to play square. **c.** *To tote tales,* to carry tales.

(**b**) **1866** C. H. Smith *Bill Arp* 147, I don't think you tote fair. **1898** *Chi. Times-Herald* 6 April 3/3 Mr. Yerkes will have to tote fair with the city. **1948** Dick *Dixie Frontier* 127 From such good-natured pranks arose such expressions as 'tote fair,' meaning to do one's honest part. — (**c**) **1901** Harben *Westerfelt* ii. 27, I never was much of a hand to tote tales.

totem ˈtotəm, *n.* ["Irregularly derived from the term *ototeman* of the Chippewa and other cognate Algonquian dialects, . . . of which *ote* is the grammatic stem" (Hodge).] Among the American Indians, something, as an animal or plant, associated with and identifying a specific group of persons, or, loosely, an individual; also, the group so designated, or a representation or symbol of the identifying object.

[**1609** P. Erondelle tr. Lescarbot *Nova Francia* 178 Memberton . . . carrieth hanged at his neck . . . a purse . . . within which there is I know not what as big as a small nut, which he saith to be his devil called Aoutem.] **1791** J. Long *Voyages* 86 [Each Indian has] his *totam,* or favourite spirit, which he believes watches over him. **1829** *Western Souvenir* 1830 217 Around his neck was hung a broad ornament . . . upon which was engraved the totem of his father. **1901** White *Westerners* 336 A brave from among us arose and took the sacred totem, the great Turtle, from the lodge of his chief. **1949** *Nat. Hist.* May 201/1 Wooden totems have not been carved on the Charlottes since 1880.

attrib. **1876** *Harper's Wkly.* 11 Nov. 909/4 Just behind the tent is shown a 'totem' post, from Alaska. **1892** *Rep. Comm. Educ. 1891–2* 890 The [Tchuktchi] women have their faces covered with totem marks. **1938** Thompson *High Trails* 39 The prohibition to kill the totem animal or plant comes from the belief that the individuals of the clan have descended from the totem animal.

transf. and *fig.* **1855** *Putnam's Mag.* May 530/2 Wisconsin has taken the badger for its emblem or 'totem' as the Indians denominate it. **1890** Howells *Boys' Town* 132 The fox was the emblem (*totem*) of the Democrats in the campaigns of 1840 and 1844. **1927** Benét *J. B.'s Body* 158 A flag is a piece of cloth and a word is a sound, But we make them something neither cloth nor a sound, Totems of love and hate.

b. totem pole, a pole covered, as by carving or painting, with totemic symbols, usu. placed before an Indian house. Also transf. and attrib.

[**1880** Jackson *Alaska* 81 These [poles] are the genealogical records of the family. The child usually takes the *totem* of the mother.] **1897** James *Alaska* 75 It has ever been an unanswerable question as to the origin of these totem poles. **1949** *Nat. Hist.* May 199/2 Of all artistic productions of North American Indians, totem poles, perhaps, have aroused the greatest public interest and curiosity.

totem ˈtotəm, *v. tr.* To apply, as by painting or tattooing (a totem symbol). *Rare.* — **1892** *Rep. Comm. Educ. 1891–2* 890 Some [Tchuktchi men] have a small mark or figure totemed on their cheek.

totemic təˈtɛmɪk, *a.* Of or pertaining to totems.

1846 Schoolcraft *Notes on Iroquois* 79 It will be necessary to go back, and examine . . . the curious and intricate principles of the Totemic Bond. *Ib.* 81 What was true of the totemic organization of the Senecas, was equally so of the Mohawks. **1880** Jackson *Alaska* 8 They have a great variety of household utensils made from the horns of mountain sheep and goats, . . . elaborately carved with their *totemic* or heraldic signs. **1938** Thompson *High Trails* 40 The culture of the Blackfeet is very definitely totemic.

totemism ˈtotəmˌɪzəm, *n.* The customs and traditions connected with the use of totems.

1791 J. Long *Voyages* 87 This idea of destiny, or, if I may be allowed the phrase, 'totamism,' . . . is not confined to the Savages. **1908** *Amer. Anthropologist* Oct. 559 Clan totemism is . . . obviously only higher development of personal totemism. **1938** Thompson *High Trails* 39 The Blackfeet Indians . . . practiced totemism, which as a matter of fact is common to all primitive peoples.

toter ˈtotɚ, *n.* [f. **tote,** *v.*] **1.** (See quot. 1891.) **2.** One who totes or carries.

(1) **1891** *N. & Q.* VI. 190 Roads . . . over which the supplies for the camps are carried, are always called 'tote roads,' and the teamsters are called 'toters.' **1895** *Cent. Mag.* July 478/2 Every one of the hundreds of logging-camps . . . over all parts of our great Maine woods . . . [is] furnished with its separate 'tote road,' 'tote team,' and 'toter.' — (2) **1908** *Country Life* July 786/1 'Toters' carry the baskets from the pickers to the 'floats,' which are flat-topped spring wagons used to carry the precious fruit to the packing shed. **1946** *Agric. Hist.* Oct. 234/2 A few days later a crew set to work to tote the shingles back to shore. It was no small task, for the toters had to wade a distance of 30 or 40 yards through water up to their waists.

As the last term in **ball, dope, gun, Ohio, stone, water toter.**

toting ˈtotɪŋ, *n.* The action of carrying. Also attrib. Cf. **gun toting, pistol toting.**

*a*1862 [see **tote road**]. **1887** Craddock *Keedon Bluffs* 165 He could not refuse his assistance in a mere matter of 'toting.' **1948** *Sat. Ev. Post* 23 Oct. 30/1 The nation's chief parcel boy, Railway Express Agency, Inc., maintains America's 109-year-old express tradition by toting considerably more than 200,000,000 packages a year across the face of this country.

* **touch,** *n.*

1. (*cap.*) (See quot.) *Obs.*

1823 *N. Eng. Farmer* II. 85/3 [New York City] has been much amused with a low tripod-kind of a hat, made of fine beaver, and worn by our Bang-ups. Some call them the *Touch,* others the *Gape and Stare,* the real name is the Bolingbroke.

2. In negative comparisons to show the preëminence of something. *Colloq.*

1835–7 HALIBURTON *Clockmaker* 1 Ser. iii. 20 A school come out of the little boys . . . [is] no touch to it. **1843** STEPHENS *High Life N.Y.* I. 152, I never did see a table so set off. . . . Cousin Beebe's warn't a touch tu it. **1846** FARNHAM *Prairie Land* 23 The bugs ain't a touch in *hyur* to what they be in yander.

3. *attrib.* Of or pertaining to the ability to use a typewriter without looking at the keys.

1897 in *Story of Typewriter* (Herkimer Co. Hist Soc., 1923) 113 Omaha has become the storm center of the commotion over the touch method of typewriting. **1918** OWEN *Typewriting Speed* 147 Do not try to apply the touch system . . . until you have thoroughly mastered it. **1949** *Reader's Digest* April 145/1, I could teach even a child to type touch system in two weeks.

* **touch,** *v.*

1. *intr.* To make an attempt *to* do something, to make a beginning. *Colloq. Obs.*

1813 S. SMITH *Life J. Downing* 136 He dared Mr Ingham out to fight. . . . But Mr Ingham wouldn't touch to, and told him he was crazy. **1865** TROWBRIDGE *Three Scouts* 53, I never will touch to do another stroke of work in your house. **1867** S. HALE *Letters* 23, I didn't touch to unpack the trunks.

2. *Football.* **a. touchback,** the act of a player who touches the ball to the ground on or behind his own goal line provided the impetus which sent it to or across the line was given by an opponent. Cf. * **safety 1.**

1893 CAMP *College Sports* 92 [When the ball is kicked behind the line by the enemy] it is called a 'touchback.' **1916** BANCROFT *Handbook* 22 Touchback. Ball sent over the goal line by an opponent, but in possession of a defender of the goal.

b. * **touchdown,** in football, the chief scoring play (see quot. 1899).

1876 in P. H. DAVIS *Football* 462 A match shall be decided by a majority of touchdowns. **1899** CHAMPLIN & BOSTWICK *Cyclo. Games & Sports* (ed. 2) 342/2 A *Touchdown* is made when the ball in possession of a player is declared dead by the Referee, any part of it being on, over, or behind the opponents' goal line. **1949** *Desplaines Valley News* (Summit, Ill.) 28 Oct. 7/3 Harvard could not push across a touchdown in the first half.

3. touch-monk, a local name for the red-throated loon, *Gavia stellata.*

1875 *Fur, Fin & Feather* (ed. 3) 119 The smaller species of loon I have heard variously called the spike-bill, the cape-race, the touch-monk [etc.].

tough tʌf, *n.* [f. the adj.] A ruffian or hoodlum. — **1866** HOWELLS *Venet. Life* ii, The toughs of the distant alleys. **1950** *Chi. Tribune* 2 Aug. 11/3 A young tough, held to the grand jury for strong-arm robbery, yesterday lashed out at his three guards . . . and fled into Ogden av.

* **tough,** *a.*

1. Vicious, rowdyish, frequented by toughs.

1884 MILLER *Memorie & Rime* 9 This is a tough town! **1910** *Morrison's Chi. Wkly.* 24 Nov. 5/1 Carlin had basked in the reputation of being the 'toughest' burg between Great Salt Lake and the Cascades. **1948** *Savings News* May 17/1 That boy Joe used to brag he was the toughest kid in town.

2. Imposing hardship or difficulty *on* (a person, etc.).

1890 *Stock Grower & Farmer* 8 March 4/2 The recent blizzard . . . was pretty tough on range cattle. **1932** *K.C. Times* 26 Jan. 16 It seems to have been tough on Clara Bow to sober up and get married. **1948** *Carthaginian* (Carthage, Miss.) 19 Aug. 2/5 If one of them when the going gets tough, takes a club from the side, all of us would rush to the aid of the one against whom the unfair advantage was taken.

3. Designating a species of ironwood (see quots.).

1813 MUHLENBERG *Cat. Plants* 24 *Bumelia tenax,* Ironwood, silvery-leaved, (tough) Car[olina]. **1897** SUDWORTH *Arborescent Flora* 318 *Bumelia tenax.* . . . Tough Buckthorn (S.C.).

4. In combs.: (1) **toughhead,** a local name for the ruddy duck; (2) **luck,** hard luck, *colloq.;* (3) **nut,** a person stubborn or otherwise difficult to deal with, a tough customer, *slang.*

(1) **1888** TRUMBULL *Names of Birds* 111 To some at Martha's Vineyard, [the name of the ruddy duck is] Tough-Head. **1889** *Cent.* 2718/1. — (2) **1918** M. B. COOKE *Cricket* 8 Poor kid, that's tough luck for her. **1932** *K.C. Times* 14 Jan. 18 It may be Mr. Hoover's tough luck to be both renominated and re-elected. — (3) **1862** E. W. PEARSON *Lett. Port Royal* 81 There are a great many men of twenty-five to forty, 'tough-nuts' many of them.

tough tʌf, *v.* [f. the adj.] *To tough it,* to undergo hardships, to rough it, also with *out. Colloq.*

1830 *Mass. Spy* 27 Jan. (Th.), Judy, with whom he had toughed it three years. **1839** *N.O. Picayune* 5 March 2/1 The markets afford good lodging, and every bale of cotton furnishes a bed; but on such a night as last we hardly know how they can 'tough it out.' **1946** BASCOM *Lett. Ticonderoga Farmer* 17 Tuppertown, more properly Toughertown, was a section of Ticonderoga where the stubborn, stony soil caused the early settlers to say that they had to 'tough it.'

b. To tax the ability of (a person). *Rare.*

1843 CARLTON *New Purchase* I. 127 If you win, which will a sort a tough you though, you may [etc.].

* **toughness,** *n.* Roughness; propensity to violence or crime. — **1895** *Pilgrim Missionary* June 11/1 You have gained a very good idea of the toughness of these mining towns. **1948** *Dly. Ardmoreite* (Ardmore, Okla.) 5 April 4/1 Neither was the decision to rebuild western Germany and make it an economic unit an example of toughness toward Russia.

* **tourist,** *n. attrib.*

1. tourist camp, a camp providing such accommodations as tourists need.

1923 *Outlook* Aug. 591/3 The University of Iowa has published a bulletin on the tourist camps of that State. **1934** *Lit. Digest* 9 June 40/2 These tourist camps . . . gradually are becoming more attractive.

2. tourist car, sleeper, sleeping car, (see quot. 1895).

1895 WAIT *Car-Builder's Dict.* 134 Tourist-car. A car roughly built and furnished for the transportation of men alone, such as bodies of troops, parties of excursionists, emigrants, etc. Frequently they are *flat* or *box-cars* furnished with roof sides, seats and doors. . . . The *emigrant sleeping-car* is now usually called a *tourist-car,* the latter being preferred by those who patronize them. **1898** *Chi. Times-Herald* 4 April 9/3 The tourist sleeping car . . . was avoided by all save immigrants and homeseekers. **1929** J. PARKER *Old Army* 195 From there we journeyed on tourist sleepers.

As the last term in **commercial tourist.**

* **tout,** *v.* **1.** *intr.* To solicit votes. **2.** *intr.* and *tr.* (See quots.)

(1) **1881** *Nation* XXXII. 397 It has never occurred to him that people would be shocked to see him 'tout' at Albany. **1894** FORD *P. Stirling* 358 'Hear him talk,' jeered one of the crowd, 'and he touting round the saloons to get votes.' — (2) **1909** WEBSTER 2177/3 *Tout,* . . . to act as a tout; to tout, or give a tip on, a race horse. *Ib., Tout,* . . . To give a tip on (a race horse) to a better with the expectation of sharing in the latter's winnings.

* **tow,** *n.* In combs., in which the first element is from various sources: (1) * **towboat,** (see quots.), *obs.,* cf. **safety barge;** (2) **boy,** a boy who drives a team on a towpath, *obs.;* (3) **car,** (see quot.); (4) **cloth,** a coarse fabric spun from tow, also attrib.; (5) **comforter,** a comforter made of, or stuffed with, tow; (6) **deer,** = **towhead deer,** *obs.;* (7) **head,** see as a main entry; (8) **hook,** (see quot.); (9) **linen,** (*a*) a fabric made of spun tow, (*b*) also attrib.

(1) **1835** *Letter from Tradesman* 17 The tow-boats above mentioned are large vessels, which are lashed on each side of the steam-vessels, and to the stern of the former are frequently two heavy canal-boats. **1836** W. O'BRYAN *Travels* 294 Tow-boats are large boats with decks; these are tied to, and towed by the Steamers; sometimes one or more each side. They carry heavy luggage, and passengers too, who choose to save money at a small inconvenience. — (2) **1887** *Cent. Mag.* Aug. 493/1 The Patriarch stepped ashore and arranged for an extra team of mules and a tow-boy. — (3) **1895** *Stand.* 1908/2 *Tow-car,* a street railway-car drawn by a grip- or motor-car; trail-car. — (4) **1706** *Boston News-Letter* 18 Nov., The uppermost [jacket is] . . . lined with brown linen called western Tow-cloth. **1746** *Ib.* 17 July, A Negro Man Servant . . . had on . . . a good Tow cloth Shirt. **1866** A. D. WHITNEY *Goldthwaite* x, I want some tow-cloth to sew on immediately. (5) **1897** *Scribner's Mag.* XXII. 728/2 On top . . . are four or five thicknesses of coarse blankets and tow comforters. — (6) *a***1846** *Quarter Race Ky.* 45, I wuz tellin the fellars 'bout Reub.'s eatin a hole tow deer. — (8) **1876** KNIGHT 2604/2 *Tow-hook,* an artilleryman's hook, used in unpacking ammunition-chests. — (9) (*a*) **1779** *N.J. Archives* 2 Ser. III. 154 [A] blue long elk saddle cloth lined with tow linen [was stolen]. **1900** H. ROBERTSON *Red Blood & Blue* 132 I've got a suit of tow-linen that the ladies think irresistible. (*b*) **1812** PAULDING *J. Bull & Bro. Jon.* 98 He wore . . . a pair of tow linen trowsers. **1881** *Chi. Tribune* 8 July 11/3, I was supplied every year with . . . two pairs of tow-linen pantaloons.

As the last term in **gun, swingle, swingling tow.**

towboating ˈtoˌbotɪŋ, *n.* The piloting or operation of a towboat. *Rare.* — **1887** *Courier-Journal* 7 Feb. 3/3 Theodore Brooks . . . will try his hand at towboating this season.

* **towel,** *n.* As the last term in **bath, hickory, rolling towel.**

* **tower,** *n. Railroad.* A tall structure containing controls governing switches or signals. Also attrib.

1895 *Chi. Strike of 1894* 214 A number of switch tenders, yard clerks, flagmen, tower men, and roundhouse men left their work. **1900** *Everybody's Mag.* II. 442/2 The tower from which the traffic entering and leaving the Grand Central Station in New York city is directed, is located just outside the station itself. **1946** THOMPSON *Amer. Daughter* 124 We climbed the little ladder to the railroad tower house.

As the last term in **fire, ivory, signal, switch, water tower.**

towhead ˈtoˌhɛd, *n.*

1. (See quot. 1884.) Also in proper names.

The term in this sense poss. developed from the use of "tow" shown in quot. 1841. Cf. in the same connection quot. 1836.

1829 CUMINGS *Western Pilot* 7 There are . . . a great number of tow-heads and sand-bars. **1836** J. HALL *Statistics of West* 26 Sometimes they [*sc.* islands in the Ohio R.] are mere sandbanks, covered with thick groves of the melancholy willow. . . . The term *tow-head,* is significantly applied . . . by the boatmen. [**1841** ELIZA A. STEELE *Summer Journey in West* 223 Fairy isles are . . . fringed with the soft bushy willow called here [on Ohio R.] *tow.*] **1884** MARK TWAIN *H. Finn* xii, A towhead is a sand-bar that has cottonwoods on it as thick as harrow-teeth. **1928** A. S. TOSSLEY *Where Goes River* 236 The boat was tied up at Glasscock Towhead, one of the largest towheads on the river, fifteen miles below Natchez Island Towhead. **1945** FUGINA *Upper Miss.* 65 The raft was caught in a cross-current and saddle-bagged (piled up) on the towhead.

2. A person, esp. a child, with white or whitish hair.

1830 ROYALL *Southern Tour* I. 92 One insolent little tow-head . . . came in upon parole. **1885** SIRINGO *Texas Cow Boy* 14 We little tow-heads, sister and I. **1949** *Minot* (N.D.) *D. News* 22 July 4/6, I began as a towhead, . . . but now I guess I'm a salt and pepper brunette.

Hence **towheaded,** *a.*

1850 JUDD *R. Edney* 450 Bronze-faced and tow-headed Wild Olive boys . . . were there. **1949** *Reader's Digest* April 67 We have a big towheaded son by the name of Tony.

b. towhead deer, a young deer. *Rare.*

*a*1846 *Quarter Race Ky.* 44 We killed a mitey fine tow hed deer.

3. =**hooded merganser.**

1888 TRUMBULL *Names of Birds* 75 The name Tow-Head . . . was heard in one of our Southern States. **1917** *Birds of Amer.* I. 112.

towhee ˈtauhi, ˈtohi, *n.* [Imitative.] Any one of various American finches of the genera *Pipilo* and *Oberholseria,* esp. the chewink, *P. erythrophthalmus,* of the eastern states. Also **towhee bird.**

*c*1729 CATESBY *Carolina* I. 34 The Towhe-bird . . . is about the size of, or rather bigger than a Lark. **1808** WILSON *Ornithology* II. 36 In Virginia he is called the Bullfinch; in many places the Towhè-bird. **1858** BAIRD *Birds Pacific R.R.* 512 Ground Robin; Towhee; Chewink. . . . Eastern United States to the Missouri river. **1949** HADLEY *Indiana Birds* 42/2 The towhee is for the most part a ground feeding bird.

b. Preceded by a specifying term, as **chestnut-crowned, green-tailed, long-clawed, spotted towhee.**

1878 *Nat. Museum Proc.* I. 419 *Pipilo chlorurus.*—Green-tailed Towhee. This bird is a common summer resident at Big Trees, Soda Springs, and Summit Meadows. *Ib.,* The Long-clawed Towhee . . . is a common constant resident of the valleys and foot-hills. **1917** *Birds of Amer.* III. 62 [The] Chestnut-crowned Towhee . . . has the peculiar trait of running along the ground when he is surprised instead of taking wing. **1948** *Pacific Discovery* March–April 16/1 The spotted towhee's vigorous scratching in the dead leaves beneath the shrubs is a frequent sound.

c. towhee bunting, =**towhee.**

1810 WILSON *Ornithology* II. 35 [The] Towhe Bunting . . . is a very common, but humble and inoffensive species. **1903** *N.Y. Ev. Post* 12 Sep., Still another shy visitor . . . was the cheewink, or towhee bunting, whose cheerful cry announced his presence every morning.

* **town,** *n.*

1. A local community of Indians.

1638 *Mass. H.S. Coll.* 4 Ser. VI. 251 With Onkace at his towne Monahiggin, a great number mingled. **1725** in *Travels Amer. Col.* 98 [He] took away what skins he could get from the people of the Town. **1844** GREGG *Commerce of Prairies* II. 259 With some tribes, and particularly among the lower classes of the Creeks, they are inclined to settle in 'towns,' as they are called,—making large fields, which are cultivated in common, and the produce proportionately distributed. **1947** MARTIN *Indians* 146 All the large towns in the areas just mentioned were abandoned.

b. (See quot. and cf. * **township 3.**)

1907 HODGE *Amer. Indians* I. 364/2 At present the Creek Nation in Indian Ter. is divided into 49 townships ('towns'), of which 3 are inhabited solely by negroes.

2. *N. Eng.* A local administrative unit exercising self-government through a town meeting *q.v.* and having selectmen as its chief executive officers. Cf. note under * **township 1.**

1658 *Portsmouth Rec.* 361 A pearsall of Land containinge Sixe acres Lijnge within the boundes of portsmouth Towne. **1704** *Conn. Rec.* IV. 474 The said tract of land shall . . . be an intire township and town of itselfe. **1808** WILSON *Prose* I. 148 The people here make no distinction between *town* and *township;* and travellers frequently asked the driver of the stagecoach, 'What town are we now in?' when perhaps we were upon the top of a miserable barren mountain, several miles from a house. **1946** *New Yorker* 23 Feb. 23/3 The U.N.O. site in Westchester and Fairfield Counties . . . includes . . . sections of five townships (quaintly called towns in Connecticut).

b. In other states, an administrative unit more or less like that of a New England town. Also attrib. Cf. * **township,** *n.* **1. b.**

1870 *Rep. Comm. Agric. 1869* 398 County commissioners are the fence-viewers in counties [in Minn.] not divided into towns. **1891** *Cent.* 6407/3 The townships of Wisconsin are more often called *towns.* **1950** *Chi. D. News* 29 March 2/5 If past meetings are a criterion, attendance will be such that town officials will have to go out in front of the town hall and ask passersby to come into the meeting.

3. A collection of prairie-dog burrows.

1810 PIKE *Sources Miss.* 156 (*footnote*), The Wishtonwish of the Indians . . . reside on the prairies of Louisiana in towns or villages. **1881** MARSHALL *Through Amer.* (1882) 125 The prairie-dog is a very sociable and hospitable animal. He lives underground in a 'town' or 'village' (as his home is called). **1949** *Time* 24 Jan. 1/3 Prairie dogs live in great 'towns' often covering hundreds of square miles.

4. In special combs.: (1) **town ball,** see as a main entry; (2) **boomer,** one who booms a town; (3) **brand,** (see quot.), *obs.;* (4) **company,** (*a*) the militia company of a town, *obs.,* (*b*) a group of persons organized or incorporated to establish a town; (5) **fair,** a fair at which the products of a town are exhibited; (6) **farm,** a poor farm maintained by a town or township; (7) * **house,** (*a*) a house, as a parsonage, supplied at the expense of a town, *obs.,* (*b*) in an Indian village, the building in which public business is conducted, (*c*) a town poorhouse; (8) * **land,** land belonging to, or within the jurisdiction of, a N. Eng. town, also attrib., *obs.;* (9) **line,** the boundary line of a town, *obs.;* (10) **lot,** (*a*) a parcel of land within a town, also attrib., (*b*) an area of land owned by a town, *obs.;* (11) **marshal,** (*a*) in colonial times, a town official having various duties, as to levy and collect fines, (*b*) a police officer or policeman in a town; (12) **meeting,** see as a main entry; (13) **order,** (*a*) an ordinance passed by a town or township, (*b*) a draft on the treasury of a town or township, both *obs.;* (14) **pew,** ?a pew for the poor of a town, *obs.;* (15) **plat, plot,** a town site, the plan of such a site, also attrib.; (16) **plattings,** laying out the site of a town; (17) **ship,** see as a main entry; (18) **site,** a tract of land set apart by legal authority for the location of a town, esp. one surveyed and laid out with streets and lots, also attrib.; (19) **-sman,** a selectman, *obs.*

(2) 1891 *Harper's Mag.* Aug. 485/2 The Western town-boomer is a silky man and wide between the eyes. — **(3) 1727** *Conn. Col. Rec.* (1873) VII. 111 Be it enacted. . . . That the towns hereafter mentioned shall have a town brand, to brand their horses and other creatures. — **(4)** (*a*) **1723** *N. Eng. Courant* 4 Feb. 2/2 The Town-Company of English, and a considerable Number of Indians under Arms attended at his Funeral. (*b*) **1860** in JOHNSON *Anderson Co., Kans.* 170 [We have] organized ourselves into a town company, under the general incorporation act of the Territory. **1894** ROBLEY *Bourbon Co., Kans.* 71 A 'Town Company' had already . . . formed a 'curbstone' organization.

(5) 1860 W. H. COOK *Lett.* (1946) 21 Oct. 66 Our town fair went of verry respectable. — **(6) 1880** *Harper's Mag.* Dec. 86/2 She would rather have taken her children to the town farm. **1899** JEWETT *Queen's Twin* 225 Her nearest neighbor . . . wished her to go to the town farm. — **(7)** (*a*) **1672** *Huntington Rec.* I. 186 The towne hous or parsonadge hous and land and fence. (*b*) **1725** in *Travels Amer. Col.* 108 About Eight of clock at night I went to the Town House. **1819** *Niles' Reg.* XVI. (Supp.) 101/2 The singer has proclaimed, with his song, on the top of the Town House, '*Hayan wah, Yauth caunu.*' (*c*) **1889** Cooke *Steadfast* 28 Just as soon as the road settled she should 'cart her off to the town-house.' — **(8)** **1639** *Boston Rec.* 1 For the entrying of the Towne Lands and other weighty businesses. **1670** *Braintree Rec.* 9 The towne land meadow and upland should be disposed off by the Select-men then in being. **1738** *Brookhaven Rec.* 141 All that I request of you . . . is one acre & half of land joining to me, of the town land. — **(9)** **1645** *Suffolk Deeds* I. 67 Gregory Stone of Cambridge granted unto Nathaniell Sparhawke . . . two Acres of Meddowe . . . laying by Cambridge towne line. **1840** *Knickerb.* XVI. 206 Such searching of trees for town lines! **1947** *Chi. Sun Book Week* 13 July 3/1 The group of industrious topers and jesters who daily congregate at the Massasoit Bar just across the Linden town line may have been a thorn in the side of the churchgoing residents of the community.

(10) (*a*) **1671** *S.C. Hist. Soc. Coll.* V. 284 We were forced to grant them towne lotts. **1860** *Harper's Mag.* Oct. 581/1 Town lot speculators striving to have the Capital elsewhere than at St. Paul. **1948** *Dly. Ardmoreite* (Ardmore, Okla.) 1 April 10/4 Land owners in the state of Maryland do not sell town lots. (*b*) **1713** *Providence Rec.* XVI. 131 To makeing and maintaining fence in the Town Lott, [£]04. — **(11)** (*a*) **1683** *Derby Rec.* 132 Ye fines [are] to be to the town marshall. (*b*) **1903** *N.Y. Sun* 16 Nov. 1 The town marshal arrested him on a charge of murder. **1949** *Chi. Tribune* 27 Sep. 1/3 Bodies of at least five persons . . . are discernible in the wreckage, . . . Town Marshal Jack Bishop reported. — **(13)** (*a*) **1659** *Dedham Rec.* IV. 7 The Constable . . . desbursed . . . the remaynder for killing black birds according to Towne order. **1719** *Boston Rec.* 138 It [shall] be Left to ye Sel[ect]men to draw up a Town order relating to ye marking Baggs, Sent to mill. (*b*) **1833** *Niles' Reg.* XLIV. 347/1 If I do not get a town order for your board, I must make a journey to Portland. — **(14)** **1799** *Hist. Pelham Mass.* (1898) 121 It was voted that the Town Pew be moved to where it first stood.

(15) **1637** *Watertown Rec.* I. 1. 4 Those Freemen of the Congregation shall build and dwell upon their Lotts at the Towne plott. **1656** *Conn. Col. Rec.* I. 282 Thos persons that cohabitt in the towne platte. **1723** *Waterbury Prop. Rec.* 121 A committe perticularly to settle the old Town platt Lotts. **1877** Hale *G.T.T.* 72 At one time he owned half of the original town plot. — **(16)** **1895** *Cent. Mag.* Aug. 638/2 The troop of boom-makers has actively given its perennial leisure to extravagant schemes of town-platting. — **(18)** **1831** Peck *Guide* 8 Having no connection with the business of land speculation or of town sites [etc.]. **1889** *N.Y. Herald* 17 April 6/1 The land . . . is fully up to the standard of excellence described in the circulars sent out by the sundry land speculators and town site sharks. **1942** Stegner *Mormon C.* 204 Then he laid out a townsite. — **(19)** **1634** *Cambridge Rec.* 11 Whatsoever these Townsmen . . . shall doe . . . sha[ll] stand in as full force as if the whole to[wn] did the same. **1705** *Boston News-Letter* 19 March 2/2 There was Chosen to Serve as Select or Townsmen, Mesieurs, Timothy Clark, . . . and Joseph Prout. *a*1817 Dwight *Travels* I. 243 The inhabitants choose, not exceeding seven men . . . to be Selectmen, or Townsmen, to take care of the order, and prudential affairs of the town.

Also in sense **2.** in such expressions as *town bounds*, **charge*, **clerk*, *common*, *council*, *court*, *debt*, *dock*, *fence*, *measurer*, **officer*, *pasture*, *rate*, *representative*, *schoolmaster*, *way*, etc.

As the last term in **air, back, banner, boom, cattle, China, college, coon, county, courthouse, cow, cowboy, cross, cross-road, Dark, dog, down, end, federal, frontier, German, ghost, gumbo, head, hick, home, hunting, Indian, log, lumber, lumbering, mill, mining, mob, Moravian, mountain, mud, mushroom, no-license, old, one-horse, out, panhandle, paper, prairie-dog, praying, river, Santa Fe, sawmill, school, shanty, shoe, show, small, sugar, tank town.**

town ball. [See quot. 1909.] A form of ball game somewhat resembling baseball in that bases were used and the players consisted of a pitcher, catcher, batter, and fielders.

1852 *Calif. Dispatch* (S.F.) 18 Jan. 2/4 A game of 'town ball' which was had on the Plaza during the week, reminded us of other days and other scenes. **1867** *Ball Players' Chron.* 18 July 4/2 Sometimes the name of 'town ball' was given to it, because matches were often played by parties representing different towns. **1909** *Collier's* 8 May 12/1 In America the corresponding game generally went under the name of 'rounders,' and because it was played at the time of town meetings, 'townball.' **1946** *Greenville* (Ala.) *Adv.* 26 Sep., The same game, with variations, was known in other Alabama communities as 'Town Ball.'

attrib. **1903** *Outing* July 455/1 Before the collegians the stalwart citizens organized baseball, the first recorded body for the pure purpose of contest being that of the 'Town Ball' Club . . . in Philadelphia, 1831.

town-ho 'taun,ho, *interj.* Also **townor, town-at.** [Origin unknown.] (See quots.)

1791 *Mass. H.S. Coll.* 1 Ser. III. 154 *Townor* . . . is an Indian word, and signifies that they have seen the whale twice. **1848** Mitchell *Nantucketisms* 40 *Town-at*, exclamation when a whale is seen. **1851** Melville *Moby-Dick* 269 Town-Ho . . . [is] the ancient whale-cry upon first sighting a whale from the mast-head, still used by whalemen in hunting the famous Gallipagos terrapin.

town meeting. *N. Eng.* A formal assembly of the voters in a town for the transaction of public business. Cf. **public town meeting.**

"In the southern and the middle colonies, also, there were assemblies of voters; but nowhere outside of the New England group was there a mass meeting of voters who could not only elect officers, but could legislate for their community" (*Cyclo. Amer. Govt.* III. 542).

1636 *Salem Rec.* I. 16 At a generall Court or towne meeting of Salem held the second of . . . May A[nn]o 1636. **1770** Hiltzheimer *Diary* (1893) 27 Sep. 22 Went to the town meeting at the State House, where it was agreed that further non-importation was necessary, a few articles only excepted. **1873** Lunt *Old N. Eng. Traits* 51 A noted magistrate . . . served many years as town-clerk, and was an energetic orator at town-meetings. **1945** Webster *Town Meeting Country* 228 Nowadays we hold two regular town meetings each year, one in the fall, the other in February. **1950** *Chi. D. News* 29 March 2/5 At 2 p.m. next Tuesday, under the laws of Illinois, it will be the duty of several hundred thousand citizens of Cook County to attend their town meeting.

transf. **1947** *Time* 27 Jan. 49/1 What we tend to have in our journalism is not a town meeting . . . but a pitched battle of propagandas. **1949** *Lisle* (Ill.) *Eagle* 10 March 6/5 Congress is, as it should be, but a national town meeting.

attrib. **1683** *Southold Rec.* I. 129 Stephen Bayly [shall be] the Town Clark to keep the Town meeting book. **1817** J. M. Scott *Blue Lights* 40 There is one. . . . Such would you see, in grave debate, Attend town-meeting day sedate. **1916** Eaton *Idyl of Twin Fires* 243 You are in the Town Meeting belt here, Mr. Upton, and you've got to get your arguments through the skulls of every voter in the place before we can have any money to work with. **1944** Holton *Yankees* 35 Of course you remember you did help elect somebody called a town meeting member back in November, and that he was expected to get together with other similarly chosen men and hold a dull evening session with the finances committee.

***Townsend,** *n.* [In **1.** f. J. K. *Townsend* (1809–51), Amer. naturalist.]

1. In the possessive in the names of birds, as (1) **Townsend's bunting,** (2) **cormorant,** (3) **flycatcher,** (4) **flycatching thrush,** (5) **fox sparrow,** (6) **mocking thrush,** (7) **solitaire,** (8) **sparrow,** (9) **warbler.**

(1) **1887** Ridgway *Man. N. Amer. Birds* 452 Chester County, Pennsylvania (only one specimen known) . . . *S[piza] townsendii* Townsend's Bunting. — **(2)** **1839** Audubon *Ornith. Biog.* V. 149 Townsend's Cormorant. *Phalacrocorax Townsendi.* — **(3)** **1869** *Amer. Naturalist* III. 34 Townsend's Flycatcher (Myiadestes Townsendii) . . . was pursuing insects from bush to bush in a small prairie. — **(4)** **1874** Coues *Birds N.W.* 93 *Myiadestes Townsendii.* Townsend's Flycatching Thrush . . . Middle and Western Provinces of the United States.

(5) **1917** *Birds of Amer.* III. 57/2 In western North America . . . [is] Townsend's Fox Sparrow (*Passerella iliaca townsendi*). — **(6)** **1839** [see **mocking thrush**]. — **(7)** **1887** Ridgway *Man. N. Amer. Birds* 572 Western United States (in mountains), north to British Columbia east to and including Rocky Mountains (casually to Illinois) . . . *M[yadestes] townsendii* (Aud.) Townsend's Solitaire. **1946** Stanwell-Fletcher *Driftwood Valley* 194 Between five and six thousand feet, Townsend's solitaires were nesting and singing in full glory. — **(8)** **1887** Ridgway *Man. N. Amer. Birds* 434 Pacific coast, breeding from southern Alaska . . . to Unalashka; south, in winter, to southern California. . . . *P[asserella] iliaca unalaschcensis.* . . . Townsend's Sparrow. — **(9)** **1839** Audubon *Ornith. Biog.* V. 36 Townsend's Warbler . . . was procured about the Columbia River. **1948** *Pacific Discovery* March–April 17/1 An Audubon warbler came down to the New Zealand beech and drove the thrush and Townsend warbler away.

2. *attrib.* Of or pertaining to a plan projected by Dr. F. E. Townsend for giving a pension of $200 a month to every person sixty years of age or over. Cf. *ham-and-egg(s) pension s.v.* ***ham,** *n.* **4. b.**

1939 Webster (*New Words*). **1943** *Greeley* (Colo.) *D. Tribune* 23 Feb. 7/4 Plans were completed for attending the Townsend convention in Loveland on Sunday. **1950** *Time* 3 April 23/3 And to win favor with Florida's numerous old folks, Pepper backed the Townsend Plan, lock, stock & barrel.

Hence **Townsendism, Townsendite.**

1936 *Rocky Mt. News* (Denver) 3 May 7/3 (*heading*), Townsendites Back Men in Both Parties. **1939** White *One Man's Meat* 94 He sounded as though this was the first time he had ever expounded Townsendism. **1949** *L.A. Times* 5 July 16/4 'End of Poverty' Political Party to be Launched by Townsendites.

Townsendia taun'zendɪə, *n.* [f. David *Townsend* (1787–1858), of Pa.] A genus of western plants of the thistle family, or a plant belonging to this genus. — **1871** *Amer. Naturalist* V. 65 There appears [in Colo.] a real beauty, which, as it yet lacks an English name, may bear its Latin one, Townsendia (*T. sericea*). **1872** TICE *Over Plains* 64 Here were . . . white and purple *Anemones;* the gaudy *Gaillordia aristata* . . . ; the white Townsendia [etc.].

***township,** *n.*

1. *N. Eng.* A local area or political unit governed by means of a town meeting; the jurisdiction of a New England town. Cf. ***town,** *n.* **2.**

It has been pointed out that the germ of the township with its local governmental powers is of Dutch origin. De Tocqueville is credited with having first pointed out the Dutch source of this peculiarity of American government. See *N.Y. Hist. Soc. Col.* II. (1848) 20 ff.

1635 *Watertown Rec.* I. I. 1 Two Hundred Acres of vpland . . . shalbe reserved as most convenient to make a Towneship. **1789** ANBURY *Travels* II. 261 Most of the places you pass through in Connecticut are called townships . . . which are not regular towns as in England, but a number of houses dispersed over a large tract of ground. **1828** COOPER *Notions* I. 94 Each township, as parishes, or *cantons,* are here called, has the entire control of all the routes within its own limits. **1884** *Cent. Mag.* Jan. 443/2 In some parts of Massachusetts a 'hayward' was employed to attend the cattle of a whole township, which were kept together in one drove. **1949** *House & Garden* July 63/2 Its largest township has a voting population under three hundred persons.

b. Elsewhere, as in the states of the Northwest Territory, a similar political unit set up by or under the influence of early settlers from New England and New York. Cf. ***town,** *n.* **2. b.**

As the present time Illinois has 1,444 such townships, chiefly in the northern part of the state settled largely by New Englanders.

1769 *Phila. Ordinances* (1812) 26 The waggon, wain or cart . . . within the district of Southwark, or the townships of Moyamensing or Passyunk, shall travel . . . on any of the paved parts of the said city. **1846** *Mich. Gen. Statutes* I. (1882) 261 Debts owing to a township . . . shall be apportioned in the same manner as the personal property of such township. **1888** BRYCE *Amer. Commonw.* II. II. xlviii. 240 The words 'town' and 'township' signify [in Ill. and other western and northwestern states] a territorial division of the county, incorporated for purposes of local government. **1950** *Chi. D. News* 29 March 2/5 The citizens of the various townships [in Ill.] at that time will set the course of their township government.

2. Any one of various tracts, differing in size, into which public land is surveyed.

"An 'original surveyed township' or 'congressional township' . . . should be distinguished from both the 'civil township' and the 'school township' which may or may not coincide with the thirty-six square mile tracts" (*Cyclo. Amer. Govt.* III. 544/2).

1759 *Newport Mercury* 3 July 3/2 Said Proprietors, for the further Encouragement of the Settlement of their Land, have agreed to grant Six Townships of five Miles Square each. **1891** *N. & Q.* VI. 264 In Maine, the unsettled lands are surveyed into townships. . . . When the Maine township becomes settled, it receives a name, and organizes a local 'plantation' government. **1909** WEBSTER 2178/3 In Maine, New Hampshire, and Vermont there are unorganized subdivisions of the county called townships, which are simply tracts of land laid off by the State authorities. **1949** *Boston Globe Mag.* 18 Sep. 5/1 On the edge of No. 3 Burn in Township 4, County of Hancock, State of Maine, a boy sat on a log, waiting.

b. Under the public-land ordinance of 1785, one of the tracts, approximately six miles square (containing thirty-six sections) in area, into which the public lands of the U.S. were divided before sale was permitted.

In states surveyed into geographical townships, the political township is usually based upon the geographical one.

1785 *Jrnls. Cont. Congress* XXVIII. 378 There shall be reserved the lot N 16, of every township, for the maintenance of public schools, within the said township. **1815** DRAKE *Cincinnati* 129 Cincinnati is built upon one entire and two fractional sections . . . in the fourth township. **1825** *New-Harmony* (Ind.) *Gaz.* 1 Oct. 7/2 A number of gentlemen are now in the New Purchase selecting a township of land, in which to form a community agreeably to Mr. Owen's plan. **1950** *Chi. Tribune* 28 Feb. 12/3 You are in township 39 north, range 14 east of the third principal meridian.

3. *W.* (See quots.)

1907 [see ***town 1. b.**]. **1947** O. LAFARGE *Santa Eulalia* xv, *Townships* are the Spanish *municipios,* to which our cognate, 'municipality' does not apply so well as does the Anglo-Saxon term. They are the units of government and a subdivision under the department.

4. Attrib., chiefly in senses **2.** and **2. b.** with (1) **high school,** (2) **land,** (3) **line,** (4) **meeting,** (5) **school,** (6) **supervisor,** (7) **treasurer,** (8) **trustee.**

(1) **1914** *Cyclo. Amer. Govt.* III. 260/3 The township high school has been organized to bring secondary education nearer to all pupils of the public schools. — (2) **1647** *Watertown Rec.* I. I. 12 The Land giuen in liew of the Towneship; is not a Just satisfaction for the Towneshipp Land. **1940** *Sat. Ev. Post* 30 March 40/3 The phone, mind you, is on township land, not on Amish property. — (3) **1814** *Niles' Reg.* V. 321/2 Our very intelligent principal surveyor . . . has been running township lines. **1949** *Surveying & Mapping* Jan.–Mar. 31/2 In the north and south directions the divisions are known as township lines. — (4) **1849** *Will Co. Telegraph* (Lockport, Ill.) 270 Sep. 2/2 Annual township meetings are to be held on the first Tuesday in April.

(5) **1816** *Ind. Constitution* ix. § 2 It shall be the duty of the General Assembly, as soon as circumstances will permit, to provide, by law, for a general system of education, ascending in a regular gradation from township schools to a State University. **1949** *Ward Co. Independent* (Minot, N.D.) 21 July 11/4 Freedom township school 12 miles south and three miles west of Minot was nearly burned to the ground last week. — (6) **1947** *Chi. Tribune* 10 July 17/5 If the commissioner is not known to the property owner, he should get in touch with his township supervisor and report the weeds. — (7) **1838** *Indiana H. Rep. Jrnl.* 23 Sess. 114 [It shall be] the duty of the township treasurer to divide and distribute the school funds. — (8) **1836** *New-Yorker* 30 April 92/1 The vote (by general ticket) for Township Trustees is stated as follows. **1851** CIST *Cincinnati* 335 Longworth is a supernumerary township trustee.

As the last term in **banner, basswood, college, Congressional, fractional, post, timber township.**

***towny,** *n.* A citizen of a college town, as distinguished from a student or a teacher. *Obs.* — **1852** *Deseret News* (Salt Lake City) 7 Aug. 1/1 'O, nothing,' replied the 'towney.' **1892** *Outing* July 323/1 The 'townies' joined in the cause of the latter, and it was now 'Yale against the town.'

toyon 'tojən, *n.* Also **tollon.** *W.* [Amer. Sp. *toyon, tollon* (prob. f. Nahuatl) in sense shown here.] The evergreen California holly, *Heteromeles arbutifolia,* cultivated as an ornamental plant because of its white blossoms and subsequent red berries.

1848 *Californian* (S.F.) 26 April 2/1 Woods, . . . willow, madrona, tyon, laurel, ash, cotton-wood, &c. **1884** SARGENT *Rep. Forests* 84 Toyon. Tollon. California Holly. . . . Wood . . . susceptible of a beautiful polish. **1949** *L.A. Times Home Mag.* 20 Nov. 35/3 Toyon is comfortably at home in its native setting.

***trace,** *n.*[1] (See quot. c1662.) *Obs.* Cf. ***braid,** *n.*, ***trace,** *v.* — **c1662** JOHN WINTHROP in *N. Eng. Quart.* X. (1937) 127 But the Common way [of keeping Indian corn] is to weave it together in long traices by some parts of the husks left upon the Eare (this worke they call traicing) and these traices they hang upon Stayes or other bearers without doors, or within, for it will keepe good and sweete hung in that manner all the Winter after. **1753** E. CHAMBERS *Cyclo. Supp. s.v. Tracing,* These traces of corn they hang up within doors.

***trace,** *n.*[2]

1. A path, trail, or road made by the passage of men or animals.

1783 in W. FLEMING *Travels Amer. Col.* 673 Started in the morning, went the old trace, got alarmed, several fresh horse tracts before us. **1851** *S. Lit. Messenger* XVII. 571/1 The 'trace' is growing a frequented highway. **1945** KENNEY *West Va. Place Names* 23 The earliest road was the footway called trace or trail.

Also **traceway,** *rare.*

1857 *Ladies' Repository* April 235/2 'There,' pointing to what had once been a traceway, 'that will take you down to the river.'

2. Preceded by a descriptive or specifying term.

1807 in PIKE *Sources Miss.* II. App. 24 [We] took the large Spanish beaten trace for the Arkansaw river. **1870** NOWLAND *Indianapolis* 14 Berry's Trace crossed that of Whetzell's. **1946** *Sat. Ev. Post* 3 Aug. 81/2 Two days later and eleven miles east of Black Cloud Agency, they crossed the Comanche trace.

As the last term in **buffalo, deer, game, Indian, Natchez, Osage, river, wagon trace.**

***trace,** *n.*[3] In fig. and colloq. phrases: (1) *To force into the traces,* to force into regular or humdrum work; (2) *to break* (or *burst*) *a trace,* to exert oneself to the utmost; (3) *to get one leg over the traces,* to misdirect one's efforts, as to get out of line with the interests of one's party or group; (4) *to work in the traces,* to work or proceed in a regular or uniform manner.

(1) **1824** IRVING *Tales of Traveller* I. 203 He was too fond of my genius to force it into the traces. — (2) **1839** *Spirit of Times* 13 July 223/3 (We.), I told him I'd go, or bust a trace trying. **1845** *Big Bear Ark.* 101 You must marry that gal and no mistake, or brake a trace! — (3) **1871** *Harper's Mag.* Dec. 155/2, I may have got one leg over the traces, but I was in the harness all the while. — (4) **1881** in McCABE *New York* 129 This whole system was founded on . . . the tendency of every voter to work in the traces, and vote for any man ostensibly nominated by the party.

* **trace,** *v. tr.* To form (ears of corn) into traces by plaiting their husks. Also with *up.*

*c***1662** [see * **trace,** *n.*[1]]. **1772** PATTEN *Diary* 290, I gathered and traced some corn. **1884** *Vt. Agric. Rep.* VIII. 285 The ears thus selected should be 'traced up' and hung away to dry.

* **tracer,** *n.* **1.** An inquiry sent from one place to another to find out the whereabouts of a person or thing. **2.** (See quot.)

(1) **1884** *Cent. Mag.* May 159/1 (*title*), A Tracer for J[ohn] B[urroughs]. **1932** *K.C. Star* 21 April 30 The Atchison Globe has sent out a tracer for the old-fashioned young man who . . . told her he was not good enough for her. — (2) **1888** *Scientific Amer.* LIX. 217/1 Nearly all the great roads employ a corps of what are known as 'lost car searchers' or 'tracers.'

* **track,** *n.*

1. (See quots.)

1850 *Western Journal* IV. 96 The common track of wagons measured 'from inside to outside,' which is the same as from centre to centre, is four feet eight inches in the State of New York. In New Jersey and the Southern States, it is five feet. In Connecticut it varies from three feet eight inches, for light wagons, to five feet two inches for heavy ones. In Wisconsin it is five feet four inches. **1948** RITTENHOUSE *Vehicles* 1 Track. The term 'track' refers to the extreme width of the vehicle as measured from outside rim of one wheel to the outside of the rim of the opposite wheel, measured at the bottom of the wheel.

2. In combs.: (1) **track clearer,** (see quot. 1876); (2) **dog,** = **track hound;** (3) **force,** a group of laborers who maintain a portion of a railroad track; (4) **hound,** a hound that hunts and follows a track by scent; (5) **layer,** (*a*) one skilled or employed in laying a railroad track, (*b*) (see quot.); (6) **laying,** the laying of the rails on a railway line; (7) **man,** one engaged in laying railroad track; (8) **master,** one responsible for the inspection and repair of a section of railroad track; (9) **sprinkler,** (see quot. 1848), *obs.;* (10) **walker,** a person employed to walk along and inspect a certain length of railroad track regularly, also transf.

(1) **1859** *Rep. Comm. Patents 1858* I. 433 Improvement in Track Clearers for Mowing Machines. **1876** KNIGHT 2608/1 *Track-clearer.* 1. (*Railway.*) *a.* A cow-catcher in front of, or bars extending down from the front frame of the locomotive, to push objects from the track. *b.* A track-sweeper to remove snow. . . . 2. (*Harvesting.*) A triangular frame on the outer end of the cutter-bar of a mowing or reaping machine to draw the grain toward the cutter. — (2) **1836** HOWARD *Stewart* 243 They soon started him with *track-dogs.* **1884** HARRIS *Mingo* 188 The next day Bill Brand and his track dogs put in an appearance. — (3) **1866** *39th Cong.* 2 Sess. H.R. Rep. No. 34, 1026, I found the road in bad condition; the track force had been over it two weeks at work repairing. — (4) **1865** *Jamestown* (N.Y.) *Jrnl.* 13 Jan. 4/1 No more flying fugitives, white men or negroes, shall be followed by track hounds. **1893** ROOSEVELT *Wilderness Hunter* 45 The cowboy and our one trackhound plunged into the young cottonwood.

(5) (*a*) *a***1861** WINTHROP *Open Air* 234 'Wanted, experienced track-layer!' was the word along the files. **1898** KING *Warrior Gap* 12 He and his troop . . . were busy scouting the neighborhood, guarding the surveyors, the engineers, and finally the track-layers. **1941** DICK *Vanguards of Frontier* 374 The track-layers advanced a mile or more a day during the summer months. (*b*) **1876** KNIGHT 2608/1 *Track-layer,* . . . a carriage provided with apparatus for placing the rails in their proper positions . . . as the machine advances. — (6) *a***1861** WINTHROP *Open Air* 234 *Track-laying* was the business on hand. **1890** *Stock Grower & Farmer* 21 June 5/1 Track-laying on the Pecos Valley railroad commenced this week, and will be pushed rapidly. — (7) **1872** HUNTINGTON *Road-Master's Ass't* iv, They are mainly of a technical nature, and not adapted to the wants or capacities of the average *track-man.* **1929** *Randolph Enterprise* 21 Nov. 1/1 A hand-car with some track-men on it going to work ran across a drove of wild turkeys crossing the track. — (8) **1866** in FULTON *Sam Hobart* 103 The track-master failed to ascertain the fact. — (9) **1848** BARTLETT 362 *Track-Sprinkler,* a contrivance recently invented in Providence, R.I., and now in use on the railroads in that State, for sprinkling railroad tracks.

(10) **1872** *Chi. Tribune* 14 Oct. 3/2 The attempt would have been successful but for its discovery by a track-walker. **1949** *Reader's Digest* July 99/2 Pipe lines have their 'track walkers'—except that they ride in planes.

b. Of or pertaining to athletic activities, such as running, jumping, etc., performed on a track, or to athletes who engage in such sports, as (1) **track athlete,** (2) **athletics,** (3) **meet,** (4) **season,** (5) **team.**

(1) **1888** *Pall Mall Gaz.,* 27 Aug. 14/1 The baseball and track athletes graduated 34 per cent of their number. **1902** *Outing* June 267/2 And the perfect track athlete is the one who joys in his work. — (2) **1890** *Cent. Mag.* June 204/2 'Track athletics' are walking, running, jumping [etc.]. — (3) **1904** *Cap & Gown* (Chi.) IX. 215 Track Meets and Scores, 1903. . . . Second Annual Interscholastic Meet, at Marshall Field. **1950** *Chi. Tribune* 27 April IV. 3/4 Record breaking is not required proof for the excellence of any track meet, of course.— (4) **1899** QUINN *Pa. Stories* 218 That was the way things were when the track season opened.

(5) **1907** *St. Nicholas* XXXIV. 693/2 Hammond has a track team, but we have n't. **1929** *Wisconsin Alumni Mag.* April 229 Tom Jones brought his track team along slowly.

c. In phrases: (1) *To make tracks,* to depart in haste, to hurry, *colloq.;* (2) *to plumb a track,* to follow out a road or track, *colloq.;* (3) *in one's tracks,* on the spot where one is at the moment, *colloq.;* (4) *to fly the track,* to depart from or leave a usual or prescribed course, usu. fig.; (5) *to cover up one's tracks,* to conceal one's actions or motives; (6) *to lose track of,* to fail to keep up with or follow the course of; (7) *to jump the track,* of a railway car, to leave the rails; (8) *the right* (or *wrong*) *side of the tracks,* (see quot. 1929).

(1) **1827** *Spirit of 'Seventy-Six* (Frankfort, Ky.) 29 March 4/2 Another made up his mind to bow his neck and make tracks. **1948** DICK *Dixie Frontier* 313 When one wanted to send a person away, one might say: 'Make Tracks!' — (2) **1844** M. C. HOUSTOUN *Texas* (1845) 230 *Plumbing the track,* the Texan term for tracing a road, is, at all times, a slow and tedious operation. **1892** *Country Church* (Buckland, Mass.) 16 March, When Old Rover took one track and plumbed it through, he holed the game. — (3) **1824** JAMES *Andrew Jackson* (1937) 156 (We.), He failed to shoot 'Jackson dead in his tracks.' **1883** HARTE *In Carquinez Woods* 180 You'd have dropped in your tracks. **1945** G. BROWN *Murder in Plain Sight* 97 (We.), He reeled, stopped in his tracks. — (4) **1847** *Cong. Globe* 4 Feb. 322/2, I had been accused of flying the track on the creed of the Democratic party. **1910** C. HARRIS *Eve's Husband* 85 No man ever gets too old to fly the track in some way.

(5) **1865** RICHARDSON *Secret Service* 57 In corresponding, I endeavored to cover my tracks as far as possible. **1878** *Masque of Poets* 244 Whatever else he lacks, He has the art of covering up his tracks. — (6) **1871** EGGLESTON *Hoosier Schoolm.* 83 May be God lost track of my father. **1907** LILLIBRIDGE *Trail* 271 We got too far apart and lost track of each other. — (7) **1872** *Harper's Mag.* Dec. 152 The ladies' car on an express train on the Paducah and Elizabethtown Railroad jumped the track. **1904** *Newark Ev. News* 14 June 5 Trolley car 415 . . . jumped the track. — (8) **1929** SMITH *Stray Lamb* (1938) 21 In most commuting towns of any recognized worth there are always two sides of which the tracks serve as a line of demarcation. There is the right side and the wrong side. Translated into terms of modern American idealism, this means, the rich side and the side that hopes to be rich. **1949** *Social Studies* May 215/1 These refined individuals who lived on the right side of the tracks were chilled to the bone in 1896 at the Bryan movement.

d. In less common phrases, chiefly obs.: (1) *To beat* (someone) *out of his track,* to force (someone) from his course; (2) *to yield the track to,* to give way or submit to; (3) *to keep out of* (someone's) *tracks,* to avoid (someone); (4) *to take one's track,* (see quot.); (5) *to run off the track, fig.* = *to fly the track;* (6) *to go back on one's tracks,* to give up one's intentions.

(1) **1833** FLINT *D. Boone* 28 He was remarkable for the backwoods attribute of *never being beaten out of his track.* — (2) **1847** FIELD *Drama in Pokerville* 41 Mr. Busby Case . . . had entirely yielded the track to his formidable rival. — (3) **1847** ROBB *Squatter Life* 122 As for that sarpent with her, he'd better keep out of my tracks. — (4) **1861** CAPT. MORTON PRICE *Theatrical Trip* 126 When there's one, who can give them a 'stun' Take their track from, and beat them easy. [Note to *take their track:*] A Yankee term signifying Going a-head.

(5) **1875** LOWELL *Spenser Prose Wks.* (1890) IV. 277 The result was a series of jolts and jars, proving that the language had run off the track. — (6) **1878** STOWE *Poganuc People* 158 He'll put it through, though; he won't go back on his tracks.

As the last term in **back, bridle, cow, creeping, crow, dirt, double, flatbar, hen's, moccasin, narrow, one, shoe, side, single, sleigh, squirrel, stock track.**

* **track,** *v.*

1. a. *tr.* To soil or mark (a floor, etc.) with tracks, also with *up.* **b.** To bring (snow or mud) into a place on one's feet, often with *in.*

(**a**) **1832** *Jamestown* (N.Y.) *Jrnl.* 1 Aug. 3/2 The gardens and roads about the city were 'tracked up' with [rats and mice]. **1869** STOWE *Oldtown Folks* 21 Don't come in to track my floor. — (**b**) **1866** *Harper's Mag.* Jan. 271/2 The snow had been tracked in till it lay pretty thick on the floor. **1901** MERWIN & WEBSTER *Calumet 'K'* 117 There's going to be a law passed about tracking mud inside the railing.

2. To provide (a region) with railroad tracks. *Obs.*

1846 *Niles' Reg.* XX. 64/2 We would compete with England for the supplies which the continents of Europe and Asia will soon require, of railroad iron—beside *tracking* our own 'wilderness' with iron highways in all directions.

3. *intr.* In walking, to place one foot in the same straight line with the other.

1857 GLISAN *Jrnl. Army Life* 382, I observed to-day that he does not 'track' (step his hind foot straight after the fore one). **1897** HOUGH *Story of Cowboy* 34 His feet, in the vernacular of the range, do not 'track,' but cross each other weakly.

trackage ˈtrækɪdʒ, *n.*

1. *collect.* The tracks of a railroad or railroad system.

1880 *Bradstreet's* 24 Nov. 2/4 The Reading will receive compensation on two-thirds of the trackage. **1946** *Trail & Timberline* May 67/1 Up behind the Front Range lies almost as much abandoned trackage as there is in operation today, abandoned because of heavy snows, grades which were too steep, diminishing population, exhausted mines or lack of traffic. **1949** *Lubbock* (Tex.) *Morn. Avalanche* 23 Feb. II. 8/5, I have the best business and trackage locations in town—also business buildings.

2. a. trackage charge, a charge for the use of a railway line by another company. **b. trackage rights,** certain rights secured by one railway company of making use, esp. at terminals, of the tracks of another company.

(**a**) **1884** *Morning Herald* (Reading, Pa.) 17 April, Our general agent has, therefore, advanced this trackage charge. — (**b**) **1898** *K.C. Star* 21 Dec. 1/4 Trackage rights will be obtained over roads entering Chicago. **1947** *Time* 3 Feb. 80/2 As for trackage rights to San Francisco, he said airily: 'There's always ways of picking them up.'

***tract** *n.* As the last term in **bounty, half-breed, lumber, manual labor, military tract.**

* **traction,** *n. attrib.* Of or pertaining to city transportation systems.

1897 *Kissimmee* (Fla.) *Valley Gaz.* 31 Dec. 1/5 A trolley car on the Schuylkill Valley Traction Company line at Norristown, Pa. was held up by four highwaymen. **1904** *N.Y. Tribune* 27 March 12 The reservoir broke, flooding paper mills and tying up railway and traction lines. **1903** *Boston Transcript* 20 Aug., Plans are being worked out for the consolidation of the traction systems of this city.

tractor ˈtræktɚ, *n.* [f. L. *trahere, tractum,* to draw. In **2.** prob. a new formation without regard to **1.**]

1. *pl.* A pair of slightly pointed bars (see quot. 1949), supposed to give relief by electricity or magnetism

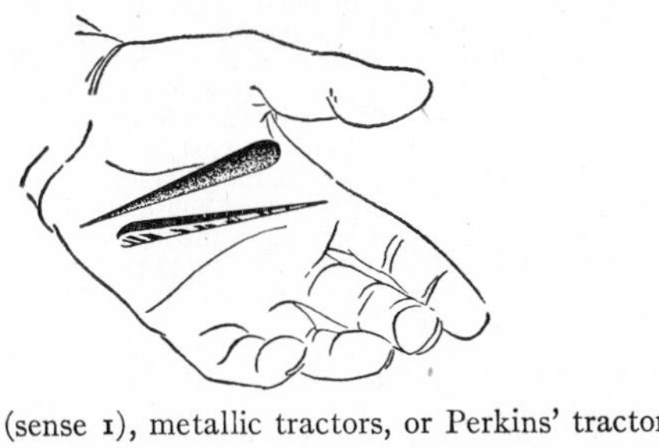

Tractors (sense 1), metallic tractors, or Perkins' tractors

when drawn over affected parts of the body. Also **metallic tractors,** and (after the inventor, Dr. Elisha Perkins (1741–99) of Norwich, Conn.), **Perkins' tractors.** Now *hist.* Cf. **Perkinism.**

These bars were always used in pairs, chiefly for local inflammations and pains. They were hailed as a great medical advance in this country and abroad. In 1802 they sold for about twenty-five dollars a pair in London.

1796 *Aurora* (Phila.) 29 March (Th.), [Notice of] Metallic Tractors. **1800** *Lancaster* (Pa.) *Jrnl.* 20 Dec. (Th.), The Turkey-cock and Tractors. **1804** *Balance* 10 Jan. 9 (Th.), There are Perkins's Tractors. They will cure everything. **1842** O. W. HOLMES *Medical Essays* (1892) IX. 15 Most of those present have at some time in their lives heard mention made of the Metallic Tractors. *Ib.* 27 Among the risks of infancy I had to encounter Perkins's Tractors. **1949** GORDON *Æsculapius Comes to Colonies* 228 Perkins' tractors consisted of two small rods, about three inches long, one of brass, one of steel, which had to be drawn downward for twenty minutes over the affected parts.

2. a. (See quot. 1909.) **b.** (See quots.)

(**a**) [**1900** HISCOX *Horseless Vehicles* 41 A number of [vehicles] . . . were built extending over the time for 1830 to 1840, carriages, omnibuses and tractors being seen on the roads about London.] **1909** *Cent. Supp.* 1366/2 *Tractor*. . . . 2. A traction-engine for use on streets and highways. Such tractors may be used to drag loaded vehicles, to drag plows in a gang, or to haul artillery-wagons and field-pieces. 3. The frame and steel rope by which a gang of plows is drawn across a field by a traction-engine. — (**b**) **1917** *Lit. Digest* 29 Dec. 73/1 Benjamin Holt started his factory at Stockton in 1883 to supply . . . the ranchers of California. . . . Over a dozen years ago Holt discarded driving wheels entirely and produced the first flexible self-laying track which both supported and propelled the tractor under all conditions. **1949** *Prairie Farmer* 4 June 17/2 The tractor, known as old Hart-Parr Number Three, was made in 1903 with 14 others just like it, by a Charles City, Iowa, manufacturing company. At first called a farm traction machine, its title was simplified to the term 'tractor' by the Hart-Parr Co., which is the first known use of the term.

tractoration ˌtræktəˈreʃən, *n.* The use of metallic tractors. *Obs.* — **1803** T. G. FESSENDEN (*title*), Terrible Tractoration! **1861** in HOLMES *Medical Essays* 9 Homœopathy has not died out so rapidly as Tractoration.

tractoring ˈtræktərɪŋ, *a.* Using metallic tractors. *Obs.* — **1803** T. G. FESSENDEN *Terrible Tractoration!* 132 You'll confound the tractoring folks By Haygarth's tale.

tractorize ˈtræktəˌraɪz, *v. intr.* and *tr.* To use metallic tractors, to attract by the use of these. Also **tractorizing,** *a. Obs.* — **1803** T. G. FESSENDEN (*title*), A Poetical Petition against Tractorising Trumpery. **1803** ——— *Terrible Tractoration!* 104 A spruce young patent-monger Contrives to wheedle simple ninnies, And *tractorise* away our guineas.

tract society. A society for distributing religious literature, usu. in the form of tracts. Often in the names of particular societies.

1760 J. ADAMS *Diary* Wks. II. 97, I should be very sorry to see the Tract Society dissolved. **1820** FLINT *Lett. from Amer.* 214 Cincinnati has . . . two tract societies, (one of them for distributing Bibles and tracts amongst boatmen on the river). **1885** BAYLOR *On Both Sides* 221, I am the agent of the American Tract Society, madam.

* **trade,** *n.*

1. Commodities or produce used in barter.

*a*1655 BRADFORD *Hist.* 153 This ship had store of English-beads (which were their good trade). **1800** TATHAM *Agric. & Commerce* 81 Such a one wishes to give you trade for your horse. **1931** *Randolph Enterprise* (Elkins, W.Va.) 29 Oct. 1/2 We note that Morris-Harvey College . . . is offering to take trade from students to help them out.

b. *in trade,* in barter, designed for barter.

1802 ELLICOTT *Jrnl.* 15 They . . . made about 30 bushels of salt per day, which sold for a dollars cash per bushel, or 3 dollars in trade, as they term it. **1847** PALMER *Rocky Mts.* 127 The value of fourteen dollars in trade would buy an ordinary horse. **1884** ROE *Nature's Story* 73 I've brought you a fair lot of things, but they are in trade.

2. A business deal or transaction involving barter. *Colloq.*

1772 in *Travels Amer. Col.* 533 He would not give them such a good Trade as the people of the Puckantallahassie did. **1883** HARRIS *Mingo* 137 Teague wore the air of awkward, recklessly, helpless independence which so often deceives those who strike the Mountain men for a trade. **1903** A. ADAMS *Log of Cowboy* 331 Our foreman thought he could effect a trade for a serviceable wagon.

b. *To make trade,* to barter. *Obs.*

1823 I. HOLMES *Account* 215 If a farmer goes to a country shopkeeper with flour, beef, mutton, &c. the common question is—'Will you make trade?'

c. *Polit.* = * **deal.**

1888 *Cent. Mag.* Dec. 313/2 We should be rid at one stroke . . . of 'deals' and 'dickers' and 'trades' at the polls. **1910** *Springfield W. Republican* 8 Dec. 8 Trade and dicker between the two leading political parties.

3. *collect.* Customers, those who come to trade. *Colloq.*

1901 DUNCAN & SCOTT *Allen & Woodson Co., Kans.* 409 It was no uncommon thing to toll grists from Independence and to wait on trade from Eureka.

4. In combs.: (1) **trade ball,** a rifle ball or bullet used in trade with the Indians, *obs.;* (2) **boom,** a boom or upswing in trade; (3) **bullet,** = **trade ball,** *obs.;* (4) **dollar,** a dollar having 420 grains of standard silver authorized in 1873 and not coined after 1885—so called because it was coined for use in Oriental trade, cf. **silver trade dollar;** (5) **goods,** commodities designed for trade with the Indians, *obs.;* (6) **gun,** a cheap gun designed for trade with the Indians, now *hist.,* cf. **Indian trader;** (7) **house,** = **trading house,** *obs.;* (8) **in,** that which has been given in a trade, usu. attrib., *colloq.;* (9) **last,** (see quots.), *colloq.;* (10) **rat,** a pack rat *q.v.;* (11) **store,** = **trading post;** (12) **vehicle,** a commercial vehicle.

(1) **1859** G. A. JACKSON *Diary* 523 Bringing back ten pounds of trade balls, ten pounds of powder, 2,000 waterproof caps, with some extra caps. **1868** M. J. CARRINGTON *Absaraka* 189 Rifles, both English and American, abound. The 'Hawkins' is a favorite, carrying what is called the 'trade ball,' and requiring a patch. — (2) **1925** *Scribner's Mag.* Oct. 69/1 What we call a 'trade boom' would undoubtedly be facilitated by abnormally easy credit. — (3) **1859** G. A. JACKSON *Diary* 9 Came up bringing 50 lbs of trade bullets. — (4) **1873** *Statutes at Large* XVII. 427 The silver coins of the United States shall be a trade-dollar, a half-dollar [etc.]. **1887** *Courier-Journal* 17 Feb. 1/6 The House to-day insisted upon its amendments to the Senate Trade-dollar Bill. **1942** LILLARD *Desert Challenge* 49 The 'trade dollar' . . . was for use in Oriental trade.

(5) **1633** *N.H. Prov. P.* I. 73 The intermixing of all the trade goods in my care. . . . I cannot give you any satisfaction for. — (6) **1873** R. F. BURTON in Lady B. *Life* (1893) II. 20 Those who must often expose themselves . . . to Anglo-Ashanti trade-guns. **1903** S. E. WHITE *Forest* x. 126 Everything here was meant for the Indian trade. Bolts of bright-patterned ginghams, . . . stacks of long brass-bound 'trade-guns.' — (7) **1668** *N.H. Hist. Soc. Coll.* III. 216 Ye sayd Capt. did at the very first tyme of settling ye Trade house aforesaide loade four Indians with Liquors. — (8) **1927** *Ladies' Home Jrnl.* Dec. 65/1 Buyers . . . took prompt advantage of the liberal trade-in allowance on their old equipment. **1929** *Collier's* 12 Jan. 9/2 More than one third of his gross financial transactions . . . is represented by trade-in cars. — (9) **1895** *D.N.* I. 426 trade-last, -lassie, me lass: a complimentary remark reported by one person to another. 'I've got a *trade-last* for you' (the speaker then reports the complimentary remark by a third person). Sometimes also a somewhat uncomplimentary remark. **1948** *Amer. Sp.* XXIII. 301/1 A friend of seventy-odd tells me that she has known *trade last* in Kansas as far back as she can remember.

(10) **1912** WASON *Friar Tuck* xxiv, Either the pack-rat reformed into a trade-rat, or else he sold out his claim to a trade-rat. **1950** *Nat. Hist.* May 214/2 Wood rats are also known as trade rats because of their habit of stealing something and then leaving a stick or other worthless object in its place. — (11) **1881** *Rep. Indian Affairs* 30 Two other Indians of the tribe are preparing to open trade stores. — (12) **1865** *Atlantic Mo.* Jan. 83/1 Central Park . . . contains . . . four subways for the passage of trade-vehicles across the Park.

As the last term in **back, beaver, cattle, dry-goods, fall, forced, horse, Indian, jug, lumber, Mormon, notion, overland, package, skin, spring, Superintendent of Indian, truck, wagon trade.**

* **trade,** *v.*

1. *tr.* To obtain or dispose of by barter. Also with *away, for, off.*

1636 *Conn. Rec.* I. 1 Henry Stiles . . . had traded a piece . . . with the Indians for Corne. **1793** *Mass. H.S. Coll.* 1 Ser. III. 1 Their land . . . produces good crops of corn and rye, which they trade off for spirituous liquors. **1802** *Steele P.* 250, [I] have not traded the mare away yet. **1939** PINKERTON *Wilderness Wife* 162 Now he saw one already killed and at once offered to trade a large lake trout he had just landed for a haunch of meat.

2. a. *To trade in,* to give an automobile, radio, etc., as part payment for another, also **trading in. b.** *To trade out,* to take commodities to the amount of a sum due.

(a) **1927** *Observer* 21 Aug. 19/2 Americans . . . call him the 'junk' man because he buys what they call 'traded-in' cars for the purpose of scrapping them. *Ib.,* Dealers . . . who have taken old cars in part purchase of new ones, which is called trading-in. **1931** *Randolph Enterprise* (Elkins, W.Va.) 1 Jan. 3/6 The old pieces which you trade in will be new to the one who buys them. — (b) *c***1847** WHITCHER *Bedott P.* xi. 109, I make a practice o' lettin' on 'em *trade* it out.

* **trader,** *n.*

1. a. = **Negro trader.** *Obs.* **b.** A horse kept for trading. *Colloq.*

(a) **1724** in A. BENEZET *Caution to Gt. Britain* (1767) 22 Our Traders came on board to-day . . . so that to-morrow we expect slaves. **1852** STOWE *Uncle Tom* xi, The enlightened, cultivated, intelligent man . . . supports the system of which the trader is the inevitable result. **1869** TOURGEE *Toinette* (1881) 150 He hoped they would go into the hands of traders so that you might never see them again. — (b) **1902** MCFAUL *Ike Glidden* 66 All prosperous people there keep a 'driver' and a 'trader.'

2. a. **tradership,** the position or office of a trader or storekeeper on an Indian reservation. **b. trader's store,** = **trading post.**

(a) **1877** *Rep. Indian Affairs* 8 A very important subject for consideration is that of traderships. — (b) **1881** *Ib.* 41 The same was true with the trader's store.

As the last term in **country, fair, fall, free, fur, gopher, horse, independent, Indian, mountain, Negro, river, room, Santa Fe, skin, whisky, Yankee trader.**

* **trading,** *n.* and *a.* In combs.: (1) **trading boat,** a boat used in trading, esp. among Indians and frontiersmen; (2) **camp,** an encampment of traders; (3) **clerk,** one employed in trade among the Indians, *obs.;* (4) **depot,** a place where trade with the Indians is carried on; (5) **establishment,** = **trading house,** *obs.;* (6) **expedition,** a trip among Indians for purposes of trade, *obs.;* (7) **fort,** = **trading post;** (8) **girl,** (see quot.), *obs.;* (9) **house,** a house in which barter trade with the Indians is carried on; (10) **lodge,** the lodge of an Indian engaged in trading, *obs.;* (11) **party,** a party engaged in Indian trade; (12) **path,** a path or way used by those engaged in trade with the Indians, *obs.;* (13) **pit,** = * **pit,** *n.*[1] **1;** (14) **point,** a place where trade is carried on, cf. * **point,** *n.*[1] **8;** (15) **post,** a place where a trader or a group of traders carries on barter trade with the Indians; (16) **road,** a trading path *q.v.,* or a road often used by those engaged in trade; (17) **schooner,** a schooner used by traders; (18) **scow,** a scow used by traders along rivers; (19) **stamp,** (see quot. 1909); (20) **store,** a store at a trading post; (21) **wagon,** a wagon used by traders among the Indians, cf. **peddler's wagon.**

(1) **1738** W. STEPHENS *Proc. Georgia* I. 156 An Indian Trading Boat arrived. **1867** J. N. EDWARDS *Shelby* xx. 364 Marmaduke . . . hoped to capture a trading-boat and thus put a quietus on the cotton trade. — (2) **1821** J. FOWLER *Journal* 31 A great many trees appeer to Have been Cut down by White men and a french trading Camp Have been latly burned down. — (3) **1834** *Amer. R.R. Jrnl.* III. 587/3 Canadians resided in the capacity of trading clerks at the principal villages. — (4) **1907** C. C. ANDREWS *Recoll.* (1928) 121 Crow Wing had been . . . the principal trading-depot for all the Chippewas.

(5) **1804** LEWIS in *L. & Clark Exped.* VI. (1905) 55 The mountains, salines, trading establishments, and all the other remarkable places . . . are also laid down on this map. **1849** PARKMAN *Ore. Trail* 25 Westport, where he owns a trading establishment. — (6) **1791** W. BARTRAM *Travels* 227 In these large canoes they descend the river on trading and hunting expeditions. **1845** FRÉMONT *Exped.* 120 Solitary trading expeditions among the Indians. — (7) **1847** PARKMAN in *Knickerb.* XXX. 235 It was a little trading fort, belonging to two private traders. — (8) **1709** LAWSON *Carolina* 183 As for the Trading Girls, which are those design'd to get Money by their Natural Parts, these are discernable by the Cut of their Hair; their Tonsure differing from all others, of that Nation, who are not of their Profession; which Method is intended to prevent Mistakes. — (9) **1637** in *Mass. H.S. Coll.* 4 Ser. VI. 215 He came from a trading house which Plymouth men have at Qunnihticut. **1791** W. BARTRAM *Travels* 18, I sat off early in the morning for the Indian trading-house. **1902** WHITE *Conjuror's House* 38 The great trading-house attracted his attention, with its narrow picket lane leading to the door.

(10) **1850** GARRARD *Wah-To-Yah* ix. (1927) 115, I took my rifle, and, skirting the village, crossed to Williams Tharpe's trading lodges. — (11) **1837** IRVING *Bonneville* I. 66 He was on his way . . . with reinforcements and supplies for . . . trading parties beyond the mountains. — (12) **1775** ADAIR *Indians* 195 He accordingly pretended to have held for a long time a continual intercourse with their subterranean progenitors in a cave, above 600 miles to the westward of Charles-town in South-Carolina, adjoining to the old Chikkasah trading path. **1853** RAMSEY *Tennessee* 143 He returned with his furs, but left the main trading path and came up the Nottichucky Trace.— (13) **1903** *N.Y. Ev. Post* 25 Sep. 11 The offerings were small in all trading pits. — (14) **1873** *Newton Kansan* 3 April 3/2 The country people who make this their trading point ask [etc.]. **1899** H. B. CUSHMAN *Hist. Indians* 391 Mobile was then a small town and trading point of the Choctaws.

(15) **1796** HAWKINS *Letters* 15 The land . . . has been recommended . . . as proper for a trading post. **1860** GREELEY *Overland Journey* 194

There are . . . two or three trading-posts, somewhat frequented by Indians of the Snake tribe. **1950** *Nat. Hist.* Feb. 73/1 The settlement supports no trading post to dispense those outward manifestations of civilization that might tend to disrupt the fine balance of their tranquil existence. — **(16) 1791** BARTRAM *Travels* 54 This trading road runs nearly two miles through ancient Indian fields. **1905** VALENTINE *H. Sandwith* 107 Leaving Dunkirk they struck the great 'trading road' over which in spring and fall Conestoga wagons lumbered. — **(17) 1791** BARTRAM *Travels* 63 Our captain knew it to be the trading schooner from the stores on St. John's. *c***1856** *Kit Carson's Life* 17 At the Mission we found a trading schooner. — **(18) 1875** MARK TWAIN *Old Times on Miss.* 219 (R.), He ran over the steering-oar of a trading-scow. **1883** ——— *Life on Miss.* xxviii, We should have passed . . . occasional little trading-scows, peddling along from farm to farm, with the peddler's family on board. — **(19) 1898** *Kissimmee* (Fla.) *Valley Gaz.* 11 Feb. 1/4 A bill placing a privilege tax of $500 on trading stamp agencies . . . was vetoed by the governor. **1909** WEBSTER 2181/3 *Trading stamp*, a printed stamp, with a certain value, given as a premium by a dealer to a customer, and usable instead of money in procuring articles from the issuers of the stamps. **1947** PAUL *Linden* 389 Luke first thought of 'trading-stamps'; he had a Punch and Judy show in his children's book department; and a monkey who used a toothbrush in the drug department.

(20) 1902 S. E. WHITE *Conjuror's House* xii. 162 Once the voices moderated, when McDonald, the Chief trader, walked rapidly from the barracks building to the trading store. — **(21) 1848** PARKMAN in *Knickerb.* XXXI. 492 This functionary was a new acquisition, having lately come from Fort Pierre with the trading wagons.

As the last term in **fur, horse, Indian, short trading.**

traditionate trəˈdɪʃəˌnet, *v.* [f. **tradition*+ **-ate.*] *tr.* To indoctrinate or teach by tradition. Also **traditionated,** *a.*

The *OED* has one example, 1593, of this term and accordingly marks it rare and obs. The word was app. formed anew here.

1856 G. A. SMITH in *Jrnl. of Discourses* III. 282 (Th.), They have been traditionated to run over a great quantity of ground, and to not half cultivate it. **1862** YOUNG in *Ib.* IX. 193 Had we been brought up and traditionated to burn a wife upon the funeral pile, we should [do it]. **1924** F. S. HARRIS *Scientific Research* 12 He was so traditionated in the old theories and treatments that he did not finally abandon them until 1552.

* **traffic,** *n.* **1. traffic artery,** a road over which much traffic passes. (Cf. ***artery 2.**) **2. traffic cop,** a policeman who enforces laws regulating road and street traffic.

(1) 1927 *New Masses* June 7/4 In a side street, close to one of the main traffic arteries of the City of the Angels, hangs a sign which reads: 'Arcadia Dairy Lunch.' **1948** *Chi. Tribune* 1 April 1. 20/2 Chicago is already choking to death because of long failure to provide traffic arteries within the city. — **(2) 1915** *Chi. Herald* 18 Nov. 11/4 If a traffic cop bawls you out, you speak to him gently. **1943** DAMON *Sense of H.* 24 Samule and his Fanny surprise the traffic cop so much that he can't think of anything to say.

As the last term in **freight, local, through, way, whisky traffic.**

* **trail,** *n.*

1. A more or less permanent path or road made by the repeated passage of people or animals.

1807 GASS *Journal* 237 We went off the path or trail. **1846** THORPE *Myst. Backwoods* 84 In their wanderings about the prairies, they will leave trails, worn like a long-travelled road. **1907** *St. Nicholas* Oct. 1142/1 The mountains are honeycombed with trails which early prospectors and railroad builders have made. **1949** *Sky Line Trail* Oct. 18/1, I enjoyed ten camping trips on trails between South Kananaskis Pass and Red Deer River.

b. With a defining term, as **Arkansas, California, Ute trail.**

1847 PALMER *Rocky Mts.* 44 This day [13 Aug.] we traveled about eight miles, to Cassia creek; here the California trail turns off. **1849** PARKMAN in *Knickerb.* XXXIII. 111 The Pawnees and the Comanches began a regular series of hostilities on the Arkansas trail. **1858** in F. HALL *Hist. Colo.* II 519 [We] took the old Ute trail with cart and one yoke of cattle. **1860** GREELEY *Overland Journey* 22 The great California trail, like the Santa Fé and all other primitive roads through this prairie country, keeps along the highest 'divides.'

2. *W.* =**cattle trail.**

1880 *Cimarron News & Press* 17 June 1/4 Cow-boys . . . will immediately start some thirty thousand head on the trail. *c***1908** CANTON *Frontier Trails* 6 Our cattle were now well broken to the trail. **1934** *Rocky Mt. News* (Denver) 30 Jan. 9/4 Blazed by vaqueros who 'would charge hell with a bucket of water,' . . . the trail, like a shimmying snake, twisted over plains and mountains, thru canons, under boiling sun or biting blizzard.

3. In combs. of obvious meaning or sufficiently explained in the quots., as (1) **trail blazer,** (2) **boss,** (3) **broke(n),** (4) **camp,** (5) **car,** (6) **cattle,** (7) **crew,** (8) **crossing,** (9) **cutter,** (10) **drive,** (11) **driver,** (12) **drover,** (13) **herd,** (14) **herder,** (15) **hunter,** (16) **man,** (also **trailsman**), (17) **outfit,** (18) **rider,** (19) **rope,** (20) **steer,** (21) **waddy,** (22) **wagon,** (23) **work.**

(1) 1932 HARRY WILLIAMS *Legends Gt. Southwest* p. vii, At conventions of the Trail Drivers . . . and other places where those worthy trail blazers congregated. **1948** *Syracuse* (N.Y.) *Herald-Journal* 16 Oct. 9/1 Watt, in his role of trail blazer, had one great aid two years ago. — **(2) 1890** *Stock Grower & Farmer* 21 Jan. 6/3 Trail bosses bronzed from exposure . . . are familiar sights. **1943** DALE *Cow Country* 35 The trail boss usually rode ahead to survey the ground and search out watering places and good grazing grounds. — **(3) 1903** A. ADAMS *Log of Cowboy* 296 The cattle were well trail-broken. **1943** L. V. HAMNER *Short Grass* 50 In a few days the herd was 'trail broke.' — **(4) 1902** LONDON *Daughter of Snows* 137 This came about in a trail-camp on the way to Miller Creek.

(5) 1891 *Cent.* 6421/2 trail-car. . . . A street railway-car which is not furnished with motive power, but is designed to be pulled or trailed behind another to which the power is applied. — **(6) 1887** *Scribner's Mag.* II. 509/1 Common [cowboy] terms are . . . trail cattle, trail-cinch. — **(7) 1906** *McClure's Mag.* XXVI. 518 So he collected a trail crew, brought some Oregon cattle across [etc.]. — **(8) 1903** A. ADAMS *Log of Cowboy* 121 At this and lower trail crossings on Red River, the lives of more trail men were lost. — **(9) 1891** *Harper's Mag.* Nov. 884/1 There was little more than the trail-cutters' path to mark what had been determined as the 'right of way.' **1944** ADAMS *W. Words* 168/1 trail cutter A man employed, usually by stock associations, to halt marching herds and inspect them for cattle which did not properly belong with them.

(10) 1927 SIRINGO *Riata* 37 Wichita lost the trail drive through the 'fool hoe-man' settling up the cattle range to the westward. — **(11) 1931** DOBIE *Coronado's C.* 102 The last time I saw him, which was at a meeting of trail drivers in San Antonio, I asked him if oil-leasing was very lively down in his country. **1941** FERGUSSON *Southwest* 32 As a rule he started as a 'hand' and a trail driver. — **(12) 1903** A. ADAMS *Log of Cowboy* 121 This boundary river on the northern border of Texas was a terror to trail drovers. [**1942** DALE *Cow Country* 41 The first drovers who started north from Texas with herds of cattle knew comparatively little of trail driving and had neither an exact objective to be reached nor a definite trail to follow.] — **(13) 1885** *Wkly. New Mexican Rev.* 18 June 1/3 The trail herds in Colfax county must go forward or turn back at once. **1944** ADAMS *W. Words* 168 trail herd. A bunch of cattle, guarded day and night, being trailed from one region to another. A trail herd usually traveled in single file, or in twos, and threes, forming a long, sinuous line, which, if seen from above, would look like a huge serpent in slow motion. **1949** *Sat. Ev. Post* 14 May 40/1 [There was] bustling preparation for the latest trail herd. — **(14) 1890** *Stock Grower & Farmer* 19 April 3/3 Cattle inspectors of New Mexico were holding up trail herders for one and one-half cents per head.

(15) 1859 W. P. TOMLINSON *Kansas in 1858* 78 This scout . . . bore moreover the reputation of being one of the best trail-hunters in the Territory. — **(16) 1885** *Wkly. New Mexican Rev.* 5 March 2/3 Little hopes of driving cattle north or west this season are entertained by the trail men there. **1943** L. V. HAMNER *Short Grass* 51 He was a master trailsman. — **(17) 1893** ROOSEVELT *Wilderness Hunter* 419 The riders of a huge trail-outfit from Texas . . . abandoned themselves to a night of roaring and lethal carousal. **1942** DALE *Cow Country* 43 The making up of a herd for the drive north and the assembling of a trail outfit and a suitable crew of men was neither a short nor an easy task. — **(18) 1937** *Lit. Digest* 5 June 36/2 Dude wranglers . . . have to know the country and their horses to be of any service in guiding trail-riders on pack-trips through the mountains. **1947** *Nat. Geog. Mag.* June 745/1 My father . . . had given me . . . vivid impressions of . . . camp cooks, and 'Trail Riders.' — **(19) 1848** PARKMAN in *Knickerb.* XXXI. 3 A long trail-rope was wound round poor Pauline's neck. **1851** M. REID *Scalp Hunters* xviii, We ran our animals out on their trail-ropes to feed.

(20) 1927 SIRINGO *Riata* 24 It was against the rules to hog-tie a trail steer, as it caused stiffness in his legs. —**(21) 1923** J. H. COOK *On Old Frontier* 39 Mr. Roberts informed me that I was to be one of his trail waddies. — **(22) 1903** AUSTIN *Land of Little Rain* 17 You should hear Salty Williams tell how he used to drive eighteen and twenty-mule teams from the borax marsh to Mojave, ninety miles, with the trail wagon full of water barrels. **1944** ADAMS *W Words* 168/2 trail wagon One fastened behind another wagon in moving camp. — **(23) 1888** T. ROOSEVELT in *Cent. Mag.* April 849/2 More important than herding is 'trail' work; cattle, while driven from one range to another, or to a shipping point for beef, being said to be 'on the trail.'

b. trail bridge, a bridge sufficient for a horse to cross, a pole bridge (see also quot. 1909 and cf. **rope ferry**).

1909 WEBSTER, trail bridge. A ferry formed of a boat attached to a pulley running on a rope stretched across the stream, and moved from side to side by the action of the current. **1946** *Mazama* Dec. 23/1 We . . . crossed the Little Yoho river on a trail bridge.

c. *Trail of Tears*, (see quots.).

1930 FERBER *Cimarron* 40 Tears came to his own eyes when he spoke of that blot on southern civilization, the Trail of Tears, in which the Cherokees, a peaceful and home-loving Indian tribe, were torn [1838–39] from the land which a government had given them by sworn treaty, to be sent far away on a march which, from cold, hunger, exposure, and heartbreak, was marked by bleaching bones from Georgia to Oklahoma. **1948** *D. Oklahoman* (Okla. City) 16 May E. 31/1 The trail of tears, used during the Indian removal in 1830–40, ended at Eagletown near the state's biggest tree.

4. In colloq. phrases, chiefly western or orig. western: (1) *To take the trail (for)*, (*a*) to depart or set out for, (*b*) (see quot.); (2) *to camp on the trail of*, to follow persistently; (3) *to cut the trail (of)*, (*a*) to come upon, meet up with, (*b*) to block temporarily a cattle trail so as to inspect a trail herd using it, see **trail cutter,** quot. 1944; (4) *to hit the trail*, (*a*) to set out, depart, also fig., (*b*) short for "to hit the sawdust trail," cf. * **sawdust,** *n.* **1. b,** quot. 1913; (5) *to ride (on) trail*, see * **ride,** *v.* **4.** (3); (6) *to break trail*, to make a road or path through obstructions.

(1) (*a*) **1850** GARRARD *Wah-To-Yah* viii. 105 Well old Kurnel Price wanted some one to take the trail for the States on express. **1895** *Outing* XXVI. 452/1 My friend . . . decided to have some sport in the mountains before he took the long steel trail for New York. (*b*) **1944** JOHNSON *As I Dare* 201 The members of the congregation . . . pleading with them in whispers to take the trail—in other words, to go up and sit in a front pew and receive the much more pointed prayers of the minister. — **(2) 1882** BAILLIE-GROHMAN *Camps in Rockies* p. v, I shall have to ask him to camp, to use another Western expression, on the trails of all sorts of beasts and uncouth characters. **1895** *Outing* XXVI. 452/1 Had we followed out the first idea, and to use the Western phrase, 'camped on their trail,' we would doubtless have slept better. — **(3)** (*a*) **1883** *Terr. Rep. N. Mex.* (1884) 110, I learned that night of the killing of Judge McComas . . . intending to cut the trail of the Indians as they left the Burro mountains. **1925** OWEN P. WHITE *Them Was Days* 86 When we again 'cut his trail' we find him wearing the badge of a peace officer in . . . El Paso. (*b*) **1903** A. ADAMS *Log Cowboy* 90 If you have no authority to cut this trail, then you don't cut this herd. — **(4)** (*a*) **1897** *Outing* XXX. 374/1 Men can pass out the church door, shoulder their packs of general cussedness, and unconcernedly hit the trail to the lower [regions]. **1907** WHITE *Arizona Nights* 87 'Well,' says Larry, still laughin', 'I must hit the trail.' **1949** *Sat. Ev. Post* 9 July 37/1 Orders were to hit the trail as soon as possible. (*b*) **1913** *Lit. Digest* 15 March 576/2 'At least one saloonist hit the trail,' we are told.

(6) 1893 *Outing* Dec. 204/2 The Indians took turn about in 'breaking trail' in the soft, deep snow. **1904** WHITE *Silent Places* 181 The bending figure of the man breaking trail, his head low.

b. Also, often fig., in phrases of obvious meaning, as (1) *on the wrong trail*, (2) *off the trail*, (3) *to keep one on the trail*, (4) *on the opposite side of the trail*, (5) *to strike the trail of*, (6) *to strike the long trail*, (7) *on the* (or *one's*) *trail*, (8) *to make trail*.

(1) 1833 COKE *Subaltern's Furlough* xv, Though the Yankees are so notoriously inquisitive, . . . [I never felt] annoyed by their asking such prying questions, generally leading them 'considerably on the wrong trail,' as they would say. — **(2) 1834** CARUTHERS *Kentuckian* I. 23 You are off the trail for once in your life. — **(3) 1834** CARUTHERS *Kentuckian* I. 25 He couldn't keep me on the trail,—I was for ever slipping into Yankee Doodle. — **(4) 1844** LEE & FROST *Oregon* 97 Now the facts in the premises lie upon the opposite side of the '*trail*.'

(5) 1883 *Terr. Rep. N. Mex.* (1884) 112 Next morning [I] struck the trail of the Indians going south. — **(6) 1895** REMINGTON *Pony Tracks* 43 He 'struck the long trail to the kingdom come,' as the cowboys phrase it. — **(7) 1888** T. ROOSEVELT in *Cent. Mag.* April 849/2 Cattle, while driven from one range to another, or to a shipping point for beef . . . are said to be 'on the trail.' **1947** *Sat. Ev. Post* 8 March 117/3 He got away with it in 1920, but by 1926 the inflamed Drys were really on his trail. — **(8) 1894** *Harper's Mag.* Feb. 359/2 We 'make trail fast' for the Neuearachie ranch.

As the last term in **back, bear, Big Bend, broken, buffalo, by, car, cattle, Chisholm, cow, crew, crossing, cutter, drive, driver, drover, fire, foot, game, grass, gulch, herd, hog, horse, hunter, hunting, Indian, iron, lodge, lodgepole, moccasin, moose, Mormon, mule, mustang, open, Oregon, Osage hunting, outfit, pack, pole, rope, Santa Fe, Spanish, steer, sunset, Texas, waddy, wagon, war, work trail.**

* **trail,** *v.*

1. *tr.* (See quot.) *Rare.*

1828 WEBSTER, *Trail*, . . . in America, to tread down grass by walking through; to lay flat; as, to *trail* grass.

2. *intr.* To troll.

1857 TOMES *Amer. in Japan* 308 Another cluster of fishing-boats was . . . trailing for fish. *a***1862** THOREAU *Maine Woods* 176 My companion trailed for trout as we paddled along.

3. *W. tr.* To drive or send (livestock) over a trail, also with *through*.

1906 *N.Y. Ev. Post* 27 Oct. (Sat. Supp.) 1, I determined to have the sheep 'trailed through' to Nebraska, which, in Western parlance, means driving them overland. **1910** *Pacific Mo.* Feb. 143/1 Legally the sheepman trails where it pleases him. **1948** *Sierra Club Bul.* Feb. 14/2 The privilege of trailing cattle across the monument still exists as always.

4. *To trail in*, to come or go in. *Colloq.*

1875 *Fur, Fin & Feather* (ed. 3) 112/1 Light and drink; drop off and trail in. **1907** WHITE *Arizona Nights* 234 With exultant cackles of joy they'd trail in, reachin' out like quarter-horses.

T rail. A railway rail a section of which has the shape of a T, said to have been devised by Robert L. Stevens, president of the Camden and South Amboy Railroad in N.J. See **crosstie.**

1837 *Civil Engineer* I. 39/2 The pattern . . . is by American engineers called the inverted T rail. **1880** *Boston Soc. Nat. Hist. Mem.* 14 The edge is rendered stiff by its shape, which in section is much like that of a T-rail of a railroad. **1945** *Newsweek* 2 April 9 Stevens at the same time [*c*1830] designed the 'T' type rail used today by railroads all over world.

fig. **1883** *Cent. Mag.* Nov. 87 That is the sort of T-rail I am. That young gentleman voted agin me, on the ground I wasn't high-toned enough.

b. Also **T railroad iron,** iron used for T rails. *Obs.*

1845 *Xenia Torch-Light* 4 Dec. 1/4 The usual T railroad iron, as imported into this country under the present tariff, costs not less than $2,000 per mile for the duty.

* **trailer,** *n.*

1. One skilled in following a trail.

1855 SIMMS *Forayers* 252 He's the 'Trailer,' and a mighty good scout, but a great rascal. **1904** WHITE *Silent Places* 59 The expert trailers took pains to obliterate the most characteristic indications of their stay. **1915** YOUNG *Hard Knocks* 33 Sutherland . . . was a wonderful trailer, and by signs and foot prints, with which he was thoroughly accustomed, accomplished what to me seemed an utter impossibility.

transf. = * **roper 2.** *Slang.*

1890 DAVIS *Gallegher* 128 The 'trailer' for the green-goods men who rented room No. 8 in Case's tenement, had had no work to do for the last few days. **1891** QUINN *Fools of Fortune* 215 The other is what is technically known as a 'trailer,' whose duty it is to follow the 'sucker' wherever he goes, keeping him continually in sight and noting his every movement.

b. *W.* One who trails cattle (see * **trail,** *v.* **3.**) or journeys along a trail. Cf. **Oregon trailer.**

1912 DAWSON *Pioneer Tales* 102 Nebraska City early became quite an outfitting place for trailers. **1945** MARSHALL *Santa Fe* 13 The crack of bullwhips, the groan of wagon wheels, the prayers and shouts of the trailers were waking it slowly.

2. a. = **trail car. b.** (See quot.) **c.** In motion pictures a short film attached to the end of a long reel—hence the name—often to advertise a coming attraction.

(a) 1890 *Columbus* (O.) *Dispatch* 5 Aug., The line is to start with five motor cars for winter service, with some 'trailers' for excursion business. — **(b) 1891** *Cent.* 6421/2 *Trailer*, . . . an old style of vessel employed in mackerel-fishing about 1800 . . . [having] outriggers or long poles on each side, . . . to the ends of which were fastened lines. — **(c) 1929** *Variety* 17 April 31/5 Virtually every theatre is using trailers announcing the referendum conducted by the Times-Union and asking patrons to vote. **1948** *Dly. Ardmoreite* (Ardmore, Okla.) 5 May 6/2 The trailer for 'Miracle of the Bells,' with Frank Sinatra in his role as a priest, is playing in Los Angeles to mixed reactions.

3. A vehicle drawn behind another, often a small mobile house used by tourists. Cf. **b.** below.

1926 *K.C.* (Mo.) *Star* 11 June, On the Victory highway most any day now one may see the migratory harvesters—a few walking, others in old motor cars, and still more with their families in cars, and a trailer behind, carrying tents, bedding, and cooking utensils. **1949** *Desplaines Valley News* (Summit, Ill.) 28 Oct. 1/2 Two trailers carrying high test gas . . . caught fire . . . at Archer and Kean avenues in Willow Springs.

Also **trailer camp,** such a vehicle equipped for camping out.

1921 *Outing* April 39/2 (*advt.*), Union Trailer Camp.... Whether a week-end jaunt or a vacation tour, this outdoor palace makes it a real one.... Your car can draw it easily.

b. Designating places composed of or appealing to those, usu. tourists, who travel with or live in trailers.

1945 *Boulder* (Colo.) *D. Camera* 1 Nov. 8/4 A Message to Students Living in the University Trailer Village. *Ib.* 30 Nov. 3/3 Arrangements are being made... to feed all veterans from the trailer camp. **1947** *Dly. Oklahoman* (Okla. City) 21 Sep. D-6/1 The verdict may well point to a bust in the boom enjoyed this year by the nation's tourist camps, hotels, motels, trailer parks, cafes, inns and restaurants.

* **trailing,** *a.*

1. trailing arbutus, the mayflower or ground laurel, *Epigaea repens*, the state flower of Mass.

1785 MARSHALL *Amer. Grove* 42 Trailing Arbutus... grows naturally upon northern hills, or mountains. **1893** DANA *Wild Flowers* 173 Trailing Arbutus. Mayflower. Ground Laurel.... In New England they are called Mayflowers, being peddled about the streets of Boston every spring. **1950** *Nat. Hist.* April 174/1 He came to a large tract... covered with young jack pines and a low growth of sweet fern, blueberries, and trailing arbutus.

2. In colloq. names for various other plants, as **trailing clover, cockspur, evergreen, hemlock, honeysuckle, pine, willow,** (see quots.).

1840 DEWEY *Mass. Flowering Plants* 67 *L[espedeza] prostrata*. Trailing Clover. — **1784** *Amer. Acad. Mem.* I. 413 *Cuscuta*.... Trailing Cockspur.... Borders of brooks and ditches. — **1899** GOING *Flowers* 251 The lycopodiums... under the name of 'ground-pine,' 'club-moss,' or 'trailing-evergreen,' are familiar to almost every one who has summered in New England. — *Ib.* 269 Those cousins of the ferns which look so confusingly like evergreens... have received the names of 'ground-pine' and 'trailing-hemlock.' — **1833** EATON *Botany* (ed. 6) 48 *Azalea procumbens*, trailing honeysuckle. — **1878** COOKE *Happy Dodd* 347 A profusion of trailing pine had been stored away in the barn cellar, before frost came. — **1813** MUHLENBERG *Cat. Plants* 91 *Salix prostrata*, Trailing willow.

traill trel, *n.* [T. S. *Traill* (1781–1862), a British writer on scientific subjects.] **1.** =next. **2. Traill's flycatcher,** a flycatcher, *Empidonax traill*i, of western North America.

(1) **1891** *Cent.* 6421/2. **1892** TORREY *Foot-Path Way* 9 The phœbe-like cry of the traill was to be heard constantly from the hotel piazza. — (2) **1831** AUDUBON *Ornith. Biog.* I. 236 Traill's Fly-Catcher. *Muscicapa Traillii*.... This is a species... closely allied to the Wood Pewee. **1870** *Amer. Naturalist* IV. 539 Traill's Flycatcher... [is] a very restless, wild bird, remaining among the topmost branches of tall trees. **1941** LOFBERG *Sierra Outpost* 41 In mid-April came the specialists: sulphur-bellied flycatchers, Traill flycatchers, Western flycatchers.

* **train,** *n.* [In sense **1.** f. Can. F. *traîne*, a large sled. Cf. **dog train.**]

1. (See quot. 1848.) *Obs.*

1835 HOFFMAN *Winter in West* I. 178 At last a *train* and a couple of carioles drove up to the door. **1848** BARTLETT 362 *Train*,... a peculiar kind of sleigh used for the transportation of merchandise, wood, &c., in Canada.

2. In combs.: (1) **train agent,** =**baggage agent,** *rare;* (2) **air signal,** a signal device operated by air enabling the conductor of a train to communicate with the engineer; (3) ***boy,** (*a*) = ***butcher 2,** (*b*) (see quot.); (4) **butcher,** = ***butcher 2;** (5) **car,** (see quot.); (6) **conductor,** = ***conductor 3;** (7) **dispatcher,** a railroad official who issues orders controlling the movement of trains; (8) **gambler,** a gambler who rides trains in search of victims, *rare;* (9) **holdup,** the act on the part of criminals of stopping a train and robbing it or its passengers; (10) **man,** a man employed on a railway train; (11) **master,** (*a*) the man in general charge of a wagon train, now *hist.*, (*b*) a railroad official in charge of train operations on a division or subdivision of a line; (12) **robber,** one who robs trains or their passengers; (13) **shed,** that part of a railway station extending over the tracks, also a structure to protect trains from the weather; (14) **starter,** a railroad employee who gives the signal for trains to start; (15) **way,** (see quot.).

(1) **1879** STOCKTON *Rudder Grange* vii, The train-agent... began to declare that he would not have the fellow in his car. — (2) **1898** *Boston & Maine R.R. Ann. Rep.* 10 (Ernst), All the Company's passenger cars and passenger locomotives have been equipped with the train air signal. — (3) (*a*) **1869** *Atlantic Mo.* July 73/2 [He] prevailed upon me to be his train-boy. **1899** MUIRHEAD *Baedeker's U.S.* p. xx, The incessant visitation of the train-boy... renders a quiet nap almost impossible. (*b*) **1883** GRESLEY *Gloss. Coal-mining*, *Trainboy*, a boy who rides upon the *train*, to attend to the rope attachments, etc. — (4) **1903** ADE *In Babel* 347 Don't buy nothin' of the train butcher.

(5) **1895** WAIT *Car-Builder's Dict.* 22 Caboose-car.... A car attached to the rear of all freight trains, for the accommodation of the conductor and trainmen, and for carrying the various stores, tools, etc., required on freight trains. Also, but rarely, called *conductor's car* or *train-car*. — (6) **1849** *Hunt's Merch. Mag.* XX. 656 State... the annual amount paid out for... train conductors, baggage and brakeman. **1894** WISTER in *Harper's Mag.* Aug. 386/2 The train conductor, the Pullman conductor, the engineer, and fireman abandoned their duty. — (7) **1857** *Mich. Gen. Statutes* I. (1882) 863 No person shall be employed as an engineer, train dispatcher, fireman... or other servant upon any railroad... who uses intoxicating drinks as a beverage. **1949** *Chi. D. News* 8 Aug. 5/1 A train dispatcher with 500 passengers on a single train may have only 20 seconds at his disposal. — (8) **1896** FREDERIC *Damnation of T. Ware* 265 The money that bought the vote was put up by the smartest and most famous train-gambler between Omaha and 'Frisco. — (9) **1907** WHITE *Arizona Nights* 89 He was killed finally in the train hold-up of '97.

(10) **1877** MCCABE *Hist. Great Riots* 48 These motives have been misunderstood, and in a great degree produced the present troubles amongst our trainmen. **1948** *Chi. D. News* 17 Aug. 1/3 Passengers and trainmen agreed that the train was running rather slowly. — (11) (*a*) **1859** *Kansas in 1858* 22 The Spaniards gazed stupidly at me from beneath their broad hats, but the train-master proved to be an American. **1890** LANGFORD *Vigilante Days* (1912) 352 'We have none to spare,' said the train master. (*b*) **1880** *Cimarron News & Press* 9 Sep. 3/2 Mr. Frank Fulton, train master on this Division,... gave the following information concerning the damage. **1949** *Harvard Alumni Bul.* 24 Sep. 34 He was appointed assistant trainmaster. — (12) **1887** *Courier-Journal* 21 Jan. 9/6 A Crank or a Train-robber? **1948** *U-High Midway* (Chi.) 17 May 1/1 Everybody is to look as much like a cowboy or trainrobber as possible when they come to the party around the bonfire in Jackson Field on May 21. — (13) **1892** *Pall Mall Gaz.* 21 Nov. 7/3 The great iron and glass portal [in Phila.]... will constitute the most extensive railway train-shed in existence. **1948** *Time* 12 Jan. 20/1 In the echoing train shed.... Driver Ambrose Grant climbed into the cab of locomotive *Number 5508*. — (14) **1925** *Scribner's Mag.* Oct. 372/1 The Secretary, important as a train-starter, sat at a table.

(15) **1877** KNIGHT, *Train-way*, a hinged platform which forms a bridge leading from a wharf to the deck of a ferry boat.

As the last term in **accommodation, bobtail, bull, car, cattle, coal, construction, dog, elevated, emigrant, emigration, extra fare, freight, fruit, gospel, government, gravel, gravy, huckleberry, immigrant, lightning, lightning express, limited, local, local accommodation, log, mail, material, meat, merchant's, milk, mixed, Mormon trading, mule, observation, oil, overland, owl, ox, pack, palace, provision, Pullman, saddle, scoot, service, shuttle, silk, sleeper, solid, steamboat, stock, tank, through, transportation, wagon, way, wild, wood, work, wrecking train.**

* **train,** *v.* **1.** *intr.* To associate *with* (or *along of*). *Colloq.* **2.** *N. Eng.* To romp or "carry on."

(1) **1871** HAY *Pike Co. Ballads* 22 It gravels me like the devil to train Along o' sich fools as you. **1907** *Methodist Rev.* Nov. 984 He does not train with the extreme radical theologians. — (2) **1877** BARTLETT 717 Almost peculiar to girls in New England. 'She's an awful one to train.' **1889** HOWELLS *Hazard of New Fortunes* I. 205 Oh, I guess you love to train!

* **trainer,** *n.* A member of a gun crew who keeps the gun trained on its target. — **1904** *Scientific Amer.* 18 June 475/1 The turrets are trained by one man, the trainer.

* **training,** *n.* In combs.: (1) **training camp,** a place where athletes, athletic teams, or soldiers train; (2) **field,** a field or open area where militiamen train, *obs.;* (3) **lot,** =prec., *obs.;* (4) **table,** the table at which members of an athletic team eat while in training.

(1) **1913** LONDON *Valley of Moon* 405 They would... rub each other down in training camp style. **1948** *Green Bay* (Wis.) *Press-Gaz.* 30 June 22/1 The tract which comprises Fort Knox was purchased by the United States government in 1917 for a World War I training camp. — (2) **1670** *Charlestown Land Rec.* 187 From Shepie into the Training field, the way is Eleven foot. **1713** *Duxbury Rec.* 219 He will grant as much of his land to the town of Duxbury... to be a perpetual common for a training field &c. **1800** *Mass. H.S. Coll.* 1 Ser. VI. 235 They assigned as a training field, what is now called the Common. — (3) *c*1880 HAZARD *Jonny-Cake P.* (1915) 179–80 Wm. Carter was hanged for the murder of Jackson about the year 1742, on

a little mound in the training lot (so called) [in Rhode Island]. — (4) **1893** POST *Harvard Stories* 260 He hardly talks at all at the training table. **1903** ADE *People You Know* 59 We keep about 40 at the Training Table all of the time.

trampage ˈtræmpɪdʒ, *n.* The habit or condition of a tramp, tramping. — **1894** *Advance* 3 May, A menace, a nuisance all along the line of their trampage. **1897** *Plantation Missionary* (Oberlin, O.) Dec., The poor [may be] rescued from pauperism, trampage and crime.

trampdom ˈtræmpdəm, *n.* The state or condition of a tramp or tramps, the domain of tramps. — **1895** *Cent. Mag.* Oct. 945/1 The love of liquor brings more men and women into trampdom than anything else. **1896** *Atlantic Mo.* Jan. 61/2, I know of no sadder sight than this in all trampdom.

tramphood ˈtræmphʊd, *n.* The state of being a tramp. *Rare.* — **1904** O. HENRY *Heart of West* ix. 132 Fifteen years of tramphood . . . had hardened the fibres of his spirit.

* **tramway,** *n. Mining.* A system of transportation consisting essentially of a cable or cables from which cars are suspended. — **1870** *Overland Mo.* Dec. 516/2 The ore extracted from the Brown is brought down on an aerial tramway. **1871** RAYMOND *3d. Rep. Mines* 318 All the ore will be sent to the base of the mountain by the tramway.

* **trans-,** *prefix.*

1. In substantival formations: (1) **trans-Alleghenian,** one living west of the Allegheny Mountains; (2) **fusionist,** one who believes in or practices blood transfusion; (3) **Mississippi,** the region beyond the Mississippi as viewed from the eastern states; (4) **Mississippian,** one who lives west of the Mississippi River; (5) **planter,** (see quots.).

(1) **1774** J. ADAMS *Diary* Wks. II. 401, I went to the Baptist Church, and heard a trans-Alleghanian, a preacher from the back parts of Virginia. **1794** JEFFERSON *Writings* VI. (1895) 516 Make friends with the trans-Alleganians. — (2) **1889** *Pop. Sci. Mo.* April 808 The early transfusionists reasoned . . . that the blood is the life. — (3) **1883** *Cent. Mag.* Nov. 142/1 If the President was to attempt to reach the Trans-Mississippi at all, . . . he should move on at once. **1949** BEEBE & CLEGG *U.S. West* 10 Anyone approaching the *matière* of the trans-Mississippi in the nineteenth century as an exploiter of new material is either deluded or an imposter. — (4) **1898** *Cent. Mag.* Oct. 844/2 The trans-Mississippians have entered upon no line of rural industry with a more intelligent determination to make it a great success than upon dairying.

(5) **1828** WEBSTER, *Transplanter*, . . . a machine for transplanting trees. **1909** *Cent. Supp.* 1370/1 *Transplanter*, a horse-power machine used in setting out tobacco or other field plants.

2. In adjectival formations: (1) **trans-Alleghenian,** situated west of the Allegheny Mountains; (2) **Allegheny,** situated in or pertaining to the region west of the Allegheny Mountains; (3) * **Atlantic,** coming from, situated in, or pertaining to a region beyond the Atlantic as viewed from the U.S.; (4) **continental,** extending or passing across a continent, also fig.; (5) **isthmian,** crossing or extending across an isthmus, esp. the isthmus of Panama; (6) **Mississippian,** denoting the region west of the Mississippi River; (7) **Missouri,** lying, extending, or operating west of the Missouri River; (8) **Sierran,** denoting a road across the Sierra Nevada Mountains; (9) **state,** designating a road that crosses several states.

(1) **1814** *Ann. 13th Cong.* 1 Sess. 1422 Even then the trans-Alleganean wilderness was rustling with the preparation of the savage. **1826** MITCHILL *Discourse on Jefferson* 25 The order of an intendant [at New Orleans] had . . . thrown our citizens inhabiting the trans-alleghanian lands into serious alarm. — (2) **1825** in *Amer. Sp.* XXI. (1946) 306/2 Why should the trans-Allegany States have remained united with those on the Atlantic, when the mountains rendered all profitable intercourse between them impracticable? **1873** *Harper's Mag.* March 572/2 The subdivision adopted in the revision of the Constitution of Virginia in 1829–30 into the Trans-Alleghany, Valley, Middle, and Tide-water districts proved a fertile source of discontent. **1950** *Pacific Discovery* March–April 20/1 The buffalo along the eastern seaboard vanished in the trans-Allegheny migration as settlements sprang up after the American Revolution. — (3) **1782** JEFFERSON *Writings* III. (1894) 193 To suggest a doubt . . . whether nature has enlisted herself as a cis- or trans-Atlantic partisan. **1891** *Harper's Wkly.* 19 Sep. 705/1 The aristocrats of Salem were proud of their transatlantic ancestries. **1950** *Chi. Tribune* 29 April 9/7 He popped the question 13 months ago in one of the first trans-Atlantic telephone calls completed between Austria and the United States. — (4) **1853** *Harper's Mag.* Feb. 550/2 A company, embracing the wealthiest of New York capitalists [was proposed], to construct a trans-continental railroad. **1889** MARK TWAIN *Conn. Yankee* 279 She pulled out . . . and got her train fairly started on one of those horizonless transcontinental sentences of hers. **1944** KAHN *Cable Car Days* 77 Chinese immigrants who contributed by their hard labor to the mining of gold and silver, the building of the transcontinental railroads.

(5) **1885** CLEVELAND in *Pres. Mess. & P.* VIII. 328 The construction of three transcontinental lines of railway . . . has been accompanied by results . . . [which] increase our interests in any transisthmian route which may be opened. **1899** *Boston Jrnl.* 28 Nov. 4/1 Senator Frye's long and earnest advocacy of an American transisthmian canal is now very near its fulfillment. — (6) **1831** WILSON *Ornithology* IV. 31 In the trans-Mississippian territories of the United States, the burrowing owl resides. **1867** *Amer. Naturalist* I. 394 They are known in the vernacular as 'Kangaroo' or 'Jumping' Rats and Mice, and are entirely confined to Transmississippian regions. — (7) **1879** WILLIAMS *Pacific Tourist* 24/1 Many scientists who are familiar with the circumstances attending the rapid development of the trans-Missouri plains . . . assert that this vast region of country is gradually undergoing important climatic changes. **1903** E. JOHNSON *Railway Transportation* 244 Agreements [were] entered into . . . by the roads which formed the Trans-Missouri Freight Association. — (8) **1935** BUCKBEE *Saga Old Tuolumne* 385 In spite of neglect the road survived until the State of California came to look with favor upon its possibilities as a tran-Sierran [*sic*] road. **1950** *Pacific Discovery* March–April 4/1 Did you know that a trans-Sierran highway is now being built in Madera County? — (9) **1917** *Outlook* 23 April 740/1 It is becoming of greater interest to the people of the crowded East that the trans-State roads in Montana, Wyoming and Nevada be improved than it possibly is to the inhabitants of those States themselves.

3. In obs. verbal expressions: **transboard, transboat,** to transfer from one ship or boat to another.

1807 BARLOW *Columbiad* 38 Barks after barks the captured seamen bear, Transboard and lodge thy silent visitors there. **1838** F. HALL *Lett.* (1840) 104 It must be a place of business—and important depot for the commodities, which pass through this channel, from the one part of the State to the opposite, for they must all here be *transboated.* **1899** *Scribner's Mag.* July 69/1 The boat . . . is equipped with spacious mail-rooms, chutes for transboarding sacks [etc.].

* **transcendentalism,** *n.* The teaching or philosophy of Emerson and others who regarded the interrogation of the subjective consciousness as the best approach to the study of objective realities. Now *hist.*

1827 EMERSON in *N. Eng. Quart.* II. (1929) 252 Transcendentalism. Metaphysics and Ethics look inwards—and France produces Mad. de Staël; England, Wordsworth; America, Sampson Reed. **1841** *Niles' Reg.* LX. 240/3 Transcendentalism is making quite a sensation in some places. **1887** CABOT *Memoirs Emerson* I. 248 The Boston or New England Transcendentalism had, . . . no very direct connection with the transcendental philosophy of Germany. **1950** *Harvard Alumni Bul.* 8 April 540/1 Any beginner in philosophy can tell you what is wrong with transcendentalism.

* **transcendentalist,** *n.* An adherent of the transcendentalism of Emerson and his followers. Now *hist.*

1838 LONGFELLOW in S. Longfellow *H. W. Longfellow* I. 306 He is something of a Transcendentalist, and a friend of Emerson. **1843** *N.Y. Wkly. Tribune* 11 Feb. 2/5 Mr. Emerson is known, here and elsewhere, as a 'transcendentalist,' deeply imbued with the philosophy of the school thus denominated. **1893** *Harper's Mag.* May 849/1 Lowell shared in the efforts of the Transcendentalists to enlarge the bounds of spiritual freedom. **1950** *Harvard Alumni Bul.* 8 April 540/1 The reasons for Emerson's current lack of favor are understandable. He was a transcendentalist.

* **transfer,** *n.*

1. *ellipt.* = **transfer tobacco.** *Obs.*

1800 TATHAM *Tobacco* 80 All under that weight are considered to be *transfer*, or parcels which may be transferred to make full hogsheads.

2. A ferry boat for trains. In full **transfer boat.** *Obs.*

1882 *Uncle Rufus & Ma* 52 We ferried over in a transfer-boat, and in due time arrived at the Town of Mandan, D.T. **1883** RITTENHOUSE *Maud* 187 It was a delightful trip—the sun was just coming up as we crossed the river on the transfer. **1888** *Daily News* (London) 10 Dec. 6/8 The transfer boat Maryland was conveying a section of a train from Washington to Boston across the Haarlem River, at midnight.

3. *ellipt.* = **transfer ticket.**

1892 S. HALE *Letters* 269, I mounted a cable, took a transfer [etc.]. **1949** *Chi. Tribune* 1 Sep. III. 6/1 The CTA regards transfers as white paper money, which explains the care with which it prints, stores, and distributes them.

4. A certificate enabling a pupil to transfer from one school to another.

1911 PERSONS *Mass. Labor Laws* 199 He presented a transfer from the East Boston parochial school.

5. In special combs.: (1) **transfer company,** a draying company, esp. one that transfers passengers, trunks, etc., to and from railway stations; (2) **man,** a man who transfers baggage from one place to another; (3) **note,** a note serviceable in commercial transactions, issued to a tobacco planter for tobacco deposited in a warehouse, *obs.;* (4) **ticket,** a ticket given with or without extra cost to a passenger on a streetcar or other medium of transportation, entitling him to change to another conveyance and continue his journey on another route; (5) **tobacco,** (see quot. 1800), *obs.*

(1) **1879** WILLIAMS *Pacific Tourist* 262/1 The Transfer Company will carry baggage alone for 50 cents. **1948** *Dly. Ardmoreite* (Ardmore, Okla.) 12 May 3/5 A 58-year-old transfer company employe was killed here yesterday when a crate of plate glass fell from a truck fracturing his skull. — (2) **1899** ADE *Fables in Slang* 188 He would be arranging for her Baggage with the Transfer Man. **1911** *Masses* Jan. 14/3 Some five thousand of their drivers, transfer men, schedule men and helpers in New York and Jersey City went on strike this fall. — (3) **1748** *Md. Gazette* 23 Nov., He will . . . furnish each Inspection in the respective counties with Transfer Notes. **1784** SMYTH *Tour* II. 138 The last [bad tobacco] is immediately committed to the flames, and for the first [good tobacco] he receives a Transfer note, specifying the weight, quality, &c. — (4) **1861** *Mass. Acts & Resolves* 521 The city of Boston . . . shall establish the terms and conditions on which commutation, transfer, or exchange tickets shall be issued. **1900** *Everybody's Mag.* II. 192/1 The object of the remarkable transfer ticket of which we give a photograph is the proper identification of the holder, to prevent the abuse of the transfer privilege.

(5) **1740** *Va. State P.* 234 The said Anderson is very much Involved in debt, and . . . the Transfer Tobacco will be subject to the Discharge thereof. **1800** TATHAM *Tobacco* 84 *Transfer* tobacco is that collection in leaf, bundle, or hand, which arises from the aggregate stock of remnants which remain from hogsheads that are reduced by wastage and refusal beneath the standard weight of . . . what is commonly termed, a *crop,* hogshead.

b. Designating a check or draft drawn by the Secretary of the Treasury at the time of the removal of public funds to state banks by President Jackson. *Obs.*

1834 C. A. DAVIS *Lett. J. Downing* 213 The game they had been playin most at latterly was . . . showing how to use the *'transfer checks'* and *'contingent drafts,'* so as to puzzle folks in time and need. **1834** BENTON *30 Years' View* I. 409/1 The difference between a transfer draft and a treasury warrant was a thing necessary to be known by every man.

c. Designating vehicles used in transferring passengers and goods to and from railway stations.

1870 MEDBERY *Men Wall St.* 167 [In] theatrical and operatic magnificences, in ferry-boats and transfer-coaches, . . . Mr. Fisk has obtained a splendor of reputation which will make him forever memorable. **1892** GUNTER *Miss Dividends* 48 He almost misses the last transfer omnibus. **1909** *Forward* (Phila.) 2 Oct. 317 In the place stood a depot hack with an omnibus behind, and a transfer wagon on the other side.

* **transient,** *n.*

1. One who passes through a place, or stays at a hotel or boardinghouse for a short time only.

1748 in EARLE *Curious Punishments* 41 The officer shall take the said transient forth-with to some publick place in this town and . . . whyp him twenty strypes well layd on his naked back. **1880** ROLLINS *N. Eng. Bygones* 60 Sudden showers brought over willing neighbors and now and then a traveller would stop a day or two to lend a helping hand. My grandmother held these 'transients' in low esteem. **1948** *Chi. D. News* 13 Jan. 12/7 The hayseed jaypees work in the South exclusively for Yankee transients.

2. A steamboat not belonging to a regular line or not having a fixed route.

[**1841** in ALBION *Square-Riggers* (1938) 261 Our packet ships will continue to receive their share of the traveling community, so long as they continue to run regularly. But if they make themselves 'transient' they must lose thereby ultimately.] **1893** MARK TWAIN *P. Wilson* i, The big Orleans lines stopped for hails only or to land passengers or freight; and this was the case also with the great flotilla of transients.

* **transient,** *a.*

1. Of a guest at a hotel or boardinghouse: Staying for a short time.

1818 FEARON *Sketches* 44 Boarding at a moderately respectable house is 8 dollars a week, for what is termed 'a transient man.' **1887** WARNER *Their Pilgrimage* vi, Occasionally transient guests appear with flash manners. **1949** *D. Oklahoman* (Okla. City) 13 Feb. D. 6/2 The feed bill for transient, four-footed guests at the 'hotel' is around $5,000 to $6,000 a day.

b. Designated or designed for those wishing hotel accommodations for a brief period.

1884 CRADDOCK *Where Battle Was Fought* 70 The 'elevator boy' knew the number of Estwicke's room on the transient floor. **1891** *Fur, Fin & Feather* 185/1 The transient rate for travelers at the Hilsabeck Hotel in Springfield is $1 a day. **1903** *N.Y. Ev. Post* 19 Oct. 3 Charles F. Rogers will build a 12-story transient hotel.

2. Of newspapers or other printed matter: Not mailed regularly or in quantities, as by the publishers, but occasionally and individually.

1841 *Lowell Offering* I. 245 The clerk asked her if it was a transient paper. **1857** *Harper's Mag.* Feb. 403/1 The prepayment of postage on transient printed matter has been made compulsory.

b. transient advertisement, a newspaper advertisement that appears for a short time only. Also **transient advertiser, advertising.**

1831 *Boston Transcript* 18 April 2/3 In the observance of this regulation, we shall use all patrons alike, whether they are annual or transient advertisers. **1857** *Lawrence* (Kans.) *Republican* 4 June 1 All transient advertisements must be paid for in advance. **1868** *Ore. State Jrnl.* 8 June 1/1 Transient Advertising. For first insertion, three Dollars per square. **1904** *Friends' Intelligencer* (Phila.) 15 Oct. p. ii, For transient advertisements, 5 cents per line. For longer insertion reduced rate.

Transition zone. One of the biogeographical zones into which North America is divided on the basis of principles worked out by Clinton Hart Merriam (1855–1942), an American biologist. — **1907** MEARNS *Mammals Mex. Boundary* 135 This station lies in the Transition Zone, the highest peaks extending well into the Canadian or lowest section of the Boreal Zone. **1948** *So. Sierran* March 2/2 The Upper Sonoran zone . . . extends from the mountain base to the beginning of the Transition zone of the conifers.

transmission line. A line consisting of insulated cables along which electricity is conveyed. — **1901** *World's Work* May 743/2 When the Niagara transmission line was built, it was thought that its chief office would be the supplying of electric light to Buffalo. **1949** *Ill. State Reg.* 1 Feb. 6/2 As a result the primary line came into contact with and shorted a transmission line carrying 23,000 volts.

* **transom,** *n.* **1.** A seat at the side of a cabin or stateroom aboard a ship. **2.** A window above a door.

(1) **1851** MELVILLE *Moby Dick* 88 To my astonishment, he sat down again on the transom very quietly. **1883** CRAWFORD *Dr. Claudius* ix, He sat down on the transom. — (2) **1880** HEALY *Lett. & Leaders* I. 141 Get a step ladder to reach over the 'transom.' **1932** *Atlantic Mo.* CXLIX. 600 One will often need . . . a small can of thick black paint to smear over the transom to keep the hall light out.

* **transpire,** *v. intr.* To occur or happen. — **1775** A. ADAMS *Familiar Lett.* 91 There is nothing new transpired since I wrote you last. **1871** BURROUGHS *Wake-Robin* (1886) 75 On a bank of club-moss . . . I recline to note what transpires. **1948** GILBRETH *Cheaper by the Doz.* 228 Ern's sheik was so interested in what seemed about to transpire in her bedroom that he didn't notice us at first.

* **transportation,** *n.*

1. Means of conveyance, also the cost or expense of this.

1853 MCCONNEL *Western Char.* 163 He furnished his own 'transportation,' and selected his own encampment. **1890** *Wis. Hist. Soc. Prospectus,* Upon any gift to the Society, transportation will be cheerfully paid. **1894** *Outing* XXIV. 234/2 Transportation is furnished for the horses of mounted officers.

b. (See quot.)

1909 *Cent. Supp.* 1370/2 *Transportation,* . . . railway tickets or other permits for travelling.

2. In combs. that designate persons, things, etc., having to do with conveying persons or things from one place to another, as **transportation agent, car, interests, master, train, wagon.**

1825 in MCKENNEY *Memoirs* I. 299 About nine years ago, I was appointed transportation agent for the United States at St. Louis. — **1883** GOODE *Fishery Industries U.S.* 67 The construction of refrigerating transportation cars, . . . are forms of activity only attainable by government aid. — **1905** *N.Y. Ev. Post* 25 Jan. 7 If the transportation interests can induce Mr. Roosevelt to withdraw his idea of an extra session, the victory will be with them. — **1887** GEORGE *40 Years on Rail* 56 Dunlap was assistant superintendent, or what was then called transportation-master. — **1862** *Harper's Mag.* Sep. 561/2 On Monday, the 30th, the last of our army, with the transportation train, crossed the White Oak swamp. — **1819** QUITMAN in Claiborne *Life Quitman* I. 36, I went to the agent of a train of transportation-wagons.

***trap,** *n.*

1. =**trap net.**

1888 GOODE *Amer. Fishes* 216 The Tunny is taken in large nets, . . . similar in many respects to the so-called 'traps' of Seconnet River in Rhode Island. **1911** *Rep. Fisheries 1908* 315 Sea Bass . . . are caught with hand lines, and in pounds and traps.

2. *pl. Music.* A group of percussion instruments.

1920 SANDBURG *Smoke & Steel* 63 You jazzmen, bang . . . drums, traps, banjoes.

3. In combs.: (1) **trap dialect,** trappers' jargon or speech, *obs.;* (2) **drummer,** a musician who plays a set of traps, cf. sense **2.** above; (3) **fishing,** fishing by means of a line of baited hooks sunk in the water and anchored in place; (4) **hook,** (see quot.), *rare;* (5) **land,** ?land upon which trapping is carried on, *obs.;* (6) **line,** see as a main entry; (7) **log,** (see quot.), *obs.;* (8) **net,** (see quot. 1876); (9) **piles,** piling for use in making fish traps; (10) ***tree,** (see quot.); (11) **weir,** (see quot.).

(1) **1850** COLTON *Deck & Port* 392 They looked at our frowning battery with a wonder for which their trap dialect had no expression. — (2) **1903** *Medical Rec.* 14 Feb. 268/1 Trap drummer's neurosis. . . . The man's occupation was to beat a drum by the operation of a pedal which is manipulated with the right foot, while with his hands he plays the other drum, triangle, and the various traps. — (3) **1877** BARTLETT 718 Trap-Fishing . . . is now much practised on our coast. — (4) **1883** *Cent. Mag.* April 899, I discard all trap-hooks, infernal machines working with springs, as only adapted for the capture of land animals.

(5) **1751** in *Amer. Sp.* XV. 405/1 A Tract containing 1000 Acres, lying . . . on the South Side by Mr. Gibson's Trap Land. — (7) **1843** *Amer. Pioneer* II. 445 The trap logs [of a log cabin] are those of unequal length above the eave bearers, which form the gable ends, and upon which the ribs rest. — (8) **1865** *Mich. Acts* 717 The size of the meshes of all the . . . trap nets, used in the waters of this State, . . . shall not be less than five inches in extension, knot to knot. **1876** KNIGHT 2617/1 *Trap-net,* a fishing-net in which a funnel-shaped piece leads the fish into a pound from which extrication is not easy. — (9) **1910** *Haines* (Alaska) *Pioneer Press* 18 March 3/3 [He] was in Haines last Saturday making arrangements to get trap piles for the Columbia Canning company.

(10) **1905** *Forestry Bureau Bul.* No. 61, 25 *Trap tree,* a tree deadened or felled at a time when destructive bark beetles will . . . enter the bark. . . . The bark is peeled and exposed to the sun, burned or buried, . . . to destroy the insect. — (11) **1891** *Cent.* 6443/2 *Trap-weir,* a trap-net.

As the last term in **bear, beaver, box, clam, dandy, death, falling, fish, goose, gopher, land, log, mash, muskrat, painter, partridge, pen, quail, skunk, soul, wolf trap.**

***trap,** *v.*

1. *intr.* To practice catching wild animals in traps for their furs.

1806 ORDWAY in *Journals of Lewis & O.* 391 Three frenchmen . . . have been trapping as high as the river Roshjone. **1832** WYETH *Journal* 171 Crossed by fording to the other side of the river intending to . . . trap up three streams. **1916** EASTMAN *From Deep Woods* 57 My immediate kindred hunted all kinds of game, and trapped and fished as well. **1947** *Harper's Mag.* Jan. 67/1 As a boy he trapped along Indian Creek and Ghost Creek and Jurdon Creek.

2. *tr.* To clear or partially clear (a river, region, etc.) of animals by catching them in traps.

1833 PATTIE *Personal Narr.* 142 We set 40 traps, and . . . caught 36 beavers. . . . We concluded . . . to travel slowly, and in hunters phrase, trap the river clear; that is, take all that could be allured to come to the bait. **1847** *Santa Fe Repub.* 20 Nov. 2/4 Mr. Kirker . . . remained for a period of eight years, trapping the Rio Gila every winter.

3. *Baseball.* To catch (a ball) immediately after it has hit the ground.

1892 *Chi. Herald* 16 May (E. J. Nichols). **1912** MATHEWSON *Pitching* 181 A Boston batter tapped one to Merkle which I thought he trapped. **1949** PARKE CUMMINGS *Dict. Sports* 472/2 Sometimes an outfielder deliberately traps a ball he could catch on the fly in order to force a runner who has held his base fearing a caught fly.

4. *To trap a squaw,* of a man, to get married. *Jocular.*

1848 RUXTON *Life Far West* i, Many's the time I've said I'd strike for Taos, and trap a squaw. **1946** *This Week Mag.* 8 June 10/2 I've trapped a squaw.

trapiche tra'pitʃe, *n. S.W.* [Sp. in Amer. Sp. sense shown here.] (See quot.) *Obs.* — **1851** *S.F. Picayune* 24 Nov. 2/3 Their machinery consists of a very large roller or wheel, weighing ten tons, which rolls over the quartz. This crusher is called a *trapicha.*

trap line. a. ?A line used in trap fishing. *Obs.* **b.** The filament in a spider web that ensnares the prey. **c.** The route along which traps are set in trapping.

(a) **1647** *Conn. Rec.* I. 478 Goods att Totokett of the sd Tho: Fenners . . . 11 traplines. — (b) **1889** McCOOK *Amer. Spiders* I. 134 The trapline of the Labyrinth spider differs . . . in being composed of several threads instead of a single line. **1907** *St. Nicholas* July 848/1 The architect, with fore feet clasping what we call the 'trap line,' is waiting for some night-flying insect to strike the snare. — (c) **1922** CURWOOD *Country Beyond* 198 Then he cut wood, and made his strychnine poison baits, and marked out his trap-lines. **1950** *Boston Globe Mag.* 5 March 1/1, I finished settin' the river trap line today.

***trapper,** *n.* As the last term in **canoe, free, mountain, muskrat, Rocky Mountain, skin trapper.**

***trapping,** *n.*

1. Of a log cabin: (See quot.) *Obs.*

1843 *Amer. Pioneer* II. 445 The trapping is the roof timbers, composing the gable end and the ribs, the ends of which appear in the drawing, being those logs upon which the clapboards lie.

2. trapping ground, the area selected by a trapper or trappers for the setting of traps for game.

1837 IRVING *Bonneville* I. 118 Those doughty rivals . . . started off for the trapping grounds to the north-northwest. **1903** WHITE *Forest* 207 The Ojibway family . . . searches out new trapping-grounds, new fisheries. **1939** PINKERTON *Wilderness Wife* 93 His catch was so good that Mr. Shields had once snowshoed to the trapping ground to buy the fur.

3. Also **trapping canoe, company, depot, expedition, party.**

1853 RAMSEY *Tennessee* 105 [They] built two boats and two trapping canoes. — **1837** IRVING *Bonneville* II. 214 Part of the goods . . . were . . . to supply the trapping companies. — **1842** *S. Lit. Messenger* VIII. 64/1, I shaped my course to the nearest trapping dépot, and soon obtained a new outfit and supply. — **1806** CLARK in *Lewis & C. Exped.* V. (1905) 329 Those men are on a trapping expedition. — **1837** IRVING *Bonneville* I. 224 In company with Campbell's convoy, was a trapping party of the Rocky Mountain Company.

As the last term in **beaver, gopher trapping.**

***trappy,** *a.* Of a horse: Having a quick, short, high gait. *Colloq.* — **1872** *Vt. Bd. Agric. Rep.* I. 207 Cross a large, roomy, strong-boned, coarse mare with a smooth, stylish, trappy little horse. **1902** McFAUL *Ike Glidden* 108 Ben had a nice smooth, slick mare, what wuz trappy and smart.

***traps,** *n. pl.* **1.** (See quot. 1870.) **2.** ?Commodities used in trade. *Rare.*

(1) **1870** MEDBERY *Men Wall St.* 138 *Traps,* an almost obsolete phrase for broken fancy stocks, depreciated railroad securities, etc. **1885** *Harper's Mag.* Nov. 842/2 Sometimes the broker or operator is caught by 'traps,' or worthless securities. — (2) **1875** WINANS *Reminiscences* 69, I couldn't afford it unless you would take your pay in 'Traps.'

***trash,** *n.*

1. a. =**trash tobacco.** *Obs.* **b.** =**trash ice. c.** (See quot.)

(a) **1732** in *Amer. Sp.* XX. (1945) 275 Some of the most turbulint among the planters, rather than their tobacco should be inspected burnt some of the warehouses, upon the presumption that if they could by that means put a stop to our proceedings, their trash which would not pass under the law, they might sell as usual. **1909** *Cent. Supp.* 1355/2 The leaves of white Burley tobacco are thus classified: lowest two, 'fliers'; next two, 'common lugs' ('trash' apparently the same). — (b) **1856** KANE *Arctic Explor.* I. 342 Warped about one hundred yards into the trash. — (c) **1881** INGERSOLL *Oyster Industry* 249 *Trash,* all cullings, small oysters, refuse, etc., thrown over from the oyster gathering on to idle ground.

2. In combs.: (1) **trash barrel,** a barrel for trash or rubbish; (2) **basket,** (see quot.); (3) **cleaner,** =**trasher,** *obs.;* (4) **gang,** *S.* a group of laborers who remove the litter from fields before a new crop is begun, cf. ***trashy,** *a.* **2;** (5) **hogshead,** a hogshead of trash tobacco; (6) **ice,** (see quot.); (7) **tobacco,** leaf tobacco of a poor grade, *obs.*

(1) **1885** CABLE *Dr. Sevier* 143 He must be expected to come fishing them out of their hole, like a rag-picker at a trash-barrel. — (2) **1895** *D.N.* I. 395 *Trash-basket,* waste-paper basket. N.Y. City. — (3) **1882** *Cent. Mag.* Feb. 563/2 Trash-cleaners, for saving the waste or total loss of storm-beaten cotton, . . . cannot now be made fast enough to supply the demand. — (4) **1854** DAVIS *Farm Bk.* 18 The trash gang spread manure for Potatoes. **1866** W. REID *After War* 492 The horizon was blue and misty with the columns of smoke from the trash-gangs on the plantations.

(5) **1772** *Md. Hist. Mag.* XIV. 281 Two Trash hgds [of tobacco] . . . are not yet sold. — (6) **1864** WEBSTER 1407/1 *Trash-ice,* crumbled

ice mixed with water. — (7) **1784** SMYTH *Tour U.S.* II. 135 The whole [is] covered with trash tobacco, or straw.

As the last term in **corn, old field, poor, poor white, white trash.**

***trash,** *v. To trash a trail,* (see quot.). *Obs.* — **1859** BARTLETT 487 *To Trash a Trail,* an expression used at the West, meaning to conceal the direction one has taken by walking in a stream, or, in fact, taking to water in any way.

trasher ˈtræʃɚ, *n.* (See quot. 1865.) *Obs.* — **1846** *De Bow's Review* 11 Sep. 154 As respects use of trashers, I am decidedly of the opinion that they ought not to be used until after frost kills the cotton. **1865** TURNER *Cotton* 135 Some run it [cotton] through a machine called a 'trasher,' that whips it up and takes out sand and loose dirt.

***trashy,** *a.* **1.** Of persons: Of poor physical constitution or inferior social standing. **2.** Of land: Covered with refuse, as the waste and discarded matter from an earlier season.

(1) **1852** STOWE *Uncle Tom* xxxi, Stout fellers last six or seven years; trashy ones get worked up in two or three. **1862** E. KIRKE *Among Pines* 167 He regarded the white man as altogether too 'trashy' to be treated with much ceremony. — (2) **1861** *Ill. Agric. Soc. Trans.* IV. 250 The wheat drill . . . is designed to do this work rapidly and perfectly, on ground however rough and trashy. **1905–6** *Trade Cat.* (*Cent. Supp.*), The high curve of the beam prevents fouling in trashy land.

travail trəˈvel, *n.* Also **travée.** [Can. F. An Amer. borrowing.] (See quot. 1941 and cf. **travois.**)

[*a***1814** in COUES *Henry & Thompson Jrnls.* I. 142 We saw also poles on which they had stretched beaver skins, old broken horse-travailles, some tent-poles, and plenty of horsedung.] **1846** SAGE *Scenes Rocky Mts.* xi, Dogs, harnessed to travées, had their part to perform. **1857** *Harper's Mag.* Oct. 647/1 The working horses were led up, ready to be harnessed into the *travees.* **1941** MCDERMOTT *Glossary* 143 Travail, n. m. A sled commonly drawn by dogs. Often written by the English and Americans *travail, travaille, travee, traverse, travois.*

***travel,** *n.*

1. ?A gait of a horse. *Obs.*

1750 *N.J. Archives* XII. 643 The one about 14 hands high, a natural pacer, but goes no faster than a travel. **1751** *Ib.* XIX. 84 Taken out of the pasture . . . a black gelding, six years old, paces a good travel. **1777** *Ib.* 2 Ser. I. 460 The gelding is a jet black, trots and paces a travel.

2. Tourists collectively. Also the distance traveled. *Rare.*

1892 *Vt. Agric. Rep.* XII. 136 At Fairlee Lake something is done in the way of attracting this travel. **1903** E. JOHNSON *Railway Transportation* 174 If each car carrying the mails be taken as a unit, the 'annual travel' or car mileage aggregated 302,613,325.

***travel,** *v. intr.* Of an animal: To go on to new feeding grounds, to move on while browsing. *Colloq.* — **1839** MARRYAT *Diary in Amer.* 1 Ser. I. 199 Bears . . . do not come down to the shores, (or travel, as they term it here,) until the huckleberries are ripe. **1877** C. HALLOCK *Sportsman's Gaz.* 88 If the deer is 'travelling,' as it is called, one has to walk much faster.

***traveled,** *a.* Of a road or place: Used or frequented by travelers.

1843 FRÉMONT *Exped.* 163 [To Fort Hall] along the travelled road from the town of Westport . . . is 1,323 miles. **1874** *Vt. Bd. Agric. Rep.* II. 658 If the hill is heavy clay, it may be much improved, . . . by covering the traveled portion with gravel or sand. **1882** HARTE *Flip* 106 [The dawn came with] voices in the traveled roads and trails.

***traveler,** *n.*

1. An itinerant preacher. *Rare.*

1813 ASBURY *Journal* III. 346 The increase . . . in preachers seventy-nine; but of these there are only thirty-three travellers.

2. In the possessive in combs.: (1) **traveler's check,** (see quot. 1909); (2) **credit,** a letter of credit; (3) ***delight,** (see quot.).

(1) **1909** WEBSTER, traveler's, or traveller's, check. . . . A check issued by a banker and payable by any of the correspondents of the issuing banker. **1949** *Dly. Ardmoreite* (Ardmore, Okla.) 4 Dec. 8/3 Exchange National Bank . . . offers. . . . Loans of all types, and Travelers Checks. — (2) **1879** *Bradstreet's* 4 Oct. 8/2 Kountze Brothers . . . issued commercial and Travelers' credits. — (3) **1892** *Amer. Folk-Lore* V. 94 *Apios tuberosa,* traveller's delight, New Albany, Miss.

As the last term in **Arkansas, through traveler.**

Travelers' Aid. An organization which extends aid to travelers in need of help. Often attrib.

1895 *Y.W.C.A. Rep. 1894* 5 Travelers' Aid Department. . . . North-Western Depot. **1911** *Rep. Travelers' Aid Soc. N.Y.C.* No. 6, 5 The Travelers' Aid Society was incorporated under the laws of the State of New York in January, 1907. **1921** *National Travelers Aid Bul.* IV. Nov.–Dec. 3/2 They were . . . obviously leaving the responsibility entirely to the Travelers Aid. **1950** *Chi. Tribune* 16 May II. 5/1 The enterprising woman's board of the Travelers Aid society will stage it Dec. 15 in the Drake hotel as its annual benefit.

***traveling,** *a.* and *n.* In combs.: (1) **traveling grasshopper, =Rocky Mountain locust,** *obs.;* (2) **mail agent,** ?a mail clerk on a steamer carrying mail, *obs.;* (3) **man,** a drummer or commercial traveler; (4) **minister,** an itinerant preacher; (5) **outfit,** a supply of clothing or equipment for travel; (6) **passenger agent,** a representative of a transportation company who travels from place to place; (7) **plan,** in the Methodist Church, the plan or system of having circuit riders, *obs.;* (8) **public,** those who travel; (9) **salesman, =traveling man;** (10) **stone,** (see quot.), *obs.;* (11) **store,** a store of goods carried from place to place as on a store boat *q.v.*

(1) **1909** J. A. HART *Pioneer Days* 167 Every two or three years we had in the fall . . . the traveling grasshopper. — (2) **1850** *Hunt's Merch. Mag.* XXII. 50 The remedy is, to require the traveling mail agents to sort and arrange all those mails during the passage from New York. — (3) **1879** *Bradstreet's* 17 Dec. 2/4 Traveling men say that this is one of the most energetic and prosperous southern cities. **1919** LEWIS *Free Air* 244 She got a great deal of satisfaction and horror out of watching two traveling-men after dinner. — (4) **1741** HEMPSTEAD *Diary* 384 Traveling ministers . . . in Some places promote the withdrawing from the Settled ministers & Set up Separate meetings. **1848** *Indiana Mag. Hist.* XXIII. 2 That same territory . . . contains . . . more than 2,000 local preachers, besides the traveling ministers.

(5) **1886** RITTENHOUSE *Maud* 377 Both milliner and dress-maker thought they were doing my traveling out-fit. *a***1918** G. STUART *On Frontier* I. 218 They had six good horses, but very little in the shape of a traveling outfit. — (6) **1944** JOHNSON *As I Dare* 272 Then a traveling passenger agent called upon me at my home and wanted the full account of my unfortunate experience. — (7) **1794** in W. W. SWEET *Religion on Amer. Frontier* IV. (1946) 203 Entered on the traveling plan. — (8) **1843** *Hunt's Merch. Mag.* IX. 291 It is not perhaps generally known to the travelling public, that the 'Express' . . . leaves Norwich every morning. **1851** *N. Amer. Misc.* I. 93/1 We trust that the managers of the Collins Line . . . will be more careful of the interests of the travelling public. — (9) **1885** *South Fla. Sentinel* (Orlando) 1 July 3/3 The popular traveling salesman, . . . will leave in a few days. **1944** *New Yorker* 11 Nov. 87 It is the story of three little girls, the children of a travelling salesman.

(10) **1877** WRIGHT *Big Bonanza* 38 Traveling stones . . . were almost perfectly round. . . . When scattered . . . on a table . . . they immediately began traveling toward a common centre. — (11) **1831** PECK *Guide* 60 Some [boats] have travelling stores.

travelogue ˈtrævl̩ˌɔg, *n.* [f. **travel* + **-logue.*] An illustrated lecture descriptive of travel, or a motion picture depicting travel.

1903 *Daily Chron.* 16 April 6/7 Mr. Burton Holmes, an American entertainer new to London, delivered last evening, the first of a series of 'Travelogues.' **1922** WILSON *Merton of Movies* 301 There ensued the annoying delays of an educational film and a travelogue. **1946** *So. Sierran* Sep. 3/3 There is little of the usual travelogue, but the impressions of a colorful land recorded by a sensitive and eager mind.

transf. **1950** *Time* 6 March 50/3 High on his villain list: public schoolteachers whose pharasaical travelogues in 'music appreciation' often bypass U.S. music completely.

traverse ˈtrævɝs, trəˈvɝs, *n.* [In **1,** f. Can. F. in the same sense; in **2,** one of the numerous variants of **travail;** in **3,** a new comb. of **traverse.*]

1. (See quots. 1941, 1945.)

1841 NICOLLET *Report* 12 One miles from the *Traverse des Sioux,* and on the bank of the river, are the remains of an Indian camp. **1850** JOHNSTON *Notes* I. 380 Here, at a place called the Traverse or Narrows, about fifty-five miles below Quebec, though the river is there thirteen miles wide, the channel usually selected by pilots is only 1800 yards in width, and, to add to the difficulty, the ebb-tide runs through it at the rate of seven, and the flood of five or six miles an hour, and there is no anchorage. **1941** MCDERMOTT *Glossary* 143 Traverse, n. f. In the language of the *voyageur,* a traverse was any large open body of water to be crossed in canoes. **1945** STEWART *Names on Land* 212 Where, canoeing on a lake, they [the French] left the shore and steered across the mouth of a bay for the point on the other side, they called it a *traverse.*

2. *N. Eng.* **=double ripper, double runner.** In full **traverse sled.**

In the *Linguistic Atlas of New England,* maps 573, 574, the prevalence of this term is well shown.

1886 *Boston Globe* 20 Dec., The man who doesn't own a toboggan, [or] a traverse . . . , stands a good chance of getting through the winter without an accident policy. **1887** *Courier-Journal* 16 Jan. 2/6 Twenty boys were coasting down South Main Street on a traverse sled. [**1941** McDermott *Glossary* 143 *Traverse* is also a variant spelling of *travail.*]

3. traverse-table, (see quot.).

1864 Webster 1407/3 *Traverse-table,* . . . (Railways), a platform with one or more tracks, and arranged to move laterally on wheels, for shifting cars, etc.; a traverser.

travois trəˈvɔɪ, *n.* Also **travoy.** [Variant of **travail.**]

1. = **travail.** Now *hist.*

1847 K. Carson in Cody *Wild West* 349 The Klamaths . . . prevented his body from falling into our hands by drawing it away on a travoi. **1893** *Outing* Oct. 11/2 The women and children pulled down the tepees, bundled up the canvas, and piled it and the camp furniture into the wagons or upon the travois. **1927** Walgamott *Remin. Early Days* II. 55 He saddled his horse, fastened a trivoy to the horn of his saddle and bid the squaw get on. **1947** Price *Trails I Rode* 173 Some of those Indians rode and took their travois fifty miles to the agency and just got a handful of grub.

attrib. **1891** *Harper's Mag.* Dec. 32/1 He came and hitched the required number of horses to her mother's travois poles beside her tent. **1901** White in *Munsey's Mag.* (Eng. ed.) XXV. 387/2 The travoy road is in the process of construction. **1907** Cook *Border & Buffalo* 207 Not a lodge-pole had been dragged travois-fashion to here, but from here a travois trail started northeast toward Fort Sill. **1948** *Sat. Ev. Post* 16 Oct. 151/2 No marks of travois poles in the hoof marks. No women then. A war party.

2. A go-devil or sled used for dragging logs. Also attrib.

1878 *Lumberman's Gaz.* 2 Feb. 87 The haul . . . is too long to use travoys. **1902** White *Blazed Trail* 52 A number of pines had been felled out on the ice . . . and left in expectation of ice thick enough to bear the travoy 'dray.' **1903** —— *Blazed Trail Stories* 49 The scaler swung leisurely down the travoy trail.

travoy trəˈvɔɪ, *v. tr.* To transport by means of a travois (sense 2.). — **1878** *Lumberman's Gaz.* 2 Feb. 86 Travoying can be carried on to good advantage. **1902** White *Blazed Trail* 13 When Nolly and Fabian had travoyed the log to the skidway, they drew it with a bump across the two parallel skids.

* **trawl,** *n.* (See quot. 1860.)

1860 Worcester 1536/2 *Trawl,* . . . a line, sometimes a mile or more in length, with short lines and baited hooks suspended from it at frequent intervals;—now much used in fishing for cod, haddock, and mackerel. *Gilbert.* **1896** Jewett *Pointed Firs* 52 It was her brother's trawl, and she meant to just run her eye along for the right sort of a little haddock. **1914** Steele *Storm* 71, I shook a thumb at the tubs of baited trawl.

attrib. **1876** Knight 2621/1 Trawl-roller, a roller . . . over which the trawls are drawn into the boat. **1884** *Nat. Museum Bul.* No. 27, 756 Trawl anchor. . . . Used for anchoring trawl-lines, boats, and nets. *Ib.* 965 Trawl-buoy. Five glass balls . . . covered with netting, and lashed around a series of cork floats strung on a staff.

* **trawler,** *n.* A person engaged in fishing with a trawl line; a vessel used in fishing with such a line.

1864 Webster 1408/1 *Trawler,* . . . one who, or that which, trawls. **1880** *Harper's Mag.* Aug. 340/1 In other departments [of fishing] there were . . . trawlers, draggers, . . . and the bankers before mentioned. **1884** *Nat. Museum Bul.* No. 27, 715 In the foreground is a Grand Bank cod-trawler being towed out of the [Gloucester] harbor by a steam tug.

* **tray,** *n.* As the last term in **bread, dough, Indian tray.**

treacle berry. (See quot. 1672.)

1634 Wood *N. Eng. Prospect* (1865) 15 There bee . . . Treacleberies, Hurtleberries, Currants. **1672** Josselyn *N. Eng. Rarities* 45 Treacle Berries, having the perfect taste of Treacle when they are ripe. **1931** Clute *Plants* 118.

tread soft(ly). = **spurge nettle.** Also attrib. *Colloq.*

1814 Pursh *Flora Amer.* II. 603 *Jatropa stimulosa* . . . ruins the Negroes' feet when they tread upon it; from which it is known by the name of Tread-softly. **1884** Harris *Mingo* 105 The man what's stobbed by a pitchfork hain't much better off'n the man that walks bar' footed in a treadsaft patch. **1894** Coulter *Bot. W. Texas* III. 397 Tread softly. Spurge nettle. . . . Sandy plains along the Rio Grande.

* **treasure,** *n.* In combs.: (1) **treasure bag,** a bag in which a housewife keeps scraps of cloth, lace, etc.; (2) **-box,** (*a*) a strongbox or receptacle on a stagecoach in which valuables, esp. gold from mining camps, were carried, *obs.*, (*b*) a box in which one keeps things that are treasured; (3) **coach,** a stagecoach transporting treasure from a gold-mining region, *obs.;* (4) **State,** Montana, a nickname.

(1) 1887 Alden *Little Fishers* xv, With some pieces of lace from her mother's old treasure bag, she meant to make herself a bonnet. — **(2)** (*a*) **1879** Vivian *Wanderings Western Land* 122 On these occasions passengers and 'treasure-box' have alike been lightened of their valuables. **1893** *Chi. Tribune* 24 April 3/1 Among the articles of greatest historical value . . . [is] the treasure-box, a memento of the attack on the Redding and Alturas stage in 1892. (*b*) **1881** Stoddard *E. Hardery* 20 She picked up the miniature . . . and carefully locked it away again in its ebony treasure-box. **1907** *St. Nicholas* July 813/1 His 'ditty-box,' . . . is the sailor's work-basket, writing-desk, treasure-box, and camp-stool all in one. — **(3) 1880** Ingham *Digging Gold* 288 Only one treasure coach has ever been robbed. — **(4) 1934** [see **Stubtoe State**]. **1950** *Nat. Geog. Mag.* June 693/2 The commonwealth that was lawless wilderness 85 years ago is aptly nicknamed the 'Treasure State.' Beneath its mountains still lies untold mineral wealth, though its mines have already disgorged billions of dollars.

* **treasurer,** *n.* (*cap.*) An officer of the U.S. Treasury Department in charge of all government funds and of disbursements.

[**1777** *Jrnls. Cont. Congress* VII. 40 The continental treasurer shall be empowered and directed to borrow money on the loan office certificates.] **1790** Hamilton *Works* VII. 52 The treasurer of the United States shall be the receiver of all payments for sales at the general land-office. **1834** Jackson in *Pres. Mess. & P.* III. 112 The power of Congress to direct in what places the Treasurer shall keep the moneys in the Treasury . . . is unlimited. **1900** *Cong. Rec.* 16 Jan. 876/1 This Treasurer of the United States walks in and fills the coffers with free money that they may lend it at a high rate of interest. **1950** *Time* 8 May 32/1 Treasurer of the U.S. Mrs. Georgia Neese Clark confessed that life in Washington had played hob with her private budget.

As the last term in **country, county, general, leg, state, sub, town treasurer.**

* **treasury,** *n.* In combs., chiefly obs.: (1) **treasury agent,** an agent appointed to dispose of U.S. Government securities; (2) **bill,** a bill in Congress relating to the U.S. Treasury; (3) **board,** a board, consisting originally of five congressmen, established by the Continental Congress in 1776 to serve chiefly as a ways and means committee, *obs.;* (4) **Department,** the financial department of the U.S. Government, now having the Secretary of the Treasury at its head; (5) **greenback,** = **greenback 1;** (6) **note,** see as a main entry; (7) **ring,** a clique of politicians particularly interested in congressional legislation affecting the U.S. Treasury; (8) **scrip,** scrip issued by the U.S. Treasury; (9) **shinplaster,** = **shinplaster;** (10) * **warrant,** a land warrant issued by the treasury of a state, in full **treasury land warrant,** also a warrant for the payment of money into or from the U.S. Treasury cf. **land office (treasury) warrant.**

(1) 1842 *Niles' Reg.* 16 July 307/2 T. F. Robinson, Esq. of Harrisburg, Pa. has been appointed as treasury agent of the U. States. — **(2) 1846** Polk *Diary* I. 368, I feared . . . that both the Treasury Bill & the reduction of the tariff would be postponed. — **(3) 1776** *Jrnls. Cont. Cong.* VI. 1038 Two members [shall] be added to the committee appointed on the 17 October for the better regulating the Treasury Board. **1787** Jefferson *Writings* VI. 128 This has prevented the treasury board from remitting any money to this place. — **(4) 1784** *Jrnls. Cont. Cong.* XXVI. 357 A motion of the delegates of Massachusetts, to revise the institution of the treasury department, . . . was read a first time. **1900** *Cong. Rec.* 14 Feb. 1794/2 The Treasury Department of the United States . . . will figure for untold hours to disallow every cent that does not come within the red tape of that organization.

(5) 1862 *N.Y. Tribune* 30 May 3/4 He has plenty of Treasury 'greenbacks,' but he very prudently never spends any of them. — **(7) 1868** *N.Y. Herald* 14 July 4/3 This would tend to break up the Wall street den and Treasury ring. — **(8) 1849** *31st Congress* 1 Sess. H.R. Ex. Doc. No. 5, II. 1178 The ninth section of the act . . . gives bounty land or treasury scrip, at the claimant's option, to non-commissioned officers . . . who served in the late Mexican war. *Ib.,* The act of March 3, 1849, prohibits the issue of treasury scrip. — **(9) 1838** *Jamestown* (N.Y.) *Jrnl.* 18 July 1/6 The new 'money bill' or act, authorizing a new issue of Treasury shinplasters, . . . has been vetoed. **1846** *Xenia Torch-Light* 2 July 3/1 Mr. Polk will pay the fiddlers in Treasury shin-plasters.

(10) 1784 *Ky. Petitions* 73 [The] House did . . . pass a Resolution forbidding the issuing any Treasury Land Warrants. **1784** Filson *Kentucke* 37 Treasury warrants were afterwards issued, authorizing their possessor to locate the quantity of land mentioned in them. **1834** C. A. Davis *Lett. J. Downing* 217 Pieces of paper all full of figerin, and some on 'em marked . . . 'Treasury Warrants.'

As the last term in **county, Evangelical, national, Secretary of the, state, sub-treasury.**

* **treasury note.**

1. A note or interest-bearing certificate issued by the treasury department of a colony. *Obs.*

1756 *Lett. to Washington* I. 202 The Treasurer . . . is hereby required to pay the same in Treasury Notes. **1778** *Ann. S.W. Va.* 988 Francis Hopkins was guilty of passing Treasury Notes knowing the same to be bad. **1894** LEAVITT *Our Money Wars* 13 In 1723, Pennsylvania . . . issued treasury notes, and kept them in use until 1773.

2. A currency bill or note issued by the Treasury Department of the U.S. Government. Also attrib.

The first notes of this kind were issued to meet the expenses of the War of 1812, and many issues subsequently appeared. Cf. **greenback 1.**

1812 *Statutes at Large* III. 767 The said treasury notes . . . shall be every where received in payment of all duties and taxes laid by the authority of the United States. **1842** *Whig Almanac 1843* 35/2 A Loan Bill, Treasury Note Bill, and Provisional Tariff were passed, to preserve the Treasury from dishonor. **1911** VANCE *Cynthia* 78 He smoothed the Treasury note out between his fingers.

b. Such notes issued by the Republic of Texas or by the Southern Confederacy. *Obs.*

1836 *Diplom. Corr. Texas* I. (1908) 71 We have concluded to adopt the plan of issuing treasury notes. **1852** GOUGE *Fiscal Hist. Texas* 73 Treasury notes should be issued only to defray the expenses of the civil department. **1861** *Vanity Fair* 27 April 195/2 The treasury notes of the Confederate States have at the end the Goddess of Liberty in starry drapery.

***treat,** *n.* As the last term in **Dutch, Dutchman's, general treat.**

***treatment,** *n.* As the last term in **absent, gold treatment.**

* **treaty,** *n.*

1. A formal meeting of representatives of the U.S. and Indian tribes looking to the drawing up of an agreement to govern future relations. Now *hist.*

1690 in B. CHURCH *Hist. Philip's War* (1867) II. 73 The discourse I made with them . . . I knew would have that Effect as to bring them to a treaty. **1788** PUTNAM in *Life & Corr. Cutler* I. 377 Congress had promised them a treaty, which was to have been holden about this time. **1843** *Civilian* (Galveston, Tex.) 18 Feb. 1/3 The Commissioners were to have started on Sunday last for the Waco village, to complete the treaties with the Indians. **1949** *Hist. & Philos. Soc. Ohio Bul.* Jan. 14 Harrison enlarged the area open to settlement by means of socalled treaties with the Indians.

2. In combs.: (1) **treaty cup,** ?a large coffee cup, *obs.;* (2) **fund,** a fund to be paid to Indians in accordance with a treaty; (3) **ground,** a place designated for holding a treaty conference with Indians, *obs.;* (4) **Indian,** an Indian belonging to a tribe which has signed a treaty with the U.S., hence **non-treaty Indian,** both *obs.;* (5) **line,** a boundary line agreed upon by treaty between whites and Indians, *obs.;* (6) **-making power,** the power or authority to make treaties; (7) **party,** a group of Indians interested in a treaty, *obs.*

(1) **1859** G. A. JACKSON *Diary* (MS) 4 Panned out eight treaty cups of dirt. — (2) **1871** *Rep. Indian Affairs* (1872) 306, I would recommend . . . a pro rata division of the Klamath and Modoc treaty-funds for employes and annuities. — (3) **1832** *Polit. Examiner* (Shelbyville, Ky.) 24 Nov. 3/2 The Pottawattamie treaty, recently held at the treaty ground near Logansport, has resulted in the cession to the United States of . . . six millions of acres. **1851** *Oquawka* (Ill.) *Spectator* 22 Oct. 2/6 They left the Treaty Ground on the 24th. — (4) **1876** DODGE *Black Hills* 139 Every year since the treaty was signed has witnessed more or less pillage, depredation, and murder, by the treaty Indians. **1877** *Rep. Indian Affairs* 12 The three chief leaders of all the non-treaty Indians agreed to go upon the reservation with their several bands.

(5) **1797** HAWKINS *Letters* 148 The line run between the Indians and the white inhabitants . . . was for the express purpose of ascertaining a line of accommodation for the settlers who were then over the treaty line. — (6) **1796** WASHINGTON *Writings* XIII. 178 It is thus that the treaty-making power has been understood by foreign nations. **1870** *Nation* 10 Feb. 86/1 An amendment may readily be such as most materially to affect our foreign relations . . . as in the treaty-making power. **1900** *Cong. Rec.* 19 Jan. 980/2 The President is a part of the treaty-making power, but not the whole of it. — (7) **1842** *S. Lit. Messenger* VIII. 578/2 We were often visited by deputations and treaty parties of the many wilder tribes of Indians.

As the last term in **beef, Indian, Louisiana, walking treaty.**

* **tree,** *n.* In combs.: (1) **tree agent,** one who sells young trees; (2) **box,** a boxlike wooden frame for protecting a tree, esp. when it is young, cf. **b.** (2) below; (3) **claim,** =**timber claim;** (4) **coral,** (see quot. 1891); (5) **Day,** an annual outdoor pageant held at Wellesley College in May for which event "Mistresses" are chosen and class trees are set out or decorated; (6) **line,** =**timberline** (*a*); (7) **looker,** (see quot.); (8) **molasses,** =**maple sirup;** (9) **peddler,** =**tree agent;** (10) **Planters State,** (see quot. 1895); (11) **scraper,** (see quot. 1876); (12) **sirup,** =**maple sirup;** (13) **sugar,** (see quot. 1859), *obs.;* (14) **surgeon,** one trained in the operative treatment of tree diseases; (15) **sweetening,** maple sugar or maple sirup; (16) **warden,** one who has the oversight of trees in a given place.

(1) **1879** STOCKTON *Rudder Grange* xii, I invited the tree-agent to get down out of the tree. — (2) **1876** MARK TWAIN *Tom Sawyer* ii. 27 Tom sat down on the tree-box discouraged. **1896** HARRIS *Sister Jane* 157, I looked back and saw him whittling away with his pocket knife on the tree-box. — (3) **1884** N. D. WOODWARD in *Checkered Yrs.* (1937) 37 He started a tree claim. **1949** *World-Herald* (Omaha) 15 May F. 8/3 The government meanwhile was allowing settlers to make preemption filings of 160 acres plus an additional 'tree claim' filing of 160 acres. — (4) **1871** *Harper's Mag.* June 28 On the confines of this channel may be seen in clear water a perfect forest of coral—tree-coral, we call it, on account of its great size. **1891** *Cent.* 6453/3 *tree-coral.* . . . An arborescent polypidom, as madrepore.

(5) **1906** *Boston Transcript* 9 June I. 3/5 Tree Day has by honored tradition been the one great fete day which Wellesley aims to keep entirely to herself. **1946** *Chi. Tribune* 2 June (Picture Sect.) 12 (*caption*), 'Tree Day Mistresses' in the spring outdoor pageant at Wellesley college — (6) **1893** *Outing* Aug. 346/1 We struck the tree-line again in the immense ravine between them. **1903** AUSTIN *Land of Little Rain* 9 South-looking hills are nearly bare, and the lower tree-line higher here by a thousand feet. — (7) **1913** *D.N.* IV. 28 *Tree looker,* . . . a timber estimater, cruiser, etc. — (8) **1880** *Harper's Mag.* Dec. 89 There's a kag of tree molasses down cellar. **1947** *Amer. Sp.* XXII. 307 My grandparents . . . made hundreds of gallons of tree molasses in some seasons. — (9) **1861** *Ill. Agric. Soc. Trans.* IV. 511 The regular Nurseryman does not make a large profit out of him, whatever the tree peddler may do.

(10) **1895** *Neb. Laws* 441 Nebraska shall hereafter in a popular sense be known and referred to as the 'Tree Planters State.' **1949** *Sun. World-Herald Mag.* (Omaha) 10 April 23/2 Later, when trees were planted as windbreakers, the nickname was changed to Tree Planter's State. — (11) **1856** *Mich. Agric. Soc. Trans.* VII. 54 D. O. & W. S. Penfield . . . [exhibited] 3 tree scrapers. **1876** KNIGHT, Tree-scraper, a tool hare [*sic*], usually a triangular blade, to remove old bark and moss from trees. Also used in gathering turpentine. — (12) **1932** *Randolph Enterprise* (Elkins, W.Va.) 18 Feb. 5/2 The weather hasn't been cold enough yet to make much success in making tree syrup and sugar. — (13) **1859** BARTLETT 488 *Tree-Sugar,* sugar made from the maple-tree. Western. **1901** *Everybody's Mag.* April 333/2 Coffee . . . was new to the Western settler at the time of which I write, milk and water sweetened with 'tree-sugar' being the usual table-drink. — (14) **1934** WEBSTER **1947** *Denver Post* 15 Feb. 16/2 It would be best to have a tree surgeon remove the maple.

(15) **1893** LELAND *Memoirs* 294 There was no sugar at his supper-table, but he had three substitutes for it—'tree-sweetnin', bee-sweetnin', and sorghum'—that is, maple sugar, honey, and the molasses made from Chinese maize. **1944** W. BLAIR *Tall Tale Amer.* 206 And bring me thirty-three buttermilk biscuits and tree-sweetnin' for them, for to finish off with. — (16) **1910** *Springfield W. Republican* 8 Dec. 3 One of the things to be seriously considered by tree wardens is the disturbing intelligence that the gypsy moth is making its way into the western counties.

b. In the names of plants: (1) **tree azalea,** (see quot. 1891); (2) **box,** the common bushy box used for hedges, cf. (2) above; (3) **cactus,** a species of *Opuntia;* (4) **cholla,** a spiny arborescent cactus of the Southwest; (5) **corn,** an especially prolific variety of corn, *obs.*, cf. **Baden corn;** (6) **cranberry,** the high or bush cranberry, *Viburnum opulus;* (7) **huckleberry,** =**farkleberry;** (8) **poppy,** a California shrub, *Dendromecon rigidum,* having large yellow flowers; (9) **primrose,** the common evening primrose, *Oenothera biennis.*

(1) **1847** WOOD *Botany* 376 *R*[*hododendron*] *arborescens.* . . . Tree Azalea. . . Flowers large, rose color. **1891** *Cent.* 6453/3 tree-azalea. . . . A shrub or small tree, *Rhododendron arborescens,* of the *Azalea* section of that genus, found in the mountains from Pennsylvania to Georgia. It has very fragrant rose-colored flowers. Also *smooth azalea.* — (2) **1785** WASHINGTON *Diaries* II. 360 Received . . . an equal number of cuttings of the Tree Box. **1858** WARDER *Hedges & Evergreens* II. 240 Where a moderate or low hedge is needed, . . . nothing can be better than the Tree-box. — (3) **1890** *Chivington*

(Colo.) *Chief* 17 Jan. 1/2 The canes referred to . . . were of a species of tree cactus that grows in our Colorado mountains; and were just as Nature had 'designed' and 'carved' them. **1905** *Bur. Plant Industry* Bul. 74, 15 The species of cactus which is fed in southeastern Colorado is one of the so-called tree cacti. — **(4) 1908** HORNADAY *Camp Fires on Desert* 224 The Tree Choya is . . . less of a curse than Bigelow's.

(5) 1848 C. L. FLEISCHMANN *Nordamerikanische Landwirth* 114 De Baden- und Burdenmais, Baden-Corn (Tree-Corn) Burden-Corn, sind durch sorgfältige Pflege erzielte Abarten des Kürbiskernmais, dessen Fruchtbarkeit von drei bis vier Aehren bis zur Hervorbringung von sechs bis zehn Aehren an einem einzigen Halme gesteigert worden is. **1848** *Rep. Comm. Patents 1847* 129 The tree corn is highly recommended by some, to be sown broad-cast for fodder. — **(6) 1846** BROWNE *Trees Amer.* 353 This edible-fruited guilder rose or tree-cranberry . . . is found from York to Canada. **1866** LOSSING *Hudson* 35 Here and there among the rocks . . . the tree-cranberry appeared. — **(7) 1897** SUDWORTH *Arborescent Flora* 312 *Vaccinium arboreum*, . . . Tree Huckleberry, . . . Bluet (La.). **1909** *Cent. Supp.* 602/2. — **(8) 1866** LINDLEY & MOORE *Treas. Botany* 392/2 *Dendromecon*, literally Tree Poppy, is a most appropriate name, the plant having all the aspect and character of the poppy tribe, combined with a woody stem and branches. **1915** ARMSTRONG & THORNBER *Western Wild Flowers* 166 [The] Tree Poppy *Dendromecon rigida* . . . is a handsome and decorative shrub, both in form and color. — **(9) 1629** PARKINSON *Paradisus* 264 *Lysimachia lutea siliquosa Virgiana.* The tree Primrose of Virginia. **1785** MARTYN *Rousseau's Bot.* (1794) xix. 256 Tree Primrose, a Virginian plant. . . . The corolla is a fine yellow. **1840** DEWEY *Mass. Flowering Plants* 47 Tree Primrose. . . . Found in fields, and flowers from June to September.

c. In the names of animals: (1) **tree civet,** =**cacomistle;** (2) **cricket,** any one of various whitish American crickets of the genus *Oecanthus;* (3) **fish,** a rockfish of the Pacific Coast, *Sebastocarus serriceps;* (4) **mouse,** (see quot.), cf. **arse-up;** (5) **peck,** a woodpecker, *obs.;* (6) ∗**sparrow,** a sparrow, *Spizella arborea*, resembling the chipping sparrow but larger and more northerly in habitat; (7) **swallow,** a widely distributed North American swallow, *Iridoprocne bicolor*, which nests in holes in trees; (8) **toad,** any arboreal toad, usu. of the family Hylidae.

(1) 1893 ROOSEVELT *Wilderness Hunter* 355 On the walls were nailed the skins of . . . raccoons, wild cats, and the tree-civet. — **(2) 1859** *Amer. Cyclo.* VI. 63/1 They form the genus *œcanthus*, and are called tree or climbing crickets. **1877** *Vt. Bd. Agric. Rep.* IV. 154 The tree cricket . . . is sometimes very troublesome to the raspberry. — **(3) 1884** GOODE *Fishes* I. 263 Wherever this species [of rock cod] receives a distinctive name, it is known as the 'Tree-fish,' an appellation originating with the Portuguese at Monterey. **1911** *Rep. Fisheries 1908* 314/2. — **(4) 1897** BLANCHAN *Bird Neighbors* 84 White-breasted Nuthatch (*Sitta carolinensis*). . . . Called also Tree-mouse.

(5) 1806 *Balance* V. 265/1 It was nothing, as he afterwards expressed himself, but 'a—tree-peck.' — **(6) 1810** WILSON *Ornithology* II. 123 The Tree Sparrow, *Fringilla Arborea*, . . . frequents sheltered hollows, thickets, and hedgerows, near springs of water. **1949** *Dly. Oklahoman Mag.* (Okla. City) 4 Dec. 16/3 A season's tally will average about equal numbers of Harris' sparrows, tree sparrows and juncos. — **(7) 1892** TORREY *Foot-Path Way* 183 Our Ipswich birds were all tree swallows. **1950** *World-Herald Mag.* (Omaha) 28 May 3/2 Only the tree swallow is uncommon. — **(8) 1778** CARVER *Travels* 489 Among the reptiles of North America there is a species of the toad termed the Tree Toad, which is nearly of the same shape as the common sort, but smaller and with longer claws. **1886** BYNNER *Agnes Surriage* 196 Tree-toads filled the air with twilight clamor. **1945** MATHEWS *Talking* 42 The tree toads set up a chorus, then stopped abruptly just as the coyotes had done.

d. In phrases: (1) *Tree of Liberty*, a tree selected as a symbol of freedom; (2) *to be up a tree*, to be in a difficult or embarrassing position, *colloq.;* (3) *to a man up a tree*, to an impartial observer, *colloq.;* (4) *tree of friendship*, (see quot.), *obs.*

(1) 1765 *Universal Mag.* XXXVII. 376/2 The great tree at the south part of the town [of Boston is] . . . known by the name of the Tree of Liberty. **1868** BEECHER *Norwood* 328 We are agreed, then, the elm is the Tree of Liberty. **1947** COFFIN *Yankee Coast* 109 Once we had thrown George's tea and him overboard, and turned many a tall pine into a Tree of Liberty, we Yankees started building ships hand-over-fist all up and down the Atlantic shoreline. — **(2) 1825** NEAL *Bro. Jonathan* I. 112 If you don't, says I, I'm up a tree, says I. **1925** *Sat. Ev. Post* 95/4 Make him come to you fellers. If ye go to him, he'll see he's got ye up a tree. **1950** *Chi. Tribune* 19 May 10 Poor Pop—now he's really up a tree. — **(3) 1835** LONGSTREET *Ga. Scenes* 230 It may be funny, . . . but it looks mightily like yearnest to a man up a tree. — **(4) 1846** BROWNE *Trees Amer.* 507 [About 1722] a deputation of Indians came to their newly-settled minister, . . . requesting permission to plant [two elms] . . . before his door, as a mark of their regard, or as the 'Tree of Friendship.'

As the last term in **alligator, American plane, angelica, balsam, bay, bean, bear, bearing, beaver, bee, beginning, benjamin, big, black, board, buckeye, buckwheat, buffalo, butterfly, butternut, button, calico, California, candle, candleberry, canoe, castor, Catawba, catclaw, China, Christmas, cigar, clapboard, coffee, corner, cotton, cranberry, cucumber, custard, dogwood, double, eastern plane, elk, European ash, European lime, fate, fever, fore-and-aft, Franklin, fringe, gift, great, gum, hack, hall, hat, head, honey, hop, hornbound, husbandman's, Joshua, large-leaved cucumber, large-leaved umbrella, large-leaved Virginian mulberry, liberty, line, live oak, locust, long-leaved cucumber, lumber, McClellan, mahogany, mammoth, medicine, mesquite, Mississippi cotton, Missouri silver, mole, Montana, moose, mountain bird cherry, navel orange, nave wood, New Jersey fir, Newton pippin, nicker, noble laurel, nooning, northern strawberry, nutmeg, occidental plane, officer, Osage orange, palmetto, papaw, peach, pecan nut, penny, pepper, pepperidge, persimmon, photograph, pine, piñon, planer, plum, poison, poison berry, polecat, princess, pump, rail, saddle, saddleleaf, salad, sap, sassafras, seed, Sequoia, service, shad, shade, shagbark, Shawnee, shoemaker's, shooting, sight, silk tassel, silver bell, snow drop, sorrel, spice, spikenard, spoon, state, station, strawberry, stump, sugar, swallow, tar, tea, Texas, Texas umbrella, toothache, trap, tulip, tupelo, umbrella, varnish, vinegar, wayfarer's, whiffle, wine, witness tree.**

∗**tree,** *v.*

1. *tr.* To cause (a hunted animal) to take refuge in a tree. Also absol.

1733 BYRD *Journey to Eden* (1901) 304 In our way to this place we treed a Bear, of so mighty a Bulk that when we fetcht her down she almost made an Earthquake. **1832** KENNEDY *Swallow Barn* I. 91 It was as good as a dozen dogs treeing an opossum. **1895** *Outing* XXVI. 439/2 The old man advised that we should wait till the dogs treed. **1948** *Democrat* 4 Nov. 8/5 He was treed about daylight.

transf. **1831** DOWNING *Lett.* 38 Cousin Nabby hopped right up and down, like a mouse treed in a flour barrel.

b. *fig.* To stump, corner, or catch (a person).

1834 CARUTHERS *Kentuckian* I. 97, I thought I would tree him next time. **1881** *Harper's Mag.* May 884/1 Though not exactly able to tree him, . . . they did go on about the prospect of the old bachelor . . . being caught at last.

2. *intr.* To take refuge behind a tree when fighting or skirmishing in wooded country. Also reflex. and **treed,** *a.*

1712 in *Va. Mag. Hist. & Biog.* V. 401 Seeing them so inconsiderable I ordered a halt, & to tree it as they call it. **1755** *N.Y. Gazette* 28 April 3/2 To rush in upon them wou'd avail but little, because they [Indians] will be ready to give you a second Fire before you can reach them; and then the Word is, *Tree all;* when each takes to a Tree or some other Cover. **1852** WATSON *Nights in Block-House* 141, The Indians treed themselves. **1886** Z. F. SMITH *Kentucky* 296 Crist and Cripps stood over him, keeping the Indians *treed*, while the release was made. **1948** DICK *Dixie Frontier* 41 Then the Indian 'treed' (hid behind a tree).

transf. **1853** P. PAXTON *Yankee in Texas* 325 When . . . knife and pistol flash in the sun, the hangers on about town . . . 'tree' in the first store or 'grocery' convenient.

Hence **treeing,** *n. Obs.*

1777 HADDEN *Journal* 133 Dragoons cannot be expected to march or manouvre well on Foot and expert at Treeing or Bush fighting, a task the British Light Infantry of this Army are not fully equal to. **1797** PRIEST *Travels* 131 They should be encamped as much as possible in a woody country, as the art of *freeing* [*sic*], as the back woodsmen call it, is one of their best manoeuvres.

tree toad, *v. intr.* To make a noise resembling that of a tree toad. Also **tree-toading,** *n. Rare.* — **1866** A. D. WHITNEY *L. Goldthwaite* x, They tree-toaded, they cat-called, they shouted, they cheered. *Ib.* vii, What a 'howl' was, superlative to 'tree-toading,' 'owl-hooting,' and other divertisements, did not appear.

∗ **trembler,** *n.* **1.** (*cap.*) *pl.* (See quots.) **2.** =**temblor,** cf. **tremblor.**

(1) 1847 EMORY *Mil. Reconn.* 70 They [Indians in valley of Gila R.] were supposed by some to be the Cayotes, a branch of the Apaches but Londeau thought they belonged to the Tribe of Tremblers, who acquired their name for their emotions at meeting the whites. **1910** HODGE *Amer. Indians* II. 814/1 Tremblers. An unidentified branch of the Apache of Arizona, 'who acquired their name from their emotions at meeting the whites.' — **(2) 1892** *N.Y. Herald* 25 Feb. 7/6 The shock was followed by light tremblers all night.

∗**trembles,** *n. pl.* (See quot. 1857.) *Obs.* — **1857** DUNGLISON *Dict. Med. Sci.* 1529 Milk sickness . . . is attributed in cattle to something eaten or drunk by them; and in man to the eating of the flesh of animals labouring under the disease. Owing to the tremors that characterize it in animals, it is called the *Trembles.* **1887** *Buck's Handbk. Med. Sci.* V. 9/1 The flesh of an animal suffering from trembles . . . would also produce the disease [milk-sickness].

∗ **trembling,** *a.* **trembling aspen, land, prairie,** (see quots.).

1897 SUDWORTH *Arborescent Flora* 128 *Populus tremuloides,* Aspen. . . . Called Trembling Aspen (Iowa). — **1834** PECK *Gaz. Ill.* 368 Trembling Lands. . . . On Rock river [Wisconsin], . . . is a tract of country for thirty or forty miles in extent . . . made up of alternate sand ridges covered with shrubs and quagmires, and swamps, that shake for some distance around when the traveler attempts to pass over them. — [**1807** C. C. ROBIN *Voyages* II. 457 (McDermott), Sur les lieux marécageux, les massettes, les souchets se sèment de graines avec plus de profusion, jettent des racines plus longues, plus multipliées, plus entrelacées, et élèvent des touffes plus larges et plus fournies, jusqu'à former sur la surface de ces eaux marécageuses d'immenses plaines de verdures, nommées prairies tremblantes.] **1828** *Spirit of 'Seventy-Six* (Frankfort, Ky.) 3 Jan. 3/4 The spot where the negroes had located themselves, is situate in what is called the Trembling Prairie. **1861** W. H. RUSSELL *Pictures Southern Life* 81 Through miles of cypress swamps the train passes on to what is called the 'trembling prairie,' where the sleepers are laid upon a tressel-work of heavier logs. **1947** *Sat. Ev. Post* 17 May 19/1 The Cajuns had a name for this wet southwestern country—they called it the Trembling Prairie.

tremblor ˈtremblɚ, tremˈblɔr, *n.* Orig. *S.W.* [Erroneous, prob. through analogy with *tremble,* f. Sp. *temblor,* in sense shown here.] An earthquake. Cf. ∗**trembler 2.** — **1913** GOODWIN *As I Remember Them* 193 He gave a series of lectures in California and received the sobriquet of 'Earthquake' Stewart, because of the theory that he put out, that the tremblors in California were caused, not by displacements below the surface of the earth, but because of electrical disturbances in the air and in the earth near the surface. **1925** *N.Y. Times* 1 July 2/2 Dr. U. S. Grant . . . does not agree with Prof. Goode that the same tremblores shook Montana and California.

∗**trencher,** *n.* (See quot.) *Obs.* — **1889** *Harper's Mag.* Jan. 238/2 The next binds his [beaver] trap to a flat stone 'about the size of a teakettle,' opens the jaws, and arranges the 'trencher,' as the pan is called, pressure on which springs the trap.

Trenton limestone. (See quot. 1890.) — **1843** *Nat. Hist. N.Y., Geology* III. 38 At Fort-Plain, . . . the change from Birdseye to Trenton limestone is perfectly abrupt. **1890** *Cent.* 3457/3 *Trenton limestone,* a rock of Lower Silurian age, finely exhibited at Trenton Falls, New York.

trestlework ˈtrɛslˌwɝk, *n.* A structure, esp. a railroad bridge, supported by trestles. Also transf.

Trestlework on railway

1848 *Knickerb.* XVIII. 153 The thick tressel-work of an hundred Lombardy poplars screened it. **1863** F. MOORE *Rebellion Rec.* V. I. 29 A force from Gen. Sherman's command . . . destroyed several pieces of tressel-work on the Mississippi Central Railroad. **1896** SHINN *Story of Mine* 210 Nothing better can be found in the way of concrete illustration than the . . . trestle works, machinery, and all.

∗ **tri-,** *prefix.* In combs.

1. trimountain, with reference to Boston, Mass.: **a.** *n. pl.* A group of three hills. **b.** *a.* Having, or related to, three hills, esp. **Trimount(ain) City,** Boston, Mass., also **trimontane.**

(a) 1838 HAWTHORNE *Twice-told Tales* II. 10 From this station, . . . Gage may have beheld his disastrous victory on Bunker Hill (unless one of the tri-mountains intervened). — **(b) 1840** ——— *Works* XII. 219 The dusk has settled heavily upon the woods, the waves, and the Trimountain peninsula. **1851** WORTLEY *Travels in U.S.* 62 For Instance this [Boston] I believe, is not only called the Granite City, but the Trimountain City. **1858** *Spirit of Times* 13 Feb. 378/1 The dwellers by the shores of the Hudson . . . are wont to look upon the inhabitants of the Tri-mount City as goodly, straight-laced plodders in the old beaten pathways. **1885** *Cent. Mag.* Feb. 511/2 It has required some independence for . . . a trimontane poet to be a progressive and speculative thinker. **1904** *Brooklyn Standard Union* 15 Aug. 6 There is much in the Tri-mountain City and its environs to interest a patriotic American—old Bunker Hill, for instance.

2. tri-weekly, a. *n.* A newspaper issued three times a week. **b.** *a.* Operating three times a week.

(a) 1851 CIST *Cincinnati* 74 Those are all dailies, tri-weeklies and weekly reissues of dailies. **1884** S. N. O. NORTH *Hist. Newspaper Press* 111 The *Spy* ran as a tri-weekly. — **(b) 1832** *Amer. State P.: Post Office* 348 The line of stages . . . has been increased from a bi-weekly to a tri-weekly line to Eastville. **1877** HODGE *Arizona* 204 It is a tri-weekly route, and is made in eight days from San Diego to Mesilla.

∗ **trial,** *n.* In combs.: (1) **trial judge,** a judge who presides at the trial of a case; (2) **justice,** a justice of the peace or other subordinate magistrate empowered to try certain types of cases; (3) **lawyer,** a lawyer chiefly engaged in the trial of cases in court as distinguished from an office lawyer; (4) **sermon,** a sermon delivered by a ministerial candidate seeking ordination or by a minister complying with an invitation extended him by a congregation considering engaging him.

(1) 1896 *Internat. Typog. Union Proc.* 11/1 The trial judge has publicly expressed his lack of confidence in his construction of the statute. — **(2) 1869** *Mass. Acts & Resolves* 556 Whoever, without a written license . . . , takes any trout . . . , shall forfeit and pay a fine of twenty-five dollars for every such offence, to be recovered before any trial justice. **1906** *Ib.* 676 Police, district and municipal courts and trial justices shall have jurisdiction of offences arising under the provisions of this act. — **(3) 1929** R. R. MORTON *What Negro Thinks* 146 His practice is seldom that of a trial lawyer, but rather as an adjuster of cases and an adviser in civil processes. **1947** *Reader's Digest* Jan. 11/2 He would have been one of the greatest trial lawyers in the country. — **(4) 1801–3** J. LYLE *Diary* (MS) 98 Mr. Stuart preached his trial sermon before ordination. **1863** P. S. DAVIS *Young Parson* 9 The Rev. Petit Meagre had accepted an invitation to preach a *trial sermon* before the Gainfield congregation.

∗**triangle,** *n.* What is now Erie County, Pa. *Obs.* — **1789** *Jrnl. of Wm. Maclay* 120 Mr Izard informed me of the attempt of Gorham to get the land commonly called the triangle from Pennsylvania.

∗**tribe,** *n.* As the last term in **blanket, border, Five Civilized, Flathead, Miami, Nez Percé, Osage, plains, prairie, Sac, seated, Seminole, Seneca, Snake tribe(s).**

∗ **trick,** *n.*

1. A small article or one of little worth, a personal belonging or effect.

1869 *Overland Mo.* III. 131 In Texas you never have *things* in your house, or *baggage* on your journey, but 'tricks.' **1906** O. HENRY *Trimmed Lamp* 77 Here's a little trick I picked out for you on my way over.

2. A playful term of praise or affection used of a child, horse, etc.

1887 *Cent. Mag.* May 113/1 We uns played tergether w'en we wuz little tricks. **1890** *Stock Grower & Farmer* 29 March 7/1 Down in the Panhandle . . . I used to ride a little trick named Dandy. **1934** VINES *Green Thicket World* 93 Cindy called her a cute little trick.

3. A device used in conjuring. Also attrib. Cf. ∗**trick,** *v.*

1893 M. A. OWEN *Voodoo Tales* 209 The aunties searched under every doorstone for 'tricks.' **1893** *Ib.* 174 Tow Head . . . [repeated] the formula she had learned from Aunt Mymee, for preparing a 'tricken-bag.'

b. trick doctor, a conjurer or sorcerer.

1889 BRUCE *Plantation Negro* 116 The trick doctor . . . employs the arts of the Obeah practitioners . . . With the arts of the Myal. **1898** PAGE *Red Rock* 161 The trick-doctor . . . bowed himself off.

4. *how's tricks,* what is the condition of things in general, often as a friendly greeting. *Colloq.*

1920 LEWIS *Main Street* 12 Oh quit fussing now. Come over here and sit down and tell us how's tricks. **1928** *Hearst's International* Aug. 100/2 'How's tricks, Steve?' said the second man.

As the last term in **lobster, Yankee trick.**

∗**trick,** *v. tr.* To bewitch. *Colloq. Obs.* — **1829** *Va. Lit. Museum* 384 And, amongst the degraded and ignorant part of our own population, the notion of 'tricking' or bewitching is universally and implicity received, rendering the miserable victim of the fancied 'tricking' wretched to himself and useless to his master. **1888** in FLEMING *Hist. Reconstruction* II. 448 When a person is said to be 'tricked,' it means the same as good old Dr. Mather would have called bewitched.

triddler ˈtrɪdlɚ, *n. local.* [The reason for the name is not known.] (See quot. 1888.) — **1888** TRUMBULL *Names of Birds* 176 Pectoral

Sandpiper. . . . Known also to some Atlantic City gunners as Triddler. **1917** *Birds of Amer.* I. 233.

* **triennial,** *n.* A college catalogue or list of alumni issued every three years. In full **triennial catalogue.**

1847 J. MITCHELL *Reminisc. College* 198 The Triennial Catalogue becomes increasingly a mournful record . . . to survivors. **1864** in *Mass. Hist. Soc. Proc.* VIII. 37 The earliest Harvard Triennial, in the octavo form with a titlepage, was printed at Boston 'Typis Thomae & Johannis Fleet, Academiae Typographorum,' in 1776. **1890** HOLMES *Over Teacups* 28 The class of 1829 at Harvard College, of which I am a member, graduated, according to the triennial, fifty-nine in number.

* **trigger,** *n.*

1. In occasional colloq. combs.: (1) **trigger eye,** the eye one sights with in shooting; (2) **finger,** the finger used in pulling the trigger in shooting; (3) **itch,** eagerness to use a gun; (4) **thumb,** the thumb used in cocking a single action revolver.

(1) **1837** NEAL *Charcoal Sk.* (1838) 63 He agreed to keep his trigger eye on the dog. — (2) **1940** *Pop. Sci. Mo.* May 113 His trigger finger 'squeezes the lemon' with speed and deadly accuracy. — (3) **1914** BOWER *Flying U Ranch* 154 The man who feels the trigger-itch had better throw his gun away. — (4) **1928** FOY & HARLOW *Clowning Thro' Life* 110 It's a wonder his trigger thumb didn't work out of sheer annoyance.

2. *quick on the trigger*, quick to act, impetuous; *easy on the trigger*, easily moved to action. Both *colloq.*

1808 WEEMS *Lett.* II. 377, I trust that all your Aids will be quick on the trigger. **1884** CRADDOCK *Where Battle Was Fought* 47 You are quick on the trigger. — **1853** P. PAXTON *Yankee in Texas* 121 I'm mighty easy on the trigger, and the next mornin' I were done gone.

* **trillium,** *n.* As the last term in **painted, red trillium.**

* **trim,** *n.* **1.** "The visible woodwork or finish of a house, as the baseboards, door- and window-casings, etc." (*Cent.*). Cf. **door trim. 2.** A window display of goods.

(1) **1884** *N.Y. Ev. Post* 14 April (*Cent.*), No wood having been used in construction except for floors, doors, and trim. **1946** *Coronet* Dec. 146/2 Yet the strongest lock is useless if it is set in a rotten door jamb or a thin piece of trim with nothing behind it. — (2) **1926** *Publishers' Wkly.* 30 Jan. 328/1 A large red ribbon rosette, from which radiated white satin ribbons to a number of stands at each side of the trim. *Ib.* 10 July 119/2 When Stone's trim was removed, Wheatly did his 'stuff.'

* **trim,** *v.* **1.** *tr.* = * **neck,** *v.* **1.** *Obs.* **2.** *To trim one's corners*, see * **corner,** *n.* **5. b.** (4). — (1) **1776** *Essex Hist. Coll.* LIII. 91 Nov. 4, 5, 6, 7, 8, 9. Trimming balls and making cartridges.

* **trimmer,** *n.* A dishonest or unscrupulous lawyer. *Colloq.* See also **timothy, window trimmer.** — **1891** S. M. WELCH *Recoll. 1830–40* 293 There was an *esprit de corps* of reliability and honor in their practice; excluding such characters as are known as 'Shysters,' 'Tombs Lawyers,' 'Trimmers,' and lawyers guilty of 'sharp practice.'

trinchera trɪnˈtʃɛrə, *n. S.W.* [Sp., fort, entrenchment.] (See quot.) — **1906** *Out West* Jan. 28 Laboratory Mountain is of considerable interest to the ethnologist as being a *trinchera*, or fortified place of refuge from predatory savages.

* **trip,** *n.*

1. (See quot.)

1891 *Cent.* 6485/2 *Trip*, . . . in the fisheries, the catch, take, or fare of fish caught during a voyage; the proceeds of a trip in fish.

2. In combs.: (1) **trip book,** (see quot.); (2) **card,** a card giving route information for cyclists; (3) **hammer,** a heavy machine hammer which is raised by mechanical means and allowed to fall by gravity; (4) **pass,** ?a complimentary pass, *obs.*; (5) **slip,** (see quot. 1891).

(1) **1891** *Cent.* 6486/1 *Trip-book*, . . . a book in which the account of a voyage of a fishing-vessel is made up, showing the shares belonging respectively to the vessel and the crew. — (2) **1897** *Outing* XXX. 492/2 These trip-cards . . . have been adopted by many other clubs for the information of riders. — (3) **1781** PETERS *Hist. Conn.* (1829) 199 Anchor making is done by water and trip hammers. *a***1819** DWIGHT *Travels* II. 15 Here he built a shop, and set up the first trip-hammer in this part of the country. **1922** PARRISH *Case & Girl* 251 His heart [was] beating like a trip-hammer. — (4) **1890** BIFF HALL *Turnover Club* 156 This landlord had visited the show on a trip-pass, and therefore didn't hesitate to give his opinion.

(5) **1876** *Scribner's Mo.* April 910/2 The conductor, when he receives a fare, will immediately punch in the presence of the passenger, A Blue trip slip for an 8 cent fare. **1891** *Cent.* 6488/3 *Trip-slip*, a slip of paper in which the conductor of a horse-car punches a hole as record of each fare taken.

b. In phrases: (1) *To get a trip*, of a steamboat, to get enough freight, passengers, etc., to justify a run; (2) *trip and twitch*, a hold or maneuver in wrestling, also transf.

(1) **1883** MARK TWAIN *Life on Miss.* xxiii, This calm craft would go as advertised, 'if she got her trip.' — (2) **1746** *N.H. Hist. Soc. Coll.* II. 88 He tried his strength, and skill, in his favorite mode of 'trip and twitch.' **1876** *Cong. Rec.* 8 Aug. 5302/2 In this body, . . . there is none of that trip and twitch by which legislation is jerked through so quickly that you cannot see it go.

As the last term in **pack, round, tote trip.**

tripas ˈtripəs, *n. pl. S.W.* [Sp. in sense shown here.] (See quot. 1932.) — **1929** DE CASTRO *Portrait* 330 (Bentley), He promised to speed a bullet into my tripas for the fine things I wrote about his enemies. **1932** BENTLEY 211 The word is also used by Americans who would not say 'entrails' and prefer not to use the unmentionable 'guts.' *Tripas* is convenient as a respectable medium.

* **triple,** *n.*

1. In baseball, a three-base hit.

1880 *N.Y. Press* 3 June. **1887** *Chi. Tribune* 3 May 3/1 He made in succession a single, double, triple, and home run. **1949** *Milwaukie* (Ore.) *Rev.* 4 Aug. 4/4 The hard working first sacker collected his first triple of the year.

2. a. triple letter, a letter three times as heavy as one regarded as usual or standard. *Obs.* **b. triple play,** in baseball, a play in which three men are put out.

(a) **1792** *Ann. 2nd. Congress* 60 Every triple letter, [shall pay] triple [the said rates]. — (b) **1870** *De Witt's Base-Ball Guide* 42 The remarks concerning double and triple plays will apply to the third baseman. **1950** *Chi. Tribune* 29 March III. 4/3 Cincinnati pulled a triple play in the first inning.

* **triplet,** *n. Baseball.* A three-base hit. — **1883** *Chi. Inter-Ocean* 9 June 3/1 In the seventh and ninth innings Radbourne hit for a triplet and a four-bagger. **1893** *Chi. Tribune* 23 April 3/3 Harvard got in two triplets, one double, and a single in the first inning.

* **tripper,** *n.* (See quot. 1891.) Also attrib.

1882 MCCABE *New York* 244 The 'trippers,' as those men are called who only run three-quarters of a day, get $1.50. **1891** *Cent.* 6488/2 tripper. . . . A street-railroad conductor or driver who is paid according to the number of trips which he makes, or who is employed to make special trips, as in the place of others who are laid off for any cause. **1950** *Reading Times* 28 Feb., They had refused to operate 'tripper' or extra, runs because five members of the union had been furloughed. The company said this situation resulted in the failure of nine 'tripper' runs to be made.

Triune Immersionists. (See quot.) — **1909** *Springfield W. Republican* 30 Sep. 14/1 The 300 or more members of 'The Latter Reign of the Apostolic Church,' who called themselves 'Triune Immersionists,' and are popularly known as 'Holy Rollers' . . . held a long watch meeting Friday night.

* **Trojan,** *n.* A native or inhabitant of Troy, N.Y.

1824 *Microscope* (Albany, N.Y.) 22 May 43/1 (Th.), Ye dull-minded Trojans . . . you must now hide your diminished heads. **1888** *Troy* (N.Y.) *D. Times* 25 Aug., Among the Trojans who went to the state firemen's convention at Cortland was Orange S. Ingram. **1948** *Amer. Sp.* XXIII. 163 The inhabitants . . . of Troy, N.Y., are *Trojans.*

* **trolley,** *n.*

1. A device for collecting electric current from a wire, a trolley pole.

1890 *N. & Q.* IV. 275 A motorneer is the man who rides on the front of an electric car and handles the trolly, which runs on the wires overhead. **1902** SLOANE *Stand. Electrical Dict. s.v.*, Trolleys are principally used on electric railroads.

b. *To be off* (or *slip*) *one's trolley, fig.* to be (or become) mentally deranged. *Slang.*

1908 DAVENPORT *Butte Beneath X-Ray* 24 The medium is clear off her trolley, for my father has been dead three years. **1945** *Amer. Sp.* April 83 When a person does slip his trolley in Texas, they fall back on euphemism.

2. = **trolley car.**

1891 *Month* LXXIII. 24, I jumped off the trolley. **1912** *Out West* April 267/1 The summits of Mt. Lowe and Mt. Wilson, nearly one mile high, are easily reached by trolley or auto. **1950** *Pacific Spectator* Winter 84 I've ridden only in private cars, busses, and trolleys.

3. In combs.: (1) **trolley bus,** a bus that operates on the trolley system; (2) **car,** an electric streetcar or tram, also attrib.; (3) **line,** a line of streetcars propelled on the trolley system; (4) **party,** (see quot.); (5) **pole,** (*a*) a pole placed along a street or way to support a wire for a trolley line, (*b*) (see quot.); (6) **stagecoach,** a coach or bus that operates on the trolley system, *obs.*

(1) **1946** *Chi. D. News* 23 Dec. 8/4 Trolley buses and motor coaches are suitable to the lighter traffic routes. — (2) **1894** *Life* 8 March 147/1 Death and the Devil met . . . to discuss the way That each would like to travel. . . . Said Death, . . . 'Ha, ha! Oh! Give me a

Brooklyn trolley car!' **1949** *Pa. Dutchman* 26 May 1/1 He was about to get on a trolley car, over in South Allentown. — **(3) 1894** *Life* 13 Dec. 382/2 A selected choir of motormen from the Brooklyn trolley lines then sang a hymn describing the massacre of the innocents by King Herod. **1949** *Dly. Ardmoreite* (Ardmore, Okla.) 23 Feb. 3/6 Trolley lines in the United States once had special cars to carry milk and mail, also street sprinkling cars. — **(4) 1896** *Harper's Wkly.* I Aug. 758/1 In some cities they have what they call 'trolley parties,' where a group of persons will charter a car, ornament it with flowers, flags, or Chinese lanterns, and go riding for an evening all over the system of connecting lines.

(5) (*a*) **1894** *Harper's Mag.* June 4/1 The new town . . . has seen fit to . . . erect red trolley poles on the most exclusive streets. (*b*) **1895** *Standard* 1935/1 *T[rolley]-pole*, a pole, on a trolley-car, carrying the trolley-wheel. — **(6) 1897** *Voice* 16 Sep. 5/5 In Greenwich, Conn., . . . the people . . . are able to ride in a trolley stage-coach that needs no rails for its operation.

trolleyize 'tralɪˌaɪz, *v. tr.* To convert (a tramway) into an electric trolley railroad. *Rare.* — **1895** *Pop. Sci. Mo.* April 751 Every species of tramway spins its overhead wires and becomes trolleyized.

***trolling line. = *trawl,** *n.*

1801 Morris in Sparks *Life G. Morris* III. 140, I took with a trolling line above fifty [trout and perch in Lake George]. **1875** *Chi. Tribune* 30 Aug. 7/2 Fishing with a trolling line on horseback is a novel sport. **1939** Pinkerton *Wilderness Wife* 25 If you'll drop the trolling line, we'll have lake trout for supper.

troll line. = *trawl, *n.* — **1855** Oliphant *Minnesota* 177 We tried the St. Louis with fly, bait, and troll lines, but without the slightest success. **1911** *Rep. Fisheries 1908* 316/2 Monterey Spanish mackerel . . . are caught on troll lines and in gill nets and pound nets.

***Trollope,** *n.* [Frances Milton *Trollope* (1780–1863), an English visitor to this country who sharply criticized some of the manners of the Americans.] (See quots.) *Obs.* — **1834** C. D. Arfwedson *United States* II. 177 Whenever an individual in a playhouse happens, when seated in the boxes, to turn his back towards the pit, or, occupying a front seat, to put his feet on the benches, (a want of decorum severely censured by Mrs. Trollope) a general outcry of 'Trollope, Trollope' is heard from every part of the house. **1896** Haswell *New York* 276 Whenever one in public fell within the range of her [i.e., Mrs. Trollope's] criticism, . . . the cry of 'Trollope! Trollope! Trollope!' was immediately vociferated.

Trollope 'traləp, *v.* [See prec. and cf. **trollop, v.*] *intr.* To emulate Mrs. Trollope. *Obs.* — **1848** *De Bow's Review* V. 283 Travelers, male and female . . . come *Trolloping* over our country, to seek what blemishes they may descry.

Trollopize 'traləpˌaɪz, *v.* [See ***Trollope,** *n.*] *tr.* To ridicule or criticize as crude or unrefined. *Obs.* — **1834** *N.Y. Mirror* 12 July 16/1 The right honourable secretary of the colonial department, Mr. Stanley, has been *Trollopized.* **1838** A. Bell *Men & Things* (1862) 210 They now stand in awe, under a dread, as they say, of being *Trollopised.*

trompillo trɔm'pijo, *n. S.W.* [Amer. Sp. name for various plants, including the one here defined.] A nightshade, *Solanum elaeagnifolium.* — **1885** Havard *Flora W. & S. Texas* 512 *Solanum elaeagnifolium.* . . . Trompillo. . . . One of the most common of weeds in all valleys of Southern and Western Texas. **1892** *D. N.* I. 253 *Trompillo*, a common weed of the nightshade family in southern and western Texas. The berries . . . are used for curdling milk.

troop fowl. *local.* (See quot. 1891.) Cf. **flocking fowl.** — **1876** *Forest & Stream* 9 Nov. 212/3 *Fulix marila.* Troop fowl. **1891** *Cent.* 6498/3 *Troop-fowl*, the American scaup. . . . (Massachusetts.) **1917** *Birds of Amer.* I. 135.

***troops,** *n. pl.* As the last term in **convention, government, palace, polka, provincial, state troops.**

***trot,** *n.* A translation of a text in a foreign, esp. a classical, language. *Slang.*

1891 *Cent.* 6501/1. **1893** Post *Harvard Stories* 235 The mucker was put in the middle of the room with the 'trot'; the students . . . followed the translation in their Greek texts. **1941** Skinner *Soap behind Ears* 40 The next is a literal translation, nostalgically reminiscent of my old Horace trot.

As the last term in **county, dog, fall, fox, horse, Irish, Negro, turkey trot.**

***trotter,** *n.* As the last term in **raw, road, square trotter.**

***trotting,** *n.*

1. a. The racing of trotters. **b.** Using a trot *q.v.* in preparing one's lessons.

(a) 1846 *Spirit of Times* (N.Y.) 11 July 234/1 The legislative Solons of Massachusetts have prohibited trotting and racing. **1883** *Harper's Mag.* Oct. 416/2 The running track, commonly used for trotting as well, has . . . seen some notable achievements. — **(b) 1940** *Amer. Mercury* Dec. 450/2 Cribbing, cramming, and trotting have become fixed if 'sub rosa' practices at our colleges.

2. a. trotting buggy, a light vehicle drawn by a trotter. **b. trotting turf,** the course used in a trotting race, hence, *fig.*, the institution of trotting races.

(a) 1866 W. Reid *After War* 99 The roads were alive with a gaily-dressed throng, . . . wending their way, . . . in Northern trotting buggies. — **(b) 1856** *Porter's Spirit of Times* 25 Oct. 128/2 Nothing would have given the lovers of the trotting turf more pleasure than to witness a trot of three miles. **1893** *Outing* May 98/2 Glancing at the kings and queens of the trotting turf,—the most memorable events of the trotting turf will pass in review.

***trouble,** *n.*

1. Disorderly festivity. *Colloq.*

1884 C. T. Buckland *Sk. Social Life India* 66 A day of rest comes in between each day of pleasure, or 'trouble' as the Yankees more rightly call it. **1897** Flandrau *Harvard Episodes* 313 There is always more or less, what is technically known as 'trouble' in Claverly [Hall] and its vicinity on Class Day afternoon.

2. In combs.: (1) **trouble man,** (see quot. 1909); (2) **shooter,** =prec., also transf., *colloq.;* (3) **shooting,** the work of a trouble shooter, also attrib., *colloq.*

(1) 1889 *Cassell's Family Mag.* 410/1 What the Americans call 'Trouble-men.' **1909** *Cent. Supp.* 1381/3 *Trouble-man*, . . . an expert, familiar with the working of any apparatus or process, who is able to locate the cause of 'trouble' (unsatisfactory operation) and remedy it. — **(2) 1931** B. Starke *Touch & Go* xv. 248 A trouble-shooter for the telephone lines. **1947** *Hyde Park Herald* (Chi.) 29 May 3/3 At any hour of day or night, if something in your home interrupts your electric service, these 'trouble shooters' hasten to the rescue. **1950** *Dly. Oklahoman Mag.* (Okla. City) 7 May 3/1 Mrs. Paine is the Camp Fire Girls troubleshooter. — **(3) 1929** *Sat. Ev. Post* 7 Dec. 70/3 A trouble-shooting car . . . is ready to dash out on short notice to service or replace a set that has gone dead. **1949** *L.A. Times Home Mag.* 11 Dec. 37/2 When trouble-shooting the ills of house foliage plants in terrariums you sometimes run out of guesses.

b. *To look for* (or *seek*) *trouble*, to risk involvement in difficulty or danger. *Colloq.*

1901 Merwin & Webster *Calumet 'K'* 134 We've got to build the belt gallery—and we'll have no end of a time doing it if the C. & S. C. is still looking for trouble. **1905** *N.Y. Ev. Post* 29 Aug. 2 In the possible chance of rounding up all who might be seeking trouble, the police temporarily sequestered and searched 140 Chinamen. **1947** Motley *Knock on Any Door* 152 Swollen out in their own importance they walked along West Madison looking for trouble.

As the last term in **double, Mormon trouble.**

***trough,** *n.*

1. *To walk up to the trough, fodder or no fodder*, and variants, to accept one's lot or responsibilities. *Colloq.* Cf. *To stand up to the rack, s.v.* ***rack,** *n*[1].

1843 Stephens *High Life N.Y.* II. 45 If that don't bring him up to the trough, fodder, or no fodder, I don't know what will. **1871** Eggleston *Hoosier Schoolm.* 43 Walk up to the trough, fodder or no fodder, as the man said to his donkey.

2. troughsman, (see quot.). *Obs.*

1904 *Nation* 23 June 500/2 The grafters . . . comprise the executive of a Western State, a judge, a working majority of the Senate and House of Assembly, and a number of inferior persons spoken of as 'troughsmen.' These used to be called 'henchmen,' then 'heelers,' but the newer word may be accepted without cavil.

As the last term in **basswood, bread, eaves, feed, feeding, sap, sluice, store, sugar, wash trough.**

troupe trup, *n.* [F. in the sense shown here.] A company or band, esp. one of performers or entertainers. Cf. **minstrel, variety troupe.**

1825 *N.Y. Ev. Post* 6 Dec. 2 The whole troupe were equally excellent. **1885** *Life* 2 April 186/1 Bob Ingersoll has found his level as a side show to a Burlesque Troupe. **1946** *This Week Mag.* 10 Aug. 5/1 Both he and his troupe took their art in deadly earnest.

troupe trup, *v.* [f. the noun.] *intr.* To travel as a member of a troupe of entertainers. Also **trouping,** *n.* — **1900** *Everybody's Mag.* II. 586/2 One hesitates to say which impresses a novice in 'trouping' the most—the seeming omnipotence of the manager, or the social sets into which the travelling troupe divides itself. **1925** Cooper *Lions 'n' Tigers* 33 He was a menagerie superintendent, she a trainer of lions, tigers and elephants. But they troupe no more.

trouper 'trupɚ, *n.* An actor or performer belonging to a troupe.

1890 Biff Hall *Turnover Club* 160 As the 'troupers' come into the station where I sat, they were a sorry-looking lot. **1912** Vance *Destroying Angel* vi, I'm as superstitious as any trooper in the profession. **1946** *Boston Transcript* Sep. 6/2 A little knot of interested troupers were looking on as Joe and I met.

***troupial,** *n.* As the last term in **cow, yellow-headed troupial.**

***trousers,** *n. pl.* As the last term in **bellows, Cape Cod, knee, mosquito, over, petticoat, sub trousers.**

*** trout,** *n.*

1. Any one of various American fishes, esp. one of the genus *Salvelinus* or *Cristivomer*, resembling or confused with the European trout.

It is not possible from the quots. to tell which of the fishes mentioned belong to American genera.

1685 BUDD *Pa. & N.J.* 80 In the said River and Cricks are many other sorts of good Fish . . . some of which are Cat-fish, Trout, Eales [etc.]. **1709** LAWSON *Carolina* 158 Trouts . . . are in the Salts, and are not red within, but white. **1772** ROMANS in P. L. Phillips *Notes B. Romans* (1924) 123 The Rivers have . . . the Chab or Chevin, here Miscalled a Trout. **1831** PECK *Guide* 47 The streams . . . are alive with trout and other fish. **1902** W. D. HULBERT *Forest Neighbors* (1903) 68 The last trout went in search of better feeding grounds. **1950** *Nat. Hist.* April 173/3 In open stretches he got out his tackle and caught trout and grayling as he drifted along.

b. With specifying terms.

1879 *Scribner's Mo.* Nov. 17/1 A white-meated fish . . . was known to them [Mich. hunters] as 'Crawford County trout.' **1884** GOODE *Fisheries* I. 475 The Black spotted Trout . . . is known as the . . . 'Black Trout,' 'Silver trout,' etc., in the mountains. **1909** *Cent. Supp.* 1381/3 *Coast Range trout, Salmo irideus,* found in coastwise streams of the western United States.

2. In the names of various fishes.

1814 MITCHILL *Fishes N.Y.* 442 Trout Pike. (*Esox salmoneus.*) . . . Length eight or nine inches, and figured somewhat like the eel. **1820** RAFINESQUE in *Western Rev.* II. 52 Trout River-Bass. *Lepomis Salmonea.* . . . Vulgar names White Trout, Brown Trout, Trout Pearch, Trout Bass [etc.]. **1890** *Cent.* 4474/1 *Trout-pickerel,* the banded pickerel, *Esox americanus.* **1891** *Cent.* 6503/3 *Trout-shad,* . . . the squeteague.

b. trout perch, a bass, as *Micropterus dolomieu,* or the sand roller, *Percopsis omiscomaycus.*

1820 RAFINESQUE in *Western Rev.* II. 52 Trout River-Bass. *Lepomis Salmonea.* . . . Vulgar names White Trout, Brown Trout, Trout Pearch. **1883** *Nat. Museum Bul.* No. 27, 472 The trout-perch spawns in spring. **1888** *Wildwood's Mag.* (Chi.) June 64 In southern Virginia the large-mouthed bass is known as the 'chub,' as in North Carolina it is called 'white salmon,' 'welchman,' or 'trout-perch.'

3. In the names of plants.

1892 *Amer. Folk-Lore* V. 96 *Begonia maculata,* trout begonia. Bedford, Mass. **1894** *Ib.* VII. 101 *Erythronium Americanum,* trout-flower (local) N.Y. **1909** *Cent.* 729/2 *Trout-lily,* the yellow dog-tooth violet or adder's-tongue, *Erythronium Americanum.* **1943** PEATTIE *Great Smokies* 275 Late in the month it may fall on the spring beauties and trout lilies which herald the blooming season above 5,000 feet.

As the last term in **bastard, black, brook, cousin, creek, cutthroat, Dolly Varden, Gila, golden, gray, Lewis, mackinaw, mountain, Oquassa, rainbow, red, red-spotted, red throat, Rio Grande, salmon, salt-water, sea, Sebago, shad, shoal water, speckled, speckled brook, speckled mountain, sun, Tahoe, water trout.**

trowel bayonet. (See quot. 1876.) *Obs.* — **1876** KNIGHT 2631/1 *Trowel-bayonet,* a bayonet resembling a mason's trowel, used as a weapon, and as a light intrenching-tool, or as a hatchet when detached from the rifle. **1884** *Cent. Mag.* May 137/2 Each man had protected himself by earth thrown up with his trowel bayonet.

trouserloons ˈtrauzəˌlunz, *n.* [f. **trousers* + **panta-loons.*] Trousers. *Jocular. Obs.*

1827 *Beacon* (Norfolk, Va.) 13 Oct. 2/2 (Th. Supp.), [One shot] glanced and passed through the trowsaloons of the Jackson man. **1847** *Ore. Spectator* 7 Jan. 3/1 His *trowserloons,* the lower extremities of which, only reached the top of his socks, gave him the appearance of being much taller than he really was. **1858** *Calif. Spirit of Times* (S.F.) 7 Aug. 1/6 The money was safe—safe in the left hand pocket of Wildes' trouserloons, and the 'bulk' concealed by the old gray shirt which hung over it.

*** Troy,** *n.*

1. A coach of a type built at Troy, N.Y. In full **Troy coach.** Now *hist.*

1834 *Western Mo. Mag.* II. 589 Here is the Harrodsburg stage driving up, and an elegant affair it is—a new Troy coach, of the latest construction, drawn by four fine horses. **1859** in *So. Calif. Hist. Soc. Pub.* XVII. 104 They are of the build of the common Troy coach, and the body is hung upon the same kind of springs and in a similar manner. **1950** *Hobbies* May 23/3 The 'Troy' was lighter than the Concord, and the favorite passenger coach in America prior to the building of railroads.

2. Troy laundry, ?a laundry using equipment manufactured at Troy, N.Y.

1900 *Everybody's Mag.* II. 37/2 Four barbers' shops had been established, and what is more extraordinary, half a dozen 'Troy' laundries and a bath-house had also sprung into existence.

truant officer. An officer charged with investigating the absence of children from school.

1872 BRACE *Dangerous Classes N.Y.* 348 The Massachusetts system of 'Truant-schools'—that is Schools to which truant officers could send children habitually truant—does not seem so applicable to New York. **1911** PERSONS *Mass. Labor Laws* 181 The truant officer finds that no certificate has been issued from the central office. **1950** *Desplaines Valley News* (Summit, Ill.) 7 April 2/1 Our Platform. . . . Employ a truant officer, school doctor and dentist.

*** truck,** *n.*[1]

1. *local.* Medicine.

*c***1775** BOUCHER *Glossary* p. l, Till now ne'er *crazy,* in my bones no pains, I *never took no truck,* nor doctor's means. **1831** *Boston Transcript* 22 July 2/3 Well, the Docktur, he giv'ur some white truck in a spoon, with sum swurrup. **1880** NYE *B. Nye & Boomerang* 26 Just squeeze a little of your truck into a tumbler, and flavor it to suit the boys.

2. Vegetables, garden produce. Also **truck and trade.** *Colloq.*

1805 PARKINSON *Tour* 161, I thought nothing in the farming-line likely to be profitable, except . . . what in that country is called truck,—which is garden produce, fruits, &c. **1848** *Oquawka* (Ill.) *Spectator* 5 April 4/1 He was compelled to receive 'truck and trade,' as the western phrase is, for his admission fee, such as onions, potatoes, eggs and the like. **1895** *Dept. Agric. Yrbk. 1894* 26 Such soils are naturally adapted to the forcing of early 'truck' and vegetables.

3. In combs.: (1) **truck house,** see as a main entry; (2) **man,** (see quot.); (3) **master,** in colonial times, a man appointed to have charge of trade with the Indians, *obs.;* (4) **store,** (*a*) a store at which vouchers given instead of wages may be exchanged for goods, (*b*) a store at which truck trade is carried on, both *rare;* (5) **trade,** bartering, exchange of commodities, *obs.*

(2) **1864** WEBSTER 1419/2 *Truckman,* . . . one who does business in the way of barter or exchange. — (3) **1637** MORTON *New Canaan* 159 Two truckmasters were chosen; wages prefixed. **1640** *New Haven Col. Rec.* 43 Mr. Gregson shall be Truck ma[ste]r of this towne . . . to truck with the Indians for venison. **1700** SEWALL *Diary* II. 10 Mr. Turfrey is made. . . . Truck-master with the Indians. **1767** HUTCHINSON *Hist. Mass.* II. 318 The charge of trading houses, truckmasters, garrisons, and a vessel employed in transporting goods was deducted. — (4) (*a*) **1886** *Appleton's Ann. Cyclo.* 84/1 In Liége . . . employers compelled the laborers to purchase supplies from their Truck stores, at prices from 50 to 90 per cent. above . . . retail rates. (*b*) **1907** WHITE *Arizona Nights* 33 'Well,' says the man, still reasonable, 'I ain't got no money, but I'll give you six bits' worth of flour or trade or an'thin' I got.' 'I don't run no truck store,' snaps Texas Pete, and turns square on his heel and goes back to his chair.

(5) **1720** *Mass. Bay Currency Tracts* 357 Were this Truck Trade at an end, and the Trader Sold all for Money, . . . I should think it a more proper time to propose such Laws. **1832** W. WILLIAMSON *Maine* II. 202 A vessel, the Snow, was likewise built, for the protection of the coasting and truck trade.

b. In combs. (sense **2.**) of obvious meaning, as (1) **truck crop,** (2) **farm,** (3) **farmer,** (4) **farming,** (5) **garden,** (6) **gardener,** (7) **gardening,** (8) **grower,** (9) **patch,** (10) **soil.**

(1) **1895** *Dept. Yrbk. Agric. 1894* 133 Soils having over 10 or 12 per cent of clay are too heavy and too retentive of moisture for the early truck crops. **1949** *Nat. Geog. Mag.* Aug. 145/2 'Truck crops' we call our vegetables. The expression has no connection with the fact that they are commonly hauled to market in motor trucks. — (2) **1866** *N. & Q.* 3 Ser. IX. 323/1 A truck garden, a truck farm, is a market-garden or farm. **1949** *Nat. Geog. Mag.* Aug. 172/2 On one truck farm I saw a beautiful 10-acre field of collards. — (3) **1877** A. DOUAI *Better Times* (1884) 7 The truck-farmers from Virginia down to Florida. **1903** *N.Y. Ev. Post* 27 Nov. 6 Until 1898 all the land included in these limits was still cultivated by truck farmers. —(4) **1870** *Rep. Comm. Agric. 1869* 447 Truck Farming in New Jersey. **1949** *Sat. Ev. Post* 5 March 24/1 Truck farming is a poor second, railroading a poor third.

(5) **1866** LOSSING *Hudson* 394 From the road . . . stretch away numerous 'truck' gardens, from which the city draws vegetable supplies. **1945** *Greeley* (Colo.) *Tribune* 6 Jan. 2/2 Doi grew a truck garden before the war. — (6) **1922** CATHER *One of Ours* 110 The rich bottom land about the Trevor place had been rented out to a truck gardener for years now. **1924** FERBER *So Big* 18 Julie had suddenly come upon her stepping agilely out of a truck gardener's wagon on Prairie Avenue. — (7) **1890** *Boston Jrnl.* 12 April 2/4 During their two years' residence they have done all of their own work and truck-gardening. **1949** *Dly. Ardmoreite* (Ardmore, Okla.) 25 Jan. 2/1 Truck gardening may become a reality in Southern Oklahoma! — (8) **1897** *Kissimmee* (Fla.) *Valley Gaz.* 1 Dec. 2/1 His long experience

as a truck grower here will, we hope, make his advice valuable to our readers. — (9) **1819** *Ky. Alman. 1820* (Lexington) 30 He had a fence round a bit of ground for a truck patch. **1948** DICK *Dixie Frontier* 289 The little truck patch was often neglected.
(10) **1895** *Dept. Agric. Yrbk. 1894* 132 The heavy grass and wheat lands will produce three or four times as great a yield of truck as the truck soils do.

As the last term in **garden, market, spun truck.**

***truck,** *n.*[2] As the last term in **auto, baggage, block, Boston, hook-and-ladder, ladder, mail, pony, wrecking truck.**

truck cloth. =**trucking cloth.** *Obs.* — **1637** *Md. Council Proc.* 57 Shipped for the Isle of Kent . . . ; three pieces of blew truck cloth. **1642** *Md. Archives* IV. 100, 10. yards ½ of blew truck cloth.

***trucker,** *n.* A truck farmer.

1868 *Norfolk* (Va.) *Jrnl.*, The truckers in this neighborhood. **1887** J. E. MCGOWAN *Chattanooga & Tenn.* 35 The fruiters, farmers and truckers have now more capital for their business. **1897** *Kissimmee* (Fla.) *Valley Gaz.* 1 Dec. 2/3 A portion of this column is to be devoted to the interests of the farmer and trucker. **1911** JENKS & LAUCK *Immigration Problem* 83 The truckers and small fruit growers are doing exceptionally well.

truck house. [The two senses shown here derive from ***truck,** *n.*[1] and ***truck,** *n.*[2]]

1. A building used as a store for trading with the Indians. Also attrib. *Obs.*

1720 *Mass. H. Rep. Jrnl.* II. 236 It would be very much for the Interest of the Government . . . if there were set up . . . a few Truck-houses, where the Indians might be supplied at reasonable Rates with what they want. **1753** FRANKLIN *Writings* III. 163 If you can procure and send me your truckhouse law, and a particular account of the manner of executing it, . . . you will much oblige me. **1832** WILLIAMSON *Maine* II. 200 The Indian trade at the truck houses was revised.

2. A building used to house fire trucks.

1854 *S.F. Whig* 28 July 1/1 The sum of ten thousand dollars . . . is hereby appropriated out of the Fire Department Fund . . . in erecting and towards the completion of a Truck House for Sansome Hook and Ladder Co. No. 3. **1904** *Baltimore News* 18 May 6 He wished to erect a Fire-Department truckhouse on the little grass plot.

***trucking,** *n.*

1. Truck farming. Also attrib.

1897 *Jrnl. Fine Arts* (Phila.) June, About one half [of the grounds] is used for trucking and pasture purposes. **1947** *Chi. Tribune* 3 July 27/5 This 200 acres is located near Fort Lauderdale, has been cleared and irrigated, . . . suitable for trucking or orange groves.

2. In combs.: (1) **trucking cloth,** cloth used in trade with the Indians, *obs.*; (2) **farm,** =**truck farm;** (3) **house,** =**truck house 1,** *obs.*; (4) **stuff,** articles used in trade with the Indians, *obs.*

(1) **1638** *New Haven Col. Rec.* 4 Twelve coates of English trucking cloath. **1682** *Mass. H.S. Coll.* 4 Ser. V. 63 [They] have sent their good mother a pound of hops, with the hat, bonnets, trucking-cloth, and other things mentioned. — (2) **1865** *Nation* I. 200 Free nigger labor may do on a trucking farm. — (3) **1631** in *N.H. Hist. Soc. Coll.* IV. 240 One man . . . fell lame by the way, and . . . stopped at a trucking house. **1668** *Ib.* III. 214, I went to the Trucking house of Capt. Richard Walderne . . . to make enquiry . . . concerning the killing of an Englishman. **1755** in E. ARBER *Eng. Garner* II. 619 There shall be a Trucking House in every Plantation, whither the Indians may resort to trade. — (4) **1619** *Va. House of Burgesses* 5 The Indians refusing to sell their Corne, those of the shallop . . . tooke it by force, . . . given [*sic*] them satisfaction in Copper, Beads, and other trucking Stuffe. **1674** *Mass. H.S. Coll.* 1 Ser. I. 159 To this end they must be furnished with such Indian trucking stuff, as may be suitable.

truck wagon. A heavy, clumsy vehicle, esp. a home-made one with wheels sawed from the trunk of a large tree, as a sycamore or blackgum.

1805 *Lewis & Clark Exped.* VII. (1905) 106 They had Some difficulty with their truck waggons as they broke Sundry times. **1857** *Ill. Agric. Soc. Trans.* II. 361 Truck wagons, the wheels being made of large sycamore logs, sawed off, were frequently used. **1913** O. A. ROTHERT *Hist. Muhlenberg Co.* (Ky.) 113 The so-called 'truck wagon' was also frequently seen in the olden days. Its wheels were discs sawed from a solid black gum log, and were about two and a half feet high. It was usually drawn by a yoke of oxen.

Trudeau's tern. [Jean Baptiste *Trudeau* (1748–1827), explorer and Indian trader.] A South American tern, *Sterna trudeaui*, once observed in New Jersey and erroneously supposed to occur also in the U.S. — **1839** AUDUBON *Ornith. Biog.* V. 125 Trudeau's Tern. . . . This beautiful Tern . . . was procured at Great Egg Harbour in New Jersey, by my . . . friend, J. Trudeau, Esq. of Louisiana. **1887** RIDGWAY *Man. N. Amer. Birds* 41 Casual on Atlantic coast of United States (New Jersey). *S[terna] trudeaui.* Trudeau's Tern.

***true,** *a.* **1. true grit,** *fig.* one of unfaltering devotion, courage, loyalty, also attrib. Cf. ***grit,** *n.*[2] **2. True Wesleyan Church,** (see quot. 1846). Both *obs.*

(1) **1840** KENNEDY *Quodlibet* 127, I am . . . a True Grit, a whole True Grit, and nothing but a True Grit. **1846** *Knickerb.* XXVIII. 63 We don't like to leave a real true-grit American . . . among a lot of cowardly Diegos. — (2) **1844** RUPP *Relig. Denominations* 484 Statistics of the True Wesleyan Church. **1846** in *Indiana Mag. Hist.* XXIII. 262 He was in what is very improperly called, the 'True Wesleyan Church,' the organization effected by Scott, Lee and others, who erroneously supposed the Methodist Episcopal Church to be proslavery.

One type of truck wagon

***trumpet,** *n.*

1. *S. pl.* The yellow trumpetleaf, *Sarracenia flava.*

1857 GRAY *Botany* 24 Trumpets. . . . Bogs, Virginia and southward. **1891** *Cent.* 6509/1. **1898** CREEVEY *Flowers of Field* 26 A larger pitcher-plant . . . is *Trumpets* . . . , with a large, drooping, yellow flower.

2. In combs.: (1) **trumpet creeper,** a vine, *Campsis radicans*, having red trumpet-shaped flowers; (2) **gall,** (see quot. 1891); (3) **gourd,** (see quot.); (4) **honeysuckle,** an American honeysuckle, *Lonicera sempervirens*, with red or orange flowers; (5) **leaf,** any one of several varieties of pitcher plant of the genus *Sarracenia*, also with specifying terms; (6) ***vine,** the trumpet creeper or the trumpet honeysuckle; (7) ***weed,** any one of several American plants, esp. the joe-pye weed and the wild lettuce.

(1) **1834** *Western Mo. Mag.* II. 574 The sides [are] ornamented with beautiful bunches of the trumpet-creeper. **1943** PEATTIE *Great Smokies* 178 Virginia creeper, trumpet creeper, Carolina jessamine, wild hydrangea, sassafras, persimmon and witch hazel have their counterparts in eastern Asia. — (2) **1891** *Cent.* 6509/3 *Trumpet-gall*, a small trumpet shaped gall occurring commonly upon grape-vines in the United States. **1908** KELLOGG *Amer. Insects* 470 Trumpet-galls on leaves of California white oak. — (3) **1901** MOHR *Plant Life Ala.* 831 *Lagenaria vulgaris clavata*, Trumpet Gourd. Louisianian area. — (4) [**1731** MILLER *Gardeners Dict. s.v. Periclymenum*, Trumpet Honeysuckle. . . . We have but one species of this Plant at present, *viz.* . . . Virginian Scarlet Honeysuckle.] **1941** R. S. WALKER *Lookout* 58 Trumpet, or coral honeysuckle with its scarlet and yellow flowers that open in April and May, is one of the most popular wild flowers in the mountain.
(5) **1861** WOOD *Botany* 222 *S. Gronovii.* Trumpet-leaf. . . . In swampy pine woods, Va. to Fla. and La. **1901** MOHR *Plant Life Ala.* 530 *Sarracenia rubra.* . . . Red-flowered Trumpet-leaf or Pitcher Plant. — (6) **1709** [in scarlet trumpet-vine *q.v.*]. **1883** *Peterson Ladies' Nat. Mag.* June 460/2 The great porch in front . . . [was] destitute of railing or ornament, but the creeping trumpet vine. **1948** *Our Dumb Animals* May 7/1 His interest centered on a flock of hummingbirds that were whirring about the trumpet vine. — (7) **1830** *Huntingdon* (Pa.) *Courier* 15 Sep. 4/5 American Remedies Wanted. . . . Gravel Wort or Trumpet Weed, (Eupatorium Purpurum.) **1913** N. L. BRITTON & A. BROWN *Flora N. Amer.* III. 357 *Eupatoreum purpureum.* Joe-Pye or Trumpet-weed. . . . Indian gravel-root. Marsh-milk weed. Nigger-weed.

As the last term in **deck, desert, horse, hummingbird's, moose trumpet.**

***trumpeter,** *n.*

1. =next.

1709 LAWSON *Carolina* 146 Of the Swans we have two sorts; the one we call Trompeters; because of a sort of trompeting Noise they make. **1874** LONG *Wild-Fowl* 230 Their notes . . . resemble greatly those of a trumpet; and because of this peculiarity of note the name 'trumpeter' was given them. **1946** STANWELL-FLETCHER *Driftwood Valley* 177 On the southern sky appeared a gigantic 'V' of trumpeters—seventy or more—the dazzling sun lighting their white bodies as they passed low just above us.

2. trumpeter swan, the largest American swan, *Cygnus buccinator*, found chiefly in the western part of the continent.

1834 NUTTALL *Man. Ornith.* II. 371 The length of the Trumpeter Swan is about 70 inches. **1917** *Birds of Amer.* I. 167 The Trumpeter Swan, the largest of North American wild fowl, represents a vanishing race. **1949** *Chi. D. News* 22 Nov. 12/7 He . . . was allowed to fire at anything save wood-duck and trumpeter swans.

truncheon snake. The banded water-snake, *Natrix sipedon fasciatus.*

1709 LAWSON *Carolina* 126 Red-back'd Snake. Black Truncheon Snake [etc.]. **1736** CATESBY *Carolina* II. 45 *Vipera fusca.* The Brown Viper. . . . They are found in Virginia and Carolina, in the last of which Places they are called the Trunchion Snake. **1838** J. E. HOLBROOK *N. Amer. Herpetology* II. 95.

* **trunk,** *n.*

1. Short for "trunk line railroad."

1847 *Hunt's Merch. Mag.* XVII. 70 And upon a trunk so important . . . there would seem to be an evident propriety in embracing at once a completeness of execution.

b. Often attrib. as **trunk railroad, railway, road.**

1851 CIST *Cincinnati* 312 Here are four trunk roads. **1884** *Cong. Rec.* 10 Dec. 163/1 Here are eight or ten . . . great trunk railroads running eastward from Chicago to the New York market. **1893** *Harper's Mag.* Feb. 382/1 [New Orleans] is the seaport terminus of several great trunk railway lines and supply depot for Texas, the Southwest, Mexico, and Central America. [**1949** *Democrat* 22 Sep. 4/5 The road . . . has been designated a state trunk highway.]

Esp. **trunk line,** a main line, esp. of a railroad, from which branch lines diverge. Also attrib.

1851 CIST *Cincinnati* 311 The railroad is a costly structure . . . —its true and legitimate use is the extended trunk line between great points. **1868** *Rep. Comm. Agric. 1867* 109 The location of the main trunk-line railroad from the northern lakes to the Gulf of Mexico has advanced the price of lands generally. **1949** J. MONAGHAN *This is Ill.* 119 Chicago in 1871 served as the junction point for thirteen trunk-line railroads.

2. *pl.* Short, close-fitting breeches worn by athletes, bathers, etc.

1883 *Pall Mall Gaz.* 26 July 7/1 Captain Webb attempted his perilous feat of swimming Niagara Rapids. . . . He wore a pair of silk trunks. **1894** *Harper's Mag.* Aug. 341/1 The use of tights or 'trunks' [by bathers] will not be allowed. **1946** *Chi. D. News* 26 July 4/5 Swim Trunks, play shorts, robes, sox, sweaters, ties (what do you need for your vacation?).

3. In special combs.: (1) **trunk back,** (see quot.); (2) **cabin,** in a ship, a cabin partly above and partly below the upper deck; (3) **check,** a check or ticket given to one who has intrusted a trunk to a railroad or other transportation system; (4) **minder,** on a rice plantation, one who has charge of a main irrigation ditch; (5) **nail,** (see quot.); (6) **rod,** a fishing rod made in sections to permit carrying in a trunk.

(1) **1883** GARMAN *Reptiles N. Amer.* p. vi, 'Trunk-backs' or 'Leather-backs,' *Sphargis*, are the largest [of the sea turtles off coasts of Fla.]. — (2) **1886** *Outing* April 11/2 In the second class I put regular decked vessels . . . which have trunk cabins. — (3) **1874** B. F. TAYLOR *World on Wheels* I. 58 He has . . . shown his ticket and his trunk check, and asked if this is the right train. — (4) **1856** in COMMONS *Doc. Hist.* I. 120 Trunk-minders undertake the whole care of the trunks. **1904** PRINGLE *Rice Planter* 80 Foreman, trunk minder, and hands were all . . . sure it could never make a crop, being mill-threshed seed.

(5) **1876** KNIGHT 2635/2 Trunk-nail. A nail with a head shaped like a segment of a sphere, so as to make a rounded boss when driven. Used for ornamenting coffins and trunks. — (6) **1893** *Outing* XXII. 121/2 Trunk rods made to pack in small space often have six or seven [joints].

b. *To play at trunk loo,* (see quot.). *Obs.* Cf. **crack-loo.**

1849 W. BROWN *America* 4 These men live partly . . . by stealing trunks from passengers which they call *playing at Trunk loo.*

As the last term in **box, camphor, dresser, hand, sample, Saratoga, steamer, wardrobe trunk.**

truss bridge. A bridge in which support is secured by the use of trusses or frames of wood or metal. Also with defining proper name.

1840 *Civil Eng. & Arch. Jrnl.* III. 125/2 On the Pottsville and Sunbury Railway, in Pennsylvania, the wood for small truss bridges, for crossing roads [etc.]. **1875** *Chi. Tribune* 11 Sep. 2/5 [A part of the Santa Fé line] has stone culverts, and the streams are spanned by Howe truss bridges. **1907** *St. Nicholas* Aug. 919/2 The bridge is what is known as a 'truss' bridge, like most railroad and highway bridges.

* **trust,** *n.*

1. (*cap.*) Used in place-names. *Obs.*

1700 *Md. Hist. Mag.* XX. 189 Harrises Trust, 300 acr. Sur. the 5 August 1684 for William Harris. *Ib.* 193 Hathways Trust, 150 acr Sur. the 28 of March 1685 for John Hathaway. *Ib.* XXI. 345 Cockeys Trust, 300 acr Sur. the 8 of Aprill 1696.

2. (*cap.*) *Hist. collect.* The board of trustees in whose hands was placed the government of the colony of Georgia, 1732–52. *Obs.*

1739 W. STEPHENS *Proc. Georgia* I. 314 All [cattle] found without any Mark, were to be judged unquestionably to belong to the Trust. **1741** *Ib.* II. 216 And I was with good Reason grown averse to any more retailing work at the Stores, more especially knowing the Trust's opinion therein, which nothing should occasion us to vary from.

3. In combs.: (1) **trust buster,** a public officer who seeks, under antitrust laws, to secure the dissolution of trusts, also **trust busting;** (2) **company,** a company specifically empowered to act as a trustee, often in titles of banking institutions; (3) **land,** (*a*) land belonging to the board of trustees governing the colony of Georgia, *obs.*, cf. **2.** above, (*b*) reservation lands held in trust for Indians by the federal government; (4) **lot,** a piece of land held in trust by the trustees of the colony of Georgia, *obs.*, cf. **2.** above; (5) **patent,** a patent issued to an Indian; (6) **plank,** a plank in a political platform dealing with the regulation of trusts; (7) **scrip,** paper promises circulated as money; (8) **stock,** (see quot.).

(1) **1903** *Chi. Chronicle* 11 April 2 Mr. Knox is surprising everybody by his zeal as a trust-buster. **1944** *Chi. D. News* 8 May 10/1 So we have a faint revival of 'trust busting' to give color to the stuff. **1949** *Time* 9 May 34/3 U.S. trustbusters were still locked in stalemate with the Zaibatsu. — (2) **1834** *Jamestown* (N.Y.) *Jrnl.* 29 Jan. 2/3 You may not, from the but recent existence of the Trust Company, have as perfect a knowledge of their powers and operations. **1888** *Economist* 3 Nov. 5/3 The Merchants' Loan and Trust Company . . . has openly declared in favor of the gas bonds. **1914** *Cyclo. Amer. Govt.* III. 245/1 In recent years trust companies have established departments with safety deposit vaults for this service. **1950** *Chi. Tribune* 8 May 1. 6/5 The source of the money is concealed behind the trust agreement in which the Chicago Title and Trust company is trustee. — (3) (*a*) **1738** W. STEPHENS *Proc. Georgia* I. 67 Jones the Surveyor Came at Mr. Bradley's Call, in order to run out some of the Trust-Land for the Germans to work on. (*b*) **1857** in *36th Cong.* 1 Sess. H.R. Rep. 648, 172 The trust lands . . . include the eastern part of the Delaware lands. **1866** *Rep. Indian Affairs* 262 The 'trust lands' are nearly all sold. — (4) **1739** W. STEPHENS *Proc. Georgia* I. 469, I proposed it to Mr. Jones to send down a few German Families to work on the Trust Lots there.

(5) **1909** *Indian Laws & Tr.* III. 389 [For] delivery of trust patents, so far as allotments shall have been selected under said act, ninety thousand dollars. — (6) **1925** BRYAN *Memoirs* 125 The trust plank was given second place of importance. — (7) **1862** G. K. WILDER *Diary* (MS) 23 May, We received from 16–18 in specie, 23–25 in Trust scrip. — (8) **1900** NELSON *A B C Wall St.* 17 The Industrial group of stocks . . . includes the so-called Trust stocks, representative of industrial enterprises.

As the last term in **anti-, brain, sugar trust.**

* **trustee,** *n.*

1. An official having governing powers of general scope, as a selectman in a town or a councilman in a city.

1662 *Maine Hist. Soc. Coll.* 2 Ser. IV. 246 Resolved by the Trustees of Fardin [etc.]. **1791** *East-Hampton Rec.* IV. 269 If any person shall cut any beach grass on any of the beaches belonging to this town without liberty from the trustees [etc.]. **1827** DRAKE & MANSFIELD *Cincinnati* 50 This instrument vests the municipal power of the city in a City Council, which is to consist of three Trustees. **1900** GOODLANDER *Fort Scott* 65 Years later he was trustee of Scott Township.

b. An officer of a superior court.

1709 *Md. Hist. Mag.* IV. 384 March Court 1709, March the Elevent The Trustees again were present.

2. One of the administrative officials controlling the property and directing the policy of an organization or institution. **a.** An official of a school or college.

1705 BEVERLEY *Virginia* IV. 31 Their Majesties granted a Power to certain Gentlemen, and the Survivors of them, as Trustees, to build and establish the College by the Name of William and Mary College. **1722** in CLAP *Ann. Yale-Coll.* 34 Upon just Ground of Suspicion of the Rector or Tutor's Inclination to Arminian or Prelatic principles, a Meeting of the Trustees shall be called. **1807** *Ann. 10th Cong.* 1 Sess. 1206 The petition of the Board of Trustees of the University of Vincennes. **1943** *U. of Chi. Announcements* 6 As the University developed, the number of Trustees was increased.

b. An official of an organized religious society or congregation.

1806 *N.Y. Laws 1804–6* 395 It shall be lawful for the mayor, aldermen and commonalty of the city of New-York, to pay to the trustees of the Roman catholic congregation . . . , the like sum as was paid to the other congregations [for the support of free schools]. **1903** *Evanston* (Ill.) *Press* 11 April, Mr. Kedzie was for many years a trustee of the Congregational church.

c. An official of the communistic society at Brook Farm. *Obs.*

1842 in Codman *Brook Farm* 14 The Chairman of the General Direction shall be presiding officer in the Association, and together with the Direction of Finance, shall constitute a Board of Trustees, by whom the property of the Association shall be managed. **1897** *McClure's Mag.* X. 193 Before he [Charles A. Dana] had been there [at Brook Farm] many weeks he was elected a trustee.

3. *local.* A person in whose hands another person's property is attached in a trustee process.

1708 *Mass. Prov. Acts* I. 630 Such attourny, factor, agent or trustee, . . . shall be admitted to defend the suit on behalf of his principal. **1799** *Mass. Supreme Ct. Rep.* III. 558 The plaintiff, a creditor of Martin, summoned Welles, one of the underwriters, as trustee of Martin. **1883** Howells *Woman's Reason* ix, [The paper] makes a personal appeal to me, in the name of the Commonwealth of Massachusetts, to become your trustee.

b. trustee process, legal attachment without seizure, in the interests of a creditor, of a debtor's properties in the hands of a third party, garnishment.

1810 W. C. White *Compendium Laws Mass.* 1268 In what case, and against whom, a trustee process will lie. **1833** L. S. Cushing (*title*), A Practical Treatise on the Trustee Process, or Foreign Attachment of the Laws of Massachusetts, or Maine; with . . . the Statutes of the Eastern States on that Subject. **1891** *Cent.* 6513/3.

As the last term in **alumni, district, school, town trustee.**

* **trustee,** *v. local. tr.* To attach the property of (a debtor) in the hands of a third person, to make (a third person) a trustee in a trustee process.

1879 Webster *Supp.* 1582/3. **1883** Howells *Woman's Reason* ix, You don't say you never was trusteed before? **1902** McFaul *Ike Glidden* 38 Yer know if I want ter trustee any one I have ter send ter Debtor's.

* **trusty,** *n.* A convict regarded as trustworthy and hence eligible for special duties and extra privileges.

1855 *S.F. Citizen* 2 Oct. 2/3 Two 'trusties' named Scottie and Greene, escaped in a whale boat from the State Prison grounds on Sunday night. **1889** *Portland* (Ore.) *Intelligencer* 12 Feb. 3/1 Worley . . . enjoyed the confidence of the sheriff to such an extent that he was made a 'trusty.' **1949** *L.A. Times* 16 May 5/4 Both men were trusties and were housed in a dormitory outside the penitentiary wall, *attrib.* **1855** *S.F. Citizen* 2 Oct. 2/3 They had numerous opportunities of escaping previously . . . which certainly does not accord with the preconceived view of the 'trustie' system, by those now in charge at the Prison. **1856** *Dem. State Journal* (Sacramento) 28 Oct. 2/3 The 'trusty guards,' (commanded by Pete, Scotty acting as first lieutenant,) have recovered from the effects of their stolen debauch of Saturday.

* **try,** *v.*

1. *tr.* To submit (a case) for the judgment of a court of law.

1905 Mitchell *Constance Trescot* 166, I am instructed to try the case. **1931** *N. Amer. Rev.* Jan. 22 This is one of his jokes; he knows I can't afford to try criminal cases.

2. In noun combs.: (1) **try house,** a shed or other structure in which whale oil is extracted from blubber, or lard or a similar substance is rendered; (2) **out,** an experimental test.

(1) **1792** *Mass. H.S. Coll.* III. 157 The blubber was brought home in large square pieces, and *tried* or boiled in try-houses. **1895** *Cent. Mag.* Aug. 575/1 The men and their wives and children begin to come up the crooked road by the clump of willows, past the try-house. — (2) **1903** *Scientific Amer.* 30 May 414/1 Cup challengers in their try-outs in British waters.

3. In phrases: (1) *To try* (something) *on a dog,* to find out the effectiveness of something by submitting it to those regarded as of lesser consequence than the ones for whom it is designed, *slang;* (2) *to try out,* (*a*) to experiment with or test (a person, thing, etc.) in order to determine value, (*b*) (see quot. 1891), (*c*) to come forward as a candidate, esp. in competition for a place on an athletic team.

(1) **1888** *Sporting Times* (B. and L.), 'Bootle's Baby' will on the 7th of May be produced somewhere in the provinces. This is what the Americans call trying it on a dog. — (2) (*a*) **1888** *Judge* 29 Dec. 190/1 Tried Out by Fire. **1922** Z. Grey *To Last Man* 199, I reckon we'd better try it [a plan] out, for a while. **1932** Tarbell *O. D. Young* Here was a situation in which he could try out, under limitations of course, his ideas of what ought to be. (*b*) **1891** *Cent.* 6515/1 The grease *tries out* of ham in cooking. . . . The perspiration is *trying out* of him. (Low, New Eng.) **1941** Farmer *Boston Cook Book* 428 Try out fat, strain, and cook onion and carrot in fat, stirring constantly until brown. (*c*) **1909** *N.Y. Ev. Post* 25 Feb. 7 Because of the small number of men trying out for winter track practice, Coach Moakley has issued another call for candidates.

tsuppitch salmon. (See quot.) — **1878** *U.S. Nat. Museum Proc.* I. 72 *Salmo Tsuppitch,* Tsuppitch Salmon. Black Trout of Lake Tahoe.

T.T.T. (See quot.) *Obs.* — **1841** *Niles' Reg.* 21 Feb. LIX. 400/3 T T T. They have temperance wagons in the west, marked with three Ts, to denote that the owner is a tee-to-taller.

* **tub,** *n.* **1. tub mill,** a grain mill in which a tub wheel is used. Now *hist.* **2. tub sugar,** maple sugar allowed to harden in tubs or tublike containers.

(1) **1775** Cresswell *Journal* 66 He has got a small tub mill. **1824** Doddridge *Notes* 143 Our first water mills were of that description denominated tub mills. **1940** Wright *Pioneer Life* 75 The tub mill was a water mill; consequently it could be used only so long as the spring freshets were strong enough to supply power. — (2) **1892** *Vt. Agric. Rep.* 156 Nice tub sugar or cakes [sell] at eight to fifteen cents per pound.

As the last term in **bath, cheese, draw, line, sap, sit tub.** See also **Blood Tubs.**

* **tube,** *n.* **1.** An electron tube somewhat resembling a small electric light bulb, used chiefly in radios. **2. tube well,** (see quot. 1876).

(1) **1929** *N.Y. Times* 13 Oct., Bottles: Audio frequency amplifier tubes. **1946** *Chi. D. News* 17 Dec. 3/4 (*advt.*), An attractive little . . . receiver with 5 tubes. — (2) **1876** Knight 2645/2 *Tube-well,* an iron pipe of small diameter, pointed, and having a number of lateral perforations near the end, driven into the earth by a small pile-driver hammer until a water-bearing stratum is reached. **1884** *Gringo & Greaser* 1 Feb. 2/1 Messrs. Houck and Morrow have gone to Las Lunas and Albuquerque to buy casing &c. for some tube wells.

* **tuck,** *n.*

1. tuck comb, =**tucking comb.**

1824 *Mo. Intelligencer* 8 May 3/3 Tortoise Shell, Tuck and Side Combs. **1870** Eggleston *Queer Stories* 63 Sukey's way of doing up her hair in a great knot, behind, with an old-fashioned tuck comb, was not pretty. **1886** *Amer. Philol. Assoc. Trans.* 42 Redding-comb . . . is the opposite of tuck-comb.

2. *To take the tuck out of, fig.* to take the toughness, stamina, or determination away from (one). *Slang.*

1878 Mark Twain *Punch Brothers* 87 We had an iron-clad chicken that ought to have been put through a quartz mill until the 'tuck' was taken out of him, and then boiled till we came again. **1910** *N.Y. Ev. Post* 10 Nov. 1 The sight of a wounded man lying on the pavement seemed to take the tuck out of the mob.

* **tuck,** *v. To tuck it on to* (a person), to overreach, get the better of in a trade. *Slang. Obs.* — **1877** Bartlett 722 That horse is not worth half what you gave for him. The dealer has tucked it on to you pretty well.

tuckahoe ˈtʌkəˌho, *n.* [Algonquian, f. a word meaning globular and applied by Indians to various bulbous roots used as food.]

1. One of several vegetables used as food by Indians, esp. the floating arum and the Virginia wake-robin.

1612 Smith *Virginia* I. 22 In June, Julie, and August, they feed vpon the rootes of Tocknough, berries, fish, and greene wheat. **1770** Forster tr. Kalm *Travels* II. 389 To judge by these qualities, the Tuckahoe may very likely be the *Arum Virginicum.* **1816** *Mass. Spy* 23 Oct. (Th.), The name of Tuckahoe is supposed to be of Indian origin. **1895** *Amer. Antiq. Soc. Proc.* April 167 There were certain natural products, as *e.g.,* wild oats, tuckahoe, and koonti, of which extensive use was made. **1946** *Nat. Geog. Mag.* Jan. 55/1 From June through August their diet consisted mainly of fish, berries, green corn, and roots of the tuckahoe, or Indian bread.

2. (*cap.*) As the name of a town or region. Cf. quot. 1877 in **b.** below.

*c***1797** Latrobe *Jrnl.* 61, I promised to send him [i.e., Gen. Washington] one of Mr. Richardson's plows of Tuckahoe, which he accepted with pleasure. **1815** *Salem Gaz.* 1/4, I confess I began to wish the war and they that declared it in Tuckahoe together. **1828** RICE *Jim Crow* i, Come listen all you galls and boys, I'm just from Tuckyhoe. **1890** *N. & Q.* IV. 25 Jan. 151 We have towns and villages called Tuckahoe in New York, New Jersey and North Carolina, beside Tuckahoe creeks and rivers without number.

b. (See quots.)

1817 PAULDING *Lett. from South* I. 112 The people [west of the Blue Ridge] called those east of the mountain Tuckahoes. **1877** BARTLETT 722 The term *tuckahoe* is often applied to an inhabitant of Lower Virginia, and to the poor land in that portion of the State. **1945** *Christian Sci. Mon.* 25 April 8/2 A *Tuckahoe* is a Virginian.

* **tucker,** *n.* [All the senses shown here may not be of the same word.]

1. *mad as tucker*, extremely angry. *Colloq.*

1846 *Spirit of Times* (N.Y.) 9 May 125/2 Old Bill got mad as 'tucker' because the boys left him.

2. (See quot. 1943.) Also *to dance Tucker. Colloq.*

1881 RITTENHOUSE *Maud* 25 It was a tucker and I danced it with Mr. B. **1891** *Harper's Mag.* Jan. 215/2 The fun was waxing fast and furious with the added and unique diversion known as 'Dancin' Tucker.' **1943** POWELL *Home Again* 93 We were not allowed to dance —that was against the rules of the churches—but we played 'Tucker' and 'twistification.' The former was simply the old fashioned square dance under another name, and the latter a somewhat modified version of the Virginia Reel.

b. (See quot.)

1940 *Square Dance* 211 Miss Tucker or Old Dan Tucker. This is a mixer in which the two step is the basic dance. One extra gent representing Old Dan Tucker, or an extra lady called Miss Tucker stands in the center of the floor.

3. An attachment to a sewing machine for making tucks in cloth.

1882 PECK *Sunshine* 84 A sewing machine, complete, with cover, drop leaf, hemmer, tucker [etc.]. **1920** *Sears Cat.* No. 141D, 517 The set [of sewing-machine attachments] consists of one tucker, one ruffler, one shirring blade . . . and one set of four hemmers of different widths.

tucker ˈtʌkɚ, *v.* [Origin not clear. Cf. *OED* and Webster and see *EDD tucked up*, exhausted, worn out, and *twickered out*, tired, done up.] *tr.* To tire, weary, exhaust (a person). Usu. **tuckered out.** *Colloq.*

1833 S. SMITH *Life J. Downing* 204 If this aint enough to tucker a fellow out I don't know what is. *a***1848** in BARTLETT 366 We sot and sot, and waited for her, till we got eenamost tuckered out. **1907** G. M. WHITE *Boniface to Burglar* 134, 'I can't, I'm tuckered,' he gasped; 'you fellers better go on, if you're in a hurry.' **1950** *Newsweek* 10 April 75/1 They were, he admitted, tuckered.

Hence **tuckering,** *a.*, wearying, exhausting. *Colloq.*

1893 HOLLEY *Samantha at World's Fair* 304 Some of the snortin' and prancin' of the horses of the Ocean—wuz meant, I spoze, to represent how awful tuckerin' it is for humanity to control the forces of Natur.

b. To supply with tucker or food. *Colloq.* [In this sense f. * *tucker*, food, and prob. a different word from above.]

1920 B. CRONIN *Timber Wolves* 40, I got a friend hereabouts that tuckers me when I'm along this way.

tucket ˈtʌkɪt, *n. local.* [Prob. f. Algonquian and poss. related to **tuckahoe.**] (See quots.) Also **tucket corn.** *Obs.*

1856 *Mich. Agric. Soc. Trans.* VII. 528 The committee notices other samples: . . . Wm. Knowles, bushel tucket corn. Good sample. **1858** *Harper's Mag.* May 763/1 [In] a certain barrel in the barn . . . , he had made . . . frequent deposits of green corn, of the diminutive species called *tucket*. **1871** DE VERE 39 The *tucket*, as the green ear is called as long as it is soft and milky, is quite a delicacy to some palates.

* **tucking,** *n.* and *a.* **1. tucking bush,** (see quot.). **2. tucking comb,** (see quot. 1909). **3.** *the whole twist and tucking*, the entire group or company. *Colloq.*

(1) 1890 SHIELDS *Big Game N. Amer.* 88 Large patches of 'tucking-bushes,' or dwarf juniper, which grow about breast-high, with strong branches stiffly interlaced. — **(2) 1822** *Receipt by Daniel McDowell* 11 April (Pettigrew P.), Bot of D McDowell one tucking Comb at $4.50. **1895** *Outing* XXVII. 11/2 He stopped and held up a gold-tipped tucking comb. **1909** *D.N.* III. 384 tuck(ing)-comb, *n.* A comb used to hold the hair on the back of the head. [e. Ala.] — **(3) 1835** LONGSTREET *Ga. Scenes* 124 No man's to make a grab till all's been once round— . . . then the whole twist and tucking of you grab away, as you come under.

tuft-eared squirrel. *S.W.* A large tree squirrel having long and noticeably tufted ears. — **1867** *Amer. Naturalist* I. 355 The most characteristic, as well as most abundant, species of Squirrel, is the Tuft-eared (*Sciurus Abertii*), discovered by Dr. Woodhouse in the San Francisco Mountains. **1917** *Mammals of Amer.* 175/1 The Tuft-eared Squirrel is characteristic of the stately yellow-pine forests.

* **tufted,** *a.* In combs.: (1) * **tufted duck,** the American ring-necked duck; (2) **partridge,** the California quail, *Lophortyx californica;* (3) **titmouse,** a crested titmouse, *Baeolophus bicolor*, found chiefly south of N. Eng.

(1) 1813 WILSON *Ornithology* VIII. 60 [The] Tufted Duck: *Anas fuligula;* . . . is a plump, short bodied Duck; its flesh generally tender, and well tasted. **1874** LONG *Wild-Fowl* 16 In the deep water varieties. . . . I shall treat of the . . . tufted duck, and buffle-head or butter ball. — **(2) 1839** ALEX. FORBES *California* 178 The small tufted partridges peculiar to California are most plentiful in the plains. They keep together in large flocks of three or four hundred, and are excellent eating. **1850** *Three Yrs. Calif.* 361 The quail, or tufted partridge, abounds in California, and is a delicious bird. — **(3) 1832** NUTTALL *Man. Ornith.* I. 236 Tufted Titmouse . . . *Parus bicolor.* . . . The crest high and pointed, like that of the common Blue Jay. **1949** HADLEY *Indiana Birds* 43/2 The tufted titmouse ranges throughout Eastern United States north to the southern part of New England and to southern Michigan and west to Nebraska and central Texas.

tufting button. "A style of button used in upholstery" (*Cent.*). — **1882** *Rep. Indian Affairs* 450. **1884** FORNEY *Car-Builder's Dict.* (*Cent.*).

Tukuarika ˌt(j)uˈkwɑrɪkə, *n.* (See quot. 1910.)

[**1870** in CRAMTON *Early Hist. Yellowstone Nat. Pk.* 84 On the eighth day we encountered a band of Indians—who, however, proved to be Tonkeys, or Sheepeaters, and friendly.] **1910** HODGE *Amer. Indians* II. 835/1 Tukuarika ('sheep-eaters,' referring to the mountain sheep). A division of Shoshoni said to have lived in Yellowstone park, subsequently in w. central Idaho on the Lemhi fork of Salmon r., and on the Malade. They were subsequently on the Lemhi res., Idaho, but in 1907 they were removed to the Ft Hall res. They numbered 90 in 1904, but are no longer separately enumerated.

tuladi ˈtulədɪ, *n.* [Can. F. *touladi, touradi*, from a Montagnais name of the fish. (Clapin.)] The namaycush or a variety of this. — **1884** GOODE *Fisheries* I. 486 [The] 'Tuladi' of the Maine and New Brunswick Indians and lumbermen [is a variety of lake trout]. **1911** *Rep. Fisheries 1908* 311/2 In different localities the individuals . . . are known by the local names 'salmon trout,' 'namaycush,' 'togue,' 'tuladi.'

tulare tuˈlɑrɪ, *n. S.W.* [See note.]

Tulare is a sing. from Amer. Sp. *tulares*, meaning regions overgrown with tules. Santamaría records *tulares* as applied to the Indians of upper California (see sense **2.** below), but does not list it in our sense **1.** This signification is, however, a quite normal development in Sp. from *tule.*

1. A region overgrown with the bulrushes known as tules. Usu. *pl.* Cf. **tule,** *n.* **1.**

1831 BEECHEY *Voyage to Pacific* II. 79 The rein-deer also is found inland, particularly upon a large plain named Tuluravos, on account of the number of bulrushes growing there. **1845** SUTTER *MS Corr.* (Bancroft Lib.) 21 April, I travelled now a whole Month through the Tular coming from Los Angeles. **1912** LUMHOLTZ *New Trails* 255 The many clumps of bulrushes (*tulares*) observed from there, growing down on the great mud-flat near the edges are a curious feature. **1934** WHITE *Folded Hills* 139 There were bear, there might even be Indians from the *tulares.* **1947** *Westerners' Brand Book* 113 The Indians from the Tulares were going to descend upon that pueblo while the Yuma and Cocopahs were going . . . to raid San Diego.

attrib. **1846** *Californian* (Monterey) 22 Aug. 2/1 A division of that company will be sent down the Toolary valley, . . . to meet the emigration on the 10th of September, at Trucky's lake. **1847** *Californian* (S.F.) 26 June 3/2 If the Straits of Carquinez was then open, it formed a narrow connexion between this arm, and the sea which must have covered the great Tulary Plains. **1850** *Calif. Courier* 3 Dec. 2/2 A party of our citizens, destined for the quartz region east of Los Angelos [*sic*], were attacked, a few days since, in the tulare plain beyond the Mariposa, by the Indians.

2. (*cap.*) *pl.* (See quot. 1910.) Also **Tulares Indians.**

1831 BEECHEY *Voyage to Pacific* II. 51 The party strolled over the ground, and visited about thirty huts belonging to some newly converted Indians of the tribe of Tooleerayos (*bulrushes*). **1848** *30th Cong.* 1 Sess. Sen. Rep. No. 75, 53 We undertook to cross the mountains nearly east, into the San Joaquin valley, and through the Tulares (Bullrush) Indians. **1910** HODGE *Amer. Indians* II. 835/2 Tulares. A band, probably of the Olamentke, formerly living on the N. coast of San Francisco bay, Cal., but nearly extinct in 1853.

attrib. **1903** JAMES *Indian Basketry* 209 The basket to the left is by a Tulare weaver, and shows the general method followed by these people to represent the human figure.

tularemia ˌtuləˈrimɪə, *n.* [Coined by Dr. Edward Francis. See quot. 1921.] An acute infectious disease of animals and man caused by *Bacterium tularense* and transmitted by the bites of blood-sucking ticks and flies, esp. the deer fly *q.v.*, and by contact with the raw flesh and blood of infected animals.

1921 EDWARD FRANCIS in *Public Health Rep.* 29 July 1731 (*footnote*), The name tularæmia is based on the specific name *Bacterium tularense*, plus *æmia*, from the Greek, and has reference to the presence of this bacterium in the blood, on the analogy of leukæmia or bacteræmia, etc. The names thus far used for this disease are strictly vernacular and do not lend themselves to international usage as easily as a name in Latin form. Accordingly, the name tularæmia is proposed as a technical international name. **1942** *Keeping Livestock Healthy, Yrbk. Agric.* 1219 Among the diseases of wildlife transmissable to man, tularemia, caused by the organism *Pasteurella tularense*, has attracted Nation-wide attention. **1949** *Reader's Digest* April 54/2 He proved for the first time that the lemming, that prodigiously spawning ground rat of the north, was the source of a mysterious ailment, which he also proved to be tularemia.

tule ˈtulɪ, *n. S.W.* [Amer. Sp. (< Nahuatl) in sense **1.**]

1. Either of two large bulrushes of the genus *Scirpus*, found in overflowed marshy regions.

1838 TEXIAN *Mexico v. Texas* 249 It was a little *Jacal*, or cabin . . . thatched over with *tule*, a kind of rushes that grow in the swampy bottoms of the Rio Bravo. **1892** *Outing* Jan. 329/2 Arriving at a small patch of tuleys about the middle of the lake, we decided to tie up there for the night. **1949** *Nat. Hist.* March 134/2 Most marsh areas overgrown with cattails or tules have numerous rafts of rotting vegetation lodged on the surface of the water and held in place by growing stalks.

2. A region or tract overgrown by tules. Cf. **tulare 1.**

1847 *Californian* (S.F.) 15 Sep. 3/1 Charley pointed out to me in the Tule an animal, which, he said was a bear. **1900** F. NORRIS *Blix* 213 They . . . held on down through the low reach of *tulles* and sand-dunes that stretch between the barracks and the old red fort.

3. In combs.: (1) **tule balsa,** a crude raft made of tules; (2) **elk,** (see quot. 1947); (3) **fog,** *W.* a low-lying fog; (4) **hut,** a hut made of tules; (5) **potato, root,** = **wappato;** (6) **wren,** a marsh wren found in California.

(1) **1926** CURTIS *N. Amer. Indians* XV. 159 The coastal bands used water craft, both dugout canoes and tule *balsas.* — (2) **1942** Nat. Pk. Service *Fading Trails* 8 The larger wild animals, such as the tule elk, pronghorn, bighorn sheep, and deer, were regarded as most important food supplies. **1947** CAHALANE *Mammals N. Amer.* 23 The tule, dwarf, or California elk (*C*[*ervus*] *nannodes*) is a much smaller and paler animal than the wapiti of the Rockies. — (3) **1926–7** EDWARD FRANCIS in *De Lamar Lectures* (Johns Hopkins) 100 To-day, in San Francisco, an old-timer refers to fogs in the direction of the San Joaquin river and Sacramento river as tule fogs. **1934** WHITE *Folded Hills* 340 A *tule* fog lay thick over the bottomlands. — (4) **1847** *Californian* (S.F.) 25 Sep. 4/1 A substantial Anglo New Yorker at my side, says, any one with a tule hut and a square, calls it a 'rancho.' **1883** *Cent. Mag.* May 9/1 The Indians . . . [tore] off the clothes of the sick lying helpless in the tents or tule huts on the beach.

(5) **1888** SHERIDAN *Memoirs* I. 49 The pots [were] filled with camas and tula roots. **1903** AUSTIN *Land of Little Rain* 163 The land filled with cattle-men and adventurers for gold: this while Seyavi and the boy lay up in the caverns of the Black Rock and ate tule roots and fresh-water clams that they dug out of the slough bottoms with their toes. **1915** ARMSTRONG & THORNBER *Western Wild Flowers* 2 Arrowhead. *Sagittaria latifolia.* . . . The tubers are edible and hence the plant is often called Tule Potato and they are much eaten by the Chinese in California. — (6) **1891** *Cent.* 6525/2 *Tule-wren*, a kind of marsh-wren, . . . *Telmatodytes palustris*, var. *paludicola*, which abounds in the tule-marshes of California. **1917** *Birds of Amer.* III. 198 In the Pacific coast district the markings vary slightly and it [the long-billed marsh wren] is known as the Tulé Wren or California Marsh Wren (*Telmatodytes palustris paludicola*).

b. Designating places and areas overgrown with tules, as (1) **tule bottom,** (2) **farm,** (3) **lake,** (4) **land,** (5) **marsh,** (6) **swamp.**

(1) **1847** *Californian* (S.F.) 15 Sep. 3/1 Our road now lay among the hills, bordering for some distance on an immense Tule bottom. — (2) **1891** A. WELCKER *Wild West* 64 A cabin on a swampy tule farm. — (3) **1873** MILLER *Amongst Modocs* 363 The few remaining Modoc warriors now returned to their sagebrush plains and tule lakes. **1900** DRANNAN *Plains & Mts.* 506 The first thing I heard when I got into camp was that the Indians had tried to run off into the tules while coming down Tule Lake. — (4) **1854** *Alta California* 4 Feb., Mr. Jones introduced a bill to reclaim tule lands. **1942** LILLARD *Desert Challenge* 116 Near the river sinks, tule land, cleared and drained, became bumper-crop alfalfa land.

(5) **1847** *Californian* (S.F.) 26 June 3/2 The other 25 miles, is a Tuly marsh, which at very high water, is overflown. **1948** *Desert Mag.* Aug. 21/1 White faced Herefords . . . dotted the green of the tule marshes with generous splashes of red. — (6) **1850** KINGSLEY *Diary* 100 Our boat went out back in the tula swamp. **1891** *Cent. Mag.* March 647 The stream had expanded into a tule swamp.

c. Also (1) **tule boat,** (2) **gnat,** (3) **raft,** (4) **roof,** (5) **sail.**

(1) **1848** BRYANT *California* xxx. 360 The tule-boat consists of bundles of tule firmly bound together with willow withes. When completed, in shape it is not unlike a small keel-boat. — (2) **1897** *Kissimmee* (Fla.) *Valley Gaz.* 26 May 3/3 Remarkable in many ways, the tule gnat of the Far West is the most curious for its almost total lack of weight. — (3) **1907** WHITE *Arizona Nights* 165 We all set to building a tule raft like the others. — (4) **1883** *Cent. Mag.* Aug. 515/1 They took the tule roofs off the little houses.

(5) **1876** JOAQUIN MILLER *Unwritten Hist.* 284 We . . . sailed on little mountain lakes with grass and tule sails.

* **tulip,** *n.* In combs.: (1) **tulip laurel,** the evergreen magnolia, *Magnolia grandiflora, obs.;* (2) **poplar,** = next; (3) **tree,** a large deciduous North American tree, *Liriodendron tulipifera*, having tulip-shaped flowers. Cf. **bay tulip tree.**

(1) **1765** ROGERS *Acct. N. Amer.* 120 Here [in Va.] is the large tulip laurel, the bark of whose roots, in intermitting fevers, has been found to answer all the purposes of the famous Peruvian Bark. **1797** IMLAY *Western Territory* (ed. 3) 270 Among the laurels the preference should be given to the tulip laurel (magnolia), which is not known in Europe. — (2) **1843** TORREY *Flora N.Y.* I. 28 Tulip poplar. . . . The bark is a stimulating tonic and diaphoretic. **1949** *Sat. Ev. Post* 12 March 17/2 In the swales and close to rushing water the trunks of tulip poplars grow fat, and spindling saplings climb high. — (3) **1705** BEVERLEY *Virginia* II. iv. 25 The large Tulip-Tree, which we call a Poplar [perfumes the woods]. **1832** *Boston Transcript* 23 June 2/3 A branch of the Liriodendron Tulipfera commonly called the 'Tulip Tree,' attracted attention. **1950** *Amer. Forests* Feb. 28/1 The natural forest climax is . . . a forest of deciduous trees dominated by such species as beech, maple, basswood, oak, red gum and tulip tree.

tullibee ˈtʌləˌbi, *n.* [f. Can. F. *toulibi* (<a Cree Indian word meaning "mouth water" and thought to allude to the unpalatable taste of the fish.] A species of whitefish found in the Great Lakes.

1822 in MORSE *Rep. Indian Affairs* II. 31 A fish called . . . by the English and French 'Telibees,' not equal to, but greatly resembling, the white fish. **1888** GOODE *Amer. Fishes* 93 Tautog, chogset, . . . tullibee . . . are among the best. **1947** *Field & Stream* June 16/2, 1947 Fish Laws. . . . Tullibee. . . . Dec. 16.–Oct. 14.

Tulpehocken ˌtʌlpəˈhɑkən, *n.* [The name of a creek and region in eastern Pa.] (See quots. and cf. **Fallawater,** quot. 1867.)

[**1797** BÜLOW *Freistaat* I. 297 Diejenigen Deutschen, welche meinen Nachrichten nicht trauen . . . mögen immerhin sehr schlechtes Land sehr theuer bezahlen, und in dem elegantesten Tulpehakken (eigentlich Tulpehaccon, die Amerikaner sprechen es aber so aus,) . . . wonnevolle Tage verträumen.] **1857** E. J. HOOPER *Western Fruit Book* 35 Fallowater, or Fallenwalder, or Apple of the Fallen Timber, called, also, Tulpehocken, from the creek of that name. **1867** WARDER *Pomology* 495 Tulpehocken. . . . A native of Pennsylvania, where it is a great favorite; extensively cultivated through the West.

* **tumble,** *v.* The verb stem in combs.: (1) **tumble beetle,** a tumblebug; (2) **bug,** see as a main entry; (3) **over,** a toy so weighted at the bottom that it always assumes an upright position; (4) **turd,** = **tumblebug,** *colloq.*, cf. **king tumbleturd;** (5) **weed,** any one of various branching plants whose globular tops become detached from the roots and are tumbled about by the winds.

(1) **1860** *Ladies' Repository* XX. 265/1 The tumble beetle in vain tries to roll its little ball up a hill. — (3) **1895** *Outing* XXVI. 380/1 She stood there with two-thirds of her weight at the bottom of her fin, like one of those lead-weighted, pith 'tumble-overs,' with which we played when children. — (4) **1737** BRICKELL *N. Carolina* 161 The Tumble-turds, are a species of the Beetles, and so called, from their constant rowling the Horse-dung (whereon they feed) from one place to another, 'till it is no bigger than a small Bullet. **1758** CATESBY *Carolina* App. 11 *Scarabaeus pilaris americanus.* The Tumble-Turds. This is the most numerous and remarkable of the Beetle kind of any in North America.

(5) **1887** *Amer. Naturalist* XXI. 929 A nearly spherical plant body . . . at the end of the season breaks away at the root, thus forming a tumble-weed. **1949** *Reader's Digest* Aug. 128/2 It was a waste of sage and greasewood and tumbleweed.

b. *To tumble to, to take a tumble,* to get wise, change one's mode of behavior, turn over a new leaf. *Slang.*

1877 in H. ASBURY *Underworld of Chi.* (1941) 80 May Willard, why don't you take a tumble to yourself and not be trying to put on so much style around the St. Mark's Hotel. **1884** *Boston Jrnl.* 23 Aug., I guess I'd better take this fifty and skip up to Portland before that Sheeny tumbles to that counterfeit. **1939** ABBOTT-SMITH *We Pointed* 87 We were strangers up North, and winter was coming on. We were getting big wages. We had to take a tumble.

tumblebug 'tʌmbḷ,bʌg, *n.*

1. Any one of various scarabaeid beetles which fashion dung into balls to serve as depositories for their eggs.

1805 PARKINSON *Tour* 362 There is a kind of beetle, called a tumble-bug. **1946** *Reader's Digest* Jan. 119/1 A tumblebug by instinct tries to bury a little ball in the sand.

b. (*cap.*) A derisive nickname applied to the Whigs in the presidential campaign of 1840 because of their ball-rolling (see ***ball,** ***n.***[1] **3. b.**) activities. Also attrib. Now *hist.*

1840 *Louisville Pub. Adv.* 30 July 2/2 We don't belong to the Tumble Bug Party. *Ib.* 24 Aug. 2/2 The Tumble Bugs evince great nervous anxiety and try to keep the ball moving—but it is evidently up-hill work. **1950** *Chi. Tribune* 28 Feb. 12/3 When it reached Louisville, July 29, the Public Advertiser ridiculed the 'Whiggies' for their 'great tumblebug procession.'

2. A farm machine of some kind. *Rare.*

1945 *Hardin* (Mont.) *Tribune-Herald* 15 Feb. 7/5 Machinery—1 Moline tumble bug.

***tumbler,** *n.*

1. (*cap.*) =**Dunker.**

1788 SCHÖPF *Reise* I. 180 Auch von einer andern Sekte, Tumblers genannt, wohnen einige Familien hier; sie tragen Bärte und einfache Kleidung, aber doch nicht auf Quäkermanier. **1796** MORSE *Univ. Geog.* I. 281 Tumblers . . . perform baptism, . . . by putting the person, while kneeling, head first under water. **1883** SCHAFF *Religious Encycl.* III. 2401 The candidate kneeling . . . was plunged by a forward movement under the water, from which they were sometimes called 'Tumblers.'

2. A tumblebug or the pupa of a mosquito.

1807 IRVING *Salmagundi* xv. 403 That indefatigable insect, called the tumbler, . . . the only industrious animal in Virginia, . . . works ignobly in the dirt. **1859** *New Amer. Cyclo.* VIII. 317/1 They are changed into pupæ, called tumblers from the manner in which they roll over and over in the water by means of the fin-like paddles at the end of the tail.

2. In combs.: (1) **tumbler dam,** =**tumbling dam;** (2) **light,** ?a light in a fixture somewhat resembling a tumbler, *rare;* (3) **quilt,** a patchwork quilt the shape of

Portion of a tumbler quilt

the principal pieces of which was apparently suggested by the base of a glass tumbler.

(1) **1779** *N.J. Archives* 2 Ser. III. 184 A tumbler dam was erected . . . sufficient to vent the water in the time of great freshes. — (2) **1877** in McCABE *Hist. Great Riots* 307 When the tumbler lights were started on the stand where the speakers of English were expected, the crowd surged forward. — (3) **1895** A. BROWN *Meadow-Grass* 181 Where's that piece o' chalk you had when you marked out your tumbler-quilt? [**1927** *Old-Time N. Eng.* April 173 (*caption*), Patchwork Quilt—Tumbler Pattern Made About 1826.]

As the last term in **ground, straw tumbler.**

***tumbling,** *a.* In combs.: (1) **tumbling brand,** *W.* (see quot. 1944); (2) **bug,** =**tumblebug,** *colloq.;* (3) **dam,** a dam over the top of which excess water passes, cf. **tumbler dam.**

(1) [**1939** ROLLINS *Gone Haywire* 62 Tumblin' K seems to be settin' pretty regardin' grass.] **1944** ADAMS *W. Words* 169/2 tumbling brand A brand leaning in an oblique position. — (2) **1898** MARK TWAIN *Mysterious Stranger* 40 (R.), He could not be insulted by Ursula any more than the king could be insulted by a tumbling-bug. — (3) **1760** WASHINGTON *Diaries* I. 139 Dogue Run carried of[f] the Tumbling Dam of my Mill. **1788** *Ib.* III. 329 The heavy rain of last Night had blown up my lower tumbling dam, or waste.

tump tʌmp, *n.* [f. an Algonquian word meaning a pack strap. Cf. Mass. *tâmpân*, Abnaki *mádûmbi.*] (See quot. 1848.) In full **tumpline.**

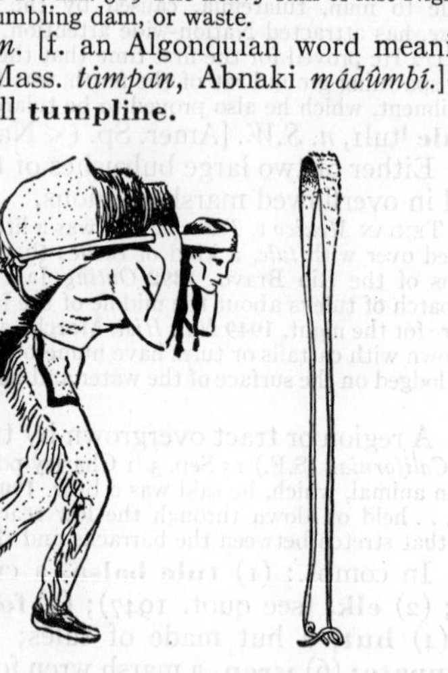

Tumpline in use and in detail

1796 *Captivity of Mrs. Johnson* 66, I was a novice at making canoes . . . and tumplines, which was the only occupation of the squaws. **1848** BARTLETT 367 *Tumpline,* a strap placed across the forehead to assist a man in carrying a pack on his back. Used in Maine, where the custom was borrowed from the Indians. **1917** KEPHART *Camping* II. 121 The tump or head-band is a good addition not only to a pack harness but to almost any other kind of pack used for carrying heavy weights. . . . When fording a swift stream, crossing on a foot-log or fallen tree, going over windfalls . . . the shoulder straps may be dropped.

Also **tump-pack, tumpstrap.**

1939 PINKERTON *Wilderness Wife* 26 The heavier [packsack], with cooking kit and grub, hung on his back, supported by leather bands over his shoulders and steadied by a tumpstrap across his forehead. **1949** *Boston Globe* 15 May (Fiction Mag.) 7/1 He nodded, tapping a small pack of furs which he had unslung from his tump-pack.

tump tʌmp, *v.* [See **tump,** ***n.***] *tr.* (See quot. 1848.) *Obs.* — **1848** BARTLETT 366 *To Tump.* . . . It means to draw a deer or other animal home through the woods, after he had been killed. . . . Used in Maine. **1855** HALIBURTON *Nature & Human Nat.* I. 268 A man passed the barrack-gate, tumping . . . an immense bull moose on a sled.

tum-tum 'tʌm,tʌm, *n. N.W.* [Chinook, in allusion to the beating of the heart.] The heart, mind, intellect. *Colloq.* — **1876** *Silver City* (Ida.) *Avalanche* 6 March 2/2 To describe the really delightful, warm, sunshiny weather . . . would create envious feeling in the *tum-tums* of the denizens of old War Eagle, therefore I will refrain. *a***1915** MUIR *Travels Alaska* (1917) 277 Tyeen said, 'Your friend has klosh tumtum.'

tuna 'tunə, *n.* [App. f. **tunny*, but cf. Sp. *atún*, in the sense shown here.] A fish of the family Thunnidae, a tunny. Also **tuna clipper.**

1884 JORDAN in Goode *Fisheries* I. 319 The names 'Spanish Mackerel,' 'Skipjack,' and 'Tuna' are also sometimes applied to [the California bonito]. **1932** MILLER *I Cover Waterfront* 31 A Portuguese tuna-clipper returned to port today after riding out a chabasco storm off the Mexican coast. **1949** *Fishing Gaz.* Sep. 98/2 Another tuna clipper, the Santa Anita, will be launched in the near future.

tuna cactus. *S.W.* [Amer. Sp. *tuna,* in the same sense.] Any one of various prickly pears of the genus *Opuntia.* — **1875** BOURKE *Journal* 30 May, A plant, plentiful in this country [along the South Cheyenne R.], called the nopal, or Tuna cactus, . . . is employed with success to clarify water for drinking purposes. **1898** A. M. DAVIDSON *Calif. Plants* 189 The prickly pear, or tuna cactus, so common in Southern California on dry hillsides and sandy wastes.

tune book. A hymn book. — **1848** *Ladies' Repository* VIII. 286 We advise all our Churches, east and west, to patronize our new and excellent tune-book. **1887** *Nation* 19 June 427/1 A hymn and tune-book for Congregational use.

Tunker ˈtʌŋkɚ, *n.* =**Dunker.** Also attrib.

1789 MORSE *Amer. Geog.* 324 They appear to be humble, well-meaning christians, and have the character of the *Harmless* Tunkers. **1864** *Commonwealth* (Boston) 19 Aug., John Kline, an aged Tunker preacher . . . , has been assassinated solely for being a good Anti-Slavery Unionist. **1940** *Sat. Ev. Post* 30 March 37/4 What sticks is their nickname, the Tunkers, or Dunkards.

tunket ˈtʌŋkɪt, *n.* [Origin obscure.] A euphemism for *hell.* Usu. *what* (or *where*) *in tunket.*

1871 *Scribner's Mo.* II. 630 What in tunket are you making such a to-do about it for? **1894** *Life* 4 Jan. 13/2 What in the name o' Tunkett makes all boys so crazy to leave the old farm? **1948** *Yankee* Sep. 18/1, I sent an SOS to Yankee, asking where in tunket I could find wooden clothespins.

tupelo ˈtjupəˌlo, *n.* [f. Creek Indian *ito*, tree, +*opilwa* swamp, lit. swamp tree.] Any one of various trees of the genus *Nyssa*, as the black or sour gum. Also **tupelo gum, tree.**

*c***1730** CATESBY *Carolina* I. 41 The Tupelo Tree . . . the Grain of the Wood is curled and very tough, and therefore very proper for Naves of Cart-Wheels, and other Country-Uses. **1816** W. DARBY *Geog. Descr. La.* 130 The tupeloo is known in Louisiana by the popular name of olive. **1885** *Milnor Free Press* 25 April 5/5 The tupelo-gum and the willow-oak are timbers that are destined to a commercial value never until recently dreamed of. **1949** *Charleston* (S.C.) *News & Courier* 6 Feb. D. 7 Cypress, sweet gum and tupelo gum, not seen farther north, are common trees there.

attrib. **1765** in STORK *Acct. E. Fla.* 79 The low lands are partly cypress and tupelow swamps. **1917** *House Beautiful* March 246 Tupelo flooring does not splinter or sliver. **1950** *Nat. Geog. Mag.* April 518 Living chiefly in tupelo and cypress swamps from Georgia to Louisiana, *avivoca* is hard to find.

As the last term in **large, sour tupelo.** See also **upland tupelo, water tupelo (tree).**

turban squash. A squash the shape of which suggests a cap or turban. — **1909** WEBSTER. **1949** *Nat. Geog. Mag.* Aug. 162 Several years ago a North Dakota horticulturalist bred a small variety of turban squash.

∗**Turk,** *n.*

1. Used in the possessive in the names of plants: (1) ∗**Turk's cap,** (*a*) the American swamp lily, *Lilium superbum*, (*b*) (see quot. 1891); (2) **head,** (*a*) (see quots.), (*b*) (see quot. and cf. ∗**Turk's cap** (*a*)).

(1) (*a*) **1890** *Cent.* 3454/2 The American Turk's-cap or swamp-lily, . . . found on low grounds at the north. **1943** PEATTIE *Great Smokies* 281 The wild Turk's-cap lily, which may attain a height of seven or eight feet, reaches its blooming peak during the second or third week of the month. (*b*) **1847** WOOD *Botany* 275 Turk's Cap. Melon Thistle. . . . This remarkable plant appears like a large, green melon, with deep furrows and prominent ribs. **1891** *Cent.* 6537/1 Turk's-cap. . . . A species of melon-cactus, *Melocactus communis.* — (2) (*a*) **1854** WHIPPLE *Explor. Ry. Route* I. 102 There are . . . various kinds of Echino cactus, the most conspicuous being that named Wislizenus, and sometimes called the 'Turk's Head.' **1895** *Amer. Folk-Lore* Jan.–Apr. 47 The *Allicôchis* . . . is a cactus, resembling the Biznaga, or Turk's Head, but much smaller. (*b*) **1892** *Ib.* V. 104 *Lillium superbum*, nodding lilies; Turk's head. Mass.

2. a. Turk's money, =next. **b. Turk's rate,** (see quot. 1887). Both *obs.*

(**a**) **1684** *Huntington Rec.* I. 384 Thos men how war bee hind of the payment of the: turkes money: ar now to pay the remaindar in Speshy. — (**b**) *Ib.*, Thos men . . . are behind of the turks Ratte. **1887** *Ib.* 383 (*footnote*), The 'Turks Rate' was a term used to denote a tax levied by the British Government to provide funds for ransoming prisoners taken by Algerian pirates in the Mediterranean Sea and other waters.

As the last term in **Grand, little Turk.**

∗**turkey,** *n.*

1. A large, well-known North American bird belonging to either of two species of the family Meleagridae.

The turkey, *Meleagris gallopavo*, of which several subspecies are recognized, is a distinctly North American bird. The common domestic turkey is thought to derive from the Mexican subspecies.

[**1587** HAKLUYT tr. Laudonnière *Notable Historie* 6r As we passed throw these woods we saw nothing but Turkeycocks flying in the forests.] **1607** in SMITH *Works* (1910) I. p. xli, We found an Ilet, on which were many Turkeys. **1701** WOLLEY *Journal N.Y.* 40 They have great store of wild-fowl, as Turkys, Heath-hens, Quails, Partridges, Pigeons. **1891** O'BEIRNE *Leaders Ind. Territory* 209/2 In these parts deer, turkey and beaver are plentiful. **1950** *Chi. Tribune* 17 Jan. 14/3 Judging from its prominence in everyday slang terms, the turkey, rather than the vaunted eagle, might well be considered the national bird of the United States.

2. A fit or spell of intoxication. *Slang. Obs.*

1846 DURIVAGE *Stray Subjects* 116 'It's a turkey I've got on,' hiccuped Tom Links, as he noticed a singular disposition on the part of the *pavé* to rise up and impede his progress. **1853** *Lantern* (N.Y.) III. 23/1 Him shall no Oysters from the Stews of Sliddon, Nor Pork and Beans, so fat . . . arouse, till he's got rid on That Turkey in his hat.

3. *fig.* Advantage or profit. *Slang.*

1873 *Ill. Dept. Agric. Trans.* X. 14, I do not . . . oppose the colleges in their legitimate work, but I do object to the *turkey* being all on the College side. **1899** BREEN *Thirty Years* 185 They thought it a still better idea when the hotel-keeper said he 'would treat them right,' which of course, the Aldermen believed meant 'turkey,' (as they sometimes called money,) or 'a divvy.'

4. (See quot. 1905.) [Cf. *EDD turkeyhide*, ?a bag or wallet, a pocketbook.]

1893 *Scribner's Mag.* June 715/2 [With] his 'turkey,' a two-bushel bag in which he carries his belongings, strung over his shoulder, the shanty boy starts . . . for town. **1905** *Forestry Bureau Bul.* No. 61, 52 *Turkey*, a bag containing a lumberjack's outfit. To 'histe the turkey' is to take one's personal belongings and leave camp. (N[orth] W[oods], L[ake] S[tates].) **1944** NUTE *Lake Superior* 210 One would appear with his turkey (luggage sack), apply for work [etc.].

5. *Theatr.* A play or motion picture that is a failure. *Slang.*

1943 *Copper Camp* 279 Many a manager of an unlucky venture or 'turkey' and many a stranded actor could tell you how he reached Butte and got out of the hole through Uncle Dick's devotion to the 'perfesh.' **1948** MENJOU & MUSSELMAN *It Took 9 Tailors* 92 Whenever there is a lot of fuss and turmoil in making a picture, it usually turns out to be a 'turkey.' **1950** *Chi. Tribune* 17 Jan. 14/3 In the cant of today the word 'turkey' may mean . . . a show that is a flop.

6. In miscellaneous combs.: (1) **turkey bump,** =**goose pimple,** *rare;* (2) **dance,** a ceremonial dance practiced by certain American Indians, *obs.;* (3) **Day,** =**Thanksgiving Day;** (4) **feather fan,** a fan made from the wing or tail of a turkey, cf. **turkey tail (fan);** (5) **match,** =**turkey shoot,** *obs.;* (6) **range,** an area over which turkeys range; (7) **roost,** a place in the forest where wild turkeys customarily roost; (8) **shoot,** a shooting match at which turkeys serve as targets and prizes; (9) **shooting,** =prec., also attrib.; (10) **tail (fan),** the tail feathers of a turkey made into a fan; (11) **trot,** see as a main entry; (12) **walk,** a performance in which two persons, chosen by lot, imitate the strutting, wing flapping, etc., of turkeys; (13) **wallow,** ?a place where turkeys take dust baths, *rare;* (14) ∗**wing,** see as a main entry.

(**1**) **1866** C. H. SMITH *Bill Arp* 85 For three days and nights fresh troops from the South poured into our streets with shouts that made the welkin ring, and the turkey bumps rise all over the flesh of our people. — (**2**) **1800** HAWKINS *Sk. Creek Country* 76 The pin-e-bun-gau, (turkey dance,) is danced by the women of the turkey tribe. *a***1820** in *Western Rev.* II. 161 There are a number of other dances, such as the . . . turkey dance. — (**3**) **1945** *Boulder* (Colo.) *D. Camera* 24 Nov. 3/6 It is doubtful if anyone seeing the University of Colorado Band stunts at the Turkey Day game realized [etc.]. **1950** *Chi. Tribune* 17 Jan. 14/3 'Turkey day'—Thanksgiving—has numerous advocates as the most typically American festival. — (**4**) **1869** STOWE *Oldtown Folks* 88 Here's a turkey-feather fan to fan her with. **1889** MELLICK *Story Old Farm* 2 She wades to the door, dragging after her a large newspaper parcel, a spreading turkey-feather fan, and a huge paper bandbox.

(**5**) **1863** E. KIRKE *Southern Friends* 49 About a hundred men, women and children were . . . witnessing a turkey match. — (**6**) **1946** *N. Eng. Homestead* 9 Feb. 6/1 The limestone soil, plus its water holding capacity, plus the cool growing season, makes for an ideal turkey range. — (**7**) **1870** KEIM *Sheridan's Troopers* 303 Towards dusk, considerably to our enjoyment, we discovered we had encamped near a turkey-roost. **1946** *Democrat* 21 Nov. 4/1 'Wild Turkey Roost in Butler Town Limits' says headline in Choctaw Advocate. Well, why not? — (**8**) **1845** JUDD *Margaret* I. 62 Its succedanea . . . were a turkey shoot the next day, and a ball. **1950** *Newsweek* 20 Feb. 6/2 Sometimes we have turkey shoots, dog races, and dances. — (**9**) **1844** *N.O. Picayune* 19 Feb. 1/2 In one day they recently had two street fights, . . . got up a turkey shooting, a gander pulling, a match dog fight. **1930** FERBER *Cimarron* 161 They got a feud with the Kid and his outfit, and [if] the Kid sees 'em he'll drop 'em like a row of gobblers at a turkey shootin'.

(**10**) **1839** *S. Lit. Messenger* V. 375/2 The more useful and enduring turkey-tail fan had not given place to the delicate pink and white plumage of these aquatic birds. **1851** HOOPER *Widow Rugby* 84 Betsy dodged behind the wild turkey-tail which she carried by way of a fan. **1896** HARRIS *Sister Jane* 232, I noticed her turkey-tail fan, which she always carried with her on occasions of moment, was swinging in the adjoining pew. — (**12**) **1901** WHITE *Westerners* xxx. 283 A happy combination of these two effects brought about the proposal of a turkey walk. A ring was formed on the instant. — (**13**) **1893** *Outing* Feb. 366/2 We have seen several turkey wallows [in La.], but so far no 'hog signs.'

b. In expressions relating chiefly to hunting wild turkeys: (1) **turkey buster,** a hunter's favorite gun for shooting turkeys; (2) **call,** (*a*) =**turkey yelper,** also **turkey call quill,** (*b*) the note or cry of a turkey; (3) **caller,** one who is proficient at calling turkeys, also a turkey yelper *q.v.;* (4) **dog,** a dog useful in hunting turkeys; (5) **hound,** =prec.; (6) **hunter,** one who hunts turkeys; (7) **pen,** a pen for turkeys, esp. one serving as a trap for wild turkeys; (8) **roosting,** ascertaining where wild turkeys roost, so as to slip up on and kill them at dawn; (9) **runner,** ?a turkey hunter, *rare;* (10) **yelper,** an instrument used by a hunter for calling a wild turkey by imitating its yelp.

(**1**) **1869** J. R. BROWNE *Adv. Apache Country* 462 Chiv he looked back, but Pop had his turkey-buster well in hand. — (**2**) (*a*) **1857** *Spirit of Times* 19 Dec. 256/3 Turkey Yelpers.—A Turkey Call of my own make and pattern, can be mailed to any State in the Union, by enclosing one dollar. **1900** DRANNAN *Plains & Mts.* 35 Uncle Kit . . . loaned me his turkey-call quill. **1950** *Democrat* 30 March 6/2 Turkey calls—Small cedar box type. Effective, especially in gobbling season. (*b*) **1873** *Forest & Stream* 2 Oct. 123/1 A turkey-call is easily imitated by using the hollow bone of the leg or wing of the same. **1943** BENÉT *Western Star* 3 Where the forgotten wampum slowly drowns, Cow-horn and turkey-call, And last, purest of all, The spell of peace. — (**3**) **1934** VINES *Green Thicket World* 184 Cal was a good turkey caller. *Ib.* 57 They had saved all of the turkey callers. **1948** *Chi. Tribune* 5 Dec. (*comics*) 8 Sittin' dead still and workin' away with his turkey caller. — (**4**) **1895** *Outing* XXVI. 231/1 This setter, Blank, was an excellent turkey dog.

(**5**) **1834** AUDUBON *Ornith. Biog.* I. 5 A slow turkey-hound has led me miles before I could flush the same bird. *c***1845** *Big Bear Ark.* 148 You must hav a turky hown az is bout 3 parts Dear Hown and the tother pinter, tho sumtimes haf and haf will doo. — (**6**) **1846** THORPE *Myst. Backwoods* 62 The implements of the turkey-hunter are few and simple. **1895** *Outing* XXVII. 231/1 Nearly every negro man and boy on the plantation came up to have a look at the famous turkey hunter. **1948** *Democrat* 13 May 4/1 When a Butler County turkey hunter kills a big tom, he goes quietly home. — (**7**) **1843** *Amer. Pioneer* II. 57 In respect to turkey pens, as they were called, the more southern pioneers constructed them as above described. **1855** P. PAXTON *Capt. Priest* 164 It was a huge turkey-pen, in which were confined at least an hundred fine, fat birds. **1913** O. A. ROTHERT *Hist. Muhlenberg Co.* (Ky.) 115 My grandfather . . . had cleared a small field, in which he built a turkey-pen for the purpose of trapping wild turkeys. — (**8**) **1877** CAMPION *On Frontier* 233 The diversion of turkey-roosting, as it is called, is not without its attractions for the sportsman. — (**9**) *c***1845** W. T. PORTER *Big Bear Ark.* 118 It is then the 'Turkey Runner,' . . . sallies forth in quest of a drove, from which he selects some master spirit, and flushes him.

(**10**) **1857** [see **turkey call** (*a*)]. **1887** in *Md. Conservationist* (1945) 13/2 With great care and a show of affection he took from an inner pocket his turkey yelper. . . . He breathed on it to impart the right degree of moisture and tone, like a musician tuning some precious instrument. **1895** *Outing* XXVII. 231/2 Matt drew from his pocket a 'turkey yelper' and began to call.

7. In the names of, or with reference to, plants: (1) **turkey acorn,** an acorn of a turkey oak; (2) **beard,** (see quot.); (3) **corn,** =**squirrel corn;** (4) **mullein,** (see quot. 1909); (5) **oak,** an oak, *Quercus catesbaei*, found chiefly in the sandy barrens of the South, also a red oak, *Q. rubra*, found in the southern states; (6) **pea,** any one of various plants (see quots.).

(**1**) **1709** LAWSON *Carolina* 141 They are the same we call Turkey-Acorns, because the wild Turkies feed very much thereon; And for the same Reason those Trees that bear them, are call'd Turkey-Oaks. — (**2**) **1938** THOMPSON *High Trails* 86 The bear grass flower . . . is also listed as pine grass, . . . and turkey beard. — (**3**) **1843** TORREY *Flora N.Y.* I. 46 Squirrel Corn. Turkey Corn. . . . Rather common in the western and northern counties. — (**4**) **1894** *Amer. Folk-Lore* VII. 98 *Eremocarpus setigerus*, turkey mullein, Santa Barbara Co., Cal. **1909** *Cent. Supp.* 837/1 Turkey mullen, a low, heavy-scented annual herb, *Piscaria setigera*, belonging to the spurge family. It is very abundant on the Pacific coast from southern California to the Columbia river. **1939** PICKWELL *Deserts* 13/1 Turkey Mullein and many another plant shows leaves gray-woolly, hairy, or prickly to the blazing sun.

(**5**) **1709** LAWSON *Carolina* 92 Turkey-Oak is so call'd from a small Acorn it bears, which the wild Turkeys feed on. **1901** MOHR *Plant Life Ala.* 96 The turkey or barren oak and the blue jack . . . are frequent companions of the long-leaf pine. — (**6**) **1891** *Cent.* 6536/3 *Turkey-pea.* 1. Same as *squirrel-corn*. . . . 2. The hoary pea, *Tephrosia Virginiana*. . . . (Southern U.S.) **1915** ARMSTRONG & THORNBER *Western Wild Flowers* 332 Turkey Peas. *Orogenia linearifolia*. White. Spring. Northwest and Utah. A quaint little plant, only about three inches high, with a tuberous root, spreading, slanting stems, and smooth leaves, all from the root. **1938** *Range Plant Handbook* W186 Mountain goldenpea [*Thermopsis montana*], variously known as buffalo pea, devil's shoestring, Montana-pea, prairie-bean, turkeypea [etc.].

8. In the names of, or with reference to, animals: (1) **turkey buzzard,** see as a main entry; (2) **dog,** see **6. b.** (4) above; (3) **gnat,** (see quot. 1909); (4) **gobbler,** a turkey cock; (5) **hound,** see **6. b.** (5) above; (6) **snake,** a fictitious snake alleged to call up turkeys by imitating their note and kill them, *rare;* (7) **vulture,** =**turkey buzzard.**

(**3**) **1889** *Cent.* 2553/2. **1909** WEBSTER, turkey gnat. A small black fly (*Simulium meridionale*) that attacks and injures poultry in the southern and western United States. — (**4**) **1833** JONES *Green Mt. Boys* I. v, I feel about as grand as a large-sized turkey-gobbler, when his hen is settin'. **1945** *New Yorker* 10 March 40 A queer bird . . . whose call . . . is a cross between that of a whippoorwill and a turkey gobbler.

(**6**) **1791** J. LONG *Voyages* 160 The turkey snake . . . takes its name from its voice which resembles the note of a wild turkey. **1800** D. R. D'ERES *Memoirs* 175 The Turkey-Snake is about six feet in length, proportionally large in its body. — (**7**) **1823** JAMES *Exped.* I. 4 At evening we heard the cry of the whip-poor-will; and among other birds saw . . . several turkey vultures. **1947** *So. Sierran* May 1/3 Turkey vultures, eagles and large hawks may be mistaken for condors.

9. In colloq. phrases: (1) *To talk turkey*, (*a*) to speak with the utmost plainness, (*b*) to invite to partake of Thanksgiving turkey; (2) *as proud as a lame turkey*, ?exceedingly humble; (3) *to catch a turkey*, to get drunk, *obs.*, cf. **2.** above; (4) *to say turkey*, (*a*) in negative contexts, to say anything, to say a word, also *to say pea-turkey*, (*b*) *to say turkey to* (one) *and buzzard to* (another), to give (one) the advantage over (another); (5) *month of turkeys*, (see quot.), *rare;* (6) *to walk turkey*, of a ship, to pitch and roll.

(**1**) (*a*) [**1830** *N.Y. Mirror* 8 July 16/2 'You may have your choice, you take the crow and I'll take the turkey, or if you'd rather, I'll take the turkey and you take the crow.' Wampum reflected a moment on the generous alternative thus offered and replied—'Ugh! you no talk turkey to me a bit.'] **1950** *Florida Grower* Feb. 13 Let's talk turkey about this threat to your welfare. (*b*) **1856** *Spirit of Age* (Sacramento) 22 Nov. 3/2 He has so little to be thankful for, that he didn't feel called upon to make any great display of gratitude, no one having 'talked turkey' to him even once. **1866** *Eastern Slope* (Washoe, Nev.) 24 Nov. 3/2 As yet no one has talked turkey to us, and thanksgiving is rapidly approaching. — (**2**) **1838** *Lexington* (Ky.) *Observer & Rep.* 2 June, The critter . . . got as proud as a lame turkey. — (**3**) **1841** *N.O. Picayune* 20 April 2/3 A chap . . . caught the largest kind of a 'turkey' while visiting the different bar-rooms. — (**4**) (*a*) **1845** in BLAIR *Amer. Humor* 319 'Bet two to one old splinter-legs thar,' nodding at one of the ministers—'won't git a chance to say turkey to a good-lookin gal today!' **1849** *Placer Times* (Sacramento) 29 Dec. 1/4 I've never said turkey about eating oysters since. **1909** *D.N.* III. 356 She never said pea-turkey to me about it. (*b*) **1896** *Cong. Rec.* 22 Dec. 409/2 That is a sort of civil service that says 'turkey' to every Democrat and 'buzzard' to every Republican. **1899** *Ib.* 25 Jan. App. 108/1 Why do these professed champions of liberty insist on saying 'turkey' to the Filipinos and 'buzzard' to the negroes?

(**5**) **1876** HALE *P. Nolan's Friends* x, The Americans found them in this 'month of turkeys.' — (**6**) **1888** *S.F. Wkly. Examiner* 22 March (F.), The north wind commenced to make the Yaquina walk turkey, standing her up on either end alternately and rolling her both ways at once.

As the last term in **Cape Cod, Cherokee, cold, Colorado, gentleman, Job's, Marblehead, prairie, Taunton, Thanksgiving, Vermont, water, western, wild turkey.**

turkey buzzard.

1. An American blackish-brown vulture or variety of vulture, *Cathartes aura septentrionalis*, found chiefly in southern states. Cf. ∗**buzzard 2.**

1672 JOSSELYN *N. Eng. Rarities* 12 The Turkie Buzzard, a kind of Kite, but as big as a Turkie. **1779** ANBUREY *Travels* II. 434 There is in this province [i.e., Virginia], . . . a large ravenous kind of bird that feeds on carrion, nearly as big as an eagle, called a turkey-bustard, from having red gills, resembling those of a turkey, whence it derives its name. **1818** PALMER *Journal* 96 We saw several of a large species of vulture (called here turkey-buzzard) hovering over a dead carcase . . . the people never kill these birds on account of their usefulness. **1945** BOTKIN *My Burden* 56 Yes sir, that's the way turkey buzzards does.

attrib. and *transf.* **1854** *Spirit of Times* (N.Y.) 448/1 Thar was dad's bald head, for all the yearth like a peeled onion, a bobbin up an' down, an' the hornets sailin' an' a circlin' round, turkey buzzard fashion. **1857** STROTHER *Virginia* 66 Ha, you ole turkey-buzzard!

b. The figure of an eagle formerly used on a one-cent piece. *Derisive. Obs.* Cf. **buzzard dollar.**

1861 *Vanity Fair* 9 March 117/1, I remember . . . in 1858 . . . how bitterly you laughed at the Turkey-Buzzard stamped on the cent coin of that date.

2. turkey buzzard dance, (see quots.). *Obs.*

1845 GREEN *Texian Exped.* 134 Among their other dances they have one called the zopilote, or turkey-buzzard dance. *c*1860 in STERLING *Belle* (1904) 217 There is a tall black man, called Robin, on this plantation [in S.C.], who has originated a dance which he calls the turkey-buzzard dance. He holds his hands under his coat-tails, which he flirts out as he jumps, first to one side, and then to the other, and looks exactly like the ugly bird he imitates.

turkey trot.

1. A fast jogging trot like that of a turkey.

1839 *S. Lit. Messenger* V. 377/1 May-be I didn't set up a high turkey trot, and peeled it like thunder. **1895** REMINGTON *Pony Tracks* 187 He would run me off the plantation at a turkey-trot if I did shoot.

Hence **turkey-trotting,** *a.*

1859 TALIAFERRO *Fisher's R.* 36 You're a purty set uv ill-begotten, turkey-trottin' pukes, to raise a quarrel with a peaceubble man, and then run like a gang uv geese.

2. A ragtime dance performed with the feet wide apart and characterized by recurring risings on the balls of the feet.

1908 DAVENPORT *Butte Beneath X-Ray* 42 The light fantastic, the turkey trot and the pazamala were indulged in by all to a late hour. **1947** *Reader's Digest* Feb. 185/2 Those who first did the 'turkey trot' were depraved beings, and conservatives sighed for the discarded waltz. **1949** *Sat. Ev. Post* 16 April 108/3 The country knocked itself out whirling to the turkey trot, the maxixe, the bunny hug and the tango.

Hence **turkey-trotting.**

1913 *Current Opinion* Oct. 263/1 The University of Wisconsin proposes to expel any students guilty of 'turkey-trotting,' which it puts on the same plane as drunkenness.

b. A tune for such a dance.

1916 EATON *Idyl of Twin Fires* 158, I bet that tune beats any o' these new-fangled turkey trots!

3. (See quot.) *Rare.*

1931 *Durant* (Okla.) *D. Democrat* 13 Nov. 3/4 The annual turkey trot here, when thousands of turkey gobblers flocked through the main streets of this town on their way to Thanksgiving markets, has fallen a victim to progress.

turkey wing.

1. A brush consisting of the wing of a turkey.

1871 STOWE *Sam Lawson* 4 'I'll sweep up the coals now,' he added, vigorously applying a turkey-wing to the purpose. **1896** E. HIGGINSON *Land of Snow Pearls* 60 She dropped the turkey-wing with which she was polishing the stove. **1919** CADY *Rhymes of Vt.* (1923) 249 I'm pretty sure I recollect. . . . The turkey wings for oven use That smelt of sulphur jest a trifle. **1939** HARRIS *Purslane* 58 With a turkey wing John brushed the compact cluster from the limb upon the table.

b. Also **turkey-wing brush, fan.**

1884 MARK TWAIN *H. Finn* xvii, There was a couple of big wild-turkey-wing fans spread out behind those things. **1888** *Cent. Mag.* XXXVI. 769/2 Turkey-wing fans and fans of peacock feathers supplanted those of a more or less artistic and elaborate design and finish. **1904** M. E. WALLER *Wood-carver* 140 [She] 'redded up,' as she says, the hearth with the turkey-wing brush.

2. a. turkey-wing cradle, a reaper's cradle suggestive in shape of the wing of a turkey. **b. turkey-wing plow,** ?= ∗**sweep 1.**

(a) 1884 *Canon City* (Colo.) *Mercury* 22 Aug. 1/5 'Grapevine' and 'Turky wing' cradles are the ones that cut most of the Hawes' grain. **1923** ADAMS *Pioneer Hist.* 319 Until I was seven years old the sickle cut all the grain in the neighborhood; then the turkey-wing cradle, the grape-vine, the mully, the man rake-off reaper, the self raking reaper, the dropper, the marsh harvester, the wire binder, then the twine binder—ten jumps, or to make the term more modern, we'll call them improvements instead of 'jumps.' — **(b) 1854** *Mich. Agric. Soc. Trans.* V. 53, 1 turkey wing plow.

∗**turn,** *n.*

1. (See quot. 1864.)

1864 DICK *Amer. Hoyle* (1866) 207 The two cards drawn from the dealer's box—one for the bank and the other for the player, which thus determine the events of the game, constitute a turn. **1901** JAMES *Sacred Fount* 44 The gentleman close to her . . . offered us the face of Guy Brissenden, as recognizable at a distance as the numbered card of a 'turn.'

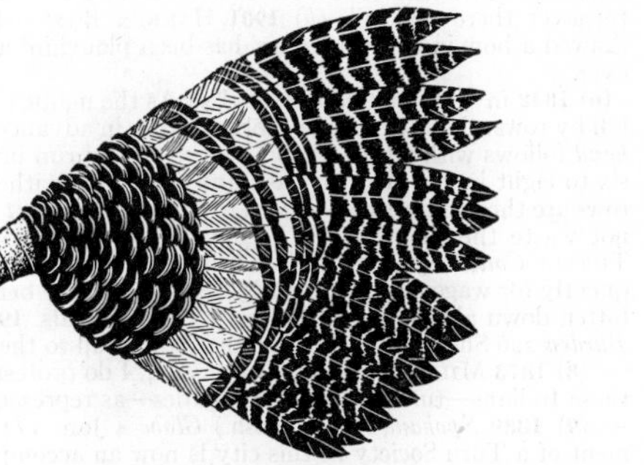

Turkey-wing fan

b. *To call the turn,* in faro (see quot. 1889). Also transf.

1889 *Cent.* 2144/2 After each turn new bets are made for another, down to the last three cards of the pack; the only betting allowed after this is on 'calling the turn,' or guessing which will show first. **1898** *N.Y. Jrnl.* 17 Aug. 6/6 He called the turn on all of them. **1908** *Sat. Ev. Post* 5 Dec. 18/2 'Ye-e-es, but this Wallingford person called the turn,' insisted Phelps. **1938** ASBURY *Sucker's Prog.* 15 Calling the turn—To guess correctly the order in which the last three cards in the box would appear.

2. A transaction involving the buying and selling of securities, or the profit so made. Also any business transaction or chance to make money.

1870 MEDBERY *Men Wall St.* 78 This neat profit is called a 'turn.' **1913** WHARTON *Custom of Country* 449 The sum his wife demanded could be acquired only by 'a quick turn.'

∗**turn,** *v.*

1. *tr.* (See quots.)

1865 *Harper's Mag.* April 619/2 Application was made to several leading bear houses to 'turn' Hudson; that is to say, to buy it for cash from the cornering party, and to sell it back to them on buyer's option. **1870** W. W. FOWLER *Ten Yrs. Wall St.* 65 A broker is said to *turn* stock when he sells it out for cash, i.e. deliverable and payable the same day, and buys it back *regular*, i.e. deliverable and payable the next day.

2. (See quot. and cf. **9. c.** below.)

1890 *N. & Q.* V. 35 Turn for Pour.—During a sojourn in New England, I often heard the word *turn* used for *pour*, especially at table. 'Will your *turn* me a cup of coffee?' 'Mr. Smith, will you please *turn* the water?' So far as I know, this is a strictly local use of the word.

3. *intr.* Of a commodity: To sell, go off. *Colloq.*

1928 *Publishers' Wkly.* 30 June (Inset), Your Star Dollar Series is the fastest turning merchandise that we have ever had in our store.

4. In noun and adj. combs.: (1) ∗**turnabout,** a merry-go-round, *rare;* (2) **off,** (*a*) on a plank road, that part of the road not covered by planks, and used by one of two meeting vehicles, *obs.*, (*b*) a place where one turns off another road, path, etc., on a journey, *colloq.;* (3) ∗**out,** the barring out of a schoolmaster by his pupils, *obs.*, cf. **9. b.** below; (4) ∗**over,** (*a*) a shift of votes from one party to another, (*b*) =**turning plow,** *rare;* (5) ∗**pike,** see as a main entry; (6) **plow,** = ∗**twister 1,** cf. **turning plow;** (7) **row,** a row, or an area about sufficient for a row, at which rows in a field come up to others running or extending in a different direction; (8) *skin, a renegade Indian, *obs.;* (9) **society,** a Turnverein *q.v.*

(1) **1889** *Harper's Mag.* Sep. 560/1 Here were found the hundreds of neat stalls . . . , the high swings and the turnabouts. — (2) (*a*) **1852** MacKinnon *Atlantic Sk.* II. 276 Running parallel to the planks the road is carefully made, and the name by which it is now known indicates its use. It is called the 'turn-off.' (*b*) **1894** J. Winsor *Cartier to Frontenac* 151 The turn off at Lake Athabasca . . . would have conducted him to the northern tributaries of the Columbia. **1948** *Sierra Club* (So. Calif. Chap.) *Sched.* 128, 43 Meet at the Angeles Crest turnoff in La Canada. — (3) **1835** Longstreet *Ga. Scenes* 78 The Boys always conceive a holiday gained by a 'turn out,' as a sole achievement of their valor. — (4) (*a*) **1895** *Forum* Oct. 160 It represents, of course, no very sweeping change of opinion—no very considerable turnover of votes. **1903** *N.Y. Times* 16 Aug., The best-informed sentiment of Union County is looking for a Democratic turnover there this fall. (*b*) **1901** Harben *Westerfelt* 59 He hain't drawed a bow in two weeks, an' has been ploughin' a two-hoss turnover.

(6) **1842** in Turner *Cotton* (1865) 54 As the manure is placed in the hill by rows, the wide way, a short distance in advance, a *good plough-hand* follows with a turn-plough, which should run into the soil from six to eight inches deep at least, and turn well, with which four furrows are thrown together on each row. **1948** *Democrat* 13 May 2/4 Do not waste the time barring cotton with a turn plow. — (7) **1865** Turner *Cotton* 25 Sometimes it will bear fruit in turnrows used frequently for wagons, while it really seems to derive benefit from being bitten down almost to the ground by the animals. **1945** Botkin *My Burden* 226 She dropped her hoe and danced up to the turn road [*sic*]. — (8) **1873** Miller *Amongst Modocs* 104, I do protest against taking these Indians—turn-skins and renegades—as representative Indians. — (9) **1889** *Spokane Falls* (Wash.) *Globe* 4 Jan. 1/4 The establishment of a Turn Society in this city is now an accomplished fact.

5. **To turn back*, to hand back, return.

1927 *Publishers' Wkly.* 12 Feb. 610 We felt that the only course open to us in view of the author's feelings in the matter was to offer to turn back the book to them, subject to their disposal.

6. **To turn down*, in a spelling class, to spell a word another has missed and so pass above him. Cf. **trap, v.*[1] **1. c.** in *OED.*

1876 Mark Twain *Tom Sawyer* vi, He took his place . . . in the spelling class, and got 'turned down,' by a succession of mere baby words. **1946** Wilson *Fidelity* 136 We had regular places in the line and turned down those who could not spell a word.

b. (See quot. 1891.)

1891 *Cent.* 6538/2 *To turn down*, . . . to snub; to suppress. **1894** *Cong. Rec.* 10 Aug. 8393/2 As soon as any one of these parties or societies . . . has shown signs of anarchy, communism, or oppression, . . . such parties have been 'turned down' and relegated to their proper place.

c. To refuse or deny.

1897 *Boston Jrnl.* 14 Jan. 7/6 Secretary Olney was turned down by the Senate . . . in his effort to have the vote on the extradition treaties . . . reconsidered. **1907** London *Road* 3 Something to eat was a hard proposition. I was 'turned down' at a dozen houses.

7. **To turn in*, to enter with vigor upon some activity, to work energetically.

1822 Woods *English Prairie* (1904) 345, I calculated to sell my creature there, and then . . . to turn in and earn some money to get me another. **1882** *Harper's Mag.* Sep. 601/1 Two leading doctors turned in on me.

b. To deliver, give.

1844 Featherstonhaugh *Slave States* 81 He is 'to turn in' 15 gallons of *bar* (bear) oil, the current value of which is one dollar per gallon. **1903** A. Adams *Log of Cowboy* 12 A number of different rancheros had turned in cattle in making up the herd.

8. **To turn loose*, to fire or discharge (a gun).

1851 A. T. Jackson *Forty-niner* (1920) 59, I hadn't gone forty feet away when he turned loose his gun. **1903** A. Adams *Log of Cowboy* 206 Somebody . . . turned his gun loose into the air.

b. To open fire with a gun. Also transf. *Colloq.*

1868 *All Year Round* 31 Oct. 491/2 It was etiquette to tell him [an armed man] to 'turn loose.' **1903** A. Adams *Log of Cowboy* 137 The chief could not speak a word of English, but . . . when I turned loose on him in Spanish, however, he instantly turned his horse. **1907** White *Arizona Nights* 14, I made up my mind that when the star was darkened I'd turn loose.

c. To break loose from the customary restraints upon conduct. *Colloq.*

1880 *Scribner's Mo.* March 771/1 Once arrived in New Sharon, the herder, or 'cow-boy,' . . . 'turns loose,' as he calls it, and . . . becomes a spendthrift, a drunkard, a gambler, a libertine. **1883** Mark Twain *Life on Miss.* iii, Lay low and hold your breath, for I'm 'bout to turn myself loose!

9. **To turn out*, to put out of cultivation or use, usu. with reference to land.

1814 J. Taylor *Arator* 107 The phrase 'the land is killed and must be turned out,' has become common over a great portion of the United States. **1883** Smith *Geol. Survey Ala.* 445 Such turned-out lands will produce well if Japan clover cover them one or two years. **1934** Vines *Green Thicket World* 66 Not far from the spring was an old turned-out house.

b. Of pupils desirous of a holiday: To prevent a schoolmaster from entering a schoolhouse by fastening the door or by other means (see also quot. 1857). *Obs.* Cf. ***turnout,** *n.*

1835 Longstreet *Ga. Scenes* 78 The boys . . . are going to turn out the schoolmaster to-morrow. **1857** *Quinland* I. 274 He says I must look out for the large boys, or they will knock me down and drag me out of the school-house, which they call 'turning-out' the master.

c. To pour out. Cf. **2.** above.

1864 in M. Todd *Life S. Jex-Blake* [In America] they ask if they shall 'turn out the tea.'

d. To release the logs of (a boom).

1905 Wiggin *Rose* 60 The boom above the falls would be 'turned out,' and the river would once more be clear.

10. **To turn over*, to deliver (property, a business, etc.) *to* another.

1882 Mark Twain *Life on Miss.* App. A, As soon as the *Susie* reached Troy she was turned over to General York. **1930** *Publishers' Wkly.* 5 April 1896 By retiring and turning the business over to his son.

11. In phrases: (1) *To turn up jack*, =*to tear up jack*, *q.v. s.v.* **jack,** *rare;* (2) *to turn the Bible*, to use a Bible suspended from a freely turning key ring supported on the finger tips of two persons as a means of fortune telling; (3) *to turn the paunch*, (see quot.).

(1) **1828** *Yankee* I. 227/1 Everything is pell-mell, helter-skelter, pig-corn, baskets, and all, are upside-down; or as they have it, they 'turn up jack.' — (2) **1887** Eggleston *Graysons* i, In gossip and banter the time went by, until some one proposed to 'turn the Bible.' — (3) **1891** *Cent.* 6538/3 *To turn the paunch*, to vomit; disgorge, as fish. (New Eng.)

For *to turn up missing*, see ***missing 2;** *to turn the double corner*, see ***corner,** *n.* **5. b.** (1).

***turned-(a)round,** *a.* Confused as to one's whereabouts. — **1877** R. I. Dodge *Plains of Gt. West* 46 To me, Detroit is always in Canada, and New Orleans always on the right bank of the Mississippi, because I happened to be 'turned round' when I first arrived in those cities. **1880** Mark Twain *Tramp Abroad* 119, I could see the dim blur of the windows, but in my turned-around condition they were exactly where they ought not to be.

Turner ˈtɜnɚ, *n.* [G.] A gymnast, esp. a member of a society of Germans or German-Americans organized for performing gymnastic exercises.

[**1853** *Alta California* (S.F.) 2 May 2/3 The *Turner Gesang Verein*, (the Gymnastic Musical Union,) the principal movers in the festivities, were early astir.] **1854** *Calif. Chronicle* (S.F.) 16 May 7/3 Yesterday we again paid a hasty visit to Russ' Gardens, where the Turners and their compatriots had resumed the sports of the previous day. **1913** *N.Y. Times* 13 Oct. 12/4 There was a big gathering of Hoboken Turners and guests at the North German Lloyd Line Pier.

attrib. **1876** *Sutro* (Nev.) *Independent* 24 June 3/2 The Turners' picnic, last Sunday, was not a very successful affair. **1880** *Dly. Inter-Ocean* (Chi.) 1 June 7/6 The next biennial convention of the Turner Bund will be held in Newark, N.J. **1949** *Minn. Hist.* March 26 The Cincinnati Turnverein built the first Turner Hall in the United States in 1850.

b. turnerfeste, and variants (see quot. 1871). Cf. **fest.**

1856 *S.F. Bulletin* 1 May 1/2 This Turner feast takes place only once a year . . . and interferes with and disturbs in no way the American church-goers. **1871** De Vere 141 *Turnerfeste*, as their annual festivals are designated, excite the utmost interest. **1892** *Chi. Tribune* 24 July 10/2 The second day of the Minnesota Turnfest passed off pleasantly.

***turning,** *n.* and *a.* In combs.: (1) ***turning out,** designating the action of releasing logs in a boom; (2) ***over,** a scathing condemnation, *rare;* (3) **plow,** a moldboard plow, cf. **pony turning plow,** ***twister 1;** (4) **row,** (see quot. and cf. **turn row**); (5) ***up,** (see quot.), *obs.*

(1) **1905** Wiggin *Rose* 29 Thousands of logs lay quietly 'in boom' until the 'turning out' process, on the last day of the drive, should

release them. — **(2) 1895** *N.Y. Dramatic News* 9 Nov. 2/3, I don't think I ever heard such a 'turning-over' extended to a production. — **(3) 1850** in TURNER *Cotton* (1865) 118, I deem it proper to say, that many planters here say they scrape with the turning-plough as well. **1950** *Democrat* 9 March 8/5 For Sale . . . fertilizer distributors, turning plows, scooter stocks. — **(4) 1890** *D.N.* I. 66 turning row, n. A row unplanted in a corn or tobacco field, where the horses turn around in plowing.

(5) 1800 TATHAM *Tobacco* 77 Turning-up, is a technical term which signifies the act of replacing the tobacco in the hogshead after it has passed the inquest of inspection.

* **turnip,** *n.* **1. turnip grass,** (see quot.). **2. turnip of the plains,** (see quot.). **3. turnip patch,** a small area in which turnips are planted.

(1) 1909 *Cent. Supp.* 1462/1 The bulbous panic grass, *Panicum bulbosum*, native in cañons from Texas to Arizona and in Mexico . . . has a stem with a bulbous base (hence called *turnip grass*). — **(2) 1827** D. DOUGLAS *Jrnl.* (1914) 284 *Psoralea* sp.; this is the Turnip of the Plains of the voyageurs, the roots of which are used by the Indians both boiled and raw. — **(3) 1773** in FITHIAN *Journal* I. 40 His turnip-patch and corn-gardens seem . . . to have put on a fresh bloom. **1828** *Central Watchtower* (Harrodsburg, Ky.) 3 Sep. 3/1 About July the men in the garrison, determined upon clearing a piece of ground . . . for a turnip patch.

As the last term in **blood, cabbage, Dakota, prairie, Russia, wild turnip.**

* **turnpike,** *n.*

1. A small cake made of meal that has been scalded and allowed to ferment, used to raise bread. Also **turnpike cake, emptins.** *Obs.*

1843 STEPHENS *High Life N.Y.* II. 78 Her face begun to swell and puff up, like a baking of bread wet with turnpike emptins. **1850** S. WARNER *Wide, Wide World* xiv, I am scalding this meal with it to make turnpikes. . . . Turnpike cakes—what I raise the bread with. **1850** *Knickerb.* XXXVI. 83 The old aunt . . . had borrowed some little yellow cakes, called *turnpikes*, and used, I believe, for some purpose or other in baking bread.

2. In special obs. combs.: (1) **turnpike company,** a group of persons organized to construct or to control the use of a turnpike road or roads; (2) **grade,** a turnpike, cf. * **grade,** *n.* **1. c;** (3) **schooner,** (see quot.).

(1) 1806 *Balance* V. 37/1 Those for the incorporation of turnpike companies occupy many pages. **1866** *Internal Revenue Guide* 133 Any railroad, canal, turnpike [etc.] . . . company . . . shall be subject to . . . a tax. — **(2) 1844** *Indiana Senate Jrnl.* 29 Sess. 272 The State of Indiana hereby gives to said company . . . the use of the present turnpike grade, in getting on and off from said bridges. — **(3) 1913** *Proc. Pa.-Ger. Soc.* XXII. 55 'Turnpike Schooners' or 'Pitt teams' were supposed to carry thirty barrels of flour or three tons.

As the last term in **National turnpike.**

turnpike 'tɜnˌpaɪk, *v. tr.* To build (a road) in the manner of construction characteristic of turnpike roads.

1791 HILTZHEIMER *Diary* (1893) 17 Sep. 172, I took Mr. Francis in my chair to view the road, from Vine Street to Vanderen's Mill, six miles, which it is proposed to turnpike. **1806** WEBSTER 320/1 *Turnpike*, to form or erect a turnpike. **1861** *Ill. Agric. Soc. Trans.* IV. 202 There were worked streets, back-furrowed or turnpiked, . . . traversing the fields. **1939** *L. A.* Map 42 The verb turnpike (up) is still used in the sense of 'crown (a road).'

turnpiker 'tɜnˌpaɪkɚ, *n.* One who travels on a turnpike (see also quot. 1819). *Obs.* — **1812** *Boston Gaz.* 27 Aug. (Th.), The heroes, who were to have mounted the heights of Abram, are yet in the garb of turnpikers, unaccoutered and undisciplined. **1819** *Niles' Reg.* XVI. 440/1 A mob of Irishmen, calling themselves turnpikers, armed with axes, mattocks, &c. . . . in a ruffian-like manner demanded toll, and exacted it at their own rate, when there was no right at all to demand any.

turnus 'tɜnəs, *n.* [f. *turnus*, the specific name (<*Turnus*, the name of a character in Vergil's *Aeneid*).] A northern variety, *Papilio glaucus turnus*, of the tiger swallowtail, a large, yellow, black-striped butterfly common in the U.S. — **1890** WEBSTER 1455/3 The tiger swallowtail, or turnus . . . , and the zebra swallowtail, or ajax . . . are common American species [of swallowtail]. **1904** KELLOGG *Amer. Insects* 449 The tiger swallowtail, or Turnus butterfly . . . , is another common species, with a striking 'negro' form.

Turnverein 'turnfəˌraɪn, *n.* [G. in same sense.] A club or society of turners. Also attrib.

1852 *S.F. Herald* 1 Nov. 2/2 The Turnverein Society held another of their fetes yesterday. **1893** *Outing* Oct. 70/1 [His] school days had been supplemented by the training of the German Turnverein. **1949** *Chi. Tribune* 7 Sep. 24/1 The latest of these ornaments of the Germania club and various sangerbunds and turnvereins is the Hon. John Haderlein.

* **turpentine,** *n.* In combs.: (1) **turpentine barrel,** a heavy, especially well-made barrel for holding turpentine; (2) **box,** = * **box,** *n.* **1;** (3) **clearing,** ?a **turpentine orchard,** *rare;* (4) **farm,** = **turpentine orchard;** (5) **farmer,** one who operates a turpentine orchard; (6) **gin,** = **turpentine whisky;** (7) **orchard,** a pine forest or extent of forest from which turpentine is obtained; (8) **still,** a still in which turpentine is refined; (9) **weed,** any one of various herbs, as various species of *Silphium*, which possess, or are thought to possess, some of the characteristics of turpentine; (10) **whisky,** whisky of an inferior grade.

(1) 1862 E. KIRKE *Among Pines* 100 The foreman . . . seated himself on a turpentine barrel. **1904** TARBELL *Hist. Standard Oil Co.* I. 12 Turpentine barrels, molasses barrels, whiskey barrels . . . were added to new ones made especially for oil. — **(2) 1893** *Outing* Jan. 275/2 What's gwinter come 'uv Viry, an' Zeke's corn crap, an' his tu'pentine boxes? — **(3) 1858** THOREAU *Maine Woods* 125, I have been in the lumber-yard, and . . . the turpentine clearing. — **(4) 1867** H. LATHAM *Black & White* 124 They led our cavalry in file through the woods, along the paths which lead among the turpentine farms. **1897** *Kissimmee* (Fla.) *Valley Gaz.* 23 June 2/8 A turpentine farm is to be conducted on the land secured.

(5) 1856 OLMSTED *Slave States* 350 The majority of what I have termed turpentine-farmers . . . [are] small proprietors of the long-leaved pine forest land. **1906** BELL *C. Lee* 196 Let's see what I have to sell my turpentine farmers. — **(6) 1848** JUDSON *Mysteries N.Y.* 76 (We.), Turpentine gin. **1855** P. PAXTON *Capt. Priest* 53 The odor of 'New England' and 'Turpentine Gin' that pervaded the atmosphere . . . induces me to suppose, that nothing like Maine law was recognized in the establishment. — **(7) 1856** OLMSTED *Slave States* 339 If we enter, in the winter, . . . a 'turpentine orchard,' we come upon negroes engaged in making boxes, in which the sap is to be collected the following spring. **1884** SARGENT *Rep. Forests* 518 Their owners oftener . . . employing them [Negroes in N. Carolina] in turpentine orchards than in the cotton-fields. — **(8) 1797** *Wilmington* (N.C.) *Gaz.* 12 Dec., Two Turpentine Stills. **1950** *Chi. D. News* 6 Feb. 26/1 In a natural quail field near an old turpentine still the field trials finally get under way. — **(9) 1819** *Western Rev.* I. 95 Among the most remarkable and singular [plants of Ky. is] . . . *Silphium therebinthaceum*, Turpentine weed. **1913** BARNES *Western Grazing Grounds* 236 In the southwest and on some of the ranges in the northern regions there is a little green weed (*Guttierrezia*) known locally as snakeweed, fireweed, turpentine weed, and possibly by other names. **1931** VANSELL *Nectar & Pollen Plants Calif.* 14 Turpentine weed, *T. laxum*, is also visited freely by bees for nectar.

(10) 1869 *Overland Mo.* III. 120 'Pinetop' is a kind of mean turpentine whisky of North Carolina. **1877** BARTLETT 125 Clay-Eaters. otherwise Dirt-Eaters. A miserable set of people inhabiting some of the Southern States, who subsist chiefly on turpentine whiskey.

b. Also in combs. of obvious meaning, as (1) **turpentine business,** (2) **camp,** (3) **country,** (4) **distillery,** (5) **district,** (6) **factor,** (7) **land,** (8) **pine,** (9) **region,** (10) **State,** (11) **wagon,** (12) **woods.**

(1) 1856 OLMSTED *Slave States* 338 There are very large forests of this tree [*Pinus palustris*] in North and South Carolina, Georgia, and Alabama; and the turpentine business is carried on, to some extent. **1899** CHESNUTT *Conjure Woman* 2, I wrote to a cousin who had gone into the turpentine business in central North Carolina. — **(2) 1901** *Westm. Gaz.* 16 March 4/1 A turpentine camp in Baldwin County, Alabama. — **(3) 1848** *N.Y. Tribune* 22 May (B.), From Petersburgh I railed it through the North Carolina pitch, tar, turpentine, and lumber country. **1899** M. GOING *Flowers* 283 We realize that when we see the pitch-pines at home, in the 'turpentine country' of Georgia. — **(4) 1854** in EASTERBY *S.C. Rice Plant.* (1945) 119 He is to put up Saw Mills (4) there and . . . Turpentine Distillery on the other side. **1862** E. KIRKE *Among Pines* 190 A half-hour found me near one of the turpentine distilleries.

(5) 1888 *Fort Smith Tribune* Feb. (F.), He came originally from the clay-eating and turpentine district of South Carolina. **1901** *Westm. Gaz.* 4 May 5/2 The turpentine district along the St. John's River has been completely wiped out. — **(6) 1906** BELL *C. Lee* 282 It was . . . a tract she intended leasing to some orchard turpentine factors in Jacksonville. — **(7) 1848** in COMMONS *Doc. Hist.* I. 197 Burn over turpentine land. — **(8) 1897** SUDWORTH *Arborescent Flora* 30 *Pinus palustris*, Longleaf Pine. . . . [Also called] Turpentine Pine (N.C.). — **(9) 1856** OLMSTED *Slave States* 325, I was now fairly in the Turpentine region of North Carolina.

(10) 1850 M. REID *Rifle Rangers* vi, The danger is, we may stick in the Turpentine State. **1886** *Chi. W. News* 29 April 4/3 North Carolina is the Turpentine state, its people being Tuckahoes or Tar-Boilers. **1907** *Boston Transcript* 9 Nov. II. 9. — **(11) 1942** RAWLINGS *C. Creek* 51 There were trails used by . . . the lurching turpentine wagons. **1948** RITTENHOUSE *Vehicles* 59 Turpentine wagon. Used in the South for hauling barrels of turpentine. A platform was added to suit, and the wagon was painted with a special mixture which withstood the turpentine. Four feet between bolster standards (corner posts); wheels 44 and 54 inches. Could haul up to 7500 lbs. — (12) **1892** *Pall Mall Gaz.* 15 Nov. 2/3 The Florida convicts . . . were mostly put to work in the turpentine woods. **1942** RAWLINGS *C. Creek* 6 The wagon . . . turns off toward the turpentine woods to collect the resin.

As the last term in **gum, orchard, scrape, tar and turpentine.**

***turpentine,** *v. tr.* and *intr.* (See 1st quots.)

1909 *Cent. Supp.* 1390/2 turpentine. . . . To make or gather turpentine. **1909** WEBSTER 2219/1 turpentine. . . . To extract turpentine from (a tree). *Southern U.S.* **1950** *Amer. Forests* Feb. 12/1 The rudimentary system of turpentining longleaf pine in the South had killed one fifth of the trees worked.

***turret,** *n.* (See quot.) — **1876** KNIGHT 2665/1 Turret. . . . (*Railway.*) The elevated central portion of a passenger-car, whose top forms an upper story of the roof, and whose sides are glazed for light and pierced for ventilation.

Turpentine wagon showing running gear (sense 3)

***turtle,** *n.*[1]

1. =next.

1631 *N.H. Hist. Soc. Col.* IV. 246 They were all turtles, as appeared by diverse of them wee killed flying. *c*1729 CATESBY *Carolina* I. 24 The Turtle of Carolina . . . is somewhat less than a Dove-house Pigeon. **1789** MORSE *Amer. Geog.* 60 Turtle of Carolina.

2. *turtledove, =mourning dove. Cf. **Carolina turtledove.**

1674 *Cal. State P., Amer. & West Indies* VII. 581 [In] Maine . . . the islands and woods yield swarms of birds, . . . turtle-doves, swans, geese [etc.]. **1709** LAWSON *Carolina* 142 Turtle Doves are here very plentiful. **1808** IRVING *Salmagundi* xx. 541 The turtle-dove, the timid fawn, . . . joy in the sequestered haunts of nature. **1945** *Md. Conservationist* 3 We have the bob-white (known to our natives as the bird with the cheery call), turtledove, imported pheasants [etc.].

***turtle,** *n.*[2]

1. A crude form of submarine invented by David Bushnell (*c*1742–1824). Now *hist.*

1813 JEFFERSON *Writings* XIII. 263 Bushnel's Turtle is mentioned slightly [in Clarke's sketches of U.S. naval history]. **1876** *Wide Awake* 140/1 Paddle, paddle, toward the river-bank came the Turtle, David Bushnell's head rising out of its shell. **1947** *Life* 13 Jan. 82/2 The *Turtle*, of which he became captain, was made of oak frame timber in the shape of a round clam.

b. During the Civil War, an ironclad ship having an upper deck suggestive of a turtle's back. *Obs.*

The 1861 quot. has reference to an ironclad invented by John A Stevenson and built for the Confederate navy in the summer of 1861, before Ericsson's monitor. See ***monitor,** *n.* **2.**

1861 in *N.O. Times-Picayune Mag.* (1949) 18 Sep. 32/3 When the turtle invited the Prebel to dine The Toast must have been quite a stumper [etc.]. **1868** *Putnam's Mag.* II. 117 Experiment succeeded experiment, and rams, mortar-schooners, iron monitors, and 'turtles,' were all brought into use under the ever-varying circumstances of the campaign, while the close of the naval war in the west was marked by one of the most brilliant engineering feats on record, the building of the Red River dam. **1897** C. A. DANA *Recoll. Civil War* 37 It was Admiral Porter's fleet of ironclad turtles, steamboats, and barges. . . . First came seven ironclad turtles and one heavy armed ram. **1949** *N.O. Times-Picayune Mag.* 18 Sep. 32/3 The turtle refers to the strangest-looking craft ever to slip down the ways of a shipyard, particularly an Algiers, La., shipyard. . . . That dream boat was the ironclad-battering ram Manassas, a converted tugboat.

2. In printing, a curved box into which type or plate matter is locked for attaching to the cylinder of a rotary press.

1860 *Ure's Dict. Arts* (ed. 5) III. 540 An American printing machine, the invention of R. Hoe and Company. . . . Each page is locked up upon a detached segment of the large cylinder, called by the compositors a 'turtle.' **1873** *Harper's Mag.* July 235/2 The Washington news goes through the hands of the compositors, the proof-readers, and the makers-up, to be rattling away in type or in stereotype on the 'turtles' of a Hoe's lightning press. **1891** *Memphis Appeal-Avalanche* 23 April 8/1 Type, iron stands, brass galleys, turtles, stones, etc., everything to run a large daily newspaper.

3. In combs.: (1) **turtle-back scale,** a common brown scale that infests orange trees; (2) **entertainment,** =next, *obs.;* (3) **frolic,** a dinner at which the main dish is turtle, a festive occasion featuring such a dinner; (4) ***head,** any one of various American plants of the genus *Chelone*, cf. **balmony, *chelone, *snakehead;** (5) **soup bean,** a bean or variety or bean now unidentifiable, *obs.;* (6) **step,** a slow step like that of a turtle, *rare.*

(1) **1884** *Rep. Comm. Agric.* 355 In Florida [this insect] destroys . . . the common 'Turtle-back scale.' — (2) **1769** SINGLETON *Social N.Y.* 370 Contiguous to the Garden there is a very good Long Room convenient for a Ball or Turtle Entertainment. — (3) **1750** in *Amer. Sp.* XV. 231/1 Had an Invitation to day to Go to a Turtle Frolick with a Comp[an]y of Gent[leme]n and Ladies. **1787** CUTLER in *Life & Corr.* I. 205, I received a polite invitation from Governor Bowen . . . to join them in a Turtle frolic. **1886** BYNNER *A. Surriage* xv, There was a turtle-frolic at Cambridge. — (4) **1857** GRAY *Botany* 285 *Chelone* Turtle-head. Snake-head. . . . The corolla resembling in shape the head of a reptile. **1943** PEATTIE *Great Smokies* 173 Characteristically Appalachian are our dainty species of bluet in the spring, our striking sorts of turtlehead in autumn.

(5) **1849** EMMONS *Agric. N.Y.* II. 280. **1856** *Rep. Comm. Patents 1855: Agric.* 287, I have tried the 'Turtle-soup Bean' you sent me, and find it very productive. — (6) **1877** HABERTON *Jericho Road* 7 Lively, boys, lively! Trot along! 'Taint no time to try the turtle-step.

As the last term in **alligator, American, box, gopher, loggerhead, mud, musk, prairie, salt-marsh, sea, snap, snapping, soft-back turtle.**

Tuscaloosa ˌtʌskəˈlusə, *n.* [*Tuscaloosa*, Ala., named for Tascalusa, an Indian chief who fought De Soto.] **Tuscaloosa Roarers,** (see quot.). *Obs.* Cf. **old Tuscaloosa.** — **1822** *Amer. Beacon* (Norfolk, Va.) 6 Sep. 4/1 (Th. Supp.), The bargemen . . . are divided into classes, such as Tuscaloosa Roarers, Alabama Screamers, Cahawba Scrougers, and the like gentle names.

Tuscarora ˌtʌskəˈrorə, *n.* [f. a native name, meaning "hemp gatherers," Indian hemp, *Apocynum cannabinum*, being much used by them.]

1. An Indian of an Iroquoian tribe first encountered by Europeans in what is now eastern North Carolina; also, *pl.*, the tribe itself.

1713 *N.C. Col. Rec.* II. 2 An order from ye Governm[en]t of New Yorke to Caution ye Tuscaroras ag[ains]t going to warr w[i]th ye English here. **1800** JEFFERSON *Notes* 99 The *Monacans* and their friends, better known latterly by the name of *Tuscaroras*, were probably connected with the Massawomees, or Five Nations. **1840** COOPER *Pathfinder* 1, There must be Oneidas or Tuscaroras near us, Arrowhead. **1906** REID *Old Ft. Johnson* 106 The persuasive power of Thomas Spencer, the Oneida half-breed, however, kept the Oneidas and Tuscaroras in line to the end of the war. **1948** *Ann. Rep. Smithsonian Inst.* 411/2 This area . . . has some 430 Tuscaroras living on it as farmers.

attrib. **1650** ALVORD & BIDGOOD *Trans-Allegheny Region* (1912) 116 An Englishman, a Cockarous hard by Captain Floods, gave this Indian Bells . . . to lay downe to the Tuskarood King. **1709** LAWSON *Carolina* 163 Craw-Fish, in the Brooks, and small rivers of water, amongst the Tuskeruro Indians, . . . are found very plentifully. **1832** *Boston Transcript* 21 Jan. 1/1 The Western papers announce the marriage of Mr Levi Williams to Miss Nancy Twenty Canoes, of the Tuscarora tribe of Indians. **1948** *Ann. Rep. Smithsonian Inst.* 411/2 The Tuscarora Indian Reservation is located in Niagara County about 4 or 5 miles to the northeast of Niagara Falls, N.Y.

2. A variety of Indian corn. Also attrib. *Obs.*

1850 JOHNSTON *Notes* I. 154 Hence the white Tuscarora corn . . . gives a whiter flour than almost any other variety. **1856** *Rep. Comm.*

Patents 1855: Agric. 162 [There is] generally some appreciable quantity of this element [oil], the 'Tuscarora,' the 'White-flour,' and the 'Wyandotte' being among the exceptions. *Ib.* 166 Analysis of the Ashes of the 'Tuscarora' Corn-cob.—This corn was grown . . . in Massachusetts.

3. Tuscarora rice, (*a*) (see quot.), *obs.*, (*b*) a wild aquatic grass, *Zizania aquatica*, the edible grains of which somewhat resemble rice, cf. **wild rice 1.**

(*a*) **1830** WATSON *Philadelphia* 616 Mrs. Sybilla Masters . . . went out to England in 1711–12, to make her fortune abroad by the patent and sale of her 'Tuscarora rice,' so called. It was her preparation from our Indian corn, made into something like our hominy. (*b*) **1843** TORREY *Flora N.Y.* II. 416 Tuscarora Rice. Water Oats. Indian Rice. . . . The grain of this plant is a favorite article of food among the Indians.

Tusks tʌsks, *n. pl.* Short for *Tuscaroras. Obs.* — **1713** *N.C. Col. Rec.* II. 26 [The traders] engaged to go so strong & to march so far wide of the Tusks, as not to be in danger of any attack. **1714** *Ib.* 140 He is further advised that ye said Order is passed Since ye Tusks Articles w[i]th ye Governm[en]t.

tusk shell. Any one of various mollusks, esp. of the genus *Dentalium*, having a shell shaped like the tusk of an elephant. — **1861** *Smithsonian Rep. 1860* 222. **1884** GOODE *Fisheries* I. 703 This mollusk . . . occurs all along the northern Pacific coast of America, and is known to Americans as the 'Tuskshell.'

Tutelo tuˈtelo, *n.* [Native name of unknown significance.] (See quot. 1910.) — **1910** HODGE *Amer. Indians* II. 855/1 Tutelo. One of the eastern Siouan tribes, formerly living in Virginia and North Carolina, but now extinct. **1917** MOOREHEAD *Stone Ornaments Amer. Indian* 177 We then pause to inquire if the Catawba, Tutelo and Saponi do not represent the survivors of the vanquished people.

***tutor,** *n.* Formerly at Harvard a faculty member. Also in some colleges a teacher giving individual instruction, and often ranking below an instructor. Cf. **class tutor.**

Since the duties and responsibilities of tutors differ from college to college both here and in Great Britain, it is difficult to make a clear-cut distinction between American and British usage. At Harvard the appointment is academic, and a tutor may be either a member of the regular teaching faculty or one who does tutorial work only.

1687 *Harvard Rec.* I. 81 Ordered by the Rector & Tutors, that Rogers be appointed the Colledge Butler. **1707** SEWALL *Diary* II. 183, I go to Cambridge and carry Joseph a small piece of Plate to present his Tutor with. **1851** HALL *College Words* 304 In the American colleges, tutors . . . have a share, with the president and professors, in the government of the students. **1941** *Gen. Inf. Harvard Coll.*, The relation of the student with his tutor has little of the compulsory in it.

For **tutor's freshman,** see ***freshman,** *n.* **1.**

***tutor,** *v. intr.* To act or serve as a tutor, to study under a tutor.

1892 *Nation* 11 Aug. 116/2 Graduate . . . of experience wishes to tutor for the September examinations. **1900** MUNN *Uncle Terry* 55, I tutored some, read law, and was admitted to the bar. **1921** PAINE *Comr. Rolling Ocean* 99 He tutored for Princeton and flunked in freshman year.

tutti-frutti (ice cream). A kind of ice cream containing mixed chopped fruits. Also attrib. in the sense of ornate or "ritzy."

1876 M. J. HENDERSON *Cooking* 313 *Tutti Frutti.* When a rich vanilla cream is partly frozen, candied cherries, English currants, chopped raisins, . . . or any other candied fruits chopped rather fine, are added. **1905** SCOTT *Walking Delegate* 13 The boss 'ud buy a tutti-frutti yacht, or a few more automobiles, or mebbe a college or two, where they learn you how to wear your pants turned up. **1919** FRANDSEN & MARKHAM *Manufacture Ice Cream* 110 Tutti Frutti Ice Cream. . . . Colored pineapple cubes are now used to a considerable extent.

Tuxedo tʌkˈsido, *n.* Also **tuxedo.** [*Tuxedo* (f. the name of a subtribe of Algonquian Indians) Park, N.Y., a fashionable resort and country club where this article was first worn.] A tailless dinner jacket less formal than a full dress coat. In full **Tuxedo coat.** Also a suit of which such a coat or jacket forms a part.

1894 *Harper's Mag.* Sep. 589/1 There were a few men in sacks and cut-aways; but the most of them had dressed for the occasion, some . . . with the black cravat and the hybrid jacket which is known as a 'Tuxedo coat.' **1906** *Harper's Mag.* July 310 No white male citizens should sit at dinner there unless clothed . . . at least in the smoking-jacket known to us as a Tuxedo. **1949** *Nat. Geog. Mag.* Dec. 825/1 At a dinner party you'll find tuxedos and cowboy shirts, evening gowns and tweed suits.

Hence **tux, tuxedoed.** *Colloq.*

1946 THOMPSON *Amer. Daughter* 181 They filed up to the front of the room . . . and the ex-boxer, resplendent in tux and banjo. **1948** *Time* 23 Feb. 74/2 As the tuxedoed old judge bent down to peer at the odd little creature, a child shrilled: 'What is it, momma, a lamb?' **1949** *Ib.* 27 June 39/1 The tuxedoed and evening-gowned audience . . . was beginning to feel self-conscious and uncomfortable.

***twain,** *n.* In river navigation, two fathoms. Used in various phrases, as **mark twain.**

1863 MARK TWAIN in Paine *Biog. Mark Twain* I. 221, I want to sign my articles . . . 'Mark Twain.' It is an old river term, a leadsman's call, signifying two fathoms—twelve feet. **1867** RICHARDSON *Beyond Miss.* 22 Every minute or two, he reports, in drawling sing-song, . . . 'F-i-v-e feet,' 'Quarter less t-w-a-i-n,' (a quarter fathom less than two fathoms,) 'M-a-r-k twain,' 'N-o bottom.' **1875** MARK TWAIN *Old Times* ii. 39 M-a-r-k three! Quarter-less-three! Half twain! Quarter twain! M-a-r-k twain! **1947** MACK *Mark Twain in Nevada* 228 How many times when he was on the River had he heard the leadsman . . . call out, 'By the mark, twain!'

b. (*cap.*) As a pseudonym for Samuel L. Clemens (1835–1910).

1863 *Terr. Enterprise* (Virginia, Nev.) 2 Feb. [Signature thus appeared for first time.] **1866** *Eastern Slope* (Washoe, Nev.) 24 Feb. 3/2 When he came in there and took them on tick, Johny used to sing out to the barkeeper, who carried a lump of chalk in his weskit pocket and kept the score, 'mark twain,' whereupon the barkeeper would score two drinks to Sam's account—and so it was, d'ye see, that he came to be called 'Mark Twain.'

Tweedian ˈtwidɪən, *a.* [See **Tweed Ring.**] Characteristic of the rule of the Tweed Ring. *Obs.* — **1878** *N. Amer. Rev.* Nov.–Dec. 491 Our fellow-citizens of the South . . . are resolved not to submit to Tweedian government.

Tweedism ˈtwidɪzəm, *n.* [See next.] The rule of the Tweed ring, or boss political control of a similar character. *Obs.* — **1876** *Harper's Wkly.* 12 Aug., [Label within cartoon:] Tweedism. **1881** *Harper's Mag.* Jan. 201/1 Tweedism was not rampant in those days.

Tweed Ring. [f. W. M. *Tweed* (1823–78), a notorious Democratic boss in N.Y. City.] The group comprising W. M. Tweed and his associates, who, from 1858 to 1871, controlled the municipal government of N.Y. City. Now *hist.*

1882 MCCABE *New York* 297 It was the chief means used by the Tweed Ring in carrying out their stupendous frauds. **1899** BREEN *Thirty Years* 37 Shortly after the close of the Civil War, when what is known as the 'Tweed Ring' was being formed, it was found necessary by the members of that combination, in order to secure absolute control of the Democratic organization, and to promote their schemes, to capture the Tammany Society. **1946** ADAMS *Album Amer. Hist.* III. 269 In New York City the Tweed Ring robbed the municipality of over $100,000,000.00 through padded payrolls, fraudulent contracts and the sale of political favors.

tweeg twig, *n.* (See quot. 1910.) — **1825** *Amer. Jrnl. Science* XI. 278 *Menopoma Alleghaniensis.* . . . Hell-bender. . . . Tweeg . . . the Menopoma always resides in the water. **1910** HODGE *Amer. Indians* II. 859/1 Tweeg. A large North American batrachian (*Menopoma alleghanensis*), called also hell-bender, mud-devil, ground-puppy, spring-keeper, man-eater, etc. The name is from Lenape (Delaware) *twe'kw*, a radical word.

tweezer,** *n.* **1.** *local.* The American merganser, *Mergus americanus.* **2. tweezer bird,** the kingfisher. — (1) **1888** G. TRUMBULL *Names & Portraits of Birds* 65 Another form of it, or I should say a name that immediately suggests the other [i.e., weaser], is heard at Shinnecock Bay (designating same species), viz.: tweezer. I can hardly believe that this last is the original form, though the bird's beak is easily likened to a pair of tweezers. — (2) *a1862** THOREAU *Maine Woods* 207, I heard a . . . kingfisher (tweezer bird), or parti-colored warbler, and a night-hawk.

***twelve,** *n.*

1. (*cap.*) =**Twelve Apostles.** *Obs.*

1844 *Maysville* (Ky.) *Eagle* 4 Sep. 3/4 Sidney Rigdon, who claimed the leadership of the church on the ground of his being the only survivor of the first Presidency, . . . has had his claims rejected by the twelve. **1871** *Harper's Mag.* Sep. 606/1 At last Brigham [Young] came to his rivals, whom he and his counselors had foredoomed; while they, on their part, had resolved to force a controversy with the president and the Twelve.

2. In combs.: (1) **Twelve Apostles,** one of the governing bodies of the Mormon Church; (2) **men,** in colonial Massachusetts, a town-governing body; (3) **-rowed,** designating a variety of Indian corn the ears of which had twelve rows of kernels, *obs.;* (4) **United Colonies,** the Thirteen Colonies *q.v.* with the exception of New York, *obs.* or *hist.*

(1) **1861** REMY *Journey to Gt.-Salt-Lake City* II. 51 There are three high-priests, presidents. . . . Then come twelve travelling councillors, who are no other than the twelve apostles, or special witnesses to the

name of Jesus Christ throughout the world. **1950** *Time* 20 March 42/3 The official voice of the church, the *News* is run by Editor and General Manager Mark Edward Peterson, 49, who is also one of the Twelve Apostles (a high governing body) of the Mormon Church. — (2) **1636** *Dorchester Rec.* 21 One acre . . . the sayd Bray is to have upon Condition he remayne in the Plantation, . . . and not to alienate it without app[ro]bation of the Twelve men. **1637** *Essex Inst. Coll.* IX. 50 A towne meeting of the 12 men appoynted for the business thereof. — (3) **1838** *Mass. Agric. Survey 1st Rep.* 25 The Dutton or Sioux corn, a twelve-rowed variety, has likewise ripened in favourable locations. **1888** *Vt. Agric. Rep.* X. 30 He had tried both the 8 and the 12-rowed, and had decided that for him the 12-rowed was the better. — (4) **1775** *Pa. Ev. Post* 8 July (Supp.) 295/1 *The* Twelve United Colonies, *by their* Delegates *in* Congress, *to the* Inhabitants *of* Great-Britain. **1775** *Mass. H.S. Coll.* 3 Ser. V. 75 By the authority of the Twelve United Colonies dwelling upon this island of America. [**1948** O. H. CHITWOOD *Hist. Colonial Amer.* 657 On July 4, 1776, the Declaration was adopted by that body by a vote of twelve colonies.]

Twelveite ˈtwɛlvaɪt, *n.* (See quot. 1890.) *Obs.* — **1847** HOWE *Hist. Coll. Ohio* 284 The Mormons . . . [are] now divided into three factions, viz.: the Rigdonites, the Twelveites, and the Strangites. **1890** *N. & Q.* V. 184 The main body of Mormons are sometimes called *Twelveites*, probably as being followers of the Twelve Apostles.

*** twenty,** *a.* and *n.*

1. A twenty-dollar bill or gold piece.

1839 *Spirit of Times* 8 June 162/2 (We.), We had the gratification of seeing his [jockeyship] rewarded by more presents of odd fifties and twenties than probably Daniel ever saw in his lifetime. **1842** *Wasp* (Nauvoo, Ill.) 2 July 4/2 Three dollar notes of the Chautauque Co. Bank, *altered to* $20's, have made their appearance. **1903** *Mo. Maroon* (Chi.) June 447 He threw down two twenties. **1949** *Courier-Journal* (Louisville, Ky.) 3 Sep. 9/5 Look not only for bad $10 notes, but also for $20's.

b. A tract of land comprising twenty acres.

1899 *Mo. So. Dakotan* I. 198, I bought this 'twenty' of timber.

2. In combs.: (1) **twenty-card poker,** =next; (2) **deck poker,** (see quots. 1857, 1887); (3) **mule team,** a team made up of twenty mules, usu. in allusion to such a team that formerly hauled borax from Death Valley, etc.; (4) *** one,** see as a main entry; (5) *** three,** as a command, be off, beat it, also **twenty-three skiddoo,** *slang.*

(1) **1851** GREEN *Twelve Days* 141, I was surprised by an invitation to visit the 'Kangaroo,' and take a game at twenty card poker. — (2) *a***1846** *Quarter Race Ky.* 66 [Officers were] all going it like forty at twenty-deck poker. **1857** *Hoyle's Games* (Amer. ed.) 289 Twenty-Deck Poker . . . is played and governed precisely in the same manner that 'Bluff' is, with the exception that only twenty cards are used. **1887** *Courier-Journal* 23 Jan. 15/7 Twenty-deck poker came first in the order of time, when all the cards below the ten were discarded from the pack. Only four could play it. — (3) **1930** FERBER *Cimarron* 322 Boilers loaded on two wagons were hauled by twenty-mule-teams. **1950** *L.A. Times* 22 Jan. VI. 4/1 The 20-mule team borax wagons were responsible for building a firm roadbed down to Mojave through Red Rock Canyon.

(5) **1906** *Cin. Enquirer* 1 April IV. 1/1. **1945** MENCKEN *Supp.* 333 Dorgan, who died in 1929, is said to have invented or introduced *skiddoo, twenty-three, drug-store cowboy, nobody home.* **1948** *Houston* (Tex.) *Post* 14 June 2/3 When she swished past this leering beast in human form would boldly accost her with such brilliant greetings as 'Oh, you kid!' or 'Twenty-three skiddoo.'

b. Used in expressions relating to money, as (1) **twenty-cent piece,** *obs.*, (2) **-dollar bill,** (3) **-dollar gold piece,** (4) **-five cent piece.**

(1) **1875** *Statutes at Large* XVIII. 479 The twenty cent piece shall be a legal tender at its nominal value for any amount not exceeding five dollars in any one payment. **1882** C. B. LEWIS *Lime-Kiln Club* 113 We took advantage of a cloudy day to pass a twenty-cent piece off for a quarter. — (2) **1829** *Va. Herald* (Fredericksburg) 18 April 3/3 Over the letter K, in the word Bank, in the genuine twenty dollar bills, there is a small flourish, which does not appear in the counterfeits. **1950** *Nature Mag.* March 168/3 One form of monetary forgery is the attempt to raise a bill, such as making a $2 bill appear to be a $20 bill by altering the numerals. — (3) **1867** RICHARDSON *Beyond Miss.* 58 They would cancel the debt from pockets burdened with twenty-dollar gold pieces. **1949** *Sat. Ev. Post* 5 Feb. 33/1 Here is a rare 1855 United States twenty-dollar gold piece that sold for seventeen hundred and fifty dollars. — (4) **1875** *Statutes at Large* XVIII. 478 The twenty-five cent piece shall be a legal tender at its nominal value for any amount not exceeding five dollars in any one payment. **1891** *Boston Jrnl.* 25 Sep. 2/3 He kissed a silver twenty-five cent piece and threw it as far as he could out upon the sea.

c. *like twenty,* used as an intensive. *Colloq.* Cf. ** like forty, * like sixty.*

1839 *S. Lit. Messenger* V. 377/2 Lord, how scared she was—she jumped and kicked and hollared like twenty.

*** twenty-one,** *n.*

1. Vingt-et-un, a card game in which each player tries to obtain cards the sum of whose spots is as near twenty-one as possible but not exceeding it. Also **twenty-one game.** Cf. **vantoon.**

1843 GREEN *Exposure Gambling* 285 The game of Vingt-un . . . is better known by the name of Twenty-one, or Van-tu-ann. **1915** YOUNG *Hard Knocks* 196 We had in operation two faro games, a chuckaluck game and a twenty-one game. **1948** *Sat. Ev. Post* 10 July 78/3 It is difficult to figure the house advantage in twenty-one because it varies with the player.

Also **twenty-one dealer.**

1922 *Sunset* Dec. 74/3 You know Matthews, the twenty-one dealer, don't you? **1948** *Sat. Ev. Post* 10 July 76/3 He indicated another young twenty-one dealer.

2. twenty-one aces, formerly in baseball, the number of points or scores that determined a game (see quots.). *Obs.*

1856 *Spirit of Times* 6 Dec. 229/1 The game to consist of 21 counts or aces; but, at the conclusion, an equal number of hands must be played—that is, the last to go in at the commencement of the game shall have the last innings, the total score to decide the game. **1857** *Ib.* 7 March 5/2 Sec. 26 was adopted, . . . making the game . . . 'nine innings,' instead of the old game of twenty-one Aces. **1867** *Ball Players' Chron.* 21 Nov. 4/1 This contest [baseball game of 21 Oct., 1855] took place when 'twenty-one aces up' was the game, the party first closing their innings with a score of 21 or over being declared the victors, provided even innings have been played.

b. Also **twenty-one points.** *Obs.*

[**1856** *Spirit of Times* 13 Sep. 28/1 The Gotham Club being the first to take the bat, and winning the match by a large majority of runs, the relative difference being 21 runs in the 7 innings for the Gotham, and 7 runs only for the Knickerbockers.] **1868** *N. Eng. Base Ballist* 6 Aug. 2/2 Games were played of 21 points, even innings, instead of nine innings as at present.

twid-line, *n.* [Origin unknown.] ?A heavy cord suitable for flying a kite. *Rare.* — **1844** *Knickerb.* XXIV. 258 In his hand is a great ball of twine containing three skeins of 'twid-line.'

*** twig,** *n. attrib.*

1. Designating various small insects that bore into or otherwise injure the twigs of trees.

1874 *Dept. Agric. Rep. 1873* 153 The twig-girdler, *Oncideres cingulatus.* . . . The insects girdle the twig before depositing their eggs. **1891** *Cent.* 5943/1 *Diapheromera femorata* . . . is also called *twig-bug, twig-insect.* **1909** *Cent. Supp.* 1391/3 Twig beetle, a twig-borer.

b. twig blight, (see quot.).

1889 *Cent.* 587/1 Pear-blight, an epidemic disease attacking pear trees, also known as *fire-blight,* and when affecting the apple and quince as *twig-blight.*

2. twig broom, a broom made of twigs, esp. hemlock twigs.

1851 JUDD *Margaret* (ed. 2) I. 10 In one corner stood a twig-broom. **1863** HAWTHORNE *Our Old Home* 194 There was a much greater variety of mechandise: . . . twig-brooms, beehives, oranges, rustic attire.

As the last term in **limber, mesquite twig.**

Twightwees ˈtwɪtwiz, *n. pl.* (See quot. 1907 and cf. **Miami 1.**) Also attrib.

1751 in *Mass. H.S. Coll.* 1 Ser X. 147 The French are now gone from Canada . . . to destroy the nation of the Tooweehtoowees, that are very friendly to the English. **1754** *Ib.* V. 119 The French army went through the country against the Twightwees. **1759** *Newport Mercury* 4 Sep. 3/1 Forty Indians, of the Twigthwee and Kuskuski Nations, were on their Way to that Fort, sent by their Chiefs to learn in what Manner the Peace was settled between us and the Western Indians. **1907** HODGE *Amer. Indians* I. 852/1 Miami. . . . An Algonquian tribe, usually designated by early English writers as Twightwees (*twanh twanh,* the cry of a crane.—Hewit), from their own name.

*** twin,** *n.*

1. One of two neighboring cities that are in some respects similar, as Superior, Wis., and Duluth, Minn. Cf. **twin cities.**

1944 NUTE *Lake Superior* 277 Superior had hoped to be the terminus of the first railroad to the head of the lake, but when one came, in 1870, its terminal was Duluth rather than the other twin.

2. In combs.: (1) **twin bed,** one of a pair of single beds that are alike; (2) **berry,** one of various plants, esp. the honeysuckle, *Lonicera involucrata,* and the partridge-berry; (3) **boat,** (see quots.), *obs.;* (4) **cities,** see as a main entry; (5) **flower,** a plant of the genus *Linnaea,* which produces flowers in pairs, also attrib.; (6) **leaf,** (see quot. 1931); (7) **States,** North and South Dakota.

(1) **1920** LEWIS *Main Street* 211 She ran about, . . . trying the rose-shaded light between the twin beds. **1947** *Democrat* 2 Oct. 8/2 Wanted to Buy—Twin bed in good condition. — (2) **1821** *Mass. H.S. Coll.* 2 Ser. IX. 158 Plants, which are indigenous in the township of Middlebury, [Vt., include] . . . Clott-bur, Twinberry, Prickly ash [etc.]. **1871** DE VERE 402 In the New England States . . . it [the partridge-berry] is often called *twin-berry,* from its uniformly double scarlet-berry. **1938** DAMON *Grandma* 73 On the left against the house [were] lilacs and twinberry and honeysuckle. — (3) *c***1816** REES *Cyclo.* XXXV. *s.v. Steam-engine,* In 1811 and 1812 two steam-boats. were built . . . as ferry-boats for crossing the Hudson river. . . . These boats are what are called twin-boats; each of them being two complete hulls united by a deck or bridge. **1876** KNIGHT 2667/1 *Twin-boat,* a boat or deck supported on two parallel floating bodies, which are placed some distance asunder.

(5) **1817–8** EATON *Botany* (1822) 338 *Linnaea borealis,* twin flower:—branches erect, each bearing 2 flowers. **1948** *Green Bay* (Wis.) *Press-Gaz.* 13 July 11/4 Such wildflowers as twinflowers, clintonia, bunchberry and others grew out of the soft spongy moss. — (6) **1817–8** EATON *Botany* (1822) 321 Twin leaf. . . . Leaves in pairs. **1863** *Rep. Comm. Agric. 1862* 157 One of these plants . . . , named by a botanist in honor of President Jefferson, . . . is commonly known as the 'twin leaf.' **1931** CLUTE *Plants* 40 The twin-leaf (*Jeffersonia diphylla*) with two equal leaflets that make the blade look as if cut in half, almost named itself. — (7) **1899** *Mo. So. Dakotan* I. 184 Mellette [was] Governor of Dakota territory . . . until the admission of the twin states November 2nd.

twin cities. Two somewhat similar cities situated near each other, often (*cap.*) as a nickname for St. Paul and Minneapolis, Minn.

1856 *Rock Island* (Ill.) *D. Argus* 23 April, The church bells of the twin-cities [Rock Island, Ill. and Davenport, Iowa] rang out their joyous notes in honor of the achievement [bridging the Mississippi]. **1883** *Harper's Mag.* June 73/2 The twin cities [St. Paul and Minneapolis, Minn.] . . . emulate each other in metropolitan airs. **1948** *News-Palladium* (Benton Harbor, Mich.) 14 Aug. 1/1 One of the objects of the club is to promote better music for the young Negro youth of the twin cities [Benton Harbor and St. Joseph, Mich.]. **1949** *St. Paul Pioneer Press* 12 Aug. 1/3 Fog and clouds gave the Twin Cities respite from the hot weather for a few hours Thursday morning.

attrib. in sing. **1894** *Chi. Rec.* 1 May 2/4 The twin-city commercial bodies were busy all day trying to bring about arbitration. **1923** *Nation* 5 Sep. 239/1 For years there has been the customary twin-city rivalry.

***twine,** *n.* **1. twine binder,** a harvesting machine that uses twine instead of wire for binding the sheaves, also **twine binding.** *Obs.* **2. twine store,** a store which specializes in various kinds of twine. *Rare.*

(1) **1885** *Rep. Indian Affairs* 47 There are twelve twine binding harvesters . . . owned by members of the tribe. **1902** *Scientific Amer. Supp.* 20 Dec. 22546/3 He would have done much to solve the problem of a practical twine binder. . . . He established twine binding machines as the grain harvesters of the time. — (2) **1894** WARNER *Golden House* xxiii, He was going with nothing, humiliated, a clerk in a twine store.

As the last term in **binder, binding, gilling twine.**

***twirl,** *v. Baseball. tr.* and *intr.* To pitch. — **1883** *Chi. Inter-Ocean* 26 June 2/2 Shaw . . . twirled the sphere with his left hand to excellent purpose. **1921** *N.Y. Times* 2 Oct. IX. 1/1 (*heading*), No Homers for Ruth, but he Twirls a Little.

Hence ***twirling,** pitching. — **1898** *Outing* June 308/2 Miller continues to do effective twirling for Michigan. **1950** *Keowee Courier* (Walhalla, S.C.) 31 Aug. 1/1 The Walhalla team trounce[d] the Georgians handily behind the airtight twirling of Spec Jamison.

***twirler,** *n. Baseball.* A pitcher.

1883 *Sporting Life* 15 April 2 (E. J. Nichols). **1890** *Oaksdale* (Wash.) *Sun* 3 Oct. 7/6 Maxwell is a dandy 'twirler,' but the team did not support him. **1905** *Denver Republican* 6 Sep. 8/2 The celebrated little twirler was thereupon banished to the bench. **1948** *Green Bay* (Wis.) *Press-Gaz.* 12 July 2/4 Neidl was the winning twirler.

***twist,** *n.*

1. Tobacco formed into a thick rope, a rope of tobacco.

1748 WEISER *Journal* 32, I made a Present to the old Shawonese Chief . . . [of] a large twist of Tobacco. **1862** *Statutes at Large* XII. 463 On tobacco, cavendish, plug, twist, fine cut, and manufactured of all descriptions . . . there shall be a tax of thirty cents per pound. **1925** TILGHMAN *Dugout* 32 Ballard was shredding up several huge bunches of tobacco twist, into their large bean kettle.

2. twist bud, a variety of tobacco. *Obs.*

*c***1775** BOUCHER *Glossary* p. l, In *twist-bud, thick-joint, bull-face, leather-coat,* I'd toil all day.

3. a. *the whole twist and tucking,* (see ***tucking 3.**). **b.** *a twist on the shorts,* exaction of a high price for stock or commodities sold short.

(b) **1870** MEDBERY *Men Wall St.* 138 Twist on the shorts. A clique phrase used where the shorts have undersold heavily, and the market has been artificially raised, compelling them to settle at ruinous rates. **1885** *Harper's Mag.* Nov. 842/1 He groans lustily when the bulls get a 'twist on the shorts' by artificially raising prices, and 'squeezing,' or compelling the bears to settle at ruinous rates.

As the last term in **buttonhole, Kentuck, lady's, machine, stub and, tobacco twist.**

***twist,** *v.*

1. *tr.* **a.** To draw (a rabbit or opossum) from a hole by twisting a forked stick into its fur and skin. *Colloq.* Cf. **twisting stick. b.** On the stock exchange, to compel (an adversary) to meet his obligations on ruinous terms. Cf. ***twist,** *n.* **3. b.**

(a) **1838** GOSSE *Letters* 44 The pupils are . . . incomparably more at home in 'twisting a rabbit,' or 'treeing a 'possum,' than in conjugating a verb. **1948** *Democrat* 2 Dec. 1/6 One of the dogs bayed an o'possum in a gopher hole. The boys twisted it out and came leading it to the house with a rope. (b) **1870** W. W. FOWLER *Ten Yrs. Wall St.* 31 The bears found themselves troubled to make their deliveries. Now the ring prepare to 'twist' their antagonists.

2. a. *twist me!* a mild imprecation. *Rare.* **b.** *To twist the tail of, fig.* to apply severe pressure to, to annoy. *Slang.*

(a) **1834** CARUTHERS *Kentuckian* I. 29 Twist me, if I didn't feel as if I was about to be nicked. — (b) **1902** O. HENRY *Roads of Destiny* 259 [He] twisted the tail of a Connecticut insurance company that was trying to do business contrary to the edicts of the great Lone Star State.

***twisted,** *a.* **1. twisted(-branched) pine,** a form, *Pinus contorta,* of the lodgepole pine found on the Pacific Coast, or the ocote, *P. montezumae,* a resinous Mexican pine. **2. twisted stalk,** a plant of the genus *Streptopus,* having a slightly twisted stem, or an orchid of the genus *Spiranthes.* Cf. **white twisted stalk.**

(1) **1869** *Amer. Naturalist* III. 409 Twisted Pine (*Pinus contorta*). I first met with this pine at the east base of Mullan's Pass. **1892** APGAR *Trees Northern U.S.* 177 Twisted-branched Pine . . . has an irregular shape, and crooked branches. **1897** SUDWORTH *Arborescent Flora* 23. — (2) **1857** GRAY *Botany* 474 Twisted-Stalk. . . . S[*treptopus*] *amplexifolius.* . . . Cold and moist woods, Northern New England. **1890** *Harper's Mag.* April 709/2 The twisted-stalk hangs its rosy cups. **1945** MCATEE *Nomina Abitera* 8 Twisted Stalk (Streptopus roseus)—Scoot-berry, because it acts as a physic.

***twister,** *n.*

1. *S.* A moldboard plow in which the cutting share and the moldboard are one solid piece of metal. Also **muley twister,** such a plow without the upper part of the moldboard. Cf. **turn plow.**

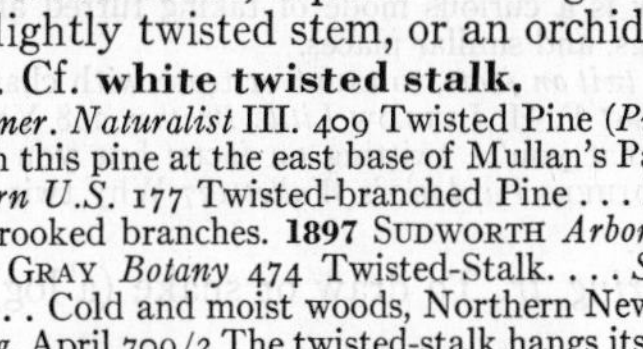

Twister (sense 1) and shovel plows

1865 TURNER *Cotton* 44 A substitute may be made by using a large twister, drawn by two horses, and passing up and down until the furrow is opened. **1944** CLARK *Pills* 281 By colloquial designations the various strange shapes were known to the trade as sweeps, shovels, scooters, twisters, half shovels, muley twisters, half sweeps, bull tongues, buzzard wings, scrapers and subsoilers.

2. In baseball, a curved pitched ball, or a pitcher capable of throwing curves.

1867 *Ball Players' Chron.* 21 Nov. 1/4 The pitching of Burk was excellent, his slow twisters proving very effective. **1887** *Courier-Journal* 20 Feb. 9/1 Stearns wants to trade Corkhill for the big twister.

3. (See quots. and cf. ***twisting 1.**)

1895 *Standard,* twister . . . *Insur.* A policy-holder who drops a policy in one company to take out a new one in another. **1932** *Sat. Morn. Advt.* (Durant, Okla.) 6 Feb. 8/5 [He] sounds a warning against the life insurance 'twister'—the salesman who attempts to make a prospect drop a policy he has in order to take out a new one.

4. A tornado.

1897 *Strand Mag.* Sep. 266/1 Kansas . . . is a favourite spot of the 'twister,' as the Westerners playfully term their windy enemy. **1922** *Dly. Ardmoreite* (Ardmore, Okla.) 21 March 1/2 The twisters worked the greatest havoc in the region of Gowen, Okla. **1949** *Chi. D. News* 24 Dec. 4/3 A freak twister swept in off the Pacific, tearing the roof off one house.

5. A doughnut.

1908 *N.Y. Ev. Post* 21 Dec. (Th.), I had only time to drink half my coffee, to seize a perfectly unmanageable thing called a '*twister*' . . . and to spring aboard the train, *twister* in hand. **1944** DUNCAN *M. Graham* 153 The children's lunch baskets held white bread and plum jam, twisters (doughnuts), apples, and hard-boiled duck eggs.

6. A bronco buster. *Slang.*

1908 *Sat. Ev. Post* 4 July 22/2 Had they only appreciated Blackie they would never have permitted a Mexican 'twister' to top him, but only the professional buster of the range.

As the last term in **Labrador, neck, prairie, storm twister.**

twistical ˈtwɪstɪkl̩, *a.* Crooked, tortuous, untrustworthy. *Colloq.*

1806 FESSENDEN *Democracy Unveiled* II. 114 Certain sages, learn'd and *twistical*, . . . Have prov'd what's wonderful. **1855** P. PAXTON *Capt. Priest* 233 He was rather twistical or so. **1883** *Remin. Rev. George Allen* 69 Godward he is a very good man, but manward he's rather *twistical!*

***twisting,** *n.* **1.** (See quots. and cf. ***twister 3.**) **2. twisting stick,** a forked stick used in drawing rabbits, etc., from holes. Cf. ***twist,** *v.* **1. a.**

(1) 1906 *N.Y. Ev. Post* 20 Jan., By 'twisting' is meant the persuading of policy holders in one company to transfer their insurance to another. **1931** *Chi. Sun. Tribune* 18 Jan. II. 8/4 'Twisting' is the term also applied to the activities of companies or salesmen of securities who use their knowledge of an investor's holdings to induce him through misrepresentation to turn over his investment for something else in order that the company or salesman may make a profit from the exchange. — **(2) 1838** GOSSE *Letters* 50 The twisting-stick I mentioned just now is a curious mode of taking furred animals out of hollow trees, logs, and similar places.

***twit,** *v. To twit on facts,* to taunt or tease with charges based on fact. *Obs.* — **1867** F. H. LUDLOW *Little Brother* 268 You've no idea, Uncle Teddy, that you're twitting on facts; but you hit the truth there. **1905** CROTHERS *Pardoner's Wallet* 127 Why twit on facts?

***twitch,** *v.*

1. *Lumbering. tr.* To draw or snake (a log) along the ground.

1773 PATTEN *Diary* 299 My bror Samuell and I and our boys and oxen went and Twitched in what logs we had at Major Goffes saw Mill. **1838** HALIBURTON *Clockmaker* 2 Ser. xiii. 187 He is a giant that's a fact and can twitch a mill-log as easy as a yoke of oxen can. **1905** *Forestry Bureau Bul.* No. 61, 41 *Skid*, . . . to draw logs from the stump to the skidway, landing, or mill. . . . Syn.: snake, twitch. **1942** RICH *We Took to Woods* (1948) 75 One of the men cuts down the trees and limbs them, one drives the twitch horse, dragging—or 'twitching'—the entire trunk of the tree to a cleared space called a yard, where the third man saws it up with a buck saw and piles it.

2. twitch-up, a trap for small game, esp. rabbits, consisting of a noose attached to a bent stick or sapling. Cf. **yank-up.**

1893 *Outing* Nov. 139/1 For the taking of poor bunny there is no trap superior to the old reliable 'twitch-up.' **1949** R. J. SIM *Pages from Past* 57 The snood or 'twitch-up' was a slipnoose of fine brass wire set in a runway and attached to an upright spring-pole.

***two,** *a.* and *n.*

1. a. A two-dollar bill. **b.** A two-year old beef.

(a) 1849 *Bankers' Mag.* IV. 490 About two years ago, a batch of counterfeited bills . . . (tens, fives, twos,) made their appearance. **1853** *Ib.* VIII. 270 The twos have upon the face of the vignette two gold dollars. **1861** *Alexandria* (Va.) *Gaz.* 4 May 4/6 The Farmers' bank on yesterday circulated a portion of its 'ones' and 'twos.' — **(b) 1890** *Stock Grower & Farmer* 19 April 4/4 Maisch & Driscoll . . . deliver at this point 2,000 head of twos, and as many threes as they find.

2. In miscellaneous combs.: (1) **two blues calico,** app. a dress of calico in two shades of blue, *rare;* (2) **book system,** (see quot.); (3) **-by-four,** see as a main entry; (4) **-eyed plow,** some now indefinable type of plow, *obs.;* (5) **-fisted,** *a.* strong, vigorous, determined, *colloq.;* (6) **forty,** see as a main entry; (7) **gun,** *a.* designating one who carries two pistols, also **two-gunned,** *a.;* (8) **horse (top) buggy,** a (top) buggy drawn by two horses; (9) **nines,** see as a main entry; (10) **-scatter shotgun,** a double-barrelled shotgun, *rare;* (11) **Seed,** see as a main entry; (12) **shoot,** designating a double-barrelled gun, hence **two-shooter,** *obs.;* (13) **spot,** (*a*) a two of any suit of cards, (*b*) an insignificant person, (*c*) a two-year prison term, *slang,* cf. **d.** (5) below; (14) **store front,** ?a store front as large as two of usual size; (15) ***thirds,** see as a main entry; (16) **-up,** (see quot.).

(1) 1839 KIRKLAND *New Home* 289 Miss Arethusa was a strapping damsel, in a 'two-blues' calico, and a buff gingham cape. — **(2) 1910** BOSTWICK *Amer. Pub. Library* 41 The allowance of two books, known as the two-book system, originated in an effort to stimulate the circulation of nonfiction, and previous to its general adoption, about 1895, restriction to a single book was quite customary. — **(4) 1760** WASHINGTON *Diaries* I. 135 Fitted a two Eyed Plow Instead of a Duck Bill Plow.

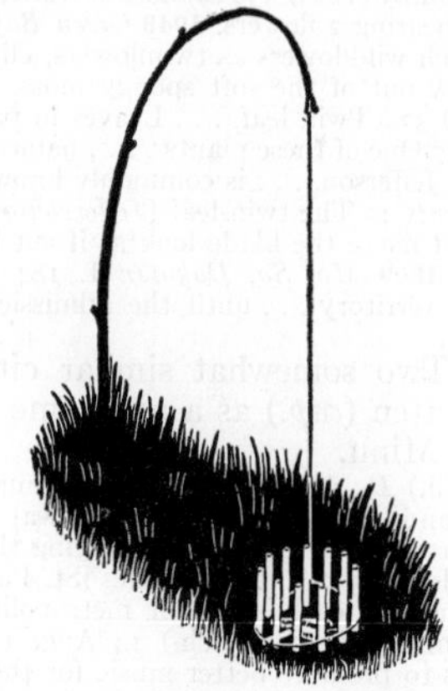

Twitch-up or yank-up

(5) 1774 FITHIAN *Journal* I. 223 [He] appointed a sturdy two fisted Gentleman to open the Ball with Mrs. Tayloe. **1852** STOWE *Uncle Tom* xvii, Phineas had been a hearty, two-fisted backwoodsman. **1920** WILSON *Somewhere* 133 No meal can ever be like breakfast to them that's two-fisted. — **(7) 1913** MULFORD *Coming of Cassidy* 90 Longhorn . . . was being shot to pieces by a two-gun man. **1948** *Popular Western* June 13/1 The town knew him as a fighting two-gun marshal. **1949** *Time* 10 Oct. 47/2 Last week, accompanied by a grim, 200-lb., two-gunned Big Spring sheriff, R. E. Wolf , . . . Composer Grandstaff was flown to Texas by private plane to hear his cantata sung. — **(8) 1880** MARK TWAIN *Tramp Abroad* 358 (R.), I hired a two-horse top-buggy for the first third of the journey. **1944** CLARK *Pills* 109 The drummer involved in the story wore away his life traveling in a two-horse buggy calling on country storekeepers.

(10) 1886 *Milnor* (Dak.) *Teller* June, Guess I'll go for the galoot with a two-scatter shotgun. — **(12) 1848** RUXTON in *Blackw. Mag.* LXIII. 732 The three had come to the resolution to join company—the owner of the 'two-shoot' gun volunteering to fill their horns. **1873** *Harper's Mag.* March 639/1, I had loaded the two-shooter as soon as I got it. — **(13)** (*a*) **1885** *Narragansett Hist. Reg.* III. 213 We were shown a play-card, the two-spot of clubs. **1897** GUNTER *Don Balasco* vii, Señor Balasco builds up in his vivid imagination a palace of cards that will some day fall down and crush him as fatally as if each two-spot were a great marble column. (*b*) **1896** ADE *Artie* 50 You're nothin' but a two-spot. (*c*) **1901** FLYNT *World of Graft* 184 They convicted me at last and I got a two-spot. — **(14) 1903** LEWIS *Boss* 42 We stopped before a grocery. It was a two-store front, and of a prosperous look.

(16) 1931 *Amer. Sp.* Oct. 47 The men [among the lumberjacks] who drive the 'four-up,' the four mule teams, are 'higher' than the 'two-up drivers.'

b. In expressions relating to ball games: (1) **two bagger,** =next; (2) **-base hit,** in baseball, a hit which enables the batter to reach second base safely; (3) **-baser,** =prec.; (4) **-cornered cat,** (see quot. and cf. next); (5) **old cat,** =prec.

(1) 1880 *S.F. Globe* 16 May 1/4 Willigrod, Smith and J. Whitney led at the bat, the two former getting in each a two-bagger. **1946** *This Week Mag.* 23 March 14/1, I hit a two-bagger with the bases full. — **(2) 1874** *N.Y. Sun* 24 July (E. J. Nichols). **1946** *Sat. Ev. Post* 3 Aug. 27/1 Call it a two-base hit. You're not married. But you used to be, and it wasn't happy. — **(3) 1874** *Chi. Inter-Ocean* 14 July

5/1 [He] was credited with four base hits, including one two-baser. **1879** *Chi. Tribune* 3 May 5/1 The Buffalos . . . tied the game by two singles and a two-baser by Galvin. — **(4) 1890** HOWELLS *Boy's Town* 83 Two-cornered cat was played by four boys: two to bat, and two behind the batters to catch and pitch.

(5) 1854 TROWBRIDGE *M. Merrivale* 295 Then there were . . . fox-and-geese in winter, and round-ball, two-old-cat, and 'old red lion, come out of your den,' in summer. **1903** *Outing* July 454/1 'Two old cat' and 'every man for himself' . . . are still in vogue among juveniles. **1948** *Ann. Iowa* July 391 'Two ol' Cat,' 'Blind Man's Buff,' 'Pussy Wants a Corner,' 'Drop the Handkerchief,' and 'Hide and Seek' might have been found among the games and activities of any group of boys and girls.

c. In expressions relating to plants and animals: (1) **two days grass,** (see quot.), *obs.;* (2) **-eyed berry,** the partridgeberry; (3) **-headed snake,** =**double-headed snake,** *obs.;* (4) **thorn acacia,** (see quot.).

(1) 1876 BOURKE *Journal* 28 July–8 Sep., Our Indians said it was called 'two days' grass because if a tired, hungry pony got a belly-full of it, he would be able to keep up two (2) days longer. It looked to me like a variety of grama. — **(2) 1832** WILLIAMSON *Maine* I. 128 Another [plant], called *Two-eyed berry,* is wild, and its fruit has two dimples, or eyes, and in other respects it resembles a chequerberry. — **(3) 1778** CARVER *Travels* 487 The Two-Headed Snake . . . was found about the year 1762, near Lake Champlain, by Mr. Park, a gentleman of New England. **1806** ASHE *Travels* II. 287 We called the following at least to our attention. Rattle Snake. . . . Two Headed Ditto. — **(4) 1782** CRÈVECOEUR *Letters* 204 The locust . . . I am persuaded would have grown here. [Note to *locust:*] A species of what we call here [in Mass.] the two-thorn acacia; it yields the most valuable timber we have.

d. In expressions relating to money; (1) **two-copper,** designating something bought for two cents; (2) **-dollar,** (*a*) designating one who receives two dollars in pay, (*b*) designating a bill for two dollars, (*c*) designating a "big" or pretentious word; (3) **for** (or **fer**), (see quot. 1948), also attrib. in the sense of cheap or contemptible, esp. with reference to cigars two of which may be had for a nickel, *slang,* cf. **two-center;** (4) **-shilling,** ?designating the side of Broadway opposite the shilling side *q.v., obs.;* (5) **spot,** a two-dollar bill, *colloq.,* cf. **2.** (13) above.

For **two bits, two-cent** see as main entries.

(1) 1814 *Niles' Reg.* V. 330/1 A penny biscuit and a 2 copper candle. — **(2)** (*a*) **1793** *Ann. 2d Cong.* 788 The miserable two-dollar men who were raised for a six months' service—their fate is too well known. (*b*) **1813** in HAZARD *Nailer Tom's Diary* (1930) 414/2 Went to Thomas Rodmans Store to get a two dollar bill changed. **1950** *Chi. D. News* 24 May 18/1 The $2 bill was chosen . . . because it carries a picture of Thomas Jefferson. (*c*) **1929** *Cent. Mag.* (Autumn) 68 He hated what he called 'two-dollar words' and 'high hat' manners. — **(3) 1892** *Chi. Tribune* 5 April 4/5, I have shaked 1356 dirty hands today, distributed thirty-six boxes of two-fer cigars, . . . kissed twenty-seven babies, and bought a walking delegate. **1894** *Puck* 26 Sep. 87/1 For him, a quarter-of-a-dollar cigar would be . . . an ostentatious extravagance, while a 'fiver' or a 'two-fer' would be altogether too democratic. [**1912** BOWER *Flying U* 97 Andy interrupted crisply, 'a Montgomery Ward two-for-a-quarter cowpuncher?'] **1931** *K.C. Times* 31 Oct., Two-fer-a-quarter and so on for sox and so forth, and now the two-fer cigar is with us. **1948** in *Amer. Sp.* XXV. (May, 1950) 147/2 Two-for-ones, or 'twofers,' in theatre jargon, are pairs of tickets sold at the box-office price of a single seat. — **(4) 1850** GREELEY *Hints Toward Reforms* 358 Fair maidens (and eke observing bachelors) throng the two-shilling sidewalk, glad to enjoy and not unwilling to be admired.

(5) 1904 O. HENRY *Roads of Destiny* 305 We get the heelers out with the crackly two-spots, and coal-tickets.

3. In phrases: (1) *To be mad with* (someone) *for two,* to be as angry as two ordinarily angry people, *rare;* (2) *two decks and a passage,* a double log house (*q.v.*) with a passage in the middle.

(1) 1890 CUSTER *Following Guidon* 121, I took hold of his chain and yanked him down, and Dixie was 'mad with me for two.' — **(2) 1879** TOURGEE *Fool's Errand* 33 An old family . . . had erected the usual double log-house (or 'two-decks-and-a-passage,' as it is still called).

two bits, *n. pl.*

1. Orig. two pieces of money each valued at a bit, later a quarter of a dollar.

1730 JOHN COMER *Diary* (1893) 117, I saw peach trees in ye blossom and many delightful varieties. Cost me two bitts. **1844** HOUSTOUN *Texas* (1845) 72 From the lady who kept the cows, we procured a small bottle of milk, for which we paid two *bits.* **1950** *So. Wkly.* 15 March 8/2 You bet your two-bits on 'em and know the jury can't convict you for gambling when you collect.

2. *attrib.* Backward, out of the way; venal, cheap. Also in sing. *Colloq.*

1904 *N.Y. Ev. Post* 12 Feb. 5 Out in the 'two-bits' country, on the other side of the Rocky Mountains, it is still possible to pass Confederate paper money if the swindler goes about it in a cool, nonchalant way. **1945** *Somerset News* 22 March 1/2 The two-bit politicians of Maryland who can pass or block almost any legislation still jump through hoops for men like O'Connor and Tawes. **1949** *Sat. Ev. Post* 12 Feb. 24/1, I admit that two-bit judge is short on ritual sense.

b. Designating saloons, grog shops, etc., where liquor is sold for twenty-five cents a drink. Cf. **bit house.**

1856 *S.F. Call* 4 Dec. 1/1 The only 'let up' to their speed was when they stopped to 'smile,' which they did at every 'two bit house' on the road. **1875** *Scribner's Mo.* July 274/2 There are two classes of saloons where these midday repasts are furnished—'two bit' places and 'one bit' places. **1928** FOY & HARLOW *Clowning Thro' Life* 164 There were two classes among the leading ones—the 'one-bit' and the two-bit' kind which served regular meals.

two-by-four.

1. A board or timber measuring two inches by four.

1884 NYE *Baled Hay* 23 The managing editor of the mill lays out the log in his mind, and works it into dimension stuff, shingle bolts, slabs, edgings, two by fours. **1926** *Ladies' Home Jrnl.* June 15 Stiff and unyielding as a two-by-four.

2. *attrib.* Small, trifling. *Colloq.*

1897 THANET *Missionary Sheriff* 13 'That how she makes a living?' 'Yes—little two-by-four bakery.' **1917** MCCUTCHEON *Green Fancy* 45 You'd be surprised to know how many great generals we have running two by four farms and choppin' wood for a livin' up here.

Also **two-by-nine, -seven, -twice.**

1893 *Cong. Rec.* 13 Dec. 211/1 Men call him a crank, and all the little two by seven newspapers and all the little two by nine politicians in the country jump onto him. **1911** HARRISON *Queed* 236 This little two-by-twice grammar school . . . tries to pass itself off for a college.

two-cent, *attrib.* Sold for two cents, of the value of two cents.

1859 WILMER *Press Gang* 42 The Express was a two-cent cash paper. **1883** RITTENHOUSE *Maud* 226 To-day the 2-cent stamp-law goes into operation. **1902** BANKS *Newspaper Girl* xiv, Dinah got a letter through the American mail. . . . Only a common two-cent stamp had been stuck on it.

Also **two-cent piece.**

1864 *Wkly. New Mexican* 27 May 1/4 The new two cent piece . . . resembles, as much as anything can, a gold coin. **1883** J. S. DYE *Coin Encycl.* 1137 No change whatever was made in this coinage down to 1873, when, by act of Congress, the issue of the Two Cent Bronze Piece was discontinued.

b. A very small amount, often **two-cents' worth.** Cf. ***cent,** *n.* **1. b.**

1947 *Atlantic Mo.* June 41/1, I think it is fun to have an Atlantic Town Meeting to discuss the momentous subject proposed by Mrs. Cyrus: 'Why Mothers Fail.' I hasten to put in my two cents' worth. **1949** *Amer. Wool & Cotton Reporter* 14 April 41/1 We wouldn't give two cents for the President's Committee of Economic Advisors.

c. two-center, a cigar that sells for two cents. *Obs.*

1834 *Boston Post* 6 Aug. 2/2 Durant was in the habit of peddling water for rum-traps, and taking his pay in two-centers. **1883** H. J. WARNER *New Lett. Idle Man* (1913) 21 'Two-centers' are really made of tobacco and are not bad.

***two-forty,** *n.*

1. Two minutes and forty seconds, formerly in horse racing the trotting record for a mile. Also with adverbial force.

1855 *Knickerb.* XLV. 634, I commenced, therefore, the process of sliding my legs out from under him—not, to be sure, at a pace of two-forty—but imitating more the speed of the snail. **1866** GREGG *Life in Army* 102 Our lieutenant-colonel spurred his fine cream-colored steed, moving forward . . . at the rate of two-forty on a plank road. **1904** WALLER *Wood-Carver* 132 He's going it two-forty a minute.

attrib. or as *adj.* **1851** *Knickerb.* XXXVII. 279 It is only the steam-whistle of the iron-horse on the Hudson River rail-road, rushing into the Great Metropolis, at a 'two-forty' pace. **1857** *Spirit of Times* 24 Jan. 332/2 The agony of his life is the shell road, with a 2:40 nag, and 'a chance to lift somebody out of their boots.' **1896** *Advance* 26 March 450/3 Get a two forty move on you, Nags!

2. A horse that attains this speed. Also transf.

1856 *Harper's Mag.* April 620/2 He knew men by their horses, and designated them thus—'The fellow that drives the sorrel mare.' . . . 'The bird that trots the two-forty.' **1866** J. KENNAWAY *On Sherman's Track* 243 When a lady is inclined to go ahead she is spoken of sometimes as 'a two-forty.' **1867** *Harper's Wkly.* 23 Feb. 119/4 'Two-forties' Dash us over roads of pleasure.

two nines. (See quot. 1909.)

1903 *N.Y. Tribune* 22 Dec., Acting Chief K—— arrived a few minutes later and ordered the fourth [alarm], and then the two nines, calling out every piece of apparatus on the island. **1904** *N.Y. Tribune* 27 March 1 Summoned by the dreaded 'two nines,' the signal used only in extreme need, every fireman and every piece of apparatus available fought for hours yesterday an ugly blaze. **1909** *Cent. Supp.* 868/3 The two nines, a fire-alarm signal, used only in an emergency, which calls out all the fire-fighting apparatus, and every available fireman. New York City.

Two-Seed, *attrib.*

1. Of or pertaining to Two-Seed Baptists.

1844 *Indiana Mag. Hist.* XXII. 407, I promised to try to shew that the two seed doctrine was a hethan opinion. **1873** Z. N. MORRELL *Flowers from Wilderness* (Boston) 72 There was an organization of some ten or twelve members east of the Trinity, near Nacogdoches, under the pastoral care of Daniel Parker, of 'two-seed' notoriety. **1944** DUNCAN *M. Graham* 59 As Johnson Graham reported, they replied with the 'two-seed doctrine.'

2. Two-Seed Baptists, and variants, an extremely anti-missionary sect of Baptists whose doctrine of the presence in individuals of the divine seed and the seed of the serpent was expounded in a pamphlet by Daniel Parker, the founder of the sect, in 1826 (see quot. 1931). Cf. **Seed Baptist.**

1893 *Census Bul.* No. 375, 38 The Old Two-Seed-in-the-Spirit Predestinarian Baptists . . . are not in fellowship with the Regular or Missionary, nor with the Primitive or any other body of Baptists. *Ib.* 39 Many of the Two-Seed Baptists are strongly opposed to a paid ministry. **1919** *Census: Religious Bodies 1916* II. 151/2 In their church government the Two-Seed Baptists are thoroughly independent. **1931** SWEET *Religion on Amer. Frontier* 75 Daniel Parker's Two-Seed-in-the-Spirit doctrine was the most extreme expression of the anti-mission theology. . . . Briefly it is this. God created Adam and Eve and endowed them with an emanation from himself, which is the good seed. After the fall of man there was also planted in Eve and all the daughters of Eve the 'seed of the serpent.' All children born of the divine seed are the children of God, while all children born of the evil seed are the children of the devil. **1949** *Newsweek* 18 July 62/3 The Old Catholic Churches, branches of Judaism, the Mennonites, Two-Seed-in-the-Spirit Predestinarian Baptists, Dunkers, and River Brethren are objectivistic.

* **two-thirds,** *n. pl.* **1.** (See quot.) *Rare.* **2. two-thirds rule,** a rule enforced in Democratic national conventions after 1832 but now abolished, requiring a candidate to secure the votes of two thirds of the delegates to secure the nomination.

(1) **1844** BROWN in *Edin. Jrnl.* II. 175 We set out in a body to raise the log-house, accompanied by the two boys, each of whom bore a large jug of whisky-punch, of the kind generally known by the name 'two-thirds' (referring to the whisky, not the water). — (2) **1844** *Talladega* (Ala.) *Dem. Watchtower* 12 June 2/3 The discussion of the two thirds rule was renewed. *a*1859 PRENTICE *Prenticeana* (1860) 187 (We.), The democrats established the two-thirds rule, and made next to no nomination at all. **1948** *Sat. Ev. Post* 10 July 18/1 The Democrats' old 'two-thirds rule' alone contributed to starting the Mexican War and the Civil War.

tycoon taɪˈkun, *n.* [See note.]

This term seems to have come into use in this country as a direct borrowing from Japanese *taikun*, great lord or prince.

1. (*cap.*) (See quot. 1945.) *Obs.* or *hist.*

1861 HAY *Lincoln & Civil War* 11 At the request of the Tycoon, . . . I went down to the Navy Yard. *Ib.* 12 Gen. Butler has sent an imploring request to the President to be allowed to bag the whole nest of traitorous Maryland legislators. This the Tycoon . . . forbade. **1861** *N.Y. Tribune* 19 Oct. 4/3 No Tammany candidate has a shadow of a chance for election unless he has the Tycoon's indorsement. **1945** MENCKEN *Supp.* I. 438 *Tycoon* was brought in by the Perry expedition of 1852–54 and seems to have come into use in the United States before the English became aware of it. It was used as an affectionate nickname for Abraham Lincoln by the members of his secretariat, and has been worked to death in recent years by *Time.*

2. One who has a dominant position in business, industry, etc. *Colloq.* Cf. **railroad tycoon.**

1886 *Outing* Nov. 164/1 The tycoon of the baggage car objected to handling the boat. **1938** HART *New Yorkers* 40 One tycoon on Robinson Street had paved the thoroughfare in front of his house with blocks of marble. **1949** *Sun. World-Herald Mag.* (Omaha) 22 May 2/1 We were joined by a man who, by Nebraska standards, is a tycoon.

tyee ˈtaɪˌi, *n.* [Chinook Jargon (<Nootka *taiyi*), chief, boss, king, etc.]

1. A chief or person of great importance.

1811 tr. HUMBOLDT *Political Essay* II. 247 It was only by the destruction of the establishment founded at the island of *Quadra and of Vancouver* that Maciuna, the *Tays* or prince of Nootka, was enabled to preserve his independence. **1856** in *34th Cong.* 3 Sess. H.R. Ex. Doc. 37, 75 The chief . . . [seems] to have more *real* influence than any of the so-called 'tyhees' on the Sound. **1877** *Puget Sound Argus* 23 Nov., With the coming of the military among us came a big church 'tyhee,' who told us that the soldiers were come to protect us. **1950** *Amer. Sp.* May 82 Prolongation of a main vowel intensified meaning; thus *tyee* meant chief, *hyas tyee* a big chief, but *hya-a-a-s tyee* a very great chief or politician.

2. = Chinook salmon. In full **tyee salmon.** Cf. **spring salmon.**

1863 BRIGGS *Dict. Chinook* 28 Tyee salmon, *the spring salmon.* **1940** SMITH *Puyallup-Nisqually* 236 Dried salmon was made from the tyee and the summer and early fall salmons. **1945** *Md. Conservationist* 8/1 There are five species of Pacific salmon: the chinook or king, also sometimes called tyee.

3. tyee grouse, (see quot.).

1917 *Birds of Amer.* II. 16 Franklin's Grouse. . . . Other Names. . . . Fool Hen; Mountain Grouse; Wood Grouse; Tyee Grouse.

* **Tyler,** *n.* **1. Tyler grippe,** (see quot. 1891). **2. Tyler man,** a supporter of John Tyler, President of the U.S. (1841–45). Both *obs.*

(1) **1843** in THOMPSON *M. Jones* (1872) 162 Old Miss Stallins . . . has had the Tyler Grip. . . . She ses she always did consider old Tiler a cuss sent on the country. **1891** WELCH *Recoll. 1830–40* 35 That severe and virulent form of Influenza, which appeared soon after the elevation of John Tyler to the Presidency, when he abandoned his party platform and principles, and the disease was named in grim satire, the *Tyler Grippe.* — (2) **1842** *Whig Almanac 1843* 5 Recapitulation.—Whigs 133; Loco Focos 102; distinctive Tyler men 6; Vacancy 1. **1843** *Quincy* (Ill.) *Herald* 30 June 2/5 One and all,—Democrats, Whigs, Tyler men and neutrals, come and hear the candidates on Monday.

Tylerism ˈtaɪləˌrɪzəm, *n.* [John *Tyler* (1790–1862).] The political practices and methods of President Tyler. *Obs.* — **1843** *Alton* (Ill.) *Telegraph* 2 Sep. 2/4 The leprosy of Tylerism which had commenced its desolating ravages upon his body must be eradicated. **1859** WILMER *Press Gang* 46 When the presidential election came off, . . . the *Philadelphia Evening Mercury*, and all the other organs of Tylerism found it necessary to change their tune.

Tylerite ˈtaɪləˌraɪt, *n.* A supporter of President John Tyler. *Obs.*

1845 *Ohio State Jrnl.* (Columbus) 3 April 2/5 The Tylerites are getting it all around. **1848** *Field Piece* (Chi.) 5 July 2/2 'They are Whigs,' rejoined another;—'Abolitionists,' exclaimed a third;—'Tylerites, by G—d,' said a fourth. **1859** L. WILMER *Press Gang* 45 The Tylerites regarded him as a man of stupendous abil'ties.

Tylerize ˈtaɪləˌraɪz, *v. intr.* To forsake the party or side to which one owes office or allegiance as President Tyler did. Also *tr.* and **Tylerizing,** *n. Obs.*

1848 *Campaign Flag* (Maysville, Ky.) 8 Sep. 3/5 You can't come it—we've been *Tylerized* once! **1851** *Ore. Statesman* 6 June 2/6 It will be seen from our Telegraphic despatch that the President has *Tylerized* at last, and in earnest. **1867** *Harper's Wkly.* 26 Jan. 50/1 The present President can not be fairly impeached for Tylerizing.

* **type,** *n.*

1. = typo. *Obs.*

1763 *Boston Gaz.* 7 Feb. 2/3 Dear Brother Types, to us are Scriblers Fate, More than the Fall of Pup Dogs, and of Cate. **1771** in *Pub. Col. Soc.* XXVI. 8, I never knew that Mr. D. ever presumed on any Powers, or claimed any abilities superior to his Brother Types. **1924** *Ib.* XXVI. 8 R. H. Thornton, though citing examples of 'typo' dated 1816 and 1902, does not recognize 'type.' Both words were in more or less common use in this country before 1800.

2. Short for tintype *q.v. Rare.*

1878 RUEDE *Sod-House Days* 231 When I got to town Tuesday I discovered an 'Art Gallery' below Fritchey's, so I had a type taken for you.

3. In combs.: (1) **type girl,** a girl who operates a typewriter, *obs.;* (2) **machine,** a typewriter, *obs.;* (3) **sticker,** a compositor, *slang.*

(1) **1905** MARK TWAIN *First Writing-Machines* 167 (R.), He put his type-girl to work, and we timed her by the watch. — (2) **1905** MARK TWAIN *First Writing-Machines* 167 (R.), I saw a type-machine for the first time in—what year?—I suppose it was 1873. — (3) **1842** GREELEY in *Corr. R. W. Griswold* (1898) 105 You will keep this lec-

ture out of the dirty hands of all type-stickers, for the present. **1896** *Typog. Jrnl.* IX. 298 Charley was a 'type-sticker.'

b. *To put the types onto,* (see quot.). *Obs.*

1849 Willis *Rural Lett.* 94, I presume, that 'to put the types on to' a man, is to send the constable to him with a printed warrant.

As the last term in **Boston, ivory, Pennsylvania, studhorse, tintype.**

typer ˈtaɪpɚ, *n.* (See quots.) *Obs.* — **1892** *People's Press* (S.F.) 10 Sep. 6/7 Typine—A typewriting machine. The accent falls on the last syllable.... Typer—A male operator on the typine. **1909** *Cent. Supp.* 1393/3 *Typer,* a type-writer.... A person who uses a type-writer.

typescript ˈtaɪpˌskrɪpt, *n.* Typewritten matter.

[**1892** *People's Press* (S.F.) 10 Sep. 6/7 To type—To write on the typine. Typoscript—Typewritten, or typewritten manuscript.] **1893** A. Estoclet in *Nation* 6 July 16/1 Writing . . . concerning a type-written document . . . , I half apologetically used the word 'type-script.' **1948** *Time* 2 Feb. 16/1 He read his speech from typescript.

typewriter ˈtaɪpˌraɪtɚ, *n.*

1. A machine for writing by means of type characters similar to those of printers.

1868 C. Latham Sholes Specifications accompanying application for patent 11 May 14 Thus made, the Type-Writer is the simplest, most perfectly adapted to its work. **1876** Knight 2677/1 The Sholes type-writer . . . is about the size of the sewing-machine, and is worked with keys arranged in four banks or rows. **1923** Dutton *Shadow on Glass* 76 The only thing that seemed to have caused it was the type-writer. **1949** *New Yorker* 9 July 54/3 They seem so good partly, I think, because of Mr. Mencken's advantages . . . of hitting a type-writer fast to make an edition.

attrib. **1884** Howells *Silas Lapham* 24, I want you should put these in shape, and give me a type-writer copy to-morrow. **1902** Mark Twain in *Harper's Mag.* CIV. 258/1 She took from the drawer of the type-writer table several squares of paper. **1903** *Christendom* 13 June 393 Please furnish . . . 12 typewriter ribbons. **1918** M. B. Owen *Typewriting Speed* 115 The typewriter cabinet is one of the things that should receive attention.

2. A typist. Now *hist.*

1884 *N.Y. Herald* 27 Oct. 7/2 Situation Wanted—By Lady, Rapid Stenographer, and typewriter. **1901** *Denver Republican* 26 Aug. 8/5 That the company should get no more than the customer is hardly fair; because it has to pay office rent and typewriters' salaries. **1947** *Newsweek* 10 Feb. 94/2 She was one of the world's first 'female typewriters.'

Also **typewriter girl.** *Obs.*

1884 Howells *Silas Lapham* xxiii. 410 One of them was Miss Dewey, the type-writer girl. **1904** A. Dale *Wanted, a Cook* 82 Have you ever heard of a typewriter girl who has come to grief, and who wasn't beautiful?

typewriting machine. A typewriter (sense **1.**). — **1868** *Rep. Comm. Patents* II. 175, 79,265 . . . Type-Writing Machine. **1902** Banks *Newspaper Girl* 8, I would be bidden . . . to return and write on my typewriting machine all about the things I had seen and heard.

Early (*c*1884) form of typewriter (sense 1)

typo ˈtaɪpo, *n.* A typographer or typesetter.

1816 *Mass. Spy* 7 Aug. (Th.), [Printers] will confer a favour on a brother typo [by publishing an advertisement of a runaway apprentice]. **1872** *Chi. Tribune* 21 Oct. 7/3 Governor Warmouth . . . became a typo in the St. Louis Republican office. **1948** *Chi. D. News* 20 Aug. 12/1 (*heading*), Typos Act On New Processes.

tyrotoxicon ˌtaɪrəˈtɑksəkən, *n.* [f. Gk. *tyro-* (<*tyros,* cheese), +Gk. *toxicon,* poison.] (See quot.) — **1886** *Scientific Amer.* 21 Aug. 112/3 About a year ago, Dr. Victor C. Vaughan, of the University of Michigan, succeeded in isolating from some samples of cheese . . . a highly poisonous ptomaine, which he named tyrotoxicon.

U

Uchee ˈjutʃi, *n.* Also **Euchee, Yuchi.** [f. a native word meaning "situated yonder" and prob. given by some member of the tribe in answer to some such question as "Who are you?" or "Where do you come from?" See Hodge.] An Indian of a tribe first encountered by Europeans in eastern Carolina or Georgia; also, *pl.*, the tribe of such an Indian.

1738 W. STEPHENS *Proc. Georgia* 75 He understood they were a Party of the Euchies. **1818** *Lynchburg* (Va.) *Press* 25 Dec. 3/1 The captain . . . reports to have taken three warriors, a Creek, a Choctaw, and a Uchee. **1851** DRAKE *Indians N. Amer.* 16 The *Uchees* are said to speak a primitive language. **1910** HODGE *Amer. Indians* II. 1005/1 In material culture the Yuchi are typical of the agricultural hunting tribes of the S.E. Atlantic and Gulf coast area.

attrib. **1744** F. MOORE *Voy. Georgia* 102 Part of these cattle belonged to the Saltzburghers, who had passed over the Ebenezer river into the Uchee lands. **1746** *Ga. Col. Rec.* VI. 170 [They] had petitioned the Trustees to obtain for them a Tract of Land said to belong to the Uchee Indians.

Hence **Uchean,** *a.*

1910 HODGE *Amer. Indians* II. 861/2 Uchean Family. A linguistic family limited, so far as is positively known, to a single tribe, the Yuchi.

* **ugly,** *a.* and *n.* **1.** *n.* The quality of ugliness. *Colloq. Obs.* **2. ugly man contest,** a jocular contest in which the man who is selected as the homeliest present receives an award. *Colloq.* Cf. * **wolf b.**

(1) **1835** LONGSTREET *Ga. Scenes* 63, I want to get in the breed of them sort o' men to drive ugly out of my kin folks. **1845** HOOPER *Taking Census* (1928) 121 The *ugly's* out on her wuss nor the small-pox! — (2) **1944** *Democrat* 27 April 1/2 The address was postponed until after the ugly man contest. [**1947** *Dly. Oklahoman* (Okla. City) 5 Nov. 8/5 There will be contests to select the 'prettiest girl' and the 'ugliest man,' a cake walk, grab bag and other traditional carnival activities.]

uinta(h)ite juˈɪntəˌaɪt, *n.* [See def. and quot. 1910.] A black, lustrous native hydrocarbon, deposits of which are found in the Uintah Mountains in Utah. — **1891** Union Pac. R.R. *Utah* (ed. 4) 75 Uintahite occurs in the bad lands of the lower Duchesne and the lower White, in veins or lodes striking straight through the sandstone formation. **1910** HODGE *Amer. Indians* II. 863/2 Uintahite. A certain mineral: from the place name *Uintah* and the English suffix *-ite*. The word Uintah, or Uinta, applied to a tribe and a mountain range in Utah, is derived from the Ute dialect of the Shoshonean stock.

Ukiah. See **Yokaia.**

ukulele ˌjukəˈlelɪ, *n.* [Hawaiian, "flea," so named because the rapid movements of the player's fingers suggested the insect.] A small guitar, usu. having four strings, of a type introduced in Hawaii by the Portuguese *c*1877.

1900 *Cent. Mag.* June 164/2 Kilomono . . . holds the ukulele, a stringed instrument which may or may not be indigenous to the island. **1916** *Chi. Tribune* 3 Oct. 8/3 Those who first brought the word to this country adopted 'ukulele' [and] . . . it is rapidly becoming standard. **1950** *Life* 2 Jan. 49 The raccoon coat . . . like mah-jongg, the ukulele and the crystal set . . . has become a symbol of the '20s.

Hence **uke.** *Colloq.*

1929 H. L. GATES *Lipstick* 12 The uke fairly wept. Then there was hilarious pandemonium.

Umatilla ˌjuməˈtɪlə, *n.* [App. a native name.] *collect.* or *pl.* (See quot. 1910.)

1842 WILLIAMS *Tour to Ore.* (1921) 70 Those Indians are the Umatilla's. **1857** NESMITH in *Indian Aff. Rep.* 323 The treaties negotiated in 1855 with the Nez Percés, Walla-Wallas, Cayuses, Umatilas, and Yakimas, I regard as of great importance. **1910** HODGE *Amer. Indians* II. 866/1 Umatilla. A Shahaptian tribe formerly living on Umatilla r. and the adjacent banks of the Columbia in Oregon. They were included under the Wallawalla by Lewis and Clark in 1805, though their language is distinct. . . . They are said to number 250, but this figure is doubtful.

attrib. **1900** *Cong. Rec.* 8 Jan. 667/1 Mr. Simon introduced a bill . . . to provide for the sale of the unsold portion of the Umantilla Indian Reservation. **1948** *Trail Riders Bul.* Jan. 23/2 The Umatilla Indians from the reservations around Pendleton take great pride in putting on this show.

* **umbrella,** *n.*

1. a. Short for **umbrella tree.** *Obs.* **b.** (See quot. 1893.)

(**a**) **1775** BURNABY *Travels* 12 They are likewise adorned and beautified with . . . flowering poplars, umbrellas, magnolias. **1809** ASHE *Travels in Amer.* 50, I confine myself to native plants. . . . Popular Name. . . . Umbrella. — (**b**) **1893** DANA *Wild Flowers* 30 'The umbrellas are out!' cry the children, when the great green leaves of the May apple first unfold themselves in spring. **1950** *Chi. Tribune* 16 May 6/3 The mandrakes have sprung their umbrellas to be ready for the spring rains.

2. a. umbrella laurel, magnolia, =**umbrella tree. b. umbrella leaf,** (see quots.).

(**a**) **1838** GOSSE *Letters* 289 These are the Big Laurel (*M. grandiflora*), and the Umbrella Laurel (*M. tripetala*). **1846** BROWNE *Trees Amer.* 10 The Umbrella Magnolia. . . . The leaves are eighteen or twenty inches long. — (**b**) **1866** *Treas. Bot.* 412/1 The only species, *Diphylleia cymosa*, a native of Japan, and of the southern United States, is there called the Umbrella Leaf. **1931** CLUTE *Plants* 40 The twin-leaf . . . almost named itself, but the name of umbrella leaf for *Diphylleia cymosa* was not so fortunate a choice.

3. umbrella tree, a magnolia or species of magnolia, *Magnolia tripetala*. Also the China tree *q.v.* Cf. **large-leaved umbrella tree.**

1738 CATESBY *Carolina* II. 80 The Umbrella Tree. . . . The leaves . . . grow in horizontal circles, representing somewhat the appearance of an Umbrella. **1838** GOSSE *Letters* 290 The Umbrella-tree is so called from its leaves, which are of extraordinary appearance; they are eighteen or twenty inches long, and six or eight broad. **1903** FOX *Little Shepherd* ii, Here and there was a blossoming wild cucumber and an umbrella-tree with huger flowers and leaves. **1950** *Chi. Tribune* 18 May 6/2 When it is in full bloom, as it will be soon, the flowers of the umbrella tree fill the arboretum with their rich fragrance.

Umpqua ˈʌmpkwə, *n.* [App. a native name.] *collect.* or *pl.* (See quot. 1910.)

1838 PARKER *Exploring Tour* 242 The principal nations are the Chenooks, the Klicatats, the Callapooahs, and the Umbaquâs. **1910** HODGE *Amer. Indians* II. 866/2 Umpqua. An Athapascan tribe formerly settled on upper Umpqua r., Oreg., E. of the Kuitsh. **1942** STEGNER *Mormon C.* 244 They had almost reached the Willamette Valley when they were again attacked by Indians, this time the Umpquas.

attrib. **1826** DAVID DOUGLAS in *Ore. Hist. Soc. Quart.* VI. 83 He speaks a few words of Chenook and understands the Umptqua tongue. **1849** in *31st Cong.* 1 Sess. 1850 Sen. Ex. Doc. 52, 172 The *Ump-qua* Indians occupy a valley of that name and are much scattered.

unabridged ˌʌnəˈbrɪdʒd, *n.* [f. the adj.] An unabridged dictionary, usu. Webster's.

[**1848** *Scientific Amer.* 23 Sep. 7/1 The publishers of Webster's Unabridged Dictionary, in crown quarto, received an order for 12 copies of that work lately from Ceylon.] **1875** MARK TWAIN in *Lotus Leaves* 28, I had the Unabridged and I was ciphering around in the back end, hoping I might tree her among the pictures. **1902** HARBEN *Abner Daniel* 58 Well, the unabridged does not furnish it. **1950** *Dly. Oklahoman Mag.* (Okla. City) 7 May 8/3 Every dictionary needs at least one such error to put its readers at ease (Remember 'Dord.' in the unabridged?).

unaker ˈjunəkɚ, *n.* [App. the same native Indian word seen in *Unaka* Mountains between N.C. and Tenn. See note below.] A form of porcelain clay found in western North Carolina, esp. in what is now Macon County.

"The 'fogg or smoke' which these early travelers observed cloaked the peaks known today as the Great Smoky Mountains, called by the Cherokee the Unakas, meaning in their language White Mountains,—the home of the God of all Indians, Michabo who was sometimes called The Ancient White One" (1950 *Asheville Citizen-Times* 26 March III. 2/5).

1744 in *D.N.B.* (1889) XX. 300/1 The material [for making china-ware] is an earth, the produce of the Cherokee nation in America, called by the natives *unaker.* **1881** *Harper's Mag.* Feb. 358/1 Wedgwood . . . made arrangements for a regular supply of 'unaker' or Pensacola clays. **1885** *Encycl. Brit.* XIX. 641/1 The clay, which was called 'unaker,' was brought from America, and was probably an impure kind of kaolin. [**1950** *Asheville* (N.C.) *Citizen-Times* 26 March VIII. 2/6 [Josiah] Wedgewood, as early as 1766, had obtained specimens of porcelain clay from the mountains of the Cherokee country, and to these had later added several varieties of the steatites peculiar to the country.]

unappropriated land. Public land not sold or set aside for a particular purpose. *Obs.*

1717 *Mass. H. Rep. Jrnl.* I. 196 A Petition . . . praying that 600 Acres of Land . . . may be laid out in some Unappropriated Land of this Province. **1780** in *Pres. Mess. & P.* III. 59 Unappropriated lands which may be ceded or relinquished to the United States by any particular State . . . shall be disposed of for the common benefit of the United States. **1836** *Mich. Gen. Statutes* (1882) I. 37 Five entire sections of land . . . from any of the unappropriated lands . . . are hereby granted to the state for the purpose of completing the public buildings of the said state.

unassimilable ˌʌnəˈsɪmləbl̩, *a.* Not capable of being assimilated. — **1873** E. H. Clarke *Sex in Educ.* 23 Our girls revel in those unassimilable abominations. **1900** *Cong. Rec.* 30 Jan. 1303/1 There is no possibility that we should ever admit to an equal participation in our Government these Asiatic people . . . so utterly unassimilable to ourselves.

***unavailable,** *a.* Not available as a political candidate. Cf. ***available,** *a.* — **1888** Bryce *Amer. Commonw.* II. III. lxx. 558 The larger delegations hold meetings to determine their course in the event of the man they chiefly favour proving 'unavailable.' **1904** *N.Y. Ev. Post* 26 Oct. 6 He now comes forward with an elaborate statement to show that he is not 'Odell's candidate,' that Mr. Odell regarded him as unavailable.

Hence ***unavailability,** *n.* — **1930** Mark Sullivan *Our Times* iii. 281 Root's speech put an additional weight of unavailability on Root as a Presidential possibility.

unbank ʌnˈbæŋk, *v.*[1] *tr.* To deprive a bank of its functions—used with reference to the second Bank of the U.S. *Obs.* — **1834** Calhoun *Works* II. 363 We must . . . use a bank to unbank the banks, to the extent that may be necessary. **1854** Benton *30 Years' View* I. 434/1 [Mr. Calhoun's] frequent expression was, that his plan was to 'unbank the banks.'

***unbank,** *v.*[2] *tr.* To free or clear (a fire) from the material used in banking it. — **1890** *Scientific Amer.* 17 May 315/3 The first duty of an engineer . . . is to ascertain how many gauges of water there are in his boilers. Never unbank or replenish the fires until this is done.

unbankable ʌnˈbæŋkəbl̩, *a.* Not suitable for depositing in a bank. — **1855** *Knickerb.* XLV. 469 Kin you let me have four hundred and fifteen dollars, unbankable money? **1890** Gildersleeve *Essays & Studies* 55 All the gold that France has paid, or can pay, were a poor exchange for the treasure of German idealism, unbankable as it is.

* **unbleached,** *a.* (See quots.) *Slang.*

1846 *Yankee Doodle* (N.Y.) I. 4/1 While in Europe our specimen of Unbleached American Domestics was invited to address Every Body's Convention. **1872** De Vere 281 In familiar intercourse, he [the Negro] appeared . . . humorously as an unbleached American. **1942** Berrey & Van den Bark *Amer. Thesaurus Slang* 360 Negro . . Aframerican, Africamerican, unbleached American, *an American Negro.*

***unbutton,** *v. fig. tr.* To kill, also *to unbutton the collar of. Slang. Obs.* — **1834** Caruthers *Kentuckian* I. 20, I think no more of taking my jack-knife and unbuttoning the collar of a Creek Injin, than I would of takin the jacket off a good . . . bell-wether. **1845** Simms *Cabin & Wigwam* 64, I had but one shoot, and if I didn't unbutton him in that one, it would be a bad shoot for poor Lucy.

unchinked ʌnˈtʃɪŋkt, *a.* Of logs or cabins: Not provided with chinking or daubing. Cf. * **chink,** *v.*

1819 *Niles' Reg.* XVII. 30/2 A year ago there were only 'five or six unchinked cabins' on the town plot. **1843** Carlton *New Purchase* I. 107 As to the cabin it was as yet unchinked, undaubed, and without its stack chimney. **1905** *Forestry Bureau Bul.* No. 67, 80 There are over a hundred cabins without door, floor, windows, or chimney, built, pen like, of unchinked logs.

* **uncle,** *n.*

1. Applied to Negroes, esp. an elderly slave or servant. Also **unkey.** *Colloq.*

1830 S. P. Holbrook *Sketches* 111 In many families, however, the children are taught to address the older servant as *uncle* or *auntee,* and this is sometimes more than a form of speech. **1835** J. H. Ingraham *South-West* II. 241 Nor are planters indifferent to the comfort of their gray-headed slaves. . . . They always address them in a mild and pleasant manner as 'Uncle' or 'Aunty.' **1861** W. H. Russell *My Diary* I. 144 We passed through the market [at Charleston, S.C.], where the stalls are kept by fat negresses and old 'unkeys.' **1947** Lumpkin *Southerner* 155 If I knew their names I at once forgot them, contenting myself with 'Sally' or 'Jim,' or if they were old, perhaps 'Uncle' or 'Auntie'—generic terms we were wont to use for Negroes whose names we did not know.

2. = **Uncle Sam.**

1849 *Placer Times* (Sacramento) 1 Sep., Two Express Lines have been established between our City and San Francisco. Our old Uncle will have to 'stir his stumps' else his 'regular' arrangements will become a *dead letter.* **1873** D. M. Berry *MS Corr.* (Huntington Lib.) 1 Sep., It is very kind in our good Uncle to allow these hopefuls to experiment with appropriations to build this uncertain wall. **1948** *Chi. Tribune* 21 Nov. (Comics) 12 This once all Indian country—Uncle Sam takum—but Uncle no mind Indian shoot one turkey.

3. In nicknames of obvious meaning or sufficiently explained in the quots., as (1) **Uncle Abe,** (2) **Jonathan,** (cf. **Brother Jonathan**), (3) **Ned,** (4) **Robert,** (5) **Samuel,** (cf. **Uncle Sam**).

For **Uncle Sam, Uncle Tom,** see as main entries.

(1) 1860 *Charleston* (S.C.) *Mercury* 20 Dec. 4/2 Now he enters the arena as chief Union-saver to his Majesty, 'Uncle Abe.' **1886** Logan *Great Conspiracy* 613 In response to the loud and jubilant cries of 'Lincoln!' 'Lincoln!' 'Abe Lincoln!' 'Uncle Abe!' and other affectionate calls . . . he appeared at an open window. — **(2) 1800** *Aurora* (Phila.) 14 July (Th.), I have heard that uncle Jonathan and some of the rest of 'em say [etc.]. — **(3) 1850** Weir *Lonz Powers* 32 Old Uncle Ned,—every family in Kentucky has some old family servant bearing this endearing title. — **(4) 1870** MacRae *Americans* I. 175 The men used to call him [Robert E. Lee] 'Uncle Robert.' They loved him as if he had been a father.

(5) 1816 Fidfaddy *Adv. Uncle Sam* 11 Behold said Thomas [Jefferson], how mine Uncle Samuel hath fought in times past against John Bull. **1876** *Stockton* (Calif.) *Wkly. Herald* 5 Aug. 1/4 Don't they wish that Uncle Samuel would send out that cash?

b. As a word of surrender, usu. in phrases. *Colloq.*

1918 *Chi. Herald-Examiner* 1 Oct. 11 Sic him Jenny Jinx—make him say 'Uncle.' **1949** *Chi. D. News* 7 Oct. 1/1 When his foe cries 'uncle' and the occupation begins, the warrior gets flabby in mind and body.

Uncle Sam. [See note.]

The statement often made that this expression was inspired by or had reference to one Samuel Wilson of Troy, N.Y., lacks confirmation. Albert Matthews in *Amer. Antiq. Soc. Proc.* n.s. XIX. (1908) 21–65 favors the view that the expression originated as a jocular expansion of the initials U.S. meaning United States.

1. The United States. A nickname. Cf. **U. Sam.**

1813 *Troy Post* 7 Sep. 3/3 'Loss upon loss,' and 'no ill luck stir[r]ing but what lights upon Uncle Sam's shoulders,' exclaim the Government editors, in every part of the Country. . . . This cant name for our government has got almost as current as 'John Bull.' The letters U.S. on the government waggons, &c are supposed to have given rise to it. **1838** A. Bell *Men & Things* (1862) 282, I ought to mention that the sobriquet 'Uncle Sam' (equivalent to our John Bull) is a popular filling up the initials U.S., abbreviation of 'United States.' **1873** *Newton Kansan* 19 June 3/2 Let patriots everywhere . . . prepare to do the clean thing by Uncle Sam and his bald headed eagle. **1949** *Chi. D. News* 23 July 6/2 Uncle Sam won't be left holding the sack.

b. Also **Uncle Samdom.** *Rare.*

1860 *Mountaineer* (Salt Lake City) 17 March 118/6 He treats upon . . . the bill . . . to punish polygamy in the Territories!!! by which they propose to rid Uncle Samdom of the Mormons.

2. Often, in the possessive, in combs. of obvious meaning.

1846 McCarty *National Songs* 101 Now I [Texas] take my station, As Uncle Sammy's child. **1867** *Atlantic Mo.* April 426/1 The Rebels used to taunt us with the assistance the gunboats gave our armies,—what dear old Abe called Uncle Sam's web-feet. **1947** *Christian Sci. Mon.* 1 March 13/6 The Ides of March coincide with fateful March 15 on Uncle Sam's calendar.

b. Uncle Sam's men, men employed in some civilian capacity by the U.S. Government. *Obs.*

1813 in *Amer. Antiq. Soc. Proc.* No. XIX. 34 A recent battle . . . between what are called in this part of the country [near Lansingburg, N.Y.], *Uncle Sam's Men* and the *Men of New-York.* **1826** Royall *Sketches* 195 In Washington . . . , I met with 'uncle Sam's' men, as they call themselves. **1893** *Harper's Mag.* Feb. 462/1 Uncle Sam's men, with a-plenty o' greenbacks.

c. Uncle Sam's Ice-box, (see quot.).

1897 Leonard *Gold Fields Klondike* 206 The matter was allowed to drop as a subject of discussion, and the allusions to 'Uncle Sam's Ice-Box,' as the country [Alaska] had been called, became infrequent.

3. Gen. Ulysses S. Grant. A nickname. *Obs.*

1866 W. F. G. Shanks *Personal Recoll. Dist. Generals* 117 The patriotic friends of the general have given the name several facetious variations, such as 'Uncle Sam,' 'Unconditional Surrender,' and 'United We Stand.' **1884** Blaine *20 Years Congress* I. 356 The initials of his name were seized upon. . . . He was 'Unconditional Surrender,' he was 'United States,' he was 'Uncle Sam.'

Uncle Tom. [The Negro hero of Harriet Beecher Stowe's antislavery novel *Uncle Tom's Cabin* (1851–52).] **1.** Used as the root of several words coined by adding suffixes (see quots.). *Obs.* **2.** A Negro thought of as having the humble, pious, long-suffering attitude of Uncle Tom of Stowe's novel.

(1) 1853 in T. S. Perry *Life F. Lieber* 257 Our papers have coined a word—*Uncle-Tomitude*—to sneer at the sympathy with the African. **1853** *Putnam's Mo.* Jan. 99/2 India, and Mexico, and South America, have yet to be Uncle Tomitized. *Ib.* 100/1 One of our newspaper critics compares the Uncle Tomific, which the reading world is now suffering from, to the yellow fever. — **(2) 1927** Benét *J. B.'s Body* 18 The South, that languorous land where Uncle Toms Groaned Biblically underneath the lash, And grinning Topsies mopped and mowed behind Each honeysuckle vine. **1943** Ottley *New World* 238 The followers of the Tuskegee educator today are mainly Southerners. . . . These Southern leaders, sometimes called 'Uncle Toms' by the more radical Negroes, apparently have not made up their minds which way to turn in the present crisis.

* **unconditional,** *a.* **1. Unconditional Surrender,** Gen. U.S. Grant, a nickname. **2. Unconditional Union man,** in the campaign of 1864, a supporter of the administration, a member of the National Union party professing the ideal of "the unconditional maintenance of the Union." *Obs.*

(1) [1862 Grant *Memoirs* I. 255 No terms except an unconditional and immediate surrender can be accepted. I propose to move immediately upon your works.] **1864** *Harper's Mag.* March 568/1 If that butter don't outrank old Unconditional Surrender by a great sight, then I'll never draw trigger on another reb! **[1944** Pennell *Rome Hanks* 39 The very officers and the very unlicked rookies . . . began to wish for Old Sam Grant before he came back to them (Good Old Unconditional, they said!).] **1946** Adams *Album Amer. Hist.* III. 122 When the defenders of Fort Donelson asked for terms, Gen. U.S. Grant offered only 'Unconditional surrender,' which expression, coupled with his initials, gave him the nickname of 'Unconditional Surrender' Grant. — **(2) 1864** *Rio Abajo Press* 12 April 1/3 The Unconditional Union Men of this Territory are respectfully requested to send Delegates to a Territorial Convention.

* **unconstitutional,** *a.* At variance with the provisions of the Federal Constitution of 1787.

1789 *Jrnl. of Wm. Maclay* (1927) 86, I read the Constitution by which the affirmation is left open to every one, and called the whole clause unconstitutional. **1890** *Stock Grower & Farmer* 31 May 3/3 The meat inspection law has been declared unconstitutional by the supreme court of the United States. **1949** *Chi. D. News* 12 March 8/7 The Supreme Court . . . ruled that any law which discriminates against the press as such is unconstitutional.

Also **unconstitutionable.** *Rare.*

1825 *Nat. Crisis* (Cin.) 8 Aug. 3/2 It is *unconstitutionable*, and therefore it is only a decree.

unconstitutionality ʌnˌkɑnstəˌt(j)uʃəˈnælɪtɪ, *n.* The quality of not being in accordance with the Federal Constitution of 1787.

[**1782** *Boston Rec.* 283 These Circumstances . . . are sufficient to demonstrate its Unconstitutionality in the Mode of Procedure should it [an act for more effectual observance of the Sabbath] be adopted.] **1795** Washington *Writings* XIII. 73 Any further sentiment now on the unconstitutionality of the measure would be received too late. **1862** *Harper's Mag.* Aug. 368/1 The new scheme . . . ingrafted upon that old system of duties on imports the policy of protection in such a form that it was not obnoxious to the charge of unconstitutionality. **1894** *Columbus* (O.) *Dispatch* 6 June, Judge Ricks' decision seems to prepare the way for the departure of the law from the statute books by the pathway of unconstitutionality.

Uncpapa ˈʌnkˌpɑpə, *n.* Variant of Hunkpapa *q.v.* — **1947** *Westerners' Brand Book* 29 Sitting Bull with his following of Uncpapas was in camp near the river away from the others.

undemocratize ʌndəˈmɑkrəˌtaɪz, *v. tr.* To make undemocratic. *Rare.* — **1876** *N. Amer. Rev.* Oct. 255 Its consequence was to undemocratize the Democratic party and secure its final defeat.

* **under.** Used with the force of an adj., adv., or prep., and also as a prefix, in compounds and combs.: (1) **underbill,** *v. tr.* to bill (goods) at less than the proper measure or amount, also **underbilling,** *n.;* (2) **brush,** see as a main entry; (3) **classman,** *n.* a student in one of the lower classes in a school or college; (4) **cleats,** *n. pl.* a dance or dance step, *rare;* (5) **clerk,** a subordinate clerk on a river steamboat, cf. **mud clerk;** (6) **cover agent,** one who secures evidence against criminals by associating with them or by working where those with whom he comes in contact do not know his real status or purpose; (7) * **current,** *n.* in mining, a shallow receptacle into which water is diverted from a sluice, with the object of catching the finer material; (8) * **cut,** (*a*) *n.* (see quot. 1905), (*b*) *v. tr.* to make an undercut in (a tree), hence **undercutter,** *n.;* (9) **dog,** the loser in a dog fight, also *fig.*, a person in a position of inferiority, esp. a victim of misfortune or injustice; (10) * **foot,** *adv., fig.* in the way, *colloq.;* (11) **go,** *n.* (see quot.), *rare;* (12) * **ground,** see as a main entry; (13) **hew,** *v. tr.* (see quot.); (14) **hold,** *n.* (and, perhaps, *adv.*), a wrestling hold in which one man grasps the other below the arms; (15) **keel,** (*a*) *n.* an earmark denoting ownership cut in the lower edge of the ear of a domestic animal, *obs.*, (*b*) also **underkeeled,** *a.*, marked with an underkeel, *obs.;* (16) **pass,** *n.* (see quot. 1909); (17) **rake,** (see quot. 1890); (18) * **take,** *v. intr.* (see quot. 1891); (19) **waist,** a waist worn beneath another garment.

(1) 1872 *Chi. Tribune* 20 Nov. 4/4 A committee of the Chicago Board of Trade appointed to investigate the abuse of the 'underbilling' of grain when shipped in bulk by rail have made a report. **1872** *Ib.* 20 Nov. 4/4 The shippers and interior points have thus been tempted to 'underbill' the quantity or weight in order to save railroad freights. **1889** *Advance* 17 Jan., The bribing of a railroad servant to underbill goods or in some other way to give an advantage to a shipper. — **(3) 1871** Bagg *At Yale* 490 Under-class men and graduates can enjoy much that is beyond the reach of others. **1904** *N.Y. Ev. Post* 4 May 4 In Cambridge—unless we are underclassmen—we walk more slowly than in New York. — **(4)** *a***1846** *Quarter Race Ky.* 178 When my time came [in the dance] therefore, I . . . commenced . . . 'Pete Jonson's knock,' 'the under cleets,' and other *refined* steps.

(5) 1883 Mark Twain *Life on Miss.* xix. 227 But that was his way: he never condescended to take notice of an under-clerk. — **(6) 1929** *Variety* 10 April 6/1 It was originally designed by the inventor for under-cover agents and prohibition tipsters looking for evidence. — **(7) 1876** Raymond *8th Rep. Mines* 95 The company has this season added a series of under-currents near the point where the washings empty into the river. — **(8)** (*a*) **1883** *Harper's Mag.* Jan. 201/1 In about an hour the undercut had approached the heart of the tree. **1905** *Forestry Bureau Bul.* No. 61, 52 *Undercut*, the notch cut in a tree to determine the direction in which the tree is to fall, and to prevent splitting. (*b*) **1851** Springer *Forest Life* 52 A smaller tree is undercut and lodged against it. **1905** *Forestry Bureau Bul.* No. 61, 52 *Undercutter*, a skilled woodman who chops the undercut in trees so that they shall fall in the proper direction. — **(9) 1879** B. F. Taylor *Summer-Savory* 140 It smells of old geographies . . . and readers with ragged edges like the ears of 'the under dog' in the fight. **1904** *N.Y. Ev. Post* 12 May 7 Ever since the period of chaos known as the Reconstruction era, the negro has been the under dog in Southern Republicanism. **1946** *Casper* (Wyo.) *Tribune-Herald* 29 March 9/3 The underdog won once and the other two bouts ended in draws.

(10) 1891 *Harper's Mag.* June 62/1 He muttered something about children being underfoot and staring at such times. **1946** *This Week Mag.* 7 Sep. 29/3 When the men came back some months ago they found it necessary to move in also. Everybody got underfoot. — **(11) 1875** Holland *Sevenoaks* 123 They were blue undergoes—in other words, blue flannel shirts. — **(13) 1841** Webster II. 855/1 *Underhew*, to hew a piece of timber which should be square, in such a manner, that it appears to contain a greater number of cubic feet than it really does. *Haldiman* [*sic*]. — **(14) 1835** Longstreet *Ga. Scenes* 62 Before Billy could recover his balance—Bob had him 'all under-hold.' **1880** N. Brooks *Fairport Nine* 116 Tom Tilden . . . invited the captive to a rough-and-tumble wrestle, no tripping, underhold, and no biting nor pulling hair.

(15) (*a*) **1677** *New Castle Court Rec.* 68 John Street in oppoquenemen his marke—a Crop on Each Eare and underkiell on the Right Eare. **1773** in Summers *Ann. S.W. Va.* 596 It is ordered that his Mark be Recorded a small fork in the Right ear and under keel in the left ear. (*b*) **1648** *Md. Archives* IV. 379 One blackish pyed browne Cow . . . slit on the left eare & underkeeld. **1681** *New Castle Court Rec.* 448 Twoo Cropps and underkeeld on ye Left Eare. — **(16) 1909** Webster, under-pass. . . . A passage beneath, as where a road goes under a railroad. **1949** *Chi. D. News* 16 Dec. 3/1 Mayor Kennelly will open the 83d st. underpass under the Illinois Central tracks at Dorchester av. — **(17) 1879** *R.I. Acts & Resolves* Jan. Sess. 180 Nothing in the next preceding section shall be construed to prevent any citizen of this state from taking oysters in Point Judith ponds, . . . by a certain instrument . . . known by the name of an under-rake. **1890** *Cent.*

4946/1 *Under-rake*, a kind of oyster-rake, used mostly through holes in the ice, with handle 15 to 20 feet long, head 1 to 2 feet wide, and iron teeth 6 to 10 inches long. — **(18)** [**1786** *Boston Rec.* 293 The names of the Persons who are willing to Undertake the charge of Funerals.] **1891** *Cent.* 6599/3 *Undertake*, . . . to manage funerals, and arrange all the details for burying the dead. (Colloq.) — **(19) 1857** in A. ALLEN *Life P. Brooks* I. 209 Thick winter underwaists and socks. **1906** FREEMAN *By Light of Soul* 333 Maria had a beautiful neck showing above the lace of her underwaist.

underbrush ˈʌndɚˌbrʌʃ, *n.* In a forest, the shrubs and low trees forming the undergrowth.

1775 *Essex Inst. Coll.* L. 107 The fire ran among the leaves & dry underbrush for upwards of a mile. **1870** KEIM *Sheridan's Troopers* 302 Suddenly a crashing of underbrush was heard not more than twenty feet off. **1904** GLASGOW *Deliverance* 47 The dogs . . . started a rabbit once from the close cover of the underbrush.

transf. **1888** *Kans. Hist. Coll.* IV. (1890) 274 Yet the underbrush of forgetfulness has so grown that but few in Kansas know that Joel K. Goodin ever lived.

Also as a verb, sometimes fig.

1832 TRAILL *Backwoods* 100 Those that understand the proper management of uncleared land, usually underbrush (that is, cut down all the small timbers and brushwood), while the leaf is yet on them. **1896** *Home Missionary* Jan. 461 The minister . . . begins to underbrush and cut down the giant sins that have grown.

∗ **underground,** *n.*

1. = **underground railroad.** Now *hist.*

1852 STOWE *Uncle Tom* vii, I know the way of all of 'em,—they makes tracks for the underground. **1946** ADAMS *Album Amer. Hist.* III. 51 Levi Coffin of Wayne County, Ind., was a typical operator of the 'Underground.'

attrib. **1852** STOWE *Uncle Tom* viii, The gal's been carried on the underground line up to Sandusky or so. **1883** *Harper's Mag.* Aug. 331/1 The Rev. Robert W. Oliver . . . helped a number of fugitive slaves to freedom by the underground route.

b. *transf.* Any secret or surreptitious means of communication. Also attrib.

1859 J. REDPATH *Roving Editor* 287 The Canadian fugitives understand it; and are thoroughly systematizing this Underground Telegraph. **1945** *Chi. D. News* 20 Jan. 4/6 Our underground reports that federal probation officers have granted unusual dispensations.

2. In special combs.: (1) **underground forest,** (see quot.); (2) **moon,** (see quot.); (3) **railroad,** see as a main entry; (4) **railway,** = **underground railroad,** also transf. and attrib.

(1) 1890 *Cent.* 3727/1 Under the action of prairie fires it [*sc.* mesquite] is reduced to a low shrub, developing then an enormous mass of roots, locally known as *underground forest*, of great value as fuel. — **(2) 1905** *Boston Herald* 6 July 7/5 An 'underground moon' is simply one which makes its change at 'no hours'—between 12 and 1 o'clock—according to the traditions of Nantucket. The 'underground moon' is a seafaring phrase. — **(4) 1856** FERGUSSON *America* 439 This is called 'the underground railway.' It consists of persons who are prepared to hide such fugitives during the day, and assist them on, from one to another, under cover of the night. **1910** *Pacific Mo.* Feb. 185/2 Knowing all the ins and outs of the 'Underground Railway Systems,' it was an easy matter for the smugglers to bring in Chinese by the boat-load along with opium. **1949** *Chi. Tribune* 25 Sep. 28/5 Slaves were taken under the building to be hidden and cared for until they could be safely passed along on the 'Underground Railway' to the north and freedom.

underground railroad. (Also *cap.*) A system of coöperation brought into existence *c*1832 by those actively opposed to slavery whereby they secretly assisted fugitive slaves to reach the North or Canada. Also attrib. Now *hist.*

1842 *N.Y. Semi-Wkly. Express* 28 Sep. 1/5 We passed 26 prime slaves to the land of freedom last week. . . . All went by 'the underground railroad.' **1857** *Lawrence* (Kans.) *Republican* 11 June 2 He is . . . charged with being in correspondence with underground railroad directors. **1946** ADAMS *Album Amer. Hist.* III. 51 'The Underground Railroad' a system by which runaway slaves were passed from one friendly Northern hideout to another until they were beyond capture, irritated the South.

transf. **1949** *Sat. Ev. Post* 4 June 29/2, I was escorted by a leader of a Russian underground railroad which helps escapees in their flight.

Also **U.G.R.R.** in transf. use. *Obs.*

1862 *Dly. Richmond* (Va.) *Enquirer* 3 Feb. 3/4 (*heading*), Our 'Local' Visits Lincolndom—A Trip to Baltimore and Back by the 'U.G.R.R.'

unearned run. In baseball, a run scored because of an error on the part of the side scored against. Cf. **earned run.** — **1875** *Chi. Tribune* 16 Sep. 8/4 The Athletics made four unearned runs by the errors of McMullin, Meyerle, and Fulmer. **1949** *Telephone Reg.* (McMinnville, Ore.) 4 Aug. 2/1 In the eighth Willamette tallied four unearned runs off Dick Ridgeway.

unfair ball. *Baseball.* (See quot.) *Obs.* — **1867** *Ball Players' Chron.* 4 July 1/2 Both in regard to 'strikes' and 'called' balls, the umpire in a match can neither call a 'strike' or a 'ball' until he has first *warned* the pitcher, and the pitcher has *repeatedly* pitched unfair balls. *Ib.* 5/1 Unfair balls are those out of the legitimate reach of the batsman.

∗ **ungraded,** *a.* **1.** Not laid out in, or brought to, proper gradients, used esp. of roads. **2. ungraded school,** an elementary school in which the pupils are not grouped into grades according to their advancement. Cf. **grade school, graded school.**

(1) 1845 JUDD *Margaret* I. 33 The roads rough, ungraded, and divided by parallel lines of green grass. **1885** *Atlantic Mo.* April 467/1 These roadways [are] ungraded, unsewered, and unpaved. — **(2) 1904** *Jrnl. Educ.* 26 May 331 Henry Sabin knows that need of the common schools, especially the ungraded schools, as well as any man in America. **1907** *Chi. Ev. Post* 4 May 3 Yesterday was the annual visiting day for the teachers in the ungraded schools of Cook County.

ungranted land. Public land that has not been disposed of to individual owners. *Obs.*

1715 *Mass. H. Rep. Jrnl.* I. 62 All the ungranted land lying between the two rivers and the frontier towns. **1798** I. ALLEN *Hist. Vermont* 111 It was thought good policy . . . to raise a sufficient revenue out of the property confiscated and the ungranted land. **1834** *N.H. Hist. Soc. Coll.* IV. 217 Between Hillsborough . . . and New Boston . . . lay a large tract of ungranted land.

unhandselled ʌnˈhænsl̩d, *a.* Untouched, unimproved. *Obs.* — **1837** EMERSON *Works* I. (1903) 99 Not out of those on whom systems of education have exhausted their culture, comes the helpful giant to destroy the old or build the new, but out of unhandselled savage nature. **1848** THOREAU *Maine Woods* 70 Here was no man's garden, but the unhandselled globe.

∗ **unicorn,** *n.*

1. A colicroot, *Aletris farinosa.*

1784 *Amer. Acad. Mem.* I. 435 Unicorn. On high land in Killingfly in the state of Connecticut. It is said to be useful in chronic rheumatism. **1795** WINTERBOTHAM *Hist. View* III. 397 Among the . . . plants of New-England, the following have been employed for medicinal purposes: . . . Adder's tongue, *Convallaria bifolia.* Unicorn, *Aletris farinosa.*

2. In combs.: (1) **unicorn plant,** an annual, *Martynia louisiana*, the fruit of which ends in long beaklike processes, or a plant resembling this; (2) **root,** (see quot. 1891); (3) **-'s horn,** = prec.

(1) 1817–8 EATON *Botany* (1822) 349 Unicorn plant. Western states. . . . Fruit somewhat gourd-like, with one long horn. **1942** CASTETTER & BELL *Pima & Papago Agric.* 113 Pima and Papago anciently utilized the pods of devil's claw or unicorn plant (*Martynia louisiana*) in basketry. — **(2) 1817–8** EATON *Botany* (1822) 166 False aloe, unicorn root, false star grass . . . [is used] as a moderate cathartic. **1891** *Cent.* 6615/3 unicorn-root. . . The blazing-star, *Aletris farinosa.* **1901** MOHR *Plant Life Ala.* 436 *Chamaelirium luteum.*—Devil's Bit. . . . The root, called 'starwort,' or 'unicorn root,' is used medicinally. — **(3) 1840** DEWEY *Mass. Flowering Plants* 205 *Helonias dioica.* Blazing Star, Devil's Bit, Unicorn's Horn; . . . wet situations on hills. **1891** *Cent.* 6615/3.

unicycle ˈjunɪˌsaɪkl̩, *n.* (See quot. 1883.)

1869 *Velocipede* (N.Y.) April 76 Hemming's Unicycle or 'Flying Yankee Velocipede.' **1883** KNIGHT *Supp.* 913/1 *Unicycle*, a one-wheeled vehicle for propulsion by foot-power. **1949** *Time* 16 May 71/2 Berle can sing, dance, juggle, act, do card tricks, imitations and acrobatics, ride a unicycle and mug under water.

unicyclist ˈjunɪˌsaɪklɪst, *n.* A circus performer who rides a unicycle. — **1881** *Sells Bros. Show Bill*, Celebrated Russian Bicyclists, Unicyclists, and Roller Skaters. **1949** *Newsweek* 16 May 56 Acrobats and unicyclists also get in the act.

∗ **uniform,** *v. tr.* To dress or put in uniform.

1861 NORTON *Army Lett.* 12 We are to be uniformed and equipped immediately. **1884** *Harper's Mag.* April 752/1 At one of their gatherings in 1789, there was a company of 'School-boy Federalists' to the number of 250, uniformed in blue and white. **1902** *Munsey's Mag.* 504/2 He established an élite cavalry corps and uniformed it in the most dazzling creation.

unimproved land. Land not in use, esp. land not used for farming.

1679 *Providence Rec.* VIII. (1895) 43 The quantity of their Land & Meadows Layd out to them, jmproved & vnjmproved. **1815** DRAKE *Cincinnati* 53 The prices of good unimproved land, are between fifty and one hundred and fifty dollars per acre. **1881** *Mich. Gen. Statutes* (1882) I. 391 Commissioners shall also have power to lay out and establish highways on section lines, through uninclosed and unimproved lands.

* **union,** *n.* and *a.*

1. *n.* A number of American colonies or states united into one national confederation, esp. (*cap.*) the United States.

1754 *Mass. H.S. Coll.* 3 Ser. V. 27 A motion was made that the Commissioners deliver their opinion whether a Union of all the Colonies is not at present absolutely necessary for their security and defence. **1775** JEFFERSON *Writings* IV. 251 A committee of Congress is gone to improve circumstances, so as to bring the Canadians into our Union. **1862** LINCOLN in Kettell *Hist. Rebellion* II. 638 My paramount object is to save the Union, and not either to save or destroy slavery. **1950** *Newsweek* 20 March 96/2 At this critical juncture, the impetuous Texans threatened to join England unless they were admitted to the Union.

One form of unicycle

b. The Northern, as distinguished from the Confederate, states.

[**1861** *Charleston* (S.C.) *Mercury* 4 Jan. 1/2 *Resolved*, That our Representatives . . . call a Convention of the people of the State to determine . . . whether North Carolina shall become the degraded member of a Northern Union, or a sovereign State in a Southern Confederacy.] **1885** *Harper's Mag.* Aug. 364/2 'Most of these mountaineers were stanch toh the Union,' said the Virginian, with a shrug. **1947** *True* Nov. 40/2 The Union had its hands full with the Civil War.

c. *pl.* Union soldiers during the Civil War. *Rare.*

1874 MARK TWAIN *Sk. New & Old* 204 When de Unions took dat town, dey all run away an' lef' me all by myse'f.

2. *a.* (*cap.*) Designating religious principles, activities, etc., relating to two or more coöperating religious sects. Cf. **Union church** as a main entry.

1834 PECK *Gaz. Illinois* 203 There are three lawyers, . . . a good English school, a Sunday school and Bible class, conducted on union principles. **1878** COOKE *Happy Dodd* 15 These were not the days of Union lessons, or Sunday-school papers, or helps. **1896** *Home Missionary* (N.Y.) Oct. 233 The Congregationalists . . . join leadingly in the Union Sunday-school. **1949** *Reading* (Pa.) *Times* 21 Dec. 25 St. Thomas Union Sunday School elected officers for the next year.

b. Union meeting, a religious meeting participated in by people of different sects (see also quot. 1884).

1871 DE VERE 246 It is gratifying to think . . . how triumphantly the fraternal love among all Christians has been proven by the Union meetings held in all the States. **1884** *Schaff's Relig. Encycl.* III. 2169/2 Meetings are held [by the Shakers] . . . for social converse, called 'Union Meetings.'

3. Loyal to the U.S., or to the Union cause during the Civil War. Now *hist.* Cf. **4. b.** below.

1836 *New-Yorker* 26 Nov. 155/1 The only political changes are the success of Hon. Hugh S. Legare, over Mr. Pinckney . . . , and of Mr. Clowney, 'State Rights,' over Gen. Rogers, 'Union.' **1861** *Alexandria* (Va.) *Gaz.* 2 May 4/5 The county . . . gave Early and Sands, Union, over Dillard and Hamilton, Secessionists, more than a thousand majority. **1863** BOUDRYE *Fifth N.Y. Cavalry* (1868) 339 An oyster man. . . . Was Union on the York, but Secesh on James river. **1883** BAGBY *Old Va. Gentleman* 148 His auditors [were] in doubt whether he was Union or secesh, or simply a crank. **1927** BENÉT *J. B.'s Body* 104 A british steamer . . . stopped by a Captain Wilkes and a Union cruiser.

4. In special combs.: (1) **unionalls,** =**overalls;** (2) **ball,** (see quot.), *obs.;* (3) **card,** a card issued to one who is a member of a labor union; (4) **catalogue,** a library catalogue formed by combining catalogues of different libraries; (5) **church,** see as a main entry; (6) **depot,** a railroad depot that serves two or more lines; (7) **garment,** (see quot.); (8) **high school,** (see quot. 1948 and cf. **consolidated school**), also attrib.; (9) **Labor party,** a minor political party organized in 1887 by farm and labor groups and elements of the Greenback party, *obs.;* (10) **leather,** (see quot.); (11) **linen,** (see quot.), *obs.;* (12) **pope,** (see quot.), *obs.;* (13) **school,** see as a main entry; (14) **station,** =**union depot;** (15) **stockyards,** stockyards maintained by several packing houses for their mutual convenience; (16) **suit,** an undergarment of which the upper and lower portions are together in one piece; (17) **ticket,** see as a main entry; (18) **undergarment,** an undergarment of which the upper and the lower portions are in one piece.

(1) 1927 EUBANK *Horse & Buggy Days* 32 His boy was . . . riding under the shade of a silk umbrella smoking a cigarette and wearing balloon unionalls, on a cushioned seat of a combine pulled by a tractor. — **(2) 1844** *Lowell Offering* IV. 90 There was to be a 'Union ball;' or an assembly in which the 'different classes' should meet. — **(3) 1874** *Internat. Typog. Union Proc.* 84 The International Typographical Union shall issue . . . a card, with appropriate designs, to be called the 'Union Card.' **1947** MOTLEY *Knock on Any Door* 135 There was a billfold. It had fifty-four dollars in it. And pictures, a union card, a social security card. — **(4) 1910** BOSTWICK *Amer. Pub. Library* 250 A good interbranch loan system requires a union catalogue.

(6) 1862 *Dinsmore's R.R. Guide* No. 101 All changes by this route, from New York to the Mississippi river, made in union depots. **1948** *Minneapolis Star* 17 Sep. 28/2 St. Paul is promoting railroads today with displays in the Union depot there which depict rail services to towns. — **(7) 1904** *Nation* 21 Jan. 51 [Overalls are] what would be called nowadays a 'union garment,' lacking the sleeves. — **(8) 1936** *Univ. Ariz. Gen. Bul.* No. 3, 267 The union high-school districts came into existence with a law passed in 1917. **1948** *Dly. Ardmoreite* (Ardmore, Okla.) 11 July 21/4 In the south, many rural schools are 'consolidated schools,' . . . while in the west such schools are known as 'union high schools.' — **(9) 1891** in B. S. HEATH *Labor & Finance Rev.* p. xxxvi, The proceedings of this convention . . . have gone into the history of the Union Labor party there organized.

(10) 1885 *Harper's Mag.* Jan. 279/2 'Union' leather designates a combination of oak and hemlock tannage. — **(11) 1830** *Coshocton* (Ohio) *Spy* 12 May 1/2 The editor of the Wheeling Gazette, mentions having lately purchased . . . a parcel of 'union linen' (cotton chain and flax filling) at 25 cents per yard, . . . and adds: . . . it is very far superior to any *imported* linen . . . at the same price. — **(12) 1823** TUDOR *Otis* 29 [The factions of 'Pope Day'] had what was called an *Union Pope*, when the two parties, after great preparations, met with their pageants, and . . . proceeded to make a common bonfire. — **(14) 1901** ADE *40 Modern Fables* 224 Farmers . . . come out of the Union Station carrying . . . Shoe Boxes full of Lunch. **1948** *Our Sunday Visitor* 3 Oct. 8/3 In the large union station where we had coffee and the substantials, groups of young men thronged.

(15) 1867 *Chi. Times* 15 July 5/1 The new mission building just completed at the Union stock-yards, and to be known as the 'Union Stock-Yards Mission,' was dedicated yesterday. **1900** *Kans. Gazetteer* 1298 The Union Stock Yards of Chicago receive the greatest number of animals. — **(16) 1901** GRINNELL *Gold Hunting in Alaska* 54 The union suit is an awkward thing to handle in washing. **1944** *Sears Cat.* (ed. 189) 175 Pilgrim lightweight cotton Union Suits. — **(18) 1896** *Godey's Mag.* Feb. 218/2 Union undergarments of silk or wool are often substituted.

b. (*cap.*) In combs., now obs. or hist., pertaining to the Federal Union, esp. during the Civil War: (1) **Union anaconda,** = * **anaconda;** (2) **army,** an army of the U.S. during the Civil War; (3) **cause,** the Northern or federal cause during the Civil War; (4) **cockade,** a cockade signifying loyalty to the Union during the Revolution; (5) * **flag,** (*a*) the flag of the federated American colonies during the Revolutionary War, cf. **rattlesnake flag,** (*b*) during the Civil War the flag of the U.S. as distinguished from that of the Confederate States; (6) **gun,** (see quot.), *obs.*, cf. **Gatling gun;** (7) **League,** see as a main entry; (8) **man,** see as a main entry; (9) **money,** money issued by the federal government; (10) **party,** (*a*) in South Carolina, the political party composed of those who opposed the nullifiers, (*b*) a political party formed at the beginning of the Civil War by a fusion of Republicans and War Democrats in the Ohio Valley states; (11) **people,** those who favored the Union cause during the Civil War; (12) **Republican,** a member of the Republican party who gave staunch support to the war policy of President Lincoln, also attrib.; (13) **Saver,** (see quot. 1914); (14) **Scout,** (see quot.), *rare;* (15) **shrieker,** (see quot.), *rare;* (16) **soldier,** a soldier who served on the Northern or Union side during the Civil War, cf. **ex-Union soldier;** (17) **Whig,** a member of one of the factions of the Whig party.

(1) 1861 NEWELL *Orpheus C. Kerr* I. 312 'Surrender to the Union Anaconda and the United States of America,' thundered Villiam. — **(2) 1866** F. KIRKLAND *Bk. Anecdotes* 376 Colonel Bailey . . . [believed] that their capture or destruction would involve the destruction of the Union army. **1948** *Norman* (Okla.) *Transcript* 4 July 5/4 The native of Tennessee was 'drafted' into the Union army when the blue-clad army invaded the state. — **(3) 1862** GREELEY in Logan *Great Conspiracy* 432 There is not one . . . intelligent champion of the Union Cause who does not feel . . . that every hour of deference to Slavery is an hour of added and deepened peril. **1890** LANGFORD *Vigilante Days* (1912) 514 Early in the Summer of 1861 he espoused the Union cause. — **(4) 1798** DUNLAP *André* p. viii, Bland . . . [is] in the uniform of a Captain of horse—dress, . . . a horseman's helmet on the head, decorated as usual, and the union cockade affixed.

(5) (*a*) **1776** *Pa. Ev. Post* 28 May 266/2 The Union Flag of the American States waved upon the Capitol. (*b*) **1861** NORTON *Army Lett.* 14 He had a big fuss with the boys who put up a Union flag near his house. **1887** CUSTER *Tenting on Plains* 219 The girl had known of a Union flag in the State House, held in derision and scornfully treated by the extremists. — **(6) 1867** LATHAM *Black & White* 76 There were in the museum two very remarkable guns for keeping up a perpetual fire of rifle-balls upon an advancing enemy; the Gatling gun, . . . the other, the Nugent or Union gun, a somewhat similar single-barrelled revolver on wheels. — **(9) 1840** in *Nation* 85 (1907) 540/2, I met one man who offered to pay $3,000 in Union money, which could not be sold for more than 40c in the dollar.

(10) (*a*) **1831** J. Q. ADAMS *Memoirs* VIII. 449 Mr. James Blair, a member of the House of Representatives from South Carolina, . . . is of what they call the Union party. **1846** MANSFIELD *Winfield Scott* 231 The name of the party of the majority was known as the nullification party, and that of the minority as the Union party. **1851** *Miss. Palladium* (Holly Springs) 30 May 2/1 'W.' insists, first, that all who do not unite with the (Foote, *alias*) Union party, are Disunionists. (*b*) **1861** MRS. S. COWELL *Diary* 351 It is said that the Governors of Indiana and Illinois have made similar pledges to the Union party in Kentucky and Missouri. **1868** *Ore. State Jrnl.* 25 July 2/1 The great Union party was formed in 1861, for the purpose, in the first place, of saving the Republic from destruction at the hands of the conspirators. — **(11) 1865** KELLOGG *Rebel Prisons* 51 Among them were many Union people whose unmistakable expressions of sympathy did us much good. **1907** ANDREWS *Recoll.* 155 At Pikeville we were in the midst of Union people who wanted to take the oath of allegiance. — **(12) 1867** *Cong. Globe* 12 April 835/3 [These offices] were filled by Mr. Lincoln with good, responsible, reliable Union Republicans. **1886** LOGAN *Great Conspiracy* 599 The victory of the Union-Republican Party at this election was an amazing one. — **(13) 1860** *Charleston* (S.C.) *Mercury* 17 Nov. 2/4 Our enemies make endeavors to inundate the whole South with a flood of Union-savers. **1914** *Cyclo. Amer. Govt.* III. 594/1 *Union Saver,* the element of the Whig party during the two decades preceding the Civil War, which advocated compromising measures in dealing with slavery. — **(14) 1866** in *Sherman Lett.* (1894) 273 'Union Scouts' (alias Confederate jayhawkers and deserters) two years after kidnapped me.

(15) 1876 *S.F. Wkly. Examiner* 24 Aug. 2/5 The real boys in blue and boys in gray having long since fraternized, and all are now Union men, but not 'Union shriekers,' who live by fomenting a spirit of sectionalism and discord. — **(16) 1864** PENNIMAN *Tanner-Boy* 99 Only a short distance off was a large body of well-armed rebel troops ready, it was reported, to turn back on the entering Union soldiers at a given signal. **1945** *Time* 27 Aug. 75/2 Union soldiers harmonized *My Old Kentucky Home* around their campfires. — **(17) 1852** *Nat. Intelligencer* 26 July, Union Whigs and Southern Rights Whigs, Scott Whigs and anti-Scott Whigs, Pierce Whigs and anti-Pierce Whigs, stand still Whigs or those who wash their hands of both candidates.

Also, with reference to the Northern as opposed to the Southern cause during the Civil War, *Union fleet, lady, lines, lover, prisoner, refugee, sentiment, troops, woman, voter,* etc.

As the last term in **anti-, company, Constitutional, farmer's, Federal, labor, sister union.**

Union church. Orig. a church building used either by formal agreement or informally by several regularly organized congregations. In later use, a church maintained by members of various denominations each one of which is only weakly represented in the community.

In its earliest use this expression was a translation of the German *gemeinschaftliche Kirche.* See quot. 1841 below. Such use of a building in common by different congregations, esp. Lutheran and Reformed, goes back in eastern Pa. to *c*1741.

[**1841** in IRWIN H. DELONG *Early Nineteenth Cent. Constitution of a Union Church* (1931) 5 Urkunde von der Declaration, bei der Ecksteinlegung der Gemeinschaftlichen Kirche [St. Paul's Union Church, Fleetwood, Pa.], in Richmond Township, Berks County, Pennsylvania.] **1847** HOWE *Hist. Coll. Ohio* 24 Washington . . . has 1 Lutheran, 1 Presbyterian, 1 Methodist, 1 Union and 1 Catholic church. **1904** TARBELL *Hist. Standard Oil Co.* I. 35 It was not long . . . before there was a church, a union church. **1950** *Chi. D. News* 22 March 33/2 She became the wife of John E. Date Jr. in the Union Church of Hinsdale.

Unioner ˈjunjənɚ, *n.* An adherent of the Union cause during the Civil War. *Rare.* — **1879** TOURGEE *Fool's Errand* 99, I first heard of it in the mountains of East Tennessee, as instituted for self-protection and mutual support among the sturdy Unioners there in those trying times.

***Unionism,** *n.* Advocacy of, or allegiance to, federal union between states or to the Union cause during the Civil War. — **1861** COX *8 Yrs. in Congress* 23 In this work no one gave to General Millson more effective aid than Sherrard Clemens, of Wheeling, . . . whose Unionism never wavered. **1883** *American* VI. 92 The obstinate Unionism of the mountaineer farmers.

* **Unionist,** *n.*

1. A supporter of the Federal Union of the U.S., esp. with reference to nullification in South Carolina, and to the secession of the southern states. Now *hist.*

1830 D. WEBSTER *Works* III. 259, I am a unionist, and, in this sense, a national republican. **1861** *N.Y. Tribune* 26 Nov. 4/5 It was the cowardice of the Unionists of the South that created the seeming unanimity there for Secession. **1948** *Sat. Review* 24 July 11/2 Anna Carroll, with the aid of a Texas Unionist, had drawn up the plan for the Tennessee campaign which was accepted by the President and the War Department.

b. (See quot.) *Obs.*

1888 M. LANE in *America* 8 Nov. 15 *Unionists.*—The name assumed by the Woolly-heads after the split in the old Whig party in 1850. Also the name of the party that met at Baltimore and nominated Everett and Bell in the campaign of 1860.

2. One who belongs to a Union church. *Rare.*

1837 W. JENKINS *Ohio Gaz.* 416 The public buildings [include] . . . six houses of public worship, one belonging . . . to the unionists.

As the last term in **constitutional, Johnson, slave-owning Unionist.**

***Unionist,** *a.* Loyal to the Union cause during the Civil War. *Obs.* — **1863** DICEY *6 Mo.* II. 187 The Atlantic Monthly, the great New England Review, is very . . . staunchly Unionist, and more or less anti-slavery. **1865** *Atlantic Mo.* April 441/2 He found us thorough Unionist.

unionite ˈjunjənˌaɪt, *n.* [*Union*ville, Pa.] A silicate of alumina and lime occurring in various crystalline forms. — **1849** SILLIMAN in *Amer. Jrnl. Science* 2 Ser. VIII. 384 Unionite . . . in general appearance . . . somewhat resembles scapolite or spodumene. **1873** *Amer. Philos. Soc. Proc.* XIII. 374 Silliman described it under the name of *unionite.*

Union League.

1. A society established in the North in 1862 to stimulate and cultivate loyalty to the Union. Also attrib. *Obs.*

1863 in H. W. BELLOWS *Hist. Sk. Union League Club N.Y.* 37 The Union League . . . shall be [formed] to discountenance and rebuke by moral and social influences all disloyalty to the Federal Government. **1904** FLEMING *Documents re. Reconstruction* No. 3, 3 In 1862 when the outlook was gloomy for the Northern cause, the Union League movement began. . . . All resulted in the low ebb of loyalty to the government and caused the formation of 'Union Leagues' among those who were devoted to the Union.

2. A secret political organization among the newly freed Negroes just after the Civil War. Now *hist.*

1867 in FLEMING *Hist. Reconstruction* II. 18 You should organize Union Leagues and Republican clubs. **1893** *Harper's Mag.* Dec. 22/1 The negroes were enrolled by the carpetbag leaders in what was known as the Union League. **1947** LUMPKIN *Southerner* 81 But chiefly, Southern men cast the blame for the solid vote against them . . . on the Union or Loyal Leagues.

union man.

1. A man who places his loyalty to the Federal Union above that to any state or section; esp., during the Civil War, one in sympathy with the North. Often *cap.* Cf. **Unconditional Union man.**

1837 SHERWOOD *Gaz. Georgia* (ed. 3) 245 None but 'Union men reside in it,' i.e. Union men in contradistinction to States' right men or nullifiers. **1861** *Chi. Tribune* 26 May 1/3, 2,500 Secession troops are stationed there, for the express purpose of overawing the Union men. **1901** MONTGOMERY *Reminiscences* 9 A wealthy gentleman . . . named Batcheldor, was as ardent a secessionist as the doctor was a union man.

2. One who is a member of a trade union.

1885 *Bradstreet's* 26 Dec. 409/1 The company has never discharged any of its employes for being union men. **1916** WILSON *Somewhere* 168 A union man nowadays would do just enough to keep within the law.

union school. A school serving two or more contiguous school districts (see also quots. 1852, 1867). Also **union school district.**

1851 QUENTIN *Reisebilder* II. 56 Ich benutzte daher meine Anwesenheit an jenem Orte [N.Y. City], um die dortige 'Union-School' zu besuchen. **1852** *Ind. Hist. Soc. Pub.* III. 615 Union, or graded schools, for the terms are synonymous, are simply the schools of a given township, village or city, classified and arranged according to the attainments of the pupils. **1867** *Ore. State Jrnl.* 12 Jan. 2/3 In Michigan every town of 3,000 inhabitants is required to establish a Union school for both sexes. **1945** C. V. GOOD *Dict. Educ.* 138/1 district, union school: a type of local school unit formed by the uniting of two or more contiguous school districts for the purpose of providing elementary or secondary education, or both.

union ticket.

1. App. a political ticket which includes candidates of different political views. *Obs.*

1813 *Mass. H.S. Coll.* 2 Ser. II. 176 [In] the years 1809 and 1812 . . . a union ticket prevailed. **1837** *New-Yorker* 30 Sep. 442/2 The 'Union' (Adm.) ticket prevails throughout the Charter Elections, as it always does. **1850** LOWELL *Letters* I. 188, I shall vote the 'Union' ticket (half Free-soil, half Democrat). **1856** *Jackson Picket Guard* (Elkton, Md.) 24 Sep. 2/5 Come up to the chalk line, Fillmore men, and vote the 'Union' State ticket in Pennsylvania.

2. The ticket of the Constitutional Union (*q.v.* sense 2.) party, or of any one of various groups or parties purporting to support the Union. *Obs.*

1862 KETTELL *Hist. Rebellion* I. 37 The election was still further complicated by the nomination of a Union ticket. **1868** *Ore. State Jrnl.* 8 June 2/4 In Washington county the whole Union ticket is elected by an increased majority.

3. =**union card.**

1891 THANET *Otto the Knight* 19, I went to two or three cities, but I couldn't get work, having no union ticket.

* **unit,** *n.*

1. A group that is united or agreed in sentiment, opinion, determination, etc.

1903 D. M. DEWITT *Impeachment Andrew Jackson* 76 Trumbull and his Republican colleagues were a unit against his right to vote. **1932** GRAYSON *Leaders* 108 The people of the United States were by no means a unit as to the advisability or necessity of waging this war.

2. *Educ.* (See quot. 1906.)

1894 *U. of Chi. Wkly.* 4 Oct. 4/1 The system of majors and minors, units and flunks, is harder to understand than any other 'credit' method in operation among educational institutions. **1906** *1st Ann. Rep. Carnegie Foundation* 38 College entrance requirements are designated in terms of units, a unit being a course of five periods weekly throughout an academic year of the preparatory school. **1945** *Mt. Holyoke College Bul.* 24 The requirements for admission to the freshman class include subjects aggregating sixteen units.

3. unit rule, a rule whereby in a political convention a majority of a delegation casts the entire vote of that delegation.

This method of voting is a characteristic of Democratic national conventions. It is said to have originated in the Massachusetts delegation to the Whig convention of 1839, its purpose being to secure the defeat of Clay and the nomination of Harrison. See J. B. Bishop, *Our Political Drama* (1904) 32–3.

1884 *Cent. Mag.* Nov. 125 A device called the 'unit rule,' whereby the whole vote of the delegation is thrown by a majority of its members. **1896** *Cin. Enquirer* 10 July 9/9 In behalf of Alabama Chairman Bankhead announced that but for the unit rule five delegates would vote for the substitute. **1949** *Dly. Ardmoreite* (Ardmore, Okla.) 23 Feb. 11/4 The amendment would mean 'a real two-party system in the south and in other so-called solid areas where the unit rule has perpetuated one party government.'

* **United,** *a.* In combs.: (1) **United Baptists,** (see quot.), *obs.;* (2) **Brethren,** (*a*) the Moravians, (*b*) a denomination which was organized in Maryland in 1800 under the leadership of the Rev. P. W. Otterbein and Martin Boehm, in full **United Brethren in Christ,** cf. **Otterbein Methodist;** (3) **Colonies,** (*a*) the New England colonies of Massachusetts Bay, Plymouth, Connecticut, and New Haven which bound themselves together in 1643 for protection against the Indians, French, and Dutch, (*b*) the colonies or states which united against Great Britain at the opening of the Revolutionary War; (4) **Nations,** =**Five Nations,** *obs.*, cf. **Six United Nations;** (5) **Order,** (see quot.); (6) **ranger,** a U.S. ranger, *rare;* (7) **Republic,** the U.S.; (8) **States,** see as a main entry; (9) **Zion's Children,** an offshoot of the River Brethren *q.v.*

(1) **1889** P. BUTLER *Recollections* 253 'Hardshell' Baptists . . . wish to be known as Old Baptists, or United Baptists, for they allege that they are the lineal descendants of the United Baptists, and that the Missionary Baptists have apostatized. — (2) (*a*) **1753** in *Mem. of Monuments Erected by Moravian Hist. Soc.* (1860) 67 [We are] confirmed in the choice we have made of one of the United Brethren to be our minister. **1876** *Moravian Hist. Soc. Trans.* I. 11 The Nazareth congregation of the United Brethren presented us with a room in the old stone mansion. (*b*) [**1800** in DRURY *Hist. Church United Brethren in Christ* 183 Von Die Vereinigte Bruederschaft zu Christo.] **1822** *Discipline United Brethren in Christ* (1895) 70 They there united themselves into a society, which bears the name of *'The United Brethren in Christ'*; and elected William Otterbein and Martin Bœhm as superintendents or bishops. **1919** *Census: Religious Bodies 1916* II. 696 The polity of the United Brethren is similar to that of the Methodist Episcopal Church. **1949** *Pa. Dutchman* 30 June 1/4 Then there was *Philip William Otterbein,* that warm-hearted Pietist who helped to found the great United Brethren Church. — (3) (*a*) **1643** *Plymouth Laws* 309 They all be and henceforth bee called by the Name of *The United Colonies of New-England.* **1682** RAWLINSON *Narr. Captivity* Pref. 1 The Narrhagansets quarters . . . were the second time beaten up by the Forces of the united Colonies. **1949** *Hobbies* Oct. 132/2 The doubloon is credited with being the first gold piece struck by the United Colonies. (*b*) **1775** *Mass. H.S. Coll.* 3 Ser. V. 75 We acquainted you yesterday from whence we came, and by whose authority; namely, by the authority of the Twelve United Colonies dwelling upon this island of America. **1866** LOWELL *Biglow P. Introd.* Poems (1890) II. 195 *To fix,* in the American sense, I find used by the Commissioners of the United Colonies as early as 1765. — (4) **1745** *Pa. Col. Rec.* V. 8 We were inclinable to speak to the Indians of the United Nations separately.

(5) **1905** *Out West* Sep. 244 One of the first steps taken by the Prophet, after the establishment of headquarters at Kirtland, was the institution of what Latter-day Saints call the 'United Order,' a religio-social system, communal in its character, designed to abolish poverty, monopoly, and kindred evils, and to bring about unity and equality in temporal and spiritual things. — (6) **1857** *Ill. Agric. Soc. Trans.* II. 362, I was a private united ranger during the year 1813. — (7) **1832** DUNLAP *Hist. Amer. Theatre* 36 [Boston] now holds but a third place in the scale of political importance among the cities of the United Republic. — (9) **1909** WEBSTER. **1938** HARK *Hex Marks Spot* 101 Mathias Brinser . . . and his followers promptly started a sect of their own known as the United Zion's Children—or Brinserites, as they're commonly called—and that made still another faction.

* **United States.**

1. The republic or Federal Union of North America. Cf. **U.S.**

1776 *Jrnls. Cont. Congress* VI. 865 Resolved, That the inhabitants of Canada, captivated by the United States . . . be released and sent home. **1810** PIKE *Sources Miss.* 97 The crime was committed long before the United States assumed its authority, and . . . no law of theirs could affect it. **1900** *Cong. Rec.* 20 Feb. 2004/2 Chief Justice Marshall used language which implies that the 'United States' means the States and Territories. **1950** *Time* 8 May 19/3 The United States needs to know who are with us.

b. In full **United States of America.**

1776 *Battle of Brooklyn* I. iv, My dear General, the great the important day advances; big with the fate of empire, in the United States of America. **1806** FESSENDEN *Democracy Unveiled* I. 121 (*footnote*), Freedonia is a cant phrase, which certain small poets or prosaic scribblers . . . would have us adopt as an appellative to designate the United States of America. **1917** in SCOTT *Wilson's Foreign Policy* 274 The Imperial German Government has committed repeated acts of war against the Government and the people of the United States of America.

2. The English language as written and spoken in the U.S. *Colloq.*

1879 BURDETTE *Hawkeyes* 248 There should be a law compelling railroad people to speak United States. **1900** *Cong. Rec.* 5 Feb. 1516/2 Suppose the appointee is simply a good American citizen who speaks only good 'United States.' **1949** *Chi. D. News* 19 Nov. 6/5 He says the new party declaration should be rewritten in plain United States.

b. *To talk United States,* to use plain and forceful language. *Colloq.*

1883 *Harper's Mag.* Sep. 561/1 The architects are still sometimes exhorted, to 'talk United States.' **1898** HAMBLEN *Gen. Manager's Story* 134 If he made any disparaging comments . . . , I vowed to myself that I'd talk United States to him if I lost my job by it.

3. In combs.: (1) **United States bank,** either one of two banks chartered by Congress in 1791 and 1816, also **United States Bank Agency,** now *hist.;* (2) **eagle,** the bald eagle, the symbol of the U.S., cf. ∗**eagle 1;** (3) **Grant,** (see quot.), *obs.;* (4) **marshal,** a federal officer serving by appointment in a judicial district of the U.S. and executing the processes of U.S. courts; (5) **regular,** a soldier in the regular army of the U.S.

(1) **1819** MCMURTRIE *Sk. Louisville* 116 Upon the location of a Branch of the United States Bank here, . . . these same lots . . . rose to 800 dollars per foot. **1837** in MACKENZIE *Van Buren* (1846) 178 The amount of payments to the Morris Canal and United States Bank Agency, as I am informed, would be about $12,000,000. **1913** A. C. COLE *Whig Party in South* 25 Jackson's war on the United States Bank stirred up general excitement throughout the country. — (2) **1847** ROBB *Squatter Life* 97 Sich a yell as that would scar an inimy into ager fits, and make the United States Eagle scream 'Hail Columby.' — (3) **1866** W. F. G. SHANKS *Personal Recoll. Dist. Generals* 117 'United States Grant' is an appellation much more common than Ulysses S. Grant. — (4) **1885** *Wkly. New Mexican Rev.* 16 April 1/2 Sheriff Romulo Martinez is to be United States Marshall. **1947** CHALFANT *Gold, Guns, & Ghost Towns* 75 Governor Nye . . . came to Aurora, accompanied by a United States Marshal.

(5) **1865** PIKE *Scout & Ranger* (1932) 24 Captain Ross, the sub agent, and Captain Plummer, commanding the United States regulars, at the post, had mistaken us.

Also *United States army, artillery, attorney, bond, citizen, commissioner, court, flag, homestead law, land office, land sale, mail, mint, money, note, officer, Sanitary commission, scrip, security, Senate, soldier, title, troops, uniform, volunteer, wagon,* etc.

∗ **universal,** *a.*

1. (*cap.*) =**Universalist,** *a. Obs.*

1840 *Niles' Reg.* 8 Aug. 368/3 The rev. Mr. Smith, late minister of the Universal church in Hartford, Connecticut, and the rev. Mr. Whittaker, . . . have both declared their solemn convictions that Universalism is not a scripture doctrine. **1868** W. C. FOWLER *Eng. Language* 122 Classification of Americanisms. . . . Ungrammatical expressions, disapproved by all; as, . . . *Universal preacher* for Universalist preacher.

2. In combs.: (1) **universal (compulsory) education,** the provision of free school instruction for all children, freq. with attendance required by law; (2) **Empire,** a secret organization in the South after the Civil War similar in purpose to the Ku-Klux Klan, *obs.;* (3) **Yankee nation,** New England, the North, or the U.S. as a whole, *obs.;* (4) **world,** the entire world, *obs.*

(1) **1867** *Nation* V. 192/1 Universal compulsory education is at first costly, but it is, in the long run, the truest economy. **1873** *Republic* I. 34 Its receipt by any State [is] conditioned on the support of free schools for universal education. — (2) **1880** *46th Congress* 2 Sess. Sen. Rep. No. 693, p. xvii, The distrust of Democracy . . . was inspired during the days when the 'Kuklux,' the 'White Brotherhood,' the 'Universal Empire,' and the 'Stonewall Guard' spread terror and desolation over the State. — (3) **1830** *Mass. Spy* 6 Jan. (Th.), It will probably light up a smile in the features of 'the universal Yankee nation' [N. Eng.]. **1893** *Harper's Wkly.* 7 Oct. 963/2 The universal Yankee nation has an opportunity [at the World's Columbian Exposition] to observe that part of the world who does not wear a Derby hat. — (4) **1823** FAUX *Memorable Days* 212 Were I a young man, I would live no where else [than Indiana] in all the Universal world. **1843** CARLTON *New Purchase* I. 175, I wouldn't a had you there for the universal world.

Universalian ˌjunəvɚˈselɪən, *a.* Relating to theological universalism. *Obs.* — **1837** W. JENKINS *Ohio Gaz.* 357 Perrysburg . . . has . . . three houses for public worship, (methodist, presbyterian, and universalian). *Ib.* 457 The religious sects in this county are composed of the presbyterian, . . . universalian, and christians, or free-will baptists. **1853** E. G. HOLLAND *Mem. J. Badger* (1854) 205 [Calvinism's] bold premises were the foundation of the plea of its opposite extreme —the Universalian statement.

∗ **Universalist,** *n.* A member of a sect or church which maintains that everybody will be saved. Also, *pl.,* the sect composed of such believers.

[**1782** CHASTELLUX *Voyages dans l'Amérique* (1786) II. 183 Un particulier, appellé je crois André, s'est avisé de prêcher une doctrine qu'on appelle celle des *Universalistes.*] **1786** BENTLEY *Diary* I. 36 Attended the association at Cape Ann . . . so much agitated by the controversy between Mr. Forbes, & J. Murray the Universalist. **1801** *Hist. Rev. & Directory* II. 39 A new sect has lately started, called the Universalists. **1844** *Jrnl. Wanderer* 213 Among the passengers there is a young lady who belongs to the sect called Universalists. . . . The Universalists believe in universal salvation. **1944** *Christian Cent.* 27 Dec. 1505/2 (*heading*), Universalists 'Belong' in Connecticut!

∗ **Universalist,** *a.* Belonging to or representing the denomination made up of Universalists.

1819 *Universalist Mag.* 21 Aug. 32/2 Pastor of the First Independent Church of Christ, called Universalist, in Philadelphia. **1870** *Nation* 27 Jan. 59/1 In Maine, at the end of 1868 there were forty Universalist clergymen. **1877** W. WRIGHT *Big Bonanza* 33 A. B. Grosch, a Universalist clergyman of considerable note, and editor of a Universalist paper at Utica, New York. **1950** *Chi. D. News* 17 April 4/7 [He] is under fire from a Universalist minister.

∗ **Universaller,** *n.* A member of the Universalist Church. *Colloq. Obs.* — **1846–51** WHITCHER *Bedott P.* ix. 87, I don't care if he is a Universaler nother. **1867** *Harper's Mag.* Aug. 408/2 The old Universaller was not entirely sure but that there might be [some catch in it].

∗ **university,** *n.*

1. An institution of higher learning comprising, usu., a college and one or more graduate or professional schools. Also **American university.**

Often used loosely for a college, but since *c*1876, when Johns Hopkins was founded, in more careful use applied only to those institutions where some emphasis is placed on graduate work and the granting of advanced and professional degrees.

1873 W. S. TYLER *Hist. Amherst Coll.* 437 But there is no disposition in any of the present Faculty to make the College an American University (sit venia verbo!) or to sacrifice the humanities or the disciplinary studies which constitute the essential characteristics of the American College. **1895** C. E. NORTON in *Four Amer. Universities* 23 The last twenty-five years have been a period of transition for her [Harvard] from the traditional narrow academic system to a new, liberal and comprehensive system, in which the ideal of an American university—a different ideal from the English or the German—has been gradually working itself out. **1902** *Science* 28 Feb. n.s. XV. 330/2 The American University as distinguished from the College is a comparatively recent product of evolution. . . . One of the young universities [Johns Hopkins] is celebrating in a quiet way the twenty-fifth anniversary of its foundation. **1946** *Newsweek* 12 Aug. 72/3 He went to the University of North Carolina.

b. (See quot.) *Obs.*

1856 HALL *College Words* (ed. 2) 472 *University* . . . at some American colleges, a name given to a university student.

2. In combs.: (1) **university campus,** the grounds about a university; (2) **fund,** a fund with which to establish or maintain a university; (3) **land,** public land set aside for the use of a university.

(1) **1895** *Univ. Nebraska Cal. 1895–6* 33 The Experiment Station Farm . . . [is] northeast of the University campus and connected with it by electric cars. — (2) **1868** *Rep. Comm. Agric. 1867* 331 A 'University Fund' of $300,000 had been realized. — (3) **1905** *Bureau of Forestry Bul.* No. 62, 36 Of these latter grants there are four classes—public school lands, university lands, asylum lands, and county school lands.

As the last term in **black, National, state university.**

unleached (wood) ashes. Ashes that have not been leached, used as fertilizer.

1804 in J. ROBERTS *Pa. Farmer* 111 Are leeched or unleeched ashes most beneficial as a manure? **1850** *Rep. Comm. Patents 1849: Agric.* 318 This manure should be composed of half a bushel of unleached ashes. **1884** R. L. ALLEN *New Amer. Farm Bk.* 81 Eight bushels of unleached wood ashes.

unlimited ticket. (See quot.) *Obs.* — **1888** LINDLEY *Calif. of South* 376 There is also an unlimited ticket, costing twenty dollars more, that allows the passenger to stop as he pleases between New York and the Pacific coast.

unlocated land. (See quot. 1763.) *Obs.*

1757 *N.J. Archives* XX. 95 At the same time will be sold, a Warrant for 250 acres of unlocated land. **1763** BOUCHER *Causes Amer. Revolution* (1797) 32 The Indians . . . already have a better title to any of our *un-located* lands, than we can possibly give any new comers. [Note to *unlocated lands:*] An American term, denoting unoccupied lands. **1792** IMLAY *Western Territory* 13 A land office was opened by the state, granting warrants for any quantity of unlocated land. [**1801** W. STRICKLAND *Agric. U.S.* 8 Much of it is yet barely known, and much of it is either yet *unlocated,* or if *located,* only by those land jobbers who have purchased from the government of the state, vast tracts at very low prices, with a view to sell them again as soon as population should approach their districts.]

***unlotted,** *a.* Of land: Owned by a colonial town and not allotted to individual settlers, also with *out. Obs.* — **1637** *Dedham Rec.* III. (1892) 33 Ther are about 16: acres of land Remayne lying at the Southermost corner of the mydle playne as yet vnlotted out. It is ordered yt it shalbe layd out into 2: acre lotts to set houses vpon. **1673** *Braintree Rec.* 15 The Towne of Boston still retaining the right and power of allotting and disposing of all these lands to ytickler [i.e., particular] persons yt are yet vnlotted out.

unmailable ʌnˈmeləbl, *a.* Not suitable for mailing, concerned with matter unsuitable for sending through the mail. — **1874** *Official Postal Guide* p. xvii, Such matter must be forwarded to the Dead-Letter Office, marked as 'unmailable.' **1896** *Columbus* (O.) *Dispatch* 17 Dec. 7 Inquiries have been made of the department as to the correct treatment of registered articles . . . found to be unmailable.

***unorganized,** *a.* **1.** Of a county or other area: Not having local governing officers or not formally organized as a government. **2.** Characterized by the presence of non-union workingmen.

(1) **1850** FILLMORE in *Pres. Mess. & P.* V. 67 The governor of Texas . . . dispatched a special commissioner with full power and instructions to extend the civil jurisdiction of the State over the unorganized counties of El Paso, Worth, Presidio, and Santa Fe. **1873** *Mich. Gen. Statutes* (1882) I. 270 The governor [shall] appoint marshals to take the census in the unorganized territory not otherwise provided in this act. — (2) **1896** *Internat. Typog. Union Proc.* 27/2 Complaints were frequent from other parts of the state on account of the unorganized condition of Rochester.

***unpleasantness,** *n.* The Civil War, freq. *the late unpleasantness. Colloq.*

1868 *Cong. Globe* 14 Feb. 1174/1 Leaving out of view 'the late unpleasantness.' *Ib.* 9 July 3880/2 The rebel generals . . . think the 'little unpleasantness' did not amount to much, after all. **1908** LORIMER *J. Spurlock* 123, I suppose, Major, that the late unpleasantness, which had so much to do with changing conditions in the South, cost you your property? **1930** HENRY *Conquer. Plains* 33 When 'the late unpleasantness' [Civil War] terminated, the Texan drover lacked a satisfactory market.

transf. **1903** *N.Y. Times* 19 Sep. 3 The only soldier to be killed from Orange during the late unpleasantness with the Filipinos. **1928** A. G. HAYS *Let Freedom Ring* 158 In time of war, when a free press in a democracy would be a real safeguard, there is repression. During the recent unpleasantness, this repression was practiced sometimes directly by the Federal Government. **1948** *Amer. Jrnl. Nursing* Dec. 770/2 Among the stamps of particular interest to nurses to come out of the 'late unpleasantness,' are a Hungarian Red Cross series, a German Red Cross and a German child welfare series.

unpledged ticket. (See quot.) *Obs.* — **1824** *Commentator* (Frankfort, Ky.) 2 Oct. 3/1 This opposition consists of a large portion of the democratic party, who support an '*unpledged ticket*,' by which we understand a ticket opposed to Mr Adams.

***unprotected,** *a.* Not protected or favored by a tariff. — **1820** *Ann. 16th Cong.* 2 Sess. 2311 The unprotected state of American manufactures. **1885** CRAWFORD *Amer. Politician* 225 We both agree in saying that it is great nonsense to leave iron unprotected.

unreconstructed ʌnˌrikənˈstrʌktɪd, *a.*

1. Not reconciled to the results of the Civil War. Also absol.

1867 *Harper's Wkly.* 9 Nov. 707/2 The Democratic candidates in Maryland are, of course, of the 'unreconstructed' kind. **1884** CRADDOCK *Where Battle Was Fought* 5, 'I thank the Federal army for nothing,' declared the unreconstructed, bitterly. **1948** *Green Bay* (Wis.) *Press-Gaz.* 13 July 1/7 Some unreconstructed southerners were suggesting that it might be a good idea to run Barkley against Mr. Truman.

transf. **1944** *U. of Chi. Mag.* May 6 So the young are in increasing numbers not only in Oklahoma but in much of the vast inland region of our republic, moving to the cities, leaving the unreconstructed small towns to their elders and to decay. **1949** *Time* 21 March 75/1 When it finally made peace with the Unionists and emerged, the *Gazette* was still unreconstructed.

b. (See quot.)

1891 *Cent.* 6640/1 *Unreconstructed*, . . . not yet reorganized as a State of the Union: applied to seceded States after the civil war.

2. unreconstructed rebel, a former Confederate who has not accepted as permanent the conditions imposed upon the South after the Civil War. Also transf.

1877 LONGFELLOW in S. Longfellow *H. W. Longfellow* III. 277 A letter from Mr.——, of Washington, a fierce and 'un-reconstructed' rebel. **1897** in W. C. CHURCH *U. S. Grant* 346 The feeling against the President was heightened by the appearance, at the doors of Congress, of what were known as 'unreconstructed rebels' arrogantly demanding to be admitted. **1947** *Chi. Tribune* 21 Dec. IV. 4/3 For 41 years the LaFollettes, father and son, served in the United States senate, where they were regarded by the majority of their Republican colleagues as unreconstructed rebels.

unscalped ʌnˈskælpt, *a.* Not scalped, used esp. of Indians. *Obs.* — **1726** PENHALLOW *Indian Wars* 37 We found seven dead upon the spot: six of whom we scalped, and left the other unscalped. **1890** *Buckskin Mose* 163 The unscalped Indian is supposed . . . to hold a higher rank in the Happy Hunting grounds . . . than the one who has lost his hair.

***unseated,** *a.* Of land: Unsettled, not occupied. *Obs.*

1662 *Va. Statutes at Large* II. 98 The greatest part of the country [will be left] unseated and unpeopled, noe man knowing how or of whome either to purchase or take lease. **1816** U. BROWN *Journal* II. 357 Makes Search after James Gillmore, Collector of the Direct Tax on unseated Lands for the years 1815 & 1816. **1877** W. H. BURROUGHS *On Taxation* 208 In Pennsylvania, prior to 1844, . . . unseated lands, that is lands unoccupied or vacant, were alone liable to be sold for taxes.

***unsettled,** *a.* Not occupied by settlers. Also **unsettledness,** *n. Obs.*

*c***1695** J. MILLER *Descr. N.Y.* 20 There is something to be said in excuse hereof, that is, the unsettledness of the country for a long time. **1724** *Pa. Assembly Acts* I. 102 Exempting . . . all unsettled Tracts or Parcels of Land, That is to say, such Tracts of Land as . . . are unseated. **1816** U. BROWN *Journal* I. 272 Thence 16 Miles through an Ugly hilly unsettled Country in the night to the Town of Bath.

***unspeakable,** *a.* Unwilling or unable to speak. — **1888** *Advance* (Chi.) 29 Nov., The distinguished but unspeakable witness. **1890** LOWELL *Lett.* (1894) II. 465 My dog . . . looks up at me as one who should say, 'You are become unspeakable as one of us, poor old fellow!'

***unterrified,** *a.* **1.** Rock-ribbed, staunch, unswervingly loyal. Applied, often derisively, to Democrats and the Democratic party. **2.** *absol.* Democrats. Both *obs.*

(1) **1832** S. SMITH *Lett. J. Downing* (1860) 169 (Th.), Mr. Van Buren was taken up by the 'unterrified Democracy' to run as Vice-President on the ticket of 'old Hickory.' **1848** *Wilmington* (N.C.) *Commercial* 2 Sep. 2/1 (*Th. Supp.*), The 'unterrified democracy' are very hard pushed to understand the character of the Oregon Bill. **1890** *Cong. Rec.* 12 Feb. 1253/1 The Democracy has always . . . stood rock-ribbed and unterrified for . . . the eternal principles of truth and justice. — (2) **1851** *S.F. Herald* 30 April 2/4 Long faces and sorrowful looks, through which an air of forced contentment would occasionally break, characterized the 'unterrified.' **1866** *Ore. State Jrnl.* 5 May 3/1 The 'unterrified' meet here to-day to 'liquor up'—and make nominations.

***untimbered,** *a.* Not wooded.

1805 LEWIS in *L. & Clark Exped.* II. (1904) 74 An untimbered Island [is] situated in the middle of the river. **1808** PIKE *Sources Miss.* App. II. 8 The vast tract of untimbered country . . . lies between the . . . Missouri, Mississippi, and the western Ocean. **1905** *Indian Laws & Tr.* III. 149 Untimbered lands so purchased are not susceptible of cultivation.

unvented brand. *W.* A brand which has not been nullified by a sale brand. *Obs.* Cf. **vent,** *v.* — **1844** GREGG *Commerce of Prairies* I. 186 Should they by chance discover any *unvented* brand, they immediately set to work to find some one with a branding-iron of the same shape, by which the beast is at once claimed.

unwashed democracy. The common people. *Contemptuous. Obs.* Cf. **great unwashed.** — **1848** BURNHAM *Stray Subjects* 177 A score of loafers from the 'unwashed democracy' had got together for the purpose of seeing a live President. **1882** *Cong. Rec.* 9 March 1759/1 If that shirt has been on that fellow these whole twelve years, I think he would be a good representative of the unwashed Democracy.

unwhisperables ʌnˈhwɪspərəblz, *n. pl.* Trousers. *Slang. Obs.* — **1837** *Knickerb.* March 288 [He could] see about procuring himself a new pair of unwhisperables from his host. **1869** *New North West* (Deer Lodge, Mont.) 17 Sep. 1/3 Fashionable tailors inform us that it will be *en regle* next winter to associate white cassimer 'unwhisperables' with a blue dress suit at the opera.

***up,** *adv., a.,* and *prep.* Used, often as a prefix, in combs. and phrases.

1. In expressions alluding to places further up toward the head of a stream, or a part of the country remote from a coast or more in the interior of a region, as (1) **up-boat,** (2) ***bound,** (3) **cargo,** (4) **country,** see as a main entry, (5) **creek,** (6) **freight.**

(1) **1857** WILLIS *Convalescent* 154 The '*up*-boat' . . . reaches Poughkeepsie . . . a few minutes before the '*down*-boat' touches at the same place. — (2) **1884** MARK TWAIN *H. Finn* xii, Up-bound steamboats fight the big river in the middle. — (3) **1879** BAGBY *Old Va. Gentleman* 232 The up-cargo . . . afforded good pickings.

(5) **1864** *Harper's Mag.* Dec. 58/2 At the point of the bluff where the up-creek mud ran into . . . the mud of the town. — (6) **1824** *Catawba Journal* 30 Nov., Up freights will be insured at one fourth of one per

cent on their value. **1833** *Amer. R.R. Jrnl.* II. 482/1, 6000 tons up freight, at $3 00.

2. Used with *south, north, east,* in the sense of "in the south," "north," "east." *Colloq.* Cf. **Down East.**

1835–7 HALIBURTON *Clockmaker* I Ser. viii. 51, I've been away up south, a speculating in nutmegs. **a1870** CHIPMAN *Notes on Bartlett* 494 *Up North,* used instead of North, *n.,* and adverbially. **1906** LYNDE *Quickening* 209 Money is tighter than a shut fist—up East.

3. a. Of a player in poker: In the position of having staked an amount equal to the ante. **b.** Of money: At stake.

(a) 1844 J. COWELL *Thirty Years* 94 The dealer makes the game, or value of the beginning bet, and called *the anti* . . . and then everybody stakes the same amount, and says, *'I'm up.'* — **(b) 1867** MARK TWAIN *Sk. New & Old* 32 But as soon as money was up on him he was a different dog; his underjaw'd begin to stick out like the fo'-castle of a steamboat.

4. *Baseball.* At bat.

1862 *N.Y. Sun. Mercury* 13 July (E. J. Nichols). **1909** BARBER *Double Play* 208 The fourth man up chose a ball to his liking and sliced it down the first-base line. **1912** MATHEWSON *Pitching* 23, I was the first man up and started the eighth inning with a single. **1949** *Oregonian* (Portland) 10 Aug. III. 4/2 Larry Herns drew a base on balls as first up.

5. In rare substantival formations: (1) **up-bring,** upbringing, rearing; (2) **up-comer,** =**up-boat.**

(1) 1898 *Advance* (Chi.) 5 May 609/1 Carl showed his 'up bring' for the first time when he deposited the cherry stones on the carpet under his chair! — **(2) 1847** FIELD *Drama in Pokerville* 175 In the mean time, round the point below, sweeps the up-comer . . . moving over the water like a rushing fire-palace.

6. In colloq. expressions: (1) *To be up against it,* to be confronted with difficulties; (2) *up creek,* used allusively with reference to "row up Salt River," see **salt river 3;** (3) *up garret,* up into, or up in, the garret; (4) *up to* (one), incumbent upon one; (5) *up to the minute,* up to date; (6) *up with the times,* =prec.

(1) 1896 ADE *Artie* 7, I saw I was up against it. **1945** BOTKIN *My Burden* 73 So because they was up against it and never had any money or nothing. — **(2) 1843** CARLTON *New Purchase* I. 261 Happily, my complimentary neighbour had no wish for that pleasant little excursion—'up crick,' and no further disturbance ensued. — **(3) 1775** *Essex Inst. Coll.* XLVIII. 48 Stevens ordered us out of our Chamber . . . & so we moved up garret. **1845** JUDD *Margaret* II. 344 You will find . . . in the bottom of my chest, up garret, five dollars and a quarter. **1899** WILKINS *Jamesons* 88 Jest old andirons like mother keeps up garret. — **(4) 1896** ADE *Artie* 11 Up to me—see! **1900** NORRIS *Blix* 151 It's up to you. **1921** PAINE *Comr. Rolling Ocean* 110 It's up to me to stay as dry as a covered bridge.

(5) 1909 WASON *Happy Hawkins* 322 They had stopped for over a month with his friends in England, an' was posted up to the minute. **1931** *K.C. Times* 25 July, At last we have seen the up-to-the-minute in sports—a turtle race. — **(6) 1893** SANBORN *S. Calif.* 4, I know of bright people who actually carried their favorite matches from an eastern city to Tacoma, . . . only to find the best of everything in that brilliant and up-with-the-times city.

For other "up" formations see as main entries. For *up to Green River,* etc., see **Green River 2.** and **2. b,** and for *up a stump* see ***stump 5. c.** (3).

As the last term in **away, back, ball, bang, banking, beat, blow, break, bust, catch, catching, check, checker, civilize, clean, cleaning, close, cut, cutting, die, dry, frame, hands, haul, higher, hitch, hold, hook, jump, look, paid, pass, pick, picked, put, rest, resting, right, round, rounding, set, setting, seven, shake, slicking, spang, stand, stick, stock round, tank, tanked, ten, three, throw, tie, tilt, turn, two, using, wake, walk, warm, wash, way, writeup.**

up and coming, *a.* Energetic, capable, aggressive or pushing. *Colloq.*

1848 D. P. THOMPSON *L. Amsden* 78, I saw a little *up-and-coming* sort of a fellow . . . fairly scare from the ground a fellow . . . as big as two of him. **1926** F. N. HART *Bellamy Trial* i. 10 Redfield's pretty up and coming for a place of its size.

Hence **up-and(-a)-comingness.**

1890 *Advance* (Chi.) 24 April, There is about our Methodist brethren . . . an up-and-a-comingness . . . that is delightful. **1899** HOWELLS *Ragged Lady* 59 The *chef* bore their mirth stoically, but not without a personal relish of the shoeman's up-and-comingness.

***up-and-down,** *a.* and *adv.* **1.** *a.* Direct or straightforward. **2.** *adv.* Directly, without attempt at concealment. Both *colloq.*

(1) 1837 *Knickerb.* X. 379 He was remarkable for his independence and fearlessness; for his up-and-down dealing, and for the originality of his figures. **1896** *Peterson Mag.* Jan. 94/2 The two women folks, . . . finally had an up-and-down row. — **(2) 1854** O. OPTIC *In Doors & Out* (1876) 30, I told her, up and down, that she was not what she used to be. **1886** ALTON *Among Law-Makers* 274, 'I will recognize the higher authority of the Constitution!' That is what . . . [the President] told [Congress], up and down!

up and up. *on the up and up,* honestly, above board. *Colloq.*

1863 *Humboldt Reg.* (Unionville, Nev.) 4 July 2/1 Now that would be business, on the dead up-and-up. **1929** *Variety* 10 July 1/3 The show is run on the up and up. Six will not stand for any graft. **1948** *Time* 1 March 51/3 As proof that everything was on the up & up, Promoter Jack Harris pointed to the heavy side-betting between Riggs and Kramer.

upasian juˈpeziən, *a.* As deadly as the upas tree. *Rare.* — **1841** *Niles' Reg.* 17 July 320/3 The New Orleans Advertiser . . . speaks of that city suffering under the blasts of the upasian winds, the forerunners of epidemic disease, unless they are driven back by the south winds. They blow from the northeast.

upcountry ˈʌpˈkʌntrɪ, ˈʌpˌkʌntrɪ, *adv.* and *n.*

"As adv. and adj. the phrase is current in English dialects (cf. quot. 1688), but the general 19th century use originated partly in India and partly in the United States; from c1875 it has also been employed in, or with reference to, Australia, South Africa, etc." (*OED*).

1. *n.* That part of a country away from the seaboard, the backwoods. *Colloq.*

1817 WEEMS *Letters* III. 176, I have a number due in the up country. **1887** *Harper's Mag.* April 666 The spring and fall freshets . . . brought down . . . fleets of flat boats from the 'up-country.'

attrib. or as *adj.* **1810** WEEMS *Letters* III. 27 Not thinking the little up country post offices safe, . . . I thought it my duty to you to concentrate all my monies into good drafts. **1861** *New Haven Palladium* 30 Nov. (Chipman), As the up-country editor [said, etc.]. **1899** JEWETT *Queen's Twin* 5 There's a path leadin' right over to it that . . . belonged to the up-country Indians.

2. *adv.* In or into the interior. *Colloq.*

1815 HUMPHREYS *Yankey* 40 Afore I was born he moved up country, into the back part. **1883** HOWELLS *Woman's Reason* xv, One girl . . . writes for two or three papers up-country, and out West. **1907** WHITE *Arizona Nights* 36, I'll march you up country and see that Geronimo gets you.

upgrade ˈʌpˌgred, *n.* and *adv.*

1. *n.* A slope upward.

1873 BEADLE *Undevel. West* 257 Forty miles of staging over boulders and rocky up-grade. **1923** WATTS *L. Nichols* 314 The steady up-grade to the North Hill [was] accomplished without incident. **1949** *Sky Line Trail* Oct. 18/1 On the upgrades I'd slither backward, frantically grabbing the pony's tail to keep from falling off.

b. *To be on the up-grade, fig.* to be improving, to be on the mend. *Colloq.*

1926 *Ladies' Home Jrnl.* Oct. 143 Monty's been the hardest child we've had to handle, . . . but I believe he's on the up-grade. **1945** FUGINA *Upper Miss.* 46 As the packet business began to wane, the rafting business was on the up-grade.

2. *adv.* Upward on an incline. *Colloq.*

1893 *Outing* XXII. 133/2 The twelve miles up-grade to Alto station . . . consumed just three hours' time. **1941** LEE *Stagecoach North* 3 The coach rounded the corner at the town park, and headed upgrade toward the Vermont Hotel.

up-head ˈʌpˌhɛd, *attrib.* Of or pertaining to a person or animal holding the head erect. Also **up-headed,** *a.,* **up-header,** *n. Colloq.*

1845 GREEN *Texian Exped.* 224 They seemed to know that we were Texians . . . from our national *up-head* appearance. **1875** *Ill. Dept. Agric. Trans.* XIV. 210 [The Siamese swine] had a fine, high-bred, up-headed style, especially in their walk. **1893** *D.N.* I. 334 *Upheader,* a horse that holds his head high. Applied figuratively to men. [N.J.]

upholster ʌpˈholstɚ, *v.* [f. ***upholsterer.**]

1. *tr.* To cover (a piece of furniture) with fabric, stuffing, etc., to equip (a car, etc.) with such furniture. Also transf.

1853 LOWELL *Fireside Trav.* (1864) 45 The dull weed upholstered the decaying wharves. **1882** MCCABE *New York* 184 The cars. . . though neatly upholstered and decorated are not as ornamental as those of the Sixth avenue line. **1944** *Sears Cat.* (ed. 179) 685B Upholstered all over in rich, deep-pile angora mohair woven on sturdy cotton back. **1950** *Chi. Tribune* 15 April, A well upholstered gent may be regarded as one who has 'plenty to eat.'

2. *intr.* To make coverings of fabric, as for furniture; to stuff cushions, etc.

1861 STOWE *Pearl Orr's Isl.* I. 21 Miss Roxy and Miss Ruey . . . could upholster and quilt.

3. *tr.* To equip (a person) with clothes. *Humorous.*

1873 MARK TWAIN & WARNER *Gilded Age* 300 It had cost something to upholster these women. **1897** FLANDRAU *Harvard Episodes* 305 Celestial companies of maidens . . . floated past Beverly, in the wake of panting but determined ladies richly upholstered.

* **upland,** *n.* and *a.*

1. *n.* = **upland cotton.**

1819 *Niles' Reg.* XVII. 9/2 Bengal cotton . . . heretofore paid the same duty as uplands. **1824** *Shipping & Commercial List* 31 July (Pettigrew P.), A lot of 300 bales of Upland was sold at 14⅝ cents, cash. **1864** *Maine Agric. Soc. Returns 1863* 48 The great cotton dearth . . . has caused that production to go up from 9 cents for middling Uplands . . . to 90 cents.

2. In combs.: (1) **upland claim,** (see quot.), *obs.;* (2) **corn,** corn grown on uplands; (3) **cotton,** short-staple cotton grown on uplands, also attrib.; (4) **cranberry,** the trailing evergreen bearberry, *Arctostaphylos uva-ursi,* having glossy red berries; (5) **flake,** (see quot.); (6) **hickory,** (see quot.); (7) **Indian,** an Indian living inland, esp. an Indian of one of the Algonquian tribes of New England and New York, as a Mohegan, *obs.;* (8) **lot,** a lot of relatively high land, *obs.;* (9) **maple,** (see quot.), *obs.;* (10) **moccasin,** (see quot. and cf. **highland moccasin**); (11) **plover,** a large sandpiper, *Bartramia longicauda,* found in fields and uplands; (12) **prairie,** a level, treeless area of elevated ground; (13) **rice,** rice of a kind that can be grown on elevated land without irrigation; (14) **sumac,** (see quot.); (15) **tupelo-tree,** (see quot.); (16) **willow (oak),** the bluejack, *Quercus cinerea,* an oak of the southern states.

(1) **1877** RUEDE *Sod-House Days* 12 An upland claim lies on top of a divide, and it is hard to find water sometimes. A bottom claim is one along a creek or river. — (2) **1785** in *S. Lit. Messenger* XXVIII. 40/1 The effect of it on upland corn has been favourable. **1945** *Democrat* 22 March 1/1 Upland corn should be planted by April 10 and bottom land by May 10. — (3) **1819** *Niles' Reg.* XVII. 9/1 Hitherto our cottons, sea island and upland, . . . have been subject to a specific duty. **1910** *Dept. Agric. Yrbk.* 57 Several new types of Upland cotton . . . introduced from Mexico and Central America . . . have now become as productive and as uniform as any of the United States Upland varieties that are being tested in the same places. **1947** *Sat. Ev. Post* 8 March 79/2 He was born in 1890 in the upland cotton town of York, South Carolina. — (4) **1860** DARLINGTON *Weeds & Plants* 211 *A[rctostaphylos] Uva-ursi.* . . . Bearberry. Upland Cranberry.

(5) **1889** *Cent.* 2250/1 *Upland flake,* a flake for drying codfish, built permanently upon the shore. It differs from the ordinary pattern in not being movable. — (6) **1897** SUDWORTH *Arborescent Flora* 113 *Hicoria ovata.* . . . Shagbark (Hickory). . . . Upland Hickory (Ill.). — (7) **1656** *Mass. H.S. Coll.* 4 Ser. VII. 75, I feare nothing soe much as warres with our Indianes about vs, who stands ready to encounter with the vpland Indianes. **1716** CHURCH *Philip's War* 27 Some . . . [were] Narraganset Indians, and some other Upland Indians, in all about 300. [**1790** UMFREVILLE *Hudson's Bay* 56 In the month of March, the Upland Indians assemble on the banks of a particular river or lake, the nomination of which had been agreed upon by common assent.] — (8) **1639** *N.H. Prov. P.* I. 138 All the inhabitants of the towne of Exeter shall [have] their uplands lotts for planting laid outt. — (9) **1720** DUDLEY in *Phil. Trans.* XXXI. 27 Maple Sugar is made of the juice of the Upland Maple, or Maple Trees that grow upon the Highlands.

(10) **1891** *Cent.* 6660/3 *Upland moccasin,* a venomous serpent of the southern United States. — (11) **1832** WILLIAMSON *Maine* I. 147 The upland Plover is larger than a robin. **1945** MATHEWS *Talking* 53, I simply get up . . . and listen for . . . the doleful whistling of the upland plover. — (12) **1817** S. BROWN *Western Gazetteer* 45 There are two kinds of these meadows—the river and upland prairies. **1912** BLACKMAR *Kansas* 50 The soil of the upland prairies is usually a deep, rich clay loam of a dark color. — (13) **1772** FRANKLIN *Writings* VIII. 21, I send you enclosed a small box of Upland Rice, brought from Cochin China. **1847** DARLINGTON *Weeds & Plants* 370 There are several varieties of cultivated Rice; some, called Upland or Mountain Rice, usually awnless. — (14) **1836** WOOD & BACHE *Dispensatory* 544 *Rhus glabrum* . . . , called variously *smooth sumach, Pennsylvania sumach,* and *upland sumach.*

(15) **1785** MARSHALL *Amer. Grove* 97 *Nyssa sylvatica.* Upland Tupelo-Tree, or Sour Gum. This grows naturally in Pennsylvania. — (16) **1765** J. BARTRAM *Diary* 31 July, Thay have ye upland willow oak with A hoary leaf, & y^e swamp willow with A narrow leaf. **1901** MOHR *Plant Life Ala.* 91 The upland willow oak or blue jack, common in the lower Coast Pine belt, in this isolated pine forest reaches its most northern station.

As the last term in **hickory, prairie upland(s).**

* **uplander,** *n.* = **upland plover.** — **1888** TRUMBULL *Names of Birds* 172 [At] Salem, Mass., Pasture Plover; at Provincetown, Uplander. **1917** *Birds of Amer.* I. 247 Upland Plover. *Bartramia longicauda.* . . . [Also called] Uplander.

uplift ˈʌpˌlɪft, *n.*

1. Elevation, lifting up.

1844 WILLIS *Poems* 12 His brow Had the inspired up-lift of the king's. **1890** STANLEY *In Darkest Africa* I. 413 There was uniform uplift and subsidence of the constantly twirling spear blades.

b. Esp. an upheaval, a lifting or rising of the surface of the earth.

1853 KANE *Grinnell Exped.* 128 The false horizon, which I had selected as an index of the uplift, rose as it receded from the sun. **1923** J. H. COOK *On Old Frontier* 105 Gullies cut into both sides of this channel-bed through a little high uplift of country.

c. *fig.* Spiritual elevation, the improvement and ennobling of the mind. Also attrib.

1873 HOLLAND *A. Bonnicastle* 22 It is impossible that he could know what an uplift he gave to the life to which he ministered. **1912** G. M. HYDE *Newspaper Reporting* 236 One of these is the 'up-lift run' for cub reporters—a round of philanthropic news sources to teach them the business of reporting before they become cynical. **1935** WEEKLEY *Something About Words* 63 *Uplift,* with which neither the Dictionary nor the Supplement deals quite satisfactorily, is now rather ironical.

d. *on the uplift,* improving. *Colloq.*

1904 *N.Y. Ev. Post* 11 June, The summer season is on the uplift, and the outlook is for record-breaking crowds.

2. A curb or low wall. *Rare.*

1896 ADE *Artie* 183 Mamie sat with him on the stone uplift dividing the park driveway from the slope toward the water.

up-offering. An offering up. *Rare.* — **1829** COOPER *Wish-ton-Wish* v, Mark was on the point of making . . . an up-offering of thanks, when Whittal Ring broke rudely into the room.

* **upper,** *a.* and *n.*

1. *n.* "A log or piece of sawed lumber of superior grade" (*OED*).

1877 *Lumberman's Gaz.* 24 May 357/1 There are about 100,000 feet [of lumber] on dock, mostly uppers.

2. In combs.: (1) **upper classman,** a member of one of the upper classes, junior and senior, in a college or high school; (2) **Coos,** see quot. *a*1817 *s.v.* **Coos;** (3) **Creeks,** "a term applied to that division of the Creeks formerly living about Coosa and Tallapoosa rs., N.E. Ala., and for a short distance below their junction" (Hodge), also **Upper Creek Indians;** (4) * **crust,** the highest social class, *colloq.;* (5) **house,** the superior branch of a colonial or state council or senate; (6) **keel,** a mark of ownership made in the ears of domestic livestock, *obs.;* (7) **party,** (see quot.), *obs.;* (8) **river,** (see quot. 1876); (9) **Sonoran,** in biogeography, that zone in the western U.S. which borders the Transition Zone *q.v.*, also attrib.; (10) **ten,** short for **upper ten thousand,** also attrib., *colloq.;* (11) **-tendom,** the world of the upper ten thousand, *colloq.;* (12) **ten thousand,** the people belonging to the highest social class, the aristocracy, also, rarely, **upper ten thousander, thousandist.**

(1) **1871** BAGG *At Yale* 70 Only a few upper-class men will be found there. **1948** *Lisle* (Ill.) *Eagle* 21 Oct. 10/2 Bewildered freshmen and astonished upperclassmen wondered what their lot would be. — (3) **1739** W. STEPHENS *Proc. Georgia* 421 He had the Friendship of the Lower and Upper Creek Indians secured to us. **1945** BOTKIN *My Burden* 132 Most of the Creeks . . . belonged to the Lower Creeks and sided with the South, but down below us along the Canadian River they were Upper Creeks. — (4) **1835–7** HALIBURTON *Clockmaker* 1 Ser. xxviii. 274 It was none o' your skim-milk parties, but superfine uppercrust real jam. **1946** *Newsweek* 1 July 25/3 He took a fashionable house and hobnobbed lavishly with Washington's tight-ringed upper crust.

(5) **1666** *Md. Archives* II. 20 The Upper House do think that the 1400 lb. powder . . . [is] very necessary. **1709** *Mass. H.S. Coll.* 3 Ser. VII. 69 Two Gentlemen of the upper house . . . were ordered to confer with me about it. *a*1817 DWIGHT *Travels* I. 270 The Legislature [of Conn.] is formed of two Houses, the Council and Representatives: customarily called the Upper and Lower Houses. — (6) **1773** in SUMMERS *Ann. S.W. Va.* 607 His Mark is ordered to be recorded a Swallow Fork in the right ear a Crop in the Left Ear and an Upper Keel. — (7) **1780** in ANBUREY *Travels* II. 479 The Upper Party con-

stituted of the partizans of the Americans, and the Lower Party of the American Loyal Refugees, they reside in New York. *Ib.* 482 What are termed these Upper and Lower Parties are mostly known to each other, and possess great inveteracy on both sides. — **(8) 1876** MARK TWAIN *Old Times* ii. 33 What is called the 'upper river' (the two hundred miles between St. Louis and Cairo, where the Ohio comes in) was low. **1896** ——— in *Harper's Mag.* Aug. 346 We was four days getting out of the 'upper river.' — **(9) 1916** *Iowa Acad. Sci. Proc.* XXIII. 323 Omitting the vegetation of the river banks and cultivated ground, the flora is pronouncedly Upper Sonoran. **1921** HALL *Yosemite Nat. Park* 128 A few Upper Sonoran birds and mammals reach up into the Transition. **1947** *Sierra Club* (So. Calif. Chap.) *Sched.* 126, 47 Be sure and come out on the January and February trips into the chaparral of the Upper Sonoran Life Zone.

(10) *a***1848** *N.Y. Herald* (B.), The seats for the first night are already many of them engaged . . . by the very cream of our 'upper ten.' **1850** *Quincy* (Ill.) *Whig* 7 May 1/3 The beauty of the whole thing was, that subsequently, the 'upper ten' negro, indignantly refused to sit at the same table and eat with the stewards and other colored servants. **1947** *Chi. D. News* 22 Oct. 46/8 Do the members of the 'upper ten' in New York City tend strongly to marry exclusively in the 'upper tens'? — **(11) 1851** *S. Lit. Messenger* XVII. 180/1 We love to meet . . . [at] the soiree of a fresh aspirant for the honors of Upper Tendom. **1904** *Amer. Hist. Rev.* IX. 838 The plantation and slave-owning aristocrat was more akin to the ideal of the British upper-tendom than the prosaic Northerner. — **(12) 1844** *N.Y. Ev. Mirror* 11 Nov. 2/1 At present there is no distinction among the upper ten thousand of the city. **1848** NEAL *Charcoal Sk.* 161 (We.), As if you were one of the upper ten-thousanders. **1849** *Bellville* (O.) *Rainbow* 30 Nov. 2/4 [One] of several growing evils . . . is the spirit of Monied Aristocracy, a class of persons that are more particularly known as the 'Upper Ten Thousandists.' **1882** MCCABE *New York* 320 With the Upper-Ten-Thousand it is made the occasion of displaying the wealth and style of the family.

b. In colloq. phrases: (1) *To be on one's uppers,* (see quot. 1891); (2) *to walk on one's uppers,* to wear shoes with holes in the soles; (3) *to keep a stiff upper lip,* see ∗**keep,** *v.* **2.** (1).

(1) 1891 *Cent.* 6661/2 *To be on one's uppers,* to be poor or in hard luck: referring to a worn-out condition of one's shoes. **1949** *N.Y. Times Bk. Review* 10 April 12/2 When Jimmy was on his uppers, President Roosevelt . . . got him the post of impartial chairman of the New York clothing industry. — **(2) 1891** *Fur, Fin, & Feather* 195 An old pair in which one is just ready 'to walk on his uppers,' . . . will serve admirably after they have been half-soled. **1917** MORGAN *Recollections* 236 Then Mrs. Davis arrived with her ragged and mud-stained escort, most of whom by this time were walking on their 'uppers,' or the bare soles of their poor bruised feet.

uppity ˈʌpɪtɪ, *a.* Uppish. *Colloq.* — **1934** WEBSTER. **1947** *Newsweek* 24 Feb. 29/1 He asks little of the world, so long as the 'damyankee' lets him alone and the 'nigger' doesn't get uppity.

uppowoc ʌˈpowɑk, *n.* Also **apooke.** [Virginian *uppôwoc, uhpooc.*] Tobacco. *Obs.* Cf. **poke,** *n.*[1]

1588 T. HARRIOT *Briefe Rep. Va.* C3 This *Uppówoc* is of so precious estimation amongst them, that they thinke their gods are maruelously delighted therwith. *c***1618** STRACHEY *Virginia* 121 There is here great store of tobacco which the salvages call apooke. **1919** R. D. W. CONNOR *Hist. N.C.* I. 13 Though now masquerading under other names we have no difficulty in recognizing in 'uppowac' our tobacco.

upraise ˈʌpˌrez, *n. Mining.* A steep shaft driven upward. *Colloq.* — **1876** RAYMOND *8th Rep. Mines* 158 A drift . . . has been run through the . . . ground, and an upraise commenced. **1900** GARLAND *Eagle's Heart* 234 All the talk was of 'pay-streaks,' 'leads,' 'float,' 'whins,' and 'up-raises.'

∗**upright,** *n.* **1.** (See quot.) **2.** A kind of artificial trout fly. Both *rare.* — **(1)** *a***1870** CHIPMAN *Notes on Bartlett* 495 *Upright,* a leg. Western U.S. — **(2) 1878** NASH *Oregon* 135 The lawyer put on a 'black palmer' and a 'blue upright.'

∗**uprise,** *n.* **1.** *Mining.* =**upraise. 2.** (See quot.) *Colloq.* — **(1) 1876** RAYMOND *8th Rep. Mines* 174 Fifty feet in from the mouth of the tunnel an uprise was made, which finally ran into wall-rock. — **(2) 1891** *Cent.* 6662/2 *Uprise,* . . . rise; development; advance; augmentation, as of price or value. (Colloq.)

up-river ˈʌpˈrɪvɚ, *a., adv.,* and *n.*

1. *n.* A region or area situated farther upstream.

1902 WHITE *Blazed Trail* 143 If the men from up-river come by, . . . don't act mysterious. **1907** LONDON *Road* 153, I had come down from 'up river' some time before.

2. *a.* Going upstream, living in or situated in a place farther upstream.

1836 *S. Lit. Messenger* II. 968/1, I had never imagined that any thing half so grand . . . awaited us on our up-river jaunt. **1857** CHANDLESS *Visit Salt Lake* 1, I passed a few days there, waiting for an up-river boat. **1915** *Lit. Digest* 4 Sep. 467/1 The second stampede of the Klondikers from up-river points.

3. *adv.* Toward the source of a river, farther upstream.

1848 THOREAU *Maine Woods* 83 Only a few axe-men have gone 'up river,' into the howling wilderness which feeds it. **1902** WHITE *Blazed Trail* 123 They're getting this stuff out up-river first. **1943** MENEFEE *Assignment* 57 Just upriver in the Delta cotton region, they added, the colored population is over 90 percent of the total.

∗**upshoot,** *n. Baseball.* An upward-curving pitched ball. Cf. **rise ball.** — **1885** CHADWICK *Art of Pitching* 14 It is essential to change the direction of the curve . . . from an 'up-shoot' to a 'down-shoot.' **1907** *St. Nicholas* June 720/1 The umpire . . . could throw an 'up shoot' and a 'snake curve' and never half try.

upside-down cake. A cake containing fruit ingredients as sliced apples, pineapple, nuts, etc., which are placed in the bottom of the cake pan with the batter on top, served with the bottom side up. Also attrib.

1930 *Canning Trade* 9 Feb. 119/2 Dessert: Apple meringue pudding. Norwegian apple pie. Up-side-down cake. **1936** *Sears Cat.* (ed. 173) 653/2 Tin Upside Down Cake Pan. **1949** *L.A. Times* 3 April (Home Mag.) 12/3 A packaged cake mix enables the working girl to serve a warm upside-down cake for a company dessert with a minimum amount of effort.

∗**upstander,** *n.* An upright post or handlebar on a sledge. — **1856** KANE *Arctic Explor.* II. 98 It has two standards, or, as we call them, 'upstanders.' **1903** PEARY in *McClure's Mag.* Feb. 419/2, I had scarcely time to seize the upstanders when my dogs were off.

upstate ˈʌpˈstet, *n.* A region in a state that is away from, and usu. north of, some large city. Used esp. in the state of New York. Also as adj. and adv.

1901 *Everybody's Mag.* March 242/1 The farmers up State would give a good deal to have the Gulf Stream flowing past their acres. **1938** DANIELS *Southerner* 247, I hear that it already has one of the most remarkable small town plants in the country. I heard about it upstate. **1949** *So. Wkly.* 16 Nov. 3/2 This is the figure with complete returns from Greater New York and 19 up-State districts missing.

Hence **upstater,** *n.*

1944 HOLTON *Yankees* 202 The Cape Codder and the Up-Stater are blood brothers with only the difference in the backdrops of sea or mountain. **1949** *L.A. Times* 8 May 26/8 Fielder held the upstaters scoreless till the ninth.

∗**uptown,** *n.* The residential part of a city. Also attrib. or as adj.

1838 STEPHENS *Travels Greece* I. 83 Even I, . . . a quondam speculator in 'up-town lots.' **1844** *Ev. Mirror* (N.Y.) 12 Nov. 2/2 'Up-Town' and 'Down-Town.'—We see that these names of the different halves of the city are becoming the common language of advertisements, notices, etc. **1891** WELCH *Recoll. 1830–40* 27 It was a Saturday afternoon play-ground for the youngsters from up-town.

b. *adv.* In the residential part of a city.

1833 *Niles' Reg.* XLIV. 177/2 The property-holders, up-town would have the site of the building a mile or so from the present chief seat of business. **1917** MATHEWSON *Sec. Base Sloan* 57 They parted, agreeing to meet uptown at noon.

urban ˈɜbən, *n.* A city dweller. *Colloq.* — **1891** *Cent.* 6666/1. **1896** *Vt. Agric. Rep.* XVI. 123 Vermonters are learning that scenery has economic value, and urbans of wealth are gaining footholds all over her fair domain.

∗**urbaniste,** *n.* A variety of medium-large pear. — **1851** BARRY *Fruit Garden* 308 *Urbaniste* (Beurre Picquery of the French.)—A large, melting, buttery pear, a tardy bearer on the pear, but succeeds well on the quince. **1913** *Standard* 1817/2.

∗**urchin,** *n.* (See quot.) *Obs.* — **1796** MORSE *Amer. Geog.* I. 201 The Urchin, or Urson, . . . is commonly called Hedgehog or Porcupine, but differs from both those animals.

urette juˈret, *n.* [f. ∗*urine*+*poudrette,* dried night-soil.] (See quot.) *Obs.* — **1839** BUEL *Farmer's Companion* 72 Urette is animal urine, absorbed and rendered dry by mixture with calcareous earth.

∗**Urim and Thummim.** [See Exod. 28:30.] Two small transparent stonelike objects which Joseph Smith said he found with the plates of the *Book of Mormon* and which he used somewhat as spectacles in translating that work (see quots. 1830, 1843). *Obs.* Cf. **peepstone.**

1830 J. SMITH *Book of Mormon* (1920) iv. There were two stones in silver bows and these stones, fastened to a breastplate, constituted what is called the Urim and Thummim. **1843** CASWALL *Prophet of 19th Cent.* 77 The mystic Urim and Thummim . . . appeared in the form of two transparent stones, set in the rim of a bow, like a pair of spectacles, and fastened to a golden breastplate. **1867** DIXON *New Amer.* I. 239 You may smile at Joseph's gift of tongues; his discovery of Urim and Thummim (which he supposed to have been a pair of spectacles!)

urinalysis ˌjurəˈnæləsɪs, *n.* [f. ∗*urine*+∗*analysis.*] Analysis of the urine.

1889 *Buck's Handbk. Med. Sci.* VII. 416/1 Processes to be found in large works on urinalysis. 1897 *Columbus* (O.) *Dispatch* 18 June 5/2 He . . . was familiar with the term urinalysis. 1949 *Time* 17 Oct. 84/2 With it ['Selftester'], any man can begin his own urinalysis.

U.S. Abbreviation of United States (of America).

1791 Washington *Writings* XII. 66 A great quantity of bonds, thrown suddenly into the market, . . . could not but have effects the most injurious to the credit of the U.S. 1843 Oliver *Eight Months* 241 Never cutting a stick of their own for any purpose so long as there is any suitable that can be stolen from U.S. or Uncle Sam as they facetiously term the United States government. 1950 *Time* 8 May 19/3 He warned the U.S. against making the same mistake.

attrib. 1826 *Va. Herald* 27 Sep. 3/1 The query . . . has been frequently advanced in conversation, why vessels, purporting to be national ships should be sold by the U.S. Marshal. 1840 *Boston Transcript* 14 April 2/3 Company A of the 1st Regiment of U.S. Artillery . . . will leave this city. 1947 *Time* 21 July 20/2 But, good or bad, polygamy was doomed. U.S. agents came in to hunt down 'cohabs.'

b. Often designating highways in the building or maintenance of which the federal government had or has a part.

1927 *Ariz. Highways* May 13/1 Leaving California traveling U.S. Route 80 you cross the Colorado River bridge at Yuma. 1937 *Southwestern Lore* Sep. 35 Thirty-two miles southwest from La Junta on U.S. Highway 350, is the little town of Bloom. 1948 *News-Dispatch* (Michigan City, Ind.) 3 April 5/4 Visitors to Danville will use U.S. 36 from the east and west, and State Road 39 from the north and south.

U.S.A. Abbreviation of United States of America and of United States Army.

1795 *Pittsburgh Gaz.* 16 Dec. 1/3 U.S.A. Congress. 1828 Sherburne *Memoirs* 68 On the forehead of some of her [a ship's] carved images, the letters U.S.A. were carved. 1848 *Santa Fe Repub.* 24 Aug. 2/1 Maj. Weightman, Pay Master U.S.A. arrived in this city a few days since. 1946 *So. Sierran* Dec. 3/3 Back to the U.S.A. along the picturesque Hood Canal and down the rugged Oregon coast with its miles of unsurpassed sea vistas.

b. American English. Cf. ***American**, *n.* **2**, ***United States 2.**

1916 Eaton *Idyl of Twin Fires* 64 'Peter may have a predisposition to follow in father's footsteps, which I infer led toward the little green swinging doors,' I protested. 'Speakin' U.S.A., tommyrot!' said Mrs. Temple.

U. Sam. Abbreviation of Uncle Sam. *Rare.* — 1814 *Columbian Centinel* 3 Dec. 2/5 U. Sam pays his soldier-servants in Paper Money.

***use,** *n.* **To have no use for*, and variants: To dislike or distrust. *Colloq.* — 1872 *Harper's Mag.* June 158/2 He was an obstinate fellow . . . and, moreover, he 'had no use for' the defendant any way. 1921 Paine *Comr. Rolling Ocean* 11, I felt acquainted with you . . . though you seemed to have no great use for me.

***use,** *v.* **To use up*, to subject to thorough discussion or unfavorable criticism. Also **using up,** *n. Obs.*

1837 *Russellville* (Ky.) *Advt.* 27 Oct. 3/1 The way they 'use up' an Ex-Governor in the Buck Eye State. 1844 *S. Lit. Messenger* X. 720/2 Each and every one of the Magazines in question, gave Mr. 'Oppodeldoc' a complete using-up. 1855 Barnum *Life* 358 An article in the Tribune, which we know to be by his vigorous pen, by the summary and effectual manner in which the argument is put and his opponent 'used up.'

used-to-be. Someone or something past its period of power or influence, a has-been. *Colloq.* — 1853 B. F. Taylor *Jan. & June* 206 [They] consign them [*sc.* poets] to that grand receptacle of dilapidated 'has beens' and despised 'used-to-be's'—the old garret. 1911 Lincoln *Cap'n Warren's Wards* 237 One of 'em's a used-to-be, and the other's a never-was.

***ush,** *v. intr.* To act as usher. *Colloq.* — 1890 *Harper's Mag.* Dec. 160/2 The six gentlemanly cow-boys . . . swore that whoever should prove to be the lucky man, the others would ush for him at the ceremony. 1910 *Ib.* March 613/1 Man alive, you've crossed half a continent to 'ush' at that wedding!

***usher,** *n. specif.* A man, usu. an intimate friend of the bride or the bridegroom, serving as an usher at a wedding.

1894 *Life* 19 April 254/2, I wanted the ushers at my wedding to have their pictures taken right after the breakfast. 1923 Wiggin *My Garden of Memory* 379 Four of the bride's summer friends were the ushers. 1949 *Gladewater* (Tex.) *Times-Tribune* 31 July II. 2/3 Mert Starnes of Lubbock attended the groom as best man. Ushers were Royce Blankenship [etc.].

using-ground. An area frequented by game. — 1893 *Harper's Mag.* Oct. 681 The 'using-grounds' of the coveys [of quail] are generally known or suspected by the farmer who is fond of shooting.

U.S.N. Abbreviation of United States Navy. — 1862 Moore *Rebellion Rec.* V. II. 177 All our fleet, (except the Pittsburgh,) under Commodore Davis, U.S.N., . . . was under way. 1881 *Naval Encycl.* p. v, List of Contributors and Articles. Ammen, Daniel, Rear-Admiral U.S.N. 1950 *Chi. Tribune* 9 Aug. 22/3 In 1859, Commodore Josiah Tattnall, U.S.N., flag officer of the Asiatic squadron, added his ships to a British fleet in an attack upon Chinese forts defending the harbor of Tientsin.

U. States. Abbreviation of United States.

1787 in *Sp. & Doc. Amer. Hist.* I. (1944) 67 Resd. that the U. States in Congs. be authorized to elect a federal Executive. 1832 *Amer. Traveller* (Boston) 18 Dec. 2/2, 735 Shares in the U. States Bank, sold In New York, Tuesday noon, at 108½ to 109. 1897 *Current Hist.* (Buffalo, N.Y.) VII. 119 A treaty with Nicaragua for the construction of an isthmian canal under the control of the U. States government.

Utah ˈjutɔ, ˈjutɑ, *n.* [See **Ute.**]

1. =**Ute.**

[1720 in *Archæological Inst. Papers* V. 183 En que doi quenta . . . de la Jornada que acauaua de ejecutar en poz de la Nazion Yutta y Cumanche.] 1808 Pike *Sources Miss.* 222 Well the Utah are Indians also? 1851 Howe *Hist. Coll. Great West* 379 The *Eutaws* or *Yutas*, are scattered from the north of New Mexico to the borders of Snake River and Rio Colorado. 1862 *Harper's Mag.* Sep. 450/1 The Eutaws had encamped for the night.

b. The language of these Indians.

1853 Brewerton *With Kit Carson* (1930) 137, I will speak to this warrior in Eutaw, and if he understands me it will prove that he belongs to a friendly tribe.

2. *attrib.* Designating persons belonging to, or groups composed of, the Utes.

1822 Fowler *Jrnl.* 122 The Indeans. . . . Ware of the utaws nation. 1825 in Dale *Ashley-Smith Explor.* (1918) 150, I met a part of the Eutau tribe of Indians, who appeared very glad to see us and treated us in the most respectful and friendly manner. 1837 Irving *Bonneville* II. 219 A pert little Eutaw wench . . . had been taken prisoner . . . by a Shoshonie. 1862 *Harper's Mag.* Sep. 450/1 A conflict had just taken place between a band of Eutaw braves . . . and a war party of Comanches.

3. In special combs. with reference to the state of Utah: (1) **Utah juniper,** (see quot. 1940); (2) **mullet,** (see quot.); (3) **route,** =**Mormon trail,** *obs.*; (4) **War,** the trouble between the federal government and the Mormons in 1857.

(1) 1909 *Univ. Ariz. Agric. Exp. Sta. Timely Hints* No. 79, 5 Of the evergreen trees that may be recommended for planting above altitudes of 4000 feet, the following list is suggested: One-seeded juniper, . . . Utah juniper, . . . alligator bark juniper. 1940 R. J. Preston *Rocky Mt. Trees* 85 Utah Juniper *Juniperus utahensis*. . . . A spreading shrub or small tree; rarely over 20 feet high or 12 inches in diameter. — (2) 1884 *Nat. Museum Bul.* No. 27, 488 *Squalius atrarius*. . . . Utah Mullet; Chub of Utah Lake. — (3) 1857 *Cong. Globe* 24 Feb. 289/3 Many California emigrants have disappeared on the Utah route. — (4) 1944 *Utah Hist. Quart.* Jan.–Apr. 10 The Carson Mission was called home as a result of the outbreak of the 'Utah War.'

Utahan ˈjutɔ·ən, ˈjutɑ·ən, *n.* Also **Utahian, Utahn.** A native or resident of Utah.

1855 Whitman *Leaves of Grass* 58 Not only the free Utahan, Kansian, or Arkansian. 1864 *Sacramento Union* 11 Jan. 3/2 We Utahians have become robust in health and strong in the cunning and power of brawny arms. 1922 *Nation* 28 June 167/1 Here one sees the Utahn in his native setting. 1948 *Utah Humanities Rev.* April 263 Some Utahns are sensitive lest some of their material be used to ridicule or misinterpret our pioneers.

Ute jut, ˈjutɪ, *n.* [See note.]

Thought to be f. a native word meaning "person," or "people." See J. P. Harrington in *Amer. Anthropologist* n.s. XIII. (1911) 173–4.

An Indian belonging to a group of primitive, warlike Shoshonean tribes formerly occupying a large territory in Colorado, Utah, and New Mexico. Also, usu. *pl.*, the group or subdivision itself.

[1776 in W. R. Harris *Catholic Church in Utah* (1909) 227 The Coward Utes are divided into Huascaris, who dwell in the valley of San José and its vicinity; the Parusis . . . join them on the south and southwest.] 1821 J. Fowler *Journal* 53 Conl. Glann . . . was told by the Ietan cheef that the ware reedey to receve the goods. 1846 in *S.W. Hist. Ser.* IV. (1936) 212 Major Gilpin . . . made a long and arduous journey through the country of the Ute and Navajo. 1947 B. Haile *Prayer Stick Cutting* 43 Neckbands . . . should be of otter or beaver skin obtained from the Utes.

b. Also attrib., esp. **Ute Indian.**

1846 in *S.W. Hist. Ser.* III. (1935) 252 About fifty Ute Indians came in and held a council with Colonel Doniphan. 1888 Lee *Plains to Peaks* 73 The Ute ponies recently ranging in this territory were always in very good condition and were very much above the average Indian pony. 1949 *Rocks & Minerals* March–April 124/2 At the end of this road we had a chance to visit the Garden of the Gods, an area of 770 acres set aside as the worshipping grounds of the Ute Indians.

c. Ute Diggers, the Paiute Indians.

1876 SIMPSON *Rep. Explor. Utah* 460 These mixed bands are known as the Diggers, and commonly called Snake Diggers and Ute Diggers.

d. The language used by the Ute Indians.

1937 *Southwestern Lore* Sep. 22 The name Yampa is Ute for bear, so the river is variously called the Yampa or Bear River.

uthlecan ˈjuθləkən, *n.* Variant of **eulachon.** *Obs.* — **1836** IRVING *Astoria* II. 79 A small kind of fish, . . . called by the natives the uthlecan, . . . made its appearance at the mouth of the [Columbia] river. *Ib.*, The sturgeon makes its appearance in the river shortly after the uthlecan.

utility man. (See quot. 1909.) — **1909** WEBSTER 2260/1 utility man . . . a member of a professional baseball team who plays various positions in the absence of regular players. **1928** *Chi. Tribune* 1 June II. 1/2 Playing with four utility men in their lineup the Yankees made it three out of four from the Senators today, 4 to 0.

Utonian juˈtonɪən, *n.* [Irreg. f. Utah+-*ian.*] =**Utahan.** — **1881–89** (*title*), South Utonian (pub. at Beaver City, Utah). **1893** *Chi. Record* 3 July 9/6 As a people none are more sound than the Utonians.

***uvularia,** *n.* An herb of the genus *Uvularia*, a bellwort. — **1818** *Mass. H.S. Coll.* 2 Ser. VIII. 168 At the same time appear the blossoms of the alder, hazel, and poplar; soon after those of the uvularia or bellwort. **1850** S. WARNER *Wide, Wide World* xl, Wild columbine, the delicate corydalis, and more uvularias, which she called yellow bells, were added to her handful.

V

V, *n.

1. In colonial times used as a badge to be worn by those convicted of venery (see also quot. 1947). Now *hist.* Cf. ***A, *n.* 1.**

1638–9 in *Pub. Col. Soc.* III. 58, 5 March, 1638–9. John Davies, 'for grosse offences in attempting lewdness wth divers weomen,' 'to bee severely whipped' '& to weare the letter V. vpon his breast, vpon his vppermost garment, untill the Court do discharge him.' **1947** Downey *Lusty Forefathers* 123 *T* marks a thief, and *V* those guilty of vulgarity or viciousness.

2. A five-dollar bill. Also **V spot.** *Colloq.*

1837 *New-Yorker* 3 June 161/3 The possession of a 'V' was a subject matter for rejoicing. **1848** Lowell *BiglowP.* 1 Ser. vi. 103, I vow my holl sheer o' the spiles wouldn't come nigh a V spot. **1865** *Republican Banner* (Nashville, Tenn.) 5 Nov. 3/2 The Court took her down to the tune of a V. **1919** Morley *Haunted Bookshop* (1921) 239 I'll lend you my last V.

3. In various uses, now obs.: **a. V-flume,** a flume in the shape of a **V. b. V-plow,** a plow or road scraper having the shape of a **V. c. V-rail,** a railroad rail a cross section of which has a **V**-shape. **d. V-trick,** a trick or formation in football in which the players outline a **V.**

(a) 1896 Shinn *Story of Mine* 119 A single form of trough . . . has since been adopted in every mountainous region of the Pacific coast—the famous V-flume. — **(b) 1902** White *Blazed Trail* 73 The V plough was now put in action. Six horses drew it down the road, each pair superintended by a driver. The machine was weighted down by a number of logs laid across the arms. — **(c) 1856** Olmsted *Journey Slave States* 317 The [rail-]road was excellent and speed good, a heavy V rail having lately been substituted for a flat one. — **(d) 1899** A. H. Quinn *Pa. Stories* 21 They commenced with the 'V-trick' in those days.

vaca ˈvɑkə, *n. S.W.* [Sp. in same sense.] A cow.

1846 Magoffin *Down Santa Fé Trail* 91 They are inhabited by rancheros as they are called, who attend solely to raising of vacas. **1897** Hough *Story of Cowboy* 26 Even cattle are sometimes called *vacas,* though this is not usual. **1944** Adams *W. Words* 172.

***vacant,** *a.* **1. vacant land,** public land which through an error was not included in the regular government survey of a state. *Obs.* **2. vacant lot,** a lot on which there is no building.

(1) 1829 Brauns *Belehrungen* 96 Nicht aufgenommenes Land (Vacant Lands) nennt man in Amerika das bei der Vermessung des Staats von dem Landmesser aus Versehen übergangene und nicht eingetragene Land. — **(2) 1648** *New Haven Col. Rec.* 95 He shall build a dwelling house vpon it, . . . so it may not lye as a vacant lott. **1885** Howells *Silas Lapham* x, The frying of the grasshopper in the blossomed weed of the vacant lots in the Back Bay is intershot with the carol of crickets. **1949** *Milwaukie* (Ore.) *Rev.* 28 July 1/6 A staff of Portland experts has been quietly at work . . . counting every dwelling unit, business establishment and even vacant lots in the community.

***vacate,** *v.* **1.** *intr.* To spend a vacation. *Colloq.* **2.** *tr.* To cause the occupants of (a house) to move from it.

(1) 1836 *Knickerb.* VII. 15 Ned and I were vacating . . . at his father's charming residence. **1885** *Advance* 23 July 476 One thing he [a Chinese] can never learn and that is how to vacate. — **(2) 1904** *N.Y. Ev. Post* 14 May 7 His system of vacating unlivable houses is less drastic. He does not summarily turn families out.

***vacation,** *n.* A period of relaxation from one's customary occupation, a holiday. Also attrib.

1844 *Lowell Offering* IV. 237, I wish they would have a vacation in 'dog days.' **1882** Lathrop *Echo of Passion* i, They had but just come to Tanford, to spend the first vacation which the young chemist . . . had allowed himself since his marriage. **1950** *Chi. Tribune* 21 May vii. 6/4 Visitors to Oregon have a wide choice of attractions from which to supplement sightseeing and other vacation activities in Oregon's cool, green vacationlands.

vacation veˈkeʃən, *v. intr.* To take a vacation or holiday. Also *to go* (or *be*) *vacationing.*

1896 *Advance* (Chi.) 27 Aug. 273 Despite hard times, people will go vacationing. **1934** in Mencken *Supp.* I. 386 Mrs. Williams vacationed for a month at Hotel Laguna. **1947** *Chi. D. News* 16 June 8/3 It took place about 10 years ago, when I was vacationing at Mackinac Island.

***vacationer,** *n.* One who is on a vacation from business or other occupation.

1890 *Advance* (Chi.) 28 Aug., The 'swallows homeward fly,' and so, by sea and land, do vacationers and tourists. **1905** *Springfield W. Republican* 28 July 2 Any vacationer may easily extend the bounds of his knowledge by drinking in what the natives may have to tell him. **1950** *Chi. Tribune* 21 May vii. 1/1 Vacationers in the west Michigan area this year will have the best time of their lives.

vacationless veˈkeʃənləs, *a.* Without a vacation. — **1891** *Advance* (Chi.) 25 June, I dislike to go away leaving people vacationless who deserve an outing more than I do. **1911** Harrison *Queed* 202 The Colonel . . . gave an account of his vacationless summer.

vacher ˈvɑʃɚ, *n. S.W.* [F.] A cowboy. *Obs.* Cf. **vaquero. — 1826** Flint *F. Berrian* 39 Then we traversed the belt of vachers and shepherds, with their blanket-capotes. **1848** Bartlett 373 *Vacher,* . . . the stock or cattle keeper on the prairies of the South-west.

vachery ˈvɑʃərɪ, *n. S.W.* [F. *vacherie,* in same sense. An Amer. borrowing.] A stock farm. *Obs.* — **1818** Darby *Emigrant's Guide* 76 Many of the richer planters on the Teche, Vermilion, and other agricultural districts, have stock farms, or as they are termed in the country, 'vacheries.' **1846** Thorpe *Myst. Backwoods* 14 Among the *vacheries* of New Spain, they [cattle] are killed for their skins alone.

vacquero, see **vaquero.**

***vacuum,** *n.* Short for "vacuum cleaner." — **1934** Webster. **1947** *Chi. Sun* 3 April 8/2 As I crammed the junk back into the closet, I heard the vacuum start up in another part of the house.

vag væg, *n.* A vagrant or vagabond. *Slang.*

1868 *Terr. Enterprise* (Virginia, Nev.) 1 Feb. 3/1 The authorities have a big crowd of 'vags' spotted, and are determined to make them travel. **1922** *Dly. Press* (Ardmore, Okla.) 23 May 1/6 (*heading*), New Law To Make 'Vags' Work Streets. **1949** *L.A. Times* ii. 2/5 (*heading*), Vice Squad Keeps Tabs on Haunts of Hollywood Back-Alley 'Vags.'

vag væg, *v.*[1] [Origin obscure.] *intr.* A mild oath. Also **vaggers,** an exclamation. *Colloq. Obs.* — **1814** *Conn. Courant* 8 March 1/4 'Is my corn fan here,' said the man at the door in a loud voice. 'Fan, fan?' said Timothy, 'I *vags,* I don't know!' **1815** in *D.N.* V. 380 *van,* exclamation. *vaggers,* do.

vag væg, *v.*[2] [f. **vag,** *n.*] *tr.* (See quot. 1891.) *Slang.*

1876 Hearn *Amer. Miscellany* (1924) I. 177 If you keep on this way, Dolly, . . . I'll 'vag' you. **1891** C. Roberts *Adrift Amer.* 169, I was arrested as a vagrant. As the popular expression went, I got 'vagged.' **1908** Davenport *Butte Beneath X-Ray* 46 If the Kalispell police had done their duty she would have been 'vagged' years ago.

vagarist vəˈgɛrɪst, *n.* One given to vagaries, a faddist. *Rare.* — **1888** *Voice* (N.Y.) 24 May, The Prohibition party are now free from that suspicion of being vagarists, which led to the invention of the word crank.

valda ˈvɑldə, *n. W.* A spelling variant of falda *q.v.* — **1871** Harte *Luck of Roaring Camp* 228 But I . . . soon prepared myself to take a boat to the lower 'valda' of the foot-hills. **1877** ——— *Story of Mine* (1896) 1 It was a sterile waste bordered here and there by arable fringes and valdas of meadow land.

valedictorian ˌvælədɪkˈtorɪən, *n.* [f. **valedictory*+-*an.*] A college or high-school senior, usu. the one of highest academic standing in his class, who delivers the valedictory oration at the graduation of his class.

1759 *Holyoke Diaries* 20 Officers of the Sophisters chose Valedictorians. **1852** *Harper's Mag.* Aug. 335/1, [I was] pointed out, to the classes, just entered, as the valedictorian. **1949** *Chi. Maroon* 4 Oct. 7/2 The college should be large and not limited to high-school valedictorians.

valedictory ˌvæləˈdɪktərɪ, *n.* [f. **valedictory, a.*]

1. A student's valedictory oration.

1779 *N.J. Archives* 2 Ser. III. 670 The six undergraduates pronounced, orations, . . . Stephan Renselaer the valedictory in English. **1893** Thanet *Stories Western Town* 99 Tommy's valedictory scored a success that is a tradition of the High School.

b. The privilege of delivering the valedictory.

1830 *Collegian* 118, I was thinking you were in the Senior Class; at any rate, when you do leave, I suppose you'll carry the day in the Valedictory of course. **1843** Stowe *Mayflower* 36 They say that your son is going to have the valedictory in college. **1893** Thanet *Stories Western Town* 96 Tommy's father . . . thinks everything of his getting the valedictory, and Tommy, he worked nights studying to get it.

2. An address delivered or printed by one leaving a public office or a private position.

1824 Marshall *Kentucky* II. 199 President Washington published his valedictory; in which he declined further service. **1863** Lincoln in Barnes *Mem. T. Weed* 433 Your valedictory to the patrons of the Albany 'Evening Journal' brings me a good deal of uneasiness. **1945** *Newsweek* 1 Jan. 36/3 The Dean of the lame ducks, . . . made his valedictory a message of gloom.

***valentine,** *n.* A variety of string bean. In full **valentine bean.** *Obs.* — **1850** *Rep. Comm. Patents 1849: Agric.* 158 [Some peas are] speckled, like the valentine bean. **1859** *Ill. Agric. Soc. Trans.* III. 503 Early yellow six-weeks and early Valentine (long red mottled,) are excellent for snaps.

As the last term in **comic valentine.**

***valerian,** *n. local.* (See quots.) — **1894** *Amer. Folk-Lore* VII. 100 *Cypripedium acaule,* valerian, Franconia, N.H. **1899** *Animal & Plant Lore* 115 *Cypripedium acaule* . . . is called valerian from its supposed efficacy in nervous disorders.

valgame Dios. [Sp. in same sense.] God help me! For heaven's sake! *Colloq.* — **1873** Lew Wallace *Fair God* 291 (Bentley), What an exchange. *Valgame Dios!* **1931** Mary Austin *Starry Adventure* 150 (Bentley), Pablo began talking as soon as he came within reach, and you said . . . *Valgame Dios* or whatever was required.

Vallandighamer vəˈlændɪŋˌæmɚ, *n.* [f. Clement L. *Vallandigham* (1820–71), Ohio Copperhead leader arrested for treason in 1863 and sentenced to prison.] (See quot.) *Obs.* — **1862** *Lawrence* (Kans.) *Republican* 11 Sep. 4/1 That faction of the Democracy who sympathise with the rebels are known in Ohio as 'Vallandighamers,' in Illinois as 'guerillas,' in Missouri as 'butternuts,' in Kansas as 'jayhawkers,' in Kentucky as 'bushwhackers,' and in Indiana as 'copperheads.'

*** valley,** *n.*

1. (*cap.*) The Shenandoah Valley, a great valley between the Allegheny and the Blue Ridge Mountains, drained by the Shenandoah River. Also attrib.

[**1832** *Amer. R.R. Jrnl.* I. 563/2 A route of equal distance cannot be found . . . as that through 'the Valley of Virginia.'] **1833** J. Hall *Harpe's Head* 9 A solitary horseman might have been seen slowly winding his way along a narrow road, in that part of Virginia which is now called the Valley. **1850** Foote *Virginia* 377 The call of General Greene for aid . . . aroused the Valley-men to come out of their quiet abode. **1894** *Harper's Mag.* Sep. 622/1 There are main roads and there are wagons to use upon then, but they are both 'valley improvements.'

b. The Mississippi Valley.

1840 *Zanesville* (O.) *Gaz.* 8 July, Louisiana.—Great outlet of the Great Valley—will soon be lost to Van Burenism. **1845** *S. Lit. Messenger* XI. 582/1 The steam power of the 'Valley' might be expanded, in case of war. **1883** Mark Twain *Life on Miss.* 289 (R.), It would not be fair to exact grammatical perfection from the peoples of the Valley.

2. *transf.* The inhabitants of a valley.

1881 Stoddard *E. Hardery* 288 All the valley came, . . . and for once the roomy, rambling old parsonage was none too large.

3. In special combs.: (1) **valley bottom,** bottomland in a valley; (2) **cottonwood,** one of various species of cottonwood found in the West; (3) **mahogany,** the feather tree, *Cercocarpus montanus;* (4) **oak,** the valley white oak, *Quercus lobata,* of California; (5) **partridge,** =next; (6) **quail,** (see quot. 1917); (7) **state,** one of the states in the Mississippi Valley; (8) **tan,** see as a main entry.

(1) **1864** Taylor *H. Thurston* 373 The elms . . . had grown up since the valley-bottom was cleared. — (2) **1913** Wooton *Trees & Shrubs N. Mex.* 39 The Valley Cottonwood . . . forms much the greater part of the 'bosques' of the Rio Grande, the Gila and the lower Pecos valleys. — (3) **1905** *Forestry Bureau Bul.* No. 66, 33 Valley mahogany, western serviceberry, buffalo berry, and dwarf maple have, without doubt, come down from the Rocky Mountains. — (4) **1897** Sudworth *Arborescent Flora* 152 *Quercus lobata*. . . . Weeping Oak (Cal.). Valley Oak (Cal.). **1949** Howell *Marin Flora* 15 There is frequently a scattered occurrence of valley oaks.

(5) **1887** Ridgway *Man. N. Amer. Birds* 192 C[*yrtonyx*] *californica vallicola,* Valley Partridge. — (6) **1858** *S.F. Bulletin* 21 May 2/1 The flesh of this bird is delicious, and is greatly preferable to that of the little valley quail. **1917** *Birds of Amer.* II. 8 The California quail . . . is known commonly in California as the Valley Quail . . . ; but ornithologists now recognize two subspecies, the California Quail and the Valley Quail (*Lophortyx californica vallicola*). *Ib.* 9 Gambel's Quail. *Lophortyx gambeli*. . . . [Also called] Arizona Quail; Gambel's Valley Quail. **1950** *Nat. Geog. Mag.* March 412 Despite Its Museum-like Pose, This Valley Quail Is Very Much Alive. — (7) **1845** *S. Lit. Messenger* XI. 584/2, I propose to show . . . how all the Valley States . . . may be benefitted, by restoring the commerce of the country to its natural channels.

As the last term in **dry, irrigation, mesquite, Mississippi, poor valley.**

valley tan.

1. (See quots.)

1858 *Kirk Anderson's Valley Tan* (Salt Lake City) 5 Nov. 2/1 Valley Tan was first applied to the leather made in this Territory in contradistinction to the imported articles from the States; it gradually began to apply to every article made, or manufactured, or produced in the Territory, and means in its strictest sense, *home manufactures.* **1859** *Ib.* 25 Jan. 2/5 [We] herewith present you with a regular Valley Tan knife, believing you are eminently entitled to it. **1942** Stegner *Mormon C.* 70 'Valley Tan,' a term of derision first applied to the inferior grades of leather made in Salt Lake, later came to be a blanket epithet for anything home-made and hence inferior.

2. (See quot. 1890.) In full **valley tan whisky.**

1860 *Mountaineer* (Salt Lake City) 16 June 169/3 Which food do you prefer, rum, mixed drinks or Valley Tan? **1884** Hill *Colo. Pioneers* 45 We handed the old man the bottle containing about a quart of 'valley tan' whisky. **1890** Langford *Vigilante Days* (1912) 272 The entire party joined in a pledge of amity over a bottle of 'Valley Tan,' a liquor well known throughout the mountains, and a production of the Mormons of Salt Lake Valley. **1942** *Ore. Hist. Quart.* Dec. 339 Only among his cronies could he crack a quart of valley tan and spin a whopper with any freedom.

valorization ˌvælərəˈzeʃən, *n.* [Prob. f. **valor,* value, worth + *-*ization,* but cf. Pg. *valorização.*] The act or fact of fixing the value or price of some commercial commodity. Also attrib. — **1907** *Amer. Polit. Sci. Rev.* Feb. 249 (*Cent. Supp.*), The financing of the valorization scheme is provided for by the issuing of bonds by the three coffee producing States, guaranteed by the general government. **1908** *Nation* 22 Aug. 730/1 He read about a coffee valorization scheme that is not working as it should.

Valparaiso oak. The canyon oak, a California evergreen. Cf. **maul oak.** — **1884** Sargent *Rep. Forests* 146 Quercus chrysolepis. . . . Live Oak. Maul Oak. Valparaiso Oak. **1897** Sudworth *Arborescent Flora* 164 *Quercus chrysolepis*. . . . Valparaiso Oak (Cal.).

vamoose væˈmus, *v.* Orig. *S.W.* [Sp. *vamos,* let us go.] *intr.* To go, depart. *Colloq.*

[**1844** G. W. Kendall *Narrative* 390 (Bentley), The Mexican now pointed to his horse, and uttered the well known bamanos (Come, let us be moving—a word we heard forty times a day.)] **1868** *Ore. State Jrnl.* 18 July 1/6 The young Lieutenant vamoosed at the next stopping place. **1949** *Sky Line Trail* Oct. 18/2 Shouts, rather than causing 'em to vamoose, brought Mama Bruin shuffling toward me.

Hence **vamoosing,** *n.*

1862 Lowell *Biglow P.* 2 Ser. v. 75 Or, when the vamosin' come, ever, to find [etc.].

b. *To vamoose the ranch,* to leave the ranch, depart.

1847 McHatton E. Ripley *Rough & Ready* 245 (Bentley), On the morning after I wrote the letter to father . . . they stacked their arms and colors and 'vamoosed the ranch.' **1891** Sloan *Fogy Days* 134, [I] soon had the pleasure of thinking I had paralyzed the whole party, and was now ready to vamose the ranche, cursing (in my mind) the unreliability of the entire fair sex. **1947** Chalfant *Gold, Guns, & Ghost Towns* 16, I proposed to quietly 'vamoose the ranch.'

Also *to vamoose the camp, the kitchen.*

1939 Rollins *Gone Haywire* 126 Vamoose the kitchen an' find ef yer saddle fits. **1950** *Boston Globe Mag.* 8 Jan. 11/2 That would have fixed us up so we could have vamoosed the camp.

*** van,** *n. Lumbering.* (See quots. 1893, 1946.) Also attrib.

1893 *Scribner's Mag.* June 710/2 There is the dealing out of tobacco and clothing to the men from the camp supply-chest, called the 'Van.' **1902** White *Blazed Trail* 61 His wages were twenty-five dollars a month, which his van bill would reduce to the double eagle. *Ib.* 196 He would have to figure on blankets, harness, . . . [and] van-goods. *Ib.* 218 Thorpe looked through the ledger and van book, and finally handed the man a slip. **1946** Newton *P. Bunyan* 67 A van is the camp store maintained by every owner or manager of logging operations at his camp in the woods.

As the last term in **baggage, moving van.** See also **Little Van.**

van væn, *v.* [Origin obscure. Cf. **swan,** *v.*] *intr. I van (you),* I swear, used as a mild imprecation. *Obs.* — **1790** *Mass. Spy* 30 Dec. (Th.), In one village you will hear the phrase 'I snore,'—in another, 'I swowgar,'—and in another, 'I van you, I wunt do it.' **1815** Humphreys *Yankey* 97, I can hardly hold my hair on, I van.

Van- væn, *prefix.* [Martin *Van* Buren (1782–1862), eighth President of the U.S. (1837–41).] In obs. compounds denoting a political follower or adherent of Martin Van Buren, as **Vanite, Vanjack, Vanocrat.**

1838 *Lexington* (Ky.) *Observer* 9 May, The Vanite leaders at Richmond give it up. **1840** *Log Cabin Song Book* 43 He makes the Vanocrats look rather slim. *Ib.* 52 The great Twenty-Second is coming And the Vanjacks begin to look blue. **1844** *Henry Clay Bugle* (Maysville, Ky.) 2 May 4/1 And Brother Swartwout, noble soul! A Vanite to the core.

Van Buren. *attrib.* Of or pertaining to Martin Van Buren (1782–1862), as (1) **Van Buren convention,** (2) **democrat,** (3) **man.** All *obs.*

(1) **1832** *Western Citizen* (Paris, Ky.) 15 June 2/6 That State is in the field against the rejected minister, and will laugh to scorn the doings of the 'Van Buren Convention at Baltimore.' — (2) **1855** *N.Y. Herald* 17 Nov. 4/4 Is not Marcy a veteran legitimate Van Buren democrat of the Albany Regency? — (3) **1879** *Chi. Tribune* 5 May 4/4 He was 'a Van Buren, Anti-Slavery war man,' who was not allowed to come forward until the Pro-Slavery programme was played out.

Van Burenism. *Polit.* The methods or principles of Martin Van Buren (1782–1862), eighth President of the U.S. (1837–41), and his followers. Now *hist.*

1835 *Franklin Repository* (Chambersburg, Pa.) 25 Aug. 3/5 Pennsylvania [must be] held more closely in the gripe of Van Burenism, by the elevation of any man to the gubernatorial chair . . . who is not openly hostile to the elevation of the President's own nominated successor. **1859** GRATTAN *Civilized Amer.* II. 302 [It] might justify the displacing the word 'Jesuitism' from the American language, and substituting 'Van Burenism' in its stead. **1935** ALEXANDER *Amer. Talleyrand* 125 It was during this period of building the dynasty that he started earning his reputation for vanburenism.

Van Burenite. A political supporter of Martin Van Buren. Now *hist.* Cf. **Van Burenism.**

1836 *Wkly. Advt.* (Russellville, Ky.) 21 Jan 3/1 And yet, the Van Burenites have the ridiculous impudence to say that all the people should vote for him to prevent the election from going into the house of Representatives. **1856** *Western Citizen* (Paris, Ky.) 13 June 1/6 Sumner was a Polk man in 1844; a Van Burenite in 1848. **1929** LYNCH *Epoch & Man* 238 Judge Joseph C. Yates . . . had the united support of the Clintonians and the Van Burenites.

Vandevere ˈvændəˌvɪr, *n.* [Poss. the name of the originator.] A variety of apple. *Obs.*

1786 WASHINGTON *Diaries* III. 24 Adjoining the cross walk, are 2 Apple trees taken from the middle walk in the No. Garden—said to be Vandiviers. **1859** ELLIOTT *Western Fruit Book* 113 Vandervere . . . American. Native of Delaware. **1875** BURROUGHS *Winter Sunshine* 155 Now a Vandevere or a King rolls down from the apex above.

vandoo, see **voodoo.**

* **vanilla,** *n.*

1. vanilla grass, holy grass, *Hierochloe borealis.*

1857 GRAY *Botany* 574. **1884** VASEY *Agric. Grasses* 55 Vanilla or Seneca grass . . . is very sweet scented and is often used to perfume drawers, &c. **1949** HOWELL *Marin Flora* 7 Other herbs that are lovely in flower or in leaf are the vanilla grass (*Hierochloe occidentalis*), fairy lantern (*Disporum Smithii*), . . . and others.

2. vanilla plant, the wild vanilla, *Trilisa odoratissima.*

1857 GRAY *Botany* 185 *L[iatris] odoratissima,* Vanilla-plant. . . . Leaves exhaling the odor of Vanilla when bruised. **1901** MOHR *Plant Life Ala.* 768 *Trilisa odoratissima,* . . . Vanilla Plant. . . . Carolinian and Louisianian areas.

As the last term in **Florida, wild vanilla.**

vantoon vænˈtun, *n.* The card game vingt-et-un. Also allusive. *Obs.* Cf. ***twenty-one.** — **1839** BRIGGS *Harry Franco* I. 33 He exclaimed, 'Vantoon,' and without more ceremony, he caught up a little heap of sixpences and shillings, and rose up from the table. **1888** PERRIN *Ky. Pioneer Press* 35 By 'vantoon' it is presumed that he meant the old French game of cards, *vingt-un.*

vaquero vəˈkɛro, *n. W.* [Sp. in same sense.] A cowboy, esp. one of Mexican nationality. Cf. **bukcaroo.**

1831 BEECHEY *Voyage to Pacific* II. 40 Intrusting their baggage to the care of two vaqueros (Indian cattle drivers) who were to accompany them . . . they set off. **1888** LINDLEY *Calif. of South* 211 A fat, young steer was then lassoed by a *vacquero.* **1949** *L.A. Times Home Mag.* 11 Dec. 20/2 Vaqueros roamed the folded hills amid bawling calves and bleating sheep.

attrib. **1844** GREGG *Commerce of Prairies* I. 214 The shanks of the vaquero spurs are three to five inches long, with rowels sometimes six inches in diameter. **1877** HARTE *Story of Mine* (1896) 203 Having caparisoned himself and charger in true vaquero style, . . . [he] put a sombrero rakishly on his curls. **1934** WHITE *Folded Hills* 136 He could throw a knife not by the blade, *vaquero* fashion, but from the flat of his hand.

vara ˈvɑrə, *n. W.* [Sp. in both the senses shown here. An Amer. borrowing.] **1.** A linear measure, usu. about 33 inches. **2.** A stick or cane used as an emblem of authority. *Obs.*

(1) **1831** DEWEES *Lett. from Texas* 139 One labor shall be composed of one million square varas. **1869** BROWNE *Adv. Apache Country* 259 This palatial edifice occupies a square of several hundred varas. **1910** J. HART *Vigilante Girl* 153 In the centre of the walled enclosure was a great plaza or rectangle of open ground, some two hundred varas square. — (2) **1864** *Wkly. New Mexican* 27 May 2/1 Each vara is silver mounted, and has the name of the pueblo it is intended for engraved on the head, together with the name of President Lincoln.

* **varied,** *a.* In the names of birds: (1) **varied bunting,** a bunting, *Passerina versicolor,* allied to the painted bunting, and found in the Southwest; (2) **creeping warbler,** the black and white warbler; (3) **thrush,** a conspicuously marked thrush, *Ixoreus naevius,* of the Northwest and Alaska.

(1) **1844** *Nat. Hist. N.Y., Zoology* II. 157 The Varied Bunting . . . has been noticed in Georgia, Kentucky, Alabama, Louisiana, Florida and New-Jersey. **1917** *Birds of Amer.* III. 74/2 The Varied Bunting is of accidental occurrence in Michigan. — (2) **1844** *Nat. Hist. N.Y., Zoology* II. 52 The Varied Creeping Warbler . . . is highly useful in destroying the various insects which hide themselves in the crevices of the bark of trees. **1917** *Birds of Amer.* III. 112 Black and White Warbler. . . . Other Names.— . . . Striped Warbler; Varied Creeping Warbler. — (3) **1839** AUDUBON *Ornith. Biog.* V. 284. **1948** *Pacific Discovery* March–April 17/2 The varied thrush pauses soberly in the dense foliage as it waits for a rainstorm to spend itself.

variegated goby. (See quots.) — **1814** MITCHILL *Fishes N.Y.* 379 Variegated Goby. *Gobius viridipallidus.* . . . Is about two inches and a half long. **1855** BAIRD in *Smithsonian Rep. 1854* 339 The variegated Goby. . . . A few specimens only of this rare fish were taken in the grass along the beach of the river.

* **variety,** *n.* **1. variety shop,** =next. **2. variety store,** a general store keeping a wide variety of articles for sale. **3. variety troupe,** a group of actors and actresses who put on variety shows.

(1) **1824** SINGLETON *Lett. South & West* 84 One indication of a new country is that the shops are variety-shops; each one keeping piece-goods, groceries, cutlery [etc.]. **1861** WINTHROP *Open Air* 220 But there were parting gifts showered on the regiment enough to establish a variety shop. — (2) **1768** *Boston Ev.-Post* 21 Nov. 3/3. **1879** B. F. TAYLOR *Summer-Savory* 138 The variety store of a hundred years ago, where needles and crowbars, goose-yokes and finger-rings, liquorice-sticks and leather are to be had for cash or 'dicker.' **1945** *Greeley* (Colo.) *D. Tribune* 18 Aug. 1/2 Mr. Quigley established a variety store. — (3) **1868** *Ore. State Jrnl.* 17 Oct. 3/1 Variety Troupe.—This troupe gave an entertainment at the Court House.

* **varnish,** *n.* As the last term in **coffin, desert varnish.**

* **varnish tree.** The poison sumac, *Toxicodendron vernix.*

[**1758** *Phil. Trans.* L. 448, I suppose he means by this true varnish-tree, the Carolina pennated Toxicodendron.] **1785** MARSHALL *Amer. Grove* 130 Varnish-Tree, or Poison Ash . . . is allowed to be the same with the true Varnish-tree of Japan. **1807** J. SCOTT *Md. & Del.* 27 There is also another species of sumach, supposed to be the rhus vernix, or varnish tree.

vaseline ˈvæslˌin, *n.* [See note.]

"*Vaseline* was coined by Robert A. Chesebrough in 1870 or thereabout. It was made of the German *wasser,* meaning water, and the Greek *elaion,* meaning oil. . . . *Vaseline* now appears in all the German and French dictionaries, but all rights to the name are still vested in the Chesebrough Company" (Mencken, *American Language,* 4th ed. 172).

A semisolid yellow-whitish petroleum product marketed under the trade-mark Vaseline and used as an ointment and for other medicinal purposes.

1874 *Eng. Mech.* 25 Sep. 36 A new petroleum product has been introduced into the trade under the name of vaseline. **1921** *Outing* Sep. 266/3 Thinner oil, as it is most frequently mixed, runs at the least provocation on the part of a heat ray; while the heavier vaseline will stay put. **1949** *Hoard's Dairyman* 25 Nov. 837/1 A ring of vaseline about an inch wide is then smeared completely around the clipped areas.

attrib. **1935** LINCOLN *Cape Cod Yesterdays* 164 There were at least half a dozen 'vaseline yellow' candlesticks pushed back out of the way in our closet, discarded, of course, when kerosene came to be burned for lighting purposes.

vastate ˈvæstet, *v.* [Cf. next.] *tr.* To make unsusceptible to evil impulses. *Rare.* — **1892** Howells in *Harper's Mag.* March 608/1 That long passion of his early youth, which seemed to have vastated him before he came here.

∗ **vastation,** *n.* Purification by destruction of evil impulses.

1850 Emerson *Representative Men* 132 He was let down through a column that seemed of brass, . . . that he might descend safely among the unhappy, and witness the vastation of souls. **1887** J. Ellis *New Christianity* 290 Spirits [are] preparing for heaven, or undergoing vastation. **1892** Howells in *Harper's Mag.* March 608/1 He was rather proud of his vastation.

vaudoux, see **voodoo.**

∗ **vault,** *n.* An underground room strongly walled and provided with heavy doors and complicated locks, used for storing money or other valuables.

1791 in *Jrnl. of Wm. Maclay* (1927) 360 Suppose the vault's empty, and a note presented for payment: would the bearer take certificates as specie? **1838** *Speeches of D. Barnard* 186 The theory in regard to bank paper is, that the coin is supposed to be all in vault. **1898** Westcott *D. Harum* 137 Everything had been put away, the safe and vault closed, and Peleg had departed with the mail. **1949** Vestal *Non-Fiction Writing* 35 It is small enough to be stored in the vault at the bank while the writer is on vacation.

As the last term in **bank, receiving vault.**

Vaux's swift. A swift (see quot. 1917) named by J. K. Townsend for a friend, W. S. Vaux (1811–82), of Philadelphia. — **1887** Ridgway *Man. N. Amer. Birds* 303 Western United States (chiefly Pacific coast), north of British Columbia. . . . *C[hætura] vauxii.* Vaux's swift. **1917** *Birds of Amer.* II. 178/2 Vaux's swift (*Chætura vauxi*) is the western representative of the Chimney Swift.

V.C. (See quot.) *Obs.* — **1881** M. Hardy *Through Cities & Prairie Lands* 150 Here and there we decipher an English name, and, beneath, the information: 'Died by the hands of the V.C.' . . . The V.C. means the Vigilance Committee, who, in the early, lawless days, executed justice swift and sure upon proven criminals.

*∗***veal,** *n.* As the last term in **bob, deacon veal.**

vealer ˈvilɚ, *n.* A calf fit or intended for veal. *Colloq.*

1895 *Standard.* **1931** *Daily News-Journal* (Murfreesboro, Tenn.) 17 April 4/1 Better grade vealers around 50¢ higher. **1949** *Oregonian* (Portland) 10 Aug. III. 4/8 A few too many 'poor calves' were in evidence, while good light vealers were a little short of needs.

*∗***veals,** *n. pl.* App. some now obsolete form of feminine adornment. — **1868** Pomeroy *Nonsense* (1870) 36 (We.), I had her curls, her frizzle, her rats, her waterfall! I had her spiral palpitators, her bird's-nest, her veals.

∗ **vealy,** *a.* Youthful, imperfect, immature. Also **vealiness,** *n.*

1890 *Columbus* (O.) *Dispatch* 17 July, A vealy medical-school graduate, whose employment is an insult to intelligent people. **1895** *Standard* 1995/2 *Vealiness,* . . . want of maturity. **1907** *Outlook* 19 Jan. 80/1 The sylvan thief shared our vealy homage with moonlighters, smugglers [etc.].

veery ˈvɪrɪ, *n.* [Imitative.] The tawny thrush, *Hylocichla fuscescens.*

1845 Judd *Margaret* II. 187 Deep in the forest [are] olive-backs, veeries, oven-birds. **1917** *Birds of Amer.* III. 228/1 The Veery is essentially a bird of the deep woods and the 'silent places.' **1943** Damon *Sense of H.* 6 Twilight is quiet to hear the wood thrush distinctly fluting his three rich notes, the veery whirling his silvery circle.

vega ˈvegə, *n. S.W.* [Sp. in same sense. An Amer. borrowing.] An extensive plain or valley. *Obs.*

1850 Taylor *Eldorado* vii, The grass on the vega before the house was still thick and green. **1888** Wallace *Land of Pueblos* 80 A plateau, the highest of equal area on the globe, varied with sterile *vegas* and dreary sierras, . . . had once been the home of wandering tribes. **1949** *Sat. Ev. Post* 9 April 132/4 There was loose horses and cattle in the *vegas.*

*∗***vegetable,** *n.* **1. vegetable canner,** one who cans vegetables. (Cf. **canner 1.**) **2. vegetable doctor,** an herb doctor. *Obs.* — **(1) 1904** *N.Y. Tribune* 17 July 8 Now even many rural districts are as dependent on the beef packer, the vegetable canner, . . . as the veriest cockney. — **(2) 1840** Dewey *Mass. Flowering Plants* 110 Indian Tobacco . . . operates as a violent emetic, and is the dangerous medicine of many who are called vegetable doctors.

As the last term in **salt-water, Shaker vegetable.**

Veiled Prophet. A member of a Masonic order for pleasure and social fellowship formally organized at Hamilton, N.Y., Sep. 10, 1889, under the name Mystic Order of the Veiled Prophets of the Enchanted Realm.

1885 Rittenhouse *Maud* 361 It is *the* week in St. Louis. Expo., Fair, Veiled Prophets, Trades, Flambeaux [etc.]. **1887** *Ib.* 400 All day Tuesday we were getting ready for the Veiled Prophets ball. **1904** *Daily Chron.* 27 April 7/6 There is a great gathering of Freemasons in Washington to-day in order to be present at the initiation of President Roosevelt to-night into the Mystic Order of the Veiled Prophets.

∗ **vein,** *n.* A stretch, strip, or extent of timber. *Obs.*

1671 *S.C. Hist. Soc. Coll.* V. 333 A mile from the River side you will finde A veine of pines. **1800** Hawkins *Sk. Creek Country* 20 These fifteen miles [of river bank] is waving, with some good oak in small veins. *a***1862** Thoreau *Maine Woods* 215 White and red pines . . . [grow] in 'veins,' 'clumps,' 'groups,' or 'communities.'

As the last term in **fissure, pay, rabbit vein.**

veloce vəˈlɑs, *n.* A velocipede. Also **veloce-riding.** *Obs.* — **1869** *Velocipede* (N.Y.) 31 It was found very difficult to construct a veloce sufficiently steady. **1896** *Godey's Mag.* April 348/1 The winter season is not favorable to veloce-riding.

∗ **velvet,** *n.*

1. Profit or gain beyond what is usual or expected, orig. the cash or chips a player was ahead in a gambling game. *Slang.*

1901 White *Westerners* xxiii. 228 Let that go for now. . . . We can call that 'velvet.' **1931** Ira L. Reeves *Ol' Rum River* 106 Any operating time over this period represents 'velvet' profits. **1946** *Harper's Mag.* Oct. 276/2 Whenever the animals manage to trade off some grain to human beings for whisky, the pigs seem to get the velvet.

2. In combs.: (1) **velvet ant,** (see quot. 1891); (2) **bean,** (see quot. 1909), also attrib.; (3) *∗* **duck,** the white-winged scoter, *Melanitta deglandi;* (4) **grass,** a coarse European grass, *Holcus lanatus,* naturalized in the U.S.; (5) *∗* **leaf,** = **Mormon-weed;** (6) **ore,** (see quot.), *obs.;* (7) **sumac,** the staghorn sumac.

(1) 1748 Catesby *Carolina* App. 13 *Formica villosa coccinea.* The Velvet Ant. . . . [Except] the thorax, . . . the whole body and head resembled crimson velvet. **1891** *Cent.* 6715/1 *Velvet ant,* a solitary ant, of the family *Mutilidae:* a spider-ant; so called from the soft hairy covering. **1947** *Desert Mag.* May 9/1 It is called a Velvet ant, but it really isn't an ant at all. — **(2) 1898** *Dept. Agric. Yrbk. 1897* 504 The velvet bean [is a widely grown forage crop] for Florida orange groves. **1909** *Cent. Supp.* 121/2 Velvet-bean, *Stizolobium utilis* (*Mucuna utilis* of Wallich), widely grown in the tropics and much cultivated in the southern United States as a forage and green-mature crop. **1950** *Democrat* 30 March 8/2 For Sale—Limited amount of good, clean velvet bean seed. — **(3) 1844** *Nat. Hist. N.Y., Zoology* II. 337 The White-winged Coot . . . is described in the books under the name of Velvet Duck. **1917** *Birds of Amer.* I. 150 White-winged Scoter. . . . Other Names.—Velvet Scoter; Velvet Duck. — **(4) 1840** Dewey *Mass. Flowering Plants* 242 *Velvet Grass* . . . [is] a grass little desired by animals. **1935** H. L. Davis *Honey in Horn* 1 Outside. . . was a ten-mile stretch of creek-meadow with wild vetch and redtop and velvet-grass reaching clear to the black-green fir timber of the mountains.

(5) 1837 Darlington *Flora Cestrica* 397 Indian Mallow. Dewitt weed. Velvet leaf. **1939** *Nat. Geog. Mag.* Aug. 229/2 Velvet Leaf Eastern, Central, and Southern States. — **(6) 1814** *Amer. Mineral. Jrnl.* I. 261 Argillaceous Iron stone . . . is generally nodular, in concentric layers, between two of which it occurs crystallized in minute crystals of a blackish brown, known by the name of velvet ore. — **(7) 1934** Webster. **1945** Pearson *Country Flavor* 78 The velvet, or staghorn, sumac lifts its scarlet foliage.

vendue vɛnˈdju, *n.* Also **vandue, vaandoo.** [Du. *vendue* in same sense.]

1. A public sale or auction, orig. *at* (*a*) *vendue.* Cf. **public vendue.**

(1) **1680** *Huntington Rec.* I. 262 [The] lot was formerly in the teniur or ocopation of trustam hoges and sould to the above sd finch at a vandue. **1726** *Smithtown Rec.* 81 After 6 hours they are to be sold at vandue for the charge being payed, one horse one shilling for pounding. **1817** Paulding *Lett. from South* II. 165 His farm is soon to be sold at vendue. **1860** Holmes *E. Venner* vii, I don't mean to set *her* up at vaandoo.

(2) **1704** S. Knight *Journal* 52 Mr. Burroughs went with me to Vendue where I bought about 100 Rheem of paper. **1786** *Old Records of the Town of Fitchburgh* (1898) 332 The second article taken in hand the vandue opned Proceded as follows [etc.]. **1897** Howells *Landlord at Lion's Head* ii, [We must] have a vendue, and sell out everything . . . , and let the State take the farm. **1950** *Pa. Dutchman* July 7/4 While the vendue was going on in some other spot the older boys would strew straw or hay on the manure pile in front of the barn.

attrib. **1668** *New Castle Court Rec.* 314 The Purchazers were obliged to pay all the vendu Charges etc. **1799** *Aurora* (Phila.) 10 April (Th.), By profession he is a vendue crier. He said he would cry the vendue in spite of the Standing Army. **1855** *Harper's Mag.* X. 853/1 The bow was bid off by a by-stander, who sold it to him at 'a quarter's' advance over the vendue-price!

b. (See quot.) *Obs.*

1885 *Mag. Amer. Hist.* May 495/1 *Vendue*, . . . a shameless assignment of offices to the highest bidders.

2. In special combs.: (1) **vendue master,** one in charge of a vendue, an auctioneer, *obs.;* (2) **note,** a note given in payment of something bought at a vendue, *obs.;* (3) **Range,** (see quot.); (4) **store,** a store in which goods are sold at or by vendue, *obs.*

(1) **1677** *New Castle Court Rec.* 53 The Pl[ain]t[iff] demands of the def[endant] as Vendu Master of the Land & houses of Capt John Carr the sume of 1962 gilder ten stivers. **1708** *R.I. Col. Rec.* IV. 49 There shall be a vendue allowed in the town of Newport, and a vendue master chosen and engaged by the townsmen. **1832** DUNLAP *Hist. Amer. Theatre* 49 This was the place for auctioneers, then called vendue-masters, to cry and sell their wares. — (2) **1809** *Steele P.* II. 610 The Board of Directors would have approved of your taking the Vendue Notes. — (3) **1843** *Knickerb.* XXI. 446, I remember stepping last summer, into the 'Vendue Range,' (the chief market for slaves in Charleston). — (4) **1774** *Pa. Packet* 19 Sep. 1/3 He is removed to his new vendue-store. **1798** *S.C. Superior Ct. Rep.* (Bay) I. 103 The goods were in a vendue store, a common market, a public place known and established in law.

vendue vɛnˈdju, *v. tr.* To sell by vendue. *Obs.* — **1764** OTIS in Tudor *Life J. Otis* 32, I was only to act in my profession as a lawyer, and not as a merchant or factor, to settle accounts and vendue goods. **1804** FESSENDEN *Orig. Poems* (1806) 164 Have pretty nymphs expos'd to sale, And ladies vendued off by tale.

veneerer vəˈnɪrɚ, *n.* A workman who applies or fits veneer. *Rare.* — **1863** HALE *If, Yes, & Perhaps* 14, I was at work as a veneerer in a piano-forte factory.

* **venire,** *n.*

1. A group of persons legally summoned to serve as a jury or a group from which a jury is selected.

1807 *Ann. 10th Cong.* 1 Sess. 391 The names of the *venire*, summoned in pursuance of the *venire facias*, . . . were accepted by the prisoner. **1905** N. DAVIS *Northerner* 217 We had a special venire of sixty, county men most of them. **1947** *Chi. D. News* 17 June 1/6 The jurymen who decided against his client . . . were chosen from a venire with a higher-than-average educational background.

2. venireman, one of those on a venire.

1776 *Va. House of Delegates Jrnl.* 17 Oct., The several venire-men and witnesses attending for the trial of criminals [shall] be discharged. **1895** *Wkly. Examiner* (S.F.) 5 Sep. 2/1 Sheriff Whelan's deputies had apparently summoned most all of the veniremen from the foreign sections of the city. **1947** *Chi. D. News* 17 June 1/6 Attorney Royal Irwin today attacked the method of picking veniremen for the U.S. District Court.

* **venison,** *n.* **1. venison bird,** = **Canada jay. 2. venison hawk,** = prec.

(1) **1885** *Outing* VII. 75/1 The venison birds fill the woods with their peculiar cry. **1950** *Skyline Trail* March 19/2 From the circumstance that it often perches upon the backs of animals, helping rid them of ticks, come such other names as *moose* (or *caribou*, or *venison*) *bird*, *venison hawk* (or *heron*). — (2) **1889** *Internat. Ann., Anthony's Photog. Bul.* II. 223 About our door the venison hawks came flitting.

vent vɛnt, *n. W.* [See **venta.**] (See quot. 1944.) In full **vent brand.** Cf. **sale brand.**

1849 *Alta California* (S.F.) 18 Jan. 2/3 The Indian said he had bought the horse from a white man, and didn't like to give him up—showed the fresh '*vent*' &c. **1912** E. HOUGH *Story of Cowboy* 113 (Bentley), Here was the original of the bill of sale, and also of the counter-brand or the 'vent brand,' as it is known on the upper ranges. **1944** ADAMS *W. Words* 172/1 vent brand From the Spanish *venta* (*ven'tah*), meaning *sale*. When used as a noun, it means a brand placed upon an animal that has been given an ownership brand and later sold, and has the effect of cancelling the ownership brand, thus serving as the acknowledgment of a sale.

vent vɛnt, *v. W.* [f. **vent,** *n.* See **venta.**] *tr.* To nullify an ownership brand on (an animal) by adding a sale brand. Cf. **cross-brand,** *v.,* **unvented brand.**

1844 GREGG *Commerce of Prairies* I. 186 It [is] impossible for persons not versed in this species of 'heraldry,' to determine whether the animal has been properly *vented* or not. **1846** *Californian* (Monterey) 17 Sep. 1/1 The Spaniards explained their laws and showed the animals not to be vented, . . . and told the Indians they must give them to the rightful owners. **1929** A. J. DICKSON *Across Plains* 91 And furthermore the brand on this one had not been 'vented,' so that it could not have been a legal transfer anyway.

venta ˈvɛntə, *n. W.* [Sp. *venta*, inn, sale.]

1. An inn. *Obs.*

1828 W. IRVING *Life & Lett.* (1864) II. 300 We took a repast together in a little venta in a deep gorge of the mountains. **1863** *Rio Abajo Press* 12 May 1 Patricio also related to him the occurrences at the gaming table at the venta within the last three weeks.

2. A vent or vent brand. Cf. **cross-brand,** *v.*

1844 FARNHAM *Travels in Calif.* 347 If a person buys an animal or hide without having it first branded with the '*venta*,' the former owner, if inclined to be rascally, can reclaim his property. **1852** *L.A. Star* 3 April 2/3 It is believed that a caballada of thirteen horses . . . are also stolen by him, as his account is unreasonable, and the horses all have different brands without 'venta.'

* **Venus,** *n.*

1. Venus' flytrap, an insectivorous plant, *Dionaea muscipula*, that grows wild on the coast of the Carolinas.

1770 J. ELLIS *Botanical Descr.* 39, I shall now give you a general description of the species of *Dionæa* before us, called *Muscipula*, or *Venus's Fly-trap*. **1802** DRAYTON *S. Carolina* 70 Venus's fly trap . . . grows near the sea shore road on the borders of North Carolina. **1949** *Nat. Hist.* June 278/3 The leaves of Venus's-flytrap are more spectacular, larger, and much more rapid in action than Drosera's apparatus.

2. Venus'-pride, (see quots.).

1784 *Amer. Acad. Mem.* I. 409 Venus Pride . . . spreads over pastures and fields, in large beds, and gives them a white appearance. **1829** EATON *Botany* (ed. 5) 246 *Houstonia cœrulea*, Venus' pride, forget-me-not. **1931** CLUTE *Plants* 75 We have a number of other plants in our flora which escaped the notice of the devout entirely, among them. . . . Venus' pride (*Houstonia angustifolia*).

verbarium vɚˈbɛrɪəm, *n.* [f. L. *verb*um + * *-arium.*] (See quot. 1891.)

1891 *Cent.*, verbarium. . . . A game played with the letters of the alphabet. (a) A game in which the player strives to make out a word when all the letters that compose it are given to him indiscriminately. (b) A game in which the player tries to form from the letters that compose a long word as many other words as possible. **1906** MARK TWAIN in *Autobiog.* (1924) II. 58 (R.), The game of Verbarium . . . was brand new at the time. A text word was chosen. . . . The player could begin with the first letter of that text word and build words out of the text word during the two minutes by the watch.

verdant zone. (See quot. and cf. **thermal belt.**) — **1862** *Rep. Comm. Patents 1861: Agric.* 146 The beautiful phenomenon of the 'Verdant Zone' or 'Thermal Belt' exhibits itself upon our mountain sides, commencing about three hundred feet vertical height above the valleys, and traversing them . . . like a vast green ribbon upon a black ground.

verdin ˈvɝdn̩, *n.* [F., yellowhammer.] A small yellow-headed titmouse, *Auriparus flaviceps*, of the Southwest.

1881 *Amer. Naturalist* XV. 217 Another minute species of the titmouse family [is] the verdin or yellow-headed titmouse. **1903** *Atlantic Mo.* July 103 The same fretful verdin was talking about something with the old emphatic monotony. **1939** PICKWELL *Deserts* 139/2 This is the voice of the Verdin, a true bird of the desert.

Verein fəˈraɪn, *n.* A Turnverein. Cf. **turn society.** — **1853** *Alta California* (S.F.) 20 May 2/3 May the Verein long flourish to be an ornament to our city and an honor to its members.

vergaloo ˈvɝgəˌlu, *n.* Also **virgalieu, bergaloo.** [F. *virgouleuse*, in same sense.] A variety of pear, the White Doyenné, of French origin. In full **vergaloo pear.**

1806 *Webster* 341/2 *Vergâloo*, a very rich pear. **1845** DOWNING *Fruits Amer.* 378 Virgalieu, of New York. . . . Virgaloo, Bergaloo, of some American gardens. **1877** BARTLETT 734 *Virgalieu Pear.* So called in New York. . . . It is the *Doyenné Blanc* of French authors, the *Butter Pear* of Philadelphia, and the St. Michael of Boston.

verge staff. (See quot. 1938.)

1873 MARK TWAIN & WARNER *Gilded Age* 43 [They] . . . tried to make friends with a passenger-bear fastened to the verge staff. **1938** RAMSAY *Mark Twain* 250/1 verge-staff. . . . The term is not used on present-day steamboats. Capt. Heckmann thinks it must have been what is now called the forward jack-staff, on which the insignia of the line are carried. Cf. *OED* Verge, sb. 4a. A rod or wand carried as an emblem or authority or symbol of office.

Veriscope ˈvɛrəˌskop, *n.* [f. L. *verus*, true, + * *scope.*] The trade-mark name of an early form of moving picture machine. Also attrib. *Obs.* — **1897** *Columbus* (O.) *Dispatch* 2 July, There remain but three more exhibitions of the veriscope. **1898** *Boston Transcript* 25 April 5/7 Veriscope Pictures of Corbett-Fitzsimmons Contest.

veritism ˈvɛrəˌtɪzəm, *n.* [App. coined by Hamlin Garland (1860–1940), and used only by him.] Realism. Also **veritist,** *n.,* **veritistic,** *a.* All *rare.*

1894 *Nation* LIX. 53/2 Veritism is the name by which devils are to be cast out, and the artist himself is to be a veritist. **1894** GARLAND in *Forum* Aug. 690 My own conception is that realism (or veritism) is the truthful statement of an individual impression corrected by reference to the fact. **1894** *Forum* Aug. 690 The veritist chooses for his subject not the impossible, not even the possible, but always the probable. *Ib.* 693 The critic cannot distinguish between the entirely fictitious characters of the veritistic novel and characters drawn from life.

vermiculite vɚˈmɪkjʊˌlaɪt, *n.* [L. *vermiculus*, a little worm, + * *-ite.*] (See quot. 1891.)

1824 T. H. WEBB in *Amer. Jrnl. Sci. & Arts* VII. 55 If subjected to the flame of a blowpipe, . . . it expands and shoots out into a variety of fanciful forms, resembling most generally small worms. . . . If this proves to be a new variety . . . I term it Vermiculite (worm breeder). **1891** *Cent.* 6730/2 vermiculite. . . . In *mineral.*, one of a group of hydrous silicates having a micaceous structure, and in most cases derived from the common micas by alteration. When heated nearly to redness they exfoliate largely, and some kinds project out with a vermicular motion, as if they were a mass of small worms (whence the name). **1950** *L.A. Times Home Mag.* 12 Feb. 38/3 Vermiculite is one of the finest storage materials for bulbs, tubers and corms as it insulates them from sudden temperature changes.

Vermont vɚˈmɑnt, *n.* [The name of a N. Eng. state, prob. f. a rendering into English of F. *Les Monts Verts.* See G. R. Stewart, *Names on the Land* 166 f.]

1. A horse raised in Vermont.

1885 HOWELLS *Silas Lapham* i, I don't ride behind anything but Vermont; never did.

Also **Vermont horse, Vermont Morgan.**

1857 *Spirit of Times* 23 May 181/3 'Young Morrill' is a Vermont horse, raised from three generations of Vermont horses. *Ib.*, The contestants are both Vermont Morgans, although of different branches. **1894** *Vt. Agric. Rep.* XIV. 93 Vermont horses have always been in good demand for road purposes. **1908** *Sat. Ev. Post* 29 Aug. 32/1 The late Senator Proctor and Mr. Battel, of Vermont, . . . have started to establish a renaissance of the Vermont Morgan horse.

2. In special combs.: (1) **Vermont granite,** granite obtained from Vermont; (2) **gray,** (see quot.), *obs.;* (3) **turkey,** (see quot.), *colloq.*

(1) 1916 *Confederate Veteran* Feb. 52/1 The tablet is of 'imperial blue' Vermont granite, eight feet high and ten inches thick. — **(2) 1884** *Cent. Mag.* Feb. 519/2 The 'tag-locks' and pulled wool were mostly worked up in the neighboring small factories into . . . the then somewhat famous 'Vermont gray,' which was the common cold-weather outer clothing of New England male farm folk. — **(3) 1935** MITCHELL *America* 216 The turkey is usually called Vermont turkey, just as the duck is always Long Island duckling.

Vermonter vɚˈmɑntɚ, *n.* Also †**Vermonteer, Varmounter.** A native or resident of Vermont.

1778 in *Amer. Sp.* XX. (1945) 275 We may hence learn that we are not to flatter ourselves with the hope of winning over the Vermonters to the Crown side. **1782** FRENEAU *Poems* (1903) II. 181 The Sage who took the wrong sow by the ears, And more than kingdoms claimed for Vermonters. **1801** *Hist. Rev. & Directory* II. 346 Great numbers of the *Vermonteers* bring their produce here. **1834** *Vt. Free Press* 7 June (Th.), A Varmounter never uses a dog. **1948** *Time* 12 Jan. 64/1 Early Vermonters learned many skills to provide for their families and found it a thrifty sport to shoot pickerel with an Indian bow and arrow.

b. A Vermont horse.

1858 *Spirit of Times* 30 Jan. 347/1 All the distinct breeds, as Canadians, Vermonters, *quasi* identical with Cleveland bays, and Conestogas, *quasi* identical with the English dray horses, should be preserved distinct by breeding the mares to stallions of their own families.

Vermontese ˌvɜmɑnˈtiz, *n.* and *a.* **1.** *n.* A Vermonter, or Vermonters collectively. **2.** *a.* Resident in Vermont, characteristic of Vermont.

(1) 1783 *Polite Traveller* 100 The persons, manners, and customs, of the Vermontese, are nearly the same with those provinces from whom they emigrated. **1845** *Knickerb.* XXVI. 583 We should be pleased to hear these lines applauded by the Vermontese. — **(2) 1798** I. ALLEN *Hist. Vt.* 280 Our Vermontese house-wives are not a little vain of their knowledge in making home-made wines. **1851** *S.F. Picayune* 20 Sep. 2/4 On a late visit to an ancient Vermontese lady, he was asked, 'Did you see Professor Webster hung?'

vernaculate vɚˈnækjəˌlet, *v.* **1.** *tr.* To name in the vernacular. **2.** *intr.* (See quot.) Both *rare.* — **(1) 1887** *N.Y. Semi-Weekly Tribune* 15 July (*Cent.*), Very large Antwerp 'patches,' as they are vernaculated by the average fruit-grower. — **(2) 1895** *Standard* 2003/2 *Vernaculate,* . . . to use vernacular language.

* **vesper,** *n.* In combs.: (1) **vesper bird,** = **vesper sparrow;** (2) **mouse,** the white-footed (prairie) mouse *q.v.;* (3) **sparrow,** = **grass finch.**

(1) 1858 *Atlantic Mo.* Oct. 595/1 The usual resorts of the Vesper-bird are the pastures and the hay-fields. **1884** COUES *Key to Birds* 364 *Passerculus gramineus.* . . . Grass Finch. Bay-winged Bunting. Vesper-Bird. — **(2) 1857** S. F. BAIRD *Mammals N. Amer.* 455 A striking feature of the North American vesper mice . . . is their diminutive size compared with the South American. **1891** *Cent.* 6739/2. — **(3) 1865** *Atlantic Mo.* XV. 515/1, I suspect . . . that the high pasture-lands begot the Vesper-Sparrow. [**1913** EATON *Barn Doors & Byways* 253 Wait a day or two and you will see, among the red fox-sparrows, the white tail feathers of a vesper, and hear his lovely song at twilight.] **1945** MATHEWS *Talking* 105 The vesper sparrow stops his evening song, the blue grosbeak becomes silent.

* **vessel,** *n.* As the last term in **bay, lumber, single stick, snag vessel.**

* **vest,** *n.*

1. a. vest-pattern, enough material to make a vest. Cf. * **pattern. b. vest-pocket voter,** (see quot.). *Obs.*

(a) [**1782** *Essex Inst. Coll.* XXXVIII. 54 A Patton for two Pare of overalls and two Westcoats.] **1804** *Austin P.* I. (1924) 108, 1 Vest Pattern, [$]1.75. **1867** *Ore. State Jrnl.* 25 May 4/1 The one that sells the most 'twixt now and Christmas, gets a vest pattern as a present. — **(b) 1883** in BRYCE *Amer. Commonw.* III. v. lxxxix. 217 They . . . created the class of 'vest-pocket voters'—men who come to the polls with their tickets made up to the confusion of 'the boys.'

2. In slang phrases (see quots.). *Obs.*

1876 *Wkly. Bee* (Portland, Ore.) 14 Sep. 1/1 Pull down your chin and wipe off your vest. *c*1877 in *Burton's Events of 1875–76* (B.), The latest flash saying with which we are blest Is to tell a man quietly, 'Pull down your vest.' **1877** BARTLETT 502 *Pull down your Vest,* a curious flash expression of recent origin, without meaning. It is heard on all occasions . . . ; yet no man can tell whence it came. **1892** WALSH *Lit. Curiosities* 923 *Pull down your vest,* an American colloquialism, meaning, originally, 'Attend to your own business,' but now used as a mere senseless exclamation.

vestee vɛsˈti, *n.* [* *vest* + *-ee,* with dim. force.] Any one of various ornamental adjuncts of dress suggestive of, or worn in the place of, a vest or waistcoat. — **1930** *Ladies' Home Jrnl.* Dec. 36 With soft georgette vestee crossing diagonally to pass through a straight band of the material on the left.

* **vestibule,** *n.* An elastic diaphragm on steel frames, with side doors and a roof, fitted to the end of a passenger coach in such a way that a protected passageway is pro-

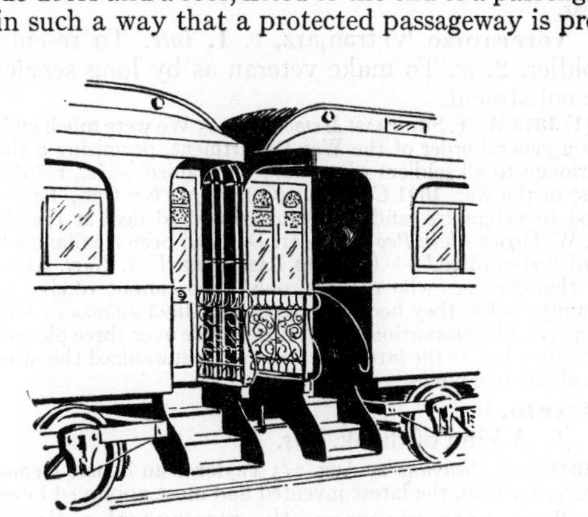

Early form of vestibule cars

vided through all the coaches of a train made up of cars equipped with this device.

1890 *Railways of Amer.* 246 A perfectly enclosed vestibule of handsome architectural appearance [runs] between the cars. **1900** *Everybody's Mag.* II. 444/2 One railway device that has increased the safety of passengers is the 'vestibule,' which connects coaches by a closely fitting covered hood over the platforms. **1949** *Chi. Tribune* 17 Nov. III. 4/6 Entrances and exits are thru two sets of pneumatically controled doors at each side of the cars, instead of thru end vestibules.

attrib. **1887** GEORGE *40 Years on Rail* 243 On this vestibule train are all the luxuries and conveniences a millionaire could desire at home. **1888** LEE *Plains to Peaks* 76 They are almost exact duplicates of the luxurious Pullman vestibule cars. **1947** *Westerners' Brand Book* 44 Some nasty minded white man invented vestibule platforms, and that fixed Mr. Indian's free rides. **1950** *Chi. Tribune* 2 April 39/3 The railroads instead advertised 'vestibule' trains and trains which had electric lights, sleeping cars with private rooms and steam heat.

vestibule ˈvɛstəˌbjul, *v. tr.* To provide (a railroad car) with a vestibule. Hence **vestibuled,** *a.*

1890 *Railways of Amer.* 249 The first of the vestibuled trains went into service on the Pennsylvania Railroad in June, 1886, and they are rapidly being adopted by railway companies. **1891** *Cent.* 6741/2 *Vestibule,* . . . to provide with a vestibule. **1903** A. J. BEVERIDGE *Russian Advance* 7 You may now board a vestibuled train of sleeping-cars at Port Arthur. **1906** *McClure's Mag.* XXVI. 92 Nor do we much better realize, in our vestibuled habit, what railroading *was.*

transf. **1911** *Everybody's Mag.* April 473/1 Similarly, one of these through vestibuled names, such as J. Mozart Chatterton-Chatterton

Hamiltonian-Wilkes Jones, is funny because it is long enough to let the last half run as a second section and still have enough name left over to satisfy the wants of almost any ordinary person.

vet vɛt, *n.* Short for veteran *q.v.* (sense **1.**). *Colloq.*

1867 DEVENS *Pictorial Bk.* 452 Colonel A. . . . took it upon himself to chide the exasperated and unfortunate 'vet' for using such unchristianlike language. **1904** *Richmond Wkly. Times-Dispatch* 22 June 4 All the old vets have returned from the reunion, some never to attend another, perhaps. **1949** *Chi. D. News* 7 March 10/6 Vet's Chance For Pension Slim.

* **veteran,** *n.*

1. An ex-service man. Cf. **banner veteran.**

1798 DUNLAP *André (preface)*, The Author has gone near to offend the veterans of the American army who were present on the first night. **1838** *S. Lit. Messenger* IV. 796 A majority of the war-worn veterans had travelled . . . beyond the reach of human reward. **1949** *Chi. D. News* 7 March 10/6 A veteran of the past conflict would stand as much chance of benefitting . . . as he would playing a slot machine.

b. (See quot. and cf. **veteranize,** *v.* **1.**) *Obs.*

1877 BARTLETT 733 *Veteran*, a term applied during the late civil war to soldiers, who, at the termination of the period for which they had enlisted, enlisted again.

c. (See quot.)

1905 *Forestry Bureau Bul.* No. 61, 26 *Veteran*, a tree over 2 feet in diameter breasthigh.

2. veteran camp, an organization composed of veterans.

1896 *N.Y. Dramatic News* 4 July 16/2 Benefits of various kinds will be given for several of the Confederate veteran camps. **1904** HARBEN *Georgians* 132 The general is invited to address nearly all the veteran camps over the State when the badges of honor are presented once a year.

veteranize ˈvɛtrənˌaɪz, *v.* **1.** *intr.* To re-enlist as a soldier. **2.** *tr.* To make veteran as by long service or by re-enlistment.

(**1**) **1875** W. T. SHERMAN *Memoirs* I. 395 We were much embarrassed by a general order of the War Department, promising a thirty-days furlough to all soldiers who would 'veteranize'—viz., reënlist for the rest of the war. **1891** *Columbus* (O.) *Dispatch* 7 Oct., They were the first to veteranize, and this signified a good deal at the time. **1929** E. W. HOWE *Plain People* 70 Mr. Day had been a gallant soldier, and had 'veteranized.' — (**2**) **1880** LAMPHERE *U.S. Govt.* 92/1 Soldiers of this class . . . who received only $300 cannot receive additional bounty, unless they became veteranized. **1893** *Johnson's Univ. Cyclo.* I. 355/2 The proportion was at first a little over three pieces for 1,000 infantry, but as the latter became more veteranized this was reduced to about two pieces.

* **veto,** *n.*

1. A kind of drink. *Obs.*

1841 *N.O. Picayune* 22 Aug. 2/3 Taylor is an honest Democrat—he ordered a veto, the latest invented and most approved beverage.

2. a. veto message, the message of a President of the U.S. or the governor of a state, informing a legislative body of his rejection of a bill and his reasons therefor. **b. veto power,** the power vested in a chief executive to veto legislation. Cf. **pocket veto.**

(**a**) **1836** *Jamestown* (N.Y.) *Jrnl.* 6 April 1/5 In General Jackson's Veto Message the use of Foreign Capital was denounced as dangerous to Liberty. **1914** *Cyclo. Amer. Govt.* III. 613/2 If Congress adjourns *sine die* within the period and thus prevents the President from sending his veto message, the bill does not become law. — (**b**) **1838** MAYO *Polit. Sk. Washington* 13 [The president] has the further power . . . under the protecting Ægis of the veto power to prevent the restoration of the treasury deposites to the legitimate control of the Legislature. **1904** *N.Y. Ev. Post* 19 Jan. 6 His bid is evidently for a veto power.

vetoer ˈvitoɚ, *n.* An executive who vetoes. — **1888** *N.Y. Wkly. Tribune* 24 Oct. 1/2 President Cleveland's ambition to go down to fame as the Great Vetoer does not wane. **1892** *Columbus* (O.) *Dispatch* 27 Sep., Cleveland's record as a vetoer of pension bills has given him . . . an unsavory reputation among the ex soldiers.

vetoite ˈvitoˌaɪt, *n.* One who was in sympathy with President Jackson's veto of the bill to re-charter the Bank of the U.S. *Obs.* — **1833** *Polit. Examiner* (Shelbyville, Ky.) 22 June 4/2 I'll try to make that national withdraw, and if I do I'll bring out another man and a full blood vetoite at that.

Vevay vəˈve, *n.* [Origin obscure. ?f. *Vevay*, Switzerland Co., Indiana.] *attrib.* Designating a kind of staw hat. *Obs.* — **1829** FLINT *G. Mason* 72 George and the boys concluded to try their skill upon the coarse manufacture of Vevay straw-hats.

* **vice,** *n.* In combs. of obvious meaning, as **vice boss, crusader, grafter.**

1903 STEFFENS in *McClure's Mag.* Nov. 89 In New York, Croker has failed signally to maintain vice-bosses whom he appointed. **1904** *Ib.* April 587/1 No wonder Minneapolis, having cleaned out its police ring of vice grafters, now discovers boodle, in the council! **1915** *Scientific Amer.* 30 Jan. 98/3 The Puritan conception of life, like that of vice-crusaders, suffragettes, and most crusaders, scorns all trifling with its weighty realities.

* **vice-,** *prefix.* **1. Vice-Presidency,** *n.* the office of Vice-President of the U.S. **2.** * **Vice-President,** *n.* the government official ranking next to the President of the U.S. **3. Vice-Presidential,** *a.* pertaining to the Vice-Presidency of the U.S.

(**1**) **1804** *Guardian of Freedom* (Frankfort, Ky.) 28 July 2/3 He is charged with having been long intriguing for the vice-presidency. **1900** *Cong. Rec.* 17 Feb. 1899/2, I am not a candidate for the Vice-Presidency of the United States. **1950** *So. Wkly.* 22 March 2/1 It was for political expedience, and for no other reason, that Hillman selected Truman for the Vice Presidency instead of Wallace. — (**2**) **1787** *Constitution* ii. § 4 The President, Vice-President and all civil officers of the United States. **1803** *12th Amendment,* The electors shall meet in their respective states, and vote by ballot for president and vice-president. **1949** J. MONAGHAN *This is Ill.* 76 He was nominated for President, with Hannibal Hamlin for Vice-President. — (**3**) **1854** BENTON *30 Years' View* I. 45/1 Mr. Calhoun was the only substantive vice-presidential candidate before the people. **1949** *Sat. Ev. Post* 2 July 66/3 If Barkley cherished any resentment because of his failure to get the vice-presidential nomination in '44, he never showed it publicly.

* **viceroy,** *n.* "The archippus, a handsomely colored American butterfly, *Basilarcha archippus*" (*Cent.*). — **1881** S. H. SCUDDER *Butterflies* 103 The caterpillar of the Viceroy signifies its displeasure at any disturbance by tossing the head upward.

vici kid. [?L. *vici*, I have conquered (cf. "veni, vidi, vici.") and *kid*.] A trade-mark name for chrome-tanned, glazed kid leather. Also attrib.

1902 *Sears Cat.* 911/2 We make our special . . . shoes from the very finest selection of vici kid stock. **1909** O. HENRY *Roads of Destiny* 297 He was the colour of vici kid, and his whiskers was like excelsior. **1936** KROLL *Share-cropper* 193, I had a pair of vici kid shoes for two dollars and a half. [**1946** *Harper's Mag.* Oct. 311/1 There, . . . would be Pa in his Sunday clothes and vici shoes.]

vicissitous vɪˈsɪsətəs, *a.* Vicissitudinous. — **1865** BURRITT *Walk to Land's End* 165 A city set upon such a hill could not have been hidden in the vicissitous experiences of a nation. **1892** *Columbus* (O.) *Dispatch* 9 June, All of them reach their affluence . . . along the same vicissitous road.

Vicksburger ˈvɪksˌbɜgɚ, *n.* A hat of a type associated in some way with Vicksburg, Miss. *Obs.* — **1836** in *Amer. Sp.* XXIV. (1914) 151/1 He . . . stuck his large white Vicksburger conceitedly on his bushy head.

* **Victoria,** *n.* **1.** ?A kind of cigar. **2.** (See quots.) Both *obs.*

(**1**) **1847** *De Bow's Review* IV. 263 There are . . . many staid and solemn people, who are perfectly satisfied to sit in their balconies, to smoke their Victorias. — (**2**) **1872** in G. W. CURTIS *Horses, Cattle* 310 The family of pigs known as Victorias originated with Col. Frank D. Curtis, Kirby Homestead, Charlton, Saratoga Co., N.Y. *Ib.* 312 Victorias [are] . . . a new breed produced within the last decade, by a judicious blending of the blood of four different breeds—Poland-China, Chester-White, Berkshire and American or White Suffolk.

Victrola vɪkˈtrolə, *n.* Also **victrola.** [f. *Victor* Talking Machine Co., a trade-mark.] A phonograph bearing the trade-mark Victrola.

1917 LEACOCK *Frenzied Fiction* v. 70 The others were dancing the fox-trot to the victrola on the piazza. **1922** *Frontier* May 21 She likes to hear the victrola, and while it plays, she sits quietly. **1949** *Prairie Schooner* Spring 48 He put away the pistol and bought a Victrola for the bunkhouse.

Vienna bentwood. *attrib.* Designating furniture of a type made in Vienna, or after the pattern of such furniture. — **1876** *Scribner's Mo.* April 809/2 Even chairs so ostentatiously bare and matter-of-fact as . . . the Vienna bent-wood chairs, cost as much as some to be found in the fashionable shops. **1887** *Courier-Journal* 3 May 3/8 So as to include the manufacture and sale of Vienna Bent-wood Furniture.

* **view,** *v. local. tr.* To apply a beech seal *q.v.* to (a person). *Obs.* Cf. **New Hampshire grants.** — **1798** I. ALLEN *Hist. Vermont* 35 All civil and military officers who had acted under authority of the Governor or Legislature of New York, were required to suspend their functions on pain of being viewed. **1840** THOMPSON *Green Mt. Boys* I. iii. 40 So I think, considering, I shall vote to have him viewed.

* **viewer,** *n.* As the last term in **chimney, fence viewer.**

vig vɪdʒ, *n.* Short for vigilante *q.v.* *Obs.* — **1879** *Bradstreet's* 10 Dec. 1/3 It is supposed by the law-abiding part of the community that the action of the 'vigs' will have a very salutary effect.

viga ˈvigə, *n. S.W.* [Sp. in same sense.] A beam or log used to support the roof in Indian and Spanish types of houses in the Southwest.

1844 GREGG *Commerce of Prairies* I. 284 Rooms which are still covered with the *vigas* and joists, remaining nearly sound under the *azoteas* of earth. **1881** MORGAN *Houses Amer. Aborigines* 164 Many of the *vigas* are still in place, and are large and perfectly smooth and straight undressed logs of pine, averaging ten inches in thickness. **1948** *Southwestern Rev.* Winter 32/1 Logs for vigas average six to ten inches in diameter and are sixteen to twenty feet long.

* **vigilance,** *n.*

1. *Committee of vigilance.* **a.** =**vigilance committee a. b.** =**vigilance committee c.** *Obs.*

(**a**) **1837** MARTINEAU *Society* II. 139 He was brought to trial by the Committee of Vigilance; seven elders of the presbyterian church at Nashville being among his judges. **1857** GIHON *Geary & Kansas* 35 A committee of vigilance, consisting of thirty persons, was appointed, whose duty it was to observe and report all such persons [i.e., abolitionists]. — (**b**) **1851** *Harper's Mag.* Sep. 559/1 A large number of most valuable citizens organized themselves into a Committee for Vigilance, for the purpose of securing the punishment of criminals. **1856** in H. H. BANCROFT *Works* XXXVII. 185 You are hereby required to surrender forthwith the possession of the county jail.... [Signed] Committee of Vigilance.

2. In combs.: (1) **vigilance association,** =**vigilance committee a.** and **c.,** *obs.;* (2) **committee,** see as a main entry; (3) **man,** =**vigilante,** *obs.;* (4) **police,** the police force of a vigilance committee (sense **c.**).

(**1**) **1831** *Boston Transcript* 17 Oct. 2/2 The 'Vigilance Association of Columbia,' (South Carolina) . . . have offered a reward of *fifteen hundred dollars* for the apprehension and prosecution to conviction of any white person who may be detected in distributing . . . [abolitionist literature]. **1851** in H. H. BANCROFT *Works* XXXVI. 469 The courts under the new criminal organization are fast superseding the want of a vigilance association. — (**3**) **1887** H. H. BANCROFT *Works* XXXVI. 314 It was not law and government that the vigilance men complained of, but the lack of these. **1892** GUNTER *Miss Dividends* 85 The best citizens of these places were Vigilance men. — (**4**) **1887** H. H. BANCROFT *Works* XXXVI. 373 Mrs. Hogan . . . was seized by the Vigilance police and brought to the Committee-rooms.

vigilance committee. a. In the South, an organization of citizens using extralegal means to control or intimidate Negroes and abolitionists and, during the Civil War, to suppress loyalty to the Union. *Obs.* **b.** In the North, an organization designed to aid fugitive slaves. *Obs.* **c.** A voluntary association of men professing to supplement the efforts of the police and the courts in maintaining order, punishing crime, etc.

(**a**) **1835** GARRISON in W. J. & F. J. Garrison *W. L. Garrison* I. 519 The slave States . . . have organized Vigilance Committees and Lynch Clubs. **1865** PIKE *Scout & Ranger* (1932) 134 Vigilance committees were organized in every town and village [in Texas], and their motto was: 'No mercy to traitors,' meaning those who were true to their country and the old flag. — (**b**) **1842** J. STURGE *Visit to U.S.* 53 They were unacquainted with the existence of vigilance committees, to facilitate the escape of runaway slaves. **1852** in STOWE *Key* 51/2 There was no Vigilance Committee at the time,—there were but anti-slavery men. — (**c**) **1851** *S.F. Herald* 1 July 2/2 A large number of the Vigilance Committee proceeded yesterday to the County Prison, by invitation of the Sheriff. **1948** JOHNSTON *Gold Rush* 20/1 The condition of things became so desperate that a vigilance committee was resolved upon.

vigilancism ˈvɪdʒələnˌsɪzəm, *n.* The principle of vigilance committees. *Obs.* — **1856** *Dem. State Journal* (Sacramento) 7 July 3/2 Col. C. E. Pickett on Vigilanceism. *Ib.* 29 July 2/2 Vigilanceism has broken out in Calaveras county. **1857** *S.F. Call* 31 May 1/1 There has been very little discussion thus far on the subject of Vigilancism—less in fact than was expected.

* **vigilant,** *a.* and *n.*

1. *n.* =**vigilante.** *Obs.*

1867 in H. H. BANCROFT *Works* XXXVI. 703 In no instance did any of the many lawless characters arrested by the vigilants ever fire a pistol in their own defence. **1895** S. R. HOLE *Little Tour in Amer.* 67 A fight occurred there yesterday between vigilants and horse-thieves. **1920** R. M. JONES *Later Periods Quakerism* II. 581 William C. Faber and Joseph Ricketson . . . were co-labourers with the abolitionists and with the 'Vigilants' or underground committees.

2. *a.* Designating a committee of vigilants, pertaining to a vigilance committee.

1824 *Mo. Intelligencer* 12 Feb. (Th.), We hate what are called vigilant men; they are a set of suspicious, mean spirited mortals, that dislike fun. **1856** in H. H. BANCROFT *Works* XXXVII. 643 You are hereby appointed . . . to take charge of the vigilant police force which will be detailed to preserve the public peace. **1873** *Newton Kansan* 13 Feb. 2/3 Threats of vigilant committees . . . have started the vicious crowd eastward.

b. vigilant flesh-fly, a blowfly. *Rare.*

1862 *Harper's Mag.* Nov. 741/2 The *Sarcophaga vigilans*—'Vigilant flesh-fly'—is one of the most watchful detectives.

vigilante ˌvɪdʒəˈlæntɪ, *n.* [Sp., watchman, policeman.] A member of a vigilance committee. Cf. **mountain vigilantes.**

[**1862** *Rocky Mountain News* (Denver) 31 May (Bentley), The vigys pointed to an empty saddle and gave him just ten minutes to skedaddle.] **1867** RICHARDSON *Beyond Mississippi* 487 The power [in Montana] has vested in the 'Vigilantes,' a secret tribunal of citizens. **1950** *Chi. D. News* 6 Feb. 12/3 A committee of Vigilantes is being formed up there.

attrib. and *transf.* **1890** LANGFORD *Vigilante Days* (1912) 90 In the name of Vigilante justice [some men] committed crimes which on any principle of ethics were wholly indefensible. **1910** HART *Vigilante Girl* 273 With some difficulty he cut the Vigilante red tape sufficiently to obtain for them a pass. **1948** *Time* 13 Dec. 76/3 He thinks of himself as the conscience of government, a Vigilante riding herd on Washington.

Also **vigilante committee.**

1949 *No. Dak. Hist.* Jan. 21 The homesteaders had a vigilante Committee who watched out for claim jumpers.

vigilanter ˌvɪdʒəˈlæntɚ, *n.* =**vigilante.** *Obs.* — **1873** *Newton Kansan* 13 Feb. 3/3 The vigilanters extend from Dodge City to Pueblo. *c***1900** R. L. HALE *Log of Forty-Niner* 120 The 'Vigilanters' were a law unto themselves, ferreting out criminals, and meting out punishments severe and sudden.

vigilantism ˌvɪdʒəˈlæntɪzəm, *n.* The principle of vigilance committees. — **1942** STEGNER *Mormon C.* 96 Perhaps even those incidents were purely unofficial and spontaneous acts of devout Mormons, the Mormon equivalent of lynch law and vigilantism. **1950** *Chi. Tribune* 23 May 19/3 Yet we have not adopted lynch law as a proper antidote; for we know that vigilanteism threatens all our civilization.

vigintial crop. A crop produced in twenty years, used esp. with reference to slave-breeding. *Obs.* — **1832** C. J. FAULKNER *Sp. Va. Legislature* (Chipman), Shall society suffer that the slaveholder may continue to gather his vigintial crop of human flesh? **1848** W. H. CHANNING *Mem. W. E. Channing* I. 84 Not then, either, had speculators discovered how to postpone the destructive effects of slave cultivation, by breeding children, like cattle, for the south-west market, and replenishing exhausted coffers by the profits of the 'vigintial crop.'

vigorite ˈvɪgəraɪt, *n.* (See quot. 1884.) *Obs.* — **1879** WEBSTER *Supp.* 1584/2 *Vigorite,* . . . a preparation of nitroglycerine used in blasting. **1884** KNIGHT *Supp.* 928/1 *Vigorite,* a nitro-glycerine explosive, manufactured at Marquette.

* **Vigors,** *n.* [N. A. *Vigors* (1785–1840), a British naturalist.] **1. Vigors' vireo,** =next. **2. Vigors' warbler,** (see quot. 1891). **3. Vigors' wren,** (see quot.).

(**1**) **1833** NUTTALL *Man. Ornith.* 318 Vigor's Vireo. *Vireo Vigorsii* . . . An individual of this very rare bird was shot by its discoverer many years ago on an island in Perkiomen creek, in Pennsylvania, and has never been seen since by any naturalist. — (**2**) **1831** AUDUBON *Ornith. Biog.* I. 153 Vigors's Warbler. *Sylvia Vigorsii.* **1891** *Cent.* 6820/3 *Vigors's warbler,* . . . the pine-creeping warbler as mistaken for another species. — (**3**) **1917** *Birds of Amer.* III. 192 In the coast region of middle California is Vigors's Wren (*Thryomanes bewicki spilurus.*)

vilfa ˈvɪlfə, *n.* [Origin obscure.] A variety of pasture or forage grass. Also **hidden-flowered vilfa.** *Obs.* — **1843** TORREY *Flora N.Y.* II. 438 *Vilfa vaginaeflora.* Hidden-flowered Vilfa. . . . Sandy arid fields and barren hill sides. **1857** *Ill. Agric. Soc. Trans.* II. 494 The vilfa is a general favorite, both for grazing and for hay.

* **village,** *n.*

1. *W.* An aggregation of prairie-dog burrows.

1774 in PEYTON *Adv. Grandfather* (1867) 121 One of the singular and interesting sights on my route was the villages of the Prairie dogs. **1881** MARSHALL *Through Amer.* (1882) 125 The prairie-dog is a very sociable and hospitable animal. He lives underground in a 'town' or a 'village' (as his home is called).

2. (See quot. 1837.) Also **village Indian.**

1837 IRVING *Bonneville* I. 98 A *village* of Indians, in trappers' language, does not always imply a fixed community; but often a wandering horde or band. **1906** *Out West* Jan. 28 It was the home of the Papagos, who were peaceable village Indians.

3. (See quot. 1883.)

1850 *Elgin* (Ill.) *Gaz.* 19 Oct. 2/3 We learn from the Marshal that he has just completed the Census of the village of St. Charles. **1883** in BRYCE *Amer. Commonw.* II. II. xlviii. 240 A minimum population of three hundred, occupying not more than two square miles in extent, may by popular vote become incorporated [in Ill.] as a 'village.' **1950** *Chi. Tribune* 5 March III. 5/3 John W. Rust, president of Willow Springs, said he could foresee no objection from trustees of that village.

4. In obs. combs.: (1) **Village-city,** (see quot.); (2) **land,** land owned by a colonial village; (3) **lot,** a lot owned by a colonial village.

(1) **1851** Lewis *Across Atlantic* 49 The name of the 'Village-city,' which I heard given to it by some gentleman, seems the most appropriate to Philadelphia. — (2) **1757** *Waterbury Prop. Rec.* 190 Ye meeting . . . was to Consider about Remeasuring our Lands & also of Disposing of ye village Land. — (3) **1746** *Waterbury Prop. Rec.* 164 The Setling the line between Woodbury and Waterbury Against the Village Lots has Altered the Highwayes there. **1817** *Ann. 14th Cong.* 2 Sess. 772 That the Committee on the Public Lands be instructed to inquire into the expediency of prohibiting, by law, the location of any floating claim . . . on any town lot, village lot, out lot, or common field lot, or commons.

b. Designating a (1) **bookstore,** (2) **calaboose,** (3) **grocery,** (4) **store,** such as are found in a village.

(1) **1907** Andrews *Recoll.* 165, I obtained permission to send to the village bookstore for a copy of Shakespeare. — (2) **1908** White *Riverman* 32, I'll just get along and bail the boys out of that village calaboose. — (3) **1920** Howells *Vacation of Kelwyns* 106 Her cooking could be ignored in the supplies of canned foods and of baker's bread from the village grocery. — (4) **1874** Howells *Chance Acquaintance* 38 Under the porch of the village store some desolate idlers . . . had clubbed their miserable leisure. **1892** *Harper's Mag.* Dec. 160, I got the presents at the village store for fifty cents in cash.

c. *Village of Magnificent Distances*, Washington, D.C. *Obs.* Cf. *City of Magnificent Distances* (*a*).

1867 *Chi. Times* 27 July 5/1 The Excelsiors have been generally accepted as the best nine in the west, and the believers in western muscle and agility were desirous of pitting them against the club from the 'village of magnificent distances.'

As the last term in **factory, farm, frontier, Indian, Indian praying, log, Miami, Mohawk, Moravian, Osage, post, prairie-dog, Shaker, shanty village.**

vim vɪm, *n.* [Usu. regarded as f. L. *vim*, acc. sing. of *vis*, strength, energy, but poss. of imitative or interjectional origin.] Force, energy, dash. Also as adv.

1843 *Yale Lit. Mag.* VIII. 406 He would have acted out his real nature with all the *vim* and pathos which heroes always manifest in like circumstances. **1850** Lewis *La. Swamp Doctor* 51 Sudden he thought of his spurs, so he ris up, an' drove them *vim* in his hoss's flanx. **1931** *Randolph Enterprise* (Elkins, W.Va.) 12 Nov. 1/4 The local post of the Legion is tackling the unemployment situation with a vim.

***vine,** *n.* In combs.: (1) ***vine dresser,** (see quot.); (2) **maple,** (*a*) a small tree, *Acer circinatum*, of the Pacific Northwest, the stems of which are often prostrate, cf. **bois de diable, devil wood,** (*b*) (see quot.); (3) **mesquite (grass),** (see quots.); (4) **rake,** (see quot.).

(1) **1891** *Cent.* 6758/2 *Vine-dresser*, . . . the larva of a sphingid moth *Ampelophaga* (*Darapsa* or *Everyx*) *myron*. It cuts off the leaves of the vine in the United States, and also sometimes severs half-grown bunches of grapes. — (2) (*a*) **1850** Glisan *Jrnl. Army Life* 27 When in Oregon and California, the forests of the stately fir, and the majestic redwood perish by fire, they are succeeded by thickets of hazel, vine maple and scrub oak. **1872** McClellan *Golden State* 163 In the State are the wild nutmeg, . . . vine-maple, and sequoia. **1949** Kitchin *Birds Olympic Peninsula* 2 Such deciduous growth as the alder, broad-leafed maple, vine maple, and willows common. (*b*) **1909** *Cent. Supp.* 770/1 *Vine-maple*, . . . the Canada moonseed, *Menispermum Canadense*. — (3) **1910** Thornber *Grazing Ranges Ariz.* 275 Vine mesquite (*Panicum obtusum*) forms a turf under favorable conditions of growth. **1912** Wooton & Standley *Grasses N. Mex.* 39 Vine Mesquite Grass (*Panicum obtusum*) is a species which is common on the plains. — (4) **1876** Knight 2710/2 Vine-rake, an implement for pulling sweet-potato or other vines off from the ridges preparatory to the digging of the ground.

As the last term in **balloon, Baltimore, bean, bullace, cane, cross, cypress, devil's hop, Elsanborough grape, flax, gourd, kudzu, Madeira, mealplum, moon, partridge, partridgeberry, pea, pipe, poison, potato, pumpkin, scarlet trumpet, scuppernong, sorrel, squaw, trumpet, wild pea vine.**

***vinegar,** *n.* In combs.: (1) **vinegar nubbin,** (see quot.), *obs.;* (2) **peach,** (see quot.), *obs.;* (3) **pie,** a pie in which a generous amount of vinegar is used; (4) **plant,** (see quot. and cf. **vinegar tree**); (5) **store,** a store where vinegar is sold; (6) **tree,** (see quot. 1891).

(1) **1880** *Harper's Mag.* Nov. 863/2 In a corner by themselves we see the pile of 'vinegar nubbins'—a tanned and soft variety of apple. — (2) **1709** Lawson *Carolina* 110 Of this sort we make Vinegar; wherefore we call them Vinegar-Peaches, and sometimes *Indian* Peaches. — (3) **1884** F. E. Owens *Cook Book* 185 [Recipe for] Vinegar Pie. **1932** Wilder *Little House* 45 She baked vinegar pies and dried-apple pies, and filled a big jar with cookies. — (4) **1797** *Encycl. Brit.* (ed. 3) XVI. 228/1 [The] Virginian sumach, or vinegar plant, grows naturally in almost every part of North America.

(5) **1883** Peck *Bad Boy* 41 His breath smelled all the time like in front of a vinegar store, where they keep yeast. — (6) **1763** tr. DuPratz *Hist. Louisiana* (1758) II. 34 The *Machonchi*, or *Vinegar tree*, is a shrub with leaves, somewhat resembling those of the ash; but the foot-stalk from which the leaves hang is much longer. [**1874** Lindley & Moore *Treas. Botany* 1350/2 Vinegar-tree, *Rhus typhina*.] **1891** *Cent.* 6758/3 *Vinegar-tree*, . . . the stag-horn sumac, *Rhus typhina*, the acid fruit of which has been used to add sourness to vinegar.

vinegarroon ˌvɪnəgəˈrun, *n.* Also **vinegerone.** *S.W.* [See note.]

From Amer. Sp. *vinagrón*, f. *vinagre*, vinegar, + the augmentative (and depreciative) *-ón*. See quot. 1853 below and cf. Amer. Sp. *vinagrillo*, used of this scorpion. The "mato venado" of **b.** below is app. a rendering of Amer. Sp. *matavenado*, used of a large poisonous ant.

A whip scorpion, esp. one of a large species, *Mastigoproctus giganteus*, popularly regarded as poisonous.

1853 Sitgreaves *Exped. Zuni & Colo. Rivers* 34 Frequently did I find in the road that disagreeable-looking object known to the Mexicans as the vinagron, (*Telephonis giganteus*,) and by them much dreaded. **1891** *Cent.* 6758/3 *Vinegerone* . . . : so called on account of the strong vinegar-like odor of an acid secretion noticeable when the creature is alarmed. **1948** *Pacific Discovery* March–April 8/2 The, vinegaroons, those queer, eight-legged devils of the desert night, raced at top speed in and out of the shadows to gather insect prey.

transf. **1914** *Blackw. Mag.* July 123/1 His late breaking-in, the lengthy vacation [etc.], . . . keep the 'vinegarone' in his [a bronco's] composition.

b. (See quot. and cf. note above.)

1925 Bryan *Papago Country* 53 The 'mato venado,' or killdeer, is also called vinegarroon—a name correctly used only for the scorpion.

viner ˈvaɪnɚ, *n.* A machine for removing peanuts from the "vines" or tops of the plant. — **1902** *Encycl. Brit.* (ed. 10) XXVI. 558/1 By the aid of modern machinery, the [pea-]pods are gathered by a viner. **1945** *Pueblo* (Colo.) *Chieftain* 8 June 10/1 New machinery includes a washer, grader, filler and viner, with the viner acting as a thresher.

***vinery,** *n.* Vines collectively. — **1883** *Cent. Mag.* Sep. 729 Latticed porticoes . . . , overgrown with masses of vinery—feign romance rather than [realism]. **1895** *Outing* XXVI. 445/1 Its ruins . . . are overgrown with vinery and bushes.

vineyardist ˈvɪnjɚdɪst, *n.* One who cultivates a vineyard — **1848** *Rep. Comm. Patents 1847* 199 A French wine maker and vineyardist came from Kentucky, where he had long been living. **1897** L. H. Bailey *Prin. Fruit-Growing* 291 Careful vineyardists are able to continue the practice [of girdling] year after year without apparent injury to the vine.

vining ˈvaɪnɪŋ, *a.* Of a plant: Growing in the manner of a vine, twining.

1804 Lewis in *L. & Clark Exped.* VI. (1905) 148 The vining honesuccle which bears a red flour is also common to the Illinois. **1806** Clark in *Ib.* IV. (1904) 13 The Vineing or low brown berry, a light brown berry rather larger and much the Shape of a black haw. **1897** *Voice* 4 March 5/3 The vining maples twined in so close . . . that we had to get right in the water and follow up the stream.

Violent Whig. A member of a group opposed to the Federalists at the end of the American Revolution. *Obs.* — **1872** *Harper's Mag.* April 692/2 The Liberty Boys, or 'Violent Whigs,' as they were called, [constituted the Anti-Federalists].

***violet,** *n.* As the last term in **bird foot, bird's-eye, Canada, dog, dog's tooth, English, false, ground, hand, horseshoe, kidney leaf, mad, rattlesnake, reddish, round-leaved, sand, Selkirk's, snake violet.**

violet-green swallow. A swallow, *Tachycineta thalassina lepida*, of western North America.

1874 Coues *Birds of Northwest* 88 The Violet-green Swallows resided during the summer in small, loose colonies, in high, open pine woods. [**1928** Bailey *Birds of N. Mex.* 455 In the Zuni Mountains, Major Goldman found the Violet-greens quite common and generally distributed.] **1950** *World-Herald Mag.* (Omaha) 28 May 3/1 In the Pine Ridge country of Northwestern Nebraska are found the white-throated swift, violet-green swallow, rock wren and house finch.

***viper,** *n.* As the last term in **blowing, spreading, water viper.**

vireo ˈvɪrɪˌo, *n.* [L. *vireo, -eonis* (Pliny) some small bird, perhaps the greenfinch. See also quot. 1917.] Any one of various small American birds constituting the family Vireonidae.

1834 AUDUBON *Ornith. Biog.* II. 287 The Vireos quench their thirst with the drops of dew or rain that adhere to the leaves or twigs. **1917** *Birds of Amer.* III. 102 Vireos are sometimes called Greenlets; the Latin word *Vireo* means 'I am green.' **1948** *Pacific Discovery* March–April 17/1 The vireo flitted away.

As the last term in **brotherly-love, Philadelphia, plumbeous, red-eyed, solitary, Vigors', warbling, white-eyed, yellow-throated vireo.**

vireosylvia ˌvɪrɪoˈsɪlvɪə, *n.* [**vireo** + **Sylvia* (genus name). See quot. 1891].—**1871** BURROUGHS *Wake-Robin* (1886) 59 The vireosylvia is classed among the fly-catchers by some writers. **1891** *Cent.* 6764/1 Vireosylvia. . . . A genus of vireos, or section of *Vireo*, including the larger greenlets with comparatively slender bill, as the common red-eyed vireo, the black-whiskered vireo, the whip-tom-kelly, and others.

virgilia vɚˈdʒɪlɪə, *n.* [f. *Virgilia* (<Virgil, the poet), a genus name.] The yellowwood, *Cladrastis lutea*, formerly referred to the genus *Virgilia*. Also the Kentucky coffee tree.

1846 BROWNE *Trees Amer.* 192 *Cladrastis tinctoria*, The Virgilia, or Yellow-Wood. **1883** *Harper's Mag.* April 732/1 On this third lawn is a collection of magnolias, a fine specimen of virgilia, a tall tulip-tree [etc.]. **1897** SUDWORTH *Arborescent Flora* 255 *Gymnocladus dioicus*. . . . Coffee tree. . . . Virgilia (Tenn.).

* **virgin,** *n.* In combs.: (1) **virgin cane,** a small cane, *Arundinaria tecta;* (2) **dance,** (see quot. and cf. **virgin feast**), *obs.;* (3) **dip,** (see quots.); (4) **feast,** (see quot.), *obs.;* (5) **-'s bower,** the American wistaria, *Wistaria frutescens;* (6) **timberland,** timberland from which none of the timber has been cut.

(1) **1863** *Ill. Agric. Soc. Trans.* V. 866 The smaller variety or perhaps species [of cane] . . . was called the Virgin Cane, and its slender culms furnished pipe rods for the pioneer and his hardy wife. — (2) **1847** LANMAN *Summer in Wild.* 106 There had been a Virgin Dance. . . . All the virgins of the [Indian] village assemble together. . . . If . . . one of the men stops suddenly and points his finger at a particular girl, she is at once looked upon as having lost her virginity. — (3) **1856** OLMSTED *Slave States* 343 The flow of the first year . . . is of higher value than the ordinary dip. It is called 'virgin dip.' [**1948** YOUNGKEN *Pharmacognosy* 115 The turpentine collected from the first year's tapping is known as 'virgin' turpentine.] — (4) **1839** MARRYAT *Diary* II. 96 They [Sioux] hold what they term Virgin Feasts, and when these are held, should any young woman accept the invitation who has by her misconduct rendered herself unqualified for it, it is the duty of any man who is aware of her unfitness, to go into the circle and lead her out.

(5) **1866** *Land We Love* (Charlotte, N.C.) May 80 Virgin's Bower. . . . Flowers purplish blue, pea-shaped. — (6) **1920** F. E. MCCLINCHEY *Joe Pete* 162 Wilson owned two hundred acres of the best virgin timberland remaining on the Island.

* **Virginia,** *n.*

1. Tobacco produced in Virginia. *Obs.* Cf. **Virginia tobacco.**

[**1624** SMITH *Gen. Hist. Va.* IV. 126 There are so many sofisticating Tobaco-mungers in England, were it neuer so bad, they would sell it for Verinas, and the trash that remaineth should be Virginia.] **1835–7** HALIBURTON *Clockmaker* 170 (We.), I got some real good Varginy. **1872** HAWTHORNE *S. Felton* (1883) 301 [A] German pipe . . . puffed out volumes of smoke, filling the pleasant western breeze with the fragrance of some excellent Virginia.

2. English as spoken in Virginia. *Obs.* Cf. **Virginia Americanism, Virginianism.**

1825 NEAL *Bro. Jonathan* I. 179 Why do you talk 'Virginny'—that vile gibberish?

3. In the names of plants: (1) **Virginia bluebell,** = **Virginia cowslip;** (2) **catchfly,** the fire pink of the eastern states; (3) **corn,** Indian corn or maize produced in Virginia, *obs.;* (4) **cowslip,** a lungwort, *Mertensia virginica,* of eastern North America; (5) **creeper,** an American climbing vine, *Parthenocissus quinquefolia;* (6) **seedling,** a variety of strawberry, also a variety of grape; (7) **snakeroot,** a birthwort, *Aristolochia serpentaria,* also a medicinal preparation made from this; (8) **thyme,** a fragrant perennial herb, *Pycnanthemum virginianum,* found in the eastern states; (9) **truffle,** a subterranean fungus, *Poria cocos,* often found in light loamy soils in the southern states; (10) **wake-robin,** the green arrow arum, *Peltandra virginica;* (11) **wheat,** corn, also wheat, grown in Virginia, *obs.,* cf. **early Virginia wheat.**

(1) **1934** WEBSTER. **1939** *Nat. Geog. Mag.* Aug. 236/2 The pale-blue flowers and rosy-pink buds of the Virginia bluebells . . . are clustered on slender branches. — (2) **1843** TORREY *Flora N.Y.* I. 102 *Silene Virginica.* Virginia Catchfly. . . . Sometimes employed in the Western States (where it is common) as an anthelmintic. — (3) **1624** SMITH *Gen. Hist. Va.* IV. 564 Whatsoeuer is said against the Virginia Corne, they finde it doth better nourish than any prouision is sent thither. **1772** PATTEN *Diary* 287, I got a bushell of Verginia corn from Mr Right for which I paid 1–12–0 bay old tenor. **1835–7** HALIBURTON *Clockmaker* 1 Ser. xvi. 133 Oatmeal . . . tante even as good for a horse as real yaller Varginy corn. — (4) **1909** WEBSTER. **1944** NUTE *Lake Superior* 293 By July 1 the Virginia cowslips are coming into bloom.

(5) **1704** PETIVER *Gazophyl.* II. xiv, This adheres to Trees by its hoary fibres, as our Virginia Creeper does to Walls by its tendrels. **1850** S. F. COOPER *Rural Hours* 90 Many a time our little friend, perched on a waving branch of the Virginia creeper, would sing his sweetest song. **1950** *Amer. Forests* Jan. 27/1 New leaves of oak and Virginia creeper show a liberal sprinkling of red coloring apparent before the green chlorophyll has reached its summer peak. — (6) **1853** FOWLER *Home for All* 140 The Virginia seedling is an early variety [of strawberry], and good to intermingle with the Hovey. **1864** *Ohio Agric. Rep.* XVIII. 25 A premium of $20 shall be offered for the best three samples of pure Ohio wine, made from the Catawba, Virginia Seedling or Delaware grape. — (7) **1694** SALMON *Bate's Dispens.* (1713) 258/2 The Sudorifick Tincture, or Tincture of Virginia Snake-root. **1796** *Hodge's N.C. Almanack* 46 For the Putrid Sore-Throat—Take of . . . Virginia snake root, the roots of aromatick calamus and wild valerian, . . . each one ounce. **1941** R. S. WALKER *Lookout* 48 Among the wild plants once employed as antidotes for the bites of poisonous reptiles are . . . Samson snakeroot, . . . Virginia snake-root, button snakeroot, and rattlesnake-root. — (8) **1814** BIGELOW *Florula Bostoniensis* 146 Virginia thyme . . . [has a] taste like penny-royal. — (9) **1848** BARTLETT 366 *Tuckahoe.* . . . The Virginia truffle. A curious vegetable, sometimes called by the name of Indian bread, or Indian Loaf, found in the Southern States. **1902** *Amer. Folk-Lore* 263 The name Tuckahoe is also applied to a sort of fungus called also 'Virginia truffle,' 'Indian bread,' 'Indian loaf.'

(10) **1883** *Smithson. Rep. 1881* 690 This name [Tuckahoe] . . . belonged to all esculent bulbous roots used by the Indians, among which are these: *Orontium aquaticum,* Golden Club, and *Pentandria virginica,* Virginia Wake Robin. **1902** *Amer. Folk-Lore* 261 A name formerly much in use in New Jersey and parts of Pennsylvania for the 'golden club' (*Orontium aquaticum*) and the 'Virginia wake-robin' (*Pentandria Virginica*). — (11) **1651** R. CHILD in Hartlib *Legacy* (1655) 36 The hill where their Corn is planted, called Virginia-Wheat. **1688** *Phil. Trans.* XVII. 978 English Wheat (as they call it, to distinguish it from Maze, commonly called Virginia Wheat). **1709** *Essex Inst. Coll.* VIII. 19 In the Weare Hows . . . [were] 500 butchells of Vorginiy Whet, . . . 203 butchells of Engen Corn.

b. In the names of, or with reference to, other plants, of obvious meaning or sufficiently explained in the quots., as (1) **Virginia crab,** (2) **gourdseed,** (cf. * **gourdseed**), (3) **knotweed,** (4) **mulberry tree,** (cf. **Virginian mulberry**), (5) **pine,** (6) **poke,** (cf. **pokeweed**), (7) **silk,** (8) **sumac,** (cf. **staghorn sumac**), (9) **tea,** (cf. **Virginia willow**), (10) **thorn,** (cf. **Washington thorn**), (11) **willow,** (12) **winterberry.**

(1) **1811** SUTCLIFF *Travels* (1815) 273 He gave us a taste of his cyder, made from a species of apple, called the Virginia crab. — (2) **1825** LORAIN *Pract. Husbandry* 203 The ears of the Virginia gourdseed are not very long. **1848** C. L. FLEISCHMANN *Nordamerikanische Landwirth* 114 Virginia White Gourdseed-Corn. — (3) **1901** MOHR *Plant Life Ala.* 486 *Polygonum virginianum.* . . . Virginia Knotweed. . . . Ontario, southern New England, west to Nebraska, south to Florida, Louisiana, Arkansas, and Missouri. — (4) **1897** SUDWORTH *Arborescent Flora* 186 *Morus rubra,* Red Mulberry. . . . Common names [include] . . . Virginia Mulberry Tree (Tenn.).

(5) **1897** SUDWORTH *Arborescent Flora* 26 *Pinus taeda.* Loblolly Pine. . . . Virginia Pine. **1943** PEATTIE *Great Smokies* 168 The scrub or Virginia pine, a weed of a tree, . . . slowly takes over from the broom sedge. — (6) **1769** STORK *Descr. E. Fla.* 19 *Phytolocca octandra* . . . in Mexico, like Virginia poke. **1840** DEWEY *Mass. Flowering Plants* 100 Poke, or Virginia Poke, or Poke Weed . . . is a favorite food of robins and other birds. **1909** WEBSTER 2287/1 V[irginia] poke, . . . the Indian poke, or false hellebore. — (7) **1891** *Cent.* 5630/1 Virginia silk, the silk-vine, *Periploca Graeca;* so called from the silky tuft of the seed. — (8) **1629** PARKINSON *Paradisus* 611 *Rhus Virginiana.* The Virginia Sumack, or Buckes horne tree of Virginia. — (9) **1931** CLUTE *Plants* 48 Virginia tea is a transposition of the technical name, *Itea Virginica.*

(10) 1860 DARLINGTON *Weeds & Plants* 131 *C[rataegus] cordata*. ... Washington Thorn. Virginia Thorn. ... It makes a handsome hedge, but not a very substantial one. — **(11) 1891** *Cent.* 3203/1 Itea. ... A small genus of plants of the natural order *Saxifragaceae*. ... Five species are known, of which one, *I. Virginica*, called the *Virginia willow*, is common in the eastern United States from New Jersey southward. — **(12) 1891** *Cent.* 6943/3 The winterberry especially so named is *I. verticillata*, otherwise called *black alder*, sometimes distinguished as *Virginia winterberry*.

c. With reference to tobacco grown in Virginia as (1) **Virginia fine cut,** (2) **honeycomb,** (3) **plug,** (4) **seed,** (5) **tobacco,** (6) **twist,** (7) **weed.**

(1) 1866 MOORE *Women of War* 506 A young lady of the city made him a present in the form of a pretty bag filled with 'Virginia fine cut.' — **(2) 1878** DALY in J. F. Daly *A. Daly* 250 The little tobacco shop ... where you invested Santa Claus's money that fatal Christmas in your first & *last* plug of Virginia Honey-Comb. — **(3) 1871** *Atlantic Mo.* Nov. 566 The circle enjoyed itself specially, — taciturnity and clouds of Virginia plug reigning supreme. — **(4) 1867** J. O. PHILSTER *Mason Co. Tobacco* 14 If you were to get the Virginia or Clarksville seed ... and cure by fire [etc.].

(5) 1655 *Suffolk Deeds* II. 191 Verginia tobacco at fower pence per pownd to be deliuered at Boston. **1705** *Va. State P.* I. 98 It will oblige the Planters to make only that which is good, whereby the reputation of the Virginia tobacco will be again advanced. **1748** *N. Eng. Hist. & Gen. Reg.* IV. 176 She continues to sell the best Virginia Tobacco, Cut, Pigtail and spun, of all Sorts. — **(6) 1859** *Harper's Mag.* April 611/1 While he vigorously executed the Virginia reel, they devoted themselves to 'Virginia twist.' — **(7) 1833** COKE *Subaltern's Furlough* xv, Several of his guests were enjoying 'a *drink*' and a mouthful of *the Virginia weed*. **1845** *S. Lit. Messenger* XI. 667/1 Left ... only with the sweet companionship of the 'Virginia weed,' what 'strange vagaries' did my imagination pursue!

4. In the names of animals, esp. birds: (1) **Virginia bat,** the whippoorwill, *obs.;* (2) **bell,** (see quot. and cf. **Virginia frog**), *obs.;* (3) **blackfish,** (see quot.); (4) **cardinal,** the Kentucky cardinal *q.v.;* (5) **deer,** (see quots.); (6) **frog,** a bullfrog; (7) **nightingale,** the Kentucky cardinal *q.v.;* (8) **partridge,** (see quot. 1917); (9) **plant,** (see quot.); (10) **quail,** = **Virginia partridge;** (11) **rail,** a long-billed wading bird, *Rallus virginianus*, similar to, but smaller than, the king rail *q.v.;* (12) **redbird,** the Kentucky cardinal *q.v.*

(1) 1688 in FORCE *Tracts* III. No. 12, 29 The night Raven, which some call the Virginia Bat, is about the Bigness of a Cuckow, feathered like them but very short. — **(2) 1708** E. COOK *Sot-Weed Factor* 9 Frogs are called *Virginea* Bells and make (both in that country and *Mary-Land*) during the Night, a very hoarse ungrateful Noise. — **(3) 1884** *Nat. Museum Bul.* No. 27, 633 The Virginia Blackfish is believed by Professor Cope to be a distinct species, which he has designated as *G. brachypterus*. — **(4) 1917** *Birds of Amer.* III. 63 Novels have been written in which the Virginia Cardinal and the Kentucky Cardinal ... have given a tone of aristocratic elegance.

(5) 1917 *Mammals of Amer.* 8/2 *Virginia Deer, or White-tailed Deer*. ... The middle and eastern United States and Canada. *Northern Virginia Deer*. ... Northern part of United States and southern Canada west to Rockies. **1945** *Nat. Geog. Mag.* Jan. (*advt.*), The Virginia or White tail Deer (*Odocoileus virginianus*) has as wide a range as any game animal in the United States. — **(6) 1706** PHILLIPS (ed. Kersey), Virginia-Frog, a kind of Frog that ... makes a noise like the bellowing of a Bull. **1827** WILLIAMS *W. Florida* 29 The Bell or Virginia frog, is only found in the eastern district; and there they are not numerous. — **(7) 1688** *Phil. Trans.* XVII. 995 Of Virginia Nightingale, or red Bird, there are two sorts. **1841** GURNEY *Journey* 62 The Virginia nightingale, of a bright red, was also observed, and on one occasion, I thought I heard his lively song. **1917** *Birds of Amer.* III. 63 Cardinal. ... Other Names.—Cardinal Grosbeak; ... Virginia Nightingale. — **(8) 1852** MARCY *Explor. Red River* (1854) 13, I observed ... the Virginia partridge (*Ortyx Virginianus*). **1917** *Birds of Amer.* II. 2 Bob-White. *Colinus virginianus virginianus*. ... [Also called] Virginia Partridge. ... Northerners call him Quail; Southerners, Partridge. — **(9) 1881** INGERSOLL *Oyster Industry* 248 *Soft Oyster*.—The 'Virginia plant,' or southern oyster (Staten Island sound), as distinguished from the 'hard' native oyster.

(10) 1897 *N.Y. Forest, Fish, & Game Comm.* 2 Rep. 317 Popular synonyms [for the bobwhite]. ... Virginia quail; partridge or colin. — **(11) 1828** BONAPARTE *Synopsis* 334 The Virginia Rail ... inhabits throughout North America; extending its migrations far to the north. **1945** *Mass. Audubon Soc. Bul.* March 63 At the Sanctuary on this date we might get the Virginia Rail, Blue-winged Teal, and, of course, the Black Ducks and Wood Ducks probably nesting. — **(12) 1789** in BANCROFT *N.W. Amer.* (1888) I. 714 In the woods are woodpeckers, robins, Virginia red-birds, snow-birds. **1810** WILSON *Ornithology* II. 40 Cardinal grosbeaks are generally known by the names Red-bird, Virginia Red-bird, ... and Crested Red-bird.

5. In miscellaneous combs.: (1) **Virginia abstraction,** (see quots. and cf. next), *obs.;* (2) **abstractionist,** a strict constructionist, *obs.* or *hist.;* (3) **Americanism,** an Americanism such as occurs in the English used by Virginians, *obs.;* (4) **and Kentucky Resolutions,** the Kentucky and Virginia Resolutions, cf. **Kentucky Resolutions;** (5) **break-down,** a kind of dance, *obs.*, cf. * **break-down,** *n.* **1;** (6) **fence,** see as a main entry; (7) **hoedown,** a kind of dance, *obs.*, cf. **hoedown;** (8) **line,** (*a*) the Virginia division of the Continental forces in the Revolution, *obs.*, (*b*) the boundary line of the state of Virginia; (9) **reel,** a country-dance for an indefinite number of participants, also the music accompanying such a dance or, rarely, the dancers themselves, cf. **six-handed Virginia reel;** (10) **Resolutions,** a set of resolutions drawn up by James Madison and passed in 1798 by the legislature of Virginia, declaring the Alien and Sedition Laws to be unconstitutional, and laying down a strict-contructionist interpretation of the relative powers of the states and the national government, now *hist.*, cf. **Kentucky Resolutions;** (11) **school,** those who upheld or favored the views concerning state rights that were popular among Virginia statesmen before the Civil War; (12) **worm fence,** = **Virginia fence,** also in fig. or allusive contexts, cf. **worm fence** and see **stake and rider(ed) fence.**

(1) 1843 in HAMBLETON *H. A. Wise* 41 'No longer embarrassed by her peculiar opinions,' by which he intended contempt and derision of 'Virginia abstractions,' or of a strict construction of our glorious Federal Constitution. **1852** *Yankee Notions* April 119/1 'And pray what is a Virginia abstraction?' asked the Court. — **(2) 1886** POORE *Reminiscences* I. 71 Senator Tazewell ... was a first-class Virginia abstractionist and an avowed hater of New England. **1913** A. C. COLE *Whig Party in South* 65 Even should Tyler, as a state rights man and a 'Virginia abstractionist,' offer opposition ... it would be but to detach himself from the great body of the Whig party. — **(3) 1855** *Herald of Freedom* 21 July 4/7 The Richmond Post is the organ of the 'American' party in Virginia. We copy from it a few specimens of Virginia Americanisms, or American Virginianisms, whichever they may be. — **(4) 1829** *Va. Herald* (Fredericksburg) 21 March 3/4, I remember the famous Alien and Sedition Laws, passed by Congress, and the Virginia and Kentucky Resolutions, which grew out of them.

(5) 1841 *N.O. Picayune* 12 Jan. 2/2 In a corner a fellow was giving a regular old Virginia 'break down' on his own account. — **(7) 1846** *N.O. Picayune* 31 Aug. 648/2 In slang parlance he was great on 'Virginia hoe-downs' and 'old corn-field shuffles.' **1894** SEARIGHT *Old Pike* 142 After supper and attention to the teams, the wagoners would gather in the bar room and ... have a 'Virginia hoe-down.' — **(8)** (*a*) **1779** HAMILTON *Works* VII. 576 Some folks in the Virginia line, jealous of his glory, had the folly to get him arrested. **1790** *Ann. 1st Cong.* 1685 The engrossed bill to enable officers and soldiers of the Virginia line ... to obtain titles to certain lands. (*b*) **1792** *Ann. 2d Cong.* 1036 These were to be located within a district bounded northwardly by the Virginia line. — **(9) 1817** PAULDING *Lett. from South* I. 151 One of the favourite Virginia reels is, 'Fire in the Mountains, run, boys, run.' **1896** WILKINS *Madelon* 33 A smothered titter ran down the files of the Virginia reel. **1949** *Sky Line Trail* March 18/1 In such-like regalia, denim pants et al they could dance the Virginny reel right round the campfire mighty sprightly.

(10) 1854 BENTON *30 Years' View* I. 139/1 The third resolve of the Virginia resolutions of the year 1798. **1934** WINSTON *Robert E. Lee* 13 At this session the famous Virginia Resolutions were offered by John Taylor, Jefferson's lieutenant. — **(11) 1833** *Cong. Deb.* 24 Jan. 1338 Whenever the doctrines of 'State rights,' as insisted upon by the Virginia school, are acted out, they must necessarily end in nullification and State rebellion. — **(12) 1809** CUMING *Western Tour* 34 Two very beautiful red foxes playfully crossed the road ... leaping with ease a Virginia worm fence above six feet high. **1858** *Yale Lit. Mag.* XXIII. 183 (Th.), I was constrained to lay out the ground plan of a Virginia worm fence every time I went to Post. **1868** *Ore. State Jrnl.* 21 Nov. 1/5 Greeley can lay Virginia worm-fences in ink faster than any other editor in New York city.

b. In combs., usu. obs. or hist., of obvious meaning or sufficiently explained in the quots., as (1) **Virginia bacon and greens,** (2) **cloth,** (3) **coal,** (4) **coupon cases,** (5) **croppings** [in allusion to Virginia City, Nevada], (6) **currency,** (7) **dynasty,** (8) **fodder house,** (9)

gaps, (10) **gouger,** (cf. **gouger 1.**), (11) **ham,** (12) **hoe,** (13) **jig,** (14) **lead,** (15) **long tails,** (16) **(paper) money,** (17) **picklet,** (18) **planter,** (19) **poke,** (cf. **3. b.** (6) above), (20) **rail fence,** (21) **ranger,** (22) **rocker,** [in allusion to Virginia City, Nevada, cf. **rocker**], (23) **stone,** (24) **style,** (25) **walk-around,** (cf. **walk-around**), (26) **Yankee.**

(1) *c***1866** BAGBY *Old Va. Gentleman* 68 He will be able to give his friends . . . a dish of real old Virginia 'Bacon and Greens.' — **(2)** [**1775** BURNABY *Travels* 21 They made a kind of cotton-cloth, which they clothe themselves with in common, and call after the name of their country.] **1818** *Norfolk* (Va.) *Herald* 22 July 4/6. **1897** TERHUNE *Old Field* 16 She had outgrown her frock of mixed blue homespun, 'Virginia cloth,' as it was called. — **(3) 1790** *Pa. Packet* 1 Jan. 4/2 Just Arrived by the Mary Ann. . . . Virginia coal. . . . Copper in sheets and bottoms. **1888** *Cong. Rec.* 12 May 4040/2, I am a free-trader . . . but not in Virginia coal. — **(4) 1889** *Cent.* 841/2 *Virginia coupon cases,* the generic name under which are known a number of suits determined by the United States Supreme Court in 1884, enforcing a Virginia statute which declared coupons on bonds of that State receivable in payment of State taxes, notwithstanding the repeal of that statute.

(5) 1877 W. M. WRIGHT *Big Bonanza* 53 This vein is known as the Virginia lead or Virginia croppings. — **(6) 1732** in *Amer. Sp.* XX. (1945) 276 Taking to himself 2s 6d in silver or gold Virginia currency for every 50 acres. **1861** *Alexandria* (Va.) *Gaz.* 27 April 3/1 Said coupons will be paid in Virginia currency at the office of the company. **1949** *Hist. & Philos. Soc. Ohio Bul.* Jan. 30. — **(7) 1812** *Columbian Centinel* 7 Nov. 2/3 They now perceive that those who pourtrayed the characters and exposed the plots of the *Virginia Dynasty,* understood their men, and were Oracles of truth. **1914** *Cyclo. Amer. Govt.* III. 622 *Virginia Dynasty,* a name given by opponents of Virginia's domination of national affairs to the men from Virginia (Jefferson, Madison, Monroe) who filled the presidency from 1801 to 1825. **1944** *Newsweek* 28 Feb. 104 So it was with the Virginia dynasty in 1824 with the Democratic party in 1860 and in 1920, and with the Republican party in 1912 and 1932. — **(8) 1807** GASS *Journal* 209 This lodge is built much after the form of the Virginia fodder houses. — **(9) 1823** COOPER *Pioneers* xvi, You must go into the Virginy gaps, if you want them [*sc.* wild turkeys] now.

(10) 1787 in *Mag. Amer. Hist.* I. 433 One of the officers being in a public house in Louisville, was grossly insulted by one of these Virginia Gougers, a perfect bully. — **(11) 1824** *Shipping & Commercial List* 31 July (Pettigrew P.). **1861** *Alexandria* (Va.) *Gaz.* 11 May 1/2 Here a slab of bacon, there a quarter of beef or a saddle of mutton, or Virginia hams. **1946** *This Week Mag.* 16 Feb. 28/3 Virginia hams were so prized in the colony that they held a place of honor as a 'standing dish.' — **(12) 1790** *Pa. Packet* 31 May 3/4 Nicodemus Loyd, . . . has now for sale . . . large Virginia hoes, suitable to hoe rice or tobacco. — **(13) 1803** DAVIS *Travels* 414 *Pat Hickory* could tire him at a *Virginia Jig.* — **(14) 1877** [see **Virginia croppings**].

(15) 1839 MARRYAT *Diary in Amer.* 1 Ser. II. 172 There is no want of handsome equipages, many four in hand (Virginny long tails). — **(16) 1757** *Lett. to Washington* II. 36 The Owner would not Take Virginia Paper money at more than Maryland. **1777** *Jrnls. Cont. Congress* VII. 43 There is due to Abraham Simons, for the hire of Ludwick Neal's wagon, in the service of the Virginia light horse, the sum of £15, Virginia money, equal to 50 dollars. **1834** *Pres. Mess. & P.* III. 96 The troops, it seems, were paid off in Virginia money, which is below *par* in our State. — **(17) 1897** *Voice* 9 Sep. 7/3 Virginia picklet is made of four heads of cabbage, chopt fine, and a quart of white onions. — **(18) 1724** H. JONES *Virginia* 38 The Virginia Planters readily learn to become good Mechanicks in Building. **1800** TATHAM *Communications* 55 Now one of these boys and one little horse are generally sufficient for the *flook* plough; which is almost universally in use among those called *Virginia planters.* — **(19) 1887** *Cent. Mag.* 549/1 He gave the cards a Virginia poke whenever it came his turn to cut them; that is to say, he pushed one card out of the middle of the pack, and put it at the back.

(20) 1864 NORTON *Army Lett.* 293 There were miles of Virginia rail fence. **1939** *L.A.* Map 117. — **(21) 1808** WEEMS *Washington* (1840) 42 The Virginia Rangers discovered signs of the Indians. — **(22) 1849** WIERZBICKI *California* 47 They are getting out from $1500 to $2,000 per week, working with mercury in the Virginia rocker. — **(23) 1676** GLOVER *Va.* in *Phil. Trans.* XI. 627, I have seen several Rings of Virginia stones, which in my judgment have equalled Diamonds in lustre. — **(24) 1880** *Fergus' Hist. Series* XIV. 107 The fences were . . . laid up, in what was called the 'worm' or 'Virginia' style.

(25) 1869 *Atlantic Mo.* July 72/2 When I executed my 'Juba' dance, or in company with others performed the Virginia Walk-around, these honest Germans would . . . rush precipitately into the middle of the street. — **(26) 1839** BIRD *Robin Day* 56 They were beef-eating Britons and not fever and aguy Virginee Yankees.

Also *Virginia bread, bred, convention, delegation, granite, Huguenot, legislature, poorhouse, pork, race horse, venison, wagon,* etc.

Virginiad vɚˈdʒɪnɪˌæd, *n.* (See quot. 1807.) *Obs.* — **1807** in *S. Lit. Messenger* XXIV. 311/1 *Resolved,* That there be a quinquennial Festival kept at James Town . . . and That each portion of five years be called a Virginiad. **1857** *S. Lit. Messenger* XXIV. 311/2 The first 'Virginiad' of five years rolled by and found the country on the eve of a war.

Virginia fence.

1. A zigzag fence made of rails split from trees and laid so as to cross each other at the ends. Cf. **snake fence, stake and rider(ed) fence, worm fence.**

1671 *Portsmouth Rec.* 160 For post and rayles it Shall be of the Same hight of the Virginia ffence. **1790** DEANE *N. Eng. Farmer* 92/1 A Virginia fence . . . [is] made by lapping the ends of rails or poles on each other, turning alternately to the right and left. **1843** *Farmers' Cabinet* 15 Sep. 61/1 The first field . . . consists of five hundred acres, under what is sometimes called Virginia or worm fence. **1948** DICK *Dixie Frontier* 104 The commonest fence was that variously known as the worm, snake, or Virginia fence. It was made in a zigzag pattern.

attrib. **1835** *Knickerb.* VI. 176 Hawk-nosed speculators already rode beside lawyers through the muddy, Virginia-fence lands of these squatments.

2. In phrases in allusion to the uncertain course of one who is intoxicated. *Colloq. Obs.*

1737 *Pa. Gazette* 13 Jan. 2 He makes Virginia Fence. **1774** J. ANDREWS *Lett.* 21 A few steps further, another [man] came running, as the only expedient to avoid making *Virginia fences.* **1800** TATHAM *Tobacco* 11 It is in allusion to this zigzag foundation that a drunken man is said to be *laying out Virginia fences.* **1867** LOWELL *Biglow P.* 2 Ser. p. lix, *Virginia fence, to make a:* to walk like a drunken man.

b. (See quot.)

1865 TROWBRIDGE *Three Scouts* x. 96 No use of yer denying what's as plain as daylight through a Virginny fence.

Virginiaism, see **Virginianism.**

* **Virginian,** *n.* and *a.*

1. *n.* A native or resident, other than an Indian, of Virginia.

1634 in C. C. HALL *Narr. Early Md.* 38 By noone we came before Monserat, where is a noble plantation of Irish Catholiques whome the virginians would not suffer to live with them because of their religion. **1755** in FRANKLIN *Works* (1887) VII. 97 No notice had ever been given of their wanting any more carriages, than the Virginians and Marylanders had undertaken to furnish. **1825** NEAL *Bro. Jonathan* I. 245 The Virginians are called Buckskins. **1949** *So. Wkly.* 21 Dec. 6/2 The Virginian minces no words in expressing the belief that 1950 will be a year of crisis.

2. *a.* In the names of plants and birds: (1) **Virginian (eared) owl,** the American long-eared owl, *Asio wilsonianus;* (2) **pine,** (see quots. and cf. **Virginia pine**); (3) **stonecrop,** the ditch stonecrop, *Penthorum sedoides;* (4) **weed,** tobacco.

(1) 1823 JAMES *Exped.* 262 *Strix Virginiana*—Virginian-eared owl. **1835** AUDUBON *Ornith. Biog.* III. 170 Besides man, the enemies of the Mallard are the White-headed Eagle, . . . the Virginian Owl . . . , and the snapping turtle. — **(2) 1775** BURNABY *Travels* 80 It becomes beautifully covered with Virginian pine. **1785** MARSHALL *Amer. Grove* 102 *Pinus virginiana.* Two-leaved Virginian, or Jersey Pine. This is generally of but low growth, but divided into many branches. **1890** *Cent.* 4496/2 *Virginian pine,* an old name of the long-leafed pine. — **(3) 1837** DARLINGTON *Flora Cestrica* 281 Sedum-like Penthorum. Vulgo—Virginian Stone-crop. **1843** TORREY *Flora N.Y.* I. 253 *Penthorum sedoides.* . . . Virginian Stonecrop. . . . Low wet places; Comm. July–September. — **(4) 1821** COOPER *Spy* iii, He took from his mouth a large allowance of the Virginian weed.

b. Used in combs. corresponding to those under * **Virginia** *q.v.*, as (1) **Virginian cowslip,** (2) **creeper,** (3) **deer,** (4) **fence,** (5) **mulberry,** (6) **partridge,** (7) **redbird,** (8) **snakeroot,** (9) **thyme,** (10) **tobacco,** (11) **wake-robin,** (12) **winterberry.**

(1) 1843 TORREY *Flora N.Y.* II. 85 *Pulmonaria Virginica.* . . . Virginian Cowslip. Virginian Lungwort. . . . Borders of Oneida creek and Fish creek, Oneida county. **1890** *Cent.* 3721/1 The Virginian cowslip or lungwort is a fine spring wild flower of the eastern United States, also in gardens. — **(2) 1843** TORREY *Flora N.Y.* I. 148. — **(3)** [**1781** PENNANT *Hist. Quadrupeds* I. 104 Virginian Deer with slender horns.] **1823** JAMES *Exped.* I. 262 *Cervus Virginianus*—Virginian deer. — **(4) 1842** *Lowell Offering* II. 129 He had surrounded his fields and pastures with stone walls, in lieu of Virginian, stump, brush, and board fence. **1852** REGAN *Emigrant's Guide* 348 For the Virginian fence, the timber is cut in the winter, when the sap is somewhat frozen. The trees are cut in lengths of ten or twelve feet. . . . They are commonly built seven rails high.

(5) [**1731** P. Miller *Gardeners Dict. s.v. Morus,* The broad-leav'd Virginian Mulberry.] **1846** Browne *Trees Amer.* 457 The Red-fruited Mulberry-Tree. . . . Red mulberry-tree, Virginian mulberry-tree. — (6) **1813** Wilson *Ornithology* IX. (index), Virginian Partridge. — (7) **1874** Coues *Birds N.W.* 172 *Cardinalis Virginianus.* . . . Cardinal Grosbeak; Virginian Redbird. — (8) **1791** *Amer. Philos. Soc.* III. 114 Virginian Snake-root. — (9) **1817–8** Eaton *Botany* (1822) 415 *Pycnanthemum linifolium,* virginian thyme. **1901** Mohr *Plant Life Ala.* 698 *Koellia flexuosa.* . . . Virginian Thyme. . . . The herb known as 'mountain mint' or 'Pycnanthemum' is used medicinally.

(10) **1817–8** Eaton *Botany* (1822) 362 *Nicotiana tabacum,* virginian tobacco. — (11) **1770** Forster tr. Kalm *Travels* I. 125 The Virginian Wake robin, or *Arum Virginicum,* grows in wet places. **1891** *Cent.* 6807/1 *Virginian wake-robin,* the arrow-arum, *Peltandra undulata.* — (12) **1785** Marshall *Amer. Grove* 110 *Prinos verticillatus.* Virginian Winter-Berry. The inner bark of this shrub is very good to make poultices of for ripening tumors.

Virginianism vəˈdʒɪnjənˌɪzəm, *n.*

1. A word, phrase, or manner of expression characteristic of the English spoken in Virginia. Also **Virginiaism.** *Obs.*

[**1588** Harriot *Briefe & True Report* D3v There are many other strange trees whose names I knowe not but in the *Virginian* language.] **1815** in *Amer. Sp.* XXII. 280, I send you instead of a copy the original of a note on *Virginianisms,* which I procured for your amusement from the most intelligent *young* man, I saw during an absence of three months at the South. **1825** Neal *Bro. Jonathan* I. 46 Only break yourself, will you, of those execrable Virginia-isms— . . . I *reckon—jest*—mighty bad—leave me *be* [etc.]. **1855** *Herald of Freedom* 21 July 4/7 We copy from it a few specimens of Virginia Americanisms, or American Virginianisms, whichever they may be.

2. The mode of life and attitude of mind thought of as characteristic of a Virginian.

1848 *S. Lit. Messenger* XIV. 635/1, I did not come to the State to see northern improvements, . . . but to get a glimpse of the genuine, unsophisticated, old Virginianism. **1855** *N.Y. Wkly. Tribune* 14 July 4/3 He outgrew his Virginianism and his Southernism and became a finished American.

Virginia's warbler. [Named by Baird for Mrs. W. W. Anderson.] The Rocky Mountain warbler, *Vermivora virginiae.* — **1860** Baird *Birds N. Amer.* p. xi, *Helminthophaga virginiae,* Virginia's Warbler. . . . N[ew] M[exico]. **1874** Coues *Birds N.W.* 51 Virginia's Warbler. . . . Southern Rocky Mountain region.

∗**vis-à-vis.** = **tête-à-tête.** — **1851** Cist *Cincinnati* 202 Dressing bureaus, sociables, and *vis-à-vis* are sure to catch the visitor's eye, and to open the visitor's purse.

visible admixture. A mixture of races resulting in obvious Negroid features. Also attrib. *Obs.*

1831 *S.C. Ct. Appeals Rep.* (Bailey) II. 558 Where there is a *distinct* and *visible* admixture of negro blood, the individual is to be denominated a mulatto, or a person of color. **1868** *Cong. Globe* 13 May 2452/2 The whole question of the 'visible admixture' law . . . is one of the most . . . characteristic chapters in modern Democratic history. **1870** *Ib.* 23 Feb. 1510/2 The Democratic party [in Ohio] endeavored to exclude [from citizenship] what are called 'visible admixture' persons—persons who had a visible admixture of black blood.

∗**visit,** *n.* A chat or talk. Cf. **donation, scalp, sitting up, spinning visit.** — **1890** *Harper's Mag.* Dec. 147/2 I've had a real nice visit with you . . . an' I wish I could ask you to stay longer.

∗**visit,** *v. intr.* To talk or chat. *Colloq.* — **1879** Tourgee *Fool's Errand* 111 He . . . stopped at the Mission-House, visiting with the teachers. **1942** Cannon *Mountain* 59 Whit happened by and Mr. Gowan spoke to him. So Whit stopped, and they visited.

∗**visitation,** *n.* (See quot. 1851.) *Obs.*

1650 *Harvard Rec.* I. 28 There shall bee three weeks of visitation yearly . . . between the tenth of June & the Commencement. **1766** *Holyoke Diaries* 29 To warn ye Cambridge School. Master of the Visitation of his School. **1851** Hall *College Words* 279 It was customary, in the early days of Harvard College, for the graduates of the year to attend in the recitation-room on Mondays and Tuesdays, for three weeks, during the month of June, subject to the examination of all who chose to visit them. This was called . . . the *Weeks of Visitation.*

∗**visor,** *n.* The stiff forepiece of a cap.

1847 Parkman in *Knickerb.* XXIX. 504 The water dropped from the vizors of our caps, and trickled down our cheeks. **1911** Lincoln *Cap. Warren's Wards* 2 He was a big man . . . wearing a cloth cap with a visor. **1944** *Sears Cat.* (ed. 189) 355 The soft, thick shearling wool pelt on the visor adds the extra smart touch.

∗**visualist,** *n.* One whose mental imagery is predominantly visual. — **1895** *Pop. Sci. Mo.* April 731 Charcot . . . classified people into 'visualists'—those whose recollections were chiefly of things seen, who had to read a name in order to remember it; 'audists' [etc.]. **1902** *Amer. Jrnl. Psychol.* XIII. 544 The visualist probably proceeds more from the standpoint of the object and the enumeration of qualities.

vitascope ˈvaɪtəˌskop, *n.* An early form of moving pictures or the machine which projected them. *Obs.*

1896 *N.Y. Herald* 4 April 5/6 Mr. Edison calls his latest invention the Vitascope, which he says means a machine showing life. **1901** *World's Work* Aug. 1057/2 In the last few years the biograph, cinematograph, the vitascope have become comparatively common. **1914** Grau *Theatre of Science* 5 The Latham Eidoloscope and the Edison Vitascope, . . . were first exhibited at Keith's Philadelphia Vaudeville Theatre.

vitascope ˈvaɪtəˌskop, *v. tr.* To take moving pictures of (a place). *Obs.* — **1896** *N.Y. Dramatic News* 11 July 10/2 Niagara having been vitascoped, Coney Island has now fallen before the camera.

viva ˈvivɑ, *n. S.W.* [Sp. in same sense.] A shout or cry of approval. *Colloq.*

1836 Parker *Trip to West & Texas* 276 (Bentley), By and by there will be a reading of the Declaration of Independence and an address punctured by vivas. **1844** G. W. Kendall *Narrative* 311 (Bentley), Instantly the air was filled with *vivas,* and in ten minutes we received a visit from the governor's secretary. [**1923** Wallace Smith *Little Tigress* 74 (Bentley), I wonder if he still *vivas* for Madero?]

vixen sister. (See quot.) *Obs.* — **1883** *Harper's Mag.* Feb. 425/1 After the union of the States . . . the political conduct of South Carolina was so imperious and so unreasonable that she was not uncommonly known as . . . the 'vixen sister.'

vly vlaɪ, flaɪ, *n. local.* [Du. dial. *vlei* (<*vallei*), valley.] Low ground, sometimes under water, a marsh or creek, often in place-names. Cf. **fly,** *n.*[1]

[**1679** tr. Danckaerts *Jrnl.* (1913) 60 There is towards the sea a large piece of low flat land which is over-flowed at every tide. . . . Such a place they [i.e., Dutch on Long Island] call *valeu* and mow it for hay, which cattle would rather eat than fresh hay or grass.] **1803** *Med. Repository* 6 About two miles S.E. from town there is another considerable extent of bog, called the *Long-Vlie.* **1877** Bartlett 734 *Vly,* . . . in New York, a swamp, a marsh. **1904** Chambers in *Harper's Mag.* May 933/1 Have you reason to believe that an attempt has been made to fire the Owl Vlaie?

vocabulation vəˌkæbjəˈleʃən, *n.* The use or choice of words. *Rare.* — **1891** Eggleston *Faith Doctor* 162 A mind . . . felicitous in vocabulation and ingenious in the construction of sentences.

∗**vocational,** *a. Educ.* Guiding or preparing for a vocation, concerned with such guidance or preparation.

1909 *Nat. Conservation Cong. Proc.* 164 In conclusion . . . the remedies: Vocational training in high schools. **1946** *Reader's Digest* Jan. 18/1 And the vocational agriculture teacher was getting the farm equipment shop ready for his evening group of adult farmers. **1947** *Democrat* 18 Dec. 1/5 (*heading*), Vocational Teachers Organize in Clarke.

volante voˈlɑnte, *n. S.W.* [Sp. in both senses, though in sense **1.** only with reference to a New World vehicle. An Amer. borrowing.]

1. A light, two-wheeled covered vehicle with long shafts. **2.** A kind of loose ornamental veil-like head covering. Both *obs.*

(1) **1805** in *Amer. Pioneer* II. (1843) 231 Ladies frequently ride abroad in a chair, (volante,) managing the horse themselves. Their volante carriages are very ugly. Often they drive mules, and sometimes horses and mules are driven three or four abreast. **1858** Vielé *Following Drum* 54 The volante, the vehicle of this country, is at the door before six o'clock. **1880** G. W. Cable *Grandissimes* xlix. 378 They agreed upon one bold outlay—a volante. — (2) **1894** Chopin *Bayou Folk* 76 Maman Chavan laughed, and her fat shoulders quivered under the white *volante* she wore.

∗**volcano,** *n.* **a.** An alcohol lamp. *Obs.* **b.** (See quot.) See also ∗**mud volcano.** — (**a**) **1861** Winthrop *C. Dreeme* 160, I'll run down and get Mr. Stillfleet's volcano and stew-pan to stew the Blue-Pointers. — (**b**) **1889** *Cent.* 2245/2 *Fizgig,* a firework, made of damp powder, which makes a hissing or fizzing noise when ignited; in one form called by boys a *volcano.*

volleyball ˈvɑlɪˌbɔl, *n.* (See quot. 1896.) Also a ball for use in this game. Also attrib.

1896 *Phys. Ed.* V. 50/1 During the past winter Mr. W. G. Morgan of Holyoke, Mass. has developed a game in his gymnasium which is called Volley Ball. . . . The play consists in keeping a ball in motion over a high net, from one side to the other, thus partaking of the character of two games,—tennis and hand ball. **1936** *Sears Cat.* (ed. 173) 827 High Quality 'Y' Volley Ball. . . . Rubber valve bladder. Double leather laced effect . . . $3.59. **1949** *Dziennik Zwiazkowy* (Chi.) 19 Nov. 6/3 Last year two of our volleyball teams finished in a tie for second place.

Hence **volleyballer.**

1948 *Chi. Maroon* 23 April 14/3 (*heading*), Phi Gam and Mathews top volleyballers.

∗ **Volstead,** *n.* [Andrew J. *Volstead*, representative from Minn.] *attrib.* Designating or pertaining to an act of Congress of Oct. 28, 1919, providing for the enforcement, under stringent penalties, of the prohibition laws, and defining intoxicating liquors as those containing more than one-half of one per cent, by volume, of alcohol.

1920 *Harvey's Wkly.* 23 Oct. 14/2 Those who do not believe in national prohibition and who opposed the adoption of the Eighteenth Amendment and the enactment of the Volstead law [etc.]. **1921** *Municipal Jrnl.* (S.F.) 30 June 2/2 The new Volstead bill has been blocked in committee, and not merely by the 'wets,' but by the 'drys.' **1949** *Chi. Tribune* 8 Sep. 22/2 In the Volstead era, corrupt politicians talked to exactly the same effect with the leaders of the Anti-Saloon league.

Hence **a. Volsteadian days. b. Volsteadism.**

(a) 1923 Cobb *Kansas* 53 Well, still and yet, even in these Volsteadian days, Maine, she says it with hiccoughs! **1950** *Chi. Tribune* 29 April, Unlike the word 'speakeasy,' so common in Volsteadian days, the etymology of which is obvious, these picturesque phrases are of rather obscure origin. — **(b) 1920** *Harvey's Wkly.* 27 March 11/2 The Republicans would have to stand for Volsteadism or incur defeat. **1947** *Chi. D. News* 23 Jan. 14/1 Volstead didn't write the law. Nor was he an apostle of the fanaticism called 'Volsteadism.'

∗ **Voltaire,** *n.* A chair having a low seat and a high back. *Obs.* — **1870** Tomes *Decorum* 97 It is not becoming to throw themselves at once on the sofa and stretch their legs, or into the Voltaire or easy-chair.

∗ **volunteer,** *a.* In combs.: (1) **volunteer crop,** a crop that comes up and grows spontaneously; (2) **fire company,** a company of fire-fighters made up of volunteers; (3) **fire department,** a fire department the personnel of which is made up of volunteers, cf. **paid fire department;** (4) **post office,** see ∗ **post office 3. b;** (5) **State,** Tennessee, so called because of the large number, 30,000, who volunteered from that state for service in the Mexican War.

(1) [**1823** in Easterby *S.C. Rice Plant.* (1945) 248, 15 acker Betwen it an the River is hangin & is vary yallow & is Excelant Good Rice clear of voluntier.] **1857** Glisan *Jrnl. Army Life* 387 Many of the farmers depend on their volunteer crops for two years in succession. [**1950** *Lincoln Co. Advt.* (Brookhaven, Miss.) 12 Jan. 10/3 A good volunteer stand of Wild Winter Peas was seen growing on the farm of L. R. Brown.] — **(2) 1841** *N.O. Picayune* 22 April 2/5 Volunteer Fire Company, No. 1. The members of this Company are requested to attend an extra meeting on Friday evening next. **1901** Jameson & Buel *Encycl. Dict. Amer. Ref.* I. 254 The first volunteer fire company in America was organized in Philadelphia, 1736. — **(3) 1876** Ingram *Centennial Exp.* 662 Parade of Volunteer Fire Department. **1949** *News-Reporter* (McMinnville, Ore.) 4 Aug. 6/4 The scene was the annual volunteer fire department picnic to which 60 or 70 Newberg citizens came for fun, frolic and gossip.

(5) 1853 Ramsey *Tennessee* 116 Thus early did the 'Volunteer State' commence its novitiate in arms. **1950** *Newsweek* 20 March 96/2 A call for 2,800 volunteers in Tennessee brought out 30,000 men and gave Tennessee its nickname, 'The Volunteer State.'

∗ **volunteer,** *v. intr.* Of plants: To come up without having been planted. Cf. **volunteer crop.** — **1889** Union Pac. R.R. *Ore. & Wash.* 17 Wheat and rye volunteer, and volunteer crops of these have yielded 35 bushels to the acre. **1948** *Capital-Democrat* (Tishomingo, Okla.) 17 June 3/3 The crotalaria has been volunteering after each plowing of corn.

vomit grass. Meaning obscure. Cf. Webster *vomitwort*, =Indian tobacco. *Rare.* — **1808** Jefferson *Writings* IV. (1830) 119 Your presence will be to them what the vomit-grass is to a sick dog.

vomito ˈvɑmɪto, *n. S.W.* [Sp. *vómito* in same sense. An Amer. borrowing.] A violent form of yellow fever, usu. accompanied by black vomit.

1836 D. B. Edward *Hist. Texas* vii. 140 The Vomito prieto, of this zone, is a kind of yellow fever, modified by the climate. **1844** G. W. Kendall *Santa Fé Exped.* II. xxi. 395 Judge Ellis found letters awaiting him which gave the information that the vomito, or yellow fever, had broken out. **1885** Baylor *On Both Sides* 416, I have added to my circle some very valuable acquaintances . . . notably a medical man who confirms my germ-propagation theory of the 'vomito.'

voodoo ˈvudu, *n.* Also †**vandoo,** †**vaudoux, voudou.** Orig. *La.* [African. Cf. Jeji (Dahomey) and Ewe (Togo and Dahomey) *vodu*, a spirit (good or bad) intermediary between God and man, tutelary deity, demon, fetish.]

1. An African deity, or a system of defensive, amatory, or soothsaying charms, spells, secret rites, etc., practiced by so-called conjurers, witch doctors, etc., among Negroes and Creoles; also a spell or charm used in such a system. Cf. **hoodoo,** *n.*

1820 *Western Carolinian* 26 Sep., For sometime past [in New Orleans], a house in the suburb T—— . . . has been used as a kind of temple for certain occult practices and the idolatrous worship of an African deity, called *Vandoo.* **1871** De Vere 108 *Vandoux*, a French term, designating a certain form of worship and the object of this worship alike, introduced from the Island of Santo Domingo. **1880** Cable *Grandissimes* 90 Do this much for me this one time and then I will let voudou alone as much as you wish. **1902** G. C. Eggleston *D. South* 216, I'll put a Voodoo on anybody I ever heahs a callin' you a ole maid, Miss Mony. **1948** *Chi. D. News* 23 Feb. 12/7, I still think that the South might have won that war if it hadn't been weakened by generations of hawg-and-hominy, dished up by vengeful slave mammies who had discarded voodoo in favor of diet.

b. Short for voodoo dance *q.v.*

1886 *Cent. Mag.* Feb. 527 There were other dances. . . . Then there were the Voudou, and the Congo, to describe which would not be pleasant.

2. One who practices voodooism.

1871 *N.O. Picayune* 10 May, This woman is Marie Laveau, better known as priestess of the Voudous. **1906** Bell *C. Lee* 235 Carolina looked just in time to see a dark face disappear from view. . . . 'It is the voodoo!' whispered Flower. **1947** Graham *There Was Once Slave* 58 He's the one they call a voodoo.

3. In combs. of obvious meaning, as (1) **voodoo dance,** (2) **doctor,** (3) **land,** (cf. **hoodoo 2.**), (4) **queen,** (5) **woman.**

(1) 1882 Buel *Metropolitan Life Unveiled* 534 The old Congo dance was very similar to the Voudou dance, minus the scandalous features. **1897** Gunter *S. Turnbull* 277 Jemima's only seen a Voodoo dance before! — **(2) 1875** Hearn *Amer. Miscellany* (1924) I. 128 The Voudoo doctor who cured him gave him only internal medicine. **1949** *Chi. Tribune* 25 Sep. 37/1 In the better Negro neighborhoods it's an unwise voodoo doctor who tries to open shop. — **(3) 1904** Stuart *River's Children* 74 They told amazing mammy-tales of voodoo-land and the ghost country. — **(4) 1872** *N.O. Times* 28 June, Soon there arrived a skiff containing ten persons, among which was the Voudou queen. **1882** Buel *Metropolitan Life Unveiled* 525 At a given signal the four initiates formed a crescent before Dede, who was evidently the high priestess or Voudou queen.

(5) 1850 *N.O. Picayune* 3 July, Marie Laveaux, otherwise Widow Paris, f.w.c., the head of the Voudou women, yesterday appeared before Recorder Seuzeneau. **1886** *Chi. W. News* 5 Aug. 7/4 This is the mansion of Aunt Polly, the voodoo woman.

Also *voodoo carnival, man, murder, orgy, powwow, priestess,* etc.

voodoo ˈvudu, *v.* Also **voudou.** *tr.* To bewitch or put a spell upon (someone) by the arts of voodooism. Cf. **hoodoo,** *v.* — **1880** Cable *Grandissimes* 242 Maybe, too, it is true as he says, that he is voudoued. **1906** Bell *C. Lee* 199 They think the baby is bewitched,—that he has been voodooed.

voodooism ˈvuduˌɪzəm, *n.* Also **voudouism.** The body of beliefs and practices making up voodoo.

1865 *Cairo* (Ill.) *D. Democrat* 29 Sep. 2/1 (*heading*), Vondooism in Memphis—Old Superstitions Revived. **1870** *N.Y. Herald* 12 July 6/1 Voudouism is the name given to the horrible superstition that exists among the negroes down South. **1942** Kennedy *Palmetto Country* 165 Voodooism is seldom an organized religious ideology, but, as an initial attempt to understand phenomena, it is religion in one of its most primitive forms.

voodooite ˈvuduˌaɪt, *n.* One accustomed to dealing with voodoos. *Rare.* — **1870** *N.Y. Herald* 12 July 6/1 The correspondent . . . recounts the fact of Parson Turner having this baleful spell cast upon him by some enemy exorcised by some Voudouites in his own Christian church in the French quarter.

V.O.P. Abbreviation of "Very Old Pale," used with reference to the age of brandy. — **1863** *Harper's Mag.* April 715/2 In our camp a peculiar kind of brandy, marked V.O.P. is much used by the officers. What V.O.P. stands for no man can tell.

∗ **vote,** *n.* In combs.: (1) **vote-broker,** one who buys and sells votes; (2) **-buyer,** one who purchases votes; (3) **-buying,** the purchasing of votes; (4) **-distributor,** ?one who hands out tickets or ballots at an election; (5) **-dodger,** one who, for ulterior motives, avoids voting; (6) **-getter,** one who is successful in getting votes; (7) **-getting machine,** a political clique or faction designed to secure votes; (8) **-monger,** one who deals or traffics in votes; (9) **-recorder,** (see quot.).

(1) 1875 *Chi. Tribune* 11 Nov. 4/2 The gentlemen . . . must be prepared to meet a powerful influence in his behalf,—the influence of the gamblers, confidence-men, thieves, roughs, plug-uglies, and vote-brokers. — (2) **1890** *Nation* 10 April 287/3 The vote-buyers were thrown out of business. — (3) **1905** *McClure's Mag.* 342 Bribe-giving is 'not so bad.' Some men who talked to me of their vote-buying, knew and said, and one of them plainly felt, that it was a shameful practice, but they all regarded it as necessary. — (4) **1877** *Harper's Mag.* Sep. 614/1 I might have risen to be vote distributor, or fence viewer, or selectman.

(5) **1852** J. W. BOND *Minnesota* 293 A wily sort of politician in Indian tactics, it seems, like some of our own vote-dodgers. — (6) **1906** *Springfield W. Republican* 1 Nov. 3 He is also a strong campaigner, and has proved himself a vote-getter. **1949** *Western Polit. Quart.* March 114 Russell was conceded to be still a popular vote-getter in spite of his support of the Taft-Hartley Act. — (7) **1892** *Courier-Journal* 3 Oct. 3/3 Mr. Needy . . . was made a victim of the vote-getting machine. — (8) **1887** *Amer. Missionary* July 195 [Negroes are] made tools of by wily politicians among the whites, and by corrupt vote-mongers among themselves. — (9) **1876** KNIGHT 2715/1 *Vote-recorder*, an apparatus in which, by an impulse given by each member of a body at his desk, upon the 'aye' or 'no' lever or button, the indication is made at the clerk's or president's desk, and the record counted or sum shown.

b. *To dodge a vote*, to fail to vote through motives of evasion; *to get out the vote*, to see that all those entitled to vote on a particular matter do so.

1846 *Cong. Globe* 20 July 1118/1 [It has been suggested] that I dodged the vote. — **1905** *Springfield W. Republican* 10 Nov. 3 No one outside the inner councils knows what it costs Tammany to get out the vote.

As the last term in **bullet, electoral, floating, hand, handy, joint, Mormon, Negro, paper, party, popular, scalp, scratch, silent, soldier, solid, straw, test vote.**

* **vote,** *v. tr.* To cause to vote.

1859 BARTLETT 98 They are treated with good living and liquors, and at a proper day are taken to the polls and 'voted,' as it is called, for the party. **1904** *N.Y. Ev. Post* 8 Nov. 1, 25 men were in line in many places, and they were voted at a rate of nearly one a minute.

b. In a political convention, to call out or announce at the proper time the vote of (a delegation).

1904 *N.Y. Ev. Post* 18 May 1 Many announced an intention of going home, leaving a few of their associates to vote their respective delegations. **1935** SULLIVAN *Our Times* VI. 54 (*footnote*), 'Vote' as a transitive verb, in the sense of a manager 'voting' his delegates, is not recognized by the dictionary but is familiar in the terminology of conventions.

* **voter,** *n.* As the last term in **absentee, cooped, drift, floating, vest-pocket voter.**

* **voting,** *a.* and *n.* In combs.: (1) **voting juice,** liquor used to influence voting, *slang, rare;* (2) **-list,** a list of the names of those entitled to vote in a particular ward or precinct; (3) **machine,** a machine for recording and counting votes; (4) **precinct,** =**election district** (*a*).

(1) **1919** C. R. RAHT *Romance of Davis Mts.* 196 By the time the first barrel of 'voting juice' was empty, all had voted. — (2) **1859** HALE *If, Yes, & Perhaps* 187, [I told] Dennis that he might use the record on the voting-list. **1889** *Cent. Mag.* Feb. 626/2 Might it not be practicable to forbid the board to enter upon the voting-lists the name of any man . . . habitually violating the law? — (3) **1901** *Everybody's Mag.* Oct. 489/1 There you see in operation the electrograph, the machine which transmits pictures by wire; . . . the voting-machine, the entertaining mutoscopes. **1947** *Chi. Sun.* 28 Jan. 3/1 The City Council's sub-committee on voting machines yesterday recommended that one of the machines be installed in each of the city's 50 wards. — (4) **1872** *Chi. Tribune* 9 Oct. 1/6 About 200 voting precincts heard from. **1949** *Summit Valley Times* (Argo, Ill.) 9 Nov. 7/1 For the purpose of said election said Pleasantview Fire Protection District has been constituted two voting precincts.

voyageur ˌvwɑjəˈʒɝ, *n.* [Can. F. in same sense.] A man, usu. a French Canadian or half-breed, engaged in transporting people or goods in the Northwest, a boatman. Also attrib. Now *hist.* Cf. **Canadian voyageur.**

1809 A. HENRY *Travels* 18 My canoes were three times unladen, and . . . carried on the shoulders of the *voyageurs.* **1846** BRYANT *California* (1848) 83 The company of *voyageurs* consisted of Mr. Bourdeau, . . . an Indian, and several creole Frenchmen, of Missouri. **1949** *Boston Globe* 14 Aug. (fiction mag.) 2/1 She could travel through the bush like a voyageur.

* **vulgate,** *n.* Common or everyday speech.

1854 COOKE *Va. Comedians* I. 75 'Here's a pretty mess,' returned the pompous gentleman, descending to the vulgate. **1883** D. H. WHEELER *By Ways of Lit.* 176 There is always 'a free and easy' vulgate for the street, the market, and the fireside. **1939** P. G. PERRIN *An Index to English* 632 In the lower schools, where the pupils are likely to be in daily contact with vulgate, it forms a serious problem for teachers.

* **vulture,** *n.* The turkey buzzard or the California vulture *qq.v.*

1806 CLARK in *Lewis & C. Exped.* IV. (1905) 79 Shannon and Labiesh brought in to us today a Buzzard or *Vulture* of the Columbia which they had wounded and taken alive. **1850** BURKE *Reminisc. Ga.* 135 The most useful bird in all the South, is the buzzard, more properly called the vulture. **1916** THOBURN *Stand. Hist. Okla.* I. 346 After removing a few choice pieces that were desired for the day, [they] left the rest for vultures and wolves.

b. vulture buzzard, the turkey buzzard; **vulture eagle,** (see quot.).

1846 *Knickerb.* XXVII. 252 A huge vulture-buzzard, with wide-extended wings, sailed slowly by. — **1869** *Amer. Naturalist* III. 480 Among these have been seen [in the Colorado Valley] the strange Vulture-eagles (*Polyborus Audubonii* and *Craxirex unicinctus*), . . . and the quaint Wood Ibis, called there 'Colorado Turkey.'

vum vʌm, *n.* [f. next.] A use of the expression *I vum. Colloq.* — **1881** *Harper's Mag.* Jan. 249 Darius was piqued, and he said, with a *vum*, 'I'll pay for the wood, if *you'll* send it hum.'

vum vʌm, *v.* [?f. * *vow.*] *intr.* To vow, swear. *Colloq.*

1785 *Mass. Spy* 13 Oct. 2/2 We all must dreadful mindful be That we must fight for liberty And vum we'll 'fend it, if we die. **1839** *Havana* (N.Y.) *Republican* 21 Aug. (Th.), I vum I cant contrive who *you* be. **1948** *Sat. Review* 26 June 26/1 In the Gadsooks novels, atmosphere is as thick as a London fog, with dialogue full of 'La, sir,' 'Gadsooks,' and 'I vum.'

b. *To be vummed*, to be darned or doggoned. *Colloq.*

1881 M. J. HOLMES *Madeline* 282 'She'd be vummed,' the indignant old lady said, 'if she would not write to Lucy herself.'

vumper ˈvʌmpɚ, *v. intr.* =**vum,** *v. Rare.* — **1815** HUMPHREYS *Yankey* 70, I don't care a cent for you and all your close, I vumpers.

W

wabana wɔˈbænə, *n.* [Cf. Ojibway *wâbanow*, lit. "I am a sorcerer."] (See quot. 1886.) *Obs.*

1807 *Staunton* (Va.) *Eagle* 28 Aug. 2/3 You are no more to dance the *Wabano*, nor the *Poigan*, or *pipe dance.* **1826** McKenney *Tour to Lakes* (1827) 206 The *wa-ba-na* was, sure enough, danced last night, and I witnessed it. **1886** Z. F. Smith *Kentucky* 385 The wabana is an offering to the devil, and, like some others, the green-corn dance, for example, winds up with a feast.

Wabash ˈwɔbæʃ, *n.* [App. f. the native name, the meaning of which is not clear.] *attrib.* Of or pertaining to the Wabash River or country, as **Wabash corn, Indian, pearl, poor land, squash, water.**

1789 *Ann. 1st Congress* 80 The Governor of the Western Territory has made a statement to me of the reciprocal hostilities of the Wabash Indians, and the people inhabiting the frontiers bordering on the river Ohio. **1838** Ellsworth *Valley of Wabash* 46 It produced 120 bushels to an acre, and this on 'Wabash poor land,' which had supported successive exhausting crops without manure. **1843** Marryat *M. Violet* 204 The general was free with his 'Wabash water' [i.e., whisky.] **1852** Fleischmann *Wegweiser* 171 Ein Kern von dem obern Theile einer Maisähre, *Wabashcorn.* **1940** Wilson *Wabash* 7 It flows over limestone or gravel and sand, yielding the famous Wabash pearls. *Ib.* 13 Near their homes, grew the first of the famous Wabash squash, pumpkins, and beans.

b. Used as an ejaculation. *Rare.*

1787 in G. O. Seilhamer *Hist. Amer. Theatre* II. (1888) 231 *Jonathan* He was going to ask a young woman to spark it with him, and—the Lord have mercy on my soul—she was another man's wife. *Jessamy* The Wabash!

wabash ˈwɔbæʃ, *v.* [f. **Wabash,** *n.*] *tr.* To get the better of, beat soundly, cheat. *Slang. Obs.*

1837 *Chi. Theol. Sem. Home Missions Coll.* 23 Jan., My wife says she feels that we have got thoroughly *Wabashed* [i.e., attacked by bilious fever on the banks of the Wabash]. **1839** *Logansburg* (Ind.) *Herald* 17 Sep., Two men at Vincennes, suspected of overzealousness in the cause of Abolitionism, were recently taken out of their beds, severely scourged, Wabashed, and coated with indelible paste, as a remembrancer of their evil doings. **1859** Bartlett 498 *To Wabash.* 'He's *Wabashed,*' meaning he is cheated, is an expression much used in Indiana and other parts of the West. **1902** *Amer. Folk-Lore* 264 The term *wabashed* ('cheated') from the river-name *Wabash* (='dirty white') was once much used in the West.

Waco ˈweko, *n.* [Native name.] An Indian belonging to one of the divisions of the Tawakoni, whose chief village (*c*1830) was on the site of the present city of Waco, Texas. Usu. *pl.* or *collect.* with reference to the division to which such an Indian belonged. Also attrib.

1822 Dewees *Letters* (1852) 25 We generally go up as high as we dare go, on account of the Whaco Indians. **1830** *Boston Transcript* 2 Sep. 1/1 War has broken out between the Cherokees, Shawnees, Delawares, . . . and the Tahuacanies, Wacos and Comanches. **1865** Pike *Scout & Ranger* 20–21 He was met about a mile from the agency by a small body of Coddres, Tonchnes, and Wacoes, and a skirmish ensued. **1870** Duval *Big-Foot Wallace* 73 Ben and I were on a spying expedition in one of the Waco villages. **1910** Hodge *Amer. Indians* II. 888/2 The Waco were included in the treaties made between the United States and the Wichita in 1835 and 1846. . . . In 1902 they received allotments of land and became citizens.

* **wabble,** *v.* **1.** *intr.* (See quot.) *Obs.* **2.** *tr.* To crumple *up. Colloq.*

(1) 1848 Bartlett 374 *To Wabble,* in the Western States, to make free use of one's tongue; to be a ready speaker. — **(2) 1870** A. D. Whitney *We Girls* vi. 95 Kitchens are horrid when girls have . . . left the dish-towels dirty, and the dish-cloth all wabbled up in the sink. **1884** *Harper's Mag.* June 88/1 The great point is to keep the net straight, and not all tangled and wobbled up.

* **wad,** *n.* A roll of bills. *Colloq.* Cf. **tightwad.**

1814 *Niles' Reg.* VII. 205/2 He then rammed both hands into his trowsers' pockets, and drew out handfulls of notes ruffled into *wads.* **1891** *Memphis Appeal-Avalanche* 22 April 5/4 He would not swear that either of them had been connected with the poker game at which he lost his wad. **1948** *Duncan* (Okla.) *D. Banner* 1 July 5/1 Out popped a fistsized wad of bills—$2,000 worth.

waddy ˈwɑdɪ, *n.* Also **waddie.** *W.* [See note.]

The origin of this term is not clear. S. J. Baker, *Australian Language* (1945), 193, has a *waddy* resulting from an aboriginal corruption of "wood" and occurring as early as 1804 in the sense of a club or stick.

Orig. a cattle rustler, later a cowboy. Cf. **cow waddy, top waddy.**

1897 Hough *Story of Cowboy* 279 A genuine rustler was called a 'waddy,' a name difficult to trace to its origin. **1929** Dobie *Vaquero* 255 Barnes tells how a waddie out in Arizona lost a fifty-dollar saddle by roping one of the camels. . . . The tried and true prescription for sobering up a drunken cowboy was to rope him and jerk him off his horse. **1949** *Sat. Ev. Post* 15 Jan. 42/3 High prices have toned the waddies down. They drank beer instead of bourbon, and were much better behaved.

* **wade,** *v. To wade in, into,* to attack, go to work upon vigorously. *Colloq.*

1872 Powers *Afoot & Alone* 130 We waded into 'em, and skinned 'em out mighty sudden. **1883** *Albany* (Tex.) *Echo* 12 Dec., Build a Chinese wall around Coleman County, put all the fence-cutters inside it, furnish them with wire fence and nippers, and tell them to wade in. **1904** Stratton-Porter *Freckles* 365 You waded single-handed into a man almost twice your size.

wading river. ?A river that can be waded. Also **wade river.** *Obs.*

1644 *R.I. Col. Rec.* I. 82 William Almy, and John Roome . . . are to have lande at the wading river. **1664** *Brookhaven Rec.* 12 The felde and timber of all the lands, . . . from the ould manes to the wadeing river. **1728** *Ib.* 118 Layd oute a highway from the Olde man's . . . to the wade River.

* **wafer,** *n.* **1. wafer ash,** (*a*) the hop tree, cf. **penny tree,** (*b*) a tea or tonic made from the roots of this, in full **wafer-ash tea. 2. wafer card,** an extremely thin calling card. *Rare.*

(1) (*a*) **1884** Sargent *Rep. Forests* 31 Hop Tree. Shrubby Trefoil. Wafer Ash. **1931** Clute *Plants* 61 The wafer ash (*Ptelea trifoliata*) is not an ash, but the fuits [*sic*] are like wafers and may suggest other objects, as the name penny-tree clearly shows. (*b*) **1872** Eggleston *End of World* 140 She should have a corn-sweat and some wafer-ash tea. *Ib.* The wafer-ash would cause a tendency of blood to the head, and thus relieve pressure on the juggler-vein. Cynthy Ann . . . set the wafer-ash to draw. — **(2) 1896** *Godey's Mag.* Feb. 220/1 The wafer card has only one thing to recommend it, and that is, that a greater number of cards may be compressed into a small space.

waffle ˈwɑfl̩, ˈwɔfl̩, *n.* [Du. *wafel,* in same sense.]

1. A crisp kind of battercake cooked in a waffle iron *q.v.*

1817 Birkbeck *Notes Journey in Amer.* (1818) 64 Waffles (a soft hot cake of German extraction, covered with butter). **1857** *Knickerb.* XLIX. 98 Coffee and milk-toast, waffles and honey, disappeared. **1948** *Savings News* Jan 15/2 Frozen waffles which need only 60 seconds heating in a toaster or hot oven will eliminate the necessity for a waffle iron.

b. *transf.* A piece of broiled beef. *Rare.*

1840 Kennedy *Quodlibet* 104 Take a plate on your knee, and fork up one of them warfields—and take care of your gown, they're dripping with butter.

2. In combs.: (1) **waffle frolic,** =**waffle party,** *obs.;* (2) **iron,** a utensil for making waffles, consisting of two patterned iron griddles hinged together [cf. Du. *wafelijzer*]; (3) **mould,** =prec., *rare;* (4) **party,** a party at which waffles are served; (5) **wagon,** the wagon of an itinerant vendor of waffles.

(1) 1744 in Earle *Colonial Days N.Y.* 216 We had the wafel-frolic at Miss Walton's talked of before your departure. — **(2) 1794** *S.C. State Gaz.* 30 Aug. 1/2 (Th. Supp.), Woffle irons [advertised]. **1828** E. Leslie *Receipts* 71 Heat your waffle-iron. . . . Shut the iron tight, and bake the waffle on both sides. **1949** *Chi. Tribune* 2 Oct. 20/1

The consequences of the strike will soon be felt in every fabricating business from automobiles to waffle irons. — (3) **1864** Mark Twain *Sketches* (1926) 139 His face was pitted like a waffle-mould. — (4) **1808** in *Scribner's Mag.* II. 183/1 They are going to have a fine waffle party on Tuesday. **1882** *Harper's Mag.* April 666/1 She tells him of 'little waffle parties' formed by her intimates.

(5) **1908** A. Ruhl *Other Amer.* vi. 90 Crowding round the pay-window just as boys at home might crowd round a waffle-wagon or hokey-pokey ice-cream cart. **1949** *Chi. Tribune* 23 Sep. III. 1/2 The waffle wagon came around on summer evenings and you could buy crisp, sugar coated waffles for a penny each.

As the last term in **apple, rice, sweet potato, wheat waffle.**

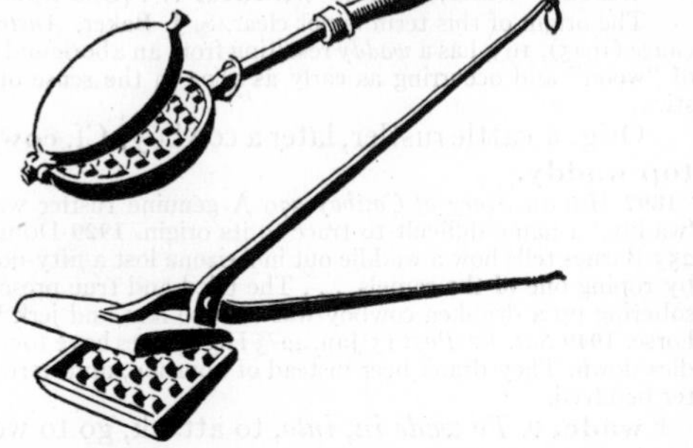

Early types of waffle irons

wageworker, *n.* One who works for wages, a wage-earner. Also transf.

1876 *Mass. Labor Statistics 7th Rep.* 9 Wage Workers from whom Schedules were received. **1899** Going *Flowers* 19 These insect visitors, however, are respectable wage-workers. **1904** *Boston Transcript* 11 June 18 The speaker went further than was necessary in his effort to do justice to the wage-worker.

waggletail ˈwægl̩tel, *n.* (See quots. and cf. **wiggletail.**) *Obs.* — **1859** Bartlett 498 *Waggletail,* the larva of the mosquito, etc.; also called a wiggler. *a***1870** Chipman *Notes on Bartlett* 498 *Waggletail* . . . wheel-insect.

waggloper ˈwæg̩lopɚ, *n.* [?Du. *weglooper,* a runaway.] (See quot. 1788.) *Rare.* — **1788** J. May *Jrnl.* (1873) 40 All sorts of superstitious traditions prevail here among the people, being Dutch. Among which the following extraordinary one was much believed in by the wagglopers. **1876** *N. Eng. Hist. & Gen. Reg.* XXX. 45/2.

wagh wɔ, *interj.* Also **wa.** An exclamation imitative of an Indian's grunt of anger, disgust, etc. *Colloq.*

1791 J. Long *Voyages* 164 *Wa! wa!* or Oh! oh! replied the Savage, but what is the warrior tied up for? **1848** Ruxton *Adventures* 292 'Wagh!' exclaimed one raw-boned young giant, as a bee flew past. **1850** Garrard *Wah-To-Yah* xiii. 166 Thar's two or three in this crowd—wagh!—howsomever, the green is 'rubbed out' a little.

∗wagon, *n.*

1. A carriage or other light vehicle, usu. for passengers and pleasure.

1799 Weld *Travels* 15 The carriages made use of in Philadelphia consist of coaches, chariots, chaises, coachees, and light waggons. **1815** Sutcliff *Travels* p. xi, The open carriages described in this plate, are called waggons. **1904** M. D. Conway *Autobiog.* 196 They appeared in a handsome wagon, all in pretty gowns.

2. A baby carriage. Also attrib.

1847 Emerson *Poems* 238 [They] let the world's affairs go by, Awhile to . . . mend his wicker wagon-frame. **1868** A. D. Whitney *P. Strong* 139 A basket as big as a baby's wagon. **1887** Cabot *Mem. Emerson* II. 282 The whole town assembled, down to the babies in their wagons.

3. A vehicle used to convey arrested persons to a police station.

1891 Quinn *Fools of Fortune* 404 When a raid is made . . . enough 'pluggers' are captured to fill one or two wagons and are driven to the nearest police station with much clatter and display. **1915** *Chi. Herald* 18 Nov. 11/7 He heard through the crack that if he and McKenna didn't clear out the wagon would be called. **1948** *Dly. Oklahoman* (Okla. City) 8 March 1/4 The wagon had been called to aid officers holding a 'customer.'

4. *To be* (or *go*) *on the wagon,* to abstain from liquor. *Colloq.* Cf. **∗water,** *n.* **3.** (3).

1944 *Reader's Digest* April 125 Jack could have been cured if he could once and for all have gone on the wagon. **1949** *Chi. D. News* 17 Dec. 6/7 Mr. Johnson is lean and saturnine and on the wagon.

5. In special combs., chiefly obs. or hist.: (1) **wagon board,** a board laid across the body of a wagon as a seat; (2) **body,** =next; (3) **box,** a large boxlike structure resting on the bolsters of a wagon, cf. **wagon box rod** *s.v.* **wagon rod;** (4) **camp,** a place where a wagon train is encamped; (5) **cistern,** a container for carrying water on a wagon; (6) **company,** a company engaged in transporting freight and passengers by wagons; (7) **cover,** a covered shed for wagons; (8) **gate,** a gate sufficiently wide to permit the passage of wagons; (9) **grease,** a lubricant prepared esp. for use on wagons; (10) **guard,** a man or detail of men to protect a wagon; (11) **hoop,** =**wagon bow;** (12) **ironing,** providing or repairing the ironwork of a wagon; (13) **jack,** a jack made for raising the wheels of a wagon clear of the ground; (14) **mound,** *W.* a mound or hillock resembling the top of a covered wagon, as a place-name; (15) **rod,** one of the rods serving to hold the two sides of a wagon body snugly in place, in full **wagon**

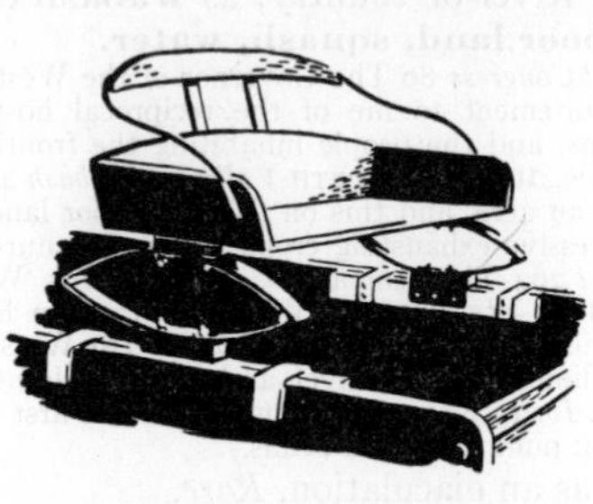

Wagon seat or spring seat

box rod; (16) **saddle,** a saddle for use on a draft animal ridden by the driver; (17) **seat,** a detachable seat for use on a wagon body; (18) **service,** postal delivery service in which wagons are used; (19) **sheet,** a large piece of canvas serving as the cover for a covered wagon; (20) **stand,** an inn having a wagon yard situated on a road where teamsters stop for the night, usu. providing their own food and sleeping accommodations; (21) **tavern,** =prec.; (22) **tobacco,** ?tobacco brought to market in wagons, *obs.;* (23) **trade,** trade of rural customers who come to stores in wagons; (24) **train,** a number of wagons traveling together while transporting goods and settlers into a newly settled region, esp. the West, also attrib.

(1) **1901** Churchill *Crisis* 99, 'I reckon I know,' said Brent, bringing down his fist on the wagon board. — (2) **1768** in Chalkley *Scotch-Irish Settlement Va.* I. 458 Credit by one wagon body at 6/. **1916** Porter *David* 26 Together they aided his father to climb into the roomy wagon-body. — (3) **1825** *Vt. Aurora* (Vergennes) 25 Aug. 4/3 He had on hand, a complete assortment of . . . Cart and Waggon Boxes. **1946** Foreman *Last Trek* 250 The camp was devastated by a tornado that carried wagon boxes, camp equipage, and some of the people through the air. — (4) **1854** Whipple *Explor. R.R. Route* I. 79 Having sent messengers to the wagon camp, . . . we recrossed Colorado Chiquito. **1867** Crawford *Mosby* 193 At midnight we started out to find the wagon-camp.

(5) **1895** Wister *Red Men & White* 167 When you see the Black Cross dry, Fill the wagon cisterns high. — (6) **1825** *Nat. Intelligencer* 8 July 2/4 The wagon company [of Santa Fe adventurers] will proceed separately, and under a different organization. — (7) **1858** *Atlantic Mo.* Aug. 336/2 At one end projects a kitchen; from the kitchen projects a wood-shed and wagon-cover, occupied at night by hens. — (8) **1879** Stockton *Rudder Grange* xii, There was a wagon-gate at one side of the front fence. **1900** Dix *Deacon Bradbury* 221 The other sleigh turned in at the wagon-gate. — (9) **1862** Browne *A. Ward: His Book* 49, [I] had a lot of sweet-scented wagon grease on my hair. **1882** Sweet & Knox *Texas Siftings* 69, [I] actually captured a lot of wagon-grease, and a dozen monkey-wrenches.

(10) **1852** Watson *Nights in Block-House* 229 The wagon-guard had also been attracted by the firing. **1862** Norton *Army Lett.* 39 [H.] will go as a wagon guard. — (11) **1891** *Scribner's Mag.* Sep. 309/1 A blanket is hung in the doorway, or the cotton from the wagon hoops will serve, and there is the dugout home. — (12) **1864** *Ore. State Jrnl.* 10 Dec. 3/5 Luckey Bros., Are prepared to do all kinds of

Blacksmithing, Horseshoeing, Wagon Ironing, etc. **1892** *York Co. Hist. Rev.* 61 Wagon ironing is done with special attention paid to horseshoeing. — **(13) 1856** *Mich. Agric. Soc. Trans.* VII. 510 Best wagon jack, $0.50. **1919** CADY *Rhymes of Vt.* (1923) 20 Other 'toys' that help him do His work. . . . Are . . . A sprayer, sprinkler, wagon-jack. — **(14) 1846** MAGOFFIN *Down Santa Fé Trail* 78 The 'wagon mound' . . . derives its name from its resemblance to the top of a covered wagon. **1888** J. WEBB *Adventures* 149 The first day we drove to a camp a few miles from Wagon Mound, and stayed all night.

(15) 1931 DOBIE *Coronado's C.* 137, $18,000 is in a bean-pot, the depth of a wagon rod with half the ring sticking out of the ground an three small rocks piled against the ring. **1936** *Sears Cat.* (ed. 173) 943 Steel Wagon Box Rods 3/8 in. . . . 3 feet 3 in. long. For narrow box . . . 3 feet 7 inches long. For wide box . . . 15c. — **(16) 1785** WASHINGTON *Diaries* II. 438 A Waggon Saddle and Gier for 4 Horses. **1851** HOOPER *Widow Rugby* 121 Save me his years for skearts to my old wagin saddle. — **(17) 1852** STOWE *Uncle Tom* x, Haley, drawing out from under the wagon-seat a heavy pair of shackles, made them fast around each ankle. **1943** *Reader's Digest* Dec. 122/2 The only chair was the wagon seat, taken from their wagon. — **(18) 1893** CUSHING *Story of P.O.* 38 The 'regulation wagon service' is performed in some forty of the chief cities of the country. — **(19)** *a***1846** *Quarter Race Ky.* 176, I histed the waggin-sheet, and looked out at him. **1926** O. L. SHIPMAN *Taming Big Bend* 30 About forty armed men were in the wagons, covered with the wagon sheets.

(20) 1864 *Harper's Mag.* Dec. 41/1 The one tavern in the town was only a wagon-stand. **1913** *Proc. Pa.-Ger. Soc.* XXII. 29 A curious tale is told in connection with one of these old wagon stands which was up for sale. — **(21) 1913** *Proc. Pa.-Ger. Soc.* XXII. 30 Three of the houses mentioned . . . ranked as stage taverns . . . the others were what were known as Wagon Taverns or Drove stands. — **(22) 1819** *Amer. Farmer* I. 135 Fine wagon Tobacco sold yesterday, for $14. — **(23) 1851** *De Bow's Review* XI. 429 How much the present wagon trade will be increased by plank roads, is a fruitful and interesting theme for speculation. **1879** *Bradstreet's* 24 Dec. 3/1 A falling off in the wagon trade with people living near was noticed. — **(24) 1849** PARKMAN in *Knickerb.* XXXIII. 111 A wagon train, with some twenty Missourians, came out from among the trees. **1950** *Chi. Tribune* 21 May VII. 5/2 Emigrant wagons halted here until men enough (38 to a wagon train) were assembled to fight off Indians.

For **wagon boss, bow, boy,** see as main entries.

b. In combs. of obvious meaning or sufficiently explained in the quots.: (1) **wagon bonnet,** (2) **factory,** (3) **ford,** (4) **freighter,** (5) **outfit,** (6) **path,** (7) **portage,** (8) **road,** (9) **route,** (10) **shop,** (11) **show,** (12) **sled,** (13) **soldier,** (14) **sugar,** (15) **top,** (16) **trace,** (17) **trail.**

(1) 1832 WATSON *Hist. Tales N.Y.* 149 The 'wagon bonnet' . . . was deemed to look on the head, not unlike the top of the 'Jersey wagons.' — **(2) 1827** DRAKE & MANSFIELD *Cincinnati* 65 Eight carriage and Wagon Factories. **1901** *Harper's Mag.* Dec. 211/1 Miles and his partner were driving to the wagon-factory. — **(3) 1793** in SUMMERS *Ann. S.W. Va.* 840 Gordon Cloyd appointed overseer of the road from top of Brushy Mountain to the wagon ford on Back Creek. — **(4) 1946** *Reader's Digest* March 104/2 Wagon freighters had invented the drag brake years before. **1948** *Time* 13 Sep. 23/2 He had been a wagon freighter, merchant, attorney, bank president, rancher.

(5) 1895 REMINGTON *Pony Tracks* 1, I had asked the general quietly if this was a 'horseback' or a 'wagon outfit.' — **(6) 1845** SIMMS *Wigwam & Cabin* 1 Ser. 75, I suddenly caught a glimpse of an opening on my right, a sort of wagon-path. — **(7) 1865** *Ore. State Jrnl.* 18 Nov. 1/4 By building a wagon portage . . . the stream is again struck at a navigable point. — **(8) 1738** *Md. Hist. Mag.* XV. 219 The old Indian Road . . . intersects the waggon road. **1824** DODDRIDGE *Notes* 187 The horse paths, along which our forefathers made their laborious journies . . . were soon succeeded by waggon roads. **1925** BRYAN *Memoirs* 285 We found the distance by wagon road some 85 or 90 miles. — **(9) 1849** *31st Cong.* 1 Sess. Sen. Ex. Doc. No. 64, 135 We left Algadones for Santa Fe, . . . taking . . . the usual wagon-route between the two places. **1856** WHIPPLE *Explor. R.R. Route* I. 93 They walked to the wagon-camp of night before, . . . finding among the low hills an excellent wagon route.

(10) 1849 CHAMBERLAIN *Ind. Gazetteer* 175 There are in the county . . . two wagon shops. **1897** *Atlantic Mo.* May 589/2 There is a sleigh and wagon shop a couple of miles out of the village. — **(11) 1895** *N.Y. Dramatic News* 6 July 3/2 The Keystone colossal circus . . . started from the East end as a wagon show. **1907** STEWART *Partners* 236 Stubbs . . . told me not to go into the show business . . . he said it took the constitution of a horse, especially with a wagon show. — **(12) 1905** *Forestry Bureau Bul.* No. 61, 42 *Logging sled,* the heavy double sled used to haul logs from the skidway or yard to the landing. (N[orthern] F[orest]) Syn.: twin sleds, two sleds, wagon sled. — **(13) 1917** J. A. MOSS *Officers' Man.* 485 *Wagon-soldier*—light or field artilleryman. — **(14) 1892** *Mod. Lang. Notes* Nov. 394 The mass [of sirup] thus reduced is emptied into wagons and run into a hot room, where it is allowed to crystallize slowly; this process is generally followed for all sugars except first sugars . . . and they are often called *wagon sugar.*

(15) 1887 *Courier-Journal* (Louisville) 5 Feb. 6/1 The boiler is fifty-four inches in diameter at the smoke-stack, with a wagon top. [**1891** *Cent.* 6802/1 wagon-top. . . . The part of a locomotive-boiler, over the fire-box, which is elevated above the rest of the shell. Its purpose is to provide greater steam room. — **(16) 1821** NUTTALL *Travels Arkansa* 164 [We] had, at last, the unexpected satisfaction of entering upon, and pursuing the wagon trace. **1852** MARCY *Explor. Red River* (1854) 88 We started on, keeping the old wagon trace through the timber for eight miles. — **(17) 1848** BRYANT *California* ix. 126 Following the wagon-trail we left the river about nine o'clock. **1950** *Nat. Hist.* May 229/3 The 'invasion' was no sinecure; not even a wagon trail had been built into the region.

c. Designating races in which horses draw light wagons, or the horses participating in such races.

1857 *Porter's Spirit of Times* 3 Jan. 292/2 Thus were disposed of the pretensions of the great wagon trotter. **1868** WOODRUFF *Trotting Horse* 265 After that wagon-race, Flora was deemed the mistress of any thing out in that way of going. *Ib.* 362 In a week after the time-race, Dexter trotted his first wagon-match with Gen. Butler.

As the last term in **auto, baby, baggage, band, beach, beer, bench, berry, box, buckboard, buffalo, buggy, bull, California, cane, celerity, chuck, chug, cigar, commissary, Concord, Conestoga, continental, cook, cotton, covered, cracky, dead, Dearborn, democrat, democratic, depot, devil's, dirt, Dougherty, dump, electric, emigrant, express, factory, family, feed, fore-and-aft, freight, furniture, gig, gospel, government, grub, hoodlum, hunting, hurry, hurry-up, ice, immigrant, jail, Jersey, Jerusalem, Kimball, lager beer, log, lumber, lunch, Macy, mail, market, mountain, mover's, moving, mud, mule, oil, Paddy, passage, patrol, peach, peddler's, Pennsylvania, pie, Pittsburgh, plains, plantation, pleasure, pole, prairie, rubbernecking, saleratus, Santa Fe, school, schooner, scoop, sheep, smoke, speed, station, steamboat, Studebaker, Tennessee, tented, Texas, tilt, tin, trading, transportation, turpentine, waffle, Washoe, wind, Yankee, York wagon.**

* **wagon,** *v. tr.* To transport or convey by wagon. *Obs.*

1755 WASHINGTON *Writings* I. 187 The quantity is too great for the present consumption, and to wagon it up can never answer the expense. **1819** SCHOOLCRAFT *Mo. Lead Mines* 58 Goods are now wagoned over from St. Genevieve. **1895** CRADDOCK *Witch-Face Mt.* 62 In the fall of the year the folks would kem wagonin' their chestnuts over ter sell in town.

* **wagonage,** *n.* Money charged or paid for conveyance by wagon. *Obs.*

1757 WASHINGTON *Writings* I. 491 The amount of waggonage and other charges of transporting these provisions . . . will exceed the whole cost of the provisions. **1816** *Ann. 14th Cong.* 1 Sess. 113 It became necessary to use four distinct lines of transportation . . . an expense of wagonage estimated at . . . not less than four hundred and fourteen thousand dollars. **1845** *Cincinnati Misc.* 125 The high rates of wagonage across the mountains, led many persons early . . . to engage in the taking up in keel-boats . . . various articles [from New Orleans].

wagon boss. *W.* A man in charge of a wagon train. Now *hist.*

1873 BEADLE *Undevel. West* 98 Our 'wagon-boss,' absolute monarch of a train while on the road, rejoiced in the name of John Monkins. **1924** MCCONNELL *Frontier Law* 15 Before leaving Atchison I asked the wagon boss how many pairs of blankets I would need, and he told me that one pair would be plenty, as I could double up with one of the other drivers. **1949** *10 Story Western* May 9/1 Big Rafe Rattery, ramrod and wagon boss, rode the point with Les Manders, his cronie and side-pardner.

wagon bow. One of the arched supports for the canvas cover of a covered wagon.

1844 GREGG *Commerce of Prairies* II. 287 Some give their lodges a round wagon-top shape, as those of the Osages, which commonly consist of a frame of bent rods, resembling wagon-bows. **1891** SWASEY *Early Days Calif.* 163 They took some of our wagon-bows, which were made of hickory, and bent them into an oblong shape. **1910** A. SANTLEBEN *Texas Pioneer* 110 Wagon-bows were attached . . . and over them two heavy tarpaulins were stretched.

wagon boy.

1. A wagoner or teamster.

1836 *S. Lit. Messenger* II. 78 Seek them who will, they have no joys For mountain lads, and Wagon-boys. **1883** FULTON *Sam Hobart* 143 He looked at the weeping women and tear-dimmed eyes of the wagon-boys.

2. (See quot. 1885.)

[**1840** *Niles' Reg.* 12 Sep. 21/3 All the counties contiguous, both in Ohio and Pennsylvania, poured out their thousands to hear Ohio's favorite wagon boy.] **1847** *Whig Almanac 1848* 32/1 At the time the 'Wagon Boy' was first sent to the Legislature by the good people of

Warren, he found a law on the statute-book providing for the punishment of certain offences by public whipping. **1885** *Mag. Amer. Hist.* May 495/1 *Wagon boy.*—The popular nickname of the Hon. Thomas Corwin, of Ohio. In his youth he earned his living by driving a team on a Kentucky farm.

* **wagtail,** *n.*

1. a. =**wiggletail.** *Obs.* **b.** Any one of various American birds, esp. the oven bird and water thrushes of the genus *Seiurus* that bob their tails as they walk. Also with specifying terms.

(**a**) **1851** Wm. Kelly *Across Rocky Mts.* 71 A large flash of water, round which there was glorious feed; but the liquid was green and full of wagtails. — (**b**) **1868** *Amer. Naturalist* II. 181 Audubon placed them [i.e., water thrushes] among his *Motacillinoe* or wagtails. **1917** *Birds of Amer.* III. 156 The Kentucky Warbler, like many other ground birds, . . . bobs his tail in that peculiar manner which has given them the vernacular name of Wagtail.

2. wagtail warbler, (see quots.).

1884 Coues *Key to Birds* (ed. 2) 309 *Siurus nævius.* Wag-tail Warbler. *Siurus motacilla.* Large-billed Wagtail Warbler. **1917** *Birds of Amer.* III. 149 Palm Warbler. *Dendroica palmarum palmarum.* . . . [Also called] Wagtail Warbler; Tip-up Warbler.

As the last term in **water, wood wagtail.**

wahoo wɑˈhu, ˈwɑhu, *n.*[1] [f. Creek *ŭhawhu,* in same sense.] The cork or wing elm, *Ulmus racemosa* or *U. alata,* or any one of various other trees of other genera similar to these. Also attrib.

1770 Mease *Narrative* 62 The Trees which I remark'd to be the largest were Oaks of different Kinds, Wahoos, Button Wood [etc.]. **1802** Drayton *S. Carolina* 65 [The] *wahoo,* affords a pliable bark, which when strypped, and soaked in water, is made sometimes into strings and ropes. **1829** Eaton *Botany* (ed. 5) 428 *Ulmus alata,* whahoo. **1948** *Chi. Tribune* 20 Nov. 10/3 The southern winged elm is also called wahoo, but it is a regular tree, 40 or 50 feet high.

attrib. **1873** *Newton Kansan* 27 March 1/7 One ounce of wahoo (winged-elm) bark, added to a quart of pure whiskey . . . is very excellent in dyspepsia. **1881** Marshall *Through Amer.* 337 We Take Wahoo Bitters.

wahoo ˈwɑhu, *n.*[2] [f. Dakota *wanhu,* arrowwood.] (See quot. 1931.)

1857 Gray *Botany* 81 *E*[*uonymus*] *atropurpureus,* Burning-Bush. Waahoo. . . . Ornamental in autumn, by its copious crimson fruit. **1903** N. H. Banks *Round Anvil Rock* 158 The bright wahoo with its graceful cluster of flame-coloured berries. **1931** Clute *Plants* 26 The plant usually regarded as the true wahoo, is the plant often called the burning-bush (*Euonymus atropurpureus*).

b. (See quot. Poss. a different word.) *Obs.*

1843 Torrey *Flora N.Y.* I. 141 From this shrub [Indian arrow] is prepared the '*Wa-a-hoo,*' a quack medicine of some reputation.

wahoo wɑˈhu, *n.*[3] [Origin unknown.] (See quot. 1909.) — **1909** *Cent. Supp.* 1429/2 wahoo. . . . A common name of *Acanthocybium solandri,* a scombroid fish of tropical seas. **1920** *Outing* July–Aug. 248/3 He has fished for—and caught—many a most unheard of species, as well as sharks, sword-fish, wahoo, etc.

* **wait,** *v.* **1.** * **wait-a-bit,** (*a*) (see quot. 1897), also attrib., (*b*) the greenbrier, *Smilax rotundifolia.* **2. wait bill,** in theatrical parlance, a poster or bill announcing in advance a performance or appearance. **3.** *To wait around,* to wait about, to remain at a place in expectation of some occurrence. *Colloq.* **4.** *To wait on* (or *upon*), to court (a lady). *Colloq.*

(**1**) (*a*) **1889** Farmer 550/1 *Wait-a-Bit Trees,* a facetious term given to a kind of bush. **1897** Sudworth *Arborescent Flora* 265 *Xanthoxylum clava-herculis.* Prickly Ash. . . . Wait-a-bit, Tear-blanket (Ark.). [**1940** Jaeger *Calif. Deserts* 185 The cat's-claw . . . , most appropriately called 'tear-blanket' by John W. Audubon and 'wait-a-minute' by some of the other early travelers, is our only native acacia.] (*b*) **1892** *Amer. Folk-Lore* V. 104 Wait-a-bit. E. Mass. — (**2**) **1896** *N.Y. Dramatic News* 4 July 12/3 Several months ago we put up a few 'wait' bills in these cities, and the size of the audience [this week] in both places was evidence that the people heeded the instructions. — (**3**) **1895** M. Halstead *Hundred Bear Stories* 37 It grew sort of monotonous waiting around. **1899** Williams *Stolen Story* 175, I suppose they're waiting around till it stops raining. — (**4**) **1877** Bartlett 735 *To wait upon,* to pay attention to a lady with a view to matrimony. **1880** *Harper's Mag.* Oct. 690/1, He was waiting on that pretty Becket girl. **1887** Wilkins *Humble Romance* 160 Benny Field was waiting on Jenny. **1898** ——— *People of Our Neighborhood* (1902) 59 He never waited on her, never spoke to her.

waiter girl. A girl who waits table, esp. in a restaurant or hotel dining room. Also **pretty waiter girl.**

1861 E. Cowell *Diary* 393 The conduct of the 'waiter girls' with the frequenters of the place is simply shocking. **1875** *Scribner's Mo.* July 277/1 In the slang vernacular . . . a 'pretty waiter girl' is a 'beer-slinger.' **1902** White *Blazed Trail* 183 Dozens of 'pretty waiter girls' served the customers.

* **wake,** *v.* For *to wake snakes, to wake the wrong passenger,* see the nouns.

* **wake-robin,** *n.* Any one of various American plants, as the arrow arum, *Peltandra virginica,* the jack-in-the-pulpit, *Arisaema triphylla,* or any one of various species of *Trillium.*

*c***1711** J. Petiver *Gazophyl. Nat.* I. i, In South Carolina . . . it Flowers in June and July, and is called by them Wake-Robin. **1778** Carver *Travels* 519 Wake Robin is an herb that grows in swampy lands. **1850** S. F. Cooper *Rural Hours* 80 Some are called nightshades; others wake-robins. **1945** McAtee *Nomina Abitera* 8 Hence Wake-Robin in the names of a number of American plants and used as the title of a book by John Burroughs.

b. With specifying adjective.

1821 *Mass. H.S. Coll.* 2 Ser. IX. 157 Plants . . . indigenous in the township of Middlebury [Vt., include] . . . *Trillium cernuum,* Nodding wake-robin. **1839** in *Mich. Agric. Soc. Trans.* VII. 421 *Trillium erectum.* False wake-robin. **1938** *Chi. Tribune* 2 April 15/1 Most common on the farm is the purple variety, sometimes called the birthroot, or ill-scented wake-robin. **1939** *Nat. Geog. Mag.* Aug. 267 Snowy Wake-Robin, *Trillium nivale,* and . . . Nodding Wake-Robin, *Trillium cernuum,* so named because they sometimes bloom before the robins arrive in spring.

As the last term in **Virginia, Virginian wake-robin.**

wake-up ˈwekˌʌp, *n.* A local name for the flicker, in allusion to its note.

1844 *Nat. Hist. N.Y., Zoology* II. 192 This species . . . is called High-hole, Yucker, Flicker, Wake-up and Pigeon Woodpecker. **1869** Muir *First Summer in Sierra* (1911) 233 The waycup, or flicker, so familiar to every boy in the old Middle West States, is one of the most common of the woodpeckers hereabouts, and makes one feel at home. **1893** *Scribner's Mag.* June 773/2 The flicker has a long array of names, . . . like flicker, clape, wake-up, . . . derived from his notes.

wakiup, see **wickiup.**

Wakon wɑˈkɑn, *n.* [f. Dakota *wakan, n.* and *a.,* a spirit, something sacred; spiritual, sacred, from the verb *wakanda, wakonda,* see **Wakonda.**]

1. =**Wakonda.**

1778 Carver *Travels* 381 The Chipeways call this being Manitou or Kitchi-Manitou; the Madowessies, Wakon or Tongo-Wakon, that is, the Great Spirit. **1809** A. Henry *Travels* 299 They believe . . . in the spirits, gods, or manitos, whom they denominate wakons. *c***1837** Catlin *Indians* II. 166 On the surface of the rocks, [are] various marks and their sculptured hieroglyphics—their wakons, totems, and medicines.

2. Wakon bird, prob. the quetzal, a Central American bird worshipped by the Aztecs and Mayas. Now *hist.*

1778 J. Carver *Travels* 472 The Wakon bird, as it is termed by the Indians, appears to be of the same species as the birds of paradise. **1789** Morse *Amer. Geog.* 60 The Wakon-bird . . . is nearly the size of the swallow. **1947** McAtee in *Nature Mag.* April 210 Doubtless the myth of the wakon bird existed before any tradeskin of a quetzal had arrived, but when it came, more gorgeously colored than any bird previously known to the northern Indians, it was recognized as a fitting embodiment of the revered bird of the Great Spirit.

Wakonda wɑˈkɑndɑ, *n.* [f. Dakota *wakonda, wakanda, v.,* to reckon as holy or sacred, to worship. For a full discussion of the word see Hodge.] (See quots.) *Obs.*

1823 James *Exped.* I. 184 They have ample cause to return thanks to the great Wahconda or Master of life. **1830** *Western Mo. Rev.* III. 563 Maize, squashes, melons, and beans they supposed they had received as direct gifts from the Wahcondah, or Master of Life **1910** Hodge *Amer. Indians* II. 897/1 Wakonda. . . . A term employed by the Omaha, Ponca, Osage, Quapaw, Kansa, Oto, Missouri, and Iowa tribes of the Siouan family when the power believed to animate all natural forms is spoken to or spoken of in supplications or rituals.

Walapai ˈwɑləˌpaɪ, *n.* Also **Hualapai.** [f. the native name signifying "pine-tree folk."] (See quot. 1910.) Also attrib.

1858 Ives *Colo. River* (1861) 94 In a few days we shall strike the Colorado and come to a large settlement of Hualpais Indians. **1882** *Atlantic Mo.* Oct. 543/2 The nearest neighbors of the Ha-va-su-paí are the Hua-la-pai, who roam over the great plains west of the cañon. **1893** *Outing* July 261/1 The actual scene itself was absolutely forlorn from the standpoint of modern civilization—no trees, no grass, saloons with the dreadful 'palisade' front, a crowd of very filthy

Hualapais Indians, the usual frontier station loafers. **1903** JAMES *Indian Basketry* 67 The Wallapias occupy their reservation adjoining that of the Havasupai on the west. **1910** HODGE *Amer. Indians* II. 899/1 Walapai. . . . A Yuman tribe originally living on middle Colorado r., above the Mohave tribe, from the great bend eastward, well into the interior of Arizona. **1947** CHALFANT *Gold, Guns, & Ghost Towns* 160 The Piute and Wallapi Indians began to resent the invasion by white men.

Waldorf salad. A salad usu. made of cubed apples, celery, nuts, and mayonnaise, so called in allusion to the old Waldorf-Astoria Hotel in N.Y. City. — **1930** FERBER *Cimmarron* 300 She was the first to electrify the ladies of the Twentieth Century Culture Club by serving them Waldorf salad—that abominable mixture of apple cubes, chopped nuts, whipped cream, and mayonnaise. **1948** *So. Sierran* Feb. 3/1 A scrumptious meal of roast beef, baked potatoes, peas, waldorf salad and mince pie was served.

*** walk,** *n.*

1. (See quot.) *Obs.*

1705 BEVERLEY *Virginia* IV. 208 Besides this Division into Counties, and Parishes, . . . two other Sub-divisions . . . are subject to the Rules and Alterations made by the County-courts; namely into Precincts or Burroughs, for the Limits of Constables; and into Precincts or Walks, for the Surveyors of High-ways.

2. (See 1st quots.) Now *hist.* Cf. **walking purchase, walking treaty.**

1762 *Pa. Archives* IV. (1853) 85 As to the Walk the prop'y Commr insist that it was reasonably performed, but we think otherwise. *Ib.* 86 As to the Walk, you say you think it was not reasonably performed, and the Proprietary Commissioners on the contrary contend that it was. **1809** KENDALL *Travels* II. 282 Lands were sometimes to be measured by *walks* performed against time. **1901** P. FOUNTAIN *Great Deserts* 118 The Indians . . . sold it [*sc.* land] by the 'walk.'

3. *N. Eng.* = **widow's walk.** Cf. *** observatory 2.**

1775 *Holyoke Diaries* 88 (*footnote*), A fine walk on the top . . . commands the prospect of the whole Island. **1876** *Wide Awake* III. 17/2 On Aunt Eliza's house-top was 'a walk,' an appendage to every mariner's home. **1939** CHAMBERLAIN *Nantucket* 36 Its picket fence and wooden trim are sparkling white, and it is crowned with a 'walk' overlooking the harbor.

4. (See quot.)

1877 BARTLETT 736 *Walk.* As 'Ladies' Walk,' 'Gentlemen's Walk,' *i.e.* a privy. This absurd piece of squeamishness is common at hotels and at railroad-stations.

5. *Baseball.* A base on balls.

1934 WEBSTER. **1948** *Dly. Ardmoreite* (Ardmore, Okla.) 21 March 4/6 Rice, on second from a walk and a sacrifice, crossed the home plate on a fly which Charley Gilbert misjudged. **1949** *Fargo* (N.D.) *Forum* 23 July 8/1 The Cards grabbed the lead for keeps in the third on a single, error, walk and fielder's choice.

6. In colloq. phrases: (1) * *To take a walk,* to depart, get out; (2) *to win in a walk,* to win without much effort.

(1) 1871 MARK TWAIN *Sk. New & Old* 248 The first time he opened his mouth and was just going to spread himself his breath took a walk. **1892** ——— *Amer. Claimant* 184 (R.), Their position was turned, and they had to take a walk. — **(2) 1896** ADE *Artie* 106 (We.), Two years ago he win in a walk. **1903** LEWIS *Boss* 138 He won in a walk.

As the last term in **board, cable, cake, captain's, cow, fox, herd, lover's, plank, road, Saratoga, shell, side, turkey, widow's walk.**

*** walk,** *v.*

1. *intr.* Of a batter in baseball: To secure a base on balls.

1867 *Ball Players' Chron.* 14 Nov. 2/4 Goodrich walked to the first on called balls. **1912** C. MATHEWSON *Pitching* 202, I lost Evers, because I was afraid to put the ball over the plate for him, and he walked. **1948** *Chi. Tribune* 7 March II. 1/4 Baker walked, filling the bases.

b. *tr.* Of a baseball pitcher: To give (a batter) a base on balls.

1913 *Chi. Record-Herald* 20 March 10/5 Lange walked Kores in the hostile part, then disposed of the next pair on easy infield flies. **1938** *Chi. Tribune* 5 April 19/2 Dobernic walked three batsmen in a row. **1948** *Ponca City* (Okla.) *News* 4 July 13/3 Hall's control was top-grade, as he walked only one and fanned five.

2. In colloq. verbal phrases: (1) *To walk around,* to perform a walk-around; (2) *to walk out,* (*a*) to go on strike, (*b*) *to walk out on,* to desert; (3) *to walk over,* to cheat, beat easily; (4) *to walk round,* to cheat, get the better of; (5) *to walk Spanish,* to walk under, or as under, compulsion (see quot. 1928), to decamp, make off.

(1) 1888 *Cent. Mag.* Jan. 468 The dancer held her dress back and 'walked around,' turning her toes in. — **(2)** (*a*) **1894** CARWARDINE *Pullman Strike* 37 The men passed the word from one to another to 'walk out,' which they did orderly and deliberately. **1946** *Newsweek* 28 Jan. 19/1 The 750,000 men who worked its furnaces walked out. (*b*) **1896** *Typog. Jrnl.* IX. 232 The Review, Republican daily, 'walked out' on the St. Louis platform. **1932** *K.C. Times* 28 March 18 It would greatly displease me if she should walk out on me because of my laziness. — **(3) 1852** STOWE *Uncle Tom* xvi, St. Clare wouldn't raise his hand, if every one of them walked over him. **1908** WHITE *Riverman* 10 Are you going to let that old high-banker walk all over you? — **(4) 1844** *Edinburgh Jrnl.* I. 302 Her husband . . . gave an account of how he had 'walked round'—alias cheated—another gentleman in the matter of a cord of wood. **1859** HALIBURTON *Sam Slick's Wise Saws* 20 My ambassadors may not dance as elegantly as European courtiers, but they can walk round them in a treaty.

(5) 1815 *Amer. Republican* (Downington, Pa.) Feb., The vet'ran troops who conquer'd Spain, Thought they our folks would banish; But Jackson settled half their men, And made the rest *walk Spanish!* **1890** *Voice* 14 Aug., [They] were hustled out of the country on an hour's notice, made to 'walk Spanish' in fact. **1920** LINCOLN *Mr. Pratt* 257 He moved then, 'walking Spanish,' like the boy in the school-yard. **1928** *Chi. Tribune* 24 June II. 2/2 'To walk Spanish,'—to walk on tiptoe involuntarily through another's lifting one by the seat of the trousers and the scruff of the neck, as in boy sport.

b. walk jawbone, (see quots.).

1832 *Polit. Examiner* (Shelbyville, Ky.) 7 July 3/1 Tune, Walk jaw-bone. **1949** *Amer. Sp.* April 151/1 The expression *walk jawbone to Tennessee* is the refrain of a popular song, to the accompaniment of music for square dances.

3. In noun and adjectival expressions: (1) **walk-along-Joe,** a dance similar to a walk-around, *obs.;* (2) *** -around,** see as a main entry; (3) **-athon,** a walking marathon, *colloq.;* (4) **-down,** an occasion upon which relays of walkers capture wild horses by walking after and exhausting them, *obs.*, cf. *** walking,** *n.* **1;** (5) **-in-the-waters,** *pl.* overshoes, *rare;* (6) **out,** a strike; (7) **round,** = *** walk-around 1;** (8) **-up,** an apartment on an upper floor of an apartment building having no elevator, also attrib.; (9) **-way,** a sidewalk.

(1) 1862 E. KIRKE *Among Pines* 283 Jim danced breakdowns, 'walk-along-Joes,' and other darky dances. — **(3) 1932** *K.C. Times* 20 Feb. 26 Sure a hick town is a place where they have enough superhicks to put on a walkathon. *Ib.* 26 Feb. 18 Now eyes are on the 'walkathon' in Kansas City. — **(4) 1907** J. R. COOK *Border & Buffalo* (1938) 358, I by previous arrangement joined in the walk-down.

(5) 1834 LONGFELLOW *Outre-Mer* 317 The pale invalid may go about without his umbrella, or his India-rubber walk-in-the-waters. — **(6) 1888** *Chi. Inter-Ocean* (F.), The walk out of brewery employés, decided upon at last night's meeting of the union, was considerable of a fizzle. **1950** *Chi. Tribune* 11 May 1/1 The walkout affected other rail workers whose number is expected to reach 200,000 by the end of the week. — **(7) 1861** *Temple Bar* May 199 The 'Jim Crow dance' . . . soon gave place to better tunes . . . and 'walk rounds.' **1895** *Cent. Mag.* Oct. 958/1 His work with the caravan was to sing songs, chiefly darky songs, accompanied by 'hoe-downs' and 'walk rounds.' **1943** *Life* 5 July 80 After the 'walk-round,' which served as an entrance for the black-faced showmen, they stood before a semicircle of chairs and waited for the interlocutor's: 'Gentlemen, be seated.' — **(8) 1919** MENCKEN 111 (*footnote*), In New York such apartments are commonly called *walk-up apartments.* **1948** *Time* 1 March 13/1 It is a disheartening area of crowded walk-up tenements, blackened blind-walled factories and littered streets. **1949** *Prairie Schooner* Spring 47 He had rented a third-floor walkup on soot-laden Biddle Street. — **(9) 1792** *Essex Inst. Coll.* VII. 37 John Saunders jr. . . . agrees to pave the Walk Way in front of his Father's Estate. **1816** BENTLEY *Diary* IV. 405 A walkway for the first time has been raised in the principal streets in the eastern part of the Town. **1911** H. S. HARRISON *Queed* xvi, He went down the broad steps of the Capitol, and out the winding white walkway through the park.

*** walk-around,** *n.*

1. A dance, or part of a dance, of Negro origins, in which the dancers move in a large circle. Also as a stage performance and fig.

1869 *Atlantic Mo.* July 72/2 We were constrained, however, to forego our jig and Walk-around. **1882** PECK *Sunshine* 30 The synod of Hayes and Sherman had bounced him from the Custom House for dancing the great spoils walk around. **1901** *Cosmopolitan* Sep. 635/1 The walk-around was always made the finale of the first part, and was usually repeated at the end of the show as a spectacle on which to drop the curtain. It was intended to be written in march-time, and to its spirited strains the whole company would circumnavigate the stage, in a dance-step that was little more than a jerky elevation of the legs below the knees, much like the 'buck and wing' dances of the present day.

2. The music for such a dance as performed on the stage.

1888 B. MATTHEWS *Pen & Ink* 153 'Dixie' was composed in 1859, by Mr. Dan D. Emmett, as a 'walk-around' for Bryant's minstrels. **1915** ——— in *Scribner's Mag.* June 755/2 'Dixie' . . . had begun life . . . humbly as a walk-around in a minstrel show in New York. **1936** *Etude* Dec. 809/1 The third part was written as a 'walk around,' and had no words, simply action, when the singer could strut, twirl his cane, or mustache, and perhaps slyly wink at a girl on the front row.

As the last term in **Virginia walk-around.**

∗**walker,** *n.* =**floor walker.** *Rare.* — **1882** *Harper's Mag.* Oct. 760/2 As I walked down the shop one of the individuals popularly known as 'walkers' approached me.

As the last term in **baby, cake, floor, jay, side, track walker.**

Walker ˈwɔkɚ, *v.* [App. f. a personal name.] *tr.* (See quot.) *Obs.* — **1882** SALA *Amer. Revisited* (1885) 382 'Hock my sparks,' 'soak my gems,' and 'Walker my diamonds' . . . American euphemisms for the act of pawning your jewellery.

∗**walking,** *n.* and *a.*

1. *W.* (See quots.) Cf. **walk-down.**

1929 DOBIE *Vaquero* 243 There is a tradition that a party of forty-niners lost their teams while crossing the plains and, in order to replace them, followed afoot after mustangs until they were able to catch some of them; hence, tradition adds, the technical use of the word *walking* among mustangers. **1944** ADAMS *W. Words* 173/2 walking down A method of capturing wild horses which calls for following them in relays fast enough to keep them in sight and give them no chance to rest or eat.

2. In combs.: (1) **walking beam,** an oscillating beam, pivoted in the center, for the transmission of power; (2) **board,** a board along the side of a keelboat to enable the crew members to walk back and forth in poling the boat, *obs.;* (3) **boss,** a foreman; (4) **-cane chair,** a chair that can be collapsed and carried conveniently, *rare;* (5) **chalk,** =**walking papers,** *rare;* (6) **cultivator,**

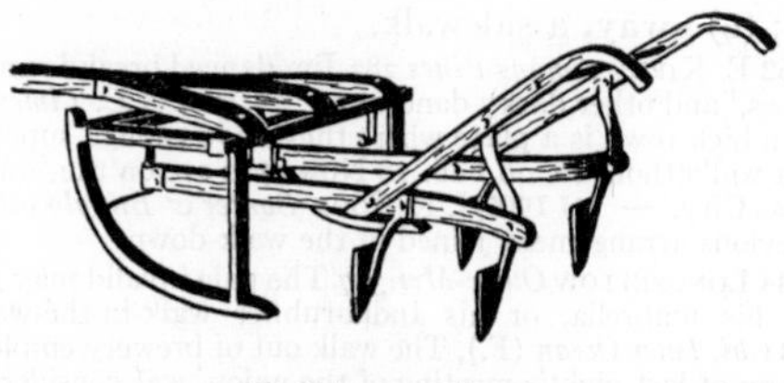

Walking cultivator

(see quot. 1876); (7) **delegate,** an official of a labor union who sees that union rules are enforced and that membership is kept up, and who presents grievances to employers; (8) ∗**fern,** (see quot. 1891); (9) **orders,** *pl.* =next; (10) **papers,** *pl.* notice of dismissal, discharge, also transf., *colloq.;* (11) **plow,** a plow the operator of which walks behind it; (12) **purchase,** a particular purchase of land, the extent being determined by a walk, cf. ∗**walk,** *n.* **2;** (13) **ticket,** =**walking papers,** *colloq.;* (14) **treaty,** (see quot.), *obs.;* (15) **typo,** short for "walking typhoid fever," an insidious form of typhoid in which the patient may go about his usual duties.

(1) **1845** *Knickerb.* XXV. 63 Some . . . climbed up the chain and up the machinery to the walking-beam. **1949** *Sat. Ev. Post* 18 June 108/3, I remember how I marveled at the 'walking beam' as it cranked the paddle wheels. — (2) **1855** *Harper's Mag.* Dec. 29/2 The crew, divided equally on each side, took their places upon the 'walking-boards,' extending along the whole length of the craft. — (3) **1891** *Harper's Mag.* Nov. 888/1 Hence the presence of Dan Dunn, his walking boss or general foreman. **1902** WHITE *Blazed Trail* 25 I'm walkin'-boss there. — (4) **1846** *Spirit of Times* (N.Y.) 18 April 94/2 On hand, walking-cane chairs—the Neplus Ultra of convenience to the invalid pedestrian.

(5) **1896** E. HIGGINSON *Land of Snow Pearls* 97, I'll give him his walking-chalk when he comes tonight. — (6) **1869** *Rep. Comm. Agric. 1868* 417 Field No. 3, . . . [was] cultivated but once, when about a foot high, with a five-toothed walking cultivator. **1876** KNIGHT 2721/1 *Walking-cultvivator,* one in which the operator walks behind, as distinguished from the *riding* or *sulky* cultivator. **1948** *Life* 23 Aug. 103 You used to start out in the morning with a team of horses and a walking cultivator and if you got through six acres it was a pretty good go. — (7) **1892** HOWELLS *Quality of Mercy* 131 She decided that he must be a walking-delegate, and that he had probably come on mischief from some of the workpeople in her father's employ. **1948** *Sat. Ev. Post* 9 Oct. 144/2 Then the communist walking delegates showed up to needle them into complaints. — (8) **1843** TORREY *Flora N.Y.* II. 494 *Antigramma rhizophylla.* . . . Walking-fern. **1891** *Cent.* 6809/2 Walking-fern. . . . A small tufted evergreen fern, *Camptosorus rhizophyllus,* native of eastern North America having the fronds heart-shaped or hastate at the base, and tapering above into a slender prolongation, which frequently takes root at the apex (whence the name). **1943** PEATTIE *Great Smokies* 178 It is true too of ferns like our dainty little walking fern, the stately cinnamon fern, our maidenhair and the ostrich fern. — (9) **1835** CROCKETT *Tour* 170 He got his walking orders, and Taney was taken into his place.

(10) **1825** WOODWORTH *Forest Rose* I. iv, As for the bumpkin, her lover, he must take his walking papers. **1850** LEWIS *La. Swamp Doctor* 71 The department gave him his walking-papers. **1950** *Dly. Worker* 4 May 12/2 Despite the haste with which the A's handed him his walking papers, the five foot nine inch, 180-pound infielder . . . was the hardest hitting third baseman in the league as recently as 1948. — (11) **1868** *Iowa State Agric. Soc. Rep. 1867* 161 [The] ground [is] plowed and harrowed, . . . and cultivated with riding and walking-plows. **1947** *Democrat* 30 Oct. 5/2 Apparently Walking Plows will be very scarce again next year. — (12) **1756** FRANKLIN *Writings* X. 185 It is said by many here that the Delawares were grossly abused in the Walking Purchase. **1895** J. WINSOR *Miss. Basin* 239 A scandalous act of Thomas Penn . . . had asserted inordinate claims by virtue of what was known as the 'Walking Purchase.' **1944** ADAMS *Album Amer. Hist.* I. 231 Lappawinsoe . . . [was] one of the signers of the Walking Purchase. — (13) **1835** CROCKETT *Tour* 162 He received his walking ticket. His services were no longer required. **1902** PIDGIN *Quincy* 337 If I git her off this bed she'll git her walkin' ticket. — (14) **1889** MELLICK *Story Old Farm* 57 Discontent . . . was greatly increased, a few years later [than 1728], by what was known as the 'Walking Treaty,' they [i.e., the Leni-Lenape Indians] claiming to have been swindled by the English in the great area of territory acquired by the Europeans in that famous bargain.

(15) **1908** GALE *Friendship Village* 230 Two cases of typhoid fever [had] recently developed in the town. (The Fire Chief had died of 'walking typo.')

As the last term in **jay walking.**

∗**wall,** *n.* In combs.: (1) ∗**wall-eye,** see as a main entry; (2) ∗**paper,** designating an edition of a newspaper brought out on wallpaper in Vicksburg, Mississippi, during the siege of that place in the Civil War, *obs.;* (3) **rock,** (*a*) (see quot.), *obs.,* (*b*) *mining,* the rock which constitutes the wall of a vein; (4) **spring,** (see quot.); (5)

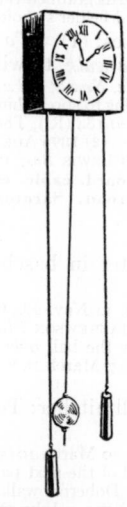

Wall-sweep clock

Street, see as a main entry; (6) **-sweep clock,** a wall clock with a long pendulum; (7) **tent,** a tent with vertical walls or partitions of canvas.

(2) **1863** *Vicksburg* (Miss.) *D. Citizen* 2 July 1/4 This is the last wall-paper edition, and is, excepting this note, from the types as we found them. **1885** *Santa Fe Wkly. New Mexican* 6 Aug. 4/7 A facsimile of the last 'wall-paper' edition of the Vicksburg Daily Citizen, issued July 2, 1863, . . . is sent out printed on modern style wallpaper as a

supplement to that enterprising journal the Chicago Herald. — (3) (a) **1859** BARTLETT 499 *Wall Rock*, granular limestone, used in the building of walls. (b) **1876** RAYMOND *8th Rep. Mines* 86 The hardness of the wall-rock has proved an obstacle to successful mining. **1883** BEADLE *Western Wilds* (1878) 582 The enclosing rocks, known in reference to the vein as 'wall rock,' . . . are somewhat more simple in construction. — (4) **1891** *Cent.* 6812/2 *Wall-spring*, . . . a spring of water issuing from stratified rocks.

(6) **1873** BEADLE *Undevel. West* 449 A great grinning demon, top-ornament to an old Spanish wall-sweep clock. **1878** —— *Western Wilds* 42 The old wall-sweep clock struck nine in a loud, aggressive tone. — (7) **1842** *S. Lit. Messenger* VIII. 409/1, I had previously ripped a wall-tent and converted it into a sail. **1936** *Sears Cat.* (ed. 173) 832 The finest wall tents you can buy at anywhere near these low prices.

As the last term in **canyon, face, fire, half high, log, stone, tariff wall.**

Wallawalla ˈwɑləˈwɑlə, *n.* [f. a native word signifying "little river."] An Indian of a Shahaptian tribe now on the Umatilla Reservation in Oregon. Also *pl.*, the tribe of such an Indian. Also attrib.

1807 GASS *Journal* 205 We then set out from Wal-la-wal-la river and nation. **1843** MARRYAT *M. Violet* ii, His leggings and mocassins were sewn with the hair of the Wallah Wallahs. **1855** *Santa Barbara* (Calif.) *Gaz.* 15 Nov. 2/4 The Walla Wallas, Nez Perces, Umatillas, Cayuses and Palouses have united, and together they can bring five or six thousand warriors into the field. **1894** *Messenger Sacred Heart Jesus* April 264 The mixed bloods on the reservation are generally related to the Walla Walla Indians. **1947** DEVOTO *Across Wide Missouri* 258 He had talked with the Cayuses, the Pend d'Oreilles, the Walla Wallas, and the Spokanes.

b. The language of these Indians.

1850 G. HINES *Voyage* 31 Mr. Perkins . . . applied himself to the acquirement of the Walla-Walla.

c. (See quot. 1890 and cf. **Cayuse 3.**)

1890 *Oregonian* (Portland) 17 Jan. 5/2 A cold easterly wind coming from the direction of Walla Walla is generally known among the Eastern Oregon Indians as a 'Walla Walla Chinook.' **1950** *Amer. Sp.* May 85 He had encountered new varieties of weather and had named a warm, thawing wind the 'Chinook' and a cold one the 'Walla Walla.'

walled lake. A shallow lake, occupying a depression in the surface of glacial drift, surrounded by embankments of boulders and similar matter. — **1868** *Amer. Naturalist* II. 143 [In] stories of the 'walled lakes' of Iowa . . . the wondrous handiwork of a departed race of men is described, consisting of walls of huge stones encircling the lakes like that of an artificial fish-pond.

* **wallet,** *n.* A billfold or flat container for carrying money or papers in the pocket.

1834 C. A. DAVIS *Lett. J. Downing* 39, I out with my seal-skin wallet. **1880** *Harper's Mag.* June 28/1 This wholly objectionable person . . . opens a well-filled wallet. **1950** *Dixie Roto. Mag.* 14 May 5/2 His cardboard wallet had $500 in it.

* **wall-eye,** *n.* **1.** = **wall-eyed pike. 2.** A fish, *Hyperprosopon argenteus*, of the Pacific Coast. Also **wall-eye surf fish. 3.** = **wall-eyed herring.**

(1) **1876** *Fur, Fin & Feather* Sep. 163/1 All along the Minnesota Division are numerous clear lakes and ponds, teeming with . . . 'walleyes' or pike-perch, tarred-perch [etc.]. **1949** *St. Paul Pioneer Press* 12 Aug. 17/3 From Mille Lacs Lake and the White fish chain, walleyes were being taken but in smaller numbers. — (2) **1884** GOODE *Fisheries* I. 278 Wall-eye Surf-fish. . . . This species is usually known as the 'Wall-eye,' in allusion to the great size of its eyes. — (3) **1891** *Cent.* 6811/1 *Walleye*, . . . the alewife, or wall-eyed herring.

* **wall-eyed,** *a.* **1. wall-eyed herring,** the alewife, *Pomolobus pseudoharengus*. **2. wall-eyed pike,** a fresh-water food fish, *Stizostedion vitreum*, common in the Great Lakes and the upper Mississippi.

(1) **1884** GOODE *Fisheries* I. 580 *C. vernalis* is known . . . on the Albemarle River as the 'Big-eyed' Herring and the 'Wall-eyed' Herring. **1891** [see * **wall-eye 3.**]. — (2) **1867** DE VOE *Market Ass't* 208 Yellow Pike perch, glass-eyed pike, big-eyed pike, pike of the lakes, or Ohio salmon. This fine and truly American fish is sometimes known as 'wall-eyed pike,' in consequence of their large eyes becoming white or clouded after death. **1946** *Chi. D. News* 14 Sep. 6/7 John caught one walleyed pike.

* **walloon,** *n.* **1.** ?Heavy cloth or leather imported from Belgium or the neighboring regions. *Obs.* **2.** (See quot. 1917.) **3.** (See quot. 1891.)

(1) **1794** *Steele P.* I. 118, I have also sent you some Cloth & such trimmings as I cou'd get—there is no Walloon of the Colour to be had. *Ib.* 120 There is no Buff Walloon in Town, but I presume the Durants will answer any purpose that Walloon would. — (2) **1851** *De Bow's Review* XI. 56 *Warloon*, or *Walloon*, a brown-colored water bird, making a noise which sounds like the name. **1917** *Birds of Amer.* I. 12 Loon. *Gavia immer*. . . . [Also called] Ember-Goose; Walloon; Ring-necked Loon. — (3) **1868** BANCROFT *Hist. U.S.* II. 279 They were chiefly Walloons, Protestant fugitives from Belgian provinces. **1891** *Cent.* 6811/3 *Walloon*, . . . in America, especially colonial New York, one of the Huguenot settlers from Artois, in northern France, etc.

* **wallow,** *n.* A place to which animals resort for rolling or wallowing; a depression in the earth caused by this (see quot. 1947).

1796 in *Amer. Sp.* XV. 407/1 To four Chesnuts in the head of a deep Wallow by a water Slip. **1827** WILLIAMS *W. Fla.* 27 But it is in the wallows, large mud holes among the rushes, that the alligator appears herself. **1876** J. A. ALLEN *Amer. Bisons* 65 These wallows thus become characteristic marks of a buffalo country. **1947** CAHALANE *Mammals* 78 After a few dust baths, the wallow is a saucerlike depression from eight to fifteen feet across and as much as sixteen or eighteen inches deep toward the center.

attrib. **1787** in *Amer. Sp.* XV. 407/2 At white oak & red oak near a wallow Hole. **1861** in *Ib.*, To a sugar tree (now fallen) by the Big wallow hole. **1882** BAILLIE-GROHMAN *Camps in Rockies* 37 All three [saddle blankets] were well soaked in the copper-coloured wallow water.

As the last term in **bear, buffalo, elk, hog, shad, turkey wallow.**

Wall Street. [So called because of a wall which extended along this street in Dutch times.] A street in lower Manhattan in which the principal financial institutions of New York City are located. Often regarded as the financial center of the country and as the aggregate of financial interests of the U.S.

1806 *Balance* V. 228/1 Walking thro' Wall street yesterday morning, I saw a large crowd. **1841** *Week in Wall St.* p. ix, In the expressive language of Wall-street, he has himself been 'flunked.' **1890** *Cong. Rec.* 5 June 5608/1 'Wall street' is a term supposed to suggest conscienceless greed for and criminal methods to obtain money, and has been applied to the investors and creditor class of our people indiscriminately. **1949** *Chi. D. News* 31 May 1/6 Wall street traced liquidation to the many new uncertainties created by declining production.

Hence **Wall Streeter,** a member of the financial community of Wall Street, a financier.

1885 *Wkly. New Mexican Rev.* 15 Jan. 2/2 The Wall streeters and money changers want less money that they may have a better chance to grind the borrowers. **1948** *New Republic* 2 Feb. 8/1 The Herter Committee on European Aid . . . called in other like-minded Wall Streeters to help.

b. Attrib. with **broker, farmer, note-shaving, plunger, ring, shark.**

1836 *Jamestown* (N.Y.) *Jrnl.* 16 March 1/2 A company—Wall street brokers and speculators—are the applicants for the loan to the New York and Erie Railroad. **1862** *N. Amer. Rev.* July 113 This Wall-Street note-shaving life is a new field, a very peculiar field. **1868** *N.Y. Herald* 7 July 6/4 The 'honesty' of our New York politicians of both parties . . . is the honesty of our Wall street rings. **1893** *Chi. Tribune* 25 April 12/1 With gold at a premium, . . . the speculators, or . . . Wall Street sharks, would have been in clover. **1903** *N.Y. Ev. Post* 19 Sep., The disrespectful term of 'Wall Street farmer' . . . embraces a large number of people who would not know the condition of a wheat or cotton field if they saw it. **1928** FOY & HARLOW *Clowning Thro' Life* 47 The . . . Wall Street plunger . . . was a queer mixture of good and bad.

Also *Wall Street bull, capitalist, method, office, operator, panic, phrase, speculation*, etc.

* **walnut,** *n.*

1. *local.* A hickory nut. Also, *ellipt.*, a walnut grove or walnut timber.

1894 *Cent. Mag.* April 850 About Lake George, I find 'shuck' used . . . for the outer covering of the hickory-nut—called here and in some other Northern districts 'walnut.' **1897** BRODHEAD *Bound in Shallows* 165 Would there be anything wrong in me selling the walnut and building me a house?

2. In combs.: (1) **walnut bottom,** a level extent of low land where walnut trees are the prevailing growth; (2) **fern,** a local name for some now unidentifiable plant, *obs.;* (3) **fudge,** fudge having walnut kernels in it; (4) **moth,** any one of various moths the larvae of which feed on walnut leaves, cf. **regal walnut moth** (*s.v.* **regal moth**) and **royal walnut moth;** (5) **plain,** a plain upon which there are walnut trees; (6) **prairie land,** prairie land upon which walnut is the prevailing growth.

(1) **1774** D. Jones *Jrnl.* (1865) 47, I . . . lost myself on the largest walnut bottom I ever met with before. — (2) **1824** Doddridge *Notes* 149 A kind of fern which from its resemblance to the leaves of walnut, was called walnut fern, was another remedy [for snake bite]. — (3) **1920** Lewis *Main Street* 1 She was meditating upon walnut fudge. — (4) **1892** Kellogg *Kansas Insects* 98 Walnut moth (*Datana angusii*). . . . Infesting walnut and hickory; large, blackish caterpillars, feeding on the leaves.

(5) **1816** U. Brown *Journal* I. 148 The Walnut-planes . . . are Dry rich Land without any Timber or wood growing on the same. — (6) **1883** Smith *Geol. Survey Ala.* 468 A loose walnut prairie land makes up a small proportion of the country about Faunsdale.

As the last term in **black, California, English, Gloucester, large-fruited shagbark, large-fruited shellbark, round black Virginia, satin, shagbark, white walnut.**

Walrussia ˈwɔlˌrʌʃə, *n.* [?f. **walrus*+ **Russia.*] One of the names suggested for what is now Alaska. *Obs.* or *hist.*

1867 *N.Y. Tribune* 9 Nov. 3/2 (*heading*), Walrussia. **1868** Whymper *Alaska* 127 Redoubt St. Michael's, or *Michaelovski*, the principal station of the Russian American Fur Company in this northern section of 'Walrus-sia,' deserves something more than a passing notice. **1897** Leonard *Gold Fields Klondike*, The names of 'Polario,' 'American Siberia,' 'Zero Islands' and 'Walrussia' were suggested, but Charles Sumner advocated the name 'Alaska' from the aboriginal 'Al-ak-shak' meaning 'the great country' or 'the continent.' **1935** *Glimpses of Alaska* 17 Some idea of the general ignorance regarding Alaska exhibited by the United States is gained from the terms applied to the Territory when its purchase was considered. 'Walrus-sia,' 'American Siberia,' 'Zero Island,' 'Polaria,' and 'Icebergia' are among the list.

* **waltz,** *v. tr.* To transport or convey (something heavy or clumsy). *Colloq.* — **1884** Mark Twain *H. Finn* iii, They've got to waltz that palace around over the country wherever you want it. **1901** Merwin & Webster *Calumet 'K'* 197 He'd call the men off just the same, and leave us to waltz the timbers around all by ourselves.

wammikin ˈwɑməkɪn, *n.* [Variant of wanigan *q.v.*] (See quots.) — **1877** *Scribner's Mo.* Dec. 151 At night, the men seek their several *Wammikins* for supper, sleep, and breakfast: and, when the 'drive' finally arrives at its destination, the timber of these portable hotels comes into good use. **1910** Hodge *Amer. Indians* II. 903 *Wammikan*, a raft of hewed logs, upon which is constructed a shanty, provided with cooking and sleeping arrangements.

Wampanoag ˌwɑmpəˈnoæg, *n.* [f. the native name meaning "eastern people."] *pl.* or *collect.* (See quot. 1910.) Also an Indian of this tribe. Also attrib.

1677 R. Williams *Unpublished Lett.* (1881) 54, I was known to all the Wampanogs . . . to be public speaker. **1818** Eastburn *Yamoyden* (1834) I. 177 The Wampanoag from the height Of Haup, who strained his anxious sight [etc.]. **1910** Hodge *Amer. Indians* II. 903/2 Wampanoag. . . . One of the principal tribes of New England. Their proper territory appears to have been the peninsula on the E. shore of Narragansett bay now included in Bristol co., R.I., and the adjacent parts in Bristol co., Mass. **1948** *Sat. Ev. Post* 26 June 23/3 The township of Dartmouth had been purchased from Chief Massasoit, of the Wampanoag tribe.

wampee wɑmˈpi, *n.* [Prob. f. Shawnee *wapa*, white.] **1.** The jack-in-the-pulpit, *Arisaema triphyllum.* **2.** The pickerel weed, *Pontederia cordata.* Also attrib.

(1) **1802** Drayton *S. Carolina* 8 [Here grow] quantities of wampe (a species of arum). — (2) **1910** Hodge *Amer. Indians* II. 904/2 *Wampee*, a name used in parts of the Southern states for the pickerel-weed (*Pontederia caudata.*) **1945** R. M. Harper in letter to the editor 13 Sep., In Okefinokee Swamp, and perhaps also in northern Florida, the name 'wampee' is applied to certain aquatic plants with arrow-shaped leaves, perhaps mostly to *Pontederia cordata*, which is called 'pickerel weed' in northern books, but apparently not in the South.

wampum ˈwɑmpəm, *n.* [See next.]

1. Short for **wampumpeag.** Now *hist.* Cf. **allocochick, mowhackees, peag, pook, porcelain, roanoke 1.**

1638 *R.I. Col. Rec.* I. 33 He desired to have commodities and wampum. **1789** Morse *Amer. Geog.* 349 Wampum was, at this time [*c*1670], the principal currency of the country. **1880** *Harper's Mag.* May 818/2 He and his fellow-sachem . . . [receive] long strings of wampum. **1949** *Chi. Tribune* 18 Dec. 24/5 Wampum figured importantly in diplomatic relations among tribes.

transf. and *attrib.* **1816** *Adventures of Uncle Sam* 43 Do not arm these cursed savage Wampums against us, blood and vengeance betide ye if ye do. **1948** *So. Weekly* 3 July 5/1 She said that . . . its center was run by the 'wampum and boodle boys.' **1949** *Chi. D. News* 13 Oct. 1/8 They play the machines to win what they call heap of wampum—the jackpot.

b. Preceded by a term denoting color.

1638 *R.I. Col. Rec.* I. 33 At last we agreed upon ten fathom of white wampum. **1748** Weiser *Jrnl.* 24 Hired a Cannoe; paid 1,000 Black Wampum for the loan of it. **1851** Schoolcraft *Information resp. Indian Tribes* I. 88 It appears from ancient documents . . . that about 1640, three beads of purple or blue wampum, and six of white wampum were equivalent to a styver or to one penny English. **1946** Foreman *Last Trek* 48 Lewis was deputized to carry the white wampum to his tribe in Ohio.

2. In combs. now obs. or hist.: (1) **wampum belt,** a belt made of wampum, often arranged in mnemonic figures or shapes, and used in ratifying treaties, confirming alliances, etc.; (2) **grass,** ?ribbon grass; (3) **maker,** one who makes wampum; (4) **snake,** the horn snake *q.v.*, so called from its colors.

Wampum belt

(1) **1676** B. Thompson *Poetical Works* 91 All up in Wampum Belts, most richly drest. **1809** Weems *Marion* (1833) 22 The Cherokees . . . sent on a deputation with their wampum belts and peace-talks to bury the hatchet. **1945** F. Rowe *Chapin Sisters* 131 Charlotte was very nice with children . . . letting small boys actually hold the wampum belts. — (2) **1852** Moodie *Roughing It* 84 There is one island among these groups (but I never could light upon the identical one) where the Indians yearly gather their wampum-grass. — (3) **1755** *N.J. Archives* XIX. 457 Broke out of Cap May county goal, . . . a man, named Jacon Bennet, . . . He is a Wampum maker by trade. — (4) **1736** Mortimer in *Phil. Trans.* XXXIX. 258 The *Wampum* Snake; so called from the Resemblance it hath in its Colours to the *Wampam*, or *Indian* Money, made of Pieces of Shells blue and white, strung together. **1791** W. Bartram *Travels* 273 They seem to be a species, if not the very same snake which in Pennsylvania and Virginia, are called wampom snake. **1808** Ashe *Travels* 243 We called the following to our recollection: . . . green snake, wampum snake.

b. Also **wampum bead, center, mill, necklace.**

1796 Hawkins *Letters* 30 He gave half a pint of salt, or 3 strans of mock wampum beads a basket. **1847** Parkman in *Knickerb.* XXIX. 590 Calico shirts, red and blue blankets, . . . wampum necklaces, appeared in profusion. **1906** *N.Y. Ev. Post* 21 Aug. 12 Alonzo Campbell has offered a reward for the arrest of any person caught despoiling the old wampum mill in the Paskack Valley. . . . The wampum business was started here by the four Campbell brothers, the last of whom died six years ago. . . . The wampum was made of clam shells, and was sold to New York traders, who in turn disposed of it to the Indians in Canada and the Northwest. **1946** *New Yorker* 23 Feb. 24/2 Westchester was a big wampum center, and the Indians called it Laaphawachking, or Place of Stringing Beads. Armonk, in fact, means Place Where Wampum Is Made. **1948** *Democrat* 11 March 4/3 The black wampum beads of Indians were made from the eyes of hen clams.

wampumpeag ˈwɑmpəmˌpig, *n.* [See note.]

Algonquian *wampŭmpeage, wampŏmpeag*, strings of shell beads. "As the native expression was too cumbersome for ready utterance by the New England colonists, the sentence-word was divided by them into *wampum*, and *peak* or *peage*" (Hodge).

Shell beads used by the Indians as ornaments and serving as a medium of exchange in early colonial trade. Now *hist.*

1627 in Bradford *Hist.* 273 Ye above-said parties are to have . . . whole stock of . . . wampampeak, hatchets, knives, &c. **1723** *N.-Eng. Courant* 4 Feb. 2/2 The Narragensets have a Crown among them made of Wampumpeeg. **1859** Campbell *Hist. Va.* 295 Around her head she wore a plait of black and white wampum-peake. **1944** Footner *Rivers of East. Shore* 138 For currency, the Naticokes used 'roanoke' and 'peake,' sometimes called 'wampum-peake,' two kinds of shell.

wamus ˈwɑməs, *n.* Also **waumus, warmus.** [f. dial. G. *wammes*, a jumper or blouse.] (See quots. 1847, 1948.) *Colloq.*

1805 *Lancaster* (Pa.) *Intelligencer* 12 Nov. (Th.), I got up, and found that my waumus was bloody, which I had not observed before. **1841** *S. Lit. Messenger* VII. 525/1 His long, matted locks overhung the back of a red flannel *warm-us*. **1847** HOWE *Hist. Coll. Ohio* 254 (*footnote*), The '*warmus*' is a working garment, similar in appearance to a 'roundabout,' but more full, and being usually made of red flannel, is elastic and easy to the wearer. **1872** EGGLESTON *End of World* 40 Instead of a coat he wore that unique garment of linsey-woolsey known in the West as wa-mus (warm us?), a sort of over-shirt. **1948** DICK *Dixie Frontier* 297 Boys until they were in their teens wore nothing but a single garment, a 'wamus' or shirt that reached down nearly to the ankles.

wanga ˈwɑŋgə, *n.* [f. an African term meaning witchcraft, fetish. Cf. Kimbundu *wanga*, witchcraft.] Witchcraft, a magic charm. Also attrib.

1882 BUEL *Metropolitan Life Unveiled* 532, I will make a wanga-charm to charm him with; I will make him a phantom, a ghost. **1883** *Harper's Wkly.* 17 Jan. 43/4 So likewise . . . are transmitted the secrets of . . . the composition of those love philters hinted at in creole ballads, and the deadly ouanga art as bequeathed to modern Voudooism by the black Locustas of the eighteenth century. **1946** TALLANT *Voodooism in N.O.* 91 Another sort held gunpowder and red pepper; these were *wangas* to be thrown into somebody's path to cause them to get into fights.

wangan ˈwɑŋgən, *n.* [See **wanigan.**] (See quots. and cf. next.)

1848 BARTLETT 377 *Wangan.* (Indian.) In Maine, a boat for carrying provisions. **1895** GERARD in *N.Y. Sun* 30 July, Wangan, a name among the lumbermen of Maine for a boat used chiefly for carrying provisions, tools, &c. **1942** RICH *We Took to Woods* (1948) 154 There is a sign in the bunk-house that reads, 'Wangan open an hour after supper.' That refers to the store where the cook sells candy, tobacco, snuff, and clothing. . . . The cook may say, 'I lost my wangan when the work boat swamped,' and that means that his dishes are at the bottom of the lake. Or he may complain, 'The wangan's runnin' low,' meaning this time that he's short of food. Or a man may take his wangan and fly—leave the job with his little bundle of personal belongings. You can tell only by the context what the word means. **1947** *Harper's Mag.* July 82/1 He could pack his 'wangan' into the woods for a camp.

attrib. **1902** *Outing* Jan. 459/1 While Harry was overhauling the 'wangan' box, it was ascertained that the Professor had almost forgotten to bring the cooking kit. **1907** *Black Cat* June 19 Abe, limping about, bustled over to an ancient Wangan-chest, relic of his father's river-days.

b. *running the wangan*, (see quot. 1910).

1895 GERARD in *N.Y. Sun* 30 July, 'Running the wangan' is a phrase well understood on the rivers of Maine. **1910** HODGE *Amer. Indians* II. 910/2 'Running the *wangan*' is the act of taking a loaded boat down a river, from station to station, particularly in swiftly flowing water.

wanigan ˈwɑnəgən, *n.* [f. Abnaki *waniigan*, trap, a receptacle for stray objects.] (See quots.) Cf. prec. and see **wammikin.**

1902 WHITE *Blazed Trail* 323 Outside, the cook and cookee were stowing articles in the already loaded wanigan. **1910** HODGE *Amer. Indians* II. 910 *Wanigan.* A receptacle in which small supplies or a reserve stock of goods are kept; also a large chest in which the lumbermen of Maine and Minnesota keep their spare clothing, pipes, tobacco, etc. Called also *wongan*-box, and spelled *wangun* and *wangan.* (2) A boat used on the rivers of Maine for the transportation of the entire personnel of a logging camp, along with the tools of the camp and provisions for the trip. . . . (3) A place in a lumber camp where accounts are kept and the men paid. **1945** FUGINA *Upper Miss.* 221 Wanigans were small flatboats, built of natural crook knees and planked lengthwise. **1949** *Survey* June 303/2 The industry is based no longer in isolated logging camps, with lonely men living in 'wannigans' dragged through the forests on sled-like runners.

attrib. **1901** *Everybody's Mag.* June 565/2 The night, the wongan boat with its food and camp-kit for the men fell far behind the crew.

wankapin ˈwɑŋkəpɪn, *n.* Also **yonkapin.** [See quot. 1910.] The water chinquapin. Also attrib.

1832 KENNEDY *Swallow Barn* 232 The heirs of Swallow Barn . . . are hereafter to be pestered with this fine garden of wankopins and snake-collards. **1872** *Amer. Naturalist* VI. 726 Very curious peltate leaves, looking somewhat like miniatures of the great lotus or 'yonkapins' (Nelumbium) beside them. **1910** HODGE *Amer. Indians* II. 904/1 Wampapin. A name for the water chinquapin, *Nelumbo lutea*, corrupted from *wankipin*, 'crooked root,' the Chippewa name for the long, nodose rootstock of the plant, which after being boiled to destroy its acidity is used as food. **1920** COOPER *Under Big Top* 73 Hard, black affairs, such as we knew in kid-hood days as 'yonkypin nuts.' **1949** *N.O. Times-Picayune Mag.* 16 Oct. 20/3 The red men loved it so much that they extended its range north, calling it in various regions the yonka nut, yonapin, and yonkapin.

* **want,** *n.*

1. =next. *Colloq.*

1855 BARNUM *Life* 143 My eyes were running over the columns of 'Wants' in the New York 'Sun.' **1897** *Scribner's Mag.* XXII. 459 'Wants' bring in a large, sure income directly.

2. want ad, a notice in a newspaper stating that something is wanted, in full **want advertisement.**

1887 *Courier-Journal* (Louisville) 12 Jan. 5/3 The *World* is treating Mr. Conkling as it treats its circulation and its 'want' advertisements upon occasion. **1897** *Chi. Record* 1 March 10/4 Record 'want ads' bring results. **1948** *Democrat* 2 Dec. 8/1 Want Ads are charged for at the rate of one cent a word.

3. want column, a column in a newspaper taken up with want ads.

1884 NYE *Baled Hay* 239 The want column of the Chicago *News* . . . has the following: 'Twelve "frightful examples" wanted, to travel with Scott Marble's new drama and appear in the realistic bar-room scene of the "Drunkard's Daughter." ' **1931** *K.C. Star* July, Our want column, as we have long and vigorously contended, will sell anything if given a chance.

* **want,** *v. tr.* With a clause as object: To desire (that someone do something). Now *colloq.*

1745 BRAINERD *Journal* (1902) 19 They wanted Christ should wipe their hearts quite clean. **1882** THAYER *From Log-Cabin* 347 Everybody wants you should answer him. **1920** HOWELLS *Vacation of Kelwyns* 188 Want I should drive ye home?

For *I want to know*, see * **know,** *v.*

wantage ˈwɑntɪdʒ, *n.* **1.** (See quot. 1828.) **2. wantage rod,** a gauged rod used in determining the wantage of a cask, etc.

(1) 1828 WEBSTER, *Wantage*, deficiency; that which is wanting. **1889** *N.Y. Produce Exch. Rep.* 256 Inspectors and Gaugers shall make a detailed return . . . of each lot inspected, showing . . . the gauge, wantage, proof, and number of proof gallons. — **(2) 1861** *Ill. Agric. Soc. Trans.* V. 166 Our other implements, except the saccharometer, gauge-rod and wantage-rod, were the common utensils. **1886** *Harper's Mag.* July 215/1 Inspectors and gaugers . . . must make their returns . . . in accordance with the straight gauge rod, wantage rod, the hydrometer used by the government.

wapacuthu ˌwɑpəˈkuθu, *n.* [Algonquian. Cf. Cree *wapiskisiw*, Montagnais *wapukulu*, it is white.] "A large white spotted owl, about 2 feet long and without ear-tufts, believed to be the common snowy owl" (*Cent.*). — **[1785** PENNANT *Arctic Zool.* II. 231 Red, Mottled, and Wapacuthu Owl. *Ib.* 232 Called by the Indians, Wapacuthu, or the Spotted Owl.] **1917** *Birds of Amer.* II. 115 *Nyctea nyctea.* . . . Great White Owl; Ermine Owl; Harfang; Wapacuthu; Arctic Owl.

wapanock ˈwɑpəˌnɑk, *n.* (See quots.) Also attrib. *Obs.* — **1721–2** in TEMPLE & SHELDON *Hist. Northfield, Mass.* (1875) 160 To a wapanock skin. . . . 0 3 8. **1875** *Ib.* 162 *Wapanock* or wogernock, was the Indian name for the sable or martin.

wapatoo ˈwɑpəˌtu, *n.* [f. Chinook Jargon *wappatoo*, in the use shown here.] A name used of various edible roots, esp. those of either of two species of arrowhead, *Sagittaria latifolia* and *S. cuneata*. Also attrib.

1805 CLARK in *Lewis & C. Exped.* III. (1905) 196 This root they call *Wap-pa-to*. . . . It has an agreeable taste and answers verry well in place of bread. **1872** DE VERE 401 In Oregon the Chinook Indians live largely on an edible bulb called *Wapatoo.* **1944** ROSS *Westward Ho!* 176 Some pioneer women . . . took lessons in making bread . . . from the wappato roots that naked squaws deftly gathered with their toes in the sloughs of the Columbia River.

b. (See quots.)

1888 *Puget Sound Gazetteer* July 12/1 Canvasback ducks . . . on the Columbia river . . . get an excellent flavor from the wapato, a sort of white water lily, upon the roots of which they feed. **1910** HODGE *Amer. Indians* II. 913 The Chippewa name *wâpato* has been applied to some plant called rhubarb.

wapiti ˈwɑpətɪ, *n.* [Algonquian. Cf. Shawnee *wapiti*, white rump, and see quot. 1895.] The North American stag or elk, *Cervus canadensis*. Also attrib. Cf. * **elk,** *n.* **1.**

1806 B. S. BARTON in *Scientific Mo.* XLIV. (1937) 162/1 As the Elk has not to my knowledge been described by any systematic writer on Zoology, I have assumed the liberty of giving it a specific name. I have called it Wapiti, which is the name by which it is known among the Shawnees or Shawnese Indians. **1817** *Thomson's Ann. Philos.* IX. 325 At the same meeting [of the Linnaean Society] was read a description, by Dr. Leach, of the Wapiti deer, a species of animal from the banks of the Missouri. **1827** W. BULLOCK *Journey* p. xxi, A pair of the gigantic elk, or wappetti (nearly the size of horses), ranged through the meadows. **1895** GERARD in *N.Y. Sun* 30 July, Wapiti, a name for the American elk or stag, from Cree 'wapitayoo,' 'it is pale,' as distinguished from the common moose, which is of a very dark color. **1948** *Pacific Discovery* Jan.–Feb. 11/1 The Jackson Hole country harbored the largest remaining nucleus of wapiti in the country, where the species was making its last stand.

Wappo ˈwɒpo, *n.* [Prob. f. Sp. *Wapos* (<*guapo*, brave) in the same sense.] *pl.* or *collect.* "A small detached portion of the Yukian family of N. California, separated from the Huchnom, the nearest Yuki division, by 30 or 40 m. of Pomo territory" (Hodge). Also attrib.

1856 *Indian Affairs Rep.* 257 The Wapo Indians . . . are a remnant of a tribe that once inhabited the country about the Geisers. **1877** *Contrib. N. Amer. Ethnology* III. 198 The Wappo presents a finer physique than the lowland Gallinomero. **1886** BANCROFT *Hist. Calif.* IV. 71 For their service in returning stolen horses they got into trouble with the Satiyomis, or Sotoyomes, generally known as Guapos, or 'braves.' **1903** JAMES *Indian Basketry* 57 The Ashochimi, commonly known as the Wappos, were once a powerful people inhabiting the region of the Geysers and Calistoga.

* **war,** *n.*

1. The American Civil War, as a point of reference, esp. *before the War.*

1883 MARK TWAIN *Life on Miss.* xlv, In the South, the War is what A. D. is elsewhere; they date from it. All day long you hear things 'placed' as having happened since the War; or 'du'in' the War,' or befo' the War.' **1943** *Chi. D. News* 12 June 6/1 In reading a mention of them, one has a faint hint of 'Gone with the Wind' or the works of Thomas Nelson Page on 'Befoh de Wah.' **1949** *Nat. Hist.* Dec. 460/3 The little mills to which small growers take their canes still use the iron presses that have been handed down from the 'yeahs befo' the wah.' Only an ignorant damyankee would ask 'Which war?'—there has been only one in these parts.

2. In combs., now obs. or hist., relating to Indians: (1) **war bag,** see as a main entry; (2) **belt,** among the North American Indians, a belt of wampum used as a means of conveying a declaration of war or summoning or winning help in the conduct of a war; (3) **budget,** a

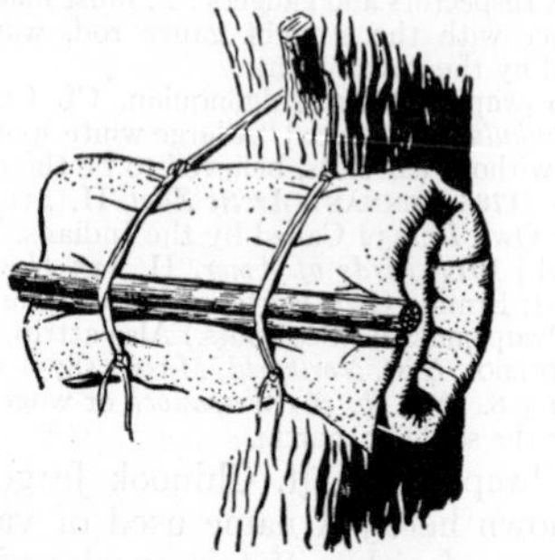

War budget of a type used by Sac Indians

packet containing amulets and military trophies; (4) **cabin,** a cabin in which an Indian war council met; (5) **hatchet,** a hatchet or tomahawk used in war, or as a ceremonial symbol of a state of war, also in phrases; (6) **kettle,** a kettle used in war ceremonies by the Indians; (7) **medicine,** see **4.** (9) below; (8) **path,** see as a main entry; (9) * **pipe,** a pipe smoked in an Indian war ceremonial; (10) **pole,** = **war post,** also *to strike the war pole,* to go on the warpath; (11) **post,** a post, frequently painted red, put up by Indians for use in public ceremonies connected with war; (12) **whoop,** see as a main entry; (13) **woman,** (*a*) among the Indians, a priestess or female councilor, (*b*) Nancy Hart, a Revolutionary heroine of Georgia, known for her courage and resourcefulness in fighting the Tories.

(2) **1763** *Ga. Gazette* 7 July 3/1 An Indian has brought a war belt to Tusquerora, who says Detroit was invested. **1847** LANMAN *Summer in Wild.* 17 Captain James Clarke, . . . when about to be murdered by a council of Indians . . . threw the war-belt in the midst of the savages, with a defying shout. — (3) **1813** STUART *Narratives* 236 A Pole surpassing in height any put in the roof, is put out at the chimney where are suspended their Medecine Bags and War Budgets carefully concealed in innumerable wrappers. **1920** *Western Rev.* II. 48 The war budget is then hung in front of the door of the person that carried it on the march. — (4) **1772** in *Travels Amer. Col.* 451 After he had Smoked with me he went to the head war Cabin where he Called two warriours to him.

(5) **1760** CROGHAN *Jrnl.* (1904) 116 You [chiefs and warriors may] . . . bury the War Hatchet in the Bottomless Pit. **1776** *N.H. Hist. Soc. Coll.* IX. 94 They have been . . . solicited by our most cruel unnatural Enemies to take up the War Hatchet against us. **1907** ANDREWS *Recoll.* 122 Full dress required his war-hatchet and weapons. — (6) **1754** *World* (London) 12 Dec. 615 At a meeting of Sachems it was determined *to take up the hatchet,* and *make the war-kettle boil.* **1791** J. LONG *Voyages* 146 [They] brought him to the war-kettle to make his death-feast: which consisted of dog, tyger-cat, and bear's grease [etc.]. — (9) **1775** ADAIR *Indians* 7 The beaus used to fasten the like [*sc.* pieces of tinkling metal] to their war pipes, with the addition of a piece of an enemy's scalp. **1899** CUSHMAN *Hist. Indians* 492 Some celebrated . . . old warrior, with the war-pipe in his hand, . . . delivered a speech.

(10) **1775** ADAIR *Indians* 162 And after they return home, hang it [their ark] on the leader's red-painted war pole. *Ib.* 187 The war-pole is a small peeled tree painted red, the top and boughs cut off short: it is fixt in the ground opposite to his [a war leader's] door, and all his implements of war are hung on the short boughs of it. **1847** in HOWE *Hist. Coll. Ohio* 422 Some time in September, 250 warriors *struck the war pole,* and took up their line of march. — (11) **1779** *Mass. Hist. Soc. Proc.* 2 Ser. II. 463 [We] found a war post which the Indians had put up with marks cut in the same in token of their Scalps. **1899** CUSHMAN *Hist. Indians* 493 The 'war-post,' painted red, was set up. — (13) (*a*) **1765** TIMBERLAKE *Memoirs* 71 Old warriors likewise, or war-women . . . have the title of Beloved. **1786** FERRIAR in *Mem. Lit. & Philos. Soc. Manch.* (1790) III. 28 In every Indian village, the war-woman also is a kind of oracle; by dreams and presages, she directs the hunters to their prey, and the warriors to the enemy. (*b*) **1857** *Ladies' Repository* XVII. 81/1 The stream, called from her, 'War-Woman's Creek,' empties into it. *Ib.* 83/1 The 'war-woman's' skill in strategy and courage in action now appeared.

b. In combs. of obvious meaning, or sufficiently explained in the quots.: (1) **war bell,** (2) **bonnet,** (3)

Form of war bonnet used by Crow Indians

captain, cf. **Mingo war captain,** (4) **chief,** (also transf.), (5) **club,** (6) **council,** (7) **dance,** (also transf.), (8) **dress,** (9) **eagle,** (10) **feast,** (11) **hoop,** (12) **name,** (13) **paint,** (also transf.), (14) **party,** (15) **road,** (16) **shout,** (17) **signal,** (18) **song,** (19) **squaw,** (20) **talk,** (also transf.), (21) **trail,** also *to go on the war trail.*

(1) **1797** F. BAILY *Tour* 367 The war bells . . . are formed of a hollow nut, about as big as one's fist, in which was a stone, which made a hollow dismal sound. — (2) **1845** FRÉMONT *Exped.* 134 Indians . . . with the long red streamers of their war bonnets reaching nearly to the ground. **1949** *Nat. Hist.* May 195/2 Chief Hind Bull is wearing a typical war bonnet of the Blood Tribe, made of eagle feathers and tipped with horsehair. — (3) **1709** LAWSON *Carolina* 174 Some one of the Nation . . . is appointed by their King, and war-Captains, to make these Songs [for their feasts]. **1871** *Rep. Indian Affairs* (1872) 392 The officers consist of a governor, . . . war captains, lieutenants, and constables. — (4) **1775** ADAIR *Indians* 292 The war-chiefs and beloved men were grown very poor. **1813** *Steele P.* II. 704 The proferred mediation of the Emperor of Russia has been acceeded [*sic*] to by our War Chief. **1947** DEVOTO *Across Wide Missouri* 81 It was to gain time that a war chief rode out from the tribe toward the trapper.

(5) **1776** in Rauck *Boonesborough* 251 The war club we got was like those I had seen of that nation [i.e., the Shawnese]. **1943** Peattie *Great Smokies* 24 The Cherokee weapons were the ball-headed war club, spears and bows and arrows. — (6) **1775** Adair *Indians* 156 The Chikkasah war-council, . . . [condemned] two pretended friends to death. **1884** *Cent. Mag.* April 805/1 There have been [in the White House] . . . war councils that flashed forth orders, . . . which moved great armies. — (7) **1711** *N.C. Col. Rec.* I. 813 The Baron de Graftenried . . . was still alive but supposed only reserved for a more solemn execution, to be tomahawked and tortured at their first publick War Dances. **1768** *N.Y. Journal* 7 April, The cherokee chiefs and Warriors . . . have offered to entertain the Public with the War Dance. **1851** *S.F. Picayune* 24 Oct. 2/2 Having thus satisfied his taste for hat smashing, the tiles were kicked into a heap, and the six joining hands around them went through an extemporary war dance. **1946** Thompson *Amer. Daughter* 147, I loved the Indian war dances. — (8) **1825** Neal *Bro. Jonathan* II. 16 He had been sent by the prophet with a command . . . for Eagle to put on his war-dress. **1887** *Cent. Mag.* May 51/1 The war-dress of these warm-weather warriors [*sc.* Apaches] . . . is not so resplendent in buckskin and beads. — (9) **1821** Nuttall *Travels Arkansa* 88 The large feathers of the war-eagle . . . are sometimes distributed throughout the nation, as sacred presents. **1916** Seton *Woodcraft Man.* 305 The only other eagle found in the United States (beside the Bald Eagle) is the *Golden or War Eagle* (*Aquila chrysaetos*). This is a little larger . . . the two species may always be distinguished by the legs. The War Eagle wears leggings—his legs are feathered to the toes. . . . The Bald Eagle has the legs bald, or bare on the lower half. **1942** Nat. Pk. Service *Fading Trails* 260 The great American golden eagle, war eagle of the Indians, seems to be gone as a breeding bird from the western Great Plains.

(10) **1809** A. Henry *Travels* 105 It had been the custom, among all the Indian nations, . . . to make a war-feast, from among the slain. **1899** Cushman *Hist. Indians* 254 Then followed war-feasts, scalp-dances, accompanied with war-songs, and shouts of victory. — (11) **1804** Ordway in *Jrnls. of Lewis & O.* 119 Each of those Musicians had War hoop . . . made of thickest buffelow hides dressed white covered with thin Goat Skin dress[e]d white & ornamented with porcupine quills & feathers. — (12) **1800** Hawkins *Sk. Creek Country* 70 All who go to war, and are in company, when a scalp is taken, get a war name. The leader reports their conduct, and they receive a name accordingly. — (13) **1826** Cooper *Mohicans* xxiii, The young Huron was in his war paint. **1869** Mark Twain *Sk. New & Old* 50 All the blackguards in the country arrive in their war-paint, and proceed to scare me to death with their tomahawks. **1869** Harte *Luck of Roaring Camp* 84 The stranger . . . [brightened] through the color which Red Gulch knew facetiously as her 'war paint.' **1948** *Sat. Ev. Post* 23 Oct. 128/3, I am sorry to see he did not wear a feather bonnet and war paint. — (14) **1755** in J. W. Lydekker *Faithful Mohawks* (1938) 84 He had ye care of providing for all ye War-parties of Indians that went thro' that place [Albany]. **1946** *Sat. Ev. Post* 3 Aug. 81/2 Pass the word back to Mr. Topliff at the gallop! Here's his war party!

(15) **1782** V. B. Howard *Heroes* (1932) 144 On the Southward side below where the War road crosses the said fork. **1822** J. Fowler *Jrnl.* 75 We are now in the Hart of the Inden Country and Emedetly on the great Ware Road. — (16) **1830** Cooper *Water Witch* III. v, I am . . . fitter for the zephyr than the gale—the jest, than the war-shout. **1847** Coyner *Lost Trappers* 174 They raised a dreadful war-shout, and came bounding down the hill. — (17) **1775** Adair *Indians* 386 If they make a plain discovery, either of fresh tracks or of the enemy, they immediately pass the war-signal to each other. **1808** Barker *Indian Princess* II. iii, Tell our chiefs to assemble; and show them the war-signal. — (18) **1775** Adair *Indians* 159 The leader . . . goes three times round his dark winter-house . . . singing the war-song. **1949** *Canadian Alpine Jrnl.* May 32 A quaint old jester . . . enlivened the bivouac by various devices: scalp-dances around a kettle, Cree war songs, wrestling, or jokes in broken English. — (19) **1812** in *Amer. Hist. Rev.* XVII. (July, 1912) 803, I am told that one squaw always goes into a battle and fights as a man, and is denominated the War Squaw.

(20) **1800** Hawkins *Sk. Creek Country* 72 It is not recollected, that more than one half the nation have been for war at the same time; or taken, as they express it, the war talk. **1833** *Sk. D. Crockett* 185 His public harangues, or his war talks, as electioneering speeches are called in the west. **1859** Taliaferro *Fisher's R.* 120 This scrape made me mighty oneasy, and I 'cluded that night to make the big war-talk to Sally, hit ur miss. — (21) **1840** Cooper *Pathfinder* III. iv, Warrior eat, drink, sleep, all time, when don't fight and go on war-trail. **1893** *Harper's Mag.* Dec. 54/2 About young bucks goin' on the war-trail? **1948** Dick *Dixie Frontier* 268 Such training enabled James Robertson to make fourteen round trips from Nashville to North Carolina . . . crossing and recrossing the numerous war trails.

Also *war ax, canoe, chieftain, company, drink, encampment, ford, gourd, ground, halloo, jacket, lock, lodge, mallet, parade, physic, pony, shirt, speech, stick, stone, town, trace, whistle, yell,* etc.

3. In combs. not relating to Indians: (1) * **war baby,** a stock, bond, etc., the value of which is increased as a result of a state of war; (2) **bird,** (*a*) the scarlet tanager, (*b*) prob. an eagle, both *obs.*, cf. **war eagle, warhawk** (*b*); (3) **boom,** an industrial boom brought on by war; (4) **chest,** the funds of a political party available for campaign purposes; (5) **College,** (*a*) a college for giving advanced instruction to experienced U.S. Army officers, also **Army, National War College,** (*b*) **Naval War College,** a similar institution for senior naval officers; (6) **correspondent,** a news reporter with an army during war who reports news from the front, also **war correspondence;** (7) **crop,** a crop calculated to meet wartime needs, *rare;* (8) **daily,** a daily newspaper containing news of a war, *rare;* (9) **Democracy,** *collect.* the War Democrats, *obs.*, cf. next; (10) **Democrat,** one of the Democrats of the North who supported the policies of the administration during the Civil War; (11) **Department,** the military division of the executive branch of the U.S. Government under the charge of the Secretary of War, the Department of War or its headquarters; (12) **dog,** (*a*) (*cap.*) *pl.* a term of abuse for those favoring the War of 1812 (see also quot. 1846), *obs.*, (*b*) a seasoned fighter, a veteran; (13) **fever,** an enthusiasm for war; (14) **governor,** (*a*) a fiery, warlike governor, *obs.*, (*b*) a governor of a state during wartime; (15) **hawk,** see as a main entry; (16) **-making power,** (*a*) the right of Congress, under the provisions of the Constitution (I. viii.), to declare war and to make provisions for the carrying on of war, (*b*) the right of the federal government, as distinguished from the government of an individual state or territory, to declare and carry on war; (17) **man,** one who favored the War of 1812, *obs.*, cf. **war dog** (*a*); (18) **measure,** a law passed, an action taken, or a procedure adopted because of the needs and requirements of war; (19) **office,** the U.S. War Department, *obs.;* (20) **President,** a President of the U.S. during a war; (21) **record,** the facts known or recorded concerning the part played by an individual or a group in a war, a record of success in war; (22) **shark,** = **war man,** *obs.;* (23) **ticket,** a political party ticket indorsed by those favoring war, *obs.*

(1) **1921** *Unpartizan Rev.* Jan.–Mar. 209 Protection for war-babies and organized labor is good old-fashioned Republican doctrine. **1948** *Green Bay* (Wis.) *Press-Gaz.* 13 July 4/2 The idle rich of Europe . . . clamored for war while they invested great amounts in American war babies and reaped superlative profits. — (2) (*a*) **1836** Traill *Backwoods* 214, I was a little amused by the appearance of one of these Indian Cupids, adorned with the wings of the American war-bird; a very beautiful creature, something like our British bullfinch, only far more lively in plumage: the breast and under-feathers of the wings being a tint of the most brilliant carmine, shaded with black and white. This bird has been called the 'war-bird,' from its having first made its appearance in this province during the late American war; a fact that I believe is well authenticated, or at any rate has obtained general credence. (*b*) **1855** Longfellow *Hiawatha* 120 Then began the greatest battle. . . . That the war-birds ever witnessed. — (3) **1891** *Cent. Mag.* Jan. 426/1 In a sagging market the colonel would be better than a war boom. **1947** *Christian Sci. Mon.* 1 March 6/1 A war-boom shipyard city, Richmond's elementary school enrollment has risen. — (4) **1901** *Nation* 21 Nov. 389/1 A corporation has no politics. If it pretends to have, the politics is clearly only a form of business, and gifts to the party war-chest are merely an investment. **1948** *Time* 9 Feb. 38/1 Delegates also started a war chest to buy newspaper space and radio time.

(5) (*a*) **1903** Roosevelt in *Laying Cornerstone Army War College Bldg.* 9 The Secretary of War [took] . . . the first practical step toward giving the Army a war college. **1946** *Newsweek* 16 Sep. 34/1 One of the most important new institutions in Washington is the National War College. **1948** *Chi. D. News* 12 Oct. 12/7 The Soviets certainly have plans—as we do—in case of war with any specific enemy. Both states maintain war colleges. (*b*) **1894** *Naval War Coll. Abstract of Courses* 3 The summer course at the Naval War College began on the 13th of June. — (6) **1861** Browne *Four Years in Secessia* (1865) 15 Since the first gun discharged at Fort Sumter awoke the American world to arms, War Correspondence on this side of the Atlantic has been as much an avocation as practising law or selling dry goods. *Ib.* 14 The War Correspondent is the outgrowth of a very modern civilization. **1950** *Sat. Ev. Post* 4 Feb. 58/4 Soon El Paso, from which war correspondents had long been date-lining their dispatches, found itself flooded by some 40,000 National Guardsmen. — (7) **1862** *N.Y.*

Tribune 28 June 8 He has planted a 'war crop' consisting of . . . twenty acres in potatoes, and half an acre in the Texas Mosquit or Musketo Grass. — **(8) 1896** *Typog. Jrnl.* IX. 263 Selling 'war' dailies at 25 and 50 cents a copy, he next entered a district printing concern. — **(9) 1864** in LOGAN *Great Conspiracy* 576 We are told . . . of a War Democracy . . . found in the Union ranks bearing arms in support of the Government.

(10) 1863 *Chi. Tribune* 7 Jan. 2/2 We have yet to see the 'copperhead' journal that is not filled, day after day, with articles bitterly denunciatory of the President, his Cabinet, the Republican Party, the War Democrats, and the Abolitionists. **1896** *Cong. Rec.* 24 March 3159/1 As a War Democrat I voted for General Grant, the nominee for the Presidency in 1868. — **(11) 1789** *Ann. 1st Congress* 369 We may then go to the consideration of the War Department and the Department of Foreign Affairs. **1944** *Time* 2 Oct. 19/1 This was strictly a military document drafted by the War Department. — **(12)** *(a)* **1813** *Columbian Centinel* 23 Oct. 2/1 His reward from the War-dogs will be, that he will be hurled from office without concern or ceremony. **1846** *Cong. Globe* 18 April 687/1 The gentleman regarded 54° 40′ men as 'war-hawks' and 'war dogs!' *(b)* **1825** COOPER *L. Lincoln* viii, A great war-dog is that old man, your honour. **1895** REMINGTON *Pony Tracks* 33 'Stand 'em off,' replies the war-dog. — **(13) 1812** *Steele P.* II. 668 The late report of the Secty. of the Treasy. will probably cool the war fever in some [people]. **1884** *Cent. Mag.* Nov. 107 It was the news that the Sixth Massachusetts regiment had been mobbed by roughs on their passage through Baltimore which gave me the war fever. — **(14)** *(a)* **1775** ADAIR *Indians* 144 One [white man] . . . was deputed by the whimsical war-governor of Georgia, to awe the traders into an obedience of his despotic power. *(b)* **1884** BLAINE *20 Years of Congress* I. 305 The governors of the free States . . . became popularly known as the 'War Governors,' and they exercised a beneficent and decisive influence upon the fortunes of the Union. **1925** BRYAN *Memoirs* 72 Richard Yates, son of Illinois' 'war governor,' . . . was the city attorney.

(16) *(a)* **1833** *Niles' Reg.* XLIV. 148/1 Very few persons questioned the right of congress to lay an embargo, under the war-making power. **1859** BUCHANAN in *Pres. Mess. & P.* V. 569 The grant of this authority . . . would be a transfer of the war-making, or, strictly, the war-declaring, power to the Executive. *(b)* **1848** POLK in *Ib.* IV. 598 The General Government, possessing exclusively the war-making power, had the right to take military possession of this disputed territory. — **(17) 1814** *Columbian Centinel* 11 June 2/4 The War-men in Washington appear determined to have some more blood shed before Peace takes place. — **(18) 1808** W. EATON in *Life* (1813) 414 The Embargo was contemplated as a war measure. **1918** *New Internat. Yrbk.* 716/1 The chief war measure of the government introduced in Congress was a bill 'to increase temporarily the military establishment of the United States.' — **(19) 1776** *Jrnls. Cont. Congress* IV. 85 Resolved, That a committee of 7 be appointed to consider the propriety of establishing a war office. **1808** *Ann. 10th Congress* 1 Sess. 2081, I was referred from the War office to the Treasury Office.

(20) 1886 LOGAN *Great Conspiracy* 644 The early beams of the morrow's sun touched . . . the lifeless remains of the great War-President and Liberator. — **(21) 1890** CUSTER *Following Guidon* 2 They longed individually and as a regiment for a war 'record.' **1904** TARBELL *Hist. Standard Oil Co.* I. 31 The soldier . . . was welcomed into oil companies, stock being given him for the value of his war record. — **(22) 1813** *Columbian Centinel* 1 Sep. 2/1 The whole [story] has been published, republished, and swallowed as matter of fact by our war sharks. — **(23) 1812** *Salem Gaz.* 20 Oct. 3/2 The Hon. Mr. Goddard, of Portsmouth, was at first placed upon the *War Ticket* for Election.

b. Also (1) **war star,** (2) **tent,** (3) **widow,** (4) **woman,** (see **2.** (13) *(b)* above).

(1) 1890 J. JEFFERSON *Autobiog.* 322 A 'war star' . . . was the technical term given by the old legitimate stars and actors to satirize those self-lighted luminaries who had flickered during the national strife and who had gone out after the cessation of hostilities. — **(2) 1895** REMINGTON *Pony Tracks* 50 The Sibley tepees or the 'white man's war tents,' as the Indians call them. — **(3) 1877** BARTLETT 261 During the rush to California, 1850 to 1860, . . . the new-found treasures of that country separated . . . many husbands from their wives. During the late war such were termed war-widows.

4. In phrases: (1) *War between the North and South, War between the States, War for Southern Independence,* the American Civil War; (2) *War of 1812,* the war between the U.S. and Great Britain, 1812–1815; (3) *War of* (or *for*) *Independence,* *(a)* the American Revolution, *(b)* the struggle of the Spanish possessions in North America for independence from Spain, *(c) second War of Independence,* the American Civil War; (4) *War of the gauges,* the controversy concerning the merits of the standard gauge and the narrow gauge in railroad track, *humorous;* (5) *War of Iniquity,* the War of 1812, *obs.;* (6) *War of Secession,* the American Civil War; (7) *War of the Rebellion,* =prec.; (8) *War of the Revolution,* the Revolutionary War; (9) *to make war medicine,* of an Indian, to engage in a ceremonial calculated to secure supernatural assistance in war, *transf.,* to become belligerent and aggressive, also allusive; (10) *to strike the war pole,* see **2.** (10) above; (11) *to go on the war trail,* see **2. b.** (21) above.

(1) 1900 *Cong. Rec.* 9 Feb. 1674/2 [There is not] the slightest feeling on my part against the men who fought on the Northern side in the war between the North and South. **1900** H. ROBERTSON *Red Blood & Blue* 283 Since the war between the States, until now, the Stars and Stripes had been rarely seen in the town. **1949** *Fla. Hist. Quart.* Jan. 216 Bloxham enlisted first in the War for Southern Independence on April 2, 1861, as a private in Captain R. B. Hilton's company. **1949** *Ward Co. Independent* (Minot, N.D.) 21 July 12/7 A Republican president, William Howard Taft, . . . elevated to the chief justiceship, Justice White—not only a Democrat but a man who had served in the Confederate army during the War Between the States. — **(2) 1833** T. DWIGHT *Hist. Hartford Convention* 233 Such is a brief history of the origin and causes of the war of 1812. **1948** *Sat. Review* 19 June 25/1 In that curious struggle known as the War of 1812, America's mediocre record in land battles was offset by the brilliant performance of her small navy. — **(3)** *(a)* **1832** DUNLAP *Hist. Amer. Theatre* 45 The rocky foundation protruded, until the earth of the hill . . . was brought down, since the war of independence, to cover [the ramparts]. **1944** JOHNSON *As I Dare* 4 She remembered her Grandmother Mead in Connecticut, whose husband fought in the war for independence. *(b)* **1848** *Santa Fe Repub.* 3 May 1/2 It was not until the mother country, herself, became temporarily subjected to a foreign power, that the war of Independence was successfully commenced in her possessions on this continent. *(c)* **1861** *Alexandria* (Va.) *Gaz.* 2 May 3/1 This old flag, especially, can never serve again so good a purpose in this, our second War of Independence. — **(4) 1854** *La Crosse Democrat* 14 Feb. 2/5 It is hoped that the war of the gauges is ended.

(5) 1813 *Columbian Centinel* (Boston) 7 April 2/2 Mr. Gallatin's second attempt to obtain cash to carry on the War of Iniquity, has confirmed him that the money holders are determined to let his Loan alone. — **(6) 1868** *N.Y. Herald* 31 July 4/5 M. Chevnier . . . [attempted] a parallel between the War of Independence and the War of Secession. **1907** *Harper's Mag.* Feb. 380 The War of Secession . . . [caused] a large number of Southern officers to leave the service. — **(7) 1873** *Newton Kansan* 6 March 2/2 The Committee did not underrate the great services of the soldiers and sailors of the war of the rebellion in preserving our free-institutions. **1948** *Chi. Tribune* 29 Feb. 1. 6/3 The library has the 127 volumes of the War of the Rebellion Official Records. — **(8) 1833** P. HONE *Diary* I. (1889) 77 He was a gallant and distinguished officer in the War of the Revolution. **1943** A. E. LOMAX *Old Washington Diary* (Preface) (We.), He served in the army of the war of the Revolution without pay. — **(9) 1805** CLARK in *Lewis & C. Exped.* I. (1904) 247 Some of our Men go to See a War Medeson made at the Village. **1893** *Chi. Tribune* 28 April 4/1 Gov. Altgeld . . . proceeded to administer a dose of war medicine he had been making for some time. **1906** *N.Y. Ev. Post* 8 May 1 Senator Dolliver was outside the breastworks, making war-medicine and refusing to be pacified.

As the last term in **alum, ante-, Broad-seal, Buckshot, cattle, Civil, Creek, Dorr, fence, Florida, Helderberg, hot water, Indian, Kansas, Madison's, Messiah, Mexican, Mormon, Navaho, Nez Percé, race, range, rate, Revolutionary, schooner-of-, Secretary of, Seminole, Sioux, Spanish-American, Spanish-Cuban, tong, Utah war.**

war bag. 1. =**war budget.** *Obs.* **2.** Among cowboys and lumbermen, a bag for supplies, money, etc., a duffle bag *q.v.* Also transf.

(1) 1820 *Western Rev.* II. 48 After the action is over, each person returns his war bag to the commander of the party. — **(2) 1897** A. H. LEWIS *Wolfville* 33 S'pose you-alls gropes about in your war-bags an' sees. **1908** MCGAFFEY *Show-Girl* 197, I plant one century in my war bag [i.e., stocking] and seven to two on the next with the other three. **1949** *Boston Globe Mag.* 25 Dec. 1/4, I don't want to pack this war-bag along.

***warble,** *v. intr.* (See quot. 1890.) Also **warbling,** *n.* — **1880** MARK TWAIN *Tramp Abroad* 289 The famous Alpine *jodel* . . . was that sort of quaint commingling of baritone and falsetto which at home we call 'Tyrolese warbling.' **1890** WEBSTER 1626/3 *Warble,* . . . to sing with sudden changes from chest to head tones; to yodel.

* **warbler,** *n.* Any one of numerous small, insect-eating birds of the family Compsothlypidae.

1835 AUDUBON *Ornith. Biog.* III. 177 Some of the Warblers had begun to think of removing farther south. **1907** *St. Nicholas* May 648/2 Whether the bird to be sketched be the laziest heron or the most animated warbler it is always best to allow for its changing position or flying away. **1917** *Birds of Amer.* III. 111 As a rule the Warblers are birds of beautiful plumage. **1950** *Chi. Tribune* 8 May 1/6 The warblers, tiny, brightly colored mites that seem to flit to another twig before anyone can get a good look, are beginning to go thru in numbers, too.

As the last term in **Audubon's, autumnal, azure, bay-breasted, black and white creeping, blackburnian, blue, blue yellow-backed, Canada, Cape May, carbonated, cerulean, Children's, Connecticut, golden, Grace's, hemlock, hermit, hooded, Kentucky, Kirtland's, Lawrence's, Lucy's, MacGillivray's, magnolia, mourning, mourning ground, myrtle, Nashville, New York, orange-crowned, palm, parula, pine, prairie, prothonotary, red poll, rose, ruby-crowned, small-headed, speckled Canada, spotted Canada, summer, swamp, sycamore, Townsend, Vigors', Virginia, wagtail, western palm, Wilson's, Wilson's black cap, wood, worm-eating, yellow, yellow-backed, yellow-crowned, yellow palm, yellow-throat, yellow-throated warbler.**

warbling vireo. A sweet-singing vireo, *Vireo gilvus.* Cf. **western warbling vireo.**

1839 PEABODY *Mass. Birds* 299 The Warbling Vireo . . . [is] unwearied in its various and animated warble. **1878** COUES *Birds Colo. Valley* 503 The Warbling Vireo is no less agile a bird than his cousin the Red-eye, and equally tireless in the pursuit of his insect prey. **1940** TODD *Birds Western Pa.* 483/2 The winter range of the Warbling Vireo has not been fully determined.

* **ward,** *n.*

1. "A territorial division in the Mormon Church for purposes of ecclesiastical government. It is the administrative unit, with an executive head called a bishop" (*Cent. Supp.*). Also attrib.

1859 *Mountaineer* (Salt Lake City) 27 Aug. 2/4 If the water-masters of our district or ward will see that we have a double portion of water during the ensuing week for our garden, we will now agree not to mention them again. **1878** BEADLE *Western Wilds* 332 The ward teachers had reported every case of real or supposed heresy. *Ib.* 348 Bishop Warren was . . . thanking the Mormon 'Lord,' in the ward assembly rooms. **1947** *This Week Mag.* 18 July 4/3 You can always spot a Mormon community by the long, straight rows of Lombardy poplars the pioneers brought West . . . and by the big Church with its adjoining 'Ward House'—a combination social hall, dance floor, baseball court, concert hall, and little theater.

2. In special combs.: (1) **ward boss,** a political party henchman in charge of the party's interests in a ward; (2) **bummer,** =**ward heeler;** (3) **chap,** =prec.; (4) **club,** a place where ward meetings are held; (5) **committee,** a group of persons representing the party organization in a ward, also **ward committeeman;** (6) **convention,** =**ward meeting;** (7) **heeler,** a political hanger-on of a ward boss; (8) **man,** (see quot.); (9) **meeting,** a meeting of the party members or party workers of a ward; (10) **politician,** one who takes part in the political activities of a ward; (11) **politics,** the political activities and interests of a ward, participation in such activities; (12) **porterhouse,** =**ward club,** *rare;* (13) * **room,** a room used for meetings or political activities of a ward, also attrib.; (14) **school,** a public school which serves the needs of a ward; (15) **striker,** a thug employed by the political leaders in a ward.

(1) 1890 T. ROOSEVELT *Wks.* XIV. (1926) 110 Many forces . . . combine to produce the ward boss, the district heeler, the boodle alderman. **1948** *Sat. Ev. Post* 3 July 16/2 When one ward boss heard the decision, he remarked, 'Well, half a loaf is better than none.' — **(2) 1872** *Chi. Tribune* 18 Oct. 4/3 Nor is the fact that a ward-bummer is in favor of suppressing the Rebellion . . . any proof that he will not steal the city's money if he gets a chance. — **(3) 1872** *Chi. Tribune* 17 Oct. 2/3, I do not mean any person in responsible management, but the ward-chaps, and those who run for the Legislature and expect no higher. — **(4) 1883** HAY *Bread-Winners* 247 There was not an Irish laborer . . . but knew his way to his ward club as well as to mass.

(5) 1807 IRVING *Salmagundi* xi. 267 The secretaries of the ward committees strut about looking like wooden oracles. **1922** MERRIAM *Amer. Party System* 70 Each of the thirty-five wards [in Chicago] elects by direct vote of the party in a primary a ward committeeman for a term of four years. — **(6) 1882** MCCABE *New York* 124 The immense Irish population . . . controls the primary meetings, the ward conventions, and even the greater political bodies. — **(7) 1888** *N.Y. Herald* 1 Nov. 9/4 A band succeeded them and preceded . . . a lot of ward heelers and 'floaters in blocks of five.' **1950** *Chi. Tribune* 27 March 1/2 He said that the census bureau is violating the constitutional rights of the American people when it 'sends 168,000 political hacks and ward heelers . . . to snoop into the people's finances.' — **(8) 1909** *Cent. Supp.* 1430/3 *Wardman,* . . . a precinct detective, particularly in New York City. — **(9) 1806** *Balance* V. 362/1 The sentiments . . . have met the approbation of the several federal ward meetings. **1883** HAY *Bread-Winners* 247 Hardly a millionaire . . . knew where the ward meetings of his party were held.

(10) 1807 IRVING *Salmagundi* iv. 84 He, however, maintained as mysterious a countenance as a Seventh Ward politician. **1904** *N.Y. Ev. Post* 27 July 2 The new chairman is a magnificent ward politician of much native ability and considerable personal magnetism. — **(11)** *Cent. Mag.* Aug. 581/2 He had been a little alarmed at the sudden irruption of such men as Farnham and his associates into the field of ward politics. **1923** HERRICK *Lilla* 103 He's quite a figure in ward politics. — **(12) 1807** IRVING *Salmagundi* xv. 409 Dabble was now very frequent . . . in his visits to those temples of politicks, popularity and smoke, the ward porter-houses. — **(13) 1872** HOLMES *Poet* 218 When they become voters, if they ever do, it may be feared that the pews will lose what the ward-rooms gain. *Ib.* 323 The sting which would be fatal to a literary *debutante* only wakes the eloquence of the pachydermatous ward-room politician to a fiercer shriek of declamation. **1889** BRAYLEY *Boston Fire Dept.* 154 The inhabitants had been warmed to the matter by the patriotic harangues in the ward-rooms. — **(14) 1818** *Niles' Reg.* XIV. 174/1 Neither the people, nor their representatives, would agree to the plan of assessment on the wards for the expenses of the ward schools. **1904** STRATTON-PORTER *Freckles* 15 They sent me out to the nearest ward school as long as the law would let them.

(15) 1894 *S.F. Midwinter Appeal* 27 Jan. 2/1 Spreckels, a ward-striker and ballot-stuffer in S.F., came down here and had a confab with Joe Harvey, the faro man.

As the last term in **fire, fish, police-jury ward.**

war-dance, *v. intr.* To engage in actions resembling those of an Indian war dance.

1894 *Outing* XXIV. 446/2 Bond an' the Injun sorter war-danced round it fur quite a spell. **1895** *Ib.* XXVI. 441/2 We swung the fire-sticks and war-danced wildly around the fight. **1923** *Nation* 29 Aug. 218/2 Those who have seen his descendants, war-dancing at hotels in Glacier Park . . . should read this beautiful and Arcadian story.

* **warden,** *n.*

1. *Rhode Island.* A town officer having duties similar to those of a justice of the peace.

1662 *Providence Rec.* XV. 88 To the Warden or Deputty Warden of The Towne of Prouidence. **1672** *R.I. Col. Rec.* II. 467 The said elected and engadged persons shall be called Wardens. **1842** *R.I. Constitution* X. § 7, The towns of New Shoreham and Jamestown may continue to elect wardens as heretofore.

2. A representative or an official of a ward.

1763 J. ADAMS *Diary* Wks. II. 144 Selectmen, assessors, collectors, wardens, fire-wards, and representatives, are regularly chosen [by the Caucus Club] before they are chosen in the town. **1789** MORSE *Amer. Geog.* 428 Charleston was . . . divided into 13 wards, who choose as many wardens, who, from among themselves, elect an intendant of the city. **1822** *Boston Charter* § 3 It shall be the duty of such warden to preside at all meetings of the citizens of such ward.

3. One of several officials in Philadelphia with responsibilities including the supervision of the night watch. *Obs.*

1771 *Phila. Ordinances* 36 Jacob Winey, Moore Furman, and Joshua Humphreys, gentlemen, . . . are hereby styled wardens. **1789** *Ib.* 74 The city wardens . . . [and] the commissioners . . . shall no longer continue in office.

4. *Conn.* The chief executive officer in a borough.

1841 *Conn. Public Acts* 7 The Warden and Burgesses of said Borough shall have power to form and continue an additional Fire Company for the further protection of the property of said Borough. **1904** *Hartford Courant* 18 Aug. 9 No other democrat in town can carry the borough for warden.

5. =**firewarden.**

1852 *Conn. Public Acts* 60 All persons who shall be engineers or wardens of any fire department . . . [shall] be exempt from serving as jurors. **1905** *Forestry Bureau Bul.* No. 60, 28 The ranger or warden could do much work on the trails when there was no danger from fires.

6. An official responsible for the enforcement of laws respecting game, a fish or game warden.

1870 *Dept. Agric. Rep. 1869* 520 The State commissioners on the fisheries recommend . . . the appointment of . . . a board of wardens for each river basin. **1883** GOODE *Fishery Industries U.S.* 83 It was impossible for any warden under the statute of the State of Maine to approach him.

As the last term in **county, fire, fish, fishing, moose, Sabbath, state game, tree warden.**

wardrobe trunk. An upright trunk having space to hang garments, and drawers or compartments for other articles.

1890 BIFF HALL *Turnover Club* 221 In Matt's wardrobe trunks there are very many suits. **1923** WATTS *L. Nichols* 242 Wardrobe-trunks and hat-boxes were hauled from the attic. **1947** *Reader's Digest* Oct. 155/1 And in the middle of it all sat an expensive wardrobe trunk.

Ward('s) willow. A small broad-leaved tree discovered about 1880 near Washington, D.C., by L. F. Ward and now recognized as a variety of the coastal plain willow, *Salix longipes wardi.*

[**1881** L. F. WARD *Flora of Washington* 114, I have observed this variety of *S. nigra* as far up the river as Great Falls.] **1897** SUDWORTH *Arborescent Flora* 119 *Salix wardi.* . . . Ward Willow. **1901** MOHR *Plant Life Ala.* 465 *Salix wardi.* . . . Ward's Willow. . . . District of Columbia west to Missouri, south to western Florida and Indian Territory.

∗**ware,** *n.* As the last term in **flat, hard, stem, tin, willow ware.**

∗**warehouse,** *n.* As the last term in **cotton, fish, log, seed, slave, tobacco warehouse.**

war hawk.

1. One who is eager for war. Also attrib.

1798 JEFFERSON *Writings* X. 33 At present, the war hawks talk of septembrizing, deportation, and the examples for quelling sedition set

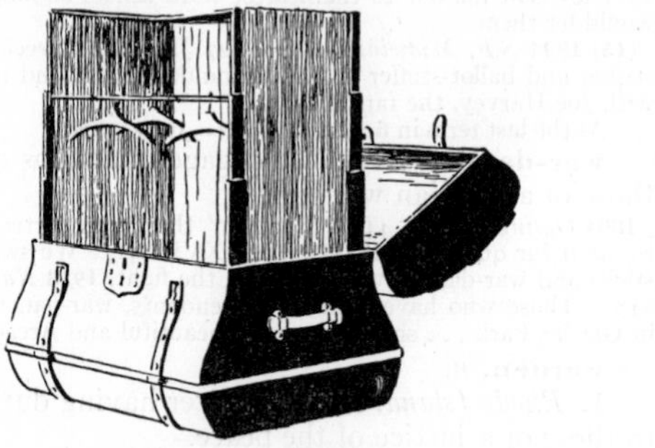

Wardrobe trunk *c*1875

by the French executive. **1846** *Cong. Globe* 18 April 687/1 The gentleman regarded 54° 40′ men as 'war-hawks' and 'war-dogs!' **1950** *Time* 6 March 98/3 In 1811 he became Henry Clay's lieutenant in the raucous young 'War Hawk' faction which whooped for war against Britain.

2. A bird of war. Also transf.

1829 IRVING *Conquest of Granada* (1850) 350 These fierce warriors were nestled, like so many war-hawks, about their lofty cliff. **1865** PARKMAN *Pioneers of France* 308 The Indian tribes, war-hawks of the wilderness, . . . infested with their scalping parties the streams and pathways of the forest.

∗**warm,** *a.* In combs.: (1) **warm air furnace,** a furnace which gives out heat by causing the circulation of heated air; (2) **blood,** unmixed thoroughbred blood, pure descent; (3) **slaw,** (see quot. and cf. "cold slaw," variant of **coleslaw**); (4) **spring,** see as a main entry.

(**1**) **1846** *Catholic Herald* (Phila.) 30 Aug. 272/3 Warm Air Furnaces, Kitchen Ranges, Gas Ovens, Bath Boilers, Grates, Stoves, &c. **1886** J. A. PORTER *New Stand. Guide Washington* 208 Chas. G. Ball & Son, . . . Warm-Air Furnaces. — (**2**) **1868** *Iowa State Agric. Soc. Rep. 1867* 120 With the exception of the one [stallion], there is not a drop of 'warm blood' in them. **1883** *Harper's Mag.* Oct. 724/2 The descendants of these [thoroughbred horses] constituted a stock of 'warm blood.' — (**3**) **1796** F. BAILY *Tour* 136 A dish of stewed pork was served up, accompanied with some hot pickled cabbage, called in this part of the country [a Dutch household in Pa.] 'warm slaw.'

warm spring.

1. A spring the water of which is exceptionally warm. Usu. *pl.* and often as a place-name.

1748 WASHINGTON *Diaries* I. 6 We this day call'd to see y. Fam'd Warm Springs. **1776** in *Amer. Sp.* XV. 407/2 A town at Warm Springs. **1837** A. SHERWOOD *Gaz. Georgia* (ed. 3) 203 The largest warm spring flows out of a spur of the Pine mountain. **1885** *Wkly. New Mexican Rev.* 16 April 4/3 The city of Socorro has been restrained . . . from using or interfering with the ojo caliente or warm spring there. **1950** *Asheville* (N.C.) *Citizen-Times* 26 March III. 2/8 The Warm Springs in Madison County were bought in 1886 by the Southern Improvement Company and the name was officially changed to Hot Springs.

2. Warm Springs Apache(s), (see quot. 1910).

1886 *Outing* April 53 Ka-e-te-na or Gait-en-eh, head chief Warm Springs Apaches. **1910** HODGE *Amer. Indians* II. 916/2 Warm Spring Apache. So called from their former residence at the Ojo Caliente, or Warm Springs, in s.w. N. Mex., near the extreme headwaters of Gila r. . . . Some of them are on the Mescalero res., N. Mex.

3. Warm Springs Indians, tribes, (see quot. 1910).

1910 HODGE *Amer. Indians* II. 916/2 Warm Springs Indians. A term used to denote the different tribes resident on Warm Springs res., Oreg., most of whom were placed there under the Wasco treaty of 1855. The chief tribes of the reservation are Wasco, Paiute, Tenino, and Tygh. **1948** *Sat. Review* 15 May 30/2 There are also a number of Indians of the Nez Perce, Warm Springs, and Umatilla tribes who . . . still fish in Celilo Falls for chinook salmon.

∗**warm,** *v.* **1.** *To warm over,* to heat again cooked food that has become cold; also, *fig.*, to revive or reinvigorate, also **warmed-over,** *a.* **2.** ∗*To warm up,* (see quot.). *Obs.* **3. warm-up,** *n.* the power of generating enthusiasm. *Rare.*

(**1**) **1879** HOLMES *J. L. Motley* 162 [They] took up the old exceptions, [and] warmed them over into grievances. **1887** *Nation* 2 June 465/3 They will be spared the future bitterness of finding . . . themselves treated to insult and warmed-over excuses. **1916** BOWER *Phantom Herd* 246 He had a midnight supper of warmed-over coffee and cold bean sandwiches. — (**2**) **1874** McCOY *Cattle Trade* 244 This style, or manner of wintering cattle, is called 'Roughing,' and the feeding of corn in the spring is termed 'Warming up.' — (**3**) **1883** MARK TWAIN *Life on Miss.* iii, The song didn't seem to have much warm-up to it.

∗**warmer,** *n.* As the last term in **bed, bench, pulse warmer.**

warmouth ˈwɔrˌmauθ, *n.* [Origin unknown.] A fresh-water fish, *Chaenobryttus gulosus,* of the eastern states. Also attrib. and with defining term.

1883 *Nat. Museum Bul.* No. 27, 461 War-mouth; Red-eyed Bream. War-mouth Perch; Yaw-mouth. Eastern United States from Virginia to Florida. **1884** GOODE *Fisheries* I. 405 The Black Warmouth . . . abounds in the tributaries of the Upper Mississippi. **1903** T. H. BEAN *Fishes N.Y.* 470 The body of the warmouth is heavy and deep. **1948** *Dly. Ardmoreite* (Ardmore, Okla.) 23 April 7/3 Dressing pan fish (crappie, calico bass, warmouth bass, rock bass or goggle-eyes, blue-gill, red ears, perch and small bass) is no trick at all if you follow these suggestions.

∗**warn,** *v.* ∗*To warn out,* of a N. Eng. town government: To serve official notice upon (a person) to withdraw from a town (see quot. 1911). *Obs.*

1758 in G. SHELDON *Hist. Deerfield, Mass.* (1895) I. 592 Voted that the Selectmen be directed to warn the two children of Margaret Choulton out of Town Immediately. **1770** in *Pub. Col. Soc.* XXVI. 20 November 14, 1770, Moses McEntosh Last from the Castel he has lived in Several towns in the Country or Provance But has been warned in his Majestys Name out of them all He says he was warned out of Boston abote 17 years ago By 2 men in Boston But he says he was born in Dedham warned in his Majestys name to Depart this town of Boston in 14 Days. **1911** J. H. BENTON *Warning Out* 116 The effect of warning out as thus practised upon persons who remained in the town after being warned was to relieve the town from all obligation to aid them if they became poor and in need of help or support.

∗**warning,** *n.* **1.** (See quot. 1851.) *Obs.* **2.** A drink. *Rare.*

(**1**) **1836** *Harvardiana* III. 98 Sadly I feel I should have been saved by numerous warnings. **1851** HALL *College Words* 309 When it is ascertained that a student is not living in accordance with the laws of the institution, he is usually informed of the fact by a *warning,* as it is called, from one of the faculty, which consists merely of friendly caution and advice. — (**2**) **1908** LORIMER *J. Spurlock* 245 The Major looked out at the suburbs of Baltimore over his before-luncheon 'warning.'

warpath ˈwɔrˌpæθ, *n.*

1. A path or way regularly used by Indians in going to war. *Obs.*

1755 L. EVANS *Anal. Map Colonies* 29 Canoes may come up to the Crossing of the War Path. **1821** NUTTALL *Travels Arkansa* 104 These extensive and convenient routes . . . were their war and hunting-paths. **1852** WATSON *Nights in Block-House* 148 They travelled all that night on the war-path leading towards Wheeling.

b. *fig.* War, a war expedition. Now *hist.*

1808 BARKER *Indian Princess* II. iii, I bring my father to the bloody war-path. **1881** *Rep. Indian Affairs* 127 The war-path will thus be abandoned, and the white and red man be at peace. **1948** *Nat. Geog. Mag.* Aug. 216/2 A party of thirty odd Indians returning from the warpath also were at Cresap's.

c. (See quot.)

1907 *Springfield W. Republican* 14 March 1 The freak thoroughfare, which was called 'the midway' at Chicago and 'the pike' at St. Louis, will be called at Jamestown 'the warpath.'

2. (1) *on the warpath,* of Indians: on a war expedition, also transf.; (2) *to go* (or *be out*) *on the warpath,* to engage in war, to begin hostilities.

(1) **1827** COOPER *Prairie* viii, Their discretion was still too doubtful to permit them to be trusted on the war-path. **1880** MARK TWAIN *Tramp Abroad* 345 (R.), She was on the war-path all the evening. **1948** *Chi. D. News* 18 March 20/7 We perpetually try to transfix ourselves on bigger and better warpaths. — (2) **1826** COOPER *Mohicans* xxviii, His nation would not go on the war-path, because they did not think it well. **1871** DE VERE 36 [The word] war-path . . . has led to the use of the phrase, he is out on the war-path, for a man who is about to make a deliberate attack on an adversary or a measure. **1929** J. PARKER *Old Army* 152 On May 17 at sunset came the news that he had gone on the Warpath.

* **warrant,** *n.*

1. =**land warrant.** Also attrib.

1636 *Md. Hist. Mag.* III. 158 A warrant to Capt. Henry ffleete for the 4000 Acres of Land due to him. **1783** in *Travels Amer. Col.* 669 The 1000 acre warrant survey . . . nearly joined Spangliss line. **1792** IMLAY *Western Territory* 13 After this period (i.e. 1781), a land office was opened by the state, granting warrants for any quantity of unlocated land. **1812** MARSHALL *Kentucky* 113 The warrant, in every instance, was an order to the surveyor, to lay off the quantity of land expressed, for the party.

2. A formal notice of the calling of a town meeting, with a statement of the business to be considered.

1644 *Portsmouth Rec.* 32 It is ordered . . . that the business of such meetinge dayes shalbe specified in the warrant of warninge to the meetinge. **1875** HOLLAND *Sevenoaks* 23 He read this article of the warrant, posted in the public places. **1914** *Cyclo. Amer. Govt.* III. 542/2 A warrant . . . is posted in a public place, or mailed to the voters before the meeting; and no business can be transacted which is not mentioned in the warrant.

3. a. warrant machinist, in the U.S. Navy, a warrant officer serving as assistant to the engineer officer. *Obs.* **b. warrant trying,** (see quot. 1859).

(**a**) **1899** *U.S. Navy Dept. Ann. Rep.* 19 Section 14 . . . authorized the appointment of 100 warrant machinists. **1902** *Mo. Rev.* Aug. 93 Admiral Melville, in his report dealing with the warrant machinists of the U.S. Navy, says [etc.]. — (**b**) **1829** *Va. Lit. Museum* 185 His compliance was used as a justification for his attending a quarter race, a shooting match, a warrant trying, or a deer hunt. **1859** BARTLETT 502 *Warrant-Trying*, the magistrates' monthly courts at the cross-roads. Virginia. **1877** BAGBY *Old Va. Gentleman* 11 Of church-going on Sunday, when the girls kept the carriage waiting; of warrant-tryings, vendues, election and general muster days.

As the last term in **land, land office, land office treasury, military land, soldier's, state, treasury warrant.**

* **warrant,** *v.* **1.** *tr.* To issue a warrant against (a person). **2. warranted land,** land held by virtue of a land warrant. Both *obs.* or *rare.* — (1) **1818** *Niles' Reg.* XIII. 406/1 You would be warranted or sued one hundred times every day. — (2) **1774** *Pa. Gazette* 14 Dec. Supp. 2/3 To be sold. . . . Four tracts of warranted land . . . about 25 miles from Pittsburgh.

warranty ˈwɔrəntɪ, *v. tr.* To convey (land) with a covenant of warranty. *Rare.* — **1742** *Md. Hist. Mag.* XX. 264 Being obliged to Warrantee the Land called Hampton Court to Edward Flannigan [etc.].

warranty deed. A deed in which there is a covenant of warranty. Also fig. — **1779** E. PARKMAN *Diary* 106 His son in law had beguiled him to give a Warrantee Deed of his Place. **1866** RICHARDSON *Secret Service* 188 Think of giving a man a warranty-deed for his own body and soul.

* **warrior,** *n.*

1. *pl. transf.* The members of Tammany Hall. *Obs.*

1812 *Salem Gaz.* 5 June 3/3 The Warriors of the Democratic Tribe will hold a powow at Agawam on Tuesday next. **1861** *N.Y. Herald* 4 July 5/3 The chiefs, sachems and warriors will assemble in the Great Wigwam at twelve o'clock, noon, precisely, for the transaction of business.

2. Warriors' Path, any one of various paths (see quots.) used by Indian warriors. Now *hist.*

1770 WASHINGTON *Diaries* I. 425 At the Mouth of this Ck . . . is the Warriors Path to the Cherokee Country. **1910** HODGE *Amer. Indians* II. 801/1 The great highway leading from Cumberland gap to the mouth of the Scioto was known as the Warriors' Path. **1943** PEATTIE *Great Smokies* 27 One [trading path] led from Virginia west of the mountains, to the Overhill Cherokees by a 'warriors' path' that ran from present-day Roanoke, Virginia, and the Shenandoah, to Chattanooga, Tennessee.

As the last term in **black, buck, dog, great, head, Indian, Mohawk, Snake warrior.**

warsaw ˈwɔrsɔ, *n.* [Sp. *guasa*, in Amer. Sp. sense shown here.] (See quot.) — **1884** GOODE *Fisheries* I. 411 The Black Grouper . . . is at Pensacola known by the name 'Warsaw,' evidently a corruption of the Spanish name 'Guasa.'

warted squash. A variety, *Cucurbita verrucosa*, of winter squash having a warted rind. — **1834** DARLINGTON *Flora Cestrica* 556 Warted Squash. Long Squash. **1847** ——— *Weeds & Plants* 143 Warted Squash. Long-necked Squash. . . . Apt to produce worthless Hybrids among Pumpkins, when growing near them.

war whoop.

1. =**Indian war whoop.**

The meaning of the term as used in the first quot. is uncertain.

[**1725** in *Travels Amer. Col.* 143 About seven of the clock in the Evening came in here the Warr hoop with the peice of a Scalp.] **1739** [see **2.** (1) below]. **1775** ADAIR *Indians* 159 The leader . . . goes three times round his dark winter-house, . . . sounding the war-whoop, singing the war-song. **1806** *Balance* V. 217/3 The war-whoop no longer resounded on the continent. **1949** *10 Story Western* May 39/1 No fierce countenance, yells and warwhoops could cow this foe.

transf. **1837** J. Q. ADAMS *Diary* (1928) 491, I said this amidst a perfect war-whoop of 'Order!' **1881** *Harper's Mag.* April 661/2 The inmates were roused . . . by a steamboat's war-whoop. **1946** *Chi. D. News* 29 June 6/3 Soon, though, Pegler vented another war whoop.

2. In phrases: (1) *To set up the* (or *a*) *war whoop*, to give a war cry, to go on the war path, also transf.; (2) *to give the* (or *a*) *war whoop*, =prec.; (3) *to raise a* (or *the*) *war whoop*, to utter a war cry, transf., to raise an outcry, to clamor for war; (4) *in the name of the war whoop*, an exclamation of astonishment, *rare.*

(1) **1739** W. STEPHENS *Proc. Ga.* 474 In marching our Indians set up the war whoop. **1775** *S.C. Hist. Soc. Coll.* II. 33 If they are so foolish as to set up the war-whoop, . . . we can send a great many [warriors] into their country. **1876** MARK TWAIN *Tom Sawyer* xvi, Then they set up a war-whoop of applause, and said it was 'splendid!' — (2) **1757** J. CARVER in *Arminian Mag.* XVII. (1794) 35 By this time the war-hoop was given, and the Indians began to murder those that were nearest to them. **1836** IRVING *Astoria* I. 184 One of them suddenly leaped up and gave a war-whoop. **1916** EASTMAN *From Deep Woods* 53, I was followed on the streets by gangs of little white savages, giving imitation war whoops. — (3) **1834** CARUTHERS *Kentuckian* I. 65, I jumped up and raised a warwhoop. **1836** EDWARD *Hist. Texas* 233 The Texian Representatives . . . raised the war-whoop. . . . To arms! To arms! **1851** MELVILLE *Moby Dick* 318 'Woo-hoo! Wa-hee!' screamed the Gay-Header in reply, raising some old war-whoop to the skies. — (4) **1837** *S. Lit. Messenger* III. 663 In the name of the warwhoop, only to think, board $200 per day at Buffaloe!

war-whoop ˈwɔrˌhup, *v. intr.* To utter a war whoop. Also **war-whooping,** *a.*

1837 *S. Lit. Messenger* III. 237 The Creeks war-whooped—the Cherokees were silent. **1883** MARK TWAIN *Life on Miss.* 11, A tribe of war-whooping savages swarmed out to meet and murder them. *Ib.* lx, The lover goes war-whooping home. **1947** PAUL *Linden* 333 They sang songs, war-whooped and did Indian dances.

Warwickite ˈwɔrwɪkˌaɪt, *n.* [f. *Warwick*, N.Y.] A titanate and borate of iron and magnesium, occurring in dark crystals. — **1838** C. U. SHEPARD in *Amer. Jrnl. Science* XXXIV. 314 A new species, which I designate Warwickite, from its original locality. **1857** DANA *Mineralogy* 212 *Warwickite* . . . occurs in prismatic crystals, of a brownish to an iron-gray color.

Wasco ˈwasko, *n.* [f. a native name or word of unknown significance.] *pl.* or *collect.* A Chinookan tribe of Indians formerly living in the neighborhood of the Dalles in Oregon. Also attrib.

1851 HINES *Oregon* 30 The Indians are known by the name of the Wasco tribe. **1903** JAMES *Indian Basketry* 189 In the Wascos, besides the conventional designs, . . . representations of fish, birds, dogs, . . . frogs, men and women are prominent. **1910** HODGE *Amer. Indians* II. 917/2 The Wasco were a sedentary people, depending for their subsistence mainly upon fish, . . . to a less extent upon edible roots, berries, and, least important of all, game.

* **wash,** *n.*

1. The underground den of a beaver or bear.

1809 A. HENRY *Travels* 130 Their washes . . . are to be discovered by striking the ice along the bank, and where the holes are, a hollow sound is returned. **1877** COUES *Fur-Bearing Animals* ii. 52 They [wolverines] bring forth in burrows under ground, probably old bear washes.

2. The erosion of topsoil and upper layers of earth by rain or running water, a place where such erosion has taken place.

1835 INGRAHAM *South-West* II. 88 Bermuda grass is used with great success to check the progress of a *wash*. **1877** *Cin. Commercial* 6 May, The dump at the foot of Smith street is regarded as valuable as having saved an extensive and injurious 'wash.'

b. (See quot. 1865.) Also attrib. Cf. **wash gold.**

1852 *Alta California* (S.F.) 18 May, The wash dirt is six feet deep, and all of it pays well. **1865** STUART *Montana as It Is* 14 The round smooth boulders and gravel commonly known as the 'wash,' that are always found in placer diggings, have evidently been caused by the grinding, pulverizing action of these glaciers. **1873** BEADLE *Undevel. West* 514 The soil is the richest kind of 'wash' earth, composed of the detritus of the volcanic hills.

c. *W.* (See quots. 1861, 1887.) Also in place-names.

1861 NEWBERRY *Geol. Rep.* 16 The flanks of the mountains . . . are marked by these dry water-courses, which have received from those who are most familiar with this region the technical name of 'washes.' **1879** WILLIAMS *Pacific Tourist* 290/2 Near San Fernando, at the Tehunga Wash., are beautiful specimens of the Agave Americana, the most remarkable of all the agaves. **1887** *So. Calif. Practitioner* Feb. 42 A large portion of the town is built upon a broad, sandy slope or 'wash' which seems to be the bed of a mountain stream that was long ago diverted to other channels. **1950** *Amer. Forests* Jan. 19/2 This rare tree is found . . . on the sides of deep ravines and washes leading to the coast.

attrib. **1930** *Denver Post* 22 June II. 9/3 It was a wash country full of arroya. **1949** *Rocks & Minerals* March–April 131/2 Danger. Flash Flood Area. 60 Wash Crossings next 18 Miles.

3. (See quots. and cf. **wash sale.**)

1859 *Watertown* (Wis.) *Democrat* 30 June, A Wash is a pretended sale, by special agreement between the seller and the buyer, for the purpose of getting a quotation reported. **1891** *Cent.* 6830/3 *Wash,* a fictitious kind of sale, . . . in which a broker who has received orders from one person to buy and from another person to sell a particular . . . quantity of some particular stock or commodity simply transfers the stock or commodity from one principal to the other and pockets the difference.

4. wash basket, (see quot.).

1881 E. INGERSOLL *Oyster Industry* 249 *Wash-basket,* a rude splint basket, circular, shallow, holding about a peck, and with a high bale-handle.

As the last term in **dry, family, sand, water, white wash.**

* **wash,** *v.*

1. *Stock Exchange. tr.* To enhance or endeavor to enhance the value of (stock) by fictitious sales. Also in phrases.

1870 M. H. SMITH *20 Years Wall St.* 74 *Washing the Market:* . . . Two parties make an agreement to buy and sell from each other. The transaction is bogus. **1873** *Newton Kansan* 9 Jan. 1/6 Several brokers . . . are employed to 'wash' the stagnant stock. **1903** S. S. PRATT *Work of Wall St.* 146 The syndicate may be washing sales by matched orders through curb brokers in order to market watered stock.

Hence **washed sale,** (see quot. 1886 and cf. **wash sale**).

1886 *Harper's Mag.* July 205/1 Washed or fictitious sales, or false reports of sales are also penal offences. **1900** NELSON *A B C Wall St.* 70 It will also be readily seen that the opportunity for washed sales is a very open one.

2. In noun combs.: (1) **wash barrel,** (*a*) a pounding barrel *q.v.*, (*b*) (see quot. 1909); (2) **bench,** a bench upon which clothes are washed; (3) **bill,** a laundry bill; (4) **bluing,** laundry bluing; (5) **boiler,** a large, strong metal container, usu. oval in shape, in which clothes are boiled in washing them, also attrib.; (6) **cloth,** a small square cloth for use in bathing; (7) **dish,** a wash basin; (8) **foot,** designating a Primitive Baptist, *jocular;* (9) **gold,** gold that occurs in alluvial deposits, as contrasted with that found in veins or lodes; (10) * **house,** a laundry, esp. one operated by a Chinese, *colloq.;* (11) **kettle,** a large open pot or cauldron in which water is heated for washing purposes; (12) **kitchen,** a kitchen or room in which clothes are washed; (13) **lady,** a washerwoman, also **washer-lady;** (14) **man,** a washerman, *obs.;* (15) **pan,** a wash basin, a pan for washing out gold; (16) **pitcher,** a pitcher or ewer for the toilet, usu. accompanying a washbowl *q.v.* (sense **1.**); (17) **pond,** a pond where washing is done, *obs.;* (18) **rag,** = **wash cloth;** (19) **room,** (*a*) a room in which things, usu. clothes, are washed, (*b*) a lavatory; (20) **sink,** a sink or washbowl at which one washes; (21) **trough,** a trough in which washing is done; (22) **-up,** the act of washing oneself.

(1) (*a*) **1846** *Knickerb.* XXVII. 511 The 'doctor' . . . relieves his culinary labors by pounding away at some shirts and other 'duds' that are smoking in the wash barrel. (*b*) **1854** *Harper's Mag.* IX. 676/1 'How many mackerel did you get today?' 'About twenty wash-barrels, mostly large.' **1909** WEBSTER, wash barrel. *Fisheries.* A barrel in which split mackerel are washed with salt water to extract the blood before salting. — (2) **1861** *Chi. Tribune* 15 April 1 We have sold the right to manufacture and sell Cram's Patent Folding Furniture, comprising Ironing Tables, Wash Benches [etc.]. **1944** *Sears Cat.* (ed. 189) 750 Folding Wash Bench . . . Sturdy wood bench holds 2 round or square wash tubs. Size about 18×47×19 inches. . . . $1.49. — (3) **1848** E. BRYANT *California* App. 478, I have just seen upon his [a clerk's] table a wash bill, made out and paid, at the rate of eight dollars per dozen. **1901** C. MORRIS *Life on Stage* 44 The three of us . . . set to work trying to solve the riddle how a girl was to pay . . . her wash-bill, and all the expenses of the theatre . . . all out of $5 a week. — (4) **1889** in J. F. DALY *Life A. Daly* 476, I wrote up the bill with a bottle of wash-blueing.

(5) **1853** FOWLER *Home for All* 119 A wash-boiler is stationed in the adjoining room. **1878** RUEDE *Sod-House Days* 201 The wash boiler lid has not arrived, so Jake Getz said if I brought the boiler he would make me a lid. **1928** *Collier's* 29 Dec. 9/4 That fellow could turn out six dollars' worth of whisky an hour with that wash boiler. — (6) **1904** STERLING *Belle* 227 For the making our toillette we discovered the value of certain gourds, when used as wash cloths. Their wearing qualities were wonderful; the more one used them the softer they became. **1936** *Sears Cat.* (ed. 173), Extra Heavy Washcloths 13×13 Inch extra size thick, soft, absorbent cotton terry washcloths . . . 6 for 49c. — (7) **1805** *Austin P.* I. (1924) 140, 1 Wash dish. **1891** WILKINS *N. Eng. Nun* 271, I've got my tin wash-dish there on the bench. — (8) **1889** MARGARET DELAND *Fla. Days* 135 The Wash-foot Baptists worship in a single room which is made of rough planks put together so carelessly that one can look out between the boards. **1890** *Harper's Mag.* May 894/1, I take you to be a wash-foot Baptist. — (9) **1873** ARNY *Items regarding N. Mex.* 84 In Pinos Altos the main lead from which most of the wash-gold came has not been discovered yet. **1901** GRINNELL *Gold Hunting in Alaska* 87 The gold on the beach is not 'wash' gold.

(10) **1856** *Dem. State Journal* (Sacramento) 4 Aug. 3/2 There is a washhouse on Front street which seems to imbrue its occupants with a desire to quarrel. **1877** MCCABE *Hist. Great Riots* 422 A portion of the crowd wrecked a Chinese wash-house in the neighborhood. [**1943** *Copper Camp* 115 Not all the washee-washee houses received the respect accorded Fun Gee's establishment.] — (11) **1787** *Ky. Gaz.* 24 Nov. 2/3 Samuel Blair, Has for sale, . . . a Quantity of excellent . . . copper and brass wash kettles. **1836** CROCKETT *Exploits* 91 He was possessed of considerable address, and had brass enough in his face to make a wash-kettle. **1944** WILSON *Passing Inst.* 5 The larger ones were picked up by the youngsters of the family and stored away for winter use as kindling or to help start the fire around the wash-kettle. — (12) **1836** GILMAN *Recoll.* (1838) 206 Preparations were made for the wedding, which she chose to have performed in the wash-kitchen instead of our parlour. **1853** FOWLER *Home for All* 90 A wash-kitchen for the rough work of the family is much needed in every house. — (13) **1882** SWEET & KNOX *Texas Siftings* 196 A 'culled wash lady' told her that the 'white woman what lived here wanted to hire a cook.' **1901** GREENOUGH & KITTREDGE *Words & Their Ways* 322 It is the courtesy of democracy . . . that brings about the results which amuse us in 'saleslady' or 'washerlady' or the 'gentleman' who sweeps the crossing. **1904** *Brooklyn Standard Union* 29 May 4 'Blanchisseuses,' what some folks here call 'washladies.' — (14) **1879** *Harper's Mag.* Nov. 894/2 We saw in turn the smoke of a smelting works, a China 'washman's' shanty, a derrick by means of which some one hoped to 'strike ile.'

(15) **1857** BORTHWICK *3 Years in Calif.* 124 A 'prospecter' goes with a pick and shovel, and a wash-pan. **1884** MARK TWAIN *H. Finn* xxxvii, [We] scratched around and found an old tin washpan. **1946** WILSON *Fidelity* 175 The tin washpan or the creek was good enough for that. — (16) **1852** STOWE *Uncle Tom* i, Eliza had upset the wash-pitcher. **1920** HOWELLS *Vacation of Kelwyns* 6 She had . . . often undergone the hardship of making Kelwyn hurry out untimely in the morning to fill the wash-pitcher. — (17) **1741** *N.H. Probate Rec.* III. 66, I give . . . my Son Jonathan The farm he lives on near the wash pond. — (18) **1890** E. L. BYNNER *Begum's Daughter* iv, She employed the interval while her guests were at their luncheon in plying the wash-rag and comb. **1945** MENCKEN *Supp.* I. 486 Several English corespondents say that the English for *wash-rag* is really *flannel,* but others deny it. — (19) (*a*) **1806** *Mass. H.S. Coll.* 1 Ser. X. 77 They have usually two good rooms in front, bed-rooms, kitchen, wash-room, and other convenient apartments in the rear. **1878** *Vt. Bd. Agric. Rep.* 79 At the end from the road were the press and wash rooms. (*b*) **1853** *So. Ladies Bk.* 217 Tabby came from the wash-room just then. **1927** *Sat. Ev. Post* 24 Dec. 59/3, I knew the washroom was at the back of the house.

(20) **1857** *Lawrence* (Kans.) *Republican* 2 July 4 'Here are all the conveniences for washing,' said the landlord, stepping to a mahogany wash sink and raising the lid. **1878** MARK TWAIN & WARNER *Gilded Age* 270 It was a small room, with a stove in the middle . . . and a wash-sink in one corner. — (21) **1902** WISTER *Virginian* 16 It was not much of a toilet that I made in the first wash-trough of my experience. — (22) **1887** HARTE *Millionaire & Devil's Ford* 176 You boys can go then for a general wash-up. **1917** MATHEWSON *Sec. Base Sloan* 64 They . . . dropped from the car and went back to the station for a wash-up.

Also in combs. sufficiently explained in the quots., as (1) **wash sale,** (2) * **stand,** (3) **still.**

(1) **1848** W. ARMSTRONG *Stocks* 19 These wash sales are of course void between parties. **1900** NELSON *A B C Wall St.* 163 Wash sales. A violation of the rules of all exchanges, where one broker arranges with another to pretend to buy a certain stock when he offers it for sale. The bargain is fictitious, and the effect, when not detected, is to keep it quoted, or, if the plotters buy and sell the stock at a high figure to afford a basis for bona fide sales. — (2) **1909** WEBSTER 2307/1 Wash stand, . . . in stables, a place in the floor prepared so that carriages may be washed there and the water run off. — (3) **1816** *Ann. 14th Cong.* 2 Sess. 1204 A wash still is used of one hundred and twenty gallons. **1909** *Cent. Supp.* 1277/1 *Wash still,* a still for the distillation of the original fermented liquor, as distinguished from one used to redistil the condensed product from the former.

For **washboard,** * **washbowl,** * **washout,** see as main entries.

b. Denoting goods and garments that are washable.

1878 *Decorum* 271 This . . . may be of . . . wash-goods. **1888** *Boston Jrnl.* 23 June 6/3 [In] rural retreats . . . she can . . . wear wash-gowns, and live out of doors all day long. **1905** *N.Y. Ev. Post* 19 May 12 Their May Sale of Girls' Summer Wash Frocks. **1943** DAMON *Sense of H.* 56 In the morning she wears a 'wash dress.'

c. *To wash gold,* to obtain gold by washing auriferous sand, earth, etc.

1863 *Rio Abajo Press* 5 May 2/1, I left him well and hearty at Real de San Francisco, day before yesterday washing gold. **1907** WHITE *Arizona Nights* 164, I camped a while, washing gold, getting friendly with the Yumas. **1948** WESTON *Mother Lode* 154 Several miners had been washing gold in Steep Hollow since 'forty-eight.

washboard ˈwɑʃˌbord, *n.* [See note.]

This term may have been suggested by Du. *waschbord.* Cf. *was(ch)berd* in Cornelissen en Vervliet, *Idioticon van het Antwerpsch Dialect.*

A board having a ribbed or fluted surface upon which clothes are rubbed when being washed.

[**1844** *Edinburgh Jrnl.* I. 412 When washing clothes, they [i.e., American women] spare their fingers by using a fluted board, against which they rub the linen; and some make a still farther improvement by churning the clothes.] **1845** J. W. NORRIS *Chi. Directory* 95 Manufacturer of the Improved Zinc Washboards. **1902** BANKS *Newspaper Girl* 163 Clothes washed by her own hands on an American washboard in a big wooden tub. **1949** *This Week Mag.* 10 Sep. 5/1 Modern husbands don't often find themselves bent over a washboard.

transf. and *attrib.* **1949** *Consumer Rep.* Jan. 8/1 Pick out a hubbly surface or a 'washboard' gravel road, drive over it at about 30 to 35 mph and keep your eye on that nifty plastic hood ornament.

* **washbowl,** *n.*

1. A large bowl, often of earthenware, for washing, esp. the face and hands. Often **washbowl and pitcher.**

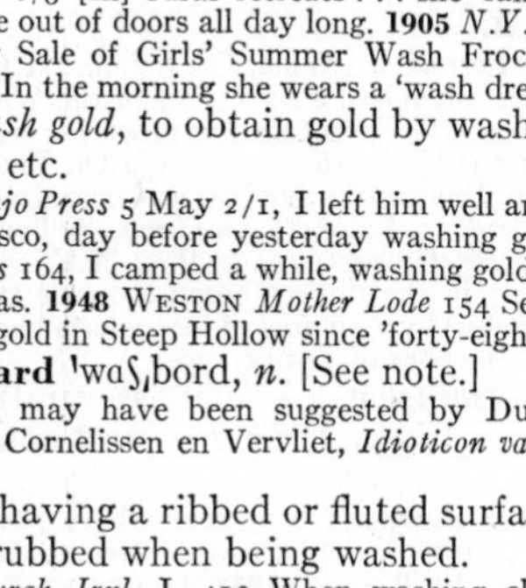

Washbowl and pitcher

1816 U. BROWN *Journal* I. 369 His wash-Bowl [is] the Knot of a tree. **1856** M. J. HOLMES *L. Rivers* 17 Now-a-days we allers has a wash-bowl and pitcher. **1883** MARK TWAIN *Life on Miss.* xxxviii, Sometimes there was a wash-bowl and pitcher. **1929** SHELTON *Salt-box House* xxiii. 186 Wash-bowls and pitchers of blue and white English pottery were a marked advance over the coarse earthen-ware.

2. *W.* A utensil in which gold is washed, a prospector's pan. *Obs.*

1848 *Essex Inst. Coll.* XII. 106, I came from Salem City, With my washbowl on my knee. **1850** in *One Man's Gold* (1930) 131, I am standing in a hole to the depth of my knees, with my pick raised high in the air; my spade and washbowl are lying upon the ground by my side. **1854** BUSH *Wanderungen* I. 168 Andere sangen draussen mit aller Anstrengung ihrer Kehlen den Gassenhauer: *I come from Salem City With my washbowl on my Knee.*

* **washer,** *n.* **1.** = **wash,** *n.* **2.** *Rare.* **2.** = **gold washer.** *Obs.* **3. washerwoman's gig,** (see quot.).

(1) **1846** *Spirit of Times* 18 April 89/3 The second subject of moment connected with ploughing is, to manage so as to prevent washers. — (2) **1850** TYSON *Diary in Calif.* 9 You will soon become accustomed to the mode of proceedings, either with a shovel, pickax, pan, or washer. **1885** *Wkly. New Mexican Rev.* 28 June 4/4 This washer of the 'Porter' pattern, does not operate well on anything but very dry dust or dry, fine tailings. **1901** WHITE *Westerners* 210 You has to have yore stamp mill and washer for all the group of claims. — (3) **1890** *Cong. Rec.* 16 Aug. 8713/2 The 'washerwoman's gig'—4–11–14—[is] the chance that these three, or any other three numbers, will, in any order, be the first three numbers out of the thirteen taken from the wheel.

As the last term in **blanket, dry, foot, gold, gully, root, steam washer.**

* **washery,** *n.* (See quot. 1909.) — **1895** *Columbus* (O.) *Dispatch* 6 May 7/6 The destruction of the washery and machinery was complete. **1909** *Cent. Supp.* 1432/3 *Washery,* . . . a place where coal is sorted and sized by the use of flowing water, and by the same process is concentrated and freed from dirt and incombustible gangue.

Washinango ˌwɑʃɪˈnaŋgo, *n. S.W.* [See note.] (See quot.) *Obs.*

Santamaría lists *guachinango* with the variant *huachinango,* undoubtedly the source of **Washinango,** as a nickname given to Mexicans from the interior. He also records the adjectival meaning in Cuba and Puerto Rico of astute, clever.

1836 EDWARD *Hist. Texas* 120 Their offspring [those of Indians and Negroes], called Washinangoes or *Zambos,* are very hardy and clever.

* **washing,** *n.*

1. *Stock Exchange.* (See quot. 1894 and cf. **wash sales.**)

1849 *Hunt's Merch. Mag.* XXI. 118 'Washing' will hardly go down at the board. **1894** S. LEAVITT *Our Money Wars* 287 In 1887 . . . by the process known as 'Washing,'—that is, by hiring one set of brokers to buy and another set of brokers to sell,—the price of shares was forced to fifteen times their value.

2. (See quot.) *Obs.*

1896 HASWELL *New York* 146 In consequence of the infrequency of fires it was customary, up to about the year 1830, for the companies to assemble once a month for the purpose of exercising the engines, to prevent the valves becoming too dry and rigid from disuse for effective operation. This meeting was termed the 'washing.'

3. In combs.: (1) **washing board,** = **washboard;** (2) **flume,** a flume used in hydraulic mining; (3) * **machine,** = **gold washer,** *obs.,* cf. **dry washing machine;** (4) **powder,** a powder, usu. saponaceous, used in washing.

(1) **1878** DRAKE *Roxbury* 59 The laundress performed her task by pounding the soiled clothes in a barrel of water with a heavy pestle, even the fluted washing-board having not yet been invented. — (2) **1876** RAYMOND *8th Rep. Mines* 103 The washing-flume is $1\frac{1}{4}$ miles long, . . . paved with blocks. — (3) **1849** WIERZBICKI *California* 40 A washing machine is used when there are two or more working in partnership. — (4) **1869** FULLER *Flower Gatherers* 182 The old Proff . . . calls salt 'chloride of Sodium' and sets me thinking of washing powders. **1896** *Internat. Typog. Union Proc.* 55/1, 1 box B.S. washing powder, $6.

As the last term in **dry, family, gold, gulch, pan, top washing(s).**

* **Washington,** *n.* [George *Washington* (1732–99).]

1. A variety of plum. Also attrib. *Obs.*

1846 BROWNE *Trees Amer.* 246 *Washington* or *Bolmar Plum-tree.* This variety may be known by its roundish, yellow fruit. **1856** *Mich. Agric. Soc. Trans.* VII. 715 A gentleman noted for his noble Washingtons and imperial Gages. **1863** *Horticulturist* XVIII. 262 Of Plums, the following will probably be best for your purpose: . . . Green Gage, McLaughlin, Washington.

2. (See quot.) *Obs.*

1913 ADAMS & WOODIN *U.S. Pattern, Trial & Exper. Pieces* 20 This was the first double eagle to be issued struck by the United States Government. . . . At the time of the issue of the coin it was suggested that it be called 'Washington.'

3. In special combs.: (1) **Washington Benevolent Society,** an organization, chiefly or entirely political, composed of those anxious to maintain the governmental policies of George Washington, *obs.* or *hist.;* (2) **cake,** (see quot. 1843), *obs.;* (3) **gun,** poss. a type of cannon, *obs.;* (4) **influenza,** (see quot.), *obs.;* (5) **lottery wheel,** a lottery wheel operated at Washington, D.C., *obs.;* (6) **Monument,** see as a main entry; (7) **penny,** (see quot.), *obs.;* (8) **pie,** a layer cake with a cream or jam filling (see also quot. 1948); (9) **press,** a type of hand-operated printing press; (10) **-'s birthday,** the day, now Feb. 22, celebrated as that upon which, in 1732, George Washington was born; (11) **territory,** the region organized as a territory in 1853 and admitted into the union as a state in 1889.

(1) **1813** (*title*), An Address Delivered Before the Washington Benevolent Society at Cambridge, 5 July, 1813. By Abdiel Holmes, D.D. **1908** *Amer. Antiq. Soc. Proc.* XIX. n.s. 26 By 'benevolents' are meant members of the Washington Benevolent Societies, then [i.e. during the War of 1812] common. — (2) **1843** *Farmers' Cabinet* 15 Jan. 179/2 Washington Cake,—So called, because it was a favourite at the table of Gen. Washington. **1856** WIDDIFIELD *New Cook Book* 254 Washington Cake. — (3) **1874** B. F. TAYLOR *World on Wheels* 72 The cylinder is trained like a Washington gun, at an angle of about thirty-three and a third degrees. — (4) **1878** DRAKE *Roxbury* 86 From some mismanagement Washington was detained at the Roxbury line nearly two hours, and exposed to a raw northeast wind, by which exposure he took a severe cold. Many others were similarly affected, and so general was the distemper that it was called the 'Washington Influenza.'

(5) **1799** *Aurora* (Phila.) 31 Jan. (Th.), The gulls and goose-traps . . . come from the shop in which the Washington Lottery wheels remain undrawn. — (7) **1888** *N. & Q.* I. 238 The so-called 'Washington pennies,' which existed previous to this date [i.e., 1793] were not issued by the Government and were models or medals. — (8) **1905** LINCOLN *Partners* 4 'Turnovers' [were] arranged cob-house fashion under a glass cover, with a dingy 'Washington' pie under another cover. **1948** MENCKEN *Supp.* II. 163 Another delicacy of the young was *Washington pie,* which was about two inches thick and was vended in blocks about two inches square. It was made of stale pies, gingercakes, etc., ground up and rebaked. — (9) **1896** SHINN *Story of Mine* 248 It contained an old-style Washington press, cases, desks, and editor's table.

(10) [**1782** *Independent Ledger* 18 Feb. 3/2 Last Tuesday a large number of Gentlemen met at Mr. Robinson's Tavern . . . to celebrate the anniversary Birth Day of His leader, General Washington.] **1829** *Va. Herald* (Fredericksburg) 7 March 3/3 During the celebration of Washington's birth day, on Monday last, . . . two persons . . . were . . . dreadfully mangled. **1841** *N.O. Picayune* 21 Feb. 2/2 Washington's Birth Day. Tomorrow will be the anniversary of the birth day of George Washington—a day hallowed in the remembrance of Americans. **1907** *St. Nicholas* July 862/2 It was on Washington's Birthday in Central Park . . . that I had my first glimpse of this beautiful bird. — (11) **1881** *Ore. State Jrnl.* 15 Jan. 4/1 The delegate from Washington Territory . . . succeeded in having two of his bills [passed].

b. In the names of, or with reference to, plants (cf. sense **1.** above) and animals: (1) **Washington canvasback,** (see quot.); (2) **cedar,** (see quot.); (3) **eagle,** the bald eagle in its immature stage; (4) **Elm,** a large elm, cut down in 1924, in Cambridge, Mass., under which Washington took command of the Continental Army on July 3, 1775; (5) **lily,** a large lily, *Lilium washingtonianum,* common on the Pacific Coast of the U.S.; (6) **navel,** the earliest and for a long time the most popular of the navel oranges, in full **Washington navel orange;** (7) **palm,** the California fan palm *q.v.,* also **Washington fan palm;** (8) **thorn,** (see quot. 1891).

(1) **1890** *Cent.* 5020/3 [An American variety of the redhead] is called more fully *red-headed duck,* . . . also *grayback, Washington canvasback,* and *American pochard.* — (2) **1889** *Cent.* 875/3 Washington cedar is the big-tree of California, *Sequoia gigantea.* — (3) **1839** PEABODY *Mass. Birds* 263 The Washington Eagle, *Falco Washingtonianus,* . . . sometimes wanders into New England. **1917** *Birds of Amer.* II. 80 Bald Eagle. . . . Black Eagle; Gray Eagle; Washington Eagle. The last three names refer to the immature Bald Eagle. — (4) **1846** BROWNE *Trees Amer.* 510 The Washington Elm. In the city of Cambridge, in Massachusetts, there stands, in the vicinity of Harvard University, a beautiful elm, named after General Washington, which has a trunk thirteen feet and three inches in circumference. **1872** HOLMES *Poet* 23 You know the 'Washington elm,' or if you do not, you had better rekindle your patriotism by reading the inscription. **1947** PAUL *Linden* 109 The Malden politicians and editors were against the big tree, on the ground that it had no definite historical or literary associations, like the Washington Elm in Cambridge.

(5) **1869** MUIR *First Summer in Sierra* (1911) 43 Here and there a Washington lily may be seen nodding above its even surface. **1915** ARMSTRONG & THORNBER *Western Wild Flowers* 36 The flowers are even more deliciously fragrant than the Washington Lily. — (6) **1888** LINDLEY *Calif. of South* 349 Popular sentiment is now practically settled in favor of the Washington navel, a strongly-marked fruit with a little protuberance (sometimes containing an aborted orange) in the blossom end. **1936** *Ariz. Agric. Exp. Sta. Bul.* No. 153, 496 In a year's time mature Washington navel orange trees will remove from the soil a bit in excess of 2½ acre-feet of water per acre. **1950** *L.A. Times Home Mag.* 26 March 4/4 These were the Washington navels and impetus for Southern California's $100,000,000 citrus industry. — (7) **1909** *Cent Supp.* 933/2 Washington palm, the desert palm, *Neowashingtonia filamentosa.* **1914** MACDOUGAL *Salton Sea* 91 Among them are well grown trees of . . . Washington palm, all of which have probably been planted by the Indians. **1948** *Pacific Discovery* March–April 11 (*caption*), In the middle distance, Washington fan palms. — (8) **1846** BROWNE *Trees* 280 [The] Washington Thorn . . . was first cultivated . . . in the District of Columbia. **1891** *Cent.* 6300/2 *Washington thorn, Cratægus cordata,* found in Virginia, and thence southward and westward. It was formerly widely planted for hedges, being disseminated from near Washington City.

c. Used to designate a temperance hotel, or in the name of a temperance society, or with reference to a plan for organizing a temperance group. Now *hist.* Cf. **Washingtonian,** *n.* **2.**

1842 *Greene Co. Torchlight* (Xenia, O.) 6 Jan. 2/1 On Wednesday evening the citizens organized a society upon the Washington plan, and have since been actively engaged in procuring signatures to the pledge. **1842** *Juliet* (Ill.) *Courier* 2 Feb. 1/2 On Thursday evening last a Washington Temperance Society was organized at Lockport. **1844** *Akron Buzzard* 25 June 4/4 (*heading*), Sullivan Washington House. **1944** MAU *Development Cent. & West. N.Y.* 274 When, a few years later, interest in the subject began to wane the Washington Society was superseded by a number of new reform bodies, prominent among which was the Sons of Temperance.

d. (1) *by Washington,* a jocular asseveration, *rare;* (2) *Washington and Adams Federalist,* =**Washingtonian,** *n.* **1.** *Obs.*

(1) **1827** AUDUBON *Journal* (1930) 207, I have powerfully in my mind to give my picture of the 'Trapped Otter' to Mrs. Basil Hall, and, by Washington, I will. — (2) **1858** WOODWARD *Reminisc.* (1939) 134 All were the sons of William Fitzpatrick, a good old Washington and Adams Federalist.

Washingtonia ˌwɑʃɪŋˈtonɪə, *n.*

1. A suggested name for the U.S. and for the Southern Confederacy. *Obs.* or *hist.*

1860 *Charleston* (S.C.) *Mercury* 8 Dec. 1/3, I would suggest that the new Confederacy be called Washingtonia, in honor of that Southerner, Slaveholder, and Secessionist, George Washington, of Mount Vernon. **1947** *St. Louis Globe-Democrat* 14 Sep., Many and desperate were the attempts to find some other 'ersatz' name to fill a need that has always been deeply felt. Among them were Washingtonia, Usona, Appalachia, Atlantis and Fredonia.

2. A genus of fan palms found in California and Mexico, or a palm of this genus. Also **Washingtonia palm.**

1945 MARSHALL *Santa Fe* 188 There were date palms and New Washingtonia palms from the Colorado desert at Needles, but they were tricks of irrigation. **1947** *Desert Mag.* June 23/2 There are three distinct generations of palms, most of them of the *Washingtonia filifera* species, but occasionally a blue palm—Erythea armata. **1949** *L.A. Times Home Mag.* 14 Aug. 32/4 There is today an impressive row of Washingtonias . . . standing like sentinels to direct the way to the ocean's cove park.

Washingtonian ˌwɑʃɪŋˈtonɪən, *n.*

1. A believer in the political principles of George Washington, a Federalist. *Obs.*

1789 *Mass. Centinel* 11 Feb. 172/3 The following gentlemen are chosen Electors. . . . All firm federalists—and Washingtonians. **1806** FESSENDEN *Democracy Unveiled* I. 142 The measures by the imps are made A handle, plausible no doubt, To turn the Washingtonians out. **1816** in M. BAYARD SMITH *Washington Society* (1906) 134 If I was a Washingtonian you might say I worshipped the rising sun.

2. A member of a Washington Temperance Society. Now *hist.* Cf. ∗**Washington 3. c.**

1842 *Juliet* (Ill.) *Courier* 2 Feb. 1/4 A meeting of Washingtonians was held at the methodist church on tuesday evening the 18th inst. **1854** SIMMS *Southward Ho!* 218 Because thou art a Washingtonian, shall there be no wine? **1891** *Cyclo. Temp. & Prohib.* 203/1 The 'Washingtonians' originated in the conversion into a temperance society in April, 1840, of a Baltimore drinking club . . . of six men. **1947** DOWNEY *Lusty Forefathers* 299 The fervor of the Washingtonians, founded by self-redeemed drunkards, felled thousands of apple trees, the fruits of which might otherwise . . . have become hard cider.

3. One who lives in Washington, D.C.

1852 EASTMAN *Aunt Phillis's Cabin* 234 The beautiful prospect, to which Washingtonians are so much accustomed that they are too apt not to notice it. **1861** *Alexandria* (Va.) *Gaz.* 2 May 3/4 Among the

Washingtonians, who have been compelled to leave this city, is Mr. George M. Thompson. **1945** *Md. Conservationist* 7/2 The Potomac River . . . is very heavily fished by Washingtonians.

Also an inhabitant of the state of Washington.

1892 *Irrigation Age* 1 May 31/3 Washingtonians know a blessing when they see it. **1948** *Pauls Valley* (Okla.) *D. Democrat* 2 July 4/1 Few Washingtonians see an oar before matriculating, with the result that they are properly taught from taw.

Washingtonian ˌwɑʃɪŋˈtonɪən, *a.*

1. Emanating from, or resembling qualities of, George Washington.

1812 *Salem Gaz.* 22 May 3/1 The political character of Vermont is really Washingtonian. **1876** *Wide Awake* III. 137/2 The little fishing band was now sadly broken and lessened by one of the Washingtonian demands upon Brother Jonathan. **1902** MARK TWAIN *Defence of Gen. Funston* 614 (R.), The Washingtonian character would not have been built.

2. Of or pertaining to temperance. *Obs.* Cf. * **Washington 3. c.**

1842 *Columbus* (Ill.) *Adv.* 17 Feb. 2/5 Levi Palmer . . . has opened a Washingtonian House, where he furnishes all kinds of *refreshments*, but nothing which *enfeebles* or *intoxicates*. **1844** *Akron Buzzard* 25 June 4/4 He has hoisted the Washingtonian flag, and nailed it at mast head. **1851** GREEN *Twelve Days* 218, I am honored by the Washingtonian Societies to present them to him, which I now do with pleasure and with pride. **1880** *Harper's Mag.* Jan. 191/2 Its influence is still visible in the Washingtonian homes which usefully supplement the charities of our large cities.

Washingtonianism ˌwɑʃɪŋˈtonɪənˌɪzəm, *n.* **1.** Enthusiasm for the political principles of George Washington or for his memory. Also **Washingtonism. 2.** The principles of the Washington Temperance Society. Both *obs.*

(1) **1814** M. CAREY *Olive Branch* (1815) 285 She [Massachusetts] cannot suffer the punishment due to her folly, her arrogance, her restlessness, her faction, her jacobinism, her anti Washingtonism, without inflicting an equal degree of misfortune on her innocent neighbors. **1852** *Harper's Mag.* 266/2 We suffer a kind of intermittent Washingtonianism, which now and then shows a very fever of drawings, and of small subscriptions. — (2) **1842** *Columbus* (Ill.) *Adv.* 17 Feb. 2/4 We find that Washingtonianism makes the newspaper market decidedly more active. **1859** *Harper's Mag.* Jan. 278/1 When Washingtonianism swept over the Western country he joined the army of its converts.

Washington Monument. 1. A monument at Baltimore in honor of George Washington. Also attrib. **2.** A marble obelisk in Washington, D.C., erected as a national memorial to George Washington. Also attrib.

(1) **1811** *Federal Republican* (Balt.) 5 Oct. 4/3 Tickets and Shares in the . . . Washington Monument Lottery. **1824** CANDLER *Summary View of Amer.* 147 We walked to the Washington Monument and ascended it. — (2) **1834** *Advocate* (Shelbyville, Ky.) 8 Feb. 2/2 A 'Washington national monument society' has been established at Washington to raise funds for a monument to the memory of the 'Father of his country,' which, it is hoped, will be without an equal in the world. **1844** *N.O. Picayune* 18 March 36/5 A lithographed plan of the Washington Monument . . . has been submitted to the committee appointed to superintend the work. **1948** *Chickasha* (Okla.) *D. Express* 4 July 7/3 The Washington Monument society had had so much trouble collecting funds that in 1855 it asked congress to take over the project.

Washoe ˈwɑʃo, *n.* [f. a native term meaning "person."]

1. *pl.* "A small tribe, forming a distinct linguistic family . . . which, when first known to Americans, occupied Truckee r., Nev., as far down as the Meadows" (Hodge).

1860 DEGROOT *Washoe Mines* 15/2 To this place, on the approach of cold weather, not only the Washoes, whose territory lies adjacent, but also bands of the Pah-Utahs, from a greater distance repair. **1868** *Terr. Enterprise* (Virginia, Nev.) 8 Feb. 3/1 The Washoes, as a rule, are smaller, darker, dirtier, more rugged and more addicted to carrying guns into towns than the Piutes. **1947** *Desert Mag.* Dec. 32/3 The Washoes, of whom less than 1,000 remain, live in valleys along the Sierra Nevada.

attrib. **1865** *Carson* (Nev.) *Appeal* 24 Oct. 3/1 Two Washoe Indians made their triumphant entry on horseback into our city from their *wickee* on the mountainside. **1879** MIGHELS *Sagebrush Leaves* 225 We saw . . . a . . . young Washoe brave escorting his wife and mother-in-law up towards the campoody. **1903** *Out West* April 439 The colors in Washoe baskets are all natural. **1949** *L.A. Times* 10 April II. 5/2 It has been deduced that it is the Washoe Indian word for water and that hah-oo or ta-au means lake and sheet of water.

2. A name for the territory or region which became the state of Nevada.

1856 *S.F. Bulletin* 26 May 3/2 The rumored trouble from the Indians of Carson, Wash-hoe and Walker's valley, is entirely without foundation. **1860** *No. Californian* (Union) 21 March 2/2 Every little town or village throughout the State has its ambitious 'parties' . . . awaiting to swell the immigration to Washoe. **1863** *Humboldt Reg.* (Unionville, Nev.) 9 May 2/3 For our own part, we are decidedly and emphatically in favor of creating the State of Washoe. **1947** *Amer. Wkly.* 2 Nov. 21/3 Back in Washoe, later to become the state of Nevada, the Comstock Lode waited—waited to be discovered.

3. In special combs.: (1) **Washoe canary,** a burro; (2) **process,** (see quot. 1909); (3) **zephyr,** a strong west wind that blows in Nevada in the fall and spring.

(1) **1867** *Terr. Enterprise* (Virginia, Nev.) 8 March 3/1 The discouraged 'Washoe canary' refuses to cheer us with its tuneful warblings. **1947** [see **Washoe zephyr**]. — (2) **1876** POWELL *Nevada* 55 The mode of treating ores in vogue in the neighborhood of the Comstock Lode is called the *Washoe* process. **1909** WEBSTER 2307/1 Washoe process . . . the process of treating silver ores by grinding in pans or tubs with the addition of mercury, and sometimes of chemicals such as blue vitriol and salt. **1942** LILLARD *Desert Challenge* 296 They worked out two early Western achievements: the wet-silver mill, or Washoe process, and the dry-silver mill, or Reese River process. — (3) **1865** *Washoe* (Nev.) *Times* 4 March 3/2 We have heard of hail and chain-lightning, etc., but ye gentle Washoe zephyr can discount all and everything in that line. **1947** *Sat. Review* 10 May 32/2 He is . . . discoursing on the Washoe zephyr and the Washoe canary.

b. In occasional, now obs., expressions, as **Washoe bubble, diggings, excitement, fever, mine, pick, Seeress, silver mine, wagon, weather.**

1896 SHINN *Story of Mine* 138 They were 'stuffing each other' after every conceivable manner and diligently blowing 'Washoe bubbles.' — **1859** *S.F. Bulletin* 20 Oct. 3/6 The steamer *Uncle Sam* carried, as a portion of her cargo to-day, four tons of silver ore from the Washoe diggings. — **1868** *Dispatch & Vanguard* (S.F.) 5 Dec. 1/7 The Washoe excitement turned the heads of the soberest and most discreet of our citizens. — **1863** *Humboldt Reg.* (Unionville, Nev.) 23 May 3/1 Californians have caught the Washoe fever, and are flocking here in immense numbers. — **1860** DEGROOT *Washoe Mines* 3/1 The recently discovered silver lodes, constituting what are known as the Washoe Mines, like on the western verge of Utah Territory. — **1880** *Cimarron News & Press* 13 May 3/2 Washoe Picks, . . . Hammers and Gold pans at Carey's. — **1877** WM. WRIGHT *Big Bonanza* 100 Mrs. L. S. Bowers—one of the early settlers at Johnstown and at Gold Hill, and now known as the 'Washoe Seeress,' on account of her many predictions about fires in the mines and rich bodies of ore—is a Spiritualist, and many of the early settlers . . . were Spiritualists. — **1860** *S.F. News Letter* 20 Jan. 6/1 The excitement with respect to the Washoe silver mines seems to gain ground day by day. — **1896** SHINN *Story of Mine* 110 Not merchants these . . . but a brave, honest outdoor race whose huge Washoe wagons were the forerunners of the railroads. — **1868** *Terr. Enterprise* (Virginia, Nev.) 10 Oct. 3/1 Whether a storm will come or not remains to be seen—Washoe weather is mighty uncertain.

Washoeite ˈwɑʃoˌaɪt, *n.* [See **Washoe.**] One of those who flocked to the silver mines in the Washoe district upon the discovery of the Comstock lode in 1859. Also a Nevadan. *Obs.*

1860 *Harper's Mag.* Dec. 12/1 An almost continuous string of Washoeites stretched . . . as far as the eye could reach. **1867** *Terr. Enterprise* (Virginia, Nev.) 9 Feb. 3/1 Mr. L. Winn, so well known to all of us Washoeites, . . . is now once more manufacturing candy for the sweet-toothed residents of the Bay City. **1869** *Ib.* 24 Jan. 3/2 A brass band enlivened the scene, and the Washoeites had a 'rare old time.'

* **washout,** *n.* The washing away by heavy rains of a part of a road, railroad, etc. Also a gully or depression resulting from this.

1873 *Newton Kansan* 29 May 3/2 Owing to a wash out on the Cottonwood last Sunday night, we had no train from the east until Tuesday afternoon. **1877** CAMPION *On Frontier* 20 It was . . . seamed with deep narrow gullies, 'wash-outs' of rain storms. **1891** *Appeal-Avalanche* (Memphis) 26 April 9/4 The work done so far has been the closing of 1,600 feet of washouts in the levee, which averaged six feet in depth. **1949** *Canadian Alpine Jrnl.* May 53 A washout had kept the jeep nine miles down the road.

attrib. **1882** *Golden* (N.M.) *Retort* 28 July 1/1 As the washout season approaches through travel over the Santa Fe road becomes light, but it catches on again in the winter.

b. *transf.* A failure; in baseball, a rained-out game.

1931 SMITH *Turnabout* (1938) 233 And that part about making a night of it is all wet. It's a washout. **1944** STOUT *Not Quite Dead Enough* 51 If anyone else . . . had beat me to it and called the cops or a doctor or even the neighbors, . . . my plan was a washout. **1950** *Chi. Tribune* 27 April IV. 1/5 But there's a redeeming feature about the washouts, etc. The Wrigley field tenants still have their perfect percentage based on three straight victories.

*wasp, *n.* As the last term in **black, burrowing, mud, paper, paper-making, yellow wasp.**

***waste,** *n.* In combs.: (1) **waste grounds,** land not used for farming or grazing, *obs.;* (2) **room,** a room in a gin house where cotton refuse collects; (3) **way,** a channel or outlet for surplus water.

(1) **1686** in *Amer. Sp.* XV. 408/1 Noe person . . . shall . . . put to feed into or upon any woodland grounds, marches or other waste grounds . . . any ston'd horse. **1711** *Ib.* Lawless persons . . . taking advantage of the large wast and uninhabited grounds and woods. — (2) **1852** STOWE *Uncle Tom* xxxvi, 'In the waste-room of the gin-house,' said Cassy. — (3) **1882** THAYER *From Log-Cabin* 184 There was a waste-way just ahead. **1884** *Harper's Mag.* Sep. 621/2 Above these . . . is a wasteway . . . over which the surplus water can pour should the supply exceed the capacity of the dam. **1940** WILSON *Wabash* 9 The wasteweir—or 'wasteway,' as some of the people there call it—that empties its parsimonious trickle into the sluggish and unromantic beginnings of Beaver Creek is fitted with heavy screens.

***wastebasket,** *v. tr.* To put into a wastebasket. — **1889** MARK TWAIN *Letters* (1917) II. 514 (R.), Send me the pages with your corrections on them, and waste-basket the rest. **1900** ——— *Man That Corrupted H.* 127 Indefinite testimonies might properly be waste-basketed, since there is evidently no lack of definite ones procurable.

watap wæ'tɑp, *n.* [f. Can. F. (<Indian term) in sense shown in quot. 1789.] (See quot. 1910.)

1789 A. MACKENZIE *Voyage from Montreal* (1801) 37 (*footnote*), Watape is the name given to the divided roots of the spruce-fir, which the natives weave into a degree of compactness that renders it capable of containing a fluid. **1806** LEWIS in *L. & Clark Exped.* (1905) IV. 84 We were visited by eight Cla[t]sops and Chinooks from whom we purchased . . . two hats made of waytape and white cedar bark. **1889** *Outing* Aug. 369/2 Dig up a fir root and pound it on a stone until you can draw out the long cord-like fibres, which the Indians and voyageurs call *watape.* **1910** HODGE *Amer. Indians* II. 921/1 Watap, roots of the pine, spruce, tamarack, etc., used to sew birch-bark for canoes and other purposes.

***watch,** *n.* In combs.: (1) **watch care,** watchful care; (2) **club,** ?a club composed of those interested in watches that are raffled off, *obs.;* (3) **fob,** a short chain, ribbon, or other ornamental appendage to a watch [in quot. 1834 app. a watch pocket], cf. ***fob,** *n.*²; (4) ***house,** (see quots.); (5) **stuffer,** one who hoodwinks those who purchase watches of him (see *Amer. Sp.* Dec. 1945, 308–9); (6) **stuffing,** the practice of selling cheap or worthless watches at high prices to unwary purchasers, *slang.*

(1) **1845** *Indiana Mag. Hist.* XXIII. 152 Very much, also, depends on the kind of preachers and leaders, who have the after watch-care of the persons that are brought into the church. **1896** *Peterson Mag.* March 253/1 The years of watch care which she had given to the child left in her charge. — (2) **1890** *Ann Arbor Rec.* 13 March, A drawing of the first watch club organized in the City, was held at Watts' jewelry store, . . . and George Krauth became the possessor of a $30 watch which cost him but $1. — (3) **1834** C. DAVIS *Letters of Downing* 124 (We.), He had no less than 7 pockets besides his watch fob. **1864** *Hist. North-Western Soldiers' Fair* 124 [Donations include] 1 watch fob. **1947** *Chi. Tribune* 23 Nov. VII. 2 (*advt.*), This replica of grandfather's watch fob [etc.]. — (4) **1836** in *Amer. Sp.* XVI. (1941) 234 The Tavern at which I staid during the night is called a Watch House. It is immediately on the banks of the River, and keeps . . . a look out for Boats for Passengers. **1881** INGERSOLL *Oyster Industry* 249 *Watch House.*—A shanty built on the shore, or near the planted oyster beds, from which they may be guarded. (Massachusetts.)

(5) **1840** in *Amer. Sp.* XVI. 231 A notorious watch stuffer . . . undertook yesterday to cheat and defraud Mr. Joseph Thompson . . . by palming off upon him a worthless brass watch as a gold one. **1929** in *Ib.* XX. (1945) 309/1 To provide for the punishment of vagrants, tramps or common street beggars . . . burglars, watch stuffers . . . and suspicious persons. — (6) **1840** in *Amer. Sp.* XVI. 231 More Watch Stuffing.—One would suppose so many cases of this description had been published that [etc.]. **1860** *Atlantic Mo.* Dec. 671 Dog-smudging, ring-dropping, watch-stuffing . . . are all terms which have more or less outgrown the bounds of their Alsatia of Thieves' Latin and are known of men.

b. (1) *watchdog of the Treasury,* a person, usu. a member of Congress, who consistently tries to check expenditure of public money; (2) *on the watch-out,* on the alert, *colloq.*

(1) **1827** *Spirit of Seventy-Six* (Frankfort, Ky.) 29 March 3/4 The watch-dogs of the Treasury . . . have made loud and grievous complaints about the waste of public money in purchasing a Billiard Table. **1872** *Chi. Tribune* 20 Nov. 1/6 In Congress he was the watch-dog of the Treasury. [**1949** *Newsweek* 23 May 70/2 He suggested reforms . . . to make these the real watchdogs they were originally intended to be.] — (2) **1884** MARK TWAIN *H. Finn* iv, I never tried to do anything, but just poked along low-spirited and on the watch-out. **1902** HARBEN *A. Daniel* 16 Peter Mosely is a man on the watch-out fer rail soft snaps.

As the last term in **dumb, gold, log, merchants', patrol, select watch.**

***watch,** *v. To watch out,* to be on one's guard, to take care. *Colloq.* — **1845** HOOPER *Simon Suggs' Adv.* 115 He determined therefore to 'watch out.' **1903** *N.Y. Sun* 16 Nov. 4 We advise the golfers to watch out, or else they may find themselves locked up.

***watcher,** *n.* In an election, a party representative authorized to be present at a polling-place to watch the conduct of officials and voters. See also **clock watcher, posy watcher.** — **1911** *Okla. Session Laws* 3 Legisl. 82 The challenger, pool book holder and watcher shall perform duties as provided by law, governing any general election. **1948** *New Yorker* 25 Sep. 25/3 Each party is entitled to have two watchers at each polling place.

***water,** *n.*

1. In miscellaneous combs.: (1) **water bar,** a ridge or low barrier slanting across a hill or mountain road to deflect water flowing down; (2) **battery,** *Mil.* a battery nearly on a level with the water of an adjacent river, lake, etc.; (3) ***bound,** confined or detained by high water; (4) **burner,** (see quot. 1818), *obs.;* (5) **call,** a signal for soldiers to assemble to get water or to water their horses; (6) **cracker,** (*a*) (see quot. 1835), (*b*) (see quot.), both *obs.;* (7) ***fall,** (*a*) a mass or bunch of hair, usu. artificial, worn by women at the back of the head, also attrib., (*b*) (see quot.); (8) **fence,** (*a*) "a fence extend-

One form of water fence

ing from a shore out into a lake or other body of water so that animals in pasture may not pass around its end" (*Cent. Supp.*), (*b*) (see quot.); (9) **gristmill,** a gristmill driven by water power; (10) **haul,** in fishing, a haul of the net which takes no fish, hence, fruitless effort of any kind [cf. *EDD watery-haul* in about the same sense]; (11) ***line,** a river or rivers regarded as a means of transportation, also attrib.; (12) **privilege,** see as a main entry; (13) **right,** the right to use the water in a particular region or place; (14) **scrape,** *W.* a drive across a region where water is not to be had, *obs.;* (15) **set,** a water pitcher and accompanying glasses; (16) **sign,** among Plains Indians, a sign showing where water may be had; (17) **wave,** a wave or undulation made in the hair when wet, also attrib.; (18) **witching,** the locating of an underground water supply by a water finder.

(1) **1850** *N.H. Hist. Soc. Coll.* VI. 220 In passing a water bar, he was thrown from his carriage and killed. **1939** GILBERT *Forty Yrs.* 65 It had rained and the road was rough, with sandy spots and water bars. — (2) **1817** *Ann. 14th Congress* 2 Sess. 983 There may be a

water battery on Craney Island, erected during the war, but it is not necessary to garrison it in time of peace. **1893** *Harper's Mag.* April 761/2 [Fort San Marco's] water-battery, where once stood the Spanish cannon, looks out to sea. — **(3) 1862** *N.Y. Tribune* 30 April 1/3 While water-bound, it [a foraging party] was attacked by guerrillas. **1919** Cady *Rhymes of Vt.* (1923) 140 Oh! yes; they jest was 'water-bound.' — **(4) 1818** *N. Amer. Rev.* Sep. 428 Much attention has recently been excited by an apparatus called the 'American Water Burner.' . . . The construction of this machine is very simple; by means of it tar is intimately mixed with steam or vapour of water, and made to issue from a small orifice, like that in the jet of a blow-pipe, and is there fired. **1833** *Amer. R.R. Jrnl.* II. 823/3 An apparatus, called the American Water-Burner, has been invented.

(5) 1781 E. Denny *Mil. Jrnl.* 35 About eight or nine o'clock, as we found water, a short halt was made, the water-call beat. **1868** *Harper's Mag.* Feb. 303/2 When the men mounted at the 'water-call,' some were seen to mount from the right-hand side, Indian fashion. — **(6)** *(a)* **1825** *Mo. Intelligencer* 4 June 3/4 Ward and Parker Have Just Received For Sale at their Grocery and Liquor Store Molasses, Water

One form of water set

Crackers [etc.]. **1835** H. C. Todd *Notes* 65 Here [Albany] I first ate the American biscuit called a water-cracker, which I found excellent, size of a crown piece, and three for a cent. **1877** *Harper's Mag.* Feb. 448/1 Aunt Helen threw her a bit of water-cracker. *(b)* **1887** *Scientific Amer.* LVI. 181/1, I have taken a water cracker, as they [Prince Rupert drops] are called in the factory, several feet long, and broken it four or five times. — **(7)** *(a)* **1864** Stowe *House & Home P.* 165 The one I wore yesterday was my waterfall-hat, with the green feather. **1865** *Carson* (Nev.) *Appeal* 2 Nov. 3/1 The waterfall, or *chignon*, is abolished by a decree of fashion. **1919** Cady *Rhymes of Vt.* (1923) 259 He'd . . . comb and braid a lady's switch Or steam her 'waterfall.' *(b)* **1950** *New Yorker* 25 March 84/2 What she calls 'waterfalls'—cascades of bustle drapery—add interest to the backs of all types of clothes. — **(8)** *(a)* **1644** *Southampton Rec.* I. 34 Yt is ordered that the little common shall be sufficiently fenced against all sorts of cattell and Goats by those that have fences upon the said common . . . both for land fence and for water fence. **1791** *Huntington Rec.* III. 160 He petitions the Trustees to Grant him toleration to Run a water fence. . . . Down to the Channel, with his erecting and keeping a Good & Convenient Swing Gate. *(b)* **1880** *Scribner's Mo.* XIX. 509/2 Of all fences, none is so simple as the water fence, only a pole spanning a stream, perhaps fastened at the larger end by a stout link and staple to a great water-maple, ash or buttonwood-tree. — **(9) 1723** *Amer. W. Mercury* 19 Sep. 2/2 To be Sold . . . , the Farm, late of Thomas Stevenson, . . . with a Water Grist-Mill upon it. **1831** Peck *Guide* 318 Vandalia contains . . . one water grist mill, one water saw mill [etc.].

(10) 1823 in Sweet *Religion* 130 The whole of this tour, disagreeable as it was, I considered an entire water haul. **1871** *Cong. Globe* 17 Feb. 1356/1 It occurred to me, at all events, the gentleman from California had made what fishermen call a 'water haul.' **1898** R. M. Johnston *P. Amerson's Will* 221, I 'tended to that business dilicate as I knowed how; but no use: a waterhaul, out an' out. — **(11) 1852** in *Amer. Sp.* XV. 382/2 The stimulating effect of a water line transportation . . . will be soon and sensibly felt. **1881–5** McClellan *Own Story* 343 The water line of transportation would have insured the prompt and safe arrival of the 1st corps. — **(13) 1793** *Columbian Museum* (Phila.) Jan. 16 The purchase of the land, including the farm buildings which may be on it, and water rights, &c. would probably be at fifteen dollars per acre. **1813** *Ann. 13th Cong.* 1 Sess. 50 Feeder, (nearly completed,) reservoirs, lock at the feeder, purchase of water-rights and land . . . [$]230,000. **1947** *Sierra Club Bul.* May 37 The big cattlemen squeezed out the little ones wherever possible, grabbing the water rights, foreclosing small holdings, frequently hiring gunmen to murder them. — **(14) 1834** A. Pike *Prose Sk. & Poems* 18 This is the beginning of what Lewis calls the water scrape. **1853** Brewerton *With Kit Carson* (1930) 230 As no water is to be found upon the trail, it becomes necessary to prepare the caravan previously to its setting out for encountering the difficulties of what, in prairie parlance, is usually termed a 'water-scrape.'

(15) 1904 *Cent. Mag.* Feb. 540/2 The many patches of color were subdued—a red table-cloth, a water-set of blue glass and a vase of paper roses. — **(16) 1903** Austin *Land of Little Rain* 41 Out on the Carrizo . . . is a water sign. . . . It is a laid circle of stones large enough not to be disturbed by any ordinary hap, with an opening flanked by two parallel rows of similar stones, between which were an arrow placed, touching the opposite rim of the circle . . . it would point as the crow flies to the spring. — **(17) 1882** *Harper's Mag.* Nov. 877/2 She is pasting down her wetted hair into a semblance of the 'water-waves' of fashionable society. **1931** *Chi. Tribune* 9 Feb. 4/6 Smart women adore this water wave bonnet. . . . It's very inexpensively priced at just 88c. — **(18) 1877** Ruede *Sod-House Days* 196 Talking with Hoot about digging wells etc., he told me about one new neighbor, Diegel, who has a firm faith in water witching.

b. In less frequent, chiefly obs., expressions: (1) **water biscuit,** a mass of calcareous matter, shaped somewhat like a biscuit, produced in fresh water now and in the remote past by certain blue-green algae; (2) **connection,** facilities for continuing a journey by water; (3) **dumpling,** (see quot.); (4) **football,** (see quot.), *rare;* (5) **grade,** a water level route; (6) **ground,** designating meal ground at a watermill as distinguished from that ground by steam, *colloq.;* (7) **log,** a bored log used as a section of a water main, cf. **pump log;** (8) **reading,** interpreting, for navigating purposes, the appearance of the water in a river; (9) **rot,** (see quot.); (10) **stage,** ?a water conveyance; (11) * **thief,** (see quot.).

(1) 1900 J. M. Clarke *(title)*, The Water Biscuit of Square Island, N.Y. — **(2) 1851** Cist *Cincinnati* 312 Then comes the Baltimore road, . . . to connect with this city, in almost a direct line, and without any water connection. — **(3) 1843** *Amer. Pioneer* II. 153, I got a dough-boy or water-dumpling, and proceeded. — **(4) 1891** *Triangle* I. 83 Water Foot Ball . . . as played at our summer school differs somewhat from water polo, as it was played in deep water, where the players were obliged to keep swimming.

(5) 1888 Lee *Plains to Peaks* 31 Instead of following the stream or gulch, or taking a 'water grade,' the Midland track soon leaves the gulch and proceeds on its downward course by picking its way through the mountains. — **(6) 1942** Rawlings *C. Creek* 209 When made of good sweet water-ground meal, it [i.e., a hoecake] is crisp and palatable. — **(7) 1857** E. Stone *Life of John Howland* I. 25 The next year, 1771, the water-logs were laid from Field's fountain to Weybosset bridge. — **(8) 1875** Mark Twain *Old Times* iii. 51 Mr. Bixby seemed to think me far enough advanced to bear a lesson on water-reading. — **(9) 1791** Bartram *Travels* 208 The traders and Indians call this disease [of horses and cattle] the water-rot or scald, and say it is occasioned by the warm waters of the savanna, . . . when these creatures wade deep to feed on the water-grass.

(10) 1795 *Minutes Amer. Conferences M. E. Church* (1840) I. 64/1 Too many also, in many parts of the country, profane the sacred day, by running their land and water stages, wagons, etc. — **(11) 1884** *Nat. Museum Bul.* No. 27, 778 Bung-bucket or water-thief. . . . Used instead of a pump for drawing drinking-water from the bung-hole of a cask.

c. In designations of persons and groups: (1) **Water Baptists,** ?a sect of Baptists opposed to liquor drinking, *obs.*, cf. **Whisky Baptists;** (2) **baron,** one who controls water needed for irrigation; (3) **borer,** one who bores wells for water, *rare;* (4) * **boy,** a boy who keeps workmen supplied with drinking water, also transf.; (5) **commissioner,** (see quot. 1834); (6) **finder,** one who locates or professes to locate subterranean springs or supplies of water by means of a divining rod, *colloq.;* (7) * **guard,** (see quot. 1866), *obs.;* (8) **master,** *W.* and *S.W.* one having supervision of an irrigation system; (9) **register,** (see quot.); (10) **soldier,** (see quot.), *obs.;* (11) **taker,** in a city, one who agrees to take water from a system of waterworks, *obs.;* (12) **toter,** *S.* one who supplies a group of workers with water, *colloq.;* (13) * **witch,** a water finder *q.v.*, or a contrivance used by him, cf. **2. b.** (17); (14) **wizard,** (see quot. and cf. **water finder, water witch**).

(1) **1723** *Amer. Wkly. Mercury* 12 Feb. 4/2 All serious Persons, whether.... Water-Baptists, or People called Quakers ... may advise with the said Person at his Lodgings. — (2) **1893** *Harper's Mag.* May 945/2 The annual dues (for 'maintenance,' as this Colorado method of producing water-barons is called) are from a dollar to two dollars and a half an acre. — (3) **1844** Norris *Directory* 41 Jefts, Amasa, water borer. — (4) **1859** *Harper's Mag.* April 712/1 The 'water-boy' in his first round found me standing by the stove. **1946** Wilson *Fidelity* 158 We small boys were allowed the great privilege of acting as water boys. **1950** *Chi. Tribune* 1 March 20/1 Mr. Denham, however, knew that he was not, as under the old Wagner act, simply a water boy for the board, but that his office had been vested by congress with broad powers.

(5) **1834** *N.Y. Laws* 451 The governor shall nominate ... five persons, to be known as the water commissioners for the city of New-York, ... to examine and consider all matters relative to supplying the city of New-York with ... pure and wholesome water. **1842** *Niles' Reg.* LXIII. 125/1 Samuel Stevens ... [was] president of the board of water commissioners. — (6) **1883** *Harper's Mag.* Oct. 708/2 By trade he is a well-digger, but to this commonplace occupation he has added the more unusual profession of water-finder. **1945** Pearson *Country Flavor* 86 In most rural communities there is one person who has a reputation as a 'waterfinder.' — (7) **1823** Thacher *Military Jrnl.* 103, I did not think it possible you could escape the vigilance of the water guards. **1866** Lossing *Hudson* 351 The 'water-guard' was an aquatic corps, in the pay of the revolutionary government. — (8) **1859** [see **ward 1.**]. **1902** F. H. Newell *Irrigation in U.S.* 107 He is usually known as the 'water-master' or 'ditch-rider.' **1949** *Sierra Club Bul.* June 75 Across the lake, Jean Landre, the Water Master for the Pacific Gas and Electric Company who controlled the level of the lake, was contentedly weathering the storm. — (9) **1849** *Act to Amend Charter of City of N.Y.* 11 There shall be a bureau in this department for the collection of the revenues derived from the sale of the water, and the chief officer thereof, shall be called the 'Water Register.'

(10) **1861** F. Moore *Rebellion Rec.* I. iii. 43 Three companies from Louisiana arrived today, also a hundred water soldiers (marines) from New Orleans. — (11) **1852** Tremenheere *Notes* 112 There were, in this first year, 13,463 'water-takers;' and of these, 1202 had obtained 'the right to attach a hose for washing windows, sprinkling streets, washing carriages, or other purposes.' **1853** *Inaugural Addresses Boston Mayors* II. 22 A subject which possesses as deep an interest to every water taker and tax payer in the City [etc.]. — (12) **1852** *Fla. Plantation Rec.* 549, 83 Negroes on Chemoonie and 43 Names goes into the Field, including the Driver and two water toters. **1860** Olmsted *Back Country* 48 Each gang [of cotton pickers] was attended by a 'water-toter.' — (13) **1817** S. Brown *Western Gazetteer* 96 The discovery [of a lead mine] was made by a water-witch. **1832** *Boston Transcript* 3 Feb. 1/2 The subscriber offers for sale, at his Store, ... the following articles, viz.:... Wooden Shoes, Water Witches, &c. **1890** L. C. D'Oyle *Notches* 153 Injun heap water-witch. Show white man where to dig. — (14) **1831** *Illinois Mo.* Feb. 228 Christopher Colewort had recourse to one of those men who profess to discover hidden treasures, both of water and of metals, beneath the earth's surface, by means of the hazel rod—and are denominated water-wizzards, or money-finders.

d. Designating places and areas: (1) **water camp,** a camp where water is available, cf. **dry camp;** (2) **claim,** a tract of government land petitioned for or claimed by a prospective settler because of the water on it; (3) **front,** land, usu. in a city, that fronts or abuts on a body of water; (4) **gap,** see as a main entry; (5) **lick,** prob. a suck lick *q.v.*, *obs.;* (6) **lot,** a lot or plot of ground which borders a body of water (see also quot. 1891); (7) **prairie,** an extensive low area covered to the depth of a few inches with water (see quot. 1871); (8) **privilege,** see as a main entry; (9) * **shed,** the entire gathering ground of a river system; (10) **slash,** a low, miry, swampy place; (11) **station,** a place where water for a locomotive is obtained; (12) **street,** a street that leads to or extends along a waterfront, usu. as a proper name, also attrib.; (13) **wash,** a place where water has eroded the topsoil, cf. * **wash,** *n.* **2.**

(1) **1898** King *Warrior Gap* 177 Ordinarily when making summer marches over the range, the first 'water camp' on the Sweetwater trail was here at Cañon Springs. — (2) **1896** Shinn *Story of Mine* 81 Water claims and mill sites were taken up almost as soon as work had fairly begun on the Comstock. **1942** Stegner *Mormon C.* 314 But Douglass persevered, filed a homestead claim and water claims on three springs. — (3) **1766** *Laws of N.C.* (1791) 234 According to the Plan of the said Town of Newbern, the Water Fronts of the Lots herein before mentioned are divided from the said Lots by a Street called Front Street. **1856** Emerson *Eng. Traits* 47 A people so skilful and sufficient in economizing water-front by docks, warehouses, and lighters. **1950** *Reader's Digest* April 124/1 Along the water front the dirty river stands unbearably.

(5) **1780** in *Travels Amer. Col.* 652 The Buffalo lick in No. 2 is a water lick at the foot of a hill. — (6) **1722** *Amer. W. Mercury* 2 Aug. 2/2 A Water-Lot containing 40 Feet 9 Inches, on King-Street, and about 250 Feet back from said Street into the River Delaware. **1839** C.F. Briggs *Harry Franco* II. iv. 34 'What are water lots?' I inquired. 'Some very beautiful situations,' he replied, 'which extend about two hundred yards into the river; they require nothing but merely to be filled up, to make them very desirable spots to build upon.' **1891** *Cent.* 6844/2 *Water-lot,* ... a lot of ground which is under water; specifically, one of a regular system of city lots which are partly or wholly covered by the water of a bay, lake, or river, and may be filled in and converted into made ground for the erection of buildings, docks, etc. — (7) **1871** De Vere 125 Those vast inland plains, known farther North as *salt* and *water* prairies, ... [are] covered with a thick incrustation or nitrous efflorescence, known as *tesquite,* so as to give them the appearance of a large motionless lake. **1938** Matschat *Suwannee River* 15 All day they poled and paddled through the great swamp, over the still water prairies and along the runs. — (9) **1874** E. Coues *Birds N.W.* p. vii, The Missouri Region, in its broadest sense, as embracing the whole watershed of that great river and its tributaries. **1950** *Dly. Ardmoreite* (Ardmore, Okla.) 30 April c. 18/1 Most of the watershed is privately owned.

(10) **1711** in *Amer. Sp.* XV. 409/2 Beginning at a marked Stooping white Oak.... Standing in a water Slash by ye road side. **1728** *Ib.*, Thence to a Corner Red Oak Standing in or Near the Water Slash. — (11) *Amer. R.R. Jrnl.* 533/3 Twenty turn outs with water stations. **1898** Nicholas *Idyl of Wabash* 56 If I can reach the water-station I can warn the engineer. — (12) **1642** *Cambridge Prop. Rec.* 73 Comon ground adioyninge to waterstreet East the Cricke south. **1868** Beecher *Sermons* (1869) I. 31 The Water street movement in New-York, to-day, is another such movement. **1902** White *Blazed Trail* 183 Any old logger ... will tell you of the 'Pen,' the 'White Row,' the 'Water Streets' of Alpena, Port Huron, Ludington, Muskegon, and a dozen other lumber towns. — (13) **1881** *Rep. Indian Affairs* 7 The southern part ... is rough, mountainous, and much cut up with deep arroyas or water-washes.

e. Used with reference to containers: (1) **water back,** "a permanent reservoir at the back of a stove or range, to utilize the heat of the fire in keeping a supply of hot water" (Knight); (2) **barrel,** a barrel serving as a container for water (see also quot. 1876); (3) **cooler,** a receptacle in which drinking water is kept cool; (4) * **tank,** a large reservoir erected beside a railroad track for supplying locomotives with water, also attrib. in the sense of small, insignificant; (5) * **tower,** a piece of fire-fighting equipment consisting essentially of an adjustable pipe or frame by means of which water may be delivered at a greater height than would otherwise be possible.

(1) **1864** Stowe *House & Home P.* 294 The kitchen-range with its water-back I humbly salute. **1897** *Boston Jrnl.* 26 Jan. 2/1 The fires were small affairs ... due to efforts to thaw out frozen water pipes or to explosions engendered by the bursting of water backs. — (2) **1849** *31st Congress* 1 Sess. Sen. Doc. No. 64, 205 After filling our water barrels, and giving our animals all they would drink, I made a start this evening at two o'clock. **1876** Knight 2375/2 *Water-barrel,* ... a large wrought-iron barrel with a self-acting valve in the bottom, used in drawing water where there are no pumps. **1907** *St. Nicholas* July 771/1 Two tents by a driven well, ... and a row of dusty water barrels comprised the new stage station. — (3) **1846** *Catholic Herald* (Phila.) 30 Aug. 272/4 Refrigerators, water coolers, and filterers, Safes, Ironing tables, Step-ladders. **1947** *True* Nov. 124/3 A nearby water cooler brought Buddy by for a drink. — (4) **1862** Moore *Rebellion Rec.* V. ii. 138 They got on a car, and ran up the road to cut a water-tank, and were ambushed. **1908** Davenport *Butte Beneath X-Ray* 84 Every whistling post and water tank precinct with six votes had a newspaper furnished it. **1946** *Sat. Ev. Post* 11 May 27/1 Big Pete [was] just then climbing down from the cab of his Four-Spot locomotive alongside the main-line water tank.

(5) **1894** B. Mathews in *Harper's Mag.* Jan. 227/1 The water-tower, ... was speedily erected and in service. **1911** A. B. Reeve *Poisoned Pen* 61 Four engines, two hook-and-ladders, a water-tower, the battalion chief and a deputy are hurrying to that fire.

2. In the names of plants, trees, etc.: (1) **water arum,** a bog herb, *Calla palustris,* a native of the north temperate zone; (2) **ash,** any one of several American ashes, also box elder *q.v.;* (3) **beech,** the American plane tree, also the American hornbeam; (4) **birch,** any one of various American birches as the red birch, also attrib.; (5) **bitternut (hickory),** =**water hickory;** (6) **chinquapin,** the wankapin or American lotus, *Nelumbo lutea;* (7) * **crowfoot,** an aquatic buttercup, *Ranunculus delphinifolius,* found in the northern states; (8) **elm,** (see quots.); (9) **feather,** the featherfoil, *Hottonia inflata;* (10) **flaxseed,** (see quot. 1891); (11) **hickory,** the bitter pecan, *Carya aquatica,* of the southern states; (12) **hyacinth,** an aquatic plant, *Eichhornia crassipes;* (13) **locust,** a species of honey locust, *Gleditsia aquatica,* found in moist regions in the South; (14) **maple,** any one of various American maples, as the red maple and the silver maple; (15) * **melon,** see as a main entry; (16) **moat,** (see quot. and cf. **batamote** and **water wally**); (17) * **myrtle,** the sour gum or tupelo; (18) **oak,** see as a main entry; (19) **oats,** =**water rice** (see also **wild rice**); (20) **onion,** ?a wild onion; (21) **pine,** (see quot.); (22) **red oak,** (see quot.), *obs.;* (23) **rice,** wild rice, *Zizania aquatica;* (24) * **shield,** an American aquatic plant, *Brasenia schreberi,* having large, shieldlike leaves, also with specifying term; (25) **star grass,** an American water plant, *Heteranthera dubia,* having star-shaped blossoms; (26) **suck leaves,** (see quot.); (27) **target,** =**water shield;** (28) **tupelo (tree),** (see quots.); (29) **wally,** the batamote (*q.v.*) of the Southwest; (30) **white oak,** an overcup oak *q.v.;* (31) * **willow,** a tree or shrub of the genus *Dianthera,* also with a specifying term.

(1) **1817–8** EATON *Botany* (1822) 214 Water arum . . . grows in wet places. **1919** STURTEVANT *Notes Edible Plants* 125 Water Arum. Water Dragon. . . . The rootstocks of this plant yield eatable starch. — (2) **1709** LAWSON *Carolina* 93 The Water-Ash is brittle. The bark is food for the Beavers. **1819** E. DANA *Geog. Sk.* 171 The soil is . . . thickly covered with timber; such as various species of oak and water ash. **1916** SETON *Woodcraft Man.* 295 Black Ash, Hoop Ash, or Water Ash (*Fraxinus nigra*) A tall forest tree of swampy places; 70, 80, or rarely 100 feet high. — (3) **1756** KALM *Resa* II. 198 Af de härvarande Ängelska kallades den dels *Button-wood,* dels ock most *Water-Beech.* **c1760** in WOODWARD *Ploughs* (1941) 319 The Button wood or Water Beach makes a tolerable Shade but is subject to worms or Catterpillars. **1916** SETON *Woodcraft Man.* 280 Blue Beech, Water Beech, or American Hornbeam (*Carpinus caroliniana*) A small tree, 10 to 25, rarely 40, feet high; bark smooth. Wood hard, close-grained, very strong; much like Ironwood. — (4) **1859** *S. Lit. Messenger* XXVIII. 143/1 Yisterday, I . . . had two lines out for cat, hitched to water-birch limbs. **1897** SUDWORTH *Arborescent Flora* **141** *Betula nigra,* River Birch. . . . Water Birch (W.Va., Kans.).

(5) **1810** MICHAUX *Arbres* I. 20 J[uglans] aquatica, *Water bitter nut,* nom donné par moi. **1860** CURTIS *Woody Plants N.C.* 44 Water Bitternut Hickory. . . . The timber is rather inferior. **1897** SUDWORTH *Arborescent Flora* 112 Water Bitternut (S.C., Tenn.). — (6) **1836** LINCOLN *Botany* App. 119 Water chinquepin, sacred bean, Indian lotus. . . . Flowers larger than those of any other plant in North America, except one species of magnolia. **1949** *N.O. Times-Picayune Mag.* 16 Oct. 20/2 The Indians call them water chinquapins, but they don't resemble the tree-grown variety at all. — (7) **1833** EATON *Botany* (ed. 6) 297 *Ranunculus aquatilis,* water crowfoot. **1899** M. GOING *Flowers* 112 The water-crowfoot for instance bears some floating leaves, and some which live beneath the surface. — (8) **1820** GILLELAND *Ohio & Miss. Pilot* 257 U. aquatica (water elm) in marshes, generally in the rear of rich bottoms. **1916** SETON *Woodcraft Man.* 285 White Elm, Water, or Swamp Elm (*Ulmus Americana*) A tall splendid forest tree; commonly 100, occasionally 120 feet. Wood reddish brown; hard, strong, tough, very hard to split. — (9) **1818** NUTTALL *N. Amer. Plants* I. 120. **1901** MOHR *Plant Life Ala.* 49 They are kept afloat . . . by the rosettes of their floating leaves, as in sundew (*Drosera intermedia*), water feather (*Hottonia inflata*) [etc.].

(10) **1817–8** EATON *Botany* (1822) 333 Water flaxseed. . . . The roots rarely reach the ground; but merely extend downwards a few inches into the water. **1891** *Cent.* 6842/1 *Water-flaxseed,* . . . the larger duckweed, *Lemna polyrhiza:* so called from the shape and minute size of the fronds. — (11) **1818** DARBY *Emigrant's Guide* 80 The most important vegetable productions [include]: . . . *Juglans amara,* Bitter nut hickory, *Juglans aquatica,* Water hickory [etc.]. **1947** *Democrat* 2 Oct. 4/1 Our so-called lakes, or river sloughs, are lined with the water hickory, pignut or wild pecan, as it is variously called. — (12) **1897** H. J. WEBBER in *U.S. Dept. Agric. Bul., Bot.* No. 18 (*title*), The Water Hyacinth, and its relation to navigation in Florida. **1909** *Cent. Supp.* 996/3 The water-hyacinth is most commonly known to florists as *Pontederia azurea* or *P. crassipes,* but the recently accepted disposition is to place it in the allied genus *Piaropus.* **1950** *L.A. Times* 19 Feb. (Home Mag.) 31/4 The water hyacinth is excellent for pools. — (13) **1810** MICHAUX *Arbres* I. 36 [Gleditschia] monosperma. . . . *Water Locust,* . . . nom secondaire. **1832** BROWNE *Sylva* 161 The Water Locust is first seen in the Atlantic States in the lower part of South Carolina. **1897** SUDWORTH *Arborescent Flora* 254. — (14) **1802** ELLICOTT *Jrnl.* 284 Water maple, (*acer negundo,*) . . . is met with as high as the Wabash. **1916** SETON *Woodcraft Man.* 292 Red, Scarlet, Water, or Swamp Maple (*Acer rubrum*). A fine tree the same size as [silver maple]. . . . Noted for its flaming crimson foliage in fall, as well as its red leaf-stalks, flowers, and fruit earlier.

(16) **1931** DAYTON *West. Browse Plants* 158 Emory baccharis (*B. emoryi*), locally known as water moats and water willow, is a shrub, 3 to 12 feet high, ranging from Colorado to California and New Mexico, usually along washes and in coastal or inland flood plains. — (17) **1853** SIMMS *Sword & Distaff* (1854) 93 The other is . . . somewhere among them water-myrtle and willow bushes. — (19) **1817** EATON *Botany* (1822) 519 *Zizania clavulosa,* water-oats, wild-rice. **1901** MOHR *Plant Life Ala.* 362 Water Oats. . . . Valuable for its highly nutritious seeds.

(20) **1925** HEMING *Living Forest* 143 Muskrats . . . eat . . . the stalks an' roots o' lilies, flags, bulrushes, an' water onions. — (21) **1818** DARBY *Emigrant's Guide* 33 [Among] the most common timber trees found in the basin of the Mobile [is] . . . *Pinus taeda,* Loblolly, or water pine. — (22) **1785** MARSHALL *Amer. Grove* 122 *Quercus rubra ramosissima,* Water Red Oak, . . . grows most naturally by creek sides, or in low wet places. — (23) **1878** KILLIBREW *Tenn. Grasses* 237 Water or Indian Rice . . . grows in swamps, and on borders of rivulets and lakes. **1901** MOHR *Plant Life Ala.* 49 Fresh-water plants which root in a water-soaked soil . . . include *Zizania, Zizianopsis* (water rice). — (24) **1817–8** EATON *Botany* (1822) 310 *Hydropeltis purpurea,* water shield. . . . The leaves float on the surface of the water. **1901** MOHR *Plant Life Ala.* 503 *Brasenia purpurea.* . . . Purple Water Shield.

(25) **1843** TORREY *Flora N.Y.* II. 313 *Heteranthera graminea.* Water Star-grass. . . . Flowing waters: frequent. **1898** CREEVEY *Flowers of Field* 128 Water Star-grass . . . has stamens all alike, with grass-like leaves which lie under water. — (26) **1674** JOSSELYN *Two Voyages* 80 Water-plantane, called in *New-England* water Suck-leaves, and Scurvie-leaves, you must lay them whole to the leggs to draw out water between the skin and the flesh. — (27) **1814** BIGELOW *Florula Bostoniensis* 135 *Hydropeltis purpurea.* Water target . . . an aquatic plant, . . . [growing in] stagnant waters. **1854** THOREAU *Walden* 194 A closer scrutiny . . . [detects] only a few small heart-leaves, . . . and perhaps a water-target or two. — (28) **c1730** CATESBY *Carolina* I. 60 The Water-Tupelo . . . has a large trunk, especially near the ground, and grows very tall. **1785** H. MARSHALL *Arbust. Amer.* 96 Nyssa aquatica, Virginian water tupelo-tree. — (29) **1931** DAYTON *Western Browse Plants* 158 Seepwillow (*B. glutinosa*), locally named false, Gila, or water willow, . . . water motie, and water wally, . . . has considerable value in erosion control.

(30) **1801** MICHAUX *Histoire des Chênes* 5 Chêne blanc aquatique. Chêne lyré. *Water white oak.* **1832** BROWNE *Sylva Amer.* 272 This interesting species . . . is called Swamp Post Oak, Over-Cup Oak and Water White Oak. — (31) **1838** AUDUBON *Ornith. Biog.* IV. 61 In the Lower parts of Louisiana, it breeds on low bushes of the water-willow. **1901** MOHR *Plant Life Ala.* 735 *Dianthera ovata.* . . . Low Water Willow. **1931** CLUTE *Plants* 70 The entire list of such transfers [of name] is too long to be included here, but we may add . . . the water willow (*Dianthera Americana*) an acanthus.

b. In the names of birds, snakes, etc.: (1) * **water adder,** any one of various American snakes, esp. *Natrix sipedon,* which live in or frequent fresh water; (2) * **bug,** (see quot.); (3) * **crow,** *S.* =**water turkey;** (4) * **dog,** any one of various large salamanders, as a mud puppy or hellbender, *colloq.;* (5) **flounder,** (see quot.); (6) **moccasin,** a pit viper, *Agkistrodon piscivorus,* found in or near water in the southern states, also any one of various harmless water snakes confused with this; (7) **puppy,** =**water dog;** (8) **rabbit,** (see quot.); (9) **rattlesnake,** (*a*) =**water moccasin,** (*b*) the diamondback rattlesnake, *Crotalus adamanteus,* often found in damp places near water; (10) **sheep,** (see quot.), *obs.;* (11) **terrapin,** an edible turtle of the family Testudinidae, esp. of the genus *Malaclemys,* found in fresh or brackish water; (12) * **thrush,** any one of various American warblers of the genus *Seiurus,* usu. found near streams; (13) **turkey,** the snakebird, *Anhinga anhinga,* cf. **anhinga,** * **darter,** * **water crow;** (14) **viper,** =**water moccasin;** (15) * **wagtail,** one of various American water thrushes; (16)

weevil, (see quot. 1891); (17) ∗**witch,** any one of various water birds esp. quick in diving, as the horned grebe and the pied-billed grebe, cf. **1. c.** (13) above.

(1) **1784** CUTLER in *Life & Corr.* I. 98 In [the] river we saw a very large snake swimming, which we supposed was either a black snake or a water adder. **1899** *Animal & Plant Lore* 86 The water-adder (*Tropedonotus sipedon*) carries a poisonous sting in its tail. New England. — (2) **1891** *Cent.* 6840/2 *Water-bug,* . . . the croton bug or German cockroach, *Blatta* (*Phyllodromia*) *germanica:* so called from its preference for water-pipes and moist places in houses. — (3) **1838** AUDUBON *Ornith. Biog.* IV. 138 At the mouths of the [Miss.] river it bears the name of 'Water Crow.' **1891** *Cent.* 6841/2 *Water crow,* . . . the darter, snake-bird, or water-turkey, *Plotus anhinga.* (Southern U.S.) — (4) **1859** BARTLETT 502 Water-Dogs, the western name for various species of salamanders, or lizard-shaped animals, with smooth, shiny, naked skins; sometimes called Water-puppies and Ground-puppies. **1949** *Amer. Photography* Sep. 593/1 The best known is probably the common mud puppy or water dog (*Necturus maculosus*).

(5) **1884** GOODE *Fisheries* I. 199 The Spotted Sand Flounder, *Lophopsetta maculata* . . . is variously known along the coast as Water Flounder, Window-pane, and Daylight. — (6) **1821** NUTTALL *Travels Arkansa* 154 The other [snake] frequents waters, and is called the water mockasin, and poisonous black-snake. **1882** C. C. HOPLEY *Snakes* 495 A 'water moccasin' . . . had been seen . . . unwelcomely close to a southern residence. **1949** *Scientific Mo.* Jan. 57/1 The dreaded water moccasin of our Northern states all too often turns out to be the banded water snake (*Natrix sipedon*), erroneously called the 'water rattle' and 'water pilot' in certain localities. — (7) **1859** [see **water dog**]. — (8) **1864** WEBSTER 1497/2 *Water-rabbit,* . . . an American rabbit (*Lepus aquaticus*), found in Mississippi and Louisiana, and having the peculiarity of swimming and diving. — (9) (*a*) **1736** CATESBY *Carolina* II. 43 *Vipera aquatica,* . . . in Carolina commonly goes by the Name of the Water Rattle-Snake, not that it hath a Rattle, but many of them are very large, and coloured not much unlike the Rattle-Snake, and their Bite is said to be mortal. (*b*) **1810** LAMBERT *Travels U.S.* III. 60 The shores abounded with a species of *water rattlesnake,* whose bite was also of a deadly nature. **1861** *New Amer. Cyclo.* XIII. 773 The diamond or water rattlesnake . . . is dark brown or dusky above, with a series of large rhomboidal spots continuous from head to tail.

(10) **1832** WILLIAMSON *Hist. Maine* I. 159 The *Roach* . . . has been called the 'water-sheep' for its simplicity. — (11) **1709** LAWSON *Carolina* 133 Water Terebins are small; containing about as much Meat as a Pullet, and are extraordinary Food. **1856** *Porter's Spirit of Times* 20 Sep. 43/2 Fishermen in our waters are often annoyed by the water-terrapin. — (12) **1811** WILSON *Ornithology* III. 66 The Water Thrush, *Turdus Aquaticus,* . . . is remarkable for its partiality to . . . shores, ponds, and streams of water. **1917** *Birds of Amer.* III. 154 Water-Thrush. . . . Other Names.—New York Warbler; Small-billed Water-Thrush; Northern Water-Thrush. **1950** *Nat. Hist.* April 175/3 The song of the Kirtland's Warbler has been described as resembling that of the house wren and the Northern Water Thrush. — (13) **1836** HOLLEY *Texas* 100 King-fishers and water-turkies . . . are found in great abundance. **1949** HADLEY *Indiana Birds* 45/1 It is a vision of turkey vultures soaring far aloft in the blue vault of heaven in company with stately wood ibises and water turkeys. — (14) *c*1735 CATESBY *Carolina* II. 43 *Vipera Aquatica.* The Water Viper. . . . One of these Serpents I surprized swimming a Shore with a large Cat-Fish. **1891** *Cent.* 6763/1 In the United States the name [viper] is commonly but erroneously applied to various spotted snakes, . . . as the water-viper, *Ancistrodon piscivorus,* the water-moccasin, poisonous.

(15) **1759** tr. VENEGAS *Nat. Hist. Calif.* I. 40 About the harbour of Monte-Rey are bustards, . . . quails, partridges, blackbirds, water-wagtails, . . . and other birds. **1917** *Birds of Amer.* III. 153 The Louisiana Water-Thrush . . . bobs its tail as it proceeds, a peculiarity from which it derives its popular name of Water Wagtail. — (16) **1881** *Amer. Naturalist* XV. 483, I send you by express a number of 'water-weevils' preserved in alcohol. **1891** *Cent., water-weevil.* . . . A snout-beetle, *Lissorhoptrus simplex,* which occurs in great numbers in the Georgia and South Carolina rice-fields, the adult feeding on the leaves of the rice, and the larvae feeding on the roots under water. — (17) **1789** MORSE *Amer. Geog.* 60 American Birds [include]. . . . Water-wagtail, Water-hen, Water-witch. **1835** AUDUBON *Ornith. Biog.* III. 359 'Water-witches,' as they call you, I clearly see your bills, although you have withdrawn all of you save those parts. **1917** *Birds of Amer.* I. 5 Horned Grebes are commonly known as 'Hell-divers' or 'Water-Witches.'

3. In colloq. phrases: (1) *To take water,* to retreat or back down from a position or undertaking; (2) *to go in the water,* to be baptized as a religious convert; (3) *to be on the water-cart* (or *wagon*), and variants, to be resolved to abstain from strong drink.

(1) **1853** BALDWIN *Flush Times* 275 'If it please your honor, I believe *I will take water*' (a common expression, signifying that the person using it would take a nonsuit.) **1891** C. ROBERTS *Adrift Amer.* 200 The fellow, who was really a coward, though nearly twice as big as myself, took water at once. — (2) **1863** E. W. PEARSON *Lett. Port Royal* 145 Katrine is 'going in the water.' — (3) **1901** HEGAN *Mrs. Wiggs* 123, I wanted to git him some whisky, but he shuck his head. 'I'm on the water-cart,' sez he. **1902** *Sun* Nov. 23 If a student has 'hit the benzine can' too hard on the night before he is apt to be anxious to get 'on to the water wagon,' which means he wants to swear off. **1948** *Miami* (Okla.) *D. News-Rec.* 4 July 2/4 We believed that his experience had lifted him onto the water wagon, but he was even drunker the next Fourth of July.

As the last term in **alkali, apple, ash, bad, big, boat, branch, cistern, cold, Congress, Croton, cut, easy, fire, Florida, fool's, freestone, fresh, grass, great, gum, high, jerk, jig, Manhattan, maple, maple tree, medical, peach, saleratus, salt, sandstone, Saratoga, sealing, Shaker distilled, Shaker rose, slack, slick, slough, soda, sprout, spunk, stock, stump, sugar, tea, tideland, Wabash, western, white, yellow water.**

∗**water,** *v.*

1. *tr.* To pack (a jury). *Obs.*

1792 BELKNAP *Hist. New Hampshire* III. 256 The practice of watering the jury was familiarly known to those persons who had business in the Law.

2. To supply (an engine) with water. Also with *up.*

1847 *Hunt's Merch. Mag.* XVI. 211 A refreshment house for crews of engines stopping to wood or water. **1901** MERWIN & WEBSTER *Calumet 'K'* 203 One hot day after watering up the engine him and the conductor went off to get a drink.

3. To increase the nominal capital of an enterprise by issuing additional shares of (stock) without investing more money in the business.

This use of the term may have been suggested by the dishonest practice sometimes indulged in of heavily salting and watering cattle just before weighing them for sale.

1865 SALA *Diary* II. 235 Its stock had been so systematically and so unscrupulously 'watered.' **1889** MARK TWAIN *Conn. Yankee* 335, I do not approve of watering stock, but . . . you can water a gift as much as you want to.

Hence **watered stock.**

1873 *Newton Kansan* 10 April 2/2 The only curse railroads can be to a country arises from the 'watered stock' process. **1908** LORIMER *J. Spurlock* 119 An era of dilution—watered honah; watered stocks; watered whiskey. I beg yo' pa'don, suh; I meant nothin' personal.

4. To put (logs) in the water for transport.

1877 *Lumberman's Gaz.* 24 May, There have been 257,000,000 feet of logs watered on the various branches of the Muskegon.

∗**Waterbury,** *n.* The popular name for a moderately priced watch manufactured by the Waterbury Clock Co., at Waterbury, Conn. Also attrib.

1890 BIFF HALL *Turnover Club* 16 The Reporter drew from its resting-place the Waterbury chronometer which had accompanied the suit of clothes he was wearing. **1897** MARK TWAIN *Following Equator* 89 (R.), Bright Improvement has arrived, with her civilization, and her Waterbury. **1948** *Democrat* 30 Sep. 1/6 Jesse replaced it with a genuine, non-jewel Waterbury, so Joe, too, is right where he started.

water gap.

1. A gap in a range of mountains through which a stream flows. Also transf.

1756 *N.J. Archives* XIX. 577 They are now building a Fort One Mile West of Broadhead's, Six from my House, and Four from the Water Gap. **1818** F. HALL *Travels* 164 There is a similar aperture some miles N.E. called the Water Gap. **1923** in *Amer. Sp.* XV. 409/1 Some [of these rivers] break through the Blue Ridge from the Valley, making water-gaps in that formidable mountain barrier. **1950** *Chi. Tribune* 19 May 14/3 Most of Elsah is one-house deep on either side of the road, hemmed in with steep hillsides. Let's call the place a miniature water gap.

2. A place where a fence crosses a branch or other small stream.

1926 ROBERTS *Time of Man* 31 She crawled down to the branch and went secretly over the watergap, intent on being unseen. **1934** VINES *Green Thicket World* 44 Did youns fix that water gap?

∗**watering,** *n.* In combs.: (1) **watering depot,** a station for obtaining water on a long overland journey; (2) **privilege,** a place where water in some quantity is available, *obs.;* (3) **station,** a water station or water depot.

(1) **1872** MARK TWAIN *Roughing It* 142 (R.), It was nothing but a watering-depot in the midst of the stretch of sixty-eight miles. — (2) **1848** *Santa Fe Repub.* 31 May 2/4 His pastures and grazing grounds are large, and supplied with good watering privileges. — (3) **1854** BROMWELL *Locomotive Sk.* 89 Even the little watering-stations, . . . rise far superior, in the spirit of the design, to any other on

the route. **1881** *Rep. Indian Affairs* 3 Drivers refused to engage on account of . . . the long hauls between watering stations.

As the last term in **stock watering.**

* **watermelon,** *n. attrib.*

1. a. watermelon patch, a small piece of land planted in watermelons. **b. watermelon preserves,** preserves made of the rinds of watermelons. **c. watermelon spoon,** a souvenir spoon in some way suggestive of a watermelon.

(a) 1809 IRVING *Knickerb.* 328 The Gardeniers of Hudson . . . [were] distinguished by many triumphant feats, such as robbing watermelon-patches. **1912** *Out West* April 236/2 It was like praying for rain and going out and finding a full grown water-melon patch. — **(b) 1894** *McClure's Mag.* IV. 83/2 Why, we've got corn' beef . . . an' watermelon perserves, An' you can make a custard pie. — **(c) 1896** *Godey's Mag.* Feb. 220/2 The Georgia Watermelon Spoon is the newest departure in souvenir spoons.

2. Of or pertaining to a time or social occasion when watermelons are eaten, as **watermelon cutting, day, party.**

1888 RITTENHOUSE *Maud* 412 At eight Mr. Blauvelt called to take me to the impromptu 'water-melon party.' **1890** *Stock Grower & Farmer* 9 Aug. 3/3 Mr. W. E. Anderson . . . sends a hearty invitation to be present at the novel celebration [at Rocky Ford, Colo.] . . . of 'watermelon day.' **1912** COBB *Back Home* 50 The veterans adjourned back behind Floral Hall for a watermelon cutting. **1948** *Dly. Ardmoreite* (Ardmore, Okla.) 13 July 2/1 Stewards of the First Methodist church have been invited to a watermelon cutting in Fellowship hall of the church Wednesday at 7:30 p.m.

water oak. Any one of various American oaks often found near water, esp. *Quercus nigra* of the southeastern states.

1687 in *Amer. Sp.* XV. 156/2 To a Water Oake Standing by ye side of ye black Swamp. **1765** J. BARTRAM *Jrnl.* 21 Dec. (1766) 2 So staid at Mr. Davis's, who walked with us about his land, on which grew very large evergreen and water oaks, magnolia. **1867** MUIR *Thousand-Mile Walk* (1916) 47 The Chattahoochee River is richly embanked with massive, bossy, dark green water oaks. **1950** *Amer. Forests* Jan. 29/1 It is, however, . . . considered by some to be less desirable for planting than either the water oak or willow oak.

water privilege. The right to make use of the water of, or the power generated by, a stream or other body of water; the place where such water or water power is available.

1749 *N.H. Probate Rec.* III. 755 We set off to Deborah Shackford, . . . the Water Privilege belonging to said Estate. **1815** HUMPHREYS *Yankey* 53 She must be as big as the nation, and have a wonderful water privilege into the bargain. **1833** A. FERGUSSON *Notes Tour U.S.* 267 They have here, what is called in America, a valuable *water privilege* or *fall*, and have erected flour and saw-mills to a large extent. **1892** *Vt. Agric. Rep.* XII. 128 Good water privileges may be found on the Missisquoi river.

transf. **1883** PECK *Bad Boy* 50 He was helping her put on her rubber water privilege to go home in the rain the night of the sociable.

wauregan wɔˈrigən, *a. local.* [Mohican *wŭrigĕn*, in same sense.] Good, fine. *Obs.*

[**1643** WILLIAMS *Key* (1866) 64 *Wunêgin* Well, or good.] *a***1809** in KENDALL *Travels* I. 307 For courage bold, for things *waureegan*, He was the glory of Moheagan. **1877** BARTLETT 741 *Wauregan*. . . . The word is still local in and about Norwich, Conn. **1910** HODGE *Amer. Indians* II. 923/2.

* **wave,** *n.* **1.** A natural or artificial undulation of the hair, or hair having such an undulation. Also attrib. **2. wave region,** (see quot.). *Rare.*

(1) 1866 A. D. WHITNEY *L. Goldthwaite* iv, Freedom's northern wind will take all the wave out of your hair. **1884** NYE *Baled Hay* 15 She blushed clear up under her 'wave.' **1944** *Sears Cat.* (ed. 189) 558H Rayon Mesh Wave Cap. . . . Sure protection for your waves. — **(2) 1856** OLMSTED *Slave States* 397 For an hour or two we got above the sandy zone, and into the . . . 'wave' region of the State. The surface here was extremely undulating.

As the last term in **crime, hair, hot, polar, Saratoga, water wave.**

wavey ˈwevɪ, *n.* [See def.] "A Canadian French corruption of *wehwew*, the Cree (onomatopoetic) name of the snow goose, *Chen hyperboreus*, called by the Chippewa *wewe*" (Hodge).

[**1795** S. HEARNE *Journey Northern Ocean* 329 Wavey (or white goose). *Ib.* 442 Horned wavey. . . . Common Wavey, or Snow Goose.] **1884** COUES *Key to Birds* (ed. 2) 686 *Chen rossi.* Ross' Goose. Horned Wavey. Least Snow Goose. **1925** HEMING *Living Forest* 139 White geese are the best runners, while wavey, or laughin' geese, Canada geese, an' gray geese come next. **1948** *Atlantic Mo.* Sep. 24/1 They come into Hannah Bay by the tens of thousands, the snow geese like whitecaps taking flight from the sea, the blue waveys as dark and unpredictable as the Bay's autumn storm clouds.

* **wavy,** *a.* **1. wavy oak,** (see quot.). **2. wavy-striped flea beetle,** (see quots.).

(1) 1885 HAVARD *Flora W. & S. Texas* 505 *Quercus undulata*, (Wavy Oak). Very common, scrubby Oak in foot-hills west of Devil's River. — **(2) 1868** *Amer. Naturalist* II. 514 The Wavy-striped Flea-Beetle. This beautiful little beetle, also called 'Striped Turnip-fly' . . . at the West, is well known and abundant. **1884** *Rep. Comm. Agric.* 301 The Wavy-Striped Flea-Beetle. . . . The wing-covers have each a broad, wavy, longitudinal band of a pale yellow color.

wawa ˈwɑwɑ, *n.*[1] = **wavey.**

1768 *Phil. Trans.* LX. 126 There are various sorts of the geese, as the grey-goose, the way-way, the brant, the dunter. **1855** LONGFELLOW *Hiawatha* 28 When the Wawa has departed, When the wild-goose has gone southward. [**1925** HEMING *Living Forest* 45 Not much, an' never to th' death, except once in a great while in the matin' season, which is during Wawe Pesim—the Egg Moon—or June.]

wawa ˈwɑwɑ, *n.*[2] *N.W.* [In the Chinook Jargon used as *v.* and *n.*, to talk, speak, a talk, speech.]

1. Language, speech.

1858 *Hutchings Mag.* May 527/1 White man halo kum-tux, Ingin waw-waw. **1889** *Seattle Post-Intelligencer* 7 Aug. 4/4 W. R. Andrews, who can speak the Chinook 'wa-wa' id[i]omatically, appears for Jim App. *a***1915** MUIR *Travels Alaska* (1917) 210 Toyatte also, with a teasing smile, said: 'Mr. Young, mika tillicum hi yu tola wawa' (your friend leads you far in speaking).

2. Talk, discussion, conference.

1868 WHYMPER *Alaska* 43 After a 'hyas wa-wa' (big talk) with the Indians, Brown at length succeeded in hiring a canoe. **1873** *Kalama* (Wash.) *Beacon* 14 June 1/2 Since last Wednesday, an investigation has been in a continued 'waw waw' before Justice Beall upon the charge of assault with intent to kill, prefered against Chung Kan for attacking Lo Ching with deadly weapons. [**1891–1904** (*title*) Kamloops Wawa (Newspaper pub. at Kamloops, B.C., in the Chinook Jargon.)]

* **wax,** *n.*

1. (See quot. 1879 and cf. **tacky wax.**)

1845 JUDD *Margaret* II. 185 The 'Wax' is freely distributed to be cooled on lumps of snow. **1879** WEBSTER *Supp.* 1585/1 *Wax*, . . . thick sirup made by boiling down the sap of the sugar-maple tree, and cooled by exposure to the air. *Local. N.E.* **1892** *Outing* March 462/1 When the proprietor, who has been boiling a portion of the syrup in a kettle over a brushwood fire, . . . invites us to partake of wax on snow, I gladly accept.

2. = **chewing gum.**

1909 WEBSTER. **1946** WILSON *Fidelity* 99 The sales were 240 bottles of soda pop, about two tubs of lemonade, a great lot of candy, wax (chewing gum), cigars etc.

3. wax bean, (see quot. 1909).

1909 WEBSTER, *Wax bean.* One of a race of snap or string beans with tender golden yellow pods;—called also butter bean. **1948** *Salt Lake Tribune* 29 June 20/6 Green and wax beans are available.

4. * **waxwork,** climbing bittersweet, *Celastrus scandens.* Cf. **Roxbury waxwork.**

1841 *Knickerb.* XVII. 334 The golden-berried wax-work weaves its wreath. **1860** CURTIS *Woody Plants N.C.* 119 Wax-work. Bittersweet. . . . This is to me the rarest plant in the State.

b. In phrases indicative of extreme neatness.

1803 in M. B. SMITH *Forty Yrs. Washington Soc.* (1906) 43, I found the house in perfect order, the parlour set off with oak boughs, curtains white as snow; and all neat as waxwork. **1849** KINGSLEY *Dairy* 14 Went on board the brig of war at night, found everything like waxwork. **1854** CUMMINS *Lamplighter* 34 Her rooms were like waxwork.

5. *Sons of wax*, (see quot.). *Colloq.*

1871 DE VERE 313 *Sons of wax*, is neither an uncommon nor an uncomplimentary name for them [boot and shoemakers].

As the last term in **bay, chaw, maple, myrtle, tacky wax.**

wax wæks, *v.* [Prob. f. * *wax* in the sense of beeswax.] *tr.* To defeat or get the better of. *Colloq.*

1880 *Mining News* (Ruby Hill, Nev.) 24 April 1/2 He . . . used to wax me at 'shinny-up-your-own-alley.' **1884** A. A. PUTNAM *Ten Years Police Judge* 190 Mr. Bungle . . . would in nine [out of twelve cases] be waxed but for the commiseration and the magnanimity of [etc.]. **1892** *Outing* Oct. 37/2 A great crowd of graduates from New York and Hartford and from everywhere were out at Hamilton Park to see Harvard 'waxed.'

* **waxwing,** *n.* As the last term in **Carolina, cedar, Lapland waxwing.**

* **way,** *n.*

1. In miscellaneous combs.: (1) * **waybill,** a document or label identifying and supplying information concerning a shipment of goods by freight or express, cf. **card waybill;** (2) **car,** (see quot. 1895); (3) **card,** a card or placard placed on a freight or express car showing its route and destination; (4) **farer's tree,** =**hobblebush;** (5) **line,** a light rope used for hauling a heavier one; (6) **log,** ?a log used in making a way or road, *obs.;* (7) **pocket,** a pocket in which objects of special importance or value were carried in a stagecoach or on horseback, *obs.;* (8) **wisdom,** knowledge, experience, *rare.*

(1) **1821** *Mass. Spy.* 23 May (Th.), Packages of the larger kind . . . were always entered on the way-bill. **1947** BEEBE *Mixed Train Dly.* 80 The conductor . . . prefers the Good Book to profane literature and reads it when not working on wheel reports and receipting waybills. — (2) **1879** BURDETTE *Hawkeyes* 240, I looked out of the way-car window. **1895** WAIT *Car-Builder's Dict.* 145 Way-car. A *caboose-car,* which see. Sometimes a so-called *way-car* partakes more of the character of a tool-car. The application of the term is not well defined. **1947** BEEBE *Mixed Train Dly.* 43 We carry a coach and use it for passengers when there are any and as a way car all the time. — (3) **1917** C. MATHEWSON *Sec. Base Sloan* 122 He tacked waycards to freight cars. — (4) **1858** THOREAU *Maine Woods* 88 The mountain-ash was now very handsome, as also the wayfarer's tree or hobble-bush. **1860** CURTIS *Woody Plants N.C.* 91 The branches spread upon the ground, and . . . form well secured loops for tripping the feet of inexperienced wayfarers; a habit which has been revenged . . . in the names imposed upon it of *American Wayfarer's Tree* and the *Devil's Shoestrings.*

(5) **1905** LINCOLN *Partners* 174 The smaller end of the 'way line,' a stout rope tapering from one inch to three inches in thickness, was spliced to the 'drag line.' — (6) **1716** HEMPSTEAD *Diary* 57, I was all day Getting Waylogs & Launching Timber. — (7) **1890** LANGFORD *Vigilante Days* (1912) 528, I handed the big man the way-pocket containing the way-bill. **1919** WILSON *White Indian* 140 Two large pieces of leather about sixteen inches wide by twenty-four long were laced together with a strong leather string thrown over the saddle. Fastened to these were four pockets, two in front and two behind; these hung on each side of the saddle. The two hind ones were the largest. The one in front on the left side was called the 'way pocket.' — (8) **1903** *N.Y. Times* 26 Aug., Her motives and her action, except for its lack of waywisdom, were above reproach.

b. *all the way from,* see * **all 4.** (2).

2. Of or pertaining to travel or traffic between intermediate points on a transportation line: (1) **way fare,** railroad fare to way points or stations; (2) **freight,** (*a*) goods destined for, or picked up at, an intermediate stopping place or way station, (*b*) a freight train that stops for way freight, in full **way freight train,** cf. **accommodation train;** (3) **letter,** a letter accepted by a post rider or postman en route between two post offices; (4) **mail,** mail picked up at or destined for a way station; (5) **passenger,** a passenger boarding or leaving a coach, etc., at a way station, or a point en route, also transf; (6) **point,** a stopping place on a route or during a journey; (7) **station,** a local or intermediate station in a transportation system, also transf.; (8) **train,** a train that stops at local or way stations, cf. **accommodation train.**

(1) **1846** *Hunt's Merch. Mag.* XV. 245 The through fare [was] placed at 2½ cents a mile, the way fare [was] reduced to 2¾ cents per mile. **1863** DICEY *6 Mos. Federal States* I. 55 You can go from New York to Chicago . . . for four pounds; but the way-fares are three-halfpence a mile. — (2) (*a*) **1833** *Niles' Reg.* XLIV. 260/2 The hatch . . . was open to get out a lot of way-freight. **1875** MARK TWAIN *Old Times* vii. 131 No way-freights and no way-passengers were allowed. (*b*) **1879** BURDETTE *Hawkeyes* 64 It was a way freight going south. **1903** E. JOHNSON *Railway Transportation* 135 Frequently the 'milk' trains and way-freight trains have passenger-coaches attached. — (3) **1773** FINLAY *Journal* 38 Way letters he makes his own perquisite. **1880** LAMPHERE *U.S. Govt.* 98/1 The accounts of the postal service must be kept in such manner as to exhibit separately the amount of . . . expenditure made for . . . way letters. — (4) **1818** *Amer. Mo. Mag.* II. 315 The way-mail . . . is so arranged as not to detain the coach more than three minutes at each post-office on the road. **1845** *S. Lit. Messenger* XI. 376/1 A mulatto . . . has something to do with the transfer of the way mail.

(5) **1786** *Mass. Spy* 5 Jan. (*advt.*), Way passengers will be accommodated when the stages are not full. **1879** BAGBY *Old Va. Gentleman* 236 The way-passengers . . . were dumped upon mattresses, placed on the dining tables. — (6) **1880** *Harper's Mag.* Dec. 53 The Ohio is plied by a line of Cincinnati and Pittsburgh packets, and by smaller craft earning a precarious existence between 'Way' points. **1943** *Sat. Ev. Post* 26 June 26/3 At New Orleans, Shreveport, Dallas, Tucumcari, Ogden, Portland and way points, connecting systems were pouring the war stuff onto Southern Pacific tracks. — (7) **1849** *Mass. R.R. Rep.* 21 Whole number of way stations, nineteen. **1892** *Cong. Rec.* 23 March 2462/2 'Will the gentleman allow me to ask him a question?' . . . 'The gentleman will excuse me. On a fast schedule I can not stop at way stations.' **1948** MENJOU & MUSSELMAN *It Took 9 Tailors* 10 She thought a theater was just a way station on the road to perdition. — (8) **1873** MARK TWAIN & WARNER *Gilded Age* 269 Next morning . . . he descended, sleepy and sore, from a way-train. **1920** LEWIS *Main Street* 22 The hordes of the way-train were not altogether new to Carol.

b. Also (1) **way bag,** (2) **baggage,** (3) **business,** (4) **conductor,** (5) **landing,** (6) **office,** (7) **package,** (8) **place,** (9) **ticket,** (10) **traffic,** (11) **travel.**

(1) **1864** *S.F. Bulletin* 26 Jan. 3/3 The 3 'brass bags' for San Francisco, . . . and 3 'iron' for Carson, had just been started west. (The 'brass' are the through overland bags; the 'iron' are the way ones.) — (2) **1847** WEBSTER 1253/3 *Way-Baggage,* the baggage or luggage of a way-passenger of a railroad, &c. — (3) **1850** *Hunt's Merch. Mag.* XXIII. 351 The way-business was considered of no moment. — (4) **1843** *Hunt's Merch. Mag.* VIII. 193 The freight must be paid to the way-conductor by the local agent.

(5) **1883** SWEET & KNOX *Through Texas* 42 About the time you get to know them, they begin to get off at way-landings. — (6) **1837** *Jamestown* (N.Y.) *Jrnl.* 26 July 2/2 The agents do not perform any of the duties of postmasters, other than separating the packets for each of the way offices. — (7) **1874** PINKERTON *Expressman & Detective* 11 The safe was intended for way packages. — (8) **1883** MARK TWAIN *Life on Miss.* lii, She got out of the cars at a way place. — (9) **1843** *Hunt's Merch. Mag.* IX. 388 These passengers . . . cannot convert their tickets into way-tickets.

(10) **1869** *Harper's Mag.* July 294/2 The 'way traffic' upon the line will for many years be inconsiderable. **1883** MARK TWAIN *Life on Miss.* xxii, Freight and passenger way traffic remains to the steamers. — (11) **1843** *Hunt's Merch. Mag.* IX. 388 The low fare is succeeding equally well with the way-travel on the Worcester railroad.

As the last term in **alley, American, Broad, cellar, country, cross, drift, drive, dug, entrance, entry, fall, ford, hall, head, high, hog, hoist, land, leading, log, mid, mule, park, pass, race, range, regular, roll, run, single, skid, sluice, speed, sub, trace, train, tramp, walk, waste, white way.**

* **way,** *adv.*

1. With other adverbs in the sense: At or by a considerable distance, thoroughly. *Colloq.*

1888 *Cong. Rec.* 3 Oct. 9122/1 He is way below, he is only 50 in mathematics. **1908** WHITE *Riverman* 83 You got to feeling like the thing was never going to end, and . . . you got sick of it way through.

2. In colloq., chiefly adverbial, combs. [cf. * **away**]: (1) **wayback,** (*a*) far back or off, long ago, hence **way-backer,** (*b*) *from wayback,* from the backwoods or "sticks," hence *a wayback from wayback,* a rustic, an uncouth person, (*c*) in commendatory expressions implying high ability, thoroughness; (2) **down,** far or deep down; (3) **off,** at a considerable distance, far removed, much in error; (4) **out,** far away from a point regarded as central; (5) **over,** far over, as far as (a point named or implied); (6) **up,** (*a*) *adv.* far up, very high, (*b*) *a.* of superior quality or rank, excellent.

(1) (*a*) **1906** in *Kans. Hist. Soc.* IX. 516 When we drove into Olathe we must have looked liked 'way-backers.' **1923** COOK *On Old Frontier* 227 This occurred 'way back,' when the Indians had no horses. (*b*) **1884** *Boston Globe* Oct., His unkempt hair, gawky appearance, and homespun suit . . . all bespoke the citizen from wayback. **1890** CUSTER *Following Guidon* 261 We were, in Western terms, 'waybacks from wayback.' (*c*) **1889** MARK TWAIN *Conn. Yankee* 401 (R.), He thinks he's a Sheol of a farmer; thinks he's old Grayback from Wayback. **1892** —— *Amer. Claimant* 167 (R.), I tell you, he's an artist from way back! — (2) **1851** WORTLEY *Travels in U.S.* 138 Less elaborately finished craft . . . are bound for . . . the trading and wealthy cities of far off Alabama and Louisiana, 'way down south.' **1913** LONDON *Valley of Moon* 332 Here I am, which proves that 'way down inside I must want the country. — (3) **1853** G. C. HILL *Dovecote* 29, I found her 'way off in them woods yonder!' **1892** *Harper's Mag.* Feb. 438/2 The papers are generally 'way off in some things. **1903** R. HALL *Pine Grove House* 15 Way off here we can hear the noise. — (4) **1868** G. A. CUSTER in Custer *Following Guidon* 53 They had braved the perils . . . in order to bring us, 'way out here, news from our loved ones.

1908 YESLAH *Tenderfoot S. Calif.* 139 Catalina is an island out at sea—way out.

(5) **1850** GARRARD *Wah-To-Yah* 200 Calyforny! way over yonder! **1904** *N.Y. Times* 5 April 2 A thick, pungent smoke which soon became so great a cloud as to cause a stench way over to Broadway. — (6) (*a*) **1850** S. WARNER *Wide, Wide World* xii, Do you live 'way up there? **1904** O. HENRY *Roads of Destiny* 299, I want to be manager of something way up—like a railroad or a diamond trust. (*b*) **1889** FARMER 553/2 *Way-up spread*, a good feast; something superlative in the matter of eating and drinking. **1901** H. ROBERTSON *Inlander* 72, I didn't think her one of those way-up girls that would suit a way-up fellow like Rod.

waybill 'weˌbɪl, *v.* [f. the noun.] *tr.* To list or include (goods) on a waybill. Also transf.

1843 *Hunt's Merch. Mag.* IX. 388 These passengers being way-billed . . . cannot convert their tickets into way-tickets. **1877** W. H. BURROUGHS *Taxation* 140 Freight being way-billed through. **1944** *Chi. D. News* 24 June (Pict. Sect.) 2 She begins her day here, way-billing freight and getting it ready to be loaded on trains.

W.C.T.U. Abbreviation of Woman's Christian Temperance Union, an organization founded at Cleveland, Ohio, in 1874. Also a member of this organization.

1888 LINDLEY *Calif. of South* 109 The W.C.T.U. was first organized here in 1883. **1940** EARLY *N. Eng. Sampler* 361 If you are a W.C.T.U., Stop! Because here is where I go on about Rum! **1948** *So. Bend* (Ind.) *Tribune* 3 April 3/1 An all-day county institute was held by the W.C.T.U. in the First Methodist church Friday.

attrib. **1930** *School & Society* 1 Nov. 588/1 A bootlegger doesn't feel at home at a W.C.T.U. convention.

Wea 'weə, *n.* [A contraction of some local native name of uncertain significance.] An Indian belonging to a subtribe of the Miamis. Also, *pl.*, the tribe of such an Indian. Also attrib.

1857 GIHON *Geary & Kansas* 19 These tribes are the Shawnees, . . . Kaskaskias, Weas and Piankshaws. **1946** FOREMAN *Last Trek* 131 Thirty Wea were in Indiana, all that remained of that tribe. **1949** *Midland Naturalist* Sep. 470 The Miamis (Wea band) had moved south from Green Bay, Wisconsin, and . . . were settled in Chicagoua at the south end of Lake Michigan by 1671.

***weaken,** *v. intr.* To give way, esp. to take a less firm stand in the face of opposition. *Colloq.* — **1876** MARK TWAIN *Tom Sawyer* xxvii, Don't you ever weaken, Huck, and I won't. **1890** LANGFORD *Vigilante Days* (1912) 100 If I were to leave it it would be reported that I had 'weakened' and fled from Patterson.

weakfish 'wikˌfɪʃ, *n.* [App. f. obs. Du. *weekvisch*, soft fish. See quot. 1841, which is translated from the Du. of Van der Donck, 1656.] An edible marine fish of the genus *Cynoscion* and allied genera of the family Otolithidae.

1796 MORSE *Univ. Geog.* I. 222 Bony Fish [found in the U.S. include the] . . . Minow, Week fish, King fish. **1841** *Coll. N.Y. Hist. Soc.* 2 Ser. I. 176 There are also shell-fish, week-fish, herrings, . . . and sheeps-heads. . . . There are also crabs, like those of the Netherlands, some of which are altogether soft. Those the people call weak crabs. **1949** *Fishes Western N. Atlantic* I. 373 Bonito (*Sarda*), weakfish (*Cynoscion*), mackerel, menhaden . . . are included in its known diet.

Hence **weakfishing,** *n.*

1888 GOODE *Amer. Fishes* 125 Much the same rig . . . is used in weakfishing. **1904** *Brooklyn Eagle* 30 May 3 The reports of good weak fishing to be had in Jamaica Bay brought out scores of anglers.

weak sister. A person who cannot be depended upon, esp. in time of stress. Also transf. *Colloq.*

1857 *S.F. Call* 3 May 1/1 G. W. Swerzy . . . is a 'weak sister' and a rather 'bad egg.' **1925** *Sat. Ev. Post* 10 Oct. 133/1 There is always a weak sister who turns yellow or overplays his game through nervousness. **1949** WEST *Rocky Mt. Cities* 311 The morning *Rocky Mountain News* . . . dawdled along as one of the weakest sisters in the Scripps-Howard string, maintaining an aura of shabby gentility.

we-all 'wiˌɔl, *pron.* [Prob. inspired by ***you-all.**] We. *Colloq.* Cf. **we-uns.**

1897 A. H. LEWIS *Wolfville* 81 First we-alls knows, these yere Britons would be runnin' cimmaron in the hills. **1923** MULFORD *Black Buttes* 114 We-all went an' got 'em. **1949** *Chi. Tribune* 27 Feb. VII. 6/6 Did we-all see Smokey hold?

Wealthy 'wɛlθɪ, *n.* A bright-red fall apple, or variety of apple, introduced by Peter M. Gideon, Excelsior, Minn., in 1860. Also attrib.

1928 BAILEY *Cyclo. Horticulture* 325/2 In the southern part of the Wealthy belt are grown hardy varieties of more or less local value such as Salome, Windsor, Black Annette. **1944** *Chi. D. News* 25 Sep. 13/3 Right now Wealthies or Maiden's Blush are the choice varieties for cooking or pie. **1948** *News-Palladium* (Benton Harbor, Mich.) 14 Aug. 7/1 Wealthies, No. 1, 2 1-2 inch, ranged between $1.50 and $2.00.

Weaponless Christian. (See quot.) *Obs.* — **1796** MORSE *Univ. Geog.* I. 283 [Mennonists] call themselves the Harmless Christians, Revengeless Christians, and Weaponless Christians.

* **weasel,** *n.*

1. (*cap.*) An inhabitant of South Carolina. A nickname. *Obs.*

1845 *St. Louis Reveille* 14 May 2/4 The inhabitants of . . . South Carolina [are called] Weasels. **1888** WHITMAN *Nov. Boughs* 70 Those from . . . South Carolina [were called] Weasels.

2. A purse. In full **weasel skin.** *Slang.*

1869 *Ore. State Jrnl.* 2 Jan. 1/6 Young man your weasel draw, or else prepare to die. **1887** TOURGEE *Button's Inn* 154 You're welcome to all you get out of that 'weasel-skin.' **1903** A. ADAMS *Log of Cowboy* 356 Every rascal of us got his weasel skin out.

3. weasel word, an equivocating word used to destroy the force of a statement. Also **weasel-worded, -wording.** *Colloq.* Cf. quot. 1919 *s.v.* **weasel,** *v.*

1900 *Cent. Mag.* June 306/2 'The public should be protected—' 'Duly protected,' said Gamage, 'That's always a good weasel word.' **1923** CHARNWOOD *Th. Roosevelt* x. 215 It is even comically reminiscent of the writer's own criticisms later of Mr. Wilson's 'weasel-worded' phrases. **1949** *Lubbock* (Tex.) *Morn. Avalanche* 23 Feb. II. 4/5 Its leaders insist on such 'weasel wording' that any treaty would be meaningless.

As the last term in **fisher, New York, white weasel.**

weasel 'wizl̩, *v.* [See quot. 1919.]

1. *tr.* To deprive (a word or expression) of its force or meaning. Also transf. *Colloq.*

1900 *Cent. Mag.* June 305/2 He's an expert on weasling. I've seen him take his pen, and go through a proposed plank or resolution, and weasel every flat-footed word in it. Then the weasel word pleases one man, and the word that's been weasled pleases another. **1919** ROOSEVELT in *Maine My State* 20 'His words weasel the meaning of the words in front of them,' said Dave, 'just like a weasel when he sucks the meat out of an egg and leaves nothing but the shell.' **1928** *Time* 15 Oct. 54/2 Others weasel their occupations; William Tatem Tilden, Jr. was listed as 'author' in the 1926–27 edition and now (1928–29) is simply a 'tennis player.'

2. *intr.* To equivocate, use weasel words. Also **weasel-word.** *Colloq.*

1900 [see **1.** above]. **1934** WEBSTER. **1948** *Sat. Ev. Post* 2 Oct. 40/3 Now, don't try to weasel out of it. **1948** *Salt Lake Tribune* 17 Dec. 3/3 Let's not weasel-word. Let's say just what we mean.

weaselism 'wizl̩ˌɪzəm, *n.* Mean or contemptible conduct. *Obs.* — **1844** *Henry Clay Bugle* (Maysville, Ky.) 18 April 3/3 A little more of the same sort will be the death of Locofocoism, Van Burenism, Lindenwoldism, Weaselism and Freetradeism.

Weaser 'wizɚ, *n. L.I.* [See quot. 1888.] (See quots.) Also **Weaser sheldrake.** Cf. ***tweezer,** *n.* **1.** — **1844** GIRAUD *Birds of L.I.* 340 The difference in plumage of the adult male, from the young male and female, is so strongly marked, that our gunners consider it a distinct species, called the former 'Weaser,' or large 'Swamp-Shell-Drake.' **1888** TRUMBULL *Names of Birds* 65 [*Merganser americanus*] is called on Long Island at Moriches, Weaser Sheldrake; at Bellport and Seaford (Hempstead), Weaser. . . . My idea is that early settlers on the Island associated our 'fresh-water sheldrake' with the German river, and got to calling it in consequence the *Weser* sheldrake.

* **weather,** *n.* In combs.: (1) **Weather Bureau,** a governmental agency, since 1940 a bureau of the Department of Commerce, which collects reports of weather conditions and issues predictions, also attrib.; (2) **light,** (see quot.), *obs.;* (3) * **man,** a man employed by the Weather Bureau to forecast the weather; (4) **map,** a map or chart showing the weather conditions at a particular time over an extensive area; (5) **rooster,** a weathercock, in squeamishness at the second element in that term, *jocular, obs.;* (6) **sharp,** (see quots.); (7) **skirt,** an outer skirt worn by a woman to protect her dress when riding horseback; (8) **strip,** a strip of material for covering the joint at a door, window, etc., so as to keep out rain, drafts, etc., also **weatherstripping;** (9) **telegram,** a telegram giving information about the weather.

(1) **1871** *Harper's Mag.* Aug. 401/1 In the year 1857 Lieutenant M. F. Maury . . . appealed to the public and Congress, through the press, urging the establishment of a storm and weather bureau. **1905** N. DAVIS *Northerner* 176 The weather vouchsafed to the valley of the Tennessee by the deities of the Weather Bureau was ideal Yule-tide

weather. **1950** *L.A. Times* 12 Feb. 1/4 Weather Bureau figures show that .34 inch fell during the rainstorm. — **(2) 1836** *Crockett Alman. 1837* 6 The singular light seen on the eastern horizon, and called by the settlers [of Fla.] 'weather light,' portends either terrible weather or continued dry weather. — **(3) 1859** *N.Y. Herald* 6 April 3/6 We are not disposed to prognosticate on the weather, but with patience adopt the language of the 'weather man,' and say that [it] is 'uncertain.' **1947** *Trail & Timberline* June 100/1 The weatherman co-operated by calling rain for noon and time to go home without interfering with the main business of the day. — **(4) 1871** *Harper's Mag.* Aug. 416 War Department weather-map (Signal Service, U.S.A.), Saturday, April 8, 1871, 7.35 A.M., Washington. **1950** *N.O. Times-Picayune Mag.* 12 March 17/2 No wonder the chief's been wrong—he's so nearsighted he's been basing his forecasts on our dart board instead of the weather map!

(5) 1851 *Ore. Statesman* 30 Sep. 1/7 At that instant the old man turned the corner, like a weather-rooster in a whirlwind. — **(6) 1883** SWEET & KNOX *Through Texas* 268 The weather-sharp is an alleged prophet, who tries to make people believe he is more intimate with the climate than anybody else. **1909** *Cent. Supp., weather-sharp....* One who understands the weather; a good weather forecaster; an official meteorologist. *Colloq.* **1950** *Chi. Tribune* 10 Jan. 18/3 As weather sharps well know, those favorite harbingers of the vernal season, migrant robins, are not due for some time. — **(7) 1903** EARLE *Two Cent. Costume Amer.* II. 617 Another name for a safeguard was a weather-skirt. — **(8) 1847** *Rep. Comm. Patents 1846* 94 One patent has been granted for improvements in fences, and another for a weather strip for doors. **1908** A. WARNER *Seeing England* 9 Lee wanted to put weather-strips on the baby's windows [in England] and nobody even knew what weather-strips were. **1944** *Sears Cat.* (ed. 189) 776 Kalk Kord Weatherstripping For sealing leaks and cracks around windows and doors—inside or outside. — **(9) 1871** *Scribner's Mo.* I. 402 The creation of the government Signal Service for obtaining weather telegrams . . . [will] mark a new era in American commerce.

As the last term in **God's, logging, sleighing, sugar, Washoe weather.**

weather-strip ˈwɛðɚˌstrɪp, *v. tr.* (See quot. 1909.) Also **weather-stripped,** *a.* — **1891** *Cent.* 6863/3 *weather-strip* . . . to apply weather-strips to; fit or secure with weather-strips. **1908** STEVENS *Liberators* 8 The wind that shook the windows, weather-stripped as they were, crept into the room.

* **weave,** *v.* **1. weave room,** a room in a factory in which cloth is woven, also attrib. **2. weave shop,** =prec. *Obs.*

(1) 1845 *Lowell Offering* V. 281 The weave-room overseer who has sent out the most cloth . . . is entitled to a premium. **1899** JEWETT *Queen's Twin* 92 She'll . . . be keeping her plants in the weave-room windows this winter with the rest of the girls. — **(2) 1847** *Knickerb.* XXX. 517 Most of the girls work in the 'weave-shop.'

* **weaver,** *n.* (See quot.) — **1920** *Nat. Museum Proc.* LVIII. 385 In parts of the Southern States the large dancing crane-flies pass by the name of 'weavers.'

As the last term in **shingle, stocking weaver.**

Weaverite ˈwivəˌraɪt, *n.* A political adherent of James B. Weaver of Iowa, the presidential candidate of the Greenback party in 1880 and of the People's party in 1892. *Obs.* — **1892** *Chi. Tribune* 19 July 4/1 There is not a State south of Mason and Dixon's line where the fiat Weaverites will get one-fifth the votes cast for the Democratic ticket.

* **web,** *n.* In combs.: (1) * **web-fingered,** designating various fishes (see quots.); (2) **foot,** see as a main entry; (3) **press,** a printing press supplied with paper from a roll, also **web perfecting press,** such a press with attachments for cutting, folding, etc.; (4) **saw,** a frame saw; (5) **worm,** one of various larvae which spin large webs, also attrib.

(1) 1814 MITCHILL *Fishes N.Y.* 431 Web-fingered Gurnard. *Trigla palmipes.* With bright yellow fringes on the fingers. Length eighteen inches or more. **1842** *Nat. Hist. N.Y., Zoology* IV. 46 Web-Fingered Grunter. . . . This is a very rare species. **1873** T. GILL *Cat. Fishes E. Coast N. Amer.* 21 *Prionotus carolinus....* Web-fingered sea-robin; Carolina robin. — **(3) 1876** KNIGHT 2751/2 The *web-press* is a late improvement. *Ib.*, In the Hoe web perfecting-press . . . the paper is printed from a roll containing a length of over four miles and a half. **1888** *Nation* 12 July p. iii/1 The New York Weekly Post . . . is printed . . . with new web presses. — **(4) 1876** KNIGHT 2752/2 *Web-saw,* a saw strained between points or holders; a frame-saw. **1889** *Cent. Mag.* Jan. 418/2 The web-saw, the glue-pot, the plane, and the hammer are the principal tools used.

(5) 1797 *Mass. H.S. Coll.* 1 Ser. V. 281 Having been in the habit of frequently visiting my trees, in order to destroy the canker and web worms [etc.]. **1802** *Ib.* VIII. 190 The *web worm* [is] a small taper worm, of a gray colour about a half of an inch in length. **1890** *Cent.* 3765/2 Common millers in the United States are *Spilosoma virginica,* a moth whose larva is one of the woolly-bear caterpillars, and *Hyphantria cunea,* the web-worm moth.

webb wɛb, *n. N. Eng.* [Prob. Algonquian.] An Indian woman or wife. *Obs.*

1634 WOOD *N. Eng. Prospect* (1865) 114 *Web,* a wife. **1672** JOSSELYN *N. Eng. Rarities* 62 A Fisher-man, having burnt his Knee Pan, was healed again by an Indian Webb, or Wife. **1676** I. MATHER *K. Philip's War* (1862) 141 A party of English came in a Warlike posture upon some of their *Webbs* (as they call them) *i.e. Women* as they were gathering corn.

* **webfoot,** *n.*

1. (*cap.*) A resident of Oregon. A nickname.

1863 *Walla Walla* (Wash.) *Statesman* 6 June 1/7 The inhabitants of Oregon are called Webfeet. **1882** W. NASH *Two Years Ore.* 164, I should think that no State is so much scoffed at as Oregon on the score of wet weather. Our neighbors in California call us 'Web-feet.' **1949** *Milwaukie* (Ore.) *Rev.* 28 July 7/6 (*heading*), Weather Keeps Webfoots at Home.

Hence **Web-Footer.**•

1890 *Spokane Falls* (Wash.) *Globe* 30 July 1/2 (*heading*), The Web-Footers are Playing Good Ball.

b. Oregon. A nickname. In full **Webfoot State.**

1866 *Dly. Morn. Chronicle* (Wash., D.C.) 5 Feb. 1/1 A capital country for young ducks is 'Web-foot,' in the winter season, anyway. **1873** *Kalama* (Wash.) *Beacon* 21 July 2/1 The Republican party in Webfoot might just as well act the 'Capt Scott's coon' next fall, for their 'goose is cooked.' **1882** W. NASH *Two Years Ore.* 164 The State is called 'The Web-foot State.' **1948** *Dly. Ardmoreite* (Ardmore, Okla.) 2 April 7/2 The overall outlook in the webfoot state is good.

c. Attrib. in the sense: Oregon or Oregonian.

1853 *S.F. Sun* 19 May 2/2 If you have any web-foot friends bound this way, dissuade them from putting in here, as nothing in the way of supplies can be obtained but water. **1864** *Ore. State Jrnl.* 12 March 3/1 Today the rain is coming down in real web-foot style. **1874** GLISAN *Jrnl. Army Life* 497 Those persons . . . cannot be contented in the 'webfoot' country as the Willamette Valley is derisively called, because of its frequent rains in winter.

2. An infantryman. *Colloq. Obs.*

1884 CABLE *Dr. Sevier* 421 Compliments . . . flew back and forth from the 'web-foots' to the 'critter company,' and from the 'critter company' to the 'web-foots.' **1917** MORGAN *Recollections* 210, I had heard a great deal about the marvelous marching powers of the Confederate infantry-man, and I was only a poor 'webfoot,' temporarily off his element, but I do not recall having seen any infantry-men pass me on the way to our second line of defense.

* **Webster,** *n.*

1. Used in the possessive in expressions referring to a spelling book prepared by Noah Webster (1758–1843) or to a dictionary bearing his name. Cf. * **blueback 3.**

1823 COOPER *Pioneers* vi, Elnathan, then about fifteen, was . . . furnished with a 'New Testament,' and a 'Webster's Spelling Book.' **1863** *Rio Abajo Press* 18 Aug. 3/1 Webster's Unabridged . . . spells the word Alburquerque and Albuquerque. **1916** MASSEY *Reminiscences* 49 The spelling book was Webster's blue-back. **1949** *Chi. Tribune* 22 Oct. 10/3 So far as known, it first appeared in the 1934 edition of Webster's Unabridged.

b. Short for "Webster's dictionary." Also **Webster's.**

1843 *Quincy* (Ill.) *Herald* 17 March 4/1 (*heading*), Definitions Not Found in Webster. **1945** *Sat. Review* 7 April 16 A famous term since (erroneously explained by Webster's). **1949** *Telephone Reg.* (McMinnville, Ore.) 4 Aug. 1/1 We wondered about the use of the word cinchier by the self-styled grammarian, so looked it up in our Webster.

c. Webster speller, a pupil using Webster's spelling book. *Rare.*

1846 *Dollar Newspaper* (Phila.) 10 June 4/4 Stubbs ruled them with an according severity. The Webster spellers he flogged every day of their lives.

2. a. *attrib.* Of or pertaining to Daniel Webster (1782–1852), as **Webster ticket, Whig.** *Obs.* **b. Webster fly,** *local.* A large black fly, great numbers of which were observed in the neighborhood of Pembroke, Mass., after the use by Daniel Webster of menhaden to fertilize his farm there. *Obs.*

(a) 1835–7 HALIBURTON *Clockmaker* 1 Ser. iv. 25, I love the Quakers, I hope they'll go the Webster ticket yet. **1884** BLAINE *20 Years of Cong.* I. 164 [The] conservative side [of the assemblage was typified] by the choice of an old Webster Whig. — **(b) 1877** HARVEY *Reminisc. D. Webster* 275 These insects were known in the neighborhood as Webster flies.

Websterian wɛbˈstɪrɪən, *a.*

1. Profound, impressive, suggestive of Daniel Webster (1782–1852). *Obs.*

1856 *S. Lit. Messenger* XXII. 243/1 He felt within him in embryo Websterian thoughts. **1883** *Cent. Mag.* Nov. 139/2 He was dressed in an ill-cut black Websterian coat. **1894** ALDRICH *Two Bites* 73 Among others came the Hon. Jedd Deane, with his most pronounced Websterian air.

2. Of or pertaining to Noah Webster or to a dictionary bearing his name.

1874 B. F. TAYLOR *World on Wheels* 28 Websterian 'probabilities' says that is not the derivation of 'scale' at all. **1897** *Bookman* Nov. 201 We are quite sure that if the English were to adopt the Websterian spelling, Professor Matthews would very, very soon experience a conservative reaction. **1949** *College English* Jan. 220/1 *Macmillan, Collegiate,* and *Winston* use the familiar 'Websterian' symbols to indicate pronunciation, despite the perennial objections of phoneticians.

* **wedding,** *n.* In combs.: (1) **wedding fixings,** a bride's wedding outfit, also **wedding fix,** *colloq.;* (2) **journey,** a trip taken by a married couple immediately after their wedding; (3) **journeyer,** one who goes on a wedding journey, *rare.*

(1) 1840 *Ky. Rifle* 31 Oct., Sal was makin up her weddin fixings. **1896** WILKINS *Madelon* 212 D'ye want any money to buy your wedding-fixings with? **1903** *Harper's Mag.* Dec. 28 There was poor Flora wantin' some cotton cloth for her weddin' fix. — **(2) 1871** HOWELLS (*title*), Their Wedding Journey. **1907** LILLIBRIDGE *Trail* 96 Is it to be a wedding journey? — **(3) 1871** HOWELLS *Wedding Journey* 57 Imagine the infinite comfort of our wedding-journeyers, transported . . . to the shelter and the quiet of that absurdly palatial steamboat.

As the last term in **China, linen, second-day, shotgun, tin, wooden wedding.**

* **wedge,** *n.* **1. wedge tent,** =**A tent. 2.** *To knock out the wedges,* (see quot. 1871). *Colloq.*

(1) 1862 NORTON *Army Lett.* 49 We used to sleep on the ground or on pine boughs when we had the small or wedge tents. **1913** *Outing* June 365/2 They were sheltered in 50 wedge tents. — **(2) 1848** LOWELL *Biglow P.* 1 Ser. vii. 90 You'd ough' to leave a feller free, An not go knockin' out the wedges, To ketch his fingers in the tree. **1871** DE VERE 320 To *knock out the wedges* . . . is used to express a painful embarrassment in which a man is left by his friends, after having been led into it by their urgency.

* **weed,** *n.*

1. *S.* The central stalk and the foliage, as distinguished from the fruit, of the cotton plant. *Colloq.* Cf. **cotton weed** (*b*).

1867 *Comm. & Fin. Chron.* V. 210/2 The weed is large and thrifty.

2. (See quots.)

1900 BRUNCKEN *N. Amer. Forests* 68 An area is denuded of its merchantable timber and henceforth lies as an idle waste, stocked at best with scrub and inferior species of trees—weeds, as the forester calls them. **1905** *Forestry Bureau Bul.* No. 61, 26 *Weed tree,* a tree of a species which has little or no value. **1938** JAMES R. SIMMONS *Feathers & Fur on the Turnpike* 110 In the practice of timber stand improvement foresters eliminate 'weed' trees which are undesirable in view of present or prospective markets.

3. weed boat, weed prairie, (see quots.).

1841 W. KENNEDY *Texas* I. 155 The settlers highly estimate the productive power of the weed prairies. **1844** MOORE *Texas* 112 In the bottoms of the Brazos . . . are many prairies which are covered with a dense growth of weeds, instead of grass: from this fact, they are styled weed prairies. **1942** KENNEDY *Palmetto Country* 22 Transportation through the Okefenokee is accomplished in flat-bottomed 'weed-boats' or bateaux.

As the last term in **ague, arrow, balsam, bear, bee, beggar, bishop's, bitter, breast, broom, bugle, bull, burro, butterfly, cancer, carpenter, carpet, carrot, chigger, choke, clear, coffee, convulsion, cotton, crazy, desert, devils, devils iron, door, dysentery, emetic, feather, fever, fire, frost, gopher, gravel, graveyard, gypsy, hand, heart, horse, horse fly, hutton, Indian, indigo, iodine, iron, Jamestown, jewel, jimson, joe-pye, joint, kidney, kill, Klamath, loco, mad dog, Masonic, master, mermaid, milk, million dollar, Missouri, Mohawk, moose, Mormon, musquash, neck, necklace, Negro, nettle, nit, oyster, pickerel, pigeon, pilot, pin, pine, pingue, poke, polecat, polk, poverty, pride, puke, pygmy, rabbit, rag, ranstead, rattle, rattlesnake, red, resin, rheumatism, rich, river, rolling, rosin, salt, salt rheum, scorpion, shovel, sickle, silk, skunk, slink, snake, sneeze, soap, squaw, stagger, stick, stink, tallow, tar, thimble, tickle, tory, trumpet, tumble, turpentine, Virginia, wire weed.**

weeding hoe. A light garden hoe as distinguished from a grubbing hoe *q.v.*

1638 *Md. Council Proc.* 76, I have seised . . . 6 weeding hoes. **1703** *N.C. Col. Rec.* I. 579 Grey did formerly attach . . . two weeding hoes, one hilling hoe [etc.]. **1907** *D.N.* III. 238 *Weeding-hoe* . . . common hoe; garden hoe. **1944** CLARK *Pills* 160 A farmer in Alabama wanted . . . 10 weeding hoes.

* **week,** *n.* (See quot.) *Obs.* — **1851** HALL *College Words* 279 It was customary, in the early days of Harvard College, for the graduates of the year to attend in the recitation-room on Mondays and Tuesdays, for three weeks, during the month of June, subject to the examination of all who chose to visit them. This was called the *Sitting of the Solstices.* . . . The time was also known as the *Weeks of Visitation.*

As the last term in **court, freshman, garden, inauguration, Old Home, rush, six week(s).**

* **weep,** *v. To weep a little weep,* to have a spell of crying. *Colloq.*

1869 ALCOTT *Little Women* I. 62 Being . . . a very human little girl, she often 'wept a little weep,' as Jo said. **1871** *Scribner's Mo.* II. 292 So, woman-like, I began to 'weep a little weep.' **1880** *Harper's Mag.* May 911/1, I sat down by my desk and 'wept a little weep.'

weequashing wiˈkwaʃɪŋ, *n.* Also **wigwassing.** [f. an Algonquian term of uncertain meaning.] (See quot. 1910.)

1792 *Mass. H.S. Coll.* 1 Ser. I. 231 The Indians, when they go in a canoe with a torch, to catch eels in the night, call it Weequash, or anglicised, *weequashing.* **1882–3** KNIGHT 510/2 Jack Lamp . . . for still-hunting, *weequashing* or fire-fishing. **1910** HODGE *Amer. Indians* II. 951/2 Wigwassing. A term used on the coast of New England for the operation of taking eels by torch-light; spelled also *wequashing.*

* **weevil,** *n.* As the last term in **bean, black, boll, chestnut, cotton, fly, granary, Mexican boll, Mexican cotton boll, pea, pine, red, snouted, water weevil.**

* **weigh,** *v.* **1. weigh boss,** one in charge of weighing. **2. weigh lock,** a canal-lock where barges are weighed and their tonnage ascertained.

(1) 1917 SINCLAIR *King Coal* 44 Scarcely an evening passed that some man did not break loose, shaking his fist at the sky, or at the weigh-boss. — **(2) 1833** *Niles' Reg.* XLIV. 177/2 There was weighed at the Albany weighlock . . . 882 lbs. merchandise, exclusive of 19 empty boats. **1835** LIEBER *Stranger in Amer.* II. 140 The object of the greatest interest to me, in Utica, was a weigh-lock—an American invention if I am not mistaken. The toll for freight on the canal is proportionate to weight.

* **weight,** *n.* As the last term in **carriage, fall, gold, heavy, hitching, rowing weight.**

weight pole. In a log cabin, a pole which holds the boards or clapboards in place.

1791 in JILLSON *Dark & Bl. Ground* 109 The weight poles are those small logs on the roof which weigh down the clapboards upon which they lie. **1859** TALIAFERRO *Fisher's R.* 165 When I saw my friend's cabin in 1857, I took it to be in size about ten feet by eighteen; the board roof was fastened on by 'weight-poles,' somewhat after the Indian fashion. **1944** DUNCAN *M. Graham* 239 The pilgrim to New Salem today finds on the flat top of the high bluff overlooking the Sangamon the little village complete to the last weight-pole and roof-shake.

wejack ˈwidʒæk, *n.* [f. Algonquian, cf. Ojibway *otchig,* Cree *otchek,* and see **woodchuck.**] **1.** = * **fisher 1. 2.** = **woodchuck.**

(1) 1784 THOMAS PENNANT *Arctic Zoology* I. 82 This animal inhabits *Hudson's Bay,* and is found in *New England,* and as low as *Pennsylvania.* About *Hudson's Bay* they are called *Wejacks* and *Woodshocks* . . . and, notwithstanding, they are not amphibious, are called *Fishers.* **1829** J. RICHARDSON *Fauna Bor.-Amer.* I. 52 *Mustela Canadensis.* The Pekan, or Fisher. . . . Wejack, or Fisher [of the] Fur Traders. — **(2)** *c***1849** PAIGE *Dow's Sermons* I. 178 The poor man . . . feels as safe as a wejag in his winter's burrow. **1945** PEARSON *Country Flavor* 31 Beneath the wall is the home of Wejack, the philosophical, bewhiskered chuck.

* **welfare,** *n. attrib.* Of or pertaining to the welfare of children, workers, etc. Also **Welfare Administrator.**

1904 *Cent. Mag.* Nov. 61 The welfare manager . . . who may be either a man or a woman, is a recognized intermediary between the employers and employees of mercantile houses and manufacturing plants. **1905** *Westm. Gaz.* 28 Jan. 11/1 The home of 'the welfare policy' is the city of Dayton, Ohio. **1935** WEEKLEY *Something About Words* 63 Not that the American contribution is purely slang. *Welfare,* as in 'child welfare,' 'welfare centre,' and so forth, was first used in this special sense in Ohio in 1904. **1950** *World-Herald Mag.* (Omaha) 8 May 4/3 A year later, he was back, this time as County Welfare Administrator.

* **well,** *n.* In combs.: (1) **well auger,** a large iron or steel cylinder, one end of which is provided with boring plates, for use in boring wells for water; (2) **driller,** one who drills wells; (3) **driver,** one who makes driven wells;

(4) **pole,** =**well sweep;** (5) **post,** a post upon which a well sweep is mounted; (6) **rig,** (see quot.); (7) **sweep,** a long pole, pivoted on the top of a high post, by means of which water is raised in a bucket attached to the end of the pole.

(1) **1877** RUEDE *Sod-House Days* 41 Tomorrow Jim and L. are going to Osborne and Schweitzer's for the well auger. **1890** *Stock Grower & Farmer* 22 Feb. 1/1 Rust's well drilling machinery, steam and horse power, for deep and shallow wells. . . . *Empire Well auger company.* — (2) **1945** MATHEWS *Talking* 4, I talked with several well-drillers about the possibility of finding water on a ridge several feet above the thousand-foot contour. — (3) **1884** *Gringo & Greaser* 1 Feb. 1/1 We are connected with the only practical Tube Well-Drivers in the West. — (4) **1775** *Mass. H.S. Coll.* 1 Ser. I. 260 Seeing the well-pole drawing down, [an Indian] took aim at the place where he thought the man must stand. **1867** HARRIS *Sut Lovingood* 87 Du yu see these yere well-poles what I uses fur laigs?

(5) **1849** G. G. FOSTER *N.Y. in Slices* 8 An interminable line of crooked well-posts, . . . meets your gaze. — (6) **1876** KNIGHT 2759/1 *Well-rig* is the term applied to the whole *plant* for well-boring, consisting of the *derrick,* its engine [etc.]. — (7) **1840** WEBSTER II. 947/2. **1857** *Harper's Mag.* May 746/1 There are four characteristic indispensables to every cottage: a well-sweep with a cypress-knee bucket [etc.]. **1903** K. M. ABBOTT *Old Paths N. Eng.* 281 Children jumped for the long arm of the well-sweep.

As the last term in **bore, drive, driven, drove, dry, dug, gas, ice, oil, sweep pole, test, tube, wildcat well.**

* **well,** *adv.* In combs.: (1) * **wellborn,** used, with the definite article, for the Federalists, a derisive nickname alluding to John Adams' use of the term (see quot. 1787), *obs.;* (2) **fixed,** well-to-do, *colloq.;* (3) **taken,** suitably chosen, reasonable.

(1) [**1787** J. ADAMS *Defence of Constitution* I. p. x, The rich, the well-born, and the able, acquire an influence among the people.] **1788** *Amer. Museum* June (1792) 527 Under such a government, men of education, abilities, and property, commonly called *the well born,* will be the most likely to get into places of power and trust. **1883** MCMASTER *People U.S.* I. 469 In most of the squibs and pasquinades that filled the papers the Federalists were reviled under the name of 'the well-born.' — (2) **1822** *Murphey P.* I. 263 His brother is well fixed. **1925** TILGHMAN *Dugout* 70 You'll be well fixed. — (3) **1903** A. T. HADLEY *Freedom & Responsibility* 165 To a certain extent this point is well taken. **1907** *Nation* 14 Feb. 146 One of Mr. Heart's points seems to us well taken.

Wells-Fargo. A firearm issued to its guards by the well-known express company. *Rare.* — **1898** *Scribner's Mag.* XXIII. 86/2 Into the face the messenger fired one barrel of his Wells-Fargo.

* **Welsh,** *a.* **1. Welsh Indians,** Indians thought to be descended from Welshmen who allegedly came to America in 1170. *Obs.* [See Hodge, *Amer. Indians* II. 931 f.] **2.** * **Welshman,** a name given locally to various fish, esp. to the large-mouthed black bass.

(1) **1804** JEFFERSON in *Lewis & Clark Exped.* VII. (1905) 292 Mr. Evans, a Welshman, was employed by the spanish government . . . to go in search of the Welsh Indians said to be up the Missouri. **1805** ORDWAY in *Journals of Lewis & O.* 282 We think that they [the Flatheads] are the welch Indians. — (2) **1709** LAWSON *Carolina* 159 The brown Pearch, which some call Welch-men, are the largest sort of Pearches that we have. **1896** JORDAN & EVERMANN *Check-List Fishes* 338 Matejuelo; Squirrel-fish; Welshman. . . . Florida to St. Helena.

Welsher ˈwɛlʃɚ, *n.* A Welsh Indian. *Rare.* — **1827** COOPER *Prairie* xviii, There was a story of a nation of Welshers, that lived here—away in the prairies.

* **wench,** *n.* A female Negro slave or servant, a Negro girl. *Obs.*

1717 *N.C. Col. Rec.* II. 310 A Wench for the House I want sore. **1830** NEILSON *Recollections* 285 In most cases the slaves who are exposed for sale seem to feel the ignominy. . . . Females, who are invariably styled 'Wenches,' seldom standing the exhibition without tears. **1909** *D.N.* III. 393 *Buck* . . . now applied almost exclusively to male negroes as the opposite of *wench.*

Wenham ice. Ice from a pond in the township of Wenham, near Boston, Mass., formerly an article of export. Also **Wenham lake ice.** *Obs.*

1846 *Niles' Reg.* 2 May 144/1 The barque Hannah Sprague, . . . has been chartered to carry a cargo of Wenham Lake ice from Boston to London. **1860** HOLMES *Professor* 103 'The Model of all the Virtues' had a pair of searching eyes as clear as Wenham ice. **1885** HOWELLS *Silas Lapham* 178 They were so many blocks of Wenham ice for purity and rectangularity.

werowance ˈwɛrəˌwæns, *n.* [f. Algonquian in the same sense, thought to be based upon *wirowántĕsu,* he is rich.] A chief or headman among the Indians in Maryland and Virginia. Now *hist.*

1588 HARIOT *Briefe & True Report* E2[r] The greatest *Wiróans* that yet we had dealing with had but eighteene towns in his gouerment. **1650** *Md. Archives* I. 330 Provided that no one Copyhold Exceed above fifty Acres unless it be to the Werrowance or chief head of every of the said Six Nations. **1705** BEVERLEY *Virginia* III. 57 A *Werowance* is a Military Officer, who of course takes upon him the command of all Parties. **1899** *Atlantic Mo.* June 725/2, I drove my boat in between the sloop of the commander of Shirley Hundred and the canoe of the Nansemond werowance. **1943** BENÉT *Western Star* 69 This is the doom of werowance and chief.

transf. **1847** *Yankee Doodle* 17 April 17/1 Perhaps, had Werowance Smith lived in these latter days he would have excepted the election of John Young Governor of the Empire State.

* **Wesson,** *n.* Short for Smith and Wesson *q.v. Obs.* — **1856** *Spirit of Times* 20 Sep. 40/1 Wesson's rifles are the best we know of, but they are very rarely to be met with. *Ib.* 25 Oct. 129/2 Send in your orders, then, and from a stallion to a stop-watch, a Wesson rifle to a Kirby fish-hook, the requisition will be answered with rapidity and dispatch.

* **west,** *n., a., adv.*

1. *n.* (*cap.*) At any particular time, that part of the U.S. west of the earlier settled regions; now, roughly, the region west of the Mississippi River, esp. the Rocky Mountain region.

1798 WASHINGTON in *Sp. & Doc. Amer. Hist.* I. (1944) 224 The West receives from the East supplies requisite to its growth and comfort. **1820** *Niles' Reg.* XVIII. 386/1 Are all the people of the 'west'—of the many highly important states beyond the mountains, to be thus traduced by wholesale? **1903** AUSTIN *Land of Little Rain* 107 The road to Jimville is the happy hunting ground of old stage-coaches bought up from superseded routes the West over. **1948** *Shelby* (Mont.) *Promoter* 16 Sep. 1/1 Army and navy engineers have urged that the government allocate $67,000,000,000 for the 'development of the west.'

2. *adv.* Toward the western part of the U.S.

1836 DUNLAP *Mem. Water Drinker* (1837) I. 52 A Connecticut settler . . . was very glad to sell his buildings and go west. **1856** E. H. HALL *Ho! for the West!* (1858) 4 If bound still further west he has at Chicago a choice of several roads. **1908** PHILLIPS *Old Wives* 315 Murdock's threat struck such terror into Henrietta Hastings's soul that she did not go West by the train Sophy and Florence took.

b. In the West. Cf. **out west.**

1889 HOWELLS *Annie Kilburn* xi, One of 'em married West, and her husband left her.

c. *go west, young man,* and variants: Settle in the West as the place of greatest opportunity—an admonition commonly ascribed to Horace Greeley. *Colloq.*

[**1834** *Sangamo Jrnl.* (Springfield, Ill.) 18 Nov. 3/2 Where are you going? The reply we received, 'Going West.'] [**1837** GREELEY in *New-Yorker* 3 June 169/1 We say, then, Mechanics, artisans, laborers. . . . Fly—scatter throughout the country—go to the Great West—rather than remain here, consuming the pittance which is left of your earnings in better days.] **1851** J. L. B. SOULE in *Terre Haute Express,* Go West, young man! Go West! **1879** W. SAUNDERS *Through Light Continent* 35 'Go West, young man' was Horace Greeley's advice, and West I went accordingly. **1947** DEVOTO *Across Wide Missouri* 4 The boys and girls who would go West . . . were studying maps whose information was grotesque.

3. In combs.: (1) **west-bound,** of railroad trains or traffic, going westward, also absol.; (2) **Coast,** the Pacific Coast of the U.S.; (3) * **country,** =**west 1,** also attrib.; (4) **Floridan, Floridian,** a resident of West Florida; (5) **Point,** see as a main entry; (6) **Side,** that part of a city, esp. N.Y. and Chicago, located in or towards the West, also attrib., cf. **East Side;** (7) **Sider,** one who lives on the West Side; (8) **Virginian,** one who lives or was born in West Virginia.

(1) **1881** *Chi. Times* 12 March, The west-bound express was laid up all night at Kearney. **1909** WASON *Happy Hawkins* 222 The west-bound had to take a sidin' and wait twenty minutes for the east-bound. **1948** *Popular Western* June 17/2 He'll probably leave the train and flag the next west-bound back to Caprock. — (2) **1850** *Calif. Courier* (S.F.) 2 Dec. 2/1 Our position here on the West Coast has been and still is a peculiar one. **1948** *Sierra Club Bul.* Feb. 10/2 It will be necessary for some of the problems to be handled by mail because of the distance from the West Coast of Washington. — (3) **1829** FLINT *G. Mason* 10 These consisted of the substantial materials of a west country-man's diet, corn, bacon, and sweet potatoes. **1839** C. A. MURRAY *Travels* II. 122, I heard this day a west-country phrase that was perfectly new to me. **1852** J. H. EAGLE *Corr.* (Huntington Lib.) 14 Nov. 2 Our shanty is as good as any you will find in the west

country. — (4) **1775** ADAIR *Indians* 140 The West-Floridans, in order to keep their women subject to the law of adultery, bring some venison or buffalo's flesh to the house of their nominal wives, at the end of every winter's hunt. **1883** *Cent. Mag.* June 311/2 'Jools,' said the West-Floridian, . . . 'do you think you have any shore hopes of heaven?'

(6) **1858** *Harper's Mag.* July 283/2 As our friend entered the door a well-known 'West side' operator made his bid. **1903** *Harper's Mo.* July 213 The abysmal craving of New Yorkers—West Side or East Side—is for friends. **1946** *Chi. D. News* 21 Dec. 3/5 With many a whoop and holler, 1,300 West Side kids greeted Santa Claus today. — (7) **1903** *N.Y. Ev. Post* 14 Nov. 4 The persistence with which the West Siders have followed up this question of the Broadway trees. **1946** *Newsweek* 21 Oct. 40/2 No West Sider will touch a single bough in my woods. — (8) **1881–5** MCCLELLAN *Own Story* 149 The executive never disowned my proclamation to the West Virginians. **1950** *Southwest Rev.* Spring 88/2, I asked why a certain towering West Virginian is called 'Tex.'

As the last term in **Far, Great, mid, Middle, north, out, Silver Knight of the, South, wild, woolly West.**

***Western,** *n.*

1. = **Westerner.**

1835 H. C. TODD *Notes* 8 *Buckskin* is the nickname for Southerns and Westerns. **1888** BRYCE *Amer. Commonw.* II. III. lxv. 480 He [Jackson] was a raw rude Western, a man of the people.

2. An animal bred and raised in the West for meat.

1890 *Stock Grower & Farmer* 26 April 7/3 The fed Westerns are about out of the way, while of fat native sheep we are not now receiving any considerable number.

3. A motion picture or a novel dealing with western scenes and characters.

1929 *Variety* 3 April 1/4 (*heading*), Decline in Westerns Sending Screen Cowboys Abroad With Own Rodeos. **1946** HOLBROOK *Lost Men* 235 On his return East he took lodgings in rural Peekskill, New York, a quiet, sleepy village that would be a fine place, so Alger thought, to write his Westerns. **1948** *Time* 24 May 77/2 The most ancient Western will bring in neighborhoods of bug-eyed, awestruck kids.

***western,** *a.*

1. In combs.: (1) **western comfort,** whisky, *obs.;* (2) **country,** = ***west 1;** (3) **desert,** = **Great American Desert,** *obs.;* (4) **fever,** the desire to migrate westward, *obs.;* (5) **Reserve,** a tract of nearly four million acres now forming the northwestern part of the state of Ohio but formerly claimed by Connecticut and reserved by that state at the time of the cession of the lands in the Northwest Territory to the U.S., also attrib.; (6) **saddle,** a heavy saddle having a high cantle and steel fork and horn; (7) **shore,** that part of Maryland and Virginia on the western side of the Chesapeake Bay, cf. **Eastern Shore;** (8) **slope,** the slope of a mountain range, esp. of the Rocky Mountain and Sierra Nevada ranges, west of the crest; (9) **territory,** land in the West, esp. land northwest of the Ohio River and east of the Mississippi River together with an area south of the Ohio which was ceded to the national government by various states, also a portion of this, *obs.*

(1) **1827** COOPER *Prairie* xxxi, I will engage to get the brats acclimated to a fever-and-ague bottom in a week, and not a word shall be uttered harder to pronounce than the bark of a cherry-tree, with perhaps a drop or two of western comfort. — (2) **1780** in S. K. PADOVER *Jefferson* (1942) 89 It becomes necessary that we aim the first stroke in the western country and throw the enemy under embarrassment of a defensive war. **1894** *Harper's Mag.* May 909/2 When you kids have travelled this Western country awhile you'll keep your cards locked. — (3) **1834** A. PIKE *Sketches* 50 A part of the western desert is common ranging ground for both nations. — (4) **1835** A. PARKER *Trip to Texas* 20 The 'western fever' rages here [in New York] as violent as on the sterile hills of New-Hampshire. **1858** *So. Cultivator* XVI. 376 (*heading*), The 'Western Fever'—Moving.

(5) **1800** *Statutes at Large* II. 56 All that territory commonly called the Western Reserve of Connecticut . . . was excepted by said state of Connecticut out of the cession by the said state heretofore made to the United States. **1847** HOWE *Hist. Coll. Ohio* 255 There were 24000 acres of choice land scattered about the county of the Connecticut Western Reserve school land. **1949** *Chi. Tribune* 18 Sep. IV. 15/1 The Western Reserve was originally that part of Northern Ohio which the state of Connecticut reserved for herself in 1786, after ceding the rest of her colonial grant . . . to the Congress. — (6) **1911** WRIGHT *Winning Barbara Worth* 117 He watched . . . that young woman . . . with her khaki divided skirt, wide sombrero, fringed gauntlets and the big western saddle, coming there on a horse whose feet seemed scarcely to touch the ground as he plunged and pranced impatiently along. **1949** *Trail Riders Bul.* March 2/2 Seated in a big western saddle with hand resting on saddle horn, even the greenest dude can watch the landscape in complete comfort and security. — (7) **1624** SMITH *Gen. Hist. Va.* IV. 143 Cleane contrary they on the Westerne shore, the younger bears the charge, and the elder the dignitie. **1746** E. KIMBER *Itinerant Observer* 51 The Inhabitants on the *Western Shore* are supply'd with prodigious Quantities of Beef, Pork and Grain. **1948** MENCKEN *Supp.* II. 128 On the Western Shore, below Annapolis, it [dialect] is predominantly General Southern. — (8) **1853** *Alta California* (S.F.) 5 April 1/6 It must be, or the Administration will hear a howl from the golden land as if all the *cayotes* and *lupos* of the western slope had united in a general cry of execration. **1911** *Country Life* 15 Nov. 3/3 Being on the western slope of the Great Divide, it has sufficient rain-fall for the growth of almost anything. **1947** *Time* 13 Jan. 69/1 Skidom's newest center is on the Rockies' western slope. — (9) **1789** *Ann. 1st Congress* 63 In conformity to the law re-establishing the Western Territory, I nominate Arthur St. Clair, Governor. **1794** *U.S. Reg. 1795* 17, 220,000,000 of acres, lying west of the northern and middle states, and northwest of the river Ohio . . . together with an extensive territory south of the Ohio . . . forms what is usually denominated the Western Territory. **1855** *S. Lit. Messenger* XXI. 669/1 The tide of emigration now set steadily towards the Western Territories.

b. In expressions, often obs., of obvious meaning or sufficiently explained in the quots.: (1) **western Americanish,** (2) **Exchange,** (3) **farmer,** (4) **frontier,** (5) **Indian,** (6) **life,** (7) **man,** (8) **nightingale,** (9) **paper,** (10) **people,** (11) **prairie,** (12) **road,** (13) **settler,** (14) **states,** (15) **swing,** (16) **Virginian,** (17) **waters,** (18) **wilds.**

(1) **1853** *Alta California* (S.F.) 20 April 2/1 This is very Western Americanish! — (2) **1827** J. BERNARD *Retrospection of Amer.* (1887) 182, I found the town [Pittsburgh], which was called the Western Exchange, a reflex of New York. — (3) **1812** *Niles' Reg.* III. 53/1 The unnatural trade which we carry on with Philadelphia and Baltimore . . . affords not the least encouragement to the western farmer. **1909** PARKER *G. Cleveland* 134 He should be invited to speak at the banquet upon the relation of the tariff to the Western farmer. — (4) **1721** *Mass. H. Rep. Jrnl.* III. 104, 50 more good Effective men [shall] be employed as Scouts for securing the Western Frontiers. **1883** SWEET & KNOX *Through Texas* 504 The past history of the western frontier is nothing more nor less than the history of one unending Indian war.

(5) **1713** *N.C. Col. Rec.* II. 26 The Tuscaroras have surprised and rob'ed our Traders going to the Western Indians. **1731** *Cal. State P., Amer. & W. Indies* (1732) 32 Six Acts of the Massachusetts Bay 1731 . . . for allowing necessary supplies to the Eastern and Western Indians and for regulating trade with them. — (6) **1850** GARRARD *Wah-To-Yah* ii. 37 We crowded together, listening with much interest to tales of western life. **1883** *Harper's Mag.* Jan. 283/1 The great festivals of Western life are camp-meetings, barbecues, and log-rollings. — (7) **1822** *Argus of Western Amer.* 1 March, The importance of having western men in the national councils . . . was never so strongly exemplified as in the transactions attending the treaty at Ghent. **1911** WRIGHT *Winning Barbara Worth* 404 At last . . . the western man broke the long silence. — (8) **1903** *N.Y. Ev. Post* 24 Oct. (*heading*), Problems which enter into the Management of the 'Western Nightingale' [i.e., a burro]. — (9) **1806** *Balance* V. 366 The following curious suggestions . . . are extracted from the file of western papers. **1902** BANKS *Newspaper Girl* 8, I would be bidden by the proprietor of the bustling Western paper to think up things for newspaper stories.

(10) **1806** *Balance* V. 366/1 A letter from a gentleman of Frankfort . . . declares the western people to be indissolubly attached to the union. **1895** G. KING *New Orleans* 154 The Western people saw themselves deprived of an outlet without which they could not exist. — (11) **1806** in *Ann. 9th Cong.* 2 Sess. 1134 Very different are the western prairies, which expression signifies only a country without timber. **1907** *St. Nicholas* May 599/1 Dick [was] accustomed . . . to the intense cold of the western mountains and prairies. — (12) **1883** *Cent. Mag.* Sep. 796/2 In railway circles, all roads east of Buffalo, Pittsburg, Wheeling, Bristol (Tennessee), etc., are distinctively known as Eastern roads, and the lines west of these points as Western roads. — (13) **1784** WASHINGTON *Diaries* II. 326 The Western Settlers—from my own observation—stand as it were on a pivot. **1913** BARNES *Western Grazing Grounds* 87 One peculiar class of western settler was the nester. — (14) **1794** T. COOPER *America* 8 These parts . . . furnish yearly a very considerable number of emigrants to the middle and western states. **1829** *Free Enquirer* (N.Y.) 31 Oct. 1/3, I have myself witnessed the kidnapping of freed negros in the nonslave-holding western states. **1948** *So. Bend* (Ind.) *Tribune* 3 April 6/6 Stewart Riley . . . is on a tour through the western states.

(15) **1847** in HOWE *Hist. Coll. Ohio* 121 [They] danced the scamper-down, double-shuffle, western-swing and half-moon, forty-six years

ago in the log cabin of Major Carter. — **(16) 1861** *Alexandria* (Va.) *Gaz.* 4 May 3/1 A delegation of Western Virginians arrived here on Wednesday. — **(17) 1777** in *Amer. Sp.* XV. 410/1 All persons who . . . had bona fide settled themselves . . . upon any waste and ungranted lands on the said Western Waters . . . shall be allowed for every family so settled four hundred acres of land. **1827** COOPER *Prairie* vii, What will the Yankee Choppers say, when they have cut their path from the eastern to the western waters? — **(18) 1786** HUMPHREYS *Anarchiad* (1861) 20 O'er Western wilds, the tawny bands allied, Insult the States. **1878** BEADLE (*title*), Western Wilds, and the Men Who Redeem Them.

Also *western America, bacon, beef, border, born, civilization, empire, farm, highway, hunter, lake, land, language, locust, mail, mining camp, phrase, phraseology, plain, preacher, sociability, sport, tour, town, trade, type, whisky, Yankee, youth,* etc.

2. In the names of birds: (1) **western bluebird,** the California bluebird, *Sialia mexicana occidentalis;* (2) **meadowlark,** the common meadowlark, *Sturnella neglecta,* characteristic of the western prairies, also known as western field lark; (3) **palm warbler,** the palm warbler, *Dendroica palmarum;* (4) **red-tail hawk,** =**red-tailed hawk.**

(1) 1839 AUDUBON *Ornith. Biog.* V. 41 The Western Blue Bird possesses many of the habits of our common kind. **1917** *Birds of Amer.* III. 243. — **(2) 1891** *Cent.* 6881/2. **1943** PEATTIE *Journey into Amer.* 89 The very calls of the birds, mocker and western meadowlark and wren-tit, are now the sounds of home. — **(3) 1934** WEBSTER. **1944** *Mass. Audubon Soc. Bul.* Dec. 261, I got 'kicks' out of seeing the following. . . . Western Palm Warbler. — **(4) 1881** *Amer. Naturalist* XV. 209 The hawks are very numerous in the vicinity of Los Angeles, Cal., and are represented by many species, the most common of which is the western red-tail hawk (Buteo montanus).

b. Also (1) **western black pewee** (or **phoebe**), (2) **duck,** (3) **flicker,** (4) **grass bunting,** (5) **gull,** (6) **mockingbird,** (7) **robin,** (8) **snowbird,** (9) **turkey,** (10) **warbling vireo,** (11) **wood pewee,** (see quots.).

(1) 1906 *Out West* May 416 This is the hunting-station of a Western Black Phœbe. **1917** *Birds of Amer.* III. 201 Black Phoebe. *Sayornis nigricans.* . . . Western Black Pewee. — **(2) 1828** BONAPARTE *Synopsis* 394 The Western Duck . . . inhabits the Western coast of North America. — **(3) 1869** *Amer. Naturalist* III. 183 The Western Flicker (*Colaptes Mexicanus*) was the only one of the tribe observed in this nearly woodless plain. — **(4) 1878** *Nat. Museum Proc.* I. 415 *Poœcetes gramineus* [var.] *confinis.*—Western Grass Bunting.

(5) 1839 AUDUBON *Ornith. Biog.* V. 320 [The] Western gull . . . is especially remarkable for the great depth and comparative shortness of its bill. **1949** *Nat. Hist.* Oct. 361/1 The slate-backed Western Gull and the pearl-gray-backed Herring Gull are much in evidence, too, as is the red-billed Heermann's Gull. — **(6) 1944** *Nat. Geog. Mag.* June 694/1 There were . . . western mockingbirds and Arizona cardinals; Bullock's orioles [etc.]. — **(7) 1878** *Nat. Museum Proc.* I. 395 The Western Robin . . . visits the valleys only in winter, when it is sometimes abundant. — **(8) 1868** *Amer. Naturalist* II. 161 Western Snow-bird (*Junco Oregonus*). A specimen [was] shot at Fort Whipple, Arizona. — **(9) 1846** CORCORAN *Pickings* 57 Western turkeys were never known to thrive when they came south.

(10) 1878 *Nat. Museum Proc.* I. 409. **1917** *Birds of Amer.* III. 105/2 In western North America there is a smaller and darker form of this bird, known as the Western, or Swainson's, Warbling Vireo (*Vireosylva gilva swainsoni*). — **(11) 1874** COUES *Birds N.W.* 248 The Western Wood Pewee is exceedingly abundant in Arizona. **1944** CARRIGHAR *Beetle Rock* 66 The Chickaree . . . had remembered a western wood pewee in the adjoining fir.

3. In the names of plants and trees: (1) **western catalpa,** a catalpa, *Catalpa speciosa,* often cultivated for its beautiful flowers; (2) **chinquapin,** "on the Pacific coast of the United States, the *Castanopsis chrysophylla,* a tree or shrub of the Sierra Nevada and Cascade mountains . . . more nearly allied to the oak than to the chestnut" (*Cent.*); (3) **daisy,** (see quot. 1891); (4) **larch,** a larch or species of larch found in western North America and valued as a timber tree; (5) **red cedar,** the western cedar or red cedar, *Thuja plicata,* of western North America; (6) **sugar maple,** a maple, *Acer grandidentatum,* found in western North America and characterized by leaves that are hairy underneath; (7) **wallflower,** (see quot. 1891); (8) **yellow pine,** the Arizona pine or bull pine, *qq.v.*

(1) 1884 SARGENT *Rep. Forests* 115 *Catalpa speciosa.* . . . Western Catalpa. Valley of the Vermilion river, Illinois [etc.]. — **(2) 1897** SUDWORTH *Arborescent Flora* 149 Goldenleaf chinquapin. . . . Common names [include] chinquapin (Cal., Oreg.), . . . Western chinquapin. — **(3) 1891** *Cent.* 6881/2 Western daisy, a plant, *Bellis integrifolia,* found from Kentucky southwestward, the only species of the true daisy genus native in the United States. **1901** MOHR *Plant Life Ala.* 778. — **(4) 1869** *Amer. Naturalist* III. 412 Western Larch (*Larix occidentalis*). I found this fine Larch first near Bitterroot valley. **1948** *Hungry Horse News* (Columbia Falls, Mont.) 17 Sep. 1/5 Present are autumn yellows and reds, with aspen turning, and western larch starting to show golden needles.

(5) 1905 *Bureau of Forestry Bul.* No. 66, 33 The rock pine, western red cedar, . . . have, without doubt, come down from the Rocky Mountains. **1948** *Mazama* Dec. 6/1 Huge western red cedars, several feet in diameter, caught our attention. — **(6) 1897** SUDWORTH *Arborescent Flora* 286 Large-tooth Maple. . . . Common names. Western Sugar Maple, Hard Maple. — **(7) 1891** *Cent.* 6811/2 Western wallflower of the United States, *Erysimum asperum,* a plant found in Ohio, and more commonly westward, with orange-yellow flowers of the size of and like those of the wallflower. **1939** *Nat. Geog. Mag.* Aug. 227/2 Western Wallflower Manitoba to Okla.; west to N.M. and Montana. — **(8) 1901** *World's Work* July 888/2 The wood of the western yellow pine . . . is used by them for mine timbers and for fuel. **1948** *So. Sierran* Feb. 1/1 Included among them are superb specimens of . . . western yellow pines and white fir.

b. Also (1) **western azalea,** (2) **black ash,** (3) **iron weed,** (4) **pennyroyal,** (5) **white pine,** (see quots.).

(1) 1946 *Sierra Club Bul.* Dec. 21 Vigorous sprouts growing from the crowns of shrubs . . . were seen in the following species: California hazel, . . . silk-tassel bush, western azalea. **1949** HOWELL *Marin Flora* 7 The western azalea (*Rhododendron occidentale*) forms open graceful thickets along the stream. — **(2) 1813** MUHLENBERG *Cat. Plants* 96 *Fraxinus sericea,* Western black ash. — **(3) 1870** *Amer. Naturalist* IV. 582 Prominent among these are . . . sunflowers of several species . . . ; the western iron weed (*Vernonia fasciculata*). — **(4) 1915** ARMSTRONG & THORNBER *Western Wild Flowers* 436 Western Penny-royal, Mustang Mint. *Monardella lanceolata.* . . . An attractive plant, pretty in color and form.

(5) 1869 *Amer. Naturalist* III. 410 Western White Pine (*Pinus monticola*). I found scattered trees of this beautiful species on the highest parts of the Rocky Mountains. **1948** TRESIDDER *Trees of Yosemite* 27 This tree . . . is locally known as Mountain Pine or Little Sugar Pine rather than by its more formal titles, Silver Pine and Western White Pine.

As the last term in **great, mid, middle, south, wild western.**

Westerner ˈwɛstənə, *n.* Also **westerner.** One who lives in the West.

1837 MARTINEAU *Society* III. 21 'We are apt to think,' said a westerner to me, 'that however great and good another person may be, we are just as great and good.' **1849** AUDUBON *Western Jrnl.* 186 The tall, raw-boned Westerner [was] bearded and moustached. **1944** JOHNSON *As I Dare* 279 My true Westerner thinks of every man as a neighbor and friend until the contrary has been proved, and usually addresses him as such.

As the last term in **far, mid, southwesterner.**

* **Westernism,** *n.* **1.** A word or expression supposed to be peculiar to the West. **2.** The character and spirit of the West.

(1) 1838 *Knickerb.* XI. 447, I now recollect but few specimens of Jacks *westernisms.* **1886** *Harper's Mag.* Oct. 773 'It hasn't—ah—panned out.' He involuntarily made a droll face as he uttered the Westernism. **1948** MENCKEN *Supp.* II. 114 Haliburton's Yankee clock-maker in 'Sam Slick' interspersed a good many Westernisms and much general slang with his Yankeeisms. — **(2) 1934** WEBSTER. **1948** *Miss. Valley Hist. Rev.* Dec. 425 Not even the most articulate advocates of 'Westernism' in literature were quite sure what they wanted.

westernite ˈwɛstəˌnaɪt, *n.* A Westerner. *Rare.* — **1886** *West Chester* (Pa.) *Republican,* The westernites are ahead of us.

* **westernize,** *v. tr.* To make American or like the American West in manner or character, to settle or travel in the West. *Colloq.*

1837 PECK *New Guide* 107 Emigrants from Europe . . . are fast losing their national manners and feelings, and to use a provincial term, will soon become 'westernized.' **1882** *Advance* 22 June, After a month's residence [in Lawrence, Kans.], I have come to feel that it was a New England town *westernized.* **1902** *Nation* 23 Jan. 77/1 Its sphere will be wider than its own West, and it will win many to Westernize. **1949** *Trail Riders Bul.* March 7/1 A number [of dudes] go to nearby Kananaskis Ranch to get completely 'westernized' before the ride.

West Point. The U.S. Military Academy, located at West Point, N.Y. Also attrib.

1827 in *Aristocratic Journey* [Letters of Mrs. Basil Hall from U.S.] (1931) 112 Here there is a military college on the same plan as West Point but a private institution not patronized by the government as West Point is. **1841** *N.O. Picayune* 3 Sep. 1/6 [The expedition] numbered about 450 men, . . . under the command of Hugh McLeod, a West Point graduate. **1946** *Chi. D. News* 10 Oct. 12/1 The Army team is composed of West Point cadets. **1950** *Dly. Ardmoreite* (Ardmore, Okla.) 15 Jan. 20/3 Last year the Air Force got only West Point graduates.

transf. **1948** MENJOU & MUSSELMAN *It Took 9 Tailors* 26 Culver is a miniature or junior-size West Point. **1949** *Chi. Tribune* 11 Oct. 1/7 The government . . . plans to found a 'West Point of the air' somewhere in the West.

Hence **West Pointer.** Also attrib.

1861 *Charleston* (S.C.) *Mercury* 8 Jan. 1/6 (*heading*), The West Pointers Coming. **1884** RITTENHOUSE *Maud* 282 [He] led me about in true West Pointer style, by my finger tips. **1950** *Time* 24 April 23/1 He stood erect as a West Pointer.

wet wet, *n.* [f. the adj.] A person who is opposed to prohibiting the legal sale of alcoholic liquors. *Colloq.* Cf. ***dry,** *n.* — **1888** *Battle Creek Wkly. Jrnl.* 29 Feb., This is the first victory for the 'wets.' **1949** *Time* 10 Oct. 27/3 For the fifth time in 41 years, Oklahoma's wets did their doggondest to repeal the state prohibition law.

***wet,** *a.*

1. Permitting or in favor of permitting the sale and consumption of intoxicating liquors. *Colloq.*

1888 *Battle Creek Wkly Jrnl.* 3 July, A seemingly senseless rumor is afloat to the effect that since the county has gone 'dry' the Michigan Central dining car headquarters will be transferred to a 'wet' point. **1890** *Cong. Rec.* 12 March 2172/1 Every spring election there is a contest as to whether the town is to be 'wet' or 'dry.' **1946** *Life* 18 Nov. 20/2 By that standard . . . freshmen have been wet since 1902, when the first nightshirt parade was held.

2. *W.* (See quots.) *Colloq.* Cf. **wetback.**

1926 BRANCH *Cowboy* 35 Pierce once brought three hundred Mexican ponies, 'wet ponies,' into Texas, at a cost of two dollars and fifty cents a head. **1929** DOBIE *Vaquero* 81 The code of these ranchers . . . forbade stealing from a neighbor, but it generally permitted trading in 'wet' horses—horses stolen in Mexico and smuggled across the Rio Grande. **1944** ADAMS *W. Words* 176/1 wet stock Cattle or horses which had been smuggled from across the Rio Grande River after having been stolen from their rightful owners in Mexico or Texas. Later the term was used to refer to any stolen stock.

3. *To be all wet,* to be quite wrong or mistaken. *Slang.*

[**1792** BRISSOT *Reise* 209 (*footnote*), *Wet quakers* bedeutet wörthlich: nasse Quäker. *Wet* mag also in dieser Verbindung ungefähr eben so gebraucht werden, wie das Wort nass auf den Universitäten in Nord-Deutschland, wo die jungen Studierenden den Begriff schlecht damit ausdrucken.] **1931** *K.C. Times* 29 Aug., Alfalfa Bill Murray may be 'all wet' in his state-line bridge and oil production controversies. **1946** *Chi. D. News* 16 Sep. 12 (*cartoon*), Truman's foreign policy is all wet!

4. In special combs.: (1) **wetback,** a Mexican who gains entrance into the U.S. by swimming the Rio Grande River, *slang;* (2) **diggings,** *W.* (see quots.); (3) **down,** a wetting, *rare;* (4) **goods,** (*a*) liquids, esp. alcoholic liquors, *colloq.*, (*b*) ?goods damaged by water, *obs.;* (5) **Grave,** (see quot.), *obs.;* (6) **groceries, =wet goods** (*a*); (7) **hawk,** a nighthawk, *obs.;* (8) **keys,** in Florida (see quot.); (9) **norther,** (see quot. 1845); (10) **prairie,** a prairie on which water stands during part of the year (see also quot. 1817); (11) **season,** *v.* (see quot.); (12) **store,** a store that sells wet goods, *obs.;* (13) **swamp,** a swamp that is wetter than most; (14) **weather pond,** a pond that exists only in wet weather; (15) **(weather) spring,** a spring that exists only in wet weather, also transf.

(1) **1948** *Amer. Butter Rev.* April 10/2 The so-called 'wetbacks,' who may illegally cross the border, hire out almost exclusively in Washington, Maine and California. **1950** *Newsweek* 8 May 10/2 How do those 'wetbacks' who slip across the border near Calexico, Calif. manage to swim the Rio Grande? — (2) **1850** *Hunt's Merch. Mag.* XXIII. 684 They are called 'dry' in contra-distinction to the 'wet' diggings, or those lying directly on the banks of streams. **1889** MUNROE *Golden Days* 111 The wet or placer diggings were those in, or in the vicinity of, flowing streams. **1935** BUCKBEE *Saga of Old Tuolumne* 11 He worked ceaselessly throughout the day lifting gold from the 'wet diggings.' — (3) **1891** *Boston Jrnl.* 6 May 4/6 The bursting of a water-pipe caused a heavy wet-down at Miss Nellie H. Bonney's millinery establishment. — (4) (*a*) **1775** *Pa. Ev. Post* 9 March 80/2 To Be Let, A little above the Drawbridge, A Vault, . . . very fit and convenient for Liquors or Wet Goods. **1881** ALCOTT *New Conn.* 122 The largest items in the bills for such occasions [i.e., weddings] being for what were called 'wet goods.' **1917** MCCUTCHEON *Green Fancy* 73 Two or three men visitors have come down from the place to sample our stock of wet goods. (*b*) **1858** *S. Lit. Messenger* XXVII. 31/2 It haunts places where what are called 'wet goods' are disposed of.

(5) **1833** J. E. ALEXANDER *Transatlantic Sk.* II. 30 New Orleans is called the 'Wet Grave,' because, in digging 'the narrow house,' water rises within eighteen inches of the surface. — (6) **1866** W. REID *After War* 136 Coarse dry goods were plenty, and so were what, I believe, are technically called 'wet groceries.' **1894** *Cong. Rec.* 6 April 3527/1 I do not know whether they were 'dry' groceries or 'wet' groceries that were sold there. — (7) **1781–2** JEFFERSON *Notes Va.* (1788) 77 Besides these, we have . . . [the] Wet hawk, which feeds flying. **1808** ASHE *Travels* 162. — (8) **1834** AUDUBON *Ornith. Biog.* II. 356 Groups of such trees [i.e., trees whose roots are constantly immersed] occur of considerable extent, and are called 'Wet Keys.' — (9) **1845** in G. A. MCCALL *Lett. from Frontiers* (1868) 431 If the Norther is accompanied by rain in the form of sleet, it is of course the more severe. Not a fortnight since, we had one of these Wet Northers, as they are called. **1871–3** *Texas Almanac* 97 The people here in Texas divide these winter storms into 'wet northers' and 'dry northers.'

(10) **1817** BROWN *Western Gazeteer* 23 Wet prairie, which are found remote from streams, or at their sources, the soil is generally cold and barren, abounding with swamps, ponds, and covered with a tall coarse grass. **1940** DEAM *Flora Indiana* 1127 Wet prairies have a black, sandy, muck soil, and during the winter months, are usually covered with water which disappears by late spring. **1949** HADLEY *Indiana Birds* 17/1 Its favorite haunts are marshes and wet prairies. — (11) **1834** in *Atlantic Mo.* XXVI. 485 Pine timber for ships is *docked*, or *wet-seasoned;* i.e. put under water 2 years, then sunned so as merely to dry the outside, and oiled superficially; then handed over to the carpenter. — (12) [**1776** *N.J. Archives* 2 Ser. I. 190 John Shields Has opened a new store . . . where he proposes to keep a neat Assortment of Dry and Wet Goods.] **1788** *Md. Jrnl.* 25 July (Th.), [Notice] to those who would wish for the best stand for a Dry or Wet Store. — (13) **1654** *Hartford Land Distrib.* 112 One parcell of land . . . abutting . . . upon a wett swamp ioyning to the neck of land on the west. — (14) **1925** in *Amer. Sp.* XV. 410/2 On the divide, which is so flat that a wet weather pond exists there.

(15) **1844** in *Filson Club Quart.* IX. 232 There was . . . a wet spring, at times. **1916** MASSEY *Reminiscences* 39 His religious zeal, however, was no mere 'wet-weather spring,' but flowed on through the times of spiritual drought as well as through the flush times of revival. **1934** VINES *Green Thicket World* 111 The syrup mill was stationed at the edge of a swamp which held a large wet-weather spring.

***wet,** *v.* **1.** *To wet one's jacket,* (see quot.). *Rare.* **2.** *To wet the colors,* to furnish liquor to a ship's crew. *Colloq.* — (1) **1856** CARTWRIGHT *Autobiog.* 149 He took a great deal of pleasure in . . . making them members of his church . . . by 'wetting their jackets,' that is, immersing them. — (2) **1884** *Nat. Museum Bul.* No. 27, 717 The bridegroom is generally supposed to 'wet the colors' by furnishing his shipmates with a liberal supply of whatever beverages they may prefer.

we-uns ˈwiənz, *pron. S.* We or us. Also attrib. *Colloq.* Cf. **we-all.**

1864 *Harper's Mag.* Dec. 16/2 'What for you uns,' said they, in their barbaric dialect, 'come down here to fight we uns?' **1912** *Out West* March 179/2, I thought mebbe yer town gal'd like to see how we-uns has fun. **1922** WILSON *Merton of Movies* 70 It's one of those we-uns mountaineers plays with revenooers and feuds. **1942** in WENTWORTH.

***whack,** *n.* In colloq. uses.

1. A chance, turn, or time, often in phrases as *to have* (or *take*) *a whack at.*

1884 *Cent. Mag.* Nov. 60 Lucky whack it was for me that I got here to-day, and in time to save the mine! **1890** *Stock Grower & Farmer* 17 May 3/1 We have first whack at the water and intend to take out all we need. **1900** *Cong. Rec.* 5 Feb. 1522/1 Senator Carter of Montana took a whack at this business not long ago. **1941** STUART *Men of Mts.* 168 Hang around and watch people flock in at a quarter a whack to see this tonight. **1949** *Boston Globe* 3 July (Fiction Mag.) 9/5 He even took a whack at a dish of lettuce salad.

2. a. *that's* (or *it's*) *a whack,* it's a deal or bargain. **b.** *out of whack,* out of order.

(**a**) **1860** in *Adventure* (1924) 10 Sep. 191/2, I axed her for to marry me, she said it was a whack. **1876** MARK TWAIN *Tom Sawyer* vi. 70 'I'll stay if you will.' 'Good—that's a whack.' [**1929** *Amer. Sp.* V. 21 *whack, n.* A bargain, an agreement . . . [Ozark Mts.].] — (**b**) **1899** ADE *Doc' Horne* 78, I don't know what's the matter with me this morning. . . . My stomach seems to be out of whack. **1949** *Time* 30 May 53/2 With normal vibration a lot of them would have gone out of whack.

As the last term in **bull, bush, paddy whack.**

***whack,** *v. tr.* To drive (mules or oxen). *Colloq.* — **1873** BEADLE *Undevel. West* 691 One ought to be a 'Pioneer'—one of those who whacked mules or oxen across the Plains in the olden time. **1874** MCCOY *Cattle* 336 He took in his own hands one of the ox whips, and, to use the parlance of early days 'whacked bulls' many trips to Denver and Salt Lake.

***whacker,** *n.* A driver of a team. *Colloq.* Cf. **bull-whacker, mule-whacker.**

1827 C. BRYANT *Letter* 1 Jan. (MS), If our doors were closed, the country whackers who bring in cotton, corn and other produce for sale, would never find the way in. **1886** *Kans. Hist. Coll.* III. 544 One distinguished freighter . . . went so far as to furnish his 'whackers' with Bibles, but the effort was a religious and financial failure. **1943** L. V. HAMNER *Short Grass & Longhorns* 163 Long, snakelike whips carried by the whackers.

whafler ˈhwæflɚ, *n.* [Cf. *EDD waffler*, a sandpiper, from its undulating flight.] The flicker, *Colaptes auratus*, of eastern North America. *Obs.* — **1807** *Mass. H.S. Coll.* III. 54 The birds, which frequent this and the adjacent islands, are the crow, . . . the woodpecker, two species, the red-headed, and the speckled or whafler.

∗**whale,** *n.* In combs.: (1) ∗**whaleback,** a steamer having a cigar-shaped hull and a curved upper deck, formerly used chiefly on the Great Lakes for carrying grain, also attrib.; (2) **boat,** a long, narrow rowboat sharp at both ends, used orig. in whaling and later for many

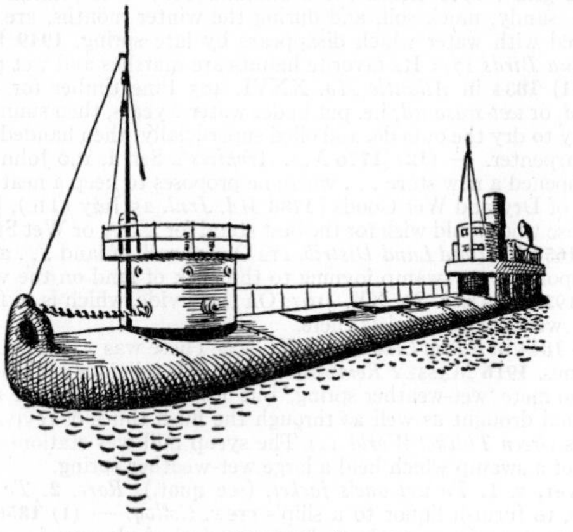

Whaleback

purposes, esp. as a lifeboat on a steamer; (3) ∗**bone,** designating a type of bonnet (see quot.), *obs.;* (4) **man,** a man engaged in whaling.

(1) **1891** *Pall Mall Gaz.* 10 June 2/2 The Americans claim that, in Captain Macdougall's steel 'whalebacks,' they possess the universal ship of the future. **1945** FUGINA *Upper Miss.* 134 Boats of the whaleback and gas-producer type were tried out. **1947** *N. & Q.* March 187/2 He afterward returned to the Great Lakes and became commander of the first of the whaleback steamers. **1949** *Sat. Ev. Post* 16 April 162/2 The whalebacks eventually gave way to the straight-sided, shallow-draft, flat-bellied ore boats of today. — (2) **1682** *Conn. Rec.* III. 318 How cam you up into these parts? In a whale boat. **1712** *Boston News-Letter* 8 Dec. 2/2 Six Men going off the Gurnet Beach in a Whale-Boat . . . after a Whale, by reason of the Boisterousness of the Sea, . . . they were all Drowned. **1886** *Outing* VIII. 45/2 I've been into a whaleboat, fast to a whale, and him a runnin' some fifteen or twenty miles a hour. — (3) **1830** WATSON *Philadelphia* 176 The 'mush-mellon' bonnet, used before the Revolution, had numerous whale-bone stiffeners in the crown . . . the next bonnet was the 'whale-bone bonnet,' having only the bones in the front as stiffeners. — (4) **1665** *East-Hampton Rec.* I. 230 The whaleman might strike a whale, and bringe her ashore at the said place. **1791** *Mass. H.S. Coll.* III. 154 The seamen are the most expert whalemen in the world. **1944** HOLTON *Yankees* 3 They were most of them whalemen in the great days of that industry.

b. Old whale, a sailor. *Colloq. Obs.*

1861 *New Haven Palladium* 27 Dec. (Chipman), We 'Old whales' or, as we are sometimes termed, 'Sardines,' are not supposed by some 'land crabs,' to have much of a taste for the feathery tribe 'done up brown.'

c. *a whale of a*, an intensive. *Colloq.*

1913 *Cent. Mag.* Sep. 621 [They] had what the Americans call 'a whale of a good time.' **1932** *K.C. Star* 30 April, What a whale of a difference a few sounds can make in the debt! **1950** *Time* 14 Aug. 50/3 His work had a whale of a lot of work in it, and that seemed a good thing to the Victorian eye.

As the last term in **drift, gray, humpback, scrag, scrag right, scrag-tail whale.**

∗**whale,** *v.* **1.** ∗*To whale away, fig.* to talk continuously and violently. **2.** *To whale it at,* to pitch into (something or someone) energetically, to whale away at. Both *colloq.*

(1) **1846** WHITCHER *Bedott P.* vi. 67 You remember that one that come round a spell ago, a whalin' away about human rights. **1890** BARRERE & LELAND (1897) II. 394/1. — (2) **1873** MARK TWAIN & WARNER *Gilded Age* 47 Spread her wide open! Whale it at her! **1886** *Harper's Mag.* July 322/1 In tones of wrath . . . he whaled it at his opponent throughout the fifteen minutes allotted to him.

∗**whaling,** *n.* In combs.: (1) **whaling gun,** a gun for shooting whales; (2) **schooner,** a schooner used in taking whales; (3) **station,** (see quot.).

(1) **1852** *S.F. Herald* 7 Aug. 4/7 Mr. Oliver Allen, the inventor of 'Allen's Patent Whaling Guns,' . . . gave us a description . . . of his modus operandi of dispatching grizzly bears. **1884** *Nat. Museum Bul.* No. 27, 302 Whaling-gun. Brand gun No. 2; muzzle-loading, skeleton iron stock. New Bedford, Massachusetts. — (2) **1884** *Nat. Museum Bul.* No. 27, 352 Whaleman's 'Bell.' . . . Gift of Captain Henry Clay. Obtained from the whaling schooner Golden Eagle. — (3) **1874** C. M. SCAMMON *Marine Mammals* 247 At the point where the enormous carcass was stripped of its fat, arose the 'whaling station,' where try-pots were set in rude furnaces . . . and capacious vats were made of planks, to receive the blubber.

whang hwæŋ, *n.* [In **1. a.** a variant of ∗*twang*. The source or sources of the other uses shown are obscure.]

1. a. Sound or twang. **b.** (See quot.)

(a) 1875 MARK TWAIN *Old Times Miss.* iv. 68 An agonized voice, with the backwoods 'whang' to it, would wail out. — **(b) 1891** *Cent.* 6885/3 whang. . . . Formerly, in Maine and some other parts of New England, a house-cleaning party; a gathering of neighbors to aid one of their number in cleaning house.

2. whangdoodle, a fabulous animal of ludicrous but undefined characteristics. *Jocular.* Cf. **guyascutus,** ∗**sidehill 2.**

1858 *Salem* (Ill.) *Adv.* 27 Jan. 1/2 They shall . . . flee unto the mountains of Hepsidam, where the lion roareth and the wang-doodle mourneth for his first-born! **1870** *Punchinello* (N.Y.) 9 April 30/1 In his own State the Ku-Klux raged, together with the fierce whang-doodle. **1950** *Chi. Tribune* 20 March 22/3 Along with the gyascutus, whangdoodle, sidehill gouger, and others, [it] is one of American folklore's great menagerie of imaginary animals.

attrib. and *transf.* **1859** *Harper's Mag.* March 568/1, I send you an anecdote of a whang-doodle hard-shell preacher. **1890** *Boston Jrnl.* 23 July, The rougher element among the boys . . . formed the 'Whang Doodle' Club for the purpose of settling him. **1923** *Nation* 22 Aug. 179 The downtrodden and oppressed force on the *Gazette* . . . has to live with this old whangdoodle and listen to his preterbacious scandulations. **1926** *Amer. Mercury* Feb. 236/2 The old Latin whangdoodle about a healthy mind in a healthy body.

b. *W.* A brand of a fantastic shape.

1939 ROLLINS *Gone Haywire* 144 It [i.e., a road brand] was artistically inconspicuous amid a volley of Flying Ws, Buckle Eights, Tincup Ms, . . . Crazy Twos, and Whangdoodles.

3. Whangdoodlers, (see quot.). *Obs.*

1890 *Boston Jrnl.* 23 July, Whang Doodlers. A Band of Youths Organized to Assault a Judge.

whapperknocker ˈhwɑpɚˌnɑkɚ, *n.* [Origin unknown.] ?A large weasel. *Rare.* — **1781** PETERS *Hist. Conn.* (1829) 189 The whapper-knocker is somethat bigger than a weazel, and of a beautiful brown-red color.

∗**wharf,** *n.* **1. wharf boat,** a boat used instead of a wharf at a place where the height of the water is too variable to permit use of a wharf. **2. wharf rat,** *(a)* the common brown rat often seen about wharves, *(b)* one who is frequently found on or near wharves, esp. a vagrant or petty criminal who haunts wharves.

(1) **1838** *Peoria* (Ill.) *Reg.* 15 Dec. 2/4 Several *citizens of Helena were killed* by the explosion, who were standing on shore and on the wharf-boat. **1911** SAUNDERS *Col. Todhunter* 39 A mighty cheer rose from the crowd assembled on the Nineveh wharf-boat. — (2) *(a)* **1823** COOPER *Pilot* II. 12 To burrow like a rabbit, or jump from hole to hole, like a wharf-rat! **1917** *Mammals of Amer.* 222 House Rat. *Epimys norvegicus*. . . . Barn Rat, Wharf Rat. . . . The common Rat to be seen about cities. *(b)* **1836** *Franklin Repository* (Chambersburg, Pa.) 4 Oct. 1/3 I've an idea, my man, that you are one of the wharf rats; and, if so, the less lip you give me the better. **1903** HARTE *Writings* XIX. 12 The fateful wharf [was] still deserted except by an occasional 'wharf-rat,'—as the longshore vagrant or petty thief was called.

∗**what,** *pron.*

1. ∗**what cheer** [the English words of greeting used by Indians upon the arrival of Roger Williams at the site of Providence, R.I.], in allusive use in Rhode Island, esp. in place-names.

1657 *Providence Rec.* III. 111 The two Indian Fields Calld whot cheare & Saxifrax hill. **1662** *Ib.* 14 The East end of that parcel of ground called What Cheere. **1832** DURFEE *Whatcheer* 159 Their shouts embodied sought the joyous sky With open arms, and greeting of Whatcheer. **1859** BARTLETT 506 There is in Providence a 'Whatcheer Bank,' a 'Whatcheer Church,' 'Whatcheer hotels' [etc.]. **1896** *N. Eng. Mag.* Feb. 771/1 The rock on the Seekonk has always been known as 'What Cheer,' while the city seal embodies a representation of this legendary event.

2. ***what-is-it,** a curiosity, a thing for which there is no suitable name. Also **whassit.** *Colloq.*

*a***1882** *Phila. Times* (Th. Supp.), The two negro girls, who figure as 'what-is-its,' are paid $200 a week. **1920** SANDBURG *Smoke & Steel* 53 There were. . . . Hound dogs with bronze paws looking to a long horizon with a shivering silver angel, a creeping mystic what-is-it. **1931** *K.C. Times* 29 Sep., A Whassit. Excitement on the south side of the square Friday afternoon was caused by the appearance of an insect which [etc.].

3. what-say, used interrogatively or as an interj., what? what do (or did) you say or think?

1825 NEAL *Bro. Jonathan* I. 357 'Was he hurt, uncle Harwood?' 'What-say?' **1891** WILKINS *N. Eng. Nun* 31 Well, what say!

***wheat,** *n.* In combs.: (1) **wheat banking,** ?holding wheat off the market until a certain time; (2) **belt,** a region where wheat is the prevailing crop; (3) **clay,** (see quot.); (4) **corner,** a condition produced by stock exchange operators' securing all or practically all the wheat available at a particular time; (5) **country,** a section or region in which considerable wheat is or may be raised; (6) **king,** one who has become rich by dealing in wheat; (7) **patch,** a small area upon which wheat is grown; (8) **pit,** the part of an exchange devoted to trading in wheat; (9) **ranch,** *W.* a large farm upon which wheat is grown, also **wheat rancher;** (10) **sand,** (see quot.); (11) **separator,** (see quot. 1883); (12) **yard,** ?a yard where wheat is threshed, *obs.*

(1) 1887 *Courier-Journal* 4 May 4/1 It is given out that all the contract wheat in Chicago is now cliqued, which implies the successive sacrifice of outside speculators every month until August by the process of wheat-banking. — **(2) 1863** *Harper's Mag.* Oct. 718/1 The enterprising town . . . is the wheat-market for a considerable section of the wheat-belt of the state. **1948** *Durant* (Okla.) *D. Democrat* 1 July 1/2 A symposium of reports from Santa Fe agents throughout the wheat belt indicates an average yield of slightly more than 16 bushels. — **(3) 1846** EMMONS *Agric. N.Y.* I. 293 Above it a soil is not uncommon, which is called locally a wheat sand, in contradistinction to a wheat clay. — **(4) 1893** M. HOWE *Honor* 264 In his calculations he omitted . . . the number of children robbed of their birthrights, that the great wheat corner might be responsible for.

(5) 1776 *N.J. Archives* 2 Ser. I. 133 To be Sold, . . . a very good Grist-Mill, . . . in a very good wheat country. **1890** *Stock Grower & Farmer* 29 March 5/3 The panhandle country . . . is a fine wheat country. — **(6) 1888** *Troy D. Times* 7 Feb. (F.), They heard of Cattle Kings and Wheat Kings. **1948** *Time* 23 Feb. 24/2 Montana's 'Wheat King,' Thomas Campbell, . . . said last week that the wise farmer would still hold on. — **(7) 1688** in *Phil. Trans.* XVII. 987 They might preserve their weakest Cattle, by these Methods, and help of the Wheat-patch. — **(8) 1884** in *Harper's Mag.* XII. 217 In the Wheat Pit at Chicago in a single year was buried more of the future prosperity of this republic than the sum of all the traffic which flows through that great city in a decade. **1949** *Time* 20 June 77/1 Tense and nervous, speculators crowded the Chicago wheat pit . . . , waiting for the opening gong. — **(9) 1883** JACKSON *Ramona* 237 He has the biggest wheat-ranch in Cajon. **1947** *Mazama* Dec. 1/1 Twenty-five blithe and kindred spirits hied themselves to . . . central Oregon on October 25th for an overnight trip to the 500-acre wheat and stock ranch . . . near Wamic. **1947** *Chi. Tribune* 1 Nov. 11/4 A former life term prisoner . . . admitted the hitch hike slaying of a retired Canadian wheat rancher in a holdup that netted $34.

(10) 1846 [see **wheat clay**]. — **(11) 1859** *Rep. Comm. Patents 1858* I. 500 Improvement in Wheat Separators. **1883** KNIGHT *Supp.* 946/1 *Wheat separator.* The separation of mustard, cockle, and grass seed from the wheat is effected by passing the mixed grains over inclined plates perforated with holes. — **(12) 1788** WASHINGTON *Diaries* III. 397 The other hands, except the Carter, who was drawing rails to the Wheat yard, were Hoeing Corn.

b. In the names of birds, insects, etc.: (1) ***wheat bird,** a bird, as the horned lark, which feeds on wheat; (2) **bulb worm,** (see quot. 1891); (3) **cutworm,** (see quot.); (4) **duck,** (see quots.); (5) **fish,** (see quot.), *obs.;* (6) **fly,** a Hessian fly or a wheat midge; (7) **-head army worm,** (see quot. 1892); (8) **insect,** =**Hessian fly,** *obs.*

(1) 1747 CATESBY in *Phil. Trans.* XLIV. 444 They arrive [in Va.] annually at the time that Wheat . . . is at a certain Degree of Maturity. . . . They have attain'd the Name of Wheat-Birds. **1858** *Texas Almanac 1859* 67 The wheat-bird and rust also injured the crop to some extent in places. **1917** *Birds of Amer.* II. 212 Horned Lark. *Otocoris alpestris alpestris.* . . . [Also called] Prairie Bird; Road Trotter; Wheat Bird. — **(2) 1883** *Amer. Naturalist* XVII. 1073 The wheat-bulb worm . . . generally affects the base of the terminal joint. **1891** *Cent.* 6888/3 Wheat bulb-worm, the larva of an oscinid fly, *Meromyza americana,* which affects the stems of wheat in the United States and Canada, stunting the ears, and prematurely ripening the kernels. — **(3) 1891** *Cent.* 6888/3 Wheat-cutworm, the larva of an American noctuid moth, *Laphygma frugiperda.* — **(4) 1888** TRUMBULL *Names of Birds* 21 While shooting in Benton Co., Oregon, in 1885, he found this species [the American widgeon] in enormous flocks on the wheat-fields, and . . . it was there called the wheat-duck. **1917** *Birds of Amer.* I. 120 Baldpate. *Mareca americana.* . . . Smoking Duck; Wheat Duck; Poacher. . . . The species is very fond of wild celery.

(5) 1845 J. J. BROWN *Amer. Angler's Guide* (1850) 170 It takes the various names of weak-fish, wheat-fish, and squeteauge [*sic*]. . . . The second name has its origin from the fact of its having made its appearance always at harvest time. — **(6) 1786** *Columbian* (Phila.) Sep. 38 [Premiums proposed] The best information, founded on actual experience, for preventing damage to crops by insects; especially the wheat-fly, . . . a gold medal. **1798** NEMNICH *Polygl.-Lex., Virginian Wheat fly,* a mischievous insect in the American state: It eats the grain, and is a moth in a perfect state. — **(7) 1890** *Cent.* 3422/3 *L[eucania] albilinea* is the adult of the wheat-head army-worm. **1892** V. KELLOGG *Kansas Insects,* Wheat-head army-worm (*Leucania albilinea*). . . . The worms come up after dark, and feed upon the [wheat] heads. — **(8) 1792** *N.Y. State Soc. Arts* I. 57 The wheat insect, or Hessian fly, as it is commonly called, put an end to this kind of husbandry. **1838** *Mass. Agric. Survey* 1st Rep. 98 Late sowing of wheat . . . has carried the season of flowering beyond the time of the wheat insect.

c. Used with reference to foods and drinks, as (1) **wheat and Indian,** (2) **cake,** (3) **coffee,** (4) **doings,** (5) **fixings,** (6) **waffle,** (7) **whisky,** (see quots.).

(1) 1641 *Dorchester Rec.* 286, I Re[ceive]d in wheate and Indein 3l. 8s. **1859** BARTLETT 506 *Wheat and Indian,* a mixture of wheat flour and the meal of Indian corn. **1873** LELAND *Sketch Bk.* 16 It seemed to be coarse macaroni in hard grains, as if made by rubbing a paste of 'wheat and Indian' through a sieve. — **(2) 1772** PATTEN *Diary* 293 Robt Forsiths gave me about 1¼ bushell of Wheat and his wife baked a parcel of Wheat Cakes for me when I went up to Cockermouth. **1865** A. D. WHITNEY *Gayworthys* 218 There are wheat-cakes and maple syrup for your breakfast. — **(3) 1840** DANA *Two Years* 203 Finding wheat-coffee and dry bread rather poor living, we clubbed together, and I went up to the town. — **(4) 1846** *Knickerb.* XXVIII. 314 John has got all my wheat-doin's away from me!

(5) 1853 *Harper's Mag.* July 279/2 A relative in Galveston, . . . knowing the rarity of wheat fixings in his visitor's location, presented him with a genuine wheat biscuit. — **(6) 1846** BEECHER *Domestic Receipt-Book* 96 Wheat Waffles. — **(7) 1867** CRAWFORD *Mosby* 186 [They] had nothing to drink . . . but new wheat whiskey and apple brandy just from the still.

d. In colloq. phrases: (1) *good as wheat,* very good; (2) *it is (all) wheat,* (see quot. 1865).

(1) 1851 *Polly Peablossom* 150 'Spose we make it up!' 'Good as wheat,' sez he. **1876** MARK TWAIN *Tom Sawyer* xxviii. 215 Agreed, and good as wheat. — **(2) 1865** S. BOWLES *Across Continent* 129 Porter . . . mutters that he supposes 'it is all wheat,' this being Utah idiom for all right. **1882** WAITE *Adv. Far West* 260 Anything that is all right with Rockwell, is 'on the square.' It is 'wheat.'

As the last term in **all, banner, barrel, buck, cape, China, club, early Virginia, English, fall, hardware, Jerusalem, Kentucky white-bearded, May, Mediterranean, red straw, robin, rock, sod, tea, Virginia, white, white-bearded wheat.**

***wheel,** *n.*

1. A dollar. *Slang.* Cf. ***cart wheel.**

1807 TUFTS *Autobiog. of Criminal* (1930) 293 Quid, a guinea. Wheel, a dollar. **1857** *Spirit of Times* 10 Oct. 91/2 We have looked in vain for the man who had the pluck and 'wheels' (cash) to come amongst us. **1906** *Harper's Mag.* Feb. 34 He brought out a silver dollar, called a 'wheel' in the language of the camp.

2. The cylinder containing the chambers of a revolver (see also quot. 1945). Now *hist.*

1857 GOVE *Letters* 73 All remarked, when the letter was read, and on being asked if they were ready to deliver up their revolvers that was on their belts, that they should turn the wheel 6 times before they did so. **1945** *Everybody's Digest* Aug. 89 A gun battle used to bring a puncher out 'a-smokin.' An empty gun has 'no beans in the wheel.'

3. (*cap.*) Any one of various political organizations of farmers. Also **National Agricultural Wheel, State Wheel.** Cf. ∗**Wheeler,** *n.*

1882 in W. S. MORGAN *Hist. of Wheel* 62 [Our organization] was named the Wheel. . . . Every editor who is opposed to our principles raises a pitiful little wail, O Wheel, keep out of politics. **1886** in *Appletons' Ann. Cyclo. 1886* 42/1 We have formed the National Agricultural Wheel of the United States of America, for the purpose of organizing and directing the powers of the industrial masses, but not as a political party. **1891** MORGAN *Hist. of Wheel* 81 A committee was appointed to assist the colored Wheelers to organize a State Wheel [in Tenn.].

4. A bicycle. *Colloq.*

1882 *Wheelman* I. 13, 'I love my wheel,' he said, 'as the yachtsman loves his boat.' **1914** ELIOT in James *C. W. Eliot* 249 This morning we had to walk instead of riding our wheels. **1948** *Chi. D. News* 20 Sep.

Early form of wheel (sense 4)

14/5 At long, long last the frantic automobile speeder has met his master, the 'jay walker' on a wheel.

attrib. **1882** *Wheelman* I. 115 This is a great country, and its railroads are better than its wheel-roads. **1897** *Outing* XXX. 277/2 One manufacturer [supplies] . . . drop-forgings, . . . another tires, . . . and so on all through the arts of the wheel-assemblers. **1903** R. HALL *Pine Grove House* 259 Surely that was Winifred Stowe in her new wheel suit.

b. A ride on a bicycle. *Obs.*

1880 *Scribner's Mo.* Feb. 483/1 A few . . . enjoyed a 'wheel around the Hub.' **1893** *Outing* XXII. 140/2 It would have been a lovely wheel had we chosen to explore it on bicycles.

5. In special combs.: (1) ∗**wheelbarrow,** see as a main entry; (2) **bug,** a large insect, *Arilus cristatus,* with a wheel-like crest; (3) **cultivator,** a cultivator having a small wheel (cf. **foot wheel** (*b*)) for regulating the depth at which it should be run, also **wheeled cultivator;** (4)

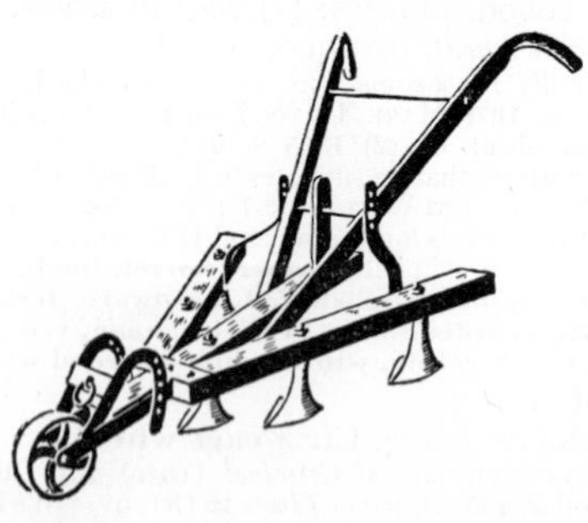

Wheel cultivator (*c*1848) showing foot wheel (sense (*b*))

guard, (*a*) = ∗**guard,** *n.* **1,** *obs.,* (*b*) ?the mudguard of a buggy; (5) **hoe,** ?a hoe supported by a wheel or wheels, *obs.;* (6) ∗**horse,** *transf.* a strong person, one taking a dominant or commanding part, also attrib., *colloq.;* (7) **house,** see as a main entry; (8) ∗**man,** a steersman, helmsman, or pilot, also **wheelsman** and transf.; (9) **scraper,** a scrape, esp. for road work, mounted on wheels, cf. ∗**scraper 1;** (10) **shed,** on a plantation, a shed where spinning wheels were used or stored, *obs.*

(2) [**1815** KIRBY & SPENCE *Introd. Entomology* I. 110 *Reduvius serratus,* F., commonly known in the West Indies by the name of the *wheel-bug.*] **1904** KELLOGG *Amer. Insects* 204 Another fairly well-known member of this family is the wheel-bug, *Prionidus cristatus,* especially common in the South. — (3) **1850** *Rep. Comm. Patents 1849* 156, I do not claim in this application the invention of a wheeled cultivator. **1868** *Mich. Agric. Rep.* VII. 345 Fords & Howe, Oneonta, N.Y., [exhibited] 1 two-horse wheel cultivator, or horse-hoe. — (4) (*a*) **1838** STEVENSON *Sk.* 129 The part of the deck overhanging the water is called the wheel-guards, and in some vessels it has a projection of 18 or 20 feet from the sides. (*b*) **1840** *Boston Transcript* 19 June 3/1 Fall back top, elliptic springs, wheel guards.

(5) **1858** C. FLINT *Milch Cows* 193 In weeding, a little wheel-hoe is invaluable. — (6) **1845** HOOPER *Suggs* (1928) 129 I'm jist a hunderd and forty seving pound neat weight, and I'm a wheel horse! **1906** LYNDE *Quickening* 213 His first care was to assure the 'wheel-horse' member of the municipal purchasing board that he was ready to talk business. — (8) **1865** *Ore. State Jrnl.* 12 Aug. 2/5 The wheelman says that large fragments of the bottom and a part of the rudder were afterwards seen alongside the wreck. **1885** *Harper's Mag.* March 643/1 She is everybody's pet, from the rather dandy wheelsman . . . down to the grizzled, grimy deck hands. **1887** *Courier-Journal* 4 May 4/6 A young farmer, seeing the peril of the wheelsman, plunged into the waves. **1947** MOTLEY *Knock on Any Door* 284 Butch is coming by in his car. He's going to work with us—he's a good wheelman. — (9) **1888** *Harper's Mag.* March 566/1 Shovels, carts, and wheelbarrows are of a past age; the big wheel-scraper does the business. **1920** *Outing* Oct. 18/3 Also free were the use of four scoops, two wheel scrapers, . . . and two plows. **1949** *Sat. Ev. Post* 15 Jan. 20/3, I took along a wheel scraper, a portable drill rig, and a lot of supplies.

(10) **1865** *Harper's Mag.* April 664/1 The meeting was held in the wheel-shed.

As the last term in **agricultural, bark, big, brake, bull, chariot, Chinese, common, driving, Ferris, fish, flutter, foot, fortune, jury, kick, logging, pilot, pin, side, side-paddle, stern, timber, tobacco wheel.**

∗**wheelbarrow,** *n.*

1. =**wheelbarrow kiss.** *Obs.*

1847 LANMAN *Summer in Wild.* 190 The forfeits are redeemed by making 'wheelbarrows,' 'measuring tape and cutting it off' [etc.].

2. In obs. or hist. combs.: (1) **wheelbarrow bet,** a bet in which the loser obligates himself to give the winner a ride in a wheelbarrow; (2) **boat,** (see quot.); (3) **fashion,** (see quot.); (4) **government,** a government pushed or goaded into action by the people; (5) **kiss,** a kiss given wheelbarrow fashion; (6) ∗**man,** a convict engaged in labor on the roads; (7) **style,** = **wheelbarrow fashion.**

(1) **1869** *Ore. State Jrnl.* 2 Jan. 1/4 Two Germans of Louisville, Ky., were arrested by the Police for attempting to fulfill the conditions of a wheelbarrow bet on the Presidential election. **1948** *Chesterton* (Ind.) *Tribune* 28 Oct. 3/4 (*heading*), Valparaiso's Great Wheelbarrow Bet. — (2) **1877** BARTLETT 748 *Wheelbarrow-Boat,* a steamboat with a stern-wheel, used on some of the Western rivers, as well as in Canada and Oregon. — (3) **1828** *Yankee* April 106/2 They were . . . ordered to kiss each other 'wheelbarrow fashion.' You would then see a . . . young man, and a . . . girl meet on the floor; close their right and left hands, on both sides; and with a whirl . . . turn through their arms, bring the back part of their shoulders in contact—each with the head resting upon the other's right shoulder, their mouths meeting. — (4) **1885** CRAFTS *Sabbath for Man* 288 The political code now in vogue . . . leads to a wheelbarrow government, carried on . . . by the people pushing them [i.e., the legislators] from behind.

(5) **1828** *Yankee* Sep. 288/1 As for their delightful good old fashioned wheel-barrow kisses I think they are all of a piece with red-ear kisses, field-beds and bundling. **1947** DOWNEY *Lusty Forefathers* 112, I heard you ask about a wheelbarrow kiss. — (6) **1788** *Mass. Spy* 26 Nov. 2/1 It is said the perpetrators were of that class called wheel-barrow men. **1860** *Ladies' Repository* XX. 4/2 *Wheel-barrow* man was the name for a convict. — (7) **1828** *Yankee* July 227/2 When a select party have met together, and they play button, roll the plate, chase the lady, and many other romping plays then they kiss wheelbarrow style—measure and cut off tape.

∗**Wheeler,** *n.* A member of an Agricultural Wheel. *Obs.* See ∗**wheel,** *n.* **3.** — **1890** *Cong. Rec.* 30 June 6802/2 [He] never left the Democratic party until he began his race for Congress, and even then he claimed to be a Democratic 'Wheeler.'

Wheelerite ˈhwilə,raɪt, *n.* (See quot.) *Obs.* — **1874** *Amer. Jrnl. Science* 3 Ser. VII. 571 Wheelerite, a new Fossil Resin. . . . I have taken the liberty of naming this new mineral after Lieutenant George M. Wheeler, Corps of Engineers, U.S. Army.

Wheeler pan. *Metallurgy.* A container invented by Zenas Wheeler for the grinding and amalgamating of ores. *Obs.* — **1869** BROWNE *Adv. Apache Country* 396 The Real del Monte contains . . . thirty-six Wheeler pans, and other machinery in proportion.

wheelhouse ˈhwil,haus, *n.*

1. (See quot. 1946.)

1835 INGRAHAM *South-West* I. 247 The pilot (as the helms-man is here called) stands in his lonely wheel-house. **1946** *Amer. Sp.* Oct. 236/1 So far as my knowledge goes, on eastern waters the 'wheel-house' on a paddle-wheel steamer has always been the pilot house, never a paddle box; and I suspect that the sense 'paddle box' is confined to the western rivers.

2. (See quots. 1860, 1938.)

1860 WORCESTER 1662/2 *Wheel-House*, a structure or box over a wheel in a steam-vessel; paddle-box. **1906** MARK TWAIN *Autobiog.* (1924) I. 310 (R.), Rush astern to one of the life-boats lashed aft at the wheel-house. **1938** RAMSAY *Mark Twain Lexicon* 257/1 The pilot-house encloses the steering-wheel and is placed forward on the upper deck, whereas the paddle-box, or wheel-house as the term is used by M.T., is over the paddle-wheel, at the stern in a stern-wheel steamboat, or at the sides in a side-wheel. **1946** [see **1.** above].

∗**Whelp,** *n.* A native or inhabitant of Tennessee, a nickname. *Obs.* — **1872** *Harper's Mag.* Jan. 318/1 Below will be found a careful compilation of the various nicknames given to the States and people of this republic . . . Tennessee, Whelps.

whetsaw ˈhwɛt,sɔ, *n.* The saw-whet owl *q.v.* [The association with the cuckoo in quot. 1815 is in error.] *Obs.* — **1778** CARVER *Travels* 475 The Whetsaw . . . makes a noise like the filing of a saw; from which it receives its name. **1815** *Mass. H.S. Coll.* 2 Ser. IV. 273 The birds noticed thereabout are, the crow, . . . whetsaw (a bird of the cuckoo kind, always heard, but seldom seen in the groves,) grous.

∗**which,** *pron.* [Poss. an Irishism, see quot. 1910.] (See quots.)

1835 A. PARKER *Trip to Texas* 88 Ask a question, and if they do not understand you, they reply '*which?*' **1859** BARTLETT 507 *Which?* An absurd word used by some persons instead of *What?* in asking for a repetition of what has been said. **1910** JOYCE *English* 348 Which. When a person does not quite catch what another says, there is generally a query:—'eh?' 'what?' or 'what's that you say?' Our people often express this query by the single word 'which?' I knew a highly educated and highly placed Dublin official who always so used the word.

whiffet ˈhwɪfɪt, *n.*[1] [Var. of ∗*whippet.*]

The alternation of *f* and *p*, seen in such pairs of words as *riffle, ripple; whiffet, whippet; whiffletree, whippletree*, is not uncommon. Sometimes, as in the case of *whiffet* and *whiffletree*, the *f* forms have so far been found only in American use and regarded, no doubt erroneously, as having originated here.

1. A small dog. Also **whiffet dog.**

1801 *Olio* (Phila.) 41 (Th.), Who heeds the Whiffit's bark, when tempests howl? **1820** *Mass. Spy* 13 Sep. (Th.), Yelping like a whiffet in pursuit of some game of which it appeared to be on the track. **1879** BURROUGHS *Locusts & Wild Honey* 30 The king-bird will worry the hawk as a whiffet dog will worry a bear.

2. An insignificant man, a whippersnapper. *Colloq.*

1839 *Cong. Globe* App. 17 Jan. 105/3 There was not a Whig whiffet in the country but could ask [etc.]. **1883** L. A. LAMBERT *Notes on Ingersoll* 200 We hold ourselves responsible to him, and to all the glib little whiffets of his shallow school.

whiffet ˈhwɪfɪt, *n.*[2] [f. ∗*whiff*+-*et.*] (See quot. 1864.) — **1864** WEBSTER 1508/2 *Whiffet*, . . . a little whiff or puff; a whiff. **1910** J. HART *Vigilante Girl* 14 At last, of the heavy fog-bank there remained nothing but whiffets and rings and wreaths of mist.

whiffletree ˈhwɪfl̩,tri, *n.* [See note to **whiffet,** *n.*[1]] A whippletree.

*a***1841** HAWES *Sporting Scenes* II. 69 Our whiffle-tree became detached from the vehicle, and fell upon the horse's heels. **1884** *Lisbon* (Dak.) *Star* 18 July, While they were driving along one of the whiffletrees suddenly broke. **1920** SANDBURG *Smoke & Steel* 255 The rings in the whiffletree count their secrets. **1939** *L.A.* Maps 172–3.

∗**Whig,** *n.*

1. A colonist who opposed the measures of the royal governors in the American colonies, esp. during the Revolutionary War.

1711 *N.C. Col. Rec.* I. 768 Sr. Nathaniel Johnson being put out by the Whigs [etc.]. **1774** J. ADAMS *Familiar Lett.* 7 Dr. Gardiner . . . brings us news of a battle at the town meeting, between Whigs and Tories. **1888** M. LANE *Pol. Catch-Words* 16 Whigs.—The name given to the adherents of the colonial cause during the Revolutionary War.

attrib. **1776** TRUMBULL *M'Fingal* 70, I see afar the sack of cities, The gallows strung with Whig-committees. **1854** SIMMS *Southward Ho!* 299 The British conquerors . . . regarded [with perfect recklessness] . . . the interests, the rights, or the affections of the whig inhabitants of South Carolina. **1922** *Friends Hist. Soc. Jrnl.* XIX. 12 While in New York he [Samuel Shoemaker] exerted himself for the relief of the Whig prisoners.

2. One politically opposed to Andrew Jackson, a member of the Whig party. Now *hist.*

1834 *Boston Ev. Transcript* 10 April 2/2 The Anti-Jackson men, or Whigs, as they are now called. **1884** BLAINE *20 Years of Congress* I. 104 For the first few weeks of the canvass the Whigs had strong hope of success. **1950** *Chi. Tribune* 28 Feb. 12/3 The Zanesville, O. Gazette . . . described a huge leather ball that some stalwart Whigs proposed to push to Nashville, Tenn., 500 miles south.

attrib. **1825** *Harbinger* (Frankfort, Ky.) 20 April 3/4 [He] has turned his intriguing and caucussing talents towards introducing . . . 'Jacobin' or democratic societies, under the specious name of 'whig clubs' or societies. **1834** C. A. DAVIS *Lett. J. Downing* 316 Masonry and Anti-Masonry was pretty much all one, and goin to vote the entire Whig Ticket all over the country. **1840** *Niles' Reg.* 2 May 136/1 The young men's national whig convention . . . is to meet on Monday. **1855** in HAMBLETON *H. A. Wise* 152 The majority of Whig Know-Nothings who affected the Winchester nominations were too keen for the spoils. **1949** *Chi. Tribune* 22 Oct. 10/3 A Whig campaign broadside of 1848 contained the lines [etc.].

b. ∗**Whig party,** the political party made up originally of those opposed to the principles and practices of Andrew Jackson and his followers. Now *hist.*

1834 HONE *Diary* I. 101 This was the day of the great fete at Castle Garden to celebrate the triumph gained by the Whig Party in the late charter election in this city. **1856** *Democratic Conv. Proc.* 69 In many a tough contest, the old Whig party, . . . have encountered the Democracy.

3. Whig plant, Whig Quaker, (see quots.). Both *obs.*

1811 MEASE *Philadelphia* 201 A party of the society of Friends, who . . . [thought] it lawful to take up arms in defence of American liberty, . . . separated from the main body of Friends. . . . This society is styled 'Whig, or Free Quakers.' **1847** DARLINGTON *Weeds & Plants* 187 Noble Anthemis. Chamomile. Garden Chamomile. . . . It is an old and still prevalent opinion, that this plant thrives better for being trampled upon or kept prostrate, whence it was popularly called '*the Whig Plant*' during the revolutionary contest in the United States.

As the last term in **Bank, Clay, Conscience, Cotton, Democratic, Free Soil, Henry Clay, Old, Outside, Seward, Tariff, Union, Violent, Webster Whig.**

∗**Whiggery,** *n.* The principles or doctrines of the American Whig party. Now *hist.*

1835 C. P. BRADLEY *I. Hill* 163 Wherever there still lives a man, who was a prominent member of the old federal party, that man is an adherent of modern Whiggery. **1851** *Miss. Palladium* (Holly Springs) 23 May 1/5 History shows the remarkable affinities of *Whiggery* for *No-Party* hobbies. **1950** *Chi. Tribune* 28 Feb. 12/3 The Public Advertiser . . . thought the ball 'characteristic of Whiggery in every particular—so hollow, so empty, so foolish, so dependent upon uphill work.'

b. *collect.* The members of the Whig party. *Obs.*

1837 *New-Yorker* 2 Dec. 587/2 The oddest affair . . . appears to have been conducted altogether by the 'rank and file' of the Whiggery of the Metropolis.

Whiggy ˈhwɪgɪ, *n.* A member of the Whig party. Now *hist.* — **1843** *Quincy* (Ill.) *Herald* 3 Feb. 2/2 The communication . . . appears to have kicked up quite a spree among the whiggies in that state. **1950** *Chi. Tribune* 28 Feb. 12/3 The Public Advertiser ridiculed the 'Whiggies' for their 'great tumblebug procession.'

Whigism ˈhwɪgɪzəm, *n.* The principles of the Whig party. *Obs.* — **1837** *New-Yorker* 2 Sep. 381/3 Its advocacy of this project is inconsistent with Whigism. **1844** *Henry Clay Bugle* (Maysville, Ky.) 25 April 2/1 (*heading*), Whigism vs Locofocoism.

∗**whip,** *n.* In combs.: (1) **whip grass,** (see quot.); (2) ∗**snake,** the coachwhip snake, cf. **coppery whipsnake;** (3) ∗**tail,** see as a main entry; (4) **thong,** the thong or lash of a whip.

(1) 1891 *Cent.* 6902/3 *Whip-grass*, an American species of nut-grass, *Scleria triglomerata.* — **(2) 1835** LATROBE *Rambler N. Amer.* II. 46 He would tell us . . . of the whip-snake, which would take hold of a tuft of grass with its mouth as you approached, and scutch you with its tail, till you removed yourself out of the way! **1898** *Smithsonian Rep.* 802 *Zamenis flagellum Shaw.* . . . This is a swift species, and is generally known everywhere as the 'whip snake.' This species ranges south into Mexico on the plateau, and southward on the western slope. **1949** *Scientific Mo.* Jan. 54/1 The only element of truth in the account is the fact that whip snakes do occasionally attack and devour rattlesnakes. — **(4) 1827** *Hallowell* (Me.) *Gaz.* 20 June 4/5 They have also received a large supply of . . . Whips and Whip-thongs. **1897** *Outing* XXX. 252/2 If your whip thong gets caught in the harness drop your hand and push the stick forward, and the thong will, invariably, release itself.

As the last term in **blacksnake, bow, buggy, bull, Californian, coach, cow, cowhide, hickory, Loudon, party, pig whip.**

* **whip,** *v.*

1. *tr.* To surpass. *Colloq. Obs.*

1835 HOFFMAN *Winter in West* II. 119 Old Kaintuck . . . whips all 'Out-West' in prettiness. **1850** HOUSTOUN *Hesperos* II. 54 It's a glorious place—and an ex-pansive country, I reckon! It can swaller Mexico, gouge both eyes out of Great Britain, and whip all creation!

2. To bring (moss or hemp) into a desired condition by threshing or beating. *Obs.*

1841 W. KENNEDY *Texas* I. 101 Let it [Spanish moss] remain in cold water to rot, like flax or hemp, after which it is dried, whipped, and put into the tick. **1850** *Rep. Comm. Patents 1849: Agric.* 331 It is an easy matter for one hand to clean 500 to 600 pounds [of hemp] per day, on the hand-brake; either by scutching or by whipping and shaking.

3. To thresh out (rice) by beating.

1903 PRINGLE *Rice Planter* 44 The hands now are whipping out the seed rice, which is a tedious business.

4. In colloq. phrases: (1) *To whip one's weight in wildcats,* and variants, to fight with uncommon ferocity and effectiveness; (2) *to whip the devil (a)round a stump,* see * **devil,** *n.* **5.** (1).

(1) **1828** *Spirit of Seventy-Six* (Frankfort, Ky.) 17 Jan. 3/5, I can ride upon a streak of lightning, whip my weight in wild cats, and if any gentleman choose for a twenty dollar bill he may throw in a panther. **1830** *Amer. Democrat* (Lebanon, Ohio) 14 Aug. 3/3 The old *Sargeant* . . . is so much excited at the result of the late elections, that he positively declares, he can 'whip his weight in wild cat skins.' **1846** *Spirit of Times* (N.Y.) 16 May 133/2 Courage enough to whip an acre of wild cats.

* **whipper,** *n.* A device for whipping or beating the dirt, trash, etc., from seed cotton. Also attrib. *Obs.*

1850 *Fla. Plantation Rec.* 61 Your overseers are using the whippers. **1863** E. W. PEARSON *Lett. Port Royal* 234 It was a busy scene—a whipper on each arbor with a child atop to fill the machine, which is used to lash the dirt out of the cotton before ginning. **1882** *Cent. Mag.* Jan. 477/1 A comparatively new machine . . . consists of a suction fan, a 'whipper-wheel,' or light paddle, for stirring up the cotton.

* **whipping,** *n.* In combs.: (1) **whipping bee,** an occasion upon which a party of ruffians beats someone, *rare;* (2) **boss,** one in charge of the whipping of prisoners or slaves; (3) **house,** a house to which slaves were sent to be punished, *obs.*

(1) **1922** *Daily Mail* 29 Nov. 9 Members of this secret organization . . . in the last 18 months in Texas alone have conducted no fewer than 500 tar and feather parties and whipping-bees. — (2) **1931** *New Republic* 8 April 201/2 Several hundred whites and blacks were ruled by an undersized 'whipping boss' who strutted among the prisoners with a loaded pistol and six-foot thong of rawhide. **1942** KENNEDY *Palmetto Country* 67 My whippin-boss was Mister Joe Sylvester. He had his pets among the women, and let em off light. — (3) **1852** STOWE *Uncle Tom* xxix, It was the universal custom to send women and young girls to whipping houses. **1865** *Atlantic Mo.* April 510/2 Without thought of nine o'clock, pass, patrol, or whipping-house, [he was] rushing on the road . . . to Tallahassee.

whippoorwill ˌhwɪpəˈwɪl, ˈhwɪpəˌwɪl, *n.* [Echoic.]

1. A nocturnal bird, *Antrostomus vociferous,* noted for its insistent call. Also, by confusion, the chuck-will's-widow, and the nighthawk. Cf. **muckawis.**

1709 LAWSON *Carolina* 146 Whippo-Will, so nam'd, because it makes those Words exactly. **1805** LEWIS in *L. & Clark Exped.* II. (1904) 200 We have not the whip-poor-will either. This last is by many persons in the U' States confounded with the large goat sucker or night-hawk as it is called in the Eastern States. **1846** *Dollar Newspaper* (Phila.) 24 June 4/2 The 'whip-poor-will' pours forth his noisy song during the evening and before daybreak. **1950** *Democrat* 30 March 4/1 We heard a whippoorwill Tuesday morning.

b. Often regarded as a bird of ill omen.

1783 ASBURY *Jrnl.* I. 459 Here was a young woman in deep distress of mind, occasioned by the flight of a whip-poor-will close to her. **1872** W. J. FLAGG *Good Investment* 901/1 The evil-omened whip-poor-will wailed. **1920** THOMAS *Ky. Superstitions* 270 If a whippoorwill sings in a tree near the house, a death will follow. You will have bad luck if you kill a whippoorwill. . . . Mountains.

c. As influencing folk practice.

1863 in HOLLANDER *Arme Blanken* 51 When the whippoorwill is first heard in the spring, they [poor whites] turn head over heels thrice, to prevent back-ache during the year. **1920** THOMAS *Ky. Superstitions* 20 When you hear the first whippoorwill of the year, walk three steps back, pick up whatever is under your left heel, spit on it, and make a wish. **1942** RAWLINGS *C. Creek* 248 We say at the Creek [in n. central Fla.], 'When the first whippoorwill calls it's time for the corn to be in the ground.'

2. A variety of speckled cowpea, or a pea of such a variety. In full **whippoorwill pea.**

1909 *Cent. Supp.* 308/3 The cow-pea is a bean rather than a pea. . . . It . . . includes . . . the mottled and speckled 'whippoorwills.' **1946** *Democrat* 25 April 8/2 For Sale—Nice clean bunch Whippoorwill peas, 20c per pound.

3. whippoorwill('s) shoe(s), any plant of the genus *Cypripedium.* Also the pitcher plant, *Sarracenia purpurea.*

1832 W. D. WILLIAMSON *Maine* I. 126 Meadow-cup, called forefathers' pitcher, or Whippoorwill's shoes. **1869** FULLER *Flower Gatherers* 182 Didn't I just tell you it is a '*Whippoor-Will's Shoe?*' **1896** *Amer. Antiquarian* XVIII. 40 An orchid growing in Southern New Jersey, *Cypripedium acaule,* or lady's slipper, is called by the Jersey farmers, *whip-poor-will shoe.* **1902** *Amer. Folk-Lore* 99 Yellow moccasin flower is kwe-ko-heah-o-tah'kwa, or 'whip-poor-will shoe.' The latter is also a Connecticut name.

As the last term in **Dutch, Nuttall's whippoorwill.**

whipsaw ˈhwɪpˌsɔ, *v.* [f. the noun.]

1. *tr.* To cut or get out (timber, plank, etc.) with a whipsaw; also, *fig.,* to get the better of.

1842 *Amer. Pioneer* I. 83 Dwelling houses, made of wood, whipsawed into timbers four inches thick, and of the requisite width and length. **1884** *Hartford* (Conn.)*Post* Sep., Had Braddock been half as prudent as he was brave, he could . . . have whipsawed the French and Indians in that campaign. **1906** *Out West* Feb. 110 The first lumber made in Arizona was whip-sawed in the Santa Rita mountains in 1856. **1948** *Time* 12 Jan. 40/1 They were just hoodwinked and whipsawed by Michigan's slickers.

2. whipsawyer, one who whipsaws.

1855 *So. Californian* (L.A.) 28 March 2/4 Lumber is being furnished in abundance by whipsawyers. **1881** *Lumber World* March, Some of the first saw mills built in England . . . were destroyed . . . on the ground that it would ruin the occupation of the whip sawyers.

3. whipsawing, a. Using a whipsaw to procure lumber. **b.** (See quots.)

(**a**) **1847** *Santa Fe Repub.* 23 Oct. 2/2 In addition to the great cost of procuring lumber by whip-sawing. — (**b**) **1885** *Mag. Amer. Hist.* May 496/1 *Whip-sawing,* the acceptance of fees or bribes from two opposing persons or parties. **1903** *N.Y. Sun* 8 Nov. 10 These speculators have subjected themselves to the process known in Wall Street as whipsawing; that is, they have bought when the market was strong and sold when the market was weak, and found each time that they bought at the top and sold at the bottom.

* **whiptail,** *n.* A lizard of the genus *Cnemidophorus.* Also **whiptail(ed) lizard.**

1933 DITMARS *Reptiles of World* pl. 20 Whip-tailed Lizard *Cnemidophorus bocurti.* **1949** *Nat. Hist.* May 209/2 The tracks of the whiptail, Cnemidophorus, which are thin and rather sharply cut, are made up of toe markings separated by the groove of the lizard's trailing tail. **1950** *Ib.* May 234/1 Also there is a whiptail lizard (*Cnemidophorus*), which is considerably paler than those immediately outside the dunes.

* **whirl,** *n.* **1.** A spinning bait used in fishing. *Obs.* **2.** *To give* (someone or something) *a whirl,* to give a trial or test. *Colloq.*

(**1**) **1888** GOODE *Amer. Fishes* 71 People who live near the lake, . . . using two lines with spoon-baits or 'whirl,' . . . frequently take two hundred or more Crappies in a day. — (**2**) **1887** *Outing* X. 112/1 Bill will want to give Old Prince a whirl. **1928** *Chi. Tribune* 28 July 10/3 If we don't hear from Uncle Dick by the end of the week we'll give it a whirl. **1948** *News-Dispatch* (Michigan City, Ind.) 3 April 1/1, I still think it won't hurt to give 'em a whirl and see.

As the last term in **sand whirl.**

* **whirligig,** *n.* **1.** An ice sport in which sleds attached to a sweep pole are drawn swiftly in a large circle. *Obs.* See *Amer. Sp.* Feb. 1946, 21 f. **2. whirligig seat,** (see quot. and cf. **swivel chair**).

(**1**) **1823** COOPER *Pioneers* (1832) xx. 213 Then the exciting and dangerous 'whirligig' would be suffered to possess its moment of notice. *c*1830 in *N.Y. Hist. Soc. Bul.* Jan. (1939) 10 Half a century ago they had there a sport called 'the Whirlagig,' which was formed by sinking a stout post upright in the ice the night previous, so as to leave about six or seven feet above the surface. — (**2**) **1946** *Pageant* Sep. 88 The first swivel chair was invented by Thomas Jefferson, who called it a 'whirligig seat.'

whirling exercise. A fit of whirling or spinning around under the stress of religious excitement. *Obs.* Cf. ***exercise 2.** — **1834** *Biblical Repertory* VI. 345 One young woman had what I would call the *whirling exercise.* **1871** DE VERE 235 *Whirling Exercises* were still more grotesque affections, in which, during a sermon, persons spun round like a top for upward of an hour, without experiencing any fatigue.

whiskerino 'hwɪskəˌrino, *n. local.* A competition in growing whiskers, usu. in connection with some approaching festival, as a Pioneer Day celebration. Also attrib. — **1924** *Placer Herald* (Auburn, Calif.) 6 Sep. 1/4 Whiskerino Clubs are being organized at Newcastle and Lincoln. **1948** *P.C.C. Chronicle* (Pasadena, Calif.) 31 March 1/4 The Whiskerino is slated for the latter part of April.

*** **whiskers,** *n. pl.* As the last term in **Bowie, chin, side-bar whiskers.**

*** **whisky,** *n.* In combs.: (1) **Whisky Baptists,** (see quot.), *obs.*, cf. **Water Baptists;** (2) **bloat,** a disreputable whisky drinker, *slang, obs.;* (3) **boys,** the insurrectionists in the Whisky Insurrection, *obs.;* (4) **cherry,**

Whirligig

=**rum cherry;** (5) **cramp,** cramp or poisoning brought on by whisky drinking, *rare;* (6) **Democrat,** a Democrat who participated in the Whisky Insurrection in Pennsylvania, *obs.;* (7) **fraud,** evasion by distillers (*c*1865–75), often with the assistance of conniving politicians and officials, of the internal revenue duties on whisky, *obs.;* (8) **Indian,** an Indian given to strong drink, *obs.;* (9) **insurgent,** one who participated in the Whisky Insurrection; (10) **Insurrection,** an outbreak in western Pennsylvania in 1794 against the enforcement of a federal tax on domestic liquors, also attrib., now *hist.;* (11) **man,** a man engaged in or sympathetic toward the liquor traffic; (12) **peddler,** =**whisky trader;** (13) **poker,** poker in which the loser pays for the drinks (see also quots. 1878, 1909); (14) **pole,** a pole set up by participants in the Whisky Insurrection, *obs.;* (15) **pool,** a game of pool in which the loser pays for the drinks; (16) **rebellion,** =**Whisky Insurrection;** (17) **ring,** a combination for fraudulently furthering the whisky interests, esp. a group of distillers and revenue officers who, during Grant's administration, conspired to defraud the government of part of the tax on distilled spirits, now *hist.;* (18) **root,** (see quot. and cf. **peyote**); (19) **trader,** one who sells whisky, esp. in trade with the Indians; (20) **traffic,** trade in whisky.

(1) **1871** EGGLESTON *Hoosier Schoolm.* 102 The 'Hardshell Baptists' or, as they are otherwise called, the 'Whiskey Baptists' . . . exist in all the old Western and South-western States. — (2) **1862** *N.Y. Tribune* 28 March 4/5 Private pilferers—the whisky-bloats—the bullies in ward elections . . . were out in full force. **1872** MARK TWAIN *Roughing It* lxxi. 513 The red sun looked . . . through the tall, clean stems of the cocoanut trees, like a blooming whisky bloat through the bars of a city prison. — (3) **1799** FRENEAU *Letters* 27 If Washington had drawn and quartered thirty or forty of the whisky boys, we would not have had this rumpus. **1850** FOOTE *Sk. Virginia* 560 The insubordinate, commonly called the Whiskey Boys, were many of them members of Presbyterian congregations. — (4) **1897** SUDWORTH *Arborescent Flora* 245 *Prunus serotina.* . . . Common Names. . . . Whisky Cherry (Minn.).

(5) **1883** BEADLE *Western Wilds* 608 He looked upon the Valley Tan when it was red and died suddenly, in 1875, of whisky cramp. — (6) **1863** *Rio Abajo Press* 4 Aug. 2/2 If the editor of the Gazette intends to insinuate that Jefferson countenanced the Whiskey Democrats in their rebellion against the laws of the United States [etc.]. — (7) **1867** *Comm. & Fin. Chron.* V. 70/1 The House on Thursday refused to commit itself . . . relative to the whisky frauds. **1900** *Cong. Rec.* 17 Jan. 913/2 One of the most discreditable things that has happened in the administration of public affairs in this country since the Belknap scandal and the whisky frauds. — (8) **1883** WRIGHT *Among Alaskans* 169 Captain Jack, having been married by Mr. Brady, declared that the ceremony had made him a Christian: his notion of Christianity was to cease being 'a whisky-Indian.' — (9) **1804** *Fredericktown* (Md.) *Herald* 25 Feb. 3/1 If our correspondent should hear it even whispered that Gallatin . . . was not secretary to the Whiskey Insurgents in 1794 . . . he will please let us know.

(10) **1804** *Fredericktown* (Md.) *Herald* 22 Sep. 3/1 The worst men have been put in, . . . persons such as Albert Gallatin, the Secretary of the Treasury, whose tongue even breaks our language, as in the whiskey insurrection of '94 he helped break our laws. **1824** *Mass. Spy* 28 July (Th.), In the whole country, we doubt whether there are an hundred individuals who are tinctured with the duelling or whiskey-insurrection mania. **1945** ADAMS *Album Amer. Hist.* II. 85 The President selected his Secretary of the Treasury, Albert Gallatin, whose home was in western Pennsylvania where the Whiskey Insurrection had occurred. — (11) **1887** *Voice* 11 Aug., The whiskey men of this city [Louisville] put up piles of money . . . to defeat Prohibition in Texas. — (12) **1886** *Rep. Ind. Affairs* 157 There are the intruding cowmen, farming intruders, coal and timber thieves . . . and whisky-peddlers. — (13) **1856** *Dem. State Jrnl.* (Sacramento) 19 Aug. 1/6 The Court has been playing 'old sledge' and 'whisky poker' with Ben for the last two years. **1878** J. S. CAMPION *On Frontier* 25 Whisky-poker, a harmless non-gambling game, in which the winner gets a drink and the loser a smell at the cork of the bottle. **1909** *Cent. Supp.* 1444/2 *whisky-poker*. . . . A variation of poker in which an extra hand, or 'widow,' is dealt face down and each player in turn can exchange his hand for it. — (14) **1794** *Mass. Spy* 19 Nov. 3/1 The whiskey poles are all cut down [at Pittsburgh]. **1808** *Ib.* 21 Dec. (Th.), Albert Gallatin . . . kindled the flame of insurrection around a whiskey pole.

(15) **1860** *Marysville* (Calif.) *Appeal* 30 March 3/3 Upon entering, I see several 'individuals' participating in a game of 'whisky pool.' — (16) **1863** *Cong. Globe* 31 Jan. 662/2 We now look [with amazement] upon those who, in the last century, maligned the great Washington for his efforts to suppress the whisky rebellion of Pennsylvania. **1947** *Chi. Tribune* 21 Dec. IV. 4/5 He tells for the first time many incidents in the boyhood lives of his characters in Virginia and Kentucky, in the Indian Wars with Mad Anthony Wayne, [and] in the Whisky Rebellion. — (17) **1868** *Cong. Globe* 9 July 3865/2 It is the 'money ring' which controls on that side, which has been charging that the 'whisky ring' controls on the other. **1946** ADAMS *Album Amer. Hist.* III. 303 One of these [scandals] revolved around the 'Whiskey Ring.' — (18) **1871** DE VERE 399 The Whiskey-root . . . is a cactus, growing on the sandy hills along the Rio Grande . . . and known to the Indians as *Pieoke*. The latter dig up the root, slice it, chew the pieces, and swallow the juice, which has a powerful intoxicating effect. — (19) **1822** MORSE *Rep. Indian Affairs* I. 48 The business done in the factory at Chicago . . . does not average two hundred dollars a year, in consequence of the whiskey traders at that place. *a***1918** G. STUART *On Frontier* I. 186, I wish those whiskey traders would go on to the Blackfoot country.

(20) **1846** McKENNEY *Memoirs* I. 25, I had . . . urged the passage of laws for the protection of the system from the inroads made upon it by the whiskey traffic of traders. **1885** *Rep. Indian Affairs* 5 The whiskey traffic continues.

b. Designating places where whisky is sold, as (1) **whisky hole,** (2) **house,** (3) **joint,** (4) **mill,** (5) **ranch,** (6) **saloon.**

(1) **1889** *Alamosa* (Colo.) *Independent* 8 Aug. 1/5 Charley Johnson proprietor of the Iron Roof Whisky hole on Apache Avenue, was driven out of Tucson for his general bad character. — (2) **1835** BIRD *Hawks* II. 6 You would have some of the wherewithall smuggled up to this identical old woman's whiskey-house! — (3) **1901** WHITE *Westerners* 2 Here and there a straight Indian, stalking solemnly towards some one of the numerous 'whiskey joints.' **1941** SETON *Trail of Artist-Naturalist* 325 She had been brought up in a whiskey joint among the gold fields of the Colorado foothills. — (4) **1856** *Butte Rec.* (Oroville, Calif.) 13 Sep. 3/1 He of course wanted *quid pro quo*, in lawful U.S. currency—something that would pass current at whiskey mills. **1949** *10 Story Western* May 50/1 A pair of gunshots spattered on the moon-dyed night from the honky tonk and whiskey mill section of the town.

(5) **1924** BECHDOLT *Tales* 100 He had established what was then known as a whisky ranch. — (6) **1873** *Newton Kansan* 14 Nov. 2/3 [Money] can buy whisky saloons and perhaps a few whiskey votes.

c. Designating drinks of which whisky is the chief ingredient, as (1) **whisky cobbler, cocktail,** (2) **skin,** (3)

sling, (4) **smash,** (5) **soda,** (6) **sour,** (7) **straight,** see ***straight 5. c.**

(1) **1862** JERRY THOMAS *How to Mix Drinks*, Contents, Whiskey Cobbler, Cocktail. — (2) **1856** *Yale Lit. Mag.* XXI. 146 (Th.), Nine whiskey skins, and our spirits rushed together. **1891** SALA in *Times* (London) 22 Feb. 2/3 The scheme of [the London American club] . . . seemed to comprise unlimited cocktails, whiskey skins, corpse revivers [etc.]. — (3) **1928** *Chi. Tribune* 25 April 10/4 Mother cured our 'tummy' aches with 'whisky slings.' — (4) **1870** STEPHENS *Married in Haste* 339, I can get him a splendid whisky smash.

(5) **1915** WILSON *Ruggles* 50 Here, Charley, veesky-soda! — (6) **1891** *Cent.* 6906/1 *Whisky sour*, a beverage consisting chiefly of whisky and water, acidulated with lemon-juice. **1904** LOVETT *R. Gresham* 186 Bring a couple o' whisky sours there, bar-keep.

As the last term in **apple, argee, bald-faced, blockade, brush, bumblebee, corn, cornstalk, crooked, forty rod, grape, grapevine, Jersey, lightning, maize, molasses, Monongahela rye, moonshine, Ohio, pass, potato, redeye, rifle, rotgut, rye, sagebrush, straight, strychnine, tangle-foot, turpentine, wheat, wildcat whisky.**

whisky-jack 'hwɪskɪˌdʒæk, *n.* [Amer. Indian. Cf. Cree *wiskatjân.*] The Canada jay, *Perisoreus canadensis.*

1839 AUDUBON *Ornith. Biog.* V. 208 The description of the habits of the Canada Jay or 'Whiskey-Jack.' **1870** *Amer. Naturalist* IV. 596 The Canada jay, known all over the northern country by the less euphonious name of 'whiskey jack,' had already laid and almost hatched its eggs. **1949** *Sky Line Trail* Oct. 5/2 The larches were becoming increasingly numerous and whisky-jacks were peering curiously about their earth-bound visitors.

b. Also **whisky-john.**

1895 GERARD in *N.Y. Sun* 30 July, Whiskey John, a popular name for the Canada jay, from Cree 'wiskatjân,' an untranslatable word. The name has been further corrupted to Whiskey Jack. **1950** *Skyline Trail* March 19/2 Another name, *Whisky Jack* (or *John*) is corrupted from an old Indian word, *wiskatjan*, meaning 'bird of old camping places.'

whispering bells. California yellow bells, *Emmenanthe penduliflora.* — **1910** PAYNE *Calif. Wild Flowers* 8 The flowers dry intact on the plants and with a slight breeze cause a delicate rustling sound, hence the name of 'Whispering Bells.' **1947** *Atlantic Mo.* Dec. 110/1 You mean my Whispering Bells are dead?

***whistle,** *n.* In combs., some of which are based on the verb: (1) **whistle pig,** a local name for the ground hog *q.v.;* (2) **stop,** a small, insignificant railroad town, also attrib.; (3) **willow,** the striped maple (see next); (4) **wood,** (see quots.).

(1) **1929** *Randolph Enterprise* (Elkins, W.Va.) 28 Nov. 8/2 The whistle pig is taking his nap of six months. **1943** PEATTIE *Great Smokies* 271 Whether the ground hog (called 'whistle-pig' by the mountain people of the Smokies) does or does not see his shadow on Candlemas Day isn't important. — (2) **1944** *Sat. Review* 2 Sep. 2/4 The frank, humorous, and, at the same time, challenging story of the men of the U.S. Foreign Service who represent America in the whistle-stops of the world. **1950** *Chi. Tribune* 15 May 16/3 The whistle-stop political orator says he stands for 'a bold, expanding economy.' — (3) **1935** H. L. DAVIS *Honey in Horn* 1 Around the springs were thickets of whistle-willow and wild crabapple. — (4) **1891** *Cent.* 6908/1 *Whistle-wood*, the striped maple, *Acer Pennsylvanicum*, thus named because used by boys to make whistles. . . . The name is also given to the basswood, *Tilia Americana.* **1931** CLUTE *Plants* 42 The willow has always been a favorite material with children for making whistles, but the striped maple (*Acer Pennsylvanicum*) is the real whistlewood because its bark is so easily loosened in spring when whistles are in season.

b. *To pay too dear for one's whistle,* and variants, to pay more for a thing than it is worth, to "pay the piper." *Colloq.*

1779 FRANKLIN *Writings* VII. 416 Poor man, said I, you pay too much for your whistle. **1837** *S. Lit. Messenger* III. 176 That, rejoined he, would be paying too dear for the whistle. **1878** *Harper's Mag.* Jan. 199 When respectable people like the Mayor of the city of Hot Springs and his friends got drunk, they should pay for their whistle. **1914** *Amer. City* Jan. 43/2 Lack of knowledge or care on the part of officials as to matters determinable only in the laboratory is the greatest reason why so many of our cities 'pay too much for their whistle.'

As the last term in **basswood, fog, papaw, Pawnee, penny, steam whistle.**

***whistle,** *v.*

1. *intr.* Of deer and moose: To utter a characteristic short, loud whistle or cry.

1839 HOFFMAN *Wild Scenes* 59 They were bent upon having a shot at the game, which dashed to and fro, snorting and whistling. **1891** *Scribner's Mag.* X. 447 A little later, about September 7th, the bulls begin to challenge each other, in hunting parlance, whistling. **1947** *Democrat* 26 June 2/1 Glen also reported hearing a deer 'whistle.'

2. *To whistle* (brakes) *down* (or *off*), of a railroad engineer: To instruct the brakeman by means of the locomotive whistle.

1869 HARTE *Poems* (1871) 37 Said the Engine from the East, . . . 'S'pose you whistle down your brakes.' **1891** C. ROBERTS *Adrift Amer.* 172 The engineer whistled the brakes off.

***whistler,** *n.*

1. The golden-eye duck.

1709 LAWSON *Carolina* 149 Whistlers. These are called whistlers, from the whistling Noise they make, as they fly. **1832** WILLIAMSON *Maine* I. 142 A Whistler is about as large as a Dipper. **1945** *Md. Conservationist* 17/2, I refer to the goldeneye, or whistler. Incidentally it is one of our ducks that nest in trees.

2. (See quot. 1917 and cf. **siffleur.**)

1820 HARMON *Jrnl.* 427 A small animal, found only on the Rocky Mountain, denominated by the Natives, Quis-qui-su, or whistlers, from the noise which they frequently make. **1842** DE SMET *Letters* (1843) 181 They abound in bucks, buffaloes, and sheep . . . also in all kinds of bears, wolves, panthers . . . tiger cats, wild cats, and whistlers, a species of mountain rat. **1917** *Mammals of Amer.* 202 The Hoary Marmot is also called the Whistler, from its call—a shrill whistle used not only as a danger signal but as a means of communication at all times.

3. =**blue whistler** (*a*). *Colloq.*

1857 *Spirit of Times* 17 Oct. 98/2 Walking back to my stand, I sounded the 'buck-load' of sixteen whistlers in my right-hand barrel.

***whistling,** *n.* and *a.*

1. The characteristic cry made by a male moose or elk. Also attrib.

1882 BAILLIE-GROHMAN *Camps in Rockies* 123 It was 'whistling time,' as the rutting season is called. **1886** *Outing* IX. 51/2 [The elk] moved away up the hill, uttering a whistling as they went. **1893** ROOSEVELT *Wilderness Hunter* 164 During the rut the bulls are very noisy; and their notes of amorous challenge are called 'whistling' by the frontiersman. **1922** W. STONE & W. E. CRAM *Amer. Animals* 33 From a distant ravine comes the shrill sweet whistle of a great bull elk.

2. In special combs.: (1) **whistling bird,** ?a bird-like device on a tea kettle that gives off a note as the water in the kettle boils; (2) **bob,** =**whisky-jack;** (3) **Jack,** (see quot.); (4) **marmot,** =***whistler 2;** (5) **post,** a post beside a railroad track as a signal to the engineer to blow for a nearby station, crossing, etc., also transf.; (6) **squirrel,** a gopher or ground squirrel of the genus *Citellus;* (7) ***swan,** the common American swan, *Cygnus columbianus.*

(1) **1776** *Pa. Ledger* 20 April, Joseph Stansbury . . . is selling off . . . his baking dishes, compotiers, pudding dishes . . . children's tea sets, whistling birds, &c. — (2) **1880** *Rep. Supt. Yellowstone Nat. Pk.* (1881) 45 The gaudy blue-jay, the camp-pest of the mountains [is] here called whistling-bob. — (3) **1892** TORREY *Footpath-Way* 93, I heard a white-throated sparrow singing outside. . . . A sweet and home-felt strain is this of 'Whistling Jack.' — (4) **1906** *Out West* May 373 (*caption*), The 'Whistling Marmot.' **1949** *Nat. Geog. Mag.* Dec. 830/1 He could scarcely avoid seeing black bears, bobcats, coyotes, or whistling marmots.

(5) **1898** HAMBLEN *Gen. Manager's Story* x. 140, I managed to see most of the whistling-posts . . . and . . . I blew the crossing signal anyway. **1941** FERGUSSON *Southwest* 33 It was still a whistling-post. — (6) **1806** CLARK in *Lewis & C. Exped.* V. (1905) 59 Labiech also brought a whisteling squirel which he had killed in it's hole on the high plains. — (7) **1806** LEWIS in *L. & Clark Exped.* III. (1905) 307 The large, and small or whistling swan . . . still remain with us. **1948** *So. Sierran* March 2/3 Scott reports two pairs of Whistling Swans and cygnets apparently wintering on Silver Lake in the heart of Los Angeles.

***white,** *a.* and *adv.*

1. Honest, fair, decent. Also *to act* (or *treat*) *white. Colloq.*

1865 MARK TWAIN *Sk. New & Old* 74 The parson . . . was one among the whitest men I ever see. **1907** COOK *Border & Buffalo* (1938) 156 Although your color is cinnamon, and you may have Spanish, Navajo, or even Apache blood in your veins, you treated me white all the same. **1913** EDITH WHARTON *Cust. Country* ix, Well—this is white of you. *Ib.* xviii, I mean to act white by you. **1949** *Boston Sun. Globe Mag.* 3 April 1/2 It's mighty white of you to put it that way, Tandy.

2. American. *Rare.*

1902 WISTER *Virginian* 158 But us folks have been white for a hundred years.

3. In miscellaneous combs.: (1) **white ash,** *attrib.* (see quot. 1920); (2) **Charlie,** (see quot.), *obs.;* (3) **Christmas,** a Christmas when there is snow; (4) **face(d) clay,** ?white clay, *obs.;* (5) ***head,** used in phrases to indicate something in the extreme, *colloq.;* (6) ***horse,** (*a*) vitality, *colloq., obs.,* (*b*) among lumberers, an order given to a workman by his foreman that he be paid for the time he has worked, *colloq.;* (7) **meadow,** prob. a meadow having whitish soil, *obs.;* (8) ***wash,** a defeat in a game, as baseball, in which the losing side fails to score, *colloq.;* (9) ***water,** *attrib.* designating a lumberer or boatman accustomed to rapids and rough water; (10) **way,** a brilliantly lighted way, street or avenue, usu. in the business or theatrical district of a city, cf. **Great White Way;** (11) ***wing,** a street sweeper, in allusion to the white uniform he wears, cf. **e.** (10) and **5.** (29) below.

(1) 1857 *Harper's Mag.* Sep. 460/2 The veins of the first, second, and third axes are of the white-ash variety. **1920** FAY *Glossary* 740/2 White-ash coal. Coal leaving a white ash. (Chance). — **(2) 1842** *Cong. Globe* App. 28 Dec. 74/2 There seems to me as much prospect of the ultra Whigs—'the white Charlies'—coalescing with the Democrats, as there is of Tyler and his friends. — **(3) 1913** *Collier's* 13 Dec. 8 (*heading*), A White Christmas. **1949** *Chi. Tribune* 27 Dec. 18/3 A white Christmas came as ordered and now, what color do you prefer for New Year's eve? — **(4) 1819** *Plough Boy* I. 190 My garden is what we call *white face clay*, though not quite the hardest kind. **1880** *Vt. Agric. Rep.* VI. 29 'White-faced' clay, not even discolored by the slightest amount of vegetable mould, is found everywhere.

(5) 1830 *Mass. Spy* 28 July (Th.), 'Clear out like a whitehead.' Given as a Southernism. **1882** PECK *Sunshine* 179 If a boy knows that there will be no school on the afternoon of circus day, he will study like a white-head all the forenoon. **1917** MCCUTCHEON *Green Fancy* 129 It doesn't seem reasonable that they'd run like whiteheads with guns in. — **(6)** (*a*) **1833** GREENE *Dod. Duckworth* I. 73 'A pretty, smart, playful, active rogue,' his mother would exclaim, 'how full of the white hoss it is!' (*b*) **1893** *Scribner's Mag.* June 710/2 Jack, if you don't show up better than this to-morrow night I will have to send you to town on the 'white horse.' This 'white horse' is the time order already described. — **(7) 1658** in *Amer. Sp.* XV. 411/2 Beginning at the North West end of a white Meadow by a branch. **1683** *Ib.*, Beginning att a Corner Pockery standing nigh a place known by ye name of ye white medow. — **(8) 1867** *Ball Players' Chron.* 20 June 4/3 A blank score at Albany, N.Y., is called 'a blind;' in Connecticut it is a 'white wash.' **1946** *Oregonian* (Portland) 22 July II. 1/4 Ferriss' fine job was his fifth whitewash trick of the season and his fifteenth victory. — **(9) 1902** WHITE *Blazed Trail* 334 Here were the best of the Fighting Forty,—men with a reputation as 'white-water birlers'—men afraid of nothing. **1905** *Forestry Bureau Bul.* 61 White water man. A log driver who is expert in breaking jams of rapids or falls. **1949** *Life* 16 May 119 The river . . . was thought so dangerous that only two dozen of the most daring white-water boatmen in the U.S. had ever tackled it.

(10) 1920 LEWIS *Main Street* 416 Then, glory of glories, the town put in a White Way. **1948** *Dly. Ardmoreite* (Ardmore, Okla.) 15 July 14/1 The Oklahoma Gas and Electric is installing the white way in Sulphur's main thoroughfare. — **(11) 1898** *K.C. Star* 21 Dec. 4/1 Alderman Herman Gerhart would have the white wings paid every Saturday night. **1950** *Time* 3 April 44/2 Dressed as whitewings, Godfrey, Crooner Morton Downey and Hollywood Comic Jack Carson appeared on the screen pushing street cleaners' brooms.

b. In other expressions, usu. less frequent and often obs.: (1) ***white dog,** (see quot. and cf. **red dog**); (2) **-face act,** an act on the stage not done in black face; (3) ***metal,** silver; (4) ***night,** (see quot. and cf. **white Christmas**); (5) **oaker,** =**white oak cheese;** (6) **sulphur,** app. a spring the waters of which are impregnated with sulphur; (7) **Templar,** (see quot.).

(1) 1875 *Chi. Tribune* 24 Aug. 6/1 'White Dog' was a State issue to pay for canal repairs. — **(2) 1895** *N.Y. Dramatic News* 9 Nov. 14/4 Lew Dockstader, in his new white-face act, . . . will be seen at Keith's. — **(3) 1900** *Cong. Rec.* 14 Feb. 1773/2 You come to us with your hands reeking with the blood of the white metal and ask us solemnly to go into an arrangement to revivify it and make it standard money? — **(4) 1835** H. C. TODD *Notes* 22 In the Pennsylvania section originated . . . *white* for snowy night.

(5) 1845 *Lowell Offering* V. 271 But I have not told you about the cheese. This was a real 'white oaker.' — **(6) 1837** W. JENKINS *Ohio Gaz.* 63 The spring is of the class denominated *White Sulphur*, in the United States. — **(7) 1944** DUNCAN *M. Graham* 122 A temperance society, the White Templars, had now become a reality.

For ***Whiteboys, *collar, *hall, *House, *man, marsh, plague, *ribbon, trash,** see as main entries.

c. In expressions, chiefly southern and often obs. or hist., designating Negroes or with reference to persons, things, etc., having to do with, or distinguished from, Negroes: (1) **white basis,** the white population thought of as serving as a basis for representation in a legislative assembly, cf. **federal number;** (2) **Brotherhood,** in some southern states after the Civil War, an organization of white men seeking to regain white political supremacy; (3) **buckra,** (see quot.); (4) **Camellias,** (see quot.); (5) **folks' Negro,** a Negro devoted to the interests of white people and a favorite with them, *colloq.;* (6) **help,** hired helpers who are white as distinguished from those who are colored; (7) **hope,** orig. any white man whose chances appeared good for winning the world's heavyweight boxing championship from Jack Johnson, a celebrated Negro champion (cf. **white man's hope** *s.v.* ***white man** as a main entry, poss. the orig. form of this expression), now anyone of whom much is expected (see *Amer. Sp.* April, 1943, 156–7); (8) **labor,** labor performed by a white person or persons as distinguished from that of those who are colored; (9) **Line,** a secret political organization formed about 1875 in some of the southern states to assist in securing white supremacy, also attrib.; (10) **Liner,** a member of the White Line organization; (11) **Republican,** a white man, as distinguished from a Negro, who is a member of the Republican party; (12) **rule,** rule or government exercised by white people as distinguished from Negroes, also **white-ruled,** *a.;* (13) **supremacy,** the social and political dominance of white people, also attrib.

(1) 1830 *Va. Lit. Museum* 509/1 Supposing . . . that there would be a few slave holding counties in the west, there was no danger that the 'white basis,' would carry power into unfriendly hands. — **(2) 1870** W. W. HOLDEN *Proclamations* 31 For be it known to your honor that there is a widespread and secret organization in this State, partly political and partly social in its objects; that this organization is known, first, as 'The Constitutional Union Guard,'—secondly, as 'The White Brotherhood,'—thirdly, as 'The Invisible Empire.' **1880** *Sen. Rep.* No. 693, 400 Who were going to massacre him? . . . The White Brotherhood. There were several associations of them. The White Brotherhood, the Invisible Empire, and the Stonewall Guard. — **(3) 1859** MACKAY *Tour* II. 46 'A white Buckra' is the most opprobrious epithet that a negro can make use of; for in his eyes, wealth, authority, power, and white blood should always be found together. — **(4) 1877** BEARD *K.K.K. Sketches* 137 The K.K.K. . . . underwent a very positive metempsychosis, and became, thereafter, the White League, or White Camelias.

(5) 1892 HARRIS *U. Remus & Friends* 266 He is known as 'a white-folks' nigger,' which, in the kitchen, is intended to be a term of very severe reproach. — **(6) 1904** PRINGLE *Rice Planter* 127, I think the time has come when I really must try and 'get white help.' — **(7) 1912** I. COBB *Back Home* 233 Judge Priest was a celebrity, holding the limelight to the virtual exclusion of grand opera stars, favourite sons, white hopes, [and] debutantes. **1921** *Double Dealer* Feb. 37/2 Passes, March 4th, beyond public appeal and scorn, from out the cartoonist's brain and politician's head, one Woodrow Wilson, erst-while Coiner of Catchwords, moral White Hope of the World and President of these United States of America. **1948** *Time* 5 July 40/2 Idol of the Negro race, and so popular with the whites that the old cry for a 'white hope' never came up, Joe Louis . . . was a champion the whole U.S. was proud of. — **(8) 1848** *De Bow's Review* V. 532 White labor is alone employed in the establishment. **1879** *Bradstreet's* 10 Dec. 2/3 The supply of white labor is sufficient. — **(9) 1875** *Chi. Tribune* 6 Nov. 3/6 These figures teach the docility and gentleness of the colored race, all white line documents and lies to the contrary notwithstanding. **1876** *Cong. Rec.* 4 Aug. 5183/2 In their party pow-wow . . . [Mr. Lamar and his friends] declared by formal resolution against the white-line policy. **1880** E. KIRKE *Garfield* 54 The horrors of the Ku-klux and the White-Lines should not run riot at the polls.

(10) 1875 *Chi. Tribune* 2 Nov. 4/7 The white-liners of Mississippi . . . expect to carry the election to-day. *Ib.* 6 Nov. 8/7 The White-Liners having carried Mississippi, it remains to be seen what they will do. **1876** *Harper's Wkly.* 2 Sep. 712 The White Liners were here. — **(11) 1863** HOPLEY *Life in South* I. 5 'Black and white republicans,' 'new and old line whigs,' 'fire-eaters' and 'democrats,' were given up in despair. **1903** *Forum* Oct. 177 Many white Republicans are already leaving that party because they do not desire to affiliate themselves with the negro. — **(12) 1868** *N.Y. Herald* 4 July 4/3 The Texan delegates observe these instructions in their intercourse with representatives from the white-ruled States. **1884** *Cent. Mag.* April 863/2 There is a strong sentiment which would crystallize . . . the present condition of absolute white rule and negro subjection in political affairs. — **(13) 1867** in EASTERBY *S.C. Rice Plant.* (1945) 234 The reports are that in all the Elections where the question of negro suffrage was submitted the proposition has been rejected by very large majorities and the principle of 'white supremacy' been significantly triumphant at the polls. **1950** *Chi. D. News* 16 Feb. 8/1 A man . . . is operating a 'white supremacy' organization.

For ∗**Whiteboys,** ∗**Caps, League, Negro,** see as main entries.

d. Designating Indians, or used in expressions alluding to them: (1) **white aborigine,** =**white Indian** (*a*); (2) **Cherokee,** (see quot. and cf. **white Choctaw**); (3) ∗**children,** used fig. in speaking to Indians, with reference to white people; (4) **Choctaw,** a Choctaw having considerable white blood, cf. **white Cherokee;** (5) **doctor,** an Indian who has taken a medical course and become a doctor, as distinguished from a "medicine man"; (6) **dog feast,** a new year feast or ceremony among the Iroquois involving the sacrifice of dogs; (7) **father,** a white man regarded by the Indians as a friend and protector, also transf., often *cap.;* (8) **flesh,** white people—used by Indians or in imitation of their speech; (9) **gift,** a natural gift or endowment characteristic of white people, *obs.;* (10) **Indian,** (*a*) an Indian belonging to certain plains tribes of relatively light color or to other tribes, as the Zuñi and Menominee, also as name of a tribe, (*b*) a white man living among the Indians; (11) **musket,** in Indian speech, a rifle, *rare;* (12) **settlement,** (*a*) a settlement or community of white people, (*b*) settlement or occupancy by white settlers; (13) **skin,** =**paleface,** also attrib.; (14) **squaw,** a white woman.

(1) 1846 SAGE *Scenes Rocky Mts.* xxiv. 251 The Munchies are a nation of white aborigines actually existing in a valley among the Sierra de los Mimbros chain. — **(2) 1873** BEADLE *Undevel. West* 358 The phrase 'White Cherokee' is generally applied to those of less than half Indian blood. — **(3) 1849** *31st Cong.* 1 Sess. Sen. Doc. No. 64, 188 Their Great Father, the President, having such a multitude of white children in the . . . East that there was not room sufficient for all of them. — **(4) 1873** J. H. BEADLE *Western Wilds* 407 Occasionally appears a cattle corral, and near it a stylish log-house or rude cabin, from which 'White Choctaws' peer out at the train.

(5) 1916 C. A. EASTMAN *From Deep Woods* (1929) 76/6 In 1890 a 'white doctor' who was also an Indian was something of a novelty. — **(6) 1907** HODGE *Amer. Indians* I. 460/2 New fire was made in . . . the White-dog feast of the Iroquois. — **(7) 1835** HOFFMAN *Winter in West* I. 251 We have no longer any white father. **1894** WISTER in *Harper's Mag.* Sep. 516/2 The White Father has sent me. **1947** *Dly. Oklahoman* (Okla. City) 21 Sep. 1-D/6 When the 'White Fathers' in Washington heard the cry of economy after World War II, that economy began with the Indian services. — **(8) 1784** FILSON *Kentucke* 82 The White Flesh, the Americans, French, Spaniards, Dutch and English, this day smoke out of the peace-pipe. — **(9) 1841** COOPER *Deerslayer* ix, That I *will* maintain . . . is ag'in white gifts!

(10) (*a*) **1765** ROGERS *Acct. N. Amer.* 191 This fruitful country [upper Missouri] is at present inhabited by a nation of Indians, called by the others the White Indians, on account of their complexion, they being much the fairest Indians on the continent. **1800** D. R. D'ERES *Memoirs* 50 This nation was called the White Indians. (*b*) **1837** *S. Lit. Messenger* III. 256 To his amazement, the proposal is rejected, and the savage rage of the 'white Indian' is awakened by the insult. — **(11) 1864** *Virginia* (Nev.) *Bul.* 29 April 3/2 There did not happen to be some of 'Uncle Sam's' blue coats aboard [the stagecoach] with the 'white muskets,' as they call them, for its protection. — **(12)** (*a*) **1822** in MORSE *Rep. Indian Affairs* II. 199 Their [the Cherokees'] present 'city of refuge for the manslayer,' is in the vicinity of a white settlement, where the guilty must stay till after corn-planting. (*b*) **1878** *Rep. Indian Affairs* p. xxxviii, Pleas, mainly intended to act as an entering-wedge to open it to white settlement. **1899** CUSHMAN *Hist. Indians* 145 Open up to white settlement! **1901** DUNCAN & SCOTT *Allen & Woodson Co., Kans.* 9 The first white settlements in the county were made in the spring and summer of 1855. — **(13) 1772** in *Travels Amer. Col.* 525 There was a talk from the Quapas with a White Skin. **1840** COOPER *Pathfinder* I. 34 Though these torments belong only to the red-skin natur', . . . whiteskin natur' may be, and often has been, agonized by them. — **(14) 1837** IRVING *Bonneville* II. 174 They . . . were especially eloquent about the white squaws. **1947** DEVOTO *Across Wide Missouri* 353 The white squaws had odd but admirable equipment for dressmaking: emery bags in the shape of strawberries, needles of many sizes [etc.].

e. In colloq. and slang designations for foods and drinks: (1) **white bacon,** (see quot. and cf. **white side**); (2) ∗**eye,** (see quots.); (3) ∗**face,** (see quots.), *obs.;* (4) **-faced New England,** New England rum; (5) **lightning,** illicit whisky, cf. next; (6) ∗**mule,** whisky or gin, esp. that of an illicit or virulent kind, in full **white mule whisky,** cf. **white lightning;** (7) **nose,** a kind of whisky, *obs.*, cf. ∗**bald face 2;** (8) **side,** =**white bacon;** (9) **wheat,** (see quot.); (10) ∗**wings,** an egg fried on one side only, cf. **3.** (11) above.

(1) 1942 RAWLINGS *C. Creek* 213 'Meat' in Florida is one thing—white bacon. We call it white bacon to distinguish it from breakfast bacon, or side meat, and it is, simply, salt pork, or, to the army, sow belly. — **(2) 1827** *Western Mo. Rev.* I. 320 They found by experience that it [whisky] made them . . . more frisky than 'white eye,' as they call New England rum. **1845** JUDD *Margaret* I. 31 She will bring home some of . . . the real white-eye. **1944** *D.N.* Nov. 14 In Va., N.C.: *white-eye,* strong whisky. — **(3) 1855** BARNUM *Life* 79 It is the meanest kind of New-England rum . . . real white-face. **1921** *Pub. Col. Soc.* XXIV. 195 It was always found necessary to substitute for 'White-face' a mixture called 'rum-punch.' — **(4) 1848** *Knickerb.* XXXII. 276 In a certain town in New-Hampshire, a certain inhabitant thereof required for his comfortable enjoyment at least a pint of 'white-faced New England,' daily.

(5) 1921 *Double Dealer* July 20/1 The men lean or sit on the counter and talk politics, hard times . . . and more enthusiastically, the devastating and withering qualities of the current 'white lightning,' 'white mule,' or just plain 'corn,' as the local moonshine whiskey is called. **1948** *Washington Post* 5 Dec. 15M/3 McRae eased the minds of bootleggers about how long they stay in jail when they're caught with 'white lightning' . . . 30 days to the gallon. — **(6) 1889** H. H. MCCONNELL *Five Years a Cavalryman* 60 About this time I first became acquainted with a . . . drink known as 'pine-top' or 'white-mule' whiskey. **1915** *N. & Q.* 11 Ser. XII. 219 *White horse* or *mule* (n. phr.), diluted alcohol used as a beverage. **1949** *Southwest Rev.* Summer 235/2 The cowboys got drunk on the newfangled 'white mule.' — **(7) 1857** *Santa Barbara* (Calif.) *Gaz.* 29 Jan. 4/3 The drinks ain't no good here —there ain't no variety in them, neither; no white-nose, apple-jack, stone-wall, chain-lightning, railroad, hailstorm. — **(8) 1936** MCKENNA *Black Range* 143 One day the four Neals pulled into the section with all their belongings—a burro loaded with a frying pan, a coffee pot, and an old Dutch oven; a scanty supply of thin blankets; a piece of whiteside, a sack of flour, a can of coffee, and a few packs of tobacco. — **(9) 1839** MARRYAT *Diary* II. 35 In the West, when you stop at an inn, they say—'What will you have? Brown meal, and common doings, or white wheat and chicken fixings;' that is 'Will you have pork and brown bread, or white bread and fried chicken?'

(10) 1893 *Alameda* (Calif.) *Lantern* 23 Dec. 1/1 [They] were invited to call for sausage, ham and eggs (either 'white wings' or turned over), buckwheat cakes and coffee, and all the etceteras which go up to make a square meal for 25 cents.

4. In the names of plants and trees: (1) **white apple,** the prairie potato, *Psoralea esculenta;* (2) **balsam,** properly, either of two western firs, but sometimes used of various spruces; (3) **basswood,** a basswood, *Tilia heterophylla,* found in the Allegheny region; (4) **bay,** the sweet bay, an American magnolia, *M. virginiana,* also attrib.; (5) **-bearded wheat,** a variety of wheat having white awns; (6) ∗**bent grass,** =∗**redtop 2;** (7) **cypress,** =**bald cypress;** (8) **dent,** a variety of white corn, cf. **dent corn;** (9) **iron oak,** the postoak; (10) **lime (tree),** any one of various lime trees the leaves of which are white or whitish underneath; (11) **linn,** =prec.; (12) ∗**locust,** a local name for the common American locust, *Robinia pseudoacacia,* or a variety of this having white heartwood; (13) **mahogany tree,** =**mountain mahogany;** (14) **maple,** any one of several maples, as the red maple or silver maple, the bark of which is pale or whitish in appearance; (15) **plantain,** =**rattlesnake plantain;** (16) ∗**poplar,** the aspen, *Populus tremuloides,* or a variety of this, also the tulip tree; (17) **potato,** the common Irish potato; (18) ∗**root,** =**butterfly weed** or **nondo;** (19) **snakeroot,** wild ginger, also an American plant, *Eupatorium urticaefolium,* having small white flowers; (20) **top (grass),** any one of various pasture grasses, as fowl meadow grass and redtop; (21)

walnut, the butternut or shagbark *qq.v.;* (22) * **wood,** any one of various American trees, esp. the tulip tree, having white or light-colored wood.

(1) 1805 Lewis in *L. & Clark Exped.* II. (1904) 10 The white apple . . . is confined to the highlands principally. **1846** Sage *Scenes Rocky Mts.* xii. 147 The *pomme blanc,* or white apple, is a native of the prairies and mountains. — **(2) 1883** Zeigler & Grosscup *Alleghanies* 57 Every grove is composed of both black and white balsam. — **(3) 1884** Sargent *Rep. Forests* 28 White Bass Wood. . . . Most common . . . along the western slopes of the southern Alleghany mountains. **1897** Sudworth *Arborescent Flora* 302. — **(4) 1810** Michaux *Arbres* I. 33 *White Bay,* nom tombé en désuétude, autrefois dans le *New Jersey.* **1901** Mohr *Plant Life Ala.* 505 White Bay. . . . The bark is used medicinally under the name of 'white bay bark.'

(5) 1788 Washington *Diaries* III. 417 Also sowing . . . one bushel of the White bearded Wheat sent me by Beale Boardly. **1850** *Rep. Comm. Patents 1849: Agric.* 132 The white-bearded wheat, a valuable kind less liable to total failure than almost any other. — **(6) 1868** Gray *Field Botany* 543 *Agrostis alba,* White Bent-Grass. . . . Moist meadows and fields. **1901** Mohr *Plant Life Ala.* 370 White Bent Grass. . . . Extensively naturalized from Canada to the Mexican Gulf. — **(7) 1810** Michaux *Arbres* I. 30 Cupressus disticha. . . . *White Cypress,* . . . en égard à la qualité et à la couleur du bois. **1832** Browne *Sylva* 143 The names of Black and White Cypress, in the Carolinas and Georgia, are founded only on the quality and color of the wood. — **(8) 1873** *Ill. Dept. Agric. Trans.* X. 77 The Dent Corns—White and Yellow Dent. **1878** *Rep. Indian Affairs* 47 The barley crop is fair; also the white-dent corn, considering it was so late planted. — **(9) 1709** Lawson *Carolina* 92 White Iron, or Ring-Oak, is so call'd, from the Durability and lasting Quality of this Wood. It chiefly grows on dry, lean Land, and seldom fails of bearing a plentiful Crop of Acorns. **1775** *Amer. Husbandry* I. 377 *White iron oak,* very durable, is reckoned the best of all for ship-building.

(10) 1810 Michaux *Arbres* I. 40 *Tilia alba,* White lime. **1832** Browne *Sylva* 305 The height of the white lime tree rarely exceeds 40 feet. — **(11) 1883** Hale *Woods & Timbers N.C.* 130 White linn (*T. heterophylla*). . . . The young branches have a smooth silver-gray bark, by which it can be distinguished in Winter from other species. — **(12) 1832** Browne *Sylva* 298 From this variety in the color of the wood, . . . are derived the names of Red, Green and White Locust. **1893** *Amer. Folk-Lore* VI. 140. — **(13) 1864** *N.Y. Herald* 2 Nov. 1/5 Cedar, pine, and white mahogany trees are our wood. — **(14) 1806** Lewis in *L. & Clark Exped.* V. (1905) 137 A small speceis of white maple are beginning to put fourth their leaves. **1916** Seton *Woodcraft Man.* 291 Silver Maple, White or Soft Maple (Acer. saccharinum). Usually a little smaller than the Sugar Maple and much inferior as timber. . . . This tree produces a little sugar.

(15) 1687 Clayton *Virginia* 145 They [i.e., the Indians] are generally most famed for curing of Wounds, and have indeed various very good Wound-herbs. . . . They also use the *Gnafalium Americanum,* commonly called there *White Plantain.* **1824** J. Doddridge *Notes* 149 A number of native plants were used for the cure of snake bites. Among them the white plantain held high rank. — **(16) 1774** in Peyton *Adv. Grandfather* (1867) 127 The forest of Kentucky consists of yellow and white poplar. **1810** Michaux *Arbres* I. 37 *Poplar,* dénomination générale dans tous les Etats-Unis. *Tulip Tree,* . . . nom peu en usage. *Yellow* or *White Poplar,* en égard à la couleur du bois. *White wood,* nom le plus en usage dans le Gennessée. **1897** Sudworth *Arborescent Flora* 128 f., 136, 194. — **(17) 1895** *Dept. Agric. Yrbk. 1894* 211 In the true agricultural part of our country, . . . white potatoes, barley and oats attain their highest perfection. — **(18) 1791** Bartram *Travels* 47 (*footnote*), [The carminative *Angelica lucida* is] called Nondo in Virginia: by the Creek and Cherokee traders, White Root. **1822** Woods *English Prairie* 230 There is [in Illinois] a small shrub, named white-root, which must be grubbed up before it can be ploughed. **1894** *Amer. Folk-Lore* VII. 94 *Asclepias tuberosa,* white root, Mass. — **(19) 1817–8** Eaton *Botany* (1822) 184 *Asarum canadense,* white snakeroot, wild ginger. Root aromatic and stimulant. **1871** *Ill. Agric. Soc. Trans.* VIII. 7 Mr. William Jerry . . . claims to have discovered the cause of Milk-sickness in the plant *Eupatorium ageratoides* (or white Snake-root).

(20) 1819 Warden *Statist. Acct. U.S.* II. 8 The grasses are: White clover, white top and red top. **1877** *Vt. Bd. Agric. Rep.* IV. 169 White-top Grass, (*Danthonia spicata,*) makes unwholesome hay. — **(21) 1743** Clayton *Flora Virginica* 190 *Juglans alba,* . . . White Walnuts. **1916** Seton *Woodcraft Man.* 275 White Walnut, Oil Nut, or Butternut (*Juglans cinerea*) Much smaller than (Black Walnut), rarely 100 feet high; with much smoother bark . . . the new twigs are covered with sticky down. — **(22) 1663** *Plymouth Rec.* 66 Lott . . . bounded with . . . a great white wood tree. **1832** D. J. Browne *Sylva* 202 In Connecticut, New York and New Jersey, it is known by the name of White Wood, and of Canoe Wood, and more rarely by that of Tulip Tree. **1916** Seton *Woodcraft Man.* 293 Basswood, White-Wood, Whistle-Wood, Lime, or Linden (Tilia americana).

For **white alder, ash, beech, birch, cedar, corn, elm, fir, flint, hickory, oak, pine, sage, spruce,** see as main entries.

For **white Burley, crowder,** see the second elements.

b. In combs. of obvious meaning or sufficiently explained in the quots.: (1) **white-bark(ed) pine,** (2) **cucumber tree,** (3) * **devil,** (4) **grass,** (5) **gum,** (6) **loco,** (see **crazy weed**), (7) **twisted stalk.**

(1) 1909 *Cent. Supp.* 1004/1 *White-barked* or *white-stemmed pine, Pinus albicaulis,* often forming the timber-line in the Rocky, Sierra Nevada, and other Western mountains. It is marked by the brown or creamy-white plate-like scales of its bark. Its timber is of little value. Its large sweet seeds are eaten by the Indians. **1946** *Sierra Club Bul.* Dec. 24 Not being a John Muir, I knew I could not get any sleep just by crawling under the low branches of a white-bark pine. **1949** *Ib.* June 6 Singing birds and scampering chipmunks, rocky cliffs, white-barked pines and white, dancing water—all familiar elements of the mountain scene—pass slowly behind and below the travelers. — **(2) 1831** Audubon *Ornith. Biog.* I. 198 This species [Magnolia auriculata], which is remarkable for the beauty of its foliage, is known in America by the names of *White Cucumber Tree, Long-leaved Cucumber Tree,* and *Indian Physic.* — **(3) 1894** *Amer. Folk-Lore* VII. 91 *Aster diffusus.* . . . Gray, white devil, wire-weed, devil weed, . . . West Va. **1931** Clute *Plants* 85 Those which especially bother the farmer are likely to be consigned to the devil. . . . The white devils is, or are, *Aster lateriflorus.* — **(4) 1891** *Cent. s.v. Leersia,* Three species occur in the United States, and are known as white-grass, especially *L. Virginica.*

(5) 1743 Clayton *Flora Virginica* 41 *Acer Virginianum* [etc.]. . . . Sweet-gum; White-gum. **1909** *Cent. Supp.* 554/3 *White gum.* . . . The sweet gum, *Liquidambar Styraciflua.* — **(6) 1909** Longyear *Rocky Mt. Wild Flower Studies* 98 One of the most showy and common of the locos is the white loco or 'Crazy weed.' — **(7) 1915** Armstrong & Thornber *Western Wild Flowers* 46 White-Twisted Stalk. *Streptopus amplexifolius.* Whitish. Spring, summer. U.S. except Southwest. This grows in moist soil, in cold mountain woods, up to an altitude of ten thousand feet and across the continent.

5. In the names of birds: (1) * **whiteback,** the canvasback duck; (2) * **-backed,** designating one of several regional American varieties of three-toed woodpeckers, esp. *Picoides americanus dorsalis;* (3) **-bellied nuthatch,** = **white-breasted nuthatch;** (4) **-bellied swallow,** a tree swallow, *Iridoprocne bicolor;* (5) **bill,** (*a*) the coot, (*b*) the slate-colored junco; (6) **-bill(ed) woodpecker,** = **ivory-billed woodpecker;** (7) * **bird,** the snow bunting; (8) **brant,** the snow goose, *Chen hyperboreus;* (9) **-breasted (chicken) hawk,** the red-tailed hawk; (10) **-breasted nuthatch,** an American nuthatch, *Sitta carolinensis,* having bluish-gray and black upper parts and a white breast; (11) **crane,** (see quots. 1872, 1949); (12) **-crowned sparrow,** a crown sparrow, *Zonotrichia leucophrys,* found throughout the greater part of the U.S.; (13) **curlew,** the white ibis, *Guara alba,* of the southern states; (14) **egret,** a large American egret, *Casmerodius albus egretta,* formerly abundant in the Gulf States, also **great white egret;** (15) **-eyed flycatcher,** = next; (16) **-eyed vireo,** a vireo, *Vireo griseus,* found chiefly in the eastern U.S.; (17) **-fronted owl,** = **Kirtland's owl;** (18) **-headed eagle,** = **bald eagle;** (19) **-headed woodpecker,** a woodpecker, *Dryobates albolarvatus,* found in the mountains of California, Oregon and Washington; (20) **ibis,** = **Spanish curlew;** (21) **-necked raven,** (see quot. 1891); (22) **pelican,** a large American pelican, *Pelecanus erythrorhynchos;* (23) **rock,** a white Plymouth Rock chicken; (24) **-rumped,** designating various American birds (see quots.); (25) **snipe,** (see quot.); (26) * **-tailed,** see as a main entry; (27) * **throat,** = next; (28) **-throated sparrow,** a brown sparrow, *Zonotrichia albicollis,* of eastern North America having a conspicuous white square on the throat; (29) * **wing,** (see quot. 1891), cf. **3.** (11) above; (30) **-winged,** see as a main entry.

(1) 1813 Wilson *Ornithology* VIII. 104 At the Susquehannah they are called *Canvas-backs,* on the Potowmac *White-backs.* **1917** *Birds of Amer.* I. 133 Canvas-back. *Marila valisineria.* . . . [Also called] White-back. — **(2) 1891** *Cent.* 691/10 *White-backed woodpecker,* a three-toed woodpecker of North America. *Picoides dorsalis* of Baird, having a long white stripe down the middle of the black back. **1917** *Birds of Amer.* II. 149. — **(3) 1858** Baird *Birds Pacific R.R.* 374 *Sitta Carolinensis.* White-bellied Nuthatch. . . . Eastern North America to the high central plains. **1869** *Amer. Naturalist* III. 556

The eggs [of the worm-eating warbler] most nearly resemble those of the White-bellied-Nuthatch. — **(4) 1812** WILSON *Ornithology* V. 44 The White-Bellied Swallow . . . often takes possession of an apartment in the boxes appropriated to the Purple Martin. **1917** *Birds of Amer.* III. 88/1 The Tree, or White-bellied, Swallow is the first of the Swallows to arrive from the south in the spring.

(5) *(a)* **1844** *Nat. Hist. N.Y., Zoology* II. 273 The American Coot . . . [or] Whitebill . . . frequents low marshy spots near the coast. *(b)* **1917** *Birds of Amer.* III. 45 Slate-colored junco. . . . [Also called] White Bill. — **(6)** *c***1728** CATESBY *Carolina* I. 16 The largest white-bill Woodpecker. Weighs twenty ounces. *Ib.* opp. p. 16 Largest White Bill'd Woodpecker. **1782** LATHAM *Gen. Syn. Birds* I. II. 553 White-billed W[oodpecker]. . . . This bird inhabits Carolina, Virginia, New Spain. — **(7) 1844** *Nat. Hist. N.Y., Zoology* II. 178 The White Snow-Bird . . . is called White-bird [in some parts of the U.S.]. **1917** *Birds of Amer.* III. 19. — **(8) 1805** LEWIS in *L. & Clark Exped.* I. (1904) 370 Saw a great number of white brant. **1872** *Amer. Naturalist* VI. 400 The snow goose or 'white-brant' began to arrive in considerable numbers about October 1st. **1950** *Nat. Geog. Mag.* March 407 Lesser snow geese . . . probably the most abundant goose in North America, it is often called 'white brant' in the West. — **(9) 1828** BONAPARTE *Synopsis* 32 [The] White-breasted Hawk, *Falco borealis*, . . . inhabits throughout North America. **1917** *Birds of Amer.* II. 71 Red-tailed Hawk. *Buteo borealis borealis*. . . . [Also called] White-breasted Chicken Hawk.

(10) 1808 WILSON *Ornithology* I. 41 The White-breasted nuthatch is common almost everywhere in the woods of North America. **1949** HADLEY *Indiana Birds* 27/1 The white-breasted nuthatch is a bird of autumn days and bare and leafless winter woodlands. — **(11) 1846** THORPE *Myst. Backwoods* 156 The angler resumes his sport, and the flocks of white crane settle down in the shallow. **1872** COUES *Key to Birds* 271 White or Whooping Crane. . . . Adult plumage pure white. **1949** A. SPRUNT & E. B. CHAMBERLAIN *S.C. Bird Life* 81 American Egret. . . . Local Names: White Heron; White Crane. — **(12) 1839** PEABODY *Mass. Birds* 32 The White-crowned sparrow, *Fringilla leucophrys*, is one of the finest of this family of birds. **1949** *Dly. Oklahoman Mag.* (Okla. City) 4 Dec. 16/3 The regal little white-crowned sparrows in both the handsome black and white striped cap of the adult and the chestnut and tan of the immature bird, seem to be erratic in their appearance. — **(13) 1731** CATESBY *Carolina* I. 82 The White Curlew . . . frequent[s] the low watery lands. **1917** *Birds of Amer.* I. 177/1 The old birds . . . are usually referred to as 'Spanish Curlews' or 'White Curlews.' — **(14) 1835** AUDUBON *Ornith. Biog.* III. 137 [The Louisiana Heron] is at all seasons a social bird, moving about in company with the Blue Heron or the White Egret. **1872** COUES *Key to Birds* 267 Great White Egret. White Heron. No obviously lengthened feathers on the head at any time.

(15) 1810 WILSON *Ornithology* II. 166 [The] White-Eyed Flycatcher . . . has been observed in the neighborhood of Savannah, so late as the middle of November. **1865** *Atlantic Mo.* May 520/1 One of the most marvellous little songsters . . . is the White-Eyed Flycatcher. — **(16) 1831** AUDUBON *Ornith. Biog.* I. 328 The White-eyed Flycatcher, or Vireo, *Vireo Noveboracensis*. **1949** A. SPRUNT & E. B. CHAMBERLAIN *S.C. Bird Life* 426 White-Eyed Vireo. . . . Breeds north to central eastern Texas and northeastern North Carolina. — **(17) 1872** *Amer. Naturalist* VI. 283. **1917** *Birds of Amer.* II. 107. — **(18) 1811** WILSON *Ornithology* IV. 89 White-headed, or bald eagle. . . . This distinguished bird . . . is the most beautiful of his tribe in this part of the world. **1946** *Reader's Digest* Jan. 39/1 He is king of the air, undisputed ruler of the sky, the American, or white-headed, eagle. — **(19) 1858** BAIRD *Birds Pacific R.R.* 96 *Picus albolarvatus*. White-headed Woodpecker. . . . Cascade mountains of Oregon and southward into California. **1940** GABRIELSON & JEWETT *Birds Ore.* 386 The curiously colored Northern White-Headed Woodpecker, . . . is a regular permanent Oregon resident wherever the yellow pine is found in good stands.

(20) 1813 WILSON *Ornithology* VIII. 43 [The] White Ibis . . . [is] pretty numerous on the borders of lake Ponchartrain. **1917** *Birds of Amer.* I. 175 The White Ibis is in no sense a Curlew, but its long, rounded, curved bill has doubtless suggested this name to many interested but unscientific observers. — **(21) 1887** RIDGWAY *Man. N. Amer. Birds* 362. **1891** *Cent.* 6911/3 The *white-necked* raven, *Corvus cryptalenus*, a small raven found in western parts of the United States, having the concealed bases of the feathers of the neck fleecy-white. **1917** *Birds of Amer.* II. 228. — **(22) 1817** S. BROWN *Western Gazetteer* 146 Those of the feathered tribe which may be considered as local, consist of the white pelican, . . . sandhill crane, great white owl [etc.]. **1940** GABRIELSON & JEWETT *Birds Ore.* 90 The White Pelican, one of the largest and most majestic birds of Oregon, arrives in March and remains until November. — **(23) 1945** *Boulder* (Colo.) *D. Camera* 28 Nov. 7/3 White Rocks, April roasters and Aug. fries . . . 2 Doz. White Rock pullets, ready to lay. **1948** *Pauls Valley* (Okla.) *D. Democrat* 2 July 3/6 Pat took the prize with six white rock broilers. — **(24) 1858** BAIRD *Birds Pacific R.R.* 113 *Melanerpes erythrocephalus*. . . . Red-headed woodpecker. . . . White-rumped woodpecker. **1874** COUES *Birds N.W.* 487 *Fringa fuscicollis*. Bonaparte's Sandpiper; White-rumped Sandpiper. **1881** *Amer. Naturalist* XV. 210 One of the earliest birds to nest in the vicinity of Los Angeles, was the white-rumped Shrike (*Collyrio excubitoroides*). **1917** *Birds of Amer.* II. 164 Marsh Hawk, *Circus hudsonius*. . . . White-rumped Hawk.

(25) 1872 *Amer. Naturalist* VI. 400 The avocet, and the black-necked stilt . . . are called 'white snipes.' — **(27)** *a***1862** THOREAU *Maine Woods* 198 We heard the white throats along the shore. **1939** LINCOLN *Migration* 111 The White-throat is one of the most abundant members of its family. — **(28) 1811** WILSON *Ornithology* III. 51 [The] White-Throated Sparrow . . . [winters] in most of the states south of New England. **1949** *Chi. Tribune* 14 Oct. 12/4 One of the pleasures of hiking . . . during early October is to strike a day when the hermit and white throated sparrows can be seen in numbers. — **(29) 1891** *Cent.* 6912/3 *Whitewing*, . . . The white-winged or velvet scoter, sea-coot, or surf-duck. **1917** *Birds of Amer.* I. 150 Black White-wing; . . . May White-wing; . . . Eastern White-wing.

b. In the names of fishes: (1) **white bass,** one of several American fishes, esp. *Lepibema chrysops*, of the Great Lakes and midwestern rivers; (2) **cat(fish),** a catfish, *Haustor catus*, found chiefly in the eastern and southern states, also the channel cat *q.v.;* (3) **-eyed shad,** see *∗***shad 3;** (4) **lake bass,** =**white bass;** (5) **mullet,** one of several suckers found in coastal streams of the south Atlantic states or a marine mullet, *Querimana curema*, of silvery appearance, found along the Atlantic and Pacific coasts; (6) **perch,** any one of various American fishes, as the silver perch, calico bass, crappie, etc.; (7) *∗***salmon,** the silver salmon, *Oncorhynchus milktschitsch*, or one of various other fishes, as the large-mouthed black bass, of a white or silvery appearance.

(1) 1813 *Niles' Reg.* IV. 317/1 Among those, not known in the Eastern states, is the *White Bass*, a fish resembling the herring but considerably larger. **1911** *Rep. Fisheries 1908* 317 The name is sometimes applied to the white bass (*Roccus chrysops*) of the Great Lakes region. — **(2) 1804** CLARK in *Lewis & C. Exped.* I. (1904) 90 This evening Guthrige Cought a White Catfish, it's eyes Small & tale much like that of a Dolfin. **1884** *Nat. Museum Bul.* No. 27, 491 *Ictalurus punctatus*. . . . White Cat. . . . That is a valuable food-fish. **1909** *Cent. Supp.* 1145/1 *white-cat*. . . . A name applied to the fork-tailed catfish of the Potomac river, *Amiurus catus*, found from Maryland to Texas. — **(4) 1842** *Nat. Hist. N.Y., Zoology* IV. 13 The White Lake Bass . . . is a very common fish in Lake Erie, and is known at Buffalo under the name White Bass.

(5) 1839 KEMBLE *Residence in Ga.* 53 Had I been the ingenious man who wrote a poem upon fish, the white mullet of the Altamaha should have been at least my heroine's cousin. **1911** *Rep. Fisheries 1908* 312 Many suckers of the genus *Moxostoma* are called 'mullet,' 'white mullet,' 'sucking mullet' [etc.]. — **(6) 1775** BURNABY *Travels* 15 These waters are stored with incredible quantities of fish, such as sheeps-heads, rock-fish, drums, white pearch. **1884** GOODE *Fisheries* I. 370 In the Ohio River it [the Fresh-Water Drum] is usually called 'White Perch' or 'Gray Perch.' **1949** *Sat. Ev. Post* 12 March 46/4 About the best fun was going out to the pond after white perch. — **(7) 1612** SMITH *Virginia* I. 15 Of fish we were best acquainted with . . . mullets, white Salmonds, Trowts, Soles [etc.]. **1856** *Porter's Spirit of Times* 25 Oct. 129/2 One or the other of these fish [the pike-perch and the growler] . . . is also, it is presumed, the *white salmon*, which Capt. John Smith describes. **1911** *Rep. Fisheries 1908* 315 The silver salmon, or white salmon . . . is found in all rivers from the Sacramento River to Bering Strait.

c. In the names of other animals: (1) *∗***white bear,** the grizzly bear, now *hist.*, cf. **silvertip;** (2) **buffalo,** see as a main entry; (3) **-faced hornet,** =**bald-faced hornet,** also **white-faced wasp;** (4) *∗***-footed (prairie) mouse,** any one of various mice of the genus *Peromyscus;* (5) **goat,** =**mountain goat;** (6) **grub,** a grub or larva which is white, esp. that of the June bug; (7) **miller,** *(a)* any one of various clothes moths, or an American tiger moth, *Diacrisia virginica*, *(b)* an artificial fly used by anglers; (8) **rabbit,** any one of various American hares, as the snowshoe rabbit, that have white fur in winter; (9) *∗***tail,** =next, also attrib.; (10) **-tailed deer,** see *s.v.* *∗***white-tailed;** (11) **weasel,** an ermine or species of ermine found in the Northwest; (12) **wolf,** (see quot. 1891).

(1) 1791 J. LONG *Voyages* 95 The large white bear commonly called the grizly bear, is a very dangerous animal. **1852** REYNOLDS *Hist. Ill.* 172 He was destroyed there [in the Rocky Mts.] by a white bear. **1940** *Ore. Guide* 25 In rare instances is found the fierce grizzly bear or silvertip, the great 'white bear' of Lewis and Clark. — **(3) 1891** *Cent.* 6739/1 *V[espa] maculata* of North America is the so-called *white-faced hornet*. **1939** *L.A.* Map 240–1. **1949** *Time* 11 July 1/1 The white markings on face and body and the characteristic 'wasp waist' of this insect identify it as a white-faced wasp. — (4) **1857** *Rep. Comm. Patents 1856: Agric.* 86 The food . . . consists almost wholly of arvicolae and a few white-footed prairie mice. **1884** MERRIAM *Mammals of Adirondacks* 265 In personal appearance the White-footed Mouse is far more attractive than the other members of the family. **1949** *Chi. Tribune* 30 Dec. 10/3 His pink nose and paws, pure white vest and golden brown body with a chocolate streak down the back proclaimed him the white-footed or deer mouse of the outdoors.

(5) **1884** *Cent. Mag.* Dec. 193 The *Aplocerus montanus*, known to the frontiersman and to the fur-trader of the extreme North-west as the white goat of the Rocky Mountains. **1888** ROOSEVELT in *Cent. Mag.* June 206/2 White goats have been known to hunters ever since Lewis and Clarke crossed the continent. — (6) *a***1817** DWIGHT *Travels* I. 77 The white-grub has . . . very extensively injured meadows and pastures. **1871** *Ill. Agric. Soc. Trans.* VIII. 172 The manure is . . . instrumental in breeding the white-grub (May-beetle) which often ruins our meadows and strawberry beds. — (7) (*a*) **1854** EMMONS *Agric. N.Y.* V. 229 White Miller. . . . Abdomen marked with three rows of black dots. **1899** *Animal & Plant Lore* 41 A white 'miller' coming into the house is a sign of bad news. New England. (*b*) **1897** *Outing* XXX. 294/1 Useful trout-flies for the month [June] include: the hackles, white miller, alder [etc.]. — (8) **1789** MORSE *Amer. Geog.* 198 In this country are brown squirrils, white rabbits, bears [etc.]. **1805** SIBLEY in *Ann. 9th Congress* 2 Sess. 1082 Wild hogs are likewise plenty in their country, and white rabbits, or hares. **1917** *Mammals of Amer.* 276 Varying Hare. *Lepus americanus*. . . . [Also called] White Hare (or 'Rabbit'). — (9) **1872** MCCLELLAN *Golden State* 241 There are several varieties: the mule-deer, black-tail, antelope, and white-tail. **1907** WHITE *Arizona Nights* 68 We succeeded in killing a nice, fat white-tail buck. **1949** *Chi. D. News* 21 Dec. 37/1 Put into effect to control the herd of whitetails and reduce serious damage to orchards, . . . the special . . . season ended with an estimated kill of 3,200 deer.

(11) **1805** LEWIS in *L. & Clark Exped.* II. (1904) 379 The ermin[e] whic[h] is known to the traiders of the N.W. by the name of the white weasel is the genuine ermine. **1840** EMMONS *Mass. Quadrupeds* 45 There is no occasion for mistaking this species for its cogenor, commonly called the White Weasel, as the latter is always larger. — (12) **1807** GASS *Journal* 37 Here we found a white wolf dead. **1891** *Cent.* 6959/3 *White wolf*, a whitish variety of the common wolf of North America.

As the last term in **bob, Boston, Chester, free, half, lily, mean, poor white.**

* **white alder.** A plant of the genus *Clethra.* Also any one of various alders, as *Alnus rhombifolia*, found in the West.

1857 GRAY *Botany* 254 *Clethra*, White Alder. Sweet Pepperbush. **1899** A. BROWN *Tiverton Tales* 320 The white alder crept farther and farther from its bounds. **1949** HOWELL *Marin Flora* 17 Along streams farther inland the white alder (*A. rhombifolia*) takes its place.

* **white ash.**

1. An American ash, *Fraxinus americana*, having leaves with whitish or pale green undersides, or the wood of such a tree. Also attrib.

1683 *N.H. Hist. Soc. Coll.* VIII. 146 [They] did feloniously . . . use about one cord of white ash. **1684** *Duxbury Rec.* 42 [The line runs] unto a white ash tree marked by the brook side. **1820** FLINT *Lett. from Amer.* 229 White and blue ash trees are easily split, pliant, and readily smoothed. **1950** *Chi. Tribune* 27 April III. 10/1 Under each cutting spindle is placed a block of white ash.

2. An oar, in allusion to the use of this wood for making oars.

1851 MELVILLE *Moby Dick* 394 This clumsy lubber was trying to free his white-ash. **1866** MARK TWAIN in *Harper's Mag.* Dec. 105 Each boat took to the 'white ash'—that is, to the oars.

b. white-ash breeze. *local.* A calm during which oars would be needed by a boat's crew.

1937 EDWARD M. CHAPMAN *N. Eng. Village Life* 135 A 'white-ash breeze' has on the coast become a synonym of calm.

* **white beech.** The common American beech.

1810 MICHAUX *Arbres* I. 27 Fagus sylvestris, *White beech*, . . . dans les Etats les plus septentrionaux et le District de Maine. **1832** BROWNE *Sylva* 153 On the banks of the Ohio the white beech attains the height of more than 100 feet. **1894** *Amer. Folk-Lore* VII. 99.

* **white birch.** The North American paper birch, *Betula papyrifera*, or the gray birch, *B. populifolia.* Also attrib. Cf. **European white birch.**

1789 MORSE *Amer. Geog.* 197 On the high lands are . . . beech and white birch. **1868** *Amer. Naturalist* II. 178 After haunting . . . the white-birch swamps, it [the warbler] moves southward. **1916** SETON *Woodcraft Man.* 278 White, Canoe, or Paper Birch (*Betula papyrifera*). . . . Besides canoes, wigwams, vessels, and paper from its bark, it furnishes syrup from its sap and the inner bark is used as an emergency food. **1948** *Pacific Discovery* March–April 14/2 A male Anna hummer has maintained its territory from the topmost branch of the white birch tree for three consecutive years.

* **Whiteboys,** *n. pl.* **1.** A partisan group during the Revolution. **2.** (See quot. 1868.) Both *obs.*

(1) **1825** J. NEAL *Jonathan* III. 290 Who knows but you are one o' the tories yourself, or one o' the whiteboys—or cowboys—or skinners. — (2) **1865** SALA *Diary* II. 50 What manner of folk are the Whiteboys? **1868** ROSE *Great Country* 382 'White Boys in Blue' are organising as an opposition to the G.A.R., while the Ku-Klux will attend to the Lie-all League.

white buffalo. The Rocky Mountain goat or sheep. Also, rarely, an albino buffalo. Also attrib.

[**1801** A. MACKENZIE *Voyages* (1802) I. 202 Our conductor informed us that great numbers of bears, and small white buffaloes, frequent those mountains.] **1806** LEWIS in *L. & Clark Exped.* V. (1905) 165 The indians inform us that there is . . . an abundance of the mountain sheep or what they call white buffaloes. **1888** *Outing* May 130 The 'white buffaloes' alluded to by Mackenzie could not have been mountain sheep, as this species is dark brown. **1947** CAHALANE *Mammals* 76 A Mandan would offer the equivalent of ten to fifteen horses for a white buffalo hide, and consider himself lucky to close the deal.

whitecap ˈhwaɪtˌkæp, *v.* [See next.] *tr.* To subject (a person) to lynch law. Hence **whitecapism, whitecapping.** *Colloq.*

1900 NICHOLSON *Hoosiers* 45 The milder form of outlawry, known as 'white-capping,' has also been practised in Indiana occasionally, and sometimes with barbarous cruelty; but it, like lynching, is not peculiar to the State, and its extent has been greatly exaggerated by Eastern newspapers. **1904** *N.Y. Ev. Post* 21 Dec. 3 The disgrace of whitecapism, which has retarded the development of the State of Mississippi. **1908** PHILLIPS *Old Wives* 68 If he wasn't such a wonderful doctor he'd have been white-capped long ago—tarred and feathered and railed out of town. **1943** POWELL *Home Again* 167 During the short time I served as county judge, a series of 'white-cappings,' directed against Negroes, occurred in the lower part of the county.

* **White Caps.** A voluntary group formed ostensibly for punishing offenders not adequately dealt with by law. Also **Whitecapper.**

1888 *Battle Creek Jrnl.* 12 Dec., The White Caps left notices at several other saloons Saturday night. **1895** in *Works of T. Roosevelt* XIV. (1926) 250 The lawbreaker, whether he be lyncher or whitecapper, or merely the liquor-seller who desires to drive an illegal business. **1907** WHITE *Boniface to Bank Burglar* 89 For our safety he must be made to believe that we were actually a band of whitecaps, and not a lot of hungry bank looters.

attrib. **1891** ADAMS *Sexual Morality Col. N. Eng.* 38 The result of my inquiries seems to indicate a state of affairs . . . very suggestive of those 'White-cap' and 'Moonshiner' proceedings in the western and southern States. **1894** *Chi. Record* 13 April 3/3 The people in the 'White-Cap belt' [of Indiana] . . . came originally from the South.

white cedar. Any one of various North American coniferous trees, esp. one of the genus *Chamaecyparis.* Also the common arborvitae (see quot. 1942).

1675 JOSSELYN *Two Voyages* 27 We had the sight of an *Indian-*Pinnace sailing by us made of *Birch-bark*, sewed together with the roots of *spruce* and white *cedar*. **1807** GASS *Jrnl.* 167 One of them had a hat made of the bark of white cedar and bear-grass. **1942** PEATTIE *Friendly Mts.* 151 Anyone who drives across northern New Hampshire and Vermont will be impressed by the way in which the white cedar (*Thuja occidentalis*) appears as soon as the limestone region is reached.

attrib. **1931** VANSELL *Nectar & Pollen Plants Calif.* 43 White cedar honey is of light color, granulates snow white, and enjoys a good local demand. **1944** MORRIS *They Hop & Crawl* 218 It appears to favor white cedar swamps.

* **white collar.** *attrib.* Of or pertaining to one who performs work of a non-manual kind, or designating a *job* of this nature.

1921 *Ladies' Home Jrnl.* May 98/4 Restaurants have accustomed white-collar boys and girls [etc.]. **1928** *Collier's* 10 Nov. 49/2 The . . . people at work in factories . . . in white-collar jobs, and in the professions. **1948** *Chi. Tribune* 3 April II. 1/4 The modern white collar girl wants a job which not only offers opportunities but advances as well.

Also ellipt., and **white collarism.**

1938 SMITTER *F.O.B. Detroit* 32 It wasn't long before the white-collars up front began taking notice of what was going on on the floor **1945** SERVICE *Ploughman* 284 From a blanket-stiff I had climbed to white-collarism. **1949** *Boston Globe* 12 June (Fiction Mag.) 1/5 The white collars in the office don't know what's going on.

* **white corn.** Indian corn the grains or kernels of which are white.

1789 Washington *Diaries* IV. 4 Finished gathering . . . White Corn of the kind had in 1787 from Colo. Richard Henry Lee. **1805** Parkinson *Tour* 329 The white corn is much higher than the yellow: but the yellow is by far the sweetest, although the tops and blades are not so abundant. **1927** Benét *J. B.'s Body* 119 In her pot she cooked, . . . grains of white corn.

white elm. The American elm or cork elm. Also attrib. Cf. **corky white elm.**

1770 Forster tr. Kalm *Travels* I. 67 *Ulmus Americana*, the white elm. **1916** Seton *Woodcraft Man.* 285 White Elm, Water, or Swamp Elm (*Ulmus Americana*). A tall splendid forest tree; commonly 100, occasionally 120 feet. Wood reddish brown; hard, strong, tough, very hard to split. **1948–9** *N.W. Ohio Quart.* Winter 10 It was made of a strip of white elm bark about one foot wide and six or seven feet long.

white fir. Any one of various firs of the western states, esp. *Abies concolor*. Cf. **Colorado white fir.**

1884 Sargent *Rep. Forests* 9 The bottoms of the streams are lined with . . . an open growth of the white fir. **1897** Sudworth *Arborescent Flora* 53 ff. **1948** *Pacific Discovery* March–April 7/2 Sequoias become established most easily along moist flats or on cool north and east slopes with sugar pine and white fir.

***whitefish,** *n.* As the last term in **lake, Menominee, Rocky Mountain, round whitefish.**

white flint. 1. A variety of hard wheat, the kernels of which are whitish in color. In full **white flint wheat. 2.** = **flint corn.** In full **white flint corn.**

(1) **1826** *Va. Herald* (Fredericksburg) 30 Aug. 2/1, I apprehend that our expectations from the 'white flint,' will prove equally fallacious. **1849** *N. Eng. Farmer* I. 291 We have in our office a fine specimen of the White Flint wheat. — (2) **1843** Oliver *Eight Months* 85 The kind almost invariably planted in the district to which I refer, and over a large portion of Illinois, is the white flint, which appears best to suit the climate. . . . From fifty to eighty bushels an acre is reckoned a good crop on most prairie; but on the Ohio and Mississippi bottoms, 100 and even 120 bushels are sometimes raised. **1868** *Mich. Agric. Rep.* VII. 349 Wm. Hall, Greenfield, [exhibited a] variety [of] white flint corn.

* **Whitehall,** *n.* **Whitehall boat,** prob. a boat built at Whitehall near the head of Lake Champlain. *Obs.*

1850 C. Mathews *Moneypenny* 161 Marking the course in which she disappeared, . . . he seized a Whitehall boat near by, and pursued. **1857** *S.F. Call* 16 Jan. (Th.), Three persons who had been laboring on Alcatras Island, started in a whitehall boat for the shore. **1890** N. P. Langford *Vigilante Days* II. 129 To attempt the passage . . . in a whitehall boat would be madness.

Hence **Whitehaller,** one who uses a Whitehall boat. *Obs.*

1828 Cooper *Notions* I. 40 The latter [New York boatmen], it appears, are of a class of watermen, that are renowned in this country, under the name of Whitehallers. **1835** C. J. Latrobe *Rambler* I. 25 (Th.), The light skilfully managed wherry of the Whitehaller.

white hickory. Any one of various hickories, as the bitternut or shellbark hickory. Also a tree of one of these species.

1750 T. Walker *Explor. Kentucky* 54 On the Lower Side . . . is . . . a white Hiccory. **1814** Pursh *Flora Amer.* II. 638 Juglans amara. . . . This is known by the name of Bitter Nut, White or Swamp Hickory. **1916** Seton *Woodcraft Man.* 276 Shagbark, Shellbark, or White Hickory (*Hicoria ovata*). A tall forest tree up to 120 feet high.

Also **white heart hickory.**

1810 Michaux *Arbres* I. 20 J[uglans] tomentosa. . . . *White heart hickery*, . . . usité dans ces deux Etats [N.Y. & N.J.]. **1916** Seton *Woodcraft Man.* 276 Mockernut, White Heart, or Big-bud Hickory (*Hicoria alba*). A tall forest tree, up to 100 feet.

* **White House.**

1. The residence in Washington, D.C., occupied by the Presidents of the U.S. while in office. Cf. **summer White House** and see **Executive Mansion.**

1811 F. J. Jackson in H. Adams *N.-Eng. Federalism* (1877) 385 [Foster] goes . . . to act as a sort of political conductor to attract the lightning that may issue from the clouds round the Capitol and the White House at Washington. **1840** *Ill. State Reg.* (Springfield) 13 March 2/5 If he did live in a log cabin, that's no reason I should vote for him to go live in the white house. **1913** La Follette *Autobiog.* 448, [I] called at the White House to pay my respects. **1950** *Reader's Digest* June 9/1 General Vaughan was handing out favors under the very roof of the White House.

attrib. **1868** *Terr. Enterprise* (Virginia, Nev.) 18 June 3/1 'General Grant's the man!' and will 'fill the White House Chair.' **1949** *Time* 7 Nov. 8/3 The White House spokesman, with both feet soberly planted on the ground, says: 'Prime Minister Nehru did not, so far as we know, stand on his head for President Truman.'

b. The office of the President of the U.S.

1946 *Chi. D. News* 5 March 8/6 There is a real, imperative need of vigorous leadership and firm statesmanship in the Department of State and the White House to assume moral leadership. **1950** *Dly. Ardmoreite* (Ardmore, Okla.) 14 Feb. 1/7 The White House said no further action on its part is contemplated at this time.

2. *transf.* (See quots.)

1860 *So. Enterprise* (Thomasville, Ga.) 3 Oct. 2/5 He announces himself, in the event of Lincoln's election, as candidate for '*the White House*' of the independent State of Georgia! **1860** *Charleston* (S.C.) *Mercury* 11 Dec. 1/5 On entering the Home Department, a building set apart for Georgia's contributions, I met, first, the 'President's Mansion' of *the Southern Confederacy*, a miniature White House of beautiful design. **1871** Cooke *R. E. Lee* 60 When General Lee left Washington to repair to Richmond, he removed the ladies of his family from Arlington to the 'White House' on the Pamunkey, near the spot where that river united with the Mattapony to form the York River. **1878** *Ill. Dept. Agric. Trans.* XIV. 146 Tecumseh had his thousands of braves encamped above and below Vincennes, Indiana, where Gen. Harrison occupied the 'White House' of this great Northwest. **1947** Downey *Lusty Forefathers* 101 George Washington had been elected President, inaugurated in New York, and had established his 'White House' at No. 3 Cherry Street. **1950** *Chi. Tribune* 15 Feb. 20/7, I never pass thru Vincennes that I do not feel a personal disgrace that the ground of the Harrison home, the old 'White House of the Northwest Territory' has been given over to factories.

White League. An organization formed in the South just after the Civil War to maintain white supremacy. *Obs.* or *hist.*

*c***1862** Sheridan in Bartlett *Americanisms* (1877) 321 The terms Jayhawker and Banditti were employed [by me] to distinguish them from the White League, a secret military organization. **1888** M. Lane *Pol. Catch-Words* 16 White League.—An Order formed in the South in 1874 in nominal opposition to the Union Leagues, but really as a kind of successor to the Kuklux Klan.

Hence **White Leaguer.**

1874 in Fleming *Hist. Reconstruction* II. 145, I told him . . . the Democrats or white leaguers would not hurt the negroes if they could help it. **1884** Morgan *Yazoo* 485 One organized a company, and took his place in line with the white leaguers, 'to kill negroes when necessary.' **1950** *N.O. Times-Picayune Mag.* 19 Feb. 27/1 Gen. Philip H. Sheridan had repeatedly urged Congress to declare the White Leaguers 'banditti,' and leave the rest to him.

* **white man.**

1. A Southerner as distinguished from a Yankee or Northerner. *Obs.*

1835 Hoffman *Winter in West* II. 204 Is he a Yankee or a white man? **1887** J. C. Harris in *Cent. Mag.* Aug. 545/2 Yonder's the Yankees on one side, and here's the blamed niggers on t'other, and betwixt and betweenst 'em a white man's got mighty little chance.

b. A white citizen of the U.S. as distinguished from a German, Spaniard, or Mexican. *Slang.*

1855 Büchele *Land und Volk* 279 Und so kommt es wohl am Ende noch dahin, dass man auf die Frage: 'was he a white man?' ('war er ein Weisser?') so hören bekommt: 'No, Sir, he was a Dutchman.' **1857** Chandless *Visit Salt Lake* 316 The term 'a white man,' as distinctive from a Spaniard, shows how much more likely it is that the latter race should remain abject and die out. **1905** O. Henry *Roads of Destiny* 135, I got into a little gun frolic down in Laredo and plugged a white man. There wasn't any Mexican handy.

c. The English language. *Rare.*

1878 Beadle *Western Wilds* 28, I'd never heard of any language but white man and Injin.

2. A man of honorable, dependable character. *Colloq.* Cf. * **white,** *a.* **1,** and **white man's chance, country.**

1865 *Atlantic Mo.* April 405/2 After spending the night at a 'white man's' hotel in Buffalo, the next morning found her standing . . . before one of the world's great wonders. **1885** Siringo *Texas Cow Boy* 100 His brother was a white man.

3. In the possessive in combs.: (1) **white man's chance,** a decent chance, one thought of as befitting a white man, *colloq.*, cf. **Chinaman's chance;** (2) **country,** a region in which white people are dominant; (3) **dish,** (see quot.), *obs.;* (4) **fly,** in Indian speech, a bee, *obs.;* (5) **foot,** (see quots.); (6) **foot grass,** (see quots.); (7) **government,** in the South during Reconstruction times, government by white southerners as distinguished from that by carpetbaggers, *obs.*, cf. **white man's party;** (8) **hope,** = **white hope,** and prob. the orig. form of that expression; (9) **party,** a political faction or group in the South particularly zealous for the maintenance of white supremacy, *obs.;* (10) **plant,** (see quot.); (11) **road,** in Indian speech, the civilization of white people, *obs.*

(1) **1845** *Big Bear Ark.* 37 To give him a white man's chance, I proposed alternatives to him. **1880** TOURGEE *Bricks* 349 It was right and fair to free the niggers and let them have a fair show and a white man's chance. — (2) **1863** in CHESNUT *Diary* 243 They were up at Shelby, Ala., a white man's country, where negroes are not wanted. **1900** *Cong. Rec.* 1 Feb. 1404/2 This is a white man's country . . . and the white people intend to rule it now and forever. — (3) **1791** W. BARTRAM *Travels* 241 Venison, varieties of fish, roasted turkies (which they call the white man's dish). — (4) **1796** LATROBE *Jrnl.* 19 Wild bees . . . are called by the Indians the white man's fly. **1845** *S. Lit. Messenger* XI. 9/2 The bee, whose busy hum is so sure a herald of civilization, that it is known among the Indians as the 'white man's fly.'

(5) **1840** DEWEY *Mass. Flowering Plants* 114 *Plantago major.* . . . The Indians called it White Man's Foot. **1860** HOLMES *Professor* 296 The broad, flat leaves of the plantain,—'the white man's foot,' as the Indians called it. — (6) **1801** W. STRICKLAND *Agric. U.S.* 62, I have been told, that by some tribes of Indians it [i.e., white clover] is called *white man's foot grass;* from an idea, that wherever he has trodden, it grows. [**1897–8** *Rep. Bur. Amer. Ethnol.* I. 421 Of the white clover, the Cherokee say that 'it follows the white man.'] — (7) **1882** COOPER *Amer. Pol.* I. 193 Later on, several Southern States imitated this form of political sagacity, and soon those in favor of 'a white man's government,' (the popular battle cry of the period) had undisputed control in Virginia, Alabama, Mississippi, Arkansas and Texas—States which the Republicans at one time had reason to believe they could control. — (8) **1911** *Chi. D. News* 2 March 6/6 Another 'White Man's Hope' has been unearthed. — (9) **1860** GREELEY *Overland Journey* 37 They must be as harsh, and cruel, and tyrannical, toward the unfortunate blacks as possible, in order to prove themselves 'the white man's party.' **1884** *Judge* 19 Nov. 162/2 We shall see . . . the white man's party triumphant in the Southern States.

(10) **1893** DANA *Wild Flowers* 103 Thorn-Apple. Jamestown-Weed. . . . The plant is a rank, ill-scented one, which was introduced into our country from Asia. It was so associated with civilization as to be called the 'white man's plant' by the Indians. — (11) **1871** *Rep. Indian Affairs* (1872) 470 He was the first one to come to the agency last year, and openly avowed his determination to follow the 'white man's road.'

white marsh.

1. *Va.* App. a place or region overgrown with the plant known locally (see next) as white marsh. Also attrib.

1635 in *Amer. Sp.* XV. 411/1 Butting . . . Southerly upon the white marsh. **1702–3** *Ib.*, Along ye sd Road to the white Marsh Vally ye westward Side bounded by ye Beaver Damms ye North Side by ye head of ye Creek. **1771** *Ib.*, Beginning at a large white Oak on the side of the white Marsh swamp. **1808** *Ib.*, Beginning at a stake by the canal of the white marsh corner to the land of Thomas Evans at the mouth or commencement of the sunken Land of the said white Marsh (Swamp).

2. A local name for the southern wild rice (see quots.).

1913 *Torreya* Oct. 227 *Zizaniopsis miliacea* (Michx.) . . . Cut grass, Mississippi Delta, La.; white marsh, Santee Club, S.C. **1939** MCATEE *Wildfowl Food Plants* 115 Cut-grass (*Zizaniopsis miliacea*). . . . water millet, white marsh (S.Car.).

white Negro.

1. A Negro of an exceptionally light, often albinic, complexion.

1775 J. WARREN in *Warren-Adams Lett.* I. 77 The [New] York troops . . . will amount to 9,000 at least, . . . including the black and white negroes engaged in their service. **1824** DODDRIDGE *Notes* 52 Mulattoes . . . are denominated white negroes. **1850** LEWIS *La. Swamp Doctor* 76 He was one of that peculiar class called Albinoes, or White negroes.

2. A white person who does hard manual labor, a drudge. *Slang.* [In this use spelled "nigger" to intensify the disrespect intended.]

1835 BIRD *Nick of Woods* I. 170 Hanging too good for him, white niggah t'ief, hah! **1871** EGGLESTON *Hoosier Schoolm.* 52 'Ole Miss Meanses' white nigger,' as some of them called her, in allusion to her slavish life.

white oak.

1. Any one of various species of American oak of which *Quercus alba* of the eastern half of the U.S. is typical, a tree of one of these species. Also attrib.

1635 *Relat. Maryland* iii. 22 The White Oake is good for Pipe-staves, the red Oake for wainescot. **1648** *Providence Rec.* XV. 21 The Southeast corner is bounded with a gully and a white Oake tree. **1724** in *Amer. Sp.* XV. 296 To a small white oak Standing on the Side of a large pocosin or Great Swamp calld the Marsh run. **1861** *N.Y. Herald* 11 July 1/1 The beds for the pivot guns are to be of white oak. **1950** *Chi. Tribune* 11 March 8/3 Four miles farther on, at Crooked creek, there flitted into the white oaks some other migrants: . . . the season's first bluebirds.

2. In combs. denoting soil, land, regions, etc., where white oak is the prevailing growth, as (1) **white oak clay,** (2) **flat,** (3) **ground,** (4) **land,** (5) **opening,** (6) **swamp.**

(1) **1847** *Rep. Comm. Patents* (1848) 112 The soil being stiff white-oak clay. — (2) **1891** RYAN *Pagan* 179 A big drove of hogs on a white-oak flat, when the acorns are a good crop. — (3) **1770** WASHINGTON *Diaries* I. 433 Some tolerable good white oak Ground, level, and meadowey. — (4) **1751** J. BARTRAM *Observations* 72 We rode over some . . . white oak, and some middling land. **1882** *Econ. Geol. Ill.* II. 21 These white oak lands are reckoned among the most fertile lands in the county.

(5) **1840** *S. Lit. Messenger* VI. 605/1 A great portion of Michigan is covered by *white-oak openings.* **1947** *Mich. Hist.* Sep. 268 There were certain Michigan newcomers who definitely preferred the bur and white oak openings. — (6) **1720** in *Amer. Sp.* XV. 290/2 Lying and being on the North side of the white Oake Swamp. **1788** *N.C. State Gaz.* (New Bern) 27 March, 3000 acres; part of which is white-oak swamp of the best quality. **1862** *Va. State P.* XI. 217 You would . . . prevent a move to intercept me from the direction of the white oak swamp.

b. white oak cheese, "tough, hard cheese made from skimmed milk" (B. '77).

1842 *People's Adv.* (Carrollton, Ill.) 19 Feb. 4/1 Happening to turn his head . . . , he saw a stout arm reach up and take from the shelf a heavy white oak cheese. **1889** *Harper's Mag.* LXXIX. 694/2 They had . . . the greatest app'tite for old-fashioned, hum-made white-oak cheese. **1927** RICHARDSON WRIGHT *Hawkers & Walkers in Early Amer.* 22 Madam, are you in need of any pocket saw-mills? Horn gun flints? Basswood hams? Wooden nutmegs? White oak cheeses? Tin bungholes?

c. white oak ham, allegedly an imitation ham carved out of white oak and disposed of by New England peddlers. *Obs.* Cf. **basswood ham, wooden ham.**

1852 *Yankee Notions* July 215/2 Next to wooden nutmegs and white oak hams, that's just a leetle the cutest speculation as ever tuk place in my neighborhood.

As the last term in **barren, box, chestnut, Texas, water white oak.**

white pine. A species of pine, *Pinus strobus,* found in the East and Middle West; one of several other species of pine, as the sugar pine and the lodgepole pine. Also a tree, or its wood, of one of these species. Cf. **western white pine.**

1682 *Providence Rec.* XIV. 113 [The boundary is] from ye said heape of stones . . . to a great white pine. **1723** *Doc. Hist. N.Y. State* I. 720 But suppose the People could be restrained from cutting any White Pines. **a1797** in IMLAY *Western Territory* (ed. 3) 149 The sap . . . is carried and poured into store troughs, . . . made of . . . white pine. **1815** DRAKE *Cincinnati* 83 The white pine . . . is said to be occasionally seen on the waters of the Muskingum. **1948** *Reader's Digest* Jan. 68/2 But of all American woods none has been more significant than white pine.

attrib. **1734** *Jrnl. Mass. H. Rep.* 120 The Acts of Parliament, . . . reserve and secure to His Majesty, the right of the White Pine Trees. **1771** *N.H. Gaz.* 30 Aug. (Ernst), This is to inform such persons as are desirous of contracting for white pine masts, yards and bowsprits, . . . to apply to me. **a1817** DWIGHT *Travels* II. 160 The white-pine plains are of stiff loam. **1868** *Rep. Comm. Agric. 1867* 73 The white pine worm, *Lophyrus abbottii,* . . . lives principally on white pine. **1905** *Forestry Bureau Bul.* No. 63, 14 The white pine weevil (*Pissodes strobi*) is a reddish-brown snout beetle. **1950** *Amer. Forests* Jan. 21/2 For the first time a helicopter has been used to spray from the air in an attempt to control white pine blister rust.

Also *white pine block, board, bucket, land, log, plank, timber.*

white plague. Tuberculosis of the lungs. Cf. **Great White Plague.**

1869 O. W. HOLMES *Medical Essays* (1892) IX. 352 Two diseases especially have attracted attention, above all others, with reference to their causes and prevention; cholera, the 'black death' of the nineteenth century, and consumption, the white plague of the North. **1909** *LaFollette's Wkly. Mag.* 16 Oct. 71 Every citizen ought to be a crusader against the White Plague. **1950** *Time* 20 March 55/1 In the long war against the white plague, medicine's two most useful search tools have had a grave defect.

* **white ribbon.** A piece of ribbon of a white color worn by one who is in favor of prohibiting the sale of alcoholic liquors. Also attrib. and fig.

1893 HOLLEY *Samantha at World's Fair* 275 Denmark has a display of seven little wimmen a-wearin' the white ribbon. **1945** WEBSTER *Town Meeting Country* 129 A real nice White Ribbon girl begged that his name be taken off the rolls. **1949** *Newsweek* 1 Aug. 37/1 Of the four major chains only Mutual kept its white ribbon pinned prominently on its bosom.

Hence **white ribboner.**

1881 *Voice* (N.Y.) 15 Dec., Brother Finch endeared himself to all White Ribboners. **1950** *Chi. D. News* 15 Jan. 12/3 The present white ribboners . . . have developed no such channel for their impressive moral fervor.

white sage. *W.* One of various western American shrubs having whitish leaves, as the sagebrush, *Artemisia mexicana.* Also attrib.

1870 BEADLE *Utah* 457 Grease-wood . . . is succeeded in time by whitesage brush. **1898** A. M. DAVIDSON *Calif. Plants* 148 The white sage has a curiously folded lower lip that seems designed to bar out all but the strongest bees. **1927** JAMES *Cow Country* 7, I ran acrost him out on a bare white sage flat, and he was the sorriest sight I ever seen a living animal in.

white spruce. Any one of various American spruces, esp. *Picea glauca.*

1803 LAMBERT *Descr. Genus Pinus* 39 *Pinus alba.* White Spruce Fir. . . . In Canada, Nova Scotia, and the northern parts of New England, it grows in perfection. **1860** CURTIS *Woody Plants N.C.* 27 White spruce (*A. alba*). This has about the same range in the United States as the *Black Spruce*, but does not extend quite so far to the northward. **1949** *Sat. Ev. Post* 12 March 50/3 These were monster alders and grew in a run between banks that were covered with a growth of fir and white spruce.

* **white-tailed,** *a.* In the names of birds: (1) **white-tailed grouse,** (see quot.); (2) **hawk,** a hawk, *Buteo albicaudatus,* found in the Southwest; (3) **kite,** a kite, *Elanus leucurus majusculus,* of the southern and central parts of the U.S.; (4) **ptarmigan,** a ptarmigan, *Lagopus leucurus,* found in the summit regions of the Rocky Mountains.

(1) 1839 AUDUBON *Ornith. Biog.* V. 200 [The] White-tailed Grous, *Tetrao Leucurus,* . . . is an inhabitant of the Rocky Mountains. — **(2) 1828** BONAPARTE *Ornithology* II. 18 [The] White-Tailed Hawk, *Falco Dispar,* . . . we recently discovered to be an inhabitant of North America. — **(3) 1872** COUES *Key to Birds* 211 White-tailed Kite. . . . Head, tail and under parts white. — **(4) 1858** BAIRD *Birds Pacific R.R.* 636 White-tailed Ptarmigan. . . . Northern America to the west. **1946** STANWELL-FLETCHER *Driftwood Valley* 221 Except for small flocks of white-tailed ptarmigan and clouds of sweet-voiced larks there was hardly any bird life at this late season.

Also **white-tailed deer,** the Virginia deer and allied species or varieties.

1849 *31st Congress* 1 Sess. Sen. Doc. No. 64, 204 [Along the Pecos] we saw for the first time since leaving the Rio Grande the white-tailed or common deer of the States! **1949** *Mazama* Jan. 3/2 Only here is the white-tailed deer to be found in considerable numbers.

white trash. Poor white trash *q.v.*, or one belonging to this class. Also attrib.

1855 in *Amer. Sp.* XII. 116/2 The appointments generally at this place might not be considered very tasteful by the *white trash.* **1868** *Dispatch & Vanguard* (S.F.) 28 Nov. 2/7 He ain't nothin' but white trash. **1945** *Newsweek* 10 Dec. 92/3 The bewildered Southerner is killed by his sweetheart's brother and a white-trash mob lynches the innocent houseboy.

* **whitewash,** *v. tr.* In baseball, to prevent (an opposing team) from scoring in an inning or in a game.

1867 *Chi. Republican* 6 July 2/6 The Unions were whitewashed 3 times, and the Forest Citys 5 times. **1884** *Boston Jrnl.* 2 Oct., Buffalo Whitewashes Providence. **1948** *Dly. Ardmoreite* (Ardmore, Okla.) 5 May 10/8 Gene Costello pitched a three-hitter in whitewashing Beaumont with only two men getting as far as third base.

* **white-winged,** *a.* In the names of birds: (1) **white-winged blackbird,** (see quot.); (2) **coot,** =**white-winged scoter;** (3) **crossbill,** a crossbill, *Loxia leucoptera,* of eastern North America; (4) **dove,** a pigeon, *Melopelia asiatica,* of the southern states; (5) **scoter,** a large and quite common American scoter, *Melanitta deglandi.*

(1) 1917 *Birds of Amer.* II. 241 Bobolink. . . . White-winged Blackbird. . . . United with various species of Blackbirds, it pillages the [rice] fields. — **(2) 1844** *Nat. Hist. N.Y., Zoology* II. 337 The White-winged Coot . . . is much prized for the quantity and quality of its down. — **(3) 1787** BERESFORD *N.W. Coast Amer.* 358 White Winged Cross Bill. . . . I have received this both from Hudson's Bay and New-York. **1811** WILSON *Ornithology* IV. 48 The White-winged Cross-bill is five inches and a quarter long. **1945** *Mass. Audubon Soc.* Jan. 288 White-winged Crossbills have been present in the State. — **(4) 1852** STANSBURY *Gt. Salt Lake* 326 *Columba Leucoptera.*—White-winged Dove. **1917** *Birds of Amer.* II. 50 The White-winged Dove [is] perhaps the best known bird of the torrid cactus deserts and mesquite valleys of the southwest.

(5) 1891 *Cent.* 5412/3. **1940** GABRIELSON & JEWETT *Birds Ore.* 169 In common with other scoters the White-winged Scoters display an uncanny power to handle themselves even in the heaviest surf.

* **whiting,** *n.* Any of several American fishes, esp. the hake and any species of *Menticirrhus.*

1790 *Pa. Packet* 3 March 3/2 Mr. Maxwell, at one haul, took up as many bass, drum, trout, mullet, and whiting, . . . as filled a six oared boat. **1888** GOODE *Amer. Fishes* 81 The Norfolk Hog-fish, *Pomodasys fulvomaculatus,* . . . is the . . . 'Pork-fish' and 'Whiting' at Key West. **1911** *Rep. Fisheries 1908* 311 It is called . . . 'whiting' in the South.

As the last term in **bullhead, lake, New England, sand, silver, surf whiting.**

* **Whitman,** *n.* A saddle of a now undefinable pattern (see also quot. 1909). — **1889** *Outing* June 205/2, I like a Whitman or a McClellan better than I do a Mexican. **1909** *Cent. Supp.* 138/1 *Whitman bit,* a bit invented by Colonel R. E. Whitman, U.S.A., characterized by a snap-hook which revolves on the outside of the head of the cheek-piece. The hook is used to attach the bit to the bridle. It can be attached or released quickly.

Whitmanesque ˌhwɪtməˈnɛsk, *a.* In the manner of Walt Whitman (1819–92). Also absol. — **1903** *Nation* 12 Nov. 388/3 None of the pieces are in any recognized metre, not even blank verse, and one of them 'Wherefore,' is at best in Whitmanesque. **1904** *Ib.* 22 Dec. 506/1 'Just as the facts were, I will relate them to you,' our author says in a Whitmanesque strain at the opening.

Whitmanite ˈhwɪtmənˌaɪt, *n.* An admirer of Walt Whitman (1819–92). — **1906** *Chi. Dial* 1 March 144/2 Much of the conversation reported is trivial to all but ardent Whitmanites.

* **Whitney,** *n.* **Whitney's rifle,** a rifle of a type devised by Eli Whitney (1765–1825). *Obs.* — **1853** *Harper's Mag.* VII. 310/1 All well mounted and armed for the most part with 'Whitney's rifle,' a weapon which I can not too strongly recommend for every description of frontier service.

whitneyite ˈhwɪtnɪˌaɪt, *n.* (See quot. 1891.) — **1862** *Amer. Jrnl. Sci. & Arts* 2 Ser. XXXIV. 223 The whitneyite is compact, with a fine grained structure, and a reddish to grayish white color. **1891** *Cent.* 6913/3 *whitneyite.* . . . [Named after J. D. *Whitney,* an American geologist (born 1819).] A native arsenide of copper, occurring massive, of a reddish-white color and metallic to sub-metallic luster, and found in the copper region of Lake Superior.

* **whiz,** *n.*

1. A celebration. *Slang.*

1892 *Harper's Mag.* March 650/1 The prevailing American desire to indulge in what is widely known as an electoral whiz, accompanied by high stepping and a feeling of great wealth. **1905** O. HENRY *Trimmed Lamp* 244 He's going on a whiz to-night.

2. =**wiz.** *Slang.*

1924 *S.F. Herald* 3 May 17/3, I suppose your Ethelbert's sister Dorothy's a whiz on highbrow stuff. **1949** *News-Herald* (Marshfield, Wis.) 16 July 9/2 Since that loss to the Dodgers he has been a whiz, winning 11 of 13 including three shutouts.

* **whole,** *a., n.,* and *adv.*

1. In colloq. and slang combs.: (1) * **whole-hearted,** of a person, earnest, good-hearted, kind; (2) * **hog,** see as a main entry; (3) **souled,** hearty, generous, noble-minded; (4) **team,** =see * **team 1.**

(1) 1840 CHANNING *Lett. to Miss Aikin* 18 July, What a whole-hearted man! as we Yankees say. **1894** MARK TWAIN *Pudd'nhead Wilson* 779 (R.), The sort of whole-hearted peal of laughter which God has vouchsafed to the black slave. — **(3) 1834** CARUTHERS *Kentuckian* I. 190 [The New Yorkers] are a whole-souled people, and I like 'em. **1908** *N.Y. Ev. Post* 22 Oct. (Th.), One of the things Mr. Taft does best is to smile upon people in a genuinely friendly, whole-souled, frank spirit, and make them like him.

Also **whole biling, caboodle,** or **works,** the "whole kit and biling." *Colloq.* Cf. * **kit,** *n.*

1922 SANDBURG *Slabs Sunburnt West* 8 It is easy to come here a stranger and show the whole works, write a book, fix it all up. **1926** *Sunset Mag.* July 28/2, I let the whole biling go to the dance at

Willow Springs. **1948** *Popular Western* June 46/1 'Outsmarted the whole caboodle of 'em!' he told himself triumphantly.

2. In colloq. phrases, app. in allusion to **to go the whole hog:* (1) *to go (for) the whole*, to go the entire way, to accept to the fullest extent; (2) *to go the whole animal, creature*, etc., to do a thing fully, heartily.

(1) **1821** *Mass. Spy* 10 Jan. (Th.), Going for the whole. **1830** *Scioto Gaz.* (Chillicothe, Ohio) 1 Sep. 2/5 We go the whole for McArthur, against caucus-mongers, caucus-intriguers and caucus-candidates. **1910** J. W. TOMPKINS *Mothers & Fathers* 79 We went the whole—I mean, we gave the baby the full Suzanna McMoogle. — (2) **1833** *Sketches D. Crockett* 40 But didn't I go the whole animal? **1834** CARUTHERS *Kentuckian* I. 188, I'm flabbergasted! if that ain't what I call goin the whole cretur. **1840** *Valentine Vox* xlii. (Th.), Then of course you mean to go the whole quadruped. **1848** BURTON *Waggeries* 22 We go the hull shoat with them.

b. *To make* (or *manufacture*) *out of whole cloth, fig.* to fabricate or invent without the slightest warrant. Usu. passive.

1840 HALIBURTON *Clockmaker* 3 Ser. iii, All that talk about her timper was made out of whole cloth, and got up a-purpose. *Ib.* xx, What a fib! . . . it's all made out of whole cloth. **1847** *Spirit of Times* 24 April 105 However big or tough the stories he manufactured out of 'whole cloth,' no one could ever detect in his countenance the slightest indication that he was conscious of cutting off even 'a hem . . . from truth's garment.' **1896** *Boston Journal* 29 Dec. 2/2 This report is positively denied in official circles, who affirm that nothing of the kind occurred, but that the story is made out of whole cloth. **1950** *Ark. Gazette* (Little Rock) 10 Sep. 2B/1 The book is told in diary form by somebody's grandson, whose grandfather may have been making the entire yarn out of whole cloth.

* **whole hog.** In slang uses, chiefly attrib. and often political.

1. Designating a political enthusiast of an indicated bent.

1833 *Cong. Deb.* 11 Feb. 1676 The gentleman from Kentucky . . . was designated by many as 'a whole hog' nullifier. **1837** *New-Yorker* 5 Aug. 314/3 Now this same Patriot, &c. is zealously upholding the Banks, and stigmatising the whole hog Anti-Bankers as agrarians, jacobins, Fanny Wright men, &c. &c. **1912** *Cong. Rec.* 1 Jan. 4/2 Whole-hog standpatters are about as scarce as whole-hog progressives. **1948** *Sat. Ev. Post* 10 July 68/4 More importantly, by clearing the path for Polk, called by his supporters 'a whole-hawg Democrat,' it greased the ways for the Mexican War.

b. Designating a town of an indicated political bias.

1839 *Columbian Reg.* (New Haven, Conn.) 19 Feb. 3/3 Bethany is a 'whole hog' town, with now and then a streak of whiggery.

c. In fig. or allusive use as a symbol of entireness, completeness, acceptability, etc.

1832 CLAY *Speeches* (1860) II. 114 The senator modestly claimed only an old smoked, rejected joint; but the stomach of his excellency yearned after the whole hog! **1883** in FLEMING *Hist. Reconstruction* II. 434 Some of them . . . proved better men than the Republicans, but still we don't put the whole hog on them. **1948** *New Republic* 2 Feb. 11/1 The report went whole-hog for the theory that air power is the perfect complement to atomic power and that the next war will be fought in terms of those weapons.

2. whole hog man, an enthusiastic, unswerving political partisan.

1829 *Va. Herald* (Fredericksburg) 28 March 2/3 We all know that of late he has shown a disposition to become 'a whole hog man,' but if he can swallow this, he can swallow anything. **1838** HONE *Diary* I. 308 Three other thorough whole-hog men . . . have no . . . notion of political honesty. [**1839** *N.O. Picayune* 11 April 2/4 If I aint a man now, and a whole hog one too, I think it darn'd strange.]

b. With reference to a particular political leader.

1830 *Working-man's Gaz.* (Woodstock, Vt.) 18 Nov. 62/3 The printer suddenly became a whole hog Clay man. **1832** *Polit. Examiner* (Shelbyville, Ky.) 2 June 3/2 You will universally find them belonging to one of two classes: either *whole-hog* Jackson men, or *half-way* Clay men. **1855** I. C. PRAY *Mem. J. G. Bennett* 141 James Gordon Bennett . . . is a thorough-going, 'whole-hog' Jackson man.

* **whoop,** *n.* In colloq. and slang uses.

1. In allusive use, with reference to the enthusiasm or triumph manifested by a whoop.

1889 MARK TWAIN *Conn. Yankee* 110 This . . . report lacked whoop and crash and lurid description. **1900** G. ADE *More Fables in Slang* 64 With the return of Prosperity and the Formation of the Trust and the Whoop in all Stocks he made so much Money that he was afraid to tell the Amount.

b. *with a whoop*, with éclat.

1911 HARRISON *Queed* 318 If you'll only let her stand two years, take my word for it, she'll go through with a whoop.

2. In combs.: (1) **whoop boy,** a whippoorwill, *obs.;* (2) **hymn,** "a weird melody chanted by the colored fishermen of the Potomac river while hauling the seine: more fully called *fishing-shore whoop-hymn*" (*Cent.*); (3) **jamboree, jamboreehoo,** high-flown, also a noisy demonstration or outcry, *obs.*

(1) **1831** FOWLER *Jrnl.* 187 The most enlivening bird which I took notice of was the *whoop-boy*, which cries in the woods in the fine summer evenings. It derives its name from the monotony of the three words which its notes seem to express. — (3) **1873** MARK TWAIN & WARNER *Gilded Age* 21 He's come back to the Forks with jist a hell's-mint o' whoop-jamboree notions. **1884** MARK TWAIN *H. Finn* xxix, If you do, they will suspicion something and raise whoop-jamboreehoo. **1894** ——— in *St. Nicholas* March 399 Me and Jim went all to pieces with joy, and began to shout whoop-jamboreehoo.

b. *not to care* (or *be worth*) *a whoop*, not to care at all, to be worthless.

1904 *Baltimore Amer.* 30 Aug. 6 The voting public as a whole doesn't care a whoop about the question. **1945** *Las Animas* (Colo.) *Leader* 25 July 1/1 So far they have not had an item worth a whoop.

c. *a whoop and a holler*, a comparatively short distance.

[**1753** GIST *Journals* 85 We grew uneasy, and then he said two whoops might be heard to his cabin.] **1920** in WENTWORTH 708/1 He lives a whoop & holler down the road. **1950** *Boston Globe* 14 May (Comics) 2 'Tain't but a whoop and a holler after we round the bend!

As the last term in **death, Indian, news, scalp, war whoop.**

* **whoop,** *v. To whoop it* (or *something*) *up*, or variants: **a.** To indulge in noisy revelry, make things hum. **b.** To praise immoderately, arouse to enthusiastic support. *Slang.*

(a) **1884** *Harper's Mag.* Aug. 472/2 He whoops it up with the plain people. **1903** *N.Y. Sun* 18 Nov. 4 Three boys broke into the Garden and began to whoop things up. **1947** *Time* 17 March 23/1 On the floor, members whooped it up on a vote to change the name of Boulder Dam back to Hoover Dam. — (b) **1885** *South Fla. Sentinel* (Orlando) 5 Aug. 3/3 Whoop up Florida to those Yankees. **1908** YESLAH *Tenderfoot S. Calif.* iv. 42 These Californians who are eternally hooping up the glorious climate.

whoopee ˈhwupi, ˈhupi, *n.* and *interj.* Also **hoopee.**

1. *n.* An instance of exclaiming "whoopee!"

The noun use of this term is not assuredly American in origin. See *Amer. Sp.* VI, 234; VII, 44, 313, and *Standard Dict.* (1935) *s.v. whoopee.*

1880 MARK TWAIN *Tramp Abroad* 80 Then I propped myself against M. Gambetta's back, and raised a rousing '*Whoop-ee!*' **1895** *Outing* XXVI. 428/2 John's 'whoopee' had caused a little ebon . . . to set open the gates.

2. Noisy, unrestrained revelry, hilarity. Also attrib. and *to make whoopee*, to have a hilarious good time. *Slang.*

1928 GUS KAHN (song) *Makin' Whoopee*, Another bride, another June, Another sunny honeymoon, Another season, another reason for making whoopee! **1941** *Amer. Guardian* (Okla. City) 15 Oct. 7/1 Then came years of high pressure whoopee. **1949** *Chi. D. News* 28 July 10/1 The people have not forgotten the District's scandalous record of extravagance and graft during the 'whoopee period.' **1950** *Chi. Tribune* 17 May 18/3 The buncombe and the whoopee end, the whistle stopper's gang departs.

3. *interj.* An exclamation of strong emotion. *Colloq.*

1845 HOOPER *Simon Suggs' Adv.* iii, Hoop-ee! won't they roll over the floor, and have chicken fits, a dozen at a time! **1862** *Harper's Mag.* July 282/1 He yelled at the top of his voice, 'Whoopee! Whiskey only twenty-five cents a gallon!' **1906** O. HENRY *Heart of West* 82 You eat chili-concarne-con-huevos and then holler 'Whoopee!'

* **whooper,** *n.* = **whooping crane.**

1860 *So. Cultivator* XVIII. 324 Here [in Fla.] is found every grade, kind, size, and color . . . from the beautiful little morning Dove . . . to the tall Whooper, of 5 or 6 feet high. **1938** MATSCHAT *Suwannee River* 286 It is the favorite haunt of the gray whoopers. **1948** *Chi. Tribune* 24 Oct. 30/4 Biologists for the fish and wildlife service flew 16,000 miles this summer . . . , but did not come across the whooper's nesting ground.

As the last term in **buffalo, sand-hill whooper.**

* **whooping,** *a.*

1. whooping crane, the large white crane, *Grus americana*, or a related species, so called because of its loud raucous cry.

*c*1730 CATESBY *Carolina* I. 75 *Grus Americana Alba*, The hooping Crane, is about the Size of the common Crane. . . . A white man . . .

[told me] that he hath seen them at the Mouths of the Savanna, Aratamaha, and other Rivers nearer St. Augustine, but never saw any so far North as the Settlements of Carolina. **1828** BONAPARTE *Synopsis* 302 The Hooping Crane, *Ardea americana*, . . . inhabits throughout North America and the West Indies. **1879** BISHOP *4 Months in Sneak-box* 108 Whooping-cranes . . . and Sand-hill cranes . . . in little flocks, dotted the grassy prairies. **1950** *New Yorker* 8 April 23/1 One of thirty-six whooping cranes known to be extant was recently spotted in that vicinity [Lafayette, La.].

2. whooping owl, a hoot owl.

1781 S. PETERS *Hist. Conn.* (1829) 197 The tree-frogs, whipperwills, and whooping-owls, serenade the inhabitants every night with music. **1837** WILLIAMS *Florida* 73 There are many birds in Florida, . . . Marsh Hawk, . . . Horned Owl, . . . Whooping Owl [etc.].

whoop-la ˈhupˌlɑ, *interj.* and *n.* An exclamation of delight, a noisy outburst, a jamboree. *Slang.*

1874 *Silver City* (Ida.) *Avalanche* 4 March 2/4 Whoop-La! There will be three hundred wild, wicked-eyed, scalp-yanking, entrail-eating, long-haired, blanketed Indians camped upon the Centennial ground at Philadelphia. **1948** *Denison* (Tex.) *Herald* 1 July 4/1 The whoop-la on the convention floor was carefully rehearsed and controlled. **1950** *Boston Globe Mag.* 12 Feb. 2/5 All I'm takin' is enough fer a ten-day whoop-la.

Whore Fair. (See quot.) *Obs.* — **1699** E. WARD *Trip N.-Eng.* 11 Their Lecture-Days [in N. Eng.] are call'd by some amongst them, *Whore Fair*, from the Levity and Wanton Frollicks of the Young People.

***whortleberry,** *n.* The fruit of any one of various species of *Gaylussacia*, or the plant bearing such fruit.

In some of the quots. the reference may not be to this plant.

1702 C. MATHER *Magnalia* (1853) II. 357 Sometimes we liv'd on whortle berries, sometimes on a kind of wild cherry. **1853** *Harper's Mag.* VI. 586/1 The whortleberries, which are large and fine, are contained in large baskets. **1898** *Maine Exp. Sta. Ann. Rep.* 164 The terms whortleberry and bilberry, which are given prominence in American references to plants of this class, are never heard among the 'common people.' **1941** LEE *Stagecoach North* 113 Their real unconfessed interest was focused on maple sugar cakes, dried whortleberries, fiddle music, and wild geese.

attrib. **1830** *Bell's Life in N.Y.* 14 Sep. 1/1 We reached the village of Caldwell in safety, after a travel of several miles through pine woods and whortleberry swamps.

As the last term in **black, blue, choke, squaw whortleberry.**

***why,** *interj. Why, certainly,* (see quot. 1889). — **1889** FARMER 558/2 *Why, Certainly!*—An Eastern phrase—one of the more delicate American catch-phrases, signifying either acquiescence, or employed as a variant of 'Well, really!' **1903** HALL *Pine Grove House* 93 Harold gave the American assent, 'Why certainly.'

Whyo ˈhwaɪˌo, ˈwaɪo, *n. local.* A ruffian or holdup man, so called from the signal cry "Oh why-oh-why-oh" formerly used by a N.Y. City gang of such characters. Also attrib. *Obs.*

1889 FARMER 195 These nicknames are, like other fashions, continually changing, the *dead-rabbits* of the last decade being now called Whyos. **1901** *Making of American* 240, I knew them—the Why-os, the worst cutthroats in the city. *Ib.* 279 Headquarters of the Whyo Gang.

Wichita ˈwɪtʃəˌtɔ, *n.* [Origin obscure.] *pl.* "A confederacy of Caddoan stock, closely related linguistically to the Pawnee, and formerly ranging from about the middle Arkansas r., Kansas, southward to Brazos r., Texas" (Hodge).

1852 MARCY *Explor. Red River* (1854) 85 The old chief of the Witchitas (To-se-quash) informed us that Pah-hah-en-ka's band of the 'Middle Comanches,' . . . were much exasperated. **1926** COOPER *Oklahoma* 299 In a year more, the same would be true of the vast regions, now uselessly occupied by the Wichitas, the Cheyennes and the Arapahoes. **1947** DEVOTO *Across Wide Missouri* 292 Their close relatives the Wichitas were in fact the people of Quivira.

attrib. **1846** *Dollar Newspaper* (Phila.) 8 July 4/3 After leaving the Wichita village, Col. Eldrege proceeded in company with the celebrated Chief of the Wacoes (A-cah-quash). **1901** *World's Work* Sep. 1127/1 On July 4th President McKinley issued a proclamation opening to white settlers the lands in Indian Territory purchased by Congress from the Kiowa, Comanche, Apache and Wichita tribes. **1934** *So. Calif. Hist. Soc. Pub.* XVI. 139 He found his rainbow end in a grass thatched Wichita village many weary miles out on the plains.

***wicket,** *n.* **1.** One of the hoops or arches used in croquet. **2.** (See quot.)

(1) 1866 A. D. WHITNEY *L. Goldthwaite* vi, Leslie came in and found her at her window that overlooked the wickets. **1890** *Cent. s.v. croquet.* Each person in turn strikes his own ball once; if his ball passes through a wicket . . . he is allowed another stroke. — **(2) 1891** *Amer. Folk-Lore* IV. 230 The boy who is 'it' places the wicket, which is sometimes made of wood, and sometimes of a piece of old rubber hose, against the tree or post chosen as home, and then stations himself at some distance from it, ready to catch it when it is kicked by the other players.

wickiup ˈwɪkɪˌʌp, *n.* ["The name is of disputed origin, but apparently is from the Sauk, Fox, and Kickapoo *wikĭyapi*, 'lodge,' 'dwelling,' 'house' " (Hodge).]

1. A brush hut or mat-covered house used by Indians in the West.

1852 *Oregonian* (Portland) 7 Feb. 1/2 This band of Indians . . . left their Wick-ey-ups at the Ogden and came and camped right by the side of us. **1923** SAUNDERS *So. Sierra Calif.* 93 It bore upon it the wickiup and bean-patch, together with the circumjacent wild preserves, of an old Indian, one Juan José. **1949** *Sat. Ev. Post* 2 July 29/1 The Goshutes cooked on campfires in the wickiups.

attrib. **1925** *Sat. Ev. Post* 4 July 53/1 There's sign of Injun at every water hole . . . and new wikiup shelters in the junipers.

b. wickiup fashion, (see quot.). *Obs.*

1861 *Sacramento Union* 21 Dec. 7/6 A few of our most reverend, sagacious gentlemen . . . speak of going it wick-a-up fashion, or betaking to the caves and dens of the mountains, with blankets and a barrel of flour.

2. A temporary abode, or crude brush shelter made by white people. Also, deprecatory, a house or dwelling.

1874 ALDRICH *P. Palfrey* vii, On one side of an impetuous stream . . . lay a city of tents, pine-huts, and rude brush wakiups. **1876** *Sun* (N.Y.) 10 May 2/6 Come up and see me at my wickiup in Montana. **1890** LANGFORD *Vigilante Days* (1912) 208 The Temple of Justice was a wakiup of brush and twigs. **1947** PRICE *Trails I Rode* 97 A hell of a wickiup for you to be living in.

***wicky,** *n.* Sheep laurel, *Kalmia angustifolia*, or hairy laurel, *K. hirsuta.* — **1860** CURTIS *Woody Plants N.C.* 99 Wicky . . . is a poisonous plant, especially to sheep, and in some places is called *Sheep Laurel.* **1901** MOHR *Plant Life Ala.* 654 Wicky. . . . Louisianian area. . . . Low sandy pine barrens.

wicopy ˈwɪkəpɪ, *n.* Also **wickupp, wickopick,** etc. [f. an Indian word used for the stringy bark of the whitewood or basswood. Cf. Massachuset *wik'pi*, Abnaki *wighebi*, Delaware *wikbi*, used for inner bark, esp. of the linden.]

1. The leatherwood or the basswood *qq.v.* Also attrib. Cf. **suckwick.**

1704 *Providence Rec.* V. 244 Two trees growing out of one Roote called Wickupp trees. **1778** CARVER *Travels* 499 The Wickopick or Suckwick appears to be a species of the white wood. **1842** BUCKINGHAM *E. & W. States* I. 159 The leatherwood, or wickape of the Indians, is a remarkable and useful tree. It has a smooth tough outside bark. **1894** ROBINSON *Danvis Folks* 27 Sam saw a sprawling moose-wood or wicopy close at hand. **1949** E. P. PALMER *Fieldbk. Nat. Hist.* 274/1 Leatherwood. . . . Moose and deer sometimes use it as forage. . . . Known also as wicopy, wickup, and leatherbark.

2. Some species of willow herb, fireweed.

1844 S. M. FULLER *Summer on Lakes* 33 The flame-like flower I was taught afterward by an Indian girl to call the Wickapee. **1891** *Amer. Folk-Lore* IV. 148 *Epilobium angustifolium* we only knew by the name our grandmother taught us, *Wickup.* **1949** E. P. PALMER *Fieldbk. Nat. Hist.* 275/2 Fireweed. . . . Plant well known, as is indicated by many common names such as . . . great willow herb, Indian wickup.

***wide,** *a.* and *adv.* **1. wide loop,** *W.* used of the loop of a lariat in allusion to cattle stealing, also *to swing a wide loop.* **2.** ***wide open,** without concealment, openly, characterized by overt lawbreaking. *Slang.* **3. wide open spaces,** regions, as the Great Plains, of ample room. *Colloq.*

(1) 1924 BECHDOLT *Tales* 4 It was . . . the era of a 'wide loop' and a Winchester. **1944** ADAMS *W. Words* 160/2 swing a wide loop To live a free life, to steal cattle. — **(2) 1896** *Works of T. Roosevelt* XIV. (1926) 216 By February everything would again 'be running wide open' . . . the gambler, the disorderly-house keeper, and the law breaking liquor-seller would be plying their trades once more. **1905** *St. Louis Globe-Democrat* 1 July 1/3 Under the license of several years of 'wide-open' sentiment in this country, gamblers . . . have sought to make betting open to all classes. **1949** *World-Herald Mag.* (Omaha) 12 June 4/1 In the field of municipal government, a myth has been developed and sustained in many cities that a wide-open town policy is good business. — **(3) 1935** *Denver Post* 4 June 7B/8 The wide open spaces and the open range are not mere picturesque phrases of western fiction. **1949** *L.A. Times* 10 May II. 4/4 We live out in the wide open spaces.

As the last term in **county, state-wide.**

∗ **wide-awake,** *a.* and *n*

1. (*cap.*) In the political campaign of 1860 and later, a supporter of Abraham Lincoln. Often, in *pl.*, an organization of such supporters. Also attrib. Now *hist.*

1860 E. Cowell *Diary* 203 Mr. Lincoln arrived on Tuesday last and was serenaded by a Band of Wideawakes. **1867** *Atlantic Mo.* June 662/1 The Wide-Awake Club . . . issued, in due time, in sixty-six regiments of loyal Missouri volunteers. **1917** B. Mathews *These Many Years* 47 The torchlight procession of Lincoln's supporters, the glittering parade of the 'wide-awakes,' as they were called. **1946** Adams *Album Amer. Hist.* III. 91 Under the name of 'Wide-Awake Clubs' Lincoln supporters organized processions.

2. The sooty tern. Also attrib.

1917 *Birds of Amer.* I. 68 Sooty Tern, *Sterna fuscata*. . . . [Also called] Egg Bird; Wide-awake. **1947** *Nat. Geog. Mag.* Feb. 230/1 No wonder they are known as 'wide-awakes'!

∗ **widgeon,** *n.* As the last term in **California, European widgeon.**

∗ **widow,** *n.*

1. *card playing.* (See quots.)

1864 Dick *Amer. Hoyle* (1866) 182 Five cards are dealt to each player, one at a time, and an extra hand is dealt on the table, which is called the 'widow.' **1887** Keller *Draw Poker* 12 Widow, or *Kitty*—A percentage taken out of the pool to defray the expenses of the game or the cost of refreshments. **1898** Dick *Amer. Hoyle* (ed. 17) 228 [In] the game of cinch . . . after the draw, the card or cards remaining undealt must be placed, face down, on the table, This is called the 'widow.'

2. In the possessive in combs.: (1) **widow's cross,** a local name for *Sedum pulchellum,* esteemed for its ornamental rosy purple flowers; (2) **perch,** (see quot.), *obs.;* (3) **walk,** a local name in some places on the seacoast in New England for an elevated observatory on a dwelling, affording a good view of the ocean. Cf. **Captain's walk,** ∗ **observatory 2.**

(1) **1890** *Cent.* 5463/1 *S[edum] pulchellum* of the southern United States is sometimes cultivated under the name of *widow's cross.* — (2) **1819** *Western Rev.* I. 371 Black dotted Perch. . . . The vulgar names of this fish are black perch, widow's perch, dotted bass [etc.]. — (3) **1939** Chamberlain *Nantucket* 25 Variously termed a 'Captain's Walk,' or the 'Widow's Walk,' it is just 'The Walk' in Nantucket. **1950** *N.Y. Folklore Quart.* Spring 38 It is topped by a watchtower familiar to homes of colonial origin and called by the natives of this port the 'Widow's Walk.'

As the last term in **black, California, chuck-will's-, college, squaw, war widow.**

wiener 'winɚ, *n.* Also **wienie.** = **wienerwurst.** Also attrib. *Colloq.*

1867 J. Christison *Crime & Criminals* 37 For a week longer he served at his usual business, which was that of peddling 'winnies,' mostly among the saloons. **1904** H. R. Martin *Tillie* 34 I'm havin' fried smashed potatoes and wieners. **1947** *Amer. Wkly.* 2 Nov. 39/5 Mix cream cheese with chopped dried beef, chopped chives and celery. Fill hot buttered wiener rolls generously.

b. wiener roast, a social gathering at which wieners are roasted and eaten.

1920 *Outing* July–Aug. 245/1 All over France they introduced the women war workers to American hikes, wiener roasts, camping in the open, and games of all sorts. **1950** *Democrat* 2 March 1/5 A large crowd enjoyed a weiner roast at Union Baptist Church on Friday night.

wienerwurst 'winɚˌwɝst, *n.* [G. *Wienerwurst,* Vienna sausage.] A sausage, usu. of mixed beef and pork, smaller than a frankfurter *q.v.* and often served with garnish in a small roll of bread.

1889 *Gallup* (N.M.) *Gleaner* 27 March 3/3 We . . . are willing to bet our unpaid debts, against a weiner-wurst that the modest local of the *Democrat* blushed more than the bride when he saw her in the diaphanous costume he describes. **1901** *Everybody's Mag.* Oct. 433/1 He hadn't the price of a . . . weiner wurst or bun. **1949** *L.A. Times* 15 May II. 5/2 I've never lamped a crooked dime, not e'en a wiener-wurst.

∗ **wife,** *n.* As the last term in **farm, old, spiritual, squaw wife.**

∗ **wiggle,** *n.* **1.** Short for next. *Rare.* **2. wiggletail,** the larva or pupa of a mosquito.

(1) **1831** Buttrick *Travels* 78 The water was very bad. . . . After straining it would still exhibit live insects, which they call wiggles. — (2) **1855** *Chi. Times* 9 Aug. 4/6 The mosquito proceeds from the animalculae commonly termed the wiggle-tail. **1945** Botkin *My Burden* 34 There was a lot of little things that looked like wiggle tails swimming around in it.

∗ **wigwag,** *n.* A signal flag. Also transf. and attrib. *Colloq.*

1886 *Scientific Amer.* LIV. 16/2 In the army wig-wag system, a flag moved to the right and left during the day. **1888** Dorsey *Midshipman Bob* 42 The blood went a hummin' up inter his face, till it looked like a wig-wag. **1910** J. Hart *Vigilante Girl* 15 The arrival of the steamer was being telegraphed by its wooden wigwags throughout the city.

wigwam 'wɪgwɑm, *n.* [f. Algonquian. Cf. Ojibway *wigiwam,* a dwelling.]

1. An Indian house or tent, constructed of poles and covered with skins, mats, bark, or other material, a tepee.

1628 *Mass. H.S. Coll.* 3 Ser. VIII. 177 When any dies, they [Sagamores] say Tanto carries them to his *wigwam,* that is his house. **1724** Kidder *Exped. Lovewell* (1865) 17 [We] came upon a Wigwam that the Indians had lately gone from. **1872** Powers *Afoot & Alone* 215 Each wigwam . . . is composed of a wickerwork frame, thatched with straw and covered with a layer of common earth a foot thick. **1947** Downey *Lusty Forefathers* 128 Here came the Indians direct from their wigwams.

transf. **1816** *Adventures of Uncle Sam* 38 Now war, with all its horrors began to stalk before the *rarified* imaginations of the knowing ones as they collected spontaneously about the great Wigwam. **1829** in M. Bayard Smith *Forty Yrs. Washington Soc.* (1906) 283 Everyone thinks there is great confusion and difficulty, mortification and disappointment—at the Wigwam—as they call the General's [Jackson's] lodgings. **1861** *Harper's Mag.* Aug. 311/2 There was a good deal of trouble in the Wigwam of the Great Chief [office of the President of the U.S.]. **1947** Cahalane *Mammals* 200 In the flat marshes and the 'tules' of California, where a suitable tree is not available, the mother [otter] makes a wigwam.

Also an Indian family. *Obs.*

1845 De Smet *Ore. Missions* 169 The Cree nation is considered very powerful, and numbers more than six hundred wigwams.

b. A hut or temporary shelter used by white people.

*a***1649** Winthrop *Hist.* I. 53 Finch of Watertown, had his wigwam burnt and all his goods. **1773** Finlay *Journal* 5 We made a *wigwam* or hut of branches open in front. **1883** Mark Twain *Life on Miss.* iii, Three or four wigwams [were] scattered about the raft's vast level space for storm quarters.

2. One of several buildings erected successively to serve as headquarters for the Tammany Society in New York.

1787 in Kilroe *St. Tammany* 120 The members of St. Tammany's Society in the City of New York are requested to meet at their wigwam. . . . By order of the Sachem. **1868** *N.Y. Herald* 3 July 4/1 Prominent is the new wigwam of the Tammany Society, Columbian Order, in East Fourteenth Street. **1947** *Chi. D. News* 10 June 12/6 This relieves him of some hallowed odium attached to the old wigwam.

b. One of various other buildings used by political groups, esp. a large temporary structure erected to house a national political convention.

1860 *Charleston* (S.C.) *Mercury* 27 Nov. 1/3 The Republican 'wigwam' in Philadelphia has been sold at auction for $210. **1896** *Chi. Record* 12 Feb. 6/3 Kerens . . . is against a wigwam [for a convention]. He says it is impossible to keep the heat out of a temporary building, constructed of thin boards. **1900** Rhodes *Hist. U.S.* II. 456 Wigwam . . . is still applied in Western cities by Republicans to buildings used for party purposes. **1949** J. Monaghan *This is Ill.* 76 He was nominated for President, with Hannibal Hamlin for Vice-President, in the Wigwam, a new frame building constructed especially for the Republican National Convention at the corner of Lake and South Water streets in Chicago.

3. (See quot. 1889.)

1887 *Milwaukee Sentinel* 12 Aug. 7/1, I am Sole Agent for Milwaukee for Philbrook's Waterproof Wigwams. **1889** *N. & Q.* III. 285

Wigwams (sense 3)

Wigwam as a name for a kind of shoe, is often called a *wigwam slipper,* or *wigwam moccasin;* meaning a moccasin to be worn in the wigwam. I have been told that the wigwam slipper was invented and first manufactured at Orono, Maine; as to the correctness of this statement

I can say nothing. **1902** *Amer. Folk-Lore* 266 Of recent years a *wigwam* shoe has appeared on the market.

As the last term in **bark, birchbark, English, gin, Indian, pole, Tammany wigwam.**

Wilburite wɪlbəˌraɪt, *n.* (See quot.) *Obs.* — **1861** TALLACK *Friendly Sk.* 12 Thus commenced the separation of the Orthodox American Friends into the two divisions of 'Evangelical' and 'Wilburite' Friends; those who sympathized with Joseph John Gurney being called by the former appellation for distinction, and the friends of John Wilbur being styled after himself.

* **wild,** *a.* and *n.*

1. In the names of plants and trees: (1) **wild comfrey,** a perennial blue-flowering herb found in the eastern states; (2) **grass,** any one of various grasses or sedges which grow wild; (3) ***hyacinth,** (*a*) the camass, *Camassia esculenta,* (*b*) the squirrel corn, *Dicentra canadensis;* (4) **ipecac,** (*a*) the ipecac spurge, *Tithymalopsis ipecacuanhae,* having a root used as an emetic and purgative, (*b*) =**wild coffee 1;** (5) ***olive,** any one of various American plants or trees resembling the cultivated olive, or bearing a somewhat similar fruit; (6) ***onion,** *W.* =**death camass;** (7) **peach,** =**laurel cherry;** (8) **peanut,** a vine, *Amphicarpa comosa,* found in the eastern states, which produces pods under the earth as the peanut; (9) ***pear (tree),** (*a*) *N. Eng.* the shadbush, *Amelanchier canadensis,* (*b*) (see quot.); (10) **pumpkin,** *W.* the calabazilla, *Cucurbita foetidissima,* having a very large root; (11) **snakeroot,** (*a*) the black cohosh, *Cimicifuga racemosa,* (*b*) the ground ivy, *Glecoma hederacea;* (12) **squash,** =**calabazilla** [the identity of the plant in quot. 1791 is not clear]; (13) **sweet potato,** the manroot, *Ipomoea pandurata,* having a large starchy root resembling a potato; (14) **tea,** a lead plant *q.v.;* (15) **tomato,** any one of various plants resembling or suggestive of the common cultivated tomato; (16) ***turnip,** the jack-in-the-pulpit, *Arisaema triphyllum;* (17) ***vetch,** the prairie bird's-foot trefoil, *Hosackia americana;* (18) ***yam (root),** a twining vine, *Dioscorea paniculata,* growing wild in North America, also the root of this used medicinally.

(1) 1857 GRAY *Botany* 325 *C. Virginicum,* L. (Wild Comfrey.) . . . Rich woods, Vermont to Virginia along the mountains, and westward. **1901** MOHR *Plant Life Ala.* 690 Wild comfrey [grows in] New England west to Minnesota, Ohio Valley to Missouri, Kansas, and Arkansas, south along the mountains from New York to Tennessee and North Carolina. — **(2) 1748** ELIOT *Field-Husb.* i. 5 There was . . . a great burthen of poor wild Grass. **1872** *Vt. Bd. Agric. Rep.* I. 288 Under the popular name of 'Wild Grass,' they [species of sedge] are much cut for hay. — **(3)** (*a*) **1847** DARLINGTON *Weeds & Plants* 353 Wild Hyacinth . . . is the celebrated Quamash, or Camass, which serves as food for some of the Indian tribes of the far west. **1909** C. H. STERNBERG *Life of Fossil Hunter* 225 The Indians were roasting camus, the bulb of the wild hyacinth. (*b*) **1893** *Amer. Folk-Lore* VI. 137 *Dicentra Canadensis,* wild hyacinth, N.Y. — **(4)** (*a*) **1815** DRAKE *Cincinnati* 87 Emetics. . . . *Euphorbia ipecacuanha*—wild ipecac, the root. **1843** TORREY *Flora N.Y.* II. 177 Wild Ipecac . . . is emetic and sometimes used as a substitute for Ipecacuaha. **1857** GRAY *Botany* 387. (*b*) **1832** WILLIAMSON *Maine* I. 129 Also, we may mention *Fever-root,* which is perennial, and called *wild Ipecac.*

(5) 1806 in *Ann. 9th Cong.* 2 Sess. 1142 The silk plant, wild endive, wild olive, [grow in the vicinity of the Washita R.]. **1813** MUHLENBERG *Cat. Plants* 96 *Nyssa tomentosa,* . . . Wild olive. **1919** STURTEVANT *Notes Edible Plants* 297 *Halesia tetraptera.* . . . Silver-Bell Tree. Wild Olive. . . . The ripe fruit is eaten by some people and when green is sometimes made into a pickle. — **(6) 1934** WEBSTER. **1945** MATHEWS *Talking* 47 That includes . . . the gathering of wild onions, and the preparation of the symbolic robes for the children. **1948** *Chi. Tribune* 2 July 6/3 If he got really hard up for something to eat he could turn to the wild onion, the bulbs of the spring beauty flower, the shoots and roots of the Solomon's seal. — **(7) 1831** HOLLEY *Texas* (1833) 50 The leaves resemble those of the peach tree. Hence it is called by the colonists, wild peach. **1901** MOHR *Plant Life Ala.* 552 *Prunus caroliniana* . . . is known as Mock Orange. Laurel Cherry. Wild Peach. — **(8) 1934** WEBSTER. **1941** R. S. WALKER *Lookout* 58 The hog or wild peanut clings closely to waste places where moisture and rich soil are abundant. — **(9)** (*a*) **1810** MICHAUX *Arbres* I. 32 Mespilus arborea, *June berry.* . . . *Wild pear* . . . , dans le district de Maine. **1832** BROWNE *Sylva* 216 In the northern section of the Union, it is called *Wild Pear Tree* and *Sugar Plum.* (*b*) **1897** SUDWORTH *Arborescent Flora* 310 *Nyssa sylvatica.* Black Gum. . . . [Also called] Wild Peartree.

(10) 1927 CATHER *Death Comes* 88 It was like a country of dry ashes; . . . nothing but thickets of withered, dead-looking cactus, and patches of wild pumpkin. — **(11)** (*a*) **1743** CLAYTON *Flora Virginica* 58 *Actaea racemis longissimis.* . . . Black or Wild-Snake-root. (*b*) **1892** *Amer. Folk-Lore* V. 102 *Nepeta Glechoma,* wild snake-root. Cambridge, Mass. — **(12) 1791** W. BARTRAM *Travels* 137 It is exceedingly curious to behold the Wild Squash climbing over the lofty limbs of the trees, its yellow fruit, somewhat of the size and figure of a large orange. **1844** FARNHAM *Travels in Calif.* 315 Over these dreadful wastes . . . is however everywhere found a scanty supply of the wild squash . . . the *cucumis colocynthis,* which serves only to tantalize the perishing traveller with the remembrance of fruitful fields and pleasant homes. — **(13) 1894** *Amer. Folk-Lore* VII. 95 *Ipomœa pandurata* . . . wild sweet potato, West Va. mechoacanna, N.Y. **1941** R. S. WALKER *Lookout* 57 Wild sweet-potato rambles over the ground adding a singular beauty to the semi-shaded woodlands with its large white flowers. — **(14) 1847** EMORY *Military Reconn.* 11 In the uplands the grass is luxuriant, and occasionally is found the wild tea, (*Amorpha canescens*).

(15) 1873 BEADLE *Undevel. West* 708 After strawberries and wild tomatoes came in the whole family usually took to the prairie on Sunday and 'browsed.' **1894** *Scribner's Mag.* May 603/1 'Cabrito,' or goat meat, is made into a stew with frijoles and the wild tomato. — **(16) 1869** FULLER *Flower Gatherers* 73 Botanists call this plant *Arisoema triphyllum,* but common country people are content with the name of 'Wild Turnip.' — **(17) 1851** WM. KELLY *Across Rocky Mts.* 80 The vegetation, too, began to improve; rich clover and grasses, commingled with wild vetch, now forming its pod. — **(18) 1843** TORREY *Flora N.Y.* II. 293 *Dioscorea villosa.* Wild Yam-root. . . . Thickets, borders of woods, etc. **1901** MOHR *Plant Life Ala.* 449 *Dioscorea villosa.* . . . Wild Yam. . . . The root, under the name of 'wild yam root,' is used nonofficially in medicine. **1941** R. S. WALKER *Lookout* 58 Wild yam is a common vine and is quite ornamental.

b. In similar expressions sufficiently defined in the quots.: (1) **wild balsam apple,** (2) **bergamot,** (3) **buckwheat,** (4) **cabbage,** (5) **calla (lily),** (6) **caper,** (7) **China (tree),** (8) **columbine,** (9) **-goose plum,** (10) **honeysuckle,** (11) **hydrangea,** (12) **jalop,** (13) **pecan,** (14) ***pink,** (15) **silk,** (16) **timothy,** (17) **vanilla.**

(1) 1843 TORREY *Flora N.Y.* I. 250 Wild balsam-apple . . . [is] an ornamental plant when in full flower. **1917** EATON *Green Trails* 236 The opposite bank shows no exposed soil, being exquisitely draped with . . . great masses of wild balsam apple (*Echinocystis lobata*) with its delicate white blooms, its light green foliage, and prickly fruit gourds. — **(2) 1843** TORREY *Flora N.Y.* II. 59 *Monarda Fistulosa.* . . . Horse-mint. Wild Bergamot. . . . Hill-sides, and rocky banks of rivers. **1947** *Nat. Geog. Mag.* July 62/1 Among the many useful plants they found . . . were two of this same Mint Family, Oswego Tea, (*Monarda didyma*), and Wild Bergamot (*Monarda fistulosa*). — **(3) 1878** JACKSON *Travel at Home* 186 There are solid knitted and knotted banks of vine on either hand,—woodbine, groundnut vine, wild or 'false' buckwheat [etc.]. **1898** A. M. DAVIDSON *Calif. Plants* 191 One of the Eriogonums, or wild buckwheats, is shrubby enough to be classed as chaparral. **1909** WEBSTER 2335/1 *W*[*ild*] *buckwheat,* . . . the heath aster. *Local, U.S.* **1948** *So. Sierran* Feb. 2/2 The hills were already covered with blooming Ceanothus, . . . with wild buckwheat and black sage beginning. — **(4) 1806** in *Ann. 9th Cong.* 2 Sess. 1142 Wild carrot, wild onion, ginger, wild cabbage [grow in the vicinity of the Washita R.]. **1878** ROTHROCK *Geog. Survey Botany* 41 Caulanthus crassicaulis, . . . Wild Cabbage.—Sometimes used as food.

(5) 1885 *Outing* VII. 178/2 An interesting plant is the wild calla (*Peltandra sagittifolia*), growing in cold, wet places. **1901** MOHR *Plant Life Ala.* 425 *Peltandra sagittifolia.* . . . White Arrow-Arum, Wild Calla Lily. . . . North Carolina to Florida, along the Gulf coast to Mississippi. — **(6) 1900** WEBSTER *Supp.* 34/3 *Wild caper,* . . . a wild plum (*Prunus Pennsylvanica*) of the Eastern United States. — **(7) 1836** EDWARD *Hist. Texas* 70 There are some peculiar kinds of trees, indigenous to the soil and climate — such as for instance the wild China. **1889** *Cent.* 962/2 *Wild china-tree,* the soapberry, *Sapindus marginatus,* a native of northern Mexico, the West Indies, and adjacent United States: so called from its resemblance to the cultivated china-tree. **1907** MEARNS *Mammals Mex. Boundary* 64 The wild china tree was found along Las Moras Creek at Fort Clark and on the San Pedro River in Texas. — **(8) 1814** BIGELOW *Florula Bostoniensis* 133 Wild columbine. . . . This early flower is more delicate in its habits and colours than the common garden species. **1898** CREEVEY *Flowers of Field* 277 Wild Columbine. . . . Insects find sweet honey at the end of the tiny horns. — **(9) 1890** *Cent.* 4566/1 *Wild-goose plum,* an improved variety of the Chickasaw, said to have been raised from a stone found in the crop of a wild goose.

(10) 1761 KALM *Resa* III. 109 Af Ängelsmännerna heta de wild Honeysuckle, emedan de äro på långt håll mycket like *Periclymenum* eller *Caprifolium.* **1832** S. J. HALE *Flora* 73 Honeysuckle, wild. . . . *Azalea procumbens*. . . . This species, so much esteemed for the beauty and fragrance of its flower, exists chiefly in North America. **1946** *N. & Q.* Aug. 80/2 It should be noted that the pinkster flower (*Azalea nudiflora*) is widely known as wild honeysuckle. — **(11) 1889** *Cent.* 2932/2 *H. arborescens*, the wild American hydrangea, was introduced into European cultivation from Virginia in 1736; it is not much cultivated in the United States. **1941** R. S. WALKER *Lookout* 61 Wild hydrangea grows profusely on Little River and other places of similar kind of soil and moisture. — **(12) 1863** PORCHER *Resources So. Fields* 21 *Podophyllum peltatum.* Wild jalap; May-apple; wild lemon; duckweed. Diffused in rich swamp lands. — **(13) 1947** *Democrat* 2 Oct. 4/1 Our so-called lakes, or river sloughs, are lined with the water hickory, pignut or wild pecan, as it is variously called. — **(14) 1814** BIGELOW *Flora Bostoniensis* 110 *Silene Pennsylvanica*. . . . Sometimes called *wild pink*, from its similarity in habit to some of that genus. **1893** *Amer. Folk-Lore* VI. 138 *Silene laciniata*, wild pink, S. Barbara Co., Cal. **1894** *Ib.* VII. 100 *Arethusa bulbosa*, wild pink, Atlantic City, N.J.

(15) 1800 TATHAM *Agric. & Commerce* 136 There is a species of wild plant, which, among the people of the country, is vulgarly called *wild hemp*, sometimes *wild silk, Indian hemp, Indian silk, silk grass*, &c. — **(16) 1804** CLARK in *Lewis & C. Exped.* I. (1904) 79 In those small Praries or Glades I saw wild Timothy, lambs-quarter, Cuckle burs, & rich weed. **1872** TICE *Over Plains* 137 There is a wild timothy in the mountain peaks, . . . which is said to yield heavily and to make a better hay than the tame on the plains below. **1909** *Cent. Supp.* 1231/3 *slough-grass.* It bears narrow one-sided spikes suggesting the rattle of a rattlesnake, whence sometimes called *rattlesnake grass.* Also called *nit-grass* and *wild timothy. Ib.* 1352/3 *Wild timothy.* . . . A satin-grass, *Muhlenbergia racemosa*, with somewhat the appearance of timothy, found in moist ground from New England to the Rocky Mountains, northward and southward. It is not valued in the eastern United States, but is esteemed a good hay-grass in the Northwest and in Texas. — **(17) 1877** *Rep. Comm. Agric. 1876* 69 *Liatris odoratissima* . . . is locally known [in Fla.] as wild vanilla, but it has no relation whatever to the vanilla-plant that produces the fragrant pods of that name. **1891** *Cent.* 6695/2 *Wild vanilla*, a composite plant, *Trilisa (Liatris) odoratissima*, found from North Carolina to Florida and Louisiana. It is a rather tall erect plant with numerous small rose-purple heads. . . . The leaves have a persistent vanilla-like fragrance, and are considerably used to improve the odor of tobacco.

2. In the names of birds: (1) **wild canary,** (*a*) (see quots.), (*b*) (see quot. 1917); (2) **dove,** the mourning dove; (3) ***goose,** the Canada goose; (4) ***pigeon,** any native American, undomesticated pigeon, esp. the now extinct passenger pigeon; (5) **turkey,** =**turkey 1,** also the flesh of this bird cooked as food.

(1) (*a*) **1891** *Cent.* 6924/2 *Wild canary*, the American goldfinch, *Spinus* or *Chrysomitris tristis.* **1917** *Birds of Amer.* III. 14/1 The male is such a bright yellow bird with black wings and tail that he readily becomes known as the Wild Canary in any community where he is commonly seen. (*b*) **1893** *Standard* 274/1. **1917** *Birds of Amer.* III. 126 Yellow Warbler. *Dendroica aestiva aestiva*. . . . [Also called] Wild Canary (incorrect). — **(2) 1891** *Cent.* 6924/2 *Wild dove*, in the United States, the common Carolina dove, or mourning-dove, *Zenaidura Carolinensis.* The implied antithesis is *wild pigeon*, namely, the passenger-pigeon. — **(3) 1845** WHITTIER *Lumbermen* ii, O'er us, to the southland heading, Screams the gray wild-goose. **1869** MARK TWAIN *Innocents Abroad* 92 (R.), George returned with his dreadful wild-goose stop turned on. — **(4) 1738** BYRD *Dividing Line* (1901) 156 A Prodigious Flight of Wild Pigeons . . . flew high over our Heads to the Southward. **1805** CLARK in *Lewis & C. Exped.* II. (1904) 226 A fiew wild pigions about our camp. **1891** [see **wild dove**].

(5) 1612 SMITH *Virginia* I. 15 Wilde Turkies are as bigge as our tame. **1833** FLINT *D. Boone* 115 Venison and wild turkey, sweet potatoes and pies, smoked on their table. **1948** *Sierra Club Bul.* March 17 Correlations between soil type and the distribution of muskrat, prairie chicken, wild turkey and bighorn sheep have been demonstrated.

b. Also, chiefly obs., in the names of, or pertaining to, other animals: (1) **wild beef,** an American bison or its meat; (2) ***cat,** see as a main entry; (3) **cow,** a buffalo; (4) ***hog,** see as a main entry; (5) **ox,** a buffalo; (6) **sheep,** a Rocky Mountain sheep.

(1) 1709 LAWSON *Carolina* 115 The Beasts of Carolina are the Buffelo, or wild Beef. Bear. Panther [etc.]. **1827** COOPER *Prairie* xxvi, It abounded in neither venison nor the wild beef of the prairies. — **(3) 1727** C. COLDEN *Hist. Five Indian Nations* 4 They soon arrived loaded with the flesh of Wild Cows. *Ib.* 18 He return'd from Hunting loaded with the Tongues of wild Cows. **1809** FRENEAU *Poems* I. 257 On A Man Killed by a Buffaloe (or wild Cow).

(5) 1809 HENRY *Travels* 247 Their clothing is of leather, or dressed skins of the wild ox and the elk. — **(6) 1807** GASS *Journal* 197, I saw the skin of a wild sheep, which had fine beautiful wool on it.

3. In miscellaneous expressions: (1) **wild area,** (see quot. 1947), also attrib.; (2) **Bill,** (see quot.); (3) **catting,** see as a main entry; (4) **cherry bark,** (see quots. 1836, 1901); (5) **engine,** (see quot.), cf. **wild train;** (6) **hay,** hay made from wild grass; (7) **Indian,** see as a main entry; (8) **land,** land either uncultivated or uncultivable, unsettled or unoccupied land, forest; (9) **lemon,** the fruit of the May apple; (10) **lot,** an area of uncultivated or unoccupied land, *obs.;* (11) **meadow,** a meadow overgrown by wild grass, *obs.;* (12) **pitch,** *baseball* (see quot. 1910); (13) **play,** in baseball, an erroneous play; (14) **throw,** in baseball, a ball thrown beyond the reach of a fielder or baseman, cf. **wild pitch;** (15) **train,** (see quot. 1877), cf. **wild engine.**

(1) 1946 *Sierra Club Bul.* Oct. 3/2 No specific plans have yet been formulated for the development which would be permitted if Wild Area boundaries were to be modified. **1947** *So. Sierran* Feb. 3/3 Wilderness Areas (over 100,000 acres) and Wild Areas (5000 acres to 100,000 acres) are designated by the Secretary of Agriculture upon recommendation of the Chief of the Forest Service. — **(2) 1886** *Harper's Mag.* June 61/1 'A wild Bill' [in the usage of Ky. mountaineers] is a bed made by boring auger-holes into a log, driving sticks into these, and overlaying them with hickory bark and sedge-grass—a favorite couch. — **(4) 1829** FLINT *G. Mason* 98 He gave an infusion of Dog Wood, Wild Cherry, and Yellow Poplar bark. **1836** WOOD & BACHE *Dispensatory* 525 *Prunus Virginiana.* U.S. Wild-cherry Bark. . . . The inner bark is the part employed in medicine. **1901** MOHR *Plant Life Ala.* 552 The inner bark [of the black cherry, *Padus serotina*] is the 'wild cherry bark, *Prunus virginiana*,' of the United States Pharmacopeia.

(5) 1891 *Cent.* 6924/2 *Wild engine.* (*a*) A locomotive running over a railway without regard to schedule time. (*b*) A locomotive which by some accident or derangement has escaped from the control of its driver. — **(6) 1835** HOFFMAN *Winter in West* I. 163 Settlers . . . for the sake of the wild hay, locate themselves near the great marshes. **1942** CANNON *Mountain* 87 The first three had some wild hay—although no great amount of it. — **(8) 1813** J. ADAMS *Works* X. 26 We had so much wild land, . . . that many years must pass before we should be ambitious of power upon the ocean. **1905** VALENTINE *H. Sandwith* 418 The coal mining company would make you a good offer for the wild land you own. — **(9) 1893** DANA *Wild Flowers* 30 The fruit, which ripens in July, has been given the name of 'wild lemon,' in some places on account of its shape.

(10) 1848 *Whig. Almanac 1849* 46/1 If the poor man with a large family could but get rid of the $100 tax on his 80 acres wild lot. — **(11) 1748** WASHINGTON *Jrnl. Journey over Mts.* 50 We camped this Night in ye Woods near a Wild Meadow where was a Large Stack of Hay. — **(12) 1867** *Ball Players' Chron.* 4 July 1/2 Zeller, . . . getting round on a passed ball and wild pitch, came home on another passed ball. **1910** *Spaulding's Base Ball Guide* 383 A wild pitch is a legally delivered ball, so high, low or wide of the plate that the catcher cannot or does not stop and control it with ordinary effort. **1949** *Fargo* (N.D.) *Forum* 23 July 8/8 Two wild pitches netted the Merchants a pair of runs in the first canto. — **(13) 1857** *Spirit of Times* 24 Oct. 117/3 The playing was, for the Enterprise, rather poor, and a good many wild plays were made. — **(14) 1866** *N.Y. Herald* 28 Aug. 8/2 The latter . . . [was] helped by . . . a wild throw by Osborne to Brentnall. **1948** *Chi. Tribune* 7 March II. 1/4 Zernial was safe at first on Jackson's wild throw.

(15) 1877 BARTLETT 760 *Wild Train*, a railroad train not on the timetables of the road, and therefore irregular, and 'not entitled to the track,' as the railroad phrase is, as against a regular train. **1881** *Chi. Tribune* 14 March 4/1 A 'wild' freight train ran into a yard train on the Pan-Handle bridge, throwing several cars off the track. **1945** MARSHALL *Santa Fe* 171 The last rail was laid to the crossing August 8, 1883. 'Wild' trains were run over the river on the ninth and tenth.

4. In colloq. phrases: (1) *To play the wild* (*with*), to upset, confound, to behave recklessly or without restraint; (2) *wild and woolly*, crude or unrefined, unpolished, suggestive of the lawless frontier; (3) *wild and woolly West*, the West when it was sparsely settled and lawless, also *wild and lawless West.*

(1) 1856 J. B. JONES *Wild West Scenes* 1 Ser. 10 Love can play the 'wild' with any young man. **1911** SAUNDERS *Col. Todhunter* 143 I'm shorely glad to get home. I been playin' the wild in St. Louis. — **(2) 1885** SIRINGO *Texas Cow Boy* 95 We had the eleven hundred head of wild and wooly steers ready. **1891** *Outing* Dec. 185/1 Of all the charasteristic scenes of Western life the 'wild and woolly' round up alone had eluded the fixed and glassy stare of his portable camera. **1948** *Democrat* 22 July 4/3 Clarke is a wild and wooly county, where bob cats roam the streets of its largest community. — **(3) 1886** *Boston Herald* 16 July, One of the most annoying things to be met with in the wild and woolly West is an 'alkali sink.' **1890** *Cong. Rec.* 20 June 6304/1, I had supposed . . . that these denunciations of culture and of scientific investigations were confined to the wild and lawless West. . . . It might be said for the 'wild and woolly West' [etc.]. **1949** *N.O. Times-Picayune Mag.* 4 Dec. 20/3 How did this relic of the wild and woolly West find its way to tradition-steeped New Orleans?

wild apple. Any one of various apples, as the Oregon crab apple, found growing wild in this country. Also **wild crab apple** and attrib.

1799 J. Smith *Acct. Captivity* 17 There is a large quantity of wild apple. **1849** Parkman in *Knickerb.* XXXIII. 112 The young apple trees . . . were now hung thickly with ruddy fruit. **1950** *Chi. Tribune* 16 May 6/4 Every spring the wild crab apple trees furnish touches of splendor to the woods.

wild bean. Any one of various wild plants of the pea family, esp. the wild pea, *q.v.* as a main entry.

1778 Carver *Travels* 515 Herbs [include]. . . . Noble Liverwort, Bloodwort, Wild Beans [etc.]. **1859** Bartlett 512 Wild Bean. (*Phaseolus diversifolius.*) A plant common in the alluvial bottoms of the West, the Wild Potato of the Sioux Indians, much used as food. **1900** Jared G. Smith *Fodder & Forage Plants* 51 Wild Bean. A climbing perennial bean with trifoliate leaves and numerous clusters of straight four- to eight-seeded pods. It grows in woodlands and along streams from New York to Texas. . . . The forage approaches that of the cowpea in feeding value. **1949** E. L. Palmer *Fieldbk. Nat. Hist.* 235/1 Groundnut, Wild Bean *Apios americana*. . . . Was used by early settlers as a basis for bread. . . . Pilgrims used tubers as food the first winter.

* **wildcat,** *n.* In colloq. uses.

1. (*cap.*) **a.** One favoring the War of 1812. Cf. **war hawk. b.** A member of a proslavery faction in Maine. Both *obs.*

(a) 1812 *Columbian Centinel* 6 June 2/5 Some of the Wildcats of Congress have gone home, unable to incur the awful responsibility of unnecessary *War.* — **(b) 1853** *Whig Almanac 1854* 40/1 Election Returns. . . . Maine. . . . Legislature. . . . House—Whigs, 65; Democrats, 58; Wildcats, 18. **1855** Weld *Vacation Tour* 282 The number of political associations in America is as extraordinary as the strange names which they bear. Here are a few of them:—Wild Cats, Woolly Heads, Hunkers, Straight-out Whigs [etc.].

2. = **wildcat bank.** *Obs.*

1838 Benton *30 Years' View* II. 92 Those called wild cats—The progeny of a general banking law in Michigan. [**1859** Bartlett 512 *Wild-cat.* A bank in Michigan had a large vignette on its notes representing a panther, which animal is familiarly called there a Wild-cat.] **1896** *Nation* 3 Dec. 417/2 The question now coming up is whether this feature of our banking system can be amended without giving the field to wildcats.

b. A mine of doubtful value or one serving as the basis of fraudulent transactions. *Obs.*

1863 *Napa Co.* (Calif.) *Reporter* 28 March 1/3 There have been so many claims turned out well recently, that were termed 'wild-cat,' that the question arises in my mind whether there is any such thing as 'wild-cat' east of the Sierra Nevada. **1896** Shinn *Story of Mine* 70 These 'wild-cats' . . . were bought and sold with increasing energy for months.

c. A boring for oil in a region not previously regarded as productive. In full **wildcat well.** Cf. **wildcatter, wildcatting.**

1883 *Cent. Mag.* July 331/2 When he begins to put down a wild-cat well, he usually leases all the land in the vicinity. **1903** *McClure's Mag.* Feb. 399/1 New territory had been opened up by unexpected wildcats. **1950** *Reader's Digest* Jan. 124/1 In some later years only one out of 25 random wildcats made a well.

3. *collect.* Unsound money or financially precarious undertakings. *Slang.*

1838 *N.Y. Advt. & Exp.* 10 March 2/4 'Wild Cat' will buy provisions of no kind. **1853** *La Crosse Democrat* 26 July 3/2 More than half his money was Wild Cat and counterfeit. **1894** Harte *Protégée of Jack Hamlin's* 142 Who'd have thought of your . . . ever doing anything but speculate in wild-cat or play at draw poker.

4. *local.* A train not operating on schedule time, or one out of control. Also attrib. Cf. **wild engine, wild train.**

1870 *Terr. Enterprise* (Virginia, Nev.) 22 Oct. 3/1 In company with four or five others, he had gone out on the road upon a hand car, when a 'wild cat train' (an extra train running on no regular time) overtook them. **1888** *Mo. Republican* 23 Feb. (F.), The Montreal night express was thrown from the track . . . by a wild cat engine that had been turned loose at the Mechanicsville yards by an evil-disposed person. **1891** Ellis *Check 2134* 88 There was just one chance in a hundred of a wild cat engine approaching.

5. In special combs.: (1) **wildcat bank,** a bank issuing notes in excess of its ability to redeem them, esp. one of various western banks organized under lax state legislation in the period preceding the establishment (1863–64) of the national banking system, now *hist.;* (2) **boom,** a boom having no sound economic basis; (3) **man,** a "half horse, half alligator," one capable of "whipping his weight in wildcats," *obs.;* (4) **still,** a still where moonshine whisky is made; (5) **strike,** a strike not authorized by union officials, hence **wildcat striker.**

(1) 1838 *N.Y. Advt. & Exp.* 14 Feb. 1/2 These institutions have very properly received the *soubriquet*, of 'wild cat banks.' **1882** G. A. Sala *Amer. Revisited* I. 284 Protested cheques, torn-up notes on 'wild-cat' banks. — **(2) 1890** *Utah Valley Gaz.* (Provo) 3 Jan. 2/2 A boom for this city is at hand—not a wild cat boom either, but a solid and rapid growth. — **(3) 1830** *Portland* (Me.) *Advt.* 7 Sep. 2/2 Col. Crockett, *the wild cat man*, is open-mouthed against Jackson, and it is said will sustain himself. — **(4) 1883** S. Bonner *Dialect Tales* 143 You're up the Cumberland spyin' for wild-cat stills. **1938** Matschat *Suwannee River* 135 Cane beer, with a sweet-sour taste, would be made from the fermented skimmings and, later, would form excellent 'buck' for a wildcat still.

(5) 1943 Menefee *Assignment* 105 It told how bad morale, wildcat strikes, material shortages, poor planning by industry and Government indecision were holding up war production. **1945** *Chi. D. News* 10 Dec. 1/9 (*caption*), Would Fire or Fine Wildcat Strikers. **1949** *Va. Quart. Rev.* Winter 41 In 1944 . . . restive auto workers began a series of 'wildcat strikes.'

b. Designating worthless currency or securities issued by a wildcat bank or in connection with other fraudulent concerns, as (1) **wildcat banknote,** (2) **bill,** (3) **currency,** (4) **money,** (5) **shinplaster,** (6) **stock.**

(1) 1888 *Cent. Mag.* XXXVI. 763/2 State treasury-notes were circulated in profusion, while 'wild-cat' bank-notes of all sorts, shapes, and sizes vied with the 'shinplaster' utterances. — **(2) 1838** *Jeffersonian* (Albany) 15 Sep. 244/1 We shall have. . . . *Lumbermen's bills,* and *Wild-cat Bills,* that nobody knows who the father or the maker is. **1894** Mark Twain *P. Wilson* viii, He held out the wild-cat bill. — **(3) 1858** *Baltimore Sun* 8 July (B.), We are overrun with a wild-cat currency from all God's creation. **1898** *Mo. So. Dakotan* I. 15 Those were the days of 'wild cat' currency when a man might be rich at sunrise, and a pauper at sunset. — **(4) 1838** *N.Y. Advt. & Exp.* 14 Feb. 1/2 Our almost entire circulation is now in 'wild cat money.'

(5) 1853 *Dly. Morning Herald* (St. Louis) 5 Feb. (Th.), [We hope gold will] take the place of 'Wild-cat' shinplasters. — **(6) 1871** Daly *Divorce* 53, I invested in some wild-cat stock.

Also *wildcat note, paper, paper bill, rag, security.*

c. Designating things of a fraudulent or highly speculative kind, as (1) **wildcat claim,** (2) **ground,** (3) **liquor,** (4) **mine,** (5) **oil company, oils,** (6) **project,** (7) **property,** (8) **shop,** (9) **state,** (10) **whisky.**

(1) 1862 *Union* (Sacramento) 11 Jan. 6/7 Candidates are plentiful as 'wild cat claims in the Flowery District.' **1902** McKee *Land of Nome* 225 Its assets consisted of forty-seven wildcat claims upon which the prospectus dwelt at length in golden praise. — **(2) 1862** *Alta California* (S.F.) 10 Nov. 1/3 Certain parties from your city have thought proper to come to this district and locate a large quantity of 'wild cat' ground, and incorporate companies at very astonishingly large figures, where the ground is not worth the paper that the certificates are printed upon. — **(3) 1945** *Chi. Tribune* 18 Nov. vii. 1/2 Ma . . . went on week-end sprees with wildcat likker. — **(4) 1872** Mark Twain *Roughing It* 307 Not a wildcat mine . . . yielded a ton of rock worth crushing. **1880** Ingham *Digging Gold* 447 A Very Common Swindle is from what are called 'Wild-Cat Mines.'

(5) 1924 *Collier's* 2 Feb. 12/1 Now don't you go in for these wildcat oils. **1938** Thompson *High Trails* 123 Altogether eleven wildcat oil companies were incorporated to operate between the railroad and the Canadian line. — **(6) 1911** Wright *Winning Barbara Worth* 309 The S. & C. is not spending money to help out wild-cat projects promoted by eastern capital. — **(7) 1859** *N. Californian Union* 13 July 1/4, I would not take it as a gift were I compelled to keep it. . . 'Twould be worse than 'Wild Cat' property in paper cities in California. — **(8) 1842** *Cong. Globe* App. 13 Jan. 65/3 It is the old, worn out . . . slang upon which every red dog, wild cat, owl creek, coon box, and Cairo, swindling shop which has disgraced our country, obtained their charters. — **(9) 1872** *Chi. Tribune* 27 Dec. 4/7 Wild-cat States in the West have been created for the seeming purpose of giving two ambitious politicians seats in the Senate.

(10) 1881 T. Hughes *Rugby, Tenn.* 64 They are sadly weak when wild-cat whisky—or 'moonshine,' as the favourite illicit beverage of the mountains is called—crosses their path. [**1928** Bradford *Ol' Man Adam* 20, I drunk some of dat new wildcat yistiddy, and hit burnt de skin off of my th'oat so I can't drink no more.]

d. Designating individuals engaged in fraudulent or highly speculative enterprises, as **wildcat banker, broker, businessman, mining promoter, operator.**

*a***1859** *Cin. Enquirer* (B.), Our banks are always willing to offer loans and facilities to speculators and wild-cat business men to operate with. **1881** *N.Y. Sun* 16 Nov. (Th.), Walsh next turned up in Washington as a wildcat banker. **1888** *Puck* (F.), This was a wild cat broker. **1909** *N.Y. Ev. Post* 22 Feb. (Th.), The wild-cat mining promoter . . . flourished successfully in the old days of boom mining camps. **1943** *Democrat* 4 Nov. 1/5 Oil men, both representatives of the 'wild cat' or independent operators and of the old line companies are active in Clarke county.

wildcat ˈwaɪldˌkæt, *v. intr.* (See quot. 1903 and cf. **wildcatting b.**) — **1903** *D.N.* II. 345 Wild-cat, . . . to prospect [for oil] in territory not known to be good. **1948** *Time* 8 March 23/3 Besides practicing law, he wildcatted for oil with moderate success.

wildcatter ˈwaɪldˌkætɚ, *n.*

1. (See quots.)

1883 *Cent. Mag.* July 327/2 The 'wild-catters,' as the prospectors are called who take the risks of sinking wells in unknown territory. **1904** *Scientific Amer.* 18 June 474/2 Large oil producers do not prospect; they leave that dangerous business to the professional 'wildcatter,' and when he has located a new, rich territory, they buy him out. **1950** *Dly. Ardmoreite* (Ardmore, Okla.) 30 April c. 8/1 He began his oil operations as a wildcatter in 1933.

2. One who operates a wildcat still or promotes a wildcat mine.

1892 *Columbus* (O.) *Dispatch* 11 March, One of the moonshiners . . . was shot in the affray. . . . Three more of the wild catters . . . are seriously hurt. **1909** *N.Y. Ev. Post* 22 Feb. 6 The wildcatter would have few victims if the intended victim had the common-sense foresight to appeal to the mining engineer. **1942** LILLARD *Desert Challenge* 239 As villain, the wildcatter replaced the gun fighter and the crooked mine superintendent.

3. One who goes out on a wildcat strike.

1947 *Time* 27 Jan. 26/3 The strike's end came after several meetings in which the wildcatters flatly refused to return to work.

wildcatting ˈwaɪldˌkætɪŋ, *n.* Engaging in an enterprise of a surreptitious, highly venturesome, or unauthorized kind.

1858 *Varieties* (S.F.) 21 Feb. 5/1 No more 'Wild-cat-ing' with either line [they] now work for the mutual benefit of each other. **1890** *Stock Grower & Farmer* 4 Jan. 3/2 We want no wild-catting in irrigating enterprises such as we had in the cattle business a few years ago. **1923** BOWER *Parowan Bonanza* 132 He's a fine, straight fellow and everybody knows he wouldn't stand for any wildcatting. **1947** *Time* Jan. 26/3 One such success would inevitably lead to more wildcatting.

b. (See quots.)

1883 *Cent. Mag.* July 331/1 'Wild-catting' is the name applied to the venturesome business of drilling wells on territory not known to contain oil. **1897** *Boston News Bureau* 22 June, 'Wildcatting' . . . consists in leasing lands and sinking wells with the expectation of making a lucky strike.

wild coffee.

1. (See quot. 1949.)

1833 EATON *Botany* (ed. 6) 372 *Triosteum perfoliatum*, fever root, horse-ginseng, wild coffee. . . . Berries purple or yellow. **1898** CREEVEY *Flowers of Field* 364 Feverwort. Horse-gentian. Wild Coffee. . . . Canada and New England to Minnesota and southward. **1949** E. L. PALMER *Fieldbk. Nat. Hist.* 314/1 Horse Gentian, Wild Coffee *Triosteum perfoliatum*. . . . Native of North America. . . . Reported by many quacks to have medicinal value.

2. (See quots.)

1890 *Cong. Rec.* 12 June 5991/1 In California . . . this wild silkworm feeds upon . . . the cascara sagrada, or wild coffee. **1897** SUDWORTH *Arborescent Flora* 299 *Rhamnus purshiana*. Bearberry. . . . [Also called] Wild Coffeebush (Cal.) . . . Wild Coffee (Cal.)

* **wilderness,** *n.*

1. Used to designate specific areas: **a.** An unsettled mountainous region along the eastern border of Kentucky. *Obs.*

1792 IMLAY *Western Territory* 9 These mountains . . . ramify into a country 200 miles over from east to west, called the wilderness. **1829** *Va. Lit. Museum* 85 This elevated tract, . . . from its dreariness and want of improvement, or population, was called 'the wilderness.'

b. (*cap.*) A forested region of Virginia south of the Rapidan River, famous as the scene of a battle in the Civil War.

1799 *Phenix* (Staunton, Va.) 13 Feb. 2/4 On Friday the 14th ult. two men coming through the Wilderness, discovered on the road side several bits of a human scull, freshly mangled. **1865** *Atlantic Mo.* June 744/1 An article . . . gives an outline of the operations of the Army of the Potomac . . . through the tangled thickets of the Wilderness. **1946** ADAMS *Album Amer. Hist.* III. 165 At the same time that Grant was fighting his way through The Wilderness toward Richmond, Gen. Sherman . . . began a push toward Atlanta.

c. (*cap.*) The difficult terrain along the Mississippi River near Vicksburg, or a remote mountainous area in West Virginia near the Maryland boundary. *Obs.*

1864 PENNIMAN *Tanner-Boy* 282 He left Grand Gulf to plunge into the 'Wilderness' of Mississippi. **1880** *Harper's Mag.* July 171/1 The Wilderness comprises seven hundred square miles of virgin forest.

2. In combs.: (1) **wilderness area,** an area, over 100,000 acres in extent, of national forest land which is set aside by the government for scientific or recreational purposes; (2) **cure,** ?a method of treating illness by life in the open air, *obs.*; (3) **Road, Trail,** the historic route from Virginia into Kentucky by way of the Cumberland Gap.

(1) **1934** WEBSTER. **1948** *Pacific Discovery* Jan.–Feb. 12/1 The national forest's Teton Wilderness Area has been threatened with similar exploitation. — (2) **1881** *Harper's Mag.* May 868/1 The Reporter pitched his tent and began the trial of the wilderness cure. — (3) **1831** A. S. WITHERS *Chron. Border Warfare* 285 The 'Wilderness Road' (or 'trace') was the overland highway through Cumberland Gap. It was sometimes called 'Boone's trace.' **1886** SPEED *Wilderness Road* 75 It is not the Kentucky people alone who have reason to study . . the history of the Wilderness Road. **1943** PEATTIE *Great Smokies* 325 Through this gap came the Wilderness Road, blazed by Daniel Boone along an old Indian and buffalo trail. **1948** DICK *Dixie Frontier* 204 The most famous of these trails were the Wilderness Trail, beginning in northeastern Tennessee and running through Cumberland Gap out onto the blue-grass area of Kentucky [etc.].

* **wild hog.**

1. A peccary. Also as an opprobrious term.

1805 in *Ann. 9th Cong.* 2 Sess. 1082 Wild hogs are likewise plenty in their country. **1884** *Cong. Rec.* 4 June 4821/1 A distinguished railroad king, who talks about this House as 'wild hogs' in letters which are of record—I refer to Mr. Huntington. **1916** THOBURN *Stand. Hist. Okla.* I. 47 Wild hog (peccary) was reported to be quite common in the valley of the Red River.

2. a. wild hog claim, = **hog claim. b. wild hog sense,** common sense. Cf. **horse sense.**

(a) **1932** RANDOLPH *Ozark Mts.* 86 If a furriner or a newcomer wanted a hawg or two he'd jest buy him a wild-hawg claim off'n some ol' residenter. — (b) **1886** *Cong. Globe* App. 18 March 286/2 This common perception is called by the 'old settlers' 'wild-hog sense.' **1903** O. HENRY *Roads of Destiny* 374 Be intelligent, now, and use at least wild-hog sense.

wild Indian. An Indian regarded as primitive, savage, or roving rather than settled; esp., in the Southwest, an Indian not a Pueblo. Also transf.

1840 *Texas Sentinel* (Austin) 22 Jan. 4/2 The wild Indians committed the depredations. **1851** *N. Mex. H. Rep. Jrnl.* 86 There are other persons who are opposed to all amicable relations with the wild Indians. **1866** *Rep. Indian Affairs* 78 The 'wild' Indian never thinks of owning any particular spot of ground. **1873** ARNY *Items regarding N. Mex.* 64 The wild Indians of New Mexico number. . . . Navajos, 8,500 Apaches, 4,502 Utes, 1,347. **1913** LONDON *Valley of Moon* 295 He cut a swath through the Johnny Rebs . . . yellin' like a wild Indian. **1946** *Life* 29 July 101 He's a regular Wild Indian, but *my* floor can take it!

wild indigo. Any one of various American plants of the genus *Baptisia*. Also a false indigo of the genus *Amorpha*.

1744 *S.C. Gazette* 220 ct. The true Wild Indigo Plant. [usu. spelling here *indico*]. **1889** *Cent.* 180/2 The false indigo, *A*[*morpha*] *fruticosa*, is occasionally cultivated for ornament. . . . Also called *bastard* or *wild indigo*. **1939** *Nat. Geog. Mag.* Aug. 244/2 The wild indigos are most abundant in the southern States, where one species was formerly used in dyeing. **1949** E. L. PALMER *Fieldbk. Nat. Hist.* 231/3 Wild Indigo. . . . Height to 4 ft. Root is used sometimes as source of dye material.

wild lily of the valley. Any one of various plants, as (*a*) the yellow clintonia, *Clintonia borealis*, or a related species, (*b*) the shinleaf, *Pyrola elliptica*, (*c*) the bead ruby *q.v.*

(*a*) **1829** EATON *Botany* (ed. 5) 184 *Convalaria borealis*, wild lily of the valley, dragoness-plant. **1909** WEBSTER 2385/2 *W*[*ild*] *lily of the valley*, . . . the lilaceous plant *Clintonia umbellata*. (*b*) **1894** *Amer. Folk-Lore* VII. 93 *Pyrola elliptica*, wild lily-of-the-valley, Concord, Mass. (*c*) **1909** WEBSTER 2335/2 *W*[*ild*] *lily of the valley*, . . . the bead-ruby (*Unifolium canadense*).

wild lime. A name given locally to various plants, as the mountain plum, *Ximenia americana*, the laurel cherry, *Laurocerasus caroliniana*, etc.

1767 in DARLINGTON *Mem. Bartram & Marshall* 292 The Wild Lime is a singular plant. **1791** W. BARTRAM *Travels* 94 These shelly ridges have a vegetable surface of loose black mould . . . which naturally produces. . . . Tallow-nut or Wild Lime. **1813** MUHLENBERG *Cat. Plants* 48 *Prunus Caroliniana*. . . . Wild lime. **1897** SUDWORTH *Arborescent Flora* 266 *Xanthoxylum fagara*. . . . Wild Lime. *Ib.* 311 *Nyssa ogeche*. Sour Tupelo. . . . Wild Limetree.

* **wild oat.**

1. Any one of various native American grasses, as wild rice *q.v.*, that somewhat resemble oats. Cf. **Pennsylvania wild oat.**

1705 BEVERLEY *Virginia* III. 14 They make their Bread of the Indian Corn, Wild Oats, or the Seed of the Sun-flower. **1775** CRESSWELL *Journal* 76 Wild Oats and Wild Rye in such plenty it might be mown and would turn out a good crop. **1884** VASEY *Agric. Grasses* 75 *Avena fatua*. (Wild oats.) This species is very common in California. **1949** E. L. PALMER *Fieldbk. Nat. Hist.* 114/2 Wild Oat *Avena fatua*. . . . Wild oats occupy land used better by cultivated species.

attrib. **1857** *Harper's Mag.* Nov. 817 He built a cabin of cedar logs in the 'wild oats country.' **1890** HARTE *Waif of Plains* 154 He was forced to defer his first self-prepared breakfast until he had reached . . . a less dangerous place than the wild-oat field to build his first camp fire.

2. * **wild oat grass,** (*a*) any one of various species of *Danthonia*, (*b*) (see quots.).

(*a*) **1843** TORREY *Flora N.Y.* II. 454 *Danthonia spicata*. Wild Oat-grass. . . . Dry open woods and in fields. **1901** MOHR *Plant Life Ala.* 373 *Danthonia compressa*. . . . Mountain Wild Oat Grass. . . . *Danthonia glabra*. . . . Smooth Wild Oat Grass. . . . *Danthonia sericea*. . . . Silky Wild Oat Grass. (*b*) **1909** *Cent. Supp.* 882/1 *Wild oat-grass* . . . the wild oat, *Avena fatua*. *Ib.*, *Wild oat-grass*, . . . the Indian grass, *Sorghastrum avenaceum*. *Ib.*, *Wild oat-grass*, . . . same as *feather bunch-grass*.

wild pea.

1. Any one of various plants, esp. the wild pea vine (see next), or their fruits, of the pea family.

1778 CARVER *Travels* 515 Herbs [include:] . . . Scabious, Mullen, Wild Pease. **1808** PIKE *Sources Miss.* 104 Their craws were filled with acorns and the wild pea. **1893** *Amer. Folk-Lore* VI. 140 *Crotalaria sagittalis*, wild pea. Ia.

2. wild pea vine, a trailing plant, *Strophostyles helvola*, found from New York to Texas, the foliage and pods of which supplied abundant and nutritious forage to cattle and sheep in pioneer times.

1786 WASHINGTON *Diaries* III. 123 Some of the Wild Pea vine . . . had been pulled. **1851** *S. Lit. Messenger* XVII. 565/1 We will . . . let the horses eat the luxuriant wild pea-vine until the wagons come up. **1950** *Asheville* (N.C.) *Citizen-Times* 26 March VII. 12/5 His horse . . . had been turned out to graze during the night on cane and the wild peavines.

wild potato. In local use any one of various plants, as man of the earth, *Ipomoea pandurata*, the groundnut, *Apios tuberosa*, the spring beauty, *Claytonia virginica*, and the arrowhead.

1772 ROMANS in P. L. Phillips *Notes B. Romans* (1924) 124 The Savages are not so well provided with Bread as the Spaniards. . . . But both . . . [use] a species of Convolvulus known by the Name of Wild Potatoe. **1778** CARVER *Travels* 511 Wild Potatoes, Liquorice, Snake Root [etc.]. **1803–4** LEWIS in *L. & Clark Exped.* VI. (1905) 138 The common wild pittatoe also forms another article of food in savage life. **1892** *Amer. Folk-Lore* V. 93 *Claytonia Virginica*, wild potatoes. Union Co., Pa. **1939** W. L. MCATEE *Wildfowl Food Plants* 115 *Delta potato* (*Sagittaria platyphylla*). . . . wild potato (La.)

wild red cherry. The pin cherry, *Prunus pennsylvanica* (see also quot. 1897).

1847 WOOD *Botany* 240 *C[erasus] Pennsylvanica*. . . . Wild Red Cherry. . . . This tree is of rapid growth, and quickly succeeds a forest-clearing if neglected. **1897** SUDWORTH *Arborescent Flora* 237 *Prunus angustifolia*. Chickasaw Plum. . . . Wild Red Cherry (La.) **1919** STURTEVANT *Notes Edible Plants* 462 Wild Red Cherry. . . . The fruit is sour and unpleasant. **1949** E. L. PALMER *Fieldbk. Nat. Hist.* 221/3 Wild Red Cherry. . . . Common in rich soils, in mixed forests.

wild rice.

1. A tall aquatic grass, *Zizania aquatica*, or its edible seeds. Also attrib. Cf. **Menominee,** * **oat 1, Tuscarora rice** (*b*).

1778 CARVER *Travels* 522 Wild Rice . . . grows in the greatest plenty throughout the interior parts of North America. **1824** KEATING *Narrative* (1825) I. 177 The Menomone, or wild rice eaters . . . [appear] to be fast decreasing in numbers. **1897** *Outing* XXX. 544/1 The duck find snails, wild rice, etc. **1939** PINKERTON *Wilderness Wife* 33 Robert tested the wild rice and changed it to a shorter hook for steaming. *Ib.* 179 He had been attending the festivities following the wild rice harvest.

2. = **rice cut-grass.**

1847 DARLINGTON *Weeds & Plants* 369 False or wild Rice . . . is in the Northern States considered not only worthless, but rather a nuisance.

* **wild sage.** *W.* Any one of various species of *Artemisia*, esp. sagebrush. Also attrib.

1807 GASS *Jrnl.* 127 A kind of wild sage, . . . as high as a man's head . . . grows in these bottoms. **1849** PARKMAN *Ore. Trail* 146 The restless young Indians . . . galloped over the hills, . . . often starting a wolf or an antelope from the thick growth of wild-sage bushes. *a***1918** G. STUART *On Frontier* I. 20 Now I see fields of alfalfa and mowing grain where were once the bunch grass and wild sage.

wild tobacco. A name given locally to (*a*) Indian tobacco, *Lobelia inflata*, (*b*) any one of various uncultivated plants of the genus *Nicotiana*, (*c*) the toad flax, *Linaria vulgaris*.

(*a*) **1817–8** EATON *Botany* (1822) 340. **1832** WILLIAMSON *Maine* I. 125 The *Lobelia, wild*, or *Indian tobacco*, . . . is a powerful emetic. (*b*) **1885** HAVARD *Flora W. & S. Texas* 513 Wild Tobacco . . . [does] not seem of much account for smoking. **1894** *Amer. Folk-Lore* VII. 95 *Nicotiana Bigelovii*, wild tobacco, Santa Barbara Co., Cal. (*c*) **1894** *Amer. Folk-Lore* VII. 96 *Linaria vulgaris*, . . . wild tobacco, Indian hemp.

wild West.

1. The western part of the U.S., regarded as the scene of lawlessness and primitive ways of life. Also attrib.

1851 B. ALCOTT *Journals* 257 Metropolitan New York were fitter, or the wild West [for one of his mettle]. **1887** *Courier-Journal* 18 Feb. 1/1 Their gang played before the members of the 'Wild West' organization of cowboys and Indians. **1949** *Reader's Digest* Aug. 129/2 [It is] a neon-lit reproduction of an old Wild West town.

Hence **wild western,** *a.*, of or pertaining to the wild West.

1872 *Chi. Ev. Jrnl.* 3 July, The spirit of the wild Western piece is the same as that . . . of the Bret Harte and John Hay school of verse. **1901** WHITE *Claim Jumpers* 27 In the afternoon the young man took a vacation and hunted Wild Western adventure.

2. Wild West Show, a circus specializing in cowboy and Indian feats, orig. applied to such a show organized by William F. (Buffalo Bill) Cody, which opened May 17, 1883, at Omaha, Nebraska.

1887 *Courier-Journal* 18 Feb. 5/4 Nate Salisbury, one of the proprietors of the Wild West show, was playing at the queer audience. **1929** *Variety* 3 April 1/5 Buck Jones will tour America this summer with a 15-car wild west show. **1947** *Democrat* 16 Oct. 1 (*caption*), Wild West Show Here Wednesday Radio And Rodeo Cowboys And Cowgirls Are Coming. [**1948** *Popular Western* June 15/2 He objects to my tryin' to make an honest dollar in their little Wild West carnival.]

willet ˈwɪlɪt, *n.* [Imitative, see quot. 1808–14.] The semipalmated snipe *q.v.*

[**1709** LAWSON *Carolina* 147 Will Willet is so called from his Cry, which he very exactly calls Will Willet, as he flies.] **1791** BARTRAM *Travels* 70 [We] procured plenty of sea fowl, such as curlews, willets, snipes, sand birds, and others. **1808–14** WILSON *Ornithology* VII. 27 Its common name is the Willet, by which appellation it is universally known along the shores of New York, New Jersey, Delaware and Maryland. . . . Its loud and shrill reiterations of Pill-will-willet, Pill-will-willet, resound, almost incessantly, along the marshes. **1941** SETON *Trail of Artist-Naturalist* 171 On this [alkali flat], we started a willet from its nest, which was merely a slight hollow between a bunch of grass and a buffalo bone.

* **William,** *n.* **1.** In jocular use any "bill" of paper money. Cf. **Blue William. 2. William Poole Association,** a short-lived political organization of a Know-Nothing, anti-foreign kind growing out of the murder in New York City of one Wm. Poole, a prize fighter. *Obs.*

(1) 1865 *Republican Banner* (Nashville, Tenn.) 5 Oct. 3/1 Will. had to remember the Workhouse in his will to the tune of a 'ten dollar William.' **1912** *Amer. Mag.* 306/1 Do I like New York, . . . Why, honey, I would give a five dollar William for just one breath from that dear desert, . . . or a neigh from old Black Eye. **1927** SIRINGO *Riata* 10 Mr. Myers wrote me . . . to buy a suit of clothes with the twenty-dollar *william*. — **(2) 1856** FERGUSSON *America* 57 'The

William Poole Association' . . . is a new society, political, of course, formed on the circumstance of this murder.

williamsite ˈwɪljəmzˌaɪt, *n.* (See quot. 1909.) — **1848** *Amer. Jrnl. Science* 2 Ser. VI. 249 New Minerals. . . . Williamsite. . . . This mineral was sent to me by L. White Williams, . . . of West Chester, Chester Co., Penn. **1909** *Cent. Supp.* 1446/2 *williamsite.* . . . [Named after L. W. Williams, from whom it was received.] An apple-green or oil-green variety of serpentine which has lamellar to massive granular structure, from Pennsylvania.

* **Williamson,** *n.* [Lt. R. S. *Williamson* (1824–82), a topographical engineer on the Pacific Railroad survey.] **Williamson's sapsucker, woodpecker,** a western sapsucker, *Sphyrapicus thyroideus,* discovered about 1850, the male of which is characterized by the absence of red feathers on the head and neck.

1858 BAIRD *Birds Pacific R.R.* 105 Williamson's Woodpecker . . . has as yet only been found in the Rocky Mountains. **1917** *Birds of Amer.* II. 152 Williamson's Woodpecker . . . has no red feathers on the top of his head. **1939** LINCOLN *Migration* 92 It has been noted that such species as the Williamson's Sapsucker . . . move down to the lower regions in August.

willies ˈwɪlɪz, *n. pl.* [Origin unknown.] A spell of nervousness, usu. *the willies. Colloq.*

1896 *D.N.* I. 427 willies: 'To have the *willies,*' to be nervous. **1900** BONNER *Hard Pan* 99 It just gives me the willies to think of your being down on your luck. **1949** *Sat. Ev. Post* 4 June 144/4 This damned country gives me the willies.

* **willow,** *n.* In combs.: (1) **willow batture,** a batture *q.v.* overgrown with willows; (2) **bottom,** an area of bottom land where willows abound; (3) **fence,** a fence composed of willows planted close together; (4) **goldfinch,** (see quot.); (5) **grouse,** the willow ptarmigan, *Lagopus lagopus;* (6) **hat,** ?a hat of willow withes, *obs.;* (7) **island,** an island upon which willows abound; (8) **oak,** an oak of the eastern states, *Quercus phellos,* or the laurel oak, *Q. laurifolia;* (9) **ptarmigan,** =**willow grouse;** (10) **rocker,** a rocking chair made of willow osiers; (11) **stateroom,** a type of willow furniture, *obs.;* (12) **swamp,** a swamp in which willows grow, also attrib.; (13) **tail,** (see quot. 1944); (14) **ware,** (*a*) articles made from willow osiers, (*b*) crockery decorated with a well-known willow pattern.

(1) **1843** *Niles' Reg.* 18 Nov. 179/1 From present appearances, I cannot help thinking there will be a willow batture in five years or so, directly across the mouth of Red River. — (2) **1807** GASS *Jrnl.* 51 We passed a willow bottom. — (3) **1919** CADY *Rhymes of Vt.* (1923) 184 The willow fence begins to grow. — (4) **1917** *Birds of Amer.* III. 15 On the Pacific coast the differences are . . . great enough to make a separate variety called the Willow Goldfinch (*Astragalinus tristis salicamans*).

(5) **1825** RICHARDSON in Wilson & Bonaparte *Amer. Ornith.* IV. 327 The willow grouse inhabits the fur countries . . . breeding in the valleys of the Rocky Mountains. **1902** WISTER *Virginia* 142 He had showed her where a covey of young willow-grouse were hiding as their horses passed. — (6) **1793** *Mass. Spy* 19 Sep. 4/3 John Nazro . . . will sell . . . chip and willow Hats. **1837** MARTINEAU *Soc. in Amer.* I. 317 He was furnished in a trice with a willow-hat. — (7) **1804** CLARK in *Lewis & C. Exped.* I. (1904) 47 Behind a Small Willow Island in the bend is a Prarie. **1807** GASS *Jrnl.* 23 We . . . passed high yellow banks . . . opposite a willow island. — (8) **1709** LAWSON *Carolina* 93 Willow-Oak is a sort of Water-Oak. **1832** BROWNE *Sylva* 279 The willow oak in favorable situations, attains the height of 50 or 60 feet. **1949** *Amer. Forests* Sep. 18/3 A tall willow oak drips slender verdant fingers. — (9) **1872** COUES *Key to Birds* 235 *Lagopus albus.* Willow Ptarmigan. **1947** BROWN *Outdoors Unlimited* 314 Among the game birds of Alaska there is none bolder nor more liked by the old-time sourdoughs than the male willow ptarmigan.

(10) **1887** *Courier-Journal* 6 Feb. 3/6 For Sale . . . willow rockers and settees. — (11) **1899** *Boston Traveller* 25 July, No one seems to know how the name of 'Willow Stateroom' first came to this piece of furniture. — (12) **1644** *R.I. Col. Rec.* I. 83 No more landes shall be layed out . . . from the brooke to the great swamp; that is to say, the willow swamp footpath. **1883** *Cent. Mag.* Oct. 922/1 Occasionally in the spring . . . they [snipe] may be found in alder or willow swamps near their usual haunts. — (13) **1929** DOBIE *Vaquero* 192 One old 'willow tail' had got the limb of a blackjack fastened into her long mane. **1944** ADAMS *W. Words* 177/2 willow tail A horse, usually a mare, which has a loose, long, coarse, heavy tail—never an indication of good breeding. — (14) (*a*) **1851** CIST *Cincinnati* 172 Baskets, Cradles, Wagons, and other willow-ware. **1892** *York Co. Hist. Rev.* 43 The premises are conveniently arranged . . . with two warehouses, one for the storage of crockeryware wood and willow-ware. (*b*) *c***1885** R. COLLYER in J. H. Holmes *Life & Lett.* (1917) I. 24 A great rack for the pewter dishes and willowware. **1904** GLASGOW *Deliverance* 58 The china consisted of some odd, broken pieces of old willow-ware.

As the last term in **ball, black, bog, Cutler's, desert, desert flowering, glaucous, gray, Kilmarnock, longstalk, prairie, red root, sage, sand bar, swamp, trailing, Virginia, Ward's, water, whistle willow.**

Wilmot Proviso. *Hist.* An amendment, offered in 1846 by David Wilmot of Pa., to an appropriation bill for two million dollars to pay for territory to be purchased from Mexico.

This amendment was in the nature of a proviso that slavery should not be extended into the territory to be acquired. It passed the House but was defeated in the Senate.

1847 in *Amer. Hist. Assoc. Rep.* II. 1138 If the Wilmot proviso . . . should receive the sanction of Congress, it will strongly tend to favor the views which we entertain. **1857** BENTON *Exam. Dred Scott Case* 117 They deemed it the best kind of a Wilmot proviso. **1943** DEVOTO *Yr. of Decision* 290 This is the Wilmot Proviso. It fastened the slavery question to Polk's request for two million dollars for the purchase of territory.

* **Wilson,** *n.* [Alexander *Wilson* (1766–1813), Scottish-born Amer. ornithologist.] Used in the possessive in the names of various birds: (1) **Wilson's black-cap warbler,** =**Wilson's warbler;** (2) **bluebird,** (see quot.); (3) **owl,** (see quot.); (4) **petrel,** the common stormy petrel, *Oceanites oceanicus;* (5) **phalarope,** a rather large phalarope, *Steganopus tricolor,* found in the West; (6) **plover,** a ring plover, *Pagolla wilsonia,* found in the southern states; (7) **sandpiper,** "the American least sandpiper, peep, or stint" (*Cent.*); (8) **snipe,** a common snipe of the U.S., *Capella delicata,* also **Wilson snipe;** (9) **tern,** (see quot.); (10) **thrush,** =**veery;** (11) **warbler,** a small black-crowned warbler, *Wilsonia pusilla,* found in the eastern and northern states.

(1) **1892** TORREY *Foot-path Way* 186 Wilson's black-cap warbler is one of the less common of our regular Massachusetts migrants. — (2) **1891** *Cent.* 6930/3 *Wilson's bluebird,* the common eastern bluebird of the United States, *Sialia sialis.* — (3) **1869** *Amer. Naturalist* II. 597 Wilson's Owl (*Otus Wilsonianus*). . . . It seems to be generally distributed across the continent. — (4) **1844** *Nat. Hist. N.Y., Zoology* II. 290 Wilson's Petrel, . . . occurs commonly along our coast from Mexico to high northern latitudes. **1917** *Birds of Amer.* I. 85/1 Leach's Petrel and Wilson's Petrel are supplementary each of the other.

(5) **1828** BONAPARTE *Synopsis* 342. **1940** GABRIELSON & JEWETT *Birds Ore.* 275 Townsend (1839) first discovered Wilson's Phalarope, as he did so many other species, as an Oregon bird. — (6) **1838** BONAPARTE *Synopsis* 297 Wilson's Plover . . . inhabits the sea shores of the southern and middle states during summer. **1917** *Birds of Amer.* I. 266 Wilson's Plover looks like a bleached and faded copy of the Semipalmated. — (7) **1839** PEABODY *Mass. Birds* 368 Wilson's Sandpiper . . . is found, in its season, on all the shores and in all the markets of the Union. — (8) **1857** *Rep. Comm. Patents: Agric. 1856* 159 The summer range of Wilson's snipe . . . extends northward far beyond the limits of the United States. **1883** *Cent. Mag.* Aug. 485/2 The woodcock and Wilson snipe are fated to disappear as civilization robs them of their restricted feeding-grounds. *c***1945** HOPKINS *Okefenokee* 46 There are many areas in Okefenokee suitable for and occupied by Wilson's snipe . . . but pursuing snipe in any area in Okefenokee is an arduous task. — (9) **1917** *Birds of Amer.* I. 60 Common Tern. . . . Sea Swallow; Wilson's Tern.

(10) **1839** PEABODY *Mass. Birds* 306 Wilson's Thrush . . . is described by Nuttall as a common bird, resembling the wood thrush in its voice and song. **1941** SETON *Trail of Artist Naturalist* 185 Beyond any doubt now, it was Wilson's thrush, the veery. — (11) **1902** WHITE *Blazed Trail* 296 Wilson's warblers, pine creepers, black-throats . . . passed silently or noisily, each according to his kind. **1949** *Amer. Forests* Sep. 44/3 Warblers range from Lucy's . . . to the black-capped, bright yellow pileated warbler, which is relative to the eastern Wilson warbler.

Wilsonian wɪlˈsonɪən, *a.* Of or pertaining to Woodrow Wilson (1856–1924), 28th President (1913–21) of the U.S. Also **Wilsonism,** *n.*

1920 *Harvey's Wkly.* 16 Oct. 13/1 No more time need be lost in following the slush-fund herring trail away from the vital issue of Wilsonism. **1924** *Amer. Mercury* Jan. 53/1 It was at this precise moment in his career that the Wilsonian storming of Valhalla began. **1948** *Ga. Review* Spring 3 We followed the Wilsonian leadership in the crusade to make the world safe for democracy.

∗**win,** *v.* In colloq. phrases: (1) *To win beef*, to shoot so well at a shooting match as to secure beef as a prize, *obs.;* (2) *to win out*, to be successful (see also quot. 1938); (3) *to win hands down*, to win decisively; (4) *to win by a nose*, to win by a narrow margin; (5) *to win in a walk*, see ∗**walk,** *n.* **6.** (2).

(1) **1835** Longstreet *Ga. Scenes* 217 He called his rifle the Soap-stick, and . . . he was very confident of winning beef with her. — (2) **1896** *Voice* 9 April 4/5 McKinley will lead on the first ballot, but 'who will win out' is a different question. **1923** Herrick *Lilla* 72 'Old Lil' had won out! **1938** Asbury *Sucker's Prog.* 17 Winning out—Betting on a card which won four times in one deal. — (3) **1896** *Internat. Typog. Union Proc.* 24/2 A cut down of about 25 per cent . . . was successfully resisted by me winning 'hands down.' — (4) **1907** *St. Nicholas* Sep. 997 (*legend*), Won By a Nose! Score 10 to 9.

∗**Winchester,** *n.* [Oliver F. *Winchester* (1810–80), Amer. manufacturer.] A breech-loading rifle, usu. of a lever-loading, tubular magazine type, manufactured by the Winchester Arms Co. In full **Winchester (repeating) rifle.**

1871 *Standard* 1 Feb., The arms . . . being the Remington and the Chassepot, with some few Winchesters. **1877** in Fleming *Hist. Reconstruction* II. 79 There was issued . . . a large number of Winchester rifles. **1885** *Outing* VII. 18/1 From the dead Chircahuas had been taken four nickel-plated, breech-loading Winchester repeating rifles. **1947** *Sat. Ev. Post* 14 June 20/2 [He] denounces railroads, barbed wire fences and the Winchester rifle.

b. *attrib.* Denoting particular makes of Winchesters or ammunition for such guns.

1886 *Outing* April 7/1, [I] had with me, the little forty-sixty Winchester saddle gun. **1902** White *Blazed Trail* 148 Wallace's rifle chambered the .38 Winchester cartridge. **1945** *New Yorker* 25 Aug. 19 Across his lap was an old .22 rifle, a Winchester octagonal-barrel pump gun.

∗**wind,** *n.* In combs.: (1) **wind auger,** a wind laden with sand that bores holes in a bluff or cliff; (2) **break,** any one of various obstacles or barriers, as a row of trees, a hill, etc., that break the force of the wind or give protection from it; (3) **breaker,** (*a*) =prec., (*b*) a jacket, usu. of leather, having elastics at the hips and cuffs, also (*cap.*) a trade-mark name for such a jacket; (4) ∗**fall,** a heap of blown-down trees, a tract upon which the trees have been leveled by a tornado; (5) **fish,** (*a*) (see quot.), (*b*) the fallfish, *Leucosomus corporalis;* (6) **gap,** a gap or notch in a mountain ridge not occupied by a stream; (7) **jammer,** (*a*) a loquacious person, hence **wind-jamming,** *slang*, (*b*) a sailing vessel; (8) **pox,** ?chicken pox, *obs.;* (9) **reef,** an appearance on the surface of a river like that of a reef but caused merely by the wind; (10) ∗**row,** =**windfall;** (11) ∗**screen,** =**windbreak;** (12) **shield,** in automotive vehicles, a shield, usu. of glass, extending across the vehicle in front to protect the occupants from wind, rain, etc., also attrib.; (13) **ship,** (see quot.), *obs.;* (14) **slash,** =**windfall;** (15) **splitter,** a thing so shaped or so rapid in its movements as to suggest cleaving the wind, also **wind-splitting,** *a.*, *jocular*, cf. **b.** (2) below; (16) **-town,** a nickname for Chicago, *obs.*, cf. **Windy City;** (17) **wagon,** =**wind ship,** *obs.;* (18) **work,** talk, discussion, planning, etc., that precedes active work on an undertaking.

(1) **1870** F. H. Ludlow *Heart of Continent* 170 Second, as to the force of the wind-auger. — (2) **1861** *Ill. Agric. Soc. Trans.* IV. 449 These trees, which are valuable as shade and as wind-breaks, should be planted. **1948** *Democrat* 19 Aug. 7/4 The planting of tree wind-breaks is one practice of many used for control of wind erosion. — (3) (*a*) **1873** Beadle *Undevel. West* 730 If there is any wind-breaker northwest, between there and Alaska, I had no evidence of it. **1893** *D.N.* I. 334 *Wind breaker:* a screen or the like used to break the force of the wind. [N.J.] (*b*) **1934** Webster. **1949** *Trail Riders Bul.* March–April 14/2 For this added protection we suggest a stout leather jacket or windbreaker. — (4) **1816** D. Thomas *Travels Western Country* (1819) 157 Though *windfalls* would let in the sun and air, and be attended by a similar diminution of moisture, we recollect no such tracts in the Western Country. **1948** *Sierra Club Bul.* March 17 Whenever the way was lost in windfalls, we dropped our packs and ranged up and down hill until another promising game trail was located.

(5) (*a*) **1842** *Nat. Hist. N.Y., Zoology* IV. 192 The Variegated Bream. *Abramis versicolor.* . . . The name of Wind-fish is derived from one of its habits. Whenever a light flaw of wind ruffles the water, thousands of these fish may be seen darting to the surface, and as suddenly disappearing. (*b*) **1891** *Cent.* 6935/2 *Windfish*, the fall-fish, or silver chub, . . . the largest cyprinoid of eastern North America. **1896** Jordan & Evermann *Check-List Fishes* 246 Wind-fish; Corporal. Abundant from St. Lawrence River to the James, east of the Alleghanies. — (6) **1769** Smith *Tour* 78 Leaving Otters at 7 oCloc we passed thro the Wind Gap and stopt at Easton. **1836** W. O'Bryan *Travels* 98 We passed through what is called the *wind gap*, a chasm in the same ridge of mountains before spoken of. **1949** *Nat. Geog. Mag.* July 8/1 And today 'wind gaps' through the Blue Ridge are monuments to the Shenandoah's piracy. — (7) (*a*) **1893** *Columbus* (O.) *Dispatch* 7 Aug., The few workers present are effectually playing the part of windjammers and many rumors are afloat. *Ib.* Oct. 5 Could this power of wind-jamming have been saved there would have been some good accruing from the extra session. (*b*) **1899** *Harmsworth's Mag.* March 102 A large three-masted wind-jammer was caught by the gale and disabled. **1904** Dolf Wyllarde *Captain Amyas* vi. (*Cent. Supp.*), I went for a voyage in a sailing-ship once, for my health. What is it you call them? Windjammers? — (8) **1868** *N.Y. Herald* 1 July 5/6 The children were all well, with the exception that they had the wind pox and were weakly. — (9) **1876** Mark Twain *Old Times* iii. 56 It wasn't a bluff reef. . . . It wasn't anything but a wind reef. The wind does that.

(10) **1829** Cooper *Wish-ton-Wish* ii, Here and there [was] a wind-row, along which trees had been uprooted by the furious blasts which sometimes sweep off acres of our trees in a minute. **1942** Rich *We Took to Woods* (1948) 25 Acres of trees are piled up like jackstraws in windrows forty feet high and half a mile long. — (11) **1858** Warder *Hedges & Evergreens* 240 The common Cedar is . . . much used . . . where a quick, permanent, and effective wind-screen is wanted. **1887** *Cent. Mag.* March 740/2 That department . . . was nearly surrounded by a wind-screen of hemlock boughs and odd pieces of canvas. — (12) **1927** *Sat. Ev. Post* 24 Dec. 56/2 Each has extra wide windshield . . . and windshield wiper. **1950** *Chi. D. News* 12 Jan. 20/7 You are sitting behind a flimsy windshield, strapped to a cushion. — (13) **1847** *Sangamo Jrnl.* (Springfield, Ill.) 22 April 2/3 'The 'Wind Ship,' or a large schooner, is nearly completed at Independence. What will the Indians say when they see the Land Schooner blowing along over the prairies? — (14) **1886** *N.Y. Times* 13 April (*Cent.*), All persons having occasion to . . . start a fire in any old chopping, wind-slash, bush or berry lot, . . . shall give five days' notice. **1905** *Forestry Bureau Bul.* No. 61, 53 Windfall, an area upon which the trees have been thrown by wind. . . . Syn.: blow down, wind slash.

(15) **1890** Allen in *Harper's Mag.* Dec. 58/2 A tall thinnish man, with . . . a white wind-splitting face. **1893** M. A. Owen *Voodoo Tales* 28, I seed dem ole win'-splittehs (wind-splitter)—(the name in the vernacular of a species of long, lean hog that ranges half-wild). [**1900** *Daily Express* (London) 13 July 6/6 The 'wind-splitting train was tested over the line between Baltimore and Washington recently. *Ib.*, The wind-splitter . . . keeps up a wonderful pace, but glides along as if on glass.] — (16) **1903** *Cin. Enquirer* 2 Jan. 3/1 The majority of Windtown's baseball writers doubted the possibility of peace when the project was broached. — (17) **1884** Hill *Colo. Pioneers* 34 As it gracefully approached us we saw that it was what was called in those days a 'wind wagon'—a wagon fitted out with sails and rudder like a ship. — (18) **1873** Beadle *Undevel. West* 130 The wind-work is all done, and grading will commence about September first. **1888** J. Kirkland *McVeys* 56 Do you know what the natives call 'the wind-work' of a railroad? . . . Talk, talk, talk about funds, about legislation, about right of way.

b. In colloq. phrases: (1) *To throw up in(to) the wind*, to bring into an unsettled state; (2) *to split the wind*, to go with great speed, cf. *to burn the wind*, *s.v.* ∗**burn,** *v.* **2.** (3), and see **wind-splitter.**

(1) **1809** *Steele P.* II. 612 Sectry Smith has quarrelled with Jackson, and thrown the whole business '*again up in the wind.*' **1810** *Ib.* 640 [He] proceeded from a disposition to . . . throw the whole business *up into the wind again.* — (2) **1856** *Porter's Spirit of Times* 27 Sep. 55/3 The veteran 'Columbus' . . . was there, and split the wind, showing the crowd that age had not crept into his heels.

winding blade(s). A step in dancing. *Obs.* — a**1846** *Quarter Race Ky.* 179 He even introduced a *new* step, which would be as difficult to describe as to perform. He called it the *windin blades.* **1848** Judson *Mysteries N.Y.* I. 91 Every step in the hornpipe, fling, reel, &c., was brought in . . . and, then, to close up, the richest step of all . . . the winding-blade.

∗**window,** *n.*

1. An opening in a canebrake. *Rare.*

1855 *Harper's Mag.* Oct. 604/1 After crossing one or two lagoons, the hunters came to a 'window,' and among the matted limbs of trees and cane the dogs halted.

2. In combs.: (1) **window casing,** a window frame or case, cf. ∗**casing 2;** (2) ∗**pane,** an exceptionally thin, translucent flounder, *Lophopsetta maculata*, cf. **New York plaice;** (3) * **sash,** (see quot.); (4) * **screen,** a screen, consisting usu. of mesh wire mounted on a light frame, placed in a window frame to bar out flies, mosquitoes, etc., when the window is open; (5) **shade,** = * **shade,** *n.* **2;** (6) **trimmer,** a window dresser, also **window trimming.**

(1) **1848** JUDSON *Mysteries N.Y.* 448 (We.), The flowers were twining up around the window casings. **1906** GUNTER *Prince in Garret* ix, The gaunt Ambigue slips an agile leg over the window casing, and climbs into his own apartment. — (2) **1873** T. GILL *Cat. Fishes E. Coast N. Amer.* 17 *Lophopsetta maculata.* . . . Spotted turbot; window-pane (New Jersey). **1884** GOODE *Fisheries* I. 199 The Spotted Sand Flounder, . . . variously known along the coast as Water Flounder, Window-pane, and Daylight. — (3) **1903** ADAMS *Log Cowboy* 92 [We] cut out three head in the blotched brand called the 'Window Sash.' — (4) **1892** *Vt. Agric. Rep.* XII. 135 [There are] mills manufacturing . . . furniture and window screens. **1907** *St. Nicholas* May 614/1 We tried to buy wire netting—the sort we use for window screens at home.

(5) **1827** *Norfolk* (Va.) *Herald* 8 Aug. 1/1 A Few of the above very neat and convenient Window Shades are still remaining on hand. **1944** *Sears Cat.* (ed. 189) 684 How to measure for window shades. — (6) **1910** *Chambers's Jrnl.* Aug. 512/1 Mr. W. W. Sawyer . . . was originally a window-trimmer in the cities of Chicago, Milwaukee, and Portland. **1926** *Publishers' Wkly.* 22 May 1676/1 Window-trimming.

As the last term in **bay, doghouse, show, store window.**

* **windowy,** *a.* Having many or large windows. — **1863** G. HAMILTON *Gala-Days* 353 The homes of the students . . . [were] formal, stiff, windowy, bricky. **1888** *Harper's Mag.* June 130/2 Several large, ugly, windowy wooden bulks grew up for shoe shops.

Windsor tie. A broad silk double-bow tie. — **1912** LONDON *Smoke Bellew* 147 He went on dressing, with fingers that had lost their deftness, tying a Windsor tie in a bow-knot at the throat of his soft cotton shirt. **1913** ——— *Valley of Moon* II. xii, The Windsor tie had disappeared from under his soft turned-down collar.

Windy City. Chicago, Ill., a nickname. Cf. **Windtown.** — **1887** *Courier-Journal* 31 Jan. 5/1 A Gauzy story of an Alleged Anarchist Dynamite Plot from the Windy City. **1948** *News-Dispatch* (Michigan City, Ind.) 3 April 9/3 The handsome Windy City youngster has an enormous following.

* **wine,** *n.* In combs.: (1) **wine brick,** in prohibition (*q.v.*) days, dehydrated grapes pressed into the shape of a brick to be used in making home-brew; (2) * **bush,** (see quot.); (3) **card,** a list of wines available in a hotel, restaurant, etc., *obs.;* (4) * **grape,** any one of various grapes used in making wine, also attrib.; (5) **room,** = next, *obs.;* (6) **saloon,** a saloon where wine is sold, *obs.;* (7) **sap,** a variety of medium-sized, roundish, deep-red winter apple, or a tree bearing such apples; (8) * **tree,** a local name for mountain ash.

(1) **1932** *K.C. Star* 7 Jan. 20 The story is told that a Larned citizen, importuned to buy a wine brick because it was indorsed by Mabel Willebrandt. — (2) **1921** HALL *Yosemite Nat. Park* 251 Along the streams at the same altitudes is the Wine Bush or Sweet Shrub (*Calycanthus occidentalis*). — (3) **1851** M. REID *Scalp Hunters* ii, Whenever I took up a wine-card or a pencil, these articles were snatched out of my fingers. **1852** *Harper's Mag.* V. 267/1 Summer visitors to the favorite watering places are not unapt to call for a wine-card. — (4) **1775** ADAIR *Indians* 228 Hemp, and wine-grapes grow there [340 miles n.w. of Charleston] to admiration. **1869** *Rep. Comm. Agric. 1868* 212 What varieties are in highest repute as wine grapes? **1913** LONDON *Valley of Moon* 509 This is a wine-grape valley.

(5) **1903** *Nation* 20 Aug. 144/1 The campaign has begun with the 'wine rooms,' which in St. Louis represent the means of approach to vice of all sorts. — (6) **1851** HALL *Manhattaner* 99 They are all among the notable characters of New Orleans most seen at the opera, . . . who, for the gratification of curiosity neglect the commodious wine-saloon up-stairs. — (7) **1817** W. COXE *Fruit Trees* 153 Winesap. This is one of our best cider fruits. **1895** CRADDOCK *Mystery Witch-Face Mt.* 111 The red-freighted boughs of an old winesap bent above the girl's head. **1945** *Sat. Review* 5 May 7/2 Winesaps sirupt and seared with sun. — (8) **1860** CURTIS *Woody Plants N.C.* 70 Mountain Ash . . . is called *Wine Tree* (from a kind of liquor said to be made from it). **1897** SUDWORTH *Arborescent Flora* 211 *Pyrus americana* . . . , Mountain Ash. . . . [Also called] Wine Tree (N.C.).

As the last term in **California, Catawba, eclipse, maple, mustang, Ohio, Pomona, scuppernong wine.**

Winebrennerians ˌwaɪnbrəˈnɛrɪənz, *n. pl.* [Named for the founder, Rev. John *Winebrenner* (1797–1860).] (See quot. 1884.) — **1867** DIXON *New Amer.* II. 309 No sect escaped this rage for separation, . . . neither River Brethren, nor Winebrennarians. **1884** SCHAFF *Religious Encycl.* III. 2538 Winebrennerians, the popular designation of a Baptist denomination officially called 'The Church of God.'

winery ˈwaɪnərɪ, *n.* An establishment for making wine. — **1882** *Harper's Mag.* Dec. 55/1 The road to the large substantial buildings of the winery was bordered by a deep orchard of oranges. **1950** *Chi. Tribune* 9 Oct. 1/1 Six wineries and one of the world's largest grape juice plants . . . are operating 24 hours a day to catch up with the bumper crop of grapes.

* **wing,** *n.* **1.** *Baseball.* A pitcher's pitching arm. *Slang.* **2. wing dam,** a dam or barrier built out into a stream to deflect or deepen the current, also attrib. and fig. **3. wing sweep,** a plow which has winglike extensions for increasing the width of furrow cut, cf. * **sweep,** *n.* **1.**

(1) **1912** C. MATHEWSON *Pitching* viii, 169 Always he wears on his right hand, which is his salary or decision wing, a large diamond. — (2) **1809** FESSENDEN *Pills Poetical* 36 His rhetorick was directed towards . . . wingdam bills. **1836** J. HALL *Statistics of West* 45 Wing-dams [thrown] from each side of the river . . . confine the current within narrow bounds. **1945** FUGINA *Upper Miss.* 1 The boat was sent to Winona to get provisions and to bring a barge load of brush for use in the construction of wing dams. — (3) **1854** *Fla. Plantation Rec.* 553/1, 5 Wing Sweapes.

As the last term in **blue, broad, buck and, duck, gay, golden, machine, May, pigeon, red, salary, turkey, white wing(s).**

wing-dam, *v. tr.* To provide (a mining claim or river) with a wing dam. Hence **wingdamming,** *n. Obs.*

1853 *Mt. Echo* (Downieville, Calif.) 12 Feb. 2/4 It was dammed and wing-dammed in '50 and '51, and in '52 it was flumed and mostly worked, yielding good wages. **1856** *Spirit of Times* 6 Sep. 13/1 The bar opposite the city presents . . . [a] lively appearance . . . [with] fluming, wingdamming, and Chinamen washing with rockers. **1882** *47th Cong.* 1 Sess. H.R. Ex. Doc. 223 Other attempts to flume or wing-dam the river have been only partially successful.

* **winged,** *a.* **1. winged dam,** = **wing dam. 2. winged elm,** the cork elm, *Ulmus alata.*

(1) **1850** *S.F. Picayune* 31 Aug. 3/1 From a winged dam, which was worked last year, and had filled up again, $6 to $10 a day was taken. — (2) **1820** GILLELAND *Ohio & Miss. Pilot* 257 *U. alata* (winged elm) peculiar to the shores of French Broad river in Tennessee. **1901** MOHR *Plant Life Ala.* 89 Box elder, winged elm, willow, . . . shade the rocky banks of the swift mountain stream.

winklehawk. *local.* [Du. *winkelhaak,* in same sense.] A right-angled tear in cloth. *Obs.* — **1848** BARTLETT 386 *Winkle-Hawk.* (Dutch *winkel-haak.*) A rent in the shape of the letter L, frequently made in cloth. **1850** JOHNSTON *Notes* II. 297 A lady will also lament that she has got a *winkelhawk* in her gown.

wink-up ˈwɪŋkˌʌp, *n.* A kind of party game. *Obs.* — **1825** *Lincoln Intelligencer* (Wiscasset, Me.) 24 June, All things become dull by satiety So for *wink-up* they cried one and all.

Winnebago ˌwɪnəˈbego, *n.* [Thought to be f. some native term suggestive of "filthy water." Cf. Sac and Fox *winnĭpyägohagi,* "people of the filthy water." But see quot. 1640.] An Indian of a Siouan tribe first encountered by Europeans in Wisconsin, on Green Bay; *collect.* or *pl.* the tribe of such an Indian. Cf. **Puants.**

[**1640** *Jesuit Rel. & Allied Doc.* XVIII. 230 Ces peuples se nomment Ouinipigou, pource qu'ils viennent des bords d'vne mer dont nouns n'auons point de cognoissance.] **1778** CARVER *Travels* 37 The Winnebagoes raise on it a great quantity of Indian corn, beans, pumpkin, squash, and water melons. **1812** *Niles' Reg.* II. 6/2 Two young Winibiegoes . . . went near some of the American sentinels, and were shot at. **1888** WHITMAN *Nov. Boughs* 409 There were Omahas, Poncas, Winnebagoes. **1910** HODGE *Amer. Indians* II. 958/1 The Winnebago have been known to the whites since 1634, when the Frenchman Nicollet found them in Wisconsin, on Green bay. *a***1947** MARTIN *Indians* 317 The Oneota Indians have been identified with the Winnebago in Wisconsin.

attrib. **1827** *Spirit of Seventy-Six* (Frankfort, Ky.) 2 Aug. 2/1 An express reached here this moment from Galena . . . with information of hostilities having been commenced by the Winnebago Indians, on the settlers. **1855** OLIPHANT *Minnesota* 228 We passed the Winnebagoe village of Watab. **1945** *This Week Mag.* 14 April 11/3 He was born near Millston, Wis., a member of the Winnebago tribe. **1948** *Highway Traveler* Aug. 43/1 The Winnebago Indians hold their ceremonial dances nightly at the Stand Rock Amphitheater.

For **Winnebago courting flute,** see **courting flute** (quot. 1833).

b. The language of this tribe. *Obs.*

1860 *Harper's Mag.* Sep. 568/2 As he could not speak Winnebago, the first thing to be done was to find an interpreter. **1945** RADIN *Road to Life & Death* vii, I need hardly stress the difficulty attendant upon a translation of Winnebago.

*** winter,** *n.* In attrib. or adjectival uses.

1. Designating places occupied by, or involved in trading operations with, Indians in winter. *Obs.*

1775 ADAIR *Indians* 322 A hunting camp of the Chikkasah went out to the extent of their winter-limits. **1835** HOFFMAN *Winter in West* I. 189 Several winter lodges of the Pottawattamies . . . were plainly perceptible over the plain. **1877** *Rep. Indian Affairs* 15 The winter camp of this chief was about two hundred miles north. **1912** *Out West* Feb. 110/1 Here the winter hogan is built, circular in form, constructed of logs and the limbs of trees, banked with earth with a doorway opening towards the East, and a smoke vent in the roof. **1948** *Trailways Mag.* Fall 30 Behind them is a winter hogan.

2. In the names of, or with reference to, plants: (1) **winter bell,** (see quot.), *obs.;* (2) **berry,** (see quot. 1891), cf. **Virginia, Virginian winterberry;** (3) **cane,** ?the small cane, genus *Arundinaria,* found in the South, *obs.,* cf. **winter reed;** (4) **clover, =partridgeberry;** (5) **fat,** sweet sage, *Eurotia lanata,* a small shrub of the Southwest, valued as forage in winter; (6) **grape,** the chicken grape, *Vitis cordifolia;* (7) **grass,** a specific variety of grass that grows in winter, or any winter-growing grass; (8) ***-green,** see as a main entry; (9) **huckleberry, =farkleberry;** (10) **reed, ?=winter cane,** *obs.;* (11) **squash,** any one of various squashes, as the crook-necked and Hubbard *qq.v.,* grown to be kept for winter use.

(1) 1855 *Amer. Inst. N.Y. Trans. 1854* 430 Rarely does any but the winter bell [a pear] . . . hang upon its branches. — **(2) 1759** MILLER *Garden Dict.* (ed. 7), *Prinos.* Winterberry. **1891** *Cent.* 6943/3 *Winterberry,* . . . a name of several shrubs of the genus *Ilex,* belonging to the section (once genus) *Prinos,* growing in eastern North America. **1930** *Sat. Ev. Post* 13 Dec. 37/1 Quantities of delicate asparagus ferns come up from the South, as well as . . . bayberry from Cape Cod; winterberry and the black-green inkberry—both holly relatives from other parts of the East. — **(3) 1797** B. HAWKINS *Letters* 88 We encamped near a small branch, the north side of which was well stored with winter cane. — **(4) 1846** SAGE *Scenes Rocky Mts.* xxvii, The larb-berry is . . . a small ground-vine of evergreen, with a leaf assimilating the winter-clover in shape, and is found only in mountainous regions.

(5) 1909 SCHNEIDER *Woody Plants Pike's Peak* 144 The most conspicuous and often the largest of the plains' woody plants is the winter fat. **1948** *Ecological Monographs* April 171/1 Winterfat, *Eurotia lanata,* with its silvery-gray foliage, is found in scattered areas. — **(6) 1771** WASHINGTON *Diaries* II. 43 Began to Plant Cuttings of the Winter Grape. **1862** *Rep. Comm. Patents 1861: Agric.* 484 The Winter grape is frequently a high climber. **1949** *Amer. Photography* April 244/2 Winter grape (*Vitis bicolor*), is one of our commonest species from northern New York to Michigan and North Carolina. — **(7) 1794** S. WILLIAMS *Hist. Vt.* 24 Trees thus diminished . . . and a species of grass called winter grass, . . . are all the vegetable productions, which nature brings forth on the tops of our highest mountains. **1850** *Rep. Comm. Patents 1849: Agric.* 157 The 'winter-grass' of this region [Washington, Miss.], the nearly universal *Poa annua,* . . . [reaches] a height of from four to eight inches. — **(9) 1934** WEBSTER. **1941** R. S. WALKER *Lookout* 60 Farkleberry, or winter huckleberry, is a common shrub whose wood is close-grained, hard, and whose limbs are contorted.

(10) 1800 HAWKINS *Sk. Creek Country* 44 They call this the winter reed, as it clusters like the cane. — **(11) 1775** *Boston Transcript* 26 April III. 12/7, I have a fine prospect of a Crop of Rusty Coats Portators and winter Squashes this fall. **1809** E. A. KENDALL *Travels* III. 109 The vine of a species of pompion, called by the colonists *winter squash,* (*cucurbita melopepo,*) yielded last year a hundred and fifty-five pounds. **1949** *Hist. & Philos. Soc. Ohio Bul.* April 70 Corn and winter squash he planted on May 16.

3. In the names of birds and other animals: (1) **winter chip-bird,** (see quot.); (2) **flounder,** a small, edible American flounder, *Pseudopleuronectes americanus;* (3) **hawk, =red-shouldered hawk;** (4) **shad,** see ***shad 3;** (5) **snipe,** the dunlin or the purple sandpiper; (6) **wren,** a small American wren, *Nannus hiemalis hiemalis,* cf. **eastern winter wren;** (7) **yellowleg(s),** the greater yellowlegs, *Totanus melanoleucus.*

(1) 1891 *Cent.* 6943/3 *Winter chip-bird,* the tree-sparrow, *Spizella monticola,* which comes into the United States in the fall. — **(2) 1814** MITCHILL *Fishes N.Y.* 387 [The] New-York Flatfish . . . is called the winter flounder. **1911** *Rep. Fisheries 1908* 310/1. — **(3) 1831** AUDUBON *Ornith. Biog.* I. 364 The Winter Hawk is not a constant resident in the United States. **1917** *Birds of Amer.* II. 74.

(5) 1844 *Nat. Hist. N.Y., Zoology* II. 240 In the autumn, . . . its plumage is so changed that it obtains another name, and is then called Winter Snipe. **1917** *Birds of Amer.* I. 232, 237. — **(6) 1808** WILSON *Ornithology* I. 139 [The] Winter Wren . . . frequents the projecting banks of creeks. **1942** WEYGANDT *Plenty of Penna.* 107 It is not a loud song, this of the ruby-crown, incredible in a small bird, as is the song of the winter wren. — **(7) 1844** *Nat. Hist. N.Y., Zoology* II. 250 The Varied Tatler . . . is the Big Yellow-leg, or Winter Yellow-leg of our sportsmen. **1917** *Birds of Amer.* I. 244/1 There is a widespread idea that these birds appear later in the autumn than the Lesser Yellow-legs, so that they are much called 'Winter Yellow-legs.'

4. In miscellaneous combs.: (1) **winter comfortable,** a comfortable or comforter *qq.v.;* (2) **count,** a pictographic historic record, usu. painted on hide and consisting of a series of symbolic figures, made by Plains Indians; (3) **dairy,** a dairy operated in winter; (4) **fever,** some now unidentifiable fever prevailing in winter, *obs.,* cf. **winter sickness;** (5) **kill,** plant death caused by the cold of winter, also attrib., cf. **winterkill,** *v.;* (6) **pemmican,** (see quot. and cf. **pemmican**); (7) **privilege,** (see quot.), *obs.;* (8) **rancheria,** the winter home of Indians in the Southwest; (9) **range,** an area that affords grazing for cattle in winter; (10) **saint,** one of those who stopped over during the winter among the Mormons rather than risk crossing the Sierra Nevada mountains at that season, *obs.;* (11) **sickness,** ?influenza, *obs.,* cf. **winter fever;** (12) **succotash,** (see quot.); (13) **yard, =moose yard.**

(1) 1878 R. T. COOKE *Happy Dodd* 42 Mrs. Dodd made a bed for them out of her winter comfortables in the little attic. — **(2) 1901** *Smithsonian Rep. 1900* 67 The calendars, or winter-counts . . . play so large, yet so obscure a role in Indian life. **1937** *Southwestern Lore* Sep. 39 Three of the figures from the 'Winter Counts' have left hand pointing down, a sign of death. — **(3)** *a***1858** in C. FLINT *Milch Cows* 233 The process for the winter dairy is similiar [*sic*] to that of the summer. **1894** *Vt. Agric. Rep.* XIV. 37, I would not know how to manage a winter-dairy without a winter silo. — **(4) 1874** GLISAN *Jrnl. Army Life* 444 They would be prostrated by various forms of malarious fever—such as . . . winter-fever. **1932** JAMES BUCKNER BARRY *Texas Ranger* 167 The company was further handicapped [in 1864] by sickness of some thirty men with typhoid and winter fevers.

(5) 1845 *Farmers' Cabinet* 15 Feb. 202/2 It is not so hardy as some varieties: it is more subject to winter-kill. **1947** *Chi. Tribune* 18 Oct. 1/7 Crop experts in each state reported a serious danger of a heavy winter kill this year. **1950** *Ib.* 12 July 19/2 In the area south of Carbondale they have had nine peach crops free of winterkill damage. — **(6) 1944** *Military Surgeon* Aug. 90/2 Winter pemmican was made in the autumn when it was hard to dry the meat and when usually the people were not planning to travel, so that weight and bulk did not matter. — **(7)** *a***1870** CHIPMAN *Notes on Bartlett* 514 Winter-Privileges, separate meetings from those in the central parochial church, allowed to be held by the people in out-districts—Former usage in Conn. — **(8) 1912** LUMHOLTZ *New Trails* 26 The winter rancherias are called *kihim,* where there are houses, (*ki*), and these might be called villages. **1925** BRYAN *Papago Country* 27 San Antone, a winter ranchería with a few Papago families, remains as the successor of Weldon. — **(9) 1874** J. C. MCCOY *Hist. Sk. Cattle Trade* 217 A large adjacent tract of land, embracing many thousands of acres, will be 'fire-guarded,' in order to secure a winter range from the ravages of prairie fires. **1948** *Sierra Club Bul.* May 11/1 Wildlife, for which there is already a deficiency in winter range, would be drastically affected.

(10) 1851 *Deseret News* (Salt Lake City) 25 Jan. 198/1 Afterwards the subject of those men who had come into our midst and become as the President observed 'winter saints' was taken up, and on motion [the following] were cut off from the church of Jesus Christ of L. D. S., for conduct unbecoming the character of saints. — **(11) 1847** DEWEES *Lett. From Texas* 303 The winter sickness . . . generally commences with a bad cold and terminates in pneumonia. — **(12) 1850** *N. Eng. Farmer* II. 66 Winter Saccatash.—This is made of dried shelled beans, and hard corn. — **(13) 1893** ROOSEVELT *Wilderness Hunter* 215 The winter-yard is usually made . . . on high ground, away from the swamps.

As the last term in **blackberry, dogwood, shad, squaw winter.**

*** wintergreen,** *n.* Any one of various American evergreen shrubs of the genus *Gaultheria,* esp. *G. procumbens.*

1817–8 EATON *Botany* (1822) 287 *Gaultheria hispidula,* creeping wintergreen—stem creeping. **1876** T. HILL *True Order of Studies* 81 Our American plant Gaultheria is called in some sections Wintergreen. **1949** *Jrnl. Mammalogy* Aug. 227 Wintergreen (*Gaultheria procumbens*) and partridgeberry (*Mitchella repens*) are also common.

b. wintergreen berry, the edible scarlet berry of *Gaultheria procumbens.*

1810 M. DWIGHT *Journey to Ohio* 46 We found winter green berrys in abundance. **1938** DAMON *Grandma* 62 Sometimes a shingle vessel, heavily laden with a priceless cargo of wintergreen berries sagaciously commanded by a June bug.

As the last term in **common, false, flowering, spotted wintergreen.**

* **wintering,** *n. attrib.*

1. Designating places occupied in the winter by Indians. *Obs.*

1804–5 CLARK in *Lewis & C. Exped.* VI. (1905) 61 [From Fort Mandan] to Menatarras Wintering Village. **1807** GASS *Journal* 51 At the mouth of this river is a wintering camp of the Rickarees of 60 lodges. **1817** BRADBURY *Travels* 51, I set out . . . at sunrise, for the wintering house.

2. a. wintering ground, the ground or place where an individual or party spends the winter. **b. wintering post,** a post or station at which a military force spends the winter. Both *obs.*

(a) 1808 PIKE *Sources Miss.* 33 This day's march made me think seriously of our wintering ground. **1852** REYNOLDS *Hist. Illinois* 190 Mr. Hay got out into the wintering ground, and erected his quarters for winter. — **(b) 1823** in *S. Dak. Hist. Coll.* I. 192 Part of the men . . . deserted from their wintering post at the Big Horn. *c***1836** CATLIN *Indians* II. 149 [Camp Des Moines] is the wintering post of Colonel Kearney.

winterkill ˈwɪntɚˌkɪl, *v.*

1. *tr.* To kill (plants) by exposure to the cold of winter.

1817 S. BROWN *Western Gazetteer* 49 That wheat . . . never gets winter-killed or smutty. **1918** *Nation* 7 Feb. 129/2 Though the farmers sowed a million acres more winter wheat than ever before, . . . much has been winter-killed. **1946** PEASE *Sequestered Vales* 73 Where the scrub has been winterkilled . . . the blanched skeletons become horny, weird, and ghostly in shape and color.

b. Also used of animals.

1860 *Mountaineer* (Salt Lake City) 30 June 178/1 Should we indulge our feeling in a few remarks on the cause of *winter-killed* stock, our readers would not be benefitted by our reflections.

2. *intr.* Of plants or crops: To die from exposure to the cold of winter.

1846 EMMONS *Agric. N.Y.* I. 281 The grain very rarely winter-kills. **1918** VISHER *So. Dakota* 56 Red clover is not a success in most of South Dakota largely because it winter-kills in this manner.

Hence **winterkilling,** *n.*

1845 *Farmers' Cabinet* 15 Jan. 195/1 This blight is not to be confounded with *winter-killing.* **1876** *Ill. Dept. Agric. Trans.* XIII. 308 The young growth [of wheat] was less luxuriant, . . . and winter-killing became more common.

Wintun wɪnˈtun, *n.* [Native word meaning "Indians," "people."] *collect.* or *pl.* One of the two divisions of the Copehan family of Indians in California.

1874 in *Overland Mo.* 1 Ser. XII. 530 Their name Wintoon (accent the ultimate) denotes 'Indians,' or 'people,' and it is one of which they are somewhat proud. **1903** JAMES *Indian Basketry* 57 On the upper Sacramento and upper Trinity still remain the Wintuns, many of whom are known as Pitt River Indians. **1910** HODGE *Amer. Indians* II. 963/1 Powers thought the Wintun were originally a sort of metropolitan tribe for the whole of N. California below Mt Shasta.

* **wire,** *n.*

1. =**barbed wire.** Also *under wire,* fenced with barbed wire.

1885 *South Fla. Sentinel* (Orlando) 8 April 2/2 J. M. Bryan, M. C. Osborn and W. D. Moore have received 6 tons of wire with which to fence in a large portion of their 2000 A. ranch. **1919** HOUGH *Sagebrusher* 6 She's all under wire—the Swede done that before I bought his quit claim. **1927** RUSSELL *Trails* 86 There ain't no wire in the country them days an' it's smooth sailin.' **1947** PRICE *Trails I Rode* 222 He grabbed the wire, trying, and cut his hand on the wire.

2. In horse racing, an imaginary line marking the finish, usu. in phrases.

1887 *Courier-Journal* 5 May 1/1 Eva K., Little Munch . . . were first under the wire. **1920** SANDBURG *Smoke & Steel* 138 He flashed his heels to other ponies . . . and hardly ever came under the wire behind the other runners. **1948** *Dly. Racing Form* (Chi.) 29 June 1/4 The Headleyite . . . began to falter when nearing the wire.

Also *transf.* **1950** *Keowee Courier* (Walhalla, S.C.) 31 Aug. 2/2 Baseball season is coming down to the wire, and the leading teams in the American league are about as close as two Scotchmen on bargain day.

3. A telegraphic dispatch, a telegram. Also attrib. *Colloq.*

1930 FERBER *Cimarron* 368 She made a practice of . . . scanning the A.P. wires. **1950** *Time* 1 May 17/1 The three wire-service men jumped up, and pushed their way to the door.

4. In combs.: (1) **wire binder,** a harvesting binder using wire instead of twine to bind sheaves, *obs.;* (2) **clipper,** =**wire cutter** (*a*); (3) **cutter,** (*a*) pliers for cutting wire, (*b*) one who cut wire fences in the West during the fence war *q.v.*, *obs.;* (4) * **edge,** *fig.* initial embarrassment or enthusiasm; (5) **ferry,** a ferryboat making use of a wire in crossing a river, cf. **rope ferry;** (6) **gold,** native gold in the form of wires or threads, cf. **wire silver;** (7) * **grass,** see as a main entry; (8) **house,** a brokerage house which has private telegraph wires connecting it with exchanges and perhaps with branches; (9) **jerker,** a telegrapher, *slang, obs.;* (10) **puller,** one who "pulls wires," esp. one who uses underhanded methods of political manipulation; (11) **pulling,** intrigue, underhanded manipulation, freq. in political affairs; (12) **silver,** native silver in the form of threads or wires, cf. **wire gold;** (13) **spool,** a wooden structure somewhat like a large spool upon which wire, esp. barbed wire, is wound, also such a structure made of wire; (14) **stretcher,** (see quot. 1876); (15) **tapper,** one who taps, or pretends to tap, a telegraph or telephone wire for the purpose of getting prior information as to the results of races, thus being able, or pretending to be able, to bet on a sure thing; (16) **taste,** a tape with fine wire woven into it, used in millinery work, *obs.;* (17) * **weed,** (see quot. 1894); (18) **worker,** a wirepuller, a party worker.

(1) 1902 *Scientific Amer.* (Supp.) 20 Dec. 22546/3 It would cost more to harvest grain with a wire binder. — **(2) 1920** WILSON *Somewhere* 109 That fresh bunch of campers . . . had a pair of wire clippers in the whip socket. — **(3)** (*a*) **1876** KNIGHT 2790/1 *Wire-cutter,* a nippers for cutting off wire. **1936** *Sears Cat.* (ed. 173) 887 Staple puller, wire splicer, pincher, cutter and hammer . . . 67c. (*b*) **1888** in WEBB *Great Plains* (1931) 314 While a man was putting up his fence one day in a hollow a crowd of wire-cutters was cutting it behind him in another hollow. — **(4)** *c***1804** BRACKENRIDGE *Mod. Chivalry* (1926) 214 In the course of mixing with good company, the wire edge of art would wear off, and an ease of demeanor be attained. **1838** COOPER *Home as Found* 352 [It was formerly] much in a rule for the legal tyro to take off the wire-edge of his wit in a Fourth of July oration. **1903** A. ADAMS *Log Cowboy* 203 Most of the boys had worn off the wire edge for gambling.

(5) *a***1918** G. STUART *On Frontier* II. 102 Went down ten miles to Huntley and crossed the river on a wire ferry. — **(6) 1880** *Cimarron News & Press* 9 Sep. 2/3 The rock is . . . full of wire gold. **1949** *10 Story Western* May 73/2 It's rich diggin's. Lumps of free gold. Wire gold shooting through all the quartz. — **(8) 1904** *N.Y. Ev. Post* 18 June, The so-called 'wire house' . . . is a product of the boom times. — **(9) 1875** *Chi. Tribune* 22 Aug. 16/1 A slim-looking, smooth faced individual . . . informed him that he was the wire-jerker [in a telegraph office].

(10) 1832 *Boston Transcript* 24 Jan. 2/1 Every thing went on swimmingly, till it occurred to the 'wire pullers' to hand round the hat, for the purpose of obtaining the wherewith to defray contingent expenses. **1889** *Cent. Mag.* March 791/2 The choice of a Senate . . . can generally be fixed by wire-pullers in advance. — **(11) 1847** *Cong. Globe* 26 Jan. 262/3 Neither by demonstrations here, nor by figuring and wire-pulling at home, am I engaged to the support of this bill. **1911** HARRISON *Queed* 220 Through much subtle wire-pulling, he got himself put on the toast list. **1949** *Time* 12 Sep. 19/1 It was much lower-grade stuff—a record of bumbling, chiseling, and shabby wire-pulling. — **(12) 1878** BEADLE *Western Wilds* 483 Wire silver . . . looks like a mass of tangled hair turned to pure silver. **1926** LORD *Frontier Dust* 168, I saw one bunch or mass of wire silver at Creede. — **(13) 1936** BARNARD *Rider* 207 We rustled some wire spools as we had no chairs. **1936** *Sears Cat.* (ed. 173) 953 Every spool guaranteed to contain full 80 rods. . . . Wire spools do not break or come apart like wooden spools. **1950** *Nat. Geog. Mag.* Jan. 77/2 A wire spool hanging on a fence post spelled out 'Chicago, Illinois.' — **(14) 1876** KNIGHT 2797/2 *Wire-stretcher,* a tool for straining lightly telegraph or fence wires. **1949** *Democrat* 8 Dec. 8/4 See if you can find part of my wire stretcher.

(15) 1894 *Columbus* (O.) *Dispatch* 5 Jan., The wire tappers escaped. **1910** O. HENRY *Strictly Business* 36 Who wears the diamonds in this town? Why, Winnie, the Wiretapper's wife, and Bella, the Buncosteerer's bride. — **(16) 1820** *Columbian Centinel* 1 April 4/3 Wire Taste for Millinery, will be sold . . . at reduced prices. — **(17) 1884** CRADDOCK *Where Battle Was Fought* 75 [She] gazed far away at the billowy sweep of the wire-weeds. **1894** *Amer. Folk-Lore* VII. 91 *Aster* *diffusus*, . . . Gray, white devil, wire-weed, devil weed, . . . West Va. — **(18) 1835** *Jamestown* (N.Y.) *Jrnl.* 10 June 1/3 The wire workers lacked sense. **1883** WILDER *Sister Ridnour* 130 The politician grasps the hand of his wire-worker and tool.

b. In colloq. phrases: (1) *To pull* (*the*) *wires*, or variants, to manipulate or control as one does puppets attached to wires, to exert influence, usu. in political contexts; (2) *to lay wires for*, to make preparations for.

(1) 1813 *Ann. 12th Congress* 2 Sess. 562 When those who pulled the wires saw fit, they passed away. **1894** ROBLEY *Bourbon Co., Kans.* 180 Political meetings and conventions caucused and pulled wires. **1913** LA FOLLETTE *Autobiog.* 46 There was no influence they did not use; no wires they did not pull. — **(2) 1908** *N.Y. Ev. Post* (s.-w. ed.) 12 Nov. 1 Woodruff began to lay wires for the coming Senatorial vacancy.

As the last term in **baling, barbed, bob, bonnet, cap, cattle, fencing, hay, hog, live, monkey, party, picket wire.**

*** wire grass.**

1. A European meadow grass, *Poa compressa*, naturalized in the U.S.

1751 ELIOT *Field-Husb.* iii. 61 The Land that you would improve this way, must be intirely free from Blue Grass, called by some Dutch Grass, or Wire Grass. **1878** KILLEBREW *Tenn. Grasses* 163 Wire Grass . . . is very hardy, and, even in paths that are trodden it does well.

2. *S.* Anyone of several coarse grasses, esp. *Aristida stricta.*

1775 ROMANS *Nat. Hist. Fla.* 16 The most natural grass on this soil is of a very harsh nature, and . . . is known by the name of wire grass. **1883** SMITH *Geol. Survey Ala.* 540 Coarse tufts of wire-grass form the undergrowth almost universally. **1947** *Jrnl. Wildlife Management* 53/2 And 'wiregrass' has some value as food, but is used more extensively for muskrat lodges or 'houses.'

attrib. **1847** *Knickerb.* XXIX. 202 Let him go . . . into the 'wire-grass' region. **1893** *Outing* Jan. 270/2 Shilling is a diminutive plow-horse of the wire-grass breed. *c***1945** HOPKINS *Okefenokee* 51 In this wire grass predominantly open woods section of Georgia, the fearfulness of forest fires is overestimated.

b. (*cap.*) The region in Georgia and Alabama where this grass abounds. Also attrib.

1905 *Montgomery Wkly. Advt.* 17 Feb. 3 The main run of land throughout the Wiregrass is clayed and sandy. **1946** *Nat. Speleological Soc. Bul.* July 45/2 It cost the humorist five dollars . . . , this amount being paid to a local Wire Grass doctor.

3. (*a*) A cultivated grass, *Eleusine indica*, (*b*) (see quot. 1885).

(*a*) **1840** DEWEY *Mass. Flowering Plants* 245 *Eleusine.* . . . Wire Grass. . . . From Eleusis, a name of Ceres, the goddess of grasses. **1894** *Amer. Folk-Lore* VII. 104. (*b*) **1878** *Rep. Indian Affairs* 157 The land is . . . full of alkali with flats of wire-grass. **1885** HAVARD *Flora W. & S. Texas* 529 The most common grass on bottoms and low prairies is *Hilaria mutica*, sometimes called Wire-Grass.

4. Soil that produces wire grass.

1869 *Overland Mo.* III. 130 In Texas . . . there is . . . the 'hummock,' (yielding principally small honey-locusts) and the 'wire-grass.'

wirework ˈwaɪrˌwɜk, *v. tr.* To persuade or make use of (a person) by wirepulling methods. Also **wire-working,** *a.* and *n.*, conniving, obtaining ends by underhanded means. *Obs.*

1831 *American* (Harrodsburg, Ky.) 28 Jan. 3/2 One of the *wire-working* writers in the Union, seems disposed to consider it a little less than treason. **1843** J. Q. ADAMS *Diary* 547 Mr. James Monroe was recalled by President Washington through Thomas Pickering, wireworked by Alexander Hamilton. **1857** HAYES *Pioneer Notes* (1929) 167, I have kept aloof from the wire-working as well as from the more stormy scenes of politics.

***wiry,** *a.* **1. wiry edge,** =**wire edge. 2. wiry grass region,** a region in the Southeast where wire grass grows. Both *rare.* — **(1) 1833** CROCKETT *Sketches* 93 The fight had just taken off the wiry edge. — **(2) 1887** *Courier-Journal* 12 Jan. 2/6 The wiry-grass region is infested by a band which has stolen millions of acres of the finest timber lands in the State.

Wisconsin wɪsˈkɑnsn̩, *n.* [See note.]

The origin of this state and river name is not clear. Webster derives it from Algonquian and cites Ojibway *Wishkonsing*, place of the beaver or muskrat hole. Stewart, in *Names on the Land*, p. 88, thinks it is an English form of the French *Ouisconsing*, f. the Indian name of the Wisconsin River. A Smithsonian Institution release for July 25, 1937, says the word is impossible of explanation.

1. In combs.: (1) **Wisconsin drift,** *geol.* drift deposited during the glacial epoch known as the Earlier or Later Wisconsin; (2) **gravy,** (see quot.), *obs.*

(1) 1915 LEVERETT & TAYLOR *Pleistocene of Ind. & Mich.* 27 In the Green Bay lobe of Wisconsin the Wisconsin drift overlaps the border of the Illinoian. **1948** *Iowa State Coll. Jrnl. Science* Oct. 104 Beneath the Wisconsin drift lies blue clay. **1950** *Ill. State Hist. Soc. Jrnl.* Spring 29 The Wisconsin Drift, however, did not benefit all parts of the state equally. — **(2) 1877** in *Amer. Sp.* XXII. 300 Johnny cake for supper, with its usual concomitant, 'Wisconsin gravy.' This was manufactured by taking a little flour or meal and stirring it in water, making a thin paste, which they spread on the corn bread.

2. Wisconsinite, Wisconsinonian, a native or inhabitant of the state of Wisconsin.

1861 *Dly. Dispatch* (Richmond, Va.) 1 Aug. 3/2 It extends its impulse to the Gaelic column in advance, and likewise set the Wisconsinonians on fire, and the three regiments went forward from that moment with one continuous shout. **1934** WEBSTER. **1949** *Reader's Digest* May 37/1 My husband and I . . . had always been impressed by the state pride of . . . Wisconsinites.

*** wise,** *a.*

1. *To be* (or *get*) *wise to*, to be or become aware of. *Slang.* For *to put* (someone) *wise*, see *** put,** *v.* **3. b.** (12).

1896 G. ADE *Artie* ii. 14, I told him that when he wanted to get wise to what was in my hand all he had to do was to dig up his bit and come in. **1901** H. MCHUGH *John Henry* 69 When I hear a poolroom comedian speaking lines about getting seasick on the B. & O., I'm wise to the fact that he dips in the Farmers' Almanac for his comedy stuff.

2. a. wisecrack, a silly, smart-alecky remark. **b. wise guy,** a know-it-all, a smart aleck. Both *slang.*

(a) 1926 *Scribner's Mag.* Aug. 117/2 They have been makin' wisecracks about His Majesty. **1947** *Dly. Oklahoman* (Okla. City) 5 Nov. 5/4 What wisecrack would he have shot at us on a dozen differences in the United Nations. — **(b) 1896** G. ADE *Artie* xvi. 150 He was the wise guy and I was the soft mark. **1949** *Democrat* 2 June 2/4 Why don't you call up your friend, . . . wise guy?

As the last term in **bridle, saddle wise.**

wise waɪz, *v.* [f. *** wise,** *a.* **1.**] *To wise up*, to "get" or "put" wise. *Slang.*

1905 REX BEACH *Pardners* iv. (1912) 107, I cast the bad eye on the boys to wise 'em up. **1923** J. L. VANCE *Baroque* vii. 40, I ain't sayin' who wised us up. **1950** *World-Herald* (Omaha) 23 April 1/2 Don't even have to shoot anymore. They've wised up.

wisecrack ˈwaɪzˌkræk, *v. intr.* To make wisecracks. Also **wisecracking,** *n.*

1928 *Chi. Tribune* 13 Dec. 12/4 The editor . . . wisecracked as follows. **1932** *K.C. Times* 15 April 20 The old bus drew . . . comment and wisecracking from his friends. **1948** *Sat. Ev. Post* 23 Oct. 132/3 There wasn't any horseplay or wisecracking now.

wishtonwish ˈwɪʃtənˌwɪʃ, *n.* ["The name . . . was applied by the Caddoan tribes of Louisiana from the cry uttered by the animals" (Hodge).]

1. =**prairie dog.**

1808 PIKE *Sources Miss.* (1810) ii. 156, I have seen the Wishtonwish, the rattle snake, the horn frog, . . . and a land tortoise all take refuge in the same hole. **1895** GERARD in *N.Y. Sun* 30 July, Wishtonwish, a Western Algonquian name for the prairie dog. The name implies an animal that burrows in company with others, that is, in communities.

2. =**whippoorwill.** *Obs.*

It is thought that Cooper was in error in applying this name to the whippoorwill. The quot. from De Vere may be based on Cooper.

1826 COOPER *Last of Mohicans* xxii, ''Tis a pleasing bird, . . . and has a soft and melancholy note,' . . . 'He speaks of the wish-ton-wish,' said the scout. **1829** ——— *Wish-ton-Wish* xvii, The Whip-poor-Will; a name that the most unlettered traveller in those regions would be likely to know was vulgarly given to the Wish-Ton-Wish or the American nighthawk. **1872** DE VERE 375 Thus also *Whip-poor-will*, universally pronounced *Whipperwill*, is an adaptation rather than an imitation of the original sound, like the Wish-ton-wish, Willy-come-go, and Who-are you, all names applied to various species.

Wistaria wɪsˈtɪrɪə, *n.* [Caspar *Wistar* (1761–1818), Amer. anatomist.] A small genus of large woody vines belonging to the pea family. Also (not *cap.*) a plant or flower of this genus. Cf. **American wistaria.**

Nuttall (see 1st. quot.) through an error used the spelling *Wisteria*, which still sometimes occurs.

1818 NUTTALL *Genera N. Amer. Plants* II. 115 Wisteria. . . . In memory of Caspar Wistar, M.D. late professor of Anatomy in the University of Pennsylvania. **1833** EATON *Botany* (ed. 6) 259 *Wistaria tuberosa*, ground-nut. . . . Root very nutritious. . . . Ought to be generally cultivated. **1842** LOUDON *Suburban Hort.* 376 Vines, roses, Wistarias, or other luxuriant climbers. **1943** PEATTIE *Great Smokies*

166 Some, like . . . the black locust with its drooping clusters of flowers like some white wisteria's, are tall foresters. **1950** *Reader's Digest* Jan. 84/1 Their loud-speakers blared boogie-woogie into the jasmine and wistaria.

Also **wistaria vine.**

1888 HARRIS *Free Joe* 199 A wistaria vine running helter-skelter across the roof of the little cabin. **1950** *Newsweek* 10 April 77/1 It thereupon occurred to Logan to capitalize on the analogy between the disintegration of the Czarist Russia and the passing of the Old South, and substitute wisteria vines.

Wistar party. [See prec.] In Philadelphia, a social gathering of men for the discussion of current subjects.

1829 B. HALL *Travels N. Amer.* II. 340, I shall never forget these agreeable and instructive Wistar parties at Philadelphia. **1918** H. L. CARSON *Centenary Wistar Party* 1 This evening's gathering commemorates the Centenary of the Wistar Party, a purely voluntary association of twenty-four gentlemen, without a charter, without a club house, without even a club room or club possessions, but held together by the mysterious and potent charm of a distinguished name, and a fixed rule that eligibility to membership requires an existing membership in The American Philosophical Society. **1942** WEYGANDT *Plenty of Penna.* 138 There was Joseph Dennie's Tuesday Club. There were the Wistar parties.

***witch,** *n.* In combs.: (1) **witch alder,** (see quot. 1895); (2) **City,** Salem, Mass., in allusion to the witchcraft delusion in 1692; (3) **grass,** the quitch-grass or couch-grass, *Agropyrum repens*, also tumble grass, *Panicum capillare*, also attrib., cf. **old witch grass;** (4) **hazel,** see as a main entry; (5) **hopple,** =**hobblebush;** (6) **stick,** a divining rod, cf. **doodle-bug b, hoodoo stick.**

(1) **1817–8** EATON *Botany* (1822) 282 *Fothergilla alnifolia*, witch alder. **1895** *Stand. Dict.* 2073/2 Witch-alder, a shrub (*Fothergilla Gardeni* or *alnifolia*) of the witch-hazel family. — (2) **1910** *Boston Sun. Globe* 3 July 32/1 Captain William Driver of Salem, . . . sailed from the port of the Witch City in December of 1831. — (3) **1790** S. DEANE *N.-Eng. Farmer* 230/2 Quitch-Grass, called also Witch-Grass, Twitch-Grass, Couch-Grass, Dutch-Grass, and Dogs-Grass, a most obstinate and troublesome weed. **1833** A. GREENE *Life D. Duckworth* II. 71 All their writin is like pussly and witch-grass—you never can know where to find it. **1946** *Progress* March 43/1 Probably the most troublesome weed, quack grass—also called witch grass or couch grass—makes a nourishing hay that is relished by cattle.

(5) **1840** HOFFMAN *Greyslaer* II. 44 Tangled thickets of moss wood and wytch-hopple gave now the springy footing the tired hunter loves. **1943** PEATTIE *Great Smokies* 283 This is the hobblebush or witch hobble, an abundant high-mountain shrub whose large rounding leaves reach their color peak in September. — (6) **1930** FERBER *Cimarron* 320 Men prowled the plains with divining rods, with absurd things called witch sticks, hoping thus to detect the precious stuff beneath the earth's surface.

witch hazel.

1. An American shrub, *Hamamelis virginiana.* Also the bark of this or an extract made from it.

1588 HARIOT *Briefe & True Report* Elv Those weapons y they haue, are onlie bowes made of Witch hazle, & arrowes of reeds. **1671** *S.C. Hist. Soc. Coll.* V. 333 Here is some holly, elder, & witch hazell. **1778** CARVER *Travels* 508 The Witch Hazle grows very bushy, about ten feet high. **1850** *Knickerb.* XXXVI. 388 Get out in the woods and scrape enough witch-hazel to make you some more ink. **1919** HOUGH *Sagebrusher* 70 Can't you put some witch hazel on your knee?

2. Attrib., esp. with reference to the use of parts of the shrub in locating water, gold, etc. Cf. **doodle-bug b, hoodoo stick.**

1847 DARLINGTON *Weeds & Plants* 144 Hamamelaceae. (Witch-hazel Family.) Shrubs or trees with alternate, simple leaves. **1848** PARKMAN in *Knickerb.* XXXI. 400, I would like to have one of those fellows . . . go about with his witch-hazel rod . . . [to locate] a gold mine. **1873** MARK TWAIN & WARNER *Gilded Age* 272 A witch-hazel professor . . . could walk over the land with his wand and tell him infallibly whether it contained coal. **1894** ROBINSON *Danvis Folks* 179, I should admire tu know if he ever tried the myraculous paower of a witch hazel crotch. . . . I c'n find veins of water with 'em. **1904** TARBELL *Hist. Standard Oil Co.* I. 24 In January there had suddenly been struck on Pithole Creek . . . a well, located with a witch-hazel twig.

withdrawal card. A card made out when one withdraws from a union. — **1874** *Internat. Typog. Union Proc.* 15 A member taking a Withdrawal Card severs his connection with the Union, and vacates any office he may hold in the Union. **1895** *Ib.* 35/1, [I] settled by having these proprietors take out withdrawal cards.

withe rod. An American shrub, *Viburnum nudum.* Also attrib.

1847 WOOD *Botany* 302 Withe Rod. . . . A shrub or small tree, 10–15 f[eet] high. **1943** PEATTIE *Great Smokies* 265 We recognize the . . . withe rod, trailing arbutus, chokeberry and wintergreen. **1949** *Sat. Ev. Post* 12 March 50/4 We would get out the dinner and look for some little withe-wood forks to impale our slices of fresh pork or mutton on, and soon dinner would be ready.

***witness,** *n.* In combs.: (1) **witness corner,** in surveying, a tree, post, rock, etc., having a recorded bearing on the corner of a tract; (2) **stand,** in a court room, the place, usu. a somewhat elevated stand beside the judge's bench, occupied by a witness when giving testimony; (3) **tree,** (see quot. 1845).

(1) **1917** KEPHART *Camping* II. 68 Witness corners bear the same marks as those of true corners, plus the letters *W. C.* — (2) **1885** CABLE *Dr. Sevier* 208 The arresting officer mounts to the witness-stand. **1947** MOTLEY *Knock on Any Door* 377 Gleason put his big hand on the rail of the witness stand and ignored Nick's hating eyes. — (3) **1845** KIRKLAND *Western Clearings* 3 The corners [are] especially distinguished by stakes whose place is pointed out by trees called

Witness tree or bearing tree

Witness-trees. **1947** *Harper's Mag.* July 85/1 About the corner he blazed witness trees in a circle facing the post and inscribed on them the date and his mark.

wiz WIZ, *n.* Short for "wizard." *Slang.*

1915 *Chi. Herald* 2 Nov. 4/2 Palmer, you know, had shown himself a regular wiz. **1924** W. M. RAINE *Troubled Waters* xiii. 142 Millie done fixed my game laig up with that ointment good as new. I want to tell you-all that girl is a wiz. **1928** SINCLAIR LEWIS *Man Who Knew Coolidge* I. 36 Cousin Ed—he thinks he's such a wiz at cars, but Lord love you, he couldn't locate that squeak.

***wizard,** *n.* As the last term in **Grand, hazel, water wizard.**

wob wɑb, *n.* [Short for **wobbly.**] *collect.* The members of the I.W.W. Also attrib. *Slang.* — **1923** *Nation* 29 Aug. 217 Send it to *The Nation*, where it will reach people who need to understand the Wob. **1926** *Amer. Mercury* Jan. 65/2, I got canned for selling wob papers.

wobbly ˈwɑblɪ, *n.* [Origin obscure. The suggested derivation f. Chinese distortion of *I.W.W.* into *I wobbly wobbly* lacks confirmation.] A nickname for a member of the I.W.W. *Slang.*

1914 *Voice of People* (Portland, Ore.) 1 Oct. 2/4 The workers are . . . asking why the wobblies are not holding meetings. **1948** *Houston* (Tex.) *Post* 14 June 6/5 The I.W.W. (or 'Wobblies' 'I Won't Work'), were outright exponents of class warfare.

attrib. and *transf.* **1921** *Outing* Nov. 94/3, I saw an angel and the devil standing side by side. The devil wore a 'Wobbly' (I.W.W.) button. **1929** ZORBAUGH *Gold Coast & Slum* 114 Chicago is the 'wobbly' capital of America. **1947** *Harper's Mag.* Nov. 468/2 The [conscientious objectors'] camp was thought of as divided between the 'politically-conscious' and the 'religious wobblies.'

wo-haw ˈwoˌhɔ, *n. W.* Beef or cattle for beef, orig. so called by the Indians from the "whoa! haw!" of the drivers of ox teams across the plains. *Colloq.*

1885 SIRINGO *Texas Cow Boy* 124 They used to try and scare Asa into giving them 'wo-ha's (cattle).' **1929** *Texas Mo.* Jan. 124 They would ask for 'wo-hah,' by which they meant beef. **1944** ADAMS *W. Words* 179/1 Rarely did a trail herd pass through the Indian country on its march north that it was not stopped to receive a demand for *wohaw.* This demand became so common that the cattlemen themselves began to use the word and it became a part of their vocabulary.

Also **wo-haw John.**

1936 BARNARD *Rider* 43 Thirty Indians rode up as we started and said they wanted 'wo-haw John!'

wokas ˈwokəs, *n.* [f. a name used by some of the Indians in Oregon for the great yellow water-lily or its seed.] The seeds of a yellow water-lily of the West,

Nuphar polysepalum, dried and roasted for use as food by the Indians.

1878 *Rep. Indian Affairs* 114 By the time this crop is harvested and put away, the wookes (the seed of the pond-lily) is ripe and ready for them. **1881** *Ib.* 144 This lake . . . produces in abundance a small seed known by the name of 'wocus.' **1902** *Nat. Museum Rep.* 728 The Indians harvest their crop of wokas, or waterlily seed.

* **wolf,** *n.* In combs.: (1) **wolfberry,** (see quot. 1891); (2) **bullet,** ?a bullet for shooting wolves, *obs.;* (3) **castle,** an area inclosed by dense and nearly impenetrable shrubbery, *obs.;* (4) **dance,** an Indian dance in which the participants imitate the actions of wolves, *obs.;* (5) **eel,** a long wolf fish, *Anarhichthys felis,* found on the California coast; (6) **hook,** a device for catching wolves, now *hist.;* (7) **Pawnee,** one of the tribes of the Pawnee confederacy, so called from their tribal name "Skidi" *q.v.;* (8) **pen,** an inclosure made of logs for trapping wolves, a cage or inclosure for the exhibition of wolves; (9) **pit,** a pit prepared as a trap for wolves; (10) **robe,** (see quot. 1891), also **wolf's robe;** (11) **scalp,** a portion of skin from a wolf's head, taken as evidence of the killer's claim to a bounty, also **wolf scalp hunter;** (12) **tail,** a disease of cattle; (13) * **trap,** a dive where greenhorns are fleeced, *obs.*

(1) [**1834** G. DON *Gen. System Gardening* III. 451.] **1847** WOOD *Botany* 300. **1891** *Cent.* 6959/3 *Wolfberry,* a shrub, *Symphoricarpos occidentalis,* of northern North America, in the United States ranging from Michigan and Illinois to the Rocky Mountains. **1940** CASSADY & GLENDENING *Revegetating Semidesert Range Lands* 1 These areas are often characterized by . . . a rather sparse stand of . . . southwestern jujube, wolfberry, . . . chollas and burroweed. — **(2) 1636** *Mass. H. S. Coll.* 2 Ser. VIII. 229 An account of certain ammunition . . . 6 wolf bullets with adders tongues. — **(3) 1853** SIMMS *Sword & Distaff* (1854) 81 The place in which the latter found himself was a sort of wolf-castle. — **(4) 1908** *Sunset Mag.* April 566/1 [He went] among the Shoshone tepees to an unexpected entertainment—a wolf-dance. **(5) 1884** GOODE *Fisheries* I. 250 This species is commonly known as the 'Eel,' or 'Wolf-eel,' the latter name probably having been given by some one familiar with the Atlantic Wolf-fish. — **(6) 1636** *Mass. H.S. Coll.* 2 Ser. VIII. 229 An account of certain ammunition . . . 200 wolfhooks, 20 wolfhooks to hang. **1891** A. M. EARLE *Sabbath* 12 This was a great number, for the wary wolf was not easily destroyed either by musket or wolf-hook. — **(7) 1818** *Lynchburg* (Va.) *Press* 7 Aug. 2/6 The Wolf Pawnees are the only tribe who offer up human sacrifices to the object of their worship. **1910** HODGE *Amer. Indians* II. 216/1 Four tribes of the Pawnee confederacy still survive: the Chaui or Grand Pawnee, the Kitkehahki or Republican Pawnee, the Pitahauerat or Tupage Pawnee, and the Skidi or Wolf Pawnee. **1946** FOREMAN *Last Trek* 302 The Skidi (Pani Loups, Panimaha) was one of the tribes of the Pawnee Confederacy sometimes called Wolf Pawnee, and by the French, Pawnee Loup. — **(8) 1647** *Watertown Rec.* I. I. 12 The Towne gaue: to John Witherll: there Right in the palisado that inclosed the woulfe pen. **1835** A. PARKER *Trip to Texas* 52 A man on Fox river . . . made a wolf pen over a cow that got accidentally killed, and caught twelve wolves in one week! **1876** INGRAM *Centennial Exp.* 106 The places of interest are . . . the Aviary, the Fox-Pens, the Wolf-Pens. — **(9) 1658** *Norwalk Hist. Rec.* 47 [They] have undertaken to make and provide a good and sufficient wolfe-pitt. **1835** AUDUBON *Ornith. Biog.* III. 339 Mine host . . . asked if I should like to pay a visit to the wolf-pits. **1948** DICK *Dixie Frontier* 106 The men were accustomed to dig a wolf pit and rid the country of 'varmints' before trying to raise sheep and tame hogs. **(10) 1857** GOVE *Letters* 12, I will send you a box, if I go on the plains, with the wolf robe and otter skins and such stuff as I think you will want. **1873** PHELPS *Trotty's Wedding* xix, Deb drew the great gray wolf's-robe over her face and head. **1891** *Cent.* 6960/1 *Wolfrobe,* . . . the skin or pelt of a wolf made into a robe for use in carriages, etc. — **(11) 1800** in ROTHERT *Muhlenberg Co.* 116 Sharp Garness Brought before me . . . four Groan Wolf Sculps and proved them as the Law directs. **1847** ROBB *Squatter Life* 70 Among the wolf-scalp hunters of the western border of Missouri, . . . *Hoss* Allen is all *powerful* popular. **1891** *Fur, Fin & Feather* 187 One dollar each [is paid] for wolf scalp and fifty cents for coyotes. — **(12) 1879** *Diseases of Swine* 195 Cattle are afflicted with wolf-tail and hollow-horn. — **(13) 1938** ASBURY *Sucker's Prog.* 271 By 1832 half a dozen Wolf-Traps were in operation in Cincinnati, most of them near the steamboat landing and designed especially to ensnare the river men. *Ib.,* The Wolf-Traps gradually decreased in numbers, and by the early 1850's . . . dens of this character had well-nigh vanished from the city of their origin. **1948** DICK *Dixie Frontier* 165 While some establishments were run honestly, others were what came to be known as 'dead falls' or 'wolf traps.'

b. *ugly enough to tree a wolf,* quite homely. *Colloq.*

1830 ROYALL *Southern Tour* I. 133 She was small and ugly enough to tree a wolf.

As the last term in **barking, brush, buffalo, curly, gray, loafer, prairie, she, timber, white wolf.**

Wolfe hat. A kind of cocked hat, prob. so called from the frequent appearance, esp. in school histories, of the picture of Gen. James Wolfe (1727–59), wearing such a hat. *Obs.* — **1889** *Cent. Mag.* April 861/1 [Washington in his portrait] wears the cocked hat usually called the Wolfe hat.

wolfer ˈwʊlfɚ, *n.* A wolf hunter. *Colloq.* — **1871** *Rep. Indian Affairs* (1872) 410 A regular stampede took place out of that section of the country of 'wolfers' and whisky traders. **1947** *True* Nov. 91/1 With his camp established, the wolfer set out his baits.

wolfing ˈwʊlfɪŋ, *n.* **1.** Becoming a prey of wolves. *Rare.* **2.** The hunting of wolves. Also attrib.

(1) 1848 RUXTON *Life Far West* i, Some of 'em got their flints fixed this side of Pawnee Fork, and a heap of mule-meat went wolfing. — **(2) 1875** BUCKLAND *Log-Book* 109 When the wolfing season has commenced on the prairies, the hunter impregnates the carcase of a buffalo . . . with strychnine and places it in a likely position. *a***1918** G. STUART *On Frontier* II. 172 Wolfing became quite an important industry in Montana. **1943** L. V. HAMNER *Short Grass* 27 They had given up buffalo hunting . . . and were 'wolfing.'

* **wolfish,** *a.* Ravenously hungry, insatiable. *Colloq.*

1806 WEBSTER 352/2 *Wolfish* or *Wolvish,* like a wolf, ravenous. *a***1848** PORTER *Tales of Southwest* 121 (B.), They'd been fightin' the barrel of whisky mightily comin' up, and were perfectly wolfish arter some har of the dog. **1895** REMINGTON *Pony Tracks* 125 By 12 M. we acquire a wolfish yearning for the 'flesh-pots.'

wolfy ˈwʊlfɪ, *a.* Abounding in wolves, wolflike. Also *wolfy about the head and shoulders,* said of a "half horse half alligator." *Colloq.* or *slang.*

1828 *Western Souvenir 1829* 314 'Couldn't you take a pack or two of wolves along?' said Pete, sneeringly. 'We can spare you a small gang. It's mighty wolfy about here.' **1831** in MATHEWS *Beginnings* (1931) 116 Felt as tho' I should have to kiver myself up in a salt barrel to keep'—so Wolfy about the head and shoulders. **1839** PLUMBE *Sk. Iowa* 59, I might find some of the law-makers of Wisconsin . . . rather 'wolfy about the head and shoulders.' **1927** RUSSELL *Trails* 114 This talk makes the whole bunch wolfy.

* **wolverine,** *n.*

1. (*cap.*) A native or resident of Michigan, the Wolverine State. A nickname.

1834 *Sun* (N.Y.) 23 Aug. 3/2 In Kentucky they are called Corn Crackers. Ohio Buckeyes. . . . Missouri Pukes. Michigan T. Woolverines. **1904** *Grand Rapids Ev. Press* 23 June 3 Wolverines At Fair Many Michigan Persons Enjoy the St. Louis Show. **1949** *Amer. Sp.* XXIV. 300/1 As a Wolverine myself I am interested in information concerning it.

2. *attrib.* Designating things relating or pertaining to Michigan.

1843 CARLTON *New Purchase* II. 239 Like all hoosiery and woolverine things, they are regardless of dignities. **1847** *Cong. Globe* 5 Feb. 332/2 Set up a great Government bank — . . . a full-grown undeniable Wolverine wild-cat. **1852** *Mich. Agric. Soc. Trans.* III. 332 We have . . . about 10,000 things which Wolverine audacity have denominated swine.

3. Wolverine State, Michigan, a nickname.

The reason for the application of this nickname is not altogether clear. Wolverines, now extinct in Michigan, were never numerous there, if indeed there were any at all. See *Amer. N. & Q.,* March, 1944, 181–2, and cf. Wm. H. Burt, *The Mammals of Michigan* (1946) 143 ff.

1846 *Knickerb.* XXVII. 360 In the Wolverine state, on one occasion, Judge M— . . . was alone upon the bench. **1948** *Chi. Tribune* 8 Aug. 1/6 Eight railroads serving the Wolverine state will sponsor the day-long celebration.

* **woman,** *n.* **1. womanalls,** overalls for women. *Obs.* **2. woman's aid society,** a Ladies' Aid Society *q.v.,* also **women's-aid society. 3. women's department,** a part of a newspaper devoted to matters of interest to women. **4.** *To make a woman of,* to force someone to do the work of a woman, in allusion to an Indian's conception of a woman's role.

(1) 1917 *New Republic* 1 Sep. 132/1 The newspapers were photographing 'farmerettes,' and the department stores advertised a strange garment called 'womanalls.' — **(2) 1865** *Atlantic Mo.* June 676/2 Their names appeared . . . as liberal contributors to . . . women's-aid societies, to the sick and wounded soldiers. **1879** BURDETTE *Hawkeyes* 56 The woman's aid society . . . had been unable to fulfill their pledge to pay for the pew cushions. — **(3) 1875** C. F. WINGATE *Views & Interviews* 146, I . . . asked the editor to make a 'women's department' and give me charge of it. — **(4) 1742** *Pa. Col.*

Rec. IV. 579 We conquer'd You, we made Women of you. **1836** IRVING *Astoria* I. 221 Where was his squaw, that he should be obliged to make a woman of himself?

As the last term in **bird, breeding, buckra, bushel, business, club, Congo, conjure, end, fine, little, medicine, old, scrub, sucker, voodoo, war, yellow woman.**

* **wonder,** *n.*

1. *N. Eng.* (See quot. 1923.)

1845 *Knickerb.* XXV. 447, I gave my good aunt ocular assurance that her . . . 'wonders' were as acceptable as they used to be. **1859** STOWE *Minister's Wooing* iv, A plate of crullers or wonders, as a sort of sweet fried cake was commonly called. **1923** J. E. C. FARNHAM *Brief Hist. Data* 180 'Wonders' . . . were simply doughnuts made in a certain prescribed regulation form—cut out round, jagged across and separated in the center two or three times, but not cut through to the edge; made in that way the fat, while they were frying, passed between these jagged cuts, with the result of crisp, deliciously browned cross-pieces, so that the 'wonder' easily broke into such separate sections, or bars, and was peculiarly appetizing. **1944** DUNCAN *M. Graham* 4 She made wonders (doughnuts) to delight the tired children.

2. Wonder State, Arkansas, a nickname.

1927 *Haldeman-Julius Quart.* Jan. 80/2 In 1923 the general assembly passed an act proclaiming it to be the 'Wonder State.'

wonderation ˌwʌndəˈreʃən, *n.* Wondering, amazement. Also used in a mild oath. *Colloq.* — **1824** *Old Colony Memorial* (Plymouth) 6 March (Th.), O the wonderation, what a nation sight of jiggermarees! **1857** *Knickerb.* XLIX. 35, I passed the time in wonderation.

* **wood,** *n.*

1. *the woods,* the backwoods or "sticks." *Colloq.*

1845 COOPER *Chainbearer* xviii, What has an attorney to do with me and mine, out there in the woods? **1889** MARK TWAIN *Conn. Yankee* 309 You have lived in the woods, and lost much by it. **1916** EASTMAN *From Deep Woods* 152, I should have long ago gone back to the woods. **1942** RICH *We Took to Woods* (1948) 84 Housekeeping in the woods is —for me—not at all difficult.

transf. **1942** RICH *We Took to Woods* (1948) 17 Very often, in winter, woodsmen who are leaving the lumber camps call on us to take them and their turkeys—woods for knapsacks—up to Middle Dam.

2. In the names of birds: (1) **woodcock,** see as a main entry; (2) **duck,** the summer duck, *Aix sponsa,* also, locally, the hooded merganser; (3) **grouse,** (see quot. 1917); (4) **hen,** (see quot. 1891); (5) **ibis,** a bird of the stork kind, *Mycteria americana,* found in the swamps and bayous of the southern states; (6) **pelican,** =**wood ibis;** (7) **pewee,** an American tyrant flycatcher, *Myiochanes virens;* (8) **robin,** =**wood thrush;** (9) **sparrow,** =**field sparrow;** (10) * **thrush,** the swamp robin, *Hylocichla mustelina;* (11) **wagtail,** =**ovenbird;** (12) **warbler,** any one of various American warblers, esp. of the genus *Dendroica;* (13) * **wren,** (see quot. 1891).

(2) 1777 J. ADAMS in *Familiar Lett.* 272 Mr. Arnold's collection of . . . mooses, wood-ducks, . . . have all been thought of. **1815** *Lit. & Phil. Soc. N.Y. Trans.* I. 63 The wood duck, and prairie hen, have in many instances, been tamed. **1950** *Chi. Tribune* 17 May 6/2 The boxes attracted wood ducks to the ponds. — **(3) 1862** WINTHROP *J. Brent* 245 The brace of wood grouse he had shot that morning . . . had never made journey in a crowded box. **1917** *Birds of Amer.* II. 14 Hudsonian Spruce Partridge. *Canachites canadensis canadensis.* . . . [Also called] Wood Grouse; Wood Partridge. — **(4) 1891** *Cent.* 6965/3 The woodcock . . . also called *snipe . . . red woodcock, . . . wood-hen . . . bog-sucker* [etc.]. **1934** VINES *Green Thicket World* 49 Some folks call 'em wood hens.

(5) 1785 LATHAM *Gen. Synopsis Birds* V. 104 Wood Ibis. . . . Found in Carolina. **1813** WILSON *Ornithology* VIII. 39 The Wood Ibis inhabits the lower parts of Louisiana, Carolina, and Georgia; is very common in Florida. **1949** *Amer. Forests* Sep. 44/3 Flocks of wood ibises spend their post-nuptial season at Havasu each midsummer. — **(6)** *c***1731** CATESBY *Carolina* I. 81 *Pelicanus Americanus.* The Wood Pelican. *Ib., Pelicanus Sylvaticus.* The Wood Pelican. **1918** *Cambridge Hist. Amer. Lit.* I. 197 We see the solitary, dejected 'wood-pelican,' alone on the topmost limb of a dead cypress. — **(7) 1810** WILSON *Ornithology* II. 81 Wood Pewee Flycatcher. *Muscicapa rapas.* I have given the name Wood Pewee to this species. **1945** PEARSON *Country Flavor* 19 The wood peewees seem to sing more sweetly on fence-mending days. — **(8) 1808** WILSON *Ornithology* I. 29 Wood Thrush, *Turdus Melodus,* . . . is called by some the Wood Robin. **1890** *Harper's Mag.* Dec. 148/1 His voice was like a wood-robin. — **(9) 1858** *Atlantic Mo.* Dec. 864/2 While listening to the notes of the Wood-Sparrow, we are continually saluted by the . . . song of the chewink, or the Ground Robin. **1917** *Birds of Amer.* III. 43.

(10) 1791 W. BARTRAM *Travels* 181 How harmonious the shrill tuneful songs of the wood-thrush! *Ib.* 288 Turdus melodes; the wood thrush. **1948** *Green Bay* (Wis.) *Press-Gaz.* 13 July 11/4 In the evening the wood thrushes across the river sent out flutey calls to tell us about the shady woods there. — **(11) 1869** BURROUGHS *Wake-Robin* (1886) 198 The well-known golden-crowned thrush (*Seiurus aurocapillus*) or wood-wagtail. **1917** *Birds of Amer.* III. 152/1 The Ovenbird is known as the Wood Wagtail. — **(12) 1883** *Cent. Mag.* Sep. 727/2 [Striking color] is easily observable . . . in the . . . quill-feathers of the wood warbler. **1891** *Cent.* 6819/3 The Cape May warbler . . . in full plumage . . . is one of the handsomest of the wood-warblers. — **(13) 1839** AUDUBON *Ornith. Biog.* V. 469. **1891** *Cent.* 6970/3 *Wood-wren,* . . . a supposed species of true wren, described by Audubon in 1834 as *Troglodytes americanus,* but not different from the common house-wren of the United States. **1917** *Birds of Amer.* III. 192 House Wren. . . . Wood Wren. . . . Hollow limbs or trunks of fruit trees are also often utilized [for nesting].

b. Also in the names of other animals: (1) **wood bison,** (see quot. 1917), also **woodland bison;** (2) **buffalo,** =prec.; (3) **gray fox,** (see quot.); (4) **hog,** (see quot. 1805), *obs.;* (5) * **horse,** (see quot.), cf. **4.** (8); (6) **lizard,** ?a California newt, *rare;* (7) **pussy,** (see quot. 1899); (8) **rat,** any one of various native American rats of the genus *Neotoma,* found in the woods, cf. **Rocky Mountain wood rat;** (9) **rattlesnake,** prob. the timber rattlesnake *q.v.;* (10) **-s colt,** (see quot.), cf. **4. g.** (5) below; (11) **terrapin,** =next; (12) **tortoise,** a common North American tortoise, *Clemmys insculpta.*

(1) 1895 *Harper's Mag.* Dec. 10/2, I must pass on my way to the Barren Grounds; and *en route* to hunt wood-bison, undoubtedly now become the rarest game in the world. **1917** *Animals of Amer.* 41/2 Woodland Bison.—*Bison bison athabascae.* . . . Larger and darker than the typical Bison with longer, more slender horns. Found formerly in the wooded uplands from Great Slave Lake south probably to the United States. **1950** *Pacific Discovery* March–April 118/1 The North American bison is variously classified as Athabasca or wood bison, mountain, and plains bison. — **(2) 1820** HARMON *Journal* 366 Those that remain in the country between the Sisiscatchwin and Peace rivers, are called the wood buffaloes, because they inhabit a woody country; and they are considerably smaller than those, which inhabit the plains. They are, also, more wild and difficult to approach. **1892** *Scribner's Mag.* Sep. 277/1 The 'mountain' and 'wood' buffalo seem to be very much alike in habit and appearance. **1947** CAHALANE *Mammals* 81 The wood buffalo (*Bison bison athabascae*), which some authorities say is larger and darker in color, while others claim that the two cannot be distinguished. It was once found over a considerable area around Great Slave Lake and Peace River in Northwest Territories and northern Alberta. — **(3) 1840** EMMONS *Mass. Quadrupeds* 31 *Vulpes Virginianus* . . . is termed by furriers the Wood-gray Fox. — **(4) 1805** PARKINSON *Tour* 290 The real American hog is what is termed the wood-hog; they are long in the leg; narrow on the back, short in the body [etc.]. **1840** *Cultivator* VII. 81 The next fall, mast was plenty, and 'wood hogs' were fat.

(5) 1891 *Cent.* 5943/1 *Stick-bug,* . . . any orthopterous insect of the family *Phasmidæ:* particularly applied to *Diapheromera femorata,* . . . also called *wood-horse.* — **(6) 1850** in *One Man's Gold* (1930) 143 The day previous I killed two very ugly wood lizards [in California]. — **(7) 1899** *Animal & Plant Lore* 61 Wood pussy, skunk, *Mephitica mephitica.* Craigville, Mass. **1950** *Chi. D. News* 16 Feb. 5/1 Miss Bennet paid $35 for the deodorized house-broken wood pussy. — **(8) 1763** tr. DUPRATZ *Hist. Louisiana* II. 65 The *Wood-Rat* has the head and tail of a common rat, but has the bulk and strength of a cat. **1835** AUDUBON *Ornith. Biog.* I. 486 In search of small birds, field-mice, moles, or wood-rats. **1950** *Nat. Hist.* May 213/1 With his big ears, fluffy fur, and bushy tail, the wood rat is a captivating member of the alpine quartet. — **(9) 1843** OLIVER *Eight Months* 150 The inhabitants recognize two kinds of rattlesnakes, to wit, the wood- and the prairie-rattlesnake, or mississauga, of which the latter is much the smaller and less dangerous.

(10) 1903 *D.N.* II. 357 *woods-colt, n.* A horse of unknown paternity. [s.e. Mo.] — **(11) 1774** FITHIAN *Journal* I. 198 Tom the Coachman came in with a wood Tarripin. **1842** *Nat. Hist. N.Y., Zoology* III. 14 The Wood Terrapin . . . is a harmless species. — **(12) 1839** STORER *Mass. Reptiles* 209 E[mys] *insculpta.* Le Conte. The wood Tortoise, . . . This, our most beautiful tortoise . . . wanders a great distance from, and remains a long time out of the water; and being oftentimes found in woods and pastures, has received the common name of wood tortoise.

3. In the names of plants: (1) **wood aster,** any one of several asters, as *Aster cordifolius,* that grow in the woods of the eastern states; (2) **hair grass,** a wiry perennial grass, *Deschampsia flexuosa;* (3) **nettle,** an American herb, *Laportea canadensis,* found in fertile woods, cf. **Canada nettle.**

(1) 1833 EATON *Botany* (ed. 6) 37 *Aster ledifolius,* wood aster. . . . About a foot high. **1883** THAXTER *Poems for Children* 73 Where hides the wood-aster? — **(2) 1870** *Rep. Comm. Agric. 1869* 89 Wood hair grass . . . [is] of no agricultural value. **1878** Killebrew *Tenn. Grasses* 197 Wood Hair Grass . . . is readily eaten by cattle and sheep. — **(3) 1857** Gray *Botany* 398. **1882** *Harper's Mag.* Nov. 847/2 A nodding leaf upon the wood-nettle arrested my attention. **1901** Mohr *Plant Life Ala.* 477.

4. In miscellaneous combs.: (1) **wood-and-water station,** a place where a railway train stops for wood and water; (2) **camp,** a camp of woodcutters; (3) **chimney, =stick-and-clay chimney,** *obs.*, cf. **wooden chimney;** (4) **cutting,** cutting down trees for logs or firewood; (5) **fence,** a rail fence, *rare;* (6) ∗**fire, =forest fire;** (7) **-grinding mill,** ?a mill for grinding dyewood, *obs.*, cf. **wood mill;** (8) ∗**horse, =sawhorse,** cf. **2. b.** (5) above; (9) **mill,** prob. a mill for grinding dyewood, *obs.*, cf. Du *houtmollen* in this sense; (10) ∗**pile,** for *nigger in the woodpile* see ∗**Negro 6. d;** (11) **rank,** one length of corded wood; (12) **road,** an unimproved road through a wooded region or forest, also **woods road,** cf. G. *Holzweg*, Du. *houtweg;* (13) **room,** a room in which firewood is kept; (14) **saw,** a saw, as a bucksaw, for sawing wood; (15) ∗**shed,** *fig.* a place where (parental) punishment is administered; (16) **station,** a place where a train stops for wood for the locomotive, cf. **wooding station;** (17) **stove,** a stove adapted for burning wood; (18) ∗**tick,** a deathwatch or some other insect that makes a ticking sound; (19) ∗**yard,** a place on the bank of a river where firewood for steamboats is kept for sale.

(1) 1873 Mark Twain & Warner *Gilded Age* 270 Ilium . . . [had been] made a wood-and-water station of the new railroad. — **(2) 1866** *Wkly. New Mexican* 28 Feb. 1/4 At a wood camp (Oak Grove) . . . six soldiers were stationed cutting wood. **1908** S. E. White *Riverman* vii, Still lingering at the woods camps, . . . five hundred woods-weary men. — **(3) 1848** *Knickerb.* XVIII. 137 Here and there a log-house appeared in the midst of a clearing, its wood chimney . . . looking cheerless enough. — **(4) 1683** *Harvard Rec.* I. 75 The cook [shall] be allowed . . . what he shall expend annually for Wood-cutting. **1784** Ellicott in Mathews *Life A. Ellicott* 23 We finished the Wood Cutting of the 5° West Longitude. **1905** Wiggin *Rose* 171 Logging was to begin that day; then harvesting; then woodcutting.

(5) 1849 F. Douglass *Life* 61 You would see him coiled up in the corner of a wood-fence. — **(6) 1942** Rawlings *C. Creek* 4 We . . . meet only when . . . wood fires come too close, or when a shooting occurs. **1949** *Democrat* 28 July 4/2 Woods fires have now been practically eliminated throughout the length and breadth of the county. — **(7) 1884** *Rep. Comm. Agric.* 176 A very excellent model of a wood-grinding mill was shown. — **(8) 1845** F. Douglass *Narrative* 116 Mr. Johnson kindly let me have his wood horse and saw. **1879** Stockton *Rudder Grange* xiii, They knocked over the wood-horse. — **(9) 1768** John Lees *Jrnl.* 15 The Settlers hereabouts [near Schenectady, N.Y.] are chiefly low-Dutch. . . . He has already built a Church . . . and has a Wood and flour Mill erected.

(11) 1884 Mark Twain *H. Finn* xviii, Then up gets one of the boys, draws a steady bead over the wood-rank, and drops one of them out of his saddle. — **(12) 1821** Cooper *Spy* vii, Finding a wood-road, . . . [he] turned down its direction. **1904** Waller *Wood-carver* 4 Here and there in a woods'-road or on a hilltop the driver draws rein and winds a blast on his tin horn. **a1918** G. Stuart *On Frontier* II. 101 We wandered around on an old wood road. — **(13) 1855** *Trans. Mich. Agric. Soc.* VI. 161 Adjoining the woodroom, in an outdoor wood-shed where a year's supply of wood is stored and prepared for the wood-room as occasion may require. — **(14) 1816** *Austin P.* I. (124) 264, 1 Wood Saw. **1845** in *Tall Tales S.W.* (1930) 26, I would sooner have my leg taken off with a wood-saw. **1876** Knight 2035/2 Wood-saw.

(15) 1907 *St. Nicholas* July 826/2 He could save himself and most of his companions from unpleasant reckonings in various and sundry woodsheds. **1949** *Time* 18 April 22/2 If you don't do what we tell you to do we are going to take you out into the woodshed. — **(16) 1847** *Hunt's Merch. Mag.* XVI. 211 Attached to this station, are also . . . two wood and water stations. **1912** Crumpton *Two Boys* 157 You are lying anyhow and now get off at the wood station. — **(17) 1847** *Rep. Comm. Patents 1846* 304 The common wood stove and cylindrical coal stove [are combined]. **1898** Westcott *D. Harum* xxiii, His appliance for warmth consisted of a small wood stove. — **(18) 1891** *Harper's Mag.* Oct. 815/1 The wood-tick was held to be a deathwatch. *Ib.* 825/2 There was a long silence broken only by the wood-ticks. — **(19) 1837** Featherstonhaugh *Canoe Voyage* II. 125 We moored at a wood-yard on the left bank to repair it. **1883** Shields *S.S. Prentiss* 14 If he would cut across the neck of the peninsula he might head the boat at the wood-yard below. **1950** *Chi. Tribune* 20 May 10/3 The phrase may have reference to the dependence of early steamboat captains upon woodyards.

b. Denoting persons who have to do with wood or with the woods: (1) **wood butcher,** (see quots.); (2) **chopper,** one who chops wood, usu. as a vocation, a lumberer, also attrib., cf. ∗**chopper 1** and Du. *houtkapper;* (3) **contractor,** one who is under contract to supply wood; (4) **corder, =corder 1,** *obs.*, cf. Du. *houtmeter*, one charged with measuring up firewood; (5) **cutter, =wood chopper;** (6) **hauler,** one who hauls wood; (7) **ranger,** a member of a military force operating in the woods or forest, a scout or woodsman; (8) **runner,** (see quots.), *obs.;* (9) **sawyer,** see as a main entry; (10) **-s boss,** a foreman of those who work in the woods getting out timber, *colloq.;* (11) **-s runner,** app. a lumberer or logger.

(1) 1888 M. Stewart *From Nile to Nile* 75 Every jackleg carpenter, or, to use the wild western nomenclature, 'wood butcher,' . . . had been set to work. **1917** J. A. Moss *Officers' Man.* 485 *Wood-butcher*—company artificer. — **(2) 1779** *Mass. H.S. Coll.* 2 Ser. II. 458 The Century discov[er]ed a man creeping towards the wood choppers. **1881** *Rep. Indian Affairs* 39 The axes of the Indian, the wood-chopper, and military wood-contractor have nearly cleared all. **1940** Hatcher *Buckeye Country* 7 He, (Colonel Poage) generously sent two of his best Negro men to help him erect what is known in our furnace region as a good 'wood chopper shanty.' — **(3) 1881** [see **wood chopper**]. **1882** *Rep. Indian Affairs* 21 They have also worked for the military post-trader and hay and wood contractor. — **(4) 1681** *Boston Rec.* 144 If the ouerseers of wood cordrs finde any corders unfaithfull or defective [etc.]. **1850** *Knickerb.* XXXVI. 105 When he has the long wand, he is a wood-corder; when he has the old gun, he is a dog-killer.

(5) 1761 Niles *Indian Wars* II. 417 A party of men were appointed to cover some bateaux and wood-cutters. **1800** in *Harper's Mag.* VI. 7 No woodcutters or carters are to be had at any rate. **1905** Valentine *H. Sandwith* 178 Work among the wood-cutters and charcoal-burners . . . took him on rides. — **(6) 1897** *Outing* Feb. 438/2 Jean walked down by an old wood-hauler's road. **a1918** G. Stuart *On Frontier* II. 166 It was decided to pay . . . the wood hauler out of the roundup funds. — **(7) 1734** *Ga. Col. Rec.* III. 414 [The French] have Five hundred men in pay, constantly employed as Wood-Rangers, to keep their neighboring Indians in subjection. **1757** E. Burke *Acct. Settlement Amer.* VII. II. 270 A company of wood rangers . . . scour the country near our settlements. **1896** *Harper's Mag.* April 712/1 The white wood-rangers were as ruthless as their red foes. — **(8) 1743** in A. Dobbs *Hudson's Bay* (1744) 106 No Europeans could undergo such Hardships as those French that intercept the English Trade, who are inur'd to it, and are called by us Wood-runners, or Coureurs de Bois. **1752** *Importance of Gaining & Preserving Friendship of Indians* 42 By this means a number of wood-runners would be form'd, well acquainted with the country, and of great use in the war time, as guides of parties and scouts, &c.

(10) 1929 *Randolph Enterprise* (Elkins, W.Va.) 21 Nov. 7/1 Abe Helmick is woods boss for Wilson Lumber Company. **1948** *Sat. Ev. Post* 24 Jan. 47/2 We usually topped a tree—selected beforehand by the engineers and the woods boss. — **(11) 1946** Richter *Fields* 20 It hadn't much danger to a master woods-runner and boatman.

c. In the names of groups or tribal divisions of Indians: (1) **Wood Cree(s),** (see quot. 1910); (2) **Indians,** (see quot.), *obs.;* (3) **-s Chippewas,** Chippewas living in wooded regions.

(1) 1885 *Boston Jrnl.* 23 June 1/8 The Wood Crees have gone back to get a cache of provisions. **1910** Hodge *Amer. Indians* II. 414/1 *Sakawithiniwuk* ('people of the woods'). The Wood Cree, one of the several divisions of the Cree. **1947** *Beaver* June 15/1 The Wood Crees, who were in the minority, were, in general, less troublesome. — **(2) 1809** Henry *Travels* 62 At the south are also seen a few of the wandering *O'pimittish Ininiwac*, literally, Men of the Woods, and otherwise called Wood-Indians. — **(3) 1849** *31st Cong.* 1 Sess. H.R. Ex. Doc. No. 5 II. 1030 The Chippewas are small in person, (this remark . . . does not apply exactly to the woods Chippewas west of the Mississippi).

d. Designating wooded areas or tracts: (1) **wood field,** ?a wood lot, *obs.;* (2) **lawn,** a portion of level land overgrown with trees, also attrib., now common in place-names; (3) **lot,** a piece of land upon which wood for fuel, etc., grows, also attrib.; (4) **pasture,** (see quot.); (5) **patch, =wood lot,** *obs.;* (6) **prairie,** (see quot.); (7) **ranch,** *W.* an area where wood can be obtained; (8)

range, an area in the woods over which cattle range; (9) **swamp,** (see quot.), *obs.*

(1) **1698** *N.H. Probate Rec.* I. 438 My wood fields lying on the Creek behind my house. — (2) **1815** DRAKE *Cincinnati* 43 On the western side, it is principally wood-lawn. **1871** *Ill. Agric. Soc. Trans.* VIII. 80 Mr. Sodowsky's farm is located in one of the finest woodlawn blue-grass regions of the State. **1946** *Chi. D. News* 8 Oct. 8/1 Along with a copy of the Woodlawn Community Association report . . . he is sending . . . the following. — (3) **1643** *N. Eng. Hist. & Gen. Reg.* II. (1848) 262 To my younger daughter, my woodlot & my part of the 4000 Acres. **1886** *Cent. Mag.* April 863/1, I can't bear any of your cheap wood-lot stuff. **1949** *Hoard's Dairyman* 25 Nov. 830/4 The income from the woodlot has been fairly large. — (4) **1845** LYELL *Travels* II. 62 These forests [in Ky.] where there is no undergrowth, are called 'wood pastures.' Originally the cane covered the ground, but when it was eaten down by the cattle, no new crop could get up, and it was replaced by grass alone.

(5) **1856** *Mich. Agric. Soc. Trans.* VIII. 754 His wood patch is nicely cleaned up and saved for future use. — (6) **1883** SMITH *Geol. Survey Ala.* 474 The post-oak Prairie soil [is] . . . sometimes also distinguished as 'woods prairies.' — (7) **1869** *Terr. Enterprise* (Virginia, Nev.) 30 March 3/4 A gentleman named Zivits, owning a wood ranch south of Empire, several times brought in rock for assay. **1947** CHALFANT *Gold, Guns, & Ghost Towns* 47 A citizen . . . took advantage of the anti-Chinese feeling by 'jumping' a Chinese contractor's wood ranch. — (8) **1824** DODDRIDGE *Notes* 105 The wood range was eaten out. — (9) **1765** J. BARTRAM *Diary* 1 Sep. Great part of ye countrey is what we call A rich wood swamp produceing very thick timber consisting of white oak hicory horn beam elm.

e. Denoting vehicles, etc., engaged in hauling wood, as (1) **wood car,** (2) **flat,** (3) **float,** (4) **sled,** (5) **sleigh,** (6) **train.**

(1) **1863** CUMMING *Hospital Life* 59/2 We came up to town on a wood-car. **1864** *Ib.* 146/2 About 3 P.M., a wood-car came from Columbus, on which we all got. — (2) **1785** *Md. Hist. Mag.* XX. 42 He hath gone up and down frequently in . . . wood-flats. **1883** MARK TWAIN *Life Miss.* xx. 237 The Pennsylvania was creeping along, . . . towing a wood-flat which was fast being emptied. — (3) **1847** H. HOWE *Hist. Coll. Ohio* 224 There was no boats at hand, except a few large and unmanageable wood-floats. — (4) **1856** HALE *If, Yes, & Perhaps* 147 The sledge . . . is in general contour not unlike a Yankee wood-sled, about eleven feet long. **1904** M. E. WALLER *Wood-carver* 63 She took the small wood-sled, for the crust holds, and there is a fine coast for good two thirds of the way.

(5) **1784** HILTZHEIMER *Diary* (1893) 16 Feb. 61, I observed a large number of wood sleighs crossing [the Delaware]. — (6) **1872** HUNTINGTON *Road-Master's Ass't* 107 He is frequently expected to act as conductor of a gravel or wood train.

f. In expressions denoting occasions upon which neighbors assemble to cut a supply of wood for one of their number, as (1) **wood bee,** (2) ***chopping,** (3) **frolic,** (4) **spell.**

(1) **1857** *Quinland* I. 91 The whole neighbourhood would assemble to prepare for each other the wood necessary to keep such a fire going during the winter as we have described at the beginning of this narrative; hence a 'wood bee.' — (2) **1872** EGGLESTON *End of World* 51, I never went to a wood-chopping. **1944** WILSON *Passing Inst.* 46 There were wood-choppings and corn-huskings and quiltings. — (3) **1889** MELLICK *Story Old Farm* 239 The 'wood frolic' was also an institution which brought together most of the people of the congregations annually at the parsonages. While the men occupied themselves during the day hauling the minister's yearly supply of wood, the wives and daughters came in the late afternoon and prepared a bountiful supper, to which the tired wood-haulers doubtless brought excellent appetites. — (4) **1864** WEBSTER 1269/2 *Spell,* a gratuitous helping forward of another's work; as, a wood-*spell.* (U.S.) **1869** STOWE *Oldtown Folks* 478 The minister's 'wood-spell' . . . was a certain day set apart in the winter, . . . when every parishioner brought the minister a sled-load of wood. *Ib.,* Tina, Harry, and I had been busy . . . in helping Esther create the wood-spell cake. **1880** S. PERLEY *Hist. Boxford, Mass.* 177 The 'wood-spell' was recognized as one of the few holiday seasons of our ancestors.

g. In expressions, usu. obs., sufficiently explained by the quots.: (1) **wood cry,** (2) **hanging,** (3) **meeting,** (4) **right,** (cf. *right in the woods s.v.* ***right 6. b.** (1)), (5) **-s colt,** (cf. **2. b.** (10) above), (6) **tag.**

(1) **1852** WATSON *Nights in Block-House* 340, I was struck with the greatest terror at hearing the wood-cry, as it is called, which the savages I had left were making, upon missing their charge. — (2) **1868** *Rep. U.S. Comm. Agric.* (1869) 15 The American wood-hanging . . . has been applied for the finish of the suite of rooms. **1876** KNIGHT 2809/1 *Wood-hanging.* Thin veneer on a paper backing, to be used as wall-paper. — (3) **1859** BARTLETT 66 Camp-meeting. A meeting held in the wood or field for religious purposes, where the assemblage encamp and remain several days. These meetings are generally held by the Methodists. The Mormons call it a *Wood-meeting.* — (4) **1788** SCHÖPF *Reise* II. 172 In einigen Gegenden aber ist ein sogenanntes Waldrecht (Wood-right) eingeführt, nach welchem eine jede Plantage einen gewissen Antheil an allen wilden Heerden hat, welche sich in solchen Bezirken befinden; und dieses Recht kann, wie anderes Eigenthum, nach Belieben veräussert oder verkauft werden.

(5) **1895** *D.N.* I. 395 *woods colt:* foundling. Winchester, Ky. **1949** *Sat. Ev. Post* 16 April 146/4 He raved, swore, called the boy a wood's colt and his instrument a thump keg. — (6) **1891** *Amer. Folk-Lore* IV. 222 Wood-Tag. . . . In this game, the one who is 'it' tries to tag any player who is not touching wood, objects of wood being regarded as a 'home' or 'hunk.'

5. In colloq. phrases: (1) *To take in wood,* to take firewood aboard a steamboat, also transf.; (2) *to go where the woodbine twineth,* to pass off the scene, to come to naught; (3) *to take to the woods,* to run off into the woods, also fig.; (4) *to be in the wood,* to be destined or fated, *rare;* (5) *to the woods for it,* out with it; (6) *to saw wood,* see ***saw,** *v.* (3).

(1) **1823** JAMES *Exped.* I. 31 We left Shawneetown . . . and stopped three miles below, to take in wood. **1839** MARRYAT *Diary* 1 Ser. II. 36 In the West, where steam-navigation is so abundant, when they ask you to drink they say, 'Stranger, will you take in wood?' — (2) **1870** *N.Y. Tribune* 24 Jan. 1/4 'What became of the $50,000,000 gold carried for Mrs. Grant [etc.]'? [Jim Fisk:] 'Oh! that has gone with all the rest. Where the woodbine twineth!' **1897** *Cong. Rec.* 18 Jan. 907/1 The bill . . . goes 'where the woodbine twineth.' **1920** *Collier's* 20 March 41/2 He's gone where the woodbine twineth, and the like, get me? — (3) **1854** *Yankee Blade* 16 Dec., The inn-keeper . . . finally agreed to give the painter fifteen dollars to paint him a wild bear with a chain, that would not take to the woods in the next storm. **1894** MARK TWAIN *Those Twins* iii, Negroes and farmers' wives took to the woods when the buggy came upon them suddenly. **1945** *Nation* 18 March 291/2 William C. Morland, Idaho Republican, took to the woods in 1932 because Hoover was defeated by Roosevelt. — (4) **1904** *Hartford Courant* 24 June 10 Probably if it were in the wood for the Russians to defeat the Japanese where the two sides are fairly well matched, he would have won it.

(5) **1906** *N.Y. Ev. Post* 10 Feb., Many publishers as far back as five or six years ago were in the habit of saying, 'We'll give rag-time a few months more, and then to the woods for it. It's worn out.'

As the last term in **acid, arrow, back, basket, bass, bear, beaver, beetle, big, bird, black, blue, bow, box, brass, brick, brittle, buck, bum, burnt, button, candle, canoe, castor, china, cotton, cow, crab, cucumber, dead, devil, dog, elk, fish, flat, flood, fox, front, gopher, grease, gum, hard, hobble, hoop, iron, kitchen, leather, lever, light, lightning, log, mesquite, moose, naked, north, northern yellow, nut, Osage orange, papaw, pecker, pigeon, pine, piny, pipe stem, pitch, poison, polecat, pop gun, pork, post oak, punk, robin, rosin, round, salt, screw, Shawnee, shin, shittim, slab, soap, sour, spice, spoon, steamboat, stem, stink, stinking, stove, sugar, swamp, tangle, tea, turpentine, whistle, white, yellow wood(s).**

***wood,** *v.*

1. *tr.* To provide (a plow) with suitable wooden parts. *Obs.*

1830 *Cortland Observer* (Homer, N.Y.) 2 July 1/3 Ploughs, of almost all patents, . . . are cast and wooded by a first rate workman from Log City. **1831** *Workingman's Gaz.* (Woodstock, Vt.) 19 April 239/3 Said Ploughs are well wooded and a iron cleves and pin attached to them.

2. *intr.* With reference to a steamboat or train: To take on wood as fuel, usu. with *up.*

1845 in *Amer. Sp.* XXII. 206/2 We had been wooding all night at the same wood-yard! **1858** W. P. SMITH *Railway Celebration* II. 47 This requires . . . a special stoppage of the passenger train . . . in order to 'wood up.' **1947** BEEBE *Mixed Train Dly.* 12 We have no fueling platforms for her to wood up at anywhere along the line; so she sticks pretty much to the yards nowadays.

transf. **1840** *N.O. Picayune* 22 Oct. 2/4 A Van Buren paper in New York calls on the party in the Tenth Ward to 'wood up,' and says 'register your brothers, uncles, aunts,' &c. **1843** *N.Y. Semi-Weekly Express* 4 Jan. 3/2 Another editor invites his Subscribers to 'wood up' while the sleighing lasted.

b. Of a person: To take a drink of liquor. *Obs.*

1840 *N.O. Picayune* 31 Oct. 2/3 He 'wooded up' as he came along. *a*1855 KELLEY *Humors* 175 [He] made a straight bend for Sander's 'Grocery,' and began to 'wood up.'

c. *tr.* To supply (a stove) with wood.

1850 JUDD *R. Edney* 52 Richard . . . very quietly went to wooding up the stove.

woodchuck ˈwʊdˌtʃʌk, *n.* [f. Algonquian. See **we-jack** and cf. Cree *otchek*, Chippewa *otchig*, the name for the fisher (see ∗**fisher 1.**) but transferred by white traders to the ground hog.] =**ground hog.** Cf. **eastern, rock woodchuck.**

1674 *Cal. State P., Amer. & West Indies* VII. 581 The natural inhabitants of the woods, hills, and swamps, are . . . rabbits, hares, and woodchucks. **1778** CARVER *Travels* 454 The Wood-chuck is a ground animal of the fur kind. **1938** *N.O. Picayune* 17 Feb. 2/4 A man wasn't born like a *woodchuck* to live in the airth. **1946** *Democrat* 6 June 4/6 One woodchuck may eat as much as two pounds of greens in a day.

attrib. **1817** *Mass. Spy* 18 June (Th.), Woodchuck Hunt. Woodchucks have appeared in great numbers. **1845** JUDD *Margaret* I. 17 Vigorously plied he his whip of wood-chuck skin on a walnut stock. **1919** CADY *Rhymes of Vt.* (1923) 105 You've never peeled a hemlock log Or set a woodchuck trap.

b. In phrases of comparison.

1835 BIRD *Hawks* I. 170 Here's a dose for the dog will make him sleep like a woodchuck at Christmas. **1860** HOLMES *Professor* 104 He will come all right by-and-by, sir,—as sound as a woodchuck—as sound as a musquash! **1937** COFFIN *Kennebec* 229 Some have . . . the 'Old Boy in them bigger than a woodchuck.'

c. *land of woodchucks*, a country area.

1851 ROSS *In New York* 46 But what could a 'greenhorn,' right from the land of woodchucks do?

∗**woodcock,** *n.* The common American woodcock, *Philohela minor*. Also the ivory-billed woodpecker and the pileated woodpecker *qq.v.* Cf. **timberdoodle 2.**

1666 ALSOP *Maryland* (1869) 41 The Turkey, the Woodcock, . . . the Pigeon, and others . . . I have seen in whole flights in the Woods of Mary-Land. **1709** LAWSON *Carolina* 139 The Woodcocks live and breed here. **1824** J. DODDRIDGE *Notes* 69 The different kinds of woodpeckers still remain . . . with the exception of the largest genus . . . the wood-cock which is now very scarce. **1948** *Chesterton* (Ind.) *Tribune* 28 Oct. 2/5 A possession limit of eight, only one of which can be wood cock, has been set.

attrib. **1835** HOFFMAN *Winter in West* I. 17 [There was] no woodcock-ground within five miles of the court-house. **1844** *Knickerb.* XXIV. 192 Pleasant was . . . our friend the captain's woodcock supper. **1891** *Cent.* 6965/2 The woodcock . . . is found in bogs and . . . alder-brakes (sometimes called *woodcock-brakes* in consequence).

As the last term in **black, ivorybill woodcock.**

∗**wooden,** *a.*

1. Wooded or forested, as **wooden country.** *Obs.*

1816 U. BROWN *Journal* I. 358 To Smith field a Wooden Town in a Wooden Country & a wooden bred set of Tavern-keepers. **1843** CARLTON *New Purchase* I. 62 Our wooden country's mighty rough. **1891** RYAN *Pagan* 130 Many people from the 'wooden' country tramped over the mountain.

2. In combs.: (1) **wooden bottom,** a form of shoe the entire bottom of which is a shaped piece of wood, *obs.;* (2) **chimney,** =**stick-and-clay chimney,** *obs.*, cf. **wood chimney;** (3) **clock,** a clock the mechanism of which is of wood, cf. **Connecticut wooden clock, timber clock;** (4) **Indian,** a wooden image of an Indian in a standing posture, formerly used as a sign before a cigar store, also transf., cf. **cigar-store Indian;** (5) **island,** (see quot. 1806 and cf. ∗**raft 2.**), now *hist.;* (6) **(over) coat,** a coffin, *slang, obs.* [cf. ∗*wooden breeks*, ∗*doublet*, ∗*sark*, in same sense]; (7) **slate,** (see quot.), *obs.;* (8) **tongue,** (see quots. and cf. **lumpy jaw**); (9) **wedding,** (see quots.).

(1) **1888** *Cent. Mag.* XXXVI. 769/2 The slave population in the farther South went barefoot in the summer and wore 'wooden bottoms' in the winter. . . . Their novelty . . . made captive the fancy of the children of both races; and juvenile wooden bottoms were the rage for a long time. — (2) **1836** J. HALL *Statistics of West* 104 Great wooden chimnies . . . occupy nearly the whole gable end of a house. — (3) **1827** *Western Mo. Rev.* June 85 The *tin-wagon, pit-coal-indigo, wooden nutmeg and wooden clock* missionaries find the harvest beginning to fall short, in consequence of the wariness of the chaps of former speculations. **1856** TAYLOR *Gold Digger's Song Book* 19 Old P. T. Barnum had the rocks. . . . But lost them all on wooden clocks. [**1945** ADAMS *Album Amer. Hist.* II. 166 In 1814, Terry devised his 'perfected wood clock.'] — (4) **1879** *Amer. Punch* Oct. 113/2 The tramp looked at him with a face as full of expression as a wooden Indian. **1907** *St. Nicholas* May 607/1 I've been hibernating over at Hammond for two whole days with a dozen wooden Indians who wouldn't even say 'Good Morning' to me until I shouted it! **1949** *Nat. Geog. Mag.* Dec. 806 (*legend*), This Wooden Indian Sells No Cigars.

(5) **1806** CRAMER *Navigator* 18 Wooden-Islands are places where by some cause or other, large quantities of drift wood, has through time, been arrested and matted together in different parts of the river. **1846** LEVINGE *Echoes from Backwoods* II. 20 The Mississippi is obstructed by *planters, sawyers,* and *wooden islands,* which are frequently the cause of injury. **1941** BALDWIN *Keelboat Age* 77 Floating logs and the loose, floating masses of debris known as 'wooden islands' were dangerous. — (6) **1859** MATSELL *Vocabulum* 96 *Wooden coat.* A coffin. **1871** J. H. BROWNE *Sights & Sensations in Europe* 21 Anything, from an infant's robe to a wooden overcoat, as they used to call it in the army, can be supplied. — (7) **1863** BOOTH *N.Y.* 99 The roof was covered with split oaken shingles, then called wooden slates. — (8) **1913** BARNES *Western Grazing Grounds* 286 Big jaw, also called lumpy jaw and wooden tongue, is an infectious disease found generally all over the West. **1921** *Farmer's Bul.* No. 1155, 17 Actinomycosis, (Lumpy jaw, wooden tongue,) . . . is a disease rare in sheep. — (9) **1870** MACRAE *Americans* II. 293 The fifth anniversary is called the wooden wedding, and the invitations are often issued on wooden cards, thin as paper, and beautifully ornamented. The presents suitable to this anniversary are of wood. **1888** *Girl's Own Papers* 24 March 407/3 In America, too, the fifth anniversary of the marriage ceremony is known as the 'wooden wedding.'

Wooden Indian or cigar-store Indian

b. Designating alleged articles of wood jocularly said to have been part of the stock in trade of Yankee peddlers, as **wooden cucumber seed, wooden ham.** Cf. next and **2.** (3) above. See **pit-coal indigo.**

1831 *Workingman's Gaz.* (Woodstock, Vt.) 19 Jan. 129/1 He was of Canadian descent, and was brought to the States by a Vermont pedlar, who took him in barter for wooden cucumber-seed. **1832** *Boston Transcript* 23 Jan. 2/2 We recently read of wooden hams in some parts of the west neatly sowed up in canvass, said to have their origin with the same ingenious people who invented wooden nutmegs. **1850** *Deseret News* (Salt Lake City) 13 July 34/1 It is time for wooden nutmeg, and wooden cucumber seed peddlers to quit the business, while copper can so easily be converted into gold. **1940** [see next].

wooden nutmeg.

1. Allegedly, an imitation nutmeg made of wood, facetiously ascribed to the inventive genius of sharp Yankee traders of New England, particularly Connecticut. Now *hist.*

1825 *Mem. Charles Mathews* III. (1839) 520 The other [saddlebag] crammed, of course, with wooden nutmegs, horn gunflints . . . and a sort of patent medicine. **1859** HILL *Elements Algebra* 124 A Yankee mixes a certain number of wooden nutmegs, which cost him 1–4 cents apiece, with a quantity of real nutmegs, worth 4 cents apiece, and sells the whole assortment for $44; and gains $3.75 by the fraud. **1940** *Amer. Mercury* Nov. 331/1 People said he cheated, that he sold wooden nutmegs, wooden pumpkin seeds and wooden hams painted to look real.

b. *land of wooden nutmegs*, New England or Connecticut.

1826 *Mass. Spy* 6 Sep. (Th.), The land of 'wooden nutmegs' and horn gun-flints. **1868** *N.Y. Herald* 2 July 4/1 From the land of wooden nutmegs, and humbugs, generally, they have winged their way.

c. Used attrib. in various expressions referring to New England and New Englanders.

1827 *Western Mo. Rev.* June 85 The *tin wagon, . . . wooden nutmeg, and wooden clock* missionaries find the harvest beginning to fall short. **1857** *Spirit of Times* 28 Feb. 414/1 We have a representative of the 'wooden nutmeg country' on board. **1859** TALIAFERRO *Fisher's R.* 202 Not even a wooden-nutmeg Yankee could make any thing from off them. They knew nothing but downright honesty. **1883** in WELLS *Practical Economics* (1885) 125 The brass and German-silver business paid the canny wooden-nutmeg men better.

2. A New Englander, esp. one from Connecticut. A nickname.

1830 *Providence Free Press* 6 May 3/2 *Masonic* Republicans are hooted at, however, as so many wooden nutmegs. **1839** *Jamestown* (N.Y.) *Jrnl.* 24 July 1/5 Do you mean to insinuate, you Yankee peddler—you infernal wooden nutmeg, that I have cheated? **1888** WHITMAN *November Boughs* 406 Those from . . . Connecticut . . . [were called] Wooden Nutmegs.

3. Wooden Nutmeg State, Connecticut, a nickname. Cf. **Nutmeg State.**

1855 BARNUM *Life* 295 The New Orleans purchasers . . . little dreamed that it was raised in the 'wooden-nutmeg' State. **1867** *Ore. State Jrnl.* 18 May 2/2 They only carried the 'wooden nutmeg state' by a few hundred. [**1927** SIRINGO *Riata* 13 Shanghai Pierce had drifted from the State where they make wooden nutmegs.]

* **wooding,** *n.* **1. wooding place,** a place where a steamboat stops for firewood, cf. **wood yard. 2. wooding station,** =prec.

(1) **1828** *Western Souvenir 1829* 110 A few hours brought us to one of those stopping points, known by the name of 'wooding places.' **1850** HOUSTON *Hesperos* II. 22 This process often proved ineffectual, and we were frequently reduced to the necessity of sending to the nearest *wooding place* in order to procure a flat or raft, for the purpose of getting out a part of the cargo. — (2) **1829** B. HALL *Forty Etchings* No. XXXIII. (*caption*), Wooding Station on the Mississippi. **1863** RUSSELL *Diary North & South* I. 269 The scenery and the scenes were just the same as yesterday's—high banks, cotton-slides, wooding stations.

* **woodland,** *n.* **1. woodland caribou,** "the common caribou of North America, as found in wooded regions, and as distinguished from the *barren-ground reindeer*, which occurs beyond the limit of trees" (*Cent.*). Also **woodland reindeer. 2. woodland star,** (see quot.).

(1) **1859** BARTLETT 69 There are two species [of American reindeer], the Barren Ground, and the Woodland, Caribou. **1868** *Amer. Naturalist* Dec. 536, I noticed . . . a pair of decayed and broken horns, which looked like those of the Woodland Reindeer. **1925** HEMING *Living Forest* 166 The woodland caribou, though they're next in size, have the smallest horns, an' they live in the Strong Woods Country. — (2) **1915** ARMSTRONG & THORNBER *Western Wild Flowers* 198 Woodland Star, *Lithophragma heterophylla*, . . . is sometimes called Star of Bethlehem.

* **woodpecker,** *n.* As the last term in **Arizona, banded, cactus, California, Canadian, downy, French, Gairdner's, Gila, golden-shafted, golden-winged, hairy, Harris's, ivory-billed, Lewis('), Mexican, Nuttall's, pigeon, pileated, red-bellied, red-breasted, red-cockaded, red-headed, red-shafted, saguaro, sap-sucking, speckled, speckled-cheek, striped-back, Texas, white-bill(ed), white-headed, Williamson's, yellow-bellied woodpecker.**

wood sawyer.

1. One whose occupation is sawing wood.

1815 *N. Amer. Rev.* II. 143 Mr. John Wood, killed in the street by Patrick Hart, a wood-sawyer. **1891** WILKINS *N. Eng. Nun* 43 Matilda's antecedents had come of wood-sawyers and garden-laborers.

b. A make or brand of tobacco. *Obs.*

1835 *Vade Mecum* (Phila.) 23 May 3/2 A pocket full of cavendish, dandy twist, lady's twist, Lorrillard, nigger-head, wood-sawyer, is the sign of a tender heart.

c. wood sawyer's buck, a sawbuck.

1867 *Ball Players' Chron.* 14 Nov. 5/1 Just think of the B. B. clubs all over the country, issuing broad and high sounding challenges to the Y.M.C.A., and *vice versa*—champion wood-sawyer's buck, silver mounted, &c, &c.

2. Used in phrases indicative of independence on the part of the wood sawyer or (facetiously) his clerk (see quots.).

Prob. in allusion to the advantageous position of the wood sawyer with reference to steamboat traffic on the western rivers, wood as fuel being essential.

1832 *Boston Transcript* 7 Jan. 2/1 'Independent as a wood-sawyer' is a common expression. **1840** in *Amer. Sp.* IV. 155 But if you live in the forecastle, you are 'as independent as a woodsawyer's clerk.' **1846** *Dollar Newspaper* (Phila.) 23 Sep. 4/2 The cap'n has been as saucy as a wood-sawyer's clerk on half pay, to me. **1928** *Amer. Sp.* IV. 155, I used to hear the expression 'as independent as a woodsawyer's clerk' many times along the Missouri river in the Nebraska City region in the late nineteenth century. I never hear it now in any part of the country. **1950** *Chi. Tribune* 20 May 10/3 An old expression, 'independent as a wood sawyer,' still occasionally heard in the midwest, goes unnoticed.

woodsy ˈwʊdzɪ, *a.* Of or pertaining to the woods, sylvan.

1860 in BREWSTER *Life J.D. Whitney* 179 Your gallery would be rather monotonously 'lake and wood'sy. **1883** MARK TWAIN *Life on Miss.* xxx, Ship Island region was as woodsy and tenantless as ever. **1917** *Ladies' Home Jrnl.* July 33/2 In woodsy browns and greens the Camp Fire Girls' booth, with its . . . paper-bead chains, attracts attention. **1949** *Nat. Hist.* Nov. 386/3, I retired to a woodsy, flat-floored dell in quest of the Dutchman's-breeches.

woohoo ˌwuˈhu, *n.* [Derived by Webster f. Amer. Sp. *guebucú*, but this term is not recorded in Santamaría. Cf. Sp. *aguja* in Amer. Sp. sense shown here.] A sailfish of the genus *Istiophorus.* — **1884** GOODE *Fisheries* I. 337 The 'Sail-fish,' *Histiophorus americanus*, is called by sailors in the south the 'Boohoo' or 'Woohoo.'

* **wool,** *n.* In combs.: (1) * **wool-dyed,** =**dyed-in-the-wool,** *colloq.;* (2) **grass,** "a rush-like plant, *Eriophorum cyperinum* (*Scirpus Eriophorum*), common in low grounds through the eastern half of North America" (*Cent.*); (3) * **hat,** one who wears a wool hat, a yokel or rustic, also **wool-hat boy;** (4) **head,** (*a*) a Negro, *slang*, (*b*) an addle-pate, *slang*, (*c*) *local*, the bufflehead duck, cf. **woollyhead;** (5) **picking,** (see quot. 1817), in full **wool-picking frolic,** now *hist.;* (6) **pulling,** pulling the wool over people's eyes, used attrib., *colloq.;* (7) **sower,** (see quot.); (8) **sponge,** (see quot. 1891).

(1) **1832** *Niles' Reg.* LXIII. 65/2 Messrs. Randolph and Ritchie . . . are chiefs of the 'wool-dyed democrats' of the present day. **1904** *Charlotte* (N.C.) *Observer* 19 June 2 Higginson is one of the old abolition gang, is wool-dyed and blind. — (2) **1854** THOREAU *Walden* 331, I am particularly attracted by the arching and sheaf-like top of the wool-grass. **1899** GOING *Flowers* 191 One of the stateliest of native sedges is the so-miscalled 'wool-grass.' — (3) **1830** *Amer. Sentinel* (Phila.) 27 Aug. 2/2 Formerly the supporters of General Jackson were said to be the rowdies, the wool hats, the filthy mechanics, &c. **1927** EUBANK *Horse & Buggy Days* 170, I was a smart boy from town, and this particular guy thought I was a wool-hat boy. **1950** *Chi. Tribune* 25 May 14/2 Whether a wool hat boy would know the requirements of old time courtesy is not within our knowledge. — (4) (*a*) **1828** COOPER *Red Rover* I. 218 Yonder is a slaver, off the fort, if you like a cargo of wool-heads for your money. (*b*) **1887** DALY *Railroad of Love* 64 Oh, you poor, dear wool-head! (*c*) **1888** TRUMBULL *Names of Birds.*

(5) **1817** BIRKBECK *Notes Journey Amer.* (1818) 58 The wife was at a neighbour's on a 'wool-picking frolic,' which is a merry meeting of gossips at each other's houses, to pick the year's wool and prepare it for carding. [In Ohio.] **1872** *Harper's Mag.* June 33/1 Zed had a wool-pickin' . . . and all the gals and fellers was there. **1943** HOLT *Carver* 17 More often than not they consisted of . . . wool pickings, or quilting parties. — (6) **1847** ROBB *Squatter Life* 16 In short I'm up to the whole 'wool pulling' system. — (7) **1891** *Cent.* 6972/2 *wool-sower.* . . . A woolly many-celled cynipid gall occurring on white-oak twigs in the United States, and made by the gall-fly *Andricus seminator.* — (8) **1877** HYATT *Revision N. Amer. Poriferæ* 16 The grades [of American sponges] are Glove Sponge . . . , Wool Sponge . . . , and Yellow and Hard Head. **1891** *Cent.* 6972/3 *wool-sponge.* . . . A kind of bath-sponge, more fully called *lamb's-wool-sponge.*

b. In colloq. phrases: (1) *To pull the wool over* (someone's) *eyes*, or variants, to deceive (someone); (2) *all wool and a yard wide*, see * **all 4.** (5).

(1) **1839** *Jamestown* (N.Y.) *Jrnl.* 14 April 1/6 That lawyer . . . has been trying to spread wool over your eyes. **1936** MCKENNA *Black Range* 284 Some claims he had the wool pulled over his eyes by a friend of his who had brought back some diamonds from the African fields. **1949** *St. Paul Pioneer Press* 19 June 10/1 He said his only purpose was to 'cite substantial evidence that will show just who is trying to pull the wool over the eyes of the American people.'

As the last term in **carpet, pulled, sheep's wool.**

woolenet ˌwʊləˈnɛt, *n.* (See quot. 1846.) Also attrib.

1820 *Columbian Centinel* 3 June 4/2 Just received . . . a few pieces of Woolinetts. **1825** MOTLEY *Correspondence* I. 3, I wish you would send me up some nankeen pantaloons, as my woolenet ones are so tight that they are uncomfortable. **1846** WORCESTER, *Woollenette*, a thin woollen stuff.

woolery ˈwʊlərɪ, *n.* The wool-growing interest. *Rare.* — **1890** *Columbus* (O.) *Dispatch* 2 Sep., The head of the Ohio woolery is here.

***woolly,** *a.* and *n.*

1. *n.* In colloq. uses: **a.** (*cap.*) *pl.* A nickname for the Republicans, in allusion to the woolly horse *q.v. Obs.* **b.** (See quot.) **c.** *W.* A sheep, usu. pl.

(a) **1856** *Dollar Times* (Cin.) 18 Sep. 1/1 He'll use up Fremont head and tail, He'll ride the Woolies round and round. — (b) **1897** *Outing* XXX. 263/1 We're going to have a 'woolly,' sure. . . . These winds, sudden and strong, beat the water into wool-white foam; hence their name. — (c) **1914** Bower *Flying U. Ranch* 101 Who owns these woollies? **1939** Rollins *Gone Haywire* 7 Voices occasionally would rise, either in profanity against the 'woolies' or in guffaws when an obscene joke was told.

2. *a.* Of a westerner or of the West: rude, untutored, also **woolly West,** in allusion to *wild and woolly West q.v. Colloq.*

1891 Ryan *Told in Hills* 191 Let us 'move our freight,' 'hit the breeze,' or any other term of the woolly West that means action. **1904** *N.Y. Ev. Post* 22 June 7 A young woman who ropes steers with as much ease and expedition as the 'wooliest' cowboy. **1930** Henry *Conquer. Plains* 58 This was roughing it, was it? Life in the woolly West!

3. In combs.: (1) **woollyhead,** see as a main entry; (2) **horse,** a horse discovered by John C. Frémont in the West and exhibited by P. T. Barnum [commonly regarded as a fraud, this creature became a campaign symbol in 1856, Republicans being stigmatized as "woollies," the "woolly horse clique," etc.], *obs.;* (3) **locust,** *W.* a sheep, cf. **hoofed locust;** (4) **pate,** =**woollyhead a,** *slang, obs.;* (5) **sheep,** a variety of Rocky Mountain sheep, *obs.;* (6) **worm,** (see quot. 1909).

(2) **1854** *Maysville Eagle* 2 Nov. 2/1 There is a little of the 'Woolly horse' about this story. **1856** *Western Citizen* (Paris, Ky.) 8 Feb. 1/5 The great shoman [*sic*] is left without a penny in his own name—his New York investments, 'Iranistan,' the woolly horse and all, having gone by the board. **1856** *Dollar Times* (Cin.) 18 Sep. 3/1 One of the transparencies . . . had Fremont and Jessie sloping on a Woolly Horse. — (3) **1869** Muir *First Summer in Sierra* (1911) 77 The high ridges and hilltops beyond the woolly locusts are now gray with monardella, clarkia, coreopsis, and tall tufted grasses. — (4) **1868** *N.Y. Herald* 1 Aug. 8/3 This representative of his Satanic majesty . . . created . . . a consternation among the little wooly pates. (5) **1837** Irving *Bonneville* I. 47 The mountain sheep . . . is often confounded with another animal, the 'woolly sheep' found more to the northward. — (6) **1909** Webster 2349/1 *Wooly worm.* . . . The larva of any sawfly that covers itself with a white woolly secretion, as the larva of *Selandria caryae,* which feeds upon the hickory and butternut. . . . A woolly bear [a larva of one of the several bombycid moths]. **1911** Ferber *Dawn O'Hara* ii. 19 I'd eat wooly worms if I thought they might benefit me.

woollyhead ˈwʊlɪˌhɛd, *n.* **a.** A Negro. *Slang.* **b.** (*cap.*) *pl.* (See quot. 1898.) Also attrib. Now *hist.* **c.** (See quot. and cf. Wentworth *s.v.*)

(a) **1827** Cooper *Prairie* xv, Some people think woolly-heads are miserable, working on hot plantations under a broiling sun. **1856** Stowe *Dred* II. 23 I'm all eaten up with woolly-heads, like locusts. — (b) **1853** *Knickerb.* XLIII. 653 'Woolly-Heads' were 'about,' and 'far-off the coming shone' of dignified 'Silver-Grays.' **1898** *N.Y. Wkly. Tribune* 16 Feb. 7/4 The Woolly Heads were the faction of the old Whig party which espoused the cause of negro liberation. **1949** *Pa. Dutchman* 7 July 1/1 He . . . incidentally drifted into active politics, with the 'Wooley Head' element of the Whig Party and against the 'Silver Greys.' — (c) **1917** Kephart *Camping* II. 24 Those great tracts of rhododendron . . . cover mile after mile of steep mountainside where few men have ever been. The natives call such wastes 'laurel slicks,' 'woolly heads,' 'lettuce beds,' 'yaller patches,' and 'hells.'

woolyneag ˈwʊlɪˌnig, *n.* Also **woolang.** [Abnaki *wulanikw,* "handsome squirrel."] (See quot. 1910.) Also attrib. *Obs.*

1722 in Temple & Sheldon *Hist. Northfield, Mass.* 160 To 3 fox skins and 1/2 a woolang skin, £0 13 6. **1875** *Ib.* 162 *Woolang* or *woolaneaque,* was the name for the fisher, which is the largest of the mink family. **1910** Hodge *Amer. Indians* II. 974/2 *Woolyneag,* a name in the northern parts of New England for the fisher or pekan. . . . The name . . . is evidently a misapplication.

woozy ˈwuzɪ, *a.* [Prob. a variant of **oozy,* muddy.] **1.** Befuddled or intoxicated. **2.** Fuzzy. Both *colloq.*

(1) **1897** Lewis *Wolfville* 66 When Jim says all this it seems like I'm in a daze an' sorter woozy. **1945** *Nation* 17 March 295/1 Preliminary rumblings from the Senate, as in the extraordinarily woozy speech made by Bushfield of South Dakota Tuesday. — (2) **1903** *N.Y. Sun* 29 Nov. 27 He has a whole lot of woozy hair.

wop wɑp, *n.* [App. f. Italian dial. *guappo,* often used as a greeting by Neapolitans. See Mencken *Supp.* I. 604.] An Italian of low class, a "dago." *Slang.*

1908 K. McGaffey *Show-Girl* 17, I don't know who or what this old wop is that made this crack. **1917** Sinclair *King Coal* 64 That's the way you have to manage them wops. **1949** *Reader's Digest* April 69/1 And she asked her Maker if He wouldn't please try to make American children understand her children, and not call them 'Wops.'

wopse wɑps, *v. N. Eng.* [Origin obscure.] *tr.* To wrap up hastily, to entangle.

1875 Holland *Sevenoaks* 60 We'll wopse 'im up in some blankits. **1897** Robinson *Uncle Lisha* 45 There's a poor leetle muskrat . . . wopsed up in a mess o' weeds. **1946** *Amer. Sp.* Oct. 233 If a shawl was wopsed up it was in an irregular pile.

***word,** *n.* **1.** *S.* In special senses (see quots.). **2. word firing,** in duelling with firearms, the firing at the word or words of the referee. *Obs.* **3. word method,** a method of teaching pupils to read by having them learn words as wholes before their attention is directed to the letters.

(1) **1836** *Quarter Race* (1846) 19 Crump . . . had won the word—that is, he was to ask 'are you ready?' and if answered 'yes!' it was to be a race. **1881** *Harper's Mag.* Aug. 395/1 [Whoever was] overcome and prostrate, cried 'Enough!' Such conduct was understood merely as an admission, technically termed 'word,' that the defeated yielded for the present only. — (2) **1856** *Porter's Spirit of Times* 22 Nov. 192/3 By the ordinary rule of word-firing, for instance, between the words 'one' and 'three,' it would be impossible for such skilful shots as Mr. Travis and Mr. Snydam to miss. — (3) **1882** in F. W. Parker in *Notes of Talks on Teaching* (1883) 34 Learning the word as a whole, without trying to fix the child's attention upon its parts before it becomes a clear object in the mind, is called the 'word method.' **1945** C. V. Good *Dict. of Education* 452/2.

As the last term in **check, swear, weasel word.**

***work,** *n.* In combs.: (1) **work boss,** one in charge of work, *obs.,* cf. Du. *werkbaas;* (2) ***house,** a house of correction for minor offenders; (3) ***out,** a spell of intense application, usu. with reference to athletic activities, *colloq.;* (4) **train,** a railroad train used in building or maintaining a roadbed.

(1) *a*1649 Winthrop *Hist.* I. 166 Here arrived a small Norsey bark . . . with one Gardiner, an expert engineer or work base, and provisions. — (2) **1653** *Boston Rec.* X. 26 My thoughts . . . have beene about . . . the setting up of a Bridewell or Workehouse for Prisonrs Malefactors & some sort of poore people. **1772** Habersham *Letters* 178 The Work House . . . for confining and punishing fugitive and Criminal Slaves, is also in the same Condition with the Goal. **1907** *Springfield W. Republican* 18 July 1 Twenty-three leading business men of the city have been . . . sentenced to six months in the workhouse. — (3) **1909** R. A. Wason *Happy Hawkins* 105 Well, we sure had a work-out. **1932** *Atlantic Mo.* CXLIX. 665 It would give two strong men a workout even to crack the door open six inches against that 120-miles-per-hour slip stream from the propellers. — (4) **1884** *Lisbon* (Dak.) *Star* 10 Oct., The work-train is again engaged in hauling gravel. **1949** *L.A. Times* 7 June 1/6 Explosion of the locomotive of a work train at Serra . . . early yesterday killed one man.

As the last term in **barrel, beaver, blank, bottling, breast, bright, cabinet, car, cob, country, custom, cutting, earth, fire, graduate, head, hoist, hoisting, horseback, indigo, laid, log, lumber, maple sugar, monkey, nail, picket, piece, porcupine-quill, prospect, public, reduction, river, rush, sand, sap, sawmill, second, section, slit, squaw, team, top, trestle, wax, whole, wind work(s).**

***work,** *v.* In colloq. phrases: (1) *To work oneself off as* (someone), to impersonate (someone) for some fraudulent purpose; (2) *to work out,* (*a*) to work away from home as a hired helper, (*b*) (see quot.); (3) *to work over, W.* to go over (a cattle brand) so as to disguise or change it; (4) *to work up,* to move, as a result of one's own effort, into a position of greater importance or to a higher salary.

(1) **1897** Thanet *Missionary Sheriff* 7 The lightning-rods ain't in it with this last scheme—working hisself off as a Methodist parson. — (2) (*a*) **1842** *Letter* 31 Jan. (MS), Chloe works out. **1858** Weed *Autobiog.* 18, I had 'worked out,' and earned leather . . . enough for a pair of shoes. (*b*) **1905** *Harper's Wkly.* 28 Jan. 136/1 The ship had returned to Liverpool, where the whole crew was 'worked out,' as the process of getting rid of men in foreign ports is termed. *Ib.,* The officers had quit after working out the crew. — (3) **1927** Russell *Trails* 157 A cowpuncher might work a brand over or steal a slick ear, but he wouldn't steal milk from a calf. — (4) **1850** Mitchell

Lorgnette I. 77 They say she wants to 'work up.' **1902** LORIMER *Lett. Merchant* 109 He was . . . drawing ten thousand a year, which was more than he could have worked up to in the leather business in a century.

* **worker,** *n.* One who works for a political party, a minor member of a political machine. *Colloq.*

1873 MARK TWAIN & WARNER *Gilded Age* 399 In Washington he was . . . a 'worker' in politics. **1886** ROOSEVELT in *Cent. Mag.* Nov. 78/1 The 'heelers,' or 'workers,' who stand at the polls . . . form a large part of the rank and file composing each organization. **1905** *McClure's Mag.* XXIV. 338 'Workers' are paid 'to get out the vote.'

As the last term in **conjure, shell, wage, wire worker.**

workeyism 'wɜkɪˌɪzəm, *n.* A social or political theory emphasizing the rights of labor. *Rare.* Cf. **worky.** — **1835** *N. Eng. Mag.* VIII. 143 They who get up the cry of workeyism, as if, forsooth, every man in New England did not work.

* **working,** *n.* **1.** An occasion upon which neighbors assemble to perform some work in common. Also **working frolic.** *Colloq.* **2. working card,** = **union card.** Also attrib.

(1) **1852** REYNOLDS *Hist. Illinois* 167 The neighbors . . . organized themselves into a kind of working frolic. **1947** *Democrat* 16 Oct. 1/4 There will be a cemetery working at Salem on Saturday. — (2) **1872** *Pacific States Enterprise* (S.F.) 16 March 3/1 They have adopted the 'working card' system. **1896** *Internat. Typog. Union Proc.* 35/2 It was agreed to issue him a working card.

workinger 'wɜkɪŋɚ, *n.* A workingman. *Rare.* — **1866** *Ore. State Jrnl.* 1 Dec. 2/3 How much contempt he always entertained for that class of beings whose very instinct seemed to condemn it to be a 'workinger.'

worky 'wɜkɪ, *n.* A worker, esp. a factory worker or operative; in *pl.*, an organization of workpeople. Also transf. Now *rare.* Cf. **workeyism.**

1830 *Scioto Gaz.* (Chillicothe, O.) 1 Sep. 2/5 He has been a '*workie*' from his boyhood upward. **1939** *Knickerb.* XIV. 138 [The woodpecker] is a practical body—a regular 'worky.' **1894** *Sunday Reform Leaflet* (Columbus, O.) Sep. 5 Take away this rest-day, and you . . . turn us into a nation of mere 'workies.'

* **world,** *n.* In combs.: (1) **world-beater,** a champion, a prize-winner, *colloq.;* (2) **premiere,** the first performance of a theatrical production or motion picture; (3) **-'s Columbian Exposition,** = **Columbian Exposition;** (4) **Series,** in baseball, a succession of post-season games played between the champion teams of two professional major leagues, also attrib., also **World's Championship series;** (5) **-'s Exposition,** the Centennial Exposition held at Philadelphia in 1876; (6) **-'s Fair,** see as a main entry.

(1) **1893** *Outing* XXII. 103/1 The master of Palo Alto believed that the filly would prove to be a world-beater. **1929** *Strand Mag.* May 498 That girl's face is a world-beater. — (2) **1934** WEBSTER. **1948** *Dly. Ardmoreite* (Ardmore, Okla.) 7 July 1/5 'Return of the Bad Man' will open a three day engagement in Ardmore . . . just one day after its world premier, it has been announced. — (3) **1890** HARRISON in *Pres. Mess. & P.* IX. 140, I do hereby invite all the nations of the earth to take part in . . . the World's Columbian Exposition. **1950** *Chi. Tribune* 4 March, Taylor claimed the word [ballyhoo] originated at the 1893 World's Columbian exposition. — (4) **1888** *Spalding's Base Ball Guide* 47 In 1887 the world's championship series had become an established supplementary series of contests. **1889** *Sporting Life* (Phila.) 14 Aug. 5/3 Boston . . . will also win the world's series from the club that comes out first in the Association race. **1913** *Collier's* 4 Oct. 5/1 In this next impending world-series carnival between Giants and Athletics we have had the hunch [etc.]. **1948** *New Yorker* 25 Sep. 55/1 Boston hopes to regain its old position as Hub of the Universe by having a World Series between the Braves and the Red Sox. — (5) **1877** E. C. BRUCE *Century* 60 [Philadelphia has become] comparable to Vienna as a site for a World's Exposition.

As the last term in **business, universal world.**

World's Fair. An international exposition, containing exhibits from various countries.

The first two examples refer to the International Exposition held in London in 1851.

1850 *N. Eng. Farmer* II. 413 The State Board of Agriculture are making up a collection of samples of Indian corn for the World's Fair. **1851** GREELEY *Glances at Europe* 29 'The World's Fair,' as we Americans have been accustomed to call it, has now been open five days. **1876** INGRAM *Centennial Expos.* 18 The story of the grandest World's Fair that has ever been held. **1949** *Time* 25 July 13/1 Musicians swung informally into *The Hootchy-Kootchy,* Little Egypt's tune at the 1893 World's Fair.

attrib. **1893** *Chi. Tribune* 21 April 4/3 The bonded debt of Chicago, including the World's Fair bonds, is but eighteen and a half millions. **1909** O. HENRY *Options* 279, I rang the door-bell of that World's Fair main building. **1931** CLUTE *Plants* 55 During the first World's Fair in Chicago, the standing cypress (*Kochia scoparia*), with foliage that turns scarlet in autumn, was largely used for garden decorations. . . . Those who were attracted by its trim shape and brilliant coloring began to speak of it as the World's Fair plant.

* **worm,** *n.*

1. The zigzag line of rails first laid down in building a rail fence.

1760 WASHINGTON *Diaries* I. 128 Laid in part the Worm of a fence round my Peach Orchard. **1800** TATHAM *Tobacco* 10 The worm (as it is called) being thus laid, the same process is repeated until the fence rises to the height of nine or ten rails. **1946** *Atlanta Jrnl. Mag.* 3 March 8/2 Neighbors usually help each other lay the worm for a new fence. A fence worm is the first rails forming the pattern of a fence.

attrib. **1846** *Xenia Torch-Light* 23 July 4/1, I found a single log cabin, surrounded by a low fence of rails, wormlaid. **1862** *Ill. Agric. Soc. Trans.* V. 209 Fourteen miles of fence . . . laid in the worm form with stakes and riders. **1880** *Fergus' Hist. Ser.* No. 14, 107 The fences were made of rails, . . . laid up, in what was called the 'worm' or 'Virginia' style.

b. App. the length of a panel of worm fence between the corners. *Rare.*

1855 *Mich. Agric. Soc. Trans.* VI. 177 The fence is laid with seven feet worm, and one foot lap at each end.

2. In special combs.: (1) **worm-eater,** a bird that feeds on worms, as the worm-eating warbler, also with specifying term; (2) **-eating warbler,** a bird of the genus *Helmitheros,* esp. the common worm-eater, *H. vermivorus,* of the eastern states; (3) **fashion,** the manner of construction characteristic of a worm fence, also as adv.; (4) **fence,** see as a main entry; (5) **People,** a division of the Piegan, a tribe related to the Blackfoot tribe of Indians, so called as a translation of their native name, *Esksinaitupiks;* (6) **punch,** (see quot.); (7) **rail fence,** = **worm fence;** (8) **snake,** (*a*) the ground snake, *Carphophis amoena,* (*b*) = **snakeworm;** (9) **tea,** (see quot.), *obs.*

(1) **1760** G. EDWARDS *Gleanings Nat. Hist.* II. 200 The Worm-eater's bill is pretty sharp-pointed. **1831** SWAINSON & RICHARDSON *Fauna Bor.-Amer.* II. 221 *Sylvicola* (*Vermivora*) *peregrina.* . . . Tennessee Worm-eater. **1917** *Birds of Amer.* III. 116/1 The Worm-eater is a quiet bird that spends most of his time on the ground or within a few feet of it. — (2) **1811** WILSON *Ornithology* III. 74 [The] Worm-Eating Warbler. . . . *Sylvia Vermivora,* . . . is remarkably fond of spiders. **1917** *Birds of Amer.* III. 116/1 The Worm-eating Warbler is distinctly a ground Warbler. — (3) **1819** FAUX *Memorable Days* 320 All the wood to be cut down and burnt, save what is wanted for fencing the land with rails in the worm fashion. **1880** MARK TWAIN *Tramp Abroad* 245 Lucerne is a charming place . . . with here and there a bit of ancient embattled wall bending itself over the ridges, worm-fashion.

(5) **1892** GRINNELL *Blackfoot Lodge Tales* 225 Gents of the Pi-kun-i [include] . . . Worm People. — (6) **1891** *Cent.* 6981/1 *Worm-punch* . . . a small, rather slender punch, used by coopers for clearing out worm-holes in staves or heads of casks, for the purpose of stopping the holes with wooden plugs to prevent leaking. — (7) **1818** FORDHAM *Narr. Travels* 163 The worm railfences running in straight-lines . . . have little of beauty. — (8) (*a*) **1885** J. S. KINGSLEY *Stand. Nat. Hist.* III. 362 The genus *Carphophis* is very generally distributed; in the United States, the species *amoena,* . . . as the thunder, ground, or worm-snake, is most familiar. (*b*) **1891** *Cent.* 6981/1. — (9) **1850** PEREIRA *Elem. Mat. Med.* (ed. 3) II. 1478 A preparation kept in the shops of the United States . . . under the name of *worm tea,* consists of spigelia root, senna, manna, and savine, mixed together.

As the last term in **apple, army, bag, basket, black, boll, bonnet, bore, bot, buckwheat, bud, canker, chestnut rail, corn, cotton, cotton army, cotton boll, cranberry, drop, fall army, fall web, fence, fever, fire, fish, grape, grass, gray, green-striped maple, gulf, half-hill, heart, hook, horn, inch, joint, maple, measuring, peach, pickle, poplar, potato, red, roller, rose, saw, screw, shelf, snake, sod, span, speckled cut, spindle, split, straw, strawberry, tape, tobacco, tomato, top, web, wheat bulb, wheat head army, woolly worm.**

* **worm,** *v. tr.* To rid (tobacco plants) of worms or grubs.

1624 SMITH *Virginia* v. 172 Wormes in the earth also there are but too many, so that to keepe them from destroying their Corne and Tobacco, they are forced to worme them euery morning . . . else all would be destroyed. **1649** W. BULLOCK *Virginia* 11 The poore

Servant goes daily through the rowes of Tobacco stooping to worme it. **1779** J. Carver *Treat. Culture Tobacco* iv. 23 This is termed 'worming the tobacco.' **1864** De Coin *Cotton & Tobacco* 274 The plants ought to be wormed—which means searched and cleared of worms—at least once a week. **1931** *Golconda* (Ill.) *Herald-Enterprise* 5 March 6/2 Oh! how I disliked cultivating and worming the tobacco.

***wormer,** *n.* A screw attached to the end of a rod, used for withdrawing a charge or some other obstruction from the barrel of a gun. — **1702** *Essex Inst. Coll.* XLII. 162 A gunne mallet, two formers, . . . a wormer, & scourer for small arms. **1891** *Cent.* 6980/3.

worm fence. A zigzag Virginia rail fence. Cf. **staked and ridered.**

1652 *East-Hampton Rec.* I. 22 It is ordered that Thomas Baker shall have . . . 7 akers . . . within the worme fence on the litel plaine. **1724** Jones *Present State of Va.* 39 *Tobacco* and *Indian Corn* are planted in *Hills* as *Hops*, and secured by *Wormfences*, which are made of Rails supporting one another very firmly in a particular Manner. **1802** Davis *Travels* (1803) 343 You must keep *strait* along the worm (i.e. *crooked*) fence, till you come to a barn. **1946** Nixon *Va. Words* 43 worm fence. . . . A zigzag rail fence; fairly common in the northern Piedmont and on the Eastern Shore.

attrib. and *transf.* **1836** Simms *Mellichampe* xx, A little cornfield, with its worm-fence enclosure, lay on one hand. **1867** Harris *Sut Lovingood* 41 The road wer sprinkled worm fence fashun. **1897** Lewis *Wolfville* 193 That Remorse pony . . . gives way to sech a fit of real old worm-fence buckin' as lands Slim Jim on his sombrero. **1946** Stoddard *Horace Greeley* opp. 241 Extract from a Letter to Helen R. Marshall Dated February 6, 1868; a Good Example of Greeley's 'Worm Fence' Handwriting.

b. Hence **worm-fenced, worm fencing.**

1789 *Amer. Philos. Soc.* III. p. lx, Worm-fencing and similar expedients of infant cultivation, should never be seen. **1904** T. E. Watson *Bethany* 8 [It] was striving, unsuccessfully, to look at ease among . . . negro cabins, and worm-fenced cotton fields.

***worry,** *v.* **1.** *tr.* (See quot. 1828.) *Obs.* **2.** *To worry along*, to manage to keep going. *Colloq.*

(1) 1828 Webster, Worry, . . . to fatigue; to harass with labor; a popular sense of the word. **1875** Holland *Sevenoaks* 66 For three steady hours he went on, the horse no more worried than if he had been standing in the stable. — **(2) 1871** Mark Twain *Sk. New & Old* 296 You seem to have pretty much all the tunes there are, and you worry along first rate. **1885** Howells *Silas Lapham* 214, I think I can manage to worry along.

***worst,** *a.*

1. *(The) worst kind*, the severest, most extreme, or most drastic kind; as adverbial phrase, to an extreme, as much as possible. Also *worse kind. Colloq.*

1839 Marryat *Diary in Amer.* 1 Ser. II. 227 He loves Sal, the worst kind. **1859** Bartlett 517 *Worst Kind.* Used in such phrases as, 'I gave him the worst kind of a licking.' **1892** *Harper's Mag.* Feb. 437/2, I want something to read the worst kind. **1893** Post *Harvard Stories* 140 Then he begged worse kind just to let him look out of a window where he could see you. **1904** *N.Y. Tribune* 26 June, 'So you want to go to Cuba, do you?' asked Colonel Roosevelt. 'I do, worst kind.'

2. *(In) the worst way*, as much as possible. *Colloq.*

c1870 Chipman *Notes on Bartlett* 517 *Worst way;* very much; very. 'It was wanted in the worst way.' Said July 18, 1860, with reference to a shower which, after a drought, fell the night before. **1908** Yeslah *Tenderfoot S. Calif.* 32 Jones . . . needed that diamond scarf-pin the worst way. **1946** *Reader's Digest* Jan. 71/1, I wanted to wear it the worst way.

***wort,** *n.* As the last term in **bell, blood, fever, frost, master, Saint Peter's, sneeze, soap, spider, thoroughwort.**

***worth,** *a. for all it is worth*, or variants, with the utmost effort, with all of which one is capable. *Colloq.*

1874 Mark Twain *Sk. New & Old* 310 We shall fly our comet for all it is worth. **1889** Gunter *That Frenchman* 298 [The steamer] is driving, for everything she is worth, down the waters of the Finnish Gulf. **1897** Thanet *Missionary Sheriff* 19 Paisley played his cough and his hollow cheeks for all they were worth.

wow waʊ, *n.* [f. **wow, interj.*] Something striking or sensational. Also attrib. and as verb. *Slang.*

1927 E. Wallace in *Morn. Post* 20 Dec., I am told this [a melodrama] was a 'wow' in America; and a 'wow,' as we all know, is American for sensational success. **1949** *Time* 19 Sep. 45/3 She wowed them with a dramatic reading of the death scene from *Romeo and Juliet. Ib.* 10 Oct. 47/2 They had a wow comic-hat routine to go with *I Wish I Was in Peoria.*

***wrangle,** *v. W. tr.* To take charge of (horses), to herd. Also transf.

1903 A. Adams *Log Cowboy* xiii. 197 Forrest detailed Rod Wheat to wrangle the horses, for we intended to take Honeyman with us. **1913** Bower *Parowan Bonanza* vii. 83 Time Tommy wrangles the burros and does the dirty work . . . crime won't look half so good to him. **1938** *Cattleman* May 5/1 Them Dutch Oven biscuits he wrangled Was somethin' that couldn't be beat. **1941** Fergusson *Southwest* 339 Then while you wrangle your dudes, I'll see what I can round up for the baile at night.

Hence **wrangling,** *n.*

1889 *Boston Jrnl.* 29 April 2/2 Two days of wrangling on the prairie . . . were sufficient. **1949** *Sierra Club Bul.* June 24 Then there was *Brownie*, one of Bud Steele's stalwart string, who was a distinguished renegade in 1946 because he continually eluded wrangling.

wrangler ˈræŋglɚ, *n. W.* [f. **caballerango.**] = **horse wrangler.** Also attrib.

1892 *Outing* Jan. 272/1 Our wrangler had been unhorsed during his wild ride of the morning, and was laid up with a badly-sprained knee joint. **1944** Clark *Pills* 177 It was thrilling to travel with Chinese junks down Oriental rivers, to catch wild horses around Turkomen wrangler camps, to stalk the wild animals of Africa. **1948** *Sky Line Trail* Nov. 4/1 Teepee Town, with tents for cook staff and wranglers, is at the base of Citadel Peak.

As the last term in **day, freight, horse, night wrangler.**

***wrapper,** *n.* In various colloq. uses (see quots.).

1808 Pike *Sources Miss.* iii. App. 36 The lower class of men are generally dressed in . . . a kind of leather boot or wrapper. **c1870** Chipman *Notes on Bartlett* 517 *Wrapper*, . . . an under-shirt. **1901** *Munsey's Mag.* XXV. 391/2 Two men cautiously unhook the 'wrappers'—chains whose function it is to bind on the load. **1905** *Forestry Bureau Bul.* No. 61, 30 *Binding chain*, a chain used to bind together a load of logs. . . . Syn.: wrapper chain. (N[orthern] F[orest].)

As the last term in **Florida wrapper.**

***wrapping,** *n.* **1. wrapping boot,** a kind of leather boot. *Obs.* **2. wrapping silk,** (see quot.). — **(1) 1808** Pike *Sources Miss.* iii. App. 41 Their dress is . . . the wrapping boot with the jack boot, and permanent spur over it. — **(2) 1891** *Cent.* 5630/1 *Wrapping-silk*, a fine strong floss employed in the manufacture of artificial flies.

***wreck,** *n.* In combs.: (1) **wreck heap,** = **rack heap,** *obs.*, cf. **wooden island;** (2) **master,** a person appointed to take charge of a wreck or of wreckage; (3) **train,** = ***wrecker 2,** cf. **wrecking train.**

(1) 1826 Flint *Recoll.* 92 These wreck-heaps are immense piles of trees, amassed by the waters, at points, and in difficult places. **1868** *Putnam's Mag.* May 596/1 The bars, the 'tow-heads,' the wreck-heaps, . . . phenomena of the Mississippi. — **(2) 1799** *Md. Laws* lxxxii, The governor . . . shall appoint one discreet and sensible person . . . to act in the office of a wreck-master. **1904** *Booklovers Mag.* May 665 When the wreck-master and his gang reach the scene this is the first question that arises: Is there anyone, living or dead, under the debris? — **(3) 1900** *Dly. Ardmoreite* (Ardmore, Okla.) 7 May 4/2 By seven o'clock this morning a wreck train and crew from Gainesville were on the scene.

***wrecker,** *n.* **1.** One appointed to recover as much as possible of the assets of insolvent firms. *Obs.* **2.** (See quot. 1904.)

(1) 1846 Lyell *Second Visit* II. 39 'A wrecker' . . . [had] the unenviable task . . . of seeking out and recovering bad debts. — **(2) 1904** *Booklovers Mag.* May 663 The special train . . . dubbed the 'Wrecker' . . . is a relief train, ready to respond to any call for aid in case of accident. **1948** *Chesterton* (Ind.) *Tribune* 28 Oct. 7/5 It took a wrecker to dislodge the car and a cutting torch to free the bent wreckage so the locomotive could continue its run.

***wrecking,** *n.* and *a.* In combs.: (1) **wrecking car,** a railroad car used in clearing the tracks after wrecks; (2) **company,** a company that engages in tearing down and removing buildings preparatory for new construction work; (3) **crane,** a railroad crane for use in case of wrecks; (4) **gang, outfit,** a group of workers who clear up train wrecks; (5) **train,** = ***wrecker 2;** (6) **truck,** a truck for towing wrecked automobiles to a repair shop.

(1) 1862 *Ashcroft's Railway Directory* 76 No. of . . . Wrecking Cars [on the Central Railroad of New Jersey], 1. **1899** *Railroad Gaz.* 29 Sep. 679/3 The name of the wrecking car has been changed to tool car. — **(2) 1898** *K.C. Star* 20 Dec. 9/1 The board of construction has had under consideration several propositions from engineers and wrecking companies. — **(3) 1874** Knight 644/1 Fairbairn's travelling crane . . . is adapted for a wrecking-crane for railroad use. — **(4) 1898** *Engineering Mag.* XVI. 68 The wrecking outfit should be immediately available. **1901** Merwin & Webster *Calumet 'K'* 8 Bannon . . . was chief of the wrecking gang on a division of the Grand Trunk.

(5) 1887 *Courier-Journal* 17 Jan. 1/7 Wrecking trains have arrived. **1947** *Chi. D. News* 17 Jan. 1/6 A wrecking train reached the scene and began clearing away the debris. — **(6) 1930** *Randolph Enter-*

prise (Elkins, W.Va.) 20 Nov. 5/3 A wrecking truck from the Randolph garage towed the car.

*wren, *n.* As the last term in **Baird's, Bewick's, cactus, Californian Bewick's, canyon, Carolina, fiery-crowned, Florida, fresh-water marsh, golden-crown(ed), house, long-billed marsh, marsh, Mexican, mocking, Parkman's, ruby-crowned, short-billed marsh, spruce, tule, Vigors', winter, wood wren.**

wren-tit, *n.* "A bird, *Chamaea fasciata*, peculiar to California, of uncertain relations, usually made the type and sole member of a family Chamæidæ: so called from its uniting, to some extent, the habits of a wren and of a titmouse" (*Cent.*). — **1872** Coues *N. Amer. Birds* 79 *Chamæidæ;* Wren-tits . . . much like a titmouse in general appearance, . . . with the general habits of wrens. **1944** *Nat. Geog. Mag.* June 694/2 Chestnut-backed chickadees, hermit thrushes, . . . and kinglets live almost side by side with such hot-country birds as mocking birds, . . . California quail, wren-tits, and road-runners.

***wrestle,** *v.* **1.** *tr.* To eat or devour (food). *Slang. Obs.* **2.** *W.* To throw or hold down (a calf) for branding. Cf. ***flank,** *v.* **3.**

(1) **1871** Hay *Pike Co. Ballads* 24 He'll wrastle his hash to-night in hell. **1897** Lewis *Wolfville* 82 The O.K. House, where them Britons has been wrastlin' their chuck. — (2) **1888** Roosevelt in *Cent. Mag.* April 861/2 A fire is built, the irons heated, and a dozen men dismount to, as it is called, 'wrastle' the calves. **1944** Adams *W. Words* 181/1 wrastlin' calves A common expression for flanking.

wring-jaw, *n.* (See quot. 1800.) *Slang. Obs.* — **1800** Boucher *Glossary* p. l, Wring-jaw; hard cider. **1845** Cooper *Chainbearer* iii, His weakness in favor of 'wring-jaw' . . . [was] a well-established failing.

***wrist,** *n.* **1.** A pin or projection from the side of a wheel, crank, etc., to which a connecting rod is attached. **2.** The grip of a gunstock.

(1) **1864** Webster 1529/3 *Wrist,* . . . a stud or pin. **1883** Knight *Supp.* 229/2 A wrist on a driving wheel. — (2) **1867** G. W. Harris *Sut Lovingood* 77 Not much bigger nor the wrist ove a rifle-gun. **1874** Long *Wild-Fowl* 27 The stock should be of English or German Walnut, with a strong thick wrist.

wrister ˈrɪstɚ, *n.* A knitted covering for the wrist.

1879 Webster *Supp.* 1585/3. **1896** *Chautauquan* Oct. 83/1 The old lady wore gray yarn wristers. **1945** Pearson *Country Flavor* 94 In the present stage of clothing styles, the wrister has been sadly neglected since the first decade of the century.

***write,** *v.* **1. write-in,** *Polit.* a name not on a ballot but written in by a voter at the time of voting. Also the action of inserting such a name. (Cf. ***paster 1,** ***sticker 1.**) **2. write-up,** a somewhat extended newspaper account of a person, place, etc.

(1) [**1944** *Greeley* (Colo.) *D. Tribune* 16 Sep. 2/2, I greatly appreciate the good will expressed and effort expended by the friends who wrote in my name as candidate for County Judge on the Republican primary ballot.] **1948** *Dly. Ardmoreite* (Ardmore, Okla.) 27 June 1/1 Mr. Truman's name is the only one on the ballot in Monday's voting here although a space will be left for write-ins. **1950** *Chi. Tribune* 2 April 40/1 Such an attempted write-in for any candidate might result in many spoiled ballots. — (2) **1885** *Wkly. New Mexican Rev.* 19 Feb. 4/1, I have prepared quite an extensive 'write-up' of the resources of this country. **1948** *Redbook Mag.* April 83/1, I got myself a press card and have gone in to plays and opera and concerts this winter and did a write-up job for them.

***writer,** *n.* As the last term in **crop, editorial, ghost, sheet, sight writer.**

***wrong,** *a.* *To get one in wrong,* to bring one into disfavor. *Slang.* — **1917** *War Birds* (1927) 30 There are a few roughnecks in every outfit that will cause trouble and get the whole bunch in wrong. **1925** Joan Sutherland *Circle of Stars* xxii, He's got you in wrong with the Governor while you were away.

***wrymouth,** *n.* A large blenny, *Cryptacanthodes maculatus.* — **1839** Storer *Mass. Fishes* 28 *Cryptacanthodes maculatus.* The spotted Wry-mouth. **1890** *Science* April 212/1 The sea-raven, the rock-eel and the wry-mouth, which inhabit these brilliant groves are all colored to match their surroundings.

wurtzilite ˈwɜtsl̩ˌaɪt, *n.* [Named after Dr. Henry *Wurtz* (b. 1828) of N.Y.] (See 1st quot.) — **1891** *Cent.* 6996/2 *wurtzilite.* . . . A kind of solid bitumen found in the Uintah Mountains, Utah. **1891** Union Pac. R.R. *Utah* (4th ed.) 76 A kindred substance to these, which Prof. Blake, of New Haven, names 'Wurtzilite,' has been found about the divide between the Strawberry and the Price.

W X Y Z, see **X.**

Wyandot ˈwaɪənˌdɑt, *n.* Also **Wyandotte.** [f. Huron *Wendat* (becoming in Eng. *Yendat, Guyandotte, Wyandot*) app. meaning "islanders" or "dwellers on a peninsula." See Hodge.]

1. An Indian of a once powerful Iroquoian tribe at one time included in the Huron confederacy; *pl.*, the tribe of such an Indian.

[**1640** *Relations des Jésuites* (1858) 35/2 Depuis le sault S. Louis montant tousiours sur ce grand fleuue, on trouue . . . les Ouendat [etc.].] **1749** *Doc. Col. Hist. N.Y.* VI. 531 The Twitchwees & Wyandotts . . . for two or three years past have dealt largely with our Traders. **1867** Parkman *Jesuits N. Amer.* xxxii. (1879) 426 Thus it appears that the Wyandots . . . are descendants of the ancient Hurons, and chiefly of that portion of them called the Tobacco Nation. **1945** *Chi. D. News* 2 Aug. 10/2 The Indians—Delawares, Shawnees, Wyandots and those of the Miami Confederacy—gave up all title to lands in southern Ohio.

attrib. **1789** *Ann. 1st Cong.* 72 The Governor of the Western Territory . . . entered into a treaty . . . with the sachems and warriors of the Wyandot, Delaware, Ottawa . . . nations. **1837** *New-Yorker* 29 April 90/2 The Wyandot reservation of lands in Ohio was offered for sale two weeks since at Marion. **1847** Parkman in *Knickerb.* XXX. 126 His sturdy Wyandot pony stood quietly behind him.

For **Wyandot float** see ***float 1. b.**

b. (See quots.) *Obs.*

1856 *Rep. Comm. Patents 1855: Agric.* 173 The 'Wyandotte' is certainly the most prolific corn I have ever grown. **1856** *Western Citizen* (Paris, Ky.) 7 March 2/1 Three of the average sized ears of the Wyandot corn would make one quart, or ninety-six ears per bushel.

c. (See quot. 1910.)

1884 *Bazaar* 12 Sep. 866/1 Wyandottes. Wanted a few early pullets, pure bred. **1910** Hodge *Amer. Indians* II. 977/2 Wyandotte. An American breed of fowls, earlier known as Sebright Cochins, said to have sprung from the mating of a Sebright bantam cock and a Cochin hen. The name was proposed at Worcester, Mass., in 1883, by Mr Houdette, and after some opposition it has been accepted. **1927** *Cornell Rural School Leaflet* XX. No. 4, 15 Thus we have produced the general-purpose breeds, the Plymouth Rocks, the Wyandottes, and the Rhode Island Reds.

2. Wyandotte Constitution, the constitution drafted for the state of Kansas in 1859 by a convention in Wyandotte, now Kansas City. Cf. **Lecompton Constitution.**

1877 Johnson *Anderson Co., Kans.* 128 On the first Tuesday of July, the delegates elected assembled at Wyandotte to frame the Constitution, afterwards known as the Wyandotte constitution.

***wye,** *n.* See ***Y.**

X

X,** ***n.

1. *Hist.* Used, in conjunction with 'W,' 'Y,' and 'Z,' to indicate one of certain French emissaries engaged in negotiations with three envoys sent to Paris by the U.S. Government in 1797. Also attrib.

1797 *Amer. State P.: For. Relations* II. 158 M. X. . . . said his communication was not immediately with M. Talleyrand but through another gentleman in whom M. Talleyrand had great confidence. This proved to be M. Y. **1798** *Ib.* 157 The names designated by the letters W. X. Y. Z. in the following copies of letters. **1841** TRUMBULL *Autobiog.* 222, [I] visited the American X, Y, Z negotiators, Pinckney, Marshall, and Gerry. **1945** ADAMS *Album Amer. Hist.* II. 82 As a result of the XYZ episode of 1797, came an outburst of patriotic feeling.

2. A ten-dollar bill. *Colloq.*

1834 *Richmond* (Ind.) *Palladium* 18 Jan. 4/2 Have you got ten dollars in small bills you will exchange for an X? **1840** *Louisville Pub. Adv.* 21 Aug. 2/1 Is there not a V or an X left to redeem the MSS? **1893** POST *Harvard Stories* 295 Perhaps you had better lend me an X now.

b. XX, a twenty-dollar bill. Also **double X.**

1852 *Yankee Notions* July 214/1 Seeing these dashing young fellows sporting their double X's in careless profusion, . . . one of them bantered B. for a game of poker. **1883** CRAWFORD *Dr. Claudius* 346 The Custom-House officials . . . know the green side of a XX.

3. X rail, a railroad rail or section of a rail shaped like an X, for use at switches or crossovers. *Obs.*

1832 *Amer. R.R. Jrnl.* I. 227/2 This takes place to a great extent upon the crossing or X rail.

xerga ˈksegɑ, *n. S.W.* [f. Sp. *jerga,* (formerly, and still occasionally in Amer. Sp., spelled *xerga*) in Amer. Sp. sense shown here.] (See quots.) Cf. **gerga.**

1897 INMAN *Old Santa Fe Trail* 56 A *salea,* or raw sheep-skin, made soft by rubbing, was put on the animal's back, to prevent chafing, and over it the saddle-cloth, or *xerga.* **1944** ADAMS *W. Words* 181 Xerga (csay′ gah) A saddle cloth placed between the salea and the packsaddle. **1946** MCWILLIAMS *So. Calif. Country* 32 Believing that the possession of finery had a tendency to induce the Indians to run away, the padres clothed them in a coarse frieze (*xerga*), made at the Missions.

Y

∗**Y,** *n.* Also ∗**wye.**

1. Used to indicate a person: See ∗**X.**

2. =**switchback.** (See also quot. 1864.)

1858 W. P. Smith *Railway Celebrations* 42 Mr. Engineer Latrobe's original triumph in crossing great elevations with locomotive and cars, by means of a series of steep inclines, called Y's. **1864** Webster 1532/1 Y, . . . a portion of track consisting of two converging tracks connected by a cross-track. **1947** Beebe *Mixed Train Dly.* 286 There were the roads . . . which possess neither wye nor turntable, with the results that an even fifty percent of their operations are accomplished backwards while the other half of the time the engines run pilot first as their builders intended.

b. A branching highway. Also as a place-name.

1926 Roberts *Time of Man* 72 At noon they stopped at a store set in front of valley fields where the roads went off in a Y. **1938** Thompson *High Trails* 109 At present the St. Mary end is being improved, and a new wye has been constructed at the junction with the Blackfeet Highway. **1948** *Calif. Highways* July–Aug. 9/1 This structure will be located at the Vallejo Wye, or Fifth Street entrance to Vallejo.

3. Abbreviation for Yale.

1892 *Outing* March 455/1 The old 'Y' rule . . . required a man to win a point either in the Yale or Harvard games, or at the Intercollegiate meeting, before he could wear the university 'Y.' **1894** *Harper's Mag.* July 184/1 As the Yale crew have not arrived, no large blue flag with a white 'Y' in the center graces the top of the staff.

4. Abbreviation for Y.M.C.A. or Y.W.C.A.

1920 *Outing* July–Aug. 245/1 They say it is almost entirely due to this recreation work at our Y. foyers and to the influence of the sportive doughboy. **1948** *Chelsea* (Mass.) *Rec.* 30 Nov. 8/1 Ladies night will be observed this evening at the Community Y.

yager ˈjegɚ, *n.* [Introduced into American use by German settlers and gunmakers. Cf. G. *Jägerbusche*, a sharpshooter's rifle.] A short-barrelled large-bore rifle of a type formerly popular in the South and Southwest. *Obs.* Cf. **Mississippi jager.**

[**1777** in *Jrnl. of Nicholas Cresswell* (1925) 231 A number of Hessian Chasseurs or Yaugers arrived in green uniforms and boots, all armed with rifles.] **1818** *Miss. Republican* (Natchez) 23 July 4/3 A. Griswold . . . has just received . . . 20 Yaugers 50 Muskets with bayonets. **1890** Langford *Vigilante Days* (1912) 410 My armory consisted of one rifle, fifteen United States yagers [etc.].

b. In full **yager rifle.**

1817 E. P. Fordham *Narr. Travels* 141 Sent the two P——s . . . for the yager rifle, and the Wallet, containing my blanket and plunder, and the spade. *a***1918** G. Stuart *On Frontier* I. 187 Nine Pipes, a Flathead, came to get a nipple put on his Yager rifle.

∗**Yahoo,** *n.* **1.** (See quot. 1855.) **2.** An early settler in California. Both *obs.* — (1) **1855** Simms *Forayers* 203 The Yahoos were another tory banditti; their name, with a strange taste, self-chosen. — (2) **1872** Powers *Afoot & Alone* 282 It is not these Yahoos alone who find themselves without wives, for the best old Spanish blood goes a begging.

Yakima ˈjækəmə, *n.* [A native word meaning "runaway."] *pl.* or *collect.* A Shahaptian tribe formerly occupying both sides of the Columbia River in Washington.

1838 Parker *Exploring Tour* 304 South of the Long Rapids, and to the confluence of Lewis' river with the Columbia, are the Yookoomans, a more active people, numbering about seven hundred. **1857** *Spirit of Times* 4 July 277/3, I have abandoned the quiet paths of Themis . . . to become a sub in one of Uncle Sam's regular regiments engaged in the late campaigns against the Yakima. **1946** Adams *Album Amer. Hist.* III. 84 In 1855 the Yakimas attacked parties of prospectors.

attrib. **1855** *N.Y. Herald* 15 Nov. 2/3 All the Yacama Indians are in the field, and the war has fairly begun. **1949** *Travel* Oct. 34/3 A salmon feast is held annually by the Yakima tribe at their 'longhouse' near Wapato on the Yakima Reservation.

b. The language of these Indians.

1940 Smith *Puyallup-Nisqually* 20 There were two other Salish groups, the Chehalis and the Twana, and the two Sahaptin dialects, Kittitas and Iakima.

∗**Yale,** *n.* [f. Linus *Yale* (1821–68), a New England locksmith.] A trade-mark name applied to locks, esp. to a type having a revolving barrel. Hence **Yale key.**

1882 *Encycl. Brit.* XIV. 751/1. **1909** O. Henry *Options* 113 His name sounded like a Yale key when you push it in wrong side up. **1946** *Coronet* Dec. 144/2, I began with three Yale locks and waited a month to sell the first one.

Yaleite ˈjelaɪt, *n.* A student at Yale. — **1867** *Harper's Wkly.* 3 Aug. 487/2 A few mishaps to the Yaleites put Harvard in possession, and the game at this juncture looked very dubious on both sides.

Yalensian jeˈlɛnzɪən, *n.* A student or graduate of Yale.

1852 Bristed *5 Years Eng. Univ.* II. 153 The necessary expenses of a Cantab will . . . be brought very nearly on a par with those of a Yalensian. **1906** *N.Y. Ev. Post* 24 April 8 Secretary Taft, speaking at New Haven last night, exhorted all fledgling Yalensians to avoid morbid social pity. **1912** Nicholson *Hoosier Chron.* 219 Dan, finding several Yalensians in the company, . . . made them all acquainted with Sylvia and her friends.

∗**yaller,** see ∗**yellow.**

yam jæm, *n. S.* [See note.]

In its Amer. use this word is app. of African origin. Cf. Gullah *jambi*, a reddish sweet potato, and Vai *dzambi*, wild yam, sweet potato.

A moist yellow or orange-colored tuber of a vine, *Dioscorea sativa.* Also attrib. Cf. **buckra yam, wild yam.**

1676 Glover *Va.* in *Phil. Trans.* XI. 629 Their Gardens have . . . Carrets, Potatoes, and Yams. **1748** Catesby *Carolina* II. p. xix, The Yam. . . . Carolina is the farthest North I have known them to grow, and there more for curiosity than advantage. **1844** *Lexington* (Ky.) *Observer* 9 Oct. 3/6 Our friend . . . left upon our table a potatoe of the yam species. **1949** *Hoard's Dairyman* 10 Nov. 803/3 A 75-day feeding test . . . proved that dried 'yams' were worth 91.4 per cent as much as ground yellow corn.

Yamassee ˈjaməˌsi, *n.* ["A name of uncertain etymology, and evidently an abbreviated form" (Hodge).] (See quot. 1910.)

1699 J. Dickenson *God's Protecting Providence* 84 The Carolina-Indians, called the Yammasees, . . . [were] Trading for Deer-Skins. **1741** *S.C. Hist. Soc. Coll.* IV. 14 The Yemassee Indians . . . had lived in amity with the Government at St. Augustine. **1871** Fairbanks *Hist. Fla.* 179 It was perhaps at this period that Capt. T. Nairn, of South Carolina, with a party of Yemassee Indians, penetrated to the headwaters of the St. John's. **1910** Hodge *Amer. Indians* II. 986 Yamasee. . . . A former noted tribe of Muskhogean stock, best known in connection with early South Carolina history. . . . They were said to be darker than the Creeks, and 'flat-footed.' **1947** Martin *Indians* 382 The Irene culture was contemporary with the Lamar culture of central Georgia. Probably the Irene Indians were Guale (Yamassee) or Cusabo, and most likely they spoke a Muskhogean language.

b. Yamassee stroke, (see quot. 1744).

1744 Moore *Voy. Georgia* 107 The Indians . . . rowed . . . by taking a short and long stroke alternately, which they called the Yamassee stroke. **1910** Hodge *Amer. Indians* II. 987 From their proficiency as canoe men [they] gave name to a particular method of rowing known as the 'Yamasee stroke.'

Yamel ˈjaməl, *n.* Also **Yam-hill.** [Native name of unknown significance.] (See quots.) *Obs.*

1844 Lee & Frost *Oregon* vii. 90 This part of the valley is inhabited by a small remnant of the Yam-hill clan of Indians only; but as it is the most inviting portion of the Walamet Valley [etc.]. **1849** *31st Cong.* 1 Sess. 1850 Sen. Ex. Doc. 52, 172 The *Yam Hill* Indians are a small tribe who claim the country drained by a river of that name, which is mostly taken up by whites. **1910** Hodge *Amer. Indians* II. 987 Yamel. A Kalapooian tribe formerly living on Yamhill cr., a w. tributary of the Willamette in Oregon. They are now under the Siletz school and numbered only 5 in 1910.

yamp jæmp, *n.* Also **yampa.** [f. Shoshonean. Cf. Ute *yămpă*, the name of this plant.] Either of two western herbs of the genus *Atenia*, or the edible potato-like tuber of these. Also attrib.

1845 FRÉMONT *Exped.* 158 This morning we breakfasted on *yampah.* **1847** *Adv. Rocky Mts.* (1848) 258 A large grizzly bear [was] . . . searching for yampa-roots or pig-nuts. **1874** *Field & Stream* 13 Aug. 1/2 Properly, the 'Yampericos' or 'Yampe-tethkis,' are eaters of 'yampe root.' **1927** WALGAMOTT *Remin. Early Days* II. 44 The Yampa was abundant along Snake river. **1937** *Range Plant Handbook* w48 Yampa is not usually abundant on the range but occasionally occurs in small rather thick stands.

Yamparika ˌjæmpəˈrikə, *n.* [See **yamp.**] (See quot. 1907.) — **1874** [see **yamp**]. **1907** HODGE *Amer. Indians* I. 393/1 Ditsakana. . . . A Comanche division. . . . They also were popularly known as Yamparika, from their habit of eating yampa root.

Yank jæŋk, *n.*[1] Short for Yankee *q.v. Colloq.* Cf. **galvanized Yank.**

1778 *Conquerors* 14 Give me five hundred brave and chosen men, I'll drive the Yanks from north to south again. **1862** *Phila. Inquirer* March (Chipman), The 'Yank' has got up a superior article, which it is very difficult to detect. **1945** *Greeley* (Colo.) *D. Tribune* 18 Aug. 1/8 (*heading*), Black and White Yanks in Battle On London Street.

yank, *n.*[2] A sudden jerk, pull, or tug. Also fig. *Colloq.* — **1885** *Milnor* (Dak.) *Free Press* 28 March 1/5 The other shoe pulled hard, and . . . Mr. Crane gave it a sudden yank. **1906** *N.Y. Globe* 20 Aug. 6 A fantastic proposition from Germany . . . takes one back with an unpleasant yank into the middle ages.

Hence **yank-up,** =**twitch-up.** — **1875** TEMPLE & SHELDON *Hist. Northfield, Mass.* 46 They were wonderfully expert in killing game . . . and in capturing both larger and smaller sorts by means of driveways and in rude traps and yank-ups.

* **Yankee,** *n.* and *a.* Also **Yankey.** [See note.]

A satisfactory origin for this term cannot be made out from the available evidence. The *OED* shows the word in British use as a surname or nickname, with Du. associations, as early as 1683. The first to apply it, in contempt, to New Englanders were app. British soldiers. In the first quot. 1758, below, Gen. Wolfe referred to New England troops serving under him. It was applied freely during the Yankee and Pennamite War (see **5.** (5) below) to those from Connecticut and was similarly used of New Englanders during the troubles between the "Yorkers" and the "Green Mountain Boys" over land titles in Vermont.

Use of the term by New Englanders has not been found prior to the battle of Lexington. After that engagement, the New Englanders began the process of dignifying the nickname. A mythical tribe of Mass. Indians, the Yankos (i.e., Invincibles), was invented and alleged to have been conquered in colonial times by the valorous New Englanders. The beaten Yankos, so it was claimed, gave their own name to their conquerors. By way of retort from the Va. side there was brought forward the Cherokee word *eankke*, coward, slave, which was said to have been early applied to the New Englanders by the Virginians for not assisting them against the Cherokees.

The theory first advanced by the Rev. John Heckewelder in 1819, explaining *Yankee* as resulting from the Indians' effort to pronounce "English" has obtained wide currency.

These and most of the other theories about the origin of the word are admirably discussed—and discarded—in O. G. T. Sonneck, *Report on "The Star Spangled Banner" . . . and "Yankee Doodle"* (1909) 79 ff. See also the *OED s.v.*, and Henri Logeman in *Studies in English Philology in Honor of F. Klaeber* (1929) pp. 403–13.

1. A nickname for New Englanders, at first and for a long time afterwards applied with extreme contempt.

1758 JAMES WOLFE in Beckles Willson *Life & Letters of James Wolfe* (1909) 376 My posts are now so fortified that I can afford you two companies of Yankees, and the more as they are better for ranging and scouting than either work or vigilance. [*Ib.* 392 The Americans are in general the dirtiest most contemptible cowardly dogs that you can conceive. There is no depending on them in action. They fall down dead in their own dirt and desert by battalions, officers and all. Such rascals as those are rather an encumberance than any real strength to an army.] **1765** *Oppression,* From meanness first this Portsmouth Yankey rose, And still to meanness all his conduct flows. **1775** *First Book Amer. Chron.* 14 By night they [British soldiers] abused the watch-men on duty, and the young children of Boston by the wayside, making mouths at them, calling them Yankeys, shewing their posteriors, and clapping their hands thereon. **1784** SMYTH *Tour* II. 366 The New Englanders are disliked by the inhabitants of all the other provinces, by whom they are called *Yankeys,* by way of derision. **1883** SWEET & KNOX *Through Texas* 18, I can lick daylight out'n the biggest Yankee ever grew in New England.

b. Used in contexts showing the rise in respectability of this originally derisive epithet. See note above.

1775 in WILLARD *Letters* 85 We have by this action [at Concord and Lexington] got in reality the term Yankee, which is an Indian word, and was given our forefathers, signifying Conquerors, which these ignoramuses [i.e., the British] give us by way of derision. **1775** *N.Y. Hist. Soc. Coll.* I. (1887) 52 Not only the name of a *Yankee,* but of a Connecticut man in particular, is become very respectable. **1807** C. JANSON *Stranger in Amer.* 8 This is so far from being considered a term of reproach by the inhabitants of New England, that it is employed by them in the same manner, and perhaps with greater complacency, than a native of Old England applies to his countrymen the appellation of 'John Bull.' It should likewise be observed, that the term is confined only to the people of the New England states, who are even called Yankees by those of the southern states. **1841** BUCKINGHAM *America* II. 271 It may be added that this term is not deemed reproachful here; persons often boast of their being Yankees, as implying a more thorough English descent, with a less admixture of foreign blood.

c. Extended in application, at first by British writers and speakers, to Americans in general.

*c***1784** NELSON in A. Duncan *Life Nelson* 321, I . . . am determined not to suffer the Yankies to come where the ship is. *a***1800** TWINING *Visit* 385 Their wit was particularly directed against a '*Yankee.*' We apply this designation . . . to the inhabitants of all parts of the United States . . . but the Americans confine its application to their countrymen of the Northern or New England States. **1828** COOPER *Notions* I. 72 At home, the native of even New York, though of English origin, will tell you he is not a Yankee. . . . But, out of the United States, even the Georgian does not hesitate to call himself a 'Yankee.' **1874** *Cong. Rec.* App. 7 May 357/2 When I say a Yankee, I mean an American. **1949** *Chi. D. News* 29 Nov. 18/5 Wake up sleeping Yankees, wake up!

d. In the South, esp. since the Civil War, often restricted in application to Northerners.

1817 FORDHAM *Narr. Travels* 64 Of the Inhabitants of the North States, or Yankees, I have seen nothing. **1833** CROCKETT *Sketches* 205 The Yankees, as all men north of the Potomac are here termed, are generally well educated. **1861** NORTON *Army Lett.* 27 The soil may be sacred, but we sacrilegious Yankees can't help observing that it is awfully deficient in manure. **1947** *Newsweek* 27 Jan. 22/2 He chawed tobacco and gave Yankees and 'niggers' unshirted hell.

Preceded by epithets, esp. "damned."

1812 *Niles' Reg.* III. 45/1 Take the middle of the road or I'll hew you down, you d'——d Yankee rascal. **1850** *Quincy* (Ill.) *Whig* 16 April 3/3 Dog my eternal cats, if I hain't been tricked by that confounded Yankee. **1862** NORTON *Army Lett.* 79 She [a Va. woman] wasn't going to have the d——d Yankees drink out of her well. **1909** O. HENRY *Options* 95 You've had to go to work just as we 'damyankees,' as you call us, have always been doing. **1948** *Atlantic Mo.* Nov. 62/2 An inferiority complex justifying itself in excuses or in futile talk about the 'damn Yankee.'

2. The English used by Yankees, American English. Cf. **Yankee dialect** in **4.** (7) below, and see **4. e.**

In the 1st group of quots. more specific characteristics of this form of English are given.

(1) **1772** in *Hist. Mag.* I. (1859) 92/1 The writer makes mention of a New England man who left a certain advertisement 'with a tavern-keeper; in the *Yankee* phraseology, vulgarly termed Landlord Benedict.' **1825** JOHN NEAL *Bro. Jonathan* I. 103 Keep in mind, however, that, when a fellow talks Yankee, it is always through the nose, with a sort of swing to his voice. **1835** *S. Lit. Messenger* I. 422 He left Athens à la Yankee he *left.* He conducted well for he conducted *himself* well. Considerable *of* a place, considerable place. Shall where English would use will. Shall you visit Boston during your tour? **1864** T. L. NICHOLS *Amer. Life* I. 386 He [a Yankee] describes a man . . . as a thunderin' fool, but a clever critter as ever lived—ugly being Yankee for wicked, and clever for good-natured.

(2) **1824** J. GILCHRIST *Etymologic Interpreter* 8 The naked savages of Indiana already speak a corrupt English (or Yankee). **1843** HALIBURTON *Attaché* 1 Ser. xv, Curb him [a horse] up, talk Yankee to him, and get his ginger up. **1866** LOWELL *Biglow P.* 2 Ser. p. xix, I should be half inclined to name the Yankee a *lingo* rather than a dialect. **1935** MITCHELL *America* 19 They waved and shouted to the Americans on board and we heard some of the stevedores talking their rich Yankee.

3. New England or Yankee rum. *Obs.* Cf. **4. c.** below.

1804 FESSENDEN *Orig. Poems* (1806) 78 Call on me, when you come this way, And take a dram of *Yankee.* **1843** MARRYAT *M. Violet* xxviii. After having drained half-a-dozen cups of 'stiff, true, downright Yankee No. 1,' we all of us took our blankets.

4. In special combs., chiefly obs.: (1) **Yankee ax,** a form of ax weighing usu. from five to nine pounds, having a relatively wide cutting edge and heavy poll, esp. suitable for heavy chopping, cf. **Collins ax;** (2) **bummer,** =**bummer 2;** (3) **bundler,** one who bundles, i.e., lies dressed in bed with his or her sweetheart during courting visits; (4) **Catchers,** a company of Confederate soldiers organized in Virginia; (5) **colonist,** see quot. 1901 *s.v.*

colonist **1. b**; (6) **comfort,** =***comforter;** (7) **dialect,** the dialect or variety of English used by Yankees, esp. those of New England; (8) **Doodle,** see as a main entry; (9) **grit,** unflinching, persevering courage; (10) **jacket,** (see quot.); (11) **jumper,** (see quot.); (12) **land,** the land of the Yankees, esp. New England, also **Yankee-lander;** (13) **leave,** =**French leave;** (14) **nation,** =**universal Yankee nation;** (15) **notion,** (*a*) a small article of merchandise, often a piece of tinware, of the kind sold by Yankee peddlers, usu. *pl.*, (*b*) **Notion State,** (see quot.); (16) **screw,** (see quot.); (17) **shilling,** (see quot.); (18) **state,** see as a main entry; (19) **trick,** a trick, fraud, or deception thought to be typical of a Yankee, also **Yankee trickery.**

(1) *c***1845** *A True Picture* 32 We likewise obtained a little coffee, two or three hoes, and a Yankee axe, which is much larger and broader than the one used in this country, and better adapted for the every-day business of hewing large blocks of timber for fuel and other purposes. [**1848** C. L. FLEISCHMANN *Nordamerikanische Landwirth* 306 Sie werden von verschiedener Grösse, Schwere und Form gemacht; die sogenannte Kentucky-Axt . . . und die Yankee Heavy-Ax . . . sind die besten und gesuchtesten.] — **(2) 1865** in CHESNUT *Diary* 389 [He] invested some thousands of dollars in New York, where Confederate moth did not corrupt nor Yankee bummers break through and steal. — **(3) 1784** A. ADAMS *Lett.* (1848) 161 We have curtains [on shipboard], it is true, and we only in part undress, about as much as the Yankee bundlers. — **(4) 1861** MOORE *Rebellion Rec.* I. III. 71 The Yankee-Catchers will report and be ready to enter service in a few days.

(6) 1834 *S. Lit. Messenger* I. 168 A lady of our party . . . aptly compared it to a Yankee comfort. — **(7) 1832** DUNLAP *Hist. Amer. Theatre* 71 'The Contrast' . . . [has] a degree of humour and knowledge of what is termed Yankee dialect. **1881** *Harper's Mag.* Jan. 258/2 Mr. Lowell wrote a letter to the Boston *Courier*, . . . inclosing a poem in the Yankee dialect. — **(9) 1865** BOUDRYE *Fifth N.Y. Cavalry* 178 With trusty carbines and Yankee grit, our boys scattered the enemy before them. **1894** *Vt. Agric. Rep.* XIV. 125 That Yankee grit . . . will see us through this blight of one of our greatest industries.

(10) 1816 SCENE PAINTER *Emigrant's Guide* 52 He commanded some of the crew to furnish the d——d English rascal with a *good Yankee Jacket*, which in plain English is a quantity of tar besmeared over the naked body, upon which an abundance of feathers is immediately strewed. — **(11) 1931** *Randolph Enterprise* (Elkins, W.Va.) 1 Jan. 1/1 We had to do that [open the roads] ourselves with big sleds, . . . 'Yankee Jumpers,' and 'Go Devils.' — **(12) 1788** FRENEAU *Misc. Works* 69 In Yanky land there stands a town Where learning may be purchas'd low. **1813** PAULDING *J. Bull & Bro. Jonathan* (ed. 2) 93 The Southlanders came at last to consider all the Yankey-landers downright cheats. **1946** DORSON *Jonathan Draws Long Bow* 88 One form of 'saw' common in Yankeeland relied on the literal statement of a contractual agreement. — **(13) 1853** STRICKLAND *Twenty-seven Yrs.* I. 211 His best plan was to take a Yankee leave, and clear out, leaving his unfinished home as a legacy to his creditors. — **(14) 1859** *Ladies' Repository* XIX. 507/1 In other portions of the 'Yankee nation' [than Boston], ingenuity is tasked chiefly to advance material gains. **1870** O. LOGAN *Before Footlights* 236 The rebel prisoners . . . [were] rather sarcastic when referring to the Yankee nation.

(15) (*a*) *c***1815** PAULDING *Amer. Comedies* (1847) 51, I suppose these are what they call Yankee notions. **1911** Williams Pub. Lib. Assoc. *Ariz. Cook Book* 423 (*advt.*), A Full Line of General Merchandise Consisting of . . . Shirts, Collars, Neckware, Yankee Notions, Post Cards, . . . Etc. (*b*) **1904** *Hartford Courant* 29 Oct. 25 The 'Yankee Notion' state, as it [Conn.] has often been called, earned its title in the early part of the 19th century, when there was a great impetus given to the manufacture of almost all sorts of useful implements for the farm and for the household. — **(16) 1815** in *Amer. Sp.* XXII. 284 In such cases the waggoner takes the rails from the fences to pry it out, & these rails are called, in such cases, in Kentucky, Ohio, & the Western parts of Pennsylvania 'Yankee screws.' — **(17) 1891** WELCH *Recoll. 1830–40* 168 The common silver coin known as Pistareen . . . was worth sixteen and two-thirds cents and halves of it, eight and one-third cents, a Yankee shilling, or sixpence. **1935** BUCKBEE *Saga of Old Tuolumne* 13 Six 'Yankee' shillings, an Englishman said, were charged for unprepared coffee. — **(19) 1776** TRUMBULL *M'Fingal* 62 Was there a Yanky trick you knew, They did not play as well as you? **1845** *Quincy* (Ill.) *Whig* 4 Nov. 1/4 Gordon tricked his inner self with the conceit that he would make our hero suffer for all the wrongs he had endured from Yankee trickery. **1947** *Life* 13 Jan. 84/2 The enemy, 'after approaching within 50 or 60 yards of the machine, and seeing the magazine suddenly detached, began to suspect a *Yankee trick*, took alarm, and returned to the Island.'

b. In expressions alluding to New Englanders as peddlers, esp. in the southern states, and to their wares: (1) **Yankee cart,** (2) **clock,** (3) **nutmeg,** (4) **peddler,** (5) **trader,** (6) **wagon.**

(1) 1834 CARUTHERS *Kentuckian* I. 26 When he come to them parts, he drove what we call a Yankee cart, half wagon and half carriage. — **(2) 1839** *Chemung* (N.Y.) *Democrat* 17 April (Th.), A 'Notion seller' was offering Yankee clocks, &c. **1867** E. KIRKE *On Border* 57 [On] a broad mantle of unpainted oak . . . a Yankee clock is ticking. — **(3) 1830** *Freeman's Sentinel* (Greenfield, Mass.) 6 July 3/4 A 'notion' has been invented in Kentucky as an offset to Yankee nutmegs. — **(4) 1820** MEAD *Travels* 51 A few years since a northern travelling merchant, or as they are called in Carolina, a Yankee pedlar, was overtaken by a shower near a wealthy planter's house. **1870** *Scribner's Mo.* I. 122 [He] won much reputation as a genuine 'Yankee peddler.' **1949** *Time* 16 May 94/3 The famed Hitchcock chairs, sold from door to door by Yankee peddlers more than 100 years ago, were back in production.

(5) 1946 *Boston Transcript* 4 Sep., Too long have we been living under the delusion that our nation is made up of Kentucky Colonels, Iowa farmers, Georgia crackers, and Yankee traders. — **(6) 1818** PALMER *Travels U.S.* 188 Their pleasure waggons, called Yankee waggons, are in miniature on four wheels, neatly painted, and drawn by one horse. **1847** *Santa Fe Repub.* 17 Sep. 2/4 For Sale, A strong and well finished Yankee Wagon and Harness.

c. In the names of foods and drinks: (1) **Yankee beverage,** (2) **chowder,** (3) **nut cake,** (4) **rum,** (5) **switchel.**

(1) 1830 PICKERING *Inquiries Emigrant* 26 Vinegar and water, sweetened with molasses, is much drank in this hot weather, and called switchel, or 'Yankee beverage.' — **(2) 1858** *Spirit of Times* 27 Feb. 403/1 Being a very firm fish, we made him into a regular Yankee chowder, or stew, with pork and potatoes. — **(3) 1835** WEBSTER *Improved Housewife* 122 Yankee Nut Cakes. — **(4) 1777** CRESSWELL *Journal* 263 They [the people of New England] import large quantities of Molasses from the West Indies, which they distill and sell to Africa and the other Colonies, which goes by the name of Yankee Rum or Stink-e-buss. **1842** UNCLE SAM *Peculiarities* I. 43 On the outside . . . is printed the following thirsty announcement. . . . Yankee Rum [etc.].

(5) 1832 *Boston Transcript* 4 Jan. 2/1 The Yankee switchell preserved the health of the men in Calcutta, while half the rum drinking crews there were in the hospital.

d. Designating a Yankee, esp. one from New England, of a particular profession, as (1) **Yankee preacher,** (2) **schoolma'am, schoolmarm,** (3) **schoolmaster.**

(1) 1822 DEWEES *Letters* (1852) 25 Our little yankee preacher seemed to enjoy himself very well during the trip. — **(2) 1871** *Cong. Globe* 5 April 205/3 A Yankee school-marm was stoned and murdered by her own pupils. **1886** *Leslie's Pop. Mo.* Jan. 66/1 A severe . . . Yankee school-ma'am. — **(3)** *a***1841** HAWES *Sporting Scenes* II. 44, I think Yankee schoolmasters ought to be taken up as vagrants. **1871** EGGLESTON *Hoosier Schoolmaster* 39 Squire Hawkins was a poor Yankee school-master.

e. In expressions alluding to Yankee speech. Cf. **2.** above.

1803 *Balance* 15 Nov. 363 It would (to use a Yankee phrase) puzzle a dozen Philadelphia lawyers to unriddle the conduct of the democrats. **1828** ROYALL *Black Book* II. 323, I arrived at Thomastown in the evening—not the *yankee* evening—I mean about sundown. **1847** WHITTIER *Writings* V. 391 Small, squeaking voices spoke in a sort of Yankee-Irish dialect. **1866** LOWELL *Biglow P.* 2 Ser. p. xxvi, Of Yankee preterites I find *risse* and *rize* for *rose* in Middleton and Dryden. **1880** *Harper's Mag.* Sep. 613/1 The familiar twang given to the Yankee speech of words like *now* and *cow* . . . was extended beyond the limits of perversion.

f. In obs. nicknames of persons: (1) **Yankee Hastings,** a farmer, Jonathan Hastings, living at Cambridge, Mass., early in the 18th century, whose frequent use of "yankee" in the sense of good, excellent, led, according to one theory, to the widespread use of the word as a nickname for New Englanders, also **Yankee Jonathan;** (2) **Yankee Hill,** (see quots. 1896, 1947).

(1) 1775 THACHER *Mil. Jrnl.* (1823) 19 The students at college [i.e., Harvard], having frequent intercourse with Mr. Hastings, and hearing him employ the term on all occasions, adopted it themselves, and gave him the name of Yankee Jonathan. **1795** *Mass. Mag.* VII. 302/1 It [letter dated Sep. 27, 1728] is a most humorous narrative of the fate of a goose roasted at 'Yankee Hastings's,' and it concludes with a poem on the occasion, in the mock heroic. **1854** *Father Abbey's Will* (Camb.) 7/8 Jonathan Hastings, Steward of the College from 1750–1779, . . . was a son of Jonathan Hastings, a tanner, who was called 'Yankee Hastings,' — **(2) 1846–7** *Yankee Doodle* I. 175/2 Yankee Hill and Jim Crow, as well as the Messieurs the Congo Minstrels and the sable professors of flip-flappery, will be accommodated upon reasonable terms. **1896** HASWELL *New York* 259 The summer of 1831 witnessed the success at the Chatham Garden Theatre of George Handel Hill [1809–49] ('Yankee Hill'), who, in his Yankee delineations, made for himself a wide reputation. **1947** BOTKIN *Treasury N. Eng. Folklore* 3 The comic Yankee became a stock figure on the stage . . . through such characters as Jonathan Ploughboy, Hiram Dodge, . . . and Sam Patch, acted by George Handel ('Yankee') Hill, James H. Hackett, and Dan Marble.

In occasional uses with merely adjectival force in such expressions as *Yankee army, banner, conservatism, engineer, farmer, ingenuity, journal, like, lover, music, reel, sled, straw hat, town, vessel,* etc.

5. In obs. colloq. phrases: (1) *To catch a Yankee*, to catch a tartar; (2) *to come Yankee over*, to humbug, cheat; (3) *to play Yankee with*, to cheat (see also quot. 1896); (4) *Yankee cheese-box on a raft*, (see quot.); (5) *Yankee and Pennamite War*, a series of disputes and armed clashes beginning about 1769 in the Wyoming Valley of Pennsylvania between settlers holding Connecticut and those holding Pennsylvania titles to land.

(1) **1811** *Niles' Reg.* I. 71/2 The irritation in England on account of the attack of the *Little Belt* on our Frigate the *President*, in which the former 'caught a yankee,' still continues. — (2) **1834** SIMMS *G. Rivers* I. 65 Jared Bunce goes about, living on everybody, and coming Yankee over everybody. — (3) **1841** G. POWERS *Hist. Sk.* 202 He thought, if they were disposed to play Yankee with him, he would take a game with them at that. **1896** *Cong. Rec.* 30 March 3366/1 Now I will play Yankee with my friend. . . . I will answer his question by asking another. — (4) **1868** *Putnam's Mag.* II. 116 The Merrimac was damaged and repulsed by the Monitor, and the greatest power for both attack and defence was shown to be possessed by an insignificant-looking craft, whose appearance fully justified the rebel description of 'a Yankee cheese-box on a raft.'

(5) [**1771** in *Pa. Archives* IV. (1853) 415 As Mr. Stewart order'd . . . to let you know if the Yankys were coming Soon, these are to acquaint you that they are upon their March. *Ib.* 420 We have received an Account this Morning from Wioming that the Block house is invested by four different camps of the Yankees.] **1873** WRIGHT *Sk.* 79 And here began that long and bitter conflict between the Connecticut and Pennsylvania men, known as the 'Yankee and Pennamite War,' which never became finally settled till the passage of the compromise law of 1799, by the Legislature of Pennsylvania.

As the last term in **Anglo-, carpetbag, Connecticut, galvanized, homemade, John Virginia, western Yankee.**

Yankee ˈjæŋkɪ, *v. tr.* To defraud, cheat, outsmart. Now *hist.* Cf. **out-Yankee.**

1801 in CIST *Cincinnati* (1841) 177, I generally yankees them once a month, and they stand that like lambs. **1859** BARTLETT 220 To *Jew* a person, is considered, in Western parlance, a shade worse than to 'Yankee' him. **1947** BOTKIN *Treasury N. Eng. Folklore* 5 To *yankee* . . . meant to cheat.

Also **Yankeed,** *a.* =**Yankeefied.** *Rare.*

1881 CARLETON *Farm Festivals* 78 'That was a sudden death, 'twill be allowed,' Said a half-Yankeed Scotchman in the crowd.

Yankeedom ˈjæŋkɪdəm, *n.* The realm of the Yankees. *Colloq.*

1839 *N.O. Picayune* 9 April 2/4 Taglionis and Eslers can come from Yankeedom, as well as from lands where the worship of Terpsichore is a regular system. **1888** AUGHEY *Tupelo* 32 The scum of Europe and mudsills of Yankeedom shall never be permitted to advance a step south of 36°30′. **1947** BOTKIN *Treasury N. Eng. Folklore* 2 In the fabulous country of Yankeeland, Yankeedom, or Down East lives a fabulous creature known as the Yankee.

Yankee Doodle ˈjæŋkɪˈdudl, *n.* [Origin unknown. Sonneck (see ***Yankee,** *n.*, note) has discussed the problem thoroughly without positive results.]

1. The title of a well-known American song and air.

1767 in SONNECK *Report* (1909) 110 Air IV, Yankee Doodle. **1775** in WILLARD *Letters* 112 When the second [British] brigade marched out of Boston to reinforce the first, nothing was played by the fifes and drums but *Yankee Doodle*. . . . Upon their return to Boston, one asked his brother officer how he liked the tune now. . . . Since then *Yankee Doodle* sounds less sweet in their ears. **1863** HOPLEY *Life in South* I. 172 The tune of 'Yankee Doodle' was hissed, and forbidden at the Mobile Theatre. **1944** JOHNSON *As I Dare* 4 The British commander . . . asked that his troops should not be humiliated by the playing of 'Yankee Doodle.'

b. *To give Yankee Doodle*, to give Hail Columbia *q.v. Rare.*

1866 MOORE *Women of War* 102 Sheridan gave the rebs 'Hail Columbia' and 'Yankee Doodle' combined, . . . and I do not think their army will trouble us again this winter.

2. A Yankee or Yankees collectively. *Obs.*

1770 *R.I. Commerce* I. 330 The many favours allready conferred on Poor Old yankey dodle. **1846–7** *Yankee Doodle* I. 100/2 The *Harbinger* says that . . . the Yankee Doodles in general, are 'a sneaky, base, hypocritical set.' **1869** *Harper's Mag.* Sep. 619/1 Here's Yankee Doodle's been and come And beat your crackest yatches.

attrib. **1825** NEAL *Bro. Jonathan* II. 319 One of your yankee doodle invitations, that—happy to see you *another* time. **1846** *Knickerb.* XXVII. 50 The writer of this was educated at a Yankee-Doodle College at New Haven. **1894** *Scribner's Mag.* May 605/2 There is little of the Yankee-Doodle business about [the music].

Also as adj. in the predicate.

1950 *Chi. Tribune* 3 April IV. 4 They're as Yankee Doodle as apple pie and baseball—it's just plain American.

b. The North in the Civil War. *Rare.*

1861 *Richmond* (Va.) *Examiner* 6 Sep. 1/3 Yankee Doodle, he went forth To conquer the Seceders.

3. In colloq. combs. and derivatives, chiefly rare or obs.: (1) **Yankee-Doodle dandeeism,** the pluck and go-ahead quality of Yankees; (2) **Dandy,** =**Yankee Doodle 1,**—from the recurrence of this expression in the song; (3) **-dom,** the home or realm of the Yankee Doodles, esp. N. Eng. or the northern states; (4) **-ism,** the characteristic quality or spirit of the Yankee Doodles.

(1) **1946** *Progress* March 121/1 We have managed to survive by dint of some elusive quality described as yankee-doodle-dandee-ism. — (2) **1944** *Chi. D. News* 20 Nov. 4/6 Then they played. The tune was 'Yankee Doodle Dandy.' **1948** *Reader's Digest* May 66/1 Other soldiers marching at the command of U.S. officers, armed with U.S. tommy guns, and singing the 'Yankee Doodle Dandy.' — (3) **1845** HONE *Diary* II. 248 The ladies of this family (natives though they be of Yankee-doodle-dom) seem to possess, in a high degree, the power of capturing the aristocracy of England. **1861** in BARTLETT (1877) 769 Abe Lincoln, and all his Northern scum, Shall own our independence of *Yankee Doodledom.* — (4) **1846–7** *Yankee Doodle* I. 3/2 The object of any paper bearing my name shall be *the propagation of true, genuine Yankee-Doodelism.*

Yankeefied ˈjæŋkɪˌfaɪd, *a.* Made or become like the Yankees. *Colloq.*

1775 in *Boston Transcript* 13 Dec. 1831 2/1 Ye tar-barrel law-givers, Yankefied prigs, . . . May I see you all hanged upon Liberty Tree. **1826** *Liberty Hall* (Cin.) 29 Aug. 2/2 If I may make use of a Yankified Galic idea, the *march of mind* is to the *westward.* **1897** *Voice* 14 Jan. 8 Japan is getting Yankeefied in more ways than one. **1948** *Southwestern Rev.* Winter 10 It's coming . . . from the nigger-loving, FEPC-CIO-Yankeefied red Communists.

Yankeeish ˈjæŋkɪ·ɪʃ, *a.* Resembling a Yankee, or suggestive of Yankee manners and customs. *Colloq.* — **1830** *Collegian* 117 Comparisons are generally 'odorous,' particularly Yankeeish, and decidedly condemned by Captain Basil Hall. **1852** *Knickerb.* XXXIX. 152 The inhabitants of that part of the world [near Cape Cod], being somewhat Yankeeish, called it 'Eating Hall.'

Yankeeism ˈjæŋkɪˌɪzəm, *n.*

1. A trait, whim, peculiarity, etc., characteristic of Yankees.

1792 *New York Mag.* III. 244 Yankeyism [title of an anecdote showing New England character]. **1890** MRS. B. HARRISON *Anglomaniacs* i. 27, I had feared that Lily's impetuous ways—her—her—'Flamboyant Yankeeism,' Mr. Gore-Thompson called it. **1946** *Boston Transcript* 4 Sep., It is high time we in New England stopped trafficking in the myth of Yankeeism.

2. A word or expression characteristic of Yankee speech; an Americanism.

1806 FESSENDEN *Democracy Unveiled* II. 177 *Twistical* is a *Yankeyism.* **1858** *Spirit of Times* 27 Feb. 403/2 It is generally acknowledged, to use a Yankeeism, that 'Censor' is 'some punkins.' **1948** MENCKEN *Supp.* II. 113 The second [error] was that of listing as Yankeeisms peculiarities of pronunciation and accidence which really belonged to the common stock of ignorant English.

3. A typical Yankee dish. *Rare.*

1848 *Spirit of Times* 12 Feb. 598 He fixed upon a plate of these delicious Yankeeisms his avid and devouring eyes . . . he 'knew' doughnuts as well as he 'knew beans.'

Yankeeness ˈjæŋkɪnɪs, *n.* The quality of being like a Yankee. *Colloq.* — **a1909** O. HENRY *Roads of Destiny* xxi. 352 Don't reopen the chasm, Doc. Any Yankeeness I may have is geographical. **1943** DE VOTO *Year of Decision* 155 An incurable Yankeeness extemporized debates, political forums, and lectures on the flora of the new country or the manifest destiny of the American nation.

Yankee State.

1. *pl.* The northern, esp. the New England, states.

1842 *Amer. Sentinel* (Georgetown, Ky.) 8 Oct. 3/2 He has no probable support from any other than the Yankee States. **1857** *Spirit of*

Times 19 Dec. 243/3 There was a feller come down to those parts from one of them cussed Yankee States—Bosting, I think it was. **1948–9** *N.W. Ohio Quart.* Winter 12 We of the Mission sent our gatherings to the friends of the Mission . . . in the then far off Yankee States.

2. Ohio, many of whose early settlers came from New England.

1826 Flint *Recoll.* 45 This is properly designated 'the Yankee state.' **1884** *Harper's Mag.* June 125/1 Ohio was called 'the Yankee State.'

Yankton 'jæŋktən, *n.* [f. a native word signifying "end village."] An Indian belonging to one of the seven divisions of the Dakota, or a related division sometimes confounded with it. Also *pl.*, the tribe of such an Indian.

1708 in Neill *Hist. Minn.* 164. **1836** *New-Yorker* 7 May 102/2 Next to them sat the stern and repulsive looking warriors of the Yanctons. **1894** Eggleston in *Harper's Mag.* Feb. 469/1 The Yanktons, Yantonnais, and Tetons . . . seem to have been scouring the Coteau in hope of slaughtering some Cree or Assiniboin hunting party.

attrib. [**1817** *Guardian of Liberty* (Cynthiana, Ky.) 15 Feb. 3/4 A Soix chief (French Crow) of the Yatoan tribe, with fifty of his warriors, was here on the 5th inst.] **1827** *Spirit of 'Seventy-Six* (Frankfort, Ky.) 8 Nov. 1/4 His dress consisted of a *Yankton dress*, new, rich, and beautiful. **1867** *Harper's Wkly.* 5 Oct. 629/2 The Commission . . . held a council, on the steamer, at Fort Thompson, with the head chiefs of the . . . Yankton tribes of Sioux.

b. Yankton Sioux, (see quot. 1910 and cf. next).

1910 Hodge *Amer. Indians* II. 991/1 The so-called 'Yankton Sioux' under the Ft. Peck agency, Mont., are in reality chiefly Yanktonai. **1947** DeVoto *Across Wide Missouri* 242 A party of Mandans, including the famous Four Bears, . . . had started for the Yankton Sioux to avenge a murder.

Yanktonia ˌjæŋk'tonɪə, *n.* [f. a dim. of the native word from which **Yankton** is derived, "little end village."] "One of the 7 primary divisions or subtribes of the Dakota, speaking the same dialect as the Yankton and believed to be the elder tribe" (Hodge). — **1838** Parker *Exploring Tour* 43 The region . . . is inhabited by the following bands of Sioux, viz: the Yanktons, . . . Santas, Yanktonas, Tetons, Ogallallahs, Siones, and the Hankpapes. **1894** [see **Yankton**].

Yannigans 'jænɪˌgənz, *n. pl.* [Origin obscure. Poss. suggested by or based upon *young'uns.*] *Baseball.* Players who are members of scrub teams. *Slang.*

1911 *Chi. D. News* 4 April 6/1 The teams resumed play in two divisions yesterday, the regulars playing in the inclosed park and the Yannigans performing in a scrub game on the second grounds. **1913** *Ib.* 8 March 1/1 The Yannigans made their run in the fourth inning. **1950** *Chi. Tribune* 8 March III. 1/8 The Yannigans' lone run was the first tally of the game.

yant jant, *n. S.W.* [Prob. f. Sp. *yanta*, noonday meal, *yantar*, to eat.] (See quot.) — **1933** Harrington *Gypsum Cave, Nev.* 82 Among traces of wild plants used as food the most numerous were the quids or 'chews' of mescal, sometimes called 'yant' (*Agave utahensis*), which grows on the higher mountains in southern Nevada.

yapon, see **yaupon.**

***yard,** *n.*

1. =college yard. Often *cap.*

1660 *Harvard Coll. Rec.* I. 193 Where any dammage is done to . . . the Colledge fences about the yard, pump, Bell or clock &c: the same shall be made good again by all the Students (then) resident in the Colledge. **1841** *Harvard Faculty Orders & Reg.* 6 Collecting in groups round the doors of the College buildings or in the yard [shall be considered a violation of decorum]. **1871** Bagg *At Yale* 27 Besides the fourteen buildings already described, the only others within the yard . . . were the two wooden dwelling-houses. **1950** *Harvard Alumni Bul.* 25 March 505 The championship was won by Adams House, and the Yard unlimited class title went to Arnold Horween, Jr.

2. In a forest, a place where moose or deer herd, esp. in winter. Cf. **moose yard.**

1834 Audubon *Ornith. Biog.* II. 431 A Moose, which had been driven from its haunt or yard by Indians. *Ib.* 433 A 'yard' for half a dozen Moose would probably contain about twenty acres. **1893** Roosevelt *Wilderness Hunter* 223 A 'yard' is . . . the spot which a moose has chosen for its winter home, . . . because it contains plenty of browse in the shape of young trees and saplings, and perhaps also because it is sheltered to some extent. **1945** *Nat. Geog. Mag.* Jan. (*advt.*), There they make a 'yard,' packing down the snow over a small area.

3. a. =woodyard. b. (See quot. and cf. ***landing 1.**)

(**a**) **1851** *Polly Peablossom* 121 Mr. T. incidentally mentioned the bursting of a steamboat at his yard. **1950** *Chi. Tribune* 20 May 10/3 Franklin J. Meine . . . has an amusing story of a steamboat wooding up at one yard all thru a foggy night, the owner boosting his prices to suit the occasion. — (**b**) **1905** *Forestry Bureau Bul.* No. 61, 41 *Landing*, . . . a place to which logs are hauled or skidded preparatory to transportation by water or rail. . . . [Also called] log dump, rollway, yard.

4. An inclosure for animals which are to be shipped or slaughtered for meat. Often *pl.*

1865 *Atlantic Mo.* Jan. 83/2 The average weekly expenditure by butchers at the New York yards during the year 1863 was $328,865. **1879** *Cimarron News & Press* 27 Nov. 3/2 The company will at once build suitable yards at Dorsey station.

5. In combs.: (1) **yard boss, =yard master;** (2) **conductor,** a railroad conductor whose duties in switching, making up trains, etc., are restricted to the limits of a railway yard; (3) **grass,** any one of various grasses, esp. crab grass, *Eleusine indica*, often found in yards; (4) **hog,** (see quot.); (5) **limit,** (see quot. 1891), also attrib.; (6) **master,** on a railroad, an official in charge of a yard; (7) **stick,** see as a main entry.

(1) **1891** Roberts *Adrift Amer.* 144, I went at once to the yard boss asking him for a job. — (2) **1878** Pinkerton *Strikers* 227 'Number Fifteen' through Chicago freight train was about to depart for the West, when a gang of yardmen comprising about a dozen firemen and brakemen, led by . . . a yard conductor on the night transfer runs, boarded the engine. — (3) **1822** Woods *English Prairie* 199 Yard-grass comes on land that has been much trodden; it is something like cock's-foot-grass. **1901** Mohr *Plant Life Ala.* 135 Far the largest part of the cultivated fields, however, is left to a luxuriant growth of weedy grass, chiefly . . . yard grasses. — (4) **1879** *Diseases of Swine* 214, Yard hogs—*i.e.* that are fed on dish-water and kitchen slops—seldom or never take the cholera.

(5) **1891** *Cent.* 7010/1 *Yard-limit*, . . . on a railway, the extreme end of the yard-space occupied by sidings and switches: usually indicated by a sign beside the track. **1898** *McClure's Mag.* X. 396 [The] switch to the outward or downhill track . . . came under the 'yard-limit' rule. **1947** Beebe *Mixed Train Dly.* 74 The last southbound local on the S.A.L. whistles for the yard limit about eight-thirty. — (6) **1872** *Newton Kansan* 10 Oct. 3/3 Geo. McCutcheon, yard-master. **1949** *Harvard Alumni Bul.* 24 Sep. 34 He had taken his turn as brakeman, . . . and yardmaster.

b. *liberty of the yard,* (see quot. 1828). *Obs.*

1777 *N.H. Comm. Safety Rec.* 97 Ordered Simeon Ladd, Gaol keeper, to give Jno Powell the Liberty of the yard. **1828** Webster *s.v. Yard, Liberty of the yard*, is a liberty granted to persons imprisoned for debt, of walking in the yard, or within any other limits prescribed by law.

As the last term in **barn, board, boat, boiler, bone, brick, bull, burying, cabbage, cane, cattle, chicken, chip, chunk, clothes, college, cotton, courthouse, deer, door, elk, feed, flake, freight, front, goose, hen, junk, log, lumber, mahogany, marble, mill, moose, Negro, oak, packing, picket, seed, sheep, shingle, side, slave, steamboat, stock, stump, switch, tan, wheat, winter, woodyard.**

***yard,** *v.* **1.** *intr.* Of moose or deer: To occupy or spend time in a yard (sense **2.**). **2.** *tr.* (See quot.)

(1) **1841** *Spirit of Times* 6 Feb. 583/2 (We.), He would soon 'yard' and lie down. **1947** Cahalane *Mammals* 29 It is said casually that deer 'yard' in the north because it is easier for a number of deer to break trails through the snow between feeding grounds and to keep these places accessible. — (2) **1878** *Lumberman's Gaz.* 12 Jan. 35/3 The logs . . . have been yarded or piled up in the woods during the fall.

yardage 'jardɪdʒ, *n.* The charge made for the use of a yard. Also attrib.

1868 *Ill. Agric. Soc. Trans.* VI. 322 Net cash receipts for yardage, and profit on feed, 1866. **1889** *Public Opinion* 16 Feb., The furnace-master paying the company yardage at the rate of 25 cents per ton. **1903** Adams *Log Cowboy* 201, I'll not ship any more cattle to your town, . . . until you adjust your yardage charges.

***yarding,** *n.*

1. (See quots.)

1840 Buel *Farmer's Companion* 315 *Summer yarding*, stuff carted into the yard, and trodden by the cattle, for manure. **1843** *Amer. Pioneer* II. 172 We were not expecting then to chase them, but merely to find their place of yarding, and then wait until the snow became deeper before we disturbed them. **1887** H. Hall *Tribune Bk. of Sports* 432 'Pot-hunters' have other methods of shooting the Adirondack deer, such as 'yarding' . . . in which the deer are traced to their winter herding grounds and are then shot down.

2. In lumbering, the bringing of logs together in a yard (sense **3. b.**). Also attrib.

1942 Rich *We Took to Woods* (1948) 75 A yarding crew consists of three men and a twitch horse. **1949** *Sat. Ev. Post* 12 March 64/2 We had to do a lot of chasing to get the money, as the man said that he had bad luck with his yarding and wanted father to allow him a discount.

yardstick ˈjɑrdˌstɪk, *n.*

1. A stick a yard in length, suitably marked off into subdivisions, for use in measuring.

1816 PICKERING 206 *Yard-wand* . . . is still sometimes used, by *old* people, for what we now call a *yard-stick.* **1907** *St. Nicholas* June 735 She's sure that the yardsticks buy shoes for their feet.

b. *fig.* A standard of measure.

1844 EMERSON *Miscellanies* 352 The railroad . . . has great value as a sort of yard-stick, and surveyor's line. **1878** *N. Amer. Rev.* CXXVI. 507 Senator Thurman was content to measure the Bland Bill with the yard-stick of the constitutional lawyer. **1893** *Doc. & Sp. Amer. Hist.* III. (1943) 175 The Congress came to formulating the prohibition which is the yardstick for measuring the complainant's right to injunction.

c. In quasi-adverbial use.

1884 MARK TWAIN *H. Finn* xl, She was just in a sweat about every little thing that warn't yardstick straight.

2. In figurative expressions.

1848 MITCHELL *Nantucketisms* 42 'He looks as if he had swallowed a yardstick.' Stiff, reserved. **1870** F. FERN *Ginger-Snaps* 72, I know of a merchant, helplessly fastened to the yardstick, who should be an editor. **1887** TOURGEE *Button's Inn* 133 Now you're talking by the yardstick. . . . If you only had nerve to practise what you preach!

yarner ˈjɑrnɚ, *n.* (See quot. and cf. **Llano Estacado.**) *Colloq.* — **1907** COOK *Border & Buffalo* (1938) 295 We were now on the Llano Estacado, or yarner, as the old Texans call it.

yarrup ˈjɑrəp, *n.* [Imitative.] =**flicker.** — **1865** *Atlantic Mo.* May 517/1 Another April comer . . . is the Golden-Winged Woodpecker, *alias,* 'High-Hole,' *alias,* 'Flicker,' *alias,* 'Yarup.' **1917** *Birds of Amer.* II. 164/2 Another person has heard the bird calling its *Yarrup-yarrup* while flying about . . . in quest of food; hence the common name of Yarrup.

yaupon ˈjɔpən, *n.* [Catawba *yopún,* little bush, small leaves.]

1. A holly, *Ilex vomitoria,* of the southern states, or a closely related plant. Also attrib. Cf. **cassine 1.**

1709 LAWSON *Carolina* 90 This *Yaupon,* call'd by the South-Carolina Indians, *Cassena,* is a Bush, that grows chiefly on the Sand Banks and Islands. **1837** WILLIAMS *Fla.* 29 Scrub oaks and yapon bushes, tangled with vines, form impenetrable thickets. **1948** *N.O. Times-Picayune Mag.* 5 Dec. 2/2 That the black drink could knock a healthy Indian six ways from Sunday is evident from the yaupon's botanical name—Ilex vomitoria.

2. Tea brewed from the leaves of such a plant, in full **yaupon tea.** Cf. **black drink, cassine 2.**

1709 LAWSON *Carolina* 221 As for Purging and Emeticks . . . they never apply themselves to, unless in drinking vast Quantities of their *Yaupon* or Tea. **1839** BRIGGS *H. Franco* I. 168 They called the tea 'Water bewitched,' and one of them swore it was the regular 'Yawpon,' which he had seen sold for sixpence the bushel. **1895** *Advance* 19 Dec. 909/1 The very sight of that horrid yupon and sassafras tea makes me fairly sick.

Yavapai ˌjɑvəˈpaɪ, *n.* Also **Yampai.** [Said to be f. a native expression meaning "people of the sun." The immediate source may have been Sp. Cf. Santamaría *s.v. yavipais.*] *pl.* A Yuman tribe of Arizona Indians now numbering only a few hundred, known also as Apache Mohave or Mohave Apache. Also attrib.

1852 SITGREAVES *Exped. Zuni & Colo. Rivers* (1853) 15 A band of Yampais were found encamped upon it. **1858** IVES *Colo. River* (1861) 108 The Yampais did not differ much from the Jualpais in general appearance. **1933** SPIER *Yuman Tribes* 1 The mountains . . . rising north of the Salt and lower Gila contained Yavapai bands. **1948** *Southwestern Jrnl. Anthrop.* Winter 374 In even more recent times trade relations were established with . . . the Northeastern and Western Yavapais.

Yazoo ˈjæzu, *n.* [Name of an Indian tribe on the Yazoo River in Mississippi, but of unknown significance.] *attrib.* Of or pertaining to the sale (1795) by Georgia of lands in the Yazoo River region to four companies and to the subsequent collection by these companies and their henchmen of ten times the alleged purchase price from the U.S. Government.

[**1770** PITTMAN *Present State* 3 The river Yazous comes from the north-east, and discharges itself into the Mississippi, sixty leagues from the Arkansas: formerly a nation of Indians of the same name had their villages on it.] **1796** *Aurora* (Phila.) 5 Dec. (Th.), The Yazoo men (as they are called in this place [Savannah, Ga.]) were making every exertion to prevent General Jackson from being elected a representative. **1805** *Ann. 8th Congress* 2 Sess. 1148 The Legislature of Georgia . . . made the fraudulent and villainous contract with the Yazoo speculators of 1795. *Ib.* 1156, I shall now proceed to a brief investigation of the legality of the Yazoo claims. *Ib.*, Now, if the sale to the Yazoo companies was just and valid, . . . any subsequent purchase by Congress must be invalid. **1850** BUCKINGHAM *Newspaper Lit.* II. 203 A three-act comedy, called 'The Georgia Spec, or Land in the Moon,' . . . censured the wickedness of the speculators in what was called the Yazoo purchase. **1932** C. C. LOVELL *Golden Isles Ga.* 78 Mr. Couper . . . was a member of the state legislature and assisted in defeating the Yazoo Fraud. **1948** DICK *Dixie Frontier* 64 The Georgia Legislature in 1789 made large grants of land in the Mississippi country to the so-called Yazoo Land Company.

Yazooism ˈjæzuˌɪzəm, *n.* The type of political thievery exhibited in the case of the Yazoo lands. *Obs.* Cf. prec. — **1806** *Western World* (Frankfort, Ky.) 7 July 4/5 May those officers of government who tolerated fraud & speculation, & hugged putrefaction to their bosoms in the form of Yazooism, never enjoy the confidence of an honest people. **1813** *Aurora* 16 Jan. 2/1 It is with pain we perceive that *Yazooism* has again begun to assail the senate of the United States. The idle . . . politician, general Bradley, . . . has reported a bill . . . in favor of the Yazoo speculators.

***year,** *n.* As the last term in **boom, campaign, dry, fiscal, freshman, grasshopper, junior, locust, mid, off, presidential, seed, senior year.**

***yearling,** *n.* **1.** A young bear. *Obs.* **2.** *Vt.* **yearling squire,** a squire or magistrate appointed for one year. *Obs.* **3. yearling tick,** (see quot. 1838). *Colloq.*

(1) 1787 ATTMORE *Jrnl.* 41 Soon after another Bear called a Yearling came out descended. — **(2) 1831** *Boston Transcript* 22 Dec. 1/1 The Governor. . . . Made him a yearling 'squire. — **(3) 1838** GOSSE *Letters* 220 The first season they are called Seed-ticks—the minute ones mentioned above; the next year they become Yearling-ticks. **1869** *Amer. Naturalist* III. 51 When ready for a new meal or a new transformation (now called 'yearling ticks'), they again ascend bushes.

yedra ˈjɛdrə, *n.* *S.W.* [f. Sp. (also *hiedra*), ivy. Cf. Santamaría *hiedra venenosa* used in Mexico for *Rhus radicans,* and see quot. 1856 below.] Poison ivy or poison oak, esp. *Rhus diversiloba.*

1831 BEECHEY *Voyage to Pacific* II. 84 The most remarkable shrub in this country is the yedra, a poisonous plant affecting only particular constitutions of the human body, by producing tumours and violent inflammations upon any part with which it comes in contact. **1844** FARNHAM *Travels in Calif.* 401 Perhaps the most remarkable shrub here is the *Yedra,* a poisonous plant, which, however, affects some particular constitutions only. **1856** *Hutching's Mag.* Dec. 258/1, I should be very much pleased if some of your readers would throw a little more light on the subject of curing or *preventing* the evil effects of *La Yedra.*

yegg ˈjɛg, *n.* [Origin uncertain. One theory attributes it to an alleged John Yegg, a safeblower. G. *jäger* has been suggested. See quot. 1926.] A tramp, thief, safebreaker, or criminal. In full **yeggman.** *Slang.*

1901 FLYNT *World of Graft* 27 The great majority are what certain detectives call 'yegg-men,' . . . the average tramp seldom uses the word. **1906** *Charities* 17 Feb. 695/2 The Goat is famous wherever panhandlers, plain hoboes and yeggmen do congregate. **1926** J. BLACK *You Can't Win* 172 In speaking of the cook ovens I may say that it was there the word 'yegg' originated. . . . It is a corruption of 'yekk,' a word from one of the many dialects spoken in Chinatown, and it means beggar. **1949** *Chi. Tribune* 20 Dec. 20/3 Still other 'explanations' link the phrase [the real McCoy] . . . with an oil field wildcatter who supplied yeggs with nitroglycerin.

***yell,** *n.* **1.** (See quots. and cf. **rebel yell.**) **2.** A rhythmical cheer having a fixed order of syllables, shouted in chorus by college students. **3.** *To raise the yell,* to protest or complain. *Slang.*

(1) 1864 POLLARD *So. Hist. of War: 3d Year* 89 Our men . . . gave a Southern yell in response to the Yankee cheer. **1914** BOWER *Flying U Ranch* 219 He fired again and again, and gave the range-old cattle-yell; the yell which had sent many a tired herd over many a weary mile. — **(2) 1890** *St. Nicholas* Aug. 837/2 The young men . . . are giving the mountain calls or 'yells,' cries adopted [for the different resort hotels] according to the well-known college custom. **1903** *N.Y. Ev. Post* 30 Sep. 2 The students sang the college song and gave the 'varsity yell from the steps of the library. — **(3) 1903** A. H. LEWIS *Boss* 197 It's water on your wheel, so you oughtn't to raise th' yell.

As the last term in **cattle, college, Comanche, Indian, painter, rebel, scalp, Texas yell.**

***yellow,** *a.* and *n.*

1. *pl.* =**peach yellows.**

1843 *Farmers' Cabinet* 15 Jan. 181/1 His trees, therefore, were as effectually destroyed by the disease called the *yellows,* as his neighbour's were by the worms. **1886** *Harper's Mag.* June 48/2, I can almost taste the yellows in much of the fruit bought in market.

2. *fig.* Cowardice. *Slang.* Cf. **d.** below.

1896 ADE *Artie* 57 This is how I found the streak o' yellow in him. **1914** BOWER *Flying U Ranch* 146 Honest to grandma, I was just b'ginnin' to think this bunch was gitting all streaked up with yeller.

b. Also as an adj.: Mean-spirited, cowardly, of poor quality. *Slang.*

1856 in BARNUM *Struggles* 400 Though you thought our minds were green, We never thought your heart was yellow. **1901** NORRIS *Octopus* 123 This business we talked over to-night—I'm out of it. It's yellow. **1947** MOTLEY *Knock on Any Door* 22 One thing you never did; you never let the fellows think you were yellow.

Also *yellow behind the gills. Slang.*

1878 BEADLE *Western Wilds* 26 He was, in local phrase, 'yaller behind the gills.'

c. With reference to baseball. *Obs.*

1889 *S.F. Bulletin* 19 July 1/6 Barry was hit much more freely than Fudger, the support of both pitchers being of the 'yellowest' description. **1907** *McClure's Mag.* April 684/1 Outside of a few . . . 'yellow' plays . . . [the game] was a good one.

d. Also **yellow streak, stripe,** a cowardly characteristic. *Slang.*

1911 FERBER *Dawn O'Hara* 96 I'll swear there is no yellow streak. **1948** *Popular Western* June 12/1 He was always a tinhorn troublemaker with a yellow stripe a yard wide running down his back.

3. *pl.* Publications depending for effect upon the exploitation of sensational aspects of the news. *Colloq.*

1898 *Daily News* (London) 27 July 5/7 This deliberate attempt to stir up animosities . . . is worthy of 'the yellows' at their worst. **1903** *N.Y. Times Sat. Rev.* 7 Nov. 796 A pretty Southern widow who did newspaper work for the yellows.

b. Used as an adj., orig. with reference to sensational books and magazines issued in inexpensive form, often in yellow covers.

1846 POE *Works* (1902) XV. 112 [Fashion has condemned] her more modern rivals . . . to the eternal insignificance of the yellow-backed pamphleteering. **1855** CARLTON *New Purchase* (ed. 2) 3 Although published near the noon of the Yellow Literature Day, the First Edition of the Work was all immediately sold. **1943** OTTLEY *New World* 32 The metropolitan press rose in all its 'yellow' might and denounced the 'black invasion.'

c. Of a writer or publisher: Connected in some way with yellow journals, unscrupulously sensational in method. Cf. **3. b.** above.

1902 PHILLIPS *Woman Ventures* 248 Gammell was a sensationalist—'the yellowest yet.' **1906** *Times* (London, wkly. ed.) 9 Nov. 714 The President of the United States sent his Secretary of State to New York to throw the whole weight of Mr. Roosevelt's . . . authority and influence against the 'yellow' candidate [*sc.* Hearst]. **1909** *N.Y. Ev. Post* (s.-w. ed.) 15 Feb. 4 Our morals are . . . under the management . . . of yellow editors.

d. yellow journal, a newspaper or similar publication depending upon sensational reporting to attract readers. Also attrib.

[**1846** *Quincy* (Ill.) *Whig* 14 March 3/1 The St. Louis papers appear to be in a flourishing condition, except the 'Organ,' which looks as yellow and nasty as ever.] **1898** *Land of Sunshine* Jan. 85 It proves anew the folly of basing our foreign policy on the ignorance and mendacity of yellow journals. **1948** *Sat. Ev. Post* 4 Sep. 31/1 Abruptly a yellow-journal voice on the radio began, 'That mad-dog killer, Morgan Dane, has begun his fifth day of liberty by adding another name to his mounting list of victims.'

e. yellow journalism, the use of sensational reporting and conspicuous display as means of attracting readers to a newspaper or journal.

1898 BANKS in *19th Cent.* Aug. 328 All American journalism is not 'yellow,' though all strictly 'up-to-date' yellow journalism is American! **1948** *Time* 8 March 48/2 The story she was playing up was a natural for yellow journalism: a messy divorce case involving some of Arizona's best people.

4. a. Gold. **b.** A yellow poker chip. Both *obs.*

(**a**) **1901** RYAN *Montana* 227 She would watch some strange miner dig and wash the soil in his search for the precious 'yellow.' **1901** GRINNELL *Gold Hunting in Alaska* 3 That not more than one of us has ever set eyes on a real, live nugget passes for nothing; we shall naturally recognize 'the yellow' when we see it. — (**b**) **1908** LORIMER *J. Spurlock* 184 Each time I would find . . . that his stack of yellows had a new bay-window or cupola on it.

5. In the names of birds: (1) **yellow-backed warbler,** =**blue yellow-back(ed) warbler;** (2) **-billed cuckoo,** a North American arboreal cuckoo, *Coccyzus americanus;* (3) **-billed magpie,** (see quot. 1917); (4) ***bird,** the goldfinch or summer yellowbird, cf. **7.** (2) below; (5) **-breasted chat,** (see quot. 1917); (6) ***hammer,** the flicker or golden-winged woodpecker, *Colaptes auratus,* or a related bird (see also quot. 1948); (7) **-headed blackbird,** a large blackbird, *Xanthocephalus xanthocephalus,* common in western North America; (8) **-headed troopial,** =prec.; (9) **-palm warbler,** a subspecies of the palm warbler *q.v.;* (10) **plover,** a golden plover; (11) **poll,** the yellow warbler, *Dendroica aestiva;* (12) **red-poll (warbler),** a subspecies, *Dendroica palmarum hypochrysea,* of the palm warbler, or the palm warbler itself; (13) **rump,** the myrtle bird, *Dendroica coronata,* having a yellow patch on the rump, or a related species; (14) **-rumped warbler,** =prec.; (15) **shank,** =**yellowleg 1,** freq. *pl.,* also attrib.; (16) **warbler,** a small bird of a bright-yellow color, *Dendroica aestiva,* also with defining terms, any one of various other yellow or yellowish birds of the family Compsothlypidae, cf. **blue-eyed yellow warbler.**

(**1**) **1783** LATHAM *Gen. Synopsis Birds* IV. 440 Yellow-backed Warbler. **1838** GOSSE *Letters* 295 Such are the Maryland Yellow-throat (*Sylvia trichas*), the Yellow-backed Warbler (*S. pusilla*) [etc.]. — (**2**) **1811** WILSON *Ornithology* IV. 13 Yellow-billed cuckoo: *Cuculus carolinensis* . . . is both shy and solitary, seeking always the thickest foliage for concealment. **1950** *Chi. Tribune* 6 July 8/5 Another insect on which the yellow billed cuckoo (the more common variety around here) feeds is the locust. — (**3**) **1858** BAIRD *Birds Pacific R.R.* 578 The restriction of the yellow billed magpie to the coast region of California . . . is an interesting fact. **1917** *Birds of Amer.* II. 216/2 Down in the San Joaquin and Sacramento valleys of California dwells a cousin of the American magpie. His name is Yellow-billed Magpie (*Pica nuttalli*). — (**4**) **1775** BURNABY *Travels* 17 In the woods [of Va.] there are . . . the blue-bird, the yellow-bird. **1836** *N.Y. Mirror* 23 July, 'I'll come see, I will, I will,' sings the yellow bird. **1892** *Outing* Aug. 348/1 One of the prettiest sights in the world is a flock of yellow-birds descending suddenly on a group of thistles.

(**5**) **1730** MORTIMER in *Phil. Trans.* XXXVI. 432 *Oenantha Americana pectore luteo,* the Yellow-breasted Chat. This bird I never saw in the inhabited Parts [of Carolina]: It flies with the Legs extended behind it (like an Heron.) **1917** *Birds of Amer.* III. 162 Yellow-breasted Chat. *Icteria virens virens.* . . . [Also called] Yellow Mockingbird. **1945** *Mass. Audubon Soc. Bul.* Feb. 35 An outstanding winter stray in eastern Massachusetts was the Yellow-breasted Chat that visited the premises of Dr. Charles F. Walcott of Cambridge in January and was seen by many observers. — (**6**) **1801** PEYROUSE *Voyage* 70 Sparrows, nightingales, black-birds, and yellow-hammers, filled the thickets, singing with a delightful melody. **1874** BAIRD *N. Amer. Birds* II. 581 This bird [*sc.* Colaptes Mexicanus], in some parts of California, is known as the Yellow-Hammer. **1948** *Democrat* 23 Sep. 4/4 There are many versions of how Alabama became tabbed as the 'Yellowhammer State.' — (**7**) **1846** *30th Cong.* 1 Sess. H.R. Ex. Doc. No. 41, [We saw] large flocks of the yellow headed black bird, or troopial. **1950** *Chi. Tribune* 8 May 1/5 There are the melodious long billed marsh wrens, the cheerful red winged blackbirds, and the spectacular yellow headed blackbirds. — (**8**) **1825** BONAPARTE *Ornithology* I. 29 The Yellow-headed Troopials assemble in dense flocks. **1858** *New Amer. Cyclo.* III. 283/1 The yellow-headed troopials of North America. — (**9**) **1934** WEBSTER. **1942** WHITE *One Man's Meat* 287 There goes one of those damned little Yellow Palm Warblers.

(**10**) **1838** J. HALL *Statistics of West* 124 The yellow plover frequents the prairies in the spring in immense flocks. — (**11**) [**1783** LATHAM *Gen. Synopsis Birds* IV. 515 Yellow-Poll. . . . This species is found in America.] **1867** LACKLAND *Homespun* I. 72 Perhaps a bustling little yellow-poll answers in the copse. **1917** *Birds of Amer.* III. 126. — (**12**) [**1764** G. EDWARDS *Gleanings Nat. Hist.* III. 295 The Yellow Red-pole . . . hath its upper mandible dusky.] **1811** WILSON *Ornithology* IV. 19 [The] Yellow-Red-poll Warbler: *Sylvia petechia* . . . [frequents] low swampy thickets. **1868** *Amer. Naturalist* II. 171 Soon after the pine-warbler has arrived, . . . the Yellow Red-polled Warbler . . . makes his appearance. — (**13**) *c***1730** CATESBY *Carolina* I. 58 The Yellow-rump . . . is a creeper. . . . They are found in Virginia. **1892** TORREY *Foot-Path Way* 96 This yellow-rump, or myrtle bird, is one of the thrifty members of his great family. — (**14**) **1783** LATHAM *Gen. Synopsis Birds* II. 481 Yellow-rumped w[arbler]. . . . Throat, breast, and rump, fine yellow. . . . Inhabits Pensylvania. **1917** *Birds of Amer.* III. 130 Because of its resemblance to the Myrtle Warbler . . . Audubon's Warbler is often called the Western Yellow-rumped Warbler.

(**15**) [**1785** PENNANT *Arctic Zool.* II. 468 Yellow-shanks Sn[ipe]. With a slender black bill. . . . Legs yellow.] **1844** *Nat. Hist. N.Y., Zoology*

II. 248 This small species . . . is described under the name of *Yellow-shank Tatler.* **1874** Coues *Birds N.W.* 496 The Yellowshank . . . nests only in high latitudes. — **(16) 1783** Latham *Gen. Synopsis Birds* II. 482 Spotted Yellow Warbler. **1917** *Birds of Amer.* III. 127/2 Regional varieties of the Yellow Warbler are [etc.]. **1938** Thompson *High Trails* 153 The trail winds through glacial meadows where the yellow warbler . . . and many other birds fill the air with their songs.

For **yellow-bellied, belly, crowned, leg, throat,** see as main entries.

b. In the names of fishes: (1) **yellow-backed rockfish,** a rockfish, *Pteropodus maliger,* of the Pacific Coast; (2) **bass,** (*a*) the small-mouthed black bass, *Micropterus dolomieu,* (*b*) a yellow fresh-water fish, *Chrysoperca interrupta,* found in the lower Mississippi; (3) * **belly,** see as a main entry; (4) * **cat,** a species of catfish found in the eastern and southern states; (5) **fin,** (see quot.); (6) **fish,** (*a*) the niggerfish, *Cephalopholis fulvus,* (*b*) the Atka fish, *Pleurogrammus monopterygius;* (7) **mackerel,** either one of two cavallas, the jurel or hardtail, *Paratractus crysos,* of the related species *Caranx hippos;* (8) **perch,** any one of various American fresh-water fishes, esp. the common perch, *Perca flavescens,* and the small-mouthed black bass, *Micropterus dolomieu* (see also quot. 1903); (9) **pickerel,** (see quot.); (10) **pike,** (see quot.); (11) * **tail,** any one of various American fishes having a yellow or yellowish tail, cf. **yellow-tailed shad** *s.v.* * **shad 3;** (12) **-tailed roncador,** (see quot.).

(1) 1884 Goode *Fisheries* I. 264 Yellow-backed Rock-fish. . . . It ranges from Monterey to Puget Sound. — **(2)** (*a*) **1820** Rafinesque in *Western Rev.* II. 50 *Pale River-Bass. Lepomis pallida.* . . . Vulgar name yellow Bass, common Bass, &c. (*b*) **1884** Goode *Fisheries* I. 431 The Yellow Bass . . . is found throughout the lower course of the Mississippi. — **(4) 1815** Drake *Cincinnati* 141 Yellow-cat and sword-fish are most esteemed.

(5) 1884 Goode *Fisheries* I. 362 About Buzzard's Bay and in the vicinity the largest [of the squeteagues] are known as 'Yellow-fins.' — **(6)** (*a*) *c***1733** Catesby *Carolina* II. 10 The Yellow Fish. . . . This had small thin scales of a reddish yellow colour. (*b*) **1884** *Nat. Museum Bul.* No. 27, 392 The 'Atka fish,' 'Atka Mackerel,' or 'Yellow fish' (*Pleurogrammus monopterygius*), . . . is extremely plentiful off Atka and the Shumagin islands and elsewhere in Alaska. — **(7) 1814** Mitchill *Fishes N.Y.* 424 Yellow Mackerel. . . . A marine fish, taken in the bay of New-York. **1911** *Rep. Fisheries 1908* 311 Jurel. . . . [Known] about New York and on the coast of New Jersey as the 'yellow mackerel.' — **(8) 1805** Parkinson *Tour* 311 The Baltimore market consists of rock perch, white and yellow [etc.]. **1855** Longfellow *Hiawatha* 67 [He] saw the yellow perch, the Sakwa, Like a sunbeam in the water. **1903** T. H. Bean *Fishes N.Y.* 529 In Great Egg Harbor bay individuals [of *Morone americana,* the white perch] taken from salt water are sometimes called yellow perch or peerch. — **(9) 1884** Goode *Fisheries* I. 421 At Cleveland and Dover, Ohio, this species [the wall-eyed pike] is known as 'Yellow Pickerel.'

(10) 1856 *Porter's Spirit of Times* 20 Sep. 40/3 The Pike-perch, *Lucioperca Americana,* . . . [is known as] the Yellow Pike. — **(11) 1775** Romans *Nat. Hist. Fla.* App. 19 A little to the north hereof is a small reef . . . where vast quantities of groopers . . . , yellow-tails, . . . may be taken. **1838** Gosse *Letters* 18 Another kind, which they called, though by a misnomer, a yellow-tail, had its body marked with longitudinal bands of delicate pink and yellow alternately. **1903** T. H. Bean *Fishes N.Y.* 309 The striped killifish, also known as the . . . mayfish, yellow-tail, and New York gudgeon, is the largest member of its family known on our eastern coast. — **(12) 1884** Goode *Fisheries* I. 379 *Umbrina roncador* . . . is generally known as the 'Yellow-tailed' or 'Yellow-finned Roncador.'

c. In the names of other animals: (1) **yellow bear,** (*a*) =**grizzly bear,** *obs.,* (*b*) the yellow larva of the Virginia tiger moth, *Diacrisia virginica;* (2) **-bellied terrapin,** see *s.v.* **yellow-bellied** as a main entry; (3) **jacket,** see as a main entry; (4) **moccasin,** prob. a copperhead *q.v.* (sense **1.**); (5) **-necked caterpillar,** (see quot.); (6) **terrapin,** =**yellow-bellied terrapin;** (7) **wasp,** =**yellow jacket 1.**

(1) (*a*) **1805** Whitehouse in *Lewis & Clark Exped.* VII. (1905) 93 Towards evening the hunters killed a yellow bear in a bottom of cotton wood. (*b*) **1867** *Amer. Naturalist* I. 162 Many winter in the caterpillar or larva state, such as the larvæ of several Noctridæ and the 'yellow-bear,' and other caterpillars. — **(4) 1828** Mrs. Hall *Letters* 235 In the course of this day's travelling we saw, not 'stuffed' but all alive, two very large snakes, one of a poisonous kind called the yellow moccassin, and one black, not venomous. **1851** *Polly Peablossom* 69 She got onto the whappinest, biggest, rustiest yaller moccasin.

(5) 1891 *Cent.* 7016/3 The yellow-necked caterpillar, the larva of a common North American bombycid moth, *Datana ministra,* which feeds in communities on the foliage of apple, hickory, and walnut in the United States. — **(6) 1857** *Spirit of Times* 25 April 116/3 Since that time I have . . . caught seven yellow terrapins. — **(7) 1782** Crèvecoeur *Letters* 43 The yellow wasps, which build under ground, in our meadows, are much more to be dreaded.

6. In the names of, or with reference to, plants and trees: (1) **yellow ash,** a local name for any one of various trees having light-colored or yellowish wood; (2) **birch,** a North American tree, *Betula lutea,* having a yellow or gray bark, also attrib.; (3) **buckeye,** =**sweet buckeye;** (4) **corn,** a variety of corn the kernels of which are yellow, also attrib., and **yellow bantam corn;** (5) **cotton,** a variety of cotton the fiber of which is of a yellowish tinge, also attrib., *obs.;* (6) **cypress,** the yellow cedar or bald cypress *qq.v.;* (7) * **daisy,** a local name for the black-eyed Susan *q.v.;* (8) **-eyed grass,** any one of various plants of the genus *Xyris;* (9) **fir,** the Douglas fir or the white fir; (10) **flint corn,** an especially productive variety of corn having yellow kernels; (11) **honeysuckle,** the trumpet honeysuckle, or a related plant, also the flame azalea; (12) * **jessamine,** the American Carolina jessamine, *Gelsemium sempervirens,* also attrib.; (13) **lady's slipper,** any one of various orchids of the genus *Cypripedium* having yellow flowers, as the species *C. parviflorum;* (14) **lily,** any one of various lilies, esp. the meadow lily, *Lilium canadense;* (15) **locust,** (*a*) the common American locust, *Robinia pseudoacacia,* (*b*) (see quot.); (16) **oak,** any one of various American oaks, as the black or quercitron oak, *Quercus velutina,* or the chinquapin oak *q.v.;* (17) **pine,** see as main entry; (18) * **plum,** the common wild plum, *Prunus americana,* or a variety of this; (19) **pond lily,** any plant of the genus *Nuphar,* also with defining adjective; (20) **poplar,** any one of various soft-wood trees, esp. the tulip tree, *Liriodendron tulipifera,* also attrib.; (21) **puccoon,** = * **goldenseal;** (22) * **root,** any one of various plants having yellow roots as goldenseal and gold thread *qq.v.,* cf. **shrub yellowroot;** (23) * **wood,** any one of various American trees having yellow wood as Osage orange, gopher wood, sweetleaf *qq.v.,* cf. **northern yellow-wood.**

(1) 1778 Carver *Travels* 497 The yellow ash . . . is only found near the head branches of the Mississippi. **1832** Williamson *Maine* I. 106 Of this species [the black ash], the *red* and *yellow* are only varieties. **1884** Sargent *Rep. Forests* 57 Yellow Wood. Yellow Ash . . . yielding a clear yellow dye. — **(2) 1787** *Amer. Acad. Mem.* II. I. 158 Black and Yellow Birch. . . . The bark of the latter is used by the Indians for making canoes. *c***1840** Neal *Beedle's Sleigh Ride* 15 Nothing was heard but a cricket under the hearth, keeping tune with a sappy yellow birch forestick. **1943** Peattie *Great Smokies* 156 A yellow birch on Whitetop Mountain was found to be seven feet three inches thick. — **(3) 1909** *Cent. Supp.* 171/3 Yellow buckeye, *Aesculus octandra,* a large tree of the eastern United States, with yellow flowers. **1942** Peattie *Great Smokies* 277 Silverbell, flowering dogwood, black locust, fire cherry, yellow buckeye, and many trees with relatively less conspicuous flowers will be in bloom at this time. — **(4) 1738** W. Stephens *Proc. Georgia* I. 200, I planted almost wholly with that yellow Corn. **1927** Benét *J. B.'s Body* 141 But this is the last . . . [of the] yellow corn meal. **1949** *Democrat* 30 June 4/1 He had cleaned up a whole row of yellow bantam corn.

(5) [**1829** B. Hall *Travels N. Amer.* III. 220 The different kinds of cotton are, 'first quality white,' 'second quality white,' and 'yellow.'] **1865** E. W. Pearson *Lett. Port Royal* 300 Celia wanted her 'yellow-cotton-money' 'by himself.' — **(6) 1812** Stoddard *Sk. Louisiana* 161 No other wood than white and yellow cypress, was sawed. **1940** *Mt. Hood Guide* 12 A prominent species in the higher altitudes is the Alaska cedar or yellow cypress. — **(7) 1891** *Amer. Folk-Lore* IV. 147 The only Buttercup we then knew . . . we called *Yellow Daisy.* — **(8) 1814** Bigelow *Florula Bostoniensis* 13 Yellow eyed grass. . . . Small yellow florets. **1899** Going *Flowers* 187 The seeds of both water-rushes and yellow-eyed-grass are small and light. — **(9) 1882** *Garden* 30 Sep. 301/3 The principal tree in these forests [near Puget Sound] is the yellow Fir. **1884** Sargent *Rep. Forests* 209 Two varieties [of the Douglas fir], red and yellow fir, are distinguished by lumbermen, dependent probably upon the age of the tree. **1897** Sudworth *Arborescent Flora* 54 *Abies grandis.* Great Silver Fir. . . . [Also called] Yellow Fir (Mont., Idaho).

(10) *a*1817 DWIGHT *Travels* I. 81 Even the proper maize of New-England, commonly styled the *yellow flint corn*, . . . [yields] but an indifferent harvest. 1848 C. L. FLEISCHMANN *Nordamerikanische Landwirth* 113 Golden Sioux, oder Northern Yellow Flint-Corn. — (11) 1836 LINCOLN *Botany* App. 113 *Lonicera . . . flava*, (yellow honeysuckle,) . . . ; flowers bright yellow. 1850 S. F. COOPER *Rural Hours* 70 The yellow honeysuckle grows in the Catskill Mountains. 1860 CURTIS *Woody Plants N.C.* 98 Yellow Honeysuckle, . . . is found only at a considerable elevation on our mountains. — (12) 1709 LAWSON *Carolina* 89 The yellow Jessamin is wild in our Woods. 1894 TORREY *Fla. Sketch-Book* 105 Here and there in the undergrowth were Yellow jessamine vines. 1949 *Democrat* 17 Feb. 4/1 The red bud, the yellow jessamine and other of the early spring flowers have been blooming for two weeks or more. — (13) 1738 CATESBY *Carolina* II. 73 The Yellow Lady's Slipper. . . . These grow on the sandy banks of rivers in Carolina, Virginia and Pensylvania. 1869 *Amer. Naturalist* III. 8 Raising their heads above the foliage of that miniature grove of wild mandrakes are a few specimens of the Yellow Ladies' Slipper. 1939 *Nat. Geog. Mag.* Aug. 271/2 The yellow ladyslipper *C. parviflorum*, occasionally found in the forests of the West and Northwest, has smaller flowers than those of this yellow ladyslipper. — (14) 1784 *Amer. Acad. Mem.* I. 433 Yellow Lily. Blossoms Yellow, with black spots. 1843 TORREY *Flora N.Y.* II. 305 *Lilium Canadense.* Wild Yellow Lily. . . . Moist meadows. 1939 *Nat. Geog. Mag.* Aug. 264/2 The stately plants of the western yellow lily (*L. parryi*) seek moisture on the middle slopes of the mountains in southern California.

(15) (*a*) 1810 MICHAUX *Arbres* I. 38 *Yellow Locust* (Acacia jaune) . . . [nom donné] à cet arbre sur les bords de la rivière Susquehannah. 1884 SARGENT *Rep. Forests* 55 Yellow Locust. . . . Widely and generally naturalized throughout the United States. (*b*) 1897 SUDWORTH *Arborescent Flora* 257 *Cladrastis lutea.* . . . Yellow-wood. . . . [Also called] Yellow locust (Ky., Tenn.). — (16) 1686 *Topsfield Rec.* 59 A heape of rocks [is] near to a . . . yealow oack at the southwesterly corner [of the parsonage land]. [1778 CARVER *Travels* 495 There are several sorts of oaks in these parts; the black, the white, the red, the yellow, the grey.] 1916 SETON *Woodcraft Man.* 281 Yellow Oak, Chestnut Oak, or Chinquapin Scrub Oak (*Quercus Muhlenbergii*) A great forest tree; up to 160 feet high; . . . It is much like the chestnut oak but its leaves are narrower, more sharply saw-edged, and its acorns much smaller. — (18) 1785 MARSHALL *Amer. Grove* 111 Prunus americana. Large Yellow Sweet Plumb. This generally rises to the height of twelve or fifteen feet. 1813 MUHLENBERG *Cat. Plants* 48 *Prunus nigra* (*Americana*), Yellow plumb. 1885 HAVARD *Flora W. & S. Texas* 512 *Prunus Americana*, var. *Mollis.* Wild Yellow Plum. . . . Yellow fruit, smaller and less palatable than that of the species in the Northern States. — (19) 1821 *Mass. H.S. Coll.* 2 Ser. IX. 152 *Nuphar advena*, Yellow pond lily. . . . [*Nuphar*] *kalmiana*, . . . Little yellow pond lily. 1898 HARPER *S. B. Anthony* I. 50 Here and there [is] a large patch of yellow pond lilies. 1931 [see **yellow lantern**].

(20) 1774 in PEYTON *Adv. Grandfather* (1867) 127 The forest of Kentucky consists of yellow and white poplar, walnut, red bud, hiccory. 1829 FLINT *G. Mason* 98 He gave an infusion of Dog Wood, Wild Cherry, and Yellow Poplar bark. 1943 PEATTIE *Great Smokies* 170 At first, about sixty years ago, only the most precious cabinet woods were culled—walnut, cherry, and magnolia, with a selection of the choicest construction timber from yellow poplar (lumberman's name for tulip tree) and white pine and basswood. — (21) 1889 *Cent.* 2933/1 It is sometimes used in dyeing, and gives a beautiful yellow color; hence the common names *yellowroot*, . . . and *yellow puccoon*. 1941 R. S. WALKER *Lookout* 50 Yellow puccoon whose thick roots were once used for painting Easter eggs thrives in the limestone area near the foot of the mountain, where Amsonia's blue flowers come in early springtime. — (22) [1796 NEMNICH *Allg. Lexicon Naturgeschichte* III. 944 Yellow root, *Hydrastis canadensis*.] 1804 LEWIS in *L. & Clark Exped.* VI. (1905) 143 This plant is known in Kentuckey and many other parts of this western country by the name of the yellow root. 1815 DRAKE *Cincinnati* 88 Yellow root [is used in dyeing]. 1948 *Hoosier Folklore* March 6 Find yellow root growing, wash it and dry it. — (23) 1806 in *Ann. 9th Cong.* 2 Sess. 1138 At this place Mr. Dunbar obtained one or two slips of the 'bois d'arc,' (bow wood, or yellow wood). 1853 SITGREAVES *Exped. Zuni & Colo. Rivers* 38 At the spot where we halted to rest the mules, we procured a number of berries of the yellow-wood, (*Berberis pennata*) which . . . assisted to quench our thirst. 1897 SUDWORTH *Arborescent Flora* 274 *Cotinus cotinoides.* . . . American Smoke-tree. . . . [Also called] Yellowwood (Ala.).

Also (1) **yellow bell flower,** (2) **cedar,** (3) **lantern,** (4) * **top,** (see quots.).

(1) 1817 W. COXE *Fruit Trees* 118 Monstrous Bellflower. A very large fair, and beautiful apple; of an oblong shape resembling the yellow Bellflower. 1849 *N. Eng. Farmer* I. 54 He sent us some as large and fine Yellow Bellflowers as we have ever seen in this market. . . . When raised in Maine they proved to be a winter apple. — (2) 1891 *Cent.* 7015/2 *Yellow cypress*, a tree, *Chamæcyparis Nutkaensis*, of northwestern North America . . . is somewhat used in boat- and ship-building. . . . Also *Sitka cypress, yellow cedar.* — (3) 1931 CLUTE *Plants* 61 The globular flowers of the yellow pond lily (*Nymphaea advena*) riding on the water are yellow lanterns. — (4) 1846 WORCESTER 833/1 *Yellow-Top*, a species of grass; called also *white-top. Farm. Ency.* 1891 *Cent.* 7017/1 Yellow-top; . . . a variety of turnip: so called from the color of the skin on the upper part of the bulb. 1909 *Cent. Supp.* 1460/1 *Yellow-top*, . . . a reed-grass, *Calamagrostis hyperborea Americana*, common in low meadows and on shady river-banks throughout the northwestern United States.

7. In miscellaneous combs.: (1) **yellowback,** (*a*) a legal-tender note the back of which is printed in a yellowish color, cf. **goldback,** (*b*) a sneak, coward, *slang*, (*c*) (see quot. 1937); (2) * **bird,** a gold coin, *obs.*, cf. **5.** (4) above; (3) **cover,** see as a main entry; (4) **day,** (see quot.), *obs.;* (5) **dip,** crude turpentine that has remained in the "boxes" on the trees all winter, in full **yellow dip turpentine;** (6) * **dog, fever,** see as main entries; (7) * **flower,** (see quot. 1833), *obs.* or *hist.;* (8) **jack,** =**yellow fever,** *colloq.;* (9) **patch,** (see quot.); (10) **pup,** (see quot.), *obs.;* (11) **slip,** (see quot.), *obs.;* (12) **water,** (see quot.), *obs.*

(1) (*a*) 1902 WILSON *Spenders* 150 She was dead in love with the nice long yellow-backs that I've piled up. 1943 *Copper Camp* 37 Bills of large denominations mysteriously appeared under the politicians' pillows and mattresses, . . . on arising in the morning they occasionally found yellowbacks tucked in their shoes. (*b*) 1922 CURWOOD *Country Beyond* 143 The world would call him a lying yellow-back if he betrayed what had actually happened on the trail between Cragg's Ridge and Mooney's cabin. (*c*) 1937 *Literary Digest* 10 July 25/2 The real dime novels began with the Beadle series, paper-covered booklets bound in orange paper and known as 'yellow-backs.' This was in November, 1860. 1950 *Time* 10 July 82/2 The first dime novel that really cost a dime was published by Beadle in 1860. *Malaeska: The Indian Wife of the White Hunter* came out in the yellowback that was to become the trademark of infamy to U.S. parents. — (2) 1853 SIMMS *Sword & Distaff* 469 Set you down quiet, and think over the different draws, or holes, whar' you hides away your yellow-birds. — (4) 1881 *Harper's Mag.* Dec. 944/1 [On] the 'yellow day' of 1881 in America . . . the sun rose clear, but within an hour the moist air . . . seemed to thicken into a heavy screen of mist, that . . . was of a strange yellow hue.

(5) 1859 G. W. PERRY *Turpentine Farming* 123 'Yellow dip' . . . makes more spirits than any other turpentine. 1861 *Charleston* (S.C.) *Mercury* 8 Jan. 3/5 Turpentine—Sales this morning of 125 bbls., at $2 for Yellow Dip, $1.60 for Virgin. 1948 YOUNGKEN *Pharmacognosy* 115 That collected during subsequent years supplies the so-called 'yellow dip' turpentine which is somewhat darker in color. — (7) 1832 *Boston Transcript* 10 May 2/1 After the first representation of the 'Lion of the West,' certain 'yellow flowers of the forest' got the skiff ready to 'row him up salt river.' 1833 COKE *Subaltern's Furlough* I. 35 The effect of his performance in the West . . . incensed the 'half-horse, half-alligator boys,' 'the yellow flowers of the forest,' as they call themselves. 1857 *Spirit of Times* 10 Oct. 81/3 The gist of the discourse was, that he, the Hoosier, was 'the yaller flower of the forest,' and the 'snappin' turkle of the Wabash.' [1944 SHAPIRO *Yankee Thunder* 39 I'm the yaller blossom of the forest, and I'll double you up like a spare shirt.] — (8) 1836 E. HOWARD *R. Reefer* xxxiii, Misgivings about Yellow Jack [in West Indies]. 1840 MAXWELL *Run* II. 169 Philadelphia used to have a fever commonly called 'Yellow Jack.' 1950 *N.O. Times-Picayune Mag.* 19 Feb. 28/3 Then Yellow Jack struck again in 1878. — (9) 1917 KEPHART *Camping* II. 24 Those great tracts of rhododendron . . . cover mile after mile of steep mountainside. . . . The natives call such wastes 'laurel slicks,' 'woolly heads,' 'lettuce beds,' 'yaller patches,' and 'hells.'

(10) 1893 *Cong. Rec.* 25 Aug. 936/2 Then we had the Michigan wild-cat money, then we had throughout Indiana, Illinois, and Ohio what is known as blue-dog and yellow-pup. — (11) 1900 NELSON *A B C Wall St.* 154 The news slips of the New York News Bureau are known as the 'yellow slips.' — (12) 1796 HAWKINS *Letters* 46 The distemper which has for 3 or 4 years past destroyed the horses in the Southern States . . . called there the yellow water, was introduced into this country from St. Antoine, and Appaluca.

b. In designations, usu. contemptuous and slang, of Negroes and Indians of a brown or mulatto color, as (1) * **yellow boy,** (2) **darky,** (3) **girl,** (4) **man,** (5) **Negro,** (6) **skin,** (7) **woman.**

(1) 1833 NEAL *Down-Easters* I. 65 Thats what they call gettin' the yeller-boys, I spose. 1936 MCKENNA *Black Range* 257 The sergeant . . . threw an armload of greasewood on the fire, which flared up, showing the white face of the yellow boy, who was chattering and weeping. — (2) 1912 *Out West* April 256/2 The little yellow darkey, who was driving, listened in silence. — (3) 1834 *Sun* (N.Y.) 20 March 2/2 A huge looking 'yaller gall' was hammering away at the eyes of a small white man in Anthony st., because he called her a *snow* ball. 1913 *Chattanooga* (Tenn.) *News* 20 Sep. 8/3 Dinah was a

product of New Orleans, a big fat 'yellow gal.' **1949** *Time* 14 March 114/3 One day a disgruntled and sulking yellow girl flavors the family tea with a dash of king's yellow, or orpiment, an arsenious pigment. — (4) **1814** *Niles' Reg.* VII. 284/2 The owner, a yellow man, not liking to lose his all without a struggle, made for a small creek. **1934** LOMAX *Amer. Ballads* 14 One of their number, a handsome yellow man, when he was sure that they were ready to heave, threw back his head and sang.

(5) **1867** LOCKE *Swingin' Round* 287 The per cent. uv yeller niggers in this State attests how faithful Kentucky hez bin. **1943** POWELL *Home Again* 101, I tuk 'er ter de bush-arber meetin', an' a big yaller nigger preached de mos' pow'rfulest sermin I ever heared. — (6) **1840** *Crockett's Harrison Alm. 1841* 4 He war a roarer of the true Varginny breed. He that treed Old Proctor, and the pesky yaller skins that war with him. **1851** M. REID *Rifle Rangers* (1853) 89, I was in hopes we'd have a brush with the yellow-skins. — (7) **1831** PECK *Guide* 72 Much has been said about certain connections that are winked at with the yellow women of [New Orleans]. **1873** BEADLE *Undevel. West* 302 We plunge into the dark alleys lined by little cubby-holes alive with yellow women.

c. In expressions alluding to the "yellow peril." *Obs.*

1876 W. M. FISHER *Californians* 62 Even as far east as Massachusetts the advancing yellow wave is creating a 'bore' in the mouth of some of the largest white rivers of trade. *Ib.*, Men laughed a long time at the *ifs* advanced regarding 'the negro question.' . . . The yellow comedy has now the boards as a kind of after-piece.

As the last term in **Baltimore, high, spruce yellow.**

***yellow-bellied,** *a.* In the names of birds: (1) **yellow-bellied flycatcher,** a small flycatcher, *Empidonax flaviventris,* of eastern North America; (2) **sapsucker,** =next; (3) **woodpecker,** a sapsucker, *Sphyrapicus varius* of the eastern states.

(1) **1827** WILLIAMS *W. Florida* 30 Black-head fly catcher. . . . Yellow-bellied do. *M[uscicapa] cristata.* **1939** LINCOLN *Migration* 63, I have in my collection a fine specimen of the Yellow-bellied Flycatcher. — (2) **1909** WEBSTER. **1942** PEATTIE *Friendly Mts.* 210, I came to a sweet or black birch tree that had been tapped by a yellow-bellied sapsucker. — (3) **c1729** CATESBY *Carolina* I. 21 *Picus Varius Minor, Ventre Luteo.* The Yellow belly'd Wood-pecker. Weighs one ounce thirteen penny weight. **1825** BONAPARTE *Ornithology* I. 75 [The] Young Yellow-Bellied Woodpecker, *Picus Varius,* . . . is introduced on account of its anomalous plumage. **1892** TORREY *Foot-Path Way* 190 The first yellow-bellied woodpecker of the season was hammering in a tree over my head.

b. yellow-bellied marmot, terrapin, (see quots.).

1884 GOODE *Fisheries* I. 155 *Pseudemys scabra,* a species which occurs in the Carolinas, Georgia, and northern Florida, . . . is known popularly as the 'Yellow-bellied Terrapin.' **1917** *Mammals of Amer.* 301/2 Yellow-bellied Marmot—*Marmota flaviventer flaviventer* (Audubon and Bachman). . . . Western Texas, New Mexico and Arizona north to 49°.

***yellowbelly,** *n.* **1.** *S.W.* A Mexican. *Contemptuous* and *obs.* **2.** (See quot.) *Obs.* **3.** =**yellow-bellied flycatcher. 4.** (See quot.)

(1) **1842** *N.O. Crescent* 16 March (Extra) 1 God send that they bayonet every 'yellow belly' in the Mexican army. **1853** C. W. WEBBER *Shot in Eye* (1855) 132 He had a hatred for the 'yaller bellies,' and 'copper heads,' as he called the Mexicans and Indians, which was refreshingly orthodox. — (2) **1865** SALA *Diary* I. 102 Don't lay out the most insignificant 'yellow-belly'—the smallest change for a 'greenback'—on it. — (3) **1892** TORREY *Foot-Path Way* 9 In his notes, the yellow-belly may be said to take after both the least flycatcher and the wood pewee. — (4) **1896** JORDAN & EVERMANN *Check-List Fishes* 247 *Ptychocheilus oregonensis.* . . . Yellow-belly; Sacramento Pike. Rivers of Oregon and Washington. *Ib.* 355 *Lepomis auritus.* . . . Yellowbelly; Redbreast Bream. Maine to Louisiana.

***yellow cover.**

1. a. A Whig songbook. **b.** (See quot. 1859.) **c.** (See quot. 1864.) All *obs.*

(a) **1844** *Republican Sentinel* (Richmond, Va.) 20 July 3/5 What cold ingratitude to the able orators, who have been imported for the purpose of making converts; to the famed 'Glee Club', with their *splendid* text book 'The Yaller Kiver!' **1848** *Field Piece* (Chi.) 16 Aug. 2/5 But if the Whigs *will* sing, the 'Yaller Kiver' is just the thing they want. — (b) **1856** *Town Talk* (S.F.) 13 June 2/1 Several of the individuals who have lately been honored by a 'yellow cover' from The Vigilance Committee, have signified their intention of waiting until the Committee order them under arrest. **1859** BARTLETT 520 *Yellow Cover,* . . . a notice of dismissal from government employment. So called from its being usually enclosed in a yellow envelope. — (c) **1858** *Calif. Spirit of Times* (S.F.) 7 Aug. 1/2 *He* was 'laying back' in an attitude of dreamy repose, poring over the nonsensical sentimentality of a 'yaller kiver,' and making a world for himself. **1864** LELAND *Art of Conversation* 234 *Yellow cover.* Applied to cheap and vulgar literature; so called first in 1840, from the twenty-five cent editions of Paul de Kock's novels, and similar works. **1950** *Chi. Tribune* 24 Aug. 20/3 The phrase 'to bite the dust,' appears to have been adopted by writers of the 'yaller kiver' school from the speech of frontiersmen.

2. yellow-covered, *a.* of a literary production: Having a yellow cover, depending for effect upon sensation or cheap thrills. *Colloq.*

1849 *Hunt's Merch. Mag.* XX. 118 Hard by them the yellow-covered literature of the day—translations from the French. **1888** *Seattle Post-Intelligencer* 20 Oct. 1/4 She is a victim of yellow-covered literature and says she wants to be a cowboy. **1915** YOUNG *Hard Knocks* 23, [I was] ashamed to acknowledge that the little yellow covered novels were the cause of it.

***yellow-crowned,** *a.* **1. yellow-crowned (night) heron,** a heron, *Nyctanassa violacea,* of the southern states, the crest of which has a pale tawny tinge. **2. yellow-crowned warbler,** (*a*) the chestnut-sided warbler, *Dendroica pennsylvanica,* (*b*) the myrtle bird, *Dendroica coronata.*

(1) **1813** WILSON *Ornithology* VIII. 26 [The] Yellow-crowned Heron: *Ardea violacea* . . . inhabits the lower parts of South Carolina, Georgia, and Louisiana. **1844** *Nat. Hist. N.Y., Zoology* II. 228 The Yellow-Crowned Night Heron . . . is no where very abundant. **1917** *Birds of Amer.* I. 195/1 [The] Yellow-crowned Night Heron . . . is quite as diurnal in its habits as any of the more common Herons. — (2) (*a*) **1817** SHAW *Gen. Zool.* X. 623 Yellow-crowned Warbler. (*Sylvia icterocephala.*) . . . This inhabits the continent of North America, appearing in . . . Pennsylvania in April. **1917** *Birds of Amer.* III. 133. (*b*) **1839** PEABODY *Mass. Birds* 307 The Yellow-crowned Warbler . . . is quite common here for two or three weeks in May. **1868** *Amer. Naturalist* II. 171 The Yellow-crowned Warbler . . . [arrives] from the fifteenth to the twentieth of April. **1917** *Birds of Amer.* III. 128.

***yellow dog.** Chiefly in slang uses.

1. A cur or mongrel, usu. in transf. uses as a symbol of utter worthlessness. Also attrib.

1833 J. S. JONES *Green Mt. Boys* II. iv, That yaller dog has broke his chain, and bit a nigger! **1895** HARTE *Clarence* III. iii, In Illinois we wouldn't hang a yellow dog on that evidence. **1903** *Everybody's Mag.* Oct. 562 If there are five magazines in the [cut-rate] combination, two of them are good. The rest are 'yellow dogs.' **1909** O. HENRY *Options* 299 I'll buy . . . a shotgun and a yellow dog. **1949** *Boston Globe* 17 July (Fiction Mag.) 4/1 It's a yellow dog trick.

b. A contemptuous designation for a person.

1880 NYE *B. Nye & Boomerang* 166 The presiding officer had lost control, and a surging crowd of yellow dogs had the floor. **1945** SERVICE *Ploughman* 217 Every one was handing me a dirty deal, and I was taking it like a yellow dog.

2. Used in combs. with reference to notes issued by wildcat banks. *Obs.* Cf. **red dog.**

[**1830** NEILSON *Recollections* 140–41 In some States, notes for such small sums as $6\frac{1}{4}$ and $12\frac{1}{2}$ cents . . . are issued. . . . In the Southern States, where the Negroes cannot read, these small notes are ornamented with the figure of a pig, a dog, or a cock, and accordingly receive these appellations from the blacks.] **1875** *Chi. Tribune* 26 Aug. 4/1 The grand mass-meeting in Detroit in favor of cheap imitation money of the 'blue-pup' and 'yellow dog' variety proved to be a wretched failure. **1906** *Cin. Enquirer* 1 April 2/2 To-day we found several entries in 'yellow dog' accounts.

b. With reference to politics, esp. **yellow dog ticket,** a ticket that a loyal party member is expected to support even though a yellow dog were running on it.

1894 *Democratic Guardian* (S.F.) 28 June 1/2 His universal popularity would carry even a 'yaller dog' ticket to success. **1903** *Outlook* 15 Aug. 931/2 In preference to a Tammany 'yellow dog' ticket his organization [*sc.* the German-American Reform Union] would support the fusion candidate. **1933** *Durant* (Okla.) *D. Democrat* 24 April 1/5 The state supreme court today knocked out the 1933 yellow dog election pledge law.

c. yellow-dog contract, an employment contract in which the employee agrees not to join a labor union.

1920 *Motorman & Conductor* Oct. 34/1 Yellow dog contracts . . . provide that the miner shall not join a union while in the employ of the company. **1949** *Chi. Tribune* 20 Feb. 34/8 Permit legislative prohibition of 'yellow dog' contracts.

d. yellow-dog lease, a lease regarded as unfair to the lessee.

1902 *U.M.W. Jrnl.* 3 July 1/1 (*heading*), Below is an Exact Copy of the Housing Lease, Better Known as the 'Yellow Dog' Lease, Which is Creating Such a Stir Among the Miners on Loup Creek.

3. *yellow dog under the wagon*, and variants (see quots. and cf. * **team,** *n.* **1.**).

1857 *Spirit of Times* 19 Dec. 248/1 For Potomac's pedigree, see page 407 of 'Edgar's General Stud Book,' which is about as long and reliable as that of 'the big yellow dog under the wagon.' **1865** BROWNE *A. Ward; His Travels* 49 Columbus was a four-horse team fillibuster, and a large yaller dog under the waggin.

yellow fever. An infectious tropical or semi-tropical fever characterized by jaundice, hemorrhages, vomiting, etc. Cf. **bronze John, dock fever, Orleans fever, Panama fever, stranger's fever, vomito, yellow jack.**

1739 *Boston News Letter* 8 Nov. 2/1 A terrible Sickness has rag'd here, which the Doctors call a yellow billious Fever, of which we bury 8 or 10 in a Day; the like never known among us; but seems to abate as the cold Weather advances. **1740** W. STEPHENS *Proc. Georgia* II. 17 From *Charles-Town* we hear of a dangerous Distemper raging there, which they call the Yellow Fever, from the Corpse immediately so changing, after Death. **1800** *Columbian Centinel* 2 July 4/1 The Pestilence known by the name of the Yellow Fever, has excited the attention of the learned in Medicine. **1949** *Friends* April 16/2 Major Walter Reed deservedly is honored for his work in conquering yellow fever; but John R. Kissinger, the first volunteer to submit to the bite of the germ-carrying mosquitoes, is forgotten.

attrib. **1833** J. E. ALEXANDER *Transatlantic Sk.* II. 16 The only chance I had was a yellow-fever captain, that is, an enterprising fellow, who ventures down the river from Cincinnati, or St. Louis, in the fall, to see if he can pick up a few stray passengers or freight at a time when others are afraid to venture. **1860** ABBOTT *South & North* 113 The yellow-fever epidemic is a very serious drawback to the idea of a residence in Mobile. **1880** *Psyche* III. 111/1 At Norfolk in 1855, a fly appeared in swarms, which the people . . . called the yellow fever fly. **1881** *Harper's Mag.* Jan. 204/2 The last entertainment [was] . . . a concert, in aid of the yellow-fever sufferers.

b. *transf.* **1.** (See quot.) **2.** =**gold fever.** Both *obs.*

(1) 1835 INGRAHAM *South-West* II. 282 One half [of the cotton] in the rows, and sometimes whole acres together, die with the 'rust,' 'sore skin,' or 'yellow fever.' — **(2) 1849** *Boston Traveller* 29 Jan. 2/6 A clerk in a Wall street bank . . . caught the 'yellow fever' so suddenly . . . that he was carried off by it before he could procure a change of raiment or take parting leave of her who had borne him. **1852** *Ore. Statesman* 8 June 1/3 In this deposite of rock and gravel is found the gold, and for the benefit of those who now have the *yellow* fever, I will add, more often than otherwise in exceedingly small quantities.

yellow jacket.

1. Any one of various American wasps having yellow markings. Also attrib.

1796 LATROBE *Journal* 106 The yellow jacket . . . appears to be on the wing very like the common wasp. **1817** PAULDING *Lett. from South* I. 228 Oliver's horse being stung by a yellow-jacket hornet. **1949** *Democrat* 25 Aug. 4/3 We had driven it directly over a yellow jacket nest.

transf. **1823** DODDRIDGE *Logan* I. i, Why so large an encampment of Indians? . . . Why do these yellow jackets come so near us?

2. a. A fish of the genus *Oligoplites*, a leather jacket. **b.** A gold coin. *Obs.*

(a) 1883 *Nat. Museum Bul.* No. 27, 440 *Oligoplites occidentalis*. . . . Yellow Jacket; Yellow Tail. — **(b) 1884** MARK TWAIN *H. Finn* 250 (R.), He begun to haul out yaller-jackets [i.e., gold coins] and stack them up.

* **yellowleg,** *n.*

1. Either of two American shore birds having long yellow legs, the lesser yellowlegs, *Totanus flavipes*, and the greater yellowlegs, *T. melanoleucus*. Also with specifying terms. Usu. *pl.*

1772 FORSTER in *Phil. Trans.* LXII. 410 *Scolopax, Totanus.* Spotted Woodcock. . . . This bird is called a yellow leg at Albany fort. **1844** *Nat. Hist. N.Y., Zoology* II. 248 The Yellow-Legs . . . [eats] insects, worms, and small aquatic animals. **1884** *Nat. Museum Bul.* No. 27, 151 Greater Yellow-legs; Tell-tale. . . . Breeding in colder portions of North America. **1950** *Dly. Oklahoman Mag.* (Okla. City) 7 May 7/2 One of the larger shore birds, yellowlegs are among the migrating horde that delights the bird watcher during the month of May.

2. A Confederate soldier. *Rare.*

1869 *Harper's Mag.* April 716/1 If you will be kind enough to bring out one of those 'yellow legs' [Confederates] in the guard-house, and let me shoot him, I can *die in peace!*

3. A mounted representative of government authority, as a cavalryman or a forest ranger. Also attrib. *Slang.*

1895 REMINGTON *Pony Tracks* 174 'We can catch him before he pulls out in the morning, I think,' said the yellow-leg. *c***1917** in *D.N.* V. 59 The detachment of Yellow Legs imported at the behest of the Commercial Club. **1924** R. CUMMINS *Sky-high Corral* 25 They come in an' . . . set yeller-leg kids in here to tell us how to raise cows.

As the last term in **bastard, winter yellowlegs.**

* **yellow-legged,** *a.* Designating various American birds having long yellow legs.

1781–2 JEFFERSON *Notes Va.* (1788) 77 Yellow-legged snipe. **1805** LEWIS in *L. & Clark Exped.* VI. (1905) 133 [*Symphemia semi-palmata*] is about the size of the yellow leged plover. **1870** *Amer. Naturalist* IV. 547 Yellow-legged Sandpiper (*Gambretta flavipes*). **1889** *Cent.* 2576/1 *Yellow-legged goose*, the American white-fronted goose. (San Diego, California, U.S.)

Also **yellow-legger,** (see quots.).

1891 *Cent.* 7016/3 *Yellow-legger*, . . . the yellowlegs. *Ib.*, *Yellow-legger*, . . . a fisherman from Eastham, (Provincetown, Massachusetts).

yellow pine. Any one of various American pines.

Among the pines thus referred to are the **bull, Georgia, Jeffrey, loblolly, long leaf, pitch,** and **short leaf pine.**

1709 LAWSON *Carolina* 89 Ever-Greens are here plentifully found . . . the yellow Pine, the white Pine [etc.]. **1878** WHEELER *Geog. Survey Rep.* VI. 260 *Pinus Arizonica* . . . [is found] on the Santa Rita Mountains, in Southern Arizona. . . . 'There called yellow pine.' **1916** SETON *Woodcraft Man.* 267 Long-leaved Pine, Georgia Pine, Southern Pine, Yellow Pine, or Hard Pine (*Pinus palustris*) A fine tree, up to 100 feet high; evergreen; found in great forests in the Southern states; it supplies much of our lumber now; and most of our turpentine, tar, and rosin. **1949** *Pacific Discovery* May–June 16/2 There are thousands of square miles of virgin forest composed of Engelmann spruce, . . . yellow pine, western red cedar, western larch, and other conifers.

attrib. **1755** PATTEN *Diary* 12 Had Willm Holms & Willm Petersons oxen helping me Haul Logs to the river and got 4 yelow pine logs and one white pine. **1792** HASWELL *Journal* in Bancroft *N.W. Amer.* (1888) I. 729 This place affords great abundance of good yellow pine timber and spars. **1858** WARDER *Hedges & Evergreens* 246 This tree furnishes the yellow-pine lumber much used in civil and naval architecture. **1872** MARK TWAIN *Roughing It* 171 It was yellow-pine timberland.

b. With defining terms.

1834 A. PIKE *Sketches* 37, I observed that it was only one particular kind of pine which they used, viz. the rough yellow pine. **1849** *31st Congress* 1 Sess. Sen. Doc. No. 64, 97 The *sylva*, to-day, has been the large yellow pine and the piñon. **1892** APGAR *Trees Northern U.S.* 174 *Pinus ponderosa.* (Western Yellow or Heavy-wooded Pine.) . . . A large Pacific coast species. **1897** SUDWORTH *Arborescent Flora* 20 *Pinus ponderosa scopulorum.* Rock Pine. . . . [Also called] Rocky Mountain Yellow Pine (lit.).

c. The wood of a yellow pine, or a yellow pine considered with reference to its value as timber.

1812 STODDARD *Sk. Louisiana* 123 They produce vast quantities of yellow and pitch pine. **1832** WILLIAMSON *Maine* I. 110 The *yellow Pine* . . . is used for flooring and for planking vessels. **1880** *Cimarron News & Press* 18 March 2/3 More than one million feet of yellow pine and seven or eight hundred thousand feet of oak will be called for. **1891** *Cent.* 4496/3 *Yellow pine*, . . . a commercial name of the common white pine. **1948** *Life* 13 Sep. 36/1 The price of yellow pine is off at the mill.

As the last term in **foothills, Georgia, long leaf, western yellow pine.**

Yellowstone trout. The cutthroat trout, *Salmo clarki*, found in the headwaters of the Yellowstone River and in Yellowstone Lake. — **1870** in CRAMTON *Early Hist. Yellowstone Nat. Pk.* 115 The Yellowstone trout are peculiar, being the largest variety of the genus caught in waters flowing east. **1884** *Nat. Museum Bul.* No. 27, 426 *Salmo purpuratus*. . . . Yellowstone Trout; Rocky Mountain Brook Trout.

* **yellowthroat,** *n.*

1. Any one of various warblers of the genus *Geothlypis*.

1844 *Nat. Hist. N.Y., Zoology* II. 80 The Yellow Throat. *Trichas Marilandica.* **1873** in COUES *Birds N.W.* 67 The Yellow-throat prefers the trees along the banks of streams. **1904** F. S. MATHEWS *Field Book of Wild Birds* 158 The Yellow-throat has a violin quality to his voice. **1949** *Dly. Oklahoman Mag.* (Okla. City) 13 Nov. 15/5 The comical yellowthroat with its trim black mask, [is] . . . common in ravines and fencerows.

b. yellowthroat warbler, =**yellow-throated warbler.**

1810 WILSON *Ornithology* II. 64 [The] Yellow-Throat Warbler, *Sylvia Flavicollis*, . . . pass[es] the summer in Virginia, and in the southern parts of Maryland.

2. yellow-throated, *a.* In the names of various American birds (see quots.).

*c***1730** CATESBY *Carolina* I. 62 *Parus Americanus gutture luteo.* The Yellow-throated Creeper. . . . The feet . . . have very long claws, which assist them in creeping about Trees in search of Insects, on which they feed. **1808** WILSON *Ornithology* I. 117 [The] Yellow-Throated Flycatcher, *Muscicapa Sylvicola*, . . . is found chiefly in the woods, hunting among the high branches. **1844** *Nat. Hist. N.Y., Zoology* II. 120 The Yellow-Throated Greenlet, *Vireo flavifrons*, . . . winters in Texas and Mexico.

b. yellow-throated vireo, a greenlet, *Vireo flavifrons,* in which the throat and breast are of a canary-yellow color.

1839 AUDUBON *Ornith. Biog.* V. 428 Yellow-Throated Vireo. *Vireo Flavifrons.* **1878** COUES *Birds Colo. Valley* 489 Most of the Greenlets, including . . . the Yellow-throated, and the Warbling Vireos, inhabit high open woods. **1945** *Mass. Audubon Soc. Bul.* Feb. 18 This may account for the Yellow-throated Vireo, the Worm-eating Warbler and the Sycamore Warbler which have been seen recently or in years past.

c. yellow-throated warbler, a wood warbler, *Dendroica dominica.*

1828 BONAPARTE *Synopsis* 80 The Yellow-throated Warbler . . . inhabits the northern parts of the United States. **1917** *Birds of Amer.* III. 139/1 The Yellow-throated and Sycamore Warblers are geographical variations of the same species of Warbler. **1942** WHITE *One Man's Meat* 287 The Sycamore Warbler, he says, is almost identical with the Yellow-throated Warbler.

As the last term in **Maryland, northern, Roscoe's yellow-throat.**

***yelp,** *v.* and *n.* **1.** *n.* The short, repetitious, staccato note of the turkey hen, or a call imitative of this. **2.** *v. tr.* and *intr.* To imitate the note of a turkey hen, to call *up* (a wild turkey) by this means.

(1) **1846** THORPE *Myst. Backwoods* 63, I knew the critter's [a wild turkey's] 'yelp' as well as I know Music's, my dear old dog. **1885** *Outing* VII. 65/1 The yelp, or call, was answered by a gobbler. — (2) **1838** GOSSE *Letters* 301 He [i.e., the turkey hunter] suffers five minutes to elapse in silence, then 'yelps' again. **1894** *Harper's Mag.* Nov. 885/2 The hunter hastily improvises a 'blind' of pine boughs, and 'yelps them up' if he can.

***yelper,** *n.* =**turkey yelper.** — **1838** GOSSE *Letters* 301 The probabilities of success are much heightened by the use of the contrivance called the 'yelper.' This is a pipe, made of reed,—or, better still, of the thigh-bone of a turkey. **1945** *Md. Conservationist* 13/2 Old Steen Friend went along . . . carrying a hollow bone . . . used to call turkeys. Friend called it his 'yelper.'

yen jɛn, *n.* [Prob. an alteration of the noun **yearn*, or **yearning.*] An intense desire. *Slang.*

1908 K. MCGAFFEY *Show-Girl* 117 One old frump that must have been tramming a mace in the Roman Hanging Gardens got a yen that was doing imitations. **1920** SANDBURG *Smoke & Steel* 206 Six bits got us snow and stopped the yen. **1948** *Capital-Democrat* (Tishomingo, Okla.) 24 June 4/5 Ever get a yen to 'take off' a day or two and see the country?

Also as a verb.

1921 MENCKEN *Amer. Lang.* 108 A great many of them have remained California localisms, among them such verbs as *to yen* (to desire strongly, as a Chinaman desires opium).

Yengee ˈjɛŋgi, *n.* [Often said to be the result of the Indians' attempt to pronounce "English," but Sonneck (see ***Yankee,** *n.* note) 86–9 shows the improbability of this theory.] A white person as distinguished from an Indian. Alleged to have been used orig. by Indians. *Obs.*

1818 HECKWELDER *Acct. Ind. Nations* 133 What a number of people are coming along! . . . Not one *long knife.* All *Yengees!* **1840** *N.Y. Mirror* 11 July 17/2 Depend upon it, were we sufficiently near, we should surprise the hated name of Yengee on the lips of these little copper-skinned imps. **1851** *Ore. Statesman* 23 May 1/7 A live and veritable specimen of the genus *yengese* (the latter phrase is aboriginal, I believe,) was to be seen, driving a wagon and an old gray mare on the highway. **1867** DIXON *New Amer.* I. 68 The Yengee has taught the Indian to drink whisky.

***yeoman,** *n. yeoman of the gun room,* formerly in the U.S. Navy, a petty officer having charge of the gun room on a warship. *Obs.* — **1794** *Ann. 3d Cong.* 1426 The following petty officers . . . shall be appointed by the captains of the ships . . . two gunner's mates, one yeoman of the gun room. **1796** *Ann. 4th Cong.* 2 Sess. 2787 Pay of the officers, seamen, and marines [per month] . . . 2 Yeomen of the Gun Rooms, [$]13.

yep jɛp, *adv.* Yes. *Colloq.* Cf. **nope, yup.**

1891 *Harper's Mag.* Nov. 970/1 He gently and peacefully murmured, 'Yep.' **1914** STEELE *Storm* 45 'Tobacco?' asked one of the whisperers. 'Yep,' another answered. **1949** *Newsweek* 14 Nov. 80/3 Do I apologize? Yep. Can I ever make it up to them? I'll try.

yerba buena. *W.* and *S.W.* [Sp., lit. "good herb," used of various plants.]

1. (*cap.*) A name formerly given to San Francisco. Now *hist.*

1836 COULTER *Adventures* (1847) I. 147 We sailed in between the two high bluffs into the great bay of San Francisco, and came to an anchor off the town of 'Yerba buena,' or, in plain English, 'Good Grass;' and indeed it deserves the name, for the undulating ground in the rear of it is covered with a luxuriant herbage that affords rich pasturage for the domesticated animals. **1847** *Calif. Star* (S.F.) 30 Jan. 2/3 The town takes its name from an herb to be found all around it which is said to make good tea; and possessing medicinal qualities; it is called good herb or Yerba Buena. **1875** *Scribner's Mo.* July 266/2 Its [San Francisco's] very name—'Yerba Buena'—was strange to American ears. **1949** *Highway Traveler* Feb. 21/1 An English lad named John Read ran a little ferry service across the Golden Gate, carrying water and lumber to the hamlet of Yerba Buena that was soon to be fantastic San Francisco.

b. (See quot.)

1872 MCCLELLAN *Golden State* 196 Directly in the line between San Francisco and Oakland, midway in the bay is *Yerba Buena*, or *Goat island.*

2. (See quot. 1915.)

1882 HARTE *Flip* 15 He seized a few of the young tender green leaves of the yerba buena vine . . . and ate them. **1915** ARMSTRONG & THORNBER *Western Wild Flowers* 436 Yerba Buena, Tea-vine. *Micromeria Chamissonis.* . . . It was used medicinally by California Indians, so it was called 'good herb' by the Mission Fathers, and is still used as a tea by Spanish-Californians. **1949** HOWELL *Marin Flora* 14 The spread of the shrubs is anticipated by dense growths of bracken, rush, blackberry, potentilla, yerba buena, and other herbaceous or suffrutescent perennials in the midst of grassland.

yerba del sapo. *S.W.* [Amer. Sp. in same sense.] A plant of the genus *Tournefortia. Obs.* — **1853** SITGREAVES *Exped. Zuni & Colo. Rivers* 34 We rapidly descended to the Rio Puerco, having passed over a barren waste upon which little was growing excepting grease-weed (*Obione canescens,*) *Franseria acanthocarpa*, or Yerba del sapo, . . . and a few cacti.

yerba del vaso. *S.W.* [Amer. Sp. *yerba del bazo,* in same sense.] =**brittlebush.** — **1912** LUMHOLTZ *New Trails* 10 The Mexicans call it *herba del vaso*, because the gum is supposed to cure pain in the *vaso* (the left side below the ribs). [**1942** SANTAMARÍA, yerba del bazo. . . . Úsase también este nombre en Arizona (Estados Unidos).]

yerba mansa. *W.* [f. Amer. Sp. *yerba del manso,* in same sense.] (See quot. 1891.)

1886 VAN DYKE *So. Calif.* 45 The dry sandy wastes are relieved by the . . . tall form of the *yerba mansa.* **1891** *Cent.* 7018/3 Yerba mansa, a Californian herb, *Anemopsis Californica*, of the *Piperaceae.* **1912** LUMHOLTZ *New Trails* 264 A plant (*anemopsis californica*) called by the Mexicans *herba del manso* was a singular growth in these pozos. **1949** *Nat. Hist.* Oct. 358/2 The most conspicuous plant in these moist meadows is the least important one, yerba mansa.

yerba santa. *W.* [Sp. in Amer. Sp. sense shown here.] Any one of several shrubs of the genus *Eriodictyon.* Cf. **bear-weed.**

1887 *Overland Mo.* Aug., The low growth . . . is made up of . . . cherry, manzanita, *herba santa*, of 'mountain balm,' from which a medicine is prepared for pulmonary affections, and a few others. **1910** J. HARTE *Vigilante Girl* 344 The keener odor of the yerba santa reached her nostrils. **1948** *So. Sierran* March 2/2 Others as the Yerba Santa evolve in one species a heavily-varnished leaf, in another a woolly-coated leathery leaf defies the heat.

***yes,** *adv.* **1. yes man,** one who curries favor by always agreeing with whatever an associate, esp. a superior, says. *Slang.* **2. yes sir-ee,** an emphatic form of yes. *Colloq.* Cf. **no sir-ee.**

(1) **1929** WITWER (*title*), Yes Man's Land. **1932** GRAYSON *Leaders* 230 The people of the country became convinced that he was nothing more than Jackson's 'yes man.' **1949** *Desplaines Valley News* (Summit, Ill.) 8 April 8/2, I . . . have never been known as a 'Yes Man' under any conditions. — (2) **1846** *Dollar Newspaper* (Phila.) 1 July 3/4 'Will you take this man to be your lawful husband?' said the Justice; to which she responded with breathless haste, '*Yes, sir-ee.*' **1947** *Trail Riders Bul.* Feb. 20/1 Sluefoot had quite a thinker on 'im, yes-siree.

yeso ˈjeso, *n. S.W.* [Sp. in same sense. An Amer. borrowing.] Gypsum.

1844 GREGG *Commerce of Prairies* I. 205 The interior of each apartment . . . is then white washed with calcined *yeso.* **1888** WALLACE *Land of Pueblos* 65 If the walls crack, they are daubed by Magdalena Rosalia with a fresh plaster of *yeso.* **1897** *Land of Sunshine* Dec. 17 Facing the dwellings stood the church, . . . with its inner walls whitened with *yeso.*

∗**yew,** *n.* As the last term in **Canadian, European, Florida, Pacific, stinking yew.**

yip jɪp, *n.* and *v.* [Echoic.] **1.** *n.* A short, high-pitched cry, also a cheep, murmur, the slightest sound. **2.** *v. intr.* To utter a yip. Also **yipping.** Both *colloq.*

(1) **1911** H. QUICK *Yellowstone N.* xii. 303 They chase 'em, with wild whoops an' yips over the undulatin reservation. **1928** *Hearst's International* Aug. 74/1 At the first yip out of Babe or Cheeky he would yank two triggers. — (2) **1907** KATE D. WIGGIN *New Chron. Rebecca* 199 He would walk right up close and cuff 'em if they dared to yip. **1927** *Sat. Ev. Post* 24 Dec. 84/2 'Hey!' Jim yipped, . . . 'Get away from there!'

yo-hah ˈjoˌhɑ, *adv.* [Imitative.] (See quots.) *Obs.* — **1751** J. BARTRAM *Observations* 22 They gave us the *Yohay*, a particular *Indian* expression of approbation. **1791** J. LONG *Voyages* 56 These gifts were received with a full yo-hah, or demonstration of joy.

Yokaia joˈkaɪə, *n. Calif.* [f. a native expression meaning "lower valley," or "down the valley."] (See quot. 1910.)

1881 MORGAN *Houses Amer. Aborigines* 108 The Yo-kai'-a inhabit a section of the northwest part of the state. **1896** *Amer. Anthrop.* Feb. 61, I find that the weaving is precisely similar to that of the Yokaia and other basketry from northern and middle California. **1910** HODGE *Amer. Indians* II. 999/1 Yokaia ('south valley'). An important division of the Pomo, formerly inhabiting the southern part of Ukiah valley, Mendocino co., Cal. The town and valley of Ukiah are named from them. Not to be confused with Yuki.

attrib. **1851** in SCHOOLCRAFT *Indian Tribes* (1853) III. 113 Near the houses stood the rancheria of the Yukai band. **1903** JAMES *Indian Basketry* 55 There are a few Indians left of the Yokaia tribe, from which we get the corrupted Ukiah.

∗**yoke,** *n.* As the last term in **canoe, goose, neck, sap, sap neck yoke.**

yokeage ˈjokɪdʒ, *n.* [Said by Hodge to be f. Pequot-Mohegan *yok'hig*, a shortened form of an expression meaning "(what is) made soft."] =**rokeage.** *Obs.*

1697 SEWALL *Letter-Book* I. 188, I pray your acceptance of a little Boston Yokeheag. **1701** ——— *Diary* II. 27 Eat Yokeheg in Milk. **1910** HODGE *Amer. Indians* II. 999/1 *Yokeag* . . . is still prepared by the Pequot-Mohegan of the Indian reservation on Thames r., Conn., and is sometimes sold by them to their white neighbors, who eat it with milk and sometimes with ice cream.

Yokut ˈjoˌkʌt, *n.* [See quot. 1873.] *pl.* Indians of a Mariposan family in California now numbering about 500.

1873 *Overland Mo.* Aug. 105/1 In the language of this nation, *yocut* is a collective word signifying 'people' in the aggregate, while *myu* or *nono* denotes 'man.' **1903** JAMES *Indian Basketry* 57 A few Yokets are still to be found on the San Joaquin and Kings Rivers, the Kaweah and a portion of Tule River. **1921** HALL *Yosemite Nat. Park* 59 The Yokuts, to the south of Yosemite, did not erect earth lodges.

yonkapin, see **wankapin.**

Yorick breed. (See quot.) *Obs.* — **1852** G. W. L. BICKLEY *Hist. Tazewell Co., Va.* 104 The *Yorick* breed, are generally black, rather small, well muscled, fiery, and make excellent saddle-horses. They are remarkable for having sprung from Yorick, the bitter foe of the Indians.

∗ **York,** *n.*

1. Short for New York, referring either to the city or to the state. *Colloq.* Cf. **York state.**

1838 MATHEWS *Motley Book* 42 (We.), I'll go to York, in a new dress. **1855** BARNUM *Life* 22 He had been to 'York.' **1901** FLYNT *World of Graft* 91 York has always been my hang-out.

attrib. **1705** *Boston News-Letter* 12 March 2/2 A French Privateer . . . supposed the York man to be a Merchant man. **1868** *N. Eng. Base Ballist* 6 Aug. 1/2 When it was first started it was the intention of the members to play the Massachusetts Game, but they concluded to give the York game a trial. **1894** FORD *P. Stirling* 73 His mother . . . had always known her Peter was a hero, and needed no 'York papers' to teach her the fact.

b. Short for New York currency *q.v. Obs.* Cf. **York shilling,** and **2. b.** below.

1845 COOPER *Chainbearer* xxviii, The lot's worth forty pounds York.

2. In special combs., often sufficiently explained in the quots., and usu. obs.

In these expressions *York* refers to various places. In (2) and (3) the allusion may well be to Yorkshire, Eng. Cf. *EDD s.v. York.*

(1) **York cheat;** (2) **fixings;** (3) **reel;** (4) **River,** an oyster from the York River in Virginia; (5) **shilling,** =**New York shilling,** also attrib.; (6) **sixpence,** a sixpence in New York currency *q.v.;* (7) **State,** see as a main entry; (8) **wagon,** a light vehicle of a kind built at York, Pa.

(1) **1834** *Amer. R.R. Jrnl.* III. 184/3 This corn was named York Cheat, because it was said to have been ground with wheat . . . when it could not be detected by the color of the flour. — (2) **1855** BESTE *Wabash* II. 209, I was much amused by the lists of spiceries and grocery wares hung outside the doors of many little shops here and at the several villages we passed, and that were all headed 'York fixings and Yankee notions.' — (3) **1873** WRIGHT *Sk.* 230 Where four [prisoners of war during the Revolution] were ironed to one bar, they could dance the cross-handed, or what we called the York reel. — (4) **1839** *S. Lit. Messenger* V. 837/1 A Steak—a dozen of 'York River,' done with a pinch of salt, but no butter, in their own liquor, over a slow fire—and the repast crowned with a bunch of Grapes. **1844** *Knickerb.* XXIII. 500 Here we are with . . . our York-rivers.

(5) **1824** *Mass. Spy* 8 Sep. (Th.), This remark quickly brought a York shilling out of my pocket for toll. **1898** HARPER *S. B. Anthony* I. 123 At the evening session a 'York shilling' admittance fee was charged. **1950** *Chi. Tribune* 3 May 22/3 In the early 19th century a coin passing current at $12\frac{1}{2}$ cents was known in . . . New York as a

One form of York wagon

shilling or York shilling. — (6) **1837** *New-Yorker* 7 Jan. 241/3 Around her neck was a bracelet . . . studded with bright pieces of metal resembling York six-pences. — (8) **1824** *Mass. Yeoman* 11 Feb. (Th.), In an instant he capsized a York-waggon, threw out the riders, and threw down the horse. **1856** *Porter's Spirit of Times* 4 Oct. 67/1 They didn't have no York waggins and the likes at that time [1835].

b. Designating units or systems of exchange acceptable in, or belonging to, New York. *Obs.*

1688 *N.J. Archives* 1 Ser. II. 31, I have secured yo[u]r money & have got it payed in this day being 26 lib . . . 2d York money. **1758** *Lett. to Washington* II. 279 The York Bill you Inclosed will over pay the postage of your Letter. **1765** ROGERS *Journals* 161 My own sley was taken with 1196 l. York currency in cash. **1846** DURIVAGE *Stray Subjects* 150 A very soft-spoken and very verdant gentleman . . . parts with an excellent pair of doe-skins, which he has worn but once, for an article dear at four shillings—York currency.

∗ **Yorker,** *n.* **1.** A person born in, living in, or coming from New York City or New York State, a New Yorker. **2.** (See quot. and cf. **York shilling.**)

(1) **1755** *N.H. Prov. P.* VI. (1872) 440 In the Engagement with Genl Diecsau about eighty of our men with about 40 Yorkers. **1862** *Harper's Mag.* July 282/2, I, as a Yorker, of course claimed the premium for my State. **1942** CANNON *Mountain* 204 Then the Yorkers, their Governor, tried to do the same thing—only he was a little mite late. — (2) **1909** *D.N.* III. 418 Yorker . . . twelve and a half cents. [Aroostook, Me.]

Yorkino jɔrˈkino, *n.* (See quot.) *Obs.* — **1836** EDWARD *Hist. Texas* 125 The Creole party is divided into several factions. First, the Aristocratic. . . . They are also called *Yorkinos* and *Anglicans* because under English influence, and leaning towards European connections.

Yorkite ˈjɔrkaɪt, *n.* =**Yorker 1.** *Obs.* — **1773** in *N. Eng. Hist. & Gen. Reg.* XXIV. (1880) 365 For his valor in cutting the head of Esquire Munroe the Yorkite.

York State. The state of New York. Also attrib.

1823 *Nat. D. Intelligencer* 1 May 1/4. **1828** J. HALL *Lett. from West* 170 On arriving at an inn . . . in New England I answered the tedious inquiries whether I was a *southerner*, or a *York-state man.* **1889** *Tombstone* (Ariz.) *Prospector* 22 Nov. 4/1 New Orleans Molasses and York State cider at Walcott's. **1940** THOMPSON *Body, Boots* 18 She is depicting York State manners as truly as if her father had never migrated from us.

Hence **York Stater.**

1945 *Amer. Mercury* June 725/2 If you're a York Stater, as you claim, I wonder you've never heard of Paul Bunyan.

Yosemite joˈsɛmətɪ, *n.* [See note.]

"Powers states that the name Yosemite is a distorted form of the Miwok *uzumaiti*, 'grizzly bear,' a term never used by the Indians to designate the valley itself or any part of it" (Hodge *s.v. Awani*).

"To the Miwok Indians, yosemite is a word which when applied to animals means 'grizzly,' and when applied to humans, means 'killer' or 'murderer' " (1949 *L.A. Times* 10 April II. 5/2).
See also Stewart, *Names on the Land*, pp. 280 ff.

1. *pl.* The Awani, a division of the Miwok Indians living in Yosemite Valley, Calif. Also (*sing.*) attrib.

1851 *Alta California* (S.F.) 12 June, One of them proved to be the son of the old Yosemite chief. **1873** *Overland Mo.* April 325/1 The Yosemite Indians despised the Wallies because they could not make bows (having no suitable timber), and had no pluck. **1903** JAMES *Indian Basketry* 257 Most of them are baskets collected in the Sierra Nevada region, and were woven by Yo-ham-i-ties, Monos, Yokuts and Paiutis. **1921** HALL *Yosemite Nat. Park* 14 The remainder of the Yosemites with their old chief Tenaya made their escape. **1947** PEATTIE *Sierra Nevada* 227 Only the Indians, the Yosemites, could have stumbled upon the scene of devastation when it still was fresh.

2. A U-shaped valley with steep cliffs and flat floor, formed by glacial action, and typified by the Yosemite Valley.

1868 MUIR *Thousand-Mile Walk* (1916) 196 The hollow canons, cut in soft lavas, are not so deep as to require a single earthquake at the hands of science, much less a baker's dozen of those convenient tools demanded for the making of mountain Yosemites. **1902** *Out West* Nov. 576 He firmly believes that all the Sierra Yosemites were formed by glacier action. **1930** F. E. MATTHES *Geological History of the Yosemite Valley* 89/1 Some of the greatest yosemites were the pathways of only moderately large glaciers.

3. *attrib.* Designating or pertaining to the well-known valley of this name in California.

1852 *Alta California* (S.F.) 3 Oct. (Supp.)1/2 From the head of the Yo-semite valley, . . . the trail leads about east. **1881** *Ore. State Jrnl.* 1 Jan. 5/5 Our enterprising druggist . . . has secured the agency for Slaven's Famous Yosemite Cologne. **1915** ARMSTRONG & THORNBER *Western Wild Flowers* 192 Yosemite Stonecrop. *Sedum Yosemitense.* Yellow. Summer. . . . On moss-covered rocks, moistened by the glistening spray blowing from the Yosemite waterfalls, we find these beautiful plants. **1947** PEATTIE *Sierra Nevada* 193 The South Fork Canyon, popularly known as 'Kings River Canyon,' also is of the Yosemite type.

Yosemitic ˌjosəˈmɪtɪk, *a.* [f. prec.] Of or pertaining to a Yosemite (sense **2.**). — **1894** MUIR *Mountains of Calif.* 276, [I have found] countless waterfalls . . . in the Sierra, . . . among the icy peaks, or warm foot-hills, or in the profound yosemitic cañons of the middle region. **1902** *Out West* Nov. 567 Its huge granite yosemitic walls and domes rise sheer on either side from 2,000 feet to a mile in height.

***you-all,** *pron.* Also **you-alls.** You. Allegedly used colloquially in the South as a singular. See note and cf. **you-uns.**

"It is commonly believed in the North that Southerners use *you-all* in the singular, but this is true, if it is ever true at all, of only the most ignorant of them. The word may be addressed to individuals, but only when they are thought of as representative of a group. . . . The literature of the subject is extensive and full of bitterness" (1936 Mencken *Amer. Language* (ed. 4) 449 note). Cf. quot. 1947 below and see *Amer. Sp.* Oct., 1938, 163–8.

1824 SINGLETON *Letters* 82 They [Virginians] say . . . madam and mistress, instead of our abbreviations. Children learn from the slaves some odd phrases; as, every which way; will you *all* do this? for, will *one* of you do this? **1901** WHITE *Westerners* 8 Reckon you-all fills the bill. **1947** *Amer. Mercury* Jan. 69/1 As a matter of fact, the uneducated Southerner's feeling for the plurality of the expression is so strong that he sometimes says *you-alls.*

b. Used as an indefinite pronoun.

1897 LEWIS *Wolfville* 54 When you-all stampedes a bunch of ponies that a-way they don't hold together like cattle. *Ib.* 179 You-alls can't run no brand on melodies.

***young,** *a.* (Chiefly *cap.*) In combs.: (1) **Young America,** see as a main entry; (2) **American,** (*a*) *n.* a representative or symbol of the idealism characteristic of the Young America (*q.v.*) movement, (*b*) *a.* progressive, enterprising; (3) **Democracy,** the radical faction of the Democratic party in the state of New York in the period following the nomination of Polk, *obs.*, cf. **Barnburner;** (4) **Hickory,** (*a*) (see quot. 1844), (*b*) (see quot. 1914); (5) **Napoleon,** Gen. George B. McClellan (1826–85), a nickname; (6) **Scratcher,** in the Republican party in New York State, a member of a faction expressing its disapproval of party leadership by scratching certain candidates' names from the ticket, *rare.*

(2) (*a*) **1844** R. W. EMERSON (*title*), The Young American. **1870** ——— *Soc. & Solitude* 135 They are so many Young Americans announcing a better era,—more bread. (*b*) **1856** *Merry's Museum* XXXI. 79 If ever a city had any reason to be called 'Young American' in its character, that city is St. Paul. — **(3) 1851** J. F. W. JOHNSTON *Notes N. Amer.* I. 218 Radical Democrats are stigmatised as *Barnburners*, but call themselves the 'Young Democracy,' or the '*Progressive Young Democracy.*' — **(4)** (*a*) **1844** *Cong. Globe* App. 3 June 598/2 In consequence of the intimate personal relations between them [*sc.* Jackson and Polk], as well as the perfect concurrence in their political opinions, and principles, and action, he [*sc.* Polk] has been called the 'Young Hickory.' **1864** NICHOLS *Amer. Life* I. 255 The President—the veritable Young Hickory, sixty years old, I think, . . . received me with dignified politeness. **1949** *Tenn. Hist. Quart.* March 95, I have tried to see 'Young Hickory's' world through his own eyes. (*b*) **1885** *Mag. Amer. Hist.* XIII. 496/2. **1914** *Cyclo. Amer. Govt.* III. 704 Young Hickory. A sobriquet given Martin Van Buren . . . about 1836 when as Democratic presidential candidate he became the political heir to 'Old Hickory,' Andrew Jackson.

(5) 1862 JOHN H. MORGAN *Proclamation* 22 Aug., The so-called 'Young Napoleon' McClellan has retreated from the Peninsula. **1871** COOKE *R. E. Lee* 51 He accepted command, and fought a successful campaign in Western Virginia. From that moment his name became famous; he was said to have achieved 'two victories in one day,' and he received from the newspapers the flattering name of 'the Young Napoleon.' — **(6) 1879** *Nation* 9 Oct. 233/3 These young Scratchers will not be stopped from scratching by hearing that the venerable editor of the *Tribune* . . . thinks it foolishness.

b. Used locally in the names of various animals and plants (see quots.).

1814 MITCHILL *Fishes N.Y.* 405 Grunts. *Labrus grunniens.* . . . This fish is called, by the fishermen, *young sheep's head*, and young drum, from its resemblance to those creatures. **1825** *Amer. Jrnl. Science* XI. 278 *Menopoma Alleghaniensis.* . . . Hell-bender. . . . Young Alligator. **1892** *Amer. Folk-Lore* V. 100 *Gaultheria procumbens*, young plantlets; . . . young chinks; . . . young ivories.

Young America. An American youth, or American youth collectively. Orig. a political name or slogan used with reference to a wave of expansionist sentiment beginning in the 1840's and culminating in a movement within the Democratic party characterized by desire to spread American ideals and institutions and to extend American influence.

1844 *St. Louis Reveille* 30 Nov. 2/2 No mammoth bank . . . can form any part of the creed of the *Young America!* **1852** in *Amer. Hist. Rev.* XXXII. 45 The grand ideas which are the most potent in the election are . . . the ideas for which the term *Young America* is the symbol. **1873** *Newton Kansan* 10 July 3/4 Young America's [*sic*], like small armies in battle, assisted in the grand jubilee. **1924** *Outlook* 10 Sep. 45/1 Young America could with profit leave such affairs well alone and confine its efforts to contests in which the development of character, courage, and skill is the reward won by those who do not attain the coveted first prize. **1948** *Chesterton* (Ind.) *Tribune* 28 Oct. 15/3 We think as long as young America is reading one of the great Hoosier authors, that all will remain well with Indiana and the rest of the Union.

Also in derivative and combinative expressions.

1852 *Harper's Mag.* Dec. 128/1 There is . . . the absurd yet dangerous spirit of 'Young-America-ism.' **1855** M. THOMPSON *Doesticks* 325 The waxen boy in a scratch wig and full suit of Young America clothes. **1886** *Outing* April 94/2 One of the most flourishing base-ball clubs in the country is the Young America Base-Ball Club of Philadelphia.

younker ˈjʌnkɚ, *n.* [Du. *jonker, jonkheer*, young lord, master. An Amer. borrowing.] A man of property and position in society, a patroon. Also **Yonkers** as a place-name.

1666 *N.Y. Council Minutes* I. 234 Commonly called ye Younckers Land . . . [and] brought severall Indians before ye Governor to acknowledg the purchase of ye said Lands by Vander Dunck commonly called ye Younker. **1734** in E. H. HALL *Philipse Manor Hall* 107 From the country seat of Fred. Philipse Esq. in Westchester County, commonly called the Yonkers, we hear that [etc.]. **1754** *Doc. Col. Hist. N.Y.* VI. 839 Even if the real line of Jersey is to run from the Forks of Delaware . . . to the Station on Hudson's River opposite to the lower Yonkers. **1870** *Putnam's Mag.* Sep. 243/1 Before the Revolution, Mr. Phillipse . . . was always spoken of by his tenantry as 'the Yonker'—*the* gentleman—*par excellence.*

youth-and-old-age. (See quot. 1891.) — **1891** *Cent.* 7035/3 They have been called *youth-and-old-age*, from the lasting and somewhat rigid rays and the continued production of new disk-flowers; but are more usually known by the generic name *zinnia*, especially in the common double form. **1949** *Courier-Journal* (Louisville, Ky.) 3

Sep. 6/4 Normally fresh and faded flowers are found on the same plant, hence its common name, 'Youth and Old Age.'

you-uns ˈjuənz, *pron. S.* You, esp. you, *pl. Colloq.* Cf. ∗**you-all.**

This expression may not have originated in this country. Cf. *you yins* (*EDD s.v. One* 8) and *you-ones* in *EDD.*

1810 M. DWIGHT *Journey to Ohio* 37 Youns is a word I have heard used several times, but what it means I don't know. **1885** CRADDOCK *Prophet* 7, I hev no call ter spen' words 'bout sech ez that, with a free-spoken man like you-uns. **1933** T. WILLIAMSON *Woods Colt* 171 *You-uns* open your trap an' say somethin'. **1944** PENNELL *Rome Hanks* 36 Whut ah you'uns comin' down heah to take ouah niggahs away from us foh?

Yo-Yo ˈjoˌjo, *n.* [f. "*you-you,*" often used by children at play.] The trade-mark name of a form of top having a cord about its spindle by means of which it is automatically brought back to the operator's hand when thrown, popular *c*1800 as a ∗*bandalore.* Also **yo-yo.**

[**1932** Application for registration of trade-mark 300,504, The trade-mark has been continuously used and applied to said goods in applicant's business since January 1, 1928.] **1932** *K.C. Star* 27 Jan. 22 Just when we were trying to forget our cigarette-rolling machine, the yo-yo attempts a comeback. **1948** *Chi. D. News* 20 Feb. 18/1 A cafe socialite's gift to the boy friend is a solid gold yo-yo.

transf. **1949** *Sat. Ev. Post* 9 April 82/4 Luck was fiddling with the Jordans like a Yo-yo, snapping them back to a humdrum and skimpy life every time they tried for something brighter.

∗**yucca,** *n.*

1. In combs., as **yucca borer, cactus, -leaved rattlesnake master, moth,** (see quots.).

1891 *Cent.* 7026/2 *Yucca-borer.* 1. A large North American castnioid moth, *Meganthymus yuccæ,* whose larva bores into the roots of plants of the genus *Yucca.* 2. A Californian weevil, *Yuccaborus frontalis.* — **1897** SUDWORTH *Arborescent Flora* 106 *Yucca arborescens.* . . . Joshua Yucca. . . . [Also called] *Yucca cactus* (Cal.). — **1870** *Amer. Naturalist* IV. 581 Other remarkable forms are . . . the yucca-leaved rattlesnake master, or button snakeroot (*Ceryngium yuccaefolium*). — **1873** *Amer. Naturalist* VII. 475 The yucca is incapable of self-fertilization, and . . . the yucca moth [*Pronuba yuccasella*] . . . effects it. **1946** *So. Sierran* July 2/1 The larva of the yucca moth bores its way out thru the walls of the dry pod.

2. yucca palm (tree), = ∗**Joshua.**

1851 M. REID *Scalp Hunters* xviii, She was standing near one of the yuca palm trees that grew up from the azotea. **1886** *Graphic News* (Chi.) 10 April 86/1 Then there is the product of the yucca palm of Antelope Valley, from which the paper is made on which the London *Times* is printed. **1940** JAEGER *Calif. Deserts* 190 Today it is often erroneously brigaded with the palms under the name of 'yucca palm.'

Yuchi, see **Uchee.**

yucker ˈjʌkɚ, *n.* [Imitative of the bird's note. Cf. *EDD yuckel* for the green woodpecker, nearest European relative of the American bird.] =**flicker.** Also **yawker bird.**

1808 WILSON *Ornithology* I. 53 It [the golden-winged woodpecker] . . . has numerous provincial appellations . . . such as . . . 'Yucker,' 'Piut,' 'Flicker.' **1844** *Nat. Hist. N.Y., Zoology* II. 192 The Clape, or Golden-Winged Woodpecker, *Picus Auratus,* . . . is called High-hole, Yucker, Flicker [etc.]. **1917** *Birds of Amer.* II. 163 Flicker. . . . [Also called] Yawker Bird; Walk-up.

Yukon stove. (See quot. 1898.) — **1898** W. B. HASKELL *2 Yrs. in Klondike* 75 The 'Yukon stove' . . . is a small sheet iron box with an oven at the back and a telescope pipe. **1908** CANTON *Frontier Trails* 156 Buy a Yukon stove and take it with you.

Yuma ˈjumə, *n.* [Thought to be f. a title, *Yah-may-o,* "Son of the Captain," misunderstood and applied by early Spanish missionaries to the tribe.] *pl.* and *collect.* (See quot. 1910.)

1831 PATTIE *Personal Narr.* 91 The point of junction is inhabited by a tribe of Indians called Umene. *Ib.* 137 Here we found the tribe of Umeas. **1849** HAYES *Pioneer Notes* (1929) 45 The Yumas attack only in the night, to steal the mules. **1864** *Harper's Mag.* Oct. 569/2 Heretofore the Yumas have supported themselves without much difficulty. **1910** HODGE *Amer. Indians* II. 1010/1 Yuma. . . . One of the chief divisions, or tribes, of the Yuman family . . . formerly residing on both sides of the Rio Colorado next above the Cocopa. **1949** *Chi. D. News* 2 Sep. 1/4 He called the find one of the most important ever made in connection with the culture of the Yuma, the nomadic group who disappeared centuries ago as a cultural unit.

Also **Yumas Indians.**

1848 in *Calif. Hist. Quart.* XXI. 299 In camp gathering Musquite Beans and buying pumpkins and mellons of the Humas Indians. **1850** *Calif. Courier* (S.F.) 3 July 2/3 Unless the Yumas Indians are promptly punished for these outrages, every small party of Americans will be robbed or murdered, that pass the Colorado.

b. *attrib.* Of or pertaining to some of the early prehistoric inhabitants of the New World.

1947 MARTIN *Indians* 84 A very small percentage of the points found were typical oblique Yuma points—long and narrow, with sides parallel most of the way. . . . Yuma points had a wider distribution than Folsom points and probably survived them. **1949** *Time* 12 Sep. 69/1 Not much is known about Yuma Man, for no Yuma skeleton has yet been found. He may or may not have been an ancestor of modern Indians. He made beautiful and characteristic stone weapons, and seems to have lived not long after the glacial period.

Yuman ˈjumən, *a.* [See **Yuma.**] Of or pertaining to the Yuma Indians.

1903 JAMES *Indian Basketry* 161 One of the most interesting specimens . . . is the carrying frame and net of the Mohave Indians, of the Yuman stock, dwelling about the mouth of the Colorado River. **1933** SPIER *Yuman Tribes* 151 The Maricopa have transposed the normal Yuman word for south to west. **1950** *Nat. Hist.* Feb. 76/3 They speak essentially the same language—a dialect of the Yuman tongue.

yup jʌp, *adv.* Variant of yep *q.v. Colloq.* — **1906** *Cent. Mag.* Jan. 410/2 'Will you go—if I swear?' 'Yup,' said Pinchas, airing his American. **1923** E. F. WYATT *Invis. Gods* II. iv. 78 'Paul as mean as ever?' 'Yup,' replied Hancock . . . 'and a little meaner.'

Yurok ˈjurɑk, *n.* [See quot. 1851.] Indians, or a tribe of Indians, poss. an isolated branch of the Algonquians, living on the lower Klamath River and the adjacent coast of northwestern California.

1851 in SCHOOLCRAFT *Indian Tribes* (1853) III. 151 They do not seem to have any generic appelation for themselves but apply the term 'Kahruk,' up and 'Youruk,' down, to all who live above or below themselves. **1910** HODGE *Amer. Indians* II. 1013/1 The Yurok are fairly tall for Pacific Coast Indians (168 cm.) and considerably above the average Californian in stature. **1948** *Amer. Folk-Lore* Oct.–Dec. 350 These events took place among the neighboring Yurok.

Z

***Z,** *n.* Used to indicate a person: See ***X.**

zaguan sɑˈgwɑn, *n. S.W.* [Sp. in same sense.] An entrance or vestibule. Also attrib.

1851 *Harper's Mag.* III. 465/2 Don Pedro was heard within, moving toward the 'Saguan.' **1863** *Rio Abajo Press* 28 April 1/2 She had just seen Juanito's ghost in the saguan door. **1880** CABLE *Grandissimes* 131 It was a long, narrowing perspective of arcades, lattices, balconies, *zaguans*, dormer windows, and blue sky.

Zambo ˈzæmbo, *n. S.W.* [Sp. in Amer. Sp. sense shown here. An Amer. borrowing.] A person of mixed Negro and Indian blood. *Obs.* — **1836** EDWARD *Hist. Texas* 120 Their offspring [those of Indians and Negroes], called Washinangoes or *Zambos*, are very hard and clever. **1850** COLTON *Deck & Port* 279 Zambos are generally employed as household servants.

zanja ˈsɑnhə, *n. S.W.* [Sp., ditch. In Amer. Sp. use as shown here.] An arroyo, an irrigation ditch. Cf. **acequia.**

[**1848** *Archives Los Angeles Co., Calif.* II. 692 Y estos señores nos manifestaron la sanja y toma de agua que forma la cuestión.] **1850** HAYES *Pioneer Notes* (1929) 70, I rode on and encamped for the night upon the thin *zanja* that flows through the place, under some large evergreen oaks. **1888** LINDLEY *Calif. of South* 89 The tourist who has leisure will be well repaid by visiting one of the open zanjas in the suburbs, . . . and watch the señoras doing their weekly washing. **1950** *L.A. Times* Midwinter No. 3 Jan. 21/1 A gurgling zanja—a water-ditch—trickled through the city.

b. zanja madre, (see quot.). Cf. **acequia madre.**

1877 *So. Calif. Hist. Soc.* XVI. 96 The zanja madre or main ditch some 12 or fifteen miles in length, was plainly visible. **1950** *Amer. Forests* Feb. 22/3 They were also required to construct communal public works, the most important of which were the Mother Ditch, or 'Zanja Madre,' and a reservoir.

zanjero sɑnˈhero, *n. S.W.* [Amer. Sp. (<Sp. *zanja*, ditch), one who digs irrigation ditches.] (See quots.)

1877 BARTLETT 771 *Zanjero*, . . . one whose duty it is to take charge of ditches, when used for purposes of irrigation. **1888** LINDLEY *Calif. of South* 87 The irrigating ditches are called *zanjas*, and the superintendent of them is the *zanjero*. **1909** *Sunset* Feb. 100/1 One day his *zanjero* brought the news that the flow in the ditch had dropped over three inches within a few hours. **1949** *L.A. Times* 1 June 24/4 He was also zanjero for the Lugonia Water Co. for 21 years but gave up that work some time ago.

zapato səˈpɑto, *n. S.W.* [Sp. in same sense.] A shoe or boot.

1849 T. T. JOHNSON *Sights Gold Region* 70 He was dressed with loose gay linen pants, yellow leather, or buckskin zapatos, or shoes. **1887** *Scribner's Mag.* II. 510/1 The true cow-boy . . . will hop and roll about until he has worn out his *zapatos*. **1907** WHITE *Arizona Nights* 168 He had on . . . the rawhide home-made zapatos the Mexicans wore then instead of boots.

***zebra,** *n.*

1. (See quot.) *Slang. Obs.* Cf. **zebra suit.**

1882 SALA *Amer. Revisited* I. 255 For awhile I was puzzled; but he went on to explain that a 'Zebra' was a humorous nickname for a convict. [Richmond, Va.]

2. In combs.: (1) **zebra caterpillar,** the striped larva of an American moth, *Ceramica picta;* (2) **suit,** a striped suit worn by a convict, *obs.;* (3) **swallowtail,** a large swallow-tailed butterfly, *Iphiclides marcellus*, found in the eastern states.

(1) 1891 *Cent.* 7030/3 *Zebra-caterpillar*. . . . It feeds on clover, peas, beans, cabbages [etc.]. **1925** HERRICK *Man. Injurious Insects* 253 The Zebra Caterpillar . . . occurs occasionally in sufficient numbers to cause injury to garden crops. — **(2) 1885** *Rep. Indian Affairs* 105 There are over twenty prisoners who are required to work and who wear the zebra suit. — **(3) 1891** *Cent.* 7031/1. **1904** KELLOGG *Amer. Insects* 448 One of the best-known butterflies of the east is the zebra swallowtail. [**1950** *Ark. Gazette* (Little Rock) 10 Sep. 3B/6 Zebra-striped Swallow-tails search out the wild ageratums.]

Zenaida dove. (See quots.)

1828 BONAPARTE *Ornithology* III. 23 [The] Zenaida Dove, *Columba Zenaida*, . . . inhabits the Florida keys. **1839** AUDUBON *Ornith. Biog.* V. 558 Zenaida Dove, *Columba Zenaida*, . . . is raised with ease in aviaries. **1895** *Dept. Agric. Yrbk. 1894* 211 Among the birds [in southern Fla.] may be mentioned the white-crowned pigeon, Zenaida dove, quail doves [etc.].

***zephyr,** *n.* A Kansas zephyr or Washoe zephyr *qq.v.* Also **Zephyr State,** (see quot. 1888), *obs.*

1877 W. WRIGHT *Big Bonanza* 253 The 'zephyr' is one of the peculiar institutions of Washoe. **1888** *Texas Siftings* (N.Y.) 29 Dec. 11/2 When North Dakota is admitted her popular name will be 'the Zephyr State.' **1942** LILLARD *Desert Challenge* 115 A warm, fructifying sun shone down, and though 'zephyrs' blew there were no tornadoes.

***zigzag,** *n.* and *a.*

1. a. Short for **zigzag fence.** *Colloq. Obs.* **b.** (See quot.)

(a) 1832 TROLLOPE *Domestic Manners* I. 144 And what does a broken zig-zag signify? **1867** *Atlantic Mo.* Jan. 103/1 Git together enough to make about ten rods o' zigzag, two rails high. — **(b) 1876** KNIGHT 2829/1 *Zigzag*, a winding chute on the face of a dam to enable fish to ascend.

2. zigzag fence, =worm fence, in full **zigzag rail fence.**

1835 INGRAHAM *South-West* II. 107 The natural loveliness of this state is disfigured by zigzag, or Virginia fences. **1898** CANFIELD *Maid of Frontier* 102 The zigzag rail fences looked as straight as a rule. **1908** PHILLIPS *Old Wives* 1 Quail were gleaning in the stubble, with a pause now and then to whistle from the gray zigzag fence.

zinfandel ˈzɪnfən͵dɛl, *n.* [Origin unknown. Poss. f. some European place-name.] A California wine made from a Hungarian grape imported into that state by Col. Agostan Harazthy. — **1908** in *Westerners' Brand Book* (1948) 88 Zinfandel, Private Stock .50. **1949** HERTRICH *Huntington Bot. Gardens* 55 These included port, sherry, tokay, sauterne and the noted California wine, zinfandel, as well as a few others.

zinkite ˈzɪŋkaɪt, *n.* (See quot. 1891.) — **1854** DANA *Mineralogy* (ed. 4) II. 100 Zincite Group. **1891** *Cent.* 7035/2 *Zinkite*, . . . a native oxid of zinc, found at Franklin Furnace and Stirling Hill, . . . in Sussex county, New Jersey.

zip zɪp, *v.*[1] [f. the noun.] *intr.* To go rapidly or with a zip. Also **zipping,** *n. Colloq.*

1852 *Knickerb.* XL. 182 How we did '*z-i-p!*' Seven miles, at one time, in less than seven minutes. **1881** BATTEN *Reminisc. U.S. Navy* 72, I heard the zipping of bullets in the air close to my head. **1947** *Dly. Oklahoman* (Okla. City) 5 Nov. 1/4 The lowest early morning temperature for the Oklahoma City area this autumn was predicted Tuesday night in the wake of a cool front that earlier zipped through the state.

zip zɪp, *v.*[2] *tr.* To finish dressing (a person) by the proper manipulation of a zipper *q.v. Colloq.* — **1936** *Sears Cat.* (ed. 173) 163/4 Easy to 'Zip' baby in and out! **1948** *Chi. Tribune* 28 March (Comics) 4 Stand still, now, while I zip you up!

Zip Coon. Also **Old Zip Coon.**

1. A jocular term for a coon. Also transf.

1834 *Zip Coon* (Pub. Atwill's Music Saloon, N.Y.), An de bery nex President, will be Zip Coon. **1834** in TOWNSEND *Narrative* (Thwaites) 86 This evening, our pet antelope, poor little 'Zip Koon,' met with a serious accident. **c1845** *Big Bear Ark.* 98 In sittin' down agin I lik'd to have sot on Barbry's tom cat, which if I had, I shoulder bin like Kurnel Zip Coon's wife, who jump'd into a holler log to mash two young panters to deth, and they scratched her so bad she couldn't set down for two munse! **1892** HARRIS *Plantation* 84 If you go into the woods an' fetch a whoop or two before you strike a light, they won't notice no 'possum; but you better believe they'll make old Zip Coon lift hisself off'n the ground.

2. The name of a minstrel song and dance. Now *hist.*

1834 *Sun* (N.Y.) 20 March 2/2 [They] were . . . accompanied . . . by the 'man wot sings Zip Coon.' **1856** *Spirit of Times* 13 Dec. 238/2 The following was the programme of dancing:—Part the First—French Four, Money Musk, Zip Coon, Scotch Reel. **1880** NYE *B. Nye & Boomerang* 124 Bye and bye the band comes down the street playing 'Old Zip Coon,' with variations. **1945** *Christian Sci. Mon.* 25 April 8/1 Nothing could be more racy of the American scene than 'Turkey in the Straw,' whose tune is borrowed from the early minstrel song of 'Zip Coon.'

zipper ˈzɪpɚ, *n.* [f. *Zipper*, a trade-mark name for the article.] A form of slide fastener used in the place of buttons or lacings. Also attrib. and transf.

1925 *Scribner's Mag.* Oct. 22/2 (*advt.*), No fastening is so quick, secure, or popular as the 'zipper.' **1944** LANKS *Alaska* 40 The grown daughter, who had disappeared inside the house, now emerged in a zipper jacket. **1949** *Reader's Digest* Aug. 34/1 In 1921 B. F. Goodrich Company thought that overshoes equipped with slide fasteners would create a sensation and in 1923 hit upon the word 'zipper' as the trademark for the new galoshes.

Zoarites ˈzoraɪts, *n. pl.* =**Separatists 2.** Also **Zoar Society.** Now *hist.* — **1901** *World's Work* Oct. 1256/2 The Zoar Society came from Germany at the beginning of the last century and settled near Pittsburg, later moving to Ohio. **1937** NOYES *John Humphrey Noyes* 159 The Ephratists were established in 1732, the Rappites in 1805, the Zoarites in 1819.

zombi ˈzɑmbɪ, *n.* Also **zombie.** [Of African origin. Cf. Kimbundu, Kongo, *zambi*, god, and Kongo *zumbi*, a good-luck fetish.] In the voodoo cult, the snake deity (see quot. 1946 below), or a supernatural force which on occasion reanimates corpses (see also quot. 1871).

1871 DE VERE 138 *Zombi*, a phantom or a ghost, not unfrequently heard in the Southern States in nurseries and among the servants. **1880** CABLE *Grandissimes* 234 Bras-Coupé hears the voice of zombis. **1943** OTTLEY *New World* 46 Besides adding the zombies, jumbies, and obeah men to the gallery of voodoo characters, a number of tropical items found their way to the tables of American Negroes. **1946** TALLANT *Voodooism in N.O.* 63 She had a snake she called 'Zombi.' It was her god, and could do things that brought sickness or health, good luck or bad luck, life or death.

transf. **1947** *Chi. D. News* 5 April 4/7 You will be mentally obsolete, a moral zombie, and a mere nuisance to your informed friends. **1950** *Time* 13 March 19/3 He still thought that the Byrd committee was 'a sort of political zombie.'

***zone,** *n.* As the last term in **Canal, thermal, transition, verdant zone.**

zoot suit. [Origin unknown.] A suit, usu. of flashy materials and extreme pattern, having a knee-length coat with padded shoulders and close-fitted waist, and peg-top trousers coming well up under the arms. Also **zoot-suiter, zooter.** *Slang.*

1943 MENEFEE *Assignment* 187 In 1941 the zoot suit made its appearance and achieved great popularity among Mexicans and Negroes. *Ib.* 189 The zooters, who earlier in the day had spread boasts that they were organized to 'kill every cop' they could find. **1943** *Chi. D. News* 12 June 6/2 A new human variety has excited the populace [in Calif.]—the 'zoot suiters.' **1948** *Miss America* June 18/2, I thought you'd begin to like me again if I changed into a zoot-suiter.

* **Zouave,** *n.* In the Civil War, a member of any one of various volunteer regiments, chiefly in the North, adopting features of the dress and the drill of the French Zouaves. Now *hist.* Cf. **fire Zouave.**

1860 *Chi. Tribune* 23 Feb. 1/4 The gallant Zouaves were out in the afternoon and attracted much attention and admiration by their fine appearance and exact drills. **1860** *Charleston* (S.C.) *Mercury* 25 Dec. 1/3 The Washington Artillery, the Zouaves, the Palmetto Riflemen, . . . the Minute Men and citizens generally, participated. **1861** *Ib.* 26 Jan. 3/1 The Chicago Zouaves have offered their services to the United States government. **1926** *Chi. Drovers' Jrnl.* 24 April 4/3 The Streator, Ill., Zouaves made a fine impression.

attrib. **1862** NORTON *Army Lett.* 77 That Zouave cap . . . is dark blue, and, of course, it has no front, that's Zouave style. **1863** RUSSELL *Diary* I. 255 The Zouave mania is quite as rampant here as it is in New York, and the smallest children are thrust into baggy red breeches, which the learned Lipsius might have appreciated, and are sent out with flags and tin swords to impede the highways.

zucchini ˌzuˈkinɪ, *n.* [It. *zucchino*, dim. of *zucca*, squash.] (See quot. 1950.) Also attrib.

1929 *Sunset* Feb. 58/2 Wash the succini and slice thinly into a baking pan. **1948** *N.O. Times-Picayune Mag.* 24 Oct. 2/2 Dem, the vegetable donkey, . . . has onion-top ears, zucchini squash head, summer squash body, fava bean pod legs, carrot fringe. **1950** *Chi. Tribune* 28 July 14/3 Zucchini . . . is a small Italian squash, shaped and colored much like a cucumber. . . . As a word, zucchini is a diminutive form of 'zucca,' a gourd or squash. A big pumpkin is 'zuccone,' a little pumpkin is 'zucchetta,' and a small vegetable marrow is 'zucchettino.' The latter word, we think, has been whittled by menu makers into 'zucchini.'

Zuñi ˈzunjɪ, *n. S.W.* [Amer. Sp. f. a Pueblo Indian term of unknown meaning. The pl. is *Zuñi*, or *Zuñis.*]

1. An Indian of a tribe residing in a pueblo of the same name in western New Mexico. Also *pl.*, the tribe.

1834 A. PIKE *Sketches* 200 The Moqui (pronounced *Mokee,*) and the Suni (Sunee) live near the Nabajo. **1897** *Outing* XXIX. 345/2 The Zuñis were then a mighty people. **1910** HODGE *Amer. Indians* II. 1017/2 Fray Martin de Arvide . . . was killed by 5 Zuñi. **1942** STEGNER *Mormon C.* 152 A Mormon missionary named Llewellyn Harris went among the Zuñi and found new hope.

attrib. **1852** SITGREAVES *Exped. Zuni & Colo. Rivers* (1853) 5 The cornfields of the Zuni Indians extended at intervals for several miles down the stream. **1883** *Cent. Mag.* Dec. 201 He regarded . . . Zuñi food prepared in Zuñi fashion as worthy of emphatic recommendation. **1933** HARRINGTON *Gypsum Cave, Nev.* 15 On March 1 three Zuñi Indians from New Mexico arrived.

2. The language of these Indians.

1882 *Atlantic Mo.* Sep. 365/2, I was awakened next morning by a chorus composed of Zuñi, Navajo, broken English, and Cheyenne imprecations. *Ib.* 367/2 Then I spoke in Zuñi. **1893** DONALDSON *Moqui Pueblo Indians* 91 The Zuñi is used by the Pueblos of Zuñi, who are of Zuñian stock.

Zuñian ˈzunjən, *n.* A Zuñi Indian. Usu. *pl.*, with reference to the tribe.

1848 ROBINSON *Santa Fe Exped.* (1932) 53 The Zunians are a tribe somewhat similar in their habits to the Lagoonies, living still more by themselves. **1855** WHIPPLE *Explor. Ry. Route* III. 40 The Zuñians that escaped built the town . . . upon a high mesa. **1858** IVES *Colo. River* 127 They want force of character and the courageous qualities which the Zuñians and some other Pueblo Indians have the credit of possessing. **1881** MORGAN *Houses Amer. Aborigines* 137 Their extreme exclusiveness has preserved to the Zuñians their strong individuality, and kept their language pure.

Zu-Zu ˈzuˌzu, *n.* Also **Zou-Zou.** (See quot. 1909.) Also attrib. Now *hist.*

1863 *Harper's Mag.* March 569/2 A zou-zou . . . found himself arrested by the guard. **1884** *Cent. Mag.* Oct. 814/2 You shall have your rations, Zou Zous, to-night. **1909** WEBSTER 2373 *Zu-Zu*, . . . a familiar nickname for the Zouaves in the Union Army. **1944** PENNELL *Rome Hanks* 70 Tom thought it was the boy who sang the Zu-Zu song at the creek.

zwieback ˈzwaɪˌbæk, *n.* Also **zweiback.** [G., "twice-baked."] A form of bread made in small loaves, cut into small pieces and toasted until quite brown and crisp.

1894 *N.Y. Wkly. Tribune* 14 March 5/3 These Zweiback will keep for a long time if put in a dry place. **1903** *Harper's Bazaar* Oct., At one year you can commence to give him gruels, broth, a little well-cooked cereal, and zwieback. **1917** *Ladies' Home Jrnl.* Nov. 62/2 He should be taught to eat dry bread, zweiback, or dry whole-wheat crackers. **1947** BEROLZHEIMER *Regional Cook Book* 535 Mix zwieback with ½ cup sugar, cinnamon and butter.

BIBLIOGRAPHY

NOTES

THIS is not a complete bibliography of the works quoted in the Dictionary. It is designed, primarily, to facilitate identification of such sources as may be obscure in the forms cited. Newspapers and periodicals are not included, except for a few of the less familiar, and those that might be confused through similarity of their titles. Serial publications of societies have also been excluded, as well as official reports, laws and statutes, and journals of legislative bodies. But, published records of cities and towns, etc., are entered, since these are extensively quoted under short titles that are often modified considerably from their full forms.

In the interest of simplicity, certain niceties of standard bibliographic practice have been ignored. Because the Dictionary cites authors under their best-known names, as "Mark Twain" or "O. Henry," their works have been listed under such pseudonyms, followed by the authors' actual names. Titles appearing under maiden names are similarly treated. Works published by historical societies and governmental agencies, etc., ordinarily gathered under institutional heads through cross-references, are indexed under the authors and titles as cited by the Dictionary, and the nominal catalogue entry is supplied in parentheses. Certain fictitious titles, used for convenience, are bracketed and followed by their proper titles, e.g. [*Annals of Congress*], for *The Debates and Proceedings in the Congress of the United States.*

The research incidental to collection of this information has shown that some dates assigned in the Dictionary are in error. These have largely been explained, as well as certain other discrepancies, such as incorrect titles and erroneous ascriptions of authorship.

A list of abbreviations is appended as a further aid to identification of the material quoted.

STYLE AND ABBREVIATIONS

1. Arrangement is in alphabetical order of authors' names or titles of works. Each title is followed by the place and date of publication of the edition used, or conjectured to have been used. No effort has been made to list every edition drawn upon in the Dictionary, owing to the difficulty of determining the origins of material gathered from a multitude of sources, over many years. In particular, inclusion of the editions used in the *DAE* has been curtailed, since it is doubtful whether all of these could have entered the one-fourth or so of that work embodied in the present Dictionary.

2. Dates in boldface are those assigned in the Dictionary to quoted matter, with **v.d.,** for "various dates," being substituted in the case of diaries, volumes of short stories, etc. Publication dates, when different, remain in lightface.

3. When necessary to give a limiting date, as of an author's death, this is preceded by *a.*, *ante.* Where a date is not precisely known, *c.*, *circa*, is employed.

4. The sign of equality (=) denotes that the editions referred to are alike in pagination.

5. Brackets are used to inclose information ascertained elsewhere than from the title-pages of the works in question. Fictitious titles and interpolated matter are also bracketed.

6. A question mark is prefixed in cases of uncertainty as to reliability of information.

7. "(*OED*)" indicates that material from the source named was requoted from the *Oxford English Dictionary* or its *Supplement*.

LIST OF BIBLIOGRAPHIC ABBREVIATIONS

a.	*ante*, before
Acad.	Academy
Acc.	Account
adds.	additions
Adv.	Adventure(s); Advertiser; Advocate
Advt.	Advertiser
Aff.	Affairs
Agric.	Agricultural; Agriculture
A.L.A.	American Library Association
Alman.	Almanac
Am. R. R. Jrnl.	*American Railroad Journal*
Am. Sp.	*American Speech* (*q.v.*)
Amer. N. & Q.	*American Notes and Queries* (*q.v.*)
Amer. Sp.	*American Speech* (*q.v.*)
Ann.	Annals; Annual
Antiq.	Antiquarian
app.	appendix
Arch.	Archeological; Architecture; Archives
Assn.	Association
Autob.	Autobiography
B.	Bartlett, *Dictionary* (*q.v.*)
Balt.	Baltimore
B. & L.	Barrère and Leland (*q.v.*)
Bd.	Board (of)
Biog.	Biography
Bk.	Book
Blackw.	*Blackwood's Edinburgh Magazine*
Bot.	Botanical; Botany
Br. Wtb.	(Bibliography, *s.v.*)
Bull.	Bulletin
c.	*circa*, about
©	copyrighted
C.	Chicago
C. A. Jrnl.	*Canadian Alpine Journal* (*q.v.*)
Cal.	Calendar (of)
Cat.	Catalogue
Cent.	*Century Dictionary* (*q.v.*)
Cent. Mag.	*Century Magazine*
Chi.	Chicago
Chr. Sci. Monitor	*Christian Science Monitor*
Chron.	Chronicle(s)
Cin(ci).	Cincinnati
Co.	Company; County
Col.	Colonial; Colonies; Colony
Coll(s).	Collections; College
Comm.	Commercial; Commission(er)
Comm. & Fin. Chron.	*Commercial and Financial Chronicle*
comp.	compiled (by); compiler
Cong(r).	Congress(ional)
Cong. Rec.	*Congressional Record*
corr.	corrected
Corr.	Correspondence
Ct.	Court
Cyclo.	Cyclopedia
D.	Daily
DAB	*Dictionary of American Biography* (*q.v.*)
DAE	*Dictionary of American English* (*q.v.*)
Dept.	Department
Descr.	Description (of)
Dial.	Dialect
Dict.	Dictionary
Diplom.	Diplomatic
Dly.	Daily
DN	*Dialect Notes* (*q.v.*)
DNB	*Dictionary of National Biography* (*q.v.*)
Doc.	Documentary; Documents
E.	East
Econ.	Economics; Economy
ed.	edited (by); edition; editor
EDD	*English Dialect Dictionary. See* Wright
Educ.	Educational
Emig.	Emigrant; Emigrating; Emigration
Encycl.	Encyclopedia
Eng.	Engineering; England; English
enl.	enlarged
Entom.	Entomological; Entomology
Ess.	Essay(s)
Ethnol.	Ethnological; Ethnology
Ev.	Evening
Ex.	Examiner; Executive; Express
Exped.	Expedition
Exper.	Experiment(al)
Explor.	Exploration(s)
F.	Farmer, *Americanisms* (*q.v.*)
For.	Foreign
Gaz.	Gazette(er)
Geog.	Geographical; Geography
Geol.	Geological; Geology
Gloss.	Glossary
H.C.	Historical Commission
H. Rep.	House of Representatives
H.S.	Historical Society
Hunt's Merch. Mag.	*Hunt's Merchant's Magazine*
Ill(ustr).	Illustrated
impr.	improved
Ind.	Indian; Industrial
Int.	International
Intell.	Intelligencer
Jrnl(s).	Journal(s)
K.C.	Kansas City
Knickerb.	*Knickerbocker*
L.A. (L.A.)	*Linguistic Atlas* (*q.v.*); Los Angeles
Ladies' H. Jrnl.	*Ladies' Home Journal*
Lang.	Language
Lect.	Lecture(s)
Let(t).	Letter(s)
Lib.	Library
Ling. Atlas	*Linguistic Atlas* (*q.v.*)
Lit. Digest.	*Literary Digest*
Mag.	Magazine
Man.	Manual
Mem.	Memoirs; Memorial
Merc.	Mercantile
Mess.	Messages; Messenger
Misc.	Miscellaneous
Mo.	Monthly
Morav.	Moravian
Morn.	Morning
MS(S).	Manuscript(s)
Mt(s).	Mountain(s)
Mus.	Museum
N.	North
N.A.; N. Amer.	North America
Narr.	Narrative
Nat.	National; Natural

Nat. Geog. Mag. . . . . . *National Geographic Magazine*
Nat. Hist. . . . . *Natural History*
Nat. Pk. . . . . National Park
n.d. . . . . no date
N. Eng. . . . . New England
No. . . . . North; Number
N.O. . . . . New Orleans
North. . . . . Northampton (Mass.)
n.p. . . . . no place
n.s. . . . . new series
Ornith. . . . . Ornithological; Ornithology
P. . . . . Papers
Pac. . . . . Pacific
perf. . . . . performed
Phil. . . . . Philological
Phila. . . . . Philadelphia
Phil(os). . . . . Philosophical; Philosophy
Phil. Trans. . . . . . . *Philosophical Transactions* (Royal Society, London)
PMLA . . . . *Publications of the Modern Language Association*
Polit. . . . . Political
Pop. Sci. Mo. . . . . *Popular Science Monthly*
p(p). . . . . page(s)
pref. . . . . preface
Pres. . . . . President(ial)
Presby. . . . . Presbyterian
priv. pr. . . . . privately printed
Proc. . . . . Proceedings
Prog. . . . . Progress
Prov. . . . . Provincial
Pseud. . . . . Pseudonym (of)
pub. . . . . published (by); publisher
Pub. . . . . Public
q.v. . . . . *quod vide*, which see
R. . . . . Ramsay and Emberson, *Mark Twain Lexicon* (*q.v.*); River
Rec. . . . . Record(s)
Recoll. . . . . Recollections
Reg. . . . . Register; Regulations
Rel. . . . . Relating (to); Relations
Relig. . . . . Religious
Reminisc. . . . . . . Reminiscences
Rep. . . . . Report(er); Republican
repr. . . . . reprint(ed)
Repr. . . . . Representatives
Repub. . . . . Republic(an)
rev. . . . . revised
Rev. . . . . Review
Sat. Ev. Post . . . . . *Saturday Evening Post*
Sched. . . . . Schedule
Sci. . . . . Science; Scientific
Sci. Amer. . . . . . . *Scientific American*
Sen. . . . . Senate
sep. . . . . separately
ser. . . . . series
Sess. . . . . Session
S.F. . . . . San Francisco
Shop. . . . . Shopping
Sk. . . . . Sketches
S. Lit. Mess. . . . . . *Southern Literary Messenger*
So. . . . . Southern
Soc. . . . . Society
South. . . . . Southampton (N.Y.)
Sta. . . . . Station
Standard . . . . *Standard Dictionary* (*q.v.*)
Stats. . . . . Statutes
St. P. . . . . State Papers
Sun. . . . . Sunday
Supp. . . . . Supplement; Supply
Supt. . . . . Superintendent
Surv. . . . . Survey
s.v. . . . . *sub verbo*, under the word
S.W. . . . . Southwest
Syd. Soc. Lex. . . . . (Bibliography, *s.v.*)
Syn. . . . . Synopsis
Tel. . . . . Telegraph
Terr. . . . . Territorial; Territory
Th., Th. Supp. . . . . Thornton (*q.v.*)
tr. . . . . translated (by); translation (of)
Trav. . . . . Travels
U. . . . . University
Univ. . . . . Universal; University
usu. . . . . usually
v.d. . . . . various dates
Ver. . . . . Verwijs and Verdam (*q.v.*)
vol(s). . . . . volume(s)
W. . . . . Webster, Noah (*q.v.*); Weekly; West(ern)
Wash. . . . . Washington
We. . . . . Weingarten (*q.v.*)
Westm. Gaz. . . . . . *Westminster Gazette*
Wks. . . . . Works
WNT . . . . (Bibliography, *s.v.*)
Yr.(s) . . . . Year(s)
Zool. . . . . Zoological; Zoology

A

ABBOTT, CARLISLE S. *Recollections of a California Pioneer*. New York, **1917**

ABBOTT, CHARLES C. *Primitive Industry*. Salem, Mass., **1881**

ABBOTT, EDWARD C., and SMITH, HELENA H. *We Pointed them North*. New York, **1939**

ABBOTT, JACOB. *New England and Her Institutions*. Hartford, 1847. =**1835**

ABBOTT, JOHN S. C. *Christopher Carson*. New York, 1875 [c**1873**]
South and North. New York, **1860**

ABDY, EDWARD S. *Journal of a Residence and Tour in the United States*. London, **1835**

ABERT, JAMES W. *Report . . . of His Examination of New Mexico*. Washington, 1848. **v.d.**

ADAIR, JAMES. *The History of the American Indians*. London, **1775**

ADAMS, ANDY. *Cattle Brands*. Boston, **1906**
The Log of a Cowboy. Boston, **1903**

ADAMS, CHARLES FRANCIS. *Some Phases of Sexual Morality and Church Discipline in Colonial New England*. Cambridge, **1891**

ADAMS, EPHRAIM D., and ALMACK, JOHN C. *A History of the United States*. New York, **1931**

ADAMS, MRS. FRANC L. *Pioneer History of Ingham County*. Lansing, Mich., **1923**

ADAMS, JAMES TRUSLOW, ed. *Album of American History*. I, *Colonial Period;* II, *1783–1853;* III, *1853–1893*. New York, **1944–46**

ADAMS, JOHN. *Works*. Boston, 1850–56. **v.d.** Includes I, *Life of John Adams* by Charles Francis Adams; II, *Diary*. **v.d.**

ADAMS, JOHN, and ADAMS, ABIGAIL. *Familiar Letters . . . during the Revolution*. Boston, 1875. **v.d.**

ADAMS, JOHN QUINCY. *Diary. . . , 1794–1845*. Ed. Allan Nevins. New York, 1928. **v.d.**
Memoirs. Ed. Charles Francis Adams. Philadelphia, 1874–77. **v.d.**

ADAMS, RAMON F. *Western Words: a Dictionary of the Range, Cow Camp and Trail*. Norman, Okla., **1944**

ADAMS, SAMUEL H. *The Clarion*. Boston, **1914**

ADAMS, WILLIAM T. *Field and Forest*. Boston, 1874. =**1870**
In Doors and Out. Boston, 1876. =**1875**

ADE, GEORGE. *Artie*. Chicago, **1896**
Doc Horne. Chicago, **1899**
Fables in Slang. London, 1902. =**1899**
Forty Modern Fables. New York, **1901**
In Babel. New York, 1906. =**1903**
More Fables. Chicago, **1900**
People You Know. New York, [**1903**]
Pink Marsh. New York, [c**1897**]

Advance. Chicago, **1867–1917**

Adv. of Uncle Sam. See FIDFADDY.

AGASSIZ, LOUIS. *Contributions to the Natural History of the United States*. Boston, **1857–62**

AGRICOLA. *A Series of Essays on Agriculture & Rural Affairs*. Raleigh, N.C., **1819**

Agricultural Museum. Georgetown, D.C., **1810–12**

ALBION, ROBERT G. *Square-Riggers on Schedule*. Princeton, **1938**

ALCOTT, A. BRONSON. *The Journals of Bronson Alcott*. Ed. Odell Shepard. Boston, 1938. **v.d.**
New Connecticut. An Autobiographical Poem. Ed. Franklin B. Sanborn. Boston, 1887. **v.d.**

ALCOTT, LOUISA MAY. *Jo's Boys*. Boston, 1899. =[**1886**]
Little Women. 2 vols. Boston, **1869**. Vol. I first pub. **1868**
Under the Lilacs. Boston, **1887**

ALDEN, ISABELLA (MCDONALD). *Little Fishers and Their Nets*. Boston, **1887**

ALDRICH, THOMAS BAILEY. *Marjorie Daw, and other People*. Boston, **1873**
Ponkapog Papers. Boston, **1903**
Prudence Palfrey. Boston, **1874**
The Queen of Sheba. Boston, **1877**
A Sea Turn, and Other Matters. Boston, **1902**
The Stillwater Tragedy. Boston, **1880**
The Story of a Bad Boy. Boston, 1877, 1911. = 1870. First pub. in *Our Young Folks*, V. Jan.–Dec., **1869**
Two Bites at a Cherry, with Other Tales. Boston, **1894**

ALDRIDGE, REGINALD. *Life on a Ranch*. New York, **1884**

ALEXANDER, MRS., pseud. HECTOR, ANNIE (FRENCH). *Going West*. Indianapolis, **1881**

ALEXANDER, HOLMES M. *The American Talleyrand*. New York, **1935**

ALLAN-OLNEY, MARY. *The New Virginians*. Edinburgh, **1880**

ALLARDICE, ROBERT B. *Agricultural Tour in the United States and Upper Canada*. Edinburgh, **1842**

ALLEN, MISS A. J. *Ten Years in Oregon*. Ithaca, N.Y., **1850**

ALLEN, ALEXANDER V. G. *Life and Letters of Phillips Brooks*. 3 vols. New York, 1901. **v.d.**

ALLEN, FREDERICK L. *Only Yesterday*. New York, **1931**

ALLEN, IRA. *The Natural and Political History of the State of Vermont*. Montpelier, 1870. **1798**

ALLEN, JAMES LANE. *The Blue-Grass Region of Kentucky*. New York, **1892**
The Choir Invisible. New York, **1897**
A Kentucky Cardinal. New York, [c**1894**]

ALLEN, RICHARD L. *The New American Farm Book*. New York, **1883**

ALLEY, FELIX E. *Random Thoughts and the Musings of a Mountaineer*. Salisbury, N.C., **1941**

ALLIGHAN, GARRY. *The Romance of the Talkies*. London, **1929**

ALSAKER, RASMUS L. *Eating for Health and Efficiency*. New York, **1920**. First pub., 5 vols., New York, 1917.
Maintaining Health. New York, **1920**. First pub. as *Health and Efficiency*. New York, 1914.

ALSOP, GEORGE. *A Character of the Province of Maryland*. Ed. John G. Shea. New York, 1869. **1666**

Alta California. San Francisco, **1849–91**. (Cited, without special identification, from dly. and other eds.)

ALTON, EDMUND. *Among the Law-Makers*. New York, 1900. =**1886**

ALVORD, CLARENCE W., and BIDGOOD, LEE. *The First Explorations of the Trans-Allegheny Region by the Virginians, 1650–1674*. Cleveland, 1912. **v.d.**

ALWOOD, WILLIAM B. *The Chemical Composition of American Grapes Grown in the Central and Eastern States*. Washington, **1916**

America; a Catholic Review of the Week. New York, **1909–**

America; a Journal for Americans. Chicago, **1888–91**

American; a National Journal. Philadelphia, **1880–1900**

The American Almanac and Repository of Useful Knowledge . . . for [1830–61]. Boston, **1829–60**

American Almanac and Treasury of Facts . . . for [1878–89]. Ed. Ainsworth R. Spofford. New York, **1878–89**

American Annual Cyclopædia. See *Appletons' Annual Cyclopædia*.

American Archives. [Comp.] Peter Force. 4th Ser., 6 vols. [Washington, 1837–46.] **v.d.** 5th Ser., 3 vols. [Washington, 1848–53.] **v.d.**

The American Home Cook Book. By Ladies of Detroit and Other Cities. Detroit, **1878**

American Husbandry. London, 1775

American (Illustrated) Magazine. New York, **1905–**

American Magazine of Useful and Entertaining Knowledge. Boston, **1834–37**

American Magazine, or a Monthly View of the Political State of the British Colonies. Philadelphia, **1741**

The American Mercury; a Monthly Review. New York, **1924–**

American Monthly Magazine and Critical Review. New York, **1817–19**

American Museum, or, Universal Magazine. Philadelphia, 1787–92. **v.d.**

American Natural History. See GODMAN.

American Nicknames. See SHANKLE.

American Notes and Queries; a Medium of Intercommunication for Literary Men, General Readers, Etc. I–IX. Philadelphia, **1888–92**. (See note to next.)

American Notes and Queries; a Journal for the Curious. I–VIII. New York; North Bennington, Vt., **1941–50**. (Often cited as *N. & Q.* May be distinguished from *Notes and Queries* (London) *q.v.*, by noting date and vol. no.)

The American Pioneer. Cincinnati, **1842–43**

American Punch. Boston, **1879–81**

American Speech. Baltimore; New York, **1926–**

American State Papers. (U.S. Congress.) Washington, 1832–61. **v.d.**

American Weekly Mercury. Philadelphia, **1719–46**

Américas. (Organ of Pan-American Union.) Washington, **1949–**

America's Cook Book. New and rev. ed. New York, **1941**

AMES, NATHAN. *Childe Harvard*. Boston, **1848**

AMHERST, MASS. *Records of the Town . . . from 1735 to 1788*. Ed. John F. Jameson. Amherst, 1884. **v.d.**

AMPHLETT, WILLIAM. *The Emigrant's Directory to the Western States of North America*. London, **1819**

ANBUREY, THOMAS. *Travels through the Interior Parts of America*. London, **1789**. (Purported dates of letters, occasionally cited, are invalid, work being largely a compilation.)

ANDREAS, ALFRED T. *History of the State of Kansas*. Chicago, **1883**

ANDREWS, CHRISTOPHER C. *Recollections*. Cleveland, 1928. **1907**

ANDREWS, EDWARD D. *The Community Industries of the Shakers*. Albany, **1933**

ANDREWS, JOHN. *Letters . . . , 1772–1776*. Ed. Winthrop Sargent. Cambridge, 1866. **v.d.**

ANDREWS, MARIETTA (MINNEGERODE). *Scraps of Paper*. New York, [c**1929**]

Animal and Plant Lore. Ed. Fanny (Dickerson) Bergen. (American Folk-Lore Society. *Memoirs*. VII.) **1899**

Animals of America: "Mammals of America." Ed. Harold E. Anthony. Garden City, N.Y. [1937]. First pub. as *Mammals of America*. New York, [c**1917**]

Ann Arbor (Mich.) *Register*. **1872–99**

[*Annals of Congress*.] *The Debates and Proceedings in the Congress of the United States*. (U.S. Congress.) Washington, 1834–56. **v.d.**

Annual Cyclopædia. See *Appletons' Annual Cyclopædia*.

Anthony's Photogr. Bul. See *International Annual*.

APGAR, AUSTIN C. *Trees of the Northern United States*. New York, [c**1892**]

APPEL, JOSEPH H. *The Business Biography of John Wanamaker*. New York, 1930. **v.d.**

APPLEGATE, JESSE H. *A Day with the Cow Column in 1843*. Chicago, 1934. **1876**. Includes *Recollections of My Boyhood*, first pub. **1914**

Appletons' Annual Cyclopædia. 1861–1902. New York, 1862–1903. **v.d.** Also cited as (*American*) *Annual Cyclopædia*.

ARCHDALE, JOHN. *A New Description of that Fertile and Pleasant Province of Carolina*. London, **1707**

Archives of Maryland. Baltimore, 1883–. **v.d.**

ARFWEDSON, CARL D. *The United States and Canada*. London, **1834**

ARMSTRONG, MARGARET N., and THORNBER, JOHN J. *Field Book of Western Wild Flowers*. New York, **1915**

ARMSTRONG, WILLIAM. *Stocks and Stock-Jobbing in Wall Street*. New York, **1848**

[*Army Regulations*.] *Revised Regulations for the Army of the United States, 1861*. (U.S. War Dept.) Philadelphia, [**1861**]

ARNETT, LONNA D. *Elements of Library Methods*. New York, **1925**

ARNOLD, JOHN R. *Hides and Skins*. Chicago, **1925**

ARNY, WILLIAM F. M. *Interesting Items Regarding New Mexico*. Santa Fe, **1873**

Arrow Points. Montgomery, Ala., **1920–**

ARTHUR, STANLEY C. *The Birds of Louisiana*. [New Orleans, **1918**]
Old New Orleans. New Orleans, **1936**

ASBURY, FRANCIS. *Journal*. New York, 1921. **v.d.**

ASBURY, HERBERT. *The French Quarter*. New York, **1936**
The Gangs of New York. New York, **1928**
Gem of the Prairie, an Informal History of the Chicago Underworld. New York, **1940**. (Cited also as fictitious *Underworld of Chi.*)
Sucker's Progress. New York, **1938**

ASH, THOMAS. *Carolina*. London, **1682**

ASHE, THOMAS. *Travels in America*. 3 vols. London, **1808**

ASHER, LOUIS E., and HEAL, EDITH. *Send No Money*. Chicago, **1942**

Ashley-Smith Explor. See DALE, H. C.

ASPINWALL. See BOSTON, MASS. REGISTRY DEPT.

ATHERTON, GERTRUDE F. (HORN). *The Californians*. London, **1898**
The Doomswoman. Philadelphia, **1892**
Perch of the Devil. [London, 1924.] =**1914**
The Travelling Thirds. New York, **1905**

ATKINSON, ELEANOR (STACKHOUSE). *Johnny Appleseed*. New York, **1915**

ATKINSON, JOSEPH. *A Match for a Widow*. London, **1788**

ATTMORE, WILLIAM. *Journal of a Tour to North Carolina*. Ed. Lida T. Rodman. Chapel Hill, 1922. **1787**

AUDUBON, JOHN JAMES. *Ornithological Biography*. Boston; Philadelphia; Edinburgh, **1831–39**

AUDUBON, JOHN J., and BACHMAN, JOHN. *The Viviparous Quadrupeds of North America*. New York, **1845–48**

AUDUBON, JOHN WOODHOUSE. *Audubon's Western Journal: 1849–1850*. Cleveland, 1906. **v.d.**

Auk. (Pub. Amer. Ornithologists' Union.) Boston, etc. **1876–**

AULD, JOSEPH. *Picturesque Burlington*. Burlington, Vt., **1893**

AURAND, AMMON M. *The "Pow-wow" Book*. Harrisburg, Pa., **1929**. Includes *An Account of the "Witch" Murder Trial*.

Aurora. (Newspaper.) Philadelphia, **1790–1835**

Austin, Benjamin. *Constitutional Republicanism, in Opposition to Fallacious Federalism.* Boston, **1803**

Austin, Mary. *The Land of Little Rain.* Boston, **1903**

Austin, Moses, and Austin, Stephen C. *The Austin Papers.* Ed. Eugene C. Barker. Washington, 1924–28. **v.d.**

Avery, Ephraim K., defendant. *Trial of Rev. Mr. Avery.* Reported by Benjamin F. Hallett. Boston, **1833**

Avery, Isaac W. *The History of the State of Georgia from 1850 to 1881.* New York, [c**1881**]

B

Baber, Mary F. (Sauer), and Walker, William. *The Longest Rope.* Caldwell, Ida., **1940**

Babson, John J. *History of the Town of Gloucester.* Gloucester, Mass., **1860**

Babson, Roger W. *Business Barometers and Investment.* New York, **1940**

Bachellor, Irving. *Eben Holden.* Boston, [c**1900**]

Baedeker, Karl, pub. *The United States.* By James F. Muirhead. 2d rev. ed. Leipzig, **1899**

Bagby, George W. *The Old Virginia Gentleman, and Other Sketches.* Ed. Thomas Nelson Page. New York, 1910. **v.d.**

Bagg, Lyman H. *Four Years at Yale.* New Haven, **1871**

Bailey, Eli S. *The Sand Dunes of Indiana.* Chicago, **1917**

Bailey, Florence M. *Birds of New Mexico.* [Santa Fe], **1928**

Bailey, James M. *Folks in Danbury; or, Mr. Miggs and His Neighbours.* London, [**1877**]. Also pub. as *They All Do It, or, Mr. Miggs of Danbury and His Neighbors.* Boston, **1877**
Life in Danbury. Boston, **1873**

Bailey, Liberty Hyde. *Cyclopedia of American Agriculture.* 4 vols. New York, **1907–9**
Cyclopedia of American Horticulture. 4 vols. New York, **1900–1902.** Rewritten, enl. 3 vols. New York, 1935 [c**1928–30**]
The Principles of Fruit-Growing. New York, **1897**

Bailey, Vernon. *The Mammals and Life Zones of Oregon.* Washington, **1936**

Baillie-Grohman, William A. *Camps in the Rockies.* London, **1882**

Baily, Francis. *Journal of a Tour in Unsettled Parts of North America in 1796 & 1797.* London, 1856. **v.d.**

Baird, Robert. *Impressions and Experiences of the West Indies and North America in 1849.* Philadelphia, **1850**
View of the Valley of the Mississippi. Philadelphia, **1832.** 2d ed. Philadelphia, **1834**

Baird, Spencer F. *The Birds of North America.* Philadelphia, **1860**
[*Birds of the Pacific Railway Routes.*] *Reports of Explorations and Surveys, . . . for a Railroad Route from the Mississippi River to the Pacific Ocean.* Vol. IX. Washington, **1858**
The Mammals of North America. Philadelphia, [**1857**]**–59**

Baird, Spencer F., *et al. A History of North American Birds.* Boston, **1905.** [?App. same as Boston, 1874.]

Baker, Benjamin A., attrib. author. *A Glance at New York.* New York, [n.d.]. First perf. **1848.** (Not to be confused with like title, 1837, by Asa Greene.)

Baker, Dorothy (Dodds). *Trio.* New York, 1946. **1943**

Baker, Hugh P. *Native and Planted Timber of Iowa.* Washington, **1908**

Baker, LaFayette C. *History of the United States Secret Service.* Philadelphia, **1867**

Baker, Louise. *Party Line.* New York, **1945**

Baker, William M. *The New Timothy.* New York, **1870**

Balance (and *Columbian Repository*). Hudson, N.Y., **1801–8**

Baldwin, Joseph G. *The Flush Times of Alabama and Mississippi.* Americus, Ga., 1908. = New York, **1853**

Baldwin, Leland D. *The Keelboat Age on Western Waters.* Pittsburgh, **1941**

The Ball Players' Chronicle. New York, **1867–68**

Ballantyne Robert M. *Hudson's Bay.* London, 1890. **1848**

Ballard, Julia P. (Pratt). *Among the Moths and Butterflies.* New York, **1890**

Ballou, Maturin M. *The New Eldorado.* 5th ed. Boston, **1890**

Baltimore, Md. [*Baltimore Rec.*] *First Records of Baltimore Town and Jones' Town, 1729–1797.* Baltimore, 1905. **v.d.**

Bancroft, George. *History of the United States.* Boston, 1852–74 [c**1834–74**]. Rev. ed. Boston, **1876**

Bancroft, Jessie H. *Handbook of Athletic Games for Players, Instructors, and Speculators* [*sic*]. New York, **1916**

Bandelier, Adolf F. *The Delight Makers.* New York, **1890**

Banks, Elizabeth L. *The Autobiography of a Newspaper Girl.* 328 pp. London, **1902.** 317 pp. New York, **1902**

Banning, William, and Banning, George H. *Six Horses.* New York, **1930**

Barbour, Ralph Henry. *The Book of School and College Sports.* New York, **1904**
Weatherby's Inning. New York, **1903**

Barbour, Thomas. *That Vanishing Eden, a Naturalist's Florida.* Boston, **1944**

Barcia Carballido y Zuniga, Andrés G. *Ensayo cronológico para la historia general de la Florida, 1512–1722.* Madrid, **1723**

Barker. See Moses. *Representative Plays.*

Barkins, Evelyn (Werner). *The Doctor Has a Baby.* New York, **1947**

Barlow, Joel. *The Columbiad.* Philadelphia, **1807**
Hasty Pudding: a Poem in Three Cantos, Written . . . 1793. New Haven, 1796. **1793**

Barnard, Evan G. *A Rider of the Cherokee Strip.* Boston, **1936**

Barnes. *Life T. Weed.* See Weed.

Barnes, Homer F. *Charles Fenno Hoffman.* New York, 1930. Includes letters and poems, **v.d.**

Barnes, William C. *Arizona Place Names.* Tucson, **1935**
Western Grazing Grounds and Forest Ranges. Chicago, **1913**

Barnett, Evelyn S. (Snead). *The Dragnet.* New York, **1909**

Barnum, Phineas T. *The Life of P. T. Barnum.* New York, **1855**
Struggles and Triumphs. New York, 1871. pp. 25–780 = 1st ed., 1869. **v.d.**

Barrère, Albert and Leland, Charles G. *A Dictionary of Slang, Jargon and Cant.* London, **1889–90.** Also pub. London, 1897.

Barrows, John H. *The World's Parliament of Religions.* Chicago, **1893**

Barrows, John R. *Ubet.* Caldwell, Ida., [c**1934**]

Barrows, Walter B. *Michigan Bird Life.* Lansing, **1912**

Barry, Patrick. *The Fruit Garden.* New York, **1851**

Bartholow, Roberts. *A Practical Treatise on Materia Medica and Therapeutics.* 3d ed. rev. New York, 1879. (Erroneously dated **1876.**)

Bartlett, John Russell. *Dictionary of Americanisms.* New York, 1849. = **1848.** 3d ed. Boston, 1860. = 2d ed., **1859.** 4th ed. Boston, 1896. = **1877**
Personal Narrative of Explorations. . . . Connected with the United States and Mexican Boundary Commission. New York, **1854**

Barton, Andrew, ?pseud. *The Disappointment; or, The Force of Credulity.* 2d ed., rev. and corr. Philadelphia, 1896. First perf. **1767**

Barton, Benjamin S. *Fragments of the Natural History of Pennsylvania.* Philadelphia, **1799**
New Views of the Origin of the Tribes and Nations of America. Philadelphia, **1797**

Barton, William E. *A Hero in Homespun.* Boston, **1897**
Sim Galloway's Daughter-in-Law. Boston, **1897**
The Truth about the Trouble at Roundstone. Boston, **1897**

Bartram, John. *Diary of a Journey through the Carolinas, Georgia, and Florida.* (American Philosophical Society. *Transactions.* XXXIII, part 1.) **v.d.**
Journal. See Stork.
Observations on the Inhabitants, Climate, Soil, . . . in His Travels Travels from Pensilvania to . . . Lake Ontario. London, **1751**

Bartram, William. *Travels in Georgia and Florida, 1773–74.* (American Philosophical Society. *Transactions.* XXXIII, part 2.) **v.d.**
Travels through North and South Carolina, Georgia, East & West Florida. Philadelphia, **1791**

Bassett, John S. *A Short History of the United States.* New York, **1913**
The Southern Plantation Overseer as Revealed in His Letters. Northampton, Mass., 1925. **v.d.**

Bastian, George C. *Editing the Day's News.* New York, **1923**

Bates, Charles A., ed. *The Clothing Book.* New York, **1898**

Bates, Mrs. D. B. *Incidents on Land and Water; Four Years on the Pacific Coast.* 10th ed. Boston, 1860. [c**1857**]

Batten, John M. *Reminiscences of Two Years in the United States Navy.* Lancaster, Pa., **1881**

The Battle of Brooklyn. Brooklyn, 1873. First pub. **1776**

Bauer, Edward E. *Highway Materials.* 1st ed. New York, **1928**

Baxley, Henry W. *What I Saw on the West Coast of South and North America.* New York, **1865**

Baxter, Richard, and Eliot, John. *Some Unpublished Correspondence.* Ed. Frederick J. Powicke. Manchester, Eng., 1931. **v.d.**

Baxter, William E. *America and the Americans.* London, **1855**

Baylor, i.e., Barnum, Frances C. (Baylor). *On Both Sides.* Philadelphia, **1885**

Beach, Rex E. *The Barrier.* New York, **1908**
Pardners. New York, **1905**

Beadle, Erastus F. *To Nebraska in '57.* New York, 1923. **1857**

Beadle, John H. *Life in Utah.* Philadelphia, **1870**
The Undeveloped West. Philadelphia, **1873**
Western Wilds, and the Men Who Redeem Them. Philadelphia, 1878 [c**1877**]

Beadle & Co., pub., New York. *Beadle's Dime Base-Ball Player.* [c**1860–81**]
Beadle's # 1 Ten Cent Songbook. **1863**

Beal, William J. *Grasses of North America.* New York, **1887–96**

Beard, Charles A. *American Government and Politics.* New York, **1931**

Beard, Daniel Carter. *The American Boys Handy Book.* New York, **1882**

Beard, James M. *K. K. K. Sketches.* Philadelphia, **1877**

Beauchamp, William M., ed. *Moravian Journals Relating to Central New York, 1745–66.* Syracuse, [1916] **v.d.** Contains *Diary of the Journey of Br. Cammerhoff and David Zeisberger to the Five Nations.* **1750.** *Journey to Onondaga and Cayuga, by David Ziesberger* [sic] *and Gottlob Sensemann, October, 1766.* **1766**

Beaudry, Louis N. *Historic Records of the Fifth New York Cavalry.* 4th ed., Albany, **1874**

Beaufoy, M. *Tour through Parts of the United States and Canada. By a British Subject.* London, 1828. **1827**

The Beaver. Winnipeg, **1920–**

Bechdolt, Frederick R. *Tales of the Old-Timers.* New York, **1924**

Beck, James M. *Our Wonderland of Bureaucracy.* New York, **1932**

Beckwith, Hiram W. *The Illinois and Indiana Indians.* Chicago, 1884. **v.d.**

Beckwourth, James P. *The Life and Adventures of James P. Beckwourth, Edited by T. D. Bonner.* Ed. Bernard DeVoto. New York, 1931. 1st pub. **1856**

Beebe, Lucius M. *Mixed Train Daily, a Book of Short-Line Railroads.* New York, **1947**

Beebe, Lucius M., and Clegg, Charles. *U.S. West, the Saga of Wells Fargo.* New York, **1949**

Beecher, Catherine E. *Miss Beecher's Domestic Receipt Book.* New York, **1846**

Beecher, Henry Ward. *Life Thoughts, Gathered from the Extemporaneous Discourses of Henry Ward Beecher.* By Edna D. Proctor. New York, 1860. = **1858**
Norwood. New York, **1868**
Notes from Plymouth Pulpit: a Collection of Memorable Passages from the Discourses of Henry Ward Beecher. By Augusta Moore. New York, **1859**
Sermons . . . in Plymouth Church. New York, 1869. **v.d.**
Yale Lectures on Preaching. 1st ser. New York, **1872**

Beechey, Fred W. *Narrative of a Voyage to the Pacific and Beering's Strait.* London, **1831**

Beer, Thomas. *The Mauve Decade.* New York, **1926**

Belasco. See Moses. *Representative American Dramas.*

Belcher, Jonathan. *The Belcher Papers.* (Massachusetts Historical Society. *Collections.* 6th Ser., VI–VII.) **v.d.**

Belknap, Jeremy. *Belknap Papers.* (Massachusetts Historical Society. *Collections.* 5th Ser., II–III; 6th Ser., IV.) **v.d.**
The History of New-Hampshire. Boston, **1784–92**
Journal of a Tour to the White Mountains in July, 1784. Boston, 1876. **1784**

Bell, Andrew. *Men & Things in America.* Southampton, Eng., 1862. First pub. **1838,** signed A. Thomason.

Bell, Lillian L. *Carolina Lee.* Boston, **1906**
Hope Loring. Boston, **1908**
A Little Sister to the Wilderness. Chicago, **1895**

Bell, Margaret V. (Dwight). *A Journey to Ohio in 1810.* Ed. Max Farrand. New Haven, 1920. = 1912. Written **1810**

BELL, WILLIAM A. *New Tracks in North America.* London, **1869**

BELLAMY, EDWARD. *Looking Backward.* Boston, **1888**

BELTRAMI, GIACOMO C. *A Pilgrimage in Europe and America, leading to the Discovery of the Sources of the Mississippi and Bloody River.* London, **1828.** Vol. II first pub. New Orleans, **1824**

BENEFIELD, BARRY. *The Chicken-Wagon Family.* New York, [c**1925**]

BENÉT, STEPHEN VINCENT. *John Brown's Body.* Garden City, N.Y., 1928. =**1927**

Listen to the People, Independence Day, 1941. New York, [**1941**]

Western Star. New York, **1943**

BENÉT WILLIAM ROSE. *Wild Goslings; a Selection of Fugitive Pieces.* New York, [c**1927**]

BENJAMIN, PARK. *The United States Naval Academy.* New York, **1900**

BENNETT, DANIEL K. *Chronology of North Carolina, . . . from the Year 1584 to the Present Time.* New York, **1858**

BENNETT, EMERSON. *Mike Fink: a Legend of the Ohio.* Rev. ed., Cincinnati, [**1852**]

BENSE, JOHAN FREDERICK. *A Dictionary of the Low-Dutch Element in the English Vocabulary.* The Hague, **1939**

BENSON, LYMAN. *The Cacti of Arizona.* Tucson, [c**1940**]

BENT, ARTHUR C. *Life Histories of North American Jays, Crows, and Titmice.* Washington, **1946**

Life Histories of North American Marsh Birds. Washington, **1926**

BENTLEY, HAROLD W. *A Dictionary of Spanish Terms in English, with Special Reference to the American Southwest.* New York, **1932**

BENTLEY, WILLIAM. *Diary.* Salem, Mass., 1905–14. **v.d.**

Bentley's Miscellany. London, **1837–68.** Also Amer. ed., New York, **1837–68**

BENTON, THOMAS HART. *Historical and Legal Examination . . . of the Decision of the Supreme Court of the United States in the Dred Scott Case.* New York, **1857**

Thirty Years' View. New York, 1854–56, **v.d.**

BENWELL, J. *An Englishman's Travels in America.* London, **1853**

BERESFORD, WILLIAM. *A Voyage Round the World; but more particularly to the North-West Coast of America.* London, **1789**

BERKELEY, GEORGE C. G. F. *The English Sportsman in the Western Prairies.* London, **1861**

BERKENHOUT. See MERENESS.

BERNARD, JOHN. *Retrospections of America, 1797–1811.* Ed. Mrs. Bayle Bernard. New York, 1887. **1827**

BERNHARD, HERZOGS. *Reise Sr. Hoheit der Herzogs Bernhard zu Sachsen-Weimar-Eisenach durch Nord-Amerika in den Jahren 1825 und 1826.* Weimar, **1828**

BEROLZHEIMER, RUTH, ed. *The United States Regional Cook Book.* Chicago, **1947**

BERRY, LESTER, and VAN DEN BARK, MELVIN. *The American Thesaurus of Slang.* New York, **1942**

BESANT, SIR WALTER, and RICE, JAMES. *The Golden Butterfly.* New York, [**1878**]

BESTE, J. RICHARD. *The Wabash.* London, **1855**

BEVERLEY, ROBERT. *The History and Present State of Virginia.* London, **1705.** 2d ed. London, **1722**

BIDDLE, CHARLES. *Autobiography.* Philadelphia, 1833. *a***1821**

BIDWELL, JOHN. *A Journey to California.* [?Liberty, Mo.], 1842. **1841**

Big Bear Ark. See PORTER, WILLIAM T.

BIGELOW, HORATIO. *Scattergun Sketches.* Springfield, Ill., **1922**

BIGELOW, JACOB. *American Medical Botany.* Boston, **1817–20**

BIGGERS, EARL DERR. *Seven Keys to Baldpate.* Indianapolis, [c**1913**]

BIGGS, WILLIAM. *Narrative of the Captivity of of William Biggs among the Kickapoo Indians in Illinois in 1788.* [New York], 1922. **1825**

BILL, JOHN. *The English Party's Excursion to Paris, . . . to which is Added, a Trip to America, etc., etc., etc.* London, **1850**

BILLINGS, JOHN D. *Hardtack and Coffee.* Boston, 1888. =**1887**

BINGLEY, WILLIAM. *Animal Biography.* 4th ed., with an addition of more than 140 sp. London, 1813. (Cited, erroneously, as **1802.**)

BINNS, ARCHIE. *The Timber Beast.* New York, **1944**

BIRD, i.e., BISHOP, ISABELLA L. (BIRD). *A Lady's Life in the Rocky Mountains.* London, 1879. New York, 1879–80. First pub. *Leisure Hour,* **1878**

BIRD, ROBERT M. *The Hawks of Hawk-Hollow.* Philadelphia, **1835**

Nick of the Woods. Philadelphia, **1837**

Robin Day. London, 1840. **1839**

Birds of America. Ed. T. Gilbert Pearson. Garden City, N.Y., 1936 [c**1917**]

BIRGE, JULIUS C. *The Awakening of the Desert.* Boston, [c**1912**]

BIRKBECK, MORRIS. *Letters from Illinois.* Philadelphia, **1818**

Notes on a Journey in America. London, 1818. First pub. **1817**

BIRKET, JAMES. *Some Cursory Remarks Made by James Birket in His Voyage to North America, 1750–1751.* New Haven, 1916. **1750–51**

BIRKMIRE, WILLIAM H. *The Planning and Construction of American Theatres.* New York, **1896**

Birmingham Emig. Co. Jrnl. See LOOMIS.

BIRNEY, HOFFMAN. *King of the Mesa.* Philadelphia, **1927**

BISHOP, JOSEPH B. *Our Political Drama Conventions Campaigns Candidates.* New York, **1904**

BISHOP, NATHANIEL H. *Four Months in a Sneak-Box.* Boston, **1879**

Voyage of the Paper Canoe. Boston, **1878**

BISHOP, ROBERT H. *An Outline of the History of the Church in the State of Kentucky.* Lexington, **1824**

BISHOP, SHERMAN C. *Handbook of Salamanders.* Ithaca, N.Y., **1943**

BITTINGER, JOHN Q. *History of Haverhill, N.H.* Haverhill, **1888**

BLACK, CARL E. *From Pioneer to Scientist.* St. Paul, **1940**

BLACK, JACK. *You Can't Win.* New York, **1926**

BLACK, JOHN, ed. *Scaffolding.* London, **1901**

Black Cat. Boston [etc.] **1895–1920**

BLAIKIE, WILLIAM G. *Summers' Suns in the Far West.* New York, **1890**

BLAINE, JAMES G. *Twenty Years in Congress.* Norwich, Conn., **1884–86**

BLAIR, WALTER. *Native American Humor.* New York, **1937**

Tall Tale America, a Legendary History of Our Humorous Heroes. New York, [**1944**]

BLAIR, WALTER, and MEINE, FRANKLIN J. *Mike Fink, King of Mississippi Keelboatmen.* New York, [c**1933**]

BLAISDELL, THOMAS C., JR. *The Federal Trade Commission.* New York, 1932. (Erroneously cited as **1923.**)

BLAKE, MORTIMER. *A Centurial History of the Mendon Association of Congregational Ministers.* Boston, **1853**

BLANCHAN, NELTJE, pseud. NELLIE B. (DE GRAFF) DOUBLEDAY. *Bird Neighbors.* New York, **1897**

BLANCHE, ERNEST E. *You Can't Win.* Washington, **1949**

BLAND, THEODORICK, JR. *The Bland Papers.* Ed. Charles Campbell. Petersburg, Va., 1840–43. **v.d.**

BLANE, WILLIAM N. *An Excursion through the United States and Canada during the Years 1822–23.* London, **1824**

BLOME, RICHARD. *The Present State of His Majesties Isles and Territories in America.* London, **1687**

BLOODGOOD, SIMEON D. *An Englishman's Sketch-Book.* New York, **1828**

BLYTHE, SAMUEL. *The Fakers.* New York, [c**1914**]

BOARDMAN, JAMES. *America, and the Americans.* London, **1833**

BOAS, FRANZ. *Handbook of American Indian Languages.* Washington, **1911**

BOHN, HENRY G. *Bohn's New Handbook of Games.* Philadelphia, **1850**

BOK, EDWARD W. *The Americanization of Edward Bok.* New York, 1921. =**1920**

BOLLER, HENRY A. *Among the Indians.* Philadelphia, **1868**

BONAPARTE, CHARLES L. *American Ornithology.* Philadelphia, **1825–33**

The Genera of North American Birds, and a Synopsis of the Species Found within the Territory of the United States. New York, **1828**

BOND, JOHN W. *Minnesota and its Resources.* New York, **1853**

BONNER, i.e., MACDOWELL, KATHERINE S. (BONNER). *Dialect Tales.* New York, **1883**

BONNER, GERALDINE. *Hard-pan; a Story of Bonanza Fortunes.* New York, **1900**

BONNYCASTLE, SIR RICHARD H. *The Canadas in 1841.* London, **1841**

BOOTH, MARY L. *History of the City of New York, from its Earliest Settlement to the Present Time.* New York, **1863**

BORNEMANN, MRS. MARY. *Madame Jane Junk and Joe.* San Francisco, **1876**

BORTHWICK, J. D. *Three Years in California.* Edinburgh, **1857**

BOSTON, MASS. CITY COUNCIL. *Documents of the City of Boston.* Boston, **v.d.**

BOSTON. REGISTRY DEPT. *Records Relating to the Early History of Boston.* Boston, 1876–1909. (Vols. I–XXVIII pub. as *Report of the Record Commissioners, 1876–1898.*) **v.d.** Individual vols. of series cited by specific titles as follows:

ASPINWALL, WILLIAM. *Notarial Records from 1644 to 1651.* **v.d.** (XXXII.)

BOSTON SELECTMEN. *Records of Boston Selectmen.* **1701–15** (XI); **1716–36** (XIII); **1736–42** (XV). *Selectmen's Minutes.* **1742/3–53** (XVIII); **1754–63** (XIX); **1764–68** (XX); **1769–75** (XXIII); **1776–86** (XXV); **1787–98** (XXVII); **1799–1810** (XXXIII); **1811–18** (XXXVIII); **1818–22** (XXXIX).

Boston (Town) Records. **1634–61** (II); **1660–1701** (VII); **1700–28** (VIII); **1729–42** (XII); **1742–57** (XIV); **1758–69** (XVI); **1770–77** (XVIII); **1778–83** (XXVI); **1784–96** (XXXI); **1796–1813** (XXXV); **1814–22** (XXXVII).

Charlestown Land Records. **v.d.** (III).

Dorchester Records. **v.d.** (IV).

Miscellaneous Papers. (X). Includes *Boston Directory q.v.* **1789, 1796**

Roxbury Land and Church Records. **v.d.** (VI.)

Boston (Commercial) Gazette. Wkly., semiwkly. **1800–15**

BOSTON. DIRECTORY. Boston, **1789**–. Also as *Stimpson's Boston Directory.* See also BOSTON. REGISTRY DEPT. *Records. Miscellaneous Papers.*

Boston Gazette or Country Journal. Wkly. **1719–98**

[*Boston Orations.*] *Orations Delivered at the Request of the Inhabitants of . . . Boston, to Commemorate the Evening of the Fifth of March, 1770.* Boston. [1785] **v.d.**

A. BOSTON TILICUM, pseud. *A Monograph on the Puyallup Indians of the State of Washington.* Tacoma, **1892**

BOSTWICK, ARTHUR E. *The American Public Library.* Boston, **1910**

BOTKIN, BEN A. *Lay My Burden Down.* Chicago, **1945**

A Treasury of New England Folklore. New York, **1947**

BOUCHER, CHAUNCEY C., and BROOKS, ROBERT P., eds. *Correspondence Addressed to John C. Calhoun, 1837–1849.* Washington, 1930. **v.d.**

BOUCHER, JONATHAN. *Boucher's Glossary of Archaic and Provincial Words, A Supplement to the Dictionaries of the English Language, Particularly those of Dr. Johnson and Dr. Webster.* Ed. Joseph Hunter and Joseph Stevenson. London, 1832–33. **v.d.**

A View of the Causes and Consequences of the American Revolution. London, 1797. **v.d.**

BOURKE, JAMES G. *Journals.* MS., West Point Military Academy. **v.d.**

On the Border with Crook. New York, 1892. **1891**

BOUVIER, JOHN. *Bouvier's Law Dictionary and Concise Encyclopedia.* 3d revision, ed. Francis Rawle. St. Paul, **1914**

A Law Dictionary, Adapted to the Constitution and Laws of the United States of America. Philadelphia, **1839.** 6th ed. Philadelphia, **1856.** 14th ed., rev. and enl., Philadelphia, **1872**

BOWDITCH, VINCENT Y. *Life and Correspondence of Henry Ingersoll Bowditch.* Boston, 1902. **v.d.**

BOWEN, CATHERINE (DRINKER). *Yankee from Olympus.* Boston, **1944.** (Author erroneously cited as "BROWN.")

BOWER, B. M., pseud. BERTHA (MUZZEY) SINCLAIR. *Flying U Ranch.* New York, **1914**

The Parowan Bonanza. Boston, **1923**

The Phantom Herd. Boston, **1916**

BOWLES, SAMUEL. *Our New West.* Hartford, **1869**

A Summer Vacation in the Parks and Mountains of Colorado. Springfield, Mass., **1869**

BOWNE, ELIZA (SOUTHGATE). *A Girl's Life Eighty Years Ago.* New York, 1887. **v.d.**

BOYCE, JOHN S. *Forest Pathology.* 2d ed., New York, **1948**

BOYD, BELLE. *Belle Boyd in Camp and Prison.* New York, **1865**

Boyd's Business Directory of over One Hundred Cities and Villages in New York State. 1869–70. Albany, **1869**

BOYNTON, CHARLES B., and MASON, TIMOTHY B. *A Journey through Kansas.* Cincinnati, **1855**

[*Br. Wtb.*] *Versuch eines Bremischniedersächsischen Wörterbuchs.* 5 vols. Bremen, **1767–71**

BRACE, CHARLES LORING. *The Dangerous Classes of New York and Twenty Years' Work Among Them.* New York, **1872**

BRACKENRIDGE, HENRY M. *Recollections of Persons and Places in the West.* Philadelphia, [**1834**]

Views of Louisiana together with a Journal of a Voyage up the Missouri River, in 1811. Pittsburgh, **1814**

BRACKENRIDGE, HUGH H. *Bunkers-Hill.* See MOSES. *Representative Plays.*

Modern Chivalry or the Adventures of Captain Farrago and Teague O'Reagan. Ed. Hugh M. Brackenridge. Philadelphia, [©1846] v.d.
BRACKETT, GEORGE E. *Farm Talk*. Boston, 1868
BRADBURY, JOHN. *Travels in the Interior of America*. London, 1817
BRADFORD, JOHN. *Historical Notes on Kentucky*. San Francisco, 1932. 1826
BRADFORD, ROARK. *Ol' Man Adam an' His Chillun*. New York, 1928
BRADFORD, WILLIAM. *Bradford's History "Of Plimoth Plantation." From the Original Manuscript*. Boston, 1899. =1898. Also pub. as *History of Plymouth Plantation 1620–1647*. 2 vols. Boston, 1912. *a*1656
BRADLEY, CYRUS P. *Biography of Isaac Hill, of New-Hampshire*. Concord, N.H., 1835
BRADY, CYRUS T. *The Bishop*. New York, 1903
BRAINERD, DAVID. *Diary* [and *Journal*]. London, 1902. v.d.
BRAINTREE, MASS. *Records of the Town . . . 1640 to 1793*. Ed. Samuel A. Bates. Randolph, Mass., 1886. v.d.
BRAMAN, D. E. E. *Braman's Information about Texas*. Philadelphia, 1857
BRANCH, DOUGLAS. *The Cowboy and His Interpreters*. New York, 1926
BRANDE, WILLIAM T., ed. *A Dictionary of Science, Literature, and Art*. New York, 1843
BRANT, IRVING. *James Madison* Indianapolis, [©1921]
BRAUNS, ERNST L. *Praktische Belehrungen und Rathschläge für Reisende und Auswanderer nach Amerika*. Braunschweig, 1829
BRAY, WILLIAM L. *Vegetation of the Sotol Country in Texas*. Austin, 1905
BRAYLEY, ARTHUR W. *A Complete History of the Boston Fire Department*. Boston, 1889
BREAKENRIDGE, WILLIAM M. *Helldorado, Bringing the Law to the Mesquite*. Boston, 1928
BREARLEY, HARRINGTON C. *Homicide in the United States*. Chapel Hill, 1932
BREAZEALE, JOHN M. *Color Schemes of Cacti*. Tucson, [1930]
BRECK, SAMUEL. *Recollections . . . , with Passages from His Notebooks, (1771–1862)*. Ed. Horace E. Scudder. Philadelphia, 1877. v.d.
BRECKENRIDGE, SOPHONISBA P., and ABBOTT, EDITH. *The Delinquent Child and the Home*. New York, 1912
BREEN, MATTHEW P. *Thirty Years of New York Politics Up-to-date*. New York, 1899
BRERETON, JOHN. *A Briefe and True Relation of the Discouerie of the North Part of Virginia*. London, 1602. (Facs. repr. in *The Bibliographer*, New York, Oct.–Dec. 1902.)
BREVARD, JOSEPH. *Brevard Papers*. MSS., N.C. Historical Commission, Raleigh, v.d.
Diary, 1791. MS., University of N.C., 1791
BREWER, WILLIAM H. *Rocky Mountain Letters, 1869*. Ed. Edmund B. Rogers. Denver, 1930. 1869
BREWERTON, GEORGE D. *Overland with Kit Carson*. New York, 1930. 1853
The War in Kansas. New York, 1856. Repr. 1859 as *Wars on the Western Border*.
BREWSTER, EDWIN T. *Life and Letters of Josiah Dwight Whitney*. Boston, 1909. v.d.
BRICE, JOHN J. *Report on the Fisheries of Indian River, Florida*. Washington, 1897
BRICE, WALLACE A. *History of Fort Wayne*. Fort Wayne, Ind., 1868
BRICKELL, JOHN. *The Natural History of North-Carolina*. Raleigh, 1911. 1737
BRIGGS, CHARLES F. *The Adventures of Harry Franco*. New York, 1839
The Trippings of Tom Pepper. 2 vols. New York, 1847–50
BRIGHAM YOUNG ACADEMY, Provo, Utah. *17th Circular, 1892–3*. Salt Lake City, 1892
BRIMLEY, CLEMENT S. *The Insects of North Carolina*. Raleigh, 1938
BRININSTOOL, EARL A. *Trail Dust of a Maverick*. New York, 1914
BRISSOT DE WARVILLE, JACQUES PIERRE. *Neue Reise durch die Nordamerikanischen Freistaaten im Jahr 1788*. Berlin, 1792
BRISTED, CHARLES A. *The English Language in America*. (In *Cambridge Essays, Contributed by Members of the University*.) London, [?1855] 1855
Five Years in an English University. 2d ed. New York, 1852
The Upper Ten Thousand: Sketches of American Society. 2d ed. rev. New York, 1852
BRISTED, JOHN. *The Resources of the United States of America*. New York, 1818
BRISTOL, VA. *Vestry Book and Register . . . 1720–1789*. Transcribed and pub. by Churchill G. Chamberlayne. Richmond, 1898. v.d.
BRITTON, NATHANIEL L., and BROWN, ADDISON. *An Illustrated Flora of the Northern United States*. New York, 1896–98
BRITTON, WILTON E. *Check-List of the Insects of Connecticut*. Hartford, 1920
Broadside Verse. See WINSLOW, O. E.
BROCKETT, LINUS P. *Our Country's Wealth and Influence*. Hartford, 1882
BRODHEAD, EVA W. (MCGLASSON). *Bound in Shallows*. New York, 1897
BROMME, TRAUGOTT. *Neustes vollständigestes Hand- und Reisebuch für Auswanderer*. Bayreuth, 1846
BROMWELL, WILLIAM. *Locomotive Sketches, with Pen and Pencil*. Philadelphia, 1854
BRONSON, EDGAR B. *The Red-Blooded Heroes of the Frontier*. New York, [©1910]
Reminiscences of a Ranchman. Rev. ed., Chicago, 1910
BROOKHAVEN, N.Y. *Records . . . Up to 1800*. Patchogue, N.Y., 1880. v.d.
BROOKS, HENRY M. *The Olden Time Series: Gleanings Chiefly from Old Newspapers of Boston and Salem, Massachusetts*. 6 vols. Boston, 1886. v.d.
BROOKS, NOAH. *The Boys of Fairport*. New York, 1924. =1898. First pub., in part, as *The Fairport Nine*. New York, 1880
BROOKS, VAN WYCK. *The World of Washington Irving*. New York, [1944]
[*Brother Bull-us*.] *The Beauties of Brother Bull-us, by His Loving Sister Bull-a*. (By James K. Paulding.) New York, 1812
BROTHERS, THOMAS. *The United States of North America as They Are*. London, 1840. v.d.
BROWN, ALICE. *Meadow-Grass*. Boston, 1895
Old Crow. New York, 1922
Tiverton Tales. Boston, [©1899]
BROWN, CHARLES BROCKDEN. *Arthur Mervyn*. Philadelphia, 1887. First pub. 1799–1800
Wieland; or, The Transformation. Philadelphia, 1887. 1798
BROWN, GARRETT. *How to Beat the Game*. New York, 1903
BROWN, HARRY P. *Trees of Northeastern United States Native and Naturalized*. Rev. ed., Boston, 1938
BROWN, HELEN D. *Two College Girls*. Boston, 1886
BROWN, J. HAMMOND. *Outdoors Unlimited*. New York, 1947
BROWN, JAMES. *The Letter Book of James Brown of Providence*. Providence, 1929. v.d.
BROWN, SAMUEL R. *The Western Gazetteer; or Emigrant's Directory*. Auburn, N.Y., 1817
BROWN, THOMAS. *A Plain Narrative of the Uncommon Sufferings, and Remarkable Deliverance of Thomas Brown*. Boston, 1760
BROWN, URIA. *Journal*. (Maryland Historical Magazine, X–XI.) v.d.
BROWN, WILLIAM. *America: A Four Years' Residence in the United States and Canada*. Leeds, Eng., 1849
BROWNE, CHARLES FARRAR. *Artemus Ward: His Book*. New York, 1864. =1852
Artemus Ward: His Travels. New York, 1865
BROWNE, DANIEL J. *The American Poultry Yard*. New York, 1855. =1850
The Sylva Americana. Boston, 1832
The Trees of America. New York, 1846
BROWNE, JOHN ROSS. *Adventures in the Apache Country*. New York, 1867
Resources of the Pacific Slope. New York, 1869
BROWNE, JUNIUS H. *Four Years in Secessia*. Hartford, 1865. v.d.
The Great Metropolis; a Mirror of New York. Hartford, 1869
BROWNELL, CHARLES D. *The Indian Races of North and South America*. Hartford, 1853
BROWNELL, WILLIAM L. *The Horse and Buggy Philosopher*. Kalamazoo, Mich., 1939
BROWNLOW, WILLIAM G. *Sketches of the Rise, Progress, and Decline of Secessionism*. Philadelphia, 1862
BRUCE, PHILIP A. *Economic History of Virginia in the Seventeenth Century*. New York, 1895
The Plantation Negro as a Freeman. New York, 1889
BRUNCKEN, ERNEST. *North American Forests and Forestry*. New York, 1900
BRYAN, KIRK. *The Papago Country, Arizona*. Washington, 1925
BRYAN, WILLIAM JENNINGS. *Memoirs*. Philadelphia, [©1925]
BRYANT, EDWIN. *What I Saw in California*. New York, 1848. Also pub. as *Rocky Mountain Adventures*. New York, [?1885].
BRYANT, WILLIAM CULLEN. *Poetical Works*. Roslyn Ed. New York, 1925. =1903. v.d. (Poems occasionally cited by individual titles and line numbers.)
BRYANT, WILLIAM CULLEN, and GAY, SYDNEY H. *A Popular History of the United States*. New York, 1876–81
BRYCE, JAMES, VISCOUNT. *The American Commonwealth*. 3 vols. London, 1888
BÜCHELE, KARL. *Land und Volk der Vereinigten Staaten von Nord-Amerika*. Stuttgart, 1855
BUCK, ALBERT H., ed. *A Reference Handbook of the Medical Sciences*. New York, 1885–93
BUCKBEE, EDNA B. *The Saga of Old Tuolumne*. New York, 1935
Buckeye Informer. Delphos, O., 1906–15
BUCKINGHAM. *Journals*. See KNIGHT, S.
BUCKINGHAM, JAMES S. *America, Historical, Statistical, and Descriptive*. 3 vols. London, [1841]. Also 2 vols. New York, 1841
The Eastern and Western States of America. London, [1842]
The Slave States of America. London, [1842]
BUCKINGHAM, JOSEPH T. *Specimens of Newspaper Literature; with Personal Memoirs, Anecdotes, and Reminiscences*. Boston, 1850. v.d.
BUCKMASTER, pseud. HENRIETTA HENKLE. *Let My People Go; the Story of the Underground Railroad and the Growth of the Abolition Movement*. New York, [©1941]
Buckskin Mose. See PERRIE.
BUDD, THOMAS. *Good Order Established in Pennsilvania & New-Jersey in America, Being a True Account of the Country*. Philadelphia, 1685
BUEL, JAMES W. *The Border Outlaws*. St. Louis, 1881. Includes, with sep. paging *The Border Bandits . . . Jesse and Frank James, and Their Bands of Highwaymen*.
Metropolitan Life Unveiled. Philadelphia, 1882
BUEL, JESSE. *The Farmer's Companion*. 2d ed. Boston, 1840. 1839
BULKELEY, GERSHOM. *Will and Doom*. (Connecticut Historical Society. *Collections*. III.) 1692
BULLARD, FANNIE J. (CURTIS). *Now-a-Days*. Bangor, Me., 1854
BULLOCK, WILLIAM. *Sketch of a Journey through the Western States of North America*. London, 1827
BUMP, GARDINER, *et al. Ruffed Grouse*. New York, 1947
BUNGAY, GEORGE W. *Off-Hand Takings*. New York, 1857
BUNN, ALFRED. *Old England and New England*. London, 1853
BUNNER, HENRY CUYLER. *Zadoc Pine, and Other Stories*. New York, 1891
BURDETTE, ROBERT J. *Hawk-Eyes*. New York, 1879
The Rise and Fall of the Mustache and other "Hawk-Eyetems." Burlington, Iowa, 1877
BURDICK, ARTHUR J. *The Mystic Mid-Region, the Deserts of the Southwest*. New York, 1904
BURDICK, USHER L. *History of the Farmers' Political Action in North Dakota*. Baltimore, 1944
BURGESS, GELETT. *Find the Woman*. Indianapolis, [©1911]
BURK, JOHN D. *The History of Virginia, from Its First Settlement to the Present Day*. Petersburg, Va., 1804–16
BURKE, EMILY P. *Reminiscences of Georgia*. [Oberlin, O.], 1850
BURKE, THOMAS A., ed. *Polly Peablossom's Wedding; and Other Tales*. Philadelphia, [©1851]
BURNABY, ANDREW. *Travels Through the Middle Settlements in North-America*. 2d ed., London, 1775
BURNETT, PETER H. *Recollections and Opinions of an Old Pioneer*. New York, 1880
BURNHAM, CLARA L. (ROOT). *Jewel: a Chapter in Her Life*. New York, [1903]
BURNHAM, GEORGE P. *Stray Subjects*. See DURIVAGE AND BURNHAM.
Three Years with Counterfeiters. Boston, [1875]
BURNS, WALTER NOBLE. *Tombstone, an Iliad of the Southwest*. Garden City, N.Y., 1927
BURR, GEORGE L., ed. *Narratives of the Witchcraft Cases, 1648–1706*. New York, 1914
BURRITT, ELIHU. *A Walk from London to Land's End, and Back*. 2d ed. London, 1868. 1864
BURROUGHS, JOHN. *Birds and Poets; with Other Papers*. Boston, 1893. =1877
Fresh Fields. Boston, 1885 [1884]
In the Catskills. Boston, New York, 1910
Locusts and Wild Honey. Boston, 1879
Pepacton. Boston, [©1909] 1881
Riverby. Boston, 1904. 1895
Wake-Robin. 2d ed. Boston, 1886. 1871
Winter Sunshine. Edinburgh, 1883. 1875
BURROUGHS, WILLIAM H. *A Treatise on the Law of Taxation*. New York, 1877
BURTON, WILLIAM E. *Burton's Comic Songster*. Pittsburgh, 1838
Waggeries and Vagaries. Philadelphia, 1848
BUSCH, MORITZ. *Wanderungen zwischen Hudson und Mississippi 1851 und 1852*. Stuttgart; Tübingen, 1854

BUSHNELL, HORACE. *Forgiveness and Law*. New York, **1874**
Work and Play. New York, 1864. **v.d.**
BUTLER, PARDEE. *Personal Recollections*. Cincinnati, **1889**
BUTTRICK. See THWAITES.
BYNNER, EDWIN L. *Agnes Surriage*. Boston, [c**1886**]
BYRD, WILLIAM. *Writings*. Ed. John S. Bassett. New York, 1901. **v.d.**
History of the Dividing Line, and Other Tracts. Ed. Thomas H. Wynne. Richmond, Va., 1866. Includes *History of the Dividing Line*. **1738.** *A Journey to the Land of Eden*. **1733.** *A Progress to the Mines*. **1732.** (Each cited also from his *Writings*.)
William Byrd's Histories of the Dividing Line Betwixt Virginia and North Carolina. Raleigh, N.C., 1929. Contains *The Secret History of the Line*. c**1738**
BYRDSALL, F. *The History of the Loco-Foco, or Equal Rights Party*. New York, 1842. **v.d.**
BYRN, MARCUS L. *The Life and Adventures of an Arkansaw Doctor*. Philadelphia, **1851**

C

CABLE, GEORGE WASHINGTON. *Bonaventure, a Prose Pastoral of Acadian Louisiana*. London, **1888**
Dr. Sevier. New York, 1889. =1885. First pub. 1883–84. **v.d.**
The Grandissimes. New York, 1922. =**1880**
John March, Southerner. New York, **1894**
CABOT, JAMES E. *A Memoir of Ralph Waldo Emerson*. Boston, **1887**
CADY, DANIEL L. *Rhymes of Vermont Rural Life*. 5th ed., Rutland, Vt., 1923. **1919.** 2d series. 2d ed., Rutland, Vt., 1926. **1922**
CAHALANE, VICTOR H. *Mammals of North America*. New York, **1947**
Meeting the Mammals. New York, **1943**
CAHAN, ABRAHAM. *The Rise of David Levinsky*. New York, [**1917**]
CALDWELL, ERSKINE. *American Earth*. New York, **1931**
You Have Seen Their Faces. New York, [c**1937**]
Calendar of State Papers, Colonial Series. America and West Indies. (Great Britain Public Record Office.) **v.d.**
Calendar of Virginia State Papers and Other Manuscripts . . . Preserved in the Capitol at Richmond. Richmond, 1875–93. **v.d.**
CALHOUN, FRANCES B. *Miss Minerva and William Green Hill*. Chicago, **1909**
California Chronicle, Daily. San Francisco, **1853–58**
California Claims. In 30th Cong., 1 Sess. Senate Rep. No. 75. 23 Feb., 1848. **v.d.**
CALKINS, EARNEST ELMO, and HOLDEN, RALPH. *Modern Advertising*. New York, **1905**
CAMBRIDGE, MASS. PROPRIETORS. *The Register Book of the Lands and Houses . . . , with the Records of the Proprietors of the Common Lands*. Cambridge, 1896. **v.d.**
[*Cambridge Rec.*] *The Records of the Town of Cambridge (formerly Newtowne) Massachusetts. 1630–1703*. Cambridge, 1901. **v.d.**
Cammerhoff & Zeisberger Diary. See BEAUCHAMP.
CAMP, WALTER C. *Walter Camp's Book of College Sports*. New York, **1893**
CAMPBELL, DAISY R. *The Proving of Virginia*. Boston, **1915**
CAMPBELL, PATRICK. *Travels in the Interior Inhabited Parts of North America*. Edinburgh, **1793**
CAMPION, J. S. *On the Frontier*. 2d ed. London, 1878. **1877**
CANDLER, ISAAC. *A Summary View of America*. London, **1824**
Canebrake Herald. Uniontown, Ala., **1886–1914**
CANFIELD, CHAUNCEY DE LEON, ed. *The Diary of a Forty-Niner*. [Alfred T. Jackson.] Boston, 1920. **v.d.** (The **1850–52** dates herein assigned are invalid, since Jackson's "Diary" is now known to be but a clever fiction of Canfield's. First pub. San Francisco, 1906.)
CANFIELD, HENRY S. *A Maid of the Frontier*. Chicago, [c**1898**]
CANNON, LEGRAND, JR. *Look to the Mountain*. New York, **1942**
The Canteen Songster. Philadelphia, **1866**
CANTON, FRANK M. *Frontier Trails*. Boston, 1930. Written *c***1908**
The Cap and Gown. Chicago, **1895–**
Cape-Fear Recorder. Wilmington, N.C., **1816–**
CAREW, HAROLD D. *History of Pasadena and the San Gabriel Valley*. [Chicago], **1930**
CARLETON, HENRY G. *Lectures Before the Thompson Street Poker Club*. New York, [c**1889**]
The Thompson Street Poker Club. First pub., in part, 1884. **v.d.**
CARLETON, WILL. *Farm Ballads*. New York, [c1882], **1873**
Farm Festivals. New York, **1881**
Farm Legends. New York, [c**1875**]
CARLTON, ROBERT, pseud. BAYNARD R. HALL. *The New Purchase*. 2 vols. New York, **1843.** 2d ed. rev. New Albany, Ind. [c**1855**]. Indiana Centennial Ed., ed. James A. Woodburn. Princeton, 1916.
CARMER, CARL. *Stars Fell on Alabama*. New York, **1934**
Carolina, The Fundamental Constitutions of. See *Old South Leaflets*.
The Carolina Housewife; or, House and Home: By a Lady of Charleston. Charleston, S.C., **1847**
CARPENTER, FRANCIS B. *Six Months at the White House with Abraham Lincoln*. New York, **1866**
CARPENTER, RALPH G., and SIEGLER, HILBERT R. *A Sportsman's Guide to the Fresh-Water Fishes of New Hampshire*. Concord, **1947**
CARRIGHAR, SALLY. *One Day on Beetle Rock*. New York, 1945 [c**1944**]
CARRINGTON, WILLIAM J. *Safe Convoy*. Philadelphia, [**1944**]
CARROLL, BARTHOLOMEW R. *Historical Collections of South Carolina*. New York, 1836. Vol. II contains THOMAS ASH. *Carolina; or, a Description of the Present State of that Country*, **1682;** JOHN ARCHDALE. *A New Description of that Fertile & Pleasant Province of Carolina*, **1707;** JAMES GLEN. *A Description of South Carolina*, **1761**
CARROLL, CHARLES. *Extracts from the Carroll Papers*. (Maryland Historical Magazine, X–XVI.) **v.d.**
CARROLL, EDWARD, JR. *Principles and Practice of Finance*. New York, 1902. =**1895**
CARSON, CHRISTOPHER. *Kit Carson's Own Story of His Life, as Dictated to Col. and Mrs. D. C. Peters about 1856–57, and Never Before Published*. Ed. Blanche C. Grant. Taos, N.M., 1926. *c***1857**
CARSON, RACHEL L. *Food from the Sea; Fish and Shellfish of New England*. Washington, **1943**
Carson Valley News. Genoa, Nev., **1875–80**
CARTWRIGHT, GEORGE. *Captain Cartwright and His Labrador Journal*. Ed. Charles W. Townsend. Boston, 1911. **v.d.**
CARTWRIGHT, PETER. *Autobiography*. Ed. William P. Strickland. New York, 1857 [c**1856**]
CARUTHERS, WILLIAM A. *The Kentuckian in New-York*. New York, **1834**
CARVER, JONATHAN. *Travels through the Interior Parts of North America*. London, **1778**
CARWARDINE, WILLIAM H. *The Pullman Strike*. 4th ed. Chicago, **1894**
CARY, ALICE. *Ballads, Lyrics, and Hymns*. New York, **1866**
Clovernook, or, Recollections of Our Neighborhood in the West. New York, 1852 [c**1851**]
Married, not Mated. New York, **1856**
Pictures of Country Life. New York, **1859**
CASEY, CHARLES. *Two Years on the Farm of Uncle Sam*. London, **1852**
CASON, CLARENCE. *90° in the Shade*. Chapel Hill, **1935**
The Casquet of Literature: Being a Selection . . . from the Works of the Most Admired Authors. Ed. Charles Gibbon. London, 1873–74. **v.d.**
CASSADY, JOHN T., and GLENDENING, GEORGE F. *Revegetating Semidesert Lands in the Southwest*. Washington, **1940**
CASSIN, JOHN. *Illustrations of the Birds of California, Texas, Oregon, British and Russian America. Intended to Contain. . . . A General Synopsis of North American Ornithology*. Philadelphia, **1856.** (Cited as *N. Amer. Birds*.)
CASTETTER, EDWARD F., and BELL, WILLIS H. *Pima and Papago Indian Agriculture*. Albuquerque, **1942**
CASTLE, VERNON. *Modern Dancing*. New York, **1914**
CASWALL, HENRY. *America, and the American Church*. London, **1839**
The Prophet of the Nineteenth Century. London, **1843**
Catawba Journal, Charlotte, N.C., **1824–27**
CATE, WIRT ARMISTEAD, ed. *Two Soldiers: the Campaign Diaries of Thomas J. Key, C.S.A., . . . and Robert J. Campbell, U.S.A.* Chapel Hill. **v.d.**
CATESBY, MARK. *The Natural History of Carolina, Florida, and the Bahama Islands*. London, *c***1727–1743;** app. **1748**
CATHER, WILLA S. *Death Comes for the Archbishop*. New York, **1927**
A Lost Lady. New York, **1923**
My Ántonia. New York, [**1918**]
One of Ours. New York, **1922**
O Pioneers! Boston, **1913**
CATHERWOOD, MARY (HARTWELL). *Mackinac and Lake Stories*. New York, **1899**
CATLIN, GEORGE. *Illustrations of the Manners, Customs, and Condition of the North American Indians*. 8th ed. London, 1851. Also pub. as *Letters and Notes on the Manners, Customs, and Condition of the North American Indians*. 3d ed., New York, 1844. =**1841. v.d.** (Eds. cited indifferently as *Indians*.)
CATTERALL, MRS. HELEN H. (TUNNICLIFF), ed. *Judicial Cases Concerning American Slavery and the Negro*. Washington, **1926–37**
CAUGHEY, JOHN W. *Gold is the Cornerstone*. Berkeley, **1948**
CAULKINS, FRANCES M. *History of Norwich, Connecticut*. Hartford, **1866**
[*Causes Reduct. Tonnage*.] *Causes of the Reduction of American Tonnage and the Decline of Navigation Interests*. (U.S. Congress. House Committee on Causes of Reduction of American Tonnage.) Washington, **1870**
CAZNEAU, MRS. WILLIAM L. *Eagle Pass; or, Life on the Border*. New York, **1852**
Centennial Exposition. See INGRAM.
[*Centennial West Point*.] *The Centennial of the United States Military Academy*. Washington, 1904. **v.d.**
Central Watchtower and Farmer's Journal. Harrodsburg, Ky., **1827–30**
The Century Dictionary: An Encyclopedic Lexicon of the English Language. Prepared under superintendence of William Dwight Whitney. 6 vols. [1889–91] **v.d.** *Supplement*. 2 vols. **1909**
CHADWICK, HENRY. *The Art of Batting and Base Running*. New York, [c**1886**]
The Art of Pitching and Fielding. Chicago, [c**1885**]
[*Base Ball Player*.] (Occasional citation for Beadle & Co.'s *The Dime Base Ball Player q.v.*)
The Base Ball Player's Book of Reference. New York, **1867**
The Game of Base Ball. New York, [c**1868**]
CHALFANT, WILLIE ARTHUR. *Death Valley; the Facts*. Stanford University, **1930**
Gold, Guns and Ghost Towns. Stanford, **1947**
Outposts of Civilization. Boston, **1928**
The Story of Inyo. Rev. ed. Los Angeles, **1933**
CHALKLEY, LYMAN. *Chronicles of the Scotch-Irish Settlement in Virginia; Extracted from the Original Court Records*. Rosslyn, Va., [c1912–13]. **v.d.**
CHALKLEY, THOMAS. *A Journal or, Historical Account of the Life, Travels and Christian Experiences, of . . . . Thomas Chalkley*. 2d ed., London, 1751. **v.d.**
CHAMBERLAIN, E., comp. *The Indiana Gazetteer*. 3d ed. Indianapolis, **1849**
CHAMBERLAIN, RICHARD. *Lithobolia, or The Stone-Throwing Devil*. In BURR *q.v.* **1698**
CHAMBERLAIN, SAMUEL. *Nantucket, a Camera Impression*. New York, [c**1939**]
CHAMBERLIN, THOMAS C., and SALISBURY, ROLLIN D. *Geology*. New York, **1904–06**
Chambers's Journal. Edinburgh; London, **1832–**
CHAMBLISS, WILLIAM H. *Chambliss Diary; or, Society as It Really Is*. New York, **1895**
CHAMPLAIN, SAMUEL DE. *Œuvres*. 2d ed. Quebec, 1870. Vol. II includes *Des Savages*. **1603**
CHAMPLIN, JOHN D., and BOSTWICK, ARTHUR E. *The Young Folks' Cyclopædia of Games and Sports*. 2d ed. rev. New York, **1899**
CHANDLESS, WILLIAM. *A Visit to Salt Lake, being a Journey across the Plains, and a Residence in the Mormon Settlements at Utah*. London, **1857**
CHANNING, GEORGE G. *Early Recollections of Newport, . . . 1793 to 1811*. Newport, R.I., **1868**
CHANNING, WILLIAM ELLERY. *Complete Works*. New and complete ed., rearranged. London, 1884. =Boston, 1886. **v.d.**
CHAPLIN, RALPH. *Wobbly: The Rough-and-Tumble Story of an American Radical*. Chicago, **1948**
CHAPMAN, ALVAN W. *Flora of the Southern United States*. New York, **1860**
CHAPMAN, FRANK M. *Bird Life*. New York, **1897**
Handbook of Birds of Eastern North America. New York, **1895**
Charlestown Land Rec. See BOSTON. REGISTRY DEPT.
Charlotte (N.C.) *Observer*. **1886–**
CHASE, ANNIE, and CLOW, E. *Stories of Industry*. Boston, [**1891**]
CHASE, CHARLES M. *The Editor's Run in New Mexico and Colorado*. [Montpelier, Vt., 1882.] **1881**
CHASE, FREDERICK. *A History of Dartmouth College and the Town of Hanover, New Hampshire*. Cambridge, 1891–1913. **v.d.**
CHASE, JOSEPH SMEATON. *California Desert Trails*. Boston, **1919**
Yosemite Trails. Boston, **1911**

Chastellux, François Jean. *Voyages de m. le Marquis de Chastellux dans l'Amérique Septentrionale dans les années 1780, 1781, & 1782.* Paris, 1786. v.d.

Chauncy, Charles. *A Letter to a Friend, Containing Revelations on Certain Passages in a Sermon Preached . . . February 20, 1767.* Boston, 1768. 1767

Cheever, Henry T. *The Whale and His Captors; or, The Whaleman's Adventures.* New York, 1850 [©1849]

Cheley, Frank H. *Camping Out.* New York, 1933

Cheney, Mary A. (Bushnell). *Life and Letters of Horace Bushnell.* New York, 1880. v.d.

Chesnut, Mary B. (Miller). *A Diary from Dixie.* Ed. Isabella D. Martin and Myrta L. Avary. New York, 1906. v.d.

Chesnut, Victor K. *Plants Used by the Indians of Mendocino County, California.* Washington, 1902

Chesnutt, Charles W. *The Conjure Woman.* Boston, 1900. 1899

The Wife of His Youth, and Other Stories of the Color Line. Boston, 1899

Chetwood, William R. *The Voyages, Dangerous Adventures and Imminent Escapes of Captain Richard Falconer.* London, 1720

Chicago Strike of June–July, 1894, Report on the. (U.S. Strike Commission, 1894.) Washington, 1895

Chicken. See Mereness.

Child, Lydia M. (Francis). *The American Frugal Housewife.* Boston, 1832

Fact and Fiction. New York, 1846

Letters from New York. 3d ed., New York, 1846. =1845. v.d.

A Romance of the Republic. Boston, 1867

Chipman, Richard M. MS notes in a copy of 2d ed. (1859) Bartlett's *Dictionary of Americanisms.* Lent through courtesy of its owner, Professor Richard H. Shyrock, Duke University. [*c*1870]

Chittenden, William L. *Ranch Verses.* New York, 1893

Chittick, Victor L., ed. *Ring-Tailed Roarers; Tall Tales of the American Frontier.* Caldwell, Ida., 1941. v.d.

Chitwood, Oliver P. *John Tyler, Champion of the Old South.* New York, [1939]

Chopin, Kate (O'Flaherty). *Bayou Folk.* Boston, 1894

Christian, Ella Storrs. *The Days That Are No More.* Unpub. MSS in possession of Mrs. Arthur Stewart, Marion, Ala., [*c*1898]

Christian Banner. Fredericksburg, Va., 1848–62

Christison, John S. *Crime and Criminals.* Chicago, 1897

Christman, Enos. *One Man's Gold. The Letters and Journal of a Forty-Niner.* ed. Florence M. Christman. New York, 1930. v.d.

Christy, George Nathan. *George Christy's Ethiopian Joke Book, No. 3.* Philadelphia, 1860

Chronicles of Oklahoma. Oklahoma City, 1921–

Chunkey's Fight. See Porter, William T.

Church, Benjamin. *Entertaining Passages Relating to Philip's War.* Boston, 1716

Church, William C. *The Life of John Ericsson.* New York, 1890

Churchill, Winston. *The Crisis.* New York, 1901

Cimarron (N.M.) *News and Press.* 1870–1910

Cincinnati Misc. See Cist.

Cist, Charles. *Cincinnati in 1841.* Cincinnati, 1841

Comp. *The Cincinnati Miscellany, or, Antiquities of the West.* Cincinnati, 1845–46. v.d.

Sketches and Statistics of Cincinnati in 1851. Cincinnati, 1851

Claiborne, John F. H. *Life and Correspondence of John A. Quitman.* New York, [1860] v.d.

Life and Times of Gen. Sam. Dale, the Mississippi Partisan. New York, 1860

Clap, Thomas. *The Annals or History of Yale-College.* New Haven, 1766. v.d.

Clapin, Sylva. *A New Dictionary of Americanisms being a Glossary of Words Supposed to be Peculiar to the United States and Canada.* New York, [1902]

Clappe, Louise A. K. (Smith). *The Shirley Letters from California Mines in 1851–52.* San Francisco, 1922. (First pub. in *The Pioneer,* Jan., 1854–Dec., 1855, from which also cited.) v.d.

Clark, Frederick T. *On Cloud Mountain.* New York, 1894

Clark, Thomas D. *Pills, Petticoats and Plows; the Southern Country Store, 1865–1915.* Indianapolis, 1944

Clarke, Clinton C. *The Pacific Crest Trailway.* Pasadena, Calif., 1945

Clarke, Thomas W. *The Bloody Mohawk.* New York, 1940

Clarke County Democrat. Grove Hill, Ala., 1856–

Clay, Henry. *Life and Speeches.* Philadelphia, 1860. v.d.

Speeches. [Comp.] Richard Chambers. Cincinnati, 1842. v.d.

Clayton, John. *Flora Virginica.* See Gronovius.

A Letter from Mr. John Clayton . . . Giving an Account of Several Observables in Virginia. (Royal Society. *Philosophical Transactions.* XVII–XVIII.) v.d. Also in Force. *Tracts.* III. No. 12

Clayton, William. *The Latter-day Saints' Emigrants' Guide.* St. Louis, 1848

Cleaves, Freeman. *Old Tippecanoe.* New York, 1939

Cleland, Robert G. *The Cattle on a Thousand Hills.* San Marino, Calif., 1941

Clements, Frederick E. *Rocky Mountain Flowers.* White Plains, N.Y., 1914

Clendenin, William W. *A Preliminary Report upon the Florida Parishes of East Louisiana and the Bluff, Prairie and Hill Lands of Southwest Louisiana.* Baton Rouge, 1896

Clover, Samuel T. *Paul Travers' Adventures.* Chicago, 1897

Clute, Willard N. *The Common Names of Plants and Their Meanings.* Indianapolis, 1931

Cobb, Irvin S. *Back Home.* New York, [©1912]

Kansas. New York, [©1924]

Cobbett, William. *A Treatise on Cobbett's Corn.* London, 1828

A Year's Residence in the United States of America. New York, 1818

Coburn, Foster D. *Swine Husbandry.* 3d ed., rev. and enl. New York, 1903

Cockrum, William M. *History of the Underground Railroad.* Oakland City, Ind., [©1915]

Cody, Louisa (Frederici), and Cooper, Courtney Ryley. *Memories of Buffalo Bill.* New York, 1919

Cody, William F. *Story of the Wild West and Camp-Fire Chats.* Philadelphia, [1888]

Coffin, Joshua. *A Sketch of the History of Newbury, Newburyport, and West Newbury, from 1635 to 1845.* Boston, 1845. v.d.

Coffin, Robert P. Tristram. *Kennebec: Cradle of Americans.* New York, [1937]

Yankee Coast. New York, 1947

Cohen, Alfred J. *Wanted: A Cook.* Indianapolis, [©1904]

Coke, Edward T. *A Subaltern's Furlough.* New York, 1833

Colcord, Joanna C. *Sea Language Comes Ashore.* New York, 1945

Cole, Arthur C. *The Whig Party in the South.* Washington, 1913. v.d.

Cole, George E. *Early Oregon.* [Spokane, ©1905]

Coles. See Harris, M.

Collegian. Cambridge, 1830

Collender, Hugh W., ed. *Modern Billiards.* New York, 1881

Collingwood, George H., and Brush, Warren D. *Knowing Your Trees.* 11th print. Washington, 1949

Collins, Mrs. A. M. *Table Receipts, Adapted to Western Housekeeping.* New Albany, Ind., 1851

Collins, Lewis. *Historical Sketches of Kentucky.* Maysville, Ky., 1847

Collins Historical Sketches of Kentucky. Rev. by Richard H. Collins. Covington, Ky., 1874

Collins, S. H. *The Emigrant's Guide to and Description of the United States of America.* 4th ed. Hull, Eng., [1830]

Collyer, Robert H. *Lights and Shadows of American Life.* Boston, [?1844]

Colman, Henry. *European Life and Manners.* Boston, 1849

The Colonial Records of the State of Georgia. [Ed.] Allen D. Candler. Atlanta, 1904–. v.d.

Colony of Connecticut. (74th Cong., 1st Sess., Senate Doc. 53.) 1935

Colo. Gazetteer. See Wallihan.

Colt, Miriam (Davis). *Went to Kansas.* Watertown, N.Y., 1862

Colton, Joseph H. pub. *The State of Indiana Delineated.* New York, 1838

Colton, Walter. *Deck and Port.* New York, 1850

Three Years in California. New York, 1850

Columbian Centinel. Boston, 1784–1840. (Also cited as *Mass. Centinel.*)

Columbian Magazine, or Monthly Miscellany. Philadelphia, 1786–92. (From March, 1790 as *Columbian Museum; or, Universal Asylum.*)

Colville, Frederick V. *Botany of the Death Valley Expedition.* Washington, 1893

Combe, George. *Notes on the United States of America, during a Phrenological Visit in 1838–9–40.* Philadelphia, 1841

Comer, John. *The Diary of John Comer.* Ed. C. Edwin Barrows. Providence, 1893. v.d.

Commager, Henry Steele, ed. *Documents of American History.* New York, 1934. v.d.

Commercial Advertiser. New York, 1797–1904

Common Sense Cook Book. New York, 1867

Commoner. Lincoln, Neb., 1901–23

Commons, John R., *et al.,* eds. *A Documentary History of American Industrial Society.* Cleveland, 1910–11. v.d.

Comstock, Harriet T. (Smith). *The Man Thou Gavest.* Garden City, N.Y., 1917

Condict, Adelaide (Burnet). *Philip Eckert's Struggles and Triumphs.* New York, 1869 [1868]

The Condor; a Magazine of Western Ornithology. Santa Clara, [etc.] Calif. 1899–

Congregational Churches in Massachusetts, Cambridge Synod, 1648. *The Original Constitution, Order and Faith of the New-England Churches.* Boston, 1812. Includes *The Platform of Church Discipline.* 1648. *Propositions. . . . Answered by the Synod of 1662.* 1662. *A Confession of Faith, Adopted . . . 1680.* 1680. *A Platform of Church-Discipline.* Boston, 1772. 1648. See also Wise.

[*Congressional Debates.*] *Register of Debates in Congress.* (U.S. Congress.) Washington, 1825–37. v.d.

Conklin, Enoch. *Picturesque Arizona.* New York, 1878

Conkling, Roscoe P., and Conkling, Margaret B. *The Butterfield Overland Mail, 1857–1869.* Glendale, Calif. 1947

Connecticut (Colony). *Public Records.* Hartford, 1850–90. v.d.

Connecticut Courant. Hartford, 1764–1914

[*Conn. Particular Court Rec.*] *Records of the Particular Court of Connecticut.* (Connecticut Historical Society. *Collections.* XXII.) v.d.

Conn. Probate Rec. See Manwaring.

Conroy, Jack. *Midland Humor.* New York, 1947

Conway, H. J. *Hiram Hireout; or, Followed by Fortune.* New York, [18—?] 1852

Cook, Ebenezer. *The Sot-weed Factor.* New York, 1865. 1708

Sotweed Redivivus. In *Early Maryland Poetry.* Ed. Bernard C. Steiner. Baltimore, 1900. 1730

Cook, James Henry. *Fifty Years on the Old Frontier, as Cowboy, Hunter, Guide, Scout, and Ranchman.* New Haven, 1923

Cook, John R. *The Border and the Buffalo.* Topeka, Kans., 1907. Rep., ed. Milo M. Quaife, Chicago, 1938.

Cook, William H. *Letters of a Ticonderoga Farmer.* Ed. Frederick G. Bascom. Ithaca, N.Y., 1946. v.d.

Cooke, Edmund V. *Baseballogy.* Chicago, 1912

Cooke, John E. *Beatrice Hallam.* New York, 1892. =Vol. I of his *The Virginia Comedians.* New York, 1854

Ellie; or, the Human Comedy. Richmond, Va., 1855

A Life of Gen. Robert E. Lee. New York, 1871

Surry of Eagle's-Nest. New York, 1866

Cooke, Rose (Terry). *The Deacon's Week.* Boston, [n.d.] 1885

Happy Dodd. Boston, 1878

Huckleberries Gathered from New England Hills. Boston, 1896. =1891. v.d.

Somebody's Neighbors. Boston, 1881. v.d.

Steadfast: the Story of a Saint and a Sinner. Boston, 1889

Coolidge, Dane. *Texas Cowboys.* New York, [©1937]

Cooper, Courtney Ryley. *Lions 'n' Tigers 'n' Everything.* Boston, 1924

Oklahoma, a Novel. Boston, 1926

Under the Big Top. Boston, 1923. (Erroneously dated 1920, work first having been pub. serially, ©1920, 1921, 1923.)

Cooper, James Fenimore. *Afloat and Ashore.* Philadelphia, 1844

The Chainbearer. 1845

The Deerslayer. 1841

Gleanings in Europe. Ed. Robert E. Spiller. London, 1928–30. v.d. First pub. as *Recollections of Europe,* London, 1837

Home as Found. New York, 1873. 1838

Homeward Bound. New York, 1860. 1838

The Last of the Mohicans. 1826

Lionel Lincoln. 3 vols. London, [n.d.]. 1825

The Monikins. New York, 1860. 1835

Notions of the Americans. London, 1828

The Oak Openings. 2 vols. New York, 1848

The Pathfinder. Philadelphia, 1840

The Pilot. New York, 1823

The Pioneers. London, 1832. 1823

The Prairie. Boston, 1879. 1827

Recollections of Europe. See above *Gleanings in Europe.*

The Red Rover. 3 vols. London, 1827

The Redskins. 1846

The Sea Lions. 1849

The Spy. London, 1831. 1821

The Water Witch. London, 1830

The Wept of Wish-ton-Wish. New York, 1859. **1829**
The Wing-and-Wing. 2 vols. Philadelphia, **1842**
COOPER, JAMES GRAHAM. *On the Distribution of the Forests and Trees of North America.* Washington, **1859**
COOPER, SUSAN F. *Rural Hours.* New York, **1830**
COOPER, THOMAS. *Some Information respecting America.* London, **1794**
COOPER, THOMAS V., and FENTON, HECTOR T. *American Politics (Non-Partisan) from the Beginning to Date.* Philadelphia, **[1882]**
COPLEY, JOHN S., and PELHAM, HENRY. *Letters and Papers . . . , 1739–1776.* [Boston], 1914. **v.d.**
Copper Camp. (Writers' Program. Montana.) New York, **[1943]**
CORBIN, DIANA FONTAINE (MAURY). *A Life of Matthew Fontaine Maury.* London, **1888**
CORBIN, JOHN. *An American at Oxford.* New York, **1902**
CORCORAN, DENIS. *Pickings from the Portfolio of the Reporter of the New Orleans "Picayune."* Philadelphia, 1846 **[c1845]**
COUES, ELLIOTT. *Birds of the Colorado Valley.* Washington, **1878**
Birds of the Northwest. Washington, **1874**
Key to North American Birds. Salem, Mass., **1872.** 2d ed. Boston, **1884.** 3d ed. Boston, **1887**
COULTER, JOHN, M.D. *Adventures in the Pacific.* Dublin, **1845**
Adventures on the Western Coast of South America, and the Interior of California. London, 1847. **v.d.**
COULTER, JOHN MERLE. *Botany of Western Texas.* Washington, **1891–99**
COULTER, THOMAS. *Notes on Upper California.* London, **1835**
Country Life in America. Garden City, N.Y., and New York City, **1901–17**
Courier-Journal. Louisville, Ky., **1868–**
COURTENAY, FLORENCE. *Physical Beauty, How to Develop and Preserve It.* New York, **[c1922]**
COWELL, EMILIE M. (EBSWORTH). *The Cowells in America, Being the Diary of Mrs. Sam Cowell.* London, 1934. **v.d.**
COWELL, JOSEPH. *Thirty Years Passed among the Players in England and America.* New York, **1844**
COWLES, JULIA. *Diaries . . . 1707–1803.* Ed. Laura H. Moseley. New Haven, 1931. **v.d.**
COX, FRANCIS A., and HOBY, J. *The Baptists in America.* New York, **1836**
COX, ROSS. *Adventures on the Columbia River.* London, **1831**
COX, SAMUEL S. *Eight Years in Congress, from 1857 to 1865.* New York, 1865. **v.d.**
COX, SANDFORD C. *Recollections of the Early Settlement of the Wabash Valley.* Lafayette, Ind., **1860**
COXE, DANIEL. *A Description of the English Province of Carolana.* London, **1722**
COXE, TENCH. *A View of the United States of America.* Philadelphia, **1794**
COXE, WILLIAM, 1747–1828. *Account of the Russian Discoveries Between Asia and America.* London, **1780**
COXE, WILLIAM, pomologist. *A View of the Cultivation of Fruit Trees.* Philadelphia, **1817**
COYNER, DAVID H. *The Lost Trappers.* Cincinnati, 1859. **=1847**
COZZENS, FREDERIC SWARTHWOUT. *Prismatics.* New York, **1853**
The Sayings of Dr. Bushwhacker and Other Learned Men. New York, **1867**
Sparrowgrass Papers. New York, 1860. **=1856**
COZZENS, SAMUEL W. *Crossing the Quicksands.* Boston, **1877**
The Marvellous Country. Boston, [c1876] **1873**
CRABB, GEORGE. *Universal Technological Dictionary.* London, **1823**
CRADDOCK, CHARLES EGBERT, pseud. MARY N. MURFREE. *The Despot of Broomsedge Cove.* Boston, 1889 **[c1888]**
In the Tennessee Mountains. Boston, **1884**
The Mystery of Witch-Face Mountain. Boston, **1895**
The Prophet of the Great Smoky Mountains. Boston, **1885**
The Story of Keedon Bluffs. Boston, 1891 **[c1887]**
Where the Battle Was Fought. Boston, 1885. **=1884**
CRAFTS, ELIZA P. (RUSSELL) ROBBINS. *Pioneer Days in the San Bernardino Valley.* Redlands, Calif., **1906**
CRAFTS, WILBUR F. *The Sabbath for Man.* New York, **1885**
CRAMER, PIETER. *De Uitlandsche Kapellen . . . Papillons exotiques des trois partes du monde l'Asie, l'Afrique et l'Amerique.* Amsterdam, **1775–82**
CRAMTON, LOUIS C. *Early History of Yellowstone National Park.* Washington, 1932. **v.d.**
CRANE, MILTON. *Sins of New York.* New York, **[c1947] v.d.**
CRANE, STEPHEN. *George's Mother.* New York, **1896**
Maggie: A Girl of the Streets. New York, 1896. **1892**
The Third Violet. New York, **1897**
CRAPSEY, EDWARD. *The Nether Side of New York.* New York, **1872**
CRAWFORD, F. MARION. *An American Politician.* Boston, **1885**
CRAWFORD, J. MARSHALL. *Mosby and His Men.* New York, **1867**
CRAWFORD, MEDOREM. *Journal.* Eugene, Ore., 1897. **1842**
CREEVEY, CAROLINE A. (STICKNEY). *Flowers of Field, Hill, and Swamp.* New York, **1897**
CRESSWELL, NICHOLAS. *Journal . . . , 1774–1777.* New York, 1924. **v.d.**
CRÈVECŒUR, MICHAEL GUILLAUME ST. JEAN DE, *called* Saint John de Crèvecœur. *Letters from an American Farmer.* London, **1782**
Sketches of Eighteenth Century America. Ed. Henri L. Bourdin *et al.* New Haven, 1925. **v.d.**
CREW, BENJAMIN J. *A Practical Treatise on Petroleum.* Philadelphia, **1887**
Crisis. Columbus, O., **1861–71**
CRISSEY, FORREST. *Alexander Legge, 1866–1933.* Chicago, **1936**
Tattlings of a Retired Politician. Chicago, **1904**
CRISWELL, ELIJAH H. *Lewis and Clark: Linguistic Pioneers.* (*University of Missouri Studies.* XV, No. 2.) **v.d.**
CROCKETT, DAVID. *An Account of Col. Crockett's Tour to the North and Down East, in the Year of the Lord One Thousand Eight Hundred and Thirty-four.* Philadelphia, **1835**
Col. Crockett's Exploits and Adventures in Texas. Philadelphia, **1836.** (Pseudo-autobiography attrib. to Richard Penn Smith.)
[*Crockett Almanacs, 1835–52.*] (Pub. Nashville, etc., under varying titles: *Davy Crockett's Almanac; Crockett's Yaller Flower Almanac;* etc.)
The Life and Adventures of Colonel David Crockett of West Tennessee. Cincinnati, **1833**
A Narrative of the Life of David Crockett. Philadelphia, **1834**
Sketches and Eccentricities of Col. David Crockett, of West Tennessee. Louisville, [n.d.] **=1833**
CROFUTT, GEORGE A. *Trans-continental Tourist.* New York, **1876**
CROGHAN, GEORGE. *Journal.* [Burlington, N.J., 1875.] **1765.** See also THWAITES.
CROLY, HERBERT D. *Marcus Alonzo Hanna; His Life and Work.* New York, **1912**
CRONEIS, CAREY, and KRUMBEIN, WILLIAM C. *Down to Earth: an Introduction to Geology.* Chicago, **[1936]**
CRONISE, TITUS F. *The Natural Wealth of California.* San Francisco, **1868**
CROW, CARL. *The Great American Customer.* New York, **1943**
CROY, HOMER. *Corn Country.* New York, **[1947]**
How Motion Pictures are Made. New York, **[c1918]**
R. F. D. No. 3. New York, **1924**
CRUMPTON, HEZEKIAH, and CRUMPTON, W. B. *The Adventures of Two Alabama Boys.* Montgomery, **1912**
CULLOM, RIDGWELL. *The Watchers of the Plains.* Philadelphia, **1909**
Cultivator. Albany, **1834–65**
CUMING, FORTESCUE. [*Western Tour.*] *Sketches of a Tour to the Western Country.* Pittsburgh, **1810**
CUMINGS, SAMUEL. *The Western Pilot.* Cincinnati, **1829.** Other eds. **1832; 1843**
CUMMING, KATE. *A Journal of Hospital Life.* Louisville, **[c1866] v.d.**
CUMMINGS, HORACE S. *Dartmouth College. Sketches of the Class of 1862.* Washington, **1909**
CUMMINGS, RICHARD O. *The American and His Food.* Chicago, **1940–41**
CUMMINS, MARIA S. *The Lamplighter.* Boston, 1890. **=1854**
CUMMINS, RALPH. *Sky-high Corral.* London, **[c1924]**
CUNNINGHAM, ALBERT B. *The Chronicle of an Old Town.* Cincinnati, **[1919]**
CURTIS, EDWARD S. *The North American Indian.* [Seattle], **1907–30**
CURTIS, GEORGE W. *Horses, Cattle, Sheep and Swine.* 2d ed., rev. and enl. New York, **1893**
CURTIS, GEORGE WILLIAM. *Nile Notes of a Howadji.* New York, **[c1851]**
Prue and I. New York, 1892. **1856**
CURTIS, MOSES A. *Botany: containing a Catalogue of . . . the Trees, Shrubs and Woody Vines.* Raleigh, N.C., **1860.** (Cited by cover title *The Woody Plants of North-Carolina.*)
CURWOOD, JAMES OLIVER. *The Country Beyond.* New York, **1922**
CUSHING, FRANK H. *Zuñi Breadstuff.* New York, **1920**
CUSHING, MARSHALL H. *The Story of Our Post Office.* Boston, **1893**
CUSHMAN, HORATIO B. *History of the Choctaw, Chickasaw and Natchez Indians.* Greenville, Tex., **1899**
CUSTER, ELIZABETH (BACON). *Boots and Saddles.* New York, **1885**
Following the Guidon. New York, **1890**
Tenting on the Plains. New York, 1889. **=1887**
CUTLER, CARL C. *Greyhounds of the Sea.* New York, London, **1930**
CUTLER, JERVIS. *A Topographical Description of the State of Ohio.* Boston, **1812**
CUTLER, WILLIAM P., and CUTLER, JULIA P. *Life, Journals and Correspondence of Rev. Manasseh Cutler, LL.D.* Cincinnati, 1888. **v.d.**
CUTTING, GEORGE R. *Student Life at Amherst College.* Amherst, Mass., **1871**

D

Daily Chronicle. London, **1869–1930**
Daily Express. London (*OED*)
Daily News. London (*OED*)
DALE, EDWARD E. *Cow Country.* Norman, Okla., **1942**
DALE, EDWARD EVERETT, and RADER, JESSE L. *Readings in Oklahoma History.* Evanston, Ill., **[c1930]**
DALE, HARRISON C., ed. *The Ashley-Smith Explorations and the Discovery of a Central Route to the Pacific 1822–1829.* Cleveland, 1918. **v.d.**
DALL, WILLIAM H. *Alaska and Its Resources.* Boston, **1870**
DALRYMPLE, BRYON W. *Panfish.* New York, **[1947]**
DALRYMPLE, LUCINDA L. *Journal of a Young Lady of Virginia.* [Ed. Emily V. Mason.] Baltimore, 1871. **1782**
DALTON, WILLIAM. *Travels in the United States of America, and Part of Upper Canada.* Appleby, Eng., **1821**
DALY, AUGUSTIN. (Dates in boldface usu. those of first perf.) *After Business Hours.* New York: Priv. pr. **1886**
The Big Bonanza. New York: Priv. pr. 1884. **1875**
Divorce. New York: Priv. pr. 1884. **1871**
The Great Unknown. New York: Priv. pr. 1890. **1889**
A Legend of "Norwood." New York: Priv. pr. **1867**
Little Miss Million. [New York] Priv. pr. 1893. **1892**
The Lottery of Love. [New York] Priv. pr. 1887. **1888**
Love in Harness. [New York] Priv. pr. 1887. **1886**
Nancy and Company. New York: Priv. pr. **1886**
Our English Friend. New York: Priv. pr. 1884. **1882**
Pique. New York: Priv. pr. 1884. **1875**
The Railroad of Love. [New York] Priv. pr. **[1887]**
A Test Case; or, Grass versus Granite. New York: Priv, pr. 1893. **1892**
Under the Gaslight. New York: Author's ed. **1867**
DALY, JOSEPH F. *The Life of Augustin Daly.* New York, 1917. **v.d.**
DAMON, BERTHA. *Grandma Called it Carnal.* New York, **1938**
A Sense of Humus. New York, **1943**
DANA, C. W. *The Great West, or, The Garden of the World.* Boston, 1857. =his *The Garden of the World, or, The Great West.* **1856**
DANA, CHARLES A. *Recollections of the Civil War.* New York, 1902 [c1898] **1897**
DANA, EDMUND. *Geographical Sketches on the Western Country.* Cincinnati, **1819**
DANA, FRANCES T. (SMITH). *How to Know the Wild Flowers.* 3d ed. New York, **1893**
DANA, JAMES DWIGHT. *Geology.* Philadelphia, **1849**
Manual of Geology. Philadelphia, 1863 **[c1862]**
Manual of Mineralogy. New ed., rev. and enl. London, **1873.** New ed. first pub. New Haven, 1857. (Other eds. also cited.)
DANA, RICHARD HENRY. *The Seaman's Manual.* London, **1841**
Two Years before the Mast. New York, 1862. **=1840.** New ed., Boston, 1884. **=1869**

DANIEL, LIZZIE (CARY). *Confederate Scrap-Book.* Richmond, Va., 1893. **v.d.**
DANIELS, JONATHAN. *Tar Heels.* New York, **1941**
DARBY, WILLIAM. *The Emigrant's Guide to the Western and Southern Territories.* New York, **1818**
A Geographical Description of the State of Louisiana. Philadelphia, **1816.** 2d ed., enl., and impr. New Orleans, **1817**
DARLINGTON, WILLIAM. *Agricultural Botany.* Philadelphia, **1847**
American Weeds and Useful Plants: Being a Second and Illustrated Edition [of above]. Rev. by George Thurber. New York, 1860. =**1859**
Flora Cestrica. The Flowering and Filicoid Plants of Chester County. Philadelphia, **1837**
DARROW, CLARENCE S. *Farmington.* Chicago, **1904**
Dartmouth. Hanover, N.H., **1839–44**
DARTON, NELSON H. *Preliminary Report on the Geology and Water Resources of Nebraska West of the One Hundred and Third Meridian.* Washington, **1899**
DAVENPORT, WARREN G. *Butte and Montana beneath the X-Ray.* Butte, **1908**
DAVIDGE, WILLIAM P. *Footlight Flashes.* New York, **1866**
DAVIDSON, ALICE M. *California Plants in Their Homes.* Los Angeles, **1898**
DAVIDSON, JAMES W. *Florida of To-day.* New York, **1889**
DAVIDSON, ROBERT. *History of the Presbyterian Church in the State of Kentucky.* New York, **1847**
DAVIES, EBENEZER. *American Scenes and Christian Slavery.* London, **1849**
DAVIES, MARY CAROLYN. *The Skyline Trail, a Book of Western Verse.* Indianapolis, **1924**
DAVIS, ANDREW McF., ed. *Tracts Relating to the Currency of the Massachusetts Bay, 1682–1720.* Boston, 1902. **v.d.**
DAVIS, BRITTON. *The Truth about Geronimo.* New Haven, **1929**
DAVIS, CHARLES AUGUSTUS. *Letters of J. Downing.* New York, **1834.** (Not to be confused with Seba Smith's *The Select Letters of Major Jack Downing q.v.* 1834.)
DAVIS, CHARLES B. *The Borderland of Society.* Chicago, **1898**
DAVIS, CHARLES HENRY, ed. *Narrative of the North Polar Expedition . . . U.S. Ship Polaris.* Washington, **1876**
DAVIS, HUGH. *Farm Book.* (A plantation diary kept on Beaver Bend Farm, near Cahaba River, Alabama, during 1854–55; in private ownership of the Davis family, Marion, Alabama.) **v.d.**
DAVIS, JOHN. *Travels of Four Years and a Half in the United States of America.* London, **1803**
DAVIS, MARY L. (CALDWELL). *We Are Alaskans.* Boston, [c**1931**]
DAVIS, NORAH. *The Northerner.* New York, **1905**
DAVIS, PARKE H. *Football, the American Intercollegiate Game.* New York, 1911. **v.d.**
DAVIS, PETER S. *The Young Parson.* Philadelphia, **1863**
DAVIS, RICHARD HARDING. *Gallegher, and Other Stories.* New York, 1913. First pub. 1891. **v.d.**
DAVIS, WILLIAM HEATH. *Seventy-Five Years in California.* Ed. Douglas S. Watson. San Francisco, 1929. **v.d.**
DAVIS, WILLIAM MORRIS. *Physical Geography.* Boston, **1898**
DAVIS, WILLIAM W. H. *El Gringo.* New York, **1857**
DAVY, JOSEPH B. *Investigations on the Natural Vegetation of Alkali Lands.* Sacramento, **1898**
DAWSON, CHARLES. *Pioneer Tales of the Oregon Trail and of Jefferson County.* Topeka, Kans., **1912**
DAWSON, SAMUEL E. *Hand-book for the Dominion of Canada,* Montreal, **1884**
DAY, HOLMAN F. *Kin o' Ktaadn.* Boston, **1904**
King Spruce. New York, **1908**
DAYTON, WILLIAM A. *Important Western Browse Plants.* Washington, **1931**
DEAM, CHARLES C. *Flora of Indiana.* Indianapolis, **1940**
Grasses of Indiana. Indianapolis, **1929**
Shurbs of Indiana. Indianapolis, **1924**
Trees of Indiana. Fort Wayne, **1921**
DEANE, JOHN. *Deane's Manual of the History and Science of Fire-arms.* London, **1858**
DEANE, SAMUEL. *Diary; Journal.* See SMITH, THOMAS.
The New-England Farmer; or, Georgical Dictionary. Worcester, **1790.** 2d ed., corr., impr., enl. Worcester, **1797**
DEANE, SILAS. *Correspondence . . . , 1774–1776.* (Connecticut Historical Society. *Publications.* II.) **v.d.**
The Deane Papers, . . . 1771–1795. Hartford, 1930. **v.d.**
DEARBORN, BENJAMIN. *The Columbian Grammar.* Boston, **1785**
[*Debates in Mass. Conv.*] *Debates and Proceedings in the Convention. . . . Held in the Year 1788.* Ed. Bradford K. Peirce and Charles Hale. (Massachusetts Convention, 1788.) Boston, 1856. **1788**
DE CASTRO, ADOLPHE D. *Portrait of Ambrose Bierce.* New York, [c**1929**]
DECOIN, ROBERT L. *History & Cultivation of Cotton and Tobacco.* London, **1864**
Decorum: A Practical Treatise on Etiquette and Dress of the Best American Society. New York, 1880. **1878**
DEDHAM, MASS. *The Early Records of the Town.* Dedham, 1886–99. **v.d.**
DE GROOT, HENRY. *Sketches of the Washoe Silver Mines.* San Francisco, **1860**
DE KRUIF, PAUL H. *Microbe Hunters.* New York, [**1926**]
DELAND, MARGARET. *Florida Days.* Boston, **1889**
John Ward, Preacher. Boston, **1888**
Old Chester Tales. New York, [c**1898**]
DELANEY, MATILDA J. (SAGER). *A Survivor's Recollections of the Whitman Massacre.* Spokane, Wash., [c**1920**]
Delaware County (N.Y.) *Deeds.* (In *Dialect Notes.* II. 132.) **v.d.**
DEMING, PHILANDER. *Adirondack Stories.* Boston, **1880**
[*Democrat.*] *Clarke County Democrat.* Grove Hill, Ala., **1856–**
DENNY, EBENEZER. *Military Journal.* Philadelphia, 1859. **v.d.**
DENTON, DANIEL. *A Brief Description of New-York.* Facsimile, New York, 1937. **1670**
DENTON, SHELLEY W. *Pages from a Naturalist's Diary.* Ed. Vanessa Denton. [Wellesley, Mass., 1949] **v.d.**
DEPEW, CHAUNCEY M. *Orations, Addresses and Speeches,* New York, 1890. **v.d.**
DERBY, CONN. *Town Records.* Derby, 1901. **v.d.**
DERBY, GEORGE H. *Phœnixiana.* New York, 1859. =**1856**
D'ERES, i.e., ROUSO D'ERES, CHARLES D. *Memoirs.* Exeter, N.H., **1800**
DERVILLE, LESLIE. *The Other Side of the Story.* New York, [**1904**]
A Description of Kentucky. See TOULMIN.
A Description of South Carolina. See GLEN.
Description of Virginia, A Perfect. See FORCE.
DE SMET, PIERRE J. *Letters and Sketches.* Philadelphia, **1843**
Oregon Missions and Travels over the Rocky Mountains, in 1845–46. New York, 1847. **v.d.**
DE VERE, i.e., SCHELE DE VERE, MAXIMILIAN R. B. *Americanisms; the English of the New World.* New York, 1872 [c**1871**]
DEVINS, JOHN B. *An Observer in the Philippines.* Boston, [**1905**]
DE VOE, THOMAS F. *The Market Assistant.* New York, **1867**
The Market Book. New York, 1862. **v.d.**
DEVOTO, BERNARD. *Across the Wide Missouri.* Boston, **1947**
The Year of Decision: 1846. Boston, **1943**
DEWEES, MARY (COBURN). *Journal of a Trip from Philadelphia to Lexington in Kentucky.* MS, University of Chicago Library. **1788.** (Subsequently pub. at Crawfordsville, Ind., 1936.)
DEWEES, WILLIAM B. *Letters from an Early Settler of Texas.* Comp. Cara Cardelle [pseud.]. Louisville, 1852. **v.d.**
DEWEY, CHESTER. [*Mass. Flowering Plants.*] *Report on the Herbaceous Flowering Plants of Massachusetts.* Cambridge, **1840**
De Witt's Base-Ball Guide for 1878. Ed. Henry Chadwick. New York, [c**1878**]
Dialect Notes. Norwood, Mass., etc., **1890–1939**
Diary of a Day Debutante. See RANOUS.
The Diary of a Forty-Niner. See CANFIELD, C. D.
DIBBLE, HENRY C. *Why Reconstruction Failed.* New Orleans, **1877**
DICE, GEORGE W. *Life of George W. Dice, Called the King of Counterfeiters.* Chicago, **1896.** (Presumably the work cited as *Counterfeiting Exposed.*)
DICE, LEE R. *The Biotic Provinces of North America.* Ann Arbor, Mich., **1943**
DICEY, EDWARD. *Six Months in the Federal States.* London, **1863**
DICK, EVERETT N. *The Dixie Frontier.* New York, **1948**
The Sod-House Frontier. New York, **1938**
DICK, WILLIAM B. *The American Hoyle.* 2d ed. New York [?1866; c**1864**]; 13th ed. New York, **1880;** 17th ed. New York, **1898**
DICKENS, CHARLES. *American Notes for General Circulation.* New York: Harper, **1842.** Also 2 vols. London, **1842**
DICKERSON, MARY C. *The Frog Book.* New York, **1906**
Moths and Butterflies. Boston, [c**1901**]
DICKINSON, JONATHAN. *God's Protecting Providence Man's Surest Help and Defence.* Philadelphia, **1699**
DICKSON, ALBERT J. *Covered Wagon Days, . . . from the Private Journals of Albert Jerome Dickson.* Ed. Arthur J. Dickson. Cleveland, 1929. **v.d.**
Dictionary of American Biography. New York, **1928–36**
Dictionary of American English. Chicago, [c**1944**]
Dictionary of National Biography. London, **1885–1901.** (Cited also from several supplements and reissues.)
DIETZ, AUGUST. *The Postal Service of the Confederate States of America.* Richmond, Va., **1929**
DILLIN, JOHN G. W. *The Kentucky Rifle.* Washington, **1924**
DIMAGGIO, JOSEPH P. *Baseball for Everyone.* New York, [**1948**]
Diplomatic Correspondence of the Republic of Texas. (American Historical Association. *Annual Report,* 1907, Vol. II; *Annual Report,* 1908, Vol. II, parts 1–2.) **v.d.**
[*Diseases of Swine.*] *Special Report, No. 12. Investigation of Diseases of Swine* [etc.]. (U.S. Dept. of Agriculture.) Washington, **1879**
DITMARS, RAYMOND L. *The Reptile Book.* New York, **1907**
Reptiles of the World. New York, **1933**
DIX, EDWIN A. *Deacon Bradbury.* New York, **1900**
DIX, JOHN. *Transatlantic Tracings.* London, **1853**
DIXON, JAMES. *Personal Narrative of a Tour through a Part of the United States and Canada.* New York, **1849**
DIXON, THOMAS. *The Clansman.* New York, **1905**
DIXON, WILLIAM H. *New America.* 6th ed. London, **1867**
DOBBS, ARTHUR. *An Account of the Countries Adjoining to Hudson's Bay.* London, **1744**
DOBIE, JAMES FRANK. *Coronado's Children.* New York, 1931. **1930**
A Vaquero of the Brush Country. Dallas, **1929**
The Documentary History of the State of New-York. By Edmund B. O'Callaghan. Albany, 1849–51. **v.d.**
Documents Relating to the Colonial, Revolutionary and Post-Revolutionary History of the State of New Jersey. (Archives of the State of New Jersey. 1st Ser.) Newark, 1880–. **v.d.**
Documents Relating to the Revolutionary History of the State of New Jersey. (Archives of the State of New Jersey. 2d Ser.) Trenton, 1901–17. **v.d.**
Documents Relative to the Colonial History of the State of New-York. Albany, 1853–87. **v.d.**
DODD, WILLIAM E. *Expansion and Conflict.* Boston, [c**1915**]
DODDRIDGE, JOSEPH. *Logan . . .* Buffalo Creek, Va., **1823.** Cincinnati, 1868. Contains *The Dialogue of the Backwoodsman and the Dandy.* First perf. **1821**
Notes on the Settlement and Indian Wars, of the Western Parts of Virginia & Pennsylvania. Wellsburgh, Va., **1824**
DODGE, RICHARD I. *The Black Hills.* New York, **1876**
DODWORTH, ALLEN. *Dancing and Its Relations to Education and Social Life.* New York, **1885**
DOESTICKS, Q. K. ALEXANDER, P. B., pseud. MORTIMER THOMSON. *Doesticks' Letters; And What He Says.* Philadelphia, [c**1855**]. Also as *Doesticks: What He Says.*
Plu-ri-bus-tah. A Song that's-by-no-author. New York, **1856**
DOMENECH, EMMANUEL. *Seven Years' Residence in the Great Deserts of North America.* London, **1860**
DONALDSON, THOMAS. *The Moqui Indians of Arizona and Pueblo Indians of New Mexico.* Washington, **1893**
DONDORE, DOROTHY. *The Prairie and the Making of Middle America.* Cedar Rapids, Ia., **1926**
DORCHESTER, DANIEL. *Christianity in the United States.* New York, **1890**
DORCHESTER REC. See BOSTON. REGISTRY DEPT.
DORLAND, WILLIAM A. N. *The American Illustrated Medical Dictionary.* 7th ed., rev. and enl. Philadelphia, **1913**
DORRIS, JONATHAN T. *Old Cane Springs; a Story of the War Between the States in Madison County, Kentucky.* Rev. and supp., from original by John C. Chenault. Louisville, **1936**
DORSEY, ELLA L. *Midshipman Bob.* New York, **1888**
DORSEY, FLORENCE L. *Master of the Mississippi.* Boston, **1941**
DORSEY, GEORGE A. *Traditions of the Caddo.* Washington, **1905**

DORSON, RICHARD M. *Jonathan Draws the Long Bow.* Cambridge, **1946**
DOS PASSOS, JOHN. *Manhattan Transfer.* New York, **1925**
DOUGLAS, DAVID. *Journal Kept by David Douglas During His Travels in North America 1823–1827.* London, 1914. **v.d.**
DOUGLAS, GEORGE W. *The American Book of Days.* New York, **1937**
DOUGLASS, FREDERICK. *Narrative of the Life of Frederick Douglass.* Boston, 1849. =**1845**
DOUGLASS, WILLIAM. *A Summary, Historical and Political, of the First Planting, Progressive Improvements, and Present State of the British Settlements in North-America.* Boston, 1847–52. **v.d.**
DOW, JR., pseud. ELBRIDGE G. PAIGE. *Dow's Patent Sermons. First Series.* Philadelphia, [c1857]. *c***1849**
DOW, GEORGE F. *Every Day Life in the Massachusetts Bay Colony.* Boston, **1935**
DOW, LORENZO. *History of Cosmopolite; or, The Four Volumes of Lorenzo's Journal.* New York, 1814. 3d ed. rev. and corr. Wheeling, 1848. **v.d.**
DOWNEY, FAIRFAX D. *Our Lusty Forefathers.* New York, **1947**
DOWNING, MAJOR JACK, pseud. (See also DAVIS, C. A.; SMITH, SEBA.) *The Life of Andrew Jackson.* Philadelphia, **1834**
D'OYLE, LYNN C, ?pseud. *Notches on the Rough Edge of Life.* [London, 1890.] **v.d.**
DRAKE, BENJAMIN. *Tales and Sketches, from the Queen City.* Cincinnati, **1838**
DRAKE, BENJAMIN, and MANSFIELD, EDWARD D. *Cincinnati in 1826.* Cincinnati, **1827**
DRAKE, CHARLES D. *A Treatise on the Law of Suits by Attachment.* 5th ed., rev., cor., enl. Boston, **1878**
DRAKE, DANIEL. *Natural and Statistical View, or Picture of Cincinnati and the Miami Country.* Cincinnati, **1815**
Pioneer Life in Kentucky. Ed. Charles D. Drake. Cincinnati, 1870. **v.d.**
DRAKE, FRANCIS S. *The Town of Roxbury.* Roxbury, Mass., **1878**
DRAKE, SAMUEL G. *The Aboriginal Races of North America.* 15th ed., rev. New York, [c**1880**]
Tragedies of the Wilderness. Boston, **1841**
Dramatic Compositions Copyrighted . . . 1870 to 1916. (U.S. Copyright Office.) Washington, 1918. **v.d.**
DRANNAN, WILLIAM F. *Thirty-One Years on the Plains and in the Mountains.* Chicago, **1900**
DRAPER, JOHN W. *History of the American Civil War.* New York, [c**1867–70**]
DRAYTON, JOHN. *Letters Written during a Tour through the Northern and Eastern States of America.* Charleston, **1794**
A View of South-Carolina, as Respects Her Natural and Civil Concerns. Charleston, **1802**
DREISER, THEODORE. *The Financier.* New York, **1912**
DRINKER, ELIZABETH (SANDWITH). *Extracts from the Journal. . . .* Ed. Henry D. Biddle. Philadelphia, 1889. **v.d.**
DROEGE, JOHN A. *Freight Terminals and Trains.* New York, **1912**
Yards and Terminals and Their Operation. New York, **1906**
DRURY, WELLS. *An Editor on the Comstock Lode.* New York, [**1936**]
DUANE, WILLIAM, ed. *Letters to Benjamin Franklin.* New York, 1859. **v.d.**
DUBKIN, LEONARD. *Enchanted Streets.* Boston, **1947**
DU BOIS, WILLIAM E. B. *A Select Bibliography of the Negro American.* Atlanta, 1905. **v.d.**
DUMONT, FRANK. *Lew Benedict's Congress Broke Loose Songster.* New York, 1869
DUNAWAY, WAYLAND F. *A History of Pennsylvania.* New York, **1935**
DUNBAR, PAUL LAURENCE. *Folks from Dixie.* New York, **1898**
DUNBAR, SEYMOUR. *A History of Travel in America.* Indianapolis, **1915**
DUNCAN, KUNIGUNDE, and NICKOLS, D. F. *Mentor Graham, the Man Who Taught Lincoln.* Chicago, **1944**
DUNCAN, LEW W., and SCOTT, CHARLES F. *History of Allen and Woodson Counties, Kansas.* Iola, Kans., **1901**
DUNCAN, MARY (GREY) L. *America as I Found It.* New York, **1852**
DUNGLISON, ROBLEY. *Medical Lexicon.* Philadelphia, 2d ed., **1839**; 7th ed., rev. and enl., **1848**; 8th ed., **1851**; 11th ed., **1854**. First pub. as *A New Dictionary of Medical Science and Literature.* Boston, **1833**
DUNLAP, JAMES. *A Book of Forms.* 4th ed. Philadelphia, **1857**
DUNLAP, WILLIAM. *André.* See MOSES. *Representative Plays.*
Darby's Return. New York, **1789**
The Father. New York, 1887. **1789**
A History of the American Theatre, New York, **1832**
The Memoirs of a Water Drinker. New York, 1837. **1836**
DUNMORE, JOHN MURRAY, Earl of. *Correspondence.* Colonial Office Papers, Class 5, No. 1353. MS, Great Britain Public Record Office. **v.d.**
DUNN, JACOB P. *Indiana and Indianans.* Chicago, **1919**
DUNN, JOHN. *History of the Oregon Territory and British North-American Fur Trade.* London, **1844**
DUNSHEE, KENNETH H. *Enjine!—Enjine! A Story of Fire Protection.* New York, **1939**
DU PRATZ, i.e., LE PAGE DU PRATZ, ANTOINE S. *Histoire de la Louisiane.* Paris, **1758**. Cited also from tr. *The History of Louisiana.* London, **1763**
DU PUY, WILLIAM A. *Uncle Sam, Detective.* New York, [**1916**]
DURELL, EDWARD H. *New Orleans As I Found It.* New York, **1845**
DURFEE, CALVIN. *A History of Williams College.* Boston, **1860**
DURIVAGE, FRANCIS A., and BURNHAM, GEORGE P. *Stray Subjects, Arrested and Bound Over; being the Fugitive Offspring of the "Old 'Un"* [Durivage] *and the "Young 'Un"* [Burnham]. Philadelphia, **1848**. (Usu. cited by individual author.)
DUTTON, CHARLES J. *The Shadow on the Glass.* New York, **1923**
DUVAL, JOHN C. *The Adventures of Big-foot Wallace, the Texas Ranger and Hunter.* Macon, Ga., **1870**
Early Times in Texas. Austin, [c**1892**]. Contains *The Young Explorers.*
DUXBURY, MASS. *Copy of the Old Records of the Town. . . . From 1642 to 1770.* Plymouth, 1893. **v.d.**
DWIGHT, TIMOTHY. *Travels; in New-England and New-York.* New Haven, 1821–22. *a***1817**

E

EARLE, ALICE (MORSE). *Colonial Days in Old New York.* New York, 1896. **v.d.**
Curious Punishments of Bygone Days. New York, 1907. =1896. **v.d.**
Customs and Fashions in Old New England. New York, **1893**
Home Life in Colonial Days. New York, **1898**
The Sabbath in Puritan New England. New York, **1891**
Two Centuries of Costume in America, MDCXX–MDCCXX. New York, **1903**
EARLY, ELEANOR. *New England Sampler.* Boston, **1940**
EARLY, JUBAL A. *The Heritage of the South.* Lynchburg, Va., [c**1915**]
Early Conn. Probate Rec. See MANWARING.
EAST HAMPTON, N.Y. *Records of the Town.* Sag Harbor, 1887–1905. **v.d.**
EASTBURN, JAMES W., and SANDS, ROBERT C. *Yamoyden.* New York, **1820**
EASTBURN, ROBERT. *A Faithful Narrative of the Many Dangers and Sufferings . . . of Robert Eastburn during His Late Captivity among the Indians.* Philadelphia, **1758**
EASTERBY, JAMES H., ed. *The South Carolina Rice Plantation as Revealed in the Papers of Robert F. W. Allison.* Chicago, [**1945**]
EASTMAN, CHARLES A. *From the Deep Woods to Civilization.* Boston, **1916**
EASTMAN, HUBBARD. *Noyesism Unveiled.* Brattleboro, Vt., **1849**
EASTMAN, MARY (HENDERSON). *Aunt Phillis's Cabin.* Philadelphia, **1852**
EASTMAN, NICHOLSON J. *Expectant Motherhood.* Boston, **1940**
EASTON, JOHN. *A Narrative of the Causes Which Led to Philip's Indian War of 1675 and 1676 . . . with Other Documents.* [Ed.] Franklin B. Hough. Albany, 1858. **1675**
EATON, AMOS. *A Manual of Botany for the Northern and Middle States.* 3d ed. Albany, 1822. **1817–18.** 5th ed., **1829.** 6th ed., **1833.** 7th ed., **1836**
EATON, WALTER PRITCHARD. *Barn Doors and Byways.* Boston, [**1913**]
Green Trails and Upland Pastures. Garden City, N.Y., **1917**
The Idyl of Twin Fires. Garden City N.Y., **1915**
EATON, WALTER PRITCHARD, and UNDERHILL, ELISE M. *The Runaway Place.* New York, **1909**
EBBUTT, PERCY G. *Emigrant Life in Kansas.* London, **1886**
Economical Geology of Illinois. Ed. A. H. Worthen. Springfield, [**1882**]
Economist. Chicago, **1888–**
EDDY, MARY (BAKER). *Church Manual of the First Church of Christ, Scientist.* 3d ed. Boston, **1895.** 10th ed. Boston, **1899.**
Science of Man. Lynn, Mass., **1876.** Boston, 1883.
EDWARD, DAVID B. *The History of Texas.* Cincinnati, **1836**
EDWARDS, GEORGE. *A Natural History of Uncommon Birds, and of Some Rare and Undescribed Animals.* London, [**1743**]–**51**
EDWARDS, JOHN N. *Shelby and His Men.* Cincinnati, **1836**
EDWARDS, JONATHAN. *The Works of President Edwards.* 1st Amer. ed. Worcester, 1808–9. **v.d.**
A Faithful Narrative of the Surprizing Work of God in the Conversion of Many Hundred Souls in . . . New-England. 3d ed. Boston, **1738**
EGGLESTON, EDWARD. *The Book of Queer Stories, and Stories Told on a Cellar Door.* New York, 1871. **1870**
The Circuit Rider. New York, **1874**
Duffels. New York, **1893**
The End of the World. New York, [**1872**]
The Graysons. (*Century Magazine.* XXXV–XXXVI.) **v.d.**
The Hoosier School-Boy. New York, 1899. =**1883**
The Hoosier Schoolmaster. New York, [c**1871**]
Mr. Blake's Walking-Stick. Chicago, 1872. =**1870**
The Mystery of Metropolisville. New York, [c**1873**]
EGGLESTON, GEORGE C. *Dorothy South.* Boston, [**1902**]
The First of the Hoosiers. Philadelphia, [**1903**]
A Rebel's Recollections. New York, **1874**
The Wreck of the Red Bird. New York, **1882**
EILMANN, HENRY J. *Medicolegal and Industrial Toxicology.* Philadelphia, [**1940**]
ELIOT, JARED. *Essays upon Field-Husbandry in New-England.* Boston, 1760. First pub. New London, Conn. and New York, **1748–59**; app. Boston, **1761**
ELIOT, JOHN. *A Brief Narrative of the Progress of the Gospel among the Indians of New England.* [Ed.] William T. R. Marvin. Boston, 1868. **1670**
Day-Breaking. (Massachusetts Historical Society. *Collections.* 3d Ser., IV.) **1647**
The Glorious Progress of the Gospel, amongst the Indians in New England. Manifested by Three Letters, under the Hand of . . . Mr. John Eliot [etc.] Ed. Edward Winslow. London. **1649**
ELIOT, SAMUEL A. *A Sketch of the History of Harvard College.* Boston, **1848**
ELLET, ELIZA F. (LUMMIS). *The Pioneer Women of the West.* Philadelphia, 1873. =**1852**
ELLICOTT, ANDREW. (See also MATHEWS, CATHERINE V.) *Journal.* Philadelphia, 1814. =1803. **v.d**
ELLIOT, JONATHAN, ed. *The Debates . . . on the Adoption of the Federal Constitution.* Washington, 1827–45. **v.d.**
ELLIOTT, CHARLES W. *Winfield Scott, the Soldier and the Man.* New York, **1937**
ELLIOTT, FRANKLIN R. *The Western Fruit Book.* Rev., enl., and impr. New York, [**1859**]
ELLIS, ANNE. *The Life of an Ordinary Woman.* Boston, **1929**
ELLIS, EDWARD S. *Check 2134.* New York, [c**1891**]
ELLIS, JOHN BRECKENRIDGE. *Lahoma.* Indianapolis, [c**1913**]
ELLSWORTH, HENRY W. *Valley of the Upper Wabash, Indiana.* New York, **1838**
ELMORE, FRANCIS H. *Ethnobotany of the Navajo.* Albuquerque, **1943**
ELMWOOD, ELNATHAN, pseud. See GREENE, ASA.
ELWYN, ALFRED L. *Glossary of Supposed Americanisms.* Philadelphia, **1859**
ELY, RICHARD T. *French and German Socialism in Modern Times.* New York, **1883**
Studies in the Evolution of Industrial Society. New York, **1903**
EMERSON, ALICE B. *Ruth Fielding at Snow Camp.* New York, **1913**
EMERSON, GEORGE B. *A Report on the Trees and Shrubs . . . of Massachusetts.* Boston, **1846**
EMERSON, RALPH WALDO. *Complete Works.* [Ed.] Edward Waldo Emerson. 12 vols. Centenary Ed. Boston, 1903–4. **v.d.**
The Conduct of Life. Boston, **1860**
English Traits. Boston, **1856**
Essays. [1st Ser.] Boston, **1841.** [2d Ser.] Boston, 1854. **v.d.**
Letters and Social Aims. 314 pp. Boston, 1876 [**1875**]. Also new and rev. ed., 285 pp., **1876**

Miscellanies. Boston, 1892. =**1883**
Miscellanies: Embracing Nature, Addresses, and Lectures. 383 pp., Boston, **1856.** Also new and rev. ed., 315 pp., Boston, 1876. **v.d.**
Nature, Addresses, and Lectures. Boston, 1849. **v.d.**
Representative Men. Boston, **1850**
Society and Solitude. 300 pp., Boston, 1870. Also 269 pp., Boston, 1876. **v.d.**
EMMONS, EBENEZER. *Agriculture of New-York.* Albany, **1846–54**
[*Mass. Quadrupeds.*] *A Report on the Quadrupeds of Massachusetts.* Cambridge, Mass., **1840**
EMORY, WILLIAM H. *Notes of a Military Reconnoisance.* Washington, 1848. **v.d.**
Report on the United States and Mexican Boundary Survey. Washington, 1857–59. (34th Cong., 1 Sess. House. Ex. Doc. 135.) **v.d.**
Emporium of Arts and Sciences. Philadelphia, **1812–14**
Encyclopaedia Americana. Ed. Francis Lieber. Philadelphia, **1829–33**
The Encyclopedia Americana; a General Dictionary of the Arts and Sciences.... Ed. Frederick C. Beach, *et al.* New York, [c**1903–4**]
The Encyclopedia Americana; a Library of Universal Knowledge. New York, 1918–20. **v.d.**
The Encyclopaedia Britannica. 9th ed. [American] *Supplement.* Also issued as *Encyclopaedia Americana. A Supplementary Dictionary of Arts, Sciences, and General Literature.* New York, 1884 [c**1883**]–**88**
Epworth League Cook Book. (Portland Methodist Church.) Louisville, **1898**
ERNST, CARL W. Marginalia in his set of the *OED*, furnished by courtesy of the owners, the Delegates of the Oxford University Press.
Essays on Christian Union. By Thomas Chalmers, *et al.* London, **1845**
Essays on Various Subjects. Written for the Amusement of Everybody, by One who is considered Nobody. New York, **1835**
ESSEX CO., MASS. PROBATE COURT. *The Probate Records.* Salem, 1916–20. **v.d.**
ESSIG, EDWARD O. *Injurious and Beneficial Insects of California.* Sacramento, **1913**
Estate of Virginia, A True Declaration of the. See FORCE.
ESTLAKE, ALLAN. *The Oneida Community.* London, **1900**
EUBANK, KENT. *Horse and Buggy Days.* Kansas City, Mo., [c**1927**]
EVANS, i.e., WILSON, AUGUSTA J. (EVANS). *Vashti.* New York, 1859. **1867**
EVANS, ESTWICK. *A Pedestrious Tour of Four Thousand Miles.* Concord, N.H., **1819**
EVANS, GEORGE H. *Pigwacket.* Conway, N.H., **1939**
EVANS, LEWIS. *Geographical, Historical, Political, Philosophical, and Mechanical Essays.* Includes *An Analysis of a General Map of the Middle British Colonies in America.* Philadelphia, **1755**
EVARTS, HAL G. *Tumbleweeds.* Boston, **1923**
EVELYN, JOHN. *Silva; a Discourse of Forest Trees.* London, 1664. Written **1662**
Evening Standard. London, **1827–**
Examiner. London, **1808–81**

F

FAIR, A. A., pseud. ERLE STANLEY GARDNER. *Fools Die on Friday.* New York, **1947**
Famous Trees. (U.S. Dept of Agriculture. Miscellaneous Pub. No. 295) Washington, **1938**
FANNING, DAVID. *Narrative ... as Written by Himself.* New York, 1865. **1790**
FARMER, FANNIE MERRITT. *The Boston Cooking-School Cook Book.* Rev. ed. Boston, **1909.** 9th rev. ed. Boston, **1941**
[*Farmington T.-Hustler.*] *The Times-Hustler.* Farmington, N.M., **1890–**
FARNHAM, ELIZA W. *Life in Prairie Land.* New York, **1846**
FARNHAM, THOMAS J. *Travels in the Californias, and Scenes in the Pacific Ocean.* New York, **1844**
Travels in the Great Western Prairies, the Anahuac and Rocky Mountains. Poughkeepsie, N.Y., **1841**
FARRAR, J. MAURICE. *Five Years in Minnesota.* London, **1880**
FARROW, EDWARD S. *Mountain Scouting.* New York, **1881**
FASSETT, NORMAN C. *A Manual of Aquatic Plants.* New York, **1940**
FAST, HOWARD. *Freedom Road.* New York, **1944**
Father Abbey's Will. See WINSLOW, O. E.
FAUX, WILLIAM. *Memorable Days in America.* London, **1823**
FAY, ALBERT H. *A Glossary of the Mining and Mineral Industry.* Washington, **1918**
FEARON, HENRY B. *Sketches of America.* London, **1818**
FEATHERSTONHAUGH, GEORGE W. *Excursion through the Slave States.* New York, **1844;** 2 vols. London, **1844**
The Federalist: a Collection of Essays Written in Favour of the new Constitution. New York, **1788**
FELTON, CORNELIUS C. *Greece, Ancient and Modern.* Boston, 1867. *a***1862**
FERBER, EDNA. *Cimarron.* New York, **1930**
Dawn O'Hara, the Girl who Laughed. New York, [**1911**]
So-Big. Garden City, N.Y., **1924**
FERGUSON, CHARLES D. *The Experiences of a Forty-Niner ... in California and Australia.* Cleveland, **1888**
FERGUSSON, ADAM. *Practical Notes Made During a Tour in Canada, and a Portion of the United States.* Edinburgh, **1833**
FERGUSSON, ERNA. *Our Southwest.* New York, **1940**
FERGUSSON, WILLIAM. *America by River and Rail.* London, **1856**
FERNOW, BERTHOLD, ed. *Documents Relative to the Colonial History of the State of New-York.* Albany, 1853–87. **v.d.**
FESSENDEN, THOMAS G. *Democracy Unveiled.* 3d ed. New York, **1806**
The Ladies Monitor. Bellows Falls, Vt., **1818**
Original Poems. Philadelphia, 1806. **v.d.**
Pills, Political, Poetical, and Philosophical. Philadelphia, **1809**
Terrible Tractoration! 1st Amer., from 2d London ed., rev. and corr. New York, **1804**
FEWKES, JESSE W. *Casa Grande, Arizona.* Washington, **1912**
FIDFADDY, FREDERICK AUGUSTUS, pseud. *The Adventures of Uncle Sam, in Search after His Lost Honor.* Middletown, Conn., **1816**
FIELD, EDWARD S. *The Sapphire Bracelet.* New York, [c**1910**]
A Six-Cylinder Courtship. New York, [**1907**]
FIELD, HENRY M. *Birght Skies and Dark Shadows.* New York, **1890**
FIELD, JOSEPH M. *The Drama in Pokerville.* Philadelphia, **1847**
Field and Forest. Washington, **1875–78**
FILLSON, JOHN. *The Discovery, Settlement, and Present State of Kentucke.* Wilmington, Del., **1784**
FINCH, JOHN. *Travels in the United States of America and Canada.* London, **1833**
FINDLEY, RUTH (EBRIGHT). *The Lady of Godey's, Sarah Josepha Hale.* Philadelphia, **1931**
FINN, HENRY J., ed. *American Comic Annual.* Boston, **1831**
First Book of the American Chronicles of the Times. Boston, **1775**
First Impressions of the New World on Two Travellers from the Old, in the Autumn of 1858. London, **1859**
[*First Planters N.-Eng.*] *Massachusetts; or, The First Planters of New-England.* Boston 1696. **v.d.**
FISCHER, ANTON OTTO. *Focs'le Days.* New York, **1947**
FISHER, DOROTHEA F. (CANFIELD). *Rough-Hewn.* New York, [c**1922**]
FISHER, WALTER M. *The Californians.* London, **1876**
FISHER, WILLIAM A. *Ye Old New-England Psalm-Tunes, 1620–1820.* Boston, [c1930] **v.d.**
[*Fisheries Exhib. Cat.*] *Official Catalogue.* (London. International Fisheries Exhibition, 1883.) **1883**
Fisheries of the United States, 1908. (U.S. Bureau of the Census.) Washington, **1911**
Fishes of the Western North Atlantic. (Sears Foundation for Marine Research. *Memoir No. 1.*) New Haven, **1948**
FISK, JAMES L. *Expedition ... to the Rocky Mountains.* [Washington, 1864.] **1863**
FITCH, ASA. *Report on the Noxious, Beneficial and Other Insects of the State of New York.* Albany, **1865**
FITCH, CLYDE. *Captain Jinks of the Horse Marines.* New York, 1902. First perf. **1901**
The City. See MOSES. *Representative American Dramas.*
FITCH, TOBIAS. See MERENESS.
FITHIAN, PHILIP VICKERS. *Journal and Letters, 1767–1774.* Ed. John R. Williams. Princeton, 1900–1934. **v.d.**
FITZGERALD, F. SCOTT. *Tales of the Jazz Age.* New York, **1922**
FITZGERALD, HUGH. *Sam Steele's Adventures on Land and Sea.* Chicago, [c**1906**]
Five Fur Traders. See GATES.
FLAGG, EDMUND. *The Far West.* New York, **1838**
FLAGG, WILLIAM J. *A Good Investment.* (*Harper's Magazine.* XLIV–XLV.) **v.d.**
Flags of Five Nations. Being a Collection of Historical Sketches, Legends and Stories of The Golden Isles of Guale. Sea Island, Ga., [*c***1943**]
FLANDRAU, CHARLES M. *Harvard Episodes.* Boston, **1897**
FLAVIN, MARTIN. *Journey in the Dark.* New York, [**1943**]
FLEISCHMANN, CARL L. *Wegweiser und Rathgeber nach und in den Vereinigten Staaten von Nord-Amerika.* Stuttgart, **1852**
FLEMING, WALTER L., ed. *Documentary History of Reconstruction.* Cleveland, 1906–7. **v.d.**
FLEMING, WILLIAM. See MERENESS.
FLEMMING, LOUIS A. *Practical Tanning.* Philadelphia, **1903**
FLICK, ALEXANDER C., ed. *History of the State of New York.* New York, 1933– **v.d.**
FLINT, CHARLES L. *Milch Cows and Diary Farming.* Boston, **1858**
FLINT, JAMES. *Letters from America.* Edinburgh, 1822. **v.d.**
FLINT, TIMOTHY. *Biographical Memoir of Daniel Boone, the First Settler of Kentucky.* Cincinnati, **1833**
A Condensed Geography and History of the Western States of the Mississippi Valley. Cincinnati, **1828**
Francis Berrian. Boston, **1826**
George Mason, the Young Backwoodsman. Boston, **1829**
Florida Plantation Records. Ed. Ulrick B. Phillips and James D. Glunt. St. Louis, 1927. **v.d.**
FLOWER, RICHARD. See THWAITES.
FLYNT, i.e., WILLARD, JOSIAH FLYNT. *Notes of an Itinerant Policeman.* Boston, **1900**
Tramping with Tramps. New York, 1900. =**1899**
The World of Graft. New York, **1901**
FOBES, SIMON. *Journal of a Member of Arnold's Expedition to Quebec.* (*Magazine of History, with Notes and Queries.* Extra No. 130.) *c***1835**
FOLSOM, GEORGE. *History of Saco and Biddeford.* Saco, Me., 1830. **v.d.**
FOOTE, HENRY S. *Texas and the Texans.* Philadelphia, **1841**
FOOTE, MARY (HALLOCK). *The Led-Horse Claim.* Boston, [c**1883**]
FOOTE, WILLIAM H. *Sketches of Virginia, Historical and Biographical.* Philadelphia, **1850**
FOOTNER, HULBERT. *Rivers of the Eastern Shore.* New York, **1944**
FORBES, ALEXANDER. *California: a History of Upper and Lower California.* London, **1839**
FORBES, ESTHER. *Johnny Tremain.* Boston, **1943**
FORBES, ROBERT H. *Irrigation in Arizona.* Washington, **1911**
FORBES, STEPHEN, and RICHARDSON, ROBERT E. *Fishes of Illinois.* 2d ed. Springfield, **1920.** =Danville, Ill., 1908.
FORBES, WILLIAM T. M. *The Lepidoptera of New York and Neighboring States.* Ithaca, **1923**
FORBUSH, EDWARD H. *A History of the Game Birds, Wild-Fowl and Shore Birds of Massachusetts and Adjacent States.* [Boston, **1912**]
FORCE, PETER, comp. *Tracts and Other Papers Relating ... to ... the Colonies.* Washington, 1836–46. Contents include: Vol. I, No. 7. ROBERT JOHNSON. *The New Life of Virginea.* **1612.** No. 12. FRANCIS HIGGINSON. *New Englands Plantation q.v.* **1630.** Vol. II, No. 1. JOHN SMITH. *A Description of New England q.v.* **1616.** No. 5. THOMAS MORTON. *New English Canaan q.v.* 1632, [i.e.,] **1637.** Vol. III, No. 1. *A True Declaration of the Estate of the Colonie in Virginia.* **1610.** No. 7. NATHANIEL SHRIGLEY. *A True Relation of Virginia and Mary-land.* [**1669.**] No. 11. EDWARD WILLIAMS. *Virginia: more especially the Southern Part thereof, Richly and Truly Valued.* **1650.** Vol. IV, No. 1. RICHARD HAKLUYT. tr. *Virginia Richly Valued.* **1609**
FORD, EMILY E. (FOWLER). *Notes on the Life of Noah Webster.* New York, 1912. **v.d.**
FORD, LESLIE, pseud. ZENITH (JONES) BROWN. *Honolulu Story.* New York, **1946**
FORD, PAUL LEICESTER. *The Honorable Peter Stirling and What People Thought of Him.* New York, 1899. =**1894**
Ed. *The New-England Primer; a Reprint of the Earliest Known Edition.* New York, **1899**
FORD, THOMAS. *A History of Illinois, from ... 1818 to 1847.* Chicago, 1859. =1854. *a***1850**
FORDHAM, ELIAS P. *Personal Narrative of Travels.* Ed. Frederic A. Ogg. Cleveland, 1606. **v.d.**
FOREMAN, GRANT. *The Last Trek of the Indians.* Chicago, **1946**
FOREMAN, SAMUEL S. *Narrative of a Journey down the Ohio and Mississippi in 1789–90.* Cincinnati, 1888. **v.d.**
FORNEY, MATTHIAS P. *Catechism of the Locomotive.* New York, 1877. =**1874**

FORREST, EARLE R. *Missions and Pueblos of the Old Southwest*. Cleveland, **1929**
FORT, CHARLES. *The Outcast Manufacturers*. New York, **1909**
FORTIER, SAMUEL. *Use of Water in Irrigation*. New York, **1915**
FOSSETT, FRANK. *Colorado: a Historical, Descriptive and Statistical Work on the Rocky Mountain Gold and Silver Mining Regions*. Denver, **1876**
FOSTER, GEORGE E. *Se-quo-yah, the American Cadmus and Modern Moses*. Philadelphia, **1885**
FOSTER, GEORGE G. *New York in Slices*. New York, **1849**
FOSTER, HANNAH (WEBSTER). *The Coquette*. Boston, **1797**
FOSTER, HARRY L. *The Adventures of a Tropical Tramp*. New York, **1922**
FOSTER, JOHN W., and WHITNEY, JOSIAH D. *Report on the Geology and Topography of a Portion of the Lake Superior Land District, in the State of Michigan*. Washington, **1850–51**
FOSTER, LARIMORE. *Larry; Thoughts of Youth*. New York, 1930. Written **1924–25**
FOWLER, GEORGE L. *Locomotive Dictionary; an Illustrated Vocabulary of Terms Which Designate American Railway Locomotives*. New York, **1909**
FOWLER, JACOB. *Journal*. Ed. Elliott Coues. New York, 1898. **v.d.**
FOWLER, ORSON S. *A Home for All*. New York, **[c1853]**
FOWLER, WILLIAM WORTHINGTON. *Ten Years in Wall Street*. Hartford, **1870**
FOY, EDDIE, and HARLOW, ALVIN F. *Clowning through Life*. New York, **[c1928]**
The Fra. East Aurora, N.Y., **1908–17**
FRANCIS. *Frauds*. See REDMOND.
FRANCIS, FRANCIS, JR. *Saddle and Mocassin* [*sic*]. London, **1887**
FRANKLIN, BENJAMIN. *Complete Works*. Comp. and ed. John Bigelow. New York, 1887–88. **v.d.**
Writings. Ed. Albert H. Smyth. New York, 1905–7. **v.d.**
An Account of the New Invented Pennsylvanian Fireplaces. Philadelphia, **1744**
Autobiography. (*Writings*. I.) **v.d.**
Dogood Papers. (*Writings*. II.) **1722**
Experiments and Observations on Electricity. London, **1751–53**. [4th ed.], corr. and impr., 1769. **v.d.**
An Historical Review of the Constitution and Government of Pennsylvania, from Its Origin. London, 1759. **v.d.**
A Modest Enquiry into the Nature . . . of a Paper Currency. (*Writings*. II.) **1729**
Plain Truth. [Philadelphia], **1747**
Poor Richard, 1733. Philadelphia, [1732]. Other issues, to **1743**
Poor Richard Improved . . . 1748. Philadelphia, **[1747]**
Proposals Relating to the Education of Youth in Pensilvania. (*Writings*. II.) **1749**
FREDERIC, HAROLD. *The Damnation of Theron Ware*. Chicago, 1900. **=1896**
The Deserter, and Other Stories. Boston, **[c1898]**
The Lawton Girl. New York, 1899. **=1890**
Seth's Brother's Wife. New York, **1887**
FREEBURG, VICTOR O. *The Art of Photoplay Making*. New York, **1918**
FREEMAN, MARY E. (WILKINS). *By the Light of the Soul*. New York, **1906**
The Copy-Cat, & Other Stories. New York, 1914. **v.d.**
The Debtor. New York, **1905**
Edgewater People. New York, **[c1918]**
Giles Corey, Yeoman. New York, **1893**
A Humble Romance and Other Stories. New York, **[c1887**, 1915]
In Colonial Times. Boston, **1899**
Jane Field. New York, 1893. **1892**
Jerome, a Poor Man. New York, **1897**
Madelon. New York, **1896**
A New England Nun and Other Stories. New York, **[c1891]**
Pembroke. New York, **1894**
The People of Our Neighborhood. New York, 1901. **=1898**
The Portion of Labor. New York, **1901**
The Pot of Gold, and Other Stories. Boston, **[c1892]**
The Shoulders of Atlas. New York, **1908**
Six Trees. New York, **1903**
The Winning Lady, and Others. New York, 1909. **v.d.**
Young Lucretia, and Other Stories. New York, **1892**
FREEMAN, MARY E. (WILKINS), and KINGSLEY, FLORENCE M. *An Alabaster Box*. New York, **1917**
Free Press. Halifax, N.C.; Tarboro, N.C., **1824–**. Title varies.
FRÉMONT, JOHN C. *Report of the Exploring Expedition to the Rocky Mountains in the Year 1842, and to Oregon and North California in the Years 1843–'44*. Washington, 1845. **v.d.**
FRENCH, ALICE. *The Missionary Sheriff*. New York, **1897**
Otto the Knight, and Other Trans-Mississippi Stories. Boston, **1891**
Stories of a Western Town. New York, 1897. **=1893**
FRENEAU, PHILIP. *Miscellaneous Works*. Philadelphia, **1788**
Poems. Ed. Fred L. Pattee. Princeton, 1902–7. **v.d.**
Poems Written and Published during the Revolutionary War. Philadelphia, 1809. **v.d.**
Poems Written between the Years 1768 & 1794. New ed. Monmouth, N.J., **1795**
Poems . . . Written Chiefly during the Late War. Philadelphia, **1786**
FRIEDERICI, GEORG. *Amerikanistisches Wörterbuch*. Hamburg, **1947**
FRIEND, W. H. *Plants of Ornamental Vólue for the Rio Grande Valley of Texas*. College Station, Tex., **1942**
FRIES, ADELAIDE L. *Records of the Moravians in North Carolina*. Raleigh, 1922–. **v.d.**
FRITZ, PERCY S. *Colorado the Centennial State*. New York, **1941**
Frontier. Missoula, Mont., **1920–39**
FROTHINGHAM, RICHARD. *The History of Charlestown, Massachusetts*. Charlestown, 1845–49. **v.d.**
FUGINA, FRANK J. *Lore and Lure of the Upper Mississippi*. Winona, Minn., **1945**
FULLER, ARCHELAUS. *Journal . . . in the Expedition Against Ticonderoga*. (Essex Institute. *Historical Collections*. XLVI.) **1758**
FULLER, JANE G. *Uncle John's Flower-Gatherers*. New York, **1869**
FULLER, SARAH M., later MARCHESA D'OSSOLI. *Summer on the Lakes, in 1843*. Boston, **1844**
FULTON, JUSTIN D. *Sam Hobart, the Locomotive Engineer*. New York, **[c1883]**
FULTON, ROBERT. *Torpedo War, and Submarine Explosions*. New York, **1810**
The Fundamental Constitutions of Carolina. See *Old South Leaflets*.
FUNK, CHARLES E. *A Hog on Ice and Other Curious Expressions*. New York, **1948**
Fur, Fin, and Feather, . . . A Compiliation of the Game Laws of the Principal States. Title varies; pub. at varying intervals. New York, **v.d.**
FURMAN, GABRIEL. [*Customs*.] *Winter Amusements in New York in the Early 19th Century*. (New York Historical Society. *Bulletin*. XXIII.) Written about 1830, additions interpolated about 1845. **c1830–45**

G

GABRIEL, RALPH H. *The Pageant of America*. II: *The Lure of the Frontier*. New Haven, **1929**. III: *Toilers of Land and Sea*. New Haven, **1926**
GABRIELSON, IRA N. *Wildlife Refuges*. New York, **1943**
GABRIELSON, IRA N., and JEWETT, STANLEY G. *Birds of Oregon*. Corvallis, Ore., **1940**
GALE, ZONA. *Friendship Village*. New York, 1910. **=1908**
GALL, LUDWIG. *Meine Auswanderung nach den Vereingten-Staaten in Nord Amerika*. Trier, **1822**
GALLAHER, JAMES. *The Western Sketch-Book*. Boston, 1850. **v.d.**
Gallinipper. New Haven, **1846–58**
GALT, JOHN. *Lawrie Todd*. New York, **1830**
GANN, THOMAS. *Discoveries and Adventures in Central America*. London, **[1928]**
GANN, WALTER. *Tread of the Longhorns*. San Antonio, **[1949]**
GARCÉS, FRANCISCO. *On the Trail of a Spanish Pioneer; the Diary and Itinerary of Francisco Garcés*. Ed. Elliott Coues. New York, 1900. **1776**
GARCIA, FABIÁN. *Shade Trees and Other Ornamentals*. Santa Fe, **1903**
Garden and Forest. New York, **1888–97**
GARDNER, ERLE STANLEY. *The Case of the Black-Eyed Blonde*. New York, **1944**
The Case of the Golddigger's Purse. New York, **1945**
The Case of the Lonely Heiress. New York, **[1948]**
The D.A. Breaks a Seal. New York, **1946**
GARLAND, HAMLIN. *The Book of the American Indian*. New York, **1923**
The Eagle's Heart. New York, **1900**
A Son of the Middle Border. New York, **1917**
GARLAND, HUGH A. *The Life of John Randolph of Roanoke*. New York, 1851. **=1850. v.d.**
GARNER, BESS (ADAMS). *Windows in an Old Adobe*. Pomona, Calif., **1939**
GARRARD, LEWIS H. *Wah-to-yah and the Taos Trail*. Ed. Walter S. Campbell. Oklahoma City, 1927. **1850**
GARRISON, WENDELL PHILLIPS, and GARRISON, FRANCIS J. *William Lloyd Garrison, 1805–1879: The Story of His Life Told by His Children*. New York, 1885–89. **v.d.**
GASS, PATRICK. *A Journal of the Voyages and Travels of a Corps of Discovery, under the Command of Capt. Lewis and Capt. Clarke*. Pittsburgh, **1807**. 3d ed. Philadelphia, 1811. Also pub. as *Lewis and Clarke's Journal to the Rocky Mountains . . . .* Dayton, O., 1847.
GATES, CHARLES M., ed. *Five Fur Traders of the Northwest; Being the Narrative of Peter Pond and the Diaries of John MacDonnell, Archibald N. McLeod, Hugh Faries, and Thomas Connor*. [Minneapolis], 1933. **v.d.**
GATSCHET, ALBERT S. *The Klamath Indians of Southwestern Oregon*. Washington, **1891**
GAYARRE, CHARLES E. A. *History of Louisiana*. New York, 1854–66. I: *Louisiana: Its Colonial History and Romance*. New York, **1851**. II: *Louisiana: Its History as a French Colony*. New York, **1852**
Gazette of the United States. New York, **1789–90**; Philadelphia, **1790–1804**
GEIST, ROLAND C. *Hiking, Camping and Mountaineering*. New York, **[1943]**
GEORGE, CHARLES B. *Forty Years on the Rail*. Chicago, **1887**
GEORGE, HENRY. *Progress and Poverty*. London, 1881. **=1879**
The Georgians. Boston: Osgood, **1881**. (Not to be confused with Harben's *The Georgians*, 1904.)
GERRY, MARGARITA (SPALDING). *The Masks of Love*. New York, **1914**
GESNER, ABRAHAM. *A Practical Treatise on Coal, Petroleum, and Other Distilled Oils*. New York, **1861**. 2d ed. New York, **1865**
GIBBONS, PHEBE H. (EARLE). *"Pennsylvania Dutch," and Other Essays*. 3d ed., rev. and enl. Philadelphia, **1882**
GIDDINGS, DANIEL. *Journal . . . during the Expedition against Cape Breton in 1744–5*. (Essex Institute. *Historical Collections*. XLVIII.) **v.d.**
GIHON, JOHN W. *Geary and Kansas*. Philadelphia, **1857**
GILBERT, BENJAMIN. *A Narrative of the Captivity and Sufferings of Benjamin Gilbert and His Family*. By William Walton. Philadelphia, **1784**
GILBERT, GEORGE B. *Forty Years a Country Preacher*. New York, **1939**
GILBRETH, FRANK B., and CAREY, ERNESTINE G. *Cheaper by the Dozen*. New York, **1948**
GILLELAND, J. C. *The Ohio and Mississippi Pilot*. Pittsburgh, **1820**
GILLIAM, ALBERT M. *Travels over the Table Lands and Cordilleras of Mexico*. Philadelphia, **1846**
GILMAN, CAROLINE (HOWARD). *Recollections of a Southern Matron*. New York, 1838. **1836**
GILMAN, CHANDLER R. *Life on the Lakes*. New York, **1836**
GIRARD, STEPHEN. *Biography of Stephen Girard, with His Will Affixed*. By Stephen Simpson. Philadelphia, 1832. **v.d.**
GIRAUD, JACOB P. *The Birds of Long Island*. New York, **1844**
GIST, CHRISTOPHER. *Christopher Gist's Journals*. Pittsburgh, 1893. **v.d.**
Journal of a Tour through Ohio and Kentucky. (*Filson Publications*. No. 13.) **1751**
GITTINGER, ROY. *The Formation of the State of Oklahoma*. Berkeley, **1917**
GIVEN, JOHN L. *Making a Newspaper*. New York, **1907**
GLADDEN, WASHINGTON. *Applied Christianity: Moral Aspects of Social Questions*. Boston, **1886**
Working People and Their Employers. Boston, 1885. **=1876**
GLASGOW, ELLEN. *The Deliverance*. New York, **1904**
GLAZIER, WILLARD. *Peculiarities of American Cities*. Philadelphia, 1886. **1883**
GLEN, JAMES. See CARROLL, B. R.
Glimpses of Alaska as It was and as It is. [Juneau], **1935**
GLISAN, RODNEY. *Journal of Army Life*. San Francisco, 1874. **v.d.**
GLOUCESTER, MASS. *Records of the Fifth Parish of Gloucester, now Rockport*. (Essex Institute. *Historical Collections*. XXI–XXII.) **v.d.**
GLOVER, THOMAS. *An Account of Virginia*. (Royal Society, London. *Philosophical Transactions*. XI.) **1676**
GODDARD, HENRY H. *The Kallikak Family; a Study in the Heredity of Feeble-Mindedness*. New York, **1912**

GODFREY, EDWARD K. *The Island of Nantucket.* Boston, 1882

GODLEY, JOHN R. *Letters from America.* London, 1844

GODMAN, JOHN D. *American Natural History.* Philadelphia, 1826–28

God's Protecting Providence. See DICKINSON, JONATHAN.

GOING, MAUD. *Field, Forest, and Wayside Flowers.* New York, [1899]

GOODE, GEORGE BROWN. *American Fishes.* New York, 1888

The Fisheries and Fishery Industries of the United States. Washington, 1884

A Review of the Fishery Industries of the United States and the Work of the U.S. Fish Commission. London, 1883

GOODLANDER, CHARLES W. *Memoirs . . . of the Early Days of Fort Scott.* Fort Scott, Kan., 1900

GOODRICH, SAMUEL G. *Recollections of a Lifetime.* New York, 1856

A System of Universal Geography. Cincinnati, 1832

The Travels, Voyages, and Adventures of Gilbert Go-Ahead, in Foreign Parts. New York, 1859. =1856

GOODSPEED, THOMAS W. *A History of the University of Chicago.* Chicago, [1916] v.d.

GOODWIN, CHARLES C. *As I Remember Them.* Salt Lake City, 1913

GOODWIN, HENRY K., defendant. *The Official Report of the Trial of Henry K. Goodwin for the Murder of Albert D. Swann.* Reported by James M. W. Yerrinton. Boston, 1887

GOOKIN, DANIEL. *Historical Collections of the Indians in New England.* (Massachusetts Historical Society. *Collections . . . for the Year 1792.*) 1674

GORDON, HARRY. See MERENESS.

GORDON, MAURICE B. *Æsculapius Comes to the Colonies.* Ventnor, N.J., [1949]

GORDON, WILLIAM. *The History of the Rise, Progress, and Establishment of the Independence of the United States of America.* New York, 1789. 1788

GORDON, WILLIAM S. [*Recoll. Lynchburg.*] *Recollections of the Old Quarter.* Lynchburg, Va., 1902

GORE, WILLARD C. *Student Slang.* (In *Contributions to Rhetorical Theory.* Ed. by Fred. N. Scott.) Ann Arbor, Mich., 1895

GORGES, SIR FERDINANDO. *A Briefe Narration of the Original Undertakings of the Advancement of Plantations into the Parts of America.* (Prince Society. *Publications.* XIX.) a1647. Cited from running title, as *Descr. N.-Eng.*

GOSNELL, H. ALLEN. *Guns on the Western Waters.* Baton Rouge, 1949

GOSS, WARREN L. *Recollections of a Private.* New York, 1890

The Soldier's Story of His Captivity. Boston, 1867 [©1866]

GOSSE, PHILIP H. *Letters from Alabama.* London, 1859. v.d.

GOUGE, WILLIAM M. *The Fiscal History of Texas.* Philadelphia, 1852

GOULD, GEORGE M. *An Illustrated Dictionary of Medicine, Biology and Allied Sciences.* Philadelphia, 1894

GOVE, JESSE A. *The Utah Expedition 1857–1859. Letters of Capt. Jesse A. Gove, 10th Inf., U.S.A.* (New Hampshire Historical Society. *Collections.* XII.) v.d.

GRAHAM, MARGARET (COLLIER). *Stories of the Foot-Hills.* Boston, 1895

Graham's American Monthly Magazine of Literature, Art, and Fashion. Philadelphia, 1826–58

GRAINGER, JAMES. *The Sugar-Cane.* (In ALEXANDER CHALMERS. *The Works of the English Poets.* XIV. London, 1810.) Written 1763

GRANT, ANNE (MACVICAR). *Memoirs of an American Lady.* London, 1808

GRANT, ROBERT. *The Little Tin Gods-on-Wheels.* Cambridge, 1879

Unleavened Bread. New York, 1900

GRANT, ULYSSES S. *Personal Memoirs.* New York, 1885–86

The Granville Centennial Cook Book. Newark, O., [1905]

GRATTAN, THOMAS C. *Civilized America.* London, 1859

GRAU, ROBERT. *The Theatre of Science.* New York, 1914

GRAY, ASA. *Field, Forest, and Garden Botany.* New York, [©1868]

First Lessons in Botany and Vegetable Physiology. New York, 1856. =1857

Letters. Ed. Jane L. Gray. Boston, 1893. v.d.

Manual of the Botany of the Northern United States. New York, 1857

GRAY, JAMES. *Pine, Stream and Prairie.* New York, 1945

GRAY, JOHN C., and ROPES, JOHN C. *War Letters, 1862–1865.* Boston, 1927. v.d.

GRAYDON, ALEXANDER. *Memoirs of His Own Time.* Philadelphia, 1846. 1811

GRAYSON, THEODORE J. *Leaders and Periods of American Finance.* New York, 1932

GREATREX, CHARLES B. *Whittlings from the West.* London, 1854

GREELEY, HORACE. *Autobiography.* New York, 1872 [©1868]

Glances at Europe; in a Series of Letters from Great Britain, France, Italy, Switzerland, &c. New York, 1851

An Overland Journey, from New York to San Francisco, in the Summer of 1859. New York, 1860

GREEN, BENNETT W. *World-Book of Virginia Folk-Speech.* Richmond, 1899

GREEN, JONATHAN H. *Twelve Days in the Tombs.* New York, 1851

GREEN, SAMUEL B. *Forestry in Minnesota.* Delano, Minn., 1898

GREEN, THOMAS J. *Journal of the Texian Expedition against Mier.* New York, 1845

GREENE, ASA. *The Life and Adventures of Dr. Dodimus Duckworth, A.N.Q.* New York, 1833

The Perils of Pearl Street. New York, 1834

A Yankee among the Nullifiers: an Autobiography. New York, 1833

GREENE, SARAH P. (MCLEAN). *Cape Cod Folks.* Boston, 1881

GREENLEAF, MOSES. *A Survey of the State of Maine.* Portland, 1829

GREENOUGH, JAMES B., and KITTREDGE, GEORGE LYMAN. *Words and Their Ways.* New York, 1901

GREER-PETRIE, CORDIA. *Angeline at the Seelbach.* Louisville, 1923. =1921

GREGG, ALEXANDER. *History of the Old Cheraws.* New York, 1867

GREGG, JOHN C. *Life in the Army, in the Departments of Virginia, and the Gulf.* Philadelphia, 1866

GREGG, JOSIAH. *Commerce of the Prairies.* New York, 1844

Diary. Ed. Maurice G. Fulton. Norman, Okla., 1941–. v.d.

Grey Towers; a Campus Novel. Chicago, 1923

GRIFFITH, i.e., BROWNE, MARTHA (GRIFFITH). *Autobiography of a Female Slave.* New York, 1857

GRIFFITHS, D. *Two Years' Residence in the New Settlements of Ohio.* London, 1835

GRIGSBY, MELVIN. *The Smoked Yank.* 3d ed. Chicago, 1899 [©1888]. =1891.

GRIMSTON, EDWARD, tr. *The Natvrall and Morall Historie of the East and West Indies.* London, 1604

Gringo and Greaser. Manzano, N.M., 1883–84

GRINNELL, GEORGE BIRD. *Blackfoot Lodge Tales.* New York, 1892

GRINNELL, JOSEPH. *Gold Hunting in Alaska.* Elgin, Ill., [©1901]

Review of the Recent Mammal Fauna of California. Berkeley, 1933

GRISWOLD, RUFUS W. *Passages from the Correspondence and Other Papers of Rufus W. Griswold.* Ed. William M. Griswold. Cambridge, 1898. v.d.

GRONLUND, LAURENCE. *The Coöperative Commonwealth in Its Outlines.* Boston, 1884.

GRONOVIUS, JOANNES FREDERICUS. *Flora Virginica, Exhibens Plantas Quas V. C. Johannes Clayton in Virginia Observavit atque Collegit.* Lugdoni Batavorum, 1743. First pub. 1739–43

GROSE, FRANCIS. *A Classical Dictionary of the Vulgar Tongue.* London, 1785

GROSVENOR, WILLIAM M. *Does Protection Protect?* New York, 1871

GROTON, MASS. *Early Records . . . 1662–1707.* Ed. Samuel A. Green. Groton, 1880, v.d.

GRUND, FRANCIS J. *Aristocracy in America.* London, 1839

A Guide to the City of Chicago. (Chicago Association of Commerce.) [Chicago, ©1909]

GUILD, JOSEPHUS C. *Old Times in Tennessee.* Nashville, 1878. v.d.

GUNN, THOMAS B. *The Physiology of New York Boarding-Houses.* New York, 1857

GUNTER, ARCHIBALD C. *Miss Dividends.* London, 1892

Miss Nobody of Nowhere. 1890

GURNEY, JOSEPH J. *A Journey in North America.* Norwich, Eng., 1841

GWINNETT, BUTTON. *Letters.* (In Charles F. Jenkins. *Button Gwinnett.*) Garden City, N.Y., 1926. v.d.

GYLES, JOHN. *Memoirs of Odd Adventures, Strange Deliverances, &c. in the Captivity of John Gyles.* Boston, 1736

H

HABBERTON, JOHN. *Bowsham Puzzle, a Novel: also My Friend Moses, a Story.* New York, 1884

The Jericho Road. Chicago, 1877 [©1876]

HABERSHAM, JAMES. *Letters . . . 1756–1775.* (Georgia Historical Society. *Collections.* IV.) v.d.

HADDEN, JAMES M. *A Journal Kept in Canada and upon Burgoyne's Campaign in 1776 and 1777.* Albany, 1884. v.d.

HADFIELD, JOSEPH. *An Englishman in America, 1785, being the Diary of Joseph Hadfield.* Ed. Douglas S. Robertson. Toronto, 1933

HAEBERLIN, HERMANN, and GUNTHER, ERNA. *The Indians of Puget Sound.* Seattle, 1930

HAGEMAN, JOHN F. *History of Princeton and Its Institutions.* Philadelphia, 1879

HAILE, BERARD. *Prayer Stick Cutting in a Five Night Navaho Ceremonial of the Male Branch of Shootingway.* Chicago, [1948, ©1947]

HAINES, ELIJAH M. *The American Indian.* Chicago, 1888. v.d.

HALDEMAN, SAMUEL S. *Pennsylvania Dutch: a Dialect of South German with an Infusion of English.* Philadelphia, 1872

HALE, EDWARD EVERETT. *G.T.T.; or, The Wonderful Adventures of a Pullman.* Boston, 1877

If, Yes, and Perhaps. Boston, 1868. v.d.

The Ingham Papers. Boston, 1869. v.d.

Kansas and Nebraska. Boston, 1854

Margaret Percival in America. Boston, 1850

A New England Boyhood. Boston, [1893]

A New England Boyhood, and Other Bits of Autobiography. Boston, 1905 [pref. 1899.] =1900. v.d.

Philip Nolan's Friends. (*Scribner's Monthly,* XI–XIII.) v.d.

Sybaris and Other Homes. Boston, 1879

Ten Times One Is Ten. Boston, 1871 [©1870]

HALE, NANCY. *Between the Dark and the Daylight.* New York, 1943

HALE, PETER M., comp. *The Woods and Timbers of North Carolina.* Raleigh, 1883. Part I comprises M. A. Curtis. *The Woody Plants.* 1860

HALE, RICHARD L. *The Log of a Forty-Niner.* [Ed.] Carolyn H. Russ. Boston, 1923. c1900

HALE, SARAH J. (BUELL). *Flora's Interpreter.* Boston, 1832; 14th ed. impr. Boston, [n.d.]. (Last wrongly cited as 1832.)

HALE, SUSAN. *Letters.* Ed. Caroline P. Atkinson. Boston, 1919. v.d.

HALIBURTON, THOMAS CHANDLER. *The Clockmaker.* [1st Ser.] London, 1838. 1835–37. 2d Ser. London, 1838. 3d Ser. London, 1852. 1840

Nature and Human Nature. 344 pp. London, 1859. 1st ed. 2 vols. London, 1855

Sam Slick in England; or, The Attaché. London, 1858. 1843–44. Cited by running title *The Attaché*

Ed. *Traits of American Humor.* 3 vols. London, 1852

HALL, ABRAHAM OAKEY. *The Manhattaner in New Orleans.* New York, 1851

HALL, ANSEL F. *Handbook of Yosemite National Park.* New York, 1921

HALL, BASIL. *Travels in North America, in the Years 1827 and 1828.* Edinburgh, 1829

HALL, BENJAMIN H. *A Collection of College Words and Customs.* Cambridge, 1851. [2d ed.] rev. and enl. Cambridge, 1856

HALL, BERT, and NILES, JOHN J. *One Man's War; the Story of the Lafayette Escadrille.* New York, [©1929] v.d.

HALL, E. RAYMOND. *The Mammals of Nevada.* Berkeley, 1946

HALL, EDWIN. *The Ancient Historical Records of Norwalk, Conn.* Norwalk, 1874. v.d.

HALL, ELIZA CALVERT, pseud. ELIZA C. (CALVERT) OBENCHAIN. *Aunt Jane of Kentucky.* Boston, 1907. v.d.

HALL, FRANCIS. *Travels in Canada and the United States, in 1816 and 1817.* Boston, 1818

HALL, FREDERICK. *Letters from the East and from the West.* Washington, [1840]

HALL, JAMES. *The Harpe's Head, a Legend of Kentucky.* Philadelphia, 1833

Legends of the West. 2d ed. Philadelphia, 1833. 1832

Letters from the West. London, 1828

Notes on the Western States. Philadelphia, 1838

Sketches of History, Life, and Manners, in the West. Philadelphia, 1835. (Vol. I pub. Cincinnati, 1834.)

Statistics of the West. Cincinnati, 1836

HALL, RUTH. *The Pine Grove House.* Boston, 1903

HALLIBURTON, RICHARD. *The Glorious Adventure.* Indianapolis, [©1927]

HALLIDAY, EVELYN G., and NOBLE, ISABEL T. *Hows and Whys of Cooking.* 3d rev. ed. Chicago, 1946

HALLOCK, CHARLES. *The Sportsman's Gazetteer and General Guide*. Rev. and enl. New York, **1883**. Includes his *Sportsman's Glossary*. **1878**

HALSEY, MARGARET. *Some of My Best Friends Are Soldiers*. New York, **1944**

HAMBLEN, HERBERT E. *The General Manager's Story*. New York, **1898**

Tom Benton's Luck. New York, **1898**

HAMBLETON, JAMES P. *A Biographical Sketch of Henry A. Wise*. Richmond, 1856. **v.d.**

HAMILTON, ALEXANDER. *Works*. Ed. Henry Cabot Lodge. New York, 1885–86. **v.d.**

HAMILTON, GAIL, pseud. MARY A. DODGE. *Country Living and Country Thinking*. Boston, 1865. =**1862**

Gala-Days. Boston, 1865. =**1863**

A New Atmosphere. Boston, **1865**

Skirmishes and Sketches. Boston, 1866. =**1865**

Twelve Miles from a Lemon. New York, **1874**

HAMILTON, THOMAS. *Men and Manners in America*. London, **1833**

HAMILTON, WILLIAM J. *American Mammals*. New York, **1939**

HAMMOND, JABEZ D. *The History of Political Parties in the State of New-York*. Albany, **1842**

HAMMOND, SAMUEL H. *Hills, Lakes, and Forest Streams*. New York, **1854**

Wild Northern Scenes. New York, **1857**

HAMMOND, WILLIAM G. *Remembrance of Amherst, an Undergraduate's Diary, 1846–1848*. New York, 1946. **v.d.**

HAMNER, LAURA V. *Short Grass & Longhorns*. Norman, Okla., **1943**

HAMOR, RALPH. *A True Discovrse of the Present Estate of Virginia*. London, **1615**

HANCOCK, HARRIE I. *Life at West Point*. New York, **1902**

HANCOCK, WILLIAM. *An Emigrant's Five Years in the Free States of America*. London, **1860**

HANDLEY, DANIEL. *Prison Echoes of the Great Rebellion*. New York, 1874. **v.d.**

HANDSAKER, SAMUEL. *Pioneer Life*. Eugene, Ore., 1908. **v.d.**

HANGER, GEORGE. *The Life, Adventures, and Opinions of Col. George Hanger*. London, **1801**

HANKINS, CHARLES A. *Dakota Land*. New York, **1868**. 2d ed. New York, **1869**

HANSON, ELIZABETH. *An Account of the Captivity of Elizabeth Hanson*. London, **1769**. First pub. Philadelphia, 1728, as *God's Mercy Surmounting Man's Cruelty, Exemplified in the Captivity . . . of Elizabeth Hanson*.

HAPGOOD, HUTCHINS. *The Autobiography of a Thief*. New York, **1903**

HARBEN, WILLIAM N. *Abner Daniel*. New York, **1902**

The Georgians. New York, **1904**

Westerfelt. New York, **1901**

HARGIS, MRS. LAVINIA. *The Graded Cook Book*. Chicago, **1888**

HARK, ANN. *Hex Marks the Spot, in the Pennsylvania Dutch Country*. New York, **[1938]**

HARLAN, JACOB W. *California '46 to '88*. San Francisco, **1888**

HARLAND, MARION, pseud. MARY V. (HAWES) TERHUNE. *Common Sense in the Household*. New York, 1884. =**1881**

The Empty Heart; or, Husks. "For Better, for Worse." New York, 1871. Includes *Husks*, **1863**. *For Better, for Worse*, **1870**

Eve's Daughters. New York, **1882**

HARLOW, WILLIAM M. *Trees of the Eastern United States and Canada*. New York, **1942**

HARMON, DANIEL W. *A Journal of Voyages and Travels in the Interiour of North America*. New York, 1903. **1820**

HARPER, IDA HUSTED. *The Life and Work of Susan B. Anthony*. Indianapolis, **1898**

HARPER, ROLAND M. *Preliminary Report on the Weeds of Alabama*. University, Ala., **1944**

HARRELL, JOHN M. *The Brooks and Baxter War; a History of the Reconstruction Period in Arkansas*. St. Louis, 1893. **v.d.**

HARRIGAN, EDWARD. *The Mulligans*. New York, **1901**

HARRINGTON, MARK R. *Gypsum Cave, Nevada*. Los Angeles, **1933**

HARRIOT, THOMAS. *A Briefe and True Report of the New Found Land of Virginia*. London, **1588**. Also facsimile, Ann Arbor, 1931.

HARRIS, BERNICE K. *Purslane*. Chapel Hill, **1939**

HARRIS, CORRA MAY. *Eve's Second Husband*. Philadelphia, **1910**

HARRIS, GEORGE WASHINGTON. *Sut Luvingood. Yarns Spun by a "Nat'ral Born Durn'd Fool."* New York, [°1867]. **v.d.**

HARRIS, JOEL CHANDLER. *Balaam and His Master, and Other Sketches and Stories*. Boston, **1891**

Mingo and Other Sketches in Black and White. Boston, 1884. **v.d.**

Mr. Rabbitt at Home. Boston, **1895**

Nights with Uncle Remus. Boston, 1911 [°**1883**]

On the Plantation. New York, **1892**

On the Wing of Occasions. New York, **1900**

Tales of the Home Folks in Peace and War. Boston, **1898**

Uncle Remus and His Friends. Boston, **1892**

Uncle Remus, His Songs and His Sayings; the Folk-Lore of the Old Plantation. New York, **1880**

HARRIS, JOHN. *Navigantium atque itinerantium bibliotheca; or, a Compleat Collection of Voyages and Travels*. London, **1705**

HARRIS, MIRIAM (COLES). *Louie's Last Term at St. Mary's*. New York, **1864**

The Tents of Wickedness. New York, **1907**

HARRIS, THADDEUS MASON. *The Journal of a Tour into the Territory Northwest of the Alleghany Mountains. . . . With a Geographical and Historical Account of the State of Ohio*. Boston, **1805**

HARRIS, THADDEUS WILLIAM. *A Treatise on Some of the Insects of New England Which Are Injurious to Vegetation*. Cambridge, **1842**. 2d ed. Boston, **1852**. New ed. as *A Treatise on Some of the Insects Injurious to Vegetation*. **1862**

HARRISON, WILLIAM HENRY. *Messages and Letters*. Ed. Logan Esarey. (*Indiana Historical Collections*. VII, IX.) **v.d.**

HARROWER, JOHN. *Diary . . . , 1773–1776*. (*American Historical Review*. VI.) **v.d.**

HART, ALBERT BUSHNELL. *Actual Government as Applied under American Conditions*. New York, **1903**

HART, FRED H. *The Sazerac Lying Club*. San Francisco, **1878**

HART, JEROME A. *A Vigilante Girl*. Chicago, **1910**

HART, SMITH, *The New Yorkers*. New York, [°**1938**]

HARTE, BRET. *Writings*. Standard Library Ed. [Boston, °1896–1903]. **v.d.**

The Argonauts of North Liberty. Boston, **1888**

Barker's Luck, and Other Stories. Boston, **1896**

The Bell-Ringer of Angel's, and Other Stories. Leipzig, **1894**

Clarence. Boston, **1895**

Colonel Starbottle's Client, and Some Other People. Boston, **1892**

Condensed Novels. And Other Papers. New York, **1867**

Drift from Two Shores. Boston, **1879**. =1878.

East and West Poems. Boston, **1871**

A First Family of Tasajara. Boston, 1892. First pub. Leipzig, **1891**

Flip and Found at Blazing Star. Boston, **1882**

Gabriel Conroy. (*Scribner's Monthly*. XI–XII.) Also Hartford, 1876. **v.d.**

The Heritage of Dedlow Marsh, and Other Tales. Boston, 1890. **1889**

In the Carquinez Woods. Boston, 1884. First pub., copyright ed., Hamburg, **1883**

The Luck of Roaring Camp, and Other Sketches. Boston, 1871. =1689. **v.d.**

Maruja. Boston, **1885**

A Millionaire of Rough-and-Ready and Devil's Ford. Boston, **1887**

Mr. Jack Hamlin's Mediation, and Other Stories. Boston, **1899** =[°1889].

Mrs. Skaggs's Husbands, and Other Sketches. Boston, **1873**

On the Frontier. Boston, **1884**

Poems. Boston, **1884**

Poetical Works. Complete Ed. Boston, **1882**

Poetical Works. Household Ed. Boston, [°1912]. **v.d.**

A Protégée of Jack Hamlin's, and Other Stories. Boston, **1894**

A Sappho of Green Springs, and Other Stories. Boston, **1894**

Snow-bound at Eagle's. Boston, **1886**

The Story of a Mine, and Other Tales. (*Writings*, III.) **1896**. First pub., authorized ed., Leipzig, 1877.

Susy, a Story of the Plains. Boston, **1893**

Tales of the Argonauts, and Other Sketches. Boston, 1875. **v.d.**

HARTE, BRET, and TWAIN, MARK. *Sketches of the Sixties*. San Francisco, 1926. **v.d.**

[*Hartford Land Distrib.*] *Distribution of Lands in Hartford*. (Connecticut Historical Society. *Collections*. XIV.) **v.d.**

Hartford Town Votes. (Connecticut Historical Society. *Collections*. VI.) **v.d.**

Harvard College Records. (Colonial Society of Massachusetts. *Publications*. XV–XVI, XXXI.) **v.d.**

The Harvard Register. Cambridge, **1827–28**

HARVARD UNIVERSITY. *The Constitution of the University at Cambridge*. Cambridge, **1812**

The Laws of Harvard College. Boston, **1790**. Also Boston, **1798**; Cambridge, **1807, 1814, 1816, 1820**

Laws of Harvard University, Relative to Undergraduates. Cambridge, **1841**. Also Cambridge, **1845**. Includes *Orders and Regulations of the Faculty of Harvard University*.

Statutes and Laws of the University in Cambridge, Massachusetts. Cambridge, **1825**. Also: Cambridge, **1826, 1828**

Harvardiana. Cambridge. **1834–38**

HASKELL, WILLIAM B. *Two Years in the Klondike and Alaskan Gold-fields*. Hartford, **1898**

HASKIN, FREDERIC J. *The American Government*. Philadelphia, **1912**

HASKINS, C. W. *The Argonauts of California*. New York, **1890**

HASWELL, CHARLES H. *Reminiscences of an Octogenarian of the City of New York (1816 to 1860)*. New York, **1896**

HATCHER, HARLAN H. *The Buckeye Country; a Pageant of Ohio*. New York, **1940**

HAUSMAN, LEON A. *Field Book of Eastern Birds*. New York, **1946**

HAVARD VALERY. *The Report on the Flora of Western and Southern Texas*. Washington, **1885**

Haverly's Genuine Colored Minstrels' Songster. New York, **[1879]**

HAWEIS, HUGH R. *American Humorists*. New York, [°**1883**]. Consisting in part of lectures delivered **1881**

HAWES, WILLIAM P. *Sporting Scenes and Sundry Sketches*. New York, 1842. *a***1841**

HAWKINS, BENJAMIN. *Letters, 1796–1806* (Georgia Historical Society. *Collections*. IX.) **v.d.**

A Sketch of the Creek Country, in 1798 and 99. (*Ib.*, III.) **1800**

HAWKINS, PLINY H. *The Trees and Shrubs of Yellowstone National Park*. Menasha, Wis., **1924**

HAWKS, FRANCIS L. *The Adventures of Daniel Boone, the Kentucky Rifleman*. New York, **1843**

The History of the Western States. Boston, 1844. =**1835**

HAWLEY, ZERAH. *A Journal of a Tour through Connecticut* [etc.]. New Haven, 1922. **v.d.**

HAWORTH, PAUL L. *George Washington, Farmer*. Indianapolis, [°**1915**]

HAWTHORNE, JULIAN. *Fortune's Fool*. London, **1883**

Nathaniel Hawthorne and His Wife: A Biography. Boston, 1885. =1884. **v.d.**

HAWTHORNE, NATHANIEL. *Works*. Standard Library Ed. Boston, 1891. =1883–89. **v.d.**

American Notebooks. Ed. Randall Stewart. New Haven, 1932. **v.d.**

The Blithedale Romance. Boston, **1852**

The House of the Seven Gables. Boston, **1851**

Mosses from an Old Manse. New York, **1846**

Our Old Home. Boston, **1863**

Passages from the American Note-Books. [Ed. Sophia Hawthorne.] 2 vols. Boston, **1868**

Passages from the English Note-Books. [Ed. Sophia Hawthorne.] 2 vols. Boston, 1870. **v.d.**

Passages from the French and Italian Note-Books of Nathaniel Hawthorne. 2 vols. Boston, 1872. **v.d.**

The Scarlet Letter. Boston, **1850**

Twice-told Tales. Rev. ed. Boston, 1851. 13th ed. Boston, [1879]. **v.d.**

HAY, JOHN. *The Bread-Winners: A Social Study*. New York, [°**1883**]

Pike County Ballads and Other Pieces. Boston, **1871**

Little-Breeches. New York, **1871**

HAYAKAWA, SAMUEL ICHIYÉ. *Language in Action*. New York, **1941**

HAYCRAFT, SAMUEL. *A History of Elizabethtown, Kentucky, and its Surroundings*. Elizabethtown, Ky., 1921. First pub. *Elizabethtown News*, 1869, and repr. 1889–90. **v.d.**

HAYDEN, ARTHUR. *Chats on English China*. London, **1904**

HAYES, BENJAMIN I. *Pioneer Notes from the Diaries. . . . 1849–1875*. Ed. Marjorie T. Walcott. Los Angeles, 1929. **v.d.**

HAYWARD, JOHN. *Hayward's Gazetteer of Maine*. Portland, **1843**

HAZARD, CAROLINE. *Thomas Hazard son of Robt, call'd College Tom*. Boston, 1893. **v.d.**

HAZARD, EBENEZER. *Historical Collections; Consisting of State Papers and Other Authentic Documents*. Philadelphia, 1792–94. **v.d.**

HAZARD, THOMAS B. *Nailer Tom's Diary: otherwise, The Journal of Thomas B. Hazard, . . . 1778 to 1840*. Boston, 1930. **v.d.**

HAZARD, THOMAS R. *The Jonny-Cake Papers of "Shepherd Tom."* Boston, 1915. *c***1880**

HAZLITT, MARGARET. *Diary*. (In WILLIAM C. HAZLITT, *Four Generations of a Literary Family*. I. London, 1897.) Written 1783–87, rewritten *c***1837**

HEAD, SIR GEORGE. *Forest Scenes and Incidents, in the Wilds of North America*. London, **1829**

HEALY, TIMOTHY M. *Letters and Leaders of My Day*. New York, [1928]. **v.d.**

HEALY & BIGELOW, firm. New Haven, Conn. *Life and Scenes among the Kickapoo Indians, Their Manners, Habits and Customs*. New Haven, [189–?]

HEARN, LAFCADIO. *American Miscellany*. New York, 1924. **v.d.**

La Cuisine Creole. New Orleans, **1885**

HEATH, WILLIAM. *Heath Papers*. (Massachusetts Historical Society. *Collections*. 5th Ser., IV; 7th Ser., IV–V.) **v.d.**

HEBARD, GRACE R. *The Bozeman Trail*. Cleveland, **1922**

Washakie, Cleveland, **1930**

HEBERT, FRANK. *40 Years Prospecting and Mining in the Black Hills of South Dakota*. [Rapid City, S.D., ©**1921**.]

HECTOR, ANNIE (FRENCH). *Going West; or, Homes for the Homeless*. Indianapolis, **1881**

HEDLEY, FENWICK Y. *Marching through Georgia*. Chicago, 1890 [©**1884**]

HELPER, HINTON R. *The Impending Crisis of the South: How to Meet It*. New York, **1860**. =1857.

The Land of Gold. Baltimore, **1855**

Nojoque. New York, **1867**

HEMING, ARTHUR. *The Living Forest*. New York, **1925**

HEMPSTEAD, JOSHUA. *Diary . . . from September, 1711, to November, 1758*. New London, Conn., 1901. **v.d.**

HEMPSTEAD, N.Y. *Records of the Towns of North and South Hempstead, Long Island, N.Y.* Ed. Benjamin J. Hicks. Jamaica, N.Y., 1896–1904. **v.d.**

HENDERSON, GEORGE C. *Keys to Crookdom*. New York, **1924**

HENDERSON, MARY N. (FOOTE). *Practical Cooking and Dinner Giving*. New York, 1883 [©**1876**]

HENDRICK, BURTON J. *Lincoln's War Cabinet*. Boston, **1946**

HENFREY, ARTHUR H. *An Elementary Course of Botany*. 2d ed. rev. and rewritten by Maxwell T. Masters. London, **1870**

HENNEPIN, LOUIS. *A New Discovery of a Vast Country in America*. London, **1698**

HENRY, ALEXANDER. *The Manuscript Journals of Alexander Henry Fur Trader of the Northwest Company and of David Thompson Official Geographer and Explorer of the Same Company 1799–1814*. Ed. Elliott Coues. New York, 1897. **v.d.**

Travels and Adventures in Canada and the Indian Territories between the Years 1760 and 1776. New York, **1809**. New ed., ed. James Bain. Toronto, 1901. **v.d.**

HENRY, JOHN J. *An Accurate and Interesting Account . . . of that Band of Heroes, Who Traversed the Wilderness in the Campaign against Quebec in 1775*. Lancaster, Pa., 1812. *a***1811**

HENRY, O., pseud. See O. HENRY.

HENRY, STUART. *Conquering Our Great American Plains*. New York, **1930**

HENRY, WILLIAM S. *Campaign Sketches of the War with Mexico*. New York, **1847**

Herald of Freedom. Edenton, N.C., **1799**. (Similar citations, 1854–60, refer to *Kansas Herald of Freedom q.v.*)

Herb Magic and Wisconsin Ferns and Wild Flowers. (Nursery Catalogue of Mr. and Mrs. W. A. Toole, Baraboo, Wis.) **1944**

HERBERT, HENRY W. *Forester's Horse and Horsemanship of the United States and British Provinces of North America*. New York, **1857**

HERGESHEIMER, JOSEPH. *The Bright Shawl*. New York, **1922**

HERIOT, GEORGE. *Travels through the Canadas*. London, **1807**

HERRICK, CHARLES J. *The Brain of the Tiger Salamander:* Ambystoma tigrinum. Chicago, [**1948**]

HERRICK, ROBERT. *Homely Lilla*. New York, [**1823**]

HERRMANN, FRIEDERICH. *Die Deutschen in Nordamerika*. Lüben, **1806**

HERTRICH, WILLIAM. *The Huntington Botanical Gardens, 1905–1949*. San Marino, Calif., **1949**

HEWETT, EDGAR L. *Pajarito Plateau and Its Ancient People*. Albuquerque, **1938**

HEWETT, EDGAR L., and FISHER, REGINALD G. *Mission Monuments of New Mexico*. [Albuquerque], **1943**

HEWITT, RANDALL H. *Across the Plains and Over the Divide*. New York, [©1926] **1862**

HEYLYN, PETER. *Cosmography*. London, **1703**

HIBBEN, SHEILA. *American Regional Cookery*. Boston, **1946**

HIBERNICUS, pseud. DE WITT CLINTON. *Letters on the Natural History and Internal Resources of the State of New-York*. New York, 1822. **1820**

HICKMAN, WILLIAM A. *Brigham's Destroying Angel; Being the Life of . . . the Notorious Bill Hickman*. New York, **1872**

HICKS, JOHN D. *A Short History of American Democracy*. Boston, **1943**

HIGGINSON, FRANCIS. *New-Englands Plantation*. [1st ed.] London, **1630**

HIGGINSON, THOMAS WENTWORTH. *Army Life in a Black Regiment*. Boston, **1870**

Oldport Days. Boston, **1873**

Outdoor Studies. Boston, **1900**

HILDRETH, JAMES. *Dragoon Campaigns to the Rocky Mountains*. New York, **1836**

HILL, ALICE (POLK). *Tales of the Colorado Pioneers*. Denver, **1884**

HILL, JIM D. *Sea Dogs of the Sixties*. Minneapolis, **1935**

HILTON, JOHN W. *Sonora Sketch Book*. New York, **1947**

HILTZHEIMER, JACOB. *Extracts from the Diary . . . , 1765–1798*. Ed. Jacob C. Parsons. Philadelphia, 1893. **v.d.**

HINDS, WILLIAM A. *American Communities*. Rev. ed. Chicago, **1902**

HINES, GUSTAVUS. *Wild Life in Oregon*. New York, [n.d.]. =his *A Voyage round the World*. Buffalo, 1850. **v.d.**

HINTON, RICHARD J. *Hand-book to Arizona*. San Francisco, **1878**

Hist. Charlestown. See FROTHINGHAM.

Hist. Coll. Ohio. See HOWE, HENRY.

Hist. Coll. S.C. See CARROLL, B. R.

Hist. Northampton. See TRUMBULL, J. R.

Hist. Pelham, Mass. See PARMENTER.

Hist. Saco. See FOLSOM.

History of Congress. Philadelphia, **1834**

History of the North-western Soldiers' Fair. Chicago, **1864**

HITCHCOCK, ALBERT S. *Manual of the Grasses of the United States*. Washington, **1938**

HITCHCOCK, ETHAN ALLEN. *A Traveler in Indian Territory: The Journal of Ethan Allen Hitchcock*. Ed. Grant Foreman. Cedar Rapids, Ia., 1930. **v.d.**

HITTELL, JOHN S. *The Resources of California*. San Francisco, **1874**

HOBART, GEORGE V. *It's Up to You*. New York, [**1902**]

John Henry. New York, [©**1901**]

HOBBS, CHARLES E. *C. E. Hobbs' Botanical Hand-book of Common Local, English, Botanical and Pharmacopœial Names*. Boston, **1876**

HODGE, FREDERICK WEBB, *et al. Handbook of American Indians North of Mexico*. Washington, **1907–10**

HODGE, HIRAM C. *Arizona as It Is*. Boston, **1877**

HODGINS, ERIC. *Mr. Blandings Builds His Dream House*. New York, **1946**

?HODGKINSON. *Letters of Emigration. By a Gentleman, Lately Returned from America*. London, **1794**

HODGSON, ADAM. *Letters from North America, Written During a Tour in the United States and Canada*. London, **1824**. Reissue, in part, of *Remarks During a Journey . . .* New York, 1823.

HOFFMAN, MRS. C. O. *The Night Watch*. Cincinnati, **1856**

HOFFMAN, CHARLES FENNO. *Greyslaer: A Romance of the Mohawk*. New York, **1840**

Wild Scenes in the Forest. London, [**1839**]

A Winter in the West. New York, **1835**

HOLBROOK, JAMES. *Ten Years among the Mail Bags*. Philadelphia, **1855**

HOLBROOK, JOHN E. *North American Herpetology*. Enl. ed. Philadelphia, **1842**

HOLBROOK, STEWART H. *Lost Men of American History*. New York, **1946**

HOLDEN, WILLIAM C. *Alkali Trails*. Dallas, [©**1930**]

HOLDER, CHARLES F. *The Channel Islands of California*. Chicago, **1910**

Marvels of Animal Life. New York, **1885**

HOLDING, ELIZABETH (SANXAY). *The Innocent Mrs. Duff*. New York, **1946**

HOLLAND, JOSIAH G. *Arthur Bonnicastle*. **1873**

The Bay-Path. New York, **1857**

Miss Gilbert's Career. New York, 1866. =**1860**

Sevenoaks, a Story of To-day. New York, 1901. =**1875**

HOLLAND, WILLIAM J. *The Moth Book*. New York, **1903**

HOLLANDER, ARIE N. J. DEN. *De landelijke arme blanken in het Zuider der Vereenegde Staten*. Groningen, **1933**

HOLLEY, MARIETTA. *My Opinions and Betsey Bobbet's*. Hartford, 1901. =**1873**

Samantha at the St. Louis Exposition. New York, [**1904**]

Samatha at the World's Fair. New York, **1893**

HOLLEY, MARY (AUSTIN). *Texas. Observations. . . . 1831*. Baltimore, 1833. **1831**. Also, greatly enl. *Texas*. Lexington, Ky., **1836**

HOLLISTER, OVANDO J. *The Mines of Colorado*. Springfield, Mass., **1867**

HOLMES, ABIEL. *The Life of Ezra Stiles*. Boston, **1798**

HOLMES, EZEKIEL. *Report of an Exploration and Survey of the Territory on the Aroostook River*. Augusta, Me., **1839**

HOLMES, ISAAC. *An Account of the United States of America, Derived from Actual Observation*. London, [**1823**]

HOLMES, MARY J. (HAWES). *Aikenside*. New York, [n.d.]. *c***1900**. Rewritten from *Madeline q.v.*

Cousin Maude. New York, **1860**

The Homestead on the Hillside, and Other Tales. New York, 1897. **1856**. Cited by story titles *The Gable-roofed House at Snowdon. The Gilberts; or, Rice Corner Number Two. Glen's Creek. The Homestead on the Hillside. The Old Red House among the Mountains. Rice Corner. The Thanksgiving Party and Its Consequences.*

'Lena Rivers. New York, 1870. =**1856**

Madeline. New York, **1881**

Meadow-Brook. New York, **1857**

Tempest and Sunshine. New York, 1860. =**1854**

HOLMES, OLIVER WENDELL. *The Autocrat of the Breakfast Table*. Boston, **1858**

Complete Poetical Works. Cambridge Ed. [©1908]. =1895. **v.d.**

Elsie Venner. Boston, **1861**. First pub. as *The Professor's Story*. (*Atlantic Monthly*. Jan., 1860–April, 1861.)

The Guardian Angel. Boston, **1867**

Humorous Poems. Boston, 1865. **v.d.**

Medical Essays, 1842–1882. 2d ed. Boston, 1883. **v.d.**

A Mortal Antipathy. Boston, **1885**

Over the Teacups. Boston, **1891**

Pages from an Old Volume of Life. Boston, 1883. **v.d.**

The Professor at the Breakfast Table, with the Story of Iris. Boston, 1880. =**1860**. First pub. *Atlantic Monthly*, Jan.–Dec., 1859.

Wit & Humour: Poems. London, **1867**

HOLT, RACKHAM. *George Washington Carver*. New York, **1943**

HOLTEN, SAMUEL. *Journal . . . , May, 1778, to August, 1780*. (Essex Institute. *Historical Collections*. LV–LVI.) **v.d.**

HOLTON, EDITH A. *Yankees Were like This*. New York, [**1944**]

The Holyoke Diaries, 1790–1856. Ed. George F. Dow. Salem, Mass., 1911. **v.d.**

The Home Missionary. New York, **1829–1909**

HONE, PHILIP. *Diary . . . , 1828–1851*. Ed. Bayard Tuckerman. New York, 1889. **v.d.**

HONYMAN, ROBERT. *Colonial Panorama, 1775. Dr. Robert Honyman's Journal*. Ed. Philip Padelford. San Marino, Calif., 1939. **1775**

HOOKER, SIR WILLIAM J. *Flora Boreali-Americana*. London, [**1829**]–**40**

HOOPER, EDWARD J. *The Practical Farmer, Gardener and Housewife*. Cincinnati, **1839**

HOOPER, JOHNSON J. *The Adventures of Captain Simon Suggs . . . together with "Taking the Census" and Other Alabama Sketches*. Americus, Ga., 1928. **1845**

The Widow Rugby's Husband. Philadelphia, [n.d.] =**1851**

HOPKINS, ANDREW D. *Contributions toward a Monograph of the Scolytid Beetles*. Washington, **1909**

HOPKINS, ESEK. *Correspondence*. Ed. Alverda S. Beck. Providence, 1933. **v.d.**

HOPKINS, JOHN M. *Forty-Five Years with the Okefenokee Swamp 1900–45*. (Georgia Society of Naturalists. *Bulletin*. No. 4.) *c***1945**

HOPLEY, CATHERINE C. *Life in the South*. London, **1863**

HOPPE, ALEXANDER. *Englisch-Deutsches Supplementlexicon*. Berlin, **1871**

HORN, STANLEY. *Invisible Empire*. Boston, **1939**

HORNADAY, WILLIAM T. *Campfires on Desert and Lava*. New York, **1908**

HORNBLOW, ARTHUR. *The Profligate*. New York, [©**1908**]

Horticulturist and Journal of Rural Art and Rural Taste. Albany, **1846–75**

HORWILL, HERBERT W. *A Dictionary of Modern American Usage*. Oxford, **1935**

HOSMER, JOHN A. *A Trip to the States in 1865*. Ed. Edith M. Duncan. Missoula, Mont., 1932. **1867**

HOSTETTER, GORDON L., and BEESLEY, THOMAS Q. *It's a Racket!* Chicago, **1929**

HOUGH, EMERSON. *The Sagebrusher*. New York, **1919**

The Story of the Cowboy. New York, **1897**

HOUSE, HOMER D. *Wild Flowers of New York*. Albany, **1918**

HOUSTOUN, MATILDA C. (JESSE) F. *Hesperos: or Travels in the West*. London, **1850**

Texas and the Gulf of Mexico. Philadelphia, 1845. First pub. **1844**

HOVEY, CARL. *The Life Story of J. Pierpont Morgan*. New York, 1911

HOVEY, HORACE C., and CALL, RICHARD E. *Mammoth Cave of Kentucky*. Louisville, 1897

How Gamblers Win.... By a Retired Professional. New York, [c1868]

HOWARD, H. R., comp. *The History of Virgil A. Stewart, and His Adventure in Capturing and Exposing the Great "Western Land Pirate" and His Gang*. New York, 1836

HOWARD, JOSEPH K. *Montana: High, Wide, and Handsome*. New Haven, 1943

HOWE, EDGAR W. *A Moonlight Boy*. Boston, 1886
Plain People. New York, 1929
The Story of a Country Town. New York, 1926. =1884. First pub. 1883

HOWE, ELIAS. *The Ethiopian Glee Book, Complete*. Boston, 1849

HOWE, HELEN. *We Happy Few*. New York, 1946

HOWE, HENRY. *Historical Collections of Ohio*. Cincinnati, 1847. v.d.

HOWELL, ARTHUR H. *Florida Bird Life*. New York, 1932

HOWELLS, WILLIAM DEAN. *A Boy's Town*. New York, 1890
A Chance Acquaintance. Boston, 1873
The Coast of Bohemia. New York, 1893
A Hazard of New Fortunes. New York, [c1889]
An Imperative Duty. 1891
Impressions and Experiences. New York, 1896
The Lady of the Aroostook. Boston, [c1879]
Literary Friends and Acquaintances. New York, 1902. First pub. 1900
The Minister's Charge. Boston, [c1886]
A Modern Instance. 1882
An Open-eyed Conspiracy. 1897
Out of the Question. 1877
The Quality of Mercy. New York, 1892
The Rise of Silas Lapham. Boston, 1885. First pub. 1884–85
The Shadow of a Dream. 1890
The Undiscovered Country. Boston, 1880
The Vacation of the Kelwyns. New York, [c1920]
Venetian Life. New York, 1866
The Wedding Journey. Boston, 1874 [c1871]

HOWISON, JOHN. *Sketches of Upper Canada ... and Some Recollections of the United States of America*. Edinburgh, 2d ed. 1822. 1821

HOWLAND, ESTHER (ALLEN). *The New England Economical Housekeeper, and Family Receipt Book*. Worcester, 1845

HOWLAND, S. A. *Steamboat Disasters and Railroad Accidents in the United States*. Worcester, 1846. =1840. v.d.

HOYLE, EDMOND. *Hoyle's Games.... With American Additions*. Philadelphia, 1882. [advt. 1857]
Hoyle's Games. Rev. and enl. New York, 1907

HOYT, CHARLES H. See MOSES. *Representative American Dramas*.

HUBBARD, LUCIUS L. *Hubbard's Guide to Moosehead Lake and Northern Maine*. 3d ed., rev. and enl. Boston, [c1882]

HUBBARD, WILLIAM. *A General History of New England*. (Massachusetts Historical Society. *Collections*. 2d Ser., V–VI.) a1704
A Narrative of the Troubles with the Indians in New-England. Boston, 1677. Also pub. as *The Present State of New-England*. London, 1677

HUDSON, ARTHUR P., ed. *Humor of the Old Deep South*. New York, 1936. v.d.

HUDSON, FREDERIC. *Journalism in the United States*. New York, 1873

HUGHES, JOHN TAYLOR. *Doniphan's Expedition*. Cincinnati, 1848. Also repr., with extensive additions [ed. William E. Connelley] Topeka, Kans., 1907. Includes his *Diary*. v.d.

HUGHES, THOMAS, ed. *G. T. T. Gone to Texas; Letters from Our Boys*. New York, 1884

HULBERT, WILLIAM D. *Forest Neighbors*. New York, 1902

HULL, JOHN. *Diaries*. (American Antiquarian Society. *Archæologia Americana*. III.) v.d.

HULME, THOMAS. See THWAITES.

HULTON, ANN. *Letters of a Loyalist Lady ... 1767–1776*. Cambridge, 1927. v.d.

HUMBOLDT, FREIHERR ALEXANDER VON. *Personal Narrative of Travels to the Equinoctial Regions of the New Continent*. Tr. Helen M. Williams. Philadelphia, 1805
Political Essay on the Kingdom of New Spain. Tr. John Black. New York, 1811

HUME, JOHN F. *The Abolitionists*. New York, 1905

HUMPHREYS, DAVID. *A Poem on Industry*. Philadelphia, 1794
The Yankee in England. [n.p. 1815]

HUMPHREYS, DAVID, *et al*. *The Anarchiad: A New England Poem*. Ed. Luther G. Riggs. New Haven, 1861. 1786–87

HUNGERFORD, EDWIN. *Wells Fargo. Advancing the American Frontier*. New York, [1949]

HUNT, JAMES H. *History of the Mormon War*. St. Louis, 1844

HUNTER, JOHN MARVIN., comp. and ed. *The Trail Drivers of Texas*. [San Antonio, [c1920]–23

HUNTINGTON, N.Y. *Huntington Town Records*. [Ed.] Charles R. Street. [Huntington], 1887–89. v.d.

HUNTINGTON, WILLIAM S. *The Road-Master's Assistant and Section-Master's Guide*. 2d ed. New York, 1872

HUNTLEY, SIR HENRY V. *California; Its Gold and Its Inhabitants*. London, 1856. v.d.

HUTCHINGS, JAMES M. *In the Heart of the Sierras*. Oakland, Calif., 1886

Hutchings' Illustrated California Magazine. San Francisco, 1856–61

HUTCHINS, THOMAS. *An Historical Narrative and Topographical Description of Louisiana and West-Florida*. Philadelphia, 1784
A Topographical Description of Virginia, Pennsylvania, Maryland, and North Carolina. London, 1778

HUTCHINSON, JOHN W. *The Free Soil Minstrel*. Buffalo, 1848

HUTCHINSON, THOMAS. *A Collection of Original Papers Relative to the History of the Colony of Massachusetts-Bay*. Boston, 1769. v.d.
Diary and Letters. Comp. Peter O. Hutchinson. London, 1883–86. v.d.
The History of the Colony of Massachusetts-Bay. 3 vols. Boston, 1764–1828. (3d vol. comp. John Hutchinson.) 3d ed. Vols. I–II. Salem, 1795. v.d.

HUTT, FREDERICK B. *Genetics of the Fowl*. New York, 1949

HUYSHE, GEORGE L. *The Red River Expedition*. New York, 1871

HYATT, ALPHEUS. [*Biological Lectures*.] *Some Governing Factors usually Neglected in Biological Investigations*. (Woods Hole Marine Biological Laboratory. *Lectures*.) 1899

HYDE, GEORGE E. *Red Cloud's Folk*. Norman, Okla., 1937

HYDE, GRANT M. *Newspaper Reporting and Correspondence*. New York, 1912

I

IDE, WILLIAM B. *California History*. Claremont, N.H., 1880. v.d.

ILGEN, WILLIAM L. *Forge Work*. New York, [c1912]

Illinois Central (*Employes'*) *Magazine*. Chicago, 1909–

IMLAY, GILBERT. *A Topographical Description of the Western Territory of North America*. London, 1792. 3d ed. London, 1797. v.d.

Imperial Night-Hawk. Atlanta, 1923–24

The Importance of Gaining and Preserving the Friendship of the Indians to the British Interest Consider'd. By Archibald Kennedy. London, 1752. First pub. New York, 1751.

The Importance of Jamaica to Great-Britain, Consider'd. London, [1740]

Independent Chronicle. Boston, 1776–1840

[*Index to Patents*.] *Subject-Matter Index of Patents from 1790 to 1873*. (U.S. Patent Office.) Washington, 1874. v.d.

Indian Affairs. Laws and Treaties. Comp. Charles J. Kappler. Washington, 1903–. v.d.

INGERSOLL, ERNEST. *The Oyster-Industry*. Washington, 1881

INGERSOLL, LUTHER A. *Ingersoll's Century History, Santa Monica Bay Cities*. Los Angeles, 1908

INGHAM, GEORGE T. *Digging Gold among the Rockies*. Philadelphia, [1880]

INGRAHAM, JOSEPH H. *Burton; or, The Sieges*. New York, 1838
The South-West. New York, 1835

INGRAM, J. S. *The Centennial Exposition*. Philadelphia, [c1876]

INMAN, HENRY. *The Old Santa Fe Trail*. New York, 1897

Inter-Ocean. Chicago, 1872–1914

Internal Revenue Guide. Ed. Charles N. Emerson. Springfield, Mass., 1866. v.d.

International Annual of Anthony's Photographic Bulletin and American Process Yearbook. New York, 1888–1902

IPSWICH, MASS. *The Ancient Records of the Town of Ipswich*. Ed. George A. Schofield. Ipswich, 1899. v.d.

IRVING, PIERRE M. *The Life and Letters of Washington Irving*. New York, 1862–64. v.d.

IRVING, WASHINGTON. *Adventures of Captain Bonneville*. London, 1837
Astoria. 2 vols. Philadelphia, 1841. =1836.
A History of New York, from the Beginning of the World to the End of the Dutch Dynasty. 2 vols. New York, 1809. (Also cited from others of numerous eds.)
The Rocky Mountains. 2 vols. Philadelphia, 1843. =his *Adventures of Captain Bonneville*. 1837. Usu. cited as *Bonneville*.
The Sketch Book of Geoffrey Crayon. [2d ed.] New York, 1819–20
Tales of a Traveller. London, 1824
A Tour on the Prairies. London, 1835

IRVING, WASHINGTON, *et al*. *Salmagundi*. Pub. serially, 20 nos., New York, Jan. 1807–Jan. 1808. Cited also from various later eds.

IRWIN, WILLIAM H. *The Red Button*. Indianapolis, [c1912]

IVES, J. M. *New England Book of Fruit*. Salem, Mass., 1847

IVES, JOSEPH C. *Report upon the Colorado River of the West, Explored in 1857 and 1858*. Washington, 1861

J

JACKSON, ALFRED T. *Diary of a Forty-Niner*. See CANFIELD, C. D.

JACKSON, GEORGE A. *Diary*. In HALL, FRANK. *History of the State of Colorado*, Vol. II. Chicago, 1889–95. v.d.

JACKSON, GEORGE P. *White Spirituals in the Southern Uplands. The Story of the Fasola Folk, Their Songs, Singings, and "Buckwheat Notes."* Chapel Hill, 1933

JACKSON, HELEN M. (FISKE) HUNT. *Between Whiles*. Boston, 1887
Bits of Travel at Home. Boston, 1878
A Century of Dishonor. New enl. ed. Boston, 1885
Ramona. Boston, 1884

JACKSON, MARY A. (MORRISON). *Life and Letters of General Thomas J. Jackson* (*Stonewall Jackson*). New York, 1892. [2d ed.] entitled *Memoirs of Stonewall Jackson*. Louisville, [1895].

JACKSON, SHELDON. *Alaska, and Missions on the North Pacific Coast*. New York, [c1880]

JACOBS, HARRIET (BRENT). *Incidents in the Life of a Slave Girl*. Ed. L. Maria Child. Boston, 1861

JACOBS, HERBERT A. *We Chose the Country*. New York, [1948]

JAEGER, EDMUND C. *The California Deserts*. Rev. ed. Stanford University, 1940
Desert Wild Flowers. Stanford University, [c1940]
Mountain Trees of Southern California. Pasadena, Calif., [c1920]

JAMAICA, N.Y. *Records of the Town of Jamaica, Long Island, New York, 1656–1751*. Ed. Josephine C. Frost. Brooklyn, 1914. v.d.

JAMES, BUSHROD W. *Alaska, Its Neglected Past, Its Brilliant Future*. Philadelphia, 1897

JAMES, ED. *The Amateur Negro Ministrel's Guide*. New York, 1880

JAMES, EDWIN, comp. *Account of an Expedition from Pittsburgh to the Rocky Mountains, Performed in the Years 1819, 1820*. 3 vols. London, 1823. 2 vols. New York, 1823

JAMES, GEORGE WHARTON. *Indian Basketry*. 3d ed., rev. and enl. Pasadena, Calif., 1903
The Wonders of the Colorado Desert. Boston, 1906

JAMES, HENRY. *The Bostonians*. London, 1886
The Ivory Tower. New York, 1917. Written 1914
The Portrait of a Lady. Boston, [c1881]
Roderick Hudson. Boston, 1876. 1875
The Sacred Fount. New York, 1901

JAMES, JAMES A. *The First Scientific Exploration of Russian America*. Evanston, Ill., 1942

JAMES, MARQUIS. *Cherokee Strip*. New York, 1945

JAMES, THOMAS H. *Rambles in the United States and Canada During the Year 1845*. London, 1846

JAMES, W. S. *Cow-boy Life in Texas*. Chicago, [c1898]

JAMES, WILL. *Cow Country*. New York, 1927

JAMESON, JOHN F. *Dictionary of United States History*. Rev. ed., Philadelphia, 1931. (Erroneously cited as 1893.)

JAMESON, JOHN F., and BUEL, J. W. *Encyclopedic Dictionary of American Reference*. [Boston], [c1901]

JANSON, CHARLES W. *The Stranger in America*. London, 1807

JAY, JOHN. *Correspondence and Public Papers*. Ed. Henry P. Johnston. New York [1890–93]. v.d.

JEFFERSON, JOSEPH. *Autobiography*. New York, [1890]

JEFFERSON, THOMAS. *Writings*. v.d. Ed. Henry A. Washington. 9 vols. New York, 1853–54. I. in-

cludes *Autobiography*. **v.d.** Ed. Paul Leicester Ford. 10 vols. New York, 1892–99. Ed. Andrew A. Lipscomb and Albert E. Bergh. 20 vols. Washington, 1906. =1903–4. (Citations from above eds. not always clearly distinguished.)
Memoir, Correspondence, and Miscellanies. Ed. Thomas J. Randolph. Charlottesville, Va., 1829. **v.d.**
Notes on the State of Virginia. 1st Amer. ed. Philadelphia, 1788. Written **1781**; corr. **1782**
Jefferson Papers. (Massachusetts Historical Society. *Collections*. 7th Ser., I.) **v.d.**
JENKINS, WARREN. *The Ohio Gazetteer, and Traveler's Guide*. Columbus, O., **[1837]**
JENKS, JEREMIAH W., and LAUCK, WILLIAM J. *The Immigration Problem*. New York, 1912 **[1911]**
JENNESS, JOHN S., ed. *Transcripts of Original Documents in the English Archives Relating to the Early History of New Hampshire*. New York, 1876. **v.d.**
JEPSON, WILLIS LINN. *Manual of the Flowering Plants of California*. Berkeley, **1925**
The Silva of California. Berkeley, [©**1910**]
The Jesuit Relations and Allied Documents. Ed. Reuben Gold Thwaites. Cleveland, 1890–1901. **v.d.**
JEWETT, SARAH ORNE. *Betty Leicester*. New York, 1890 [©**1889**]
Country By-Ways. Boston, **1881**
A Country Doctor. Boston, **1884**
The Country of the Pointed Firs. Boston, **1896**
Deephaven. Boston, **1877**
King of Folly Island, and Other Stories. Boston, **1899**
Life of Nancy. Boston, **1895**
Marsh Island. Boston, **1885**
The Mate of the Daylight and Friends Ashore. Boston, **1883**
Old Friends and New. Boston, **1879**
Play Days. Boston, **1878**
JILLSON, WILLARD R. *Tales of the Dark and Bloody Ground*. Louisville, **1930**
JOHNSON, BURGES. *As Much As I Dare*. New York, **1944**
JOHNSON, CHARLES BRITTEN. *Letters from the British Settlement in Pennsylvania*. Philadelphia, **1819**
JOHNSON, CLIFTON. *Highways and Byways of the Pacific Coast*. New York, **1908**
Highways and Byways of the South. New York, **1905**
JOHNSON, EDWARD. *Wonder-working Providence of Sions Saviour in New England*. [Ed.] William F. Poole. (Repr. of original ed. *A History of New-England*. London, **1654**.)
JOHNSON, EMORY R. *American Railway Transportation*. New York, **1903**
JOHNSON, JOSEPH. *Traditions and Reminiscences chiefly of the American Revolution in the South*. Charleston, S.C., **1851**
JOHNSON, OVERTON, and WINTER, WILLIAM H. *Route Across the Rocky Mountains, with a Description of Oregon and California*. Lafayette, Ind., **1846**
JOHNSON, OWEN. *Stover at Yale*. New York, **[1912]**
JOHNSON, THEODORE T. *Sights in the Gold Region and Scenes by the Way*. New York, **1849**
JOHNSON, WILLIAM A. *The History of Anderson County, Kansas*. Garnett, Kans., **1877**
JOHNSTON, JAMES F. W. *Notes on North America*. Edinburgh, **1851**
JOHNSTON, PHILIP. *Lost and Living Cities of the California Gold Rush*. Los Angeles, **[1948]**
Jonathan's Visit. (In *Poor Will's Almanac. 1839*.) Philadelphia, **[?1838]**
JONES, DAVID. *A Journal of Two Visits Made to Some Nations of Indians on the West Side of the River Ohio, in the Years 1772 and 1773*. Burlington, N.J., **1774**
JONES, HUGH. *The Present State of Virginia*. London, **1724**
JONES, JOHN B. *Adventures of Col. Gracchus Vanderbomb*. Philadelphia, **1852**
Wild Southern Scenes. Philadelphia, [©**1859**]
Wild Western Scenes. [1st. ser.] New Stereotype ed. Philadelphia, 1865. =1856. First pub. **1841**
JONES, NELSON E. *The Squirrel Hunters of Ohio*. Cincinnati, 1898. **1897**
JONES, THELMA *Skinny Angel*. New York, **1946**
JORDAN, DAVID STARR, and EVERMANN, BARTON W. *American Food and Game Fishes*. New York, **1902**
A Check-List of the Fishes and Fishlike Vertebrates of North and Middle America. Washington, **1896**
JORDAN, PHILIP D. *The National Road*. Indianapolis, **[1948]**
JOSSELYN, JOHN. *An Account of Two Voyages to New-England*. London, **1674**
New Englands Rarities Discovered. London, **1672**
Journal of an Excursion to the United States and Canada in the Year 1834. Edinburgh, **1835**
Journals of the American Congress: from 1774 to 1778. Washington, 1823. **v.d.**
Journals of the Continental Congress, 1774–1789. Washington, 1904–37. **v.d.**
JOUTEL, HENRI. *A Journal of the Last Voyage Perform'd by Monsr. de La Sale, to the Gulph of Mexico*. London, **1714**
JOYCE, PATRICK W. *English as We Speak It in Ireland*. London, **1910**
JUDD, SYLVESTER. *History of Hadley*. Springfield, Mass. 1905. =**1863**
Margaret. Boston, **1845** 2d ed. Boston, **1851**
Richard Edney and the Governor's Family. Boston, **1850**
JUDSON, EDWARD Z. C. *The Mysteries and Miseries of New York*. New York, **1848**
Junius Tracts. New York, 1844. **1843–44**

K

KAHN, EDGAR M. *Cable Car Days in San Francisco*. Rev. ed. Stanford University, **1944**
KALM, PEHR. *En Resa til Norra America*. Stockholm, **1753–61**
Travels into North America. Tr. John Reinhold Forster. 3 vols. London, **1770–71**. 2d ed. **1772**
KANE, ELISHA K. *Arctic Explorations: The Second Grinnell Expedition in Search of Sir John Franklin*. Philadelphia, **1856**
The U.S. Grinnell Expedition in Search of Sir John Franklin. New York, **1853**
Kansas Herald of Freedom. Lawrence, **1854–60**
KEARNEY, THOMAS H., and PEEBLES, ROBERT H. *Flowering Plants and Ferns of Arizona*. Washington, **1942**
KEATE, JAMES H. *The Destruction of Mephisto's Greatest Web*. Salt Lake City, **1914**
KEATING, WILLIAM H. *Narrative of an Expedition to the Source of St. Peter's River, Lake Winnepeek, Lakes of the Woods, etc*. Philadelphia, **1824**
KEIM, DEBENNEVILLE R. *Sheridan's Troopers on the Borders*. Philadelphia, [©1885]. =**1870**
KELLER, GEORGE. *A Trip Across the Plains, and Life in California*. Massillon, O., **1851**
KELLER, JOHN W. *The Game of Draw Poker*. New York, **1887**
KELLOGG, CHARLES. *Trails and Tales*. In his *Charles Kellogg, The Nature Singer, His Book*. Morgan Hill, Calif., **1929**
KELLOGG, MARY F. *Trails of Adventure*. Pasadena, Calif., [©**1927**]
KELLOGG, ROBERT H. *Life and Death in Rebel Prisons*. Hartford, **1864**
KELLOGG, VERNON L. *American Insects*. New York, **1905**
Common Injurious Insects of Kansas. Lawrence, Kans., **1892**
KELLY, JONATHAN F. *The Humors of Falconbridge*. Philadelphia, [©1856]. =*a***1855**
KELLY, MYRA. *Little Citizens*. New York, **1904**
KELLY, WELLBOURN. *Inchin' Along*. New York, **1932**
KELLY, WILLIAM. *Across the Rocky Mountains. from New York to California*. London, **1852**. (See note, below.)
A Stroll through the Diggings of California. London, **1852**. (Above titles = Vols. I–II of his *An Excursion to California*. London, 1851.)
KEMBLE, FRANCES A. *Journal*. London, 1835. **v.d.**
Journal of a Residence on a Georgian Plantation in 1838–39. New York, 1863. **v.d.**
KENDALL, EDWARD A. *Travels through the Northern Parts of the United States*. New York, **1809**
KENDALL, GEORGE W. *Narrative of the Texan Santa Fé Expedition*. New York, **1844**
KENNEDY, JOHN P. *Horse Shoe Robinson*. Philadelphia, **1835**
Memoirs of the Life of William Wirt. Philadelphia, 1860. =1850. First pub. **1849**
Quodlibet: Containing Some Annals Thereof. Philadelphia, **1840**
Rob of the Bowl. Philadelphia, **1838**
Swallow Barn. Philadelphia, **1832**
KENNEDY, PHILIP P. *The Blackwater Chronicle*. New York, **1853**
KENNEDY, STETSON. *The Palmetto Country*. New York, **1942**
KENNEDY, WILLIAM. *Texas: The Rise, Progress, and Prospects of the Republic of Texas*. London, **1841**
KENNY, HAMILL. *West Virginia Place Names*. Piedmont, W.Va , **1945**
Kentucky Gazette. Lexington, **1787–1848**
Kentucky Rifle. Danville, **1840**
KEPHART, HORACE. *Camping and Woodcraft*. 2 vols. New York, **1916–17**. New York, 1921 [©**1917**]
Our Southern Highlanders. New York, **1913**. Also new and enl., New York, **1922**
KER, HENRY. *Travels through the Western Interior of the United States*. Elizabethtown, N.J., **1816**
KERCHEVAL, SAMUEL. *A History of the Valley of Virginia*. Winchester, Va., **1833**
KERSEY, JOHN. *Dictionarium Anglo-Britannicum*. London, **1708**
KERWIN, JEROME G., ed. *Civil-Military Relationships in American Life*. Chicago, **1948**
KETTELL, THOMAS P. *History of the Great Rebellion*. Worcester, 1862–63. **v.d.**
Key Reporter. New York, **1936—**
KIDDER, ALFRED V. *The Pottery of Pecos*. New Haven, **1931–36**
KIDDER, DANIEL P. *Mormonism and the Mormons*. New York, **1842**
KIDDER, FREDERIC. *The Expeditions of Capt. John Lovewell, and His Encounters with the Indians*. Boston, 1865. **v.d.**
KILBOURN, JOHN. *The Ohio Gazetteer*. 8th ed. Columbus, **1826**. 10th ed. **1831**. 11th ed. **1833**
KILLEBREW, JOSEPH B. *The Grasses of Tennessee; including Cereals and Forage Plants*. Nashville, **1878**
KILROE, EDWIN P. *Saint Tammany and the Origin of the Society of Tammany*. New York, 1913. **v.d.**
KIMBALL, SIDNEY F. *Domestic Architecture of the American Colonies*. New York, **1922**
KIMBER, EDWARD. *Itinerant Observations in America*. Savannah, 1878. **1745–46**
KING, CAROLINE H. *When I Lived in Salem*. Brattleboro, Vt., **1937**
KING, CHARLES. *Fort Frayne*. London [n.d.]. First pub. New York, **[1895]**
Sunset Pass. New York, [©**1890**]
A Trooper Galahad. Philadelphia, **1899**
Warrior Gap. New York, [©**1897**]
KING, CLARENCE. *Mountaineering in the Sierra Nevada*. Boston, **1872**
[*Rep. Precious Metals*.] Erroneous citation for *Report of the Director of the Mint upon the Statistics of the Production of the Precious Metals [1881]*. (U.S. Bureau of the Mint.) Washington, **1882**
KING, DAN. *The Life and Times of Thomas Wilson Dorr*. Boston, **1859**
KING, GRACE E. *New Orleans; the Place and the People*. New York, 1904. =**1895**
KING, RUFUS. *Life and Correspondence*. Ed. Charles R. King, New York, **1894–1900**. **v.d.**
KINGSBURY, GEORGE W. *History of Dakota Territory*. Chicago, **1915**
KINGSLEY, JOHN S., *et al. The Standard Natural History*. Boston, **1884–85**. Also pub. as *The Riverside Natural History*. Boston, [©**1888**]
KINGSLEY, NELSON. *Diary*. Ed. Frederick J. Teggart. Berkeley, 1914. **v.d.**
KIPLING, RUDYARD. *"Captains Courageous," a Story of the Grand Banks*. Copyright Ed. Leipzig, **1897**
KIRKE, EDMUND, pseud. JAMES R. GILMORE. *Among the Pines*. New York, **1862**
My Southern Friends. New York, **1863**
On the Border. Boston, **1867**
KIRKLAND, CAROLINE M. (STANSBURY). *Forest Life*. New York, **1842**
A New Home—Who'll Follow? 2d ed. New York, 1840. First pub. **1839**
Western Clearings. New York, 1845. **v.d.**
KIRKLAND, FRAZAR, pseud. RICHARD M. DEVENS. *The Pictorial Book of Anecdotes and Incidents of the War of the Rebellion*. Hartford, **1867**
KIRKLAND, JOSEPH. *The McVeys (An Episode)*. Boston, **1888**
Zury: The Meanest Man in Spring County. Boston, **1887**
Kissimmee Valley (Gazette). Kissimmee, Fla., **1894–**
KITCHIN, EDWARD A. *Birds of the Olympic Peninsula*. Port Angeles, Wash., **1949**
KITTREDGE, GEORGE L. *The Old Farmer and His Almanack*. Boston, **1904**
Klondike. The Chicago Record's Book for Gold Seekers. Chicago, **1897**
KNIGHT, EDWARD H. [Vols. I–II.] *The Practical Dictionary of Mechanics*., London, [n.d.]. [Vol. III.] *Knight's American Mechanical Dictionary*. Set first pub. under latter title, New York, **1874–76**. [*Supp*.] Citation for *Knight's New Mechanical Dictionary*. Boston [pref. **1883**]
KNIGHT, HENRY C. *Letters from the South and West*. Boston, 1824. **v.d.**
KNIGHT, ORA W. *The Birds of Maine*. Bangor, **1908**
KNIGHT, RICHARD P. *The Symbolical Language of the Ancient Art and Mythology*. Ed. Alexander Wilder. New ed., New York, **1876**
KNIGHT, SARAH (KEMBLE). *The Journals of Madam Knight, and Rev. Mr. Buckingham*. Includes KNIGHT. *The Private Journal Kept*

. . . on a Journey from Boston to New-York. **1704.** *The Private Journals Kept by Rev. John* [i.e., Thomas] *Buckingham of the Expedition against Canada,* [etc.] **1710, 1711**

Koch, Charles R. E. *History of Dental Surgery.* Chicago, **1909**

Krapp, George P. *The English Language in America.* New York, **1925**

Kroll, Harry H. *I Was a Sharecropper.* Indianapolis, **[1937]**

Krug, Merton E. *History of Reedsburg and Upper Baraboo Valley.* Madison, Wis., **1926**

[*Ku Klux Klan Rep.*] (Joint Select Committee on the Condition of Affairs in the Late Insurrectionary States.) *Report.* Washington, 1872. **v.d.**

Kunz, George F. *Gems and Precious Stones of North America.* New York, **1890**

L

Lackland, Thomas, pseud. George C. Hill. *Homespun; or, Five and Twenty Years Ago.* New York, **1867**

La Cuisine Creole. See Hearn, Lafcadio.

Ladies' Repository. Cincinnati; New York, **1841–76**

Lady's Magazine and Repository of Entertaining Knowledge. Philadelphia, **1792–93**

LaFollette, Robert M. *Autobiography.* Madison, Wis., **1913**

Lahontan, Louis A., Baron de. *New Voyages to North-America.* London, **1703**

Lambert, Aylmer B. *A Description of the Genus* Pinus. London, **1803**

Lambert, John. *Travels through Lower Canada, and the United States of North America.* London, **1810.** 2d ed. as *Travels through Canada,* [etc.]. London, **1813**

Lambert, Marcus B. *A Dictionary of the Non-English Words of the Pennsylvania-German Dialect.* [Lancaster, Pa., **©1924**]

Lamborn, Leeburt L. *Cottonseed Products.* New York, **1904**

Lamphere, George N. *The United States Government: Its Organization and Practical Workings.* Philadelphia, **1880**

Lamson, Alvan. *The Church of the First Three Centuries.* 2d ed. rev. and enl. Boston, **1875**

Lancaster, Mass. *Early Records . . . 1643–1725.* Ed. Henry S. Nourse. Lancaster, 1884. **v.d.**

Land of Nakoda; the Story of the Assiniboine Indians. (Montana Writers' Program.) Helena, **1942**

The Land of Sunshine. Los Angeles, **1894–1901**

Landon, Melville D. *Eli Perkins (At Large): His Sayings and Doings.* New York, **1875**

Lane, Marcus. *American Political Catch-Words, Names, and Phrases.* (*America: A Journal for Americans.* 13 Sep.–8 Nov., **1888**)

Langdon, William C. *Everyday Things in American Life.* New York, **1937**

Lange, Dorothea, and Taylor, Paul S. *An American Exodus.* New York, **[©1939]**

Langford, Nathaniel P. *Diary of the Washburn Expedition to the Yellowstone and Firehole Rivers in the Year 1870.* [?St. Paul, **©1905**]
Vigilante Days and Ways. Chicago, 1912. **1890**

Langsdorff, Georg H., Freiherr von. *Voyages and Travels in Various Parts of the World.* Carlisle, Pa., **1817**

Lanks, Herbert C. *Highway to Alaska.* New York, **1944**

Lanman, Charles. *Letters from the Alleghany Mountains.* New York, **1849**
A Summer in the Wilderness. New York, **1846**

La Perouse, Jean F. G., Comte de. *A Voyage Round the World.* Boston, **1801**

Latham, Henry. *Black and White.* London, **1867**

Latham, John. *A General Synopsis of Birds.* London, **1781–85.** *Supplement.* London, **1787–1801**

Lathrop, George P. *An Echo of Passion.* Boston, **1882**

Latrobe, Benjamin H. *Journal.* New York, 1905. **v.d.**

Latrobe, Charles J. *The Rambler in Mexico.* New York, **1836**
The Rambler in North America. London, **1835**

Laudonnière, René G. de. *A Notable Historie Containing Foure Voyages . . . into Florida.* Tr. Richard Hakluyt. London, 1810. **1587**

Lawrence, Amos. *Extracts from the Diary and Correspondence of the Late Amos Lawrence.* Ed. William R. Lawrence. Boston, 1855. **v.d.**

Lawrence George A. *Silverland.* London, **1873**

Lawrence, William, bishop. *Life of Amos A. Lawrence, with Extracts from His Diary and Correspondence.* Boston, 1889. **v.d.**

Lawrence (Kans.) *Republican.* **1857–69**

Lawson, John. *A New Voyage to Carolina.* London, **1809.** Also cited from *Lawson's History of North Carolina.* Ed. Frances L. Harriss. Richmond, Va., 1937.

Leacock. See Moses. *Representative Plays.*

Leavitt, Samuel. *Our Money Wars.* Boston, 1896. **=1894**

Lechford, Thomas. *Note-Book . . . June 27, 1638, to July 29, 1641.* (American Antiquarian Society. *Archæologia Americana.* VII.) **v.d.**
Plain Dealing. (Massachusetts Historical Society. *Collections.* 3d Ser., III.) **1642**

Leconte, Joseph. *Elements of Geology.* New York, **1878**

Lee, Daniel, and Frost, Joseph H. *Ten Years in Oregon.* New York, **1844**

Lee, W. Storrs. *Stagecoach North.* New York, **1941**

Left Handed. *Son of Old Man Hat; A Navaho Autobiography Recorded by Walter Dyk.* New York, **[©1938]**

Leggett, William. *Tales and Sketches.* New York, **1829**

Lehmann, Valgene W. *Atwater's Prairie Chicken: Its Life History and Management.* Washington, **1941**

Leisure Hour. London, **1852–**

Leland, Charles Godfrey. *The Art of Conversation.* New York, **1864**
Memoirs. 2 vols. London, **1893**

Leonard, Delevan L. *A Century of Congregationalism in Ohio.* Oberlin, O., **1896**

Leonard, John W. *The Gold Fields of the Klondike.* Chicago, **1897**

Leonard, Mary F. *The Story of the Big Front Door.* Boston, **[©1898]**

Leonard, Zenas. *Narrative of the Adventures of Zenas Leonard.* Clearfield, Pa., **1839**

Lerch, Otto. *A Preliminary Report upon the Hills of Louisiana.* [Baton Rouge, **1893**]

Lescarbot, Marc. *Nova Francia.* Tr. Pierre Erondelle. London, **[1609]**

Leslie, Eliza. *Seventy-Five Receipts for Pastry, Cakes, and Sweetmeats.* Boston, **1828**

Lester, Francis E. *A Southern New Mexico Flower Garden.* Santa Fe, **1901**

Lester, John C., and Wilson, Daniel L. *Ku Klux Klan, Its Origin, Growth and Disbandment.* New York, 1905. **v.d.**

L'Estrange, R., licenser. *A Relation of the Invasion and Conquest of Florida . . . under the Command of Ferdinand de Soto.* London, **1686**

Letter from a Tradesman Recently Arrived from America. London, **1835**

Letters to Benjamin Franklin. Ed. William Duane. New York, 1859. **v.d.**

Letters to Washington, and Accompanying Papers. Ed. Stanislaus M. Hamilton. Boston, 1898–1902. **v.d.**

Leupp, Francis E. *Walks about Washington.* Boston, **1915**

Leverett, Frank, and Taylor, Frank B. *The Pleistocene of Indiana and Michigan.* Washington, **1915**

Levett, Christopher. *A Voyage into New England.* (Massachusetts Historical Society. *Collections.* 3d Ser., VIII.) **1628**

Levinge, Sir Richard. *Echoes from the Backwoods.* London, **1846**

Lewinson, Paul. *Race, Class, and Party.* New York, **1932**

Lewis, Alfred Henry. *The Apaches of New York.* New York, **[©1912]**
The Boss, and How He Came to Rule New York. New York, **1903**
Wolfville. New York, **[©1897]**

Lewis, Charles B. *Brother Gardner's Lime-Kiln Club.* Chicago, **1882**
Quod's Odds. Detroit, **1865**

Lewis, George. *Impressions of America and the American Churches.* Edinburgh, **1845**

Lewis, Henry Clay. *Odd Leaves from the Life of a Louisiana "Swamp Doctor."* Philadelphia, **1850.** [©1849]. Also included, separately paged, in
The Swamp Doctor's Adventures in the South-West. Philadelphia, **[©1858]**

Lewis, John D. *Across the Atlantic.* London, **1851**

Lewis, Meriwether, and Clark, William. *History of the Expedition . . . to the Sources of the Missouri.* [Written by Nicholas Biddle; ed. Paul Allen.] Philadelphia, 1814. Ed. Elliott Coues. New York, 1893. **v.d.**
Original Journals of the Lewis and Clark Expedition, 1804–1806. Ed. Reuben Gold Thwaites. New York, 1904–5. **v.d.** (Cited as Lewis & Clark. *Exped.*)

Lewis, Meriwether, and Ordway, John. *Journals . . . Kept on the Expedition of Western Explorations, 1803–1806.* Ed. Milo M. Quaife. Madison, Wis., 1916. **v.d.**

Lewis, Sinclair. *Babbitt.* New York, **[©1922]**
Free Air. New York, **1919**
Main Street, the Story of Carol Kennicott. New York, **1920**

Lewis, William N. *The People's Practical Poultry Book.* New York, **[©1871]**

Library of Universal Knowledge. New York, 1881 **[©1880]**

Lieber, Francis. *The Stranger in America.* London, **1835.** Reissue of *Letters to a Gentleman in Germany.* Philadelphia, 1834.

Life & Adv. Arkansaw Doctor. See Byrn.

Life in the West: Back-Wood Leaves and Prairie Flowers. London, **1842**

Lillard, John F. *Poker Stories.* New York, **1896**

Lillard, Richard G. *Desert Challenge, an Interpretation of Nevada.* New York, **1942**

Lillibridge, William O. *Where the Trail Divides.* New York, **1907**

Limerick, Oliver V. *Billy Burgundy's Letters.* New York, **1902**

Limpus, Lowell M. *History of the New York Fire Department.* New York, 1940. **v.d.**

Lincoln, i.e., Phelps, Almira (Hart) L. *Familiar Lectures on Botany.* 5th ed., rev. and enl. New York, **1837.** New ed., rev. and enl. **1850**

Lincoln, Anna T. *Wilmington, Delaware.* Rutland, Vt., **1937**

Lincoln, Frederick C. *The Migration of American Birds.* New York, **1939**

Lincoln, Joseph C. *Cape Cod Yesterdays.* Boston, **[1935]**
Cap'n Warren's Wards. New York, **1911**
Kent Knowles; Quahaug. New York, **1914**
The "Old Home House." New York, **1907**
Partners of the Tide. New York, **1905**
Shavings. New York, **[©1918]**

Lindley, John, and Moore, Thomas, eds. *The Treasury of Botany.* London, **1866**

Lindquist, Gustavus E. *The Red Man in the United States.* New York, **[©1923]**

Linguistic Atlas of New England. Directed and ed. by Hans Kurath. Providence, **1939–43**

Linsdale, Jean M. *The California Ground Squirrel.* Berkeley, **1946**

Lippincott, Horace M. *Early Philadelphia.* Philadelphia, **1917**

L'Isle, Guillaume de. *Atlas nouveau, contenant toutes les parties du monde.* Amsterdam, **[1741]**

Literary Magazine and American Register. Philadelphia, **1803–7**

Livingston, Robert R. *Essay on Sheep.* 2d ed., much enl. New York, 1810. **1809**

Locke, David Ross. *The Struggles (Social, Financial and Political) of Petroleum V. Nasby.* Boston, **1872**
Swingin' Round the Cirkle. Boston, **1867**

Locke, J. *Fundamental Constitutions.* See *Old South Leaflets.*

Lockwood, George B. *The New Harmony Movement.* New York, **1905**

Lodge, Henry Cabot. *Daniel Webster.* Boston, **1883**

Lofberg, Lila. *Sierra Outpost.* New York, **[1941]**

The Log Cabin & Hard Cider Melodies. Boston, **1840**

Logan, James. *Notes of a Journey through Canada, the United States of America, and the West Indies.* Edinburgh, **1838**

Logan, John A. *The Great Conspiracy.* New York, 1886. **v.d.**

Logan, Olive. *Before the Footlights.* Philadelphia, **1870**

Lomax, John A. *American Ballads and Folk Songs.* New York, **1934**

London, Jack. *A Daughter of the Snows.* Philadelphia, **1902**
The Road. New York, 1916. **=1907**
Smoke Bellew. New York, 1912 **[©1911–12]**
The Valley of the Moon. New York, **1913**

Long, John. *Voyages and Travels of an Indian Interpreter and Trader.* London, **1791**

Long, Joseph W. *American Wild-Fowl Shooting.* New York, **1874**

Long Lance, i.e., Chief Buffalo Child Long Lance. *Long Lance.* New York, **1928**

Longfellow, Henry Wadsworth. *Complete Poetical Works.* Cambridge Ed., ed. Horace E. Scudder. Boston [©1893]. **v.d.**
The Courtship of Miles Standish, and Other Poems. Boston, **1838**
Evangeline. Boston, 1848. **=1847**
Hyperion. New York, **1839**
Kavanagh. Boston, **1849**
The Song of Hiawatha. Boston, **1855**
Tales of a Wayside Inn. Boston, **1863**

Longfellow, Samuel, ed. *Life of Henry Wadsworth Longfellow, with Extracts from His Journals and Correspondence.* Boston, 1896. =1891. **v.d.**

Longstreet, Augustus B. *Georgia Scenes.* Augusta, Ga., **1835.** 2d ed. New York, 1843. =1840.

Longyear, Burton O. *Rocky Mountain Wild Flower Studies*. Denver, **[1909]**

Loomis, Leander V. *A Journal of the Birmingham Emigrating Company; the Record of a Trip from Birmingham, Iowa, to Sacramento, California, in 1850*. Edgar M. Ledyard, ed. Salt Lake City, 1928. **1850**

Lorain, John. *Nature and Reason Harmonized in the Practice of Husbandry*. Philadelphia, **1825**

Lord, John. *Frontier Dust*. Hartford, **1926**

Lorimer, George Horace. *Letters from a Self-Made Merchant to His Son*. Boston, **1902**

Lossing, Benson J. *The Hudson, from the Wilderness to the Sea*. New York, **[1866]**

Lovell, Solomon. *Original Journal . . . Kept during the Penobscot Expedition, 1779*. [Boston], 1881. **1779**

Lovett, Richard. *United States Pictures Drawn with Pen and Pencil*. [London], **1891**

Lovett, Robert Morss. *Richard Gresham*. New York, **1904**

Lowell, James Russell. *Writings*. Riverside Ed., Boston, 1890. **v.d.**

Among My Books. Boston, **1870**

The Biglow Papers. [1st Ser.] Boston, 1876. =1848. **v.d.** 2d Ser. Boston, 1867 [c1866]. **v.d.**

Complete Poetical Works. Cambridge Ed. Boston, [c1924]. =1896. **v.d.**

Democracy, and Other Addresses. Boston, 1887 [1886]. **v.d.** Includes his [*On*] *Democracy* q.v. **1884**

Fireside Travels. Boston, **1864**

The Independent in Politics. New York, **1888.** Also in *Writings*, VI.

Letters. Ed. Charles E. Norton. New York, 1894. **v.d.**

Literary and Political Addresses. (*Writings*, VI.) **v.d.**

A Moosehead Journal. (*Putnam's Monthly Magazine*, II.) **1853**

My Study Windows. Boston, 1871. **v.d.**

On Democracy. Birmingham, Eng., **[1884]**

Poetical Works. Complete Ed. Boston, 1882 [c1876]. **v.d.**

[*Prose Works*.] Citation for *Writings*, I–VI.

Lowell Offering. Lowell, Mass., **1840–45**

Ludlow, Fitzhugh. *Little Brother; and other Genre Pictures*. Boston, **1867.** Contains *Fleeing to Tarshish*.

Lumberman's Gazette. Bay City, Mich., **1871–86**

Lumholtz, Karl S. *New Trails in Mexico*. New York, **1912**

Lummis, Charles F. *The Land of Poco Tiempo*. New York, **1893**

A Tramp across the Continent. New York, **1892**

Lumpkin, Katharine D. *The Making of a Southerner*. New York, **1947**

Lundberg, Ferdinand. *Imperial Hearst; a Social Biography*. New York, **[c1936]**

Lunenberg, Mass. *Early Records of the Town . . . 1719–1764*. Ed. Walter A. Davis. Fitchburg, 1896. **v.d.**

Proprietors. *The Proprietors' Records . . . 1729–1833*. Ed. Walter A. Davis. Fitchburg, 1897. **v.d.**

Lunt, George, ed. *Old New England Traits*. New York, **1873**

Lutes, Della (Thompson). *The Country Kitchen*. Boston, **1936**

Home Grown. Boston, **1937**

Luttig, John C. *Journal of a Fur-Trading Expedition on the Upper Missouri 1812–1813*. Ed. Stella M. Drumm. St. Louis, 1920. **v.d.**

Lyell, Sir Charles. *A Second Visit to the United States of North America*. New York, 1849. **v.d.**

Travels in North America. London, 1845. **v.d.**

Lyman, George D. *Ralston's Ring*. New York, **1937**

The Saga of the Comstock Lode. New York, **1934**

Lynch, Denis T. *An Epoch and a Man*. New York, **1929**

Lynde, Benjamin. *The Diaries of Benjamin Lynde and of Benjamin Lynde, Jr.* Boston. Priv. pr. 1880. **v.d.**

Lynde, Francis. *The Grafters*. Indianapolis, **1904**

The Quickening. Indianapolis, **1906**

Lyon, Marguerite. *And So to Bedlam*. New York, **[1943]**

Take to the Hills. New York, **1941**

Lyon, T. T. *Fruits*. (Mich. Agricultural Experiment Station. *Bulletin* No. 80.) **1892**

Lyons, Albert B. *Plant Names, Scientific and Popular*. 2d ed., rev. Detroit, **1907**

M

McAllister, Ward. *Society as I Have Found It*. New York, **[c1890]**

McArthur, Lewis A. *Oregon Geographic Names*. Portland, **1928**

McAtee, Waldo L. *John and Joe*. [?Chicago] Priv. pr., **1945**

Local Names of Migratory Game Birds. Washington, **1937.** =1923.

Nomina Abitera. [?Chicago] Priv. pr., **1945**

Plants Useful in Upland Wildlife Management. Washington, **1941**

Ed. *The Ring-Necked Pheasant and Its Management in North America*. Washington, **1945**

Rural Dialect of Grant County, Indiana, in the 'Nineties. [?Washington] Priv. pr., **1942**

Some Local Names of Plants—IX. [?Chicago] Priv. pr., **1946**

Wildfowl Food Plants. Ames, Ia., **1939**

McCardell, Ray L. *Conversations of a Chorus Girl*. New York, **[1903]**

McClellan, Elisabeth. *Historic Dress in America, 1607–1800*. Philadelphia, **[1904]**

McClellan, George B. *McClellan's Own Story*. New York, 1887 [1886] **v.d.**

McClellan, Rolander G. *The Golden State*. Philadelphia, 1874. First pub. **1872**

McClinchey, Florence E. *Joe Pete*. New York, **1929**

McClung, John A. *Sketches of Western Adventure*. Maysville, Ky., **1832**

McClung, John W. *Minnesota as It Is in 1870*. [St. Paul], **1870**

McClure, Alexander K. *Three Thousand Miles through the Rocky Mountains*. Philadelphia, **1869**

McConnel, John L. *Western Characters*. New York, **1853**

McConnell, William J. *Frontier Law*. Yonkers-on-Hudson, N.Y., **1924**

McCook, Henry C. *Tenants of an Old Farm*. New York, 1885 **[1884]**

McCormac, Eugene I. *James K. Polk, a Political Biography*. Berkeley, **1922**

McCowan, Dan. *A Naturalist in Canada*. Toronto, **1941**

McCoy, Joseph G. *Historic Sketches of the Cattle Trade of the West and Southwest*. Kansas City, Mo., **1874.** Repr. Washington, 1932.

McCutcheon, George Barr. *Graustark*. New York, 1903. =**1901**

Green Fancy. New York, **1917**

The Rose in the Ring. New York, **1910**

McDanield, H. F., and Taylor, Nathaniel A. *The Coming Empire; or, Two Thousand Miles in Texas on Horseback*. Rev. ed. Dallas, [c1936]. First pub. **1877**

McDermott, John F. *A Glossary of Mississippi Valley French 1673–1850*. (Washington University Studies, n.s., *Language and Literature*, No. 12.) St. Louis, **1941**

MacDonald, Betty. *The Egg and I*. New York, **1945**

McDonald, Philip, and McLeod, Alexander. *A Surprising Account of the Captivity and Escape of Philip M'Donald & Alexander M'Leod, of Virginia, from the Chickemogga Indians*. Keene, N.H., **1794**

MacDougal, Daniel T. *The Salton Sea*. Washington, **1914**

McElrath, Thomson P. *The Yellowstone Valley*. St. Paul, **1880**

McFarland, J. Horace, *et al*. *Garden Bulbs in Color*. New York, **1938**

McFaul, Alexander D. *Ike Glidden in Maine*. Boston, [c1903]. **1902**

McGaffey, Kenneth. *The Sorrows of a Show Girl*. Chicago, **1908**

MacGowan, Alice. *The Last Word*. Boston, 1903, **[1902]**

McGregor, John. *British America*. Edinburgh, **1832**

McHatton-Ripley, Eliza M. (Chinn). *From Flag to Flag*. New York, **1889**

McIlwaine, Shields. *The Southern Poor-White from Lubberland to Tobacco Road*. Norman, Okla., **1939**

MacKaye, Harold S. *The Panchronicon*. New York, **1904**

McKee, Lanier. *The Land of Nome*. New York, **[1902]**

McKenna, James A. *Black Range Tales*. New York, **1936**

McKenney, Thomas L. *Memoirs, Official and Personal; with Sketches of Travel*. New York, **1846**

Sketches of a Tour to the Lakes. Baltimore, **1827**

Mackensen, Bernard. *The Trees and Shrubs of San Antonio and Vicinity*. San Antonio, **1909**

MacKenzie, William L. *The Life and Times of Martin Van Buren*. Boston, 1846. **v.d.**

Mackey, Albert G. *An Encyclopedia of Freemasonry and Its Kindred Sciences*. Philadelphia, **1874**

MacKinnon, Lauchlan B. *Atlantic and Transatlantic; Sketches Afloat and Ashore*. New York, **1852**

McLaughlin, Andrew C., and Hart, Albert Bushnell. *Cyclopedia of American Government*. New York, **1914**

McLean, John. *Notes of a Twenty-Five Years' Service in the Hudson's Bay Territory*. London, **1849.** Repr. Toronto, 1932.

McLean, Sydney R. *A Moment of Time*. New York, **1945**

McLeod, George A. *History of Alturas and Blaine Counties, Idaho*. Hailey, Ida., **1930**

MacLeod, Xavier D. *Biography of Hon. Fernando Wood, Mayor of the City of New-York*. New York, 1856. **v.d.**

McLoughlin, John. *Letters . . . from Fort Vancouver to the Governor and Committee*. Ed. Edwin E. Rich. Toronto, 1941–44. **v.d.**

McMahon, Bernard. *The American Gardener's Calendar*. Philadelphia, **1806**

MacMaster, John Bach. *A History of the People of the United States, from the Revolution to the Civil War*. New York, **1883–1913**

McMinn, Howard E., and Maino, Evelyn. *An Illustrated Manual of Pacific Coast Trees*. Berkeley, **1935**

McMurtrie, Henry. *Sketches of Louisville and Its Environs*. Louisville, **1819**

McNeal, Thomas A. *When Kansas was Young*. New York, **1922**

McNemar, Richard. *The Kentucky Revival*. Cincinnati, **1807**

McPherson, Charles. *Memoirs of the Life and Travels of the Late Charles McPherson, Written by Himself Chiefly between the Years 1773 and 1790*. Edinburgh, 1800. **v.d.**

McPherson, Edward. *A Handbook of Politics for 1868* [to 1894]. Washington, **1868–94.** (Issued bimonthly.)

MacRae, David. *The Americans at Home*. Edinburgh, **1870**

M'Robert, Patrick. *A Tour through Part of the Northern Provinces of America*. Edinburgh, **1776**

MacSparran, James. [*Diary.*] *A Letter Book and Abstract of Out Services, . . . 1743–1761*. Ed. Daniel Goodwin. Boston, 1899. **v.d.**

MacTaggart, John. *Three Years in Canada*. London, **1829**

McWilliams, Carey. *Southern California Country*. New York, **[1946]**

Madison, James. *Writings*. Ed. Gaillard Hunt. New York, 1900–10. **v.d.**

Magoffin, Susan (Shelby). *Down the Santa Fe Trail and into Mexico*. Ed. Stella M. Drumm. New Haven, 1926. **v.d.**

Maillard, Antoine S. *An Account of the Customs and Manners of the Micmakis and Maricheets Savage Nations*. London, **1758.** Letts. dated 1755–56.

[*Maine Doc. Hist.*] *Documentary History of the State of Maine*. Portland, 1869–1916. **v.d.**

Maine, My State. (Maine Writers Research Club.) [Lewiston, c**1919**]

[*Maine Prov. Rec.*] *Province and Court Records*. Portland, 1928–. **v.d.**

Maine Wills. By William M. Sargent. Portland, 1887. **v.d.**

Maitland, James. *The American Slang Dictionary*. Chicago, **1891**

Major Jack Downing. (*Northern Humor*.) Author's unabridged ed. London, [?1867]. **v.d.**

Majors, Alexander. *Seventy Years on the Frontier*. Chicago, **1893**

Makemie, Francis. *A Plain and Friendly Persuasive to the Inhabitants of Virginia and Maryland, for Promoting Towns and Cohabitation*. London, **1705.** Also facs. repr. Boston, 1942.

The Making of an American. See Riis.

A Man of Destiny. Siva . . . By Norman C. Perkins. Chicago, **1885**

Manchester, Mass. *Town Records*. Salem, 1889–91. **v.d.**

Manning, William. *The Key of Libberty, Shewing the Cause why a Free Government has always Failed, and a Remidy against It*. Billerica, Mass., 1922. **1798**

Manring, Benjamin F. *The Conquest of the Coeur d'Alenes, Spokanes and Palouses*. [Spokane, **1912**]

Mansfield, Edward D. *The Life of General Winfield Scott*. New York, **1846**

A Manual of Style. (University of Chicago Press.) 10th ed. Chicago, **1937.** 11th rev. ed. Chicago, **1949**

Manwaring, Charles W., comp. *A Digest of the Early Connecticut Probate Records*. Hartford, 1904–6. **v.d.**

Marbois, i.e. Barbé-Marbois, François, Marquis de. *The History of Louisiana*. Philadelphia, **1830**

March, Daniel. *Yankee Land and the Yankee*. Hartford, 1840. Contains *The Iron Horse*, written **1839**

MARCY, RANDOLPH B. *Exploration of the Red River of Louisiana, in the Year 1852.* Washington, 1854. 1852
The Prairie Traveller. New York, 1859
Report of Route from Fort Smith to Santa Fé. (31st Cong., 1 Sess. Senate Ex. Doc. No. 64.) Washington, 1850. 1849
MARGRY, PIERRE. *Découvertes et établissements des Français dans l'Ouest et dans le Sud de l'Amérique Septentrionale (1614–1734).* Paris, 1875–86. v.d.
MARKS, PERCY. *The Plastic Age.* New York, [©1924]
MARLOWE, GEORGE F. *Coaching Roads of Old New England.* New York, 1945
MARRYAT, FRANCIS (FRANK) S. *Mountains and Molehills.* New York, 1855
MARRYAT, FREDERICK. *Frank Mildmay.* New York, 1877. First pub. London, 1829 as *The Naval Officer; or, Scenes and Adventures in the Life of Frank Mildmay.*
Travels and Adventures of Monsieur Violet in California, Sonora, and Western Texas. London, 1874. =1843. Also issued under several variant titles.
MARSHALL, CHRISTOPHER. *Excerpts from the Diary . . . Kept . . . during the American Revolution.* Ed. William Duane. Albany, 1877. v.d.
MARSHALL, HUMPHREY. *The History of Kentucky.* Frankfort, 1812. [2d ed.] Frankfort, 1824
MARSHALL, HUMPHRY, comp. *Arbustrum Americanum; the American Grove, or, an Alphabetical Catalogue of Forest Trees and Shrubs.* Philadelphia, 1785
MARSHALL, JAMES L. *Santa Fe, the Railroad that Built an Empire.* New York, [1945]
MARSHALL, JOHN. *Writings . . . upon the Federal Constitution.* Boston, 1839. v.d.
MARSHALL, WALTER G. *Through America.* London, 1882. 1881
MARTIN, EDWARD WINSLOW, pseud. JAMES D. MCCABE. *The History of the Great Riots.* Philadelphia, [1877]
New York by Sunlight and Gaslight. Philadelphia, 1882
MARTIN, JOSEPH, ed. *A Comprehensive Description of Virginia, and the District of Columbia. . . . To Which is Added a History of Virginia, . . . to the Year 1754.* By William H. Brockenbrough. Richmond [n.d.] =his *A New and Comprehensive Gazetteer of Virginia.* Charlottesville, 1835
MARTIN, PAUL S., *et al. Indians Before Columbus.* Chicago, 1947
MARTINEAU, HARRIET. *Autobiography.* Ed. Maria W. Chapman. London, 1877. Written 1855
Illustrations of Political Economy. London, 1834
Retrospect of Western Travel. London, 1838
Society in America. London, 1837
MARTYN, CARLOS. *Wendell Phillips: the Agitator.* New York, [©1890]
Maryland Gazette. Wkly. (Pub. Parks.) Annapolis, 1727–34
Maryland Gazette. Wkly. (Pub. Green.) Annapolis, 1745–1839
Maryland Gazette. Wkly., semi-wkly. Baltimore, 1778–91
MASKELYNE, JOHN N. *Sharps and Flats.* New York, 1894
MASON, COL. R. B. *Report* [on Gold-Mining in California.] In 30th Cong., 2 Sess. House Ex. Doc. No. 1. 1848
[*Mass. Bay Rec.*] *Records of the Governor and Company of the Massachusetts Bay in New England.* Ed. Nathaniel B. Shurtleff. Boston, 1853–54. v.d. Vol. I. includes *Mass. Charter.* 1629
Massachusetts (Body of) Liberties. (Massachusetts Historical Society. *Collections,* 3d Ser., VIII.) 1641
Massachusetts Centinel. Continuation of *Columbian Centinel q.v.* 1784–90
[*Mass. Charters & Laws.*] *The Charters and General Laws of the Colony and Province of Massachusetts Bay.* Boston, 1914. v.d.
[*Mass. Court Rec.*] *Records of the Court of Assistants of the Colony of Massachusetts Bay.* [ed.] John Noble and John F. Cronin. Boston, 1901–28. v.d.
[*Mass. Gen. Court Rec.*] *Journals of the House of Representatives of Massachusetts.* [Cambridge,] 1919–. v.d.
[*Mass. Prov. Acts.*] *The Acts and Resolves, Public and Private, of the Province of Massachusetts Bay.* Boston, 1869–1922. v.d.
Massachusetts Spy. Boston; Worcester, 1770–1904
MASSETT, STEPHEN C. *Drifting About.* New York, 1863
MASSEY, JOHN. *Reminiscences.* Nashville, 1916
MASSON, LOUIS F. R. *Les Bourgeois de la Compagnie du Nord-Ouest.* Quebec, 1889–90. v.d.
MATHER, COTTON. *Diary.* (Massachusetts Historical Society. *Collections.* 7th Ser., VII–VIII.) v.d.
Magnalia Christi Americana. Hartford, 1853. 1702
The Wonders of the Invisible World. London, 1862. 1693
MATHER, INCREASE. *Cases of Conscience.* (In C. MATHER. *The Wonders* [etc.].) 1693
An Essay for the Recording of Illustrious Providences. Boston, 1684
A Further Account of the Tryals of the New-England Witches. (In C. MATHER. *The Wonders* [etc.].) 1693
The History of King Philip's War. Ed. Samuel G. Drake. Boston, 1862. 1676
MATHEWS, ANNE (JACKSON). *Memoirs of Charles Mathews, Comedian.* London, 1839. v.d.
MATHEWS, CORNELIUS. *Moneypenny.* New York. 1850
The Motley Book. 3d ed. New York, 1840. =1838
The Politicians. (In *Various Writings.* New York, 1863 [i.e., 1843].) 1840
MATHEWS, JOHN J. *Talking to the Moon.* Chicago, 1945
Wah'Kon-tah; the Osage and the White Man's Road. Norman, Okla., 1932
MATHEWS, LYMAN. *Lectures on Eloquence and Style.* Andover, Mass., 1836
MATHEWS, MITFORD M., ed. *The Beginnings of American English; Essays and Comments.* Chicago, [©1931]. v.d.
Some Sources of Southernisms. University, Ala., 1948
MATHEWSON, CHRISTOPHER. *Pitching in a Pinch.* New York, 1912
Second Base Sloan. New York, [©1917]
MATSCHAT, CECILE H. *Suwanee River.* New York, 1938
MATSELL, GEORGE W. *Vocabulum; or, The Rogue's Lexicon.* New York, 1859
MATTHEWS, BRANDER. *These Many Years.* New York, 1914
MATTHEWS, BRANDER, and BUNNER, HENRY C. *In Partnership; Studies in Story-Telling.* New York, 1884
MATTHEWS, FRANCES A. *Billy Duane.* New York, 1905
MATTHEWS, WILLIAM. *Getting on in the World.* Chicago, 1873
MATTOON, WILBUR R., *et al. Forest Trees of Oklahoma.* Oklahoma City, 1930
MAU, CLAYTON C. *The Development of Central and Western New York.* Rochester, [1944]
MAUDE, JOHN. *Visit to the Falls of Niagara in 1800.* London, 1826. 1800
MAURY, SARAH M. (HUGHES). *An Englishwoman in America.* London, 1848
MAVERICK, AUGUSTUS. *Henry J. Raymond and the New York Press, for Thirty Years.* Hartford, 1870
MAXWELL, ARCHIBALD M. *A Run through the United States, During the Autumn of 1841.* London, 1841
MAXWELL, WILLIAM. *The Folded Leaf.* New York, 1945
MAY, JOHN. *Journal and Letters . . . 1788 and '89.* Cincinnati, 1783. v.d.
MAYO, ROBERT. *Political Sketches of Eight Years in Washington.* Baltimore, 1839. v.d.
Mazama. A Record of Mountaineering in the Pacific Northwest. Portland, Ore., 1896–
MEAD, MARGARET. *The Changing Culture of an Indian Tribe.* New York, 1932
MEANY, EDMOND S. *Origin of Washington Geographic Names.* Seattle, 1934
MEARNS, EDGAR A. *Mammals of the Mexican Boundary of the United States.* Washington, 1907
MEASE, EDWARD. *Narrative of a Journey through Several Parts of the Province of West Florida.* (Mississippi Historical Society. *Publications.* V.) 1771
MEASE, JAMES. *The Picture of Philadelphia.* Philadelphia, 1811
MECKLIN, JOHN M. *The Ku Klux Klan.* New York, 1924
MEDBERY, JAMES K. *Men and Mysteries of Wall Street.* Boston, 1870
MEINE, FRANKLIN J., ed. *Tall Tales of the Southwest.* New York, 1930. v.d.
MEINZER, OSCAR E. *Plants as Indicators of Ground Water.* Washington, 1927
MEINZER, OSCAR E., and KELTON, F. C. *Geology and Water Resources of Sulphur Springs Valley, Arizona.* Washington, 1913
MELINE, JAMES F. *Two Thousand Miles on Horseback. Santa Fé and Back.* New York, 1867
MELISH, JOHN. *Travels in the United States of America.* Philadelphia, 1812
MELLICK, ANDREW D. *The Story of an Old Farm.* Somerville, N.J., 1889
MELVILLE, HERMAN. *Moby Dick; or, The Whale.* New York, 1851
Typee: A Peep at Polynesian Life. London, 1846
MELVIN, JAMES. *A Journal of the Expedition to Quebec.* New York, 1857. 1775
MENCKEN, HENRY L. *The American Language.* 1st ed. New York, 1919. 4th ed., corr., rev. and rewritten, New York, 1936. *Supplement I,* New York, 1945. *Supplement II,* New York, 1948
Happy Days 1880–1892. New York, 1940
Treatise on the Gods. 2d ed., corr. and rev. New York, 1946
MENEFEE, SELDEN. *Assignment: U.S.A.* New York, 1943
MENKE, FRANK G. *Encyclopedia of Sports.* Rev. and enl. New York, [1944]
MERENESS, NEWTON D., ed. *Travels in the American Colonies.* New York, 1916. v.d. Includes *Dr. John Berkenhout's Excursion from New York to Philadelphia.* 1778. *Journal of Colonel George Chicken's Mission from Charleston, S.C., to the Cherokees.* 1726. *Colonel William Fleming's Journal of Travels in Kentucky.* 1779–88. *Colonel William Fleming's Journal of Travels in Kentucky.* 1783. *Journal of Captain Harry Gordon's Journey from Pittsburg down the Ohio and the Mississippi to New Orleans, Mobile, and Pensacola.* 1766. *Journal of Captain Phineas Stevens' Journey from Charlestown, N.H. to Canada.* 1752. *David Taitt's Journal of a Journey through the Creek Country.* 1772
MERRIAM, CHARLES E. *The American Party System.* New York, 1922
Chicago. New York, 1929
MERRIAM, CLINTON HART. *The Mammals of the Adirondack Region.* New York, 1884
MERRIAM, GEORGE S. *The Life and Times of Samuel Bowles.* New York, 1885
MERWIN, SAMUEL. *Temperamental Henry.* Indianapolis, [©1917]
MERWIN, SAMUEL, and WEBSTER, HENRY K. *Calumet 'K.'* New York, 1905. =1901
MEYER, ERNST C. *Nominating Systems.* Madison, Wis., 1902
MICHAUX, ANDRÉ. *Histoire des Chênes de l'Amérique.* Paris, 1801
MICHAUX, FRANÇOIS A. *Histoire des arbres forestiers de l'Amérique septentrionale.* Paris, 1810–13
The North American Sylva. [Tr. Augustus L. Hillhouse.] Notes by John J. Smith. Philadelphia, 1817–19
Voyages à l'Ouest des Montes Alléghanys, dans les États de l'Ohio, du Kentucky, et du Tennessée, et Retour à Charleston par les Hautes-Carolines. Paris, 1804
Midland Naturalist, American. Notre Dame, Ind., 1909–
Midwinter Appeal and Journal of Forty-Nine. San Francisco, 1894
MIGHELS, HENRY R. *Sage Brush Leaves.* San Francisco, 1879
MILES, WILLIAM, of Carlisle, Pa. *Journal of the Sufferings and Hardships of Captain Parker H. French's Overland Expedition to California.* [New York, 1916.] =1851. 1850
MILLER, HENRY. *The Cosmological Eye.* Norfolk, Conn., [©1939]
MILLER, JOAQUIN. *First Fam'lies of the Sierras.* Chicago, 1876
Life Amongst the Modocs: Unwritten History. London, 1873
Memorie and Rime. New York, 1884
MILLER, JOHN. *A Description of the Province and City of New York.* London, 1843. c1695
MILLER, JOHN G. *The Black Patch War.* Chapel Hill, 1936
MILLER, MAX. *I Cover the Waterfront.* New York, [©1932]
MILLER, WADE, pseud. *Fatal Step.* New York, 1948
MILLER, WILLIAM. *A Dictionary of English Names of Plants.* London, 1884
MILLS, WILLIAM C. *Exploration of the Tremper Mound.* Columbus, O., 1916
MINOR, LUCIAN. [*Diary.*] *A Virginian in New England Thirty-Five Years Ago.* (*Atlantic Monthly.* XXVI–XXVII.) v.d.
MINOT, HENRY D. *The Land-Birds and Game-Birds of New England.* Salem, Mass., 1877
MINTURN, WILLIAM. *Travels West.* London, 1877
MITCHELL, DONALD G. *Dream Life.* New York, 1852. =1851
Fudge Doings. New York, 1855
The Lorgnette. New York, 1850
My Farm of Edgewood. New York, 1863
Reveries of a Bachelor. New York, 1850
MITCHELL, EDWIN V. *The Horse and Buggy Age in New England.* New York, 1937
MITCHELL, JAMES. *Nantucketisms of 1848.* (*American Speech,* IX.) 1848

Mitchell, John. *Reminiscences of Scenes and Characters in College: by a Graduate of Yale.* New Haven, 1847

Mitchell, Ronald E. *America; a Practical Handbook.* London, [1935]

Mitchell, Silas Weir. *Constance Trescot.* New York, 1905
Roland Blake. New York, 1895. =1886

Mitchill, Samuel L. *The Fishes of New York.* (Literary and Philosophical Society of New-York. *Transactions.* I.) 1814

Moe, Alfred K. *A History of Harvard.* Cambridge, Mass., 1896

Mohr, Charles T. *Plant Life of Alabama.* Washington, 1901

Moldenke, Harold N. *American Wild Flowers.* New York, [1949]

Molloy, Robert. *Pride's Way.* New York, 1945

Monaghan, James. *This is Illinois.* Chicago, 1949

Monardes, Nicolás. *Ioyfvll Nevves ovt of the Nevve Founde World.* Tr. John Frampton. London, 1577

Monette, John W. *History of the Discovery and Settlement of the Valley of the Mississippi.* New York, 1846

Monroe, Day, and Stratton, Lenore M. *Food Buying and Our Market.* Boston, 1925

Monroe, Kirk. *Dorymates.* New York, [c1889]
The Golden Days of '49. New York, [1889]

Montgomery, David H. *The Student's American History.* 2d rev. ed. Boston, 1916

Montgomery, Frank A. *Reminiscences of a Mississippian in Peace and War.* Cincinnati, 1901

Montgomery Ward & Co., firm. *Catalogue.* Chicago, 1935

Moodie, Susannah (Strickland). *Roughing It in the Bush; or, Life in Canada.* New York, 1852

Moore, Francis. *fl.* 1744. *A Voyage to Georgia.* London, 1744

Moore, Francis. *Description of Texas.* 2d ed. New York, 1844

Moore, Francis C. *How to Build a Home.* New York, 1897

Moore, Frank, ed. *Rebel Rhymes and Rhapsodies.* New York, 1864. v.d.
Ed. *Songs and Ballads of the American Revolution.* New York, 1856. v.d.
Women of the War. Hartford, 1866

Moore, John T. *Ole Mistis: and Other Songs and Stories from Tennessee.* Nashville, 1925

Moore, Mabel R. *Hitchcock Chairs.* [New Haven], 1933

Moorehead, Warren K. *Primitive Man in Ohio.* New York, 1892
Stone Ornaments Used by Indians in the United States and Canada. Andover, Mass., 1917

Moravian Jrnls. See Beauchamp.

Mordecai, Samuel. *Virginia, Especially Richmond, in By-gone Days.* Richmond, 1860

Morehead, Albert H., and Mott-Smith, Geoffrey, eds. *The Penguin Hoyle.* New York, [c1946]

Morgan, Albert T. *Yazoo.* Washington, 1884

Morgan, Dale L. *The Humboldt, Highroad of the West.* New York, [1943]

Morgan, James M. *Recollections of a Rebel Reefer.* Boston, 1917

Morgan, Lewis H. *Houses and House-Life of the American Aborigines.* Washington, 1881

Morison, Samuel E. *The Life and Letters of Harrison Gray Otis, . . . 1765–1848.* Boston, 1913. v.d.

Morley, Christopher. *The Haunted Bookshop.* Garden City, N.Y., 1921. Pref. 1919
Shandygaff. Garden City, 1918
Swiss Family Manhattan. Garden City, N.Y., 1932

Morley, Margaret W. *The Carolina Mountains.* Boston, 1913

Morrell, William. *New England.* London, 1625

Morrell, Z. N. *Flowers and Fruits from the Wilderness.* 2d ed., rev. Boston, 1873. =1872

Morris, Ann (Axtell). *Digging in the Southwest.* Garden City, N.Y., 1933

Morris, Clara. *Life on the Stage.* New York, 1901
Stage Confidences; Talks about Players and Play Acting. Boston, [1902]

Morris, Percy A. *They Hop and Crawl.* Lancaster, Pa., 1944

Morris, William G. *Report upon the Customs District, the Public Service, and the Resources of Alaska.* Washington, 1878. v.d.

Morse, Frances C. *Furniture of the Olden Time.* New ed. New York, 1936. =1917.

Morse, Jedidiah, comp. *The American Gazetteer.* Boston, 1797. 2d ed. 1798
The American Geography. Elizabethtown, N.J., 1789. New ed. London, 1794
The American Universal Geography. 3d ed. Boston, 1796
A Report to the Secretary of War . . . on Indian Affairs. New Haven, 1822. v.d.

Morse, John T. *John Quincy Adams.* Boston, 1892. =1882
Life and Letters of Oliver Wendell Holmes. Boston, 1896. v.d.

Morton, Nathaniel. *New-Englands Memoriall.* Cambridge, 1669. 6th ed. Boston, 1855.

Morton, Samuel G. *Crania Americana.* Philadelphia, 1839

Morton, Thomas, of Clifford's Inn. *New English Canaan.* 1632 [i.e., 1637] in Force. *Tracts.* Vol. II, No. 5. 1637

Moses, Belle. *Franklin Delano Roosevelt.* New York, 1933

Moses, Montrose J., ed. *Representative American Dramas.* Boston, 1925. v.d. Contents include David Belasco. *The Girl of the Golden West.* 1905. Clyde Fitch. *The City.* 1909. Charles H. Hoyt. *A Texas Steer.* 1894. Augustus Thomas. *The Witching Hour.* 1907
Representative Plays by American Dramatists. 3 vols. New York, 1918–[25]. v.d. Contents include James N. Barker. *The Indian Princess.* 1808. Hugh H. Brackenridge. *The Battle of Bunkers-Hill.* 1776. William Dunlap. *André.* 1798. John Leacock. *The Fall of British Tyranny.* 1776. Samuel Low. *The Politician Out-witted.* 1789. Mordecai M. Noah. *She Would be a Soldier q.v.* 1819. Robert Rogers. *Ponteach.* 1766. Royall Tyler. *The Contrast q.v.* 1787

Motley, John Lothrop. *Correspondence.* Ed. George W. Curtis. New York, 1889. v.d.

Motley, Willard. *Knock on Any Door.* New York, 1947

Mott, Frank L. *American Journalism.* New York, 1941

Mount Hood. A Guide. (Oregon Writers' Project.) [New York], 1940

Mourt's Relation or Journal of the Plantation at Plymouth. Ed. Henry M. Dexter. Boston, 1865. 1622

Mowry, Harold. *Ornamental Vines.* (Agricultural Experiment Station. Gainesville, Fla. *Bulletin* No. 188.) 1927

Mowry, Sylvester. *Arizona and Sonora.* New York, 1864

Mudd, William S. *The Old Boat Rocker.* New York, 1935

Muhlenberg, Henry. *Catalogus Plantarum Americae Septentrionalis.* Lancaster, Pa., 1813
Index Florae Lancastriensis. (American Philosophical Society. *Proceedings.* Old ser. III.) 1791

Muir, John. *John of the Mountains. Unpublished Journals of John Muir.* Ed. Linnie Marsh Wolfe. Boston, 1938. v.d.
The Mountains of California. New York, 1894
My First Summer in the Sierra. Boston, 1911. =1869
Our National Parks. Boston, 1901
Ed. *Picturesque California and the Region West of the Rocky Mountains from Alaska to Mexico.* San Francisco, 1888
A Thousand-Mile Walk to the Gulf. Boston, 1916. 1867
Travels in Alaska. Boston, 1915. *a*1915

Mulford, Clarence E. *Bar-20.* New York, 1907
Black Buttes. Garden City, N.Y., 1923
The Coming of Cassidy—and the Others. Chicago, [1913]
Cottonwood Gulch. Garden City, N.Y., 1925
Johnny Nelson. New York, 1920
The Orphan. New York, 1908

Mulford, Clarence E., and Clay, John W. *Buck Peters, Ranchman.* New York, 1912

Mulhall, Michael G. *Mulhall's Dictionary of Statistics.* New York, 1884

Munn, Charles C. *Uncle Terry.* New York, 1900

Munsell, Joel. *The Annals of Albany.* Albany, 1850–59. v.d.

Murphey, Archibald D. *Papers.* (N.C. Historical Commission. *Publications.* IV–V.) v.d.

Murphy, John M., comp. *Oregon Business Directory and State Gazetteer.* Portland, 1873

Murray, Amelia M. *Letters from the United States, Cuba, and Canada.* London, 1856. v.d.

Murray, Sir Charles A. *Travels in North America.* New York, 1839. 3d ed. London, 1854.

Murray, William H. H. *Adventures in the Wilderness.* Boston, 1869

Muzzey, David S. *History of the American People.* New York, 1927
James G. Blaine. New York, 1934

Myers, Allen O. *Bosses and Boodle in Ohio Politics.* Cincinnati, 1895

Myers, Gustavus. *The History of Tammany Hall.* New York, 1901. v.d.

Myers, Walter. *The "Guv" A Tale of Midwest Law and Politics.* New York, 1947

Myrick, Herbert. *The Federal Farm Loan System.* New York, 1916

N

Nadal, Ehrman S. *Impressions of London Social Life.* New York, 1875

Narragansett Historical Register. Providence, 1882–91

Narratives of Early Maryland, 1633–1684. Ed. Clayton C. Hall. New York, 1910. v.d.

Nash, Wallis. *Two Years in Oregon.* New York, 1882

Nason, Daniel. *A Journal of a Tour from Boston to Savannah.* Cambridge, 1849

National Intelligencer. Washington, 1800–1869

National Park Service. (U.S. Dept. Interior.) *Fading Trails; the Story of Endangered American Wildlife.* New York, 1942

Nature and Science on the Pacific Coast. Ed. Joseph Grinnell. San Francisco, 1915

A Naval Encyclopædia. Philadelphia, 1861

[*Naval War Rec.*] *Official Records of the Union and Confederate Navies in the War of the Rebellion.* (U.S. Navy Dept.) Washington, 1894–1922. v.d.

Neal, Daniel. *The History of New-England.* London, 1720

Neal, John. *Brother Jonathan.* Edinburgh, 1825
The Down-Easters. New York, 1833
John Beedle's Sleigh Ride, Courtship, and Marriage. First pub. anonymously in *Portland Courier.* Attrib. also to "Capt. M'Clintock." New York, 1841. *c*1840
Rachel Dyer. Portland, Me., 1828

Neal, Joseph C. *Charcoal Sketches.* Philadelphia. 1838. 1837

Neill, Edward D. *The History of Minnesota.* Philadelphia, 1858
Virginia Carolorum . . . 1625–1685. Albany, 1886. v.d.

Neilson, Peter. *Recollections of a Six Years' Residence in the United States of America.* Glasgow, 1830

Nelson, Edward W. *The Rabbits of North America.* Washington, 1909
Wild Animals of North America. Washington, 1918

Nelson, Samuel A. *The A B C of Wall Street.* New York, [1909]

Nesbit, Wilbur D. *The Trail to Boyland, and Other Poems.* Indianapolis, [1904]

Nevins, Allan. *Henry White; Thirty Years of American Diplomacy.* New York, 1930

The New American Encyclopædia. Ed. George Ripley and Charles A. Dana. New York, 1869–72. =1858 [1857]–63. Revised as *The American Cyclopædia.* With supp. New York, 1883–84. First pub., without supp. 1873–76

New Castle, Del. Court. *Records . . . , 1676–1681.* Lancaster, Pa., 1904. v.d.

New-England Magazine. Boston, 1831–35

New England Magazine: An Illustrated Monthly. Boston, 1884–88. New ser. Boston, 1889–1917

New England's First Fruits. London, 1643

[*N.H. Docs. & Recs.*] New Hampshire. (Colony.) [*Provincial, State, Town and Revolutionary Papers.*] Ed. Nathaniel Boulton, *et al.* Concord; Manchester, 1867–. (Titles vary greatly.) Vols. XXXI–XXXIX have title *Probate Records of the Province of New Hampshire.*

N.H. Orig. Docs. See Jenness.

N.H. Probate Recs. See *N.H. Docs. & Recs.*

New Haven (Colony). *Records of the Colony and Plantation . . . , from 1638 to 1640.* Ed. Charles J. Hoadly. Hartford, 1857. v.d.
Records of the Colony or Jurisdiction . . . , from May, 1653, to the Union. Ed. Charles J. Hoadly. Hartford, 1858. v.d.

New Haven, Conn. *New Haven Town Records, 1640–1684.* (New Haven Colony Historical Society. *Ancient Town Records* I–II.) New Haven, 1917–19. v.d.

New Mexico Press. Albuquerque, 1864–67. (Preceded by *Rio Abajo Weekly Press.*)

The New Negro Forget-me-not Songster. Cincinnati, 1848

New Plymouth Colony. *Records.* Ed. Nathaniel B. Shurtleff [and David Pulsifer]. Boston, 1855–61. v.d.
Laws, Statutes, etc. *The Compact with the Charter and Laws of the Colony of New Plymouth.* Boston, 1836. v.d.

(*New*) *Voice.* New York; Chicago, 1884–1906. Also as *New York Voice.*

A New Voyage to Georgia. 2d ed. London, 1737. =1735

[*N.Y. Wills.*] *Abstracts of Wills on File. 1665–1800.* (New York (County). Surrogate's Court.) In New York Historical Society. *Collections.* XXV–XLI. **v.d.**
Newberry, John S. *Geological Report.* (36th Cong., 1st sess. House Ex. Doc. 90.) Washington, **1861**
Newell, Chester. *History of the Revolution in Texas.* New York, **1838.** Also facs. repr., Austin, 1935.
Newell, Frederick H. *Irrigation in the United States.* New York, **[1902]**
Newell, Robert H. *The Orpheus C. Kerr Papers.* 1st Ser. New York, 1863. =**1862. v.d.**
Newmark, Harris. *Sixty Years in Southern California, 1853–1913.* Eds. Maurice H. and Marco R. Newmark. New York, **1916**
Newton, Alfred. *A Dictionary of Birds.* London, **1896**
Newton, Stan. *Paul Bunyan of the Great Lakes.* Chicago, **1946**
Nichol, Andrew A. *The Natural Vegetation of Arizona.* Tucson, **1937**
Nicholas, Anna. *An Idyl of the Wabash, and Other Stories.* Indianapolis, **1899**
Nichols, Edward J. *An Historical Dictionary of Baseball Terminology.* [State College Pa., 1939]. Microfilm copy of Ph.D. thesis. **v.d.**
Nichols, James L. *The Business Guide.* 28th ed. Naperville, Ill., **1891**
Nichols, Thomas L. *Forty Years of American Life.* London, **1864**
Nicholson, Meredith. *A Hoosier Chronicle.* London, **1912**
The Hoosiers. New York, **1900**
Nicklin, Philip H. *Letters Descriptive of the Virginia Springs.* Philadelphia, **1835**
A Pleasant Peregrination through the Prettiest Parts of Pennsylvania. Philadelphia, **1836**
Nicollet, Joseph. *Report Intended to Illustrate a Map of the Hydrographical Basin of the Upper Mississippi River.* Washington, **1843**
Nixon, Herman C. *Forty Acres and Steel Mules.* Chapel Hill, **1938**
Nixon, Phyllis J. *A Glossary of Virginia Words.* (American Dialect Society. *Publication No. 5.* **1946.)**
Noah, Mordecai M. *Gleanings from a Gathered Harvest.* **1845**
She Would Be a Soldier. New York, **1819.** See also Moses. *Representative Plays.*
Noble Rec. Included in *Florida Plantation Records q.v.*
Noll, Henry R. *The Botanical Class Book, and Flora of Pennsylvania.* Lewisburg, Pa., **1852**
Nordhoff, Charles. *The Communistic Societies of the United States.* New York, **1875**
The Cotton States in the Spring and Summer of 1875. New York, **1876**
Nordyke, Lewis. *Cattle Empire.* New York, **1949**
Norris, Charles G. *Bricks Without Straw.* New York, **1938**
Norris, Frank. *Blix.* New York, 1900. =**1899**
McTeague. New York, 1904. =**1899**
The Octopus. New York, **1901**
The Pit. New York, 1922. =1903 **[c1902]**
The Third Circle. New York, 1909. **v.d.**
Vandover and the Brute. Garden City, N.Y., 1914. *c***1895**
Norris, J. Wellington. *A Business Adviser and General Directory for the City of Chicago, for the Year 1845–6.* Chicago, **1845**
Norris, Kathleen (Thompson). *Certain People of Importance.* New York, **1922**
North Carolina. (Colony). *Colonial Records.* Ed. William L. Saunders. Raleigh, 1886–90. **v.d.**
Northall, William K. *Before and Behind the Curtain.* New York, 1851. **v.d.**
Ed. *Life and Recollections of Yankee Hill.* New York, 1850. **v.d.**
Northern Vindicator. Estherville, Iowa, **1868–1902**
Norton, Anthony B. *The Great Revolution of 1840. Reminiscences of the Log Cabin and Hard Cider Campaign.* Mt. Vernon, O.; Dallas, Tex., 1888
Tippecanoe Songs of the Log Cabin Boys and Girls of 1840. Mt. Vernon, O.; Dallas, 1888. =**1840**
Norton, Charles B., and Valentine, William J. *Report to the Government of the United States on the Munitions of War.* New York, **1868**
Norton, Charles L. *Political Americanisms.* (*Magazine of American History.* XII–XIII.) **1884–85**
Norton, John. *The Redeemed Captive.* Boston, **1748**
Norton, Oliver W. *Army Letters, 1861–1865.* [Chicago, 1903] **v.d.**
Notes and Queries; for Readers and Writers, Collectors and Librarians, Etc. London, **1849–** (Note: Used also as citation for *The Bizarre. Notes and Queries.* Manchester, N.H., **1886–91.** See also note to *American Notes and Queries.*)
Nott, Henry J. *Novellettes of a Traveller.* New York, **1834**
Nowland, John H. *Early Reminiscences of Indianapolis.* Indianapolis, **1870**
Noyes, Pierrepont B. *My Father's House; an Oneida Boyhood.* New York, **1937**
Nute, Grace L. *Lake Superior.* New York, **1944**
Nuttall, Thomas. *The Genera of North American Plants.* Philadelphia, **1818**
Nutting, Wallace. *Furniture of the Pilgrim Century, 1620–1720, (of American Origin), with Maple and Pine to 1800.* Rev. and enl. ed., Framingham, Mass., **[c1924]**
Massachusetts Beautiful. Framingham, **[c1923]**
Nye, Edgar W. *Baled Hay.* New York, **[c1884]**
Bill Nye and Boomerang. Chicago, **1894**

O

O'Beirne, Harry F. *Leaders and Leading Men of the Indian Territory.* Chicago, **1891**
Obenchain, Eliza C. (Calvert). *Aunt Jane of Kentucky.* Boston, 1907. **v.d.**
O'Bryan, William. *A Narrative of Travels in the United States of America.* London, **1836**
Odell, George C. D. *Annals of the New York Stage.* New York, 1927–. **v.d.**
Ogilby, John. *America.* London, **1671**
O. Henry, pseud. William Sydney Porter. *Cabbages and Kings.* London, 1916. First pub. 1904. **v.d.**
The Four Million. New York, 1915. =1913 [c1906]. **v.d.**
Heart of the West. New York, 1927. =1913. First pub. 1907. **v.d.**
Options. New York, [1909]. **v.d.**
Roads of Destiny. New York, 1909; New York, 1913. **v.d.**
Rolling Stones. New York, 1920. =1912. **v.d.**
Strictly Business. London, [n.d.]. First pub. 1910. **v.d.**
The Trimmed Lamp. New York, 1915. =1907. **v.d.**
Whirligigs. New York, 1920 [c1910]. **v.d.**
Old South Leaflets. [General Series.] Boston, [1896—.] Contents include Vol. I, No. 21. John Eliot. *Brief Narrative q.v.* **1670.** Vol. III, No. 51. *New England's First Fruits q.v.* **1643.** Vol. VI, No. 143. John Eliot. *The Day-breaking of the Gospel q.v.* **1647.** Vol. VII, No. 172. John Locke. *The Fundamental Constitutions of Carolina.* **1669**
Oldmixon, John. *The British Empire in America.* London, **1708**
Oliphant, Laurence. *Minnesota and the Far West.* London, **1855**
Olmsted, Frederick Law. *A Journey in the Back Country.* London, **1860**
A Journey in the Seaboard Slave States. New York, 1861. =**1856**
Omwake, John. *The Conestoga Six-Horse Bell Teams of Eastern Pennsylvania.* Cincinnati, **1930**
Onderdonk, James L. *Idaho.* San Francisco, **1885**
One Man's Gold. See Christman.
O'Neall, John B., and Chapman, John A. *The Annals of Newberry.* Newberry, S.C., 1892. **v.d.**
Onward. New York, **1869–70.** Cover-title *Mayne Reid's Magazine: Onward.*
Oregon State Journal. Eugene, **1864–1909**
Orne, Henry. *Letters of Columbus* [pseud.]. Boston, **1829**
Ostrander, Isabel E. *How Many Cards?* New York, **1920**
Otis, James. *The Rights of the British Colonies Asserted and Proved.* 3d ed. London, 1766. **1764**
Ottley, Roi. *New World A-Coming.* Boston, **1943**
Ouseley, Sir William G. *Remarks on the Statistics and Political Institutions of the United States.* Philadelphia, **1832**
Out West. Los Angeles, **1902–10**
Overland to the Pacific. Colorado Springs, Colo., [c1932]–. **v.d.**
Owen, Margaret B. *The Secret of Typewriting Speed.* Chicago, 1918. =**1917**
Owen, Mary A. *Voodoo Tales, as Told among the Negroes of the Southwest.* New York, **1893**
Owen, William. *Private Diary, November 1824–April 1825.* (Indiana Historical Society. *Publications.* IV.) **v.d.**
Owens, Frances E. (Johnston). *Mrs. Owens' Cook Book.* Chicago, **1882.** Rev. ed. 1888. =**1884**
Oyster Bay, N.Y. *Oyster Bay Town Records.* New York, 1916. **v.d.**

P

Pacific Discovery. Berkeley, **1947–**
[*Pacific R.R. Rep.*] *Reports of Explorations and Surveys, to Ascertain the Most Practicable and Economical Route from the Mississippi River to the Pacific Ocean.* (U.S. War Dept.) Washington, 1855–60. **v.d.**
Paddlford. See Honyman.
Padover, Saul K. *The Complete Jefferson.* New York, **1943**
Page, David. *Handbook of Geological Terms.* 2d ed. rev. and enl. Edinburgh, **1865**
Page, Thomas Nelson. *Red Rock.* New York, **1898**
Paine, Ralph D. *Comrades of the Rolling Ocean.* Boston, 1923 [c**1921**, 1923]
Palache, Charles. *The Minerals of Franklin and Sterling Hill, Sussex County, N.J.* Washington, **1935**
Pall Mall Gazette. London, **1865–**
Palmer, E. Laurence. *Fieldbook of Natural History.* New York, **1949**
Palmer, George H. *The Life of Alice Freeman Palmer.* Boston, **1908**
Palmer, Harry C. *Stories of the Base Ball Field.* Chicago, **1890**
Palmer, Howard. *Mountaineering and Exploration in the Selkirks.* New York, **1914**
Palmer, Joel. *Journal of Travels over the Rocky Mountains, to the Mouth of the Columbia River.* Cincinnati, **1847**
Palmer, John. *Journal of Travels in the United States of North America, and in Lower Canada.* London, **1818**
Park, Roswell. *Pantalogy; or, A Systematic Survey of Human Knowledge.* Philadelphia, **1841**
Parker, Amos A. *Trip to the West and Texas.* Concord, N.H., **1835**
Parker, George F. *Recollections of Grover Cleveland.* New York, 1911. =**1909**
Parker, James. *The Old Army.* Philadelphia, **[c1929]**
Parker, Samuel. *Journal of an Exploring Tour beyond the Rocky Mountains.* Ithaca, N.Y., **1838**
Parker, William B. *Notes Taken During the Expedition Commanded by Capt. R. B. Marcy, U.S.A., through Unexplored Texas, in the Summer and Fall of 1854.* Philadelphia, **1856**
Parkinson, John. *Paradisi in Sole Paradisus Terrestris.* Repr. London, 1904. **1629**
Theatrum Botanicum: The Theater of Plants. London, **1640**
Parkinson, Richard. *A Tour in America, in 1798, 1799, and 1800.* London, **1805**
Parkman, Ebenezer. *Diary.* Ed. Harriette M. Forbes. [Westborough, Mass.], 1899. **v.d.**
Parkman, Francis. *The California and Oregon Trail.* (*Knickerbocker Magazine.* XXIX–XXXIII.) **1847–49**
Champlain and His Associates. New York, [c1890]. From *Pioneers . . .*, **1865**
Pioneers of France in the New World. Boston, **1865**
Parks, H. B. *Valuable Plants Native to Texas.* (Texas Agricultural Experiment Station. *Bulletin.* No. 551.) **1937**
Parmenter, Charles O. *History of Pelham, Mass., from 1738 to 1898.* Amherst, Mass., 1898. **v.d.**
Parrish, Randall. *The Case and the Girl.* New York, **1922**
Parsons, Frances T. (Smith) Dana. *According to Season.* New and enl. ed. New York, **1902**
Parsons, Mary E. *The Wild Flowers of California.* 7th ed., rev. and corr. San Francisco, **1906**
Parton, Sara P. (Willis). *Ginger-Snaps.* New York, **1870**
Partridge, Bellamy, and Bettmann, Otto. *As We Were; Family Life in America, 1850–1900.* New York, **[1946]**
Pastor, Tony. *Tony Pastor's "444" Combination Songster.* New York, **[1864]**
Patten, Matthew. *The Diary of Matthew Patten of Bedford, N.H.* Concord, N.H., 1903. **v.d.**
Pattie, James Ohio. *Personal Narrative.* Ed. Timothy Flint. Cincinnati, **1831**
Paul, Elliot H. *Linden on the Saugus Branch.* New York, **[1947]**
Paul Bunyan's Quiz. (American Forest Products Industries, Inc.). Washington, **1944**
Paulding, Hiram. *Journal of a Cruise of the United States Schooner Dolphin among the Islands of the Pacific Ocean.* New York, **1831**
Paulding, James K. *The Backwoodsman.* Philadelphia, **1818**
The Beauties of Brother Bull-us. New York, **1812**
The Book of Saint Nicholas. New York, **1836**

A Book of Vagaries. New York, **1868**
Chronicles of the City of Gotham. New York, **1830**
The Diverting History of John Bull and Brother Jonathan. 2d ed. New York, **1813**. New ed. New York, **1835**. First pub. New York, 1812.
John Bull in America. New York, **1825**
The Lay of the Scottish Fiddle. 1st Amer. from 4th Edinburgh ed. London, 1814. First pub. **1813**
Letters from the South. New York, **1817**
The New Mirror for Travellers. New York, **1828**
Westward Ho! New York, **1832**
PAULDING, JAMES K., and PAULDING, WILLIAM I. *American Comedies*. Philadelphia, 1847. Includes *The Bucktails*, *c***1815**; *Antipathies*, *c***1845**; *Madmen All*, *c***1845**; and *The Noble Exile*, *c***1845**. (The first only is by J. K. Paulding.)
PAXTON, PHILIP, pseud. SAMUEL A. HAMMETT. *A Stray Yankee in Texas*. New York, **1853**
The Wonderful Adventures of Captain Priest. New York, **1855**
PAYSON, GEORGE. *Golden Dreams and Leaden Realities*. New York, **1853**
P. C. C. Chronicle. (Pub. Pasadena, Calif., City College.) **1949**
PEABODY, WILLIAM B. O. [*Mass. Birds*.] *A Report of the Ornithology of Massachusetts*. Boston, **1839**
PEARS, SARAH. *Narrative*. MS., Newberry Library, Chicago, *c***1875**
PEARSON, ELIZABETH W., ed. *Letters from Port Royal Written at the Time of the Civil War*. Boston, 1906. **v.d.**
PEARSON, HAYDN S. *Country Flavor*. New York, **1945**
PEARY, ROBERT E. *The North Pole*. New York, **1910**
PEASE, ARTHUR S. *Sequestered Vales of Life*. Cambridge, **1946**
PEASE, THEODORE C. *The United States*. New York, [c**1927**]
PEATTIE, DONALD CULROSS. *Journey into America*. Boston, **1943**
PEATTIE, RODERICK, ed. *The Berkshires: the Purple Hills*. New York, [**1948**]
The Friendly Mountains, Green, White, and Adirondacks. New York, **1942**
The Great Smokies and the Blue Ridge. New York, **1943**
The Pacific Coast Ranges. New York, [**1946**]
PECK, GEORGE W. *Peck's Bad Boy and His Pa*. Chicago, **1883**
Peck's Boss Book. Chicago, 1892. =**1884**
Peck's Sunshine. Chicago, 1883. =**1882**
PECK, JOHN M. *A Gazetteer of Illinois*. Jacksonville, Ill., **1834**. 2d ed. Philadelphia, **1837**
A Guide for Emigrants. Boston, **1831**
A New Guide for Emigrants to the West. 2d ed. Boston, **1837**
PEEL, ROY V. *The Political Clubs of New York*. New York, **1935**
Peel City Guardian. (*OED*)
PEIRCE, BENJAMIN. *A History of Harvard University, from Its Foundation . . . to the Period of the American Revolution*. Cambridge, 1833. **v.d.**
PENCIL, MARK, pseud. *White Sulphur Papers*. New York, **1839**
PENHALLOW, SAMUEL. [*Indian Wars*.] *The History of the Wars of New-England and the Eastern Indians*. (New Hampshire Historical Society. *Collections*. I.) **1726**
PENN, WILLIAM. *Select Works*. 3d ed. London, 1782. **v.d.**
[*Penn-Logan Corr*.] *Correspondence between William Penn and James Logan, . . . 1700–1750*. (Historical Society of Pennsylvania. *Memoirs*. IX–X.) **v.d.**
PENNANT, THOMAS. *Arctic Zoology*. London, **1784–85**
Synopsis of Quadrupeds. Chester, Eng., **1771**
PENNELL, JOSEPH S. *The History of Rome Hanks and Kindred Matters*. New York, **1944**
PENNIMAN, MAJOR, pseud. CHARLES W. DENISON. *The Tanner-Boy and How He Became Lieutenant-General*. Boston, **1864**
[*Pa. Colonial Rec*.] Citation for series (each specially titled) comprising [*Colonial Records of Pennsylvania. 1683–1790*.]. Harrisburg, 1851–53; Philadelphia, 1852. **v.d.**
Pennsylvania Evening Post. Philadelphia, **1775–84**
Pennsylvania Gazette. Philadelphia, **1728–1815**
Pennsylvania Journal. Philadelphia, **1742–93**
Pennsylvania Packet. Philadelphia, **1771–90**
The Penny Cyclopædia of the Society for the Diffusion of Useful Knowledge. London, **1833–43**
A Perfect Description of Virginia. (FORCE. *Tracts*. II, No. 8.) **1649**
PERRIE, GEORGE W. *Buckskin Mose*. Ed. C. G. Rosenberg. New York, 1890 [c1889.] =**1873**
PERRIN, WILLIAM H. *The Pioneer Press of Kentucky*. [Louisville], **1888**
PERROT, NICOLAS. *Mémoire sur les Mœurs, coustumes et Relligion des Sauvages de l'Amérique Septentrionale*. Paris, 1864. *a***1716**
PERRY, GEORGE SESSIONS. *Cities of America*. New York, [**1947**]
PERRY, GEORGE W. *A Treatise on Turpentine Farming*. Newbern, N.C., **1859**
PERRY, WILLIAM S., ed. *Historical Collections Relating to the American Colonial Church*. [Hartford], 1870–78. **v.d.**
PERSONS, CHARLES E., *et al*. *Labor Laws and their Enforcement with Special Reference to Massachusetts*. New York, **1911**
PETERS, DE WITT C. *The Life and Adventures of Kit Carson*. New York, **1858**
PETERS, SAMUEL. *A General History of Connecticut*. London, **1781**
PETERSON, ROGER TORY. *A Field Guide to Western Birds*. Boston, **1941**
PETERSON, THOMAS GILBERT. *Adventures in Bird Protection*. New York, **1937**
PETIVER, JAMES. *Gazophylacii naturæ et artis Deces prima (-quinta)*. London, **1702–6**
PETRULLO, VINCENZO. *The Diabolic Root*. Philadelphia, **1934**
PETTIGREW PAPERS. Various letters by or to members of the Pettigrew family, in the Library of the University of North Carolina, Chapel Hill. **v.d.**
PEYTON, JOHN L. *The Adventures of My Grandfather*. London, **1867**
The Pharmacopaeia of the United States of America. Boston, **1820**
PHELAN, MICHAEL. *The Game of Billiards*. New York, **1857**
PHILIPS, MELVILLE, ed. *The Making of a Newspaper*. New York, **1893**
PHILIPS, SHINE. *Big Spring, the Casual Biography of a Prairie Town*. New York, [c**1942**]
The Philistine. East Aurora, N.Y., **1895–1915**
PHILLIPS, DAVID GRAHAM. *Old Wives for New*. New York, 1920. =**1908**
The Plum Tree. New York, **1905**
The Social Secretary, New York, **1905**
A Woman's Ventures. New York, [c**1902**]
PHILLIPS, DAVID L. *Letters from California*. Springfield, Ill., **1877**
PHILLIPS, HENRY. *Historical Sketches of the Paper Currency of the American Colonies, Prior to the Adoption of the Federal Constitution*. Roxbury, Mass., **1865–66**
PHILLIPS, JOHN C., and LINCOLN, FREDERICK C. *American Waterfowl*. Boston, **1930**
PHILLIPS, MICHAEL J. *History of Santa Barbara County, California*. Chicago, **1927**
PHILLIPS, PHILIP L. *Notes on the Life and Works of Bernard Romans*. Deland, Fla., 1924. **v.d.**
PHILLIPS, WENDELL. *Speeches, Lectures, and Letters*. Boston, 1863. **v.d.**
PHILLIPS, WILLIAM. *The Conquest of Kansas by Missouri and Her Allies*. Boston, **1856**
PHILLIPS-WOLLEY, CLIVE. *The Trottings of a Tenderfoot*. London, **1884**
PHILOPOLITES [?Cotton Mather]. *A Memorial of the Present Deplorable State of New-England*. [London], **1707**
PHOEBUS, WILLIAM. *Memoirs of the Rev. Richard Whatcoat*. New York, 1828. **v.d.**
PICKERING, JOHN. *A Vocabulary; or, Collection of Words and Phrases, which Have Been Supposed to be Peculiar to the United States of America*. Boston, **1816**. Repub., with corr. and adds., from American Academy of Arts and Sciences. *Memoirs*. 1815.
PICKERING, JOSEPH. *Inquiries of an Emigrant*. New ed. London, 1831. 3d ed., 1832. First pub. as *Emigration, or No Emigration*. London, 1830. **v.d.**
PICKWELL, GAYLE B. *Deserts*. New York, [c**1939**]
PIDGIN, CHARLES F. *Blennerhassett*. New York, [c**1901**]
Quincy Adams Sawyer and Mason's Corner Folks. Rev. ed. Boston, **1902**
Stephen Holton. Boston, **1902**
PIERSON, HAMILTON W. *In the Brush*. New York, **1881**
PIKE, ALBERT. *Prose Sketches and Poems*. Boston, **1834**
PIKE, JAMES. *Scout and Ranger*. Princeton, 1932. **1865**
PIKE, ZEBULON M. *An Account of Expeditions to the Sources of the Mississippi*. Philadelphia, 1810. **v.d.** Pub. also as *The Expeditions of Zebulon Montgomery Pike, to Headwaters of the Mississippi River*. Ed. Elliott Coues. New York, 1895.
PILLING, JAMES C. *Bibliography of the Chinookan Languages*. Washington, **1893**
PINCHOT, GIFFORD. *The Adirondack Spruce*. New York, **1898**
The Fight for Conservation. New York, **1910**
PINE, GEORGE W. *Beyond the West*. 2d ed. Utica, N.Y., 1871. **1870**
PINKERTON, ALLAN. *The Expressman and the Detective*. Chicago, 1875. =**1874**
Strikers, Communists, Tramps and Detectives. New York, 1884. =**1878**
PINKERTON, JOHN J. *A Practical Guide to Administrators, Guardians and Assignees*. West Chester, Pa., **1870**
PINKERTON, KATHRENE S. (GEDNEY). *Wilderness Wife*. Philadelphia, **1939**
Pioneer Days in the Southwest from 1850 to 1879. Guthrie, Okla., **1909**
PITTENGER, WILLIAM. *Daring and Suffering: A History of the Great Railroad Adventure*. Philadelphia, 1864. =**1863**
PITTMAN, HANNAH (DAVIESS). *The Belle of the Blue Grass Country*. Boston, **1906**
PITTMAN, PHILIP. *The Present State of the European Settlements on the Mississippi*. London, **1770**
A Platform of Church Discipline. See CONGREGATIONAL CHURCHES.
PLAYFAIR, HUGO. *The Hugo Playfair Papers; or, Brother Jonathan, the Smartest Nation in All Creation*. London, **1841**
Plough Boy, and Journal of the Board of Agriculture. Albany, **1819–23**
PLUMBE, JOHN. *Sketches of Iowa and Wisconsin*. St. Louis, **1839**
PLUMMER, FRED G. *Chaparral*. Washington, **1911**
PLUMMER, JONATHAN. *Sketches of the History of the Life and Adventures of Jonathan Plummer*. [?Boston, *c***1800**]
PLYMOUTH, MASS. *Records of the Town*. Plymouth, 1889–1903. **v.d.**
Plymouth Church Records, 1620–1859. (Colonial Society of Massachusetts. *Publications*. XXII–XXIII.) **v.d.**
[*Plymouth Col. Rec*.] See NEW PLYMOUTH COLONY.
[*Plymouth Laws*.] See NEW PLYMOUTH COLONY.
POAGE, GEORGE R. *Henry Clay and the Whig Party*. Chapel Hill, **1936**
The Pocumtuc Housewife. [Deerfield, Mass., 1906.] First pub. **1805**
POE, EDGAR ALLAN. *Complete Works*. Ed James A. Harrison. [Virginia Ed.] New York, [1902]. Also Ed. Edmund C. Stedman and George E. Woodberry. New York, 1914. =1894–95. **v.d.** (Poems sometimes cited by individual titles.)
POE, SOPHIE (ALBERDING). *Buckboard Days*. Caldwell, Ida., **1936**
The Polite Traveller, being a Modern View of the Thirteen United States of America. London, [**1783**]
POLK, JAMES K. *Diary*. Ed. Milo M. Quaife. 4 vols. Chicago, 1910. **v.d.**
Polk: The Diary of a President, 1845–1849. Ed. Allan Nevins. London, 1929. **v.d.**
POLLARD, EDWARD A. *Southern History of the War*. 2 vols. in 1. New York, **1866**
Southern History of the War. The First Years of the War. New York, 1863. **1862**
Southern History of the War. The Third Year of the War. New York, 1865. **1864**
POLLARD, JOHN G. *The Pamunkey Indians of Virginia*. Washington, **1894**
Polly Peablossom. See BURKE, THOMAS A.
POMEROY, MARCUS M. *Nonsense*. New York, **1868**
POOL, MARIA L. *In Buncombe County*. Chicago, **1896**
POOLE, ERNEST. *The Harbor*. New York, **1915**
POOLE, JOHN F. *The Double-Quick Comic Songster*. New York, [**1862**]
POORE, BENJAMIN PERLEY. *Perley's Reminiscenses of Sixty Years in the National Metropolis*. Philadelphia, **1886**
POPE, JOHN. *A Tour through the Southern and Western Territories of the United States of North-America*. Richmond, Va., **1792**
POPKIN, JOHN S. *Memorial*. Ed. Cornelius Felton. Cambridge, 1852. **v.d.**
PORCHER, FRANCIS P. *Resources of the Southern Fields and Forests*. Richmond, Va., **1863**
Port Folio Philadelphia, **1801–27**
PORTER, DAVID D. *Incidents and Anecdotes of the Civil War*. New York, 1886. =**1885**
PORTER, ELEANOR (HODGMAN). *Just David*. New York, [**1916**]
PORTER, GENE (STRATTON). *The Keeper of the Bees*. Garden City, N.Y., **1925**
Laddie. Garden City, N.Y., **1913**
PORTER, HORACE. *West Point Life: An Anonymous Communication*. [New York, ?**1859**]
PORTER, WILLIAM TROTTER, ed. *The Big Bear of Arkansas, and Other Sketches*. Philadelphia, [c**1845**]. Includes *Chunkey's Fight with the Panthers*.
Ed. *A Quarter Race in Kentucky, and Other Sketches*. Philadelphia, [c1846, 1854]. **v.d.**
Porter's Spirit of the Times. New York, **1856–61**. Merged into *Wilkes' Spirit of the Times q.v.* (See also note to *Spirit of the Times*.)

PORTSMOUTH, R.I. *Early Records.* Ed. Amos Perry and Clarence S. Brigham. Providence, 1901. **v.d.**

PORY, JOHN. *John Pory's Lost Description of Plymouth Colony.* Boston, 1918. **1622. c1622**

POST, CHARLES C. *Ten Years a Cowboy.* Chicago, 1898. **=1896**

POST, WALDRON K. *Harvard Stories.* New York, **1893**

POTE, WILLIAM. *The Journal of Captain William Pote, Jr. during His Captivity in the French and Indian War.* New York, 1896. **v.d.**

POWELL, ARTHUR G. *I Can Go Home Again.* Chapel Hill, **1943**

POWELL, JOHN J. *Nevada: the Land of Silver.* San Francisco, **1876**

POWER, TYRONE. *Impressions of America.* London, **1836**

POWERS, STEPHEN. *Afoot and Alone.* Hartford, **1872**

POYAS, ELIZABETH A. *A Peep into the Past.* Charleston, **1853**

Prairie Club Bulletin. Chicago, **1908–**

The Prairie Schooner. Lincoln, Neb., **1927–**

PREMIUM, BARTON. *Eight Years in British Guiana.* London, **1850**

PRENTICE, ARCHIBALD. *A Tour in the United States.* Manchester, Eng., 1853. **1848**

PRESCOTT, DE WITT C. *Early Day Railroading from Chicago.* Chicago, **1910**

PRESCOTT, GEORGE B. *The Speaking Telephone, Electric Light, and other Recent Electrical Inventions.* New York, **1879**

[*Pres. Messages & Papers.*] *A Compilation of the Messages and Papers of the Presidents, 1780–1897.* Comp. by James D. Richardson. 10 vols. Washington, 1896–99. **v.d.**

PRESTON, RICHARD J. *Rocky Mountain Trees.* Ames, Ia., **1940**

PRICE, CON. *Trails I Rode.* Pasadena, Calif., **1947**

PRIEST, LORING B. *Uncle Sam's Stepchildren.* New Brunswick, N.J., **1942**

PRIEST, WILLIAM. *Travels in the United States of America.* London, 1802. Written **1779**

Primitive Man; Quarterly Bulletin of the Catholic Anthropological Conference. Washington, **1923–**

PRINCE, LEBARON B. *Historical Sketches of New Mexico.* Kansas City, Mo., **1883**

PRINGLE, ELIZABETH W. (ALLSTON). *A Woman Rice Planter.* New York, 1913. **v.d.**

PROGRESS, MARCH OF. Chicago, **1946**

PROVIDENCE, R.I. RECORD COMMISSIONERS. *Early Records.* Providence, 1892–1909. **v.d.**

PURCHAS, SAMUEL. *Purchas His Pilgrimage.* London, **1613**

PURDY, TRUMAN H. *Legends of the Susquehanna, and Other Poems.* Philadelphia, **1888**

PURSH, FREDERICK. *Flora Americæ Septentrionalis.* London, **1814**

PUSEY, WILLIAM A. *The Wilderness Road to Kentucky, Its Location and Features.* New York, [c1921] **v.d.**

PUTNAM, ELIZABETH, H. L. *Mrs. Putnam's Receipt Book.* New and enl. ed. New York, 1869. **=1867**

PUTNAM, RUFUS. *Memoirs.* Boston, 1903. **v.d.**

Put's Golden Songster. San Francisco, **[1858]**

Q

A Quarter Race in Kentucky, and Other Sketches. Ed. William T. Porter. Philadelphia, [c1846, 1854] 1846. **v.d.**

QUENTIN, KARL. *Reisebilder und Studien aus dem Norden der Vereinigten Staaten von Amerika.* Arnsberg, 1851. Letters and memoranda written **1850**

QUICK, HERBERT. *Double Trouble.* Indianapolis, **[1906]**
Vandemark's Folly. Indianapolis, **[1922]**
Yellowstone Nights. Indianapolis, **[c1911]**

QUINCY, JOSIAH. *Figures of the Past from the Leaves of Old Journals.* Boston, 1883. **a1882**
The History of Harvard University. Cambridge, 1840. **v.d.**

Quinland; or, Varieties in American Life. London, **1857**

QUINN, ARTHUR H. *Pennsylvania Stories.* Philadelphia, **1899**

QUINN, JOHN P. *Fools of Fortune.* Chicago, **1890**

QUINT, ALONZO H. *The Potomac and the Rapidan.* Boston, 1864. **v.d.**

Quiz on Railroads and Railroading. (Association of American Railroads.) Washington, **1940.** (Cited by question nos.)

R

R., I., pseud. MRS. ISABELLE RANDALL. *A Lady's Ranche Life in Montana.* London, **1887**

RABB, KATE M., ed. *A Tour Through Indiana in 1840. The Diary of John Parsons of Petersburgh, Virginia.* New York, 1920. **1840**

Radges' Sixth Biennial Directory . . . of the City of Topeka. Topeka, Kans., **1882**

RAE, WILLIAM F. *Westward by Rail.* 2d ed. New York, 1871. **=London, 1870**

RAFINESQUE, CONSTANTINE S. *Ichthyologia Ohioensis.* Lexington, Ky., **1820**

The Railways of America. By various writers. London, **1890**

RAINE, JAMES W. *The Land of Saddle-Bags.* New York, [c1924]

RAINE, WILLIAM MACLEOD. *Brand Blotters.* New York, **[c1912]**
Bucky O'Connor, a Tale of the Unfenced Border. New York, **[c1910]**

RAINE, WILLIAM MACLEOD, and BARNES, WILL C. *Cattle.* Garden City, N.Y., **1930**

RAINWATER, CLARENCE E. *The Play Movement in the United States.* Chicago, **[c1921]**

RAMSAY, ROBERT L., and EMBERSON, FRANCES G. *A Mark Twain Lexicon.* (*University of Missouri Studies.* XIII, No. 1.) **1938**

RAMSEY, JAMES F. M. *The Annals of Tennessee to the End of the Eighteenth Century.* Charleston, S.C., 1853. **v.d.**

RANDALL, HENRY S. *The Practical Shepherd.* Rochester, N.Y., 1864. **=1863**

RANDOLPH, VANCE. *Ozark Mountain Folks.* New York, **[c1932]**

Range Plant Handbook. (Forest Service. U.S. Dept. Agriculture.) Washington, **1937.** (Looseleaf; citations by symbols: G. Grasses; W. Weeds; B. Browse.)

RANKIN, DANIEL S. *Kate Chopin and Her Creole Stories.* Philadelphia, 1932. **v.d.**

RANOUS, DORA K. (THOMPSON). *Diary of a Daly Débutante.* New York, 1910. **v.d.**

RATTAN, VOLNEY. *West Coast Botany.* San Francisco, **1898**

RAUM, JOHN O. *The History of New Jersey.* Philadelphia, **[1877]**

RAWLINGS, MARJORIE (KINNAN). *Cross Creek.* New York, **1942**

RAWSON, MARION N. *New Hampshire Borns a Town.* New York, **1942**

RAYMOND, ROSSITER W. *A Glossary of Mining and Metallurgical Terms.* Easton, Pa., **1881**
Statistics of Mines and Mining in the States and Territories West of the Rocky Mountains. Washington, 1869–77. **v.d.**

REA, CALEB. *Journal . . . during the Expedition against Ticonderoga in 1758.* (Essex Institute. *Historical Collections.* XVIII.) **1758**

READ, OPIE P. *The Jucklins.* Chicago, **[c1896]**

READ, WILLIAM A. *Louisiana-French.* Baton Rouge, **1931**
A Score of Louisiana-French Words. (*Zeitschrift für französische Sprache und Literatur.* LXIII, pts. 1–2.) **1940**
Some Louisiana-French Words. (*Zeitschrift für französische Sprache und Literature.* LXI, pts. 1–2.) **1937**

The Rebellion Record: A Diary of American Events. Ed. Frank Moore. New York, 1862–71. **v.d.**

The Red Book. Chicago Classified Telephone Directory. **1945–50**

Redbook Magazine. Chicago, **1903–**

REDFIELD, ISAAC F. *A Practical Treatise upon the Law of Railways.* Boston, **1858**

REDFORD, ALBERT H. *The History of Methodism in Kentucky.* Nashville, **1868–70**

REDMOND, E. G. *Frauds of America.* Naperville, Ill., 1902. **[c1896 by Joseph H. Francis.]**

REED, ANDREW, and MATHESON, JAMES. *A Narrative of the Visit to the American Churches, by the Deputation from the Congregational Union of England and Wales.* New York, **1835**

REED, THOMAS B. *Reed's Rules. A Manual of General Parliamentary Law.* Chicago, **1894**

REES, JOHN E. *Idaho Chronology, Nomenclature, Bibliography.* Chicago, **1918**

REEVE, ARTHUR B. *The Golden Age of Crime.* New York, **1931**

REGAN, JOHN. *The Emigrant's Guide to the Western States of America.* 2d ed., rev. and enl. Edinburgh, **[1852]**

REICHARD, GLADYS A. *Navajo Shepherd and Weaver.* New York, **[1936]**

REID, MAYNE. *The Desert Home.* Boston, **1856**
The Scalp Hunters. Philadelphia, **1851**

REID, SAMUEL C. *The Scouting Expeditions of of McCulloch's Texas Rangers.* Philadelphia, **1847**

REID, WHITELAW. *After the War.* Cincinnati, **1866**

REID, WILLIAM M. *The Story of Old Fort Johnson.* New York, **1906**

A Relation of the Invasion and Conquest of Florida by the Spaniards. London, **1686**

A Relation of Maryland, Reprinted from the London Edition of 1635. Ed. Francis L. Hawks. New York, 1865. **1635**

A Relation of the Successefull Beginnings of the Lord Baltemore's Plantation in Mary-Land. [Albany, 1865.] **1634**

Relations des Jésuites. Quebec, 1858. **v.d.**

Remarks on the Trial of J. P. Zenger, Printer of the New York Weekly Journal. London, **1748**

REMINGTON, FREDERICK. *Pony Tracks.* New York, **1895**

Reminiscences in the Life of a Railroad Engineer. Columbus, O., **1861**

REMY, JULES. *A Journey to Great-Salt-Lake City.* London, **1861**

Republic. (Wkly., semi-wkly.) Washington, **1849–53**

Republic: A Monthly Magazine. Washington, **1873–77**

REUTER, CHRISTIAN G. *Wachau.* (In *Records of the Moravians in North Carolina.* Ed. Adelaide L. Fries. XV.) **1764**

REVELEY, WILLIAM. *An Historical Journal of the Expeditions by Sea and Land to the North of California.* London, **1790**

REVERE, JOSEPH W. *A Tour of Duty in California.* Boston, **1849**

The Reviewers Reviewed, or British Falsehoods Detected by American Truths. New York, **1815**

Revolutionary Diplomatic Correspondence of the United States. Ed. Francis Wharton. (U.S. Dept. of State.) Washington, 1889. **v.d.**

REYNOLDS, JOHN. *The Pioneer History of Illinois.* Belleville, Ill., **1852**

RHODE ISLAND (COLONY). *Records of the Colony of Rhode Island and Providence Plantations.* Ed. John Russell Bartlett. Providence, 1856–65. **v.d.**
COURT OF TRIALS. *Rhode Island Court Records.* Providence, 1920–22. **v.d.**

RICE, ALICE C. (HEGAN). *Mr. Opp.* New York, **1909**
Mrs. Wiggs of the Cabbage Patch. New York, 1913. **=1901**
Sandy. New York, **1905**

RICE, BERTHA M. and RICE, ROLAND. *Popular Studies of California Wild Flowers.* San Francisco, **[1920]**

RICE, THOMAS D. *Jim Crow. Celebrated Comic Song or Ballad.* New York: Atwill's Music Saloon, **1828**

RICH, LOUISE (DICKINSON). *We Took to the Woods.* New York, 1948. **1942**

RICH, OLIVER O. *A Synopsis of the Genera of American Plants.* Georgetown, D.C., **1814**

RICHARDS, CAROLINE C. *Village Life in America, 1852–1872.* New York, 1912. **v.d.**

RICHARDS, ELLEN H. (SWALLOW). *Euthenics, the Science of Controllable Environment.* Boston, **1910**

RICHARDS, LAURA E. (HOWE). *Mrs. Tree.* Boston, **[c1902]**

RICHARDSON, ALBERT D. *Beyond the Mississippi.* Hartford, **[c1867]**
The Secret Service, the Field, the Dungeon, and the Escape. Hartford, 1866. **=1865**

RICHARDSON, JAMES, ed. *Wonders of the Yellowstone.* New York, **1873**

RICHARDSON, SIR JOHN, *et al.* *Fauna Boreali-Americana.* London, **1829–37**

RICHARDSON, WILLIAM. *The Travel Diary of William Richardson from Boston to New Orleans by Land.* Ed. William B. Wait. New York, 1938. **1815**

RICHTER, CONRAD. *The Fields.* New York, **1946**
The Sea of Grass. New York, **1936**

RICHTER, MAX C. *Honey Plants of California.* Sacramento, **1911**

RICKABY, FRANZ. *Ballads and Songs of the Shanty-Boy.* Cambridge, **1926**

RIDEOUT, HENRY M. *The Key of the Fields, and Boldero.* New York, **1918**

RIDGWAY, ROBERT. *The Ornithology of Illinois.* Springfield, **1889–95**

RIDLEY, BROMFIELD L. *Battles and Sketches of the Army of Tennessee.* Mexico, Mo., **1906**

RIESENBERG, FELIX, JR. *Golden Gate.* New York, **1940**

RIIS, JACOB A. *The Making of an American.* New York, 1902. **=1901**

RILEY, CHARLES V. *Second Annual Report on the Noxious, Beneficial and Other Insects, of the State of Missouri.* Jefferson City, **1870**

RILEY, HENRY H. *Puddleford, and Its People.* New York, **1854**

RILEY, JAMES WHITCOMB. *Eccentric Mr. Clark.* New York, **1913**

"The Old Swimmin'-Hole," and 'Leven More Poems. Indianapolis, **1883**
Pipes o' Pan at Zekesbury. Indianapolis, **1889**
RINGWALT, JOHN L., ed. *American Encyclopaedia of Printing*. Philadelphia, **1871**
Rio Abajo Weekly Press. Albuquerque, N.M., **1863–64**. (Continued as *New Mexico Press*.)
RISTER, CARL C. *Land Hunger: David L. Payne and the Oklahoma Boomers*. Norman, Okla., **1942**
RITCH, WILLIAM G. *Illustrated New Mexico*. 4th ed. Santa Fe, **1883**
RITSON, ANNE. *A Poetical Picture of America*. London, **1809**
RITTENHOUSE, ISABELLA M. *Maud*. Ed. Richard L. Strout. New York, 1939. **v.d.**
RITTENHOUSE, JACK D. *American Horse-Drawn Vehicles*. Los Angeles, **1948**
RIVES, HALLIE E. *The Castaway*. Indianapolis, **[c1904]**
ROADS, SAMUEL. *The History and Traditions of Marblehead*. Boston, **1880**
ROBB, JOHN S. *Streaks of Squatter Life*. (Bound with H. C. LEWIS. *The Swamp Doctor's Adventures q.v.*) **1847**
ROBERTS, CECIL. *Adrift in America*. London, **1891**
ROBERTS, ELIZABETH MADOX. *The Time of Man*. New York, **1926**
ROBERTS, JOB. *The Pennsylvania Farmer*. Philadelphia, **1804**
ROBERTS, THOMAS S. *The Birds of Minnesota*. Minneapolis, **1932**
ROBERTS, WILLIAM. *An Account of the First Discovery and Natural History of Florida*. London, **1763**
ROBERTSON, HARRISON. *The Inlander*. New York, **1901**
Red Blood and Blue. New York, **1900**
ROBERTSON, JAMES, of Manchester, Eng. *A Few Months in America*. London, **1855**
ROBERTSON, MORGAN. *Land Ho!* New York, **1905**
"Where Angels Fear to Tread" and Other Tales of the Sea. New York, 1921. **=1899**
ROBIN, CLAUDE C. *Florula Ludoviciana; or, A Flora of the State of Louisiana*. Tr., rev. and impr. by C. S. Rafinesque. New York, **1817**
Voyages dans l'Intérieur de la Louisiane. Paris, **1807**
ROBINS, ELIZABETH. *The Magnetic North*. 417 pp. New York, **[c1904]**. Also (Tauchnitz Ed.) 2 vols. Leipzig, **1904**
ROBINSON, FAYETTE. *California and Its Gold Regions*. New York, **1849**
ROBINSON, HENRY MORTON. *The Great Snow*. New York, **1947**
ROBINSON, JOHN. *The Flora of Essex County, Massachusetts*. Salem, **1880**
ROBINSON, ROWLAND E. *Danvis Folks*. Boston, 1899. **=1894**
Uncle Lisha's Outing. Boston, 1898. **=1897**
ROBINSON, SARA T. D. (LAWRENCE). *Kansas: Its Interior and Exterior Life*. Boston, **1856**
ROBLEY, THOMAS F. *History of Bourbon County, Kansas*. Fort Scott, Kans., **1894**
ROBSJOHN-GIBBINGS, TERENCE H. *Good-bye, Mr. Chippendale*. New York, **1944**
ROBSON, JOSEPH. *An Account of Six Years Residence in Hudson's-Bay*. London, **1752**
ROCKFELLOW, JOHN A. *Log of an Arizona Trail-blazer*. Tucson, **[c1933]**
RODELL, MARIE (FREID). *Mystery Fiction; Theory and Technique*. New York, **[1943]**
ROE, EDWARD P. *Barriers Burned Away*. New York, **1872**
Nature's Serial Story. New York, 1885 **[1884]**
ROGERS, DAVID B. *Prehistoric Man of the Santa Barbara Coast*. [Santa Barbara, Calif.] **1929**
ROGERS, ROBERT. *A Concise Account of North America*. London, **1765**
Journals of Major Robert Rogers. London, **1765**
Ponteach. London, **1766**. See also MOSES. *Representative Plays*.
ROGERS, WOODES. *A Cruising Voyage Round the World*. London, **1712**
ROLLINS, ELLEN C. (HOBBS). *New England Bygones*. New ed. Philadelphia, 1883. **1880**
ROLLINS, PHILIP A. *The Cowboy; His Characteristics, His Equipment, and His Part in the Development of the West*. New York, **1922**
Ed. *The Discovery of the Oregon Trail. Robert Stuart's Narratives of His Overland Trip Eastward from Astoria in 1812–13*. New York, 1935. **v.d.**
Gone Haywire. New York, **1939**
ROLLINSON, JOHN K. *Wyoming Cattle Trails*. Caldwell, Ida., **1948**
ROLT-WHEELER, FRANCIS W. *The Boy with the U.S. Census*. Boston, **[1911]**
ROMANS, BERNARD. *A Concise Natural History of East and West Florida*. New York, 1776. **=1775**
ROMSPERT, GEORGE W. *The Western Echo*. Dayton, O., **1881**
ROOSA, DANIEL B. ST. JOHN. *A Practical Treatise on the Diseases of the Ear*. 2d ed. New York, **1874**
ROOSEVELT, EDITH K. (CAROW), and ROOSEVELT, KERMIT, comps. *American Backlogs: The Story of Gertrude Tyler and Her Family, 1660–1860*. New York, 1928. **v.d.**
ROOSEVELT, THEODORE. *Works*. Memorial Ed. New York, 1923–26. **v.d.**
Hunting Trips of a Ranchman. New York, **1885**
The Wilderness Hunter. New York, 1909. **=1893**
ROOT, FRANK A., and CONNELLEY, WILLIAM E. *The Overland Stage to California*. Topeka, Kans., **1901**
ROOT, NATHANIEL W. T., and LOMBARD, JAMES K., comps. *Songs of Yale*. New Haven, **1853**
ROPES, HANNAH A. *Six Months in Kansas*. Boston, **1856**
ROSE, GEORGE. *The Great Country; or, Impressions of America*. London, **1868**
ROSENBERGER, JESSE L. *The Pennsylvania Germans*. Chicago, **[c1923]**
ROSIER, JAMES. *Rosier's Relation of Waymouth's Voyage to the Coast of Maine, 1605*. By Henry S. Burrage. Portland, 1887. **1605**
ROSS, ALEXANDER. *Adventures of the First Settlers on the Oregon or Columbia River*. London, **1849**. Also repr. Cleveland, 1904.
The Fur Hunters of the Far West. London, **1855**. Also repr. ed. Milo M. Quaife, Chicago, 1924.
ROSS, JOEL H. *What I Saw in New-York*. Auburn, N.Y., **1851**
ROSS, NANCY W. *Westward the Women*. New York, **1944**
ROTHERT, OTTO A. *A History of Muhlenberg County*. Louisville, 1913. **v.d.**
ROTHROCK, JOSEPH T. *Flora of Alaska*. Washington, **[1867]**
ROWBOTHAM, FRANCIS G. *A Trip to Prairie-Land*. London, **1885**
ROWE, JOHN. *Letters and Diary . . . 1759–1762, 1764–1779*. Ed. Anna R. Cunningham. Boston, 1903. **v.d.**
ROWLEY, MASS. *Early Records . . . 1639–1672*. Rowley, 1894. **v.d.**
Roxbury Land Rec. See BOSTON. REGISTRY DEPT.
ROYALL, ANNE (NEWPORT). *The Black Book*. Washington, **1828–29**
Letters from Alabama on Various Subjects. Washington, 1830. **v.d.**
Mrs. Royall's Pennsylvania; or, Travels Continued in the United States. Washington, **1829**
Mrs. Royall's Southern Tour; or, Second Series of the Black Book. Washington, **1830–31**
RUEDE, HOWARD. *Sod-House Days. Letters from a Kansas Homesteader 1877–78*. Ed. John Ise. New York, **1937**
RUHL, ARTHUR B. *The Other Americans*. New York, **1908**
RUPP, ISRAEL D. *An Original History of the Religious Denominations at Present Existing in the United States*. Philadelphia, **1844**
Rural Organization; Proceedings of the Third National Country Life Conference, Springfield, Mass., 1920. Washington, 1921. **1920**
RUSCHENBERGER, WILLIAM S. W. *Narrative of a Voyage Round the World*. London, **1838**
RUSSELL, CHARLES M. *Trails Plowed Under*. New York, **1927**
RUSSELL, OSBORNE. *Journal of a Trapper*. [Ed. Lem A. York. 2d ed. Boise, Ida., c1921.] **v.d.**
RUSSELL, T. BARON. *Current Americanisms: A Dictionary of Words and Phrases in Common Use*. London, **[1893]**
RUSSELL, WILLIAM HOWARD. *My Diary North and South*. London, **1863**
RUTTENBER, EDWARD M. *Indian Geographical Names in the Valley of Hudson's River* [etc.]. (New York State Historical Association. *Proceedings*. VI.) **1906**
RUXTON, GEORGE F. A. *Adventures in Mexico and the Rocky Mountains*. New York, 1848. First pub. London, **1847**
Life in the Far West. (*Blackwood's Edinburgh Magazine*. LXIII–LXIV.) **1848**. Cited also from ed. New York, 1849.
Wild Life in the Rocky Mountains. Ed. Horace Kephart. New York, 1924. =1915. (pp. 182–308 are from his *Adventures in Mexico q.v.*) **1847**
RYAN, MARAH E. (MARTIN). *A Pagan of the Alleghanies*. Chicago, **[c1901]**
That Girl Montana. Chicago, **[c1901]**
Told in the Hills. Chicago, **[c1891]**
RYAN, WILLIAM R. *Personal Adventures in Upper and Lower California*. London, **1850**
RYDBERG, PER AXEL. *Flora of Colorado*. Fort Collins, Colo., **1906**
Flora of the Prairies and Plains of Central North America. New York, **1932**
RYE, EDGAR. *The Quirt and the Spur*. Chicago, **[c1909]**

S

SABINE, LORENZO. *Principal Fisheries of the American Seas*. (32d Cong., 2 Sess. House Ex. Doc. No. 23.) **1852**
SAGARD-THÉODAT, GABRIEL. *Le Grand Voyage dv pays des Hvrons*. Paris, 1865. **1632**
SAGE, RUFUS B. *Rocky Mountain Life*. Boston, 1859. First pub. as *Scenes in the Rocky Mountains*. Philadelphia, **1846**
Saginaw Courier-Herald. Wkly., semi-wkly., daily eds. Saginaw, Mich., **1859–1918**
The St. Clair Papers. by William Henry Smith. Cincinnati, 1882. **v.d.**
ST. JOHN. Occasional citation for CRÈVECŒUR *q.v.*
ST. JOHN. HAROLD. *Flora of Southeastern Washington and of Adjacent Idaho*. Pullman, Wash., **1937**
St. Nicholas. New York, **1873–1940**
SALA, GEORGE A. H. *America Revisited*. London, **1882**
My Diary in America in the Midst of War. 2d ed. London, **1865**
SALEM, MASS. *Town Records*, Salem, 1868–. **v.d.**
SALMONS, CHARLES H., comp. *The Burlington Strike: Its Motives and Methods*. Aurora, Ill., **1889**
SALTUS, EDGAR E. *The Paliser Case*. New York, **1919**
SANDBURG, CARL. *Abraham Lincoln: the Prairie Years*. New York, [c1926] **v.d.**
The American Songbag. New York, **[c1927]**
Chicago Poems. New York, **1916**
Cornhuskers. New York, **1918**
Slabs of the Sunburnt West. New York, **[c1922]**
Smoke and Steel. New York, **1920**
SANDOZ, MARI. *Crazy Horse*. New York, **1942**
Old Jules. Boston, **1935**
SANDS, ROBERT C. *Writings . . . in Prose and Verse*. New York, 1834. **v.d.** Vol. I includes EASTBURN AND SANDS. *Yamoyden q.v.* **1820**
SANFORD, PELEG. *Letter Book . . . 1666–1668*. Transcribed by Howard W. Preston. Providence, 1928. **v.d.**
SANTAMARÍA, FRANCISCO J. *Diccionario General de Americanismos*. Mexico City, **1942**
SANTLEBEN, AUGUST. *A Texas Pioneer*. New York, **1910**
SARGENT, CHARLES S. *Report on the Forests of North America*. Washington, **1884**
SARGENT, WILLIAM M. *Maine Wills. 1640–1760*. Portland, 1887. **v.d.**
SARGENT, WINTHROP, 1753–1820. *Diary . . . during the Campaign of MDCCXCI*. Wormsloe, Ga., 1851. **1791**
SARGENT, WINTHROP, 1825–70, ed. *The History of an Expedition against Fort Du Quesne, in 1755 under Major-General Edward Braddock*. Philadelphia, **1855**
SAUER, MARTIN. *An Account of Geographical and Astronomical Expedition to the Northern Parts of Russia . . . and of the Islands . . . Stretching to the American Coast*. London, **1802**
SAUNDERS, CHARLES FRANCIS. *The Indians of the Terraced Houses*. New York, **1912**
The Southern Sierras of California. New York, **1923**
Western Flower Guide. Garden City, N.Y., **1917**
With the Flowers and Trees in California. New York, **1914**
SAUNDERS, RIPLEY D. *Colonel Todhunter of Missouri*. New York, **[c1911]**
SAVAGE, RICHARD H. *The Midnight Passenger*. London, 1901 **[1900]**
SAWYER, CHARLES W. *Our Rifles*. (Vol. III of *Firearms in American History*.) Boston, **[c1920]**
SAWYER, LORENZO. *Way Sketches*. Ed. Edward Eberstadt. New York, 1926. **1850**
SAXE, JOHN G. *Progress: A Satirical Poem*. New York, **1846**
SAXON, LYLE. *Old Louisiana*. New York, **[c1929]**
SAYLES, JOHN, and SAYLES, HENRY. *Early Laws of Texas*. St. Louis, 1888. **v.d.**
SCAMMON, CHARLES M. *The Marine Mammals of the North-Western Coast of North America*. New York, **1874**
SCANLAN, PETER LAWRENCE. *Prairie du Chien*. Menasha, Wis., **1937**
SCENE PAINTER, AN OLD, pseud. *The Emigrant's Guide; or, a Picture of America*. London, **1816**
SCHAFF, PHILIP, ed. *A Religious Encyclopaedia*. Edinburgh, 1883 **[c1882]–84**

SCHAW, JENET. *Journal of a Lady of Quality*. Ed. Evangeline W. Andrews and Charles M. Andrews. New Haven, Conn., 1922. **v.d.**

SCHMIDT, CARL. *Briefe aus und uber die vereinigten Staaten von Nord-Amerika an Freunde in der Heimath*. Altenburg, [1857]. **v.d.**

SCHOCH, ALFRED D., and KRON, RICHARD. *The Little Yankee; a Handbook of Idiomatic American English*. Berlin, **1912**

SCHOOLCRAFT, HENRY R. *The American Indians*. New rev. ed. Rochester, N.Y., **1851**. First pub. in part, **1848**
Historical and Scientific Sketches of Michigan. Detroit, **1834**
Journal of a Tour into the Interior of Missouri and Arkansaw. London, 1821. **v.d.**
A View of the Lead Mines of Missouri. New York, **1819**

SCHÖPF, JOHANN DAVID. *Reise durch einige der mittlern und südlichen vereinigten nordamerikanischen Staaten nach Ost-Florida . . . in der Jahren 1783 und 1784*. Erlangen, **1788**

SCHROEDER, THEODORE A. *"Obscene" Literature and Constitutional Law*. New York, **1911**

SCHUCKERS, JACOB W. *A Brief Account of the Finances and Paper Money of the Revolutionary War*. Philadelphia, **1874**

SCHULTZ, CHRISTIAN, JR. *Travels on an Inland Voyage . . . Performed in the Years 1807 and 1808*. New York, 1810. **1807–8**

SCHURZ, CARL. *Life of Henry Clay*. Boston, **1887**

SCHUYLER, LIVINGSTON R. *The Liberty of the Press in the American Colonies before the Revolutionary War*. New York, 1905 **v.d.**

SCOTT, HENRY W. *Distinguished American Lawyers*. New York, **1891**

SCOTT, JOHN, 1820–1907. *Partisan Life with Col. John S. Mosby*. New York, **1867**

SCOTT, JOHN, of Centreville, Ind. *The Indiana Gazetteer, or Topographical Dictionary*. 2d ed. Indianapolis, **1833**

SCOTT, JONATHAN M. *Blue Lights, or, The Convention*. New York, **1817**

SCOTT, JOSEPH, geographer. *A Geographical Description of the States of Maryland and Delaware*. Philadelphia, **1807**
The United States Gazetteer. Philadelphia, **1795**

SCOTT, LEROY. *The Walking Delegate*. New York, **1905**

SCOULER, JAMES. *History of the United States of America under the Constitution*. Washington, **1880–[c1913]**

SCUDDER, HORACE E. *The Dweller in Five-Sisters Court*. New York, **1876**

SEALSFIELD, CHARLES, pseud. KARL POSTEL. *The Americans as They Are*. London, **1828**

SEARIGHT, THOMAS B. *The Old Pike: A History of the National Road*. Uniontown, Pa., **1894**

SEARS, ROEBUCK & CO., firm. *Catalogue*. Eds. 102–200. Chicago, **1902–50**
How to Get Running Water. [**c1942**]

SEDGWICK, CATHERINE M. *Tales and Sketches*. Philadelphia. **1835**. 2d Series. New York, **1844**

SEILHAMER, GEORGE O. *History of the American Theatre*. Philadelphia, **1888–91**

SEITZ, DON C. *Braxton Bragg, General of the Confederacy*. Columbia, S.C., **1924**
Training for the Newspaper Trade. Philadelphia, [**c1916**]

SERLE, AMBROSE. *American Journal . . . 1776–1778*. Ed. Edward H. Tatum. San Marino, Calif., 1940. **v.d.**

SERVICE, ROBERT W. *Ploughman of the Moon*. New York, **1945**

SETON, ERNEST THOMPSON. *Trail of an Artist Naturalist*. New York, **1940**
The Woodcraft Manual for Girls. New York, **1916**

SEWALL, SAMUEL. *Diary . . . , 1674–1729*. (Massachusetts Historical Society. *Collections*. 5th Ser., V–VII.) **v.d.**
Letter-Book [1685–1729]. (Massachusetts Historical Society. *Collections*. 6th Ser., I–II.) **v.d.**
Phænomena quædam Apocalyptica ad aspectum Novi orbis configurata. Boston, **1697**

SEWARD, WILLIAM. *Journal of a Voyage from Savannah to Philadelphia, and from Philadelphia to England*. London, **1740**

SHALER, NATHANIEL. *The Citizen*. New York, **1904**

SHALER, WILLIAM. *Journal of a Voyage between China and the Northwestern Coast of America*. Claremont, Calif., 1935. **1808**

SHANKLE, GEORGE E. *American Nicknames*. New York, **1937**
State Names, Flags, Seals, Songs, Birds, Flowers, and Other Symbols. New York, **1934**

SHANKS, WILLIAM F. G. *Personal Recollections of Distinguished Generals*. New York, **1866**

SHAPIRO, IRWIN. *Yankee Thunder, the Legendary Life of Davy Crockett*. [New York, **1944**]

SHAW, GEORGE C. *The Chinook Jargon and How to Use It*. Seattle, **1909**

SHAW, HENRY WHEELER. *Josh Billings' Farmers' Allminax. 1870–79*. New York, [**1869**]-**78**

SHECUT, JOHN L. E. W. *Flora Carolinæensis*. Charleston, **1806**

SHELDON, GEORGE. *A History of Deerfield, Massachusetts*. Deerfield, 1895–96. **v.d.**

SHELDON, HEZEKIAH S., ed. *Documentary History of Suffield, [Conn.] . . . 1660–1749*. Springfield, Mass., 1879–88. **v.d.**

SHELTON, JANE D. *The Salt-Box House: Eighteenth Century Life in a New England Hill Town*. New York, 1929. =1900. **v.d.**

SHEPARD, ESTHER. *Paul Bunyan*. Seattle, **1924**

SHEPARD, THOMAS. *The Clear Sunshine of the Gospel Breaking Forth upon the Indians in New-England*. New York, 1865. **1648**

SHEPHERD, WILLIAM. *Prairie Experiences in Handling Cattle and Sheep*. London, **1884**

SHERBURNE, ANDREW. *Memoirs*. 2d ed. Providence, 1831. **1828**

SHERIDAN, PHILIP H. *Personal Memoirs*. New York, 1888. **v.d.**

SHERMAN, WILLIAM TECUMSEH, and SHERMAN, JOHN. *The Sherman Letters: Correspondence between General and Senator Sherman from 1837 to 1891*. Ed. Rachel S. Thorndike. New York, 1894. **v.d.**

SHERWOOD, ADIEL. *Gazetteer of the State of Georgia*. Charleston, **1827**. 2d ed. Philadelphia, **1829**. 3d ed. Washington, **1837**

SHERWOOD, J. ELY. *California: Her Wealth and Resources*. New York, **1848**
Pocket Guide to California. New York, **1849**

SHIELDS, GEORGE O. *Rustlings in the Rockies*. Chicago, **1883**

SHIELDS, JOSEPH D. *The Life and Times of Sergeant Smith Prentiss*. Philadelphia, **1883**

SHILLABER, BENJAMIN P. *Life and Sayings of Mrs. Partington*. New York, **1854**

SHIMER, HERVEY W. *Origin and Significance of Plant Names*. Hingham, Mass., **1943**

SHINN, CHARLES H. *The Story of the Mine*. New York, **1897**

SHREVE, FORREST, *et al*. *The Plant Life of Maryland*. Baltimore, **1910**

SHRIGLEY, NATHANIEL. *A True Relation of Virginia and Mary-land*. London. **1669**. Also in FORCE. *Tracts*. Vol. III, No. 7.

SHUMAN, EDWIN L. *Practical Journalism*. New York, **1903**
Steps into Journalism. Evanston, Ill., **1894**

SHURTLEFF, HAROLD R. *The Log Cabin Myth*. Cambridge, **1939**

SIEBERT, WILBUR H. *The Underground Railroad from Slavery to Freedom*. New York, **1898**

Sierra Club Bulletin. San Francisco, **1893–**

SILLIMAN, BENJAMIN. *Manual on the Cultivation of the Sugar Cane*. Washington, **1833**

Silliman's Journal. Occasional citation for *American Journal of Science and Arts*. New Haven, **1818–**

SIMMONDS, i.e., (SYMONDS,) WILLIAM. See SMITH, JOHN. *A Map of Virginia*.

SIMMONDS, PETER L. *The Commercial Dictionary of Trade Products*. London, [**1867**]
A Dictionary of Trade Products. London, **1858**

SIMMS, WILLIAM GILMORE. *Border Beagles*. 2 vols. Philadelphia, **1840**
Cabin & Wigwam. Occasional citation for his *The Wigwam and the Cabin q.v.*
Charlemont. New York 1882. =**1856**
The Forayers. Chicago [n.d.] =**1855**
Guy Rivers. New York, **1834**
The Kinsmen. Philadelphia, **1841**
The Last Wager. (In his *The Wigwam and the Cabin*.) 1845. (Erroneously dated **a1870**)
Mellichampe. New York, **1836**
The Partisan. 2 vols. New York, **1835**
The Scout. (New and rev. ed. of his *The Kinsmen q.v.*) Chicago [n.d.] =**1854**
Southward Ho! New York, **1854**
The Sword and the Distaff. See his *Woodcraft*.
The Wigwam and the Cabin. 2 vols. (1st–2d Ser.) in 1. New York, **1845**
Woodcraft; or, Hawks about the Dovecote. New and rev. ed. New York, 1854. 1st ed. as *The Sword and the Distaff*. **1853**
The Yemassee. New York, **1835**

SIMONIN, LOUIS L. *Le Grand-Ouest des États-Unis*. Paris, **1869**

SIMPSON, JAMES HERVEY. *Journal of a Military Reconnaissance from Santa Fe, New Mexico, to the Navajo Country*. (In 31st Cong., 1 Sess. Senate Ex. Doc. No. 64.) **1849**

SINCLAIR, HAROLD. *Port of New Orleans*. New York, **1942**

SINCLAIR, UPTON B. *The Brass Check*. Pasadena, Calif., [**1919**]
King Coal. New York, **1917**
The Jungle. New York, **1906**
The Metropolis. New York, **1908**
Money Writes! New York, **1927**
The Wet Parade. New York, [**c1931**]

SINGLETON, ARTHUR, pseud. HENRY C. KNIGHT. *Letters from the South and West*. Boston, **1824**

SINGLETON, ESTHER. *The Furniture of Our Forefathers*. New York, 1901. **v.d.**
Social New York under the Georges, 1714–1776. New York, 1902. **v.d.**

SIPES, WILLIAM B. *The Pennsylvania Railroad*. Philadelphia, **1875**

SIRINGO, CHARLES A. *Riata and Spurs*. Boston, 1931. =**1927**
A Texas Cow-Boy. Chicago, **1885**

SITGREAVES, LORENZO. *Report of an Expedition down the Zuñi and Colorado Rivers*. Washington, **1853**

SKINNER, CORNELIA OTIS. *Soap Behind the Ears*. New York, **1941**

Skyline Trail. Winnipeg; Montreal, **1933–**

SLICK, SAM. See HALIBURTON.

SLOAN, DAVE U. *Fogy Days, and Now; or, The World Has Changed*. Atlanta, **1891**

SMALL, JOHN K. *Ferns of the Southeastern States*. Lancaster, Pa., **1938**
Manual of the Southeastern Flora. New York, **1933**

SMALLWOOD, MARY L. *An Historical Study of Examinations and Grading Systems in Early American Universities*. Cambridge, Mass., 1935. **v.d.**

SMILEY, FRANK J. *Weeds of California and Methods of Control*. Sacramento, **1922**

SMITH, CHARLES FORSTER. *On Southernisms*. (American Philological Association. *Transactions*. XIV.) **1883**

SMITH, CHARLES HENRY. *Bill Arp, So Called. A Side Show of the Southern Side of the War*. New York, **1866**

SMITH, EDWARD. *Account of a Journey through North-eastern Texas*. London, **1849**

SMITH, ELIHU H., ed. *American Poems*. Litchfield, Conn., [**1793**]

SMITH, JAMES. *An Account of the Remarkable Occurrences in the Life and Travels of Col. James Smith . . . during His Captivity with the Indians*. Lexington, [Ky.], **1799**

SMITH, JOHN. *Works*. Ed. Edward Arber. Birmingham, Eng., 1884. New ed. by Arthur G. Bradley as *Travels and Works*. Edinburgh, 1910. **v.d.**
Advertisements for the Unexperienced Planters of New-England, or Anywhere. London, **1631**
A Description of New England. In his *Works q.v.*
The Generall Historie of Virginia, New-England, and the Summer Isles. London, **1624**
A Map of Virginia. With a Description of the Countrey. Includes, Part II, W. SYMONDS. *The Proceedings of the English Colonie in Virginia*. (In *Works q.v.*) **1612**
[*Newes from Virginia*.] *A True Relation of . . . Occurrences and Accidents . . . in Virginia*. (In *Works q.v.*) **1608**

SMITH, JOSHUA T. *Journal in America*. Ed. Floyd B. Streeter. New York, 1925. **v.d.**

SMITH, MARGARET BAYARD. *Forty Years of Washington Society*. London, **1906**. Pub. also as *The First Forty Years of Washington Society*. New York, **1906**

SMITH, MARIAN W. *The Puyallup-Nisqually*. New York, **1940**

SMITH, MARTHA L. *Going to God's Country*. Boston, [**c1941**]

SMITH, MATTHEW H. *Sunshine and Shadow in New York*. Hartford, **1858**
Twenty Years among the Bulls and Bears of Wall Street. New York, 1871. =**1870**

SMITH, RICHARD, 1738–1803. *A Tour of Four Great Rivers . . . in 1769*. Ed. Francis W. Halsey. New York, 1906. **1769**

SMITH, ROBERT MILLER. *Baseball; a Historical Narrative of the Game*. New York, **1947**

SMITH, SEBA. *Jack Downing's Letters*. Philadelphia, [**c1845**]
The Life and Writings of Major Jack Downing. 2d ed. Boston, 1834. =**1833. v.d.**
May-Day in New York. New York, **1845**. (Identical with his *Jack Downing's Letters q.v.*)
My Thirty Years out of the Senate. New York, 1859. **v.d.**
The Select Letters of Major Jack Downing. Philadelphia, 1834. (pirated.) **v.d.**
'Way Down East; or, Portraitures of Yankee Life. Boston, **1854**

SMITH, SOLOMON F. [*Autobiog.*] Occasional citation for *The Theatrical Apprenticeship and Anecdotical Recollections of Sol. Smith*. Philadelphia, **1846**
Theatrical Management in the West and South for Thirty Years. New York, **1868**

SMITH, THOMAS. *Journals of the Rev. Thomas Smith, and the Rev. Samuel Deane*. [Ed.]

William Willis. [2d ed.] Portland, Me., 1849. **v.d.**
SMITH, THOMAS HENRY. *Official Basket Ball Guide and Protective Association Rules for 1907–'08.* New York, [c1907]
SMITH, THORNE. *Thorne Smith Three-Decker.* Garden City, N.Y., 1936. Contains *The Stray Lamb.* **1929.** *Turnabout.* **1931**
SMITH, WILLIAM HAWLEY. *The Promoters.* Chicago, [1904]
SMITH, WILLIAM PRESCOTT. *The Book of the Great Railway Celebrations of 1857.* New York, **1858**
SMITH, ZACHARIAH F. *The History of Kentucky.* Louisville, 1886. **v.d.**
SMITHTOWN, N.Y. *Records.* [Huntington, N.Y., 1898] **v.d.**
SMITHWICK, NOAH. *The Evolution of a State.* Austin, Tex., [c1900]
SMITTER, WESSEL. *F.O.B. Detroit.* New York, **1938**
SMYTH, JOHN F. D. *Tour in the United States of America.* London, **1784**
Snake County Talk. See TAYLOR, J. L. B.
SNEDIGAR, ROBERT. *Our Small Native Animals.* New York, [1939]
SNELLING, WILLIAM J. *Exposé of the Vice of Gaming, as It Lately Existed in Massachusetts.* Boston, **1833**
SOMERS, ROBERT. *The Southern States since the War.* New York, **1871**
Somerset News. Princess Anne, Md., **1925–**
Songs of Yale. Edward C. Porter, ed., New Haven, **1860.** (For same title, **1853**, see ROOT AND LOMBARD.)
SONNECK, OSCAR G. T. *Report on "The Star-spangled Banner"* [etc.]. Washington, **1909**
Sooner Magazine. Norman, Okla., 1922–
SOULÉ, FRANK, *et al. The Annals of San Francisco.* New York, **1855**
South Atlantic Quarterly. Durham, N.C., 1902–
South Dakotan. Mitchell, **1898–1904.** (Also as *Monthly South Dakotan.*)
SOUTHAMPTON, N.Y. *Records of the Town.* Sag Harbor, N.Y. 1874–1915. **v.d.**
Southern Literary Messenger. Richmond, Va., **1834–64**
Southern Sierran. Los Angeles, **1946–**
SOUTHOLD, N. Y. *Town Records.* [Ed.] Joseph W. Case. [New York], 1882–84. **v.d.**
Spalding's (Official) Base Ball Guide. New York, **1878–1914**
SPARKS, JARED, ed. *Correspondence of the American Revolution.* Boston, 1853. **v.d.**
The Life of Gouverneur Morris, with Selections from His Correspondence and Miscellaneous Papers. Boston, 1832. **v.d.**
SPEED, THOMAS. *The Political Club, Danville, Kentucky, 1786–1790.* Louisville, 1894. **v.d.**
SPIER, LESLIE. *Yuman Tribes of the Gila River.* Chicago, [1933]
The Spirit of the Farmers' Museum, and Lay Preacher's Gazette. Walpole, N.H., 1801. **v.d.**
Spirit of XIX. Century. Baltimore, **1842–43**
Spirit of the Times; a Chronicle of the Turf. New York, **1831–61.** (See note to next.)
Spirit of the Times and the New York Sportsman. New York, **1859–73.** Cited also as *Wilkes' Spirit of the Times.* **1859–68.** (Note: Numerous citations *Spirit of the Times,* are doubtless from the concurrent *Porter's Spirit of the Times q.v.*)
SPRING, LEVERETT W. *Kansas; the Prelude to the War for the Union.* Boston, **1885.** (A few quots. erroneously dated **1855.**)
SPRINGER, JOHN S. *Forest Life and Forest Trees.* New York, **1851**
SPRINGFIELD, MASS. *The First Century of the History of Springfield: The Official Records from 1636 to 1736.* Springfield, 1898–99. **v.d.**
Springfield (Mass.) *Wkly. Republican.* **1824–**
SPRUNT, ALEXANDER, JR., and CHAMBERLAIN, E. BURNHAM. *South Carolina Bird Life.* Columbia, S.C., **1949**
SPURR, JOSIAH E. *Through the Yukon Gold Diggings.* Boston, **1900**
The Square Dance, including Round Dances, Quadrilles, Novelties and Mixers. (Writers' Program. Illinois.) Chicago, [c1940]
SQUIERS, EPHRAIM G., and DAVIS, EDWIN H. *Ancient Monuments of the Mississippi Valley.* Cincinnati, **1848**
STAFFORD, JEAN. *Boston Adventure.* New York, **1944**
STAGG, AMOS A., and WILLIAMS, H. L. *A Scientific and Practical Treatise on American Football for Schools and Colleges.* Hartford, **1893**
A Standard Dictionary of the English Language. Ed. Isaac K. Funk, *et al.* New York, **1893–95**
Standardized Plant Names. (American Joint Committee on Horticultural Nomenclature.) Salem, Mass., **1923.** 2d ed., Harrisburg, Pa., **1942**
STANLEY, EDWARD G. G. S., earl of Derby. *Journal of a Tour in America, 1824–1825.* [London], 1930. **v.d.**
STANLEY, EDWIN J. *Rambles in Wonderland.* New York, **1878**
STANSBERY, LON R. *The Passing of 3D Ranch.* [Tulsa, Okla., 1928]
STANSBURY, HOWARD. *Exploration and Survey of the Valley of the Great Salt Lake of Utah.* Washington, 1853. **1852**
STANSBURY, JOSEPH, and ODELL, JONATHAN. *Loyal Verses.* Ed. Winthrop Sargent. Albany, 1860. **v.d.**
STANSBURY, PHILIP. *A Pedestrian Tour of Two Thousand Three Hundred Miles, in North America.* New York, **1822**
STANWELL-FLETCHER, THEODORA M. (COPE). *Driftwood Valley.* Boston, **1946**
STAPLETON, AMMON. *Flashlights on Evangelical History.* York, Pa., **1908**
STAPLETON, PATIENCE. *The Major's Christmas, and Other Stories.* Denver, **1886**
STARR, JOHN W. *One Hundred Years of American Railroading.* New York, **1928**
STARRETT, VINCENT. *Murder in Peking.* New York, **1946**
State of the British and French Colonies in North America, with Respect to Number of People [etc.]. London, **1755**
State Papers and Publick Documents of the United States. 2d [3d] ed. Boston, 1817–19. **v.d.** (Not to be confused with *American State Papers q.v.*)
The Statutes at Large of the United States of America. Boston; Washington, 1845–. **v.d.**
STEAD, WILLIAM T. *If Christ Came to Chicago!* Chicago, **1894**
Steamboat Pilot. Steamboat Springs, Colo. **1885–**
STEEDMAN, CHARLES J. *Bucking the Sagebrush.* New York, **1904**
STEELE, ELIZA R. *A Summer Journey in the West.* New York, **1841**
STEELE, JAMES W. *Frontier Army Sketches.* Chicago, **1883**
STEELE, JOHN. *Steele Papers.* (North Carolina Historical Commission. *Publications.* XIII–XI.) **v.d.**
STEELE, WILBUR DANIEL. *Storm.* New York, **1914**
STEGNER, WALLACE. *Mormon Country.* New York, **1942**
STEINBECK, JOHN. *Cannery Row.* New York, **1945**
STELZLE, CHARLES. *Why Prohibition!* New York, [c1918]
STEPHENS, ALEXANDER H. *Recollections . . . : His Diary . . . at Fort Wilson, Boston Harbour, 1865.* Ed. Myrta L. Avary. New York, 1910. **1865**
STEPHENS, ANN S. (WINTERBOTHAM). *High Life in New York.* London, 1844. **1843**
Married in Haste. New York, [c1890]. **=1870**
STEPHENS, KATE. *Life at Laurel Town in Anglo-Saxon Kansas.* Lawrence, Kans., **1920**
STEPHENS, WILLIAM. *A Journal of the Proceedings in Georgia, beginning October 20, 1737.* (In *The Colonial Records of the State of Georgia q.v.* IV.) **v.d.**
A State of the Province of Georgia. (Appendix to above.) London, **1742.** (Georgia Historical Society. *Collections.* II.) **1742**
STERLING, ADA, ed. *A Belle of the Fifties; Memoirs of Mrs. Clay of Alabama.* New York, **1904**
STEVENS, ISAAC N. *The Liberators.* New York, **1908**
STEVENS, JAMES. *Revolutionary Journal.* (Essex Institute. *Historical Collections.* LXVIII.) **v.d.**
STEVENS, P. See MERENESS.
STEVENSON, DAVID. *Sketch of the Civil Engineering of North America.* London, **1838**
STEVENSON, ROBERT LOUIS. *The Silverado Squatters. Sketches from a California Mountain.* London, **1883**
STEWART, CHARLES D. *Partners of Providence.* Boston, **1907**
STEWART, ELINORE (PRUITT). *Letters of a Woman Homesteader.* Boston, **1914**
STEWART, GEORGE R. *Names on the Land.* New York, [c1945]
STEWART, SIR WILLIAM G. D., 4th bart. *Altowan.* Ed. James Watson Webb. New York, **1846**
STILES, EZRA. *Extracts from the Itineraries and Other Miscellanies of Ezra Stiles.* Ed. Franklin B. Dexter. New Haven, 1916. **v.d.**
Literary Diary. Ed. Franklin B. Dexter. New York, 1901. **v.d.**
STILES, ROBERT. *Four Years under Marse Robert.* Washington, **1903**
STILLMAN, WILLIAM J. *The Autobiography of a Journalist.* Boston, **1901**
STIMPSON, GEORGE W. *Nuggets of Knowledge.* New York, [c1928]
Stimpson's Boston Directory. See *Boston Directory.*
Stock Grower and Farmer. Las Vegas, N.M., **1890**
STOCKTON, FRANK R. *Afield and Afloat.* New York, **1900**
The Casting Away of Mrs. Lecks and Mrs. Aleshine. (*Century Magazine.* XXXII.) **1886**
The Dusantes. (*Century Magazine.* XXXV.) **v.d.**
The Hundredth Man. (*Century Magazine.* XXXIII–XXXIV.) **v.d.**
[*Mrs. Lecks.*] Citation for his *The Casting Away. . . . q.v.*
Rudder Grange. New York, 1907. **=1879**
STODDARD, AMOS. *Sketches, Historical and Descriptive, of Louisiana.* Philadelphia, **1812**
STODDARD, HENRY L. *Horace Greeley, Printer, Editor, Crusader.* New York, [c1946]
STODDARD, WILLIAM O. *Esau Hardery.* New York, **1881**
STOKES, ANTHONY. *A View of the Constitution of the British Colonies, in North-America and the West Indies.* London, **1783**
STONE, BARTON W. *The Biography of Eld. Barton Warren Stone, Written by Himself.* [Ed.] John Rogers. Cincinnati, 1847. **v.d.**
STONE, EDWIN M. *The Life and Recollections of John Howland.* Providence, **1857**
STONE, WILLIAM LEETE. *Uncas and Minantonomok.* New York, **1842**
STONE, WITMER. *Bird Studies at Old Cape May.* Philadelphia, **1937**
STORER, DAVID H. [*Mass. Fishes.*] [*Mass. Reptiles.*] *Report on the Ichthyology and Herpetology of Massachusetts.* Boston, **1839**
STORK, WILLIAM. *An Account of East-Florida.* London, [1766]. Includes JOHN BARTRAM. *Journal.* **v.d.**
STOUT, REX. *Not Quite Dead Enough: a Nero Wolfe Double Mystery.* New York, [c1944]. Also contains *Booby Trap.*
STOWE, HARRIET BEECHER. *Dred, a Tale of the Great Dismal Swamp.* Boston, **1856**
House and Home Papers. Boston, 1865. First pub. **1864**
A Key to Uncle Tom's Cabin. Boston, **1853** London, **1853**
The Mayflower. New York, 1844. **=1843**
The Minister's Wooing. **1859**
Oldtown Folks. Boston, **1869**
The Pearl of Orr's Island. London, **1861–62**
Pink and White Tyranny. Boston, **1871**
Poganuc People. New York, [c1878]
Sam Lawson's Oldtown Fireside Stories. Boston, [c1871]
Uncle Tom's Cabin. Boston, **1852.** First pub. serially, *National Era.* June, 1851–April 1852.
We and Our Neighbors. New York, [c1875]
STRACHEY, WILLIAM. *The Historie of Travaile into Virginia Britannia.* London, 1849. Written **c1618**
STRATTON-PORTER, GENE. (See also PORTER, G.) *Freckles.* New York, **1904**
The Girl of the Limberlost. New York, **1909**
STREETER, FLOYD B. *Prairie Trails & Cow Towns.* Boston, [c1936]
STRICKLAND, SAMUEL. *Twenty-Seven Years in Canada West.* London, **1853**
STRICKLAND, WILLIAM. *Observations on the Agriculture of the United States of America.* London, **1801**
STRONG, GEORGE C. *Cadet Life at West Point.* Boston, **1862**
STROTHER, DAVID H. *The Blackwater Chronicle.* See KENNEDY, P. P. (Erroneously cited, Strother merely being illustrator.)
Virginia Illustrated. New York, **1857**
STUART. *Narratives.* See ROLLINS.
STUART, GRANVILLE. *Forty Years on the Frontier.* Ed. Paul C. Phillips. Cleveland, 1925. **a1918**
Montana as It Is. New York, **1865**
STUART, JAMES. *Three Years in North America.* Edinburgh, **1833**
STUART, JESSE. *Man with a Bull-tongue Plow.* New York, **1934**
Men of the Mountains. New York, **1941**
Tales from the Plum Grove Hills. New York, **1946**
Trees of Heaven. New York, **1940**
STUART, RUTH (MCENERY). *In Simpkinsville.* New York, **1897**
STUART-WORTLEY, EMMELINE C. E. (MANNERS). *Travels in the United States.* New York, **1851**
STURGE, JOSEPH. *A Visit to the United States in 1841.* London, **1842**
STURGIS, RUSSELL. *A Dictionary of Architecture and Building.* New York, **1901–2**
STURTEVANT, EDWARD L. *Sturtevant's Notes on Edible Plants.* Ed. U. P. Hedrick. Albany, **1919**
Suburban (Country) Life. Boston; New York, **1902–17**
The Suburban List. Essex Junction, Vt. **1875–**
SUDWORTH, GEORGE B. *Check List of the Forest Trees of the United States, Their Names and*

Ranges. Washington, 1898. Rev. ed. Washington, 1927
Forest Trees of the Pacific Slope. Washington, 1908
Nomenclature of the Arborescent Flora of the United States. Washington, 1897
Suffield Doc. Hist. See SHELDON, H. S.
SUFFOLK CO., MASS. *Suffolk Deeds*. Boston, 1880–1906. v.d.
SULLIVAN, JAMES W. *Tenement Tales of New York*. New York, 1895
SULLIVAN, MAURICE S. *Jedediah Smith, Trader and Trail Breaker* New York, 1934. v.d.
SUMMERHAYS, MARTHA. *Vanished Arizona*. Chicago, 1939. First pub. 1908
SUMMERS, LEWIS P. *Annals of Southwest Virginia, 1769–1800*. Abingdon, Va., 1929. v.d.
SUTCLIFF, ROBERT. *Travels in Some Parts of North America*. 2d ed. York, Eng., 1815. 1811
SUTHERLAND, EDWIN H. *Professional Thief, by a Professional Thief*. Annotated and interpreted by E. H. Sutherland. Chicago, 1937
SUTTER, JOHN A. *New Helvetia Diary of Events. 1845–1848*. Copy in Bancroft Library, University of California. v.d.
SWAINSON, WILLIAM, and RICHARDSON, SIR JOHN. *The Birds*. (Vol. II of latter's *Flora Boreali-Americana q.v.*) 1831
SWASEY, WILLIAM F. *The Early Days and Men of California*. Oakland, Calif., [1891]
SWEET, ALEXANDER E., and KNOX, JOHN ARMOY. *On a Mexican Mustang, Through Texas, from the Gulf to the Rio Grande*. Hartford, 1883
Sketches from "Texas Siftings." New York, 1882
SWEET, WILLIAM W. *Religion on the American Frontier*. New York, 1931
SWEETSER, MOSES F. *King's Handbook of the United States*. Buffalo, [©1891]
Picturesque Maine. Portland, Me., [©1880]
[*Syd. Soc. Lex.*] *The New Sydenham Society's Lexicon of Medicine and Allied Sciences*. London, 1879–99

T

TABER, EDWARD M. *Stowe Notes, Letters and Verses*. Boston, 1913. 1890–93
TAILFER, PATRICK. *A True and Historical Narrative of the Colony of Georgia, in America*. (Georgia Historical Society. *Collections*. II.) 1741
TAITT. See MERENESS.
TALBOT, EDWARD A. *Five Years' Residence in the Canadas: Including a Tour Through Part of the United States of America*. London, 1824
TALBOT, THEODORE. *Journals . . . , 1843 and 1849–52*. Ed. Charles H. Carey. Portland, Ore., 1913. v.d.
TALCOTT, JOSEPH. *Talcott Papers . . . 1724–41*. (Connecticut Historical Society. *Collections*. IV–V.) v.d.
TALIAFERRO, HARDEN E. *Fisher's River (North Carolina) Scenes and Characters*. New York, 1859
Tall Tales of the Southwest. See MEINE.
TALLACK, WILLIAM. *Friendly Sketches in America*. London, 1861
TALLANT, ROBERT. *Voodoo in New Orleans*. New York, 1947. First pub. 1946.
TALMAGE, THOMAS DE WITT. *The Abominations of Modern Society*. New York, 1872
Sermons . . . Delivered in the Brooklyn Tabernacle. London, 1872
TARBELL, IDA M. *The History of the Standard Oil Company*. New York, 1904. v.d.
Owen D. Young. New York, 1932
TARKINGTON, BOOTH. *Gentle Julia*. Garden City, N.Y., 1922
The Gentleman from Indiana. 1899
In the Arena. New York, 1905
TASISTRO, LOUIS F. *Random Shots*. New York, 1842
TATHAM, WILLIAM. *Communications concerning the Agriculture and Commerce of the United States of America*. London, 1800
An Historical and Practical Essay on the Culture and Commerce of Tobacco. London, 1800
TAYLOR, BAYARD. *Eldorado*. London, 1850
Hannah Thurston: A Story of American Life. New York, 1864. =1863
TAYLOR, BENJAMIN F. *Between the Gates*. Chicago, 1878
January and June. New York, 1854. =1853
Summer-Savory, Gleaned from Rural Nooks in Pleasant Weather. Chicago, 1879
The World on Wheels. Chicago, 1874
TAYLOR, JAY L. B. *Snake County Talk*. (*Dialect Notes*. V.) 1923
TAYLOR, JOHN, of Caroline, Va. *Arator, Being a Series of Agricultural Essays*. 2d ed. Georgetown, D.C., 1814. 4th–6th eds. Petersburg, Va., 1818
An Enquiry into the Principles and Tendency of Certain Public Measures. Philadelphia, 1794
TAYLOR, MART. *The Gold Digger's Song Book*. Marysville, Calif., 1856
TEHON, LEO R. *Fieldbook of Native Illinois Shrubs*. Urbana, Ill., 1942
TEMPLE, JOSIAH H., and SHELDON, GEORGE. *A History of the Town of Northfield, Massachusetts, for 150 Years*. Albany, 1875. v.d.
TERHUNE, MARY V. *An Old-Field School-Girl*. New York, 1897
TERRETT, COURTENAY. *Only Saps Work: a Ballyhoo for Racketeering*. New York, [1930]
TEXIAN, pseud. ANTHONY GANILH. *Mexico versus Texas, A Descriptive Novel*. Philadelphia, 1838
THACHER, JAMES. *A Military Journal . . . from 1775 to 1783*. Boston, 1823. v.d.
THANET, OCTAVE, pseud. ALICE FRENCH. *The Missionary Sheriff*. New York, 1897
Otto the Knight, and Other Trans-Mississippi Stories. Boston, 1891
Stories of a Western Town. New York, 1897. =1893
THAXTER, ADAM W. *A Poem Delivered before the Iadma of Harvard College*. Cambridge, 1850
THAXTER, CELIA (LAIGHTON). *Among the Isles of Shoals*. Boston, 1885. =1873
Poems for Children. Boston, 1884 [©1883]
THAYER, WILLIAM M. *From Log Cabin to the White House*. First pub. Boston, 1881. Rev. ed. Norwich, Conn., 1882
These Are Our Lives. (Federal Writers Project. North Carolina.) Chapel Hill, 1939
THOBURN, JOSEPH B. *A Standard History of Oklahoma*. 5 vols. Chicago, 1916. v.d.
THOM, CHARLES, and FISK, WALTER W. *The Book of Cheese*. New York, 1921. =1918
THOMAS, AUGUSTUS. *Arizona*. Chicago, [©1899]
The Witching Hour. See MOSES. *Representative American Dramas*.
THOMAS, DANIEL L., and THOMAS, LUCY B. *Kentucky Superstitions*. Princeton, N.J., 1920
THOMAS, DAVID. *Travels through the Western Country in the Summer of 1816*. Auburn, N.Y., 1819
THOMAS, FREDERICK W. *John Randolph, of Roanoke*. Philadelphia, 1853
THOMAS, GABRIEL. *An Historical and Geographical Account of the Province and Country of Pensilvania; and of West-New-Jersey in America*. London, 1698
THOMPSON, DANIEL P. *The Adventures of Timothy Peacock*. Middlebury, Vt., 1835
The Green Mountain Boys. Rev. ed. Boston, 1848. First pub. 1839. 1840
Locke Amsden. Boston, 1848. =1847
THOMPSON, ERA BELL. *American Daughter*. Chicago, 1946
THOMPSON, HAROLD WILLIAM. *Body, Boots and Britches*. Philadelphia, 1940
THOMPSON, MARGARET (HOLLINSHEAD). *High Trails of Glacier National Park*. Caldwell, Ida., 1938
THOMPSON, MAURICE. *Byways and Bird Notes*. New York, 1885
THOMPSON, WILLIAM TAPPAN. *Chronicles of Pineville*. Philadelphia, 1849. =1845
Major Jones's Courtship. Rev. and enl. New York, 1872. First pub., in part, 1843. v.d.
Major Jones's Courtship and Travels. Philadelphia, [1857]. Includes with separate pagination *Major Jones's Courtship q.v.; Major Jones's Sketches of Travel*. =1848
THOMPSON, WINFIELD M. *In the Maine Woods*. Bangor, 1900
THOMPSON, ZADOCK. *History of Vermont*. Burlington, 1842
Thompson Street Poker Club. See CARLETON, H. G.
THOREAU, HENRY DAVID *Writings*. Riverside Ed. Boston, 1894 [1893]. v.d.
Autumn. . . . Ed. by Harrison G. O. Blake. Boston, 1892
Cape Cod. Boston, 1865. v.d.
Excursions Boston, 1863. *a*1862
Journal, Vols. I–XIV. In *Writings*. VII–XX *q.v.* v.d.
The Maine Woods. Boston, 1864. v.d.
Walden. Boston, 1854
A Week on the Concord and Merrimack Rivers. Boston, 1862. =1849. Also new and rev. ed. Boston, 1879. =1868 [©1867].
A Yankee in Canada, with Anti-Slavery and Reform Papers. Boston, 1866. *a*1862
THORNBER, JOHN J. *The Grazing Ranges of Arizona*. Tucson, 1910
Native Cacti as Emergency Forage Plants. Tucson, 1911
THORNTON, RICHARD H. *An American Glossary*. Philadelphia, 1912. Vol. III, *Supplement*, in *Dialect Notes*, VI.
THORPE, THOMAS BANGS. *The Hive of the "Beehunter."* New York, 1854
The Mysteries of the Backwoods. Philadelphia, 1846 [1845]
Three Years among the Working Classes in the United States during the War. By James D. Burn. London, 1865
Three Years in California. See COLTON, WALTER.
THROOP, MONTGOMERY H. *The Future; a Political Essay*. New York, 1864
THURLOE, JOHN. *A Collection of the State Papers of John Thurloe*. London, 1742. v.d.
THWAITES, REUBEN GOLD, ed. *Early Western Travels, 1758–1846*. 32 vols. Cleveland, 1904–7. v.d. Many of these annotated reprints have been used, especially the following:
TILLY BUTTRICK. *Voyages, Travels, and Discoveries, 1812–1819*. 1831. (VIII.) GEORGE CROGHAN. *A Selection of Letters and Journals relating to Tours in the Western Country*. 1765. (I.) RICHARD FLOWER. *Letters from Lexington . . . and the Illinois*. v.d. (X.) THOMAS HULME. *Journal of a Tour in the Western Countries of America*. v.d. (X.) JOHN K. TOWNSEND. *Narrative of a Journey across the Rocky Mountains, to the Columbia River*. 1839. (XXI.) CONRAD WEISER. *Journal of a Tour to the Ohio, August 11–October 2, 1748*. 1748. (I.) JOHN B. WYETH. *Oregon*. 1833. (XXI.)
TICE, JOHN H. *Over the Plains*. St. Louis, 1872
TIFFANY, JOHN K. *History of the Postage Stamps of the United States of America*. St. Louis, 1887, [©1886]
TILGHMAN, ZOE A. *The Dugout*. Oklahoma City, 1925
TIMBERLAKE, HENRY. *The Memoirs of Lieut. Henry Timberlake*. London, 1765
TITTERWELL, TIMO., ESQ., pseud. SAMUEL KETTELL. *Yankee Notions. A Medley*. Boston, 1838
TITUS, HAROLD. *"—I Conquered."* Chicago [1916]
"Timber." Boston, [©1922]
TIXIER, VICTOR. *Voyage aux Prairies Osages, Louisiane et Missouri, 1839–43*. Paris, 1844
TOBIAS, NORMAN. *Essentials of Dermatology*. 2d ed. Philadelphia, [1945]
TODD, HENRY C. *Notes upon Canada and the United States of America*. Toronto, 1835
TODD, JOHN. *The Student's Manual*. 3d ed. Northampton, Mass., 1835
TODD, WALTER E. C. *Birds of Western Pennsylvania*. [Pittsburgh], 1940
TOMES, ROBERT. *The Bazar Book of Decorum*. New York, [©1870]
TOMLINSON, ABRAHAM, comp. *The Military Journals of Two Private Soldiers, 1758–1775*. Poughkeepsie, N.Y., 1855. v.d.
TOMPKINS, JULIET WILBOR. *Mothers and Fathers*. New York, 1910
TOMPSON, BENJAMIN. *Benjamin Tompson, 1642–1714 . . . His Poems Collected with an Introduction by Howard Judson Hall*. Boston, 1924. v.d. Includes *New-Englands Crisis*. 1676
TONTI, HENRY DE. *An Account of M. de la Salle's Last Expedition and Discoveries in North America*. London, 1698
Topsfield, Mass. Town Records. 1659–1778. Topsfield, 1917–20. v.d.
TORREY, BRADFORD. *A Florida Sketch-Book*. Boston, 1894
The Foot-Path Way. Boston, 1893. =1892
TORREY, JOHN. *A Flora of the State of New-York*. Albany, 1843
Plantæ Fremontianæ. Washington, 1853
TOULMIN, HARRY. *A Description of Kentucky, in North America*. London, 1792
TOURGÉE, ALBION W. *Bricks without Straw* New York, [©1880]
Button's Inn. Boston, 1887
A Fool's Errand. New, enl. ed. New York, [©1880] 1879. Part II, *The Invisible Empire*. 1880
A Royal Gentleman. . . . And *'Zouri's Christmas*. New York, [©1881]. *A Royal Gentleman* first pub. 1874 as *Toinette*. Written 1868–69. 1869
Toinette. See his *A Royal Gentleman*.
'Zouri's Christmas. See his *A Royal Gentleman*.
TOWNES, S. A. *History of Marion, Alabama*. Unpub. MS. in Perry County High School, Marion, Ala., *c*1844
TOWNSEND, GEORGE A. *The Mormon Trials at Salt Lake City*. New York, 1871
TOWNSEND, J. K., see THWAITES.
TOWNSEND, MALCOLM, comp. *U.S. An Index to the United States of America*. Boston, [©1890]
Tracks—Chesapeake & Ohio Railway Magazine. Cleveland, 1915–

Trail and Timberline. Denver, 1918–
Trail Riders Bulletin. Winnipeg; Montreal, 1924–
TRAIN, ARTHUR K. *The Story of Everyday Things*. New York, [c1941]
Travels Amer. Cols. See MERENESS.
The Travels of Capts. Lewis and Clarke. London, 1809
The Treasury of Botany. See LINDLEY and MOORE.
TREMENHEERE, HUGH S. *Notes on Public Subjects, Made during a Tour in the United States and in Canada*. London, 1852
TRENT, WILLIAM. *Journal . . . A.D. 1752*. Ed. Alfred T. Goodman. Cincinnati, 1871. 1752
TRENT, WILLIAM P., ed. *Southern Writers*. New York, 1905. v.d.
TRESIDDER, MARY (CURRY). *The Trees of Yosemite*. [Rev. ed.] Stanford University, [1948]
Triangle. Pub. by Physical Department of Y.M.C.A. Training School, Springfield, Mass. Springfield, 1891–92
Tribune Almanac. 1838–1914. New York, 1838–1913. Issues 1838–54 from photolithographic reproduction with general title-page reading *The Tribune Almanac for the Years 1838 to 1868, Inclusive*. (Almanacs for 1838, 1843–55 cited also under title *Whig Almanac*.)
TRINKA, ZENA I. *Out where the West Begins*. St. Paul, 1920
TRIPP, GEORGE H. *Student-Life at Harvard*. Boston, 1876
TROBRIAND, PHILIPPE R. D. DE K., COMTE DE. *Vie militaire dans le Dakota . . . (1867–1869)*. Paris, 1926. v.d.
TROLLOPE, ANTHONY. *North America*. London, 1862
TROLLOPE, FRANCES (MILTON). *Domestic Manners of the Americans*. London, 1832
TROWBRIDGE, JOHN T. *Cudjo's Cave*. Boston, 1864
The Kelp-Gatherers. Boston, 1890
True Democrat. Marion, Ala. 1883–84
A True Picture of Emigration. London, 1848. c1845
TRUMBULL, GURDON. *Names and Portraits of Birds Which Interest Gunners*. New York, 1888
TRUMBULL, HENRY C. *The Knightly Soldier*. Philadelphia, 1892
TRUMBULL, JAMES R. *History of Northampton, Massachusetts, from Its Settlement in 1654*. Northampton, 1898–1902. v.d.
TRUMBULL, JOHN. *Autobiography, Reminiscences and Letters*. New York, 1841. v.d.
M'Fingal. Boston, 1785. Also Ed. Benson J. Lossing. New York, 1881. v.d.
TRYON, LEWIS R. *Poor Man's Doctor*. New York, 1945
TUCKER, T. W. *Waifs from the Way-bills of an Old Expressman*. Boston, 1872
TUCKLEY, HENRY. *Under the Queen*. Cincinnati, 1891
TUDOR, WILLIAM. *Letters on the Eastern States*. New York, 1820
The Life of James Otis, of Massachusetts. Boston, 1823. v.d.
TURNBULL, DAVID. *Travels in the West*. London, 1840
TURNER, FREDERICK J. *The Significance of the Frontier in American History*. Washington, 1894. 1893
TURNER, JOSEPH A., comp. *The Cotton Planter's Manual*. New York, 1865. =1857
TURNER, LORENZO D. *Africanisms in the Gullah Dialect*. Chicago, 1949
TWAIN, MARK, pseud. SAMUEL L. CLEMENS. *Writings*. Definitive Ed. [New York, 1922–25.] v.d.
The Adventures of Huckleberry Finn. London, 1884
The Adventures of Thomas Jefferson Snodgrass. Ed. Charles Honce. Chicago, 1928. 1856–57
The Adventures of Tom Sawyer. Hartford, 1876
The American Claimant. New York, 1892
The Celebrated Jumping Frog of Calaveras County, and Other Sketches. New York, 1867. v.d.
A Connecticut Yankee in King Arthur's Court. New York, 1889
The Curious Republic of Gondour, and Other Whimsical Sketches. New York, 1919. v.d.
Following the Equator. Hartford, 1897
The Innocents Abroad. Hartford, 1869
Jumping Frog. See his *The Celebrated Jumping Frog;* also his *Mark Twain's Sketches*.
Letters from the Sandwich Islands, Written for the Sacramento Union. Stanford University, 1938. v.d.
Life on the Mississippi. New York, [c1911]. First pub. 1883. Chaps. iv–xvii as *Old Times on the Mississippi q.v.* 1875
The Man that Corrupted Hadleyburg, and Other Stories and Essays. New York, 1900. v.d.
Mark Twain's Letters. New York, 1917. v.d.
Mark Twain's Sketches, New and Old. Hartford, 1875. Also *Sketches, New and Old*. New York, [c1903.] (*Writings*, Author's National Ed., XIX.) v.d. Includes *The Celebrated Jumping Frog q.v.*. 1865
The £1,000,000 Bank-Note and Other New Stories. New York, 1893
The Mysterious Stranger. New York, [1916]. 1898
Old Times on the Mississippi. Pirated, Toronto, 1876. First pub. 1875. See also his *Life on the Mississippi*.
Pudd'nhead Wilson. (*Century Magazine*. XLVII–XLVIII.) v.d.
Punch, Brothers, Punch! and Other Sketches. New York, 1878. v.d.
Roughing It. Hartford, 1872
Screamers. 166 pp. London, [?1871] v.d.
Some Rambling Notes of an Idle Excursion. (*Atlantic Monthly*. XL–XLI.) v.d.
Those Extraordinary Twins. Pub. as *The Tragedy of Pudd'nhead Wilson, and the Comedy of Those Extraordinary Twins*. Hartford, 1894
A Tramp Abroad. Hartford, 1880
TWAIN, MARK and WARNER, CHARLES DUDLEY. *The Gilded Age*. Hartford, 1873
TWINING, THOMAS. *Travels in America 100 Years Ago*. New York, 1894. a1800
Travels in India a Hundred Years Ago, with a Visit to the United States. Ed. William H. G. Twining. London, 1893. v.d.
TWITCHELL, RALPH E. *The Leading Facts of New Mexican History*. Cedar Rapids, Ia., 1911–17
TYLER, LYON G. *The Letters and Times of the Tylers*. Richmond, 1884–96. v.d.
TYLER, WILLIAM S. *History of Amherst College during Its First Half Century. 1821–1871*. Springfield, Mass., 1873. Rev. ed. [1821–91]. 1895
TYLOR, SIR EDWARD B. *Anahuac: or Mexico and the Mexicans*. London, 1861
Researches into the Early History of Mankind. London, 1865
Typographical Journal. Indianapolis, 1889–
TYSON, JAMES L. *Diary of a Physician in California*. New York, 1850

U

ULLOA, ANTONIO DE. *Noticias Americanas*. Madrid, 1772
UMFREVILLE, EDWARD. *The Present State of Hudson's Bay*. London, 1790
"Uncle Rufus" and "Ma," the Story of a Summer Jaunt. [?Chicago], 1882
Uncle Sam, pseud. *Uncle Sam's Peculiarities*. London, [1844]. Also cited as contributor of miscellaneous articles in *Ainsworth's Magazine* (London), I–IV; and Bentley's *Miscellany* (London), IV, VI–VII.) v.d.
UNDERHILL, EDWARD F., and THOMSON, MORTIMER. *The History and Records of the Elephant Club*. New York, 1857. First pub. 1856.
UNDERHILL, JOHN. *Newes from America*. (Massachusetts Historical Society. *Collections*. 23d Ser., Vol. VI.) 1638
UNDERHILL, RUTH M. *First Penthouse Dwellers of America*. 2d ed., rev. and redesigned. Santa Fe, [1946]
[*Union Songster*.] *Tony Pastor's Union Songster*. (In *Tony Pastor's Complete Budget of Comic Songs*.) New York, [1864]
United States Magazine and Democratic Review. Washington; New York, 1837–59
Universal Asylum and Columbian Magazine. Philadelphia, 1786–92. Usually cited as *Columbian Mag. q.v.*
UPHAM, SAMUEL C. *Notes on a Voyage to California, 1849–50*. Philadelphia, 1878
URBACH, ERICH, and GOTTLIEB, PHILIP M. *Allergy*. 2d ed., New York, 1946

V

VACHELL, HORACE A. *Some Happenings*. London, 1918
[*Vade Mecum*.] *The Gentleman's Vade-Mecum; or the Sporting and Dramatic Companion*. Philadelphia, 1835–36
VALENTINE, EDWARD A. U. *Hecla Sandwith*. Indianapolis, [1905]
Valley Tan, Kirk Anderson's. Salt Lake City, 1858–60
VAN BUREN, A. DE PUY. *Jottings of a Year's Sojourn in the South*. Battle Creek, Mich., 1859
VANCE, LOUIS JOSEPH. *Baroque*. New York, [c1923]
Cynthia-of-the-Minute. New York, 1911
VANDERBILT, GERTRUDE (LEFFERTS). *The Social History of Flatbush, and Manners and Customs of the Dutch Settlers in Kings County*. 391 pp. New York, 1899. First pub. 351 pp. New York, 1881.
VAN DERSAL, WILLIAM R. *Native Woody Plants of the United States*. Washington, 1938
Ornamental American Shrubs. New York, 1942
VAN DYKE, HENRY. *Fisherman's Luck and Some Other Uncertain Things*. New York, 1900. =1899
VAN DYKE, THEODORE S. *Southern California: Its Valleys, Hills and Streams*. New York, 1886
Vanity Fair. New York, 1859–63
VAN LAER, ARNOLD J. F., tr. and ed. *Minutes of the Court of Fort Orange and Beverwyck, 1657–1660*. Albany, 1923. v.d.
VAN RENSSELAER, MAY (KING). *The Social Ladder*. New York, 1924
VAN SCHAACK, HENRY C. *The Law of Bank Checks in the United States*. Denver, 1892
The Life of Peter Van Schaack, LL.D. New York, 1842. v.d.
VANSELL, GEORGE H. *Nectar and Pollen Plants of California*. Berkeley, [1931]
VASEY, GEORGE. *The Agricultural Grasses of the United States*. Washington, 1884. New ed. Washington, 1889
Vaughan's Gardening Illustrated for 1946. (Vaughan's Seed Store.) Chicago, 1945
VAUX, CALVERT. *Villas and Cottages*. New York, 1857. [2d ed.] New York, 1864
VAWTER, JOHN B. *Prison Life in Dixie*. 3d ed. Chicago, 1881
VENEGAS, MIGUEL. *A Natural and Civil History of California*. Tr. from original Spanish, Madrid, 1758. London, 1759
Vermont State Papers. Comp. William Slade. Middlebury, 1823. v.d.
VERPLANCK, GULIAN C. *The State Triumvirate*. New York, 1819
VERRILL, ALPHEUS HYATT. *Foods America Gave the World*. Boston, [1937]
VERWIJS, EELCO, and VERDAM, JACOB. *Middelnederlandsch Woordenboek*. 's-Gravenhage, 1885–1929
VESTAL, STANLEY. *The Old Santa Fe Trail*. Boston, 1939
Sitting Bull, Champion of the Sioux. Boston 1932
Victims of Gaming. Boston, 1838
VICTOR, ORVILLE J. *The History, Civil, Political and Military, of the Southern Rebellion*. New York, [1861–68]. v.d.
VIELÉ, TERESA (GRIFFIN). *"Following the Drum."* New York, 1858
A View of North America. Glasgow, Printed by William Smith, for author, 1781
VIGNOLES, CHARLES B. *Observations upon the Floridas*. New York, 1823
VILLARD, OSWALD GARRISON. *John Brown, 1800–1859*. Boston, 1910
VINES, HOWELL. *This Green Thicket World*. Boston, 1934
A River Goes with Heaven. Boston, 1930
VIRGINIA (COLONY). CENTRAL ASSEMBLY. HOUSE OF BURGESSES. *Journals . . . 1619–1658–59*. Ed. Henry R. McIlwaine. Richmond, 1915. v.d.
[*Va. Laws*.] *The Statutes at Large; Being a Collection of All the Laws of Virginia from . . . 1619*. Ed. William W. Hening. Richmond, etc. 1819–23. v.d.
Virginia Literary Museum and Journal of Belles Lettres. Charlottesville, 1829–30
A Visit to the States. A Reprint of Letters from the Special Correspondent of the Times. London, 1887–88
A Visit to Texas: Being the Journal of a Traveller through Those Parts Most Interesting to American Settlers. New York, 1834
VISHER, STEPHEN S. *The Geography of South Dakota*. Vermillion, S.D., 1918
VISSCHER, WILLIAM L. *A Thrilling and Truthful History of the Pony Express*. Chicago, 1908
VIVIAN, SIR ARTHUR P. *Wanderings in the Western Land*. London, 1879
VOLNEY, CONSTANTIN F. C., COMTE DE. *A View of the Soil and Climate of the United States of America*. Tr. C. B. Brown, Philadelphia, 1804. Also pub. as *View of the Climate and Soil of the United States of America*. Tr. [anon.] London, 1804
Voodoo Tales. See OWEN, MARY A.

W

WADSWORTH, DANIEL. *Diary*. [Ed. George L. Walker.] Hartford, 1894. v.d.
WAGNER, LEOPOLD. *More about Names*. London, 1893

WAIT, JOHN C. *The Car-Builder's Dictionary.* 3d ed. New York, **1895**

WAITE, CATHERINE (VAN VALKENBURG). *Adventures in the Far West.* Chicago, **1882**

WAKEFIELD, JOHN A. *Wakefield's History of the Black Hawk War.* Chicago, 1907. **1834**

WALCOTT, EARLE A. *The Open Door.* New York, **1910**

Waldie's Select Circulating Library. Philadelphia, **1832–42**

WALGAMOTT, CHARLES S. *Reminiscences of Early Days.* Twin Falls, Ida., **[c1926]**

WALKER, ROBERT SPARKS. *Lookout: The Story of a Mountain.* Kingsport, Tenn., **1941**

WALKER, THOMAS, 1715–1794. *Doctor Thomas Walker's Journal of an Exploration of Kentucky in 1750.* In *First Explorations of Kentucky.* Ed. Josiah S. Johnstone. Louisville, 1898. **1750**

WALKER, TIMOTHY. *Diaries.* (New Hampshire Historical Society. *Collections.* IX.) **v.d.**

WALLACE, DILLON. *Saddle and Camp in the Rockies.* New York, **1911**

WALLACE, EDWARD T. *Barington.* New York, **1945**

WALLACE, LEWIS. *Ben-Hur, A Tale of the Christ.* 560 pp. New York, **[c1880]**

WALLACE, SUSAN (ELSTON). *The Land of the Pueblos.* New York, **1888**

WALLER, ELBERT. *Illinois Pioneer Days.* Litchfield, Ill., **1918**

WALLER, MARY E. *The Wood-Carver of 'Lympus.* Boston, **1904**

WALLIHAN & Co., S. S., comp. *Rocky Mountain Directory and Colorado Gazetteer for 1871.* Denver, **[c1870]**

WALSH, WILLIAM SHEPARD. *Handy-Book of Literary Curiosities.* Philadelphia, **[c1892]**

WANSEY, HENRY. *The Journal of an Excursion to the United States of North America in the Summer of 1794.* Salisbury, England, **1796**

War Birds. By John M. Grider. New York, 1927. **1917**

WARD, ARTEMAS. *Encyclopedia of Food.* New York, 1941. =**1923**

WARD, EDWARD. *A Trip to New-England.* London, **1699**

WARD, MARY A. (ARNOLD). *Canadian Born.* London, **1910**

WARDEN, DAVID B. *A Chorographical and Statistical Description of the District of Columbia.* Paris, **1816**

A Statistical, Political, and Historical Account of the United States of North America. **1819**

WARDER, JOHN A. *American Pomology.* New York, **[c1867]**

Hedges and Evergreens. New York, **1858**

WARE, JAMES R. *Passing English of the Victorian Era.* London, **[1909]**

WARFIELD, WILLIAM. *The Theory and Practice of Cattle Breeding.* Chicago, **1889**

WARNER, CHARLES DUDLEY. *The Golden House.* **1894**

My Summer in a Garden. **1870**

On Horseback. A Tour in Virginia, North Carolina and Tennessee. Boston, 1896. =**1888**

Studies in the South and West. New York, 1904. **1889**

Their Pilgrimage. New York, **1887**

WARNER, SUSAN B. *The Wide, Wide World.* **1850**

WARNER, SUSAN B., and WARNER, ANNA B. *The Gold of Chickaree.* New York, **1876**

WARNICK, FLORENCE. *Dialect of Garrett County, Maryland.* Priv. pr., **1942**

Warren-Adams Letters. Being Chiefly a Correspondence among John Adams, Samuel Adams, and James Warren. (Massachusetts Historical Society. *Collections.* LXXII–LXXIII.) **v.d.**

Warwick, R.I. Early Records. [Ed. Howard M. Chapin.] Providence, 1926. **v.d.**

WASHBURN, WATSON, and DE LONG, EDMUND S. *High and Low Financiers.* Indianapolis, **[c1932]**

WASHINGTON, BOOKER T. *Up from Slavery; an Autobiography.* New York, **[c1901]**

WASHINGTON, GEORGE. *Writings.* Ed. Worthington C. Ford. New York, 1889–93. **v.d.**

Diaries . . . 1748–1799. Ed. John C. Fitzpatrick. Boston, 1925. **v.d.**

Journal of My Journey over the Mountains . . . in 1747–8. Ed. Joseph M. Toner. Albany, 1892. **v.d.**

WASON, ROBERT A. *Friar Tuck.* Boston, **[1912]**

Happy Hawkins. Boston, **[c1909]**

WATERBURY, CONN. *Proprietors' Records of the Town . . . 1677–1761.* Ed. Katherine A. Pritchard. [Waterbury], 1911. **v.d.**

WATERS, WILLIAM E. *Life among the Mormons.* New York, **1868**

WATERTOWN, MASS. *Watertown Records.* Watertown, 1894. **v.d.**

WATKINS, ALBERT, ed. *Illustrated History of Nebraska.* Ed. Julius S. Morton, succeeded by Albert Watkins as ed.-in-chief. Lincoln, Neb., **1907–13**

WATKINS, SIR EDWARD W. *A Trip to the United States and Canada.* London, **1852**

WATSON, ELKANAH. *Men and Times of the Revolution.* Ed. Winslow C. Watson. 2d ed. New York, 1861. =1856. **v.d.**

WATSON, HENRY C. *Camp-Fires of the Revolution.* New York, 1874. =**1850**

Nights in a Block-House. Philadelphia, **1852**

WATSON, JOHN F. *Annals of Philadelphia.* Philadelphia, **1830**

Historic Tales of Olden Time: Concerning the Early Settlement and Advancement of New-York City and State. New York, **1832**

Historic Tales of Olden Time: Concerning the Early Settlement and Progress of Philadelphia and Pennsylvania. Philadelphia, **1833**

WATSON, THOMAS E. *Bethany: A Story of the Old South.* Thomson, Ga., 1920. =**1904**

WATTERSON, HENRY, ed. *Oddities in Southern Life and Character.* Boston, 1883. **v.d.**

WATTS, MARY (STANBERY). *Luther Nichols.* New York, **1923**

Nathan Burke. New York, **1910**

WAYLEN, EDWARD. *Ecclesiastical Reminiscences of the U.S.* New York, **1846**

WAYMOUTH, GEORGE. *Rosier's Relation of Waymouth's Voyage to the Coast of Maine, 1605.* By Henry S. Burrage. Portland, 1887. **1605**

Waynesville (N.C.) Mountaineer. **1914–**

WEBB, JAMES J. *Memoirs.* Typewritten copy, in Historical Society of N.M., Santa Fe, of original MS pub. as *Adventures in the Santa Fe Trade, 1844–1847.* Ed. Ralph P. Bieber. Glendale, Calif., 1931. **1888**

WEBB, WALTER P. *The Great Plains.* [Boston, c1931] **v.d.**

WEBBER, CHARLES W. *Old Hicks, the Guide.* New York, **1848**

Tales of the South Border. Philadelphia, **1853**

WEBNER, FRANK E. *Factory Costs.* New York, **1911**

WEBSTER, MRS. A. L. *The Improved Housewife, or Book of Receipts.* Boston, **1853**

WEBSTER, ANGUS D. *Hardy Ornamental Flowering Trees and Shrubs.* 3d ed. London, **1908**

WEBSTER, CLARENCE M. *Town Meeting Country.* New York, **1945**

WEBSTER, DANIEL. *Works.* Boston, 1851 .**v.d.**

Private Correspondence. Ed. Fletcher Webster. Boston, 1857. **v.d.**

WEBSTER, NOAH. *An American Dictionary of the English Language. . . .* 2 vols., New York, **1828.** Rev. eds. New Haven, **1841.** Springfield, Mass., 1856. **1847.** Springfield, Mass., 1884. **1864.** With *Supplement.* **1879**

A Compendious Dictionary of the English Language. [New Haven], **1806**

Dissertations on the English Language. Boston, **1789**

A Letter to the Honorable John Pickering on the Subject of His Vocabulary. Boston, **1817**

Webster's International Dictionary of the English Language. Springfield, Mass., 1900. **1890.** *Supplement.* **1900**

Webster's New International Dictionary of the English Language. Springfield, Mass., 1928. First pub. **1909**

WEED, CLARENCE, and DEARBORN, NED. *Birds in their Relations to Man.* Philadelphia, **1903**

WEED, THURLOW. *Autobiography.* Ed. Harriet A. Weed. II

Letters from Europe and America. Albany, 1866. **v.d.**

Life of Thurlow Weed. [Boston, 1883–84.] I *Memoir.* By Thurlow Weed Barnes. **v.d.**

A Week in Wall Street. New York, **1841**

(Weekly) New Mexican. Santa Fe, **1863–83**

Weekly New Mexican Review. See *New Mexican Review.*

WEEMS, MASON LOCKE. *The Drunkard's Looking Glass.* 6th ed. Philadelphia, **1818**

The Life of Benjamin Franklin. Philadelphia, **[c1829]**

The Life of Gen. Francis Marion. By Peter Horry and M. L. Weems. Philadelphia, 1833. First pub. **1809**

Life of George Washington. Philadelphia, 1867. (Erroneously cited as **1806.**)

Mason Locke Weems, His Works and Ways. New York, 1929. Vols. II–III *Letters.* **v.d.**

WEISER, see THWAITES.

WELBY, ADLARD. *A Visit to North America and the English Settlements in Illinois.* London, **1821**

WELCH, LEWIS S., and CAMP, WALTER C. *Yale, Her Campus, Class-rooms, and Athletics.* Boston, **1899**

WELCH, SAMUEL M. *Home History. Recollections of Buffalo during the Decade from 1830 to 1840.* Buffalo, **1891**

WELD, CHARLES R. *A Vacation Tour in the United States and Canada.* London, **1855**

WELD, ISAAC. *Travels through the States of North America.* London, **1799**

WELD, THEODORE D. *American Slavery as It Is.* New York, **1839**

WELLMAN, PAUL I. *The Trampling Herd.* New York, **[1939]**

WELLS, DAVID A. *Practical Economics.* New York, 1885. **v.d.**

WELSH, CHARLES. *Poker: How to Play It.* London, **1882**

WESLEY, JOHN. *Journal. . . . From October 14th, 1735, to October 24th, 1790. With Introd. Essay by Thomas Jackson.* London, 1903. Also *Journal.* Ed. Nehemiah Curnock. London, [1909–16]. **v.d.**

WEST, RAY B. *Rocky Mountain Cities.* New York, **[1949]**

WESTCOTT, EDWARD N. *David Harum.* New York, **1898**

Western Carolinian. Salisbury, N.C., **1820–44**

Western Gleaner, Or Repository for Arts, Sciences and Literature. Pittsburgh, **1813–14**

Western Journal (and Civilian). St. Louis, **1848–56**

Western Monthly Review. Cincinnati, **1827–30**

Western Review and Miscellaneous Magazine. Lexington, Ky., **1819–21**

The Western Souvenir, a Christmas and New Year's Gift for 1829. Ed. James Hall. Cincinnati, **[1828]**

Westminster Gazette. London, (*OED*).

WESTON, OTHETO. *Mother Lode Album.* Stanford University, **[1948]**

WESTON, RICHARD. *A Visit to the United States and Canada in 1833.* Edinburgh, **1836**

WETMORE, ALPHONSO, comp. *Gazetteer of the State of Missouri.* St. Louis, **1837**

WEYGANDT, CORNELIUS. *The Plenty of Pennsylvania.* New York, **1942**

WHARTON, EDITH N. (JONES). *The Custom of the Country.* New York, **1913**

The Hermit and the Wild Woman, and Other Stories. New York, **1908**

WHEELER, ARTHUR O. *The Selkirk Mountains; a Guide for Mountain Climbers and Pilgrims.* Winnipeg, **[c1912]**

The Selkirk Range. Ottawa, **1905**

WHEELER, JACOB D. *A Practical Treatise on the Law of Slavery.* New Orleans, **1837**

WHEELER, MRS. L. MAY, and CARDWILL, MARY E., comps. *W.A.W. A Souvenir of the 4th Annual Convention* [of the Western Association of Writers.] Richmond, Ind., **1890**

The Wheelman. Boston, **1882–83**

Whig Almanac. See *Tribune Almanac.*

WHILLDIN, M. comp., *A Description of Western Texas.* Galveston, **1876**

Whimwhams. [By Henry J. Finn, *et al.*] Boston, **1828**

WHIPPLE, AMIEL W., *et al. Report upon the Indian Tribes.* Washington, **1855**

WHITCHER, FRANCES M. (BERRY). *The Widow Bedott Papers.* New York, 1856. **v.d.**

WHITE, ANDREW. *A Briefe Relation of the Voyage unto Maryland.* In Clayton C. Hall. *Narratives of Early Maryland, 1633–1684.* **1634**

WHITE, CHARLES. *Oh Hush! or, The Virginny Cupids.* New York, **[1856]**

The Policy Players. New York, [c1874]. First perf. **1847**

WHITE, ELWYN B. *One Man's Meat.* New York, **1944.** First pub. [1942].

WHITE, GEORGE M. *From Boniface to Bank Burglar.* New York, 1907. =**1905**

WHITE, GRACE M. *Rose o' Paradise.* New York, **[1915]**

WHITE, STEWART EDWARD. *Adventures of Bobby Orde.* New York, **1911**

Arizona Nights. Garden City, N.Y., 1916. =**1907**

The Blazed Trail. New York, **[c1902]**

Blazed Trail Stories. Garden City, N.Y., 1916. **v.d.**

The Claim Jumpers. Garden City, N.Y., 1916. =**1901**

Conjuror's House. New York, **[c1903]**

Folded Hills. New York, **1934**

The Forest. New York, 1907. =**1903**

The Mountains. New York, **1904**

The Riverman. Garden City, N.Y., 1916. =**1908**

The Rules of the Game. New York, **1910**

The Silent Places. Garden City, N.Y., 1916. =**1904**

The Westerners. New York, **[c1901]**

WHITE, WILLIAM ALLEN. *The Real Issue.* Chicago, 1897. =**1896**

WHITLOCK, BRAND. *The Gold Brick.* Indianapolis, **[c1910]**

The 13th District. Indianapolis, **[c1902]**

WHITMAN, WALT. *Complete Prose Works.* Philadelphia, 1892. **v.d.**

Democratic Vistas. Washington, **1871**

November Boughs. Philadelphia, **1888**
Specimen Days & Collect. Philadelphia, 1882–83. **v.d.**
Whitney, Adeline D. (Train). *Faith Gartney's Girlhood*. **1863**
The Gayworthys. Boston, **1865**
Just How; a Key to Cook-Books. Boston, **1879**
Real Folks. Boston, 1872. =**1871**
Sights and Insights. Boston, **1876**
A Summer in Leslie Goldthwaite's Life. Boston, [c1894] =1893. Also New York: Hurst [n.d.] First pub. **1866**
We Girls. **1870**
Whittier, John Greenleaf. *Writings*. [Riverside Ed. Boston, 1892]. **v.d.** I–IV *Poetical Works*. V–VII. *Prose Works*, Vols. I–III.
Complete Poetical Works. Boston, 1882. Cambridge. Ed. Boston, [1894]. **v.d.**
Whymper, Frederick. *Travel and Adventure in the Territory of Alaska*. New York, **1868**
Wideawake, an Illustrated Magazine for Young People. Boston, **[1875]–93**
Wierzbicki, Felix P. *California As It Is*. (*Magazine of History*. Extra No. 126.) **1849**
Wiggin, Kate Douglas (Smith). *Polly Oliver's Problem*. Boston, 1894. =**1893**
Rebecca of Sunnybrook Farm. Boston, **1903**
Rose o' the River. Boston, **1905**
Timothy's Quest. Boston, 1892. =**1890**
The Village Watch-Tower. Boston, **1895**
Wilcox, Estelle M., comp. *Buckeye Cookery*. Rev. and enl. ed., 536 pp. Minneapolis, 1885. [c**1880**]. Enl. as *Practical Housekeeping*. 688 pp. Minneapolis, 1883 [c**1881**]
Wilder, Charlotte F. (Felt). *Sister Ridnour's Sacrifice*. Cincinnati, **1883**
Wilder, Laura I. *Little House in the Big Woods*. New York, **1932**
Little Town on the Prairie. New York, **[1941]**
Wiley, Calvin H. *Life in the South*. Philadelphia, **[1852]**
Wilkes, Charles. *Narrative of the U.S Exploring Expedition. During the Years 1838, 1839, 1840, 1841, 1842*. Philadelphia, **1844**
Wilkes' Spirit of the Times. New York, **1859–68**
Wilkie, Franc B. *Davenport, Past and Present*. Davenport, Iowa, **1858**
Will, George F., and Hyde, George E. *Corn among the Indians of the Upper Missouri*. St. Louis, **1917**
Willard, Caroline M. (White). *Life in Alaska*. Philadelphia, [c**1884**]
Willard, Emma (Hart). *Journal and Letters*. Troy, N.Y., 1833. **v.d.**
Willey, Austin. *History of the Anti-Slavery Cause in State and Nation*. Portland, Me., **1886**
Williams, Aaron. *The Harmony Society, at Economy, Penn'a*. Pittsburgh, **1866**
Williams, Annie (Keeler). *Early California Gold Rush Days*. Glendale, Calif., **1948**
Williams, Ben Ames. *Its a Free Country*. Boston. **1945**
Williams, Henry T. *The Pacific Tourist*. New York, 1880 [c**1879**]
Williams, Jesse Lynch. *Princeton Stories*. New York, **1895**
The Stolen Story and Other Newspaper Stories. New York, **1899**
Williams, John Lee. *The Territory of Florida*. New York, **1837**
A View of West Florida. Philadelphia, **1827**
Williams, Joseph. *Narrative of a Tour from the State of Indiana to the Oregon Territory*. New York, 1921. **1843**
Williams, Roger. *A Key into the Language of America*. London, **1643**. (Also cited from *Collections of Rhode Island Historical Society*. I. 1827.)
Letters. (Narragansett Club. *Publications*. VI.) **v.d.**
Roger Williams's "Christenings Make Not Christians" 1645 . . . Followed by . . . Letters Written by Roger Williams. Ed. Henry M. Dexter. Providence, 1881. **v.d.**
Williams, Samuel. *The Natural and Civil History of Vermont*. Walpole, N.H., **1794**. 2d ed. Burlington, Vt., **1809**
Williams, Samuel C. *Early Travels in the Tennessee Country*. Johnson City, Tenn., **1928**
Williamson, Charles. *Description of the Genesee Country*. Albany, **1798**. Also in *The Documentary History of the State of New York q.v.*
Williamson, Jefferson. *The American Hotel*. New York, **1930**
Williamson, Thames. *Woods Colt*. New York, **1933**
Williamson, William D. *The History of the State of Maine*. Hollowell, Me., **1832**
Willis, Henry P. *Stephen A. Douglas*. Philadelphia, **[1910]**
Willis, Nathaniel P. *À l'Abri, or The Tent Pitched*. New York, **1839**
The Convalescent. New York, **1859**
Pencillings by the Way. London, **1835**
Willison, George F. *Here They Dug the Gold*. New York, [c**1931**]
Wills, Henry O. *Twice Born*. Cincinnati, **1890**
Willughby, Francis. *The Ornithology of Francis Willughby*. Ed. and tr. John Ray. London, **1678**
Wilmer, Lambert A. *Our Press Gang*. Philadelphia, **1859**
Wilmington (N.C.) Gazette. **1797–1816. (1797–98** as *Hall's Wilmington Gazette*.)
Wilson, Alexander. *American Ornithology*. Philadelphia, 1808–14. **v.d.**
The Foresters: A Poem, Descriptive of a Pedestrian Journey to the Falls of Niagara, in the Autumn of 1804. West Chester, Pa., 1839. First pub. 1818. **a1813**
The Poems and Literary Prose of Alexander Wilson. Ed. Alexander B. Grosart. 2 vols. I, *Prose;* II, *Poems*. Paisley, Scotland, 1876. **v.d.**
Wilson, Alexander, and Bonaparte, Charles L. *American Ornithology*. Ed. Robert Jameson. Edinburgh, 1831. Also pub. London, 1832. **v.d.** See also Bonaparte.
Wilson, Augusta J (Evans). *Vashti*. **1867**
Wilson, Elijah N. *The White Indian Boy*. Rev. and ed. by Howard R. Driggs. New York, **1919**
Wilson, Gordon. *Fidelity Folks*. Cynthiana, Ky., **1946**
Passing Institutions. Cynthiana, Ky., **1944**
Wilson, Harry Leon. *Ma Pettengill*. **1919**
Somewhere in Red Gap. London, 1920. =**1916**
The Spenders. New York, **[1902]**
Wilson, John Fleming. *The Land Claimers*. Boston, **1911**
Wilson, Samuel Paynter. *Chicago and Its Cess-Pools of Infamy*. [5th ed. Chicago, **?1910**]
Wilson, William E. *The Wabash*. New York, **1940**
Winans, William H. *Reminiscences and Experiences in the Life of an Editor*. Newark, N.J., **1875**
Winchell, Alexander. *Walks and Talks in the Geological Field*. New York, **1886**
Wines, Enoch C. *Two Years and a Half in the American Navy*. Philadelphia, **1832**
Winfield (Kans.) *Courier*. **1873–1919**
Winkler, John K. *Morgan the Magnificent*. New York, **[1930]**
Winship, George P., ed. *Boston in 1682 and 1699: A Trip to New-England, by Edward Ward, and A Letter from New England, by J. W.* Providence, 1905. **v.d.**
Winslow, Anna. *Diary of Anna Green Winslow, a Boston School Girl of 1771*. Ed. Alice M. Earle. Boston, 1894. **v.d.**
Winslow, Benjamin D. *Class Poem, Delivered . . . at the Valedictory Exercises of the Class of 1835*. Cambridge, **1835**
Winslow, Ola E. *American Broadside Verse from Imprints of the 17th and 18th Centuries*. New Haven, 1930. **v.d.** Includes *Father Abbey's Will*. (Attrib. to John Seccomb). **1731**
Winsor, Justin. *Cartier to Frontenac*. Boston, **1894**
The Mississippi Basin. New York, 1895. **v.d.**
Ed. *The Narrative and Critical History of America*. Boston, 1884–89. **v.d.**
Winston, Robert W. *Robert E. Lee*. New York, **1934**
Winter, Alexander. *The New York State Reformatory in Elmira*. London, **1891**
Winterbotham, William. *An Historical, Geographical, Commercial, and Philosophical View of the American United States*. London, **1795**
Winther, Oscar O. *Express and Stagecoach Days in California*. Stanford University, **1936**
Winthrop, John, 1588–1649. *Winthrop's Journal, "History of New England," 1630–1649*. Ed. James K. Hosmer. New York, 1908. **a1649**
Winthrop, John. 1606–76. *Winthrop Papers*. Massachusetts Historical Society. *Collections*. 4th Ser., VI–VII; 5th Ser., I, VIII; 6th Ser., III, V.) **v.d.** Part IV (5th Ser., VIII) also cited as J. Winthrop. *Letters*.
Winthrop, Robert C. *Life and Letters of John Winthrop*. Boston, 1869. =1864–67. **v.d.**
Winthrop, Theodore. *The Canoe and the Saddle*. Boston, 1863. **a1861**
John Brent. Boston, 1862. **a1861**
Life in the Open Air, and Other Papers. Boston, 1863. **a1861**
Wislizenus, Frederick A. *A Journey to the Rocky Mountains in the Year 1839*. Tr. from original German, St. Louis, **1840**. St. Louis, [1912].
Wister, Owen. *How Doth the Simple Spelling Bee*. New York, **1907**
Lin McLean. New York, 1898 **[1897]**. **v.d.**
Red Men and White. New York, [c**1895**]
The Virginian. New York, **1902**
Wister, Sally. *Sally Wister's Journal*. Ed. Albert C. Myers. Philadelphia, 1902. **1777–78**
Withers, Alexander S. *Chronicles of Border Warfare*. Ed. Reuben Gold Thwaites. Cincinnati, 1895. **1831**
Witherspoon, John. *The Druid* [*Papers*]. In Mitford M. Mathews, ed. *The Beginnings of American English*. Chicago, [1931]. **1781**
Wittke, Carl. *Tambo and Bones*. Durham, N.C., **1930**
Witwer, Harry C. *Roughly Speaking*. New York, 1926 [c**1924–25**]
Yes Man's Land. New York, **1929**
[*WNT*.] *Woordenboek der Nederlandsche taal*. Ed. Matthias de Vries *et al*. 's-Gravenhage, etc., **1882–**
Wolcott, Imogene B. *The Yankee Cook Book*. New York, [c**1939**]
Wolfe, Thomas C. *Look Homeward, Angel*. New York, 1929. **1927–28**
Of Time and the River. New York, 1944. **1935**
Wolley, Charles. *A Two Years Journal in New York*. London, **1701**. Repr., ed. Edward G. Bourne, Cleveland, 1902.
Wolman, Leo. *The Growth of American Trade Unions, 1880–1923*. New York, **1924**
Wood, Alphonso. *A Class-Book of Botany*. 10th ed. Claremont, N.H., 1850 [pref. **1847**]. Also New York, 1864. **1861**
Wood, George B., and Bache, Franklin. *The Dispensatory of the United States of America*. Philadelphia, **1836**
Wood, John G. *The Illustrated Natural History*. New York, 1863. First pub **1859**
Wood, Laura N. *Walter Reed, Doctor in Uniform*. New York, **[1943]**
Wood, Lemuel. *A Journal of the Canada Expedition in Ye Year 1759*. (Essex Institute. *Historical Collections*. XIX–XXI.) **v.d.**
Wood, Samuel. *Letters from the United States*. [London, **1838**]
Wood, William Burke. *Personal Recollections of the Stage*, Philadelphia, **1855**
Woodcock, Thomas S. *New York to Niagara, 1836. The Journal of Thomas S. Woodcock*. Ed. Deoch Fulton. New York, 1938. **1836**
Woodrow, Nancy M. (Waddel). *Sally Salt*. Indianapolis, [c**1912**]
Woodruff, Hiram W. *The Trotting Horse of America*. New York, **1868**
Woods, Daniel B. *Sixteen Months at the Gold Diggings*. New York, **1851**
Woods, John. *Two Years' Residence in the Settlement on the English Prairie, in the Illinois Country*. London, **1822**. See also Thwaites.
Woodward, Calvin M. *A History of the St. Louis Bridge*. St. Louis, **1881**
Woodward, Carl R. *Ploughs and Politicks; Charles Read of New Jersey and His Notes on Agriculture, 1715–1774*. New Brunswick, N.J., 1941. **v.d.**
Woodward, Mary (Dodge). *The Checkered Years*. Ed. Mary B. Cowdrey. Caldwell, Ida., 1937. **v.d.**
Woodward, Thomas S. *Reminiscences of Life among the Creek Indians*. Tuscaloosa, Ala., 1939. **v.d.**
Woodworth, Samuel. *The Forest Rose or, American Farmers*. New York, **1825**
Woolman, John. *Journal*. Boston, 1882. =1871 **a1772**
Woolridge, Clifton R. *Grafters of America*. Chicago, **1907**
Woolsey, Theodore D. *An Historical Discourse Pronounced Before the Graduates of Yale College*. New Haven, 1850. **v.d.**
Wooton, Elmer O. *Native Ornamental Plants of New Mexico*. Santa Fe, **1904**
Wright, Harold Bell. *The Winning of Barbara Worth*. Chicago, **[1911]**
Wright, Hendrick B. *Historical Sketches of Plymouth, Luzerne Co., Penna*. Philadelphia, **1873**
Wright, Joseph, ed. *The English Dialect Dictionary*. London, **1898–1904**; *Supplement*, **1905**
Wright, Julia (McNair). *Among the Alaskans*. Philadelphia, [c**1883**]
Wright, Richard. *Black Boy, a Record of Childhood and Youth*. Cleveland, **1945**
Wright, William. *History of the Big Bonanza*. Hartford, **1877**
Wyatt, Edith F. *The Invisible Gods*. New York, **1923**
Wyckoff, Walter. *The Workers; an Experiment in Reality. The East*. New York, **1897**. *The West*. New York, **1898**
Wyeth, John A. *Life of General Nathan Bedford Forrest*. New York, **1899**
Wyeth, John B. See Thwaites.
Wyeth, Nathaniel J. *Correspondence and Journals . . . , 1831–6*. Eugene, Ore., 1899. **v.d.**
Wylie, William W. *Yellowstone National Park*. Kansas City, **1882**

Wyllys Papers. (Connecticut Historical Society. *Collections.* XXI.) v.d.
Wynn, Marcia R. *Desert Bonanza.* Culver City, Calif., 1949
Wyse, Francis. *America, Its Realities and Resources.* London, 1846

X

Xenia (Ohio) *Torch-Light.* 1838–88

Y

Yale Banger. New Haven, 1845–50, 1852. Pub. by Sigma Theta.
Yale Battery. New Haven, 1850. Pub. by Delta Kappa.
Yale Literary Magazine. New Haven, 1836–
Yankee. Portland, Me., 1828–29
The Yankee Doodle Songster. Philadelphia, [1861]
The Yankey in London. New York, 1809
Yeager, Lee E. *Contributions toward a Bibliography on North American Fur Animals.* Washington, 1941
Yeslah, pseud. Halsey, Mina D. *A Tenderfoot in Southern California.* New York, 1908
Yoakum, Henderson K. *History of Texas.* New York, 1856
York, Co., Me. Register of Deeds. *York Deeds. 1642–1737.* Portland, 1887–1910. v.d.
York Co., Va. *Records.* MS. v.d.
Youmans, E. L. *The Hand-Book of Household Science.* New York, 1881 [©1857]
Young, Andrew W. *History of Wayne County, Indiana.* Cincinnati, 1872
Young, Benjamin H. *A History of Jessamine County, Kentucky, from Its Earliest Settlement to 1898.* Louisville, 1898. v.d.
Young, Harry. *Hard Knocks.* Portland, Ore., [©1915]
Young, Levi E. *The Founding of Utah.* New York, [©1923]
Young, Marguerite. *Angel in the Forest, a Fairy Tale of Two Utopias.* New York, [1945]
Young, Stark. *Feliciana.* New York, 1935
Youngken, Heber W. *Text-book of Pharmacognosy.* 6th ed. Philadelphia, [1948]

Z

Zeigler, Wilbur G., and Grosscup, Ben S. *The Heart of the Alleghanies.* Raleigh, N.C., [©1883]
Zeisberger, David. *Diary of David Zeisberger, a Moravian Missionary among the Indians of Ohio.* Tr. and ed. Eugene F. Bliss. Cincinnati, 1885. v.d.
——— *Diary of David Zeisberger's Journey to the Ohio . . .* (In *Ohio Archæological and Historical Collections.* XXI.) v.d.
Zeisberger, David, and Zenseman, G. *Diary of Zeisberger and Gottlob Zenseman.* (*Archæological and Historical Quarterly.* XXI.) 1768–69. See also Beauchamp.
Zorbaugh, Harvey W. *Gold Coast and Slum.* Chicago, [©1929]
Zunder, Theodore A. *The Early Days of Joel Barlow, a Connecticut Wit.* New Haven, 1934. v.d.